2019
Harris
Ohio
Industrial Directory

Published July 2019 next update July 2020

WARNING: Purchasers and users of this directory may not use this directory to compile mailing lists, other marketing aids and other types of data, which are sold or otherwise provided to third parties. Such use is wrongful, illegal and a violation of the federal copyright laws.

CAUTION: Because of the many thousands of establishment listings contained in this directory and the possibilities of both human and mechanical error in processing this information, Mergent Inc. cannot assume liability for the correctness of the listings or information on which they are based. Hence, no information contained in this work should be relied upon in any instance where there is a possibility of any loss or damage as a consequence of any error or omission in this volume.

Publisher
Mergent Inc.
444 Madison Ave
New York, NY 10022

©Mergent Inc All Rights Reserved
2019 Mergent Business Press
ISSN 1080-2614
ISBN 978-1-64141-221-6

TABLE OF CONTENTS

Summary of Comtents & Explanatory Notes 4
User's Guide to Listings 6

Geographic Section
County/City Cross-Reference Index 9
Firms Listed by Location City 13

Standard Industrial Classification (SIC) Section
SIC Alphabetical Index 805
SIC Numerical Index 807
Firms Listed by SIC 809

Alphabetic Section
Firms Listed by Firm Name 1027

Product Section
Product Index 1297
Firms Listed by Product Category 1323

SUMMARY OF CONTENTS

Number of Companies 21,196
Number of Decision Makers 43,737
Minimum Number of Employees 3

EXPLANATORY NOTES

How to Cross-Reference in This Directory

Sequential Entry Numbers. Each establishment in the Geographic Section is numbered sequentially (G-0000). The number assigned to each establishment is referred to as its "entry number." To make cross-referencing easier, each listing in the Geographic, SIC, Alphabetic and Product Sections includes the establishment's entry number. To facilitate locating an entry in the Geographic Section, the entry numbers for the first listing on the left page and the last listing on the right page are printed at the top of the page next to the city name.

Source Suggestions Welcome

Although all known sources were used to compile this directory, it is possible that companies were inadvertently omitted. Your assistance in calling attention to such omissions would be greatly appreciated. A special form on the facing page will help you in the reporting process.

Analysis

Every effort has been made to contact all firms to verify their information. The one exception to this rule is the annual sales figure, which is considered by many companies to be confidential information. Therefore, estimated sales have been calculated by multiplying the nationwide average sales per employee for the firm's major SIC/NAICS code by the firm's number of employees. Nationwide averages for sales per employee by SIC/NAICS codes are provided by the U.S. Department of Commerce and are updated annually. All sales—sales (est)—have been estimated by this method. The exceptions are parent companies (PA), division headquarters (DH) and headquarter locations (HQ) which may include an actual corporate sales figure—sales (corporate-wide) if available.

Types of Companies

Descriptive and statistical data are included for companies in the entire state. These comprise manufacturers, machine shops, fabricators, assemblers and printers. Also identified are corporate offices in the state.

Employment Data

The employment figure shown in the Geographic Section includes male and female employees and embraces all levels of the company: administrative, clerical, sales and maintenance. This figure is for the facility listed and does not include other plants or offices. It should be recognized that these figures represent an approximate year-round average. These employment figures are broken into codes A through G and used in the Product and SIC Sections to further help you in qualifying a company. Be sure to check the footnotes on the bottom of pages for the code breakdowns.

Standard Industrial Classification (SIC)

The Standard Industrial Classification (SIC) system used in this directory was developed by the federal government for use in classifying establishments by the type of activity they are engaged in. The SIC classifications used in this directory are from the 1987 edition published by the U.S. Government's Office of Management and Budget. The SIC system separates all activities into broad industrial divisions (e.g., manufacturing, mining, retail trade). It further subdivides each division. The range of manufacturing industry classes extends from two-digit codes (major industry group) to four-digit codes (product).

For example:

Industry Breakdown	Code	Industry, Product, etc.
*Major industry group	20	Food and kindred products
Industry group	203	Canned and frozen foods
*Industry	2033	Fruits and vegetables, etc.

*Classifications used in this directory

Only two-digit and four-digit codes are used in this directory.

Arrangement

1. The **Geographic Section** contains complete in-depth corporate data. This section is sorted by cities listed in alphabetical order and companies listed alphabetically within each city. A County/City Index for referencing cities within counties precedes this section.

> IMPORTANT NOTICE: It is a violation of both federal and state law to transmit an unsolicited advertisement to a facsimile machine. Any user of this product that violates such laws may be subject to civil and criminal penalties, which may exceed $500 for each transmission of an unsolicited facsimile. Mergent Inc. provides fax numbers for lawful purposes only and expressly forbids the use of these numbers in any unlawful manner.

2. The **Standard Industrial Classification (SIC) Section** lists companies under approximately 500 four-digit SIC codes. An alphabetical and a numerical index precedes this section. A company can be listed under several codes. The codes are in numerical order with companies listed alphabetically under each code.

3. The **Alphabetic Section** lists all companies with their full physical or mailing addresses and telephone number.

4. The **Product Section** lists companies under unique Harris categories. An index preceding this section lists all product categories in alphabetical order. Companies can be listed under several categories.

USER'S GUIDE TO LISTINGS

GEOGRAPHIC SECTION

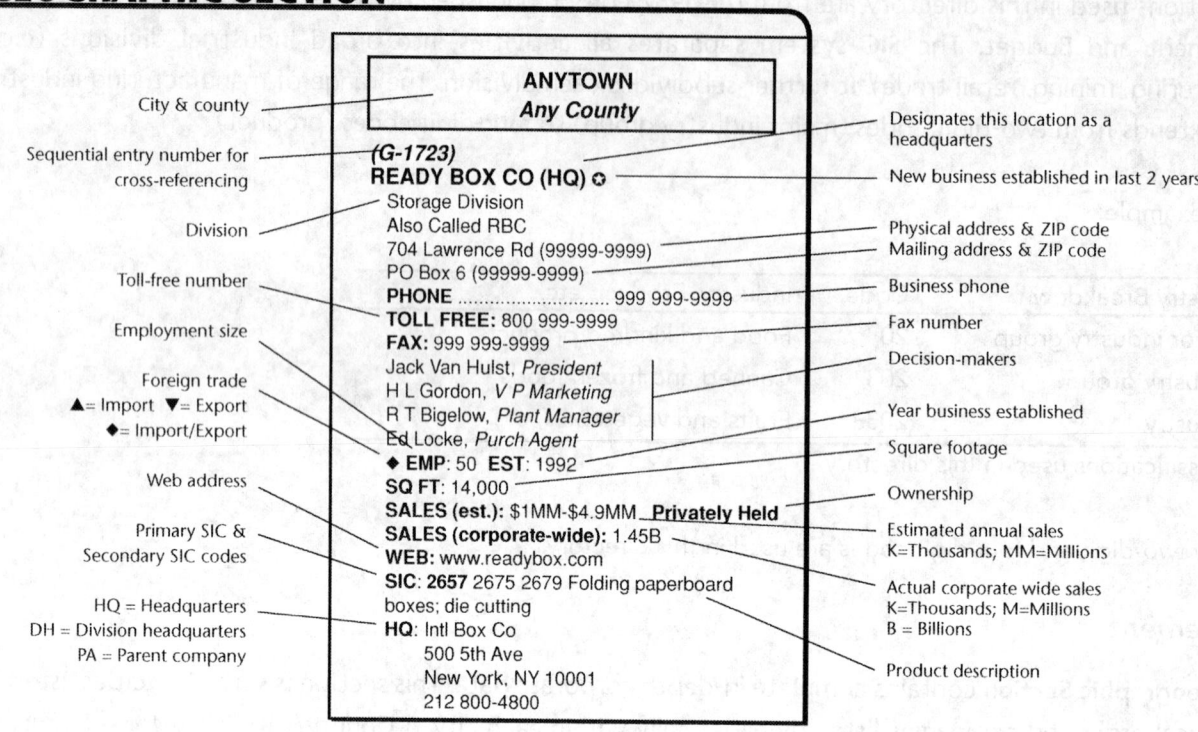

SIC SECTION

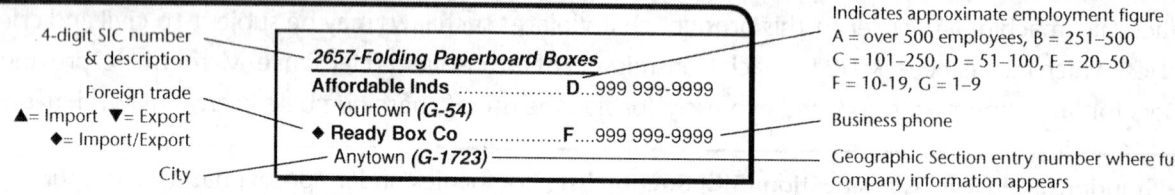

ALPHABETIC SECTION

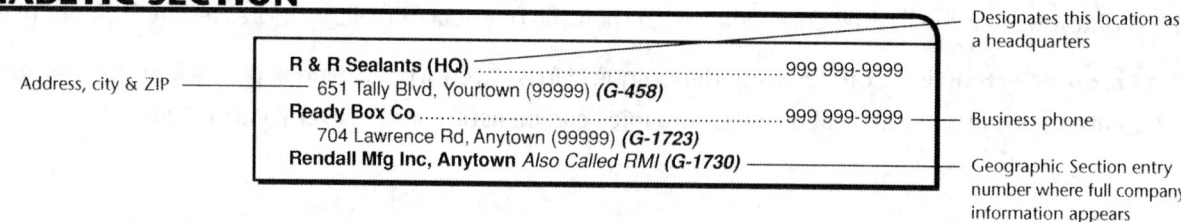

PRODUCT SECTION

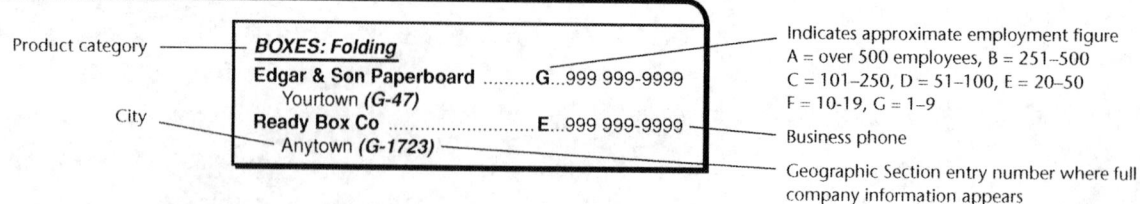

GEOGRAPHIC SECTION
Companies sorted by city in alphabetical order
In-depth company data listed

STANDARD INDUSTRIAL CLASSIFICATIONS
Alphabetical index of classifcation descriptions
Numerical index of classifcation descriptions
Companies sorted by SIC product groupings

ALPHABETIC SECTION
Company listings in alphabetical order

PRODUCT INDEX
Product categories listed in alphabetical order

PRODUCT SECTION
Companies sorted by product and manufacturing service classifications

Ohio
County Map

COUNTY/CITY CROSS-REFERENCE INDEX

Adams
Manchester .... (G-12394)
Peebles .... (G-15877)
Seaman .... (G-16882)
West Union .... (G-19959)
Winchester .... (G-20518)

Allen
Bluffton .... (G-1883)
Cairo .... (G-2402)
Delphos .... (G-8734)
Elida .... (G-9192)
Lima .... (G-11828)
Spencerville .... (G-17308)

Ashland
Ashland .... (G-675)
Hayesville .... (G-10714)
Jeromesville .... (G-11249)
Loudonville .... (G-12141)
Nova .... (G-15430)
Perrysville .... (G-16030)
Sullivan .... (G-17880)

Ashtabula
Andover .... (G-577)
Ashtabula .... (G-761)
Austinburg .... (G-918)
Conneaut .... (G-7641)
Geneva .... (G-10210)
Jefferson .... (G-11223)
Kingsville .... (G-11459)
North Kingsville ..... (G-15159)
Orwell .... (G-15630)
Pierpont .... (G-16063)
Rock Creek .... (G-16531)
Rome .... (G-16562)
Williamsfield .... (G-20259)
Windsor .... (G-20526)

Athens
Albany .... (G-442)
Amesville .... (G-551)
Athens .... (G-821)
Coolville .... (G-7672)
Glouster .... (G-10275)
Guysville .... (G-10520)
Nelsonville .... (G-14593)
New Marshfield ..... (G-14743)
Shade .... (G-16921)
Stewart .... (G-17558)
The Plains .... (G-18019)

Auglaize
Cridersville .... (G-7810)
Lima .... (G-11960)
Minster .... (G-14209)
New Bremen .... (G-14647)
New Hampshire ..... (G-14699)
New Knoxville .... (G-14703)
Saint Marys .... (G-16675)
Uniopolis .... (G-18939)
Wapakoneta .... (G-19317)
Waynesfield .... (G-19567)

Belmont
Alledonia .... (G-446)
Barnesville .... (G-1115)
Bellaire .... (G-1483)
Belmont .... (G-1564)
Bethesda .... (G-1657)
Bridgeport .... (G-2072)
Flushing .... (G-9783)
Martins Ferry .... (G-12756)
Morristown .... (G-14406)
Powhatan Point ...... (G-16341)
Saint Clairsville ..... (G-16621)
Shadyside .... (G-16922)
Somerton .... (G-17269)

Brown
Aberdeen .... (G-1)
Fayetteville .... (G-9638)
Georgetown .... (G-10237)
Mount Orab .... (G-14439)
Ripley .... (G-16513)
Sardinia .... (G-16867)

Butler
Fairfield .... (G-9477)
Fairfield Township ..... (G-9580)
Hamilton .... (G-10526)
Liberty Township .... (G-11811)
Liberty Twp .... (G-11821)
Middletown .... (G-13874)
Monroe .... (G-14254)
Okeana .... (G-15515)
Oxford .... (G-15691)
Seven Mile .... (G-16907)
Shandon .... (G-16940)
Trenton .... (G-18617)
West Chester .... (G-19635)

Carroll
Carrollton .... (G-2914)
Dellroy .... (G-8733)
Malvern .... (G-12385)
Mechanicstown ...... (G-13212)
Sherrodsville .... (G-16990)

Champaign
Mechanicsburg ...... (G-13210)
North Lewisburg ..... (G-15164)
Saint Paris .... (G-16705)
Urbana .... (G-18978)

Clark
Donnelsville .... (G-8800)
Enon .... (G-9384)
Medway .... (G-13365)
New Carlisle .... (G-14663)
South Charleston .... (G-17271)
South Vienna .... (G-17297)
Springfield .... (G-17359)
Tremont City .... (G-18616)

Clermont
Amelia .... (G-527)
Batavia .... (G-1121)
Bethel .... (G-1655)
Cincinnati .... (G-3232)
Felicity .... (G-9643)
Goshen .... (G-10285)
Loveland .... (G-12173)
Miamiville .... (G-13752)
Milford .... (G-13991)
New Richmond ...... (G-14810)
Owensville .... (G-15690)
Williamsburg .... (G-20250)

Clinton
Blanchester .... (G-1698)
Clarksville .... (G-4568)
Martinsville .... (G-12766)
New Vienna .... (G-14823)
Sabina .... (G-16615)
Wilmington .... (G-20483)

Columbiana
Columbiana .... (G-6452)
East Liverpool .... (G-9050)
East Palestine .... (G-9069)
East Rochester .... (G-9090)
Homeworth .... (G-10987)
Kensington .... (G-11284)
Leetonia .... (G-11716)
Lisbon .... (G-11963)
Negley .... (G-14589)
New Waterford ...... (G-14835)
North Georgetown .... (G-15139)
Rogers .... (G-16560)
Salem .... (G-16713)
Salineville .... (G-16785)
Washingtonville .... (G-19480)
Wellsville .... (G-19612)

Coshocton
Bakersville .... (G-1021)
Coshocton .... (G-7717)
Fresno .... (G-10066)
Walhonding .... (G-19305)
Warsaw .... (G-19475)
West Lafayette .... (G-19929)

Crawford
Bucyrus .... (G-2316)
Crestline .... (G-7793)
Galion .... (G-10119)
New Washington .... (G-14827)

Cuyahoga
Bay Village .... (G-1204)
Beachwood .... (G-1216)
Bedford .... (G-1377)
Bedford Heights ..... (G-1458)
Berea .... (G-1588)
Brecksville .... (G-2017)
Broadview Heights ..... (G-2085)
Brooklyn .... (G-2111)
Brooklyn Heights ..... (G-2115)
Brookpark .... (G-2134)
Chagrin Falls .... (G-3007)
Cleveland .... (G-4579)
Cleveland Heights ..... (G-6347)
Euclid .... (G-9400)
Gates Mills .... (G-10207)
Highland Heights .... (G-10786)
Independence .... (G-11116)
Lakewood .... (G-11507)
Maple Heights .... (G-12563)
Mayfield Heights ..... (G-13162)
Mayfield Hts .... (G-13173)
Mayfield Village ..... (G-13174)
Middleburg Heights... (G-13761)
Moreland Hills .... (G-14401)
Newburgh Heights ..... (G-14934)
North Olmsted .... (G-15180)
North Royalton .... (G-15259)
Oakwood Village ..... (G-15476)
Olmsted Falls .... (G-15527)
Olmsted Twp .... (G-15532)
Parma .... (G-15814)
Richmond Heights ..... (G-16500)
Rocky River .... (G-16543)
Seven Hills .... (G-16901)
Shaker Heights .... (G-16925)
Solon .... (G-17097)
Strongsville .... (G-17705)
University Heights ..... (G-18940)
Walton Hills .... (G-19309)
Warrensville Heights .. (G-19464)
Westlake .... (G-20086)

Darke
Ansonia .... (G-592)
Arcanum .... (G-627)
Gettysburg .... (G-10247)
Greenville .... (G-10359)
New Madison .... (G-14741)
New Weston .... (G-14845)
Osgood .... (G-15642)
Rossburg .... (G-16581)
Union City .... (G-18901)
Versailles .... (G-19173)
Yorkshire .... (G-20826)

Defiance
Defiance .... (G-8611)
Hicksville .... (G-10773)
Ney .... (G-14997)
Sherwood .... (G-16991)

Delaware
Ashley .... (G-757)
Columbus .... (G-6489)
Delaware .... (G-8648)
Galena .... (G-10111)
Lewis Center .... (G-11740)
Ostrander .... (G-15643)
Powell .... (G-16306)
Radnor .... (G-16357)
Sunbury .... (G-17883)
Westerville .... (G-19976)

Erie
Berlin Heights .... (G-1652)
Castalia .... (G-2935)
Huron .... (G-11089)
Kelleys Island .... (G-11283)
Milan .... (G-13981)
Sandusky .... (G-16791)
Vermilion .... (G-19156)

Fairfield
Amanda .... (G-523)
Baltimore .... (G-1036)
Bremen .... (G-2064)
Carroll .... (G-2898)
Lancaster .... (G-11538)
Millersport .... (G-14158)
Pickerington .... (G-16038)
Pleasantville .... (G-16228)
Rushville .... (G-16597)
Sugar Grove .... (G-17837)

Fayette
Bloomingburg .... (G-1709)
Jeffersonville .... (G-11245)
Washington Court Hou (G-19476)
Wshngtn CT Hs ..... (G-20718)

Franklin
Blacklick .... (G-1676)
Brice .... (G-2071)
Canal Winchester ..... (G-2497)
Columbus .... (G-6510)
Dublin .... (G-8870)
Etna .... (G-9388)
Gahanna .... (G-10073)
Galloway .... (G-10177)
Grove City .... (G-10410)
Groveport .... (G-10481)
Hilliard .... (G-10801)
Lockbourne .... (G-11992)
New Albany .... (G-14602)
Obetz .... (G-15506)
Reynoldsburg .... (G-16428)
Upper Arlington ...... (G-18943)
Urbancrest .... (G-19021)
Westerville .... (G-20032)
Worthington .... (G-20673)

Fulton
Archbold .... (G-634)
Delta .... (G-8765)
Fayette .... (G-9632)
Lyons .... (G-12272)
Metamora .... (G-13634)
Pettisville .... (G-16034)
Swanton .... (G-17903)
Wauseon .... (G-19509)

Gallia
Bidwell .... (G-1664)
Cheshire .... (G-3148)
Gallipolis .... (G-10160)
Patriot .... (G-15849)
Thurman .... (G-18037)
Vinton .... (G-19215)

Geauga
Burton .... (G-2357)
Chagrin Falls .... (G-3034)
Chardon .... (G-3094)
Chesterland .... (G-3149)
Middlefield .... (G-13772)
Montville .... (G-14323)
Newbury .... (G-14946)
Novelty .... (G-15437)
Parkman .... (G-15810)
Thompson .... (G-18025)

Greene
Alpha .... (G-517)
Beavercreek .... (G-1296)
Beavercreek Township (G-1369)
Bellbrook .... (G-1490)
Cedarville .... (G-2943)
Dayton .... (G-7968)
Fairborn .... (G-9450)
Jamestown .... (G-11218)

2019 Harris Ohio Industrial Directory

COUNTY/CITY CROSS-REFERENCE

	ENTRY #		ENTRY #		ENTRY #		ENTRY #		ENTRY #
Spring Valley	(G-17315)	**Highland**		Kirtland	(G-11467)	Sylvania	(G-17931)	Conover	(G-7662)
Sugarcrk Twp	(G-17879)	Greenfield	(G-10345)	Madison	(G-12339)	Toledo	(G-18150)	Covington	(G-7779)
Wilberforce	(G-20237)	Hillsboro	(G-10876)	Mentor	(G-13368)	Waterville	(G-19489)	Fletcher	(G-9782)
Wright Patterson Afb.	(G-20716)	Leesburg	(G-11708)	Mentor On The Lake	(G-13631)	Whitehouse	(G-20188)	Laura	(G-11625)
Xenia	(G-20753)	Lynchburg	(G-12271)	Painesville	(G-15704)	**Madison**		Ludlow Falls	(G-12269)
Yellow Springs	(G-20805)	**Hocking**		Perry	(G-15903)	London	(G-12047)	Piqua	(G-16098)
Guernsey		Laurelville	(G-11626)	Wickliffe	(G-20195)	Mount Sterling	(G-14460)	Pleasant Hill	(G-16224)
Byesville	(G-2379)	Logan	(G-12021)	Willoughby	(G-20263)	Plain City	(G-16168)	Tipp City	(G-18095)
Cambridge	(G-2421)	Rockbridge	(G-16536)	Willoughby Hills	(G-20466)	West Jefferson	(G-19921)	Troy	(G-18632)
Cumberland	(G-7823)	South Bloomingville	(G-17270)	Willowick	(G-20477)	**Mahoning**		West Milton	(G-19947)
Kimbolton	(G-11457)	**Holmes**		**Lawrence**		Austintown	(G-928)	**Monroe**	
Lore City	(G-12139)	Berlin	(G-1637)	Chesapeake	(G-3143)	Beloit	(G-1568)	Beallsville	(G-1288)
Old Washington	(G-15526)	Big Prairie	(G-1673)	Hanging Rock	(G-10624)	Berlin Center	(G-1645)	Clarington	(G-4566)
Pleasant City	(G-16223)	Charm	(G-3141)	Ironton	(G-11159)	Boardman	(G-1897)	Hannibal	(G-10625)
Quaker City	(G-16353)	Glenmont	(G-10274)	Kitts Hill	(G-11474)	Campbell	(G-2468)	Jerusalem	(G-11251)
Salesville	(G-16784)	Holmesville	(G-10971)	Proctorville	(G-16342)	Canfield	(G-2517)	Lewisville	(G-11802)
Senecaville	(G-16899)	Killbuck	(G-11448)	Scottown	(G-16881)	Greenford	(G-10355)	Sardis	(G-16875)
Hamilton		Lakeville	(G-11506)	South Point	(G-17278)	Lake Milton	(G-11498)	Woodsfield	(G-20542)
Addyston	(G-11)	Millersburg	(G-14053)	**Licking**		Lowellville	(G-12248)	**Montgomery**	
Blue Ash	(G-1716)	Mount Hope	(G-14436)	Alexandria	(G-443)	New Middletown	(G-14747)	Beavercreek	(G-1348)
Cincinnati	(G-3268)	Walnut Creek	(G-19307)	Brownsville	(G-2184)	New Springfield	(G-14818)	Brookville	(G-2160)
Cleves	(G-6353)	Winesburg	(G-20529)	Buckeye Lake	(G-2315)	North Jackson	(G-15140)	Centerville	(G-2995)
Harrison	(G-10627)	**Huron**		Croton	(G-7821)	North Lima	(G-15166)	Clayton	(G-4571)
Lockland	(G-12001)	Bellevue	(G-1527)	Etna	(G-9391)	Petersburg	(G-16033)	Dayton	(G-7995)
Miamitown	(G-13743)	Collins	(G-6425)	Granville	(G-10327)	Poland	(G-16236)	Englewood	(G-9349)
Montgomery	(G-14294)	Greenwich	(G-10403)	Heath	(G-10716)	Sebring	(G-16885)	Farmersville	(G-9631)
North Bend	(G-15050)	Monroeville	(G-14285)	Hebron	(G-10736)	Struthers	(G-17811)	Germantown	(G-10240)
Norwood	(G-15422)	New London	(G-14728)	Homer	(G-10985)	Youngstown	(G-20828)	Huber Heights	(G-11015)
Saint Bernard	(G-16620)	North Fairfield	(G-15138)	Johnstown	(G-11253)	**Marion**		Kettering	(G-11426)
Sharonville	(G-16956)	Norwalk	(G-15378)	Newark	(G-14846)	Caledonia	(G-2414)	Miamisburg	(G-13635)
Terrace Park	(G-18017)	Plymouth	(G-16231)	Pataskala	(G-15827)	La Rue	(G-11476)	Moraine	(G-14327)
West Chester	(G-19825)	Wakeman	(G-19282)	Saint Louisville	(G-16672)	Marion	(G-12691)	New Lebanon	(G-14706)
Wyoming	(G-20752)	Willard	(G-20238)	Utica	(G-19023)	Morral	(G-14403)	Oakwood	(G-15461)
Hancock		**Jackson**		**Logan**		New Bloomington	(G-14644)	Phillipsburg	(G-16037)
Arcadia	(G-625)	Jackson	(G-11178)	Belle Center	(G-1497)	Prospect	(G-16349)	Trotwood	(G-18627)
Findlay	(G-9645)	Oak Hill	(G-15449)	Bellefontaine	(G-1501)	Waldo	(G-19302)	Union	(G-18900)
Mc Comb	(G-13187)	Wellston	(G-19598)	De Graff	(G-8605)	**Medina**		Vandalia	(G-19112)
Mount Cory	(G-14418)	**Jefferson**		East Liberty	(G-9046)	Brunswick	(G-2185)	West Carrollton	(G-19628)
Rawson	(G-16421)	Amsterdam	(G-576)	Huntsville	(G-11085)	Hinckley	(G-10896)	**Morgan**	
Van Buren	(G-19071)	Bergholz	(G-1634)	Lakeview	(G-11504)	Homerville	(G-10986)	Malta	(G-12381)
Vanlue	(G-19153)	Bloomingdale	(G-1710)	Lewistown	(G-11800)	Litchfield	(G-11984)	McConnelsville	(G-13203)
Hardin		Brilliant	(G-2079)	Quincy	(G-16355)	Lodi	(G-12002)	Stockport	(G-17559)
Ada	(G-2)	Hammondsville	(G-10623)	Rushsylvania	(G-16595)	Medina	(G-13214)	**Morrow**	
Alger	(G-444)	Irondale	(G-11158)	Russells Point	(G-16598)	Seville	(G-16909)	Cardington	(G-2869)
Dunkirk	(G-9034)	Mingo Junction	(G-14208)	West Liberty	(G-19935)	Sharon Center	(G-16943)	Iberia	(G-11112)
Forest	(G-9785)	Rayland	(G-16423)	West Mansfield	(G-19942)	Spencer	(G-17303)	Marengo	(G-12588)
Kenton	(G-11400)	Richmond	(G-16496)	Zanesfield	(G-21089)	Valley City	(G-19030)	Mount Gilead	(G-14422)
Mount Victory	(G-14520)	Steubenville	(G-17525)	**Lorain**		Wadsworth	(G-19217)	**Muskingum**	
Harrison		Tiltonsville	(G-18093)	Amherst	(G-552)	Westfield Center	(G-20085)	Adamsville	(G-9)
Bowerston	(G-1939)	Toronto	(G-18607)	Avon	(G-936)	**Meigs**		Dresden	(G-8868)
Cadiz	(G-2397)	Wintersville	(G-20537)	Avon Lake	(G-978)	Langsville	(G-11621)	East Fultonham	(G-9045)
Freeport	(G-9984)	Yorkville	(G-20827)	Columbia Station	(G-6426)	Middleport	(G-13872)	Frazeysburg	(G-9937)
Hopedale	(G-10991)	**Knox**		Elyria	(G-9209)	Pomeroy	(G-16240)	Hopewell	(G-10992)
Jewett	(G-11252)	Bladensburg	(G-1696)	Grafton	(G-10291)	Portland	(G-16275)	Nashport	(G-14564)
Scio	(G-16877)	Brinkhaven	(G-2081)	Lagrange	(G-11478)	Racine	(G-16356)	New Concord	(G-14682)
Tippecanoe	(G-18147)	Centerburg	(G-2993)	Lorain	(G-12076)	Tuppers Plains	(G-18720)	Norwich	(G-15420)
Henry		Danville	(G-7956)	North Ridgeville	(G-15205)	**Mercer**		Roseville	(G-16574)
Deshler	(G-8787)	Fredericktown	(G-9963)	Oberlin	(G-15490)	Burkettsville	(G-2356)	South Zanesville	(G-17301)
Holgate	(G-10912)	Gambier	(G-10182)	Sheffield Lake	(G-16963)	Celina	(G-2948)	Zanesville	(G-21090)
Liberty Center	(G-11809)	Howard	(G-10995)	Sheffield Village	(G-16964)	Coldwater	(G-6398)	**Noble**	
Malinta	(G-12379)	Martinsburg	(G-12765)	Wellington	(G-19573)	Fort Recovery	(G-9812)	Caldwell	(G-2403)
Mc Clure	(G-13185)	Mount Vernon	(G-14467)	**Lucas**		Maria Stein	(G-12597)	Dexter City	(G-8791)
Napoleon	(G-14530)	**Lake**		Berkey	(G-1636)	Rockford	(G-16539)	Sarahsville	(G-16865)
New Bavaria	(G-14643)	Concord Township	(G-7640)	Holland	(G-10914)	Saint Henry	(G-16659)	**Ottawa**	
Okolona	(G-15523)	Eastlake	(G-9096)	Maumee	(G-13065)	**Miami**		Clay Center	(G-4569)
Ridgeville Corners	(G-16510)	Fairport Harbor	(G-9623)	Monclova	(G-14253)	Bradford	(G-2009)	Curtice	(G-7825)
		Grand River	(G-10322)	Oregon	(G-15551)	Casstown	(G-2933)	Elmore	(G-9203)
				Ottawa Hills	(G-15673)				

2019 Harris Ohio Industrial Directory

COUNTY/CITY CROSS-REFERENCE

	ENTRY #
Genoa	(G-10232)
Gypsum	(G-10521)
Lakeside	(G-11501)
Lakeside Marblehead	
(G-11502)	
Marblehead	(G-12584)
Oak Harbor	(G-15441)
Port Clinton	(G-16242)
Put In Bay	(G-16352)
Williston	(G-20262)

Paulding

Antwerp	(G-595)
Cecil	(G-2942)
Grover Hill	(G-10518)
Haviland	(G-10708)
Latty	(G-11624)
Oakwood	(G-15468)
Paulding	(G-15854)
Payne	(G-15872)

Perry

Corning	(G-7699)
Crooksville	(G-7814)
Glenford	(G-10270)
Junction City	(G-11275)
Mount Perry	(G-14454)
New Lexington	(G-14713)
Shawnee	(G-16961)
Somerset	(G-17264)
Thornville	(G-18029)

Pickaway

Ashville	(G-814)
Circleville	(G-4536)
New Holland	(G-14701)
Orient	(G-15574)
Williamsport	(G-20260)

Pike

Beaver	(G-1291)
Latham	(G-11622)
Piketon	(G-16067)
Waverly	(G-19541)

Portage

Atwater	(G-861)
Aurora	(G-866)
Deerfield	(G-8607)
Diamond	(G-8797)
Garrettsville	(G-10187)
Hiram	(G-10909)
Kent	(G-11288)
Mantua	(G-12541)
Mogadore	(G-14228)
North Benton	(G-15059)
Randolph	(G-16360)
Ravenna	(G-16362)
Rootstown	(G-16565)
Streetsboro	(G-17656)
Windham	(G-20524)

Preble

Camden	(G-2464)
Eaton	(G-9141)
Eldorado	(G-9189)
Gratis	(G-10340)
Lewisburg	(G-11789)
New Paris	(G-14752)
Verona	(G-19172)

	ENTRY #
West Alexandria	(G-19616)
West Manchester	(G-19940)

Putnam

Cloverdale	(G-6386)
Columbus Grove	(G-7630)
Continental	(G-7666)
Dupont	(G-9037)
Fort Jennings	(G-9791)
Gilboa	(G-10250)
Glandorf	(G-10269)
Kalida	(G-11276)
Leipsic	(G-11723)
Ottawa	(G-15647)
Ottoville	(G-15679)
Pandora	(G-15806)

Richland

Bellville	(G-1555)
Butler	(G-2375)
Lexington	(G-11804)
Mansfield	(G-12399)
Ontario	(G-15537)
Shelby	(G-16977)
Shiloh	(G-16993)

Ross

Bainbridge	(G-1015)
Chillicothe	(G-3173)
Frankfort	(G-9861)
Kingston	(G-11458)
Londonderry	(G-12073)
Richmond Dale	(G-16499)
South Salem	(G-17296)

Sandusky

Clyde	(G-6387)
Fremont	(G-9987)
Gibsonburg	(G-10248)
Helena	(G-10771)
Millersville	(G-14163)
Vickery	(G-19194)
Woodville	(G-20551)

Scioto

Franklin Furnace	(G-9933)
Haverhill	(G-10707)
Lucasville	(G-12260)
Mc Dermott	(G-13192)
Minford	(G-14207)
New Boston	(G-14645)
Otway	(G-15684)
Portsmouth	(G-16276)
South Webster	(G-17298)
Wheelersburg	(G-20179)

Seneca

Alvada	(G-519)
Attica	(G-855)
Bettsville	(G-1660)
Bloomville	(G-1712)
Fostoria	(G-9832)
Green Springs	(G-10344)
New Riegel	(G-14815)
Old Fort	(G-15524)
Republic	(G-16427)
Tiffin	(G-18039)

Shelby

Anna	(G-587)
Botkins	(G-1931)

	ENTRY #
Fort Loramie	(G-9793)
Houston	(G-10994)
Jackson Center	(G-11204)
Kettlersville	(G-11445)
Port Jefferson	(G-16265)
Russia	(G-16604)
Sidney	(G-17011)

Stark

Alliance	(G-447)
Beach City	(G-1211)
Brewster	(G-2067)
Canal Fulton	(G-2473)
Canton	(G-2554)
East Canton	(G-9038)
East Sparta	(G-9093)
Greentown	(G-10356)
Hartville	(G-10682)
Louisville	(G-12151)
Magnolia	(G-12359)
Massillon	(G-12956)
Middlebranch	(G-13758)
Minerva	(G-14175)
Navarre	(G-14571)
New Franklin	(G-14688)
North Canton	(G-15066)
North Lawrence	(G-15162)
Paris	(G-15808)
Uniontown	(G-18907)
Waynesburg	(G-19561)
Wilmot	(G-20513)

Summit

Akron	(G-13)
Barberton	(G-1047)
Bath	(G-1200)
Clinton	(G-6383)
Copley	(G-7676)
Coventry Township	(G-7760)
Cuyahoga Falls	(G-7829)
Fairlawn	(G-9589)
Green	(G-10343)
Hudson	(G-11025)
Lakemore	(G-11499)
Macedonia	(G-12275)
Munroe Falls	(G-14523)
New Franklin	(G-14689)
Northfield	(G-15313)
Norton	(G-15355)
Peninsula	(G-15888)
Richfield	(G-16461)
Sagamore Hills	(G-16619)
Stow	(G-17565)
Tallmadge	(G-17970)
Twinsburg	(G-18722)

Trumbull

Bristolville	(G-2082)
Brookfield	(G-2103)
Burghill	(G-2354)
Cortland	(G-7703)
Girard	(G-10251)
Hartford	(G-10681)
Hubbard	(G-10999)
Kinsman	(G-11463)
Masury	(G-13059)
Mc Donald	(G-13196)
Mesopotamia	(G-13633)
Mineral Ridge	(G-14165)

	ENTRY #
Newton Falls	(G-14984)
Niles	(G-14998)
North Bloomfield	(G-15063)
Southington	(G-17302)
Vienna	(G-19195)
Warren	(G-19362)
West Farmington	(G-19918)

Tuscarawas

Baltic	(G-1022)
Bolivar	(G-1906)
Dennison	(G-8781)
Dover	(G-8802)
Dundee	(G-9016)
Gnadenhutten	(G-10277)
Midvale	(G-13973)
Mineral City	(G-14164)
New Philadelphia	(G-14756)
Newcomerstown	(G-14968)
Port Washington	(G-16267)
Sandyville	(G-16864)
Stone Creek	(G-17561)
Strasburg	(G-17644)
Sugarcreek	(G-17841)
Uhrichsville	(G-18879)
Zoarville	(G-21195)

Union

Marysville	(G-12769)
Milford Center	(G-14047)
Raymond	(G-16424)
Richwood	(G-16508)
Unionville Center	(G-18938)

Van Wert

Convoy	(G-7670)
Middle Point	(G-13754)
Ohio City	(G-15514)
Van Wert	(G-19073)
Venedocia	(G-19154)
Willshire	(G-20482)

Vinton

Hamden	(G-10522)
Mc Arthur	(G-13178)
New Plymouth	(G-14809)
Ray	(G-16422)
Zaleski	(G-21088)

Warren

Carlisle	(G-2891)
Franklin	(G-9865)
Harveysburg	(G-10706)
Lebanon	(G-11628)
Maineville	(G-12364)
Mason	(G-12820)
Middletown	(G-13970)
Morrow	(G-14407)
Oregonia	(G-15573)
Pleasant Plain	(G-16225)
South Lebanon	(G-17276)
Springboro	(G-17319)
Waynesville	(G-19568)

Washington

Belpre	(G-1573)
Beverly	(G-1661)
Fleming	(G-9777)
Graysville	(G-10341)
Little Hocking	(G-11988)

	ENTRY #
Lowell	(G-12246)
Lower Salem	(G-12258)
Marietta	(G-12602)
New Matamoras	(G-14745)
Newport	(G-14983)
Reno	(G-16425)
Vincent	(G-19212)
Waterford	(G-19483)
Wingett Run	(G-20536)

Wayne

Apple Creek	(G-601)
Burbank	(G-2353)
Creston	(G-7802)
Dalton	(G-7936)
Doylestown	(G-8864)
Fredericksburg	(G-9943)
Kidron	(G-11446)
Marshallville	(G-12752)
Mount Eaton	(G-14419)
Orrville	(G-15580)
Rittman	(G-16520)
Shreve	(G-17001)
Smithville	(G-17087)
Sterling	(G-17523)
West Salem	(G-19953)
Wooster	(G-20552)

Williams

Alvordton	(G-521)
Blakeslee	(G-1697)
Bryan	(G-2257)
Edgerton	(G-9167)
Edon	(G-9183)
Montpelier	(G-14300)
Pioneer	(G-16083)
Stryker	(G-17827)
West Unity	(G-19967)

Wood

Bowling Green	(G-1943)
Bradner	(G-2012)
Custar	(G-7828)
Dunbridge	(G-9014)
Grand Rapids	(G-10314)
Millbury	(G-14048)
North Baltimore	(G-15042)
Northwood	(G-15330)
Pemberville	(G-15883)
Perrysburg	(G-15915)
Portage	(G-16269)
Risingsun	(G-16519)
Rossford	(G-16583)
Walbridge	(G-19291)
Wayne	(G-19560)
West Millgrove	(G-19946)
Weston	(G-20175)

Wyandot

Carey	(G-2877)
Harpster	(G-10626)
Mc Cutchenville	(G-13191)
Nevada	(G-14601)
Sycamore	(G-17930)
Upper Sandusky	(G-18945)

GEOGRAPHIC SECTION

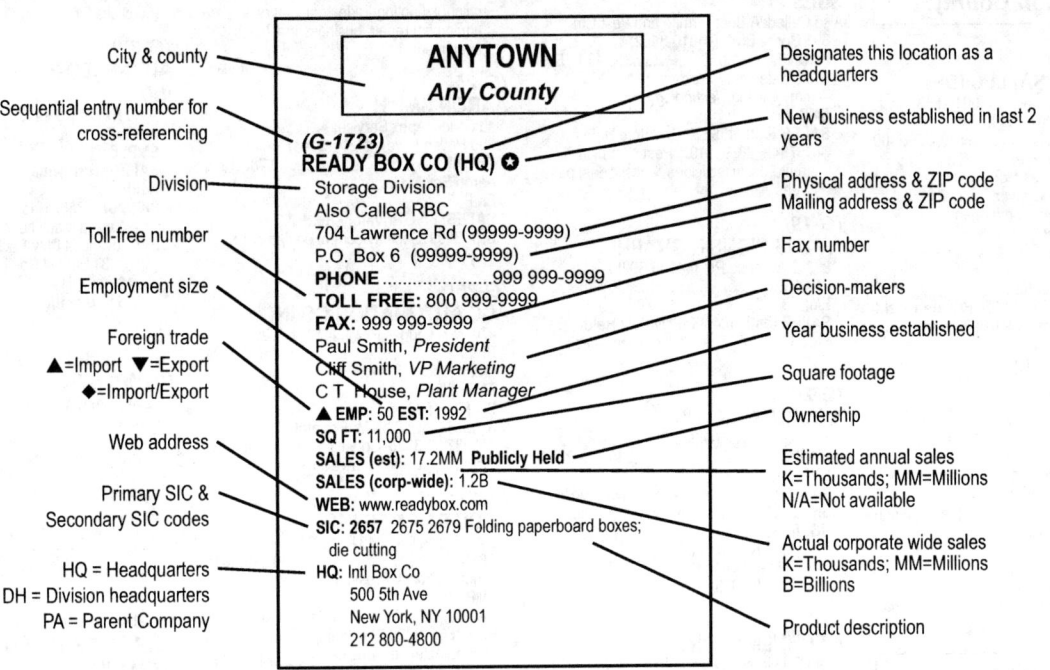

See footnotes for symbols and codes identification.
- This section is in alphabetical order by city.
- Companies are sorted alphabetically under their respective cities.
- To locate cities within a county refer to the County/City Cross Reference Index.

IMPORTANT NOTICE: It is a violation of both federal and state law to transmit an unsolicited advertisement to a facsimile machine. Any user of this product that violates such laws may be subject to civil and criminal penalties which may exceed $500 for each transmission of an unsolicited facsimile. Harris InfoSource provides fax numbers for lawful purposes only and expressly forbids the use of these numbers in any unlawful manner.

Aberdeen
Brown County

(G-1)
HILLTOP BASIC RESOURCES INC
Also Called: Maysville Ready Mix Con Co
8030 Rte 52 Us (45101)
PHONE.....................937 795-2020
John F Steele Jr, CEO
EMP: 10
SALES (corp-wide): 116.7MM Privately Held
SIC: 3273 Ready-mixed concrete
PA: Hilltop Basic Resources, Inc.
  1 W 4th St Ste 1100
  Cincinnati OH 45202
  513 651-5000

Ada
Hardin County

(G-2)
ADA HERALD
229 N Main St (45810-1109)
PHONE.....................419 634-6055
Kevin Wannemacher, Office Mgr
Virginia Bandy, Manager
Ashley Lehman, Relations
EMP: 3 EST: 2013
SALES (est): 133.3K Privately Held
SIC: 2711 Newspapers, publishing & printing

(G-3)
ADA TECHNOLOGIES INC
805 E North Ave (45810-1809)
PHONE.....................419 634-7000
Noriyuki Suzuki, President
Masakatsu Marui, Exec VP
Keith Montgomery, Vice Pres
▲ EMP: 313
SQ FT: 156,000
SALES: 145MM Privately Held
WEB: www.adatechinc.com
SIC: 3714 Motor vehicle transmissions, drive assemblies & parts

(G-4)
AMERICAN METAL SIGN
4750 State Route 309 (45810-9716)
PHONE.....................267 521-2670
Ronald Klesmit, Principal
EMP: 3
SALES (est): 311.5K Privately Held
SIC: 3993 Electric signs

(G-5)
ASSOCIATED PLASTICS CORP
502 Eric Wolber Dr (45810-1100)
PHONE.....................419 634-3910
Fred Wolber, President
Samuel W Diller, Principal
George Wolber, Vice Pres
Carie Rowe, Human Res Mgr
Vickie Wolber, Corp Comm Staff
▲ EMP: 70
SQ FT: 63,000
SALES (est): 15.4MM Privately Held
WEB: www.associatedplastics.com
SIC: 3089 Injection molded finished plastic products; injection molding of plastics

(G-6)
FRONT LINE DEFENSE
2783 Heritage Pl (45810-9483)
PHONE.....................419 516-7992
Charles Seeley, Principal
EMP: 3
SALES (est): 145.3K Privately Held
SIC: 3812 Defense systems & equipment

(G-7)
NASG OHIO LLC
Also Called: North American Stamping Group
605 E Montford Ave (45810-1804)
P.O. Box 265 (45810-0265)
PHONE.....................419 634-3125
Michael Haughey, Mng Member
EMP: 11
SALES (est): 2.4MM
SALES (corp-wide): 198.1MM Privately Held
WEB: www.adastampings.com
SIC: 3465 Automotive stampings
PA: North American Stamping Group, Llc
  119 Kirby Dr
  Portland TN 37148
  615 323-0500

(G-8)
SAY SECURITY GROUP USA LLC (PA)
520 E Montford Ave (45810-1821)
PHONE.....................419 634-0004
Jason Szuch, Mng Member
Bob Szuch,
EMP: 16
SQ FT: 10,000
SALES (est): 1.9MM Privately Held
WEB: www.saysecurity.com
SIC: 7382 3699 Security systems services; security devices

Adamsville
Muskingum County

(G-9)
HARRISON 20 MTD BOREFINERY LLC
Also Called: Harrison Ethanol
9665 Young America Rd (43802-9721)
PHONE.....................740 796-4797
Wendel E Dreve, President
EMP: 4
SALES (est): 200.2K Privately Held
SIC: 2869 Ethyl alcohol, ethanol

(G-10)
SHIRER BROTHERS MEATS
Also Called: Shirer Brothers Slaughter Hse
7805 Adamsville Otsego Rd (43802-9732)
PHONE.....................740 796-3214
Ronald Shirer, Partner
John Shirer, Partner
EMP: 5 EST: 1949
SQ FT: 2,000
SALES (est): 464K Privately Held
SIC: 2011 Beef products from beef slaughtered on site

Addyston - Hamilton County (G-11) — GEOGRAPHIC SECTION

Addyston
Hamilton County

(G-11)
INEOS ABS (USA) LLC (DH)
356 Three Rivers Pkwy (45001-2553)
P.O. Box 39 (45001-0039)
PHONE..................513 467-2400
Clint Herring, *Vice Pres*
Greg Mikut, *Facilities Mgr*
Duane Day, *Senior Buyer*
Bridget McDonagh, *Purch Agent*
Baron Wair, *Buyer*
◆ **EMP:** 203
SQ FT: 372,600
SALES (est): 84.2MM
SALES (corp-wide): 17.9B **Privately Held**
SIC: 2821 Plastics materials & resins
HQ: Ineos Group Ag
  Avenue Des Uttins 3
  Rolle VD
  216 277-040

(G-12)
KIEF SIGNS
3 E Main St (45001-2520)
P.O. Box 458 (45001-0458)
PHONE..................513 941-8800
Olivia Centrulla, *Owner*
EMP: 3
SQ FT: 2,000
SALES: 100K **Privately Held**
SIC: 3993 Signs, not made in custom sign painting shops

Akron
Summit County

(G-13)
21STCENTURY MEDICAL TECH LLC
526 S Main St (44311-4401)
PHONE..................732 310-9367
Arthur Alfaro, *CEO*
EMP: 3
SQ FT: 3,100
SALES (est): 157K **Privately Held**
SIC: 3841 Surgical & medical instruments

(G-14)
360 COMMUNICATIONS LLC
Also Called: Dbd
826 Minota Ave (44306-3420)
P.O. Box 7646 (44306-0646)
PHONE..................330 329-2013
Benita Williams,
EMP: 4
SALES: 100K **Privately Held**
SIC: 2741 Miscellaneous publishing

(G-15)
48 HR BOOKS INC
2249 14th St Sw (44314-2007)
PHONE..................330 374-6917
James Fulton, *President*
Kirby Twigg, *Manager*
▼ **EMP:** 24 **EST:** 2007
SQ FT: 33,000
SALES (est): 2.9MM **Privately Held**
SIC: 2741 Miscellaneous publishing

(G-16)
69 TAPS
374 Paul Williams St (44311)
PHONE..................330 253-4554
Susie Drandel, *Principal*
EMP: 5
SALES (est): 151.5K **Privately Held**
SIC: 2064 Candy bars, including chocolate covered bars

(G-17)
A & P TECH SERVICES INC
856 Home Ave (44310-4119)
PHONE..................330 535-1700
John Pappano, *President*
EMP: 4
SALES: 88K **Privately Held**
SIC: 3421 Knife blades & blanks

(G-18)
A BEST TRMT & PEST CTRL SUPS
Also Called: A-Best Termite and Pest Ctrl
891 Gorge Blvd (44310-3462)
PHONE..................330 434-5555
Todd Anderson, *President*
Tammy Gibson, *Technology*
EMP: 6
SALES (est): 458.5K **Privately Held**
SIC: 7342 2879 5191 Pest control in structures; insecticides & pesticides; pesticides

(G-19)
A PLUS SIGNS & GRAPHIX
833 E Waterloo Rd (44306-3925)
PHONE..................330 848-4800
EMP: 3
SALES (est): 184.9K **Privately Held**
SIC: 3993 Mfg Signs/Advertising Specialties

(G-20)
A SCHULMAN INC
1353 Exeter Rd (44306-3853)
PHONE..................330 773-2700
EMP: 124
SALES (corp-wide): 34.5B **Privately Held**
SIC: 2821 Molding compounds, plastics
HQ: A. Schulman, Inc.
  3637 Ridgewood Rd
  Fairlawn OH 44333
  330 666-3751

(G-21)
A SCHULMAN INC
790 E Tallmadge Ave (44310-3503)
PHONE..................330 630-0308
Derold Hines, *Branch Mgr*
EMP: 202
SQ FT: 104,823
SALES (corp-wide): 34.5B **Privately Held**
WEB: www.aschulman.com
SIC: 2821 Molding compounds, plastics
HQ: A. Schulman, Inc.
  3637 Ridgewood Rd
  Fairlawn OH 44333
  330 666-3751

(G-22)
A SCHULMAN INC
1183 Home Ave (44310-2508)
PHONE..................330 630-3315
Tom McQaide, *Project Mgr*
William Fedak, *Opers Staff*
Kim House, *Office Mgr*
Joe Ocampo, *Branch Mgr*
Tim Angel, *Manager*
EMP: 15
SQ FT: 52,766
SALES (corp-wide): 34.5B **Privately Held**
WEB: www.aschulman.com
SIC: 2821 Molding compounds, plastics
HQ: A. Schulman, Inc.
  3637 Ridgewood Rd
  Fairlawn OH 44333
  330 666-3751

(G-23)
A-A BLUEPRINT CO INC
2757 Gilchrist Rd (44305-4400)
PHONE..................330 794-8803
John Scalia, *President*
Daisy Scalia, *Principal*
Joseph Brown, *Production*
EMP: 32
SQ FT: 30,000
SALES (est): 5.7MM **Privately Held**
WEB: www.aablueprint.com
SIC: 2791 7334 2752 2789 Typesetting; photocopying & duplicating services; commercial printing, offset; bookbinding & related work; letterpress printing

(G-24)
A/C LASER TECHNOLOGIES INC
867 Moe Dr Ste F (44310-2531)
PHONE..................330 784-3355
Jo Ann Wilson, *President*
Gary Berginnis, *Vice Pres*
Frank Wilson, *Treasurer*
EMP: 12
SQ FT: 4,100
SALES: 1.6MM **Privately Held**
WEB: www.aclaser.com
SIC: 3555 7699 5999 Printing trades machinery; printing trades machinery & equipment repair; business machines & equipment

(G-25)
AARON SMITH
Also Called: Apex Services
385 Rutland Ave (44305-3144)
PHONE..................330 285-1360
Aaron Smith, *Owner*
EMP: 3
SALES: 60K **Privately Held**
SIC: 3699 Security control equipment & systems

(G-26)
ACC AUTOMATION CO INC
475 Wolf Ledges Pkwy (44311-1199)
PHONE..................330 928-3821
Frank Rzicznek, *Vice Pres*
EMP: 25
SQ FT: 7,500
SALES (est): 2.3MM **Privately Held**
SIC: 8711 3536 Consulting engineer; cranes, overhead traveling

(G-27)
ACCU PAK MFG INC
2422 Pickle Rd (44312-4227)
PHONE..................330 644-3015
Timothy Probst, *President*
EMP: 3
SALES (est): 220K **Privately Held**
SIC: 3565 3999 Packaging machinery; manufacturing industries

(G-28)
ACE PRECISION INDUSTRIES INC
925 Moe Dr (44310-2518)
PHONE..................330 633-8523
Jerry S Wolf, *CEO*
James S Wolf, *President*
Bill Jobe, *General Mgr*
Sandy A Di Fiore, *Principal*
Jerome S Wolf, *Vice Pres*
▲ **EMP:** 25 **EST:** 1974
SQ FT: 15,000
SALES (est): 5.7MM **Privately Held**
WEB: www.acebearings.com
SIC: 3599 Machine shop, jobbing & repair

(G-29)
ACRO TOOL & DIE COMPANY
Also Called: Landscape & Christmas Tree
325 Morgan Ave (44311-2494)
PHONE..................330 773-5173
T T Thompson, *President*
Steve Wilcox, *Purchasing*
Randy Farnsworth, *QC Mgr*
Terry Ellis, *Technology*
Pamela Perrin, *Admin Sec*
▲ **EMP:** 60
SQ FT: 27,000
SALES (est): 9.1MM **Privately Held**
WEB: www.acrotool.com
SIC: 3544 3469 0781 0811 Special dies & tools; stamping metal for the trade; landscape services; Christmas tree farm; machine tools, metal cutting type; sheet metalwork

(G-30)
ADVANCED COATINGS INTL
2990 Gilchrist Rd # 1100 (44305-4418)
PHONE..................330 794-6361
Steven M Johnson, *President*
▲ **EMP:** 7
SQ FT: 7,000
SALES: 500K **Privately Held**
WEB: www.advancedcoatingsinternational.com
SIC: 3479 Coating electrodes

(G-31)
ADVANCED CRYOGENIC ENTPS LLC
1034 Home Ave (44310-3502)
PHONE..................330 922-0750
David Norton, *Vice Pres*
EMP: 11 **EST:** 2006
SQ FT: 52,000
SALES: 1.2MM **Privately Held**
SIC: 7389 3679 Grinding, precision: commercial or industrial; cryogenic cooling devices for infrared detectors, masers

(G-32)
ADVANCED POLY-PACKAGING INC
1360 Exeter Rd (44306-3860)
PHONE..................330 785-4000
EMP: 6
SALES (corp-wide): 19.6MM **Privately Held**
SIC: 2673 3565 Plastic & pliofilm bags; packaging machinery
PA: Advanced Poly-Packaging Inc.
  1331 Emmitt Rd
  Akron OH 44306
  330 785-4000

(G-33)
AKRON BELTING & SUPPLY COMPANY
1244 Home Ave (44310-2511)
PHONE..................330 633-8212
Joe Mentzer, *President*
Joe Clark, *President*
Mark Brotherton, *Vice Pres*
EMP: 8
SQ FT: 2,500
SALES (est): 2.7MM **Privately Held**
WEB: www.akronbelting.com
SIC: 5085 3496 Hose, belting & packing; conveyor belts

(G-34)
AKRON CENTL ENGRV MOLD MCH INC
1625 Massillon Rd (44312-4204)
PHONE..................330 794-8704
John Kaeberlein, *President*
Bob Simone, *Plant Mgr*
Linda Gibson, *Manager*
Frank Muhl, *Manager*
James Muhl, *Technology*
EMP: 50 **EST:** 1969
SQ FT: 15,000
SALES (est): 10.8MM **Privately Held**
WEB: www.acemm.com
SIC: 3544 8742 4213 Industrial molds; new products & services consultants; automobiles, transport & delivery

(G-35)
AKRON COATING & ADHESIVES INC
365 Stanton Ave (44301-1468)
PHONE..................330 724-4716
John Questel, *President*
Clifford C Questel, *Shareholder*
John C Questel, *Shareholder*
Lynn Questel, *Shareholder*
EMP: 10
SQ FT: 17,000
SALES: 1.8MM **Privately Held**
SIC: 2891 Adhesives & sealants

(G-36)
AKRON COTTON PRODUCTS INC
437 W Cedar St (44307-2321)
PHONE..................330 434-7171
Michael Zwick, *President*
EMP: 9
SQ FT: 26,000
SALES: 700K **Privately Held**
WEB: www.akroncotton.com
SIC: 2211 5999 Scrub cloths; cleaning equipment & supplies

(G-37)
AKRON COUNCIL OF ENGINEERING (PA)
411 Wolf Ledges Pkwy # 105 (44311-1028)
PHONE..................330 535-8835
George Giakos, *President*
EMP: 4
SALES (est): 2.5MM **Privately Held**
SIC: 7379 3826 Computer related consulting services; spectroscopic & other optical properties measuring equipment

▲ = Import ▼ = Export
◆ = Import/Export

GEOGRAPHIC SECTION

Akron - Summit County (G-63)

(G-38)
AKRON ENT HEARING SERVICES INC
Also Called: Akron E N T Associates
395 E Market St (44304-1542)
PHONE..................................330 762-8959
Gigi A Woodruff, *Principal*
Jackie Hamilton, *Principal*
EMP: 3
SALES (est): 349.3K **Privately Held**
SIC: 8049 3842 8011 Audiologist; hearing aids; ears, nose & throat specialist: physician/surgeon

(G-39)
AKRON FELT & CHENILLE MFG CO
1205 George Wash Blvd (44312-3007)
PHONE..................................330 733-7778
Daniel J Fanelly, *President*
Dave Watson, *Sales Staff*
EMP: 10
SQ FT: 7,200
SALES (est): 1MM **Privately Held**
SIC: 2399 2396 5091 Emblems, badges & insignia: from purchased materials; printing & embossing on plastics fabric articles; tip printing & stamping on fabric; sporting & recreation goods

(G-40)
AKRON FOUNDRY CO (PA)
2728 Wingate Ave (44314-1300)
P.O. Box 27028 (44319-7028)
PHONE..................................330 745-3101
George Ostich, *President*
Ronald C Allan, *Principal*
Geraldine Ostich, *Vice Pres*
Michael Ostich, *VP Opers*
John Varga, *Supervisor*
EMP: 175 **EST:** 1969
SQ FT: 100,000
SALES: 22MM **Privately Held**
WEB: www.akronfoundry.com
SIC: 3369 5063 3365 3363 Castings, except die-castings, precision; boxes & fittings, electrical; aluminum foundries; aluminum die-castings

(G-41)
AKRON GEAR & ENGINEERING INC
501 Morgan Ave (44311-2431)
P.O. Box 269 (44309-0269)
PHONE..................................330 773-6608
W Thomas James III, *President*
Carl G James, *Vice Pres*
William Moore, *Vice Pres*
Michael Stohovitch, *VP Mfg*
John A Neuman, *Treasurer*
EMP: 21 **EST:** 1911
SQ FT: 25,000
SALES (est): 5MM
SALES (corp-wide): 549.3MM **Privately Held**
WEB: www.akrongear.com
SIC: 3568 3566 3545 3462 Sprockets (power transmission equipment); gears, power transmission, except automotive; machine tool accessories; iron & steel forgings; gray & ductile iron foundries; machine shop, jobbing & repair
PA: Forge Industries, Inc.
4450 Market St
Youngstown OH 44512
330 782-8301

(G-42)
AKRON LEGAL NEWS INC
60 S Summit St (44308-1775)
PHONE..................................330 296-7578
John L Burleson, *President*
Johm Burleson, *Publisher*
EMP: 12
SQ FT: 4,000
SALES (est): 852.8K **Privately Held**
WEB: www.akronlegalnews.com
SIC: 2711 8111 Newspapers: publishing only, not printed on site; legal services

(G-43)
AKRON LITHO-PRINT COMPANY INC
1026 S Main St (44311-2346)
PHONE..................................330 434-3145
Pete P Ripplinger, *President*
Sharon Ripplinger, *Treasurer*
EMP: 18 **EST:** 1935
SQ FT: 5,500
SALES: 1.6MM **Privately Held**
WEB: www.lithoprintco.com
SIC: 2752 2759 Lithographing on metal; commercial printing, offset; letterpress printing

(G-44)
AKRON METAL ETCHING CO
463 Locust St (44307-2592)
PHONE..................................330 762-7687
Lee Eisinger, *President*
Debbie Eisinger, *Corp Secy*
EMP: 5 **EST:** 1961
SQ FT: 10,000
SALES (est): 400K **Privately Held**
WEB: www.textureame.com
SIC: 3479 Etching on metals

(G-45)
AKRON ORTHOTIC SOLUTIONS INC
582 W Market St (44303-1839)
PHONE..................................330 253-3002
Robert McInturff, *President*
EMP: 8
SALES (est): 820.4K **Privately Held**
SIC: 3842 5999 Braces, orthopedic; orthopedic & prosthesis applications

(G-46)
AKRON PAINT & VARNISH INC
Also Called: APV Engineered Coatings
1390 Firestone Pkwy (44301-1695)
PHONE..................................330 773-8911
Dave Venarge, *President*
Ed Apsega, *Vice Pres*
Mike Summers, *Vice Pres*
Eric Rumley, *Inv Control Mgr*
Cathy Kirk, *Accounting Mgr*
◆ **EMP:** 90
SQ FT: 160,000
SALES (est): 34.6MM **Privately Held**
WEB: www.apvcoatings.com
SIC: 2851 2891 3953 Paints & paint additives; lacquers, varnishes, enamels & other coatings; adhesives & sealants; adhesives; marking devices

(G-47)
AKRON PLATING CO INC
1774 Hackberry St (44301-2493)
PHONE..................................330 773-6878
Robert Ormsby Jr, *President*
Fred Beidle, *Vice Pres*
Jennifer Ormsby, *Admin Sec*
EMP: 10 **EST:** 1948
SQ FT: 7,500
SALES (est): 1.3MM **Privately Held**
WEB: www.akronplating.com
SIC: 3471 Electroplating of metals or formed products

(G-48)
AKRON POLYMER PRODUCTS INC (PA)
571 Kennedy Rd (44305-4425)
PHONE..................................330 628-5551
Greg C Anderson, *President*
Kevin Gandee, *Vice Pres*
Jon Callander, *Controller*
▲ **EMP:** 68
SQ FT: 18,000
SALES: 13MM **Privately Held**
WEB: www.akronpolymer.com
SIC: 3089 3082 Extruded finished plastic products; tubes, unsupported plastic

(G-49)
AKRON PORCELAIN & PLASTICS CO (PA)
Also Called: Akron Porcelain & Plastic Co
2739 Cory Ave (44314-1308)
P.O. Box 15157 (44314-5157)
PHONE..................................330 745-2159
George H Lewis Jr, *Ch of Bd*
Larry Mathias, *Purchasing*
Michael B Dunphy, *Treasurer*
Jeff Combs, *Sales Engr*
Mike Gaume, *Manager*
▲ **EMP:** 140 **EST:** 1890
SQ FT: 120,000
SALES (est): 21.1MM **Privately Held**
WEB: www.akronporcelain.com
SIC: 3089 3264 Injection molded finished plastic products; porcelain electrical supplies

(G-50)
AKRON REBAR CO (PA)
Also Called: Cleveland Rebar
809 W Waterloo Rd (44314-1527)
P.O. Box 3710 (44314-0710)
PHONE..................................330 745-7100
Michael Humphrey II, *CEO*
Denise Moore, *Draft/Design*
John Tekus, *Engineer*
▲ **EMP:** 32
SQ FT: 32,600
SALES (est): 10.1MM **Privately Held**
WEB: www.akronrebar.com
SIC: 3441 3449 Fabricated structural metal; bars, concrete reinforcing: fabricated steel

(G-51)
AKRON SPECIAL MACHINERY INC (PA)
Also Called: Poling Group, The
2740 Cory Ave (44314-1396)
PHONE..................................330 753-1077
David Poling Sr, *President*
Mike Ward, *Purch Mgr*
Mike Haines, *Engineer*
Larry Swonger, *Design Engr*
Matt Blubaugh, *Electrical Engi*
▼ **EMP:** 50
SQ FT: 60,000
SALES (est): 12.9MM **Privately Held**
WEB: www.akronspecial.com
SIC: 3599 Machine shop, jobbing & repair; custom machinery

(G-52)
AKRON SPECIALIZED PRODUCTS (PA)
96 E Miller Ave (44301-1325)
PHONE..................................330 762-9269
Marilyn L Tuzzio, *President*
EMP: 5
SALES (est): 1.3MM **Privately Held**
SIC: 3542 Machine tools, metal forming type

(G-53)
AKRON STEEL TREATING CO
336 Morgan Ave (44311-2424)
P.O. Box 2290 (44309-2290)
PHONE..................................330 773-8211
Christopher Powell, *CEO*
Joseph A Powell, *President*
Jim Stewart, *Vice Pres*
Matt Moldvay, *Sales Associate*
Rick Miller, *Director*
EMP: 45 **EST:** 1943
SQ FT: 46,000
SALES (est): 10.2MM **Privately Held**
SIC: 3398 3479 Metal heat treating; painting, coating & hot dipping

(G-54)
AKRON THERMOGRAPHY INC
Also Called: BCT
3406 Fortuna Dr (44312)
PHONE..................................330 896-9712
Randal S Teague, *President*
Lisa R Teague, *Corp Secy*
EMP: 30
SALES (est): 5.4MM **Privately Held**
SIC: 2752 Commercial printing, offset

(G-55)
AKRON VAULT COMPANY INC
Also Called: Akron Crematory
2399 Gilchrist Rd (44305-4496)
PHONE..................................330 784-5475
Marty Ebie, *President*
Phil Kauffman, *Admin Sec*
EMP: 12 **EST:** 1944
SQ FT: 11,000
SALES: 1.1MM **Privately Held**
SIC: 3272 Burial vaults, concrete or pre-cast terrazzo

(G-56)
ALCO-CHEM INC (PA)
45 N Summit St (44308-1933)
PHONE..................................330 253-3535
Anthony Mandala Jr, *President*
Bart Mandala, *Vice Pres*
Robert Mandala, *Vice Pres*
▲ **EMP:** 34
SQ FT: 22,000
SALES (est): 26.7MM **Privately Held**
WEB: www.alco-chem.com
SIC: 5087 2869 2842 Janitors' supplies; industrial organic chemicals; specialty cleaning, polishes & sanitation goods

(G-57)
ALCON TOOL COMPANY
565 Lafollette St (44311-1824)
PHONE..................................330 773-9171
Charles E Conner, *CEO*
Charles F Rankin, *President*
Jared Adams, *Plant Mgr*
Ed Smith, *Traffic Mgr*
Daniel Debellis, *Engineer*
▼ **EMP:** 65 **EST:** 1946
SQ FT: 100,000
SALES (est): 13.7MM **Privately Held**
WEB: www.alcontool.com
SIC: 3541 Machine tools, metal cutting type

(G-58)
ALL-TECH MANUFACTURING LTD
1477 Industrial Pkwy (44310-2601)
PHONE..................................330 633-1095
Joseph Manijak, *Mng Member*
Frank Manijak, *Mng Member*
EMP: 40
SQ FT: 9,000
SALES (est): 6.2MM **Privately Held**
WEB: www.alltechmanufacturing.com
SIC: 3599 Machine shop, jobbing & repair

(G-59)
ALLEN RANDALL ENTERPRISES INC
70 E Miller Ave (44301-1324)
P.O. Box 1117 (44309-1117)
PHONE..................................330 374-9850
Jim Bradshaw, *President*
EMP: 10
SQ FT: 12,500
SALES (est): 750K **Privately Held**
WEB: www.allenrandall.com
SIC: 3599 Machine shop, jobbing & repair

(G-60)
ALLIANCE FORGING GROUP LLC
847 Pier Dr 1000 (44307-2267)
PHONE..................................330 680-4861
David Risher, *Mng Member*
Alissa Bryan,
EMP: 6
SQ FT: 100,000
SALES (est): 1.1MM **Privately Held**
SIC: 3462 Ornamental metal forgings, ferrous

(G-61)
AMERICAN EXECUTIVE GIFTS INC
2098 Sypher Rd Unit C (44306-4291)
P.O. Box 1524 (44309-1524)
PHONE..................................330 645-4396
Robert R Weber, *President*
EMP: 10
SQ FT: 4,000
SALES (est): 953.5K **Privately Held**
WEB: www.aegawards.com
SIC: 3993 Advertising novelties

(G-62)
AMERICAN MADE BAGS LLC
999 Sweitzer Ave (44311-2359)
PHONE..................................330 475-1385
Thomas Armour, *President*
EMP: 19
SALES (est): 241.9K **Privately Held**
SIC: 2393 Canvas bags

(G-63)
AMERICAN ORGINAL BLDG PDTS LLC
1000 Arlington Cir (44306-3973)
PHONE..................................330 786-3000
Edward West, *Controller*
Dale V Wilson, *Mng Member*

Akron - Summit County (G-64) GEOGRAPHIC SECTION

Gordon F Keeler Jr, *Mng Member*
James Neary, *Manager*
EMP: 15
SALES (est): 3MM **Privately Held**
SIC: 2952 Siding materials

(G-64)
AMERICAN PRINTING INC
1121 Tower Dr (44305-1089)
PHONE.................................330 630-1121
David Hall, *President*
Steve Spinell, *Accounts Exec*
Kim Krietz, *Admin Sec*
EMP: 10 **EST:** 1928
SQ FT: 15,000
SALES (est): 1.6MM **Privately Held**
WEB: www.americanprinting.com
SIC: 2752 Commercial printing, offset

(G-65)
AMERICAN UTILITY PROC LLC
1246 Princeton St (44301-1168)
PHONE.................................330 535-3000
Richard K Kmiecik, *Mng Member*
EMP: 34
SQ FT: 60,000
SALES (est): 4.1MM **Privately Held**
WEB: www.americanutilityprocessing.com
SIC: 3479 Coating of metals & formed products

(G-66)
AMYS BEAUTY JAMS LLC
2149 Briar Club Trl (44313-8145)
PHONE.................................330 869-8317
Amy Campbell, *Principal*
EMP: 3
SALES (est): 133K **Privately Held**
SIC: 2033 Jams, jellies & preserves: packaged in cans, jars, etc.

(G-67)
APPLE SEED LLC
305 High Grove Blvd (44312-2619)
PHONE.................................330 606-1776
Gina Gaskins, *Principal*
EMP: 5
SALES (est): 455.6K **Privately Held**
SIC: 3571 Mfg Electronic Computers

(G-68)
APTO ORTHOPAEDICS CORPORATION
47 N Main St (44308-1971)
PHONE.................................330 572-7544
John Zak, *General Mgr*
Stephen D Fening, *CTO*
Thomas Olmstead, *Director*
Ritzman M D, *Director*
Steve Fening, *Director*
EMP: 28
SQ FT: 500
SALES (est): 1.3MM **Privately Held**
SIC: 3841 Surgical & medical instruments

(G-69)
ARCHITCTRAL RFUSE SLUTIONS LLC
525 Kennedy Rd (44305-4425)
PHONE.................................330 733-3996
Michael Ennis, *CEO*
EMP: 4
SALES: 350K **Privately Held**
WEB: www.ars-llc.net
SIC: 3449 Miscellaneous metalwork

(G-70)
ARNOLDS CANDIES INC
931 High Grove Blvd (44312-3499)
PHONE.................................330 733-4022
Ted Arnold, *President*
EMP: 6
SALES (est): 40.5K **Privately Held**
SIC: 2064 Lollipops & other hard candy

(G-71)
ASH SEWER & DRAIN SERVICE
451 E North St (44304-1217)
PHONE.................................330 376-9714
Greg Ash, *Owner*
EMP: 6
SALES (est): 577.5K **Privately Held**
SIC: 3272 4959 Sewer pipe, concrete; sanitary services

(G-72)
ASTER INDUSTRIES INC
275 N Arlington St Ste B (44305-1600)
PHONE.................................330 762-7965
Kimberly Oplinger, *President*
Michael J Oplinger, *Principal*
EMP: 15
SQ FT: 14,500
SALES (est): 3.5MM **Privately Held**
WEB: www.asterind.com
SIC: 2599 3999 Bar, restaurant & cafeteria furniture; advertising display products

(G-73)
AURIS NOBLE LLC
130 E Voris St Ste C (44311-1536)
PHONE.................................330 685-3748
Lou Britton, *Manager*
EMP: 7
SQ FT: 12,000
SALES (corp-wide): 1.5MM **Privately Held**
SIC: 3341 Secondary precious metals; platinum group metals, smelting & refining (secondary); silver smelting & refining (secondary); iridium smelting & refining (secondary)
PA: Auris Noble, Llc
   3045 Smith Rd Ste 700
   Fairlawn OH 44333
   330 321-6649

(G-74)
AUTO DEALER DESIGNS INC
303 W Bartges St (44307-2205)
PHONE.................................330 374-7666
John Volpe, *CEO*
David Volpe, *President*
Paul Volpe, *Vice Pres*
Marilyn Volpe, *Treasurer*
Paula Volpe, *Admin Sec*
EMP: 22
SQ FT: 16,152
SALES (est): 2.6MM **Privately Held**
WEB: www.licenseframes.com
SIC: 3993 5199 Signs & advertising specialties; advertising specialties

(G-75)
AXIS TOOL & GRINDING LLC
895 Home Ave (44310-4115)
P.O. Box 10054 (44310-0054)
PHONE.................................330 535-4713
Thomas Burrilo, *President*
EMP: 5 **EST:** 2001
SALES (est): 478.9K **Privately Held**
SIC: 3599 Grinding castings for the trade

(G-76)
B RICHARDSON INC
Also Called: Talk of Town Silkscreen & EMB
25 Elinor Ave (44305-4005)
PHONE.................................330 724-2122
Becky Waidmann, *President*
Herb Waidmann, *Treasurer*
EMP: 18
SQ FT: 5,000
SALES (est): 1.5MM **Privately Held**
SIC: 2262 7299 Screen printing: man-made fiber & silk broadwoven fabrics; stitching, custom

(G-77)
B W T INC
353 E Cuyahoga Falls Ave (44310-2251)
PHONE.................................330 928-9107
EMP: 3
SALES (est): 270K **Privately Held**
SIC: 3691 5063 5531 5734 Mfg Storage Batteries Whol Electrical Equip Ret Auto/Home Supplies Ret Computers/Software

(G-78)
BAKER MEDIA GROUP LLC
Also Called: Akron Life
1653 Merriman Rd Ste 116 (44313-5293)
PHONE.................................330 253-0056
Don Baker Jr, *Mng Member*
EMP: 11 **EST:** 2004
SQ FT: 3,000
SALES (est): 1.2MM **Privately Held**
SIC: 2721 Magazines: publishing only, not printed on site

(G-79)
BANSAL ENTERPRISES INC
Also Called: Ink Well
1538 Home Ave (44310-1601)
PHONE.................................330 633-9355
Usha Bansal, *President*
EMP: 10
SQ FT: 3,750
SALES (est): 1.3MM **Privately Held**
SIC: 2752 7389 Commercial printing, offset; advertising, promotional & trade show services

(G-80)
BARNETT SPOUTING INC
Also Called: Barney Schoolers
204 E Ralston Ave (44301-2974)
PHONE.................................330 644-0853
Lynn Barnett, *President*
Mary Barnett, *Vice Pres*
EMP: 5
SALES (est): 350K **Privately Held**
SIC: 1761 3949 Gutter & downspout contractor; fishing tackle, general

(G-81)
BAXTERS LLC
1259 Ashford Ln (44313-6870)
PHONE.................................234 678-5484
Jerry Mallo, *Principal*
EMP: 3
SALES (est): 264.2K **Privately Held**
SIC: 2834 Pharmaceutical preparations

(G-82)
BEAVER PRODUCTIONS
2251 Cooledge Ave (44305-2162)
PHONE.................................330 352-4603
Joshua Beaver, *Principal*
EMP: 4
SALES (est): 283K **Privately Held**
SIC: 2741 Guides: publishing & printing

(G-83)
BEMIS COMPANY INC
Also Called: Bemis North America
1972 Akron Peninsula Rd (44313-4810)
PHONE.................................330 923-5281
Tom Hudson, *Branch Mgr*
Mike Hines, *Supervisor*
Jo Ellen Zilko, *Web Proj Mgr*
EMP: 20
SALES (corp-wide): 4B **Publicly Held**
SIC: 2752 5199 2759 2672 Commercial printing, lithographic; packaging materials; commercial printing; coated & laminated paper
PA: Bemis Company, Inc.
   2301 Industrial Dr
   Neenah WI 54956
   920 527-5000

(G-84)
BERINGER PLATING INC
1211 Devalera St (44310-2488)
PHONE.................................330 633-8409
James Beringer Jr, *President*
Laura Beringer, *Admin Sec*
Bruce Hogie, *Maintence Staff*
EMP: 8 **EST:** 1953
SQ FT: 21,000
SALES (est): 1.1MM **Privately Held**
WEB: www.beringerplatinginc.com
SIC: 3471 8711 Electroplating of metals or formed products; engineering services

(G-85)
BERRAN INDUSTRIAL GROUP INC
570 Wolf Ledges Pkwy (44311-1022)
PHONE.................................330 253-5800
Randy P Adair, *President*
Don Schultz, *Corp Secy*
EMP: 26
SQ FT: 18,000
SALES (est): 6.1MM **Privately Held**
WEB: www.berran.com
SIC: 3599 3441 3549 3444 Custom machinery; fabricated structural metal; metalworking machinery; sheet metalwork

(G-86)
BEST MOLD & MANUFACTURING INC
1546 E Turkeyfoot Lake Rd (44312-5350)
P.O. Box 544, Uniontown (44685-0544)
PHONE.................................330 896-9988
Dave Miller, *President*
EMP: 45
SQ FT: 26,000
SALES (est): 8.6MM **Privately Held**
WEB: www.bestmmi.com
SIC: 3599 Machine shop, jobbing & repair

(G-87)
BESTEN EQUIPMENT INC
388 S Main St Ste 700 (44311-1060)
PHONE.................................216 581-1166
Lynn Bisantz, *Principal*
EMP: 30
SALES (est): 2.7MM **Publicly Held**
WEB: www.quanex.com
SIC: 2891 Sealants
PA: Quanex Building Products Corporation
   1800 West Loop S Ste 1500
   Houston TX 77027

(G-88)
BIF CO LLC
Also Called: Bif, LLC
1405 Home Ave (44310-2514)
PHONE.................................330 564-0941
Mark Schoenbaechler, *President*
EMP: 10
SQ FT: 150,000
SALES (est): 1.5MM
SALES (corp-wide): 15.2MM **Privately Held**
SIC: 3824 Impeller & counter driven flow meters
PA: Logan Machine Company
   1405 Home Ave
   Akron OH 44310
   330 633-6163

(G-89)
BNOAT ONCOLOGY
411 Wolf Ledges Pkwy (44311-1028)
PHONE.................................330 285-2537
Joseph A Bauer PHD, *Principal*
EMP: 6
SALES (est): 473.1K **Privately Held**
SIC: 2834 Pharmaceutical preparations

(G-90)
BOB KING SIGN COMPANY INC
Also Called: Abl Lighting Service
1631 East Ave (44314-2645)
PHONE.................................330 753-2679
Kenneth King, *President*
EMP: 3
SQ FT: 2,800
SALES (est): 350.5K **Privately Held**
WEB: www.bobkingsigns.com
SIC: 3993 2759 7374 1799 Signs & advertising specialties; screen printing; computer graphics service; sign installation & maintenance

(G-91)
BODYVEGA NUTRITION LLC
3493 Torrey Pines Dr (44333-9273)
PHONE.................................708 712-5743
Ryan Daniel Moran, *Administration*
EMP: 5
SALES (est): 108.9K **Privately Held**
SIC: 2834 Pharmaceutical preparations

(G-92)
BOGIE INDUSTRIES INC LTD
Also Called: Weaver Fab & Finishing
1100 Home Ave (44310-3504)
PHONE.................................330 745-3105
Jim Lauer, *President*
Marian Lauer, *Owner*
Fuzzy Helton, *Vice Pres*
Anthony Tarulli, *Purch Agent*
EMP: 38 **EST:** 1998
SQ FT: 40,000
SALES (est): 10.7MM **Privately Held**
WEB: www.weaverfab.com
SIC: 3444 1799 3399 Sheet metalwork; coating of metal structures at construction site; powder, metal

▲ = Import ▼=Export
◆ =Import/Export

GEOGRAPHIC SECTION
Akron - Summit County (G-121)

(G-93)
BONNOT COMPANY
1301 Home Ave (44310-2654)
PHONE..................................330 896-6544
George W Bain, *President*
John Negrelli, *Vice Pres*
▼ **EMP:** 25
SQ FT: 40,000
SALES (est): 4.5MM **Privately Held**
WEB: www.thebonnotco.com
SIC: 3599 Custom machinery

(G-94)
BRIDGESTONE AMERICAS CENTER FO
1659 S Main St (44301-2035)
PHONE..................................330 379-7575
EMP: 9 **EST:** 2016
SALES (est): 1MM **Privately Held**
SIC: 2822 Automotive tires

(G-95)
BRIDGESTONE PROCUREMENT HOLDIN (HQ)
381 W Wilbeth Rd (44301-2465)
P.O. Box 26611 (44319-6611)
PHONE..................................337 882-1200
Gene Lavengco, *CEO*
Yuji Mochizuki, *Ch of Bd*
Tinus Grobbrlaar, *CFO*
Paul Huth, *Finance*
Greg Defrates, *Officer*
EMP: 594
SALES (est): 190.1MM
SALES (corp-wide): 32.4B **Privately Held**
SIC: 2822 Synthetic rubber
PA: Bridgestone Corporation
  3-1-1, Kyobashi
  Chuo-Ku TKY 104-0
  368 363-001

(G-96)
BRIGHTEYE INNOVATIONS LLC
1760 Wadsworth Rd (44320-3142)
PHONE..................................800 573-0052
Josh Lefkovitz, *President*
Mark Jenkins, *Manager*
EMP: 15
SQ FT: 35,000
SALES: 14MM **Privately Held**
SIC: 5023 3089 Kitchenware; kitchenware, plastic

(G-97)
BUCKEYE POST
1266 Grant St (44301-1847)
PHONE..................................330 724-2800
EMP: 3
SALES (est): 143.8K **Privately Held**
SIC: 2711 Newspapers-Publishing/Printing

(G-98)
BURGHARDT MANUFACTURING INC
1524 Massillon Rd (44306-4162)
PHONE..................................330 253-7590
Adam Burghardt, *President*
EMP: 9
SQ FT: 8,000
SALES (est): 1.8MM **Privately Held**
SIC: 3441 Fabricated structural metal for bridges

(G-99)
BURGHARDT METAL FABG INC
1638 Mcchesney Rd (44306-4396)
PHONE..................................330 794-1830
Craig Shuster, *President*
Cindy Archer, *Corp Secy*
EMP: 18 **EST:** 1958
SQ FT: 22,000
SALES (est): 5.4MM **Privately Held**
WEB: www.burgmetalfab.com
SIC: 3449 3441 Miscellaneous metalwork; fabricated structural metal

(G-100)
BURT MANUFACTURING COMPANY INC
Also Called: Thycurb
44 E South St (44311-2031)
PHONE..................................330 762-0061
Marvin Ricklefs, *CEO*
EMP: 210
SQ FT: 120,000
SALES (est): 14.4MM
SALES (corp-wide): 37.4MM **Privately Held**
WEB: www.thybar.com
SIC: 3564 3442 3444 Blowers & fans; metal doors, sash & trim; ventilators, sheet metal
PA: Thybar Corporation
  913 S Kay Ave
  Addison IL 60101
  630 543-5300

(G-101)
C E D PROCESS MINERALS INC (PA)
863 N Clvland Mssillon Rd (44333-2167)
PHONE..................................330 666-5500
Leland D Cole, *Vice Pres*
Nolan E Douglas, *Treasurer*
Steven Fannin, *Software Dev*
William M Douglas, *Admin Sec*
▼ **EMP:** 18
SQ FT: 2,368
SALES (est): 3.8MM **Privately Held**
WEB: www.colelpa.com
SIC: 1446 Foundry sand mining

(G-102)
CALIBER MOLD AND MACHINE INC
1461 Industrial Pkwy (44310-2601)
PHONE..................................330 633-8171
Jack Thornton, *President*
Thomas Thornton, *Vice Pres*
EMP: 40
SQ FT: 12,000
SALES (est): 6.1MM **Privately Held**
WEB: www.caliber.tiremolds.com
SIC: 3544 Industrial molds

(G-103)
CARDINAL PRINTING INC
112 W Wilbeth Rd (44301-2415)
P.O. Box 678, Green (44232-0678)
PHONE..................................330 773-7300
Vince Rosnack, *President*
Pam Rosnack, *Corp Secy*
EMP: 8
SQ FT: 6,700
SALES (est): 953.2K **Privately Held**
WEB: www.electjesus.com
SIC: 2752 Commercial printing, offset

(G-104)
CARGILL INCORPORATED
2065 Manchester Rd (44314-1770)
PHONE..................................330 745-0031
Wayne A Brown, *Manager*
EMP: 151
SALES (corp-wide): 114.7B **Privately Held**
WEB: www.cargill.com
SIC: 2048 Prepared feeds
PA: Cargill, Incorporated
  15407 Mcginty Rd W
  Wayzata MN 55391
  952 742-7575

(G-105)
CCM WELDING INC
895 Moe Dr Ste D11 (44310-2592)
PHONE..................................330 630-2521
Charles Balogh, *President*
EMP: 4
SQ FT: 4,000
SALES (est): 653.3K **Privately Held**
SIC: 3441 Fabricated structural metal

(G-106)
CCSI INC
221 Beaver St (44304-1909)
PHONE..................................800 742-8535
Frank Orlando, *Vice Pres*
EMP: 9 **EST:** 2013
SALES (est): 1.2MM **Privately Held**
SIC: 3953 Textile marking stamps, hand: rubber or metal

(G-107)
CEC ELECTRONICS CORP
1739 Akron Peninsula Rd (44313-5157)
P.O. Box 354567, Palm Coast FL (32135-4567)
PHONE..................................330 916-8100
Dan Lujan, *President*
Leslie Taylor, *Buyer*
EMP: 7
SQ FT: 3,000
SALES (est): 2.5MM **Privately Held**
WEB: www.cecelectronics.com
SIC: 3679 Electronic circuits

(G-108)
CECIL C PECK CO
1029 Arlington Cir (44306-3959)
PHONE..................................330 785-0781
Paul Stewart, *President*
▲ **EMP:** 10 **EST:** 1945
SQ FT: 8,350
SALES (est): 1.2MM **Privately Held**
WEB: www.cecilpeck.com
SIC: 3699 8711 Welding machines & equipment, ultrasonic; designing: ship, boat, machine & product

(G-109)
CENTER AUTOMOTIVE PARTS CO
274 E South St (44311-2162)
PHONE..................................330 434-2174
Randall Allen, *President*
EMP: 4
SALES: 1.3MM **Privately Held**
WEB: www.centerautomachine.com
SIC: 5531 3599 Automotive parts; machine shop, jobbing & repair

(G-110)
CENTRAL COCA-COLA BTLG CO INC
1560 Triplett Blvd (44306-3306)
PHONE..................................330 875-1487
EMP: 4
SALES (corp-wide): 35.4B **Publicly Held**
SIC: 5149 2086 8741 Soft drinks; soft drinks: packaged in cans, bottles, etc.; management services
HQ: Central Coca-Cola Bottling Company, Inc.
  555 Taxter Rd Ste 550
  Elmsford NY 10523
  914 789-1100

(G-111)
CHARLES AUTO ELECTRIC CO INC
600 Grant St (44311-1502)
PHONE..................................330 535-6269
Daniel Ardelean, *President*
Erik S Ardelean, *Vice Pres*
Mary Ardelean, *Treasurer*
EMP: 8
SQ FT: 8,000
SALES (est): 1.2MM **Privately Held**
WEB: www.charlesautoelectric.com
SIC: 3694 3621 Generators, automotive & aircraft; alternators, automotive; starters, for motors

(G-112)
CHARLES COSTA INC
Also Called: Costa Machine
924 Home Ave (44310-4108)
PHONE..................................330 376-3636
George Marino, *President*
Carl Prentiss, *Vice Pres*
EMP: 11 **EST:** 1972
SQ FT: 10,000
SALES: 1MM **Privately Held**
WEB: www.costamachine.com
SIC: 3599 Machine shop, jobbing & repair

(G-113)
CHEMIGON LLC
520 S Main St Ste 2519 (44311-1073)
PHONE..................................330 592-1875
Oliver Stahl, *Managing Prtnr*
Ann Marie Yoder, *Managing Prtnr*
EMP: 3 **EST:** 2014
SQ FT: 250
SALES: 135K **Privately Held**
SIC: 3089 8742 Plastic processing; sales (including sales management) consultant

(G-114)
CHESTNUT HOLDINGS INC (PA)
670 W Market St (44303-1448)
PHONE..................................330 849-6503
James P McCready, *Ch of Bd*
▲ **EMP:** 2
SQ FT: 12,000
SALES (est): 148.9MM **Privately Held**
SIC: 3053 5014 5013 3714 Gaskets, all materials; tires & tubes; wheels, motor vehicle; mufflers (exhaust), motor vehicle; exhaust systems & parts, motor vehicle

(G-115)
CHRISTINA A KRAFT PHD
75 Arch St Ste 410 (44304-1433)
PHONE..................................330 375-7474
Christina A Kraft, *Principal*
EMP: 3
SALES (est): 72.3K **Privately Held**
SIC: 2022 Mfg Cheese

(G-116)
CHROME DEPOSIT CORPORATIO
1566 Firestone Pkwy (44301-1626)
PHONE..................................330 773-7800
EMP: 7
SALES (est): 792K **Privately Held**
SIC: 3471 Plating & polishing

(G-117)
CHUTE SOURCE LLC
525 Kennedy Rd (44305-4425)
PHONE..................................330 475-0377
Nello Decarli, *Mng Member*
Claudio Decarli,
EMP: 15
SQ FT: 13,000
SALES (est): 2.5MM **Privately Held**
SIC: 3443 3444 Chutes & troughs; sheet metalwork

(G-118)
CITY SCRAP & SALVAGE CO
760 Flora Ave (44314-1755)
PHONE..................................330 753-5051
Steven Katz, *CEO*
Randy Katz, *Vice Pres*
EMP: 31
SQ FT: 10,000
SALES (est): 7.7MM
SALES (corp-wide): 1.3B **Publicly Held**
SIC: 5093 3341 Ferrous metal scrap & waste; nonferrous metals scrap; secondary nonferrous metals
HQ: Tsb Metal Recycling Llc
  1835 Dueber Ave Sw
  Canton OH 44706

(G-119)
CLASSIC COUNTERTOPS LLC
1519 Kenmore Blvd (44314-1661)
PHONE..................................330 882-4220
William Blackert,
Seth Wilkerson,
EMP: 6
SQ FT: 4,700
SALES (est): 758.3K **Privately Held**
SIC: 3131 1799 Counters; counter top installation

(G-120)
CONSOLIDATED PATTERN WORKS INC
754 E Glenwood Ave (44310-3452)
PHONE..................................330 434-6060
James Housley, *President*
Patricia Housley, *Admin Sec*
EMP: 4 **EST:** 1966
SQ FT: 4,000
SALES: 500K **Privately Held**
WEB: www.consolidatedpatternworksinc.com
SIC: 3999 3543 Models, except toy; industrial patterns

(G-121)
CONTI TOOL & DIE INC
1333 Devalera St (44310-2453)
PHONE..................................330 633-1414
Donald L Conti, *President*
Mary Conti, *Corp Secy*
EMP: 5 **EST:** 1961
SQ FT: 4,000
SALES (est): 747.1K **Privately Held**
WEB: www.contitool.com
SIC: 3544 Special dies & tools; jigs: inspection, gauging & checking; jigs & fixtures

Akron - Summit County (G-122)

(G-122)
COS BLUEPRINT INC (PA)
590 N Main St (44310-3145)
PHONE.....................330 376-0022
Jim Scalia, *President*
Linda Scalia, *Corp Secy*
Martin Hyatt, *Vice Pres*
EMP: 13
SQ FT: 12,000
SALES (est): 1.5MM **Privately Held**
SIC: 2752 5999 5712 5943 Commercial printing, offset; typewriters & business machines; drafting equipment & supplies; office furniture; office forms & supplies; typesetting; bookbinding & related work

(G-123)
COUNTRY PURE FOODS INC (DH)
222 W Main St Ste 401 (44308)
PHONE.....................330 848-6875
Kenny Sadai, *Ch of Bd*
James O'Toole, *President*
Randy Peck, *Prdtn Mgr*
Kofi Frimpong, *Production*
Danelle Ayotte, *QC Mgr*
◆ **EMP:** 120
SALES (est): 262.5MM
SALES (corp-wide): 4.6B **Privately Held**
WEB: www.countrypurefoods.com
SIC: 2033 2037 2086 Fruit juices: fresh; fruit juice concentrates, frozen; fruit drinks (less than 100% juice): packaged in cans, etc.

(G-124)
COUNTY OF SUMMIT
Also Called: FA Siberling Naturelm Mtro Prk
1828 Smith Rd (44313-5012)
PHONE.....................330 865-8065
Keith Shy, *Director*
EMP: 9 **Privately Held**
WEB: www.cpcourt.summitoh.net
SIC: 2531 9111 Picnic tables or benches, park; county supervisors' & executives' offices
PA: County Of Summit
650 Dan St
Akron OH 44310
330 643-2500

(G-125)
CRAIN COMMUNICATIONS INC
Also Called: Rubber & Plastics News
1725 Merriman Rd Ste 300 (44313-5283)
PHONE.....................330 836-9180
Robert S Simmons, *Vice Pres*
Christine Zernick, *Sales Mgr*
Sarah Arnold, *Marketing Staff*
EMP: 90
SALES (corp-wide): 225MM **Privately Held**
WEB: www.crainsnewyork.com
SIC: 2711 2721 7389 Newspapers: publishing only, not printed on site; periodicals; advertising, promotional & trade show services
PA: Crain Communications, Inc.
1155 Gratiot Ave
Detroit MI 48207
313 446-6000

(G-126)
CTO INC
Also Called: Surface Systems
2035 S Main St (44301-2818)
PHONE.....................330 785-1130
Tom Gutshall, *President*
EMP: 5
SQ FT: 4,000
SALES: 708.9K **Privately Held**
WEB: www.diversifiedcoatings.com
SIC: 3479 5198 Enameling, including porcelain, of metal products; paints, varnishes & supplies

(G-127)
CUSTOM APPAREL LLC
1180 Brittain Rd (44305-1034)
PHONE.....................330 633-2626
Larry Yaco,
EMP: 6
SQ FT: 3,500
SALES (est): 538.1K **Privately Held**
SIC: 2759 Screen printing

(G-128)
CUSTOM CRAFT CONTROLS INC
1620 Triplett Blvd (44306-3308)
P.O. Box 7363 (44306-0363)
PHONE.....................330 630-9599
Kenneth Mike Dunaway, *President*
Debbie Dunaway, *President*
Kevin Dunaway, *COO*
Eric Kirvel, *Purch Agent*
Barry Dicicco, *Prgrmr*
EMP: 18
SQ FT: 10,000
SALES (est): 4.3MM **Privately Held**
SIC: 3613 8711 Control panels, electric; engineering services

(G-129)
CUSTOM ENCLOSURES CORP
Also Called: Ceco Equipment Company
1951 S Main St (44301-2817)
PHONE.....................330 786-9000
Chris Ehmann, *President*
EMP: 3
SQ FT: 6,330
SALES (est): 559.6K **Privately Held**
WEB: www.cecoequipment.com
SIC: 3444 Machine guards, sheet metal

(G-130)
CUSTOM MADE PALM TREES LLC
Also Called: Custom Made Palm Trees & Tiki
1201 Devalera St (44310-2417)
PHONE.....................330 633-0063
Michael Beringer, *Vice Pres*
Paul Kresowaty, *Opers Staff*
Michael A Beringer,
EMP: 3
SQ FT: 1,722
SALES (est): 182.2K **Privately Held**
WEB: www.custompalmtrees.com
SIC: 3999 Plants, artificial & preserved

(G-131)
D & D PLASTICS INC
581 E Tallmadge Ave (44310-2402)
P.O. Box 285, Tallmadge (44278-0285)
PHONE.....................330 376-0668
Charles Hay, *President*
Terri Hay, *Treasurer*
EMP: 10 EST: 1982
SQ FT: 8,000
SALES: 600K **Privately Held**
SIC: 3089 Extruded finished plastic products; injection molding of plastics

(G-132)
D & L MACHINE CO INC
1029 Arlington Cir (44306-3959)
PHONE.....................330 785-0781
Charles Bell, *President*
Naaman Elliott, *Vice Pres*
EMP: 25 EST: 1943
SQ FT: 18,100
SALES (est): 4.5MM **Privately Held**
SIC: 3599 Machine shop, jobbing & repair

(G-133)
DATAQ INSTRUMENTS
241 Springside Dr (44333-2432)
PHONE.....................330 668-1444
John J Bowers, *President*
Karen Bowers, *Corp Secy*
Roger Lockhart, *Vice Pres*
EMP: 15
SQ FT: 4,000
SALES (est): 3.8MM **Privately Held**
WEB: www.dataq.com
SIC: 3577 Computer peripheral equipment

(G-134)
DAVID WOLFE DESIGN INC
829 Moe Dr (44310-2516)
PHONE.....................330 633-6124
David Wolfe Sr, *President*
Nancy C Wolfe, *Admin Sec*
EMP: 15
SALES (est): 2MM **Privately Held**
WEB: www.davidwolfedesign.com
SIC: 7389 3089 Design, commercial & industrial; plastic processing

(G-135)
DEBS WELDING & FABRICATION
950 Rhodes Ave (44307-2262)
PHONE.....................330 376-2242
Tanios Debs, *President*
EMP: 4
SQ FT: 7,800
SALES (est): 400K **Privately Held**
SIC: 3441 Fabricated structural metal

(G-136)
DEL-TER PRECISION MACHINE INC
1038 Triplett Blvd (44306-3001)
PHONE.....................330 724-9167
Terry Eddy, *President*
EMP: 5
SQ FT: 7,000
SALES (est): 645.9K **Privately Held**
SIC: 3599 Machine shop, jobbing & repair

(G-137)
DELCO CORPORATION
3300 Massillon Rd (44312-5389)
PHONE.....................330 896-4220
Michael Hochschwender, *CEO*
Albert Kungl, *Vice Pres*
Christian Kungl, *VP Sales*
▲ **EMP:** 40
SQ FT: 26,000
SALES (est): 11MM **Privately Held**
WEB: www.delcocorp.com
SIC: 3544 Forms (molds), for foundry & plastics working machinery; special dies & tools

(G-138)
DELCO LLC
3300 Massillon Rd (44312-5361)
PHONE.....................330 896-4220
Frank Kern,
Christian Kungl,
EMP: 35
SQ FT: 26,000
SALES (est): 1.4MM **Privately Held**
SIC: 3599 Machine shop, jobbing & repair

(G-139)
DESIGN FLUX TECHNOLOGIES LLC
526 S Main St Ste 108 (44311-4402)
P.O. Box 37092, Maple Heights (44137-0092)
PHONE.....................216 543-6066
Terence Baptiste,
Courtney Gras,
Kent Kristensen,
Tom Vo,
EMP: 4
SALES (est): 293.2K **Privately Held**
SIC: 3694 3621 Battery charging generators, automobile & aircraft; storage battery chargers, motor & engine generator type

(G-140)
DEXOL INDUSTRIES INC
844 E Tallmadge Ave (44310-3512)
P.O. Box 237, Tallmadge (44278-0237)
PHONE.....................330 633-4477
Marwan Ghosn, *President*
Ghassan Ghosn, *Vice Pres*
Denise Lieb, *Office Mgr*
Elias Ghosn, *Shareholder*
George Ghosn, *Shareholder*
▼ **EMP:** 7
SQ FT: 12,000
SALES (est): 907.7K **Privately Held**
WEB: www.dexol.com
SIC: 3714 5013 Motor vehicle engines & parts; motor vehicle supplies & new parts

(G-141)
DIAMOND AMERICA CORPORATION
520 S Main St Ste 2456 (44311-1095)
PHONE.....................330 535-3330
Jeff Schweizer, *CEO*
EMP: 9
SALES (est): 1.3MM **Privately Held**
WEB: www.diamondamericacorp.com
SIC: 3542 Extruding machines (machine tools), metal

PA: Akron Specialized Products Inc
96 E Miller Ave
Akron OH 44301
330 762-9269

(G-142)
DIDONATO PRODUCTS INC
1145 Highbrook St Ste 507 (44301-1356)
PHONE.....................330 535-1119
Rudolph Didonato, *President*
Patricia Didonato, *Vice Pres*
EMP: 3
SALES (est): 265.5K **Privately Held**
SIC: 3634 Electric household cooking appliances

(G-143)
DIGITAL COLOR INTL LLC
Also Called: D C I
1653 Merriman Rd Ste 211 (44313-5276)
PHONE.....................330 762-6959
Christopher Che, *CEO*
David Fusselman,
David Welner,
EMP: 43
SQ FT: 38,000
SALES (est): 8.5MM **Privately Held**
WEB: www.digitalcolorinternational.com
SIC: 7336 2653 7319 7331 Creative services to advertisers, except writers; display items, solid fiber: made from purchased materials; display advertising service; transit advertising services; direct mail advertising services; commercial printing, lithographic

(G-144)
DJ SIGNS MD LLC
224 W Exchange St Ste 290 (44302-1722)
PHONE.....................330 344-6643
Gary Bollin, *Principal*
EMP: 5 EST: 2010
SALES (est): 248.8K **Privately Held**
SIC: 3993 Signs & advertising specialties

(G-145)
DOWCO LLC
Also Called: Finite Fibers
1374 Markle St (44306-1801)
PHONE.....................330 773-6654
Keith Kleve, *President*
Dawn Jermont, *Accounts Mgr*
Richard Todd Downing,
William R Downing,
▲ **EMP:** 22
SQ FT: 1,500
SALES (est): 4.2MM **Privately Held**
SIC: 2824 Nylon fibers; polyester fibers

(G-146)
DP2 ENERGY LLC
697 W Market St (44303-1450)
PHONE.....................330 376-5068
Julia Norton, *Office Mgr*
EMP: 4
SALES (est): 168.7K **Privately Held**
SIC: 1389 Oil & gas wells: building, repairing & dismantling

(G-147)
DRB SYSTEMS LLC (HQ)
3245 Pickle Rd (44312-5333)
P.O. Box 550, Uniontown (44685-0550)
PHONE.....................330 645-3299
Dale Brott, *President*
William Ritter, *Project Mgr*
Kenneth Brott, *Treasurer*
Amy Abraham, *Manager*
Andy Clugston, *Manager*
EMP: 104
SALES (est): 35.9MM
SALES (corp-wide): 11.6MM **Privately Held**
WEB: www.drbsystems.com
SIC: 7373 7371 7372 Systems software development services; custom computer programming services; prepackaged software
PA: Drb Holdings Llc
3245 Pickle Rd
Akron OH 44312
330 645-3299

▲ = Import ▼ = Export
◆ = Import/Export

GEOGRAPHIC SECTION

Akron - Summit County (G-173)

(G-148)
EARTHQUAKER DEVICES LLC
350 W Bowery St (44307-2538)
PHONE.................................330 252-9220
Julie Robbins, *Vice Pres*
Jamie Stillman, *Mng Member*
▲ EMP: 15 EST: 2007
SALES: 2MM **Privately Held**
SIC: 3931 Guitars & parts, electric & non-electric

(G-149)
ELECTRO-MECHANICAL MFG CO INC
Also Called: Emmco
1351 S Clvlnd Mhlln Rd (44321)
PHONE.................................330 864-0717
John Gemind, *President*
Bennie L Gemind, *Admin Sec*
EMP: 4
SQ FT: 3,000
SALES (est): 557.6K **Privately Held**
WEB: www.emmcoinc.com
SIC: 3561 Pumps & pumping equipment

(G-150)
ELLET NEON SALES & SERVICE INC
Also Called: E S C
3041 E Waterloo Rd (44312-4058)
P.O. Box 6063 (44312-0063)
PHONE.................................330 628-9907
Gregory Peters, *President*
Mike Croston, *Principal*
Johnathan Webb, *Principal*
Amy Yelling, *Principal*
Fred Hicks, *Project Mgr*
EMP: 50 EST: 1956
SQ FT: 7,000
SALES (est): 7.5MM **Privately Held**
WEB: www.elletneon.com
SIC: 3993 Electric signs

(G-151)
ELLORAS CAVE PUBLISHING INC
1056 Home Ave (44310-3502)
P.O. Box 937, Cuyahoga Falls (44223-0937)
PHONE.................................330 253-3521
Patty L Marks, *CEO*
Tina M Engler, *President*
Christina M Brashear, *COO*
EMP: 35
SQ FT: 12,960
SALES: 7MM **Privately Held**
WEB: www.ellorascave.com
SIC: 2741 2731 Miscellaneous publishing; book publishing

(G-152)
EMERALD PERFORMANCE MTLS LLC
240 W Emerling Ave (44301-1620)
PHONE.................................330 374-2418
Jeffrey Michaels, *Principal*
EMP: 100
SALES (corp-wide): 357.2MM **Privately Held**
SIC: 2899 2821 Chemical preparations; plastics materials & resins
PA: Emerald Performance Materials Llc
1499 Se Tech Center Pl
Vancouver WA 98683
360 954-7100

(G-153)
EMERALD POLYMER ADDITIVES LLC (HQ)
240 W Emerling Ave (44301-1620)
PHONE.................................330 374-2424
Tom Holleran, *President*
EMP: 85
SALES (est): 29.4MM
SALES (corp-wide): 357.2MM **Privately Held**
SIC: 2869 Industrial organic chemicals
PA: Emerald Performance Materials Llc
1499 Se Tech Center Pl
Vancouver WA 98683
360 954-7100

(G-154)
EMERALD SPECIALTY POLYMERS LLC
240 W Emerling Ave (44301-1620)
PHONE.................................330 374-2424
Tom Holleran, *President*
EMP: 30
SALES (est): 4.1MM
SALES (corp-wide): 357.2MM **Privately Held**
SIC: 2821 Plastics materials & resins
PA: Emerald Performance Materials Llc
1499 Se Tech Center Pl
Vancouver WA 98683
360 954-7100

(G-155)
ENGINEERED PLASTICS CORP
420 Kenmore Blvd (44301-1038)
PHONE.................................330 376-7700
Jim Rauh, *President*
Joe Raugh, *Vice Pres*
▲ EMP: 34
SQ FT: 1,000,000
SALES (est): 4.4MM **Privately Held**
WEB: www.engineeredplasticscorp.com
SIC: 3052 Plastic belting

(G-156)
ENLARGING ARTS INC
2280 Tinkham Rd (44313-4426)
PHONE.................................330 434-3433
John Welsh III, *President*
Shirley Welsh, *Vice Pres*
EMP: 8
SQ FT: 10,000
SALES (est): 720K **Privately Held**
WEB: www.enlargingarts.com
SIC: 2752 7384 3993 7336 Commercial printing, lithographic; photofinish laboratories; signs & advertising specialties; commercial art & graphic design

(G-157)
ENTERASYS NETWORKS INC
1093 Corsham Cir (44312-5904)
PHONE.................................330 245-0240
Eddie Torres, *Manager*
EMP: 251 **Publicly Held**
WEB: www.enterasys.com
SIC: 3577 Computer peripheral equipment
HQ: Enterasys Networks, Inc.
9 Northsern Blvd Ste 300
Salem NH 03079
603 952-5000

(G-158)
ENZYME CATALYZED POLYMERS LLC
Also Called: Ecp
2295 W Market St Ste D (44313-6944)
PHONE.................................330 310-1072
Judit Puskas, *Mng Member*
Gabor Kaszas, *CTO*
Matthew A Heinle,
Susan Louscher,
EMP: 4
SQ FT: 1,625
SALES (est): 121.3K **Privately Held**
SIC: 2869 High purity grade chemicals, organic

(G-159)
EP TECHNOLOGIES LLC
520 S Main St Ste 2455 (44311-4425)
PHONE.................................234 208-8967
Robert Gray,
EMP: 14
SALES (est): 2MM **Privately Held**
SIC: 3845 Electrotherapeutic apparatus

(G-160)
EUCLID UNIVERSAL CORPORATION
1503 Exeter Rd (44306-3889)
PHONE.................................440 542-0960
Scott Lantzy, *Vice Pres*
▲ EMP: 5
SALES (est): 500K **Privately Held**
SIC: 3568 Power transmission equipment

(G-161)
EXCHANGE PRINTING COMPANY
969 Grant St (44311-2491)
PHONE.................................330 773-7842
Manuel Underdown, *President*
Janet Bliman, *Corp Secy*
EMP: 4 EST: 1926
SQ FT: 8,000
SALES (est): 370K **Privately Held**
SIC: 2752 2759 Commercial printing, offset; letterpress printing

(G-162)
EZ MACHINE INC
2359 Triplett Blvd (44312-2404)
PHONE.................................330 784-3363
Eugene Zemlanfky, *President*
EMP: 8
SQ FT: 10,969
SALES (est): 1.2MM **Privately Held**
SIC: 3599 Machine shop, jobbing & repair

(G-163)
F M MACHINE CO
1114 Triplett Blvd (44306-3098)
PHONE.................................330 773-8237
Robert R Christian, *President*
Danny Christian, *Vice Pres*
Joel Christian, *Vice Pres*
Shannon Adolph, *Treasurer*
EMP: 45 EST: 1963
SQ FT: 36,000
SALES (est): 12.5MM **Privately Held**
WEB: www.fmmachine.com
SIC: 3599 3441 Machine shop, jobbing & repair; fabricated structural metal

(G-164)
FALLS METAL FABRICATORS IND
760 Home Ave (44310-4104)
PHONE.................................330 253-7181
Daniel R Pugh, *President*
Stephanie Pugh, *Treasurer*
EMP: 13 EST: 2014
SALES (est): 2.9MM **Privately Held**
SIC: 3542 1542 1541 Punching, shearing & bending machines; nonresidential construction; factory construction; steel building construction; warehouse construction

(G-165)
FALLS WELDING & FABG INC
608 Grant St (44311-1502)
PHONE.................................330 253-3437
Ross R Holden, *President*
Theresa Holden, *Admin Sec*
▲ EMP: 7 EST: 1942
SQ FT: 11,000
SALES: 500K **Privately Held**
WEB: www.fallsweldingandfab.com
SIC: 3841 3537 3443 3441 Surgical & medical instruments; industrial trucks & tractors; fabricated plate work (boiler shop); fabricated structural metal

(G-166)
FAMOUS INDUSTRIES INC (HQ)
Also Called: Johnson Contrls Authorized Dlr
2620 Ridgewood Rd Ste 200 (44313-3507)
PHONE.................................330 535-1811
Jay Blaushild, *President*
Marc Blaushild, *Vice Pres*
EMP: 50
SALES (est): 69.2MM **Privately Held**
WEB: www.jfgoodco.com
SIC: 3444 5065 5074 Metal ventilating equipment; telephone equipment; intercommunication equipment, electronic; plumbing & heating valves

(G-167)
FEDEX OFFICE & PRINT SVCS INC
322 E Exchange St (44304-1761)
PHONE.................................330 376-6002
EMP: 16
SALES (corp-wide): 65.4B **Publicly Held**
WEB: www.kinkos.com
SIC: 7334 2752 Photocopying Services Lithographic Printing
HQ: Fedex Office And Print Services, Inc.
7900 Legacy Dr
Plano TX 75024
800 463-3339

(G-168)
FENIX FABRICATION INC
2689 Wingate Ave (44314-1301)
PHONE.................................330 745-8731
Christopher J Forgan, *President*
Anthony Leipold, *Vice Pres*
EMP: 37
SALES (est): 9MM **Privately Held**
SIC: 3441 Fabricated structural metal

(G-169)
FERRIOT INC
1000 Arlington Cir (44306-3973)
P.O. Box 7670 (44306-0670)
PHONE.................................330 786-3000
Gordon Keeler, *CEO*
David Ferriot, *Vice Pres*
Robert Brook, *Maint Spvr*
Dan Thompson, *Purch Agent*
Rhonda Starcher, *Purchasing*
▲ EMP: 170 EST: 1929
SQ FT: 220,000
SALES (est): 59.4MM **Privately Held**
WEB: www.ferriot.com
SIC: 3089 3544 Injection molding of plastics; injection molded finished plastic products; industrial molds

(G-170)
FINE LINE GRAPHICS INC
1972 Akron Peninsula Rd (44313-4810)
PHONE.................................330 920-6096
Ron Beauregard, *Branch Mgr*
EMP: 4
SALES (est): 303.1K **Privately Held**
SIC: 2752 Commercial printing, offset
PA: Fine Line Graphics, Inc.
90 Douglas Pike Unit 3
Smithfield RI 02917

(G-171)
FIRESTONE POLYMERS LLC (DH)
381 W Wilbeth Rd (44301-2465)
P.O. Box 26611 (44319-6611)
PHONE.................................330 379-7000
Gene Lavengco, *CEO*
◆ EMP: 73
SALES (est): 190.1MM
SALES (corp-wide): 32.4B **Privately Held**
WEB: www.firesyn.com
SIC: 3069 Latex, foamed
HQ: Bridgestone Procurement Holdings Usa, Inc.
381 W Wilbeth Rd
Akron OH 44301
337 882-1200

(G-172)
FIRST MERIT
106 S Main St Fl 6 (44308-1442)
PHONE.................................330 849-8750
Paul Greig, *CEO*
Patrick Brangle, *Vice Pres*
Lisa Hibbs, *Vice Pres*
EMP: 4
SALES (est): 611.7K **Privately Held**
SIC: 3944 6311 Banks, toy; life insurance carriers

(G-173)
FLEXSYS AMERICA LP (DH)
260 Springside Dr (44333-4554)
PHONE.................................330 666-4111
Enrique Bolanos, *CEO*
James Voss, *President*
◆ EMP: 65
SQ FT: 85,000
SALES (est): 22.7MM **Publicly Held**
SIC: 3069 8731 2899 2823 Reclaimed rubber & specialty rubber compounds; commercial physical research; chemical preparations; cellulosic manmade fibers; synthetic rubber; plastics materials & resins
HQ: Solutia Inc.
575 Maryville Centre Dr
Saint Louis MO 63141
423 229-2000

Akron - Summit County (G-174) GEOGRAPHIC SECTION

(G-174)
FLOWERS BAKERIES LLC
1500 Firestone Pkwy (44301-1677)
PHONE..................................330 724-1604
EMP: 49
SALES (corp-wide): 3.9B Publicly Held
SIC: 2051 Bread, cake & related products
HQ: Flowers Bakeries, Llc
   1919 Flowers Cir
   Thomasville GA 31757

(G-175)
FLUENCE THERAPEUTICS
526 S Main St Ste 608c (44311-4404)
PHONE..................................216 780-5220
Shauna R Brummet, Principal
Warren Goldenberg, Info Tech Mgr
Thomas McCormick, Info Tech Mgr
EMP: 3
SALES (est): 137.2K Privately Held
SIC: 2834 Pharmaceutical preparations

(G-176)
FOUNDATION INDUSTRIES INC (PA)
Also Called: F I C
880 W Waterloo Rd Ste B (44314-1519)
PHONE..................................330 564-1250
Richard Huscroft, President
▼ EMP: 75
SQ FT: 109,000
SALES (est): 27.6MM Privately Held
WEB: www.foundationindustries.com
SIC: 3089 Engraving of plastic; injection molding of plastics

(G-177)
FREEDOM FORKLIFT SALES LLC
1114 Garman Rd (44313-6614)
PHONE..................................330 289-0879
David Dye, Principal
EMP: 4
SALES (est): 523.8K Privately Held
SIC: 3537 Forklift trucks

(G-178)
FRIESS EQUIPMENT INC
2222 Akron Peninsula Rd (44313-4806)
PHONE..................................330 945-9440
James Friess, President
EMP: 4
SQ FT: 1,000
SALES (est): 670K Privately Held
SIC: 5084 3599 3589 Machine tools & metalworking machinery; custom machinery; commercial cleaning equipment

(G-179)
FUTURE POS OHIO INC
2561 S Arlington Rd (44319-2007)
PHONE..................................330 645-6623
Steve Pritchard, President
Scott Pritchard, Vice Pres
EMP: 13
SQ FT: 3,500
SALES: 2MM Privately Held
WEB: www.futurepos.com
SIC: 3695 Computer software tape & disks: blank, rigid & floppy

(G-180)
GABRIEL PERFORMANCE PDTS LLC (HQ)
388 S Main St Ste 340 (44311-1044)
PHONE..................................866 800-2436
Seth Tomasch, CEO
Vern Sebbio, CFO
▲ EMP: 17
SALES (est): 100MM
SALES (corp-wide): 1.9B Privately Held
WEB: www.gabepro.com
SIC: 2819 Chemicals, high purity: refined from technical grade
PA: Audax Group, L.P.
   101 Huntington Ave # 2450
   Boston MA 02199
   617 859-1500

(G-181)
GARRO TREAD CORPORATION (PA)
Also Called: Ace Rubber Products Division
100 Beech St (44308-1916)
P.O. Box 4567 (44310-0567)
PHONE..................................330 376-3125
Charles Garro, President
Greg Garro, Vice Pres
EMP: 9 EST: 1980
SQ FT: 100,000
SALES: 2MM Privately Held
SIC: 3069 5531 Mats or matting, rubber; stair treads, rubber; floor coverings, rubber; automotive tires

(G-182)
GATEWAY INDUSTRIES
1236 Brittain Rd (44310-3704)
PHONE..................................330 633-3700
Paul Kasmar, President
Stephen Sweezey, Treasurer
▼ EMP: 5
SQ FT: 6,000
SALES (est): 1.5MM Privately Held
WEB: www.gatewayindustriesonline.com
SIC: 3463 Aluminum forgings

(G-183)
GEAR STAR AMERICAN PERFORMANCE
132 N Howard St (44308-1937)
PHONE..................................330 434-5216
Zack Farah, President
Derek Kriebel, Principal
◆ EMP: 6
SALES: 1.5MM Privately Held
SIC: 3714 5571 5013 Motor vehicle transmissions, drive assemblies & parts; motorcycle parts & accessories; motor vehicle supplies & new parts

(G-184)
GEARHART MACHINE COMPANY
1145 Highbrook St Ste 508 (44301-1356)
PHONE..................................330 253-1880
Patrick Casto, President
Becki Casto, Admin Sec
EMP: 3
SQ FT: 4,000
SALES: 100K Privately Held
SIC: 3599 Machine shop, jobbing & repair

(G-185)
GEHM & SONS LIMITED (PA)
825 S Arlington St (44306-2498)
PHONE..................................330 724-8423
Juanita Gehm, President
EMP: 6
SQ FT: 5,780
SALES (est): 1.9MM Privately Held
SIC: 5145 2086 5169 Syrups, fountain; carbonated beverages, nonalcoholic: bottled & canned; dry ice

(G-186)
GENERAL METALS POWDER CO (PA)
Also Called: Gempco
1195 Home Ave (44310-2576)
PHONE..................................330 633-1226
Jerry Lynch, President
Barry P Alvord, Vice Pres
Louis L Cseko Jr, Vice Pres
Barbara Franz, Vice Pres
EMP: 55 EST: 1929
SQ FT: 30,000
SALES (est): 11.6MM Privately Held
WEB: www.gmpfriction.com
SIC: 3499 3714 3568 Friction material, made from powdered metal; motor vehicle parts & accessories; power transmission equipment

(G-187)
GENESCO INC
Also Called: Lids
2000 Brittain Rd Ste 681 (44310-4309)
PHONE..................................330 633-8179
EMP: 5
SALES (corp-wide): 2.9B Publicly Held
SIC: 2353 Mfg Hats/Caps/Millinery

PA: Genesco Inc.
   1415 Murfreesboro Pike
   Nashville TN 37217
   615 367-7000

(G-188)
GENTZLER TOOL & DIE CORP (PA)
3903 Massillon Rd (44312)
P.O. Box 158, Green (44232-0158)
PHONE..................................330 896-1941
David W Gentzler, President
Geraldine Gentzler, President
David Gentzler, Vice Pres
EMP: 21 EST: 1953
SQ FT: 20,000
SALES (est): 4.4MM Privately Held
SIC: 3469 3544 Stamping metal for the trade; special dies & tools

(G-189)
GOJO INDUSTRIES INC (PA)
1 Gojo Plz Ste 500 (44311-1085)
P.O. Box 991 (44309-0991)
PHONE..................................330 255-6000
Joseph Kanfer, Ch of Bd
Mark Lerner, President
Keith Dare, Vice Pres
Sharon Guten, Vice Pres
Ron Hammond, Vice Pres
◆ EMP: 200
SQ FT: 500,000
SALES (est): 373.8MM Privately Held
WEB: www.gojo.com
SIC: 2842 3586 2844 Specialty cleaning, polishes & sanitation goods; measuring & dispensing pumps; toilet preparations

(G-190)
GOODYEAR INTERNATIONAL CORP (HQ)
200 E Innovation Way (44316-0001)
PHONE..................................330 796-2121
Richard J Kramer, CEO
Damon J Audia, Vice Pres
Sylvain G Balensi, Vice Pres
CHI K Liang, Vice Pres
Richard Padante, Vice Pres
◆ EMP: 23 EST: 1922
SALES (est): 37.3MM
SALES (corp-wide): 15.4B Publicly Held
SIC: 5014 3061 Tires & tubes; mechanical rubber goods
PA: The Goodyear Tire & Rubber Company
   200 E Innovation Way
   Akron OH 44316
   330 796-2121

(G-191)
GOODYEAR TIRE & RUBBER COMPANY (PA)
200 E Innovation Way (44316-0001)
PHONE..................................330 796-2121
Richard J Kramer, Ch of Bd
Christopher R Delaney, President
Stephen R McClellan, President
Ryan G Patterson, President
Jose Asencio, District Mgr
◆ EMP: 3000 EST: 1898
SALES: 15.4B Publicly Held
WEB: www.goodyear.com
SIC: 3052 7534 7538 7539 Rubber & plastics hose & beltings; automobile hose, rubber; rubber belting; tire retreading & repair shops; rebuilding & retreading tires; general automotive repair shops; truck engine repair, except industrial; automotive repair shops; brake services; shock absorber replacement; tune-up service, automotive; motor vehicle supplies & new parts; automotive servicing equipment; automotive supplies & parts; inner tubes, all types

(G-192)
GUARI INC (PA)
2215 E Waterloo Rd # 101 (44312-3818)
PHONE..................................330 733-4005
Darrell N Guariniello, President
Gerald J Cahill, Principal
Patrick J Cahill, Principal
India A Key, Principal
EMP: 7
SALES (est): 2.2MM Privately Held
SIC: 2121 Cigars

(G-193)
H & H MACHINE SHOP AKRON INC
955 Grant St (44311-2490)
PHONE..................................330 773-3327
Henry R Haas, President
Anna Haas, Admin Sec
EMP: 21 EST: 1959
SQ FT: 24,000
SALES (est): 4.1MM Privately Held
WEB: www.hhmachineshopofakron.com
SIC: 3599 7692 Machine shop, jobbing & repair; welding repair

(G-194)
H & M METAL PROCESSING CO
1414 Kenmore Blvd (44314-1600)
PHONE..................................330 745-3075
Robert McMillen, President
Shade McMillen, General Mgr
Alexandra Evanko, Shareholder
Ben McMillen, Shareholder
Robert McMillen IV, Shareholder
EMP: 23 EST: 1942
SQ FT: 7,000
SALES: 12.2MM Privately Held
WEB: www.handmmetal.com
SIC: 3398 Metal heat treating

(G-195)
HALLER ENTERPRISES INC
1621 E Market St (44305-4210)
PHONE..................................330 733-9693
David Haller, President
Daid Haller Jr, Vice Pres
Harriet Haller, Vice Pres
EMP: 10
SQ FT: 6,000
SALES (est): 1.3MM Privately Held
WEB: www.hallerenterprises.com
SIC: 2097 5999 Manufactured ice; ice

(G-196)
HAMLIN NEWCO LLC
2741 Wingate Avo (44314 1301)
PHONE..................................330 753-7791
Lai D Teckchandani,
Charles N Biehara,
▲ EMP: 52
SQ FT: 110
SALES (est): 16MM Privately Held
SIC: 3469 Machine parts, stamped or pressed metal

(G-197)
HAMLIN STEEL PRODUCTS LLC
2741 Wingate Ave (44314-1301)
PHONE..................................330 753-7791
Lal Teckchandani,
EMP: 75 EST: 1978
SQ FT: 110,000
SALES (est): 13.6MM Privately Held
WEB: www.featherheadproductions.com
SIC: 3469 Stamping metal for the trade

(G-198)
HANGER PRSTHETCS & ORTHO INC
388 S Main St Ste 205 (44311-1035)
PHONE..................................330 374-9544
Frank Coptolino, Manager
Beth Orzell, Manager
EMP: 3
SALES (corp-wide): 1B Publicly Held
SIC: 3842 5099 Limbs, artificial; firearms & ammunition, except sporting
HQ: Hanger Prosthetics & Orthotics, Inc.
   10910 Domain Dr Ste 300
   Austin TX 78758
   512 777-3800

(G-199)
HARRY C LOBALZO & SONS INC (PA)
Also Called: Hobart Sales & Service
61 N Cleveland (44333)
PHONE..................................330 666-6758
Mike Lobalzo, CEO
Joe Saporito, President
Rick Lobalzo, Exec VP
Douglas Fox, Financial Exec
▲ EMP: 35
SQ FT: 20,000

GEOGRAPHIC SECTION

Akron - Summit County (G-227)

SALES: 6.3MM **Privately Held**
WEB: www.lobalzo.com
SIC: 5046 7699 3556 Commercial cooking & food service equipment; bakery equipment & supplies; restaurant equipment repair; food products machinery

(G-200)
HAWK MANUFACTURING LLC
Also Called: S. C. Manufacturing
2642 Gilchrist Rd (44305-4412)
PHONE.................................330 784-6234
Leonard Errington, *Manager*
EMP: 15
SALES (corp-wide): 289K **Privately Held**
SIC: 3599 Machine shop, jobbing & repair
HQ: Hawk Manufacturing, Llc
380 Kennedy Rd
Akron OH 44305
330 784-3151

(G-201)
HAWK MANUFACTURING LLC (HQ)
Also Called: S. C. Manufacturing
380 Kennedy Rd (44305-4422)
PHONE.................................330 784-3151
Carl Harbert, *Partner*
Gary Worner, *Partner*
Cheryl Fink, *Cust Mgr*
EMP: 57
SQ FT: 33,624
SALES (est): 18.2MM
SALES (corp-wide): 289K **Privately Held**
SIC: 3542 3541 3599 Mechanical (pneumatic or hydraulic) metal forming machines; machine tools, metal cutting type; drilling & boring machines; milling machines; machine & other job shop work; machine shop, jobbing & repair
PA: New Growth Capital Group, Llc
380 Kennedy Rd
Akron OH 44305
216 630-0873

(G-202)
HAWK MANUFACTURING LLC
Also Called: S. C. Manufacturing
382 Kennedy Rd (44305)
PHONE.................................330 784-4815
Luke Mitchell, *General Mgr*
EMP: 11
SALES (corp-wide): 289K **Privately Held**
SIC: 3599 3541 Machine shop, jobbing & repair; machine tools, metal cutting type
HQ: Hawk Manufacturing, Llc
380 Kennedy Rd
Akron OH 44305
330 784-3151

(G-203)
HENNACY MACHINE COMPANY INC
1209 Triplett Blvd (44306-3030)
PHONE.................................330 785-2940
James Hennacy, *President*
EMP: 4
SALES (est): 410K **Privately Held**
SIC: 3599 Machine shop, jobbing & repair

(G-204)
HERBERT USA INC
1480 Industrial Pkwy (44310-2602)
PHONE.................................330 929-4297
Mathias Walter, *President*
Todd Jarvis, *Admin Sec*
▲ **EMP:** 55 **EST:** 1974
SQ FT: 25,000
SALES (est): 8MM **Privately Held**
SIC: 3544 Industrial molds

(G-205)
HERITAGE INDUSTRIAL FINSHG INC
1874 Englewood Ave (44312-1002)
PHONE.................................330 798-9840
Nicholas Pamboukis, *CEO*
Russell Kemppel, *President*
Roland Ciha, *General Mgr*
Agathonico Pamboukis, *Chairman*
Roberta French, *Corp Secy*
▲ **EMP:** 58
SQ FT: 35,000
SALES (est): 8.2MM **Privately Held**
SIC: 3479 Painting of metal products; coating of metals & formed products

(G-206)
HERITAGE MANUFACTURING INC
Also Called: Schien Equipment Company
1600 E Waterloo Rd (44306-4103)
PHONE.................................217 854-2513
EMP: 5 **EST:** 2012
SALES (est): 1.2MM **Privately Held**
SIC: 3715 Mfg Truck Trailers

(G-207)
HICKOK AE LLC
Also Called: Air Enterprises, LLC
735 Glaser Pkwy (44306-4166)
PHONE.................................330 794-9770
Kelly Marek,
Gary Oravetz, *Technician*
Brian Powers,
◆ **EMP:** 95 **EST:** 2017
SALES: 30MM
SALES (corp-wide): 66.3MM **Publicly Held**
SIC: 3585 Heating & air conditioning combination units
PA: Hickok Incorporated
10514 Dupont Ave
Cleveland OH 44108
216 541-8060

(G-208)
HKB ENTERPRISES INC
2215 E Waterloo Rd # 303 (44312-3856)
PHONE.................................330 733-3200
Martin Tass, *President*
EMP: 4
SQ FT: 2,000
SALES (est): 678.8K **Privately Held**
SIC: 3089 Injection molding of plastics

(G-209)
HUNNELL ELECTRIC CO INC
Also Called: Hunnell Electric Motor Repair
950 Grant St (44311-2487)
PHONE.................................330 773-8278
Michael Coughenour, *President*
Gail Coughenour, *Vice Pres*
EMP: 5
SQ FT: 10,000
SALES (est): 605K **Privately Held**
SIC: 7694 5063 Electric motor repair; motors, electric

(G-210)
HYDRATECS INJECTION EQP CO
430 Morgan Ave (44311-2432)
P.O. Box 26338 (44319-6338)
PHONE.................................330 773-0491
Karl Barkey, *President*
Rebecca Barkey, *Admin Sec*
EMP: 4
SALES (est): 748.4K **Privately Held**
SIC: 3559 Rubber working machinery, including tires

(G-211)
HYDROGEN ENERGY SYSTEMS LLC
12 E Exchange St Fl 8 (44308-1541)
PHONE.................................330 236-0358
Kevin Davis, *General Counsel*
Rosemary Ohara,
Rick Saccone,
Jeffrey Wilhite,
EMP: 5
SALES (est): 187K **Privately Held**
SIC: 2813 Hydrogen

(G-212)
HYGENIC ACQUISITION CO
1245 Home Ave (44310-2510)
P.O. Box 1818 (44309-1818)
PHONE.................................330 633-8460
EMP: 125
SQ FT: 135,000
SALES (est): 6.2MM
SALES (corp-wide): 747.9MM **Privately Held**
SIC: 3061 3069 Mfg Mechanical Rubber Goods Mfg Fabricated Rubber Products
HQ: Baird Capital Partners Management Company, Iii Llc
777 E Wisconsin Ave # 2900
Milwaukee WI 53202
414 765-3500

(G-213)
HYGENIC CORPORATION (HQ)
1245 Home Ave (44310-2575)
P.O. Box 1818 (44309-1818)
PHONE.................................330 633-8460
Marshall Dahneke, *President*
Ralph Buster, *Vice Pres*
James Parchem, *Vice Pres*
Niels Lichti, *CFO*
Elizabeth Helbley, *Internal Med*
◆ **EMP:** 125 **EST:** 2000
SQ FT: 135,000
SALES: 96.5MM
SALES (corp-wide): 126MM **Privately Held**
SIC: 3069 3061 Medical & laboratory rubber sundries & related products; mechanical rubber goods
PA: Cogr, Inc.
140 E 45th St Fl 43
New York NY 10017
212 370-5600

(G-214)
IMPORTERS DIRECT LLC
1559 S Main St (44301-1632)
PHONE.................................330 436-3260
Timothy Adkins, *President*
EMP: 22 **EST:** 2008
SQ FT: 15,400
SALES (est): 4MM **Privately Held**
SIC: 1731 3648 7359 3646 Sound equipment specialization; stage lighting equipment; sound & lighting equipment rental; commercial indusl & institutional electric lighting fixtures

(G-215)
IN BOX PUBLICATIONS LLC
977 Hampton Ridge Dr (44313-5087)
PHONE.................................330 592-4288
Robert Almenar, *Owner*
EMP: 3
SALES (est): 165.7K **Privately Held**
SIC: 2721 Periodicals

(G-216)
INTEGRITY PRINT SOLUTIONS INC
567 E Turkeyfoot Lake Rd (44319-4107)
PHONE.................................330 818-0161
Gary Mosteller, *President*
EMP: 4
SALES (est): 526.5K **Privately Held**
WEB: www.integrityprintsolutions.com
SIC: 2752 Commercial printing, offset

(G-217)
INTELLIROD SPINE INC
554 White Pond Dr Ste F (44320-1146)
PHONE.................................234 678-8965
Richard Navarro, *CEO*
EMP: 4
SALES (est): 580.6K **Privately Held**
SIC: 3841 Surgical & medical instruments

(G-218)
INTERGROUP INTERNATIONAL LTD
1653 Merriman Rd Ste 211 (44313-5276)
PHONE.................................216 965-0257
Neil Gloger, *Partner*
Sarah Gatanas, *Partner*
EMP: 70
SQ FT: 130,000
SALES (est): 19.6MM **Privately Held**
SIC: 2821 Plastics materials & resins

(G-219)
INVISIBLE REPAIR PRODUCTS INC
1021 Evans Ave (44305-1020)
PHONE.................................330 798-0441
Melissa L Speer, *President*
EMP: 5
SQ FT: 15,000
SALES (est): 570K **Privately Held**
SIC: 2891 Adhesives

(G-220)
IVAN EXTRUDERS CO INC
Also Called: Siegfried
2404 Pickle Rd (44312-4227)
PHONE.................................330 644-7400
Keith Sigfreud, *President*
EMP: 4
SQ FT: 4,500
SALES (est): 420K **Privately Held**
WEB: www.ivanextruders.com
SIC: 3452 7699 3599 Screws, metal; industrial machinery & equipment repair; machine shop, jobbing & repair

(G-221)
JADLYN INC
Also Called: Today's Bride Magazine
1930 N Clvland Mssllon Rd (44333-1817)
PHONE.................................330 670-9545
Jim Frericks, *President*
Denise Frericks, *Vice Pres*
EMP: 5
SALES: 600K **Privately Held**
WEB: www.todaysbrideshows.com
SIC: 2721 Magazines: publishing only, not printed on site

(G-222)
JDA SOFTWARE GROUP INC
308 N Clvland Mssillon Rd (44333-9302)
PHONE.................................480 308-3000
Kurt Thomiet, *Branch Mgr*
EMP: 3
SALES (corp-wide): 764.5MM **Privately Held**
SIC: 7372 Prepackaged software
HQ: Jda Software Group, Inc.
15059 N Scottsdale Rd # 400
Scottsdale AZ 85254

(G-223)
JILCO PRECISION MOLD & MCH CO
1245 Devalera St (44310-2457)
PHONE.................................330 633-9645
John Shepherd, *President*
EMP: 6
SQ FT: 3,300
SALES: 250K **Privately Held**
SIC: 3599 Machine shop, jobbing & repair; custom machinery

(G-224)
JJC PRODUCTS INC
3670 Forest Oaks Dr (44333-9236)
PHONE.................................330 666-4582
James Costigan, *Principal*
Jerry Costigan, *Principal*
EMP: 3
SALES (est): 246K **Privately Held**
SIC: 3089 Plastics products

(G-225)
JONATHAN BISHOP
Also Called: Bishop International
200 Hampshire Rd (44313-4304)
PHONE.................................330 836-6947
Jonathan Bishop, *Owner*
EMP: 4
SALES: 500K **Privately Held**
WEB: www.jonathanbishop.com
SIC: 3728 Aircraft parts & equipment

(G-226)
JORDAN E ARMOUR
Also Called: Union Sewing Company
1145 Highbrook St Ste 103 (44301-1357)
PHONE.................................330 252-0290
EMP: 50
SQ FT: 700
SALES (est): 2.3MM **Privately Held**
SIC: 2393 Mfg Textile Bags

(G-227)
JRB ATTACHMENTS LLC (DH)
820 Glaser Pkwy (44306-4133)
PHONE.................................330 734-3000
Steve Andrews, *CEO*
Paul Burton, *Vice Pres*
Michael Flannery, *Vice Pres*
Wendell Moss, *Vice Pres*
John Thomas, *Vice Pres*
▲ **EMP:** 7

Akron - Summit County (G-228)   GEOGRAPHIC SECTION

SALES (est): 35.2MM
SALES (corp-wide): 2B Privately Held
WEB: www.paladinbrands.com
SIC: 3531 Construction machinery attachments
HQ: Paladin Brands Group, Inc.
2800 Zeeb Rd
Dexter MI 48130
319 378-3696

(G-228)
JSC EMPLOYEE LEASING CORP (PA)
1560 Firestone Pkwy (44301-1626)
PHONE 330 773-8971
Jack Jeter, *President*
Pam Love, *Exec VP*
Nicholas George, *Admin Sec*
EMP: 19 EST: 1971
SQ FT: 150,000
SALES (est): 25MM Privately Held
WEB: www.jetersystems.com
SIC: 2522 5021 Office cabinets & filing drawers: except wood; filing units

(G-229)
K K RACING CHASSIS
485 Taylor Ave (44312-3548)
PHONE 330 628-2930
Kenneth Kennedy, *Owner*
EMP: 3
SQ FT: 2,400
SALES (est): 214.9K Privately Held
SIC: 3711 Automobile assembly, including specialty automobiles

(G-230)
KAMAN FLUID POWER LLC
195 S Main St Ste 400 (44308-1314)
PHONE 330 315-3100
EMP: 9
SALES (corp-wide): 1.8B Publicly Held
SIC: 3492 Hose & tube fittings & assemblies, hydraulic/pneumatic
HQ: Kaman Fluid Power, Llc
1 Vision Way
Bloomfield CT 06002
860 243-7100

(G-231)
KANE SIGN CO
486 E Glenwood Ave (44310-3421)
PHONE 330 253-5263
Michael Kane, *Owner*
EMP: 3
SQ FT: 7,320
SALES (est): 223.8K Privately Held
WEB: www.kanesign.com
SIC: 3993 Signs, not made in custom sign painting shops

(G-232)
KARMAN RUBBER COMPANY (PA)
2331 Copley Rd (44320-1499)
PHONE 330 864-2161
David W Mann, *President*
G Jay Hearty, *Vice Pres*
EMP: 49 EST: 1945
SQ FT: 55,000
SALES (est): 7MM Privately Held
WEB: www.karman.com
SIC: 3069 3829 3822 3061 Molded rubber products; measuring & controlling devices; auto controls regulating residntl & coml environmt & applncs; mechanical rubber goods

(G-233)
KENMORE DEVELOPMENT & MCH CO
1395 Kenmore Blvd (44314-1658)
PHONE 330 753-2274
Richard Roten, *President*
EMP: 10 EST: 1939
SQ FT: 20,000
SALES (est): 1.4MM Privately Held
WEB: www.allwny.com
SIC: 3599 Machine shop, jobbing & repair

(G-234)
KENMORE GEAR & MACHINE CO INC
2129 Jennifer St (44313-4763)
PHONE 330 753-6671
David Ingham Jr, *President*
Pamela S Ballinger, *Vice Pres*
Gary Ballinger, *Treasurer*
EMP: 7 EST: 1926
SQ FT: 9,352
SALES (est): 1.4MM Privately Held
SIC: 3566 Speed changers, drives & gears

(G-235)
KENT STOW SCREEN PRINTING INC
Also Called: Mascot Shop, The
1340 Home Ave Ste F (44310-2570)
PHONE 330 923-5118
William C Sauders, *President*
EMP: 14
SQ FT: 3,000
SALES: 1MM Privately Held
SIC: 7336 2396 Silk screen design; automotive & apparel trimmings

(G-236)
KILLIAN LATEX INC
2064 Killian Rd (44312-4897)
PHONE 330 644-6746
Timothy J Killian, *President*
Dave Schuck, *QC Mgr*
Sara Benoit, *Executive*
Joan Killian Fisk, *Admin Sec*
EMP: 15
SQ FT: 65,000
SALES (est): 3.2MM Privately Held
WEB: www.killianlatex.com
SIC: 3069 3087 Custom compounding of rubber materials; custom compound purchased resins

(G-237)
KILTEX CORPORATION
2064 Killian Rd (44312-4830)
PHONE 330 644-6746
Timothy J Killian, *President*
Joan Killian-Fisk, *Corp Secy*
EMP: 20
SALES (est): 2.3MM Privately Held
SIC: 3060 Custom compounding of rubber materials

(G-238)
KING MODEL COMPANY
Also Called: King Castings
365 Kenmore Blvd (44301-1053)
PHONE 330 633-0491
Michael Wells, *President*
Gifford Wells, *President*
John Horrell, *Vice Pres*
John E Brown, *Plant Mgr*
Jim Moyer, *Manager*
EMP: 31
SQ FT: 15,000
SALES (est): 4.3MM Privately Held
WEB: www.kingcastings.com
SIC: 3999 Models, general, except toy

(G-239)
KIT MB SYSTEMS INC
925 Glaser Pkwy (44306-4161)
PHONE 330 945-4500
Eveline Nordhauss, *President*
Mike Nordhauss, *Vice Pres*
▲ EMP: 30
SQ FT: 50,000
SALES (est): 9.9MM Privately Held
WEB: www.itemamerica.com
SIC: 3354 Shapes, extruded aluminum

(G-240)
KNAPP FOUNDRY CO INC
1207 Sweitzer Ave (44301-1389)
P.O. Box 26304 (44319-6304)
PHONE 330 434-0916
Charles Knapp Jr, *President*
Jeffery Knapp, *Corp Secy*
EMP: 14 EST: 1910
SQ FT: 20,000
SALES (est): 2.1MM Privately Held
WEB: www.knappfoundry.com
SIC: 3321 Gray iron castings

(G-241)
KOKI LABORATORIES INC
1081 Rosemary Blvd (44306-3727)
PHONE 330 773-7669
John J Piscitelli, *Owner*
EMP: 20
SALES (est): 3.1MM Privately Held
SIC: 2992 Transmission fluid: made from purchased materials

(G-242)
KURTZ BROS COMPOST SERVICES
2677 Riverview Rd (44313-4719)
PHONE 330 864-2621
Thomas Kurtz, *President*
EMP: 30
SALES (est): 4.3MM Privately Held
WEB: www.kbcompost.com
SIC: 2875 8741 Compost; management services

(G-243)
L A PRODUCTIONS CO LLC (PA)
Also Called: L A Products Co
1333 Collier Rd (44320-2409)
PHONE 330 666-4230
Nicholas Lamonica,
Patricia L Lamonica,
EMP: 3
SQ FT: 16,000
SALES (est): 770.8K Privately Held
SIC: 7699 4213 3949 Recreational vehicle repair services; aircraft & heavy equipment repair services; heavy machinery transport; sporting & athletic goods

(G-244)
LAAD SIGN & LIGHTING INC
830 Moe Dr Ste B (44310-2569)
PHONE 330 379-2297
Linda Nichols, *Owner*
EMP: 10
SQ FT: 1,000
SALES: 1MM Privately Held
SIC: 3993 Signs & advertising specialties

(G-245)
LABABIDI ENTERPRISES INC
2167 Forest Oak Dr (44312-2234)
PHONE 330 733-2907
Wallid Lababidi, *Owner*
EMP: 20
SALES (est): 1.8MM Privately Held
SIC: 3841 8011 Anesthesia apparatus; offices & clinics of medical doctors

(G-246)
LAIRD CONNECTIVITY INC (HQ)
50 S Main St Ste 1100 (44308-1831)
PHONE 330 434-7929
Scott Lord, *CEO*
Stephen Minardi, *CFO*
Alexis Reggie, *Finance Mgr*
EMP: 500
SALES: 250MM
SALES (corp-wide): 1.2B Privately Held
SIC: 3674 Computer logic modules
PA: Laird Limited
100 Pall Mall
London SW1Y
207 468-4040

(G-247)
LAIRD TECHNOLOGIES INC
50 S Main St Ste 1100 (44308-1831)
PHONE 330 434-7929
EMP: 12
SALES (corp-wide): 1.2B Privately Held
SIC: 3679 Electronic circuits
HQ: Laird Technologies, Inc.
16401 Swingley
Chesterfield MO 63017
636 898-6000

(G-248)
LANDMARK PLASTIC CORPORATION (PA)
1331 Kelly Ave (44306-3773)
PHONE 330 785-2200
Robert G Merzweiler, *CEO*
Joe Donley, *Regional Mgr*
Steve Beall, *Vice Pres*
Steve Merzweiler, *Opers Dir*
Glen Betts, *Controller*
◆ EMP: 200
SQ FT: 200,000
SALES (est): 84.6MM Privately Held
WEB: www.landmarkplastic.com
SIC: 3089 Plastic containers, except foam

(G-249)
LAZER ACTION INC
1534 Brittain Rd (44310-2738)
PHONE 330 630-9200
Tom Frascella, *President*
Cheryl Frascella, *Vice Pres*
EMP: 5
SQ FT: 2,876
SALES (est): 611.5K Privately Held
WEB: www.lazeraction.com
SIC: 3577 5734 7378 7699 Computer peripheral equipment; computer peripheral equipment; computer peripheral equipment repair & maintenance; printing trades machinery & equipment repair

(G-250)
LEHNER SCREW MACHINE LLC
1169 Brittain Rd (44305-1004)
PHONE 330 688-6616
Thomas Bader, *President*
John Bader, *Vice Pres*
EMP: 21
SQ FT: 10,524
SALES: 680K Privately Held
WEB: www.lehnerscrewmachine.com
SIC: 3451 3599 Screw machine products; machine shop, jobbing & repair

(G-251)
LELAND-GIFFORD INC
1029 Arlington Cir (44306-3959)
PHONE 330 785-9730
Robert Hartford, *President*
EMP: 9
SQ FT: 20,000
SALES (est): 1.4MM Privately Held
WEB: www.barkermill.com
SIC: 3541 Drilling & boring machines; milling machines

(G-252)
LENA FIORE INC
2188 Majesty Ct (44333-1286)
PHONE 330 659-0020
Celeste Massullo, *President*
Mary Helene Massullo, *Co-Owner*
EMP: 15
SALES: 200K Privately Held
WEB: www.clevelandrockscandy.com
SIC: 5023 2339 Decorative home furnishings & supplies; women's & misses' accessories

(G-253)
LEVERETT A ANDERSON CO INC
1245 S Clvld Masslln Rd (44321)
P.O. Box 4400, Copley (44321-0400)
PHONE 330 670-1363
Leverett A Anderson, *CEO*
William Cole, *President*
EMP: 4
SQ FT: 1,100
SALES (est): 743.7K Privately Held
SIC: 3821 5169 Laboratory equipment: fume hoods, distillation racks, etc.; chemicals & allied products

(G-254)
LIPPINCOTT & PETO INC
Also Called: Rubber World Magazine
1741 Akron Peninsula Rd (44313-5157)
P.O. Box 5451 (44334-0451)
PHONE 330 864-2122
Joe Lippincott, *President*
EMP: 17
SQ FT: 2,500
SALES (est): 1.9MM Privately Held
SIC: 2721 Trade journals: publishing only, not printed on site

(G-255)
LOCKHEED MARTIN CORPORATION
1210 Massillon Rd (44315-0001)
PHONE 330 796-7000
Dale P Bennett, *Branch Mgr*
EMP: 500 Publicly Held
WEB: www.lockheedmartin.com
SIC: 3812 Search & navigation equipment
PA: Lockheed Martin Corporation
6801 Rockledge Dr
Bethesda MD 20817

GEOGRAPHIC SECTION
Akron - Summit County (G-280)

(G-256)
LOCKHEED MARTIN CORPORATION
1210 Massillon Rd (44315-0001)
PHONE..................330 796-2800
Jill O Reilly, *Branch Mgr*
EMP: 420 **Publicly Held**
WEB: www.lockheedmartin.com
SIC: 3721 3761 Aircraft; ballistic missiles, complete; guided missiles & space vehicles, research & development; guided missiles, complete; space vehicles, complete
PA: Lockheed Martin Corporation
6801 Rockledge Dr
Bethesda MD 20817

(G-257)
LOCKHEED MARTIN INTEG
1210 Massillon Rd (44315-0001)
PHONE..................330 796-2800
Mike Gifford, *General Mgr*
Paul Wyman, *General Mgr*
Ken Kiley, *Principal*
Douglas Cook, *Project Mgr*
Kim Smith, *Project Mgr*
▲ **EMP:** 99
SALES (est): 21.1MM **Publicly Held**
SIC: 3699 3769 3728 3812 Electrical equipment & supplies; guided missile & space vehicle parts & auxiliary equipment; aircraft parts & equipment; search & navigation equipment
PA: Lockheed Martin Corporation
6801 Rockledge Dr
Bethesda MD 20817

(G-258)
LOCKHEED MARTIN INTEGRTD SYSTM
Also Called: Aerospace Simulations
1210 Massillon Rd (44315-0001)
PHONE..................330 796-2800
Dan Fiest, *Manager*
EMP: 600 **Publicly Held**
SIC: 3812 Search & navigation equipment
HQ: Lockheed Martin Integrated Systems, Llc
6801 Rockledge Dr
Bethesda MD 20817

(G-259)
LOGAN MACHINE COMPANY (PA)
Also Called: LMC
1405 Home Ave (44310-2586)
PHONE..................330 633-6163
Mark Schoenbaechler, *President*
Kenneth Schoenbaechler, *Vice Pres*
Clint Waggle, *Plant Mgr*
Geri Holder, *Persnl Mgr*
▲ **EMP:** 74 **EST:** 1943
SQ FT: 96,000
SALES (est): 15.2MM **Privately Held**
WEB: www.loganmachine.com
SIC: 3599 3728 3544 3469 Custom machinery; machine shop, jobbing & repair; aircraft parts & equipment; special dies, tools, jigs & fixtures; metal stampings

(G-260)
LOWRY FURNACE COMPANY INC
Also Called: Hvac
663 Flora Ave (44314-1754)
PHONE..................330 745-4822
Gregory Shiflett, *President*
EMP: 6
SQ FT: 3,000
SALES (est): 428.4K **Privately Held**
SIC: 1711 3444 Warm air heating & air conditioning contractor; heating systems repair & maintenance; sheet metalwork

(G-261)
LUBRIZOL CORPORATION
1779 Marvo Dr (44306-4331)
PHONE..................216 447-6212
EMP: 4
SALES (corp-wide): 225.3B **Publicly Held**
SIC: 2899 Chemical preparations
HQ: The Lubrizol Corporation
29400 Lakeland Blvd
Wickliffe OH 44092
440 943-4200

(G-262)
LUND PRINTING CO
2962 Trenton Rd (44312-2855)
PHONE..................330 628-4047
Norman Lund, *Owner*
EMP: 3
SQ FT: 1,400
SALES (est): 170K **Privately Held**
SIC: 2759 2752 2791 2789 Letterpress printing; commercial printing, offset; typesetting; bookbinding & related work; automotive & apparel trimmings

(G-263)
M & J MACHINE SHOP INC
2420 Pickle Rd (44312-4227)
PHONE..................330 645-0042
James Kuts, *President*
Charlene Kuts, *Vice Pres*
Jonathan Kuts, *Admin Sec*
EMP: 10
SQ FT: 15,000
SALES (est): 200K **Privately Held**
SIC: 3599 Machine shop, jobbing & repair

(G-264)
MACK CONCRETE INDUSTRIES INC
Also Called: Mack Ready-Mix
124 Darrow Rd Ste 7 (44305-3835)
PHONE..................330 784-7008
Ron Blanton, *Manager*
EMP: 10
SALES (corp-wide): 170.9MM **Privately Held**
SIC: 3273 Ready-mixed concrete
HQ: Mack Concrete Industries, Inc.
201 Columbia Rd
Valley City OH 44280
330 483-3111

(G-265)
MAJESTIC TRAILERS INC (PA)
Also Called: Majestic Trailer & Hitch
1750 E Waterloo Rd (44306-4104)
PHONE..................330 798-1698
John Hughes, *Principal*
Penny Hughes, *Admin Sec*
EMP: 10
SALES (est): 1.1MM **Privately Held**
SIC: 3714 3715 Air conditioner parts, motor vehicle; truck trailers

(G-266)
MALCO PRODUCTS INC
393 W Wilbeth Rd (44301-2465)
PHONE..................330 753-0361
Todd West, *Branch Mgr*
EMP: 50
SALES (corp-wide): 92.9MM **Privately Held**
WEB: www.malcopro.com
SIC: 2842 Specialty cleaning, polishes & sanitation goods
PA: Malco Products, Inc.
361 Fairview Ave
Barberton OH 44203
330 753-0361

(G-267)
MARAZITA GRAPHICS INC
1100 Triplett Blvd (44306-3029)
PHONE..................330 773-6462
James J Marazita, *President*
James S Marazita, *Treasurer*
David Marazita, *Admin Sec*
EMP: 5
SALES: 260K **Privately Held**
WEB: www.marazitagraphics.com
SIC: 7336 2759 Silk screen design; screen printing

(G-268)
MARK-ALL ENTERPRISES LLC
Also Called: Excelsior Marking
888 W Waterloo Rd (44314-1528)
PHONE..................800 433-3615
Gwenn Bull, *CFO*
Brian Collins, *Sales Staff*
Amanda Smith, *Sales Staff*
David Sutter,
Robert Lux,
▲ **EMP:** 22 **EST:** 1905
SQ FT: 32,000
SALES (est): 5.1MM **Privately Held**
WEB: www.excelsiormarking.com
SIC: 3953 2796 3999 Figures (marking devices), metal; date stamps, hand: rubber or metal; stencils, painting & marking; platemaking services; badges, metal: policemen, firemen, etc.

(G-269)
MARKETHATCH CO INC
Also Called: J G Pads
91 E Voris St (44311-1507)
P.O. Box 1151 (44309-1151)
PHONE..................330 376-6363
Paul Joyce, *President*
EMP: 15
SQ FT: 9,400
SALES (est): 3.5MM **Privately Held**
WEB: www.jgpads.com
SIC: 5047 5122 3841 Medical equipment & supplies; pharmaceuticals; surgical & medical instruments

(G-270)
MARKHAM MACHINE COMPANY INC
160 N Union St (44304-1355)
PHONE..................330 762-7676
James M Markham, *President*
EMP: 18
SQ FT: 13,000
SALES (est): 3.7MM **Privately Held**
SIC: 3599 Machine shop, jobbing & repair

(G-271)
MARKS BREW THRU
2455 Canton Rd (44312-5050)
PHONE..................330 699-1755
Mark L Heldlick, *Owner*
EMP: 4
SALES (est): 293.8K **Privately Held**
SIC: 2082 Beer (alcoholic beverage)

(G-272)
MAXION WHEELS AKRON LLC (DH)
Also Called: Hayes Lemmerz Intl-Commrcl Hwy
428 Seiberling St (44306-3205)
PHONE..................330 794-2310
Don Polk, *President*
Steven Esau, *Vice Pres*
John A Salvette, *Vice Pres*
Ken Pavlak, *Maintence Staff*
▲ **EMP:** 47
SALES (est): 23.3MM **Privately Held**
SIC: 3714 Motor vehicle parts & accessories
HQ: Maxion Wheels U.S.A. Llc
39500 Orchard Hill Pl # 500
Novi MI 48375
734 737-5000

(G-273)
MAXION WHEELS SEDALIA LLC
428 Seiberling St (44306-3205)
PHONE..................330 794-2300
Randy Arnst, *Branch Mgr*
EMP: 9 **Privately Held**
SIC: 3714 Motor vehicle parts & accessories
HQ: Hayes Lemmerz International—Sedalia, Llc
3610 W Main St
Sedalia MO 65301
660 827-3640

(G-274)
MCMILLEN STEEL LLC
Also Called: Service Iron & Steel Company
1372 Kenmore Blvd (44314-1633)
PHONE..................330 253-9147
Frank M Bernert Jr, *President*
Tom Nader, *Mng Member*
EMP: 7 **EST:** 1945
SALES (est): 1.5MM **Privately Held**
SIC: 3441 Fabricated structural metal

(G-275)
MCNEIL & NRM INC (DH)
96 E Crosier St (44311-2342)
PHONE..................330 761-1855
Paul Yared, *CEO*
F H Yared, *Ch of Bd*
John McCormick, *Exec VP*
A Melek, *Exec VP*
Al Melek, *Exec VP*
▲ **EMP:** 65 **EST:** 1979
SQ FT: 35,000
SALES (est): 23.5MM **Privately Held**
SIC: 3559 3599 3542 Rubber working machinery, including tires; custom machinery; machine tools, metal forming type
HQ: Mcneil & Nrm Intl., Inc.
96 E Crosier St
Akron OH 44311
330 253-2525

(G-276)
MCNEIL & NRM INTL INC (HQ)
96 E Crosier St (44311-2342)
PHONE..................330 253-2525
F H Yared, *Ch of Bd*
Al M Melek, *Exec VP*
R A Nelson, *CFO*
Joel Siegfried, *Treasurer*
EMP: 75
SQ FT: 35,000
SALES (est): 31.5MM **Privately Held**
SIC: 3559 3599 Rubber working machinery, including tires; custom machinery
PA: British International Co. Sal (Off-Shore)
Christianne Fouad Yared
Beirut
702 760-47

(G-277)
MEASUREMENT SPECIALTIES INC
2236 N Cleveland Massillo (44333-1288)
PHONE..................330 659-3312
Robert Visger, *Branch Mgr*
EMP: 53
SALES (corp-wide): 13.1B **Privately Held**
SIC: 3829 Measuring & controlling devices
HQ: Measurement Specialties, Inc.
1000 Lucas Way
Hampton VA 23666
757 766-1500

(G-278)
MEGGITT AIRCRAFT BRAKING (HQ)
Also Called: Mabsc
1204 Massillon Rd (44306-4188)
PHONE..................330 796-4400
Luke Duardogan, *President*
Joseph McCutcheon, *General Mgr*
Paul Robinson, *General Mgr*
Jodi Wenzlawsh, *General Mgr*
Mario Andreou, *Regional Mgr*
▲ **EMP:** 769
SQ FT: 733,000
SALES (est): 309MM
SALES (corp-wide): 2.6B **Privately Held**
WEB: www.meggitt-mabs.com
SIC: 3728 Brakes, aircraft; wheels, aircraft
PA: Meggitt Plc
Atlantic House, Aviation Park West
Christchurch BH23
120 259-7597

(G-279)
METALICO AKRON INC (HQ)
Also Called: Metalico Annaco
943 Hazel St (44305-1609)
P.O. Box 1148 (44309-1148)
PHONE..................330 376-1400
Jeffery Bauer, *General Mgr*
EMP: 35 **EST:** 1930
SQ FT: 30,000
SALES (est): 9.5MM
SALES (corp-wide): 110.5MM **Privately Held**
WEB: www.annaco.com
SIC: 5093 4953 3341 Ferrous metal scrap & waste; nonferrous metals scrap; refuse systems; secondary nonferrous metals
PA: Metalico, Inc.
135 Dermody St
Cranford NJ 07016
908 497-9610

(G-280)
MEYER DESIGN INC
100 N High St (44308-1918)
PHONE..................330 434-9176

Akron - Summit County (G-281)   GEOGRAPHIC SECTION

Christopher Meyer, *President*
EMP: 20
SQ FT: 18,000
SALES (est): 2.5MM **Privately Held**
WEB: www.meyerdesign.com
SIC: 3949 Playground equipment

(G-281)
MIA EXPRESS INC
3238 Robins Trce (44319-3874)
PHONE..................330 896-8180
Theodore V Sokolovic, *Principal*
EMP: 4
SALES (est): 406.4K **Privately Held**
SIC: 2741 Miscellaneous publishing

(G-282)
MILESTONE SERVICES CORP
551 Beacon St (44311-1805)
PHONE..................330 374-9988
Richard Drillien, *President*
George Stanley, *Treasurer*
EMP: 6
SQ FT: 200
SALES (est): 590K **Privately Held**
WEB: www.milestoneservicescorp.com
SIC: 3471 Plating & polishing

(G-283)
MIRACLE CUSTOM AWARDS & GIFTS
Also Called: Andy's Award
565 Wolf Ledges Pkwy A (44311-4433)
PHONE..................330 376-8335
Joshua Miracle, *President*
Craig Miracle, *Owner*
EMP: 3
SQ FT: 3,960
SALES: 350K **Privately Held**
SIC: 5999 2759 Trophies & plaques; commercial printing; engraving

(G-284)
MOHICAN INDUSTRIES INC
1225 W Market St (44313-7107)
PHONE..................330 869-0500
Judy Dipaola, *President*
EMP: 12
SQ FT: 20,000
SALES (est): 996.1K
SALES (corp-wide): 6.5MM **Privately Held**
SIC: 2822 Synthetic rubber
PA: Sovereign Chemical Company
4040 Embassy Pkwy Ste 190
Akron OH 44333
330 869-0500

(G-285)
MONTGOMERY & MONTGOMERY LLC
80 N Pershing Ave (44313-6258)
PHONE..................330 858-9533
David Montgomery,
EMP: 7 EST: 2014
SALES (est): 255.4K **Privately Held**
SIC: 7692 Welding repair

(G-286)
MORE THAN GOURMET INC
929 Home Ave (44310-4107)
PHONE..................330 762-6652
Brad Sacks, *CEO*
Emily Maglott, *Vice Pres*
Jeffrey A Witherite, *VP Finance*
Barb Sacks, *Human Res Dir*
Tish Gerber, *Sales Staff*
▲ **EMP:** 45
SALES: 26MM **Privately Held**
WEB: www.morethangourmet.com
SIC: 2032 Soups & broths: canned, jarred, etc.

(G-287)
MORGAN PRECISION INSTRS LLC
3375 Miller Park Rd (44312-5341)
PHONE..................330 896-0846
Jim Geib, *General Mgr*
George Koberlein, *Principal*
EMP: 5
SQ FT: 6,000
SALES: 520K **Privately Held**
WEB: www.morgangages.com
SIC: 3545 Precision measuring tools

(G-288)
MORRIS TECHNOLOGIES
1741 S Main St (44301-2428)
PHONE..................330 384-3084
Jim Morris, *Owner*
EMP: 3 EST: 2010
SALES (est): 155.2K **Privately Held**
SIC: 8731 3999 Commercial physical research; manufacturing industries

(G-289)
MOSHER MEDICAL INC
150 Springside Dr 220b (44333-4562)
PHONE..................330 668-2252
Dan Mosher, *President*
Jill Goldinger, *Office Admin*
Dan Caton, *Executive*
EMP: 5
SALES (est): 649.5K **Privately Held**
WEB: www.moshermedical.com
SIC: 3842 Implants, surgical

(G-290)
MUELLER ELECTRIC COMPANY INC
2850 Gilchrist Rd Ste 5 (44305-4445)
P.O. Box 92922, Cleveland (44194-2922)
PHONE..................216 771-5225
Arnold Siemer, *President*
Mike Jett, *Purch Mgr*
▲ **EMP:** 30 EST: 2011
SALES (est): 1.5MM
SALES (corp-wide): 180.1MM **Privately Held**
SIC: 3644 3643 3694 3496 Insulators & insulation materials, electrical; current-carrying wiring devices; harness wiring sets, internal combustion engines; miscellaneous fabricated wire products; nonferrous wiredrawing & insulating; electrical equipment & supplies
PA: Desco Corporation
7795 Walton Pkwy Ste 175
New Albany OH 43054
614 888-8855

(G-291)
MYE AUTOMOTIVE INC
1293 S Main St (44301-1302)
PHONE..................330 253-5592
John C Orr, *President*
EMP: 4
SALES (est): 255.4K
SALES (corp-wide): 566.7MM **Publicly Held**
SIC: 3089 Pallets, plastic; stock shapes, plastic; boxes, plastic; blow molded finished plastic products
PA: Myers Industries, Inc.
1293 S Main St
Akron OH 44301
330 253-5592

(G-292)
MYERS INDUSTRIES INC (PA)
1293 S Main St (44301-1339)
PHONE..................330 253-5592
F Jack Liebau Jr, *Ch of Bd*
R David Banyard, *President*
Kevin Brackman, *Vice Pres*
Matteo Anversa, *CFO*
Kevin L Brackman, *CFO*
EMP: 50
SQ FT: 129,000
SALES: 566.7MM **Publicly Held**
WEB: www.myersind.com
SIC: 3089 3086 3069 3052 Pallets, plastic; stock shapes, plastic; boxes, plastic; blow molded finished plastic products; plastics foam products; packaging & shipping materials, foamed plastic; insulation or cushioning material, foamed plastic; padding, foamed plastic; rubber automotive products; automobile hose, rubber; tools & equipment, automotive; tire & tube repair materials

(G-293)
MYERS INDUSTRIES INC
Akro-Mils Division
1293 S Main St (44301-1339)
P.O. Box 989 (44309-0989)
PHONE..................330 253-5592
David Grider, *General Mgr*
Ron Cox, *Sales Staff*
J Dluzyn, *Sales Staff*

EMP: 50
SALES (corp-wide): 566.7MM **Publicly Held**
WEB: www.myersind.com
SIC: 3089 3443 Molding primary plastic; fabricated plate work (boiler shop)
PA: Myers Industries, Inc.
1293 S Main St
Akron OH 44301
330 253-5592

(G-294)
NATURAL COUNTRY FARMS INC (DH)
681 W Waterloo Rd (44314-1547)
PHONE..................330 753-2293
Kenny Sadai, *Ch of Bd*
James O'Toole, *President*
Thomas Kolb, *CFO*
▲ **EMP:** 2
SQ FT: 67,000
SALES: 229MM
SALES (corp-wide): 4.6B **Privately Held**
WEB: www.countrypure.com
SIC: 2033 2037 2086 Fruit juices: fresh; fruit juice concentrates, frozen; pasteurized & mineral waters, bottled & canned

(G-295)
NEW CASTINGS INC
Also Called: Quality Molded
2200 Massillon Rd (44312-4234)
PHONE..................330 645-6653
Mike Cingel, *President*
EMP: 140
SQ FT: 15,000
SALES (est): 12.4MM
SALES (corp-wide): 76.8MM **Privately Held**
WEB: www.newcastings.com
SIC: 3544 Industrial molds
PA: Saehwa Imc Na, Inc.
2200 Massillon Rd
Akron OH 44312
330 645-6653

(G-296)
NEWSOME & WORK METALIZING CO
258 Kenmore Blvd (44301-1000)
P.O. Box 27091 (44319-7091)
PHONE..................330 376-7144
Michael Newsome, *President*
EMP: 7 EST: 1958
SQ FT: 10,000
SALES (est): 1.4MM **Privately Held**
WEB: www.newsome-work.com
SIC: 3471 Sand blasting of metal parts; finishing, metals or formed products

(G-297)
NIDEC MOTOR CORPORATION
Imperial Electric
1503 Exeter Rd (44306-3889)
PHONE..................575 434-0633
Bill Kuhar, *Engineer*
Sheri Brown, *Human Resources*
Zachary Depaul, *Technology*
EMP: 125
SALES (corp-wide): 13.9B **Privately Held**
SIC: 3621 Motors, electric; generators & sets, electric
HQ: Nidec Motor Corporation
8050 West Florissant Ave
Saint Louis MO 63136

(G-298)
NORKAAM INDUSTRIES LLC
Also Called: Maple Valley Cleaners
1477 Copley Rd (44320-2656)
PHONE..................330 873-9793
Eugene Norris, *Manager*
EMP: 9
SALES (est): 349.4K **Privately Held**
SIC: 3999 Manufacturing industries

(G-299)
NORTH COAST HOLDINGS INC (PA)
768 E North St (44305-1164)
P.O. Box 9320 (44305-0320)
PHONE..................330 535-7177
H A Pendleton, *Ch of Bd*
EMP: 2
SQ FT: 50,000

SALES (est): 19MM **Privately Held**
SIC: 3423 6512 Hand & edge tools; commercial & industrial building operation

(G-300)
NORTH COAST THEATRICAL INC (PA)
2181 Killian Rd Unit A (44312-4884)
PHONE..................330 762-1768
Richard Arconti, *President*
John Kramanak, *Vice Pres*
EMP: 5
SALES (est): 763K **Privately Held**
SIC: 3993 7922 Signs & advertising specialties; theatrical production services

(G-301)
NORTH HILL MARBLE & GRANITE CO
448 N Howard St (44310-3185)
PHONE..................330 253-2179
Miles V Buzzi II, *President*
Paul Buzzi, *Admin Sec*
EMP: 10
SQ FT: 4,000
SALES (est): 890K **Privately Held**
WEB: www.exportersindia.com
SIC: 5999 1741 3993 3281 Monuments, finished to custom order; masonry & other stonework; signs, not made in custom sign painting shops; cut stone & stone products; dimension stone

(G-302)
NORTHEAST TIRE MOLDS INC (HQ)
Also Called: Southwest Tire Molds
159 Opportunity Pkwy (44307-2202)
PHONE..................330 376-6107
Christopher Sipe, *President*
▲ **EMP:** 2
SQ FT: 29,500
SALES (est): 3.5MM
SALES (corp-wide): 174.2MM **Privately Held**
SIC: 3544 Industrial molds
PA: Greatoo Intelligent Equipment Inc.
Middle Section, No.5 Road, Jiedong Economic Development Area
Jieyang 51550
663 327-4082

(G-303)
NORTHESTRN OH FOOT & ANKL ASOC
1557 Vernon Odom Blvd # 102 (44320-4061)
PHONE..................330 633-3445
Theodore Buccilli, *Owner*
Theodore A Buccilli DPM, *Principal*
EMP: 3
SALES (est): 334.9K **Privately Held**
SIC: 3842 Foot appliances, orthopedic

(G-304)
NSA TECHNOLOGIES LLC
3867 Medina Rd Ste 256 (44333-4525)
PHONE..................330 576-4600
Vincent E Fischer,
Victor J Bierman III,
Mark W Jenney,
EMP: 150
SALES (est): 6.1MM **Privately Held**
SIC: 7372 8742 8731 Publishers' computer software; marketing consulting services; commercial physical research; biological research

(G-305)
OHIO BEAUTY INC
Also Called: Ohio Beauty Cut Stone
40 W Turkeyfoot Lake Rd (44319-4012)
PHONE..................330 644-2241
Jason Berenyi, *President*
Frank J Berenyi, *President*
Sirenna Berenyi, *Vice Pres*
EMP: 7 EST: 1947
SQ FT: 8,000
SALES (est): 1.5MM **Privately Held**
SIC: 5032 3281 1411 Brick, stone & related material; cut stone & stone products; dimension stone

GEOGRAPHIC SECTION

Akron - Summit County (G-333)

(G-306)
OHIO FABRICATORS INC
1452 Kenmore Blvd (44314-1659)
PHONE..................................216 391-2400
Paul Newman, *President*
Terra Soles, *Admin Sec*
EMP: 40
SALES (corp-wide): 4MM **Privately Held**
WEB: www.tinshops.com
SIC: 3444 Ducts, sheet metal
PA: Ohio Fabricators, Inc.
   883 Addison Rd
   Cleveland OH 44103
   216 391-2400

(G-307)
OHIO GASKET AND SHIM CO INC (PA)
Also Called: Ogs Industries
976 Evans Ave (44305-1019)
PHONE..................................330 630-0626
John S Bader, *President*
Thomas Bader, *Principal*
▲ **EMP:** 45 **EST:** 1959
SQ FT: 84,000
SALES (est): 21.7MM **Privately Held**
WEB: www.ogsindustries.com
SIC: 3469 3053 3599 3499 Stamping metal for the trade; gaskets, all materials; machine shop, jobbing & repair; shims, metal; packaging & labeling services

(G-308)
OHIO MECHANICAL HANDLING CO
1856 S Main St (44301-2461)
P.O. Box 26033 (44319-6033)
PHONE..................................330 773-5165
William W Burse, *President*
Robert L Burse, *Treasurer*
EMP: 10 **EST:** 1945
SQ FT: 20,000
SALES: 205.5K **Privately Held**
SIC: 3536 5084 Cranes, overhead traveling; hoists; monorail systems; materials handling machinery

(G-309)
OHIO PURE FOODS INC (DH)
681 W Waterloo Rd (44314-1547)
PHONE..................................330 753-2293
Kenny Sadai, *Ch of Bd*
James O'Toole, *President*
Thomas Kolb, *CFO*
▲ **EMP:** 89
SQ FT: 100,000
SALES (est): 11.1MM
SALES (corp-wide): 4.6B **Privately Held**
SIC: 2033 2086 Fruit juices: fresh; fruit drinks (less than 100% juice): packaged in cans, etc.

(G-310)
OLDFORGE TOOLS INC (DH)
768 E North St (44305-1164)
PHONE..................................330 535-7177
Scott Meyer, *President*
EMP: 1
SALES (est): 3MM
SALES (corp-wide): 19MM **Privately Held**
WEB: www.kentool.com
SIC: 3423 Mechanics' hand tools
HQ: Summit Tool Company
   768 E North St
   Akron OH 44305
   330 535-7177

(G-311)
OMNOVA SOLUTIONS INC
1380 Tech Way (44306-2572)
PHONE..................................330 734-1237
EMP: 84
SALES (corp-wide): 769.8MM **Publicly Held**
SIC: 2819 Industrial inorganic chemicals
PA: Omnova Solutions Inc.
   25435 Harvard Rd
   Beachwood OH 44122
   216 682-7000

(G-312)
ORTHOHLIX SURGICAL DESIGNS INC
3975 Embassy Pkwy (44333-8320)
PHONE..................................330 869-9562
About David B Kay, *Principal*
EMP: 3
SALES (est): 146.5K **Privately Held**
SIC: 3842 Surgical appliances & supplies

(G-313)
P C R INC
Also Called: Ruber Polymer
1135 Portage Trail Ext (44313-8283)
PHONE..................................330 945-7721
EMP: 10
SALES (corp-wide): 2.2MM **Privately Held**
SIC: 2952 Asphalt Felts And Coatings
PA: P C R Inc
   5760 County Line Rd
   Cumming GA 30040
   330 945-7721

(G-314)
PALMER INDUSTRIES INC
Also Called: Palmer Products
920 Moe Dr (44310-2519)
PHONE..................................330 630-9397
Leonard Palmer, *President*
Leonard Palmer Jr, *President*
Len Senior, *President*
EMP: 7
SQ FT: 8,000
SALES (est): 1.1MM **Privately Held**
WEB: www.shaftsaver.com
SIC: 3599 Machine shop, jobbing & repair

(G-315)
PC SYSTEMS
Also Called: Sabbagh Tool and Equipment Co
307 Montrose Ave (44310-3815)
PHONE..................................330 825-7966
Dennis Sabbagh, *Owner*
EMP: 4
SQ FT: 1,200
SALES: 200K **Privately Held**
SIC: 3571 3578 5045 5734 Computers, digital, analog or hybrid; computer peripheral equipment repair & maintenance; computer peripheral equipment; computer peripheral equipment

(G-316)
PENINSULA PUBLISHING LLC
Also Called: Plastics Machinery Magazine
302 N Cleveland Massillon (44333-9303)
PHONE..................................330 524-3359
Ja Lewellenc, *CEO*
Tony Eagan,
EMP: 9
SALES (est): 371.8K **Privately Held**
SIC: 2721 Magazines: publishing & printing

(G-317)
PERFECT PRCISION MACHINING LTD
920 Clay St (44311-2214)
PHONE..................................330 475-0324
Margaret Habib, *Principal*
EMP: 9
SALES (est): 1MM **Privately Held**
SIC: 3599 Machine shop, jobbing & repair

(G-318)
PERKINELMER HLTH SCIENCES INC
520 S Main St Ste 2423 (44311-1086)
PHONE..................................330 825-4525
Susan Monaco, *Human Res Mgr*
Chritine Gradisher, *Manager*
Jim Bailey, *Manager*
Aniket Parekh, *Software Engr*
Mallory Petrolla, *Software Dev*
EMP: 32
SALES (corp-wide): 2.7B **Publicly Held**
SIC: 2835 2836 5049 In vitro & in vivo diagnostic substances; biological products, except diagnostic; laboratory equipment, except medical or dental
HQ: Perkinelmer Health Sciences, Inc.
   940 Winter St
   Waltham MA 02451
   781 663-6900

(G-319)
PFAHL GAUGE & MANUFACTURING CO
665 Harden Ave (44310-2421)
PHONE..................................330 633-8402
EMP: 4 **EST:** 1912
SQ FT: 2,000
SALES (est): 350K **Privately Held**
SIC: 3469 Mfg Metal Stampings

(G-320)
PIN OAK ENERGY PARTNERS LLC
209 S Main St Ste 501 (44308-1319)
PHONE..................................888 748-0763
Christopher T Halvorson, *CEO*
EMP: 5
SALES (est): 1.3MM **Privately Held**
SIC: 1311 Crude petroleum & natural gas production

(G-321)
PIONEER PLASTICS CORPORATION
3330 Massillon Rd (44312-5397)
PHONE..................................330 896-2356
Ralph J Danesi Jr, *President*
Jakob Denzinger, *Principal*
EMP: 125
SQ FT: 45,000
SALES (est): 26.1MM **Privately Held**
SIC: 3089 Injection molding of plastics

(G-322)
PLATE-ALL METAL COMPANY INC
1210 Devalera St (44310-2483)
PHONE..................................330 633-6166
John L Burg, *President*
Charles Killinger, *Plt & Fclts Mgr*
Irene Burg, *Office Mgr*
EMP: 8
SQ FT: 6,660
SALES (est): 925.2K **Privately Held**
WEB: www.plateallmetal.com
SIC: 3471 8711 Chromium plating of metals or formed products; engineering services

(G-323)
POLY-MET INC
1997 Nolt Dr (44312-4862)
PHONE..................................330 630-9006
Frank Moore, *President*
Laura Moore, *Vice Pres*
EMP: 14
SQ FT: 10,000
SALES (est): 500K **Privately Held**
WEB: www.poly-met.com
SIC: 3479 Hot dip coating of metals or formed products

(G-324)
PORTAGE MACHINE CONCEPTS INC
Also Called: Portage Knife Company
75 Skelton Rd (44312-1821)
PHONE..................................330 628-2343
Jeannine Lizak, *President*
Christopher Michalec, *Treasurer*
Mary Lou Govia, *Admin Sec*
W Duane Huff, *Admin Sec*
▲ **EMP:** 16 **EST:** 1981
SQ FT: 6,500
SALES (est): 3.4MM **Privately Held**
WEB: www.portageknife.com
SIC: 3549 Rotary slitters (metalworking machines)

(G-325)
POWER MEDIA INC
546 Grant St (44311-1158)
PHONE..................................330 475-0500
Jon Erisey, *President*
Mike Belofi, *Opers Staff*
Beth Milkovich, *Manager*
Michael West, *Creative Dir*
EMP: 8
SQ FT: 11,000
SALES: 1.2MM **Privately Held**
SIC: 3993 3999 Advertising novelties; advertising display products

(G-326)
PRECISION DYNAMICS INC
1270 Linden Ave (44310-1263)
PHONE..................................330 697-0611
David Burns, *President*
Lisa Burns, *Vice Pres*
EMP: 4
SALES (est): 320K **Privately Held**
SIC: 3599 Machine & other job shop work

(G-327)
PRECISION INTERNATIONAL LLC
843 N Cleveland (44322)
PHONE..................................330 793-0900
Anthony P Crisalli, *President*
Kurt Walcutt, *CFO*
EMP: 20
SALES: 6MM **Privately Held**
SIC: 3441 Fabricated structural metal

(G-328)
PREMIER SEALS MFG LLC
Also Called: Premier Seals Mfg
909 W Waterloo Rd (44314-1529)
PHONE..................................330 861-1060
Robert Shultz,
▼ **EMP:** 8
SALES (est): 764.4K **Privately Held**
SIC: 2891 Sealing compounds, synthetic rubber or plastic

(G-329)
PRESSLERS MEATS INC
2553 Pressler Rd (44312-5500)
PHONE..................................330 644-5636
Roger H Pressler, *President*
Richard Pressler, *Vice Pres*
EMP: 15 **EST:** 1944
SQ FT: 1,800
SALES (est): 1.7MM **Privately Held**
SIC: 2011 Meat packing plants

(G-330)
PRIMAL LIFE ORGANICS LLC
3637 Torrey Pines Dr (44333-9278)
PHONE..................................419 356-3843
Trina Felber Rn, *CEO*
EMP: 6
SALES (est): 782.6K **Privately Held**
SIC: 2844 Toilet preparations

(G-331)
PRINTING SYSTEM INC
Also Called: 48hr Books
2249 14th St Sw (44314-2007)
PHONE..................................330 375-9128
James Fulton, *President*
James T Pachell, *Principal*
EMP: 12
SALES (est): 1.3MM **Privately Held**
WEB: www.printingsystem.com
SIC: 2752 Commercial printing, offset

(G-332)
PRO-FAB INC
2570 Pressler Rd (44312-5554)
PHONE..................................330 644-0044
Anna Myers, *CEO*
Monroe W Townsend, *Vice Pres*
EMP: 20
SQ FT: 15,000
SALES (est): 6.2MM **Privately Held**
SIC: 3441 1791 Fabricated structural metal; structural steel erection

(G-333)
PROGRESSIVE MANUFACTURING CO
Also Called: Progrssive Mtllizing Machining
300 Massillon Rd (44312-1914)
PHONE..................................330 784-4717
Doris Datsko, *President*
George Datsko Jr, *Corp Secy*
David Datsko, *Vice Pres*
EMP: 8
SQ FT: 18,000
SALES (est): 1.2MM **Privately Held**
WEB: www.prorebuild.com
SIC: 3599 3479 5084 Machine shop, jobbing & repair; painting, coating & hot dipping; industrial machinery & equipment

Akron - Summit County (G-334)   GEOGRAPHIC SECTION

(G-334)
QT EQUIPMENT COMPANY (PA)
151 W Dartmore Ave (44301-2462)
PHONE..................................330 724-3055
Daniel Root, *President*
Dave Root, *Treasurer*
Mitch Langford, *Manager*
▼ EMP: 35
SQ FT: 20,000
SALES (est): 6.3MM Privately Held
SIC: 7532 5531 3713 Body shop, trucks; automotive tires; utility truck bodies

(G-335)
QUALITY INNOVATIVE PDTS LLC
787 Wye Rd (44333-2268)
PHONE..................................330 990-9888
Greg Cordray,
EMP: 5
SQ FT: 50,000
SALES (est): 284.7K Privately Held
SIC: 3089 Novelties, plastic

(G-336)
QUANEX IG SYSTEMS INC (HQ)
Also Called: Quanex Building Products
388 S Main St Ste 700 (44311-1060)
PHONE..................................216 910-1519
Michael Hovan, *President*
Kevin Gray, *Vice Pres*
Jim Hummel, *Vice Pres*
David Gingrich, *CFO*
Rick Mazanec, *Controller*
◆ EMP: 175
SQ FT: 400,000
SALES (est): 28.9MM Publicly Held
WEB: www.superspacer.com
SIC: 3061 3053 Mechanical rubber goods; gaskets, packing & sealing devices

(G-337)
QUIKEY MANUFACTURING CO INC (PA)
1500 Industrial Pkwy (44310-2600)
PHONE..................................330 633-8106
Michael W Burns, *President*
Patrick P Burns, *Vice Pres*
Thomas Stiller, *Vice Pres*
William B Stiller, *Vice Pres*
Tom Stiller, *VP Mfg*
▲ EMP: 125 EST: 1959
SQ FT: 50,000
SALES (est): 14.1MM Privately Held
WEB: www.quikey.com
SIC: 3993 Advertising novelties

(G-338)
R C A RUBBER COMPANY
1833 E Market St (44305-4214)
P.O. Box 9240 (44305-0240)
PHONE..................................330 784-1291
Sherry Price, *President*
Ennice Barnes, *Principal*
Paul H Taylor, *Principal*
Katherine Woodward, *Principal*
Shane Price, *Vice Pres*
▼ EMP: 80 EST: 1931
SQ FT: 40,000
SALES (est): 24.7MM Privately Held
WEB: www.rcarubber.com
SIC: 3069 Molded rubber products

(G-339)
R C MUSSON RUBBER CO
1320 E Archwood Ave (44306-2825)
P.O. Box 7038 (44306-0038)
PHONE..................................330 773-7651
Bennie D Segers, *Ch of Bd*
Frank W Rockhold, *Vice Pres*
Robert S Segers, *Vice Pres*
William J Segers, *Vice Pres*
Joseph Kostko, *Treasurer*
EMP: 20 EST: 1945
SQ FT: 40,000
SALES (est): 3.8MM Privately Held
WEB: www.mussonrubber.com
SIC: 3069 5085 Mats or matting, rubber; rubber goods, mechanical

(G-340)
R W MICHAEL PRINTING CO
665 E Cuyahoga Falls Ave (44310-1552)
PHONE..................................330 923-9277
Robert Michael, *Owner*
Evelyn Michael, *Co-Owner*
EMP: 3
SQ FT: 2,000
SALES: 25K Privately Held
SIC: 2759 2796 2791 2789 Commercial printing; platemaking services; typesetting; bookbinding & related work; commercial printing, lithographic; die-cut paper & board

(G-341)
RANDOLPH RESEARCH CO
2449 Kensington Rd (44333-2054)
PHONE..................................330 666-1667
William Hinks, *President*
Paul Ertly, *Vice Pres*
Gerald D Shook, *Vice Pres*
EMP: 3
SALES (est): 425K Privately Held
WEB: www.randolphresearch.com
SIC: 3562 Ball & roller bearings

(G-342)
RANDY LEWIS INC
Also Called: Acme Fence & Lumber
1053 Bank St (44305-2507)
PHONE..................................330 784-0456
Randy Lewis, *President*
EMP: 10
SQ FT: 10,000
SALES: 1.2MM Privately Held
SIC: 3446 2499 3315 3089 Fences or posts, ornamental iron or steel; fencing, wood; chain link fencing; fences, gates & accessories: plastic; fencing

(G-343)
RAPID MOLD REPAIR & MACHINE
813 Home Ave (44310-4105)
PHONE..................................330 253-1000
Ivan Cagaric, *President*
Zelco Tomic, *Vice Pres*
EMP: 3
SQ FT: 3,700
SALES: 250K Privately Held
SIC: 3544 3599 Special dies & tools; custom machinery

(G-344)
RAUH POLYMERS INC
420 Kenmore Blvd (44301-1038)
PHONE..................................330 376-1120
Joseph M Rauh, *President*
James T Rauh, *Vice Pres*
Jim Rauh, *Vice Pres*
Ted Rauh, *Opers Mgr*
▲ EMP: 15
SALES (est): 5MM Privately Held
WEB: www.rauhpolymers.com
SIC: 2821 Plastics materials & resins

(G-345)
RCM ENGINEERING COMPANY
2089 N Clvland Msslln Rd (44333-1258)
P.O. Box 517, Bath (44210-0517)
PHONE..................................330 666-0575
Robert C Mc Dowell, *Owner*
EMP: 9 EST: 1903
SQ FT: 2,200
SALES (est): 725.7K Privately Held
SIC: 1311 1321 Natural gas production; natural gasoline production

(G-346)
REPORTER NEWSPAPER INC
1088 S Main St (44301-1206)
P.O. Box 2042 (44309-2042)
PHONE..................................330 535-7061
William Ellis Jr, *President*
EMP: 10
SALES (est): 460K Privately Held
SIC: 2711 Newspapers: publishing only, not printed on site

(G-347)
RESOURCE EXCHANGE COMPANY INC
383 Abbyshire Rd (44319-3803)
PHONE..................................440 773-8915
Larry Burkette, *Principal*
Bob Buckley, *Agent*
EMP: 5
SALES (est): 402.3K Privately Held
SIC: 3641 7389 Electric lamps & parts for specialized applications;

(G-348)
RICHARDS WHL FENCE CO INC
Also Called: Richard's Fence Company
1600 Firestone Pkwy (44301-1659)
PHONE..................................330 773-0423
Richard Peterson, *President*
Bill Peterson, *Vice Pres*
▲ EMP: 30
SQ FT: 235,000
SALES (est): 11.1MM Privately Held
SIC: 3315 5039 Chain link fencing; wire fence, gates & accessories

(G-349)
RICKS GRAPHIC ACCENTS INC
3554 S Arlington Rd (44312-5223)
PHONE..................................330 644-4455
Rick Lang, *President*
EMP: 4
SALES (est): 300K Privately Held
SIC: 3993 Signs & advertising specialties

(G-350)
RIVERCOR LLC
1560 Firestone Pkwy (44301-1626)
PHONE..................................330 784-1113
John Sharp, *President*
EMP: 25
SQ FT: 140,000
SALES (est): 6.3MM Privately Held
SIC: 2679 Paper products, converted

(G-351)
ROBERT F SAMS
Also Called: Real Solution Communication
1148 Monteray Dr (44305-1770)
PHONE..................................330 990-0477
Robert F Sams, *Owner*
EMP: 5
SALES: 75K Privately Held
SIC: 3669 Communications equipment

(G-352)
ROCHLING AUTOMOTIVE USA LLP
2275 Picton Pkwy (44312-4270)
PHONE..................................330 400-5785
Robert Roach, *Plant Mgr*
EMP: 75
SALES (corp-wide): 1.7B Privately Held
SIC: 3714 Motor vehicle engines & parts
HQ: Rochling Automotive Usa Llp
245 Parkway E
Duncan SC 29334
864 486-0888

(G-353)
ROGERS INDUSTRIAL PRODUCTS INC
532 S Main St (44311-1018)
PHONE..................................330 535-3331
John Cole, *President*
▲ EMP: 35 EST: 1951
SQ FT: 239,000
SALES (est): 7.7MM Privately Held
WEB: www.rogersusa.com
SIC: 3542 3625 3491 3643 Presses: hydraulic & pneumatic, mechanical & manual; industrial electrical relays & switches; pressure valves & regulators, industrial; current-carrying wiring devices

(G-354)
ROTOCAST TECHNOLOGIES INC
1900 Englewood Ave (44312-1004)
PHONE..................................330 798-9091
Edward W Kissel, *President*
Bruce Kuhn, *Opers Mgr*
Mark Bradley, *Sales Engr*
Ken Herold, *Sales Engr*
EMP: 30
SQ FT: 25,000
SALES (est): 6.1MM Privately Held
WEB: www.rotocastmold.com
SIC: 3365 3544 Aluminum & aluminum-based alloy castings; special dies, tools, jigs & fixtures

(G-355)
ROYALTON MANUFACTURING INC
1169 Brittain Rd (44305-1004)
PHONE..................................440 237-2233
Kenneth Wesner, *President*
William Calfee, *Vice Pres*
Judith Wesner, *Treasurer*
EMP: 18
SQ FT: 12,000
SALES (est): 2.7MM Privately Held
SIC: 3599 Mfg Industrial Machinery

(G-356)
RUBBER CITY MACHINERY CORP
Also Called: R C M
1 Thousand Sweitzer Ave (44311)
P.O. Box 2043 (44309-2043)
PHONE..................................330 434-3500
George B Sobieraj, *President*
Daniel Abraham, *General Mgr*
Bernie Sobieraj, *Vice Pres*
Robert J Westfall, *Vice Pres*
Doug Fulwell, *Engineer*
▲ EMP: 32
SQ FT: 100,000
SALES (est): 7.7MM Privately Held
SIC: 3559 5084 7629 Rubber working machinery, including tires; plastics working machinery; industrial machinery & equipment; electrical repair shops

(G-357)
RUBBER WORLD MAGAZINE INC
1741 Akron Peninsula Rd (44313-5157)
PHONE..................................330 864-2122
Job Lippincott, *President*
EMP: 15
SALES (est): 880K Privately Held
WEB: www.rubberworld.com
SIC: 2721 Periodicals

(G-358)
RUSCOE COMPANY (PA)
485 Kenmore Blvd (44301-1013)
P.O. Box 3858 (44314-0858)
PHONE..................................330 253-8148
Paul Michalec, *President*
Larry Musci, *General Mgr*
Betty Pfaff, *Corp Secy*
John Postan, *Plant Mgr*
Bob Peterson, *Credit Mgr*
EMP: 49 EST: 1949
SQ FT: 24,000
SALES (est): 10.8MM Privately Held
WEB: www.ruscoe.com
SIC: 2891 3297 2851 Adhesives & sealants; nonclay refractories; paints & allied products

(G-359)
RUSCOE COMPANY
219 E Miller Ave (44301-1326)
P.O. Box 3858 (44314-0858)
PHONE..................................330 253-8148
Paul Michalec, *Director*
EMP: 50
SALES (corp-wide): 11.1MM Privately Held
WEB: www.ruscoe.com
SIC: 2865 Color pigments, organic
PA: The Ruscoe Company
485 Kenmore Blvd
Akron OH 44301
330 253-8148

(G-360)
RUSSELL PRODUCTS CO INC
Also Called: Akron Anodizing & Coating Div
1066 Home Ave (44310-3502)
PHONE..................................330 535-3391
Daniel Dzurovcin, *Vice Pres*
EMP: 9
SALES (corp-wide): 5.2MM Privately Held
WEB: www.russprodco.com
SIC: 3471 Finishing, metals or formed products; anodizing (plating) of metals or formed products
PA: Russell Products Co., Inc.
275 N Forge St Ste 1
Akron OH 44304
330 535-9246

(G-361)
RUSSELL PRODUCTS CO INC
Falholt Division
1066 Home Ave (44310-3502)
PHONE..................................330 434-9163
Jerry Gray, *Executive*

▲ = Import ▼=Export ◆ =Import/Export

GEOGRAPHIC SECTION
Akron - Summit County (G-387)

EMP: 4
SALES (corp-wide): 5.2MM Privately Held
WEB: www.russprodco.com
SIC: 3479 Coating of metals & formed products
PA: Russell Products Co., Inc.
275 N Forge St Ste 1
Akron OH 44304
330 535-9246

(G-362)
RUSSELL PRODUCTS CO INC
Russell Division
275 N Forge St Ste 2 (44304-1472)
PHONE..........................216 267-0880
Tim Dzurovcin, Manager
EMP: 4
SALES (corp-wide): 5.2MM Privately Held
WEB: www.russprodco.com
SIC: 3479 Painting, coating & hot dipping
PA: Russell Products Co., Inc.
275 N Forge St Ste 1
Akron OH 44304
330 535-9246

(G-363)
RUSSELL STANDARD CORPORATION
Also Called: Jasa Asphalt Russell Standard
990 Hazel St (44305-1610)
PHONE..........................330 733-9400
Robert Gunther, Manager
EMP: 6
SALES (corp-wide): 195.6MM Privately Held
WEB: www.russellstandard.com
SIC: 5032 2951 Asphalt mixture; concrete, bituminous
PA: Russell Standard Corporation
285 Kappa Dr Ste 300
Pittsburgh PA 15238
412 449-0700

(G-364)
S & A INDUSTRIES CORPORATION (DH)
571 Kennedy Rd Ste R (44305-4425)
PHONE..........................330 733-6040
Greg Anderson, President
▲ EMP: 66
SQ FT: 42,000
SALES (est): 21MM
SALES (corp-wide): 663.3MM Privately Held
SIC: 3086 Plastics foam products
HQ: Sekiso Corporation
1-3, Hinakitamachi
Okazaki AIC 444-0
564 252-121

(G-365)
S I T STRINGS CO INC
2493 Romig Rd (44320-4109)
PHONE..........................330 434-8010
Virgil Lay, President
Edwin Speedy, Exec VP
Robert C Hird, Vice Pres
EMP: 20
SQ FT: 16,000
SALES (est): 2.7MM Privately Held
WEB: www.sitstrings.com
SIC: 3931 5736 Guitars & parts, electric & nonelectric; strings, musical instrument; musical instrument stores

(G-366)
S R TECHNOLOGIES LLC (PA)
2200 N Clvland Msslln Rd (44333-1255)
PHONE..........................330 523-7184
Frank Manning, Mng Member
Thomas Tedde, Mng Member
Marilyn Close,
▲ EMP: 4
SQ FT: 2,982
SALES (est): 877.6K Privately Held
SIC: 3699 Bells, electric

(G-367)
SACO LOWELL PARTS LLC
1395 Triplett Blvd (44306-3124)
PHONE..........................330 794-1535
John Daenes, President
Bruce Weick, Vice Pres
Russell Dunlap, Vice Pres
EMP: 21
SALES (est): 3MM Privately Held
WEB: www.sacolowell.com
SIC: 3469 Machine parts, stamped or pressed metal

(G-368)
SAEHWA IMC NA INC
Also Called: Versitech Mold
2200 Massillon Rd (44312-4234)
PHONE..........................419 752-4511
Thomas Tanler, Manager
EMP: 70
SALES (corp-wide): 76.8MM Privately Held
WEB: www.qualitymold.com
SIC: 3599 3544 Machine shop, jobbing & repair; special dies, tools, jigs & fixtures
PA: Saehwa Imc Na, Inc.
2200 Massillon Rd
Akron OH 44312
330 645-6653

(G-369)
SAEHWA IMC NA INC (PA)
Also Called: Versitech Mold Div
2200 Massillon Rd (44312-4234)
PHONE..........................330 645-6653
Mike Cingel, President
Stanley B Migdal, Principal
Jerry Candiliotis, Vice Pres
Mike Politis, Vice Pres
Jim Finfield, Admin Sec
▲ EMP: 100 EST: 1978
SQ FT: 83,821
SALES (est): 76.8MM Privately Held
WEB: www.qualitymold.com
SIC: 3544 Industrial molds

(G-370)
SAFAR MACHINE COMPANY
905 Brown St (44311-2211)
PHONE..........................330 644-0155
John Safar, President
Bruce Safar, Vice Pres
Julie Salopek, Treasurer
EMP: 10 EST: 1978
SQ FT: 5,500
SALES (est): 1.9MM Privately Held
SIC: 3599 Machine shop, jobbing & repair

(G-371)
SAINT CROIX LTD
3371 W Bath Rd (44333-2105)
P.O. Box 5229 (44334-0229)
PHONE..........................330 666-1544
Jonathan Schiesswohl, President
EMP: 5
SALES (est): 423.7K Privately Held
WEB: www.saintcroix.net
SIC: 1311 Crude petroleum production; natural gas production

(G-372)
SAINT-GOBAIN PRFMCE PLAS CORP
2664 Gilchrist Rd (44305-4412)
PHONE..........................330 798-6981
Chris Mattern, Plant Mgr
EMP: 200
SQ FT: 100,000
SALES (corp-wide): 215.9MM Privately Held
SIC: 3061 3083 Medical & surgical rubber tubing (extruded & lathe-cut); laminated plastics plate & sheet
HQ: Saint-Gobain Performance Plastics Corporation
31500 Solon Rd
Solon OH 44139
440 836-6900

(G-373)
SCHOTT METAL PRODUCTS COMPANY
Also Called: Design Wheel and Hub
2225 Lee Dr (44306-4399)
PHONE..........................330 773-7873
Samuel Schott, President
F W Schott, Vice Pres
Paul Graham, Admin Sec
EMP: 100 EST: 1945
SQ FT: 90,000
SALES (est): 12.2MM Privately Held
SIC: 3469 3714 Stamping metal for the trade; motor vehicle parts & accessories

(G-374)
SEAVIVAL LLC
526 S Main St Ste 518 (44311-4403)
P.O. Box 4372, Copley (44321-0372)
PHONE..........................330 252-1151
Brian G Friedman, CEO
EMP: 5
SALES: 1,000K Privately Held
SIC: 3999 Manufacturing industries

(G-375)
SHOOK MANUFACTURED PDTS INC (PA)
1017 Kenmore Blvd (44314-2153)
P.O. Box 15058 (44314-5058)
PHONE..........................330 848-9780
Roy Knittle, President
Thomas Johns, Vice Pres
▲ EMP: 9
SQ FT: 10,000
SALES (est): 1.2MM Privately Held
SIC: 3545 5072 Chucks: drill, lathe or magnetic (machine tool accessories); hardware; screws; rivets; hand tools

(G-376)
SIMPLY CANVAS INC
1479 Exeter Rd (44306-3856)
PHONE..........................330 436-6500
Adam Fried, President
Merrie Casteel, COO
Laurie Ware, Controller
EMP: 22
SALES (est): 3.3MM Privately Held
SIC: 2396 7384 Screen printing on fabric articles; fabric printing & stamping; photofinish laboratories

(G-377)
SK MACHINERY CORPORATION
487 Wellington Ave (44305-2680)
P.O. Box 2109, Stow (44224-0109)
PHONE..........................330 733-7325
Soroosh Khoshbin, President
▲ EMP: 4
SQ FT: 15,000
SALES: 300K Privately Held
SIC: 3531 Construction machinery

(G-378)
SLICE MFG LLC
1800 Triplett Blvd (44306-3311)
PHONE..........................330 733-7600
Randy Theken, Principal
Bobi Lekic, Director
EMP: 3 EST: 2015
SALES (est): 186.3K Privately Held
SIC: 3313 Alloys, additive, except copper: not made in blast furnaces

(G-379)
SMART 3D SOLUTIONS LLC
411 Wolf Ledges Pkwy # 100 (44311-1051)
PHONE..........................330 972-7840
EMP: 4
SQ FT: 66,500
SALES (est): 136.2K Privately Held
SIC: 3949 Mfg Sporting/Athletic Goods

(G-380)
SML INC (PA)
Also Called: Primeline Industries
4083 Embassy Pkwy (44333-1781)
PHONE..........................330 668-6555
Brian Zinkan, General Mgr
Sandy Costill, Manager
Kevin Larizza, Shareholder
Jacqueline Bebczuk, Shareholder
Mary Larizza, Shareholder
▲ EMP: 5
SQ FT: 2,000
SALES (est): 19.3MM Privately Held
WEB: www.primelineindustries.com
SIC: 3069 Tubing, rubber

(G-381)
SOLDIER TECH & ARMOR RES LLC
3300 Massillon Rd (44312-5361)
PHONE..........................330 896-5217
Fred Kungl,
EMP: 5
SALES (est): 246.3K Privately Held
SIC: 3999 Manufacturing industries

(G-382)
SOUTH AKRON AWNING CO (PA)
763 Kenmore Blvd (44314-2196)
PHONE..........................330 848-7611
Ranell Minear, President
Michelle Halafa, Vice Pres
Kathleen Mueller, Admin Sec
EMP: 14
SQ FT: 19,000
SALES (est): 2MM Privately Held
WEB: www.southakronawning.com
SIC: 2394 1799 7359 Awnings, fabric: made from purchased materials; canvas covers & drop cloths; awning installation; tent & tarpaulin rental; party supplies rental services

(G-383)
SPECIALTY DRAPERY WORKROOM
50 S Frank Blvd (44313-7212)
PHONE..........................330 864-4190
Mark Ruby, President
EMP: 5
SQ FT: 4,000
SALES (est): 881.2K Privately Held
SIC: 2391 Draperies, plastic & textile: from purchased materials

(G-384)
STANDARD JIG BORING SVC LLC (HQ)
Also Called: Sjbs
3360 Miller Park Rd (44312-5388)
PHONE..........................330 896-9530
David Stuller, Controller
Ginger Townsend, Mng Member
Jeffrey R Wahl,
▲ EMP: 40 EST: 2007
SQ FT: 30,000
SALES (est): 13.5MM
SALES (corp-wide): 138.7MM Privately Held
SIC: 3599 Machine shop, jobbing & repair
PA: Ariel Corporation
35 Blackjack Road Ext
Mount Vernon OH 43050
740 397-0311

(G-385)
STANDARD JIG BORING SVC LLC
3194 Massillon Rd (44312-5363)
PHONE..........................330 644-5405
George Koberlein, Branch Mgr
EMP: 6
SALES (corp-wide): 138.7MM Privately Held
SIC: 3599 Machine shop, jobbing & repair
HQ: Standard Jig Boring Service, Llc
3360 Miller Park Rd
Akron OH 44312
330 896-9530

(G-386)
STAR PRINTING COMPANY INC
125 N Union St (44304-1390)
PHONE..........................330 376-0514
Vicki Lauck, President
Lynda Moore, Corp Secy
Paul M Lauck, Vice Pres
Robert D Lauck Jr, Vice Pres
Jill Arney, Purchasing
EMP: 22
SQ FT: 20,000
SALES (est): 3.3MM Privately Held
WEB: www.starptg.com
SIC: 2752 2759 2789 Commercial printing, offset; letterpress printing; bookbinding & related work

(G-387)
STATIONERY SHOP INC
30 N Summit St (44308-1941)
PHONE..........................330 376-2033
John E Steurer, President
EMP: 5
SQ FT: 6,000
SALES (est): 692.2K Privately Held
SIC: 2752 2759 2791 Commercial printing, offset; letterpress printing; embossing on paper; engraving; typesetting

(G-388)
STEEL STRUCTURES OF OHIO LLC
1324 Firestone Pkwy A (44301-1624)
PHONE...................................330 374-9900
James L Rench, *Mng Member*
John Young,
EMP: 40
SQ FT: 5,000
SALES (est): 6.7MM **Privately Held**
WEB: www.steel-oh.com
SIC: 3449 Bars, concrete reinforcing: fabricated steel

(G-389)
STERLING ASSOCIATES INC
Also Called: Fastsigns
1783 Brittain Rd (44310-1801)
PHONE...................................330 630-3500
Milton L Liming, *President*
Elaine Liming, *Corp Secy*
Brent B Liming, *Vice Pres*
Todd Evans, *Executive*
EMP: 8 EST: 1962
SQ FT: 2,000
SALES (est): 1MM **Privately Held**
SIC: 3993 2721 Signs, not made in custom sign painting shops; periodicals

(G-390)
SUMMIT DRILLING COMPANY INC
152 W Dartmore Ave (44301-2450)
PHONE...................................800 775-5537
EMP: 16
SQ FT: 9,000
SALES: 1.3MM **Privately Held**
SIC: 1381 8748 Environmental Drilling & Consulting

(G-391)
SUMMIT PRINTING & GRAPHICS
Also Called: Summit Printing and Graphics
1265 W Waterloo Rd (44314-1522)
PHONE...................................330 645-7644
Joe C Reinmann, *President*
EMP: 3 EST: 1976
SQ FT: 3,000
SALES (est): 240K **Privately Held**
WEB: www.summitp-g.com
SIC: 2752 Commercial printing, offset

(G-392)
SUMMIT TOOL COMPANY (HQ)
Also Called: Ken-Tools
768 E North St (44305-1164)
P.O. Box 9320 (44305-0320)
PHONE...................................330 535-7177
Douglas Romstadt, *Vice Pres*
Doug Ronstadt, *Purchasing*
Larry Sorles, *Director*
▲ EMP: 65 EST: 1932
SQ FT: 70,000
SALES (est): 19MM **Privately Held**
WEB: www.kenstool.com
SIC: 3423 Hand & edge tools
PA: North Coast Holdings Incorporated
   768 E North St
   Akron OH 44305
   330 535-7177

(G-393)
SUNOCO INC
1375 Home Ave (44310-2549)
PHONE...................................216 912-2579
EMP: 27
SALES (corp-wide): 54B **Publicly Held**
SIC: 2911 Petroleum refining
HQ: Sunoco, Inc.
   3801 West Chester Pike
   Newtown Square PA 19073
   215 977-3000

(G-394)
TALLMADGE FINISHING CO INC
879 Moe Dr Ste C20 (44310-2558)
PHONE...................................330 633-7466
David Mann, *President*
Paul Cooper, *Vice Pres*
EMP: 30
SALES (est): 3MM **Privately Held**
SIC: 3069 Hard rubber & molded rubber products

(G-395)
TALLMADGE SPINNING & METAL CO
2783 Gilchrist Rd Unit A (44305-4406)
P.O. Box 58, Tallmadge (44278-0058)
PHONE...................................330 794-2277
John Sasanecki, *President*
Jacob Sasanecki, *Vice Pres*
Jake Sasanecki, *Opers Mgr*
Linda Sasanecki, *Treasurer*
Don White, *Manager*
EMP: 15 EST: 1947
SQ FT: 15,000
SALES: 4MM **Privately Held**
WEB: www.tsm1947.com
SIC: 3449 Miscellaneous metalwork

(G-396)
TARGETING CUSTOMER SAFETY INC
Also Called: TCS
1021 Galsworthy Dr (44313-8110)
PHONE...................................330 865-9593
Benny Swigert, *Partner*
Steve Zaugg, *Partner*
EMP: 5
SALES (est): 430K **Privately Held**
WEB: www.targetingcustomersafety.com
SIC: 3842 Personal safety equipment

(G-397)
TECH PRO INC
3030 Gilchrist Rd (44305-4420)
PHONE...................................330 923-3546
John Putman, *President*
Kay Putman, *Vice Pres*
▲ EMP: 28
SQ FT: 30,000
SALES (est): 2.6MM **Privately Held**
WEB: www.techpro-usa.com
SIC: 7699 3821 3829 3825 Laboratory instrument repair; laboratory apparatus & furniture; measuring & controlling devices; instruments to measure electricity; computer peripheral equipment

(G-398)
TEMPERATURE CONTROLS COMPANY
661 Anderson Ave (44306-3101)
P.O. Box 7665 (44306-0665)
PHONE...................................330 773-6633
John Kerr, *Chairman*
Robert J Kerr Sr, *Chairman*
James Mc Clarnon, *Vice Pres*
Robert J Kerr Jr, *Treasurer*
Lawrence Simers, *Accountant*
EMP: 15 EST: 1952
SQ FT: 12,000
SALES (est): 3.1MM **Privately Held**
SIC: 1711 7692 Mechanical contractor; warm air heating & air conditioning contractor; welding repair

(G-399)
TEMPLE ISRAEL
91 Springside Dr (44333-2428)
PHONE...................................330 762-8617
Milton I Wiskind, *President*
David Lipper, *Pastor*
Dr Davis Meckler, *Vice Pres*
Henry Nagel, *Vice Pres*
Davis Unger, *Treasurer*
EMP: 9 EST: 1866
SALES (est): 440K **Privately Held**
SIC: 8661 3625 Synagogue; switches, electric power

(G-400)
THE BEACON JOURNAL PUBG CO
Also Called: Akron Beacon Journal
44 E Exchange St (44308-1510)
P.O. Box 640 (44309-0640)
PHONE...................................330 996-3000
Kirk Davis, *CEO*
Kimberly Drezdzon, *Editor*
Richard Stallsmith, *Editor*
Craig Webb, *Editor*
Drew Burge, *District Mgr*
EMP: 115
SQ FT: 250,000
SALES (est): 35.1MM
SALES (corp-wide): 1.5B **Publicly Held**
WEB: www.ohio.com
SIC: 2711 Newspapers, publishing & printing
HQ: Gatehouse Media, Llc
   175 Sullys Trl Fl 3
   Pittsford NY 14534
   585 598-0030

(G-401)
THE BOOKSELLER INC
39 Westgate Cir (44313-7401)
PHONE...................................330 865-5831
Frank Klein, *President*
Pat Klein, *Corp Secy*
Andrea A Klein, *Treasurer*
EMP: 4
SQ FT: 2,400
SALES (est): 327.3K **Privately Held**
SIC: 5932 2789 7389 Rare books; binding only: books, pamphlets, magazines, etc.; auction, appraisal & exchange services

(G-402)
THEKEN COMPANIES LLC
1800 Triplett Blvd (44306-3311)
PHONE...................................330 733-7600
Jolene Maurer, *CFO*
EMP: 25
SQ FT: 30,000
SALES (est): 1MM **Privately Held**
SIC: 3841 Surgical & medical instruments

(G-403)
THERMO-RITE MFG COMPANY
Also Called: Star Fire Distributing
1355 Evans Ave (44305-1038)
PHONE...................................330 633-8680
Roy Allen, *CEO*
Barbara Lewis, *Purchasing*
Dave Williams, *Purchasing*
Roy Repasky, *Sales Mgr*
Stephanie Stankwits, *Manager*
EMP: 35 EST: 1946
SQ FT: 120,000
SALES (est): 9.1MM **Privately Held**
WEB: www.thermo-rite.com
SIC: 3429 Fireplace equipment, hardware: andirons, grates, screens

(G-404)
THIRSTY DOG BREWING CO
529 Grant St Ste 103 (44311-1184)
PHONE...................................330 252-8740
Ulo Konsen, *President*
V Erik Konsen, *Corp Secy*
John Nhaeway, *Vice Pres*
Tim Rastetter, *Opers Staff*
EMP: 4
SALES (est): 573.5K **Privately Held**
WEB: www.thirstydog.com
SIC: 2082 Beer (alcoholic beverage)

(G-405)
TINYCIRCUITS
540 S Main St (44311-1079)
PHONE...................................330 329-5753
EMP: 5
SALES (est): 517.8K **Privately Held**
SIC: 3679 Electronic circuits

(G-406)
TJ BELL INC
1340 Home Ave Ste E (44310-2570)
PHONE...................................330 633-3644
Thomas J Bell, *President*
Roger Phillips, *Sales Staff*
Eva Bell, *Admin Sec*
EMP: 3
SQ FT: 5,000
SALES (est): 919.4K **Privately Held**
WEB: www.tjbell.com
SIC: 5084 3599 Industrial machinery & equipment; custom machinery

(G-407)
TLT-TURBO INC
2693 Wingate Ave (44314-1301)
PHONE...................................330 776-5115
John A Landis, *Director*
▲ EMP: 6
SALES (est): 1.5MM
SALES (corp-wide): 54.9B **Privately Held**
SIC: 3564 Ventilating fans: industrial or commercial
HQ: Tlt-Turbo Gmbh
   Gleiwitzstr. 7
   Zweibrucken 66482
   633 280-80

(G-408)
TRANSITWORKS LLC
1090 W Wilbeth Rd (44314-1945)
PHONE...................................855 337-9543
EMP: 5
SALES (corp-wide): 404.9MM **Privately Held**
SIC: 3465 Body parts, automobile: stamped metal
HQ: Transitworks, Llc
   4199 Kinross Lakes Pkwy
   Richfield OH 44286
   330 861-1118

(G-409)
TRELLEBORG WHEEL SYSTEMS AMERI (HQ)
1501 Exeter Rd (44306-3889)
PHONE...................................866 633-8473
Ydo Doornbos, *Managing Dir*
Adam Blooenstein, *Principal*
Gregory Hower, *Principal*
◆ EMP: 40
SQ FT: 600,000
SALES (est): 66.1MM
SALES (corp-wide): 3.7B **Privately Held**
SIC: 3011 3061 Industrial tires, pneumatic; mechanical rubber goods
PA: Trelleborg Ab
   Johan Kocksgatan 10
   Trelleborg 231 4
   410 670-00

(G-410)
TRI CAST LIMITED PARTNERSHIP
2128 Killian Rd (44312-4898)
PHONE...................................330 733-8718
John Voight, *CEO*
EMP: 24
SQ FT: 18,712
SALES (est): 3MM **Privately Held**
WEB: www.tri-cast.com
SIC: 3321 Gray iron castings

(G-411)
TRI-CAST INC (PA)
2128 Killian Rd (44312-4898)
PHONE...................................330 733-8718
John Voight, *CEO*
EMP: 30
SQ FT: 28,000
SALES (est): 2.5MM **Privately Held**
SIC: 3321 Gray iron castings; ductile iron castings

(G-412)
TRIANGLE ADHESIVES LLC
3616 Torrey Pines Dr (44333-9277)
PHONE...................................330 670-9722
EMP: 3
SALES (est): 135.6K **Privately Held**
SIC: 2891 Mfg Adhesives/Sealants

(G-413)
TRUMBULL INDUSTRIES INC
209 Perkins St (44304-1298)
PHONE...................................330 434-6174
Joe Reguerio, *Branch Mgr*
Joe Regueiro, *Branch Mgr*
EMP: 21
SALES (corp-wide): 150.3MM **Privately Held**
SIC: 5074 8711 2541 Plumbing fittings & supplies; engineering services; wood partitions & fixtures
PA: Trumbull Industries, Inc.
   300 Dietz Rd Ne
   Warren OH 44483
   330 393-6624

(G-414)
TRUSEAL TECHNOLOGIES INC (HQ)
388 S Main St Ste 700 (44311-1060)
PHONE...................................216 910-1500

▲ = Import ▼ = Export
◆ = Import/Export

GEOGRAPHIC SECTION

Albany - Athens County (G-442)

August J Coppola, *CEO*
James Baratuci, *Vice Pres*
Lee Burroughs, *Vice Pres*
David Marlar, *Vice Pres*
Louis Ferri, *Research*
◆ **EMP:** 35
SQ FT: 80,000
SALES (est): 27.3MM Publicly Held
WEB: www.swiggle.com
SIC: 2891 Sealants

(G-415)
TURKEYFOOT HILL SAND & GRAVEL
465 E Turkeyfoot Lake Rd (44319-4105)
PHONE 330 899-1997
Rick Williams, *Principal*
EMP: 3 **EST:** 2011
SALES (est): 184.2K Privately Held
SIC: 1442 Construction sand & gravel

(G-416)
TW CORPORATION
99 S Seiberling St (44305)
PHONE 440 461-3234
Thomas T Whims, *President*
Thomas M Seger, *Admin Sec*
EMP: 30
SQ FT: 28,000
SALES (est): 2.5MM Privately Held
SIC: 3365 Aerospace castings, aluminum

(G-417)
TYLER ELECTRIC MOTOR REPAIR
1888 Copley Rd (44320-1570)
PHONE 330 836-5537
Frank S Politz, *President*
Michael E Politz, *Vice Pres*
Frank J Politz, *Treasurer*
Teresa Snyder, *Admin Sec*
EMP: 5 **EST:** 1946
SQ FT: 2,700
SALES (est): 571.7K Privately Held
SIC: 7694 7699 5063 5084 Electric motor repair; pumps & pumping equipment repair; motors, electric; pumps & pumping equipment

(G-418)
UNINTERRUPTED LLC
3800 Embassy Pkwy Ste 360 (44333-8389)
PHONE 216 771-2323
Maverick Carter, *CEO*
EMP: 15
SALES (est): 6MM Privately Held
SIC: 7372 Application computer software

(G-419)
UNION PROCESS INC
1925 Akron Peninsula Rd (44313-4896)
PHONE 330 929-3333
Arno Szegvari, *President*
Emery Ll, *Vice Pres*
Anita Szegvari, *Treasurer*
Anita Goins, *Sales Staff*
Tracy Denholm, *Manager*
▲ **EMP:** 35 **EST:** 1944
SQ FT: 30,000
SALES (est): 9.1MM Privately Held
WEB: www.unionprocess.com
SIC: 3541 Grinding machines, metalworking

(G-420)
UNITED FEED SCREWS LTD
487 Wellington Ave (44305-2680)
PHONE 330 798-5532
Paul Norton, *President*
Joe Norton Sr, *Info Tech Dir*
▲ **EMP:** 10 **EST:** 1998
SQ FT: 14,500
SALES (est): 1.5MM Privately Held
WEB: www.unitedfeedscrews.com
SIC: 3061 Oil & gas field machinery rubber goods (mechanical)

(G-421)
UNIVERSAL PRECISION PRODUCTS
1480 Industrial Pkwy (44310-2602)
PHONE 330 633-6128
Jon Munson, *President*
Bob Munson, *Vice Pres*
EMP: 45 **EST:** 1946
SQ FT: 65,000
SALES (est): 7.4MM Privately Held
WEB: www.uppinc.com
SIC: 3554 3549 Paper industries machinery; metalworking machinery

(G-422)
UNIVERSAL TIRE MOLDS INC
5127 Boyer Pkwy (44312-4272)
PHONE 330 253-5101
Paul Scurei, *President*
Michael R Cingel, *Vice Pres*
Harold Vance, *Treasurer*
▲ **EMP:** 30
SQ FT: 17,000
SALES (est): 4.7MM
SALES (corp-wide): 67.1MM Privately Held
SIC: 3544 3599 Forms (molds), for foundry & plastics working machinery; machine shop, jobbing & repair
PA: Saehwa Imc Co., Ltd.
   12 Cheomdanyeonsin-Ro 29beon-Gil, Buk-Gu
   Gwangju 61089
   826 294-4616

(G-423)
VACUUM ELECTRIC SWITCH CO INC (PA)
2390 Romig Rd (44320)
PHONE 330 374-5156
Cecil C Wristen, *President*
Sandra M Wristen, *Vice Pres*
EMP: 2
SQ FT: 200
SALES (est): 1.2MM Privately Held
WEB: www.vacuumelectricswitch.com
SIC: 3613 7629 Switchboards & parts, power; electronic equipment repair

(G-424)
VALLEY RUBBER MIXING INC
4478 Regal Dr (44321-1174)
PHONE 330 434-4442
Thomas Brennan, *President*
Tom Brenan, *Owner*
EMP: 14
SALES (est): 2.1MM Privately Held
SIC: 3069 Reclaimed rubber & specialty rubber compounds

(G-425)
VERTICAL DATA LLC
Also Called: Medtrace
2169 Chuckery Ln (44333-4742)
P.O. Box 38, Bath (44210-0038)
PHONE 330 289-0313
Christopher Wolff,
EMP: 15 **EST:** 2015
SALES (est): 500K Privately Held
SIC: 7372 Application computer software

(G-426)
VINTAGE VAULT
832 Elmore Ave (44302-1206)
PHONE 330 607-0136
Carrie Shkolnik, *Principal*
EMP: 3
SALES (est): 153.1K Privately Held
SIC: 3272 Burial vaults, concrete or pre-cast terrazzo

(G-427)
VIRTUAL HOLD TECHNOLOGY LLC (PA)
3875 Embassy Pkwy Ste 350 (44333-8343)
PHONE 330 670-2200
Wes Hayden, *CEO*
Thomas Jameson, *Exec VP*
Ted Bray, *Vice Pres*
Kevin Shinseki, *Vice Pres*
Mark Williams, *Mng Member*
EMP: 80
SQ FT: 18,000
SALES (est): 19.1MM Privately Held
WEB: www.virtualhold.com
SIC: 7371 7372 Computer software development; prepackaged software

(G-428)
VULCAN MACHINERY CORPORATION
20 N Case Ave (44305-2598)
PHONE 330 376-6025
David Jacobs, *President*
Bradley J Jacobs, *Vice Pres*
Steph Wensel, *Purchasing*
EMP: 25
SALES (est): 3.9MM Privately Held
WEB: www.vulcanmachinery.com
SIC: 3559 7299 Plastics working machinery; banquet hall facilities

(G-429)
W G LOCKHART CONSTRUCTION CO
800 W Waterloo Rd (44314-1528)
PHONE 330 745-6520
Alexander R Lockhart, *President*
Richard Stanley, *Admin Sec*
EMP: 100 **EST:** 1918
SQ FT: 5,000
SALES (est): 8.1MM Privately Held
SIC: 1611 3273 Highway & street construction; ready-mixed concrete

(G-430)
W L BECK PRINTING & DESIGN
1326 S Main St (44301-1625)
P.O. Box 1257 (44309-1257)
PHONE 330 762-3020
William L Beck, *President*
Vivian Shanafelt, *Treasurer*
Shirley Beck, *Admin Sec*
EMP: 6
SQ FT: 2,000
SALES (est): 649.5K Privately Held
SIC: 2754 2791 Commercial printing, gravure; typesetting

(G-431)
WARREN ENTERPRISES
1067 Winhurst Dr (44313-5814)
PHONE 330 836-6119
Phillip Warren, *Owner*
EMP: 3
SALES: 500K Privately Held
WEB: www.internetsalesman.com
SIC: 3993 Neon signs

(G-432)
WAYMAKERS INC
Also Called: Taste of Heaven Original Gourm
628 Roscoe Ave (44306-2131)
PHONE 330 352-1096
Ben Thurman, *President*
EMP: 3
SALES (est): 210.3K Privately Held
SIC: 2035 Pickles, sauces & salad dressings

(G-433)
WESCO MACHINE INC
918 N Main St (44310-2149)
PHONE 330 688-6973
De Etta Connelly, *President*
Ronald Connelly, *Vice Pres*
EMP: 17
SQ FT: 10,000
SALES (est): 2.4MM Privately Held
SIC: 3599 3559 Machine shop, jobbing & repair; plastics working machinery

(G-434)
WEST MOTORSPORTS INC
Also Called: Weldon West
1018 Ironwood Rd Ste A (44306-4217)
PHONE 330 350-0375
Weldon West, *President*
EMP: 3
SQ FT: 8,000
SALES (est): 297.3K Privately Held
SIC: 3312 Tool & die steel

(G-435)
WHITE INDUSTRIAL TOOL INC
Also Called: White Tool
102 W Wilbeth Rd (44301-2415)
PHONE 330 773-6889
Ronald White Jr, *President*
Richard White, *Vice Pres*
Christopher White, *Treasurer*
Ronald White Sr, *Shareholder*
Robert White, *Admin Sec*
EMP: 15
SQ FT: 18,000
SALES (est): 1.2MM Privately Held
WEB: www.whitetool.com
SIC: 3546 Power-driven handtools

(G-436)
WILKES ENERGY INC
17 S Main St Ste 101a (44308-1803)
PHONE 330 252-4560
Scott Wilkes, *President*
EMP: 4
SALES (est): 442.5K Privately Held
SIC: 1382 Oil & gas exploration services

(G-437)
WINSELL INCORPORATED
1720 Merriman Rd Unit J (44313-5280)
PHONE 330 836-7421
Fred Shockey, *CEO*
EMP: 3
SALES (est): 650.5K Privately Held
SIC: 2821 Plastics materials & resins

(G-438)
YANKE BIONICS INC (PA)
303 W Exchange St (44302-1702)
PHONE 330 762-6411
Mark Yanke, *President*
Michele Hogan, *General Mgr*
Gary Charton, *Vice Pres*
Jerry Bernar, *Engineer*
Mark Clary, *Director*
EMP: 44
SQ FT: 15,000
SALES (est): 10.1MM Privately Held
SIC: 3842 Limbs, artificial; braces, orthopedic

(G-439)
YANKE BIONICS INC
3975 Embassy Pkwy Ste 1 (44333-8321)
PHONE 330 668-4070
Gary Charton, *Branch Mgr*
EMP: 5
SALES (corp-wide): 10.1MM Privately Held
SIC: 3842 Limbs, artificial; braces, orthopedic
PA: Yanke Bionics, Inc.
   303 W Exchange St
   Akron OH 44302
   330 762-6411

(G-440)
YES PRESS PRINTING CO
720 E Glenwood Ave Front (44310-3400)
PHONE 330 535-8398
Philip Freeman, *Owner*
EMP: 3
SQ FT: 2,500
SALES (est): 190K Privately Held
SIC: 2752 Commercial printing, offset

(G-441)
YUGO MOLD INC
1733 Wadsworth Rd (44320-3141)
PHONE 330 606-0710
Sam Milkovich, *Ch of Bd*
Zack Milkovich, *President*
Milo Milkovich, *Vice Pres*
EMP: 17
SQ FT: 6,050
SALES (est): 1.7MM Privately Held
SIC: 3544 Industrial molds

Albany
Athens County

(G-442)
HILL JAMES R & HILL EARLEY W
41085 Townsend Rd (45710-9067)
PHONE 740 591-4203
James R Hill, *Partner*
Early W Hill, *Partner*
Randy Hill, *Park Mgr*
EMP: 3
SALES: 110K Privately Held
SIC: 2082 Beer (alcoholic beverage)

(PA)=Parent Co (HQ)=Headquarters (DH)=Div Headquarters
✪ = New Business established in last 2 years

Alexandria
Licking County

(G-443)
SPANISH LNGAGE PRODUCTIONS INC
3017 Mounts Rd (43001-9755)
PHONE.................614 737-3424
Rocio Reyes-Moore, *President*
David R Moore, *CFO*
David Moore, *CFO*
EMP: 5
SQ FT: 11,000
SALES: 700K Privately Held
WEB: www.spanlanpro.com
SIC: 2731 Textbooks: publishing & printing

Alger
Hardin County

(G-444)
WIWA LLC
107 N Main St (45812-9738)
P.O. Box 398 (45812-0398)
PHONE.................419 757-0141
Jeffrey Wold, *General Mgr*
◆ **EMP:** 10
SQ FT: 12,000
SALES: 1.3MM
SALES (corp-wide): 21.8MM Privately Held
WEB: www.wiwa.com
SIC: 3563 Spraying & dusting equipment
PA: Wiwa Wilhelm Wagner Gmbh & Co. Kg
Gewerbestr. 1-3
Lahnau 35633
644 160-90

(G-445)
WIWA LP
107 N Main St (45812-9738)
P.O. Box 398 (45812-0398)
PHONE.................419 757-0141
Jeffrey T Wold, *Principal*
Austin Oglesbee, *Cust Mgr*
EMP: 11
SALES (est): 1.8MM Privately Held
SIC: 3563 Robots for industrial spraying, painting, etc.

Alledonia
Belmont County

(G-446)
MAPLE CREEK MINING INC (HQ)
56854 Pleasant Ridge Rd (43902-9716)
PHONE.................740 926-9205
Robert E Murray, *President*
John Ferelli, *Vice Pres*
Michael Loiacono, *Treasurer*
EMP: 1
SALES (est): 33.4MM
SALES (corp-wide): 4.8B Publicly Held
SIC: 1222 Bituminous coal-underground mining
PA: Murray Energy Corporation
46226 National Rd
Saint Clairsville OH 43950
740 338-3100

Alliance
Stark County

(G-447)
A J OSTER FOILS LLC
2081 Mccrea St (44601-2793)
PHONE.................330 823-1700
Kevin Bense, *President*
Brian Vonder Haar, *General Mgr*
Alexander B Jourdan, *General Mgr*
Robert M James, *Vice Pres*
Scott Riordan, *Plant Mgr*
▲ **EMP:** 53
SQ FT: 80,000
SALES (est): 14.9MM Publicly Held
SIC: 3341 3353 3471 3497 Secondary nonferrous metals; aluminum sheet, plate & foil; plating & polishing; metal foil & leaf; metals service centers & offices
HQ: A.J. Oster, Llc
301 Metro Center Blvd # 204
Warwick RI 02886
401 736-2600

(G-448)
A R SCHOPPS SONS INC
14536 Oyster Rd (44601-9243)
P.O. Box 2513 (44601-0513)
PHONE.................330 821-8406
Robert Schopp, *President*
Joe Russo, *General Mgr*
David Schopp, *Vice Pres*
Sandee Monte, *Office Mgr*
Mary Schopp, *Admin Sec*
▲ **EMP:** 50 **EST:** 1898
SQ FT: 3,084
SALES (est): 3.1MM Privately Held
WEB: www.arschopp.com
SIC: 3931 Organ parts & materials

(G-449)
ACME INDUSTRIAL GROUP INC
540 N Freedom Ave (44601-1816)
P.O. Box 2388 (44601-0388)
PHONE.................330 821-3900
Richard Burton Jr, *President*
Deborah Burton, *Treasurer*
Ray Maki, *Office Mgr*
EMP: 14
SALES (est): 1.7MM Privately Held
WEB: www.acme-chrome.com
SIC: 3471 Electroplating of metals or formed products; chromium plating of metals or formed products

(G-450)
ACME SURFACE DYNAMICS INC
555 N Freedom Ave (44601-1873)
P.O. Box 2388 (44601-0388)
PHONE.................330 821-3900
Dan Curry, *Maint Spvr*
Jim Householder, *Sales Staff*
Tracy Hower, *Office Mgr*
Debbie Burton,
EMP: 4
SALES (est): 695.7K Privately Held
SIC: 3312 Stainless steel

(G-451)
ALL COATINGS CO INC
510 W Ely St (44601-1610)
PHONE.................330 821-3806
Scott Brothers, *President*
Wanda Lou Brothers, *Corp Secy*
EMP: 7
SQ FT: 70,000
SALES (est): 910K Privately Held
SIC: 2951 2851 Asphalt paving mixtures & blocks; paints & paint additives

(G-452)
ALLIANCE CASTINGS COMPANY LLC
1001 E Broadway St (44601-2602)
PHONE.................330 829-5600
David Goodwin,
▲ **EMP:** 20
SALES (est): 5.7MM
SALES (corp-wide): 2.4B Privately Held
WEB: www.alliancecastings.com
SIC: 3363 Aluminum die-castings
HQ: Amsted Rail Company, Inc.
311 S Wacker Dr Ste 5300
Chicago IL 60606

(G-453)
ALLIANCE EQUIPMENT COMPANY INC
1000 N Union Ave (44601-1392)
PHONE.................330 821-2291
Patricia Antonosanti, *President*
Matthew Antonosanti, *Vice Pres*
▲ **EMP:** 11
SQ FT: 49,000
SALES (est): 1.2MM Privately Held
SIC: 3089 Plastic & fiberglass tanks

(G-454)
ALLIANCE PUBLISHING CO INC (HQ)
Also Called: Review, The
40 S Linden Ave (44601-2447)
P.O. Box 2180 (44601-0180)
PHONE.................330 453-1304
Chuck Dix, *President*
David E Dix, *Vice Pres*
R Victor Dix, *Vice Pres*
Robert C Dix, *Vice Pres*
G Charles Dix, *Treasurer*
EMP: 125 **EST:** 1888
SQ FT: 25,000
SALES (est): 32.9MM
SALES (corp-wide): 528.2MM Privately Held
WEB: www.alliancelink.com
SIC: 2711 2752 Newspapers, publishing & printing; commercial printing, lithographic
PA: Dix 1898, Inc.
212 E Liberty St
Wooster OH
330 264-3511

(G-455)
ANSTINE MACHINING CORP
15835 Armour St Ne (44601-9349)
P.O. Box 3734 (44601-7734)
PHONE.................330 821-4365
Michael Anstine, *President*
EMP: 18
SQ FT: 23,000
SALES (est): 3.6MM Privately Held
SIC: 3599 3441 Machine shop, jobbing & repair; fabricated structural metal

(G-456)
BANCO DIE INC
11322 Union Ave Ne (44601-1398)
PHONE.................330 821-8511
Michael Bresnahan, *President*
Joseph E Bender, *Vice Pres*
Patti Bresnahan, *Treasurer*
Joseph Bender, *VP Finance*
Chric Carmen, *Manager*
EMP: 15 **EST:** 1948
SQ FT: 7,500
SALES (est): 2.3MM Privately Held
SIC: 3544 Special dies & tools

(G-457)
BAYLEY ENVELOPE INC
119 E State St (44601-4933)
PHONE.................330 821-2150
Margret Mangano, *President*
Tom Babb, *Vice Pres*
Tim Vanfosson, *Vice Pres*
Michael Hoover, *Treasurer*
EMP: 5 **EST:** 1957
SQ FT: 20,000
SALES (corp-wide): 580K Privately Held
SIC: 2677 Envelopes
PA: Luzerne Company
48941 Clctta Smthferry Rd
East Liverpool OH

(G-458)
BRIAN FRANKS ELECTRIC INC
11424 Beech St Ne (44601-8705)
PHONE.................330 821-5457
Brian Frank, *President*
Tracy Frank, *Admin Sec*
EMP: 3
SALES (est): 250K Privately Held
SIC: 7694 Electric motor repair

(G-459)
C JS SIGNS
1670 Charl Ann Dr (44601-3688)
PHONE.................330 821-7446
Christopher Liebhart, *Owner*
EMP: 6 **EST:** 1998
SALES (est): 400K Privately Held
SIC: 3993 Signs & advertising specialties

(G-460)
CARNATION ELC MTR REPR SLS INC
232 N Lincoln Ave (44601-1600)
PHONE.................330 823-7116
Jim Wyman, *President*
EMP: 5
SQ FT: 3,600
SALES (est): 1.7MM Privately Held
SIC: 7694 5999 Electric motor repair; motors, electric

(G-461)
CARNATION MACHINE & TOOL INC
14632 Oyster Rd (44601-9244)
PHONE.................330 823-5352
A Edgar Smith Jr, *President*
Carol Smith, *Corp Secy*
EMP: 6 **EST:** 1965
SQ FT: 4,200
SALES: 270K Privately Held
SIC: 3599 Machine shop, jobbing & repair

(G-462)
CENTRAL COATED PRODUCTS INC
2025 Mccrea St (44601-2794)
P.O. Box 3348 (44601-7348)
PHONE.................330 821-9830
Thomas A Tormey, *President*
Nathaniel Porter, *Opers Mgr*
Steven T Porter, *Treasurer*
Cheryl Dyer, *Accounting Dir*
Jeff Porter, *Sales Mgr*
▲ **EMP:** 60
SQ FT: 77,500
SALES (est): 24.5MM Privately Held
WEB: www.centralcoated.net
SIC: 2672 2671 Coated & laminated paper; paper coated or laminated for packaging

(G-463)
DANGO & DIENENTHAL INC
21 E Chestnut St (44601-4950)
P.O. Box 2870 (44601-0870)
PHONE.................330 829-0277
Jorg Dienenthal, *President*
Rainer Dango, *Admin Sec*
EMP: 3
SQ FT: 19,000
SALES: 475K
SALES (corp-wide): 1.3MM Privately Held
SIC: 3549 Metalworking machinery
PA: Dango & Dienenthal Gmbh & Co. Kg
Hagener Str. 103
Siegen 57072
271 401-0

(G-464)
DAVIS TECHNOLOGIES INC
Also Called: Dti
837 W Main St (44601-2208)
PHONE.................330 823-2544
Robert W Dillon, *President*
Douglas E Anderson, *Vice Pres*
James R Dillon, *Treasurer*
Richard N Dillon, *Admin Sec*
EMP: 15
SQ FT: 7,500
SALES: 750K Privately Held
WEB: www.davistechnologies.com
SIC: 8711 3625 Engineering services; control equipment, electric

(G-465)
FILNOR INC (PA)
227 N Freedom Ave (44601-1897)
P.O. Box 2328 (44601-0328)
PHONE.................330 821-8731
Ronald L Neely, *CEO*
James C Neely, *President*
Craig Clarke, *Vice Pres*
Daren Szekely, *Vice Pres*
Mike Higgins, *Production*
◆ **EMP:** 50 **EST:** 1970
SQ FT: 72,000
SALES (est): 14.3MM Privately Held
WEB: www.filnor.com
SIC: 3625 5063 Electric controls & control accessories, industrial; switches, electric power; resistors & resistor units; electrical apparatus & equipment

(G-466)
FILNOR INC
181 N Arch Ave (44601-2413)
PHONE.................330 829-3180
Lottie Roach, *Manager*
EMP: 9
SQ FT: 7,854

GEOGRAPHIC SECTION

Alliance - Stark County (G-494)

SALES (corp-wide): 14.3MM **Privately Held**
WEB: www.filnor.com
SIC: 3625 Electric controls & control accessories, industrial
PA: Filnor, Inc.
227 N Freedom Ave
Alliance OH 44601
330 821-8731

(G-467)
FILNOR INC
227 N Freedom Ave (44601-1897)
P.O. Box 2328 (44601-0328)
PHONE..................330 821-7667
Lottie Roach, *Branch Mgr*
EMP: 15
SQ FT: 5,712
SALES (corp-wide): 14.3MM **Privately Held**
WEB: www.filnor.com
SIC: 3625 3676 3643 3613 Electric controls & control accessories, industrial; electronic resistors; current-carrying wiring devices; knife switches, electric
PA: Filnor, Inc.
227 N Freedom Ave
Alliance OH 44601
330 821-8731

(G-468)
FOREPLEASURE
14461 Gaskill Dr Ne (44601-1142)
PHONE..................330 821-1293
Kathleen Miller, *Principal*
EMP: 3
SALES (est): 212.3K **Privately Held**
SIC: 2252 Hosiery

(G-469)
GBC METALS LLC
Also Called: Olin Brass
2081 Mccrea St (44601-2704)
PHONE..................330 823-1700
Beth Tirey, *General Mgr*
EMP: 50 **Publicly Held**
SIC: 2812 Caustic soda, sodium hydroxide
HQ: Gbc Metals, Llc
4801 Olympia Park Plz
Louisville KY 40241

(G-470)
HAISS FABRIPART LLC
22421 Lake Park Blvd (44601-3469)
PHONE..................330 821-2028
Duane Stuckey, *Sales Executive*
Valerie G Giarrana, *Manager*
Moritz Haiss,
EMP: 30
SQ FT: 6,600
SALES: 4MM **Privately Held**
SIC: 3599 Machine shop, jobbing & repair

(G-471)
HARTLEY MACHINE INC
22640 Hartley Rd (44601-6908)
PHONE..................330 821-0343
Thomas Poto, *President*
Judy B Poto, *Vice Pres*
EMP: 4 EST: 1951
SQ FT: 5,000
SALES: 350K **Privately Held**
SIC: 3599 7692 3444 Machine shop, jobbing & repair; welding repair; sheet metalwork

(G-472)
HEBRAIC WAY PRESS COMPANY
2615 S Seneca Ave (44601-5148)
PHONE..................330 614-4872
Beverly Shaw, *President*
EMP: 4
SALES: 125K **Privately Held**
SIC: 2741 7389 Miscellaneous publishing;

(G-473)
HILLES BURIAL VAULTS INC
2145 S Union Ave (44601-4961)
PHONE..................330 823-2251
Michael Hilles, *President*
Todd Andrie, *Admin Sec*
EMP: 3 EST: 1923
SQ FT: 624

SALES (est): 390.4K **Privately Held**
SIC: 3272 Burial vaults, concrete or pre-cast terrazzo; monuments, concrete

(G-474)
HOFFMAN HINGE AND HARDWARE LLC
11750 Marlboro Ave Ne (44601-9719)
PHONE..................330 935-2240
Renee Milliken, *Principal*
EMP: 3
SALES (est): 299.9K **Privately Held**
SIC: 3429 Manufactured hardware (general)

(G-475)
HOLOPHANE LIGHTING
12720 Beech St Ne (44601-8778)
PHONE..................330 823-5535
Steve Oyster, *Principal*
EMP: 5
SALES (est): 40.7K **Privately Held**
WEB: www.holophanelighting.com
SIC: 3646 Commercial indusl & institutional electric lighting fixtures

(G-476)
HOOPES FERTILIZER WORKS INC
9866 Freshley Ave Ne # 166 (44601-8794)
PHONE..................330 821-3550
Steve Hoopes, *Manager*
EMP: 4
SALES (corp-wide): 1.8MM **Privately Held**
WEB: www.hooverfence.com
SIC: 2875 Fertilizers, mixing only
PA: Hoopes Fertilizer Works, Inc
24104 Us Route 30
East Rochester OH 44625
330 894-2121

(G-477)
HYKON MANUFACTURING COMPANY
163 E State St (44601-4933)
P.O. Box 3800 (44601-7800)
PHONE..................330 821-8889
Douglas Duchon, *President*
Brenda Duchon, *Vice Pres*
EMP: 3 EST: 1913
SQ FT: 3,000
SALES: 800K **Privately Held**
SIC: 3499 3545 Reels, cable: metal; measuring tools & machines, machinists' metalworking type

(G-478)
INNOVATIVE WLDG & DESIGN LLC
24946 Hartley Rd (44601-9015)
PHONE..................330 581-1316
Eric J Peters, *Administration*
Eric Peters,
EMP: 3
SALES (est): 66.9K **Privately Held**
SIC: 7692 Welding repair

(G-479)
JARMAN PRINTING COMPANY LLC
350 S Union Ave (44601-2664)
P.O. Box 2505 (44601-0505)
PHONE..................330 823-8585
Krista Jarvis, *Mng Member*
Randal Jarvis,
EMP: 6 EST: 1906
SQ FT: 6,500
SALES (est): 888.5K **Privately Held**
SIC: 2752 2759 Lithographing on metal; letterpress printing

(G-480)
KARRIER COMPANY INC
1065 S Liberty Ave (44601-4061)
PHONE..................330 823-9597
Bob Church, *Owner*
Wayne R Church, *Owner*
Holly Church, *Co-Owner*
EMP: 3
SQ FT: 5,000
SALES (est): 230K **Privately Held**
WEB: www.karrierco.com
SIC: 3612 Vibrators, interrupter

(G-481)
KEENER RUBBER COMPANY
14700 Commerce St Ne (44601-1099)
P.O. Box 2717 (44601-0717)
PHONE..................330 821-1880
Richard A Michelson, *CEO*
EMP: 28
SQ FT: 30,000
SALES (est): 5.2MM **Privately Held**
WEB: www.keenerrubber.com
SIC: 3069 Rubber bands

(G-482)
LEXINGTON ABRASIVES INC
Also Called: Sancap Abrasives
16123 Armour St Ne (44601-9301)
PHONE..................330 821-1166
Robert Stuhlmiller, *President*
Michael A Ogline, *Principal*
Sharon McFarland, *Controller*
▲ EMP: 80 EST: 1999
SQ FT: 540,000
SALES (est): 14.5MM **Privately Held**
WEB: www.sancapabrasives.com
SIC: 3291 Coated abrasive products

(G-483)
MAC MANUFACTURING INC (PA)
14599 Commerce St Ne (44601-1003)
PHONE..................330 823-9900
Michael Conny, *Principal*
Jenny Conny, *Corp Secy*
Dan Tubbs, *Vice Pres*
▲ EMP: 700
SALES (est): 270.9MM **Privately Held**
SIC: 3715 5012 Truck trailers; trailers for trucks, new & used; truck bodies

(G-484)
MAC STEEL TRAILER LTD
14599 Commerce St Ne (44601-1003)
PHONE..................330 823-9900
Michael A Conny, *Mng Member*
EMP: 40
SALES (est): 435.4K **Privately Held**
SIC: 3715 Truck trailers

(G-485)
MAC TRAILER MANUFACTURING INC (PA)
14599 Commerce St Ne (44601-1003)
PHONE..................330 823-9900
Mike Conny, *President*
Ben Childers, *Vice Pres*
David Sandor, *Vice Pres*
Bill Ogden, *CFO*
Jenny Conny, *Treasurer*
▲ EMP: 193
SQ FT: 220,000
SALES (est): 140.2MM **Privately Held**
SIC: 3715 5012 5013 5015 Truck trailers; trailers for trucks, new & used; truck bodies; motor vehicle supplies & new parts; motor vehicle parts, used; trailer repair

(G-486)
MAC TRAILER SERVICE INC
14504 Commerce St Ne (44601-1000)
PHONE..................330 823-9190
Michael Conny, *President*
EMP: 40 EST: 1997
SALES (est): 9.6MM **Privately Held**
SIC: 3715 Truck trailers

(G-487)
MALCO PRODUCTS INC
Also Called: Malco Products Alliance Packg
12155 Fisher Ave Ne (44601-1038)
PHONE..................330 753-0361
Ed Scheid, *Branch Mgr*
EMP: 40
SQ FT: 16,560
SALES (corp-wide): 92.9MM **Privately Held**
WEB: www.malcopro.com
SIC: 2842 Disinfectants, household or industrial plant
PA: Malco Products, Inc.
361 Fairview Ave
Barberton OH 44203
330 753-0361

(G-488)
MARLBORO MANUFACTURING INC
11750 Marlboro Ave Ne (44601-9798)
PHONE..................330 935-2221
Thomas Naughton, *President*
Renee Milliken, *President*
Daniel Lough, *Vice Pres*
Patrick Whitaker, *Vice Pres*
▲ EMP: 50 EST: 1960
SQ FT: 54,000
SALES (est): 13.1MM **Privately Held**
WEB: www.marlborohinge.com
SIC: 3429 Piano hardware

(G-489)
MILLS ALUMINUM FAB
W 23 Rd St (44601)
PHONE..................330 821-4108
Christine Miller, *Owner*
EMP: 4
SALES (est): 349.3K **Privately Held**
SIC: 3499 Fabricated metal products

(G-490)
MORGAN ENGINEERING SYSTEMS INC
1049 S Mahoning Ave (44601-3212)
PHONE..................330 823-6120
Mark Fedor, *President*
EMP: 45
SQ FT: 952
SALES (corp-wide): 27.5MM **Privately Held**
WEB: www.morganengineering.com
SIC: 3536 Hoists, cranes & monorails
PA: Morgan Engineering Systems, Inc.
1049 S Mahoning Ave
Alliance OH 44601
330 823-6130

(G-491)
MORGAN ENGINEERING SYSTEMS INC
1182 E Summit St (44601-3224)
PHONE..................330 821-4721
Beverly Montagner, *Purch Dir*
James Broch, *Branch Mgr*
EMP: 45
SALES (corp-wide): 27.5MM **Privately Held**
WEB: www.morganengineering.com
SIC: 3536 Cranes, overhead traveling
PA: Morgan Engineering Systems, Inc.
1049 S Mahoning Ave
Alliance OH 44601
330 823-6130

(G-492)
MOUNT UNION PATTERN WORKS INC
920 Auld St (44601-3239)
PHONE..................330 821-2274
Jeff Ruggles, *President*
Marjorie Ruggles, *Admin Sec*
EMP: 3
SQ FT: 10,000
SALES: 300K **Privately Held**
SIC: 3543 Industrial patterns

(G-493)
NORTH COAST PROFILE INC
255 E Perry St (44601-1774)
PHONE..................330 823-7777
Dewayne Frank, *President*
EMP: 4
SALES: 450K **Privately Held**
SIC: 3547 3444 Ferrous & nonferrous mill equipment, auxiliary; sheet metalwork

(G-494)
OUTLIER SOLUTIONS LLC
14835 Mccallum Ave Ne (44601-8868)
PHONE..................330 947-2678
Matthew Brown, *Mng Member*
John Brown,
Jorge Brown,
Rebecca Brown,
EMP: 4
SALES (est): 154.7K **Privately Held**
SIC: 3812 Defense systems & equipment

Alliance - Stark County (G-495)

(G-495)
P & E SALES LTD
1595 W Main St (44601-2104)
P.O. Box 382, North Benton (44449-0382)
PHONE..................................330 829-0100
Paul J Tatulinski, *President*
Ellen Tatulinski, *Vice Pres*
EMP: 8
SQ FT: 5,600
SALES: 550K **Privately Held**
SIC: 3053 5085 Gaskets, all materials; gaskets & seals

(G-496)
PHILLIPS MFG & MCH CORP
118 1/2 E Ely St (44601-1809)
P.O. Box 2627 (44601-0627)
PHONE..................................330 823-9178
Deborah L Williamson, *President*
EMP: 9 **EST:** 1914
SQ FT: 20,000
SALES: 364.5K **Privately Held**
SIC: 3599 Machine shop, jobbing & repair

(G-497)
SALLY BEAUTY SUPPLY LLC
2636 W State St (44601-5699)
PHONE..................................330 823-7476
Nicole Yoder, *Manager*
EMP: 4 **Publicly Held**
WEB: www.sallybeauty.com
SIC: 5087 2844 Beauty parlor equipment & supplies; toilet preparations
HQ: Sally Beauty Supply Llc
   3001 Colorado Blvd
   Denton TX 76210
   940 898-7500

(G-498)
SAMS GRAPHIC INDUSTRIES
611 Homeworth Rd (44601-9072)
PHONE..................................330 821-4710
Sam Schuette, *Owner*
EMP: 10
SQ FT: 6,000
SALES: 150K **Privately Held**
WEB: www.graphicind.com
SIC: 2796 2759 Engraving platemaking services; engraving

(G-499)
SCOTT A ZURBRUGG
Also Called: Zurbrugg Machine
6016 Union Ave Ne (44601-9449)
PHONE..................................330 821-9814
Scott A Zurbugg, *Owner*
EMP: 3 **EST:** 1990
SQ FT: 1,200
SALES (est): 159.2K **Privately Held**
SIC: 3599 Machine shop, jobbing & repair

(G-500)
SMITH MACHINE INC
20651 Lake Park Blvd (44601-3319)
PHONE..................................330 821-9898
David F Smith, *President*
Tim Smith, *General Mgr*
Eileen R Smith, *Vice Pres*
EMP: 7 **EST:** 1976
SALES: 670K **Privately Held**
SIC: 3599 Machine shop, jobbing & repair

(G-501)
STEEL EQP SPECIALISTS INC
22623 Lake Park Blvd (44601-3454)
PHONE..................................330 829-2626
Richard L Hansen, *Principal*
EMP: 25
SALES (corp-wide): 23.5MM **Privately Held**
WEB: www.seseng.com
SIC: 3599 3593 3547 Custom machinery; fluid power cylinders & actuators; rolling mill machinery
PA: Steel Equipment Specialists, Inc.
   1507 Beeson St Ne
   Alliance OH 44601
   330 823-8260

(G-502)
STEEL EQP SPECIALISTS INC (PA)
Also Called: S.E.S.
1507 Beeson St Ne (44601-2142)
PHONE..................................330 823-8260

James R Boughton, *CEO*
T Virgil Huggett, *Ch of Bd*
Doris Gulyas, *Principal*
Said S Kabalan, *Principal*
Richard G Pinkett, *Principal*
▲ **EMP:** 72 **EST:** 1976
SQ FT: 32,000
SALES (est): 23.5MM **Privately Held**
WEB: www.seseng.com
SIC: 7699 3599 7629 3593 Industrial machinery & equipment repair; custom machinery; electrical repair shops; fluid power cylinders & actuators; rolling mill machinery; fabricated structural metal

(G-503)
STUCHELL PRODUCTS LLC
Also Called: Sare Plastics
12240 Rockhill Ave Ne (44601-1064)
PHONE..................................330 821-4299
Jerome Robinson, *Project Mgr*
Bradson Ephraim, *Engineer*
Karen Roudabush, *Human Res Mgr*
Bart Stuchell,
EMP: 45
SALES (est): 3.8MM **Privately Held**
WEB: www.sareplastics.com
SIC: 3089 Injection molded finished plastic products; injection molding of plastics

(G-504)
SUNAMERICACONVERTING LLC
46 N Rockhill Ave (44601-2211)
PHONE..................................330 821-6300
Gaby Ajram,
Howard Davison,
Russ Romocean,
▲ **EMP:** 55
SQ FT: 72,000
SALES (est): 14.8MM **Privately Held**
SIC: 2656 Paper cups, plates, dishes & utensils

(G-505)
T AND W STAMPING ACQUISITION
930 W Ely St (44601-1500)
PHONE..................................330 821-5777
EMP: 12
SALES (est): 1.8MM **Privately Held**
SIC: 3469 Stamping metal for the trade

(G-506)
THOMAS ALLEN CO
1062 Parkside Dr (44601-3734)
PHONE..................................330 823-8487
Scott Celasko, *Owner*
EMP: 3
SALES (est): 216.7K **Privately Held**
SIC: 2759 Commercial printing

(G-507)
TIMKEN COMPANY
22261 Margaret Ln (44601-9099)
PHONE..................................330 471-4791
EMP: 3
SALES (corp-wide): 3.5B **Publicly Held**
SIC: 3562 Ball & roller bearings
PA: The Timken Company
   4500 Mount Pleasant St Nw
   North Canton OH 44720
   234 262-3000

(G-508)
TRANSUE & WILLIAMS STAMPG CORP (PA)
930 W Ely St (44601-1500)
PHONE..................................330 821-5777
John Staudt, *Vice Pres*
John Beringer, *Treasurer*
▲ **EMP:** 16
SALES (est): 5MM **Privately Held**
SIC: 3469 Stamping metal for the trade

(G-509)
TRANSUE WILLIAMS STAMPING INC (HQ)
930 W Ely St (44601-1500)
PHONE..................................330 829-5007
John Staudt, *President*
John C Beringer, *Treasurer*
▲ **EMP:** 4
SQ FT: 180,000

SALES (est): 728.5K **Privately Held**
WEB: www.twstamping.com
SIC: 3469 Stamping metal for the trade

(G-510)
TRI-SEAL LLC
16125 Armour St Ne (44601-9301)
PHONE..................................330 821-1166
Paul Young, *President*
Robert Larney, *CFO*
Art Richards, *Treasurer*
David Waksman, *Admin Sec*
EMP: 8
SALES (est): 309.8K
SALES (corp-wide): 1.1B **Privately Held**
SIC: 3053 Gaskets & sealing devices
PA: Tekni-Plex, Inc.
   460 E Swedesford Rd # 3000
   Wayne PA 19087
   484 690-1520

(G-511)
TRILOGY PLASTICS INC (PA)
2290 W Main St (44601-2272)
P.O. Box 2600 (44601-0600)
PHONE..................................330 821-4700
Stephen Osborn, *President*
Bruce Frank, *Vice Pres*
Rex Roseberry, *CFO*
EMP: 80
SQ FT: 90,000
SALES (est): 18.2MM **Privately Held**
WEB: www.trilogyplastics.com
SIC: 3089 Molding primary plastic

(G-512)
W J EGLI COMPANY INC (PA)
205 E Columbia St (44601-2563)
P.O. Box 2605 (44601-0605)
PHONE..................................330 823-3666
William J Egli, *President*
Cheryl A Stuffel, *Corp Secy*
Garth Egli, *Vice Pres*
Cheryl Stuffel, *Admin Sec*
▼ **EMP:** 15 **EST:** 1968
SQ FT: 100,000
SALES: 3.5MM **Privately Held**
WEB: www.wjegli.com
SIC: 2541 3496 3498 3444 Display fixtures, wood; miscellaneous fabricated wire products; fabricated pipe & fittings; sheet metalwork; partitions & fixtures, except wood; automotive & apparel trimmings

(G-513)
WEDGE HARDWOOD PRODUCTS
2137 Knox School Rd (44601-6923)
PHONE..................................330 525-7775
Michael Stahl, *Partner*
Jim Hahlen, *Partner*
EMP: 6
SQ FT: 7,200
SALES: 852.5K **Privately Held**
SIC: 2431 Planing mill, millwork

(G-514)
WERE ROLLING PRETZLE COMPANY
2500 W State St Ste 82 (44601-5607)
PHONE..................................419 784-0762
Angela Quinones, *Manager*
EMP: 6
SALES (est): 283.8K **Privately Held**
SIC: 2051 Breads, rolls & buns

(G-515)
WHITACRE GREER COMPANY (PA)
1400 S Mahoning Ave (44601-3433)
PHONE..................................330 823-1610
Janet Kaboth, *CEO*
J B Whitacre Jr, *Ch of Bd*
L A Morrison, *President*
Christopher Kaboth, *Vice Pres*
Judith Rodgers, *Accountant*
EMP: 38 **EST:** 1916
SALES (est): 14.3MM **Privately Held**
WEB: www.wgpaver.com
SIC: 3251 3255 Paving brick, clay; clay refractories

(G-516)
WINKLE INDUSTRIES INC
2080 W Main St (44601-2187)
PHONE..................................330 823-9730
Joe Schatz, *CEO*
Shawn Babington, *General Mgr*
Jeff McCartney, *Engineer*
Beth A Felger, *Treasurer*
Paul Bean, *Regl Sales Mgr*
▲ **EMP:** 55
SQ FT: 85,000
SALES (est): 12.8MM **Privately Held**
WEB: www.winkleindustries.com
SIC: 7699 3499 5063 Industrial machinery & equipment repair; magnets, permanent: metallic; control & signal wire & cable, including coaxial

Alpha
Greene County

(G-517)
UNISON INDUSTRIES LLC
2070 Heller Rd (45301)
PHONE..................................937 426-0621
Eric Christianson, *Engineer*
EMP: 11 **EST:** 1998
SALES (est): 1.1MM **Privately Held**
SIC: 7699 3315 Typewriter repair, including electric; steel wire & related products

(G-518)
UNISON INDUSTRIES LLC
Also Called: Elano Machine Operations
530 Orchard Ln (45301)
P.O. Box 135 (45301-0135)
PHONE..................................937 426-4676
EMP: 85
SALES (corp-wide): 121.6B **Publicly Held**
WEB: www.unisonindustries.com
SIC: 3498 3728 3444 Tube fabricating (contract bending & shaping); aircraft parts & equipment; sheet metalwork
HQ: Unison Industries, Llc
   7575 Baymeadows Way
   Jacksonville FL 32256
   904 739-4000

Alvada
Seneca County

(G-519)
PROFLO INDUSTRIES LLC
2679 S Us Highway 23 (44802-9707)
PHONE..................................419 436-6008
Terry N Bosserman, *President*
Terry Bosserman, *President*
Gustavo Corzo, *Sales Staff*
EMP: 20
SQ FT: 12,000
SALES: 4.5MM **Privately Held**
SIC: 3728 Refueling equipment for use in flight, airplane

(G-520)
UPM INC
4777 S Us Highway 23 (44802-9702)
PHONE..................................419 595-2600
Chad Bouillon,
EMP: 4 **EST:** 1997
SQ FT: 5,000
SALES (est): 1MM **Privately Held**
SIC: 3599 Machine shop, jobbing & repair

Alvordton
Williams County

(G-521)
PIONEER FABRICATION
17455 County Road P (43501-9734)
PHONE..................................419 737-9464
Robert Sliwinski, *Principal*
EMP: 4
SALES (est): 424.2K **Privately Held**
SIC: 3444 Sheet metalwork

▲ = Import ▼ = Export
◆ = Import/Export

GEOGRAPHIC SECTION

Amelia - Clermont County (G-548)

(G-522)
PIONEER INDUSTRIAL SYSTEMS LLC (PA)
16442 Us Highway 20 (43501-9797)
PHONE.................................419 737-9506
Todd Hendricks Sr, *President*
Steve Edwards, *Plant Mgr*
Troy Martin, *Engineer*
Amy Hendricks, *Human Res Mgr*
Lynn Parker, *Sales Associate*
▲ **EMP:** 12
SQ FT: 7,500
SALES (est): 2.6MM **Privately Held**
SIC: 3599 Custom machinery

Amanda
Fairfield County

(G-523)
BUCKEYE PRODUCTS
6745 Chillicothe Lancster (43102-9508)
PHONE.................................740 969-4718
Stuart A Wharton, *Principal*
George Wharton, *Principal*
Terrence Wharton, *Principal*
EMP: 6
SQ FT: 6,000
SALES: 200K **Privately Held**
SIC: 2431 Millwork

(G-524)
CENTRAL OHIO FABRICATION LLC
8143 Bowers Rd Sw (43102-9567)
PHONE.................................740 969-2976
Bob Brown, *Mng Member*
EMP: 4
SQ FT: 4,000
SALES: 1MM **Privately Held**
SIC: 7692 Automotive welding

(G-525)
CLEAR CREEK SCREW MACHINE CORP
4900 Julian Rd Sw (43102-9514)
PHONE.................................740 969-2113
George Bartrom, *President*
EMP: 8
SQ FT: 15,000
SALES (est): 986.8K **Privately Held**
SIC: 3599 3451 Machine shop, jobbing & repair; screw machine products

(G-526)
MID-WEST FABRICATING CO (PA)
Also Called: Mid West Fabricating Co
313 N Johns St (43102-9002)
PHONE.................................740 969-4411
Jennifer Johns Friel, *President*
Ann Custer, *Vice Pres*
Paul Salcido, *Mfg Mgr*
Doug McCafferty, *Mfg Staff*
David Whitaker, *Buyer*
◆ **EMP:** 125 **EST:** 1945
SQ FT: 280,000
SALES (est): 25.5MM **Privately Held**
WEB: www.midwestfab.com
SIC: 3714 3524 3452 Tie rods, motor vehicle; lawn & garden tractors & equipment; bolts, metal

Amelia
Clermont County

(G-527)
A & A SAFETY INC (PA)
1126 Ferris Rd Bldg B (45102-2376)
PHONE.................................513 943-6100
William N Luttmer, *President*
Billy Luttmer, *Vice Pres*
Steve Clough, *Project Mgr*
Francis Luttmer, *Treasurer*
Tom McLaughlin, *Manager*
EMP: 50
SQ FT: 12,300
SALES (est): 20.2MM **Privately Held**
WEB: www.aasafetyinc.com
SIC: 7359 3993 5084 1721 Work zone traffic equipment (flags, cones, barrels, etc.); signs & advertising specialties; safety equipment; painting & paper hanging; highway & street sign installation

(G-528)
ACREO INC
3209 Marshall Dr (45102-9213)
P.O. Box 361, New Richmond (45157-0361)
PHONE.................................513 734-3327
Roger Williams, *President*
EMP: 7
SQ FT: 10,000
SALES (est): 600K **Privately Held**
SIC: 7389 3556 Design, commercial & industrial; food products machinery

(G-529)
ALL WRITE RIBBON INC
3916 Bach Buxton Rd (45102-1014)
P.O. Box 67 (45102-0067)
PHONE.................................513 753-8300
William E Lyon, *President*
Harold Wolfe, *Vice Pres*
Bill Lyon, *CFO*
▲ **EMP:** 35
SQ FT: 20,000
SALES (est): 4MM **Privately Held**
WEB: www.allwriteribbon.com
SIC: 3955 Print cartridges for laser & other computer printers

(G-530)
AMELIA PLASTICS
3202 Marshall Dr Bldg 8 (45102-9212)
PHONE.................................513 386-4926
EMP: 3 **EST:** 2016
SALES (est): 228.2K **Privately Held**
SIC: 3089 Injection molding of plastics

(G-531)
AMON INC
3214 Marshall Dr (45102-9212)
PHONE.................................513 734-1700
Derrick Campbell, *President*
Naomi Campbell, *Corp Secy*
Greg Campbell, *Vice Pres*
Donna Hinton, *Shareholder*
EMP: 13
SALES (est): 2.1MM **Privately Held**
WEB: www.amoninc.com
SIC: 3599 Machine shop, jobbing & repair

(G-532)
ASAP READY MIX INC
250 Mount Holly Rd (45102-9740)
PHONE.................................513 797-1774
Dan Dunham, *Principal*
EMP: 3
SALES (est): 197.5K **Privately Held**
SIC: 3273 Ready-mixed concrete

(G-533)
BERRY WOODWORKING
2244 Berry Rd (45102-9174)
PHONE.................................513 734-6133
Charles Steelman, *Owner*
Elsa Steelman, *Co-Owner*
EMP: 10
SALES: 600K **Privately Held**
SIC: 2431 Staircases & stairs, wood

(G-534)
CINCINNATI PRINT SOLUTIONS LLC
4007 Bach Buxton Rd (45102-1047)
PHONE.................................513 943-9500
Mark Johnson,
EMP: 6 **EST:** 2006
SQ FT: 10,000
SALES (est): 1MM **Privately Held**
SIC: 2752 7334 2759 Commercial printing, offset; photocopying & duplicating services; commercial printing

(G-535)
DACA VENDING WHOLESALE LLC
1105b W Ohio Pike (45102-1292)
PHONE.................................513 753-1600
Dave Clair,
Dave St Clair,
▲ **EMP:** 5 **EST:** 1997
SALES (est): 237.5K **Privately Held**
SIC: 3999 3651 Slot machines; home entertainment equipment, electronic

(G-536)
DEIMLING/JELIHO PLASTICS INC
4010 Bach Buxton Rd (45102-1048)
PHONE.................................513 752-6653
William Deimling, *President*
Mary Ann Deimling, *Corp Secy*
Jennifer Miller, *Sales Staff*
Jody Bratten, *Manager*
Don Browning, *Director*
▲ **EMP:** 83
SQ FT: 60,000
SALES (est): 22.6MM **Privately Held**
WEB: www.deimling-jeliho.com
SIC: 3089 3599 Injection molding of plastics; machine shop, jobbing & repair

(G-537)
EAGLE COACH INC
Also Called: Eagle Coach Company
3344 State Route 132 (45102-2249)
PHONE.................................513 797-4100
Eric Yeager, *President*
Tim Lautermilch, *Principal*
Christy Kellerman, *Corp Secy*
Doug Cromwell, *Vice Pres*
Greg Dahnke, *Vice Pres*
EMP: 60
SQ FT: 150,000
SALES (est): 12.8MM **Privately Held**
WEB: www.eaglecoachcompany.com
SIC: 3711 Hearses (motor vehicles), assembly of

(G-538)
EAST FORK PRECISION MACHINE LL
3874 Gordon Dr (45102-1043)
PHONE.................................513 753-4157
EMP: 3 **EST:** 2001
SALES (est): 170K **Privately Held**
SIC: 3599 Mfg Industrial Machinery

(G-539)
EGER PRODUCTS INC (PA)
1132 Ferris Rd (45102-1020)
PHONE.................................513 753-4200
Dick Koebbe, *President*
EMP: 60 **EST:** 1969
SQ FT: 38,400
SALES (est): 28MM **Privately Held**
WEB: www.egerproducts.com
SIC: 3644 3544 5039 Insulators & insulation materials, electrical; forms (molds), for foundry & plastics working machinery; ceiling systems & products

(G-540)
HAMILTON SAFE AMELIA
3997 Bach Buxton Rd (45102-1013)
PHONE.................................513 753-5694
Ansil Perry, *President*
William Fennessy, *Vice Pres*
EMP: 18
SQ FT: 45,000
SALES: 3MM
SALES (corp-wide): 5.3MM **Privately Held**
SIC: 3499 Safes & vaults, metal
PA: Hamilton Safe Co.
  7775 Cooper Rd
  Cincinnati OH 45242
  513 874-3733

(G-541)
INDUCTIVE COMPONENTS MFG
Also Called: I C M I
1200 Ferris Rd (45102-1022)
P.O. Box 188 (45102-0188)
PHONE.................................513 752-4731
Dirk W Mooibroek, *President*
Sonja M Mooibroek, *Treasurer*
EMP: 25 **EST:** 1973
SQ FT: 11,000
SALES (est): 4.5MM **Privately Held**
WEB: www.icmiinc.com
SIC: 3679 Electronic circuits

(G-542)
JABCO & ASSOCIATES INC
1188 Ferris Rd (45102-1046)
PHONE.................................513 752-0600
Mike Spicer, *President*
Tom Munninghoff, *Vice Pres*
Mike Spicer, *Plant Mgr*
EMP: 5
SQ FT: 20,000
SALES (est): 900K **Privately Held**
SIC: 2841 5169 Detergents, synthetic organic or inorganic alkaline; detergents

(G-543)
MARK J MYERS (PA)
Also Called: Heritage Tool & Manufacturing
80 W Main St (45102-1736)
PHONE.................................513 753-7300
Mark J Myers, *Owner*
EMP: 2
SALES (est): 1.7MM **Privately Held**
SIC: 3599 Machine shop, jobbing & repair

(G-544)
MOBILE CONVERSIONS INC
3354 State Route 132 (45102-2249)
PHONE.................................513 797-1991
Michael G Dobbins, *President*
EMP: 14
SQ FT: 2,176
SALES (est): 1.9MM **Privately Held**
WEB: www.mobileconversions.com
SIC: 7532 2451 Van conversion; mobile homes

(G-545)
ONLINE ENGINEERING CORPORATION
3947 Bach Buxton Rd (45102-1013)
PHONE.................................513 561-8878
Richard Hittinger, *President*
Jane Hittinger, *Shareholder*
▼ **EMP:** 6
SQ FT: 4,000
SALES (est): 750K **Privately Held**
WEB: www.onlineengineeringcorp.com
SIC: 3914 Stainless steel ware

(G-546)
QUEEN CITY TOOL COMPANY INC
Also Called: Queen City Bearers
3939 Bach Buxton Rd (45102-1013)
PHONE.................................513 752-4200
James Erb, *President*
EMP: 3
SQ FT: 8,000
SALES (est): 421.3K **Privately Held**
WEB: www.bearers.com
SIC: 3599 Machine shop, jobbing & repair

(G-547)
SOLUTIONS PLUS INC
3907 Bach Buxton Rd (45102-1013)
PHONE.................................513 943-9600
Charles R Weaver, *President*
Nancy D Weaver, *Vice Pres*
Bill Sechrist, *Opers Mgr*
Mike Gwin, *VP Sales*
Scott Coate, *Sales Mgr*
EMP: 20
SQ FT: 15,000
SALES (est): 5.5MM **Privately Held**
WEB: www.spiworld.com
SIC: 2842 Industrial plant disinfectants or deodorants

(G-548)
STEWART FILMSCREEN CORP
3919 Bach Buxton Rd (45102-1013)
PHONE.................................513 753-0800
Grant Stewart, *President*
Josh Webb, *Engineer*
EMP: 30
SALES (corp-wide): 28.5MM **Privately Held**
SIC: 3861 Screens, projection
PA: Stewart Filmscreen Corp.
  1161 Sepulveda Blvd
  Torrance CA 90502
  310 326-1422

(G-549)
SUN CHEMICAL CORPORATION
Colors Dispersion Division
3922 Bach Buxton Rd (45102-1098)
PHONE..................513 753-9550
Edward Polaski, *General Mgr*
John Rozier, *Mfg Staff*
Chris Vissing, *Design Engr*
Jennifer Smith, *Controller*
Richard Krieger, *Manager*
EMP: 90
SQ FT: 7,200
SALES (corp-wide): 7.1B **Privately Held**
WEB: www.sunchemical.com
SIC: 2893 2865 Printing ink; cyclic crudes & intermediates
HQ: Sun Chemical Corporation
35 Waterview Blvd Ste 100
Parsippany NJ 07054
973 404-6000

(G-550)
TRI-STATE FABRICATORS INC
1146 Ferris Rd (45102-1020)
PHONE..................513 752-5005
Richard Mark Vogt, *President*
Jay Richard Vogt, *Principal*
Joanne Vogt, *Principal*
Jeffrey G Vogt, *VP Mfg*
EMP: 50
SQ FT: 120,000
SALES: 6.1MM **Privately Held**
SIC: 3441 3444 3471 3479 Fabricated structural metal; sheet metalwork; plating & polishing; painting of metal products; fabricated pipe & fittings

---
Amesville
Athens County

(G-551)
APPAL ENERGY
15383 E Kasler Creek Rd (45711-9448)
P.O. Box 62 (45711-0062)
PHONE..................740 448-4605
EMP: 3 EST: 2000
SALES (est): 310K **Privately Held**
SIC: 2911 Biofuel Manufacturer - Biodiesel

Amherst
Lorain County

(G-552)
ADVANCEPIERRE FOODS INC
1833 Cooper Foster Pk Rd (44001-1206)
PHONE..................580 616-4403
EMP: 3
SALES (corp-wide): 40B **Publicly Held**
SIC: 2013 Cooked meats from purchased meat
HQ: Advancepierre Foods, Inc.
9990 Prnceton Glendale Rd
West Chester OH 45246
513 874-8741

(G-553)
ALCO MANUFACTURING
105 Middle Ave (44001)
PHONE..................440 322-9166
EMP: 3 EST: 2002
SALES (est): 190K **Privately Held**
SIC: 3451 Mfg Screw Machine Products

(G-554)
BCT ALARM SERVICES INC
103 Milan Ave Ste 4 (44001-1492)
PHONE..................440 669-8153
Brian J Jankowski, *President*
EMP: 6
SALES (est): 753.4K **Privately Held**
SIC: 2752 Commercial printing, lithographic

(G-555)
BIRD LOFT
141 N Leavitt Rd (44001-1110)
PHONE..................440 988-2473
Elaine D Jameyson, *Principal*
EMP: 3
SALES (est): 110K **Privately Held**
SIC: 3999 Pet supplies

(G-556)
BRP INC
114 Hidden Tree Ln (44001-1919)
PHONE..................440 988-4398
EMP: 3
SQ FT: 4,700
SALES: 130K **Privately Held**
SIC: 3944 5531 Mfg Games/Toys Ret Auto/Home Supplies

(G-557)
CHEFS PANTRY INC (DH)
Also Called: Cloverdale Food Processing
1833 Cooper Foster Pk Rd (44001-1206)
PHONE..................440 288-0146
Richard Cawrse Jr, *President*
Richard Cecil, *Corp Secy*
EMP: 2
SALES (est): 1MM
SALES (corp-wide): 40B **Publicly Held**
WEB: www.chefspantry.com
SIC: 2053 Frozen bakery products, except bread
HQ: Advancepierre Foods, Inc.
9990 Prnceton Glendale Rd
West Chester OH 45246
513 874-8741

(G-558)
CLOVERVALE FARMS INC (DH)
Also Called: Clovervale Foods
8133 Cooper Foster Pk Rd (44001)
PHONE..................440 960-0146
Richard Cawrse Jr, *President*
Richard Cecil, *Corp Secy*
Suzanne Graham, *Vice Pres*
EMP: 100 EST: 1920
SQ FT: 38,000
SALES (est): 7.1MM
SALES (corp-wide): 40B **Publicly Held**
WEB: www.clovervale.com
SIC: 2099 2032 2033 2038 Gelatin dessert preparations; salads, fresh or refrigerated; puddings, except meat: packaged in cans, jars, etc.; fruits: packaged in cans, jars, etc.; frozen specialties
HQ: Advancepierre Foods, Inc.
9990 Prnceton Glendale Rd
West Chester OH 45246
513 874-8741

(G-559)
CURRIER RICHARD & JAMES
Also Called: Amherst Party Shop
540 Mcintosh Ln (44001-3108)
PHONE..................440 988-4132
Richard Currier, *Partner*
James Currier, *Partner*
EMP: 6
SALES (est): 760K **Privately Held**
SIC: 5921 2086 Beer (packaged); wine; bottled & canned soft drinks

(G-560)
CUSTOM ALUMINUM BOXES
210 Cooper Foster Park Rd (44001-1004)
PHONE..................440 864-2664
Mark Morales, *Principal*
EMP: 4
SALES (est): 448.6K **Privately Held**
SIC: 2631 Folding boxboard

(G-561)
DURAY MACHINE CO INC
400 Ravenglass Blvd (44001-2383)
PHONE..................440 277-4119
Wayne Duray, *President*
Janet Dadas, *Corp Secy*
EMP: 10
SQ FT: 18,000
SALES (est): 1.4MM **Privately Held**
SIC: 3599 7692 Machine shop, jobbing & repair; welding repair

(G-562)
ECO FUEL SOLUTION LLC
779 Sunrise Dr (44001-1660)
PHONE..................440 282-8592
James Bodnar, *Principal*
EMP: 3
SALES (est): 155.6K **Privately Held**
SIC: 2869 Fuels

(G-563)
JAN SQUIRES INC
7985 Leavitt Rd (44001-2709)
PHONE..................440 988-7859
Janis Squires, *President*
Robert Squires, *Vice Pres*
EMP: 4
SQ FT: 2,400
SALES: 250K **Privately Held**
SIC: 1711 3498 Mechanical contractor; fabricated pipe & fittings

(G-564)
KTM NORTH AMERICA INC (PA)
1119 Milan Ave (44001-1319)
PHONE..................855 215-6360
Di Stefan Pierer, *CEO*
Rod Bush, *President*
John S Harden, *Vice Pres*
Selvaraj Narayana, *Vice Pres*
Jon-Erik Burleson, *Treasurer*
▲ EMP: 87
SQ FT: 5,000
SALES (est): 36.8MM **Privately Held**
SIC: 5012 3751 Motorcycles; motorcycles, bicycles & parts

(G-565)
NEON BEACH TAN
2259 Kresge Dr (44001-1243)
PHONE..................440 933-3051
EMP: 3
SALES (est): 123.2K **Privately Held**
SIC: 2813 Neon

(G-566)
NORDSON CORPORATION
100 Nordson Dr Ms81 (44001-2454)
PHONE..................440 985-4000
Michael Hilton, *President*
EMP: 500
SALES (corp-wide): 2.2B **Publicly Held**
WEB: www.nordson.com
SIC: 3563 Spraying outfits: metals, paints & chemicals (compressor)
PA: Nordson Corporation
28601 Clemens Rd
Westlake OH 44145
440 892-1580

(G-567)
NORDSON CORPORATION
555 Jackson St (44001-2496)
PHONE..................440 988-9411
Mary Fuller, *Human Resources*
John Kirschner, *Manager*
EMP: 432
SALES (corp-wide): 2.2B **Publicly Held**
WEB: www.nordson.com
SIC: 3563 Spraying outfits: metals, paints & chemicals (compressor); robots for industrial spraying, painting, etc.
PA: Nordson Corporation
28601 Clemens Rd
Westlake OH 44145
440 892-1580

(G-568)
NORDSON UV INC
Also Called: Spectral Uv Systems
555 Jackson St (44001-2408)
PHONE..................440 985-4573
John Dillon, *Director*
EMP: 13
SALES (est): 5MM
SALES (corp-wide): 2.2B **Publicly Held**
SIC: 3826 Ultraviolet analytical instruments
PA: Nordson Corporation
28601 Clemens Rd
Westlake OH 44145
440 892-1580

(G-569)
PAINT BOOTH PROS INC
577 Fieldstone Dr (44001-1916)
PHONE..................440 653-3982
Pete McNamara, *CEO*
Ellie McNamara, *President*
EMP: 4
SALES (est): 492.5K **Privately Held**
SIC: 3444 Booths, spray: prefabricated sheet metal

(G-570)
PERSONAL STITCH MONOGRAMMING
924 Amchester Dr (44001-1254)
PHONE..................440 282-7707
Don Szakhes, *Owner*
Cindy Szakhes, *Co-Owner*
EMP: 4
SQ FT: 1,200
SALES: 100K **Privately Held**
SIC: 2395 Embroidery products, except schiffli machine; embroidery & art needlework

(G-571)
POLYGON SPACESHIP
Also Called: Polygon Spaceship Games
5536 Linn Dr (44001-1221)
PHONE..................440 506-0403
Anthony Calabro, *Partner*
Matthew Beckwith, *Partner*
Ian Zeigler, *Partner*
EMP: 3
SALES (est): 78.2K **Privately Held**
SIC: 7372 Home entertainment computer software

(G-572)
RCS BREWHOUSE
223 Church St (44001-2201)
PHONE..................440 984-3103
Robert Pijor, *Principal*
EMP: 7
SALES (est): 598.9K **Privately Held**
SIC: 2064 Candy bars, including chocolate covered bars

(G-573)
SC CAMPANA INC
48201 Rice Rd (44001-9400)
PHONE..................440 390-8854
Scotti Campana, *President*
Kris Camtana, *Vice Pres*
EMP: 3
SALES (est): 209.4K **Privately Held**
SIC: 2099 Food preparations

(G-574)
SILK ROAD SOURCING LLC
Also Called: SRS Worldwide
161 Charles Ave (44001-2075)
P.O. Box 37102, Rock Hill SC (29732-0535)
PHONE..................814 571-5533
Christopher Phillips, *Mng Member*
EMP: 4 EST: 2017
SALES: 10MM **Privately Held**
SIC: 2426 5023 Flooring, hardwood; wood flooring

(G-575)
SPEEDWAY LLC
Also Called: Speedway Superamerica 9975
712 N Leavitt Rd (44001-1133)
PHONE..................440 988-8014
John Petis, *Branch Mgr*
EMP: 10 **Publicly Held**
WEB: www.speedwaynet.com
SIC: 1311 Crude petroleum production
HQ: Speedway Llc
500 Speedway Dr
Enon OH 45323
937 864-3000

Amsterdam
Jefferson County

(G-576)
ALLEN HARPER
1654 Township Road 266 (43903-7919)
PHONE..................740 543-3919
Allen Harper, *CEO*
EMP: 4
SALES (est): 182.5K **Privately Held**
SIC: 1442 Construction sand & gravel

Andover
Ashtabula County

GEOGRAPHIC SECTION

(G-577)
ADVANCED TECHNOLOGY CORP
101 Parker Dr (44003-9456)
PHONE.....................................440 293-4064
Seymour S Stein, *Ch of Bd*
Sherry Epstein, *Treasurer*
Anthony Stavole, *Admin Sec*
▲ EMP: 250 EST: 1951
SQ FT: 220,000
SALES (est): 24.5MM
SALES (corp-wide): 42.1MM **Privately Held**
SIC: 3647 3469 Vehicular lighting equipment; metal stampings
HQ: Atc Lighting & Plastics, Inc.
    101 Parker Dr
    Andover OH 44003

(G-578)
ALOTERRA PACKAGING LLC
198 Parker Dr (44003-9481)
PHONE.....................................281 547-0568
EMP: 5
SALES (corp-wide): 5.8MM **Privately Held**
SIC: 2679 Food dishes & utensils, from pressed & molded pulp
PA: Aloterra Packaging Llc
    2002 Timberloch Pl # 420
    The Woodlands TX 77380
    440 689-0986

(G-579)
ATC GROUP INC (PA)
Also Called: Atc Lighting & Plastics
101 Parker Dr (44003-9456)
P.O. Box 1120 (44003-1120)
PHONE.....................................440 293-4064
Seymour S Stein PHD, *President*
Sherry Epstein, *Treasurer*
▲ EMP: 100
SQ FT: 50,000
SALES (est): 42.1MM **Privately Held**
SIC: 3647 3089 3841 Vehicular lighting equipment; injection molded finished plastic products; surgical & medical instruments

(G-580)
ATC LIGHTING & PLASTICS INC (HQ)
Also Called: Kdlamp Company
101 Parker Dr (44003-9456)
P.O. Box 1120 (44003-1120)
PHONE.....................................440 466-7670
Seymour S Stein PHD, *Ch of Bd*
▲ EMP: 155
SALES (est): 40MM
SALES (corp-wide): 41.5MM **Privately Held**
SIC: 3647 3714 3713 3648 Motor vehicle lighting equipment; motor vehicle parts & accessories; truck & bus bodies; lighting equipment; products of purchased glass
PA: Atc Group, Inc.
    101 Parker Dr
    Andover OH 44003
    440 293-4064

(G-581)
ATC NYMOLD CORPORATION
101 Parker Dr (44003-9456)
PHONE.....................................440 293-4064
Dr Seymour Stein, *Branch Mgr*
EMP: 3
SALES (corp-wide): 41.5MM **Privately Held**
WEB: www.atc-lighting-plastics.com
SIC: 3089 Injection molded finished plastic products
HQ: Atc Nymold Corporation
    101 Parker Dr
    Andover OH 44003
    440 293-4064

(G-582)
ATC NYMOLD CORPORATION (DH)
101 Parker Dr (44003-9456)
PHONE.....................................440 293-4064
Seymour S Stein PHD, *President*
EMP: 2
SQ FT: 500,000
SALES (est): 3.8MM
SALES (corp-wide): 41.5MM **Privately Held**
WEB: www.atc-lighting-plastics.com
SIC: 3089 Injection molded finished plastic products

(G-583)
K D LAMP COMPANY
Also Called: Etc Lighting and Plastic
101 Parker Dr (44003-9456)
PHONE.....................................440 293-4064
Dr Seymour Stein, *President*
Sherry Epstein, *Treasurer*
▲ EMP: 49
SALES (est): 700K
SALES (corp-wide): 41.5MM **Privately Held**
SIC: 3647 Headlights (fixtures), vehicular
PA: Atc Group, Inc.
    101 Parker Dr
    Andover OH 44003
    440 293-4064

(G-584)
LIGHTING PRODUCTS INC
101 Parker Dr (44003-9456)
P.O. Box 1120 (44003-1120)
PHONE.....................................440 293-4064
Seymour S Stein PHD, *President*
Sherry Epstein, *Corp Secy*
Denise Kahler, *Plant Mgr*
Anthony Stavole, *Admin Sec*
EMP: 84
SALES (est): 11.6MM
SALES (corp-wide): 41.5MM **Privately Held**
WEB: www.lightingproducts.com
SIC: 3647 Motor vehicle lighting equipment
HQ: Atc Lighting & Plastics, Inc.
    101 Parker Dr
    Andover OH 44003

(G-585)
MATHEW ODONNELL
Also Called: Model and Tool Making
6645 2nd Ave (44003-9668)
PHONE.....................................440 969-4054
Matthew Odonnell, *Owner*
Matthew O'Donnell, *Engineer*
EMP: 3
SALES (est): 240.5K **Privately Held**
SIC: 3549 Metalworking machinery

(G-586)
PYMATNING SPCIALTY PALLETS LLC
4683 Stanhope Klloggvl Rd (44003-9676)
PHONE.....................................440 293-3306
Alvin Lambright, *Principal*
EMP: 3
SALES (est): 119.9K **Privately Held**
SIC: 2448 Wood pallets & skids

Anna
Shelby County

(G-587)
6S PRODUCTS LLC
12800 Wenger Rd (45302-9003)
PHONE.....................................937 394-7440
Genny Schroer,
Emliy Bensman,
Tracy Platsoot,
EMP: 5
SQ FT: 4,000
SALES: 850K **Privately Held**
SIC: 3089 Bottle caps, molded plastic

(G-588)
CHILLTEX LLC
Also Called: Honeywell Authorized Dealer
7440 Hoying Rd (45302-9616)
PHONE.....................................937 710-3308
Matt Eilerman, *Principal*
EMP: 13
SALES (est): 2.1MM **Privately Held**
SIC: 3585 Heating equipment, complete

(G-589)
ELSASS FABRICATING LTD
11385 Amsterdam Rd (45302-9766)
PHONE.....................................937 394-7169
William Elsass, *President*
Bonnie Elsass, *Manager*
EMP: 4
SALES (est): 320.4K **Privately Held**
SIC: 3444 Sheet metalwork

(G-590)
HOEHNES CUSTOM WOODWORKING
9600 Amsterdam Rd (45302-9307)
PHONE.....................................937 693-8008
Susan Hoehne, *Principal*
EMP: 4
SALES (est): 335.3K **Privately Held**
SIC: 2431 Millwork

(G-591)
PANEL CONTROL INC
107 Shue Dr (45302-8402)
PHONE.....................................937 394-2201
Sandy Wells, *Principal*
EMP: 1
SQ FT: 32,000
SALES (est): 9.4MM **Privately Held**
SIC: 3613 Control panels, electric

Ansonia
Darke County

(G-592)
AFS TECHNOLOGY LLC
400 E Elroy Ansonia Rd (45303-8967)
PHONE.....................................937 669-3548
John Tiernan, *President*
Diana Szenay, *Business Mgr*
Jim Miller, *Opers Mgr*
Steve Banks, *Prdtn Mgr*
EMP: 13
SALES (est): 4.2MM **Privately Held**
SIC: 3523 Elevators, farm

(G-593)
HOFMANNS LURES INC
5350 State Route 47 (45303-9796)
P.O. Box 361, Greenville (45331-0361)
PHONE.....................................937 684-0338
Denis Short, *President*
EMP: 8
SQ FT: 7,200
SALES (est): 66.5K **Privately Held**
SIC: 3949 Masks: hockey, baseball, football, etc.

(G-594)
SHOOK TOOL INC
405 W High St (45303-5061)
P.O. Box 334 (45303-0334)
PHONE.....................................937 337-6471
David D Shook, *President*
Darin Shook, *Vice Pres*
EMP: 5
SQ FT: 4,000
SALES: 300K **Privately Held**
SIC: 3544 Industrial molds

Antwerp
Paulding County

(G-595)
ANTWERP BEE-ARGUS
Also Called: Ohio Press
113 N Main St (45813-8406)
P.O. Box 334 (45813-0334)
PHONE.....................................419 258-8161
June Temple, *Partner*
Sandra Temple, *Partner*
EMP: 3
SALES (est): 205.6K **Privately Held**
SIC: 2711 Newspapers: publishing only, not printed on site

(G-596)
ANTWERP TOOL & DIE INC
3167 County Road 424 (45813-9416)
PHONE.....................................419 258-5271
Gerald A Snyder, *President*
EMP: 15
SQ FT: 10,500
SALES: 800K **Privately Held**
SIC: 3544 3545 Special dies, tools, jigs & fixtures; machine tool accessories

(G-597)
ATWOOD MOBILE PRODUCTS LLC
5406 Us 24 (45813)
PHONE.....................................419 258-5531
Vincent Proaccina, *Principal*
EMP: 43
SALES (corp-wide): 1.6B **Privately Held**
SIC: 3714 Motor vehicle parts & accessories
HQ: Atwood Mobile Products Llc
    1120 N Main St
    Elkhart IN 46514

(G-598)
K & L TOOL INC
5141 Us 24 (45813)
P.O. Box 1086 (45813-1086)
PHONE.....................................419 258-2086
Kirk L Hopkins, *President*
Laurel Hopkins, *Vice Pres*
EMP: 18
SQ FT: 4,500
SALES (est): 2.2MM **Privately Held**
SIC: 3542 3544 Bending machines; special dies & tools

(G-599)
NEW AMERICAN REEL COMPANY LLC
5278 County Road 424 A (45813-9578)
PHONE.....................................419 258-2900
Mark Greenwood,
David Parisot,
▲ EMP: 5
SQ FT: 30,000
SALES: 400K **Privately Held**
SIC: 3499 Reels, cable: metal

(G-600)
WEST BEND PRINTING & PUBG INC
101 N Main St (45813)
PHONE.....................................419 258-2000
Bryce Steiner, *President*
EMP: 6
SQ FT: 3,000
SALES: 350K **Privately Held**
SIC: 2752 Commercial printing, offset

Apple Creek
Wayne County

(G-601)
A C PRODUCTS CO
4299 S Apple Creek Rd (44606-9680)
P.O. Box 518 (44606-0518)
PHONE.....................................330 698-1105
Don Olsen, *President*
David Reader, *Vice Pres*
Mahlon Troyer, *Opers Mgr*
Richard Bernard, *Controller*
Missy Irwin, *Manager*
▼ EMP: 60
SQ FT: 80,000
SALES (est): 9.7MM **Privately Held**
WEB: www.acproductsco.com
SIC: 3261 Bathroom accessories/fittings, vitreous china or earthenware

(G-602)
COBLENTZ BROTHERS INC
7101 S Kohler Rd (44606-9613)
PHONE.....................................330 857-7211
Wayne Liechty, *President*
Jonas Coblentz, *Vice Pres*
Ray Coblentz, *Admin Sec*
EMP: 28
SQ FT: 20,100

Apple Creek - Wayne County (G-603)

SALES: 3.9MM **Privately Held**
SIC: 2448 2421 Pallets, wood; sawmills & planing mills, general

(G-603)
DES ECK WELDING
10777 E Moreland Rd (44606-9628)
PHONE................................330 698-7271
Nelson Chupp, *Owner*
EMP: 5
SALES (est): 484K **Privately Held**
SIC: 7692 Welding repair

(G-604)
ELY ROAD REEL COMPANY LTD
9081 Ely Rd (44606-9320)
PHONE................................330 683-1818
Marvin Weaver, *Partner*
Robert Weaver, *Partner*
EMP: 25
SQ FT: 16,000
SALES (est): 7MM **Privately Held**
SIC: 2499 Spools, reels & pulleys: wood

(G-605)
FARMSIDE WOOD
11833 Harrison Rd (44606-9025)
PHONE................................330 695-5100
Crist Miller, *Owner*
EMP: 5
SALES: 1.7MM **Privately Held**
SIC: 2511 Wood bedroom furniture

(G-606)
GROSS LUMBER INC
8848 Ely Rd (44606-9799)
PHONE................................330 683-2055
Rick Grossniklaus, *President*
Don Grossniklaus, *President*
EMP: 35 EST: 1957
SQ FT: 30,000
SALES (est): 5MM **Privately Held**
SIC: 2448 5031 5099 2426 Pallets, wood; lumber: rough, dressed & finished; wood & wood by-products; hardwood dimension & flooring mills; sawmills & planing mills, general

(G-607)
HILLCREST LUMBER LTD
8669 Zuercher Rd (44606-9651)
PHONE................................330 359-5721
David Hershberger, *Partner*
Edward Hershberger, *Partner*
Henry Hershberger, *Partner*
EMP: 5
SQ FT: 400,000
SALES (est): 807.7K **Privately Held**
SIC: 2421 Sawmills & planing mills, general

(G-608)
JAE TECH INC
32 Hunter St (44606-9600)
PHONE................................330 698-2000
Ian Cameron, *Principal*
EMP: 55 EST: 2000
SQ FT: 37,500
SALES (est): 11.2MM **Privately Held**
WEB: www.jaetechinc.com
SIC: 3714 Axle housings & shafts, motor vehicle

(G-609)
JOHN J YODER LOGGING
6776 Mount Hope Rd (44606-9061)
PHONE................................330 749-6324
John J Yoder, *Principal*
EMP: 3
SALES (est): 240.5K **Privately Held**
SIC: 2411 Logging

(G-610)
LE SUMMER KIDRON INC
6856 Kidron Rd (44606-9326)
P.O. Box 230, Kidron (44636-0230)
PHONE................................330 857-2031
Glenford Steiner, *President*
EMP: 20
SALES: 11MM **Privately Held**
SIC: 2048 Livestock feeds

(G-611)
LEGGETT & PLATT INCORPORATED
Also Called: Crown North America
7315 E Lincoln Way (44606-9524)
PHONE................................330 262-6010
EMP: 9
SALES (corp-wide): 3.9B **Publicly Held**
SIC: 3714 Mfg Motor Vehicle Parts/Accessories
PA: Leggett & Platt, Incorporated
1 Leggett Rd
Carthage MO 64836
417 358-8131

(G-612)
MAYSVILLE HARNESS SHOP LTD
8572 Mount Hope Rd (44606-9495)
PHONE................................330 695-9977
Aden Yoder, *President*
EMP: 3
SALES (est): 505.5K **Privately Held**
SIC: 3199 7251 7699 Harness or harness parts; holsters, leather; straps, leather; shoe repair shop; harness repair shop

(G-613)
MCKAY-GROSS DIV
8848 Ely Rd (44606-9319)
PHONE................................330 683-2055
EMP: 3
SALES (est): 66.6K **Privately Held**
SIC: 2426 Lumber, hardwood dimension

(G-614)
MILLWOOD INC
Also Called: Litco Wood Products
8208 S Kohler Rd (44606-9420)
PHONE................................330 857-3075
Ely Miller, *Branch Mgr*
EMP: 70 **Privately Held**
WEB: www.millwoodinc.com
SIC: 2448 Pallets, wood
PA: Millwood, Inc.
3708 International Blvd
Vienna OH 44473

(G-615)
MOWHAWK LUMBER LTD
2931 S Carr Rd (44606-9306)
PHONE................................330 698-5333
Marvin H Yoder,
EMP: 24
SALES (est): 2.2MM **Privately Held**
SIC: 2421 Sawmills & planing mills, general

(G-616)
OMEGA CEMENTING CO
3776 S Millborne Rd (44606-9757)
P.O. Box 357 (44606-0357)
PHONE................................330 695-7147
Donald Gaddis, *CEO*
EMP: 7
SQ FT: 3,000
SALES (est): 2.5MM **Privately Held**
SIC: 1389 1081 7349 Well plugging & abandoning, oil & gas; cementing oil & gas well casings; metal mining exploration & development services; cleaning service, industrial or commercial

(G-617)
PRECISION PRODUCTS GROUP INC
339 Mill St (44606-9541)
PHONE................................330 698-4711
Dave Hooe, *President*
EMP: 60 **Privately Held**
SIC: 3495 3493 Wire springs; steel springs, except wire
PA: Precision Products Group, Inc.
10201 N Illinois St # 390
Indianapolis IN 46290

(G-618)
REBERLAND EQUIPMENT INC
Also Called: Firovac
5963 Fountain Nook Rd (44606-9677)
PHONE................................330 698-5883
Larry Reber, *President*
Valerie Lewis, *Treasurer*
Rebecca Reber, *Admin Sec*
▲ EMP: 18

SQ FT: 10,000
SALES: 5MM **Privately Held**
WEB: www.firovac.com
SIC: 7699 5083 3711 3713 Farm machinery repair; agricultural machinery & equipment; fire department vehicles (motor vehicles); assembly of; tank truck bodies; oil & gas field machinery

(G-619)
STEIN-WAY EQUIPMENT
12335 Emerson Rd (44606-9798)
PHONE................................330 857-8700
Oris Steiner, *Partner*
EMP: 12
SQ FT: 20,000
SALES (est): 2.5MM **Privately Held**
SIC: 3523 Barn, silo, poultry, dairy & livestock machinery

(G-620)
SUMMIT VALLEY LUMBER
6086 Fountain Nook Rd (44606-9607)
PHONE................................330 698-7781
EMP: 6
SALES: 1MM **Privately Held**
SIC: 2421 Sawmill

(G-621)
TOP NOTCH LOGGING
8242 Secrest Rd (44606-9506)
PHONE................................330 466-1780
Roy Miller, *Owner*
EMP: 3
SALES (est): 228.9K **Privately Held**
SIC: 2411 Logging

(G-622)
WAYNEDALE TRUSS AND PANEL CO
8971 Dover Rd (44606-9407)
PHONE................................330 698-7373
James Fry, *President*
Diane Fry, *Admin Sec*
EMP: 34
SQ FT: 2,000
SALES (est): 4.9MM **Privately Held**
WEB: www.waynedaletruss.com
SIC: 2439 Trusses, wooden roof; trusses, except roof: laminated lumber

(G-623)
WEAVER PALLET LTD
9380 Ely Rd (44606-9322)
PHONE................................330 682-4022
Emery Weaver,
Andrew Weaver,
EMP: 5
SALES: 1.2MM **Privately Held**
SIC: 2448 Pallets, wood

(G-624)
WEAVER WOODCRAFT L L C
9652 Harrison Rd (44606-9623)
PHONE................................330 695-2150
Dave Weaver, *Principal*
EMP: 9
SALES (est): 689.3K **Privately Held**
SIC: 2511 Wood household furniture

Arcadia
Hancock County

(G-625)
MAASS MIDWEST MFG INC
Also Called: Dickens Foundry
19710 State Route 12 (44804-9503)
PHONE................................419 894-6424
Mike Wedge, *Ltd Ptnr*
EMP: 9
SALES (corp-wide): 15.6MM **Privately Held**
WEB: www.maassmidwest.com
SIC: 3366 3491 3432 Brass foundry; industrial valves; plumbing fixture fittings & trim
PA: Maass Midwest Mfg Inc.
11283 Dundee Rd
Huntley IL 60142
847 669-5135

(G-626)
RPM CARBIDE DIE INC
202 E South St (44804-9773)
P.O. Box 278 (44804-0278)
PHONE................................419 894-6426
Eric E Metcalfe, *CEO*
Joseph E Phillips, *CFO*
Carrie Phillits, *Sales Executive*
Carrie Phillips, *Marketing Mgr*
Carrie Ritcher Phillips, *Marketing Staff*
EMP: 38
SQ FT: 18,500
SALES (est): 7MM **Privately Held**
WEB: www.rpmcarbidedie.com
SIC: 3544 Special dies & tools

Arcanum
Darke County

(G-627)
A & S INC
6 N Main St (45304-1325)
P.O. Box 189 (45304-0189)
PHONE................................866 209-1574
David Archer, *President*
EMP: 3
SALES (est): 227.5K **Privately Held**
SIC: 2395 Embroidery & art needlework

(G-628)
EMRICK MACHINE & TOOL
211 S Sycamore St (45304-1172)
PHONE................................937 692-5901
Rick Emrick, *Principal*
Dana Anderson, *Sales Engr*
EMP: 5
SALES (est): 300K **Privately Held**
SIC: 3599 Machine shop, jobbing & repair

(G-629)
J-T TOOL INC
6995 Hllnsburg Sampson Rd (45304-9654)
PHONE................................937 623-9959
Douglas G Harman, *Principal*
EMP: 3
SALES (est): 164K **Privately Held**
SIC: 3599 Machine shop, jobbing & repair

(G-630)
LAVY INC
Also Called: Lavy's Marathon
1977 Gttysburg Ptsburg Rd (45304-9442)
PHONE................................937 692-8189
Sheldon Lavy, *President*
Kimberly Lavy, *Vice Pres*
EMP: 4
SQ FT: 200
SALES (est): 684.3K **Privately Held**
SIC: 2911 5172 Gasoline blending plants; gasoline; fuel oil

(G-631)
R J COX CO
Also Called: Cox Trailer
8903 State Route 571 (45304-9741)
PHONE................................937 548-4699
Robert J Cox, *President*
John Cox, *Vice Pres*
Joseph Cox, *Treasurer*
Kelley Cox, *Admin Sec*
EMP: 5 EST: 1949
SQ FT: 8,000
SALES (est): 600K **Privately Held**
WEB: www.rjcox.com
SIC: 3715 5083 Trailer bodies; agricultural machinery & equipment

(G-632)
RED BARN CABINET CO
8046 State Route 722 (45304-9409)
PHONE................................937 884-9800
Mark Angle, *President*
EMP: 6
SALES (est): 857K **Privately Held**
SIC: 2434 Wood kitchen cabinets

(G-633)
SCHWIETERMAN CY INC
4240 State Route 49 (45304-9010)
PHONE................................937 548-3965
Michael Schwieterman, *Branch Mgr*
EMP: 5

GEOGRAPHIC SECTION
Archbold - Fulton County (G-660)

SALES (est): 623.5K
SALES (corp-wide): 6.2MM **Privately Held**
SIC: 3531 Plows: construction, excavating & grading
PA: Cy Schwieterman Inc
   1663 Cranberry Rd
   Saint Henry OH 45883
   419 925-4290

Archbold
Fulton County

(G-634)
AL MEDA CHOCOLATES INC
23050 Fulton County Rd E (43502)
PHONE..............................419 446-2676
Diane Taylor, *President*
Frank Taylor, *Vice Pres*
EMP: 5
SQ FT: 3,000
SALES (est): 399.3K **Privately Held**
SIC: 2064 Chocolate candy, except solid chocolate

(G-635)
AMERICAN COLLOID COMPANY
Also Called: Mineral Technology Metal Cast
809 Myers St (43502-1575)
P.O. Box 195 (43502-0195)
PHONE..............................419 445-9085
Greg Johnson, *Manager*
EMP: 5 **Publicly Held**
WEB: www.colloid.com
SIC: 1459 Bentonite mining
HQ: American Colloid Company
   2870 Forbs Ave
   Hoffman Estates IL 60192

(G-636)
ARCHBOLD BUCKEYE INC
207 N Defiance St (43502-1187)
PHONE..............................419 445-4466
Ross William Taylor, *President*
Sharon S Taylor, *Corp Secy*
Brent C Taylor, *Vice Pres*
EMP: 10 **EST:** 1905
SQ FT: 2,800
SALES (est): 658.4K **Privately Held**
SIC: 2711 Newspapers: publishing only, not printed on site

(G-637)
ARCHBOLD CONTAINER CORP
800 W Barre Rd (43502-9595)
P.O. Box 10 (43502-0010)
PHONE..............................800 446-2520
Lynn Aschliman, *President*
Elvin D Yoder, *Corp Secy*
EMP: 150
SQ FT: 230,000
SALES (est): 34MM
SALES (corp-wide): 1.3B **Privately Held**
WEB: www.gbp.com
SIC: 2653 3086 Boxes, corrugated: made from purchased materials; packaging & shipping materials, foamed plastic
PA: Green Bay Packaging Inc.
   1700 N Webster Ave
   Green Bay WI 54302
   920 433-5111

(G-638)
ARCHBOLD FURNITURE CO
733 W Barre Rd (43502-9304)
PHONE..............................567 444-4666
Pat McNamara, *President*
Pete Gstaldar, *Vice Pres*
◆ **EMP:** 35
SALES (est): 7MM **Privately Held**
WEB: www.archboldfurniture.com
SIC: 5712 2511 Furniture stores; unassembled or unfinished furniture, household: wood

(G-639)
ARROW TRU-LINE INC (PA)
2211 S Defiance St (43502-9151)
PHONE..............................419 446-2785
Marvin Miller, *President*
Suzie Tule, *General Mgr*
Alan Elliott, *Plant Mgr*
Jim Aschliman, *Materials Mgr*
Randy Ordway, *Opers Staff*

◆ **EMP:** 150 **EST:** 1959
SQ FT: 63,000
SALES (est): 35.5MM **Privately Held**
SIC: 3469 Metal stampings

(G-640)
BALSER INC
502 Jackson St (43502-1411)
P.O. Box 8 (43502-0008)
PHONE..............................567 444-4737
Anthony Balser, *President*
EMP: 6
SQ FT: 18,000
SALES (est): 274.8K **Privately Held**
SIC: 3479 Painting of metal products

(G-641)
CLANCYS CABINET SHOP
3751 County Road 26 (43502-9434)
PHONE..............................419 445-4455
Clancy Foor, *Owner*
EMP: 25
SQ FT: 4,000
SALES (est): 180K **Privately Held**
WEB: www.clancyscabinets.com
SIC: 2434 Wood kitchen cabinets

(G-642)
CONAGRA BRANDS INC
La Choy Food Products Division
901 Stryker St (43502-1053)
PHONE..............................419 445-8015
Ron Corkins, *Branch Mgr*
EMP: 398
SALES (corp-wide): 7.9B **Publicly Held**
WEB: www.conagra.com
SIC: 2032 2099 Chinese foods: packaged in cans, jars, etc.; food preparations
PA: Conagra Brands, Inc.
   222 Merchandise Mart Plz
   Chicago IL 60654
   312 549-5000

(G-643)
D & G WELDING INC
302 W Barre Rd (43502-1554)
PHONE..............................419 445-5751
Dan Stuckey, *President*
Julie Stuckey, *Vice Pres*
EMP: 6 **EST:** 1956
SQ FT: 2,500
SALES (est): 100K **Privately Held**
SIC: 7692 1796 Welding repair; millwright

(G-644)
F & W AUTO SUPPLY
111 Depot St (43502-1236)
PHONE..............................419 445-3350
Ronald Wyse, *Owner*
EMP: 3
SQ FT: 2,000
SALES (est): 230K **Privately Held**
SIC: 3599 5084 Machine shop, jobbing & repair; industrial machine parts

(G-645)
FARMLAND NEWS LLC
104 Depot St (43502-1235)
P.O. Box 240 (43502-0240)
PHONE..............................419 445-9456
Lisa Grisez, *Mng Member*
Jed W Grisez,
EMP: 10
SALES (est): 350K **Privately Held**
SIC: 2711 Newspapers: publishing only, not printed on site

(G-646)
FM MANUFACTURING INC
300 E Mechanic St (43502-1425)
PHONE..............................419 445-0700
Ron Rupp, *President*
EMP: 9
SQ FT: 4,000
SALES (est): 1.5MM **Privately Held**
SIC: 3699 Laser systems & equipment

(G-647)
FROZEN SPECIALTIES INC
720 W Barre Rd (43502-9305)
P.O. Box 410 (43502-0410)
PHONE..............................419 445-9015
Brian Riplogo, *Branch Mgr*
EMP: 165
SALES (corp-wide): 15.2B **Privately Held**
SIC: 2038 Frozen specialties

HQ: Frozen Specialties, Inc.
   8600 S Wilkinson Way G
   Perrysburg OH 43551
   419 445-9015

(G-648)
FSI/MFP INC
720 W Barre Rd (43502-9304)
PHONE..............................419 445-9015
Eugene Welka, *Principal*
EMP: 5
SALES (est): 263.1K **Privately Held**
SIC: 2038 Frozen specialties

(G-649)
GENDRON WHEEL LLC
400 E Lugbill Rd (43502-1564)
P.O. Box 197 (43502-0197)
PHONE..............................419 445-6060
Fred Strobel, *President*
EMP: 3
SALES (est): 295.6K
SALES (corp-wide): 3.9MM **Privately Held**
WEB: www.gendroninc.com
SIC: 3842 Surgical appliances & supplies
PA: Gendron, Inc.
   520 W Mulberry St Ste 100
   Bryan OH 43506
   419 636-0848

(G-650)
GERALD GRAIN CENTER INC
3265 County Road 24 (43502-9415)
PHONE..............................419 445-2451
Chet Phillips, *Branch Mgr*
EMP: 17
SALES (corp-wide): 35.9MM **Privately Held**
SIC: 3523 5191 Elevators, farm; animal feeds
PA: Gerald Grain Center, Inc.
   14540 County Road U
   Napoleon OH 43545
   419 598-8015

(G-651)
GRANITE INDUSTRIES INC
595 E Lugbill Rd (43502-1560)
PHONE..............................419 445-4733
Steve Wise, *President*
Keith Short, *Treasurer*
Mindy Borer, *Admin Sec*
◆ **EMP:** 80
SALES (est): 13.4MM **Privately Held**
WEB: www.graniteind.com
SIC: 3993 3446 2531 Signs & advertising specialties; architectural metalwork; public building & related furniture

(G-652)
HAULOTTE US INC (DH)
Also Called: Bil-Jax
125 Taylor Pkwy (43502-9122)
PHONE..............................419 445-8915
Mike Garvaglia, *CEO*
Lynn Yarnell, *CFO*
◆ **EMP:** 20
SQ FT: 14,700
SALES (est): 5.7MM
SALES (corp-wide): 13.8MM **Privately Held**
WEB: www.haulotteus.com
SIC: 3531 Aerial work platforms: hydraulic/elec. truck/carrier mounted
HQ: Haulotte Group
   La Peronniere
   L'horme 42152
   477 292-424

(G-653)
HIT TROPHY INC
4989 State Route 66 (43502-9362)
PHONE..............................419 445-5356
Tom Wyse, *President*
Abe Wyse, *Marketing Staff*
EMP: 6 **EST:** 1949
SALES: 400K **Privately Held**
WEB: www.hittrophy.com
SIC: 3499 5999 2499 Trophies, metal, except silver; trophies & plaques; trophy bases, wood

(G-654)
LAUBER MANUFACTURING CO
3751 County Road 26 (43502-9434)
PHONE..............................419 446-2450
Bruce Lauber, *President*
Graeme O Lauber Jr, *Treasurer*
Elizabeth Grime, *Admin Sec*
EMP: 7 **EST:** 1929
SQ FT: 43,000
SALES (est): 1.2MM **Privately Held**
WEB: www.laubermfg.com
SIC: 2511 Wood household furniture

(G-655)
LIECHTY SPECIALTIES INC
Also Called: Industrial WD Prts Fabrication
1901 S Defiance St (43502-9438)
P.O. Box 6 (43502-0006)
PHONE..............................419 445-6696
Allen K Liechty, *President*
Virgina Liechty, *Corp Secy*
EMP: 8
SQ FT: 25,000
SALES (est): 1.5MM **Privately Held**
SIC: 2431 Millwork

(G-656)
LOCKER ROOM INC
223 N Defiance St (43502-1160)
PHONE..............................419 445-9600
Kyle Brodbeck, *President*
Tara Brodbeck, *Admin Sec*
EMP: 5
SQ FT: 2,600
SALES (est): 800K **Privately Held**
WEB: www.lockerroominc.com
SIC: 5941 2759 Team sports equipment; commercial printing

(G-657)
LOGO THIS
301 Ditto St Ste E (43502-1111)
PHONE..............................419 445-1355
Dan Rychener, *President*
EMP: 6
SALES (est): 511.5K **Privately Held**
SIC: 2395 Embroidery products, except schiffli machine; embroidery & art needlework

(G-658)
MATTHEWS ART GLASS
Also Called: Mark Matthews Glass
22611 State Route 2 (43502-9452)
P.O. Box 332 (43502-0332)
PHONE..............................419 335-2448
Mark Matthews, *Owner*
Ruth Matthews, *Co-Owner*
EMP: 3
SALES (est): 146.4K **Privately Held**
SIC: 3229 Pressed & blown glass

(G-659)
MILLER BROS PAVING INC (HQ)
1613 S Defiance St (43502-9488)
P.O. Box 30 (43502-0030)
PHONE..............................419 445-1015
Dean Miller, *President*
Bradley Dmiller, *President*
Steven A Everhart, *Corp Secy*
Robert Miller, *Vice Pres*
EMP: 10
SQ FT: 48,000
SALES (est): 2.2MM **Privately Held**
SIC: 2951 Asphalt paving mixtures & blocks

(G-660)
NAPOLEON SPRING WORKS INC (HQ)
111 Weires Dr (43502-9153)
P.O. Box 160 (43502-0160)
PHONE..............................419 445-1010
Robert Shram Sr, *President*
Phil Foster, *General Mgr*
Ej Horst, *Engineer*
◆ **EMP:** 143 **EST:** 1960
SALES (est): 24.4MM
SALES (corp-wide): 15.3MM **Privately Held**
SIC: 3493 3429 Torsion bar springs; builders' hardware
PA: Industries Lynx Inc
   175 Rue Upper Edison
   Saint-Lambert QC J4R 2
   514 866-1068

Archbold - Fulton County (G-661)

(G-661)
NEF LTD
Also Called: Liechty Specialties
1901 S Defiance St (43502-9438)
P.O. Box 6 (43502-0006)
PHONE.................................419 445-6696
Nisha E Francis, President
EMP: 6
SALES: 2MM Privately Held
SIC: 2452 Prefabricated buildings, wood

(G-662)
NOFZIGER DOOR SALES INC
111 Taylor Pkwy (43502-9309)
PHONE.................................419 445-2961
Tom Rufenacht, Manager
EMP: 10
SALES (corp-wide): 35.1MM Privately Held
WEB: www.haasdoor.com
SIC: 3442 5211 Metal doors; garage doors, sale & installation
PA: Nofziger Door Sales, Inc.
   320 Sycamore St
   Wauseon OH 43567
   419 337-9900

(G-663)
P T I INC
100 Taylor Pkwy (43502-9309)
PHONE.................................419 445-2800
Charles F Lantz, President
▲ EMP: 40
SALES (est): 5.3MM Privately Held
WEB: www.inplastech.com
SIC: 3089 Plastic processing

(G-664)
PROGRESSIVE FURNITURE INC (HQ)
Also Called: Progressive International
502 Middle St (43502-1559)
P.O. Box 308 (43502-0308)
PHONE.................................419 446-4500
Kevin Sauder, President
Dan Kendrick, Exec VP
John Boring, VP Finance
Janys Etts, Credit Mgr
▲ EMP: 25
SQ FT: 8,000
SALES (est): 23.1MM
SALES (corp-wide): 500MM Privately Held
WEB: www.progressivefurniture.com
SIC: 2511 2517 5021 Bed frames, except water bed frames: wood; dressers, household: wood; home entertainment unit cabinets, wood; tables, occasional; beds; dining room furniture
PA: Sauder Woodworking Co.
   502 Middle St
   Archbold OH 43502
   419 446-2711

(G-665)
QUADCO REHABILITATION CENTER
Also Called: Northwest Products Div
600 Oak St (43502-1579)
PHONE.................................419 445-1950
Phillip Zuver, Branch Mgr
Shannon Zellers, Program Mgr
EMP: 90
SALES (corp-wide): 247.7K Privately Held
SIC: 8331 2448 Vocational rehabilitation agency; wood pallets & skids
PA: Quadco Rehabilitation Center, Inc.
   427 N Defiance St
   Stryker OH 43557
   419 682-1011

(G-666)
SAUDER MANUFACTURING CO (HQ)
Also Called: Wieland
930 W Barre Rd (43502-9385)
P.O. Box 230 (43502-0230)
PHONE.................................419 445-7670
Virgil L Miller, President
Phil Bontrager, President
Beth Ehinger, General Mgr
Willaim Ogden, Vice Pres
William Ogden, Vice Pres
◆ EMP: 220 EST: 1945

SQ FT: 300,000
SALES (est): 87.2MM
SALES (corp-wide): 500MM Privately Held
WEB: www.saudermfg.com
SIC: 2531 Church furniture; chairs, portable folding
PA: Sauder Woodworking Co.
   502 Middle St
   Archbold OH 43502
   419 446-2711

(G-667)
SAUDER WDWKG CO WELFARE TR
502 Middle St (43502-1500)
PHONE.................................419 446-2711
Doug Krieger, Director
EMP: 2
SALES: 16.8MM Privately Held
SIC: 2431 Millwork

(G-668)
SAUDER WOODWORKING CO (PA)
502 Middle St (43502-1500)
P.O. Box 156 (43502-0156)
PHONE.................................419 446-2711
Kevin J Sauder, President
Patrick Sauder, CFO
Paige Miller, Admin Sec
◆ EMP: 2100
SQ FT: 5,000,000
SALES (est): 500MM Privately Held
WEB: www.sauder.com
SIC: 2512 5021 Upholstered household furniture; wood upholstered chairs & couches; couches, sofas & davenports: upholstered on wood frames; living room furniture: upholstered on wood frames; furniture

(G-669)
SAUDER WOODWORKING CO
330 N Clydes Way (43502-9170)
PHONE.................................419 446-2711
Kevin J Sauder, President
EMP: 6
SALES (corp-wide): 500MM Privately Held
SIC: 2519 5021 Fiberglass & plastic furniture; furniture
PA: Sauder Woodworking Co.
   502 Middle St
   Archbold OH 43502
   419 446-2711

(G-670)
SYSTECH HANDLING INC
120 Taylor Pkwy (43502-9309)
PHONE.................................419 445-8226
Wendell Lantz, President
Mike Waidelich, Vice Pres
Cole Lantz, Sales Mgr
Dawn Lantz, Office Mgr
EMP: 12 EST: 1999
SQ FT: 12,500
SALES (est): 2.2MM Privately Held
WEB: www.systechhandling.com
SIC: 3599 8711 7692 3444 Custom machinery; engineering services; welding repair; sheet metalwork

(G-671)
THREE CORD LLC
203 E Lugbill Rd (43502-1568)
PHONE.................................419 445-2673
Andy Borcherdt, VP Sales
Cathy King, Mng Member
Ron King,
Ronald D King,
EMP: 3
SQ FT: 16,000
SALES (est): 220K Privately Held
WEB: www.threecord.com
SIC: 2261 Screen printing of cotton broadwoven fabrics

(G-672)
TRI-STATE GARDEN SUPPLY INC
Also Called: Gardenscape
56 State Rte 66 (43502)
P.O. Box 451 (43502-0451)
PHONE.................................419 445-6561

Timothy Kasmoch, Owner
EMP: 50
SALES (corp-wide): 75.6MM Privately Held
WEB: www.gardenscapetransport.com
SIC: 5261 2875 Nurseries & garden centers; fertilizers, mixing only
PA: Tri-State Garden Supply, Inc.
   And Sandy Pt Rd Rr 38
   Eau Claire PA 16030
   724 867-1711

(G-673)
WYSE ELECTRIC MOTOR REPAIR
2101 S Defiance St (43502-9150)
PHONE.................................419 445-5921
Richard J Wyse, President
Grace Wyse, Corp Secy
EMP: 5
SALES (est): 716.5K Privately Held
SIC: 7694 Electric motor repair

(G-674)
YODER & FREY INC
3649 County Road 24 (43502-9317)
P.O. Box 155 (43502-0155)
PHONE.................................419 445-2070
Robert Frey, President
EMP: 8 EST: 1947
SQ FT: 12,000
SALES (est): 1.2MM Privately Held
SIC: 5083 3523 Agricultural machinery & equipment; farm machinery & equipment

Ashland
Ashland County

(G-675)
ADVANCED CYLINDER REPAIR INC
Also Called: Signal Group
942 State Route 302 (44805-9577)
PHONE.................................419 289-0538
Kyle Sigley, President
EMP: 5 EST: 1978
SQ FT: 10,000
SALES (est): 686K Privately Held
SIC: 3599 7699 Machine shop, jobbing & repair; hydraulic equipment repair

(G-676)
ALTEC INDUSTRIES
1236 Township Road 1175 (44805-1979)
PHONE.................................419 289-6066
Bob Donaldson, Principal
EMP: 8
SALES (est): 638.3K Privately Held
SIC: 3531 Construction machinery

(G-677)
ART PRINTING CO INC
147 E 2nd St (44805-2396)
PHONE.................................419 281-4371
Michael B Sattler, President
Judith Staley, Corp Secy
EMP: 5 EST: 1924
SQ FT: 1,500
SALES (est): 210K Privately Held
SIC: 2752 2791 2759 Commercial printing, offset; typesetting; letterpress printing

(G-678)
ASHLAND MONUMENT COMPANY INC
34 E 2nd St (44805-2399)
PHONE.................................419 281-2688
Donald Hoffman, President
EMP: 4
SQ FT: 15,000
SALES: 600K Privately Held
SIC: 3272 5999 Grave markers, concrete; gravestones, finished

(G-679)
ASHLAND PRECISION TOOLING LLC
1750 S Baney Rd (44805-3522)
PHONE.................................419 289-1736
Steve Englet,
John Englet,
Chris Schmid,

EMP: 52
SQ FT: 56,000
SALES (est): 8.8MM Privately Held
WEB: www.aptooling.com
SIC: 3599 Machine shop, jobbing & repair

(G-680)
ASHLAND PUBLISHING CO
Also Called: Ashland Times Gazette
40 E 2nd St (44805-2304)
PHONE.................................419 281-0581
Troy Dix, General Mgr
G Charles Dix II, Treasurer
Timothy Dix, Admin Sec
EMP: 855 EST: 1850
SQ FT: 12,400
SALES (est): 32.9MM
SALES (corp-wide): 528.2MM Privately Held
WEB: www.times-gazette.com
SIC: 2711 Newspapers, publishing & printing
PA: Dix 1898, Inc.
   212 E Liberty St
   Wooster OH
   330 264-3511

(G-681)
ATLAS BOLT & SCREW COMPANY LLC (DH)
Also Called: Atlas Fasteners For Cnstr
1628 Troy Rd (44805-1398)
PHONE.................................419 289-6171
Robert W Moore, President
Robert C Gluth, Treasurer
Robert Webb, Admin Sec
▲ EMP: 175
SQ FT: 75,000
SALES (est): 30.1MM
SALES (corp-wide): 225.3B Publicly Held
WEB: www.atlasfasteners.com
SIC: 3452 5085 5051 5072 Washers, metal; screws, metal; fasteners, industrial: nuts, bolts, screws, etc.; metals service centers & offices; hardware
HQ: Marmon Group Llc
   181 W Madison St Ste 2600
   Chicago IL 60602
   312 372-9500

(G-682)
BALL BOUNCE AND SPORT INC (PA)
Also Called: Hedstrom Fitness
1 Hedstrom Dr (44805-3586)
PHONE.................................419 289-9310
David Faulkner, President
Scott Fickes, CFO
Michael Kelly, CFO
Jeremy Rohr, Associate
◆ EMP: 270
SQ FT: 187,000
SALES (est): 195.8MM Privately Held
SIC: 5092 5091 3089 Toys; fitness equipment & supplies; plastic processing

(G-683)
BANDIT MACHINE INC
261 E 8th St (44805-1803)
PHONE.................................419 281-6595
Gerald Kieft, President
Marilyn Kieft, Vice Pres
EMP: 4
SALES (est): 200K Privately Held
WEB: www.banditmachine.com
SIC: 3586 Measuring & dispensing pumps

(G-684)
BARBASOL LLC
2011 Ford Dr (44805-1277)
PHONE.................................419 903-0738
Don Buckingham,
▲ EMP: 36 EST: 2009
SQ FT: 80,000
SALES (est): 15.7MM
SALES (corp-wide): 18.9MM Privately Held
SIC: 2844 Toilet preparations
PA: Perio, Inc.
   6156 Wilcox Rd
   Dublin OH 43016
   614 791-1207

GEOGRAPHIC SECTION
Ashland - Ashland County (G-712)

(G-685)
BENDON INC (PA)
1840 S Baney Rd (44805-3524)
PHONE..............................419 207-3600
Benjamin Ferguson, *President*
Brent Bowers, *Editor*
Terry Gerwig, *Exec VP*
Jenny Hastings, *Exec VP*
Don Myers II, *Senior VP*
▲ EMP: 54
SQ FT: 220,000
SALES (est): 31.4MM **Privately Held**
WEB: www.bendonpub.com
SIC: 2731 5999 5961 5092 Books: publishing only; educational aids & electronic training materials; educational supplies & equipment, mail order; educational toys

(G-686)
BOOKMASTERS INC (PA)
Also Called: Atlasbooks
30 Amberwood Pkwy (44805-9765)
PHONE..............................419 281-1802
Tony Proe, *President*
Raymond Sevin, *President*
Karen Broach, *Publisher*
Jessica Phillips, *Publisher*
Ken Fultz, *General Mgr*
◆ EMP: 122
SQ FT: 180,000
SALES (est): 58.4MM **Privately Held**
WEB: www.atlasbooks.com
SIC: 7389 2752 2731 2791 Printers' services: folding, collating; commercial printing, lithographic; book publishing; typesetting; books, periodicals & newspapers

(G-687)
BOR-IT MANUFACTURING INC
1687 Cleveland Rd (44805-1929)
P.O. Box 789 (44805-0789)
PHONE..............................419 289-6639
Michael W Albers, *President*
Michelle Albers, *Corp Secy*
▼ EMP: 20
SQ FT: 12,500
SALES (est): 4.9MM **Privately Held**
WEB: www.bor-it.com
SIC: 3541 Drilling & boring machines

(G-688)
BYLER TRUSS
1271 State Route 96 (44805-9357)
PHONE..............................330 465-5412
Harvey Byler, *Executive*
EMP: 4
SALES (est): 274.7K **Privately Held**
SIC: 2439 Structural wood members

(G-689)
CARTER DRAPERY SERVICE INC
1301 County Road 1356 (44805-9702)
PHONE..............................419 289-2530
John Carter, *President*
Nancy Carter, *Vice Pres*
EMP: 4
SALES: 125K **Privately Held**
SIC: 2391 Curtains & draperies

(G-690)
CENTERRA CO-OP (PA)
813 Clark Ave (44805-1967)
PHONE..............................419 281-2153
Jean Bratton, *CEO*
William Bullock, *CFO*
EMP: 30
SALES: 174.6MM **Privately Held**
WEB: www.tc-feed.com
SIC: 5983 5261 5999 2048 Fuel oil dealers; fertilizer; feed & farm supply; bird food, prepared; gases, liquefied petroleum (propane)

(G-691)
CERTIFIED LABS & SERVICE INC
535 E 7th St (44805-2553)
PHONE..............................419 289-7462
Gary E Funkhouser, *President*
Michael C Huber, *Vice Pres*
Harret Funkhouser, *Treasurer*
Pam Huber, *Admin Sec*
EMP: 6

SQ FT: 5,000
SALES: 600K **Privately Held**
SIC: 7699 3822 3561 Pumps & pumping equipment repair; hydronic controls; pumps, domestic: water or sump

(G-692)
CHANDLER SYSTEMS INCORPORATED
710 Orange St (44805-1725)
PHONE..............................419 281-6829
William D Chandler III, *Principal*
EMP: 7
SQ FT: 70,000
SALES (est): 1.5MM **Privately Held**
SIC: 3699 Electrical equipment & supplies

(G-693)
CHANDLER SYSTEMS INCORPORATED
Also Called: Best Controls Company
710 Orange St (44805-1725)
PHONE..............................888 363-9434
William Chandler III, *President*
Bill Chandler, *Principal*
Polly Chandler, *Admin Sec*
▲ EMP: 65
SQ FT: 52,000
SALES (est): 25.3MM **Privately Held**
WEB: www.chandlersystemsinc.com
SIC: 5074 3625 3823 Water purification equipment; relays & industrial controls

(G-694)
CITY OF ASHLAND
City Services
310 W 12th St (44805-1756)
P.O. Box Remont Ave (44805)
PHONE..............................419 289-8728
Jerry Mack, *Director*
EMP: 9 **Privately Held**
WEB: www.ashland-ohio.com
SIC: 3589 Garbage disposers & compactors, commercial
PA: City Of Ashland
    206 Claremont Ave Ste 1
    Ashland OH 44805
    419 289-8170

(G-695)
COLORING BOOK SOLUTIONS LLC
426 E 8th St (44805-1952)
PHONE..............................419 281-9641
Kim Vogel, *Accounts Mgr*
Karen Spellman, *Cust Mgr*
Patrick Broun, *Sales Staff*
Don Myers III, *Mng Member*
Jean Myers, *Department Mgr*
▲ EMP: 11
SQ FT: 15,000
SALES (est): 820K **Privately Held**
SIC: 2759 Commercial printing

(G-696)
CONERY MANUFACTURING INC
1380 Township Road 743 (44805-8926)
PHONE..............................419 289-1444
Scott Conery, *President*
Tim Swaisgood, *General Mgr*
Chris Shafer, *Vice Pres*
Linda Brinker, *Sales Staff*
▲ EMP: 16
SQ FT: 24,000
SALES (est): 4.3MM **Privately Held**
WEB: www.conerymfg.com
SIC: 3822 Liquid level controls, residential or commercial heating

(G-697)
CONSUETUDO ABSCISUM INC
Also Called: Custom Cutting Company
921 Jacobson Ave (44805-1836)
P.O. Box 1013 (44805-7013)
PHONE..............................419 281-8002
Dwain Hochstetler, *President*
Anita Hochstetler, *Admin Sec*
EMP: 4
SQ FT: 11,000
SALES: 230K **Privately Held**
SIC: 2675 Die-cut paper & board

(G-698)
CONVERGE GROUP INC
1850 S Baney Rd (44805-3524)
PHONE..............................419 281-0000
Mike Sloan, *General Mgr*
EMP: 12
SQ FT: 25,000
SALES (est): 1.6MM **Privately Held**
SIC: 3089 Injection molding of plastics

(G-699)
CUSTOM HOISTS INC (HQ)
771 County Road 30a (44805-9227)
PHONE..............................419 368-4721
Rick Hiltunen, *President*
Mike Hayes, *Design Engr*
William Wright, *VP Sales*
Richard N Hiltunen, *Info Tech Dir*
Judd Shearer, *Technology*
▲ EMP: 165
SQ FT: 110,000
SALES (est): 40.8MM
SALES (corp-wide): 868.3MM **Publicly Held**
WEB: www.customhoists.com
SIC: 3593 Fluid power cylinders & actuators
PA: Standex International Corporation
    11 Keewaydin Dr Ste 300
    Salem NH 03079
    603 893-9701

(G-700)
DALMATIAN PRESS LLC
605 Westlake Dr (44805-4710)
PHONE..............................419 207-3600
Richard Hilicki,
▲ EMP: 25
SQ FT: 13,000
SALES (est): 1.6MM
SALES (corp-wide): 31.4MM **Privately Held**
SIC: 2731 Book publishing
PA: Bendon, Inc.
    1840 S Baney Rd
    Ashland OH 44805
    419 207-3600

(G-701)
DIAMOND PALLETS LLC
1505 Center Lane Dr (44805-3409)
P.O. Box 991 (44805-0991)
PHONE..............................419 281-2908
Susan Emmons, *Principal*
EMP: 4
SALES (est): 359.8K **Privately Held**
SIC: 2448 Pallets, wood & wood with metal

(G-702)
DR HESS PRODUCTS LLC
1000 Hedstrom Dr Ste B (44805-3587)
PHONE..............................800 718-8022
Dave Wurster, *Mng Member*
Scott Conery,
Terry Terwig,
Polly Tribe,
EMP: 5
SQ FT: 6,000
SALES: 420K **Privately Held**
SIC: 2834 Ointments

(G-703)
ECO-FLO PRODUCTS INC (PA)
1899 Cottage St (44805-1239)
PHONE..............................877 326-3561
Larry Donelson, *President*
Jody Bartter, *Treasurer*
▲ EMP: 15
SQ FT: 3,000
SALES (est): 2MM **Privately Held**
SIC: 3561 Pumps & pumping equipment

(G-704)
FLOW CONTROL US HOLDING CORP
Also Called: Pentair Water Ashland Oper
1430 George Rd 1101 (44805-8946)
PHONE..............................419 289-1144
EMP: 3
SALES (corp-wide): 17.4B **Publicly Held**
WEB: www.pentair.com
SIC: 3561 Pumps & pumping equipment
HQ: Flow Control Us Holding Corporation
    5500 Wayzata Blvd Ste 800
    Minneapolis MN 55416
    763 545-1730

(G-705)
FOLDING CARTON SERVICE INC
608 Westlake Dr (44805-1378)
PHONE..............................419 281-4099
Mina Risha, *President*
EMP: 15
SQ FT: 24,000
SALES (est): 3.3MM **Privately Held**
SIC: 2631 Folding boxboard

(G-706)
GOOD JP
Also Called: JP Good Co
854 Willow Ln (44805-9298)
PHONE..............................419 207-8484
JP Good, *Owner*
EMP: 3
SQ FT: 2,200
SALES (est): 150K **Privately Held**
SIC: 7336 2759 2395 Silk screen design; screen printing; embroidery products, except schiffli machine

(G-707)
HARRIS WELDING AND MACHINE CO (PA)
2219 Cottage St (44805-1296)
P.O. Box 317 (44805-0317)
PHONE..............................419 281-8351
John Kochenderfer, *President*
Tracy Kochenderfer, *Corp Secy*
EMP: 10
SQ FT: 7,500
SALES (est): 1.4MM **Privately Held**
SIC: 7692 3599 Welding repair; machine shop, jobbing & repair

(G-708)
HARRIS WELDING AND MACHINE CO
2219 Cottage St (44805-1296)
PHONE..............................419 281-9623
Kacey Kline, *Branch Mgr*
EMP: 9
SALES (corp-wide): 1.4MM **Privately Held**
SIC: 3599 7692 Machine shop, jobbing & repair; welding repair
PA: Harris Welding And Machine Company
    2219 Cottage St
    Ashland OH 44805
    419 281-8351

(G-709)
HERITAGE PRESS INC
Also Called: Northcoast Advertising
651 Sandusky St (44805-1524)
PHONE..............................419 289-9209
EMP: 20 EST: 1959
SQ FT: 6,000
SALES (est): 2.6MM **Privately Held**
SIC: 2752 2791 Lithographic Commercial Printing Typesetting Services

(G-710)
HESS & GAULT LUMBER CO
707 County Road 1302 (44805-9783)
PHONE..............................419 281-3105
Dan Ungerer, *Owner*
▲ EMP: 3
SQ FT: 9,000
SALES (est): 300.3K **Privately Held**
SIC: 2421 5032 Sawmills & planing mills, general; tile & clay products

(G-711)
HILLMAN PRECISION INC
462 E 9th St Ste 1 (44805-1908)
PHONE..............................419 289-1557
Geoff Hillman Sr, *CEO*
Geoff Hillman Jr, *President*
EMP: 16
SQ FT: 37,000
SALES (est): 1.5MM **Privately Held**
WEB: www.hillmanprecision.com
SIC: 3599 Machine shop, jobbing & repair

(G-712)
HYDROMATIC PUMPS INC
1101 Myers Pkwy (44805-1969)
PHONE..............................419 289-1144
Keith Lang, *President*
▼ EMP: 600

Ashland - Ashland County (G-713) GEOGRAPHIC SECTION

SALES (est): 56MM **Privately Held**
WEB: www.pentair.com
SIC: 3561 Pumps, domestic: water or sump

(G-713)
HYNEKS MACHINE AND WELDING
Also Called: Hyneks Machine & Weld Shop
1372 State Route 603 (44805-9720)
PHONE.................................419 281-7966
Mark Hynek, *President*
EMP: 3
SALES: 700K **Privately Held**
SIC: 3599 7692 Machine shop, jobbing & repair; welding repair

(G-714)
INGRAM PRODUCTS INC
1376 Township Road 743 (44805-8926)
PHONE.................................904 778-1010
William A Irvin, *President*
William English, *Vice Pres*
▲ **EMP:** 12
SQ FT: 5,000
SALES (est): 2.4MM **Privately Held**
WEB: www.ingramproducts.com
SIC: 3679 Electronic circuits

(G-715)
KAR-DEL PLASTICS INC
1177 Faultless Dr (44805-1250)
PHONE.................................419 289-9739
Scott Pay, *President*
Shari L Regan, *President*
Teresa Pay, *Admin Sec*
EMP: 8
SQ FT: 14,000
SALES: 800K **Privately Held**
WEB: www.kar-delplastics.com
SIC: 3089 Plastic & fiberglass tanks; plastic hardware & building products; laminating of plastic; thermoformed finished plastic products

(G-716)
KEEN PUMP COMPANY INC
471 E State Rte 250 E (44805)
PHONE.................................419 207-9400
Gregory W Keener, *President*
Frank Yuhafz, *Vice Pres*
Jody Barr, *Prdtn Mgr*
Drew Pollock, *Production*
Jeffrey Cox, *QC Dir*
◆ **EMP:** 35
SQ FT: 100,000
SALES (est): 9.2MM **Privately Held**
SIC: 3561 Pumps & pumping equipment

(G-717)
KEHL-KOLOR INC
824 Us Highway 42 (44805-9516)
P.O. Box 770 (44805-0770)
PHONE.................................419 281-3107
Jon B Kehl, *President*
Mark Kehl, *Vice Pres*
▲ **EMP:** 32
SQ FT: 60,000
SALES (est): 5.5MM **Privately Held**
WEB: www.kehlkolor.com
SIC: 2752 2796 2791 2789 Commercial printing, offset; lithographic plates, positives or negatives; typesetting; bookbinding & related work

(G-718)
KEN AG INC
101 E 7th St (44805-1702)
PHONE.................................419 281-1204
Doug Patton, *President*
▲ **EMP:** 21 EST: 1997
SQ FT: 35,000
SALES (est): 4.4MM **Privately Held**
SIC: 2621 5085 Milk filter disks; filters, industrial

(G-719)
KNOWLTON MACHINE INC
726 Virginia Ave (44805-1944)
P.O. Box 656 (44805-0656)
PHONE.................................419 281-6802
James Knowlton, *President*
Tammy Frontz, *Accountant*
EMP: 6
SQ FT: 6,000
SALES (est): 625.7K **Privately Held**
WEB: www.knowltonmachine.com
SIC: 3599 1799 Machine shop, jobbing & repair; welding on site

(G-720)
LAKE ERIE FROZEN FOODS MFG CO
1830 Orange Rd (44805-1335)
PHONE.................................419 289-9204
William Buckingham, *President*
Mike Buckingham, *Vice Pres*
Judy Smith, *QC Mgr*
▲ **EMP:** 40
SQ FT: 30,000
SALES (est): 9.3MM **Privately Held**
WEB: www.leffco.net
SIC: 2038 2037 2022 Snacks, including onion rings, cheese sticks, etc.; vegetables, quick frozen & cold pack, excl. potato products; cheese, natural & processed

(G-721)
LIQUI-BOX CORPORATION
1817 Masters Ave (44805-1291)
PHONE.................................419 289-9696
Dennis Rollason, *Purch Mgr*
Sheff Sweet, *Manager*
EMP: 120
SALES (corp-wide): 377.1MM **Privately Held**
WEB: www.liquibox.com
SIC: 2673 3089 3081 2671 Plastic bags: made from purchased materials; plastic processing; unsupported plastics film & sheet; packaging paper & plastics film, coated & laminated
PA: Liqui-Box Corporation
901 E Byrd St Ste 1105
Richmond VA 23219
804 325-1400

(G-722)
MAVERICK INNVTIVE SLUTIONS LLC (PA)
Also Called: Mis
532 County Road 1600 (44805-9207)
PHONE.................................419 281-7944
Keith Jackson, *President*
Todd Meldrum, *Representative*
▲ **EMP:** 45
SQ FT: 50,000
SALES (est): 17.3MM **Privately Held**
SIC: 3556 3585 Food products machinery; refrigeration & heating equipment

(G-723)
MAVERICK INNVTIVE SLUTIONS LLC
532 County Road 1600 (44805-9207)
PHONE.................................419 281-7944
EMP: 30
SALES (est): 2.4MM
SALES (corp-wide): 15.7MM **Privately Held**
SIC: 3441 Metal Fabricating
PA: Maverick Innovative Solutions, Llc
532 County Road 1600
Ashland OH 44805
419 281-7944

(G-724)
MCGRAW-HILL SCHOOL EDUCATION H
Also Called: Mc Graw-Hill Educational Pubg
1250 George Rd (44805-8916)
PHONE.................................419 207-7400
Maryellen Valaitis, *Principal*
EMP: 401
SALES (corp-wide): 158MM **Privately Held**
WEB: www.mcgraw-hill.com
SIC: 2731 5192 Books: publishing & printing; books, periodicals & newspapers
HQ: Mcgraw-Hill School Education Holdings, Llc
2 Penn Plz Fl 20
New York NY 10121
646 766-2000

(G-725)
MIDWEST CONVEYOR PRODUCTS INC
Also Called: Ashland Conveyor Products
1919 Cellar Dr (44805-1275)
PHONE.................................419 281-1235
William Waltz, *President*
Tim Swineford, *Vice Pres*
Brian Davis, *Purch Mgr*
Linda Frech, *Accounting Mgr*
Jenna Waltz, *Regl Sales Mgr*
EMP: 23 EST: 1998
SQ FT: 50,000
SALES (est): 12.9MM **Privately Held**
SIC: 5084 3535 Conveyor systems; belt conveyor systems, general industrial use

(G-726)
MORITZ MATERIALS INC (PA)
859 Faultless Dr (44805-1274)
P.O. Box 392 (44805-0392)
PHONE.................................419 281-0575
James Moritz, *President*
Joseph Moritz, *Vice Pres*
EMP: 22
SQ FT: 2,000
SALES (est): 2MM **Privately Held**
SIC: 3273 5032 Ready-mixed concrete; concrete building products

(G-727)
NATIONAL PRIDE EQUIPMENT INC
1266 Middle Rowsburg Rd (44805-2813)
P.O. Box 467 (44805-0467)
PHONE.................................419 289-2886
Charles Collins, *President*
Richard Walter, *Corp Secy*
EMP: 9
SQ FT: 11,500
SALES (est): 3.9MM **Privately Held**
WEB: www.nationalpridecarwash.com
SIC: 5046 3589 5007 Commercial equipment; car washing machinery; carwash equipment & supplies

(G-728)
NOVATEX NORTH AMERICA INC
1070 Faultless Dr (44805-1247)
PHONE.................................419 282-4264
Michael Donofrio, *Principal*
Brad Neill, *QC Mgr*
▲ **EMP:** 55
SALES (est): 12.8MM **Privately Held**
SIC: 3069 3085 3089 Nipples, rubber; plastics bottles; injection molded finished plastic products

(G-729)
OHIO CARBON COMPANY
Also Called: OCC
1201 Jacobson Ave (44805-1842)
PHONE.................................216 251-7274
Frank Harris, *Manager*
EMP: 4
SALES (corp-wide): 36.8MM **Privately Held**
SIC: 3991 Brushes, household or industrial
PA: The Ohio Carbon Company
W146n9300 Held Dr
Menomonee Falls WI 53051
262 250-4812

(G-730)
OHIO CARBON INDUSTRIES INC
1201 Jacobson Ave (44805-1842)
PHONE.................................419 496-2530
Will Reineke, *Owner*
EMP: 21
SALES (est): 4.4MM **Privately Held**
SIC: 3624 Carbon & graphite products

(G-731)
OHIO POWER TOOL BRUSH CO
Also Called: Opt Brush
1201 Jacobson Ave (44805-1842)
PHONE.................................419 736-3010
Lee Reineke, *President*
Lance Ebert, *Sales Staff*
EMP: 5
SALES (est): 613.8K **Privately Held**
SIC: 3624 5072 Brushes & brush stock contacts, electric; hardware

(G-732)
OHIO TOOL WORKS LLC
1374 Enterprise Pkwy (44805-8926)
PHONE.................................419 281-3700
John C Hovsepian, *President*
Randy Iselt, *Vice Pres*
Michael Murphy, *Vice Pres*
David McCormic, *Plant Mgr*
Sharon Parrish, *Admin Sec*
EMP: 59
SQ FT: 45,000
SALES: 12MM **Privately Held**
WEB: www.ohiotoolworks.com
SIC: 3599 Machine shop, jobbing & repair

(G-733)
PACKAGING CORPORATION AMERICA
Also Called: Pca/Ashland 307
929 Faultless Dr (44805-1246)
PHONE.................................419 282-5809
John Cooney, *Safety Dir*
Doug Huff, *Production*
Dan Stefko, *Engineer*
Jeff Kaser, *Sales Staff*
Don Haag, *Manager*
EMP: 110
SALES (corp-wide): 7B **Publicly Held**
WEB: www.packagingcorp.com
SIC: 2653 Boxes, corrugated: made from purchased materials
PA: Packaging Corporation Of America
1 N Field Ct
Lake Forest IL 60045
847 482-3000

(G-734)
PENTAIR FLOW TECHNOLOGIES LLC (DH)
Also Called: Pentair Water
1101 Myers Pkwy (44805-1969)
PHONE.................................419 289-1144
Randall J Hogan, *CEO*
Linda Thompson, *General Mgr*
John L Stauch, *Exec VP*
Todd R Gleason, *Senior VP*
Frederick S Koury, *Senior VP*
◆ **EMP:** 250
SALES (est): 223.5MM
SALES (corp-wide): 17.4B **Publicly Held**
WEB: www.aurorapump.com
SIC: 3589 3561 Water purification equipment, household type; pumps & pumping equipment
HQ: Flow Control Us Holding Corporation
5500 Wayzata Blvd Ste 800
Minneapolis MN 55416
763 545-1730

(G-735)
PENTAIR FLOW TECHNOLOGIES LLC
740 E 9th St (44805-1954)
PHONE.................................419 281-9918
Nancy Flowers, *Manager*
EMP: 5
SALES (corp-wide): 17.4B **Publicly Held**
SIC: 3589 Water purification equipment, household type
HQ: Pentair Flow Technologies, Llc
1101 Myers Pkwy
Ashland OH 44805
419 289-1144

(G-736)
PIONEER NATIONAL LATEX INC (HQ)
246 E 4th St (44805-2412)
PHONE.................................419 289-3300
Harry Gill, *Treasurer*
Nancy Hadaway, *Controller*
Karen Dravenstott, *Cust Mgr*
▲ **EMP:** 100 EST: 1999
SQ FT: 58,006
SALES (est): 83.5MM
SALES (corp-wide): 228.7MM **Privately Held**
SIC: 3069 3944 Toys, rubber; balls, rubber; balloons, advertising & toy: rubber; games, toys & children's vehicles
PA: Continental American Corporation
5000 E 29th St N
Wichita KS 67220
316 685-2266

GEOGRAPHIC SECTION

Ashtabula - Ashtabula County (G-761)

(G-737)
PRECISION DESIGN INC
Also Called: Ohio Electric Control
2395 Rock Rd (44805-9486)
PHONE..................................419 289-1553
Robert McMullen, *President*
Beth Gault, *Accounting Mgr*
EMP: 6
SQ FT: 3,000
SALES (est): 520K **Privately Held**
SIC: 3621 Control equipment for electric buses & locomotives

(G-738)
PRIMARY COLORS DESIGN CORP
1899 Cottage St (44805-1239)
PHONE..................................419 903-0403
David Vespor, *President*
David Vesper, *President*
Jody Bartter, *Treasurer*
Randy Boyd, *Art Dir*
▲ EMP: 8
SQ FT: 5,000
SALES (est): 1.1MM
SALES (corp-wide): 2MM **Privately Held**
SIC: 2678 Stationery products
PA: Eco-Flo Products, Inc.
1899 Cottage St
Ashland OH 44805
877 326-3561

(G-739)
PURVI OIL INC
654 Us Highway 250 E (44805-9755)
PHONE..................................419 207-8234
EMP: 3
SALES (est): 149.8K **Privately Held**
SIC: 1311 Crude petroleum & natural gas

(G-740)
PWP INC
532 County Road 1600 (44805-9207)
PHONE..................................216 251-2181
Micheal Hooper, *CEO*
David Agard, *General Mgr*
Cynthia Somogyi, *Office Mgr*
▲ EMP: 45
SALES (est): 9.2MM
SALES (corp-wide): 33.3MM **Privately Held**
WEB: www.progresswire.com
SIC: 3496 Miscellaneous fabricated wire products
PA: Tahoma Enterprises, Inc.
255 Wooster Rd N
Barberton OH 44203
330 745-9016

(G-741)
R & J AG MANUFACTURING INC
Also Called: All-Plant Liquid Plant Food
821 State Route 511 (44805-9562)
PHONE..................................419 962-4707
Roger D Shopbell, *President*
Joan Shopbell, *Vice Pres*
James Shopbell, *Treasurer*
Pam Tobias, *Admin Sec*
EMP: 10
SQ FT: 5,000
SALES (est): 1.7MM **Privately Held**
SIC: 2873 5999 Nitrogenous fertilizers; farm equipment & supplies

(G-742)
RAIN DROP PRODUCTS LLC
2121 Cottage St (44805-1245)
PHONE..................................419 207-1229
Mark Williams, *President*
Ross Kette, *VP Opers*
Cory Davis, *Prdtn Mgr*
Laurie Evans, *Accounting Mgr*
Jodi Holt, *Sales Mgr*
◆ EMP: 30
SQ FT: 30,000
SALES (est): 5MM **Privately Held**
SIC: 3949 Water sports equipment

(G-743)
REINEKE COMPANY LLC
1025 Faultless Dr (44805-1248)
PHONE..................................419 281-5800
Matt Reineke, *CEO*
EMP: 14
SQ FT: 144,000
SALES (est): 2.2MM
SALES (corp-wide): 29.5MM **Privately Held**
WEB: www.reinekecompany.com
SIC: 3714 Motor vehicle parts & accessories
PA: Bearing Technologies, Ltd.
1141 Jaycox Rd
Avon OH 44011
440 937-4770

(G-744)
ROSSI MACHINERY SERVICES INC (PA)
1529 Cottage St (44805-1226)
PHONE..................................419 281-4488
Michael Rossi, *CEO*
Chris Rossi, *President*
EMP: 4
SALES (est): 270K **Privately Held**
WEB: www.rossimachineryservices.com
SIC: 7349 7699 3541 3545 Building maintenance services; industrial machinery & equipment repair; machine tools, metal cutting type; machine tool accessories; rebuilt machine tools, metal forming types

(G-745)
ROTOSOLUTIONS INC
1401 Jacobson Ave (44805-1846)
PHONE..................................419 903-0800
Ralph Kirkpatrick, *CEO*
Chris Fitzcharles, *Manager*
Mark Kirkpatrick, *Software Engr*
EMP: 15
SALES (est): 3.2MM **Privately Held**
SIC: 3089 Injection molding of plastics

(G-746)
SANTMYER OIL CO OF ASHLAND
1011 Jacobson Ave (44805-1838)
PHONE..................................419 289-8815
Seth Resinger, *Branch Mgr*
EMP: 3
SALES (corp-wide): 104.2MM **Privately Held**
SIC: 2911 5983 Diesel fuels; jet fuels; fuel oil dealers
HQ: Santmyer Oil Co Of Ashland Inc
1055 W Old Lincoln Way
Wooster OH 44691

(G-747)
SCHOONOVER INDUSTRIES INC
1440 Simonton Rd (44805-1906)
P.O. Box 69 (44805-0069)
PHONE..................................419 289-8332
Robert P Schoonover, *President*
Alyxandra Schoonover, *Vice Pres*
Allen Judy, *Purch Mgr*
Judy Rebman, *Buyer*
Jenny Barack, *CFO*
EMP: 27
SQ FT: 12,000
SALES (est): 6.1MM **Privately Held**
WEB: www.schoonveronline.com
SIC: 3441 3444 Fabricated structural metal; sheet metalwork; sheet metal specialties, not stamped

(G-748)
SEPTIC PRODUCTS INC
1378 Township Road 743 (44805-8926)
PHONE..................................419 282-5933
Rod Mitchell, *President*
Doug Middleton, *Engineer*
Doug Clark, *Sales Staff*
Wendy Smith, *Manager*
EMP: 8
SALES (est): 1.4MM **Privately Held**
SIC: 3272 Septic tanks, concrete

(G-749)
STEEL CITY CORPORATION (PA)
1000 Hedstrom Dr (44805-3587)
PHONE..................................330 792-7663
Chris Shafer, *President*
Scott Vangilder, *Purch Mgr*
Jim Smith, *Sales Staff*
◆ EMP: 25 EST: 1939
SQ FT: 161,000
SALES (est): 2.1MM **Privately Held**
WEB: www.scity.com
SIC: 2678 Newsprint tablets & pads: made from purchased materials

(G-750)
STRAIGHTAWAY FABRICATIONS LTD
481 Us Highway 250 E (44805-9771)
PHONE..................................419 281-9440
David Bowles, *President*
EMP: 30
SQ FT: 1,500
SALES (est): 8.7MM **Privately Held**
WEB: www.straightawayfab.com
SIC: 3441 Fabricated structural metal

(G-751)
THIELS REPLACEMENT SYSTEMS INC
Also Called: Cabinet Restylers
419 E 8th St (44805-1953)
PHONE..................................419 289-6139
Eric Thiel, *President*
Denise Appleby, *Vice Pres*
Anthony Thiel, *Wholesale*
Bobbie Browne, *Manager*
EMP: 56
SQ FT: 50,000
SALES (est): 7.7MM **Privately Held**
SIC: 1751 2541 5211 1799 Window & door (prefabricated) installation; cabinet & finish carpentry; cabinets, lockers & shelving; cabinets, kitchen; bathtub refinishing; gutter & downspout contractor

(G-752)
TREMCO INCORPORATED
Also Called: Tremco Glazing Solutions Group
1451 Jacobson Ave (44805-1865)
PHONE..................................419 289-2050
Ray Jackenheimer, *Safety Mgr*
Shirley Towne, *Purch Agent*
Robert Gourley, *Engineer*
Sharon Gebura, *Human Res Dir*
James Mongiardo, *Manager*
EMP: 70
SALES (corp-wide): 5.3B **Publicly Held**
WEB: www.tremcoinc.com
SIC: 2891 Adhesives & sealants
HQ: Tremco Incorporated
3735 Green Rd
Beachwood OH 44122
216 292-5000

(G-753)
VISTA RESEARCH GROUP LLC
Also Called: Vistanet
1554 Township Road 805 (44805-9202)
P.O. Box 321 (44805-0321)
PHONE..................................419 281-3927
James Chandler,
Barbara Chandler,
EMP: 5
SQ FT: 1,200
SALES: 500K
SALES (corp-wide): 871.9MM **Publicly Held**
SIC: 8748 2731 4813 Business consulting; book publishing;
PA: Cantel Medical Corp.
150 Clove Rd Ste 36
Little Falls NJ 07424
973 890-7220

(G-754)
WAUGS INC
956 State Route 302 (44805-9578)
PHONE..................................440 315-4851
Richard P Ryan, *Principal*
EMP: 8
SALES (est): 1.1MM **Privately Held**
SIC: 3089 Injection molding of plastics

(G-755)
WHITTEN STUDIOS
1180 County Road 30a (44805-9424)
P.O. Box 1623, Mansfield (44901-1623)
PHONE..................................419 368-8366
George Whitten, *Owner*
EMP: 5
SALES: 300K **Privately Held**
SIC: 3952 Canvas, prepared on frames: artists'

(G-756)
ZEPHYR INDUSTRIES INC
600 Township Road 1500 (44805-9759)
PHONE..................................419 281-4485
Vincent Richilano, *President*
David E Richilano, *Corp Secy*
EMP: 8
SQ FT: 20,000
SALES: 625K **Privately Held**
WEB: www.zephyrindustries.com
SIC: 3365 3569 3599 Machinery castings, aluminum; firefighting apparatus & related equipment; machine shop, jobbing & repair

Ashley
Delaware County

(G-757)
IMPERIAL ON-PECE FIBRGLS POOLS
255 S Franklin St (43003-9749)
PHONE..................................740 747-2971
Charles Levings Jr, *President*
Glen Mash, *Principal*
John Mash, *Principal*
Carol Mash, *Vice Pres*
EMP: 10
SQ FT: 10,000
SALES (est): 700K **Privately Held**
WEB: www.imperial-1pc-pools.com
SIC: 3949 1799 Swimming pools, except plastic; swimming pool construction

(G-758)
INDUSTRIAL AUTOMATION SERVICE
4590 State Route 229 (43003-9712)
PHONE..................................740 747-2222
Thomas Greer, *President*
Martha Greer, *Admin Sec*
EMP: 6
SQ FT: 4,000
SALES (est): 740.9K **Privately Held**
SIC: 3544 Special dies, tools, jigs & fixtures

(G-759)
ROTARY PRODUCTS INC (PA)
117 E High St (43003)
P.O. Box 370 (43003-0370)
PHONE..................................740 747-2623
Christopher Buechel, *President*
EMP: 14 EST: 1958
SQ FT: 9,000
SALES (est): 2MM **Privately Held**
WEB: www.rotaryproductsinc.com
SIC: 3081 Vinyl film & sheet

(G-760)
ROTARY PRODUCTS INC
202 W High St (43003-9703)
P.O. Box 370 (43003-0370)
PHONE..................................740 747-2623
Chris Buechel, *President*
EMP: 15
SALES (corp-wide): 2MM **Privately Held**
WEB: www.rotaryproductsinc.com
SIC: 3081 Unsupported plastics film & sheet
PA: Rotary Products Inc
117 E High St
Ashley OH 43003
740 747-2623

Ashtabula
Ashtabula County

(G-761)
ARGENTIFEX LLC
4608 Main Ave (44004-6927)
PHONE..................................440 990-1108
Michael Thompson,
EMP: 3
SQ FT: 1,000
SALES: 80K **Privately Held**
SIC: 7379 5099 2844 Computer related consulting services; novelties, durable; cosmetic preparations

Ashtabula - Ashtabula County (G-762)

(G-762)
ASHTA CHEMICALS INC
3509 Middle Rd (44004-3915)
P.O. Box 858 (44005-0858)
PHONE.................................440 997-5221
Reginald Baxter, *President*
Jamison Baxter, *Corp Secy*
Bill Brodnick, *Vice Pres*
Richard Jackson, *Vice Pres*
Brad Westfall, *Vice Pres*
▲ EMP: 90
SALES (est): 47.1MM Privately Held
WEB: www.ashtachemicals.com
SIC: 2812 Caustic potash, potassium hydroxide; chlorine, compressed or liquefied; potassium carbonate

(G-763)
ASHTABULA RUBBER CO
2751 West Ave (44004-3100)
P.O. Box 398 (44005-0398)
PHONE.................................440 992-2195
Nicholas J Jammal, *President*
Jeff Marano, *Plant Supt*
David Covell, *Maint Spvr*
Janice Meade, *Purch Mgr*
Lise Hudson, *Purch Agent*
▲ EMP: 200 EST: 1945
SQ FT: 72,000
SALES (est): 42.6MM Privately Held
WEB: www.ashtabularubber.com
SIC: 3061 3069 3053 Mechanical rubber goods; hard rubber & molded rubber products; battery boxes, jars or parts, hard rubber; washers, rubber; molded rubber products; gaskets, all materials

(G-764)
CHROMAFLO TECHNOLOGIES CORP (PA)
2600 Michigan Ave (44004-3140)
P.O. Box 816 (44005-0816)
PHONE.................................440 997-0081
Scott Becker, *CEO*
Jim Hill, *Admin Soc*
▲ EMP: 160 EST: 1970
SQ FT: 175,000
SALES (est): 48MM Privately Held
SIC: 2816 3087 2865 Inorganic pigments; custom compound purchased resins; color pigments, organic

(G-765)
CHROMAFLO TECHNOLOGIES CORP
1603 W 29th St (44004-9452)
P.O. Box B (44005)
PHONE.................................440 997-5137
Jim Ogren, *Branch Mgr*
EMP: 110
SALES (corp-wide): 48MM Privately Held
SIC: 2816 Inorganic pigments
PA: Chromaflo Technologies Corporation
2600 Michigan Ave
Ashtabula OH 44004
440 997-0081

(G-766)
CICOGNA ELECTRIC AND SIGN CO (PA)
4330 N Bend Rd (44004-9797)
P.O. Box 234 (44005-0234)
PHONE.................................440 998-2637
Frank Cicogna, *President*
James M Timonere, *Principal*
Brad Petro, *VP Opers*
Mark Woodburn, *Prdtn Mgr*
George Dragon, *Sales Mgr*
EMP: 75
SQ FT: 55,000
SALES (est): 14.4MM Privately Held
WEB: www.cicognasign.com
SIC: 3993 Neon signs

(G-767)
COMMUNITY RE GROUP-COMVET
3220 Station Ave (44004)
PHONE.................................440 319-6714
James Brewington, *CEO*
EMP: 3
SALES (est): 63.3K Privately Held
SIC: 8211 8732 8748 1521 Specialty education; commercial sociological & educational research; testing service, educational or personnel; single-family housing construction; printed circuit boards

(G-768)
CREATIVE MILLWORK OHIO INC
1801 W 47th St (44004-5425)
P.O. Box 1157 (44005-1157)
PHONE.................................440 992-3566
Mark Estock, *President*
Cynthia Estock, *Corp Secy*
Barbara Anthony, *Vice Pres*
Joseph Lalli, *Vice Pres*
Jo Ann Anderson, *Controller*
EMP: 45
SQ FT: 67,000
SALES (est): 7.3MM Privately Held
WEB: www.creativemillwork.com
SIC: 2431 Doors, wood; windows & window parts & trim, wood

(G-769)
CRISTAL USA INC
Also Called: Millennium
2900 Middle Rd (44004-3925)
P.O. Box 160 (44005-0160)
PHONE.................................440 994-1400
Michael Sawruk, *Human Res Mgr*
Joseph Dezman, *Manager*
Mike Gurbba, *Manager*
EMP: 200
SALES (corp-wide): 646.4MM Privately Held
SIC: 2819 Industrial inorganic chemicals
HQ: Cristal Usa Inc.
6752 Baymeadow Dr
Glen Burnie MD 21060
410 762-1000

(G-770)
DALIN AUTO SERVICE
3041 3 Ridge Rd W (44004-9060)
PHONE.................................440 997-3301
Ronald Dalin Sr, *Partner*
Judy Dalin, *Partner*
Ronald Dalin Jr, *Partner*
EMP: 3
SQ FT: 9,000
SALES: 170K Privately Held
SIC: 7692 7699 7538 Welding repair; farm machinery repair; general truck repair

(G-771)
DPA INVESTMENTS INC
3050 Lake Rd E (44004-3829)
PHONE.................................440 992-3377
Brad Loejoy, *Manager*
EMP: 5
SALES (corp-wide): 150MM Privately Held
WEB: www.usalco.com
SIC: 2819 Industrial inorganic chemicals
PA: Dpa Investments, Inc.
2601 Cannery Ave
Baltimore MD 21226
410 918-2230

(G-772)
DPA INVESTMENTS INC
1741 W 47th St (44004-5423)
P.O. Box 1767 (44005-1767)
PHONE.................................440 992-7039
Bruce Wonder, *COO*
Jack Felde, *Manager*
EMP: 12
SALES (corp-wide): 150MM Privately Held
SIC: 2819 Aluminum sulfate
PA: Dpa Investments, Inc.
2601 Cannery Ave
Baltimore MD 21226
410 918-2230

(G-773)
ELCO CORPORATION
1100 State Rd (44004-3943)
PHONE.................................440 997-6131
Tom Steiv, *Manager*
Urban Meyer, *Administration*
EMP: 25
SALES (corp-wide): 571K Privately Held
WEB: www.elcocorp.com
SIC: 2869 2819 2899 Industrial organic chemicals; industrial inorganic chemicals; hydrochloric acid; chemical preparations
HQ: Elco Corporation
1000 Belt Line Ave
Cleveland OH 44109
800 321-0467

(G-774)
ESAB GROUP INCORPORATED
3325 Middle Rd (44004-3974)
P.O. Box 943 (44005-0943)
PHONE.................................440 813-2506
Cheri Houser, *Principal*
EMP: 3
SALES (est): 99.9K Privately Held
SIC: 3356 Nonferrous rolling & drawing

(G-775)
FARGO TOOLITE INCORPORATED
998 Stevenson Rd (44004-9675)
PHONE.................................440 997-2442
Larry Fargo, *President*
EMP: 10 EST: 1973
SQ FT: 13,200
SALES (est): 1.4MM Privately Held
WEB: www.fargomachine.com
SIC: 3544 3599 Special dies & tools; machine shop, jobbing & repair

(G-776)
FENTON MANUFACTURING INC
6600 Depot Rd (44004-9475)
PHONE.................................440 969-1128
Dan Fenton, *President*
Melissa Fenton, *Treasurer*
EMP: 5
SQ FT: 3,200
SALES (est): 773.1K Privately Held
SIC: 3544 Special dies, tools, jigs & fixtures

(G-777)
G M R TECHNOLOGY INC
2131 Aetna Rd (44004-6291)
PHONE.................................440 992-6003
Connie J Speakman, *Principal*
Fred English, *Engineer*
Sue Scheppelmann, *Sales Mgr*
Jackie Juliano, *Office Mgr*
Rick Wilczewski, *Consultant*
▲ EMP: 30
SQ FT: 45,000
SALES (est): 6MM Privately Held
SIC: 3089 Injection molding of plastics

(G-778)
GABRIEL PERFORMANCE PDTS LLC
725 State Rd (44004-3934)
PHONE.................................440 992-3200
Seth Tomasch, *Manager*
EMP: 4
SALES (corp-wide): 1.9B Privately Held
SIC: 2819 Chemicals, high purity: refined from technical grade
HQ: Gabriel Performance Products, Llc
388 S Main St Ste 340
Akron OH 44311
866 800-2436

(G-779)
GREAT LAKES PRINTING INC
2926 Lake Ave (44004-4964)
P.O. Box 245, Jefferson (44047-0245)
PHONE.................................440 993-8781
Jeff Lampson, *President*
EMP: 100
SQ FT: 2,460
SALES (est): 9.1MM Privately Held
SIC: 2752 2759 Commercial printing, offset; letterpress printing

(G-780)
ITEN INDUSTRIES INC (PA)
Also Called: Plant 2
4602 Benefit Ave (44004-5455)
P.O. Box 2150 (44005-2150)
PHONE.................................440 997-6134
Peter D Huggins, *CEO*
Bill Kane, *President*
Dave Zundell, *Purchasing*
Vickie N Partridge, *Human Res Mgr*
Larry Jennings, *Marketing Staff*
▲ EMP: 190 EST: 1922
SQ FT: 175,000
SALES (est): 60.9MM Privately Held
WEB: www.itenindustries.com
SIC: 3089 Laminating of plastic; injection molded finished plastic products

(G-781)
JACKS MARINE INC
2612 Arlington Ave (44004-2304)
PHONE.................................440 997-5060
Patricia Phelps, *President*
John Phelps, *Vice Pres*
Ron Phelps, *Vice Pres*
EMP: 5
SALES: 400K Privately Held
SIC: 3732 4493 5551 Boat building & repairing; boat yards, storage & incidental repair; marine supplies

(G-782)
KOSKI CONSTRUCTION CO (PA)
5841 Woodman Ave (44004-7919)
P.O. Box 1038 (44005-1038)
PHONE.................................440 997-5337
Donald R Koski, *President*
Thomas Pope, *Vice Pres*
Janet Smith, *Vice Pres*
Rachael Merlene, *Treasurer*
David C Sheldon, *Treasurer*
EMP: 6 EST: 1921
SQ FT: 3,500
SALES (est): 4.5MM Privately Held
SIC: 1611 1794 1771 2951 Surfacing & paving; excavation work; concrete work; asphalt & asphaltic paving mixtures (not from refineries); liquid waste, collection & disposal

(G-783)
KOSKI CONSTRUCTION CO
1149 E 5th St (44004-3513)
P.O. Box 1038 (44005-1030)
PHONE.................................440 964-8171
Bruce Schmidt, *Manager*
EMP: 4
SALES (corp-wide): 4.5MM Privately Held
SIC: 3531 Bituminous, cement & concrete related products & equipment
PA: Koski Construction Co (Inc)
5841 Woodman Ave
Ashtabula OH 44004
440 997-5337

(G-784)
LAKE CITY PLATING LLC
1701 Lake Ave (44004-3099)
PHONE.................................440 964-3555
Todd Bendis, *CEO*
Ryan Carroll, *President*
EMP: 18 EST: 1949
SQ FT: 60,000
SALES (est): 3.4MM Privately Held
WEB: www.lakecityplating.com
SIC: 3471 Plating of metals or formed products

(G-785)
MEESE INC
Meese Orbitron Dunne
4920 State Rd (44004-6264)
P.O. Box 607 (44005-0607)
PHONE.................................440 998-1202
Robert W Dunne Jr, *President*
Jennifer Lemponen, *Human Res Mgr*
EMP: 80
SALES (corp-wide): 119.6MM Privately Held
WEB: www.modroto.com
SIC: 3429 3089 3544 3444 Manufactured hardware (general); injection molded finished plastic products; special dies, tools, jigs & fixtures; sheet metalwork; miscellaneous fabricated wire products; plastics plumbing fixtures
HQ: Meese, Inc.
535 N Midland Ave
Saddle Brook NJ 07663
201 796-4490

Ashtabula - Ashtabula County (G-812)

(G-786)
MFG COMPOSITE SYSTEMS COMPANY
Also Called: Mfg CSC
2925 Mfg Pl (44004-9701)
P.O. Box 675 (44005-0675)
PHONE..................................440 997-5851
Richard Morrison, *President*
Andy Juhola, *Vice Pres*
Perry Bennett, *Director*
Keith Bihary, *Director*
Dan Plona, *Director*
▼ **EMP:** 350
SALES (est): 76.1MM
SALES (corp-wide): 589.3MM **Privately Held**
SIC: 3229 2823 Glass fiber products; cellulosic manmade fibers
PA: Molded Fiber Glass Companies
2925 Mfg Pl
Ashtabula OH 44004
440 997-5851

(G-787)
MODROTO
4920 State Rd (44004-6264)
PHONE..................................800 772-7659
Bob Dunne, *President*
EMP: 7 EST: 2015
SALES (est): 252.2K **Privately Held**
SIC: 2655 2599 5085 Fiber cans, drums & containers; carts, restaurant equipment; bins & containers, storage

(G-788)
MOHAWK FINE PAPERS INC
6800 Center Rd (44004-8947)
PHONE..................................440 969-2000
Thomas Oconnor Jr, *President*
EMP: 30
SALES (corp-wide): 253.1MM **Privately Held**
WEB: www.mohawkpaper.com
SIC: 2621 Paper mills
PA: Mohawk Fine Papers Inc.
465 Saratoga St
Cohoes NY 12047
518 237-1740

(G-789)
MOLDED FIBER GLASS COMPANIES (PA)
2925 Mfg Pl (44004-9445)
P.O. Box 675 (44005-0675)
PHONE..................................440 997-5851
Richard Morrison, *CEO*
Dave Denny, *President*
Greg Tilton, *COO*
David M Giovannini, *Senior VP*
Carl Lafrance, *Senior VP*
▼ **EMP:** 685
SQ FT: 265,000
SALES (est): 589.3MM **Privately Held**
WEB: www.moldedfiberglass.com
SIC: 3089 Molding primary plastic; boxes, plastic; injection molding of plastics

(G-790)
MOLDED FIBER GLASS COMPANIES
Also Called: Msg Premier Molded Fiber
4401 Benefit Ave (44004-5458)
P.O. Box 675 (44005-0675)
PHONE..................................440 997-5851
Richard Morrison, *CEO*
Ivan Schwarz, *Buyer*
Jane Acker, *Manager*
EMP: 300
SQ FT: 168,000
SALES (corp-wide): 589.3MM **Privately Held**
SIC: 3089 Molding primary plastic
PA: Molded Fiber Glass Companies
2925 Mfg Pl
Ashtabula OH 44004
440 997-5851

(G-791)
MOLDED FIBER GLASS RESEARCH
1315 W 47th St (44004-5403)
PHONE..................................440 994-5100
Pete Emrich, *Vice Pres*
John Oneil, *IT/INT Sup*
EMP: 20

SALES (est): 2.6MM **Privately Held**
SIC: 3229 Glass fiber products

(G-792)
NEWSPAPER HOLDING INC
Also Called: Ashtabula Star Beacon
4626 Park Ave (44004-6933)
P.O. Box 2100 (44005-2100)
PHONE..................................440 998-2323
Jim Frustere, *Branch Mgr*
EMP: 51 **Privately Held**
WEB: www.clintonnc.com
SIC: 2711 2791 2752 Newspapers, publishing & printing; typesetting; commercial printing, lithographic
HQ: Newspaper Holding, Inc.
425 Locust St
Johnstown PA 15901
814 532-5102

(G-793)
NORTHEAST BOX COMPANY
1726 Griswold Ave (44004-9213)
P.O. Box 370 (44005-0370)
PHONE..................................440 992-5500
Ronald Marchewka, *President*
Bryon Perry, *Plant Mgr*
Mike Johnson, *Sales Mgr*
Susan Selman, *Manager*
Robert Jessup, *Shareholder*
EMP: 55
SQ FT: 110,000
SALES (est): 15.2MM **Privately Held**
WEB: www.northeastbox.com
SIC: 2653 Boxes, corrugated: made from purchased materials

(G-794)
OUTDOOR ARMY STORE OF ASHTBULA
Also Called: Outdoor Army Navy Stores
4420 Main Ave (44004-6923)
PHONE..................................440 992-8791
William Hyland, *President*
Harmon Lustig, *Corp Secy*
EMP: 18
SQ FT: 17,000
SALES (est): 2MM **Privately Held**
SIC: 2329 5661 5941 Athletic (warmup, sweat & jogging) suits: men's & boys'; shoe stores; camping equipment

(G-795)
PENCO TOOL LLC
2621 West Ave (44004-3115)
P.O. Box 429 (44005-0429)
PHONE..................................440 998-1116
Brian Lewis, *President*
Steve Berndt, *Vice Pres*
EMP: 23
SQ FT: 18,450
SALES (est): 5.5MM **Privately Held**
WEB: www.deephole.com
SIC: 3544 3599 7692 Industrial molds; special dies & tools; machine shop, jobbing & repair; welding repair

(G-796)
PENDLETON MOLD & MACHINE LLC
4624 State Rd (44004-6292)
PHONE..................................440 998-0041
Steven Pendleton,
EMP: 5
SALES (est): 300K **Privately Held**
SIC: 3544 3312 Industrial molds; blast furnaces & steel mills

(G-797)
PESKA INC (PA)
Also Called: Sports & Sports
3600 N Ridge Rd E (44004-4316)
PHONE..................................440 998-4664
Steve Reichert, *President*
Edith M Reichert, *Principal*
Paul A Reichert, *Principal*
EMP: 10 EST: 1983
SQ FT: 6,000
SALES (est): 2MM **Privately Held**
SIC: 5941 2396 Sporting goods & bicycle shops; screen printing on fabric articles

(G-798)
PINNEY DOCK & TRANSPORT LLC
1149 E 5th St (44004-3513)
P.O. Box 41 (44005-0041)
PHONE..................................440 964-7186
Lee Demers,
Bradley Frank,
◆ **EMP:** 33 EST: 1953
SQ FT: 20,000
SALES (est): 36.1MM **Publicly Held**
SIC: 3731 4491 5032 Drydocks, floating; docks, piers & terminals; limestone
PA: Kinder Morgan Inc
1001 La St Ste 1000
Houston TX 77002

(G-799)
PLAY ALL LLC
Also Called: Playall Trophies Awards Engrv
4542 Main Ave (44004-6925)
PHONE..................................440 992-7529
Robert Simpson, *President*
EMP: 3
SQ FT: 2,000
SALES (est): 200K **Privately Held**
SIC: 3479 5999 Etching & engraving; trophies & plaques

(G-800)
PRAXAIR INC
3102 Lake Rd E (44004-3829)
PHONE..................................440 994-1000
J J Redmond, *Branch Mgr*
EMP: 99 **Privately Held**
SIC: 2813 Oxygen, compressed or liquefied; nitrogen
HQ: Praxair, Inc.
10 Riverview Dr
Danbury CT 06810
203 837-2000

(G-801)
REESE MACHINE COMPANY INC
2501 State Rd (44004-5235)
P.O. Box 1396 (44005-1396)
PHONE..................................440 992-3942
Dale Reese, *President*
EMP: 10
SALES (est): 1.5MM **Privately Held**
WEB: www.reesemachinecompany.com
SIC: 3599 Machine shop, jobbing & repair

(G-802)
RELOADING SUPPLIES CORP
Also Called: Ohio Guns
1040 Devon Dr (44004-2100)
PHONE..................................440 228-0367
Daryl Upole, *President*
Daryl G Upole III, *Administration*
EMP: 3
SALES (est): 227.3K **Privately Held**
SIC: 3484 5941 Machine guns & grenade launchers; ammunition; firearms

(G-803)
REX INTERNATIONAL USA INC
Also Called: Wheeler Manufacturing
3744 Jefferson Rd (44004-9601)
P.O. Box 688 (44005-0688)
PHONE..................................800 321-7950
John Miyagawa, *President*
Tim Bowler, *Vice Pres*
▲ **EMP:** 28
SQ FT: 22,000
SALES (est): 6.2MM
SALES (corp-wide): 50.1MM **Privately Held**
WEB: www.wheelerrex.com
SIC: 3423 3546 3545 3541 Hand & edge tools; power-driven handtools; machine tool accessories; pipe cutting & threading machines
PA: Rex Industries Co.,Ltd.
1-9-3, Hishiyahigashi
Higashi-Osaka OSK 578-0
729 619-887

(G-804)
SHORT RUN MACHINE PRODUCTS INC
4744 Kister Ct (44004-8974)
PHONE..................................440 969-1313
Scott Ray, *President*

EMP: 12
SALES (est): 675.1K **Privately Held**
SIC: 3599 3544 Machine shop, jobbing & repair; special dies, tools, jigs & fixtures

(G-805)
SQUIRE SHOPPE BAKERY
511 Lake Ave (44004-3261)
P.O. Box 3126 (44005-3126)
PHONE..................................440 964-3303
Dennis Peters, *Owner*
EMP: 4
SQ FT: 4,800
SALES (est): 290.9K **Privately Held**
SIC: 2051 Bread, cake & related products

(G-806)
TDM LLC
1303 W 38th St (44004-5433)
PHONE..................................440 969-1442
Charles Tanzola,
EMP: 4 EST: 2014
SALES (est): 425K **Privately Held**
SIC: 3549 3442 Marking machines, metalworking; molding, trim & stripping

(G-807)
TENAN MACHINE & FABRICATING
6002 State Rd Bldg A (44004-6248)
PHONE..................................440 997-5100
Patrick Tenan, *President*
Janice Tenan, *Vice Pres*
EMP: 3
SALES (est): 200K **Privately Held**
SIC: 3599 Machine shop, jobbing & repair

(G-808)
THOMAS J RAFFA DDS INC
355 W Prospect Rd Ste 120 (44004-5830)
PHONE..................................440 997-5208
Thomas Raffa, *President*
EMP: 6
SQ FT: 1,200
SALES (est): 696.2K **Privately Held**
SIC: 3843 8021 Orthodontic appliances; offices & clinics of dentists

(G-809)
ULTIMATE CHEM SOLUTIONS INC
1800 E 21st St (44004-4012)
P.O. Box 1768 (44005-1768)
PHONE..................................440 998-6751
Yogi V Chokshi, *President*
EMP: 20 EST: 2010
SALES (est): 3.8MM **Privately Held**
SIC: 2869 Industrial organic chemicals

(G-810)
USALCO LLC
3050 Lake Rd E (44004-3829)
PHONE..................................440 993-2721
EMP: 4
SALES (corp-wide): 150MM **Privately Held**
SIC: 2911 Oils, fuel
HQ: Usalco, Llc
2601 Cannery Ave
Baltimore MD 21226
410 918-2230

(G-811)
VEITSCH-RADEX AMERICA LLC
4741 Kister Ct (44004-8975)
PHONE..................................440 969-2300
David Lawrie, *Branch Mgr*
EMP: 65
SALES (corp-wide): 351.2MM **Privately Held**
WEB: www.rhi-ag.com
SIC: 3297 Graphite refractories: carbon bond or ceramic bond
PA: Veitsch-Radex Gmbh & Co Og
WienerbergstraBe 9
Wien 1120
502 130-

(G-812)
WITT ENTERPRISES INC
2024 Aetna Rd (44004-6260)
PHONE..................................440 992-8333
Ron Kister Jr, *President*
EMP: 25
SQ FT: 600

Ashtabula - Ashtabula County (G-813)

SALES: 2MM **Privately Held**
SIC: 3471 Sand blasting of metal parts

(G-813)
ZEHRCO-GIANCOLA COMPOSITES INC (PA)
1501 W 47th St (44004-5419)
PHONE.....................................440 994-6317
Anthony Giancola, *President*
Edward Brashear, *General Mgr*
John Berwald, *Manager*
Ted Washburn, *Director*
▲ EMP: 105
SQ FT: 150,000
SALES: 26MM **Privately Held**
WEB: www.zehrco-giancola.com
SIC: 3089 Plates, plastic; injection molding of plastics

Ashville
Pickaway County

(G-814)
ALERIS ROLLED PRODUCTS INC
1 Reynolds Rd (43103-9204)
P.O. Box 197 (43103-0197)
PHONE.....................................740 983-2571
EMP: 59 **Privately Held**
SIC: 3341 3444 Secondary nonferrous metals; sheet metalwork
HQ: Aleris Rolled Products, Inc.
25825 Science Park Dr # 400
Beachwood OH 44122
216 910-3400

(G-815)
ALSCO METALS CORPORATION
1 Reynolds Rd (43103-9204)
PHONE.....................................740 983-2571
Mark Schiffman, *Regl Sales Mgr*
Sheri Moore, *Cust Mgr*
Bill Easton, *Branch Mgr*
EMP: 3 **Privately Held**
SIC: 3444 Siding, sheet metal
HQ: Alsco Metals, Llc
1309 Deer Hill Rd
Dennison OH 44621

(G-816)
COLUMBUS INDUSTRIES INC (PA)
2938 State Route 752 (43103-9543)
P.O. Box 257 (43103-0257)
PHONE.....................................740 983-2552
Harold T Pontius, *Ch of Bd*
Jeffrey Pontius, *President*
Wayne Vickers, *Exec VP*
April Brokaw, *Vice Pres*
Marvin Lampi, *Vice Pres*
◆ EMP: 900 EST: 1965
SQ FT: 78,000
SALES: 228.8MM **Privately Held**
WEB: www.colind.com
SIC: 3569 Filters

(G-817)
DAILY NEEDS PERSONAL CARE LLC
11560 State Route 104 (43103-9642)
PHONE.....................................614 598-8383
Suzanne Pettigrew, *Principal*
EMP: 3
SALES (est): 153.1K **Privately Held**
SIC: 2711 Newspapers, publishing & printing

(G-818)
H O FIBERTRENDS
235 State Route 674 S (43103-9794)
PHONE.....................................740 983-3864
Dave Lanman, *Managing Prtnr*
James Wickline, *Partner*
EMP: 3
SALES: 130K **Privately Held**
WEB: www.hofibertrends.com
SIC: 3714 5013 Motor vehicle parts & accessories; automotive supplies & parts

(G-819)
OWENS CORNING SALES LLC
1 Reynolds Rd (43103-9204)
P.O. Box 197 (43103-0197)
PHONE.....................................740 983-1300
Rodney Sawall, *Opers-Prdtn-Mfg*
EMP: 5 **Publicly Held**
WEB: www.owenscorning.com
SIC: 3444 3354 Siding, sheet metal; aluminum extruded products
HQ: Owens Corning Sales, Llc
1 Owens Corning Pkwy
Toledo OH 43659
419 248-8000

(G-820)
PRODUCTION PLUS CORP
Also Called: Magic Rack
101 S Business Pl (43103-6502)
PHONE.....................................740 983-5178
Jeremy Davitz, *President*
EMP: 16
SALES: 2.6MM **Privately Held**
WEB: www.magicrack.com
SIC: 3496 Miscellaneous fabricated wire products

Athens
Athens County

(G-821)
ADAMS PUBLISHING GROUP LLC (HQ)
Also Called: Apg Media of Ohio
9300 Johnson Hollow Rd (45701-9028)
PHONE.....................................740 592-6612
Mark Adams, *CEO*
Robert Wallace, *CFO*
EMP: 11 EST: 2013
SALES (est): 28.9MM
SALES (corp-wide): 268.7MM **Privately Held**
SIC: 2711 Newspapers, publishing & printing
PA: Adams Publishing Group, Llc
103 W Summer St
Easton MD 21601
218 348-3391

(G-822)
ALL POWER EQUIPMENT LLC (PA)
Also Called: Kubota Authorized Dealer
8880 United Ln (45701-3667)
PHONE.....................................740 593-3279
Gil Elmore, *Mng Member*
EMP: 19
SQ FT: 6,000
SALES (est): 7.3MM **Privately Held**
SIC: 5261 5561 3799 5083 Lawnmowers & tractors; camper & travel trailer dealers; all terrain vehicles (ATV); farm & garden machinery

(G-823)
ATHENS MOLD AND MACHINE INC
180 Mill St (45701-2627)
PHONE.....................................740 593-6613
Jack D Thornton, *President*
Mark Thornton, *Vice Pres*
EMP: 81
SQ FT: 70,000
SALES (est): 11.5MM **Privately Held**
SIC: 3544 3599 7692 Special dies & tools; machine shop, jobbing & repair; welding repair

(G-824)
ATHENS TECHNICAL SPECIALISTS
Also Called: Atsi
8157 Us Highway 50 (45701-9303)
PHONE.....................................740 592-2874
Ted Gilfert, *CEO*
James Gilfert, *President*
Una Gilfert, *Corp Secy*
▲ EMP: 14
SQ FT: 6,000
SALES (est): 3.1MM **Privately Held**
WEB: www.atsi-tester.com
SIC: 3669 8748 Traffic signals, electric; traffic consultant

(G-825)
CITY OF ATHENS
395 W State St (45701-1527)
PHONE.....................................740 592-3344
Shawn Beasley, *Plant Mgr*
Crystal Kynard, *Branch Mgr*
EMP: 23 **Privately Held**
SIC: 3589 4941 Water treatment equipment, industrial; water supply
PA: City Of Athens
8 E Washington St Ste 101
Athens OH 45701
740 592-3338

(G-826)
CRUMBS INC
Also Called: Crumbs Bakery
94 Columbus Rd (45701-1312)
PHONE.....................................740 592-3803
Jeremy Bowman, *President*
EMP: 10
SALES (est): 716.4K **Privately Held**
WEB: www.crumbs.net
SIC: 2051 5461 Bakery: wholesale or wholesale/retail combined; bakeries

(G-827)
DEMEL ENTERPRISES INC
10980 Northpoint Dr (45701-8760)
PHONE.....................................740 331-1400
Chris Demel, *President*
▲ EMP: 5
SALES (est): 513.4K **Privately Held**
SIC: 3991 0139 Brooms & brushes; herb or spice farm

(G-828)
DIAGNOSTIC HYBRIDS INC
2005 E State St Ste 100 (45701-2125)
PHONE.....................................740 593-1784
David R Scholl PHD, *President*
James L Brown, *COO*
Gail Goodrum, *Vice Pres*
Paul D Olivo PHD, *Vice Pres*
Geoff Morgan, *CFO*
EMP: 220
SQ FT: 25,000
SALES (est): 52.2MM
SALES (corp-wide): 522.2MM **Publicly Held**
WEB: www.dhiusa.com
SIC: 2835 3841 In vitro & in vivo diagnostic substances; diagnostic apparatus, medical
PA: Quidel Corporation
12544 High Bluff Dr # 200
San Diego CA 92130
858 552-1100

(G-829)
DOUBLE B PRINTING LLC
Also Called: Minuteman Press
17 W Washington St (45701-2433)
PHONE.....................................740 593-7393
William Bowers Jr,
Eric Bobo,
EMP: 4
SQ FT: 4,000
SALES (est): 385K **Privately Held**
SIC: 2752 Commercial printing, offset

(G-830)
FUSION NOODLE CO
30 E Union St (45701-2911)
PHONE.....................................740 589-5511
EMP: 8
SALES (est): 582.6K **Privately Held**
SIC: 2098 Noodles (e.g. egg, plain & water), dry

(G-831)
G & J PEPSI-COLA BOTTLERS INC
2001 E State St (45701-2125)
PHONE.....................................740 593-3366
Curt Allison, *Branch Mgr*
EMP: 51
SALES (corp-wide): 418.3MM **Privately Held**
WEB: www.gjpepsi.com
SIC: 4225 5149 2086 General warehousing; beverages, except coffee & tea; carbonated beverages, nonalcoholic: bottled & canned
PA: G & J Pepsi-Cola Bottlers Inc
9435 Waterstone Blvd # 390
Cincinnati OH 45249
513 785-6060

(G-832)
GEM COATINGS LTD
5840 Industrial Park Rd (45701-8736)
PHONE.....................................740 589-2998
Karry Gemmell, *Partner*
EMP: 35
SQ FT: 55,000
SALES (est): 4.6MM **Privately Held**
SIC: 3479 Coating of metals with plastic or resins

(G-833)
GLOBAL COOLING INC
Also Called: Stirling Ultracold
6000 Poston Rd (45701-9051)
PHONE.....................................740 274-7900
Neill Lane, *President*
David Berchowitz, *Senior VP*
Brett Harris, *Vice Pres*
Yong-Rak Kwon, *Vice Pres*
Jeremy King, *Prdtn Mgr*
◆ EMP: 32
SQ FT: 15,000
SALES (est): 10.2MM **Privately Held**
WEB: www.globalcooling.com
SIC: 3821 Freezers, laboratory

(G-834)
GUITAR DIGEST INC
23 Curtis St (45701-3724)
P.O. Box 66, The Plains (45780-0066)
PHONE.....................................740 592-4614
Marc Newman, *President*
Marc Wayner, *Vice Pres*
EMP: 15
SALES (est): 854.8K **Privately Held**
WEB: www.guitardigest.com
SIC: 2721 Magazines: publishing only, not printed on site

(G-835)
INDIE-PEASANT ENTERPRISES
Also Called: Shagbark Seed & Mill
88 Columbus Cir (45701-1370)
PHONE.....................................740 590-8240
Michelle Ajamian, *Principal*
Brandon Jaeger, *Principal*
Shagbark Mill, *Principal*
EMP: 3 EST: 2012
SALES (est): 216.8K **Privately Held**
SIC: 2099 2041 Tortillas, fresh or refrigerated; flour & other grain mill products

(G-836)
JACKIE OS PUB BREWERY LLC
25 Campbell St (45701-2616)
PHONE.....................................740 274-0777
Art Oestrike, *President*
Andrew A Oestrike, *Principal*
Laura Winch, *Administration*
EMP: 61
SALES (est): 7MM **Privately Held**
SIC: 2082 Beer (alcoholic beverage)

(G-837)
JACQUELINE L VANDYKE
Also Called: Performance Lettering & Signs
10414 State Route 550 (45701-9705)
PHONE.....................................740 593-6779
Jacqueline Vandyke, *Owner*
Jackie Vandyke, *Owner*
EMP: 5
SALES: 250K **Privately Held**
SIC: 3993 5999 Electric signs; awnings

(G-838)
MCHAPPYS DONUTS OF PARKERSBURG
Also Called: Mc Happys Donuts
384 Richland Ave (45701-3204)
PHONE.....................................740 593-8744
Bonnie Boring, *Manager*
EMP: 4

▲ = Import ▼ = Export ◆ = Import/Export

SALES (corp-wide): 45.5MM **Privately Held**
WEB: www.mchappys.com
SIC: **5461** 2051 Doughnuts; doughnuts, except frozen
HQ: Mchappys Donuts Of Parkersburg Inc
2515 Washington Blvd
Belpre OH 45714
740 423-6351

(G-839)
MESSENGER PUBLISHING COMPANY
Also Called: Athens Messenger, The
9300 Johnson Hollow Rd (45701-9028)
PHONE.................................740 592-6612
Clarence Brown Jr, *Ch of Bd*
Mark Policinski, *President*
Kathy Kerr, *Editor*
Chana Powell, *Business Mgr*
Glenn Christensen, *Vice Pres*
EMP: 125 EST: 1825
SQ FT: 25,000
SALES (est): 28.9MM
SALES (corp-wide): 268.7MM **Privately Held**
WEB: www.athensmessenger.com
SIC: **2711** 2752 Newspapers, publishing & printing; commercial printing, offset
HQ: Adams Publishing Group, Llc
9300 Johnson Hollow Rd
Athens OH 45701
740 592-6612

(G-840)
MILOS WHOLE WORLD GOURMET LLC
94 Columbus Rd (45701-1312)
PHONE.................................740 589-6456
Jonathan Leal, *Mng Member*
EMP: 9
SALES (est): 1.4MM **Privately Held**
SIC: **1541** 2033 Food products manufacturing or packing plant construction; canned fruits & specialties

(G-841)
MINUTEMAN PRESS OF ATHENS LLC
17 W Washington St (45701-2433)
PHONE.................................740 593-7393
William Bowers Jr,
Eric Bobo,
EMP: 3 EST: 1930
SQ FT: 7,000
SALES (est): 350.2K **Privately Held**
SIC: **2752** 2759 Commercial printing, offset; letterpress printing

(G-842)
MITCHELL ELECTRONICS INC
1005 E State St Ste 5 (45701-2151)
P.O. Box 2626 (45701-5426)
PHONE.................................740 594-8532
Lawrence Mitchell, *President*
Brett Martz, *Sales Staff*
Linda W Mitchell, *Admin Sec*
EMP: 5
SQ FT: 2,000
SALES (est): 820.4K **Privately Held**
WEB: www.mitchell-electronics.com
SIC: **3679** 8711 Electronic circuits; engineering services

(G-843)
OHIO UNIVERSITY
Also Called: Post, The
28 Union St Ground Fl (45701)
PHONE.................................740 593-4010
Jim Rodgers, *Manager*
EMP: 130
SALES (corp-wide): 531.5MM **Privately Held**
WEB: www.zanesville.ohiou.edu
SIC: **2711** 8221 Newspapers, publishing & printing; university
PA: Ohio University
1 Ohio University
Athens OH 45701
740 593-1000

(G-844)
PETRO QUEST INC (PA)
3 W Stimson Ave (45701-2679)
P.O. Box 268 (45701-0268)
PHONE.................................740 593-3800
Paul J Gerig, *President*
Christian Gerig, *Vice Pres*
Debora Jarvis, *Admin Sec*
EMP: 8
SQ FT: 2,200
SALES (est): 961.7K **Privately Held**
SIC: **1381** 8111 Drilling oil & gas wells; general practice attorney, lawyer

(G-845)
POTENTIAL LABS LLC
101 S May Ave (45701-2016)
PHONE.................................740 590-0009
Benjamin L Lachman, *Mng Member*
Robin Kinney,
EMP: 2
SQ FT: 1,500
SALES: 1.5MM **Privately Held**
SIC: **3571** Electronic computers

(G-846)
PRECISION IMPRINT
26 E State St (45701-2540)
PHONE.................................740 592-5916
Randy Shoup, *Owner*
EMP: 8
SQ FT: 5,000
SALES (est): 380K **Privately Held**
WEB: www.precisionimprint.com
SIC: **2261** 5136 5137 2759 Screen printing of cotton broadwoven fabrics; sportswear, men's & boys'; sportswear, women's & children's; screen printing; embroidery products, except schiffli machine

(G-847)
QUIDEL CORPORATION
1055 E State St Ste 100 (45701-7911)
PHONE.................................740 589-3300
EMP: 56
SALES (corp-wide): 522.2MM **Publicly Held**
SIC: **2835** In vitro & in vivo diagnostic substances
PA: Quidel Corporation
12544 High Bluff Dr # 200
San Diego CA 92130
858 552-1100

(G-848)
QUIDEL DHI
2005 E State St (45701-2125)
PHONE.................................740 589-3300
Chris Ridgway, *Manager*
EMP: 28
SALES (est): 204.8K
SALES (corp-wide): 522.2MM **Publicly Held**
SIC: **3829** Medical diagnostic systems, nuclear
PA: Quidel Corporation
12544 High Bluff Dr # 200
San Diego CA 92130
858 552-1100

(G-849)
STEWART-MACDONALD MFG CO (PA)
Also Called: Stewart McDnalds Guitar Sp Sup
21 N Shafer St (45701-2304)
PHONE.................................740 592-3021
Kay Tousley, *Principal*
Jay Hostetler, *Vice Pres*
John A Woodrow, *CFO*
Angie Hayes, *Controller*
▲ EMP: 40
SQ FT: 12,000
SALES (est): 7.8MM **Privately Held**
WEB: www.banjoparts.com
SIC: **3931** 5736 Banjos & parts; mandolins & parts; violins & parts; guitars & parts, electric & nonelectric; musical instrument stores

(G-850)
STICKY PETES MAPLE SYRUP
18216 S Canaan Rd (45701-9465)
PHONE.................................740 662-2726
Laura McManus-Berry, *Principal*
EMP: 3

SALES (est): 121.3K **Privately Held**
SIC: **2099** Maple syrup

(G-851)
SUNPOWER INC
2005 E State St Ste 104 (45701-2125)
PHONE.................................740 594-2221
Jeffrey Hatfield, *Vice Pres*
Douglas Richards, *Vice Pres*
Mike Blair, *Info Tech Mgr*
EMP: 95
SQ FT: 16,000
SALES (est): 15.6MM
SALES (corp-wide): 4.8B **Publicly Held**
WEB: www.sunpower.com
SIC: **8731** 8711 8733 3769 Commercial physical research; engineering services; physical research, noncommercial; scientific research agency; guided missile & space vehicle parts & auxiliary equipment
HQ: Advanced Measurement Technology, Inc.
801 S Illinois Ave
Oak Ridge TN 37830
865 482-4411

(G-852)
TS TRIM INDUSTRIES INC
10 Kenny Dr (45701-9406)
PHONE.................................740 593-5958
Keith Mills, *Manager*
Gary Griggs, *Training Dir*
EMP: 360
SALES (corp-wide): 4.5B **Privately Held**
WEB: www.tstrim.com
SIC: **2399** 3714 Seat covers, automobile; motor vehicle parts & accessories
HQ: Ts Trim Industries Inc.
6380 Canal St
Canal Winchester OH 43110
614 837-4114

(G-853)
UPTOWN DOG THE INC
9 W Union St (45701-2819)
PHONE.................................740 592-4600
Mary Swintek, *President*
EMP: 8
SQ FT: 1,000
SALES (est): 750K **Privately Held**
WEB: www.uptowndogtshirts.com
SIC: **5699** 2261 2759 Sports apparel; screen printing of cotton broadwoven fabrics; screen printing

(G-854)
YORK PAVING CO (PA)
758 W Union St (45701-9408)
P.O. Box 2450 (45701-5250)
PHONE.................................740 594-3600
Cindy L Hayes, *CEO*
James Hayes, *President*
EMP: 15 EST: 1997
SALES (est): 3.2MM **Privately Held**
WEB: www.yorkpaving.com
SIC: **1771** 2951 Blacktop (asphalt) work; asphalt paving mixtures & blocks

Attica
Seneca County

(G-855)
BLOOMVILLE GAZETTE INC
Also Called: Attica Hub Office
26 N Main St (44807-9001)
P.O. Box 516 (44807-0516)
PHONE.................................419 426-3491
Deb Cook, *President*
EMP: 3
SALES (est): 162K **Privately Held**
WEB: www.atticahub.com
SIC: **2711** Newspapers, publishing & printing

(G-856)
EITLE MACHINE TOOL INC
6036 Coder Rd (44807-9638)
PHONE.................................419 935-8753
Jerrold Eitle, *President*
EMP: 7
SALES (est): 1MM **Privately Held**
SIC: **3599** Machine shop, jobbing & repair

(G-857)
KF TECHNOLOGIES AND CUSTOM MFG
12178 E County Road 6 (44807-9793)
P.O. Box 122 (44807-0122)
PHONE.................................419 426-0172
Ron Waldock, *Owner*
EMP: 3
SALES (est): 52.9K **Privately Held**
SIC: **8731** 3999 Commercial physical research; manufacturing industries

(G-858)
OMAR ASSOCIATES LLC
625 N State Route 4 (44807-9533)
PHONE.................................419 426-0610
Eric J WI, *Owner*
Heather Auburn, *Sales Staff*
Jane Wise,
EMP: 8 EST: 2001
SALES (est): 1.6MM **Privately Held**
SIC: **3556** Food products machinery

(G-859)
SENECA TILES INC
7100 S County Road 23 (44807-9796)
PHONE.................................419 426-3561
James D Fry, *President*
◆ EMP: 55
SQ FT: 150,000
SALES (est): 6.3MM **Privately Held**
WEB: www.senecatile.com
SIC: **3253** Ceramic wall & floor tile

(G-860)
WALDOCK EQP SLS & SVC INC (PA)
12178 E County Road 6 (44807-9793)
P.O. Box 122 (44807-0122)
PHONE.................................419 426-7771
Ronald D Waldock, *President*
Karla Waldock, *Vice Pres*
EMP: 3
SQ FT: 1,800
SALES: 100K **Privately Held**
SIC: **7692** Welding repair

Atwater
Portage County

(G-861)
HR PARTS N STUFF
2002 Industry Rd (44201-9354)
P.O. Box 67 (44201-0067)
PHONE.................................330 947-2433
Paul Ferry, *Partner*
▼ EMP: 3
SQ FT: 3,680
SALES: 170K **Privately Held**
SIC: **3599** 3561 Grinding castings for the trade; machine shop, jobbing & repair; cylinders, pump

(G-862)
MALCOLM HYDRAULICS
6581 Waterloo Rd (44201-9508)
PHONE.................................330 819-2033
James Malcolm, *Owner*
EMP: 5
SALES (est): 345.4K **Privately Held**
SIC: **3593** Fluid power cylinders, hydraulic or pneumatic

(G-863)
PYRAMID TREATING INC
3031 Sanford Rd (44201-9338)
PHONE.................................330 325-2811
Roy E Kommel Jr, *President*
Kathy Kommel, *Corp Secy*
EMP: 4
SALES (est): 463.9K **Privately Held**
SIC: **1389** Servicing oil & gas wells

(G-864)
VICTORIAN FARMS
1375 Aberagg Rd (44201-9743)
PHONE.................................330 628-9188
Kathy Cruise, *Principal*
EMP: 4

Atwater - Portage County (G-865)   GEOGRAPHIC SECTION

SALES (est): 341.5K Privately Held
SIC: 3799 4789 7999 Carriages, horse drawn; horse drawn transportation services; saddlehorse rental

(G-865)
WATERLOO MANUFACTURING CO INC
6298 Waterloo Rd (44201-9702)
PHONE..................................330 947-2917
Thomas Ludlam, *President*
EMP: 4
SQ FT: 51,200
SALES: 150K Privately Held
WEB: www.waterloomanufacturing.com
SIC: 3629 5084 Blasting machines, electrical; industrial machinery & equipment

Aurora
Portage County

(G-866)
ADIDAS NORTH AMERICA INC
Also Called: Adidas Outlet Store Aurora
549 S Chillicothe Rd (44202-7848)
PHONE..................................330 562-4689
Amanda, *Branch Mgr*
EMP: 6
SALES (corp-wide): 25B Privately Held
SIC: 2329 Athletic (warmup, sweat & jogging) suits: men's & boys'; men's & boys' athletic uniforms; knickers, dress (separate): men's & boys'
HQ: Adidas North America, Inc.
3449 N Anchor St Ste 500
Portland OR 97217
971 234-2300

(G-867)
ADVANCED INNOVATIVE MFG INC
Also Called: A.I.M.
116 Lena Dr Operator (44202)
PHONE..................................330 562-2468
Joseph A Hawald, *President*
Mark J Hawald, *CFO*
EMP: 15
SQ FT: 29,120
SALES: 3.8MM Privately Held
SIC: 3541 Machine tools, metal cutting type

(G-868)
ALUMINUM FENCE & MFG CO
189 New Castle Dr (44202-6731)
PHONE..................................330 755-3323
Edward C Joseph, *President*
Maureen Joseph, *Vice Pres*
EMP: 6
SQ FT: 12,000
SALES (est): 1.2MM Privately Held
WEB: www.aluminumfencemfg.com
SIC: 3315 3599 3544 Chain link fencing; machine shop, jobbing & repair; special dies & tools

(G-869)
ARGOSY WIND POWER LTD
70 Aurora Industrial Pkwy (44202-8086)
P.O. Box 113, Chesterland (44026-0113)
PHONE..................................440 539-1345
Jeffrey B Milbourn, *President*
Gerard J Sposato, *Exec VP*
John C Rexford, *Senior VP*
Raphael J Omerza, *Vice Pres*
▲ EMP: 7 EST: 2011
SALES (est): 867.1K Privately Held
SIC: 3511 Turbines & turbine generator sets

(G-870)
ATRIUM AT ANNA MARIA INC
849 N Aurora Rd (44202-9537)
PHONE..................................330 562-7777
Aaron Baker, *Administration*
EMP: 4
SALES (est): 274.5K Privately Held
SIC: 2711 Newspapers, publishing & printing

(G-871)
AUTOMATION PLASTICS CORP
150 Lena Dr (44202-9202)
PHONE..................................330 562-5148
Harry Smith, *President*
Will Wilke, *Prdtn Mgr*
Tressa Dewitt, *QC Mgr*
Alan Higgs, *Engineer*
Chris Miller, *Engineer*
EMP: 60
SQ FT: 43,000
SALES (est): 16.2MM Privately Held
WEB: www.automationplastics.com
SIC: 3089 3544 Injection molding of plastics; special dies, tools, jigs & fixtures

(G-872)
BARRACUDA TECHNOLOGIES INC
2900 State Route 82 (44202-9395)
PHONE..................................216 469-1566
Kris Santin, *CEO*
EMP: 12
SALES (est): 724.9K Privately Held
SIC: 3644 Noncurrent-carrying wiring services

(G-873)
BERRY PLASTICS FILMCO INC
1450 S Chillicothe Rd (44202-9282)
PHONE..................................330 562-6111
David Meldren, *President*
Judy Ciocca, *Principal*
▲ EMP: 100
SQ FT: 85,000
SALES (est): 13.2MM Publicly Held
SIC: 3081 Plastic film & sheet
HQ: Berry Global, Inc.
101 Oakley St
Evansville IN 47710
812 424-2904

(G-874)
CANTEX INC
11444 Chamberlain Rd 1 (44202-9306)
PHONE..................................330 995-3665
Kevin McNamara, *Plant Mgr*
Mike Schafer, *Branch Mgr*
John Gerbec, *Maintence Staff*
EMP: 60
SALES (corp-wide): 71B Privately Held
WEB: www.cantex.com
SIC: 3084 3089 Plastics pipe; fittings for pipe, plastic
HQ: Cantex Inc.
301 Commerce St Ste 2700
Fort Worth TX 76102

(G-875)
CORROSION RESISTANT TECHNOLOGY
560 Club Dr (44202-6305)
PHONE..................................800 245-3769
Scott Henry, *Principal*
EMP: 7
SALES (est): 470.1K Privately Held
SIC: 3296 Mineral wool

(G-876)
CUSTOM PULTRUSIONS INC (HQ)
1331 S Chillicothe Rd (44202-8066)
PHONE..................................330 562-5201
Jay Lund, *CEO*
EMP: 29
SALES (est): 15.5MM
SALES (corp-wide): 2.9B Privately Held
SIC: 3089 Injection molding of plastics
PA: Andersen Corporation
100 4th Ave N
Bayport MN 55003
651 264-5150

(G-877)
EATON CORPORATION
Synflex Division
115 Lena Dr (44202-9202)
PHONE..................................330 274-0743
Daniel Gomez, *Sales Mgr*
Phil Corvo, *Manager*
Christopher Fletcher, *Manager*
EMP: 210
SQ FT: 7,568 Privately Held

SIC: 3089 3494 3429 3052 Plastic containers, except foam; valves & pipe fittings; manufactured hardware (general); rubber & plastics hose & beltings
HQ: Eaton Corporation
1000 Eaton Blvd
Cleveland OH 44122
440 523-5000

(G-878)
ELECTROVATIONS INC
350 Harris Dr (44202-7536)
PHONE..................................330 274-3558
R Charles Vermerris, *President*
EMP: 25
SQ FT: 4,500
SALES (est): 1.9MM Privately Held
SIC: 8711 7389 3357 Electrical or electronic engineering; design, commercial & industrial; nonferrous wiredrawing & insulating

(G-879)
EPG INC
500 Lena Dr (44202-9245)
PHONE..................................330 995-5125
Michael Orazen, *Manager*
EMP: 80
SALES (corp-wide): 3.7B Privately Held
WEB: www.epgcando.com
SIC: 3053 3061 Gaskets, all materials; mechanical rubber goods
HQ: Epg, Inc.
1780 Miller Pkwy
Streetsboro OH 44241
330 995-9725

(G-880)
FREEDOM HEALTH LLC
65 Aurora Industrial Pkwy (44202-8088)
PHONE..................................330 562-0888
John Hall, *President*
Stephen Willey, *COO*
Stephen A Willey, *COO*
Steve Willey, *COO*
Vincenzo Franco, *Vice Pres*
▲ EMP: 20
SQ FT: 50,000
SALES (est): 3.6MM Privately Held
WEB: www.freedomhealth.com
SIC: 2023 Dietary supplements, dairy & non-dairy based

(G-881)
GODFREY & WING INC (PA)
220 Campus Dr (44202-6663)
PHONE..................................330 562-1440
Christopher Gilmore, *President*
Brad Welch, *Corp Secy*
Karen Gilmore, *Vice Pres*
▲ EMP: 50 EST: 1947
SQ FT: 68,000
SALES (est): 19.3MM Privately Held
SIC: 3479 8734 Coating of metals with plastic or resins; testing laboratories

(G-882)
HEINENS INC
Also Called: Heinen's 8
115 N Chillicothe Rd (44202-7797)
PHONE..................................330 562-5297
Paul Otoole, *Manager*
EMP: 60
SALES (corp-wide): 393.3MM Privately Held
SIC: 5411 2051 Supermarkets, chain; bread, cake & related products
PA: Heinen's, Inc.
4540 Richmond Rd
Warrensville Heights OH 44128
216 475-2300

(G-883)
HOLM INDUSTRIES INC (PA)
1300 Danner Dr (44202-9284)
PHONE..................................330 562-2900
Ted McQuade, *Principal*
EMP: 5
SALES (est): 3.6MM Privately Held
SIC: 3089 Plastics products

(G-884)
ILPEA INDUSTRIES INC
OEM/Miller
1300 Danner Dr (44202-9284)
PHONE..................................330 562-2916

Ken Chenoweth, *Manager*
EMP: 135 Privately Held
WEB: www.holmindustries.com
SIC: 3089 5162 3083 Plastic containers, except foam; plastics sheets & rods; laminated plastics plate & sheet
HQ: Ilpea Industries, Inc.
745 S Gardner St
Scottsburg IN 47170
812 752-2526

(G-885)
JIT PACKAGING INC (PA)
Also Called: Jit Milrob
250 Page Rd (44202)
PHONE..................................330 562-8080
Dan Harrison, *General Mgr*
David R Jones, *Chairman*
Elaine Jones, *Vice Pres*
Marian Maulis, *Purchasing*
EMP: 34
SQ FT: 60,000
SALES (est): 11.7MM Privately Held
SIC: 2448 5113 5085 2653 Pallets, wood; corrugated & solid fiber boxes; industrial supplies; corrugated & solid fiber boxes

(G-886)
KAPSTONE CONTAINER CORPORATION
Also Called: Filmco
1450 S Chillicothe Rd (44202-9282)
P.O. Box 239 (44202-0239)
PHONE..................................330 562-6111
Richard Pohland, *Branch Mgr*
EMP: 106
SQ FT: 20,000
SALES (corp-wide): 16.2B Publicly Held
SIC: 3081 5199 2671 Packing materials, plastic sheet; packaging materials; packaging paper & plastics film, coated & laminated
HQ: Kapstone Container Corporation
1601 Blairs Ferry Rd Ne
Cedar Rapids IA 52402
319 393-3610

(G-887)
KARL INDUSTRIES INC
11415 Chamberlain Rd (44202-9306)
P.O. Box 181 (44202-0181)
PHONE..................................330 562-4100
Paul Tornstrom, *President*
Karen Tornstrom, *Treasurer*
EMP: 3
SQ FT: 7,000
SALES: 200K Privately Held
WEB: www.karlindustries.com
SIC: 2869 Industrial organic chemicals

(G-888)
KENT PAVERBRICK LLC
11437 Chamberlain Rd (44202-9306)
PHONE..................................330 995-7000
James Wasas, *CEO*
Robert Schultz, *Director*
EMP: 5
SQ FT: 6,000
SALES (est): 373.8K Privately Held
SIC: 3299 Blocks & brick, sand lime

(G-889)
KING SOFTWARE SYSTEMS
680 Briarcliff Dr (44202-9212)
PHONE..................................330 562-1135
John King, *Owner*
EMP: 3
SALES (est): 294.6K Privately Held
WEB: www.kingsoftwaresystems.com
SIC: 7372 Business oriented computer software

(G-890)
LAYERZERO POWER SYSTEMS INC
1500 Danner Dr (44202-9298)
PHONE..................................440 399-9000
Milind Bhanoo, *President*
James M Galm, *Vice Pres*
Linda Bell, *Controller*
Jeff Maass, *Marketing Mgr*
Ryan Fenik, *Manager*
EMP: 25 EST: 2001

GEOGRAPHIC SECTION

Aurora - Portage County (G-915)

SALES (est): 10.5MM **Privately Held**
WEB: www.layerzero.com
SIC: **3613** Power switching equipment

(G-891)
LINDSEY GRAPHICS INC
112 Parkview Dr (44202-8043)
PHONE..................................330 995-9241
Robert Nelson Jr, *President*
EMP: 3
SQ FT: 2,000
SALES (est): 385.2K **Privately Held**
WEB: www.lindseygraphics.com
SIC: **5112** **2752** Business forms; color lithography

(G-892)
MERIDIAN LLC
325 Harris Dr (44202-7539)
PHONE..................................330 995-0371
Larry Cornell, *Principal*
EMP: 12
SALES (est): 1.3MM **Privately Held**
SIC: **3841** Surgical & medical instruments

(G-893)
MULCH MADNESS LLC
8022 S Riverside Dr (44202-8619)
PHONE..................................330 920-9900
EMP: 10
SALES (est): 1.5MM **Privately Held**
SIC: **2499** **4212** Mfg Wood Products Local Trucking Operator

(G-894)
MYTEE PRODUCTS INC
1335 S Chillicothe Rd (44202-8066)
PHONE..................................440 591-4301
Vick Agarwalla, *President*
Prabhav Agarwalla, *Vice Pres*
Natasha Thomason, *Office Mgr*
▲ EMP: 14
SQ FT: 28,000
SALES (est): 4.2MM **Privately Held**
SIC: **5013** **2824** Truck parts & accessories; vinyl fibers

(G-895)
NATURAL ESSENTIALS INC
Also Called: Bulk Apothecary
1199 S Chillicothe Rd (44202-8001)
PHONE..................................330 562-8022
Gary Pellegrino, *President*
Leonard Marsden, *General Mgr*
Dan Frenz, *Vice Pres*
Sheldon Triplett, *Purch Agent*
Michael Cutlip, *QA Dir*
◆ EMP: 30
SQ FT: 22,000
SALES (est): 24.5MM **Privately Held**
SIC: **2844** **2899** Cosmetic preparations; oils & essential oils

(G-896)
ODYSSEY SPIRITS INC
Also Called: Odyssey Printwear
7286 N Aurora Rd (44202-9627)
PHONE..................................330 562-1523
Mark Hoehn, *President*
Laura Hoehn, *Vice Pres*
EMP: 12
SQ FT: 7,500
SALES (est): 1.6MM **Privately Held**
WEB: www.odysseyprintwear.com
SIC: **2759** **5651** **5699** **5947** Screen printing; family clothing stores; T-shirts, custom printed; gift shop

(G-897)
OMEGA POLYMER TECHNOLOGIES INC (PA)
Also Called: Opti
1331 S Chillicothe Rd (44202-8066)
PHONE..................................330 562-5201
Ronald Baker, *President*
Donald Smith, *Vice Pres*
Bob Jackson, *Admin Sec*
EMP: 6
SALES (est): 32.5MM **Privately Held**
SIC: **3089** Injection molding of plastics

(G-898)
OMEGA PULTRUSIONS INCORPORATED
1331 S Chillicothe Rd (44202-8066)
PHONE..................................330 562-5201
Donald F Borraccini, *President*
EMP: 140
SQ FT: 95,000
SALES (est): 23.6MM **Privately Held**
SIC: **3089** Injection molding of plastics
PA: Omega Polymer Technologies, Inc.
1331 S Chillicothe Rd
Aurora OH 44202

(G-899)
PHILPOTT RUBBER LLC
Also Called: Philpott Rubber and Plastics
375 Gentry Dr (44202-7540)
PHONE..................................330 225-3344
Mike Baach, *President*
EMP: 8
SALES (corp-wide): 9MM **Privately Held**
SIC: **3069** Medical sundries, rubber
HQ: Philpott Rubber Llc
1010 Industrial Pkwy N
Brunswick OH 44212
330 225-3344

(G-900)
PVH CORP
Also Called: Van Heusen
549 S Chilcthe Rd Ste 340 (44202-6519)
PHONE..................................330 562-4440
Stephanie Lottig, *Manager*
EMP: 9
SALES (corp-wide): 9.6B **Publicly Held**
WEB: www.pvh.com
SIC: **2321** **2326** Men's & boys' dress shirts; work shirts: men's, youths' & boys'
PA: Pvh Corp.
200 Madison Ave Bsmt 1
New York NY 10016
212 381-3500

(G-901)
PYROTEK INCORPORATED
Metaullics Systems Division
355 Campus Dr (44202-6662)
PHONE..................................440 349-8800
EMP: 133
SALES (corp-wide): 588.8MM **Privately Held**
SIC: **3569** **3624** **3295** **3561** Mfg General Indstl Mach Mfg Carbon/Graphite Prdt Mfg Minerals-Earth/Treat Mfg Pumps/Pumping Equip
PA: Pyrotek Incorporated
705 W 1st Ave
Spokane WA 99201
509 926-6212

(G-902)
RADIX WIRE COMPANY
350 Harris Dr (44202-7536)
PHONE..................................330 995-3677
Craig Hines, *Manager*
EMP: 25
SQ FT: 10,000
SALES (corp-wide): 21.5MM **Privately Held**
WEB: www.radix-wire.com
SIC: **3357** Nonferrous wiredrawing & insulating
PA: Radix Wire Co
26000 Lakeland Blvd
Cleveland OH 44132
216 731-9191

(G-903)
ROBECK FLUID POWER CO
350 Lena Dr (44202-8098)
PHONE..................................330 562-1140
Peter Becker, *President*
Ken Traeger, *Corp Secy*
Don Louis, *Opers Mgr*
Sherri Meloy, *Purchasing*
Bob Long, *Engineer*
▲ EMP: 65
SQ FT: 6,000
SALES (est): 71.1MM **Privately Held**
WEB: www.robeckfluidpower.com
SIC: **5084** **3593** **3594** **3494** Hydraulic systems equipment & supplies; fluid power cylinders & actuators; fluid power pumps & motors; valves & pipe fittings

(G-904)
ROTEK INCORPORATED (DH)
1400 S Chillicothe Rd (44202-9299)
P.O. Box 312 (44202-0312)
PHONE..................................330 562-4000
Mike Drobik, *President*
Jackie Nuber, *General Mgr*
Tom Code, *Vice Pres*
Michael Blanton, *Maint Spvr*
Donald Basham, *Production*
▲ EMP: 160 EST: 1962
SQ FT: 132,000
SALES (est): 70.6MM
SALES (corp-wide): 39.8B **Privately Held**
WEB: www.rotek-inc.com
SIC: **3562** **3462** **3463** **3321** Ball bearings & parts; roller bearings & parts; iron & steel forgings; nonferrous forgings; gray & ductile iron foundries
HQ: Thyssenkrupp North America, Inc.
111 W Jackson Blvd # 2400
Chicago IL 60604
312 525-2800

(G-905)
RP GATTA INC
435 Gentry Dr (44202-7538)
PHONE..................................330 562-2288
Raymond P Gatta, *President*
Katherine E Gatta, *Corp Secy*
◆ EMP: 46
SQ FT: 28,000
SALES (est): 10.1MM **Privately Held**
WEB: www.rpgatta.com
SIC: **3559** Automotive related machinery

(G-906)
SACO AEI POLYMERS INC
Also Called: Macro Meric
1395 Danner Dr (44202-9273)
PHONE..................................330 995-1600
Matt McLaughlin, *Manager*
EMP: 16
SQ FT: 28,829
SALES (corp-wide): 35.1MM **Privately Held**
WEB: www.padanaplastusa.com
SIC: **2821** Plastics materials & resins
PA: Saco Aei Polymers, Inc.
3220 Crocker Ave
Sheboygan WI 53081
920 803-0778

(G-907)
SATELLITE GEAR INC
130 Idlewood Ln (44202-8046)
PHONE..................................216 514-8668
John R Papesh, *President*
John R Papesh Jr, *Admin Sec*
EMP: 15
SQ FT: 12,000
SALES (est): 2.9MM **Privately Held**
SIC: **3462** **2833** Gears, forged steel; drugs & herbs: grading, grinding & milling

(G-908)
THORNCREEK WINERY & GARDEN
155 Treat Rd (44202-8704)
PHONE..................................330 562-9245
David Walker, *General Mgr*
David Thorn, *Principal*
EMP: 4
SALES (est): 270K **Privately Held**
SIC: **2084** Wines

(G-909)
TRANSCONTINENTAL OIL & GAS
1509 Page Rd (44202-6644)
PHONE..................................330 995-0777
Calvin R Marks, *President*
EMP: 3
SQ FT: 1,800
SALES (est): 2.5MM **Privately Held**
SIC: **1381** Drilling oil & gas wells

(G-910)
TRELLBORG SLING PRFILES US INC
285 Lena Dr (44202-9247)
PHONE..................................330 995-5125
Smitty McKee, *President*
EMP: 30

SALES (corp-wide): 3.7B **Privately Held**
SIC: **3053** Gaskets, packing & sealing devices
HQ: Trelleborg Sealing Profiles U.S. Inc.
285 Lena Dr
Aurora OH 44202
330 995-9725

(G-911)
TRELLBORG SLING PRFILES US INC (DH)
285 Lena Dr (44202-9247)
P.O. Box 639, Bristol IN (46507-0639)
PHONE..................................330 995-9725
Smitty McKee, *President*
Tom Layton, *Business Mgr*
Michael Scanlon, *Vice Pres*
Gary Salter, *Opers Mgr*
Melinda Gruber, *QC Mgr*
EMP: 30
SQ FT: 48,588
SALES (est): 18.6MM
SALES (corp-wide): 3.7B **Privately Held**
SIC: **3089** **3465** Extruded finished plastic products; automotive parts, plastic; body parts, automobile: stamped metal
HQ: Trelleborg Corporation
200 Veterans Blvd Ste 3
South Haven MI 49090
269 639-9891

(G-912)
UNDER ARMOUR INC
549 S Chillicothe Rd # 355 (44202-8843)
PHONE..................................330 995-9557
EMP: 6
SALES (corp-wide): 5.1B **Publicly Held**
SIC: **2329** Men's & boys' sportswear & athletic clothing
PA: Under Armour, Inc.
1020 Hull St Ste 300
Baltimore MD 21230
410 454-6428

(G-913)
USA INSTRUMENTS INC
Also Called: GE
1515 Danner Dr (44202-9273)
PHONE..................................330 562-1000
Eric Stahre, *President*
Vivek Bhatt, *General Mgr*
Donald Moon, *Plant Mgr*
Yun-Jeong Stickle, *Engineer*
Scott Danna, *Manager*
▲ EMP: 250
SQ FT: 58,000
SALES (est): 43.1MM
SALES (corp-wide): 121.6B **Publicly Held**
SIC: **3677** Electronic coils, transformers & other inductors
HQ: Ge Healthcare Inc.
100 Results Way
Marlborough MA 01752
800 526-3593

(G-914)
VIBRATION TEST SYSTEMS INC
Also Called: V T S
10246 Clipper Cv (44202-9043)
PHONE..................................330 562-5729
Christopher Hunt, *President*
Carol Hunt, *Vice Pres*
EMP: 4
SALES (est): 495.4K **Privately Held**
SIC: **3829** Vibration meters, analyzers & calibrators

(G-915)
VIDEO PRODUCTS INC
Also Called: VPI
1275 Danner Dr (44202-8054)
PHONE..................................330 562-2622
Carl Jagatich, *President*
Tammy Kuhn, *COO*
Alan Willis, *Production*
Carl Jackson, *Engineer*
Michelle Deeter, *Bookkeeper*
EMP: 60
SQ FT: 8,000
SALES: 3MM **Privately Held**
WEB: www.nti1.com
SIC: **3577** Computer peripheral equipment

Aurora – Portage County (G-916)

(G-916)
WILLIAM THOMPSON
Also Called: Custom Boat Covers
11304 Chamberlain Rd (44202-9360)
PHONE.................. 440 232-4363
William Thompson, *Owner*
EMP: 4
SQ FT: 2,500
SALES (est) 280.3K **Privately Held**
SIC: 2394 3732 Convertible tops, canvas or boat: from purchased materials; boat building & repairing

(G-917)
WORKSHOP WIRE CUT AND MCH INC
100 Francis D Kenneth Dr (44202-9275)
PHONE.................. 330 995-6404
Michael W Meredith, *President*
EMP: 4
SALES (est) 614.3K **Privately Held**
SIC: 3599 Machine shop, jobbing & repair

Austinburg
Ashtabula County

(G-918)
AUSTINBURG MACHINE INC
2899 Industrial Park Dr (44010-9764)
PHONE.................. 440 275-2001
Richard Pildner, *President*
Lynetta Pildner, *Corp Secy*
John Pildner, *Vice Pres*
EMP: 8
SQ FT: 8,200
SALES: 750K **Privately Held**
SIC: 3599 Machine shop, jobbing & repair

(G-919)
COLORAMIC PROCESS INC
2883 Industrial Park Dr (44010-9764)
P.O. Box 12 (44010-0012)
PHONE.................. 440 275-1199
Donald Pikounik, *President*
Robert Pikounik, *President*
Fred Zust, *President*
Marilyn Pikounik, *Admin Sec*
EMP: 15 EST: 1959
SALES (est): 1.9MM **Privately Held**
WEB: www.coloramic.com
SIC: 2752 Cards, lithographed

(G-920)
EUCLID REFINISHING COMPNAY INC (PA)
Also Called: Surftech
2937 Industrial Park Dr (44010-9763)
PHONE.................. 440 275-3356
Nicholas Cottone, *CEO*
EMP: 10
SQ FT: 15,000
SALES: 876.5K **Privately Held**
SIC: 3471 Polishing, metals or formed products; finishing, metals or formed products

(G-921)
FARIN INDUSTRIES INC
2844 Industrial Park Dr (44010-9764)
P.O. Box 185 (44010-0185)
PHONE.................. 440 275-2755
Michael F Farinacci, *President*
EMP: 15
SQ FT: 10,000
SALES (est): 2.4MM **Privately Held**
SIC: 3714 Motor vehicle parts & accessories

(G-922)
FUTURE CONTROLS CORPORATION
1419 State Route 45 (44010-9749)
P.O. Box 130 (44010-0130)
PHONE.................. 440 275-3191
John Williams, *President*
Philip Bunnell, *Vice Pres*
Jeremy Sutch, *Vice Pres*
Phil Bunnell, *Human Res Mgr*
Edward Kuehn, *Info Tech Mgr*
EMP: 41
SQ FT: 33,000
SALES (est): 7.7MM **Privately Held**
SIC: 3823 3625 3822 Temperature instruments: industrial process type; relays & industrial controls; auto controls regulating residntl & coml environmt & applncs

(G-923)
MULTI-DESIGN INC
Also Called: Twin Fin
2844 Industrial Park Dr (44010-9764)
P.O. Box 185 (44010-0185)
PHONE.................. 440 275-2255
Michael F Farinacci, *President*
EMP: 4
SQ FT: 10,000
SALES (est): 336.3K **Privately Held**
WEB: www.twinfin.com
SIC: 3751 3714 Brakes, friction clutch & other: bicycle; motor vehicle parts & accessories

(G-924)
PAINESVILLE PUBLISHING CO
2883 Industrial Park Dr (44010-9764)
P.O. Box 12 (44010-0012)
PHONE.................. 440 354-4142
Don Tiknovnik, *President*
Marie Baker, *Treasurer*
Tom Bain, *Manager*
EMP: 7 EST: 1941
SQ FT: 3,000
SALES (est): 1MM **Privately Held**
SIC: 2752 2791 2789 Commercial printing, offset; typesetting; bookbinding & related work

(G-925)
RTS COMPANIES (US) INC
2900 Industrial Park Dr (44010-9763)
PHONE.................. 440 275-3077
Graham Lobban, *President*
▲ **EMP:** 40 EST: 2008
SALES (est): 8.5MM **Privately Held**
SIC: 3089 Plastic & fiberglass tanks

(G-926)
SPRING TEAM INC
2851 Industrial Park Dr (44010-9764)
P.O. Box 215 (44010-0215)
PHONE.................. 440 275-5981
Russ Bryer, *President*
Robert Schultz, *Principal*
Richard Kovach, *Vice Pres*
Gary Van Buren, *Vice Pres*
Ed Hall, *Treasurer*
▼ **EMP:** 67
SQ FT: 42,000
SALES (est): 13.5MM **Privately Held**
WEB: www.springteam.com
SIC: 3496 3495 Miscellaneous fabricated wire products; wire springs

(G-927)
SURFTECH INC
2937 Industrial Park Dr (44010-9763)
PHONE.................. 440 275-3356
June E Yusko, *President*
Edward Yusko Jr, *Vice Pres*
EMP: 6
SQ FT: 12,000
SALES (est): 287.1K
SALES (corp-wide): 876.5K **Privately Held**
WEB: www.ercsurftech.com
SIC: 3479 Coating of metals with plastic or resins
PA: Euclid Refinishing Compnay, Inc.
2937 Industrial Park Dr
Austinburg OH 44010
440 275-3356

Austintown
Mahoning County

(G-928)
ADYL INC
Also Called: Party On
6000 Mahoning Ave Ste 230 (44515-2225)
P.O. Box 4327 (44515-0327)
PHONE.................. 330 797-8700
Debbie Simon, *President*
Kathy Lyda, *Corp Secy*
Jeffrey T Lyda, *Vice Pres*
EMP: 3
SQ FT: 10,000
SALES (est): 428.8K **Privately Held**
WEB: www.adyl.com
SIC: 2759 5699 5947 7299 Invitation & stationery printing & engraving; costumes, masquerade or theatrical; party favors; party planning service

(G-929)
BARTELLS CUPCAKERY
4555 Norquest Blvd (44515-1629)
PHONE.................. 330 957-1793
EMP: 3
SALES (est): 137.9K **Privately Held**
SIC: 2053 Mfg Frozen Bakery Products

(G-930)
BOJOS CREAM
1412 S Raccoon Rd (44515-4525)
PHONE.................. 330 270-3332
Bob McCalster, *Owner*
EMP: 3
SALES (est): 225.9K **Privately Held**
SIC: 2024 Ice cream, bulk

(G-931)
CAPITAL OIL & GAS INC
6075 Silica Rd (44515-1081)
PHONE.................. 330 533-1828
Bruce Brocker, *President*
EMP: 6
SALES (est): 169.4K **Privately Held**
SIC: 1382 Oil & gas exploration services

(G-932)
COWLES INDUSTRIAL TOOL CO LLC
185 N Four Mile Run Rd (44515-3006)
PHONE.................. 330 799-9100
David Smith, *President*
EMP: 35 EST: 2012
SQ FT: 30,000
SALES (est): 5.6MM **Privately Held**
SIC: 3545 Tools & accessories for machine tools

(G-933)
HAZ-SAFE LLC
3850 Hendricks Rd (44515-1528)
P.O. Box 181, Sistersville WV (26175-0181)
PHONE.................. 330 793-0900
Chuck Lisman,
Ronald L Larson,
Michael P Lewis,
EMP: 15 EST: 2008
SALES (est): 1MM **Privately Held**
SIC: 3448 Prefabricated metal buildings
PA: Precision, L.L.C.
843 N Cleveland Massillon
Akron OH 44333

(G-934)
MAHONING VALLEY FABRICATORS
3697 Oakwood Ave (44515-3030)
PHONE.................. 330 793-8995
Donald J Zeisler, *President*
Donald C Zeisler, *President*
EMP: 15
SQ FT: 10,000
SALES (est): 3.2MM **Privately Held**
SIC: 3441 3599 Fabricated structural metal; machine shop, jobbing & repair

(G-935)
TRANSUE WILLIAMS STAMPING INC
207 N Four Mile Run Rd (44515-3008)
PHONE.................. 330 270-0891
EMP: 4 **Privately Held**
SIC: 3469 Stamping metal for the trade
HQ: Transue & Williams Stamping Co., Inc.
930 W Ely St
Alliance OH 44601

Avon
Lorain County

(G-936)
A J ROSE MFG CO (PA)
38000 Chester Rd (44011-4022)
PHONE.................. 216 631-4645
Daniel T Pritchard, *President*
Michael Nejman, *Business Mgr*
Douglas E Krzywicki, *Vice Pres*
Terry Sweeney, *Vice Pres*
Gary Sluss, *Maint Spvr*
◆ **EMP:** 200 EST: 1922
SQ FT: 270,000
SALES (est): 99.5MM **Privately Held**
WEB: www.ajrose.com
SIC: 3465 3568 3469 Automotive stampings; pulleys, power transmission; metal stampings

(G-937)
ACCEL CORPORATION
Also Called: Accel Color
38620 Chester Rd (44011-1074)
PHONE.................. 440 327-7418
Dwight Morgan, *Manager*
EMP: 19
SALES (corp-wide): 35.7MM **Privately Held**
WEB: www.accelcolor.com
SIC: 2865 Dyes & pigments
HQ: Accel Corporation
38620 Chester Rd
Avon OH 44011

(G-938)
ACCEL CORPORATION (DH)
Also Called: Accel Color
38620 Chester Rd (44011-1074)
PHONE.................. 440 934-7711
Dwight Morgan, *CEO*
David Knowles, *President*
Mike Clabough, *Vice Pres*
Mike Gross, *Vice Pres*
▲ **EMP:** 60
SALES (est): 11.4MM
SALES (corp-wide): 35.7MM **Privately Held**
WEB: www.accelcolor.com
SIC: 3087 Custom compound purchased resins
HQ: Techmer Pm, Llc
1 Quality Cir
Clinton TN 37716
865 457-6700

(G-939)
ADVANCED POLYMER COATINGS LTD
951 Jaycox Rd (44011-1351)
P.O. Box 269 (44011-0269)
PHONE.................. 440 937-6218
Donald Keehan, *Chairman*
Denise Keehan, *COO*
James Machnauer, *Accountant*
Arthur Marshall, *Sales Staff*
▲ **EMP:** 26
SQ FT: 35,000
SALES: 5.9MM **Privately Held**
WEB: www.adv-polymer.com
SIC: 3081 Plastic film & sheet

(G-940)
AIRTUG LLC
1350 Chester Indus Pkwy (44011-1082)
PHONE.................. 440 829-2167
David Scholtz,
▲ **EMP:** 4
SALES (est): 524.5K **Privately Held**
SIC: 3728 Aircraft parts & equipment

(G-941)
AVON CONCRETE CORPORATION
930 Miller Rd (44011-1032)
PHONE.................. 440 937-6264
Brock Walls, *President*
Sam Walls, *Owner*
EMP: 5
SQ FT: 8,000

GEOGRAPHIC SECTION
Avon - Lorain County (G-966)

SALES: 1MM
SALES (corp-wide): 1MM Privately Held
SIC: 3273 5211 Ready-mixed concrete; lumber & other building materials
PA: The Brock Corporation
26000 Sprague Rd
Olmsted Falls OH 44138
440 235-1806

(G-942)
BLUE RIBBON SCREEN GRAPHICS
1473 Hollow Wood Ln (44011-1094)
PHONE..................216 226-6200
EMP: 4
SQ FT: 8,000
SALES (est): 240K Privately Held
SIC: 2759 Screen Printing

(G-943)
BUDERER DRUG COMPANY INC
38530 Chester Rd Ste 400 (44011-4048)
PHONE..................440 934-3100
Rebecca Arcaro, *Branch Mgr*
EMP: 5
SALES (corp-wide): 9.5MM Privately Held
SIC: 5122 2834 Drugs & drug proprietaries; animal medicines; proprietary (patent) medicines; proprietary drug products
PA: Buderer Drug Company, Inc.
633 Hancock St
Sandusky OH 44870
419 627-2800

(G-944)
CLEVELAND WHEELS
Also Called: Aircraft Wheels and Breaks
1160 Center Rd (44011-1208)
PHONE..................440 937-6211
Manny Nnay Bajakfoujian, *CEO*
EMP: 99
SALES (est): 6.5MM Privately Held
SIC: 5088 3799 Aircraft equipment & supplies; transportation equipment

(G-945)
COMPREHENSIVE LOGISTICS CO INC
1200 A Chester Indus Pkwy (44011-1081)
PHONE..................440 934-3517
Daryl Legg, *Branch Mgr*
EMP: 45 Privately Held
SIC: 3714 Motor vehicle transmissions, drive assemblies & parts
PA: Comprehensive Logistics, Co., Inc.
4944 Belmont Ave Ste 202
Youngstown OH 44505

(G-946)
CORE TECHNOLOGY INC
1260 Moore Rd Ste E (44011-4021)
PHONE..................440 934-9935
Jack A Redilla, *President*
Shujaat Lakhani, *Purch Mgr*
Donna Dolezal, *Office Mgr*
Leslie Dewitt, *Manager*
▲ EMP: 10
SQ FT: 5,500
SALES: 1MM Privately Held
SIC: 3629 Power conversion units, a.c. to d.c.: static-electric

(G-947)
CUTTING DYNAMICS INC (PA)
Also Called: CDI
980 Jaycox Rd (44011-1352)
PHONE..................440 249-4150
William V Carson Jr, *President*
Marie Carson, *Corp Secy*
Wilbur S Kohring, *Vice Pres*
Wayne Beadnell, *Plant Mgr*
Nader Youssef, *QC Mgr*
▲ EMP: 140 EST: 1985
SQ FT: 50,000
SALES (est): 41.3MM Privately Held
WEB: www.cuttingdynamics.com
SIC: 3599 Machine & other job shop work

(G-948)
ECP CORPORATION
Also Called: Polycase Division
1305 Chester Indus Pkwy (44011-1083)
PHONE..................440 934-0444
Steven Began, *President*
Natasha Dean, *Vice Pres*
Michelle Mather, *Controller*
Michael Hess, *Department Mgr*
Jim Brightbill, *Technology*
▲ EMP: 48 EST: 1951
SQ FT: 40,000
SALES (est): 10.4MM Privately Held
WEB: www.polycase.com
SIC: 3469 Electronic enclosures, stamped or pressed metal

(G-949)
FLAVORSEAL LLC
35179 Avon Commerce Pkwy (44011-1374)
PHONE..................440 937-3900
Chris Carroll, *President*
Ken Hynes, *Vice Pres*
Corey Raub, *VP Opers*
Kevin Johnson, *Sales Staff*
Storch Julie, *Sales Staff*
◆ EMP: 99
SQ FT: 40,000
SALES (est): 34.9MM Privately Held
SIC: 2673 Bags: plastic, laminated & coated
PA: M&Q Acquisition Llc
3 Earl Ave
Schuylkill Haven PA

(G-950)
FREEMAN MANUFACTURING & SUP CO (PA)
1101 Moore Rd (44011-4043)
PHONE..................440 934-1902
Gerald W Rusk, *Ch of Bd*
Lou Turco, *President*
Mike Porter, *Business Mgr*
Jon Hofener, *Export Mgr*
Ben Inman, *Export Mgr*
EMP: 50
SQ FT: 110,000
SALES (est): 70.2MM Privately Held
WEB: www.freemansupply.com
SIC: 5084 3087 3543 2821 Industrial machinery & equipment; custom compound purchased resins; industrial patterns; plastics materials & resins

(G-951)
GREEN ACQUISITION LLC
Also Called: Green Bearing Co
1141 Jaycox Rd (44011-1366)
PHONE..................440 930-7600
Laszlo Tromler,
EMP: 50
SALES (est): 3.7MM
SALES (corp-wide): 29.5MM Privately Held
SIC: 3714 Bearings, motor vehicle
PA: Bearing Technologies, Ltd.
1141 Jaycox Rd
Avon OH 44011
440 937-4770

(G-952)
JLW - TW CORP
Also Called: Suntan Supply
35350 Chester Rd (44011-1255)
PHONE..................216 361-5940
William Gallagherr, *President*
William Gallagher, *President*
Martin F Gallagher, *Exec VP*
Jamie Carlson, *Vice Pres*
Nicole Bynaker, *Sales Associate*
EMP: 7 EST: 2007
SALES (est): 1.8MM Privately Held
SIC: 3711 Mfg Motor Vehicle/Car Bodies

(G-953)
L & W INC
Also Called: L&W Cleveland
1190 Jaycox Rd (44011-1313)
PHONE..................734 397-6300
Steve Schafer, *Manager*
EMP: 55
SALES (corp-wide): 679.8MM Privately Held
SIC: 3469 3465 3441 3429 Stamping metal for the trade; automotive stampings; fabricated structural metal; manufactured hardware (general)
PA: L & W, Inc.
17757 Woodland Dr
New Boston MI 48164
734 397-6300

(G-954)
MC KINLEY MACHINERY INC
1265 Lear Industrial Pkwy (44011-1364)
PHONE..................440 937-6300
Scott Mc Kinley, *President*
EMP: 20
SALES (est): 4.3MM Privately Held
SIC: 3554 5084 Die cutting & stamping machinery, paper converting; folding machines, paper; industrial machinery & equipment

(G-955)
P M R INC
4661 Jaycox Rd (44011-2499)
PHONE..................440 937-6241
Robert W Younglas, *President*
John Lucas, *Vice Pres*
Gay L McViegh, *Treasurer*
EMP: 6 EST: 1966
SQ FT: 25,000
SALES (est): 954.8K Privately Held
SIC: 3541 Machine tools, metal cutting type

(G-956)
PARKER-HANNIFIN CORPORATION
Parker Hannifin Corp
1160 Center Rd (44011-1297)
P.O. Box 158 (44011-0158)
PHONE..................440 937-6211
Donald Washkewics, *CEO*
Tom Dorinsky, *General Mgr*
David Cinadr, *Materials Mgr*
Michael Phillips, *Buyer*
Wylie Riggle, *Buyer*
EMP: 110
SALES (corp-wide): 14.3B Publicly Held
WEB: www.parker.com
SIC: 3728 Wheels, aircraft; brakes, aircraft
PA: Parker-Hannifin Corporation
6035 Parkland Blvd
Cleveland OH 44124
216 896-3000

(G-957)
PILGRIM-HARP CO
35050 Avon Commerce Pkwy (44011-1374)
PHONE..................440 249-4185
William Carson, *President*
Chris Foertch, *Vice Pres*
▲ EMP: 3
SALES (est): 559.1K Privately Held
WEB: www.pilgrimharp.com
SIC: 3541 3312 Machine tools, metal cutting type; forgings, iron & steel

(G-958)
PIN HIGH LLC
37040 Detroit Rd (44011-1702)
PHONE..................216 577-9999
EMP: 3
SALES (est): 195.7K Privately Held
SIC: 3452 Pins

(G-959)
PROTEC INDUSTRIES INCORPORATED
Also Called: Protech Industries
1384 Lear Industrial Pkwy (44011-1368)
PHONE..................440 937-4142
Kurt F Van Luit, *President*
Jeff Leonard, *Vice Pres*
EMP: 6
SQ FT: 6,000
SALES (est): 785.7K Privately Held
SIC: 3089 Plastic hardware & building products

(G-960)
QUAL-FAB INC
34250 Mills Rd (44011-2471)
PHONE..................440 327-5000
Brice Blackman, *President*
Craig Hartzell, *Vice Pres*
Gary Vanek, *Vice Pres*
David Peter, *Project Mgr*
Jim Chapek, *Opers Mgr*
▼ EMP: 50
SQ FT: 80,000
SALES (est): 16.7MM Privately Held
WEB: www.qual-fab.net
SIC: 3312 3498 3433 Stainless steel; fabricated pipe & fittings; heating equipment, except electric

(G-961)
RAILROAD BREWING COMPANY
1010 Center Rd (44011-1206)
PHONE..................440 723-8234
Thomas R Wagner, *President*
Thomas Wager, *President*
Jerome Moore, *Vice Pres*
Tom Culler, *Treasurer*
EMP: 9
SQ FT: 4,000
SALES (est): 98.9K Privately Held
SIC: 5813 3556 Tavern (drinking places); brewers' & maltsters' machinery

(G-962)
RDA GROUP LLC
2131 Clifton Way (44011-2809)
PHONE..................440 724-4347
Robert Desmarais, *Principal*
EMP: 3
SALES (est): 256.4K Privately Held
SIC: 3559 Sewing machines & attachments, industrial

(G-963)
RETEK INC
34550 Chester Rd (44011-1300)
P.O. Box 359 (44011-0359)
PHONE..................440 937-6282
Daniel L Green, *President*
Richard L Green, *Admin Sec*
EMP: 4
SQ FT: 5,000
SALES (est): 2.1MM Privately Held
WEB: www.retekinc.com
SIC: 5084 3625 5085 3548 Industrial machine parts; welding machinery & equipment; resistance welder controls; resistors & resistor units; welding supplies; spot welding apparatus, electric

(G-964)
RICHTECH INDUSTRIES INC
34000 Lear Indus Pkwy (44011-1375)
PHONE..................440 937-4401
Kurt Van Luit, *CEO*
Bill Drockton, *Accounts Exec*
Jeremy Haag, *Manager*
EMP: 9
SALES (est): 1.2MM Privately Held
WEB: www.richtech-industries.com
SIC: 3299 1799 Moldings, architectural: plaster of paris; waterproofing

(G-965)
S & A PRECISION BEARING INC (PA)
1050 Jaycox Rd (44011-1312)
PHONE..................440 930-7600
William Hagy, *President*
▼ EMP: 5
SQ FT: 20,000
SALES (est): 550.4K Privately Held
SIC: 3714 Bearings, motor vehicle

(G-966)
SHURTAPE TECHNOLOGIES LLC
32150 Just Imagine Dr (44011-1355)
PHONE..................440 937-7000
John M Kahl, *Branch Mgr*
EMP: 350
SALES (corp-wide): 695.6MM Privately Held
SIC: 3083 2672 2671 3442 Laminated plastics plate & sheet; tape, pressure sensitive: made from purchased materials; masking tape: made from purchased materials; adhesive papers, labels or tapes: from purchased material; packaging paper & plastics film, coated & laminated; metal doors, sash & trim; narrow fabric mills
HQ: Shurtape Technologies, Llc
1712 8th Street Dr Se
Hickory NC 28602

Avon - Lorain County (G-967)

(G-967)
SHURTECH BRANDS LLC (DH)
Also Called: Duck Tape
32150 Just Imagine Dr (44011-1355)
P.O. Box 2228, Hickory NC (28603-2228)
PHONE..................440 937-7000
Stephen Shuford, *CEO*
C Hunt Shuford Jr, *Principal*
James B Shuford, *Principal*
Don Pomeroy, *CFO*
◆ **EMP:** 155
SQ FT: 644,000
SALES (est): 124.7MM
SALES (corp-wide): 695.6MM **Privately Held**
SIC: 2671 Plastic film, coated or laminated for packaging

(G-968)
TECHNIFAB INC
38600 Chester Rd (44011-1074)
PHONE..................440 934-8324
Jeff Petras, *President*
John Cehovic, *Controller*
Travis Gift, *Manager*
EMP: 29
SALES (est): 3.2MM **Privately Held**
SIC: 3086 Insulation or cushioning material, foamed plastic
PA: Technifab, Inc.
1355 Chester Indus Pkwy
Avon OH 44011

(G-969)
TECHNIFAB INC
1300 Chester Indus Pkwy (44011-1165)
PHONE..................440 934-8324
Jeff Petras, *President*
EMP: 99
SALES (est): 3.9MM **Privately Held**
SIC: 3086 Insulation or cushioning material, foamed plastic

(G-970)
TECHNIFAB INC (PA)
Also Called: Technifab Engineered Products
1355 Chester Indus Pkwy (44011-1083)
PHONE..................440 934-8324
Jeffrey L Petras, *President*
◆ **EMP:** 30
SQ FT: 40,000
SALES (est): 8.9MM **Privately Held**
WEB: www.technifabfoam.com
SIC: 3086 Insulation or cushioning material, foamed plastic; packaging & shipping materials, foamed plastic

(G-971)
TOMS COUNTRY PLACE INC
3442 Stoney Ridge Rd (44011-2210)
PHONE..................440 934-4553
William Hricovec, *President*
EMP: 35
SQ FT: 500
SALES (est): 4.3MM **Privately Held**
WEB: www.tomscountryplace.com
SIC: 2099 Food preparations

(G-972)
TRI-TECH MEDICAL INC
35401 Avon Commerce Pkwy (44011-1374)
PHONE..................800 253-8692
Don L Daviess, *CEO*
Don Simo, *President*
Donald M Simo, *President*
Susie Wolf, *Buyer*
Bob Gehrke, *Manager*
◆ **EMP:** 40
SQ FT: 26,500
SALES (est): 4.4MM **Privately Held**
WEB: www.tri-techmedical.com
SIC: 3841 Surgical & medical instruments

(G-973)
VALENSIL TECHNOLOGIES LLC
34910 Commerce Way (44011)
PHONE..................440 937-8181
Richard A West, *Principal*
EMP: 8 **EST:** 2014
SALES (est): 1.3MM **Privately Held**
SIC: 3841 8733 Surgical & medical instruments; medical research

(G-974)
WEBER ORTHOPEDIC INC
Also Called: Hely & Weber Orthopedic
1324 Chester Indus Pkwy (44011-1082)
P.O. Box 612956, Dallas TX (75261-2956)
PHONE..................440 934-1812
Dave Ferrier, *Manager*
EMP: 7
SALES (corp-wide): 5.9MM **Privately Held**
SIC: 3842 Braces, orthopedic
PA: Weber Orthopedic, Inc.
1185 E Main St
Santa Paula CA 93060
805 525-8474

(G-975)
WONDER MACHINE SERVICES INC
35340 Avon Commerce Pkwy (44011-1374)
PHONE..................440 937-7500
George Woyansky, *President*
Diane Woyansky, *Corp Secy*
Jeanine Woyansky, *Vice Pres*
Christopher Williams, *QC Mgr*
EMP: 30
SQ FT: 22,500
SALES (est): 5.5MM **Privately Held**
WEB: www.wondermachine.com
SIC: 3599 3541 Machine shop, jobbing & repair; machine tools, metal cutting type

(G-976)
WOODMAN AGITATOR INC
1404 Lear Industrial Pkwy (44011-1363)
PHONE..................440 937-9865
James Bielozer, *President*
Keith M Bielozer, *Vice Pres*
Mary Bielozer, *Vice Pres*
◆ **EMP:** 17
SALES (est): 3.7MM **Privately Held**
WEB: www.woodmanagitator.com
SIC: 3559 Paint making machinery

(G-977)
WTD REAL ESTATE INC
1280 Moore Rd (44011-1014)
P.O. Box 240 (44011-0240)
PHONE..................440 934-5305
Seamus E Walsh, *President*
Theresa Walsh, *Vice Pres*
EMP: 60
SQ FT: 65,100
SALES (est): 13.3MM **Privately Held**
SIC: 3469 Stamping metal for the trade; utensils, household: metal, except cast; machine parts, stamped or pressed metal

Avon Lake
Lorain County

(G-978)
ADVANCED WLDG FABRICATION INC (PA)
648 Moore Rd (44012-2315)
PHONE..................440 724-9165
Scott J Cornelius Jr, *President*
Scott Corneilus, *Manager*
EMP: 7
SALES (est): 600.9K **Privately Held**
SIC: 7692 Welding repair

(G-979)
AVON LAKE PRINTING
227 Miller Rd (44012-1004)
PHONE..................440 933-2078
Thomas Brock, *Owner*
EMP: 9
SQ FT: 8,000
SALES (est): 1MM **Privately Held**
WEB: www.avonlakeprinting.com
SIC: 2752 5943 Commercial printing, offset; office forms & supplies

(G-980)
AVON LAKE SHEET METAL CO
33574 Pin Oak Pkwy (44012-2320)
P.O. Box 64 (44012-0064)
PHONE..................440 933-3505
Carl Wetzig Jr, *President*
Gary Wightman, *Corp Secy*
Dennis Lightfoot, *Draft/Design*
EMP: 38
SQ FT: 32,000
SALES (est): 8.8MM **Privately Held**
WEB: www.avonlakesheetmetal.com
SIC: 3444 1761 Sheet metalwork; sheet metalwork

(G-981)
CATANIA MEDALLIC SPECIALTY
Also Called: Catania Medallic Specialities
668 Moore Rd (44012-2315)
PHONE..................440 933-9595
Vince Frank, *President*
Trisha Frank, *Vice Pres*
▲ **EMP:** 25
SQ FT: 12,000
SALES (est): 4.9MM **Privately Held**
WEB: www.cataniainc.com
SIC: 3469 3965 3369 2395 Ornamental metal stampings; fasteners, buttons, needles & pins; nonferrous foundries; pleating & stitching

(G-982)
COLORMATRIX
33587 Walker Rd (44012-1145)
PHONE..................440 930-1000
Bjoern Klaas, *President*
EMP: 3
SALES (est): 608.4K **Privately Held**
SIC: 2821 Plastics materials & resins

(G-983)
CUSTOM ENGRAVING & SCREEN PRTG
690 Avon Belden Rd Ste 1b (44012-2255)
PHONE..................440 933-2902
Gary Randall, *President*
Rebecca Randall, *Vice Pres*
EMP: 3
SALES (est): 156.1K **Privately Held**
SIC: 5947 3993 Gift shop; signs & advertising specialties

(G-984)
EMPIRE SYSTEMS INC
33683 Walker Rd (44012-1044)
PHONE..................440 653-9300
Jeffery Eagens, *CEO*
Cheryle Hayley, *CFO*
EMP: 10
SQ FT: 41,000
SALES: 4MM **Privately Held**
SIC: 8711 3559 Consulting engineer; foundry machinery & equipment

(G-985)
ERIE SHORE INDUSTRIAL SVC CO
683 Moore Rd Ste A (44012-3504)
PHONE..................440 933-4301
John Schmitt, *President*
Tracy Birney, *Vice Pres*
EMP: 4
SALES: 250K **Privately Held**
SIC: 3568 Bearings, plain

(G-986)
FORD MOTOR COMPANY
650 Miller Rd (44012-2398)
PHONE..................440 933-1215
Deborah S Kent, *Engineer*
Dale Daniels, *Engineer*
Vern Meyers, *Engineer*
Mike Spencer, *Engineer*
Thomas Van Hoose, *Supervisor*
EMP: 2693
SALES (corp-wide): 160.3B **Publicly Held**
WEB: www.ford.com
SIC: 3713 3711 Van bodies; motor vehicles & car bodies
PA: Ford Motor Company
1 American Rd
Dearborn MI 48126
313 322-3000

(G-987)
GOODMAN DISTRIBUTION INC
760 Moore Rd (44012-2317)
PHONE..................440 324-4071
Alan Fayer, *Manager*
EMP: 5
SALES (corp-wide): 21.5B **Privately Held**
SIC: 3585 Heating & air conditioning combination units

HQ: Goodman Distribution, Inc.
1426 Ne 8th Ave
Ocala FL 34470
352 620-2717

(G-988)
HASHIER & HASHIER MFG
644 Moore Rd (44012-2315)
PHONE..................440 933-4883
Frank Hashier, *President*
EMP: 6 **EST:** 1976
SQ FT: 6,000
SALES: 400K **Privately Held**
SIC: 3599 Machine shop, jobbing & repair

(G-989)
HELICAL LINE PRODUCTS CO
659 Miller Rd (44012-2306)
P.O. Box 217 (44012-0217)
PHONE..................440 933-9263
Albert C Bonds, *President*
William T Bonds, *Corp Secy*
Robert S Bonds, *Vice Pres*
▼ **EMP:** 23 **EST:** 1964
SQ FT: 33,000
SALES: 3MM **Privately Held**
WEB: www.helical-line.com
SIC: 3644 Pole line hardware

(G-990)
JMJ PAPER INC
Also Called: Wolfe Paper Co.
681 Moore Rd Ste D (44012-2365)
PHONE..................216 941-8100
Jerry Jazwa, *President*
EMP: 11
SALES: 18.3K **Privately Held**
SIC: 2621 Packaging paper

(G-991)
JOHN CHRIST WINERY INC
32421 Walker Rd (44012-2226)
PHONE..................440 933-9672
Dean Gunter, *General Mgr*
EMP: 8
SALES (est): 479K **Privately Held**
SIC: 2084 Wines

(G-992)
KLINGSHIRN WINERY INC
33050 Webber Rd (44012-2330)
PHONE..................440 933-6666
Lee Klingshirn, *President*
Nancy Klingshirn, *Vice Pres*
EMP: 8
SQ FT: 3,850
SALES (est): 973.5K **Privately Held**
WEB: www.klingshirnwine.com
SIC: 2084 Wines

(G-993)
LUBRIZOL ADVANCED MTLS INC
Also Called: LUBRIZOL ADVANCED MATERIALS, INC.
550 Moore Rd (44012-2313)
P.O. Box 134 (44012-0134)
PHONE..................440 933-0400
Joeri Plusnin, *Engineer*
Dmitry Shuster, *Engineer*
Stan Biel, *Project Engr*
Meredith Bruder, *Marketing Staff*
Joseph Lazeunick, *Branch Mgr*
EMP: 50
SALES (corp-wide): 225.3B **Publicly Held**
WEB: www.pharma.noveoninc.com
SIC: 8731 2821 2899 Commercial physical research; plastics materials & resins; chemical preparations
HQ: Lubrizol Global Management, Inc
9911 Brecksville Rd
Brecksville OH 44141
216 447-5000

(G-994)
M S K TOOL & DIE INC
685 Moore Rd Ste B (44012-3507)
PHONE..................440 930-8100
Mark Roth, *President*
Michael Roth, *Vice Pres*
EMP: 6
SQ FT: 1,500
SALES: 800K **Privately Held**
SIC: 3544 Special dies & tools

▲ = Import ▼=Export
◆ =Import/Export

GEOGRAPHIC SECTION

Baltic - Tuscarawas County (G-1022)

(G-995)
MARKERS INC
33490 Pin Oak Pkwy (44012-2318)
P.O. Box 330 (44012-0330)
PHONE..................................440 933-5927
Dale Hlavin, *Shareholder*
Meja Gillett, *Executive Asst*
Meja Tansey, *Executive Asst*
EMP: 6
SALES (est): 480K **Privately Held**
WEB: www.markersinc.com
SIC: 2399 5261 Banners, pennants & flags; lawn & garden supplies

(G-996)
MEXICHEM SPECIALTY RESINS INC (HQ)
33653 Walker Rd (44012-1044)
P.O. Box 277 (44012-0277)
PHONE..................................440 930-1435
Frank Tomaselli, *General Mgr*
Joe Harkelroad, *Director*
Joanne Spikowski, *Admin Sec*
◆ EMP: 27 EST: 2013
SALES (est): 76.4MM **Privately Held**
SIC: 2822 2821 Ethylene-propylene rubbers, EPDM polymers; polymethyl methacrylate resins (plexiglass)

(G-997)
NATIONAL FLEET SVCS OHIO LLC
607 Miller Rd (44012-2306)
P.O. Box 338 (44012-0338)
PHONE..................................440 930-5177
Tim Lariviere, *President*
EMP: 12
SALES (est): 504.1K **Privately Held**
SIC: 3089 7532 Automotive parts, plastic; van conversion

(G-998)
NEXJEN TECHNOLOGIES LTD
362 Bethany Ct (44012-2614)
PHONE..................................781 572-5737
EMP: 5 EST: 2008
SALES (est): 624.4K **Privately Held**
SIC: 3677 Electronic coils, transformers & other inductors

(G-999)
OCEANSIDE FOODS
32859 Lake Rd (44012-1521)
PHONE..................................440 554-7810
Rich Klotz, *Principal*
EMP: 3
SALES (est): 84K **Privately Held**
SIC: 2099 Food preparations

(G-1000)
PIN OAK DEVELOPMENT LLC
32329 Orchard Park Dr (44012-2167)
PHONE..................................440 933-9862
David Rickey, *Owner*
EMP: 3
SALES (est): 210.4K **Privately Held**
SIC: 3452 Pins

(G-1001)
POLYONE CORPORATION (PA)
33587 Walker Rd (44012-1145)
PHONE..................................440 930-1000
Robert M Patterson, *Ch of Bd*
Richard N Altice, *President*
Robert Bindner, *President*
Mark D Crist, *President*
Michael A Garrett, *President*
◆ EMP: 73
SALES: 3.5B **Publicly Held**
WEB: www.polyone.com
SIC: 2821 3087 5162 3081 Thermoplastic materials; polyvinyl chloride resins (PVC); vinyl resins; custom compound purchased resins; resins; plastics basic shapes; unsupported plastics film & sheet

(G-1002)
POLYONE CORPORATION
33587 Walker Rd Rdb-418 (44012-1145)
P.O. Box 31480, Cleveland (44131-0480)
PHONE..................................440 930-3817
EMP: 16 **Publicly Held**
SIC: 2821 Plastics materials & resins

PA: Polyone Corporation
33587 Walker Rd
Avon Lake OH 44012

(G-1003)
POLYONE FUNDING CORPORATION
33587 Walker Rd (44012-1145)
PHONE..................................440 930-1000
EMP: 3 EST: 2002
SALES (est): 168.9K **Publicly Held**
SIC: 2821 Thermoplastic materials
PA: Polyone Corporation
33587 Walker Rd
Avon Lake OH 44012

(G-1004)
POLYONE LLC
33587 Walker Rd (44012-1145)
PHONE..................................440 930-1000
Robert M Patterson, *President*
EMP: 5
SALES (est): 108.9K **Publicly Held**
SIC: 2821 Thermoplastic materials
PA: Polyone Corporation
33587 Walker Rd
Avon Lake OH 44012

(G-1005)
RELIACHECK MANUFACTURING INC
Also Called: Ecil Met TEC
33554 Pin Oak Pkwy (44012-2320)
P.O. Box 303 (44012-0303)
PHONE..................................440 933-6162
Luis Antonio Srerie, *President*
David Updegraff, *President*
▲ EMP: 26
SQ FT: 53,000
SALES: 6MM
SALES (corp-wide): 2.2B **Privately Held**
WEB: www.reliacheck.net
SIC: 3317 Seamless pipes & tubes
PA: Vesuvius Plc
165 Fleet Street
London EC4A
207 822-0000

(G-1006)
RYKON PLATING INC
555 Miller Rd (44012-2304)
PHONE..................................440 933-3273
Carl Kulas, *President*
EMP: 5 EST: 1949
SQ FT: 17,500
SALES (est): 581.9K **Privately Held**
WEB: www.rykon.net
SIC: 3471 Electroplating of metals or formed products

(G-1007)
SCOTT FETZER COMPANY
Also Called: Western Entps A Scott Fetzer
33672 Pin Oak Pkwy (44012-2322)
PHONE..................................440 871-2160
Craig Wallskerry, *Branch Mgr*
EMP: 200
SALES (corp-wide): 225.3B **Publicly Held**
SIC: 3635 Household vacuum cleaners
HQ: The Scott Fetzer Company
28800 Clemens Rd
Westlake OH 44145
440 892-3000

(G-1008)
SOLUTION VENTURES INC
Also Called: Proforma Solution Ventures
31728 Commodore Ct (44012-2902)
PHONE..................................440 242-1658
EMP: 3 EST: 2006
SALES: 300K **Privately Held**
SIC: 2759 Commercial Printing

(G-1009)
SOUTHWIRE COMPANY LLC
Also Called: Southwire Avon Lake Plant
567 Miller Rd (44012-2304)
PHONE..................................440 933-6110
Peter Carroll, *Manager*
EMP: 6
SALES (corp-wide): 2.3B **Privately Held**
SIC: 3355 Aluminum rolling & drawing

PA: Southwire Company, Llc
1 Southwire Dr
Carrollton GA 30119
770 832-4242

(G-1010)
SOVEREIGN STITCH
701 Jockeys Cir (44012-4042)
PHONE..................................440 829-0678
Aaron Fenton, *Mng Member*
EMP: 4
SALES: 200K **Privately Held**
SIC: 2395 Embroidery products, except schiffli machine

(G-1011)
THOGUS PRODUCTS COMPANY
33490 Pin Oak Pkwy (44012-2318)
P.O. Box 330 (44012-0330)
PHONE..................................440 933-8850
Helen Thompson, *CEO*
Matthew Grantson, *President*
Kim Tackett, *Materials Mgr*
Geno Isabell, *Production*
Jeff Hanigan, *Engineer*
▲ EMP: 96 EST: 1958
SQ FT: 50,000
SALES (est): 39MM **Privately Held**
WEB: www.thogus.com
SIC: 3089 3494 3492 Injection molding of plastics; valves & pipe fittings; fluid power valves & hose fittings

(G-1012)
VOODOO INDUSTRIES
33640 Pin Oak Pkwy Ste 4 (44012-3510)
PHONE..................................440 653-5333
Robert Ueker, *Principal*
▲ EMP: 3
SALES (est): 209.7K **Privately Held**
SIC: 3999 Manufacturing industries

(G-1013)
WATTEREDGE LLC (DH)
567 Miller Rd (44012-2304)
PHONE..................................440 933-6110
Joseph P Langheny, *President*
Craig Smith, *Engineer*
George Sass, *Project Engr*
Janet Collins, *Human Res Mgr*
Brenda Westfall, *Sales Staff*
◆ EMP: 64
SQ FT: 65,000
SALES (est): 41.1MM
SALES (corp-wide): 2.3B **Privately Held**
WEB: www.watteredge.com
SIC: 5085 3643 5051 3052 Industrial supplies; current-carrying wiring devices; metals service centers & offices; rubber & plastics hose & beltings; miscellaneous metalwork
HQ: Coleman Cable, Llc
1 Overlook Pt
Lincolnshire IL 60069
847 672-2300

(G-1014)
WOLFF TOOL & MANUFACTURING CO
Also Called: O G Bell
139 Lear Rd (44012-1904)
PHONE..................................440 933-7797
Alan Wolff, *President*
Barbara Wolff, *Vice Pres*
EMP: 10
SQ FT: 1,610
SALES (est): 1.4MM **Privately Held**
WEB: www.ogbell.com
SIC: 3545 Machine tool accessories

Bainbridge
Ross County

(G-1015)
COUNTRY CRUST BAKERY
4918 State Route 41 S (45612-9613)
PHONE..................................888 860-2940
EMP: 8
SALES (est): 504K **Privately Held**
SIC: 2051 Bread, cake & related products

(G-1016)
J D KNISLEY LOGGING
112 W 3rd St (45612)
PHONE..................................740 634-3207
J D Knisley, *Owner*
EMP: 5
SALES (est): 335.8K **Privately Held**
SIC: 2411 Logging

(G-1017)
JEFFREY ADAMS LOGGING INC
3656 Us Highway 50 W (45612-7504)
P.O. Box 47 (45612-0047)
PHONE..................................740 634-2286
Jeffrey A Adams, *President*
EMP: 3
SALES: 320K **Privately Held**
SIC: 2411 Logging

(G-1018)
KNAUFF BROS LOGGING & LUMBER
Also Called: Knauff Logging
494 Houseman Town Rd (45612-9408)
PHONE..................................740 634-2432
Joyce Knauff, *President*
Jonathan Knauff, *Vice Pres*
EMP: 18
SALES (est): 1.6MM **Privately Held**
SIC: 2411 Logging camps & contractors

(G-1019)
KNISLEY LUMBER
160 Potts Hill Rd (45612-9768)
P.O. Box 488 (45612-0488)
PHONE..................................740 634-2935
Mark A Knisley, *Owner*
Chris Knisley, *Director*
EMP: 15
SQ FT: 4,000
SALES: 1MM **Privately Held**
SIC: 2421 2435 2426 Sawmills & planing mills, general; hardwood veneer & plywood; hardwood dimension & flooring mills

(G-1020)
RANDY CARTER LOGGING INC
1100 Schmidt Rd (45612-9762)
PHONE..................................740 634-2604
Randy L Carter, *Principal*
EMP: 6
SALES (est): 402.4K **Privately Held**
SIC: 2411 Logging camps & contractors

Bakersville
Coshocton County

(G-1021)
MULLET ENTERPRISES INC
28003 Adams Twp Rd 101 (43803)
PHONE..................................330 897-3911
Mike Myers, *Branch Mgr*
EMP: 6
SALES (corp-wide): 8.9MM **Privately Held**
WEB: www.tmkvalley.com
SIC: 5153 2041 Grain elevators; flour & other grain mill products
PA: Mullet Enterprises, Inc
138 2nd St Nw
Sugarcreek OH 44681
330 852-4681

Baltic
Tuscarawas County

(G-1022)
ANDAL WOODWORKING
1411 Township Road 151 (43804-9627)
PHONE..................................330 897-8059
Andrew Yoder, *Principal*
EMP: 10 EST: 2008
SALES: 1.8MM **Privately Held**
SIC: 2511 Wood bedroom furniture

Baltic - Tuscarawas County (G-1023)

(G-1023)
BALTIC COUNTRY MEATS
Also Called: Baltic Meats
3320 State Route 557 (43804-9609)
PHONE..................................330 897-7025
Susie Raber, *Owner*
Dan Miller, *Owner*
EMP: 6
SALES (est): 523.6K **Privately Held**
SIC: 2011 5411 Meat packing plants; delicatessens

(G-1024)
COUNTRY FREEZER UNITS LLC
Also Called: Country Ice Cream Freezer
50938 Township Road 220 (43804-9502)
PHONE..................................740 623-8658
Roy M Hershberger,
EMP: 3
SALES (est): 471.7K **Privately Held**
WEB: www.countryfreezerunits.com
SIC: 3556 Ice cream manufacturing machinery

(G-1025)
COUNTY LINE WOOD WORKING LLC
1482 County Road 600 (43804-9642)
PHONE..................................330 316-3057
Marvin Miller, *Principal*
EMP: 3
SALES (est): 50.2K **Privately Held**
SIC: 2499 Wood products

(G-1026)
CRAWFORD MANUFACTURING COMPANY
Also Called: Miller Leasing
52496 State Route 651 (43804-9505)
PHONE..................................330 897-1060
Dan J Miller, *President*
Mary Miller, *Admin Sec*
EMP: 18
SQ FT: 2,500
SALES (est): 3.8MM **Privately Held**
WEB: www.cmcservice.net
SIC: 3493 Steel springs, except wire

(G-1027)
ES STEINER DAIRY LLC
115 S Mill St (43804-9204)
PHONE..................................330 897-5555
Stanley Mullet, *President*
EMP: 18
SALES: 4.6MM **Privately Held**
SIC: 2022 Mfg Cheese

(G-1028)
FARMERSTOWN AXLE CO
2816 State Route 557 (43804-9672)
PHONE..................................330 897-2711
Emanuel H Yoder, *Owner*
▲ EMP: 5 EST: 1962
SQ FT: 8,500
SALES (est): 362.7K **Privately Held**
SIC: 3599 3799 Machine shop, jobbing & repair; carriages, horse drawn

(G-1029)
FLEX TECHNOLOGIES INC
Also Called: Poly Flex
3430 State Route 93 (43804-9705)
P.O. Box 300 (43804-0300)
PHONE..................................330 897-6311
Gglenn Burket, *Division Mgr*
Brian Harrison, *Manager*
Ken Ziegembusch, *Info Tech Mgr*
EMP: 35
SQ FT: 20,000
SALES (corp-wide): 6MM **Privately Held**
WEB: www.flextechnologies.com
SIC: 2821 5169 3087 Molding compounds, plastics; synthetic resins, rubber & plastic materials; custom compound purchased resins
PA: Flex Technologies, Inc.
5479 Gundy Dr
Midvale OH 44653
740 922-5992

(G-1030)
GERBER & SONS INC (PA)
201 E Main St (43804)
PHONE..................................330 897-6201
Thomas Gerber, *President*
Michael Gerber, *President*
Steven Gerber, *Principal*
Wayne Young, *Production*
Douglas A Davis, *Admin Sec*
EMP: 32 EST: 1905
SQ FT: 7,200
SALES (est): 9.8MM **Privately Held**
SIC: 2048 5999 Livestock feeds; farm equipment & supplies

(G-1031)
HOLMES PANEL
3052 State Route 557 (43804-7504)
PHONE..................................330 897-5040
Junior Keim, *Partner*
Dan Hershberger, *Partner*
Wayne Hershberger, *Partner*
EMP: 9
SQ FT: 600
SALES (est): 1.1MM **Privately Held**
SIC: 5211 2511 Lumber & other building materials; wood household furniture

(G-1032)
POLYNEW INC
3557 State Route 93 (43804-9705)
P.O. Box 318 (43804-0318)
PHONE..................................330 897-3202
Robert Burket, *President*
Gail Burket, *Admin Sec*
EMP: 6
SQ FT: 12,000
SALES: 300K **Privately Held**
WEB: www.polynew.com
SIC: 2821 Plastics materials & resins

(G-1033)
TBONE SALES LLC
410 N Ray St (43804-8901)
P.O. Box 75 (43804-0075)
PHONE..................................330 897-6131
Michael J Young,
Chad Schilling,
EMP: 22
SQ FT: 7,500
SALES (est): 2.8MM **Privately Held**
SIC: 5411 7549 5531 5511 Convenience stores; automotive maintenance services; automobile & truck equipment & parts; trucks, tractors & trailers: new & used; filling stations, gasoline; welding repair

(G-1034)
TRI STATE DAIRY LLC
Also Called: Es Steiner Dairy
115 S Mill St (43804-9204)
PHONE..................................330 897-5555
Stanley Mullet,
EMP: 15
SALES (est): 1.7MM **Privately Held**
SIC: 2022 Cheese, natural & processed

(G-1035)
WOODLAND WOODWORKING
2586 Township Road 183 (43804-9613)
PHONE..................................330 897-7282
EMP: 4 EST: 2008
SALES (est): 353.9K **Privately Held**
SIC: 2431 Mfg Millwork

Baltimore
Fairfield County

(G-1036)
BALTIMORE FABRICATORS INC
9420 Lancaster Krkersvlle (43105-9621)
P.O. Box 147 (43105-0147)
PHONE..................................740 862-6016
Michael Stanley, *President*
EMP: 4
SALES (est): 568.8K **Privately Held**
SIC: 3444 Sheet metalwork

(G-1037)
CARAUSTAR INDUSTRIES INC
Ohio Paperboard
310 W Water St (43105-1276)
PHONE..................................740 862-4167
Jeff Peters, *Manager*
EMP: 100
SALES (corp-wide): 3.8B **Publicly Held**
WEB: www.newarkgroup.com
SIC: 2631 2611 Paperboard mills; pulp mills
HQ: Caraustar Industries, Inc.
5000 Austell Powder Sprin
Austell GA 30106
770 948-3101

(G-1038)
GREEN GOURMET FOODS LLC
515 N Main St (43105-1214)
P.O. Box 206 (43105-0206)
PHONE..................................740 400-4212
Jeffrey Ware, *CFO*
Mitchell Adams,
Dennis Logan,
Cameron Smith,
Murray Stroud,
EMP: 30 EST: 2011
SQ FT: 150,000
SALES (est): 6.4MM **Privately Held**
SIC: 2034 Potato products, dried & dehydrated

(G-1039)
MARCUM CREW CUT INC
6080 Fisher Rd Nw (43105-9617)
PHONE..................................740 862-3400
Mike Marcum, *President*
EMP: 3
SALES (est): 235.2K **Privately Held**
SIC: 2499 Decorative wood & woodwork

(G-1040)
PROGRESSIVE AUTOMOTIVE INC
125 W Rome St (43105-1256)
PHONE..................................740 862-4696
Robert F Shetrone, *President*
EMP: 5
SQ FT: 9,500
SALES (est): 762.9K **Privately Held**
WEB: www.progressiveautomotive.com
SIC: 3711 Chassis, motor vehicle

(G-1041)
RAYMOND W REISIGER
11885 Paddock View Ct Nw (43105-9556)
PHONE..................................740 400-4090
Ray Reisiger, *Principal*
EMP: 4
SALES (est): 270K **Privately Held**
SIC: 3569 Filters

(G-1042)
SAKAS INCORPORATED
312 Bltmore Smerset Rd Ne (43105-9400)
P.O. Box 98 (43105-0098)
PHONE..................................740 862-4114
Dan Sakas, *CEO*
Lora Sakas, *President*
EMP: 29 EST: 1955
SQ FT: 30,000
SALES (est): 5.2MM **Privately Held**
WEB: www.sakas.com
SIC: 3469 Machine parts, stamped or pressed metal

(G-1043)
SAWDUST
4799 Refugee Rd Nw (43105-9424)
PHONE..................................740 862-0612
James Wagenbrenner, *Owner*
EMP: 8
SALES: 250K **Privately Held**
WEB: www.sawdust.com
SIC: 2431 Woodwork, interior & ornamental

(G-1044)
TIMBERMILL LTD
11015 Stoudertown Rd Nw (43105-9315)
PHONE..................................740 862-3426
Randy Smith, *Principal*
EMP: 3
SALES (est): 219.5K **Privately Held**
SIC: 2421 Sawmills & planing mills, general

(G-1045)
TRI-TECH LED SYSTEMS
600 W Market St (43105-1176)
PHONE..................................614 593-2860
EMP: 7
SQ FT: 2,000
SALES (est): 65.8K **Privately Held**
SIC: 3674 Mfg Semiconductors/Related Devices

(G-1046)
WOODEN HORSE
204 N Main St (43105-1212)
PHONE..................................740 503-5243
Wade Messmer, *Owner*
Barbara Messmer, *Partner*
EMP: 6
SQ FT: 2,400
SALES (est): 254.2K **Privately Held**
SIC: 5947 5092 2426 8299 Gift, novelty & souvenir shop; toys & hobby goods & supplies; hardwood dimension & flooring mills; arts & crafts schools

Barberton
Summit County

(G-1047)
11AM INDUSTRIES LLC
1297 Noble Ave (44203-7805)
PHONE..................................330 730-3177
Andrew Subotnik,
EMP: 14
SALES (est): 1.2MM **Privately Held**
SIC: 3999 Atomizers, toiletry

(G-1048)
ACE BOILER & WELDING CO INC
2891 Newpark Dr (44203-1047)
PHONE..................................330 745-4443
Robert Kille, *President*
Cynthia Kille, *Shareholder*
EMP: 8
SQ FT: 15,000
SALES (est): 1.1MM **Privately Held**
SIC: 3599 3441 Machine shop, jobbing & repair; fabricated structural metal

(G-1049)
ADVERTISING IDEAS OF OHIO INC
Also Called: 1 Stop Graphics
833 Wooster Rd N (44203-1664)
PHONE..................................330 745-6555
Robert W Jacob, *President*
Gene McMullen, *Vice Pres*
EMP: 9
SALES: 600K **Privately Held**
WEB: www.weinstallanywhere.com
SIC: 3993 Signs & advertising specialties
PA: International Installations Inc
833 Wooster Rd N
Barberton OH 44203

(G-1050)
AKRON FOUNDRY CO
Also Called: Akron Electric
1025 Eagon St (44203-1603)
PHONE..................................330 745-3101
Mike Pancoe, *General Mgr*
Sukhwant Puri, *Mfg Mgr*
EMP: 40
SALES (corp-wide): 22MM **Privately Held**
WEB: www.akronfoundry.com
SIC: 1731 3699 3644 3444 Electrical work; electrical equipment & supplies; noncurrent-carrying wiring services; sheet metalwork; aluminum foundries
PA: Akron Foundry Co.
2728 Wingate Ave
Akron OH 44314
330 745-3101

(G-1051)
AMERICAN MOLDING COMPANY INC
711 Wooster Rd W (44203-2444)
PHONE..................................330 620-6799
Laverne J Strohfus, *Principal*
EMP: 4
SALES (est): 338.2K **Privately Held**
SIC: 3089 Molding primary plastic

(G-1052)
ANDERSON GRAPHICS INC
711 Wooster Rd W (44203-2444)
PHONE..................................330 745-2165

GEOGRAPHIC SECTION — Barberton - Summit County (G-1078)

John Anderson, *President*
Larry Okolish, *Treasurer*
EMP: 30 **EST**: 1979
SALES: 1.8MM **Privately Held**
SIC: 2752 2759 2789 2791 Commercial printing, offset; commercial printing; bookbinding & related work; typesetting; manifold business forms

(G-1053)
ARCONIC INC
Also Called: Alcoa
842 Norton Ave (44203-1715)
PHONE...................330 848-4000
Victor Marquez, *General Mgr*
Ryan Behenna, *VP Opers*
Michael Lucek, *Project Mgr*
Daron Langdon, *Opers Staff*
Rick Aspiras, *QC Mgr*
EMP: 135
SALES (corp-wide): 14B **Publicly Held**
SIC: 3353 Aluminum sheet & strip
PA: Arconic Inc.
   390 Park Ave Fl 12
   New York NY 10022
   212 836-2758

(G-1054)
ASB INDUSTRIES INC
1031 Lambert St (44203-1689)
PHONE...................330 753-8458
Albert Kay, *President*
Charles Kay, *Vice Pres*
John Lindeman, *Vice Pres*
EMP: 23
SQ FT: 90,000
SALES (est): 4.8MM **Privately Held**
WEB: www.asbindustries.com
SIC: 1799 3599 3542 4215 Coating, caulking & weather, water & fireproofing; machine shop, jobbing & repair; presses: hydraulic & pneumatic, mechanical & manual; courier services, except by air

(G-1055)
AUSTIN ENGINEERING INC
Also Called: Austin Engineering Group
834 Promenade Cir (44203-4445)
PHONE...................330 848-0815
William Babbin, *President*
EMP: 4
SALES (est): 380K **Privately Held**
SIC: 3443 Jackets, industrial: metal plate

(G-1056)
B & C RESEARCH INC
842 Norton Ave (44203-1750)
PHONE...................330 848-4000
Bob Clements, *Ch of Bd*
Louis Bilinovich, *President*
▲ **EMP**: 500
SQ FT: 100,000
SALES (est): 70.1MM
SALES (corp-wide): 14B **Publicly Held**
WEB: www.bcresearch.com
SIC: 3599 Machine shop, jobbing & repair
HQ: Arconic Securities Llc
   101 Cherry St Ste 400
   Burlington VT 05401
   802 658-2661

(G-1057)
B & P POLISHING INC
123 9th St Nw (44203-2455)
P.O. Box 408 (44203-0408)
PHONE...................330 753-4202
Louie Vilinovach, *President*
▲ **EMP**: 11
SALES (est): 1.3MM **Privately Held**
SIC: 3291 Buffing or polishing wheels, abrasive or nonabrasive

(G-1058)
B&C MACHINE CO LLC
401 Newell St (44203-2018)
P.O. Box 345 (44203-0345)
PHONE...................330 745-4013
Peter Bilinovich,
Tonya Becker,
Brandon Bilinovich,
Eric Bilinovich,
Paul Bilinovich,
EMP: 300
SQ FT: 300,000
SALES: 20MM **Privately Held**
SIC: 3599 3714 3743 3398 Jobbing & Repair Machine Shop Mfg Motor Vehicle Parts Accessories Locomotives Parts & Metal Heat Treating

(G-1059)
BABCOCK & WILCOX COMPANY (HQ)
20 S Van Buren Ave (44203-3585)
P.O. Box 351 (44203-0351)
PHONE...................330 753-4511
Gregory Calvin, *President*
Pete Campanizzi, *General Mgr*
Kevin Brolly, *Regional Mgr*
Mark S Low, *Senior VP*
Jenny L Apker, *Senior VP*
◆ **EMP**: 1000 **EST**: 1867
SQ FT: 16,000
SALES (est): 1.3B
SALES (corp-wide): 1B **Publicly Held**
SIC: 1629 1711 3443 7699 Industrial plant construction; power plant construction; plumbing, heating, air-conditioning contractors; fabricated plate work (boiler shop); boilers: industrial, power, or marine; boiler & heating repair services; management services; auto controls regulating residntl & coml environmnt & applncs
PA: Babcock & Wilcox Enterprises, Inc.
   20 S Van Buren Ave
   Barberton OH 44203
   330 753-4511

(G-1060)
BABCOCK & WILCOX COMPANY
Also Called: Barberton Facility
91 Stirling Ave (44203-2600)
PHONE...................330 753-4511
Rich Conrad, *Purchasing*
Katie McVan, *Purchasing*
Shawn Vessalo, *Purchasing*
Jeremy Albright, *Engineer*
Keith Curtis, *Engineer*
EMP: 20
SALES (corp-wide): 1B **Publicly Held**
SIC: 3511 Turbines & turbine generator sets
HQ: The Babcock & Wilcox Company
   20 S Van Buren Ave
   Barberton OH 44203
   330 753-4511

(G-1061)
BABCOCK & WILCOX ENTPS INC (PA)
20 S Van Buren Ave (44203-3522)
PHONE...................330 753-4511
Kenneth Young, *CEO*
J Andre Hall, *Senior VP*
James J Muckley, *Senior VP*
Daniel W Hoehn, *Vice Pres*
Jimmy B Morgan, *Vice Pres*
EMP: 2208
SALES: 1B **Publicly Held**
SIC: 3621 3829 Power generators; nuclear instrument modules

(G-1062)
BARBERTON MAGIC PRESS PRINTING
Also Called: Magic Press Printery
699 Wooster Rd N (44203-1849)
PHONE...................330 753-9578
Richard Law, *Owner*
EMP: 4 **EST**: 1975
SQ FT: 4,000
SALES: 500K **Privately Held**
SIC: 2752 2754 Commercial printing, offset; letter, circular & form: gravure printing

(G-1063)
BARBERTON MOLD & MACHINE CO
465 5th St Ne (44203-2754)
PHONE...................330 745-8559
Helen P Adair, *President*
Harold W Adair, *Consultant*
EMP: 4
SQ FT: 1,200
SALES: 200K **Privately Held**
SIC: 3544 Industrial molds

(G-1064)
BARBERTON PRINTCRAFT
520 Wooster Rd W (44203-2549)
PHONE...................330 848-3000
Thomas Schleicher, *Owner*
EMP: 5 **EST**: 1975
SQ FT: 7,500
SALES (est): 472.7K **Privately Held**
SIC: 2752 Commercial printing, offset

(G-1065)
BARBERTON STEEL INDUSTRIES INC
240 E Huston St (44203-3044)
P.O. Box 350 (44203-0350)
PHONE...................330 745-6837
Jim Kotarski, *CEO*
Jim Cecconi, *Vice Pres*
EMP: 48
SALES (est): 16.8MM **Privately Held**
SIC: 3321 Gray & ductile iron foundries

(G-1066)
BOOKBINDERS INCORPORATED
90 16th St Sw Ste C (44203-7070)
PHONE...................330 848-4980
Steve Heim, *President*
EMP: 6
SQ FT: 7,000
SALES (est): 794K **Privately Held**
WEB: www.bookbindersinc.com
SIC: 2789 Bookbinding & related work

(G-1067)
BUCKEYE ABRASIVE INC
1020 Eagon St (44203-1604)
PHONE...................330 753-1041
Robert J Armour, *President*
EMP: 10
SQ FT: 14,400
SALES (est): 1.2MM **Privately Held**
SIC: 3291 Wheels, abrasive

(G-1068)
BWXT NCLEAR OPRTIONS GROUP INC
91 Stirling Ave (44203-2615)
P.O. Box 271 (44203-0271)
PHONE...................330 860-1010
Rod Woolsey, *Branch Mgr*
Todd Locke, *Manager*
EMP: 15 **Publicly Held**
SIC: 3443 Nuclear reactors, military or industrial
HQ: Bwxt Nuclear Operations Group, Inc.
   2016 Mount Athos Rd
   Lynchburg VA 24504

(G-1069)
CARDINAL RUBBER COMPANY INC
939 Wooster Rd N (44203-1698)
PHONE...................330 745-2191
Diane McConnell, *President*
Thomas R Schnee, *Vice Pres*
Tom Schnee, *Engineer*
Diane Schnee, *VP Mktg*
Robert F Schnee Jr, *Shareholder*
▲ **EMP**: 30
SQ FT: 80,000
SALES: 5MM **Privately Held**
SIC: 3069 3061 3479 2891 Molded rubber products; automotive rubber goods (mechanical); bonderizing of metal or metal products; adhesives & sealants; synthetic rubber

(G-1070)
FLOHR MACHINE COMPANY INC
Also Called: Flohrmachine.com
1028 Coventry Rd (44203-1636)
PHONE...................330 745-3030
Ivan W Flohr, *President*
Joseph Flohr, *Principal*
Jude Flohr, *Principal*
William Flohr, *Principal*
EMP: 18 **EST**: 1966
SQ FT: 6,000
SALES (est): 3MM **Privately Held**
WEB: www.flohrmachine.com
SIC: 3599 Machine shop, jobbing & repair

(G-1071)
FLORENCE ALLOYS INC
Also Called: Hard Drive Co
121 Snyder Ave (44203-4007)
PHONE...................330 745-9141
Jim Federan, *President*
EMP: 7
SQ FT: 7,700
SALES: 300K **Privately Held**
SIC: 3714 5013 Transmissions, motor vehicle; automotive supplies & parts

(G-1072)
GARDEN ART INNOVATIONS LLC
30 2nd St Sw (44203-2620)
PHONE...................330 697-0007
William Marthaler,
EMP: 3 **EST**: 2011
SALES (est): 330.8K **Privately Held**
SIC: 2844 Toilet preparations

(G-1073)
GENERAL PLASTEX INC
35 Stuver Pl (44203-2417)
PHONE...................330 745-7775
Renee Hershberger, *President*
EMP: 31
SQ FT: 52,500
SALES (est): 5.1MM **Privately Held**
SIC: 7699 3452 Industrial machinery & equipment repair; screws, metal

(G-1074)
GLAS ORNAMENTAL METALS INC
1559 Waterloo Rd (44203-1335)
PHONE...................330 753-0215
Rita Glas, *Ch of Bd*
John Glas, *President*
Karol Glas, *Admin Sec*
EMP: 9
SQ FT: 6,300
SALES (est): 825K **Privately Held**
SIC: 3446 Railings, prefabricated metal

(G-1075)
GLASS SURFACE SYSTEMS INC
Also Called: G S S
24 Brown St (44203-2315)
PHONE...................330 745-8500
Barry Jacobs, *President*
EMP: 75
SQ FT: 17,000
SALES (est): 9.4MM **Privately Held**
WEB: www.glasscoat.com
SIC: 3231 Strengthened or reinforced glass

(G-1076)
HYCOM INC
374 5th St Nw (44203-2127)
PHONE...................330 753-2330
Thomas J Bilinovich, *CEO*
Ralph Bowling, *President*
Joseph Hufgard, *Project Mgr*
EMP: 45
SQ FT: 126,684
SALES: 2.7MM **Privately Held**
SIC: 3498 Tube fabricating (contract bending & shaping)

(G-1077)
INTERNATIONAL INSTALLATIONS (PA)
Also Called: A Plus Signs & Graphics
833 Wooster Rd N (44203-1664)
PHONE...................330 848-4800
Gene McMullen, *President*
Robert W Jacob, *Vice Pres*
EMP: 8
SALES (est): 1.1MM **Privately Held**
SIC: 3993 Signs & advertising specialties

(G-1078)
JOHNDOW INDUSTRIES INC
151 Snyder Ave (44203-4007)
PHONE...................330 753-6895
Drew Dawson, *President*
Dean Jones, *Warehouse Mgr*
Christine Brown, *Purchasing*
Robert Christy, *VP Sales*
Gary Church, *Sales Staff*
▲ **EMP**: 24
SQ FT: 120,000

Barberton - Summit County (G-1079)

SALES (est): 7.7MM **Privately Held**
WEB: www.johndow.com
SIC: 3559 Automotive maintenance equipment

(G-1079)
JR ENGINEERING INC (PA)
Also Called: J R Engineering
123 9th St Nw (44203-2455)
P.O. Box 1497, Norton (44203-8497)
PHONE.................................330 848-0960
Louis Bilinovich Jr, *President*
Louis Bilinovich Sr, *Corp Secy*
John Callan, *QC Mgr*
Greg Roehrich, *Sls & Mktg Exec*
Darin Nist, *Info Tech Mgr*
◆ EMP: 215
SQ FT: 242,000
SALES (est): 70.6MM **Privately Held**
WEB: www.jr-engineering.com
SIC: 3714 Motor vehicle parts & accessories

(G-1080)
KEM ADVERTISING AND PRTG LLC
564 W Tuscarawas Ave # 104 (44203-8213)
PHONE.................................330 818-5061
Kimberly Okolish, *Principal*
EMP: 3
SALES (est): 214.1K **Privately Held**
SIC: 2752 Commercial printing, lithographic

(G-1081)
LITTLERN CORPORATION
77 2nd St Sw (44203-2645)
PHONE.................................330 848-8847
Ernest L Puskas Jr, *President*
EMP: 9
SALES (est): 1.4MM **Privately Held**
WEB: www.littlern.com
SIC: 2869 2819 4226 Industrial organic chemicals; industrial inorganic chemicals; special warehousing & storage

(G-1082)
MADGAR GENIS CORP
Also Called: Medkeff-Nye
131 Snyder Ave (44203-4007)
P.O. Box 287 (44203-0287)
PHONE.................................330 848-6950
Normand J Madgar, *President*
James Genis, *Vice Pres*
EMP: 5
SQ FT: 7,000
SALES (est): 786.8K **Privately Held**
WEB: www.medkeff-nye.com
SIC: 3565 Packaging machinery

(G-1083)
MAG RESOURCES LLC
711 Wooster Rd W (44203-2444)
P.O. Box 590 (44203-0590)
PHONE.................................330 294-0494
Peggy Giovanini, *Office Mgr*
Joseph Giovanini, *Mng Member*
Michael Giovanini,
▲ EMP: 5
SQ FT: 3,300
SALES: 700K **Privately Held**
SIC: 5719 5023 2431 2591 Venetian blinds; venetian blinds; blinds (shutters), wood; window blinds

(G-1084)
MAGIC CITY MACHINE INC
21 4th St Nw (44203-2503)
P.O. Box 488 (44203-0488)
PHONE.................................330 825-0048
Sandor Baksa, *President*
Michael A Stobaugh, *Corp Secy*
EMP: 10
SQ FT: 11,000
SALES: 1.2MM **Privately Held**
WEB: www.magiccitymachine.com
SIC: 3599 Machine shop, jobbing & repair

(G-1085)
MAY LIN SILICONE PRODUCTS INC
955 Wooster Rd W (44203-7149)
P.O. Box 335 (44203-0335)
PHONE.................................330 825-9019
Linda Weaver, *President*
Dave Weaver, *Vice Pres*
EMP: 6 EST: 1958
SQ FT: 1,800
SALES: 500K **Privately Held**
WEB: www.may-lin.com
SIC: 3069 3053 Molded rubber products; rubber hardware; gaskets, all materials; gaskets & sealing devices

(G-1086)
MITCHELL PLASTICS INC
130 31st St Nw (44203-7238)
PHONE.................................330 825-2461
Mitchell E Volk, *President*
EMP: 22
SQ FT: 15,000
SALES (est): 4.4MM **Privately Held**
WEB: www.mpicase.com
SIC: 3069 3993 Laboratory sundries: cases, covers, funnels, cups, etc.; signs & advertising specialties

(G-1087)
MODEL ENGINEERING COMPANY
800 Robinson Ave (44203-3725)
PHONE.................................330 644-3450
Eugene Sanders, *President*
Jeff Sanders, *Vice Pres*
EMP: 4
SALES: 150K **Privately Held**
WEB: www.modelengineeringco.com
SIC: 3543 3999 Industrial patterns; models, general, except toy

(G-1088)
NEIDERT FABRICATING INC
712 Wooster Rd W (44203-2420)
PHONE.................................330 753-3331
Paul Neidert, *President*
Carol Neidert, *Admin Sec*
EMP: 8
SQ FT: 9,000
SALES (est): 1.2MM **Privately Held**
SIC: 3599 3441 Machine shop, jobbing & repair; fabricated structural metal

(G-1089)
NORTHCOAST PRFMCE & MCH CO
1190 Wooster Rd N (44203-1254)
PHONE.................................330 753-7333
James Sibbio, *Owner*
EMP: 3
SALES: 150K **Privately Held**
SIC: 3599 Industrial machinery

(G-1090)
NOVATION SOLUTIONS LLC
30 2nd St Sw (44203-2620)
PHONE.................................330 620-1189
Thomas J Tupa, *Principal*
EMP: 6
SALES (est): 840.2K **Privately Held**
SIC: 2869 Industrial organic chemicals

(G-1091)
OHIO PRECISION MOLDING INC
Also Called: Opm
122 E Tuscarawas Ave (44203-2628)
PHONE.................................330 745-9393
Bruce Vereecken, *President*
Joe Vereecken, *Vice Pres*
Melissa Garrett, *Office Mgr*
Karen Vereecken, *Shareholder*
David Vereecken, *Admin Sec*
▲ EMP: 30
SQ FT: 30,000
SALES (est): 7.6MM **Privately Held**
WEB: www.ohioprecisionmolding.com
SIC: 3089 Injection molding of plastics

(G-1092)
OLSON SHEET METAL CNSTR CO
465 Glenn St (44203-1499)
PHONE.................................330 745-8225
John Sveda, *President*
Joanne Sveda, *Admin Sec*
EMP: 6
SALES: 250K **Privately Held**
SIC: 3441 Fabricated structural metal

(G-1093)
PARATUS SUPPLY INC
635 Wooster Rd W (44203-2440)
PHONE.................................330 745-3600
John Sesic, *General Mgr*
Craig Cutcher, *Vice Pres*
EMP: 10
SALES (est): 1.7MM **Privately Held**
SIC: 3563 3086 Spraying & dusting equipment; insulation or cushioning material, foamed plastic

(G-1094)
PATHFINDER COMPUTER SYSTEMS
345 5th St Ne (44203-2863)
PHONE.................................330 928-1961
Rodney Starcher, *President*
Chuck Rainer, *Vice Pres*
EMP: 7
SALES (est): 705.7K **Privately Held**
WEB: www.pathfindercs.com
SIC: 7372 7371 Prepackaged software; custom computer programming services

(G-1095)
PLASTIC MOLD TECHNOLOGY INC
40 Stuver Pl (44203-2416)
PHONE.................................330 848-4921
Damir Petkovic, *President*
Robin Petkovic, *Corp Secy*
EMP: 8
SQ FT: 6,500
SALES (est): 1MM **Privately Held**
WEB: www.pmtmolds.com
SIC: 3544 Industrial molds

(G-1096)
PPG INDUSTRIES INC
Also Called: P P G Chemicals Group
4829 Fairland Rd (44203-3905)
PHONE.................................330 825-0831
Carl E Johnson, *Manager*
EMP: 24
SQ FT: 306
SALES (corp-wide): 15.3B **Publicly Held**
WEB: www.ppg.com
SIC: 2851 Paints & paint additives
PA: Ppg Industries, Inc.
1 Ppg Pl
Pittsburgh PA 15272
412 434-3131

(G-1097)
PPG INDUSTRIES INC
900 Columbia Ct At 16th & (44203)
PHONE.................................330 825-6328
Ted Ladd, *Branch Mgr*
EMP: 4
SALES (corp-wide): 15.3B **Publicly Held**
SIC: 2851 Paints & allied products
PA: Ppg Industries, Inc.
1 Ppg Pl
Pittsburgh PA 15272
412 434-3131

(G-1098)
PRAXAIR INC
4805 Fairland Rd (44203-3913)
PHONE.................................330 825-4449
David Corley, *Plant Mgr*
Dave Corly, *Manager*
EMP: 6 **Privately Held**
SIC: 2813 Industrial gases
HQ: Praxair, Inc.
10 Riverview Dr
Danbury CT 06810
203 837-2000

(G-1099)
PRO GRAM ENGINEERING CORP
475 5th St Ne (44203-2754)
P.O. Box 472 (44203-0472)
PHONE.................................330 745-1004
Kenneth Anderson, *President*
Dadan Anderson, *Vice Pres*
EMP: 9
SQ FT: 5,500
SALES (est): 1.6MM **Privately Held**
WEB: www.pro-gram.com
SIC: 3599 Machine shop, jobbing & repair

(G-1100)
Q MODEL INC
711 Wooster Rd W (44203-2444)
P.O. Box 25, Mogadore (44260-0025)
PHONE.................................330 673-0473
Todd Strohfus, *President*
Laverne Strohfus, *CFO*
Paul Proctor,
EMP: 30
SQ FT: 35,000
SALES (est): 6.8MM **Privately Held**
WEB: www.qmodel.com
SIC: 3469 3069 Patterns on metal; molded rubber products

(G-1101)
REVLIS CORPORATION
Also Called: Revlon
2845 Newpark Dr (44203-1047)
PHONE.................................330 535-2108
Brad Wehman, *Sales/Mktg Mgr*
EMP: 24
SQ FT: 10,000
SALES (corp-wide): 5.1MM **Privately Held**
SIC: 2816 Inorganic pigments
PA: Revlis Corporation
255 Huntington Ave
Akron OH 44306
330 535-2108

(G-1102)
RICHARDSON PUBLISHING COMPANY
Also Called: Barberton Herald
70 4th St Nw Ste 1 (44203-8283)
P.O. Box 830 (44203-0830)
PHONE.................................330 753-1068
Dave Richardson, *President*
Cathy Robertson, *Vice Pres*
EMP: 13 EST: 1923
SALES: 650K **Privately Held**
WEB: www.barbertonherald.com
SIC: 2711 Newspapers, publishing & printing

(G-1103)
RISE N SHINE YARD SIGNS
606 Grandview Ave (44203-2941)
PHONE.................................330 745-5868
Mike Beal, *Principal*
EMP: 3 EST: 2010
SALES (est): 250.7K **Privately Held**
SIC: 3993 Signs & advertising specialties

(G-1104)
S P Z MACHINE CO
2871 Newpark Dr (44203-1047)
PHONE.................................330 848-3286
Peter Zarkovacki, *Owner*
David Scott Zarkovacki, *Vice Pres*
EMP: 8
SQ FT: 50,000
SALES (est): 895.3K **Privately Held**
WEB: www.spzmachine.net
SIC: 3599 Machine shop, jobbing & repair

(G-1105)
SLOGANS LLC
Also Called: Indoor Dog Litter
234 W State St (44203-1372)
PHONE.................................330 942-9464
Duane P McCann,
EMP: 3
SALES (est): 105.4K **Privately Held**
SIC: 3999 Pet supplies

(G-1106)
SPECIFIED STRUCTURES INC
643 Holmes Ave (44203-2181)
PHONE.................................330 753-0693
Grant Senn, *President*
EMP: 8
SQ FT: 10,000
SALES (est): 1MM **Privately Held**
WEB: www.specifiedstructures.com
SIC: 2434 Wood kitchen cabinets

(G-1107)
STADVEC INC
Also Called: Esssco Aircraft
579 W Tuscarawas Ave (44203-2521)
PHONE.................................330 644-7724
Michael Stadvec, *President*
Marjorie Stadev, *COO*

▲ = Import ▼=Export
◆ =Import/Export

Franca Stadvec, *CFO*
Braxton Carter, *Finance Mgr*
EMP: 3
SQ FT: 11,000
SALES (est): 1.4MM **Privately Held**
WEB: www.esscoaircraft.com
SIC: 5961 7389 2759 Books, mail order (except book clubs); packaging & labeling services; laminating service; commercial printing

(G-1108)
TAHOMA ENTERPRISES INC (PA)
255 Wooster Rd N (44203-2560)
PHONE.................................330 745-9016
William P Herrington, *CEO*
EMP: 100
SALES (est): 33.1MM **Privately Held**
SIC: 3069 3089 5199 5162 Reclaimed rubber (reworked by manufacturing processes); plastic processing; foams & rubber; plastics products

(G-1109)
TAHOMA RUBBER & PLASTICS INC (HQ)
Also Called: Rondy & Co.
255 Wooster Rd N (44203-2560)
PHONE.................................330 745-9016
William P Herrington, *CEO*
Mary Wilcox, *Manager*
▼ **EMP:** 100
SQ FT: 750,000
SALES (est): 23.8MM
SALES (corp-wide): 33.1MM **Privately Held**
WEB: www.rondy.net
SIC: 3069 3089 5199 5162 Reclaimed rubber (reworked by manufacturing processes); plastic processing; foams & rubber; plastics products
PA: Tahoma Enterprises, Inc.
 255 Wooster Rd N
 Barberton OH 44203
 330 745-9016

(G-1110)
TENNEY TOOL & SUPPLY CO
973 Wooster Rd N (44203-1625)
PHONE.................................330 666-2807
David Masa, *President*
Daniel Braun, *Vice Pres*
Donald Kepple, *Admin Sec*
EMP: 16 EST: 1947
SQ FT: 11,000
SALES (est): 2.9MM **Privately Held**
WEB: www.tenneytool.com
SIC: 5085 3599 Industrial tools; machine shop, jobbing & repair

(G-1111)
TERRA COMP TECHNOLOGY
449 4th St Nw (44203-2051)
PHONE.................................330 745-8912
Terry Silvester, *Owner*
EMP: 5
SALES (est): 462K **Privately Held**
WEB: www.terracomptech.com
SIC: 7378 3571 Computer maintenance & repair; computer & data processing equipment repair/maintenance; computer peripheral equipment repair & maintenance; computers, digital, analog or hybrid

(G-1112)
VILLAGE PLASTICS CO
Also Called: 3d Systems
100 16th St Sw (44203-7004)
PHONE.................................330 753-0100
Kevin Gerstenslager, *Principal*
EMP: 8
SQ FT: 22,000
SALES (est): 1.2MM **Publicly Held**
SIC: 3544 Extrusion dies
PA: 3d Systems Corporation
 333 Three D Systems Cir
 Rock Hill SC 29730

(G-1113)
WINERY AT WOLF CREEK
2637 Clvland Massillon Rd (44203-6417)
PHONE.................................330 666-9285
Andrew Troutman, *Owner*
EMP: 10

SALES (est): 1.2MM **Privately Held**
WEB: www.wineryatwolfcreek.com
SIC: 2084 Wines

(G-1114)
WRIGHT TOOL COMPANY
1 Wright Pl (44203-2798)
P.O. Box 512 (44203-0512)
PHONE.................................330 848-0600
Richard Wright, *Ch of Bd*
Terry G Taylor, *President*
Al Ryding, *Vice Pres*
Brent Smith, *Plant Supt*
Brian Hale, *Foreman/Supr*
▲ **EMP:** 160 EST: 1927
SQ FT: 124,000
SALES (est): 53.4MM **Privately Held**
WEB: www.wrighttool.com
SIC: 3462 3423 Iron & steel forgings; wrenches, hand tools

Barnesville
Belmont County

(G-1115)
ART WORKS
119 E Pike St (43713-1539)
PHONE.................................740 425-5765
Ann Hudson, *Owner*
Brad Hudson, *Owner*
EMP: 6
SALES (est): 380K **Privately Held**
SIC: 2396 Screen printing on fabric articles

(G-1116)
BUCKEYE STEEL INC
607 Watt Ave (43713-1272)
P.O. Box 458 (43713-0458)
PHONE.................................740 425-2306
Richard W Pryor, *President*
Douglas E Kriechbaum, *Vice Pres*
EMP: 10
SQ FT: 34,000
SALES (est): 2.9MM **Privately Held**
SIC: 3441 Fabricated structural metal

(G-1117)
K & J MACHINE INC
326 Fairmont Ave (43713-9669)
PHONE.................................740 425-3282
Homer Luyster, *President*
Martha L Luyster, *Vice Pres*
Sharon Lucas, *Admin Sec*
EMP: 17 EST: 1971
SQ FT: 3,300
SALES (est): 1.6MM **Privately Held**
SIC: 7699 3599 7692 Aircraft & heavy equipment repair services; machine shop, jobbing & repair; welding repair

(G-1118)
RODNEY WELLS
Also Called: Rods Welding and Rebuilding
34225 Holland Rd (43713-9602)
PHONE.................................740 425-2266
Rodney Wells, *Owner*
EMP: 7
SALES (est): 280K **Privately Held**
SIC: 7692 Welding repair

(G-1119)
SUN SHINE AWARDS
36099 Bethesda Street Ext (43713-9619)
PHONE.................................740 425-2504
Danny Kimble, *Owner*
EMP: 10
SALES (est): 453.3K **Privately Held**
WEB: www.sunshineawards.com
SIC: 5999 2395 Trophies & plaques; embroidery & art needlework

(G-1120)
W O HARDWOODS INC
58098 Wright Rd (43713-9540)
PHONE.................................740 425-1588
Lowell Bahmer, *President*
EMP: 3 EST: 1986
SALES (est): 245K **Privately Held**
SIC: 2421 Sawmills & planing mills, general

Batavia
Clermont County

(G-1121)
A N H
4065 Clough Woods Dr (45103-2587)
PHONE.................................513 576-6240
EMP: 3
SALES (est): 174.7K **Privately Held**
SIC: 3255 Clay refractories

(G-1122)
A-1 FABRICATORS FINISHERS LLC
4220 Curliss Ln (45103-3276)
PHONE.................................513 724-0383
Joseph Strack, *Senior Engr*
Stacy Lanter, *Human Res Dir*
Jason Robinson, *Sales Staff*
Jamie Doane, *Office Mgr*
Dennis Doane, *Mng Member*
EMP: 78
SQ FT: 80,000
SALES (est): 11MM **Privately Held**
SIC: 3441 Fabricated structural metal

(G-1123)
AUTO TEMP INC
Also Called: ATI
950 Kent Rd (45103-1738)
P.O. Box 631690, Cincinnati (45263-1690)
PHONE.................................513 732-6969
Frank Lauch, *CEO*
Doug Fassler, *Vice Pres*
Matt Fassler, *Vice Pres*
Jim Elcook, *Opers Staff*
John Day, *Production*
◆ **EMP:** 155
SQ FT: 210,000
SALES (est): 27.9MM **Privately Held**
WEB: www.autotempinc.com
SIC: 3231 Tempered glass: made from purchased glass

(G-1124)
AVENUE FABRICATING INC
1281 Clough Pike (45103-2501)
PHONE.................................513 752-1911
Gretchen Nichols, *President*
Adrian Nichols, *Vice Pres*
Lauren Nichols, *Vice Pres*
Robert Nichols, *Vice Pres*
Jeff Huseman, *Project Mgr*
EMP: 41
SQ FT: 17,800
SALES (est): 16MM **Privately Held**
WEB: www.avenuefabricating.com
SIC: 3499 3441 Metal ladders; fabricated structural metal

(G-1125)
B C METALS INC
4484 Hartman Ln (45103-1905)
PHONE.................................513 732-9644
Harold Gatts, *President*
Kathy Gatts, *Vice Pres*
EMP: 4
SQ FT: 8,500
SALES (est): 380K **Privately Held**
SIC: 3599 Machine shop, jobbing & repair

(G-1126)
BALTA TECHNOLOGY INC
4350 Batavia Rd (45103-3342)
PHONE.................................513 724-0247
Andy Weidner, *President*
EMP: 4
SALES (est): 59.9K **Privately Held**
SIC: 3822 Auto controls regulating residntl & coml environmt & applncs

(G-1127)
BECKMAN ENVIRONMENTAL SVCS INC
Also Called: Besco
4259 Armstrong Blvd (45103-1697)
PHONE.................................513 752-3570
Joan Beckman, *President*
John Beckman, *Vice Pres*
Eddie Shepherd, *Opers Staff*
EMP: 12
SQ FT: 6,700

SALES (est): 3.5MM **Privately Held**
WEB: www.beckmanenvironmental.com
SIC: 3589 7699 Sewage treatment equipment; sewer cleaning & rodding

(G-1128)
BLACK MACHINING & TECHNOLOGY
4020 Bach Buxton Rd (45103-2525)
PHONE.................................513 752-8625
Frank Black, *President*
Stephanie Standring, *Corp Secy*
Margaret Lynn Black, *Vice Pres*
EMP: 10
SALES (est): 660K **Privately Held**
SIC: 3599 Machine shop, jobbing & repair

(G-1129)
CINCHEMPRO INC
Also Called: Cincinnati Chemical Processing
458 W Main St (45103-1712)
PHONE.................................513 724-6111
John Glass, *CEO*
Mary Hucke, *Executive*
EMP: 105
SQ FT: 22,000
SALES (est): 19.9MM **Privately Held**
WEB: www.cinchempro.com
SIC: 2899 Chemical preparations

(G-1130)
CINCINNATI MACHINES INC
4165 Half Acre Rd (45103-3247)
PHONE.................................513 536-2432
Rose Acree, *Supervisor*
▲ **EMP:** 900
SALES (est): 64.1MM **Privately Held**
WEB: www.cinmac.com
SIC: 3088 Plastics plumbing fixtures

(G-1131)
CLERMONT STEEL FABRICATORS LLC
2565 Old State Route 32 (45103-3205)
PHONE.................................513 732-6033
Robert Mampe, *CEO*
Ken Miller, *Vice Pres*
Lisa Brann, *Executive*
◆ **EMP:** 70
SQ FT: 144,000
SALES (est): 17.8MM **Privately Held**
WEB: www.clermontsteel.com
SIC: 3441 Fabricated structural metal

(G-1132)
COLLOTYPE LABELS USA INC
4053 Clough Woods Dr (45103-2587)
PHONE.................................513 381-1480
David Buse, *President*
EMP: 100
SALES (est): 3.6MM
SALES (corp-wide): 1.3B **Publicly Held**
SIC: 2759 Labels & seals: printing
PA: Multi-Color Corporation
 4053 Clough Woods Dr
 Batavia OH 45103
 513 381-1480

(G-1133)
CORE COMPOSITES CINCINNATI LLC
4174 Half Acre Rd (45103-3250)
PHONE.................................513 724-6111
John Glass, *Principal*
EMP: 21
SALES (est): 428.6K **Publicly Held**
SIC: 3089 Molding primary plastic
PA: Core Molding Technologies, Inc.
 800 Manor Park Dr
 Columbus OH 43228

(G-1134)
CURTISS-WRIGHT FLOW CONTROL
Also Called: Qualtech NP
750 Kent Rd (45103-1704)
PHONE.................................513 735-2538
EMP: 85
SALES (corp-wide): 2.1B **Publicly Held**
SIC: 3491 3443 3599 1799 Mfg Industrial Valves Mfg Fabricated Plate Wrk Mfg Industrial Machinery Special Trade Contractor

Batavia - Clermont County (G-1135)

HQ: Curtiss-Wright Flow Control Service
Corporation
2950 E Birch St
Brea CA 92821
714 982-1898

(G-1135)
D&D DESIGN CONCEPTS INC
Also Called: W.T.nickell Co.
4360 Winding Creek Blvd (45103-1729)
PHONE..................513 752-2191
Rick Meyer, *President*
Ray Meyer, *President*
EMP: 10
SQ FT: 8,000
SALES: 1.5MM **Privately Held**
WEB: www.wtnickell.com
SIC: 2759 Labels & seals: printing

(G-1136)
DELTEC INCORPORATED
4230 Grissom Dr (45103-1669)
PHONE..................513 732-0800
Jason Dugle, *President*
Chris Dugle, *Chairman*
EMP: 46
SQ FT: 42,000
SALES: 6.2MM **Privately Held**
WEB: www.deltec-inc.com
SIC: 3441 Fabricated structural metal

(G-1137)
EARTHGANIC ELEMENTS LLC
1150 Nature Run Rd (45103-1040)
PHONE..................513 430-0503
Erin L Christen,
EMP: 4
SALES (est): 135.6K **Privately Held**
SIC: 2819 Mfg Industrial Inorganic Chemicals

(G-1138)
EAT MOORE CUPCAKES
1212 Forest Run Dr (45103-2554)
PHONE..................513 713-8139
Jodye Moore, *Principal*
EMP: 4
SALES (est): 164.7K **Privately Held**
SIC: 2051 Bread, cake & related products

(G-1139)
EGER PRODUCTS INC
4226 Grissom Dr (45103-1669)
PHONE..................513 735-1400
Scott McLarin, *Branch Mgr*
EMP: 40
SQ FT: 2,128
SALES (corp-wide): 28MM **Privately Held**
WEB: www.egerproducts.com
SIC: 3089 Plastic processing
PA: Eger Products, Inc.
1132 Ferris Rd
Amelia OH 45102
513 753-4200

(G-1140)
ELECTRODYNE COMPANY INC
4188 Taylor Rd (45103-9736)
P.O. Box 321 (45103-0321)
PHONE..................513 732-2822
Scott Blume, *President*
Cathy Brinkman, *Treasurer*
▲ EMP: 14
SQ FT: 22,000
SALES (est): 1.9MM **Privately Held**
WEB: www.edyne.com
SIC: 3264 Porcelain electrical supplies

(G-1141)
ELECTROFUEL INDUSTRIES INC
77 N Depot Rd (45103-2951)
PHONE..................937 783-2846
Jerry Rearick, *President*
EMP: 3
SQ FT: 24,000
SALES: 280K **Privately Held**
SIC: 3545 Cutting tools for machine tools

(G-1142)
ELLIS & WATTS GLOBAL INDS INC
4400 Glen Willow Lake Ln (45103-2379)
PHONE..................513 752-9000
Gina Cottrell, *President*
EMP: 20
SALES (est): 4.1MM
SALES (corp-wide): 225.3B **Publicly Held**
SIC: 3585 Refrigeration & heating equipment
HQ: Mitek Industries, Inc.
16023 Swinly Rdg
Chesterfield MO 63017
314 434-1200

(G-1143)
ELLIS & WATTS INTL LLC
4400 Glen Willow Lake Ln (45103-2379)
PHONE..................513 752-9000
Richard D Porco, *President*
Richard Porco, *COO*
Jean Brown, *CFO*
Andrew J Pike, *Mng Member*
Pamela Abrams, *Manager*
▲ EMP: 3
SQ FT: 172,000
SALES (est): 1.2MM **Privately Held**
WEB: www.elliswatts.com
SIC: 3585 3713 3625 3564 Air conditioning units, complete: domestic or industrial; dehumidifiers electric, except portable; heating equipment, complete; van bodies; relays & industrial controls; blowers & fans; fabricated plate work (boiler shop); mobile homes

(G-1144)
ENGINEERED MBL SOLUTIONS INC
Also Called: E M S
4350 Batavia Rd (45103-3342)
PHONE..................513 724-0247
Bryce Johnson, *Vice Pres*
An Nguyen, *Vice Pres*
EMP: 15
SALES: 950K **Privately Held**
SIC: 3715 Truck trailers

(G-1145)
FOSTER MANUFACTURING
4283 Armstrong Blvd (45103-1697)
P.O. Box 458 (45103-0458)
PHONE..................513 735-9770
Gary Foster, *President*
EMP: 4
SQ FT: 1,824
SALES (est): 348.4K **Privately Held**
WEB: www.bowholder.com
SIC: 3949 Archery equipment, general

(G-1146)
FOSTER PRODUCTS INC
Also Called: Mobile Office Solutions
4283 Armstrong Blvd (45103-1697)
P.O. Box 458 (45103-0458)
PHONE..................513 735-9770
Gary D Foster, *President*
EMP: 4
SQ FT: 7,300
SALES (est): 639.2K **Privately Held**
SIC: 3441 Fabricated structural metal

(G-1147)
FREEMAN ENCLOSURE SYSTEMS LLC
4160 Half Acre Rd (45103-3250)
PHONE..................877 441-8555
Dale Freeman, *President*
EMP: 210
SQ FT: 120,000
SALES (est): 31.2MM **Publicly Held**
SIC: 3444 Sheet metalwork
HQ: Ies Infrastructure Solutions, Llc
800 Nave Rd Se
Massillon OH 44646
330 830-3500

(G-1148)
FREEMAN SCHWABE MACHINERY LLC
Also Called: F S
4064 Clough Woods Dr (45103-2586)
PHONE..................513 947-2888
Greg Defisher, *CEO*
▲ EMP: 30
SALES (est): 7.7MM **Privately Held**
WEB: www.freemanschwabe.com
SIC: 3559 Automotive related machinery

(G-1149)
GEORGIA-PACIFIC LLC
4225 Curliss Ln (45103-3217)
PHONE..................513 536-3020
Ed Ford, *Manager*
EMP: 130
SALES (corp-wide): 42.4B **Privately Held**
WEB: www.gp.com
SIC: 2653 Corrugated & solid fiber boxes
HQ: Georgia-Pacific Llc
133 Peachtree St Nw
Atlanta GA 30303
404 652-4000

(G-1150)
GUTTER TOPPER LTD
4111 Founders Blvd (45103-2534)
P.O. Box 349, Amelia (45102-0349)
PHONE..................513 797-5800
Anthony Iannelli, *Partner*
Phyllis Iannelli, *Partner*
EMP: 7
SALES: 5MM **Privately Held**
SIC: 3444 5033 1521 Gutters, sheet metal; roofing, siding & insulation; single-family housing construction

(G-1151)
HAMILTON FABRICATORS INC
4008 Borman Dr (45103-1681)
PHONE..................513 735-7773
Ken Murry, *President*
Jeffrey Gileen, *Vice Pres*
EMP: 23
SALES (est): 3MM **Privately Held**
SIC: 3499 Mfg Misc Fabricated Metal Products

(G-1152)
HARBISONWALKER INTL INC
4065a Clough Woods Dr (45103-2587)
PHONE..................513 576-6240
Annette Kreiner, *Branch Mgr*
EMP: 22
SALES (corp-wide): 703.8MM **Privately Held**
WEB: www.hwr.com
SIC: 3255 Clay refractories
HQ: Harbisonwalker International, Inc.
1305 Cherrington Pkwy # 100
Moon Township PA 15108

(G-1153)
HUHTAMAKI INC
1985 James E Sauls Sr Dr (45103-3246)
PHONE..................513 201-1525
EMP: 320
SALES (corp-wide): 35.2B **Privately Held**
SIC: 3565 2656 Labeling machines, industrial; ice cream containers: made from purchased material
HQ: Huhtamaki, Inc.
9201 Packaging Dr
De Soto KS 66018
913 583-3025

(G-1154)
INGREDIENT MASTERS INC
Also Called: Manufacturing Animal Food Phrm
377 E Main St (45103-3001)
PHONE..................513 231-7432
Scott Culshaw, *President*
Cheryl Culshaw, *Corp Secy*
Jennifer Brogan, *Opers Staff*
▼ EMP: 7 EST: 1980
SALES: 5MM **Privately Held**
SIC: 3556 3559 Bakery machinery; refinery, chemical processing & similar machinery; chemical machinery & equipment; foundry machinery & equipment

(G-1155)
J O Y ALUMINUM PRODUCTS INC
4111 Founders Blvd (45103-2534)
P.O. Box 349, Amelia (45102-0349)
PHONE..................513 797-1100
Anthony Iannelli, *President*
EMP: 15
SALES (est): 2.3MM **Privately Held**
WEB: www.guttertopper.com
SIC: 3444 Gutters, sheet metal

(G-1156)
KABLER FARMS
4529 Elmwood Rd (45103-9495)
PHONE..................513 732-0501
Beverly Kabler, *Owner*
Randall Kabler, *Owner*
EMP: 3
SALES (est): 160K **Privately Held**
SIC: 3949 7999 Hunting equipment; zoological garden, commercial

(G-1157)
KENNEDY CATALOGS LLC
4177 Knollview Ct (45103-2557)
PHONE..................513 753-1518
Stuart Kennedy,
Julie Kennedy,
EMP: 3
SALES (est): 141.3K **Privately Held**
SIC: 2741 Catalogs: publishing only, not printed on site

(G-1158)
KENNETH HICKMAN CO
4266 Tranquility Ct (45103-3152)
PHONE..................513 348-0016
Kenneth Hickman, *Owner*
EMP: 15
SALES (est): 999.3K **Privately Held**
SIC: 3571 Electronic computers

(G-1159)
KEY RESIN COMPANY (DH)
4050 Clough Woods Dr (45103-2586)
PHONE..................513 943-4225
Jeff Cain, *President*
David Coleman, *Opers Mgr*
Joe Larger, *Finance Mgr*
Michelle Frambes, *Human Resources*
Mike Flanagan, *Sales Staff*
◆ EMP: 16
SQ FT: 18,000
SALES (est): 4.1MM
SALES (corp-wide): 5.3B **Publicly Held**
WEB: www.keyresin.com
SIC: 2821 2822 Epoxy resins; acrylic resins; polyurethane resins; ethylene-propylene rubbers, EPDM polymers
HQ: The Euclid Chemical Company
19218 Redwood Rd
Cleveland OH 44110
800 321-7628

(G-1160)
KIPPS GRAVEL COMPANY INC
4987 State Route 222 (45103-9782)
PHONE..................513 732-1024
Melvin M Kipp, *President*
Judy King, *Admin Sec*
EMP: 12 EST: 1967
SQ FT: 5,000
SALES (est): 1.7MM **Privately Held**
SIC: 1442 1794 Gravel mining; excavation work

(G-1161)
L & F LAUCH LLC
950 Kent Rd (45103-1738)
PHONE..................513 732-5805
Frank Lauch, *Vice Pres*
Matt Fassler, *Vice Pres*
EMP: 6
SALES: 100K **Privately Held**
WEB: www.mootechnologies.com
SIC: 2023 2086 Concentrated milk; bottled & canned soft drinks

(G-1162)
L A EXPRESS (PA)
1148 Marian Dr (45103-2378)
PHONE..................513 752-6999
Mike Mueller, *Principal*
EMP: 8
SALES (est): 1MM **Privately Held**
SIC: 3589 Car washing machinery

(G-1163)
LOUIS G FREEMAN CO
4064 Clough Woods Dr (45103-2586)
PHONE..................513 263-1720
Louis Freeman, *Principal*
EMP: 3 EST: 2010
SALES (est): 201.5K **Privately Held**
SIC: 3089 Plastics products

▲ = Import ▼ = Export
◆ = Import/Export

GEOGRAPHIC SECTION
Batavia - Clermont County (G-1191)

(G-1164)
MET FAB FABRICATION AND MCH
2974 Waitensburg Pike (45103)
P.O. Box 363 (45103-0363)
PHONE..................513 724-3715
Rod Stouder, *President*
Debbie Stouder, *Treasurer*
EMP: 6
SQ FT: 14,000
SALES: 460K **Privately Held**
WEB: www.met-fabinc.com
SIC: 3535 3599 Conveyors & conveying equipment; machine & other job shop work

(G-1165)
MIDWEST MOLD & TEXTURE CORP
4270 Armstrong Blvd (45103-1670)
PHONE..................513 732-1300
Katsumi Kawaguchi, *President*
Yoji Tatematsu, *Chairman*
Jerry Boehm, *Manager*
Susumu Kitsuta, *Manager*
Mervin Senters, *Manager*
▲ **EMP**: 38
SQ FT: 20,000
SALES: 14.9MM
SALES (corp-wide): 43.4MM **Privately Held**
WEB: www.mmtcorp.com
SIC: 3544 Forms (molds), for foundry & plastics working machinery; industrial molds
PA: Tmw Co. Ltd.
 27-1, Okudaosawacho
 Inazawa AIC 492-8
 587 326-281

(G-1166)
MILACRON LLC
4165 Half Acre Rd (45103-3247)
PHONE..................513 536-2000
Tom Goeke, *CEO*
Dean Roberts, *President*
Ron Krisanda, *COO*
Thomas Brown, *Vice Pres*
Mark Dixon, *Vice Pres*
▲ **EMP**: 37
SALES (est): 6.8MM
SALES (corp-wide): 1.2B **Publicly Held**
SIC: 3089 Plastic processing
HQ: Milacron Llc
 10200 Alliance Rd Ste 200
 Blue Ash OH 45242

(G-1167)
MILACRON MARKETING COMPANY LLC (DH)
Also Called: Wear Technology
4165 Half Acre Rd (45103-3247)
PHONE..................513 536-2000
Tom Goeke, *CEO*
Brian Bish, *Vice Pres*
Robert C McKee, *Vice Pres*
Ben Waldman, *Engineer*
John Francy, *CFO*
◆ **EMP**: 39
SQ FT: 275,000
SALES (est): 928.4MM
SALES (corp-wide): 1.2B **Publicly Held**
SIC: 3541 Machine tools, metal cutting type

(G-1168)
MILACRON PLAS TECH GROUP LLC (DH)
4165 Half Acre Rd (45103-3247)
PHONE..................513 536-2000
Tom Goeke, *CEO*
Dave Lawrence, *President*
Ron Krisanda, *COO*
Mark Dixon, *Vice Pres*
Richard A Oleary, *Vice Pres*
▲ **EMP**: 156
SALES: 235.4MM
SALES (corp-wide): 1.2B **Publicly Held**
SIC: 3544 Forms (molds), for foundry & plastics working machinery

(G-1169)
MOO TECHNOLOGIES INC
950 Kent Rd (45103-1738)
PHONE..................513 732-5805
Frank Lauch, *Vice Pres*
EMP: 5
SALES (est): 405K **Privately Held**
SIC: 2023 Dry, condensed, evaporated dairy products

(G-1170)
MULTI-COLOR AUSTRALIA LLC
4053 Clough Woods Dr (45103-2587)
PHONE..................513 381-1480
Nigel A Vinecombe, *CEO*
Mary T Fetch, *Vice Pres*
Sharon E Birkett, *CFO*
EMP: 388
SALES (est): 13.6MM
SALES (corp-wide): 1.3B **Publicly Held**
SIC: 2754 2752 2759 Commercial printing, gravure; commercial printing, lithographic; advertising literature: printing; laser printing
PA: Multi-Color Corporation
 4053 Clough Woods Dr
 Batavia OH 45103
 513 381-1480

(G-1171)
MULTI-COLOR CORPORATION (PA)
4053 Clough Woods Dr (45103-2587)
PHONE..................513 381-1480
Nigel A Vinecombe, *Ch of Bd*
Michael J Henry, *President*
Sharon E Birkett, *CFO*
Hal Hunt, *Manager*
Rick Ball, *Director*
▲ **EMP**: 16
SQ FT: 277,730
SALES: 1.3B **Publicly Held**
WEB: www.multicolorcorp.com
SIC: 2759 2679 2672 Labels & seals: printing; labels, paper: made from purchased material; labels (unprinted); gummed: made from purchased materials

(G-1172)
MULTI-COLOR CORPORATION
4053 Clough Woods Dr (45103-2587)
PHONE..................513 943-0080
Ken Pizzuco, *Branch Mgr*
EMP: 60
SALES (corp-wide): 1.3B **Publicly Held**
WEB: www.multicolorcorp.com
SIC: 2759 2671 2754 Labels & seals: printing; packaging paper & plastics film, coated & laminated; commercial printing, gravure
PA: Multi-Color Corporation
 4053 Clough Woods Dr
 Batavia OH 45103
 513 381-1480

(G-1173)
NEWACT INC
2084 James E Sauls Sr Dr (45103-3259)
PHONE..................513 321-5177
Rodney J Newman, *President*
Ennes Ireton III, *Vice Pres*
Tom Vale, *VP Mktg*
EMP: 17
SQ FT: 16,000
SALES (est): 10.1MM **Privately Held**
WEB: www.newactinc.com
SIC: 5085 3643 3069 Industrial supplies; electric connectors; molded rubber products

(G-1174)
ON DISPLAY LTD
1250 Clough Pike (45103-2502)
PHONE..................513 841-1600
Dave Downey,
Donald Miller,
EMP: 20
SQ FT: 35,000
SALES (est): 4.5MM **Privately Held**
WEB: www.ondisplay.net
SIC: 3999 Advertising display products

(G-1175)
ORBIT MANUFACTURING INC
4291 Armstrong Blvd (45103-1697)
P.O. Box 144 (45103-0144)
PHONE..................513 732-6097
James S Paul, *President*
Kathy Paul, *Corp Secy*
EMP: 25
SQ FT: 10,000
SALES (est): 3.9MM **Privately Held**
WEB: www.orbitman.com
SIC: 3089 Injection molding of plastics; plastic processing

(G-1176)
PLASTIKOS CORPORATION
Also Called: Multi-Form Plastics
700 Kent Rd (45103-1704)
P.O. Box 138 (45103-0138)
PHONE..................513 732-0961
Richard Bates, *Chairman*
EMP: 22
SQ FT: 48,000
SALES (est): 4.4MM **Privately Held**
SIC: 3089 Thermoformed finished plastic products; injection molding of plastics

(G-1177)
POWER SOURCE SERVICE LLC
5400 Belle Meade Dr (45103-8549)
PHONE..................513 607-4555
Pamela K Silvers,
Richard Silvers,
EMP: 7
SQ FT: 5,000
SALES (est): 250K **Privately Held**
SIC: 3629 3646 Electronic generation equipment; commercial indusl & institutional electric lighting fixtures

(G-1178)
PRECISE PALLETS LLC
4211 Curliss Ln (45103-3221)
PHONE..................513 560-8236
David Eyles, *Principal*
EMP: 4
SALES (est): 289.9K **Privately Held**
SIC: 2448 Pallets, wood

(G-1179)
PROCOAT PAINTING INC
601 W Main St Unit B (45103-1705)
PHONE..................513 735-2500
Steve Hickey, *Principal*
EMP: 6 **EST**: 2014
SALES (est): 297.4K **Privately Held**
SIC: 1721 3479 Painting & paper hanging; painting of metal products

(G-1180)
ROCKWELL AUTOMATION INC
1195 Clough Pike (45103-2307)
PHONE..................513 943-1145
Fax: 513 943-7438
EMP: 20 **Publicly Held**
SIC: 3625 Mfg Relays/Industrial Controls
PA: Rockwell Automation, Inc.
 1201 S 2nd St
 Milwaukee WI 53204

(G-1181)
ROSS TMBER HARVSTG FOR MGT INC
5300 Rapp Ln (45103-9403)
PHONE..................513 383-6933
Earnie Ross III, *President*
EMP: 4
SALES (est): 215.1K **Privately Held**
SIC: 2411 Logging

(G-1182)
S & K METAL POLSG & BUFFING
4194 Taylor Rd (45103-9736)
PHONE..................513 732-6662
Aldena Sons, *President*
Everett J Sons, *Vice Pres*
EMP: 7 **EST**: 1971
SQ FT: 17,500
SALES (est): 739.9K **Privately Held**
SIC: 3471 Buffing for the trade; polishing, metals or formed products; finishing, metals or formed products

(G-1183)
SAVOR SEASONINGS LLC
4292 Armstrong Blvd (45103-1600)
PHONE..................513 732-2333
Jeff Higgins,
Shelly Higgins,
EMP: 5
SQ FT: 10,000
SALES (est): 709.9K **Privately Held**
SIC: 2099 Seasonings & spices

(G-1184)
SMOOTHIE-LICIOUS
1325 Quail Ridge Rd (45103-9537)
PHONE..................513 742-2260
Chris Zerhusen, *Administration*
EMP: 3
SALES (est): 132.8K **Privately Held**
SIC: 2037 Frozen fruits & vegetables

(G-1185)
SOUTHERN OHIO MFG INC
1147 Clough Pike (45103-2307)
PHONE..................513 943-2555
Dave Rechtin, *President*
EMP: 21
SQ FT: 13,500
SALES (est): 1.5MM **Privately Held**
WEB: www.sommfginc.com
SIC: 3599 Machine shop, jobbing & repair

(G-1186)
SPECTRA-TECH MANUFACTURING INC
4013 Borman Dr (45103-1684)
PHONE..................513 735-9300
Scott Reilman, *President*
Jason Jasper, *Vice Pres*
Shirley Reilman, *Vice Pres*
Craig Wilson, *Vice Pres*
▲ **EMP**: 47
SQ FT: 18,000
SALES (est): 21.4MM **Privately Held**
WEB: www.spectratechmfg.com
SIC: 3613 Panelboards & distribution boards, electric

(G-1187)
STRAIGHT CREEK BUSHMAN LLC
202 E Main St (45103-2905)
PHONE..................513 732-1698
Robert Stearns, *Principal*
EMP: 3 **EST**: 2013
SALES (est): 161.3K **Privately Held**
SIC: 1221 Bituminous coal & lignite-surface mining

(G-1188)
SUPERIOR STEEL SERVICE LLC
2760 Old State Route 32 (45103-3210)
PHONE..................513 724-0437
Jeffrey A Brewsaugh, *Mng Member*
EMP: 15
SQ FT: 12,000
SALES (est): 3.6MM **Privately Held**
SIC: 3449 Bars, concrete reinforcing: fabricated steel

(G-1189)
TEN DOGS GLOBAL INDUSTRIES LLC
4400 Glen Willow Lake Ln (45103-2320)
PHONE..................513 752-9000
Andrew J Pike,
Jean Brown,
Richard D Porco,
EMP: 100
SALES (est): 10MM **Privately Held**
SIC: 3585 Refrigeration & heating equipment

(G-1190)
TIPTON ENVIRONMENTAL INTL INC
4446 State Route 132 (45103-1229)
PHONE..................513 735-2777
Fred Tipton, *President*
Scott Tipton, *Vice Pres*
EMP: 10
SQ FT: 3,600
SALES: 4MM **Privately Held**
WEB: www.tiptonenv.com
SIC: 3589 Water treatment equipment, industrial

(G-1191)
TSP INC
2009 Glenn Pkwy (45103-1676)
PHONE..................513 732-8900
J Stuart Newman, *President*
EMP: 25
SQ FT: 30,000

(PA)=Parent Co (HQ)=Headquarters (DH)=Div Headquarters
✿ = New Business established in last 2 years

2019 Harris Ohio Industrial Directory

Batavia - Clermont County (G-1192)

SALES (est): 16.2MM **Privately Held**
WEB: www.tspinc.com
SIC: **3479** 3089 3081 Painting, coating & hot dipping; windows, plastic; thermo-formed finished plastic products; lenses, except optical: plastic; plastic film & sheet

(G-1192)
UNILOY MILACRON INC
4165 Half Acre Rd (45103-3247)
PHONE 513 487-5000
John C Francy, *President*
Ron ABT, *Engineer*
Dave Esposito, *Electrical Engi*
Tim Goertemiller, *Sales Dir*
Catherine Butcher, *Marketing Staff*
◆ EMP: 42
SALES (est): 10.6MM
SALES (corp-wide): 1.2B **Publicly Held**
SIC: **2821** Plastics materials & resins
HQ: Milacron Llc
  10200 Alliance Rd Ste 200
  Blue Ash OH 45242

(G-1193)
UNIVERSAL PACKG SYSTEMS INC
Also Called: Paklab
5055 State Route 276 (45103-1211)
PHONE 513 732-2000
Richard Burton, *Branch Mgr*
EMP: 388
SALES (corp-wide): 399.6MM **Privately Held**
SIC: **2844** 7389 3565 2671 Cosmetic preparations; packaging & labeling services; bottling machinery: filling, capping, labeling; plastic film, coated or laminated for packaging
PA: Universal Packaging Systems, Inc.
  380 Townline Rd Ste 130
  Hauppauge NY 11788
  631 543-2277

(G-1194)
UNIVERSAL PACKG SYSTEMS INC
5069 State Route 276 (45103-1211)
PHONE 513 735-4777
Rick Zellen, *Site Mgr*
EMP: 40
SALES (corp-wide): 423.8MM **Privately Held**
SIC: **2844** 7389 3565 2671 Cosmetic preparations; packaging & labeling services; bottling machinery: filling, capping, labeling; plastic film, coated or laminated for packaging
PA: Universal Packaging Systems, Inc.
  380 Townline Rd Ste 130
  Hauppauge NY 11788
  631 543-2277

(G-1195)
VERSTRAETE IN MOLD LAB
Also Called: Multi-Color
4101 Founders Blvd (45103-3616)
PHONE 513 943-0080
Mike Henry, *President*
Sharon Birkett, *CFO*
EMP: 15
SQ FT: 115,000
SALES (est): 469.5K
SALES (corp-wide): 1.3B **Publicly Held**
SIC: **2759** 2679 Labels & seals: printing; labels, paper: made from purchased material
PA: Multi-Color Corporation
  4053 Clough Woods Dr
  Batavia OH 45103
  513 381-1480

(G-1196)
WHITEWATER FOREST PRODUCTS LLC
Also Called: White Water Forest
2720 Moraine Way (45103-3201)
P.O. Box 429 (45103-0429)
PHONE 513 673-7596
Dan Shiels, *Mng Member*
EMP: 4
SQ FT: 60,000
SALES (est): 101.1K **Privately Held**
SIC: **2421** Sawmills & planing mills, general

(G-1197)
WILSON SEAT COMPANY INC
199 Foundry Ave (45103-2606)
P.O. Box 323 (45103-0323)
PHONE 513 732-2460
Michael A Wilson, *President*
Mark Wilson, *Vice Pres*
EMP: 25 EST: 1961
SQ FT: 33,000
SALES (est): 4MM **Privately Held**
SIC: **3713** 3993 Truck bodies & parts; signs, not made in custom sign painting shops

(G-1198)
X-TREME SHOOTING PRODUCTS LLC
2008 Glenn Pkwy (45103-1620)
P.O. Box 829, Milford (45150-0829)
PHONE 513 313-3464
C Thomas Myers, *President*
EMP: 5
SALES (est): 200K **Privately Held**
SIC: **3484** Guns (firearms) or gun parts, 30 mm. & below

(G-1199)
XOMOX CORPORATION
4576 Helmsdale Ct (45103-4000)
PHONE 513 947-1200
J T Williams, *Branch Mgr*
EMP: 25
SALES (corp-wide): 3.3B **Publicly Held**
SIC: **3491** Industrial valves
HQ: Xomox Corporation
  4526 Res Frest Dr Ste 400
  The Woodlands TX 77381
  936 271-6500

Bath
Summit County

(G-1200)
ETS SOLUTIONS USA LLC
3900 Ira Rd (44210)
PHONE 330 666-8696
James H Rothwell, *President*
Mark Davey, *Principal*
Jim H Rothwell, *Principal*
Karen Parker, *Info Tech Mgr*
▲ EMP: 5
SALES (est): 75.4K **Privately Held**
SIC: **3829** Measuring & controlling devices

(G-1201)
LUND EQUIPMENT CO INC
2400 N Clvlnd Mssllon Rd (44210)
P.O. Box 213 (44210-0213)
PHONE 330 659-4800
John Skeel, *President*
Rebecca Skeel, *Regional Mgr*
Raymond Smiley, *Vice Pres*
EMP: 20
SQ FT: 5,000
SALES (est): 3.2MM **Privately Held**
WEB: www.lundkeycab.com
SIC: **3444** Sheet metalwork

(G-1202)
MOLLARD CONDUCTING BATONS INC
Also Called: Lancio
2236 N Clvlnd Mssllon Rd (44210)
P.O. Box 178 (44210-0178)
PHONE 330 659-7081
Robert Mollard, *President*
EMP: 13
SALES (est): 654.5K **Privately Held**
SIC: **2499** Carved & turned wood

(G-1203)
WARMUS AND ASSOCIATES INC
Also Called: Smith Carl E Cnslting Engneers
2324 N Clvlnd Mssllon Rd (44210)
PHONE 330 659-4440
Alfred T Warmus, *President*
Roy P Stype III, *Vice Pres*
Brain Warmus, *Admin Sec*
EMP: 17
SQ FT: 7,000
SALES (est): 2.2MM **Privately Held**
SIC: **8711** 3441 5063 Consulting engineer; tower sections, radio & television transmission; electrical apparatus & equipment

Bay Village
Cuyahoga County

(G-1204)
ACOUSTICAL PUBLICATIONS INC
Also Called: Sound and Vibration
27101 E Oviatt Rd (44140-3307)
P.O. Box 40416 (44140-0416)
PHONE 440 835-0101
Jack K Mowry, *President*
Lois Mowry, *Corp Secy*
EMP: 5 EST: 1966
SQ FT: 900
SALES (est): 732.1K **Privately Held**
SIC: **2721** Magazines: publishing only, not printed on site

(G-1205)
BAY WEST PRODUCTS
31008 Walker Rd (44140-1405)
PHONE 440 835-1991
Wayne Smith, *Owner*
EMP: 5 EST: 1978
SQ FT: 3,200
SALES (est): 290K **Privately Held**
SIC: **3599** Machine shop, jobbing & repair

(G-1206)
CONCENTRIC CORPORATION
27101 E Oviatt Rd Ste 8 (44140-3301)
PHONE 440 899-9090
Marc R Klecka, *President*
Matt Klecka, *Vice Pres*
Rick Klecka, *Parts Mgr*
EMP: 10
SALES (est): 1.8MM **Privately Held**
WEB: www.citizenmachines.com
SIC: **3599** Machine shop, jobbing & repair

(G-1207)
RANIR DCP
4701 E Paris (44140)
PHONE 616 698-8880
Rich Sorota, *Principal*
EMP: 3
SALES (est): 308.8K **Privately Held**
SIC: **2834** Pharmaceutical preparations

(G-1208)
RESERVE INDUSTRIES INC
386 Lake Park Dr (44140-2963)
PHONE 440 871-2796
John Megyimori, *President*
John Ruminsky, *Vice Pres*
EMP: 32
SQ FT: 26,000
SALES (est): 3.8MM **Privately Held**
SIC: **3089** 3544 Injection molding of plastics; special dies & tools

(G-1209)
ROBERT TUNEBERG
Also Called: Villager Newspaper, The
27016 Knickerbocker Rd # 1 (44140-2386)
PHONE 440 899-9277
Robert Tuneberg, *Owner*
EMP: 4
SALES (est): 190K **Privately Held**
SIC: **2711** Newspapers, publishing & printing

(G-1210)
SWEET MOBILE CUPCAKERY
428 Walmar Rd (44140-1518)
PHONE 440 465-7333
EMP: 3
SALES (est): 94.5K **Privately Held**
SIC: **2051** Bread, cake & related products

Beach City
Stark County

(G-1211)
DANIEL MEENAN
Also Called: Corell's Potato Chips
614 Pine St Nw (44608-9580)
P.O. Box 255 (44608-0255)
PHONE 330 756-2818
Dan Meenan, *Owner*
EMP: 5 EST: 1939
SQ FT: 4,000
SALES: 300K **Privately Held**
SIC: **2096** 2099 Potato chips & other potato-based snacks; food preparations

(G-1212)
MERIDIAN INDUSTRIES INC
Also Called: Kleen Test Products
9901 Chestnut Ridge Rd Nw (44608-9417)
PHONE 330 359-5809
Peter Morton, *Manager*
EMP: 50
SQ FT: 15,000
SALES (corp-wide): 379.3MM **Privately Held**
WEB: www.meridiancompanies.com
SIC: **2299** 2844 Pads, fiber: henequen, sisal, istle; toilet preparations
PA: Meridian Industries, Inc.
  735 N Water St Ste 630
  Milwaukee WI 53202
  414 224-0610

(G-1213)
MILLER CORE 2 INC
9823 Chestnut Ridge Rd Nw (44608-9480)
PHONE 330 359-0500
Joseph Miller, *President*
Reuben Miller, *Vice Pres*
Sue Duffield, *Office Mgr*
Linda Miller, *Admin Sec*
EMP: 8
SALES (est): 1.2MM **Privately Held**
SIC: **3567** Core baking & mold drying ovens

(G-1214)
PROGRESSIVE FOAM TECH INC
6753 Chestnut Ridge Rd Nw (44608-9464)
PHONE 330 756-3200
Patrick Culpepper, *President*
Richard Wilson, *Vice Pres*
Bryan Groff, *Plant Mgr*
Kenny Albrecht, *Prdtn Mgr*
Scott Foreman, *Mfg Staff*
▲ EMP: 120
SQ FT: 100,000
SALES (est): 31.3MM **Privately Held**
WEB: www.fullback.com
SIC: **2821** Polystyrene resins

(G-1215)
STARK TRUSS COMPANY INC
Also Called: Stark Truss Beach City Lumber
6855 Chestnut Ridge Rd Nw (44608-9462)
PHONE 330 756-3050
Jay Dickey, *Branch Mgr*
EMP: 32
SALES (corp-wide): 186.7MM **Privately Held**
WEB: www.starktruss.com
SIC: **2439** 2421 Trusses, wooden roof; sawmills & planing mills, general
PA: Stark Truss Company, Inc.
  109 Miles Ave Sw
  Canton OH 44710
  330 478-2100

Beachwood
Cuyahoga County

(G-1216)
6062 HOLDINGS LLC
Also Called: Sure To Grow
23366 Commerce Park 100b (44122-5850)
PHONE 216 359-9005
Eric Senders, *Mng Member*
Cary Senders,
EMP: 3

GEOGRAPHIC SECTION
Beachwood - Cuyahoga County (G-1244)

SALES (est): 296.5K **Privately Held**
SIC: 3295 Minerals, ground or treated

(G-1217)
ABB INC
23000 Harvard Rd (44122-7234)
PHONE.....................440 585-8500
Steve Hawkins, *Principal*
EMP: 5
SALES (corp-wide): 34.3B **Privately Held**
WEB: www.elsterelectricity.com
SIC: 3823 Industrial instrmnts msrmnt display/control process variable
HQ: Abb Inc.
   305 Gregson Dr
   Cary NC 27511

(G-1218)
ALERIS INTERNATIONAL INC (HQ)
25825 Science Park Dr # 400 (44122-7392)
PHONE.....................216 910-3400
Sean M Stack, *CEO*
Christopher R Clegg, *Exec VP*
Steven A Faas, *Senior VP*
Eric M Rychel, *CFO*
Stephen Stone, *Marketing Staff*
▲ EMP: 225
SQ FT: 43,000
SALES (est): 1.3B **Privately Held**
SIC: 3355 Bars, rolled, aluminum

(G-1219)
ALERIS RECYCLING INC
25825 Science Park Dr # 400 (44122-7392)
PHONE.....................216 910-3400
EMP: 3
SALES (est): 147.1K **Privately Held**
SIC: 3554 Mfg Paper Industrial Machinery

(G-1220)
ALERIS RM INC
25825 Science Park Dr # 400 (44122-7323)
PHONE.....................216 910-3400
EMP: 238
SALES (est): 163K **Privately Held**
SIC: 3355 Aluminum rolling & drawing
PA: Aleris Corporation
   25825 Science Park Dr # 400
   Cleveland OH 44122

(G-1221)
ALERIS ROLLED PRODUCTS INC (DH)
25825 Science Park Dr # 400 (44122-7323)
PHONE.....................216 910-3400
Sean M Stack, *CEO*
EMP: 300 EST: 2010
SALES (est): 511.6MM **Privately Held**
SIC: 3341 Secondary nonferrous metals

(G-1222)
ALEX AND ANI LLC
26300 Cedar Rd Ste 1120 (44122-1184)
PHONE.....................216 378-2139
EMP: 5 **Privately Held**
SIC: 3915 Jewelers' materials & lapidary work
PA: Alex And Ani, Llc
   2000 Chapel View Blvd # 360
   Cranston RI 02920

(G-1223)
AMPERSAND INTERNATIONAL INC
23775 Commerce Park (44122-5836)
PHONE.....................216 831-3500
Ilya Vetrov, *President*
EMP: 4
SALES (est): 592.3K **Privately Held**
WEB: www.ampersand-intl.com
SIC: 7372 Prepackaged software

(G-1224)
AUFBACKGROUNDSCREENING COM
26101 Village Ln (44122-8522)
PHONE.....................216 831-4113
Marvin Goldfarb, *Principal*
EMP: 4 EST: 2010

SALES (est): 159.4K **Privately Held**
SIC: 2899

(G-1225)
BIP PRINTING SOLUTIONS LLC
24755 Highpoint Rd Ste 1 (44122-6050)
PHONE.....................216 832-5673
Nancy McGraw, *President*
EMP: 10
SQ FT: 13,000
SALES (est): 831.4K **Privately Held**
SIC: 2732 2789 Books: printing & binding; pamphlets: printing & binding, not published on site; trade binding services

(G-1226)
CIPAR INC (HQ)
3601 Green Rd Ste 308 (44122-5719)
PHONE.....................216 910-1700
Morris Wheeler, *President*
EMP: 4
SALES (est): 420.7K **Privately Held**
SIC: 3563 Spraying & dusting equipment

(G-1227)
CLEVELAND JEWISH PUBL CO FDN
23800 Commerce Park (44122-5828)
PHONE.....................216 454-8300
Barry Chesler, *Principal*
EMP: 3
SALES (est): 40.9K **Privately Held**
SIC: 2711 Newspapers: publishing only, not printed on site

(G-1228)
COHESANT INC (PA)
3601 Green Rd Ste 308 (44122-5719)
PHONE.....................216 910-1700
Morton A Cohen, *Ch of Bd*
Morris H Wheeler, *President*
J Stewart Nance, *President*
David Dunn, *Opers Staff*
Robert W Pawlak, *CFO*
EMP: 45
SALES (est): 20.9MM **Privately Held**
WEB: www.cohesant.com
SIC: 3563 3559 3586 Spraying outfits: metals, paints & chemicals (compressor); paint making machinery; measuring & dispensing pumps

(G-1229)
COMMONWEALTH ALUMINUM MTLS LLC
25825 Science Park Dr # 400 (44122-7323)
PHONE.....................216 910-3400
EMP: 5
SALES (est): 1MM **Privately Held**
SIC: 3555 Printing trades machinery

(G-1230)
CONCEPT XXI INC
23600 Merc Rd Ste 101 (44122)
PHONE.....................216 831-2121
Irving Kaplan, *President*
Irving Sayers, *Info Tech Dir*
Jaime Rogers, *Director*
EMP: 18
SQ FT: 2,000
SALES (est): 1.2MM **Privately Held**
WEB: www.cxxi.com
SIC: 7379 7372 Computer related consulting services; prepackaged software

(G-1231)
CORCADENCE INC
26701 Bernwood Rd (44122-7135)
PHONE.....................216 702-6371
Eugene Jung, *Principal*
Subbakrishna Shankar, *COO*
EMP: 3
SALES (est): 271.6K **Privately Held**
SIC: 3829 7389 Thermometers, including digital; clinical;

(G-1232)
DIALOGUE HOUSE ASSOCIATES INC
23400 Mercantile Rd Ste 2 (44122-5948)
PHONE.....................216 342-5170
Jonathan Progoff, *President*
Jonathan Progoff, *Director*
EMP: 4

SQ FT: 1,200
SALES: 175K **Privately Held**
WEB: www.intensivejournal.org
SIC: 8299 2731 Personal development school; religious school; books: publishing only

(G-1233)
EATON CORPORATION
Also Called: Fluid Power Plant
1000 Eaton Blvd (44122-6058)
PHONE.....................440 523-5000
Ali Vakili, *District Mgr*
Ram Ramakrishnan, *Senior VP*
Alberto Garcia, *Vice Pres*
Scott Hughes, *Project Mgr*
Daniel Kalka, *Project Mgr*
EMP: 500 **Privately Held**
WEB: www.eaton.com
SIC: 3714 3824 Motor vehicle electrical equipment; mechanical & electromechanical counters & devices
HQ: Eaton Corporation
   1000 Eaton Blvd
   Cleveland OH 44122
   440 523-5000

(G-1234)
EATON CORPORATION
Eastlake Office
1000 Eaton Blvd (44122-6058)
PHONE.....................216 523-5000
Manuel Prieto, *Project Mgr*
Keith Cozart, *Purch Mgr*
Bernie Beier, *Engineer*
Sell Craig, *Engineer*
Doug Koch, *Manager*
EMP: 260 **Privately Held**
WEB: www.eaton.com
SIC: 3714 5084 Hydraulic fluid power pumps for auto steering mechanism; hydraulic systems equipment & supplies
HQ: Eaton Corporation
   1000 Eaton Blvd
   Cleveland OH 44122
   440 523-5000

(G-1235)
EATON LEASING CORPORATION (DH)
1000 Eaton Blvd (44122-6058)
PHONE.....................216 382-2292
Richard Fearon, *President*
Lisa Trombo, *Principal*
Billie Rawot, *Vice Pres*
EMP: 9
SQ FT: 1,200
SALES (est): 10.1MM **Privately Held**
SIC: 7359 3612 3594 3593 Equipment rental & leasing; transformers, except electric; fluid power pumps & motors; fluid power cylinders & actuators; speed changers, drives & gears; turbines & turbine generator sets
HQ: Eaton Corporation
   1000 Eaton Blvd
   Cleveland OH 44122
   440 523-5000

(G-1236)
ENVISION RADIO MII
3733 Park East Dr Ste 222 (44122-4334)
PHONE.....................216 831-3761
Danno Wolkoss, *Owner*
Gary James, *Manager*
Ryan Verardi, *Manager*
EMP: 12
SALES (est): 1.5MM **Privately Held**
WEB: www.envisionradio.com
SIC: 3663 Radio receiver networks

(G-1237)
ETS SCHAEFER LLC (DH)
3700 Park East Dr Ste 300 (44122-4399)
PHONE.....................330 468-6600
Terrance Hogan, *CEO*
Michael Hobey, *CFO*
EMP: 5
SALES (est): 3.1MM
SALES (corp-wide): 78MM **Privately Held**
SIC: 3297 3433 Nonclay refractories; heating equipment, except electric

HQ: Real Alloy Recycling, Llc
   3700 Park East Dr Ste 300
   Beachwood OH 44122
   216 755-8900

(G-1238)
EUCLID CHEMICAL COMPANY
3735 Green Rd (44122-5705)
PHONE.....................216 292-5000
Moorman L Scott Jr, *President*
EMP: 10
SALES (corp-wide): 5.3B **Publicly Held**
SIC: 2899 Chemical preparations
HQ: The Euclid Chemical Company
   19218 Redwood Rd
   Cleveland OH 44110
   800 321-7628

(G-1239)
GENERAL ENVIRONMENTAL SCIENCE
3659 Green Rd Ste 306 (44122-5715)
PHONE.....................216 464-0680
Barton Gilbert, *President*
Elaine Gilbert, *Vice Pres*
EMP: 8
SALES (est): 166.4K **Privately Held**
SIC: 2836 Bacteriological media

(G-1240)
HELIX LINEAR TECHNOLOGIES INC
23200 Commerce Park (44122-5802)
PHONE.....................216 485-2263
Jaseph Nook, *Principal*
EMP: 35
SALES (est): 8MM **Privately Held**
SIC: 3451 3549 Screw machine products; screw driving machines

(G-1241)
INDUSTRIAL TIMBER & LUMBER CO
23925 Commerce Park (44122-5821)
PHONE.....................800 829-9663
Larry Evans, *President*
EMP: 5
SALES (est): 479.3K **Privately Held**
SIC: 2421 Sawmills & planing mills, general

(G-1242)
ITL LLC
Also Called: Industrial Timber and Lbr LLC
23925 Commerce Park (44122-5821)
PHONE.....................216 831-3140
Larry Evans,
Rich Craxton, *Administration*
EMP: 325
SALES (est): 10.1MM **Privately Held**
SIC: 2426 Lumber, hardwood dimension
HQ: Northwest Hardwoods, Inc.
   1313 Broadway Ste 300
   Tacoma WA 98402

(G-1243)
JMC STEEL GROUP
3201 Entp Pkwy Ste 150 (44122)
PHONE.....................216 910-3700
Frank A Riddick III, *CEO*
Barry Zekelman, *CEO*
David W Seeger, *President*
Michael P McNamara Jr, *Vice Pres*
John C Higgins, *Opers Staff*
EMP: 31 EST: 2010
SALES (est): 15.4MM **Privately Held**
SIC: 3317 Steel pipe & tubes

(G-1244)
KIRTLAND CAPITAL PARTNERS LP (PA)
Also Called: K C P
3201 Entp Pkwy Ste 200 (44122)
PHONE.....................216 593-0100
Corrie Menary, *Partner*
John Nestor, *Principal*
◆ EMP: 23
SQ FT: 4,031
SALES (est): 119.6MM **Privately Held**
SIC: 5051 3312 3498 3494 Metals service centers & offices; tubes, steel & iron; fabricated pipe & fittings; valves & pipe fittings; fluid power valves & hose fittings; steel pipe & tubes

Beachwood - Cuyahoga County (G-1245)

(G-1245)
LASTING IMPRESSION DIRECT
23500 Mercantile Rd (44122-5930)
PHONE..................................216 464-1960
EMP: 4
SALES (est): 360.4K Privately Held
SIC: 2752 Commercial printing, offset

(G-1246)
MAKERGEAR LLC
23632 Merc Rd Unit G (44122)
PHONE..................................216 765-0030
Richard Pollack, Mng Member
▲ EMP: 25
SALES (est): 2.8MM Privately Held
SIC: 3999 Education aids, devices & supplies

(G-1247)
MASTER BUILDERS LLC (DH)
Also Called: Degussa Construction
23700 Chagrin Blvd (44122-5506)
PHONE..................................216 831-5500
John Salvatore, President
Michael Pelsozy, Research
Donald Kehr, Treasurer
◆ EMP: 50
SALES (est): 336.8MM
SALES (corp-wide): 71.7B Privately Held
WEB: www.basf-admixtures.com
SIC: 2899 2851 1799 Concrete curing & hardening compounds; epoxy coatings; caulking (construction)
HQ: Basf Corporation
   100 Park Ave
   Florham Park NJ 07932
   973 245-6000

(G-1248)
MILES PK VNTIAN BLIND SHDS MFG
Also Called: Miles Park Window Treatments
23880 Commerce Park # 100 (44122-5830)
PHONE..................................216 239-0850
Robert M Bernstein, President
Bonnie Bernstein, Treasurer
EMP: 3 EST: 1936
SQ FT: 4,000
SALES (est): 454.6K Privately Held
SIC: 2591 5719 7699 Venetian blinds; window shades; venetian blinds; window shades; venetian blind repair shop

(G-1249)
MILICOM LLC
23307 Commerce Park (44122-5810)
PHONE..................................216 765-8875
Jason Banera, Director
James Harris,
EMP: 5
SALES (est): 500K Privately Held
SIC: 3669 Intercommunication systems, electric

(G-1250)
MIM SOFTWARE INC (PA)
25800 Science Park Dr # 180 (44122-7339)
PHONE..................................216 896-9798
Dennis Nelson, President
Peter Simmelink, General Mgr
Pete Zimmelink, COO
Kelly Mastromonaco, Vice Pres
Aaron Greene, Opers Staff
EMP: 49
SALES (est): 16.3MM Privately Held
WEB: www.mimvista.com
SIC: 7372 Application computer software

(G-1251)
MK GLOBAL ENTERPRISES LLC
23980 Chagrin Blvd # 204 (44122-5548)
PHONE..................................440 823-0081
Michael Krasnyansky,
EMP: 4
SQ FT: 2,000
SALES (est): 309.3K Privately Held
SIC: 3541 Machine tool replacement & repair parts, metal cutting types

(G-1252)
NATIONAL BIOLOGICAL CORP
23700 Mercantile Rd (44122-5900)
PHONE..................................216 831-0600
Kenneth Oif, President
Michael Kaufman, Vice Pres
David Richmond, Opers Mgr
Kathy Puskar, Buyer
Patti Palmer, Controller
▲ EMP: 50
SQ FT: 36,000
SALES (est): 9.3MM Privately Held
WEB: www.natbiocorp.com
SIC: 3841 3648 Surgical & medical instruments; ultraviolet lamp fixtures

(G-1253)
NICHOLS ALUMINUM-ALABAMA LLC
25825 Science Park Dr # 400 (44122-7392)
PHONE..................................256 353-1550
Sean M Stack, CEO
EMP: 130
SALES (est): 18.9MM Privately Held
SIC: 3353 Aluminum sheet, plate & foil
HQ: Uwa Acquisition Co.
   397 Black Hollow Rd
   Rockwood TN 37854
   865 354-3626

(G-1254)
NOVACARE INC
24400 Highpoint Rd Ste 10 (44122-6027)
PHONE..................................216 704-4817
George Shamp, President
Margaret Shamp, Vice Pres
EMP: 3
SQ FT: 4,800
SALES (est): 270K Privately Held
SIC: 3842 5999 7991 Limbs, artificial; artificial limbs; physical fitness facilities

(G-1255)
OHIO CLLBRTIVE LRNG SLTONS INC (PA)
Also Called: Smart Solutions
24700 Chagrin Blvd # 104 (44122-5647)
PHONE..................................216 595-5289
Anand Julka, President
Frank Hanis, Purchasing
Stephanie Green, Accountant
Ray Baumiller, Comp Tech
EMP: 50
SQ FT: 6,000
SALES (est): 15MM Privately Held
WEB: www.smartsolutionsonline.com
SIC: 7372 8741 Business oriented computer software; business management

(G-1256)
OLD RAR INC (PA)
3700 Park East Dr Ste 300 (44122-4399)
PHONE..................................216 910-3400
Terry Hogan, President
Michael Hobey, CFO
EMP: 20
SQ FT: 7,000
SALES (est): 273.3MM Privately Held
SIC: 3341 Secondary nonferrous metals

(G-1257)
OMNOVA SOLUTIONS INC (PA)
25435 Harvard Rd (44122-6201)
PHONE..................................216 682-7000
William R Seelbach, Ch of Bd
Anne P Noonan, President
James C Lemay, Senior VP
Marshall D Moore, Senior VP
Andy Steranka, Project Engr
EMP: 140 EST: 1952
SALES: 769.8MM Publicly Held
WEB: www.omnova.com
SIC: 2819 2211 3069 3081 Industrial inorganic chemicals; decorative trim & specialty fabrics, including twist weave; roofing, membrane rubber; unsupported plastics film & sheet; plastic film & sheet; vinyl film & sheet

(G-1258)
OMNOVA WALLCOVERING USA INC (HQ)
25435 Harvard Rd (44122-6201)
PHONE..................................216 682-7000
Kevin Mc Mullin, CEO
Jonathan Pollock, Production
EMP: 4
SALES (est): 5MM
SALES (corp-wide): 769.8MM Publicly Held
SIC: 2819 Industrial inorganic chemicals
PA: Omnova Solutions Inc.
   25435 Harvard Rd
   Beachwood OH 44122
   216 682-7000

(G-1259)
ONE WISH LLC
Also Called: Audimute Soundproofing & Medic
23945 Mercantile Rd Ste H (44122-5924)
PHONE..................................800 505-6883
Mitchell Zlotnik,
Amy Zlotnik,
EMP: 18
SALES (est): 4MM Privately Held
WEB: www.medicbatteries.com
SIC: 5063 5999 8742 1742 Batteries; batteries, non-automotive; marketing consulting services; acoustical & insulation work; acoustical & ceiling work; building materials, except block or brick; concrete; acoustical suspension systems, metal

(G-1260)
ORACLE AMERICA INC
Also Called: Sun Microsystems
3333 Richmond Rd Ste 420 (44122-4198)
PHONE..................................513 381-0125
Joe Otto, Manager
EMP: 15
SALES (corp-wide): 39.8B Publicly Held
SIC: 7372 Prepackaged software
HQ: Oracle America, Inc.
   500 Oracle Pkwy
   Redwood City CA 94065
   650 506-7000

(G-1261)
ORACLE CORPORATION
3333 Richmond Rd Ste 420 (44122-4198)
PHONE..................................513 826-6000
Andrea Klein, Manager
Shekar Ramanathan, Consultant
Katrina Hardwick, Admin Asst
Jeff Dean, Sr Consultant
Jeff Campbell, Fellow
EMP: 4
SALES (corp-wide): 39.8B Publicly Held
WEB: www.oracle.com
SIC: 7372 Prepackaged software
PA: Oracle Corporation
   500 Oracle Pkwy
   Redwood City CA 94065
   650 506-7000

(G-1262)
ORACLE SYSTEMS CORPORATION
3333 Richmond Rd Ste 420 (44122-4198)
PHONE..................................513 826-6000
Carol Beebe, Manager
EMP: 50
SALES (corp-wide): 39.8B Publicly Held
WEB: www.forcecapital.com
SIC: 7372 Prepackaged software
HQ: Oracle Systems Corporation
   500 Oracle Pkwy
   Redwood City CA 94065
   650 506-7000

(G-1263)
PCC AIRFOILS LLC
25201 Chagrin Blvd # 290 (44122-5633)
PHONE..................................216 766-6206
Todd Kestranek, Facilities Mgr
Sharon Czeck, Purch Mgr
Bruno Durigon, Purch Mgr
Lynn Connell, Purchasing
Anthony Vecchio, Engineer
EMP: 14 EST: 2017
SALES (est): 786.8K Privately Held
SIC: 3369 Nonferrous foundries

(G-1264)
PEARLWIND LLC
Also Called: Pearl Lighting
24800 Chagrin Blvd # 101 (44122-5648)
PHONE..................................216 591-9463
Jonathan Kaplan, Mng Member
EMP: 5
SALES: 2MM Privately Held
SIC: 3646 1731 Commercial indusl & institutional electric lighting fixtures; lighting contractor

(G-1265)
PFIZER INC
2000 Auburn Dr Ste 200 (44122-4328)
PHONE..................................216 591-0642
Andrea Maxwell, Branch Mgr
Denise Knecht, Regional
EMP: 60
SALES (corp-wide): 53.6B Publicly Held
WEB: www.pfizer.com
SIC: 2834 Pharmaceutical preparations
PA: Pfizer Inc.
   235 E 42nd St
   New York NY 10017
   212 733-2323

(G-1266)
POWERTECH INC
25805 Frmunt Blvd Apt 203 (44122)
PHONE..................................901 850-9393
Danny Holmes, President
Barbara Gross, Exec VP
◆ EMP: 12 EST: 1999
SQ FT: 10,000
SALES (est): 1.7MM Privately Held
WEB: www.powertechinc.com
SIC: 3648 Flashlights

(G-1267)
PREMIER METAL TRADING LLC (PA)
26949 Chagrin Blvd # 306 (44122-4230)
PHONE..................................440 247-9494
David Glassman, Director
EMP: 3
SALES (est): 2.7MM Privately Held
SIC: 5051 3312 Ferrous metals; nonferrous metal sheets, bars, rods, etc.; sheets, metal; stainless steel

(G-1268)
PRESQUE ISLE ORTHOTICS
Also Called: Presque Isle Medical Tech
2101 Richmond Rd Ste 1000 (44122-1390)
PHONE..................................216 371-0660
Solomon Heifetz, COO
EMP: 5
SQ FT: 1,200
SALES: 1.2MM Privately Held
SIC: 8011 5999 3842 Primary care medical clinic; orthopedic physician; orthopedic & prosthesis applications; prosthetic appliances

(G-1269)
PRIME CONDUIT INC (PA)
23240 Chagrin Blvd # 405 (44122-5468)
P.O. Box 22897 (44122-0897)
PHONE..................................216 464-3400
Jim Abel, President
James Rajecki, General Mgr
John Lomoro, Vice Pres
Renee Bruno, Export Mgr
Lisa Denham, Buyer
◆ EMP: 18
SALES (est): 13.1MM Privately Held
SIC: 2821 3312 Polyvinyl chloride resins (PVC); pipes & tubes

(G-1270)
REAL ALLOY HOLDING LLC (PA)
3700 Park East Dr Ste 300 (44122-4399)
PHONE..................................216 755-8900
Terry Hogan, President
EMP: 1
SQ FT: 7,000
SALES (est): 78MM Privately Held
SIC: 6719 3341 Investment holding companies, except banks; secondary nonferrous metals

(G-1271)
REAL ALLOY RECYCLING LLC
3700 Park East Dr Ste 100 (44122-4339)
PHONE..................................346 444-8540
Daniel Rangel, Branch Mgr
EMP: 25

GEOGRAPHIC SECTION

Beavercreek - Greene County (G-1298)

SALES (corp-wide): 85.8MM **Privately Held**
SIC: 3341 Secondary nonferrous metals
HQ: Real Alloy Recycling, Llc
 3700 Park East Dr Ste 300
 Beachwood OH 44122
 216 755-8900

(G-1272)
REAL ALLOY RECYCLING LLC (HQ)
Also Called: Ra Recycling, LLC
3700 Park East Dr Ste 300 (44122-4399)
PHONE..................216 755-8900
Terry Hogan,
▲ EMP: 100
SQ FT: 7,000
SALES (est): 115MM
SALES (corp-wide): 78MM **Privately Held**
SIC: 3341 Secondary nonferrous metals
PA: Real Alloy Holding, Llc
 3700 Park East Dr Ste 300
 Beachwood OH 44122
 216 755-8900

(G-1273)
REAL ALLOY SPECIALTY PDTS LLC
3700 Park East Dr Ste 300 (44122-4399)
PHONE..................216 755-8836
Terry Hogan, *President*
EMP: 1000
SALES (est): 29.8MM
SALES (corp-wide): 78MM **Privately Held**
SIC: 3341 3313 3334 Secondary nonferrous metals; ferromanganese, not made in blast furnaces; pigs, aluminum
HQ: Real Alloy Recycling, Llc
 3700 Park East Dr Ste 300
 Beachwood OH 44122
 216 755-8900

(G-1274)
REAL ALLOY SPECIALTY PRODUCTS (DH)
3700 Park East Dr Ste 300 (44122-4399)
PHONE..................216 755-8836
Terry Hogan, *President*
Jeffrey Slavin, *Production*
Kenny Webster, *Buyer*
Michael Hobey, *CFO*
Kim Samuels, *Manager*
EMP: 159
SQ FT: 36,500
SALES (est): 197MM
SALES (corp-wide): 1.3B **Publicly Held**
WEB: www.alumitechinc.com
SIC: 3355 Aluminum rolling & drawing; slugs, aluminum

(G-1275)
REAL ALLOY SPECIFICATION LLC (DH)
3700 Park East Dr Ste 300 (44122-4399)
PHONE..................216 755-8900
Terrance J Hogan, *President*
EMP: 7
SALES (est): 1.5MM
SALES (corp-wide): 78MM **Privately Held**
SIC: 3334 3341 3313 Pigs, aluminum; secondary nonferrous metals; ferromanganese, not made in blast furnaces
HQ: Real Alloy Recycling, Llc
 3700 Park East Dr Ste 300
 Beachwood OH 44122
 216 755-8900

(G-1276)
RELIABLE WHEELCHAIR TRANS
28899 Harvard Rd (44122-4741)
PHONE..................216 390-3999
Lapetha Ruffin, *Principal*
EMP: 3
SALES (est): 182.6K **Privately Held**
SIC: 3842 Wheelchairs

(G-1277)
RSI COMPANY (PA)
Also Called: Worthington
24050 Commerce Park # 200 (44122-5833)
PHONE..................216 360-9800
Steve Sords, *President*
Robert Sords, *CFO*
▼ EMP: 19
SQ FT: 60,000
SALES (est): 3.2MM **Privately Held**
WEB: www.rsicomp.com
SIC: 3559 3585 Recycling machinery; refrigeration & heating equipment

(G-1278)
SIATA DS INC (PA)
24665 Greenwich Ln (44122-1650)
PHONE..................216 503-7200
Naum Simkhovich, *President*
Leible Simkhovich, *Vice Pres*
▲ EMP: 3
SALES (est): 407.6K **Privately Held**
SIC: 3444 Pipe, sheet metal

(G-1279)
SINGER PRESS
23500 Mercantile Rd Ste A (44122-5927)
PHONE..................216 595-9400
Andrew Press, *Principal*
EMP: 4 EST: 2007
SALES (est): 302.4K **Privately Held**
SIC: 2741 Miscellaneous publishing

(G-1280)
THE CLEVELAND JEWISH PUBL CO
23880 Commerce Park Ste 1 (44122-5830)
PHONE..................216 454-8300
Rob Certner, *Principal*
EMP: 10
SALES: 32.9K **Privately Held**
SIC: 2711 Newspapers

(G-1281)
TRAPEZE SOFTWARE GROUP INC
23215 Commerce Park # 200 (44122-5803)
PHONE..................905 629-8727
EMP: 3
SALES (corp-wide): 2.1B **Privately Held**
SIC: 7372 Prepackaged software
HQ: Trapeze Software Group, Inc.
 5265 Rockwell Dr Ne
 Cedar Rapids IA

(G-1282)
TREMCO INC
23150 Commerce Park (44122-5807)
PHONE..................216 514-7783
Anne Manno, *Principal*
Marilyn Nativio, *Project Mgr*
Erik Hilston, *Planning*
EMP: 4
SALES (est): 290.7K **Privately Held**
SIC: 2891 Adhesives & sealants

(G-1283)
TREMCO INCORPORATED (HQ)
3735 Green Rd (44122-5730)
PHONE..................216 292-5000
Jeffrey L Korach, *CEO*
Randall J Korach, *President*
Donna Teffer, *President*
Deryl Kratzer, *Division Pres*
Moorman Scott, *Division Pres*
◆ EMP: 300
SQ FT: 93,000
SALES (est): 581.4MM
SALES (corp-wide): 5.3B **Publicly Held**
WEB: www.tremcoinc.com
SIC: 2891 2952 1761 1752 Sealants; caulking compounds; adhesives; epoxy adhesives; roofing materials; coating compounds, tar; asphalt saturated board; roofing contractor; floor laying & floor work; paints & allied products; specialty cleaning, polishes & sanitation goods
PA: Rpm International Inc.
 2628 Pearl Rd
 Medina OH 44256
 330 273-5090

(G-1284)
UVISIR INC
23600 Merc Rd Ste 102 (44122)
PHONE..................216 374-9376
Guilin Mao, *President*
EMP: 3
SALES (est): 200K **Privately Held**
SIC: 3827 Optical instruments & lenses

(G-1285)
WALTER H DRANE CO INC
23811 Chagrin Blvd # 344 (44122-5525)
PHONE..................216 514-1022
William Kenneweg, *President*
Karen Kelly, *CFO*
Marie Skory-Ingalls, *Senior Editor*
EMP: 8 EST: 1955
SALES (est): 560K **Privately Held**
WEB: www.walterdrane.com
SIC: 2741 Technical manual & paper publishing

(G-1286)
WEATHERPROOFING TECH INC
3735 Green Rd (44122-5705)
PHONE..................281 480-7900
Marty Billingsly, *Branch Mgr*
EMP: 3
SALES (corp-wide): 5.3B **Publicly Held**
WEB: www.wtiservices.com
SIC: 2891 Mfg Adhesives/Sealants
HQ: Weatherproofing Technologies, Inc.
 3735 Green Rd
 Beachwood OH 44122
 216 292-5000

(G-1287)
ZHAO HUI FILTERS (US) INC (PA)
Also Called: Zhai Hui Filters & Home Pdts
24400 Highpoint Rd Ste 5 (44122-6027)
PHONE..................440 519-9301
Cong Lawrence Lin, *President*
EMP: 5
SALES (est): 2.6MM **Privately Held**
SIC: 3569 Filters

Beallsville
Monroe County

(G-1288)
A REED EXCAVATING LLC
52912 State Route 145 (43716-9359)
PHONE..................740 391-4985
Adam Reed, *CEO*
Meghan Williamson, *Administration*
EMP: 9 EST: 2014
SALES (est): 453.3K **Privately Held**
SIC: 3531 Plows: construction, excavating & grading

(G-1289)
AMERICAN ENERGY CORPORATION
43521 Mayhugh Hill Rd (43716-9641)
PHONE..................740 926-9152
EMP: 11
SALES (corp-wide): 4.8B **Publicly Held**
SIC: 1241 1222 Coal mining services; bituminous coal-underground mining
HQ: American Energy Corporation
 46226 National Rd
 Saint Clairsville OH 43950
 740 926-3055

(G-1290)
DONALD E DORNON
44592 Game Ridge Rd (43716-9318)
PHONE..................740 926-9144
Donald E Dornon, *Principal*
EMP: 5
SALES (est): 894K **Privately Held**
SIC: 3531 Backhoes

Beaver
Pike County

(G-1291)
A&E MACHINE & FABRICATION INC (PA)
384 State Route 335 (45613-8000)
PHONE..................740 820-4701
Arthur Doll, *Vice Pres*
EMP: 13
SALES: 500K **Privately Held**
SIC: 3499 Fabricated metal products

(G-1292)
BEAVER WOOD PRODUCTS
190 Buck Hollow Rd (45613-9498)
P.O. Box 404 (45613-0404)
PHONE..................740 226-6211
Walter Thornsberry, *Partner*
Rick Thornsberry, *Partner*
EMP: 25
SALES (est): 3.7MM **Privately Held**
SIC: 2421 2436 2435 2426 Sawmills & planing mills, general; softwood veneer & plywood; hardwood veneer & plywood; hardwood dimension & flooring mills

(G-1293)
RAMONA SOUTHWORTH
Also Called: Southworth Wood Products
2882 Adams Rd (45613-9031)
PHONE..................740 226-8202
Ramona Southworth, *Owner*
EMP: 3
SALES: 600K **Privately Held**
SIC: 2421 Sawmills & planing mills, general

(G-1294)
WAVERLY TOOL CO LTD
2596 Glade Rd (45613-9613)
PHONE..................740 988-4831
Roger Wiseman, *Partner*
Gary Miller, *Partner*
EMP: 4
SQ FT: 4,000
SALES (est): 310K **Privately Held**
SIC: 3544 Special dies & tools

(G-1295)
WISEMAN BROS FABG & STL LTD
2598 Glade Rd (45613-9613)
P.O. Box 307 (45613-0307)
PHONE..................740 988-5121
Shane Wiseman,
Derek Wiseman,
EMP: 10 EST: 1995
SQ FT: 8,000
SALES (est): 2.2MM **Privately Held**
SIC: 3441 Fabricated structural metal

Beavercreek
Greene County

(G-1296)
A C HADLEY - PRINTING INC
Also Called: Hadley Printing
1530 Marsetta Dr (45432-2733)
PHONE..................937 426-0952
Nancy Hadley, *President*
Scott Hadley, *Vice Pres*
Michael Hadley, *Treasurer*
EMP: 6
SQ FT: 4,800
SALES: 450K **Privately Held**
SIC: 2396 2759 Automotive & apparel trimmings; thermography

(G-1297)
A SERVICE GLASS INC
1363 N Fairfield Rd (45432-2693)
PHONE..................937 426-4920
Donald T Sullivan, *President*
Donald J Sullivan, *President*
Glenn Sullivan, *Corp Secy*
William C Sullivan, *Vice Pres*
EMP: 15 EST: 1959
SQ FT: 8,000
SALES (est): 1.6MM **Privately Held**
WEB: www.aserviceglass.com
SIC: 5231 3231 1793 5039 Glass; doors, glass: made from purchased glass; glass & glazing work; glass construction materials; automotive glass replacement shops

(G-1298)
ADVANT-E CORPORATION (PA)
2434 Esquire Dr (45431-2573)
PHONE..................937 429-4288
Jason K Wadzinski, *Ch of Bd*
James E Lesch, *CFO*
Jason Boone, *Accounting Dir*
EMP: 12 EST: 1994
SQ FT: 19,000

Beavercreek - Greene County (G-1299)   GEOGRAPHIC SECTION

SALES: 12.6MM **Publicly Held**
WEB: www.advant-e.com
SIC: 7372 7375 Application computer software; information retrieval services

(G-1299)
ANALOG BRIDGE INC
2897 Kant Pl (45431-8507)
PHONE 937 901-4832
Stephen Adams, *CEO*
Gregg Steinhauser, *President*
David Novak, *Vice Pres*
EMP: 3
SALES (est): 212.5K **Privately Held**
WEB: www.analogbridge.com
SIC: 3571 Electronic computers

(G-1300)
ASSISTED PATROL LLC
2130 Hedge Gate Blvd (45431-3909)
PHONE 937 369-0080
David Gasper, *Principal*
EMP: 3
SALES (est): 252.9K **Privately Held**
SIC: 7372 Business oriented computer software

(G-1301)
ASTRO INDUSTRIES INC
4403 Dayton Xenia Rd (45432-1805)
PHONE 937 429-5900
Kailash Mehta, *President*
Nina Joshi, *President*
John Gruenwald, *Vice Pres*
Thomas Stansell, *Purchasing*
William Riley, *Accounting Mgr*
EMP: 24 **EST:** 1967
SQ FT: 24,000
SALES (est): 12.6MM **Privately Held**
WEB: www.astro-ind.com
SIC: 3678 3679 5063 3357 Electronic connectors; electronic circuits; wiring devices; wire & cable; apparatus wire & cordage; building wire & cable; communication wire; current-carrying wiring devices

(G-1302)
AT&T GOVERNMENT SOLUTIONS INC
2940 Presidential Dr # 390 (45324-6762)
PHONE 937 306-3030
Kirk Dunker, *General Mgr*
EMP: 75
SQ FT: 1,500
SALES (corp-wide): 170.7B **Publicly Held**
SIC: 3829 8742 Measuring & controlling devices; management consulting services
HQ: At&T Government Solutions, Inc.
1900 Gallows Rd Ste 105
Vienna VA 22182
703 506-5000

(G-1303)
BALL AEROSPACE & TECH CORP
2875 Presidential Dr # 180 (45324-6769)
P.O. Box 1062, Boulder CO (80306-1062)
PHONE 303 939-4000
James Tribbett, *Principal*
John Godzac, *Branch Mgr*
Donn Johnson, *Branch Mgr*
EMP: 134
SALES (corp-wide): 11.6B **Publicly Held**
SIC: 3812 Aircraft/aerospace flight instruments & guidance systems
HQ: Ball Aerospace & Technologies Corporation
1600 Commerce St
Boulder CO 80301

(G-1304)
CARBIDE PROBES INC
1328 Research Park Dr (45432-2897)
PHONE 937 490-2994
Dan Shellabarger, *President*
Tom Terry, *General Mgr*
Roberta Lee Shellabarger, *Vice Pres*
Jason Black, *QC Mgr*
Cheryl Terry, *Treasurer*
EMP: 28 **EST:** 1955
SQ FT: 10,000
SALES (est): 3MM **Privately Held**
WEB: www.carbideprobes.com
SIC: 3545 Machine tool attachments & accessories

(G-1305)
CHROME & SPEED CYCLE LLC
3490 Dayton Xenia Rd C (45432-2769)
PHONE 937 429-5656
Tom Rogers, *Principal*
EMP: 3 **EST:** 2012
SALES (est): 169.8K **Privately Held**
SIC: 3471 Finishing, metals or formed products

(G-1306)
CISCO SYSTEMS INC
2661 Commons Blvd Ste 133 (45431-3704)
PHONE 937 427-4264
Helen Yep, *Principal*
EMP: 691
SALES (corp-wide): 48B **Publicly Held**
SIC: 3577 7379 Data conversion equipment, media-to-media: computer;
PA: Cisco Systems, Inc.
170 W Tasman Dr
San Jose CA 95134
408 526-4000

(G-1307)
COMMUNICATION CONCEPTS INC
508 Mill Stone Dr (45434-5840)
PHONE 937 426-8600
Rodger L Southworth, *President*
Marlis Southworth, *Corp Secy*
EMP: 6
SALES: 500K **Privately Held**
WEB: www.communication-concepts.com
SIC: 5961 3674 Mail order house; semiconductors & related devices

(G-1308)
CREATIVE ELECTRONIC DESIGN
2565 Celia Dr (45434-6815)
PHONE 937 256-5106
David Johnson, *President*
EMP: 3
SALES (est): 269K **Privately Held**
SIC: 5065 5063 3625 Electronic parts; electrical supplies; relays & industrial controls

(G-1309)
CREEK SMOOTHIES LLC
3195 Dayton Xenia Rd (45434-6390)
PHONE 937 429-1519
Creek Smoothies, *Principal*
EMP: 4
SALES (est): 311.2K **Privately Held**
SIC: 2037 Frozen fruits & vegetables

(G-1310)
DECIBEL RESEARCH INC
2661 Commons Blvd Ste 136 (45431-3704)
PHONE 256 705-3341
Bassem Mahafza, *Branch Mgr*
EMP: 48
SALES (corp-wide): 9.9MM **Privately Held**
SIC: 3812 Radar systems & equipment
PA: Decibel Research, Inc
325 Bob Heath
Huntsville AL 35806
256 716-0787

(G-1311)
DRS ADVANCED ISR LLC (DH)
Also Called: Technologies Inc Arlington VA
2601 Mission Point Blvd (45431-6600)
PHONE 937 429-7408
William J Lynn III, *CEO*
Terence J Murphy, *COO*
Jim Womble, *Vice Pres*
Sandra L Hodgkinson, *Vice Pres*
Angella Cowan, *Controller*
EMP: 150
SQ FT: 25,000
SALES (est): 95.1MM
SALES (corp-wide): 9.2B **Privately Held**
SIC: 3812 Navigational systems & instruments

(G-1312)
DRS SIGNAL TECHNOLOGIES INC
4393 Dayton Xenia Rd (45432)
PHONE 937 429-7470
Leo Torresani, *President*
EMP: 30
SALES (est): 10.3MM
SALES (corp-wide): 9.2B **Privately Held**
WEB: www.drs-st.com
SIC: 3825 7371 Electrical energy measuring equipment; custom computer programming services
HQ: Leonardo Drs, Inc.
2345 Crystal Dr Ste 1000
Arlington VA 22202
703 416-8000

(G-1313)
EDICT SYSTEMS INC
2434 Esquire Dr (45431-2573)
PHONE 937 429-4288
Ason K Wadzinski, *Ch of Bd*
David J Rike, *VP Sales*
Michael Byers, *Accounts Exec*
Derrik Moerner, *Accounts Exec*
Chuck Stuckert, *Accounts Exec*
EMP: 45
SQ FT: 12,000
SALES: 11.8MM
SALES (corp-wide): 12.6MM **Publicly Held**
WEB: www.retailec.com
SIC: 7372 Prepackaged software
PA: Advant-E Corporation
2434 Esquire Dr
Beavercreek OH 45431
937 429-4288

(G-1314)
ENVIRO POLYMERS & CHEMICALS
3045 Rodenbeck Dr Ste D (45432-2660)
P.O. Box 340278, Dayton (45434-0278)
PHONE 937 427-1315
Hamid T Abdulla, *President*
EMP: 4
SALES: 1MM **Privately Held**
SIC: 2899 Water treating compounds

(G-1315)
FLOWERS PRINT INC
Also Called: Corner Copy Shop, The
3355 Dayton Xenia Rd (45432-2728)
PHONE 937 429-3823
Vicki Flowers, *President*
Ronald Flowers, *Treasurer*
EMP: 3
SALES: 165K **Privately Held**
SIC: 2752 Commercial printing, lithographic

(G-1316)
GDC INDUSTRIES LLC
1423 Research Park Dr (45432-2842)
PHONE 937 367-7229
Louis Luedtke, *CEO*
EMP: 6
SQ FT: 1,000
SALES (est): 449.4K **Privately Held**
SIC: 3339 Tin-base alloys (primary)

(G-1317)
GENERAL DYNMICS MSSION SYSTEMS
2673 Commons Blvd Ste 200 (45431-3812)
PHONE 513 253-4770
Chris Marzilli, *President*
Bob Kiley, *Manager*
James Crown, *Director*
Lester Lyles, *Bd of Directors*
EMP: 35
SALES (corp-wide): 36.1B **Publicly Held**
SIC: 3669 3812 Transportation signaling devices; search & navigation equipment
HQ: General Dynamics Mission Systems, Inc.
12450 Fair Lakes Cir # 200
Fairfax VA 22033
703 263-2800

(G-1318)
GRAPHIC IMAGE
2210 Shumway Ct (45431-3018)
PHONE 937 320-0302
Greg Opt, *President*
Tina Opt, *Vice Pres*
EMP: 3
SQ FT: 3,500
SALES (est): 225K **Privately Held**
WEB: www.thegraphicimage.com
SIC: 7336 2791 Graphic arts & related design; typesetting

(G-1319)
GREENTEC PRECISION INC
2372 Lakeview Dr Ste F (45431-2566)
PHONE 937 431-1840
Hideki Onoda, *President*
Philip Rumme, *Vice Pres*
EMP: 9
SALES (est): 2.4MM **Privately Held**
WEB: www.greentec-precision.com
SIC: 3545 Machine tool accessories

(G-1320)
GRID SENTRY LLC
3915 Germany Ln (45431-1688)
PHONE 937 490-2101
James Stethem, *Electrical Engi*
Kim A Gilmer, *Director*
Thomas M McCann,
EMP: 13
SALES (est): 1.9MM **Privately Held**
SIC: 3822 Thermostats & other environmental sensors

(G-1321)
H R MACHINE
2972 Homeway Dr (45434-5709)
P.O. Box 213, Alpha (45301-0213)
PHONE 937 838-6289
Larry Hudson, *Owner*
EMP: 5
SALES: 160K **Privately Held**
SIC: 3599 Machine shop, jobbing & repair

(G-1322)
HARRIS CORPORATION
3500 Pentagon Blvd # 300 (45431-2374)
PHONE 973 284-2866
Jim Wantrobski, *Branch Mgr*
EMP: 195
SALES (corp-wide): 6.1B **Publicly Held**
SIC: 3823 3812 Industrial instrmnts msrmnt display/control process variable; search & navigation equipment
PA: Harris Corporation
1025 W Nasa Blvd
Melbourne FL 32919
321 727-9100

(G-1323)
HR MACHINE LLC
2972 Homeway Dr (45434-5709)
PHONE 937 222-7644
Jennifer Hudson, *President*
Larry Hudson, *Vice Pres*
EMP: 8 **EST:** 2010
SQ FT: 7,000
SALES: 450K **Privately Held**
SIC: 3441 3914 Fabricated structural metal; trophies, stainless steel

(G-1324)
KETCO INC
1348 Research Park Dr (45432-2818)
PHONE 937 426-9331
Richard D Harding, *President*
Steven Gerbic, *Vice Pres*
EMP: 20 **EST:** 1973
SQ FT: 15,000
SALES (est): 3.3MM **Privately Held**
WEB: www.ketco.com
SIC: 3543 Industrial patterns

(G-1325)
LEAR ENGINEERING CORP
2942 Stauffer Dr (45434-6247)
PHONE 937 429-0534
Dennis M Swing, *President*
EMP: 15
SQ FT: 2,400
SALES: 2.4MM **Privately Held**
WEB: www.learengineering.com
SIC: 3827 Optical test & inspection equipment

GEOGRAPHIC SECTION
Beavercreek - Montgomery County (G-1353)

(G-1326)
LEIDOS INC
Also Called: Mission Support
3745 Pentagon Blvd (45431-2369)
PHONE..................937 431-2270
Dennis Anders, *Branch Mgr*
EMP: 77
SALES (corp-wide): 10.1B **Publicly Held**
WEB: www.saic.com
SIC: **8731** 7371 7373 8742 Commercial physical research; energy research; environmental research; medical research, commercial; computer software development; systems engineering, computer related; training & development consultant; recording & playback apparatus, including phonograph; integrated circuits, semiconductor networks, etc.
HQ: Leidos, Inc.
    11951 Freedom Dr Ste 500
    Reston VA 20190
    571 526-6000

(G-1327)
LOCKHEED MARTIN CORPORATION
2940 Presidential Dr # 290 (45324-6564)
PHONE..................937 429-0100
Sandy Bunn, *Branch Mgr*
Ed Jespersen, *Manager*
EMP: 4 **Publicly Held**
WEB: www.lockheedmartin.com
SIC: **3812** Search & navigation equipment
PA: Lockheed Martin Corporation
    6801 Rockledge Dr
    Bethesda MD 20817

(G-1328)
LOCKHEED MARTIN CORPORATION
2940 Presidential Dr # 290 (45324-6564)
PHONE..................937 429-0100
Anney Harris, *Branch Mgr*
EMP: 232 **Publicly Held**
SIC: **3812** Search & navigation equipment
PA: Lockheed Martin Corporation
    6801 Rockledge Dr
    Bethesda MD 20817

(G-1329)
LOCKHEED MARTIN INVESTMENTS
2940 Presidential Dr # 290 (45324-6564)
PHONE..................937 429-0100
Joe Lanni, *Director*
EMP: 11 **Publicly Held**
SIC: **3365** Aerospace castings, aluminum
HQ: Lockheed Martin Investments Inc
    3510 Silverside Rd Ste 3
    Wilmington DE 19810
    302 478-1583

(G-1330)
MAR CHELE INC
2727 Fairfield Cmns Blvd (45431-3778)
PHONE..................937 429-2300
EMP: 11
SALES (corp-wide): 2.8MM **Privately Held**
SIC: **2052** Pretzels
PA: Mar Chele Inc
    18 Market St
    Brookville OH 45309
    937 833-3400

(G-1331)
MERKUR GROUP INC
2434 Esquire Dr (45431-2573)
PHONE..................937 429-4288
Jason Wadzinski, *CEO*
EMP: 5
SQ FT: 19,000
SALES: 959.7K
SALES (corp-wide): 12.6MM **Publicly Held**
WEB: www.merkur.com
SIC: **5734** 7372 Computer software & accessories; prepackaged software
PA: Advant-E Corporation
    2434 Esquire Dr
    Beavercreek OH 45431
    937 429-4288

(G-1332)
MINUTEMAN PRESS
2372 Lakeview Dr (45431-4202)
PHONE..................937 429-8610
EMP: 3
SALES (est): 242.3K **Privately Held**
SIC: **2752** Commercial printing, lithographic

(G-1333)
MONARCH WATER SYSTEMS INC
689 Greystone Dr (45434-4202)
PHONE..................937 426-5773
Toll Free:................888 -
Patricia A Glaser, *President*
John Glaser, *Vice Pres*
EMP: 10
SQ FT: 7,500
SALES (est): 1.5MM **Privately Held**
SIC: **3589** Water filters & softeners, household type

(G-1334)
NEW TECH WELDING INC
2972 Lantz Rd (45434-6633)
PHONE..................937 426-4801
James King, *President*
Pamela King, *Owner*
EMP: 3
SALES: 50K **Privately Held**
SIC: **7692** Welding repair

(G-1335)
ORACLE CORPORATION
3610 Pentagon Blvd # 205 (45431-6700)
PHONE..................513 826-5632
Peter Burton, *Principal*
EMP: 191
SALES (corp-wide): 39.8B **Publicly Held**
SIC: **7372** Business oriented computer software
PA: Oracle Corporation
    500 Oracle Pkwy
    Redwood City CA 94065
    650 506-7000

(G-1336)
ORACLE SYSTEMS CORPORATION
2661 Commons Blvd (45431-3704)
PHONE..................937 427-5495
Lisa Wells, *Manager*
EMP: 4
SALES (corp-wide): 39.8B **Publicly Held**
WEB: www.forcecapital.com
SIC: **7372** Prepackaged software
HQ: Oracle Systems Corporation
    500 Oracle Pkwy
    Redwood City CA 94065
    650 506-7000

(G-1337)
PROTECH ELECTRIC LLC
1632 Beaverbrook Dr (45432-2104)
PHONE..................937 427-0813
John Steelman, *Mng Member*
Janet Steelman,
EMP: 12
SALES (est): 528K **Privately Held**
SIC: **4822** 3495 Telegraph & other communications; wire springs

(G-1338)
QUALITY METROLOGY SYS & SOL LL
425 Mill Stone Dr (45434-5837)
PHONE..................937 431-1800
John Kolaczkowski, *Mng Member*
Laura Kolaczkowski,
EMP: 3
SALES (est): 457K **Privately Held**
SIC: **3823** Industrial instrmnts msrmnt display/control process variable

(G-1339)
RAYTHEON COMPANY
2970 Presidential Dr # 300 (45324-6752)
PHONE..................937 429-5429
Mike Evans, *Branch Mgr*
EMP: 10
SALES (corp-wide): 27B **Publicly Held**
SIC: **3812** Sonar systems & equipment

PA: Raytheon Company
    870 Winter St
    Waltham MA 02451
    781 522-3000

(G-1340)
SHOPS BY TODD INC (PA)
Also Called: Occassionaly Yours
2727 Fairfld Comns W273 (45431-5748)
PHONE..................937 458-3192
Todd Bettman, *President*
Danielle Bierer, *Creative Dir*
Natalie Moon, *Asst Director*
EMP: 9
SQ FT: 1,750
SALES (est): 1.2MM **Privately Held**
WEB: www.oygifts.com
SIC: **5947** 2759 Gift shop; invitation & stationery printing & engraving

(G-1341)
SIGN WRITE
3348 Dayton Xenia Rd (45432-2747)
PHONE..................937 559-4388
Kristine Sturr, *Principal*
EMP: 3
SALES (est): 204.4K **Privately Held**
SIC: **3993** Signs & advertising specialties

(G-1342)
SONALYSTS INC
2940 Presidential Dr # 160 (45324-6564)
PHONE..................937 429-9711
EMP: 23
SALES (corp-wide): 91.7MM **Privately Held**
SIC: **3211** Window glass, clear & colored
PA: Sonalysts, Inc.
    215 Parkway N
    Waterford CT 06385
    860 442-4355

(G-1343)
TERADYNE INC
Avionics Interface Tech
2689 Commons Blvd Ste 201 (45431-3822)
PHONE..................937 427-1280
Andy Kragick, *Manager*
EMP: 15
SALES (corp-wide): 2.1B **Publicly Held**
SIC: **3829** Measuring & controlling devices
PA: Teradyne, Inc.
    600 Riverpark Dr
    North Reading MA 01864
    978 370-2700

(G-1344)
THREAD WORKS CUSTOM EMBROIDERY
2630 Colonel Glenn Hwy (45324-6559)
PHONE..................937 478-5231
Toni Webb, *Owner*
Don Webb, *General Mgr*
▲ EMP: 6
SQ FT: 1,700
SALES: 330K **Privately Held**
SIC: **2395** Embroidery & art needlework

(G-1345)
UNISON INDUSTRIES LLC
Also Called: Elano Div
2070 Heller Dr (45434-7210)
PHONE..................937 427-0550
Robert Hessel, *Branch Mgr*
EMP: 400
SALES (corp-wide): 121.6B **Publicly Held**
WEB: www.unisonindustries.com
SIC: **3728** 4581 Aircraft parts & equipment; aircraft servicing & repairing
HQ: Unison Industries, Llc
    7575 Baymeadows Way
    Jacksonville FL 32256
    904 739-4000

(G-1346)
UNISON INDUSTRIES LLC
Also Called: GE
2156 Heller Dr (45434-7211)
PHONE..................937 426-0621
Robert Hessel, *Branch Mgr*
EMP: 140
SALES (corp-wide): 121.6B **Publicly Held**
SIC: **3728** Aircraft parts & equipment

HQ: Unison Industries, Llc
    7575 Baymeadows Way
    Jacksonville FL 32256
    904 739-4000

(G-1347)
YOUNGS PUBLISHING INC
2171 N Fairfield Rd (45431-2556)
PHONE..................937 259-6575
Ronald K Young Sr, *President*
Ronald K Young Jr, *Vice Pres*
EMP: 11
SQ FT: 3,000
SALES: 2MM **Privately Held**
WEB: www.reforsale.org
SIC: **2721** Magazines: publishing & printing

Beavercreek
Montgomery County

(G-1348)
A & A SAFETY INC
4080 Industrial Ln (45430-1017)
PHONE..................937 567-9781
Tim Weeks, *Manager*
EMP: 10
SALES (corp-wide): 20.2MM **Privately Held**
WEB: www.aasafetyinc.com
SIC: **7359** 1721 5084 1611 Work zone traffic equipment (flags, cones, barrels, etc.); painting & paper hanging; safety equipment; highway & street sign installation; signs & advertising specialties; transportation signaling devices
PA: A & A Safety, Inc.
    1126 Ferris Rd Bldg B
    Amelia OH 45102
    513 943-6100

(G-1349)
ALEKTRONICS INC
4095 Executive Dr (45430-1062)
PHONE..................937 429-2118
Alan Eakle, *CEO*
EMP: 16
SQ FT: 4,800
SALES (est): 3.3MM **Privately Held**
WEB: www.alektronics.com
SIC: **3672** Printed circuit boards

(G-1350)
AVASAX LTD
Also Called: Avasax Data Recovery
3895 Oakview Dr (45430-5109)
PHONE..................937 694-0807
Robert Mardis,
EMP: 3
SALES (est): 145.1K **Privately Held**
SIC: **7372** 7371 Application computer software; custom computer programming services

(G-1351)
BLUESERV REPROGRAHICS LLC
3313 Seajay Dr (45430-1365)
PHONE..................937 426-6410
Rob Mantia, *Principal*
Jack Lehman, *Manager*
EMP: 4
SALES (est): 550.8K **Privately Held**
SIC: **2752** Lithographic Commercial Printing

(G-1352)
BOKO PATTERNS MODELS & MOLDS
4130 Industrial Ln (45430-1019)
PHONE..................937 426-9667
Bob Koehler, *Principal*
EMP: 5
SALES (est): 632.6K **Privately Held**
SIC: **3553** 3543 Pattern makers' machinery, woodworking; industrial patterns

(G-1353)
CERTIFIED COMPARATOR PRODUCTS
1174 Grange Hall Rd (45430-1094)
PHONE..................937 426-9677
Rod Murch, *President*
Steve Ison, *QC Mgr*

Beavercreek - Montgomery County (G-1354)

EMP: 6
SALES (est): 692.3K **Privately Held**
SIC: 5065 3545 Electronic parts & equipment; comparators (machinists' precision tools)

(G-1354)
CLINTS PRINTING INC
Also Called: Clint's Prntng
3963 Rockfield Dr (45430-1126)
PHONE......................937 426-2771
Clinton Whittaker, *CEO*
Lucille Whittaker, *President*
Lawrence Bernard, *Vice Pres*
EMP: 6
SQ FT: 9,500
SALES (est): 906.8K **Privately Held**
SIC: 2791 2789 2752 Typesetting; bookbinding & related work; commercial printing, offset

(G-1355)
EXITO MANUFACTURING
4120 Industrial Ln Ste B (45430-1004)
PHONE......................937 291-9871
Eric Fernandez,
EMP: 7
SALES (est): 783K **Privately Held**
SIC: 3544 3542 3728 3714 Special dies, tools, jigs & fixtures; machine tools, metal forming type; aircraft parts & equipment; motor vehicle parts & accessories

(G-1356)
INNOVATIVE WELD SOLUTIONS LTD
4030 N Emerald Ct (45430-2077)
PHONE......................937 545-7695
Anthony Ananthanarayanan,
EMP: 8
SQ FT: 8,000
SALES (est): 165K **Privately Held**
SIC: 8733 3691 Scientific research agency; storage batteries

(G-1357)
MATRIX RESEARCH INC
3844 Research Blvd (45430-2104)
PHONE......................937 427-8433
James Lutz, *Ch of Bd*
Robert Hawley, *President*
Robert W Hawley, *President*
William Pierson, *Vice Pres*
EMP: 80
SQ FT: 4,000
SALES (est): 23.3MM **Privately Held**
SIC: 3829 8711 Measuring & controlling devices; engineering services

(G-1358)
MEASUREMENT SPECIALTIES INC
2670 Indian Ripple Rd (45440-3605)
PHONE......................937 427-1231
Brian Ream, *Branch Mgr*
EMP: 13
SALES (corp-wide): 13.1B **Privately Held**
SIC: 3674 3676 Diodes, solid state (germanium, silicon, etc.); thermistors, except temperature sensors; varistors
HQ: Measurement Specialties, Inc.
1000 Lucas Way
Hampton VA 23666
757 766-1500

(G-1359)
NAKED LIME
2405 County Line Rd (45430-1573)
PHONE......................937 485-1932
Brooke Wood, *Principal*
Josh Allen, *Sales Dir*
Craig Lawson, *Accounts Mgr*
Clay Luttrell, *Accounts Mgr*
Amanda Cheadle, *Marketing Staff*
EMP: 75
SALES (est): 6.8MM **Privately Held**
SIC: 3274 Lime

(G-1360)
NORTHROP GRUMMAN INNOVATION
1365 Technology Ct (45430-2212)
PHONE......................937 429-9261
Don Hairston, *Principal*
Mike Cimbalista, *Chief Engr*
Eric Vanderhorst, *Engineer*
Ash Miller, *Design Engr*
James Burns, *Finance*
EMP: 150 **Publicly Held**
WEB: www.mrcwdc.com
SIC: 3812 Search & navigation equipment
HQ: Northrop Grumman Innovation Systems, Inc.
45101 Warp Dr
Dulles VA 20166
703 406-5000

(G-1361)
RCF KITCHENS INDIANA LLC
Also Called: Really Cool Foods
87 Shelford Way (45440-3657)
PHONE......................765 478-6600
Don Gillun, *CEO*
Joe Myres, *CFO*
Joseph W Meyers,
EMP: 150
SQ FT: 1,500
SALES (est): 21.4MM **Privately Held**
SIC: 2015 Chicken, processed: fresh

(G-1362)
REYNOLDS AND REYNOLDS COMPANY
2405 County Line Rd (45430-1573)
P.O. Box 2608, Dayton (45401-2608)
PHONE......................937 485-2805
Finbarr Oneill, *Manager*
EMP: 10
SALES (corp-wide): 1.5B **Privately Held**
WEB: www.reyrey.com
SIC: 2761 7372 7371 Manifold business forms; prepackaged software; custom computer programming services
HQ: The Reynolds And Reynolds Company
1 Reynolds Way
Kettering OH 45430
937 485-2000

(G-1363)
SNI INC
75 Harbert Dr Ste A (45440-5126)
PHONE......................937 427-9447
Steven C Nuttall, *President*
EMP: 4
SQ FT: 12,000
SALES (est): 565.4K **Privately Held**
WEB: www.snitool.com
SIC: 3544 3599 Special dies & tools; machine shop, jobbing & repair

(G-1364)
SUPERIOR SODA SERVICE LLC
3626 Napanee Dr (45430-1322)
P.O. Box 341450 (45434-1450)
PHONE......................937 657-9700
Greg Gouldbourn,
EMP: 6
SALES: 75K **Privately Held**
SIC: 5963 3441 Beverage services, direct sales; fabricated structural metal

(G-1365)
TARGETED CMPUND MONITORING LLC
2790 Indian Ripple Rd A (45440-3639)
PHONE......................513 461-3535
Todd Dockum,
EMP: 4
SALES (est): 179K **Privately Held**
SIC: 3826 Automatic chemical analyzers

(G-1366)
UNMANNED SOLUTIONS TECH LLC
3908 Eagle Point Dr (45430-2085)
PHONE......................937 771-7023
Robert Barry,
Clara Tiffany,
Kent Tiffany,
EMP: 4
SALES (est): 639.2K **Privately Held**
SIC: 3721 Research & development on aircraft by the manufacturer

(G-1367)
VECTOR ELECTROMAGNETICS LLC
2670b Indian Ripple Rd (45440-3605)
PHONE......................937 478-5904
Errol English, *President*
Brian Barber, *Vice Pres*
EMP: 4
SALES: 1MM **Privately Held**
SIC: 8711 3812 Electrical or electronic engineering; mining engineer; defense systems & equipment

(G-1368)
WERNLI REALTY INC
1300 Grange Hall Rd (45430-1013)
PHONE......................937 258-7878
Richard L Schaefer, *President*
John Miltenberger, *Asst Sec*
EMP: 75
SQ FT: 20,000
SALES (est): 8.6MM **Privately Held**
SIC: 3441 6512 Building components, structural steel; nonresidential building operators

Beavercreek Township
Greene County

(G-1369)
MBM INDUSTRIES LTD
801 Space Dr (45434-7162)
PHONE......................937 522-0719
Bradley M McWilliams,
Bradley McWilliams,
EMP: 4 EST: 2001
SALES (est): 776.6K **Privately Held**
SIC: 3711 3827 Military motor vehicle assembly; gun sights, optical

(G-1370)
PHILLIPS COMPANIES (PA)
620 Phillips Dr (45434-7230)
P.O. Box 187, Alpha (45301-0187)
PHONE......................937 426-5461
Richard L Phillips II, *President*
George E Phillips, *Chairman*
Bradley Phillips, *Vice Pres*
Jason Phillips, *Treasurer*
Dennis Phillips, *Admin Sec*
EMP: 20 EST: 1942
SQ FT: 2,000
SALES (est): 13.3MM **Privately Held**
WEB: www.phillipscompanies.com
SIC: 1442 6552 1794 Sand mining; gravel mining; subdividers & developers; excavation work

(G-1371)
PHILLIPS COMPANIES
Also Called: Phillips Sand & Gravel Co
620 Phillips Dr (45434-7230)
PHONE......................937 426-5461
Richard L Phillips II, *President*
EMP: 29
SALES (corp-wide): 13.3MM **Privately Held**
WEB: www.phillipscompanies.com
SIC: 3273 1771 Ready-mixed concrete; concrete pumping
PA: Phillips Companies
620 Phillips Dr
Beavercreek Township OH 45434
937 426-5461

(G-1372)
PHILLIPS READY MIX CO
620 Phillips Dr (45434-7230)
P.O. Box 187, Alpha (45301-0187)
PHONE......................937 426-5151
Rick Phillips, *President*
Dennis Phillips, *Treasurer*
EMP: 100
SALES (est): 4.2MM **Privately Held**
SIC: 1771 3273 7353 5191 Concrete pumping; ready-mixed concrete; heavy construction equipment rental; farm supplies; excavation work; construction sand & gravel

(G-1373)
PRIORITY CUSTOM MOLDING INC
840 Distribution Dr (45434-7174)
PHONE......................937 431-8770
Carol S Williams, *President*
Dennie Williams, *Vice Pres*
Bob Abbitt, *Treasurer*
Angela Abbit, *Admin Sec*

▲ EMP: 18
SQ FT: 17,500
SALES: 2.8MM **Privately Held**
SIC: 3089 3081 Molding primary plastic; unsupported plastics film & sheet

(G-1374)
SONOCO PRODUCTS COMPANY
Sonoco Consumer Products
761 Space Dr (45434-7171)
PHONE......................937 429-0040
Norwood Bizzell, *Manager*
EMP: 60
SALES (corp-wide): 5.3B **Publicly Held**
WEB: www.sonoco.com
SIC: 2655 5113 2891 Cans, fiber: made from purchased material; paper tubes & cores; adhesives & sealants
PA: Sonoco Products Company
1 N 2nd St
Hartsville SC 29550
843 383-7000

(G-1375)
W&W AUTOMOTIVE & TOWING INC
Also Called: W & W Automotive
680 Orchard Ln (45434-7205)
PHONE......................937 429-1699
Regina White, *President*
EMP: 10
SQ FT: 16,000
SALES (est): 1.4MM **Privately Held**
SIC: 3711 7532 Chassis, motor vehicle; body shop, automotive

(G-1376)
WALLEN COMMERCIAL HARDWARE
832 Space Dr (45434-7161)
PHONE......................937 426-5711
Tim Wallen, *President*
EMP: 4
SALES: 300K **Privately Held**
SIC: 3429 Manufactured hardware (general)

Bedford
Cuyahoga County

(G-1377)
1967
594 Corkhill Rd Apt 402 (44146-3479)
PHONE......................216 882-4228
Mitch Range, *Vice Pres*
EMP: 3 EST: 2016
SALES (est): 114.3K **Privately Held**
SIC: 3421 Scissors, shears, clippers, snips & similar tools

(G-1378)
ABI INC
26000 Richmond Rd Ste 4 (44146-1420)
P.O. Box 389, Richfield (44286-0389)
PHONE......................216 378-1336
Lloyd Ray Parr, *President*
Thomas L Feher, *Admin Sec*
Thomas Feher, *Assistant*
EMP: 10
SALES (est): 1.7MM **Privately Held**
WEB: www.ultraclear.com
SIC: 2836 Biological products, except diagnostic

(G-1379)
ADEMCO INC
Also Called: ADI Global Distribution
7710 First Pl Ste A (44146-6718)
PHONE......................440 439-7002
Mark Blackburn, *Manager*
EMP: 6
SALES (corp-wide): 4.8B **Publicly Held**
WEB: www.adilink.com
SIC: 5063 3669 3822 Electrical apparatus & equipment; emergency alarms; auto controls regulating residntl & coml environmt & applncs
HQ: Ademco Inc.
1985 Douglas Dr N
Golden Valley MN 55422
800 468-1502

GEOGRAPHIC SECTION

Bedford - Cuyahoga County (G-1405)

(G-1380)
ALS HIGH TECH INC (PA)
Also Called: Al's Electric Motor Service
135 Northfield Rd (44146-4606)
PHONE 440 232-7090
Elaine Ochwat, *CEO*
Dale Ochwat, *President*
Lynn O Meffen, *Corp Secy*
Albert Ochwat, *Manager*
EMP: 11
SQ FT: 45,000
SALES: 1.2MM **Privately Held**
SIC: 7694 5063 Electric motor repair; rewinding services; electrical apparatus & equipment; motors, electric

(G-1381)
AM CASTLE & CO
Also Called: Oliver Steel Plate
26800 Miles Rd (44146-1405)
PHONE 330 425-7000
Tony Prybuto, *Transportation*
Scott J Dolan, *Branch Mgr*
EMP: 65
SALES (corp-wide): 581.9MM **Publicly Held**
SIC: 5051 3444 3443 3398 Steel; sheet metalwork; fabricated plate work (boiler shop); metal heat treating
PA: A.M. Castle & Co.
1420 Kensington Rd # 220
Oak Brook IL 60523
847 455-7111

(G-1382)
AMERICAN ACADEMIC PRESS
550 Turney Rd Apt C (44146-7328)
PHONE 216 906-2518
Michael Cikraji, *Owner*
EMP: 3
SALES (est): 95K **Privately Held**
SIC: 2731 Book publishing

(G-1383)
ANSON CO
Also Called: Effective Air
18679 Orchard Hill Dr (44146-5258)
PHONE 216 524-8838
EMP: 3
SQ FT: 1,200
SALES: 400K **Privately Held**
SIC: 5075 3634 Whol Heat Air Conditioning & Ventilation Equipment

(G-1384)
APEX WELDING INCORPORATED
Also Called: Apex Bulk Handlers
1 Industry Dr (44146-4413)
P.O. Box 46199, Cleveland (44146-0199)
PHONE 440 232-6770
D J Warner, *President*
B A Danna, *Vice Pres*
Joel Petit, *Sales Staff*
Gary Warner, *Manager*
EMP: 15 **EST:** 1947
SQ FT: 15,200
SALES (est): 2.9MM **Privately Held**
WEB: www.apexwelding.com
SIC: 3444 3443 Hoppers, sheet metal; fabricated plate work (boiler shop)

(G-1385)
ART OF BEAUTY COMPANY INC (PA)
200 Egbert Rd (44146-4221)
P.O. Box 22349, Cleveland (44122-0349)
PHONE 216 438-6363
Michael Reyzis, *President*
Leo Reyzis, *Vice Pres*
Leonid Reyzis, *Vice Pres*
Rebecca ISA, *Natl Sales Mgr*
Melissa McTee, *Mktg Coord*
◆ **EMP:** 15
SQ FT: 5,000
SALES (est): 3.5MM **Privately Held**
WEB: www.artofbeauty.com
SIC: 2844 Cosmetic preparations

(G-1386)
AUTOMATED PACKG SYSTEMS INC
Sidepouch
25900 Solon Rd (44146-4788)
PHONE 330 342-2000
Bob Stinger, *Manager*
EMP: 75
SQ FT: 59,780
SALES (corp-wide): 225.2MM **Privately Held**
WEB: www.autobag.com
SIC: 3565 2673 Packaging machinery; bags: plastic, laminated & coated
PA: Automated Packaging Systems Inc.
10175 Philipp Pkwy
Streetsboro OH 44241
330 528-2000

(G-1387)
BARTA VIOREL
Also Called: Cabinet Studio
26245 Broadway Ave (44146-6523)
PHONE 440 735-1699
Viorel Barta, *Owner*
EMP: 4
SALES (est): 240K **Privately Held**
SIC: 3281 Granite, cut & shaped

(G-1388)
BASWA ACOUSTICS NORTH AMER LLC
Also Called: Sound Solutions Cnstr Svcs
21863 Aurora Rd (44146-1201)
PHONE 216 475-7197
Ed Sellers, *Managing Prtnr*
Matt Townsend, *Partner*
Eric Sulzer, *Managing Dir*
▲ **EMP:** 12
SQ FT: 3,000
SALES (est): 3.3MM **Privately Held**
SIC: 5082 3272 General construction machinery & equipment; building materials, except block or brick: concrete

(G-1389)
BEAUTY CFT MET FABRICATORS INC
5439 Perkins Rd (44146-1856)
PHONE 440 439-0710
Ronald Walnsch, *President*
Brian Walnsch, *Vice Pres*
Mary Walnsch, *Admin Sec*
EMP: 10
SQ FT: 7,000
SALES (est): 1.6MM **Privately Held**
WEB: www.beautycraftmetal.com
SIC: 3441 Fabricated structural metal

(G-1390)
BOEHRINGER INGELHEIM USA CORP
Also Called: Ben Venue Laboratories
300 Northfield Rd (44146-4650)
P.O. Box 2075, Ridgefield CT (06877-6675)
PHONE 440 232-3320
Gary Price, *CFO*
Paul Kersten, *Marketing Staff*
▲ **EMP:** 17
SALES (est): 2.6MM
SALES (corp-wide): 21.2B **Privately Held**
SIC: 2834 Pharmaceutical preparations
PA: C.H. Boehringer Sohn Ag & Co. Kg
Binger Str. 173
Ingelheim Am Rhein 55218
613 277-0

(G-1391)
BRAINMASTER TECHNOLOGIES INC
195 Willis St 3 (44146-3508)
P.O. Box 46725 (44146-0725)
PHONE 440 232-6000
Thomas F Collura, *President*
Terri Collura, *Exec VP*
William Mrklas, *Vice Pres*
EMP: 9 **EST:** 1999
SALES (est): 1.5MM **Privately Held**
WEB: www.brainmaster.com
SIC: 3845 7371 Electromedical equipment; computer software development

(G-1392)
CANNON SALT AND SUPPLY INC
26041 Cannon Rd (44146-1835)
PHONE 440 232-1700
Robert Foster, *President*
Todd Kling, *Vice Pres*
EMP: 6
SALES (est): 1.2MM **Privately Held**
SIC: 3524 3423 Lawn & garden equipment; garden & farm tools, including shovels

(G-1393)
CAR BROS INC
7177 Northfield Rd (44146-5403)
PHONE 440 232-1840
Duane A Carr Jr, *Administration*
EMP: 4
SALES (est): 397.6K **Privately Held**
SIC: 3273 Ready-mixed concrete

(G-1394)
CARR BROS INC
7177 Northfield Rd (44146-5403)
P.O. Box 46387 (44146-0387)
PHONE 440 232-3700
Mike Carr, *Owner*
EMP: 25
SALES (est): 4.6MM **Privately Held**
SIC: 3273 Ready-mixed concrete

(G-1395)
CERTON TECHNOLOGIES INC (PA)
Also Called: Har Adhesive Technologies
60 S Park St (44146-3635)
PHONE 440 786-7185
Joseph Cerino, *President*
Keith Nagy, *Division Mgr*
Joe Cerino, *Principal*
Diane Cerino, *Vice Pres*
Geri Horvath, *Purchasing*
EMP: 15
SQ FT: 30,000
SALES (est): 4.6MM **Privately Held**
SIC: 2891 2851 7699 7359 Adhesives; paints & paint additives; professional instrument repair services; home cleaning & maintenance equipment rental services

(G-1396)
CLOSETTEC OF NORTH EAST OHIO
5222 Richmond Rd (44146-1333)
PHONE 216 464-0042
Don Cussari, *Principal*
EMP: 4
SALES (est): 474.2K **Privately Held**
SIC: 3553 Cabinet makers' machinery

(G-1397)
COMBINE GRINDING CO INC
7005 Krick Rd Ste C (44146-4447)
PHONE 440 439-6148
Charles Musgrave III, *President*
EMP: 3
SQ FT: 3,200
SALES (est): 410.1K **Privately Held**
SIC: 3599 Grinding castings for the trade

(G-1398)
DARKO INC
26401 Richmond Rd (44146-1443)
PHONE 330 425-9805
Dean Rinicella, *President*
Dan Rinicella Jr, *Vice Pres*
Derek Rinicella, *Vice Pres*
Dominic Dumas, *Project Mgr*
Kerry Kiser, *Project Mgr*
▲ **EMP:** 50
SQ FT: 72,000
SALES (est): 16.1MM **Privately Held**
WEB: www.darkoinc.com
SIC: 2541 2542 Shelving, office & store, wood; office & store showcases & display fixtures

(G-1399)
DENGENSHA AMERICA CORPORATION
7647 First Pl (44146-6701)
PHONE 440 439-8081
Donald Grisez, *President*
▲ **EMP:** 13
SALES (est): 3.1MM
SALES (corp-wide): 71.4MM **Privately Held**
WEB: www.dengensha.com
SIC: 3559 5084 Automotive related machinery; industrial machinery & equipment
PA: Dengensha Toa Co., Ltd.
1-23-1, Masugata, Tama-Ku
Kawasaki KNG 214-0
449 221-121

(G-1400)
DEUFOL WORLDWIDE PACKAGING LLC
19800 Alexander Rd (44146-5346)
PHONE 440 232-1100
Rich Stillman, *Branch Mgr*
EMP: 22 **Privately Held**
WEB: www.overseaspacking.net
SIC: 5113 3412 3086 Boxes & containers; corrugated & solid fiber boxes; metal barrels, drums & pails; plastics foam products
HQ: Deufol Worldwide Packaging Llc
924 S Meridian St
Sunman IN 47041
812 623-1140

(G-1401)
DIVERSIFIED BRANDS
26300 Fargo Ave (44146-1310)
PHONE 216 595-8777
Gayle Dlougon, *Principal*
EMP: 7
SALES (est): 741K **Privately Held**
SIC: 2819 Industrial inorganic chemicals

(G-1402)
DONE-RITE BOWLING SERVICE CO (PA)
Also Called: Paragon Machine Company
20434 Krick Rd (44146-4422)
PHONE 440 232-3280
Robert W Gable, *CEO*
Glenn Gable, *President*
Gale Burns, *Vice Pres*
Dave Patz, *Vice Pres*
Ann Gable, *Shareholder*
▲ **EMP:** 25 **EST:** 1950
SQ FT: 20,000
SALES (est): 2.6MM **Privately Held**
WEB: www.donerite.com
SIC: 3949 1752 5091 Bowling equipment & supplies; floor laying & floor work; bowling equipment

(G-1403)
E J SKOK INDUSTRIES (PA)
26901 Richmond Rd (44146-1416)
PHONE 216 292-7533
Edward J Skok, *President*
Richard Skok, *Corp Secy*
EMP: 20
SQ FT: 18,000
SALES (est): 1.9MM **Privately Held**
SIC: 2541 2434 Table or counter tops, plastic laminated; wood kitchen cabinets; vanities, bathroom: wood

(G-1404)
FEDERAL METAL COMPANY
Also Called: FM
7250 Division St (44146-5495)
PHONE 440 232-8700
David R Nagusky, *CEO*
Peter Nagusky, *President*
Mike Buyarski, *COO*
Chris Greendfield, *Vice Pres*
Robert I Kohn, *Vice Pres*
EMP: 65 **EST:** 1913
SQ FT: 65,000
SALES (est): 13.7MM
SALES (corp-wide): 16.2MM **Privately Held**
WEB: www.federalmetalcompany.com
SIC: 3351 3364 Copper & copper alloy sheet, strip, plate & products; copper & copper alloy die-castings
PA: Oakwood Industries Inc.
7250 Division St
Bedford OH 44146
440 232-8700

(G-1405)
FERRO CORPORATION
7050 Krick Rd (44146-4416)
PHONE 216 577-7144
Ferro Bedford, *Div Sub Head*
R Szabo, *Purchasing*
Steven Hofmeister, *Engineer*
Sally Lenhart, *Sales Mgr*
Kent Lee, *Marketing Staff*

Bedford - Cuyahoga County (G-1406)

EMP: 70
SALES (corp-wide): 1.6B **Publicly Held**
WEB: www.ferro.com
SIC: 2851 2869 2842 2836 Paint driers; industrial organic chemicals; specialty cleaning, polishes & sanitation goods; biological products, except diagnostic; industrial inorganic chemicals
PA: Ferro Corporation
6060 Parkland Blvd # 250
Mayfield Heights OH 44124
216 875-5600

(G-1406)
GREAT LAKES TEXTILES INC
11 Industry Dr (44146-4413)
PHONE................................440 201-1300
Evan Wake, *Manager*
EMP: 20
SALES (corp-wide): 15.8MM **Privately Held**
WEB: www.gltproducts.com
SIC: 3083 Laminated plastic sheets
PA: Great Lakes Textiles, Inc.
6810 Cochran Rd
Solon OH 44139
440 914-1122

(G-1407)
GROUNDHOGS 2000 LLC
33 Industry Dr (44146-4413)
PHONE................................440 653-1647
Troy H Hauff,
EMP: 6
SALES: 180K **Privately Held**
SIC: 1381 1623 7389 Directional drilling oil & gas wells; drilling water intake wells; service well drilling; water, sewer & utility lines; oil & gas line & compressor station construction; communication line & transmission tower construction; water & sewer line construction;

(G-1408)
GUILD INTERNATIONAL INC
7273 Division St (44146-5490)
PHONE................................440 232-5887
Joe Thomas, *President*
Debbie Klouda, *Purch Mgr*
Alex Uchitel, *Engineer*
Mark Wagner, *Engineer*
Bill Maruschak, *CFO*
▲ **EMP:** 28 **EST:** 1956
SQ FT: 12,000
SALES (est): 8MM **Privately Held**
SIC: 3549 Coiling machinery

(G-1409)
GVC PLASTICS & METALS LLC
7051 Krick Rd (44146-4415)
PHONE................................440 232-9360
Greg Charatian, *Owner*
EMP: 3 **EST:** 2010
SALES (est): 365.2K **Privately Held**
SIC: 2295 Resin or plastic coated fabrics

(G-1410)
HANDICRAFT LLC
26225 Broadway Ave (44146-6514)
PHONE................................216 295-1950
Eli Gunzburg,
▼ **EMP:** 5
SQ FT: 8,000
SALES (est): 588.4K **Privately Held**
SIC: 2499 Decorative wood & woodwork

(G-1411)
HAR EQUIPMENT SALES INC
60 S Park St (44146-3635)
PHONE................................440 786-7189
Dennis Grosel, *Principal*
EMP: 5
SALES (est): 701.3K **Privately Held**
SIC: 2891 Adhesives

(G-1412)
HIKMA PHARMACEUTICALS USA INC
Also Called: Research & Development Div
300 Northfield Rd (44146-4650)
PHONE................................732 542-1191
EMP: 16
SALES (corp-wide): 1.9B **Privately Held**
SIC: 2834 Pharmaceutical preparations

HQ: Hikma Pharmaceuticals Usa Inc.
246 Industrial Way W
Eatontown NJ 07724
732 542-1191

(G-1413)
HOME CITY ICE COMPANY
20282 Hannan Pkwy (44146-5353)
PHONE................................440 439-5001
Rick Wetterau, *Manager*
EMP: 11
SQ FT: 15,947
SALES (corp-wide): 232.5MM **Privately Held**
WEB: www.homecityice.com
SIC: 5999 2097 Ice; manufactured ice
PA: The Home City Ice Company
6045 Bridgetown Rd Ste 1
Cincinnati OH 45248
513 574-1800

(G-1414)
I SCHUMANN & CO LLC
Also Called: I Schumann & Co
22500 Alexander Rd (44146-5576)
PHONE................................440 439-2300
Michael A Schumann, *Ch of Bd*
Scott Schumann, *President*
David Schumann, *Exec VP*
Duke Mullins, *Maint Spvr*
Don Robertson, *CFO*
◆ **EMP:** 115 **EST:** 1917
SQ FT: 150,000
SALES (est): 46.5MM **Privately Held**
WEB: www.ischumann.com
SIC: 3341 Brass smelting & refining (secondary); bronze smelting & refining (secondary); copper smelting & refining (secondary); nickel smelting & refining (secondary)

(G-1415)
ILLINOIS TOOL WORKS INC
Anchor Fasteners
26101 Fargo Ave (44146-1305)
PHONE................................216 292-7161
Ray Belcher, *Branch Mgr*
EMP: 35
SALES (corp-wide): 14.7B **Publicly Held**
SIC: 3496 Miscellaneous fabricated wire products
PA: Illinois Tool Works Inc.
155 Harlem Ave
Glenview IL 60025
847 724-7500

(G-1416)
INNER PRODUCTS SALES INC
Also Called: Fastsigns
5221 Northfield Rd A (44146-1110)
PHONE................................216 581-4141
Janice Sims, *President*
▲ **EMP:** 4
SQ FT: 1,575
SALES (est): 300K **Privately Held**
SIC: 3993 3953 Signs & advertising specialties; marking devices

(G-1417)
INTERNATIONAL SOURCES INC
380 Golden Oak Pkwy (44146-6525)
PHONE................................440 735-9890
Gregory Neal, *President*
Andy Grice, *Opers Dir*
Carey Hamilton, *Purchasing*
▲ **EMP:** 4 **EST:** 2015
SALES (est): 225.4K **Privately Held**
SIC: 3069 Fabricated rubber products

(G-1418)
IOPPOLO CONCRETE CORPORATION
10 Industry Dr (44146-4414)
PHONE................................440 439-6606
Anthony Ioppolo Jr, *President*
EMP: 20
SQ FT: 6,000
SALES (est): 3.2MM **Privately Held**
SIC: 3273 1711 7353 4959 Ready-mixed concrete; plumbing, heating, air-conditioning contractors; heavy construction equipment rental; snowplowing

(G-1419)
K C N TECHNOLOGIES LLC
Also Called: Ace Hydraulics
20637 Krick Rd (44146-5412)
PHONE................................440 439-4219
Brian Schuster, *General Mgr*
Gary Schuster, *Principal*
EMP: 8
SQ FT: 7,000
SALES (est): 799.8K **Privately Held**
WEB: www.acehem.com
SIC: 1799 7694 7629 Hydraulic equipment, installation & service; armature rewinding shops; electrical repair shops

(G-1420)
KADEE INDUSTRIES NEWCO INC
7160 Krick Rd Ste A (44146-4438)
PHONE................................440 439-8650
Brian Mullins, *President*
Joseph Scott, *Exec VP*
Catherine Mullins, *Admin Sec*
EMP: 10
SALES (est): 1.7MM **Privately Held**
WEB: www.kadeeindustries.com
SIC: 3496 2273 Mats & matting; carpets & rugs

(G-1421)
KOLTCZ CONCRETE BLOCK CO
7660 Oak Leaf Rd (44146-5554)
PHONE................................440 232-3630
Stanley M Koltcz, *President*
EMP: 26 **EST:** 1938
SQ FT: 55,000
SALES (est): 4.8MM **Privately Held**
WEB: www.koltcz.com
SIC: 3271 5032 5211 Blocks, concrete or cinder: standard; masons' materials; masonry materials & supplies

(G-1422)
LAKE SHORE ELECTRIC CORP
205 Willis St (44146-3505)
PHONE................................440 232-0200
Michael Shane, *President*
Michael Sharne, *President*
Wayne Bussard, *Vice Pres*
◆ **EMP:** 25
SQ FT: 40,000
SALES (est): 17.5MM **Privately Held**
WEB: www.lake-shore-electric.com
SIC: 3625 3613 3643 3621 Control equipment, electric; switches, electric power except snap, push button, etc.; current-carrying wiring devices; motors & generators; transformers, except electric; sheet metalwork

(G-1423)
LOVEMAN STEEL CORPORATION
5455 Perkins Rd (44146-1856)
PHONE................................440 232-6200
Anthony Murru, *CEO*
James Loveman, *COO*
David Loveman, *Exec VP*
Rob Loveman, *Vice Pres*
◆ **EMP:** 75
SQ FT: 80,000
SALES: 17MM **Privately Held**
WEB: www.lovemansteel.com
SIC: 5051 3443 Plates, metal; weldments

(G-1424)
MARLEN MANUFACTURING & DEV CO (PA)
5150 Richmond Rd (44146-1331)
PHONE................................216 292-7060
Gary Fenton, *President*
Robert L Keyes, *Principal*
David L Levine, *Principal*
R Williambashein, *Principal*
Michael Magar, *Treasurer*
▲ **EMP:** 6
SQ FT: 45,000
SALES (est): 6.1MM **Privately Held**
SIC: 3842 Surgical appliances & supplies; adhesive tape & plasters, medicated or non-medicated

(G-1425)
MARLEN MANUFACTURING & DEV CO
Medco Coated Products
5156 Richmond Rd (44146-1331)
PHONE................................216 292-7546
Mark Fenton, *Manager*
EMP: 29
SALES (corp-wide): 6.1MM **Privately Held**
SIC: 2891 3842 2672 2671 Adhesives & sealants; surgical appliances & supplies; coated & laminated paper; packaging paper & plastics film, coated & laminated
PA: Marlen Manufacturing And Development Co.
5150 Richmond Rd
Bedford OH 44146
216 292-7060

(G-1426)
MICROPLEX PRINTWARE CORP
100 Northfield Rd (44146-4640)
PHONE................................440 374-2424
Andre Fedak, *President*
Julie Swanbeck, *Accounting Mgr*
Gene Griggy, *Info Tech Mgr*
▲ **EMP:** 11
SQ FT: 12,000
SALES: 5.6MM **Privately Held**
WEB: www.microplex-usa.com
SIC: 2759 Laser printing

(G-1427)
MOLDING DYNAMICS INC
7009 Krick Rd (44146-4415)
PHONE................................440 786-8100
Charles F Connors III, *President*
Steve Walunis, *Plant Mgr*
Summer Howard, *Office Mgr*
EMP: 15
SQ FT: 14,000
SALES (est): 3.8MM **Privately Held**
SIC: 3089 Injection molding of plastics

(G-1428)
MORGAN ADVANCED CERAMICS INC
Also Called: Morgan Advanced Materials
232 Forbes Rd (44146-5418)
PHONE................................440 232-8604
Jack Gray, *Vice Pres*
Al Metcalfe, *Prdtn Mgr*
Joseph Fielding, *Research*
Gary E Stephen, *Controller*
Peter Morten, *Human Res Mgr*
EMP: 140
SALES (corp-wide): 1.3B **Privately Held**
WEB: www.morganelectroceramics.com
SIC: 2899 3251 Fluxes; brazing, soldering, galvanizing & welding; brick & structural clay tile
HQ: Morgan Advanced Ceramics, Inc
2425 Whipple Rd
Hayward CA 94544

(G-1429)
MT PLEASANT PHARMACY LLC
631 Lee Rd Apt 1228 (44146-6605)
PHONE................................216 672-4377
Michael Asiedu-Gyekye, *Principal*
EMP: 3
SALES (est): 240K **Privately Held**
SIC: 3842 Adhesive tape & plasters, medicated or non-medicated

(G-1430)
NEW YORK FROZEN FOODS INC (DH)
25900 Fargo Ave (44146-1302)
PHONE................................216 292-5655
Bruce Rosa, *President*
Donald Penn, *VP Mfg*
Brad McWithey, *Safety Mgr*
Lynette Sopko, *QC Mgr*
Brian Edwards, *Manager*
EMP: 260
SQ FT: 55,000
SALES (est): 60.8MM
SALES (corp-wide): 1.2B **Publicly Held**
WEB: www.lancaster.com
SIC: 2051 Bread, all types (white, wheat, rye, etc): fresh or frozen

HQ: T.Marzetti Company
380 Polaris Pkwy Ste 400
Westerville OH 43082
614 846-2232

(G-1431)
NOVA FILMS AND FOILS INC
11 Industry Dr (44146-4413)
P.O. Box 39055, Solon (44139-0055)
PHONE.....................................440 201-1300
Steven Wake, *President*
Marinko Milos, *CFO*
Robert Bucholz, *Manager*
▲ **EMP:** 10
SALES (est): 2.7MM **Privately Held**
WEB: www.novafilmsusa.com
SIC: 2891 Adhesives

(G-1432)
NPK CONSTRUCTION EQUIPMENT INC (HQ)
7550 Independence Dr (44146-5541)
PHONE.....................................440 232-7900
Dan Tyrell, *President*
Bob Gerhardstein, *Opers Mgr*
Robert Truelsch, *Executive*
◆ **EMP:** 60
SQ FT: 150,000
SALES (est): 45.5MM
SALES (corp-wide): 85.8MM **Privately Held**
WEB: www.npkce.com
SIC: 5082 3599 3546 3532 General construction machinery & equipment; machine shop, jobbing & repair; power-driven handtools; mining machinery; construction machinery; cutlery
PA: Nippon Pneumatic Manufacturing Co.,Ltd.
    4-11-5, Kamiji, Higashinari-Ku
    Osaka OSK 537-0
    669 739-100

(G-1433)
OAKWOOD INDUSTRIES INC (PA)
Also Called: Federal Metal Co
7250 Division St (44146-5406)
PHONE.....................................440 232-8700
David R Nagusky, *President*
Mike Naughton, *CFO*
Michael Bowman, *Manager*
Malvin E Bank, *Admin Sec*
◆ **EMP:** 60
SQ FT: 65,000
SALES (est): 16.2MM **Privately Held**
WEB: www.federalmetalcompany.com
SIC: 3341 3364 Brass smelting & refining (secondary); bronze smelting & refining (secondary); nonferrous die-castings except aluminum

(G-1434)
OVERSEAS PACKING LLC
Also Called: United Packaging Supply Co Div
19800 Alexander Rd (44146-5346)
PHONE.....................................440 232-2917
Stan Gaul, *Purchasing*
Thomas Bentley,
EMP: 15
SQ FT: 52,000
SALES (est): 2.5MM **Privately Held**
WEB: www.overseaspacking.net
SIC: 2449 3412 4783 Wood containers; metal barrels, drums & pails; packing goods for shipping; crating goods for shipping

(G-1435)
PALEOMD LLC
26245 Broadway Ave Ste B (44146-6524)
PHONE.....................................248 854-0031
Patricia Urcuyo, *Mng Member*
EMP: 7
SALES (est): 476K **Privately Held**
SIC: 2038 Pizza, frozen

(G-1436)
PINNACLE PRECISION PDTS LLC
624 Golden Oak Pkwy (44146-6504)
PHONE.....................................440 786-0248
Eric Ratiaczak, *President*
EMP: 4 **EST:** 1999
SQ FT: 3,800
SALES (est): 250K **Privately Held**
WEB: www.pinnacleprecisioninc.com
SIC: 3541 Machine tools, metal cutting type

(G-1437)
PPG INDUSTRIES INC
7650 First Pl Ste E (44146-6732)
PHONE.....................................440 232-1260
Andy Cherenfant, *Branch Mgr*
EMP: 11
SALES (corp-wide): 15.3B **Publicly Held**
SIC: 2851 Paints & allied products
PA: Ppg Industries, Inc.
    1 Ppg Pl
    Pittsburgh PA 15272
    412 434-3131

(G-1438)
PRINT SHOP DESIGN AND PRINT
366 Broadway Ave (44146-2604)
PHONE.....................................440 232-2391
Lisa M Szabo, *Manager*
EMP: 4
SALES (est): 285.5K **Privately Held**
SIC: 2752 Commercial printing, offset

(G-1439)
PUHD
20806 Aurora Rd (44146-1006)
PHONE.....................................216 244-3336
Chris Beard, *Owner*
EMP: 5
SALES: 1MM **Privately Held**
SIC: 2741 Miscellaneous publishing

(G-1440)
REA ELEKTRONIK INC
7307 Young Dr Ste B (44146-5385)
PHONE.....................................440 232-0555
Ray Turchi, *President*
MO Hassan, *Manager*
▲ **EMP:** 11
SQ FT: 5,400
SALES (est): 2.4MM **Privately Held**
WEB: www.rea-jet.com
SIC: 3953 5112 Marking devices; marking devices

(G-1441)
RESERVE MILLWORK INC
26881 Cannon Rd (44146-1851)
PHONE.....................................216 531-6982
Tony Azzolina, *President*
Virginia Azzolina, *Vice Pres*
EMP: 28 **EST:** 1980
SQ FT: 18,000
SALES (est): 5.3MM **Privately Held**
WEB: www.reservemillwork.com
SIC: 2431 2434 2541 Ornamental woodwork: cornices, mantels, etc.; wood kitchen cabinets; wood partitions & fixtures

(G-1442)
S & H INDUSTRIES INC (PA)
5200 Richmond Rd (44146-1387)
PHONE.....................................216 831-0550
Eric Turk, *CEO*
Steve Perney, *Treasurer*
EMP: 3 **EST:** 1978
SALES (est): 5MM **Privately Held**
SIC: 3423 Mechanics' hand tools

(G-1443)
S-TEK INC (PA)
26046 Broadway Ave (44146-6511)
P.O. Box 27, Tipp City (45371-0027)
PHONE.....................................440 439-8232
David Lepore, *President*
Bob Smith, *Corp Secy*
Fred B Holzworth, *Exec VP*
▲ **EMP:** 7
SQ FT: 3,000
SALES (est): 1.2MM **Privately Held**
WEB: www.s-tek.com
SIC: 3679 3826 5065 Liquid crystal displays (LCD); magnetic resonance imaging apparatus; radio & television equipment & parts; magnetic recording tape

(G-1444)
SATURN PRESS INC
177 Northfield Rd (44146-4605)
PHONE.....................................440 232-3344
Cindy Balamenti, *President*
Anthony Balamenti, *Vice Pres*
EMP: 5
SALES: 400K **Privately Held**
WEB: www.saturn-press.com
SIC: 2752 Commercial printing, lithographic

(G-1445)
SEEB INDUSTRIAL INC
5182 Richmond Rd (44146-1349)
P.O. Box 382, Twinsburg (44087-0382)
PHONE.....................................216 896-9016
Alex Nagy Jr, *President*
Judy Brunnett, *Office Mgr*
EMP: 9
SQ FT: 5,000
SALES: 880K **Privately Held**
WEB: www.seeb-sa.com
SIC: 3599 Machine shop, jobbing & repair

(G-1446)
SMITH-LUSTIG PAPER BOX MFG CO
22475 Aurora Rd (44146-1270)
PHONE.....................................216 621-0453
Richard Ames, *President*
Ann Ames, *Vice Pres*
Graham Klintworth, *Vice Pres*
Jenna Hadavny, *Manager*
▲ **EMP:** 40 **EST:** 1932
SQ FT: 75,000
SALES (est): 7.6MM **Privately Held**
SIC: 2631 2653 Folding boxboard; boxes, corrugated: made from purchased materials

(G-1447)
STEPHEN RADECKY
Also Called: Ris
659 Broadway Ave (44146-3504)
PHONE.....................................440 232-2132
Stephen Radecky, *Owner*
Sharon Radecky, *Manager*
EMP: 3
SQ FT: 1,000
SALES: 40K **Privately Held**
SIC: 7629 3699 Aircraft electrical equipment repair; flight simulators (training aids), electronic

(G-1448)
TAVENS CONTAINER INC
Also Called: Tavens Packg Display Solutions
22475 Aurora Rd (44146-1270)
PHONE.....................................216 883-3333
Richard Ames, *President*
Graham Klintworth, *VP Finance*
Benjamin Calkins, *Incorporator*
EMP: 60 **EST:** 1957
SQ FT: 87,000
SALES (est): 22.4MM **Privately Held**
WEB: www.tavens.com
SIC: 2653 3412 Boxes, corrugated: made from purchased materials; metal barrels, drums & pails

(G-1449)
THERMO FISHER SCIENTIFIC INC
1 Thermo Fisher Way (44146-6536)
PHONE.....................................440 703-1400
Rich Pallatine, *Branch Mgr*
Harold Liepert, *Project Leader*
EMP: 8
SALES (corp-wide): 24.3B **Publicly Held**
WEB: www.thermo.com
SIC: 3826 Analytical instruments
PA: Thermo Fisher Scientific Inc.
    168 3rd Ave
    Waltham MA 02451
    781 622-1000

(G-1450)
TMARZETTI COMPANY
Also Called: New York Frozen Foods
25900 Fargo Ave (44146-1302)
PHONE.....................................216 292-5655
Mike Mahon, *Managing Dir*
Bill Vandyke, *Supervisor*
EMP: 5
SALES (corp-wide): 1.2B **Publicly Held**
SIC: 2035 Pickles, sauces & salad dressings

HQ: T.Marzetti Company
380 Polaris Pkwy Ste 400
Westerville OH 43082
614 846-2232

(G-1451)
TORQ CORPORATION
32 W Monroe Ave (44146-3693)
PHONE.....................................440 232-4100
James E Taylor, *CEO*
John P Taylor, *President*
Gary Reitler, *General Mgr*
Marian Knapik, *Principal*
Gvido Kubulins, *Engineer*
▲ **EMP:** 29 **EST:** 1951
SQ FT: 22,000
SALES (est): 5.7MM **Privately Held**
WEB: www.torq.com
SIC: 3643 Current-carrying wiring devices

(G-1452)
TRUE GRINDING
20502 Krick Rd (44146-5408)
PHONE.....................................440 786-7608
Mark Kerney, *President*
Jim Orban, *Vice Pres*
EMP: 3
SALES: 300K **Privately Held**
SIC: 3599 Grinding castings for the trade

(G-1453)
VITEC INC
26901 Cannon Rd (44146-1809)
PHONE.....................................216 464-4670
Richard A Wynveen, *CEO*
Franz H Schubert, *Shareholder*
EMP: 11
SQ FT: 15,000
SALES (est): 2.2MM **Privately Held**
SIC: 3823 Industrial instrmnts msrmnt display/control process variable

(G-1454)
WALTON PLASTICS INC
Also Called: Wal Plax
20493 Hannan Pkwy (44146-5356)
PHONE.....................................440 786-7711
Steven Wake, *CEO*
Larry Crystal, *Principal*
Marinko Milos, *CFO*
John Oyster, *Sales Dir*
Ron Seese, *Accounts Mgr*
▲ **EMP:** 21
SQ FT: 44,000
SALES (est): 7.1MM **Privately Held**
WEB: www.waltonpvc.com
SIC: 3081 Vinyl film & sheet

(G-1455)
XELLIA PHARMACEUTICALS USA LLC
200 Northfield Rd (44146-4642)
PHONE.....................................847 986-7984
Niess Agerbak, *Branch Mgr*
EMP: 20
SALES (corp-wide): 20.1B **Privately Held**
SIC: 2834 Pharmaceutical preparations
HQ: Xellia Pharmaceuticals Usa Llc
    8841 Wadford Dr
    Raleigh NC 27616
    919 327-5500

(G-1456)
YOUNG REGULATOR COMPANY INC
7100 Krick Rd Ste A (44146-4443)
PHONE.....................................440 232-9452
Michael E McGuigan, *President*
Marty Gullatta, *Purch Mgr*
EMP: 20 **EST:** 1930
SQ FT: 40,000
SALES: 6.2MM **Privately Held**
WEB: www.youngregulator.com
SIC: 3822 1711 Air conditioning & refrigeration controls; plumbing, heating, air-conditioning contractors

(G-1457)
ZENEX INTERNATIONAL
7777 First Pl (44146-6733)
PHONE.....................................440 232-4155
George Kniere, *Owner*
Jason Archer, *Natl Sales Mgr*
Paul Crowther, *Regl Sales Mgr*
Scott Flowe, *Regl Sales Mgr*
▲ **EMP:** 30

Bedford Heights - Cuyahoga County (G-1458)

GEOGRAPHIC SECTION

SALES (est): 4.8MM **Privately Held**
SIC: 2813 Aerosols

Bedford Heights
Cuyahoga County

(G-1458)
ALERT STAMPING & MFG CO INC
Also Called: Paul S Blanch
24500 Solon Rd (44146-4793)
PHONE.................................440 232-5020
Paul S Blanch, *President*
Dave Collura, *Business Mgr*
James D Kovacik, *Vice Pres*
Ralph Technow, *Director*
▲ EMP: 40 EST: 1961
SQ FT: 40,000
SALES (est): 8MM **Privately Held**
SIC: 3699 3499 3641 3645 Extension cords; reels, cable: metal; lamps, fluorescent, electric; lamps, incandescent filament, electric; residential lighting fixtures

(G-1459)
ALLOY METAL EXCHANGE LLC
Also Called: Dynamic Metal Services
26000 Corbin Dr (44128)
PHONE.................................216 478-0200
Brian Ducovna, *President*
Ben Henson, *Vice Pres*
Bill Mills, *Vice Pres*
Frank Lochiatto, *Director*
EMP: 25
SQ FT: 40,000
SALES (est): 12MM **Privately Held**
SIC: 1081 Metal mining services

(G-1460)
AMERICAN SPRING WIRE CORP (PA)
Also Called: A S W
26300 Miles Rd (44146-1072)
PHONE.................................216 292-4620
Timothy W Selhorst, *CEO*
Michael L Miller, *Principal*
Greg Bokar, *COO*
Peter Anselmi, *Safety Mgr*
Jose Pineda, *Purchasing*
▲ EMP: 200
SQ FT: 360,500
SALES (est): 166.1MM **Privately Held**
WEB: www.americanspringwire.com
SIC: 3272 3315 3316 3339 Concrete products; wire products, ferrous/iron: made in wiredrawing plants; wire, flat, cold-rolled strip: not made in hot-rolled mills; primary nonferrous metals; carbon & graphite products

(G-1461)
ASWPENGG LLC
Also Called: Amrican Spring Wire
26300 Miles Rd (44146-1410)
PHONE.................................216 292-4620
Timothy W Selhorst, *President*
EMP: 3 EST: 2016
SALES (est): 234.8K **Privately Held**
SIC: 3592 3495 Valves; wire springs

(G-1462)
BRAND CASTLE LLC (PA)
5111 Richmond Rd Frnt (44146-1354)
PHONE.................................216 292-7700
Carolyn Resar, *General Mgr*
Bobbi Weissman, *Controller*
Jimmy Zeilinger, *Mng Member*
Linda Bina, *Manager*
Taylor Meadows, *Manager*
◆ EMP: 12
SQ FT: 10,000
SALES (est): 16.7MM **Privately Held**
WEB: www.brandcastle.com
SIC: 2052 Bakery products, dry

(G-1463)
BRIDGE ANALYZERS INCORPORATED
5198 Richmond Rd (44146-1331)
PHONE.................................216 332-0592
David Anderson, *Principal*
EMP: 3 EST: 2017

SALES (est): 491.8K **Privately Held**
SIC: 3826 Analytical instruments

(G-1464)
CARDINAL FSTENER SPECIALTY INC
5185 Richmond Rd (44146-1330)
PHONE.................................216 831-3800
Bill Boak, *President*
Wendy L Brugmann, *Exec VP*
Denise R Muha, *Vice Pres*
Bill Walczak, *Vice Pres*
Sarah Wieczorek, *Sales Staff*
▲ EMP: 50
SQ FT: 100,000
SALES (est): 11.8MM **Privately Held**
WEB: www.cardinalfastener.com
SIC: 3965 Fasteners

(G-1465)
CLEVELAND COCA-COLA BTLG INC
25000 Miles Rd (44146-1319)
PHONE.................................216 690-2653
Et Al, *President*
George M Gernhardt, *Principal*
Peter E Benzino, *Vice Pres*
Charles R Hanlon, *Treasurer*
Angel Hardin, *Human Resources*
EMP: 220 EST: 1911
SQ FT: 220,000
SALES (est): 38.5MM
SALES (corp-wide): 361.4MM **Privately Held**
SIC: 2086 Bottled & canned soft drinks
HQ: Wilmington Trust Sp Services
    1105 N Market St Ste 1300
    Wilmington DE 19801
    302 427-7550

(G-1466)
CLEVELAND STEEL SPECIALTY CO
26001 Richmond Rd (44146-1435)
PHONE.................................216 464-9400
Robert W Ehrhardt Sr, *President*
Robert W Ehrhardt Jr, *President*
EMP: 30 EST: 1924
SQ FT: 24,000
SALES (est): 8.1MM **Privately Held**
WEB: www.clevelandsteel.com
SIC: 3443 3429 3444 Metal parts; builders' hardware; sheet metalwork

(G-1467)
CRAFTED SURFACE AND STONE LLC
26050 Richmond Rd Ste D (44146-1436)
PHONE.................................440 658-3799
Allen Gleine, *Mng Member*
EMP: 25
SQ FT: 38,000
SALES: 7MM **Privately Held**
SIC: 1799 2541 Counter top installation; counter & sink tops

(G-1468)
CWH GRAPHICS LLC
Also Called: Ink Well
23196 Miles Rd Ste A (44128-5490)
P.O. Box 22651, Cleveland (44122-0651)
PHONE.................................866 241-8515
Kelvin Hunter Sr,
George F Voinovich,
EMP: 7
SQ FT: 4,000
SALES (est): 612.7K **Privately Held**
SIC: 2752 Commercial printing, offset

(G-1469)
ELECTRODATA INC
23400 Aurora Rd Ste 5 (44146-1738)
P.O. Box 31780, Independence (44131-0780)
PHONE.................................216 663-3333
Eddy Wright, *President*
Michael Wright, *Principal*
Jim Spoth, *Corp Secy*
James Spoth, *Admin Sec*
EMP: 15 EST: 1972
SQ FT: 11,000
SALES (est): 3.1MM **Privately Held**
WEB: www.electrodata.com
SIC: 3661 Telephone & telegraph apparatus

(G-1470)
FOOD EQUIPMENT MFG CORP
Also Called: Femc
22201 Aurora Rd (44146-1273)
PHONE.................................216 672-5859
Robert Sauer, *President*
Betty Howard, *President*
Randa Sacha, *Purchasing*
Les Weagraff, *Chief Engr*
EMP: 20
SQ FT: 65,000
SALES (est): 6.4MM **Privately Held**
WEB: www.femc.com
SIC: 3565 Packaging machinery

(G-1471)
HALEX/SCOTT FETZER COMPANY (DH)
Also Called: Halex, A Scott Fetzer Company
23901 Aurora Rd (44146-1717)
PHONE.................................440 439-1616
Gary Heeman, *President*
▲ EMP: 87
SALES (est): 16.3MM
SALES (corp-wide): 225.3B **Publicly Held**
SIC: 3699 Electrical equipment & supplies
HQ: The Scott Fetzer Company
    28800 Clemens Rd
    Westlake OH 44145
    440 892-3000

(G-1472)
HOIST EQUIPMENT CO INC (PA)
26161 Cannon Rd (44146-1896)
PHONE.................................440 232-0300
Nicholas Gambatesa, *CEO*
Jeffrey Sadar, *Vice Pres*
Thomas Gedeon, *Chief Engr*
Dina Iacano, *Admin Asst*
EMP: 30 EST: 1953
SQ FT: 40,000
SALES (est): 4.2MM **Privately Held**
WEB: www.hoistequipment.com
SIC: 3537 3535 3536 Cranes, industrial truck; engine stands & racks, metal; lift trucks, industrial; fork, platform, straddle, etc.; overhead conveyor systems; hoists

(G-1473)
MADISON ELECTRIC PRODUCTS INC (PA)
26401 Fargo Ave (44146-1311)
PHONE.................................216 391-7776
Brad Wiandt, *President*
Rob Fisher, *Vice Pres*
◆ EMP: 40 EST: 1988
SQ FT: 1,000
SALES (est): 9.6MM **Privately Held**
SIC: 3644 Electric conduits & fittings

(G-1474)
METRON INSTRUMENTS INC
5198 Richmond Rd (44146-1331)
PHONE.................................216 332-0592
David Anderson, *President*
EMP: 8
SALES (est): 1.6MM **Privately Held**
SIC: 3826 Analytical instruments

(G-1475)
MOLDED EXTRUDED
23940 Miles Rd (44128-5425)
PHONE.................................216 475-5491
Frank Novak, *Principal*
EMP: 4 EST: 2012
SALES (est): 276.6K **Privately Held**
SIC: 3089 Molding primary plastic

(G-1476)
NATIONAL PEENING
23800 Corbin Dr Unit B (44128-5454)
PHONE.................................216 342-9155
Don Kvorka, *President*
EMP: 6
SALES (est): 518.5K **Privately Held**
SIC: 3398 Shot peening (treating steel to reduce fatigue)

(G-1477)
NETWORKED CMMNCTONS SLTONS LLC
23400 Aurora Rd Ste 5 (44146-1738)
PHONE.................................440 374-4990
Eddie Wright, *President*

EMP: 3
SALES (est): 155.7K **Privately Held**
SIC: 3679 Electronic components

(G-1478)
PARAGON ROBOTICS LLC
5386 Majestic Pkwy Ste 2 (44146-6907)
PHONE.................................216 313-9299
Julian Lamb,
EMP: 3
SALES: 40K **Privately Held**
SIC: 3695 Computer software tape & disks: blank, rigid & floppy

(G-1479)
RMW INDUSTRIES INC
24869 Aurora Rd (44146-1760)
PHONE.................................440 439-1971
Robyn Mays, *Principal*
EMP: 3
SALES (est): 230.1K **Privately Held**
SIC: 3999 Manufacturing industries

(G-1480)
STUNTRONICS LLC
23020 Miles Rd (44146-5443)
PHONE.................................216 780-1413
Randy Saley, *Mng Member*
Darko Cralj,
EMP: 4
SQ FT: 1,400
SALES: 250K **Privately Held**
SIC: 3699 8748 Security devices; safety training service

(G-1481)
TPSC INC
Also Called: Perfect Score, The
25801 Solon Rd (44146-4759)
PHONE.................................440 439-9320
Fax: 440 439-9380
EMP: 15
SQ FT: 2,000
SALES: 5MM **Privately Held**
SIC: 3556 Mfg Food Products Machinery

(G-1482)
VIRCO VIRLON INDUSTRIES CORP
Also Called: Vvi Dispensers
24700 Aurora Rd Ste 3 (44146-1786)
PHONE.................................216 410-4872
Virgil Collins, *Principal*
EMP: 3 EST: 2014
SALES (est): 141.7K **Privately Held**
SIC: 3999 Barber & beauty shop equipment

Bellaire
Belmont County

(G-1483)
BELMONT COMMUNITY HOSPITAL
Also Called: Belmont Community Health Ctr
4697 Harrison St (43906-1338)
PHONE.................................740 671-1216
Garry Gould, *CEO*
KY Sohn, *Principal*
EMP: 275
SALES (corp-wide): 395.3MM **Privately Held**
SIC: 2599 Hospital beds
HQ: Belmont Community Hospital
    4697 Harrison St
    Bellaire OH 43906
    740 671-1200

(G-1484)
CHARLES WISVARI
Also Called: Vivid Graphix
3266 Guernsey St (43906-1545)
PHONE.................................740 671-9960
Charles Wisvari, *Owner*
Nancy Wisvari, *Co-Owner*
EMP: 11
SQ FT: 10,500
SALES: 500K **Privately Held**
SIC: 2396 2395 5699 Screen printing on fabric articles; embroidery products, except schiffli machine; customized clothing & apparel

GEOGRAPHIC SECTION

Bellefontaine - Logan County (G-1512)

(G-1485)
COUNTRY CLB RTRMENT CTR IV LLC
55801 Conno Mara Dr (43906-9698)
PHONE......................740 676-2300
EMP: 1
SALES: 4.3MM Privately Held
SIC: 3949 Indian clubs

(G-1486)
GUMBYS LLC
2300 Belmont St (43906-1733)
PHONE......................740 671-0818
Beau Lamotte, Branch Mgr
EMP: 8 Privately Held
SIC: 3999 Cigarette & cigar products & accessories
PA: Gumby's, L.L.C.
98 E Cove Ave Ste 1
Wheeling WV 26003

(G-1487)
KROGER CO
400 28th St (43906-1790)
PHONE......................740 671-5164
Kim Bartsch, Manager
EMP: 175
SALES (corp-wide): 121.1B Publicly Held
WEB: www.kroger.com
SIC: 5411 5912 5812 2052 Supermarkets, chain; drug stores & proprietary stores; eating places; cookies & crackers; bread, cake & related products
PA: The Kroger Co
1014 Vine St Ste 1000
Cincinnati OH 45202
513 762-4000

(G-1488)
PAUL/JAY ASSOCIATES
Also Called: Digital Solutions
3057 Union St (43906-1531)
P.O. Box 236 (43906-0236)
PHONE......................740 676-8776
Paul J Cramer, Owner
EMP: 4
SQ FT: 9,000
SALES (est): 425.8K Privately Held
WEB: www.digitalsolutionsusa.com
SIC: 2752 7311 7372 2791 Commercial printing, offset; advertising agencies; prepackaged software; typesetting

(G-1489)
XTO ENERGY INC
2358 W 23rd St (43906-9614)
PHONE......................740 671-9901
EMP: 73
SALES (corp-wide): 290.2B Publicly Held
SIC: 1311 Crude petroleum production
HQ: Xto Energy Inc.
22777 Sprngwoods Vlg Pkwy
Spring TX 77389

Bellbrook
Greene County

(G-1490)
COMPUTER ZOO INC
1930 N Lakeman Dr Ste 106 (45305-1200)
PHONE......................937 310-1474
Fax: 937 438-2027
EMP: 9 EST: 1999
SQ FT: 2,500
SALES (est): 940K Privately Held
SIC: 5734 3571 7372 3577 Ret Computers/Software Mfg Electronic Computers Prepackaged Software Svc Mfg Computer Peripherals Electrical Contractor

(G-1491)
D J DECORATIVE STONE INC
3180 Ferry Rd (45305-8926)
PHONE......................937 848-6462
Jamie Zimmer, President
EMP: 4
SALES (est): 505.2K Privately Held
SIC: 3281 Stone, quarrying & processing of own stone products

(G-1492)
DAIRY SHED
55 Bellbrook Plz (45305-1954)
PHONE......................937 848-3504
Roger McConnell, Principal
EMP: 3
SALES (est): 191.8K Privately Held
SIC: 2024 Ice cream, bulk

(G-1493)
ERNST ENTERPRISES INC
Also Called: Sugarcreek Ready Mix
2181 Ferry Rd (45305-9728)
PHONE......................937 848-6811
John Ernst Jr, President
EMP: 25
SQ FT: 5,000
SALES (corp-wide): 227.2MM Privately Held
WEB: www.ernstconcrete.com
SIC: 3273 Ready-mixed concrete
PA: Ernst Enterprises, Inc.
3361 Successful Way
Dayton OH 45414
937 233-5555

(G-1494)
FANZ STOP
63 Bellbrook Plz (45305-1954)
PHONE......................937 310-1436
Jenniffer Simpson, Partner
EMP: 6
SALES (est): 838.7K Privately Held
SIC: 2329 2339 Men's & boys' sportswear & athletic clothing; sportswear, women's

(G-1495)
GOLDEN SPRING CO INC
2143 Ferry Rd (45305-9728)
P.O. Box 244 (45305-0244)
PHONE......................937 848-2513
Paul Smith, President
Rita Treser, Corp Secy
EMP: 10 EST: 1953
SQ FT: 5,100
SALES: 1MM Privately Held
WEB: www.golden-spring.com
SIC: 3493 Coiled flat springs

(G-1496)
N S T BATTERY
4496 W Franklin St (45305-1598)
PHONE......................937 433-9222
Linda G Mem, Principal
EMP: 7
SALES (est): 696.1K Privately Held
WEB: www.nstbattery.com
SIC: 3692 5063 5531 Primary batteries, dry & wet; batteries; batteries, automotive & truck

Belle Center
Logan County

(G-1497)
BELLE CENTER AIR TOOL CO INC
202 N Elizabeth St (43310-9684)
P.O. Box 37 (43310-0037)
PHONE......................937 464-7474
Carroll Doty, President
Ruth Doty, Corp Secy
▲ EMP: 9
SQ FT: 9,500
SALES (est): 2.6MM Privately Held
SIC: 5084 3532 Pneumatic tools & equipment; drills, bits & similar equipment

(G-1498)
DAN S MILLER & DAVID S MILLER
9535 County Road 97 (43310-9598)
PHONE......................937 464-9061
Dan S Miller, Partner
EMP: 4
SALES: 500K Privately Held
SIC: 2448 Pallets, wood

(G-1499)
HIGHS WELDING INC
3065 County Road 150 (43310-1107)
P.O. Box 97, Alger (45812-0097)
PHONE......................937 464-3029
Nick S High, President
EMP: 6 EST: 1972
SALES (est): 403.9K Privately Held
SIC: 7692 Welding repair

(G-1500)
MILLER PALLET COMPANY
9216 County Road 97 (43310-9597)
PHONE......................937 464-4483
Dan Miller, Owner
David Miller, Principal
EMP: 3
SALES (est): 439.9K Privately Held
SIC: 2448 Pallets, wood

Bellefontaine
Logan County

(G-1501)
AGC AUTOMOTIVE AMERICAS
1465 W Sandusky Ave (43311-1082)
PHONE......................937 599-3131
Arkady Doorman, Vice Pres
Dean Wright, Plant Mgr
Scott Keller, Buyer
▲ EMP: 81
SALES (est): 11.4MM Privately Held
SIC: 7549 1793 1799 3231 Automotive customizing services, non-factory basis; glass & glazing work; glass tinting, architectural or automotive; products of purchased glass

(G-1502)
AGC FLAT GLASS NORTH AMER INC
31 Hunter Pl (43311-3006)
PHONE......................937 292-7784
Bade Furling, Branch Mgr
EMP: 11
SALES (corp-wide): 13.5B Privately Held
SIC: 3211 Flat glass
HQ: Agc Flat Glass North America, Inc.
11175 Cicero Dr Ste 400
Alpharetta GA 30022
404 446-4200

(G-1503)
AGC FLAT GLASS NORTH AMER INC
1465 W Sandusky Ave (43311-1082)
P.O. Box 819 (43311-0819)
PHONE......................937 599-3131
Arcadie Dorman, Branch Mgr
EMP: 5
SQ FT: 570,000
SALES (corp-wide): 13.5B Privately Held
WEB: www.aptechnoglass.com
SIC: 3231 3211 Safety glass: made from purchased glass; flat glass
HQ: Agc Flat Glass North America, Inc.
11175 Cicero Dr Ste 400
Alpharetta GA 30022
404 446-4200

(G-1504)
ARDEN J NEER SR
Also Called: Neer's Engineering Labs
4859 Township Road 45 (43311-9624)
PHONE......................937 585-6733
Arden J Neer Sr, Owner
EMP: 12
SQ FT: 7,500
SALES: 1.1MM Privately Held
SIC: 1442 Construction sand mining; gravel mining

(G-1505)
AXIS CORPORATION
314 Water Ave (43311-1734)
P.O. Box 668 (43311-0668)
PHONE......................937 592-1958
Matt Oldiges, President
Thomas Oldiges, Shareholder
Linda Luebke, Admin Sec
EMP: 10 EST: 1969
SQ FT: 20,000
SALES (est): 1.8MM Privately Held
WEB: www.axiscorporation.com
SIC: 3499 Wheels: wheelbarrow, stroller, etc.: disc, stamped metal

(G-1506)
BELLE PRINTING
118 S Main St (43311-2007)
P.O. Box 307 (43311-0307)
PHONE......................937 592-5161
Mike Joseph, Owner
EMP: 5
SQ FT: 1,500
SALES (est): 400K Privately Held
SIC: 2752 Commercial printing, offset

(G-1507)
BELLEFONTAINE EXAMINER
127 E Chillicothe Ave (43311-1957)
PHONE......................937 592-3060
Thomas Hubbard, Principal
EMP: 4
SALES (est): 314.1K Privately Held
SIC: 2711 Commercial printing & newspaper publishing combined; newspapers, publishing & printing

(G-1508)
BUCKEYE BOXES INC
1133 W Columbus Ave (43311-1076)
PHONE......................937 599-2551
Kevin Maxam, Manager
EMP: 8
SALES (est): 680K
SALES (corp-wide): 56.9MM Privately Held
SIC: 2653 Boxes, corrugated: made from purchased materials
PA: Buckeye Boxes, Inc.
601 N Hague Ave
Columbus OH 43204
614 274-8484

(G-1509)
CATHIE D HUBBARD
Also Called: Publishing Company
305 E Williams Ave (43311-2449)
PHONE......................937 593-0316
Janet Hubbard, Owner
EMP: 32
SALES (est): 612.5K Privately Held
SIC: 2711 Newspapers, publishing & printing

(G-1510)
COUNTY CLASSIFIEDS
Also Called: The County Classified's
117 E Patterson Ave (43311-1912)
P.O. Box 596 (43311-0596)
PHONE......................937 592-8847
Leah Frank, President
EMP: 8
SALES (est): 310K Privately Held
SIC: 2711 2752 2741 Job printing & newspaper publishing combined; commercial printing, lithographic; miscellaneous publishing

(G-1511)
DAIDO METAL BELLEFONTAINE LLC
1215 S Greenwood St (43311-1628)
PHONE......................937 592-5010
Mark Ikawa,
▲ EMP: 192
SQ FT: 224,000
SALES (est): 25.9MM
SALES (corp-wide): 1B Privately Held
WEB: www.daidometal.co.jp
SIC: 3366 Bushings & bearings
PA: Daido Metal Co., Ltd.
2-3-1, Sakae, Naka-Ku
Nagoya AIC 460-0
522 051-400

(G-1512)
DESIGNED HARNESS SYSTEMS INC
Also Called: Dhs Innovations
227 Water Ave (43311-1731)
P.O. Box 37 (43311-0037)
PHONE......................937 599-2485
Craig Lingon, President
EMP: 10
SALES (est): 1.1MM Privately Held
SIC: 3714 Automotive wiring harness sets

Bellefontaine - Logan County (G-1513)

(G-1513)
DEWEY SMITH QUARTER HORSES
2679 Township Road 55 (43311-9417)
PHONE.................................682 597-2424
EMP: 3
SALES (est): 292.7K Privately Held
SIC: 3131 Quarters

(G-1514)
DMG TOOL & DIE LLC
1215 S Greenwood St (43311-1628)
PHONE.................................937 407-0810
John Pope, *Mfg Staff*
Thomas D Moreland, *Mng Member*
EMP: 6
SQ FT: 10,000
SALES: 13.4K Privately Held
SIC: 3599 Machine shop, jobbing & repair

(G-1515)
EWH SPECTRUM LLC
221 W Chillicothe Ave (43311-1467)
PHONE.................................937 593-8010
Robert L Robinson, *President*
Cheryl Smucker, *General Mgr*
Jean Robinson, *Vice Pres*
Dave Shoffner, *Purch Mgr*
Nick Tillman, *Financial Exec*
EMP: 74
SQ FT: 27,500
SALES (est): 16MM Privately Held
WEB: www.ewhspectrum.com
SIC: 3679 3694 Harness assemblies for electronic use: wire or cable; engine electrical equipment

(G-1516)
GRIT GUARD INC
3690 County Road 10 (43311-9416)
PHONE.................................937 592-9003
Luan Lamb, *President*
Chris Lamb, *Director*
EMP: 5
SALES: 1.7MM Privately Held
SIC: 5084 2821 Plastic products machinery; plastics materials & resins

(G-1517)
HBD/THERMOID INC
1301 W Sandusky Ave (43311-1082)
PHONE.................................937 593-5010
R Greely, *Principal*
EMP: 7
SALES (corp-wide): 261.6MM Privately Held
SIC: 3429 3052 Manufactured hardware (general); rubber & plastics hose & beltings
HQ: Hbd/Thermoid, Inc.
5200 Upper Metro Pl
Dublin OH 43017

(G-1518)
HUBBARD PUBLISHING CO
127 E Chillicothe Ave (43311-1957)
P.O. Box 40 (43311-0040)
PHONE.................................937 592-3060
Janet Hubbard, *President*
Jon B Hubbard, *Vice Pres*
EMP: 35 EST: 1891
SQ FT: 13,000
SALES (est): 2.6MM Privately Held
SIC: 2711 2752 2791 Commercial printing & newspaper publishing combined; commercial printing, offset; typesetting

(G-1519)
IEG PLASTICS LLC
223 Lock And Load Rd (43311-2500)
PHONE.................................937 565-4211
Jim Moore, *Principal*
EMP: 14 EST: 2014
SALES (est): 2.4MM Privately Held
SIC: 3089 Injection molding of plastics

(G-1520)
INSTANT REPLAY
334 E Columbus Ave (43311-2002)
PHONE.................................937 592-0534
Helen Manns, *Prdtn Mgr*
Lisa Russell, *Office Mgr*
Nancy Evans-Donley, *Manager*
Christy McGill, *Manager*
EMP: 3
SALES (est): 247.5K Privately Held
SIC: 2752 Commercial printing, lithographic

(G-1521)
KLB INDUSTRIES INC
Also Called: National Extrusion & Mfg Co
Orchard & Elm St (43311)
P.O. Box 460 (43311-0460)
PHONE.................................937 592-9010
Christopher A Kerns, *President*
John D Bishop, *Vice Pres*
Nick Benson, *Design Engr*
Craig Johnson, *Treasurer*
John Bishop, *Manager*
▲ EMP: 45 EST: 1949
SQ FT: 41,942
SALES (est): 9.1MM Privately Held
WEB: www.nationalextrusion.com
SIC: 3354 Aluminum extruded products

(G-1522)
MAJESTIC PLASTICS INC
811 N Main St (43311-2376)
P.O. Box 47 (43311-0047)
PHONE.................................937 593-9500
Sean Ammons, *President*
EMP: 9
SQ FT: 7,800
SALES (est): 1.6MM Privately Held
WEB: www.majesticplastics.com
SIC: 3089 Injection molding of plastics

(G-1523)
OHIO WIRE HARNESS LLC
225 Lincoln Ave (43311-1717)
P.O. Box 27 (43311-0027)
PHONE.................................937 292-7355
Jerry Robinson,
Linda Botkin,
Hayden Stanley,
Kim Wilson,
EMP: 10
SALES (est): 950K Privately Held
SIC: 3679 Harness assemblies for electronic use: wire or cable

(G-1524)
REYNOLDS & CO INC
1515 S Main St (43311-1505)
P.O. Box 907 (43311-0907)
PHONE.................................937 592-8300
Thomas M Reynolds, *President*
EMP: 4
SALES (est): 1MM Privately Held
WEB: www.reynolds-co.com
SIC: 5075 3589 Warm air heating & air conditioning; water treatment equipment, industrial

(G-1525)
SIEMENS INDUSTRY INC
811 N Main St (43311-2300)
PHONE.................................937 593-6010
Chris Childs, *Purchasing*
Larry Falk, *Director*
EMP: 100
SALES (corp-wide): 95B Privately Held
WEB: www.sea.siemens.com
SIC: 3612 3613 3643 Transformers, except electric; switchgear & switchboard apparatus; current-carrying wiring devices
HQ: Siemens Industry, Inc.
1000 Deerfield Pkwy
Buffalo Grove IL 60089
800 743-6367

(G-1526)
VITAL SIGNS & ADVERTISING LLC
224 S Madriver St (43311-1936)
PHONE.................................937 292-7967
Pat Culp, *Owner*
EMP: 3
SALES (est): 252.4K Privately Held
SIC: 3993 Signs & advertising specialties

Bellevue
Huron County

(G-1527)
AMCOR RIGID PLASTICS USA LLC
975 W Main St (44811-9011)
PHONE.................................419 483-4343
Dave Hoover, *Ch of Bd*
Jeff Salmon, *Mfg Spvr*
Angelo Deblase, *Purch Agent*
Thomas Hall, *Human Res Mgr*
Lee Elftman, *Manager*
EMP: 58 Privately Held
SIC: 3089 Plastic containers, except foam
HQ: Amcor Rigid Plastics Usa, Llc
935 Technology Dr Ste 100
Ann Arbor MI 48108

(G-1528)
AMCOR RIGID PLASTICS USA LLC
Also Called: Ball Plastic Container Div
975 W Main St (44811-9011)
PHONE.................................419 483-4343
EMP: 9
SALES (corp-wide): 9.6B Privately Held
SIC: 3411 Mfg Metal Cans
HQ: Amcor Rigid Plastics Usa, Llc
10521 Mi State Road 52
Manchester MI 48108

(G-1529)
AMERICAN BALER CO
800 E Center St (44811-1748)
P.O. Box 29 (44811-0029)
PHONE.................................419 483-5790
Leland Boren, *CEO*
Dave Kowaleski, *President*
Frank B Cameron, *Principal*
Richard R Hollington, *Principal*
E E Moulton, *Principal*
EMP: 65 EST: 1945
SQ FT: 80,133
SALES: 28.5MM
SALES (corp-wide): 312.9MM Privately Held
WEB: www.avisindustrial.com
SIC: 3569 3523 Baling machines, for scrap metal, paper or similar material; farm machinery & equipment
PA: Avis Industrial Corporation
1909 S Main St
Upland IN 46989
765 998-8100

(G-1530)
BALL CORP
975 W Main St (44811-9011)
PHONE.................................419 483-4343
Bruce Zemba, *Principal*
Angelo Deblase, *Purch Agent*
EMP: 6
SALES (est): 90.5K Privately Held
SIC: 5812 3089 Eating places; plastics products

(G-1531)
BELLEVUE MANUFACTURING COMPANY (PA)
520 Goodrich Rd (44811-1139)
PHONE.................................419 483-3190
Frank A Knapp, *Incorporator*
Ralph T Wolfrom Et Al, *Incorporator*
EMP: 94 EST: 1915
SQ FT: 150,000
SALES (est): 19MM Privately Held
WEB: www.tbmc.net
SIC: 3714 Filters: oil, fuel & air, motor vehicle

(G-1532)
BELLEVUE MANUFACTURING COMPANY
300 Ashford Ave (44811-1600)
PHONE.................................419 483-3190
Charles Deluca, *Manager*
EMP: 5
SALES (corp-wide): 19MM Privately Held
WEB: www.tbmc.net
SIC: 3714 3469 Filters: oil, fuel & air, motor vehicle; metal stampings
PA: The Bellevue Manufacturing Company
520 Goodrich Rd
Bellevue OH 44811
419 483-3190

(G-1533)
BUNGE NORTH AMERICA FOUNDATION
605 Goodrich Rd (44811-1142)
P.O. Box 369 (44811-0369)
PHONE.................................419 483-5340
Ray Bowns, *Branch Mgr*
EMP: 8 Privately Held
WEB: www.bungemarion.com
SIC: 2075 2041 Soybean oil, cake or meal; lecithin, soybean; flour & other grain mill products
HQ: Bunge North America Foundation
1391 Timberlk Mnr Pkwy # 31
Chesterfield MO 63017
314 872-3030

(G-1534)
CAPITOL ALUMINUM & GLASS CORP
1276 W Main St (44811-9424)
PHONE.................................800 331-8268
Robert C Wagner, *Ch of Bd*
Gail P Coe, *President*
Tory J Woodard, *Corp Secy*
Dean Camp, *Vice Pres*
Tricia Norton, *Human Resources*
EMP: 55 EST: 1955
SQ FT: 75,000
SALES (est): 16.8MM Privately Held
WEB: www.capitol-windows.com
SIC: 3442 Metal doors; window & door frames

(G-1535)
DONALD E DIDION II
Also Called: Didion's Mechanical
1027b County Road 308 (44811-9497)
PHONE.................................419 483-2226
Donald E Didion II, *Principal*
EMP: 25
SQ FT: 20,000
SALES: 1.4MM Privately Held
WEB: www.didionsmech.com
SIC: 3499 8711 Fire- or burglary-resistive products; engineering services

(G-1536)
HURON PRODUCTS
601 E Center St (44811-1712)
PHONE.................................419 483-5608
Carey Stiles, *Principal*
EMP: 3
SALES (est): 189.3K Privately Held
SIC: 3273 Ready-mixed concrete

(G-1537)
INDUSTRIAL IMAGE
5630 State Route 113 (44811-8900)
PHONE.................................419 547-1417
Jason Holcomb, *Owner*
Ericca Holcomb, *Co-Owner*
EMP: 4
SALES (est): 347.8K Privately Held
SIC: 3993 Signs & advertising specialties

(G-1538)
MAGNESIUM REFINING TECH INC
Also Called: Magretech
301 County Road 177 (44811-8713)
PHONE.................................419 483-9199
Ken Balser, *Manager*
EMP: 50
SALES (corp-wide): 12.1MM Privately Held
SIC: 3339 Magnesium refining (primary)
PA: Magnesium Refining Technologies, Inc.
29695 Pettibone Rd
Cleveland OH 44139
419 483-9199

GEOGRAPHIC SECTION

Belmont - Belmont County (G-1566)

(G-1539)
MEC
540 Goodrich Rd (44811-1139)
PHONE..................................419 483-4852
A Wolfe, *Principal*
EMP: 3
SALES (est): 119.9K **Privately Held**
SIC: 2448 Wood pallets & skids

(G-1540)
MITSUBISHI CHLS PERF PLYRS INC
Also Called: McPp
350 N Buckeye St (44811-1208)
PHONE..................................419 483-2931
Diane Sabo, *Purch Mgr*
Anthony Piscitello, *Engineer*
Lee Wilson, *Branch Mgr*
Harry Behning, *Manager*
EMP: 95 **Privately Held**
SIC: 2821 2891 Plastics materials & resins; adhesives
HQ: Mitsubishi Chemical Performance Polymers, Inc.
2001 Hood Rd
Greer SC 29650
864 879-5487

(G-1541)
QUALITY WELDING INC
104 Ronald Ln (44811)
P.O. Box 273 (44811-0273)
PHONE..................................419 483-6067
Charles Tinnel, *President*
EMP: 25
SQ FT: 2,800
SALES: 1.5MM **Privately Held**
SIC: 7692 Welding repair

(G-1542)
R AND S TECHNOLOGIES INC
2474 State Route 4 (44811-9742)
PHONE..................................419 483-3691
Paul Ritz, *President*
Gary Shingledecker, *Vice Pres*
Ben Ritz, *Engineer*
EMP: 11
SQ FT: 2,400
SALES (est): 1.7MM **Privately Held**
WEB: www.r-s-t-inc.com
SIC: 3089 3599 Molding primary plastic; machine & other job shop work

(G-1543)
SCS GEARBOX INC
739 W Main St (44811-9312)
PHONE..................................419 483-7278
Craig Sage, *President*
EMP: 11
SQ FT: 10,000
SALES: 3.3MM **Privately Held**
WEB: www.scsgearbox.com
SIC: 3714 Gears, motor vehicle; connecting rods, motor vehicle engine

(G-1544)
SELBRO INC
555 Goodrich Rd (44811-1140)
P.O. Box 595 (44811-0595)
PHONE..................................419 483-9918
James Seliga, *President*
Gordon Seliga, *Vice Pres*
Vicki Seliga, *Admin Sec*
EMP: 10
SQ FT: 15,000
SALES (est): 1.2MM **Privately Held**
WEB: www.selbro.com
SIC: 3546 Power-driven handtools

(G-1545)
SENECA RAILROAD & MINING CO
1075 W Main St (44811-9012)
PHONE..................................419 483-7764
Raymond Wasson, *President*
Pat Mira, *Asst Sec*
EMP: 11
SQ FT: 16,300
SALES (est): 1.9MM **Privately Held**
SIC: 3312 Rail joints or fastenings

(G-1546)
SOLAE LLC
Also Called: Solae Central Soya
300 Great Lakes Pkwy (44811)
P.O. Box 369 (44811-0369)
PHONE..................................419 483-0400
Dale Perman, *Manager*
Raymond Bowns, *Director*
EMP: 150
SALES (corp-wide): 85.9B **Publicly Held**
WEB: www.solae.com
SIC: 2075 Soybean oil, cake or meal
HQ: Solae, Llc
4300 Duncan Ave
Saint Louis MO 63110
314 659-3000

(G-1547)
SOLAE LLC
605 Goodrich Rd (44811-1142)
PHONE..................................419 483-5340
Dale Hoffman, *Manager*
Kevin Hand, *Supervisor*
EMP: 8
SALES (est): 637.9K **Privately Held**
SIC: 2099 Food preparations

(G-1548)
SPIRALCOOL COMPANY
186 Sheffield St Ste 188 (44811-1528)
P.O. Box 128 (44811-0128)
PHONE..................................419 483-2510
Thomas Artino, *President*
Richard A Hopkins, *President*
EMP: 9
SQ FT: 5,000
SALES (est): 1.3MM **Privately Held**
SIC: 3069 Hard rubber & molded rubber products

(G-1549)
THOMAS STEEL INC
305 Elm St (44811-1543)
P.O. Box 343 (44811-0343)
PHONE..................................419 483-7540
Jake Thomas, *CEO*
Steve Roth, *President*
Lynn E Thomas, *Corp Secy*
Carl Koselke, *Vice Pres*
Chuck Gerber, *Plant Mgr*
EMP: 38
SQ FT: 50,000
SALES: 8MM **Privately Held**
WEB: www.tsifab.com
SIC: 3441 Building components, structural steel

(G-1550)
TOWER AUTOMOTIVE OPERATIONS I
630 Southwest St (44811-9314)
PHONE..................................419 483-1500
Chuck Beach, *Design Engr*
Mike Jenkins, *Branch Mgr*
Ken Lynch, *Technician*
Vernon Van Fleet, *Maintence Staff*
EMP: 192 **Publicly Held**
SIC: 3465 Automotive stampings
HQ: Tower Automotive Operations Usa I, Llc
17672 N Laurel Park Dr 400e
Livonia MI 48152

(G-1551)
WILBERT INC
Also Called: Wilbert Plastic Services
635 Southwest St (44811-9314)
PHONE..................................419 483-2300
Greg Botner, *Branch Mgr*
EMP: 85
SALES (corp-wide): 906MM **Privately Held**
SIC: 3089 Injection molding of plastics
PA: Wilbert, Inc.
2001 Oaks Pkwy
Belmont NC 28012
704 247-3850

(G-1552)
WINDSOR MOLD INC
Also Called: Precision Automotive Plastics
122 Hirt Dr (44811-9053)
PHONE..................................419 484-2400
Joe Giardina, *Branch Mgr*
EMP: 29

SALES (corp-wide): 796K **Privately Held**
SIC: 3089 Injection molding of plastics
HQ: Windsor Mold Inc
4035 Malden Rd
Windsor ON N9C 2
519 972-9032

(G-1553)
WINDSOR MOLD USA INC
Also Called: Autoplas Division
560 Goodrich Rd (44811-1139)
PHONE..................................419 483-0653
Brian K Moll, *President*
Bill Plate, *General Mgr*
▲ **EMP:** 50
SALES (est): 11.9MM
SALES (corp-wide): 796K **Privately Held**
SIC: 3089 Injection molding of plastics
HQ: Windsor Mold Inc
4035 Malden Rd
Windsor ON N9C 2
519 972-9032

(G-1554)
YORK FABRICATION & MACHINE
6964 County Road 191 (44811-8700)
PHONE..................................419 483-6275
Jerome Huff, *Owner*
EMP: 4
SQ FT: 2,200
SALES (est): 190K **Privately Held**
SIC: 3599 5531 Machine shop, jobbing & repair; automotive & home supply stores

---

Bellville
Richland County

(G-1555)
COLLEEN D TURNER
Also Called: Bellville Flowers and Gifts
72 Main St (44813-1021)
PHONE..................................419 886-4810
Colleen Turner, *Owner*
EMP: 4
SALES (est): 288.4K **Privately Held**
SIC: 3231 Novelties, glass: fruit, foliage, flowers, animals, etc.

(G-1556)
GATTON PACKAGING INC
99 East St (44813-1003)
PHONE..................................419 886-2577
John R Gatton, *President*
Larry Gatton, *Corp Secy*
EMP: 6
SQ FT: 10,000
SALES (est): 1.3MM **Privately Held**
SIC: 2653 Boxes, corrugated: made from purchased materials

(G-1557)
GORMAN-RUPP COMPANY
Also Called: Division Gorman-Rupp Company
180 Hines Ave (44813-1234)
PHONE..................................419 886-3001
Michael Hill, *General Mgr*
Brian Morris, *Engineer*
EMP: 46
SQ FT: 12,000
SALES (corp-wide): 414.3MM **Publicly Held**
WEB: www.gormanrupp.com
SIC: 3561 Industrial pumps & parts
PA: Gorman-Rupp Company
600 S Airport Rd
Mansfield OH 44903
419 755-1011

(G-1558)
JACKSON WELLS SERVICES
1201 Mill Rd (44813-1282)
PHONE..................................419 886-2017
Cory Jackson, *Owner*
EMP: 8
SALES (est): 591.3K **Privately Held**
SIC: 1381 Service well drilling

(G-1559)
MID-OHIO TUBING LLC
500 Main St (44813-1302)
PHONE..................................419 886-0220
EMP: 3

SALES (corp-wide): 29.9MM **Privately Held**
SIC: 3317 Tubes, seamless steel
HQ: Mid-Ohio Tubing, Llc
145 W Elm St
Butler OH 44822
419 883-2066

(G-1560)
NATURAL OPTIONS AROMATHERAPY
Also Called: Holistic Botanicals
610 State Route 97 W (44813-8813)
PHONE..................................419 886-3736
George Cox, *Principal*
EMP: 5
SALES (est): 248.9K **Privately Held**
SIC: 2833 Medicinals & botanicals

(G-1561)
NORTH CENTRAL INSULATION INC (PA)
7539 State Route 13 (44813-8943)
P.O. Box 368 (44813-0368)
PHONE..................................419 886-2030
D Brent Dudgeon, *President*
John Dudgeon, *Vice Pres*
Andrew Dungeon, *Vice Pres*
Linda Dudgeon, *Treasurer*
▲ **EMP:** 18
SQ FT: 10,000
SALES (est): 26.5MM **Privately Held**
WEB: www.nci-ins.com
SIC: 1741 1742 3231 Foundation building; insulation, buildings; products of purchased glass

(G-1562)
PJ WOODWORK LLC
16 E Ogle St (44813-1029)
PHONE..................................419 886-0008
Joel Warner, *Principal*
EMP: 4
SALES (est): 404.8K **Privately Held**
SIC: 2431 Millwork

(G-1563)
PROTEUS ELECTRONICS INC
161 Spayde Rd (44813-9011)
P.O. Box 725 (44813-0725)
PHONE..................................419 886-2296
Thomas Clabaugh, *President*
Mark Molnar, *Vice Pres*
EMP: 8
SQ FT: 3,500
SALES (est): 1.3MM **Privately Held**
WEB: www.proteuselectronics.com
SIC: 3629 Electronic generation equipment

Belmont
Belmont County

(G-1564)
ALANAX TECHNOLOGIES INC
40714 Cherrywood Dr (43718-9443)
PHONE..................................216 469-1545
Brian Barritt, *CEO*
Wesley Eddy, *Principal*
Robert Glitch, *CFO*
EMP: 5
SALES (est): 230.3K **Privately Held**
SIC: 7372 4899 7371 Business oriented computer software; communication signal enhancement network system; computer software development

(G-1565)
BAKER LOGGING
62683 Ok Rd (43718-9503)
PHONE..................................740 686-2817
Steve Baker, *Principal*
EMP: 3
SALES (est): 181.3K **Privately Held**
SIC: 2411 Logging camps & contractors

(G-1566)
GOOD WOOD INC (PA)
42591 Bina Rd (43718-9657)
P.O. Box 35 (43718-0035)
PHONE..................................740 484-1500
David Murphy, *President*
Nancy Murphy, *Admin Sec*
▲ **EMP:** 6

Belmont - Belmont County (G-1567)

SQ FT: 50,000
SALES (est): 925.8K **Privately Held**
SIC: 2499 Novelties, wood fiber

(G-1567)
STINGRAY PRESSURE PUMPING LLC (PA)
42739 National Rd (43718-9669)
PHONE..................405 648-4177
Bob Maughmer, *Mng Member*
▲ **EMP:** 42
SALES (est): 130.1MM **Privately Held**
SIC: 1389 Gas field services

Beloit
Mahoning County

(G-1568)
BENDER ENGINEERING COMPANY
17934 Mill St (44609-9512)
P.O. Box 238 (44609-0238)
PHONE..................330 938-2355
Dennis Patterson, *President*
Lois Patterson, *Vice Pres*
EMP: 7
SQ FT: 2,000
SALES (est): 759.6K **Privately Held**
SIC: 8711 3545 Engineering services; machine tool accessories

(G-1569)
DP OPERATING COMPANY INC
19220 State Route 62 (44609-9509)
PHONE..................330 938-2172
Louis Dorfman, *President*
EMP: 5
SALES (est): 708K
SALES (corp-wide): 3MM **Privately Held**
SIC: 1311 Crude petroleum production
PA: Dorfman Production Company
8144 Walnut Hill Ln # 1060
Dallas TX 75231
214 361-1660

(G-1570)
JENKINS MOTOR PARTS
Also Called: Carquest Auto Parts
38 Westville Lake Rd (44609-9402)
PHONE..................330 525-4011
Thomas W Jenkins, *Owner*
EMP: 4 **EST:** 1949
SQ FT: 3,750
SALES (est): 511.9K **Privately Held**
SIC: 5013 7538 3599 5531 Automotive supplies & parts; engine rebuilding: automotive; machine shop, jobbing & repair; automotive parts

(G-1571)
MAHONING VALLEY MANUFACTURING
17796 Rte 62 (44609)
P.O. Box 247, Damascus (44619-0247)
PHONE..................330 537-4492
Tony Sampedro, *CEO*
Susan Sampedro, *Vice Pres*
EMP: 20
SQ FT: 35,000
SALES (est): 3.4MM **Privately Held**
WEB: www.mvmi.com
SIC: 3944 3469 Strollers, baby (vehicle); stamping metal for the trade

(G-1572)
WESTERN RESERVE INDUSTRIES LLC
25933 State Route 62 (44609-9330)
PHONE..................330 238-1800
EMP: 3
SALES (est): 156.8K **Privately Held**
SIC: 3999 Manufacturing industries

Belpre
Washington County

(G-1573)
DAVES PALLETS
710 Thomas St (45714-1929)
PHONE..................740 525-4938
David Leek, *Principal*
EMP: 4
SALES (est): 206.1K **Privately Held**
SIC: 2448 Pallets, wood & wood with metal

(G-1574)
EDI HOLDING COMPANY LLC (PA)
100 Ayers Blvd (45714-9303)
PHONE..................740 401-4000
Richard Wynn, *President*
EMP: 4
SALES (est): 16.5MM **Privately Held**
SIC: 3533 5084 Oil & gas field machinery; oil refining machinery, equipment & supplies

(G-1575)
ELECTRNIC DSIGN FOR INDUST INC
Also Called: E D I
100 Ayers Blvd (45714-9303)
PHONE..................740 401-4000
Richard Wynn, *President*
Jay Pottmeyer, *Vice Pres*
Nancy Wynn, *Vice Pres*
Johnny Hendershot, *Engineer*
Sam Wynn, *Admin Sec*
EMP: 21
SQ FT: 2,700
SALES: 16.5MM **Privately Held**
SIC: 3533 5084 Oil & gas field machinery; oil refining machinery, equipment & supplies
PA: Edi Holding Company, Llc
100 Ayers Blvd
Belpre OH 45714
740 401-4000

(G-1576)
HEALTH BRIDGE IMAGING LLC
809 Farson St Unit 107 (45714-1067)
PHONE..................740 423-3300
Yale Conley,
EMP: 4
SALES (est): 420K **Privately Held**
WEB: www.healthbridgeimaging.com
SIC: 3826 Analytical instruments

(G-1577)
KRATON EMPLYEES RECREATION CLB
2419 State Route 618 (45714-2086)
P.O. Box 235 (45714-0235)
PHONE..................740 423-7571
Nanette Pettit, *Principal*
EMP: 5
SALES (est): 510.2K **Privately Held**
SIC: 2822 Synthetic rubber

(G-1578)
KRATON POLYMERS US LLC
2419 State Rd 618 (45714)
P.O. Box 235 (45714-0235)
PHONE..................740 423-7571
Robert Roesh, *Plant Mgr*
Kathleen Ervine, *Engineer*
Gabriel Guevara, *Engineer*
Ben Hayes, *Engineer*
Bob Rose, *Branch Mgr*
EMP: 400 **Publicly Held**
WEB: www.kraton.com
SIC: 2822 5169 2821 Synthetic rubber; synthetic resins, rubber & plastic materials; plastics materials & resins
HQ: Kraton Polymers U.S. Llc
15710 John F Kennedy Blvd # 300
Houston TX 77032
281 504-4700

(G-1579)
LAFARGE NORTH AMERICA INC
1684 State Route 618 (45714-2085)
PHONE..................740 423-5900
Michael Timmons, *Manager*
EMP: 4
SALES (corp-wide): 26.4B **Privately Held**
WEB: www.lafargenorthamerica.com
SIC: 3241 5211 Cement, hydraulic; masonry materials & supplies
HQ: Lafarge North America Inc.
8700 W Bryn Mawr Ave
Chicago IL 60631
773 372-1000

(G-1580)
MILLER PRSTHTICS ORTHOTICS LLC
2354 Richmiller Ln (45714-1052)
PHONE..................740 421-4211
Mark Miller, *CEO*
Nancy Miller, *COO*
EMP: 3
SALES (est): 230.4K **Privately Held**
SIC: 3842 Prosthetic appliances

(G-1581)
ORION ENGINEERED CARBONS LLC
11135 State Route 7 (45714-9496)
PHONE..................740 423-9571
Donnie Loubiere, *Plant Mgr*
EMP: 71
SALES (corp-wide): 889.5K **Privately Held**
SIC: 2869 Industrial organic chemicals
HQ: Orion Engineered Carbons Llc
4501 Magnolia Cove Dr
Kingwood TX 77345
832 445-3300

(G-1582)
PIONEER CITY CASTING COMPANY
904 Campus Dr (45714-2342)
P.O. Box 425 (45714-0425)
PHONE..................740 423-7533
Don W Simmons, *President*
EMP: 30 **EST:** 1946
SQ FT: 55,000
SALES (est): 7.1MM **Privately Held**
SIC: 3321 3322 Gray iron castings; malleable iron foundries

(G-1583)
POLYONE CORPORATION
2419 State Route 618 (45714-2086)
P.O. Box 219 (45714-0219)
PHONE..................740 423-7571
Kevin M Fogarty, *Branch Mgr*
EMP: 13 **Publicly Held**
SIC: 2821 Thermoplastic materials
PA: Polyone Corporation
33587 Walker Rd
Avon Lake OH 44012

(G-1584)
TOLL COMPACTION GROUP LLC
721 Farson St (45714-1044)
PHONE..................740 376-0511
Paul B Pritchard,
EMP: 36
SALES: 5MM **Privately Held**
SIC: 3482 Pellets & BB's, pistol & air rifle ammunition

(G-1585)
WAL-BON OF OHIO INC (PA)
Also Called: Napoli's Pizza
210 Main St (45714-1612)
P.O. Box 508 (45714-0508)
PHONE..................740 423-6351
Wayne D Waldeck, *Ch of Bd*
William D Waldeck, *President*
EMP: 15 **EST:** 1966
SQ FT: 6,000
SALES (est): 45.5MM **Privately Held**
WEB: www.napolis.com
SIC: 2051 5812 Bakery: wholesale or wholesale/retail combined; pizzeria, independent

(G-1586)
WAL-BON OF OHIO INC
Also Called: Mc Happy's Bake Shoppe
708 Main St (45714-1622)
P.O. Box 508 (45714-0508)
PHONE..................740 423-8178
William Waldeck, *Manager*
EMP: 100
SQ FT: 8,000
SALES (corp-wide): 45.5MM **Privately Held**
WEB: www.napolis.com
SIC: 5461 2051 2099 Bakeries; doughnuts, except frozen; food preparations
PA: Wal-Bon Of Ohio, Inc.
210 Main St
Belpre OH 45714
740 423-6351

(G-1587)
WEEKLY CHATTER
1564 Calder Ridge Rd (45714-9467)
PHONE..................740 336-4704
Misty Perry-Durham, *Principal*
EMP: 3
SALES (est): 113.6K **Privately Held**
SIC: 2711 Newspapers

Berea
Cuyahoga County

(G-1588)
A & F MACHINE PRODUCTS CO
454 Geiger St (44017-1392)
PHONE..................440 826-0959
Fred J Helwig Sr, *President*
Fred J Helwig Jr, *Vice Pres*
EMP: 22 **EST:** 1960
SQ FT: 12,000
SALES (est): 6.6MM **Privately Held**
WEB: www.helwigpumps.com
SIC: 3561 Industrial pumps & parts

(G-1589)
ALLOY ENGINEERING COMPANY (PA)
844 Thacker St (44017-1698)
PHONE..................440 243-6800
Lou Petonovich, *President*
Richard Turiczek, *Vice Pres*
Lee Watson, *Vice Pres*
Eric Sistek, *Plant Supt*
Jan Gomes, *Plant Mgr*
▼ **EMP:** 85 **EST:** 1943
SQ FT: 45,000
SALES: 13.9MM **Privately Held**
WEB: www.alloyengineering.com
SIC: 3443 Plate work for the metalworking trade

(G-1590)
ANGEL WINDOW MFG CORP
237 Depot St (44017-1860)
PHONE..................440 891-1006
William C Engelmann, *President*
Arthur Engelmann, *Vice Pres*
EMP: 4
SQ FT: 4,000
SALES (est): 313.6K **Privately Held**
SIC: 3442 Storm doors or windows, metal

(G-1591)
AUDION AUTOMATION LTD (PA)
775 Berea Industrial Pkwy (44017-2948)
PHONE..................216 267-1911
Mark Goldman, *CEO*
▲ **EMP:** 35
SQ FT: 64,000
SALES (est): 6.5MM **Privately Held**
WEB: www.audionautomation.com
SIC: 3565 Packing & wrapping machinery

(G-1592)
AUDION AUTOMATION LTD
Clamco
775 Berea Industrial Pkwy (44017-2948)
PHONE..................216 267-1911
Mark E Goldman, *CEO*
Gregg Hazen, *Engineer*
EMP: 25
SALES (corp-wide): 6.5MM **Privately Held**
SIC: 3565 Packaging machinery
PA: Audion Automation, Ltd.
775 Berea Industrial Pkwy
Berea OH 44017
216 267-1911

(G-1593)
BEREA MANUFACTURING INC
480 Geiger St (44017-1319)
PHONE..................440 260-0590
Ed Casper, *President*
Mike Pandoli, *Treasurer*
Earl Sunkel, *Admin Sec*
▲ **EMP:** 14

GEOGRAPHIC SECTION
Berea - Cuyahoga County (G-1620)

SALES: 1MM **Privately Held**
WEB: www.allwelding.com
SIC: 3599 Machine & other job shop work

(G-1594)
BEREA PRINTING COMPANY
1060 W Bagley Rd Ste 102 (44017-2938)
P.O. Box 38251, Olmsted Falls (44138-0251)
PHONE.....................440 243-1080
James Dettmer, *President*
Linda Dettmer, *Admin Sec*
EMP: 9 EST: 1967
SQ FT: 5,500
SALES (est): 2MM **Privately Held**
WEB: www.bereaprinting.com
SIC: 2752 2759 Commercial printing, offset; letterpress printing

(G-1595)
CLEVELAND HOYA CORP
Also Called: Advance Lens Labs
94 Pelret Industrial Pkwy (44017-2940)
PHONE.....................440 234-5703
William Bennedict, *CEO*
▲ EMP: 75
SALES (est): 9.8MM
SALES (corp-wide): 5B **Privately Held**
WEB: www.advancelens.com
SIC: 3827 3851 Optical instruments & lenses; ophthalmic goods
PA: Hoya Corporation
  6-10-1, Nishishinjuku
  Shinjuku-Ku TKY 160-0
  369 114-811

(G-1596)
CLEVELAND METAL STAMPING CO
1231 W Bagley Rd Ste 1 (44017-2911)
PHONE.....................440 234-0010
Frank Ghinga, *Vice Pres*
Florian Ghinga, *Plant Mgr*
EMP: 15 EST: 1974
SQ FT: 23,000
SALES (est): 2.4MM **Privately Held**
SIC: 3469 Stamping metal for the trade

(G-1597)
CLEVELAND SHUTTERS
204 Depot St (44017-1810)
PHONE.....................440 234-7600
Shannon Harris, *Agent*
EMP: 4
SALES (est): 305.7K **Privately Held**
SIC: 3442 Shutters, door or window: metal

(G-1598)
COLORMATRIX GROUP INC (HQ)
680 N Rocky River Dr (44017-1628)
PHONE.....................216 622-0100
Stephen Newlin, *Principal*
EMP: 1
SALES (est): 12.2MM **Publicly Held**
SIC: 2865 2816 Dyes & pigments; inorganic pigments

(G-1599)
COLORMATRIX HOLDINGS INC (DH)
680 N Rocky River Dr (44017-1628)
PHONE.....................440 930-3162
Gerry Corrigan, *Principal*
EMP: 160
SALES (est): 7.6MM **Publicly Held**
SIC: 2865 2816 Dyes & pigments; inorganic pigments

(G-1600)
DEARBORN INC
678 Front St (44017-1607)
PHONE.....................440 234-1353
Kenneth Dearborn, *President*
David Klaich, *Project Mgr*
Ron Kompa, *Site Mgr*
Mark Romelfanger, *QC Mgr*
Shawn Brown, *Engineer*
EMP: 50
SQ FT: 30,000
SALES (est): 8.6MM **Privately Held**
WEB: www.dearborninc.com
SIC: 3599 Machine shop, jobbing & repair

(G-1601)
DENTAL PURE WATER INC
336 Daisy Ave Ste 102b (44017-1729)
PHONE.....................440 234-0890
Frank Falat, *Principal*
EMP: 10
SALES: 530K **Privately Held**
WEB: www.dentalpurewater.com
SIC: 5499 3843 Water: distilled mineral or spring; dental chairs

(G-1602)
DJ INTERNATIONAL INC
35 2nd Ave (44017-1243)
PHONE.....................440 260-7593
Joseph Antal, *Principal*
EMP: 3
SALES (est): 271.8K **Privately Held**
SIC: 3842 Surgical appliances & supplies

(G-1603)
E W WELDING & FABRICATING
336 Wyleswood Dr (44017-2443)
PHONE.....................440 826-9038
Eli Waiters, *Owner*
EMP: 4
SQ FT: 2,000
SALES (est): 97.4K **Privately Held**
SIC: 7692 3441 Welding repair; fabricated structural metal

(G-1604)
EATON CORPORATION
Also Called: Hansen Coupling Division
1000 W Bagley Rd (44017-2906)
P.O. Box 805 (44017-0805)
PHONE.....................440 826-1115
Michael Fitzsimmons, *Engineer*
Brett Jaffe, *Branch Mgr*
EMP: 180 **Privately Held**
WEB: www.tuthill.com
SIC: 3494 3568 3498 Couplings, except pressure & soil pipe; pipe fittings; power transmission equipment; fabricated pipe & fittings
HQ: Eaton Corporation
  1000 Eaton Blvd
  Cleveland OH 44122
  440 523-5000

(G-1605)
ELGIN FASTENER GROUP
777 W Bagley Rd (44017-2901)
PHONE.....................440 325-4337
EMP: 6
SALES (est): 841.2K **Privately Held**
SIC: 3965 Fasteners

(G-1606)
ESTABROOK ASSEMBLY SVCS INC
Also Called: Easi
700 W Bagley Rd (44017-2900)
P.O. Box 804 (44017-0804)
PHONE.....................440 243-3350
Jeffrey W Tarr, *President*
Rich Zsigray, *Vice Pres*
Fran Torok, *Accountant*
▼ EMP: 15
SQ FT: 14,000
SALES (est): 3.9MM **Privately Held**
SIC: 3822 Energy cutoff controls, residential or commercial types

(G-1607)
FASTENER INDUSTRIES INC
Also Called: Ohio Nut & Bolt Company Div
33 Lou Groza Blvd (44017-1237)
PHONE.....................440 891-2031
Susan Croft, *Purch Mgr*
Jim Thomas, *Engineer*
Tim Morgan, *Manager*
Patrick Finnegan, *Manager*
EMP: 50
SALES (corp-wide): 42.3MM **Privately Held**
WEB: www.on-b.com
SIC: 3452 5084 Bolts, nuts, rivets & washers; lift trucks & parts
PA: Fastener Industries, Inc.
  1 Berea Cmns Ste 209
  Berea OH 44017
  440 243-0034

(G-1608)
FLAMING RIVER INDUSTRIES INC
800 Poertner Dr (44017-2936)
PHONE.....................440 826-4488
Jeanette Ladina, *President*
Jim Stanfield, *Warehouse Mgr*
Karen Raines, *Purch Agent*
Ralph A Deluca, *Treasurer*
Bradley Scott, *Accountant*
▲ EMP: 18
SQ FT: 25,000
SALES (est): 4.4MM **Privately Held**
WEB: www.flamingriver.com
SIC: 3714 Motor vehicle engines & parts; steering mechanisms, motor vehicle

(G-1609)
HORIZON METALS INC
8059 Lewis Rd Ste 102 (44017-2943)
P.O. Box 38310, Olmsted Falls (44138-0310)
PHONE.....................440 235-3338
Paul Froehlich, *President*
James Batcha, *Vice Pres*
▲ EMP: 20 EST: 1997
SQ FT: 38,000
SALES (est): 6.2MM **Privately Held**
SIC: 3441 Fabricated structural metal

(G-1610)
HOYA OPTICAL LABS
869 W Bagley Rd (44017-2903)
PHONE.....................440 239-1924
EMP: 3
SALES (est): 192.3K **Privately Held**
SIC: 8734 5049 5048 3827 Testing laboratories; optical goods; optometric equipment & supplies; optical instruments & lenses

(G-1611)
HUNT IMAGING LLC (PA)
210 Sheldon Rd (44017-1234)
PHONE.....................440 826-0433
Peter J Calabrese, *General Mgr*
Jeff Johnson, *Principal*
Vic Scigliano, *Mfg Staff*
Michael E Stanek, *CFO*
John J Margherio, *Mng Member*
▲ EMP: 31
SQ FT: 2,040
SALES (est): 5.5MM **Privately Held**
SIC: 2869 2899 Industrial organic chemicals; chemical preparations

(G-1612)
JACO MANUFACTURING COMPANY (PA)
468 Geiger St (44017-1319)
P.O. Box 619 (44017-0619)
PHONE.....................440 234-4000
Stephen C Campbell, *President*
Thomas Campell, *Exec VP*
Anthony Lamorte, *Vice Pres*
Susan Sexton, *Vice Pres*
Phil Di Masa, *Plant Mgr*
EMP: 100
SQ FT: 70,000
SALES (est): 19.5MM **Privately Held**
WEB: www.jacomfg.com
SIC: 3089 Injection molding of plastics

(G-1613)
JACO MANUFACTURING COMPANY
90 Karl St (44017-1320)
P.O. Box 619 (44017-0619)
PHONE.....................440 234-4000
Annmarie Brian, *Manager*
EMP: 12
SQ FT: 12,000
SALES (corp-wide): 19.5MM **Privately Held**
WEB: www.jacomfg.com
SIC: 3089 3559 Injection molded finished plastic products; synthetic resin finished products; plastics working machinery
PA: Jaco Manufacturing Company
  468 Geiger St
  Berea OH 44017
  440 234-4000

(G-1614)
JAMES F SEME
292 Karl St (44017-1371)
PHONE.....................440 759-6455
James F Seme, *Owner*
EMP: 4 EST: 2012
SALES (est): 367K **Privately Held**
SIC: 2434 1799 Wood kitchen cabinets; kitchen & bathroom remodeling

(G-1615)
JOYCE MANUFACTURING CO (PA)
Also Called: Joyce Windows
1125 Berea Indus Pkwy (44017-2928)
PHONE.....................440 239-9100
Russell Schmidt, *President*
John Caputo, *Corp Secy*
Gary Winkler, *Vice Pres*
Nikki Jacobs, *Manager*
EMP: 70
SQ FT: 100,000
SALES (est): 12.3MM **Privately Held**
WEB: www.joycemfg.com
SIC: 3448 3446 3444 Prefabricated metal buildings; architectural metalwork; awnings, sheet metal

(G-1616)
MACPHERSON ENGINEERING INC
Also Called: Macpherson & Company
95 Pelret Industrial Pkwy (44017-2940)
PHONE.....................440 243-6565
Bruce McPherson, *President*
EMP: 25
SALES (est): 2MM **Privately Held**
SIC: 3231 Reflecting glass

(G-1617)
MGM CONSTRUCTION INC
Also Called: MGM Roofing
1480 W Bagley Rd Ste 1 (44017-2951)
PHONE.....................440 234-7660
Michael Lyon, *President*
EMP: 15 EST: 2000
SALES (est): 3.3MM **Privately Held**
SIC: 1389 1542 1761 1799 Construction, repair & dismantling services; commercial & office building contractors; roofing contractor; athletic & recreation facilities construction

(G-1618)
MR 14K INC
Also Called: C S Johns Company
370 W Bagley Rd (44017-1348)
PHONE.....................440 234-6661
Matt Regotti, *President*
Mark Regotti, *Vice Pres*
EMP: 5
SQ FT: 1,000
SALES (est): 763.7K **Privately Held**
SIC: 3911 7631 Jewelry, precious metal; jewelry repair services; watch repair

(G-1619)
NORTH COAST MEDICAL EQP INC
96 Lincoln Ave (44017-1662)
PHONE.....................440 243-2722
Edward Gibbs, *President*
EMP: 10
SQ FT: 2,694
SALES (est): 1.4MM **Privately Held**
SIC: 3844 X-ray apparatus & tubes

(G-1620)
NOSHOK INC (PA)
1010 W Bagley Rd (44017-2906)
PHONE.....................440 243-0888
James B Cole, *CEO*
Jeff N Scott, *President*
Pierre Carmona, *Principal*
Michael Walker, *Regional Mgr*
Christian F L Cole, *Vice Pres*
▲ EMP: 33
SQ FT: 50,000
SALES (est): 7MM **Privately Held**
WEB: www.noshok.com
SIC: 3823 Industrial instrmnts msrmnt display/control process variable

Berea - Cuyahoga County (G-1621)

(G-1621)
OLMSTED PRINTING INC
1060 W Bagley Rd Ste 102 (44017-2938)
PHONE 440 234-2600
Richard Bucher, *President*
Karen Bucher, *Treasurer*
EMP: 5
SALES (est): 989K **Privately Held**
WEB: www.olmstedprinting.com
SIC: 2752 Commercial printing, offset; business forms, lithographed

(G-1622)
POLYONE CORPORATION
680 N Rocky River Dr (44017-1628)
PHONE 216 622-0100
EMP: 5 **Publicly Held**
SIC: 2821 Plastics materials & resins
PA: Polyone Corporation
33587 Walker Rd
Avon Lake OH 44012

(G-1623)
RADS LLC
Also Called: Radcliffe Steel
135 Blaze Industrial Pkwy (44017-2930)
P.O. Box 13862, Fairlawn (44334-3862)
PHONE 330 671-0464
Douglas Radcliffe,
EMP: 19
SQ FT: 16,000
SALES (est): 3.6MM **Privately Held**
SIC: 3441 Fabricated structural metal

(G-1624)
SABRE PUBLISHING
398 W Bagley Rd Ste 210 (44017-1312)
PHONE 440 243-4300
Keith Dunbar, *President*
EMP: 6
SALES (est): 651.3K **Privately Held**
WEB: www.sabrepublishing.com
SIC: 2721 Magazines: publishing & printing

(G-1625)
STANDBY SCREW MACHINE PDTS CO
1122 W Bagley Rd (44017-2908)
PHONE 440 243-8200
Frederick W Marcell, *Ch of Bd*
Sal Caroniti, *President*
J Albert Lowell, *Principal*
William F Marcell, *Principal*
E J Miller, *Principal*
▲ **EMP:** 375 **EST:** 1939
SALES (est): 88.7MM **Privately Held**
WEB: www.standbyscrew.com
SIC: 3451 Screw machine products

(G-1626)
SUN ART DECALS INC
83 Dorland Ave (44017-2801)
PHONE 440 234-9045
John J Soppelsa, *President*
Nikki Soppelsa, *Corp Secy*
James A Soppelsa, *Vice Pres*
EMP: 7
SALES (est): 690K **Privately Held**
WEB: www.sunartdecals.com
SIC: 2752 Decals, lithographed; letters, circular or form: lithographed

(G-1627)
TALENT TOOL & DIE INC
777 Berea Industrial Pkwy (44017-2948)
PHONE 440 239-8777
Tam Pham, *Ch of Bd*
Thanh Pham, *President*
Kha Vu, *Vice Pres*
Tri Pham, *Purchasing*
Linda Vanek, *Controller*
▲ **EMP:** 40
SQ FT: 80,000
SALES (est): 10.4MM **Privately Held**
WEB: www.talent-tool.com
SIC: 3469 3544 Metal stampings; special dies, tools, jigs & fixtures

(G-1628)
TELEFAST INDUSTRIES INC
777 W Bagley Rd (44017-2901)
PHONE 440 826-0011
Jeff Liter, *President*
▲ **EMP:** 65
SQ FT: 60,000
SALES (est): 20MM
SALES (corp-wide): 70MM **Privately Held**
WEB: www.telefast.com
SIC: 3452 Nuts, metal
HQ: Elgin Fastener Group, Llc
10217 Brecksville Rd # 101
Brecksville OH 44141

(G-1629)
TIMCO RUBBER PRODUCTS INC (PA)
125 Blaze Industrial Pkwy (44017-2930)
PHONE 216 267-6242
John Kuzmick, *CEO*
Joe Hoffman, *President*
Randy Dahlke, *Vice Pres*
Joe Budd, *Project Mgr*
Doug Wheatcraft, *Project Mgr*
EMP: 27 **EST:** 1956
SQ FT: 4,500
SALES: 16MM **Privately Held**
WEB: www.timcorubber.com
SIC: 3069 Bags, rubber or rubberized fabric

(G-1630)
UNITED WIRE EDM INC
777 Berea Industrial Pkwy (44017-2948)
PHONE 440 239-8777
Thanh Pham, *President*
Tam Pham, *President*
Tri Pham, *Shareholder*
Kha Vu, *Shareholder*
EMP: 4
SQ FT: 24,000
SALES (est): 460K **Privately Held**
SIC: 3541 Electrical discharge erosion machines

(G-1631)
VRC INC
Also Called: Vrc Manufacturers
696 W Bagley Rd (44017-1350)
PHONE 440 243-6666
Christopher W Lovell, *CEO*
EMP: 54
SQ FT: 42,000
SALES (est): 11.2MM **Privately Held**
WEB: www.vrcmfg.com
SIC: 3599 Machine shop, jobbing & repair; custom machinery

(G-1632)
WHISKEY FOX CORPORATION
Also Called: Csqp Quick Printing
1060 W Bagley Rd Ste 102 (44017-2938)
PHONE 440 779-6767
William McKay, *President*
EMP: 11
SALES (est): 1.3MM **Privately Held**
SIC: 2752 Commercial printing, offset

(G-1633)
WISE WINDOW TREATMENT INC
Also Called: Wise Contracts
353 Race St (44017-2331)
PHONE 216 676-4080
Jerry Lang, *President*
EMP: 12
SQ FT: 5,700
SALES (est): 785.1K **Privately Held**
SIC: 2391 2392 Curtains & draperies; bedspreads & bed sets: made from purchased materials

Bergholz
Jefferson County

(G-1634)
DENOON LUMBER COMPANY LLC (PA)
571 County Highway 52 (43908-7961)
PHONE 740 768-2220
Al Thompson, *Plant Mgr*
Janie L Denoon,
Jaime Carpenter, *Retailers*
EMP: 96
SALES (est): 11.2MM **Privately Held**
WEB: www.denoon.com
SIC: 2421 2449 2431 2426 Lumber: rough, sawed or planed; wood containers; millwork; hardwood dimension & flooring mills

(G-1635)
ROSEBUD MINING COMPANY
Also Called: Bergholz 7
9076 County Road 53 (43908-7948)
PHONE 740 768-2097
William Denoon, *Branch Mgr*
EMP: 33
SALES (corp-wide): 605.3MM **Privately Held**
SIC: 1222 1221 Bituminous coal-underground mining; bituminous coal & lignite-surface mining
PA: Rosebud Mining Company
301 Market St
Kittanning PA 16201
724 545-6222

Berkey
Lucas County

(G-1636)
STAR DOOR & SASH CO INC
4815 Kilburn Rd (43504-9760)
PHONE 419 841-3396
EMP: 10
SQ FT: 25,000
SALES (est): 1.5MM **Privately Held**
SIC: 2431 Mfg Millwork

Berlin
Holmes County

(G-1637)
BERLIN GARDENS GAZEBOS LTD
5045 State Rte 39 (44610)
PHONE 330 893-3411
Atlee Raber,
EMP: 26
SALES (est): 3.5MM **Privately Held**
SIC: 2511 Wood household furniture

(G-1638)
BERLIN NATURAL BAKERY INC
5126 County Rd 120 (44610)
P.O. Box 311 (44610-0311)
PHONE 330 893-2734
John Schrock, *President*
Joy Von Allman, *Admin Sec*
◆ **EMP:** 21
SALES (est): 3MM **Privately Held**
WEB: www.berlinnaturalbakery.com
SIC: 2051 Bakery: wholesale or wholesale/retail combined

(G-1639)
BERLIN WOOD PRODUCTS INC
5039 County Rd 120 (44610)
P.O. Box 184 (44610-0184)
PHONE 330 893-3281
John A Yoder, *President*
Arthur Yoder, *Vice Pres*
EMP: 30
SQ FT: 50,000
SALES (est): 2.9MM **Privately Held**
WEB: www.berlinwood.com
SIC: 2499 3944 Dowels, wood; tool handles, wood; wagons: coaster, express & play: children's

(G-1640)
CENTOR INC
5091 County Rd 120 (44610)
PHONE 800 321-3391
Roger Klein, *Safety Mgr*
Brent Stein, *Human Res Mgr*
Mitch Stein, *Branch Mgr*
David Borter, *Manager*
EMP: 150
SALES (corp-wide): 1.5B **Privately Held**
SIC: 2631 Container, packaging & boxboard
HQ: Centor Inc.
1899 N Wilkinson Way
Perrysburg OH 43551
567 336-8094

(G-1641)
DUTCH HERITAGE WOODCRAFT
4363 State Route 39 (44610)
P.O. Box 358 (44610-0358)
PHONE 330 893-2211
John Wengerd, *Partner*
John Schrock, *Partner*
EMP: 30
SQ FT: 20,000
SALES (est): 2MM **Privately Held**
SIC: 2511 2431 2426 Wood household furniture; millwork; hardwood dimension & flooring mills

(G-1642)
HOLMES LIMESTONE CO (PA)
4255 State Rte 39 (44610)
P.O. Box 295 (44610-0295)
PHONE 330 893-2721
Merle Mullet, *President*
William Hummel, *Treasurer*
Wade Mullet, *Admin Sec*
EMP: 7 **EST:** 1949
SQ FT: 10,000
SALES (est): 1.8MM **Privately Held**
WEB: www.holmeslimestone.com
SIC: 1221 Strip mining, bituminous

(G-1643)
J-J BERLIN WOODCRAFT INC (PA)
Also Called: J & J Woodcraft
4805 State Rt 39 Main St (44610)
PHONE 330 893-9171
Roman L Kandel Jr, *President*
Naomi Kandel, *Vice Pres*
EMP: 2
SALES (est): 1.2MM **Privately Held**
WEB: www.jjwoodcraft.com
SIC: 2511 5712 Wood household furniture; furniture stores

(G-1644)
ROBIN INDUSTRIES INC
5200 County Rd 120 (44610)
P.O. Box 330 (44610-0330)
PHONE 330 893-3501
David Theiss, *Branch Mgr*
EMP: 23
SALES (corp-wide): 81.6MM **Privately Held**
WEB: www.robin-industries.com
SIC: 3061 3069 1481 Mechanical rubber goods; molded rubber products; mine development, nonmetallic minerals
PA: Robin Industries, Inc.
6500 Rockside Rd Ste 230
Independence OH 44131
216 631-7000

Berlin Center
Mahoning County

(G-1645)
BERLIN BOAT COVERS
Also Called: Berlin Boat Covers Ulphostery
17740 W Akron Canfield Rd (44401-9769)
PHONE 330 547-7600
Toll Free: 888   -
Julie A Bowman, *Partner*
Jeffrey Bowman, *Partner*
EMP: 3
SQ FT: 3,400
SALES: 75K **Privately Held**
SIC: 2394 7641 Liners & covers, fabric: made from purchased materials; canvas boat seats; awnings, fabric: made from purchased materials; convertible tops, canvas or boat: from purchased materials; upholstery work

(G-1646)
HIGH CARD INDUSTRIES LLC
Also Called: Paragan Tool and Die
15439 W Akron Canfield Rd (44401-8766)
P.O. Box 102 (44401-0102)
PHONE 330 547-3381
Daniel F Crowe, *Mng Member*

GEOGRAPHIC SECTION

EMP: 10
SQ FT: 16,000
SALES (est): 800K **Privately Held**
SIC: 3544 Special dies, tools, jigs & fixtures

(G-1647)
MASTROPIETRO WINERY INC
14558 Ellsworth Rd (44401-9742)
PHONE..................................330 547-2151
Daniel Mastropietro, *President*
Marianne Mastropietro, *Vice Pres*
EMP: 8
SQ FT: 1,512
SALES (est): 669.8K **Privately Held**
WEB: www.mastropietrowinery.com
SIC: 2084 Wines

(G-1648)
OHIO STRUCTURES INC
6120 S Pricetown Rd (44401-9718)
PHONE..................................330 547-7705
EMP: 35
SALES (corp-wide): 13.3MM **Privately Held**
SIC: 3441 Structural Steel Fabrication
HQ: Ohio Structures, Inc.
535 N Broad St Ste 5
Canfield OH 44406
330 533-0084

(G-1649)
OHIO WINDMILL & PUMP CO INC
8389 S Pricetown Rd (44401-9701)
PHONE..................................330 547-6300
Craig Donges, *President*
EMP: 4
SALES (est): 471.7K **Privately Held**
SIC: 3523 Windmills for pumping water, agricultural

(G-1650)
PARKER-HANNIFIN CORPORATION
Also Called: Parker Hannifin
14010 Ellsworth Rd (44401-9749)
PHONE..................................330 261-1618
EMP: 4
SALES (corp-wide): 12B **Publicly Held**
SIC: 3594 Fluid power pumps & motors
PA: Parker-Hannifin Corporation
6035 Parkland Blvd
Cleveland OH 44124
216 896-3000

(G-1651)
WEBB MACHINE & FAB INC
15262 Hoyle Rd (44401-9785)
P.O. Box 1735, Murrells Inlet SC (29576-1735)
PHONE..................................330 717-5745
William Boyer, *Owner*
EMP: 3
SQ FT: 1,914
SALES (est): 306.5K **Privately Held**
SIC: 3599 Machine shop, jobbing & repair

Berlin Heights
Erie County

(G-1652)
AUTOGATE INC
7306 Driver Rd (44814-9661)
P.O. Box 50 (44814-0050)
PHONE..................................419 588-2796
Robert B Rodwancy, *Ch of Bd*
William Rodwancy, *President*
Jennifer A Kravec, *Principal*
Don Rodwancy, *Vice Pres*
Donald Rodwancy, *Vice Pres*
EMP: 34
SQ FT: 19,000
SALES (est): 9MM **Privately Held**
WEB: www.autogate.com
SIC: 3446 Gates, ornamental metal

(G-1653)
E & R WELDING INC
32 South St (44814-9320)
PHONE..................................440 329-9387
Edwin E Charles, *President*
Roberta Charles, *President*
EMP: 15
SQ FT: 28,000
SALES (est): 1.5MM **Privately Held**
SIC: 7692 Welding repair

(G-1654)
KERNELLS AUTMTC MACHINING INC
10511 State Rte 61 N (44814)
P.O. Box 41 (44814-0041)
PHONE..................................419 588-2164
Claude Kernell, *President*
Lou Gehringer, *Engineer*
Vicky Seck, *Treasurer*
Jeff Kernell, *Admin Sec*
▲ EMP: 50 EST: 1969
SQ FT: 20,500
SALES (est): 8.1MM **Privately Held**
WEB: www.kernellsautomatic.com
SIC: 3451 Screw machine products

Bethel
Clermont County

(G-1655)
AFFORDABLE CABINET DOORS
205 S Main St (45106-1327)
PHONE..................................513 734-9663
Jason Johnson, *Owner*
▲ EMP: 4
SALES (est): 180K **Privately Held**
SIC: 2434 Wood kitchen cabinets

(G-1656)
WALNUT CREEK WOODWORKING LLC
1878 Jones Florer Rd (45106-8525)
PHONE..................................513 504-3520
EMP: 4
SALES (est): 286.6K **Privately Held**
SIC: 2431 Millwork

Bethesda
Belmont County

(G-1657)
MAR-ZANE INC
Also Called: Shelly and Zans
38824 National Rd (43719-9612)
PHONE..................................740 782-1240
Richard McClone, *CEO*
EMP: 4
SALES (corp-wide): 276.3MM **Privately Held**
WEB: www.zanemar.com
SIC: 2951 Asphalt paving mixtures & blocks
HQ: Mar-Zane, Inc.
3570 S River Rd
Zanesville OH 43701
740 453-0721

(G-1658)
SMITHS SAWDUST STUDIO
206 Maple Ave (43719-9609)
PHONE..................................740 484-4656
Terry Smith, *Owner*
EMP: 3
SALES (est): 210K **Privately Held**
WEB: www.sawduststudio.net
SIC: 2452 Prefabricated buildings, wood

(G-1659)
WESTROCK USC INC
41298 Brown Rd (43719-9619)
PHONE..................................740 484-1000
Dannis Mehiel, *Branch Mgr*
EMP: 8
SALES (corp-wide): 16.2B **Publicly Held**
SIC: 2653 Boxes, corrugated: made from purchased materials
HQ: Westrock Usc, Inc.
1000 Abernathy Rd
Atlanta GA 30328
770 448-2193

Bettsville
Seneca County

(G-1660)
CARMEUSE LIME INC
Also Called: Carmeuse Natural Chemicals
1967 W County Rd 42 (44815)
P.O. Box 708 (44815-0708)
PHONE..................................419 986-5200
Thomas A Buck, *CEO*
Matt Rogish, *Safety Mgr*
Bobby Hay, *Production*
Nathaniel Freeborn, *Project Engr*
Dwayne Knee, *CFO*
EMP: 49 **Privately Held**
SIC: 1422 Crushed & broken limestone
HQ: Carmeuse Lime, Inc.
11 Stanwix St Fl 21
Pittsburgh PA 15222
412 995-5500

Beverly
Washington County

(G-1661)
GENESIS SERVICES LLC
565 Straight Run Rd (45715-5015)
PHONE..................................740 896-3734
Michael Woodford,
Pamela Woodford,
EMP: 3
SQ FT: 500
SALES: 350K **Privately Held**
SIC: 3448 3449 Docks: prefabricated metal; bars, concrete reinforcing: fabricated steel

(G-1662)
SCHILLING TRUSS INC
230 Stony Run Rd (45715-5051)
P.O. Box 187 (45715-0187)
PHONE..................................740 984-2396
Charles L Schilling, *President*
Jeff Schilling, *President*
Lori Meek, *Admin Sec*
EMP: 12
SALES (est): 1.2MM **Privately Held**
SIC: 2439 Trusses, wooden roof

(G-1663)
WATERFORD TANK FABRICATION LTD
203 State Route 83 (45715-8938)
P.O. Box 392, Lowell (45744-0392)
PHONE..................................740 984-4100
Matt Brook, *President*
Larry Lang,
▲ EMP: 80
SQ FT: 80,000
SALES (est): 28.3MM **Privately Held**
SIC: 3399 3441 Iron ore recovery from open hearth slag; building components, structural steel

Bidwell
Gallia County

(G-1664)
BOB EVANS FARMS INC
791 Farmview Rd (45614-9230)
P.O. Box 198, Rio Grande (45674-0198)
PHONE..................................740 245-5305
Rain McKinniss, *Manager*
EMP: 11 **Publicly Held**
WEB: www.bobevans.com
SIC: 2011 Sausages from meat slaughtered on site
HQ: Bob Evans Farms, Inc.
8111 Smiths Mill Rd
New Albany OH 43054
614 491-2225

(G-1665)
BUCKEYE METALS
185 Curr Rd (45614)
PHONE..................................740 446-9590
Gaylan Belville, *Owner*
EMP: 3
SALES (est): 286.7K **Privately Held**
SIC: 3499 Fabricated metal products

(G-1666)
GERALD H SMITH
670 Buck Ridge Rd (45614-9204)
PHONE..................................740 446-3455
Gerald Smith, *Owner*
EMP: 3
SALES (est): 141.7K **Privately Held**
SIC: 3443 4959 Dumpsters, garbage; sanitary services

(G-1667)
OHIO VALLEY TRACKWORK INC
39 Fairview Rd (45614-1100)
P.O. Box 153, Rio Grande (45674-0153)
PHONE..................................740 446-0181
Mike Little, *President*
Bret Little, *Vice Pres*
Adam Little, *Director*
EMP: 12
SALES (est): 2.8MM **Privately Held**
WEB: www.ohiovalleytrackwork.com
SIC: 3531 Railway track equipment

(G-1668)
R&C PACKING & CUSTOM BUTCHER
Also Called: R & C Pkg & Cstm Butchering
3836 State Route 850 (45614-9525)
PHONE..................................740 245-9440
Roger Glassburn, *Owner*
EMP: 4
SALES (est): 292K **Privately Held**
SIC: 2011 Meat packing plants

(G-1669)
RUTLAND TOWNSHIP
33325 Jessie Creek Rd (45614-9600)
P.O. Box 203, Rutland (45775-0203)
PHONE..................................740 742-2805
Opal Dyer, *Officer*
EMP: 6
SALES: 260K **Privately Held**
SIC: 2951 Asphalt paving mixtures & blocks

(G-1670)
SOUTHERN CABINETRY INC
41 International Blvd (45614-8002)
PHONE..................................740 245-5992
Don Strieter, *President*
Leah Bynum, *Admin Sec*
EMP: 35
SALES (est): 5.2MM **Privately Held**
SIC: 3083 Plastic finished products, laminated

(G-1671)
TS DEFENSE LLC
214 Buck Ridge Rd (45614-9197)
PHONE..................................740 446-7716
Anthony Simpson, *Principal*
EMP: 3
SALES (est): 150K **Privately Held**
SIC: 3812 Defense systems & equipment

(G-1672)
UPCREEK PRODUCTIONS INC
1513 Upcreek Rd (45614-9335)
PHONE..................................740 208-8124
Kendra Ward-Bence, *President*
EMP: 3
SALES: 100K **Privately Held**
WEB: www.dulcimertimes.com
SIC: 5099 2721 Compact discs; magazines: publishing only, not printed on site

Big Prairie
Holmes County

(G-1673)
DOMETIC SANITATION CORPORATION
13128 State Route 226 (44611-9522)
P.O. Box 38 (44611-0038)
PHONE..................................330 439-5550
Doug Whyte, *President*
▲ EMP: 75 EST: 1998
SALES: 11.9MM
SALES (corp-wide): 1.6B **Privately Held**
SIC: 3089 Plastic containers, except foam

Big Prairie - Holmes County (G-1674)

HQ: Dometic Corporation
1120 N Main St
Elkhart IN 46514

(G-1674)
GRACE AUTOMATION SERVICES INC
8140 State Route 514 (44611-9692)
PHONE.................................330 567-3108
Curtis W Murray Jr, *President*
EMP: 4
SALES (est): 895K **Privately Held**
WEB: www.graceautomation.com
SIC: 3663 Telemetering equipment, electronic

(G-1675)
MANSFIELD PLUMBING PDTS LLC
13211 State Route 226 (44611-9584)
P.O. Box 68 (44611-0068)
PHONE.................................330 496-2301
Paul Conrad, *Manager*
EMP: 40 **Privately Held**
SIC: 1711 3088 Plumbing contractors; plastics plumbing fixtures
HQ: Mansfield Plumbing Products Llc
150 E 1st St
Perrysville OH 44864
419 938-5211

Blacklick
Franklin County

(G-1676)
ACTION GROUP INC
411 Reynoldsburg New (43004)
PHONE.................................614 868-8868
Frank De Nutte, *President*
Tracy Garner, *Vice Pres*
Tony N Melendez, *Branch Mgr*
Tina Wilson, *Manager*
John Stevenson, *Officer*
EMP: 98
SQ FT: 155,000
SALES (est): 21.8MM **Privately Held**
WEB: www.actiongroupinc.com
SIC: 3449 2541 Bars, concrete reinforcing; fabricated steel; wood partitions & fixtures

(G-1677)
ART BRANDS LLC
225 Business Center Dr (43004-9452)
PHONE.................................614 755-4278
Larry M Levine, *Mng Member*
EMP: 45
SQ FT: 27,000
SALES: 4.8MM **Privately Held**
SIC: 2759 Screen printing

(G-1678)
AUSTINS MACHINE SHOP
4295 N Waggoner Rd (43004-9732)
PHONE.................................614 855-2525
Daniel Aldridge, *Owner*
EMP: 20
SALES (est): 1.1MM **Privately Held**
SIC: 3599 Machine shop, jobbing & repair

(G-1679)
BESA LIGHTING CO INC
6695 Taylor Rd (43004-9614)
PHONE.................................614 475-7046
Bernd Hoffbauer, *President*
▲ **EMP:** 47
SQ FT: 48,500
SALES (est): 8.1MM **Privately Held**
WEB: www.besalighting.com
SIC: 3646 3645 Commercial indusl & institutional electric lighting fixtures; residential lighting fixtures

(G-1680)
BLACKLICK MACHINE CO INC
265 North St (43004-9139)
PHONE.................................614 866-9300
John Boggs, *President*
Morgan Brooks, *Regional Mgr*
Morgan P Brooks, *Purchasing*
EMP: 7 **EST:** 1954
SQ FT: 7,200
SALES: 500K **Privately Held**
SIC: 3599 Machine shop, jobbing & repair

(G-1681)
CEDAR CRAFT PRODUCTS INC
776 Reynldsbrg New Albany (43004-9690)
P.O. Box 9 (43004-0009)
PHONE.................................614 759-1600
Rick Van Walsen, *President*
Magdlen Van Walsen, *Corp Secy*
EMP: 20
SQ FT: 4,800
SALES (est): 2.6MM **Privately Held**
WEB: www.cedar-craft.com
SIC: 2441 Boxes, wood

(G-1682)
CP TECHNOLOGIES COMPANY
6615 Taylor Rd (43004-9600)
P.O. Box 639 (43004-0639)
PHONE.................................614 866-9200
Charles D Amata Sr, *CEO*
Charles D Amata Jr, *President*
▲ **EMP:** 35
SQ FT: 31,000
SALES (est): 7.7MM
SALES (corp-wide): 632.4MM **Privately Held**
WEB: www.cptechnologies.com
SIC: 3089 3544 Injection molded finished plastic products; injection molding of plastics; molding primary plastic; air mattresses, plastic; special dies, tools, jigs & fixtures
HQ: Anomatic Corporation
8880 Innvation Campus Way
Johnstown OH 43031
740 522-2203

(G-1683)
DANA OFF HIGHWAY PRODUCTS LLC
6635 Taylor Rd (43004-9600)
PHONE.................................614 864-1116
Terry Casto, *Branch Mgr*
EMP: 20 **Publicly Held**
SIC: 3714 3599 Motor vehicle parts & accessories; machine shop, jobbing & repair
HQ: Dana Off Highway Products, Llc
3939 Technology Dr
Maumee OH 43537

(G-1684)
GREEN DOOR INDUSTRIES LLC
7844 Waggoner Trace Dr (43004-7182)
PHONE.................................614 558-1663
Nathan E Hood, *Principal*
EMP: 3
SALES (est): 209.3K **Privately Held**
SIC: 3999 Manufacturing industries

(G-1685)
HALVEY QUARTER HORSES
6230 Havens Corners Rd (43004-8728)
PHONE.................................614 648-0483
EMP: 3
SALES (est): 126.1K **Privately Held**
SIC: 3131 Quarters

(G-1686)
HUB PLASTICS INC
725 Reynoldsburg New (43004)
P.O. Box 350 (43004-0350)
PHONE.................................614 861-1791
Dennis Nielsen, *President*
Heather Blackburn, *Human Res Mgr*
Mindy Campbell, *Manager*
EMP: 70
SQ FT: 72,000
SALES (est): 12.5MM **Privately Held**
WEB: www.hubplastics.com
SIC: 3089 Plastic containers, except foam

(G-1687)
INDUSTRIAL CONTAINER SVCS LLC
1385 Blatt Blvd Gahanna A Indsutrial (43004)
PHONE.................................614 864-1900
Ron Grannan, *Principal*
EMP: 60
SALES (corp-wide): 1.1B **Privately Held**
WEB: www.iconserv.com
SIC: 3443 3412 3411 Fabricated plate work (boiler shop); metal barrels, drums & pails; metal cans
HQ: Industrial Container Services Llc
2600 Mtland Ctr Pkwy 20 # 200
Maitland FL 32751
407 930-4182

(G-1688)
LOCTOTE LLC
1010 Jackson Hole Dr (43004-6050)
PHONE.................................614 407-0882
Donald Halpern, *CEO*
Tony Robbins, *Producer*
EMP: 4
SALES (est): 169.6K **Privately Held**
SIC: 2393 5961 Textile bags; mail order house

(G-1689)
MARINE JET POWER INC
6740 Commerce Court Dr (43004-9200)
PHONE.................................614 759-9000
James Campbell, *President*
▲ **EMP:** 6
SQ FT: 7,000
SALES (est): 1MM
SALES (corp-wide): 765.5K **Privately Held**
WEB: www.ultradynamics.com
SIC: 3483 Jet propulsion projectiles
HQ: Marine Jet Power Ab
Hansellisgatan 6
Uppsala 754 5
295 244-200

(G-1690)
MCGRAW-HILL GLOBAL EDUCATN LLC
860 Taylor Station Rd (43004-9540)
P.O. Box 543 (43004-0543)
PHONE.................................614 755-4151
Charles Kunkel, *Project Mgr*
Maryjane Lampe, *Manager*
Matthew Backhaus, *Graphic Designe*
EMP: 500
SALES (corp-wide): 158MM **Privately Held**
WEB: www.mcgraw-hill.com
SIC: 2731 Book publishing
HQ: Mcgraw-Hill Global Education, Llc
2 Penn Plz Fl 20
New York NY 10121
646 766-2000

(G-1691)
PERFECTION BAKERIES INC
6720 Commerce Court Dr (43004-9200)
PHONE.................................614 866-8171
Tod Cambell, *Branch Mgr*
EMP: 57
SALES (corp-wide): 515.3MM **Privately Held**
SIC: 2051 Bakery: wholesale or wholesale/retail combined
PA: Perfection Bakeries, Inc.
350 Pearl St
Fort Wayne IN 46802
260 424-8245

(G-1692)
REYNOLDS INDUSTRIES GROUP LLC
7463 Old River Dr (43004-7126)
PHONE.................................614 864-6199
David Reynolds, *Administration*
EMP: 45 **EST:** 2010
SALES (est): 1.3MM **Privately Held**
SIC: 2731 Book publishing

(G-1693)
RICHARDSON WOODWORKING
3834 Mann Rd (43004-9741)
PHONE.................................614 893-8850
Craig Richardson, *President*
EMP: 6 **EST:** 2000
SALES: 230K **Privately Held**
SIC: 2431 Interior & ornamental woodwork & trim

(G-1694)
SCHAFER DRIVELINE LLC
6635 Taylor Rd (43004-9600)
PHONE.................................614 864-1116
EMP: 9
SALES (corp-wide): 38.3MM **Privately Held**
SIC: 3714 Axles, motor vehicle
HQ: Schafer Driveline Llc
123 Phoenix Pl
Fredericktown OH 43019
740 694-2055

(G-1695)
WIRELESS RETAIL LLC
Also Called: Cricket
6750 Commerce Court Dr (43004-9200)
PHONE.................................614 657-5182
Matt Starkin, *Mng Member*
EMP: 10
SALES: 1MM **Privately Held**
SIC: 3663 Mobile communication equipment

Bladensburg
Knox County

(G-1696)
DERRICK PETROLEUM INC
Market St (43005)
P.O. Box 145 (43005-0145)
PHONE.................................740 668-5711
Duane Dugan, *President*
Vickie Dugan, *Admin Sec*
EMP: 6
SQ FT: 500
SALES (est): 990K **Privately Held**
SIC: 1311 Crude petroleum production; natural gas production

Blakeslee
Williams County

(G-1697)
S & M PRODUCTS
County Rd 5 I (43505)
PHONE.................................419 272-2054
Steve Mohre, *Owner*
Nick Mohre, *Co-Owner*
EMP: 3
SALES: 250K **Privately Held**
SIC: 2448 Pallets, wood

Blanchester
Clinton County

(G-1698)
AMERICAN SHOWA INC
960 Cherry St (45107-7883)
PHONE.................................937 783-4961
Jim Magge, *Principal*
Adam Holthaus, *Engineer*
Adam Mooney, *Engineer*
Mitch Trimble, *Engineer*
Jim Wiebe, *VP Bus Dvlpt*
EMP: 530
SALES (corp-wide): 2.7B **Privately Held**
SIC: 3714 5812 Motor vehicle steering systems & parts; caterers
HQ: American Showa, Inc.
707 W Cherry St
Sunbury OH 43074
740 965-1133

(G-1699)
BIC PRECISION MACHINE CO INC
3004 Cherry St (45107-7915)
P.O. Box 188 (45107-0188)
PHONE.................................937 783-1406
James Bellamy Jr, *Principal*
James M Bellamy, *Principal*
Vernon L Bellamy, *Principal*
Victor Burkhart Jr, *Principal*
EMP: 12
SQ FT: 4,000
SALES (est): 2.9MM **Privately Held**
WEB: www.bicprecision.com
SIC: 3599 Machine shop, jobbing & repair

(G-1700)
BLANCHESTER FOUNDRY CO INC
214 Cherry St (45107-1217)
P.O. Box 126 (45107-0126)
PHONE.................................937 783-2091

GEOGRAPHIC SECTION

Blue Ash - Hamilton County (G-1725)

Robert H Ballinger, *President*
Greg Ballinger, *President*
Kevin Ballinger, *Vice Pres*
Mark Ballinger, *CFO*
EMP: 15 **EST:** 1947
SQ FT: 35,000
SALES (est): 1.9MM **Privately Held**
SIC: 3321 Gray iron castings

(G-1701)
CRICKET ENGINES
10810 Cincinnati Chillico (45107-8494)
PHONE 513 532-2145
EMP: 3
SALES (est): 228.6K **Privately Held**
SIC: 3519 Internal combustion engines

(G-1702)
CURLESS PRINTING COMPANY
202 E Main St Unit 1 (45107-1247)
P.O. Box 97 (45107-0097)
PHONE 937 783-2403
Donald S Hadley, *President*
Parker M Beebe, *Vice Pres*
EMP: 24
SQ FT: 23,500
SALES: 1.8MM **Privately Held**
SIC: 2752 Commercial printing, offset

(G-1703)
FULFLO SPECIALTIES COMPANY
Also Called: True Torq
459 E Fancy St (45107-1462)
PHONE 937 783-2411
Thomas Ruthman, *President*
David Locaputo, *General Mgr*
EMP: 30 **EST:** 1939
SQ FT: 30,000
SALES: 4.5MM
SALES (corp-wide): 45.4MM **Privately Held**
SIC: 3494 Couplings, except pressure & soil pipe
PA: Ruthman Pump And Engineering, Inc
1212 Streng St
Cincinnati OH 45223
513 559-1901

(G-1704)
J-C-R TECH INC
936 Cherry St (45107-1318)
P.O. Box 65 (45107-0065)
PHONE 937 783-2296
Rick Carmean, *President*
Larry Hinz, *Electrical Engi*
Caleb Maxwell, *Electrical Engi*
▲ **EMP:** 27
SQ FT: 18,000
SALES (est): 4.5MM **Privately Held**
WEB: www.jcrtech.com
SIC: 3541 7629 3544 Machine tool replacement & repair parts, metal cutting types; electrical repair shops; special dies, tools, jigs & fixtures

(G-1705)
R & R TOOL INC
1449a Middleboro Rd (45107)
PHONE 937 783-8665
Dan Reed, *CEO*
Daniel Reed, *CEO*
Bonnie Reed, *President*
▲ **EMP:** 46
SQ FT: 30,000
SALES (est): 10MM **Privately Held**
SIC: 3429 Manufactured hardware (general)

(G-1706)
RUTHMAN PUMP AND ENGINEERING
Fulflo Specialties Co
459 E Fancy St (45107-1462)
PHONE 937 783-2411
David Locaputo, *Manager*
EMP: 25
SALES (corp-wide): 45.4MM **Privately Held**
WEB: www.ruthmannpumpen.de
SIC: 3494 5085 3491 Valves & pipe fittings; valves & fittings; industrial valves
PA: Ruthman Pump And Engineering, Inc
1212 Streng St
Cincinnati OH 45223
513 559-1901

(G-1707)
UFP BLANCHESTER LLC
Also Called: Universal Forest Products
940 Cherry St (45107-7883)
PHONE 937 783-2443
Matthew J Missad, *CEO*
William G Currie, *Ch of Bd*
Patrick M Webster, *President*
Michael R Cole, *CFO*
EMP: 25
SALES (est): 3.7MM
SALES (corp-wide): 4.4B **Publicly Held**
SIC: 2491 Wood preserving
PA: Universal Forest Products, Inc.
2801 E Beltline Ave Ne
Grand Rapids MI 49525
616 364-6161

(G-1708)
WICO PRODUCTS INC
311 E Fancy St (45107-1456)
PHONE 937 783-0000
Tom Wise, *CEO*
William Wise, *President*
Joyce Wise, *Admin Sec*
EMP: 3
SALES: 300K **Privately Held**
SIC: 2493 Particleboard, plastic laminated

Bloomingburg
Fayette County

(G-1709)
BLOOMINGBURG SPRING & WIRE FOR
83 Main St (43106-9008)
P.O. Box 158 (43106-0158)
PHONE 740 437-7614
James Van Horn, *President*
Rebecca Maynard, *General Mgr*
Tim Van Horn, *Vice Pres*
Donna Vanhorn, *Office Mgr*
Donna Van Horn, *Manager*
▲ **EMP:** 20
SQ FT: 27,000
SALES (est): 3.8MM **Privately Held**
WEB: www.bloomingburgspring.com
SIC: 3495 3496 Wire springs; miscellaneous fabricated wire products

Bloomingdale
Jefferson County

(G-1710)
DIE-TECH MACHINE INC
1650 County Road 22a (43910-7966)
PHONE 740 264-2426
William D Freeland, *President*
Michele Freeland, *Corp Secy*
Brett Freeland, *Vice Pres*
EMP: 9
SALES: 750K **Privately Held**
SIC: 3599 Machine shop, jobbing & repair; machine & other job shop work

(G-1711)
J A H WOODWORKING LLC
39 Belvedere Dr (43910-7738)
PHONE 740 266-6949
John Humpe III,
Brenda Humpe,
EMP: 5
SQ FT: 4,200
SALES (est): 731K **Privately Held**
SIC: 2431 Millwork

Bloomville
Seneca County

(G-1712)
BU E COMP INC
7092 S State Route 19 (44818-9203)
P.O. Box 467 (44818-0467)
PHONE 419 284-3381
Kimberline Nelferd, *President*
EMP: 5

SALES (est): 402.3K **Privately Held**
SIC: 3089 Extruded finished plastic products

(G-1713)
BUECOMP INC
Also Called: Bucyrus Extruded Composites
7016 S State Route 19 (44818-9203)
P.O. Box 467, Bucyrus (44820-0467)
PHONE 419 284-3840
Nelfred G Kimerline, *President*
Norm Tackett, *General Mgr*
Charles W Kimerline, *Corp Secy*
EMP: 32
SQ FT: 19,000
SALES (est): 4.1MM **Privately Held**
WEB: www.buecomp.com
SIC: 3089 Extruded finished plastic products

(G-1714)
EPRO INC
10890 E County Road 6 (44818-9243)
PHONE 419 426-5053
Jim Fry, *President*
EMP: 30
SALES (est): 2.4MM **Privately Held**
SIC: 3253 Ceramic wall & floor tile

(G-1715)
HANSON AGGREGATES MIDWEST LLC
Also Called: Hanson Aggregates Mid West
4575 S County Road 49 (44818-8400)
P.O. Box 128 (44818-0128)
PHONE 419 983-2211
Dan Lepp, *Manager*
EMP: 8
SALES (corp-wide): 20.6B **Privately Held**
SIC: 2951 1422 Asphalt paving mixtures & blocks; limestones, ground
HQ: Hanson Aggregates Midwest Llc
207 Old Harrods Creek Rd
Louisville KY 40223
502 244-7550

Blue Ash
Hamilton County

(G-1716)
1 A LIFESAFER INC (PA)
Also Called: Ignition Interlock
4290 Glendale Milford Rd (45242-3704)
PHONE 513 651-9560
Richard Freund, *President*
Craig Armstrong, *President*
Glenn Kermes, *CFO*
John Collett, *Controller*
Jacqueline Boyce, *Accountant*
EMP: 9
SQ FT: 3,600
SALES (est): 3.2MM **Privately Held**
WEB: www.lifesafer.com
SIC: 3829 Measuring & controlling devices

(G-1717)
1 A LIFESAFER HAWAII INC
4290 Glendale Milford Rd (45242-3704)
PHONE 513 651-9560
Kermes Glenn, *Principal*
EMP: 14
SALES (est): 2.6MM **Privately Held**
SIC: 3829 3714 Breathalyzers; motor vehicle parts & accessories

(G-1718)
A G RUFF PAPER SPECIALTIES CO
4320 Indeco Ct (45241-2925)
PHONE 513 891-7990
Michael Ruff, *President*
Thomas Ruff, *President*
EMP: 3
SQ FT: 20,000
SALES (est): 429.8K **Privately Held**
SIC: 2675 Die-cut paper & board

(G-1719)
ABSTRACT DISPLAYS INC
6465 Creek Rd (45242-4113)
PHONE 513 985-9700
Carla Eng, *President*
Michael Eng, *Vice Pres*

Jim Pearson, *Consultant*
EMP: 4 **EST:** 2001
SALES (est): 1.4MM **Privately Held**
WEB: www.abstractdisplays.com
SIC: 5046 7389 3577 7336 Display equipment, except refrigerated; exhibit construction by industrial contractors; graphic displays, except graphic terminals; graphic arts & related design

(G-1720)
ACTEGA NORTH AMERICA INC
Also Called: Water Ink Technologies
11264 Grooms Rd (45242-1418)
PHONE 800 426-4657
Dave Carr, *Branch Mgr*
EMP: 4
SALES (corp-wide): 501.4K **Privately Held**
WEB: www.waterinktech.com
SIC: 2893 Printing ink
HQ: Actega North America, Inc.
950 S Chester Ave Ste B2
Delran NJ 08075
856 829-6300

(G-1721)
ADEMCO INC
Also Called: ADI Global Distribution
5601 Creek Rd Ste Ab (45242-4037)
PHONE 513 772-1851
Erin Fletcher, *Branch Mgr*
EMP: 10
SALES (corp-wide): 4.8B **Publicly Held**
WEB: www.honeywell.com
SIC: 5063 3669 3822 Alarm systems; emergency alarms; auto controls regulating residntl & coml environmt & applncs
HQ: Ademco Inc.
1985 Douglas Dr N
Golden Valley MN 55422
800 468-1502

(G-1722)
ADVANTAGE PRODUCTS CORPORATION (PA)
11559 Grooms Rd (45242-1409)
PHONE 513 489-2283
Robert Weber, *President*
Katherine Rolley, *VP Sales*
EMP: 10
SALES (est): 1.3MM **Privately Held**
WEB: www.treds.com
SIC: 3021 Protective footwear, rubber or plastic

(G-1723)
AERPIO PHARMACEUTICALS INC
9987 Carver Rd Ste 420 (45242-5563)
PHONE 513 985-1920
Michael Roger, *CFO*
EMP: 6
SALES: 20.1MM **Privately Held**
SIC: 2834 Pharmaceutical preparations

(G-1724)
AKKO FASTENER INC (PA)
6855 Cornell Rd (45242-3022)
PHONE 513 489-8300
Nancy Fernandez, *President*
Nestor Fernandez, *Vice Pres*
Dave Biddle, *Technology*
▲ **EMP:** 16
SQ FT: 35,000
SALES (est): 4.7MM **Privately Held**
WEB: www.akkofastener.com
SIC: 3452 5072 Screws, metal; bolts; washers (hardware)

(G-1725)
ALERT SAFETY PRODUCTS INC
11435 Williamson Rd Ste C (45241-4218)
PHONE 513 791-4790
Bill Shernick, *President*
David Fossier, *Vice Pres*
Kym Murphy, *Accounting Mgr*
EMP: 5
SALES (est): 711.1K **Privately Held**
WEB: www.alertsafetyproducts.com
SIC: 3669 Burglar alarm apparatus, electric; emergency alarms; fire alarm apparatus, electric

Blue Ash - Hamilton County (G-1726)

(G-1726)
ALIFET USA INC
Also Called: Rouse Marketing
3714 Fallentree Ln (45236-1036)
PHONE.................513 793-8033
Raymond Rouse, *President*
Pat Rouse, *Admin Sec*
EMP: 3
SQ FT: 1,500
SALES (est): 246.8K **Privately Held**
WEB: www.rousemarketing.com
SIC: 2023 Dietary supplements, dairy & non-dairy based

(G-1727)
ALL SIGNS EXPRESS INC (PA)
Also Called: Accent Signs and Graphics
6610 Corporate Dr (45242-2103)
PHONE.................513 489-7744
Robert Johnson, *President*
Earl Johnson, *Vice Pres*
Sherri Johnson, *Admin Sec*
EMP: 10
SALES: 900K **Privately Held**
WEB: www.cincinnatisigns.net
SIC: 3993 Electric signs

(G-1728)
ALL-BILT UNIFORM CORP
4545 Malsbary Rd (45242-5624)
PHONE.................513 793-5400
Fax: 513 793-2725
EMP: 20 EST: 1962
SALES (est): 2.1MM
SALES (corp-wide): 194.6B **Publicly Held**
SIC: 2326 Manufacturer Of Professional Apparel
HQ: The Fechheimer Brothers Company
4545 Malsbary Rd
Blue Ash OH 45242
513 793-7819

(G-1729)
APRECIA PHARMACEUTICALS LLC (HQ)
10901 Kenwood Rd (45242-2813)
PHONE.................513 864-4107
Tim Tracy, *CEO*
Grant Brock, *President*
Mike Rohlfs, *CFO*
EMP: 15
SQ FT: 14,000
SALES (est): 16.1MM
SALES (corp-wide): 19MM **Privately Held**
WEB: www.aprecia.com
SIC: 2834 Pharmaceutical preparations
PA: Prasco, Llc
6125 Commerce Ct
Mason OH 45040
513 204-1100

(G-1730)
ARKU COIL-SYSTEMS INC
11405 Grooms Rd (45242-1407)
PHONE.................513 985-0500
Franck Hirschmann, *President*
Stephan Robertson, *VP Sales*
Beth Frederick, *Manager*
▲ EMP: 9
SALES (est): 1.9MM
SALES (corp-wide): 65.7MM **Privately Held**
SIC: 3549 Wiredrawing & fabricating machinery & equipment, ex. die
PA: Arku Maschinenbau Gmbh
Siemensstr. 11
Baden-Baden 76532
722 150-090

(G-1731)
AULD LANG SIGNS INC
Also Called: Fastsigns
11109 Kenwood Rd (45242-1817)
PHONE.................513 792-5555
Michael Langdon, *President*
Kathryn Langdon, *Vice Pres*
EMP: 4
SQ FT: 2,000
SALES (est): 515.4K **Privately Held**
SIC: 3993 Electric signs

(G-1732)
BEAM MACHINES INC
5101 Creek Rd (45242-3931)
PHONE.................513 745-4510
Tim Bell, *General Mgr*
EMP: 3
SALES (est): 209.4K **Privately Held**
SIC: 3559 Automotive related machinery

(G-1733)
BEEBE WORLDWIDE GRAPHICS SIGN
Also Called: Worldwide Graphics and Sign
9933 Alliance Rd Ste 2 (45242-5662)
PHONE.................513 241-2726
Christian Beebe, *President*
EMP: 6
SQ FT: 6,000
SALES (est): 730.5K **Privately Held**
SIC: 3993 Signs, not made in custom sign painting shops

(G-1734)
BHA ALTAIR LLC
Also Called: Clarcor Industrial Air
4440 Creek Rd (45242-2802)
PHONE.................717 285-8040
EMP: 4
SALES (corp-wide): 12B **Publicly Held**
SIC: 3564 Mfg Blowers/Fans
HQ: Bha Altair, Llc
11501 Outlook St Ste 100
Overland Park KS 66211
816 356-8400

(G-1735)
BIOSENSE WEBSTER INC
4545 Creek Rd (45242-2803)
PHONE.................513 337-3351
EMP: 3
SALES (est): 152.9K **Privately Held**
SIC: 3845 Electromedical apparatus

(G-1736)
BLUE ASH PAPER SALES LLC
5000 Creek Rd (45242-3990)
PHONE.................513 891-9544
James Lallathin, *Mng Member*
EMP: 3
SQ FT: 100
SALES (est): 517.8K **Privately Held**
SIC: 2679 Book covers, paper

(G-1737)
BLUE ASH TOOL & DIE CO INC
4245 Creek Rd (45241-2999)
PHONE.................513 793-4530
Ronald Siderits, *President*
James Siderits, *General Mgr*
Anna Siderits, *Vice Pres*
Caroline Siderits, *Vice Pres*
Joel Donnelly, *Marketing Staff*
EMP: 15 EST: 1965
SQ FT: 20,000
SALES: 829.1K **Privately Held**
WEB: www.batd.com
SIC: 3545 3544 Gauge blocks; machine tool attachments & accessories; special dies, tools, jigs & fixtures

(G-1738)
BOB SMITH
Also Called: Docupros Digital Printing
9933 Alliance Rd (45242-5661)
PHONE.................513 242-7700
Bob Smith, *Owner*
EMP: 4
SALES (est): 321.4K **Privately Held**
WEB: www.docupros.com
SIC: 2759 Commercial printing

(G-1739)
BODOR VENTS LLC
Also Called: Vents US
11013 Kenwood Rd (45242-1842)
PHONE.................513 348-3853
Zoltan Bodor,
EMP: 7
SALES: 3MM **Privately Held**
SIC: 3585 Refrigeration & heating equipment

(G-1740)
BRAMKAMP PRINTING COMPANY INC
9933 Alliance Rd Ste 2 (45242-5662)
PHONE.................513 241-1865
Larry Kuhlman, *President*
Craig Masencamp, *President*
Kevin Murray, *CFO*
Brad Sullivan, *Sales Staff*
EMP: 26 EST: 1921
SQ FT: 200,000
SALES (est): 4.3MM **Privately Held**
WEB: www.bramkamp.com
SIC: 2759 2752 Letterpress printing; commercial printing, offset

(G-1741)
BROAN-NUTONE LLC
9825 Kenwood Rd Ste 301 (45242-6252)
PHONE.................888 336-3948
EMP: 8
SALES (corp-wide): 2.7B **Privately Held**
SIC: 3634 Fans, exhaust & ventilating, electric; household
HQ: Broan-Nutone Llc
926 W State St
Hartford WI 53027
262 673-4340

(G-1742)
BROWN PUBLISHING INC LLC
4229 Saint Andrews Pl (45236-1057)
PHONE.................513 794-5040
Roy Brown,
EMP: 6
SALES (est): 311.1K **Privately Held**
SIC: 2711 Newspapers

(G-1743)
C A I R OHIO
10999 Reed Hartman Hwy # 207 (45242-8301)
PHONE.................513 281-8200
C Cooper, *Principal*
EMP: 3
SALES (est): 127.7K **Privately Held**
SIC: 8661 2759 Churches, temples & shrines; screen printing

(G-1744)
C M M S - RE INC
Also Called: Forward Technologies
6130 Interstate Cir (45242-1425)
PHONE.................513 489-5111
Bradley Meyers, *President*
EMP: 15
SALES (corp-wide): 2.6MM **Privately Held**
SIC: 3599 Machine shop, jobbing & repair
PA: C M M S - Re, Llc
6130 Interstate Cir
Blue Ash OH 45242
513 489-5111

(G-1745)
C M M S - RE LLC (PA)
Also Called: Forward Technologies
6130 Interstate Cir (45242-1425)
PHONE.................513 489-5111
Bradley Meyers, *President*
Brian Collins, *Vice Pres*
Scott Mayson, *Vice Pres*
Andrew Schultz, *Vice Pres*
EMP: 12 EST: 2014
SQ FT: 6,500
SALES (est): 2.6MM **Privately Held**
SIC: 3365 3541 Aluminum foundries; machine tools, metal cutting: exotic (explosive, etc.)

(G-1746)
CAMARGO PHRM SVCS LLC (PA)
9825 Kenwood Rd Ste 203 (45242-6252)
PHONE.................513 561-3329
Daniel S Duffy, *CEO*
Jim Beach, *COO*
Gray Barnette, *Vice Pres*
K Gary Barnette, *Vice Pres*
Steven A Castillo, *Vice Pres*
EMP: 14
SALES (est): 1.8MM **Privately Held**
SIC: 2834 Proprietary drug products

(G-1747)
CANDLE-LITE COMPANY LLC (HQ)
10521 Millington Ct Ste B (45242-4022)
PHONE.................513 563-1113
Calvin Johnston, *CEO*
Gary Prampero, *Vice Pres*
EMP: 60
SQ FT: 900,000
SALES (est): 209.9MM
SALES (corp-wide): 259.4MM **Privately Held**
SIC: 3999 Candles
PA: Luminex Home Decor & Fragrance Holding Corporation
10521 Millington Ct
Blue Ash OH 45242
513 563-1113

(G-1748)
CECO ENVIRONMENTAL CORP
6245 Creek Rd (45242-4104)
PHONE.................513 458-2606
T Kroeger, *Branch Mgr*
EMP: 8
SALES (corp-wide): 337.3MM **Publicly Held**
SIC: 3564 Purification & dust collection equipment
PA: Ceco Environmental Corp.
14651 Dallas Pkwy
Dallas TX 75254
513 458-2600

(G-1749)
CHECK YOURSELF LLC
Also Called: Repp
4422 Carver Woods Dr # 110 (45242-5599)
PHONE.................513 685-0868
Breeanna Bergman, *Co-Owner*
Adam Daniel, *Co-Owner*
Stephen Hartz, *Co-Owner*
David Volker, *Co-Owner*
EMP: 5 EST: 2012
SALES (est): 295.7K **Privately Held**
SIC: 7372 Application computer software

(G-1750)
CINCINNATI THERMAL SPRAY INC
5901 Creek Rd (45242-4011)
PHONE.................513 793-1037
Scott Paschke, *Branch Mgr*
EMP: 110 **Privately Held**
SIC: 3479 Coating of metals & formed products
PA: Cincinnati Thermal Spray, Inc.
10904 Deerfield Rd
Blue Ash OH 45242

(G-1751)
CLARIANT CORPORATION
10999 Reed Hartman Hwy # 201 (45242-8319)
PHONE.................513 791-2964
Tim Urmstom, *Principal*
Jerry Ogrady, *Manager*
EMP: 3 EST: 2010
SALES (est): 202.2K **Privately Held**
SIC: 2869 Industrial organic chemicals

(G-1752)
COMPUTATIONAL ENGINEERING SVCS
10979 Reed Hartman Hwy # 210 (45242-2800)
PHONE.................513 745-0313
Gyan Sasmal, *President*
EMP: 4
SQ FT: 500
SALES (est): 343.5K **Privately Held**
SIC: 3369 Aerospace castings, nonferrous: except aluminum

(G-1753)
COVAP INC
10829 Millington Ct Ste 1 (45242-4023)
P.O. Box 42510, Cincinnati (45242-0510)
PHONE.................513 793-1855
Arnold Stoller, *President*
Stephanie Stoller, *Vice Pres*
EMP: 18
SQ FT: 9,000

Blue Ash - Hamilton County (G-1777)

SALES (est): 3.7MM **Privately Held**
WEB: www.covap.com
SIC: 5112 7331 2752 Stationery & office supplies; mailing service; commercial printing, lithographic

(G-1754)
CREST CRAFT COMPANY
4460 Lake Forest Dr # 232 (45242-3755)
PHONE...................513 271-4858
Jack Johnson, *President*
James Johnson, *Exec VP*
Michael Borellis, *CFO*
Barbara Gabbard, *Controller*
Linda Stanelle, *Controller*
EMP: 19
SQ FT: 44,000
SALES (est): 2.5MM **Privately Held**
SIC: 2752 3911 3499 Lithographing on metal; medals, precious or semiprecious metal; novelties & giftware, including trophies

(G-1755)
CREST GRAPHICS INC
9933 Alliance Rd Ste 1 (45242-5662)
PHONE...................513 271-2200
Robert Sparks, *President*
Andy Bregger, *Vice Pres*
Mike Hickle, *Vice Pres*
EMP: 16 EST: 1999
SQ FT: 22,000
SALES (est): 2.7MM **Privately Held**
WEB: www.crestgraphics.com
SIC: 2752 Commercial printing, offset

(G-1756)
CUMMINS - ALLISON CORP
11256 Cornell Park Dr (45242-1821)
PHONE...................513 469-2924
Jack Prather, *Manager*
EMP: 7
SALES (corp-wide): 383.8MM **Privately Held**
WEB: www.gsb.com
SIC: 5046 3519 Commercial equipment; internal combustion engines
PA: Cummins - Allison Corp.
852 Feehanville Dr
Mount Prospect IL 60056
847 759-6403

(G-1757)
CUSHMAN FOUNDRY LLC
5300 Creek Rd (45242-3936)
PHONE...................513 984-5570
Pam Fox, *Office Mgr*
John Beyersdorfer, *Mng Member*
John C Beyersdorfer, *Mng Member*
EMP: 11
SALES (est): 1.6MM **Privately Held**
SIC: 3365 Aluminum & aluminum-based alloy castings

(G-1758)
DIGITEK CORP
5665 Creek Rd (45242-4005)
PHONE...................513 794-3190
Marc E Brown, *President*
EMP: 10
SQ FT: 3,500
SALES (est): 2.6MM **Privately Held**
WEB: www.digitekcorp.net
SIC: 5136 5137 2253 Uniforms, men's & boys'; uniforms, women's & children's; T-shirts & tops, knit

(G-1759)
DSK IMAGING LLC
Also Called: Allegra Marketing Print Mail
6839 Ashfield Dr (45242-4108)
PHONE...................513 554-1797
Steve Kapuscinski, *Principal*
EMP: 10
SQ FT: 4,000
SALES (est): 1.4MM **Privately Held**
WEB: www.allegracinci.com
SIC: 8742 2752 Marketing consulting services; commercial printing, lithographic

(G-1760)
DURBIN MINUTEMAN PRESS
11130 Kenwood Rd (45242-1818)
PHONE...................513 791-9171
Jeff Bock,
EMP: 4

SQ FT: 3,000
SALES (est): 400.1K **Privately Held**
SIC: 2752 2759 2789 Commercial printing, offset; commercial printing; binding only: books, pamphlets, magazines, etc.

(G-1761)
DYVERSE ENTERTAINMENT LLC
Also Called: Dyverse Marketing Solutions
10979 Reed Hartman Hwy (45242-2800)
PHONE...................513 225-3301
Edward Cohen,
EMP: 3
SALES (est): 50K **Privately Held**
SIC: 3993 Signs & advertising specialties

(G-1762)
EAJ SERVICES LLC
Also Called: Nextstep Networking
4350 Glendale Milford Rd # 170 (45242-3700)
PHONE...................513 792-3400
Andrew Johnson, *Vice Pres*
Cindy Rolfes, *Office Mgr*
Erin Arnold,
EMP: 18
SQ FT: 5,500
SALES (est): 2.4MM **Privately Held**
WEB: www.nextstepnetworking.com
SIC: 7373 7378 3571 Computer integrated systems design; computer maintenance & repair; electronic computers

(G-1763)
EASTERN SHEET METAL INC (DH)
8959 Blue Ash Rd (45242-7800)
PHONE...................513 793-3440
William K Stout Sr, *Ch of Bd*
William K Stout Jr, *President*
Margaret Geiger, *Treasurer*
Robert Fedders, *Admin Sec*
▲ EMP: 85 EST: 1978
SQ FT: 80,000
SALES (est): 13.5MM **Privately Held**
WEB: www.easternsheetmetal.com
SIC: 3444 Ducts, sheet metal
HQ: Johnson Controls, Inc.
5757 N Green Bay Ave
Milwaukee WI 53209
414 524-1200

(G-1764)
EMPIRE BAKERY COMMISSARY LLC (PA)
11243 Cornell Park Dr (45242-1811)
PHONE...................513 793-6241
Michael Marek, *President*
EMP: 8 EST: 2015
SALES (est): 25MM **Privately Held**
SIC: 2051 Bakery: wholesale or wholesale/retail combined

(G-1765)
ETHICON ENDO-SURGERY INC (HQ)
4545 Creek Rd (45242-2839)
PHONE...................513 337-7000
Andrew K Ekdahl, *President*
RC Caldwell, *Partner*
Dawn Rauen, *Division Mgr*
Amy Maxson, *Project Mgr*
Michael Boehm, *Research*
▲ EMP: 1440
SQ FT: 31,330
SALES (est): 430.4MM
SALES (corp-wide): 81.5B **Publicly Held**
WEB: www.ethiconendo.com
SIC: 3841 5047 Surgical instruments & apparatus; medical equipment & supplies; surgical equipment & supplies
PA: Johnson & Johnson
1 Johnson And Johnson Plz
New Brunswick NJ 08933
732 524-0400

(G-1766)
ETHICON INC
Also Called: Ethicon Endo - Surgery
10123 Alliance Rd (45242-4714)
PHONE...................513 786-7000
Frank J Ryan, *Manager*
EMP: 225

SALES (corp-wide): 81.5B **Publicly Held**
WEB: www.ethiconinc.com
SIC: 3842 Surgical appliances & supplies
HQ: Ethicon Inc.
Us Route 22
Somerville NJ 08876
732 524-0400

(G-1767)
ETHICON US LLC (DH)
4545 Creek Rd 3 (45242-2839)
PHONE...................513 337-7000
Timothy H Schmid, *President*
Jeff Davis, *Materials Mgr*
James Lee, *Research*
Rudy Nobis, *Engineer*
Michael W Calvani, *Treasurer*
EMP: 33
SALES (est): 12.1MM
SALES (corp-wide): 81.5B **Publicly Held**
SIC: 3841 Surgical instruments & apparatus
HQ: Ethicon Endo-Surgery, Inc.
4545 Creek Rd
Blue Ash OH 45242
513 337-7000

(G-1768)
EVERYTHINGS IMAGE INC
9933 Alliance Rd Ste 2 (45242-5662)
PHONE...................513 469-6727
Kirk Morris, *President*
Daniel McBride, *Vice Pres*
EMP: 15
SQ FT: 5,500
SALES (est): 1.5MM **Privately Held**
WEB: www.everythingsimage.com
SIC: 2759 Promotional printing

(G-1769)
EXCEL LOADING SYSTEMS LLC
675 N Deis Dr Ste 276 (45242)
PHONE...................513 265-2936
David Shull, *President*
Alex Oswald,
Joe Williamson,
EMP: 3
SALES (est): 460.2K **Privately Held**
SIC: 3498 Pipe sections fabricated from purchased pipe

(G-1770)
F+W MEDIA INC (HQ)
Also Called: Novel Writing Workshop
10151 Carver Rd Ste 200 (45242-4760)
P.O. Box 78000, Detroit MI (48278-0001)
PHONE...................513 531-2690
Gregory J Osberg, *CEO*
David Nussbaum, *Ch of Bd*
Sara Domville, *President*
Gwenael Nicolas, *Principal*
Chris Berens, *Editor*
▲ EMP: 265 EST: 2005
SQ FT: 250,000
SALES (est): 256.7MM
SALES (corp-wide): 259.2MM **Privately Held**
WEB: www.decorativeartist.com
SIC: 2721 2731 4813 Magazines: publishing only, not printed on site; trade journals: publishing only, not printed on site; books: publishing only;

(G-1771)
F+W MEDIA INC
10151 Carver Rd Ste 200 (45242-4760)
PHONE...................603 253-8148
EMP: 8
SALES (corp-wide): 259.2MM **Privately Held**
SIC: 2731 Books: publishing only
HQ: F+W Media, Inc.
10151 Carver Rd Ste 200
Blue Ash OH 45242
513 531-2690

(G-1772)
FECHHEIMER BROTHERS COMPANY (HQ)
4545 Malsbary Rd (45242-5624)
PHONE...................513 793-5400
Dan Dudley, *CEO*
Fred Heldman, *Senior VP*
▲ EMP: 200
SQ FT: 108,000

SALES (est): 269.3MM
SALES (corp-wide): 225.3B **Publicly Held**
WEB: www.allbilt.com
SIC: 2311 2337 2339 5699 Men's & boys' uniforms; policemen's uniforms: made from purchased materials; firemen's uniforms: made from purchased materials; women's & misses' suits & coats; uniforms, except athletic: women's, misses' & juniors'; women's & misses' outerwear; uniforms
PA: Berkshire Hathaway Inc.
3555 Farnam St Ste 1140
Omaha NE 68131
402 346-1400

(G-1773)
FEINTOOL CINCINNATI INC (DH)
11280 Cornell Park Dr (45242-1888)
PHONE...................513 247-0110
Christoph Trachsler, *CEO*
Ralph Hardt, *Principal*
Paul Frauchiger, *Vice Pres*
Rolf Haag, *Vice Pres*
Steve Klaserner, *QC Mgr*
▲ EMP: 240
SALES (est): 62.7MM
SALES (corp-wide): 2.9B **Privately Held**
WEB: www.feintool-usa.com
SIC: 3465 Automotive stampings
HQ: Feintool U.S. Operations, Inc.
11280 Cornell Park Dr
Blue Ash OH 45242
513 247-4061

(G-1774)
FEINTOOL US OPERATIONS INC (DH)
11280 Cornell Park Dr (45242-1888)
PHONE...................513 247-4061
Richard Surico, *CEO*
Ralph E Hardt, *President*
Christoph Trachsler, *Principal*
Tim Runyan, *Vice Pres*
Ray Stratman, *Production*
▲ EMP: 250
SALES (est): 84.5MM
SALES (corp-wide): 2.9B **Privately Held**
SIC: 3469 3465 Metal stampings; automotive stampings
HQ: Feintool Technologie Ag
Industrierring 3
Lyss BE 3250
323 875-111

(G-1775)
FLEX PRO LABEL INC
11465 Deerfield Rd (45242-2106)
PHONE...................513 489-4417
Peter Harpen, *President*
Anthony Harpen, *Corp Secy*
EMP: 3
SQ FT: 6,000
SALES (est): 400K **Privately Held**
WEB: www.flex-pro.com
SIC: 2759 Labels & seals: printing

(G-1776)
FLEXOPLATE INC
6504 Corporate Dr (45242-2101)
PHONE...................513 489-0433
Thomas M Bock, *President*
EMP: 25
SQ FT: 10,000
SALES (est): 3.6MM **Privately Held**
WEB: www.flexoplate.com
SIC: 3555 2796 2791 Printing plates; platemaking services; typesetting

(G-1777)
FLORIDA TILE INC
Florida Tile 56
10840 Millington Ct (45242-4017)
PHONE...................513 891-1122
Ian Buttress, *Principal*
EMP: 8
SQ FT: 12,000
SALES (corp-wide): 147.6MM **Privately Held**
WEB: www.floridatile.com
SIC: 3253 Wall tile, ceramic
PA: Florida Tile, Inc.
998 Governors Ln Ste 300
Lexington KY 40513
859 219-5200

Blue Ash - Hamilton County (G-1778)   GEOGRAPHIC SECTION

(G-1778)
FORREST PHARMACEUTICALS
10901 Kenwood Rd (45242-2813)
PHONE.................................513 791-1701
EMP: 5
SALES (est): 511.8K **Privately Held**
SIC: 2834 Mfg Pharmaceutical Preparations

(G-1779)
FORWARD TECHNOLOGIES INC
6130 Interstate Cir (45242-1425)
PHONE.................................513 489-5111
EMP: 15
SQ FT: 6,500
SALES: 500K **Privately Held**
SIC: 3599 Machine shop, jobbing & repair

(G-1780)
G Q BUSINESS PRODUCTS
11380 Grooms Rd (45242-1406)
PHONE.................................513 792-4750
Diana Queen, *President*
Gordon Queen, *Treasurer*
Brenda Swoger, *Sales Associate*
EMP: 8
SQ FT: 10,000
SALES (est): 970K **Privately Held**
WEB: www.gqproducts.com
SIC: 5112 5199 2759 Business forms; advertising specialties; commercial printing

(G-1781)
GATE WEST COAST VENTURES LLC
Also Called: Tsjmedia
4412 Carver Woods Dr # 105 (45242-5539)
PHONE.................................513 891-1000
Marco Grgurevic-Pujan, *General Mgr*
Josh Guttman, *General Mgr*
Sonia Galicia, *Accounts Exec*
Elizabeth Herrera, *Manager*
Brian Wiles, *Manager*
EMP: 15 **EST:** 2005
SALES (est): 1.2MM **Privately Held**
SIC: 2711 Newspapers, publishing & printing

(G-1782)
GIS DYNAMICS LLC
11315 Williamson Rd (45241-2232)
PHONE.................................513 847-4931
Michael Rorie,
EMP: 5
SQ FT: 2,500
SALES (est): 389.8K **Privately Held**
SIC: 7372 Application computer software

(G-1783)
GT INDUSTRIAL SUPPLY INC
4350 Indeco Ct Ste B (45241-3488)
PHONE.................................513 771-7000
Michael Griffie Jr, *President*
Stephen Tino, *Vice Pres*
EMP: 10
SQ FT: 1,500
SALES: 6MM **Privately Held**
SIC: 2671 5063 5087 5199 Packaging paper & plastics film, coated & laminated; lighting fixtures; janitors' supplies; packaging materials; industrial & personal service paper; disposable plates, cups, napkins & eating utensils

(G-1784)
H & G EQUIPMENT INC (PA)
10837 Millington Ct (45242-4019)
PHONE.................................513 761-2060
Eric Kuehne, *President*
Dave Meiners, *Vice Pres*
David Meiners, *Vice Pres*
Amy Lilly, *Buyer*
EMP: 12
SQ FT: 4,400
SALES (est): 2.7MM **Privately Held**
SIC: 3565 Packaging machinery

(G-1785)
HARTMANN INCORPORATED
4615 Carlynn Dr (45241-2202)
PHONE.................................513 276-7318
Carolyn Hartmann, *President*
EMP: 12 **EST:** 2011
SALES (est): 1.3MM **Privately Held**
SIC: 2752 Commercial printing, offset

(G-1786)
HB FULLER COMPANY
Also Called: Adhesves Sealants Coatings Div
4450 Malsbary Rd (45242-5695)
PHONE.................................513 719-3600
Todd Trushenski, *Manager*
EMP: 46
SQ FT: 23,000
SALES (corp-wide): 3B **Publicly Held**
WEB: www.hbfuller.com
SIC: 2891 Adhesives
PA: H.B. Fuller Company
1200 Willow Lake Blvd
Saint Paul MN 55110
651 236-5900

(G-1787)
HB FULLER COMPANY
4440 Malsbary Rd (45242-5623)
PHONE.................................513 719-3600
Todd Trushenski, *Branch Mgr*
EMP: 9
SALES (corp-wide): 3B **Publicly Held**
SIC: 2891 Adhesives
PA: H.B. Fuller Company
1200 Willow Lake Blvd
Saint Paul MN 55110
651 236-5900

(G-1788)
HENNIG INC
11431 Williamson Rd Ste A (45241-4216)
PHONE.................................513 247-0838
Brian Smith, *Branch Mgr*
EMP: 3
SALES (corp-wide): 118MM **Privately Held**
SIC: 3444 Machine guards, sheet metal
HQ: Hennig Inc.
9900 N Alpine Rd
Machesney Park IL 61115
815 636-9900

(G-1789)
HOUSETRENDS
4601 Malsbary Rd 104 (45242-5632)
PHONE.................................513 794-4103
Jeremy Hensley, *Vice Pres*
EMP: 6
SALES (est): 370.4K **Privately Held**
SIC: 2721 Magazines: publishing & printing

(G-1790)
IACONO PRODUCTION SERVICES INC
Also Called: AVI Staging Technology
11420 Deerfield Rd (45242-2107)
PHONE.................................513 469-5095
Molly Cates, *Opers Mgr*
Tom Treer, *Manager*
EMP: 10
SALES (corp-wide): 5.1MM **Privately Held**
SIC: 3648 7359 7922 Stage lighting equipment; sound & lighting equipment rental; lighting, theatrical
PA: Iacono Production Services, Inc.
10816 Millington Ct # 100
Blue Ash OH 45242
513 621-9108

(G-1791)
ILLINOIS TOOL WORKS INC
Also Called: ITW Evercoat
6600 Cornell Rd (45242-2033)
PHONE.................................513 489-7600
Steven Levine, *General Mgr*
EMP: 130
SALES (corp-wide): 14.7B **Publicly Held**
SIC: 2821 3714 2891 Polyesters; motor vehicle parts & accessories; adhesives & sealants
PA: Illinois Tool Works Inc.
155 Harlem Ave
Glenview IL 60025
847 724-7500

(G-1792)
IMMERSUS HEALTH COMPANY LLC
4351 Creek Rd (45241-2923)
PHONE.................................855 994-4325
Brian Pavlin,
EMP: 3
SALES (corp-wide): 10MM **Privately Held**
SIC: 3841 Surgical & medical instruments
PA: Immersus Health Company, Llc
2 Hill And Hollow Ln
Cincinnati OH 45208
855 994-4325

(G-1793)
INFINIT NUTRITION LLC
11240 Cornell Park Dr # 110 (45242-1800)
PHONE.................................513 791-3500
Mark Martines, *Project Mgr*
Michael Folan, *Mng Member*
▲ **EMP:** 10
SALES (est): 2MM **Privately Held**
SIC: 2023 Dietary supplements, dairy & non-dairy based

(G-1794)
INTERWEAVE PRESS LLC
10151 Carver Rd Ste 200 (45242-4760)
PHONE.................................513 531-2690
EMP: 9
SALES (est): 683.3K **Privately Held**
SIC: 2741 Miscellaneous publishing

(G-1795)
JOB NEWS (PA)
10250 Alliance Rd Ste 201 (45242-4774)
PHONE.................................513 984-5724
Dawna Urlakis, *Owner*
EMP: 7
SALES (est): 615.2K **Privately Held**
SIC: 2711 7311 Job printing & newspaper publishing combined; advertising agencies

(G-1796)
JOE P FISCHER WOODCRAFT
4627 Carlynn Dr (45241-2202)
PHONE.................................513 530-9600
Joe P Fischer, *Owner*
EMP: 3
SALES (est): 151.1K **Privately Held**
SIC: 2431 Woodwork, interior & ornamental

(G-1797)
JPS TECHNOLOGIES INC (PA)
11110 Deerfield Rd (45242-2022)
PHONE.................................513 984-6400
Robert J Brandner, *President*
Nancy K Meyer, *Treasurer*
EMP: 10
SQ FT: 7,500
SALES (est): 10.8MM **Privately Held**
WEB: www.jpstechnologies.com
SIC: 5084 3089 Industrial machinery & equipment; plastic processing

(G-1798)
JPS TECHNOLOGIES INC
11118 Deerfield Rd (45242-2022)
PHONE.................................513 984-6400
Nancy Meyers, *Manager*
EMP: 12
SALES (corp-wide): 10.8MM **Privately Held**
WEB: www.jpstechnologies.com
SIC: 5084 3089 Industrial machinery & equipment; plastic processing
PA: Jps Technologies, Inc.
11110 Deerfield Rd
Blue Ash OH 45242
513 984-6400

(G-1799)
JZ TECHNOLOGIES LLC
3420 Aston Pl (45241-3223)
PHONE.................................937 252-5800
Jeff Samuelson,
John Buckles,
EMP: 5 **EST:** 2016
SALES (est): 239.7K **Privately Held**
SIC: 3829 Measuring & controlling devices

(G-1800)
KARDOL QUALITY PRODUCTS LLC (PA)
9933 Alliance Rd Ste 2 (45242-5662)
PHONE.................................513 933-8206
Eric Kahn, *CEO*
Mark Bedwell, *President*
Gary Harris, *Plant Mgr*
Mike Darding, *CFO*
▼ **EMP:** 33
SQ FT: 5,000
SALES (est): 9.2MM **Privately Held**
WEB: www.kardol.com
SIC: 2672 2841 2842 2821 Coated & laminated paper; soap & other detergents; specialty cleaning, polishes & sanitation goods; plastics materials & resins; paints & allied products

(G-1801)
KOLINAHR SYSTEMS INC
6840 Ashfield Dr (45242-4108)
PHONE.................................513 745-9401
Gary Jenkins, *President*
Greg Reichling, *Electrical Engi*
Andrew Stone, *Sales Dir*
Eric Hartman, *Manager*
EMP: 15
SALES (est): 6.1MM **Privately Held**
WEB: www.kolinahr.cc
SIC: 3535 5084 3565 Conveyors & conveying equipment; industrial machinery & equipment; packaging machinery

(G-1802)
LANGE PRECISION INC
6971 Cornell Rd (45242-3024)
PHONE.................................513 530-9500
Karl Lange, *President*
EMP: 15
SQ FT: 13,000
SALES (est): 3MM **Privately Held**
SIC: 3544 3599 3545 3537 Special dies, tools, jigs & fixtures; machine shop, jobbing & repair; machine tool accessories; industrial trucks & tractors; iron & steel forgings

(G-1803)
LARMAX INC
Also Called: Kwik Kopy Printing
10945 Reed Hartman Hwy # 210 (45242-2828)
PHONE.................................513 984-0783
Larry Richardson, *President*
Maxine Richardson, *Vice Pres*
EMP: 6
SQ FT: 1,500
SALES: 500K **Privately Held**
SIC: 2759 Thermography

(G-1804)
LEADEC CORP (DH)
9395 Kenwood Rd Ste 200 (45242-6819)
PHONE.................................513 731-3590
William Bell, *CEO*
Donald G Morsch, *Treasurer*
▲ **EMP:** 34
SQ FT: 18,000
SALES (est): 341.3MM **Privately Held**
WEB: www.premiermss.com
SIC: 7349 8741 3714 Building cleaning service; management services; motor vehicle parts & accessories
HQ: Leadec Holding Bv & Co. Kg
Meitnerstr. 11
Stuttgart 70563
711 784-10

(G-1805)
LEGRAND AV INC
Polacoat Divison
11500 Williamson Rd (45241-2271)
PHONE.................................574 267-8101
Keith Sterwerf, *Materials Mgr*
Bob S Martin, *Manager*
EMP: 25
SQ FT: 41,700
SALES (corp-wide): 20.7MM **Privately Held**
WEB: www.dalite.com
SIC: 3861 3643 Motion picture apparatus & equipment; current-carrying wiring devices
HQ: Legrand Av Inc.
6436 City West Pkwy
Eden Prairie MN 55344
866 977-3901

(G-1806)
LOCKES HEATING & COOLING LLC
10229 Kenwood Rd (45242-4701)
PHONE.................................513 793-1900

GEOGRAPHIC SECTION

Blue Ash - Hamilton County (G-1830)

EMP: 10
SQ FT: 1,000
SALES (est): 1.1MM **Privately Held**
SIC: 3585 Mfg Refrigeration/Heating Equipment

(G-1807)
LOROCO INDUSTRIES INC (PA)
Also Called: Royal Pad Products
5000 Creek Rd (45242-3990)
PHONE.................513 891-9544
James Lallathin, *President*
Lee Rozin, *Chairman*
Jim Myers, *CFO*
James Y Myers, *Info Tech Mgr*
◆ **EMP:** 50 **EST:** 1898
SQ FT: 125,000
SALES (est): 13.7MM **Privately Held**
SIC: 2675 2671 3479 3544 Paperboard die-cutting; chip board, pasted, die-cut: from purchased materials; packaging paper & plastics film, coated & laminated; painting, coating & hot dipping; dies, steel rule; coated & laminated paper; paperboard mills

(G-1808)
LSI INDUSTRIES INC
Abolite Lighting
10000 Alliance Rd (45242-4706)
P.O. Box 42728, Cincinnati (45242-0728)
PHONE.................513 793-3200
Larry Branham, *Manager*
EMP: 50
SALES (corp-wide): 342MM **Publicly Held**
WEB: www.lsi-industries.com
SIC: 3993 2759 3444 3646 Electric signs; screen printing; labels & seals: printing; decals: printing; sheet metalwork; commercial indusl & institutional electric lighting fixtures; residential lighting fixtures; floodlights
PA: Lsi Industries Inc.
10000 Alliance Rd
Blue Ash OH 45242
513 793-3200

(G-1809)
LSI INDUSTRIES INC
10170 Alliance Rd (45242)
PHONE.................513 372-3200
Drew Riley, *Business Mgr*
Ronald Hansel, *Plant Mgr*
Glenn Reinheimer, *Plant Mgr*
Linda Cooper, *Project Mgr*
Travis Schubert, *Research*
EMP: 4
SALES (est): 347K
SALES (corp-wide): 342MM **Publicly Held**
SIC: 3648 Outdoor lighting equipment
PA: Lsi Industries Inc.
10000 Alliance Rd
Blue Ash OH 45242
513 793-3200

(G-1810)
LSI INDUSTRIES INC
LSI Midwest Lighting
10000 Alliance Rd (45242-4706)
PHONE.................913 281-1100
Dennis Oberling, *Manager*
EMP: 200
SALES (corp-wide): 331.3MM **Publicly Held**
WEB: www.lsi-industries.com
SIC: 3646 5063 Commercial indusl & institutional electric lighting fixtures; lighting fixtures
PA: Lsi Industries Inc.
10000 Alliance Rd
Blue Ash OH 45242
513 793-3200

(G-1811)
LSI INDUSTRIES INC (PA)
10000 Alliance Rd (45242-4706)
P.O. Box 42728, Cincinnati (45242-0728)
PHONE.................513 793-3200
Wilfred T O'Gara, *Ch of Bd*
James A Clark, *President*
Howard E Japlon, *Exec VP*
Leonard Fernandez, *Vice Pres*
Bruce Frasure, *Vice Pres*
EMP: 277
SQ FT: 243,000
SALES: 342MM **Publicly Held**
WEB: www.lsi-industries.com
SIC: 3993 3663 3648 Electric signs; light communications equipment; floodlights

(G-1812)
LUMINEX HOME DECOR (PA)
Also Called: Luminex HD&f Company
10521 Millington Ct (45242-4022)
PHONE.................513 563-1113
Calvin Johnston, *CEO*
EMP: 709
SALES (est): 259.4MM **Privately Held**
SIC: 5023 2844 Decorative home furnishings & supplies; toilet preparations

(G-1813)
MASTER COMMUNICATIONS INC
Also Called: Asia For Kids
4480 Lake Forest Dr # 302 (45242-3753)
P.O. Box 9096, Cincinnati (45209-0096)
PHONE.................208 821-3473
Selina Yoon, *President*
Frederick Chen, *Vice Pres*
▲ **EMP:** 9
SALES (est): 1.4MM **Privately Held**
WEB: www.master-comm.com
SIC: 7812 2731 Video tape production; book publishing

(G-1814)
MAT BASICS INCORPORATED
4546 Cornell Rd (45241-2425)
PHONE.................513 793-0313
Suzie L Johnson, *Principal*
EMP: 7 **EST:** 2011
SALES (est): 543.4K **Privately Held**
SIC: 2273 Carpets & rugs

(G-1815)
MATDAN CORPORATION
10855 Millington Ct (45242-4019)
PHONE.................513 794-0500
David Arand, *President*
▲ **EMP:** 35
SQ FT: 10,000
SALES (est): 8.1MM **Privately Held**
WEB: www.matdanfasteners.com
SIC: 3452 3429 Bolts, metal; manufactured hardware (general)

(G-1816)
MAVERICK CORPORATION
11285 Grooms Rd (45242-1428)
PHONE.................513 469-9919
Eric Collins, *CEO*
Robert Gray, *President*
Brad Love, *General Mgr*
Hoffelder Daniel, *Vice Pres*
Ty Shah, *Facilities Mgr*
EMP: 14
SQ FT: 2,300
SALES (est): 2.9MM **Privately Held**
SIC: 3089 3299 Thermoformed finished plastic products; ceramic fiber

(G-1817)
MAVERICK MOLDING CO
11359 Grooms Rd (45242-1405)
PHONE.................513 387-6100
Traci Denny, *General Mgr*
Brad Love, *Principal*
Laurel Mesing, *Principal*
Jack Rubino, *Exec VP*
▲ **EMP:** 17
SALES (est): 60.5K **Privately Held**
SIC: 3728 Aircraft parts & equipment

(G-1818)
META MANUFACTURING CORPORATION
8901 Blue Ash Rd Ste 1 (45242-7809)
PHONE.................513 793-6382
David Mc Swain, *President*
Bruce Fille, *QC Mgr*
Jeff Theis, *Manager*
EMP: 50
SQ FT: 54,000
SALES (est): 9.2MM **Privately Held**
WEB: www.metamfg.com
SIC: 3599 7692 Machine shop, jobbing & repair; welding repair

(G-1819)
METAL IMPROVEMENT COMPANY LLC
11131 Luschek Dr (45241-2434)
PHONE.................513 489-6484
James Groark, *General Mgr*
Dan Richardson, *Manager*
Barb Pratt, *Director*
EMP: 23
SQ FT: 15,031
SALES (corp-wide): 2.4B **Publicly Held**
WEB: www.mic-houston.com
SIC: 3398 Shot peening (treating steel to reduce fatigue)
HQ: Metal Improvement Company, Llc
80 E Rte 4 Ste 310
Paramus NJ 07652
201 843-7800

(G-1820)
METALEX MANUFACTURING INC (PA)
5750 Cornell Rd (45242-2083)
PHONE.................513 489-0507
Kevin Kummerle, *CEO*
Werner Kummerle, *President*
Jeff Bruns, *General Mgr*
Rob McCabe, *Engineer*
Justin Forsberg, *Project Engr*
▲ **EMP:** 115
SQ FT: 120,000
SALES: 35.2MM **Privately Held**
WEB: www.metalexmfg.com
SIC: 3599 3511 3544 3769 Custom machinery; turbines & turbine generator sets; special dies, tools, jigs & fixtures; guided missile & space vehicle parts & auxiliary equipment; machine tool accessories

(G-1821)
MILACRON HOLDINGS CORP (PA)
10200 Alliance Rd Ste 200 (45242-4716)
PHONE.................513 487-5000
Ira G Boots, *Ch of Bd*
Thomas J Goeke, *President*
Hugh O'Donnell, *Vice Pres*
Bruce Chalmers, *CFO*
Mark Miller, *Officer*
EMP: 67
SQ FT: 22,000
SALES: 1.2B **Publicly Held**
SIC: 3544 Industrial molds; forms (molds), for foundry & plastics working machinery

(G-1822)
MILACRON LLC (DH)
10200 Alliance Rd Ste 200 (45242-4716)
PHONE.................513 487-5000
Tom Goeke, *CEO*
John Gallagher, *COO*
Ron Krisanda, *COO*
Mark Griffiths, *Vice Pres*
Rick Smith, *Vice Pres*
◆ **EMP:** 35
SALES (est): 1.4B
SALES (corp-wide): 1.2B **Publicly Held**
SIC: 3549 2899 Metalworking machinery; correction fluid
HQ: Milacron Intermediate Holdings Inc.
3010 Disney St
Cincinnati OH 45209
513 536-2000

(G-1823)
MOLDERS WORLD INC
11471 Deerfield Rd (45242-2106)
PHONE.................513 469-6653
Russell Bowen, *Principal*
Brandon Bowen, *Opers Mgr*
EMP: 9
SALES (est): 981.2K **Privately Held**
SIC: 3089 Molding primary plastic

(G-1824)
MULTI-CRAFT LITHO INC
4440 Creek Rd (45242-2802)
P.O. Box 72960, Newport KY (41072-0960)
PHONE.................859 581-2754
Deborah A Simpson, *President*
Pamela Gibbs, *Corp Secy*
Thomas Gibbs, *Vice Pres*
James Martin, *Production*
Kathy Locey, *Accounting Mgr*
EMP: 48
SALES: 8.4MM **Privately Held**
WEB: www.multi-craft.com
SIC: 2791 2789 2759 2732 Typesetting; bookbinding & related work; commercial printing; book printing; die-cut paper & board; commercial printing, offset

(G-1825)
NEW TRACK MEDIA LLC
10151 Carver Rd Ste 200 (45242-4760)
PHONE.................513 421-6500
Stephen J Kent, *President*
W Budge Wallis, *President*
Tina Battock, *Exec VP*
Mark F Arnett, *CFO*
Nicole McGuire, *Chief Mktg Ofcr*
▲ **EMP:** 10
SALES (est): 964.7K
SALES (corp-wide): 259.2MM **Privately Held**
SIC: 2721 Magazines: publishing & printing
HQ: F+W Media, Inc.
10151 Carver Rd Ste 200
Blue Ash OH 45242
513 531-2690

(G-1826)
OLAY LLC
Also Called: Procter Gamble Olay Co - Cayey
11530 Reed Hartman Hwy (45241-2422)
PHONE.................787 535-2191
AG Lafley, *CEO*
EMP: 5 **EST:** 2007
SALES (est): 559.1K
SALES (corp-wide): 66.8B **Publicly Held**
SIC: 2844 Cosmetic preparations
HQ: Procter & Gamble International Operations Sa
Route De St-Georges 47
Petit-Lancy GE 1213
800 000-884

(G-1827)
OMYA DISTRIBUTION LLC (DH)
9987 Carver Rd Ste 300 (45242-5563)
PHONE.................513 387-4600
Anthony Colak, *President*
EMP: 6
SALES (est): 4.8MM
SALES (corp-wide): 3.9B **Privately Held**
SIC: 2819 Calcium compounds & salts, inorganic
HQ: Omya Inc.
9987 Carver Rd Ste 300
Blue Ash OH 45242
513 387-4600

(G-1828)
OMYA INDUSTRIES INC (HQ)
9987 Carver Rd Ste 300 (45242-5563)
PHONE.................513 387-4600
Anthony Colak, *President*
John Suddarth, *Vice Pres*
Don Stewart, *Safety Mgr*
Roland Meier, *Facilities Mgr*
Lester Cantrell, *Buyer*
◆ **EMP:** 85 **EST:** 1977
SQ FT: 21,700
SALES (est): 279.8MM
SALES (corp-wide): 4B **Privately Held**
SIC: 1422 Crushed & broken limestone
PA: Omya Ag
Baslerstrasse 42
Oftringen AG 4665
627 892-929

(G-1829)
PAYNE FAMILY LLC II
5871 Creek Rd (45242-4009)
PHONE.................513 861-7600
Paul Keith, *Sales Executive*
EMP: 3
SALES (est): 127.2K **Privately Held**
SIC: 3399 Primary metal products

(G-1830)
PLASTIC MOLDINGS COMPANY LLC (PA)
Also Called: P M C
9825 Kenwood Rd Ste 302 (45242-6252)
PHONE.................513 921-5040
George H Vincent,
Thomas R Gerdes,
Lisa Jennings,
▲ **EMP:** 75
SQ FT: 63,500

Blue Ash - Hamilton County (G-1831)

GEOGRAPHIC SECTION

SALES (est): 32.2MM **Privately Held**
WEB: www.plasticmoldings.com
SIC: 3089 Injection molding of plastics

(G-1831)
PMC SMART SOLUTIONS LLC
9825 Kenwood Rd Ste 300 (45242-6252)
PHONE..................513 921-5040
Lisa Jennings, *President*
Deborah Gerdes,
EMP: 14
SALES (est): 2.1MM **Privately Held**
SIC: 3841 Surgical & medical instruments

(G-1832)
POKLAR POWER AND MOTION INC
Also Called: Poklar Power Motion
10979 Reed Hartman Hwy # 111 (45242-2857)
PHONE..................513 791-5009
Tom Daddario, *President*
EMP: 4
SALES (est): 319K
SALES (corp-wide): 1.2MM **Privately Held**
SIC: 3568 Power transmission equipment
PA: Poklar Power And Motion Inc
    28861 Euclid Ave
    Wickliffe OH 44092
    440 585-2121

(G-1833)
POSITECH CORP
11310 Williamson Rd (45241-2233)
PHONE..................513 942-7411
Jeff Hauck, *President*
▲ EMP: 15
SQ FT: 12,400
SALES (est): 2.8MM **Privately Held**
WEB: www.positechcorp.com
SIC: 3599 Machine shop, jobbing & repair

(G-1834)
PRECISION ANLYTICAL INSTRS INC
Also Called: P A I
10857 Millington Ct (45242-4019)
PHONE..................513 984-1600
Douglas G Frank, *President*
Gary Frank, *Manager*
EMP: 6
SQ FT: 2,100
SALES (est): 966.3K **Privately Held**
WEB: www.toolsforanalysis.com
SIC: 3826 Analytical instruments

(G-1835)
PRESTIGE ENTERPRISE INTL INC
11343 Grooms Rd (45242-1405)
PHONE..................513 469-6044
Charles Gabbour, *President*
Jeff Gabbour, *Vice Pres*
◆ EMP: 51
SQ FT: 10,000
SALES (est): 7.1MM **Privately Held**
WEB: www.prestigefloor.com
SIC: 2426 Flooring, hardwood

(G-1836)
PROCTER & GAMBLE COMPANY
11530 Reed Hartman Hwy (45241-2422)
PHONE..................513 626-2500
Howard Greg, *Research*
Rob Nemeth, *Engineer*
Gale Britton, *Manager*
EMP: 150
SALES (corp-wide): 66.8B **Publicly Held**
WEB: www.pg.com
SIC: 2844 Deodorants, personal
PA: The Procter & Gamble Company
    1 Procter And Gamble Plz
    Cincinnati OH 45202
    513 983-1100

(G-1837)
PROCTOER & GAMBLE
11530 Reed Hartman Hwy (45241-2422)
P.O. Box 5584, Cincinnati (45201-5584)
PHONE..................513 983-1100
Camille Chammas, *Manager*
EMP: 4 EST: 2010
SALES (est): 365.2K **Privately Held**
SIC: 2833 Medicinal chemicals

(G-1838)
PROTEIN EXPRESS INC
10931 Reed Hartman Hwy B (45242-2862)
PHONE..................513 769-9654
Michael L Howell, *President*
Gary Dean, *Vice Pres*
Zsolt Hertelendy, *Vice Pres*
Charles Gillespie, *Technical Mgr*
EMP: 4 EST: 1996
SQ FT: 4,537
SALES (est): 464.7K **Privately Held**
SIC: 2834 8731 Vitamin, nutrient & hematinic preparations for human use; commercial physical research

(G-1839)
PROTEIN EXPRESS LABORATORIES
Also Called: Skirdle
10931 R Hartman Hwy B (45242)
PHONE..................513 769-9654
Zsolt Hertelendy, *Vice Pres*
EMP: 3
SALES (est): 283.5K **Privately Held**
SIC: 2836 Toxins, viruses & similar substances, including venom

(G-1840)
RA CONSULTANTS LLC
10856 Kenwood Rd (45242-2812)
PHONE..................513 469-6600
John P Allen,
Marijo Flamm, *Admin Asst*
EMP: 30
SALES (est): 4.5MM **Privately Held**
WEB: www.raconsultantsllc.com
SIC: 8711 3679 Civil engineering; commutators, electronic

(G-1841)
RSW DISTRIBUTORS LLC
Also Called: Culinary Standards
4700 Ashwood Dr Ste 200 (45241-2424)
PHONE..................502 587-8877
Ronald Wilheim,
Mark A Littman,
EMP: 100 EST: 2008
SQ FT: 27,111
SALES (est): 13MM **Privately Held**
SIC: 2038 Frozen specialties

(G-1842)
SAMUELS PRODUCTS INC
9851 Redhill Dr (45242-5694)
PHONE..................513 891-4456
Millard Samuels, *President*
Thomas J Samuels, *Vice Pres*
William Fitzpatric, *Admin Sec*
EMP: 30 EST: 1903
SQ FT: 61,000
SALES (est): 4.3MM **Privately Held**
WEB: www.samuelsproducts.com
SIC: 2759 5122 Flexographic printing; bags, plastic: printing; druggists' sundries

(G-1843)
SCHOOL MAINTENANCE SUPPLY INC (PA)
10616 Millington Ct (45242-4015)
PHONE..................513 376-8670
Derrick Spruance, *President*
Vicky Spruance, *Corp Secy*
EMP: 5
SALES (est): 525K **Privately Held**
SIC: 2399 5013 Seat covers, automobile; seat covers

(G-1844)
SD IP HOLDINGS COMPANY
4747 Lake Forest Dr (45242-3853)
PHONE..................513 483-3300
Billy Cyr, *President*
William Schumacher, *Senior VP*
EMP: 1
SALES (est): 11.1MM
SALES (corp-wide): 1.3B **Privately Held**
SIC: 2086 Carbonated soft drinks, bottled & canned
HQ: Sunny Delight Beverage Co
    10300 Alliance Rd Ste 500
    Blue Ash OH 45242
    513 483-3300

(G-1845)
SECQURE SURGICAL CORP
4480 Lake Forest Dr # 414 (45242-3740)
PHONE..................513 769-1916
Rich Grant, *President*
EMP: 3
SQ FT: 13,000
SALES: 3MM **Privately Held**
SIC: 3841 Surgical & medical instruments

(G-1846)
SERV ALL GRAPHICS LLC
10901 Reed Hartman Hwy # 209 (45242-2831)
PHONE..................513 681-8883
Dennis Engel, *Vice Pres*
Pam Stephens, *Mng Member*
Don Ingle,
EMP: 3
SQ FT: 21,000
SALES (est): 361.3K **Privately Held**
WEB: www.servallgraphics.com
SIC: 2752 Commercial printing, offset

(G-1847)
SPACE DYNAMICS CORP
Also Called: Ambassador Heat Transfer
10080 Alliance Rd (45242-4706)
P.O. Box 42344, Cincinnati (45242-0344)
PHONE..................513 792-9800
Madan L Ghai, *Ch of Bd*
Rik L Ghai, *President*
James L Lyons, *Principal*
Dolores A Yackle, *Corp Secy*
Sheila Revis, *Vice Pres*
EMP: 25 EST: 1961
SQ FT: 45,000
SALES: 6MM **Privately Held**
WEB: www.ambassadorco.com
SIC: 3443 3585 Heat exchangers, condensers & components; refrigeration & heating equipment

(G-1848)
SPECTRE EDM
6082 Interstate Cir (45242-1413)
PHONE..................513 469-7700
Burt Melson, *Owner*
EMP: 5
SQ FT: 6,000
SALES: 500K **Privately Held**
SIC: 3599 Machine shop, jobbing & repair

(G-1849)
ST MEDIA GROUP INTL INC
11262 Cornell Park Dr (45242-1828)
PHONE..................513 421-2050
Murray Kasmenn, *President*
Christine Lewis, *Publisher*
Michael Schneider, *Publisher*
Grant Freking, *Editor*
Carly Hagedon, *Editor*
▲ EMP: 65 EST: 1906
SQ FT: 30,000
SALES (est): 15.6MM **Privately Held**
WEB: www.signweb.com
SIC: 2721 2731 2791 Magazines: publishing only, not printed on site; book publishing; typesetting

(G-1850)
STANDARD BARIATRICS INC
4362 Glendale Milford Rd (45242-3706)
PHONE..................513 620-7751
Matt Sokany, *CEO*
Kurt Azarbarzin, *Ch of Bd*
Jonathan Thompson, *Principal*
Adam Dunki-Jacobs, *COO*
EMP: 6
SALES (est): 631K **Privately Held**
SIC: 3841 Surgical & medical instruments

(G-1851)
STIGLERS WOODWORKS
9358 Opal Ct (45242-6712)
PHONE..................513 733-3009
Robert Stigler, *Owner*
EMP: 3
SQ FT: 6,000
SALES: 250K **Privately Held**
WEB: www.stiglerswoodworks.com
SIC: 2512 5712 Upholstered household furniture; furniture stores

(G-1852)
STOLLE PROPERTIES INC
6954 Cornell Rd Ste 100 (45242-3001)
P.O. Box 815, Lebanon (45036-0815)
PHONE..................513 932-8664
William Faulkner, *President*
EMP: 580
SQ FT: 1,876
SALES (est): 42.2MM
SALES (corp-wide): 63.4MM **Privately Held**
SIC: 3469 Metal stampings
PA: The Ralph J Stolle Company

    Cincinnati OH 45242
    513 489-7184

(G-1853)
SUNNY DELIGHT BEVERAGE CO (HQ)
10300 Alliance Rd Ste 500 (45242-4767)
PHONE..................513 483-3300
Tim Voelkerding, *President*
Andrea Hogue, *Opers Mgr*
George Galvez, *Production*
Shelly Crawford, *Purch Agent*
Brian Grote, *CFO*
▼ EMP: 70
SQ FT: 20,000
SALES (est): 224.7MM
SALES (corp-wide): 1.3B **Privately Held**
SIC: 2086 5499 Fruit drinks (less than 100% juice): packaged in cans, etc.; soft drinks
PA: Harvest Hill Holdings, Llc
    1 High Ridge Park Fl 2
    Stamford CT 06905
    203 914-1620

(G-1854)
SUPERALLOY MFG SOLUTIONS CORP
Also Called: Aerospace Mfg Group-Ohio
11230 Deerfield Rd (45242-2024)
PHONE..................513 489-9800
Phil Swash, *CEO*
Tom Battagli, *Senior VP*
Mike Beck, *Vice Pres*
Terry Lievestro, *Engineer*
▲ EMP: 138
SQ FT: 125,000
SALES (est): 43.5MM
SALES (corp-wide): 2.7B **Privately Held**
WEB: www.teleflex.com
SIC: 3599 Electrical discharge machining (EDM); machine shop, jobbing & repair
HQ: Gkn Limited
    Po Box 55
    Redditch WORCS B98 0
    152 751-7715

(G-1855)
SUPERIOR PRINTING INK CO INC
Also Called: Mueller Color
10861 Millington Ct Ste B (45242-4035)
PHONE..................513 221-4707
Ed Bradley, *Principal*
EMP: 17
SQ FT: 20,000
SALES (est): 2.6MM **Privately Held**
SIC: 2893 Printing ink

(G-1856)
SURGRX INC
4545 Creek Rd (45242-2803)
PHONE..................650 482-2400
David Clapper, *President*
Edward Unkard, *CFO*
EMP: 14 EST: 2000
SQ FT: 20,000
SALES (est): 832.6K
SALES (corp-wide): 81.5B **Publicly Held**
WEB: www.surgrx.com
SIC: 3841 Surgical & medical instruments
HQ: Ethicon Endo-Surgery, Inc.
    4545 Creek Rd
    Blue Ash OH 45242
    513 337-7000

(G-1857)
TECHNOSOFT INC
11180 Reed Hartman Hwy # 200 (45242-1824)
PHONE..................513 985-9877

GEOGRAPHIC SECTION

Blue Ash - Hamilton County (G-1882)

Adel Chemaly, *President*
Nabil Khater, *Vice Pres*
Alok Mathur, *CIO*
Mahesh Naphade, *Director*
Kenneth Rojas, *Associate*
EMP: 12
SALES (est): 1.5MM **Privately Held**
SIC: 7372 7371 Prepackaged software; custom computer programming services

(G-1858)
TEKWORX LLC
4538 Cornell Rd (45241-2425)
PHONE 513 533-4777
Mike Flaherty, *Managing Dir*
Larry Tillack, *Research*
EMP: 15
SALES (est): 2.2MM **Privately Held**
SIC: 8748 8711 1731 3625 Systems analysis & engineering consulting services; energy conservation engineering; energy management controls; electric controls & control accessories, industrial

(G-1859)
TESLA INC
Also Called: Tesla Motors
9111 Blue Ash Rd (45242-6821)
PHONE 513 745-9111
EMP: 7
SALES (corp-wide): 21.4B **Publicly Held**
SIC: 3711 Motor vehicles & car bodies
PA: Tesla, Inc.
3500 Deer Creek Rd
Palo Alto CA 94304
650 681-5000

(G-1860)
TOYO SEIKI USA INC
11130 Luschek Dr (45241-2434)
PHONE 513 546-9657
Nobukaizu Kaike, *Principal*
EMP: 5
SALES (est): 482.4K
SALES (corp-wide): 43.7MM **Privately Held**
SIC: 2822 Ethylene-propylene rubbers, EPDM polymers
PA: Toyo Seiki Seisaku-Sho, Ltd.
5-15-4, Takinogawa
Kita-Ku TKY 114-0
339 168-181

(G-1861)
TRANS-ACC INC (PA)
11167 Deerfield Rd (45242-2021)
PHONE 513 793-6410
John Weinkam, *President*
Mary Weinkam, *Vice Pres*
Wayne Wood, *Purchasing*
Douglas Miller, *Controller*
EMP: 35
SQ FT: 27,000
SALES (est): 4.4MM **Privately Held**
SIC: 3471 3479 Finishing, metals or formed products; coating of metals & formed products

(G-1862)
TYTEK INDUSTRIES INC (PA)
4700 Ashwood Dr Ste 445 (45241-2684)
PHONE 513 874-7326
Chris C Tyler, *President*
Terry Mistler, *Manager*
▲ **EMP:** 4
SQ FT: 210,000
SALES (est): 798.6K **Privately Held**
WEB: www.tytekindustries.com
SIC: 3674 Photoelectric magnetic devices

(G-1863)
US INC
10937 Reed Hartman Hwy (45242-2858)
PHONE 513 791-1162
Charles Davis, *Branch Mgr*
EMP: 4 **Privately Held**
SIC: 1711 5023 3263 Heating & air conditioning contractors; kitchenware; commercial tableware or kitchen articles, fine earthenware
PA: Us, Inc.
6890 Distribution Dr
Beltsville MD 20705

(G-1864)
VALENTINE RESEARCH INC
10280 Alliance Rd (45242-4710)
PHONE 513 984-8900
Michael Valentine, *President*
Stephen Scholl, *Vice Pres*
Margaret Valentine, *Vice Pres*
Frank Maher, *Purch Mgr*
EMP: 45
SQ FT: 11,000
SALES (est): 10.8MM **Privately Held**
WEB: www.valentine1.com
SIC: 3812 Radar systems & equipment

(G-1865)
VORTEC AND PAXTON PRODUCTS
10125 Carver Rd (45242-4719)
PHONE 513 891-7474
David Spears, *CEO*
William Ooh, *General Mgr*
Jeem Newland, *Engineer*
Burdick Scott, *Sales Staff*
Steve Prows, *Technology*
EMP: 14
SQ FT: 25,000
SALES (est): 3MM **Privately Held**
WEB: www.paxtonproducts.com
SIC: 3564 Blowers & fans

(G-1866)
VORTEC CORPORATION
Also Called: Vortec-An Illinois TI Works Co
10125 Carver Rd (45242-4798)
PHONE 513 891-7485
Lois Lannigan, *President*
EMP: 22
SALES (est): 3.7MM
SALES (corp-wide): 14.7B **Publicly Held**
WEB: www.itwvortec.com
SIC: 3585 3499 3699 3498 Refrigeration & heating equipment; nozzles, spray: aerosol, paint or insecticide; electrical equipment & supplies; fabricated pipe & fittings; fabricated plate work (boiler shop); auto controls regulating residntl & coml environmt & applncs
PA: Illinois Tool Works Inc.
155 Harlem Ave
Glenview IL 60025
847 724-7500

(G-1867)
WELDPARTS INC
6500 Corporate Dr (45242-2101)
PHONE 513 530-0064
Mikio Kusano, *President*
Emiko Kusano,
▲ **EMP:** 5 **EST:** 2000
SQ FT: 8,000
SALES (est): 2MM **Privately Held**
WEB: www.weldparts.com
SIC: 5084 3548 Welding machinery & equipment; resistance welders, electric

(G-1868)
WESTROCK CP LLC
Also Called: Smurfit-Stone
9960 Alliance Rd (45242-5643)
P.O. Box 42363, Cincinnati (45242-0363)
PHONE 513 745-2400
Pete Widollss, *Branch Mgr*
EMP: 270
SALES (corp-wide): 16.2B **Publicly Held**
WEB: www.sto.com
SIC: 2653 3993 3412 2671 Boxes, corrugated: made from purchased materials; signs & advertising specialties; metal barrels, drums & pails; packaging paper & plastics film, coated & laminated
HQ: Westrock Cp, Llc
1000 Abernathy Rd
Atlanta GA 30328

(G-1869)
WHATIFSPORTSCOM INC
10200 Alliance Rd Ste 301 (45242-4716)
PHONE 513 333-0313
Tarek Kamil, *President*
Ryan Fowler, *Manager*
Scott Eble, *Sr Software Eng*
EMP: 10
SALES (est): 82.8K **Privately Held**
WEB: www.whatifsports.com
SIC: 7372 Home entertainment computer software

(G-1870)
WHITEHOUSE BROS INC
4393 Creek Rd (45241-2923)
PHONE 513 621-2259
Joseph G Vogelsang, *President*
Gary Domsher, *Manager*
▲ **EMP:** 9 **EST:** 1906
SQ FT: 1,200
SALES (est): 1.3MM **Privately Held**
WEB: www.whitehousebrothers.com
SIC: 3911 Jewelry, precious metal

(G-1871)
WINGATE PACKAGING INC (PA)
Also Called: Wingate Packaging South
4347 Indeco Ct (45241-2925)
PHONE 513 745-8600
Robert W Braunschweig, *Ch of Bd*
John S Richardson, *President*
Rob Howe, *Vice Pres*
Lance Layman, *Vice Pres*
Richard Reese, *Plant Mgr*
EMP: 38
SQ FT: 44,000
SALES (est): 14.4MM **Privately Held**
WEB: www.wingateartcraft.com
SIC: 2759 Flexographic printing

(G-1872)
WISE CONSUMER PRODUCTS COMPANY
4729 Cornell Rd (45241-2433)
PHONE 513 484-6530
Willam S Wise, *CEO*
Pamela S Wise, *Vice Pres*
EMP: 2 **EST:** 2001
SALES (est): 1.5MM **Privately Held**
SIC: 2842 Cleaning or polishing preparations

(G-1873)
WITTROCK WDWKG & MFG CO INC
4201 Malsbary Rd (45242-5509)
PHONE 513 891-5800
David Wittrock, *President*
Christopher Wittrock, *Corp Secy*
Joseph Wittrock, *Vice Pres*
▲ **EMP:** 70 **EST:** 1963
SQ FT: 11,000
SALES (est): 14.1MM **Privately Held**
SIC: 2431 Millwork

(G-1874)
WOLF MACHINE COMPANY (PA)
5570 Creek Rd (45242-4004)
PHONE 513 791-5194
Scott E Andre, *President*
Greg Russell, *Vice Pres*
Dave Smith, *Plant Mgr*
EMP: 160
SQ FT: 50,000
SALES (est): 41.3MM **Privately Held**
WEB: www.wolfmachine.com
SIC: 5084 3552 3556 3546 Machine tools & accessories; textile machinery; food products machinery; power-driven handtools

(G-1875)
WOODLAWN RUBBER CO
11268 Williamson Rd (45241-2281)
PHONE 513 489-1718
Kirk Heithaus, *President*
Donald Heithaus, *Treasurer*
Sandy Sampson, *Office Mgr*
EMP: 18
SQ FT: 21,000
SALES (est): 2.2MM **Privately Held**
WEB: www.woodlawnrubber.com
SIC: 3069 3061 Molded rubber products; mechanical rubber goods

(G-1876)
WORNICK COMPANY (DH)
Also Called: Wornick Foods
4700 Creek Rd (45242-2875)
P.O. Box 42634, Cincinnati (45242-0634)
PHONE 800 860-4555
John Kowalchik, *CEO*
Jon P Geisler, *Principal*
Scott Kaylor, *Sr Exec VP*
Jack Fields, *Vice Pres*
Doug Herald, *Vice Pres*
▼ **EMP:** 277
SQ FT: 600,000
SALES (est): 236.1MM
SALES (corp-wide): 473.3MM **Privately Held**
SIC: 2032 Baby foods, including meats: packaged in cans, jars, etc.
HQ: Baxters Food Group Limited
Highfield House
Fochabers IV32
134 382-0393

(G-1877)
WORNICK COMPANY
Also Called: Right Away Division
4700 Creek Rd (45242-2875)
PHONE 513 552-7463
Matt Femia, *Controller*
Gail Wunderlin Beigh, *Marketing Staff*
EMP: 600
SALES (corp-wide): 473.3MM **Privately Held**
SIC: 2032 Canned specialties
HQ: The Wornick Company
4700 Creek Rd
Blue Ash OH 45242
800 860-4555

(G-1878)
WORNICK HOLDING COMPANY INC
4700 Creek Rd (45242-2808)
PHONE 513 794-9800
Jon P Geisler, *President*
Michael Hyche, *Vice Pres*
John Kowalchik, *Vice Pres*
Dustin McDulin, *CFO*
EMP: 1368
SALES (est): 85MM **Privately Held**
SIC: 2032 Canned specialties
PA: Ddj Capital Management, Llc
130 Turner St Ste 600
Waltham MA 02453

(G-1879)
XEROX CORPORATION
10560 Ashview Pl (45242-3735)
PHONE 513 554-3200
Lonnie Stiff, *Plant Mgr*
EMP: 500
SALES (corp-wide): 9.8B **Publicly Held**
WEB: www.xerox.com
SIC: 3861 5044 Photocopy machines; office equipment
PA: Xerox Corporation
201 Merritt 7
Norwalk CT 06851
203 968-3000

(G-1880)
XOMOX CORPORATION
Also Called: Crane Xomox
4477 Malsbary Rd (45242)
PHONE 513 745-6000
William Hayes, *Branch Mgr*
EMP: 6
SALES (corp-wide): 3.3B **Publicly Held**
SIC: 3491 Process control regulator valves
HQ: Xomox Corporation
4526 Res Frest Dr Ste 400
The Woodlands TX 77381
936 271-6500

(G-1881)
ZAROMET INC
10851 Millington Ct (45242-4019)
PHONE 513 891-0773
Tom Mettey, *President*
Anthony Catanzaro, *Vice Pres*
EMP: 4
SQ FT: 5,000
SALES (est): 473.9K **Privately Held**
WEB: www.zaromet.com
SIC: 3599 Machine shop, jobbing & repair

(G-1882)
ZOO PUBLISHING INC
11258 Cornell Park Dr # 608 (45242-1840)
PHONE 513 824-8297
Mark Seremet, *CEO*
David Fremed, *CFO*
▲ **EMP:** 30
SQ FT: 7,700
SALES (est): 2.1MM **Publicly Held**
SIC: 2741 Miscellaneous publishing

PA: Indiepub Entertainment, Inc.
11258 Cornell Park Dr # 608
Blue Ash OH 45242

Bluffton
Allen County

(G-1883)
A TO Z PORTION CTRL MEATS INC
201 N Main St (45817-1283)
PHONE..................................419 358-2926
Lee Ann Kagy, *President*
Leslie Barnes, *Corp Secy*
Sean Kagy, *COO*
Ed Bucher, *Engineer*
EMP: 34 **EST:** 1945
SQ FT: 20,000
SALES (est): 10.2MM **Privately Held**
SIC: 5142 2013 Meat, frozen: packaged; sausages & other prepared meats

(G-1884)
BLUFFTON NEWS PUBG & PRTG CO (PA)
Also Called: Bluffton News, The
101 S Main St (45817-1249)
P.O. Box 105, Leipsic (45856-0105)
PHONE..................................419 358-8010
Thomas M Edwards, *President*
Marilyn Edwards, *Vice Pres*
EMP: 30
SQ FT: 4,500
SALES (est): 2MM **Privately Held**
SIC: 2711 2721 Job printing & newspaper publishing combined; magazines: publishing & printing

(G-1885)
BLUFFTON PRECAST CONCRETE CO
8950 Dixie Hwy (45817-8566)
P.O. Box 161 (45817-0161)
PHONE..................................419 358-6946
David P Akin, *President*
Michael J Akin, *Vice Pres*
James D Akin, *Shareholder*
Carlin Porter, *Admin Sec*
EMP: 15 **EST:** 1963
SQ FT: 3,000
SALES (est): 3.3MM **Privately Held**
SIC: 3272 Septic tanks, concrete

(G-1886)
BLUFFTON STONE CO
310 Quarry Dr (45817)
PHONE..................................419 358-6941
Brent Gerken, *President*
Mike Gerken, *Corp Secy*
EMP: 22 **EST:** 1930
SQ FT: 1,800
SALES (est): 4.2MM **Privately Held**
SIC: 1422 3274 2951 Crushed & broken limestone; lime; asphalt paving mixtures & blocks

(G-1887)
CARPE DIEM INDUSTRIES LLC
Also Called: Diamond Machine and Mfg
505 E Jefferson St (45817-1349)
PHONE..................................419 358-0129
Ryan Smith, *Manager*
EMP: 30
SQ FT: 271,000
SALES (corp-wide): 18.1MM **Privately Held**
WEB: www.colonialsurfacesolutions.com
SIC: 3471 3398 3479 1799 Cleaning & descaling metal products; sand blasting of metal parts; tumbling (cleaning & polishing) of machine parts; metal heat treating; tempering of metal; painting of metal products; coating of metal structures at construction site
PA: Carpe Diem Industries, Llc
4599 Campbell Rd
Columbus Grove OH 45830
419 659-5639

(G-1888)
DIAMOND MFG BLUFFTON LTD
505 E Jefferson St (45817-1349)
P.O. Box 73 (45817-0073)
PHONE..................................419 358-0129
Janice Langhals,
Tom Langhals,
EMP: 95 **EST:** 2010
SQ FT: 120,000
SALES (est): 8.5MM **Privately Held**
SIC: 3441 Fabricated structural metal

(G-1889)
GROB SYSTEMS INC
Also Called: Machine Tool Division
1070 Navajo Dr (45817-9666)
PHONE..................................419 358-9015
Michael Hutecker, *CEO*
Jason Cartright, *President*
Michael Salger, *COO*
David Stephan, *Maint Spvr*
Brian Wolke, *Purch Agent*
◆ **EMP:** 198 **EST:** 1981
SQ FT: 262,000
SALES (est): 137.8MM
SALES (corp-wide): 276.6MM **Privately Held**
WEB: www.grobsystems.com
SIC: 3535 7699 Robotic conveyors; industrial equipment services
PA: Grob-Werke Burkhart Grob E.K.
Industriestr. 4
Mindelheim 87719
826 199-60

(G-1890)
JOHNS BODY SHOP
200 Lake Dr (45817-1383)
PHONE..................................419 358-1200
John Haldman, *Principal*
EMP: 4
SALES (est): 202.5K **Privately Held**
SIC: 7532 3713 3711 Body shop, automotive; truck & bus bodies; automobile bodies, passenger car, not including engine, etc.

(G-1891)
MASTERPIECE SIGNS & GRAPHICS
902 N Main St (45817-9710)
PHONE..................................419 358-0077
Tim Boutwell, *Owner*
EMP: 4
SALES (est): 77.1K **Privately Held**
SIC: 3993 Signs & advertising specialties

(G-1892)
RICHLAND TWP GARAGE
8435 Dixie Hwy (45817-9543)
PHONE..................................419 358-4897
Jim Weaver, *Principal*
EMP: 4
SALES (est): 474.2K **Privately Held**
SIC: 3531 Road construction & maintenance machinery

(G-1893)
SUMIRIKO OHIO INC (HQ)
320 Snider Rd (45817-9573)
PHONE..................................419 358-2121
M Fujiwara, *Ch of Bd*
Akira Kikuta, *President*
Yuichi Ariga, *Treasurer*
▲ **EMP:** 217
SQ FT: 240,000
SALES (est): 162.4MM
SALES (corp-wide): 4.3B **Privately Held**
WEB: www.dtroh.com
SIC: 3052 3069 3829 3714 Automobile hose, rubber; molded rubber products; measuring & controlling devices; motor vehicle parts & accessories
PA: Sumitomo Riko Company Limited
3-1, Higashi
Komaki AIC 485-0
568 772-121

(G-1894)
TIM BOUTWELL
Also Called: Golf Graphics
902 N Main St (45817-9710)
P.O. Box 124 (45817-0124)
PHONE..................................419 358-4653
Tim Boutwell, *Owner*
EMP: 4

SALES (est): 307.4K **Privately Held**
SIC: 5091 3993 Golf equipment; signs & advertising specialties

(G-1895)
TOWER AUTOMOTIVE OPERATIONS I
18717 County Road 15 (45817-9693)
PHONE..................................419 358-8966
Craig Ciola, *Engineer*
Mike Jenkins, *Manager*
EMP: 283 **Publicly Held**
SIC: 3465 Automotive stampings
HQ: Tower Automotive Operations Usa I, Llc
17672 N Laurel Park Dr 400e
Livonia MI 48152

(G-1896)
TRIPLETT BLUFFTON CORPORATION
Also Called: Lfe Instruments
1 Triplett Dr (45817-1055)
P.O. Box 13 (45817-0013)
PHONE..................................419 358-8750
Warren J Hess, *President*
Kyle Apkarian, *CFO*
▲ **EMP:** 9
SQ FT: 150,000
SALES (est): 1MM **Privately Held**
WEB: www.triplett.com
SIC: 3825 3824 Test equipment for electronic & electrical circuits; fluid meters & counting devices

Boardman
Mahoning County

(G-1897)
AGC FLAT GLASS NORTH AMER INC
365 Mcclurg Rd Ste E (44512-6452)
PHONE..................................330 965-1000
Rob Luffman, *Controller*
EMP: 3
SALES (corp-wide): 13.5B **Privately Held**
SIC: 3211 Flat glass
HQ: Agc Flat Glass North America, Inc.
11175 Cicero Dr Ste 400
Alpharetta GA 30022
404 446-4200

(G-1898)
BOARDMAN NEWS
8302 Southern Blvd Ste 2 (44512-3390)
PHONE..................................330 758-6397
Jack Darnell, *Owner*
EMP: 8
SQ FT: 3,500
SALES (est): 250K **Privately Held**
SIC: 2711 Newspapers: publishing only, not printed on site

(G-1899)
GORANT CHOCOLATIER LLC (PA)
Also Called: Gorant's Yum Yum Tree
8301 Market St (44512-6257)
PHONE..................................330 726-8821
Gary Weiss, *President*
Joseph M Miller, *Mng Member*
EMP: 120 **EST:** 1946
SQ FT: 60,000
SALES (est): 63.7MM **Privately Held**
SIC: 5441 5947 5145 3999 Candy; greeting cards; gift shop; candy; candles; chocolate & cocoa products

(G-1900)
PITA WRAP LLC
4721 Market St (44512-1526)
PHONE..................................330 886-8091
Marlene A Bassil, *President*
EMP: 7
SQ FT: 3,700
SALES (est): 175.6K **Privately Held**
SIC: 2099 Food preparations

(G-1901)
POMA GL SPECIALTY WINDOWS INC
365 Mcclurg Rd Ste E (44512-6452)
PHONE..................................330 965-1000
EMP: 7
SALES (corp-wide): 13.5B **Privately Held**
SIC: 3211 Insulating glass, sealed units
HQ: Poma Glass & Specialty Windows Inc.
11175 Cicero Dr Ste 400
Alpharetta GA 30022
404 446-4200

(G-1902)
RL BEST COMPANY
723 Bev Rd (44512-6423)
PHONE..................................330 758-8601
Ted A Best, *President*
Ted Best, *President*
Mark Best, *Vice Pres*
William Kavanaugh, *Vice Pres*
◆ **EMP:** 26
SQ FT: 35,000
SALES (est): 9MM **Privately Held**
WEB: www.rlbest.com
SIC: 3599 7539 Machine shop, jobbing & repair; machine shop, automotive

(G-1903)
STRUGGLE GRIND SUCCESS LLC ✪
6414 Market St (44512-3434)
PHONE..................................330 834-6738
Parris Brown,
EMP: 6 **EST:** 2019
SALES (est): 120.8K **Privately Held**
SIC: 7389 2211 Apparel designers, commercial; apparel & outerwear fabrics, cotton

(G-1904)
TREEMEN INDUSTRIES INC
Also Called: Tii Treemen Industries
691 Mcclurg Rd (44512-6408)
P.O. Box 3777 (44513-3777)
PHONE..................................330 965-3777
George Ogletree, *President*
Violet Ogletree, *Corp Secy*
Daniel Solmen, *Vice Pres*
EMP: 40
SQ FT: 35,900
SALES (est): 11.3MM **Privately Held**
WEB: www.treemen.com
SIC: 3479 3089 3646 3647 Aluminum coating of metal products; injection molding of plastics; commercial indusl & institutional electric lighting fixtures; vehicular lighting equipment

(G-1905)
ZIDIAN MANUFACTURING INC (PA)
Also Called: Summer Garden Food Mfg
500 Mcclurg Rd (44512-6405)
PHONE..................................330 965-8455
Tom Zidian, *CEO*
Michelle Gross, *Corp Secy*
Kenny Sung, *COO*
Aaron Stamp, *CFO*
▲ **EMP:** 7 **EST:** 2000
SALES (est): 13.5MM **Privately Held**
SIC: 2099 Sauces: gravy, dressing & dip mixes

Bolivar
Tuscarawas County

(G-1906)
AMERICAN HIGHWAY PRODUCTS LLC
11723 Strasburg Bolivar (44612-8554)
PHONE..................................330 874-3270
Scott Fier, *President*
Jason E Downing, *General Mgr*
Eric Fier, *Vice Pres*
Eric J Fier, *Vice Pres*
EMP: 10 **EST:** 1978
SQ FT: 10,400
SALES (est): 2.2MM **Privately Held**
WEB: www.ahp1.com
SIC: 3531 Road construction & maintenance machinery

GEOGRAPHIC SECTION

Botkins - Shelby County (G-1934)

(G-1907)
BLUE JAY ENTPS OF TSCRWAS CNTY
9852 Hess Mill Rd Ne (44612-8716)
PHONE...................330 874-2048
Leland Ervin, *President*
Brian Miller, *Vice Pres*
Tonya Ervin Miller, *Treasurer*
Karen Ervin, *Admin Sec*
EMP: 4
SALES (est): 159.1K **Privately Held**
SIC: 1459 Shale (common) quarrying

(G-1908)
CABLE MFG & ASSEMBLY INC (PA)
Also Called: CMA
10896 Industrial Pkwy Nw (44612-8990)
P.O. Box 409 (44612-0409)
PHONE...................330 874-2900
Robert Clegg, *CEO*
Terry Williams, *President*
▲ **EMP:** 200
SQ FT: 61,000
SALES (est): 31.1MM **Privately Held**
WEB: www.cablemfg.com
SIC: 3496 Cable, uninsulated wire: made from purchased wire

(G-1909)
CHEMPURE PRODUCTS CORPORATION
148 Central Ave (44612)
PHONE...................330 874-4300
Samuel J Lloyd, *President*
Robert Lloyd, *Vice Pres*
Karen S Lloyd, *Admin Sec*
EMP: 4
SQ FT: 10,000
SALES (est): 360K **Privately Held**
WEB: www.chempure.com
SIC: 5999 3443 Cleaning equipment & supplies; industrial vessels, tanks & containers

(G-1910)
CUSTOM DISPLAYS LLC
9838 Bimeler St Ne (44612-8805)
PHONE...................330 454-8850
Lee Hartline,
EMP: 4
SALES (est): 190K **Privately Held**
SIC: 2441 Cases, wood

(G-1911)
DAMSEL IN DEFENSE DIVA
11331 Whitetail Run St Nw (44612-9230)
PHONE...................330 874-2068
Christen Marzilli, *Principal*
EMP: 3
SALES (est): 165.9K **Privately Held**
SIC: 3812 Defense systems & equipment

(G-1912)
DIVERSIFIED HONING INC
11064 Industrial Pkwy Nw (44612-8992)
PHONE...................330 874-4663
William Blackwell, *President*
Shawn Blackwell, *Mfg Staff*
Bonnie L Blackwell, *Treasurer*
EMP: 21
SQ FT: 31,000
SALES (est): 300K **Privately Held**
WEB: www.diversifiedhoning.com
SIC: 3541 Honing & lapping machines

(G-1913)
ELEET CRYOGENICS INC (PA)
11132 Industrial Pkwy Nw (44612-8993)
PHONE...................330 874-4009
Garry Sears, *President*
Tenia Sears, *Vice Pres*
▲ **EMP:** 33
SQ FT: 47,000
SALES (est): 10.1MM **Privately Held**
WEB: www.eleetcryogenics.com
SIC: 3443 7353 2761 5088 Cryogenic tanks, for liquids & gases; oil field equipment, rental or leasing; manifold business forms; tanks & tank components; trailer rental; management services

(G-1914)
FSRC TANKS INC
11029 Industrial Pkwy Nw (44612-8992)
PHONE...................234 221-2015
Andrew Feucht, *President*
EMP: 35
SALES (est): 1.5MM **Privately Held**
SIC: 1791 3443 Storage tanks, metal: erection; reactor containment vessels, metal plate

(G-1915)
GEMINI FIBER CORPORATION
11145 Industrial Pkwy Nw (44612-8993)
P.O. Box 487 (44612-0487)
PHONE...................330 874-4131
Stanley F Lakota, *President*
▲ **EMP:** 12
SQ FT: 15,000
SALES (est): 2.9MM **Privately Held**
WEB: www.geminifiber.com
SIC: 2679 Paper products, converted

(G-1916)
HOLDSWORTH INDUSTRIAL FABG
10407 Welton Rd Ne (44612-8833)
P.O. Box 643, Zoar (44697-0643)
PHONE...................330 874-3945
Randy Holdsworth, *Owner*
EMP: 6
SQ FT: 5,000
SALES (est): 507.9K **Privately Held**
SIC: 1799 7692 Welding on site; welding repair

(G-1917)
INVENTIVE EXTRUSIONS CORP
Also Called: I E C
10882 Fort Laurens Rd Nw (44612-8942)
PHONE...................330 874-3000
Steven Martin, *President*
Stephen Martin, *Data Proc Dir*
EMP: 20
SQ FT: 12,000
SALES (est): 1.8MM **Privately Held**
SIC: 3089 3082 Extruded finished plastic products; unsupported plastics profile shapes

(G-1918)
MYERS MACHINING INC
11789 Strasburg Bolivar (44612-8555)
PHONE...................330 874-3005
David Myers, *President*
Brenda Myers, *Treasurer*
EMP: 15
SQ FT: 16,000
SALES (est): 2.4MM **Privately Held**
WEB: www.myersmachining.com
SIC: 3599 Machine shop, jobbing & repair

(G-1919)
NILODOR INC
10966 Industrial Pkwy Nw (44612-8991)
P.O. Box 660 (44612-0660)
PHONE...................800 443-4321
Les W Mitson, *President*
Jeff Wilkof, *Corp Secy*
Kurt Peterson, *Vice Pres*
◆ **EMP:** 43
SQ FT: 43,000
SALES (est): 12.2MM **Privately Held**
WEB: www.nilodor.com
SIC: 2842 Deodorants, nonpersonal

(G-1920)
OSTER SAND AND GRAVEL INC
3467 Dover Zoar Rd Ne (44612-8922)
PHONE...................330 874-3322
Dan Morrisset, *Manager*
EMP: 6
SALES (corp-wide): 4.1MM **Privately Held**
SIC: 1442 Construction sand & gravel
PA: Oster Sand And Gravel, Inc.
5947 Whipple Ave Nw
Canton OH 44720
330 494-5472

(G-1921)
PAC DRILLING O & G LLC
1037 Lawnridge St Ne (44612-8873)
PHONE...................330 874-3781
Justin L Caldwell, *Mng Member*
Jason Caldwell, *Supervisor*
EMP: 4
SALES (est): 380K **Privately Held**
SIC: 1381 Drilling oil & gas wells

(G-1922)
PREMERE ENTERPRISES INC
10882 Fort Laurens Rd Nw (44612-8942)
PHONE...................330 874-3000
Garry D Martin, *President*
Richard D Dodez, *Principal*
EMP: 6
SALES (est): 799.9K **Privately Held**
SIC: 3544 Special dies, tools, jigs & fixtures

(G-1923)
PREMIERE MOLD AND MACHINE CO
10882 Fort Laurens Rd Nw (44612-8942)
PHONE...................330 874-3000
Robert L Martin, *Ch of Bd*
Garry Martin, *President*
Richard Dodez, *Admin Sec*
EMP: 6
SALES (est): 656.6K **Privately Held**
SIC: 3544 Forms (molds), for foundry & plastics working machinery

(G-1924)
PRIMARY PACKAGING INCORPORATED
10810 Industrial Pkwy Nw (44612-8990)
PHONE...................330 874-3131
Joseph Kaplan, *CEO*
Jeffrey Thrams, *President*
Jim O'Brien, *Treasurer*
John Hiltner, *VP Finance*
EMP: 85
SQ FT: 50,000
SALES (est): 24.1MM **Privately Held**
WEB: www.primarypackaging.com
SIC: 2673 Plastic bags: made from purchased materials

(G-1925)
PROGRSSIVE MOLDING BOLIVAR INC
10882 Fort Laurens Rd Nw (44612-8942)
PHONE...................330 874-3000
Robert L Martin, *Ch of Bd*
Garry Martin, *President*
James C Dukat, *Principal*
Richard D Dodez, *Principal*
Sandra K Scott, *Principal*
EMP: 110 **EST:** 1976
SQ FT: 33,000
SALES (est): 17.1MM **Privately Held**
SIC: 3544 3089 Dies, plastics forming; thermoformed finished plastic products

(G-1926)
QUILTING CREATIONS INTL
8778 Towpath Rd Ne (44612-8556)
P.O. Box 512, Zoar (44697-0512)
PHONE...................330 874-4741
Aaron Bell, *President*
Amy Gibbons, *Assistant*
EMP: 20
SALES (est): 3.9MM **Privately Held**
WEB: www.quiltingcreations.com
SIC: 2631 5949 Stencil board; quilting materials & supplies

(G-1927)
RHC INC
Also Called: Ragon House Collection
10841 Fisher Rd Nw (44612-8487)
PHONE...................330 874-3750
Mary Ragon, *President*
Joshua Ragon, *Vice Pres*
Kerrie Thomas, *Admin Sec*
▲ **EMP:** 4
SALES (est): 284.3K **Privately Held**
SIC: 3999 5023 5999 Christmas tree ornaments, except electrical & glass; decorating supplies; Christmas lights & decorations

(G-1928)
SPEEDWAY LLC
Also Called: Speedway Superamerica 6241
11099 State Route 212 Ne (44612-8745)
PHONE...................330 874-4616
Paul Duerig, *President*
EMP: 11 **Publicly Held**
WEB: www.speedwaynet.com
SIC: 1311 Crude petroleum production
HQ: Speedway Llc
500 Speedway Dr
Enon OH 45323
937 864-3000

(G-1929)
US TECHNOLOGY MEDIA INC
509 Water St Sw (44612-8986)
PHONE...................330 874-3094
EMP: 10
SALES (est): 729.3K **Privately Held**
SIC: 3291 Abrasive products

(G-1930)
USA LABEL EXPRESS INC
11206 Industrial Pkwy Nw (44612-8994)
P.O. Box 518 (44612-0518)
PHONE...................330 874-1001
Chris Helwig, *President*
Buster Longo, *General Mgr*
Mary Seldenright, *Vice Pres*
EMP: 25
SQ FT: 25,000
SALES (est): 5.2MM **Privately Held**
SIC: 2672 Labels (unprinted), gummed: made from purchased materials

Botkins
Shelby County

(G-1931)
A METALCRAFT ASSOCIATES INC
18965 State Route 219 (45306-9582)
PHONE...................937 693-4008
Maurice Delap, *President*
EMP: 7
SALES: 300K **Privately Held**
WEB: www.metalcraftinc.net
SIC: 1542 5031 7692 7699 Nonresidential construction; lumber, plywood & millwork; welding repair; metal reshaping & replating services; fabricated plate work (boiler shop)

(G-1932)
AGRANA FRUIT US INC
16197 County Road 25a (45306-9646)
PHONE...................937 693-3821
Sean Augustus, *Opers Mgr*
Jeff Elliott, *Opers Mgr*
Salvador Vazquez, *Opers Mgr*
Salvador Alvarez, *Engineer*
Tony Kerns, *Engineer*
EMP: 150
SALES (corp-wide): 51.7MM **Privately Held**
SIC: 8734 2099 2087 Food testing service; food preparations; flavoring extracts & syrups
HQ: Agrana Fruit Us, Inc.
6850 Southpointe Pkwy
Brecksville OH 44141
440 546-1199

(G-1933)
BOOMERANG RUBBER INC
105 Dinsmore St (45306-9632)
P.O. Box 538 (45306-0538)
PHONE...................937 693-4611
Mark Sultman, *President*
Bobby Brush, *General Mgr*
Sandy Higginbotham, *Manager*
EMP: 22
SALES (est): 7.8MM **Privately Held**
SIC: 3069 Reclaimed rubber & specialty rubber compounds

(G-1934)
BROWN INDUSTRIAL INC
311 W South St (45306-8019)
P.O. Box 74 (45306-0074)
PHONE...................937 693-3838
Christopher D Brown, *President*
Ruth C Brown, *Corp Secy*
Craig D Brown, *Vice Pres*
Boyce Branscrum, *Manager*
EMP: 45
SQ FT: 32,000

Botkins - Shelby County (G-1935)

SALES (est): 12.5MM **Privately Held**
WEB: www.brownindustrial.com
SIC: **3713** 5012 5084 7692 Truck bodies (motor vehicles); truck bodies; industrial machinery & equipment; packaging machinery & equipment; automotive welding

(G-1935)
BUCKEYE ELECTRICAL PRODUCTS
100 Commerce Dr (45306-1100)
P.O. Box 124 (45306-0124)
PHONE..................................937 693-7519
Dick Platfoot, *President*
Kevin Platfoot, *Officer*
EMP: 20
SALES (est): 3.9MM **Privately Held**
SIC: **3699** Electrical equipment & supplies

(G-1936)
RIDLEY USA INC
Also Called: Hubbard Feeds
104 Oak St (45306-8031)
P.O. Box 1105, Hopkinsville KY (42241-1105)
PHONE..................................800 837-8222
Roger Allen, *Manager*
EMP: 10
SALES (corp-wide): 1.7B **Privately Held**
WEB: www.hubbardfeeds.net
SIC: **2048** 5191 Livestock feeds; animal feeds
HQ: Ridley Usa Inc.
    111 W Cherry St Ste 500
    Mankato MN 56001
    507 388-9400

(G-1937)
RIDLEY USA INC
Also Called: Hubbard Feeds
104 Oak St (45306-8031)
P.O. Box 460 (45306-0460)
PHONE..................................937 693-6393
Rick Duncan, *Manager*
EMP: 45
SALES (corp-wide): 1.7B **Privately Held**
WEB: www.hubbardfeeds.net
SIC: **2048** Livestock feeds
HQ: Ridley Usa Inc.
    111 W Cherry St Ste 500
    Mankato MN 56001
    507 388-9400

(G-1938)
T&K LASER WORKS INC
401 N Main St (45306-9547)
PHONE..................................937 693-3783
Ernest Vehorn, *Principal*
EMP: 4
SALES (est): 310.6K **Privately Held**
SIC: **3479** Etching & engraving

Bowerston
Harrison County

(G-1939)
BOWERSTON SHALE COMPANY (PA)
515 Main St (44695-9512)
PHONE..................................740 269-2921
Mark Willard, *President*
Beth Hillyer, *Vice Pres*
Edward C Milliken, *Vice Pres*
Stephanie Price, *Accounting Mgr*
EMP: 30 EST: 1929
SQ FT: 100,000
SALES (est): 36.8MM **Privately Held**
SIC: **3255** 3251 2951 Clay refractories; brick clay: common face, glazed, vitrified or hollow; asphalt paving mixtures & blocks

(G-1940)
L J SMITH INC (DH)
Also Called: Woodsmiths Design & Mfg
35280 Scio Bowerston Rd (44695-9731)
PHONE..................................740 269-2221
Craig Kurtz, *President*
Giovanni Savastano, *Foreman/Supr*
Dave Polce, *Purchasing*
Dan Tope, *Purchasing*
Sheri Pongrat, *Controller*
▲ EMP: 238

SQ FT: 180,000
SALES (est): 61.8MM
SALES (corp-wide): 300.2MM **Privately Held**
WEB: www.ljsmith.com
SIC: **2431** Staircases & stairs, wood; staircases, stairs & railings

(G-1941)
MINOVA USA INC
600 Boyce Dr (44695-9801)
PHONE..................................740 269-8100
Larry Jordan, *President*
EMP: 431 **Privately Held**
SIC: **3441** Building components, structural steel
HQ: Minova Usa Inc.
    150 Summer Ct
    Georgetown KY 40324
    502 863-6800

(G-1942)
NOLAN COMPANY
300 Boyce Dr (44695-9760)
PHONE..................................740 269-1512
Dan Chew, *Manager*
EMP: 7
SALES (corp-wide): 4MM **Privately Held**
SIC: **3743** 3532 Railroad equipment; mining machinery
PA: The Nolan Company
    1016 9th St Sw
    Canton OH 44707
    330 453-7922

Bowling Green
Wood County

(G-1943)
A SCREEN PRINTED PRODUCTS
17715 N Dixie Hwy (43402-9257)
PHONE..................................419 352-1535
David L Schumacher, *Owner*
Robb First, *Data Proc Dir*
Tricia Jackson, *Art Dir*
EMP: 5
SALES (est): 442.6K **Privately Held**
SIC: **2759** Screen printing

(G-1944)
A W S INCORPORATED
520 Hankey Ave (43402-7801)
P.O. Box 472 (43402-0472)
PHONE..................................419 352-5397
Arlyn Snyder, *President*
Judith Ann Snyder, *Corp Secy*
EMP: 2
SQ FT: 5,000
SALES: 2MM **Privately Held**
SIC: **1542** 1521 2431 General Contractor Commercial Buildings & Residential Concerns

(G-1945)
A-GAS US HOLDINGS INC (DH)
Also Called: A-Gas Americas
1100 Haskins Rd (43402-9363)
PHONE..................................419 867-8990
Monte Roach, *President*
Patricia Burns, *Vice Pres*
Jason Zilles, *CFO*
EMP: 14 EST: 2012
SALES (est): 59.6MM
SALES (corp-wide): 306.9K **Privately Held**
SIC: **5099** 2869 4953 3399 Fire extinguishers; freon; chemical detoxification; reclaiming ferrous metals from clay
HQ: A-Gas International Limited
    Banyard Road
    Bristol BS20
    127 537-6600

(G-1946)
A-GAS US INC (DH)
1100 Haskins Rd (43402-9363)
PHONE..................................800 372-1301
J Monte Roach, *CEO*
Mike Armstrong, *COO*
Michael Fox, *CFO*
Robert Hennessy, *Ch Credit Ofcr*
EMP: 4

SALES (est): 11.4MM
SALES (corp-wide): 306.9K **Privately Held**
SIC: **2869** Freon
HQ: A-Gas Us Holdings Inc.
    1100 Haskins Rd
    Bowling Green OH 43402
    419 867-8990

(G-1947)
AARDVARK GRAPHIC ENTERPRISES L
123 S Main St (43402-2910)
PHONE..................................419 352-3197
Gary Bell, *Owner*
EMP: 12
SALES (est): 887.2K **Privately Held**
SIC: **2396** Screen printing on fabric articles

(G-1948)
AARDVARK SCREEN PRTG & EMB LLC
123 S Main St (43402-2910)
P.O. Box 128 (43402-0128)
PHONE..................................419 354-6686
Toll Free:..................................888 -
Gary A Bell,
EMP: 10
SQ FT: 3,000
SALES: 400K **Privately Held**
SIC: **2759** 7311 Screen printing; advertising agencies

(G-1949)
ABSORBENT PRODUCTS COMPANY INC
2121 S Woodland Cir (43402-8832)
PHONE..................................419 352-5353
Paul Rankin, *President*
◆ EMP: 35
SQ FT: 54,000
SALES (est): 11.3MM
SALES (corp-wide): 112.5MM **Privately Held**
WEB: www.absorbent-products-company.com
SIC: **2676** Diapers, paper (disposable): made from purchased paper
PA: Principle Business Enterprises, Inc.
    20189 Pine Lake Rd
    Bowling Green OH 43402
    419 352-1551

(G-1950)
ADVANCED SPECIALTY PRODUCTS
428 Clough St (43402-2914)
P.O. Box 210 (43402-0210)
PHONE..................................419 882-6528
Kenneth T Kujawa, *President*
Eugene Kujawa, *Vice Pres*
▼ EMP: 60
SQ FT: 24,000
SALES (est): 7.8MM **Privately Held**
SIC: **5082** 7389 2759 Construction & mining machinery; packaging & labeling services; commercial printing

(G-1951)
ANGEL GLASS LOST
122 Meeker St (43402-2215)
PHONE..................................419 353-2831
Joel Odorisio, *President*
EMP: 4
SALES: 310K **Privately Held**
SIC: **3229** Glass furnishings & accessories

(G-1952)
B G NEWS
Also Called: Bg News
214 W Hall Bgsu (43403-0001)
PHONE..................................419 372-2601
Fax: 419 372-6967
EMP: 50
SALES (est): 2MM **Privately Held**
SIC: **2711** 7313 2741 Newspapers-Publishing/Printing Advertising Representative Misc Publishing

(G-1953)
BARNES INTERNATIONAL INC
Henry Filters
555 Van Camp Rd (43402)
PHONE..................................419 352-7501
Steve Volmer, *Branch Mgr*

EMP: 60
SALES (est): 11.7MM
SALES (corp-wide): 35MM **Privately Held**
WEB: www.durrautomation.com
SIC: **3677** Electronic coils, transformers & other inductors
PA: Barnes International, Inc.
    814 Chestnut St
    Rockford IL 61102
    815 964-8661

(G-1954)
BASIC COATINGS LLC
400 Van Camp Rd (43402-9062)
PHONE..................................419 241-2156
Paul C Betz,
EMP: 36
SALES (est): 333.3K
SALES (corp-wide): 138.8MM **Privately Held**
WEB: www.betco.com
SIC: **2851** Paints & allied products
PA: Betco Corporation
    400 Van Camp Rd
    Bowling Green OH 43402
    419 241-2156

(G-1955)
BETCO CORPORATION LTD (HQ)
400 Van Camp Rd (43402-9062)
PHONE..................................419 241-2156
Paul C Betz, *CEO*
Tony Lyons, *CFO*
James Betz, *Admin Sec*
◆ EMP: 250
SALES (est): 21.2MM
SALES (corp-wide): 138.8MM **Privately Held**
SIC: **2842** Specialty cleaning, polishes & sanitation goods
PA: Betco Corporation
    400 Van Camp Rd
    Bowling Green OH 43402
    419 241-2156

(G-1956)
BIO-SYSTEMS CORPORATION
Also Called: BSC Environmental
400 Van Camp Rd (43402-9062)
PHONE..................................608 365-9550
Malcolm Peacock, *President*
Marilyn Peacock, *Corp Secy*
Lisa Peacock, *Vice Pres*
EMP: 65
SALES (est): 12.1MM **Privately Held**
WEB: www.biobugs.com
SIC: **2819** Industrial inorganic chemicals

(G-1957)
BRUFIST LLC
122 1/2 S Maple St (43402-2823)
PHONE..................................330 221-4472
Martin Yungmann, *CEO*
Daniel Nawrocki,
Jeremy Rober,
EMP: 3
SALES (est): 91.3K **Privately Held**
SIC: **2082** Beer (alcoholic beverage); ale (alcoholic beverage); porter (alcoholic beverage); stout (alcoholic beverage)

(G-1958)
C & C FABRICATION INC
18237 N Dixie Hwy (43402-9322)
PHONE..................................419 354-3535
Charles H Wolford, *President*
Claudell Wolford, *Vice Pres*
EMP: 5 EST: 1969
SQ FT: 13,800
SALES: 750K **Privately Held**
SIC: **3443** 3469 Fabricated plate work (boiler shop); metal stampings

(G-1959)
CENTAUR TOOL & DIE INC
2019 Wood Bridge Blvd (43402-8913)
PHONE..................................419 352-7704
Paul E Faykosh, *President*
Jack Faykosh, *Vice Pres*
Jeff Faykosh, *Vice Pres*
EMP: 18
SQ FT: 16,400

GEOGRAPHIC SECTION
Bowling Green - Wood County (G-1983)

SALES (est): 1.6MM **Privately Held**
WEB: www.centaurtool.com
SIC: 3544 Die sets for metal stamping (presses)

(G-1960)
CENTURY MARKETING CORPORATION
1145 Fairview Ave (43402-1204)
PHONE.....................419 354-2591
EMP: 3
SALES (corp-wide): 41.9MM **Privately Held**
SIC: 2759 Labels & seals: printing
HQ: Century Marketing Corporation
12836 S Dixie Hwy
Bowling Green OH 43402
419 354-2591

(G-1961)
CENTURY MARKETING CORPORATION (HQ)
Also Called: Centurylabel
12836 S Dixie Hwy (43402-9230)
PHONE.....................419 354-2591
Albert J Caperna, *President*
Craig E Dixon, *President*
William Horner, *Corp Secy*
▼ **EMP:** 150
SQ FT: 58,000
SALES (est): 21.2MM
SALES (corp-wide): 41.9MM **Privately Held**
WEB: www.centurylabel.com
SIC: 2759 2679 5046 5199 Labels & seals: printing; flexographic printing; tags & labels, paper; price marking equipment & supplies; packaging materials; commercial printing, lithographic
PA: Cmc Group, Inc.
12836 S Dixie Hwy
Bowling Green OH 43402
419 354-2591

(G-1962)
CENTURY SIGNS
Also Called: Mason's Century Signs
169 S Main St (43402-2910)
PHONE.....................419 352-2666
Mason Brown, *Owner*
EMP: 5
SQ FT: 1,470
SALES: 260K **Privately Held**
SIC: 3993 Signs & advertising specialties

(G-1963)
CMC DAYMARK CORPORATION
Also Called: Daymark Security Systems
12830 S Dixie Hwy (43402-9697)
PHONE.....................419 354-2591
Jeffery Palmer, *General Mgr*
▲ **EMP:** 140
SALES (est): 24.9MM
SALES (corp-wide): 41.9MM **Privately Held**
WEB: www.centurylabel.com
SIC: 2679 5046 Labels, paper: made from purchased material; commercial equipment
PA: Cmc Group, Inc.
12836 S Dixie Hwy
Bowling Green OH 43402
419 354-2591

(G-1964)
CMC GROUP INC (PA)
12836 S Dixie Hwy (43402-9697)
PHONE.....................419 354-2591
Craig Dixon, *CEO*
Jeff Palmer, *President*
Albert J Caperna, *Chairman*
Tammy Corral, *Vice Pres*
Bob Copple, *CFO*
▲ **EMP:** 250 **EST:** 1999
SQ FT: 2,268
SALES (est): 41.9MM **Privately Held**
WEB: www.centurylabel.com
SIC: 2759 Labels & seals: printing

(G-1965)
COOPER-STANDARD AUTOMOTIVE INC
1175 N Main St (43402-1310)
PHONE.....................419 352-3533
Steven Ingraham, *Engineer*
Dan Stalter, *Engineer*
Pamela Russell, *Controller*
Pat Scholl, *Human Res Dir*
Holli Roller, *Human Resources*
EMP: 350
SALES (corp-wide): 3.6B **Publicly Held**
WEB: www.cooperstandard.com
SIC: 3052 Automobile hose, rubber
HQ: Cooper-Standard Automotive Inc.
207 S West St
Auburn IN 46706
248 596-5900

(G-1966)
COSMA INTERNATIONAL AMER INC
2125 Wood Bridge Blvd (43402-9164)
PHONE.....................419 409-7350
Reiko Hall, *Sales Staff*
Struart Benford, *Maintence Staff*
EMP: 4
SALES (corp-wide): 38.9B **Privately Held**
SIC: 3714 Motor vehicle parts & accessories
HQ: Cosma International Of America, Inc.
750 Tower Dr
Troy MI 48098
248 631-1100

(G-1967)
CURATION FOODS INC
12700 S Dixie Hwy (43402-9697)
PHONE.....................419 931-1029
Bill Richardville, *Vice Pres*
EMP: 6
SALES (corp-wide): 524.2MM **Publicly Held**
SIC: 2099 0723 Food preparations; vegetable packing services
HQ: Curation Foods, Inc.
4575 W Main St
Guadalupe CA 93434
800 454-1355

(G-1968)
DIAMONDBACK FILTERS
Also Called: Rinz-N-Reuz
11602 Sugar Ridge Rd (43402-9285)
PHONE.....................419 494-1156
Robert Fox, *Owner*
EMP: 3
SALES: 200K **Privately Held**
SIC: 3569 Filters

(G-1969)
DIGITAL AUTOMATION ASSOCIATES
310 W Gypsy Lane Rd (43402-4596)
P.O. Box 131 (43402-0131)
PHONE.....................419 352-6977
Gary C Border, *President*
Erica Border, *Corp Secy*
EMP: 3
SQ FT: 6,000
SALES (est): 281.7K **Privately Held**
WEB: www.digauto.com
SIC: 8711 3491 8748 Electrical or electronic engineering; process control regulator valves; telecommunications consultant

(G-1970)
DOW JONES & COMPANY INC
1201 Brim Rd (43402-9352)
PHONE.....................419 352-4696
Fred Vandermeulen, *Plant Mgr*
Nick Barbosa, *Opers-Prdtn-Mfg*
Abel Posada, *Cust Svc Dir*
Fred Van Der Meulen, *Manager*
EMP: 25
SALES (corp-wide): 9B **Publicly Held**
SIC: 2711 Newspapers, publishing & printing
HQ: Dow Jones & Company, Inc.
1211 Avenue Of The Americ
New York NY 10036
609 627-2999

(G-1971)
DOWA THT AMERICA INC
2130 S Woodland Cir (43402-8832)
PHONE.....................419 354-4144
Masanari Konomi, *President*
▲ **EMP:** 35
SALES (est): 9.6MM
SALES (corp-wide): 4.2B **Privately Held**
WEB: www.dowa-tht.com
SIC: 3398 Metal heat treating
HQ: Dowa Thermotech Co., Ltd.
19-1, Ukishimacho, Mizuho-Ku
Nagoya AIC 467-0

(G-1972)
ENVIROZYME LLC
400 Van Camp Rd (43402-9062)
PHONE.....................800 232-2847
Daniel J Lavalley,
EMP: 5
SALES (est): 592.9K **Privately Held**
SIC: 2836 Bacteriological media

(G-1973)
GKN DRIVELINE BOWL GREEN INC (DH)
2223 Wood Bridge Blvd (43402-8873)
PHONE.....................419 373-7700
Kevin Cumming, *CEO*
▲ **EMP:** 31 **EST:** 1998
SALES (est): 5.9MM
SALES (corp-wide): 2.7B **Privately Held**
SIC: 3999 Barber & beauty shop equipment
HQ: Gkn Limited
Po Box 55
Redditch WORCS B98 0
152 751-7715

(G-1974)
GKN DRIVELINE NORTH AMER INC
Also Called: GKN Driveline Bowling Green
2223 Wood Bridge Blvd (43402-8873)
PHONE.....................419 354-3955
Hideo Miyagi, *Branch Mgr*
EMP: 65
SALES (corp-wide): 2.7B **Privately Held**
WEB: www.gknai.com
SIC: 3714 Motor vehicle parts & accessories
HQ: Gkn Driveline North America, Inc.
2200 N Opdyke Rd
Auburn Hills MI 48326
248 296-7000

(G-1975)
ISHIKAWA GASKET AMERICA INC (HQ)
828 Van Camp Rd (43402-9379)
PHONE.....................419 353-7300
Toshio Matsuzaki, *President*
▲ **EMP:** 10
SQ FT: 3,000
SALES (est): 1.4MM
SALES (corp-wide): 63.5MM **Privately Held**
WEB: www.ishikawaamerica.com
SIC: 3053 Gaskets, all materials
PA: Ishikawa Gasket Co., Ltd.
2-5-5, Toranomon
Minato-Ku TKY 105-0
335 010-371

(G-1976)
ISHIKAWA GASKET AMERICA INC
828 Van Camp Rd (43402-9379)
PHONE.....................419 353-7300
Gary Stasiak, *Manager*
EMP: 190
SALES (corp-wide): 54MM **Privately Held**
WEB: www.ishikawaamerica.com
SIC: 3053 5085 3714 Gaskets & sealing devices; gaskets; motor vehicle parts & accessories
HQ: Ishikawa Gasket America, Inc.
828 Van Camp Rd
Bowling Green OH 43402

(G-1977)
J & K WADE LTD
Also Called: Environmental Water Engrg
143 E Wooster St Ste B (43402-2959)
P.O. Box 611 (43402-0611)
PHONE.....................419 352-6163
Michael McIntosh, *President*
EMP: 4
SQ FT: 4,000
SALES (est): 732K **Privately Held**
WEB: www.ewero.com
SIC: 5169 3589 Chemicals, industrial & heavy; water treatment equipment, industrial

(G-1978)
J P TOOL INC
2019 Wood Bridge Blvd (43402-8913)
PHONE.....................419 354-8696
Jack Faykosh, *President*
Paul Faykosh, *Corp Secy*
Jeff Faykosh, *Vice Pres*
EMP: 3
SQ FT: 3,200
SALES (est): 200K **Privately Held**
SIC: 3544 Special dies & tools

(G-1979)
KEL-MAR INC
436 N Enterprise St (43402-2001)
P.O. Box 424 (43402-0424)
PHONE.....................419 806-4600
Burr Sterling, *President*
EMP: 25
SALES (est): 2.4MM **Privately Held**
WEB: www.kel-mar.com
SIC: 3471 Finishing, metals or formed products

(G-1980)
LANDEC CORPORATION
12700 S Dixie Hwy (43402-9697)
PHONE.....................419 931-1095
EMP: 179
SALES (corp-wide): 524.2MM **Publicly Held**
SIC: 2033 Fruits: packaged in cans, jars, etc.
PA: Landec Corporation
5201 Great America Pkwy # 232
Santa Clara CA 95054
650 306-1650

(G-1981)
LIFEFORMATIONS INC
2029 Wood Bridge Blvd (43402-8913)
PHONE.....................419 352-2101
Rodney Hailigmann, *President*
Will Brady, *Production*
EMP: 50
SQ FT: 8,000
SALES (est): 8.8MM **Privately Held**
WEB: www.lifeformations.com
SIC: 3559 Robots, molding & forming plastics

(G-1982)
LUBRIZOL ADVANCED MTLS INC
Also Called: LUBRIZOL ADVANCED MATERIALS, INC.
1142 N Main St (43402-1309)
PHONE.....................419 352-5565
Dennis Callan, *Principal*
Scott Wagemaker, *Plant Mgr*
Dave Carter, *QC Dir*
Joe Lovell, *QC Mgr*
Clayton Salsbury, *Engineer*
EMP: 22
SALES (corp-wide): 225.3B **Publicly Held**
SIC: 2899 Chemical preparations
HQ: Lubrizol Global Management, Inc
9911 Brecksville Rd
Brecksville OH 44141
216 447-5000

(G-1983)
MACK INDUSTRIES
507 Derby Ave (43402-3973)
PHONE.....................419 353-7081
Betsie Mack, *President*
EMP: 173
SALES (est): 19.3MM
SALES (corp-wide): 170.9MM **Privately Held**
WEB: www.mackconcrete.com
SIC: 3272 5211 1711 Burial vaults, concrete or precast terrazzo; masonry materials & supplies; septic system construction
PA: Mack Industries, Inc.
1321 Industrial Pkwy N # 500
Brunswick OH 44212
330 460-7005

Bowling Green - Wood County

(G-1984)
MARTIN MACHINE & TOOL INC
435 W Woodland Cir (43402-8834)
PHONE.................................419 373-1711
Allen L Ahrens, *President*
Robb C Coffman, *Vice Pres*
Fred A Curtis, *Vice Pres*
W John Schobinger, *Vice Pres*
Robb Coffman, *VP Sls/Mktg*
EMP: 10
SQ FT: 12,000
SALES (est): 1.4MM **Privately Held**
SIC: 3599 3544 Machine shop, jobbing & repair; special dies & tools

(G-1985)
MCCORD PRODUCTS INC
Also Called: McCord Monuments
1135 N Main St (43402-1310)
P.O. Box 646 (43402-0646)
PHONE.................................419 352-3691
Kraig Hanneman, *President*
Mercene Hanneman, *Corp Secy*
Kris Hanneman, *Vice Pres*
EMP: 12 **EST:** 1941
SQ FT: 8,200
SALES (est): 1.6MM **Privately Held**
WEB: www.mccordproducts.com
SIC: 3995 Burial vaults, fiberglass

(G-1986)
NOVAVISION INC (PA)
524 E Woodland Cir (43402-8966)
PHONE.................................419 354-1427
Albert Caperna, *President*
Craig Dixon, *Vice Pres*
Mike Messmer, *Vice Pres*
Brian Cramer, *Sales Staff*
Jeff Gerwin, *Sales Staff*
▲ **EMP:** 58
SQ FT: 39,000
SALES (est): 12.6MM **Privately Held**
WEB: www.novavisioninc.com
SIC: 2759 3471 Flexographic printing; electroplating of metals or formed products

(G-1987)
ONE LIBERTY STREET
813 Hamilton Ct (43402-1206)
PHONE.................................419 352-6298
Jim Litwin, *President*
EMP: 3
SALES (est): 80K **Privately Held**
SIC: 2731 Book publishing

(G-1988)
ORTHO PROSTHETIC CENTER
1224 W Wooster St (43402-2632)
PHONE.................................419 352-8161
Roberto Vives, *Principal*
EMP: 3
SALES (est): 254.2K **Privately Held**
SIC: 3842 Prosthetic appliances

(G-1989)
PALMER BROS TRANSIT MIX CON (PA)
Also Called: Fostoria Concrete
12205 E Gypsy Lane Rd (43402-9516)
PHONE.................................419 352-4681
Randolph G Schmeltz, *President*
Jesse Schmeltz, *Vice Pres*
EMP: 15
SQ FT: 2,000
SALES (est): 7MM **Privately Held**
SIC: 3273 Ready-mixed concrete

(G-1990)
PHOENIX TECHNOLOGIES INTL LLC (PA)
Also Called: Pti
1098 Fairview Ave (43402-1233)
PHONE.................................419 353-7738
Shari McCague, *Finance*
Adam Bechstein, *Sales Staff*
Lori Carson, *Sales Staff*
Thomas E Brady, *Mng Member*
Henrey Schworm, *Maintence Staff*
▲ **EMP:** 50
SQ FT: 100,000
SALES (est): 12.3MM **Privately Held**
WEB: www.phoenixtechnologies.net
SIC: 3085 5169 Plastics bottles; synthetic resins, rubber & plastic materials

(G-1991)
PINNACLE INDUSTRIAL ENTPS INC
Also Called: Pinnacle Plastic Products
513 Napoleon Rd (43402-4822)
P.O. Box 286 (43402-0286)
PHONE.................................419 352-8688
Kevin J Tearney, *President*
Mike Hagen, *Vice Pres*
Rodney Kirkpatrick, *Purch Mgr*
John Puffenberger, *Purch Mgr*
Paul Chovanec, *Engineer*
▲ **EMP:** 125
SQ FT: 90,000
SALES (est): 24.7MM **Privately Held**
WEB: www.pinnacleplasticproducts.com
SIC: 3089 Blow molded finished plastic products; injection molding of plastics

(G-1992)
PRINCIPLE BUSINESS ENTPS INC (PA)
Also Called: Tranquility
20189 Pine Lake Rd (43402-4091)
P.O. Box 129, Dunbridge (43414-0129)
PHONE.................................419 352-1551
Carol Stocking, *CEO*
Andrew Stocking, *President*
Charles A Stocking, *President*
Luis Fuentes, *Vice Pres*
Michael Kirby, *CFO*
▲ **EMP:** 235
SQ FT: 105,000
SALES (est): 112.5MM **Privately Held**
WEB: www.pberopelock.com
SIC: 2676 3142 Diapers, paper (disposable); made from purchased paper; house slippers

(G-1993)
RAWHIDE SOFTWARE INC (PA)
Also Called: Rawhide Press
17552 W River Rd (43402-8862)
PHONE.................................419 878-0857
Steven L Mandell, *President*
EMP: 3
SALES (est): 5.1MM **Privately Held**
SIC: 7372 7371 7379 2741 Publishers' computer software; computer software development; computer related consulting services; miscellaneous publishing

(G-1994)
RECLAMATION TECHNOLOGIES INC (DH)
Also Called: Remtec International
1100 Haskins Rd (43402-9363)
PHONE.................................800 372-1301
Monte Roach, *President*
Mike Armstrong, *COO*
Jason Zilles, *CFO*
Robert Hennessy, *Ch Credit Ofcr*
▲ **EMP:** 38 **EST:** 1986
SQ FT: 148,000
SALES (est): 11.4MM
SALES (corp-wide): 306.9K **Privately Held**
WEB: www.remtec.net
SIC: 2869 Freon
HQ: A-Gas Us Inc.
1100 Haskins Rd
Bowling Green OH 43402
800 372-1301

(G-1995)
RECLAMATION TECHNOLOGIES INC
Also Called: Remtec International
1100 Haskins Rd (43402-9363)
PHONE.................................419 867-8990
Richard Marcus, *President*
EMP: 10
SALES (corp-wide): 306.9K **Privately Held**
WEB: www.remtec.net
SIC: 2869 Freon
HQ: Reclamation Technologies, Inc.
1100 Haskins Rd
Bowling Green OH 43402
800 372-1301

(G-1996)
REGAL BELOIT AMERICA INC
Marathon Special Products
427 Van Camp Rd (43402)
PHONE.................................419 352-8441
Larry Minnich, *General Mgr*
Michael Jensen, *Area Mgr*
Jeff Wood, *Area Mgr*
Bret Danks, *Vice Pres*
Donald Riley, *Purchasing*
EMP: 200
SALES (corp-wide): 3.6B **Publicly Held**
WEB: www.marathonelect.com
SIC: 3613 3644 Fuse mountings, electric power; noncurrent-carrying wiring services
HQ: Regal Beloit America, Inc.
200 State St
Beloit WI 53511
608 364-8800

(G-1997)
ROARE-Q LLC
Also Called: Porkbelly Bbq
10232 Middleton Pike (43402-9808)
PHONE.................................419 801-4040
Charles Earl, *CEO*
Rory Earl, *COO*
Patricia Earl, *CFO*
EMP: 3 **EST:** 2010
SALES (est): 207.4K **Privately Held**
SIC: 2099 2087 Food preparations; glace, for glazing food

(G-1998)
ROSENBOOM MACHINE & TOOL INC
1032 S Maple St (43402-4535)
PHONE.................................419 352-9484
Shawn Markins, *Engineer*
Derrik Fowler, *Branch Mgr*
Duane Baker, *Manager*
EMP: 50
SALES (corp-wide): 135MM **Privately Held**
WEB: www.rosenboom.com
SIC: 3593 3599 Fluid power cylinders, hydraulic or pneumatic; machine shop, jobbing & repair
PA: Rosenboom Machine & Tool, Inc.
1530 Western Ave
Sheldon IA 51201
712 324-4854

(G-1999)
SMITH SECURITY SAFES INC
17641 Tontogany Rd (43402-9782)
P.O. Box 185, Tontogany (43565-0185)
PHONE.................................419 823-1423
Doug Smith, *President*
▲ **EMP:** 5
SALES: 500K **Privately Held**
SIC: 3499 Fire- or burglary-resistive products

(G-2000)
SOUTHEASTERN CONTAINER INC
307 Industrial Pkwy (43402-1347)
PHONE.................................419 352-6300
Corey Beaber, *Project Engr*
John Johnson, *Branch Mgr*
George Gater, *Maintence Staff*
EMP: 100
SALES (corp-wide): 344.5MM **Privately Held**
SIC: 3085 3089 Plastics bottles; plastic containers, except foam
PA: Southeastern Container, Inc.
1250 Sand Hill Rd
Enka NC 28728
828 350-7200

(G-2001)
TH PLASTICS INC
843 Miller Dr (43402-8601)
PHONE.................................419 352-2770
Patrick Haas, *Owner*
EMP: 108
SALES (est): 14.6MM
SALES (corp-wide): 142MM **Privately Held**
SIC: 3089 Injection molding of plastics
PA: Th Plastics, Inc.
106 E Main St
Mendon MI 49072
269 496-8495

(G-2002)
TOLEDO MOLDING & DIE INC
515 E Gypsy Lane Rd (43402-8739)
PHONE.................................419 354-6050
Bruce Romstad, *Engineer*
Tom Pasche, *Manager*
EMP: 100
SALES (corp-wide): 309.9MM **Privately Held**
WEB: www.tmdinc.com
SIC: 3089 Injection molding of plastics
HQ: Toledo Molding & Die, Inc.
1429 Coining Dr
Toledo OH 43612
419 470-3950

(G-2003)
UNIQUE PLASTICS LLC
13350 Bishop Rd (43402)
PHONE.................................419 352-0066
EMP: 5
SALES (est): 574K **Privately Held**
SIC: 3089 Mfg Plastic Products

(G-2004)
VEHTEK SYSTEMS INC
2125 Wood Bridge Blvd (43402-9164)
PHONE.................................419 373-8741
Christian Holzer, *Principal*
Jeff Bartenslager, *Marketing Mgr*
Jeff Bible, *Info Tech Mgr*
◆ **EMP:** 700
SALES (est): 58.4MM
SALES (corp-wide): 38.9B **Privately Held**
WEB: www.magnaint.com
SIC: 3465 Body parts, automobile: stamped metal
PA: Magna International Inc
337 Magna Dr
Aurora ON L4G 7
905 726-2462

(G-2005)
WILLIAMS INDUSTRIAL SVC INC
2120 Wood Bridge Blvd (43402-9164)
PHONE.................................419 353-2120
Robert S Williams, *President*
Mary E Geremski, *Principal*
Mary Helen Nowak, *Principal*
Barry E Savage, *Principal*
Greg Raubenolt, *Purch Dir*
EMP: 22
SQ FT: 56,000
SALES (est): 8.4MM **Privately Held**
WEB: www.wisfurnaces.com
SIC: 3567 Heating units & devices, industrial: electric

(G-2006)
WIZARD GRAPHICS INC
112 S Main St (43402-2909)
PHONE.................................419 354-3098
Debra Elliott, *President*
EMP: 5
SQ FT: 3,000
SALES (est): 588.5K **Privately Held**
WEB: www.wizardgraphics.net
SIC: 2396 7299 2262 2395 Screen printing on fabric articles; stitching services; decorative finishing of manmade broadwoven fabrics; pleating & stitching

(G-2007)
WOOD COUNTY OHIO
Also Called: Laser Cartridge Express
991 S Main St (43402-4708)
PHONE.................................419 353-1227
Gaile Brooker, *Manager*
EMP: 8 **Privately Held**
WEB: www.woodmrdd.org
SIC: 3955 Print cartridges for laser & other computer printers
PA: County Of Wood
1 Courthouse Sq
Bowling Green OH 43402
419 354-9100

(G-2008)
XORB CORPORATION
455 W Woodland Cir (43402-8834)
PHONE.................................419 354-6021

Ralph Temple, *President*
Paul Dunlavey, *Corp Secy*
EMP: 7
SQ FT: 10,000
SALES (est): 1.2MM **Privately Held**
SIC: 3599 Bellows, industrial: metal

Bradford
Miami County

(G-2009)
BOSCOTT METALS INC
138 S Miami Ave (45308-1321)
P.O. Box 23 (45308-0023)
PHONE..................................937 448-2018
Mark Quinner, *President*
EMP: 12
SQ FT: 20,000
SALES (est): 1.1MM **Privately Held**
SIC: 3365 Aluminum & aluminum-based alloy castings

(G-2010)
C F POEPPELMAN INC (PA)
Also Called: Pepcon Concrete
4755 N State Route 721 (45308-9425)
PHONE..................................937 448-2191
James Poeppelman, *President*
Fred Poeppelman, *Vice Pres*
EMP: 20 EST: 1950
SQ FT: 1,500
SALES (est): 11.8MM **Privately Held**
SIC: 1411 3273 1442 Limestone, dimension-quarrying; ready-mixed concrete; construction sand & gravel

(G-2011)
PRODUCTION PAINT FINISHERS INC
Also Called: P P F
140 Center St (45308-1202)
P.O. Box 127 (45308-0127)
PHONE..................................937 448-2627
Lawrence F Francis, *President*
Kenneth L Robertson, *Principal*
Selwyn C Jackson, *Principal*
Ronald G Smith, *Principal*
Allen J Francis, *Vice Pres*
EMP: 80
SQ FT: 67,000
SALES (est): 10.3MM **Privately Held**
WEB: www.productionpaint.com
SIC: 3479 Painting of metal products; coating of metals & formed products

Bradner
Wood County

(G-2012)
LICENSED SPCIALTY PDTS OF OHIO
Also Called: Real Geese
130 Cherry St (43406-7702)
PHONE..................................419 800-8104
Darrel Wise, *Principal*
Sean Mann, *Principal*
Josh Neuwiller, *Principal*
Kevin Popo, *Principal*
EMP: 5
SALES (est): 867.1K **Privately Held**
SIC: 3949 Sporting & athletic goods

(G-2013)
LUCKEY FARMERS INC
2320 Bowling Green Rd E (43406-9731)
PHONE..................................419 287-3275
John Lintner, *Branch Mgr*
EMP: 3
SALES (corp-wide): 104.6MM **Privately Held**
WEB: www.luckeyfarmers.com
SIC: 2875 5191 Fertilizers, mixing only; farm supplies
PA: Luckey Farmers, Inc.
1200 W Main St
Woodville OH 43469
419 849-2711

(G-2014)
MCCLAFLIN MOBILE MEDIA LLC
106 Caldwell St (43406-9784)
P.O. Box 512 (43406-0512)
PHONE..................................419 575-9367
Doug McClaflin, *General Mgr*
Douglas McClaflin,
EMP: 3
SALES (est): 240.9K **Privately Held**
SIC: 3663 Radio & TV communications equipment

(G-2015)
MESTEK INC
America Warming & Ventraling
120 Plin St (43406-7735)
P.O. Box 677 (43406-0677)
PHONE..................................419 288-2703
Todd Whightman, *Branch Mgr*
EMP: 75
SALES (corp-wide): 669.8MM **Privately Held**
SIC: 3822 3564 3444 3442 Hardware for environmental regulators; blowers & fans; sheet metalwork; metal doors, sash & trim; nonferrous rolling & drawing
PA: Mestek, Inc.
260 N Elm St
Westfield MA 01085
413 568-9571

(G-2016)
TRI COUNTY TARP LLC (PA)
13100 State Rte 23 (43406)
PHONE..................................419 288-3350
Michelle Halshill, *Human Res Mgr*
Gary L Harrison, *Mng Member*
Terrence Augustin, *Executive*
EMP: 32
SQ FT: 82,000
SALES (est): 4MM **Privately Held**
WEB: www.tritarp.com
SIC: 2394 2542 3354 Tarpaulins, fabric: made from purchased materials; partitions for floor attachment, prefabricated: except wood; aluminum extruded products

Brecksville
Cuyahoga County

(G-2017)
AB RESOURCES LLC
6802 W Snowville Rd Ste E (44141-3296)
PHONE..................................440 922-1098
Gordon O Yonel,
EMP: 25
SQ FT: 7,500
SALES (est): 3.5MM **Privately Held**
SIC: 1311 Crude petroleum & natural gas production

(G-2018)
ABEON MEDICAL CORPORATION
8006 Katherine Blvd (44141-4202)
PHONE..................................440 262-6000
George Picha, *CEO*
Matt Thompson, *General Mgr*
Matthew Thompson, *General Mgr*
Dawn Thompson, *Engineer*
EMP: 5
SALES (est): 548.2K **Privately Held**
SIC: 3069 Medical & laboratory rubber sundries & related products

(G-2019)
ACHILL ISLAND COMPOSITES LLC
6981 Chapel Hill Dr (44141-2717)
PHONE..................................440 838-1746
James Sutter, *Principal*
EMP: 5
SALES (est): 229.3K **Privately Held**
SIC: 3089 Plastics products

(G-2020)
APPLIED MEDICAL TECHNOLOGY INC
Also Called: Amt
8006 Katherine Blvd (44141-4202)
PHONE..................................440 717-4000

George J Picha, *President*
Robert J Crump, *Director*
EMP: 30
SQ FT: 14,000
SALES (est): 9.5MM **Privately Held**
SIC: 3841 3083 8731 Surgical & medical instruments; laminated plastics plate & sheet; medical research, commercial

(G-2021)
BARNES GROUP INC
Also Called: Hyson Products
10367 Brecksville Rd (44141-3335)
PHONE..................................440 526-5900
Dwight Warner, *Asst Controller*
Mike Gaudiani, *Branch Mgr*
EMP: 8
SQ FT: 53,593
SALES (corp-wide): 1.5B **Publicly Held**
WEB: www.barnesgroupinc.com
SIC: 3469 3495 Metal stampings; wire springs
PA: Barnes Group Inc.
123 Main St
Bristol CT 06010
860 583-7070

(G-2022)
BENJAMIN MEDIA INC
10050 Brecksville Rd (44141-3219)
P.O. Box 190, Peninsula (44264-0190)
PHONE..................................330 467-7588
Bernard P Krzys, *President*
Russell H Frisby, *Partner*
Brittany Maurer, *Sales Staff*
Todd Miller, *Sales Staff*
Hannah Schiffman, *Sales Staff*
▲ **EMP:** 28
SQ FT: 2,744
SALES (est): 4.7MM **Privately Held**
WEB: www.ttmag.com
SIC: 2721 Trade journals: publishing & printing

(G-2023)
BLACK BOX CORPORATION
6650 W Snowville Rd Ste R (44141-4301)
PHONE..................................800 676-8850
Randy Reffert, *Branch Mgr*
EMP: 10
SALES (corp-wide): 1.8MM **Privately Held**
SIC: 3577 Computer peripheral equipment
HQ: Black Box Corporation
1000 Park Dr
Lawrence PA 15055
724 746-5500

(G-2024)
BRECKSVILLE BROADVIEW GAZETTE
Also Called: Parma Seven Hills Gazette
7014 Mill Rd (44141-1814)
PHONE..................................440 526-7977
Joyce McFadden, *President*
Joyce Mc Fadden, *Publisher*
EMP: 25
SQ FT: 816
SALES (est): 1.3MM **Privately Held**
WEB: www.gazette-news.com
SIC: 2711 Newspapers, publishing & printing

(G-2025)
BUILDING CTRL INTEGRATORS LLC
6900 W Snowville Rd (44141-3216)
PHONE..................................440 526-6660
Jim McClintock, *Branch Mgr*
EMP: 5
SALES (corp-wide): 17.1MM **Privately Held**
SIC: 3822 Temperature controls, automatic
PA: Building Control Integrators, Llc
383 N Liberty St
Powell OH 43065
614 334-3300

(G-2026)
C M STEPHANOFF JEWELERS INC
8718 Bradford Ln (44141-2056)
PHONE..................................440 526-5890
Chris Stephanoff, *President*
EMP: 5

SQ FT: 2,100
SALES (est): 580K **Privately Held**
SIC: 3911 7631 Bracelets, precious metal; earrings, precious metal; necklaces, precious metal; jewelry repair services

(G-2027)
CLINICAL SPECIALTIES INC (PA)
Also Called: Csi Infusion Services
6955 Treeline Dr Ste A (44141-3373)
PHONE..................................888 873-7888
Edward Rivalsky, *President*
EMP: 74
SQ FT: 22,000
SALES (est): 20.1MM **Privately Held**
WEB: www.csi-network.com
SIC: 2834 Intravenous solutions

(G-2028)
CURTISS-WRIGHT FLOW CTRL CORP
Also Called: Sprague Products
10195 Brecksville Rd (44141-3205)
PHONE..................................440 838-7690
Josh Kolenc, *Vice Pres*
Yvonne Denko, *Engineer*
Paul George, *Engineer*
Kelly Grudzinski, *Engineer*
Tony La Morte, *Engineer*
EMP: 30
SQ FT: 77,847
SALES (corp-wide): 2.4B **Publicly Held**
SIC: 3491 Industrial valves
HQ: Curtiss-Wright Flow Control Service, Llc
1966 Broadhollow Rd Ste E
Farmingdale NY 11735
631 293-3800

(G-2029)
DIRECT DISPOSABLES LLC
10605 Snowville Rd (44141-3446)
P.O. Box 470451, Broadview Heights (44147-0451)
PHONE..................................440 717-3335
Sharon Scott,
EMP: 7
SALES (est): 824.4K **Privately Held**
WEB: www.directdisposables.com
SIC: 2389 Disposable garments & accessories

(G-2030)
EFG HOLDINGS INC (PA)
10217 Brecksville Rd # 101 (44141-3207)
PHONE..................................812 689-8990
Brian Nadel, *President*
Bob Korbenbrock, *CFO*
EMP: 35
SALES: 70MM **Privately Held**
SIC: 3452 Bolts, nuts, rivets & washers

(G-2031)
ELGIN FASTENER GROUP LLC
Quality Bolt & Screw
10147 Brecksville Rd (44141-3205)
PHONE..................................440 717-7650
Daniel Wade, *Manager*
Paul Meister, *Info Tech Mgr*
EMP: 38
SALES (corp-wide): 70MM **Privately Held**
SIC: 3452 Bolts, metal; screws, metal
HQ: Elgin Fastener Group, Llc
10217 Brecksville Rd # 101
Brecksville OH 44141

(G-2032)
ELGIN FASTENER GROUP LLC (HQ)
10217 Brecksville Rd # 101 (44141-3207)
PHONE..................................812 689-8990
Jason Nehf, *Vice Pres*
Tena Heller, *Treasurer*
Daniel Wade, *Controller*
EMP: 14
SALES (est): 131.5MM
SALES (corp-wide): 70MM **Privately Held**
SIC: 3399 3452 Metal fasteners; bolts, metal

Brecksville - Cuyahoga County (G-2033)

PA: Efg Holdings, Inc.
10217 Brecksville Rd # 101
Brecksville OH 44141
812 689-8990

(G-2033)
EN GARDE DEER DEFENSE LLC
10292 Fitzwater Rd (44141-1341)
PHONE..................................440 334-7271
Jeffrey Ardo, *Principal*
EMP: 5
SALES (est): 512.6K **Privately Held**
SIC: 3812 Defense systems & equipment

(G-2034)
ENHANCED MFG SOLUTIONS LLC
2890 Boston Mills Rd (44141-3819)
P.O. Box 470024, Broadview Heights (44147-0024)
PHONE..................................440 476-1244
Brian Frost, *CEO*
Rick Bohn, *President*
EMP: 61
SQ FT: 2,200
SALES (est): 4.5MM **Privately Held**
SIC: 3714 Motor vehicle electrical equipment

(G-2035)
EXACT CUTTING SERVICE INC
Also Called: Experimental Machine
6892 W Snwvlle Rd Ste 108 (44141)
PHONE..................................440 546-1319
Jerry Narduzzi, *President*
▲ **EMP:** 20 **EST:** 1974
SQ FT: 20,000
SALES (est): 1.8MM **Privately Held**
WEB: www.exactcut.com
SIC: 7389 3599 Metal cutting services; machine shop, jobbing & repair

(G-2036)
FAB TECH INC
6500 W Snowville Rd (44141-3230)
PHONE..................................330 926-9556
Richard Herrilko, *President*
Gail Herrilko, *Vice Pres*
▲ **EMP:** 5
SQ FT: 12,000
SALES: 600K **Privately Held**
SIC: 3442 Store fronts, prefabricated, metal

(G-2037)
FULTON MANUFACTURING INDS LLC
6600 W Snowville Rd # 6500 (44141-3257)
PHONE..................................440 546-1435
Doug Perau, *Ch of Bd*
John Medas, *President*
Julie C Medas,
EMP: 34
SQ FT: 55,000
SALES (est): 4.6MM **Privately Held**
SIC: 3469 Mfg Metal Stampings

(G-2038)
GENERATIONS COFFEE COMPANY LLC (HQ)
60100 W Snowell (44141)
PHONE..................................440 546-0901
Michael Caruso, *General Mgr*
EMP: 9
SALES (est): 3MM
SALES (corp-wide): 90.6MM **Publicly Held**
WEB: www.coffeeholding.com
SIC: 2095 5149 5499 Roasted coffee; groceries & related products; coffee
PA: Coffee Holding Co., Inc.
3475 Victory Blvd Ste 4
Staten Island NY 10314
718 832-0800

(G-2039)
GLOBAL LIGHTING TECH INC
55 Andrews Cir Ste 1 (44141-3269)
PHONE..................................440 922-4584
Jeffery Parker, *President*
Michael Mayer, *Vice Pres*
Brett Shriver, *Vice Pres*
Melanie Gerdeman, *Engineer*
Bret Dunham, *Project Engr*
▲ **EMP:** 24

SQ FT: 16,500
SALES (est): 5.1MM **Privately Held**
WEB: www.glthome.com
SIC: 3648 3993 Lighting equipment; signs & advertising specialties
PA: Global Lighting Technologies Inc.
C/O: Maples & Calder Limited
George Town GR CAYMAN

(G-2040)
HANOVER PUBLISHING CO
7569 Sanctuary Cir (44141-3194)
PHONE..................................440 838-0911
Agnes Thomas, *Principal*
EMP: 4
SALES (est): 253.1K **Privately Held**
SIC: 2741 Miscellaneous publishing

(G-2041)
INDUSTRIAL MFG CO LLC (HQ)
8223 Brecksville Rd Ste 1 (44141-1367)
PHONE..................................440 838-4700
James Benenson Jr,
Clement Benenson,
James Benenson III,
John E Cvetic,
Nancy Lenhart,
◆ **EMP:** 10 **EST:** 1979
SQ FT: 4,700
SALES (est): 506.2MM **Privately Held**
SIC: 2542 3728 3566 Lockers (not refrigerated); except wood; aircraft body & wing assemblies & parts; speed changers, drives & gears
PA: Summa Holdings, Inc.
8223 Brecksville Rd # 100
Cleveland OH 44141
440 838-4700

(G-2042)
INTEGRATED CHEM CONCEPTS INC
Also Called: ICC
6650 W Snowville Rd Ste F (44141-4301)
PHONE..................................440 838-5666
Richard H Fagher, *President*
Christine Lease, *Admin Sec*
EMP: 9
SQ FT: 9,300
SALES (est): 980K **Privately Held**
SIC: 2821 Plastics materials & resins

(G-2043)
JCB ARROWHEAD PRODUCTS INC
8223 Brecksville Rd # 100 (44141-1371)
PHONE..................................440 546-4288
EMP: 3
SALES (est): 197.3K **Privately Held**
SIC: 3728 Aircraft parts & equipment

(G-2044)
KILN
7225 Fitzwater Rd (44141-1323)
PHONE..................................440 717-1880
Lindsey Beeson, *Owner*
EMP: 3
SALES (est): 288.2K **Privately Held**
SIC: 3559 Kilns

(G-2045)
KNIGHT ERGONOMICS INC
Also Called: Gemini Products
6650 W Snowville Rd Ste G (44141-4301)
PHONE..................................440 746-0044
Robert Haller, *President*
Nicholas Pyros, *Vice Pres*
EMP: 10
SALES: 1MM **Privately Held**
SIC: 3423 Hand & edge tools

(G-2046)
KONECRANES INC
Also Called: Crane Pro Services
6400 W Snowville Rd Ste 1 (44141-3248)
PHONE..................................440 461-8400
Denise Collins, *Administration*
EMP: 10
SALES (corp-wide): 3.7B **Privately Held**
WEB: www.kciusa.com
SIC: 3536 7389 Hoists, cranes & monorails; crane & aerial lift service
HQ: Konecranes, Inc.
4401 Gateway Blvd
Springfield OH 45502

(G-2047)
LAKE ERIE ASPHALT PAVING INC
5510 Oakes Rd (44141-2600)
PHONE..................................440 526-5191
Peter Boukis, *President*
EMP: 3
SALES (est): 455.1K **Privately Held**
SIC: 2951 Asphalt paving mixtures & blocks

(G-2048)
LUBRIZOL GLOBAL MANAGEMENT (DH)
Also Called: Lubrizol Advanced Mtls Inc
9911 Brecksville Rd (44141-3201)
PHONE..................................216 447-5000
James L Hambrick, *CEO*
Rick Tolin, *President*
John J King, *Vice Pres*
Allen Park, *Project Mgr*
Debbie McKee, *Opers Mgr*
◆ **EMP:** 10
SQ FT: 380,000
SALES (est): 999.2MM
SALES (corp-wide): 225.3B **Publicly Held**
WEB: www.pharma.noveoninc.com
SIC: 2899 2891 3088 2834 Chemical preparations; adhesives & sealants; plastics plumbing fixtures; pharmaceutical preparations; electronic generation equipment
HQ: The Lubrizol Corporation
29400 Lakeland Blvd
Wickliffe OH 44092
440 943-4200

(G-2049)
MAVERICK INDUSTRIES INC
5945 W Snowville Rd (44141-3266)
PHONE..................................440 838-5335
Jim Urbanski, *President*
Cindy Maro, *Manager*
EMP: 10
SQ FT: 24,000
SALES (est): 1.4MM **Privately Held**
WEB: www.maverickindustries.com
SIC: 3492 5074 Hose & tube fittings & assemblies, hydraulic/pneumatic; plumbing & heating valves

(G-2050)
NATURES OWN SOURCE LLC
7033 Mill Rd (44141-1813)
PHONE..................................440 838-5135
David Mansbery,
EMP: 8
SALES (est): 820K **Privately Held**
SIC: 2899 Desalter kits, sea water

(G-2051)
NAUTICUS INC
8080 Snowville Rd (44141-3413)
PHONE..................................440 746-1290
John Agro, *President*
John Deagro, *President*
Greg Schreiber, *Opers Mgr*
▲ **EMP:** 6
SALES (est): 876.5K **Privately Held**
SIC: 3732 Motorized boat, building & repairing

(G-2052)
NOVEON INCORPORATED
9921 Brecksville Rd (44141-3201)
P.O. Box 41250 (44141-0250)
PHONE..................................216 447-5000
◆ **EMP:** 3
SALES (est): 517.3K **Privately Held**
SIC: 2841 Mfg Soap/Other Detergents

(G-2053)
PHARMAZELL INC
8921 Brecksville Rd (44141-2301)
PHONE..................................440 526-6417
John Nolan, *President*
Kurt Mayrhofer, *Manager*
Kai Donsbach, *CTO*
Merita Day, *Admin Asst*
EMP: 3
SALES: 732.5K **Privately Held**
SIC: 3661 Telephone & telegraph apparatus

HQ: Pharmazell Gmbh
Rosenheimer Str. 43
Raubling 83064
803 588-0

(G-2054)
PITNEY BOWES INC
6910 Treeline Dr Ste C (44141-3366)
P.O. Box 75007, Fort Thomas KY (41075-0007)
PHONE..................................203 426-7025
Brian Philbin, *Director*
EMP: 75
SALES (corp-wide): 3.5B **Publicly Held**
SIC: 3579 7359 Postage meters; business machine & electronic equipment rental services
PA: Pitney Bowes Inc.
3001 Summer St Ste 3
Stamford CT 06905
203 356-5000

(G-2055)
PMD ENTERPRISES INC
Also Called: Caruso's Coffee
6100 W Snowville Rd (44141-3238)
PHONE..................................440 546-0901
Michael Caruso, *President*
Christopher Bertin, *Corp Secy*
Karen Anderson, *Sales Staff*
▲ **EMP:** 15
SALES (est): 3.4MM **Privately Held**
WEB: www.carusoscoffee.com
SIC: 2095 Coffee roasting (except by wholesale grocers)

(G-2056)
SCRATCH-OFF SYSTEMS INC
6600 W Snowville Rd (44141-3257)
PHONE..................................216 649-7800
Daniel Ogorek, *President*
Robert F Collett, *Principal*
Michael Hazelwood, *Principal*
Angela Jelovich, *Financial Exec*
Scott Cunningham, *Accounts Exec*
▼ **EMP:** 20
SQ FT: 10,000
SALES (est): 6MM **Privately Held**
WEB: www.scratchoff.com
SIC: 2679 5112 2759 2754 Labels, paper: made from purchased material; stationery & office supplies; labels & seals: printing; labels: gravure printing

(G-2057)
SELECTRONICS INCORPORATED
9771 Forge Dr (44141-2825)
PHONE..................................440 546-5595
Ted Liggett, *CEO*
EMP: 5
SQ FT: 600
SALES: 1MM **Privately Held**
WEB: www.selectronicsusa.com
SIC: 3674 5731 Semiconductors & related devices; radio, television & electronic stores

(G-2058)
SIEMENS INDUSTRY INC
Also Called: Rapistan Systems
6930 Treeline Dr Ste A (44141-3367)
PHONE..................................440 526-2770
Charles McBride, *Manager*
EMP: 30
SALES (corp-wide): 95B **Privately Held**
WEB: www.sea.siemens.com
SIC: 5084 3535 Industrial machinery & equipment; conveyors & conveying equipment
HQ: Siemens Industry, Inc.
1000 Deerfield Pkwy
Buffalo Grove IL 60089
800 743-6367

(G-2059)
SYNTHETIC BODY PARTS INC
6099 Warblers Roost (44141-1751)
PHONE..................................440 838-0985
Carl McMillin, *President*
EMP: 4
SALES (est): 312.4K **Privately Held**
SIC: 3842 Prosthetic appliances

GEOGRAPHIC SECTION

(G-2060)
TEREX UTILITIES INC
Also Called: Cleveland Division
6400 W Snowville Rd Ste 1 (44141-3248)
PHONE...................................440 262-3200
Mike Dallager, *Branch Mgr*
EMP: 12
SALES (corp-wide): 5.1B **Publicly Held**
WEB: www.craneamerica.com
SIC: 7699 5084 3536 1796 Industrial machinery & equipment repair; cranes, industrial; hoists; hoists, cranes & monorails; installing building equipment
HQ: Terex Utilities, Inc.
12805 Sw 77th Pl
Tigard OR 97223
503 620-0611

(G-2061)
TEST-FUCHS CORPORATION
10325 Brecksville Rd (44141-3335)
PHONE...................................440 708-3505
Peter Barnhart, *CEO*
EMP: 8
SQ FT: 168
SALES (est): 2.2MM **Privately Held**
SIC: 3826 3829 3728 Analytical instruments; measuring & controlling devices; military aircraft equipment & armament

(G-2062)
TURK+HILLINGER USA INC
6650 W Snowville Rd Ste W (44141-4301)
P.O. Box 41371 (44141-0371)
PHONE...................................440 781-1900
Michael Mann, *President*
Christopher Grolimund, *Vice Pres*
▲ **EMP:** 3
SALES (est): 421.6K
SALES (corp-wide): 66MM **Privately Held**
SIC: 3621 Generating apparatus & parts, electrical
PA: Turk & Hillinger Gmbh
Fohrenstr. 20
Tuttlingen 78532
746 170-140

(G-2063)
ZEECO EQUIPMENT COMMODITY
6581 Glen Coe Dr (44141-2883)
PHONE...................................440 838-1102
Zoran Stojkov, *CEO*
EMP: 5
SALES (est): 500K **Privately Held**
SIC: 3559 Chemical machinery & equipment

Bremen
Fairfield County

(G-2064)
STUART BURIAL VAULT COMPANY
527 Ford St (43107-1111)
P.O. Box 146 (43107-0146)
PHONE...................................740 569-4158
John A Boone, *President*
Mary Lyle Boone, *Vice Pres*
EMP: 12 **EST:** 1919
SQ FT: 16,500
SALES (est): 1.1MM **Privately Held**
SIC: 3272 Burial vaults, concrete or precast terrazzo

(G-2065)
WESTERMAN INC (DH)
245 N Broad St (43107-1003)
P.O. Box 125 (43107-0125)
PHONE...................................740 569-4143
Terry A McGhee, *President*
Barry Keller, *Exec VP*
Melissa Eaton, *CFO*
▼ **EMP:** 185 **EST:** 1957
SQ FT: 150,000
SALES (est): 75.9MM
SALES (corp-wide): 3.5B **Publicly Held**
WEB: www.westermancompanies.com
SIC: 3566 Reduction gears & gear units for turbines, except automotive

HQ: Worthington Cylinder Corporation
200 W Wlson Bridge Rd
Worthington OH 43085
614 840-3210

(G-2066)
WORTHINGTON CYLINDER CORP
245 N Broad St (43107-1003)
P.O. Box 125 (43107-0125)
PHONE...................................740 569-4143
EMP: 191
SALES (corp-wide): 3.5B **Publicly Held**
SIC: 3443 Cylinders, pressure: metal plate
HQ: Worthington Cylinder Corporation
200 W Wlson Bridge Rd
Worthington OH 43085
614 840-3210

Brewster
Stark County

(G-2067)
BREWSTER CHEESE COMPANY (PA)
800 Wabash Ave S (44613-1464)
PHONE...................................330 767-3492
Fritz Leeman, *CEO*
Thomas Murphy, *President*
Emil Aleufan, *Vice Pres*
Tom Beck, *Mfg Spvr*
James Barnard, *Purch Agent*
EMP: 200 **EST:** 1964
SQ FT: 78,914
SALES (est): 139.5MM **Privately Held**
SIC: 2022 Natural cheese

(G-2068)
BREWSTER SUGARCREEK TWP HISTO
Also Called: BREWSTER HISTORICAL SOCIETY
45 Wabash Ave S (44613-1210)
PHONE...................................330 767-0045
Robert Lucking, *Owner*
EMP: 10
SQ FT: 3,196
SALES: 21K **Privately Held**
SIC: 3732 8412 Boat kits, not models; museum

(G-2069)
L & J DRIVE THRU
212 Wabash Ave N (44613-1040)
PHONE...................................330 767-2185
Lena Porter, *Principal*
EMP: 4
SALES (est): 237.9K **Privately Held**
SIC: 2086 Carbonated beverages, nonalcoholic: bottled & canned

(G-2070)
MICRO MACHINE LTD
275 7th St Sw (44613-1457)
PHONE...................................330 438-7078
Ronald Pollock, *Partner*
Harold Byer, *Partner*
EMP: 7
SALES (est): 522.3K **Privately Held**
SIC: 3599 Machine & other job shop work

Brice
Franklin County

(G-2071)
CARL C ANDRE INC
Also Called: Andre Kitchens
2894 Brice Rd (43109)
P.O. Box 62 (43109-0062)
PHONE...................................614 864-0123
Carl C Andre, *President*
EMP: 3
SQ FT: 8,000
SALES (est): 320K **Privately Held**
SIC: 2435 5211 Hardwood veneer & plywood; cabinets, kitchen

Bridgeport
Belmont County

(G-2072)
ANGELINA STONE & MARBLE LTD
55341 W Center St (43912-1216)
PHONE...................................740 633-3360
Jack McKeever, *Branch Mgr*
EMP: 6 **Privately Held**
SIC: 3281 Granite, cut & shaped
PA: Angelina Stone & Marble Ltd
55341 W Center St
Bridgeport OH 43912

(G-2073)
CLOUD 9 NATURALLY INC
53840 National Rd (43912-7733)
PHONE...................................403 348-9704
Patricia Macdonald, *President*
EMP: 3
SALES (est): 123.2K **Privately Held**
SIC: 2834 Liniments

(G-2074)
EVERLY CONCRETE PRODUCTS
53620 Farmington Rd (43912-9779)
PHONE...................................740 635-1415
Rich Theaker, *Principal*
EMP: 3
SALES (est): 451.1K **Privately Held**
SIC: 3272 Concrete products, precast

(G-2075)
GOLD 2 GREEN LTD
319 Main St (43912-1347)
P.O. Box 3 (43912-0003)
PHONE...................................304 551-1172
Richard Lund, *Principal*
EMP: 4
SALES (est): 382.9K **Privately Held**
SIC: 3341 Secondary nonferrous metals

(G-2076)
JERRY HAROLDS DOORS UNLIMITED (PA)
415 Hall St (43912-1343)
PHONE...................................740 635-4949
Jerry Brocht, *President*
Harold Games, *Vice Pres*
EMP: 7
SQ FT: 1,600
SALES (est): 1.5MM **Privately Held**
SIC: 5031 3446 5211 Doors; architectural metalwork; garage doors, sale & installation

(G-2077)
MIKE SUPONCIC
68940 Blaine Chermont Rd (43912-9749)
PHONE...................................740 635-0654
Suponcic Mike, *Owner*
EMP: 3
SALES (est): 211.9K **Privately Held**
SIC: 3532 Mining machinery

(G-2078)
SKYLINER
225 Main St (43912-1345)
PHONE...................................740 738-0874
Donald Rhodes, *Owner*
Robyn Rhodes, *Principal*
Witney Stewski, *Principal*
EMP: 8
SALES: 100K **Privately Held**
SIC: 7299 2051 Facility rental & party planning services; bakery: wholesale or wholesale/retail combined

Brilliant
Jefferson County

(G-2079)
OPTIMUN BLINDS INC
Also Called: Optimum Blinds
204 Ohio St (43913-1125)
PHONE...................................740 598-5808
Mark Laurine, *President*
EMP: 5

SALES (est): 481.9K **Privately Held**
SIC: 2591 5719 Blinds vertical; vertical blinds; venetian blinds; window shades

(G-2080)
STEEL VALLEY TANK & WELDING
24 County Road 7e (43913-1079)
P.O. Box 8 (43913-0008)
PHONE...................................740 598-4994
Gary Kessler, *Owner*
EMP: 10
SALES (est): 1MM **Privately Held**
WEB: www.steelvalleytank.com
SIC: 3443 Industrial vessels, tanks & containers

Brinkhaven
Knox County

(G-2081)
HILLCREST
Also Called: Hw Chair
31580 Township Rd (43006)
PHONE...................................740 824-4849
Norman Yoder, *President*
EMP: 6
SALES: 400K **Privately Held**
SIC: 2426 Chair seats, hardwood

Bristolville
Trumbull County

(G-2082)
K M B INC
Also Called: King Bros Feed & Supply
1306 State Route 88 (44402-8743)
P.O. Box 240 (44402-0240)
PHONE...................................330 889-3451
Marlene King, *President*
Rex King, *Vice Pres*
EMP: 35 **EST:** 1956
SQ FT: 4,200
SALES (est): 6.2MM **Privately Held**
WEB: www.kingbrosracing.com
SIC: 3273 5211 5261 5191 Ready-mixed concrete; lumber & other building materials; fertilizer; feed; concrete products

(G-2083)
MAHAN PACKING CO INC
6540 State Route 45 (44402-9730)
PHONE...................................330 889-2454
K Ray Mahan, *President*
Nancy Mahan, *Vice Pres*
EMP: 35 **EST:** 1958
SQ FT: 15,000
SALES (est): 5.2MM **Privately Held**
SIC: 2011 Meat packing plants

(G-2084)
STRUTT PRODUCTS LLC
Also Called: Fire Pit Gallery, The
6340 State Route 45 Cd (44402-9705)
PHONE...................................330 889-2727
Jason Crisp, *President*
Melissa Crisp, *Vice Pres*
Marlene Appel, *Treasurer*
Thomas Appel, *Admin Sec*
EMP: 4
SALES: 340K **Privately Held**
SIC: 3429 Fireplace equipment, hardware: andirons, grates, screens

Broadview Heights
Cuyahoga County

(G-2085)
10155 BROADVIEW BUSINESS
10155 Broadview Rd (44147-3296)
PHONE...................................440 546-1901
David M Leneghan, *Principal*
EMP: 4
SALES (est): 290.9K **Privately Held**
SIC: 3629 Power conversion units, a.c. to d.c.: static-electric

Broadview Heights - Cuyahoga County (G-2086)

(G-2086)
ACCU-SIGN
3652 Elm Brook Dr (44147-2029)
PHONE..................................216 544-2059
Raymond C Eier, *Principal*
EMP: 3
SALES (est): 307.1K **Privately Held**
SIC: 3993 Signs & advertising specialties

(G-2087)
ACTIPRO SOFTWARE LLC
8576 Somerset Dr (44147-3422)
PHONE..................................888 922-8477
William M Henning, *President*
EMP: 3 **EST:** 1999
SALES (est): 220.5K **Privately Held**
SIC: 7372 Business oriented computer software

(G-2088)
BENJAMIN P FORBES COMPANY
Also Called: Forbes Chocolate
800 Ken Mar Indus Pkwy (44147-2922)
PHONE..................................440 838-4400
Keith Geringer, *President*
▲ **EMP:** 13 **EST:** 1913
SQ FT: 16,687
SALES (est): 3.1MM **Privately Held**
SIC: 2066 Powdered cocoa

(G-2089)
BROADVIEW HEIGHTS SPOTLIGHTS
9543 Broadview Rd (44147-2300)
PHONE..................................440 526-4404
Annette Phelps, *President*
EMP: 3
SALES: 14.9K **Privately Held**
SIC: 3648 Mfg Lighting Equipment

(G-2090)
CHICAGO PNEUMATIC TOOL CO LLC
9100 Market Pl Rear (44147-2861)
PHONE..................................704 883-3500
EMP: 3
SALES (corp-wide): 13.8B **Privately Held**
SIC: 3546 Power-driven handtools
HQ: Chicago Pneumatic Tool Company Llc
  1815 Clubhouse Dr
  Rock Hill SC 29730
  803 817-7100

(G-2091)
CLEVELAND BUSINESS SUPPLY LLC
Also Called: Total Voice Technologies
8193 Avery Rd Ste 200 (44147-1673)
PHONE..................................888 831-0088
Christopher Kikel, *President*
EMP: 5
SALES (est): 260K **Privately Held**
SIC: 8243 5044 7372 Software training, computer; typewriter & dictation equipment; business oriented computer software

(G-2092)
CLINICL OTCMS MNGMNT SYST LLC
Also Called: Coms Interactive
9200 S Hills Blvd Ste 200 (44147-3520)
PHONE..................................330 650-9900
Edward J Tromczynski, *CEO*
Libby Manthei, *Opers Staff*
Bill Stuart, *CFO*
Terry Sullivan, *Chief Mktg Ofcr*
Nichole Fetterman, *Manager*
EMP: 59
SQ FT: 1,400
SALES (est): 8.7MM
SALES (corp-wide): 77.3MM **Privately Held**
WEB: www.comsllc.com
SIC: 7372 Business oriented computer software
HQ: Pointclickcare Technologies Inc
  5570 Explorer Dr
  Mississauga ON L4W 0
  905 858-8885

(G-2093)
J & L STEEL BAR LLC
3587 Antony Dr (44147-2048)
PHONE..................................440 526-0050
EMP: 4
SALES (est): 346.7K **Privately Held**
SIC: 3312 Bars & bar shapes, steel, hot-rolled

(G-2094)
M/W INTERNATIONAL INC
Also Called: Mills Walls
2525 E Royalton Rd (44147-2840)
P.O. Box 470115 (44147-0115)
PHONE..................................440 526-6900
Joseph R Bucalo, *President*
Kathleen Bucalo, *Corp Secy*
Tom Davis, *VP Sales*
▲ **EMP:** 18
SQ FT: 1,500
SALES: 2MM **Privately Held**
SIC: 2522 Office furniture, except wood

(G-2095)
MANTRA HAIRCARE LLC
305 Ken Mar Indus Pkwy (44147)
PHONE..................................440 526-3304
Jeffery Klominek,
Amy Levak,
EMP: 18
SQ FT: 10,000
SALES: 2MM **Privately Held**
SIC: 2844 Hair preparations, including shampoos

(G-2096)
MATACO
Also Called: Machine & Tool Accessories Co
2861 E Royalton Rd (44147-2827)
PHONE..................................440 546-8355
Jeff Bubb, *Partner*
David Pajestka, *Partner*
Joseph Pajestka, *Partner*
▲ **EMP:** 4
SQ FT: 1,000
SALES (est): 544.9K **Privately Held**
WEB: www.matacoinc.net
SIC: 3541 5251 5084 3446 Machine tool replacement & repair parts, metal cutting types; tools; industrial machinery & equipment; architectural metalwork

(G-2097)
MATHEMATICAL BUSINESS SYSTEMS
1261 Valley Park Dr (44147-1643)
PHONE..................................440 237-2345
Tom Penn, *Owner*
EMP: 5
SALES: 250K **Privately Held**
SIC: 7372 Prepackaged software

(G-2098)
PROMOTIONS PLUS INC
3402 Magnolia Way (44147-3917)
PHONE..................................440 582-2855
EMP: 4
SALES (est): 280K **Privately Held**
SIC: 2329 Mfg Men's/Boy's Clothing

(G-2099)
QUALITY IMAGE EMBROIDERY & AP
2643 Royalwood Rd (44147-1756)
PHONE..................................440 230-1109
Barbara Franko, *President*
Mike Franko, *Admin Sec*
EMP: 5
SQ FT: 2,000
SALES: 125K **Privately Held**
SIC: 2395 Embroidery products, except schiffli machine

(G-2100)
SAWMILL EYE ASSOCIATES INC
8666 Scenicview Dr (44147-3476)
PHONE..................................440 724-0396
Scott P Caleodis Od, *Principal*
EMP: 3
SALES (est): 184K **Privately Held**
SIC: 2421 Sawmills & planing mills, general

(G-2101)
SEVES GLASS BLOCK INC
10576 Broadview Rd (44147-3227)
PHONE..................................440 627-6257
Anton Kava, *Managing Dir*
◆ **EMP:** 5 **EST:** 2016
SALES: 150K **Privately Held**
SIC: 3299 Ornamental & architectural plaster work

(G-2102)
STEIN STEEL MILL SERVICES INC
1929 E Royalton Rd (44147-2867)
P.O. Box 470264 (44147-0264)
PHONE..................................440 526-9301
John Desmond, *President*
EMP: 18
SALES (est): 2.6MM **Privately Held**
SIC: 3295 Blast furnace slag

Brookfield
Trumbull County

(G-2103)
CNG FUELING LLC
1266 State Route 7 Ne F (44403-9200)
P.O. Box 4 (44403-0004)
PHONE..................................330 772-2403
Robert Nemeth, *Managing Prtnr*
EMP: 3
SALES (est): 360.3K **Privately Held**
SIC: 3824 Gasoline dispensing meters

(G-2104)
D & D LANDSCAPING INC
7012 Warren Sharon Rd (44403-9601)
PHONE..................................330 507-6647
Darryl Dickson, *President*
Dennis Dickson, *Vice Pres*
EMP: 3
SALES (est): 296.7K **Privately Held**
SIC: 0781 3531 Landscape services; plows: construction, excavating & grading

(G-2105)
E-Z STOP SERVICE CENTER
Also Called: E-Z Label Co
354 Bedford Rd Se (44403-9727)
PHONE..................................330 448-2236
Frank Zurawsky, *Partner*
Dave Zurawsky, *Partner*
EMP: 60
SQ FT: 3,000
SALES (est): 5.1MM **Privately Held**
SIC: 2754 2671 Labels: gravure printing; packaging paper & plastics film, coated & laminated

(G-2106)
ENREVO PYRO LLC
6874 Strimbu Dr (44403-9526)
PHONE..................................203 517-5002
Philip Smith, *CEO*
EMP: 6 **EST:** 2012
SQ FT: 15,000
SALES (est): 217.8K **Privately Held**
SIC: 1311 2911 Coal pyrolysis; fractionation products of crude petroleum, hydrocarbons

(G-2107)
INDUSTRIAL TANK & CONTAINMENT
411 State Route 7 Se # 3 (44403-9555)
PHONE..................................330 448-4876
Raymond Graff, *President*
Steve Douty, *Buyer*
EMP: 10
SQ FT: 10,000
SALES: 2MM **Privately Held**
SIC: 3443 Fabricated plate work (boiler shop)

(G-2108)
IPSCO TUBULARS INC
6880 Parkway Dr (44403-9797)
PHONE..................................330 448-6772
EMP: 4
SALES (corp-wide): 355.8K **Privately Held**
SIC: 3498 Fabricated pipe & fittings
HQ: Ipsco Tubulars Inc.
  10120 Houston Oaks Dr
  Houston TX 77064

(G-2109)
SIGNS BY GEORGE
5815 Warren Sharon Rd (44403-9543)
PHONE..................................216 394-2095
George Hardin, *President*
Linda Hardin, *Corp Secy*
Dave Hardin, *Vice Pres*
EMP: 4
SALES (est): 408.7K **Privately Held**
SIC: 3993 2759 Electric signs; screen printing

(G-2110)
ULTRA PREMIUM OILFLD SVCS LTD
Also Called: Tmk Ipsco
6880 Parkway Dr (44403-9797)
PHONE..................................330 448-3683
Gabe Carrington, *Prdtn Dir*
Ernie Sexton, *Plant Mgr*
EMP: 10
SALES (corp-wide): 355.8K **Privately Held**
SIC: 3533 Oil field machinery & equipment
HQ: Ultra Premium Oilfield Services, Ltd.
  7501 Groening St
  Odessa TX 79765
  432 337-2109

Brooklyn
Cuyahoga County

(G-2111)
AREWAY ACQUISITION INC
8525 Clinton Rd (44144-1014)
PHONE..................................216 651-9022
John Hadgis, *President*
EMP: 99
SQ FT: 100,000
SALES (est): 8.4MM **Privately Held**
SIC: 3471 Polishing, metals or formed products

(G-2112)
AREWAY LLC
8525 Clinton Rd (44144-1014)
PHONE..................................216 651-9022
Gregory S Hadgis,
▲ **EMP:** 99
SALES (est): 25.9MM **Privately Held**
SIC: 3714 3541 Motor vehicle engines & parts; motor vehicle transmissions, drive assemblies & parts; buffing & polishing machines

(G-2113)
HMI INDUSTRIES INC (PA)
Also Called: Health Mor At Home Cbp
1 American Rd Ste 1250 (44144-2355)
PHONE..................................440 846-7800
Kirk Foley, *CEO*
John Pryor, *President*
Daniel J Duggan, *Vice Pres*
Timothy Duggan, *Vice Pres*
Joseph Najm, *Vice Pres*
◆ **EMP:** 50 **EST:** 1928
SQ FT: 73,000
SALES (est): 18.7MM **Privately Held**
WEB: www.filterqueen.com
SIC: 3634 Air purifiers, portable

(G-2114)
RHINOSYSTEMS INC
Also Called: Navage
1 American Rd Ste 1100 (44144-2355)
PHONE..................................216 351-6262
Martin Hoke, *President*
EMP: 10 **EST:** 2007
SQ FT: 9,000
SALES (est): 705.9K **Privately Held**
SIC: 3841 Inhalation therapy equipment

Brooklyn Heights
Cuyahoga County

GEOGRAPHIC SECTION

Brookpark - Cuyahoga County (G-2140)

(G-2115)
APPLIED METALS TECH LTD
1040 Valley Belt Rd (44131-1433)
PHONE..................216 741-3236
Lisa Virost, *President*
Wills Vrost, *Opers Mgr*
EMP: 47
SQ FT: 30,000
SALES (est): 6.2MM **Privately Held**
SIC: 3471 Finishing, metals or formed products

(G-2116)
BRILLIANT ELECTRIC SIGN CO LTD
4811 Van Epps Rd (44131-1082)
PHONE..................216 741-3800
Rob Kraus, *Plant Mgr*
Patty Molnar, *Project Mgr*
Jo Janos, *Accounting Mgr*
Lee Rodenfels, *Accounts Exec*
John Walsh, *Sales Staff*
EMP: 55
SQ FT: 55,000
SALES (est): 7.6MM **Privately Held**
WEB: www.brilliantsign.com
SIC: 3993 1799 Electric signs; sign installation & maintenance

(G-2117)
C T I AUDIO INC
220 Eastview Dr Ste 1 (44131-1039)
PHONE..................440 593-1111
William Ross, *Ch of Bd*
EMP: 97
SQ FT: 70,000
SALES (est): 7.7MM **Privately Held**
SIC: 3651 Microphones; audio electronic systems

(G-2118)
CI DISPOSITION CO
1000 Valley Belt Rd (44131-1433)
PHONE..................216 587-5200
Gary Tarnowski, *Vice Pres*
EMP: 38
SQ FT: 56,000
SALES (est): 8MM **Privately Held**
WEB: www.comptrolinc.com
SIC: 3699 5085 Linear accelerators; industrial supplies

(G-2119)
DIE-MATIC CORPORATION
201 Eastview Dr (44131-1074)
PHONE..................216 749-4656
Louie J Zeitler, *CEO*
John A Gorman, *Corp Secy*
James Britt, *QC Mgr*
John Kazanowski, *Engineer*
William Rambert, *Engineer*
▲ **EMP:** 55 **EST:** 1958
SQ FT: 120,000
SALES (est): 17.2MM **Privately Held**
WEB: www.die-matic.com
SIC: 3469 3544 Stamping metal for the trade; special dies, tools, jigs & fixtures

(G-2120)
DIGICOM INC
5405 Valley Belt Rd Ste A (44131-1470)
PHONE..................216 642-3838
Frank J Prucha Jr, *Principal*
Melissa Lapor, *Principal*
Nancy Prucha, *Principal*
EMP: 8
SALES (est): 429.2K **Privately Held**
SIC: 2711 2732 Commercial printing & newspaper publishing combined; pamphlets: printing only, not published on site

(G-2121)
DIVERSIFIED AIR SYSTEMS INC (PA)
4760 Van Epps Rd (44131-1014)
PHONE..................216 741-1700
Bob Lisi, *President*
Vincent Lisi, *Corp Secy*
EMP: 20 **EST:** 1995
SQ FT: 20,000
SALES (est): 13.5MM **Privately Held**
WEB: www.diversifiedair.com
SIC: 5084 5075 7694 Compressors, except air conditioning; compressors, air conditioning; armature rewinding shops

(G-2122)
GOODRICH CORPORATION
925 Keynote Cir Ste 300 (44131-1869)
PHONE..................216 429-4655
Legrave Hamilton, *Branch Mgr*
EMP: 8
SALES (corp-wide): 66.5B **Publicly Held**
WEB: www.bfgoodrich.com
SIC: 3011 Tires & inner tubes
HQ: Goodrich Corporation
2730 W Tyvola Rd
Charlotte NC 28217
704 423-7000

(G-2123)
GRAFTECH INTERNATIONAL LTD (HQ)
982 Keynote Cir Ste 6 (44131-1873)
PHONE..................216 676-2000
Denis A Turcotte, *Ch of Bd*
David J Rintoul, *President*
Quinn J Coburn, *CFO*
EMP: 98
SALES: 1.9B
SALES (corp-wide): 8.5B **Publicly Held**
WEB: www.graftech.com
SIC: 3624 Carbon & graphite products
PA: Brookfield Asset Management Inc
181 Bay St Suite 300
Toronto ON M5J 2
416 363-9491

(G-2124)
GRAFTECH INTL HOLDINGS INC
982 Keynote Cir (44131-1872)
PHONE..................216 676-2000
EMP: 3
SALES (corp-wide): 8.5B **Publicly Held**
SIC: 3624 Carbon & graphite products
HQ: Graftech International Holdings Inc.
982 Keynote Cir
Brooklyn Heights OH 44131
216 676-2000

(G-2125)
GRAFTECH INTL HOLDINGS INC (DH)
Also Called: UCAR Carbon
982 Keynote Cir (44131-1872)
PHONE..................216 676-2000
David Rintoul, *CEO*
▲ **EMP:** 197
SQ FT: 10,000
SALES (est): 233.1MM
SALES (corp-wide): 8.5B **Publicly Held**
SIC: 3624 Electrodes, thermal & electrolytic uses: carbon, graphite

(G-2126)
J & L BODY INC
4848 Van Epps Rd (44131-1016)
PHONE..................216 661-2323
Mike Litteria, *President*
Rosemary Nelson, *Corp Secy*
Robert Daley, *Vice Pres*
EMP: 10
SQ FT: 16,000
SALES: 700K **Privately Held**
SIC: 3715 7549 7539 Truck trailers; trailer maintenance; trailer repair

(G-2127)
NATIONAL FASTENERS INC
4581 Spring Rd (44131-1023)
PHONE..................216 771-6473
William Fulop, *President*
EMP: 3
SALES (est): 578.1K **Privately Held**
SIC: 3399 Metal fasteners

(G-2128)
NORTH SHORE STRAPPING INC (PA)
1400 Valley Belt Rd (44131-1441)
PHONE..................216 661-5200
Bridget A Leneghan, *President*
Kevin Leneghan, *Vice Pres*
Laurie Leneghan, *Manager*
David M Leneghan, *Admin Sec*
David Leneghan, *Admin Sec*
▲ **EMP:** 53 **EST:** 1982
SQ FT: 225,000
SALES (est): 15.2MM **Privately Held**
SIC: 3081 3499 3312 2992 Unsupported plastics film & sheet; strapping, metal; wire products, steel or iron; lubricating oils & greases; enamels; lacquer: bases, dopes, thinner; lead pencils & art goods

(G-2129)
PEN BRANDS LLC
220 Eastview Dr Ste 102 (44131-1040)
PHONE..................216 674-1430
Scott Rickert, *President*
EMP: 35
SALES (corp-wide): 7.8MM **Publicly Held**
WEB: www.nanofilm.cc
SIC: 2869 2842 2392 Industrial organic chemicals; specialty cleaning, polishes & sanitation goods; household furnishings
HQ: Pen Brands Llc
220 Eastview Dr Ste 102
Brooklyn Heights OH 44131
216 447-1199

(G-2130)
R&D MARKETING GROUP INC
Also Called: Proforma Signature Solutions
4597 Van Epps Rd (44131-1009)
PHONE..................216 398-9100
Dave Mader, *President*
Tony Zayas, *Director*
EMP: 8 **EST:** 2011
SALES (est): 1.5MM **Privately Held**
SIC: 6794 2759 2752 Franchises, selling or licensing; commercial printing; commercial printing, lithographic

(G-2131)
SIMS-LOHMAN INC
1500 Valley Belt Rd (44131-1450)
PHONE..................440 799-8285
EMP: 35
SALES (corp-wide): 127.4MM **Privately Held**
SIC: 3281 Cut stone & stone products
PA: Sims-Lohman, Inc.
6325 Este Ave
Cincinnati OH 45232
513 651-3510

(G-2132)
SPECTRUM INC
Also Called: Spectrum Infared
800 Resource Dr Ste 8 (44131-1875)
PHONE..................440 951-6061
Daniel Ross, *President*
Jay Peet, *Vice Pres*
▲ **EMP:** 12
SALES (est): 2.6MM **Privately Held**
SIC: 3433 Gas infrared heating units

(G-2133)
TRIONETICS INC
4924 Schaaf Ln (44131-1008)
PHONE..................216 812-3570
Colleen Maitino, *CEO*
Phillip Maitino, *President*
John Maitino, *Principal*
Michael Maitino, *Principal*
Sheryl Maitino, *Principal*
EMP: 14
SQ FT: 2,100
SALES: 3.6MM **Privately Held**
SIC: 3589 Water treatment equipment, industrial

Brookpark
Cuyahoga County

(G-2134)
AM INDUSTRIAL GROUP LLC (PA)
16000 Commerce Park Dr (44142-2023)
PHONE..................216 433-7171
Reginald Wyman, *Owner*
Luke Wootten, *Opers Mgr*
Ryan Wyman, *Engineer*
Jason Cottle, *Sales Staff*
Robert Wootten, *Sales Staff*
▲ **EMP:** 40
SQ FT: 5,000
SALES (est): 23.6MM **Privately Held**
WEB: www.amindustrial.com
SIC: 5084 3541 1799 Machine tools & accessories; sawing & cutoff machines (metalworking machinery); rigging & scaffolding

(G-2135)
AMERICAN SOLVING INC
6519 Eastland Rd Ste 5 (44142-1347)
PHONE..................440 234-7373
Orley Aten, *President*
Peter Bjork, *Managing Dir*
Andreas Bjork, *QC Mgr*
Julia Aten, *Treasurer*
▲ **EMP:** 6
SQ FT: 5,000
SALES (est): 1MM **Privately Held**
WEB: www.americansolving.com
SIC: 3535 5084 Pneumatic tube conveyor systems; materials handling machinery; hoists

(G-2136)
AMPEX METAL PRODUCTS COMPANY (PA)
5581 W 164th St (44142-1513)
PHONE..................216 267-9242
Andrew S Pastor, *President*
Robert Pastor, *Vice Pres*
Beverly Pavlin, *Manager*
Gail Catcher, *Executive*
EMP: 30
SQ FT: 24,000
SALES: 6.6MM **Privately Held**
WEB: www.ampexmetal.com
SIC: 3469 3544 3452 3429 Stamping metal for the trade; special dies, tools, jigs & fixtures; bolts, nuts, rivets & washers; manufactured hardware (general)

(G-2137)
AXENT GRAPHICS LLC
6270 Engle Rd (44142-2106)
PHONE..................216 362-7560
F David Weber,
EMP: 3
SALES (est): 314.5K **Privately Held**
SIC: 2759 Promotional printing; screen printing

(G-2138)
CLEVELAND INSTRUMENT CORP
6430 Eastland Rd Ste 2 (44142-1340)
PHONE..................440 826-1800
Ryan Sullivan, *President*
EMP: 4
SQ FT: 4,000
SALES: 350K **Privately Held**
WEB: www.clevelandinstrument.com
SIC: 3728 3823 8734 Aircraft parts & equipment; industrial instrmnts msrmnt display/control process variable; testing laboratories

(G-2139)
CRITERION TOOL & DIE INC
Also Called: Criterion Instrument
5349 W 161st St (44142-1609)
PHONE..................216 267-1733
Tanya Disalvo, *President*
Dennis M Ondercin, *Vice Pres*
Dennis Ondercin, *Vice Pres*
Theodore D Ward, *Council Mbr*
EMP: 40 **EST:** 1953
SQ FT: 20,000
SALES (est): 6MM **Privately Held**
WEB: www.criteriontool.com
SIC: 3599 3544 3541 Machine shop, jobbing & repair; special dies, tools, jigs & fixtures; machine tools, metal cutting type

(G-2140)
CUSTOM FLOATERS LLC
5161 W 161st St (44142-1604)
PHONE..................216 337-9118
Dianne Malone, *Administration*
EMP: 5 **EST:** 2012
SALES (est): 590.7K **Privately Held**
SIC: 3465 Body parts, automobile: stamped metal

Brookpark - Cuyahoga County (G-2141)

(G-2141)
CUSTOM FLOATERS LLC
6519 Eastland Rd Ste 101 (44142-1347)
PHONE..................................216 536-8979
EMP: 3 **EST:** 2017
SALES (est): 355.2K **Privately Held**
SIC: 3131 Quarters

(G-2142)
CUYAHOGA MACHINE COMPANY LLC
5250 W 137th St (44142-1828)
PHONE..................................216 267-3560
Irene Bogdan, *Mng Member*
Nona Betz, *Admin Sec*
EMP: 19 **EST:** 2013
SALES (est): 257.2K **Privately Held**
SIC: 7699 3599 Industrial machinery & equipment repair; machine shop, jobbing & repair

(G-2143)
DD FOUNDRY INC (PA)
15583 Brookpark Rd (44142-1618)
PHONE..................................216 362-4100
David Dolata, *CEO*
Jerry Kovatch, *President*
David Zanto, *COO*
Sandra Catlett, *CFO*
Mary Miller, *Shareholder*
▲ **EMP:** 97
SQ FT: 80,000
SALES (est): 38MM **Privately Held**
WEB: www.precisionmetalsmiths.com
SIC: 3364 3324 3369 3365 Nonferrous die-castings except aluminum; commercial investment castings, ferrous; nonferrous foundries; aluminum foundries; steel foundries; gray & ductile iron foundries

(G-2144)
DRIVE COMPONENTS
6519 Eastland Rd Ste 106 (44142-1349)
PHONE..................................440 234-6200
Bud Zollars, *Manager*
▲ **EMP:** 5
SALES (est): 632.3K **Privately Held**
SIC: 3568 Power transmission equipment

(G-2145)
E L MUSTEE & SONS INC (PA)
5431 W 164th St (44142-1586)
PHONE..................................216 267-3100
Kevin Mustee, *President*
Henry Dutton, *President*
Bob Mustee, *Plant Mgr*
Steve Chomyk, *Purch Agent*
Laura Mustee, *Marketing Staff*
◆ **EMP:** 100 **EST:** 1932
SQ FT: 140,000
SALES (est): 23.5MM **Privately Held**
WEB: www.elmustee.com
SIC: 3088 Tubs (bath, shower & laundry), plastic

(G-2146)
FIREHOUSE SIGN CO INC
5241 W 161st St (44142-1606)
PHONE..................................216 267-5300
Scott Hales, *President*
EMP: 4
SQ FT: 2,400
SALES: 200K **Privately Held**
SIC: 3993 Signs, not made in custom sign painting shops

(G-2147)
FORD MOTOR COMPANY
17601 Brookpark Rd (44142-1518)
P.O. Box 9900, Cleveland (44142)
PHONE..................................216 676-7918
Andrew Kitral, *Engineer*
Timothy M Duperron, *Branch Mgr*
Steve Flate, *Technology*
Kevin Rush, *Planning*
EMP: 2832
SQ FT: 2,320,000
SALES (corp-wide): 160.3B **Publicly Held**
WEB: www.ford.com
SIC: 3714 3321 Motor vehicle parts & accessories; gray & ductile iron foundries
PA: Ford Motor Company
 1 American Rd
 Dearborn MI 48126
 313 322-3000

(G-2148)
GREENKOTE USA INC
6435 Eastland Rd (44142-1305)
PHONE..................................440 243-2865
Dwight Hutson, *Vice Pres*
Jaime Camacho, *Plant Mgr*
James Thomson, *CFO*
Mark Gore, *Director*
▲ **EMP:** 8
SALES (est): 1.3MM **Privately Held**
SIC: 3479 Coating of metals & formed products

(G-2149)
H&M MTAL STAMPING ASSEMBLY INC
5325 W 140th St (44142-1759)
PHONE..................................216 898-9030
Kathryn Mabin, *President*
Lenny Hull, *Mfg Staff*
EMP: 11
SALES (est): 1.3MM **Privately Held**
SIC: 3469 Stamping metal for the trade

(G-2150)
K-M-S INDUSTRIES INC
Also Called: K.M.S.
6519 Eastland Rd Ste 1 (44142-1347)
PHONE..................................440 243-6680
Gerald Korman, *President*
Richard Malone Jr, *Vice Pres*
Diane Malone, *Treasurer*
EMP: 30
SQ FT: 25,000
SALES (est): 5.6MM **Privately Held**
SIC: 3599 5531 7692 Machine shop, jobbing & repair; automotive parts; automotive accessories; welding repair

(G-2151)
LAKE ERIE GRAPHICS INC
5372 W 130th St (44142-1801)
PHONE..................................216 575-1333
James K Dietz, *President*
Brain Karlak, *Prdtn Mgr*
EMP: 30
SQ FT: 25,000
SALES (est): 6MM **Privately Held**
WEB: www.lakeeriegraphics.com
SIC: 2752 Commercial printing, offset

(G-2152)
MORSELICIOUS CUPCAKES
17341 Independence Ct (44142-3532)
PHONE..................................216 408-7508
Tina Filipkowski, *Principal*
EMP: 4 **EST:** 2010
SALES (est): 216.6K **Privately Held**
SIC: 2051 Bread, cake & related products

(G-2153)
NELSON AUTOMOTIVE LLC
6430 Eastland Rd Ste 3 (44142-1340)
PHONE..................................724 681-0975
David Smoot, *CEO*
EMP: 18
SALES (corp-wide): 10.5MM **Privately Held**
SIC: 3452 Bolts, nuts, rivets & washers
PA: Nelson Automotive, Llc
 835 Poquonnock Rd
 Groton CT 06340
 724 681-0975

(G-2154)
PRINTING CONNECTION INC
5221 W 161st St (44142-1606)
PHONE..................................216 898-4878
Frank Metro, *Principal*
EMP: 7 **EST:** 2009
SALES (est): 781.2K **Privately Held**
SIC: 2752 Commercial printing, offset

(G-2155)
ROLL-IN SAW INC
15851 Commerce Park Dr (44142-2020)
PHONE..................................216 459-9001
Donald Borman, *President*
Marcus Borman, *Vice Pres*
Charmaine Kizzer, *Manager*
▼ **EMP:** 10
SQ FT: 15,000
SALES: 1.5MM **Privately Held**
WEB: www.rollinsaw.com
SIC: 3541 Sawing & cutoff machines (metalworking machinery)

(G-2156)
SUPERCHARGER SYSTEMS INC
5300 W 140th St (44142-1758)
PHONE..................................216 676-5800
Timothy Fitch, *President*
EMP: 4
SQ FT: 22,000
SALES (est): 523.5K **Privately Held**
SIC: 5531 3714 Automotive parts; automotive accessories; motor vehicle engines & parts; axles, motor vehicle; drive shafts, motor vehicle; motor vehicle body components & frame

(G-2157)
VARIETY PRINTING
5707 Van Wert Ave (44142-2575)
PHONE..................................216 676-9815
Mike Fairley, *Principal*
EMP: 4
SALES (est): 326.2K **Privately Held**
SIC: 2752 Commercial printing, offset

(G-2158)
VECTOR MECHANICAL LLC
5240 Smith Rd (44142-1768)
PHONE..................................216 337-4042
Ildiko Sarai, *Mng Member*
Roland Sarai,
EMP: 8
SALES: 1MM **Privately Held**
SIC: 1711 1799 3564 Heating & air conditioning contractors; dock equipment installation, industrial; ventilating fans; industrial or commercial

(G-2159)
WESTSIDE SUPPLY CO INC
5010 W 140th St (44142-1754)
PHONE..................................216 267-9353
William Swann, *President*
EMP: 4
SQ FT: 5,000
SALES (est): 700.9K **Privately Held**
SIC: 3548 Welding apparatus

Brookville
Montgomery County

(G-2160)
ADMARK PRINTING INC
310 Sycamore St (45309-1731)
PHONE..................................937 833-5111
Patrick J Bruchs, *President*
EMP: 6
SQ FT: 15,000
SALES (est): 853.6K **Privately Held**
SIC: 2752 Commercial printing, lithographic

(G-2161)
ANTIQUE AUTO SHEET METAL INC
718 Albert Rd (45309-9202)
PHONE..................................937 833-4422
Raymond Gollahon, *President*
Pamela Knox, *General Mgr*
Donna Gollahon, *Corp Secy*
EMP: 40
SQ FT: 21,000
SALES (est): 6.1MM **Privately Held**
SIC: 3711 3444 3465 Motor vehicles & car bodies; sheet metalwork; body parts, automobile: stamped metal

(G-2162)
BROOKVILLE ROADSTER INC
718 Albert Rd (45309-9202)
PHONE..................................937 833-4605
Ray Gollahon, *President*
EMP: 40
SALES (est): 5.8MM **Privately Held**
WEB: www.brookvilleroadster.com
SIC: 3711 5013 Automobile assembly, including specialty automobiles; automotive supplies & parts

(G-2163)
BROOKVILLE STAR
14 Mulberry St (45309-1828)
P.O. Box 100 (45309-0100)
PHONE..................................937 833-2545
John Gordon, *President*
Julie Harrison, *Corp Secy*
Jean Gordon, *Vice Pres*
EMP: 5
SQ FT: 4,800
SALES (est): 346.7K **Privately Held**
SIC: 2711 2752 Newspapers: publishing only, not printed on site; commercial printing, lithographic

(G-2164)
CSA NUTRITION SERVICES INC
10 Nutrition Way (45309-8884)
P.O. Box 69 (45309-0069)
PHONE..................................800 257-3788
Richard J Chernesky, *Principal*
EMP: 10 **EST:** 1974
SALES (est): 717.7K
SALES (corp-wide): 114.7B **Privately Held**
SIC: 2048 Prepared feeds
PA: Cargill, Incorporated
 15407 Mcginty Rd W
 Wayzata MN 55391
 952 742-7575

(G-2165)
CYCLE ELECTRIC INC
8734 Dyton Grenville Pike (45309-9232)
P.O. Box 81, Englewood (45322-0081)
PHONE..................................937 884-7300
Karl Fahringer, *President*
Roxanne Fahringer, *Vice Pres*
EMP: 15
SQ FT: 8,000
SALES: 2MM **Privately Held**
SIC: 3694 Generators, automotive & aircraft; voltage regulators, automotive

(G-2166)
D M TOOL & PLASTICS INC
11150 Baltimore (45309)
PHONE..................................937 962-4140
Pat Meyer, *Manager*
EMP: 15
SALES (est): 868.5K
SALES (corp-wide): 4.2MM **Privately Held**
WEB: www.bulldogtools.com
SIC: 3089 3599 Injection molding of plastics; machine shop, jobbing & repair
PA: D M Tool & Plastics, Inc.
 4140 Us Route 40 E
 Lewisburg OH 45338
 937 962-4140

(G-2167)
DIGISOFT SYSTEMS CORPORATION
4520 Clayton Rd (45309-9332)
PHONE..................................937 833-5016
Gary E Brazier, *President*
Betty L Brazier, *Treasurer*
Christopher F Cowan, *Admin Sec*
EMP: 7
SQ FT: 600
SALES (est): 419K **Privately Held**
SIC: 7372 Business oriented computer software

(G-2168)
FLOW DRY TECHNOLOGY INC (HQ)
379 Albert Rd (45309-9247)
P.O. Box 190 (45309-0190)
PHONE..................................937 833-2161
Douglas Leconey, *President*
Marty Kilberg, *Plant Mgr*
Csaba Gonter, *Opers Mgr*
Tim Eustache, *Maint Spvr*
Bob Swearingen, *Maint Spvr*
▲ **EMP:** 111
SQ FT: 65,000
SALES: 33.5MM
SALES (corp-wide): 35.4MM **Privately Held**
SIC: 3053 2834 Gasket materials; druggists' preparations (pharmaceuticals)

GEOGRAPHIC SECTION
Brunswick - Medina County (G-2194)

PA: Argosy Investment Partners Iv, L.P.
950 W Valley Rd Ste 2900
Wayne PA 19087
610 971-9685

(G-2169)
FTD INVESTMENTS LLC
379 Albert Rd (45309-9247)
P.O. Box 190 (45309-0190)
PHONE.................................937 833-2161
Doug Le, *Principal*
EMP: 186 EST: 2006
SQ FT: 65,000
SALES (est): 16.9MM **Privately Held**
SIC: 3714 2834 Air conditioner parts, motor vehicle; druggists' preparations (pharmaceuticals)
PA: Blackstreet Capital Management, Llc
5425 Wisconsin Ave # 701
Chevy Chase MD 20815

(G-2170)
GREEN TOKAI CO LTD (DH)
Also Called: GTC
55 Robert Wright Dr (45309-1931)
PHONE.................................937 833-5444
Daniel Bowers, *President*
Harumitsu Yamamoto, *Corp Secy*
Mary McKay, *Production*
Shiva Deshmukh, *Engineer*
Shawn Hemmerich, *Engineer*
◆ **EMP:** 525
SQ FT: 246,000
SALES (est): 169.1MM
SALES (corp-wide): 1.6MM **Privately Held**
SIC: 3714 3069 Motor vehicle body components & frame; rubber automotive products
HQ: Tokai Kogyo Co.,Ltd.
4-1, Naganecho
Obu AIC 474-0
562 441-500

(G-2171)
HELLER ACQUISITIONS INC
Also Called: Life Time Embroidery
227 Market St (45309-1818)
PHONE.................................937 833-2676
Karen Heller, *President*
Tim Heller, *President*
EMP: 3
SALES (est): 100K **Privately Held**
SIC: 7389 2395 7336 Embroidering of advertising on shirts, etc.; embroidery & art needlework; silk screen design

(G-2172)
IMAGE PAVEMENT MAINTENANCE
425 Carr Dr (45309-1935)
P.O. Box 157 (45309-0157)
PHONE.................................937 833-9200
Michael Gartrell, *President*
EMP: 42
SALES (est): 3.9MM **Privately Held**
SIC: 1611 2951 1799 1771 Surfacing & paving; asphalt paving mixtures & blocks; parking lot maintenance; driveway contractor; sweeping service: road, airport, parking lot, etc.; tennis court construction

(G-2173)
LINK-O-MATIC COMPANY INC
13359 Brkville Pyrmont Rd (45309-9703)
P.O. Box 148, Richmond IN (47375-0148)
PHONE.................................765 962-1538
Doyle L Lincoln, *President*
Connie Lincoln, *Vice Pres*
EMP: 10 EST: 1951
SQ FT: 11,000
SALES (est): 750K **Privately Held**
SIC: 3589 5999 3564 Water treatment equipment, industrial; water purification equipment; blowers & fans

(G-2174)
MAR CHELE INC (PA)
Also Called: Pretzel Fest
18 Market St (45309-1815)
PHONE.................................937 833-3400
Brad Good, *President*
Michelle Good, *Vice Pres*
EMP: 5 EST: 1964
SQ FT: 1,500

SALES (est): 2.8MM **Privately Held**
SIC: 2052 Pretzels

(G-2175)
MARIETTA MARTIN MATERIALS INC
Also Called: Phillipsburg Quarry
9843 Dyton Grenville Pike (45309-8210)
PHONE.................................919 781-4550
Rodney Wolford, *Manager*
EMP: 10 **Publicly Held**
WEB: www.martinmarietta.com
SIC: 1422 Crushed & broken limestone
PA: Martin Marietta Materials Inc
2710 Wycliff Rd
Raleigh NC 27607

(G-2176)
MARIETTA MARTIN MATERIALS INC
Also Called: Martin Marietta Aggregates
9843 State Route 49 (45309-8210)
PHONE.................................937 884-5814
Rodney Wolford, *Manager*
EMP: 12 **Publicly Held**
WEB: www.martinmarietta.com
SIC: 1422 Limestones, ground
PA: Martin Marietta Materials Inc
2710 Wycliff Rd
Raleigh NC 27607

(G-2177)
MATERIALS ENGINEERING & DEV
11150 Bltmr Phllpsburg Rd (45309)
PHONE.................................937 884-5118
Tracy Slemker, *President*
Dennis Meyer, *Vice Pres*
Dave Thompson, *Shareholder*
EMP: 3
SQ FT: 35,000
SALES (est): 150K **Privately Held**
SIC: 3842 Prosthetic appliances; limbs, artificial

(G-2178)
MC GREGOR & ASSOCIATES INC
365 Carr Dr (45309-1921)
PHONE.................................937 833-6768
Larry McGregor, *President*
Don Wurst, *Vice Pres*
Mark McGregor, *Facilities Mgr*
Greg Wartinger, *Sales Dir*
Ernie Carter, *Marketing Staff*
▲ **EMP:** 120
SQ FT: 16,000
SALES (est): 14.5MM **Privately Held**
SIC: 3679 Electronic circuits

(G-2179)
NORGREN INC
Also Called: IMI Precision
325 Carr Dr (45309-1929)
PHONE.................................937 833-4033
Michael Vinski, *Branch Mgr*
EMP: 147
SALES (corp-wide): 2.3B **Privately Held**
WEB: www.norgren.com
SIC: 3625 Actuators, industrial
HQ: Norgren, Inc.
5400 S Delaware St
Littleton CO 80120
303 794-5000

(G-2180)
PARKER AIRCRAFT SALES
212 Church St (45309-1407)
PHONE.................................937 833-4820
Jeff Parker, *Owner*
EMP: 4
SALES (est): 250K **Privately Held**
WEB: www.parkeraircraft.com
SIC: 3724 Research & development on aircraft engines & parts

(G-2181)
PETERS CABINETRY
8766 N County Line Rd (45309-9511)
PHONE.................................937 884-7514
Gary L Peters, *Owner*
EMP: 3
SALES (est): 324.1K **Privately Held**
SIC: 2434 Wood kitchen cabinets

(G-2182)
PROVIMI NORTH AMERICA INC (HQ)
Also Called: Cargill Premix and Nutrition
10 Collective Way (45309-8878)
P.O. Box 69 (45309-0069)
PHONE.................................937 770-2400
Thomas Taylor, *President*
Terrence Quinlan, *President*
Scott Swenson, *Plant Mgr*
Mark Hemrick, *Safety Mgr*
Chad Nate, *Purch Dir*
◆ **EMP:** 253
SALES (est): 516.9MM
SALES (corp-wide): 114.7B **Privately Held**
WEB: www.vigortone.com
SIC: 5191 2048 Animal feeds; prepared feeds
PA: Cargill, Incorporated
15407 Mcginty Rd W
Wayzata MN 55391
952 742-7575

(G-2183)
R & J TOOL INC
10550 Upper Lewisburg (45309)
P.O. Box 118 (45309-0118)
PHONE.................................937 833-3200
Richard Rohrer, *President*
Marilyn K Rohrer, *Vice Pres*
EMP: 10
SQ FT: 5,000
SALES (est): 1MM **Privately Held**
SIC: 3545 Cutting tools for machine tools

Brownsville
Licking County

(G-2184)
MIDLAND OIL CO
14687 National Rd Se (43721)
P.O. Box 43 (43721-0043)
PHONE.................................740 787-2557
EMP: 3 EST: 1916
SALES (est): 60K **Privately Held**
SIC: 1311 Oil & Gas Producers

Brunswick
Medina County

(G-2185)
A G INDUSTRIES INC
2963 Interstate Pkwy (44212-4327)
PHONE.................................330 220-0050
Albert Gawel, *President*
EMP: 11
SQ FT: 4,000
SALES (est): 1.8MM **Privately Held**
SIC: 3544 Special dies, tools, jigs & fixtures

(G-2186)
A RAYMOND TINNERMAN INDUS INC (DH)
1060 W 130th St (44212-2316)
PHONE.................................330 220-5100
Dan Kerr, *President*
Dan Dolan, *COO*
Jim Stith, *Plant Mgr*
Melissa Krauth, *Materials Mgr*
David Stergiou, *Buyer*
EMP: 61 EST: 2009
SALES (est): 66.4MM **Privately Held**
WEB: www.tinnermanpalnut.com
SIC: 3965 Fasteners
HQ: A Raymond Gerance
113 Cours Berriat
Grenoble 38000
476 334-949

(G-2187)
ALTERNATIVE SURFACE GRINDING
Also Called: Ring Masters
1093 Industrial Pkwy N (44212-4319)
PHONE.................................330 273-3443
Kent Shutey, *President*
Dale Jarvis, *General Mgr*
EMP: 30

SALES (est): 2.7MM **Privately Held**
SIC: 3599 Machine shop, jobbing & repair

(G-2188)
AVION MANUFACTURING COMPANY
2950 Westway Dr Ste 106 (44212-5666)
PHONE.................................330 220-1989
Mark Ratliff, *President*
EMP: 4
SQ FT: 6,000
SALES (est): 650.8K **Privately Held**
WEB: www.avionmfg.com
SIC: 2851 3469 Paints & paint additives; machine parts, stamped or pressed metal

(G-2189)
AXESS INTERNATIONAL LLC
4641 Stag Thicket Ln (44212-5800)
PHONE.................................330 460-4840
Tawfik Kashou,
EMP: 5
SALES (est): 519.8K **Privately Held**
SIC: 2522 Office furniture, except wood

(G-2190)
B & B TROPHIES & AWARDS
1317 Pearl Rd (44212-2880)
PHONE.................................330 225-6193
Michael Sinclair, *Owner*
EMP: 4 EST: 1976
SALES (est): 263.5K **Privately Held**
SIC: 3914 5999 2796 Trophies; trophies & plaques; engraving on copper, steel, wood or rubber: printing plates

(G-2191)
BARANY JEWELRY INC
3702 Center Rd (44212-4429)
PHONE.................................330 220-4367
Elizabeth A Schlauch, *President*
Melvyn Schlauch, *Admin Sec*
EMP: 4 EST: 1969
SQ FT: 1,200
SALES (est): 400K **Privately Held**
WEB: www.baranyjewelers.com
SIC: 5944 7631 3911 Jewelry, precious stones & precious metals; jewelry repair services; jewelry, precious metal

(G-2192)
BEST PROCESS SOLUTIONS INC
1071 Industrial Pkwy N (44212-4319)
PHONE.................................330 220-1440
Mike Desalvo, *President*
EMP: 30
SALES (est): 4.3MM **Privately Held**
SIC: 3441 Fabricated structural metal

(G-2193)
BULLSEYE ACTIVEWEAR INC
2947 Nationwide Pkwy (44212-2365)
PHONE.................................330 220-1720
Susan Heiser, *President*
James J Heiser, *Vice Pres*
Jim Heiser, *Vice Pres*
Debbie Bode, *Bookkeeper*
EMP: 5
SALES (est): 460K **Privately Held**
WEB: www.bullseyeactivewear.com
SIC: 2759 Screen printing

(G-2194)
CCL LABEL INC
Also Called: CCL Design
2845 Center Rd (44212-2331)
PHONE.................................440 878-7000
Dean Discenza, *Mfg Mgr*
John Walsh, *Branch Mgr*
EMP: 40
SALES (corp-wide): 3.7B **Privately Held**
WEB: www.avery.com
SIC: 2672 3081 3497 2678 Adhesive papers, labels or tapes: from purchased material; gummed paper: made from purchased materials; coated paper, except photographic, carbon or abrasive; unsupported plastics film & sheet; metal foil & leaf; notebooks: made from purchased paper
HQ: Ccl Label, Inc.
161 Worcester Rd Ste 504
Framingham MA 01701
508 872-4511

Brunswick - Medina County (G-2195)

(G-2195)
CHALFANT MANUFACTURING COMPANY (DH)
50 Pearl Rd Ste 212 (44212-5704)
PHONE...................................330 273-3510
Gloria Slaga, *CEO*
John Slaga, *President*
F A Lennie, *Principal*
Carl W Schaefer, *Principal*
Richard C Schaefer, *Principal*
◆ **EMP:** 7
SQ FT: 55,000
SALES (est): 3.1MM
SALES (corp-wide): 267.9K **Privately Held**
SIC: 3643 Current-carrying wiring devices
HQ: Obo Bettermann Holding Gmbh & Co. Kg
  Huingser Ring 52
  Menden (Sauerland) 58710
  237 389-0

(G-2196)
COLUMBIA CHEMICAL CORPORATION
1000 Western Dr (44212-4330)
PHONE...................................330 225-3200
Brett Larick, *President*
Herbert H Geduld, *Principal*
D J Hudak, *Principal*
William E Rosenberg, *Principal*
◆ **EMP:** 22
SALES (est): 8.4MM **Privately Held**
WEB: www.columbiachemical.com
SIC: 2819 Zinc chloride; tin (stannic/stannous) compounds or salts, inorganic

(G-2197)
COMPONENT MFG & DESIGN
3121 Interstate Pkwy (44212-4329)
P.O. Box 845 (44212-0845)
PHONE...................................330 225-8080
Edward C Crist, *President*
EMP: 15
SQ FT: 12,000
SALES (est): 3.3MM **Privately Held**
WEB: www.cmd-tip.com
SIC: 3559 Plastics working machinery

(G-2198)
D C SYSTEMS INC
1251 Industrial Pkwy N (44212-2341)
PHONE...................................330 273-3030
Thomas E Schira, *President*
Katherine Schira, *Corp Secy*
EMP: 10
SQ FT: 22,600
SALES (est): 3.6MM **Privately Held**
SIC: 5063 3692 7699 3629 Batteries; batteries, dry cell; dry cell batteries, single or multiple cell; battery service & repair; battery chargers, rectifying or nonrotating

(G-2199)
DESTINY MANUFACTURING INC
2974 Interstate Pkwy (44212-4323)
PHONE...................................330 273-9000
Josef Schuessler, *President*
Reinhold Rock, *Corp Secy*
Bernard Karthan, *Vice Pres*
Michael Schuessler, *VP Sales*
▼ **EMP:** 35
SQ FT: 100,000
SALES (est): 12.4MM **Privately Held**
WEB: www.destinymfg.com
SIC: 3469 3399 Appliance parts, porcelain enameled; metal powders, pastes & flakes

(G-2200)
DIE-MENSION CORPORATION
3020 Nationwide Pkwy (44212-2360)
PHONE...................................330 273-5872
Karen Thompson, *President*
Rick Thompson, *Vice Pres*
▼ **EMP:** 12
SQ FT: 14,250
SALES (est): 1.1MM **Privately Held**
WEB: www.diemension.com
SIC: 3544 3469 Special dies & tools; metal stampings

(G-2201)
DYNAMIC BAR CODE SYSTEMS INC
3139 Ipswich Ct (44212-5645)
PHONE...................................330 220-5451
Bill Gregory Jr, *President*
Leslie Gregory, *Vice Pres*
EMP: 3
SQ FT: 1,300
SALES: 455K **Privately Held**
WEB: www.dynamicbarcode.com
SIC: 3565 Labeling Barcoding And Identification Equipment And Supplies

(G-2202)
ELECTRODUCT LLC
1126 Industrial Pkwy N (44212-5606)
PHONE...................................330 220-9300
EMP: 20
SQ FT: 20,000
SALES (est): 152.1K **Privately Held**
SIC: 3315 Mfg Steel Wire/Related Products

(G-2203)
FEDERAL-MOGUL VALVE TRAIN INTE
1035 Western Dr (44212-4331)
PHONE...................................330 460-5828
EMP: 10
SALES (corp-wide): 11.7B **Publicly Held**
SIC: 3592 Valves, engine
HQ: Federal-Mogul Valve Train International Llc
  27300 W 11 Mile Rd
  Southfield MI 48034
  248 354-7700

(G-2204)
FIRSTAR PRECISION CORPORATION
Also Called: Cnc Machine Shop
2867 Nationwide Pkwy (44212-2363)
PHONE...................................216 362-7888
Dave Tenny, *President*
David Tenny, *President*
Joe Tako, *Corp Secy*
Mark Lisi, *Traffic Mgr*
Darreyl Hansard, *Engineer*
EMP: 32 **EST:** 2000
SALES (est): 7.3MM **Privately Held**
WEB: www.firstarcnc.com
SIC: 3599 Machine shop, jobbing & repair

(G-2205)
FORMATECH INC
3024 Interstate Pkwy (44212-4324)
PHONE...................................330 273-2800
Craig F Wahl, *President*
Joseph Thuener, *General Mgr*
Steve Corcoran, *Prdtn Mgr*
Steve Lampshire, *Prdtn Mgr*
Brett Garner, *Accounts Exec*
▲ **EMP:** 20
SALES (est): 4.2MM **Privately Held**
WEB: www.formatechexhibits.com
SIC: 2542 2541 Counters or counter display cases: except wood; counters or counter display cases, wood

(G-2206)
FREE BIRD PUBLICATIONS LTD
1410 S Carptr Rd Apt 238 (44212)
PHONE...................................216 673-0229
Chantelle Drake, *CEO*
EMP: 3
SALES: 10K **Privately Held**
SIC: 2741 Miscellaneous publishing

(G-2207)
FREMAR INDUSTRIES INC
2808 Westway Dr (44212-5656)
PHONE...................................330 220-3700
Marcus Bauman, *CEO*
Donald Brandt, *President*
▼ **EMP:** 30
SQ FT: 26,000
SALES (est): 5.8MM **Privately Held**
SIC: 3544 Dies, plastics forming; forms (molds), for foundry & plastics working machinery

(G-2208)
GALLEY PRINTING INC
Also Called: Galley Printing Company
2892 Westway Dr (44212-5656)
PHONE...................................330 220-5577
Richard Stitch, *CEO*
Barbara Stitch, *Corp Secy*
EMP: 25
SALES (est): 5.6MM **Privately Held**
SIC: 2752 Commercial printing, offset

(G-2209)
GEM INSTRUMENT CO
2832 Nationwide Pkwy (44212-2362)
P.O. Box 830 (44212-0830)
PHONE...................................330 273-6117
Spiras Arfaras, *President*
Joan Arfaras, *Vice Pres*
EMP: 15
SQ FT: 10,000
SALES (est): 2.3MM **Privately Held**
WEB: www.gem-instrument.com
SIC: 3823 3829 Digital displays of process variables; measuring & controlling devices

(G-2210)
GLOBAL SPECIALTIES INC
2950 Westway Dr Ste 110 (44212-5666)
PHONE...................................800 338-0814
Clyde Kanz, *Principal*
EMP: 6
SALES (est): 42.1K **Privately Held**
SIC: 3965 Fasteners

(G-2211)
GRIND-ALL CORPORATION
1113 Industrial Pkwy N (44212-2371)
PHONE...................................330 220-1600
Henry Matousek Sr, *President*
Mary Matousek, *Corp Secy*
EMP: 48
SALES (est): 9MM **Privately Held**
WEB: www.grindall.com
SIC: 3541 Grinding machines, metalworking; honing & lapping machines

(G-2212)
GROENEVELD ATLANTIC SOUTH
1130 Industrial Pkwy N # 7 (44212-5605)
PHONE...................................330 225-4949
Yan Isscs, *President*
Glenn Isscs, *President*
▲ **EMP:** 11
SALES (est): 1.2MM **Privately Held**
WEB: www.groeneveldusa.com
SIC: 3569 Lubricating equipment

(G-2213)
HYDRA-TEC INC
3027 Nationwide Pkwy (44212-2361)
PHONE...................................330 225-8797
Karl Holler, *President*
Simon J Holler, *Vice Pres*
Mary E Holler, *Treasurer*
Celeste Holler, *Admin Sec*
EMP: 4
SQ FT: 2,000
SALES (est): 475.9K **Privately Held**
SIC: 3498 Tube fabricating (contract bending & shaping)

(G-2214)
ID IMAGES INC
2991 Interstate Pkwy (44212-4327)
PHONE...................................330 220-7300
Dick Yisha, *Owner*
EMP: 3
SALES (est): 94.5K **Privately Held**
SIC: 3577 Bar code (magnetic ink) printers

(G-2215)
ID IMAGES LLC (PA)
2991 Interstate Pkwy (44212-4327)
PHONE...................................330 220-7300
Brian Gale, *President*
▲ **EMP:** 65
SQ FT: 24,200
SALES (est): 26.1MM **Privately Held**
WEB: www.idimages.com
SIC: 2672 Adhesive papers, labels or tapes: from purchased material

(G-2216)
INTERNATIONAL MACHINING INC
2885 Nationwide Pkwy (44212-4314)
PHONE...................................330 225-1963
John Strobel, *President*
Bruce Sherman, *Vice Pres*
Ryan Strobel, *Vice Pres*
EMP: 40
SQ FT: 26,000
SALES (est): 7.9MM **Privately Held**
WEB: www.imimachining.com
SIC: 3599 Machine shop, jobbing & repair

(G-2217)
KOSTER CROP TESTER INC
Also Called: Koster Moisture Tester
3077 Nationwide Pkwy (44212-2361)
PHONE...................................330 220-2116
Karl Faschian, *CEO*
Ludmilla Faschian, *President*
EMP: 4 **EST:** 1961
SQ FT: 1,440
SALES: 250K **Privately Held**
SIC: 3523 Farm machinery & equipment

(G-2218)
L & R RACING INC
Also Called: Drr
900 Theora Dr (44212-5650)
PHONE...................................330 220-3102
Louis Allan, *CEO*
▲ **EMP:** 20
SQ FT: 25,000
SALES (est): 4.6MM **Privately Held**
WEB: www.drrinc.com
SIC: 5012 5013 3799 Motorcycles; motorcycle parts; recreational vehicles; all terrain vehicles (ATV)

(G-2219)
MACK INDUSTRIES INC (PA)
Also Called: Mack Transport
1321 Industrial Pkwy N # 500 (44212-6358)
PHONE...................................330 460-7005
Betsy Mack-Nespeca, *President*
Betsy Mack Nespeca, *Corp Secy*
EMP: 1 **EST:** 1932
SQ FT: 40,000
SALES (est): 170.9MM **Privately Held**
WEB: www.mackconcrete.com
SIC: 3272 1771 Burial vaults, concrete or precast terrazzo; septic tanks, concrete; manhole covers or frames, concrete; concrete work

(G-2220)
MARTIN ALLEN TRAILER LLC
Also Called: AMG Trailer and Equipment
2888 Nationwide Pkwy (44212-2362)
PHONE...................................330 942-0217
Dean Martin, *President*
EMP: 4
SALES (est): 105.5K **Privately Held**
SIC: 3715 5084 Truck trailers; trailers, industrial

(G-2221)
MURPHY TRACTOR & EQP CO INC
Also Called: John Deere Authorized Dealer
1240 Industrial Rd Pkwy N (44212)
PHONE...................................330 220-4999
Bob Cumberledge, *Service Mgr*
EMP: 8 **Privately Held**
SIC: 3531 5082 Construction machinery; construction & mining machinery
HQ: Murphy Tractor & Equipment Co., Inc.
  5375 N Deere Rd
  Park City KS 67219
  855 246-9124

(G-2222)
NICHOLAS PRESS SALES LLC
3077 Nationwide Pkwy (44212-2361)
PHONE...................................440 652-6604
Joyce Nicholas, *Principal*
EMP: 4
SALES (est): 280K **Privately Held**
SIC: 3469 Metal stampings

(G-2223)
PACIFIC TOOL & DIE CO
1035 Western Dr (44212-4331)
PHONE 330 273-7363
Charles W Smith, *President*
Jeffrey Smith, *Vice Pres*
EMP: 14 **EST:** 1959
SQ FT: 20,000
SALES (est): 3MM **Privately Held**
SIC: 3544 Dies & die holders for metal cutting, forming, die casting; jigs & fixtures

(G-2224)
PHILPOTT INDUS PLAS ENTPS LTD
Also Called: Philpott Intl Entps Ltd
1010 Industrial Pkwy N (44212-4318)
PHONE 330 225-3344
Russell Schabel, *Manager*
EMP: 7
SALES (est): 558.2K
SALES (corp-wide): 9MM **Privately Held**
SIC: 3089 Plastic containers, except foam; plastic hardware & building products; washers, plastic
HQ: Philpott Rubber Llc
1010 Industrial Pkwy N
Brunswick OH 44212
330 225-3344

(G-2225)
PHILPOTT RUBBER LLC (HQ)
Also Called: Philpott Rubber Company
1010 Industrial Pkwy N (44212-4318)
PHONE 330 225-3344
Mike Baach, *President*
David Ferrell, *Vice Pres*
Jeffrey Rog, *Vice Pres*
Gregory C Stafford, *Vice Pres*
Russell E Schabel, *CFO*
▲ **EMP:** 28 **EST:** 1889
SQ FT: 30,000
SALES (est): 9MM **Privately Held**
WEB: www.philpottrubber.com
SIC: 3069 Medical sundries, rubber
PA: Philpott Solutions Group Inc.
1010 Industrial Pkwy N
Brunswick OH 44212
330 225-3344

(G-2226)
POMACON INC
2996 Interstate Pkwy (44212-4323)
PHONE 330 273-1576
Rodger Post, *President*
EMP: 15
SQ FT: 14,000
SALES (est): 3.5MM **Privately Held**
WEB: www.pomacon.com
SIC: 3535 5084 5999 Conveyors & conveying equipment; conveyor systems; alcoholic beverage making equipment & supplies

(G-2227)
POSITOOL TECHNOLOGIES INC
2985 Nationwide Pkwy (44212-2365)
PHONE 330 220-4002
Anthony Scardigli, *President*
EMP: 5
SQ FT: 2,500
SALES (est): 870K **Privately Held**
WEB: www.positool.com
SIC: 3544 3089 Special dies & tools; injection molding of plastics

(G-2228)
PRECISION EQUIPMENT LLC
1460 W 130th St Ste C (44212-2400)
PHONE 330 220-7600
John H Nickerson III,
EMP: 3
SALES (est): 336.5K **Privately Held**
SIC: 5046 3537 Commercial equipment; forklift trucks

(G-2229)
PRIME WOOD CRAFT INC (HQ)
Also Called: P W C
1120 W 130th St (44212-2317)
P.O. Box 807, West Salem (44287-0807)
PHONE 216 738-2222
Ansir Junaid, *President*
Ijaz SA, *President*
Robert Campbell, *Owner*
Ahad Shamsi, *Engineer*
Ej Hughes, *Natl Sales Mgr*
▲ **EMP:** 48
SQ FT: 60,000
SALES (est): 11.9MM **Privately Held**
WEB: www.primewoodcraft.com
SIC: 2448 Pallets, wood
PA: I.H.S. Enterprise, Inc.
5755 Granger Rd Ste 905
Independence OH 44131
216 588-9078

(G-2230)
PRISM POWDER COATINGS LTD
2890 Carquest Dr (44212-4352)
PHONE 330 225-5626
Alex Asour, *President*
Livio Agnoletto, *Vice Pres*
Mike Kowalsky, *Technical Mgr*
▲ **EMP:** 35
SQ FT: 4,000
SALES (est): 5.8MM **Privately Held**
SIC: 2851 Paints & allied products

(G-2231)
QUAD FLUID DYNAMICS INC
2826 Westway Dr (44212-5656)
P.O. Box 429 (44212-0429)
PHONE 330 220-3005
Kenneth H Oleksiak, *President*
Barbara Oleksiak, *Vice Pres*
David E Williams, *Vice Pres*
EMP: 10
SQ FT: 10,000
SALES (est): 4.2MM **Privately Held**
WEB: www.quadfluiddynamics.com
SIC: 5085 3594 7699 Valves & fittings; fluid power pumps & motors; hydraulic equipment repair

(G-2232)
RAINBOW CULTURED MARBLE
1442 W 130th St (44212-2320)
PHONE 330 225-3400
Carrie Fuller, *Principal*
Dale Boss, *Principal*
EMP: 13
SQ FT: 6,000
SALES (est): 1.7MM **Privately Held**
SIC: 3281 Bathroom fixtures, cut stone

(G-2233)
RBOOG INDUSTRIES LLC
Also Called: Slicksaw.com
3132 Ipswich Ct (44212-5644)
PHONE 330 350-0396
Richard Barber,
EMP: 4
SALES: 20K **Privately Held**
SIC: 3546 Saws & sawing equipment

(G-2234)
REED MACHINERY INC
629 Marsh Way (44212-5522)
PHONE 330 220-6668
John F Peterson, *Branch Mgr*
EMP: 3
SALES (est): 259.4K
SALES (corp-wide): 3.5MM **Privately Held**
SIC: 3545 Threading tools (machine tool accessories)
PA: Reed Machinery, Inc
10a New Bond St
Worcester MA 01606
508 595-9090

(G-2235)
ROCKSTEDT TOOL & DIE INC
2974 Interstate Pkwy (44212-4323)
PHONE 330 273-9000
Josef Schuessler, *President*
Bernard Karthan, *Vice Pres*
Joe Schuessler, *CTO*
Sharon Mueller, *Admin Asst*
EMP: 14
SQ FT: 100,000
SALES (est): 2.4MM **Privately Held**
WEB: www.rockstedt.com
SIC: 3544 Special dies & tools

(G-2236)
RONLEN INDUSTRIES INC
2809 Nationwide Pkwy (44212-2363)
PHONE 330 273-6468
Leonard Lutch, *President*
Ron Bryant, *Vice Pres*
Greg Lutch, *Vice Pres*
Kimberly Bowers, *Executive*
EMP: 26
SQ FT: 25,000
SALES (est): 7.9MM **Privately Held**
WEB: www.ronlen.com
SIC: 3469 3544 Stamping metal for the trade; special dies & tools

(G-2237)
SAUSAGE SHOPPE
1728 S Carpenter Rd (44212-3752)
PHONE 216 351-5213
Norm Heinle, *Owner*
Carol Heinle, *Co-Owner*
EMP: 4
SQ FT: 1,600
SALES (est): 310.6K **Privately Held**
WEB: www.sausageshoppe.com
SIC: 2013 5812 Sausages from purchased meat; eating places

(G-2238)
SCHERBA INDUSTRIES INC
Also Called: Inflatable Images
2880 Interstate Pkwy (44212-4322)
PHONE 330 273-3200
Robert J Scherba, *President*
Kerry Esposito, *General Mgr*
David M Scherba, *Vice Pres*
Emily Kuharcik, *Sales Staff*
Tammy Schebek, *Marketing Staff*
▲ **EMP:** 100
SQ FT: 63,000
SALES (est): 21.2MM **Privately Held**
WEB: www.inflatableimages.com
SIC: 3081 3069 2394 Vinyl film & sheet; balloons, advertising & toy: rubber; canvas & related products

(G-2239)
SITEONE LANDSCAPE SUPPLY LLC
2925 Interstate Pkwy (44212-4327)
PHONE 330 220-8691
Dan Codeluppi, *Manager*
EMP: 4
SALES (corp-wide): 2.1B **Publicly Held**
SIC: 5083 3494 0781 Lawn & garden machinery & equipment; sprinkler systems, field; landscape services
HQ: Siteone Landscape Supply, Llc
300 Colonial Center Pkwy # 600
Roswell GA 30076
770 255-2100

(G-2240)
STOPOL EQUIPMENT SALES LLC
1321 Industrial Pkwy N # 600 (44212-6358)
PHONE 440 499-0030
Bob Happ, *CFO*
Randall Frey, *Accounts Exec*
EMP: 3
SALES (est): 546.1K **Privately Held**
SIC: 2821 3089 Molding compounds, plastics; injection molding of plastics

(G-2241)
STRESS CON INDUSTRIES INC (PA)
1321 Industrial Pkwy N # 500 (44212-6358)
PHONE 586 731-1628
Dennis Declerk, *President*
EMP: 4
SALES (est): 112.8MM **Privately Held**
WEB: www.stressconindustries.com
SIC: 3272 Precast terrazo or concrete products

(G-2242)
SURTEC INC
3097 Interstate Pkwy (44212-4328)
PHONE 440 239-9710
Karl Lindemann, *CEO*
Ray Lindemann, *President*
Nabil Zaki, *Vice Pres*
Carlos Chaves, *Info Tech Mgr*
▲ **EMP:** 5
SALES (est): 1.3MM
SALES (corp-wide): 11B **Privately Held**
WEB: www.cstplating.com
SIC: 2899 Plating compounds
PA: Freudenberg & Co. Kg
Hohnerweg 2-4
Weinheim 69469
620 180-0

(G-2243)
SYMATIC INC
Also Called: Ancom Business Products
2831 Center Rd (44212-2331)
PHONE 330 225-1510
Walter H Tanner, *President*
Cindy Holton, *Vice Pres*
Nancy Hanshue, *Sales Staff*
Michelle McDonald, *Manager*
EMP: 35
SALES (est): 5.4MM **Privately Held**
WEB: www.ancom-filing.com
SIC: 3579 5044 2541 2521 Paper handling machines; office equipment; wood partitions & fixtures; wood office furniture

(G-2244)
TECHNICAL TOOL & GAUGE INC
2914 Westway Dr (44212-5658)
PHONE 330 273-1778
Jeff Butcher, *Owner*
EMP: 17
SALES (est): 2.7MM **Privately Held**
SIC: 3599 Machine shop, jobbing & repair

(G-2245)
TIGER CAT FURNITURE
294 Marks Rd (44212-1042)
PHONE 330 220-7232
Audrey F Bledsoe, *Owner*
Lloyd Bledsoe, *Co-Owner*
EMP: 8 **EST:** 1999
SALES (est): 150K **Privately Held**
WEB: www.therustydog.com
SIC: 3999 Novelties, bric-a-brac & hobby kits

(G-2246)
TINNERMAN PALNUT ENGINEERED PR
1060 W 130th St (44212-2316)
PHONE 330 220-5100
Jim Finley, *Principal*
Dan Dolan, *COO*
Justin McCullah, *Mfg Mgr*
Amy Jacobs, *Marketing Mgr*
Michael Brookshire, *Analyst*
◆ **EMP:** 22
SALES (est): 3MM **Privately Held**
SIC: 3452 Screws, metal

(G-2247)
TURF CARE SUPPLY CORP (HQ)
50 Pearl Rd Ste 200 (44212-5703)
PHONE 877 220-1014
William Milowitz, *President*
Mark Mangan, *COO*
Frank Vetter, *COO*
Jeffrey Bailey, *CFO*
Richard C Nihei, *CFO*
▼ **EMP:** 256
SQ FT: 5,000
SALES (est): 177.9MM **Privately Held**
WEB: www.turfcaresupply.com
SIC: 2873 Nitrogenous fertilizers

(G-2248)
VERSATILE AUTOMATION TECH LTD
Also Called: VA Technology
2853 Westway Dr (44212-5657)
PHONE 330 220-2600
James Byrne, *President*
▲ **EMP:** 6
SQ FT: 1,300
SALES (est): 1MM
SALES (corp-wide): 23.1MM **Privately Held**
SIC: 3569 5084 Robots, assembly line: industrial & commercial; robots, industrial
PA: V A Technology Limited
Halesfield 9
Telford TF7 4
195 258-5252

(G-2249)
WENTWORTH SOLUTIONS
2868 Westway Dr Ste B (44212-5661)
P.O. Box 283, Hinckley (44233-0283)
PHONE 440 212-7696
Sean Spigtle, *President*

Brunswick - Medina County (G-2250)

Jessica Spittle, *Admin Sec*
EMP: 10
SQ FT: 1,000
SALES (est): 2MM **Privately Held**
SIC: 7371 7372 Computer software writing services; prepackaged software; application computer software

(G-2250)
WENTWORTH TECHNOLOGIES LLC
2868 Westway Dr (44212-5660)
P.O. Box 283, Hinckley (44233-0283)
PHONE....................440 212-7696
Gregory Spittle, *Partner*
Sean Spittle, *Partner*
EMP: 12
SQ FT: 1,800
SALES (est): 503.2K **Privately Held**
SIC: 7379 7372 ; prepackaged software; business oriented computer software; application computer software

(G-2251)
WIFI-PLUS INC
2950 Westway Dr Ste 101 (44212-5666)
PHONE....................877 838-4195
Allen Higgins, *Managing Prtnr*
Dennis Broderick, *Partner*
Jack Nilsson, *Partner*
EMP: 6
SQ FT: 6,000
SALES (est): 1MM **Privately Held**
WEB: www.wifi-plus.com
SIC: 5063 3679 Antennas, receiving, satellite dishes; antennas, receiving

(G-2252)
WIRICK PRESS INC
Also Called: Printing Partners
839 Pearl Rd (44212-2559)
PHONE....................330 273-3488
Carl Wirick, *President*
Jerry Wirick, *Vice Pres*
EMP: 4
SQ FT: 7,000
SALES (est): 605.5K **Privately Held**
SIC: 2752 2759 Commercial printing, offset; letterpress printing; envelopes: printing; announcements: engraved; card printing & engraving, except greeting

(G-2253)
WM SOFTWARE INC
3660 Center Rd Ste 371 (44212-3620)
PHONE....................330 558-0501
Micheal Monasterio, *President*
EMP: 10
SALES (est): 1.1MM **Privately Held**
SIC: 3695 Computer software tape & disks: blank, rigid & floppy

(G-2254)
X-PRESS TOOL INC
2845 Interstate Pkwy (44212-4326)
PHONE....................330 225-8748
Bob Koch, *President*
EMP: 20
SALES (est): 436.4K **Privately Held**
SIC: 7999 3546 3545 Golf services & professionals; power-driven handtools; machine tool accessories
PA: Blackhawk Industrial Distribution, Inc.
1501 Sw Expressway Dr
Broken Arrow OK 74012

(G-2255)
YOST FOODS INC
Also Called: Food Basics
2795 Westway Dr (44212-5708)
P.O. Box 386, Hinckley (44233-0386)
PHONE....................330 273-4420
William Yost, *President*
Carol Yost, *Treasurer*
EMP: 5
SQ FT: 1,500
SALES (est): 1.1MM **Privately Held**
WEB: www.yostfoods.com
SIC: 2099 Food preparations

(G-2256)
ZEUS ELECTRONICS LLC
5083 Creekside Blvd (44212-1957)
PHONE....................330 220-1571
Dan Lion, *Principal*
Patros Gatis,
Dionysios Gatis,
Stamatia Gatis,
EMP: 4
SALES: 50K **Privately Held**
SIC: 3679 Electronic circuits

Bryan
Williams County

(G-2257)
A-STAMP INDUSTRIES LLC
633 Commerce Dr (43506-9197)
PHONE....................419 633-0451
David Vondeylen, *Mng Member*
▲ **EMP:** 92
SQ FT: 80,000
SALES (est): 20MM **Privately Held**
WEB: www.a-stamp.com
SIC: 3469 Stamping metal for the trade

(G-2258)
AIRMATE COMPANY
16280 County Road D (43506-9552)
PHONE....................419 636-3184
Carol Schreder Czech, *President*
Carol Schreder, *President*
Neil Oberlin, *Vice Pres*
Ed Dewitt, *Production*
Todd Moyer, *Purch Agent*
▲ **EMP:** 57
SQ FT: 24,000
SALES (est): 6.8MM **Privately Held**
WEB: www.airmatecompany.com
SIC: 3823 7311 Industrial instrmnts msrmnt display/control process variable; advertising consultant

(G-2259)
ALLIED MOULDED PRODUCTS INC (PA)
222 N Union St (43506-1450)
PHONE....................419 636-4217
Aaron T Herman, *President*
Karen Sims, *Senior Buyer*
Kathy Mohler, *Buyer*
Ben Bucklew, *CFO*
Terry Buntain, *Controller*
◆ **EMP:** 189 **EST:** 1958
SQ FT: 110,000
SALES: 62MM **Privately Held**
WEB: www.alliedmoulded.com
SIC: 3089 3699 Injection molded finished plastic products; electrical equipment & supplies

(G-2260)
ALLIED MOULDED PRODUCTS INC
1117 E High St (43506-9484)
PHONE....................419 636-4217
Aaron T Herman, *President*
EMP: 5
SALES (corp-wide): 62MM **Privately Held**
SIC: 3089 Injection molded finished plastic products
PA: Allied Moulded Products, Inc.
222 N Union St
Bryan OH 43506
419 636-4217

(G-2261)
ALLIED MOULDED PRODUCTS INC
2103 Industrial Dr (43506-8773)
PHONE....................419 636-4217
Aaron T Herman, *President*
EMP: 6
SALES (corp-wide): 62MM **Privately Held**
SIC: 3089 Injection molded finished plastic products
PA: Allied Moulded Products, Inc.
222 N Union St
Bryan OH 43506
419 636-4217

(G-2262)
ALTENLOH BRINCK & CO INC
2105 County Road 12c (43506-8301)
PHONE....................419 636-6715
Brian Roth, *President*
D Kip Winzeler, *CFO*
▲ **EMP:** 135 **EST:** 1981
SQ FT: 200,000
SALES (est): 33.4MM
SALES (corp-wide): 370.6MM **Privately Held**
WEB: www.trufast.com
SIC: 3452 Pins
HQ: Altenloh, Brinck & Co. Us, Inc.
2105 Williams Co Rd 12 C
Bryan OH 43506

(G-2263)
ALTENLOH BRINCK & CO US INC (DH)
Also Called: Trufast
2105 Williams Co Rd 12 C (43506-8301)
PHONE....................419 636-6715
Brian Roth, *President*
Kip Winzeler, *CFO*
▲ **EMP:** 80
SALES (est): 44.6MM
SALES (corp-wide): 370.6MM **Privately Held**
SIC: 3452 Screws, metal
HQ: Abc Finanzierungs- Und Beteiligungs Gmbh
Kolner Str. 71-77
Ennepetal
233 379-90

(G-2264)
ANDERSON & VREELAND INC
Also Called: Anderson Vreeland Midwest
15348 State Rte 127 E (43506)
P.O. Box 527 (43506-0527)
PHONE....................419 636-5002
Scott Gordon, *Vice Pres*
Graig Sanderson, *Buyer*
Gary Goll, *Purchasing*
Keith Vreeland, *Engineer*
Lauren Wenz, *Finance Mgr*
EMP: 30
SQ FT: 3,000
SALES (corp-wide): 73.7MM **Privately Held**
WEB: www.andersonvreeland.com
SIC: 5084 3555 3542 2796 Printing trades machinery, equipment & supplies; printing trades machinery; machine tools, metal forming type; platemaking services
PA: Anderson & Vreeland, Inc.
8 Evans St
Fairfield NJ 07004
973 227-2270

(G-2265)
ARROW TRU-LINE INC
720 E Perry St (43506-2223)
PHONE....................419 636-7013
Curtis Anderson, *Ch of Bd*
EMP: 100
SALES (corp-wide): 35.5MM **Privately Held**
SIC: 3429 3469 3449 Builders' hardware; metal stampings; miscellaneous metalwork
PA: Arrow Tru-Line, Inc.
2211 S Defiance St
Archbold OH 43502
419 446-2785

(G-2266)
AUTOCOAT
1900 Progress Dr (43506-9323)
PHONE....................419 636-3830
Roy Rodriguez, *Principal*
EMP: 5
SALES (est): 668K **Privately Held**
SIC: 3471 Finishing, metals or formed products

(G-2267)
BARD MANUFACTURING COMPANY INC (PA)
1914 Randolph Dr (43506-2253)
P.O. Box 607 (43506-0607)
PHONE....................419 636-1194
William Steel, *President*
Paul Matz, *Vice Pres*
Jeff Newton, *Controller*
Charles Fox, *Human Res Mgr*
▼ **EMP:** 99
SALES (est): 29.4MM **Privately Held**
SIC: 3585 Refrigeration & heating equipment

(G-2268)
BEAN COUNTER LLC
1210 W High St Ste C (43506-3521)
PHONE....................419 636-0705
Shannon Lyman, *Principal*
EMP: 3
SALES (est): 230.7K **Privately Held**
SIC: 3131 Counters

(G-2269)
BMC HOLDINGS INC (PA)
1914 Randolph Dr (43506-2253)
P.O. Box 607 (43506-0607)
PHONE....................419 636-1194
Richard O Bard, *President*
James R Bard, *COO*
Paul Matz, *Treasurer*
EMP: 2 **EST:** 1914
SQ FT: 200,000
SALES (est): 51.5MM **Privately Held**
WEB: www.bardhvac.com
SIC: 3433 3585 Gas burners, domestic; gas burners, industrial; oil burners, domestic or industrial; air conditioning units, complete: domestic or industrial; heat pumps, electric

(G-2270)
BP PRODUCTS NORTH AMERICA INC
Also Called: B P Exploration
710 E Wilson St (43506-1847)
P.O. Box 426 (43506-0426)
PHONE....................419 636-2249
Larry Thiel, *Manager*
EMP: 5
SQ FT: 400
SALES (corp-wide): 240.2B **Privately Held**
WEB: www.bpproductsnorthamerica.com
SIC: 2911 Petroleum refining
HQ: Bp Products North America Inc.
501 Westlake Park Blvd
Houston TX 77079
281 366-2000

(G-2271)
BRICKER PLATING INC
612 E Edgerton St (43506-1408)
PHONE....................419 636-1990
Tim Bricker, *President*
EMP: 6 **EST:** 1950
SQ FT: 4,800
SALES: 300K **Privately Held**
SIC: 3471 Electroplating of metals or formed products; polishing, metals or formed products

(G-2272)
BRYAN METALS LLC (DH)
1103 S Main St (43506-2440)
PHONE....................419 636-4571
Tony Norden, *Mng Member*
▲ **EMP:** 5 **EST:** 1955
SQ FT: 63,000
SALES (est): 21.8MM **Publicly Held**
SIC: 3331 3351 Blocks, copper; copper & copper alloy sheet, strip, plate & products

(G-2273)
BRYAN PACKAGING INC
620 E Perry St (43506-2221)
PHONE....................419 636-2600
Leo Deiger, *President*
Tim Haynes, *Sales Dir*
EMP: 14
SALES (est): 3.4MM
SALES (corp-wide): 35.6MM **Privately Held**
SIC: 2653 Boxes, corrugated: made from purchased materials
PA: Pro-Pak Industries, Inc.
1125 Ford St
Maumee OH 43537
419 729-0751

(G-2274)
BRYAN PUBLISHING COMPANY (PA)
Also Called: County Line
127 S Walnut St (43506-1718)
PHONE....................419 636-1111
Christopher Cullis, *President*
Tom Voight, *Vice Pres*
Elizabeth Cullis, *Admin Sec*

GEOGRAPHIC SECTION
Bryan - Williams County (G-2300)

EMP: 80
SQ FT: 12,000
SALES: 4MM **Privately Held**
WEB: www.bryantimes.com
SIC: 2711 Newspapers, publishing & printing

(G-2275)
C E ELECTRONICS INC
2107 Industrial Dr (43506-8773)
PHONE.............................419 636-6705
Garry L Courtney, *President*
Thomas Manges, *Engineer*
Robert Taylor, *Engineer*
Kevin Schroer, *Electrical Engi*
Ken Grohowski, *Sales Mgr*
EMP: 85 **EST:** 1980
SALES (est): 22.5MM **Privately Held**
WEB: www.ceelectronics.com
SIC: 3679 3672 Electronic circuits; printed circuit boards

(G-2276)
CONTINENTAL TIRE AMERICAS LLC
Also Called: Ctna Tire Plant
927 S Union Bryan (43506)
PHONE.............................419 633-4221
Steve Newell, *Branch Mgr*
EMP: 5
SALES (corp-wide): 50.8B **Privately Held**
WEB: www.continentaltire.com
SIC: 3011 Tires & inner tubes
HQ: Continental Tire The Americas, Llc
  1830 Macmillan Park Dr
  Fort Mill SC 29707
  800 847-3349

(G-2277)
COTTON PICKIN TEES & CAPS
215 W Bryan St (43506-1241)
PHONE.............................419 636-3595
June Flemming, *Partner*
Ernie Flemming, *Partner*
EMP: 4
SQ FT: 2,500
SALES (est): 250K **Privately Held**
SIC: 2759 5699 5651 Imprinting; T-shirts, custom printed; family clothing stores

(G-2278)
DAAVLIN DISTRIBUTING CO
205 W Bement St (43506-1264)
P.O. Box 626 (43506-0626)
PHONE.............................419 636-6304
David W Swanson, *President*
Traci Hartman, *Vice Pres*
Tracey McKelvey, *Vice Pres*
Sandrine Woolace, *Vice Pres*
Irma Moeller, *Opers Mgr*
▼ **EMP:** 48
SQ FT: 24,000
SALES (est): 9.9MM **Privately Held**
WEB: www.daavlin.com
SIC: 3841 Diagnostic apparatus, medical

(G-2279)
DG CUSTOM MACHINE
840 E Edgerton St (43506-1412)
PHONE.............................419 636-8059
Dave Greutman, *Owner*
EMP: 3
SALES (est): 295.2K **Privately Held**
SIC: 3599 Machine shop, jobbing & repair

(G-2280)
FAYETTE INDUSTRIAL COATINGS
533 Commerce Dr Ste A (43506-7809)
PHONE.............................419 636-1773
EMP: 25
SQ FT: 60,000
SALES (est): 1.8MM **Privately Held**
SIC: 3479 Parts Painting

(G-2281)
FLUID EQUIPMENT CORP
7671 County Road E 7g (43506-9118)
P.O. Box 689 (43506-0689)
PHONE.............................419 636-0777
Edward T Ward, *President*
EMP: 7

SALES (est): 700.2K **Privately Held**
SIC: 8748 8711 3823 Systems engineering consultant, ex. computer or professional; consulting engineer; fluidic devices, circuits & systems for process control

(G-2282)
G&M MEDIA PACKAGING INC
1 Toy St (43506-1853)
P.O. Box 524 (43506-0524)
PHONE.............................419 636-5461
Thomas P Dillon, *President*
▲ **EMP:** 15
SALES (est): 3.9MM **Privately Held**
SIC: 3411 3221 Food & beverage containers; bottles for packing, bottling & canning: glass
HQ: Glud & Marstrand A/S
  Hedenstedvej 14
  LOsning 8723
  631 242-00

(G-2283)
H MACHINING INC
720 Commerce Dr (43506-9198)
PHONE.............................419 636-6890
Denny Herman, *President*
Sherrie Herman, *Admin Sec*
EMP: 11
SQ FT: 18,000
SALES (est): 1.7MM **Privately Held**
SIC: 3545 3544 Drills (machine tool accessories); special dies & tools

(G-2284)
HABITEC SEC DIVERSFD ALARM
115 N Lynn St (43506-1213)
PHONE.............................419 636-1155
James Smythe, *Owner*
EMP: 4
SALES (est): 224.1K **Privately Held**
SIC: 3699 Security control equipment & systems

(G-2285)
HEALTH CARE SOLUTIONS INC
5673 State Route 15 (43506-8878)
PHONE.............................419 636-4189
Kari Shininger, *Manager*
EMP: 5
SALES (corp-wide): 37.7MM **Privately Held**
SIC: 3845 Respiratory analysis equipment, electromedical
HQ: Health Care Solutions Inc
  1039 Bern Rd
  Reading PA 19610
  610 373-5733

(G-2286)
HEARING AID CENTER OF NW OHIO
Also Called: Hearing Aid Ctr of NW Ohio The
1318 E High St Ste B (43506-8407)
PHONE.............................419 636-8959
Larry Hand, *Manager*
EMP: 4
SALES (est): 50K **Privately Held**
SIC: 3842 Hearing aids

(G-2287)
ILLINOIS TOOL WORKS INC
Also Called: ITW Powertrain Components
730 E South St (43506-2433)
PHONE.............................419 633-3236
Martin Collins, *Branch Mgr*
EMP: 100
SALES (corp-wide): 14.7B **Publicly Held**
SIC: 3089 Injection molding of plastics
PA: Illinois Tool Works Inc.
  155 Harlem Ave
  Glenview IL 60025
  847 724-7500

(G-2288)
ILLINOIS TOOL WORKS INC
ITW Tomco
730 E South St (43506-2433)
PHONE.............................419 636-3161
Tom Mack, *Vice Pres*
EMP: 270
SQ FT: 75,000
SALES (corp-wide): 14.7B **Publicly Held**
SIC: 3089 Injection molding of plastics

PA: Illinois Tool Works Inc.
  155 Harlem Ave
  Glenview IL 60025
  847 724-7500

(G-2289)
ILLINOIS TOOL WORKS INC
Also Called: ITW Filtration Products
730 E South St (43506-2433)
PHONE.............................262 248-8277
Bob Hamilton, *General Mgr*
EMP: 120
SALES (corp-wide): 14.7B **Publicly Held**
SIC: 3677 3714 3564 Filtration devices, electronic; motor vehicle parts & accessories; blowers & fans
PA: Illinois Tool Works Inc.
  155 Harlem Ave
  Glenview IL 60025
  847 724-7500

(G-2290)
INDUSTRIAL STEERING PDTS INC
426 N Lewis St (43506-1485)
PHONE.............................419 636-3300
John E Freudenberger, *Principal*
EMP: 4
SALES (est): 455.8K **Privately Held**
SIC: 3714 Motor vehicle steering systems & parts

(G-2291)
INGERSOLL-RAND COMPANY
209 N Main St (43506-1319)
P.O. Box 151 (43506-0151)
PHONE.............................419 633-6800
Larry White, *Manager*
EMP: 50 **Privately Held**
WEB: www.ingersoll-rand.com
SIC: 3546 4225 3823 3594 Power-driven handtools; general warehousing & storage; industrial instrmnts msrmnt display/control process variable; fluid power pumps & motors; pumps & pumping equipment; hoists, cranes & monorails
HQ: Ingersoll-Rand Company
  800 Beaty St Ste B
  Davidson NC 28036
  704 655-4000

(G-2292)
JOHNSON CONTROLS INC
918 S Union St (43506-2246)
PHONE.............................419 636-4211
Kevin Cagala, *Manager*
EMP: 94 **Privately Held**
SIC: 2531 Seats, automobile
HQ: Johnson Controls, Inc.
  5757 N Green Bay Ave
  Milwaukee WI 53209
  414 524-1200

(G-2293)
KENLEY ENTERPRISES LLC
418 N Lynn St (43506-1218)
P.O. Box 7036 (43506-7036)
PHONE.............................419 630-0921
Aaron Kendricks, *Project Engr*
Dave Franley,
EMP: 22
SALES (est): 1.4MM **Privately Held**
SIC: 3549 3498 3714 Wiredrawing & fabricating machinery & equipment, ex. die; tube fabricating (contract bending & shaping); motor vehicle parts & accessories

(G-2294)
KW SERVICES LLC
527 S Union St (43506-2248)
PHONE.............................419 636-3438
Kermit Caudill Jr, *General Mgr*
EMP: 6
SALES (corp-wide): 40MM **Privately Held**
WEB: www.koontz-wagner.com
SIC: 7694 Electric motor repair
PA: Kw Services, Llc
  3801 Voorde Dr Ste B
  South Bend IN 46628
  574 232-2051

(G-2295)
LE SMITH COMPANY (PA)
1030 E Wilson St (43506-9358)
P.O. Box 766 (43506-0766)
PHONE.............................419 636-4555
Laura Juarez, *President*
Steve Smith, *Principal*
Craig Francisco, *COO*
Mari Ivan, *COO*
Mindy Hess, *CFO*
▲ **EMP:** 100 **EST:** 1950
SQ FT: 90,000
SALES (est): 18.8MM **Privately Held**
WEB: www.lesmith.com
SIC: 2431 5072 2541 Interior & ornamental woodwork & trim; builders' hardware; wood partitions & fixtures

(G-2296)
LEADER ENGNRNG-FABRICATION INC
County Rd D 50 (43506)
PHONE.............................419 636-1731
John Hill, *Manager*
EMP: 6
SALES (corp-wide): 8.2MM **Privately Held**
WEB: www.leaderengineeringfabrication.com
SIC: 3599 Catapults
PA: Leader Engineering-Fabrication, Inc.
  695 Independence Dr
  Napoleon OH 43545
  419 592-0008

(G-2297)
LIBERTY DIE CASTING COMPANY
Also Called: Liberty Ornamental Products
872 E Trevitt St (43506-1498)
PHONE.............................419 636-3971
Larry Barr, *President*
Scott Schafer, *Vice Pres*
Keith Dart, *Treasurer*
EMP: 3 **EST:** 1972
SQ FT: 16,000
SALES (est): 438.4K **Privately Held**
SIC: 3369 Zinc & zinc-base alloy castings, except die-castings

(G-2298)
MANUFACTURED HOUSING ENTPS INC
Also Called: MANSION HOMES
9302 Us Highway 6 (43506-9516)
PHONE.............................419 636-4511
Mary Jane Fitzcharles, *CEO*
Janet Rice, *Corp Secy*
Nathan Kimpel, *Vice Pres*
Robert Confer, *Purch Agent*
John Bailey, *Engineer*
EMP: 150
SQ FT: 250,000
SALES: 28.1MM **Privately Held**
WEB: www.mheinc.com
SIC: 2451 1521 Mobile homes, except recreational; single-family housing construction

(G-2299)
NOSTRUM LABORATORIES INC
705 E Mulberry St (43506-1734)
PHONE.............................419 636-1168
Grace Shen, *President*
Gregory Reed, *Prdtn Mgr*
Jane Galliers, *Safety Mgr*
Donna Anthony, *Supervisor*
Linda Warner, *Supervisor*
EMP: 46
SQ FT: 91,100
SALES (est): 13MM **Privately Held**
SIC: 2834 Syrups, pharmaceutical
PA: Nostrum Laboratories Inc.
  1800 N Topping Ave
  Kansas City MO 64120

(G-2300)
NOVA POLYMERS INC
15348 Rt 127 E (43506)
PHONE.............................888 484-6682
Diane Millimay, *Manager*
EMP: 1
SALES (est): 2.2MM **Privately Held**
SIC: 2822 Ethylene-propylene rubbers, EPDM polymers

Bryan - Williams County (G-2301) GEOGRAPHIC SECTION

(G-2301)
OHIO ART COMPANY (PA)
1 Toy St (43506-1853)
P.O. Box 111 (43506-0111)
PHONE......................419 636-3141
William C Killgallon, *Ch of Bd*
Martin L Killgallon II, *President*
Larry Killgallon, *COO*
Martin L Killgallon III, *Senior VP*
Dave Batt, *Plant Mgr*
▲ **EMP:** 80
SQ FT: 661,000
SALES (est): 16.4MM **Privately Held**
WEB: www.world-of-toys.com
SIC: 2752 5945 Commercial printing, lithographic; toys & games

(G-2302)
OTTOKEE GROUP INC
17768 County Road H50 (43506-9429)
PHONE......................419 636-1932
Keith Krovath, *Manager*
EMP: 6
SALES (est): 340.6K
SALES (corp-wide): 2.1MM **Privately Held**
WEB: www.archbold.org
SIC: 2875 Fertilizers, mixing only
PA: Ottokee Group, Inc.
21450 County Rd J
Archbold OH 43502
419 445-0446

(G-2303)
PAHL READY MIX CONCRETE INC (PA)
14586 Us Highway 127 Ew (43506-9754)
PHONE......................419 636-4238
Thomas G Weber, *President*
Judy Weber, *Vice Pres*
EMP: 17
SQ FT: 500
SALES (est): 4.4MM **Privately Held**
SIC: 3273 Ready-mixed concrete

(G-2304)
PARAGON CUSTOM PLASTICS INC
402 N Union St (43506-1454)
P.O. Box 127 (43506-0127)
PHONE......................419 636-6060
Mark Troder, *President*
EMP: 30
SQ FT: 11,000
SALES (est): 3.7MM **Privately Held**
SIC: 3086 Plastics foam products

(G-2305)
PRECISE METAL FORM INC
810 Commerce Dr (43506-8861)
P.O. Box 764 (43506-0764)
PHONE......................419 636-5221
James Bloir, *President*
Linda Bloir, *Corp Secy*
EMP: 10
SALES (est): 1.3MM **Privately Held**
SIC: 3444 Sheet metalwork

(G-2306)
S & H AUTOMATION & EQP CO
815 Commerce Dr (43506-8862)
PHONE......................419 636-0020
Melinda Stewart, *President*
Jimmy Stewart, *President*
EMP: 20
SALES (est): 3.6MM **Privately Held**
WEB: www.autobenders.com
SIC: 3542 Bending machines

(G-2307)
STONEY RIDGE WINERY LTD
Also Called: Stoney Ridge Farm & Winery
7144 County Road 16 (43506-9080)
PHONE......................419 636-3500
Phillip Stotz, *President*
Sophia Stotz, *Vice Pres*
EMP: 4
SALES: 500K **Privately Held**
SIC: 2084 Wines

(G-2308)
SWIVEL-TEK INDUSTRIES LLC
417 N Lynn St (43506-1219)
P.O. Box 269 (43506-0269)
PHONE......................419 636-7770
Joyce F Essman, *Mng Member*
Joyce Essman,
EMP: 5
SQ FT: 18,000
SALES: 600.8K **Privately Held**
WEB: www.swivel-tek.com
SIC: 3599 3469 Custom machinery; machine shop, jobbing & repair; machine parts, stamped or pressed metal

(G-2309)
TITAN TIRE CORPORATION
Also Called: Titan Tire Corporation Bryan
927 S Union St (43506-2252)
PHONE......................419 633-4221
Ann Wirth, *Purch Dir*
Kayc Ditommaso, *Purchasing*
Thomas Ort, *Controller*
Tom Jagielski, *Manager*
Harry Dalby, *Manager*
EMP: 400
SQ FT: 750,000
SALES (corp-wide): 1.6B **Publicly Held**
SIC: 3011 Tires & inner tubes
HQ: Titan Tire Corporation
2345 E Market St
Des Moines IA 50317

(G-2310)
TWO BANDITS BREWING CO LLC
206 Scott Dr (43506-8955)
PHONE......................419 636-4045
Mark T Young, *Principal*
EMP: 3
SALES (est): 84.9K **Privately Held**
SIC: 2082 Malt beverages

(G-2311)
UNIQUE-CHARDAN INC
705 S Union St (43506-2250)
PHONE......................419 636-6900
John Weinhard, *President*
Thomas Tekiele, *CFO*
EMP: 50
SQ FT: 40,000
SALES: 4.7MM
SALES (corp-wide): 174.9MM **Publicly Held**
WEB: www.chardancorp.com
SIC: 3944 3949 3714 3086 Games, toys & children's vehicles; sporting & athletic goods; motor vehicle parts & accessories; plastics foam products; injection molded finished plastic products
HQ: Unique Fabricating Na, Inc.
800 Standard Pkwy
Auburn Hills MI 48326
248 853-2333

(G-2312)
WEBER SAND & GRAVEL INC
14586 Us Highway 127 Ew (43506-9754)
PHONE......................419 636-7920
Tom Weber, *President*
EMP: 8
SALES: 520K **Privately Held**
SIC: 1442 Gravel mining

(G-2313)
WESTAR PLASTICS LLC
4271 County Road 15d (43506-9442)
PHONE......................419 636-1333
Steve Goltare, *Mng Member*
Kerri Goltare,
EMP: 7 **EST:** 1996
SQ FT: 12,000
SALES: 800K **Privately Held**
SIC: 3089 Injection molding of plastics

(G-2314)
YANFENG US AUTOMOTIVE
918 S Union St (43506-2246)
PHONE......................419 636-4211
Kevin Cagala, *Manager*
EMP: 500
SALES (corp-wide): 55MM **Privately Held**
SIC: 3089 Molding primary plastic
HQ: Yanfeng Us Automotive Interior Systems Ii Llc
5757 N Green Bay Ave
Milwaukee WI 53209
205 477-4225

Buckeye Lake
Licking County

(G-2315)
IMPACT PUBLICATIONS
Also Called: Buckeye Lake Beacon
4675 Walnut Rd (43008-7770)
P.O. Box 1542 (43008-1542)
PHONE......................740 928-5541
Charlie Prince, *Owner*
EMP: 5
SALES (est): 215.4K **Privately Held**
WEB: www.buckeyelakebeacon.com
SIC: 2711 Newspapers: publishing only, not printed on site

Bucyrus
Crawford County

(G-2316)
A-1 PRINTING INC (PA)
825 S Sandusky Ave (44820-2633)
PHONE......................419 562-3111
Dan Price, *President*
Barbara Price, *Corp Secy*
EMP: 5
SALES (est): 1.3MM **Privately Held**
SIC: 2752 Commercial printing, offset

(G-2317)
ADVANCED FIBER LLC
100 Crossroads Blvd (44820-1361)
PHONE......................419 562-1337
Doug Leuthold, *President*
EMP: 20
SALES (est): 1MM
SALES (corp-wide): 1.3B **Publicly Held**
SIC: 2821 2951 2823 Cellulose derivative materials; asphalt paving mixtures & blocks; cellulosic manmade fibers
PA: Installed Building Products, Inc.
495 S High St Ste 50
Columbus OH 43215
614 221-3399

(G-2318)
BUCYRUS BLADES INC (DH)
260 E Beal Ave (44820-3492)
PHONE......................419 562-6015
Alvin Collins, *CEO*
Jon Owens, *President*
Kevin Thomas, *Senior VP*
Eric Blackburn, *CFO*
◆ **EMP:** 154
SQ FT: 130,000
SALES: 60MM
SALES (corp-wide): 3.1B **Privately Held**
WEB: www.bucyrusblades.com
SIC: 3531 Blades for graders, scrapers, dozers & snow plows
HQ: Esco Group Llc
2141 Nw 25th Ave
Portland OR 97210
503 228-2141

(G-2319)
BUCYRUS GRAPHICS INC
Also Called: Quality Printing Co
214 W Liberty St (44820-2639)
P.O. Box 454 (44820-0454)
PHONE......................419 562-2906
W Gary Mc Kee, *President*
Judy Mc Kee, *Corp Secy*
EMP: 10
SQ FT: 5,000
SALES (est): 1.2MM **Privately Held**
SIC: 2752 Commercial printing, offset

(G-2320)
BUCYRUS PRECISION TECH INC
Also Called: B P T
200 Crossroads Blvd (44820-1363)
PHONE......................419 563-9950
Keiji Nishio, *President*
Terry Pence, *Vice Pres*
Stephanie Hassel, *Manager*
▲ **EMP:** 189
SQ FT: 107,000
SALES (est): 53.5MM
SALES (corp-wide): 68MM **Privately Held**
WEB: www.bptus.com
SIC: 3714 3568 5531 Motor vehicle engines & parts; motor vehicle transmissions, drive assemblies & parts; power transmission equipment; automotive accessories
PA: Kaneta Kogyo Co.,Ltd.
3-18-5, Takaokahigashi, Naka-Ku
Hamamatsu SZO 433-8
534 361-211

(G-2321)
CHECKMATE MARINE INC
3691 State Route 4 (44820-9466)
PHONE......................419 562-3881
Doug Smith, *President*
EMP: 17
SALES (est): 3.9MM **Privately Held**
SIC: 3732 Boat building & repairing

(G-2322)
COOPERS MILL INC
1414 N Sandusky Ave (44820-1330)
P.O. Box 149 (44820-0149)
PHONE......................419 562-4215
Jason McMullan, *President*
Justin McMullan, *Vice Pres*
EMP: 18
SQ FT: 17,300
SALES: 1MM **Privately Held**
WEB: www.coopersmill.net
SIC: 2033 5431 5149 Jams, jellies & preserves: packaged in cans, jars, etc.; fruit butters: packaged in cans, jars, etc.; fruit stands or markets; vegetable stands or markets; pickles, preserves, jellies & jams

(G-2323)
CRAWFORD COUNTY ARTS COUNCIL
1810 E Mansfield St (44820-2083)
P.O. Box 581 (44820-0581)
PHONE......................419 834-4133
Beverly Morgan, *President*
Harold Strang, *Treasurer*
EMP: 4
SALES (est): 63.2K **Privately Held**
SIC: 5945 5719 3952 7999 Arts & crafts supplies; pottery; water colors, artists'; arts & crafts instruction

(G-2324)
D PICKING & CO
119 S Walnut St (44820-2325)
PHONE......................419 562-5016
Helen Picking Neff, *Owner*
EMP: 6 **EST:** 1874
SQ FT: 5,000
SALES (est): 577.3K **Privately Held**
SIC: 3364 3931 3366 3321 Copper & copper alloy die-castings; musical instruments; copper foundries; gray & ductile iron foundries

(G-2325)
DIAMOND WIPES INTL INC
1375 Isaac Beal Rd (44820-9604)
PHONE......................419 562-3575
Diane Belcher, *Principal*
Dave Metzger, *Maintence Staff*
EMP: 8
SALES (corp-wide): 29.5MM **Privately Held**
SIC: 3441 Fabricated structural metal
PA: Diamond Wipes International, Inc.
4651 Schaefer Ave
Chino CA 91710
909 230-9888

(G-2326)
EAGLE CRUSHER CO INC
521 E Southern Ave (44820-3258)
P.O. Box 537, Galion (44833-0537)
PHONE......................419 562-1183
Tom Cole, *Plant Mgr*
Susan Cobey, *Branch Mgr*
EMP: 50
SQ FT: 200,000
SALES (corp-wide): 59.8MM **Privately Held**
WEB: www.eaglecrusher.com
SIC: 3532 Crushing, pulverizing & screening equipment

▲ = Import ▼ = Export
◆ = Import/Export

PA: Eagle Crusher Co Inc
525 S Market St
Galion OH 44833
419 468-2288

(G-2327)
EAST SIDE FUEL PLUS OPERATIONS
1505 N Sandusky Ave (44820-1333)
PHONE...............................419 563-0777
Bridgette J Liedorff, *Principal*
EMP: 5
SALES (est): 561.1K **Privately Held**
SIC: 2869 Fuels

(G-2328)
ERS INDUSTRIES INC
Also Called: American Ohio Locomotive Crane
811 Hopley Ave (44820-2856)
P.O. Box 71 (44820-0071)
PHONE...............................419 562-6010
David Egner, *Vice Pres*
Chuck Billman, *Parts Mgr*
EMP: 26
SALES (corp-wide): 28.8MM **Privately Held**
SIC: 3531 Cranes, locomotive
PA: Ers Industries, Inc.
1005 Indian Church Rd
West Seneca NY 14224
716 675-2040

(G-2329)
ESCO GROUP LLC
260 E Beal Ave (44820-3492)
PHONE...............................419 562-6015
Mike Sparks, *Branch Mgr*
EMP: 50
SALES (corp-wide): 3.1B **Privately Held**
SIC: 3532 Mining machinery
HQ: Esco Group Llc
2141 Nw 25th Ave
Portland OR 97210
503 228-2141

(G-2330)
GANYMEDE TECHNOLOGIES CORP
Also Called: J3 Point-Of-Sale
1685 Marion Rd (44820-3116)
P.O. Box 1138 (44820-1138)
PHONE...............................419 562-5522
George Fred Fischer, *President*
Jen Fischer, *COO*
EMP: 6
SALES (est): 490.1K **Privately Held**
SIC: 7371 3578 Computer software development; calculators & adding machines

(G-2331)
GENERAL ELECTRIC COMPANY
1250 S Walnut St (44820-3266)
PHONE...............................419 563-1200
Dan Monnin, *Plant Mgr*
Randy Harriger, *Engineer*
Laszlo Ilyes, *Engineer*
David Shilling, *Design Engr*
Tyler Smolen, *Design Engr*
EMP: 325
SALES (corp-wide): 121.6B **Publicly Held**
SIC: 3641 Lamps, fluorescent, electric
PA: General Electric Company
41 Farnsworth St
Boston MA 02210
617 443-3000

(G-2332)
GOFAST LLC
963 Hopley Ave (44820-3506)
PHONE...............................419 562-8027
Shaun Frecska, *Mng Member*
Richard Szydlyk,
EMP: 3
SALES (est): 261.3K **Privately Held**
SIC: 2033 Canned fruits & specialties

(G-2333)
HEBCO PRODUCTS INC
1232 Whetstone St (44820-3539)
PHONE...............................419 562-7987
Andrew Ason, *President*
Ralph Reins, *Vice Pres*
EMP: 862
SALES (est): 73.7MM **Privately Held**
WEB: www.hebcoproducts.com
SIC: 3714 3451 3429 5013 Motor vehicle brake systems & parts; screw machine products; manufactured hardware (general); automotive supplies & parts
HQ: Qualitor, Inc.
1840 Mccullough St
Lima OH 45801
248 204-8600

(G-2334)
HOME SHEET METAL & ROOFING CO
211 W Galen St (44820-2237)
P.O. Box 66 (44820-0066)
PHONE...............................419 562-7806
Terry Barney, *Owner*
EMP: 5
SALES (est): 250K **Privately Held**
SIC: 1761 3444 Roofing contractor; sheet metalwork

(G-2335)
HORD ELEVATOR LLC
1016 State Route 98 (44820-9523)
P.O. Box 808 (44820-0808)
PHONE...............................419 562-5934
Robert D Hord, *Manager*
EMP: 12
SALES (est): 950K **Privately Held**
SIC: 3523 Elevators, farm

(G-2336)
IMASEN BUCYRUS TECHNOLOGY INC
Also Called: I B-Tech
260 Crossroads Blvd (44820-1363)
PHONE...............................419 563-9590
Katsumi Ito, *President*
Joe Downing, *Vice Pres*
Koichi Fukui, *Vice Pres*
◆ EMP: 220
SALES (est): 49.1MM
SALES (corp-wide): 1.1B **Privately Held**
SIC: 3714 Motor vehicle parts & accessories
PA: Imasen Electric Industrial Co., Ltd.
1, Kakibata
Inuyama AIC 484-0
568 671-211

(G-2337)
LAWSON PRECISION MACHINING INC
3981 Crestline Rd (44820-9573)
PHONE...............................419 562-1543
Gary Lawson, *President*
EMP: 3
SALES (est): 223.2K **Privately Held**
SIC: 3599 Custom machinery

(G-2338)
LUX CORPORATION
Also Called: C-Hawk Trailers
4613 Stetzer Rd (44820-9391)
PHONE...............................419 562-7978
Otis Shearer, *President*
Carol Shearer, *Corp Secy*
▲ EMP: 3
SALES (est): 260K **Privately Held**
WEB: www.c-hawktrailers.com
SIC: 3799 5599 Boat trailers; trailers & trailer equipment; utility trailers

(G-2339)
NATIONAL LIME AND STONE CO
4580 Bethel Rd (44820-9754)
P.O. Box 69 (44820-0069)
PHONE...............................419 562-0771
Eric Johnson, *Principal*
Rick Dehays, *Purchasing*
Roger Nye, *Maintence Staff*
EMP: 62
SALES (corp-wide): 3.2B **Privately Held**
WEB: www.natlime.com
SIC: 1411 1423 1422 Limestone, dimension-quarrying; cut stone & stone products; crushed & broken limestone
PA: The National Lime And Stone Company
551 Lake Cascade Pkwy
Findlay OH 45840
419 422-4341

(G-2340)
OAK VIEW ENTERPRISES INC
100 Crossroads Blvd (44820-1361)
PHONE...............................513 860-4446
Doug Leuthold, *President*
EMP: 20
SQ FT: 51,500
SALES (est): 5.5MM **Privately Held**
WEB: www.advancedfiber.com
SIC: 2821 5084 Cellulose derivative materials; paper manufacturing machinery

(G-2341)
OHIO FOAM CORPORATION (PA)
820 Plymouth St (44820-1641)
P.O. Box 208 (44820-0208)
PHONE...............................419 563-0399
Gail Potter, *President*
Jerry Necastro, *Vice Pres*
Terry Lady, *Treasurer*
Steve Erlsten, *Admin Sec*
EMP: 2 EST: 1972
SQ FT: 1,500
SALES (est): 11.7MM **Privately Held**
WEB: www.ohiofoam.com
SIC: 3086 Plastics foam products

(G-2342)
R L RUSH TOOL & PATTERN INC
Also Called: Rush, R L Tool & Pattern
1620 Whetstone St (44820-3557)
P.O. Box 763 (44820-0763)
PHONE...............................419 562-9849
Roger Rush, *President*
Phyllis Rush, *Admin Sec*
EMP: 7
SQ FT: 7,000
SALES (est): 888.2K **Privately Held**
SIC: 3543 3469 Industrial patterns; stamping metal for the trade

(G-2343)
RYDER-HEIL BRONZE INC
126 E Irving St (44820-1409)
P.O. Box 647 (44820-0647)
PHONE...............................419 562-2841
Herbert D Kleine, *President*
Herb Kleine, *Plant Mgr*
Aaron Atkinson, *Maintence Staff*
EMP: 35 EST: 1910
SQ FT: 39,750
SALES (est): 8.4MM **Privately Held**
WEB: www.ryderheil.com
SIC: 3364 Brass & bronze die-castings

(G-2344)
T AND D WASHERS LLC
255 E Warren St (44820-2336)
PHONE...............................419 562-5500
EMP: 3
SALES (est): 175.1K **Privately Held**
SIC: 3452 Washers

(G-2345)
TIMKEN COMPANY
2325 E Mansfield St (44820-2094)
PHONE...............................419 563-2200
Jack Yohe, *Branch Mgr*
Kimberly Hummel, *CIO*
Deb Shields, *Director*
EMP: 560
SQ FT: 400,000
SALES (corp-wide): 3.5B **Publicly Held**
SIC: 3562 Ball & roller bearings
PA: The Timken Company
4500 Mount Pleasant St Nw
North Canton OH 44720
234 262-3000

(G-2346)
VAL CASTING INC
108 E Rensselaer St (44820-2320)
P.O. Box 374 (44820-0374)
PHONE...............................419 562-2499
Val Fawley, *President*
Michael Romanoff, *Vice Pres*
EMP: 30
SQ FT: 4,500
SALES (est): 3.5MM **Privately Held**
SIC: 3911 Jewelry, precious metal

(G-2347)
VASIL CO INC
Also Called: Vasil Fashions
119 E Mary St (44820-1828)
PHONE...............................419 562-2901
Margaret Ann Vasil, *Vice Pres*
Nicholas G Vasil, *Treasurer*
EMP: 8 EST: 1958
SQ FT: 12,000
SALES (est): 804.4K **Privately Held**
SIC: 2396 2395 Screen printing on fabric articles; art goods for embroidering, stamped: purchased materials

(G-2348)
VELVET ICE CREAM COMPANY
Also Called: Bucyrus Ice Company
1233 Whetstone St (44820-3540)
PHONE...............................419 562-2009
Jack Rogers, *Manager*
EMP: 15
SALES (corp-wide): 30.3MM **Privately Held**
WEB: www.velveticecream.com
SIC: 5143 2097 Ice cream & ices; manufactured ice
PA: Velvet Ice Cream Company
11324 Mount Vernon Rd
Utica OH 43080
740 892-3921

(G-2349)
W M DAUCH CONCRETE INC
900 Nevada Rd (44820-1744)
PHONE...............................419 562-6917
William Dauch, *President*
EMP: 7
SALES (est): 580.6K **Privately Held**
SIC: 3273 1771 Ready-mixed concrete; concrete work

(G-2350)
WILLIAM DAUCH CONCRETE COMPANY
900 Nevada Wynford Rd (44820-9440)
PHONE...............................419 562-6917
Tim Corrigan, *Manager*
EMP: 10
SALES (corp-wide): 23.2MM **Privately Held**
WEB: www.dauchconcrete.com
SIC: 3273 Ready-mixed concrete
PA: William Dauch Concrete Company Inc
84 Cleveland Rd
Norwalk OH 44857
419 668-4458

(G-2351)
WOOD STOVE SHED
4602 Stetzer Rd (44820-9391)
PHONE...............................419 562-1545
Patricia Garrett, *Owner*
Charles Garrett, *Co-Owner*
EMP: 3
SALES (est): 245K **Privately Held**
SIC: 3433 5075 1711 Burners, furnaces, boilers & stokers; warm air heating equipment & supplies; heating systems repair & maintenance

(G-2352)
XT INNOVATIONS LTD
4799 Stetzer Rd (44820-9391)
PHONE...............................419 562-1989
Lane Carlisle, *Principal*
EMP: 3
SALES (est): 326.1K **Privately Held**
SIC: 2273 Carpets & rugs

Burbank
Wayne County

(G-2353)
PIPE COIL TECHNOLOGY INC
Also Called: P C T
111 Cardington Ln (44214-9426)
PHONE...............................330 256-6070
John Reece, *Chairman*
▲ EMP: 14
SALES (est): 2.1MM
SALES (corp-wide): 63.1MM **Privately Held**
SIC: 3549 Coiling machinery
PA: Reece Group Limited
Armstrong Works Scotswood Road
Newcastle-Upon-Tyne NE15
191 234-8700

Burghill
Trumbull County

(G-2354)
DESIGNER DOORS INC
4810 State Route 7 (44404-9701)
PHONE 330 772-6391
Ron Seidle Jr, *President*
Robert Seidle, *Vice Pres*
Ronald Seidle, *Project Mgr*
◆ **EMP:** 32
SQ FT: 23,500
SALES (est): 3.6MM **Privately Held**
WEB: www.cabinet-knobs.net
SIC: 2431 Doors, wood

(G-2355)
MICHAELS TOOL SERVICE CO INC
8346 Milligan East Rd (44404-9729)
PHONE 330 772-1119
Robert F Michael, *Owner*
EMP: 4
SALES: 300K **Privately Held**
SIC: 3599 Industrial machinery

Burkettsville
Mercer County

(G-2356)
WERLING AND SONS INC
Also Called: Burkettsville Stockyard
100 Plum St (45310-5017)
PHONE 937 338-3281
Edward J Werling, *President*
James R Werling, *Corp Secy*
EMP: 10 **EST:** 1886
SALES (est): 3.2MM **Privately Held**
WEB: www.werlingandsons.com
SIC: 5154 2011 Livestock; meat packing plants

Burton
Geauga County

(G-2357)
DP PRODUCTS LLC
14395 Aquilla Rd (44021-9558)
P.O. Box 1062 (44021-1062)
PHONE 440 834-9663
Ken Ashba,
EMP: 4
SQ FT: 12,000
SALES (est): 549.4K **Privately Held**
SIC: 2449 2441 Rectangular boxes & crates, wood; nailed wood boxes & shook

(G-2358)
FONTANELLE GROUP INC
Also Called: Country Savings Magazine
13199 Longwood Ave (44021-9508)
PHONE 440 834-8900
Barbara Fontanelle, *President*
Benjamin Fontanelle, *Vice Pres*
EMP: 3
SALES (est): 320K **Privately Held**
WEB: www.countrysavingsmagazine.com
SIC: 2721 Magazines: publishing only, not printed on site; magazines: publishing & printing

(G-2359)
HARVEY MILLER
Also Called: H & M Fabricating
16828 Jug Rd (44021-9443)
PHONE 440 834-9125
Harvey Miller, *Owner*
Melvin Miller, *Principal*
EMP: 3
SALES (est): 119.9K **Privately Held**
SIC: 3449 Miscellaneous metalwork

(G-2360)
HEXPOL COMPOUNDING LLC
Also Called: Burton Rubber Processing
14330 Kinsman Rd (44021-9648)
PHONE 440 834-4644
John Gorrell, *Manager*
EMP: 200
SALES (corp-wide): 1.4B **Privately Held**
SIC: 3087 2865 5162 2899 Custom compound purchased resins; dyes & pigments; resins; plastics basic shapes; chemical preparations; adhesives & sealants; paints & allied products
HQ: Hexpol Compounding Llc
14330 Kinsman Rd
Burton OH 44021
440 834-4644

(G-2361)
HEXPOL COMPOUNDING LLC (DH)
Also Called: Hexpol Polymers
14330 Kinsman Rd (44021-9648)
P.O. Box 415000, Nashville TN (37241-5000)
PHONE 440 834-4644
Tracy Garrison, *CEO*
Denise Bowers, *Buyer*
Kevin Park, *Senior Engr*
Ernie Ulmer, *CFO*
Mary Ann Devers, *Human Res Dir*
▲ **EMP:** 50
SALES (est): 438.7MM
SALES (corp-wide): 1.4B **Privately Held**
WEB: www.excel-polymers.com
SIC: 3087 2821 Custom compound purchased resins; thermoplastic materials
HQ: Hexpol Holding Inc.
14330 Kinsman Rd
Burton OH 44021
440 834-4644

(G-2362)
HEXPOL HOLDING INC (HQ)
14330 Kinsman Rd (44021-9648)
PHONE 440 834-4644
Georg Brunstam, *President*
EMP: 10
SALES (est): 550.1MM
SALES (corp-wide): 1.4B **Privately Held**
SIC: 6719 2821 3087 Investment holding companies, except banks; plastics materials & resins; custom compound purchased resins
PA: Hexpol Ab
Skeppsbron 3
Malmo 211 2
402 546-60

(G-2363)
JOES SAW SHOP
14530 Butternut Rd (44021-9528)
PHONE 440 834-1196
Joe Byler, *Principal*
EMP: 4
SALES (est): 325.6K **Privately Held**
SIC: 3425 Saw blades & handsaws

(G-2364)
K D HARDWOODS INC
14195 Kinsman Rd (44021-9650)
P.O. Box 177 (44021-0177)
PHONE 440 834-1772
Brian Snider, *President*
Cynthia Snider, *Vice Pres*
EMP: 3
SQ FT: 5,600
SALES (est): 344.2K **Privately Held**
SIC: 2431 5211 Moldings, wood: unfinished & prefinished; doors & door parts & trim, wood; staircases, stairs & railings; lumber products

(G-2365)
KEN EMERICK MACHINE PRODUCTS
14504 Main Market Rd (44021-9615)
PHONE 440 834-4501
Ken Emerick, *President*
Pam Emerick, *Vice Pres*
EMP: 8
SQ FT: 12,500
SALES: 100K **Privately Held**
WEB: www.emerickmachine.com
SIC: 3541 Screw machines, automatic

(G-2366)
OHIO BOX & CRATE INC
Also Called: Ohio Box and Crate Co
16751 Tavern Rd (44021-9605)
PHONE 440 526-3133
Sarmite S Grava, *President*
EMP: 12
SQ FT: 15,000
SALES (est): 1.8MM **Privately Held**
SIC: 2441 2448 Boxes, wood; skids, wood & wood with metal

(G-2367)
R J DOBAY ENTERPRISES INC
Also Called: Ronald J Dobay Enterprises
14704 Main Market Rd (44021-9667)
PHONE 440 227-1005
Nancy Dobay, *President*
EMP: 6
SALES (est): 527.4K **Privately Held**
SIC: 4212 1794 2421 Local trucking, without storage; excavation work; sawdust & shavings

(G-2368)
REVOLUTION MACHINE WORKS INC
14646 Ravenna Rd Unit B (44021-9713)
PHONE 706 505-6525
Kris Fugate, *President*
EMP: 8
SALES (est): 202.8K **Privately Held**
SIC: 3599 Machine shop, jobbing & repair

(G-2369)
ROTARY TECH INC
12710 Kinsman Rd (44021-9763)
PHONE 440 862-8568
Kristopher Fugate, *Principal*
Chad Derbyshire, *Vice Pres*
EMP: 5
SALES (est): 202.8K **Privately Held**
SIC: 3599 Machine shop, jobbing & repair

(G-2370)
SHALERSVILLE ASPHALT CO (PA)
Also Called: Ronyak Brothers Paving
14376 N Cheshire St (44021-9574)
P.O. Box 449 (44021-0449)
PHONE 440 834-4294
David W Ronyak, *President*
Jim Shale, *Vice Pres*
EMP: 25
SQ FT: 2,000
SALES (est): 10.8MM **Privately Held**
SIC: 2951 Asphalt & asphaltic paving mixtures (not from refineries)

(G-2371)
STEPHEN M TRUDICK
Also Called: Hardwood Lumber Co
13813 Station Rd (44021)
P.O. Box 15 (44021-0015)
PHONE 440 834-1891
Stephen M Trudick, *Owner*
Jayne Shaffer, *Director*
▲ **EMP:** 41
SQ FT: 80,000
SALES (est): 5.5MM **Privately Held**
WEB: www.hardwood-lumber.com
SIC: 3991 2426 5031 3442 Brooms & brushes; dimension, hardwood; lumber: rough, dressed & finished; metal doors, sash & trim; millwork; sawmills & planing mills, general

(G-2372)
STONEY ACRES WOODWORKING LLC
14575 Patch Rd (44021-9631)
PHONE 440 834-0717
Michael J Miller, *Principal*
EMP: 4
SALES (est): 417.8K **Privately Held**
SIC: 2431 Millwork

(G-2373)
TROY MANUFACTURING CO
17090 Rapids Rd (44021-9754)
P.O. Box 448 (44021-0448)
PHONE 440 834-8262
David Cseplo, *President*
Wynne Bogert, *Vice Pres*
Charles Fath, *Vice Pres*
Richard Taylor, *Vice Pres*
Jasen Miller, *Opers Mgr*
EMP: 30 **EST:** 1952
SQ FT: 40,000
SALES (est): 5.2MM **Privately Held**
SIC: 3451 Screw machine products

(G-2374)
TROY PRECISION CARBIDE DIE
17720 Claridon Troy Rd (44021-9658)
PHONE 440 834-4477
James Dewalt, *President*
Jeff Amon, *Corp Secy*
Kelly Amon, *Vice Pres*
EMP: 12
SQ FT: 10,000
SALES (est): 1.5MM **Privately Held**
SIC: 3544 Special dies, tools, jigs & fixtures

Butler
Richland County

(G-2375)
HIGHLINE RACEWAY LLC
1766 Cassell Rd (44822-9700)
PHONE 419 883-2042
Kelly Donaugh, *Principal*
EMP: 3
SALES (est): 211.3K **Privately Held**
SIC: 3644 Raceways

(G-2376)
MID-OHIO TUBING LLC (HQ)
145 W Elm St (44822-9783)
PHONE 419 883-2066
Jamie Feick, *CEO*
Wayne Riffe, *President*
EMP: 52 **EST:** 2013
SALES (est): 14.8MM
SALES (corp-wide): 29.9MM **Privately Held**
SIC: 3317 Tubes, seamless steel
PA: Gregory Industries, Inc.
4100 13th St Sw
Canton OH 44710
330 477-4800

(G-2377)
MOHICAN WOOD PRODUCTS
20460 Nunda Rd (44822-9400)
PHONE 740 599-5655
Ivan Miller, *Owner*
EMP: 4
SQ FT: 9,792
SALES: 750K **Privately Held**
SIC: 2431 Door trim, wood; moldings, wood: unfinished & prefinished

(G-2378)
YODER WOODWORKING
21198 Swendal Rd (44822-9214)
PHONE 740 399-9400
Mervin Yoder, *Principal*
EMP: 5
SALES (est): 438.3K **Privately Held**
SIC: 2431 Millwork

Byesville
Guernsey County

(G-2379)
CALDWELL REDI MIX COMPANY
209 Pioneer Rd (43723)
PHONE 740 685-6554
Ruben Schafer, *President*
Allen Hill, *Manager*
EMP: 5
SALES (corp-wide): 1MM **Privately Held**
SIC: 3273 Ready-mixed concrete
PA: Caldwell Redi Mix Company
45947 Marietta Rd
Caldwell OH 43724
740 732-2906

(G-2380)
CAMBRIDGE CABLE SERVICE CO
58945 Country Club Rd (43723-9763)
P.O. Box 5 (43723-0005)
PHONE 740 685-5775
Kevin G Deason, *President*
Cindy Deason, *Vice Pres*
EMP: 4
SQ FT: 5,000

GEOGRAPHIC SECTION

SALES: 1.5MM **Privately Held**
SIC: 5251 1623 5051 3315 Hardware; cable laying construction; rope, wire (not insulated); wire & fabricated wire products

(G-2381)
DAVID R HILL INC
132 S 2nd St (43723-1304)
P.O. Box 247 (43723-0247)
PHONE.................................740 685-5168
David R Hill, *CEO*
EMP: 6
SALES (est): 746.8K **Privately Held**
SIC: 1382 Geological exploration, oil & gas field

(G-2382)
DETROIT DESL RMNFCTRNG-AST INC
60703 Country Club Rd (43723-9730)
PHONE.................................740 439-7701
Roger S Penske, *Ch of Bd*
James Morrow, *President*
Mike Chuich, *Vice Pres*
Michael Chuich, *Plant Mgr*
Jessica Moore, *Engineer*
◆ **EMP:** 500
SQ FT: 128,000
SALES (est): 117.2MM
SALES (corp-wide): 191.6B **Privately Held**
SIC: 3519 Diesel engine rebuilding
HQ: Detroit Diesel Remanufacturing Corporation
100 Lodestone Way
Tooele UT 84074

(G-2383)
DETROIT DIESL SPECIALTY TL INC
60703 Country Club Rd (43723-9730)
PHONE.................................740 435-4452
Wayne Prouty, *President*
▲ **EMP:** 30
SALES (est): 4.1MM
SALES (corp-wide): 191.6B **Privately Held**
WEB: www.ddre.detroitdiesel.com
SIC: 3599 Electrical discharge machining (EDM)
HQ: Detroit Diesel Corporation
13400 W Outer Dr
Detroit MI 48239
313 592-5000

(G-2384)
FAMOUS INDUSTRIES INC
Also Called: L B Manufacturing
356 W Main St (43723-1123)
PHONE.................................740 685-2592
Bob Badnell, *Manager*
EMP: 80 **Privately Held**
WEB: www.jfgoodco.com
SIC: 3469 3585 3564 3498 Stamping metal for the trade; refrigeration & heating equipment; blowers & fans; fabricated pipe & fittings; heating equipment, except electric
HQ: Famous Industries, Inc.
2620 Ridgewood Rd Ste 200
Akron OH 44313
330 535-1811

(G-2385)
FAMOUS REALTY CLEVELAND INC
Also Called: Famous Supply
354 W Main St (43723-1123)
PHONE.................................740 685-2533
Eric St Claire, *Manager*
EMP: 11
SALES (corp-wide): 1MM **Privately Held**
SIC: 3585 5074 Heating & air conditioning combination units; plumbing fittings & supplies
PA: Famous Realty Of Cleveland, Inc.
109 N Union St
Akron OH 44304
330 762-9621

(G-2386)
HILL & ASSOCIATES INC
132 S 6th St (43723)
P.O. Box 247 (43723-0247)
PHONE.................................740 685-5168
David R Hill, *President*
EMP: 3 **EST:** 1974
SALES (est): 300K **Privately Held**
SIC: 1389 Oil & gas wells: building, repairing & dismantling

(G-2387)
INTERNATIONAL PAPER COMPANY
60700 Hope Ave (43723-9740)
PHONE.................................740 439-3527
Chuck Evans, *Safety Dir*
Risch Joe, *Prdtn Mgr*
Becky Delik, *Controller*
EMP: 45
SALES (corp-wide): 23.3B **Publicly Held**
SIC: 2621 Paper mills
PA: International Paper Company
6400 Poplar Ave
Memphis TN 38197
901 419-9000

(G-2388)
KEN HARPER
Also Called: GUERNSEY INDUSTRIES
60772 Southgate Rd (43723-9731)
PHONE.................................740 439-4452
Ken Harper, *Exec Dir*
EMP: 110
SALES: 997.3K **Privately Held**
SIC: 8331 2511 2448 Sheltered workshop; wood household furniture; wood pallets & skids

(G-2389)
KERRY INC
Also Called: Kerry Ingredients
100 Hope Ave (43723-9460)
PHONE.................................760 685-2548
EMP: 5 **Privately Held**
SIC: 2656 5149 Food containers (liquid tight), including milk cartons; condiments
HQ: Kerry Inc.
3330 Millington Rd
Beloit WI 53511
608 363-1200

(G-2390)
MAR-ZANE INC
59903 Vocational Rd (43723)
PHONE.................................740 685-5178
Robert Hamilton, *Manager*
EMP: 3
SALES (corp-wide): 276.3MM **Privately Held**
SIC: 2951 Asphalt paving mixtures & blocks
HQ: Mar-Zane, Inc.
3570 S River Rd
Zanesville OH 43701
740 453-0721

(G-2391)
PEOPLES BANCORP INC
221 S 2nd St (43723-1303)
PHONE.................................740 685-1500
Phyllis Jeffries, *Principal*
EMP: 120
SALES (corp-wide): 208MM **Publicly Held**
SIC: 3578 Automatic teller machines (ATM)
PA: Peoples Bancorp Inc.
138 Putnam St
Marietta OH 45750
740 373-3155

(G-2392)
PROFESSIONAL OILFIELD SERVICES
221 1/2 S 6th St (43723-1151)
P.O. Box 247 (43723-0247)
PHONE.................................740 685-5168
David Hill, *President*
Jerry Olds, *Treasurer*
EMP: 4
SQ FT: 1,000
SALES (est): 470K **Privately Held**
SIC: 1381 Drilling oil & gas wells

(G-2393)
TIMCO INC
57051 Marietta Rd (43723-9709)
PHONE.................................740 685-2594
Tim Brown, *President*
Mark Brown, *Vice Pres*
EMP: 12
SQ FT: 2,000
SALES (est): 1.4MM **Privately Held**
WEB: www.timcoinc.net
SIC: 1381 3533 Drilling oil & gas wells; oil & gas field machinery

(G-2394)
TIMOTHY SASSER
Also Called: Triple T Fabricating
59538 Lost Rd (43723-9543)
PHONE.................................740 260-9499
Timothy Sasser, *Owner*
EMP: 5 **EST:** 2014
SALES (est): 170K **Privately Held**
SIC: 7692 Welding repair

(G-2395)
VELOCITY CONCEPT DEV GROUP LLC
8824 Clay Pike (43723-9712)
PHONE.................................740 685-2637
Eric Fehrman, *Branch Mgr*
EMP: 8
SALES (corp-wide): 4.4MM **Privately Held**
SIC: 3544 Industrial molds; special dies & tools; jigs & fixtures
PA: Velocity Concept Development Group, Llc
4393 Digital Way
Mason OH 45040
513 204-2100

(G-2396)
W P BROWN ENTERPRISES INC
57051 Marietta Rd (43723-9709)
PHONE.................................740 685-2594
William P Brown, *President*
EMP: 6
SALES (est): 600.5K **Privately Held**
SIC: 1311 Crude petroleum production

Cadiz
Harrison County

(G-2397)
DANIEL WAGNER
39170 Welsh Rd (43907-9571)
PHONE.................................740 942-2928
Daniel Wagner, *Principal*
EMP: 4 **EST:** 2010
SALES (est): 351.4K **Privately Held**
SIC: 3713 Dump truck bodies

(G-2398)
HARRISON NEWS HERALD INC
Also Called: Schloss Media
144 S Main St Lowr (43907-1167)
PHONE.................................740 942-2118
David Schloss, *President*
Millie Pruent, *President*
EMP: 11
SALES (est): 702.4K **Privately Held**
WEB: www.harrisonnewsherald.com
SIC: 2711 Newspapers: publishing only, not printed on site

(G-2399)
MARKWEST ENERGY PARTNERS LP
Also Called: Mark West Energy
78405 Cadiz New Athens Rd (43907-9665)
PHONE.................................740 942-0463
Mark West, *Branch Mgr*
EMP: 8
SALES (corp-wide): 6.4B **Publicly Held**
SIC: 1321 Natural gas liquids
HQ: Markwest Energy Partners, L.P.
1515 Arapahoe St
Denver CO 80202
303 925-9200

(G-2400)
MIZER PRINTING & GRAPHICS
160 Cunningham Ave Ste C (43907-1032)
PHONE.................................740 942-3343
Thomas Mizer, *Owner*
EMP: 3
SQ FT: 1,440
SALES (est): 317.9K **Privately Held**
SIC: 2752 Lithographing on metal

(G-2401)
STANLEY BITTINGER
Also Called: Bittinger Carbide
81331 Hines Rd (43907-9535)
PHONE.................................740 942-4302
Stanley Bittinger, *Owner*
Sheila Bittinger, *Office Mgr*
EMP: 7
SQ FT: 1,800
SALES: 500K **Privately Held**
WEB: www.bestbur.com
SIC: 3546 5084 3545 Power-driven handtools; industrial machinery & equipment; machine tool accessories

Cairo
Allen County

(G-2402)
CHEMTRADE REFINERY SVCS INC
7680 Ottawa Rd (45820)
PHONE.................................419 641-4151
Tim Handiford, *Branch Mgr*
EMP: 10
SALES (corp-wide): 1.1B **Privately Held**
SIC: 2819 Industrial inorganic chemicals
HQ: Chemtrade Refinery Services Inc.
440 N 9th St
Lawrence KS 66044
785 843-2290

Caldwell
Noble County

(G-2403)
BEAR WELDING SERVICES LLC
18210 Myrtle Ake Rd (43724-9136)
PHONE.................................740 630-7538
Jeremy Leonard, *Mng Member*
EMP: 10
SALES: 1.2MM **Privately Held**
SIC: 7692 Welding repair

(G-2404)
CALDWELL LUMBER & SUPPLY CO
Also Called: Do It Best
17990 Woodsfield Rd (43724-9435)
PHONE.................................740 732-2306
Edward Crock, *President*
Brandon Crock, *Corp Secy*
EMP: 45 **EST:** 1948
SQ FT: 25,000
SALES (est): 5.7MM **Privately Held**
SIC: 5251 3273 Hardware; ready-mixed concrete

(G-2405)
CALDWELL REDI MIX COMPANY (PA)
Also Called: Caldwell Redi-Mix Concrete
45997 Marietta Rd (43724-9241)
PHONE.................................740 732-2906
Reuben Schafer, *President*
EMP: 4 **EST:** 1958
SQ FT: 800
SALES (est): 1MM **Privately Held**
SIC: 3273 Mfg Ready-Mixed Concrete

(G-2406)
HL OILFIELD SERVICES LLC
19797 Harl Weiller Rd (43724-9149)
PHONE.................................740 783-1156
EMP: 3
SALES (est): 164.6K **Privately Held**
SIC: 1389 Oil/Gas Field Services

(G-2407)
INTERNTNAL CNVRTER CLDWELL INC
Also Called: I-Convert
17153 Industrial Hwy (43724-9779)
PHONE.................................740 732-5665
Phil Harris, *President*
Jerry Lawrence, *Vice Pres*
Craig Lemieux, *Vice Pres*
Gerry Medlin, *Vice Pres*
Mitchell Mekaelian, *Vice Pres*

Caldwell - Noble County (G-2408)

◆ **EMP:** 241
SQ FT: 75,000
SALES (est): 45.6MM
SALES (corp-wide): 3B **Privately Held**
WEB: www.ici-laminating.com
SIC: 3089 3353 3083 Laminating of plastic; aluminum sheet, plate & foil; laminated plastics plate & sheet
HQ: Packaging Dynamics Corporation
3900 W 43rd St
Chicago IL 60632
773 254-8000

(G-2408)
KING QUARRIES INC
41820 Parrish Ridge Rd (43724-8910)
PHONE.................................740 732-2923
Mary King, *President*
EMP: 5 **EST:** 1955
SQ FT: 800
SALES (est): 765.4K **Privately Held**
SIC: 1221 Bituminous coal & lignite-surface mining

(G-2409)
MAGNUM MAGNETICS CORPORATION
17289 Industrial Hwy (43724-9779)
PHONE.................................740 516-6237
EMP: 10
SALES (est): 1.3MM **Privately Held**
SIC: 2893 Printing ink
PA: Magnum Magnetics Corporation
801 Masonic Park Rd
Marietta OH 45750

(G-2410)
R C MOORE LUMBER CO
820 Miller St (43724)
PHONE.................................740 732-4950
Chad Moore, *President*
EMP: 14
SALES (corp-wide): 3.1MM **Privately Held**
WEB: www.rcmooredoorsnmore.com
SIC: 2431 5211 Doors, combination screen-storm, wood; lumber products
PA: R C Moore Lumber Co Inc
46000 County Road 56
Caldwell OH
740 732-2326

(G-2411)
SHARON STONE INC
44895 Sharon Stone Rd (43724-9534)
P.O. Box 100, Dexter City (45727-0100)
PHONE.................................740 732-7100
John McCort, *President*
Robert Cunningham, *Corp Secy*
Carl Baker Jr, *Vice Pres*
EMP: 6
SQ FT: 980
SALES (est): 509.5K **Privately Held**
SIC: 1422 Limestones, ground

(G-2412)
SOUTHEAST PUBLICATIONS INC
Also Called: Journal Leader
309 Main St (43724-1321)
P.O. Box 315 (43724-0315)
PHONE.................................740 732-2341
David Evans, *President*
Jack Cartener, *Director*
Ann Velgari, *Director*
EMP: 10 **EST:** 1941
SQ FT: 3,360
SALES: 536.5K **Privately Held**
SIC: 2711 2752 Commercial printing & newspaper publishing combined; commercial printing, lithographic

(G-2413)
UPPER SARAHSVILLE LLC
48726 Sarahsville Rd (43724-9773)
PHONE.................................740 732-2071
Elizabeth Saling, *Principal*
EMP: 3
SALES (est): 181.1K **Privately Held**
SIC: 3131 Mfg Footwear Cut Stock

Caledonia
Marion County

(G-2414)
CLARIDON TOOL & DIE INC
Also Called: Retterer Manufacturing Company
4985 Marion Mt Gilead Rd (43314-9431)
PHONE.................................740 389-1944
Karen Retterer, *President*
EMP: 7
SALES: 600K **Privately Held**
WEB: www.retterer.com
SIC: 3544 Special dies & tools

(G-2415)
DIVERSIFIED TOOL SYSTEMS
5357 Mrion Wllmsport Rd E (43314-9527)
P.O. Box 249 (43314-0249)
PHONE.................................419 845-2143
Robert Freeman, *Owner*
EMP: 4
SQ FT: 3,500
SALES (est): 432.5K **Privately Held**
SIC: 3544 Forms (molds), for foundry & plastics working machinery; special dies & tools

(G-2416)
GLEN-GERY CORPORATION
Also Called: Glen-Gery Caledonia Plant
5692 Rinker Rd (43314-9791)
P.O. Box 398 (43314-0398)
PHONE.................................419 845-3321
Jerry Hatch, *Plant Mgr*
Ken Hagberg, *Manager*
EMP: 90
SALES (corp-wide): 1.2MM **Privately Held**
WEB: www.glengerybrick.com
SIC: 3251 5211 3255 Brick clay: common face, glazed, vitrified or hollow; brick; clay refractories
HQ: Glen-Gery Corporation
1166 Spring St
Reading PA 19610
610 374-4011

(G-2417)
INSTA-GRO MANUFACTURING INC
8217 Linn Hipsher Rd (43314-9736)
PHONE.................................419 845-3046
Allan Farrow, *President*
Pat Miller, *Manager*
EMP: 6
SALES (est): 1.2MM **Privately Held**
WEB: www.instagro.com
SIC: 2875 5261 Fertilizers, mixing only; fertilizer

(G-2418)
JEFFERY A BURNS
Also Called: R & J Contracting
7430 Linn Hipsher Rd (43314-9733)
PHONE.................................419 845-2129
Jeffery A Burns, *Owner*
EMP: 5
SALES (est): 200K **Privately Held**
SIC: 3444 Sheet metalwork

(G-2419)
NAMES UNLIMITED CORP
3787 Marion Galion Rd (43314-9495)
PHONE.................................419 845-2005
Tom Cannane, *President*
EMP: 3
SQ FT: 3,000
SALES (est): 192.3K **Privately Held**
SIC: 3993 Signs & advertising specialties

(G-2420)
PILLSBURY COMPANY LLC
4136 Martel Rd (43314-9634)
PHONE.................................419 845-3751
Heidi Duval, *QC Dir*
Craig Olinger, *Branch Mgr*
Bob Rice, *MIS Mgr*
EMP: 75
SALES (corp-wide): 15.7B **Publicly Held**
WEB: www.pillsbury.com
SIC: 2041 2033 Flour & other grain mill products; canned fruits & specialties
HQ: The Pillsbury Company Llc
1 General Mills Blvd
Minneapolis MN 55426

Cambridge
Guernsey County

(G-2421)
ACI SERVICES INC (PA)
Also Called: Gas Products
125 Steubenville Ave (43725-2212)
PHONE.................................740 435-0240
Chad Brahler, *President*
Norm Shade, *Principal*
Danny Sawyer, *Mfg Mgr*
Brett Kyle, *Opers Staff*
Lou Brahler, *Mfg Staff*
EMP: 40
SQ FT: 25,000
SALES (est): 20MM **Privately Held**
WEB: www.aciservices.net
SIC: 3563 Air & gas compressors including vacuum pumps

(G-2422)
AMERICAN CULVERT & FABG CO
201 Wheeling Ave (43725-2256)
P.O. Box 757 (43725-0757)
PHONE.................................740 432-6334
Herman Rogovin, *President*
Christian Hasel, *Project Mgr*
EMP: 15 **EST:** 1936
SQ FT: 5,000
SALES (est): 1.4MM **Privately Held**
SIC: 3444 3312 Pipe, sheet metal; blast furnaces & steel mills

(G-2423)
AMG VANADIUM LLC
60790 Southgate Rd (43725-9414)
PHONE.................................740 435-4600
Hoy Frakes, *President*
Mark Anderson, *Vice Pres*
Christy McNamee, *Safety Mgr*
Mike Ross, *Foreman/Supr*
David Wardle, *QC Mgr*
◆ **EMP:** 1
SALES (est): 3.5MM
SALES (corp-wide): 1B **Privately Held**
SIC: 1094 Vanadium ore mining
PA: Amg Advanced Metallurgical Group N.V.
Strawinskylaan 1343
Amsterdam 1077
207 147-140

(G-2424)
APPALACHIAN SOLVENTS LLC
5041 Skyline Dr (43725-9729)
PHONE.................................740 680-3649
Jonathan Hudson, *Owner*
EMP: 3
SALES (est): 310.8K **Privately Held**
SIC: 2911 Solvents

(G-2425)
APPALACHIAN WELL SURVEYS INC
10291 Ohio Ave (43725)
P.O. Box 1058 (43725-6058)
PHONE.................................740 255-7652
Jonathan W Hudson, *President*
Mary Ann Hudson, *Vice Pres*
EMP: 8
SALES (est): 1.4MM **Privately Held**
SIC: 1389 Perforating well casings; surveying wells; well logging

(G-2426)
BATTLE HORSE KNIVES LLC
700 S 9th St (43725-2818)
PHONE.................................740 995-9009
Alicia B McQuain, *Principal*
EMP: 6
SALES (est): 501.1K **Privately Held**
SIC: 3949 Sporting & athletic goods

(G-2427)
BENNETT PLASTICS INC
197 N 2nd St (43725-2222)
PHONE.................................740 432-2209
Frank J Bennett Jr, *President*
EMP: 20
SALES (est): 1.2MM **Privately Held**
SIC: 3089 Injection molding of plastics

(G-2428)
BLUE RACER MIDSTREAM LLC
11388 E Pike Rd Unit B (43725-9669)
PHONE.................................740 630-7556
EMP: 16
SALES (est): 1MM **Privately Held**
SIC: 1382 Oil & gas exploration services

(G-2429)
CAMBRIDGE OHIO PRODUCTION & AS
Also Called: Copac
1521 Morton Ave (43725-2750)
PHONE.................................740 432-6383
Mike Arent, *President*
Andrew E Yandora, *Vice Pres*
Andrew Balik, *VP Sales*
EMP: 15
SQ FT: 39,500
SALES (est): 7.8MM **Privately Held**
SIC: 3578 3643 Accounting machines & cash registers; current-carrying wiring devices

(G-2430)
CAMBRIDGE PACKAGING INC
Also Called: Cambridge Box & Gift Shop
60794 Southgate Rd (43725-9414)
PHONE.................................740 432-3351
Larry Knellinger, *President*
Bill Knellinger, *Vice Pres*
Rick Knellinger, *Vice Pres*
John Common, *Purch Mgr*
John Luskevich, *Purch Mgr*
EMP: 31
SQ FT: 26,000
SALES (est): 7.6MM **Privately Held**
WEB: www.cambridgepackaging.com
SIC: 2653 5199 Boxes, corrugated: made from purchased materials; packaging materials

(G-2431)
CENTRIA INC
Also Called: Centria Coil Coating Services
530 N 2nd St (43725-1214)
PHONE.................................740 432-7351
Kelli Hill, *Human Resources*
Charlie Hamilton, *Manager*
Matt Mallett, *Assistant*
EMP: 100
SALES (corp-wide): 2B **Publicly Held**
SIC: 3444 Sheet metalwork
HQ: Centria, Inc.
1005 Beaver Grade Rd # 2
Moon Township PA 15108
412 299-8000

(G-2432)
COLGATE-PALMOLIVE COMPANY
8800 Guernsey Indus Blvd (43725-8913)
PHONE.................................212 310-2000
Pilar Mora, *Opers Mgr*
Brent Holton, *Safety Mgr*
Rick Spann, *Opers-Prdtn-Mfg*
Tom Badertscher, *Engineer*
Mauricio Torres, *Financial Exec*
EMP: 250
SALES (corp-wide): 15.5B **Publicly Held**
WEB: www.colgate.com
SIC: 2844 Toilet preparations
PA: Colgate-Palmolive Company
300 Park Ave Fl 3
New York NY 10022
212 310-2000

(G-2433)
CRESCENT SERVICES LLC
11137 E Pike Rd (43725-8949)
PHONE.................................405 603-1200
Susan Leonard, *Principal*
EMP: 4
SALES (est): 278.2K **Privately Held**
SIC: 1389 Oil field services

(G-2434)
DETROIT DESL RMNFACTURING CORP
8475 Reitler Rd (43725)
PHONE.................................740 439-7701

GEOGRAPHIC SECTION
Cambridge - Guernsey County (G-2460)

Cheryl Meyer, *Branch Mgr*
EMP: 13
SALES (corp-wide): 191.6B **Privately Held**
SIC: 3519 Diesel engine rebuilding
HQ: Detroit Diesel Remanufacturing Corporation
100 Lodestone Way
Tooele UT 84074

(G-2435)
DONAHUES HILLTOP ICE COMPANY
Also Called: Donahue's Hilltop Supply
1112 Highland Ave (43725-8809)
PHONE 740 432-3348
John Hoffman, *Owner*
John B Hoffman, *Owner*
EMP: 12
SQ FT: 8,000
SALES (est): 1.3MM **Privately Held**
SIC: 2097 Block ice; ice cubes

(G-2436)
ENCORE PLASTICS CORPORATION
725 Water St (43725-1241)
PHONE 740 432-1652
John Wilson, *Branch Mgr*
EMP: 56
SALES (est): 10MM
SALES (corp-wide): 83.3MM **Privately Held**
WEB: www.encoreplasticscorporation.com
SIC: 3089 Plastic processing
HQ: Encore Plastics Corporation
319 Howard Dr
Sandusky OH 44870

(G-2437)
FEDERAL-MOGUL POWERTRAIN LLC
6420 Glenn Hwy (43725-9755)
PHONE 740 432-2393
Robb Junker, *Branch Mgr*
EMP: 170
SALES (corp-wide): 11.7B **Publicly Held**
SIC: 3053 3592 3562 5085 Gaskets & sealing devices; oil seals, rubber; gaskets, all materials; pistons & piston rings; ball bearings & parts; bearings; motor vehicle parts & accessories; bearings, motor vehicle; transmission housings or parts, motor vehicle; steering mechanisms, motor vehicle; motor vehicle lighting equipment
HQ: Federal-Mogul Powertrain Llc
27300 W 11 Mile Rd # 101
Southfield MI 48034

(G-2438)
FREEDOM ROAD DEFENSE
1 Orchard Ln (43725-9526)
PHONE 740 541-7467
David J Ryan, *Principal*
EMP: 3
SALES (est): 185.4K **Privately Held**
SIC: 3812 Defense systems & equipment

(G-2439)
GAMETIME APPAREL & DEZIGNS LLC
2327 E Wheeling Ave (43725-2164)
PHONE 740 255-5254
Katalin S Beck,
EMP: 3
SALES (est): 89.2K **Privately Held**
SIC: 2329 Men's & boys' sportswear & athletic clothing

(G-2440)
GEORGETOWN VINEYARDS INC
62920 Georgetown Rd (43725-9749)
PHONE 740 435-3222
John Nicolozakes, *President*
Kay Nicolozakes, *Vice Pres*
Sam Nicolozakes, *Treasurer*
Emma McVicker, *Admin Sec*
EMP: 25
SQ FT: 600
SALES (est): 113.3K **Privately Held**
SIC: 0721 2084 5812 2082 Vines, cultivation of; wine cellars, bonded: engaged in blending wines; pizza restaurants; near beer

(G-2441)
GRAHAM PACKAGING COMPANY LP
8800 Guernsey Industrial (43725-8912)
PHONE 740 439-4242
Jim Blume, *Plant Mgr*
Dave Echols, *Branch Mgr*
EMP: 43
SALES (corp-wide): 1MM **Privately Held**
WEB: www.grahampackaging.com
SIC: 3089 Plastic containers, except foam
HQ: Graham Packaging Company, L.P.
700 Indian Springs Dr # 100
Lancaster PA 17601
717 849-8500

(G-2442)
H & AN LLC
Also Called: Allegra Marketing & Printing
1224 Southgate Pkwy (43725-2945)
PHONE 740 435-0200
Thomas L Heins,
EMP: 3
SALES (est): 188.6K **Privately Held**
SIC: 2752 Commercial printing, offset

(G-2443)
HOMESTEAD LANDSCAPERS
67137 Old 21 Rd 21st (43725)
P.O. Box 81 (43725-0081)
PHONE 740 435-8480
Adam Meighen, *Owner*
EMP: 5
SALES (est): 311.4K **Privately Held**
SIC: 0782 1389 Landscape contractors; construction, repair & dismantling services

(G-2444)
KENNEDYS BAKERY INC
1025 Wheeling Ave (43725-2441)
P.O. Box 396 (43725-0396)
PHONE 740 432-2301
T Noralee Kennedy, *President*
Bob Kennedy, *Vice Pres*
EMP: 27 **EST:** 1925
SQ FT: 8,000
SALES (est): 1.2MM **Privately Held**
WEB: www.kennedysbakery.com
SIC: 5461 2052 2051 Doughnuts; cookies & crackers; bread, cake & related products

(G-2445)
KINGSLY COMPRESSION INC
3956 Glenn Hwy (43725-8575)
PHONE 740 439-0772
Jeffrey B Sable, *Branch Mgr*
EMP: 8 **Privately Held**
WEB: www.kingslycompression.com
SIC: 3563 5084 Air & gas compressors; processing & packaging equipment
PA: Kingsly Compression, Inc.
3750 S Noah Dr
Saxonburg PA 16056

(G-2446)
LILIENTHAL SOUTHEASTERN INC
1609 N 11th St (43725-1009)
P.O. Box 580 (43725-0580)
PHONE 740 439-1640
Richard W Lilienthal, *President*
EMP: 18 **EST:** 1875
SQ FT: 6,000
SALES (est): 2.2MM **Privately Held**
WEB: www.lilseinc.com
SIC: 2752 2782 2759 2789 Commercial printing, offset; blankbooks; letterpress printing; bookbinding & related work

(G-2447)
LMI CUSTOM MIXING LLC
804 Byesville Rd (43725-9327)
PHONE 740 435-0444
Jason Pierce, *Prdtn Mgr*
Chris Mears, *Production*
Garry Lute, *Plant Engr*
Maurya Shaw, *Human Res Mgr*
Greg Mealer, *Technical Staff*
▲ **EMP:** 74 **EST:** 1997
SQ FT: 15,000
SALES (est): 29.8MM
SALES (corp-wide): 3.6B **Publicly Held**
WEB: www.laureninternational.com
SIC: 2891 Rubber cement
HQ: Lauren International, Ltd.
2228 Reiser Ave Se
New Philadelphia OH 44663
330 339-3373

(G-2448)
MILLER MACHINE & MFG LLC
62056 Greendale Rd (43725-9687)
PHONE 740 439-2283
John Miller, *Mng Member*
Sherri Miller, *Mng Member*
EMP: 3 **EST:** 2002
SALES: 250K **Privately Held**
SIC: 3599 Machine shop, jobbing & repair

(G-2449)
MOSSER GLASS INCORPORATED
9279 Cadiz Rd (43725-9564)
PHONE 740 439-1827
Timmy J Mosser, *President*
Thomas R Mosser, *President*
Mindy Hartly, *Manager*
▲ **EMP:** 30
SALES (est): 3.9MM **Privately Held**
WEB: www.mosserglass.com
SIC: 3229 5199 5719 Novelty glassware; glassware, industrial; glassware, novelty; glassware

(G-2450)
MOTRIN CORPORATION
1070 Byesville Rd (43725-8403)
P.O. Box 262 (43725-0262)
PHONE 740 439-2725
Jack O Cartner, *President*
EMP: 4 **EST:** 1967
SQ FT: 8,000
SALES (est): 396.3K **Privately Held**
SIC: 3523 Farm machinery & equipment

(G-2451)
OHIO BRIDGE CORPORATION
Also Called: U.S. Bridge
201 Wheeling Ave (43725-2256)
P.O. Box 757 (43725-0757)
PHONE 740 432-6334
Daniel Rogovin, *CEO*
Jeff Lawson, *Division Mgr*
Richard Rogovin, *Chairman*
Scott Flaten, *Project Engr*
David Morgan, *Design Engr*
▼ **EMP:** 140 **EST:** 1952
SQ FT: 250,000
SALES (est): 56.6MM **Privately Held**
SIC: 1622 3449 Bridge construction; bars, concrete reinforcing: fabricated steel

(G-2452)
PACKAGING MATERIALS INC
62805 Bennett Ave (43725-9490)
P.O. Box 731 (43725-0731)
PHONE 740 439-6337
Fax: 740 439-4718
▼ **EMP:** 38 **EST:** 1970
SQ FT: 48,000
SALES (est): 6.4MM
SALES (corp-wide): 14.9MM **Privately Held**
SIC: 3081 2759 2673 Mfg Unsupported Plastic Film/Sheet Commercial Printing Mfg Bags-Plastic/Coated Paper
PA: Columbia Burlap And Bag Company, Inc.
999 Bedford Rd
North Kansas City MO 64116
816 421-4121

(G-2453)
PLASTIC COMPOUNDERS INC
1125 Utica Dr (43725-2578)
P.O. Box 664 (43725-0664)
PHONE 740 432-7371
Dick Eubanks, *President*
Phyllis Bowlin, *President*
D I C K Eubanks, *President*
Dave Carroll, *Vice Pres*
EMP: 40
SQ FT: 50,000
SALES (est): 9.3MM **Privately Held**
SIC: 2821 Melamine resins, melamine-formaldehyde

(G-2454)
QUANEX IG SYSTEMS INC
2411 E Wheeling Ave (43725-2166)
PHONE 740 439-2338
Michael Hovan, *CEO*
EMP: 175 **Publicly Held**
SIC: 3061 3053 Mechanical rubber goods; gaskets, packing & sealing devices
HQ: Quanex Ig Systems, Inc.
388 S Main St Ste 700
Akron OH 44311

(G-2455)
RIDGE TOOL COMPANY
Also Called: North American Dist Ctr
9877 Brick Church Rd (43725-9420)
PHONE 740 432-8782
Brian Shanahann, *Manager*
EMP: 81
SALES (corp-wide): 17.4B **Publicly Held**
WEB: www.ridgid.com
SIC: 3541 Machine tools, metal cutting type
HQ: Ridge Tool Company
400 Clark St
Elyria OH 44035
440 323-5581

(G-2456)
SLABE TOOL COMPANY
1300 Oxford Ave (43725-3012)
PHONE 740 439-1647
Paula Larrick, *President*
Don Larrick, *Vice Pres*
EMP: 3
SQ FT: 5,000
SALES: 300K **Privately Held**
SIC: 3544 7692 Industrial molds; dies & die holders for metal cutting, forming, die casting; welding repair

(G-2457)
SUPERIOR HARDWOODS OHIO INC
Also Called: Superior Hardwoods Cambridge
9911 Ohio Ave (43725-9307)
P.O. Box 1358 (43725-6358)
PHONE 740 439-2727
Fred Lander, *Manager*
EMP: 30
SALES (corp-wide): 9.1MM **Privately Held**
SIC: 2421 2426 Sawmills & planing mills, general; hardwood dimension & flooring mills
PA: Superior Hardwoods Of Ohio, Inc.
134 Wellston Indus Pk Rd
Wellston OH 45692
740 384-5677

(G-2458)
TAYLOR QUICK PRINT
1008 Woodlawn Ave A (43725-2951)
PHONE 740 439-2208
Brenda Taylor, *Principal*
EMP: 6
SALES (est): 844.9K **Privately Held**
SIC: 2752 Commercial printing, offset

(G-2459)
TED TIPPLE
6176 Simmons Rd (43725-9458)
PHONE 740 432-3263
Ted Tipple, *Principal*
EMP: 4
SALES (est): 218.5K **Privately Held**
SIC: 1221 Bituminous coal & lignite-surface mining

(G-2460)
TELLING INDUSTRIES LLC
2105 Larrick Rd (43725-3064)
PHONE 740 435-8900
Jon Reed, *Plant Mgr*
Deirdre McGregor, *Sales Staff*
Summer Reed, *Sales Staff*
Steve Linch, *Manager*
John Greminger, *Manager*
EMP: 70
SALES (corp-wide): 29.1MM **Privately Held**
WEB: www.tellingindustries.com
SIC: 3316 Bars, steel, cold finished, from purchased hot-rolled

Cambridge - Guernsey County (G-2461)

GEOGRAPHIC SECTION

PA: Telling Industries, Llc
4420 Sherwin Rd
Willoughby OH 44094
440 974-3370

(G-2461)
VARIETY GLASS INC
201 Foster Ave (43725-1219)
PHONE..................740 432-3643
Thomas R Mosser, *President*
Timothy J Mosser, *Vice Pres*
EMP: 10
SQ FT: 16,000
SALES (est): 2MM **Privately Held**
WEB: www.varietyglass.com
SIC: 3229 Scientific glassware

(G-2462)
W A S P INC
59100 Claysville Rd (43725-8943)
PHONE..................740 439-2398
Jeffrey L Carpenter, *Principal*
EMP: 3
SALES (est): 394.6K **Privately Held**
SIC: 5074 3432 Plumbing & hydronic heating supplies; plumbing fixture fittings & trim

(G-2463)
ZEKELMAN INDUSTRIES INC
Also Called: Wheatland Tube Company
9208 Jeffrey Dr (43725-9417)
PHONE..................740 432-2146
Ned Feeney, *President*
EMP: 104
SQ FT: 58,000 **Privately Held**
SIC: 3317 3498 5074 3644 Pipes, seamless steel; fabricated pipe & fittings; plumbing fittings & supplies; noncurrent-carrying wiring services; plumbing fixture fittings & trim; blast furnaces & steel mills
PA: Zekelman Industries, Inc.
227 W Monroe St Ste 2600
Chicago IL 60606

Camden
Preble County

(G-2464)
CAMDEN READY MIX CO (PA)
478 Cmden Cllege Cornr Rd (45311-9520)
P.O. Box 5, West Alexandria (45381-0005)
PHONE..................937 456-4539
John D Wysong, *President*
Carroll Wysong, *Vice Pres*
EMP: 10
SALES (est): 1.2MM **Privately Held**
SIC: 3273 Ready-mixed concrete

(G-2465)
OHIO SLITTING & STORAGE
7000 N Main St (45311-9503)
PHONE..................937 452-1108
Travis Hearn, *President*
Matt Lankheit, *General Mgr*
Gary Macobe, *Controller*
EMP: 20
SALES (est): 998.8K **Privately Held**
SIC: 3291 Abrasive products

(G-2466)
PRECISION WOOD PRODUCTS INC (PA)
2456 Aukerman Creek Rd (45311-9706)
P.O. Box 10 (45311-0010)
PHONE..................937 787-3523
Anthony Metzger, *President*
Lloyd W Kinzie, *President*
Glen D Knaus, *Vice Pres*
H Ronald Knaus, *Vice Pres*
Barbara Knaus, *Admin Sec*
EMP: 28 EST: 1977
SQ FT: 32,000
SALES (est): 2.6MM **Privately Held**
WEB: www.precisionwoodproducts.net
SIC: 2431 Doors, wood

(G-2467)
WYSONG GRAVEL CO INC
120 Cmden Cllege Cornr Rd (45311-9520)
P.O. Box 5, West Alexandria (45381-0005)
PHONE..................937 452-1523
Tom Caden, *General Mgr*
EMP: 7
SQ FT: 3,452
SALES (corp-wide): 3.1MM **Privately Held**
SIC: 1442 Gravel mining
PA: Wysong Gravel Co Inc
2332 State Route 503 N
West Alexandria OH 45381
937 456-4539

Campbell
Mahoning County

(G-2468)
INTERNTNAL PLSTIC CMPNENTS INC
75 Mccartney Rd (44405-1071)
P.O. Box 603 (44405-0603)
PHONE..................330 744-0625
William West, *President*
William West Jr, *Vice Pres*
EMP: 15
SQ FT: 20,000
SALES (est): 2.4MM **Privately Held**
SIC: 3089 5084 Plastic hardware & building products; industrial machinery & equipment

(G-2469)
SEACOR PAINTING CORPORATION
98 Creed Cir (44405-1277)
P.O. Box 588 (44405-0588)
PHONE..................330 755-6361
Nicholas Frangos, *President*
EMP: 8
SALES (est): 984.8K **Privately Held**
SIC: 3479 Painting of metal products

(G-2470)
SUMMER GLOBAL SYSTEMS LLC
115 Creed Cir (44405-1204)
PHONE..................330 397-1653
John Mahinis,
EMP: 4
SALES (est): 203.7K **Privately Held**
SIC: 3599 Machine & other job shop work

(G-2471)
VINDICATOR
3770 Wilson Ave (44405-1767)
PHONE..................330 755-0135
EMP: 3
SALES (est): 118.9K **Privately Held**
SIC: 2711 Newspapers-Publishing/Printing

(G-2472)
WEST EXTRUSION LLC
75 Mccartney Rd (44405-1071)
PHONE..................330 744-0625
William West, *Principal*
EMP: 5
SALES (est): 171.8K **Privately Held**
SIC: 3089 Extruded finished plastic products

Canal Fulton
Stark County

(G-2473)
AMAN & CO INC
Also Called: Met-All Industries
231 Locust St S (44614-1294)
P.O. Box 459 (44614-0459)
PHONE..................330 854-1122
John Aman, *President*
Elizabeth Aman, *Corp Secy*
Michael Aman, *Vice Pres*
EMP: 4
SQ FT: 7,500
SALES (est): 683.5K **Privately Held**
SIC: 2842 Metal polish

(G-2474)
AMERICAN TRADITIONS BASKET CO
Also Called: Bayberry Co
722 Tell Dr (44614-9324)
PHONE..................330 854-0900
▲ **EMP:** 20
SQ FT: 15,000
SALES (est): 2.1MM **Privately Held**
SIC: 3944 5947 Mfg & Ret Baskets & Accessories

(G-2475)
ASTRO-TEC MFG INC
550 Elm Ridge Ave (44614-9369)
P.O. Box 608 (44614-0608)
PHONE..................330 854-2209
Stephanie Hopper, *President*
Derl Wells, *Design Engr*
Dale Lewis, *Sales Mgr*
Heather Beichler, *Accounts Mgr*
Sophia Haines, *Office Mgr*
◆ **EMP:** 22 EST: 1963
SQ FT: 15,328
SALES (est): 5.3MM **Privately Held**
WEB: www.astro-tec.com
SIC: 3441 Fabricated structural metal

(G-2476)
BECKY KNAPP
Also Called: Deliciously Different Candies
136 N Canal St (44614-1198)
PHONE..................330 854-4400
Becky Knapp, *Owner*
EMP: 5
SQ FT: 1,400
SALES (est): 337.2K **Privately Held**
SIC: 5441 2064 2066 Candy; candy & other confectionery products; chocolate & cocoa products

(G-2477)
BIRDS EYE FOODS INC
611 Elm Ridge Ave (44614-8476)
PHONE..................330 854-0818
Bill Gaster, *Branch Mgr*
EMP: 25
SALES (corp-wide): 7.9B **Publicly Held**
WEB: www.agrilinkfoods.com
SIC: 2096 3523 Potato chips & similar snacks; peanut combines, diggers, packers & threshers
HQ: Birds Eye Foods, Inc.
121 Woodcrest Rd
Cherry Hill NJ 08003
585 383-1850

(G-2478)
C MASSOUH PRINTING CO INC
Also Called: C Massouh Printing
590 Elm Ridge Ave (44614-9369)
PHONE..................330 408-7330
Carl Massouh, *President*
Chris Massouh, *Vice Pres*
Steve Massouh, *VP Sales*
EMP: 10
SALES (est): 1.5MM **Privately Held**
SIC: 2752 Commercial printing, offset

(G-2479)
EXODUS MOLD & MACHINE INC
960 Milan St N (44614-9737)
P.O. Box 593 (44614-0593)
PHONE..................330 854-0282
Mark White, *Principal*
EMP: 4
SALES (est): 522K **Privately Held**
WEB: www.exodusmold.com
SIC: 3544 Industrial molds

(G-2480)
GLOBECOM TECHNOLOGIES INC
8542 Kepler Ave Nw (44614-8862)
PHONE..................330 408-7008
Robert Alto, *President*
EMP: 1
SALES (est): 1.1MM **Privately Held**
SIC: 3663 Radio receiver networks

(G-2481)
JONMAR GEAR AND MACHINE INC
13786 Warwick Dr Nw (44614-9738)
PHONE..................330 854-6500
Larry Murgatroyd, *President*
Brent A Murgatroyd, *Vice Pres*
EMP: 6 EST: 2000
SQ FT: 18,000
SALES (est): 302.5K **Privately Held**
SIC: 3566 7699 Gears, power transmission, except automotive; industrial machinery & equipment repair

(G-2482)
LINDSAY PACKAGE SYSTEMS INC
6845 Erie Ave Nw (44614-8509)
P.O. Box 578 (44614-0578)
PHONE..................330 854-4511
Tim Gesaman, *CEO*
EMP: 4
SALES: 1MM
SALES (corp-wide): 31.1MM **Privately Held**
WEB: www.lindsayconcrete.com
SIC: 3272 Precast terrazo or concrete products
PA: Lindsay Precast, Inc.
5820 Erie Ave Nw
Canal Fulton OH 44614
800 837-7788

(G-2483)
LINDSAY PRECAST INC (PA)
5820 Erie Ave Nw (44614-9726)
P.O. Box 578 (44614-0578)
PHONE..................800 837-7788
Roland Lindsay Sr, *President*
Timothy Gesaman, *Vice Pres*
Linda Lindsay, *Treasurer*
▼ **EMP:** 49
SQ FT: 16,400
SALES (est): 31.1MM **Privately Held**
WEB: www.lindsayconcrete.com
SIC: 3272 3699 Septic tanks, concrete; manhole covers or frames, concrete; security devices

(G-2484)
LUBE DEPOT
2185 Locust St S (44614-8437)
PHONE..................330 854-6345
Mike Primovero, *Principal*
EMP: 3
SALES (est): 243.4K **Privately Held**
SIC: 2911 Oils, lubricating

(G-2485)
MACA MOLD & MACHINE CO INC
761 Elm Ridge Ave (44614-9380)
PHONE..................330 854-0292
John J Addessi, *President*
EMP: 6
SALES (est): 767.5K **Privately Held**
SIC: 3999 Manufacturing industries

(G-2486)
MIDWEST KNIFE GRINDING INC
492 Elm Ridge Ave Ste 4 (44614-9369)
PHONE..................330 854-1030
James M Richmond II, *President*
Bobbie Stephenson, *General Mgr*
Shawna Delauder, *Engineer*
EMP: 10
SQ FT: 12,000
SALES (est): 2MM **Privately Held**
WEB: www.midwestknifegrinding.com
SIC: 7699 3541 3423 Knife, saw & tool sharpening & repair; machine tools, metal cutting type; hand & edge tools

(G-2487)
NEW IMAGE PLASTICS MFG CO
Also Called: Nipm
241 Market St W (44614-1014)
P.O. Box 550 (44614-0550)
PHONE..................330 854-3010
James E Waring Sr, *Owner*
EMP: 3
SQ FT: 9,000
SALES (est): 393.9K **Privately Held**
WEB: www.newimageplastic.com
SIC: 3082 Rods, unsupported plastic; tubes, unsupported plastic

(G-2488)
OIL & GO LLC
2185 Locust St S (44614-8437)
PHONE..................330 854-6345
Matt Farmer, *President*
EMP: 3 EST: 2017
SALES (est): 181.5K **Privately Held**
SIC: 1311 Crude petroleum production

(G-2489)
PROCESS AUTOMATION SPECIALISTS
7405 Diamondback Ave Nw (44614-8106)
PHONE...................330 247-1384
Scott Veno, *Owner*
EMP: 1
SALES: 1MM **Privately Held**
SIC: 5084 3564 Instruments & control equipment; dust or fume collecting equipment, industrial

(G-2490)
QUADCAST
6845 Erie Ave Nw (44614-8509)
P.O. Box 578 (44614-0578)
PHONE...................330 854-4511
Roland C Lindsay Jr, *Principal*
EMP: 4
SALES (est): 240.2K **Privately Held**
SIC: 3273 Ready-mixed concrete

(G-2491)
RACK COATING SERVICE INC
5760 Erie Ave Nw (44614-9726)
P.O. Box 486 (44614-0486)
PHONE...................330 854-2869
John L Hexamer, *President*
EMP: 20 EST: 1963
SQ FT: 2,500
SALES: 1.4MM **Privately Held**
SIC: 3479 Hot dip coating of metals or formed products

(G-2492)
RICHARD PASKIET MACHINISTS
468 Etheridge Blvd S (44614-9399)
PHONE...................330 854-4160
Richard Paskiet, *President*
Holly Paskiet, *Treasurer*
EMP: 4
SALES (est): 468.2K **Privately Held**
SIC: 3599 3544 Machine shop, jobbing & repair; special dies, tools, jigs & fixtures

(G-2493)
SUMMIT ENGINEERED PRODUCTS
516 Elm Ridge Ave (44614-9369)
PHONE...................330 854-5388
Dick Lutz, *Principal*
EMP: 10
SALES (est): 1.8MM **Privately Held**
SIC: 3315 Steel wire & related products

(G-2494)
TEK GROUP INTERNATIONAL INC
Also Called: Tek Manufacturing
567 Elm Ridge Ave (44614-9369)
PHONE...................330 706-0000
Chris Willison, *President*
Cliff Willison, *President*
EMP: 35
SQ FT: 12,000
SALES (est): 8.7MM **Privately Held**
WEB: www.tekintl.com
SIC: 3462 Automotive forgings, ferrous: crankshaft, engine, axle, etc.

(G-2495)
USA PRECAST CONCRETE LIMITED
801 Elm Ridge Ave (44614-9396)
P.O. Box 613 (44614-0613)
PHONE...................330 854-9600
Timothy Gesaman, *President*
Jeffrey Augustine, *Vice Pres*
Jeff Augustine, *Vice Pres*
Krista Gesaman, *Vice Pres*
Wendy Potashnik, *Vice Pres*
EMP: 7
SALES (est): 473K **Privately Held**
SIC: 3272 Concrete products, precast

(G-2496)
WELDED TUBE PROS LLC
Also Called: Wtp Engineering
215 Market St W (44614-1014)
P.O. Box 202, Doylestown (44230-0202)
PHONE...................330 854-2966
Bud Graham, *President*
Worth B Graham,
EMP: 3
SQ FT: 2,500
SALES (est): 592.9K **Privately Held**
WEB: www.weldedtubepros.com
SIC: 5084 3827 8711 Industrial machinery & equipment; optical test & inspection equipment; consulting engineer

Canal Winchester
Franklin County

(G-2497)
A K ATHLETIC EQUIPMENT INC
8015 Howe Industrial Pkwy (43110-7890)
PHONE...................614 920-3069
Angela Katz, *President*
Paige Ludwin, *Sales Staff*
EMP: 25
SQ FT: 32,000
SALES (est): 4.2MM **Privately Held**
WEB: www.akathletics.com
SIC: 3086 5091 Plastics foam products; gymnasium equipment

(G-2498)
ALBANESE CONCESSIONS LLC
6983 Greensview Vlg Dr (43110-8454)
PHONE...................614 402-4937
Bridget L Albanese,
EMP: 7
SALES (est): 749K **Privately Held**
SIC: 2064 Candy & other confectionery products

(G-2499)
BABBERT REAL ESTATE INV CO LTD (PA)
7415 Diley Rd (43110-8813)
P.O. Box 203 (43110-0203)
PHONE...................614 837-8444
Ervin C Babbert, *CEO*
Chuck Babbert, *President*
Bonnie Babbert, *Corp Secy*
Ronald Babbert, *Vice Pres*
EMP: 100
SQ FT: 20,000
SALES (est): 8.6MM **Privately Held**
SIC: 3272 Liquid catch basins, tanks & covers: concrete

(G-2500)
CAPSA SOLUTIONS LLC
8170 Dove Pkwy (43110-9674)
PHONE...................800 437-6633
David Burns, *CEO*
EMP: 90
SALES (corp-wide): 238MM **Privately Held**
SIC: 3572 Computer storage devices
HQ: Capsa Solutions Llc
    4253 Ne 189th Ave
    Portland OR 97230
    503 766-2324

(G-2501)
CATERPILLAR INC
8170 Dove Pkwy (43110-9674)
PHONE...................614 834-2400
Jay Kautz, *Engineer*
David McLay, *Engineer*
Eric Ruth, *Engineer*
Bill Schmidt, *Engineer*
Darrel Berglund, *Senior Engr*
EMP: 63
SALES (corp-wide): 54.7B **Publicly Held**
WEB: www.cat.com
SIC: 3531 Construction machinery
PA: Caterpillar Inc.
    510 Lake Cook Rd Ste 100
    Deerfield IL 60015
    224 551-4000

(G-2502)
E C BABBERT INC
7415 Diley Rd (43110-8813)
P.O. Box 203 (43110-0203)
PHONE...................614 837-8444
Ervin C Babbert, *CEO*
Charles Babbert, *President*
Chris Conkey, *Sales Staff*
EMP: 72
SALES: 950K **Privately Held**
SIC: 3272 Liquid catch basins, tanks & covers: concrete

(G-2503)
FIFTH AVENUE LUMBER CO
Lumbercraft
5200 Winchester Pike (43110-9723)
PHONE...................614 833-6655
Chris Kealey, *Manager*
EMP: 67
SALES (corp-wide): 39.1MM **Privately Held**
WEB: www.straitandlamp.com
SIC: 2431 2439 2452 2435 Millwork; trusses, wooden roof; prefabricated wood buildings; hardwood veneer & plywood
HQ: Fifth Avenue Lumber Co (Inc)
    479 E 5th Ave
    Columbus OH 43201
    614 294-0068

(G-2504)
KELLOGG CABINETS INC
Also Called: Kci Works
7711 Diley Rd (43110-9616)
PHONE...................614 833-9596
Judy A Kellogg, *CEO*
Judy Kellogg, *President*
Douglas E Kellogg, *Vice Pres*
◆ EMP: 9
SQ FT: 28,850
SALES (est): 4.4MM **Privately Held**
WEB: www.kellogcabinets.com
SIC: 2541 2542 2434 Cabinets, except refrigerated: show, display, etc.: wood; store fixtures, wood; partitions & fixtures, except wood; wood kitchen cabinets

(G-2505)
LEAF LONO EARTH ALTERNTV FUELS
4204 Town Square Dr (43110-7757)
PHONE...................614 829-7159
Patrick Hannon, *Owner*
EMP: 3
SALES (est): 200.7K **Privately Held**
SIC: 2869 Fuels

(G-2506)
MANIFOLD & PHALOR INC
Also Called: US Die & Mold
10385 Busey Rd Nw (43110-8883)
PHONE...................614 920-1200
Thomas J Creek, *President*
Chad White, *Opers Mgr*
Nancy McCoy, *Purch Mgr*
Tim Furlong, *VP Sales*
▼ EMP: 45 EST: 1946
SQ FT: 28,800
SALES (est): 13.1MM **Privately Held**
WEB: www.manifoldphalor.com
SIC: 3441 3599 3559 Fabricated structural metal; machine shop, jobbing & repair; glass making machinery: blowing, molding, forming, etc.

(G-2507)
NIFCO AMERICA CORPORATION (HQ)
8015 Dove Pkwy (43110-9697)
PHONE...................614 920-6800
Toshiyuki Yamamoto, *President*
Tom Day, *Vice Pres*
John Kosik, *CFO*
▲ EMP: 312
SQ FT: 50,000
SALES (est): 246.3MM
SALES (corp-wide): 2.5B **Privately Held**
WEB: www.nifco-us.com
SIC: 3089 Automotive parts, plastic
PA: Nifco Inc.
    5-3, Hikarinooka
    Yokosuka KNG 239-0
    468 390-225

(G-2508)
NIFCO AMERICA CORPORATION
Also Called: Canal Winchester Facility
8015 Dove Pkwy (43110-9697)
PHONE...................614 836-3808
Tom Day, *General Mgr*
EMP: 250
SALES (corp-wide): 2.5B **Privately Held**
WEB: www.nifco-us.com
SIC: 3089 Automotive parts, plastic

HQ: Nifco America Corporation
    8015 Dove Pkwy
    Canal Winchester OH 43110
    614 920-6800

(G-2509)
NURDCON LLC
Also Called: Division 20
6645 Kodiak Dr (43110-8665)
PHONE...................614 208-5898
Jack Stewart,
EMP: 3
SALES: 36K **Privately Held**
SIC: 2731 8742 Book publishing; marketing consulting services

(G-2510)
OLAN PLASTICS INC
6550 Olan Dr (43110-9685)
PHONE...................614 834-6526
Olan Long, *CEO*
James Long, *President*
Marcella Long, *Corp Secy*
EMP: 40
SQ FT: 30,000
SALES (est): 6.7MM **Privately Held**
WEB: www.olanplastics.com
SIC: 3089 Plastic containers, except foam; injection molding of plastics

(G-2511)
S & S SIGN CO
10601 Lithopolis Rd Nw (43110-8804)
PHONE...................614 837-1511
Robert Schorr, *Owner*
EMP: 3
SALES (est): 142K **Privately Held**
SIC: 3993 Signs & advertising specialties

(G-2512)
TARMAN MACHINE COMPANY INC
8215 Dove Pkwy (43110-7717)
P.O. Box 192, Pickerington (43147-0192)
PHONE...................614 834-4010
Randy Tarman, *President*
EMP: 17
SQ FT: 13,000
SALES (est): 1.8MM **Privately Held**
SIC: 3599 Machine shop, jobbing & repair

(G-2513)
TIGER OIL INC (PA)
Also Called: Tiger Construction
650 Winchester Pike (43110-9170)
PHONE...................614 837-5552
Gerald Pfeifer, *President*
Damon Pfeifer, *Vice Pres*
Henrietta Pfeifer, *Treasurer*
EMP: 3
SALES (est): 1.4MM **Privately Held**
WEB: www.tigeroil.com
SIC: 1381 Drilling oil & gas wells

(G-2514)
TS TRIM INDUSTRIES INC
6380 Canal St (43110-9640)
PHONE...................614 837-4114
Ray Davis, *Plant Mgr*
Paul Korwin, *QC Mgr*
Robyn Miller, *Human Res Mgr*
Allen Layne, *Mktg Dir*
Cliff Campbell, *Manager*
EMP: 11
SALES (corp-wide): 4.5B **Privately Held**
WEB: www.tstrim.com
SIC: 3465 Automotive stampings
HQ: Ts Trim Industries Inc.
    6380 Canal St
    Canal Winchester OH 43110
    614 837-4114

(G-2515)
WORKING PROFESSIONALS LLC
3353 Oak Bend Blvd (43110-9322)
PHONE...................833 244-6299
Monecca Webb, *Mng Member*
EMP: 5
SALES (est): 230.7K **Privately Held**
SIC: 3537 Hoppers, end dump

Canal Winchester - Franklin County (G-2516)

(G-2516)
WORLD HARVEST CHURCH INC (PA)
Also Called: Breakthrough Media Ministries
4595 Gender Rd (43110-9149)
P.O. Box 428 (43110-0428)
PHONE.................................614 837-1990
Rodney Parsley, *Pastor*
Rod Parsley, *Pastor*
Darrin Endicott, *Maintenance Dir*
Jeff Barnhart, *Director*
EMP: 300
SQ FT: 200,000
SALES (est): 14.4MM **Privately Held**
WEB: www.breakthrough.net
SIC: 7812 2731 Video tape production; books; publishing & printing

Canfield
Mahoning County

(G-2517)
ADVETECH INC (PA)
Also Called: Perfection In Carbide
445 W Main St (44406-1425)
PHONE.................................330 533-2227
David Scott Owens, *CEO*
David Smith, *President*
EMP: 30
SQ FT: 30,000
SALES (est): 7.4MM **Privately Held**
SIC: 3421 3599 3423 3541 Knife blades & blanks; shears, hand; machine shop, jobbing & repair; knives, agricultural or industrial; machine tools, metal cutting type

(G-2518)
ADVETECH INC
451 W Main St (44406-1425)
P.O. Box 163216, Columbus (43216-3216)
PHONE.................................330 533-2227
Dave Smith, *Manager*
EMP: 34
SALES (corp-wide): 7.4MM **Privately Held**
WEB: www.advetech.com
SIC: 3423 Knives, agricultural or industrial
PA: Advetech Inc
445 W Main St
Canfield OH 44406
330 533-2227

(G-2519)
AFC COMPANY
Also Called: Canfield Industrial Park
5183 W Western Reserve Rd (44406-8112)
PHONE.................................330 533-5581
Judith Raber, *President*
EMP: 13 **EST:** 1915
SQ FT: 2,500
SALES (est): 1.2MM **Privately Held**
WEB: www.afcfencing.com
SIC: 6512 7389 3255 3251 Commercial & industrial building operation; grinding, precision: commercial or industrial; clay refractories; ceramic glazed brick, clay

(G-2520)
ALLOY UNLIMITED WELD
4200 W Middletown Rd (44406-9474)
PHONE.................................330 506-8375
John Kish, *Principal*
EMP: 3
SALES (est): 265.7K **Privately Held**
SIC: 7692 Welding repair

(G-2521)
ALSTART ENTERPRISES LLC
Also Called: USA Rolls
451 W Main St (44406-1425)
P.O. Box 1076 (44406-5076)
PHONE.................................330 533-3222
Kevin M Sheldon, *President*
EMP: 18 **EST:** 2009
SQ FT: 55,000
SALES (est): 4.9MM **Privately Held**
SIC: 3559 Plastics working machinery

(G-2522)
ALUMINUM EXTRUSION TECH LLC
6155 State Route 446 (44406-9428)
PHONE.................................330 533-3994
Andrew Ruhl, *Mng Member*
EMP: 6
SALES (est): 710K **Privately Held**
SIC: 3355 Extrusion ingot, aluminum: made in rolling mills

(G-2523)
BAIRD BROTHERS SAWMILL INC
7060 Crory Rd (44406-9720)
PHONE.................................330 533-3122
Paul Baird, *President*
Roland Bundy, *Sales Staff*
C Smith, *Sales Staff*
Helen Perrine, *Admin Sec*
EMP: 115 **EST:** 1960
SQ FT: 350,000
SALES (est): 19.9MM **Privately Held**
WEB: www.bairdbros.com
SIC: 2431 Doors & door parts & trim, wood

(G-2524)
CANFIELD COATING LLC
460 W Main St (44406-1434)
PHONE.................................330 533-3311
Ron Jandrokovic,
EMP: 9
SALES (est): 16.6MM **Privately Held**
SIC: 3479 5051 Galvanizing of iron, steel or end-formed products; metals service centers & offices
HQ: Material Sciences Corporation
6855 Commerce Blvd
Canton MI 48187
734 207-4444

(G-2525)
DUNAWAY INC
Also Called: D I
5959 Leffingwell Rd (44406-9132)
P.O. Box 488 (44406-0488)
PHONE.................................330 533-7753
Michael Dunaway, *President*
Albert E Brennan, *Principal*
Catherine Dunaway, *Vice Pres*
▲ **EMP:** 20
SQ FT: 30,000
SALES (est): 3.9MM **Privately Held**
WEB: www.dunawayinc.com
SIC: 3599 Machine shop, jobbing & repair

(G-2526)
EMPYRACOM INC
6550 Seville Dr Ste A (44406-9138)
PHONE.................................330 744-5570
Shanthi Subramanyam, *President*
Viswanath Subramanya, *Vice Pres*
EMP: 20
SQ FT: 2,500
SALES (est): 3.3MM **Privately Held**
WEB: www.empyra.com
SIC: 7379 7372 7371 Computer related consulting services; prepackaged software; business oriented computer software; computer software systems analysis & design, custom; computer software development

(G-2527)
ERIC ALLSHOUSE LLC
9666 Lisbon Rd (44406-8425)
PHONE.................................330 533-4258
Eric Allshouse, *Partner*
EMP: 6
SALES (est): 157.3K **Privately Held**
SIC: 3561 8741 Cylinders, pump; construction management

(G-2528)
EVERFLOW EASTERN PARTNERS LP (PA)
585 W Main St (44406-9733)
P.O. Box 629 (44406-0629)
PHONE.................................330 533-2692
William A Siskovic, *President*
Everflow M Limited, *General Ptnr*
Brian A Staebler, *CFO*
EMP: 21
SQ FT: 6,400
SALES: 10.1MM **Privately Held**
SIC: 1382 1311 Oil & gas exploration services; crude petroleum & natural gas

(G-2529)
HAUS MATHIAS
Also Called: Haus Cider Mill & Fruit Farm
6742 W Calla Rd (44406-9453)
PHONE.................................330 533-5305
Mathias E Haus, *Owner*
Cheryl Haus, *Co-Owner*
EMP: 5
SALES (est): 366.7K **Privately Held**
SIC: 2099 0175 2086 Cider, nonalcoholic; apple orchard; bottled & canned soft drinks

(G-2530)
IES SYSTEMS INC
464 Lisbon St (44406-1423)
P.O. Box 89 (44406-0089)
PHONE.................................330 533-6683
Mark Brucoli, *President*
Kelly Weiss, *Corp Secy*
Rob McAndrew, *Exec VP*
David Wigal, *Exec VP*
Bill Yobi, *Exec VP*
EMP: 45
SQ FT: 27,000
SALES (est): 7.5MM **Privately Held**
WEB: www.ies-us.com
SIC: 7389 3821 Design, commercial & industrial; laboratory apparatus & furniture

(G-2531)
LEEBAW MANUFACTURING COMPANY
3 Industrial Park Dr (44406-9738)
P.O. Box 553 (44406-0553)
PHONE.................................330 533-3368
Jeff Raymer, *General Mgr*
John C Leek, *Sales Mgr*
John Leek, *Sales Mgr*
Pati Bevan, *Marketing Staff*
Susan Hyatte, *Marketing Staff*
EMP: 18 **EST:** 1947
SQ FT: 20,000
SALES (est): 5MM **Privately Held**
WEB: www.leebaw.com
SIC: 3537 Lift trucks, industrial: fork, platform, straddle, etc.; dollies (hand or power trucks), industrial except mining

(G-2532)
LINDE HYDRAULICS CORPORATION (DH)
5089 W Western Reserve Rd (44406-9112)
PHONE.................................330 533-6801
Frank Cobb, *CEO*
Dr Ferdinand Megerlin, *Ch of Bd*
Lewis P Kasper, *President*
John Kumler, *President*
▲ **EMP:** 38
SQ FT: 80,000
SALES (est): 4.9MM
SALES (corp-wide): 236.2K **Privately Held**
WEB: www.lindeamerica.com
SIC: 3594 3566 3714 3621 Pumps, hydraulic power transfer; motors: hydraulic, fluid power or air; gears, power transmission, except automotive; motor vehicle parts & accessories; motors & generators
HQ: Linde Hydraulics Gmbh & Co. Kg
Wailandtstr. 13
Aschaffenburg 63741
602 115-000

(G-2533)
LTF ACQUISITION LLC
Also Called: Lifetime Fenders
430 W Main St (44406-1434)
PHONE.................................330 533-0111
Marcus Shively,
EMP: 14
SQ FT: 25,000
SALES: 2.6MM
SALES (corp-wide): 77.2MM **Privately Held**
SIC: 3465 Fenders, automobile: stamped or pressed metal
PA: Betts Company
2843 S Maple Ave
Fresno CA 93725
559 498-3304

(G-2534)
MANUFACTURING DIVISION INC
445 W Main St (44406-1425)
P.O. Box 9 (44406-0009)
PHONE.................................330 533-6835
D Scott Owens, *President*
EMP: 3 **EST:** 1940
SQ FT: 2,000
SALES (est): 302.3K
SALES (corp-wide): 3.4MM **Privately Held**
WEB: www.prefcommunities.com
SIC: 3592 Valves, aircraft
PA: Owens-Ohio Corporation
2015 W 5th Ave
Columbus OH 43212
614 486-1148

(G-2535)
MATERIAL SCIENCES CORPORATION
460 W Main St (44406-1434)
PHONE.................................330 702-3882
EMP: 3 **Privately Held**
SIC: 3479 Painting of metal products
HQ: Material Sciences Corporation
6855 Commerce Blvd
Canton MI 48187
734 207-4444

(G-2536)
MERCERS WELDING INC
6336 W Calla Rd (44406-9452)
PHONE.................................330 533-3373
Glenn Wolford, *President*
Susan Wyand, *Treasurer*
EMP: 4
SQ FT: 1,000
SALES: 130K **Privately Held**
SIC: 7692 Welding repair

(G-2537)
MOLOROKALIN INC (DH)
Also Called: Carepoint Partners
4137 Boardman Canfield Rd Ll04 (44406-8087)
PHONE.................................330 629-1332
Ralph Dimuccio, *Ch of Bd*
Leonard Holman, *President*
Greg Krieger, *Vice Pres*
John Appel, *Treasurer*
Harold Cullar, *Admin Sec*
EMP: 16
SQ FT: 5,000
SALES (est): 1.5MM **Publicly Held**
SIC: 2834 Intravenous solutions

(G-2538)
MOONLIGHTING
8627 Gibson Rd (44406-9745)
PHONE.................................330 533-3324
Peter Mazar, *Owner*
EMP: 4 **EST:** 2001
SALES (est): 452.9K **Privately Held**
SIC: 3648 Outdoor lighting equipment

(G-2539)
OHIO STRUCTURES INC (HQ)
535 N Broad St Ste 5 (44406-8221)
PHONE.................................330 533-0084
John Donadee, *President*
Julie Hlebovy, *Corp Secy*
Sean Giblin, *Vice Pres*
David Spurio, *Treasurer*
Thomas Kostelic, *Admin Sec*
EMP: 50
SALES (est): 13.2MM
SALES (corp-wide): 3.6MM **Privately Held**
SIC: 3441 8711 Fabricated structural metal; engineering services
PA: J A Donadee Corporation
535 N Broad St Ste 5
Canfield OH 44406
330 533-3305

(G-2540)
PIERSANTE AND ASSOCIATES
230 Russo Dr (44406-9679)
PHONE.................................330 533-9904
Thomas S Piersante, *Principal*
EMP: 5 **EST:** 2010
SALES (est): 282.2K **Privately Held**
SIC: 3494 Valves & pipe fittings

GEOGRAPHIC SECTION
Canton - Stark County (G-2568)

(G-2541)
PROCESS SLTIONS FOR INDUST INC
Also Called: PSI Products
480 S Broad St Ste A (44406-1688)
P.O. Box 771 (44406-0771)
PHONE..................................330 702-1685
Douglas R Holt, *President*
Diane Holt, *Vice Pres*
EMP: 4 **EST:** 1997
SQ FT: 500
SALES: 250K **Privately Held**
SIC: 2819 Industrial inorganic chemicals

(G-2542)
RANGE ONE PRODUCTS & FABG
580 W Main St (44406-9740)
P.O. Box 628 (44406-0628)
PHONE..................................330 533-1151
EMP: 11
SQ FT: 7,000
SALES (est): 83K **Privately Held**
SIC: 3599 3496 3444 Mfg Industrial Machinery Mfg Misc Fabricated Wire Products Mfg Sheet Metalwork

(G-2543)
RELATED METALS INC
6011 Deer Spring Run (44406-7609)
PHONE..................................330 799-4866
Lori Dripps, *President*
Mary Dripps, *Vice Pres*
Thomas Dripps, *Treasurer*
Lawson Dripps, *Admin Sec*
EMP: 7
SQ FT: 2,000
SALES (est): 750.4K **Privately Held**
SIC: 1761 3444 Roofing contractor; sheet metalwork; sheet metalwork

(G-2544)
SCHOEN INDUSTRIES INC
290 Southview Rd (44406-1162)
PHONE..................................330 533-6659
William Schoenfeld Sr, *President*
Robert Schoenfeld, *Treasurer*
EMP: 5
SQ FT: 8,000
SALES (est): 527.5K **Privately Held**
SIC: 3469 Kitchen fixtures & equipment, porcelain enameled

(G-2545)
SPECIAL T FOODS LLC
5529 W Middletown Rd (44406-9492)
PHONE..................................330 533-9493
Bernadette Shimek,
Tony Shimek,
EMP: 3
SALES: 250K **Privately Held**
SIC: 2099 Food preparations

(G-2546)
STAR EXTRUDED SHAPES INC
7055 Herbert Rd (44406-8660)
P.O. Box 553 (44406-0553)
PHONE..................................330 533-9863
Kenneth W George, *President*
EMP: 300
SQ FT: 143,000
SALES (est): 61.6MM **Privately Held**
SIC: 3354 Aluminum extruded products

(G-2547)
STAR FAB INC (PA)
7055 Herbert Rd (44406-8660)
P.O. Box 553 (44406-0553)
PHONE..................................330 533-9863
Kenneth W George Jr, *President*
Nick Mistovich, *CFO*
▲ **EMP:** 120
SQ FT: 100,000
SALES (est): 24.2MM **Privately Held**
WEB: www.starext.com
SIC: 3354 3479 Aluminum extruded products; painting of metal products

(G-2548)
STONEFRUIT COFFEE CO
410 W Main St (44406-1434)
PHONE..................................330 509-2787
Joshua Langenhein, *Owner*
▲ **EMP:** 5
SALES (est): 142.7K **Privately Held**
SIC: 2095 Roasted coffee

(G-2549)
TETRA TECH INC
6715 Tippecanoe Rd C201 (44406-7120)
PHONE..................................330 286-3683
Dan Batrack, *CEO*
Larry Drane, *General Mgr*
EMP: 15
SALES (corp-wide): 2.9B **Publicly Held**
SIC: 8711 3822 8744 Consulting engineer; auto controls regulating residntl & coml environmt & applncs;
PA: Tetra Tech, Inc.
  3475 E Foothill Blvd
  Pasadena CA 91107
  626 351-4664

(G-2550)
THOROUGHBRED GT MFG LLC
6145 State Route 446 (44406-9428)
PHONE..................................330 533-0048
Nathan Miller, *Principal*
▲ **EMP:** 10
SALES (est): 865.4K **Privately Held**
SIC: 3999 Manufacturing industries

(G-2551)
TRAILEX INC
1 Industrial Park Dr (44406-9738)
P.O. Box 553 (44406-0553)
PHONE..................................330 533-6814
Kenneth George II, *President*
Tim Cooper, *Business Mgr*
Ken Montgomery, *Sales Staff*
▼ **EMP:** 10 **EST:** 1963
SQ FT: 20,000
SALES (est): 1.8MM **Privately Held**
WEB: www.trailex.com
SIC: 3715 Truck trailers

(G-2552)
UNITED EXTRUSION DIES INC
5171 W Western Reserve Rd (44406-8112)
P.O. Box 117 (44406-0117)
PHONE..................................330 533-2915
John Fritz, *President*
James Rektor, *Vice Pres*
Sharon Crawford, *Admin Sec*
EMP: 17
SQ FT: 8,000
SALES (est): 1.2MM **Privately Held**
SIC: 3544 Special dies & tools

(G-2553)
WRP ENERGY INC
12 W Main St (44406-1426)
PHONE..................................330 533-1921
Nils Johnsons, *CEO*
Kathleen Johnson, *Corp Secy*
Cindy Wilson, *Manager*
Scott W Johnson,
EMP: 5
SQ FT: 1,300
SALES (est): 331.5K **Privately Held**
SIC: 1382 Oil & gas exploration services

Canton
Stark County

(G-2554)
1455 GROUP LLC
Also Called: Ohio Print Source
6116 Market Ave N (44721-3123)
P.O. Box 227, Middlebranch (44652-0227)
PHONE..................................330 494-9074
Mike Dicato, *President*
EMP: 5 **EST:** 2008
SALES (est): 606.5K **Privately Held**
SIC: 2752 Commercial printing, lithographic

(G-2555)
A & M CREATIVE GROUP INC
1704 Ira Turpin Way Ne (44705-1415)
PHONE..................................330 452-8940
EMP: 20
SALES (est): 3.9MM **Privately Held**
SIC: 3578 Mfg Calculating Equipment

(G-2556)
A P O HOLDINGS INC
Also Called: Air Power of Ohio
1405 Timken Pl Sw (44706-3068)
PHONE..................................330 455-8925
Eric Dunkle, *Branch Mgr*
EMP: 22
SALES (corp-wide): 47.6MM **Privately Held**
WEB: www.airpowerofohio.com
SIC: 5084 3561 3443 Compressors, except air conditioning; pumps & pumping equipment; fabricated plate work (boiler shop)
PA: A P O Holdings Inc
  6607 Chittenden Rd
  Hudson OH 44236
  330 650-1330

(G-2557)
ACCU-RITE TOOL & DIE CO CORP
7295 Sunset Strip Ave Nw (44720-7038)
P.O. Box 2651 (44720-0651)
PHONE..................................330 497-9959
John Snyder, *President*
Susan Snyder, *Corp Secy*
EMP: 6
SQ FT: 5,000
SALES (est): 961.4K **Privately Held**
SIC: 3544 Special dies & tools

(G-2558)
ADELMANS TRUCK PARTS CORP (PA)
Also Called: Adelman's Truck Sales
2000 Waynesburg Dr Se (44707-2194)
PHONE..................................330 456-0206
Carl Adelman, *President*
Larry Adelman, *Vice Pres*
◆ **EMP:** 30
SQ FT: 120,000
SALES (est): 8.8MM **Privately Held**
WEB: www.adelmans.com
SIC: 5013 3714 Truck parts & accessories; power transmission equipment, motor vehicle; differentials & parts, motor vehicle

(G-2559)
ADELMANS TRUCK PARTS CORP
2000 Waynesburg Dr Se (44707-2194)
PHONE..................................216 362-0500
David Olsen,
EMP: 17
SALES (est): 1MM
SALES (corp-wide): 8.8MM **Privately Held**
SIC: 5013 3714 Truck parts & accessories; differentials & parts, motor vehicle
PA: Adelman's Truck Parts Corporation
  2000 Waynesburg Dr Se
  Canton OH 44707
  330 456-0206

(G-2560)
AGGREGATE TERSORNANCE LLC
Also Called: NOOTROPICS CITY DBA
455 Navarre Rd Sw Unit H (44707)
PHONE..................................330 418-4751
Kenny L James III, *Mng Member*
EMP: 5
SALES: 500K **Privately Held**
SIC: 2023 5499 Dietary supplements, dairy & non-dairy based; health & dietetic food stores

(G-2561)
AIRFASCO INC
2655 Harrison Ave Sw (44706-3047)
PHONE..................................330 430-6190
Dennis Dent, *CEO*
Jeff Parker, *Vice Pres*
Marlene Veobides, *Vice Pres*
Tim West, *Director*
EMP: 42
SQ FT: 25,000
SALES (est): 8.2MM **Privately Held**
WEB: www.airfasco.com
SIC: 3452 Bolts, metal

(G-2562)
AIRFASCO INDS FSTNER GROUP LLC
2655 Harrison Ave Sw (44706-3047)
PHONE..................................330 430-6190
Dennis Dent,
EMP: 40
SALES: 1,000K **Privately Held**
SIC: 3452 Bolts, nuts, rivets & washers

(G-2563)
AIRGAS USA LLC
2505 Shepler Ave Sw (44706)
PHONE..................................330 454-1330
Rod St John, *Branch Mgr*
Jody Engstrom, *Manager*
EMP: 50
SALES (corp-wide): 125.9MM **Privately Held**
WEB: www.us.linde-gas.com
SIC: 2813 Oxygen, compressed or liquefied; nitrous oxide; acetylene; hydrogen
HQ: Airgas Usa, Llc
  259 N Radnor Chester Rd # 100
  Radnor PA 19087
  610 687-5253

(G-2564)
AJAX TOCCO MAGNETHERMIC CORP
8984 Meridian Cir Nw (44720-8259)
PHONE..................................330 818-8080
Robert Jamison, *Project Engr*
Michele Davidson, *Human Res Dir*
Dave Flanigan, *Manager*
EMP: 53
SALES (corp-wide): 1.6B **Publicly Held**
WEB: www.ajaxtocco.com
SIC: 3567 Industrial furnaces & ovens
HQ: Ajax Tocco Magnethermic Corporation
  1745 Overland Ave Ne
  Warren OH 44483
  330 372-8511

(G-2565)
AK FABRICATION INC
1500 Allen Ave Se (44707-3768)
PHONE..................................330 458-1037
Chris Kulenics, *President*
Stacey Griffith, *Office Mgr*
EMP: 12
SQ FT: 10,000
SALES (est): 1.7MM **Privately Held**
SIC: 1751 3548 Carpentry work; welding apparatus

(G-2566)
AKERS IDENTITY LLC
Also Called: Akers Sign
4150 Belden Village St Nw # 503 (44718-3650)
PHONE..................................330 493-0055
Richard W Akers,
EMP: 3
SALES (est): 414.5K **Privately Held**
SIC: 7389 3993 8748 Lettering & sign painting services; signs & advertising specialties; systems analysis or design

(G-2567)
ALL POWER BATTERY INC
1387 Clarendon Ave Sw # 6 (44710-2190)
PHONE..................................330 453-5236
William Ferris, *President*
EMP: 6
SQ FT: 4,000
SALES: 1.5MM **Privately Held**
WEB: www.allpowerbattery.com
SIC: 7699 5013 3691 Battery service & repair; automotive batteries; lead acid batteries (storage batteries)

(G-2568)
ALLIANCE HEALTHCARE SVCS INC
5005 Whipple Ave Nw (44718-2657)
PHONE..................................330 493-6747
Howard Aihara, *CFO*
EMP: 9 **Privately Held**
SIC: 3826 Magnetic resonance imaging apparatus
HQ: Alliance Healthcare Services, Inc.
  18201 Von Karman Ave
  Irvine CA 92612
  949 242-5300

Canton - Stark County (G-2569)

(G-2569)
ALLIANCE PETROLEUM CORPORATION (HQ)
4150 Belden Village Mall (44718-2502)
PHONE...................330 493-0440
Dora L Silvis, *COO*
Martin L Miller, *VP Opers*
EMP: 61
SQ FT: 2,900
SALES (est): 75.2MM Privately Held
WEB: www.alliancepetroleumcorp.com
SIC: 1311 1382 Crude petroleum production; natural gas production; oil & gas exploration services
PA: Diversified Gas & Oil Corporation
1800 Corporate Dr
Birmingham AL 35242
205 408-0909

(G-2570)
ALRON INC
5307 Southway St Sw (44706-1943)
PHONE...................330 477-3405
Ron Gritzan, *Principal*
EMP: 3
SALES (est): 585.5K Privately Held
SIC: 3441 Fabricated structural metal

(G-2571)
AMBAFLEX INC
1530 Raff Rd Sw (44710-2322)
PHONE...................330 478-1858
David Spencer, *General Mgr*
Charles Zhu, *Area Mgr*
Andrew Hu, *Foreman/Supr*
Marcel Van Hooff, *Research*
Victor Ortiz, *Sales Mgr*
◆ EMP: 22
SALES (est): 4.9MM Privately Held
SIC: 3535 Conveyors & conveying equipment

(G-2572)
AMERICAN ALUMINUM EXTRUSIONS
Also Called: A A E
4416 Louisville St Ne (44705-4848)
PHONE...................330 458-0300
Samuel Popa, *President*
Diane Hendricks, *Mng Member*
Ken Hendricks, *Mng Member*
Barb Kepner,
▲ EMP: 105
SQ FT: 240,000
SALES (est): 26.1MM Privately Held
WEB: www.aaeo.com
SIC: 3354 Aluminum extruded products

(G-2573)
ANGELICS A QUILTERS HAVEN
3033 Cleveland Ave S (44707-3625)
PHONE...................330 484-5480
Perry Simon, *Owner*
EMP: 4
SALES (est): 99K Privately Held
SIC: 2395 Quilting & quilting supplies

(G-2574)
ARCHER CORPORATION
Also Called: Archer Sign
1917 Henry Ave Sw (44706-2941)
PHONE...................330 455-9995
Jerry Archer, *CEO*
Michael Minor, *Vice Pres*
EMP: 40
SQ FT: 70,000
SALES (est): 6.4MM Privately Held
WEB: www.archersign.com
SIC: 1799 3993 Sign installation & maintenance; signs & advertising specialties

(G-2575)
ARM OPCO INC
Also Called: American Road Machinery
3026 Saratoga Ave Sw (44706-2236)
PHONE...................330 868-7724
Nicholas W Ballas, *President*
Nick Ballas, *Vice Pres*
Matthew D H Valentine, *Vice Pres*
▲ EMP: 40
SQ FT: 30,000
SALES (est): 18.4MM Privately Held
WEB: www.amroadmach.com
SIC: 3531 Blades for graders, scrapers, dozers & snow plows

(G-2576)
ARNOLD PRINTING INC
5772 West Blvd Nw (44718-1430)
PHONE...................330 494-1191
Joe Arnold, *President*
Craig Arnold, *Vice Pres*
Sue Arnold, *Admin Sec*
EMP: 4
SQ FT: 1,500
SALES: 325K Privately Held
SIC: 2752 Commercial printing, offset

(G-2577)
ASSOCTED VSUAL CMMNCATIONS INC
Also Called: A V C
7000 Firestone Ave Ne (44721-2594)
PHONE...................330 452-4449
Raymond Gonzalez, *President*
Paul Anthony, *Vice Pres*
EMP: 25 EST: 1983
SALES: 3MM Privately Held
WEB: www.avcprint.com
SIC: 2759 Commercial printing

(G-2578)
AULTWRKS OCCUPATIONAL MEDICINE
4650 Hills And Dales Rd N (44708-6220)
PHONE...................330 491-9675
Lisa Dyer, *Director*
EMP: 15
SALES (est): 1.2MM Privately Held
SIC: 2834 Medicines, capsuled or ampuled

(G-2579)
AVONDALE PRINTING INC
2820 Whipple Ave Nw (44708-1566)
PHONE...................330 477-1180
Don Denham, *President*
Amber Rector, *Manager*
EMP: 3
SQ FT: 1,500
SALES (est): 523.6K Privately Held
WEB: www.starkrealtors.com
SIC: 2752 Lithographic Commercial Printing

(G-2580)
AZZ INC
1723 Cleveland Ave Sw (44707-3646)
PHONE...................330 456-3241
Joe Allen, *Sales Mgr*
Tim Myers, *Manager*
EMP: 33
SALES (corp-wide): 810.4MM Publicly Held
SIC: 3699 Electrical equipment & supplies
PA: Azz Inc.
3100 W 7th St Ste 500
Fort Worth TX 76107
817 810-0095

(G-2581)
AZZ INCORPORATED
1723 Cleveland Ave Sw (44707-3646)
PHONE...................330 445-2170
Michael Donley, *Branch Mgr*
EMP: 25
SALES (corp-wide): 810.4MM Publicly Held
SIC: 3479 Hot dip coating of metals or formed products
PA: Azz Inc.
3100 W 7th St Ste 500
Fort Worth TX 76107
817 810-0095

(G-2582)
B-TEK SCALES LLC
1510 Metric Ave Sw (44706-3088)
PHONE...................330 471-8900
Kraig F Brechbuhler, *President*
Rei Tritt, *Corp Secy*
Andrew Brechbuhler, *Vice Pres*
Matthew Mulinix, *Draft/Design*
Brian Wheatley, *Engineer*
◆ EMP: 50
SQ FT: 65,000
SALES (est): 18.6MM
SALES (corp-wide): 48.1MM Privately Held
WEB: www.b-tek.com
SIC: 3325 7371 Steel foundries; software programming applications
PA: Brechbuhler Scales, Inc.
1424 Scales St Sw
Canton OH 44706
330 458-3060

(G-2583)
BADBOY BLASTERS INCORPORATED
1720 Wallace Ave Ne (44705-4056)
PHONE...................330 454-2699
Andrea Bandi Cain, *President*
Mark Cain, *Vice Pres*
▲ EMP: 10 EST: 2006
SQ FT: 13,000
SALES: 1.4MM Privately Held
SIC: 3471 Sand blasting of metal parts

(G-2584)
BALL CORPORATION
2121 Warner Rd Se (44707-2273)
PHONE...................330 244-2800
EMP: 57
SALES (corp-wide): 11.6B Publicly Held
WEB: www.sonoco.com
SIC: 2631 Paperboard mills
PA: Ball Corporation
10 Longs Peak Dr
Broomfield CO 80021
303 469-3131

(G-2585)
BARNHART PRINTING CORP
Also Called: Barnhart Publishing
1107 Melchoir Pl Sw (44707-4220)
PHONE...................330 456-2279
John F Waechter, *President*
Brent A Barnhart, *Chairman*
EMP: 18 EST: 1930
SQ FT: 10,000
SALES (est): 3.5MM Privately Held
WEB: www.barnhartprinting.com
SIC: 2752 2759 2789 Commercial printing, offset; letterpress printing; bookbinding & related work

(G-2586)
BDI INC
417 Applegrove St Nw (44720-1617)
PHONE...................330 498-4980
Tom Carlouzzi, *Branch Mgr*
EMP: 12
SALES (corp-wide): 346.5MM Privately Held
SIC: 3568 Power transmission equipment
PA: Bdi, Inc.
8000 Hub Pkwy
Cleveland OH 44125
216 642-9100

(G-2587)
BEAD SHOPPE AT HOME
2872 Whipple Ave Nw (44708-1532)
PHONE...................330 479-9598
Shelley Lantz, *Owner*
EMP: 3
SALES (est): 131.9K Privately Held
SIC: 3999 Beads, unassembled

(G-2588)
BEATTY FOODS LLC
1117 Brant Ave Nw (44708-4008)
PHONE...................330 327-2442
EMP: 3 EST: 2011
SALES (est): 74K Privately Held
SIC: 2099 Mfg Food Preparations

(G-2589)
BEN JAMES ENTERPRISES INC
4110 Southway St Sw (44706-1863)
PHONE...................330 477-9353
Ben James, *President*
EMP: 4 EST: 2002
SALES (est): 739.1K Privately Held
SIC: 3499 Welding tips, heat resistant: metal

(G-2590)
BETTER LIVING CONCEPTS INC
Also Called: Compu-Print
7233 Freedom Ave Nw (44720-7123)
P.O. Box 2340, North Canton (44720-0340)
PHONE...................330 494-2213
Jeff Davies, *President*
EMP: 14
SQ FT: 5,400
SALES (est): 930.2K Privately Held
WEB: www.betterlivingconcepts.com
SIC: 2759 Imprinting

(G-2591)
BIG KAHUNA GRAPHICS LLC
1255 Prospect Ave Sw (44706-1627)
PHONE...................330 455-2625
Kyle Bradley, *President*
EMP: 9
SALES (est): 714.7K Privately Held
SIC: 2396 2395 2759 Stamping fabric articles; pleating & stitching; screen printing

(G-2592)
BIOCURV MEDICAL INSTRUMENTS (PA)
3054 Tuscarawas St W (44708-4167)
PHONE...................330 454-6621
Robert J Ripich, *President*
Richard Marks, *Vice Pres*
James Bower, *Director*
John Wirtz, *Admin Sec*
EMP: 4
SQ FT: 1,420
SALES (est): 524.6K Privately Held
WEB: www.biocurv.com
SIC: 2844 Oral preparations

(G-2593)
BLACK MCCUSKEY SOUERS (PA)
220 Market Ave S Ste 612 (44702-2171)
PHONE...................330 456-8341
Steven P Cress, *President*
Norman Jackson, *Chairman*
Lee Dicola, *Corp Secy*
Thomas Herrick, *CFO*
EMP: 4
SALES (est): 26.2MM Privately Held
SIC: 6712 3599 3441 Bank holding companies; machine & other job shop work; fabricated structural metal

(G-2594)
BOCOR HOLDINGS LLC
Also Called: Bocor Producing
7793 Pittsburg Ave Nw (44720-6947)
PHONE...................330 494-1221
Robert Hutcheson, *Manager*
EMP: 4
SALES (est): 350K Privately Held
WEB: www.bocorproducing.com
SIC: 1382 Oil & gas exploration services

(G-2595)
BOLONS CUSTOM KITCHENS INC
6287 Promler St Nw (44720-7609)
PHONE...................330 499-0092
Guy Bolon, *CEO*
Terry Bolon, *President*
EMP: 13
SQ FT: 1,500
SALES (est): 1.7MM Privately Held
SIC: 5722 2599 Kitchens, complete (sinks, cabinets, etc.); cabinets, factory

(G-2596)
BOWDIL COMPANY
2030 Industrial Pl Se (44707-2641)
PHONE...................800 356-8663
Brite Morrow, *President*
J Britton Morrow, *Corp Secy*
Dove Hout, *Purch Mgr*
EMP: 17 EST: 1923
SQ FT: 50,000
SALES: 2MM Privately Held
WEB: www.bowdil.com
SIC: 3532 3599 3398 Mining machinery; custom machinery; metal heat treating

(G-2597)
BRAHLER INC
Also Called: Wedding Pages
4041 Batton St Nw Ste 104 (44720-7158)
PHONE...................330 966-7730
Richard Brahler, *President*
EMP: 5
SALES (est): 330.5K Privately Held
SIC: 5621 2759 Bridal shops; publication printing

GEOGRAPHIC SECTION

Canton - Stark County (G-2625)

(G-2598)
BRENDEL PRODUCING COMPANY
8215 Arlington Ave Nw (44720-5111)
PHONE.....................330 854-4151
Frank Brendel Jr, *President*
Kay Morgan, *Office Mgr*
EMP: 8
SQ FT: 1,200
SALES (est): 668.3K **Privately Held**
SIC: 1381 1311 Directional drilling oil & gas wells; crude petroleum & natural gas

(G-2599)
BROOKS UTILITY PRODUCTS GROUP
Also Called: Brooks Meter Devices
3359 Bruening Ave Sw (44706-4100)
P.O. Box 6382 (44706-0382)
PHONE.....................330 455-0301
Susan Barringer, *Branch Mgr*
EMP: 15
SALES (est): 2.3MM **Privately Held**
SIC: 3643 3469 Sockets, electric; electronic enclosures, stamped or pressed metal
PA: Brooks Utility Products Group Inc
43045 W 9 Mile Rd
Novi MI 48375

(G-2600)
BUCKEYE PAPER CO INC
5233 Southway St Sw # 523 (44706-1943)
P.O. Box 711, Massillon (44648-0711)
PHONE.....................330 477-5925
Edward N Bast Sr, *President*
Edward Bast Jr, *Vice Pres*
Debby Olson, *Plant Mgr*
▼ **EMP:** 32
SQ FT: 54,000
SALES (est): 8.9MM **Privately Held**
WEB: www.buckeyepaper.com
SIC: 2679 5113 Paper products, converted; industrial & personal service paper

(G-2601)
BUGH VINYL PRODUCTS INC
8933 Cleveland Ave Nw (44720-4565)
PHONE.....................330 305-0978
Roger Bugh, *President*
Barb Bugh, *Vice Pres*
Barbara Bugh, *Vice Pres*
Kim George, *Purch Mgr*
EMP: 8
SQ FT: 3,600
SALES (est): 1.1MM **Privately Held**
WEB: www.bughvinyl.com
SIC: 5211 3089 Fencing; fences, gates & accessories: plastic

(G-2602)
BURN-RITE MOLD & MACHINE INC
2401 Shepler Ch Ave Sw (44706-4111)
PHONE.....................330 956-4143
Terry Bristow, *President*
Joan Bristow, *Corp Secy*
EMP: 4
SQ FT: 21,000
SALES (est): 535.5K **Privately Held**
WEB: www.burn-rite.com
SIC: 3312 3599 Tool & die steel; machine shop, jobbing & repair

(G-2603)
C&H INDUSTRIES
2054 Jaquelyn Dr (44720-1134)
PHONE.....................330 899-0001
EMP: 3
SALES (est): 196K **Privately Held**
SIC: 3999 Mfg Misc Products

(G-2604)
CAGE GEAR & MACHINE LLC
1776 Gateway Blvd Se (44707-3503)
PHONE.....................330 452-1532
Gary Barber, *Prdtn Mgr*
Shawn Roeder, *Sales Staff*
David Churbock,
EMP: 12
SQ FT: 22,900
SALES (est): 1.9MM **Privately Held**
WEB: www.cage-gear.com
SIC: 3599 3566 Machine shop, jobbing & repair; gears, power transmission, except automotive

(G-2605)
CAMMEL SAW COMPANY INC
4898 Hills & Dales Rd Nw (44708-1495)
PHONE.....................330 477-3764
Dennis Cammel, *President*
William Leasure, *Opers Mgr*
EMP: 14
SQ FT: 10,000
SALES (est): 1.7MM **Privately Held**
WEB: www.cammelsaw.com
SIC: 7699 5072 5251 3425 Knife, saw & tool sharpening & repair; saw blades; tools; saws, hand: metalworking or woodworking

(G-2606)
CAMPBELLS CANDIES
3074 Chaucer Dr Ne (44721-3670)
PHONE.....................330 493-1805
John Saner, *Owner*
EMP: 3 **EST:** 1969
SQ FT: 1,300
SALES (est): 137.4K **Privately Held**
SIC: 2066 5441 Chocolate candy, solid; candy

(G-2607)
CANTON CABINET CO
1415 7th St Nw (44703-2923)
PHONE.....................330 455-2585
John Haslam, *Principal*
EMP: 4
SALES (est): 319.4K **Privately Held**
SIC: 2434 Wood kitchen cabinets

(G-2608)
CANTON DROP FORGE INC
4575 Southway St Sw (44706-1995)
PHONE.....................330 477-4511
Bradly Ahbe, *President*
Dan Antos, *Vice Pres*
Bill Maykowski, *Vice Pres*
Bill Newhouse, *Vice Pres*
Brad Abhe, *VP Mfg*
◆ **EMP:** 300 **EST:** 1903
SQ FT: 245,000
SALES (est): 8.6MM
SALES (corp-wide): 1.6B **Publicly Held**
WEB: www.cantondropforge.com
SIC: 3462 3463 3356 3312 Iron & steel forgings; nonferrous forgings; nonferrous rolling & drawing; blast furnaces & steel mills
PA: Park-Ohio Holdings Corp.
6065 Parkland Blvd Ste 1
Cleveland OH 44124
440 947-2000

(G-2609)
CANTON FUEL
1600 30th St Ne (44714-1628)
PHONE.....................330 455-3400
EMP: 5 **EST:** 2011
SALES (est): 534.5K **Privately Held**
SIC: 2869 Mfg Industrial Organic Chemicals

(G-2610)
CANTON GEAR MFG DESIGN CO INC
1600 Tuscarawas St E (44707-3199)
PHONE.....................330 455-2771
Matthew Weida, *President*
Barbara Bettis, *Vice Pres*
EMP: 10
SALES (est): 2.1MM **Privately Held**
SIC: 3566 Gears, power transmission, except automotive

(G-2611)
CANTON GRAPHIC ARTS SERVICE
800 Cleveland Ave Sw (44702-2140)
PHONE.....................330 456-9868
Ronald Wertman, *President*
Tim Toolan, *Vice Pres*
Denise Dearment, *Admin Sec*
EMP: 5 **EST:** 1951
SALES (est): 390K **Privately Held**
SIC: 7389 2752 2791 Engraving service; commercial printing, lithographic; typesetting

(G-2612)
CANTON OH RUBBER SPECLTY PRODS
Also Called: Cors Products
1387 Clarendon Ave Sw (44710-2190)
P.O. Box 20188 (44701-0188)
PHONE.....................330 454-3847
Mark Lukosavich, *CEO*
EMP: 8
SQ FT: 15,000
SALES (est): 750K **Privately Held**
SIC: 3061 2869 3069 2822 Appliance rubber goods (mechanical); silicones; weather strip, sponge rubber; ethylene-propylene rubbers, EPDM polymers

(G-2613)
CANTON OIL WELL SERVICE INC
7793 Pittsburg Ave Nw (44720-6947)
PHONE.....................330 494-1221
Thomas R Hutcheson, *CEO*
Kevin W Hutcheson, *President*
Robert J Hutcheson, *Principal*
James Paumier, *Vice Pres*
Seth Kienzle, *Broker*
EMP: 12
SQ FT: 7,500
SALES (est): 2.2MM **Privately Held**
SIC: 1382 Oil & gas exploration services

(G-2614)
CANTON ORTHOTIC LABORATORY
811 12th St Nw (44703-1927)
PHONE.....................330 833-0955
Stephen T Simko, *President*
Ann Marie Simko, *Vice Pres*
EMP: 7 **EST:** 1975
SQ FT: 4,500
SALES (est): 593.3K **Privately Held**
SIC: 3842 Orthopedic appliances

(G-2615)
CANTON PATTERN & MOLD INC
Also Called: Canton Pattern and Mold
914 Sylvan Ct Ne (44705-1056)
P.O. Box 7295 (44705-0295)
PHONE.....................330 455-4316
Dan Ritz, *President*
EMP: 5
SQ FT: 4,300
SALES (est): 613.9K **Privately Held**
SIC: 3544 Industrial molds

(G-2616)
CANTON PLATING CO INC
903 9th St Ne (44704-1400)
PHONE.....................330 452-7808
Mark Kast, *President*
Denise Kast, *Admin Sec*
EMP: 6
SQ FT: 3,480
SALES: 210K **Privately Held**
SIC: 3471 Electroplating of metals or formed products

(G-2617)
CANTON SIGN CO
222 5th St Ne (44702-1262)
P.O. Box 80137 (44708-0137)
PHONE.....................330 456-7151
Timothy Franta, *President*
Mark A Franta, *Vice Pres*
EMP: 3 **EST:** 1910
SQ FT: 8,500
SALES: 400K **Privately Held**
SIC: 3993 Neon signs; name plates: except engraved, etched, etc.: metal

(G-2618)
CANTON STERILIZED WIPING CLOTH
Also Called: Sentry Products
1401 Waynesburg Dr Se (44707-2115)
PHONE.....................330 455-5179
Robert Shapiro, *President*
Ronald Shapiro, *Vice Pres*
EMP: 8 **EST:** 1924
SQ FT: 42,000
SALES (est): 1.7MM **Privately Held**
SIC: 2211 5199 5113 Scrub cloths; chamois leather; sponges (animal); napkins, paper

(G-2619)
CAPITAL CHEMICAL CO
5340 Mayfair Rd (44720-1533)
PHONE.....................330 494-9535
Lon Swinehart, *President*
EMP: 25 **EST:** 1964
SQ FT: 8,000
SALES (est): 1.8MM **Privately Held**
WEB: www.royalsheeninc.com
SIC: 2842 2899 Specialty cleaning, polishes & sanitation goods; chemical preparations

(G-2620)
CARMEL TRADER PUBLISHING INC
4501 Hills & Dales Rd Nw (44708-1572)
PHONE.....................330 478-9200
Ernie Blood, *President*
Joseph Meranto, *Principal*
Karen Hought, *Vice Pres*
Melody Blood, *Treasurer*
EMP: 30
SALES (est): 15MM **Privately Held**
SIC: 2721 2731 Magazines: publishing & printing; book publishing

(G-2621)
CASTLEBAR CORPORATION
406 15th St Sw (44707-4011)
PHONE.....................330 451-6511
Johnathan Adamski, *President*
EMP: 5
SALES (est): 1.1MM **Privately Held**
SIC: 3313 3356 Tungsten carbide powder; tungsten, basic shapes

(G-2622)
CHECKPOINT SYSTEMS INC
Alpha Security
1510 4th St Se (44707-3206)
PHONE.....................330 456-7776
Earl Williams, *Plant Mgr*
Tim Williams, *Branch Mgr*
EMP: 140
SALES (corp-wide): 3.7B **Privately Held**
WEB: www.checkpointsystems.com
SIC: 3089 Cases, plastic
HQ: Checkpoint Systems, Inc.
101 Wolf Dr
West Deptford NJ 08086
800 257-5540

(G-2623)
CHRISTMAN FABRICATORS INC
4668 Navarre Rd Sw (44706-2337)
PHONE.....................330 477-8077
Esther Christman, *President*
Kevin Christman, *Corp Secy*
Mark Christman, *Vice Pres*
EMP: 9
SQ FT: 15,000
SALES (est): 1.8MM **Privately Held**
SIC: 3441 Fabricated structural metal

(G-2624)
CINTAS CORPORATION NO 2
3865 Highland Park Nw (44720-4537)
P.O. Box 3010 (44720-8010)
PHONE.....................330 966-7800
Allen Kocsis, *Manager*
EMP: 100
SQ FT: 17,084
SALES (corp-wide): 6.4B **Publicly Held**
WEB: www.cintas-corp.com
SIC: 7218 2326 2337 Industrial uniform supply; treated equipment supply: mats, rugs, mops, cloths, etc.; wiping towel supply; work uniforms; uniforms, except athletic: women's, misses' & juniors'
HQ: Cintas Corporation No 2
6800 Cintas Blvd
Mason OH 45040

(G-2625)
CITY OF CANTON
Also Called: Traffic Engineering Department
2436 30th St Ne (44705-2568)
PHONE.....................330 489-3370
Dan Moeglin, *Administration*
EMP: 30 **Privately Held**

Canton - Stark County (G-2626)

WEB: www.cantonincometax.com
SIC: 3669 9111 Traffic signals, electric; mayors' offices
PA: City Of Canton
218 Cleveland Ave Sw
Canton OH 44702
330 438-4300

(G-2626)
CLARK & SON POOL TABLE COMPANY
Also Called: Clark & Son Billiard Supply
2737 Cleveland Ave Nw (44709-3391)
PHONE 330 454-9153
Timothy J Clark, *Owner*
Darlene Clark, *Co-Owner*
EMP: 3
SQ FT: 6,550
SALES: 250K **Privately Held**
WEB: www.clarkandson.com
SIC: 3949 Billiard & pool equipment & supplies, general

(G-2627)
CLARK OPTIMIZATION LLC
1222 Easton St Ne (44721-2455)
PHONE 330 417-2164
Steve Clark, *President*
Douglas B Crawford, *CFO*
EMP: 20
SALES (est): 1.4MM **Privately Held**
SIC: 2741

(G-2628)
CLARK SUBSTATIONS LLC
2240 Allen Ave Se (44707-3612)
PHONE 330 452-5200
Lawrence E Butts,
Ralph H Aldridge,
T Morris Hackney,
Carolyn M Smith,
EMP: 30
SALES (est): 3.6MM **Privately Held**
SIC: 3612 3699 3625 Distribution transformers, electric; electrical equipment & supplies; relays & industrial controls

(G-2629)
CLOVER PALLET LLC
5219 Violet Knoll Ave Ne (44705-3271)
PHONE 330 454-5592
Adam Rennecker, *Principal*
EMP: 3
SALES (est): 247.1K **Privately Held**
SIC: 2448 Pallets, wood & wood with metal

(G-2630)
CNC CUSTOM MACHINING INC
1314 Henry Ave Sw (44706-1750)
PHONE 330 456-5868
Theodore F Russ, *Principal*
EMP: 5
SALES (est): 486.5K **Privately Held**
SIC: 3599 Machine shop, jobbing & repair

(G-2631)
COATING CONTROL INC
825 Navarre Rd Sw (44707-4058)
PHONE 330 453-9136
Charles E Decker II, *President*
EMP: 5
SQ FT: 30,000
SALES (est): 652.9K **Privately Held**
WEB: www.coatingcontrol.com
SIC: 3549 Metalworking machinery

(G-2632)
COMBI PACKAGING SYSTEMS LLC
6299 Dressler Rd Nw (44720-7607)
P.O. Box 9326 (44711-9326)
PHONE 330 456-9333
John F Fisher, *CEO*
Bob Beasley, *Project Mgr*
Tara Withers, *Project Mgr*
Greg Duly, *Opers Mgr*
Chris Pizzedaz, *Parts Mgr*
◆ **EMP:** 70
SQ FT: 119,000
SALES (est): 35.7MM **Privately Held**
WEB: www.combi.com
SIC: 3565 Packaging machinery

(G-2633)
COMMUNICATION RESOURCES INC
4786 Dressler Rd Nw Ste 3 (44718-2555)
PHONE 800 992-2144
Randall S Coy, *President*
Robert W Fisher, *Chairman*
Georgia A Fisher, *Vice Pres*
EMP: 25 **EST:** 1979
SQ FT: 2,000
SALES (est): 1.6MM **Privately Held**
SIC: 2731 2721 Pamphlets: publishing & printing; periodicals

(G-2634)
CONCRETE LEVELING SYSTEMS INC (PA)
Also Called: CLS
5046 East Blvd Nw (44718-1212)
PHONE 330 966-8120
Suzanne I Barth, *CEO*
Edward A Barth, *President*
Eugene H Swearengin, *Admin Sec*
EMP: 3
SQ FT: 2,500
SALES: 2.8K **Publicly Held**
SIC: 3531 Construction machinery

(G-2635)
CONTINENTAL HYDRODYNE SYSTEMS
2216 Glenmont Dr Nw (44708-2036)
PHONE 330 494-2740
Theodore F Savastano, *Principal*
EMP: 11
SALES (est): 1.3MM **Privately Held**
SIC: 3821 Chemical laboratory apparatus

(G-2636)
COPLEY OHIO NEWSPAPERS INC (HQ)
Also Called: Repository
500 Market Ave S (44702-2112)
PHONE 585 598-0030
Kevin Kampman, *President*
James Porter, *Principal*
Darryl Hudson, *CFO*
Audra Boone, *Marketing Staff*
Garrett J Cummings,
EMP: 60 **EST:** 2000
SALES: 45.1MM
SALES (corp-wide): 1.5B **Publicly Held**
WEB: www.timesreporter.com
SIC: 2711 Commercial printing & newspaper publishing combined; newspapers, publishing & printing
PA: New Media Investment Group Inc.
1345 Avenue Of The Americ
New York NY 10105
212 479-3160

(G-2637)
CORDIER GROUP HOLDINGS INC
4575 Southway St Sw (44706-1933)
PHONE 330 477-4511
James J O'Sullivan Jr, *Chairman*
John Motsay, *Vice Pres*
Todd Grey, *Controller*
Bill Maykowski, *Sales Staff*
Tamara Bressanelli, *Manager*
EMP: 301
SALES (est): 20.6MM **Privately Held**
SIC: 3462 Iron & steel forgings

(G-2638)
CRAMERS INC
4944 Southway St Sw (44706-1990)
PHONE 330 477-4571
Don Hoover, *President*
E Robert Schellhase, *Principal*
R C Cramer, *Principal*
Dana Cramer, *Vice Pres*
Lynn Herdlick, *Vice Pres*
EMP: 25
SQ FT: 15,000
SALES: 5.9MM **Privately Held**
WEB: www.cramers.com
SIC: 3444 3446 3443 3441 Sheet metal specialties, not stamped; architectural metalwork; fabricated plate work (boiler shop); fabricated structural metal

(G-2639)
CROSCO
5246 18th St Sw (44706-1904)
PHONE 330 477-1999
Glenn Cross, *Principal*
EMP: 3 **EST:** 2001
SALES (est): 230K **Privately Held**
SIC: 3713 Truck beds

(G-2640)
CS PRODUCTS
1307 Gross Ave Ne (44705-1607)
PHONE 330 452-8566
Bill Stine, *Owner*
EMP: 5
SALES (est): 704.7K **Privately Held**
SIC: 2448 5169 Wood pallets & skids; chemicals & allied products

(G-2641)
CUSTOM BRASS FINISHING INC
1541 Raff Rd Sw (44710-2321)
PHONE 330 453-0888
Jack R Vogt, *President*
Nancy M Vogt, *Vice Pres*
EMP: 9
SQ FT: 24,000
SALES (est): 553.8K **Privately Held**
SIC: 3471 Plating of metals or formed products

(G-2642)
CUSTOM CLTCH JINT HYDRLICS INC
1313 15th St Sw (44706-5206)
PHONE 330 455-1202
Shawn Jackson, *Manager*
EMP: 3
SQ FT: 5,000
SALES (est): 416.2K
SALES (corp-wide): 5.9MM **Privately Held**
WEB: www.customcclutch.com
SIC: 3714 Motor vehicle parts & accessories
PA: Custom Clutch, Joint & Hydraulics, Inc.
3417 Saint Clair Ave Ne
Cleveland OH 44114
216 431-1630

(G-2643)
CUSTOM WELD & MACHINE CORP
1500 Henry Ave Sw (44706-2852)
PHONE 330 452-3935
Tom Greening, *CEO*
Tim Savage, *Vice Pres*
EMP: 15
SQ FT: 31,500
SALES: 1.5MM **Privately Held**
WEB: www.customweldcorp.com
SIC: 7692 Welding repair

(G-2644)
D & D ENERGY CO
6033 Marelis Ave Ne (44721-3160)
PHONE 330 495-1631
Bob Ditty, *Principal*
EMP: 6
SALES (est): 462K **Privately Held**
SIC: 1389 Oil & gas field services

(G-2645)
D & L ENERGY INC
3930 Fulton Dr Nw Ste 200 (44718-3040)
PHONE 330 270-1201
Ben W Lupo, *CEO*
Susan A Faith, *President*
EMP: 23
SQ FT: 13,637
SALES (est): 5.6MM **Privately Held**
SIC: 1311 Crude Petroleum/Natural Gas Production

(G-2646)
D ANDERSON CORP
6872 Glengarry Ave Nw (44718-4044)
P.O. Box 36205 (44735-6205)
PHONE 330 433-0606
Dale Anderson, *President*
Charles Brown, *Treasurer*
EMP: 2
SALES: 2MM **Privately Held**
SIC: 1381 Directional drilling oil & gas wells

(G-2647)
DANNER PRESS CORP
1411 Navarre Rd Sw (44706-1624)
PHONE 330 454-5692
James Ilundquist, *President*
EMP: 3
SALES (est): 246.9K **Privately Held**
SIC: 2759 2752 Commercial printing; commercial printing, lithographic

(G-2648)
DANSCO MFG & PMPG UNIT SVC LP
2149 Moore Ave Se (44707-2239)
PHONE 330 452-3677
Dave Send, *Owner*
Don Sibley, *Opers Mgr*
EMP: 4
SALES (est): 200K **Privately Held**
SIC: 1389 Oil field services

(G-2649)
DARTING AROUND LLC
3032 Martindale Rd Ne (44714-1444)
PHONE 330 639-3990
Jeff Bowman, *Principal*
EMP: 4
SALES (est): 456.8K **Privately Held**
SIC: 3949 Darts & table sports equipment & supplies

(G-2650)
DAS CONSULTING SERVICES INC (PA)
5178 Mayfair Rd (44720-1446)
PHONE 330 896-4064
Dennis Sklack, *President*
Lynnann Sklack, *Admin Sec*
EMP: 12
SQ FT: 3,300
SALES (est): 1.3MM **Privately Held**
SIC: 3625 8748 Control equipment, electric; systems engineering consultant, ex. computer or professional

(G-2651)
DCC CORP (PA)
5757 Mayfair Rd (44720-1546)
P.O. Box 2288 (44720-0288)
PHONE 330 494-0494
Stephen G Deuble, *President*
Andy Deuble, *Vice Pres*
EMP: 15 **EST:** 1908
SQ FT: 16,000 **Privately Held**
SIC: 6719 3999 Investment holding companies, except banks; plaques, picture, laminated

(G-2652)
DE VORE ENGRAVING CO
1017 Tuscarawas St E (44707-3154)
PHONE 330 454-6820
Alan J De Vore, *President*
Chris De Vore, *Vice Pres*
EMP: 6 **EST:** 1963
SQ FT: 400
SALES (est): 500K **Privately Held**
WEB: www.devoreengraving.com
SIC: 3479 Painting, coating & hot dipping

(G-2653)
DECISION SYSTEMS INC
Also Called: Midland Engineering
2935 Woodcliff Dr Nw (44718-3331)
PHONE 330 456-7600
Peter E Voss, *President*
E R Frederick, *Exec VP*
Kay Wieschaus, *Treasurer*
EMP: 20
SQ FT: 5,000
SALES: 49MM **Privately Held**
SIC: 3559 8711 3535 Separation equipment, magnetic; engineering services; conveyors & conveying equipment

(G-2654)
DELTA MEDIA GROUP INC
4726 Hills And Dales Rd N (44708-1571)
PHONE 330 493-0350
Mike Minard, *President*
EMP: 40
SALES (est): 4.3MM **Privately Held**
WEB: www.deltagroup.com
SIC: 7372 Application computer software

GEOGRAPHIC SECTION

Canton - Stark County (G-2681)

(G-2655)
DELTA PLATING INC
Also Called: Olymco
2125 Harrison Ave Sw (44706-3005)
PHONE..................330 452-2300
Gregory Kalikas, *President*
Alex Sklavenitis, *Vice Pres*
Stephanie Kalikas, *Admin Sec*
EMP: 43
SQ FT: 46,000
SALES (est): 7.2MM **Privately Held**
SIC: 3471 Electroplating of metals or formed products; chromium plating of metals or formed products

(G-2656)
DEVAULT INDUSTRIES LLC
3500 12th St Nw (44708-3805)
PHONE..................330 456-6070
Dennis R Devault, *Principal*
EMP: 6
SALES (est): 758.4K **Privately Held**
SIC: 3999 Manufacturing industries

(G-2657)
DI WALT OPTICAL INC
1112 12th St Ne (44705-1120)
P.O. Box 9259 (44711-9259)
PHONE..................330 453-8427
Marilyn Mc Dougal, *President*
Larry Dillworth, *Vice Pres*
EMP: 13 **EST:** 1971
SQ FT: 3,600
SALES (est): 1.7MM **Privately Held**
SIC: 3827 Optical instruments & lenses

(G-2658)
DIANO CONSTRUCTION AND SUP CO
Also Called: Diano Supply Co
1000 Warner Rd Se (44707-3398)
PHONE..................330 456-7229
Anthony Diano Jr, *President*
Darlene Guynup, *Vice Pres*
EMP: 20 **EST:** 1929
SQ FT: 1,500
SALES (est): 3.1MM **Privately Held**
SIC: 3273 Ready-mixed concrete

(G-2659)
DIEBOLD NIXDORF INCORPORATED
5571 Global Gtwy (44720-1377)
PHONE..................330 490-4000
Jim Huntsman, *Technical Mgr*
Leslie Pierce, *Controller*
Joe Oleksik, *Manager*
Michelle Seabolt, *Manager*
Jim Bambrick, *Info Tech Mgr*
EMP: 300
SALES (corp-wide): 4.5B **Publicly Held**
WEB: www.diebold.com
SIC: 3578 Automatic teller machines (ATM)
PA: Diebold Nixdorf, Incorporated
5995 Mayfair Rd
North Canton OH 44720
330 490-4000

(G-2660)
DISCHEM INTERNATIONAL INC
4252 Strausser St Nw (44720-7114)
PHONE..................330 494-5210
Raj Lakhia, *President*
Todd Lakhia, *Vice Pres*
▼ **EMP:** 4
SALES: 980K **Privately Held**
WEB: www.latexink.com
SIC: 3953 5112 Marking devices; marking devices

(G-2661)
DLHBOWLES INC (PA)
2422 Leo Ave Sw (44706-2344)
PHONE..................330 478-2503
John W Saxon, *CEO*
SRI Sridhara, *President*
Dennis Whittington, *Buyer*
Mike Ramsay, *CFO*
Matt Nyeste, *Controller*
◆ **EMP:** 450
SQ FT: 107,000
SALES (est): 271.5MM **Privately Held**
WEB: www.dlh-inc.com
SIC: 8711 3089 3082 Engineering services; injection molding of plastics; tubes, unsupported plastic

(G-2662)
DLHBOWLES INC
Also Called: Genex Mold
2422 Leo Ave Sw (44706-2344)
P.O. Box 6030 (44706)
PHONE..................330 478-2503
Tom Huskey, *Branch Mgr*
EMP: 17
SALES (corp-wide): 271.5MM **Privately Held**
WEB: www.dlh-inc.com
SIC: 2821 Molding compounds, plastics
PA: Dlhbowles, Inc.
2422 Leo Ave Sw
Canton OH 44706
330 478-2503

(G-2663)
DLHBOWLES INC
2310 Leo Ave Sw (44706)
PHONE..................330 479-7595
Tom Huskey, *Branch Mgr*
EMP: 30
SALES (corp-wide): 271.5MM **Privately Held**
WEB: www.dlh-inc.com
SIC: 3089 Injection molding of plastics
PA: Dlhbowles, Inc.
2422 Leo Ave Sw
Canton OH 44706
330 478-2503

(G-2664)
DUNCAN PRESS CORPORATION
5049 Yukon St Nw (44708-5017)
PHONE..................330 477-4529
Richard Kempthorn, *President*
Scott Duncan, *Vice Pres*
Jed Parker, *Vice Pres*
Steve Smith, *Sales Staff*
EMP: 22 **EST:** 1958
SQ FT: 20,000
SALES (est): 2MM **Privately Held**
WEB: www.duncanpress.com
SIC: 2752 Commercial printing, offset

(G-2665)
EDW C LEVY CO
3715 Whipple Ave Sw (44706-3535)
PHONE..................330 484-6328
Jack Sines, *Manager*
EMP: 20
SQ FT: 5,200
SALES (corp-wide): 368.1MM **Privately Held**
WEB: www.edwclevy.com
SIC: 5093 3295 Scrap & waste materials; minerals, ground or treated
PA: Edw. C. Levy Co.
9300 Dix
Dearborn MI 48120
313 429-2200

(G-2666)
ELCOMA METAL FABRICATING & SLS
521 Lawrence Rd Ne (44704-1007)
PHONE..................330 588-3075
Charles Robertson, *Manager*
EMP: 3
SALES (corp-wide): 7MM **Privately Held**
WEB: www.elcoma.com
SIC: 3441 Fabricated structural metal
PA: Elcoma Metal Fabricating Ltd.
878 William St
Midland ON L4R 4
705 526-9363

(G-2667)
ELECTRA TARP INC
2900 Perry Dr Sw (44706-2268)
PHONE..................330 477-7168
Betsy Paul, *President*
EMP: 14
SQ FT: 20,000
SALES (est): 1.4MM **Privately Held**
WEB: www.electratarp.com
SIC: 2394 Tarpaulins, fabric: made from purchased materials

(G-2668)
EMBROIDME
3611 Cleveland Ave S (44707-1447)
PHONE..................330 484-8484
Scott Leuenberger, *Manager*
Mike Hamsher, *Manager*
EMP: 6
SALES (est): 692.3K **Privately Held**
SIC: 2395 Embroidery & art needlework

(G-2669)
EVANS INDUSTRIES INC
606 Walnut Ave Ne (44702-1029)
PHONE..................330 453-1122
Sue Ann Evans, *President*
Bevan Evans, *Treasurer*
EMP: 18
SQ FT: 15,000
SALES (est): 3.3MM **Privately Held**
SIC: 3089 Injection molding of plastics

(G-2670)
EVERHARD PRODUCTS INC (PA)
1016 9th St Sw (44707-4100)
PHONE..................330 453-7786
G R Lucas, *Ch of Bd*
James L Anderson, *President*
Scott Anderson, *Vice Pres*
Brian Loy, *Engineer*
Larry Wise, *Engineer*
▲ **EMP:** 119
SQ FT: 154,000
SALES (est): 23.3MM **Privately Held**
WEB: www.everhard.com
SIC: 3423 Hand & edge tools

(G-2671)
FIN FEATHER FUR
4080 Belden Village St Nw (44718-2541)
PHONE..................330 493-8300
Mike Goschinski, *Branch Mgr*
EMP: 3
SALES (corp-wide): 10.8MM **Privately Held**
SIC: 3999 Furs
PA: Fin Feather Fur Outfitters-Ashland, Inc.
652 Us Highway 250 E
Ashland OH 44805
419 281-2557

(G-2672)
FINAL MACHINE
8397 Cleveland Ave Nw (44720-4819)
PHONE..................330 966-1744
Herman Bower, *Owner*
EMP: 4
SALES (est): 317.6K **Privately Held**
SIC: 3599 Machine shop, jobbing & repair

(G-2673)
FOLTZ MACHINE LLC
2030 Allen Ave Se (44707-3691)
PHONE..................330 453-9235
Lee Dicola, *Ch of Bd*
David Dicola, *President*
Linda R Polsinelli, *Vice Pres*
Brittany Barnhart, *Office Mgr*
Dan Duffy, *Manager*
EMP: 30 **EST:** 1970
SQ FT: 37,500
SALES (est): 6.6MM **Privately Held**
WEB: www.foltzmachine.com
SIC: 3599 Machine shop, jobbing & repair

(G-2674)
FORMCO INC
5175 Stoneham Rd (44720-1540)
PHONE..................330 966-2111
Richard Bourne, *President*
Christopher Bourne, *Treasurer*
Carol Bourne, *Admin Sec*
EMP: 7
SQ FT: 9,000
SALES: 500K **Privately Held**
SIC: 3069 Medical sundries, rubber

(G-2675)
FOUNDATION SYSTEMS ANCHORS INC (PA)
Also Called: F S A
2300 Allen Ave Se (44707-3673)
PHONE..................330 454-1700
Anthony Codispoti, *President*
Karen Hawk, *Corp Secy*
Dennis Dinarda, *Vice Pres*
Maria Bertram, *Traffic Mgr*
Cassie Yoder, *Sales Mgr*
▲ **EMP:** 15
SQ FT: 2,500
SALES (est): 5.1MM **Privately Held**
WEB: www.fsabolt.com
SIC: 3449 Fabricated bar joists & concrete reinforcing bars

(G-2676)
FRITO-LAY NORTH AMERICA INC
4030 16th St Sw (44710-2354)
PHONE..................330 477-7009
Mike Kulbacki, *Branch Mgr*
Kathy Foskey, *Admin Asst*
EMP: 100
SQ FT: 36,400
SALES (corp-wide): 64.6B **Publicly Held**
WEB: www.fritolay.com
SIC: 2096 2099 Potato chips & other potato-based snacks; food preparations
HQ: Frito-Lay North America, Inc.
7701 Legacy Dr
Plano TX 75024

(G-2677)
FUTURE PRODUCTIONS INC
4601 11th St Nw (44708-3561)
PHONE..................330 478-0477
Brett Huntsman, *President*
EMP: 3
SALES (est): 290.7K **Privately Held**
SIC: 1381 Directional drilling oil & gas wells

(G-2678)
GALT ALLOYS INC MAIN OFC
122 Central Plz N (44702-1448)
PHONE..................330 453-4678
Stephen R Giangiordano, *Principal*
EMP: 6
SALES (est): 376.9K **Privately Held**
SIC: 3339 Primary nonferrous metals

(G-2679)
GASPAR INC
1545 Whipple Ave Sw (44710-1373)
PHONE..................330 477-2222
Gary W Gaspar, *President*
Wesley M Morgan, *Managing Dir*
Chuck Clark, *Editor*
Rodney Shaffer, *Materials Mgr*
Bob Frederick, *Purch Mgr*
EMP: 55
SQ FT: 36,000
SALES (est): 15.6MM **Privately Held**
WEB: www.gasparinc.com
SIC: 3443 7692 3444 Tanks, standard or custom fabricated: metal plate; heat exchangers, condensers & components; welding repair; sheet metalwork

(G-2680)
GENERAL ELECTRIC COMPANY
1807 Allen Ave Se (44707-3695)
PHONE..................330 455-2140
Hughes Christensen, *Branch Mgr*
EMP: 4
SALES (corp-wide): 121.6B **Publicly Held**
SIC: 3533 Oil & gas field machinery
PA: General Electric Company
41 Farnsworth St
Boston MA 02210
617 443-3000

(G-2681)
GENERAL ELECTRIC COMPANY
5555 Massillon Rd Bldg D (44720-1339)
PHONE..................330 458-3200
June Mutter, *Manager*
EMP: 25
SALES (corp-wide): 121.6B **Publicly Held**
SIC: 3646 Commercial indusl & institutional electric lighting fixtures
PA: General Electric Company
41 Farnsworth St
Boston MA 02210
617 443-3000

Canton - Stark County (G-2682)

(G-2682)
GENERAL PUMP & EQP COMPNAY
3276 Bruening Ave Sw (44706-4190)
P.O. Box 6380 (44706-0380)
PHONE..................330 455-2100
David Lapp, *President*
Cindy A Lapp, *Vice Pres*
EMP: 5
SQ FT: 3,750
SALES (est): 73.2K **Privately Held**
WEB: www.gpequip.com
SIC: 3829 5999 5049 Anamometers; alcoholic beverage making equipment & supplies; bank equipment & supplies

(G-2683)
GERDAU MACSTEEL ATMOSPHERE ANN
Also Called: Advanced Bar Technology
1501 Raff Rd Sw (44710-2356)
PHONE..................330 478-0314
Saminathan Ramaswamy, *Principal*
Scott C Pence, *Principal*
EMP: 80
SQ FT: 31,316 **Privately Held**
WEB: www.aaimac.com
SIC: 7389 3398 Metal cutting services; metal heat treating
HQ: Gerdau Macsteel Atmosphere Annealing
209 W Mount Hope Ave # 1
Lansing MI 48910
517 782-0415

(G-2684)
GILBERT GEISER
Also Called: Protista Tool
3301 Longview Pl Nw (44720-4777)
PHONE..................330 237-7901
Gilbert Geiser, *Owner*
EMP: 5
SALES: 105K **Privately Held**
SIC: 3523 Planting, haying, harvesting & processing machinery

(G-2685)
GMELECTRIC INC
4606 Southway St Sw (44706-1935)
PHONE..................330 477-3392
George H Mountcastle, *Principal*
EMP: 6 EST: 2008
SALES (est): 687.6K **Privately Held**
SIC: 3694 5013 3679 Engine electrical equipment; automotive supplies & parts; harness assemblies for electronic use: wire or cable

(G-2686)
GONZOIL INC
5260 Fulton Dr Nw (44718-1806)
PHONE..................330 497-5888
Douglas W Gonzalez, *President*
Frank W Gonzalez, *Corp Secy*
EMP: 9
SQ FT: 1,000
SALES: 770.1K **Privately Held**
SIC: 1382 Oil & gas exploration services

(G-2687)
GRANGER PIPELINE CORPORATION
111 2nd St Nw Ste 202 (44702-1547)
PHONE..................330 454-8095
Mitchell Graham, *President*
EMP: 3
SQ FT: 6,834
SALES (est): 234.3K **Privately Held**
SIC: 1389 Oil field services

(G-2688)
GREGORY INDUSTRIES INC (PA)
4100 13th St Nw (44710-1464)
PHONE..................330 477-4800
T Stephen Gregory, *CEO*
Matt Gregory, *Exec VP*
Tim Porter, *Vice Pres*
Brian Lester, *Plant Mgr*
Judy Stenger, *Materials Mgr*
◆ EMP: 80 EST: 1957
SQ FT: 145,000
SALES (est): 29.9MM **Privately Held**
WEB: www.gregorycorp.com
SIC: 3441 Fabricated structural metal

(G-2689)
GREGORY ROLL FORM INC
4100 13th St Sw (44710-1464)
PHONE..................330 477-4800
T Stephen Gregory, *CEO*
T Raymond Gregory, *Ch of Bd*
Joseph Weaver, *CFO*
Yvonne Nichols, *Human Res Dir*
EMP: 100 EST: 1978
SQ FT: 160,000
SALES (est): 10.7MM
SALES (corp-wide): 29.9MM **Privately Held**
WEB: www.gregorycorp.com
SIC: 3312 Iron & steel: galvanized, pipes, plates, sheets, etc.
PA: Gregory Industries, Inc.
4100 13th St Sw
Canton OH 44710
330 477-4800

(G-2690)
H-W MACHINE INC
4028 Southway St Sw (44706-1801)
PHONE..................330 477-7231
Kris Houk, *President*
Joel Grissom, *Treasurer*
Millie Valentine, *Admin Sec*
EMP: 6 EST: 1944
SQ FT: 15,000
SALES (est): 600K **Privately Held**
WEB: www.hwmachine.com
SIC: 3599 Machine shop, jobbing & repair

(G-2691)
HAINES PUBLISHING INC
8050 Freedom Ave Nw (44720-6912)
P.O. Box 2117 (44720-0117)
PHONE..................330 494-9111
William Haines Jr, *President*
EMP: 65
SQ FT: 20,000
SALES: 4.1MM **Privately Held**
SIC: 2741 Directories: publishing & printing

(G-2692)
HANGER PRSTHETCS & ORTHO INC
4663 Whipple Ave Nw (44718-2615)
PHONE..................330 821-4918
George Sham, *President*
EMP: 5
SALES (corp-wide): 1B **Publicly Held**
SIC: 3842 Orthopedic & prosthesis applications
HQ: Hanger Prosthetics & Orthotics, Inc.
10910 Domain Dr Ste 300
Austin TX 78758
512 777-3800

(G-2693)
HANNON COMPANY (PA)
Also Called: Charles Rewinding Div
1605 Waynesburg Dr Se (44707-2137)
PHONE..................330 456-4728
Christopher Meister, *President*
Mike McAllister, *Superintendent*
Steven Harper, *COO*
Gary Gonzalez, *Plant Mgr*
Gary Griswold, *CFO*
EMP: 75 EST: 1926
SQ FT: 65,000
SALES (est): 25.8MM **Privately Held**
WEB: www.hanco.com
SIC: 3621 3825 5084 3699 Motors, electric; test equipment for electronic & electrical circuits; transformers, portable; instrument; industrial machinery & equipment; electrical equipment & supplies; transformers, except electric; industrial furnaces & ovens

(G-2694)
HARRISON PAINT COMPANY (PA)
1329 Harrison Ave Sw (44706-1596)
PHONE..................330 455-5120
Patrick Lauber, *President*
Guy Braun, *VP Sales*
Rhett Forkum, *Manager*
Patrick Gorman, *Manager*
Anna Krisko, *Technology*
▼ EMP: 27
SQ FT: 173,000
SALES (est): 4.3MM **Privately Held**
WEB: www.harrisonpaint.com
SIC: 2851 Paints & allied products

(G-2695)
HAZEL AND RYE ARTISAN BKG CO
220 Market Ave S Ste 110 (44702-2182)
PHONE..................330 454-6658
James Ferrero, *Owner*
EMP: 4
SALES (est): 279.1K **Privately Held**
SIC: 2051 Bread, cake & related products

(G-2696)
HENDRICKSON USA LLC
Also Called: Hendrickson Trailer
2070 Industrial Pl Se (44707-2641)
PHONE..................330 456-7288
Perry Bahr, *General Mgr*
John Falconer, *Project Mgr*
Dean Zimmerman, *Safety Mgr*
Eric Bauer, *Purch Mgr*
Eric Harkins, *Buyer*
EMP: 150
SALES (corp-wide): 916.4MM **Privately Held**
SIC: 3714 Motor vehicle parts & accessories
HQ: Hendrickson Usa, L.L.C.
500 Park Blvd Ste 450
Itasca IL 60143

(G-2697)
HERCULES POLISHING & PLATING
4883 Southway St Sw (44706-1954)
PHONE..................330 455-8871
Linda J Paxos, *CEO*
Nicholas Paxos, *Vice Pres*
EMP: 10
SQ FT: 20,000
SALES: 2MM **Privately Held**
SIC: 3471 Plating of metals or formed products; chromium plating of metals or formed products; polishing, metals or formed products

(G-2698)
HHI COMPANY INC (PA)
2512 Columbus Rd Ne (44705-3707)
P.O. Box 7117 (44705-0117)
PHONE..................330 455-3983
Larry R Hunter, *President*
Judith Kay Hunter, *Vice Pres*
EMP: 3
SQ FT: 10,000
SALES (est): 1.1MM **Privately Held**
SIC: 7699 3069 Hydraulic equipment repair; molded rubber products

(G-2699)
HILAND GROUP INCORPORATED (PA)
Also Called: Delano Foods
7600 Supreme St Nw (44720-6920)
P.O. Box 36737 (44735-6737)
PHONE..................330 499-8404
EMP: 65 EST: 1955
SQ FT: 10,000
SALES (est): 8.3MM **Privately Held**
SIC: 5149 2099 Whol Groceries Mfg Food Preparations

(G-2700)
HM WIRE INTERNATIONAL INC
2125 46th St Nw (44709-1831)
P.O. Box 2153, North Canton (44720-0153)
PHONE..................330 244-8501
Hal Marker, *President*
▲ EMP: 5
SQ FT: 10,000
SALES (est): 777.1K **Privately Held**
WEB: www.hmwire.com
SIC: 3357 5051 Magnet wire, nonferrous; miscellaneous nonferrous products

(G-2701)
HUNTER HYDRAULICS INC
Also Called: Hhi
2512 Columbus Rd Ne (44705-3707)
P.O. Box 7117 (44705-0117)
PHONE..................330 455-3983
Larry R Hunter, *President*
Judith Kay Hunter, *Treasurer*
EMP: 6 EST: 1968
SQ FT: 10,000
SALES: 999K
SALES (corp-wide): 1.1MM **Privately Held**
SIC: 3542 7699 Presses: hydraulic & pneumatic, mechanical & manual; hydraulic equipment repair
PA: The Hhi Company Inc
2512 Columbus Rd Ne
Canton OH 44705
330 455-3983

(G-2702)
HYDRODEC INC (HQ)
2021 Steinway Blvd Se (44707-2644)
PHONE..................330 454-8202
Mark McNamara, *CEO*
EMP: 17
SALES (est): 9.7MM **Privately Held**
SIC: 2911 Oils, partly refined: sold for rerunning

(G-2703)
HYDRODEC OF NORTH AMERICA LLC
2021 Steinway Blvd Se (44707-2644)
PHONE..................330 454-8202
Ian Smale, *CEO*
Moynihan Colin, *Chairman*
Ellis Chris, *CFO*
▼ EMP: 29 EST: 2007
SQ FT: 15,000
SALES (est): 9.7MM **Privately Held**
SIC: 2911 Oils, partly refined: sold for rerunning
HQ: Hydrodec Inc.
2021 Steinway Blvd Se
Canton OH 44707

(G-2704)
I SQ R POWER CABLE CO
4300 Chamber Ave Sw (44706-3376)
P.O. Box 20149 (44701-0149)
PHONE..................330 588-3000
Michael G Pinney, *President*
Mike Farber, *Engineer*
Sharon Perry, *Cust Mgr*
Karl Schwenk, *Director*
▲ EMP: 12
SQ FT: 8,000
SALES (est): 2.3MM **Privately Held**
SIC: 3643 Current-carrying wiring devices

(G-2705)
IML CONTAINERS OHIO INC
5365 E Center Dr Ne (44721-3734)
PHONE..................330 754-1066
John P Lacroix, *President*
Dora Bower, *Manager*
EMP: 15
SALES (est): 97.8K
SALES (corp-wide): 31.7MM **Privately Held**
SIC: 3089 Plastic containers, except foam; boxes, plastic
PA: Contenants I.M.L. D'amerique Du Nord Inc, Les
2625 344 Rte
Saint-Placide QC J0V 2
450 258-3130

(G-2706)
IMPERIAL TECHNOLOGIES INC (HQ)
4155 Martindale Rd Ne (44705-2727)
PHONE..................330 491-3200
Albert R Christian, *President*
Richard Tschantz, *Vice Pres*
Ronald Tschantz, *Vice Pres*
C Lynch Christian III, *Admin Sec*
EMP: 12
SALES (est): 3.8MM
SALES (corp-wide): 6.9MM **Privately Held**
WEB: www.imperial-technologies.com
SIC: 3535 Conveyors & conveying equipment
PA: Imperial Colliery Company
1000 Church St Ste 3
Lynchburg VA 24504
434 845-5918

GEOGRAPHIC SECTION
Canton - Stark County (G-2735)

(G-2707)
INDEPENDENT PARTICLE LABS
5353 Swepstone St Nw (44708-3256)
PHONE.................................330 477-2016
James Fete, *Principal*
EMP: 3 **EST:** 2016
SALES (est): 143.6K **Privately Held**
SIC: 2834 Pharmaceutical preparations

(G-2708)
INNOVATIVE PLASTIC MACHINERY
5252 Southway St Sw (44706-1961)
PHONE.................................330 478-1825
Abe J Kauffman, *President*
EMP: 9
SQ FT: 27,000
SALES: 1.2MM **Privately Held**
SIC: 3559 Plastics working machinery

(G-2709)
INTERIOR GRAPHIC SYSTEMS LLC
4550 Aultman Rd (44720-1525)
PHONE.................................330 244-0100
Deborah Weisburn, *Co-Owner*
Lisa Shanklin, *Production*
Jim Weisburn, *Mng Member*
EMP: 8
SQ FT: 10,000
SALES (est): 1.1MM **Privately Held**
WEB: www.interiorgraphicsystems.com
SIC: 3993 Signs, not made in custom sign painting shops

(G-2710)
INTERTEX WORLD RESOURCES INC
4518 Fulton Dr Nw Ste 101 (44718-2391)
PHONE.................................770 214-5551
EMP: 9 **Privately Held**
SIC: 3011 Tires & inner tubes
PA: Intertex World Resources, Inc.
225 Maple View Dr Ste 201
Carrollton GA 30117

(G-2711)
INVUE SECURITY PRODUCTS INC
1510 4th St Se (44707-3206)
PHONE.................................330 456-7776
Farrokh Abadi, *President*
Gale Essick, *Mfg Mgr*
▼ **EMP:** 200
SALES (est): 12.9MM
SALES (corp-wide): 3.7B **Privately Held**
WEB: www.checkpointsystems.com
SIC: 3699 Security devices
HQ: Checkpoint Systems, Inc.
101 Wolf Dr
West Deptford NJ 08086
800 257-5540

(G-2712)
IRONROCK CAPITAL INCORPORATED
Also Called: Metropolitan Ceramics Div
1201 Millerton St Se (44707-2209)
P.O. Box 9240 (44711-9240)
PHONE.................................330 484-4887
Guy F Renkert, *President*
J G Barbour Et Al, *Principal*
C W Keplinger, *Principal*
H S Renkert, *Principal*
Daniel Marvin, *Senior VP*
▲ **EMP:** 100 **EST:** 1866
SQ FT: 100,000
SALES (est): 20MM **Privately Held**
WEB: www.metroceramics.com
SIC: 3253 Ceramic wall & floor tile

(G-2713)
J & K PRINTING
1728 Navarre Rd Sw (44706-1652)
PHONE.................................330 456-5306
Keith Gillilan, *Owner*
Jane Vagges, *Personnel Exec*
EMP: 5
SALES (est): 385K **Privately Held**
WEB: www.jkprint.com
SIC: 2752 2759 Commercial printing, off-set; commercial printing

(G-2714)
J M SMUCKER COMPANY
Akron Canton Reg Aprt 7 (44720)
PHONE.................................330 497-0073
Hallie McGonigal, *Manager*
EMP: 3
SALES (corp-wide): 7.3B **Publicly Held**
WEB: www.smuckers.com
SIC: 2033 Canned fruits & specialties
PA: The J M Smucker Company
1 Strawberry Ln
Orrville OH 44667
330 682-3000

(G-2715)
JACODAR FSA LLC
2300 Allen Ave Se (44707-3673)
PHONE.................................330 454-1832
Vincent Codispoti, *Principal*
EMP: 21
SALES (est): 776.5K
SALES (corp-wide): 5.1MM **Privately Held**
SIC: 3452 Bolts, metal
PA: Foundation Systems And Anchors, Inc.
2300 Allen Ave Se
Canton OH 44707
330 454-1700

(G-2716)
JANSON INDUSTRIES
1200 Garfield Ave Sw (44706-1639)
P.O. Box 6090 (44706-0090)
PHONE.................................330 455-7029
Richard Janson, *Partner*
Eric H Janson, *Partner*
Tim Brindack, *Design Engr*
Will Harper, *Manager*
Lisa Whitt, *Manager*
EMP: 100
SQ FT: 120,000
SALES (est): 13.6MM **Privately Held**
WEB: www.jansonindustries.com
SIC: 1799 2391 3999 Rigging & scaffolding; curtains & draperies; stage hardware & equipment, except lighting

(G-2717)
JAZ FOODS INC
Also Called: Invisible Chef, The
1818 Hopple Ave Sw (44706-1909)
PHONE.................................800 456-7115
Jill McCauley, *Owner*
EMP: 2
SQ FT: 500
SALES: 2MM **Privately Held**
SIC: 2041 Bread & bread-type roll mixes

(G-2718)
JEBCO MACHINE COMPANY INC
1311 Greenfield Ave Sw (44706-5406)
PHONE.................................330 452-2909
Gerald E Baxter, *President*
EMP: 3
SQ FT: 4,040
SALES (est): 300K **Privately Held**
SIC: 3469 Machine parts, stamped or pressed metal

(G-2719)
JMW WELDING AND MFG
512 45th St Sw (44706-4432)
PHONE.................................330 484-2428
John Slutz, *President*
Michael Slutz, *Vice Pres*
Neal Slutz, *Treasurer*
EMP: 30
SQ FT: 12,000
SALES: 6MM **Privately Held**
SIC: 3443 7692 Industrial vessels, tanks & containers; dumpsters, garbage; welding repair

(G-2720)
JOSHUA LEIGH ENTERPRISES INC
2191 E Maple St (44720-3337)
PHONE.................................330 244-9200
Katie Marcus, *Branch Mgr*
EMP: 9
SALES (corp-wide): 1.8MM **Privately Held**
SIC: 2024 Ice cream & frozen desserts
PA: Joshua Leigh Enterprises Inc
3830 Strrs Cntre Dr Ste 2
Canfield OH 44406
330 702-8270

(G-2721)
KANEL BROTHERS SUPPLY
Also Called: Kanel Brothers Church Supplies
8280 Kent Ave Ne (44721-1303)
P.O. Box 2286 (44720-0286)
PHONE.................................330 499-4802
Thomas Kanel, *Owner*
EMP: 5 **EST:** 1924
SQ FT: 2,000
SALES (est): 273.5K **Privately Held**
WEB: www.kanelbrothers.com
SIC: 2399 Emblems, badges & insignia

(G-2722)
KEBCO PRECISION FABRICATORS
3145 Columbus Rd Ne (44705-3942)
PHONE.................................330 456-0808
Eric James Keblesh, *Principal*
Michael Todd Cogan, *Principal*
Shari Keblesh, *Manager*
EMP: 20
SALES (est): 4.2MM **Privately Held**
SIC: 3441 Fabricated structural metal

(G-2723)
KERR FRICTION PRODUCTS INC
2512 Columbus Rd Ne (44705-3707)
P.O. Box 7117 (44705-0117)
PHONE.................................330 455-3983
Larry R Hunter, *President*
Judith K Hunter, *Vice Pres*
EMP: 25
SQ FT: 10,000
SALES (est): 2.4MM **Privately Held**
SIC: 3714 Motor vehicle brake systems & parts

(G-2724)
KLEBAUM MACHINERY INC
Also Called: KMC Precision Machine
1303 13th St Se (44707-3429)
P.O. Box 6084 (44706-0084)
PHONE.................................330 455-2046
Herb Klebaum, *President*
EMP: 5
SQ FT: 6,000
SALES (est): 909.5K **Privately Held**
SIC: 3555 Printing plates

(G-2725)
KLENK INDUSTRIES INC
1016 9th St Sw (44707-4108)
PHONE.................................330 453-7857
James Andreson, *President*
EMP: 100 **EST:** 1934
SQ FT: 5,000
SALES (est): 8MM **Privately Held**
SIC: 3421 Shears, hand; snips, tinners'

(G-2726)
KLINGSTEDT BROTHERS COMPANY
425 Schroyer Ave Sw (44702-2012)
P.O. Box 6088 (44706-0088)
PHONE.................................330 456-8319
James R Cassler, *President*
Janet Cassler, *Admin Sec*
EMP: 12 **EST:** 1912
SQ FT: 15,000
SALES: 700K **Privately Held**
WEB: www.lhtp.com
SIC: 2752 2754 Commercial printing, off-set; rotary photogravure printing

(G-2727)
KMS 2000 INC (PA)
Also Called: P P I Graphics
315 12th St Nw (44703-1806)
P.O. Box 21220 (44701-1220)
PHONE.................................330 454-9444
Kevin Smith, *President*
Mark Ickes, *Prdtn Mgr*
EMP: 14
SALES (est): 2.9MM **Privately Held**
WEB: www.ppigraphics.com
SIC: 2752 2759 Commercial printing, off-set; letterpress printing

(G-2728)
KOLE INDUSTRIES
121 34th St Ne (44714-1418)
PHONE.................................330 353-1751
EMP: 3
SALES (est): 201.9K **Privately Held**
SIC: 3999 Manufacturing industries

(G-2729)
KONOIL INC
6477 Frank Ave Nw (44720-8412)
PHONE.................................330 499-9811
Paul Konovsky, *President*
Donald Konovsky, *Vice Pres*
John Konovsky, *Vice Pres*
EMP: 3
SALES (est): 306.9K **Privately Held**
SIC: 1311 Crude petroleum production; natural gas production

(G-2730)
LAKE CABLE OPTICAL LAB
Also Called: Lake Cable Optical Laboratory
4837 Frank Ave Nw (44720-7425)
PHONE.................................330 497-3022
Jeff Fisher, *CEO*
EMP: 3 **EST:** 2001
SALES (est): 220.6K **Privately Held**
SIC: 3851 Ophthalmic goods

(G-2731)
LAZARS ART GLLERY CRTIVE FRMNG
2940 Woodlawn Ave Nw (44708)
PHONE.................................330 477-8351
Lazer Tarzan, *President*
Elizabeth Tarzan, *Vice Pres*
EMP: 8
SALES (est): 918.9K **Privately Held**
SIC: 2499 5999 Picture & mirror frames, wood; art dealers

(G-2732)
LEGALCRAFT INC
302 Hallum St Sw (44720-4217)
P.O. Box 8500 (44711-8500)
PHONE.................................330 494-1261
Robert Beck, *President*
Phil Farrelly, *Senior VP*
EMP: 14
SQ FT: 2,000
SALES (est): 1.7MM **Privately Held**
WEB: www.legalcraft.com
SIC: 2752 Commercial printing, lithographic

(G-2733)
LEXINGTON RUBBER GROUP INC
Lexington Lsr Division
3565 Highland Park Nw (44720-4531)
P.O. Box 3076, North Canton (44720-8076)
PHONE.................................330 425-8352
John Miller, *Division Pres*
EMP: 50
SQ FT: 28,802
SALES (corp-wide): 1.8B **Privately Held**
SIC: 3061 Mechanical rubber goods
HQ: Lexington Rubber Group, Inc.
1700 Highland Rd
Twinsburg OH 44087
330 425-8472

(G-2734)
LINX DEFENSE LLC
2230 University Ave Nw (44709-3938)
PHONE.................................805 233-2472
Steve Olson, *Owner*
EMP: 4
SALES (est): 400.5K **Privately Held**
SIC: 3812 Defense systems & equipment

(G-2735)
LUSTROUS METAL COATINGS INC
1541 Raff Rd Sw (44710-2321)
PHONE.................................330 478-4653
Michael Paxos, *President*
Tom Vonortas, *Exec VP*
EMP: 40
SQ FT: 34,000
SALES (est): 6MM **Privately Held**
WEB: www.lustrousmetal.com
SIC: 3471 Plating of metals or formed products

Canton - Stark County (G-2736)

(G-2736)
M A C MACHINE
1111 Faircrest St Se (44707)
PHONE.....................410 944-6171
Allen Craig, *Owner*
EMP: 6
SQ FT: 5,400
SALES (est): 390.7K **Privately Held**
SIC: 3599 Machine shop, jobbing & repair

(G-2737)
M K MORSE COMPANY (PA)
1101 11th St Se (44707-3400)
P.O. Box 8677 (44711-8677)
PHONE.....................330 453-8187
Nancy Sonner, *CEO*
James Batchelder, *President*
Sally Dale, *Owner*
Jeff Guritza, *Business Mgr*
Tom Capone, *Opers Mgr*
◆ EMP: 277 EST: 1963
SQ FT: 375,000
SALES (est): 90MM **Privately Held**
WEB: www.mkmorse.com
SIC: 3425 Saw blades for hand or power saws

(G-2738)
M T SYSTEMS INC
400 Schroyer Ave Sw (44702-2013)
P.O. Box 2086, Danville IL (61834-2086)
PHONE.....................330 453-4646
Mark E Church, *President*
EMP: 8
SQ FT: 12,500
SALES: 2.1MM **Privately Held**
WEB: www.mt-systems.com
SIC: 7373 3823 3561 Computer integrated systems design; industrial instrmnts msrmnt display/control process variable; pumps & pumping equipment

(G-2739)
M TECHNOLOGIES INC
Also Called: Northern Mobile Electric
1818 Hopple Ave Sw (44706-1909)
PHONE.....................330 477-9009
Rodney McCauley, *Managing Prtnr*
Diane Broderick, *Partner*
EMP: 12
SQ FT: 6,000
SALES (est): 2.3MM **Privately Held**
SIC: 3625 5531 Starter, electric motor; automotive parts

(G-2740)
MACHINE COMPONENT MFG
Also Called: Brownlee Engineering & Mfg
3410 Perry Dr Nw (44708-1137)
PHONE.....................330 454-4566
Joseph R Gill, *President*
Jim Walsh, *Vice Pres*
Scott Gill, *Treasurer*
Steven Gill, *Asst Treas*
EMP: 12 EST: 1964
SQ FT: 12,000
SALES: 800K **Privately Held**
WEB: www.brownleemfg.com
SIC: 3491 3599 3541 3494 Industrial valves; machine shop, jobbing & repair; machine tools, metal cutting type; valves & pipe fittings

(G-2741)
MACHINE SHOP
410 Viking St Nw (44720-2466)
PHONE.....................330 494-1251
Fred Gardner, *Owner*
EMP: 4
SALES (est): 234.1K **Privately Held**
SIC: 3599 Machine shop, jobbing & repair

(G-2742)
MARCHIONE STUDIO INC
1225 Minerva Ct Nw (44703-1818)
PHONE.....................330 454-7408
Frank Marchione, *President*
EMP: 4
SQ FT: 1,200
SALES (corp-wide): 403K **Privately Held**
SIC: 3269 3231 Art & ornamental ware, pottery; ornamental glass: cut, engraved or otherwise decorated

PA: Marchione Studio Inc
5030 Gardendale Ave Ne
Canton OH 44714
330 454-7408

(G-2743)
MARIOS DRIVE THRU
914 12th St Ne (44704-1320)
PHONE.....................330 452-8793
Wayne Marion, *Principal*
EMP: 3
SALES (est): 230.9K **Privately Held**
SIC: 2082 Beer (alcoholic beverage)

(G-2744)
MARTZ WELL SERVICE
5101 Rocky Rill Ave Ne (44705-3269)
PHONE.....................330 323-7417
Gary L Martz, *Owner*
EMP: 3
SALES: 160K **Privately Held**
SIC: 1389 Swabbing wells; roustabout service

(G-2745)
MARY ANN DONUT SHOPPE INC (PA)
Also Called: Mary Ann Donuts
5032 Yukon St Nw (44708-5018)
PHONE.....................330 478-1655
Patrick J Welden, *President*
Dorothy Schweitzer, *Vice Pres*
Patrick Welden II, *Opers Mgr*
Danielle Brickwood, *Marketing Mgr*
Marie Sander, *Office Mgr*
EMP: 40 EST: 1947
SALES (est): 2.3MM **Privately Held**
WEB: www.maryanndonuts.com
SIC: 5461 2051 Doughnuts; doughnuts, except frozen

(G-2746)
MATALCO (US) INC
4420 Louisville St Ne (44705-4848)
PHONE.....................330 452-4760
Gina Mason, *Principal*
▲ EMP: 25
SALES (est): 6MM
SALES (corp-wide): 244.3MM **Privately Held**
SIC: 3363 Aluminum die-castings
HQ: Matalco Inc
850 Intermodal Dr
Brampton ON L6T 0
905 790-2511

(G-2747)
MATRIX MANAGEMENT SOLUTIONS
5200 Stoneham Rd (44720-1584)
PHONE.....................330 470-3700
Mark Terpylak, *President*
EMP: 140
SALES (est): 7.9MM
SALES (corp-wide): 531MM **Publicly Held**
SIC: 7372 7373 Prepackaged software; computer integrated systems design
PA: Nextgen Healthcare, Inc.
18111 Von Karman Ave
Irvine CA 92612
949 255-2600

(G-2748)
MC CONCEPTS LLC
2459 55th St Ne (44721-3425)
PHONE.....................330 933-6402
Manuel Chavarria,
EMP: 7
SALES (est): 461.8K **Privately Held**
SIC: 2095 Roasted coffee

(G-2749)
MC CULLY SUPPLY & SALES INC
5559 Fulton Dr Nw Ste A (44718-1728)
PHONE.....................330 497-2211
Toby Mc Cully, *President*
Glenn McCully, *Vice Pres*
EMP: 4
SQ FT: 1,800
SALES: 280K **Privately Held**
SIC: 3312 8742 Rail joints or fastenings; construction project management consultant

(G-2750)
MCCANN PLASTICS INC
5600 Mayfair Rd (44720-1539)
PHONE.....................330 499-1515
Michael A McCann, *President*
Al Imler, *Vice Pres*
Berney Villers, *Plant Mgr*
David Miller, *Opers Mgr*
Carl Schmeltzer, *Maint Spvr*
EMP: 85
SQ FT: 157,800
SALES (est): 30.4MM **Privately Held**
WEB: www.mccannplastics.com
SIC: 3087 Custom compound purchased resins

(G-2751)
MCPHERSON WIRE CUT INC
5208 Mayfair Rd (44720-1531)
P.O. Box 649, Green (44232-0649)
PHONE.....................330 896-0267
Scott Mc Pherson, *President*
Janet Mc Pherson, *Vice Pres*
EMP: 3
SQ FT: 3,000
SALES (est): 477.3K **Privately Held**
SIC: 3599 Machine shop, jobbing & repair

(G-2752)
MEDLINE INDUSTRIES INC
3800 Commerce St Sw (44706-3367)
PHONE.....................330 484-1450
Kevin Yohman, *President*
Scott Wakser, *Principal*
Robert Clark, *Vice Pres*
EMP: 5
SALES (est): 584.1K **Privately Held**
SIC: 3999 Barber & beauty shop equipment

(G-2753)
MIDLANDS MILLROOM SUPPLY INC
1911 36th St Ne (44705-5023)
P.O. Box 7007 (44705-0007)
PHONE.....................330 453-9100
Fred Clark, *President*
David Salvino, *Accounting Mgr*
John Husser, *Manager*
Dee Sohal, *Manager*
▲ EMP: 28
SQ FT: 17,000
SALES: 15MM **Privately Held**
WEB: www.batch-off.com
SIC: 5084 3061 Materials handling machinery; mechanical rubber goods

(G-2754)
MIDWEST SIGN CTR
Also Called: Midwest Sign Center
4210 Cleveland Ave Nw (44709-2350)
PHONE.....................330 493-7330
Melvin R Lloyd, *President*
Carolyn P Lloyd, *Vice Pres*
EMP: 12
SQ FT: 3,000
SALES: 1.3MM **Privately Held**
WEB: www.midwestsigncenter.com
SIC: 3993 Signs, not made in custom sign painting shops

(G-2755)
MILK & HONEY
3400 Cleveland Ave Nw # 1 (44709-2784)
PHONE.....................330 492-5884
Dwayne Cornell, *Partner*
EMP: 15
SQ FT: 2,500
SALES (est): 883.5K **Privately Held**
SIC: 5451 5812 2066 2064 Ice cream (packaged); restaurant, lunch counter; chocolate & cocoa products; candy & other confectionery products

(G-2756)
MOBILE MINI INC
8045 Dawnwood Ave Ne (44721-2164)
PHONE.....................303 305-9515
Anthony Day, *Branch Mgr*
EMP: 20
SALES (corp-wide): 593.2MM **Publicly Held**
WEB: www.mobilemini.com
SIC: 3448 Buildings, portable: prefabricated metal

PA: Mobile Mini, Inc.
4646 E Van Buren St # 400
Phoenix AZ 85008
480 894-6311

(G-2757)
MPLX TERMINALS LLC
Also Called: Marathon Canton Refinery
2408 Gambrinus Ave Sw (44706-2365)
PHONE.....................330 479-5539
Mike Armbrester, *Branch Mgr*
EMP: 350
SALES (corp-wide): 6.4B **Publicly Held**
WEB: www.mapllc.com
SIC: 5172 2951 Gasoline; asphalt paving mixtures & blocks
HQ: Mplx Terminals Llc
200 E Hardin St
Findlay OH

(G-2758)
MULTI GALVANIZING LLC
825 Navarre Rd Sw (44707-4058)
PHONE.....................330 453-1441
Charles E Decker III, *Plant Mgr*
EMP: 6
SQ FT: 30,000
SALES (est): 620K **Privately Held**
SIC: 3547 Galvanizing lines (rolling mill equipment)

(G-2759)
MURPHY TRACTOR & EQP CO INC
Also Called: John Deere Authorized Dealer
1509 Raff Rd Sw (44710-2321)
PHONE.....................330 477-9304
Chris Mears, *Branch Mgr*
EMP: 8 **Privately Held**
SIC: 3531 5082 Construction machinery; construction & mining machinery
HQ: Murphy Tractor & Equipment Co., Inc.
5375 N Deere Rd
Park City KS 67219
855 246-9124

(G-2760)
MYERS CONTROLLED POWER LLC
133 Taft Ave Ne (44720-2527)
PHONE.....................909 923-1800
Jim Tucker, *Buyer*
Adam Marvin, *Engineer*
James Fink, *Branch Mgr*
EMP: 8
SALES (corp-wide): 196MM **Privately Held**
SIC: 3629 Inverters, nonrotating: electrical
HQ: Myers Controlled Power, Llc
219 E Maple St 100-200e
North Canton OH 44720
330 834-3200

(G-2761)
NICHOLAS RAY ENTERPRISES LLC
Also Called: Olympic Enterprises
3605 Mahoning Rd Ne (44705-4005)
PHONE.....................330 454-4811
Nicholas Ray,
EMP: 4 EST: 1963
SQ FT: 5,000
SALES (est): 310K **Privately Held**
SIC: 2396 Ribbons & bows, cut & sewed

(G-2762)
NOLAN COMPANY (PA)
1016 9th St Sw (44707-4108)
PHONE.....................330 453-7922
James L Anderson, *President*
EMP: 8
SQ FT: 52,000
SALES (est): 4MM **Privately Held**
SIC: 3743 3532 Railroad equipment; mining machinery

(G-2763)
NORCIA BAKERY
624 Belden Ave Ne (44704-2229)
PHONE.....................330 454-1077
Donald C Horne, *President*
Jim Butler, *Vice Pres*
EMP: 25 EST: 1920
SQ FT: 3,200

▲ = Import ▼ = Export
◆ = Import/Export

GEOGRAPHIC SECTION
Canton - Stark County (G-2790)

SALES (est): 3MM **Privately Held**
SIC: 2051 5461 5149 2052 Bakery: wholesale or wholesale/retail combined; bread; groceries & related products; cookies & crackers

(G-2764)
NORRIS NORTH MANUFACTURING
1500 Henry Ave Sw (44706-2852)
PHONE.....................330 691-0449
Tyler Palumbo, *Principal*
EMP: 6
SALES (est): 160.1K **Privately Held**
SIC: 3999 Manufacturing industries

(G-2765)
NORTH CANTON PLASTICS INC
6658 Promway Ave Nw (44720-7316)
PHONE.....................330 497-0071
Fax: 330 497-0269
EMP: 38
SQ FT: 26,000
SALES (est): 7.3MM **Privately Held**
SIC: 3089 Mfg Plastic Products

(G-2766)
NORTH CANTON TOOL CO
1156 Marion Ave Sw (44707-4138)
PHONE.....................330 452-0545
David Pool, *President*
Rebecca Perez, *Vice Pres*
EMP: 9 EST: 1950
SQ FT: 10,000
SALES: 1MM **Privately Held**
SIC: 3599 Machine shop, jobbing & repair

(G-2767)
NORTHEASTERN OILFIELD SVCS LLC (PA)
1537 Waynesburg Dr Se (44707-2135)
PHONE.....................330 581-3304
David D Krutilek, *Principal*
EMP: 9
SALES (est): 830.2K **Privately Held**
SIC: 1389 Oil field services

(G-2768)
NORTHEASTERN PLASTICS INC
112 Navarre Rd Sw (44707-3950)
PHONE.....................330 453-5925
Allen Richards, *President*
EMP: 6
SQ FT: 4,800
SALES: 500K **Privately Held**
WEB: www.northeasternplastics.com
SIC: 2759 2396 Screen printing; automotive & apparel trimmings

(G-2769)
OBS INC
Also Called: Obs Specialty Vehicles
1324 Tuscarawas St W (44702-2036)
P.O. Box 6210 (44706-0210)
PHONE.....................330 453-3725
Robert Ferne, *President*
▲ EMP: 13
SQ FT: 28,000
SALES: 2MM **Privately Held**
SIC: 3711 7532 Mobile lounges (motor vehicle), assembly of; body shop, automotive

(G-2770)
OGC INDUSTRIES INC
934 Wells Ave Nw (44703-3500)
PHONE.....................330 456-1500
Orlando Chiarucci, *President*
EMP: 10
SQ FT: 80,000
SALES (est): 1.7MM **Privately Held**
SIC: 4731 3679 Brokers, shipping; harness assemblies for electronic use: wire or cable

(G-2771)
OHIO AUTO SUPPLY COMPANY
Also Called: Professional Detailing Pdts
1128 Tuscarawas St W (44702-2086)
PHONE.....................330 454-5105
Michael Dickson, *President*
Stanley R Rubin, *Admin Sec*
EMP: 29 EST: 1933
SQ FT: 15,000
SALES (est): 6.7MM **Privately Held**
WEB: www.ohioautosupply.com
SIC: 5013 2842 5531 3714 Automotive supplies & parts; cleaning or polishing preparations; automotive parts; motor vehicle parts & accessories

(G-2772)
OHIO GRATINGS INC (PA)
5299 Southway St Sw (44706-1992)
PHONE.....................330 477-6707
David Bartley, *Ch of Bd*
John Bartley, *President*
Ronald Lenney, *Vice Pres*
◆ EMP: 300 EST: 1970
SQ FT: 150,000
SALES (est): 98.7MM **Privately Held**
WEB: www.ohiogratings.com
SIC: 3446 3444 3441 3312 Gratings, open steel flooring; open flooring & grating for construction; sheet metalwork; fabricated structural metal; blast furnaces & steel mills

(G-2773)
OHIO METAL WORKING PRODUCTS
Also Called: American Carbide Tool Company
3620 Progress St Ne (44705-4438)
P.O. Box 288, Armstrong IA (50514-0288)
PHONE.....................330 455-2009
Paul Ernenwein, *President*
Catherine Howenstine, *Admin Sec*
EMP: 35
SALES (est): 5.8MM
SALES (corp-wide): 19.7MM **Publicly Held**
SIC: 2819 Carbides
PA: Art's-Way Manufacturing Co., Inc.
5556 Highway 9
Armstrong IA 50514
712 864-3131

(G-2774)
OHIO PAPER TUBE CO
3422 Navarre Rd Sw (44706-1856)
PHONE.....................330 478-5171
William Natale Jr, *President*
Timothy Natale, *Corp Secy*
Dennis Natale, *Vice Pres*
Kevin Reisinger, *Sales Staff*
EMP: 18
SQ FT: 46,000
SALES (est): 4.6MM **Privately Held**
WEB: www.ohiopapertube.com
SIC: 2655 Tubes, fiber or paper: made from purchased material

(G-2775)
OHIO PRECISION INC
1239 Market Ave S (44707-3968)
PHONE.....................330 453-9710
Susan Stabler, *President*
David Boord, *Vice Pres*
EMP: 8
SALES (est): 810K **Privately Held**
SIC: 3599 Machine shop, jobbing & repair

(G-2776)
OSTER SAND AND GRAVEL INC (PA)
5947 Whipple Ave Nw (44720-7692)
PHONE.....................330 494-5472
Marlene Oster, *President*
Scott Oster, *Vice Pres*
Valerie Newman, *Treasurer*
EMP: 7 EST: 1967
SQ FT: 3,000
SALES (est): 4.1MM **Privately Held**
SIC: 1442 Gravel mining

(G-2777)
P & M ENTERPRISES GROUP INC
1900 Mahoning Rd Ne (44705-1449)
PHONE.....................330 316-0387
EMP: 3
SALES (est): 123.8K **Privately Held**
SIC: 1389 5963 Construction, repair & dismantling services; home related products, direct sales

(G-2778)
PARAGRAPHICS INC
2011 29th St Nw (44709-3218)
PHONE.....................330 493-1074
James S Bosworth, *President*
Andrew Bosworth, *Vice Pres*
Peter A Bosworth, *Vice Pres*
Clark Swab, *Plant Mgr*
Judy Knapski, *Controller*
▲ EMP: 30
SQ FT: 18,000
SALES (est): 5.3MM **Privately Held**
WEB: www.para-inc.com
SIC: 2752 Commercial printing, offset

(G-2779)
PATRIOT PRECISION PRODUCTS
8817 Pleasantwood Ave Nw (44720-4759)
PHONE.....................330 966-7177
Ronald Dillard, *President*
Art Noll, *COO*
EMP: 60
SQ FT: 41,000
SALES (est): 5.2MM **Privately Held**
SIC: 3599 Machine shop, jobbing & repair

(G-2780)
PATRIOT SOFTWARE LLC
4883 Dressler Rd Nw # 301 (44718-3665)
PHONE.....................877 968-7147
Michael J Kappel, *President*
Todd Schmitt, *Treasurer*
Michele Bossart, *Marketing Staff*
Zach Masters, *Marketing Staff*
Wendy Smith, *Payroll Mgr*
EMP: 100
SQ FT: 1,120
SALES: 2.4MM **Privately Held**
WEB: www.patriothr.com
SIC: 7372 Business oriented computer software

(G-2781)
PATRIOT SPECIAL METALS INC
2201 Harrison Ave Sw (44706-3076)
PHONE.....................330 580-9600
Frank Carchidi, *CEO*
Paul Olah, *Vice Pres*
EMP: 70
SALES (est): 16.9MM
SALES (corp-wide): 51MM **Privately Held**
SIC: 3356 Nonferrous rolling & drawing
PA: Patriot Forge Co.
280 Henry St
Brantford ON N3S 7
519 758-8100

(G-2782)
PAXOS PLATING INC
4631 Navarre Rd Sw (44706-2336)
PHONE.....................330 479-0022
Mike Paxos, *President*
EMP: 25
SQ FT: 35,000
SALES (est): 2.9MM **Privately Held**
WEB: www.paxosplating.com
SIC: 3471 Plating of metals or formed products

(G-2783)
PERMAGUIDE
2427 9th St Sw (44710-1806)
PHONE.....................330 456-8519
George Springer, *Owner*
EMP: 20
SALES: 1MM **Privately Held**
SIC: 2741 Maps: publishing only, not printed on site

(G-2784)
PHASE II ENTERPRISES INC
Also Called: Marino Maintenance Co
2154 Bolivar Ave Sw (44706-3055)
PHONE.....................330 484-2113
Richard Marino, *President*
EMP: 8
SQ FT: 5,200
SALES: 1.4MM **Privately Held**
SIC: 7349 3446 Building maintenance services; stairs, fire escapes, balconies, railings & ladders

(G-2785)
PINNACLE PRESS INC
2960 Harrisburg Rd Ne (44705-2562)
PHONE.....................330 453-7060
Robert Kettlewell, *President*
Shelly Poyser, *Treasurer*
EMP: 18
SQ FT: 9,700
SALES: 1.2MM **Privately Held**
SIC: 2752 Commercial printing, offset

(G-2786)
PJS FABRICATING INC
Also Called: Pj's
1511 Linwood Ave Sw (44710-2313)
PHONE.....................330 478-1120
Francis C Bell, *President*
Kathleen Hohler, *Corp Secy*
Harry Spurrier, *Vice Pres*
EMP: 30
SQ FT: 33,000
SALES (est): 9.4MM **Privately Held**
SIC: 3441 Fabricated structural metal

(G-2787)
POWELL ELECTRICAL SYSTEMS INC
Also Called: Pemco North Canton Division
8967 Pleasantwood Ave Nw (44720-4761)
PHONE.....................330 966-1750
Randy Mulheim, *Project Mgr*
Donald Vrudney, *Mfg Staff*
Allen Marshall, *Engineer*
Kristin Heller, *Human Res Mgr*
Jarc Tana, *Department Mgr*
EMP: 92
SQ FT: 41,600
SALES (corp-wide): 395.9MM **Publicly Held**
WEB: www.powl.com
SIC: 3678 5063 3699 Electronic connectors; electrical apparatus & equipment; electrical equipment & supplies
HQ: Powell Electrical Systems, Inc.
8550 Mosley Rd
Houston TX 77075
713 944-6900

(G-2788)
PPG ARCHITECTURAL FINISHES INC
Also Called: Glidden Professional Paint Ctr
4575 Tuscarawas St W (44708-5336)
PHONE.....................330 477-8165
Joe Sonson, *Manager*
Troy Hunter, *Manager*
EMP: 3
SALES (corp-wide): 15.3B **Publicly Held**
WEB: www.gliddenpaint.com
SIC: 5231 2851 Paint; paints & allied products
HQ: Ppg Architectural Finishes, Inc.
1 Ppg Pl
Pittsburgh PA 15272
412 434-3131

(G-2789)
PRAXAIR INC
2225 Bolivar Rd Sw (44706-3056)
PHONE.....................330 453-9904
Ron Kalinooski, *Systems Mgr*
EMP: 25 **Privately Held**
SIC: 2813 Industrial gases
HQ: Praxair, Inc.
10 Riverview Dr
Danbury CT 06810
203 837-2000

(G-2790)
PRECISION COMPONENT INDS LLC
5325 Southway St Sw (44706-1943)
PHONE.....................330 477-1052
Patricia Gerak, *CEO*
George Melson, *COO*
Frank Bachman, *QC Mgr*
David Desimio, *Manager*
Tony Jerak, *Info Tech Dir*
EMP: 30 EST: 1957
SQ FT: 56,000
SALES (est): 7.7MM **Privately Held**
WEB: www.precision-component.com
SIC: 3599 3544 3545 Mfg Industrial Machinery Mfg Dies/Tools/Jigs/Fixtures Mfg Machine Tool Accessories

Canton - Stark County (G-2791)

(G-2791)
PRIME ENGINEERED PLASTICS CORP
1505 Howington Cir Se (44707-2214)
PHONE.................................330 452-5110
Patrick M Nolan, *President*
EMP: 15
SQ FT: 14,400
SALES (est): 2.9MM **Privately Held**
SIC: 3089 Injection molding of plastics

(G-2792)
PRINT SHOP OF CANTON INC
6536 Promler St Nw (44720-7630)
PHONE.................................330 497-3212
Jeff Grametbauer, *President*
Josef K Grametbauer, *President*
Joyce Grametbauer, *Treasurer*
EMP: 8 EST: 1972
SQ FT: 2,600
SALES (est): 1.3MM **Privately Held**
SIC: 2752 Commercial printing, offset

(G-2793)
PRO-DECAL INC
3638 Cleveland Ave S (44707-1448)
PHONE.................................330 484-0089
Shane Branning, *President*
Robin Branning, *Corp Secy*
Kim Schott, *Vice Pres*
Michael Nowlin, *Info Tech Mgr*
EMP: 6
SQ FT: 800
SALES (est): 650K **Privately Held**
WEB: www.prodecalinc.com
SIC: 2752 3993 Decals, lithographed; signs & advertising specialties

(G-2794)
PROFILE PLASTICS INC
1226 Prospect Ave Sw (44706-1628)
PHONE.................................330 452-7000
Bryan Knowles, *Principal*
Sandra Knowles, *Corp Secy*
Cindy Nidy, *Purchasing*
Phillip Creed, *Design Engr*
Ben Weaver, *Maintence Staff*
EMP: 21
SQ FT: 16,000
SALES (est): 5.4MM **Privately Held**
WEB: www.profileplastics.com
SIC: 3089 Extruded finished plastic products; injection molding of plastics

(G-2795)
PROFILE PRODUCTS LLC
1525 Waynesburg Dr Se (44707-2135)
PHONE.................................330 452-2630
Lloyd De Persig, *Plant Mgr*
Lloyd Deperig, *Manager*
EMP: 14
SALES (corp-wide): 92MM **Privately Held**
WEB: www.centralfiber.com
SIC: 2493 Reconstituted wood products
HQ: Profile Products Llc
750 W Lake Cook Rd # 440
Buffalo Grove IL 60089
847 215-1144

(G-2796)
QUALITY POLY CORP
3000 Atlantic Blvd Ne Rear (44705-3919)
P.O. Box 7490 (44705-0490)
PHONE.................................330 453-9559
Craig Shotwell, *President*
EMP: 16
SQ FT: 34,000
SALES (est): 2.5MM **Privately Held**
SIC: 3081 3082 Unsupported plastics film & sheet; tubes, unsupported plastic

(G-2797)
QUARRYMASTERS INC
7761 Hill Church St Se (44730-9799)
PHONE.................................330 612-0474
Joseph A Della, *President*
Jacalyn Tutthill, *Vice Pres*
▲ EMP: 9
SQ FT: 1,600
SALES: 749K **Privately Held**
SIC: 3281 8742 Granite, cut & shaped; general management consultant

(G-2798)
QUASS SHEET METAL INC
5018 Yukon St Nw (44708-5018)
PHONE.................................330 477-4841
John Angerer, *President*
Joyce Angerer, *Vice Pres*
EMP: 9 EST: 1936
SQ FT: 9,500
SALES (est): 1.3MM **Privately Held**
SIC: 3444 Sheet metalwork

(G-2799)
QUICKDRAFT INC
1525 Perry Dr Sw (44710-1098)
PHONE.................................330 477-4574
Matthew C Litler, *President*
Matthew C Litzler, *President*
William J Urban, *COO*
EMP: 45 EST: 1953
SQ FT: 45,000
SALES (est): 13.8MM
SALES (corp-wide): 36.1MM **Privately Held**
WEB: www.quickdraft.com
SIC: 3535 3564 Conveyors & conveying equipment; blowers & fans
PA: C.A. Litzler Holding Company
4800 W 160th St
Cleveland OH 44135
216 267-8020

(G-2800)
R H LITTLE CO
4434 Southway St Sw (44706-1894)
PHONE.................................330 477-3455
David Little, *President*
Robert Brady, *Vice Pres*
Genevieve Little, *Admin Sec*
EMP: 8 EST: 1940
SQ FT: 22,000
SALES (est): 2.5MM **Privately Held**
SIC: 3743 Railroad equipment

(G-2801)
R W SIDLEY INCORPORATED
7545 Pittsburg Ave Nw (44720-6943)
PHONE.................................330 499-5616
R W Sidley, *President*
EMP: 15
SALES (corp-wide): 132.6MM **Privately Held**
SIC: 3273 Ready-mixed concrete
PA: R. W. Sidley Incorporated
436 Casement Ave
Painesville OH 44077
440 352-9343

(G-2802)
RANDALL RICHARD & MOORE LLC
Also Called: Cutter Equipment Company
3710 Progress St Ne (44705-4438)
PHONE.................................330 455-8873
Gregory R Moore,
Glenn R Moore Jr,
EMP: 15 EST: 1998
SALES (est): 3.5MM **Privately Held**
WEB: www.cutteronline.com
SIC: 3523 Turf & grounds equipment; turf equipment, commercial

(G-2803)
RENEGADE WELL SERVICES LLC
215 Trump Ave Ne (44730-1627)
PHONE.................................330 488-6055
EMP: 4
SALES (corp-wide): 284.4MM **Privately Held**
SIC: 1389 Servicing oil & gas wells
HQ: Renegade Well Services, Llc
3301 E Us Highway 377 # 202
Granbury TX 76049

(G-2804)
REPUBLIC STEEL (DH)
2633 8th St Ne (44704-2311)
PHONE.................................330 438-5435
Jaime Vigil, *President*
Inigo Vigil, *Exec VP*
Noel J Huettich, *Vice Pres*
Ted Thielens, *Vice Pres*
Manny Viadero, *Vice Pres*
▲ EMP: 277
SQ FT: 800,000
SALES (est): 325.7MM **Privately Held**
SIC: 3312 Bars, iron: made in steel mills; structural shapes & pilings, steel

(G-2805)
REPUBLIC STEEL INC
Also Called: Canton Hot Rolled Plant
2633 8th St Ne (44704-2311)
PHONE.................................330 438-5533
John Ridgeway, *Manager*
EMP: 200 **Privately Held**
SIC: 3312 Bars & bar shapes, steel, cold-finished: own hot-rolled; rods, iron & steel: made in steel mills
HQ: Republic Steel
2633 8th St Ne
Canton OH 44704
330 438-5435

(G-2806)
RMI TITANIUM COMPANY LLC
Also Called: Rti Alloys Tpd
1935 Warner Rd Se (44707-2273)
PHONE.................................330 455-4010
Cheryl Lyons, *Principal*
Chris Zbuka, *Manager*
EMP: 100
SALES (corp-wide): 14B **Publicly Held**
SIC: 3499 Friction material, made from powdered metal
HQ: Rmi Titanium Company, Llc
1000 Warren Ave
Niles OH 44446
330 652-9952

(G-2807)
RMI TITANIUM COMPANY LLC
Also Called: Galt Alloys
208 15th St Sw (44707-4009)
PHONE.................................330 471-1844
Bruce Whatzel, *Manager*
EMP: 78
SALES (corp-wide): 14B **Publicly Held**
SIC: 3312 3341 Blast furnace & related products; secondary nonferrous metals
HQ: Rmi Titanium Company, Llc
1000 Warren Ave
Niles OH 44446
330 652-9952

(G-2808)
ROBERT PEREZ CARPENTRY
430 Browning Ave Nw (44720-2340)
PHONE.................................330 497-0043
Robert Perez, *Owner*
EMP: 6
SALES (est): 310.1K **Privately Held**
SIC: 1442 Construction sand & gravel

(G-2809)
ROBERT SMART INC
Also Called: Superior Machine Co
1100 High Ave Sw (44707-4116)
PHONE.................................330 454-8881
Robert Scott Smart, *President*
EMP: 12 EST: 1939
SALES (est): 1.6MM **Privately Held**
WEB: www.superior-machine.com
SIC: 3599 Machine shop, jobbing & repair

(G-2810)
RODCO PETROLEUM INC
4600 Castlebar St Nw (44708-2139)
PHONE.................................330 477-9823
Betty O'Neill-Roderick, *President*
David W Roderick, *Corp Secy*
Morgan W Roderick Jr, *Vice Pres*
EMP: 3
SALES (est): 212.2K **Privately Held**
SIC: 1311 Crude petroleum production

(G-2811)
ROSSI CONCEPT ARTS
Also Called: Mr Neon Sign
1019 Mckinley Ave Nw (44703-2054)
P.O. Box 36144 (44735-6144)
PHONE.................................330 453-6366
Kenneth Rossi, *Owner*
EMP: 3
SQ FT: 4,000
SALES: 100K **Privately Held**
SIC: 3993 7389 Signs & advertising specialties; embroidering of advertising on shirts, etc.

(G-2812)
SEASON OF WREATH
8347 Market Ave N (44721-1332)
PHONE.................................330 936-7498
Pamela Beard, *Principal*
EMP: 3
SALES (est): 100.1K **Privately Held**
SIC: 3999 Wreaths, artificial

(G-2813)
SHAHEEN ORIENTAL RUG CO INC (PA)
Also Called: Abbey Carpet
4120 Whipple Ave Nw (44718-2970)
PHONE.................................330 493-9000
Nicholas H Shaheen Jr, *President*
Dawn Shaheen, *Treasurer*
EMP: 10
SQ FT: 12,800
SALES (est): 3.8MM **Privately Held**
WEB: www.shaheenrugs.com
SIC: 5713 7217 2295 Rugs; carpet & furniture cleaning on location; tape, varnished: plastic & other coated (except magnetic)

(G-2814)
SHANAFELT MANUFACTURING CO (PA)
2600 Wnfeld Way Ne 2700 (44705)
P.O. Box 7040 (44705-0040)
PHONE.................................330 455-0315
Jon Lindseth, *Ch of Bd*
Leo Kovachic, *President*
Edwin Cassidy, *Manager*
Judy Haut, *Manager*
Joseph Sullivan, *Admin Sec*
EMP: 35
SQ FT: 50,000
SALES (est): 9.2MM **Privately Held**
WEB: www.shanafelt.com
SIC: 3537 3451 Containers (metal), air cargo; screw machine products

(G-2815)
SHOWROOM TRACKER LLC
6543 Forestwood St Nw (44718-4208)
PHONE.................................888 407-0094
Matthew Tew,
Chris Nickless,
Matthew Nickless,
EMP: 3
SALES (est): 71.1K **Privately Held**
SIC: 7372 Business oriented computer software

(G-2816)
SIGN MAKERS LLC
2417 Cleveland Ave Nw (44709-3612)
PHONE.................................330 455-0909
Glenda Akers,
EMP: 7
SQ FT: 5,800
SALES (est): 688.9K **Privately Held**
SIC: 3993 Signs & advertising specialties

(G-2817)
SIZETEC INC
4825 Higbee Ave Nw # 103 (44718-2567)
PHONE.................................330 492-9682
Mike Tsutsumi, *President*
EMP: 3
SQ FT: 1,000
SALES (est): 380K **Privately Held**
WEB: www.sizetec.com
SIC: 3559 8711 Screening equipment, electric; engineering services

(G-2818)
SLIMANS PRINTERY INC
Also Called: SPI Mailing
624 5th St Nw (44703-2625)
PHONE.................................330 454-9141
Samuel Sliman Jr, *President*
Judy Sliman Humphries, *Vice Pres*
Deanne Hoffman, *Mktg Dir*
EMP: 14 EST: 1947
SQ FT: 9,000
SALES (est): 1.4MM **Privately Held**
SIC: 2752 2759 Commercial printing, offset; letterpress printing

GEOGRAPHIC SECTION

Canton - Stark County (G-2844)

(G-2819)
SOLMET TECHNOLOGIES INC
2716 Shepler Ch Ave Sw (44706-4114)
PHONE....................330 915-4160
Joseph R Halter Jr, *President*
Matthew Halter, *Vice Pres*
E Scott Jackson, *Vice Pres*
Lee Dicola, *Treasurer*
Kyle Sheposh, *Controller*
EMP: 50
SALES (est): 9.8MM **Privately Held**
WEB: www.solmettechnologies.com
SIC: 3462 Iron & steel forgings

(G-2820)
SPECIALTY HOSE AEROSPACE CORP
7802 Freedom Ave Nw (44720-6908)
PHONE....................330 497-9650
Michael Helfer, *President*
Marjorie Onslow, *Treasurer*
EMP: 10
SALES: 1.1MM
SALES (corp-wide): 874.6K **Privately Held**
SIC: 3599 Hose, flexible metallic
PA: Specialty Hose Corporation
7800 Freedom Ave Nw
North Canton OH 44720
330 497-9650

(G-2821)
SPERLING RAILWAY SERVICES INC
4313 Southway St Sw (44706-1809)
PHONE....................330 479-2004
Fred Sperling, *President*
Nancy Sperling, *Corp Secy*
EMP: 10
SQ FT: 17,000
SALES (est): 1.1MM **Privately Held**
WEB: www.sperlingrailway.com
SIC: 3743 Railroad equipment

(G-2822)
STARK MATERIALS INC
Also Called: Northstar Asphalt
7345 Sunset Strip Ave Nw (44720-7040)
P.O. Box 2646 (44720-0646)
PHONE....................330 497-1648
Howard Wenger, *President*
Joe Chiavari, *QC Dir*
EMP: 45
SQ FT: 1,404
SALES (est): 6.1MM **Privately Held**
SIC: 2911 2951 Asphalt or asphaltic materials, made in refineries; asphalt paving mixtures & blocks

(G-2823)
STARK READY MIX & SUPPLY CO
2905 Columbus Rd Ne (44705-3938)
P.O. Box 80449 (44708-0449)
PHONE....................330 580-4307
Douglas A Woodhall, *President*
Gerald Orn, *Treasurer*
EMP: 20
SQ FT: 2,250
SALES: 5.2MM
SALES (corp-wide): 60.2MM **Privately Held**
SIC: 3273 Ready-mixed concrete
PA: Central Allied Enterprises, Inc.
1243 Raff Rd Sw
Canton OH 44710
330 477-6751

(G-2824)
STARK TRUSS COMPANY INC (PA)
Also Called: S T C
109 Miles Ave Sw (44710-1261)
P.O. Box 80469 (44708-0469)
PHONE....................330 478-2100
Abner Yoder, *CEO*
Stephen Yoder, *President*
Javan Yoder, *Exec VP*
Todd Pallotta, *Vice Pres*
Esther Yoder, *Treasurer*
EMP: 18
SQ FT: 4,300
SALES (est): 186.7MM **Privately Held**
WEB: www.starktruss.com
SIC: 5031 2439 Lumber, plywood & millwork; trusses, wooden roof

(G-2825)
STARK TRUSS COMPANY INC
Also Called: Stark Forest Products
4933 Southway St Sw (44706-1979)
PHONE....................330 478-2100
Rob Blyer, *Branch Mgr*
EMP: 100
SALES (corp-wide): 186.7MM **Privately Held**
WEB: www.starktruss.com
SIC: 2439 2511 Trusses, wooden roof; wood household furniture
PA: Stark Truss Company, Inc.
109 Miles Ave Sw
Canton OH 44710
330 478-2100

(G-2826)
STUDIO ARTS & GLASS INC
7495 Strauss Ave Nw (44720-7103)
PHONE....................330 494-9779
Robert Joliet, *President*
Wendy Warren, *Vice Pres*
EMP: 10
SQ FT: 7,000
SALES (est): 800K **Privately Held**
WEB: www.studioartsandglass.com
SIC: 3231 8299 Stained glass: made from purchased glass; arts & crafts schools

(G-2827)
SUAREZ CORPORATION INDUSTRIES
Biotech Research Division
7800 Whipple Ave Nw (44767-0002)
PHONE....................330 494-4282
Benjamin Suarez, *Manager*
EMP: 73
SALES (corp-wide): 71.8MM **Privately Held**
WEB: www.suarez.com
SIC: 3841 5091 2834 5122 Veterinarians' instruments & apparatus; fitness equipment & supplies; vitamin, nutrient & hematinic preparations for human use; vitamins & minerals
PA: Suarez Corporation Industries
7800 Whipple Ave Nw
North Canton OH 44720
330 494-5504

(G-2828)
SUAREZ CORPORATION INDUSTRIES
Edenpure Heater
7800 Whipple Ave Nw (44767-0002)
PHONE....................330 494-5504
John Carten, *Branch Mgr*
EMP: 27
SALES (corp-wide): 71.8MM **Privately Held**
SIC: 3433 Room & wall heaters, including radiators
PA: Suarez Corporation Industries
7800 Whipple Ave Nw
North Canton OH 44720
330 494-5504

(G-2829)
SUN STATE PLASTICS INC
4045 Kevin St Nw (44720-6981)
PHONE....................330 494-5220
Rick Dewees, *President*
EMP: 40
SQ FT: 37,000
SALES (est): 6.7MM **Privately Held**
SIC: 3089 Injection molding of plastics

(G-2830)
SUPER SIGN GUYS LLC
Also Called: Fww
5060 Navarre Rd Sw Ste C (44706-3320)
P.O. Box 36092 (44735-6092)
PHONE....................330 477-3887
Gregory Magee, *Principal*
EMP: 3
SALES (est): 287K **Privately Held**
SIC: 3993 Signs & advertising specialties

(G-2831)
SUSPENSION TECHNOLOGY INC
1424 Scales St Sw (44706-3081)
PHONE....................330 458-3058
David Croston, *President*
Ervin Vandenberg, *Principal*
EMP: 15
SQ FT: 12,000
SALES (est): 2.5MM **Privately Held**
WEB: www.ridesti.com
SIC: 3537 5084 Lift trucks, industrial: fork, platform, straddle, etc.; lift trucks & parts

(G-2832)
TAG SPORTSWEAR LLC
1300 Market Ave N (44714-2606)
PHONE....................330 456-8867
Richard Gattuso,
Charles Gattuso,
EMP: 5 **EST:** 2008
SALES: 120K **Privately Held**
SIC: 2395 Embroidery products, except schiffli machine

(G-2833)
TECHNIBUS INC
1501 Raff Rd Sw Ste 6 (44710-2356)
PHONE....................330 479-4202
Mike Rice, *President*
Keith Anthony, *Safety Mgr*
Howard Dyer, *Project Engr*
Tammy Orr, *Controller*
Jacob Isaacson, *Finance Dir*
▲ **EMP:** 100 **EST:** 2006
SQ FT: 150,000
SALES: 50MM **Publicly Held**
WEB: www.technibus.com
SIC: 3444 Ducts, sheet metal; radiator shields or enclosures, sheet metal
HQ: Ies Infrastructure Solutions, Llc
800 Nave Rd Se
Massillon OH 44646
330 830-3500

(G-2834)
TEK GEAR & MACHINE INC
1220 Camden Ave Sw (44706-1618)
PHONE....................330 455-3331
Kevin Aronhalt, *President*
Thomas Mertz, *Vice Pres*
Emil Bueno, *Treasurer*
EMP: 8
SQ FT: 6,000
SALES (est): 900K **Privately Held**
WEB: www.tekgear.com
SIC: 3599 Machine shop, jobbing & repair

(G-2835)
THE W L JENKINS COMPANY
Also Called: Chaplet & Chill Division
1445 Whipple Ave N (44710-1321)
PHONE....................330 477-3407
Susan E Jenkins, *President*
EMP: 18
SQ FT: 65,000
SALES (est): 3.2MM **Privately Held**
WEB: www.wljenkinsco.com
SIC: 3679 3931 3469 3699 Electronic circuits; musical instruments; metal stampings; security devices

(G-2836)
TIM L HUMBERT
Also Called: Humbert Screen Graphix
6535 Promler St Nw (44720-7626)
PHONE....................330 497-4944
Tim L Humbert, *Owner*
EMP: 11
SQ FT: 6,200
SALES (est): 897.6K **Privately Held**
SIC: 2396 2791 Screen printing on fabric articles; typesetting

(G-2837)
TIMKEN COMPANY
Also Called: Timken Aircraft Operation
5430 Lauby Rd Bldg 7 (44720-1576)
PHONE....................330 471-4300
Bob Campbell, *Manager*
EMP: 7
SALES (corp-wide): 3.5B **Publicly Held**
SIC: 3562 Ball & roller bearings
PA: The Timken Company
4500 Mount Pleasant St Nw
North Canton OH 44720
234 262-3000

(G-2838)
TIMKEN COMPANY
20th & Dueber Ave Sw (44706)
P.O. Box 6920 (44706-0920)
PHONE....................330 471-5028
Jim Wolfter, *Branch Mgr*
EMP: 4
SALES (corp-wide): 3.5B **Publicly Held**
SIC: 3562 Ball & roller bearings
PA: The Timken Company
4500 Mount Pleasant St Nw
North Canton OH 44720
234 262-3000

(G-2839)
TIMKEN COMPANY
Also Called: Roller Plant
786 Whipple Ave Sw (44710)
PHONE....................330 471-5043
Christopher Armstrong, *Branch Mgr*
EMP: 510
SALES (corp-wide): 3.5B **Publicly Held**
SIC: 3562 Ball & roller bearings
PA: The Timken Company
4500 Mount Pleasant St Nw
North Canton OH 44720
234 262-3000

(G-2840)
TIMKEN FOUNDATION
200 Market Ave N Ste 210 (44702-1437)
PHONE....................330 452-1144
Ward J Timken, *President*
EMP: 3
SALES: 6.6MM **Privately Held**
SIC: 2515 Foundations & platforms

(G-2841)
TIMKENSTEEL CORPORATION (PA)
1835 Dueber Ave Sw (44706-2728)
PHONE....................330 471-7000
Ward J Timken Jr, *Ch of Bd*
William P Bryan, *Exec VP*
Frank A Dipiero, *Exec VP*
Thomas D Moline, *Exec VP*
Paul Ward, *Mfg Staff*
◆ **EMP:** 277
SALES: 1.3B **Publicly Held**
SIC: 3312 Blast furnaces & steel mills

(G-2842)
TIMKENSTEEL CORPORATION
4511 Faircrest St Sw (44706-3513)
PHONE....................330 471-7000
Ron Balyint, *Branch Mgr*
EMP: 10
SALES (corp-wide): 869.5MM **Publicly Held**
SIC: 3317 Steel pipe & tubes
PA: Timkensteel Corporation
1835 Dueber Ave Sw
Canton OH 44706
330 471-7000

(G-2843)
TOTAL LUBRICATION MGT CO (HQ)
3713 Progress St Ne (44705-4437)
PHONE....................888 478-6996
Terry Ross, *Senior VP*
▲ **EMP:** 34 **EST:** 2011
SALES (est): 10.4MM
SALES (corp-wide): 3.6B **Publicly Held**
SIC: 3569 Lubrication machinery, automatic
PA: Colfax Corporation
420 Natl Bus Pkwy Ste 500
Annapolis Junction MD 20701
301 323-9000

(G-2844)
TRANSFORMER ASSOCIATES LIMITED
831 Market Ave N (44702-1175)
PHONE....................330 430-0750
Rodney Herndon, *President*
Tonya Cihon, *Manager*
EMP: 6

Canton - Stark County (G-2845)

SALES: 381K **Privately Held**
WEB: www.transformerassociates.com
SIC: 3612 Voltage regulating transformers, electric power

(G-2845)
TRI-K ENTERPRISES INC
935 Mckinley Ave Sw (44707-4163)
PHONE..................................330 832-7380
Robert S Black, *President*
Joan Black, *Corp Secy*
Kerry Black, *Vice Pres*
Kevin Black, *Vice Pres*
EMP: 6
SALES (est): 1.1MM **Privately Held**
SIC: 3451 3542 Screw machine products; presses: hydraulic & pneumatic, mechanical & manual

(G-2846)
UNION METAL INDUSTRIES CORP ○
1432 Maple Ave Ne (44705-1700)
PHONE..................................330 456-7653
EMP: 3 EST: 2018
SALES (est): 551.2K **Privately Held**
SIC: 3669 Traffic signals, electric

(G-2847)
UNITED ENGINEERING & FNDRY CO
1400 Grace Ave Ne (44705-2035)
PHONE..................................330 456-2761
Ronald A Martin, *President*
Jay Neisom, *Principal*
Edward Bauer, *COO*
EMP: 12
SQ FT: 5,000
SALES (est): 1.1MM **Privately Held**
SIC: 3325 Rolling mill rolls, cast steel

(G-2848)
UNITED GRINDING AND MACHINE CO
2315 Ellis Ave Ne (44705-4696)
PHONE..................................330 453-7402
Allan J Pfabe, *President*
Dennis Pfabe, *Vice Pres*
Karen Essig, *Treasurer*
▲ EMP: 75 EST: 1967
SQ FT: 65,000
SALES (est): 13.3MM **Privately Held**
WEB: www.unitedgrinding.com
SIC: 3599 Machine shop, jobbing & repair

(G-2849)
UNITED HARD CHROME CORPORATION
2202 Gilbert Ave Ne (44705-4697)
PHONE..................................330 453-2786
Robert R Horger, *President*
Beth Horger, *Vice Pres*
EMP: 13 EST: 1954
SQ FT: 18,000
SALES (est): 1.1MM **Privately Held**
WEB: www.unitedhardchrome.com
SIC: 3471 Electroplating of metals or formed products

(G-2850)
UNITED ROLLS INC (DH)
Also Called: Whemco
1400 Grace Ave Ne (44705-2035)
PHONE..................................330 456-2761
J Douglas Nesom Jr, *Ch of Bd*
Robin Ingols, *President*
Ron Wilcox, *President*
Edward Bauer, *COO*
Paula Harbaugh, *Vice Pres*
♦ EMP: 81
SQ FT: 225,000
SALES (est): 38.3MM
SALES (corp-wide): 574.3MM **Privately Held**
WEB: www.ufirolls.com
SIC: 3547 3613 Rolling mill machinery; control panels, electric
HQ: Whemco Inc.
    5 Hot Metal St Ste 300
    Pittsburgh PA 15203
    412 390-2700

(G-2851)
UNITED SURFACE FINISHING INC
2202 Gilbert Ave Ne (44705-4634)
PHONE..................................330 453-2786
Richard N Horger, *Principal*
Beulla P Bango, *Principal*
Francis L Petti, *Principal*
EMP: 3 EST: 1957
SALES (est): 421.2K **Privately Held**
SIC: 3471 Chromium plating of metals or formed products

(G-2852)
UNIVERSAL METALS CUTTING INC
2656 Harrison Ave Sw (44706)
PHONE..................................330 580-5192
Joseph Halter Jr, *President*
Lee J Dicola, *Corp Secy*
EMP: 7
SQ FT: 8,140
SALES (est): 723.6K **Privately Held**
SIC: 3312 Tubes, steel & iron

(G-2853)
US TECHNOLOGY CORPORATION
4200 Munson St Nw (44718-2981)
PHONE..................................330 455-1181
Raymond F Williams, *President*
Robert B Putnam, *Vice Pres*
Jill Aldridge, *Administration*
♦ EMP: 42
SQ FT: 2,000
SALES (est): 7.9MM **Privately Held**
WEB: www.ustechnology.com
SIC: 3291 3728 Abrasive products; aircraft parts & equipment

(G-2854)
USA QUICKPRINT INC (PA)
Also Called: Quick Print
409 3rd St Sw (44702-1910)
PHONE..................................330 455-5119
Gerald Hohler, *President*
Jocelyn Hohler, *Vice Pres*
EMP: 22
SQ FT: 2,000
SALES (est): 3.4MM **Privately Held**
SIC: 2752 Commercial printing, offset

(G-2855)
V & S SCHULER ENGINEERING INC (DH)
2240 Allen Ave Se (44707-3612)
PHONE..................................330 452-5200
Brian Miller, *President*
Paul Balster, *Controller*
EMP: 99
SQ FT: 40,000
SALES (est): 36.1MM
SALES (corp-wide): 773.1MM **Privately Held**
WEB: www.vsschuler.com
SIC: 3441 3444 Fabricated structural metal; sheet metalwork
HQ: Voigt & Schweitzer Llc
    987 Buckeye Park Rd
    Columbus OH 43207
    614 449-8281

(G-2856)
V MAST MANUFACTURING INC
1712 Kimball Rd Se (44707-3618)
PHONE..................................330 409-8116
Raymond M Valentine, *President*
EMP: 3 EST: 2009
SALES (est): 196.2K **Privately Held**
SIC: 3999 Manufacturing industries

(G-2857)
VEE GEE ENTERPRISE CORPORATION
4897 Fulton Dr Nw (44718-2337)
PHONE..................................330 493-9780
Dennis L Noland, *President*
Steven T Noland, *Vice Pres*
EMP: 4
SQ FT: 3,200
SALES (est): 200K **Privately Held**
SIC: 2673 Cellophane bags, unprinted: made from purchased materials

(G-2858)
VER MICH LTD
4210 Cleveland Ave Nw (44709-2350)
PHONE..................................330 493-7330
Melvin R Lloyd, *President*
EMP: 4
SALES (est): 279K **Privately Held**
SIC: 2399 Fabricated textile products

(G-2859)
VERSALIFT EAST INC
4884 Corporate St Sw (44706-1907)
PHONE..................................610 866-1400
Keith W Joseph, *Branch Mgr*
EMP: 8
SALES (corp-wide): 138.7MM **Privately Held**
SIC: 3534 Elevators & moving stairways
HQ: Versalift East, L.L.C.
    2706 Brodhead Rd
    Bethlehem PA 18020

(G-2860)
VERVASI VINEYARD & ITLN BISTRO
Also Called: Gervasi Vineyard
1700 55th St Ne (44721-3401)
PHONE..................................330 497-1000
Ted Swaldo, *Principal*
Paul Cincotta, *Opers Staff*
Ashley Fritz-Champine, *Sales Staff*
Jeff Hicks, *Sales Staff*
Jan Prengaman, *Director*
EMP: 23
SALES (est): 3.4MM **Privately Held**
SIC: 2084 Wines

(G-2861)
W W CROSS INDUSTRIES INC
2510 Allen Ave Se (44707-3614)
PHONE..................................330 588-8400
Thomas Trudeau, *President*
Phillip Lattavo, *Vice Pres*
Matt Mehringer, *VP Opers*
Christine Trudeau, *Treasurer*
EMP: 10
SALES (est): 1.8MM **Privately Held**
WEB: www.wwcross.com
SIC: 3965 Fasteners

(G-2862)
WACKER CHEMICAL CORPORATION
Also Called: Silmix Division
2215 International Pkwy (44720-1372)
PHONE..................................330 899-0847
Mathias Wiedemann, *Engineer*
John A Bacon, *Project Engr*
Debra May, *Human Resources*
Brian Allen, *Sales Mgr*
Angela Grim, *Office Mgr*
EMP: 30
SALES (corp-wide): 5.8B **Privately Held**
WEB: www.wackerchemicalcorporation.com
SIC: 2869 Silicones
HQ: Wacker Chemical Corporation
    3301 Sutton Rd
    Adrian MI 49221
    517 264-8500

(G-2863)
WALLACE FORGE COMPANY
3700 Georgetown Rd Ne (44704-2697)
PHONE..................................330 488-1203
Dean Wallace, *President*
Sheila A Ghezzi, *Vice Pres*
William A Peterson, *Admin Sec*
▲ EMP: 65
SQ FT: 55,000
SALES (est): 13.3MM **Privately Held**
WEB: www.wallaceforgecompany.com
SIC: 3462 3321 3463 3452 Iron & steel forgings; gray & ductile iron foundries; nonferrous forgings; bolts, nuts, rivets & washers; truck & bus bodies

(G-2864)
WESTERN BRANCH DIESEL INC
Also Called: John Deere Authorized Dealer
1616 Metric Ave Sw (44706-3087)
PHONE..................................330 454-8800
Mike McElwain, *Branch Mgr*
EMP: 28
SQ FT: 22,400

SALES (corp-wide): 84MM **Privately Held**
WEB: www.westernbranchdiesel.com
SIC: 5084 5531 5063 3714 Engines & parts, diesel; truck equipment & parts; generators; motor vehicle parts & accessories; power transmission equipment; internal combustion engines
PA: Western Branch Diesel, Incorporated
    3504 Shipwright St
    Portsmouth VA 23703
    757 673-7000

(G-2865)
WORTHIGNTON PRODUCTS INC
3405 Kuemerle Ct Ne (44705-5074)
PHONE..................................330 452-7400
Paul Meeks, *President*
Jeffrey S Sanger, *Vice Pres*
▲ EMP: 6
SQ FT: 6,000
SALES (est): 752.7K **Privately Held**
SIC: 3443 3429 3089 Buoys, metal; marine hardware; buoys & floats, plastic

(G-2866)
WYOMING CASING SERVICE INC
1414 Raff Rd Sw (44710-2320)
PHONE..................................330 479-8785
EMP: 20
SALES (corp-wide): 182.2MM **Privately Held**
SIC: 1389 Oil field services
PA: Wyoming Casing Service, Inc.
    198 40th St E
    Dickinson ND 58601
    701 225-8521

(G-2867)
XCEL MOLD AND MACHINE INC
7661 Freedom Ave Nw (44720-6987)
PHONE..................................330 499-8450
Bruce Cain, *President*
Bob Johnson, *Vice Pres*
EMP: 13
SQ FT: 25,000
SALES: 120K **Privately Held**
WEB: www.xcelmold.com
SIC: 3544 Industrial molds; special dies & tools

(G-2868)
ZEIGER INDUSTRIES
4704 Wiseland Ave Se (44707-1054)
PHONE..................................330 484-4413
Donald Zeiger, *President*
Sandi Zeiger, *Treasurer*
EMP: 22
SQ FT: 2,500
SALES (est): 5.6MM **Privately Held**
WEB: www.zeigerindustries.com
SIC: 3494 Valves & pipe fittings

Cardington
Morrow County

(G-2869)
3GC LLC
Also Called: Myairplane.com
5600 Sw Us 42 (43315)
PHONE..................................740 703-0580
Dennis Megarry, *Owner*
EMP: 4
SALES (est): 140K **Privately Held**
SIC: 3812 Aircraft control systems, electronic

(G-2870)
BJ OILFIELD SERVICES LTD
2944 County Road 186 (43315-9344)
PHONE..................................419 768-2408
Jessica Keplar, *Principal*
EMP: 3
SALES (est): 173.1K **Privately Held**
SIC: 1389 Oil field services

(G-2871)
CARDINGTON YUTAKA TECH INC (DH)
575 W Main St (43315-9796)
PHONE..................................419 864-8777
Hirokazu Kawuai, *President*

Fred Razavi, *Exec VP*
Ray Welch, *Plant Mgr*
Chariss Nelson, *Purch Mgr*
Kim Leimbach, *Buyer*
▲ **EMP:** 750
SQ FT: 300,000
SALES (est): 224.8MM
SALES (corp-wide): 144.1B **Privately Held**
SIC: 3714 Exhaust systems & parts, motor vehicle
HQ: Yutaka Giken Co., Ltd.
    508-1, Yutakacho, Higashi-Ku
    Hamamatsu SZO 431-3
    534 334-111

(G-2872)
GEOCORE DRILLING INC
2918 Us Highway 42 (43315-9790)
PHONE..................................419 864-4011
Chad Mullin, *Owner*
EMP: 4
SALES (est): 250K **Privately Held**
SIC: 1381 Service well drilling

(G-2873)
HOFFMAN MEAT PROCESSING
157 S 4th St (43315-9726)
PHONE..................................419 864-3994
Mike Hoffman, *Owner*
EMP: 7
SALES: 500K **Privately Held**
SIC: 2013 5421 Sausages & other pre-pared meats; meat markets, including freezer provisioners

(G-2874)
JACK GRUBER
Also Called: Industrial Machine Service
2606 County Rd Ste 184 (43315)
P.O. Box 104, Mount Gilead (43338-0104)
PHONE..................................740 408-2718
Jack Gruber, *Owner*
EMP: 3 **EST:** 1978
SALES (est): 169.2K **Privately Held**
WEB: www.jackgruber.com
SIC: 3089 7699 Injection molded finished plastic products; industrial machinery & equipment repair

(G-2875)
PATRIOT
217 W Main St (43315-1010)
PHONE..................................419 864-8411
Shannon Leary, *Owner*
EMP: 3 **EST:** 2014
SALES (est): 83.8K **Privately Held**
SIC: 2711 Newspapers, publishing & printing

(G-2876)
STAHL/SCOTT FETZER COMPANY
201 Cunard St (43315-1090)
PHONE..................................419 864-8045
George Kalis, *President*
EMP: 107
SALES (corp-wide): 225.3B **Publicly Held**
SIC: 3715 Trailer bodies
HQ: Stahl/Scott Fetzer Company
    3201 W Old Lincoln Way
    Wooster OH 44691

Carey
Wyandot County

(G-2877)
ANDERSON CO MFG LLC
Also Called: Anderson Company
415 W North St (43316-1033)
P.O. Box 95 (43316-0095)
PHONE..................................419 230-7332
Bethany Masquelier, *Principal*
EMP: 8
SALES (est): 662K **Privately Held**
SIC: 3999 Barber & beauty shop equipment

(G-2878)
ANDERSONS PLANT NUTRIENT LLC
Also Called: Mineral Processing
1855 County Highway 99 (43316-9722)
PHONE..................................419 396-3501
Nick Klein, *Plant Mgr*
Ron Cass, *Manager*
EMP: 5
SALES (corp-wide): 3B **Publicly Held**
SIC: 2873 Nitrogenous fertilizers
HQ: The Andersons Plant Nutrient Llc
    1947 Briarfield Blvd
    Maumee OH 43537
    419 893-5050

(G-2879)
CAREY PRECAST CONCRETE COMPANY
3420 Township Highway 98 (43316-9763)
P.O. Box 129 (43316-0129)
PHONE..................................419 396-7142
Kathryn Beck, *President*
Dean Beck, *Corp Secy*
EMP: 6
SQ FT: 2,000
SALES (est): 390K **Privately Held**
WEB: www.careyprecast.com
SIC: 3272 Concrete products, precast

(G-2880)
CONTINENTAL STRL PLAS INC
Also Called: CSP Carey
2915 County Rd 96 (43316)
PHONE..................................419 396-1980
Randi Hoyer, *Safety Mgr*
Mike Bishop, *Branch Mgr*
EMP: 390
SALES (corp-wide): 7.8B **Privately Held**
WEB: www.cs-plastics.com
SIC: 3089 3714 Injection molding of plastics; motor vehicle parts & accessories
HQ: Continental Structural Plastics, Inc.
    255 Rex Blvd
    Auburn Hills MI 48326
    248 237-7800

(G-2881)
FRUGAL SYSTEMS
21250 County Road 26 (43316-9302)
PHONE..................................419 957-7863
Timothy Lee, *Partner*
EMP: 3
SALES (est): 113K **Privately Held**
SIC: 3999 Manufacturing industries

(G-2882)
HANON SYSTEMS USA LLC
581 Arrowhead Dr (43316-7503)
PHONE..................................313 920-0583
Thomas Charnesky, *Plant Mgr*
EMP: 140
SALES (corp-wide): 10.1MM **Privately Held**
SIC: 3714 3585 3699 Air conditioner parts, motor vehicle; radiators & radiator shells & cores, motor vehicle; heaters, motor vehicle; compressors for refrigeration & air conditioning equipment; heat emission operating apparatus
HQ: Hanon Systems Usa, Llc
    39600 Lewis Dr
    Novi MI 48377
    248 907-8000

(G-2883)
MINERAL PROCESSING COMPANY
1855 County Highway 99 (43316-9722)
PHONE..................................419 396-3501
Daniel Allen, *President*
John Uliveto, *Vice Pres*
Victoria C Allen, *Treasurer*
Harry Allen, *Admin Sec*
EMP: 6
SQ FT: 15,000
SALES (est): 747.3K **Privately Held**
WEB: www.mineralprocess.com
SIC: 3275 3274 Gypsum products; lime

(G-2884)
NATIONAL LIME AND STONE CO
370 N Patterson St (43316-1057)
P.O. Box 8 (43316-0008)
PHONE..................................419 396-7671
Chris Beeman, *Exec VP*
Ron Wike, *Mktg Dir*
Ryan Phillips, *Branch Mgr*
David Beltz, *Info Tech Dir*
EMP: 130
SALES (corp-wide): 3.2B **Privately Held**
WEB: www.natlime.com
SIC: 1422 3291 3281 3274 Lime rock, ground; abrasive products; cut stone & stone products; lime; alkalies & chlorine; construction sand & gravel
PA: The National Lime And Stone Company
    551 Lake Cascade Pkwy
    Findlay OH 45840
    419 422-4341

(G-2885)
OF MACHINING LLC
2140 State Rd 568 (43316)
PHONE..................................419 396-7870
Michael T Fredritz, *Principal*
EMP: 5
SALES (est): 687.6K **Privately Held**
SIC: 3599 Machine shop, jobbing & repair

(G-2886)
OPS WIRELESS
807 E Findlay St (43316-1331)
PHONE..................................419 396-4041
Dustin Brooks, *Controller*
Michael R Brooks, *Mng Member*
EMP: 8
SQ FT: 10,500
SALES (est): 630K **Privately Held**
SIC: 3679 Video triggers, except remote control TV devices

(G-2887)
PROGRESSOR TIMES
1198 E Findlay St (43316-9760)
P.O. Box 37 (43316-0037)
PHONE..................................419 396-7567
Stephen Zender, *Owner*
Amy Yeater, *Sales Staff*
EMP: 6
SALES (est): 481.2K **Privately Held**
WEB: www.theprogressortimes.com
SIC: 7313 2711 Newspaper advertising representative; newspapers

(G-2888)
PSD PARTNERS LLC (PA)
5968 State Highway 199 (43316-9422)
PHONE..................................419 294-3838
Paul M Kalmbach, *Principal*
EMP: 4
SALES (est): 1.4MM **Privately Held**
SIC: 2048 Mfg Prepared Feeds

(G-2889)
QUALITY PLLETS RECYCLABLES LLC
410 E Findlay St (43316-1209)
PHONE..................................419 396-3244
Edward J Gretzinger, *Principal*
EMP: 4
SALES (est): 299.7K **Privately Held**
SIC: 2448 Pallets, wood & wood with metal

(G-2890)
TRANSGLOBAL INC (PA)
225 N Patterson St (43316-1053)
PHONE..................................419 396-9079
James Schroeder, *President*
John Haan, *Engineer*
John Lane, *Engineer*
Stefano Di Paco, *Sales Staff*
EMP: 7
SALES (est): 3.9MM **Privately Held**
WEB: www.transglobal.com
SIC: 3799 Trailers & trailer equipment

Carlisle
Warren County

(G-2891)
CONVERTERS/PREPRESS INC
301 Industry Dr (45005-6330)
PHONE..................................937 743-0935
Mike Zimmer, *Branch Mgr*
EMP: 12
SALES (corp-wide): 2.6MM **Privately Held**
WEB: www.4cp.net
SIC: 2796 7336 Engraving platemaking services; commercial art & graphic design
PA: Converters/Prepress, Inc.
    1070 Tower Ln
    Bensenville IL 60106
    630 860-9400

(G-2892)
DRACOOL-USA INC (PA)
30 Eagle Ct (45005-6321)
PHONE..................................937 743-5899
Javier Avendano, *CEO*
Scott Howard, *Sales Staff*
Shelly Jackson, *Sales Associate*
Donnie Mann, *Supervisor*
◆ **EMP:** 24
SQ FT: 20,000
SALES: 6MM **Privately Held**
SIC: 3441 Fabricated structural metal

(G-2893)
INDUSTRIAL ELECTRONIC SERVICE
Also Called: Dc- Digital
325 Industry Dr (45005-6309)
PHONE..................................937 746-9750
Jim Staffan, *Principal*
Pete Staffan, *Principal*
EMP: 11 **EST:** 1965
SQ FT: 3,700
SALES (est): 2.2MM **Privately Held**
WEB: www.ies-1.com
SIC: 3993 3579 7622 1731 Scoreboards, electric; time clocks & time recording devices; intercommunication equipment repair; electronic controls installation

(G-2894)
KITTYHAWK MOLDING COMPANY INC
10 Eagle Ct (45005-6321)
PHONE..................................937 746-3663
Wilbur V Wisecup Jr, *CEO*
Dave Holmes, *President*
Anita Holmes, *Vice Pres*
Sue Little, *Admin Sec*
EMP: 29
SQ FT: 20,500
SALES (est): 5.5MM **Privately Held**
SIC: 3089 Injection molding of plastics

(G-2895)
NARROW WAY CUSTOM TECHNOLOGY
100 Industry Dr (45005-6304)
PHONE..................................937 743-1611
Timothy Williams, *President*
EMP: 29 **EST:** 1998
SQ FT: 5,600
SALES (est): 5.3MM **Privately Held**
SIC: 3599 7629 Custom machinery; electrical repair shops

(G-2896)
PATRIOT MFG GROUP INC
512 Linden Ave (45005-3345)
PHONE..................................937 746-2117
Phillip Hubbell, *President*
Michael Swigert, *Principal*
Mike Skaggs, *Manager*
EMP: 54
SALES (est): 10.1MM **Privately Held**
WEB: www.patriotmms.com
SIC: 3545 Machine tool accessories

(G-2897)
QIBCO BUFFING PADS INC (PA)
Also Called: American Buffing
301 Industry Dr Ste B (45005-6330)
PHONE..................................937 743-0805
Jeff Phipps, *Vice Pres*
▲ **EMP:** 12
SALES (est): 1.4MM **Privately Held**
WEB: www.americanbuffing.com
SIC: 3291 Abrasive buffs, bricks, cloth, paper, stones, etc.

Carroll
Fairfield County

(G-2898)
ARTISAN EQUIPMENT INC
5770 Winchester Rd (43112-9204)
P.O. Box 500 (43112-0500)
PHONE................................740 756-9135
Stuart Brengman, *President*
Marsha Brengman, *Corp Secy*
Keith C Brengman, *Vice Pres*
EMP: 10
SQ FT: 12,700
SALES (est): 1.8MM Privately Held
WEB: www.artisanequipment.com
SIC: 3599 3469 3544 Custom machinery; machine parts, stamped or pressed metal; special dies, tools, jigs & fixtures

(G-2899)
BAINTER MACHINING COMPANY
2945 Carroll Eastern Rd (43112-9647)
PHONE................................740 756-4598
Dan Bainter, *Systems Mgr*
EMP: 12
SALES (est): 1.5MM
SALES (corp-wide): 600K Privately Held
PA: Bainter Machining Company
1230 Rainbow Dr Ne
Lancaster OH 43130
740 653-2422

(G-2900)
CARRIAGE HOUSE PRINTERY LLC
5458 Carroll Northern Rd (43112-9781)
PHONE................................740 243-7493
Michael Frankhauser,
EMP: 4
SALES (est): 239.8K Privately Held
SIC: 2752 Commercial printing, lithographic

(G-2901)
CRAIG BROS MACHINE CO INC
5846 Winchester Rd (43112-9203)
P.O. Box 395 (43112-0395)
PHONE................................740 756-9280
Larry E Craig, *President*
Howard W Craig, *Vice Pres*
EMP: 4
SQ FT: 3,800
SALES (est): 439.1K Privately Held
SIC: 3599 Machine shop, jobbing & repair

(G-2902)
CW MACHINE WORX LTD
4805 Scooby Ln (43112-9446)
PHONE................................740 654-5304
Shannon Heston, *Principal*
Scott Carpenter,
Cameron Gabbard,
Brad D Hutchinson,
Justin Owen,
EMP: 12
SQ FT: 15,000
SALES (est): 3.2MM Privately Held
SIC: 3531 Construction machinery

(G-2903)
DELTA H TECHNOLOGIES LLC
62 High St (43112-9018)
PHONE................................740 756-7676
Richard Conway, *Mng Member*
EMP: 9
SALES: 4.5MM Privately Held
SIC: 3567 Industrial furnaces & ovens

(G-2904)
F C BRENGMAN AND ASSOC LLC
86 High St (43112-9793)
P.O. Box 470 (43112-0470)
PHONE................................740 756-4308
Robert Mason, *President*
Bill Mason, *Owner*
Kathy Snide, *Office Mgr*
EMP: 28 EST: 1949
SQ FT: 12,000
SALES (est): 6MM Privately Held
WEB: www.fcbrengman.com
SIC: 3469 Stamping metal for the trade

(G-2905)
FAIRFIELD MACHINED PRODUCTS
5594 Winchester Rd (43112-9202)
P.O. Box 410 (43112-0410)
PHONE................................740 756-4409
David Riggenbach, *President*
Ronnie Wyne, *Corp Secy*
Frederick Marshall, *Vice Pres*
EMP: 15
SALES (est): 1MM Privately Held
SIC: 3451 Screw machine products

(G-2906)
LLOYD F HELBER
3820 Clmbus Lncster Rd Nw (43112-9720)
PHONE................................740 756-9607
Lloyd Helber, *Owner*
EMP: 20
SQ FT: 2,756
SALES (est): 742.8K Privately Held
SIC: 6531 5812 2754 7519 Real estate leasing & rentals; Italian restaurant; commercial printing, gravure; trailer rental; real property lessors

(G-2907)
MARTIN PAPER PRODUCTS INC
5907 Clmbus Lncster Rd Nw (43112-7700)
P.O. Box 102 (43112-0102)
PHONE................................740 756-9271
Robert A Martin, *President*
Clara R Martin, *Principal*
Ronald Martin, *Admin Sec*
EMP: 20 EST: 1975
SQ FT: 8,100
SALES (est): 1.7MM Privately Held
WEB: www.martinpartitions.com
SIC: 2653 2631 Corrugated boxes, partitions, display items, sheets & pad; paperboard mills

(G-2908)
RELIABLE MFG CO LLC
4411 Carroll Southern Rd (43112-9794)
PHONE................................740 756-9373
Emma Snodgrass,
Gordon Fink,
Susan Fosnaugh,
EMP: 6
SQ FT: 8,500
SALES (est): 1MM Privately Held
SIC: 2813 Industrial gases

(G-2909)
S J COX TOOL INC
Also Called: Cox Machine & Fabrication
3800 Old Columbus Rd Nw (43112-9672)
PHONE................................740 756-1100
Jim Cox, *President*
EMP: 4
SALES (est): 472.5K Privately Held
SIC: 3599 Machine shop, jobbing & repair

(G-2910)
SAFE AUTO SYSTEMS LLC
5401 Brookpark Rd (43112)
PHONE................................216 661-1166
Tara Beck,
EMP: 4
SALES: 425K Privately Held
SIC: 3714 Motor vehicle parts & accessories

(G-2911)
STERLING GRINDING COMPANY INC
62 High St (43112-9018)
PHONE................................614 836-3412
Glenna Shy, *President*
Brenda Kirk, *Vice Pres*
John S Shy, *Vice Pres*
Donald Losasso, *Plant Mgr*
EMP: 12
SQ FT: 28,000
SALES: 1MM Privately Held
SIC: 3599 Machine shop, jobbing & repair

(G-2912)
SUN CLEANERS & LAUNDRY INC
Also Called: Frsteam By Sun Cleaners
3739 Old Columbus Rd Nw (43112-9673)
PHONE................................740 756-4749
Nick Babamov, *President*
Ashley Babamov, *Admin Sec*
EMP: 4
SALES (est): 206K Privately Held
SIC: 2842 Specialty cleaning, polishes & sanitation goods

(G-2913)
TECH-BOND SOLUTIONS
3775 Columbus Lancaster (43112-9800)
PHONE................................614 327-8884
Dan Meyers, *CEO*
EMP: 5
SALES (est): 606.2K Privately Held
SIC: 2891 5169 Glue; glue

Carrollton
Carroll County

(G-2914)
A & A DISCOUNT TIRE
5125 Canton Rd Nw (44615-9015)
PHONE................................330 863-1936
Gene Dunn, *Owner*
EMP: 6
SQ FT: 34,000
SALES (est): 572.6K Privately Held
SIC: 3089 5015 5531 Automotive parts, plastic; tires, used; automotive tires

(G-2915)
ALL STEEL STRUCTURES INC
Also Called: Toibox Structuretures
755 N Lisbon St (44615-9401)
PHONE................................330 312-3131
Jeremy Athey, *President*
Judy Fieldhouse, *Treasurer*
EMP: 5
SALES (est): 401.5K Privately Held
SIC: 3317 Steel pipe & tubes

(G-2916)
ATKORE PLASTIC PIPE CORP
Also Called: Heritage Plas An Atkore Intl
861 N Lisbon St (44615-9401)
PHONE................................330 627-8002
Mitch Colly, *Plant Mgr*
EMP: 70 Publicly Held
WEB: www.heritageplastics.com
SIC: 3547 Pipe & tube mills
HQ: Atkore Plastic Pipe Corporation
1202 N Bowie Dr
Weatherford TX 76086
817 594-8791

(G-2917)
CARROLL HILLS INDUSTRIES INC
540 High St Nw (44615-1116)
P.O. Box 567 (44615-0567)
PHONE................................330 627-5524
Matt Champbell, *Superintendent*
Shannan Boone, *Administration*
Diana Strader, *Administration*
EMP: 60
SQ FT: 4,640
SALES: 499.3K Privately Held
SIC: 8331 3999 Sheltered workshop; barber & beauty shop equipment

(G-2918)
CARROLLTON PUBLISHING COMPANY
Also Called: Free Press Standard
43 E Main St (44615-1221)
P.O. Box 37 (44615-0037)
PHONE................................330 627-5591
William Peterson, *General Mgr*
Maynard Buck, *Treasurer*
EMP: 12
SQ FT: 4,800
SALES (est): 717.9K Privately Held
WEB: www.freepressstandard.com
SIC: 2711 Commercial printing & newspaper publishing combined; newspapers: publishing only, not printed on site

(G-2919)
ERNST ENTERPRISES INC
Also Called: Valley Concrete
4710 Soldiers Home Rd (44615)
P.O. Box 638 (44615-0638)
PHONE................................937 866-9441
John McAffee, *General Mgr*
EMP: 25
SALES (corp-wide): 227.2MM Privately Held
WEB: www.ernstconcrete.com
SIC: 3273 Ready-mixed concrete
PA: Ernst Enterprises, Inc.
3361 Successful Way
Dayton OH 45414
937 233-5555

(G-2920)
FUSION CERAMICS INC (PA)
160 Scio Rd Se (44615-9502)
P.O. Box 127 (44615-0127)
PHONE................................330 627-5821
Richard Hannon Jr, *President*
David Stanton, *General Mgr*
John Baker, *Vice Pres*
Dave Schneider, *Vice Pres*
Ray Stanton, *Technical Mgr*
◆ EMP: 42
SQ FT: 20,000
SALES (est): 7.1MM Privately Held
WEB: www.fusionceramics.com
SIC: 2899 Chemical preparations

(G-2921)
JOHN BYLER
Also Called: JW Log and Lumber
5130 Germano Rd Se (44615-9556)
PHONE................................330 627-7635
John W Byler, *Administration*
EMP: 3 EST: 2014
SALES (est): 244.3K Privately Held
SIC: 2411 Logging

(G-2922)
JOMAC LTD
Also Called: Jones Propane Supply
182 Scio Rd Se (44615-8521)
PHONE................................330 627-7727
Richard Jones, *President*
Fritz Ekstam, *General Mgr*
Lori Jones, *Admin Sec*
EMP: 7
SALES (est): 2.1MM Privately Held
WEB: www.jomacltd.com
SIC: 3441 5984 Fabricated structural metal; propane gas, bottled

(G-2923)
LAKOTA RACING
109 12th St Nw (44615-9456)
PHONE................................330 627-7255
Darlene Sample, *Owner*
EMP: 3
SALES (est): 269.3K Privately Held
WEB: www.lakotaracing.com
SIC: 3714 Motor vehicle engines & parts

(G-2924)
LAM WELDING & MET FABRICATION
2269 Waynesburg Rd Nw (44615-9319)
PHONE................................304 839-2404
William Niccum, *Administration*
EMP: 6
SALES (est): 166.9K Privately Held
SIC: 3499 Fabricated metal products

(G-2925)
M & M TOBACCO
701 Canton Rd Nw (44615-9447)
PHONE................................330 573-8543
Matt McCune, *Owner*
EMP: 4
SALES (est): 393.5K Privately Held
SIC: 3911 Cigar & cigarette accessories

(G-2926)
NOMAC DRILLING LLC
1258 Panda Rd Se (44615-9657)
PHONE................................330 476-7040
EMP: 4
SALES (corp-wide): 3.3B Publicly Held
SIC: 1381 Drilling oil & gas wells
HQ: Nomac Drilling, L.L.C.
3400 S Radio Rd
El Reno OK 73036
405 422-2754

(G-2927)
RCE HEAT EXCHANGERS LLC
3165 Folsam Rd Nw (44615-8201)
PHONE................................330 627-0300
Mike Earl, *Managing Prtnr*

GEOGRAPHIC SECTION

Robert Strobel, *Vice Pres*
EMP: 20
SALES (est): 4.9MM **Privately Held**
SIC: 3443 Heat exchangers, condensers & components

(G-2928)
SEVEN RANGES MFG CORP
330 Industrial Dr Sw (44615-8569)
P.O. Box 206 (44615-0206)
PHONE.................................330 627-7155
Fred D Tarr Sr, *President*
David Richard Tarr, *Vice Pres*
Mark Fichter, *Purchasing*
EMP: 26
SQ FT: 29,000
SALES (est): 5.7MM **Privately Held**
WEB: www.sevenranges.com
SIC: 3469 Stamping metal for the trade

(G-2929)
SMA PLASTICS LLC
755 N Lisbon St (44615-9401)
PHONE.................................330 627-1377
Charles McCort, *CEO*
EMP: 5 **EST:** 2015
SALES (est): 583.1K **Privately Held**
SIC: 2611 Pulp manufactured from waste or recycled paper

(G-2930)
T M INDUSTRIES INC
4082 Thrasher Rd Sw (44615-9516)
PHONE.................................330 627-4410
Mary Sowko, *President*
John Sowko, *Vice Pres*
EMP: 4 **EST:** 1975
SQ FT: 2,500
SALES: 800K **Privately Held**
SIC: 5085 7699 3545 Tools; tool repair services; cutting tools for machine tools

(G-2931)
TWIN CITIES CONCRETE CO
1031 Kensington Rd Ne (44615-9403)
P.O. Box 400, Dover (44622-0400)
PHONE.................................330 627-2158
Louis Cline, *Manager*
EMP: 5
SALES (corp-wide): 29.7B **Privately Held**
SIC: 3273 Ready-mixed concrete
HQ: Twin Cities Concrete Co
141 S Tuscarawas Ave
Dover OH 44622
330 343-4491

(G-2932)
WENDELL MACHINE SHOP
2076 Mobile Rd Ne (44615-9796)
PHONE.................................330 627-3480
Jeff Wendell, *Owner*
EMP: 3 **EST:** 1992
SALES (est): 208.8K **Privately Held**
SIC: 3599 Machine & other job shop work

Casstown
Miami County

(G-2933)
JED TOOL COMPANY
8058 E Troy Urbana Rd (45312-9729)
PHONE.................................937 857-9222
John Deford, *Owner*
EMP: 3
SALES: 100K **Privately Held**
SIC: 3599 Machine shop, jobbing & repair

(G-2934)
STEEL AVIATION AIRCRAFT SALES
4433 E State Route 55 (45312-9579)
PHONE.................................937 332-7587
Jaime Steel, *Principal*
EMP: 7
SALES (est): 837.4K **Privately Held**
WEB: www.steelaviation.com
SIC: 3721 Airplanes, fixed or rotary wing

Castalia
Erie County

(G-2935)
ABJ EQUIPFIX
202 Lucas St W (44824-9254)
PHONE.................................419 684-5236
Alan D Strause, *CEO*
EMP: 20
SQ FT: 7,000
SALES (est): 210K **Privately Held**
WEB: www.abjequipfix.com
SIC: 7699 3556 Industrial machinery & equipment repair; food products machinery

(G-2936)
CASTALIA TRENCHING & READY MIX
4814 State Route 269 S (44824-9359)
PHONE.................................419 684-5502
Francis Winkel, *President*
James Winkel, *Corp Secy*
John Winkel, *Vice Pres*
Larry Winkel, *Vice Pres*
EMP: 10 **EST:** 1954
SQ FT: 8,000
SALES (est): 1.7MM **Privately Held**
SIC: 3273 1794 Ready-mixed concrete; excavation work

(G-2937)
ECI
8802 Portland Rd (44824-9259)
PHONE.................................419 483-2738
Marvin Brenzo, *Principal*
EMP: 5 **EST:** 2010
SALES (est): 265.2K **Privately Held**
SIC: 3273 Ready-mixed concrete

(G-2938)
ERIE MATERIALS INC
Also Called: Erie Black Top
9200 Portland Rd (44824)
PHONE.................................419 483-4648
Dave Misinec, *Manager*
EMP: 5
SALES (corp-wide): 45.6MM **Privately Held**
WEB: www.eriematerials.com
SIC: 2951 5032 Asphalt paving mixtures & blocks; paving materials
PA: Erie Materials, Inc.
4507 Tiffin Ave
Sandusky OH 44870
419 625-7374

(G-2939)
HANSON AGGREGATES EAST LLC
9220 Portland Rd (44824-9260)
PHONE.................................419 483-4390
Gregory Russell, *Plant Mgr*
Tera Thornhill, *Manager*
EMP: 67
SQ FT: 3,200
SALES (corp-wide): 20.6B **Privately Held**
SIC: 1422 3274 Limestones, ground; lime
HQ: Hanson Aggregates East Llc
3131 Rdu Center Dr
Morrisville NC 27560
919 380-2500

(G-2940)
LOCKER ROOM LETTERING LTD
7316 Magill Rd (44824-9303)
PHONE.................................419 359-1761
James Barton, *President*
EMP: 4
SQ FT: 2,500
SALES (est): 210K **Privately Held**
SIC: 2759 2395 5611 5621 Screen printing; embroidery products, except schiffli machine; clothing, sportswear, men's & boys'; women's sportswear; children's wear

(G-2941)
WALLSEYE CONCRETE CORP
8802 Portland Rd (44824-9259)
PHONE.................................419 483-2738
Marvin Brenzo, *Manager*
EMP: 10 **Privately Held**
SIC: 3241 5032 Portland cement; brick, stone & related material
PA: Wallseye Concrete Corp.
26000 Sprague Rd
Cleveland OH 44138

Cecil
Paulding County

(G-2942)
BAKER-SHINDLER CONTRACTING CO
Also Called: Baker-Shindler Ready Mix
121 German St (45821)
PHONE.................................419 399-4841
John Clellan, *Manager*
EMP: 4
SALES (corp-wide): 6MM **Privately Held**
SIC: 3273 Ready-mixed concrete
PA: The Baker-Shindler Contracting Company
525 Cleveland Ave
Defiance OH 43512
419 782-5080

Cedarville
Greene County

(G-2943)
APPLIED SCIENCES INC (PA)
141 W Xenia Ave (45314-9529)
P.O. Box 579 (45314-0579)
PHONE.................................937 766-2020
Max Lake, *President*
Inga Lake, *Vice Pres*
Loren Goins, *Technician*
EMP: 29
SQ FT: 6,600
SALES (est): 4.7MM **Privately Held**
SIC: 8731 3624 Commercial research laboratory; carbon & graphite products

(G-2944)
MARIETTA MARTIN MATERIALS INC
Also Called: Martin Marietta Aggregates
3744 Turnbull Rd (45314-9429)
P.O. Box 577 (45314-0577)
PHONE.................................937 766-2351
Ken Holland, *Principal*
EMP: 21 **Publicly Held**
WEB: www.martinmarietta.com
SIC: 1422 Crushed & broken limestone
PA: Martin Marietta Materials Inc
2710 Wycliff Rd
Raleigh NC 27607

(G-2945)
MARTIN MARIETTA MATERIALS INC
Also Called: Cedarville Quarry
3744 Turnbull Rd (45314-9429)
PHONE.................................937 766-2351
Brian Parks, *Manager*
EMP: 20 **Publicly Held**
WEB: www.martinmarietta.com
SIC: 1423 Crushed & broken granite
PA: Martin Marietta Materials Inc
2710 Wycliff Rd
Raleigh NC 27607

(G-2946)
PYROGRAF PRODUCTS INC
154 W Xenia Ave (45314-9529)
P.O. Box 579 (45314-0579)
PHONE.................................937 766-2020
Max Lake, *President*
Inga Lake, *Admin Sec*
EMP: 18 **EST:** 1996
SQ FT: 6,600
SALES (est): 2.9MM
SALES (corp-wide): 4.7MM **Privately Held**
SIC: 3624 Carbon & graphite products
PA: Applied Sciences Inc.
141 W Xenia Ave
Cedarville OH 45314
937 766-2020

(G-2947)
THIRD WAVE WATER LLC
83 N Main St (45314-8635)
PHONE.................................855 590-4500
Taylor Minor,
Charles Nick,
EMP: 3
SQ FT: 400
SALES (est): 100.5K **Privately Held**
SIC: 2087 Beverage bases

Celina
Mercer County

(G-2948)
1 IRON GOLF INC
504 Maplewood Ln (45822-2964)
PHONE.................................419 662-9336
David Lake, *President*
Kathy Lake, *Vice Pres*
▲ **EMP:** 4
SALES (est): 200K **Privately Held**
SIC: 3949 Shafts, golf club

(G-2949)
ALUMACAST LLC
300 N Brandon Ave (45822-1672)
PHONE.................................419 584-1473
Richard W Kaylor,
Garry Kuess,
EMP: 5
SALES (est): 320K **Privately Held**
SIC: 3363 Aluminum die-castings

(G-2950)
B HOGENKAMP & R HARLAMERT
Also Called: Grand Slam Acres
3145 Hartke Rd (45822-9570)
PHONE.................................419 925-0526
Joseph Harlamert, *Partner*
Renea Harlamert, *Partner*
Bernard Hogenkamp, *Partner*
Christopher Miller, *Partner*
Jill Miller, *Partner*
EMP: 4 **EST:** 2017
SALES (est): 158.2K **Privately Held**
SIC: 2411 Saw logs

(G-2951)
C & M WELDING SERVICES LLC
1405 James Dr (45822-9482)
PHONE.................................419 584-0008
Charles Zehringer, *Mng Member*
Mike Huelsman,
EMP: 5
SQ FT: 800
SALES: 450K **Privately Held**
SIC: 7692 5999 Welding repair; welding supplies

(G-2952)
CABINETRY BY EBBING
5765 State Route 219 (45822-9513)
PHONE.................................419 678-2191
Michael J Ebbing, *Owner*
EMP: 5
SALES (est): 585K **Privately Held**
WEB: www.cabinetrybyebbing.com
SIC: 2434 Vanities, bathroom: wood

(G-2953)
CELINA ALUM PRECISION TECH INC
Also Called: Capt
7059 Staeger Rd (45822-9395)
PHONE.................................419 586-2278
Takenori Yamaguchi, *President*
Jay James, *Senior VP*
Shelley Young, *Safety Dir*
Christopher Nester, *Project Dir*
Jason Silliman, *Plant Supt*
▲ **EMP:** 500
SQ FT: 160,000
SALES: 130.2MM
SALES (corp-wide): 144.1B **Privately Held**
WEB: www.capt-celina.com
SIC: 3592 Pistons & piston rings
HQ: Honda Foundry Co., Ltd.
1620, Matoba
Kawagoe STM 350-1
492 311-521

Celina - Mercer County (G-2954)

(G-2954)
CELINA TENT INC
Also Called: Celina Industries
5373 State Route 29 (45822-9210)
PHONE..............................419 586-3610
Jeff Grieshop, *President*
Janice Grieshop, *Corp Secy*
▼ **EMP:** 48
SQ FT: 27,000
SALES (est): 8.3MM **Privately Held**
WEB: www.celinatent.com
SIC: 2394 Tents: made from purchased materials

(G-2955)
CHICKASAW MACHINE & TL CO INC
3050 Chickasaw Rd (45822)
PHONE..............................419 925-4325
Norbert B Tangeman, *President*
Ted Homan, *Vice Pres*
Dave Tangeman, *Vice Pres*
▼ **EMP:** 14 **EST:** 1960
SQ FT: 18,000
SALES: 4.1MM **Privately Held**
SIC: 3599 Machine shop, jobbing & repair

(G-2956)
CROWN EQUIPMENT CORPORATION
Also Called: Crown Lift Trucks
410 Grand Lake Rd (45822-1869)
PHONE..............................419 586-1100
Chuck Post, *Branch Mgr*
EMP: 719
SALES (corp-wide): 3.1B **Privately Held**
SIC: 3537 Lift trucks, industrial: fork, platform, straddle, etc.
PA: Crown Equipment Corporation
44 S Washington St
New Bremen OH 45869
419 629-2311

(G-2957)
DOLL INC
Also Called: Doll Printing
1901 Havemann Rd (45822)
PHONE..............................419 586-7880
Robert A Doll, *President*
Phyllis Doll, *Corp Secy*
EMP: 8
SQ FT: 6,200
SALES: 800K **Privately Held**
WEB: www.dollprinting.com
SIC: 2752 Commercial printing, offset

(G-2958)
E L DAVIS INC
Also Called: Davis Welding Company
6032 State Route 219 (45822-8523)
PHONE..............................419 268-2004
Edward Davis, *President*
Edward L Davis, *President*
Phillys Davis, *Vice Pres*
Phyllis Davis, *Vice Pres*
EMP: 5
SQ FT: 2,000
SALES: 550K **Privately Held**
SIC: 7692 Welding repair; aerosol valves, metal

(G-2959)
EIGHTH FLOOR PROMOTIONS LLC
Also Called: Awardcraft
1 Visions Pkwy (45822-7500)
P.O. Box 42501, Middletown (45042-0501)
PHONE..............................419 586-6433
Dave Willis, *President*
Les Dorfman, *Senior VP*
Michelle Vires, *Marketing Staff*
▲ **EMP:** 190
SQ FT: 83,000
SALES (est): 26.8MM **Privately Held**
WEB: www.awardcraft.com
SIC: 3993 Signs & advertising specialties

(G-2960)
ERGO DESKTOP LLC
457 Grand Lake Rd (45822-1839)
PHONE..............................567 890-3746
Daniel Sharkey, *Marketing Staff*
Kathy Sharkey, *Mng Member*
Derrick Walls, *Mng Member*
▲ **EMP:** 23
SQ FT: 2,500
SALES: 6MM **Privately Held**
SIC: 2522 7389 Office furniture, except wood;

(G-2961)
ESM PRODUCTS INC
5445 Behm Rd Lot 5 (45822-8146)
PHONE..............................937 492-4644
John Elliott, *President*
Tom Elliott, *Corp Secy*
Dave Elliott, *Vice Pres*
EMP: 8
SQ FT: 4,400
SALES (est): 751.7K **Privately Held**
SIC: 3312 Tool & die steel & alloys

(G-2962)
FALLEN OAK CANDLES INC
917 Lilac St (45822-1326)
PHONE..............................419 204-8162
Brian Brim, *President*
EMP: 7
SALES: 20K **Privately Held**
SIC: 3999 Candles

(G-2963)
FUEL AMERICA
204 E Market St (45822-1733)
PHONE..............................419 586-5609
Penny Zizelman, *Principal*
EMP: 3
SALES (est): 174.4K **Privately Held**
SIC: 2869 Fuels

(G-2964)
GRYPMAT INC
6886 Nancy Ave (45822-9268)
PHONE..............................419 953-7607
Tom Burden, *CEO*
EMP: 7
SALES: 400K **Privately Held**
SIC: 3069 Trays, rubber

(G-2965)
H & S COMPANY INC
7219 Harris Rd (45822-9370)
PHONE..............................419 394-4444
Kurtis Hoelscher, *President*
Kellie Hoelscher, *Finance*
EMP: 15
SQ FT: 6,480
SALES (est): 4.5MM **Privately Held**
WEB: www.wheeledtrenchers.com
SIC: 3533 3523 Oil field machinery & equipment; farm machinery & equipment

(G-2966)
HAULETTE MANUFACTURING INC
8271 Us Route 127 (45822-9416)
PHONE..............................419 586-1717
Fred Kremer, *CEO*
Steven Braun, *President*
EMP: 53
SQ FT: 50,000
SALES: 5.5MM **Privately Held**
WEB: www.haulette.com
SIC: 3599 3715 Machine shop, jobbing & repair; trailer bodies

(G-2967)
HEITKAMP & KREMER PRINTING
Also Called: Messenger Press
6184 State Route 274 (45822-9505)
PHONE..............................419 925-4121
Alan Kremer, *President*
Randy Heitkamp, *Vice Pres*
Jenny Schwenzer, *Admin Sec*
EMP: 9
SALES (est): 1.3MM **Privately Held**
WEB: www.messenger-press.com
SIC: 2752 Commercial printing, offset

(G-2968)
HOLES CUSTOM WOODWORKING
6875 Nancy Ave (45822-9268)
PHONE..............................419 586-8171
Jane Hole, *Principal*
EMP: 4
SALES (est): 343.7K **Privately Held**
SIC: 2431 Millwork

(G-2969)
HOT BRASS PERSONAL DEFENSE
101 S Sugar St (45822-2135)
PHONE..............................419 733-7400
EMP: 3
SALES (est): 209.9K **Privately Held**
SIC: 3812 Defense systems & equipment

(G-2970)
JAVANATION
108 S Main St (45822-2228)
PHONE..............................419 584-1705
Vance Nation, *Owner*
EMP: 10
SALES (est): 261.5K **Privately Held**
SIC: 3269 Pottery products

(G-2971)
JES FOODS/CELINA INC
1800 Industrial Dr (45822-1376)
PHONE..............................419 586-7446
Elaine Freed, *President*
William Freed, *Vice Pres*
EMP: 25
SQ FT: 24,000
SALES (est): 4.2MM
SALES (corp-wide): 20.6MM **Privately Held**
WEB: www.jesfoods.com
SIC: 2033 2035 2032 Canned fruits & specialties; pickles, sauces & salad dressings; canned specialties
PA: J.E.S. Foods, Inc.
4733 Broadway Ave
Cleveland OH 44127
216 883-8987

(G-2972)
M S K PARTNERSHIP
7219 Harris Rd (45822-9370)
PHONE..............................419 394-4444
Shirley Hoelsher, *Partner*
Kurt Hoelsher, *Partner*
Michael Hoelsher, *Partner*
EMP: 5
SALES (est): 683.6K **Privately Held**
SIC: 3531 Entrenching machines

(G-2973)
MACHINE-PRO TECHNOLOGIES INC
1321 W Market St (45822-9285)
PHONE..............................419 584-0086
Tim Klosterman, *President*
Scott Snethkamp, *Vice Pres*
Jeff Bunnell, *Sales Mgr*
Sandy Bettinger, *Admin Asst*
▲ **EMP:** 57
SQ FT: 24,000
SALES (est): 11.1MM **Privately Held**
WEB: www.machine-pro.com
SIC: 3599 Machine shop, jobbing & repair

(G-2974)
MCSPORTS
1945 Havemann Rd (45822-9390)
PHONE..............................419 586-5555
Tony Bidlack, *Manager*
EMP: 3 **EST:** 2009
SALES (est): 86.2K **Privately Held**
SIC: 7999 5941 5091 3949 Sporting goods rental; sporting goods & bicycle shops; sporting & recreation goods; sporting & athletic goods

(G-2975)
METAL CUTTING TECHNOLOGY LLC
5410 Golden Pond Rd (45822-7157)
PHONE..............................419 733-1236
Larry M Pond, *Mng Member*
EMP: 4
SALES: 1.5MM **Privately Held**
SIC: 3541 Machine tools, metal cutting type

(G-2976)
MIAMI VALLEY PIZZA HUT INC
1152 E Market St (45822-1934)
PHONE..............................419 586-5900
Karen Roland,
EMP: 35
SALES (corp-wide): 4.6MM **Privately Held**
SIC: 5812 2099 Pizzeria, chain; food preparations
PA: Miami Valley Pizza Hut Inc
7665 Monarch Ct Ste 111
West Chester OH 45069
513 777-8434

(G-2977)
MSK TRENCHER MFG INC
7219 Harris Rd (45822-9370)
PHONE..............................419 394-4444
Kurtis Hoelscher, *President*
Kellie Hoelscher, *Corp Secy*
EMP: 10
SALES (est): 1.7MM **Privately Held**
SIC: 3531 Construction machinery

(G-2978)
PAX MACHINE WORKS INC
5139 Monroe Rd (45822-9033)
P.O. Box 338 (45822-0338)
PHONE..............................419 586-2337
Francis J Pax, *President*
Carol Knapke, *Human Res Mgr*
Deborah Guingrich, *Admin Sec*
Michael Pax, *Admin Sec*
▼ **EMP:** 137 **EST:** 1948
SQ FT: 451,000
SALES (est): 1.8MM **Privately Held**
WEB: www.paxmachine.com
SIC: 3469 Metal stampings

(G-2979)
PAX PRODUCTS INC
5097 Monroe Rd (45822-9033)
P.O. Box 257 (45822-0257)
PHONE..............................419 586-2337
Francis J Pax, *President*
Steven Pax, *Vice Pres*
Michael Pax, *Treasurer*
Deborah Guingrich, *Admin Sec*
EMP: 11
SQ FT: 36,500
SALES (est): 2.8MM **Privately Held**
SIC: 3569 Lubricating equipment

(G-2980)
PHI WERKES LLC
1201 Havemann Rd (45822-1391)
PHONE..............................419 586-9222
Scott Hoenie,
Kevin Pohlman,
EMP: 8
SQ FT: 13,800
SALES (est): 582.1K **Privately Held**
SIC: 3599 Machine shop, jobbing & repair

(G-2981)
POTTER HOUSE
108 S Main St (45822-2228)
PHONE..............................419 584-1705
Kimberly Nation, *Owner*
EMP: 4
SALES (est): 464.4K **Privately Held**
SIC: 3269 Firing & decorating china

(G-2982)
RENOIR VISIONS LLC
Also Called: Accents By Renoir
1 Visions Pkwy (45822-7500)
PHONE..............................419 586-5679
Tom Meyer,
Kent Paxson,
Dav Willis,
EMP: 12
SQ FT: 65,000
SALES (est): 1.2MM **Privately Held**
SIC: 3993 5094 Signs & advertising specialties; jewelry & precious stones

(G-2983)
REYNOLDS AND REYNOLDS COMPANY
824 Murlin Ave (45822-2459)
P.O. Box 999 (45822-0999)
PHONE..............................419 584-7000
Michael Craig, *Plant Mgr*
Ed Hettesheimer, *QC Mgr*
Don Kramer, *Plant Engr*
Brent Koesters, *Controller*
Dennis Hirt, *Human Res Dir*
EMP: 10

SALES (corp-wide): 1.5B **Privately Held**
WEB: www.reyrey.com
SIC: 2761 2759 2752 Manifold business forms; commercial printing; commercial printing, lithographic
HQ: The Reynolds And Reynolds Company
1 Reynolds Way
Kettering OH 45430
937 485-2000

(G-2984)
SOCIETY OF THE PRECIOUS BLOOD
Also Called: Messinger Press
2860 Us Route 127 (45822-9533)
PHONE..............................419 925-4516
Fr James Seibert, *Branch Mgr*
EMP: 40
SALES (corp-wide): 741.5K **Privately Held**
WEB: www.cpps-preciousblood.org
SIC: 2732 8661 8211 Pamphlets: printing only, not published on site; Brethren Church; private elementary & secondary schools
PA: The Society Of The Precious Blood
431 E 2nd St
Dayton OH 45402
937 228-9263

(G-2985)
STANDARD PRINTING CO INC
Also Called: Daily Standard The
123 E Market St (45822-1730)
P.O. Box 140 (45822-0140)
PHONE..............................419 586-2371
Frank Snyder, *President*
Ryan Snyder, *Administration*
EMP: 45 **EST:** 1851
SQ FT: 20,000
SALES (est): 3.6MM **Privately Held**
WEB: www.dailystandard.com
SIC: 2711 Commercial printing & newspaper publishing combined; newspapers, publishing & printing

(G-2986)
TECH SOLUTIONS LLC
Also Called: Instantorder
658 N Main St (45822-1463)
PHONE..............................419 852-7190
Daniel Hierholzer, *Principal*
EMP: 8
SALES: 200K **Privately Held**
SIC: 7371 5961 7372 Computer software development & applications; food, mail order; application computer software

(G-2987)
THEES MACHINE & TOOL CO
2007 State Route 703 (45822-2525)
PHONE..............................419 586-4766
John E Thees, *President*
Carolann Thees, *Vice Pres*
EMP: 6
SQ FT: 7,000
SALES (est): 275K **Privately Held**
SIC: 3599 Machine shop, jobbing & repair

(G-2988)
THIEMAN TAILGATES INC
600 E Wayne St (45822-1566)
PHONE..............................419 586-7727
Thomas A Thieman, *President*
Todd Thieman, *Vice Pres*
David McMurray, *Purch Mgr*
Matt Butturini, *Sales Staff*
Alan Freeman, *Sales Staff*
EMP: 90
SQ FT: 130,000
SALES: 30MM **Privately Held**
SIC: 3561 Industrial pumps & parts

(G-2989)
TIN-SAU LLC
1406 Canterbury Dr (45822-1183)
PHONE..............................419 586-8886
Christopher Sauer, *Principal*
EMP: 3
SALES (est): 236.4K **Privately Held**
SIC: 3356 Tin

(G-2990)
UNIQUE WOODMASTERS LLC
6750 Guadalupe Rd (45822-9545)
PHONE..............................419 268-9663
William Schoen,
Lawrence Schoen,
Robert Schoen,
EMP: 3
SALES (est): 348.1K **Privately Held**
SIC: 2434 Wood kitchen cabinets

(G-2991)
VERSA-PAK LTD
500 Staeger Rd (45822-9373)
P.O. Box 69 (45822-0069)
PHONE..............................419 586-5466
EMP: 45
SQ FT: 23,000
SALES (est): 15.5MM **Privately Held**
WEB: www.versa-pak.com
SIC: 3089 Plastic containers, except foam

(G-2992)
WELDTEC INC
8319 Us Route 127 (45822-9416)
PHONE..............................419 586-1200
Henry B Hoskins, *President*
Anthony D Hoskins, *Treasurer*
EMP: 19
SQ FT: 76,000
SALES (est): 4.1MM **Privately Held**
SIC: 3441 Fabricated structural metal

Centerburg
Knox County

(G-2993)
DANIS SWEET CUPCAKES
283 N Clayton St (43011-7089)
PHONE..............................614 581-8978
Christina Halley, *Manager*
EMP: 4 **EST:** 2013
SALES (est): 226.7K **Privately Held**
SIC: 2051 Bread, cake & related products

(G-2994)
TRADYE MACHINE & TOOL INC
3116a Wilson Rd (43011-9467)
PHONE..............................740 625-7550
Tracy Payne, *President*
Diana Payne,
EMP: 7
SQ FT: 12,000
SALES: 900K **Privately Held**
SIC: 3544 3599 Special dies & tools; machine shop, jobbing & repair

Centerville
Montgomery County

(G-2995)
ADVANCED MEDICAL SOLUTIONS INC
Also Called: Next Step
7026 Corp Way Ste 116 (45459)
PHONE..............................937 291-0069
Mark Abraham, *President*
EMP: 3
SALES (est): 396.4K **Privately Held**
SIC: 2834 3841 Medicines, capsuled or ampuled; medical instruments & equipment, blood & bone work

(G-2996)
AEROSEAL LLC (PA)
7989 S Suburban Rd (45458-2702)
PHONE..............................937 428-9300
Amit Gupta, *CEO*
Vijay Kollepara, *Vice Pres*
Neal Walsh, *Vice Pres*
Joshua Lewis, *Production*
Brian Smith, *Marketing Staff*
▲ **EMP:** 34 **EST:** 2011
SALES (est): 7MM **Privately Held**
SIC: 3679 Hermetic seals for electronic equipment

(G-2997)
AMERICAN SPORTS DESIGN COMPANY
Also Called: Airborne
6551 Centervl Bus Pkwy (45459-2686)
PHONE..............................937 865-5431
Michael Buenzow, *President*
Nancy Michaud, *Senior VP*
EMP: 70
SALES (est): 2.3MM
SALES (corp-wide): 24.6MM **Privately Held**
WEB: www.huffy.com
SIC: 3949 Basketball equipment & supplies, general
PA: Huffy Corporation
8877 Gander Creek Dr
Miamisburg OH 45342
937 865-2800

(G-2998)
BAILEY & JENSEN INC
442 Yankee Trace Dr (45458-3980)
PHONE..............................937 272-1784
Sharon Bailey, *CEO*
Jerry Bailey, *President*
EMP: 15 **EST:** 2012
SALES: 5MM **Privately Held**
SIC: 2514 5021 Metal household furniture; mattresses

(G-2999)
BEACON AUDIO VIDEO SYSTEMS INC
155 N Main St (45459-4620)
PHONE..............................937 723-9587
Robert R Hopper, *President*
EMP: 7
SQ FT: 5,500
SALES (est): 900K **Privately Held**
SIC: 3651 Home entertainment equipment, electronic

(G-3000)
CARLY CO LLC
235 N Main St (45459-4617)
PHONE..............................937 477-6411
Robin Grushon,
Mike Grushon,
EMP: 4
SALES: 120K **Privately Held**
SIC: 3633 Laundry dryers, household or coin-operated

(G-3001)
DIMCOGRAY CORPORATION (PA)
Also Called: Dimco-Gray Company
900 Dimco Way (45458-2709)
PHONE..............................937 433-7600
Michael Sieron, *CEO*
Terry Tate, *Treasurer*
Phyllis Snell, *Director*
▲ **EMP:** 92
SQ FT: 48,000
SALES (est): 25.1MM **Privately Held**
WEB: www.dimcogray.com
SIC: 3089 3873 3965 3625 Injection molding of plastics; watches, clocks, watchcases & parts; fasteners; relays & industrial controls; bolts, nuts, rivets & washers

(G-3002)
EVOLUTION RESOURCES LLC
480 Congress Park Dr (45459-4144)
PHONE..............................937 438-2390
Donald Cain, *CFO*
Chuck Biehn Jr,
▲ **EMP:** 3
SQ FT: 10,000
SALES: 500K **Privately Held**
WEB: www.evolve-now.net
SIC: 3421 5084 Knife blades & blanks; machine tools & accessories

(G-3003)
MBENZTECH
5528 Liberty Bell Cir (45459-7913)
PHONE..............................937 291-1527
Joseph S Johnson, *Principal*
EMP: 4
SALES: 50K **Privately Held**
SIC: 5045 3571 7389 Computers, peripherals & software; electronic computers;

(G-3004)
MDFRITZ TECHNOLOGIES INC
59 E Franklin St (45459-5952)
PHONE..............................937 314-1234
Matthew Fritz, *President*
EMP: 4
SALES (est): 318.7K **Privately Held**
SIC: 3643 Connectors & terminals for electrical devices

(G-3005)
OFFENDAWAY LLC
9498 Ash Hollow Ln (45458-9313)
PHONE..............................937 232-3933
Daniel B Hock, *Mng Member*
EMP: 2
SALES: 1MM **Privately Held**
SIC: 3669 Emergency alarms

(G-3006)
TROPICAL OHIO SMOOTHIE INC
Also Called: Tropical Smoothie Cafe
988 Miamisburg (45459)
PHONE..............................937 673-6218
Chester Hakanson, *President*
Chet Hakanson, *Principal*
Christena Hakanson, *Corp Secy*
EMP: 38 **EST:** 2012
SALES (est): 341.7K **Privately Held**
SIC: 2037 Frozen fruits & vegetables

Chagrin Falls
Cuyahoga County

(G-3007)
1-2-3 GLUTEN FREE INC
125 Orange Tree Dr (44022-1560)
PHONE..............................216 378-9233
Kim Ullner, *Principal*
EMP: 6 **EST:** 2007
SALES (est): 992.3K **Privately Held**
SIC: 2041 Flour mixes

(G-3008)
11 92 HOLDINGS LLC
8 E Washington St Ste 200 (44022-3057)
PHONE..............................216 920-7790
Mike Owens, *Principal*
EMP: 30
SALES (est): 2.4MM
SALES (corp-wide): 7.1MM **Privately Held**
SIC: 2591 Blinds vertical
PA: Vertical Knowledge Llc
8 E Washington St Ste 200
Chagrin Falls OH 44022
216 920-7790

(G-3009)
BELKIN PRODUCTION
44 N Main St (44022-3023)
PHONE..............................440 247-2722
Myron Belkin, *President*
EMP: 23 **EST:** 1976
SQ FT: 4,000
SALES (est): 3.6MM **Privately Held**
SIC: 3652 Pre-recorded records & tapes

(G-3010)
BELVINO LLC
526 Manor Brook Dr (44022-4505)
PHONE..............................440 715-0076
Claudia Dilillo, *Mktg Dir*
Claudia Di Lillo,
Chris Di Lillo,
▲ **EMP:** 5
SALES (est): 438.3K **Privately Held**
SIC: 2084 Wines

(G-3011)
BREWER INDUSTRIES LLC
318 Bentleyville Rd (44022-2414)
PHONE..............................216 469-0808
Paul Seegott, *Owner*
EMP: 4
SALES: 500K **Privately Held**
SIC: 2899 Chemical preparations

(G-3012)
CHAGRIN VALLEY PUBLISHING CO
Also Called: Chagrin Valley Times
525 Washington St (44022-4455)
P.O. Box 150 (44022-0150)
PHONE..............................440 247-5335
Harold Douthit, *President*
EMP: 200 **EST:** 1971
SQ FT: 4,000

Chagrin Falls - Cuyahoga County (G-3013)

SALES (est): 9.9MM **Privately Held**
WEB: www.chagrinvalleytimes.com
SIC: 2711 Newspapers: publishing only, not printed on site

(G-3013)
CLEVELAND LETTER SERVICE INC
8351 Clover Ln (44022-3810)
PHONE.................216 781-8300
Charles E Janes, *President*
EMP: 20 EST: 1945
SQ FT: 12,000
SALES (est): 1MM **Privately Held**
WEB: www.clevelandletter.com
SIC: 7331 2752 2789 Addressing service; mailing service; commercial printing, offset; bookbinding & related work

(G-3014)
CORNERSTONE INDUS HOLDINGS (PA)
100 Park Pl (44022-4442)
PHONE.................440 893-9144
Joseph G Teague, *Ch of Bd*
Michael C Adams, *President*
Mark W Teague, *Shareholder*
EMP: 3
SALES (est): 8.5MM **Privately Held**
SIC: 3053 3644 2891 2821 Gaskets & sealing devices; gaskets, all materials; insulators & insulation materials, electrical; adhesives & sealants; plastics materials & resins; die-cut paper & board

(G-3015)
DOUGLAS W & B C RICHARDSON
62 Wychwood Dr (44022-6853)
PHONE.................440 247-5262
Barbara C Richardson, *Principal*
EMP: 3
SALES (est): 190K **Privately Held**
SIC: 2992 Lubricating oils & greases

(G-3016)
E L OSTENDORF INC
Also Called: Shuler International
3425 Roundwood Rd (44022-6634)
PHONE.................440 247-7631
Ed L Ostendorf, *President*
EMP: 7
SQ FT: 12,000
SALES (est): 340.5K **Privately Held**
SIC: 6531 3645 Real estate agent, commercial; residential lighting fixtures

(G-3017)
E-Z GRADER COMPANY
300 Industrial Pkwy Ste A (44022-4420)
PHONE.................440 247-7511
Jill Richards, *President*
Bruce Richards, *Vice Pres*
EMP: 8 EST: 1952
SALES (est): 900.7K **Privately Held**
WEB: www.ezgrader.com
SIC: 5961 2679 Educational supplies & equipment, mail order; paperboard products, converted

(G-3018)
EDMAR CHEMICAL COMPANY
539 Washington St (44022-4407)
P.O. Box 598 (44022-0598)
PHONE.................440 247-9560
Jack Binder, *President*
Jack Ahern, *Treasurer*
Dan Berick, *Admin Sec*
EMP: 9 EST: 1940
SALES (est): 1.6MM **Privately Held**
SIC: 2841 2842 Soap: granulated, liquid, cake, flaked or chip; fabric softeners

(G-3019)
EMT TRADING COMPANY LLC
Also Called: Metalmark
147 Bell St (44022-2982)
PHONE.................888 352-8000
Gary Marshall, *Vice Pres*
EMP: 3
SALES (est): 127.2K **Privately Held**
SIC: 3312 3479 Stainless steel; aluminum coating of metal products

(G-3020)
FLIPSIDE INC (PA)
44 N Main St (44022-3023)
PHONE.................440 600-7274
Angie Cancasci, *Principal*
Hunter Hoffman, *Manager*
EMP: 6 EST: 1975
SALES (est): 2.1MM **Privately Held**
SIC: 2599 Bar, restaurant & cafeteria furniture

(G-3021)
INTEGRATED DEVELOPMENT & MFG (PA)
Also Called: Environmental Growth Chambers
510 Washington St (44022-4448)
P.O. Box 390 (44022-0390)
PHONE.................440 247-5100
Adrian Rule, *President*
Tim Fanikos, *Regional Mgr*
Adrian Rule IV, *Vice Pres*
Chad Pearce, *Project Mgr*
Scott Weygandt, *Project Mgr*
EMP: 16
SQ FT: 28,000
SALES (est): 12.1MM **Privately Held**
SIC: 3822 1711 Auto controls regulating residntl & coml environmt & applncs; refrigeration contractor

(G-3022)
INVESTMENT SYSTEMS COMPANY
37840 Jackson Rd (44022-1912)
PHONE.................440 247-2865
Ronni Bialosky, *President*
EMP: 4
SALES (est): 405K **Privately Held**
WEB: www.investmentsystems.com
SIC: 7372 5045 Prepackaged software; computer software

(G-3023)
LIST MEDIA INC
Also Called: Admail.net
46 Shopping Plz Ste 122 (44022-3022)
P.O. Box 152, Aurora (44202-0152)
PHONE.................330 995-0864
Robert Hicks, *President*
EMP: 5 EST: 1990
SALES (est): 4.5MM **Privately Held**
WEB: www.dm1.net
SIC: 7374 7372 7371 7373 Computer processing services; application computer software; computer software development & applications; systems software development services

(G-3024)
MILLENNIUM ADHESIVE PDTS INC
178 E Washington St Ste 1 (44022-2978)
PHONE.................440 708-1212
Ronald Janoski, *President*
Mark Rundo, *Vice Pres*
EMP: 10
SQ FT: 7,000
SALES (est): 1.5MM **Privately Held**
WEB: www.millenniumadhesives.com
SIC: 2891 Adhesives & sealants

(G-3025)
NATIONAL DIRCTRY OF MORTS INC
Also Called: Red Book
285 Park Pl (44022-4456)
P.O. Box 73 (44022-0073)
PHONE.................440 247-3561
Jack Schmidt, *President*
EMP: 3
SALES (est): 190.3K **Privately Held**
WEB: www.funeral-dir.com
SIC: 2731 Books: publishing only

(G-3026)
P P M INC
35 High Ct (44022-2863)
PHONE.................216 701-0419
Chas Gilmore, *Principal*
Cliff Nazelli, *Principal*
EMP: 10
SQ FT: 3,600

SALES (est): 1.6MM **Privately Held**
WEB: www.ppminc.com
SIC: 3825 Instruments to measure electricity

(G-3027)
PERENNIAL SOFTWARE INC
Also Called: Sedona Office
547 Washington St Ste 11 (44022-4436)
PHONE.................440 247-5602
Michael Marks, *President*
Lisa Gambatese, *Manager*
Jim Mayes, *Manager*
Chris Williams, *Manager*
James Howe, *Senior Mgr*
EMP: 15
SALES (est): 1.7MM **Privately Held**
SIC: 7372 Business oriented computer software

(G-3028)
PERFECTION METAL CO
15085 N Deepwood Ln (44022-2637)
PHONE.................216 641-0949
David J Eget, *President*
EMP: 4 EST: 1949
SQ FT: 24,000
SALES (est): 785.7K **Privately Held**
WEB: www.pmetal.com
SIC: 3599 5051 Machine shop, jobbing & repair; metals service centers & offices

(G-3029)
SHOOK MANUFACTURED PDTS INC
3801 Wiltshire Rd (44022-1151)
PHONE.................440 247-9130
Thomas John, *Manager*
EMP: 8
SALES (corp-wide): 1.2MM **Privately Held**
SIC: 3545 Chucks: drill, lathe or magnetic (machine tool accessories)
PA: Shook Manufactured Products, Inc.
1017 Kenmore Blvd
Akron OH 44314
330 848-9780

(G-3030)
SNAPPSKIN INC
534 Manor Brook Dr (44022-4505)
PHONE.................440 318-4879
Joachim Hallwachs, *President*
EMP: 5
SQ FT: 2,000
SALES (est): 400K **Privately Held**
SIC: 3823 Digital displays of process variables

(G-3031)
THERMO KING CORPORATION
13 Orchard Cir (44022-2195)
PHONE.................478 625-7241
EMP: 11
SALES (est): 1.4MM **Privately Held**
SIC: 3585 Mfg Refrigeration/Heating Equipment
HQ: Ingersoll-Rand Company
800 Beaty St Ste B
Davidson NC 28036
704 655-4000

(G-3032)
WESTERN RESERVE FOODS LLC
325 Bell St (44022-2907)
P.O. Box 816, Middlefield (44062-0816)
PHONE.................330 770-0885
Edward Gordos, *Principal*
EMP: 3
SALES (est): 251K **Privately Held**
SIC: 2099 Food preparations

(G-3033)
YUTEC LLC (PA)
3940 Ellendale Rd (44022-1126)
PHONE.................440 725-5353
Yuri Borsch, *Partner*
Tanya Borsch,
▲ EMP: 5
SQ FT: 3,500
SALES (est): 453.2K **Privately Held**
WEB: www.yutec.com
SIC: 3575 Computer terminals, monitors & components

Chagrin Falls
Geauga County

(G-3034)
ABANAKI CORPORATION (PA)
Also Called: Aerodyne
17387 Munn Rd (44023-5400)
PHONE.................440 543-7400
Mark Thomas Hobson, *President*
▲ EMP: 15
SQ FT: 7,700
SALES (est): 2.7MM **Privately Held**
WEB: www.abanaki.com
SIC: 3569 Filters

(G-3035)
AERODYNAMIC SYSTEMS
19020 Brookfield Rd (44023-9605)
P.O. Box 143, Aurora (44202-0143)
PHONE.................440 463-8820
Patrick E Ryan, *Principal*
EMP: 4
SALES (est): 343.4K **Privately Held**
SIC: 3799 Recreational vehicles

(G-3036)
AFFORDABLE BUS SUPPORT LLC
Also Called: Minuteman Press
17800 Chillicothe Rd (44023-4868)
PHONE.................440 543-5547
Kelvin Fernandez, *Mng Member*
Jorge Fernandez,
EMP: 3
SQ FT: 2,000
SALES (est): 500K **Privately Held**
WEB: www.excelprint.net
SIC: 2752 Commercial printing, lithographic

(G-3037)
BECHEM LUBRICATION TECH LLC
8401 Chagrin Rd Ste 5a (44023-4704)
P.O. Box 23609 (44023-0609)
PHONE.................440 543-9845
Isaac Tripp IV, *Treasurer*
John S Steigerwald,
▲ EMP: 7
SALES (est): 979K **Privately Held**
SIC: 2992 Lubricating oils

(G-3038)
BUCKEYE GEAR CO
Also Called: Skidmore Engineering Div
16354 Stone Ridge Rd (44023-1117)
PHONE.................216 292-7998
Ray Skidmore, *President*
EMP: 13 EST: 1957
SQ FT: 7,200
SALES (est): 2.8MM **Privately Held**
WEB: www.skidmoreengineering.com
SIC: 3566 3423 3462 Gears, power transmission, except automotive; wrenches, hand tools; iron & steel forgings

(G-3039)
CHEMPAK INTERNATIONAL LLC (PA)
10175 Queens Way Ste 8 (44023-5435)
PHONE.................440 543-8511
Jay Hole, *Director*
Patrick McCarthy,
◆ EMP: 8
SQ FT: 1,600
SALES (est): 1.8MM **Privately Held**
WEB: www.chempakintl.com
SIC: 2869 Laboratory chemicals, organic

(G-3040)
CLEARLY VISIBLE MOBILE WASH
7302 Jackson Rd (44023-1713)
PHONE.................440 543-9299
Charlie Kiggans, *Owner*
EMP: 4
SALES (est): 386.4K **Privately Held**
SIC: 3069 7542 Washers, rubber; carwashes

GEOGRAPHIC SECTION

Chagrin Falls - Geauga County (G-3068)

(G-3041)
CONSTRUCTION POLYMERS CO
8160 Devon Ct (44023-5008)
PHONE................................440 591-9018
Ronald P Raymond, *President*
Russell Raymond, *Vice Pres*
▲ **EMP:** 8
SALES (est): 1MM **Privately Held**
WEB: www.kktechnologies.com
SIC: 3531 Construction machinery

(G-3042)
CONTROL ASSOCIATES INC
10205 Queens Way Unit 2 (44023-5409)
P.O. Box 187 (44022-0187)
PHONE................................440 708-1770
Stanley S Briggs, *President*
Steve Briggs, *Vice Pres*
Carol Abrams, *Admin Sec*
EMP: 4 **EST:** 1969
SQ FT: 2,500
SALES (est): 185.3K **Privately Held**
SIC: 8711 3823 1731 3625 Industrial engineers; industrial process control instruments; electronic controls installation; relays & industrial controls

(G-3043)
CUT OFF BLADES INC
426 Chipping Ln (44023-6713)
PHONE................................440 543-2947
Jake Boland, *President*
EMP: 3
SALES (est): 288.6K **Privately Held**
SIC: 3421 Knife blades & blanks

(G-3044)
DYNAMIC DESIGN & SYSTEMS INC
7639 Washington St (44023-4403)
PHONE................................440 708-1010
Richard E Doerr, *President*
Marilyn N Doerr, *Vice Pres*
Brad Baker, *Production*
Mark Doerr, *VP Mktg*
◆ **EMP:** 6
SQ FT: 3,000
SALES: 1.5MM **Privately Held**
SIC: 2759 2752 Screen printing; decals, lithographed; business form & card printing, lithographic

(G-3045)
ESSENTIAL SEALING PRODUCTS INC (PA)
10145 Queens Way (44023-5407)
P.O. Box 23699 (44023-0699)
PHONE................................440 543-8108
Susan Pyle, *President*
Bruce Pyle, *Vice Pres*
Pat Stipp, *Treasurer*
Bob Kauffman, *Regl Sales Mgr*
EMP: 10
SQ FT: 30,000
SALES (est): 1.7MM **Privately Held**
WEB: www.espsealing.com
SIC: 3053 Gaskets, all materials; packing materials

(G-3046)
ETNA PRODUCTS INCORPORATED (PA)
Also Called: Master Draw Lubricants
16824 Park Circle Dr (44023-4516)
P.O. Box 23609 (44023-0609)
PHONE................................440 543-9845
Isaac Tripp IV, *President*
Jeanne S Tripp, *Corp Secy*
Dennis Broadwater, *Plant Mgr*
Anne Tripp, *Asst Treas*
Ralph Noonan, *Sales Mgr*
◆ **EMP:** 30
SQ FT: 35,000
SALES (est): 5.4MM **Privately Held**
SIC: 2992 2821 2899 Oils & greases, blending & compounding; polyethylene resins; chemical preparations

(G-3047)
GEAUGA GROUP LLC
11024 Wingate Dr (44023-6181)
PHONE................................440 543-8797
Henry Milnark, *President*
James Mecsko, *Vice Pres*
Janet Mecsko, *Treasurer*

EMP: 5
SALES (est): 256.5K **Privately Held**
SIC: 2326 2339 7213 Aprons, work, except rubberized & plastic: men's; aprons, except rubber or plastic: women's, misses', juniors'; hoovers (apron): women's & misses'; apron supply

(G-3048)
GLOBAL GEAR LLC
8336 W Craig Dr (44023-4542)
PHONE................................941 830-0531
Kathleen Meyer,
EMP: 4
SALES (est): 300K **Privately Held**
SIC: 2311 Military uniforms, men's & youths': purchased materials

(G-3049)
HIGH TEMPERATURE SYSTEMS INC
16755 Park Circle Dr (44023-4562)
PHONE................................440 543-8271
Bruno Thut, *Ch of Bd*
Kristine Thut, *President*
Sherie Campbell, *Sales Staff*
Paul Meyer, *Marketing Staff*
▲ **EMP:** 9
SQ FT: 16,000
SALES (est): 1.8MM **Privately Held**
WEB: www.hitemp.com
SIC: 3559 Smelting & refining machinery & equipment

(G-3050)
HOME CARE PRODUCTS LLC (HQ)
7160 Chagrin Rd Ste 220 (44023-1135)
PHONE................................919 693-1002
Mark Howard, *Mng Member*
EMP: 18
SALES (est): 2.6MM **Privately Held**
SIC: 2674 Vacuum cleaner bags: made from purchased materials

(G-3051)
HYPER TOOL COMPANY
16829 Park Circle Dr (44023-4515)
PHONE................................440 543-5151
Morton C Mc Clennan, *President*
Donald Felton, *Vice Pres*
EMP: 18 **EST:** 1948
SQ FT: 12,000
SALES (est): 2.5MM **Privately Held**
SIC: 3541 3545 Machine tools, metal cutting type; machine tool accessories

(G-3052)
IBI BRAKE PRODUCTS INC
16751 Hilltop Park Pl (44023-4500)
P.O. Box 23547 (44023-0547)
PHONE................................440 543-7962
John Hooper, *President*
EMP: 6
SQ FT: 9,000
SALES (est): 2MM **Privately Held**
WEB: www.brakeproducts.com
SIC: 3499 5084 7389 3536 Wheels: wheelbarrow, stroller, etc.: disc, stamped metal; industrial machinery & equipment; crane & aerial lift service; hoists, cranes & monorails

(G-3053)
INTEGRATED DEVELOPMENT & MFG
8401 Washington St (44023-4511)
PHONE................................440 543-2423
Adrian O Rule III, *Manager*
EMP: 40
SALES (corp-wide): 12.1MM **Privately Held**
SIC: 3822 Auto controls regulating residntl & coml environmt & applncs
PA: Integrated Development & Mfg
510 Washington St
Chagrin Falls OH 44022
440 247-5100

(G-3054)
L HABERNY CO INC
10115 Queens Way (44023-5407)
PHONE................................440 543-5999
Dale Haberny, *President*
EMP: 12

SQ FT: 7,000
SALES (est): 2.9MM **Privately Held**
SIC: 3567 1796 Industrial furnaces & ovens; pollution control equipment installation

(G-3055)
LASER AUTOMATION INC
16771 Hilltop Park Pl (44023-4500)
PHONE................................440 543-9291
John Herkes, *President*
Carol Scerba, *Admin Sec*
EMP: 12 **EST:** 1977
SQ FT: 12,000
SALES: 950K **Privately Held**
WEB: www.laserautomation.com
SIC: 3699 5049 3535 Laser welding, drilling & cutting equipment; scientific & engineering equipment & supplies; conveyors & conveying equipment

(G-3056)
MAGNUS INTERNATIONAL GROUP INC (PA)
16533 Chillicothe Rd A (44023-4335)
PHONE................................216 592-8355
Theresa M Paicic, *President*
Sharon Sunderman, *President*
Eric Lofquist, *Principal*
Mark Allio, *Principal*
Scott Forster, *Vice Pres*
▲ **EMP:** 8
SALES (est): 60.7MM **Privately Held**
SIC: 4953 2048 2992 Recycling, waste materials; prepared feeds; rust arresting compounds, animal or vegetable oil base

(G-3057)
MAR-BAL INC (PA)
10095 Queens Way (44023-5406)
PHONE................................440 543-7526
Scott Balogh, *CEO*
Carolyn E Balogh, *Vice Pres*
Steven Balogh, *Vice Pres*
Kevin Casey, *Vice Pres*
Brian Leftwich, *Marketing Staff*
▲ **EMP:** 93 **EST:** 1970
SALES (est): 49.7MM **Privately Held**
SIC: 3089 2821 3081 Molding primary plastic; polyesters; unsupported plastics film & sheet

(G-3058)
MAR-BAL INC
10095 Queens Way (44023-5406)
PHONE................................440 543-7526
Scott Balogh, *President*
EMP: 93
SALES (corp-wide): 49.7MM **Privately Held**
WEB: www.mar-bal.com
SIC: 3089 2821 3081 Molding primary plastic; polyesters; unsupported plastics film & sheet
PA: Mar-Bal, Inc.
10095 Queens Way
Chagrin Falls OH 44023
440 543-7526

(G-3059)
MASTERS GROUP INC
7160 Chagrin Rd Ste 160 (44023-1182)
PHONE................................440 893-1900
John Dublo, *President*
EMP: 4
SQ FT: 500
SALES (est): 722.2K **Privately Held**
SIC: 1481 3399 3341 5051 Nonmetallic mineral services; iron ore recovery from open hearth slag; secondary nonferrous metals; ferrous metals; iron ore

(G-3060)
MILLENNIUM ADHESIVE PRODUCTS
17340 Munn Rd (44023-5476)
PHONE................................440 708-1212
Ron Janoski, *CEO*
EMP: 9
SALES (est): 1MM
SALES (corp-wide): 1.2MM **Privately Held**
SIC: 2891 Adhesives

PA: Millennium Adhesive Products
4401 Page Ave
Michigan Center MI 49254
800 248-4010

(G-3061)
NATIONAL POLYMER DEV CO INC
10200 Gottschalk Pkwy # 4 (44023-5470)
PHONE................................440 708-1245
Adrian De Krom, *President*
Amanda Dekrom, *Office Mgr*
EMP: 11
SALES (est): 1.6MM **Privately Held**
SIC: 2821 Plastics materials & resins

(G-3062)
NATIONAL POLYMER INC
10200 Gottschalk Pkwy (44023-5470)
P.O. Box 343, Newbury (44065-0343)
PHONE................................440 708-1245
Adrian De Krom, *President*
Daniel Bess, *Director*
EMP: 11
SQ FT: 6,000
SALES (est): 1.9MM **Privately Held**
SIC: 8734 5169 2891 Testing laboratories; adhesives & sealants; adhesives, plastic

(G-3063)
NELSON ALUMINUM FOUNDRY INC
17093 Munn Rd (44023-5412)
PHONE................................440 543-1941
Russell Nelson, *President*
EMP: 6 **EST:** 1951
SALES: 500K **Privately Held**
SIC: 3365 3369 Machinery castings, aluminum; nonferrous foundries

(G-3064)
P & T MILLWORK INC
10090 Queens Way (44023-5403)
PHONE................................440 543-2151
Joe Tesauro, *CEO*
Randall Pistone, *Vice Pres*
David Koci, *Admin Sec*
EMP: 21
SQ FT: 21,500
SALES (est): 2.6MM **Privately Held**
WEB: www.ptmillwork.com
SIC: 2499 5211 2431 Decorative wood & woodwork; door & window products; millwork

(G-3065)
PEDIAVASCULAR INC
7181 Chagrin Rd Ste 250 (44023-1130)
PHONE................................216 236-5533
Timothy Moran, *CEO*
EMP: 15
SALES (est): 1.5MM **Privately Held**
SIC: 3841 Inhalation therapy equipment

(G-3066)
PHOENIX ASSOCIATES
16760 W Park Circle Dr (44023-4550)
PHONE................................440 543-9701
Travis Hendershot, *General Mgr*
Ed McNeeley, *Sales Mgr*
Tim Reed,
Scott Janda,
EMP: 25
SQ FT: 12,000
SALES (est): 4.1MM **Privately Held**
WEB: www.intreeg.com
SIC: 3053 Gaskets, all materials

(G-3067)
POP/POS ADVANTAGE
Also Called: Poppos Advantage Group
17911 Snyder Rd Ste A (44023-1631)
PHONE................................440 543-9452
Linda White, *Owner*
EMP: 2
SALES: 1MM **Privately Held**
SIC: 3292 Asbestos textiles, except insulating material

(G-3068)
POV PRINT COMMUNICATION INC
16715 W Park Circle Dr (44023-4549)
PHONE................................440 591-5443

Chagrin Falls - Geauga County (G-3069)

Chris Yuhasz, *President*
EMP: 9
SQ FT: 3,000
SALES (est): 960.2K **Privately Held**
SIC: 2752 Commercial printing, offset

(G-3069)
PRIDE OF GENEVA
18106 Snyder Rd (44023-1628)
PHONE..................................440 466-5695
Curtis Hall, *Principal*
EMP: 5
SALES (est): 157.2K **Privately Held**
SIC: 2711 Newspapers, publishing & printing

(G-3070)
PRINTING SERVICES
16750 Park Circle Dr (44023-4563)
PHONE..................................440 708-1999
Robert Roulan, *President*
EMP: 25
SQ FT: 16,000
SALES (est): 1.2MM **Privately Held**
SIC: 7389 2752 Printers' services: folding, collating; commercial printing, lithographic

(G-3071)
QUBE CORPORATION
16744 W Park Circle Dr (44023-4550)
PHONE..................................440 543-2393
William C Mc Coy, *President*
Steve L Clark, *Vice Pres*
EMP: 12
SQ FT: 13,000
SALES (est): 930K **Privately Held**
WEB: www.qubeinc.com
SIC: 3089 Fittings for pipe, plastic

(G-3072)
RESERVE ENERGY EXPLORATION CO
10155 Gottschalk Pkwy # 1 (44023-5465)
P.O. Box 23278 (44023-0278)
PHONE..................................440 543-0770
Joseph Haas, *President*
Sean Haas, *Manager*
EMP: 8
SALES (est): 1.2MM **Privately Held**
SIC: 1382 Oil & gas exploration services

(G-3073)
ROYAL ADHESIVES & SEALANTS LLC
17340 Munn Rd (44023-5476)
PHONE..................................440 708-1212
Ron Janoski, *President*
EMP: 13
SALES (corp-wide): 3B **Publicly Held**
SIC: 2891 Sealants
HQ: Royal Adhesives And Sealants Llc
2001 W Washington St
South Bend IN 46628
574 246-5000

(G-3074)
SCHENCK PROCESS LLC
16490 Chillicothe Rd (44023-4326)
PHONE..................................513 576-9200
Graham Cooper, *Branch Mgr*
EMP: 10 **Privately Held**
SIC: 3535 3564 5084 Pneumatic tube conveyor systems; dust or fume collecting equipment, industrial; pneumatic tools & equipment
HQ: Schenck Process Llc
7901 Nw 107th Ter
Kansas City MO 64153
816 891-9300

(G-3075)
SCOTT FETZER COMPANY
Scots Tuff
16841 Park Circle Dr (44023-4515)
PHONE..................................216 228-2400
Pat McCoy, *Manager*
EMP: 30
SALES (corp-wide): 225.3B **Publicly Held**
SIC: 5999 3635 Cleaning equipment & supplies; household vacuum cleaners
HQ: The Scott Fetzer Company
28800 Clemens Rd
Westlake OH 44145
440 892-3000

(G-3076)
SHOOTERS CHOICE LLC
66 Windward Way (44023-6706)
PHONE..................................440 834-8888
Joseph Ventimiglia, *President*
Frank Ventimiglia, *Principal*
EMP: 5
SQ FT: 13,104
SALES (est): 365.2K **Privately Held**
SIC: 2992 Lubricating oils & greases

(G-3077)
SPEED SELECTOR INC
17050 Munn Rd (44023-5494)
PHONE..................................440 543-8233
George C Wick Jr, *President*
George F Howson Jr, *Vice Pres*
Craig Liechty, *CFO*
EMP: 15
SQ FT: 31,000
SALES (est): 4MM **Privately Held**
WEB: www.speedselector.com
SIC: 3566 Drives, high speed industrial, except hydrostatic

(G-3078)
STOCK FAIRFIELD CORPORATION
Also Called: Stock Equipment Company
16490 Chillicothe Rd (44023-4326)
PHONE..................................440 543-6000
Robert Ciavarella, *President*
Xitao Wang, *General Mgr*
Ihor Yakovenko, *Project Mgr*
Michal Cerych, *Prdtn Mgr*
Felipe Fonseca, *Production*
EMP: 170 EST: 2007
SALES (est): 34.3MM **Privately Held**
WEB: www.stockequipment.com
SIC: 5063 8711 3535 3823 Power transmission equipment, electric; electrical or electronic engineering; conveyors & conveying equipment; industrial instrmnts msrmnt display/control process variable; relays & industrial controls; industrial trucks & tractors
HQ: Schenck Process Llc
7901 Nw 107th Ter
Kansas City MO 64153
816 891-9300

(G-3079)
TANGENT COMPANY LLC
10175 Queens Way Ste 1 (44023-5435)
PHONE..................................440 543-2775
James Bolton, *Mng Member*
EMP: 9 EST: 2008
SALES (est): 1.4MM **Privately Held**
SIC: 3999 8711 8734 8733 Custom pulverizing & grinding of plastic materials; engineering services; testing laboratories; noncommercial research organizations; sewage & water treatment equipment

(G-3080)
TARKETT INC
16910 Munn Rd (44023-5411)
PHONE..................................440 708-9366
Mitchell Brooks, *Project Mgr*
Chris Burke, *Production*
Brad Marler, *Technical Mgr*
Anders Nilsson, *Finance Mgr*
James Beckerman, *Finance*
EMP: 3
SALES (corp-wide): 589.6K **Privately Held**
SIC: 3069 Flooring, rubber: tile or sheet
HQ: Tarkett, Inc.
30000 Aurora Rd
Solon OH 44139
800 899-8916

(G-3081)
TEWELL & ASSOCIATES
10260 Washington St (44023-5478)
PHONE..................................440 543-5190
James Tewell, *President*
Carolyn Tewell, *Corp Secy*
EMP: 8
SQ FT: 3,500
SALES (est): 3.8MM **Privately Held**
WEB: www.tewell.com
SIC: 7389 2759 Brokers, contract services; screen printing

(G-3082)
THERM-O-PACKAGING SUPPLIERS
16815 Park Circle Dr (44023-4515)
PHONE..................................440 543-5188
Fax: 440 543-9489
EMP: 14
SQ FT: 10,600
SALES (est): 1.5MM **Privately Held**
SIC: 2671 2657 Mfg Packaging Paper/Film Mfg Folding Paperboard Boxes

(G-3083)
TITANIUM TROUT LLC
18060 Birch Hill Dr (44023-5826)
PHONE..................................440 543-3187
Kevin Donovan, *Principal*
EMP: 3 EST: 2010
SALES (est): 30.6K **Privately Held**
SIC: 3356 Titanium

(G-3084)
TRIAD METAL PRODUCTS COMPANY
12990 Snow Rd (44023)
PHONE..................................216 676-6505
Patricia Basista, *President*
Richard Basista, *President*
Wally Klubert, *President*
▲ EMP: 100 EST: 1945
SQ FT: 150,000
SALES (est): 20MM **Privately Held**
WEB: www.triadmetal.com
SIC: 3469 Stamping metal for the trade

(G-3085)
TRILOGY PLASTICS INC
7160 Chagrin Rd (44023-1134)
PHONE..................................440 893-5522
EMP: 55
SALES (corp-wide): 18.2MM **Privately Held**
SIC: 3089 Molding primary plastic
PA: Trilogy Plastics, Inc.
2290 W Main St
Alliance OH 44601
330 821-4700

(G-3086)
TUNGSTEN SLTONS GROUP INTL INC
17523 Merry Oaks Trl (44023-5643)
PHONE..................................440 708-3096
Hugh McIvor, *President*
Kevin McIvor, *Vice Pres*
EMP: 3 EST: 2012
SQ FT: 10,000
SALES (est): 7MM **Privately Held**
SIC: 3313 5093 Tungsten carbide powder; metal scrap & waste materials

(G-3087)
UTILITY RELAY CO LTD
Also Called: Urc
10100 Queens Way (44023-5404)
PHONE..................................440 708-1000
Helmut Weiher, *Mng Member*
EMP: 42
SQ FT: 15,000
SALES (est): 9.2MM **Privately Held**
WEB: www.utilityrelay.com
SIC: 3625 Industrial electrical relays & switches

(G-3088)
VENTCO INC
66 Windward Way (44023-6706)
PHONE..................................440 834-8888
Joseph Ventimiglia, *President*
Frank Ventimiglia, *Vice Pres*
▼ EMP: 10
SQ FT: 15,500
SALES (est): 1.5MM **Privately Held**
WEB: www.shooters-choice.com
SIC: 2842 2992 Cleaning or polishing preparations; lubricating oils & greases

(G-3089)
VIRTUS STUNTS LLC
16320 Snyder Rd (44023-4312)
PHONE..................................440 543-0472
Ted Batchelor, *Principal*
EMP: 3 EST: 2010
SALES (est): 265.6K **Privately Held**
SIC: 2721 Television schedules: publishing only, not printed on site

(G-3090)
WHIP GUIDE CO
Also Called: Gizmo
16829 Park Circle Dr (44023-4515)
PHONE..................................440 543-5151
Morton C Mc Clennan, *Partner*
Walter C Mc Clennan, *Partner*
EMP: 10
SQ FT: 10,000
SALES (est): 899.5K **Privately Held**
SIC: 3545 3366 Drilling machine attachments & accessories; copper foundries

(G-3091)
XACT SPEC INDUSTRIES LLC
Aerospace Operations
16959 Munn Rd (44023-5410)
PHONE..................................440 543-8157
Peter Barnhart, *Managing Prtnr*
EMP: 9
SALES (est): 406.9K **Privately Held**
SIC: 3599 Machine & other job shop work
PA: Xact Spec Industries Llc
16959 Munn Rd
Chagrin Falls OH 44023

(G-3092)
XACT SPEC INDUSTRIES LLC (PA)
16959 Munn Rd (44023-5410)
PHONE..................................440 543-8157
Peter Barnhart, *Mng Member*
EMP: 42
SQ FT: 32,000
SALES (est): 14.7MM **Privately Held**
SIC: 3599 Machine shop, jobbing & repair; machine & other job shop work

(G-3093)
ZOOK ENTERPRISES LLC (PA)
16809 Park Circle Dr (44023-4515)
P.O. Box 419 (44022-0419)
PHONE..................................440 543-1010
Richard V Varos, *Mng Member*
▲ EMP: 30
SQ FT: 8,400
SALES (est): 4.4MM **Privately Held**
SIC: 3559 Petroleum refinery equipment

Chardon
Geauga County

(G-3094)
9/10 CASTINGS INC
313 Greenway Dr (44024-1481)
PHONE..................................216 406-8907
EMP: 3
SALES (est): 282.3K **Privately Held**
SIC: 3272 Concrete products

(G-3095)
ADVANCED QUARTZ FABRICATION
11920 Quail Woods Dr (44024-8648)
P.O. Box 5070, Mentor (44061-5070)
PHONE..................................440 350-4567
▲ EMP: 12
SQ FT: 26,000
SALES (est): 1.5MM **Privately Held**
SIC: 3679 Mfg Electronic Components

(G-3096)
AIR CLEANING SYSTEMS INC
12965 Mayfield Rd (44024-8923)
PHONE..................................440 285-3565
Jan C Brindo, *President*
EMP: 6
SALES (est): 1MM **Privately Held**
SIC: 3564 Blowers & fans

(G-3097)
ALTITUDE MEDICAL INC
Po Box 770 (44024-0770)
P.O. Box 770
PHONE..................................440 799-7701
Ray Dunning, *CEO*
EMP: 5
SALES (est): 544.8K **Privately Held**
SIC: 3841 Surgical & medical instruments

GEOGRAPHIC SECTION — Chardon - Geauga County (G-3126)

(G-3098)
ALVORDS YARD & GARDEN EQP
12089 Ravenna Rd (44024-7008)
PHONE 440 286-2315
William J Alvord, *Owner*
EMP: 5
SALES (est): 349.9K **Privately Held**
SIC: 5261 7699 3546 Lawnmowers & tractors; motorcycle repair service; saws & sawing equipment

(G-3099)
ARABIAN TOOLS INC
9632 Brakeman Rd (44024-8207)
PHONE 440 286-3600
Frank Janek, *President*
Theresa Janek, *Vice Pres*
EMP: 3
SQ FT: 5,000
SALES: 150K **Privately Held**
SIC: 3599 Machine shop, jobbing & repair

(G-3100)
BOEHRNGER INGLHEIM PHRMCCTCALS
11540 Autumn Ridge Dr (44024-8764)
PHONE 440 286-5667
Rick Oprzadek, *Principal*
EMP: 4
SALES (est): 400.3K **Privately Held**
SIC: 2834 Pharmaceutical preparations

(G-3101)
CHARDON CUSTOM POLYMERS LLC
373 Washington St (44024-1129)
PHONE 440 285-2161
Marian Devoe, *President*
Rich Garey, *Opers Staff*
Randy Cooke, *Engineer*
Dick Peterson, *Engineer*
Jim Knipp, *Regl Sales Mgr*
EMP: 16
SALES (est): 5.2MM **Privately Held**
SIC: 3061 3069 Mechanical rubber goods; molded rubber products

(G-3102)
CHARDON METAL PRODUCTS CO
206 5th Ave (44024-1007)
P.O. Box 67 (44024-0067)
PHONE 440 285-2147
Anderson Allyn Jr, *Ch of Bd*
Duke Allyn, *President*
Aric Allyn, *Vice Pres*
Anderson Allyn III, *CFO*
EMP: 32 EST: 1945
SQ FT: 31,000
SALES (est): 8.6MM **Privately Held**
WEB: www.chardonmetal.com
SIC: 3498 3451 3599 Tube fabricating (contract bending & shaping); screw machine products; machine shop, jobbing & repair

(G-3103)
CHARDON PLASTICS MACHINERY
11680 Butternut Rd (44024-9355)
P.O. Box 796, Newbury (44065-0796)
PHONE 440 564-5360
Don Schindelhold, *President*
EMP: 3 EST: 1998
SALES: 375K **Privately Held**
WEB: www.chardonplastics.com
SIC: 3559 Plastics working machinery

(G-3104)
CHARDON TOOL & SUPPLY CO INC
115 Parker Ct (44024-1112)
P.O. Box 291 (44024-0291)
PHONE 440 286-6440
Weldon Bennett, *President*
Donna Blewett, *Principal*
Marshall Meadows, *Principal*
Andrew O'Dell, *Principal*
EMP: 35
SQ FT: 4,800
SALES: 3MM **Privately Held**
SIC: 3545 5085 Diamond cutting tools for turning, boring, burnishing, etc.; diamonds, industrial: natural, crude

(G-3105)
CITY OF CHARDON
Also Called: Water & Sewer
201 N Hambden St (44024-1175)
PHONE 440 286-2657
David Lelkl, *Manager*
EMP: 15 **Privately Held**
WEB: www.co.geauga.oh.us
SIC: 3589 Sewage & water treatment equipment
PA: City Of Chardon
111 Water St Fl 2
Chardon OH 44024
440 286-2600

(G-3106)
COLLATED PRODUCTS CORP
8480 Brakeman Rd (44024-9229)
PHONE 440 946-1950
EMP: 10
SQ FT: 8,000
SALES (est): 1.4MM **Privately Held**
SIC: 3579 Mfg Office Machines

(G-3107)
DARK DIAMOND TOOLS INC
10319 Sawmill Dr (44024-8220)
P.O. Box 22, Montville (44064-0022)
PHONE 440 701-6424
Richard De Francesco, *President*
Andrew Kawalec, *Vice Pres*
Cheryl De Francesco, *Treasurer*
EMP: 5
SQ FT: 2,000
SALES: 750K **Privately Held**
WEB: www.darkdiamond.net
SIC: 3545 Diamond cutting tools for turning, boring, burnishing, etc.

(G-3108)
DEAKS FORM TOOLS INC
9954a Cutts Rd (44024-9182)
PHONE 440 286-2353
George Deak, *Branch Mgr*
EMP: 3
SALES (corp-wide): 703K **Privately Held**
SIC: 3312 Tool & die steel
PA: Form Deak's Tools Inc
11836 Western Ave
Stanton CA 90680
714 891-5272

(G-3109)
DND PRODUCTS INC
Also Called: Maple Valley Sug Bush & Farms
13262 Chardon Windsor Rd (44024-8975)
PHONE 440 286-7275
Donna Divoky, *President*
Dave Divoky, *Vice Pres*
EMP: 3
SQ FT: 1,390
SALES (est): 246.3K **Privately Held**
SIC: 3199 Safety belts, leather

(G-3110)
EGC ENTERPRISES INC
140 Parker Ct (44024-1112)
PHONE 440 285-5835
Bernard L Casamento, *President*
Robert R Rutherford, *Vice Pres*
Dario Ortiz, *Plant Mgr*
Michael Bartos, *Engineer*
Brian Biller, *Engineer*
▲ EMP: 47 EST: 1978
SQ FT: 49,000
SALES (est): 19.4MM **Privately Held**
WEB: www.egc-ent.com
SIC: 2891 3053 Sealants; gaskets, packing & sealing devices

(G-3111)
FABCRAFT INC
344 Center St (44024-1104)
PHONE 440 286-6700
John M Svoboda Sr, *President*
John M Svoboda Jr, *General Mgr*
EMP: 5
SQ FT: 9,600
SALES: 750K **Privately Held**
SIC: 3444 3498 Sheet metalwork; tube fabricating (contract bending & shaping)

(G-3112)
FOWLERS MILLING CO INC
12500 Fowlers Mill Rd (44024-9371)
PHONE 440 286-2024
Rick Erickson, *President*
EMP: 6
SQ FT: 4,600
SALES (est): 660K **Privately Held**
WEB: www.fowlermill.com
SIC: 2041 5947 Flour mixes; gift baskets

(G-3113)
GEAUGA COATINGS LLC
15120 Sisson Rd (44024-8507)
PHONE 440 286-5571
Brian Milks, *Principal*
EMP: 3 EST: 2011
SALES (est): 322K **Privately Held**
SIC: 3312 Chemicals & other products derived from coking

(G-3114)
GEAUGA RHABILITATION ENGRG INC (PA)
Also Called: Geauga Rehab Engineering
13376 Ravenna Rd (44024-9007)
PHONE 216 536-0826
Jonathan Naft, *President*
Sherri Morris, *Manager*
Cheryl Naft, *Info Tech Mgr*
EMP: 12
SQ FT: 4,000
SALES (est): 1.6MM **Privately Held**
SIC: 3842 Surgical appliances & supplies

(G-3115)
GEORGIA METAL COATINGS COMPANY
275 Industrial Pkwy (44024-1052)
PHONE 770 446-3930
EMP: 10
SQ FT: 24,000
SALES (est): 852.3K
SALES (corp-wide): 1.6B **Privately Held**
SIC: 3479 Coating/Engraving Service
HQ: Nof Metal Coatings North America Inc.
275 Industrial Pkwy
Chardon OH 44024
440 285-2231

(G-3116)
HI-TECH EXTRUSIONS LTD
12621 Chardon Windsor Rd (44024-8969)
PHONE 440 286-4000
Matt Michalek, *Partner*
Julius Wilson, *Partner*
Donald J Michalek, *General Ptnr*
Bonnie Cunningham, *QC Mgr*
Ed Wilson, *Manager*
EMP: 30
SQ FT: 25,000
SALES (est): 7MM **Privately Held**
WEB: www.hitechextrusions.com
SIC: 3089 Extruded finished plastic products

(G-3117)
HUTTER RACING ENGINES LTD
12550 Gar Hwy (44024-8232)
PHONE 440 285-2175
Ronald Hutter, *Partner*
Thalia Hutter, *Partner*
Trevor Hutter, *Partner*
Ron Hutter, *Executive*
EMP: 10
SQ FT: 6,000
SALES (est): 1.4MM **Privately Held**
SIC: 3599 7538 Machine shop, jobbing & repair; general automotive repair shops

(G-3118)
III WILLIAMS LLC
11993 Ravenna Rd Ste 12 (44024-9018)
PHONE 440 721-8191
William Hurt, *President*
EMP: 2
SQ FT: 2,400
SALES: 1MM **Privately Held**
SIC: 3494 5531 Valves & pipe fittings; automotive parts

(G-3119)
KEY MANEUVERS INC (PA)
Also Called: K.M.I. Printing
10639 Grant St Ste C (44024-1282)
P.O. Box 51 (44024-0051)
PHONE 440 285-0774
Randy Bennett, *President*
EMP: 15
SQ FT: 3,000
SALES (est): 1.7MM **Privately Held**
WEB: www.kmiprinting.com
SIC: 2752 Commercial printing, offset

(G-3120)
KTS CSTM LGS/XCLSVELY YOU INC
602 South St Ste C-2 (44024-1459)
PHONE 440 285-9803
Kevin R Temple, *President*
Melissa Temple, *Vice Pres*
EMP: 7
SQ FT: 2,800
SALES: 500K **Privately Held**
SIC: 2395 7389 Embroidery & art needlework; advertising, promotional & trade show services

(G-3121)
KTS CUSTOM LOGOS
602 South St Ste C-2 (44024-1459)
PHONE 440 285-9803
Kevin Temple, *President*
Ken Temple, *Principal*
Melissa Temple, *Vice Pres*
EMP: 7
SALES (est): 630.2K **Privately Held**
WEB: www.ktscustomlogos.com
SIC: 2395 Embroidery & art needlework

(G-3122)
LAMAR PROFORMA
12636 Mayfield Rd Ste 1 (44024-7978)
PHONE 440 285-2277
Kathy McClure, *Principal*
EMP: 6
SALES (est): 589K **Privately Held**
SIC: 2752 Stationery & office supplies

(G-3123)
LANXESS CORPORATION
145 Parker Ct (44024-1112)
PHONE 440 279-2367
Margie Durkos, *Safety Mgr*
Lou Mueller, *Manager*
EMP: 250
SALES (corp-wide): 8.2B **Privately Held**
SIC: 3069 5169 Reclaimed rubber & specialty rubber compounds; industrial chemicals
HQ: Lanxess Corporation
111 Ridc Park West Dr
Pittsburgh PA 15275
800 526-9377

(G-3124)
MADISON ELECTRIC (MEPCO) INC
11993 Ravenna Rd Ste 12 (44024-9018)
PHONE 440 279-0521
Bruce Barclay, *President*
James Ramsey, *Treasurer*
EMP: 4
SALES: 800K **Privately Held**
SIC: 3674 Infrared sensors, solid state

(G-3125)
MAPLEDALE FARM INC
Also Called: Mapledale Landscaping
12613 Woodin Rd (44024-9177)
PHONE 440 286-3389
David P Johnson, *President*
Judy Johnson, *Corp Secy*
Arthur L Johnson Sr, *Vice Pres*
EMP: 10
SALES (est): 560K **Privately Held**
WEB: www.mapledalelandscaping.com
SIC: 0782 4959 2087 5251 Lawn & garden services; snowplowing; beverage bases, concentrates, syrups, powders & mixes; snowblowers

(G-3126)
MUNSON SALES & ENGINEERING
13260 Crows Hollow Dr (44024-9023)
PHONE 216 496-5436
Arthur G Hollis, *Owner*
EMP: 3
SALES (est): 236.2K **Privately Held**
SIC: 3599 Machine & other job shop work

Chardon - Geauga County (G-3127)

(G-3127)
NEO TACTICAL GEAR
11540 Glenmora Dr (44024-8679)
PHONE.....................216 235-2625
David Maki, *Principal*
EMP: 4
SALES (est): 310.7K **Privately Held**
SIC: 3949 Sporting & athletic goods

(G-3128)
NOF METAL COATINGS N AMER INC (HQ)
275 Industrial Pkwy (44024-1052)
PHONE.....................440 285-2231
Shin Masuda, *President*
Kevin McCarthy, *Business Mgr*
Frederic Gheno, *Vice Pres*
Brian Straka, *Technical Mgr*
Norman Gertz, *CFO*
▲ EMP: 50
SQ FT: 20,000
SALES (est): 17.2MM
SALES (corp-wide): 1.6B **Privately Held**
WEB: www.geomet.net
SIC: 2899 Chemical preparations
PA: Nof Corporation
    4-20-3, Ebisu
    Shibuya-Ku TKY 150-0
    354 246-600

(G-3129)
NORTH AMERICAN CAST STONE INC
13271 Bass Lake Rd (44024-8321)
PHONE.....................440 286-1999
Richard T Rickelman, *Principal*
EMP: 5
SQ FT: 7,059
SALES (est): 623.4K **Privately Held**
WEB: www.northamericancaststone.com
SIC: 3272 Concrete products, precast

(G-3130)
OHIO ORDNANCE WORKS INC
310 Park Dr (44024-1057)
P.O. Box 687 (44024-0687)
PHONE.....................440 285-3481
Robert I Landies, *Owner*
Robert E Conroy Jr, *Vice Pres*
Liz Conroy, *Manager*
▼ EMP: 40
SALES (est): 9.4MM **Privately Held**
WEB: www.ohioordnanceworks.com
SIC: 3484 Guns (firearms) or gun parts, 30 mm. & below; revolvers or revolver parts, 30 mm. & below; rifles or rifle parts, 30 mm. & below

(G-3131)
ORWELL PRINTING
10639 Grant St Ste C (44024-1282)
P.O. Box 51 (44024-0051)
PHONE.....................440 285-2233
Randy Bennett, *President*
EMP: 8 EST: 1948
SQ FT: 1,900
SALES (est): 970.3K
SALES (corp-wide): 1.7MM **Privately Held**
WEB: www.orwellprinting.com
SIC: 2752 Commercial printing, offset; lithographing on metal
PA: Key Maneuvers Inc
    10639 Grant St Ste C
    Chardon OH 44024
    440 285-0774

(G-3132)
PERFORM METALS INC
124 Industrial Pkwy (44024-1049)
PHONE.....................440 286-1951
Craig Rupar, *President*
Carol Rupar, *Vice Pres*
EMP: 5
SALES (est): 460K **Privately Held**
SIC: 3599 Machine shop, jobbing & repair

(G-3133)
QUANTUM ENERGY LLC (PA)
10405 Locust Grove Dr (44024-8861)
P.O. Box 241506, Cleveland (44124-8506)
PHONE.....................440 285-7381
Paul J Mysyk,
Harrison Schumacher,
EMP: 15

SALES (est): 3.6MM **Privately Held**
SIC: 1382 Oil & gas exploration services

(G-3134)
RICHARDS MAPLE PRODUCTS INC
545 Water St (44024-1142)
PHONE.....................440 286-4160
Debra Richards, *President*
Colin Rennie, *Vice Pres*
Annette Polson, *Admin Sec*
EMP: 6 EST: 1910
SALES: 750K **Privately Held**
WEB: www.richardsmapleproducts.com
SIC: 2064 5149 Candy & other confectionery products; syrups, except for fountain use

(G-3135)
SCREEN CRAFT PLASTICS
Also Called: Great Lakes Embroidery
695 South St Ste 7 (44024-1474)
P.O. Box 612 (44024-0612)
PHONE.....................440 286-4060
Richard Lakatosh, *Owner*
Linda Lakatosh, *Co-Owner*
EMP: 3
SQ FT: 1,000
SALES: 100K **Privately Held**
SIC: 2759 Screen printing

(G-3136)
SHIFFLER EQUIPMENT SALES INC (PA)
745 South St (44024-2800)
P.O. Box 232 (44024-0232)
PHONE.....................440 285-9175
John Shiffler, *CEO*
Mark C Lewis, *President*
Duane Frager, *Manager*
Gloria S Shiffler, *Director*
▲ EMP: 50
SQ FT: 30,000
SALES (est): 11.7MM **Privately Held**
WEB: www.shifflerequip.com
SIC: 2531 School furniture

(G-3137)
SOLON MANUFACTURING COMPANY
425 Center St (44024-1054)
P.O. Box 207 (44024-0207)
PHONE.....................440 286-7149
J Timothy Dunn, *President*
Steve Fowler, *President*
Jim Young, *Principal*
David J Carpenter, *Chairman*
George Davet, *Vice Pres*
▲ EMP: 38
SQ FT: 30,000
SALES (est): 16.7MM **Privately Held**
WEB: www.solonmfg.com
SIC: 3823 3493 3643 3495 Pressure measurement instruments, industrial; cold formed springs; current-carrying wiring devices; wire springs; spring washers, metal

(G-3138)
TECHNISAND INC (DH)
Also Called: Santrol
11833 Ravenna Rd (44024-7006)
P.O. Box 87 (44024-0087)
PHONE.....................440 285-3132
Jenniffer Deckard, *President*
William Conway, *Director*
▲ EMP: 3
SQ FT: 4,500
SALES (est): 78.1MM
SALES (corp-wide): 136.2MM **Publicly Held**
SIC: 1442 Sand mining
HQ: Fairmount Santrol Inc.
    3 Summit Park Dr Ste 700
    Independence OH 44131
    440 214-3200

(G-3139)
THE Q-P MANUFACTURING CO INC
215 5th Ave (44024-1001)
PHONE.....................440 946-2120
John Chesnes, *Plant Mgr*
Joyce Richardson, *Buyer*
Paul Overberger, *Info Tech Mgr*

Mate Brkic,
Dorris Brkic,
EMP: 15
SQ FT: 74,000
SALES (est): 6.4MM **Privately Held**
SIC: 3599 Machine shop, jobbing & repair

(G-3140)
VACUUM FINISHING COMPANY
10275 Old State Rd (44024-9524)
P.O. Box 311 (44024-0311)
PHONE.....................440 286-4386
EMP: 10
SQ FT: 30,000
SALES (est): 931.7K **Privately Held**
SIC: 3944 3479 3471 Mfg Games/Toys Coating/Engraving Service Plating/Polishing Service

Charm
Holmes County

(G-3141)
CHARM HARNESS AND BOOT LTD
Also Called: Harness Shop
4432 County Road 70 (44617)
P.O. Box 114 (44617-0114)
PHONE.....................330 893-0402
Roy A Miller, *President*
EMP: 10
SQ FT: 8,000
SALES: 5MM **Privately Held**
SIC: 7251 3199 5661 7699 Shoe stores; customized clothing & apparel; shoe repair shop

(G-3142)
RABER LUMBER CO
4112 State Rte 557 (44617)
P.O. Box 26 (44617-0026)
PHONE.....................330 893-2797
Edward Raber, *Partner*
Ivan Miller, *Manager*
EMP: 7
SQ FT: 1,000
SALES (est): 1MM **Privately Held**
SIC: 2421 2448 Sawmills & planing mills, general; pallets, wood

Chesapeake
Lawrence County

(G-3143)
CABELL HUNTINGTON
29 Candy Ln (45619-7090)
PHONE.....................740 867-2665
Rhonda Crockett, *Principal*
EMP: 3 EST: 2010
SALES (est): 207.2K **Privately Held**
SIC: 2834 Medicines, capsuled or ampuled

(G-3144)
COUNTY OF LAWRENCE
Also Called: Eastern Lawrnce Cty Watr Reclm
11100 Private Dr (45619)
P.O. Box 430 (45619-0430)
PHONE.....................740 867-8700
Tim Porter, *Administration*
EMP: 10 **Privately Held**
SIC: 3589 Sewage & water treatment equipment
PA: County Of Lawrence
    115 S 5th St
    Ironton OH 45638
    740 532-3106

(G-3145)
G BIG INC (PA)
Also Called: Pickett Concrete
441 Rockwood Ave (45619-1120)
PHONE.....................740 867-5758
John W Galloway, *President*
James W Galloway, *Vice Pres*
Todd A Galloway, *Vice Pres*
Todd Galloway, *Vice Pres*
EMP: 25
SQ FT: 2,000

SALES (est): 3.8MM **Privately Held**
WEB: www.gbig.com
SIC: 3273 1771 Ready-mixed concrete; concrete work

(G-3146)
GERALD D DAMRON
197 Township Road 1156 (45619-8905)
PHONE.....................740 894-3680
Gerald Damron, *Principal*
EMP: 4
SALES (est): 327.9K **Privately Held**
SIC: 2411 Logging

(G-3147)
PRECISION COMPONENT & MCH INC
17 Rosslyn Rd (45619)
P.O. Box 580 (45619-0580)
PHONE.....................740 867-6366
Steve Chatteron, *President*
Stephanie Black, *Vice Pres*
EMP: 38
SQ FT: 24,000
SALES: 6.8MM **Privately Held**
SIC: 3069 Pump sleeves, rubber

Cheshire
Gallia County

(G-3148)
HARSCO CORPORATION
5486 State Route 7 N (45620-9522)
P.O. Box 371 (45620-0371)
PHONE.....................740 367-7322
James D Taylor, *Manager*
EMP: 9
SQ FT: 300
SALES (corp-wide): 1.6B **Publicly Held**
SIC: 3295 Slag, crushed or ground
PA: Harsco Corporation
    350 Poplar Church Rd
    Camp Hill PA 17011
    717 763-7064

Chesterland
Geauga County

(G-3149)
ABA GUTTERS INC
13046 Cherry Ln (44026-3025)
PHONE.....................440 729-2177
Bruce Bakula, *President*
EMP: 3
SALES (est): 280K **Privately Held**
SIC: 3444 Gutters, sheet metal

(G-3150)
AEROSPACE MAINT SOLUTIONS LLC
8759 Mayfield Rd (44026-2674)
PHONE.....................440 729-7703
Andrea Rillahan, *Finance*
John P Dooley, *Mng Member*
Denette Ditmer, *Manager*
Barton Spears, *Manager*
Thomas Dooley,
▲ EMP: 25
SQ FT: 7,500
SALES (est): 6.2MM **Privately Held**
WEB: www.aerospacellc.com
SIC: 3728 Aircraft parts & equipment

(G-3151)
AEROTECH ENTERPRISE
8511 Mulberry Rd (44026-1437)
P.O. Box 596 (44026-0596)
PHONE.....................440 729-2616
Mike Matic, *President*
Andrea Matic, *Corp Secy*
EMP: 15
SQ FT: 6,000
SALES (est): 1.8MM **Privately Held**
SIC: 3599 Machine shop, jobbing & repair

(G-3152)
ALL FOR SHOW INC
9321 Winchester Vly (44026-3213)
PHONE.....................440 729-7186
Elaine L Sonnie, *President*

GEOGRAPHIC SECTION

Chillicothe - Ross County (G-3183)

Wallace Sonnie, *Principal*
EMP: 4
SALES (est): 163.6K **Privately Held**
SIC: 2395 Embroidery & art needlework

(G-3153)
AMERICAN GRPHCAL SFTWR SYSTEMS
Also Called: American Grphcal Sftwr Systems
8000 Wedgewood Dr (44026-2162)
PHONE 440 729-0018
Salvatore Totino, *President*
Amy I Totino, *Corp Secy*
EMP: 3
SALES (est): 217.8K **Privately Held**
SIC: 7372 Educational computer software

(G-3154)
CHESTERLAND NEWS INC
8389 Mayfield Rd Ste B-4 (44026-2553)
PHONE 440 729-7667
Pamela Gable, *President*
EMP: 12
SALES (est): 756.2K **Privately Held**
SIC: 2711 Newspapers: publishing only, not printed on site

(G-3155)
COMPUTER AIDED SOLUTIONS LLC
Also Called: Cas Data Loggers
8437 Mayfield Rd Ste 104a (44026-2538)
PHONE 440 729-2570
Laszlo Zala, *President*
Pete Martin,
Terry Nagy,
EMP: 20
SQ FT: 2,800
SALES: 4MM **Privately Held**
WEB: www.dataloggerinc.com
SIC: 3823 Data loggers, industrial process type

(G-3156)
DEGAETANO SALES
8408 Mayfield Rd (44026-2524)
PHONE 440 729-8877
Nicholas Degaetano, *President*
EMP: 3
SALES (est): 290K **Privately Held**
SIC: 3645 Chandeliers, residential

(G-3157)
ESSENCE MAKER
12819 Opalocka Dr (44026-2613)
PHONE 440 729-3894
Tracy Knake, *Principal*
EMP: 4 **EST:** 2010
SALES (est): 304.7K **Privately Held**
SIC: 2834 Dermatologicals

(G-3158)
HF GROUP
8844 Mayfield Rd (44026-2632)
PHONE 440 729-9411
Jim Brantton, *Vice Pres*
EMP: 45
SALES (est): 1.5MM **Privately Held**
SIC: 2789 Bookbinding & related work

(G-3159)
HF GROUP LLC (PA)
8844 Mayfield Rd (44026-2632)
PHONE 440 729-2445
Tim Baker, *Plant Mgr*
Jay B Fairfield, *Mng Member*
Steve Eisenberg,
EMP: 10
SQ FT: 6,000
SALES: 28MM **Privately Held**
SIC: 2789 Bookbinding & related work

(G-3160)
HF GROUP LLC
8844 Mayfield Rd (44026-2632)
PHONE 440 729-9411
Terry Hymas, *Branch Mgr*
EMP: 550
SALES (corp-wide): 28MM **Privately Held**
SIC: 2732 Books: printing & binding
PA: Hf Group, Llc
8844 Mayfield Rd
Chesterland OH 44026
440 729-2445

(G-3161)
HF GROUP LLC
Also Called: General Book Binding
8844 Mayfield Rd (44026-2632)
PHONE 440 729-9411
Jim Bratton, *Branch Mgr*
EMP: 62
SALES (corp-wide): 28MM **Privately Held**
SIC: 2732 Books: printing & binding
PA: Hf Group, Llc
8844 Mayfield Rd
Chesterland OH 44026
440 729-2445

(G-3162)
ICIBINDING CORPORATION (PA)
8834 Mayfield Rd Ste A (44026-2696)
PHONE 440 729-2445
Jay Fairfield, *President*
EMP: 20
SALES (est): 37.8MM **Privately Held**
SIC: 2789 Bookbinding & related work

(G-3163)
MEISTERMATIC INC
12446 Bentbrook Dr (44026-2459)
PHONE 216 481-7773
Edward Kurnava, *President*
Terry Kurnava, *Admin Sec*
EMP: 68 **EST:** 1963
SQ FT: 70,000
SALES (est): 8MM **Privately Held**
SIC: 3451 Screw machine products

(G-3164)
METZENBAUM SHELTERED INDS INC
Also Called: MSI
8090 Cedar Rd (44026-3400)
PHONE 440 729-1919
Robert Preston, *Chairman*
Robert Voss, *Manager*
Diane Buehner, *Admin Sec*
EMP: 160
SQ FT: 12,000
SALES: 2.3MM **Privately Held**
SIC: 8331 7389 3672 Sheltered workshop; packaging & labeling services; pre-sorted mail service; printed circuit boards

(G-3165)
MORNING GLORY TECHNOLOGIES
12826 Morning Glory Trl (44026-2927)
PHONE 440 796-5076
Anthony May, *Owner*
EMP: 11
SALES (est): 106K **Privately Held**
SIC: 3599 Industrial machinery

(G-3166)
NITROJECTION
8430 Mayfield Rd (44026-2580)
PHONE 440 834-8790
Ana Leben, *Principal*
EMP: 8
SALES (est): 1MM **Privately Held**
SIC: 3089 Injection molding of plastics

(G-3167)
ORGANON INC
7407 Cedar Rd (44026-3464)
PHONE 440 729-2290
EMP: 4
SALES (est): 337.2K **Privately Held**
SIC: 2834 Pharmaceutical preparations

(G-3168)
PATHOS LLC
Also Called: Pathos Printing
7948 Mayfield Rd (44026-2437)
PHONE 440 497-7278
Michael Ruddock,
EMP: 3
SALES (est): 71.1K **Privately Held**
SIC: 7372 Prepackaged software

(G-3169)
T A BACON CO
Also Called: Tabco
11655 Chillicothe Rd (44026-1927)
P.O. Box 21150, Cleveland (44121-0150)
PHONE 216 851-1404
Timothy Bacon, *President*

▲ **EMP:** 18
SQ FT: 45,000
SALES (est): 3.1MM **Privately Held**
WEB: www.tabcobodyparts.com
SIC: 3465 5013 Automotive stampings; automotive stampings

(G-3170)
TDM FUELCELL LLC TDM LLC
12144 W Shiloh Dr (44026-2241)
PHONE 440 969-1442
Daniel V Judy, *President*
EMP: 3
SQ FT: 1,000
SALES (est): 297.9K **Privately Held**
SIC: 3769 Casings, missiles & missile components: storage

(G-3171)
TRULINE INDUSTRIES INC
11685 Chillicothe Rd (44026-1927)
P.O. Box 307 (44026-0307)
PHONE 440 729-0140
Court Durkalski, *CEO*
Stuart Watson, *President*
Frank Durkalski, *Chairman*
Joan Durkalski, *Corp Secy*
Alan Linnington, *Manager*
EMP: 52 **EST:** 1939
SQ FT: 24,000
SALES (est): 9.7MM **Privately Held**
WEB: www.trulineind.com
SIC: 3728 Aircraft parts & equipment

(G-3172)
WESTERN RESERVE GRAPHICS
13404 Caves Rd (44026-3421)
PHONE 440 729-9527
Charles R Damko, *Owner*
EMP: 3
SALES: 150K **Privately Held**
SIC: 2752 Commercial printing, lithographic

Chillicothe
Ross County

(G-3173)
ADVANTAGE TENT FITTINGS INC
11661 Pleasant Valley Rd (45601-8315)
PHONE 740 773-3015
Robert Hall, *Ch of Bd*
Benjamin Hall, *President*
▼ **EMP:** 10
SQ FT: 14,000
SALES (est): 944K **Privately Held**
WEB: www.aadvantagetent.com
SIC: 2431 5091 2394 Millwork; sporting & recreation goods; canvas & related products

(G-3174)
ALL SIGNS OF CHILLICOTHE INC
12035 Pleasant Valley Rd (45601-9785)
PHONE 740 773-5016
Kristine M Oliver, *Manager*
Kris Oliver, *Executive*
EMP: 9
SALES (est): 1.2MM **Privately Held**
WEB: www.allsignsofohio.com
SIC: 3993 1799 Electric signs; sign installation & maintenance

(G-3175)
ARCHER-DANIELS-MIDLAND COMPANY
Also Called: ADM
331 S Watt St (45601-3648)
P.O. Box 2070 (45601-8070)
PHONE 740 702-6179
EMP: 10
SALES (corp-wide): 60.8B **Publicly Held**
SIC: 2041 Farm Product Warehousing
PA: Archer-Daniels-Midland Company
77 W Wacker Dr Ste 4600
Chicago IL 60601
312 634-8100

(G-3176)
BBB MUSIC LLC
20 E Water St (45601-2534)
PHONE 740 772-2262
Bob Green,
Sarah Lambert,
EMP: 8
SALES: 300K **Privately Held**
SIC: 3931 5736 Musical instruments; musical instrument stores

(G-3177)
BELL LOGISTICS CO
27311 Old Route 35 (45601-8110)
P.O. Box 91 (45601-0091)
PHONE 740 702-9830
Jon Bell, *President*
Deana Bell, *Vice Pres*
EMP: 30
SQ FT: 25,000
SALES: 10MM **Privately Held**
SIC: 3715 Truck trailers

(G-3178)
BROCK RAD & WLDG FABRICATION
Also Called: Brocks RAD Wldg Fabrication I
370 Douglas Ave (45601-3662)
PHONE 740 773-2540
David J Brock, *President*
Nancy Brock, *Corp Secy*
EMP: 8
SQ FT: 12,000
SALES (est): 1.2MM **Privately Held**
SIC: 7539 7692 Radiator repair shop, automotive; automotive welding

(G-3179)
CAPITAL MACHINE & FABRICATION
162 Commercial Cir (45601-3673)
PHONE 740 773-4976
Royce Rinehart, *Owner*
EMP: 5
SALES (est): 395.7K **Privately Held**
SIC: 3599 Machine shop, jobbing & repair

(G-3180)
CHILLICOTHE PACKAGING CORP
Also Called: Churmac Industries
4168 State Route 159 (45601-8695)
P.O. Box 466 (45601-0466)
PHONE 740 773-5800
Michael McCarty, *President*
EMP: 40
SQ FT: 60,000
SALES (est): 8.8MM **Privately Held**
SIC: 2653 Boxes, corrugated: made from purchased materials

(G-3181)
CHUB GIBSONS LOGGING
391 Fyffe Hollow Rd (45601-7803)
PHONE 740 884-4079
EMP: 4 **EST:** 2005
SALES: 230K **Privately Held**
SIC: 2411 Logging

(G-3182)
CHURMAC INDUSTRIES INC
Also Called: Chillicothe Packing
4168 State Route 159 (45601-8695)
P.O. Box 205 (45601-0205)
PHONE 740 773-5800
Michael McCarty, *President*
EMP: 25
SQ FT: 60,000
SALES (est): 3.7MM **Privately Held**
SIC: 2631 Paperboard mills

(G-3183)
CRISPIE CREME OF CHILLICOTHE
Also Called: Grandpa Jack's
47 N Bridge St (45601-2615)
PHONE 740 774-3770
Richard Renison, *President*
James M Renison, *Vice Pres*
EMP: 36
SQ FT: 2,500
SALES: 500K **Privately Held**
SIC: 2051 5461 Doughnuts, except frozen; doughnuts

(PA)=Parent Co (HQ)=Headquarters (DH)=Div Headquarters
✪ = New Business established in last 2 years

Chillicothe - Ross County (G-3184)

(G-3184)
DEWARD PUBLISHING CO LTD
278 Scott Rd (45601-9183)
PHONE 800 300-9778
Daniel Degarmo, *Principal*
Dan Degarmo, *Business Mgr*
EMP: 4
SALES (est): 264.5K **Privately Held**
SIC: 2741 Miscellaneous publishing

(G-3185)
DOUGLAS INDUSTRIES LLC
379 Douglas Ave (45601-3663)
P.O. Box 6188 (45601-6188)
PHONE 740 775-2400
Gloria Eyre,
Larry Eyre,
EMP: 24
SALES (est): 4.2MM **Privately Held**
SIC: 3272 Concrete products

(G-3186)
G & J ASPHALT & MATERIAL INC
379 Seney Rd (45601-8396)
PHONE 740 773-6358
Chad Jordan, *President*
Tricia Pardfard, *Admin Sec*
EMP: 12
SALES (est): 2.3MM **Privately Held**
SIC: 3531 Asphalt plant, including gravel-mix type

(G-3187)
G & J PEPSI-COLA BOTTLERS INC
Also Called: Pepsico
400 E 7th St (45601-3455)
PHONE 740 774-2148
Henry Thrapp, *Sales & Mktg St*
John Miller, *Finance Mgr*
EMP: 45
SALES (corp-wide): 418.3MM **Privately Held**
WEB: www.gjpepsi.com
SIC: 5149 2086 Starch; bottled & canned soft drinks
PA: G & J Pepsi-Cola Bottlers Inc
9435 Waterstone Blvd # 390
Cincinnati OH 45249
513 785-6060

(G-3188)
GANNETT CO INC
Also Called: Chillicothe Gazette
50 W Main St (45601-3103)
PHONE 740 773-2111
Mike Therone, *Principal*
EMP: 108
SALES (corp-wide): 2.9B **Publicly Held**
WEB: www.gannett.com
SIC: 2711 2752 Newspapers: publishing only, not printed on site; commercial printing, lithographic
PA: Gannett Co., Inc.
7950 Jones Branch Dr
Mc Lean VA 22102
703 854-6000

(G-3189)
GILLS PETROLEUM LLC
213 S Paint St (45601-3828)
PHONE 740 702-2600
Barry Rahe, *Principal*
EMP: 4
SALES (est): 99.1K **Privately Held**
SIC: 1381 Drilling oil & gas wells

(G-3190)
GRAPHIC PLUS
712 Overlook Heights Ln (45601-8452)
PHONE 740 701-1860
Marsha Landrum, *Owner*
EMP: 3
SALES (est): 227.9K **Privately Held**
SIC: 2759 Screen printing

(G-3191)
HANSON AGGREGATES EAST LLC
Hanson Aggregates Davon
33 Renick Ave (45601-2895)
PHONE 740 773-2172
Leonard McFerren, *Manager*
EMP: 25
SALES (corp-wide): 20.6B **Privately Held**
SIC: 3273 3271 3272 1442 Ready-mixed concrete; blocks, concrete or cinder: standard; concrete products; construction sand & gravel
HQ: Hanson Aggregates East Llc
3131 Rdu Center Dr
Morrisville NC 27560
919 380-2500

(G-3192)
HERR FOODS INCORPORATED
476 E 7th St (45601-3455)
PHONE 740 773-8282
Shawn Martindale, *General Mgr*
Scott Carmenan, *Sales/Mktg Mgr*
EMP: 40
SQ FT: 1,000
SALES (corp-wide): 436.1MM **Privately Held**
WEB: www.herrs.com
SIC: 2096 Potato chips & other potato-based snacks
PA: Herr Foods Incorporated
20 Herr Dr
Nottingham PA 19362
610 932-9330

(G-3193)
HUSTON GIFTS DOLLS AND FLOWERS
Also Called: Huston Gift Shop
306 Fairway Ave (45601-1258)
PHONE 740 775-9141
Pamela Caldwell, *President*
James M Caldwell, *Vice Pres*
EMP: 3
SQ FT: 1,200
SALES (est): 160K **Privately Held**
SIC: 5947 3942 5992 5092 Gift shop; dolls, except stuffed toy animals; flowers, fresh; plants, potted; dolls, flowers, fresh

(G-3194)
INFOSIGHT CORPORATION
20700 Us Highway 23 (45601-9016)
P.O. Box 5000 (45601-7000)
PHONE 740 642-3600
John A Robertson, *CEO*
G D Hudelson, *President*
John Redfearn, *General Mgr*
Darren Givens, *Project Mgr*
Chris Speakman, *Mfg Staff*
▲ **EMP:** 65
SQ FT: 30,000
SALES: 16MM **Privately Held**
WEB: www.infosight.com
SIC: 3953 Figures (marking devices), metal

(G-3195)
INGLE-BARR INC (PA)
Also Called: Ibi
20 Plyleys Ln (45601-2005)
PHONE 740 702-6117
Jeffrey Poole, *President*
Rod Poole, *Vice Pres*
Mike Moss, *Sr Project Mgr*
Steve Bettendorf, *Technology*
EMP: 130
SQ FT: 6,500
SALES (est): 19.4MM **Privately Held**
WEB: www.4ibi.com
SIC: 1521 1541 1542 1389 General remodeling, single-family houses; renovation, remodeling & repairs: industrial buildings; steel building construction; commercial & office building, new construction; commercial & office buildings, renovation & repair; construction, repair & dismantling services; construction management

(G-3196)
JASON C GIBSON
414 Bethel Rd (45601-8060)
PHONE 740 663-4520
Jason C Gibson, *Owner*
EMP: 13
SALES (est): 900K **Privately Held**
SIC: 2411 Logging

(G-3197)
JIM BUMEN CONSTRUCTION COMPANY (PA)
3218 S Bridge St (45601-9361)
PHONE 740 663-2659
James Bumen, *President*
Jane Bumen, *Vice Pres*
Julie Stewart, *Admin Sec*
EMP: 6
SALES (est): 745.6K **Privately Held**
SIC: 3272 1542 1541 Concrete products, precast; commercial & office building, new construction; industrial buildings, new construction

(G-3198)
KITCHEN COLLECTION LLC (HQ)
Also Called: Le Gourmet Chef
71 E Water St (45601-2577)
PHONE 740 773-9150
Gregory H Trepp, *President*
Michelle Dech, *Regional Mgr*
Daniel Russeau, *Regional Mgr*
Carla Ison, *Vice Pres*
Emil Wepprich, *Vice Pres*
▲ **EMP:** 82
SQ FT: 10,000
SALES (est): 740.7MM **Publicly Held**
WEB: www.kitchencollection.com
SIC: 3634 5719 Toasters, electric: household; ovens, portable: household; irons, electric: household; coffee makers, electric: household; kitchenware
PA: Hamilton Beach Brands Holding Company
4421 Waterfront Dr
Glen Allen VA 23060
804 273-9777

(G-3199)
M & M FABRICATION INC
18828 Us Highway 50 (45601-9268)
PHONE 740 779-3071
Gary Timmons, *President*
EMP: 10
SALES (est): 2MM **Privately Held**
SIC: 3441 Building components, structural steel

(G-3200)
MISCELLNOUS MTALS FBRCTION INC
18828 Us Highway 50 (45601-9268)
PHONE 740 779-3071
Robert J Onda, *President*
EMP: 4
SALES (est): 448.9K **Privately Held**
SIC: 3499 Friction material, made from powdered metal

(G-3201)
NACCO INDUSTRIES INC
71 E Water St (45601-2535)
PHONE 740 773-9150
Alfred M Rankin Jr, *Branch Mgr*
EMP: 47
SALES (corp-wide): 104.7MM **Publicly Held**
SIC: 3634 Electric household cooking appliances
PA: Nacco Industries, Inc.
5875 Landerbrook Dr # 220
Cleveland OH 44124
440 229-5151

(G-3202)
NAW PETROLEUM SERVICE
208 Copperfield Dr (45601-8609)
PHONE 740 464-7988
Wilby A Nelson, *Owner*
EMP: 4
SALES: 830K **Privately Held**
SIC: 1389 Construction, repair & dismantling services

(G-3203)
ORBIS RPM LLC
5938 State Route 159 (45601-8956)
PHONE 740 772-6355
Scott Smittle, *General Mgr*
EMP: 5
SALES (corp-wide): 1.7B **Privately Held**
WEB: www.orbiscorporation.com
SIC: 3081 Unsupported plastics film & sheet
HQ: Orbis Rpm, Llc
1055 Corporate Center Dr
Oconomowoc WI 53066
262 560-5000

(G-3204)
P H GLATFELTER COMPANY
Also Called: Chillicothe Facility
232 E 8th St (45601-3364)
PHONE 740 772-3111
John R Blind, *Vice Pres*
Michelle Corcoran, *Safety Mgr*
Tammy Tackett, *Buyer*
Donald Kasik, *QC Mgr*
Ron Dalton, *Engineer*
EMP: 100
SALES (corp-wide): 866.2MM **Publicly Held**
SIC: 2621 Book paper; copy paper; envelope paper; filter paper
PA: P. H. Glatfelter Company
96 S George St Ste 520
York PA 17401
717 225-4711

(G-3205)
PACCAR INC
65 Kenworth Dr (45601-8829)
P.O. Box 2345 (45601-0998)
PHONE 740 774-5111
Carl Carter, *Engineer*
Doug Littick, *Manager*
Larry Jett, *Supervisor*
EMP: 2000
SALES (corp-wide): 23.5B **Publicly Held**
WEB: www.paccar.com
SIC: 3711 3715 3713 Truck & tractor truck assembly; truck trailers; truck & bus bodies
PA: Paccar Inc
777 106th Ave Ne
Bellevue WA 98004
425 468-7400

(G-3206)
PARRY CO
33630 Old Route 35 (45601-9117)
PHONE 740 884-4893
Dave Merideth, *President*
Cassandra Bolt-Merideth, *Vice Pres*
EMP: 9 **EST:** 1936
SQ FT: 30,000
SALES (est): 870K **Privately Held**
WEB: www.parryco.com
SIC: 1446 Industrial sand

(G-3207)
PEGASUS INDUSTRIES
104 S Mcarthur St (45601-3600)
PHONE 740 772-1049
Gwen Van Horn, *Principal*
EMP: 5
SALES (est): 248.7K **Privately Held**
SIC: 3999 Manufacturing industries

(G-3208)
PELLETIER BROTHERS MFG
4000 Sulphur Lick Rd (45601-8972)
PHONE 740 774-4704
Chris Pelletier, *President*
Mark Pelletier, *Vice Pres*
EMP: 16
SQ FT: 7,000
SALES (est): 2.6MM **Privately Held**
SIC: 3312 Ferroalloys, produced in blast furnaces

(G-3209)
PERKINS LOGGING LLC
361 Perkins Rd (45601-9501)
PHONE 740 288-7311
Roger Perkins,
EMP: 4
SALES: 1.8MM **Privately Held**
SIC: 2411 Logging camps & contractors

(G-3210)
PERKINS WOOD PRODUCTS
8686 Limerick Rd (45601-9508)
PHONE 740 884-4046
EMP: 8

GEOGRAPHIC SECTION

Cincinnati - Clermont County (G-3236)

SALES (est): 440K **Privately Held**
SIC: 2411 Logging

(G-3211)
PITTSBURGH GLASS WORKS LLC
850 Southern Ave (45601-9123)
PHONE.................................740 774-8762
Joe Stas, *Branch Mgr*
Gene Hoyet,
EMP: 12 **Privately Held**
SIC: 3211 5013 Flat glass; automobile glass
HQ: Pittsburgh Glass Works, Llc
30 Isabella St Ste 500
Pittsburgh PA 15212

(G-3212)
PPG INDUSTRIES INC
Also Called: PPG Chillicothe
848 Southern Ave (45601-9123)
PHONE.................................740 774-8734
Amanda Moore, *Accountant*
EMP: 9
SALES (corp-wide): 15.3B **Publicly Held**
SIC: 2851 Paints & allied products
PA: Ppg Industries, Inc.
1 Ppg Pl
Pittsburgh PA 15272
412 434-3131

(G-3213)
PPG INDUSTRIES INC
Also Called: PPG Regional Support Center
848 Southern Ave (45601-9123)
PHONE.................................740 774-7600
Melissa Wills, *Manager*
EMP: 37
SALES (corp-wide): 15.3B **Publicly Held**
SIC: 2851 Paints & allied products
PA: Ppg Industries, Inc.
1 Ppg Pl
Pittsburgh PA 15272
412 434-3131

(G-3214)
PPG INDUSTRIES INC
Also Called: P P G Regional Support Center
848 Southern Ave (45601-9123)
P.O. Box 7025 (45601)
PHONE.................................740 774-7600
EMP: 14
SALES (corp-wide): 15.3B **Publicly Held**
SIC: 2851 Paints & allied products
PA: Ppg Industries, Inc.
1 Ppg Pl
Pittsburgh PA 15272
412 434-3131

(G-3215)
PPG INDUSTRIES INC
848 Southern Ave (45601-9123)
P.O. Box 7011 (45601)
PHONE.................................740 774-7600
EMP: 6
SALES (corp-wide): 15.3B **Publicly Held**
SIC: 2851 Paints & allied products
PA: Ppg Industries, Inc.
1 Ppg Pl
Pittsburgh PA 15272
412 434-3131

(G-3216)
PRC - DESOTO INTERNATIONAL INC
Also Called: PRC Desoto International
848 Southern Ave (45601-9123)
PHONE.................................800 772-9378
EMP: 37
SALES (corp-wide): 15.3B **Publicly Held**
SIC: 2891 Adhesives & sealants
HQ: Prc - Desoto International, Inc.
24811 Ave Rockefeller
Valencia CA 91355
661 678-4209

(G-3217)
PRINTEX INCORPORATED (PA)
Also Called: Printex-Same Day Printing
185 E Main St (45601-2507)
P.O. Box 1626 (45601-5626)
PHONE.................................740 773-0088
Jeffrey G Marshall, *President*
Gene T Marshall, *Vice Pres*
Janet Fox, *Manager*
Brenda Ison, *Manager*
EMP: 10
SQ FT: 3,000
SALES (est): 1.6MM **Privately Held**
SIC: 2732 2759 2752 Books: printing only; letterpress printing; commercial printing, offset

(G-3218)
QC INDUSTRIAL INC
526 Red Bud Rd (45601-9002)
PHONE.................................740 642-5004
Cyndi Davis, *General Mgr*
EMP: 5
SALES (est): 584.7K **Privately Held**
SIC: 3441 Fabricated structural metal

(G-3219)
R L S CORPORATION
Also Called: R L S Recycling
990 Eastern Ave (45601-3658)
P.O. Box 327 (45601-0327)
PHONE.................................740 773-1440
Charles Stevens, *President*
EMP: 25 **EST:** 1923
SQ FT: 14,000
SALES (est): 3.3MM **Privately Held**
SIC: 5093 3341 Metal scrap & waste materials; waste paper; secondary nonferrous metals

(G-3220)
RIFFLE MACHINE WORKS INC (PA)
Also Called: Riffle & Sons
5746 State Route 159 (45601-8956)
PHONE.................................740 775-2838
Bob Riffle, *President*
Mark Riffle, *Vice Pres*
Mike Riffle, *Vice Pres*
Tim Riffle, *Vice Pres*
Joe Harvey, *Manager*
EMP: 12
SQ FT: 3,500
SALES (est): 2.7MM **Privately Held**
SIC: 3599 Machine shop, jobbing & repair

(G-3221)
ROSS-CO REDI-MIX CO INC (PA)
689 Marietta Rd (45601-8437)
PHONE.................................740 775-4466
Todd Wrightsel, *President*
Thomas Overly, *Principal*
Connie Wrightsel, *Corp Secy*
EMP: 35 **EST:** 1962
SQ FT: 2,400
SALES (est): 5.8MM **Privately Held**
SIC: 3273 Ready-mixed concrete

(G-3222)
SHELLY MATERIALS INC
1177 Hopetown Rd (45601-8224)
PHONE.................................740 775-4567
Rusty Scott, *Manager*
EMP: 19
SALES (corp-wide): 29.7B **Privately Held**
SIC: 1442 Gravel mining
HQ: Shelly Materials, Inc.
80 Park Dr
Thornville OH 43076
740 246-6315

(G-3223)
STANDARD CAR TRUCK COMPANY
Also Called: Barber Spring Ohio
387 Wetzel Dr (45601-2873)
P.O. Box 243 (45601-0243)
PHONE.................................740 775-6450
Scott Diehl, *Branch Mgr*
EMP: 75
SALES (corp-wide): 4.3B **Publicly Held**
SIC: 3549 3677 3743 Coil winding machines for springs; electronic coils, transformers & other inductors; freight cars & equipment
HQ: Standard Car Truck Company Inc
6400 Shafer Ct Ste 450
Rosemont IL 60018
847 692-6050

(G-3224)
STAT INDUSTRIES INC (PA)
Also Called: Stat Index Tab
137 Stone Rd (45601-9709)
PHONE.................................740 779-6561
Robert Kellough, *CEO*
Chris Kellough, *Principal*
Susanna Kellough, *CFO*
EMP: 7
SQ FT: 6,000
SALES (est): 930K **Privately Held**
WEB: www.statindex.com
SIC: 2675 Index cards, die-cut: made from purchased materials

(G-3225)
STAT INDUSTRIES INC
Also Called: Stat Index Tab Company
137 Stone Rd (45601-9709)
PHONE.................................740 779-6561
Robert Kellough, *President*
EMP: 6
SALES (corp-wide): 930K **Privately Held**
WEB: www.statindex.com
SIC: 2675 Index cards, die-cut: made from purchased materials
PA: Stat Industries, Inc.
137 Stone Rd
Chillicothe OH 45601
740 779-6561

(G-3226)
SUPER FINE SHINE INC
2806 Patton Hill Rd Lot 6 (45601-3763)
PHONE.................................740 774-1700
Philip Velez, *Principal*
EMP: 5
SALES (est): 315.5K **Privately Held**
SIC: 3471 Electroplating of metals or formed products

(G-3227)
TECHNOLOGY AND SERVICES INC
1336 Baum Hill Rd (45601-9179)
PHONE.................................740 626-2020
John Parks, *CEO*
Richmond Parks, *Treasurer*
▼ EMP: 8
SQ FT: 7,000
SALES (est): 1.4MM **Privately Held**
WEB: www.technologyandservices.com
SIC: 3953 7371 Marking devices; custom computer programming services

(G-3228)
TRIM SYSTEMS OPERATING CORP
75 Chamber Dr (45601-7612)
PHONE.................................740 772-5998
Patrick Turner, *Plant Mgr*
Eric Conley, *Branch Mgr*
EMP: 178
SALES (corp-wide): 897.7MM **Publicly Held**
SIC: 2396 Automotive & apparel trimmings
HQ: Trim Systems Operating Corp.
7800 Walton Pkwy
New Albany OH 43054
614 289-5360

(G-3229)
TRUGREEN CLEANERS LLC
1733 Anderson Station Rd (45601-7909)
PHONE.................................740 703-1063
Francis L Breeden,
EMP: 3
SALES (est): 198.2K **Privately Held**
SIC: 2869 Industrial organic chemicals

(G-3230)
TYKMA INC
Also Called: Tykma Electrox
370 Gateway Dr (45601-3976)
P.O. Box 917 (45601-0917)
PHONE.................................877 318-9562
David Grimes, *President*
Cindy Quesinberry, *COO*
Rick Weisbarth, *Vice Pres*
Chris Tipton, *Production*
Mark Bragg, *Engineer*
EMP: 53 **EST:** 2000
SQ FT: 50,000
SALES: 9.4MM
SALES (corp-wide): 66MM **Privately Held**
WEB: www.permanentmarking.com
SIC: 3541 3555 Machine tools, metal cutting type; engraving machinery & equipment, except plates

PA: 600 Group Public Limited Company(The)
Union Street
Heckmondwike WF16
192 441-5000

(G-3231)
YSK CORPORATION
1 Colomet Rd (45601-8819)
PHONE.................................740 774-7315
Kenzaburo Matsuo, *President*
Reiichi Hohda, *President*
Sandy Hoffman, *Manager*
H Naiki, *Admin Sec*
Tom Hargett, *Maintence Staff*
▲ EMP: 279
SQ FT: 200,000
SALES (est): 61.6MM
SALES (corp-wide): 301.1MM **Privately Held**
WEB: www.yskcorp.com
SIC: 3469 Machine parts, stamped or pressed metal; household cooking & kitchen utensils, metal
PA: Yanagawa Seiki Co., Ltd.
1-3-5, Shinsayama
Sayama STM 350-1
429 535-151

Cincinnati
Clermont County

(G-3232)
5ME LLC
4270 Ivy Pointe Blvd # 100 (45245-0004)
PHONE.................................513 719-1600
William A Horwarth, *President*
Jeffery Price, *Vice Pres*
Chris Chapman, *CFO*
EMP: 45
SALES (est): 9.1MM
SALES (corp-wide): 9.9MM **Privately Held**
SIC: 3544 8742 Special dies, tools, jigs & fixtures; business consultant
PA: 5me Holdings Llc
4270 Ivy Pointe Blvd # 100
Cincinnati OH 45245
859 534-4872

(G-3233)
5ME HOLDINGS LLC (PA)
4270 Ivy Pointe Blvd # 100 (45245-0003)
PHONE.................................859 534-4872
William A Horwarth, *President*
EMP: 1
SALES: 9.9MM **Privately Held**
SIC: 3544 8742 Special dies, tools, jigs & fixtures; business consultant

(G-3234)
A & P TECHNOLOGY INC
4599 E Tech Dr (45245)
PHONE.................................513 688-3200
Andrew Head, *President*
Keith Cnarr, *Manager*
EMP: 26 **Privately Held**
SIC: 2241 Webbing, braids & belting
PA: A & P Technology, Inc.
4595 E Tech Dr
Cincinnati OH 45245

(G-3235)
A & P TECHNOLOGY INC
4622 E Tech Dr (45245-1000)
PHONE.................................513 688-3200
Andrew Head, *President*
EMP: 99
SALES (est): 2.9MM **Privately Held**
SIC: 2241 Narrow fabric mills

(G-3236)
A & P TECHNOLOGY INC
4578 E Tech Dr (45245-1054)
PHONE.................................513 688-3200
Andrew Head, *President*
EMP: 99 **EST:** 2013
SALES (est): 3MM **Privately Held**
SIC: 2241 Narrow fabric mills

(PA)=Parent Co (HQ)=Headquarters (DH)=Div Headquarters
◊ = New Business established in last 2 years

Cincinnati - Clermont County (G-3237)

(G-3237)
A & P TECHNOLOGY INC
4624 E Tech Dr (45245)
PHONE.................................513 688-3200
Rhonda Slominski, *Branch Mgr*
EMP: 31
SQ FT: 1,880 **Privately Held**
WEB: www.braider.com
SIC: 2241 Narrow fabric mills
PA: A & P Technology, Inc.
  4595 E Tech Dr
  Cincinnati OH 45245

(G-3238)
A & P TECHNOLOGY INC (PA)
4595 E Tech Dr (45245-1055)
PHONE.................................513 688-3200
Andrew A Head, *President*
Timothy Lofton, *Prdtn Mgr*
Nathan Jessie, *Engineer*
David J Kehrl, *Engineer*
Brandon Strohminger, *Engineer*
▲ EMP: 20
SQ FT: 75,000
SALES (est): 49.6MM **Privately Held**
WEB: www.braider.com
SIC: 2241 Webbing, braids & belting

(G-3239)
ADGO INCORPORATED
3988 Mcmann Rd (45245-2308)
PHONE.................................513 752-6880
Robert C Reynolds, *President*
Mike Cliett, *COO*
Rick Elliott, *Vice Pres*
Lynn Green, *Sales Mgr*
Kelly Throckmorton, *Bd of Directors*
EMP: 23 EST: 1957
SQ FT: 30,000
SALES (est): 7.1MM **Privately Held**
WEB: www.adgoinc.com
SIC: 3613 Control panels, electric

(G-3240)
ALUFAB INC
1018 Seabrook Way (45245-1963)
PHONE.................................513 528-7281
Doug Nimmo, *President*
Fred Mileham, *Vice Pres*
▲ EMP: 6
SQ FT: 4,000
SALES: 2.2MM **Privately Held**
SIC: 3441 Fabricated structural metal

(G-3241)
BEACHS TREES SELECTIVE HARVEST
915 Wilma Cir (45245-2220)
PHONE.................................513 289-5976
Brian Beach, *Principal*
Mike Beach,
Steve Beach,
EMP: 15 EST: 2013
SQ FT: 2,500
SALES (est): 957.1K **Privately Held**
SIC: 2411 Logging camps & contractors

(G-3242)
CGH-GLOBAL EMERG MNGMT STRATEG
Also Called: Cgh Global
851 Ohio Pike Ste 203 (45245-2203)
PHONE.................................800 376-0655
Andrew Glassmeyer, *CEO*
Eric Mitchell, *President*
EMP: 48 EST: 2011
SALES: 180.2K
SALES (corp-wide): 8MM **Privately Held**
SIC: 8711 8322 1389 0851 Fire protection engineering; emergency social services; fire fighting, oil & gas field; fire fighting services, forest; fire prevention services, forest
PA: Cgh-Global, Llc
  851 Ohio Pike Ste 203
  Cincinnati OH 45245
  800 376-0655

(G-3243)
CLIPPER PRODUCTS INC
675 Cncnnati Batavia Pike (45245-1028)
PHONE.................................513 688-7300
Gerold J Zobrist, *Ch of Bd*
David J Durham, *President*
EMP: 6

SQ FT: 16,000
SALES: 360K **Privately Held**
WEB: www.clipperproducts.com
SIC: 3161 Cases, carrying; sample cases

(G-3244)
CURTISS-WRIGHT FLOW CONTROL
Also Called: Qualtech NP
4600 E Tech Dr (45245-1000)
PHONE.................................513 528-7900
Kurt Mitchell, *Branch Mgr*
EMP: 88
SALES (corp-wide): 2.4B **Publicly Held**
SIC: 3491 8734 3441 Industrial valves; testing laboratories; fabricated structural metal
HQ: Curtiss-Wright Flow Control Service Corporation
  2950 E Birch St
  Brea CA 92821
  714 982-1898

(G-3245)
CURTISS-WRIGHT FLOW CTRL CORP
Also Called: Qualtech NP
4600 E Tech Dr (45245-1000)
PHONE.................................513 528-7900
Wayne Laib, *Chief Engr*
David Holmes, *Controller*
Marion Mitchell, *Branch Mgr*
Michael Bell, *Supervisor*
Brett Runyon, *Administration*
EMP: 82
SALES (corp-wide): 2.4B **Publicly Held**
SIC: 3443 8734 Fabricated plate work (boiler shop); testing laboratories
HQ: Curtiss-Wright Flow Control Service, Llc
  1966 Broadhollow Rd Ste E
  Farmingdale NY 11735
  631 293-3800

(G-3246)
DRS MOBILE ENVIRONMNTL SVC
4043 Mcmann Rd (45245-1960)
PHONE.................................513 943-1111
Rich Reynolds, *Principal*
Brian Weyant, *Director*
EMP: 5
SALES (est): 442.4K **Privately Held**
SIC: 3812 Search & navigation equipment

(G-3247)
ELECTRODYNAMICS INC
Also Called: L-3 Cmmnctions Electrodynamics
3975 Mcmann Rd (45245-2307)
PHONE.................................847 259-0740
Donald A Spetter, *President*
Steven M Post, *Senior VP*
Stephen Post, *Admin Sec*
EMP: 195
SQ FT: 46,000
SALES (est): 37.6MM
SALES (corp-wide): 10.2B **Publicly Held**
SIC: 3577 3812 3824 3823 Data conversion equipment, media-to-media: computer; flight recorders; controls, revolution & timing instruments; counter type registers; industrial instrmnts msrmnt display/control process variable; relays & industrial controls
PA: L3 Technologies, Inc.
  600 3rd Ave Fl 34
  New York NY 10016
  212 697-1111

(G-3248)
ELITE BIOMEDICAL SOLUTIONS LLC
756 Old State Route 74 C (45245-1277)
PHONE.................................513 207-0602
Jeff Smith, *Mng Member*
Jeremy Borggren, *Manager*
Jeff Diesel, *Supervisor*
Nate Smith,
EMP: 13
SALES (est): 3.5MM **Privately Held**
SIC: 3841 7699 7389 Surgical & medical instruments; medical equipment repair, non-electric;

(G-3249)
EMITTED ENERGY INC
754 Cincinnati Batavia Pi (45245-1275)
PHONE.................................513 752-9999
Debbie Vanover, *Administration*
EMP: 3
SALES (corp-wide): 2.1MM **Privately Held**
SIC: 3641 Electric lamps
PA: Emitted Energy, Inc.
  6559 Diplomat Dr
  Sterling Heights MI 48314
  855 752-3347

(G-3250)
FUNTOWN PLAYGROUNDS INC
839 Cypresspoint Ct (45245-3352)
PHONE.................................513 871-8585
Orville Wright, *President*
Marty Kremer, *Vice Pres*
EMP: 25
SALES (est): 2MM **Privately Held**
SIC: 3949 Playground equipment

(G-3251)
GBC INTERNATIONAL LLC
1091 Ohio Pike (45245-2339)
PHONE.................................513 943-7283
Michael R Adams, *Principal*
EMP: 3
SALES (est): 120.7K **Privately Held**
SIC: 2653 Corrugated & solid fiber boxes

(G-3252)
GENERAL DATA COMPANY INC (PA)
4354 Ferguson Dr (45245-1667)
P.O. Box 541165 (45254-1165)
PHONE.................................513 752-7978
Peter Wenzel, *President*
Jim Burns, *Vice Pres*
Tom Maue, *Safety Mgr*
Amy Clark, *Purchasing*
Rhonda Utley, *Purchasing*
▲ EMP: 230 EST: 1980
SQ FT: 45,000
SALES (est): 62.5MM **Privately Held**
WEB: www.general-data.com
SIC: 2679 5046 5084 2759 Labels, paper; made from purchased material; commercial equipment; printing trades machinery, equipment & supplies; commercial printing; surgical & medical instruments; unsupported plastics film & sheet

(G-3253)
GENERAL DATA HEALTHCARE INC
4043 Mcmann Rd (45245-1960)
PHONE.................................513 752-7978
Peter Wenzel, *CEO*
EMP: 7
SALES (est): 927.1K **Privately Held**
SIC: 3565 Labeling machines, industrial

(G-3254)
HAWKS & ASSOCIATES INC
Also Called: Hawks Tag
1029 Seabrook Way (45245-1964)
P.O. Box 541207 (45254-1207)
PHONE.................................513 752-4311
James M Hawks, *President*
Mike Bauer, *Sales Executive*
Dave Hawks, *Info Tech Mgr*
EMP: 28 EST: 1973
SQ FT: 15,000
SALES: 5.8MM **Privately Held**
WEB: www.hawkstag.com
SIC: 2759 2752 Flexographic printing; commercial printing, lithographic

(G-3255)
HUNTER DEFENSE TECH INC
1032 Seabrook Way (45245-1963)
PHONE.................................513 943-7880
Sean Bond, *President*
Angela Cowan, *Branch Mgr*
EMP: 150 **Privately Held**
SIC: 3812 Search & navigation equipment
PA: Hunter Defense Technologies, Inc.
  30500 Aurora Rd Ste 100
  Solon OH 44139

(G-3256)
KYOCERA SENCO INDUS TLS INC (HQ)
4270 Ivy Pointe Blvd (45245-0003)
PHONE.................................800 543-4596
Benjamin C Johansen, *CEO*
Cliff Mentrup, *Vice Pres*
Mike Desmond, *Design Engr*
Eric Habermehl, *Marketing Staff*
Ken Leadmon, *Manager*
EMP: 19
SALES (est): 137.6MM
SALES (corp-wide): 14.8B **Publicly Held**
SIC: 3452 3553 Screws, metal; furniture makers' machinery, woodworking
PA: Kyocera Corporation
  6, Tobadonocho, Takeda, Fushimi-Ku
  Kyoto KYO 612-8
  756 043-500

(G-3257)
L3 FUZING AND ORD SYSTEMS INC
Also Called: L-3 Fuzing and Ord Systems Inc
3975 Mcmann Rd (45245-2307)
PHONE.................................513 943-2000
Michael T Strianese, *CEO*
Eric Ellis, *President*
Curtis Brunson, *Exec VP*
Richard A Cody, *Senior VP*
Steven M Post, *Senior VP*
EMP: 575 EST: 1967
SQ FT: 236,000
SALES: 224.8MM
SALES (corp-wide): 10.2B **Publicly Held**
SIC: 3483 Arming & fusing devices for missiles
PA: L3 Technologies, Inc.
  600 3rd Ave Fl 34
  New York NY 10016
  212 697-1111

(G-3258)
L3 TECHNOLOGIES INC
Electro Fab Division
3975 Mcmann Rd (45245-2307)
PHONE.................................513 943-2000
Charls King, *General Mgr*
EMP: 40
SALES (corp-wide): 10.2B **Publicly Held**
WEB: www.l3circuitboards.com
SIC: 3672 Printed circuit boards
PA: L3 Technologies, Inc.
  600 3rd Ave Fl 34
  New York NY 10016
  212 697-1111

(G-3259)
LINTECH ELECTRONICS LLC
4435 Aicholtz Rd Ste 500 (45245-1692)
P.O. Box 54436 (45254-0436)
PHONE.................................513 528-6190
John Rathbone, *Vice Pres*
Linda Rathbone,
EMP: 12
SALES (est): 1.8MM **Privately Held**
WEB: www.lintech-electronics.com
SIC: 8711 3679 Electrical or electronic engineering; electronic circuits

(G-3260)
ORIGINAL MATTRESS FACTORY INC
4450 Eastgate Blvd # 265 (45245-1532)
PHONE.................................513 752-6600
Dawn Hodge, *Manager*
EMP: 3
SALES (corp-wide): 26.6MM **Privately Held**
WEB: www.originalmattress.com
SIC: 2515 5712 Mattresses & foundations; furniture springs; bedding & bedsprings; mattresses
PA: The Original Mattress Factory Inc
  4930 State Rd
  Cleveland OH 44134
  216 661-8388

(G-3261)
PRO AUDIO
671 Cncnnati Batavia Pike (45245-1002)
PHONE.................................513 752-7500
Frank Marino, *Owner*
EMP: 6

GEOGRAPHIC SECTION Cincinnati - Hamilton County (G-3290)

SALES (est): 511.2K **Privately Held**
SIC: 3651 Audio electronic systems

(G-3262)
SENCO BRANDS INC (DH)
Also Called: Nexicor
4270 Ivy Pointe Blvd (45245-0003)
PHONE.................................513 388-2000
Ben Johansen, *CEO*
Ken Turner, *Maint Spvr*
Peggy Bohl, *Mfg Staff*
Vicki Fichter, *Mfg Staff*
Matt Sims, *Mfg Staff*
▲ **EMP:** 70
SALES (est): 134.3MM
SALES (corp-wide): 14.8B **Publicly Held**
SIC: 3546 Power-driven handtools
HQ: Kyocera Senco Industrial Tools, Inc.
4270 Ivy Pointe Blvd
Cincinnati OH 45245
800 543-4596

(G-3263)
SENSOURCE GLOBAL SOURCING LLC
4270 Ivy Pointe Blvd (45245-0003)
PHONE.................................513 659-8283
Glenn P Rudolph,
▲ **EMP:** 3
SALES (est): 342.5K **Privately Held**
SIC: 3546 Power-driven handtools

(G-3264)
SMASHING EVENTS AND BAKING
693 Winding Way (45245-2421)
PHONE.................................513 415-9693
Cindy King, *Principal*
EMP: 4
SALES (est): 185K **Privately Held**
SIC: 2051 Bread, cake & related products

(G-3265)
TAKE IT FOR GRANITE LLC
3898 Mcmann Rd (45245-2347)
PHONE.................................513 735-0555
Dustin Wallace, *Mng Member*
Amy Jo Wallace, *Mng Member*
Amy Wallace,
▲ **EMP:** 15
SQ FT: 12,000
SALES (est): 2.6MM **Privately Held**
SIC: 3281 Granite, cut & shaped

(G-3266)
UNITED TOOL SUPPLY INC
851 Ohio Pike Ste 101 (45245-2293)
PHONE.................................513 752-6000
Russell F Young, *President*
EMP: 6
SQ FT: 8,000
SALES: 750K **Privately Held**
SIC: 5085 3823 Industrial supplies; industrial instrmnts msrmnt display/control process variable

(G-3267)
XCITE SYSTEMS CORPORATION
675 Cncnnati Batavia Pike (45245-1028)
PHONE.................................513 965-0300
Terry A Dunlap, *President*
Gerald J Zobrist, *Chairman*
EMP: 6
SQ FT: 2,000
SALES: 950K **Privately Held**
WEB: www.xcitesystems.com
SIC: 3829 8711 Stress, strain & flaw detecting/measuring equipment; engineering services

Cincinnati
Hamilton County

(G-3268)
21ST CENTURY PRINTERS INC
326 Northland Blvd (45246-6602)
PHONE.................................513 771-4150
Cynthia Edwards, *President*
Kevin Robert Edwards, *Vice Pres*
EMP: 4 **EST:** 1973
SQ FT: 900

SALES (est): 242K **Privately Held**
SIC: 2752 2791 2789 2672 Commercial printing, offset; typesetting; bookbinding & related work; coated & laminated paper

(G-3269)
3-G INCORPORATED (PA)
Also Called: Napolitano Monument
4122 Spring Grove Ave (45223-2641)
PHONE.................................513 921-4515
Gregory Napolitano, *President*
Sandra Bender, *Corp Secy*
Gary Napolitano, *Vice Pres*
Linda Ledermeier, *Manager*
EMP: 5 **EST:** 1965
SQ FT: 5,000
SALES (est): 1.3MM **Privately Held**
SIC: 1751 3211 5999 Window & door installation & erection; insulating glass, sealed units; monuments & tombstones

(G-3270)
3D CORRUGATED LLC
5524 Goldcrest Dr (45238-3235)
PHONE.................................513 241-8126
EMP: 6
SALES (est): 377.3K **Privately Held**
SIC: 2653 Corrugated & solid fiber boxes

(G-3271)
3DLT LLC
8 Peasenhall Ln (45208-1214)
PHONE.................................513 452-3358
EMP: 11
SQ FT: 6,000
SALES (est): 1.1MM **Privately Held**
SIC: 2759 7374 Commercial Printing Data Processing/Preparation

(G-3272)
3N1 MENS FASHION
481 E Kemper Rd (45246-3228)
P.O. Box 40138 (45240-0138)
PHONE.................................513 851-3610
Vinne Spence, *Partner*
EMP: 3
SALES (est): 308K **Privately Held**
SIC: 2326 Men's & boys' work clothing

(G-3273)
80 ACRES URBAN AGRICULTURE LLC (PA)
4535 Este Ave (45232-1762)
PHONE.................................513 218-4387
Mike Zelkind, *President*
EMP: 7 **EST:** 2015
SALES (est): 1.3MM **Privately Held**
SIC: 3532 Mining machinery

(G-3274)
A & B DEBURRING COMPANY
525 Carr St (45203-1815)
PHONE.................................513 723-0444
Robert Wegman, *President*
Lance Lagaly, *Accounts Mgr*
Mike Hacker, *Manager*
EMP: 14 **EST:** 1946
SQ FT: 25,000
SALES (est): 6.8MM **Privately Held**
WEB: www.abdeburr.com
SIC: 5084 3471 Metal refining machinery & equipment; polishing, metals or formed products

(G-3275)
A & E BUTSCHA CO
110 E Seymour Ave (45216-2024)
P.O. Box 532000 (45253-2000)
PHONE.................................513 761-1919
Daniel Hoetker, *President*
REA Hoetker, *Vice Pres*
EMP: 4 **EST:** 1948
SQ FT: 30,000
SALES (est): 721.8K **Privately Held**
SIC: 3444 3446 3443 3441 Sheet metal specialties, not stamped; architectural metalwork; fabricated plate work (boiler shop); fabricated structural metal

(G-3276)
A AND V GRINDING INC
Also Called: Midwest Centerless Grinding
1115 Straight St 17 (45214-1735)
PHONE.................................937 444-4141
Albert Benedetti, *President*
Vera Benedetti, *Vice Pres*

EMP: 6 **EST:** 1982
SQ FT: 12,500
SALES (est): 786.4K **Privately Held**
SIC: 3599 Machine shop, jobbing & repair

(G-3277)
A B & J MACHINING & FABG
Also Called: AB&j Machng Fabrictn
10330 Wayne Ave (45215-1129)
PHONE.................................513 769-5900
James J Meister, *President*
Bev Meister, *Vice Pres*
EMP: 5
SQ FT: 2,000
SALES (est): 642.8K **Privately Held**
SIC: 3599 Machine shop, jobbing & repair

(G-3278)
A B C SIGN INC
38 W Mcmicken Ave (45202-7718)
PHONE.................................513 241-8884
Cliff Meyer, *President*
Tom Meyer, *General Mgr*
Thomas Meyer, *Vice Pres*
EMP: 10
SQ FT: 30,500
SALES (est): 1.2MM **Privately Held**
WEB: www.abcsign.com
SIC: 3993 2394 1799 7359 Electric signs; awnings, fabric: made from purchased materials; sign installation & maintenance; sign rental

(G-3279)
A C KNOX INC
Also Called: Helex Division
525 Purcell Ave (45205-2341)
PHONE.................................513 921-5028
Arthur C Knox Jr, *President*
Rita Knox, *Corp Secy*
Arthur Knox, *Manager*
Teri Knox, *Manager*
EMP: 4
SALES (est): 360K **Privately Held**
WEB: www.acknox.com
SIC: 3443 8742 8711 Heat exchangers, condensers & components; management consulting services; engineering services

(G-3280)
A DESIGNERS WORKROOM
3066 Madison Rd 3 (45209-1723)
PHONE.................................513 251-7396
EMP: 7
SALES: 180K **Privately Held**
SIC: 2391 Mfg Curtains/Draperies

(G-3281)
A TO Z WEAR LTD
5647 Cheviot Rd (45247-7089)
PHONE.................................513 923-4662
Donna Fenstermacher, *Partner*
Gail Gilmore, *Partner*
EMP: 3
SQ FT: 1,500
SALES (est): 238.3K **Privately Held**
WEB: www.atozwear.com
SIC: 2395 Embroidery products, except schiffli machine; embroidery & art needlework

(G-3282)
A Z PRINTING INC (PA)
Also Called: A-Z Discount Printing
10122 Reading Rd (45241-3110)
PHONE.................................513 733-3900
Bruce Hassel, *President*
EMP: 8
SQ FT: 4,000
SALES (est): 1.1MM **Privately Held**
WEB: www.azprt.com
SIC: 2752 Commercial printing, offset

(G-3283)
A Z PRINTING INC
4077 E Galbraith Rd (45236-2323)
PHONE.................................513 745-0700
Bruce Hassle, *Owner*
EMP: 4
SALES (corp-wide): 1.1MM **Privately Held**
WEB: www.azprt.com
SIC: 2759 7389 4783 Commercial printing; mailing & messenger services; packing & crating

PA: A Z Printing Inc
10122 Reading Rd
Cincinnati OH 45241
513 733-3900

(G-3284)
A2Z PALLETS LLC
1292 Glendale Milford Rd (45215-1209)
P.O. Box 18151 (45218-0151)
PHONE.................................513 652-9026
Ramonita Garcia, *Principal*
EMP: 4
SALES (est): 421.1K **Privately Held**
SIC: 2448 Pallets, wood & wood with metal

(G-3285)
AAA GALVANIZING - JOLIET INC
Also Called: Azz Galvanizing - Cincinnati
4454 Steel Pl (45209-1135)
PHONE.................................513 871-5700
Lori Wilp, *Plant Mgr*
Michele Fletcher, *Manager*
EMP: 49
SALES (corp-wide): 810.4MM **Publicly Held**
SIC: 3479 Hot dip coating of metals or formed products; coating of metals & formed products
HQ: Aaa Galvanizing - Joliet, Inc.
625 Mills Rd
Joliet IL 60433

(G-3286)
AB BONDED LOCKSMITHS INC
Also Called: Tri County Locksmith
4344 Montgomery Rd (45212-3104)
PHONE.................................513 531-7334
Russell McGurrin, *President*
Cindy McGurrin, *CFO*
EMP: 7 **EST:** 1933
SQ FT: 5,000
SALES (est): 1.4MM **Privately Held**
WEB: www.ablocks.com
SIC: 7699 3429 Locksmith shop; manufactured hardware (general)

(G-3287)
ABEL MANUFACTURING COMPANY
3474 Beekman St (45223-2425)
PHONE.................................513 681-5000
Carl Abel Jr, *President*
Mark Abel, *Vice Pres*
Michael Nagel, *Vice Pres*
Kent Smith, *Plant Mgr*
Katherine Nagel, *Treasurer*
EMP: 15 **EST:** 1966
SQ FT: 14,000
SALES (est): 3.2MM **Privately Held**
WEB: www.abel-usa.com
SIC: 3451 Screw machine products

(G-3288)
ABLE TOOL CORPORATION
617 N Wayne Ave (45215-2250)
PHONE.................................513 733-8989
Daniel R Hayes, *President*
Janice M Hayes, *Corp Secy*
Sara Hayes, *Vice Pres*
EMP: 30
SQ FT: 22,400
SALES (est): 6MM **Privately Held**
WEB: www.abletool.com
SIC: 3599 3565 3545 Machine shop, jobbing & repair; packing & wrapping machinery; machine tool accessories

(G-3289)
ABRA AUTO BODY & GLASS LP
Also Called: ABRA Autobody & Glass
6947 E Kemper Rd (45249-1085)
PHONE.................................513 247-3400
EMP: 7
SALES (corp-wide): 1.8B **Privately Held**
SIC: 5013 2851 Body repair or paint shop supplies, automotive; paint removers
HQ: Abra Auto Body & Glass Lp
7225 Northland Dr N # 110
Brooklyn Park MN 55428
888 872-2272

(G-3290)
ACCURATE GEAR MANUFACTURING CO
16 E 73rd St (45216-2038)
PHONE.................................513 761-3220

Cincinnati - Hamilton County (G-3291) GEOGRAPHIC SECTION

Dennis M Pauly, *President*
David Schacere, *Vice Pres*
EMP: 9
SQ FT: 10,500
SALES (est): 1.7MM Privately Held
SIC: 3566 Gears, power transmission, except automotive

(G-3291)
ACCUTECH SIGN SHOP
9316 Colerain Ave (45251-2012)
PHONE..................513 385-3595
Sheila Pierce, *Owner*
▲ **EMP:** 3 **EST:** 2001
SALES: 150K Privately Held
SIC: 3993 Signs, not made in custom sign painting shops

(G-3292)
ACE GASKET MANUFACTURING CO
7873 Main St (45244-3158)
P.O. Box 54367 (45254-0367)
PHONE..................513 271-6321
Gregory Dietrich, *President*
Edward Dietrich, *Vice Pres*
Judith Dietrich, *Admin Sec*
EMP: 3 **EST:** 1964
SQ FT: 6,000
SALES: 500K Privately Held
SIC: 2899 3053 Industrial sizes; gaskets, all materials

(G-3293)
ACOUFLOW THERAPEUTICS LLC
6914 Copperglow Ct (45244-3647)
PHONE..................513 558-0073
Liran Oren,
EMP: 4
SALES (est): 197K Privately Held
SIC: 3841 Surgical & medical instruments

(G-3294)
ACTION MECHANICAL REPAIR INC
7760 Harrison Ave (45247-2469)
P.O. Box 427, Miamitown (45041-0427)
PHONE..................513 353-1046
June C Retherford, *President*
Joseph H Retherford Jr, *Vice Pres*
EMP: 4
SQ FT: 5,000
SALES: 630K Privately Held
SIC: 3599 Machine shop, jobbing & repair

(G-3295)
ACTIVE DAILY LIVING LLC
3308 Bishop St (45220-1858)
PHONE..................513 607-6769
Daniel E Ansel, *Principal*
EMP: 3 **EST:** 2013
SALES (est): 123.7K Privately Held
SIC: 2711 Newspapers, publishing & printing

(G-3296)
AD-PRO SIGNS I LLC
11336 Dallas Blvd (45231-1357)
PHONE..................513 922-5046
Jim Kleemeier,
EMP: 3
SQ FT: 15,000
SALES (est): 335.1K Privately Held
SIC: 3993 Electric signs

(G-3297)
ADAMS CUSTOM WOODWORKING
324 W Wyoming Ave (45215-3035)
PHONE..................513 761-1395
EMP: 10 **EST:** 2008
SALES (est): 650K Privately Held
SIC: 2431 Mfg Millwork

(G-3298)
ADLER & COMPANY INC
Also Called: Camargo Construction
6801 Shawnee Run Rd (45243-2417)
PHONE..................513 248-1500
Harry Adler Jr, *President*
EMP: 15
SALES: 2MM Privately Held
SIC: 3272 Paving materials, prefabricated concrete

(G-3299)
ADVANCED FITNESS INC
11875 Reading Rd (45241-1545)
P.O. Box 62751 (45262-0751)
PHONE..................513 563-1000
Mark D Pittroff, *President*
Sandra Pittroff, *Corp Secy*
EMP: 3
SALES (est): 430.3K Privately Held
WEB: www.adfit.com
SIC: 7331 3949 Direct mail advertising services; sporting & athletic goods

(G-3300)
ADVANCED GROUND SYSTEMS
Also Called: Agse Tooling
1650 Magnolia Dr (45215-1976)
PHONE..................513 402-7226
Roy Stone, *Manager*
EMP: 18
SALES (corp-wide): 23.6MM Privately Held
SIC: 3724 Aircraft engines & engine parts
HQ: Advanced Ground Systems Engineering Llc
  10805 Painter Ave
  Santa Fe Springs CA 90670
  562 906-9300

(G-3301)
ADVANCED OEM SOLUTIONS LLC
8044 Montgomery Rd # 700 (45236-2926)
PHONE..................513 846-5755
Gavin Dao, *CEO*
EMP: 2
SQ FT: 3,146
SALES (est): 2.7MM Privately Held
SIC: 3829 Ultrasonic testing equipment

(G-3302)
ADVANCED ONSIGHT WELDING SVCS
5220 Globe Ave (45212-1536)
PHONE..................513 924-1400
Anthony Moore, *Owner*
Mary Moore,
Mathew Moore,
Wayne Moore,
EMP: 7
SALES: 720K Privately Held
SIC: 3441 7692 Fabricated structural metal; welding repair

(G-3303)
ADVENTUROUS CHILD INC
4781 Duck Creek Rd (45227)
PHONE..................513 531-7700
Clark Kugler, *President*
EMP: 7
SQ FT: 4,000
SALES (est): 1MM Privately Held
WEB: www.theadventurouschild.com
SIC: 3949 Playground equipment

(G-3304)
ADWEST TECHNOLOGIES INC
4625 Red Bank Rd Ste 200 (45227-1552)
PHONE..................513 458-2600
EMP: 5
SALES (corp-wide): 337.3MM Publicly Held
SIC: 3564 Air purification equipment
HQ: Adwest Technologies, Inc.
  4222 E La Palma Ave
  Anaheim CA 92807
  714 632-8595

(G-3305)
AERO PREP LLC
11584 Goldcoast Dr (45249-1640)
PHONE..................513 469-8300
Nancy Talbot, *Principal*
EMP: 5
SQ FT: 6,500
SALES (est): 754.9K Privately Held
SIC: 3599 Machine shop, jobbing & repair

(G-3306)
AFFINITY DISP EXPOSITIONS INC (PA)
Also Called: Adex International
1301 Glendale Milford Rd (45215-1210)
PHONE..................513 771-2339
Timothy Murphy, *President*
Walt Pottschmidt, *Exec VP*
Mike Pierdiluca, *Vice Pres*
Joe Rickard, *CFO*
▲ **EMP:** 150
SQ FT: 250,000
SALES (est): 24.3MM Privately Held
WEB: www.adex-intl.com
SIC: 3993 Displays & cutouts, window & lobby

(G-3307)
AFFINITY DISP EXPOSITIONS INC
Also Called: Adex International
1375 Spring Park Walk (45215-0046)
PHONE..................513 771-2339
Tim Murphy, *President*
EMP: 100
SALES (corp-wide): 24.3MM Privately Held
WEB: www.adex-intl.com
SIC: 3993 Signs & advertising specialties
PA: Affinity Displays & Expositions, Inc.
  1301 Glendale Milford Rd
  Cincinnati OH 45215
  513 771-2339

(G-3308)
AFTER WERK
3095 Glenmore Ave (45238-2270)
PHONE..................513 661-9375
Allen Anderson, *Principal*
EMP: 4
SALES (est): 316.1K Privately Held
SIC: 2599 Bar, restaurant & cafeteria furniture

(G-3309)
AG ANTENNA GROUP LLC
11931 Montgomery Rd (45249-2019)
PHONE..................513 289-6521
John Reynolds, *CEO*
James Moore, *Vice Pres*
Matt Kopeny,
EMP: 10
SQ FT: 2,500
SALES (est): 706.6K Privately Held
SIC: 3663 Antennas, transmitting & communications

(G-3310)
AGNONE-KELLY ENTERPRISES INC
Also Called: Thermalgraphics
11658 Baen Rd (45242-1600)
P.O. Box 428543 (45242-8543)
PHONE..................800 634-6503
Kevin Kelly, *President*
Elizabeth Kelly, *Vice Pres*
EMP: 6
SQ FT: 20,000
SALES: 1MM Privately Held
WEB: www.thermalg.com
SIC: 2759 Commercial printing

(G-3311)
AHALOGY
1140 Main St 3 (45202-7236)
PHONE..................314 974-5599
Michael Wohlschlaeger, *CEO*
Marc Cousineau, *Vice Pres*
Monica Murphy, *Sales Dir*
Samantha Knutson, *Accounts Mgr*
Stephanie Lutz, *Sales Staff*
EMP: 23
SALES (est): 3.5MM Privately Held
SIC: 2741

(G-3312)
AIR PRODUCTS AND CHEMICALS INC
4900 Este Ave (45232-1491)
P.O. Box 32283 (45232-0283)
PHONE..................513 242-9215
Wallace West, *Manager*
EMP: 5
SALES (corp-wide): 8.9B Publicly Held
WEB: www.airproducts.com
SIC: 2813 Oxygen, compressed or liquefied
PA: Air Products And Chemicals, Inc.
  7201 Hamilton Blvd
  Allentown PA 18195
  610 481-4911

(G-3313)
AIRECON MANUFACTURING CORP
5271 Brotherton Rd (45227-2103)
PHONE..................513 561-5522
Joseph E Gutierrez, *President*
Timothy Kidd, *Vice Pres*
Paul Bockrath, *Sales Engr*
David W Miller, *Admin Sec*
▲ **EMP:** 50
SQ FT: 30,000
SALES (est): 13.9MM Privately Held
WEB: www.airecon.com
SIC: 3564 Air purification equipment; dust or fume collecting equipment, industrial

(G-3314)
AIRTX INTERNATIONAL LTD
6320 Wiehe Rd (45237-4214)
PHONE..................513 631-0660
Michael Rawlings, *Partner*
Sandy Mayer, *Office Mgr*
EMP: 10
SQ FT: 7,500
SALES (est): 1.9MM Privately Held
WEB: www.artxltd.com
SIC: 3563 Air & gas compressors

(G-3315)
AK STEEL CORPORATION
Sawhill Tubular
1080 Nimitzview Dr (45230-4314)
PHONE..................513 231-2552
EMP: 3
SALES (corp-wide): 5.9B Publicly Held
SIC: 3312 Blast Furnace-Steel Works
HQ: Ak Steel Corporation
  9227 Centre Pointe Dr
  West Chester OH 45069
  513 425-5000

(G-3316)
AKZO NOBEL PAINTS LLC
Also Called: Glidden Professional Paint Ctr
1754 Tennessee Ave (45229-1202)
PHONE..................513 242-0530
EMP: 4
SQ FT: 2,500
SALES (corp-wide): 15.2B Publicly Held
SIC: 2891 Mfg Adhesives/Sealants
HQ: Akzo Nobel Paints Llc
  8381 Pearl Rd
  Strongsville OH 44136
  440 297-8000

(G-3317)
ALBERT BICKEL
Also Called: CCI
7116 Leibel Rd (45248-2814)
PHONE..................513 530-5700
Albert J Bickel, *Owner*
EMP: 3
SALES (est): 173.7K Privately Held
SIC: 2741 7379 Miscellaneous publishing; computer related consulting services

(G-3318)
ALBERT BRAMKAMP PRINTING CO
4501 Greenlee Ave (45217-1803)
PHONE..................513 641-1069
Dave Bramkamp, *President*
Ed Collins, *Corp Secy*
David Bramkamp Jr, *Vice Pres*
EMP: 3
SALES: 250K Privately Held
SIC: 2752 Commercial printing, lithographic

(G-3319)
ALEX AND ANI LLC
7875 Montgomery Rd # 2135 (45236-4370)
PHONE..................513 791-1480
EMP: 3 Privately Held
SIC: 3915 Jewelers' materials & lapidary work
PA: Alex And Ani, Llc
  2000 Chapel View Blvd # 360
  Cranston RI 02920

(G-3320)
ALK INDUSTRIES LLC
7178 Lamplite Ct (45244-4108)
PHONE..................513 429-3047

GEOGRAPHIC SECTION

Cincinnati - Hamilton County (G-3345)

Andrew Whitley, *Owner*
EMP: 3
SALES (est): 100.1K **Privately Held**
SIC: 3999 Manufacturing industries

(G-3321)
ALL CRAFT MANUFACTURING CO
Also Called: Talisman Racing
6500 Glenway Ave Side 2 (45211-4451)
PHONE..................................513 661-3383
Robert W Farrell, *President*
Paula Farrell, *Vice Pres*
Thomas Farrell, *Engineer*
EMP: 15
SQ FT: 3,200
SALES (est): 2MM **Privately Held**
SIC: 3599 Machine shop, jobbing & repair

(G-3322)
ALL POINTS INDUSTRIES INC
10590 Hamilton Ave (45231-1764)
PHONE..................................513 826-0681
EMP: 3
SALES (est): 105.2K **Privately Held**
SIC: 3999 Manufacturing industries

(G-3323)
ALLERGAN SALES LLC
5000 Brotherton Rd (45209-1105)
PHONE..................................513 271-6800
Doug Yelton, *Branch Mgr*
EMP: 190 **Privately Held**
WEB: www.forestpharm.com
SIC: 2834 Pharmaceutical preparations
HQ: Allergan Sales, Llc
2525 Dupont Dr Towe Fl14
Irvine CA 92612
862 261-7000

(G-3324)
ALLGEIER & SON INC (PA)
6386 Bridgetown Rd (45248-2933)
PHONE..................................513 574-3735
Michael Allgeier, *Owner*
Margaret A Steigerwald, *Treasurer*
EMP: 40
SQ FT: 800
SALES (est): 5MM **Privately Held**
SIC: 1794 1422 1795 Excavation & grading, building construction; crushed & broken limestone; wrecking & demolition work

(G-3325)
ALLIED WINDOW INC
11111 Canal Rd (45241-1861)
PHONE..................................513 559-1212
David Martin, *President*
Gregg Martin, *Vice Pres*
Sonya Martin, *Vice Pres*
Bob Schumacher, *Prdtn Mgr*
Richard Young, *CFO*
EMP: 40 **EST:** 1950
SQ FT: 15,000
SALES (est): 4.2MM **Privately Held**
WEB: www.alliedwindow.com
SIC: 3442 Metal doors, sash & trim

(G-3326)
ALTERA CORPORATION
9435 Waterstone Blvd # 140 (45249-8326)
PHONE..................................513 444-2021
Bernhard R Kiessling, *Manager*
Wit Dinh, *Manager*
EMP: 5
SALES (corp-wide): 70.8B **Publicly Held**
WEB: www.altera.com
SIC: 3674 Semiconductors & related devices
HQ: Altera Corporation
101 Innovation Dr
San Jose CA 95134
408 544-7000

(G-3327)
ALUCHEM INC (PA)
1 Landy Ln Ste 1 # 1 (45215-3489)
PHONE..................................513 733-8519
Ronald P Zapletal, *President*
Edward L Butera, *Vice Pres*
Ken Sierk, *Plant Mgr*
Charles Hawkins, *Prdtn Mgr*
Daniel Groll, *Plant Engr*
◆ **EMP:** 47
SQ FT: 200,000
SALES (est): 17.9MM **Privately Held**
WEB: www.aluchem.com
SIC: 2819 Industrial inorganic chemicals

(G-3328)
ALUMINUM EXTRUDED SHAPES INC
Also Called: AES
10549 Reading Rd (45241-2524)
PHONE..................................513 563-2205
Robert E Hoeweler, *President*
EMP: 115 **EST:** 1946
SQ FT: 130,000
SALES (est): 27.6MM **Privately Held**
SIC: 3354 3471 3444 Aluminum extruded products; plating & polishing; sheet metal-work

(G-3329)
AMERICAN BOTTLING COMPANY
125 E Court St Ste 820 (45202-1201)
PHONE..................................513 381-4891
EMP: 70
SALES (corp-wide): 6B **Publicly Held**
SIC: 2086 Mfg Bottled/Canned Soft Drinks
HQ: The American Bottling Company
5301 Legacy Dr
Plano TX 75024
972 673-7000

(G-3330)
AMERICAN BOTTLING COMPANY
Also Called: 7 Up/ Royal Crown
5151 Fischer Ave (45217-1157)
PHONE..................................513 242-5151
Mark Wendling, *Manager*
EMP: 165 **Publicly Held**
WEB: www.cs-americas.com
SIC: 2086 Bottled & canned soft drinks
HQ: The American Bottling Company
5301 Legacy Dr
Plano TX 75024

(G-3331)
AMERICAN CITY BUS JOURNALS INC
Also Called: Business Courier
120 E 4th St Ste 230 (45202-4099)
PHONE..................................513 337-9450
Douglas Bolton, *Branch Mgr*
James Smith, *Manager*
EMP: 30
SALES (corp-wide): 1.4B **Privately Held**
SIC: 2711 2741 Newspapers: publishing only, not printed on site; miscellaneous publishing
HQ: American City Business Journals, Inc.
120 W Morehead St Ste 400
Charlotte NC 28202
704 973-1000

(G-3332)
AMERICAN FOODS GROUP LLC
3480 E Kemper Rd (45241-2007)
PHONE..................................513 733-8898
Nancy Carroll, *Safety Dir*
Ken Allred, *VP Engrg*
Lee Torres, *Manager*
Alexis Harris, *Admin Sec*
EMP: 20
SALES (corp-wide): 3B **Privately Held**
WEB: www.americanfoodsgroup.com
SIC: 2011 2013 Beef products from beef slaughtered on site; sausages & other prepared meats
HQ: American Foods Group, Llc
500 S Washington St
Green Bay WI 54301
320 759-5900

(G-3333)
AMERICAN GUILD OF ENGLISH HAND
201 E 5th St 19001025 (45202-4152)
PHONE..................................937 438-0085
Jennifer Cauhorn, *Exec Dir*
EMP: 9
SQ FT: 2,253
SALES: 717.4K **Privately Held**
WEB: www.agehr.org
SIC: 8699 7929 2741 7041 Personal interest organization; entertainers & entertainment groups; musical entertainers; music, sheet: publishing only, not printed on site; membership-basis organization hotels

(G-3334)
AMERICAN ISRAELITE CO
Also Called: American Israelite Newspaper
18 W 9th St Ste 2 (45202-2037)
PHONE..................................513 621-3145
Ted Deustch, *President*
EMP: 8
SQ FT: 1,000
SALES: 240K **Privately Held**
SIC: 2711 Newspapers: publishing only, not printed on site

(G-3335)
AMERICAN LEGAL PUBLISHING CORP
1 W 4th St Ste 300 (45202-3606)
PHONE..................................513 421-4248
Stephen G Wolf, *President*
Kathy Donnermeyer, *Editor*
Joseph McDonough, *Vice Pres*
Cynthia Poweleit, *Vice Pres*
Paul Mueller, *Controller*
EMP: 40 **EST:** 1978
SQ FT: 7,800
SALES (est): 5MM **Privately Held**
WEB: www.amlegal.com
SIC: 2731 2741 Books: publishing only; miscellaneous publishing

(G-3336)
AMERICAN MTAL CLG CNCNNATI INC
475 Northland Blvd (45240-3210)
PHONE..................................513 825-1171
James Taylor, *President*
Carol Taylor, *Vice Pres*
EMP: 3
SALES: 225K **Privately Held**
SIC: 3471 Cleaning & descaling metal products

(G-3337)
AMERICAN QUICKSILVER CO
646 Rushton Rd (45226-1124)
PHONE..................................513 871-4517
Barney Pogue, *President*
Mara Pogue, *Admin Sec*
▲ **EMP:** 8 **EST:** 1993
SALES (est): 619.9K **Privately Held**
WEB: www.americanquicksilver.com
SIC: 3421 Knife blades & blanks

(G-3338)
AMERICRAFT MFG CO INC
7937 School Rd (45249-1533)
PHONE..................................513 489-1047
Erin Giblin, *President*
Dan Giblin, *Plant Mgr*
EMP: 11
SQ FT: 55,000
SALES (est): 3.9MM **Privately Held**
WEB: www.americraftmfg.com
SIC: 3564 Blowers & fans

(G-3339)
AMERIDIAN SPECIALTY SERVICES
11520 Rockfield Ct (45241-1919)
P.O. Box 62808 (45262-0808)
PHONE..................................513 769-0150
Betty Owens, *President*
EMP: 50
SQ FT: 32,000
SALES (est): 6.6MM **Privately Held**
WEB: www.ameridiansvcs.com
SIC: 8741 1761 3441 Construction management; architectural sheet metal work; gutter & downspout contractor; fabricated structural metal

(G-3340)
AMPAC HOLDINGS LLC (HQ)
Also Called: Proampac
12025 Tricon Rd (45246-1719)
PHONE..................................513 671-1777
Greg Tucker, *Mng Member*
Eric Bradford,
Jon Dill,
Tom Geyer,
◆ **EMP:** 700 **EST:** 2001
SQ FT: 220,000
SALES (est): 354.9MM
SALES (corp-wide): 1.1B **Privately Held**
WEB: www.ampaconline.com
SIC: 2673 2677 3081 2674 Plastic bags: made from purchased materials; pliofilm bags: made from purchased materials; envelopes; unsupported plastics film & sheet; shopping bags: made from purchased materials; investment holding companies, except banks
PA: Proampac Holdings Inc.
12025 Tricon Rd
Cincinnati OH 45246
513 671-1777

(G-3341)
AMPAC PACKAGING LLC (HQ)
12025 Tricon Rd (45246-1719)
PHONE..................................513 671-1777
John Baumann, *CEO*
◆ **EMP:** 6
SALES (est): 232.6MM
SALES (corp-wide): 1.1B **Privately Held**
SIC: 2673 Pliofilm bags: made from purchased materials; plastic bags: made from purchased materials
PA: Proampac Holdings Inc.
12025 Tricon Rd
Cincinnati OH 45246
513 671-1777

(G-3342)
AMPAC PLASTICS LLC
12025 Tricon Rd (45246-1792)
PHONE..................................513 671-1777
John Q Baumann, *CEO*
Jon Dill,
Tom Geyer,
▲ **EMP:** 300 **EST:** 1965
SQ FT: 210,000
SALES (est): 40.4MM
SALES (corp-wide): 1.1B **Privately Held**
WEB: www.ampaconline.com
SIC: 2621 Packaging paper
HQ: Ampac Holdings, Llc
12025 Tricon Rd
Cincinnati OH 45246
513 671-1777

(G-3343)
AMPACET CORPORATION
4705 Duke Dr 400 (45249)
PHONE..................................513 247-5400
Vicky Willsey, *Manager*
EMP: 25
SALES (corp-wide): 584.5MM **Privately Held**
WEB: www.ampacet.com
SIC: 3089 5162 Coloring & finishing of plastic products; plastics materials & basic shapes
PA: Ampacet Corporation
660 White Plains Rd # 360
Tarrytown NY 10591
914 631-6600

(G-3344)
ANCHOR FLANGE COMPANY
Also Called: Anchor Fluid Power
3959 Virginia Ave (45227-3411)
PHONE..................................513 527-4444
Robert Coffaro, *Branch Mgr*
EMP: 10
SALES (corp-wide): 18.7MM **Privately Held**
SIC: 3462 Flange, valve & pipe fitting forgings, ferrous
PA: Anchor Flange Company
5553 Murray Ave
Cincinnati OH 45227
513 527-3512

(G-3345)
ANDERSON COSMETIC & VEIN INST
7794 5 Mile Rd Ste 270 (45230-2369)
PHONE..................................513 624-7900
Joseph Russell, *Owner*
EMP: 4

(PA)=Parent Co (HQ)=Headquarters (DH)=Div Headquarters
✪ = New Business established in last 2 years

2019 Harris Ohio Industrial Directory

Cincinnati - Hamilton County (G-3346)

SALES (est): 254K **Privately Held**
SIC: **7299** 3842 Personal appearance services; cosmetic restorations

(G-3346)
ANDROMEDA RESEARCH
648 Quail Run (45244-1041)
P.O. Box 222, Milford (45150-0222)
PHONE..................513 831-9708
John Dumont, *Owner*
Adrian Rollin, *Director*
EMP: 5
SALES: 250K **Privately Held**
SIC: **3825** Test equipment for electronic & electrical circuits

(G-3347)
ANDYS MDTERRANEAN FD PDTS LLC
906 Nassau St (45206-2508)
PHONE..................513 281-9791
Therese Hajjar,
Andy Hajjar,
Majed Hajjar,
▲ EMP: 6
SQ FT: 9,000
SALES (est): 47.2K **Privately Held**
SIC: **2099** Food preparations

(G-3348)
ANNIES MUD PIE SHOP LLC
Also Called: Funke Signature Holdings
3130 Wasson Rd Unit 4 (45209-2344)
PHONE..................513 871-2529
Thomas Funke, *Mng Member*
Jen Louis,
EMP: 5
SQ FT: 24,000
SALES (est): 835.4K **Privately Held**
WEB: www.anniesmudpieshop.com
SIC: **5023** 5719 3269 Pottery; pottery; vases, pottery

(G-3349)
ANZA INC
3265 Colerain Ave Ste 2 (45225-3301)
PHONE..................513 542-7337
John Busse, *President*
David Burbink, *Vice Pres*
▲ EMP: 8
SQ FT: 6,000
SALES (est): 1.1MM **Privately Held**
WEB: www.anzadesign.com
SIC: **3999** Models, general, except toy

(G-3350)
APEX CABINETRY
4536 W Mitchell Ave (45232-1912)
PHONE..................859 581-5300
EMP: 8
SALES (est): 1.2MM **Privately Held**
SIC: **2434** Wood kitchen cabinets

(G-3351)
APPAREL IMPRESSIONS INC
Also Called: Thanks Mom Designs
11410 Gideon Ln (45249-1654)
P.O. Box 42794 (45242-0794)
PHONE..................513 247-0555
Gregg Devita, *President*
EMP: 3
SALES: 230K **Privately Held**
SIC: **2395** Embroidery products, except schiffli machine

(G-3352)
APPAREL SCREEN PRINTING INC
11255 Reading Rd Ste 1 (45241-4202)
PHONE..................513 733-9495
Ronnie Thornton, *President*
Carrie Thornton, *Corp Secy*
John Guenther, *Vice Pres*
EMP: 4
SALES: 250K **Privately Held**
SIC: **2261** Screen printing of cotton broad-woven fabrics

(G-3353)
AR JESTER CO
Also Called: Jester Jewelers
6781 Harrison Ave (45247-3239)
PHONE..................513 241-1465
Randall D Jester, *President*
Pauline A Jester, *Treasurer*
EMP: 7 EST: 1939
SQ FT: 2,500
SALES (est): 1.4MM **Privately Held**
WEB: www.arjester.com
SIC: **5094** 3911 Precious stones & metals; diamonds (gems); jewelry, precious metal

(G-3354)
ARCHER COUNTER DESIGN INC
4433 Verne Ave (45209-1223)
PHONE..................513 396-7526
Robert Lewis, *President*
Tony Williams, *Vice Pres*
▲ EMP: 9
SQ FT: 15,000
SALES: 810K **Privately Held**
SIC: **2541** Table or counter tops, plastic laminated

(G-3355)
ARCHITECTURAL ART GLASS STUDIO
6106 Ridge Ave (45213-1302)
PHONE..................513 731-7336
Richard Dunkin, *Owner*
EMP: 5
SQ FT: 3,700
SALES (est): 264.3K **Privately Held**
WEB: www.architecturalartglass.net
SIC: **7699** 3231 Customizing services; stained glass: made from purchased glass

(G-3356)
ARSCO CUSTOM METALS LLC (PA)
Also Called: Arsco Manufacturing Company
3330 E Kemper Rd (45241-1538)
PHONE..................513 385-0555
Gregory Hemmert, *Mng Member*
EMP: 10
SQ FT: 3,000
SALES (est): 2.2MM **Privately Held**
WEB: www.arscomfg.com
SIC: **3444** Sheet metalwork

(G-3357)
ARSCO CUSTOM METALS LLC
3330 E Kemper Rd (45241-1538)
PHONE..................513 563-8822
EMP: 59
SALES (corp-wide): 2MM **Privately Held**
SIC: **2542** 3599 Fixtures: display, office or store: except wood; machine shop, jobbing & repair
PA: Arsco Custom Metals Llc
5313 Robert Ave
Cincinnati OH 45241
513 385-0555

(G-3358)
ART GUILD BINDERS INC
Also Called: Happy Booker
1068 Meta Dr (45237-5008)
PHONE..................513 242-3000
Timothy Hugenberg, *President*
Gregory M Hugenberg, *Vice Pres*
Donald F Cooper, *Admin Sec*
▲ EMP: 23 EST: 1948
SQ FT: 28,000
SALES (est): 2.8MM **Privately Held**
SIC: **2782** 2675 2789 Looseleaf binders & devices; die-cut paper & board; bookbinding & repairing: trade, edition, library, etc.

(G-3359)
ART WOODWORKING & MFG CO
4238 Dane Ave (45223-1856)
PHONE..................513 681-2986
Ralph R Dickman, *President*
EMP: 30
SQ FT: 23,000
SALES: 4.5MM **Privately Held**
SIC: **2431** Millwork

(G-3360)
ASCH-KLAASSEN SONICS LLC
11711 Princeton Pike # 943 (45246-2534)
PHONE..................513 671-3226
Herbert Asch, *President*
Dan Castner, *Principal*
Rich Klaassen, *Principal*
EMP: 3
SALES (est): 178.9K **Privately Held**
SIC: **3843** Dental equipment & supplies

(G-3361)
ASHLAND LLC
3901 River Rd (45204-1033)
PHONE..................513 557-3100
EMP: 8
SALES (corp-wide): 3.7B **Publicly Held**
SIC: **1622** 2821 2911 2951 Bridge construction; plastics materials & resins; polyesters; ester gum; thermoplastic materials; heavy distillates; oils, lubricating; paving mixtures; chemicals & allied products; noncorrosive products & materials; chemical additives; alcohols & antifreeze compounds; surfacing & paving
HQ: Ashland Llc
50 E Rivercenter Blvd # 1600
Covington KY 41011
859 815-3333

(G-3362)
ASKIA INC
4303 Williamsburg Rd N (45215-5140)
PHONE..................513 828-7443
Alioune Gueye, *President*
EMP: 3
SALES (est): 85.7K **Privately Held**
SIC: **7359** 5047 5085 5063 Equipment rental & leasing; medical & hospital equipment; commercial containers; ground fault interrupters; service industry machinery

(G-3363)
ASPEC INC
5810 Carothers St (45227-2350)
PHONE..................513 561-9922
Kerry L Bollmer, *President*
EMP: 9
SQ FT: 11,000
SALES (est): 1.6MM **Privately Held**
SIC: **3089** 3544 Injection molding of plastics; forms (molds), for foundry & plastics working machinery

(G-3364)
ASTRO MET INC (PA)
9974 Springfield Pike (45215-1425)
PHONE..................513 772-1242
Donald Graham, *President*
Tom Schwetschenau, *General Mgr*
Mike Shepherd, *Mfg Mgr*
EMP: 23 EST: 1961
SQ FT: 39,000
SALES (est): 3MM **Privately Held**
WEB: www.astromet.com
SIC: **3299** Ceramic fiber

(G-3365)
AT&T CORP
7875 Montgomery Rd Ofc (45236-4305)
PHONE..................513 792-9300
Vicky Valento, *Branch Mgr*
EMP: 9
SALES (corp-wide): 170.7B **Publicly Held**
WEB: www.att.com
SIC: **4813** 3661 3357 3571 Local & long distance telephone communications; long distance telephone communications; voice telephone communications; data telephone communications; telephone & telegraph apparatus; telephone sets, all types except cellular radio; switching equipment, telephone; PBX equipment, manual or automatic; communication wire; fiber optic cable (insulated); electronic computers; mainframe computers; minicomputers; personal computers (microcomputers); computer peripheral equipment; microprocessors
HQ: At&T Corp.
1 At&T Way
Bedminster NJ 07921
800 403-3302

(G-3366)
ATK2 INC
3111 Harrison Ave (45211-5741)
PHONE..................513 661-5869
Amy Osterfeld, *Principal*
EMP: 3
SALES (est): 181.7K **Privately Held**
SIC: **2053** Cakes, bakery: frozen

(G-3367)
ATLANTIC SIGN COMPANY INC
2328 Florence Ave (45206-2431)
PHONE..................513 383-1504
William Yusko, *President*
Aleisa Yusko, *Corp Secy*
CJ McDonald, *Vice Pres*
EMP: 27
SQ FT: 15,000
SALES: 5MM **Privately Held**
SIC: **3993** Signs & advertising specialties

(G-3368)
ATLAS VAC MACHINE LLC
9150 Reading Rd (45215-3343)
P.O. Box 42633 (45242-0633)
PHONE..................513 407-3513
Mike Oliver, *Engineer*
John Abraham, *Mng Member*
Bert Bullock, *CTO*
▲ EMP: 6
SQ FT: 8,800
SALES: 1MM **Privately Held**
SIC: **3565** Packaging machinery

(G-3369)
ATR DISTRIBUTING COMPANY
Wonderware Cincinnati
11857 Tamper Springs Dr (45240)
PHONE..................513 353-1800
Joe Murray, *Branch Mgr*
EMP: 19
SALES (corp-wide): 5.2MM **Privately Held**
SIC: **7372** Prepackaged software
PA: Atr Distributing Company
9585 Cilley Rd
Cleves OH 45002
513 353-1800

(G-3370)
AUBREY ROSE APPAREL LLC
3862 Race Rd (45211-4346)
PHONE..................513 728-2681
Raymond G Hollenkamp Jr,
EMP: 6
SALES: 264.2K **Privately Held**
SIC: **7389** 2395 Advertising, promotional & trade show services; embroidery & art needlework

(G-3371)
AURAND MANUFACTURING & EQP CO
1210 Ellis St (45223-1843)
PHONE..................513 541-7200
Ray Evers, *President*
Mary Evers, *Corp Secy*
EMP: 6
SQ FT: 4,280
SALES: 1.8MM **Privately Held**
WEB: www.everterprises.com
SIC: **3589** Commercial cleaning equipment
PA: Evers Enterprises Inc
4849 Blue Rock Rd
Cincinnati OH

(G-3372)
AVERY DENNISON CORPORATION
11101 Mosteller Rd Ste 2 (45241-1882)
PHONE..................513 682-7500
Stuart Miller, *Engineer*
Dennis Cain, *Branch Mgr*
EMP: 12
SALES (corp-wide): 7.1B **Publicly Held**
SIC: **2672** Adhesive backed films, foams & foils
PA: Avery Dennison Corporation
207 N Goode Ave Ste 500
Glendale CA 91203
626 304-2000

(G-3373)
B & D GRAPHICS INC
300 Township Ave (45216-2336)
PHONE..................513 641-0855
Gregory Buchtmann, *President*
Albert W Dixon III, *Vice Pres*
EMP: 5
SQ FT: 3,000
SALES: 400K **Privately Held**
SIC: **3993** Signs & advertising specialties

GEOGRAPHIC SECTION
Cincinnati - Hamilton County (G-3402)

(G-3374)
B & J BAKING COMPANY INC
4056 Colerain Ave (45223-2561)
PHONE..................513 541-2386
Steve Toleski, *President*
Tatsa Toleski, *Treasurer*
EMP: 15
SQ FT: 10,000
SALES (est): 2.2MM **Privately Held**
SIC: 2051 Buns, bread type: fresh or frozen

(G-3375)
B & R FABRICATORS & MAINT INC
4524 W Mitchell Ave (45232-1912)
P.O. Box 17211 (45217-0211)
PHONE..................513 641-2222
Randy Allen, *President*
Bruce Allen, *Vice Pres*
EMP: 12
SQ FT: 5,000
SALES: 1MM **Privately Held**
SIC: 7692 Welding repair

(G-3376)
B P OIL COMPANY
Also Called: BP
1201 Omniplex Dr (45240-1280)
PHONE..................513 671-4107
Pat Hoelle, *Principal*
EMP: 4
SALES (est): 268.4K **Privately Held**
SIC: 2869 Fuels

(G-3377)
BAERLOCHER PRODUCTION USA LLC
5890 Highland Ridge Dr (45232-1440)
PHONE..................513 482-6300
Ray Buehler, *CEO*
Jerry Vail, *Engineer*
David Kuebel, *CFO*
Mari Newton, *Controller*
Roberto Castaneda, *Accounts Mgr*
◆ **EMP:** 50
SQ FT: 50,000
SALES (est): 12.2MM
SALES (corp-wide): 474.4MM **Privately Held**
WEB: www.baerlocher.com
SIC: 2819 Nonmetallic compounds
HQ: Baerlocher Gmbh
   Freisinger Str. 1
   UnterschleiBheim 85716
   891 437-30

(G-3378)
BALDIE CORPORATION
Also Called: James Alexander President
4520 Lucerne Ave (45227-2816)
PHONE..................513 503-0953
James S Alexander, *CEO*
▲ **EMP:** 4
SQ FT: 2,800
SALES (est): 423K **Privately Held**
SIC: 3089 Plastic processing

(G-3379)
BARDES CORPORATION (PA)
Also Called: Ilsco
4730 Madison Rd (45227-1426)
PHONE..................513 533-6200
David Fitzgibbon, *CEO*
Merrilyn Q Bardes, *Ch of Bd*
Andrew Quinn, *President*
Bruce Godleski, *Plant Engr*
Steve Mayo, *Senior Engr*
▲ **EMP:** 300
SQ FT: 300,000
SALES (est): 116.7MM **Privately Held**
WEB: www.utilco.com
SIC: 3643 Electric connectors

(G-3380)
BARR LABORATORIES INC
5040 Duramed Rd (45213-2520)
PHONE..................513 731-9900
S Goldstein, *Principal*
Patricia Barney, *Buyer*
William Bentley, *QC Mgr*
Amy Hammond, *QC Mgr*
Regina Norris, *Engineer*
EMP: 300
SALES (corp-wide): 18.8B **Privately Held**
WEB: www.barrlabs.com
SIC: 2834 Pharmaceutical preparations
HQ: Barr Laboratories, Inc.
   1090 Horsham Rd
   North Wales PA 19454
   215 591-3000

(G-3381)
BASF CORPORATION
4900 Este Ave (45232-1491)
PHONE..................513 482-3000
Tasso Rigopoulos, *Manager*
EMP: 145
SALES (corp-wide): 71.7B **Privately Held**
SIC: 2869 Industrial organic chemicals
HQ: Basf Corporation
   100 Park Ave
   Florham Park NJ 07932
   973 245-6000

(G-3382)
BAXTER BURIAL VAULT SERVICE
Also Called: Baxter-Wilbert Burial Vault
909 E Ross Ave (45217-1159)
PHONE..................513 641-1010
R Douglas Baxter, *President*
EMP: 25
SALES: 2.4MM **Privately Held**
SIC: 5087 3272 Concrete burial vaults & boxes; funeral directors' equipment & supplies; concrete products

(G-3383)
BAYSWATER BEVERAGES LLC
705 Wakefield Dr (45226-1324)
PHONE..................312 224-8012
Charles Hamman,
▲ **EMP:** 5
SALES: 80K **Privately Held**
SIC: 5963 2087 Bottled water delivery; beverage bases

(G-3384)
BEAST CARBON CORPORATION
607 Shepherd Dr Unit 9 (45215-2194)
PHONE..................800 909-9051
Trevor Holekamp, *CEO*
EMP: 3 **EST:** 2016
SALES (est): 97.8K **Privately Held**
SIC: 3089 3714 Thermoformed finished plastic products; closures, plastic; stock shapes, plastic; automotive parts, plastic; wind deflectors, motor vehicle

(G-3385)
BECKER GALLAGHER LEGAL PUBG
8790 Governors Hill Dr # 102 (45249-1307)
PHONE..................513 677-5044
B J Becker, *President*
John Gallagher, *Vice Pres*
EMP: 10
SQ FT: 3,000
SALES (est): 830K **Privately Held**
WEB: www.beckergallagher.com
SIC: 2741 Miscellaneous publishing

(G-3386)
BECKMAN MACHINE LLC
4684 Paddock Rd (45229-1002)
P.O. Box 37655 (45222-0655)
PHONE..................513 242-2700
Mary Kathryn Lynch, *President*
Charles Beckman, *Vice Pres*
EMP: 20
SALES (est): 3.3MM **Privately Held**
SIC: 3599 Machine shop, jobbing & repair

(G-3387)
BELLA STONE CINCINNATI
239 Northland Blvd (45246-3603)
PHONE..................513 772-3552
Mary De Salvo, *President*
EMP: 6
SALES (est): 771.8K **Privately Held**
SIC: 3281 Cut stone & stone products

(G-3388)
BENCH BILLBOARD COMPANY INC
6805 Cambridge Ave (45227-3227)
PHONE..................513 271-2222
Bruce Graumlich, *President*
Patsy Davis, *Office Mgr*
EMP: 3
SQ FT: 6,000
SALES (est): 366.8K **Privately Held**
WEB: www.bbcx.com
SIC: 7312 3993 Billboard advertising; signs & advertising specialties

(G-3389)
BERGHAUSEN CORPORATION
4524 Este Ave (45232-1763)
P.O. Box 43400 (45243-0400)
PHONE..................513 541-5631
Fritz Berghausen, *President*
◆ **EMP:** 20 **EST:** 1863
SQ FT: 38,000
SALES (est): 4.9MM **Privately Held**
WEB: www.berghausen.com
SIC: 2843 2087 2865 Emulsifiers, except food & pharmaceutical; extracts, flavoring; food dyes or colors, synthetic

(G-3390)
BERGSTEIN OIL & GAS PARTNR
11464 Lippelman Rd # 200 (45246-4081)
PHONE..................513 771-6220
EMP: 4
SALES (est): 330K **Privately Held**
SIC: 1382 Oil/Gas Exploration Company

(G-3391)
BERNARD LABORATORIES INC
1738 Townsend St (45223-2710)
PHONE..................513 681-7373
Boyd J Piper Jr, *President*
▲ **EMP:** 22 **EST:** 1980
SQ FT: 30,000
SALES (est): 3.5MM **Privately Held**
WEB: www.bernardlab.com
SIC: 7389 2899 Packaging & labeling services; chemical preparations

(G-3392)
BERRY COMPANY
312 Plum St Ste 600 (45202-4809)
PHONE..................513 768-7800
Pete Luongo, *President*
EMP: 6
SALES (est): 621.8K **Privately Held**
SIC: 2741 Directories, telephone: publishing & printing

(G-3393)
BINNS MACHINERY COMPANY
330 Railroad Ave (45217-1024)
PHONE..................513 242-3388
Jack N Binns Sr, *President*
Roger Heaton, *Exec VP*
EMP: 4
SQ FT: 3,000
SALES (est): 518K **Privately Held**
SIC: 3549 Metalworking machinery

(G-3394)
BIORX LLC (HQ)
Also Called: Thriverx
7167 E Kemper Rd (45249-1028)
PHONE..................866 442-4679
Al Ranz, *Partner*
Megan Champagne, *Business Mgr*
Paul Costello, *Business Mgr*
Alex Zlatanoff, *Business Mgr*
Eric Hill, *COO*
EMP: 105
SALES (est): 81.7MM
SALES (corp-wide): 5.4B **Publicly Held**
WEB: www.biorx.net
SIC: 5122 8748 2834 5047 Pharmaceuticals; business consulting; pharmaceutical preparations; intravenous solutions; medical & hospital equipment; medical equipment & supplies; skilled nursing care facilities; extended care facility; convalescent home with continuous nursing care
PA: Diplomat Pharmacy, Inc.
   4100 S Saginaw St
   Flint MI 48507
   810 768-9000

(G-3395)
BIOWISH TECHNOLOGIES INC
2724 Erie Ave Ste B (45208-2125)
PHONE..................312 572-6700
Ian Edwards, *CEO*
Richard Carpenter, *Principal*
Russell Haack, *COO*
John Schroeder, *Vice Pres*
Rod Vautier, *Vice Pres*
▲ **EMP:** 9
SALES (est): 1.8MM **Privately Held**
SIC: 2869 Enzymes

(G-3396)
BLUE CHIP PUMP INC
1045 Meta Dr (45237-5007)
PHONE..................513 871-7867
Bruce Lipe, *President*
EMP: 3
SQ FT: 2,000
SALES (est): 190K **Privately Held**
SIC: 7699 3561 Pumps & pumping equipment repair; pumps & pumping equipment

(G-3397)
BLUE CHIP TOOL INC
11511 Goldcoast Dr (45249-1620)
PHONE..................513 489-3561
William Riehle, *President*
Eileen Riehle, *Corp Secy*
John Kilgore, *VP Mfg*
EMP: 12
SQ FT: 5,000
SALES (est): 1.9MM **Privately Held**
WEB: www.bluechiptool.com
SIC: 3599 Machine shop, jobbing & repair

(G-3398)
BOCK & PIERCE ENTERPRISES
Also Called: Minuteman Press
8550 Beechmont Ave # 800 (45255-4712)
PHONE..................513 474-9500
Donald S Bock, *President*
J Joshua Pierce, *Treasurer*
EMP: 5 **EST:** 1997
SQ FT: 3,000
SALES (est): 943.9K **Privately Held**
WEB: www.mmpcincinnati.com
SIC: 2752 2796 2791 2789 Commercial printing, offset; platemaking services; typesetting; bookbinding & related work; commercial printing

(G-3399)
BODYCOTE THERMAL PROC INC
710 Burns St (45204-1904)
PHONE..................513 921-2300
Pete Putthoff, *Plant Mgr*
Kevin McCurdy, *Branch Mgr*
EMP: 46
SALES (corp-wide): 911.9MM **Privately Held**
SIC: 3398 Metal heat treating
HQ: Bodycote Thermal Processing, Inc.
   12700 Park Central Dr # 700
   Dallas TX 75251
   214 904-2420

(G-3400)
BOHLENDER ENGRAVING COMPANY
Also Called: Bohlender Engravg
1599 Central Pkwy (45214-2863)
PHONE..................513 621-4095
Randy Brunk, *President*
EMP: 11 **EST:** 1895
SQ FT: 7,500
SALES (est): 1MM **Privately Held**
SIC: 2759 2752 Commercial printing; commercial printing, lithographic

(G-3401)
BONBONNERI INC
Also Called: Bonbonneri Bakery
2030 Madison Rd Ste 1 (45208-3347)
PHONE..................513 321-3399
Mary Pat Sullivan Pace, *President*
Sharon Butler, *Vice Pres*
Sheridan Miller, *Cust Mgr*
Maureen Arata, *Marketing Staff*
Liz Beiting, *Manager*
EMP: 16
SQ FT: 2,000
SALES (est): 1.9MM **Privately Held**
SIC: 2051 Bakery: wholesale or wholesale/retail combined

(G-3402)
BONDED PALLETS
1801 John St (45214-2411)
PHONE..................513 541-1855

Cincinnati - Hamilton County (G-3403) **GEOGRAPHIC SECTION**

Tony Combs, *Owner*
EMP: 4
SALES (est): 364.4K **Privately Held**
SIC: 2448 Pallets, wood

(G-3403)
BONSAL AMERICAN INC
5155 Fischer Ave (45217-1157)
PHONE.................513 398-7300
Marshal Lewis, *Opers-Prdtn-Mfg*
EMP: 20
SQ FT: 8,100
SALES (corp-wide): 29.7B **Privately Held**
WEB: www.bonsalamerican.com
SIC: 1442 Construction sand & gravel
HQ: Bonsal American, Inc.
625 Griffith Rd Ste 100
Charlotte NC 28217
704 525-1421

(G-3404)
BORDEN DAIRY CO CINCINNATI LLC
Also Called: H. Meyer Dairy
415 John St (45215-5481)
PHONE.................513 948-8811
David R Meyer, *President*
Mike Campe, *Info Tech Mgr*
James Houchin, *Maintence Staff*
EMP: 154 EST: 1976
SALES (est): 54MM **Privately Held**
WEB: www.meyerdairy.com
SIC: 2026 2086 5143 5144 Milk processing (pasteurizing, homogenizing, bottling); bottled & canned soft drinks; dairy products, except dried or canned; poultry & poultry products
PA: Borden Dairy Company
8750 N Central Expy # 400
Dallas TX 75231

(G-3405)
BOSTON BEER COMPANY
1625 Central Pkwy (45214-2423)
PHONE.................267 240-4429
Jeremy Roza, *Principal*
▲ EMP: 12
SALES (est): 291.6K **Privately Held**
SIC: 3585 Beer dispensing equipment

(G-3406)
BOX SEAT PUBLISHING LLC
8635 Willowview Ct (45251-5810)
PHONE.................513 519-2812
Thaisa Jones, *Administration*
EMP: 3
SALES (est): 87.5K **Privately Held**
SIC: 2711 Newspapers

(G-3407)
BRACE SHOP PROSTHETIC ORTHO (DH)
111 Wellington Pl Ste 8 (45219)
PHONE.................513 421-5653
Ted Ryder, *President*
Marianne Meyer, *Business Mgr*
Patrick Flaherty, *Vice Pres*
Richard Taylor, *Vice Pres*
Douglas B Van Atta, *Vice Pres*
EMP: 15
SQ FT: 7,500
SALES (est): 1.6MM
SALES (corp-wide): 1B **Publicly Held**
SIC: 3842 Braces, orthopedic; prosthetic appliances
HQ: Hanger Prosthetics & Orthotics, Inc.
10910 Domain Dr Ste 300
Austin TX 78758
512 777-3800

(G-3408)
BRADY A LANTZ ENTERPRISES
Also Called: Artic Diamond
11242 Sebring Dr (45240-2715)
PHONE.................513 742-4921
Brady Lantz, *President*
EMP: 4
SALES: 350K **Privately Held**
SIC: 2097 Manufactured ice

(G-3409)
BRADY A LANTZ ENTERPRISES INC
Also Called: Artic Diamond
11242 Sebring Dr (45240-2715)
PHONE.................513 742-4921
Brady A Lantz, *President*
Micah Sensenig, *Treasurer*
EMP: 4
SALES (est): 193.1K **Privately Held**
SIC: 3299 Architectural sculptures: gypsum, clay, papier mache, etc.

(G-3410)
BRENT BLEH COMPANY
Also Called: Quick Sign Works
917 Vine St (45202-1112)
PHONE.................513 721-1100
Brent J Bleh, *Owner*
EMP: 5
SQ FT: 4,000
SALES (est): 350K **Privately Held**
SIC: 3993 7389 6531 Mfg Signs/Advertising Specialties Business Services Real Estate Agent/Manager

(G-3411)
BRENT CARTER ENTERPRISES INC
Also Called: Prographics Printing Center
4404 Forest Ave (45212-3302)
PHONE.................513 731-1440
Brent Carter, *President*
Denise Beets, *Manager*
EMP: 5
SQ FT: 2,200
SALES: 700K **Privately Held**
WEB: www.prographicsprinting.com
SIC: 2752 Commercial printing, offset

(G-3412)
BRENTWOOD PRINTING & STY
8630 Winton Rd (45231-4817)
PHONE.................513 522-2679
Scott Finke, *Owner*
Gaille Finke, *Co-Owner*
EMP: 8
SQ FT: 1,250
SALES (est): 712.7K **Privately Held**
WEB: www.brentwood-printing.com
SIC: 2752 Commercial printing, offset; lithographing on metal

(G-3413)
BREW MONKEYS LLC
36 E 7th St Ste 1510 (45202-4454)
PHONE.................513 330-8806
EMP: 3
SALES (est): 167.6K **Privately Held**
SIC: 2082 Malt beverages

(G-3414)
BREWER COMPANY
7300 Main St (45244-3015)
PHONE.................513 576-6300
Laura Graber, *Planning Mgr*
EMP: 7
SALES (corp-wide): 50MM **Privately Held**
WEB: www.thebrewerco.com
SIC: 2952 2891 Coating compounds, tar; adhesives & sealants
PA: The Brewer Company
1354 Us Route 50
Milford OH 45150
800 394-0017

(G-3415)
BREWPRO INC
Also Called: Brewer Products Co
9483 Reading Rd (45215-3550)
P.O. Box 62065 (45262-0065)
PHONE.................513 577-7200
David Brewer, *President*
EMP: 6
SALES (est): 1.5MM **Privately Held**
WEB: www.brewerproducts.com
SIC: 5082 3531 7353 5169 Road construction equipment; general construction machinery & equipment; airport construction machinery; heavy construction equipment rental; adhesives & sealants; sealants

(G-3416)
BRIDGETOWN WELDERS LLC
4489 Bridgetown Rd (45211-4442)
PHONE.................513 574-4851
Fred Coyle,
EMP: 4
SQ FT: 7,000
SALES (est): 200K **Privately Held**
SIC: 7692 Automotive welding

(G-3417)
BRIGHTON TECHNOLOGIES GROUP
Also Called: Btg Labs
5129 Kieley Pl Ste A (45217-1112)
PHONE.................513 469-1800
Giles Dillingham, *President*
Eric Oseas, *COO*
Alexis Liu, *Manager*
Lindsey Mathews, *Manager*
EMP: 5
SALES (est): 500K **Privately Held**
WEB: www.btgnow.com
SIC: 3823 Industrial process control instruments

(G-3418)
BRIGHTON TRUEDGE
4955 Spring Grove Ave (45232-1925)
PHONE.................513 771-2300
Mark Lang, *Principal*
EMP: 3
SALES (est): 459K **Privately Held**
SIC: 3443 Fabricated plate work (boiler shop)

(G-3419)
BROADWAY PRINTING LLC
530 Reading Rd (45202-1407)
PHONE.................513 621-3429
Don Stanley,
EMP: 6
SALES (est): 518.8K **Privately Held**
SIC: 2759 Commercial printing

(G-3420)
BROADWAY WELDING & FABRICATION
25 E 76th St (45216-1611)
PHONE.................513 821-0004
William B Schmidt, *President*
Patricia J Schmidt, *Vice Pres*
EMP: 4
SQ FT: 5,000
SALES (est): 667.5K **Privately Held**
SIC: 7692 Welding repair

(G-3421)
BROCAR PRODUCTS INC
4335 River Rd (45204-1041)
P.O. Box 42295 (45242-0295)
PHONE.................513 922-2888
EMP: 21
SQ FT: 16,000
SALES: 5MM **Privately Held**
SIC: 2531 Manufactures Baby Changing Tables And High Chairs Ems Backboards Contract Mfg

(G-3422)
BROCKMANS SIGNS INC
6041 Harrison Ave Ste 5 (45248-1645)
PHONE.................513 574-6163
Alan Brockman, *President*
Carl Brockman, *Vice Pres*
Trey Canter, *Admin Sec*
EMP: 5
SALES (est): 487.5K **Privately Held**
WEB: www.brockmansigns.com
SIC: 3993 Signs, not made in custom sign painting shops

(G-3423)
BRODWILL LLC
3900 Rose Hill Ave Ste C (45229-1454)
PHONE.................513 258-2716
Rick Williams, *President*
Broderick Williams,
EMP: 8
SALES (est): 555.5K **Privately Held**
SIC: 2599 Hospital furniture, except beds

(G-3424)
BROODLE BRANDS LLC
8361 Broadwell Rd Ste 100 (45244-1609)
PHONE.................855 276-6353
Kent Arnold, *President*
EMP: 16
SQ FT: 10,000
SALES: 1MM **Privately Held**
SIC: 3411 Food & beverage containers

(G-3425)
BROOKWOOD GROUP INC
Also Called: Schauer Battery Chargers
3210 Wasson Rd (45209-2382)
PHONE.................513 791-3030
Jonathan Chaiken, *President*
▲ EMP: 10
SQ FT: 10,000
SALES (est): 4MM **Privately Held**
WEB: www.battery-chargers.com
SIC: 3629 Battery chargers, rectifying or nonrotating

(G-3426)
BROWER PRODUCTS INC (DH)
Also Called: Cabinet Solutions By Design
401 Northland Blvd (45240-3210)
PHONE.................937 563-1111
Daniel C Brower, *Ch of Bd*
William Brower, *President*
Mark Frericks, *Vice Pres*
EMP: 65
SQ FT: 125,000
SALES (est): 11.2MM **Privately Held**
SIC: 5031 2434 5211 3281 Whol Lumber/Plywd/Millwk Mfg Wood Kitchen Cabinet
HQ: Nisbet, Inc.
11575 Reading Rd
Cincinnati OH 45241
513 563-1111

(G-3427)
BRV INC
Also Called: Boulder Daily Camera
312 Walnut St Ste 2800 (45202-4019)
P.O. Box 5380 (45201-5380)
PHONE.................513 977-3000
Ken Lowe, *President*
EMP: 15
SALES (est): 2.2MM
SALES (corp-wide): 2.9B **Publicly Held**
SIC: 2711 Newspapers
HQ: Journal Media Group, Inc.
333 W State St
Milwaukee WI 53203
414 224-2000

(G-3428)
BUCKEYE FIELD SUPPLY LTD
8190 Beechmont Ave 262a (45255-6117)
PHONE.................513 312-2343
Russell C Romme,
EMP: 3
SALES (est): 355.5K **Privately Held**
SIC: 3589 Water treatment equipment, industrial

(G-3429)
BUCKLEY MANUFACTURING COMPANY
10333 Wayne Ave Ste 1 (45215-1198)
PHONE.................513 821-4444
Michael G Strotman, *President*
Thomas M Strotman, *Treasurer*
Kathleen Strotman, *Asst Treas*
Mary Reardon, *Admin Sec*
EMP: 18 EST: 1947
SQ FT: 150,000
SALES (est): 6.4MM **Privately Held**
SIC: 3469 3714 Stamping metal for the trade; gas tanks, motor vehicle

(G-3430)
BUILDING CTRL INTEGRATORS LLC
300 E Bus Way Ste 200 (45241)
PHONE.................513 247-6154
Dave Milar, *Branch Mgr*
EMP: 6
SALES (corp-wide): 17.1MM **Privately Held**
WEB: www.bcicontrols.com
SIC: 3822 Temperature controls, automatic

GEOGRAPHIC SECTION

Cincinnati - Hamilton County (G-3456)

PA: Building Control Integrators, Llc
  383 N Liberty St
  Powell OH 43065
  614 334-3300

(G-3431)
BURNS & RINK ENTERPRISES LLC
Also Called: PES
2016 Elm St (45202-4979)
PHONE.....................513 421-7799
Chris Burns,
Tammy Burns,
EMP: 5 EST: 2009
SALES (est): 414.7K Privately Held
SIC: 2759 Commercial printing

(G-3432)
BUZZ SEATING INC (PA)
623 N Wayne Ave (45215-2250)
P.O. Box 31379 (45231-0379)
PHONE.....................877 263-5737
Dan Ohara, President
▲ EMP: 15
SQ FT: 12,982
SALES: 6.2MM Privately Held
WEB: www.buzzseating.com
SIC: 2521 Chairs, office: padded, upholstered or plain: wood

(G-3433)
BWAY CORPORATION
Also Called: Bwaypackaging
8200 Broadwell Rd (45244-1608)
PHONE.....................513 388-2200
Teri Raleigh, Safety Mgr
Leslie Bradshaw, Opers Staff
Teresa Cherry, Engineer
Allen Thornton, Engineer
Brian Wilber, Engineer
EMP: 20
SALES (corp-wide): 1.1B Privately Held
SIC: 3411 Metal cans
HQ: Bway Corporation
  375 Northridge Rd Ste 600
  Atlanta GA 30350

(G-3434)
BYER STEEL REBAR INC
200 W North Bend Rd (45216-1728)
PHONE.....................513 821-6400
Burke Byer, President
Jonas Allen, COO
Debi Debellevue, Accounts Mgr
Chris Valone, Accounts Mgr
Steve Weber, Accounts Mgr
EMP: 25
SQ FT: 48,000
SALES (est): 6.8MM Privately Held
WEB: www.abssteel.com
SIC: 3441 Fabricated structural metal

(G-3435)
C & W CUSTOM WDWKG CO INC
11949 Tramway Dr (45241-1666)
PHONE.....................513 891-6340
Dave Williams, Principal
Steven Cornett, Principal
EMP: 20
SQ FT: 3,000
SALES (est): 2.6MM Privately Held
WEB: www.candwcustomwoodworking.com
SIC: 2431 Millwork

(G-3436)
C J KREHBIEL COMPANY
Also Called: Cjk USA Print Possibilities
3962 Virginia Ave (45227-3412)
PHONE.....................513 271-6035
Tim Ruppert, CEO
Mike Donley, Safety Mgr
Doug Kohls, Purch Agent
Tim Toepfert, Controller
John D Krehbiel, Senior Mgr
▼ EMP: 62
SQ FT: 170,000
SALES: 15MM Privately Held
WEB: www.cjkusa.com
SIC: 2732 Books: printing & binding

(G-3437)
CALIFORNIA GROUNDS CARE LLC
5827 Berte St (45230-7201)
PHONE.....................513 207-0244
Roberta Christ,
EMP: 3
SALES (est): 220K Privately Held
SIC: 3524 Lawn & garden mowers & accessories

(G-3438)
CAMARGO PUBLICATIONS INC
7270 N Mingo Ln (45243-1818)
PHONE.....................513 779-7177
George Quigley Jr, President
Mary Quigley, Admin Sec
EMP: 5
SALES: 2MM Privately Held
SIC: 2721 Magazines: publishing only, not printed on site

(G-3439)
CAMPBELL HAUSFELD LLC (DH)
Also Called: Campbell Group
225 Pictoria Dr Ste 210 (45246-1616)
PHONE.....................513 367-4811
Eric Tinnemeyer, President
Frances Ann Ziemniak, Vice Pres
Dave Kohlmayer, CFO
Mary Parsell, Director
◆ EMP: 112
SQ FT: 3,000
SALES (est): 124.7MM
SALES (corp-wide): 225.3B Publicly Held
WEB: www.waynepumps.com
SIC: 3563 3546 3548 Air & gas compressors including vacuum pumps; spraying outfits: metals, paints & chemicals (compressor); power-driven handtools; welding apparatus

(G-3440)
CAPOZZOLO PRINTERS INC
4000 Hamilton Ave (45223-2602)
PHONE.....................513 542-7874
Samuel J Capozzolo II, President
Carmen L Capozzolo, Corp Secy
EMP: 4 EST: 1958
SQ FT: 13,000
SALES: 278.1K Privately Held
SIC: 2752 2791 Commercial printing, offset; color lithography; typesetting

(G-3441)
CARAUSTAR INDUSTRIES INC
Also Called: Cincinnati Paperboard
5500 Wooster Pike (45226-2227)
PHONE.....................513 871-7112
Allen Hall, Plant Mgr
Alan Hall, Facilities Mgr
Brad Toles, Sales Staff
EMP: 45
SALES (corp-wide): 3.8B Publicly Held
WEB: www.caraustar.com
SIC: 2631 Paperboard mills
HQ: Caraustar Industries, Inc.
  5000 Austell Powder Sprin
  Austell GA 30106
  770 948-3101

(G-3442)
CAREY COLOR LLC/CINCINNATI
Also Called: Carey Digital Solutions
1361 Tennessee Ave (45229-1013)
PHONE.....................513 241-5210
Stephen O'Connor, President
Jim Oconnor, Accountant
Tom Carey, Accounts Exec
Donna Stewart, Office Mgr
Beth Hogan, Manager
EMP: 5
SALES (est): 1.3MM
SALES (corp-wide): 7.2MM Privately Held
WEB: www.careydigital.com
SIC: 2759 7379 Commercial printing; computer related consulting services
PA: Tech/Iii, Inc.
  1330 Tennessee Ave Ste 2
  Cincinnati OH 45229
  513 482-7500

(G-3443)
CARGILL INCORPORATED
5204 River Rd (45233-1643)
PHONE.....................513 941-7400
Robert Mattock, Manager
EMP: 10
SQ FT: 12,000
SALES (corp-wide): 114.7B Privately Held
WEB: www.cargill.com
SIC: 2869 2899 Industrial organic chemicals; chemical preparations
PA: Cargill, Incorporated
  15407 Mcginty Rd W
  Wayzata MN 55391
  952 742-7575

(G-3444)
CARHARTT INC
2685 Edmondson Rd (45209-1910)
PHONE.....................513 657-7130
EMP: 4
SALES (corp-wide): 2.1B Privately Held
SIC: 2326 Men's & boys' work clothing
PA: Carhartt, Inc.
  5750 Mercury Dr
  Dearborn MI 48126
  313 271-8460

(G-3445)
CARLISLE AND FINCH COMPANY
4562 W Mitchell Ave (45232-1759)
PHONE.....................513 681-6080
Kurtis Finch, CEO
Brent R Finch, President
Garth Finch, Vice Pres
Andy Herring, Plant Mgr
Bob Batsche, QC Mgr
EMP: 30 EST: 1897
SQ FT: 45,000
SALES (est): 6.6MM Privately Held
WEB: www.carlislefinch.com
SIC: 3648 3471 3641 Searchlights; floodlights; plating & polishing; electric lamps

(G-3446)
CARRILLO PALLETS LLC
1292 Glendale Milford Rd (45215-1209)
PHONE.....................513 942-2210
Francisco Carrillo, Principal
EMP: 4 EST: 2010
SALES (est): 255.7K Privately Held
SIC: 2448 Pallets, wood & wood with metal

(G-3447)
CASCO MFG SOLUTIONS INC
3107 Spring Grove Ave (45225-1821)
PHONE.....................513 681-0003
Melissa Mangold, President
Thomas Mangold, Chairman
Terri Mangold, Vice Pres
Scott Clifford, CFO
David Stewart, Human Res Mgr
▲ EMP: 60 EST: 1959
SQ FT: 72,000
SALES (est): 10.6MM Privately Held
WEB: www.cascosolutions.com
SIC: 2515 7641 3841 2522 Mattresses, containing felt, foam rubber, urethane, etc.; upholstery work; surgical & medical instruments; office furniture, except wood; household furnishings

(G-3448)
CATERINGSTONE
6119 Kenwood Rd (45243-2307)
PHONE.....................513 410-1064
Dr David Pensak, CEO
EMP: 6
SALES (est): 224.6K Privately Held
SIC: 2599 Carts, restaurant equipment

(G-3449)
CBD MEDIA HOLDINGS LLC (DH)
312 Plum St Ste 900 (45202-2693)
PHONE.....................513 217-9483
Doug Myers, President
John P Schwing, CFO
EMP: 3
SALES (est): 871.9K Privately Held
SIC: 2741 Directories, telephone: publishing only, not printed on site

(G-3450)
CDS SIGNS
11024 Reading Rd (45241-1929)
PHONE.....................513 563-7446
Charles P Coburn, Owner
Charles Coburn, Owner
EMP: 3 EST: 1996
SQ FT: 2,000
SALES (est): 176K Privately Held
SIC: 3993 Signs & advertising specialties

(G-3451)
CECO FILTERS INC
4625 Red Bank Rd Ste 200 (45227-1552)
PHONE.....................513 458-2600
Mary Buckius, President
EMP: 4
SALES (est): 87.6K
SALES (corp-wide): 337.3MM Publicly Held
SIC: 3564 Filters, air: furnaces, air conditioning equipment, etc.
PA: Ceco Environmental Corp.
  14651 Dallas Pkwy
  Dallas TX 75254
  513 458-2600

(G-3452)
CECO GROUP INC (HQ)
4625 Red Bank Rd Ste 200 (45227-1552)
PHONE.....................513 458-2600
Benton Cook, CFO
◆ EMP: 4
SALES (est): 81.8MM
SALES (corp-wide): 337.3MM Publicly Held
SIC: 8711 8734 3443 3564 Engineering services; testing laboratories; industrial vessels, tanks & containers; blowers & fans; filters, air: furnaces, air conditioning equipment, etc.; sheet metalwork; sheet metal specialties, not stamped; roofing, siding & sheet metal work; sheet metalwork
PA: Ceco Environmental Corp.
  14651 Dallas Pkwy
  Dallas TX 75254
  513 458-2600

(G-3453)
CECO GROUP GLOBAL HOLDINGS LLC (HQ)
4625 Red Bank Rd Ste 200 (45227-1552)
PHONE.....................513 458-2600
EMP: 3 EST: 2015
SALES (est): 640.2K
SALES (corp-wide): 337.3MM Publicly Held
SIC: 3564 Purification & dust collection equipment
PA: Ceco Environmental Corp.
  14651 Dallas Pkwy
  Dallas TX 75254
  513 458-2600

(G-3454)
CEMEDINE NORTH AMERICA LLC
2142 Western Ave (45214-1744)
PHONE.....................513 618-4652
Takuo Ishibashi, President
Naoto Nakajima, Treasurer
EMP: 1
SALES (est): 1.3MM
SALES (corp-wide): 5.6B Privately Held
SIC: 2891 Adhesives & sealants
HQ: Kaneka Americas Holding, Inc.
  6250 Underwood Rd
  Pasadena TX 77507
  281 474-7084

(G-3455)
CENTRAL BUSINESS PRODUCTS INC
3722 Vernier Dr (45251-2433)
PHONE.....................513 385-5899
Thomas Taulbee, President
EMP: 3
SALES (est): 75K Privately Held
SIC: 3579 Perforators (office machines)

(G-3456)
CENTRAL FABRICATORS INC
408 Poplar St (45214-2481)
PHONE.....................513 621-1240
David A Angner, President
Micheal Lewis, Vice Pres
Daniel Meade, Vice Pres
EMP: 26 EST: 1945
SQ FT: 65,000

Cincinnati - Hamilton County (G-3457)

SALES: 2.5MM **Privately Held**
WEB: www.centralfabricators.com
SIC: 3443 Tanks, standard or custom fabricated: metal plate; vessels, process or storage (from boiler shops): metal plate; heat exchangers, plate type

(G-3457)
CENTRAL READY MIX LLC (PA)
6310 E Kemper Rd Ste 125 (45241-2370)
P.O. Box 70, Monroe (45050-0070)
PHONE..................513 402-5001
Toll Free:........................888 -
Robert Cherry,
EMP: 30 **EST:** 1934
SQ FT: 8,000
SALES (est): 11.1MM **Privately Held**
WEB: www.morainematerials.com
SIC: 3273 1442 Ready-mixed concrete; sand mining

(G-3458)
CENTRAL READY-MIX OF OHIO LLC
6310 E Kemper Rd Ste 125 (45241-2370)
PHONE..................614 252-3452
Mike Fox,
Joe Tanner,
EMP: 40
SALES (est): 1.9MM **Privately Held**
SIC: 3273 Ready-mixed concrete

(G-3459)
CENTRAL USA WIRELESS LLC
11210 Montgomery Rd (45249-2311)
PHONE..................513 469-1500
Angie Flottemesch, *Opers Staff*
Mike Dalton, *CFO*
Chris Hildebrant, *Sales Staff*
EMP: 28
SALES (est): 2.9MM **Privately Held**
SIC: 7622 3663 Antenna repair & installation; antennas, transmitting & communications

(G-3460)
CFM INTERNATIONAL INC
1 Neumann Way (45215-1915)
PHONE..................513 563-4180
Pierre Fabre, *Branch Mgr*
EMP: 36
SALES (corp-wide): 16.8MM **Privately Held**
SIC: 3724 Aircraft engines & engine parts
PA: Cfm International, Inc.
    6440 Aviation Way
    West Chester OH 45069
    513 552-2787

(G-3461)
CFM RELIGION PUBG GROUP LLC (PA)
8805 Governors Hill Dr # 400 (45249-3319)
PHONE..................513 931-4050
Matthew Thibeau, *President*
EMP: 31
SALES (est): 34.4MM **Privately Held**
SIC: 2721 8741 Magazines: publishing only, not printed on site; management services

(G-3462)
CHALLENGE TARGETS
2524 Spring Grove Ave (45214-1730)
P.O. Box 75040, Fort Thomas KY (41075-0040)
PHONE..................859 462-5851
Brad Brune, *Owner*
Rob Kallschmidt, *VP Opers*
EMP: 4
SALES: 600K **Privately Held**
SIC: 3949 Targets, archery & rifle shooting

(G-3463)
CHAMPION OPCO LLC (PA)
Also Called: Champion Windows Manufacturing
12121 Champion Way (45241-6419)
PHONE..................513 327-7338
Jim Mishler, *CEO*
Donald R Jones, *President*
Joe Faisant, *CFO*
▲ **EMP:** 300 **EST:** 1953
SQ FT: 500,000

SALES (est): 516.4MM **Privately Held**
WEB: www.championfactorydirct.com
SIC: 3089 1761 3442 Window frames & sash, plastic; siding contractor; storm doors or windows, metal

(G-3464)
CHARGER CONNECTION
7779 Meadowcreek Dr (45244-2956)
PHONE..................888 427-5829
Larry Morgan, *Principal*
EMP: 3
SALES (est): 179.9K **Privately Held**
SIC: 3621 Storage battery chargers, motor & engine generator type

(G-3465)
CHARLES J MEYERS
Also Called: American Custom Polishing
866 Suncreek Ct (45238-4837)
PHONE..................513 922-2866
Charles J Meyers, *Owner*
EMP: 3
SALES (est): 182.9K **Privately Held**
SIC: 3471 Polishing, metals or formed products

(G-3466)
CHATTANOOGA LASER CUTTING LLC
891 Redna Ter (45215-1110)
PHONE..................513 779-7200
Eric Hill,
EMP: 50
SQ FT: 34,000
SALES (est): 1.6MM **Privately Held**
WEB: www.chattanoogalaser.com
SIC: 3441 Fabricated structural metal

(G-3467)
CHC MANUFACTURING INC (PA)
10270 Wayne Ave (45215-1127)
PHONE..................513 821-7757
Patrick McLaughlin, *CEO*
Mark Lambert, *President*
Robert J Christen, *Treasurer*
Lonnie Reynolds, *Supervisor*
EMP: 21
SALES (est): 8MM **Privately Held**
SIC: 3446 3441 Stairs, staircases, stair treads: prefabricated metal; fabricated structural metal

(G-3468)
CHESTER LABS INC
900 Section Rd Ste A (45237)
PHONE..................513 458-3871
Robert King, *Principal*
EMP: 22
SALES (est): 3.5MM **Privately Held**
SIC: 2834 Pharmaceutical preparations

(G-3469)
CHESTER PACKAGING LLC
1900 Section Rd Ste A (45237-3308)
PHONE..................513 458-3840
Charlie Mills, *President*
Thomas L Twilling, *VP Finance*
◆ **EMP:** 120 **EST:** 1945
SQ FT: 110,000
SALES (est): 20.5MM
SALES (corp-wide): 5.9B **Privately Held**
WEB: www.chester-labs.com
SIC: 2842 2841 2834 Specialty cleaning, polishes & sanitation goods; soap & other detergents; dermatologicals
PA: Medline Industries, Inc.
    3 Lakes Dr
    Northfield IL 60093
    847 949-5500

(G-3470)
CHICA BANDS LLC
6216 Madison Rd (45227-1908)
P.O. Box 30537 (45230-0537)
PHONE..................513 871-4300
Meredith Finn, *Owner*
Marguerita Perez, *Principal*
EMP: 7
SALES (est): 548.3K **Privately Held**
SIC: 3089 Bands, plastic

(G-3471)
CHIPMAN MACHINING CO INC
2900 Spring Grove Ave (45225-2115)
PHONE..................513 681-8515

David Chipman, *President*
Richard Chipman, *Vice Pres*
EMP: 3
SALES: 250K **Privately Held**
SIC: 3599 Machine shop, jobbing & repair

(G-3472)
CHOICE BRANDS ADHESIVES LTD
666 Redna Ter Ste 500 (45215-1166)
PHONE..................800 330-5566
Jeffrey Allison, *Principal*
EMP: 5
SALES (est): 373.5K **Privately Held**
SIC: 2891 Adhesives

(G-3473)
CHRIS ERHART FOUNDRY & MCH CO
1240 Mehring Way (45203-1836)
PHONE..................513 421-6550
Daniel J Erhart, *President*
Kate Wesseling, *Purch Agent*
EMP: 30 **EST:** 1854
SQ FT: 40,000
SALES (est): 7MM **Privately Held**
WEB: www.erhart.com
SIC: 3321 Gray iron castings

(G-3474)
CHROMAFLO TECHNOLOGIES CORP
620 Shepherd Dr (45215-2104)
PHONE..................513 733-5111
Diane Wills, *Supervisor*
EMP: 110
SALES (corp-wide): 48MM **Privately Held**
SIC: 2816 2865 3087 Inorganic pigments; color pigments, organic; custom compound purchased resins
PA: Chromaflo Technologies Corporation
    2600 Michigan Ave
    Ashtabula OH 44004
    440 997-0081

(G-3475)
CIGARS OF CINCY
1467 Larann Ln (45231-5315)
PHONE..................513 931-5926
Melissa St Hilaire, *Principal*
EMP: 3
SALES (est): 184.1K **Privately Held**
SIC: 2121 Cigars

(G-3476)
CIMX LLC
Also Called: Cimx Software
4625 Red Bank Rd Ste 200 (45227-1552)
PHONE..................513 248-7700
Anthony Cuilwik, *Principal*
Kristin Cuilwik, *Manager*
Comfort Wendel, *Director*
EMP: 30
SQ FT: 12,000
SALES (est): 3.3MM **Privately Held**
WEB: www.cimx.com
SIC: 7372 7371 Prepackaged software; custom computer programming services

(G-3477)
CINCINNATI - VULCAN COMPANY
5353 Spring Grove Ave (45217-1026)
PHONE..................513 242-5300
Garry C Ferraris, *President*
Kathy Hughes, *Office Mgr*
EMP: 60
SQ FT: 6,000
SALES: 11.6MM
SALES (corp-wide): 13.4MM **Privately Held**
WEB: www.vulcanoil.com
SIC: 5983 2992 5171 2899 Fuel oil dealers; oils & greases, blending & compounding; petroleum bulk stations; petroleum terminals; chemical preparations; specialty cleaning, polishes & sanitation goods; soap & other detergents
PA: Coolant Control, Inc.
    5353 Spring Grove Ave
    Cincinnati OH 45217
    513 471-8770

(G-3478)
CINCINNATI A FLTER SLS SVC INC
Also Called: Cafco Filter
4815 Para Dr (45237-5009)
PHONE..................513 242-3400
Edward W Flick, *CEO*
Mark Flick, *President*
EMP: 21
SQ FT: 12,500
SALES (est): 10MM **Privately Held**
WEB: www.cafcoairfilter.com
SIC: 5075 7349 3564 Air filters; building component cleaning service; filters, air: furnaces, air conditioning equipment, etc.

(G-3479)
CINCINNATI ADVG PDTS LLC (HQ)
Also Called: Wear Magic
12150 Northwest Blvd (45246-1231)
PHONE..................513 346-7310
Jesse King, *Opers Staff*
Emma Pearl, *Purch Mgr*
Rick Mouty,
EMP: 46
SQ FT: 40,000
SALES: 10MM
SALES (corp-wide): 242.8MM **Privately Held**
WEB: www.profillholdings.com
SIC: 2262 Screen printing: manmade fiber & silk broadwoven fabrics
PA: Hit Promotional Products, Inc.
    7150 Bryan Dairy Rd
    Largo FL 33777
    727 541-5561

(G-3480)
CINCINNATI AIR CONDITIONING CO
Also Called: Honeywell Authorized Dealer
2080 Northwest Dr (45231-1700)
PHONE..................513 721-5622
Mark Radtke, *President*
Michael Geiger, *Corp Secy*
Bill Wolf, *Project Mgr*
Patrick Doan, *Engineer*
Chris Fahrenholz, *Engineer*
EMP: 55 **EST:** 1939
SQ FT: 30,000
SALES (est): 17.2MM **Privately Held**
WEB: www.cincinnatiair.com
SIC: 1711 3822 Warm air heating & air conditioning contractor; refrigeration contractor; auto controls regulating residntl & coml environmt & applncs

(G-3481)
CINCINNATI ASSN FOR THE BLIND
2045 Gilbert Ave (45202-1403)
PHONE..................513 221-8558
Toll Free:........................888 -
John Mitchell, *CEO*
Amy Scrivner, *Development*
Jennifer Dubois, *Finance*
Hanna Firestone, *Marketing Staff*
Judy Hale, *Info Tech Mgr*
▲ **EMP:** 120 **EST:** 1910
SQ FT: 88,000
SALES: 9.4MM **Privately Held**
SIC: 8331 8322 2891 Sheltered workshop; association for the handicapped; adhesives & sealants

(G-3482)
CINCINNATI BARGE RAIL TRML LLC
1707 Riverside Dr (45202-1710)
PHONE..................513 227-3611
Jeff Stewart, *Vice Pres*
Timothy Roddy, *Sales Staff*
Jeffrey R Stewart, *Mng Member*
Tim Roddy, *Mng Member*
James Rose, *Mng Member*
EMP: 4
SALES (est): 269K **Privately Held**
SIC: 4225 3537 1629 3312 General warehousing & storage; industrial trucks & tractors; dams, waterways, docks & other marine construction; rails, rerolled or renewed

▲ = Import ▼ = Export
◆ = Import/Export

GEOGRAPHIC SECTION
Cincinnati - Hamilton County (G-3508)

(G-3483)
CINCINNATI BELL ANY DSTNCE INC
221 E 4th St Ste 700 (45202-4118)
P.O. Box 2301 (45201-2301)
PHONE.................................513 397-9900
Theodore H Torbeck, *CEO*
David L Heimbach, *COO*
Shua T Duckworth, *Vice Pres*
Leigh R Fox, *CFO*
Kurt Freyberger, *CFO*
EMP: 615
SALES (est): 66.7MM
SALES (corp-wide): 1.3B **Publicly Held**
SIC: 3669 Mfg Communications Equipment
HQ: Cincinnati Bell Telephone Company Llc
209 W 7th St Fl 1
Cincinnati OH 45202
513 565-9402

(G-3484)
CINCINNATI BINDERY & PACKG INC
2838 Spring Grove Ave (45225-2268)
PHONE.................................859 816-0282
Emmett Grummich, *President*
EMP: 8
SALES (est): 1MM **Privately Held**
SIC: 2789 Bookbinding & related work

(G-3485)
CINCINNATI BIOREFINING CORP (HQ)
470 Este Ave (45232)
PHONE.................................513 482-8800
Gary R Heminger, *President*
EMP: 5
SALES (est): 38.3MM **Publicly Held**
SIC: 2079 Edible fats & oils

(G-3486)
CINCINNATI BLACKTOP COMPANY
4992 Gray Rd (45232-1513)
P.O. Box 141100 (45250-1100)
PHONE.................................513 681-0952
Fax: 513 681-1519
EMP: 12
SQ FT: 2,500
SALES (est): 1.3MM **Privately Held**
SIC: 3241 Mfg Hydraulic Cement

(G-3487)
CINCINNATI CONVERTORS INC
1730 Cleneay Ave (45212-3506)
PHONE.................................513 731-6600
Kristin Goltra, *President*
Angie Holt, *Admin Asst*
EMP: 12
SQ FT: 15,000
SALES: 2.5MM **Privately Held**
WEB: www.cincinnaticonvertors.com
SIC: 2759 Flexographic printing

(G-3488)
CINCINNATI CRT INDEX PRESS INC
119 W Central Pkwy (45202-1075)
PHONE.................................513 241-1450
Gregory Arvanetes, *President*
Mark Beatty, *General Mgr*
Joseph W Shea III, *Vice Pres*
EMP: 12 **EST:** 1892
SALES (est): 833.3K **Privately Held**
WEB: www.courtindex.com
SIC: 2711 Commercial printing & newspaper publishing combined

(G-3489)
CINCINNATI CTRL DYNAMICS INC
4924 Para Dr (45237-5012)
PHONE.................................513 242-7300
Jeffrey Bao, *President*
Christopher Bao, *Co-Owner*
Derick Bao, *Co-Owner*
Jeffrey Bad, *Director*
Richard Burkel, *Director*
EMP: 8 **EST:** 1976
SQ FT: 20,000
SALES (est): 1.4MM **Privately Held**
WEB: www.ccdi1.com
SIC: 3625 3829 7373 Control equipment, electric; measuring & controlling devices; systems software development services

(G-3490)
CINCINNATI DRVELINE HYDRAULICS
1220 W 8th St (45203-1005)
PHONE.................................513 651-2406
Joe Klawitter, *President*
EMP: 3
SALES (est): 498.8K **Privately Held**
SIC: 3714 Drive shafts, motor vehicle

(G-3491)
CINCINNATI ENQUIRER
312 Elm St Fl 18 (45202-2721)
PHONE.................................513 721-2700
Mike Ballman, *Principal*
Michael Kilian, *Director*
EMP: 27
SALES (est): 8.3MM **Privately Held**
SIC: 2711 Newspapers, publishing & printing

(G-3492)
CINCINNATI GASKET PKG MFG INC
Also Called: Cincinnati Gasket & Indus GL
40 Illinois Ave (45215-5512)
PHONE.................................513 761-3458
Lawrence Uhlenbrock, *President*
Barry Ruter, *General Mgr*
Frank Duttenhofer, *Principal*
Henry D Hopf, *Principal*
Becky Knecht, *Vice Pres*
▲ **EMP:** 45
SQ FT: 75,000
SALES (est): 8.1MM **Privately Held**
WEB: www.cincinnatigasket.com
SIC: 3229 3053 Glassware, industrial; gaskets, all materials

(G-3493)
CINCINNATI GEARING SYSTEMS INC (PA)
5757 Mariemont Ave (45227-4216)
PHONE.................................513 527-8600
Evans L Decamp, *President*
Walter L Rye, *Chairman*
Kenneth Kiehl, *Vice Pres*
Mark Moeves, *Plant Mgr*
EMP: 75 **EST:** 1941
SQ FT: 100,000
SALES (est): 33.5MM **Privately Held**
WEB: www.steeltreating.com
SIC: 3398 3471 Metal heat treating; plating & polishing

(G-3494)
CINCINNATI GEARING SYSTEMS INC
301 Milford Pkwy (45227)
PHONE.................................513 527-8634
Kenneth Kiehl, *Vice Pres*
EMP: 140
SALES (corp-wide): 33.5MM **Privately Held**
SIC: 3462 Gears, forged steel
PA: Cincinnati Gearing Systems Incorporated
5757 Mariemont Ave
Cincinnati OH 45227
513 527-8600

(G-3495)
CINCINNATI GEARING SYSTEMS INC
5757 Mariemont Ave (45227-4216)
PHONE.................................513 527-8600
Dan Thomas, *Plant Supt*
Kent Kiehl, *Manager*
EMP: 75
SALES (est): 11.3MM
SALES (corp-wide): 33.5MM **Privately Held**
WEB: www.steeltreating.com
SIC: 3398 Metal heat treating
PA: Cincinnati Gearing Systems Incorporated
5757 Mariemont Ave
Cincinnati OH 45227
513 527-8600

(G-3496)
CINCINNATI GEARING SYSTEMS INC
5757 Mariemont Ave (45227-4216)
PHONE.................................513 527-8600
Robert Rye, *Branch Mgr*
EMP: 102
SALES (est): 8.3MM
SALES (corp-wide): 33.5MM **Privately Held**
WEB: www.steeltreating.com
SIC: 3714 Gears, motor vehicle
PA: Cincinnati Gearing Systems Incorporated
5757 Mariemont Ave
Cincinnati OH 45227
513 527-8600

(G-3497)
CINCINNATI GILBERT MCH TL LLC
3366 Beekman St (45223-2424)
PHONE.................................513 541-4815
Rein Petry, *Vice Pres*
John Rolfes, *Project Engr*
James Malatin, *Treasurer*
Dan Randolph, *Office Mgr*
Stan Rudolph, *Info Tech Dir*
▲ **EMP:** 30 **EST:** 1995
SQ FT: 50,000
SALES (est): 4.7MM **Privately Held**
WEB: www.cincinnatigilbert.com
SIC: 3541 Drilling machine tools (metal cutting)

(G-3498)
CINCINNATI LASER CUTTING LLC
Also Called: Cincinnati Metal Fabricating
891 Redna Ter (45215-1110)
PHONE.................................513 779-7200
Eric Copeland Hill, *President*
EMP: 40 **EST:** 1999
SQ FT: 45,000
SALES (est): 5.4MM **Privately Held**
WEB: www.cincylaser.com
SIC: 3441 Fabricated structural metal

(G-3499)
CINCINNATI MAGAZINE
441 Vine St Ste 200 (45202-2039)
PHONE.................................513 421-4300
Patrice Watson, *Principal*
Chris Ohmer, *Mktg Dir*
Tammy Vilaboy, *Adv Dir*
Kathryn Landis, *Director*
EMP: 3
SALES (est): 393.6K **Privately Held**
SIC: 2721 Magazines: publishing only, not printed on site

(G-3500)
CINCINNATI MARLINS INC
616 W North Bend Rd (45224-1424)
PHONE.................................513 761-3320
Brian Bridgeford, *President*
EMP: 8
SQ FT: 500
SALES (est): 1MM **Privately Held**
SIC: 7997 2086 Country club, membership; swimming club, membership; soft drinks: packaged in cans, bottles, etc.

(G-3501)
CINCINNATI MINE MACHINERY CO
2950 Jonrose Ave (45239-5319)
PHONE.................................513 522-7777
Robert J Stenger, *President*
Ron Paolello, *General Mgr*
William D Stenger, *Treasurer*
Bobby Stenger, *Mktg Dir*
Jane Wegman, *Admin Sec*
▲ **EMP:** 55 **EST:** 1924
SQ FT: 75,000
SALES (est): 13MM **Privately Held**
WEB: www.cinmine.com
SIC: 3541 3535 Machine tools, metal cutting type; conveyors & conveying equipment

(G-3502)
CINCINNATI MOLD INCORPORATED
225 Stille Dr (45233-1646)
PHONE.................................513 922-1888
Edward Korb, *President*
James Korb, *Vice Pres*
Jim Korb, *Treasurer*
EMP: 3
SALES: 500K **Privately Held**
SIC: 3544 Industrial molds

(G-3503)
CINCINNATI PATTERN COMPANY
2405 Spring Grove Ave (45214-1727)
PHONE.................................513 241-9872
Michael J Ballard, *President*
EMP: 14
SQ FT: 8,000
SALES: 1MM **Privately Held**
SIC: 3543 Foundry patternmaking

(G-3504)
CINCINNATI PRESERVING COMPANY (DH)
Also Called: David Evans Foods
3015 E Kemper Rd (45241-1514)
PHONE.................................513 771-2000
Andrew Liscow, *CEO*
Dan Cohen, *Vice Pres*
Joe Hendricks, *Controller*
Kimberly Sueberling, *Sales Executive*
▲ **EMP:** 18 **EST:** 1924
SQ FT: 30,000
SALES (est): 10.8MM
SALES (corp-wide): 17.8MM **Privately Held**
WEB: www.clearbrookfarms.com
SIC: 2033 Fruit pie mixes & fillings: packaged in cans, jars, etc.; preserves, including imitation: in cans, jars, etc.
HQ: Glencoe Capital, Llc
200 N Lasalle St Ste 2150
Chicago IL 60606
312 795-6300

(G-3505)
CINCINNATI RECREATION COMM
Also Called: Cincinnati City Boat Ramp
3540 Southside Ave (45204-1138)
PHONE.................................513 921-5657
Kathy Lang, *Director*
EMP: 3
SQ FT: 2,048
SALES (est): 400K **Privately Held**
SIC: 3536 Boat lifts

(G-3506)
CINCINNATI RENEWABLE FUELS LLC
4700 Este Ave (45232-1415)
PHONE.................................513 482-8800
Arunas Paliulis, *CEO*
Jeffrie Defraties, *COO*
Rajive Khosla, *CFO*
◆ **EMP:** 75
SALES (est): 38.3MM **Publicly Held**
SIC: 2079 Edible fats & oils
HQ: Cincinnati Biorefining Corp
470 Este Ave
Cincinnati OH 45232

(G-3507)
CINCINNATI SPECIALTIES LLC
501 Murray Rd (45217-1014)
PHONE.................................513 242-3300
James McKenna,
EMP: 175
SQ FT: 61,020
SALES: 70MM
SALES (corp-wide): 2.5B **Privately Held**
WEB: www.pmcsg.com
SIC: 2819 Industrial inorganic chemicals
HQ: Pmc Specialties Group, Inc.
501 Murray Rd
Cincinnati OH 45217

(G-3508)
CINCINNATI VALVE COMPANY
Also Called: Cincinnati Valve Lunkenheimer
1245 Hill Smith Dr (45215-1228)
PHONE.................................513 471-8258

Cincinnati - Hamilton County (G-3509)

Suran Hegde, *President*
EMP: 14
SALES (est): 2MM **Privately Held**
SIC: 3491 Industrial valves

(G-3509)
CINCINNATI VALVE COMPANY
1245 Hill Smith Dr (45215-1228)
P.O. Box 141451 (45250-1451)
PHONE....................513 471-8258
Suran Hegde, *President*
Juan Del Rincon, *Human Res Dir*
▲ **EMP:** 13
SQ FT: 200,000
SALES (est): 2.6MM **Privately Held**
WEB: www.lunkenheimercvc.com
SIC: 3491 Industrial valves

(G-3510)
CINCINNATI WINDOW SHADE INC (PA)
Also Called: Cincinnati Window Decor
3004 Harris Ave (45212-2404)
PHONE....................513 631-7200
James G Frederick, *President*
Janet Frederick, *Treasurer*
James M Frederick, *Admin Sec*
EMP: 16
SQ FT: 15,000
SALES (est): 5.4MM **Privately Held**
SIC: 5023 5719 2591 Window furnishings; window shades; venetian blinds; vertical blinds; window shades; venetian blinds; vertical blinds; window shades; venetian blinds; blinds vertical

(G-3511)
CINCINNATI WOOD PRODUCTS CO
2644 Colerain Ave (45214-1712)
PHONE....................513 542-0569
Tim Janson, *Owner*
EMP: 3 **EST:** 1933
SALES: 100K **Privately Held**
SIC: 2431 Woodwork, interior & ornamental

(G-3512)
CINCINNATI WOODWORKS INC
2161 Elysian Pl (45219-1603)
PHONE....................513 241-6412
Charles Kussmaul, *President*
Janis Kussmaul, *Admin Sec*
EMP: 3
SQ FT: 12,000
SALES (est): 240K **Privately Held**
SIC: 2431 7532 Millwork; antique & classic automobile restoration

(G-3513)
CINCINNATTI PREMIER CANDY LLC
Also Called: Marpro
5141 Fischer Ave (45217-1157)
PHONE....................513 253-0079
Bill Ward,
Bill Clark,
Fred Runk,
Sandy Runk,
EMP: 36 **EST:** 1936
SQ FT: 30,000
SALES (est): 1.2MM **Privately Held**
WEB: www.marshmallowcone.com
SIC: 2064 2099 Candy & other confectionery products; food preparations

(G-3514)
CINCY GLASS INC
3249 Fredonia Ave (45229-3309)
PHONE....................513 241-0455
Michael T Brown, *President*
EMP: 8
SALES (est): 1.3MM **Privately Held**
SIC: 3441 Fabricated structural metal

(G-3515)
CINEX INC
2641 Cummins St (45225-2099)
PHONE....................513 921-2825
Gary R Smith, *President*
Judith A Smith, *Corp Secy*
EMP: 65 **EST:** 1966
SQ FT: 35,000
SALES (est): 8.1MM **Privately Held**
SIC: 3599 Machine shop, jobbing & repair

(G-3516)
CINFAB LLC
5240 Lester Rd (45213-2522)
PHONE....................513 396-6100
Stu Cameron, *Superintendent*
Bern Chouteau, *Vice Pres*
Mel Phillips, *Project Mgr*
Kathy Mitchell, *Safety Mgr*
Steve Merman, *Foreman/Supr*
EMP: 140
SQ FT: 36,500
SALES (est): 38MM **Privately Held**
WEB: www.cinfab.com
SIC: 3444 Sheet metalwork

(G-3517)
CINN WIRE E D M INC
6850 Colerain Ave (45239-5544)
PHONE....................513 741-5402
Judith Coster, *CEO*
Robert Coster, *President*
EMP: 3
SQ FT: 3,000
SALES (est): 343.8K **Privately Held**
SIC: 3544 Special dies, tools, jigs & fixtures

(G-3518)
CINTAS CORPORATION (PA)
6800 Cintas Blvd (45262)
PHONE....................513 459-1200
Scott D Farmer, *Ch of Bd*
Pablo Almeida, *General Mgr*
Todd Schneider, *COO*
Michael Hansen, *Exec VP*
Thomas E Frooman, *Senior VP*
◆ **EMP:** 1500
SALES: 6.4B **Publicly Held**
WEB: www.cintas-corp.com
SIC: 7218 2337 2326 5084 Industrial uniform supply; uniforms, except athletic: women's, misses' & juniors'; work uniforms; safety equipment

(G-3519)
CINTAS CORPORATION
Also Called: Cintas Uniforms AP Fcilty Svcs
5570 Ridge Ave (45213-2516)
PHONE....................513 631-5750
Marie Seng, *Branch Mgr*
EMP: 100
SALES (corp-wide): 6.4B **Publicly Held**
SIC: 2326 2337 7218 5084 Work uniforms; uniforms, except athletic: women's, misses' & juniors'; industrial uniform supply; wiping towel supply; treated equipment supply: mats, rugs, mops, cloths, etc.; safety equipment
PA: Cintas Corporation
  6800 Cintas Blvd
  Cincinnati OH 45262
  513 459-1200

(G-3520)
CINTAS SALES CORPORATION (HQ)
6800 Cintas Blvd (45262)
PHONE....................513 459-1200
Richard T Farmer, *Ch of Bd*
Robert J Kohlhepp, *Vice Ch Bd*
Scott Farmer, *President*
Arrika Garcia, *Plant Mgr*
Nick Watkins, *Plant Mgr*
EMP: 450
SALES (est): 32.2MM
SALES (corp-wide): 6.4B **Publicly Held**
SIC: 7218 2326 5136 5137 Industrial uniform supply; work clothing supply; work uniforms; uniforms, men's & boys'; uniforms, women's & children's
PA: Cintas Corporation
  6800 Cintas Blvd
  Cincinnati OH 45262
  513 459-1200

(G-3521)
CITY IRON LLC
4136 Colerain Ave (45223-2560)
PHONE....................513 721-5678
Steve Sallquist, *Principal*
EMP: 4
SQ FT: 13,266
SALES (est): 359.9K **Privately Held**
SIC: 3446 Fences or posts, ornamental iron or steel

(G-3522)
CITYWIDE MATERIALS INC
Also Called: Citywide Ready Mix
5263 Wooster Pike (45226-2228)
PHONE....................513 533-1111
Jerry Powell Jr, *Ch of Bd*
Mark Cassiere, *President*
EMP: 20
SQ FT: 560
SALES (est): 2.7MM **Privately Held**
SIC: 3273 Ready-mixed concrete

(G-3523)
CLARKE FIRE PRTECTION PDTS INC (HQ)
3133 E Kemper Rd (45241-1516)
PHONE....................513 771-2200
Dane Petrie, *Principal*
▲ **EMP:** 80
SALES (est): 19MM
SALES (corp-wide): 252.9MM **Privately Held**
SIC: 3519 Diesel, semi-diesel or duel-fuel engines, including marine
PA: Clarke Power Services, Inc.
  3133 E Kemper Rd
  Cincinnati OH 45241
  513 771-2200

(G-3524)
CLARKE POWER SERVICES INC
Also Called: Clarke Fire Protection Product
3133 E Kemper Rd (45241-1516)
PHONE....................513 771-2200
Dane Petrie, *Manager*
EMP: 35
SALES (corp-wide): 252.9MM **Privately Held**
SIC: 3463 Pump, compressor, turbine & engine forgings, except auto
PA: Clarke Power Services, Inc.
  3133 E Kemper Rd
  Cincinnati OH 45241
  513 771-2200

(G-3525)
CLASSIC RECIPE CHILI INC
Also Called: Empress Chili
10592 Taconic Ter (45215-1125)
PHONE....................513 771-1441
Jim Papakirk, *President*
EMP: 3
SQ FT: 10,000
SALES (est): 331.3K **Privately Held**
SIC: 2038 Dinners, frozen & packaged

(G-3526)
CLAYTON MANUFACTURING COMPANY
Also Called: Clayton Mfg Co
3051 Exon Ave (45241-2549)
PHONE....................513 563-1300
Ted Williams, *Engineer*
Debbie Williams, *Cust Mgr*
Todd Slieker, *Manager*
EMP: 12
SQ FT: 27,664
SALES (corp-wide): 114.2MM **Privately Held**
WEB: www.claytonindustries.com
SIC: 2842 Cleaning or polishing preparations
PA: Clayton Manufacturing Company
  17477 Hurley St
  City Of Industry CA 91744
  626 443-9381

(G-3527)
CLINE SIGNS LLC
Also Called: Fastsigns
3272 Highland Ave (45213-2508)
PHONE....................513 396-7446
Jeff Cline, *Mng Member*
EMP: 5
SALES: 600K **Privately Held**
SIC: 3993 Signs & advertising specialties

(G-3528)
CLIPSONS METAL WORKING INC
Also Called: Clipson S Metalworking
127 Novner Dr (45215-1300)
PHONE....................513 772-6393
Stuart Clipson, *President*
Patricia Clipson, *Vice Pres*
EMP: 7
SQ FT: 7,500
SALES (est): 962.4K **Privately Held**
SIC: 3599 7692 3441 Machine shop, jobbing & repair; welding repair; fabricated structural metal

(G-3529)
CLOPAY CORPORATION
1260 W Sharon Rd (45240-2917)
PHONE....................513 742-1984
William Weber, *Branch Mgr*
EMP: 5
SALES (corp-wide): 1.5B **Publicly Held**
WEB: www.clopay.com
SIC: 3081 Plastic film & sheet
HQ: Clopay Corporation
  8585 Duke Blvd
  Mason OH 45040
  800 282-2260

(G-3530)
CLOVERNOOK CENTER FOR THE BLI (PA)
7000 Hamilton Ave (45231-5240)
PHONE....................513 522-3860
Robin Usalis, *President*
Christopher Faust, *President*
Betsy Baugh, *Vice Pres*
Jacqueline L Conner, *Vice Pres*
Douglas Jacques, *Vice Pres*
EMP: 125
SQ FT: 40,000
SALES: 8.5MM **Privately Held**
WEB: www.clovernook.org
SIC: 2656 8322 7389 Paper cups, plates, dishes & utensils; rehabilitation services; fund raising organizations

(G-3531)
CLUB 513 LLC
201 E 5th St Fl 19 (45202-4152)
PHONE....................800 530-2574
Aaron R Chiles, *Mng Member*
Charles Chiles,
Jonathan Chiles,
London Chiles,
Murmith Chiles,
EMP: 6
SQ FT: 3,500
SALES: 372K **Privately Held**
SIC: 7929 2759 5099 Entertainment group; letterpress & screen printing; novelties, durable

(G-3532)
CMF CUSTOM METAL FINISHERS
7616 Anthony Wayne Ave (45216-1617)
PHONE....................513 821-8145
John Metz, *President*
EMP: 3
SALES: 600K **Privately Held**
SIC: 3471 3449 Finishing, metals or formed products; miscellaneous metalwork

(G-3533)
CNS INC (PA)
Also Called: United Graphics
3716 Montgomery Rd (45207-1131)
PHONE....................513 631-7073
Steve Siegwald, *President*
Larry Castagno, *Corp Secy*
EMP: 5
SQ FT: 3,000
SALES (est): 9.4MM **Privately Held**
SIC: 2759 2752 Business forms: printing; commercial printing, lithographic

(G-3534)
COATING APPLICATIONS INTL LLC
2860 Cooper Rd Ste 200 (45241-3368)
PHONE....................513 956-5222
Terri Coombs, *Manager*
Bruce Rowe,
Kevin Rafferty,
EMP: 5
SQ FT: 10,500
SALES (est): 510K **Privately Held**
WEB: www.caillc.com
SIC: 2672 Enameled paper: made from purchased paper

▲ = Import ▼ = Export
◆ = Import/Export

GEOGRAPHIC SECTION
Cincinnati - Hamilton County (G-3561)

(G-3535)
COCA-COLA BOTTLING CO CNSLD
5100 Duck Creek Rd (45227-1450)
PHONE..................513 527-6600
John Whitaker, *Manager*
EMP: 400
SALES (corp-wide): 4.6B **Publicly Held**
WEB: www.cokecce.com
SIC: 2086 Soft drinks: packaged in cans, bottles, etc.
PA: Coca-Cola Consolidated, Inc.
4100 Coca Cola Plz # 100
Charlotte NC 28211
704 557-4400

(G-3536)
COMBINED CONTAINER BOARD
7741 School Rd (45249-1529)
PHONE..................513 530-5700
Peter Watson, *President*
Phil Wenger, *Vice Pres*
EMP: 52
SQ FT: 162,000
SALES (est): 13.5MM
SALES (corp-wide): 3.8B **Publicly Held**
WEB: www.mpc-spc.com
SIC: 2653 Sheets, corrugated: made from purchased materials
HQ: Corrchoice, Inc.
777 3rd St Nw
Massillon OH 44647
330 833-5705

(G-3537)
COMMUNICATIONS AID INC
Also Called: University Hring Aid Assctions
222 Piedmont Ave Ste 5200 (45219-4222)
PHONE..................513 475-8453
Stephanie Lockhart, *President*
Myles Pensak, *Director*
EMP: 10
SALES (est): 800K **Privately Held**
SIC: 5999 3842 Communication equipment; hearing aids; hearing aids

(G-3538)
COMPLETE CYLINDER SERVICE INC
1240 Glendale Milford Rd (45215-1209)
PHONE..................513 772-1500
David Kleier, *Principal*
EMP: 8 **EST:** 2012
SALES (est): 1MM **Privately Held**
SIC: 3272 Cylinder pipe, prestressed or pretensioned concrete

(G-3539)
COMPLETE DRY FLOOD
6006 Madison Rd (45227-1818)
PHONE..................513 200-9274
Howard Champion, *Principal*
EMP: 3 **EST:** 2015
SALES (est): 107.4K **Privately Held**
SIC: 1799 3589 Post-disaster renovations; high pressure cleaning equipment

(G-3540)
COMPOST CINCY
5800 Este Ave (45232-1442)
PHONE..................513 278-8178
Grant A Gibson, *Principal*
EMP: 3
SALES (est): 297.2K **Privately Held**
SIC: 2875 Compost

(G-3541)
COMPUTER SYSTEM ENHANCEMENT
Also Called: Cse-Industrial Products Group
1053 Kreis Ln (45205-1523)
PHONE..................513 251-6791
Spencer Morgan, *President*
James Klein, *Vice Pres*
Patricia Morgan, *Admin Sec*
EMP: 5
SQ FT: 1,200
SALES: 150K **Privately Held**
WEB: www.cse-inc.com
SIC: 7372 5085 Prepackaged software; industrial supplies

(G-3542)
CONSOLIDATED METAL PDTS INC
1028 Depot St (45204-2073)
PHONE..................513 251-2624
John Bernloehr, *President*
Hugh M Gallagher Jr, *President*
Fred Madden, *Vice Pres*
Don Day, *QC Mgr*
Charles Schmidt, *Controller*
EMP: 130 **EST:** 1945
SQ FT: 150,000
SALES (est): 47.9MM **Privately Held**
WEB: www.cmpubolt.com
SIC: 3452 3316 3356 Bolts, metal; cold finishing of steel shapes; nonferrous rolling & drawing

(G-3543)
CONSUMER SOURCE INC
431 Elliott Ave (45215-5413)
PHONE..................513 621-7300
Carol Morgenthel, *Manager*
EMP: 7 **Privately Held**
WEB: www.apartmentguide.com
SIC: 2741 Directories: publishing only, not printed on site
HQ: Consumer Source Inc.
3585 Engrg Dr Ste 100
Norcross GA 30092
678 421-3000

(G-3544)
CONTROL CRAFT LLC
2130 Schappelle Ln (45240-2723)
PHONE..................513 674-0056
Thomas Freudiger,
Ray Buller,
EMP: 10
SQ FT: 1,600
SALES (est): 1.9MM **Privately Held**
SIC: 3613 Control panels, electric

(G-3545)
CONTROLLED RELEASE SOCIETY INC
110 E 69th St (45216-2008)
PHONE..................513 948-8000
Robert Sherwood, *Senior VP*
Bob Antenucci, *Vice Pres*
Roger Elkin, *Vice Pres*
Lisa Lewis, *Vice Pres*
Albert Lopez, *Vice Pres*
EMP: 23 **EST:** 2014
SALES (est): 1.2MM **Privately Held**
SIC: 2869 Industrial organic chemicals

(G-3546)
CONTROLS AND SHEET METAL INC (PA)
1051 Sargent St (45203-1858)
PHONE..................513 721-3610
Rick Schaible, *President*
EMP: 35 **EST:** 1983
SQ FT: 40,000
SALES (est): 10.8MM **Privately Held**
WEB: www.csm-inc.com
SIC: 5075 3444 Warm air heating & air conditioning; ducts, sheet metal

(G-3547)
COOL TIMES
6127 Fairway Dr (45212-1307)
PHONE..................513 608-5201
Calvin Lanier, *Principal*
EMP: 4
SALES (est): 438.7K **Privately Held**
SIC: 3822 Air flow controllers, air conditioning & refrigeration

(G-3548)
COOLANT CONTROL INC (PA)
5353 Spring Grove Ave (45217-1095)
PHONE..................513 471-8770
Greg Battle, *CEO*
Garry C Ferraris, *President*
Jorge Costa, *Chairman*
Kurt Maurer, *Vice Pres*
Larry Schirmann, *CFO*
▲ **EMP:** 45 **EST:** 1975
SQ FT: 30,000
SALES (est): 13.4MM **Privately Held**
WEB: www.coolantcontrol.com
SIC: 2899 2819 Chemical preparations; industrial inorganic chemicals

(G-3549)
COOPER-ATKINS CORPORATION
11353 R Hartman Hwy 110 (45241)
PHONE..................513 793-5366
David Atkin, *Owner*
EMP: 5
SALES (corp-wide): 17.4B **Publicly Held**
SIC: 3829 Measuring & controlling devices
HQ: Cooper-Atkins Corporation
33 Reeds Gap Rd
Middlefield CT 06455
860 349-3473

(G-3550)
CORNERSTONE SPCLTY WD PDTS LLC
12020 Tramway Dr (45241-1692)
PHONE..................513 772-5560
Jonathon Egbert, *Engineer*
Chad Faulkner, *Engineer*
Jim Lindner, *Engineer*
Jim Pipp, *Sales Engr*
Lisa Friemoth, *Office Mgr*
EMP: 90
SQ FT: 7,500
SALES: 18MM
SALES (corp-wide): 23.2MM **Privately Held**
WEB: www.resindek.com
SIC: 2499 Fencing, docks & other outdoor wood structural products
PA: Universal Woods, Incorporated
2600 Grassland Dr
Louisville KY 40299
502 491-1461

(G-3551)
CORNPENTRY
2122 Schappelle Ln (45240-2723)
PHONE..................513 741-0594
Dean Walters, *Owner*
EMP: 6
SALES (est): 422.6K **Privately Held**
WEB: www.cornpentry.com
SIC: 3944 Games, toys & children's vehicles

(G-3552)
CORPORATE DCMENT SOLUTIONS INC
11120 Ashburn Rd (45240-3813)
PHONE..................513 595-8200
Mary C Percy, *President*
Harold B Percy Jr, *Vice Pres*
EMP: 15
SQ FT: 15,000
SALES: 2.1MM **Privately Held**
WEB: www.cdsprint.com
SIC: 7334 2752 2759 Photocopying & duplicating services; offset & photolithographic printing; commercial printing

(G-3553)
CORRUGATED CHEMICALS INC
3865 Virginia Ave (45227-3409)
PHONE..................513 561-7773
Tod Sistrunk, *Enginr/R&D Mgr*
Tony Shoemaker, *Natl Sales Mgr*
Jan Titus, *Director*
EMP: 6
SQ FT: 23,940
SALES (corp-wide): 2.6MM **Privately Held**
WEB: www.corrugatedchemicals.com
SIC: 2869 5169 Industrial organic chemicals; chemicals & allied products
PA: Corrugated Chemicals, Inc.
5410 Homberg Dr Ste 20
Knoxville TN 37919
865 588-2471

(G-3554)
COVIDIEN HOLDING INC
2111 E Galbraith Rd (45237-1624)
PHONE..................513 948-7219
Krista Reiss, *Sales Staff*
EMP: 10 **Privately Held**
SIC: 3841 Surgical & medical instruments
HQ: Covidien Holding Inc.
710 Medtronic Pkwy
Minneapolis MN 55432

(G-3555)
CPG - OHIO LLC (PA)
470 Northland Blvd (45240-3211)
PHONE..................513 825-4800
Ben Kaufman,
Chaim Kaufman,
EMP: 51
SALES (est): 8.8MM **Privately Held**
SIC: 2671 2673 Plastic film, coated or laminated for packaging; plastic bags: made from purchased materials

(G-3556)
CRACO EMBROIDERY INC
37 Techview Dr (45215-1980)
PHONE..................513 563-6999
Bob Crable, *President*
Rick Crable, *Vice Pres*
EMP: 9
SQ FT: 1,200
SALES (est): 561.8K **Privately Held**
SIC: 2395 Emblems, embroidered

(G-3557)
CRANIAL TECHNOLOGIES INC
4030 Smith Rd Ste 105 (45209-0008)
PHONE..................844 447-5894
Tammy Jones, *Branch Mgr*
EMP: 3 **Privately Held**
SIC: 3842 Braces, orthopedic
PA: Cranial Technologies, Inc.
1395 W Auto Dr
Tempe AZ 85284

(G-3558)
CREATIVE BLAST CO
3627 Spring Grove Ave (45223-2458)
PHONE..................513 251-4177
Paul Shoemaker, *Owner*
EMP: 3
SQ FT: 9,000
SALES (est): 220K **Privately Held**
SIC: 5999 3993 Banners, flags, decals & posters; signs & advertising specialties

(G-3559)
CRITICALAIRE LLC (PA)
11325 R Hartman Hwy 100 (45241)
PHONE..................614 499-7744
Matthew W Beecroft,
EMP: 5
SALES (est): 1.3MM **Privately Held**
SIC: 3564 Exhaust fans: industrial or commercial

(G-3560)
CROWN EQUIPMENT CORPORATION
Also Called: Crown Lift Trucks
10685 Medallion Dr (45241-4827)
PHONE..................513 874-2600
Dave Kelly, *Manager*
Scott Winters, *Manager*
EMP: 85
SALES (corp-wide): 3.1B **Privately Held**
SIC: 3537 Lift trucks, industrial: fork, platform, straddle, etc.
PA: Crown Equipment Corporation
44 S Washington St
New Bremen OH 45869
419 629-2311

(G-3561)
CRYOGENIC EQUIPMENT & SVCS INC
11959 Tramway Dr Ste 1 (45241-1666)
PHONE..................513 761-4200
Hans Vanackere, *CEO*
▲ **EMP:** 10 **EST:** 1998
SQ FT: 28,000
SALES (est): 2.8MM
SALES (corp-wide): 6.6MM **Privately Held**
WEB: www.cesgroup.com
SIC: 3585 Refrigeration & heating equipment
PA: Cryogenic Equipment And Services
Vlaswaagplein 13
Kortrijk 8501
563 726-66

Cincinnati - Hamilton County (G-3562)

GEOGRAPHIC SECTION

(G-3562)
CTEK TOOL & MACHINE COMPANY
11310 Southland Rd (45240-3201)
PHONE..................513 742-0423
Phyllis Couch, *President*
James Couch, *Vice Pres*
EMP: 6
SQ FT: 6,500
SALES (est): 850.9K **Privately Held**
SIC: 3599 Machine shop, jobbing & repair

(G-3563)
CUSTOM CARVING SOURCE LLC
3182 Beekman St (45223-2422)
PHONE..................513 407-1008
Luke Bennett, *Principal*
EMP: 3
SALES (est): 235.1K **Privately Held**
SIC: 2431 Moldings, wood: unfinished & prefinished

(G-3564)
CUSTOM CAST MARBLEWORKS INC
Also Called: Vanity Classics
3154 Exon Ave (45241-2548)
PHONE..................513 769-6505
Ron Schmidt, *CEO*
Jason Sieg, *Corp Secy*
Brian Schmidt, *Vice Pres*
Brian E Schmitt, *Vice Pres*
▲ EMP: 20
SQ FT: 36,000
SALES (est): 3.7MM **Privately Held**
SIC: 3281 Marble, building: cut & shaped

(G-3565)
CUSTOM MATERIAL HDLG EQP LLC
7868 Gapstow Brg (45231-6058)
PHONE..................513 235-5336
Stephen D Maatman,
EMP: 6
SALES (est): 410.8K **Privately Held**
SIC: 2411 Logging camps & contractors

(G-3566)
CUSTOM TOOLING COMPANY INC
603 Wayne Park Dr (45215-2848)
PHONE..................513 733-5790
Thomas Brune, *President*
Charles Brune, *Vice Pres*
EMP: 10 EST: 1963
SQ FT: 5,000
SALES (est): 1.5MM **Privately Held**
WEB: www.custom-tooling.com
SIC: 3599 Machine shop, jobbing & repair

(G-3567)
D & A ROFAEL ENTERPRISES INC
Also Called: Gold Star Chili-Burnet
3026 Burnet Ave (45219-2420)
PHONE..................513 751-4929
Ron Alsaleh, *Principal*
EMP: 5
SALES (est): 395.1K **Privately Held**
SIC: 2032 Chili with or without meat: packaged in cans, jars, etc.

(G-3568)
D & M SAW & TOOL INC
Also Called: Eccles Saw & Tool
2974 P G Graves Ln (45241-3155)
PHONE..................513 871-5433
Michael Hugenberg, *President*
EMP: 9
SQ FT: 6,000
SALES (est): 930.1K **Privately Held**
SIC: 7699 5251 3423 Knife, saw & tool sharpening & repair; chainsaws; cutting dies, except metal cutting

(G-3569)
D F ELECTRONICS INC
200 Novner Dr (45215-6002)
PHONE..................513 772-7792
Laughton Fine, *President*
Rene Kennedy, *Manager*
EMP: 75 EST: 1975
SQ FT: 27,000
SALES (est): 15.2MM **Privately Held**
WEB: www.dfelectronics.com
SIC: 3674 Solid state electronic devices

(G-3570)
D J KLINGLER INC
Also Called: Montgomery License Bureau
9999 Montgomery Rd (45242-5311)
PHONE..................513 891-2284
Donna Klingler, *President*
EMP: 6 EST: 1993
SALES (est): 583.7K **Privately Held**
SIC: 3469 7299 Automobile license tags, stamped metal; personal appearance services

(G-3571)
D-G CUSTOM CHROME LLC
5200 Lester Rd (45213-2522)
PHONE..................513 531-1881
Alex Wyatt, *President*
Don Gorman, *President*
Victoria Gorman, *Vice Pres*
EMP: 58
SQ FT: 10,162
SALES (est): 7.2MM **Privately Held**
WEB: www.dgcustomchrome.com
SIC: 5013 3471 Automotive supplies & parts; plating & polishing

(G-3572)
DADCO INC (PA)
Also Called: Rpp Containers
7365 E Kemper Rd Ste C (45249-3005)
PHONE..................513 489-2244
Scott Denoma, *President*
Jim West, *President*
EMP: 17
SQ FT: 45,000
SALES (est): 19.6MM **Privately Held**
WEB: www.rppcontainers.com
SIC: 5085 3089 Bins & containers, storage; plastic containers, except foam

(G-3573)
DADCO INC
Also Called: Rpp Containers
12151 Best Pl (45241-6402)
PHONE..................513 489-2244
Scott Denoma, *Branch Mgr*
EMP: 12
SALES (est): 1.3MM
SALES (corp-wide): 19.6MM **Privately Held**
SIC: 3089 5085 Plastic containers, except foam; bins & containers, storage
PA: Dadco, Inc.
7365 E Kemper Rd Ste C
Cincinnati OH 45249
513 489-2244

(G-3574)
DALE KESTLER
Also Called: Apollo GL Mirror Win Screen Co
3475 Cardiff Ave (45209-1317)
PHONE..................513 871-9000
Dale Kestler, *President*
EMP: 8
SQ FT: 1,500
SALES (est): 1MM **Privately Held**
SIC: 5231 5719 5211 3442 Glass; mirrors; door & window products; screens, door & window; screens, window, metal; glass construction materials; interior flat glass: plate or window; exterior flat glass: plate or window; mirrors & pictures, framed & unframed

(G-3575)
DANA GRAPHICS INC
2200 Dana Ave Fl 2 (45208-1025)
P.O. Box 42219 (45242-0219)
PHONE..................513 351-4400
Jeanne M Johnson, *President*
Charles S Johnson, *CFO*
▲ EMP: 5
SALES (est): 705.2K **Privately Held**
WEB: www.danagraphics.com
SIC: 2752 2759 Commercial printing, offset; letterpress printing

(G-3576)
DARLING INGREDIENTS INC
Also Called: Darling International
3105 Spring Grove Ave (45225-1821)
PHONE..................972 717-0300
Tim Fontaine, *Manager*
EMP: 9
SALES (corp-wide): 3.3B **Publicly Held**
WEB: www.darlingii.com
SIC: 2077 Animal & marine fats & oils
PA: Darling Ingredients Inc.
251 Oconnor Ridge Blvd
Irving TX 75038
972 717-0300

(G-3577)
DAVIS MACHINING SERVICE
602 Comet Dr (45244-1304)
PHONE..................513 528-4917
EMP: 5
SALES (est): 293.9K **Privately Held**
SIC: 3599 Mfg Industrial Machinery

(G-3578)
DB PARENT INC
3630 E Kemper Rd (45241-2011)
PHONE..................513 475-3265
Tom Heintz, *CFO*
EMP: 3
SALES (est): 265.4K **Privately Held**
SIC: 2819 Industrial inorganic chemicals

(G-3579)
DEBRA-KUEMPEL INC (HQ)
Also Called: De Bra - Kuempel
3976 Southern Ave (45227-3562)
P.O. Box 701620 (45270-1620)
PHONE..................513 271-6500
Joe D Clark, *CEO*
Fred B De Bra, *Ch of Bd*
Morris H Reed, *Corp Secy*
Robert E Cupp, *Vice Pres*
John Kuempel Jr, *Vice Pres*
EMP: 80 EST: 1944
SQ FT: 20,079
SALES (est): 29.3MM
SALES (corp-wide): 8.1B **Publicly Held**
SIC: 3446 1711 3443 3441 Architectural metalwork; mechanical contractor; fabricated plate work (boiler shop); fabricated structural metal
PA: Emcor Group, Inc.
301 Merritt 7 Fl 6
Norwalk CT 06851
203 849-7800

(G-3580)
DEGUSSA INCORPORATED
620 Shepherd Dr (45215-2104)
PHONE..................513 733-5111
Probyn Forbes, *Principal*
▲ EMP: 6 EST: 2008
SALES (est): 632.7K **Privately Held**
SIC: 2816 Inorganic pigments

(G-3581)
DELTA TRANSFORMER INC
406 Blade Ave (45216-2302)
PHONE..................513 242-9400
Shannon Hackney, *President*
John H Juengst, *Manager*
EMP: 5
SQ FT: 5,000
SALES (est): 826.6K **Privately Held**
SIC: 3612 7629 Power transformers, electric; electrical equipment repair, high voltage

(G-3582)
DEODORA VINEYARDS & WINERY LLC
1071 Celestial St # 2402 (45202-1689)
PHONE..................513 238-1167
Doug Mryglod, *Mng Member*
EMP: 6 EST: 2015
SALES (est): 99.7K **Privately Held**
SIC: 2084 Wines

(G-3583)
DERRICK COMPANY INC
4560 Kellogg Ave (45226-2499)
PHONE..................513 321-8122
Gary Schmid, *CEO*
Jason Schmid, *President*
Kathie Schmid, *Treasurer*
EMP: 25
SQ FT: 170,000
SALES (est): 6.2MM **Privately Held**
WEB: www.derrickcompany.com
SIC: 3398 3471 Metal heat treating; sand blasting of metal parts

(G-3584)
DESIGN MASTERS INC
800 Redna Ter (45215-1111)
PHONE..................513 772-7175
Terry Masters, *President*
EMP: 6
SALES (est): 772.1K **Privately Held**
SIC: 3993 7532 7319 Signs, not made in custom sign painting shops; truck painting & lettering; display advertising service

(G-3585)
DESSERTS BY SANDY LLC
8071 Redhaven Ct (45247-3560)
PHONE..................513 385-8755
Sandra Maffey, *Principal*
EMP: 4
SALES (est): 120K **Privately Held**
SIC: 2051 Cakes, pies & pastries

(G-3586)
DEVICOR MED PDTS HOLDINGS INC
300 E Business Way Fl 5 (45241-2384)
PHONE..................513 864-9000
Thomas D Daulton, *CEO*
Jonathan Salkin, *Exec VP*
David Nuty, *CFO*
EMP: 550
SALES (est): 26.2MM **Privately Held**
SIC: 3841 Surgical & medical instruments

(G-3587)
DEVICOR MEDICAL PRODUCTS INC (DH)
Also Called: Mammotone
300 E Business Way Fl 5 (45241-2384)
PHONE..................513 864-9000
Tom Daulton, *CEO*
Jim Frontero, *Senior VP*
Gene Schrecengost, *Senior VP*
Chip Clark, *Vice Pres*
Robert Goss, *CFO*
EMP: 3
SALES (est): 228.6MM
SALES (corp-wide): 19.8B **Publicly Held**
SIC: 3841 Surgical & medical instruments
HQ: Leica Biosystems Richmond, Inc.
5205 Rte 12
Richmond IL 60071
815 678-2000

(G-3588)
DIE CRAFT MACHINING & ENGINEER
1705 Magnolia Dr (45215-1979)
PHONE..................513 771-1290
Justin Westerfeld, *Plant Mgr*
Brent Mayer, *Engineer*
EMP: 4
SALES (est): 100.6K **Privately Held**
SIC: 3544 Special dies & tools

(G-3589)
DIMENSION MACHINE COMPANY INC
6614 Lebanon St (45216-1931)
PHONE..................513 242-9996
Donald P Barth, *President*
EMP: 8
SQ FT: 12,000
SALES (est): 1.3MM **Privately Held**
SIC: 3599 Machine shop, jobbing & repair

(G-3590)
DISCOUNT DRAINAGE SUPPLIES LLC
Also Called: Discount Dring Sups Cincinnati
200 Cavett Ave (45215-3186)
PHONE..................513 563-8616
Larry Gorman, *Manager*
EMP: 5
SALES (corp-wide): 2.9MM **Privately Held**
SIC: 5051 3444 Pipe & tubing, steel; culverts, sheet metal
PA: Discount Drainage Supplies Llc
2600 S Arlington Rd
Coventry Township OH 44319
330 644-0114

GEOGRAPHIC SECTION
Cincinnati - Hamilton County (G-3618)

(G-3591)
DITSCH USA LLC
311 Northland Blvd (45246-3690)
PHONE.................513 782-8888
Gary Gottenbusch, *CEO*
Brian Tooley, *CFO*
EMP: 50
SQ FT: 100,000
SALES: 4MM
SALES (corp-wide): 2.1B **Privately Held**
SIC: 2052 5149 Pretzels; bakery products
PA: Valora Holding Ag
Hofackerstrasse 40
Muttenz BL
614 672-020

(G-3592)
DIVERSEY INC
200 Crowne Point Pl (45241-5426)
PHONE.................513 326-8300
Karen Aielli, *Branch Mgr*
EMP: 10
SALES (corp-wide): 14.2B **Privately Held**
WEB: www.johnsondiversey.com
SIC: 2842 Cleaning or polishing preparations
HQ: Diversey, Inc.
1300 Altura Rd Ste 125
Fort Mill SC 29708
800 842-2341

(G-3593)
DIVERSEYLEVER INC
3630 E Kemper Rd (45241-2011)
PHONE.................513 554-4200
Richard Koch, *President*
Beau Schuetz, *Manager*
EMP: 7 EST: 2017
SALES (est): 833.8K **Privately Held**
SIC: 2819 Industrial inorganic chemicals

(G-3594)
DIVERSIFIED OPHTHALMICS INC
Also Called: Diversified SE Division
250 Mccullough St (45226-2145)
PHONE.................803 783-3454
Sara Baldwin, *Manager*
EMP: 13
SALES (corp-wide): 353MM **Privately Held**
WEB: www.divopt.com
SIC: 5048 3851 5049 Contact lenses; contact lenses; optical goods
HQ: Diversified Ophthalmics, Inc.
250 Mccullough St
Cincinnati OH
800 852-8089

(G-3595)
DIVERSIFIED OPHTHALMICS INC
250 Mccullough St (45226-2145)
P.O. Box 2530, Spokane WA (99220-2530)
PHONE.................509 324-6364
Wayne Heaston, *Manager*
EMP: 13
SALES (corp-wide): 353MM **Privately Held**
WEB: www.divopt.com
SIC: 5049 5048 3851 Optical goods; ophthalmic goods; ophthalmic goods
HQ: Diversified Ophthalmics, Inc.
250 Mccullough St
Cincinnati OH
800 852-8089

(G-3596)
DIVERSIPAK INC (PA)
Also Called: Questmark
838 Reedy St (45202-2216)
PHONE.................513 321-7884
Dan Kunkemoeller, *CEO*
Jennifer Kunkemoeller, *Principal*
Douglas Hearn, *Project Mgr*
Ted Trammel, *CFO*
EMP: 125
SQ FT: 15,000
SALES (est): 22.4MM **Privately Held**
WEB: www.diversipak.com
SIC: 2631 7336 Container, packaging & boxboard; package design

(G-3597)
DIVISION OVERHEAD DOOR INC (PA)
Also Called: Cincinnati Prof Door Sls Div
861 Dellway St (45229-3305)
P.O. Box 12588, Covington KY (41012-0588)
PHONE.................513 872-0888
Robert H Mc Kibben Jr, *President*
Jim Morrison, *Corp Secy*
Pat Higgins, *Vice Pres*
EMP: 19 EST: 1942
SQ FT: 12,000
SALES (est): 1.7MM **Privately Held**
WEB: www.overheaddoors.com
SIC: 3442 2431 7699 1751 Garage doors, overhead: metal; garage doors, overhead: wood; garage door repair; garage door, installation or erection

(G-3598)
DODGE DATA & ANALYTICS LLC
Also Called: F W Dodge
7265 Kenwood Rd Ste 200 (45236-4413)
PHONE.................513 763-3660
Claire Corneau, *Opers-Prdtn-Mfg*
EMP: 40
SALES (corp-wide): 52.3MM **Privately Held**
WEB: www.mcgraw-hill.com
SIC: 2741 Miscellaneous publishing
PA: Dodge Data & Analytics Llc
830 3rd Ave Fl 6
New York NY 10022
347 620-7930

(G-3599)
DOG DEPOT
950 S Troy Ave (45246-4632)
PHONE.................513 771-9274
Natalie Lotspeich, *Owner*
EMP: 3
SQ FT: 500
SALES (est): 240K **Privately Held**
SIC: 5199 3199 Dogs; dog furnishings: collars, leashes, muzzles, etc.: leather

(G-3600)
DOMINION LIQUID TECH LLC
Also Called: D L T
3965 Virginia Ave (45227-3411)
PHONE.................513 272-2824
Charles Cain, *Mng Member*
EMP: 41
SQ FT: 54,000
SALES (est): 10.4MM **Privately Held**
SIC: 2086 2087 2033 Syrups, drink; barbecue sauce: packaged in cans, jars, etc.

(G-3601)
DORAN MFG LLC
2851 Massachusetts Ave (45225-2225)
PHONE.................513 681-5424
Tom D'Agnillo, *CFO*
EMP: 15
SQ FT: 10,000
SALES (est): 1.7MM **Privately Held**
SIC: 5013 3714 Motor vehicle supplies & new parts; sanders, motor vehicle safety
PA: Evolving Enterprises, Inc.
2851 Massachusetts Ave
Cincinnati OH 45225

(G-3602)
DOROTHY CROOKER
Also Called: Rapid Copy Printing
5984 Cheviot Rd (45247-6245)
PHONE.................513 385-0888
Dorothy Crooker, *Owner*
EMP: 3
SALES: 150K **Privately Held**
SIC: 2752 2796 2791 Commercial printing, offset; platemaking services; typesetting

(G-3603)
DOSCHERS CANDIES LLC
Also Called: Doscher's Candy Company
6926 Main St (45244-3009)
PHONE.................513 381-8656
Gregory Clark, *VP Bus Dvlpt*
Chip Nielsen, *Mng Member*
EMP: 10 EST: 1959
SQ FT: 5,000
SALES: 1MM **Privately Held**
SIC: 2064 Candy & other confectionery products

(G-3604)
DOSMATIC USA INC (PA)
3798 Round Bottom Rd (45244-2413)
PHONE.................972 245-9765
Jeff Rowe, *President*
Steve Vogel, *Vice Pres*
▲ EMP: 14
SQ FT: 25,000
SALES (est): 1.8MM **Privately Held**
SIC: 3569 Liquid automation machinery & equipment

(G-3605)
DOV GRAPHICS INC
2230 Gilbert Ave (45206-2531)
PHONE.................513 241-5150
Robert J Van Lear, *President*
Gayle Sherman, *Vice Pres*
Lisa Colegate, *Sales Staff*
EMP: 23 EST: 1963
SQ FT: 10,000
SALES (est): 4MM **Privately Held**
WEB: www.dovgraphics.com
SIC: 2791 2752 2759 Photocomposition, for the printing trade; commercial printing, offset; letterpress printing

(G-3606)
DOVER WIPES COMPANY
1 Procter And Gamble Plz (45202-3315)
PHONE.................513 983-1100
Ann McKinney,
EMP: 7
SALES (est): 1.7MM
SALES (corp-wide): 66.8B **Publicly Held**
WEB: www.pg.com
SIC: 2844 Deodorants, personal
PA: The Procter & Gamble Company
1 Procter And Gamble Plz
Cincinnati OH 45202
513 983-1100

(G-3607)
DOWNHOME INC
Also Called: Down Decor
1 Kovach Dr (45215-1000)
PHONE.................513 921-3373
Daniel Guigui, *President*
James P Mason, *Principal*
Michael G Mason, *Principal*
▲ EMP: 45
SALES (est): 6.8MM **Privately Held**
WEB: www.downdecor.com
SIC: 2392 Pillows, bed: made from purchased materials

(G-3608)
DR PEPPER SNAPPLE GROUP
Also Called: Dr Pepper
1115 Regina Graeter Way (45216-1998)
PHONE.................513 242-5151
Mark Wendling, *General Mgr*
EMP: 3
SALES (est): 177.9K **Privately Held**
SIC: 2086 Soft drinks: packaged in cans, bottles, etc.

(G-3609)
DRAPERY STITCH CINCINNATI INC
5601 Wooster Pike (45227-4120)
PHONE.................513 561-2443
Phillip Beckman, *President*
EMP: 18
SALES (est): 1.4MM **Privately Held**
SIC: 2391 Curtains & draperies

(G-3610)
DREIER TOOL & DIE CORP
2865 Compton Rd (45251-2633)
PHONE.................513 521-8200
Timmothy Dreier, *President*
EMP: 4
SQ FT: 7,020
SALES: 500K **Privately Held**
SIC: 3544 Special dies & tools

(G-3611)
DTE COOL CO
105 E 4th St Ste G100 (45202-4009)
PHONE.................513 579-0160
Tim Heineman, *General Mgr*
EMP: 3
SALES (est): 307.5K **Privately Held**
SIC: 3585 Coolers, milk & water: electric

(G-3612)
DULLE ASSOCIATES
Also Called: Dulle Printing
848 Woodshire Dr (45233-4800)
PHONE.................513 723-9600
Steve Dulle, *Owner*
Jim Dulle, *Co-Owner*
EMP: 4
SALES (est): 411.4K **Privately Held**
WEB: www.dulleandcompany.com
SIC: 2754 Commercial printing, gravure

(G-3613)
DYNAMIC INDUSTRIES INC
3611 Woodburn Ave (45207-1019)
PHONE.................513 861-6767
Phillip J Mitchell, *President*
Henry W Ochs, *Principal*
John Meyer, *CFO*
Kim Richendollar, *Executive*
EMP: 33
SQ FT: 150,000
SALES (est): 6.6MM **Privately Held**
SIC: 3599 Machine shop, jobbing & repair; custom machinery

(G-3614)
DYNEON LLC
2165 Cablecar Ct (45244-4101)
PHONE.................859 334-4500
Thomasine Miller, *Manager*
EMP: 25
SALES (corp-wide): 32.7B **Publicly Held**
WEB: www.dyneon.com
SIC: 3087 Custom compound purchased resins
HQ: Dyneon Llc
6744 33rd St N
Oakdale MN 55128

(G-3615)
E & J GALLO WINERY
125 E Court St (45202-1212)
PHONE.................513 381-4050
Holly McClelland, *Manager*
EMP: 38
SALES (corp-wide): 2.4B **Privately Held**
SIC: 2084 Wines
PA: E. & J. Gallo Winery
600 Yosemite Blvd
Modesto CA 95354
209 341-3111

(G-3616)
E C SHAW CO
1242 Mehring Way (45203-1836)
PHONE.................513 721-6334
Joseph Grome, *President*
Bob Grome, *Vice Pres*
Kenneth Grome, *Vice Pres*
Robert Grome, *Vice Pres*
Joann Denzler, *Cust Mgr*
EMP: 30
SQ FT: 12,000
SALES (est): 7.8MM **Privately Held**
WEB: www.ecshaw.com
SIC: 3555 3953 3469 2821 Printing plates; marking devices; metal stampings; plastics materials & resins; platemaking services

(G-3617)
E I CERAMICS LLC
2600 Commerce Blvd (45241-1552)
PHONE.................513 772-7001
James McIntosh, *President*
Graham J Roberts, *Mng Member*
▲ EMP: 60
SALES (est): 11.7MM **Privately Held**
SIC: 3297 Graphite refractories: carbon bond or ceramic bond
HQ: Ifgl Refractories Limited
Mcleod House
Kolkata WB 70000

(G-3618)
E P S SPECIALISTS LTD INC
7875 School Rd (45249-1531)
PHONE.................513 489-3676
Ed L Wilkson, *President*
Lee Wilkinson, *Vice Pres*
EMP: 12

Cincinnati - Hamilton County (G-3619)

GEOGRAPHIC SECTION

SALES (est): 1MM **Privately Held**
SIC: 2821 Plastics materials & resins

(G-3619)
E Z BINDERYS
10122 Reading Rd (45241-3110)
PHONE.................................513 733-0005
Bruce Hassle, *Owner*
EMP: 3
SALES (est): 102.5K **Privately Held**
SIC: 2789 Binding only: books, pamphlets, magazines, etc.

(G-3620)
EAGLE CREEK INC
9799 Prechtel Rd (45252-2117)
PHONE.................................513 385-4442
EMP: 62
SALES (corp-wide): 11.8B **Publicly Held**
SIC: 3161 Traveling bags
HQ: Eagle Creek, Inc.
   5935 Darwin Ct
   Carlsbad CA 92008
   760 431-6400

(G-3621)
EAGLE IMAGE INC
4742 Blue Rock Rd (45247-5503)
PHONE.................................513 662-3000
Richard Kessler, *President*
EMP: 10
SALES (est): 679K **Privately Held**
WEB: www.eagleimage.com
SIC: 2759 Commercial printing

(G-3622)
EAGLEBURGMANN INDUSTRIES LP
3478 Hauck Rd Ste A (45241-4604)
PHONE.................................513 563-7325
Matt Vaupel, *Manager*
EMP: 8
SALES (corp-wide): 11B **Privately Held**
SIC: 3053 Gaskets, packing & sealing devices
HQ: Eagleburgmann Industries Lp
   10035 Brookriver Dr
   Houston TX 77040
   713 939-9515

(G-3623)
EAR MEDICAL CENTER INC (PA)
Also Called: Balance Disorder Institute
2121 Alpine Pl Apt 1101 (45206-2695)
PHONE.................................812 537-0031
Claude P Hobeika, *President*
EMP: 14
SQ FT: 10,000
SALES (est): 2.3MM **Privately Held**
WEB: www.bdi1.com
SIC: 3842 Hearing aids

(G-3624)
EARL D ARNOLD PRINTING COMPANY
630 Lunken Park Dr (45226-1800)
PHONE.................................513 533-6900
Earl D Arnold Sr, *President*
Timothy A Arnold, *Vice Pres*
Bob Clements, *Accounts Exec*
Pj Schiano, *Accounts Exec*
Drew Smith, *Accounts Exec*
EMP: 35 EST: 1910
SQ FT: 30,000
SALES (est): 6.9MM **Privately Held**
WEB: www.arnoldprinting.com
SIC: 2752 2759 2796 2791 Commercial printing, offset; letterpress printing; platemaking services; typesetting; bookbinding & related work

(G-3625)
EASTGATE CUSTOM GRAPHICS LTD
Also Called: Loveland Graphics
4459 Mt Carmel Tobasco Rd (45244-2225)
PHONE.................................513 528-7922
Donald R Hall, *Partner*
EMP: 7
SQ FT: 42,000
SALES: 458K **Privately Held**
SIC: 7336 5999 2395 Silk screen design; banners; embroidery & art needlework

(G-3626)
EASY DEFENSE PRODUCTS
2660 Hummingbird Ct (45239-7227)
PHONE.................................513 258-2897
EMP: 3 EST: 2017
SALES (est): 164.5K **Privately Held**
SIC: 3812 Defense systems & equipment

(G-3627)
EASY WAY LEISURE CORPORATION (PA)
Also Called: Easy Way Products
8950 Rossash Rd (45236-1210)
PHONE.................................513 731-5640
Jon D Randman, *President*
Steve Coppel, *Vice Pres*
Scott Szymkowicz, *VP Sales*
◆ EMP: 40
SQ FT: 100,000
SALES: 45MM **Privately Held**
WEB: www.easywayproducts.com
SIC: 2392 Cushions & pillows

(G-3628)
EBEL-BINDER PRINTING CO
Also Called: Ebel Tape & Label
1630 Dalton Ave 1 (45214-2020)
PHONE.................................513 471-1067
Thomas Heidemann, *President*
Marian Dulle, *Vice Pres*
James Dulle, *Treasurer*
EMP: 7
SQ FT: 3,000
SALES (est): 930.9K **Privately Held**
SIC: 2759 Flexographic printing; labels & seals: printing

(G-3629)
ECO-PRINT SOLUTIONS LLC
6893 High Meadows Dr (45230-3802)
PHONE.................................513 731-3106
Ben Morrison,
EMP: 3
SQ FT: 2,500
SALES: 76K **Privately Held**
WEB: www.ecoprintsolutions.com
SIC: 5085 3955 Ink, printers'; print cartridges for laser & other computer printers

(G-3630)
ECU CORPORATION (PA)
7209 E Kemper Rd (45249-1030)
PHONE.................................513 898-9294
Mike Fox, *President*
Hank Worsley, *Vice Pres*
Bill Kubicki, *QC Mgr*
Mary Jo, *Controller*
Mary Kubicki, *Controller*
◆ EMP: 20
SQ FT: 25,000
SALES: 3MM **Privately Held**
SIC: 3585 Air conditioning units, complete: domestic or industrial

(G-3631)
ELA HOLDING CORPORATION
Also Called: Turnkey Technology Sales
5403 Haft Rd (45247-7421)
PHONE.................................513 200-1374
Eric Anevski, *Principal*
EMP: 3
SALES (est): 733.4K **Privately Held**
SIC: 7372 Business oriented computer software

(G-3632)
ELECTRIC SERVICE CO INC
5331 Hetzell St (45227-1513)
PHONE.................................513 271-6387
Helen Snyder, *President*
EMP: 34
SQ FT: 35,000
SALES (est): 6.1MM **Privately Held**
WEB: www.electricservice.com
SIC: 7629 3677 3621 Electronic equipment repair; transformers power supply, electronic type; phase or rotary converters (electrical equipment)

(G-3633)
ELYNX HOLDINGS LLC (DH)
11500 Northlake Dr # 200 (45249-1650)
PHONE.................................513 612-5969
Sharon Matthews, *President*
Ty Cieloha, *Partner*
Ashwin RAO, *Engineer*
Jeff Rooks, *Manager*
Kelsey Wasson, *Manager*
EMP: 1
SALES (est): 23.6MM
SALES (corp-wide): 1.1B **Publicly Held**
SIC: 7371 7373 7372 Computer software development; systems integration services; prepackaged software
HQ: Black Knight Financial Services, Inc.
   601 Riverside Ave
   Jacksonville FL 32204
   904 854-5100

(G-3634)
EMERALD PERFORMANCE MTLS LLC
Also Called: Emerald Hilton Davis
2235 Langdon Farm Rd (45237-4712)
PHONE.................................513 841-4000
Robert Culp, *President*
EMP: 93
SALES (corp-wide): 357.2MM **Privately Held**
SIC: 2899 Chemical preparations
PA: Emerald Performance Materials Llc
   1499 Se Tech Center Pl
   Vancouver WA 98683
   360 954-7100

(G-3635)
EMERSON ELECTRIC CO
6000 Fernview Ave (45212-1312)
PHONE.................................513 731-2020
Hanna Lotfy, *Engineer*
Scott Schuckmann, *Engineer*
Brent Schroeder, *Manager*
EMP: 200
SALES (corp-wide): 17.4B **Publicly Held**
WEB: www.gotoemerson.com
SIC: 3823 Industrial instrmnts msrmnt display/control process variable
PA: Emerson Electric Co.
   8000 West Florissant Ave
   Saint Louis MO 63136
   314 553-2000

(G-3636)
EMERY OLEOCHEMICALS LLC (HQ)
4900 Este Ave (45232-1491)
PHONE.................................513 762-2500
Ramesh Kana, *CEO*
Bill Kafiti, *Area Mgr*
Mark Lucke, *Business Mgr*
Joe Lynch, *Business Mgr*
Kate Willis, *Business Mgr*
◆ EMP: 270
SQ FT: 4,032
SALES (est): 94.5MM
SALES (corp-wide): 674.7MM **Privately Held**
WEB: www.emeryoleo.com
SIC: 2899 Acids
PA: Emery Oleochemicals (M) Sdn. Bhd.
   Lot 4 Jalan Perak
   Telok Panglima Garang SLG 42500
   333 268-686

(G-3637)
ENCLOSURE SUPPLIERS LLC
Also Called: Champion
12119 Champion Way (45241-6419)
PHONE.................................513 782-3900
Dennis Manes,
▲ EMP: 30
SQ FT: 160,000
SALES (est): 12.1MM
SALES (corp-wide): 516.4MM **Privately Held**
SIC: 3448 5031 3231 Prefabricated metal buildings; lumber, plywood & millwork; products of purchased glass
PA: Champion Opco, Llc
   12121 Champion Way
   Cincinnati OH 45241
   513 327-7338

(G-3638)
ENCORE DISTRIBUTING INC
Also Called: Pirtek Reading Road
8060 Reading Rd Ste 6 (45237-1423)
PHONE.................................513 948-1242
Dan Pridemore, *Vice Pres*
EMP: 5 **Privately Held**
SIC: 3492 Fluid power valves & hose fittings
PA: Encore Distributing, Inc.
   5132 White Oak Ln
   Brighton MI 48114

(G-3639)
ENERCHEM INCORPORATED
8373 Squirrelridge Dr (45243-1052)
P.O. Box 43422 (45243-0422)
PHONE.................................513 745-0580
Jerrold E Radway, *President*
Larry Radway, *Vice Pres*
EMP: 4
SALES (est): 1.5MM **Privately Held**
SIC: 2819 8742 8732 7389 Industrial inorganic chemicals; management consulting services; market analysis, business & economic research;

(G-3640)
ENERFAB INC (PA)
4955 Spring Grove Ave (45232-1925)
PHONE.................................513 641-0500
Wendell R Bell, *CEO*
Jeffrey P Hock, *President*
Dave Herche, *Chairman*
Mark Schoettmer, *Vice Pres*
Daniel J Sillies, *CFO*
▲ EMP: 330
SQ FT: 180,000
SALES (est): 621.1MM **Privately Held**
WEB: www.enerfab.com
SIC: 3443 1629 1541 1711 Tanks, standard or custom fabricated: metal plate; power plant construction; land reclamation; industrial buildings & warehouses; mechanical contractor; process piping contractor; painting, coating & hot dipping

(G-3641)
ENERFAB INC
11861 Mosteller Rd (45241-1524)
PHONE.................................513 771-2300
Steve Zoller, *General Mgr*
EMP: 6
SQ FT: 250,000
SALES (corp-wide): 621.1MM **Privately Held**
WEB: www.enerfab.com
SIC: 3559 Pharmaceutical machinery; chemical machinery & equipment
PA: Enerfab, Inc.
   4955 Spring Grove Ave
   Cincinnati OH 45232
   513 641-0500

(G-3642)
ENQUIRER PRINTING CO INC
7188 Main St (45244-3019)
PHONE.................................513 241-1956
John G Anderson, *President*
Michael W Anderson, *Vice Pres*
Steve Anderson, *Treasurer*
EMP: 10
SQ FT: 19,000
SALES: 500K **Privately Held**
SIC: 2752 Commercial printing, offset

(G-3643)
ENQUIRER PRINTING COMPANY
7188 Main St (45244-3019)
PHONE.................................513 241-1956
Steve Anderson, *Principal*
EMP: 6
SALES (est): 560K **Privately Held**
SIC: 2752 Commercial printing, lithographic

(G-3644)
ENTERTAINMENT JUNCTION
Also Called: Watson's
2721 E Sharon Rd (45241-1944)
PHONE.................................513 326-1100
Eric Mueller, *Owner*
EMP: 60
SALES (est): 5.9MM **Privately Held**
SIC: 2519 Household furniture

(G-3645)
ENVOI DESIGN INC
1332 Main St Frnt (45202-7849)
PHONE.................................513 651-4229
Denise Calmus, *President*
Phil Milligan, *Partner*
Steve Weinstein, *Partner*

▲ = Import ▼ = Export
◆ = Import/Export

GEOGRAPHIC SECTION
Cincinnati - Hamilton County (G-3673)

Wayne Park, *Director*
EMP: 7
SQ FT: 1,200
SALES (est): 873.5K **Privately Held**
WEB: www.envoidesign.com
SIC: 2752 7336 Commercial printing, lithographic; graphic arts & related design

(G-3646)
EP BOLLINGER LLC
Also Called: Myrlen
2664 Saint Georges Ct (45233-4290)
PHONE..................513 941-1101
Ed P Bollinger, *Mng Member*
Kenneth F Seibel, *Mng Member*
Edward P Bollinger,
EMP: 17006
SQ FT: 22,000
SALES (est): 429.8K **Privately Held**
SIC: 2821 Plastics materials & resins

(G-3647)
EPANEL PLUS LTD
271 Northland Blvd (45246-3603)
P.O. Box 18220 (45218-0220)
PHONE..................513 772-0888
Charles Koehler,
EMP: 12
SQ FT: 10,200
SALES (est): 95.4K **Privately Held**
WEB: www.epanelplus.com
SIC: 3613 Control panels, electric

(G-3648)
EPRINTWORKSPLUS
5846 Hamilton Ave (45224-2921)
PHONE..................513 731-3797
James Engleman, *CEO*
EMP: 3
SALES (est): 343.1K **Privately Held**
SIC: 3577 Printers & plotters

(G-3649)
EPS SPECIALTIES LTD INC
7875 School Rd 77 (45249-1531)
PHONE..................513 489-3676
Edgar L Wilkinson, *President*
Lee Wilkinson, *Vice Pres*
▲ **EMP:** 12
SALES (est): 2.5MM **Privately Held**
WEB: www.lamlite.com
SIC: 3086 Packaging & shipping materials, foamed plastic

(G-3650)
EQM TECHNOLOGIES & ENERGY INC (PA)
1800 Carillion Blvd (45240-2788)
PHONE..................513 825-7500
Jon Colin, *CEO*
Jack S Greber, *Senior VP*
Robert Galvin, *CFO*
EMP: 18
SQ FT: 1,000
SALES: 56.2MM **Publicly Held**
SIC: 2869 Industrial organic chemicals

(G-3651)
EQUISTAR CHEMICALS LP
11530 Northlake Dr (45249-1642)
PHONE..................513 530-4000
Peter Hanik, *Branch Mgr*
David Kinney, *Director*
EMP: 18
SALES (corp-wide): 34.5B **Privately Held**
SIC: 2869 Industrial organic chemicals
HQ: Equistar Chemicals, Lp
1221 Mckinney St Ste 300
Houston TX 77010

(G-3652)
ERNST CUSTOM CABINETS LLC
4686 Paddock Rd Ste 99 (45229-1042)
PHONE..................513 376-9554
Thomas Ernst, *Principal*
EMP: 4
SALES (est): 408.4K **Privately Held**
SIC: 2434 Wood kitchen cabinets

(G-3653)
ERVAN GUTTMAN CO
8208 Blue Ash Rd Rear (45236-2188)
PHONE..................513 791-0767
Fax: 513 891-0559
EMP: 3 **EST:** 1938
SQ FT: 6,000

SALES (est): 408.9K **Privately Held**
SIC: 5149 2064 5046 Mfr Candy & Baking Molds & Holiday Novelties

(G-3654)
ESTREAMZ INC
1118 Groesbeck Rd (45224-3276)
PHONE..................513 278-7836
Travis Bea, *President*
EMP: 30
SALES (est): 730.8K **Privately Held**
SIC: 7379 7372 7812 ; home entertainment computer software; motion picture production & distribution, television

(G-3655)
ETHOS CORP
1045 Meta Dr (45237-5007)
PHONE..................513 242-6336
EMP: 4
SALES (est): 401.6K **Privately Held**
SIC: 3535 Mfg Conveyors/Equipment

(G-3656)
EUROSTAMPA NORTH AMERICA INC (DH)
1440 Seymour Ave (45237-3006)
PHONE..................513 821-2275
Gian Franco Cillario, *CEO*
Vito Vicino, *Prdtn Mgr*
Ken Cione, *Opers Staff*
Bob Fenster, *Production*
Garry Lanham, *Manager*
▲ **EMP:** 95
SALES (est): 18.6MM
SALES (corp-wide): 156.4K **Privately Held**
SIC: 2752 Commercial printing, offset
HQ: Industria Grafica Eurostampa Spa
Viale Rimembranza 20
Bene Vagienna CN 12041
017 265-1811

(G-3657)
EVERS ENTERPRISES INC
Aurand Manufacturing & Eqp Co
1210 Ellis St (45223-1843)
PHONE..................513 541-7200
Ray Evers, *President*
EMP: 6
SALES (est): 561.4K
SALES (corp-wide): 1.8MM **Privately Held**
WEB: www.evertenterprises.com
SIC: 3589 Commercial cleaning equipment
PA: Evers Enterprises Inc
4849 Blue Rock Rd
Cincinnati OH

(G-3658)
EVERS WELDING CO INC
4849 Blue Rock Rd (45247-5504)
P.O. Box 53426 (45253-0426)
PHONE..................513 385-7352
Edward G Evers, *President*
Jacqueline Evers, *Corp Secy*
EMP: 40 **EST:** 1957
SQ FT: 3,000
SALES (est): 4.5MM **Privately Held**
WEB: www.verssteel.com
SIC: 1791 3441 Structural steel erection; fabricated structural metal

(G-3659)
EVOLUTION CRTIVE SOLUTIONS INC
7107 Shona Dr (45237-3808)
PHONE..................513 681-4450
Cathy Lindemann, *President*
Jeff Lack, *Plant Mgr*
Charley Lindemann, *Sales Staff*
Celia Lack,
EMP: 45
SQ FT: 22,000
SALES (est): 9.7MM **Privately Held**
WEB: www.kpbprinting.com
SIC: 2752 Color lithography

(G-3660)
EVOLUTION CRTIVE SOLUTIONS LLC
7107 Shona Dr Ste 110 (45237-3808)
PHONE..................513 681-4450
Cathy Lindemann, *President*
Cathy Welz, *Accounting Mgr*

EMP: 25
SQ FT: 14,000
SALES: 3MM **Privately Held**
SIC: 7336 2759 5199 7389 Graphic arts & related design; commercial printing; advertising specialties; embroidering of advertising on shirts, etc.; screen printing: manmade fiber & silk broadwoven fabrics

(G-3661)
EVONIK CORPORATION
Also Called: Coatings & Colorants
620 Shepherd Dr (45215-2104)
PHONE..................513 554-8969
Joseph Won, *Plt & Fclts Mgr*
EMP: 60
SALES (corp-wide): 2.4B **Privately Held**
SIC: 2819 Industrial inorganic chemicals
HQ: Evonik Corporation
299 Jefferson Rd
Parsippany NJ 07054
973 929-8000

(G-3662)
EVP INTERNATIONAL LLC
Also Called: Mn8-Foxfire
10179 Wayne Ave (45215-1555)
PHONE..................513 761-7614
Zachary Green,
EMP: 6
SQ FT: 4,000
SALES (est): 700.2K **Privately Held**
SIC: 3646 Commercial indusl & institutional electric lighting fixtures

(G-3663)
EW SCRIPPS COMPANY (PA)
312 Walnut St Ste 2800 (45202-4067)
PHONE..................513 977-3000
Richard A Boehne, *Ch of Bd*
Adam Symson, *President*
Jeff Hassan, *Managing Dir*
William Appleton, *Exec VP*
Robert Carson, *Vice Pres*
EMP: 21
SALES: 1.2B **Publicly Held**
WEB: www.scripps.com
SIC: 4841 2711 4833 7375 Cable & other pay television services; newspapers; television broadcasting stations; on-line data base information retrieval

(G-3664)
EXAIR CORPORATION (PA)
11510 Goldcoast Dr (45249-1621)
P.O. Box 00766 (45264)
PHONE..................513 671-3322
Roy O Sweeney, *CEO*
Brian Peters, *President*
Bruce Patterson, *Facilities Mgr*
Lee Evans, *Engineer*
Bob West, *CFO*
EMP: 45
SQ FT: 42,000
SALES (est): 8.4MM **Privately Held**
WEB: www.linevac.com
SIC: 3499 Nozzles, spray: aerosol, paint or insecticide

(G-3665)
EXECUTIVE SECURITY SYSTEMS INC
332 Cherry St (45246-3536)
PHONE..................513 895-2783
Gary Michael Bender, *President*
EMP: 3
SQ FT: 2,200
SALES (est): 445.3K **Privately Held**
WEB: www.executivessi.com
SIC: 3699 Security devices

(G-3666)
EXPRESS GRAPHIC PRTG & DESIGN
9695 Hamilton Ave (45231-2351)
PHONE..................513 728-3344
Craig Keller, *Owner*
Karla Roth, *Graphic Designe*
EMP: 8
SQ FT: 2,400
SALES (est): 944.3K **Privately Held**
WEB: www.davis411.com
SIC: 2752 Commercial printing, lithographic

(G-3667)
EXXCITE MARKETING INC
Also Called: Exxcite Marketing Products
7949 Graves Rd (45243-3626)
PHONE..................513 271-4550
Mary Jo Byrnes, *President*
William Stratman, *Vice Pres*
EMP: 4
SALES: 800K **Privately Held**
SIC: 2759 Promotional printing

(G-3668)
F AND W PUBLICATIONS INC
4700 E Galbraith Rd (45236-2754)
P.O. Box 36275 (45236-0275)
PHONE..................513 531-2690
Mark Arnett, *CEO*
Karen B Callard, *General Mgr*
Kristin Godsey, *Editor*
Kelly Kane, *Editor*
Phil Graham, *Senior VP*
EMP: 7
SALES (est): 89K **Privately Held**
SIC: 2741 Miscellaneous publishing

(G-3669)
FAIRY DUST LTD INC
3528 Warsaw Ave (45205-1875)
PHONE..................513 251-0065
Fax: 513 251-2525
▲ **EMP:** 15
SQ FT: 7,000
SALES (est): 3MM **Privately Held**
SIC: 2841 Manufacturer Of Soap/Other Detergents & Ret Gifts/Novelties

(G-3670)
FAME TOOL & MFG CO INC
5340 Hetzell St (45227-1541)
PHONE..................513 271-6387
EMP: 25
SQ FT: 20,000
SALES (est): 2.3MM **Privately Held**
SIC: 3544 3812 3537 Mfg Dies/Tools/Jigs/Fixtures Mfg Search/Navigation Equipment Mfg Industrial Trucks/Tractors

(G-3671)
FAMILY MOTOR COACH ASSN INC (PA)
8291 Clough Pike (45244-2756)
PHONE..................513 474-3622
Lana Makin, *CEO*
Bill Mallory, *Vice Pres*
Tina Henry, *Sales Staff*
Pamela Kay, *Comms Dir*
Barbara Greenwood, *Manager*
EMP: 111
SQ FT: 22,000
SALES: 3.1MM **Privately Held**
WEB: www.fmca.com
SIC: 8641 2721 Social associations; magazines: publishing & printing

(G-3672)
FAMILY MOTOR COACHING INC
8291 Clough Pike (45244-2756)
PHONE..................513 474-3622
Don Moore, *President*
Cindy Ackley, *Manager*
Aaron White, *Manager*
Don Eversmann, *Exec Dir*
Margie Burwinkel, *Assistant*
EMP: 57
SQ FT: 20,000
SALES (est): 7MM
SALES (corp-wide): 3.1MM **Privately Held**
WEB: www.fmca.com
SIC: 2721 Magazines: publishing only, not printed on site
PA: Family Motor Coach Association, Inc.
8291 Clough Pike
Cincinnati OH 45244
513 474-3622

(G-3673)
FARMED MATERIALS INC
300 E Business Way # 200 (45241-2389)
PHONE..................513 680-4046
Adam Malofsky, *CEO*
Steven Levin, *COO*
Katrina Cornish, *Vice Pres*
Chuck Joffe, *Vice Pres*
EMP: 4

(PA)=Parent Co (HQ)=Headquarters (DH)=Div Headquarters
✪ = New Business established in last 2 years

Cincinnati - Hamilton County (G-3674)

SQ FT: 800
SALES (est): 206K **Privately Held**
SIC: **3069** 2821 8731 0191 Type, rubber; plastics materials & resins; commercial physical research; general farms, primarily crop

(G-3674)
FASTSIGNS
12125 Montgomery Rd (45249-1730)
PHONE..................513 489-8989
William Jamison, *Principal*
EMP: 4
SALES (est): 473.7K **Privately Held**
SIC: **3993** Signs & advertising specialties

(G-3675)
FAWN CONFECTIONERY (PA)
4271 Harrison Ave (45211-3340)
PHONE..................513 574-9612
Kathy Guenther, *CEO*
Jane Guenther, *Treasurer*
Jackie Copenhaver, *Admin Sec*
EMP: 15
SALES (est): 1.5MM **Privately Held**
WEB: www.fawnconfectionery.com
SIC: **5441** 2064 2066 Candy; candy & other confectionery products; chocolate & cocoa products

(G-3676)
FAX MEDLEY GROUP INC
7754 Camargo Rd Ste 18 (45243-2661)
PHONE..................513 272-1932
Michael Lowry, *President*
Rita Burgess, *Administration*
EMP: 3 EST: 1994
SALES (est): 174.4K **Privately Held**
SIC: **2741** 7338 Miscellaneous publishing; secretarial & court reporting

(G-3677)
FAXON FIREARMS LLC
11101 Adwood Dr (45240-3235)
PHONE..................513 674-2580
Robert Faxon, *President*
Barry Faxon, *Vice Pres*
EMP: 4
SALES (est): 429.6K **Privately Held**
SIC: **3484** Guns (firearms) or gun parts, 30 mm. & below

(G-3678)
FAXON MACHINING INC
11101 Adwood Dr (45240-3235)
PHONE..................513 851-4644
Barry A Faxon, *President*
B W Faxon, *Principal*
D K Faxon II, *Principal*
David K Faxon, *Principal*
Clyde Lajoye, *COO*
▲ EMP: 135 EST: 1978
SQ FT: 155,000
SALES (est): 29.3MM **Privately Held**
WEB: www.faxon-machining.com
SIC: **3599** Machine shop, jobbing & repair

(G-3679)
FBF LIMITED
Also Called: Queen City Steel Treating Co
2980 Spring Grove Ave (45225-2146)
PHONE..................513 541-6300
Judith T Houchens, *President*
Michael E Fourney, *Vice Pres*
William L Fourney, *Vice Pres*
EMP: 35
SALES (est): 7.5MM **Privately Held**
WEB: www.qcst.com
SIC: **3398** Brazing (hardening) of metal

(G-3680)
FEDERAL EQUIPMENT COMPANY (PA)
5298 River Rd (45233-1688)
PHONE..................513 621-5260
Jack Davis, *CEO*
Doug P Ridenour, *President*
▲ EMP: 70
SALES (est): 25.2MM **Privately Held**
WEB: www.fecheliports.com
SIC: **3699** 3728 3534 3535 Electrical equipment & supplies; aircraft parts & equipment; elevators & moving stairways; conveyors & conveying equipment; hoists, cranes & monorails; manufactured hardware (general)

(G-3681)
FEINER PATTERN WORKS INC
11335 Sebring Dr (45240-2796)
PHONE..................513 851-9800
Kenneth Feiner, *President*
Jimmy Feiner, *Vice Pres*
EMP: 12 EST: 1957
SQ FT: 9,000
SALES (est): 1.7MM **Privately Held**
SIC: **3543** Industrial patterns

(G-3682)
FELD PRINTING CO
6806 Main St (45244-3435)
P.O. Box 44188 (45244-0188)
PHONE..................513 271-6806
Robert A Feld Jr, *President*
David A Feld, *Vice Pres*
William Feld, *Accounts Mgr*
Marilyn Feld Mitchell, *Admin Sec*
EMP: 7
SQ FT: 5,000
SALES (est): 797.5K **Privately Held**
WEB: www.feldprinting.com
SIC: **2752** Commercial printing, offset

(G-3683)
FES-OHIO INC
Also Called: Fes Incorporated
4030 Mt Carml Tbsc Rd # 227 (45255-3431)
PHONE..................513 772-8566
Joseph Rubino, *President*
EMP: 3
SQ FT: 1,000
SALES (est): 349.7K **Privately Held**
SIC: **3822** Air conditioning & refrigeration controls

(G-3684)
FIEDELDEY STL FABRICATORS INC
8487 E Miami River Rd (45247-2208)
PHONE..................513 353-3300
Bernard A Fiedeldey Jr, *President*
EMP: 20
SQ FT: 20,000
SALES (est): 5.9MM **Privately Held**
SIC: **3441** Fabricated structural metal

(G-3685)
FIELD APPARATUS SERVICE & TSTG
Also Called: F A S T
4040 Rev Dr (45232-1914)
PHONE..................513 353-9399
Kathy Jones, *President*
EMP: 7
SALES (est): 520K **Privately Held**
SIC: **8711** 3825 Electrical or electronic engineering; test equipment for electronic & electric measurement

(G-3686)
FIELD AVIATION INC (PA)
8044 Montgomery Rd # 400 (45236-2900)
PHONE..................513 792-2282
John Mactaggart, *CEO*
Amber Drennen, *Director*
EMP: 5
SALES (est): 38.6MM **Privately Held**
SIC: **3728** Aircraft parts & equipment

(G-3687)
FIELD DAILIES LLC
323 W 5th St Apt 3 (45202-2772)
PHONE..................859 379-2120
Jim Duff, *Mng Member*
EMP: 4
SALES (est): 230K **Privately Held**
SIC: **7372** Business oriented computer software

(G-3688)
FIELDS ASSOCIATES INC
Also Called: JCB Payroll Solutions
2134 Hatmaker St Ste 3 (45204-1948)
PHONE..................513 426-8652
Damian Fields, *CEO*
Christine Collins, *Vice Pres*
Joseph Pierce, *Vice Pres*
Mary Smith, *Exec Sec*
EMP: 4

SALES (est): 198.7K **Privately Held**
SIC: **5461** 8721 2051 Bakeries; payroll accounting service; bagels, fresh or frozen

(G-3689)
FIFTY WEST BREWING COMPANY
Also Called: Fifty West Brewing,
7668 Wooster Pike (45227-3926)
PHONE..................513 834-8789
Robert Slattery, *CEO*
Bobby Slattery, *Principal*
EMP: 58
SALES (est): 4.8MM **Privately Held**
SIC: **2082** Malt beverage products

(G-3690)
FINN GRAPHICS INC
220 Stille Dr (45233-1695)
PHONE..................513 941-6161
Robert Finn, *CEO*
Dan Finn, *President*
Jack Roch, *Vice Pres*
EMP: 40 EST: 1940
SQ FT: 30,000
SALES (est): 6.3MM **Privately Held**
SIC: **2752** 3993 2395 Commercial printing, offset; advertising novelties; pleating & stitching

(G-3691)
FIOMET LLC
2717 Erie Ave (45208-2103)
PHONE..................513 519-7622
Scott Rapp, *President*
EMP: 4
SQ FT: 2,000
SALES (est): 179K **Privately Held**
SIC: **3829** Stress, strain & flaw detecting/measuring equipment

(G-3692)
FISH EXPRESS
2463 Harrison Ave (45211-7957)
PHONE..................513 661-3000
Khaled Munjed, *Principal*
EMP: 4
SALES (est): 312.7K **Privately Held**
SIC: **2741** Miscellaneous publishing

(G-3693)
FLEXOMATION LLC
11701 Chesterdale Rd (45246-3405)
P.O. Box 40537 (45240-0537)
PHONE..................513 825-0555
Eric Lewis,
EMP: 17
SALES (est): 3MM **Privately Held**
SIC: **3549** Assembly machines, including robotic

(G-3694)
FLIGHTLOGIX LLC
4510 Airport Rd (45226-1601)
PHONE..................513 321-1200
Greg Herrmann,
Jay Schmalfuss,
EMP: 8
SALES (est): 990K **Privately Held**
SIC: **3721** Aircraft

(G-3695)
FLINT GROUP US LLC
Also Called: C D R Pigments Dispersions Div
410 Glendale Milford Rd (45215-1103)
PHONE..................513 771-1900
Michael V Luchini, *Controller*
Frank Gillette, *Manager*
Alan Burt, *Technical Staff*
EMP: 60
SALES (corp-wide): 3.2B **Privately Held**
WEB: www.flintink.com
SIC: **2865** 2893 Color pigments, organic; printing ink
PA: Flint Group Us Llc
    14909 N Beck Rd
    Plymouth MI 48170
    734 781-4600

(G-3696)
FLOTTEMESCH ANTHONY & SON
8201 Camargo Rd Ste 1 (45243-1469)
PHONE..................513 561-1212

James Flottemesch, *President*
James Flottimish Jr, *Vice Pres*
EMP: 10 EST: 1942
SQ FT: 13,000
SALES (est): 1MM **Privately Held**
SIC: **2511** 2434 2431 Wood household furniture; wood kitchen cabinets; millwork

(G-3697)
FLOTURN INC
120 Progress Pl (45246-1793)
PHONE..................513 671-0210
Fax: 513 671-7033
EMP: 4
SALES (corp-wide): 67.8MM **Privately Held**
SIC: **3599** Job Machine Shop Metal Spinning And Metal Shearing
PA: Floturn, Inc.
    4236 Thunderbird Ln
    West Chester OH 45014
    513 860-8040

(G-3698)
FLOW CONTROL US HOLDING CORP
Also Called: General Aquatics
4030 Mount Carmel Tobasco (45255-3400)
PHONE..................800 843-5628
Kevan Langner, *Principal*
EMP: 3
SALES (corp-wide): 17.4B **Publicly Held**
WEB: www.pentair.com
SIC: **3561** Pumps & pumping equipment
HQ: Flow Control Us Holding Corporation
    5500 Wayzata Blvd Ste 800
    Minneapolis MN 55416
    763 545-1730

(G-3699)
FLOW TECHNOLOGY INC
4444 Cooper Rd (45242-5615)
PHONE..................513 745-6000
Bill Hayes, *President*
Bill Hays, *President*
EMP: 200
SALES (est): 9.9MM
SALES (corp-wide): 3.3B **Publicly Held**
SIC: **3491** Valves, automatic control
HQ: Xomox Corporation
    4526 Res Frest Dr Ste 400
    The Woodlands TX 77381
    936 271-6500

(G-3700)
FLYPAPER STUDIO INC
311 Elm St Ste 200 (45202-2743)
PHONE..................602 801-2208
Patrick Sullivan, *CEO*
Greg Head, *President*
Pat Stoner, *Treasurer*
Sunil Padiyar, *CTO*
Don Perison, *Admin Sec*
EMP: 30
SQ FT: 16,778
SALES: 1.9MM **Privately Held**
WEB: www.interactivealchemy.com
SIC: **7372** Educational computer software

(G-3701)
FOOD SPECIALTIES CO (PA)
12 Sunnybrook Dr (45237-2191)
PHONE..................513 761-1242
Kenneth Troy, *Principal*
Patricia Furlong, *Principal*
Lucien G Strauss, *Principal*
EMP: 5 EST: 1956
SQ FT: 20,000
SALES (est): 2.4MM **Privately Held**
SIC: **2035** Mayonnaise; dressings, salad: raw & cooked (except dry mixes)

(G-3702)
FORCAM INC
4030 Smith Rd Ste 475 (45209-0016)
PHONE..................513 878-2780
Franz Gruber, *CEO*
EMP: 15
SQ FT: 5,000
SALES (est): 1.2MM **Privately Held**
SIC: **7371** 7372 Computer software development & applications; application computer software

GEOGRAPHIC SECTION

Cincinnati - Hamilton County (G-3727)

(G-3703)
FOREST CONVERTING COMPANY INC
4701 Forest Ave (45212-3399)
PHONE.....................513 631-4190
R Douglas Lojinger, *President*
EMP: 6 EST: 1949
SQ FT: 22,000
SALES: 500K **Privately Held**
SIC: 2675 Paper die-cutting; paperboard die-cutting; cardboard cut-outs, panels & foundations: die-cut

(G-3704)
FOREST PHARMACEUTICALS INC
3941 Brotherton Rd (45209)
PHONE.....................513 271-6800
Greg Yurchak, *Branch Mgr*
EMP: 200 **Privately Held**
WEB: www.forestpharm.com
SIC: 2834 Pharmaceutical preparations
HQ: Forest Pharmaceuticals, Inc.
400 Interpace Pkwy Ste A1
Parsippany NJ 07054
862 261-7000

(G-3705)
FORMICA CORPORATION (HQ)
10155 Reading Rd (45241-4805)
PHONE.....................513 786-3400
Frank Riddick, *President*
Mitchell P Quint, *President*
Barry Jenkinson, *Business Mgr*
Paul Nystrom, *Business Mgr*
Earl Bennett, *Senior VP*
◆ EMP: 20
SQ FT: 14,000
SALES (est): 359.7MM
SALES (corp-wide): 6.5B **Privately Held**
WEB: www.formica.com
SIC: 2541 2679 Counter & sink tops; table or counter tops, plastic laminated; paperboard products, converted
PA: Fletcher Building Limited
810 Great South Road
Auckland 1061
952 590-00

(G-3706)
FORUM III INC
436 Mcgregor Ave (45206-2364)
PHONE.....................513 961-5123
Michael Evans, *President*
Jeffrey Crosby, *Vice Pres*
EMP: 13
SQ FT: 8,800
SALES: 500K **Privately Held**
SIC: 2434 2431 2541 Wood kitchen cabinets; millwork; wood partitions & fixtures

(G-3707)
FORWARD MOVEMENT PUBLICATIONS
Also Called: Forward Day By Day
412 Sycamore St Fl 2 (45202-6202)
PHONE.....................513 721-6659
Richard Schmidt, *Director*
▲ EMP: 12
SALES (est): 960K **Privately Held**
WEB: www.forwarddaybyday.com
SIC: 2759 Publication printing

(G-3708)
FRAME USA
225 Northland Blvd (45246-3603)
PHONE.....................513 577-7107
Greg Clark, *CEO*
Daniel P Regenold, *Ch of Bd*
Dana Gore, *President*
◆ EMP: 20
SQ FT: 7,000
SALES (est): 3.9MM
SALES (corp-wide): 8.1MM **Privately Held**
WEB: www.frameusa.com
SIC: 2499 5999 3499 Picture frame molding, finished; picture frames, ready made; picture frames, metal
PA: Posterservice, Incorporated
225 Northland Blvd
Cincinnati OH 45246
513 577-7100

(G-3709)
FRANK L HARTER & SON INC
3778 Frondorf Ave (45211-4421)
PHONE.....................513 574-1330
Michael Harter, *President*
Barb Harter, *Admin Sec*
EMP: 6 EST: 1928
SQ FT: 800
SALES: 1MM **Privately Held**
SIC: 5143 5144 5148 2099 Butter; cheese; eggs; fresh fruits & vegetables; salads, fresh or refrigerated

(G-3710)
FRANKLIN COVEY CO
7875 Montgomery Rd # 1202 (45236-4344)
PHONE.....................513 792-0099
Jason Mast, *Manager*
EMP: 8
SALES (corp-wide): 209.7MM **Publicly Held**
WEB: www.franklincovey.com
SIC: 2741 Miscellaneous publishing
PA: Franklin Covey Co.
2200 W Parkway Blvd
Salt Lake City UT 84119
801 817-1776

(G-3711)
FRANKS ELECTRIC INC
Also Called: Franks Electric Motor Repair
2640 Colerain Ave (45214-1712)
PHONE.....................513 313-5883
Brian Knue, *President*
Diana Grady, *Vice Pres*
EMP: 8
SQ FT: 10,000
SALES (est): 659.5K **Privately Held**
SIC: 1731 7694 5999 General electrical contractor; electric motor repair; motors, electric

(G-3712)
FREDERICK STEEL COMPANY LLC
Also Called: Bfs Supply
630 Glendale Milford Rd (45215-1105)
PHONE.....................513 821-6400
Burke Byer, *Principal*
Mark Kurtz, *Vice Pres*
Timothy Nagy, *Asst Sec*
EMP: 60 EST: 2013
SALES (est): 8.1MM
SALES (corp-wide): 86.5MM **Privately Held**
SIC: 1791 3441 Structural steel erection; building components, structural steel
PA: Benjamin Steel Company, Inc.
777 Benjamin Dr
Springfield OH 45502
937 322-8600

(G-3713)
FRESH TABLE LLC
1801 Race St Ste 45 (45202-5917)
PHONE.....................513 381-3774
Sheila W Nolan, *Principal*
EMP: 3
SALES (est): 268.1K **Privately Held**
SIC: 2099 Food preparations

(G-3714)
FRISBIE ENGINE & MACHINE CO (PA)
2635 Spring Grove Ave (45214-1731)
P.O. Box 14568 (45250-0568)
PHONE.....................513 542-1770
Reed Lee Coen, *President*
EMP: 12
SQ FT: 22,000
SALES: 1MM **Privately Held**
SIC: 3599 8742 6411 Jobbing & Repair Machine Shop Marine Consultant And Insurance Surveyor

(G-3715)
FROST ENGINEERING INC
3408 Beekman St (45223-2425)
PHONE.....................513 541-6330
Charles E Frost, *President*
EMP: 21
SQ FT: 15,000
SALES (est): 6.4MM **Privately Held**
WEB: www.frostengineering.com
SIC: 3556 8711 Smokers, food processing equipment; engineering services

(G-3716)
FT GROUP INC
4710 Madison Rd (45227-1426)
PHONE.....................937 746-6439
Thomas C Wortley, *CEO*
Karen Bogan, *Treasurer*
EMP: 20
SQ FT: 45,993
SALES (est): 1.9MM **Privately Held**
WEB: www.ftgroup.com
SIC: 3555 3827 2796 3825 Printing trades machinery; microscopes, except electron, proton & corneal; engraving on copper, steel, wood or rubber: printing plates; measuring instruments & meters, electric

(G-3717)
FURNITURE BY OTMAR INC
9500 Montgomery Rd (45242-7204)
PHONE.....................513 891-5141
Harold James, *Manager*
EMP: 3
SALES (corp-wide): 1.1MM **Privately Held**
WEB: www.furniturebyotmar.com
SIC: 2511 5712 Wood household furniture; furniture stores
PA: Furniture By Otmar, Inc.
301 Mmsburg Cnterville Rd
Dayton OH 45459
937 435-2039

(G-3718)
G & J PEPSI-COLA BOTTLERS INC (PA)
9435 Waterstone Blvd # 390 (45249-8227)
PHONE.....................513 785-6060
Thomas D Heekin, *Vice Ch Bd*
Sydnor I Davis, *President*
George G Grubb, *Principal*
Stanley Kaplan, *Chairman*
Daniel D Sweeney, *COO*
EMP: 10
SQ FT: 8,052
SALES (est): 418.3MM **Privately Held**
WEB: www.gjpepsi.com
SIC: 2086 Soft drinks: packaged in cans, bottles, etc.; carbonated soft drinks, bottled & canned

(G-3719)
G A AVRIL COMPANY (PA)
Also Called: Brass & Bronze Ingot Division
4445 Kings Run Dr (45232-1401)
P.O. Box 32066 (45232-0066)
PHONE.....................513 641-0566
Thomas B Avril, *President*
John G Avril, *Vice Pres*
EMP: 10
SQ FT: 47,000
SALES (est): 2.3MM **Privately Held**
SIC: 3341 3356 Brass smelting & refining (secondary); bronze smelting & refining (secondary); nonferrous rolling & drawing; lead & lead alloy: rolling, drawing or extruding; tin & tin alloy: rolling, drawing or extruding; solder: wire, bar, acid core, & rosin core

(G-3720)
G A AVRIL COMPANY
White Metal Products Division
2108 Eagle Ct (45237-4754)
P.O. Box 12050 (45212-0050)
PHONE.....................513 731-5133
Philip V Schneider, *Manager*
EMP: 12
SQ FT: 66,782
SALES (corp-wide): 2.3MM **Privately Held**
SIC: 3356 Lead & lead alloy bars, pipe, plates, shapes, etc.; lead & lead alloy: rolling, drawing or extruding
PA: The G A Avril Company
4445 Kings Run Dr
Cincinnati OH 45232
513 641-0566

(G-3721)
GAITWELL ORTHOTICS PEDORTHICS
1 N Commerce Park Dr # 306 (45215-3187)
PHONE.....................513 829-2217
Michael Veder, *Principal*
EMP: 3 EST: 2010
SALES (est): 140K **Privately Held**
SIC: 3842 Orthopedic appliances

(G-3722)
GALLERIA CO (HQ)
1 Procter And Gamble Plz (45202-3315)
PHONE.....................513 983-1490
Camillo Pane, *CEO*
EMP: 5 EST: 2015
SALES (est): 2.5MM **Publicly Held**
SIC: 2844 Cosmetic preparations

(G-3723)
GANNETT CO INC
Also Called: Cincinnati Enquirer, The
312 Elm St Ste 1400 (45202-2722)
PHONE.....................513 721-2700
Kimberly Harris, *Branch Mgr*
Libby Korosec, *Director*
EMP: 78
SALES (corp-wide): 2.9B **Publicly Held**
SIC: 2711 Newspapers, publishing & printing
PA: Gannett Co., Inc.
7950 Jones Branch Dr
Mc Lean VA 22102
703 854-6000

(G-3724)
GANNETT STLLITE INFO NTWRK INC
Cincinnati Enquirer, The
312 Elm St Ste 1400 (45202-2722)
PHONE.....................513 721-2700
Margaret Buchanan, *President*
Denette Pfaffenberger, *Trustee*
H Theodore Bergh, *VP Finance*
Cheryl Norris, *Financial Analy*
Bob Strickley, *Webmaster*
EMP: 88
SALES (corp-wide): 2.9B **Publicly Held**
WEB: www.usatoday.com
SIC: 2711 Newspapers
HQ: Gannett Satellite Information Network, Llc
7950 Jones Branch Dr
Mc Lean VA 22102
703 854-6000

(G-3725)
GARDEN OF DELIGHT LLC
5540 Chandler St (45227-1636)
PHONE.....................513 300-7205
Ray Edwards, *Mng Member*
Tonia Edward,
EMP: 4
SALES: 20K **Privately Held**
SIC: 2079 7389 Edible fats & oils;

(G-3726)
GARDEN STREET IRON & METAL (PA)
2885 Spring Grove Ave (45225-2222)
PHONE.....................513 853-3700
Earl J Weber Jr, *President*
Dave Hollbroke, *General Mgr*
Margaret Weber, *Vice Pres*
Sarah Weber, *Office Mgr*
▲ EMP: 40
SQ FT: 43,000
SALES (est): 7.2MM **Privately Held**
SIC: 4953 3341 3312 Refuse System Secondary Nonferrous Metal Producer Blast Furnace-Steel Works

(G-3727)
GARDNER BUSINESS MEDIA INC
6925 Valley Ave (45244-3029)
PHONE.....................513 527-8800
Margaret Kline, *Manager*
EMP: 30
SQ FT: 17,600

Cincinnati - Hamilton County (G-3728)

SALES (corp-wide): 34.9MM **Privately Held**
WEB: www.gardnerweb.com
SIC: 2721 2731 Trade journals: publishing only, not printed on site; statistical reports (periodicals): publishing & printing; books: publishing & printing
PA: Gardner Business Media, Inc.
6915 Valley Ave
Cincinnati OH 45244
513 527-8800

(G-3728)
GARYS CHESECAKES FINE DESSERTS
5285 Crookshank Rd Side (45238-3372)
PHONE 513 574-1700
Gary Haas, *Owner*
EMP: 8
SALES (est): 580.5K **Privately Held**
SIC: 2051 Bread, cake & related products

(G-3729)
GBI CINCINNATI INC
7700 Shawnee Run Rd (45243-3120)
PHONE 513 841-8684
Kevin V Bevan, *President*
Robert Whiting, *CFO*
▲ EMP: 4
SQ FT: 16,600
SALES (est): 1MM **Privately Held**
WEB: www.gbicincinnati.com
SIC: 5084 3541 Machine tools & metal-working machinery; machine tools, metal cutting type

(G-3730)
GCI DIGITAL IMAGING INC
5031 Winton Rd (45232-1506)
PHONE 513 521-7446
Tom Bedacht, *President*
Kevin Fink, *Accounts Mgr*
Nikko Hassell, *Accounts Mgr*
Ken Naylor, *Accounts Mgr*
Michelle Prince, *Accounts Mgr*
▲ EMP: 14
SQ FT: 10,000
SALES (est): 2.6MM **Privately Held**
WEB: www.gci-digital.com
SIC: 2759 Screen printing

(G-3731)
GE AIRCRAFT ENGINES
1 Neumann Way (45215-1915)
PHONE 513 243-2000
David L Joyce, *President*
Charles Blankenship, *President*
Jean Lydon-Rodgers, *President*
Anthony Aiello, *Vice Pres*
Colleen B Athans, *Vice Pres*
EMP: 22
SALES (est): 10.2MM **Privately Held**
SIC: 3724 Aircraft engines & engine parts

(G-3732)
GE AVIATION SYSTEMS LLC
10270 Saint Rita Ln (45215-1215)
PHONE 513 470-2889
Kevin Moermond, *Engineer*
EMP: 10
SALES (corp-wide): 121.6B **Publicly Held**
SIC: 3812 Aircraft control systems, electronic
HQ: Ge Aviation Systems Llc
1 Neumann Way
Cincinnati OH 45215
937 898-9600

(G-3733)
GE AVIATION SYSTEMS LLC
Also Called: GE Aviation Services
201 W Crescentville Rd (45246-1713)
PHONE 513 977-1500
EMP: 128
SALES (corp-wide): 121.6B **Publicly Held**
SIC: 3724 Aircraft engines & engine parts
HQ: Ge Aviation Systems Llc
1 Neumann Way
Cincinnati OH 45215
937 898-9600

(G-3734)
GE AVIATION SYSTEMS LLC
Also Called: Morris Technologies
11988 Tramway Dr (45241-1664)
PHONE 513 733-1611
Gregory Morris, *Branch Mgr*
EMP: 105
SALES (corp-wide): 121.6B **Publicly Held**
SIC: 3313 Alloys, additive, except copper: not made in blast furnaces
HQ: Ge Aviation Systems Llc
1 Neumann Way
Cincinnati OH 45215
937 898-9600

(G-3735)
GE AVIATION SYSTEMS LLC
123 Merchant St (45246-3730)
PHONE 513 552-5663
David Joyce, *CEO*
EMP: 8
SALES (corp-wide): 121.6B **Publicly Held**
SIC: 3313 Alloys, additive, except copper: not made in blast furnaces
HQ: Ge Aviation Systems Llc
1 Neumann Way
Cincinnati OH 45215
937 898-9600

(G-3736)
GE AVIATION SYSTEMS LLC (HQ)
1 Neumann Way (45215-1915)
PHONE 937 898-9600
R F Ehr, *President*
J B Hines, *President*
Jeff Immelt, *Chairman*
Peter Page, *Exec VP*
Bradley D Mottier, *Vice Pres*
▲ EMP: 8
SALES (est): 1.5B
SALES (corp-wide): 121.6B **Publicly Held**
SIC: 3812 Aircraft control systems, electronic
PA: General Electric Company
41 Farnsworth St
Boston MA 02210
617 443-3000

(G-3737)
GE HEALTHCARE INC
346 Gest St (45203-1822)
PHONE 513 241-5955
Mark Nybo, *Manager*
EMP: 15
SALES (corp-wide): 121.6B **Publicly Held**
SIC: 2835 In vitro & in vivo diagnostic substances
HQ: Ge Healthcare Inc.
100 Results Way
Marlborough MA 01752
800 526-3593

(G-3738)
GE MILITARY SYSTEMS
1 Neumann Way (45215-1915)
PHONE 513 243-2000
Russ Sparks, *Vice Pres*
Andrew Marovich, *Systs Prg Mgr*
EMP: 812
SALES (est): 41.5MM
SALES (corp-wide): 121.6B **Publicly Held**
SIC: 3724 Aircraft engines & engine parts
PA: General Electric Company
41 Farnsworth St
Boston MA 02210
617 443-3000

(G-3739)
GE ROLLS ROYCE FIGHTER
1 Neumann Way 318a (45215-1915)
PHONE 513 243-2787
Robert H Griswold, *President*
Vicki Kawecki,
EMP: 3
SALES (est): 205K
SALES (corp-wide): 121.6B **Publicly Held**
SIC: 3519 Jet propulsion engines

(G-3740)
GENERAL CHAIN & MFG CORP
3274 Beekman St (45223-2423)
PHONE 513 541-6005
Eric Schaumloffel, *President*
EMP: 40 EST: 1919
SALES (est): 7.7MM **Privately Held**
SIC: 3496 Miscellaneous fabricated wire products

(G-3741)
GENERAL ELECTRIC COMPANY
201 W Crescentville Rd (45246-1733)
PHONE 513 977-1500
Josh Mason, *Engineer*
Dave Kircher, *Sales Staff*
Bill Fitzgerald, *Manager*
EMP: 500
SALES (corp-wide): 121.6B **Publicly Held**
SIC: 7629 3769 3728 3537 Aircraft electrical equipment repair; electrical equipment repair, high voltage; guided missile & space vehicle parts & auxiliary equipment; aircraft parts & equipment; industrial trucks & tractors
PA: General Electric Company
41 Farnsworth St
Boston MA 02210
617 443-3000

(G-3742)
GENERAL ELECTRIC COMPANY
445 S Cooper Ave (45215-4565)
PHONE 513 948-4170
Carol Mase, *Manager*
EMP: 8
SALES (corp-wide): 121.6B **Publicly Held**
SIC: 3724 Aircraft engines & engine parts
PA: General Electric Company
41 Farnsworth St
Boston MA 02210
617 443-3000

(G-3743)
GENERAL ELECTRIC COMPANY
1 Neumann Way (45215-1988)
PHONE 513 552-2000
Partha Sreenivasan, *Program Mgr*
Randy Bates, *Manager*
Diane Orr, *Senior Mgr*
EMP: 1000
SQ FT: 84,308
SALES (corp-wide): 121.6B **Publicly Held**
SIC: 4581 3724 Hangar operation; aircraft engines & engine parts
PA: General Electric Company
41 Farnsworth St
Boston MA 02210
617 443-3000

(G-3744)
GENERAL ELECTRIC INTL INC
191 Rosa Parks St (45202-2573)
PHONE 410 737-7228
Robert Smits, *President*
EMP: 4
SQ FT: 5,000
SALES (corp-wide): 121.6B **Publicly Held**
SIC: 8711 7629 7694 Engineering services; electrical equipment repair services; motor repair services
HQ: General Electric International, Inc.
191 Rosa Parks St
Cincinnati OH 45202
617 443-3000

(G-3745)
GENERAL MILLS INC
11301 Mosteller Rd (45241-1827)
PHONE 513 771-8200
Jerry Kelley, *Branch Mgr*
Cathy Cranfill-Parker, *Manager*
EMP: 100
SALES (corp-wide): 15.7B **Publicly Held**
WEB: www.generalmills.com
SIC: 2043 2099 Cereal breakfast foods; food preparations
PA: General Mills, Inc.
1 General Mills Blvd
Minneapolis MN 55426
763 764-7600

(G-3746)
GENERAL PLASTICS NORTH CORP
5220 Vine St (45217-1028)
PHONE 800 542-2466
Zetta Bouligaraki, *President*
EMP: 35
SQ FT: 150,000
SALES (est): 5.3MM
SALES (corp-wide): 2.5B **Privately Held**
WEB: www.generalplasticscorp.com
SIC: 3812 Aircraft flight instruments
HQ: Pmc, Inc.
12243 Branford St
Sun Valley CA 91352
818 896-1101

(G-3747)
GENERAL TOOL COMPANY (PA)
101 Landy Ln (45215-3495)
PHONE 513 733-5500
William J Kramer Jr, *CEO*
John Cozad, *COO*
Elliot Adams, *Exec VP*
William J Kramer III, *CFO*
Paul Kramer, *Treasurer*
▲ EMP: 235 EST: 1947
SQ FT: 150,000
SALES: 47.5MM **Privately Held**
WEB: www.gentool.com
SIC: 3599 3443 3444 3544 Machine shop, jobbing & repair; fabricated plate work (boiler shop); sheet metalwork; special dies & tools; welding repair

(G-3748)
GENESIS DISPLAY SYSTEMS INC
4004 Erie Ct (45227-2110)
PHONE 513 561-1440
Thomas A Bove, *President*
EMP: 4
SQ FT: 13,000
SALES (est): 389K **Privately Held**
WEB: www.genesisdisplay.com
SIC: 3993 Displays & cutouts, window & lobby

(G-3749)
GENOA HEALTHCARE LLC
5837 Hamilton Ave (45224-2923)
PHONE 513 541-0164
EMP: 9
SALES (corp-wide): 226.2B **Publicly Held**
SIC: 2834 Pharmaceutical preparations
HQ: Genoa Healthcare Llc
707 S Grady Way Ste 700
Renton WA 98057

(G-3750)
GERALD L HERMANN CO INC
Also Called: Master Print Center
3325 Harrison Ave (45211-5618)
PHONE 513 661-1818
Gerald Herrmann, *President*
Suzanne Herrmann, *Corp Secy*
Fred Krieger, *Financial Exec*
EMP: 11
SQ FT: 7,500
SALES (est): 2.1MM **Privately Held**
WEB: www.addresserbasedsystems.com
SIC: 7331 2752 Addressing service; photo-offset printing

(G-3751)
GILKEY WINDOW COMPANY INC
3528 Hauck Rd (45241-1604)
PHONE 513 769-9663
John Gilkey, *Manager*
EMP: 5
SALES (corp-wide): 16.9MM **Privately Held**
SIC: 3089 Plastic hardware & building products; windows, plastic
PA: Gilkey Window Company, Inc.
3625 Hauck Rd
Cincinnati OH 45241
513 769-4527

Cincinnati - Hamilton County

(G-3752)
GILKEY WINDOW COMPANY INC (PA)
3625 Hauck Rd (45241-1605)
PHONE.....................513 769-4527
John M Gilkey, *President*
Eric Mace, *Division Mgr*
Michael Vincent Gilkey, *General Mgr*
Sue Gilkey, *Vice Pres*
Dennis Jackson, *Opers Mgr*
▲ EMP: 98
SQ FT: 56,000
SALES (est): 16.9MM Privately Held
SIC: 3089 Plastic hardware & building products; windows, plastic

(G-3753)
GIMINETTI BAKING COMPANY
2900 Gilbert Ave (45206-1207)
PHONE.....................513 751-7655
James Ciuccio, *President*
EMP: 20
SALES (est): 2.9MM Privately Held
SIC: 2051 5461 Bakery: wholesale or wholesale/retail combined; bakeries

(G-3754)
GIVAUDAN
110 E 69th St (45216-2008)
PHONE.....................513 482-2536
Mitch Lord, *Principal*
Regina Godvin, *Vice Pres*
Mariann De Iturrondo, *Accountant*
EMP: 17 EST: 2014
SALES (est): 2.6MM Privately Held
SIC: 2869 Flavors or flavoring materials, synthetic; butadiene (industrial organic chemical)

(G-3755)
GIVAUDAN FLAVORS CORPORATION
100 E 69th St (45216-2008)
P.O. Box 17086 (45217-0086)
PHONE.....................513 948-4933
Geraldine Nicolai, *Vice Pres*
Paula Branam, *Purchasing*
Gary Francis, *Engineer*
Sherri Rose, *Accountant*
Tony Bowing, *Branch Mgr*
EMP: 300
SALES (corp-wide): 5.5B Privately Held
SIC: 2869 2087 Flavors or flavoring materials, synthetic; butadiene (industrial organic chemical); concentrates, flavoring (except drink)
HQ: Givaudan Flavors Corporation
    1199 Edison Dr
    Cincinnati OH 45216
    513 948-8000

(G-3756)
GIVAUDAN FLAVORS CORPORATION
110 E 70th St (45216-2011)
PHONE.....................513 948-8000
Ayako Hayashi, *Mktg Dir*
Jeffrey Peppet, *Marketing Staff*
Felix Mayr Harting, *Branch Mgr*
Martin Hoegee, *Manager*
Lee Rutkowski, *Senior Mgr*
EMP: 9
SALES (corp-wide): 5.5B Privately Held
SIC: 2087 Flavoring extracts & syrups
HQ: Givaudan Flavors Corporation
    1199 Edison Dr
    Cincinnati OH 45216
    513 948-8000

(G-3757)
GIVAUDAN FLVORS FRAGRANCES INC (DH)
1199 Edison Dr (45216-2265)
P.O. Box 17038 (45217-0038)
PHONE.....................513 948-8000
Stefan Giezendanner, *CFO*
EMP: 1
SALES (est): 734.2MM
SALES (corp-wide): 5.5B Privately Held
SIC: 2869 2087 Flavors or flavoring materials, synthetic; perfume materials, synthetic; flavoring extracts & syrups
HQ: Givaudan Roure (United States) Inc.
    1199 Edison Dr
    Cincinnati OH 45216
    513 948-8000

(G-3758)
GIVAUDAN FRAGRANCES CORP (DH)
1199 Edison Dr Ste 1-2 (45216-2265)
PHONE.....................513 948-3428
Gilles Andrier, *CEO*
Kasey Reed-Long, *Regional Mgr*
David Schuster, *COO*
Stephen Fenimore, *Research*
Wagner Thomaz, *Engineer*
◆ EMP: 386 EST: 2000
SQ FT: 78,000
SALES (est): 449.1MM
SALES (corp-wide): 5.5B Privately Held
SIC: 2869 Perfume materials, synthetic; flavors or flavoring materials, synthetic

(G-3759)
GIVAUDAN FRAGRANCES CORP
100 E 69th St (45216-2008)
PHONE.....................513 948-3428
Gary Schmidt, *Manager*
EMP: 260
SALES (corp-wide): 5.5B Privately Held
SIC: 2869 2087 Flavors or flavoring materials, synthetic; flavoring extracts & syrups
HQ: Givaudan Fragrances Corporation
    1199 Edison Dr Ste 1-2
    Cincinnati OH 45216
    513 948-3428

(G-3760)
GIVAUDAN ROURE US INC (HQ)
Also Called: Givaudan US
1199 Edison Dr (45216-2265)
PHONE.....................513 948-8000
Michael Davis, *President*
◆ EMP: 1
SALES (est): 754.2MM
SALES (corp-wide): 5.5B Privately Held
SIC: 2869 2087 Perfume materials, synthetic; flavors or flavoring materials, synthetic; flavoring extracts & syrups
PA: Givaudan Sa
    Chemin De La Parfumerie 5
    Vernier GE 1214
    227 809-111

(G-3761)
GLASS SEALE LTD
1700 Hunt Rd (45215-3916)
PHONE.....................513 733-1464
Deborah Seale, *Principal*
EMP: 4
SALES (est): 221.4K Privately Held
SIC: 3231 Stained glass: made from purchased glass

(G-3762)
GLOBAL BIOCHEM
8044 Montgomery Rd (45236-2919)
PHONE.....................513 792-2218
Jeffrey Mahaffey, *COO*
▲ EMP: 5 EST: 2010
SALES (est): 491.5K Privately Held
SIC: 2869 2821 Ethylene glycols; ethylene glycol terephthalic acid (mylar)

(G-3763)
GLOBAL E-LUMENATION TECH
3289 Spring Grove Ave (45225-1329)
PHONE.....................513 821-8687
EMP: 3
SALES: 500K Privately Held
SIC: 3648 Mfg Lighting Equipment

(G-3764)
GLOBAL MANUFACTURING INDS (PA)
7710 Shawnee Run Rd (45243-3176)
PHONE.....................513 271-2180
Jim Tusing, *Principal*
EMP: 9
SALES (est): 7.1MM Privately Held
SIC: 3999 Chairs, hydraulic, barber & beauty shop

(G-3765)
GLOBAL SRCING SUPPORT SVCS LLC
260 E University Ave (45219-2356)
PHONE.....................800 645-2986
David Schlegeo,
▲ EMP: 6
SALES (est): 671.6K Privately Held
SIC: 3599 Custom machinery

(G-3766)
GMP WELDING & FABRICATION INC
11175 Adwood Dr (45240-3235)
PHONE.....................513 825-7861
Leonard J Mee, *President*
Tyler Mee, *Vice Pres*
Linda Conrad, *Admin Sec*
EMP: 16
SALES (est): 1.3MM Privately Held
SIC: 7692 Welding repair

(G-3767)
GOLD STAR CHILI INC (PA)
650 Lunken Park Dr (45226-1800)
PHONE.....................513 231-4541
Roger David, *President*
Jeremy Hildebrand, *Project Mgr*
James Conover, *CFO*
Jodi Kelly, *Asst Controller*
Jenny Endres, *Credit Mgr*
EMP: 33 EST: 1965
SQ FT: 5,000
SALES (est): 61.4MM Privately Held
SIC: 2032 2099 6794 5499 Chili with or without meat: packaged in cans, jars, etc.; food preparations; franchises, selling or licensing; spices & herbs

(G-3768)
GOLD STAR CHILI INC
5420 Ridge Ave (45213-2514)
PHONE.....................513 631-1990
Rusa Abusway, *Owner*
EMP: 20
SALES (corp-wide): 61.4MM Privately Held
SIC: 5812 2099 Chili stand; food preparations
PA: Gold Star Chili, Inc.
    650 Lunken Park Dr
    Cincinnati OH 45226
    513 231-4541

(G-3769)
GOMEZ SALSA LLC
8575 Coolwood Ct (45236-1301)
PHONE.....................513 314-1978
Andrew Gomez, *Principal*
EMP: 13
SALES (est): 1.6MM Privately Held
SIC: 2099 Dips, except cheese & sour cream based

(G-3770)
GOOD DAY TOOLS LLC
4603 Carter Ave (45212-2539)
PHONE.....................513 578-2050
Matt McFarland, *Partner*
Mark Donohoe, *Partner*
Rich McFarland, *Partner*
William Potts, *Partner*
Gene Warren, *Partner*
EMP: 5
SQ FT: 800
SALES (est): 564.3K Privately Held
SIC: 3743 Industrial locomotives & parts

(G-3771)
GOOD EARTH GOOD EATING LLC
6317 Starridge Ct (45248-3928)
PHONE.....................513 256-5935
Rachel Doyle,
EMP: 3
SALES (est): 43.8K Privately Held
SIC: 8099 5149 2844 Nutrition services; specialty food items; natural & organic foods; toothpastes or powders, dentifrices

(G-3772)
GOSUN INC
1217 Ellis St (45223-1842)
PHONE.....................888 868-6154
Patrick Sherwin, *CEO*
EMP: 10 EST: 2016
SQ FT: 50,000
SALES (est): 1MM Privately Held
SIC: 3631 Barbecues, grills & braziers (outdoor cooking)

(G-3773)
GOVERNMENT ACQUISITIONS INC
720 E Pete Rose Way # 330 (45202-3583)
PHONE.....................513 721-8700
Roger Brown, *Owner*
Kathy Meece, *Project Mgr*
Bobby Brown, *CFO*
Stan Jones, *CFO*
Corliss Baker, *Accountant*
EMP: 35
SQ FT: 20,000
SALES (est): 11.8MM Privately Held
WEB: www.gov-acq.com
SIC: 7378 3577 5045 Computer maintenance & repair; computer peripheral equipment; computer software

(G-3774)
GRAETERS MANUFACTURING CO (PA)
1175 Regina Graeter Way (45216-1998)
PHONE.....................513 721-3323
Richard Graeter, *President*
Eric T Schulze, *Principal*
Chip Graeter, *Vice Pres*
Tom Kunzelman, *Vice Pres*
Penny Richmond, *Director*
EMP: 60 EST: 1870
SQ FT: 25,000
SALES (est): 121.9MM Privately Held
SIC: 2024 2051 2064 2066 Ice cream, packaged: molded, on sticks, etc.; bread, cake & related products; candy & other confectionery products; chocolate & cocoa products

(G-3775)
GRAND RAPIDS PRINTING INK CO
Also Called: Ohio Valley Ink
95 Glendale Milford Rd (45215-1142)
PHONE.....................859 261-4530
Joe Poigo, *Owner*
EMP: 4
SALES (corp-wide): 2.5MM Privately Held
WEB: www.graphicarts.org
SIC: 2893 Printing ink
PA: Grand Rapids Printing Ink Company
    4920 Starr St Se
    Grand Rapids MI 49546
    616 241-5681

(G-3776)
GRAPHIC INFO SYSTEMS INC
7665 Production Dr (45237-3208)
P.O. Box 37958 (45222-0958)
PHONE.....................513 948-1300
Walter Theiss, *President*
Edward Reilly, *Treasurer*
Doug Lindeman, *Sales Staff*
Tom Stephens, *Sales Staff*
Nancy Bose, *Manager*
EMP: 16
SQ FT: 10,000
SALES (est): 4MM Privately Held
WEB: www.graphicinfo.com
SIC: 2759 Commercial printing

(G-3777)
GRAPHIC PRINT SOLUTIONS INC
7633 Production Dr (45237-3208)
PHONE.....................513 948-3344
EMP: 4
SALES (est): 333.9K Privately Held
SIC: 2752 Commercial printing, lithographic

(G-3778)
GRAPHIC SOLUTIONS COMPANY
3438 Middleton Ave (45220-1627)
PHONE.....................513 484-3067
Ryan Gentry, *Principal*
EMP: 10
SQ FT: 40,000

Cincinnati - Hamilton County (G-3779) GEOGRAPHIC SECTION

SALES (est): 395.8K Privately Held
SIC: 2752 Offset & photolithographic printing

(G-3779)
GREAT MIDWEST TOBACCO INC
Also Called: Jnj Distributors
10825 Medallion Dr (45241-4829)
PHONE.................513 745-0450
Dennis E Harper, President
EMP: 3
SALES: 950K Privately Held
SIC: 2131 Chewing & smoking tobacco

(G-3780)
GREATER CINCINNATI BOWL ASSN
611 Mercury Dr (45244-1412)
PHONE.................513 761-7387
Willie Dean, President
Joe McFarland, Vice Pres
Tom Taylor, Vice Pres
EMP: 22
SQ FT: 1,700
SALES (est): 980K Privately Held
SIC: 8699 2721 7933 Bowling club; periodicals; bowling centers

(G-3781)
GREEN RECYCLING WORKS LLC
1530 Tremont St (45214-1432)
PHONE.................513 278-7111
Bradley Sherman, Principal
EMP: 5 EST: 2011
SALES (est): 423.4K Privately Held
SIC: 2611 Pulp mills, mechanical & recycling processing

(G-3782)
GREENDALE HOME FASHIONS LLC
5500 Muddy Creek Rd (45238-2030)
PHONE.................859 916-5475
Barry J Hackett, President
▲ EMP: 80
SALES (est): 14.1MM Privately Held
WEB: www.safegardusa.com
SIC: 3842 2392 Life preservers, except cork & inflatable; cushions & pillows

(G-3783)
GREENROCK LTD
341 W Benson St (45215-3101)
PHONE.................646 388-4281
Mary Lehrter, CTO
Adam Pacelli,
EMP: 5
SALES (est): 19.7K Privately Held
SIC: 2671 Packaging paper & plastics film, coated & laminated

(G-3784)
GREG G WRIGHT & SONS LLC
10200 Springfield Pike (45215-1116)
PHONE.................513 721-3310
Tracey A Chriske, Principal
Carl A Fries,
EMP: 30 EST: 1860
SQ FT: 34,000
SALES: 6MM Privately Held
WEB: www.gregwrightandsons.com
SIC: 3953 3993 Textile marking stamps, hand: rubber or metal; stencils, painting & marking; name plates: except engraved, etched, etc.: metal

(G-3785)
GRIFFIN FISHER CO INC
1126 Wlliam Hward Taft Rd (45206-2031)
PHONE.................513 961-2110
Whitney Fisher, CEO
Branden Fisher, President
EMP: 9
SQ FT: 3,800
SALES (est): 937.2K Privately Held
SIC: 2394 2396 2399 Convertible tops, canvas or boat: from purchased materials; automotive trimmings, fabric; seat covers, automobile

(G-3786)
GRIPPO POTATO CHIP CO INC
6750 Colerain Ave (45239-5542)
PHONE.................513 923-1900
Ralph W Pagel II, President
Linda Foster, Vice Pres
James Pagel, Vice Pres
Dorothy Saylor, Treasurer
EMP: 65
SQ FT: 27,000
SALES (est): 10.1MM Privately Held
SIC: 2096 2099 Potato chips & other potato-based snacks; food preparations

(G-3787)
GSF ENERGY LLC
10795 Hughes Rd (45251-4523)
PHONE.................513 825-0504
John Schmitt, President
Daniel Bonk, Vice Pres
Martin Ryan, Admin Sec
EMP: 5
SALES (est): 1MM Privately Held
SIC: 2813 Industrial gases

(G-3788)
GTLP HOLDINGS LLC (PA)
Also Called: Premier Southern Ticket
7911 School Rd (45249-1533)
PHONE.................513 489-6700
Phillip R Sorensen, President
Kirk Schulz, Vice Pres
Bryan Lansaw, Plant Mgr
Brenda Spears, Accounting Mgr
Dave Cropper, Manager
EMP: 28
SQ FT: 35,000
SALES: 7.9MM Privately Held
SIC: 2752 Tag, ticket & schedule printing: lithographic

(G-3789)
GUIDE TECHNOLOGIES LLC (PA)
7363 E Kemper Rd Ste Ab (45249-1097)
PHONE.................513 631-8800
Mick Pennington, Business Mgr
Fred Cramer, VP Sls/Mktg
Larry Deets, Accounts Exec
Dave Meadows,
Sheri George, Sr Consultant
EMP: 3 EST: 1997
SQ FT: 1,750
SALES (est): 4.3MM Privately Held
WEB: www.guidetechnologies.com
SIC: 7372 Prepackaged software

(G-3790)
GUS HOLTHAUS SIGNS INC
Also Called: Holthaus Lackner Signs
817 Ridgeway Ave (45229-3222)
P.O. Box 29373 (45229-0373)
PHONE.................513 861-0060
Kevin Holthaus, President
Scott Holthaus, Vice Pres
Rick Souder, Prdtn Mgr
Charlie Holthaus, Purch Mgr
Jon Holthaus, Sales Staff
EMP: 40 EST: 1929
SQ FT: 38,600
SALES (est): 6.5MM Privately Held
WEB: www.holthaussigns.com
SIC: 3993 1799 Electric signs; sign installation & maintenance

(G-3791)
H NAGEL & SON CO
Also Called: Brighton Mills
2641 Spring Grove Ave (45214-1731)
PHONE.................513 665-4550
Brian Mitchell, General Mgr
EMP: 10
SALES (est): 1.1MM
SALES (corp-wide): 30MM Privately Held
SIC: 2041 Flour: blended, prepared or self-rising
PA: H. Nagel & Son Co.
707 Harrison Brookville
West Harrison IN 47060
513 665-4550

(G-3792)
HADRONICS INC
4570 Steel Pl (45209-1189)
PHONE.................513 321-9350
Kenneth J Green, Ch of Bd
Michael G Green, President
Pat McDonough, President
Jeffrey McCarty, Vice Pres
EMP: 56
SQ FT: 38,850
SALES (est): 9MM Privately Held
WEB: www.hadronics.com
SIC: 3471 3479 3555 3366 Electroplating of metals or formed products; etching & engraving; printing trades machinery; copper foundries; blast furnaces & steel mills; platemaking services

(G-3793)
HAIR SCIENCE SYSTEMS LLC
445 Bishopsbridge Dr (45255-3951)
P.O. Box 54506 (45254-0506)
PHONE.................513 231-8284
Wm Banker, Mng Member
Raymond Bitzer,
EMP: 5
SALES (est): 303.3K Privately Held
SIC: 3845 Laser systems & equipment, medical

(G-3794)
HAMILTON SAFE CO (PA)
7775 Cooper Rd (45242-7703)
PHONE.................513 874-3733
Robert C Deluse, President
John Stroia, President
Greg Holbrock, Principal
David Vanschoik, CFO
▲ EMP: 19
SQ FT: 20,000
SALES (est): 5.3MM Privately Held
WEB: www.hamiltonproductsgroup.com
SIC: 3499 Safe deposit boxes or chests, metal; safes & vaults, metal

(G-3795)
HAMILTON SECURITY PRODUCTS CO (PA)
Also Called: Hamilton Safe
7775 Cooper Rd (45242-7703)
PHONE.................513 874-3733
Robert Leslie, CEO
John Haining, President
Robert C Deluse, Principal
Lowell E Francois, Principal
H L Henkel, Principal
▲ EMP: 2
SQ FT: 20,000
SALES (est): 7.4MM Privately Held
SIC: 3499 Safe deposit boxes or chests, metal

(G-3796)
HANCHETT PAPER COMPANY
Also Called: Shorr Packaging
12121 Best Pl (45241-6402)
PHONE.................513 782-4440
Mark Trainer, Principal
Greg Woolum, Sales Mgr
Christine Dietz, Regl Sales Mgr
Connie Gates-Williams, Sales Staff
EMP: 66
SALES (corp-wide): 353.5MM Privately Held
SIC: 2621 Wrapping & packaging papers
PA: Hanchett Paper Company
4000 Ferry Rd
Aurora IL 60502
630 978-1000

(G-3797)
HANGER PRSTHETCS & ORTHO INC
Also Called: Hanger Clinic
2135 Dana Ave Ste 100 (45207-1327)
PHONE.................513 421-5653
Vinit Asar, Branch Mgr
EMP: 4
SALES (corp-wide): 1B Publicly Held
SIC: 3842 Surgical appliances & supplies
HQ: Hanger Prosthetics & Orthotics, Inc.
10910 Domain Dr Ste 300
Austin TX 78758
512 777-3800

(G-3798)
HARLAN GRAPHIC ARTS SVCS INC
4752 River Rd (45233-1633)
P.O. Box 643806 (45264-3806)
PHONE.................513 251-5700
Larry Ehrman, President
Jeff Ehrman, Vice Pres
Jenny Marsh, Project Mgr
Kim Springer, CFO
Andy Dwyer, Sales Staff
EMP: 22 EST: 1980
SQ FT: 40,000
SALES (est): 3.7MM Privately Held
WEB: www.harlangraphics.com
SIC: 2791 Typesetting

(G-3799)
HARRAY LLC
266 W Mitchell Ave (45232-1908)
PHONE.................888 568-8371
Joseph Ray, President
Kurt Harrington, Vice Pres
EMP: 6
SALES (est): 650K Privately Held
WEB: www.archlouvers.com
SIC: 3444 Sheet metalwork

(G-3800)
HARVEY BROTHERS INC (PA)
3492 Spring Grove Ave (45223-2417)
PHONE.................513 541-2622
Stephen Kyle, President
EMP: 12
SQ FT: 5,600
SALES: 2MM Privately Held
SIC: 3449 Miscellaneous metalwork

(G-3801)
HARVEY WHITNEY BOOKS COMPANY
4906 Cooper Rd (45242-6915)
P.O. Box 42435, Blue Ash (45242-0435)
PHONE.................513 793-3555
Kim Whitney, President
EMP: 2
SQ FT: 5,000
SALES (est): 1MM Privately Held
WEB: www.hwbooks.com
SIC: 2721 2731 7389 Magazines: publishing only, not printed on site; books: publishing only;

(G-3802)
HATHAWAY STAMP & IDENT CO OF C
Also Called: Hathaway Stamp Identification
635 Main St (45202-2524)
PHONE.................513 621-1052
Ken Secor, Advt Staff
Larry Schultz, Branch Mgr
Lisa Ruttenberg,
EMP: 12
SALES (est): 1.3MM
SALES (corp-wide): 30.7MM Privately Held
SIC: 3953 3479 Marking devices; name plates: engraved, etched, etc.
PA: Volk Corporation
23936 Indl Pk Dr
Farmington Hills MI 48335
248 477-6700

(G-3803)
HATHAWAY STAMP CO
635 Main St Ste 1 (45202-2524)
PHONE.................513 621-1052
Peter Ruttenberg, President
Robert C Ruwe, Vice Pres
Jerry Braun, Accounts Exec
Lauren Schneider, Sales Staff
EMP: 15
SQ FT: 4,000
SALES (est): 1.9MM
SALES (corp-wide): 30.7MM Privately Held
WEB: www.hathawaystamps.com
SIC: 3953 3089 5999 5943 Embossing seals & hand stamps; engraving of plastic; rubber stamps; office forms & supplies; notary & corporate seals
PA: Volk Corporation
23936 Indl Pk Dr
Farmington Hills MI 48335
248 477-6700

Cincinnati - Hamilton County (G-3830)

(G-3804)
HCC INDUSTRIES
9705 Reading Rd (45215-3515)
PHONE................513 334-5585
EMP: 5
SALES (est): 518.6K **Privately Held**
SIC: 3678 Electronic connectors

(G-3805)
HCC/SEALTRON (DH)
9705 Reading Rd (45215-3515)
PHONE................513 733-8400
Wes Hausman, *Principal*
EMP: 29
SQ FT: 38,000
SALES (est): 15.7MM
SALES (corp-wide): 4.8B **Publicly Held**
SIC: 3678 Electronic connectors
HQ: Hcc Industries Inc.
4232 Temple City Blvd
Rosemead CA 91770
626 443-8933

(G-3806)
HELMART COMPANY INC
Also Called: Countertops Helmart
4960 Hillside Ave (45233-1621)
PHONE................513 941-3095
Jeff Wittwer, *President*
Mark Wittwer, *Principal*
Marlene Wittwer, *Treasurer*
EMP: 7 EST: 1979
SQ FT: 6,000
SALES (est): 1.6MM **Privately Held**
WEB: www.helmart.net
SIC: 5032 1411 2541 Marble building stone; granite dimension stone; table or counter tops, plastic laminated

(G-3807)
HEN OF WOODS LLC
1432 Main St (45202-7642)
P.O. Box 867 (45201-0867)
PHONE................513 833-7357
Nick Marckwald,
EMP: 7
SQ FT: 9,000
SALES (est): 372.9K **Privately Held**
SIC: 2052 Cookies & crackers

(G-3808)
HENKEL US OPERATIONS CORP
9435 Waterstone Blvd (45249-8226)
PHONE................513 830-0260
John Rye, *Vice Pres*
Khanh Tran, *Engineer*
Paige Scheidler, *Human Res Mgr*
Ann Sipe, *Sales Staff*
Laura Soltis, *Sales Staff*
EMP: 65
SALES (corp-wide): 22.7B **Privately Held**
SIC: 2891 Adhesives
HQ: Henkel Us Operations Corporation
1 Henkel Way
Rocky Hill CT 06067
860 571-5100

(G-3809)
HENTY USA
7260 Edington Dr (45249-1063)
PHONE................513 984-5590
Tylor Scott, *CEO*
Tyler Scott, *Principal*
▲ EMP: 10
SALES: 100K **Privately Held**
SIC: 2392 Bags, garment storage: except paper or plastic film

(G-3810)
HERMETIC SEAL TECHNOLOGY INC
Also Called: Hst
2150 Schappelle Ln (45240-4602)
PHONE................513 851-4899
John Wendeln, *President*
EMP: 10
SALES (est): 1.7MM **Privately Held**
SIC: 3643 Connectors & terminals for electrical devices

(G-3811)
HESKAMP PRINTING CO INC
5514 Fair Ln (45227-3402)
PHONE................513 871-6770
J David Heskamp, *President*
Jane Heskamp, *Corp Secy*
EMP: 6 EST: 1922
SQ FT: 7,500
SALES (est): 660K **Privately Held**
SIC: 2752 2759 Commercial printing, offset; letterpress printing

(G-3812)
HILL & GRIFFITH COMPANY (PA)
1085 Summer St (45204-2037)
PHONE................513 921-1075
David Greek, *President*
Dale Welsh, *Vice Pres*
Marylou Dempsey, *Buyer*
Sarah Dixon, *Human Res Mgr*
Mike Lawry, *Sales Mgr*
EMP: 8 EST: 1896
SQ FT: 15,000
SALES (est): 12.1MM **Privately Held**
SIC: 2899 2869 3565 3542 Chemical preparations; industrial organic chemicals; packaging machinery; machine tools, metal forming type

(G-3813)
HILLTOP BASIC RESOURCES INC (PA)
Also Called: Hilltop Concrete
1 W 4th St Ste 1100 (45202-3610)
PHONE................513 651-5000
John F Steele Jr, *CEO*
Kevin M Sheehan, *President*
Brad Slabaugh, *Vice Pres*
Paul Hennekes, *CFO*
EMP: 15 EST: 1930
SQ FT: 10,000
SALES (est): 116.7MM **Privately Held**
WEB: www.hilltopbasicresources.com
SIC: 1442 3273 Construction sand mining; gravel mining; ready-mixed concrete

(G-3814)
HILLTOP BASIC RESOURCES INC
Also Called: Hilltop Concrete
511 W Water St (45202-3400)
PHONE................513 621-1500
Mike Marchioni, *Manager*
EMP: 45
SQ FT: 1,758
SALES (corp-wide): 116.7MM **Privately Held**
WEB: www.hilltopbasicresources.com
SIC: 3273 3272 1442 Ready-mixed concrete; concrete products; construction sand & gravel
PA: Hilltop Basic Resources, Inc.
1 W 4th St Ste 1100
Cincinnati OH 45202
513 651-5000

(G-3815)
HILLTOP BIG BEND QUARRY LLC
1 W 4th St Ste 1100 (45202-3610)
PHONE................513 651-5000
John F Steele Jr, *Principal*
EMP: 6
SALES (est): 699.9K **Privately Held**
SIC: 3273 Ready-mixed concrete

(G-3816)
HILLTOP STONE LLC
1 W 4th St Ste 1100 (45202-3610)
PHONE................513 651-5000
John Steele, *Principal*
EMP: 3
SALES (est): 390K **Privately Held**
SIC: 3272 Concrete products

(G-3817)
HOLLAENDER MANUFACTURING CO
10285 Wayne Ave (45215-1199)
P.O. Box 156399 (45215-6399)
PHONE................513 772-8800
Robert P Hollaender II, *CEO*
Marc E Cetrulo, *President*
Ron Crebo, *Vice Pres*
Brent Wittmeyer, *Project Mgr*
Jim James, *Purch Agent*
▼ EMP: 51 EST: 1943
SQ FT: 33,000
SALES (est): 16.1MM **Privately Held**
SIC: 3498 Fabricated pipe & fittings

(G-3818)
HOLLAND ASSOCTS LLC DBA ARCHOU
316 W 4th St Ste 201 (45202-2675)
PHONE................513 891-0006
Murray Holland,
EMP: 10
SALES (est): 3.1MM **Privately Held**
SIC: 5065 3699 1742 Sound equipment, electronic; electric sound equipment; acoustical & insulation work; acoustical & ceiling work

(G-3819)
HOLLMANN INC
1617 W Belmar Pl (45224-1017)
PHONE................513 522-1800
Joseph L Hollmann, *President*
EMP: 5
SALES (est): 623.3K **Privately Held**
WEB: www.hollmanninc.com
SIC: 3523 Dairy equipment (farm)

(G-3820)
HOLTE EYEWARE
2651 Observatory Ave # 1 (45208-2040)
PHONE................513 321-4000
Ryan Holte, *Branch Mgr*
EMP: 5 **Privately Held**
SIC: 8042 5999 3827 Offices & clinics of optometrists; sunglasses; optical instruments & lenses
PA: Holte Eyeware
8211 Cornell Rd Ste 510
Cincinnati OH 45249

(G-3821)
HOMAN METALS LLC
1253 Knowlton St (45223-1844)
PHONE................513 721-5010
Marcia P Beckmeyer,
Jerome W Beckmeyer,
EMP: 8
SQ FT: 60,000
SALES (est): 2.4MM **Privately Held**
SIC: 5093 3334 4953 3355 Metal scrap & waste materials; aluminum ingots & slabs; ingots (primary), aluminum; recycling, waste materials; aluminum ingot

(G-3822)
HOME CITY ICE COMPANY
Also Called: Hc Transport
6045 Bridgetown Rd Ste 1 (45248-3047)
PHONE................513 941-0340
Tom Sedler, *President*
EMP: 5
SALES (corp-wide): 232.5MM **Privately Held**
WEB: www.homecityice.com
SIC: 2097 Manufactured ice
PA: The Home City Ice Company
6045 Bridgetown Rd Ste 1
Cincinnati OH 45248
513 574-1800

(G-3823)
HOME CITY ICE COMPANY
11920 Kemper Springs Dr (45240-1642)
PHONE................513 851-4040
Jason Dugas, *Branch Mgr*
Eric Geiser, *Maintence Staff*
EMP: 35
SQ FT: 14,040
SALES (corp-wide): 232.5MM **Privately Held**
WEB: www.homecityice.com
SIC: 2097 Ice cubes
PA: The Home City Ice Company
6045 Bridgetown Rd Ste 1
Cincinnati OH 45248
513 574-1800

(G-3824)
HONEYBAKED HAM COMPANY (PA)
11935 Mason Montgomery Rd # 110 (45249-3702)
PHONE................513 583-9700
Craig Kurz, *CEO*
George S Kurz, *Ch of Bd*
George J Kurz, *President*
Keith Kurz, *COO*
EMP: 25
SQ FT: 12,000
SALES (est): 78.8MM **Privately Held**
SIC: 5421 2099 2024 2013 Meat markets, including freezer provisioners; food preparations; ice cream & frozen desserts; sausages & other prepared meats

(G-3825)
HONEYWELL INC
3940 Virginia Ave (45227-3412)
PHONE................513 272-1111
EMP: 143
SALES (corp-wide): 38.5B **Publicly Held**
SIC: 3823 Mfg Process Control Instruments
HQ: Honeywell Inc.
115 Tabor Rd
Morris Plains NJ 07950
973 455-2000

(G-3826)
HONEYWELL INTERNATIONAL INC
1280 Kemper Meadow Dr (45240-1632)
PHONE................513 745-7200
Tracy Glendy, *Branch Mgr*
Bill Mc Afoos, *Manager*
EMP: 100
SALES (corp-wide): 41.8B **Publicly Held**
SIC: 7373 7372 Computer systems analysis & design; prepackaged software
PA: Honeywell International Inc.
115 Tabor Rd
Morris Plains NJ 07950
973 455-2000

(G-3827)
HORNELL BREWING CO INC
Also Called: Arizona Beverages
644 Linn St Ste 318 (45203-1734)
PHONE................516 812-0384
Francie Patton, *Vice Pres*
EMP: 6
SALES (corp-wide): 74.6MM **Privately Held**
WEB: www.arizonabev.com
SIC: 2086 Bottled & canned soft drinks
PA: Hornell Brewing Co., Inc.
60 Crossways Park Dr W # 400
Woodbury NY 11797
516 812-0300

(G-3828)
HUKON MANUFACTURING COMPANY
2111 Freeman Ave (45214-1820)
PHONE................513 721-5562
Micheal Gruenschlaeger, *Owner*
Ralph Gruenschlaeger, *Owner*
EMP: 9 EST: 1907
SALES (est): 410K **Privately Held**
SIC: 3469 Spinning metal for the trade

(G-3829)
HUNKAR TECHNOLOGIES INC (PA)
2368 Victory Pkwy Ste 210 (45206-2810)
PHONE................513 272-1010
Eric R Thiemann, *President*
Jeannine Martin, *Vice Pres*
C Kevin Whaley, *Treasurer*
Brian Fugate, *Sales Staff*
James K Rice, *Admin Sec*
EMP: 140
SQ FT: 47,000
SALES (est): 30.1MM **Privately Held**
WEB: www.hunkar.com
SIC: 3565 3823 3577 3441 Labeling machines, industrial; controllers for process variables, all types; bar code (magnetic ink) printers; fabricated structural metal

(G-3830)
HYDE PARK LUMBER COMPANY
Also Called: Do It Best
3360 Red Bank Rd (45227-4107)
PHONE................513 271-1500
Mills C Judy Jr, *President*
Greg Meyer, *Buyer*
Vicki Clephane, *CFO*
EMP: 35
SQ FT: 80,000

Cincinnati - Hamilton County (G-3831)   GEOGRAPHIC SECTION

SALES (est): 6.5MM
SALES (corp-wide): 6.9MM **Privately Held**
WEB: www.hprp.com
SIC: **5211** 2431 Lumber products; millwork
PA: The Judy Mills Company Inc
3360 Red Bank Rd
Cincinnati OH 45227
513 271-4241

(G-3831)
HYDRATECH ENGINEERED PDTS LLC
10448 Chester Rd (45215-1202)
PHONE..................513 827-9169
Peter Blais, *Mng Member*
EMP: 10
SALES (est): 2.2MM **Privately Held**
SIC: **2891** Sealing compounds for pipe threads or joints

(G-3832)
HYDRO SYSTEMS COMPANY (DH)
3798 Round Bottom Rd (45244-2498)
PHONE..................513 271-8800
Serge Joris, *CEO*
Doug Papp, *CFO*
◆ EMP: 34
SALES (est): 32.7MM
SALES (corp-wide): 6.9B **Publicly Held**
WEB: www.hydrosystemsco.com
SIC: **3586** Measuring & dispensing pumps
HQ: Opw Fluid Transfer Group
4304 Nw Mattox Rd
Kansas City MO 64150
816 741-6600

(G-3833)
I T VERDIN CO (PA)
Also Called: Verdin Company
444 Reading Rd (45202-1432)
PHONE..................513 241-4010
F B Wersel, *CEO*
Robert R Verdin Jr, *CEO*
James R Verdin, *President*
Steve Kemme, *General Mgr*
Stanley A Hittner, *Principal*
▲ EMP: 30 EST: 1842
SQ FT: 13,000
SALES (est): 20.2MM **Privately Held**
SIC: **3931** 3699 3873 Carillon bells; bells, electric; clocks, except timeclocks

(G-3834)
I T VERDIN CO
3900 Kellogg Ave (45226-1518)
PHONE..................513 559-3947
David Verdin, *Branch Mgr*
Shannon Parker, *Tech/Comp Coord*
EMP: 35
SQ FT: 24,175
SALES (corp-wide): 20.2MM **Privately Held**
SIC: **3931** 3699 3873 Carillon bells; bells, electric; clocks, except timeclocks
PA: The I T Verdin Co
444 Reading Rd
Cincinnati OH 45202
513 241-4010

(G-3835)
IDEAS & AD VENTURES INC
2614 Spring Grove Ave (45214-1732)
PHONE..................513 542-7154
Dennis P Haskamp, *President*
Patricia J Haskamp, *Corp Secy*
John H Haskamp, *Shareholder*
EMP: 6
SQ FT: 4,500
SALES (est): 530K **Privately Held**
SIC: **2752** Commercial printing, offset

(G-3836)
IFCO SYSTEMS US LLC
Also Called: I F C O Systems
10725 Evendale Dr (45241-2535)
PHONE..................513 769-0377
Matt Mallory, *General Mgr*
Kimberly Lindsay, *Office Mgr*
Hope Singleton, *Branch Mgr*
EMP: 40 **Privately Held**
SIC: **2448** Pallets, wood; skids, wood
HQ: Ifco Systems Us, Llc
3030 N Rocky Point Dr W # 300
Tampa FL 33607

(G-3837)
IGEL TECHNOLOGY AMERICA LLC
2106 Florence Ave (45206-2427)
PHONE..................954 739-9990
Jim Volpenhein, *CEO*
EMP: 13
SALES (est): 1.1MM **Privately Held**
SIC: **7372** Prepackaged software

(G-3838)
IMMERSUS HEALTH COMPANY LLC (PA)
2 Hill And Hollow Ln (45208-3317)
P.O. Box 8323 (45208-0323)
PHONE..................855 994-4325
Brian Pavlin,
EMP: 1
SALES: 10MM **Privately Held**
SIC: **3841** 7389 Surgical & medical instruments;

(G-3839)
IMPACKT
3700 Pocahontas Ave (45227-3821)
PHONE..................513 559-1488
David Haynes, *Principal*
EMP: 5
SALES (est): 441.6K **Privately Held**
SIC: **3565** Packaging machinery

(G-3840)
IMPAKT
5721 Dragon Way Ste 217 (45227-4518)
PHONE..................513 271-9191
D Bruce Freeman, *Owner*
EMP: 3
SALES (est): 221.6K **Privately Held**
WEB: www.impaktusa.com
SIC: **3544** Special dies, tools, jigs & fixtures

(G-3841)
IMPERIAL ADHESIVES
6315 Wiehe Rd (45237-4213)
PHONE..................513 351-1300
Pete Smith, *Vice Pres*
EMP: 4
SALES (est): 360.6K **Privately Held**
SIC: **2891** Adhesives

(G-3842)
IMPERIAL POOLS INC
12090 Best Pl (45241-1569)
PHONE..................513 771-1506
Mike Grant, *Branch Mgr*
EMP: 68
SALES (corp-wide): 70.3MM **Privately Held**
SIC: **3949** Swimming pools, except plastic
PA: Imperial Pools, Inc.
33 Wade Rd
Latham NY 12110
518 786-1200

(G-3843)
INDUSTRIAL CONTAINER SVCS LLC
Also Called: Ics-Cargo Clean
1258 Knowlton St (45223-1845)
PHONE..................513 921-2056
Gary Craig, *Branch Mgr*
EMP: 20
SALES (est): 1.1B **Privately Held**
WEB: www.iconserv.com
SIC: **3443** 3089 Fabricated plate work (boiler shop); plastic & fiberglass tanks
HQ: Industrial Container Services Llc
2600 Mtland Ctr Pkwy 20 # 200
Maitland FL 32751
407 930-4182

(G-3844)
INDUSTRIAL CONTAINER SVCS LLC
Also Called: Ics-Cargo Clean
837 Depot St (45204-2005)
PHONE..................513 921-8811
John Stephens, *Branch Mgr*
EMP: 20
SALES (corp-wide): 1.1B **Privately Held**
WEB: www.iconserv.com
SIC: **3443** 3412 3411 Fabricated plate work (boiler shop); metal barrels, drums & pails; metal cans
HQ: Industrial Container Services Llc
2600 Mtland Ctr Pkwy 20 # 200
Maitland FL 32751
407 930-4182

(G-3845)
INDUSTRIAL THERMAL SYSTEMS INC
3914 Virginia Ave (45227-3412)
PHONE..................513 561-2100
Robert Jackson, *President*
Susan Jackson, *Treasurer*
◆ EMP: 15
SQ FT: 34,000
SALES (est): 3.7MM **Privately Held**
SIC: **3559** 3613 Kilns; control panels, electric

(G-3846)
INDUSTRIAL WIRE ROPE SUP INC (PA)
7390 Harrison Ave (45247-2400)
P.O. Box 58149 (45258-0149)
PHONE..................513 941-2443
Barry Stroube, *President*
James Scott Lemen, *Opers Mgr*
Chris Chappell, *Sales Executive*
Matthew Hall, *Office Mgr*
John Korn, *Admin Sec*
◆ EMP: 9
SQ FT: 3,000
SALES (est): 6.7MM **Privately Held**
WEB: www.industrialrope.com
SIC: **5051** 3496 Rope, wire (not insulated); miscellaneous fabricated wire products

(G-3847)
INDY RESOLUTIONS LTD
1776 Mentor Ave Ste 130 (45212-3554)
PHONE..................513 475-6625
Christopher D Fahrmeier, *Principal*
EMP: 3
SALES (est): 181.9K **Privately Held**
SIC: **3823** Industrial instrmnts msrmnt display/control process variable

(G-3848)
INK PRODUCTION SERVICES INC
9648 Wayne Ave (45215-2259)
P.O. Box 12288 (45212-0288)
PHONE..................513 733-9338
Jeff Wilson, *President*
Betty Wilson, *Vice Pres*
EMP: 12
SQ FT: 20,000
SALES (est): 1.9MM **Privately Held**
SIC: **2893** Printing ink

(G-3849)
INNER FIRE SPORTS LLC
2558 Madison Rd Apt 18 (45208-1144)
PHONE..................719 244-6622
Joseph Carman, *Partner*
John Karaus, *Partner*
EMP: 3 EST: 2012
SALES (est): 182.8K **Privately Held**
SIC: **2389** 2329 2339 Men's miscellaneous accessories; men's & boys' sportswear & athletic clothing; women's & misses' outerwear

(G-3850)
INNOVATIVE WOODWORKING INC
1901 Ross Ave (45212-2019)
PHONE..................513 531-1940
Robert Rodenfels, *President*
Janet A Rodenfels, *President*
Robert W Rodenfels II, *President*
EMP: 9
SQ FT: 13,000
SALES (est): 1.1MM **Privately Held**
SIC: **2522** 2521 Office bookcases, wallcases & partitions, except wood; wood office filing cabinets & bookcases

(G-3851)
INSTRMNTATION CTRL SYSTEMS INC
Also Called: Ics Electrical Services
11355 Sebring Dr (45240-2796)
PHONE..................513 662-2600
John Guenther, *President*
Darrenn Pegg, *Project Mgr*
▲ EMP: 43
SQ FT: 15,500
SALES (est): 7.6MM **Privately Held**
WEB: www.icselectricalservices.com
SIC: **1731** 7629 3613 General electrical contractor; electric power systems contractors; electronic controls installation; fiber optic cable installation; electrical measuring instrument repair & calibration; control panels, electric

(G-3852)
INTEL INDUSTRIES LLC
773 Laverty Ln (45230-3552)
PHONE..................614 551-5702
Thomas J Elliott, *Principal*
EMP: 4
SALES (est): 503.9K **Privately Held**
SIC: **3674** Microprocessors

(G-3853)
INTER AMERICAN PRODUCTS INC (HQ)
Also Called: Kenlakje Foods
1240 State Ave (45204-1728)
PHONE..................800 645-2233
David B Dillon, *CEO*
Rodney McMullen, *President*
Bill Lucia, *General Mgr*
David Hipenbecker, *Director*
EMP: 28
SALES (est): 246.6MM
SALES (corp-wide): 121.1B **Publicly Held**
WEB: www.interamericanproducts.com
SIC: **2095** 2099 2033 2079 Roasted coffee; spices, including grinding; jellies, edible, including imitation: in cans, jars, etc.; preserves, including imitation: in cans, jars, etc.; salad oils, except corn: vegetable refined; concentrates, drink; processed cheese; natural cheese
PA: The Kroger Co
1014 Vine St Ste 1000
Cincinnati OH 45202
513 762-4000

(G-3854)
INTERCONTINENTAL CHEMICAL CORP (PA)
4660 Spring Grove Ave (45232-1995)
PHONE..................513 541-7100
Cameron W Cord, *President*
Paul Shaver, *Admin Sec*
EMP: 30
SQ FT: 54,000
SALES (est): 3.3MM **Privately Held**
WEB: www.icc-chemicals.com
SIC: **2842** Specialty cleaning, polishes & sanitation goods

(G-3855)
INTERLUBE CORPORATION
Also Called: Lube & Chem Products
4646 Baker St (45212-2594)
PHONE..................513 531-1777
Elmer Cleave, *President*
Elmer B Cleves, *President*
Tony Martini, *Technical Mgr*
Robert Erpenbeck, *Engineer*
EMP: 10 EST: 1969
SQ FT: 4,464
SALES (est): 1.8MM **Privately Held**
WEB: www.interlubecorporation.com
SIC: **2992** Lubricating oils & greases

(G-3856)
INTERNATIONAL BRAND SERVICES
Also Called: Graeter's Ice Cream
3397 Erie Ave Apt 215 (45208-1638)
PHONE..................513 376-8209
Kellie Manning, *General Mgr*
EMP: 15
SALES (est): 910K **Privately Held**
SIC: **2024** 5812 Ice cream & ice milk; ice cream stands or dairy bars

(G-3857)
INTERNATIONAL BUS MCHS CORP
Also Called: IBM
1 Procter And Gamble Plz (45202-3315)
PHONE..................513 826-1001

▲ = Import ▼ = Export
◆ = Import/Export

GEOGRAPHIC SECTION
Cincinnati - Hamilton County (G-3885)

Steve Parks, *Partner*
Michael Flood, *Manager*
EMP: 350
SALES (corp-wide): 79.5B **Publicly Held**
WEB: www.ibm.com
SIC: 3613 Distribution cutouts
PA: International Business Machines Corporation
1 New Orchard Rd Ste 1 # 1
Armonk NY 10504
914 499-1900

(G-3858)
INTERNATIONAL SUPPLY CORP
Also Called: International Financial Svcs
3284 E Sharon Rd (45241-1945)
PHONE 513 793-0393
Ted J Day, *President*
Theodore J Day, *President*
EMP: 3
SQ FT: 2,000
SALES (est): 350.9K **Privately Held**
SIC: 3089 7389 Injection molding of plastics; financial services

(G-3859)
IRON WIND METALS CO LLC
10488 Chester Rd (45215-1202)
PHONE 513 870-0606
Mike Noe, *Principal*
EMP: 6
SQ FT: 5,000
SALES (est): 560K **Privately Held**
WEB: www.ironwindmetals.com
SIC: 3944 7389 Games, toys & children's vehicles; packaging & labeling services

(G-3860)
IROQUOIS PALLET
9417 Bainwoods Dr (45249-3602)
PHONE 513 677-0048
Richard Friend, *Owner*
EMP: 3
SALES (est): 119.9K **Privately Held**
SIC: 2448 Wood pallets & skids

(G-3861)
J & P INVESTMENTS INC
Also Called: Advance Printing Company
8100 Reading Rd (45237-1404)
P.O. Box 37633 (45222-0633)
PHONE 513 821-2299
Paul Erdman, *President*
Thomas Schamer, *Vice Pres*
Tom Schamer, *Vice Pres*
Rob Barhorst, *Manager*
EMP: 13
SQ FT: 26,500
SALES (est): 2MM **Privately Held**
SIC: 2752 Commercial printing, offset

(G-3862)
J C EQUIPMENT SALES & LEASING
2300 E Kemper Rd Unit 11a (45241-6505)
PHONE 513 772-7612
Jeff Combs, *President*
Chris Wells, *General Mgr*
EMP: 5
SQ FT: 2,300
SALES (est): 965.4K **Privately Held**
SIC: 3829 5049 5999 Surveying & drafting equipment; drafting supplies; drafting equipment & supplies

(G-3863)
J FELDKAMP DESIGN BUILD LTD
10036 Springfield Pike (45215-1452)
PHONE 513 870-0601
Jody Feldkamp, *President*
Robert Boggs, *Principal*
Jonathan Feldkamp, *Vice Pres*
Jonathan W Feldkamp, *Vice Pres*
Elisa Feldkamp, *CFO*
EMP: 42
SQ FT: 18,000
SALES (est): 3.7MM **Privately Held**
SIC: 1711 3499 Heating & air conditioning contractors; plumbing contractors; aerosol valves, metal

(G-3864)
J II FIRE SYSTEMS INC
3628 Harrison Ave (45211-5567)
PHONE 513 574-0609

June Craynon, *President*
John Craynon, *Principal*
EMP: 5
SALES (est): 1.1MM **Privately Held**
SIC: 3699 Security devices

(G-3865)
J M SMUCKER COMPANY
5204 Spring Grove Ave (45217-1031)
P.O. Box 599 (45201-0599)
PHONE 513 482-8000
Steve Landry, *Plant Mgr*
Richard Cappola, *Purchasing*
Mike Mankus, *Engineer*
Rodney Dozier, *Sales Mgr*
E Hunter, *Branch Mgr*
EMP: 100
SALES (corp-wide): 7.3B **Publicly Held**
WEB: www.smuckers.com
SIC: 2099 Peanut butter
PA: The J M Smucker Company
1 Strawberry Ln
Orrville OH 44667
330 682-3000

(G-3866)
JACOBS MECHANICAL CO
4500 W Mitchell Ave (45232-1912)
PHONE 513 681-6800
John E Mc Donald, *President*
EMP: 125
SQ FT: 20,000
SALES (est): 24.4MM **Privately Held**
WEB: www.jacobsmech.com
SIC: 1711 3444 Ventilation & duct work contractor; sheet metalwork

(G-3867)
JAKMAR INCORPORATED
3280 Hageman Ave (45241-1907)
PHONE 513 631-4303
William Thaman, *President*
EMP: 16
SALES (est): 1.4MM **Privately Held**
SIC: 3061 Mechanical rubber goods

(G-3868)
JAMES C FREE INC
Also Called: James Free Jewellers
9555 Main St Ste 1 (45242-7670)
PHONE 513 793-0133
Zackery Karaman, *Vice Pres*
EMP: 6
SALES (corp-wide): 3.4MM **Privately Held**
WEB: www.jamesfreejewelers.com
SIC: 3911 5944 Jewelry, precious metal; jewelry, precious stones & precious metals
PA: James C. Free, Inc.
3100 Far Hills Ave
Dayton OH 45429
937 298-0171

(G-3869)
JAMES C ROBINSON
Also Called: J C Robinson Products
442 Chestnut St Apt 1 (45203-1454)
PHONE 513 969-7482
James C Robinson, *Owner*
EMP: 9
SALES: 19MM **Privately Held**
SIC: 5149 7231 2842 Dried or canned foods; beauty shops; automobile polish

(G-3870)
JAPLAR GROUP INC
Also Called: Japlar Schauer
3210 Wasson Rd (45209-2382)
PHONE 513 791-7192
Jonathan Chaiken, *President*
▲ **EMP:** 15
SQ FT: 120,000
SALES (est): 2.3MM **Privately Held**
SIC: 3629 3612 3825 Battery chargers, rectifying or nonrotating; transformers, except electric; instruments to measure electricity

(G-3871)
JERRY TOOLS INC
6200 Vine St (45216-2199)
PHONE 513 242-3211
David Inboldt, *President*
David Imholt, *President*
Don Daniels, *Vice Pres*

Debra Imholt, *Vice Pres*
EMP: 16
SQ FT: 15,625
SALES (est): 3MM **Privately Held**
WEB: www.jerrytools.com
SIC: 3545 3452 Chucks: drill, lathe or magnetic (machine tool accessories); arbors (machine tool accessories); nuts, metal

(G-3872)
JHG RETAIL SERVICES LLC
Also Called: Phg Retail Services
7951 Merrymaker Ln (45236-2748)
PHONE 216 447-0831
Joelle Hominy-Gertz, *President*
EMP: 14
SALES: 750K **Privately Held**
SIC: 2542 Racks, merchandise display or storage: except wood

(G-3873)
JJKB ENTERPRISES LLC
Also Called: Right Srce Cmmunications Group
6125 Montgomery Rd Unit 1 (45213-1454)
P.O. Box 36164 (45236-0164)
PHONE 513 731-4332
Patricia Meder, *Senior Partner*
Angela Osborne, *Editor*
Katy Bair, *Mng Member*
EMP: 4
SQ FT: 3,000
SALES (est): 356.8K **Privately Held**
SIC: 8743 7374 2759 Public relations & publicity; computer graphics service; publication printing

(G-3874)
JJS3 FOUNDATION
Also Called: Neusole Glassworks
11925 Kemper Springs Dr (45240-1643)
PHONE 513 751-3292
Debbie Bradley, *Manager*
John Schiff, *Exec Dir*
Sandy Burt, *Executive Asst*
EMP: 5
SALES (est): 828.4K **Privately Held**
WEB: www.neusole.com
SIC: 1542 3229 Nonresidential construction; pressed & blown glass

(G-3875)
JOE BAKER EQUIPMENT SALES
1000 Devils Backbone Rd (45233-4812)
PHONE 513 451-1327
Joe Baker, *Principal*
▲ **EMP:** 3 **EST:** 2007
SALES (est): 440.2K **Privately Held**
SIC: 7538 7694 7699 Engine repair; rebuilding motors, except automotive; engine repair & replacement, non-automotive

(G-3876)
JOE BUSBY
Also Called: Laces For Less
439 S Cooper Ave (45215-4565)
P.O. Box 15726 (45215-0726)
PHONE 513 821-1716
Joe Busby, *Owner*
EMP: 3
SQ FT: 800
SALES: 200K **Privately Held**
WEB: www.lacesforless.com
SIC: 5131 2241 Lace fabrics; shoe laces, except leather

(G-3877)
JOE P FISCHER WOODCRAFT
8455 Greenleaf Dr (45255-5609)
PHONE 513 474-4316
Joe Fischer, *Principal*
EMP: 3 **EST:** 2008
SALES (est): 246.2K **Privately Held**
SIC: 2511 Wood household furniture

(G-3878)
JOHN F KILFOIL CO
3799 Madison Rd (45209-1123)
PHONE 513 791-6150
Timothy M Kilfoil, *President*
Christine Bell, *Vice Pres*
EMP: 4

SALES (est): 1.1MM **Privately Held**
SIC: 5065 3544 Electronic parts & equipment; special dies, tools, jigs & fixtures

(G-3879)
JOHN FRIEDA PROF HAIR CARE INC (DH)
2535 Spring Grove Ave (45214-1729)
PHONE 800 521-3189
William J Gentner, *President*
Joseph B Workman, *Vice Pres*
EMP: 40
SALES (est): 8MM
SALES (corp-wide): 13.4B **Privately Held**
SIC: 2844 Hair preparations, including shampoos
HQ: Kao Usa Inc.
2535 Spring Grove Ave
Cincinnati OH 45214
513 421-1400

(G-3880)
JOHN S SWIFT COMPANY INC
8044 Montgomery Rd # 700 (45236-2926)
PHONE 513 721-4147
Bill Zimmerman, *Manager*
EMP: 15
SQ FT: 18,000
SALES (est): 2.1MM
SALES (corp-wide): 15.7MM **Privately Held**
WEB: www.jssco.com
SIC: 2752 Commercial printing, offset
PA: John S Swift Company Incorporated
999 Commerce Ct
Buffalo Grove IL 60089
847 465-3300

(G-3881)
JOHN STEHLIN & SONS CO INC
Also Called: Stehlin, John & Sons Meats
10134 Colerain Ave (45251-4902)
PHONE 513 385-6164
John Stehlin, *President*
Dennis Stehlin, *Vice Pres*
Ronald Stehlin, *Vice Pres*
Richard Stehlin, *Admin Sec*
EMP: 14 **EST:** 1913
SQ FT: 3,600
SALES (est): 1MM **Privately Held**
SIC: 5421 2013 2011 Meat markets, including freezer provisioners; sausages & other prepared meats; beef products from beef slaughtered on site

(G-3882)
JOHNSON CONTROLS INC
11648 Springfield Pike (45246-3019)
PHONE 513 671-6338
Lawrence W Gundler, *President*
EMP: 15 **Privately Held**
SIC: 2531 7382 Seats, automobile; security systems services
HQ: Johnson Controls, Inc.
5757 N Green Bay Ave
Milwaukee WI 53209
414 524-1200

(G-3883)
JOSEPH BERNING PRINTING CO
1850 Dalton Ave (45214-2056)
PHONE 513 721-0781
Michael Berning, *President*
Jim Lamping, *Opers Mgr*
Kim Fishback, *Human Res Mgr*
EMP: 18 **EST:** 1883
SQ FT: 11,800
SALES: 5MM **Privately Held**
WEB: www.josberningprinting.com
SIC: 2752 Commercial printing, offset

(G-3884)
JOSEPH G BETZ & SONS
4219 Saint Martins Pl (45211-5315)
PHONE 513 481-0322
EMP: 4 **EST:** 1945
SQ FT: 7,500
SALES (est): 240K **Privately Held**
SIC: 7641 2512 Reupholstery/Furniture Repair Mfg Upholstered Household Furniture

(G-3885)
JOSTENS INC
3047 Madison Rd Ste 207 (45209-1786)
PHONE 513 731-5900

(PA)=Parent Co (HQ)=Headquarters (DH)=Div Headquarters
✪ = New Business established in last 2 years

Cincinnati - Hamilton County (G-3886)   GEOGRAPHIC SECTION

Tom Jans, *President*
EMP: 3
SALES (corp-wide): 1.3B **Privately Held**
WEB: www.jostens.com
SIC: 3911 Rings, finger: precious metal
HQ: Jostens, Inc.
7760 France Ave S Ste 400
Minneapolis MN 55435
952 830-3300

(G-3886)
JSCS GROUP INC
Also Called: Market Direct
690 Northland Blvd (45240-3214)
PHONE..................513 563-4900
John Harmon, *President*
Stephanie Harmon, *President*
EMP: 5
SQ FT: 10,000
SALES (est): 550K **Privately Held**
WEB: www.marketdirectinc.com
SIC: 2759 7331 7336 8732 Commercial printing; direct mail advertising services; commercial art & graphic design; market analysis or research

(G-3887)
JUDY MILLS COMPANY INC (PA)
3360 Red Bank Rd (45227-4107)
PHONE..................513 271-4241
Mike Judy, *President*
EMP: 36 EST: 1922
SALES (est): 6.9MM **Privately Held**
SIC: 6512 5211 2431 Commercial & industrial building operation; lumber & other building materials; millwork

(G-3888)
JUSTIN P STRAUB LLC
Also Called: Automation Etc
14 De Camp Ave (45216-1624)
PHONE..................513 761-0282
Annie White,
Maggie Clezenger,
Justin Straub,
EMP: 6
SALES: 290K **Privately Held**
SIC: 3544 7699 Forms (molds), for foundry & plastics working machinery; industrial machinery & equipment repair

(G-3889)
K & H INDUSTRIES LLC
1041 Evans St Ste 2 (45204-2019)
PHONE..................513 921-6770
Jennifer Sharkey,
Tom Sharkey,
EMP: 15 EST: 1905
SQ FT: 60,000
SALES (est): 2.8MM **Privately Held**
WEB: www.kh-ind.com
SIC: 3469 Stamping metal for the trade

(G-3890)
K F T INC
726 Mehring Way (45203-1809)
PHONE..................513 241-5910
Ronald Eubanks, *President*
EMP: 60
SQ FT: 45,000
SALES (est): 6.1MM **Privately Held**
WEB: www.tkf.com
SIC: 1796 3535 Millwright; machinery installation; overhead conveyor systems

(G-3891)
K2 PETROLEUM & SUPPLY LLC
11371 Village Brook Dr # 1321 (45249-2072)
PHONE..................937 503-2614
Jeffery Pastor, *CFO*
EMP: 3
SALES (est): 200.2K **Privately Held**
SIC: 2911 5172 2899 5169 Petroleum refining; diesel fuel; jet fuel igniters; waxes, except petroleum

(G-3892)
KAFFENBARGER TRUCK EQP CO
3260 E Kemper Rd (45241-1519)
PHONE..................513 772-6800
Rodney Swigert, *Manager*
EMP: 35
SQ FT: 18,280
SALES (corp-wide): 38MM **Privately Held**
WEB: www.kaffenbarger.com
SIC: 7538 5531 3713 3532 Truck engine repair, except industrial; truck equipment & parts; truck bodies & parts; mining machinery; construction machinery
PA: Kaffenbarger Truck Equipment Co Inc
10100 Ballentine Pike
New Carlisle OH 45344
937 845-3804

(G-3893)
KAHNY PRINTING INC
4766 River Rd (45233-1633)
PHONE..................513 251-2911
John S Kahny, *President*
Linda Knierim, *Vice Pres*
Cathy Kahny, *Graphic Designe*
EMP: 25 EST: 1956
SQ FT: 14,000
SALES (est): 4.1MM **Privately Held**
WEB: www.kahny.com
SIC: 2752 Commercial printing, offset

(G-3894)
KAISER FOODS INC (PA)
500 York St (45214-2490)
PHONE..................513 621-2053
David Kaiser, *Chairman*
Donald J Kaiser, *Vice Pres*
Kim Speed, *Vice Pres*
Renee Link, *Human Res Mgr*
Nick Horton, *Sales Staff*
▲ EMP: 20
SQ FT: 50,000
SALES (est): 26.1MM **Privately Held**
WEB: www.kaiserfoods.com
SIC: 5149 2035 Pickles, preserves, jellies & jams; condiments; cookies; cucumbers, pickles & pickle salting; pickles, vinegar

(G-3895)
KAISER FOODS INC
Also Called: Kaiser Pickles
2155 Kindel Ave (45214-1841)
PHONE..................513 241-6833
Ted Kaiser, *Manager*
EMP: 16
SQ FT: 12,308
SALES (corp-wide): 26.1MM **Privately Held**
WEB: www.kaiserfoods.com
SIC: 2035 Pickles, vinegar; relishes, fruit & vegetable; relishes, vinegar
PA: Kaiser Foods, Inc.
500 York St
Cincinnati OH 45214
513 621-2053

(G-3896)
KAISER PICKLES LLC
500 York St (45214-2416)
PHONE..................513 621-2053
David Kaiser, *CEO*
Kim Speed, *President*
EMP: 25
SALES (est): 890.1K
SALES (corp-wide): 26.1MM **Privately Held**
SIC: 2035 Pickled fruits & vegetables
PA: Kaiser Foods, Inc.
500 York St
Cincinnati OH 45214
513 621-2053

(G-3897)
KAO USA INC (HQ)
2535 Spring Grove Ave (45214-1729)
P.O. Box 145444 (45250-5444)
PHONE..................513 421-1400
Bill Gentner, *President*
John Nosek, *President*
Cassandra Dunn, *General Mgr*
Mark Ciochetto, *Business Mgr*
John Hewer, *Business Mgr*
◆ EMP: 400 EST: 1882
SQ FT: 489,000
SALES (est): 544.9MM
SALES (corp-wide): 13.4B **Privately Held**
WEB: www.kaobrands.com
SIC: 2844 2841 Cosmetic preparations; face creams or lotions; soap: granulated, liquid, cake, flaked or chip
PA: Kao Corporation
1-14-10, Nihombashikayabacho
Chuo-Ku TKY 103-0
336 607-111

(G-3898)
KAWS INC
Also Called: RB Tool and Manufacturing
2680 Civic Center Dr (45231-1312)
PHONE..................513 521-8292
Kathy Schaeper, *CEO*
Al Schaeper, *President*
EMP: 39
SQ FT: 20,000
SALES (est): 6MM **Privately Held**
WEB: www.rbtoolandmfg.com
SIC: 3599 Machine shop, jobbing & repair

(G-3899)
KDM SIGNS INC
Kdm Retail
3000 Exon Ave (45241-2550)
PHONE..................513 769-3900
Lee Diss, *Branch Mgr*
EMP: 30
SALES (corp-wide): 82.2MM **Privately Held**
SIC: 2541 Display fixtures, wood
PA: Kdm Signs, Inc.
10450 Medallion Dr
Cincinnati OH 45241
513 769-1932

(G-3900)
KDM SIGNS INC (PA)
Also Called: Kdm Screen Printing
10450 Medallion Dr (45241-3199)
PHONE..................513 769-1932
Robert J Kissel, *President*
Kathy McQueen, *Corp Secy*
▲ EMP: 230 EST: 1984
SQ FT: 150,000
SALES (est): 82.2MM **Privately Held**
WEB: www.kdmpop.com
SIC: 3993 2759 Signs & advertising specialties; screen printing

(G-3901)
KEEBLER COMPANY
1 Trade St (45227-4509)
PHONE..................513 271-3500
Sam Bristle, *Manager*
EMP: 42
SALES (corp-wide): 13.5B **Publicly Held**
SIC: 2052 Cookies
HQ: Keebler Company
1 Kellogg Sq
Battle Creek MI 49017
269 961-2000

(G-3902)
KELLOGG COMPANY
1 Trade St (45227-4509)
PHONE..................513 271-3500
Jerry Morgan, *Prdtn Mgr*
Leslie Marksberry, *Plant Engr*
Tim Williams, *Manager*
EMP: 450
SALES (corp-wide): 13.5B **Publicly Held**
WEB: www.kelloggs.com
SIC: 2052 2051 Biscuits, dry; cookies; crackers, dry; bread, cake & related products
PA: Kellogg Company
1 Kellogg Sq
Battle Creek MI 49017
269 961-2000

(G-3903)
KELLOGG COMPANY
8044 Montgomery Rd # 700 (45236-2919)
PHONE..................513 792-2700
Frank Fay, *President*
EMP: 385
SALES (corp-wide): 13.5B **Publicly Held**
SIC: 2043 Cereal breakfast foods
PA: Kellogg Company
1 Kellogg Sq
Battle Creek MI 49017
269 961-2000

(G-3904)
KENDALL/HUNT PUBLISHING CO
Also Called: Rcl Benziger
8805 Governors Hill Dr # 400 (45249-3314)
PHONE..................877 275-4725
Anne Battes, *Publisher*
Sori Govin, *Sales Staff*
Peter Ashpostio, *Branch Mgr*
Angela Harner, *Manager*
Joseph Leonard, *Web Dvlpr*
EMP: 90
SALES (corp-wide): 70.4MM **Privately Held**
SIC: 2731 Books: publishing & printing
PA: Kendall/Hunt Publishing Company
4050 Westmark Dr
Dubuque IA 52002
563 589-1000

(G-3905)
KENNEDY INK COMPANY INC (PA)
5230 Wooster Pike (45226-2229)
PHONE..................513 871-2515
Jim Scott, *President*
Donald M Kennedy, *Principal*
James H Scott, *Principal*
Ralph W Wagner, *Principal*
EMP: 15
SQ FT: 8,000
SALES (est): 2.5MM **Privately Held**
SIC: 2893 Printing ink

(G-3906)
KETTERING ROOFING & SHTMTL
3210 Jefferson Ave Ste 1 (45220-2290)
PHONE..................513 281-6413
Timothy Kettering, *President*
Christina Kettering, *Corp Secy*
EMP: 12 EST: 1929
SQ FT: 5,000
SALES (est): 1.3MM **Privately Held**
SIC: 1761 3444 2952 Sheet metalwork; roofing contractor; sheet metalwork; asphalt felts & coatings

(G-3907)
KEY PRESS INC
2135 Central Pkwy (45214-3712)
PHONE..................513 721-1203
Jerry Koch, *President*
Rick Koch, *Vice Pres*
EMP: 4 EST: 1901
SQ FT: 5,000
SALES (est): 350K **Privately Held**
SIC: 2752 2759 Lithographing on metal; letterpress printing

(G-3908)
KILN OF HYDE PARK INC
1286 Herschel Ave (45208-3011)
PHONE..................513 321-3307
Carol Philpott, *Owner*
EMP: 15
SALES (est): 688K **Privately Held**
SIC: 5719 3269 Pottery; firing & decorating china

(G-3909)
KIMBERLY-CLARK CORPORATION
209 W 7th St (45202-2373)
PHONE..................513 864-3780
EMP: 213
SALES (corp-wide): 18.4B **Publicly Held**
SIC: 2621 2676 Sanitary tissue paper; infant & baby paper products
PA: Kimberly-Clark Corporation
351 Phelps Dr
Irving TX 75038
972 281-1200

(G-3910)
KING BAG AND MANUFACTURING CO (PA)
1500 Spring Lawn Ave (45223-1699)
PHONE..................513 541-5440
Connie M Kirsch, *President*
Mary Pugh, *Business Mgr*
Ronald Kirsch Sr, *Vice Pres*
Ronald Kirsch Jr, *Vice Pres*

▲ = Import ▼ = Export
◆ = Import/Export

GEOGRAPHIC SECTION

Mary Yarger, *Controller*
▲ **EMP:** 25
SQ FT: 18,000
SALES: 13.7MM **Privately Held**
WEB: www.kingbag.com
SIC: 2393 2221 Textile bags; polyethylene broadwoven fabrics

(G-3911)
KINSELLA MANUFACTURING CO INC
7880 Camargo Rd (45243-2652)
PHONE..................513 561-5285
George P Kinsella, *President*
John Kinsella, *Corp Secy*
Kevin Kinsella, *Vice Pres*
EMP: 10 **EST:** 1961
SQ FT: 10,000
SALES: 2MM **Privately Held**
WEB: www.kinsellakitchens.com
SIC: 5211 2541 2434 Cabinets, kitchen; counter tops; counters or counter display cases, wood; table or counter tops, plastic laminated; wood kitchen cabinets

(G-3912)
KIRK & BLUM MANUFACTURING CO (DH)
4625 Red Bank Rd Ste 200 (45227-1552)
PHONE..................513 458-2600
◆ **EMP:** 200 **EST:** 1907
SQ FT: 250,000
SALES (est): 78.7MM
SALES (corp-wide): 337.3MM **Publicly Held**
SIC: 1761 3444 3443 Sheet metalwork; sheet metal specialties, not stamped; fabricated plate work (boiler shop)
HQ: Ceco Group, Inc.
4625 Red Bank Rd Ste 200
Cincinnati OH 45227
513 458-2600

(G-3913)
KIRWAN INDUSTRIES INC
1964 Central Ave (45214-2264)
PHONE..................513 333-0766
Ronan Kirwan, *President*
EMP: 8
SQ FT: 20,000
SALES (est): 987.9K **Privately Held**
WEB: www.kirwanindustries.com
SIC: 3441 Building components, structural steel

(G-3914)
KITCHENS BY RUTENSCHROER INC (PA)
Also Called: Kbr
950 Laidlaw Ave (45237-5004)
PHONE..................513 251-8333
Steven Rutenschroer, *President*
Kathy Frisby, *Principal*
G Robert Hines, *Principal*
Steven D Rutenschroer, *Principal*
Missy Rutenschroer, *Vice Pres*
▲ **EMP:** 10
SQ FT: 8,000
SALES (est): 1.9MM **Privately Held**
WEB: www.kitchensbyrutenschroer.com
SIC: 5722 2519 2541 2511 Kitchens, complete (sinks, cabinets, etc.); household furniture, except wood or metal: upholstered; wood partitions & fixtures; wood household furniture; wood kitchen cabinets

(G-3915)
KLC BRANDS INC
2692 Madison Rd (45208-1321)
PHONE..................201 456-4115
Marvel Hecking, *Principal*
Robert J Hecking, *Vice Pres*
EMP: 4
SALES (est): 461.7K **Privately Held**
SIC: 2842 Specialty cleaning, polishes & sanitation goods

(G-3916)
KLOSTERMAN BAKING CO (PA)
4760 Paddock Rd (45229-1047)
PHONE..................513 242-5667
Kenneth Klosterman, *President*
Trent Doak, *President*
Dennis Wiltshire, *COO*
Ed Piasecki, *Vice Pres*
Jason Shingleton, *Vice Pres*
EMP: 30 **EST:** 1900
SQ FT: 10,000
SALES (est): 207.2MM **Privately Held**
WEB: www.klostermanbakery.com
SIC: 2051 Bakery: wholesale or wholesale/retail combined; bread, all types (white, wheat, rye, etc): fresh or frozen; cakes, bakery: except frozen; yeast goods, sweet: except frozen

(G-3917)
KLOSTERMAN BAKING CO
1000 E Ross Ave (45217-1191)
PHONE..................513 242-1004
Larry Moore, *Manager*
EMP: 85
SALES (corp-wide): 207.2MM **Privately Held**
SIC: 5149 2051 Bakery products; bread, cake & related products
PA: Klosterman Baking Co.
4760 Paddock Rd
Cincinnati OH 45229
513 242-5667

(G-3918)
KN8DESIGNS LLC
4016 Allston St (45209-1743)
PHONE..................859 380-5926
Nathan Ward, *Principal*
EMP: 3
SALES (est): 355.8K **Privately Held**
SIC: 2621 Printing paper

(G-3919)
KNOBLE GLASS & METAL INC (PA)
Also Called: K G M
8650 Green Rd (45255-5016)
PHONE..................513 753-1246
David Knoble, *President*
EMP: 9
SALES (est): 950.8K **Privately Held**
SIC: 3229 3354 Glass fibers, textile; aluminum extruded products

(G-3920)
KNOWLTON MANUFACTURING CO INC
2524 Leslie Ave (45212-4299)
PHONE..................513 631-7353
Kenneth Jenkins, *President*
John Fricker, *Vice Pres*
Allan Marcuse, *CFO*
Karen Fanroy, *Director*
EMP: 15
SQ FT: 44,000
SALES (est): 2.6MM **Privately Held**
WEB: www.knowltonmfg.com
SIC: 3469 3544 Stamping metal for the trade; special dies & tools

(G-3921)
KOEBBECO SIGNS LLC
5683 Springdale Rd (45251-1825)
PHONE..................513 923-2974
John Koebbe, *Owner*
EMP: 3
SALES (est): 153.3K **Privately Held**
WEB: www.koebbeco.net
SIC: 3993 Signs & advertising specialties

(G-3922)
KONKRETE CITY SKATEBOARDS
2109 Beechmont Ave (45230-1620)
PHONE..................513 231-0399
Maurice Richman, *Principal*
EMP: 4
SALES (est): 315.9K **Privately Held**
SIC: 3949 Skateboards

(G-3923)
KOOP DIAMOND CUTTERS INC
214 E 8th St Fl 4 (45202-2173)
PHONE..................513 621-2838
Clarence E Koop, *President*
Richard J Louis, *Treasurer*
Carol Adleta, *Marketing Staff*
EMP: 10
SQ FT: 4,300

SALES (est): 1.5MM **Privately Held**
WEB: www.koopdiamondcutters.com
SIC: 3911 7631 3915 Jewelry, precious metal; jewelry repair services; jewel cutting, drilling, polishing, recutting or setting

(G-3924)
KROGER CO
1212 W Kemper Rd Ste 1 (45240-1774)
PHONE..................513 742-9500
Leandrew Lloyd, *Manager*
EMP: 183
SALES (corp-wide): 121.1B **Publicly Held**
WEB: www.kroger.com
SIC: 5411 2051 Supermarkets, chain; bread, cake & related products
PA: The Kroger Co
1014 Vine St Ste 1000
Cincinnati OH 45202
513 762-4000

(G-3925)
KS DESIGNS INC
3636 Muddy Creek Rd Apt 1 (45238-2042)
PHONE..................513 241-5953
Steven Salling, *President*
Dennis Wall, *Vice Pres*
EMP: 5 **EST:** 1981
SQ FT: 7,400
SALES (est): 541.4K **Privately Held**
WEB: www.ksdesignsinc.com
SIC: 7389 2759 Sign painting & lettering shop; screen printing

(G-3926)
KUHLS HOT SPORTSPOT
7860 Beechmont Ave (45255-4213)
PHONE..................513 474-2282
Robert Kuhl, *Owner*
EMP: 10
SQ FT: 3,000
SALES (est): 734.8K **Privately Held**
WEB: www.kuhls.com
SIC: 2395 Embroidery products, except schiffli machine; embroidery & art needlework

(G-3927)
KW RIVER HYDROELECTRIC I LLC
5667 Krystal Ct Ste 100 (45252-1303)
PHONE..................513 673-2251
Paul R Kling,
EMP: 1
SALES: 1MM **Privately Held**
SIC: 3511 7389 Hydraulic turbine generator set units, complete;

(G-3928)
LA MFG INC
Also Called: Brewer Products
9483 Reading Rd (45215-3550)
P.O. Box 62065 (45262-0065)
PHONE..................513 577-7200
David Brewer, *President*
EMP: 6 **EST:** 1989
SALES (est): 500K **Privately Held**
SIC: 3569 5199 5082 General industrial machinery; nondurable goods; construction & mining machinery

(G-3929)
LAMBERT BROS INC
Also Called: Lambert Bros Nutangs
1337 Bates Ave (45225-1309)
PHONE..................513 541-1042
Charlie Bowlin, *President*
EMP: 5 **EST:** 1948
SQ FT: 3,000
SALES: 350K **Privately Held**
SIC: 3599 Machine shop, jobbing & repair

(G-3930)
LANGDON INC
9865 Wayne Ave (45215-1403)
P.O. Box 15308 (45215-0308)
PHONE..................513 733-5955
David Sandman, *President*
Michael Sandman, *Vice Pres*
Bill Seibert, *Project Mgr*
▲ **EMP:** 40
SQ FT: 42,000

SALES (est): 11.6MM **Privately Held**
WEB: www.langdonsheetmetal.com
SIC: 3444 1711 3564 3446 Ducts, sheet metal; warm air heating & air conditioning contractor; ventilation & duct work contractor; blowers & fans; architectural metalwork; fabricated plate work (boiler shop); fabricated structural metal

(G-3931)
LAROSA DIE ENGINEERING INC
3320 Robinet Dr (45238-2120)
PHONE..................513 284-9195
Joseph Larosa, *President*
Loretta A Larosa, *Vice Pres*
EMP: 4
SQ FT: 1,800
SALES: 231K **Privately Held**
SIC: 3469 3544 Metal stampings; special dies & tools

(G-3932)
LATE FOR SKY PRODUCTION CO
1292 Glendale Milford Rd (45215-1209)
PHONE..................513 531-4400
Cy Zack, *General Mgr*
Robyn L Wilson, *Principal*
Chris Niehaus, *Principal*
William C Schulte Jr, *Vice Pres*
Mark Hunter, *VP Mfg*
▲ **EMP:** 48
SQ FT: 60,000
SALES (est): 8MM **Privately Held**
WEB: www.lateforthesky.com
SIC: 3944 Board games, children's & adults'

(G-3933)
LATIN QUARTER
6904 Wooster Pike (45227-4427)
PHONE..................513 271-5400
Victor Kleykamp, *Principal*
EMP: 4 **EST:** 2001
SALES (est): 390.1K **Privately Held**
SIC: 3131 Quarters

(G-3934)
LAURENEE LTD LLC
Also Called: Deerfield Digital
3509 Harrison Ave (45211-5544)
PHONE..................513 662-2225
Susan Mroedersheime, *Vice Pres*
Timothy R Roedersheimer, *Mng Member*
T R Roedersheimer,
EMP: 8 **EST:** 1975
SQ FT: 8,500
SALES (est): 1.4MM **Privately Held**
WEB: www.deerfield-press.com
SIC: 2752 2791 Commercial printing, offset; typesetting

(G-3935)
LAZER SYSTEMS INC (PA)
850 E Ross Ave (45217-1129)
PHONE..................513 641-4002
Kenny D Allen, *President*
EMP: 12
SQ FT: 12,000
SALES: 4MM **Privately Held**
SIC: 2796 2759 Color separations for printing; flexographic printing

(G-3936)
LCP TECH INC
8120 Indian Hill Rd (45243-3910)
PHONE..................513 271-1389
David Ferguson, *President*
EMP: 5
SALES (est): 510.2K **Privately Held**
WEB: www.lcptech.com
SIC: 2992 Lubricating oils

(G-3937)
LEE CORPORATION
Also Called: Lee Printers
12055 Mosteller Rd (45241-1589)
PHONE..................513 771-3602
Thomas Krieg, *President*
Lee Krieg, *Vice Pres*
Ronald Krieg, *Treasurer*
Carol Krieg, *Admin Sec*
EMP: 7 **EST:** 1905
SQ FT: 35,000

Cincinnati - Hamilton County (G-3938)

SALES: 2MM **Privately Held**
WEB: www.leeprinters.com
SIC: 2752 2759 2791 2789 Commercial printing, offset; letterpress printing; typesetting; bookbinding & related work

(G-3938)
LEONHARDT PLATING COMPANY
5753 Este Ave (45232-1499)
PHONE.................513 242-1410
Kerry Leonhardt, *President*
Daniel Leonhardt, *Shareholder*
EMP: 24 **EST:** 1950
SQ FT: 20,500
SALES (est): 2.6MM **Privately Held**
WEB: www.leonhardtplating.com
SIC: 3471 2899 2851 2842 Electroplating of metals or formed products; chemical preparations; paints & allied products; specialty cleaning, polishes & sanitation goods; inorganic pigments

(G-3939)
LEYMAN MANUFACTURING CORP
Also Called: Leyman Liftgates
10335 Wayne Ave (45215-1128)
PHONE.................513 891-6210
John Mc Henry, *President*
Robert Drews Jr, *Vice Pres*
Raymond B Leyman, *Vice Pres*
William Margroum, *Vice Pres*
Jeff Morgan, *Opers Staff*
▲ **EMP:** 90 **EST:** 1940
SQ FT: 50,000
SALES (est): 22.5MM **Privately Held**
WEB: www.leymanlift.com
SIC: 3713 Truck & bus bodies

(G-3940)
LIB THERAPEUTICS LLC
5375 Medpace Way (45227-1543)
PHONE.................859 240-7764
Adam Vreeland, *Manager*
EMP: 4
SALES (est): 203.2K **Privately Held**
SIC: 2834 Pharmaceutical preparations

(G-3941)
LIFESTYLE NUTRACEUTICALS LTD
Also Called: Pun-U
5911 Turpin Hills Dr (45244-3857)
PHONE.................513 376-7218
Collin Literski, *CEO*
Sam Browstein, *Principal*
Brad Bolton, *Sales Staff*
Graham Clark, *Director*
Diane Literski, *Director*
EMP: 11
SALES (est): 900K **Privately Held**
SIC: 2023 5149 8731 Dietary supplements, dairy & non-dairy based; health foods; agricultural research

(G-3942)
LIGHT VISION
1776 Mentor Ave (45212-3554)
PHONE.................513 351-9444
Paul Graham, *Treasurer*
Mike Wodke,
Eric Begleiter,
EMP: 24
SQ FT: 3,000
SALES: 230.1K **Privately Held**
WEB: www.lightvision.com
SIC: 2064 Candy & other confectionery products

(G-3943)
LIGHTHOUSE YOUTH SERVICES INC
2522 Highland Ave (45219-2649)
PHONE.................513 961-4080
Jeoff Hollenbach, *Manager*
EMP: 17
SALES (corp-wide): 25.2MM **Privately Held**
SIC: 8322 3731 Emergency shelters; lighthouse tenders, building & repairing
PA: Lighthouse Youth Services, Inc.
401 E Mcmillan St
Cincinnati OH 45206
513 221-3350

(G-3944)
LILY TIGER PRESS
1945 Dunham Way (45238-3053)
PHONE.................513 591-0817
Andreas Lange, *Principal*
EMP: 35 **EST:** 2010
SALES (est): 1MM **Privately Held**
SIC: 2741 Miscellaneous publishing

(G-3945)
LINGER PHOTO ENGRAVING CORP
2230 Gilbert Ave (45206-2531)
PHONE.................513 579-1380
Robert Vanlear, *President*
EMP: 5
SALES (est): 370K **Privately Held**
SIC: 2796 Photoengraving plates, linecuts or halftones

(G-3946)
LISTERMANN MFG CO INC
Also Called: Listermann Brewery Supply
1621 Dana Ave (45207-1007)
PHONE.................513 731-1130
Daniel Listermann, *President*
Sue Listermann, *Vice Pres*
EMP: 8
SQ FT: 12,500
SALES: 450K **Privately Held**
WEB: www.listermann.com
SIC: 3556 Brewers' & maltsters' machinery

(G-3947)
LITHO-CRAFT LITHOGRAPHY INC
7107 Shona Dr 130 (45237-3808)
PHONE.................513 542-6404
Kimberly Pietrosky, *President*
EMP: 3
SALES (est): 392.3K **Privately Held**
SIC: 2796 Lithographic plates, positives or negatives

(G-3948)
LITTLE BUSY BODIES LLC
Also Called: Boogie Wipes
1130 Findlay St (45214-2052)
PHONE.................513 351-5700
Julie Pickin, *CEO*
Molly Wright, *Marketing Mgr*
▲ **EMP:** 50
SALES (est): 15.2MM **Privately Held**
SIC: 2676 Sanitary paper products

(G-3949)
LLOYD LIBRARY & MUSEUM
917 Plum St (45202-1081)
PHONE.................513 721-3707
Maggie Heran, *Director*
EMP: 5
SQ FT: 21,696
SALES (est): 616K **Privately Held**
WEB: www.lloydlibrary.com
SIC: 8231 2731 Specialized libraries; public library; medical library; book publishing

(G-3950)
LONG-LOK FASTENERS CORPORATION
10630 Chester Rd (45215-1249)
PHONE.................513 772-1880
Robert Bennett, *CEO*
Randy Ammon, *President*
Emilio Reyes, *QC Mgr*
James Bennett, *VP Finance*
Marsha Hassman, *Accounts Mgr*
EMP: 35
SQ FT: 33,000
SALES (corp-wide): 6MM **Privately Held**
SIC: 3452 Bolts, nuts, rivets & washers
HQ: Long-Lok Fasteners Corporation
14755 Preston Rd Ste 520
Dallas TX 75254
888 656-9450

(G-3951)
LOROCO INDUSTRIES INC
Royal Pad Products
10600 Evendale Dr (45241-2518)
PHONE.................513 554-0356
Bryan Helber, *Manager*
EMP: 21
SALES (corp-wide): 13.7MM **Privately Held**
SIC: 7389 3554 Personal service agents, brokers & bureaus; paper industries machinery
PA: Loroco Industries, Inc.
5000 Creek Rd
Blue Ash OH 45242
513 891-9544

(G-3952)
LOW STRESS GRIND INC
12077 Mosteller Rd (45241-1528)
PHONE.................513 771-7977
EMP: 19
SQ FT: 10,000
SALES (est): 1.3MM
SALES (corp-wide): 15.8MM **Privately Held**
SIC: 3829 Manufactures Mechanical Test Specimens
PA: Element Materials Technology Cincinnati Inc.
3701 Port Union Rd
Fairfield OH 45014
513 771-2536

(G-3953)
LS BOMBSHELLES
3940 Vine St (45217-1965)
PHONE.................513 254-6898
Yolanda Jackson, *Owner*
EMP: 3
SALES (est): 130.4K **Privately Held**
SIC: 2844 Toilet preparations

(G-3954)
LUCKY PAWS LLC
5541 Foley Rd (45238-4613)
PHONE.................859 620-2525
Melinda Kirk, *Mng Member*
EMP: 5
SQ FT: 1,000
SALES (est): 360.3K **Privately Held**
SIC: 2047 Dog food

(G-3955)
LUKENS BLACKSMITH SHOP
30 Compton Rd (45216-1014)
PHONE.................513 821-2308
John Luken, *Owner*
EMP: 3
SQ FT: 2,700
SALES: 90K **Privately Held**
SIC: 3599 7692 Machine shop, jobbing & repair; welding repair

(G-3956)
LUMBERJACK PALLET RECYCL LLC
81 Caldwell Dr (45216-1541)
PHONE.................513 821-7543
Denise Catanzaro, *Mng Member*
EMP: 3
SQ FT: 34,500
SALES: 135.7K **Privately Held**
SIC: 4953 2448 7699 Recycling, waste materials; wood pallets & skids; pallet repair

(G-3957)
LUNKEN CHARTS LLC
262 Wilmer Ave (45226-1679)
P.O. Box 8461 (45208-0461)
PHONE.................513 253-7615
Debbie Edwards, *Mng Member*
Thomas Edwards,
EMP: 4
SALES (est): 246.7K **Privately Held**
SIC: 3812 Search & navigation equipment

(G-3958)
LUXFER MAGTECH INC (HQ)
Also Called: Heatermeals
2940 Highland Ave Ste 210 (45212-2402)
PHONE.................513 772-3066
Brian Purves, *CEO*
Marc Lamensdorf, *President*
Tim Zimmerman, *Exec VP*
Deborah Simsen, *Treasurer*
Cindy Reinhardt, *Accountant*
EMP: 38
SALES (est): 8.5MM
SALES (corp-wide): 441.3MM **Privately Held**
SIC: 2899 5149 Desalter kits, sea water; groceries & related products; beverages, except coffee & tea
PA: Luxfer Holdings Plc
Ancorage Gateway
Salford LANCS M50 3
161 300-0611

(G-3959)
LYNC CORP
2963 Commodore Ln Apt 2 (45251-3193)
PHONE.................513 655-7286
Travis Bea,
EMP: 22
SQ FT: 5,000
SALES (est): 1.9MM **Privately Held**
SIC: 7371 7372 7379 Computer software development & applications; application computer software; computer related maintenance services; computer related consulting services

(G-3960)
LYONDELL CHEMICAL COMPANY
11530 Northlake Dr (45249-1642)
PHONE.................513 530-4000
James Simiskey, *Principal*
Michael Bridges, *Research*
Norma Maraschin, *Manager*
Anne Balthazar, *Manager*
Natalie Nichols, *Manager*
EMP: 79
SALES (corp-wide): 34.5B **Privately Held**
WEB: www.lyondell.com
SIC: 2869 2822 8731 Olefins; ethylene; polyethylene, chlorosulfonated (hypalon); commercial physical research
HQ: Lyondell Chemical Company
1221 Mckinney St Ste 300
Houston TX 77010
713 309-7200

(G-3961)
LYONDELLBASELL
11530 Northlake Dr (45249-1642)
PHONE.................513 530-4000
Dan Smith, *Principal*
Massimo Covezzi, *Vice Pres*
Francesco Svelto, *Vice Pres*
Mark Gasper, *Project Mgr*
Gregory Gray, *Opers Mgr*
EMP: 5
SQ FT: 260,000
SALES (est): 1.1MM **Privately Held**
SIC: 8732 2822 Market analysis, business & economic research; ethylene-propylene rubbers, EPDM polymers

(G-3962)
M D M GRAPHICS INC
10600 Chester Rd (45215-1206)
PHONE.................859 816-7375
Brian Garlich, *President*
EMP: 4
SQ FT: 5,000
SALES: 200K **Privately Held**
SIC: 2752 Commercial printing, lithographic

(G-3963)
M PHARMACEUTICAL USA
4030 Mount Camel Tobasco Ste 327 (45255)
PHONE.................859 868-3131
James Thompson, *COO*
EMP: 3
SQ FT: 200
SALES (est): 123.2K **Privately Held**
SIC: 2834 Pharmaceutical preparations

(G-3964)
M R I EDUCATION FOUNDATION
5400 Kennedy Ave (45213-2664)
PHONE.................513 281-3400
Steve J Pomeranz MD, *President*
James Kereiakes, *Shareholder*
EMP: 200
SQ FT: 5,600
SALES (est): 2.6MM **Privately Held**
SIC: 8249 2741 Medical training services; miscellaneous publishing

GEOGRAPHIC SECTION

Cincinnati - Hamilton County (G-3992)

(G-3965)
MACHINE DEVELOPMENT CORP
Also Called: Marine Development
7707 Affinity Dr (45231-3567)
PHONE.................................513 825-5885
Gary Fay, *President*
EMP: 8
SQ FT: 7,800
SALES (est): 890.9K **Privately Held**
SIC: 3599 Custom machinery; machine shop, jobbing & repair

(G-3966)
MACHINE DOCTORS INC
3490 Mustafa Dr (45241-1668)
PHONE.................................513 422-3060
Al Bradshaw, *President*
Trent Collier, *Manager*
EMP: 3
SQ FT: 5,000
SALES (est): 190K **Privately Held**
SIC: 7694 Electric motor repair

(G-3967)
MACHINE TL SLTONS UNLMITED LLC
8711 Reading Rd (45215-4800)
PHONE.................................513 761-0709
E Harold Schoch,
Bruce Daniels,
George Edwards,
Herb Varin,
EMP: 15
SQ FT: 22,000
SALES (est): 2.3MM **Privately Held**
SIC: 3541 Machine tools, metal cutting type

(G-3968)
MACHINE WORKS INC
979 Redna Ter (45215-1182)
PHONE.................................513 771-4600
Jerry Whitacker, *Principal*
Jerry Whitaker, *Vice Pres*
EMP: 3
SALES (est): 284.8K **Privately Held**
SIC: 3599 Machine shop, jobbing & repair

(G-3969)
MACKE BROTHERS INC
10355 Spartan Dr (45215-1220)
PHONE.................................513 771-7500
Joseph D Macke Sr, *President*
Joseph D Macke Jr, *Vice Pres*
Bill Macke, *Treasurer*
Nick Macke, *Admin Sec*
EMP: 85 **EST:** 1908
SQ FT: 43,000
SALES (est): 8.4MM **Privately Held**
SIC: 2789 7331 Pamphlets, binding; bookbinding & repairing: trade, edition, library, etc.; mailing service

(G-3970)
MAE CONSULTING
700 W Pete Rose Way 531b (45203-1896)
PHONE.................................513 531-8100
Scott Risner, *General Mgr*
Denise Bartick, *Principal*
EMP: 3
SALES: 225K **Privately Held**
WEB: www.maeconsulting.com
SIC: 7372 Prepackaged software

(G-3971)
MAGNA GROUP LLC
Also Called: Control System Upgrades
2340 Clydes Xing (45244-2839)
PHONE.................................513 388-9463
Nannette Williams, *CEO*
Richard McKenzie, *President*
Gregory Smith, *Director*
EMP: 4
SALES (est): 1MM **Privately Held**
SIC: 3531 8711 Construction machinery; machine tool design

(G-3972)
MAGNA MACHINE CO (PA)
11180 Southland Rd (45240-3202)
PHONE.................................513 851-6900
Scott Kramer, *President*
Elliot Adams, *President*
James Parker, *Vice Pres*
Greg Bodenburg, *CFO*
William Kramer Jr, *Admin Sec*
▼ **EMP:** 101 **EST:** 1953
SQ FT: 80,000
SALES (est): 25MM **Privately Held**
WEB: www.magna-machine.com
SIC: 3556 3554 3599 Bakery machinery; paper industries machinery; machine shop, jobbing & repair

(G-3973)
MAGNETIC MKTG SOLUTIONS LLC
Also Called: Decal Impressions
2111 Kindel Ave (45214-1841)
PHONE.................................513 721-3801
Bryan Vielhauer,
EMP: 3
SALES (est): 469.7K **Privately Held**
WEB: www.decalimpressions.com
SIC: 2759 3993 Screen printing; signs & advertising specialties

(G-3974)
MAIN AWNING & TENT INC
415 W Seymour Ave (45216-1862)
PHONE.................................513 621-6947
Hyman Goldfarb, *President*
Leslie Goldfarb, *President*
Robert Goldfarb, *Vice Pres*
◆ **EMP:** 9 **EST:** 1933
SQ FT: 200,000
SALES: 1.1MM **Privately Held**
WEB: www.tentsource.com
SIC: 2394 Awnings, fabric: made from purchased materials; tents: made from purchased materials; tarpaulins, fabric: made from purchased materials

(G-3975)
MALCO LAMINATED INC
4251 Spring Grove Ave (45223-1861)
PHONE.................................513 541-8300
Leo Snitzer, *President*
EMP: 4
SQ FT: 5,000
SALES (est): 409.7K **Privately Held**
SIC: 2541 2434 Sink tops, plastic laminated; vanities, bathroom: wood

(G-3976)
MALLINCKRODT LLC
2111 E Galbraith Rd (45237-1624)
PHONE.................................513 948-5751
Robert Janney, *Engineer*
EMP: 10 **Privately Held**
SIC: 2834 Pharmaceutical preparations
HQ: Mallinckrodt Llc
   675 Jmes S Mcdonnell Blvd
   Hazelwood MO 63042
   314 654-2000

(G-3977)
MANUFACTURING COMPANY LLC
3468 Cornell Pl (45220-1502)
PHONE.................................414 708-7583
Michael Fleisch, *Principal*
EMP: 3
SALES (est): 182.9K **Privately Held**
SIC: 3999 Manufacturing industries

(G-3978)
MAPES CONCRETE CONSTRUCTION
5691 Cheviot Rd Apt 3 (45247-7098)
PHONE.................................513 245-2631
Rick Mapes, *President*
EMP: 3
SALES (est): 485.4K **Privately Held**
SIC: 3271 Concrete block & brick

(G-3979)
MARCUS JEWELERS
2022 8 Mile Rd (45244-2607)
PHONE.................................513 474-4950
Mark Ogier, *Owner*
EMP: 7
SQ FT: 1,100
SALES (est): 470K **Privately Held**
SIC: 3911 5944 Jewelry, precious metal; jewelry stores

(G-3980)
MARGARET TRENTMAN
Also Called: Zip Graphics
5123 Montgomery Rd (45212-2237)
P.O. Box 12897 (45212-0897)
PHONE.................................513 948-1700
Margaret Trentman, *Owner*
Richard Trentman, *Owner*
EMP: 4
SALES (est): 394.4K **Privately Held**
SIC: 2752 2791 2759 Commercial printing, offset; typesetting; commercial printing

(G-3981)
MARINERS LANDING INC
Also Called: Mariner's Landing Marina
7405 Forbes Rd (45233-1014)
PHONE.................................513 941-3625
Pamela Tonne, *President*
David B Tonne, *Principal*
EMP: 15
SQ FT: 6,992
SALES (est): 1.7MM **Privately Held**
WEB: www.mariners-landing.com
SIC: 4493 5551 3732 Boat yards, storage & incidental repair; boat dealers; boat building & repairing

(G-3982)
MARKLEY ENTERPRISES LLC
Also Called: Die Craft Division
1705 Magnolia Dr (45215-1979)
PHONE.................................513 771-1290
Skip Markley, *President*
Joe Ramsey, *Plant Mgr*
Mary Jo Thomas, *Manager*
▲ **EMP:** 22
SQ FT: 32,000
SALES (est): 6.8MM **Privately Held**
WEB: www.diecraftmachine.com
SIC: 3449 8711 3599 Miscellaneous metalwork; mechanical engineering; machine shop, jobbing & repair

(G-3983)
MARTIN MARIETTA MATERIALS INC
Also Called: Kellogg Yard
4439 Kellogg Ave (45226-1540)
PHONE.................................513 871-7152
Harry Charles, *Manager*
EMP: 20 **Publicly Held**
WEB: www.martinmarietta.com
SIC: 1422 Crushed & broken limestone
PA: Martin Marietta Materials Inc
   2710 Wycliff Rd
   Raleigh NC 27607

(G-3984)
MARULA PUBLISHING LLC
6539 Harrison Ave Ste 154 (45247-7822)
PHONE.................................513 549-5218
Sterlin Styles,
EMP: 3
SALES (est): 112.9K **Privately Held**
SIC: 2721 Magazines: publishing & printing

(G-3985)
MASTERPIECE PUBLISHER L P
8046 Debonair Ct (45237-1106)
PHONE.................................513 948-1000
EMP: 4 **EST:** 2008
SALES (est): 150K **Privately Held**
SIC: 2741 Misc Publishing

(G-3986)
MATLOCK ELECTRIC CO INC (PA)
2780 Highland Ave (45212-2494)
PHONE.................................513 731-9600
Joseph P Geoppinger, *President*
Thomas J Geoppinger, *Chairman*
Rick Mullaney, *Controller*
Casey McKenna, *Manager*
Phil Mohr, *Manager*
EMP: 38
SQ FT: 25,000
SALES (est): 9.2MM **Privately Held**
WEB: www.matlockelectric.com
SIC: 7694 5063 3699 3612 Electric motor repair; rebuilding motors, except automotive; motors, electric; electrical equipment & supplies; transformers, except electric; speed changers, drives & gears

(G-3987)
MATRIX CABLE AND MOULD
11785 Highway Dr Ste 900 (45241-2087)
PHONE.................................513 832-2577
Kevin Meiners, *Owner*
EMP: 5
SQ FT: 5,500
SALES (est): 210.2K **Privately Held**
SIC: 3714 3613 3089 Automotive wiring harness sets; control panels, electric; injection molding of plastics

(G-3988)
MAZZELLA LIFTING TECH INC
Also Called: Mazzella Crane & Hoist Svcs
10605 Chester Rd (45215-1205)
PHONE.................................513 772-4466
John Ellsworth, *Manager*
EMP: 12
SQ FT: 5,000 **Privately Held**
WEB: www.mazzellalifting.com
SIC: 3496 Woven wire products; slings, lifting: made from purchased wire
HQ: Mazzella Lifting Technologies, Inc.
   21000 Aerospace Pkwy
   Cleveland OH 44142
   440 239-7000

(G-3989)
MCNERNEY & ASSOCIATES LLC (PA)
Also Called: P J McNerney & Associates
440 Northland Blvd (45240-3211)
PHONE.................................513 241-9951
Patrick J McNerney, *President*
Jan McNerney, *Vice Pres*
Tim McNerney, *Mktg Dir*
◆ **EMP:** 25
SQ FT: 70,000
SALES (est): 4.7MM **Privately Held**
WEB: www.pjmcnerney.com
SIC: 2752 4783 Commercial printing, lithographic; packing goods for shipping

(G-3990)
MCRON FINANCE CORP
3010 Disney St (45209-5028)
PHONE.................................513 487-5000
EMP: 1110
SALES (est): 229.9MM
SALES (corp-wide): 1.2B **Publicly Held**
SIC: 3544 Forms (molds), for foundry & plastics working machinery
PA: Milacron Holdings Inc
   10200 Alliance Rd Ste 200
   Blue Ash OH 45242
   513 487-5000

(G-3991)
MCSWAIN MANUFACTURING LLC
189 Container Pl (45246-1708)
PHONE.................................513 619-1222
Michael Meshay, *President*
Bill Michalski, *Vice Pres*
◆ **EMP:** 148
SQ FT: 70,000
SALES (est): 31.9MM **Privately Held**
SIC: 3599 Machine shop, jobbing & repair

(G-3992)
MEASURENET TECHNOLOGY LTD
4242 Airport Rd Ste 101 (45226-1615)
PHONE.................................513 396-6765
Robert Voorhees, *General Mgr*
Mark Hoffman, *President*
Beth Voorhees, *Sales Mgr*
EMP: 10
SQ FT: 3,000
SALES (est): 1.1MM **Privately Held**
WEB: www.measurenet-tech.com
SIC: 3826 Analytical instruments

Cincinnati - Hamilton County (G-3993)

(G-3993)
MECHANICAL FINISHERS INC LLC
Also Called: Mfi
6350 Este Ave (45232-1450)
PHONE.................................513 641-5419
Nico Cottone, *Principal*
EMP: 30
SALES (est): 3.6MM **Privately Held**
SIC: 3471 Decorative plating & finishing of formed products; cleaning, polishing & finishing

(G-3994)
MECHANICAL FINISHING INC
6350 Este Ave (45232-1450)
PHONE.................................513 641-5419
Jerry Stenger, *President*
EMP: 20
SQ FT: 40,000
SALES (est): 1.8MM **Privately Held**
WEB: www.mechfin.com
SIC: 3471 Finishing, metals or formed products

(G-3995)
MEDERS SPECIAL TEES
618 Delhi Ave (45204-1222)
PHONE.................................513 921-3800
Jerome A Meder, *Owner*
Brent Meder, *Manager*
EMP: 8
SQ FT: 3,000
SALES (est): 796.6K **Privately Held**
WEB: www.lux.cinti.net
SIC: 2759 Screen printing

(G-3996)
MEDIA PROCUREMENT SERVICES INC
312 Walnut St (45202-4024)
PHONE.................................513 977-3000
Kenneth Lowe, *President*
EMP: 4
SALES (est): 689.3K
SALES (corp-wide): 2.9B **Publicly Held**
WEB: www.scripps.com
SIC: 8741 5044 2679 Administrative management; office equipment; paper products, converted
HQ: Journal Media Group, Inc.
   333 W State St
   Milwaukee WI 53203
   414 224-2000

(G-3997)
MEDIA SIGN COMPANY
2111 Kindel Ave (45214-1841)
PHONE.................................513 564-9500
Joyce Mc Elroy, *President*
Robert Mc Elroy, *Vice Pres*
EMP: 4
SQ FT: 1,400
SALES: 900K **Privately Held**
WEB: www.mediasign.com
SIC: 3993 Electric signs

(G-3998)
MEDPACE HOLDINGS INC (PA)
5375 Medpace Way (45227-1543)
PHONE.................................513 579-9911
August J Troendle, *Ch of Bd*
Jesse J Geiger, *COO*
Susan E Burwig, *Exec VP*
Mark Mentzer, *Opers Staff*
Chelsea Howard, *Research*
EMP: 15
SQ FT: 332,000
SALES: 704.5MM **Publicly Held**
SIC: 2834 8731 Pharmaceutical preparations; commercial physical research; biological research

(G-3999)
MEDPACE RESEARCH INC
Also Called: Nephrogenex
5375 Medpace Way (45227-1543)
PHONE.................................513 579-9911
John P Hamill, *CEO*
Richard J Markham, *Ch of Bd*
EMP: 5 **EST:** 2004
SQ FT: 5,514
SALES (est): 1.3MM **Privately Held**
SIC: 2834 Pharmaceutical preparations

(G-4000)
MEGGITT (ERLANGER) LLC
Also Called: Edac Composites
10293 Burlington Rd (45231-1901)
PHONE.................................513 851-5550
Steve Hartke, *Branch Mgr*
EMP: 70
SALES (est): 2.6B **Privately Held**
WEB: www.parkwayproducts.com
SIC: 3089 3544 2851 2822 Molding primary plastic; special dies, tools, jigs & fixtures; paints & allied products; synthetic rubber; molding compounds, plastics
HQ: Meggitt (Erlanger), Llc
   1400 Jamike Ave
   Erlanger KY 41018
   859 525-8040

(G-4001)
MEGGITT POLYMERS & COMPOSITES
10293 Burlington Rd (45231-1901)
PHONE.................................513 851-5550
EMP: 5
SALES (est): 662.9K **Privately Held**
SIC: 3728 Aircraft parts & equipment

(G-4002)
MEIERJOHAN-WENGLER INC
10340 Julian Dr (45215-1131)
PHONE.................................513 771-6074
Steve Jones, *President*
▲ **EMP:** 15
SQ FT: 34,000
SALES (est): 2.2MM
SALES (corp-wide): 1.6B **Publicly Held**
WEB: www.plaques.net
SIC: 3366 Bronze foundry
HQ: Aurora Casket Company, Llc
   10944 Marsh Rd
   Aurora IN 47001
   800 457-1111

(G-4003)
MEIERS WINE CELLARS INC
Also Called: John C Meier Grape Juice Co
6955 Plainfield Rd (45236-3793)
PHONE.................................513 891-2900
Paul Lux, *President*
Lux Paul, *President*
Robert Manchick, *Principal*
Lucia Jack, *Vice Pres*
Jack Lucia, *Vice Pres*
▲ **EMP:** 29 **EST:** 1895
SQ FT: 20,000
SALES (est): 6MM
SALES (corp-wide): 61.9MM **Privately Held**
WEB: www.meierswinecellars.com
SIC: 2033 2084 2086 Fruit juices: fresh; wines; bottled & canned soft drinks
PA: Luxco, Inc.
   5050 Kemper Ave
   Saint Louis MO 63139
   314 772-2626

(G-4004)
MELVIN STONE CO LLC
11641 Mosteller Rd Ste 2 (45241-1520)
PHONE.................................513 771-0820
Susan B Salyer, *Principal*
Ryan Garrison, *Materials Mgr*
EMP: 8
SALES (est): 684.4K **Privately Held**
SIC: 3281 Cut stone & stone products

(G-4005)
MENARD INC
2789 Cunningham Rd (45241-1390)
PHONE.................................513 250-4566
EMP: 12
SALES (corp-wide): 12.5B **Privately Held**
SIC: 2431 Millwork
PA: Menard, Inc.
   5101 Menard Dr
   Eau Claire WI 54703
   715 876-5911

(G-4006)
MERIDIAN BIOSCIENCE INC (PA)
3471 River Hills Dr (45244-3023)
PHONE.................................513 271-3700
John Kenny, *CEO*
David C Phillips, *Ch of Bd*
Lawrence J Baldini, *Exec VP*
Susan Rolih, *Exec VP*
Lourdes G Weltzien, *Exec VP*
EMP: 277 **EST:** 1976
SQ FT: 120,000
SALES: 213.5MM **Publicly Held**
WEB: www.meridianbioscience.com
SIC: 2835 2834 In vitro & in vivo diagnostic substances; pharmaceutical preparations

(G-4007)
MERIDIAN LIFE SCIENCE INC (HQ)
Also Called: Viral Antigens
3471 River Hills Dr (45244-3023)
PHONE.................................513 271-3700
Rick Eberly, *President*
EMP: 61
SQ FT: 34,000
SALES (est): 9.6MM
SALES (corp-wide): 200.7MM **Publicly Held**
WEB: www.meridianbioscience.com
SIC: 2835 Veterinary diagnostic substances
PA: Meridian Bioscience, Inc.
   3471 River Hills Dr
   Cincinnati OH 45244
   513 271-3700

(G-4008)
MERK BLASTING
3917 Biehl Ave (45248-3203)
PHONE.................................513 813-6375
John Merk, *Owner*
EMP: 3 **EST:** 2017
SALES (est): 155.2K **Privately Held**
SIC: 3471 Plating & polishing

(G-4009)
MESA INDUSTRIES INC (PA)
Also Called: Airplaco Equipment Company
4027 Eastern Ave (45226-1747)
PHONE.................................513 321-2950
Terry S Segerberg, *CEO*
Kent Sexton, *President*
James R Sexton, *Vice Pres*
Melanie Roaden, *Buyer*
Kent Segerberg, *Director*
◆ **EMP:** 82
SQ FT: 100,000
SALES (est): 30.1MM **Privately Held**
WEB: www.mesa-ind.net
SIC: 3531 5085 5082 Bituminous, cement & concrete related products & equipment; hose, belting & packing; construction & mining machinery

(G-4010)
MET-L-FAB INC
5313 Robert Ave (45248-6214)
PHONE.................................513 561-4289
David Martin, *President*
EMP: 15 **EST:** 1959
SQ FT: 12,000
SALES (est): 2.5MM **Privately Held**
SIC: 3444 Sheet metalwork

(G-4011)
MET-PRO TECHNOLOGIES LLC (HQ)
4625 Red Bank Rd (45227-1500)
PHONE.................................513 458-2600
Dennis Sadlowski, *President*
EMP: 120 **EST:** 2013
SALES (est): 64.3MM
SALES (corp-wide): 337.3MM **Publicly Held**
SIC: 3564 Air purification equipment
PA: Ceco Environmental Corp.
   14651 Dallas Pkwy
   Dallas TX 75254
   513 458-2600

(G-4012)
METAL TECHNOLOGY SYSTEMS INC
Also Called: M T S
675 Redna Ter (45215-1108)
PHONE.................................513 563-1882
Steve Williams, *President*
Perry Joyce, *Vice Pres*
Anita Williams, *Shareholder*
EMP: 5
SQ FT: 5,000
SALES: 500K **Privately Held**
SIC: 3444 Sheet metal specialties, not stamped

(G-4013)
METALPHOTO OF CINCINNATI INC
1080 Skillman Dr (45215-1137)
PHONE.................................513 772-8281
Herbert Wainer, *President*
Michael Elter, *General Mgr*
Patrick Hollis, *Vice Pres*
Richard Doerger, *VP Opers*
Jonathan Lane, *Opers Mgr*
EMP: 26 **EST:** 1959
SQ FT: 21,000
SALES (est): 3.7MM
SALES (corp-wide): 30.4MM **Privately Held**
WEB: www.mpofcinci.com
SIC: 3993 Name plates: except engraved, etched, etc.: metal
PA: Horizons Incorporated
   18531 S Miles Rd
   Cleveland OH 44128
   216 475-0555

(G-4014)
METALWORKING GROUP HOLDINGS (PA)
Also Called: Metalworking Group, The
9070 Pippin Rd (45251-3174)
PHONE.................................513 521-4119
Mike Schmitt, *President*
Brad Brune, *Vice Pres*
Doug Watts, *CFO*
▲ **EMP:** 120 **EST:** 2000
SQ FT: 65,000
SALES (est): 29MM **Privately Held**
SIC: 3444 Sheet metalwork

(G-4015)
METCUT RESEARCH ASSOCIATES INC (PA)
3980 Rosslyn Dr (45209-1110)
PHONE.................................513 271-5100
William P Koster, *Ch of Bd*
John P Kahles, *President*
John H Clippinger, *Principal*
Robert T Keeler, *Principal*
John M More, *Principal*
EMP: 85
SQ FT: 25,000
SALES (est): 12.6MM **Privately Held**
WEB: www.metcut.com
SIC: 8734 3599 Metallurgical testing laboratory; machine & other job shop work

(G-4016)
METLWEB
3330 E Kemper Rd (45241-1538)
PHONE.................................513 563-8822
William E Ensminger, *President*
EMP: 20
SALES (est): 1.7MM **Privately Held**
SIC: 3444 3441 Sheet metal specialties, not stamped; fabricated structural metal

(G-4017)
METRO RECYCLING COMPANY
19 W Vine St (45215-3233)
PHONE.................................513 251-1800
EMP: 9 **EST:** 1978
SQ FT: 100,000
SALES (est): 1.6MM **Privately Held**
SIC: 2621 3089 4953 Paper Mill Mfg Plastic Products Refuse System

(G-4018)
METRODECK INC
4795 Day Rd (45252-1809)
PHONE.................................513 541-4370
W Ronald Trischler, *President*
EMP: 10
SQ FT: 50,000
SALES (est): 1.1MM **Privately Held**
SIC: 2542 3444 3449 5051 Shelving, office & store: except wood; sheet metalwork; lath, expanded metal; steel; sheet metalwork

GEOGRAPHIC SECTION
Cincinnati - Hamilton County (G-4047)

(G-4019)
METZGER MACHINE CO
2165 Spring Grove Ave (45214-1790)
PHONE.................513 241-3360
David L Brown, *President*
Tina Kells, *Manager*
Virginia Brown, *Admin Sec*
EMP: 10
SQ FT: 10,000
SALES (est): 1.7MM **Privately Held**
SIC: 3599 5085 Machine shop, jobbing & repair; industrial supplies

(G-4020)
MEYER TOOL INC (PA)
3055 Colerain Ave (45225-1827)
PHONE.................513 681-7362
Arlyn Easton, *President*
Daniel Godin, *President*
Larry Allen, *Vice Pres*
Jerry Flyr, *Vice Pres*
Richard Ottino, *Plant Mgr*
◆ **EMP:** 650
SQ FT: 365,000
SALES (est): 368.4MM **Privately Held**
WEB: www.meyertool.com
SIC: 3724 3599 Aircraft engines & engine parts; machine shop, jobbing & repair

(G-4021)
MIBTACH ENTERPRISES INC
2629 Lytham Ct (45233-4295)
PHONE.................513 941-0387
William J Steioff, *President*
EMP: 4
SALES (est): 252.7K **Privately Held**
SIC: 3089 3999 Molding primary plastic; novelties, bric-a-brac & hobby kits

(G-4022)
MICRO METAL FINISHING LLC
3448 Spring Grove Ave (45225-1328)
PHONE.................513 541-3095
John A Rose, *President*
Karen Lafkas,
EMP: 61 EST: 1995
SQ FT: 100,000
SALES: 6MM **Privately Held**
WEB: www.micrometalfinishing.com
SIC: 3471 Finishing, metals or formed products

(G-4023)
MICROPOWER LLC
10470 Evendale Dr (45241-2514)
PHONE.................513 382-0100
EMP: 10
SALES (est): 1MM **Privately Held**
SIC: 3621 Mfg Motors/Generators

(G-4024)
MICROPRESS AMERICA LLC
Also Called: Tachometer Press
4240 Minmor Dr (45217-1822)
PHONE.................513 746-0689
Todd Ea Larson, *Mng Member*
Chad S Beckett,
Marc T Hanger,
EMP: 3
SALES (est): 158.6K **Privately Held**
SIC: 2731 7389 Books: publishing only;

(G-4025)
MICROPYRETICS HEATERS INTL INC
Also Called: Mhi
750 Redna Ter (45215-1109)
PHONE.................513 772-0404
Anu Vissa, *COO*
▲ **EMP:** 15
SALES (est): 3.7MM **Privately Held**
WEB: www.mhi-inc.com
SIC: 3567 Industrial furnaces & ovens

(G-4026)
MICROSOFT CORPORATION
7875 Montgomery Rd # 2205 (45236-4373)
PHONE.................513 826-9650
Lane Sorgen, *Principal*
EMP: 5
SALES (corp-wide): 110.3B **Publicly Held**
SIC: 7372 Prepackaged software

PA: Microsoft Corporation
1 Microsoft Way
Redmond WA 98052
425 882-8080

(G-4027)
MICROSTRATEGY INCORPORATED
8044 Montgomery Rd # 700 (45236-2919)
PHONE.................513 792-2253
Mike Jonas, *Branch Mgr*
EMP: 5
SALES (corp-wide): 497.6MM **Publicly Held**
WEB: www.microstrategy.com
SIC: 7372 7371 Application computer software; computer software systems analysis & design, custom
PA: Microstrategy Incorporated
1850 Towers Crescent Plz # 700
Tysons Corner VA 22182
703 848-8600

(G-4028)
MIDWEST WOODWORKING CO INC
4019 Montgomery Rd (45212-3694)
P.O. Box 12047 (45212-0047)
PHONE.................513 631-6684
Frank David, *President*
EMP: 20 EST: 1946
SQ FT: 60,000
SALES (est): 2.3MM **Privately Held**
SIC: 2431 2541 2434 Millwork; display fixtures, wood; wood kitchen cabinets

(G-4029)
MILLSTONE COFFEE INC (HQ)
1 Procter And Gamble Plz (45202-3315)
PHONE.................513 983-1100
R Kerry Clark, *President*
G W Pric, *President*
Clayton C Daley Jr, *Vice Pres*
S P Donovan Jr, *Vice Pres*
H J Kangis, *Vice Pres*
▲ **EMP:** 80
SALES (est): 109.4MM
SALES (corp-wide): 7.3B **Publicly Held**
WEB: www.millstone.com
SIC: 2095 Coffee roasting (except by wholesale grocers)
PA: The J M Smucker Company
1 Strawberry Ln
Orrville OH 44667
330 682-3000

(G-4030)
MINI GRAPHICS INC
7306 Euclid Ave (45243-2548)
PHONE.................513 563-8600
EMP: 7
SQ FT: 11,000
SALES (est): 1.1MM **Privately Held**
SIC: 2621 2273 2511 2221 Paper Mill Mfg Carpets/Rugs Mfg Wood Household Furn Manmad Brdwv Fabric Mill Whol Paints/Varnishes

(G-4031)
MINUTEMAN PRESS
2312 E Sharon Rd (45241-1844)
PHONE.................513 772-0500
Julie Garrett, *Owner*
EMP: 5
SQ FT: 3,000
SALES: 500K **Privately Held**
WEB: www.mmpprints.com
SIC: 2752 Commercial printing, lithographic

(G-4032)
MINUTEMAN PRESS INC
9904 Colerain Ave (45251-1431)
PHONE.................513 741-9056
Portia Ash, *Principal*
EMP: 5
SALES (est): 390.9K **Privately Held**
SIC: 2752 Commercial printing, lithographic

(G-4033)
MIO VINO
7908 Blue Ash Rd (45236-2602)
PHONE.................513 407-0486
Tim Bryant, *Principal*
EMP: 4 EST: 2014

SALES (est): 316.2K **Privately Held**
SIC: 2084 Wines

(G-4034)
MIRACLE DOCUMENTS
2300 Montana Ave Ste 301 (45211-3890)
PHONE.................513 651-2222
Bill Tapke, *Owner*
EMP: 3 EST: 2010
SALES (est): 160.7K **Privately Held**
SIC: 2759 Commercial printing

(G-4035)
MMP PRINTING INC
Also Called: Minuteman Press
10570 Chester Rd (45215-1204)
PHONE.................513 381-0990
Melody Tuttle, *President*
William Tuttle, *Vice Pres*
EMP: 23
SQ FT: 30,000
SALES (est): 3.5MM **Privately Held**
SIC: 2752 2791 2789 2759 Commercial printing, offset; photo-offset printing; typesetting; bookbinding & related work; commercial printing

(G-4036)
MODEL PATTERN & FOUNDRY CO
3242 Spring Grove Ave (45225-1373)
PHONE.................513 542-2322
Shirley Kipp, *President*
David Kipp, *Corp Secy*
Kenneth Kipp, *Vice Pres*
EMP: 25 EST: 1943
SQ FT: 16,500
SALES: 1.5MM **Privately Held**
SIC: 3363 3364 3365 3365 Aluminum die-castings; brass & bronze die-castings; copper foundries; aluminum foundries

(G-4037)
MODERN DISPLAYS INC
4301 Schulte Dr (45205-2037)
PHONE.................513 471-1639
Raymond Hafner, *President*
Eugene Hafner, *Vice Pres*
EMP: 6
SQ FT: 18,000
SALES: 500K **Privately Held**
SIC: 2759 Screen printing; advertising literature: printing

(G-4038)
MODERN ICE EQUIPMENT & SUP CO (PA)
Also Called: Modern Tour
5709 Harrison Ave (45248-1601)
PHONE.................513 367-2101
Gary E Jerow, *President*
Shawn Messmore, *Vice Pres*
John Murphy, *Vice Pres*
Brian Bloch, *Project Mgr*
Rod Proctor, *Purchasing*
◆ **EMP:** 20
SQ FT: 12,000
SALES (est): 18.2MM **Privately Held**
WEB: www.matthiesenequipment.com
SIC: 5078 3444 Refrigeration equipment & supplies; sheet metalwork

(G-4039)
MODERN MANUFACTURING INC (PA)
Also Called: M&S Machine and Manufacturing
240 Stille Dr (45233-1647)
PHONE.................513 251-3600
Patrick Sexton, *President*
Eric Rands, *Purchasing*
EMP: 10 EST: 2001
SQ FT: 30,000
SALES (est): 1.8MM **Privately Held**
WEB: www.modmfg.com
SIC: 2531 3444 3544 Public building & related furniture; sheet metal specialties, not stamped; special dies, tools, jigs & fixtures

(G-4040)
MOLECULAR RESEARCH CENTER (PA)
Also Called: MRC
5645 Montgomery Rd (45212-1846)
PHONE.................513 841-0900
Piotr Chomczynski, *President*
Dr Joanna Rymaszewska, *Principal*
Dr Karl Mackey, *Manager*
Judith Heiny, *Executive*
▲ **EMP:** 19
SQ FT: 15,000
SALES (est): 1.8MM **Privately Held**
WEB: www.mrcgene.com
SIC: 2819 Industrial inorganic chemicals

(G-4041)
MOLEMAN
Also Called: Moleman Mole Trapping
1314 Pennsbury Dr (45238-3606)
P.O. Box 14785 (45250-0785)
PHONE.................513 662-3017
Tom Schmidt, *Partner*
David Schmidt, *Partner*
Richard Schmidt, *Partner*
Sara Schmidt, *Partner*
EMP: 5
SALES (est): 429K **Privately Held**
WEB: www.themoleman.com
SIC: 2211 Moleskins

(G-4042)
MONNIG WELDING CO
521 Harriet St (45203-1886)
PHONE.................513 241-5156
Lawrence Monnig Jr, *Partner*
EMP: 5 EST: 1875
SQ FT: 3,000
SALES (est): 300K **Privately Held**
SIC: 7692 3441 Welding repair; fabricated structural metal

(G-4043)
MONTI INCORPORATED (PA)
4510 Reading Rd (45229-1230)
PHONE.................513 761-7775
Gavin J Narburgh, *President*
Beverly Narburgh, *Vice Pres*
John Narburgh, *Admin Sec*
▲ **EMP:** 150
SQ FT: 137,000
SALES (est): 49.5MM **Privately Held**
WEB: www.monti-inc.com
SIC: 3644 3599 Insulators & insulation materials, electrical; machine shop, jobbing & repair

(G-4044)
MOONSTRUCK GAMES INC
312 Walnut St Ste 2275 (45202-4044)
PHONE.................513 721-3900
EMP: 5
SQ FT: 1,500
SALES (est): 210.2K **Privately Held**
SIC: 3944 5734 Mfg Games/Toys Ret Computers/Software

(G-4045)
MOR-LITE CO INC
2344 Wyoming Ave (45214-1062)
PHONE.................513 661-8587
Donald Lauck, *President*
EMP: 4
SQ FT: 5,000
SALES: 350K **Privately Held**
SIC: 1751 1761 3444 3089 Window & door (prefabricated) installation; siding contractor; awnings, sheet metal; awnings, fiberglass & plastic combination

(G-4046)
MORRIS CLEAN IT N SWEEP CLEAN
327 Crestline Ave (45205-2206)
PHONE.................513 200-8222
Brittani Morris, *Principal*
EMP: 3
SALES (est): 134K **Privately Held**
SIC: 2842 7389 Cleaning or polishing preparations;

(G-4047)
MORRIS TECHNOLOGIES INC
11988 Tramway Dr (45241-1664)
PHONE.................513 733-1611

Cincinnati - Hamilton County (G-4048)

Gregory M Morris, *CEO*
William G Noack, *President*
Wendell H Morris, *Treasurer*
Sharon Wray, *Human Resources*
Tom Sinnett, *Director*
EMP: 105
SQ FT: 25,000
SALES (est): 11.5MM **Privately Held**
WEB: www.morristech.com
SIC: 8711 3999 3313 8731 Mechanical engineering; models, except toy; alloys, additive, except copper: not made in blast furnaces; engineering laboratory, except testing; electrical discharge machining (EDM); surgical & medical instruments

(G-4048)
MORROW GRAVEL COMPANY INC (PA)
11641 Mosteller Rd (45241-1520)
PHONE..................513 771-0820
James P Jurgensen, *President*
Tim St Clair, *CFO*
Dave Patterson, *Manager*
EMP: 20 **EST:** 1958
SQ FT: 15,000
SALES (est): 26MM **Privately Held**
SIC: 1442 1771 2951 Construction sand mining; gravel mining; blacktop (asphalt) work; asphalt & asphaltic paving mixtures (not from refineries)

(G-4049)
MORTON INTERNATIONAL LLC
Also Called: Morton Salt
5340 River Rd (45233-1645)
PHONE..................513 941-1578
Ruben Lowrey, *Branch Mgr*
EMP: 9
SALES (corp-wide): 85.9B **Publicly Held**
SIC: 1479 Salt & sulfur mining
HQ: Morton International, Llc
400 Arcola Rd
Collegeville PA 19426
989 636-1000

(G-4050)
MOTZ MOBILE CONTAINERS INC
3153 Madison Rd Apt 1 (45209-1399)
PHONE..................513 772-6689
Marjorie Motz, *President*
James Motz, *Treasurer*
EMP: 5
SQ FT: 14,000
SALES (est): 430K **Privately Held**
WEB: www.flexamat.com
SIC: 1741 3272 Foundation & retaining wall construction; building materials, except block or brick: concrete

(G-4051)
MR LABEL INC
5018 Gray Rd (45232-1514)
PHONE..................513 681-2088
Patrick H Meehan Jr, *President*
Brigid Hoffman, *Corp Secy*
Timothy F Meehan, *Vice Pres*
EMP: 25
SQ FT: 19,200
SALES (est): 4.3MM **Privately Held**
WEB: www.mrlabel.com
SIC: 2759 2672 Flexographic printing; screen printing; coated & laminated paper

(G-4052)
MT CARMEL BREWING COMPANY
4362 Mt Carmel Tobasco Rd (45244-2338)
PHONE..................513 519-7161
Michael Dewey, *Principal*
EMP: 7
SALES (est): 746.4K **Privately Held**
SIC: 2084 Wines

(G-4053)
MUEHLENKAMP PROPERTIES INC
Also Called: Paragon Metal Fabricators
4317 Kugler Mill Rd (45236-1820)
PHONE..................513 745-0874
Joseph B Muehlenkamp III, *President*
Stanley Muehlenkamp, *Vice Pres*
Mark Muehlenkamp, *Treasurer*
Bryan Muehlenkamp, *Sales Staff*
Heather Orth, *Office Mgr*
EMP: 24
SQ FT: 20,000
SALES (est): 5.7MM **Privately Held**
WEB: www.paragonmetalfab.com
SIC: 3444 6531 Sheet metal specialties, not stamped; real estate agents & managers

(G-4054)
MULTI-COLOR CORPORATION
Also Called: Altivity Packaging
4500 Beech St (45212-3402)
PHONE..................513 396-5600
Tom Yunker, *Senior VP*
Randy James, *Traffic Mgr*
John Gaffney, *Finance Other*
Terry Skiba, *Branch Mgr*
EMP: 150
SALES (corp-wide): 1.3B **Publicly Held**
SIC: 2759 Commercial printing
PA: Multi-Color Corporation
4053 Clough Woods Dr
Batavia OH 45103
513 381-1480

(G-4055)
MURDOCK INC
7180 Anderson Woods Dr (45244-3260)
PHONE..................513 471-7700
Robert A Murdock, *President*
J Kelso Murdock, *Chairman*
Betty Jo Murdock, *Vice Pres*
EMP: 15
SQ FT: 41,730
SALES (est): 3.4MM **Privately Held**
WEB: www.murdockfountains.com
SIC: 3431 Drinking fountains, metal

(G-4056)
N M R INC
Also Called: BP
7555 Fields Ertel Rd (45241-1750)
PHONE..................513 530-9075
Mohamed Elnemr, *Owner*
Craig Whitfield, *Chief Engr*
James Asker, *Engineer*
Claire Woodcock, *Marketing Mgr*
EMP: 5
SALES (est): 417.3K **Privately Held**
WEB: www.nmr.com
SIC: 5541 2834 Filling stations, gasoline; pharmaceutical preparations

(G-4057)
NANBRANDS LLC
8405 Indian Hill Rd (45243-3703)
PHONE..................513 313-9581
Nancy Aichholz, *Principal*
EMP: 3
SALES (est): 130K **Privately Held**
SIC: 2051 7389 Cakes, pies & pastries;

(G-4058)
NATIONAL ACCESS DESIGN LLC
Also Called: N A D
1924 Losantiville Ave (45237-4106)
PHONE..................513 351-3400
Cheryl White, *President*
EMP: 13
SQ FT: 10,300
SALES: 1.2MM **Privately Held**
SIC: 3442 3089 Metal doors, sash & trim; doors, folding: plastic or plastic coated fabric

(G-4059)
NATIONAL ADHESIVES INC
Also Called: Celtic Forms
9435 Waterstone Blvd # 200 (45249-8226)
PHONE..................513 683-8650
Michael Roten, *President*
EMP: 10
SQ FT: 5,000
SALES (est): 931.4K **Privately Held**
SIC: 5085 2891 Adhesives, tape & plasters; adhesives & sealants

(G-4060)
NATIONAL BEDDING COMPANY LLC
Also Called: Serta Mattress Company
1680 Carillion Blvd (45240-4700)
PHONE..................513 825-4172
Robert Sherman, *President*
Mike Nearn, *Plant Mgr*
Ken Blier, *Purch Agent*
Lynn Zorzi, *Sales Staff*
EMP: 5
SALES (est): 513.6K **Privately Held**
SIC: 2515 Mattresses & bedsprings
PA: Serta Simmons Bedding, Llc
2451 Industry Ave
Atlanta GA 30360

(G-4061)
NATIONAL MACHINE TOOL COMPANY
2013 E Galbraith Rd (45215-5633)
PHONE..................513 541-6682
Harold J Rembold, *President*
Chris K Rembold, *Vice Pres*
EMP: 9
SQ FT: 5,998
SALES: 1MM **Privately Held**
WEB: www.keyseaters.com
SIC: 3541 Machine tools, metal cutting: exotic (explosive, etc.)

(G-4062)
NATIONAL STARCH CHEMICAL
9435 Waterstone Blvd # 200 (45249-8229)
PHONE..................513 830-0260
Michael Roten, *Principal*
EMP: 4
SALES (est): 316K **Privately Held**
SIC: 2891 Adhesives & sealants

(G-4063)
NATURE TREK
5979 Wind St (45227-1243)
PHONE..................513 314-3916
Rick Hartigan, *Principal*
EMP: 3 **EST:** 2017
SALES (est): 123K **Privately Held**
SIC: 2741 Miscellaneous publishing

(G-4064)
NAVISTAR INC
11775 Highway Dr (45241-2005)
PHONE..................513 733-8500
David Mannin, *Branch Mgr*
EMP: 6
SALES (corp-wide): 10.2B **Publicly Held**
WEB: www.internationaldelivers.com
SIC: 3711 Truck & tractor truck assembly
HQ: Navistar, Inc.
2701 Navistar Dr
Lisle IL 60532
331 332-5000

(G-4065)
NAVISTONE INC
1308 Race St Ste 103 (45202-7397)
PHONE..................844 677-3667
Larry Kavanagh, *CEO*
Allen Abbott, *COO*
Efrain Torres, *CFO*
Lori Paikin, *Risk Mgmt Dir*
EMP: 3
SALES (est): 50.7K **Privately Held**
SIC: 7371 7372 Computer software development; computer software development & applications; software programming applications; application computer software; business oriented computer software; operating systems computer software

(G-4066)
NEHEMIAH MANUFACTURING CO LLC
1907 South St (45204-2033)
PHONE..................513 351-5700
Daniel Meyer, *CEO*
Richard T Palmer, *President*
Mike Pachko, *COO*
Rich Halsey, *Vice Pres*
Eric Wellinghoff, *Vice Pres*
▲ **EMP:** 50
SQ FT: 33,706
SALES (est): 29.2MM **Privately Held**
SIC: 5122 2844 Toilet preparations; toiletries

(G-4067)
NEPTUNE EQUIPMENT COMPANY
11082 Southland Rd (45240-3713)
PHONE..................513 851-8008
Robert W Becker, *President*
Zina Mecca, *President*
Mary Ellen Shouse, *Corp Secy*
EMP: 16
SQ FT: 4,000
SALES (est): 8.1MM **Privately Held**
WEB: www.neptuneequipment.com
SIC: 3825 1623 Meters: electric, pocket, portable, panelboard, etc.; aqueduct construction

(G-4068)
NETHERLAND RUBBER COMPANY (PA)
2931 Exon Ave (45241-2593)
P.O. Box 62165 (45262-0165)
PHONE..................513 733-0883
Timothy Clarke, *President*
Robert Pater, *Vice Pres*
Sue Clarke, *Treasurer*
EMP: 17 **EST:** 1931
SQ FT: 69,000
SALES (est): 9.7MM **Privately Held**
WEB: www.netherlandrubber.com
SIC: 5085 3053 3492 5099 Rubber goods, mechanical; seals, industrial; gaskets, all materials; hose & tube fittings & assemblies, hydraulic/pneumatic; safety equipment & supplies; chemicals & allied products; manufactured hardware (general)

(G-4069)
NEURAL HOLDINGS LLC
9867 Beech St (45231-2784)
PHONE..................734 512-8865
Nicholas Shah, *CEO*
Paul Demott, *Principal*
Endel Maricq, *COO*
Kevin McHugh, *Vice Pres*
EMP: 4 **EST:** 2016
SALES (est): 106.4K **Privately Held**
SIC: 7372 Business oriented computer software

(G-4070)
NEW LIFE CHAPEL
10195 Giverny Blvd (45241-3276)
P.O. Box 62047 (45262-0047)
PHONE..................513 298-2980
Lonnie Snell, *Pastor*
EMP: 10
SALES: 1MM **Privately Held**
SIC: 8661 7372 Non-denominational church; application computer software

(G-4071)
NEW PME INC
Also Called: Plant Maintenance Engineering
518 W Crescentville Rd (45246-1222)
PHONE..................513 671-1717
Charles Walter, *President*
EMP: 30 **EST:** 1980
SALES (est): 3.9MM **Privately Held**
SIC: 3599 Machine shop, jobbing & repair

(G-4072)
NEW VULCO MFG & SALES CO LLC
Also Called: Vulcan Oil Company
5353 Spring Grove Ave (45217-1026)
PHONE..................513 242-2672
Garry Ferraris,
Larry Schirmann,
EMP: 60
SALES (est): 14.6MM **Privately Held**
SIC: 5983 2992 5171 2899 Fuel oil dealers; oils & greases, blending & compounding; petroleum bulk stations; petroleum terminals; chemical preparations; specialty cleaning, polishes & sanitation goods; soap & other detergents

(G-4073)
NEWHOUSE & FAULKNER INC
Also Called: Corporate Printing
215 E 9th St (45202-2139)
P.O. Box 3587 (45201-3587)
PHONE..................513 721-1660
George A Newhouse, *President*
Joyce Faulkner, *Vice Pres*
Joan Allen, *Manager*
EMP: 4
SQ FT: 2,500
SALES: 500K **Privately Held**
SIC: 2752 Commercial printing, offset; lithographing on metal

GEOGRAPHIC SECTION
Cincinnati - Hamilton County (G-4104)

(G-4074)
NEWMAN BROTHERS INC
5609 Center Hill Ave (45216-2305)
P.O. Box 43460 (45243-0460)
PHONE 513 242-0011
Ken Newman, *President*
Ted Oldiges, *Corp Secy*
EMP: 35 **EST:** 1882
SQ FT: 65,000
SALES (est): 6.7MM **Privately Held**
WEB: www.newmanbrothers.com
SIC: 3446 Ornamental metalwork

(G-4075)
NEXTGEN FIBER OPTICS LLC (PA)
720 E Pete Rose Way # 410 (45202-3579)
PHONE 513 549-4691
Richard Coleman,
EMP: 66
SALES (est): 3.5MM **Privately Held**
WEB: www.nextgenfiberoptics.com
SIC: 3229 Fiber optics strands

(G-4076)
NEXTMED SYSTEMS INC (PA)
16 Triangle Park Dr (45246-3411)
PHONE 216 674-0511
David Shute, *CEO*
James Bennett, *Ch of Bd*
EMP: 44
SQ FT: 3,000
SALES (est): 3.6MM **Privately Held**
SIC: 7372 Business oriented computer software

(G-4077)
NICKUM ENTERPRISES INC
Also Called: HI Tech Graphics
6105 Madison Rd (45227-1905)
PHONE 513 561-2292
Matthew Nickum, *President*
EMP: 4
SALES (est): 568.8K **Privately Held**
WEB: www.hitechgraphics.com
SIC: 5734 2752 Printers & plotters: computers; commercial printing, lithographic

(G-4078)
NIGERIAN ASSN PHARMACISTS & PH
483 Northland Blvd (45240-3210)
PHONE 513 861-2329
Nnodum Iheme, *Principal*
Charlene Mayes, *Manager*
EMP: 5
SALES: 204K **Privately Held**
SIC: 2834 Pharmaceutical preparations

(G-4079)
NIJA FOODS LLC
323 Warren Ave (45220-1134)
PHONE 513 377-7495
Kirana RAO, *Principal*
EMP: 6
SALES (est): 371.3K **Privately Held**
SIC: 2099 Food preparations

(G-4080)
NILPETER USA INC
Also Called: Next
11550 Goldcoast Dr (45249-1640)
PHONE 513 489-4400
Lenny Degirolmo, *Principal*
Timothy Taggart, *Vice Pres*
Eric Vandenburg, *Vice Pres*
Melissa Clark, *Purch Mgr*
Julie McIntosh, *Purch Mgr*
◆ **EMP:** 110
SQ FT: 35,000
SALES: 37.7MM
SALES (corp-wide): 92.3B **Privately Held**
WEB: www.nilpeter.com
SIC: 3555 3554 3565 2759 Printing trades machinery; die cutting & stamping machinery, paper converting; packaging machinery; commercial printing, coated & laminated paper; packaging paper & plastics film, coated & laminated
PA: Nilpeter-Fonden
Elmedalsvej 20-22
Slagelse
585 283-11

(G-4081)
NINE GIANT BREWING LLC
3204 Nash Ave (45226-1232)
PHONE 510 220-5104
Brandon Hughes, *Owner*
EMP: 5
SALES (est): 218.5K **Privately Held**
SIC: 2082 Malt beverages

(G-4082)
NITTO DENKO AVECIA INC
8560 Reading Rd (45215-5528)
PHONE 513 679-3000
Lindsay Biagini, *Branch Mgr*
EMP: 14
SALES (corp-wide): 8B **Privately Held**
SIC: 2834 Pharmaceutical preparations
HQ: Nitto Denko Avecia, Inc.
125 Fortune Blvd
Milford MA 01757

(G-4083)
NNODUM PHARMACEUTICALS CORP
483 Northland Blvd (45240-3210)
P.O. Box 19725 (45219-0725)
PHONE 513 861-2329
Nnodum Iheme, *President*
Peggy Iheme, *Vice Pres*
EMP: 12
SQ FT: 16,000
SALES: 3MM **Privately Held**
WEB: www.zikspain.com
SIC: 2834 Pharmaceutical preparations

(G-4084)
NOBLE DENIM WORKSHOP
2929 Spring Grove Ave (45225-2157)
PHONE 513 560-5640
EMP: 3
SALES (est): 275K **Privately Held**
SIC: 2211 Denims

(G-4085)
NORSTAR INTERNATIONAL LLC
9435 Waterstone Blvd # 290 (45249-8226)
PHONE 513 404-3543
Colleen Williams, *Mng Member*
▲ **EMP:** 5
SALES (est): 81.3K **Privately Held**
SIC: 3999 Manufacturing industries

(G-4086)
NORTH BEND EXPRESS
Also Called: BP
3295 North Bend Rd (45239-7635)
PHONE 513 481-4623
Doug Pessler, *Principal*
EMP: 4
SQ FT: 410
SALES (est): 248.1K **Privately Held**
SIC: 2741 Miscellaneous publishing

(G-4087)
NORTHEAST SUBURBAN LIFE
312 Elm St (45202-2739)
PHONE 513 248-8600
Susan McHugh, *Principal*
EMP: 20
SALES (est): 375.3K **Privately Held**
SIC: 2711 Newspapers, publishing & printing

(G-4088)
NORTHSIDE MEAT CO INC
2910 Sidney Ave (45225-2125)
PHONE 513 681-4111
Adam Nixon, *President*
Mary J Nixon, *President*
Vicki Summerly, *General Mgr*
EMP: 8
SQ FT: 5,000
SALES (est): 1.1MM **Privately Held**
SIC: 2011 Meat packing plants

(G-4089)
NORTON OUTDOOR ADVERTISING
5280 Kennedy Ave (45213-2620)
PHONE 513 631-4864
Thomas Norton, *CEO*
Daniel Norton, *President*
Mike Norton, *Exec VP*
Steve Knapp, *Vice Pres*
Michael Norton, *Vice Pres*
EMP: 24 **EST:** 1949
SQ FT: 7,500
SALES (est): 3MM **Privately Held**
WEB: www.norton-outdoor.com
SIC: 7312 3993 Poster advertising, outdoor; billboard advertising; signs & advertising specialties

(G-4090)
NOVARTIS CORPORATION
Also Called: Novartis Vaccines & Diagnostic
1880 Waycross Rd (45240-2825)
PHONE 919 577-5000
EMP: 56
SALES (corp-wide): 49.1B **Privately Held**
SIC: 2834 Pharmaceutical preparations
HQ: Novartis Corporation
1 S Ridgedale Ave
East Hanover NJ 07936
212 307-1122

(G-4091)
NOVITRAN LLC
8100 Deer Path (45243-1356)
PHONE 513 792-2727
Conrad Haupt, *Mng Member*
Lawrence Higvon, *Mng Member*
EMP: 5
SALES (est): 434K **Privately Held**
WEB: www.novitran.com
SIC: 3829 Transits, surveyors'

(G-4092)
NTS ENTERPRISES LTD (PA)
Also Called: Betula USA
1550 Magnolia Dr (45215-1914)
PHONE 513 531-1166
Stewart R Halbauer II, *CEO*
Natalie T Halbauer, *Vice Pres*
EMP: 2
SALES: 8MM **Privately Held**
SIC: 3149 5139 Athletic shoes, except rubber or plastic; footwear, athletic

(G-4093)
NURTURE BRANDS LLC
177 Wyoming Woods Ln (45215-2171)
PHONE 513 307-2338
Elizabeth Piocos,
EMP: 5
SALES (est): 217.4K **Privately Held**
SIC: 2086 Bottled & canned soft drinks

(G-4094)
NXSTAGE MEDICAL INC
12065 Montgomery Rd (45249-1728)
PHONE 513 712-1300
Jannie Heymaker, *Branch Mgr*
EMP: 6
SALES (corp-wide): 393.9MM **Privately Held**
SIC: 3845 Electromedical equipment
PA: Nxstage Medical, Inc.
350 Merrimack St
Lawrence MA 01843
978 687-4700

(G-4095)
OAK HILLS CARTON CO
6310 Este Ave (45232-1450)
PHONE 513 948-4200
Kenneth Kabel, *President*
EMP: 25
SQ FT: 40,000
SALES (est): 5.4MM **Privately Held**
WEB: www.oakhillscarton.com
SIC: 2679 2657 Paperboard products, converted; folding paperboard boxes

(G-4096)
OBRIEN INDUSTRIES LLC
2131 Oxford Ave (45230-1606)
P.O. Box 30087 (45230-0087)
PHONE 513 476-0040
EMP: 4
SALES (est): 390K **Privately Held**
SIC: 3999 Manufacturing industries

(G-4097)
OCCIDENTAL CHEMICAL CORP
4701 Paddock Rd (45229-1003)
PHONE 513 242-2900
Tom Miller, *Plant Supt*
Eugene Thomas, *Branch Mgr*
Luanne K Istre, *Clerk*
EMP: 29
SALES (corp-wide): 18.9B **Publicly Held**
WEB: www.oxychem.com
SIC: 2812 2874 2869 2821 Alkalies & chlorine; phosphatic fertilizers; industrial organic chemicals; plastics materials & resins; industrial inorganic chemicals; prepared feeds
HQ: Occidental Chemical Corporation
14555 Dallas Pkwy Ste 400
Dallas TX 75254
972 404-3800

(G-4098)
ODACS INC
8634 Reading Rd (45215-5529)
PHONE 513 761-0539
Phil Barnett, *Principal*
Tony Goecke, *Vice Pres*
EMP: 8
SALES (est): 1.2MM **Privately Held**
WEB: www.odacs.com
SIC: 2833 Drugs & herbs: grading, grinding & milling

(G-4099)
OHIO BIOFUELS
3613 Woodbridge Pl (45226-1730)
PHONE 614 886-6518
Daniel S Casey, *Principal*
EMP: 3
SALES (est): 147.6K **Privately Held**
SIC: 2911 Petroleum refining

(G-4100)
OHIO CENTECH
444 Hidden Valley Ln (45215-2542)
PHONE 513 477-8779
Jeff Weiss, *Principal*
EMP: 5
SALES (est): 376.4K **Privately Held**
SIC: 3281 Cut stone & stone products

(G-4101)
OHIO FEATHER COMPANY INC
1 Kovach Dr (45215-1000)
PHONE 513 921-3373
Gabriel Guigui, *President*
Daniel Guigui, *Vice Pres*
▲ **EMP:** 6
SALES (est): 600K **Privately Held**
SIC: 3999 Feathers & feather products

(G-4102)
OHIO FLAME HARDENING COMPANY
637 N Wayne Ave (45215-2250)
PHONE 513 733-5162
Robert Bokon, *President*
EMP: 24
SALES (corp-wide): 1.4MM **Privately Held**
SIC: 3398 Brazing (hardening) of metal
PA: Ohio Flame Hardening Company Inc
4110 Columbia Rd
Lebanon OH 45036
513 336-6160

(G-4103)
OHIO HYDRAULICS INC
2510 E Sharon Rd Ste 1 (45241-1891)
PHONE 513 771-2590
John Davis, *Ch of Bd*
Kathleen Hilliard, *President*
Tamera Fair, *Corp Secy*
Dave Davis, *Vice Pres*
Robert Farwick, *Vice Pres*
EMP: 25 **EST:** 1971
SQ FT: 13,500
SALES (est): 6.5MM **Privately Held**
WEB: www.ohiohydraulics.com
SIC: 3492 3599 5084 7699 Hose & tube fittings & assemblies, hydraulic/pneumatic; flexible metal hose, tubing & bellows; hydraulic systems equipment & supplies; tank repair & cleaning services; welding repair; manufactured hardware (general)

(G-4104)
OHIO PLYWOOD BOX
5555 Vine St (45216-2343)
PHONE 513 242-9125
Jerry Graves, *Owner*
EMP: 4
SQ FT: 3,500

Cincinnati - Hamilton County (G-4105)

SALES: 75K **Privately Held**
SIC: 2449 Wood containers

(G-4105)
OHIO TILE & MARBLE CO (PA)
3809 Spring Grove Ave (45223-2693)
PHONE..................513 541-4211
Sean Dowers, *President*
Ruth Dowers, *Vice Pres*
Lisa Weidmenn, *Controller*
Sharon Baird, *Sales Staff*
Clyde Dowers, *Shareholder*
▲ EMP: 23
SQ FT: 21,500
SALES (est): 4.5MM **Privately Held**
WEB: www.ohiotile.com
SIC: 5032 5211 3281 3253 Tile, clay or other ceramic, excluding refractory; marble building stone; tile, ceramic; masonry materials & supplies; marble, building: cut & shaped; ceramic wall & floor tile

(G-4106)
OHIO VALLEY ADHESIVES
6148 Rapid Run Rd (45233-4549)
PHONE..................513 454-1800
EMP: 3
SALES (est): 123.2K **Privately Held**
SIC: 2891 Adhesives

(G-4107)
OHIO WOODWORKING CO INC
5035 Beech St (45212-2399)
PHONE..................513 631-0870
Thomas R Frank Jr, *President*
Peggy Frank, *Admin Sec*
EMP: 8 EST: 1931
SQ FT: 17,000
SALES (est): 1MM **Privately Held**
WEB: www.ohiowoodworkingcompany.com
SIC: 2541 2431 Display fixtures, wood; store fixtures, wood; millwork

(G-4108)
OKL CAN LINE INC
11235 Sebring Dr (45240-2714)
PHONE..................513 825-1655
Anthony Lacey, *CEO*
Scott Feldmann, *Prdtn Mgr*
Richard Green, *Manager*
◆ EMP: 47
SQ FT: 50,000
SALES (est): 12.8MM
SALES (corp-wide): 3MM **Privately Held**
WEB: www.oklcan.com
SIC: 3565 7699 Bottling & canning machinery; industrial machinery & equipment repair
PA: Allcan Global Services, Inc
   11235 Sebring Dr
   Cincinnati OH 45240
   513 825-1655

(G-4109)
OLIVE SMUCKERS OIL
5204 Spring Grove Ave (45217-1031)
PHONE..................513 646-7103
EMP: 3
SALES (est): 260K **Privately Held**
SIC: 2079 Olive oil

(G-4110)
OLIVER CHEMICAL CO INC
2908 Spring Grove Ave (45225-2154)
PHONE..................513 541-4540
Thomas J Stiens, *President*
Robert O Stiens, *Vice Pres*
EMP: 7 EST: 1938
SQ FT: 25,000
SALES (est): 1.1MM **Privately Held**
SIC: 2842 3471 2992 2899 Sanitation preparations; metal polish; specialty cleaning preparations; plating & polishing; lubricating oils & greases; chemical preparations; soap & other detergents

(G-4111)
OMNICARE PHRM OF MIDWEST LLC (DH)
201 E 4th St Ste 900 (45202-1513)
PHONE..................513 719-2600
Joel Gemunder, *Principal*
EMP: 100

SALES (est): 33.5MM
SALES (corp-wide): 194.5B **Publicly Held**
SIC: 5122 5912 2834 Drugs & drug proprietaries; drug stores; pharmaceutical preparations

(G-4112)
ONE CLOUD SERVICES LLC
1080 Nimitzview Dr # 400 (45230-4314)
PHONE..................513 231-9500
Anne Zimmerman, *President*
Jason Huebner, *General Mgr*
Steve Searles, *Vice Pres*
EMP: 6
SALES (est): 148.8K **Privately Held**
SIC: 7372 Business oriented computer software
PA: Liberty Noc, Llc
   24200 Woodward Ave
   Pleasant Ridge MI 48069

(G-4113)
ONETOUCHPOINT EAST CORP
Also Called: Touch Print Solution
1441 Western Ave (45214-2041)
PHONE..................513 421-1600
Christopher A Illman, *Principal*
William Pearson, *Principal*
George Ditullio, *Purch Mgr*
Ben Griffith, *Officer*
Larry Halenkamp, *CFO*
EMP: 87 EST: 1935
SQ FT: 102,000
SALES (est): 19.1MM
SALES (corp-wide): 28.5MM **Privately Held**
WEB: www.bermanprinting.com
SIC: 2759 2752 2791 2789 Commercial printing; commercial printing, lithographic; typesetting; bookbinding & related work
HQ: Onetouchpoint Corp.
   1225 Walnut Ridge Dr
   Hartland WI 53029

(G-4114)
ONX HOLDINGS LLC (HQ)
Also Called: Onx Enterprise Solutions
221 E 4th St (45202-4124)
PHONE..................866 587-2287
Scott Seger, *President*
Laura Teigeler, *Marketing Staff*
Chris Lehotsky, *Manager*
Joshua Ramaker, *Consultant*
Denise Bell, *Director*
EMP: 13 EST: 2006
SALES (est): 79.2MM
SALES (corp-wide): 1.3B **Publicly Held**
SIC: 7379 7372 Computer related consulting services; business oriented computer software
PA: Cincinnati Bell Inc.
   221 E 4th St Ste 700
   Cincinnati OH 45202
   513 397-9900

(G-4115)
OPTIMAL OFFICE SOLUTIONS LLC
25 Merchant St Ste 135 (45246-3740)
PHONE..................201 257-8516
Ana Vivancos, *Mng Member*
Kavous Ahmadi,
EMP: 3
SQ FT: 800
SALES: 264.1K **Privately Held**
SIC: 7372 Prepackaged software

(G-4116)
OPTIMUS LLC
4623 Wesley Ave Ste B (45212-2243)
PHONE..................513 918-2320
John Brandt, *Principal*
Anita Curtis, *Manager*
Travis Barlow, *Director*
EMP: 35 EST: 2016
SALES (est): 1.4MM **Privately Held**
SIC: 3842 Surgical appliances & supplies

(G-4117)
OPTIMZED PRDCTVITY SLTIONS LLC
Also Called: Omative North America
9435 Waterstone Blvd (45249-8226)
PHONE..................513 444-2156

EMP: 3
SALES (est): 180K **Privately Held**
SIC: 7372 Prepackaged Software Services

(G-4118)
ORGANIZED LIVING INC (PA)
3100 E Kemper Rd (45241-1517)
PHONE..................513 489-9300
John D Kokenge, *CEO*
Kevin Glynn, *General Mgr*
Kevin Ball, *Principal*
Robert J Lamping, *Vice Pres*
Steve McCamley, *Vice Pres*
▲ EMP: 40 EST: 1919
SQ FT: 16,000
SALES (est): 31.8MM **Privately Held**
WEB: www.schultestorage.com
SIC: 3496 3083 3411 2542 Miscellaneous fabricated wire products; laminated plastics plate & sheet; metal cans; partitions & fixtures, except wood

(G-4119)
ORION CONTROL PANELS INC
5012 Calvert St Ste B (45209-1076)
PHONE..................513 615-6534
EMP: 3 EST: 2013
SALES (est): 290K **Privately Held**
SIC: 3625 Mfg Relays/Industrial Controls

(G-4120)
OSBORNE COINAGE COMPANY (PA)
Also Called: Doran Manufacturing Co.
2851 Massachusetts Ave (45225-2276)
PHONE..................513 681-5424
Thomas E Stegman, *President*
Ross Ormsby, *President*
Jim Samocki, *General Mgr*
Randy Caskey, *Engineer*
Todd R Stegman, *Treasurer*
▲ EMP: 70 EST: 1835
SQ FT: 40,000
SALES: 13MM **Privately Held**
WEB: www.doranmfg.com
SIC: 3999 3644 3613 Coins & tokens, non-currency; terminal boards; panelboards & distribution boards, electric

(G-4121)
OSHKOSH CORPORATION
7875 Montgomery Rd Spc 87 (45236-4374)
PHONE..................513 745-9436
Mye'shia Alexander, *President*
EMP: 3
SALES (corp-wide): 6.8B **Publicly Held**
SIC: 3711 Motor vehicles & car bodies
PA: Oshkosh Corporation
   2307 Oregon St
   Oshkosh WI 54902
   920 235-9151

(G-4122)
OSTEODYNAMICS
3130 Highland Ave Fl 3 (45219-2399)
PHONE..................405 921-9271
David Ralph, *Owner*
EMP: 4
SALES (est): 160K **Privately Held**
SIC: 3845 Electromedical equipment

(G-4123)
OTR CONTROLS LLC
40 E Mcmicken Ave (45202-6625)
PHONE..................513 621-2197
Donna Owens, *Manager*
Howard Elliott,
EMP: 5
SQ FT: 3,000
SALES: 363.7K **Privately Held**
WEB: www.otrcontrols.com
SIC: 3613 3679 Control panels, electric; harness assemblies for electronic use: wire or cable

(G-4124)
OUT ON A LIMB
5311 Springdale Rd (45251-1819)
PHONE..................513 432-5091
Michael Niehaus, *Principal*
EMP: 3
SALES (est): 351.3K **Privately Held**
SIC: 3842 Limbs, artificial

(G-4125)
OUTBACK CYCLE SHACK LLC
Also Called: Pride and True Garage
7923 Blue Ash Rd (45236-2601)
PHONE..................513 554-1048
Sean Bast, *CEO*
EMP: 3
SALES: 180K **Privately Held**
SIC: 7699 3751 Motorcycle repair service; motorcycle accessories

(G-4126)
OWEN S PRECISION GRINDING
Also Called: Owens Precisn Grindg
8383 Blue Ash Rd (45236-1986)
PHONE..................513 745-9335
Wanda Owens, *Owner*
Kathy Glassmyer, *Manager*
EMP: 3
SQ FT: 2,500
SALES: 450K **Privately Held**
SIC: 3599 Grinding castings for the trade

(G-4127)
OWL BE SWEATIN
Also Called: Hoot and Holler,
4914 Ridge Ave (45209-1035)
PHONE..................513 260-2026
Kc Debra, *Partner*
Mallory Debra, *Partner*
EMP: 3
SALES (est): 205.2K **Privately Held**
SIC: 2339 5632 Scarves, hoods, headbands, etc.: women's; women's accessory & specialty stores

(G-4128)
P & C METAL POLISHING INC
340 Glendale Milford Rd (45215-1102)
PHONE..................513 771-9143
Perry Pullum, *President*
Donna Williamson, *Vice Pres*
EMP: 20
SQ FT: 30,000
SALES (est): 2.3MM **Privately Held**
WEB: www.pandcmetalpolishing.com
SIC: 3471 Polishing, metals or formed products

(G-4129)
P-AMERICAS LLC
Also Called: Pepsico
2121 Sunnybrook Dr (45237-2107)
PHONE..................513 948-5100
Chuck Lewis, *Mfg Staff*
Sandra Moeller, *Sales Staff*
Bob Goodman, *Branch Mgr*
Priya RAO, *Info Tech Mgr*
Patricia Tully, *Technical Staff*
EMP: 400
SQ FT: 150,000
SALES (corp-wide): 64.6B **Publicly Held**
SIC: 2086 Carbonated soft drinks, bottled & canned
HQ: P-Americas Llc
   1 Pepsi Way
   Somers NY 10589
   336 896-5740

(G-4130)
PACKAGING CORPORATION AMERICA
Also Called: PCA
791 Saint Thomas Ct (45230-3873)
PHONE..................513 582-0690
Keith Ferrara, *Manager*
EMP: 3
SALES (corp-wide): 7B **Publicly Held**
SIC: 2653 Boxes, corrugated: made from purchased materials
PA: Packaging Corporation Of America
   1 N Field Ct
   Lake Forest IL 60045
   847 482-3000

(G-4131)
PALETTE STUDIOS INC
2501 Woodburn Ave (45206-2202)
PHONE..................513 961-1316
Sharon L Denight, *President*
EMP: 4
SQ FT: 3,500
SALES (est): 468.7K **Privately Held**
WEB: www.palettestudios.com
SIC: 5719 3645 Lamps & lamp shades; residential lighting fixtures

GEOGRAPHIC SECTION

Cincinnati - Hamilton County (G-4158)

(G-4132)
PANEL-FAB INC
10520 Taconic Ter (45215-1125)
PHONE.................513 771-1462
Robert A Harrison, *President*
Nancy J Shurlow, *Principal*
Stephen T Williford, *Vice Pres*
Jarrod Harrison, *Traffic Mgr*
Carolyn Zinnecker, *Purchasing*
EMP: 90
SQ FT: 25,000
SALES (est): 40.7MM **Privately Held**
WEB: www.panel-fab.com
SIC: 3613 Control panels, electric

(G-4133)
PARAGON PRESS
2239 Fulton Ave (45206-2504)
PHONE.................513 281-9911
James Fryman, *Owner*
EMP: 4
SALES (est): 274K **Privately Held**
SIC: 2759 2752 Letterpress printing; commercial printing, offset

(G-4134)
PATHEON PHARMACEUTICALS INC
2110 E Galbraith Rd (45237-1625)
P.O. Box 40017, College Station TX (77842-4017)
PHONE.................513 948-9111
Tim Edmonds, *Business Mgr*
Peter Franck, *Business Mgr*
Claudia Hayes, *Business Mgr*
Colleen Wegman, *Project Mgr*
Tom Madsen, *Opers Staff*
EMP: 277 **Privately Held**
SIC: 2834 Pharmaceutical preparations
HQ: Patheon Pharmaceuticals Inc.
4815 Emperor Blvd Ste 300
Durham NC 27703
919 226-3200

(G-4135)
PATIO ENCLOSURES (PA)
11949 Tramway Dr (45241-1666)
PHONE.................513 733-4646
Ronald J Molnar, *President*
Donna Molnar, *Corp Secy*
EMP: 19
SQ FT: 10,000
SALES (est): 2.3MM **Privately Held**
SIC: 5039 2452 1521 Prefabricated structures; prefabricated wood buildings; patio & deck construction & repair

(G-4136)
PATRICIA LEE BURD
Also Called: Crosstown Bindery
310 Culvert St (45202-2229)
PHONE.................513 302-4860
Patricia Lee Burd, *Owner*
EMP: 3
SALES (est): 110K **Privately Held**
SIC: 2789 Bookbinding & related work

(G-4137)
PATRICK J BURKE & CO
Also Called: Burke & Company
901 Adams Crossing Fl 1 (45202-1693)
PHONE.................513 455-8200
Patrick Burke, *Owner*
Eugene Schindler, *Co-Owner*
Betty Hancock, *Controller*
Monica Cradler, *Accountant*
Julie Gady, *Accountant*
EMP: 25
SALES (est): 2.9MM **Privately Held**
SIC: 8721 7372 Certified public accountant; prepackaged software

(G-4138)
PATRIOT SIGNAGE INC
10561 Chester Rd (45215-1203)
PHONE.................859 655-9009
Kevin L Keefe, *President*
Mike Maier, *Principal*
EMP: 9
SQ FT: 14,500
SALES (est): 1.4MM **Privately Held**
SIC: 3993 Signs, not made in custom sign painting shops

(G-4139)
PAUL BARTEL (PA)
Also Called: Baroque Violin Shop
1038 W North Bend Rd (45224-2241)
PHONE.................513 541-2000
Paul Bartel, *Owner*
▲ **EMP:** 9
SQ FT: 2,000
SALES (est): 1.2MM **Privately Held**
WEB: www.baroqueviolinshop.com
SIC: 3931 5736 7359 7699 String instruments & parts; musical instrument stores; musical instrument rental services; musical instrument repair services

(G-4140)
PAUL H ROHE COMPANY INC
11641 Mosteller Rd (45241-1520)
PHONE.................513 326-6789
James P Jurgensen II, *President*
EMP: 3 **EST:** 2009
SALES (est): 250.2K **Privately Held**
SIC: 3273 Ready-mixed concrete

(G-4141)
PAUL WILKE & SON INC
1965 Grand Ave (45214-1505)
PHONE.................513 921-3163
Charles S Wilke, *President*
EMP: 14
SQ FT: 22,000
SALES (est): 2MM **Privately Held**
WEB: www.paulwilkeandson.com
SIC: 3444 3599 7692 Sheet metal specialties, not stamped; machine shop, jobbing & repair; welding repair

(G-4142)
PAVESTONE LLC
8479 Broadwell Rd (45244-1693)
PHONE.................513 474-3783
Dave Lemmon, *Manager*
Dennis Potts, *Manager*
EMP: 70
SQ FT: 54,837 **Privately Held**
WEB: www.pavestone.com
SIC: 3272 3281 Paving materials, prefabricated concrete; cut stone & stone products
HQ: Pavestone, Llc
5 Concourse Pkwy Ste 1900
Atlanta GA 30328
404 926-3167

(G-4143)
PCY ENTERPRISES INC
Also Called: Young & Bertke Air Systems
3111 Spring Grove Ave (45225-1821)
PHONE.................513 241-5566
Roger Young, *President*
Michael Munafo, *Vice Pres*
Tim Rohrer, *Vice Pres*
Phillip C Young, *Shareholder*
EMP: 28
SQ FT: 51,000
SALES (est): 4MM **Privately Held**
WEB: www.youngbertke.com
SIC: 1761 3441 3564 3444 Sheet metalwork; fabricated structural metal; blowers & fans; sheet metalwork; fabricated plate work (boiler shop)

(G-4144)
PDMB INC
9600 Colerain Ave Ste 110 (45251-2014)
PHONE.................513 522-7362
Donald Peak, *President*
Will Singer, *Vice Pres*
Adam Singer, *Sales Mgr*
EMP: 5
SQ FT: 1,200
SALES (est): 516.5K **Privately Held**
WEB: www.palm-tech.com
SIC: 7372 7371 Prepackaged software; custom computer programming services

(G-4145)
PEERLESS PRINTING COMPANY
2250 Gilbert Ave Ste 1 (45206-2531)
PHONE.................513 721-4657
Ken Schrand, *President*
Paul Dimario, *Principal*
Jay Heidemann, *Principal*
Steve Lyons, *Principal*
Ryan Schrand, *Principal*
EMP: 12 **EST:** 1900
SQ FT: 4,400
SALES (est): 1.9MM **Privately Held**
SIC: 2752 Commercial printing, offset

(G-4146)
PERFECT PROBATE
2036 8 Mile Rd (45244-2607)
PHONE.................513 791-4100
Shawn Wood, *Owner*
EMP: 6
SALES (est): 318K **Privately Held**
WEB: www.perfectprobate.com
SIC: 7372 8111 Prepackaged software; legal services

(G-4147)
PERFORMANCE ABRASIVES INC
10330 Wayne Ave (45215-1129)
PHONE.................513 733-9283
Jim Meister, *President*
Beverly Meister, *Vice Pres*
▲ **EMP:** 5
SQ FT: 17,000
SALES (est): 624.6K **Privately Held**
WEB: www.performanceabrasives.net
SIC: 3291 Abrasive products

(G-4148)
PERFORMANCE ELECTRONICS LTD
11529 Goldcoast Dr (45249-1620)
PHONE.................513 777-5233
Brian Lewis, *Managing Prtnr*
Julie Lewis, *Manager*
EMP: 8
SALES (est): 3MM **Privately Held**
WEB: www.pe-ltd.com
SIC: 3679 Electronic circuits

(G-4149)
PERFORMANCE MOTORSPORTS
2545 W Galbraith Rd (45239-4206)
PHONE.................513 931-9999
Joe Leach, *Owner*
Joe Leacg, *Owner*
EMP: 3
SALES (est): 170K **Privately Held**
SIC: 3462 5531 Automotive & internal combustion engine forgings; automotive parts

(G-4150)
PERFORMANCE PLASTICS LTD
4435 Brownway Ave (45209-1264)
PHONE.................513 321-8404
Tom Mendel, *President*
Edward Schauer, *COO*
Anthony Malone, *Engineer*
Peggy Delany, *Sls & Mktg Exec*
Margaret Delany, *CTO*
EMP: 40 **EST:** 1982
SQ FT: 20,000
SALES (est): 12.2MM **Privately Held**
WEB: www.performanceplastics.com
SIC: 3089 Injection molding of plastics

(G-4151)
PERFUME COUNTER
11700 Princeton Pike (45246-2535)
PHONE.................513 885-5989
Christianene Kelly, *Principal*
EMP: 3 **EST:** 2011
SALES (est): 189.8K **Privately Held**
SIC: 3131 Counters

(G-4152)
PETE GAIETTO & ASSOCIATES INC
1900 Section Rd (45237-3308)
PHONE.................513 771-0903
Jordan Gaietto, *CEO*
▲ **EMP:** 75
SQ FT: 3,880
SALES (est): 15.4MM **Privately Held**
SIC: 2542 Office & store showcases & display fixtures

(G-4153)
PETER CREMER NORTH AMERICA LP (DH)
Also Called: Pcna
3117 Southside Ave (45204-1215)
PHONE.................513 471-7200
Raymond Bitzer, *Managing Prtnr*
Jennifer Sheffel, *Analyst*
▲ **EMP:** 60
SALES (est): 23.7MM
SALES (corp-wide): 188.6K **Privately Held**
WEB: www.petercremerna.com
SIC: 2843 Sulfonated oils, fats or greases
HQ: Peter Cremer Gmbh
GlockengieBerwall 3
Hamburg 20095
403 201-10

(G-4154)
PETNET SOLUTIONS INC
2139 Auburn Ave (45219-2906)
PHONE.................865 218-2000
Barry Scott, *CEO*
EMP: 6
SALES (corp-wide): 95B **Privately Held**
SIC: 2835 Radioactive diagnostic substances
HQ: Petnet Solutions, Inc.
810 Innovation Dr
Knoxville TN 37932
865 218-2000

(G-4155)
PFPC ENTERPRISES INC
5750 Hillside Ave (45233-1508)
PHONE.................513 941-6200
Peter F Coffaro, *Ch of Bd*
James Coffaro, *President*
Stephen Stout, *CFO*
Chuck Williams, *Manager*
EMP: 300 **EST:** 1963
SQ FT: 52,000
SALES (est): 18.1MM **Privately Held**
WEB: www.pabcofluidpower.com
SIC: 5023 5084 3594 3535 Floor coverings; industrial machinery & equipment; pumps & pumping equipment; water pumps (industrial); hydraulic systems equipment & supplies; fluid power pumps & motors; conveyors & conveying equipment; turbines & turbine generator sets

(G-4156)
PGT HEALTHCARE LLP (HQ)
1 Procter And Gamble Plz (45202-3315)
PHONE.................513 983-1100
David S Taylor, *President*
Jon Moeller, *CFO*
Linda Clement-Holmes, *CIO*
Kathleen Fish, *CTO*
Deborah Majoras,
EMP: 3
SALES (est): 1.3MM
SALES (corp-wide): 66.8B **Publicly Held**
SIC: 2676 Towels, napkins & tissue paper products
PA: The Procter & Gamble Company
1 Procter And Gamble Plz
Cincinnati OH 45202
513 983-1100

(G-4157)
PICKENS WINDOW SERVICE INC
7824 Hamilton Ave (45231-3106)
PHONE.................513 931-4432
Brian Pickens, *President*
Kendall Pickens, *Corp Secy*
EMP: 11
SQ FT: 10,000
SALES: 980K **Privately Held**
WEB: www.pickenswindowparts.com
SIC: 5211 7699 2431 Windows, storm: wood or metal; doors, storm: wood or metal; door & window repair; window screens, wood frame

(G-4158)
PIERCE GL INC
Also Called: Cincinnati Glass Block Day GL
12100 Mosteller Rd # 500 (45241-6404)
PHONE.................513 772-7202
Gregory L Pierce, *President*
EMP: 7
SALES: 200K **Privately Held**
SIC: 3229 1741 Blocks & bricks, glass; concrete block masonry laying

---

(PA)=Parent Co (HQ)=Headquarters (DH)=Div Headquarters
✿ = New Business established in last 2 years

Cincinnati - Hamilton County (G-4159) — GEOGRAPHIC SECTION

(G-4159)
PILOT CHEMICAL COMPANY OHIO (PA)
2744 E Kemper Rd (45241-1818)
PHONE.................................513 326-0600
Pamela R Butcher, *CEO*
Pam Butcher, *CEO*
Michael Scott, *President*
Mike Clark, *COO*
Glynn E Goertzen, *Vice Pres*
◆ EMP: 30
SALES (est): 108.9MM **Privately Held**
SIC: 2843 2841 Finishing agents; detergents, synthetic organic or inorganic alkaline

(G-4160)
PILOT CHEMICAL COMPANY OHIO
606 Shepherd Dr (45215-2145)
PHONE.................................513 733-4880
Thomas Melhorn, *Manager*
EMP: 25
SQ FT: 13,820
SALES (corp-wide): 109.1MM **Privately Held**
SIC: 2843 2841 2842 Finishing agents; detergents, synthetic organic or inorganic alkaline; specialty cleaning, polishes & sanitation goods
PA: Pilot Chemical Company Of Ohio
2744 E Kemper Rd
Cincinnati OH 45241
513 326-0600

(G-4161)
PILOT CHEMICAL CORP (HQ)
2744 E Kemper Rd (45241-1818)
PHONE.................................513 326-0600
Pamela R Butcher, *President*
Mike Clark, *President*
Bert Gutierrez, *General Mgr*
Susan K Leslie, *Vice Pres*
Dennis Burgess, *Mfg Staff*
◆ EMP: 13
SQ FT: 10,000
SALES (est): 12.9MM
SALES (corp-wide): 109.1MM **Privately Held**
WEB: www.pilotchemical.com
SIC: 2841 2843 Detergents, synthetic organic or inorganic alkaline; surface active agents
PA: Pilot Chemical Company Of Ohio
2744 E Kemper Rd
Cincinnati OH 45241
513 326-0600

(G-4162)
PINNACLE ROLLER CO
2147 Spring Grove Ave (45214-1721)
PHONE.................................513 369-4830
Mike Brown, *Vice Pres*
Dan Dinkelacker, *Marketing Staff*
EMP: 15
SALES (est): 2.2MM **Privately Held**
SIC: 3069 Rubber rolls & roll coverings

(G-4163)
PIQUA MATERIALS INC (PA)
11641 Mosteller Rd Ste 1 (45241-1520)
PHONE.................................513 771-0820
James Jurgensen, *President*
Tim Saintclair, *Corp Secy*
James Jurgenson II, *Vice Pres*
James P Jurgensen, *Plant Mgr*
Beth Baker, *Controller*
EMP: 100
SALES (est): 10.1MM **Privately Held**
SIC: 1422 Limestones, ground

(G-4164)
PKI INC
Also Called: Powder Kote Industries
4500 Reading Rd (45229-1230)
PHONE.................................513 832-8749
Jeff Cox, *President*
EMP: 10
SQ FT: 10,000
SALES (est): 1.2MM **Privately Held**
WEB: www.pki-inc.com
SIC: 3479 3471 Coating of metals & formed products; sand blasting of metal parts

(G-4165)
PLANK AND HIDE CO
2721a E Sharon Rd (45241-1944)
PHONE.................................888 462-6852
Amy Brown, *Principal*
Jennifer Ashby, *Business Mgr*
EMP: 11
SALES (est): 502.8K **Privately Held**
SIC: 2426 Carvings, furniture: wood

(G-4166)
PLASTIGRAPHICS INC
722 Redna Ter (45215-1109)
PHONE.................................513 771-8848
Robert Heinold, *President*
Sandy Miller, *Corp Secy*
EMP: 12
SQ FT: 6,500
SALES: 1.5MM **Privately Held**
WEB: www.plastigraphics.com
SIC: 3993 3861 Signs & advertising specialties; graphic arts plates, sensitized

(G-4167)
PLATING SOLUTIONS
871 Redna Ter (45215-1110)
PHONE.................................513 771-1941
Cris Narburgh, *Vice Pres*
EMP: 5
SALES (est): 299.5K **Privately Held**
SIC: 3471 Plating of metals or formed products

(G-4168)
PLAYGROUND EQUIPMENT SERVICE
2980 Diehl Rd (45211-2714)
PHONE.................................513 481-3776
EMP: 6
SALES (est): 532.2K **Privately Held**
SIC: 3949 Mfg Sporting/Athletic Goods

(G-4169)
PMC SPECIALTIES GROUP INC (DH)
501 Murray Rd (45217-1014)
PHONE.................................513 242-3300
Zetta Bouligaraki, *President*
▲ EMP: 24
SQ FT: 7,500
SALES (est): 70MM
SALES (corp-wide): 2.5B **Privately Held**
WEB: www.pmcspecialties.com
SIC: 2819 2816 Industrial inorganic chemicals; inorganic pigments
HQ: Pmc, Inc.
12243 Branford St
Sun Valley CA 91352
818 896-1101

(G-4170)
PMC SPECIALTIES GROUP INC
5220 Vine St (45217-1028)
PHONE.................................513 242-3300
EMP: 9
SALES (corp-wide): 2.5B **Privately Held**
SIC: 2819 2816 Industrial inorganic chemicals; inorganic pigments
HQ: Pmc Specialties Group, Inc.
501 Murray Rd
Cincinnati OH 45217

(G-4171)
PME OF OHIO INC (PA)
Also Called: PME- Babbit Bearings
518 W Crescentville Rd (45246-1222)
PHONE.................................513 671-1717
Charles Walter, *President*
Michelle Holt, *Controller*
Walter Michelle, *Controller*
Michelle McCord, *Executive*
EMP: 50
SQ FT: 20,000
SALES (est): 8.9MM **Privately Held**
WEB: www.pmebabbittbearings.com
SIC: 3599 Machine shop, jobbing & repair

(G-4172)
POROCEL INDUSTRIES LLC (PA)
1 Landy Ln (45215-3405)
PHONE.................................513 733-8519
Ronald Zapletal, *President*
Ronald L Bell, *Vice Pres*
Edward L Butera, *Vice Pres*
Terrence McHugh, *Vice Pres*
William A Kist, *CFO*
◆ EMP: 4
SALES (est): 21.6MM **Privately Held**
WEB: www.porocel.com
SIC: 2819 Bauxite, refined

(G-4173)
PORTER PRECISION PRODUCTS CO (PA)
2734 Banning Rd (45239-5504)
PHONE.................................513 385-1569
John Cipriani Jr, *President*
Mary M Cipriani, *Chairman*
Dale Warlaumont, *Corp Secy*
Vince Cipriani, *Vice Pres*
Jim Cipriani, *Safety Mgr*
EMP: 79
SQ FT: 33,200
SALES (est): 23.8MM **Privately Held**
WEB: www.porterpunch.com
SIC: 3544 Punches, forming & stamping; dies & die holders for metal cutting, forming, die casting; die sets for metal stamping (presses)

(G-4174)
PORTER-GUERTIN CO INC
2150 Colerain Ave (45214-1873)
P.O. Box 14177 (45250-0177)
PHONE.................................513 241-7663
James F Gentil, *President*
Kathleen Gentil, *Corp Secy*
EMP: 14 EST: 1953
SQ FT: 12,000
SALES (est): 1.5MM **Privately Held**
SIC: 3471 Plating of metals or formed products

(G-4175)
POSITROL INC
Also Called: Positrol Workholding
3890 Virginia Ave (45227-3410)
PHONE.................................513 272-0500
David C Weber, *President*
Jonathan T Weber, *Vice Pres*
William Lorenz, *Prdtn Mgr*
Barry Cox, *Engineer*
Josh Pocock, *Engineer*
EMP: 30 EST: 1947
SQ FT: 11,000
SALES (est): 6.4MM **Privately Held**
WEB: www.positrol.com
SIC: 3545 Machine tool attachments & accessories

(G-4176)
POSTERSERVICE INCORPORATED (PA)
225 Northland Blvd (45246-3603)
PHONE.................................513 577-7100
Dana W Gore, *President*
Daniel P Regenold, *Chairman*
Rebecca Regenold, *Corp Secy*
▲ EMP: 20
SQ FT: 30,000
SALES (est): 8.1MM **Privately Held**
WEB: www.posterservice.com
SIC: 5199 2741 Posters; posters: publishing & printing

(G-4177)
POWER ENGINEERING LLC
Also Called: Blue Machine
507 N Wayne Ave (45215-2871)
PHONE.................................513 793-5800
John H Burke,
Edmond Burke,
EMP: 3
SQ FT: 7,000
SALES (est): 273.7K **Privately Held**
SIC: 3541 Machine tools, metal cutting type

(G-4178)
POWERHOUSE FACTORIES INC
1111 Saint Gregory St (45202-1770)
PHONE.................................513 719-6417
Jim Price, *Principal*
EMP: 10 EST: 2012
SALES (est): 902.9K **Privately Held**
SIC: 2741 Art copy: publishing & printing

(G-4179)
PPG INDUSTRIES INC
Also Called: PPG 4331
7198 Beechmont Ave (45230-4115)
PHONE.................................513 231-3200
Steve Tauber, *Manager*
EMP: 24
SALES (corp-wide): 15.3B **Publicly Held**
WEB: www.ppg.com
SIC: 2851 Paints & allied products
PA: Ppg Industries, Inc.
1 Ppg Pl
Pittsburgh PA 15272
412 434-3131

(G-4180)
PPG INDUSTRIES INC
Also Called: PPG 4333
6462 Glenway Ave (45211-5222)
PHONE.................................513 661-5220
Jim Jackson, *Manager*
EMP: 24
SALES (corp-wide): 15.3B **Publicly Held**
WEB: www.ppg.com
SIC: 2851 Paints & allied products
PA: Ppg Industries, Inc.
1 Ppg Pl
Pittsburgh PA 15272
412 434-3131

(G-4181)
PPG INDUSTRIES INC
Also Called: PPG 4339
9865 Montgomery Rd (45242-6424)
PHONE.................................513 984-6761
Steve Bryson, *Branch Mgr*
EMP: 24
SALES (corp-wide): 15.3B **Publicly Held**
WEB: www.ppg.com
SIC: 2851 Paints & allied products
PA: Ppg Industries, Inc.
1 Ppg Pl
Pittsburgh PA 15272
412 434-3131

(G-4182)
PPG INDUSTRIES INC
Also Called: PPG 4332
4600 Reading Rd (45229-1232)
PHONE.................................513 242-3050
Mike Allen, *Branch Mgr*
EMP: 24
SALES (corp-wide): 15.3B **Publicly Held**
WEB: www.ppg.com
SIC: 2851 Paints & allied products
PA: Ppg Industries, Inc.
1 Ppg Pl
Pittsburgh PA 15272
412 434-3131

(G-4183)
PRACTICE CENTER INC (PA)
7621 E Kemper Rd (45249-1609)
PHONE.................................513 489-5229
Randal R Sadler, *President*
EMP: 6
SQ FT: 7,200
SALES (est): 417.1K **Privately Held**
WEB: www.tpcgolf.com
SIC: 7993 7999 7992 3949 Video game arcade; golf driving range; pool parlor; public golf courses; driving ranges, golf, electronic

(G-4184)
PRAXAIR DISTRIBUTION INC
8376 Reading Rd (45237-1407)
PHONE.................................513 821-2192
Joe R Smith, *Opers-Prdtn-Mfg*
EMP: 8 **Privately Held**
SIC: 2813 5084 5999 Carbon dioxide; dry ice, carbon dioxide (solid); oxygen, compressed or liquefied; welding machinery & equipment; welding supplies
HQ: Praxair Distribution, Inc.
10 Riverview Dr
Danbury CT 06810
203 837-2000

(G-4185)
PRECISION SWISS LLC
9580 Wayne Ave (45215-2252)
PHONE.................................513 716-7000
Ron Hinks, *Owner*
Tatyana Hinks, *CFO*
EMP: 9

GEOGRAPHIC SECTION

Cincinnati - Hamilton County (G-4209)

SQ FT: 17,000
SALES: 535K **Privately Held**
SIC: **3843** Dental equipment & supplies

(G-4186)
PREFERRED GLOBAL EQUIPMENT LLC
7800 Redsky Dr (45249-1632)
PHONE.................................513 530-5800
William A Decenso,
Mark Werner,
▲ EMP: 86
SALES (est): 43.9MM **Privately Held**
SIC: **3561** Pumps & pumping equipment

(G-4187)
PREMIER INDUSTRIES INC
5721 Dragon Way Ste 113 (45227-4518)
PHONE.................................513 271-2550
J Paul Taylor, *President*
Suzanne Gerwin, *Vice Pres*
EMP: 40 EST: 1935
SQ FT: 45,000
SALES (est): 3.4MM
SALES (corp-wide): 12.6MM **Privately Held**
SIC: **2656** 3556 Plates, paper: made from purchased material; food products machinery
PA: Taylor Company
 5721 Dragon Way Ste 117
 Cincinnati OH 45227
 513 271-2550

(G-4188)
PREMIER SOUTHERN TICKET CO INC
7911 School Rd (45249-1596)
PHONE.................................513 489-6700
Kirk Schulz, *President*
Jim Raike, *Human Resources*
▲ EMP: 38
SQ FT: 38,000
SALES (est): 3.7MM **Privately Held**
WEB: www.premiersouthern.com
SIC: **2759** Tickets: printing; tags: printing; coupons: printing
PA: Gtlp Holdings, Llc
 7911 School Rd
 Cincinnati OH 45249

(G-4189)
PRIDE CAST METALS INC
2737 Colerain Ave (45225-2263)
PHONE.................................513 541-1395
Thomas Hamm, *President*
Kenneth Bechtol, *Principal*
▲ EMP: 100
SQ FT: 150,000
SALES: 20.6MM **Privately Held**
WEB: www.pridecastmetals.com
SIC: **3365** 3366 3599 Aluminum & aluminum-based alloy castings; castings (except die): bronze; castings (except die): brass; machine shop, jobbing & repair

(G-4190)
PRIDE TOOL CO INC
10200 Wayne Ave (45215-1127)
P.O. Box 15627 (45215-0627)
PHONE.................................513 563-0070
David Draginoff, *CEO*
Sandra Draginoff, *Corp Secy*
Albert Harvey, *Vice Pres*
Mike Trovillo, *Vice Pres*
Kyle Boosveld, *CFO*
EMP: 17
SQ FT: 11,500
SALES (est): 3.7MM **Privately Held**
SIC: **3599** Machine shop, jobbing & repair

(G-4191)
PRINT CRAFT INC
8045 Colerain Ave (45239-4513)
PHONE.................................513 931-6828
Mark Schuster, *President*
Dale Schuster, *Vice Pres*
EMP: 5 EST: 1974
SQ FT: 4,400
SALES: 650K **Privately Held**
SIC: **5943** 5999 2752 Office forms & supplies; artists' supplies & materials; commercial printing, offset

(G-4192)
PRINTERS BINDERY SERVICES INC
Also Called: Printers Bindery
925 Freeman Ave (45203-1109)
PHONE.................................513 821-8039
Joyce Bowman, *President*
▲ EMP: 68
SQ FT: 80,000
SALES (est): 7.7MM **Privately Held**
WEB: www.printersbinderyohio.com
SIC: **2789** 2675 Binding only: books, pamphlets, magazines, etc.; die-cut paper & board

(G-4193)
PRINTERS EMERGENCY SERVICE LLC
2016 Elm St Side A (45202-4979)
PHONE.................................513 421-7799
Chris Burns,
EMP: 3
SQ FT: 1,500
SALES: 500K **Privately Held**
SIC: **2752** Letters, circular or form: lithographed; commercial printing, offset

(G-4194)
PRINTZONE
11974 Lebanon Rd (45241-1711)
PHONE.................................513 733-0067
B J Ariapad, *Owner*
EMP: 3
SQ FT: 1,500
SALES (est): 269.8K **Privately Held**
SIC: **2752** Offset & photolithographic printing

(G-4195)
PROAMPAC PG BORROWER LLC (PA)
12025 Tricon Rd (45246-1719)
PHONE.................................513 671-1777
Greg Tucker, *CEO*
EMP: 5
SALES (est): 316MM **Privately Held**
SIC: **2671** Paper coated or laminated for packaging

(G-4196)
PROCESSALL INC
Also Called: Mixmill
4600 N Masn Montgomery Rd (45215)
PHONE.................................513 771-2266
EMP: 10
SQ FT: 9,500
SALES (est): 1.5MM **Privately Held**
SIC: **3559** 3556 Mfg Misc Industry Mach Mfg Food Prdts Mach

(G-4197)
PROCTER & GAMBLE
1611 Northwood Dr (45237-2719)
PHONE.................................513 207-8931
Carla Cobb, *Principal*
Stephen S Hayutin, *Finance Mgr*
EMP: 3
SALES (est): 172.6K **Privately Held**
SIC: **2841** Soap & other detergents

(G-4198)
PROCTER & GAMBLE COMPANY (PA)
Also Called: P&G
1 Procter And Gamble Plz (45202-3393)
P.O. Box 599 (45201-0599)
PHONE.................................513 983-1100
David S Taylor, *Ch of Bd*
Jason J Camp, *Counsel*
Marianne Dressman, *Counsel*
John T Chevalier, *Vice Pres*
Dan Wuebbling, *Purchasing*
◆ EMP: 277 EST: 1837
SALES: 66.8B **Publicly Held**
WEB: www.pg.com
SIC: **2676** 3421 2842 2841 Towels, napkins & tissue paper products; diapers, paper (disposable): made from purchased paper; feminine hygiene paper products; razor blades & razors; specialty cleaning preparations; fabric softeners; soap: granulated, liquid, cake, flaked or chip; detergents, synthetic organic or inorganic alkaline; hair preparations, including shampoos

(G-4199)
PROCTER & GAMBLE COMPANY
6210 Center Hill Ave (45224-1708)
PHONE.................................513 983-1100
Matt Wagner, *President*
Jacob Adams, *General Mgr*
Matthew Wagner, *General Mgr*
Jodi Allen, *Vice Pres*
James Miller, *Facilities Mgr*
EMP: 150
SALES (corp-wide): 66.8B **Publicly Held**
SIC: **2844** 2676 3421 2842 Deodorants, personal; towels, napkins & tissue paper products; razor blades & razors; specialty cleaning preparations; soap: granulated, liquid, cake, flaked or chip
PA: The Procter & Gamble Company
 1 Procter And Gamble Plz
 Cincinnati OH 45202
 513 983-1100

(G-4200)
PROCTER & GAMBLE COMPANY
5280 Vine St (45217-1028)
PHONE.................................513 266-4375
Brian Schwamberger, *Engineer*
Ed Allie, *Manager*
EMP: 22
SALES (corp-wide): 66.8B **Publicly Held**
SIC: **2844** 2676 3421 2842 Deodorants, personal; towels, napkins & tissue paper products; razor blades & razors; specialty cleaning preparations; soap: granulated, liquid, cake, flaked or chip
PA: The Procter & Gamble Company
 1 Procter And Gamble Plz
 Cincinnati OH 45202
 513 983-1100

(G-4201)
PROCTER & GAMBLE COMPANY
654 Wilmer Ave Hngr 4 (45226-1860)
PHONE.................................513 871-7557
David Tobertge, *Manager*
EMP: 45
SALES (corp-wide): 66.8B **Publicly Held**
WEB: www.pg.com
SIC: **2844** 2676 3421 2842 Deodorants, personal; towels, napkins & tissue paper products; razor blades & razors; specialty cleaning preparations; soap: granulated, liquid, cake, flaked or chip
PA: The Procter & Gamble Company
 1 Procter And Gamble Plz
 Cincinnati OH 45202
 513 983-1100

(G-4202)
PROCTER & GAMBLE COMPANY
5299 Spring Grove Ave (45217-1025)
PHONE.................................513 983-1100
John E Pepper, *Ch of Bd*
Erica Linville, *Project Mgr*
Joshua Mitchell, *Purch Mgr*
Ryan Hess, *Purchasing*
Robert Higginson, *Engineer*
EMP: 49
SALES (corp-wide): 66.8B **Publicly Held**
WEB: www.pg.com
SIC: **2844** Deodorants, personal
PA: The Procter & Gamble Company
 1 Procter And Gamble Plz
 Cincinnati OH 45202
 513 983-1100

(G-4203)
PROCTER & GAMBLE COMPANY
4460 Kings Run Dr (45232)
PHONE.................................513 482-6789
Joe Kelly, *Manager*
EMP: 10
SALES (corp-wide): 66.8B **Publicly Held**
SIC: **2844** 2676 3421 2842 Deodorants, personal; towels, napkins & tissue paper products; razor blades & razors; specialty cleaning preparations; soap: granulated, liquid, cake, flaked or chip
PA: The Procter & Gamble Company
 1 Procter And Gamble Plz
 Cincinnati OH 45202
 513 983-1100

(G-4204)
PROCTER & GAMBLE COMPANY
6300 Center Hill Ave Fl 2 (45224-1795)
PHONE.................................513 634-5069
Mark Levandoski, *Engineer*
Steve McKinley, *Project Engr*
D L Miller, *Manager*
Jennifer Brenner, *Admin Asst*
EMP: 500
SALES (corp-wide): 66.8B **Publicly Held**
WEB: www.pg.com
SIC: **2844** Deodorants, personal
PA: The Procter & Gamble Company
 1 Procter And Gamble Plz
 Cincinnati OH 45202
 513 983-1100

(G-4205)
PROCTER & GAMBLE COMPANY
5348 Vine St (45217-1030)
PHONE.................................513 627-7115
Jim Blundy, *Engineer*
Joe Barbro, *Branch Mgr*
Michael Rubin, *Info Tech Mgr*
EMP: 500
SALES (corp-wide): 66.8B **Publicly Held**
WEB: www.pg.com
SIC: **2844** 2676 3421 2842 Deodorants, personal; towels, napkins & tissue paper products; razor blades & razors; specialty cleaning preparations; soap: granulated, liquid, cake, flaked or chip
PA: The Procter & Gamble Company
 1 Procter And Gamble Plz
 Cincinnati OH 45202
 513 983-1100

(G-4206)
PROCTER & GAMBLE COMPANY
2 Procter And Gamble Plz (45202-3315)
PHONE.................................513 983-1100
Sharon Shea, *Branch Mgr*
William Esterly, *Manager*
Brent Maclean, *Senior Mgr*
Vicki Wilson-Barrett, *Associate Dir*
EMP: 500
SALES (corp-wide): 66.8B **Publicly Held**
WEB: www.pg.com
SIC: **2844** Deodorants, personal; hair preparations, including shampoos; cosmetic preparations; oral preparations
PA: The Procter & Gamble Company
 1 Procter And Gamble Plz
 Cincinnati OH 45202
 513 983-1100

(G-4207)
PROCTER & GAMBLE COMPANY
5201 Spring Grove Ave (45217-1094)
PHONE.................................513 627-7779
Rich Bartonni, *Manager*
EMP: 4
SALES (corp-wide): 66.8B **Publicly Held**
WEB: www.pg.com
SIC: **2844** 2676 3421 2842 Deodorants, personal; towels, napkins & tissue paper products; razor blades & razors; specialty cleaning preparations; soap: granulated, liquid, cake, flaked or chip
PA: The Procter & Gamble Company
 1 Procter And Gamble Plz
 Cincinnati OH 45202
 513 983-1100

(G-4208)
PROCTER & GAMBLE COMPANY
6280 Center Hill Ave (45224-1708)
PHONE.................................513 945-0340
Mary McKibben, *Opers Mgr*
Sarah Dia, *Manager*
EMP: 500
SALES (corp-wide): 66.8B **Publicly Held**
WEB: www.pg.com
SIC: **2844** 2676 3421 2842 Deodorants, personal; towels, napkins & tissue paper products; razor blades & razors; specialty cleaning preparations; soap: granulated, liquid, cake, flaked or chip
PA: The Procter & Gamble Company
 1 Procter And Gamble Plz
 Cincinnati OH 45202
 513 983-1100

(G-4209)
PROCTER & GAMBLE COMPANY
5289 Vine St (45217-1027)
PHONE.................................513 242-5752
Julie Tysen, *Engineer*
Arthur Wong, *Engineer*
Tia Maurer, *Branch Mgr*

Cincinnati - Hamilton County (G-4210)   GEOGRAPHIC SECTION

EMP: 12
SALES (corp-wide): 66.8B **Publicly Held**
SIC: 2844 Deodorants, personal
PA: The Procter & Gamble Company
1 Procter And Gamble Plz
Cincinnati OH 45202
513 983-1100

(G-4210)
PROCTER & GAMBLE FAR EAST INC (HQ)
1 Procter And Gamble Plz (45202-3393)
PHONE................................513 983-1100
A G Lafley, *President*
C Daley, *Principal*
RI Antoine, *Vice Pres*
F Benvegnu, *Vice Pres*
RG Pease, *Vice Pres*
EMP: 110
SQ FT: 1,600,000
SALES (est): 117.3MM
SALES (corp-wide): 66.8B **Publicly Held**
SIC: 2842 2844 2676 Laundry cleaning preparations; fabric softeners; toilet preparations; hair preparations, including shampoos, shampoos, rinses, conditioners: hair; napkins, sanitary: made from purchased paper
PA: The Procter & Gamble Company
1 Procter And Gamble Plz
Cincinnati OH 45202
513 983-1100

(G-4211)
PROCTER & GAMBLE HAIR CARE LLC
1 Procter And Gamble Plz (45202-3393)
PHONE................................513 983-4502
David S Taylor, *Ch of Bd*
EMP: 3 EST: 2001
SALES (est): 81.8K
SALES (corp-wide): 66.8B **Publicly Held**
SIC: 2844 Shampoos, rinses, conditioners: hair
PA: The Procter & Gamble Company
1 Procter And Gamble Plz
Cincinnati OH 45202
513 983-1100

(G-4212)
PROCTER & GAMBLE MFG CO (HQ)
1 Procter And Gamble Plz (45202-3393)
P.O. Box 599 (45201-0599)
PHONE................................513 983-1100
Bob McDonald, *President*
Keith Harrison, *President*
John Jensen, *Vice Pres*
Romulo Gonzalez, *Engineer*
Michael Boyle, *Plant Engr*
▼ EMP: 15 EST: 1910
SQ FT: 1,600,000
SALES (est): 1.5B
SALES (corp-wide): 66.8B **Publicly Held**
SIC: 2841 2079 2099 2844 Soap: granulated, liquid, cake, flaked or chip; detergents, synthetic organic or inorganic alkaline; shortening & other solid edible fats; peanut butter; toilet preparations; cake mixes, prepared: from purchased flour
PA: The Procter & Gamble Company
1 Procter And Gamble Plz
Cincinnati OH 45202
513 983-1100

(G-4213)
PROCTER & GAMBLE PAPER PDTS CO (HQ)
1 Procter And Gamble Plz (45202-3393)
P.O. Box 599 (45201-0599)
PHONE................................513 983-1100
David S Taylor, *President*
Samuel Benedict, *Principal*
Richard R Deupree Jr, *Principal*
K Y Siddall, *Principal*
E G Nelson, *Vice Pres*
▼ EMP: 15
SQ FT: 1,600,000
SALES (est): 1.9B
SALES (corp-wide): 66.8B **Publicly Held**
SIC: 2676 Towels, napkins & tissue paper products
PA: The Procter & Gamble Company
1 Procter And Gamble Plz
Cincinnati OH 45202
513 983-1100

(G-4214)
PROCTER & GAMBLE PAPER PDTS CO
301 E 6th St (45202-3339)
PHONE................................513 983-2222
Linda Ambrosio, *Counsel*
Kenneth Blackburn, *Counsel*
Amy Hoekzema, *Project Mgr*
Blayne Smith, *Opers Mgr*
Mark Kostecka, *Engineer*
EMP: 25
SALES (corp-wide): 66.8B **Publicly Held**
SIC: 2676 Towels, paper: made from purchased paper
HQ: The Procter & Gamble Paper Products Company
1 Procter And Gamble Plz
Cincinnati OH 45202
513 983-1100

(G-4215)
PRODUCTIVE CARBIDES INC
10265 Spartan Dr Ste K (45215-1237)
PHONE................................513 771-7092
Lynda Wittman, *President*
Nelson Wittman, *Vice Pres*
EMP: 5 EST: 1982
SQ FT: 1,200
SALES: 200K **Privately Held**
WEB: www.productivecarbides.com
SIC: 3545 7699 Cutting tools for machine tools; knife, saw & tool sharpening & repair

(G-4216)
PROFESSIONAL AWARD SERVICE
Also Called: ID Plastech Engraving
3901 N Bend Rd (45211-4814)
PHONE................................513 389-3600
Ronald Jeremiah, *President*
EMP: 8
SQ FT: 3,818
SALES (est): 1.2MM **Privately Held**
WEB: www.awardsanddesign.com
SIC: 3914 7389 Silverware & plated ware; engraving service

(G-4217)
PROFILES IN DESIGN INC
860 Dellway St (45229-3306)
PHONE................................513 751-2212
Joe Pfaltzgraff, *President*
Gary Stacy, *Vice Pres*
Sarah Albert, *Admin Sec*
Michele Stacy, *Admin Asst*
EMP: 14
SQ FT: 20,000
SALES (est): 1.7MM **Privately Held**
WEB: www.profilesindesign.com
SIC: 2434 Vanities, bathroom: wood

(G-4218)
PROFT & GAMBLE
6280 Center Hill Ave (45224-1708)
PHONE................................513 945-0340
Debbie Schurgast, *Principal*
▲ EMP: 7
SALES (est): 1MM **Privately Held**
SIC: 2844 Shampoos, rinses, conditioners: hair

(G-4219)
PROVINCE OF ST JOHN THE BAPTIS
Also Called: St Anthony Messenger Press
28 W Liberty St (45202-6442)
PHONE................................513 241-5615
Jeremy Harrington, *Principal*
John Feister, *CIO*
EMP: 100
SQ FT: 30,514
SALES (corp-wide): 12MM **Privately Held**
WEB: www.rogerbacon.org
SIC: 2721 5942 7812 2752 Magazines: publishing only, not printed on site; book stores; motion picture & video production; commercial printing, lithographic; miscellaneous publishing; book publishing

PA: The Procter & Gamble Company
1 Procter And Gamble Plz
Cincinnati OH 45202
513 983-1100

(G-4220)
PSA CONSULTING INC
Also Called: Cincinnati Book Publischer
19 Garfield Pl Ste 211 (45202-4309)
PHONE................................513 382-4315
Anthony Braunsfel, *President*
EMP: 4
SALES: 250K **Privately Held**
SIC: 2741 Miscellaneous publishing

(G-4221)
PTC INC
625 Eden Park Dr Ste 860 (45202-6033)
PHONE................................513 791-0330
EMP: 15
SALES (corp-wide): 1.2B **Publicly Held**
SIC: 7372 Whol Engineering Software
PA: Ptc Inc.
140 Kendrick St Ste C120
Needham MA 02210
781 370-5000

(G-4222)
PURACERA 3 LLC
Also Called: European Wax Center
7466 Beechmont Ave # 409 (45255-4106)
PHONE................................513 231-7555
Dia M Rose,
EMP: 12
SALES (est): 611.6K **Privately Held**
SIC: 3952 Wax, artists'

(G-4223)
Q C A INC
2832 Spring Grove Ave (45225-2220)
PHONE................................513 681-8400
James Bosken, *President*
Andrea Winterhalter, *Vice Pres*
Amber Hines, *Sls & Mktg Exec*
EMP: 11
SQ FT: 35,000
SALES: 1MM **Privately Held**
WEB: www.go-qca.com
SIC: 3652 Master records or tapes, preparation of; magnetic tape (audio): prerecorded; compact laser discs, prerecorded

(G-4224)
QC SOFTWARE LLC
11800 Conrey Rd Ste 150 (45249-1081)
PHONE................................513 469-1424
Jerry List, *Vice Pres*
EMP: 6
SQ FT: 2,900
SALES (est): 939.3K **Privately Held**
WEB: www.qcsoftware.com
SIC: 7371 7372 Computer software development; prepackaged software

(G-4225)
QUALITY CONTROLS INC
3411 Church St (45244-3409)
PHONE................................513 272-3900
Thomas M Pulskamp, *President*
Annette Pulskamp, *Admin Sec*
EMP: 11
SQ FT: 15,000
SALES: 2.1MM **Privately Held**
WEB: www.qualitycontrolsinc.com
SIC: 3625 3829 Motor control accessories, including overload relays; measuring & controlling devices

(G-4226)
QUALITY MECHANICALS INC
1225 Streng St (45223-2642)
PHONE................................513 559-0998
Richard Doll, *President*
Denise Albright, *Treasurer*
Shad Hankins, *Manager*
EMP: 35
SQ FT: 4,000
SALES (est): 7.6MM **Privately Held**
SIC: 3498 Fabricated pipe & fittings

(G-4227)
QUALITY METAL TREATING COMPANY
2980 Spring Grove Ave (45225-2146)
PHONE................................931 432-7467

PA: The Province Of St John Baptist Order Friars Minor
1615 Vine St
Cincinnati OH 45202
513 721-4700

EMP: 3
SALES (est): 155K **Privately Held**
SIC: 3398 Metal heat treating

(G-4228)
QUALITY MFG COMPANY INC
4323 Spring Grove Ave (45223-1834)
PHONE................................513 921-4500
Edward J Bemerer, *President*
Paul A Kapper, *Corp Secy*
Richard Lipps, *Vice Pres*
EMP: 8 EST: 1975
SQ FT: 16,000
SALES (est): 1.1MM **Privately Held**
SIC: 3599 Machine shop, jobbing & repair

(G-4229)
QUALITY SPT & SILK SCREEN SP
Also Called: Quality Spt Silk Screen & EMB
9217 Reading Rd (45215-3415)
PHONE................................513 769-8300
Dean J Haralamos, *Owner*
EMP: 3
SALES (est): 260.1K **Privately Held**
WEB: www.marylandsportsapparel.com
SIC: 5941 5699 2396 Sporting goods & bicycle shops; sports apparel; screen printing on fabric articles

(G-4230)
QUANTEM FBO SERVICES
1077 Celestial St (45202-1637)
PHONE................................603 647-6763
EMP: 5 EST: 2013
SALES (est): 26.9K **Privately Held**
SIC: 3572 Computer storage devices

(G-4231)
QUARRIES LLC
12157 Brisben Pl (45249-8103)
PHONE................................513 306-2924
Metin Elmas, *Principal*
EMP: 3
SALES (est): 130.1K **Privately Held**
SIC: 1422 Crushed & broken limestone

(G-4232)
QUARTER BISTRO
6904 Wooster Pike (45227-4427)
PHONE................................513 271-5400
Adam Kleshinski, *Principal*
EMP: 3
SALES (est): 280.7K **Privately Held**
SIC: 3131 Quarters

(G-4233)
QUEBECOR WORLD JOHNSON HARDIN
3600 Red Bank Rd (45227-4142)
PHONE................................614 326-0299
Chuck Miotke, *President*
James H Bossart, *Senior VP*
Jeffery R Herman, *VP Finance*
EMP: 900 EST: 1902
SQ FT: 200,000
SALES: 100MM **Privately Held**
SIC: 2759 2752 2732 Magazines: printing; catalogs: printing; commercial printing, offset; books: printing only

(G-4234)
QUEEN CITY AWNING & TENT CO
7225 E Kemper Rd (45249-1030)
PHONE................................513 530-9660
Peter Weingartner, *President*
Chris Herrmann, *Vice Pres*
James Weingartner, *Vice Pres*
Bradley Curtis, *VP Opers*
Robert P Weingartner Sr, *CFO*
EMP: 35 EST: 1877
SQ FT: 27,000
SALES (est): 4.1MM **Privately Held**
WEB: www.queencityawning.com
SIC: 2394 5712 Awnings, fabric: made from purchased materials; outdoor & garden furniture

(G-4235)
QUEEN CITY CARPETS LLC
6539 Harrison Ave 304 (45247-7822)
PHONE................................513 823-8238
Terry Hensley, *Vice Pres*
EMP: 10 EST: 2012

GEOGRAPHIC SECTION

Cincinnati - Hamilton County (G-4265)

SALES (est): 486.8K **Privately Held**
SIC: 2393 Cushions, except spring & carpet: purchased materials

(G-4236)
QUEEN CITY FOAM INC
1000 Redna Ter (45215-1187)
PHONE..................................513 741-7722
Herbert Bevelhymer, *President*
EMP: 5
SALES (est): 407K **Privately Held**
SIC: 2821 Polystyrene resins

(G-4237)
QUEEN CITY FORGING COMPANY
Also Called: Qcforge.com
235b Tennyson St (45226-1555)
PHONE..................................513 321-2003
Howard R Mayer, *Ch of Bd*
George C Allen, *Principal*
John Mayer, *Vice Pres*
Ronnie Secen, *Vice Pres*
Andy Spires, *Prdtn Mgr*
▲ **EMP:** 16 **EST:** 1881
SQ FT: 36,000
SALES (est): 4.2MM **Privately Held**
WEB: www.qcforge.com
SIC: 3462 Iron & steel forgings

(G-4238)
QUEEN CITY OFFICE MACHINE
3984 Trevor Ave (45211-3407)
PHONE..................................513 251-7200
Ronald Swing, *Principal*
EMP: 10
SQ FT: 6,000
SALES (est): 2MM **Privately Held**
WEB: www.queencityoffice.com
SIC: 5112 7629 2759 Office supplies; business machine repair, electric; laser printing

(G-4239)
QUEEN CITY PALLETS INC
7744 Reinhold Dr (45237-2806)
PHONE..................................513 821-6700
Mike Unthank, *CEO*
Garry Unthank, *President*
EMP: 40
SQ FT: 30,000
SALES: 2.8MM **Privately Held**
SIC: 2448 Pallets, wood

(G-4240)
QUEEN CITY REPROGRAPHICS
2863 E Sharon Rd (45241-1923)
PHONE..................................513 326-2300
Joe Herbst, *CEO*
Chris Chalifoux, *President*
EMP: 105
SQ FT: 30,000
SALES (est): 16.8MM
SALES (corp-wide): 400.7MM **Publicly Held**
WEB: www.ohioblue.com
SIC: 5049 7334 7335 2752 Drafting supplies; blueprinting service; commercial photography; lithographing on metal
PA: Arc Document Solutions, Inc.
  12657 Alcosta Blvd # 200
  San Ramon CA 94583
  925 949-5100

(G-4241)
QUEEN CITY SAUSAGE & PROVISION
1136 Straight St (45214-1736)
PHONE..................................513 541-5581
Elmer J Hensler, *President*
Mark Rodgers, *Plant Mgr*
Sandy Witt, *Sales Staff*
Mark Balasa, *Marketing Mgr*
Pat Miller, *Administration*
EMP: 43
SQ FT: 17,000
SALES (est): 7.6MM **Privately Held**
WEB: www.queencitysausage.com
SIC: 2013 Sausages from purchased meat

(G-4242)
R A HELLER COMPANY
10530 Chester Rd (45215-1262)
PHONE..................................513 771-6100
Steve Heller, *President*
Laura Heller, *Admin Sec*
EMP: 11 **EST:** 1946
SQ FT: 20,000
SALES (est): 1.5MM **Privately Held**
WEB: www.raheller.com
SIC: 3471 3599 3545 Chromium plating of metals or formed products; machine shop, jobbing & repair; cutting tools for machine tools

(G-4243)
R E SMITH INC
10330 Chester Rd (45215-1225)
PHONE..................................513 771-0645
Kenneth J Koncelik, *President*
EMP: 10
SQ FT: 2,000
SALES (est): 1MM **Privately Held**
SIC: 3621 Frequency converters (electric generators)

(G-4244)
R L Y INC
Also Called: Yeager Sports
5874 Cheviot Rd (45247-6243)
PHONE..................................513 385-1950
Richard Yeager, *President*
EMP: 4
SQ FT: 3,000
SALES: 425K **Privately Held**
SIC: 3949 Sporting & athletic goods

(G-4245)
R VANDEWALLE INC
Also Called: Van Engineering Co
4030 Delhi Ave (45204-1276)
PHONE..................................513 921-2657
Robert Vandewalle, *President*
Richard Vandewalle, *Vice Pres*
EMP: 8 **EST:** 1942
SQ FT: 7,000
SALES: 400K **Privately Held**
SIC: 3599 Machine shop, jobbing & repair

(G-4246)
RAD TECHNOLOGIES INCORPORATED
Also Called: Precision Temp
11 Sunnybrook Dr (45237-2103)
PHONE..................................513 641-0523
Robert Muhlhauser, *CEO*
Gerry Wolters, *Principal*
Christopher Volz, *Safety Mgr*
Fred Rothzeid, *CFO*
Linda White, *Human Res Mgr*
▲ **EMP:** 12
SALES (est): 2.1MM **Privately Held**
SIC: 3639 Hot water heaters, household

(G-4247)
RANDALL FOODS INC (PA)
312 Walnut St Ste 1600 (45202-4038)
PHONE..................................513 793-6525
Meredith Keating, *President*
Kathy Pike, *Opers Mgr*
Scott Keating, *Treasurer*
EMP: 1 **EST:** 1890
SQ FT: 1,800
SALES (est): 2.8MM **Privately Held**
WEB: www.randallbeans.com
SIC: 2032 Beans, without meat: packaged in cans, jars, etc.

(G-4248)
RANDY GRAY
Also Called: Brat Printing
4142 Airport Rd Fl 1 (45226-1627)
PHONE..................................513 533-3200
Randy Gray, *Owner*
Trent Gray, *Manager*
EMP: 6
SQ FT: 9,000
SALES (est): 260.5K **Privately Held**
SIC: 3552 2395 2396 Textile machinery; emblems, embroidered; automotive & apparel trimmings

(G-4249)
RATECH
11110 Adwood Dr (45240-3234)
PHONE..................................513 742-2711
John Musuraca, *Owner*
▲ **EMP:** 3
SALES (est): 220K **Privately Held**
WEB: www.ratechmfg.com
SIC: 3559 Automotive maintenance equipment

(G-4250)
RBI SOLAR INC (DH)
5513 Vine St (45217-1000)
PHONE..................................513 242-2051
Rich Reilly, *President*
Jessica Abrego, *Project Mgr*
Adam Brescia, *Sales Engr*
Jodi Bielinski, *Sales Staff*
Larz Palmer, *Technical Staff*
◆ **EMP:** 1
SALES (est): 15.1MM
SALES (corp-wide): 1B **Publicly Held**
SIC: 3433 Solar heaters & collectors
HQ: Rough Brothers Holding Co., Inc
  3556 Lake Shore Rd # 100
  Buffalo NY 14219
  716 826-6500

(G-4251)
RC LONESTAR INC
6381 River Rd (45233)
PHONE..................................513 467-0430
Michael Rieger, *Branch Mgr*
EMP: 3
SALES (corp-wide): 287.7MM **Privately Held**
SIC: 3241 Portland cement
HQ: Rc Lonestar Inc.
  100 Brodhead Rd Ste 230
  Bethlehem PA 18017

(G-4252)
RCL PUBLISHING GROUP LLC
8805 Governors Hill Dr # 400 (45249-3314)
PHONE..................................972 390-6400
Rcl Benziger, *Principal*
▼ **EMP:** 7
SALES (est): 866.8K **Privately Held**
SIC: 2741 Miscellaneous publishing

(G-4253)
RECARO CHILD SAFETY LLC
4921 Para Dr (45237-5011)
PHONE..................................248 904-1570
Kai Weisskopf,
Bill Pierchala,
▲ **EMP:** 38
SQ FT: 40,000
SALES (est): 9.3MM **Privately Held**
SIC: 3944 5099 Child restraint seats, automotive; child restraint seats, automotive

(G-4254)
RECEET INC
4055 Executive Park Dr # 140 (45241-4029)
PHONE..................................513 769-1900
Omar Barkawi, *CEO*
EMP: 5
SALES: 50K **Privately Held**
SIC: 7372 Application computer software

(G-4255)
RECOV BEVERAGES LLC
331 W 4th St Apt 2 (45202-2733)
PHONE..................................513 518-9794
Patrick McGinnis, *Principal*
EMP: 3
SALES (est): 68.6K **Privately Held**
SIC: 2086 Fruit drinks (less than 100% juice): packaged in cans, etc.

(G-4256)
RECTO MOLDED PRODUCTS INC
4425 Appleton St (45209-1290)
PHONE..................................513 871-5544
Per Flem, *President*
EMP: 65
SQ FT: 65,000
SALES: 12.5MM **Privately Held**
WEB: www.rectomolded.com
SIC: 3089 3083 Injection molding of plastics; laminated plastics plate & sheet

(G-4257)
REGISTERED IMAGES INC
Also Called: Patron Graphics
6545 Wiehe Rd (45237-4217)
PHONE..................................859 781-9200
Ronald Hager, *President*
EMP: 3
SQ FT: 7,500

SALES (est): 402K **Privately Held**
WEB: www.aicinsulate.com
SIC: 2796 2791 Color separations for printing; typesetting

(G-4258)
RELADYNE INC (PA)
8280 Montgomery Rd # 101 (45236-6101)
PHONE..................................513 489-6000
Larry J Stoddard, *President*
Paul Helton, *CFO*
Krista Somershoe, *Manager*
Jeff Hart, *Security Dir*
EMP: 74
SALES (est): 389.3MM **Privately Held**
SIC: 2992 Lubricating oils & greases

(G-4259)
RENEE BARRETT WINERY
8129 Austin Ridge Dr (45247-1213)
PHONE..................................513 471-1340
Carl B Best, *Principal*
EMP: 4
SALES (est): 162.1K **Privately Held**
SIC: 2084 Wines

(G-4260)
RESOLUTE FP US INC
Also Called: Recycling Div
5535 Vine St (45217-1003)
PHONE..................................513 242-3671
Eric Vandervert, *Branch Mgr*
EMP: 434
SALES (corp-wide): 3.5B **Privately Held**
WEB: www.bowater.com
SIC: 2621 Paper mills
HQ: Resolute Fp Us Inc.
  5300 Cureton Ferry Rd
  Catawba SC 29704
  803 981-8000

(G-4261)
RESOURCE GRAPHICS
2230 Gilbert Ave (45206-2531)
PHONE..................................513 205-2686
Gregory R Cozart, *Owner*
EMP: 3
SALES: 250K **Privately Held**
SIC: 3555 Printing trades machinery

(G-4262)
REULAND ELECTRIC CO
9620 Colerain Ave Ste 22 (45251-2018)
PHONE..................................513 825-7314
Bill Kramer, *Branch Mgr*
Jeanie Brown, *Manager*
EMP: 4
SALES (corp-wide): 42.4MM **Privately Held**
WEB: www.reuland.com
SIC: 3621 Motors, electric
PA: Reuland Electric Co.
  17969 Railroad St
  City Of Industry CA 91748
  626 964-6411

(G-4263)
REYNOLDS ENGINEERED PDTS LLC
4242 Airport Rd Ste 103 (45226-1621)
PHONE..................................513 751-4400
Thomas Reynolds, *CEO*
EMP: 2 **EST:** 2017
SALES: 7MM **Privately Held**
SIC: 3714 Motor vehicle engines & parts

(G-4264)
RHI US LTD (DH)
3956 Virginia Ave (45227-3412)
PHONE..................................513 753-1254
Phil Poulin, *President*
Hans Joerg Junger, *Vice Pres*
Friedrich Schweighofer, *Vice Pres*
Julie Greger, *Purch Agent*
Carlos Ramirez, *Manager*
▲ **EMP:** 12
SALES (est): 5.7MM
SALES (corp-wide): 2.2B **Privately Held**
SIC: 3823 Refractometers, industrial process type

(G-4265)
RIBS KING INC
9406 Main St (45242-7616)
PHONE..................................513 791-1942
Thomas Gregory, *President*

(PA)=Parent Co (HQ)=Headquarters (DH)=Div Headquarters
✪ = New Business established in last 2 years

Cincinnati - Hamilton County (G-4266)

Evan Andrews, *Vice Pres*
Dean Gregory, *Vice Pres*
Victoria Siegel, *Vice Pres*
EMP: 9
SQ FT: 21,000
SALES: 7MM **Privately Held**
SIC: 2035 Seasonings & sauces, except tomato & dry

(G-4266)
RICHARD B LINNEMAN
Also Called: Sterling Industries
5642 Victory Dr (45233-4657)
PHONE................................513 922-5537
Richard B Linneman, *Owner*
EMP: 4 **EST:** 1961
SQ FT: 6,300
SALES (est): 506.6K **Privately Held**
SIC: 3556 2541 2542 Food products machinery; store fixtures, wood; fixtures, store: except wood

(G-4267)
RICHARD BENHASE & ASSOCIATES
11741 Chesterdale Rd (45246-3405)
PHONE................................513 772-1896
Richard Benhase, *President*
Linda Benhase, *Vice Pres*
EMP: 11
SQ FT: 15,000
SALES: 800K **Privately Held**
SIC: 2521 2511 2434 Cabinets, office: wood; wood household furniture; wood kitchen cabinets

(G-4268)
RICHARDS INDUSTRIES INC
Also Called: Marwin Ball Valves Div
3170 Wasson Rd (45209-2329)
PHONE................................513 533-5600
Bruce Broxterman, *President*
James R Bridgeland, *Principal*
Michelle Davis, *COO*
William Metz, *Vice Pres*
Bob Linville, *Plant Mgr*
▲ **EMP:** 150 **EST:** 1961
SQ FT: 150,000
SALES (est): 51.4MM **Privately Held**
WEB: www.richardsind.com
SIC: 3491 3494 3823 Industrial valves; pipe fittings; industrial instrmnts msrmnt display/control process variable

(G-4269)
RICKING PAPER AND SPECIALTY CO
525 Northland Blvd (45240-3233)
PHONE................................513 825-3551
Carl Ricking Jr, *President*
Preston M Simpson, *Principal*
Carla Droll, *Vice Pres*
Julie Ricking, *Vice Pres*
Joyce Ricking, *Treasurer*
EMP: 50
SQ FT: 84,000
SALES (est): 13.4MM **Privately Held**
WEB: www.ricking.com
SIC: 5141 2656 5113 Groceries, general line; cups, paper: made from purchased material; bags, paper & disposable plastic

(G-4270)
RINA SYSTEMS LLC
8180 Corp Pk Dr Ste 140 (45242)
PHONE................................513 469-7462
Leo G Samasqui, *President*
Meg Dunn, *Opers Mgr*
Meg Petric, *Opers Mgr*
Terry Carr, *Info Tech Mgr*
EMP: 6
SALES (est): 97.7K **Privately Held**
SIC: 7372 Prepackaged software

(G-4271)
RIVER CITY BODY COMPANY
2660 Commerce Blvd (45241-1552)
PHONE................................513 772-9317
John Mc Henry, *President*
Mark Zembrodt, *General Mgr*
EMP: 11
SQ FT: 10,000
SALES (est): 2.4MM **Privately Held**
WEB: www.rivercitybody.com
SIC: 3537 5531 Trucks, tractors, loaders, carriers & similar equipment; truck equipment & parts

(G-4272)
RIVER CORP
32 W Mitchell Ave (45217-1526)
P.O. Box 20206 (45220-0206)
PHONE................................513 641-3355
Edgar Ragouzis, *President*
EMP: 3
SQ FT: 3,500
SALES (est): 296.4K **Privately Held**
SIC: 2731 2791 Books: publishing only; pamphlets: publishing only, not printed on site; typesetting

(G-4273)
RIVERSIDE CNSTR SVCS INC
218 W Mcmicken Ave (45214-2314)
PHONE................................513 723-0900
Robert S Krejci, *President*
Timothy L Pierce, *Vice Pres*
EMP: 32
SQ FT: 21,000
SALES (est): 5.2MM **Privately Held**
WEB: www.riversidearchitectural.com
SIC: 2431 1751 2434 Millwork; carpentry work; wood kitchen cabinets

(G-4274)
RM ADVISORY GROUP INC
5300 Vine St (45217-1030)
PHONE................................513 242-2100
Robert Moskowitz, *President*
Ira Moskowitz, *Principal*
Mark Moskowitz, *Vice Pres*
Linda Curtis, *VP Human Res*
EMP: 35 **EST:** 1901
SQ FT: 70,000
SALES (est): 13.1MM **Privately Held**
WEB: www.moskowitzbros.com
SIC: 5093 3341 Ferrous metal scrap & waste; nonferrous metals scrap; secondary nonferrous metals

(G-4275)
RME MACHINING CO
2900 Spring Grove Ave (45225-2115)
PHONE................................513 541-3328
Robert Enderle, *President*
EMP: 5
SQ FT: 10,000
SALES (est): 480K **Privately Held**
SIC: 3599 3544 Machine shop, jobbing & repair; special dies & tools

(G-4276)
ROBBINS INC (PA)
Also Called: Robbins Sports Surfaces
4777 Eastern Ave (45226-2339)
PHONE................................513 871-8988
Dave Fulton, *CEO*
James H Stoehr III, *Chairman*
Mike Niese, *Vice Pres*
Beth Smith, *Vice Pres*
Jonathan Turner, *Vice Pres*
◆ **EMP:** 35 **EST:** 1970
SQ FT: 3,000
SALES (est): 71.2MM **Privately Held**
WEB: www.robbinsfloor.com
SIC: 2426 Flooring, hardwood

(G-4277)
ROBERT ESTERMAN
Also Called: Esterman Printing Services
2929 Spring Grove Ave # 100 (45225-2157)
PHONE................................513 541-3311
Robert Esterman, *Owner*
EMP: 3
SQ FT: 5,000
SALES (est): 288.8K **Privately Held**
WEB: www.estermanprinting.com
SIC: 2759 2791 2789 Commercial printing; typesetting; bookbinding & related work

(G-4278)
ROBERT J & CINDY K HARTZ
8734 Woodview Dr (45231-5031)
P.O. Box 62046 (45262-0046)
PHONE................................513 521-6215
Robert Hartz, *Owner*
EMP: 3
SALES: 200K **Privately Held**
SIC: 3599 Water leak detectors

(G-4279)
ROBERT ROTHSCHILD FARM LLC
Also Called: Robert Rothschild Market Cafe
3015 E Kemper Rd (45241-1514)
P.O. Box 767, Urbana (43078-0767)
PHONE................................937 653-7397
Andy Beister, *President*
Heather Mader, *Human Res Mgr*
▲ **EMP:** 18
SQ FT: 45,000
SALES (est): 10.8MM
SALES (corp-wide): 17.8MM **Privately Held**
SIC: 0171 2035 2033 2032 Raspberry farm; pickles, sauces & salad dressings; canned fruits & specialties; canned specialties
HQ: Cincinnati Preserving Company
3015 E Kemper Rd
Cincinnati OH 45241
513 771-2000

(G-4280)
ROCKDALE SYSTEMS LLC
6 Rowley Ct (45246-3851)
PHONE................................513 379-3577
Ganesh Balasubramanian, *CEO*
Adrian Thompson, *Principal*
EMP: 3
SALES (est): 234.4K **Privately Held**
SIC: 3841 Veterinarians' instruments & apparatus

(G-4281)
ROLCON INC
510 Station Ave (45215-5439)
PHONE................................513 821-7259
Don Mileham, *Administration*
EMP: 10
SALES (corp-wide): 2.9MM **Privately Held**
WEB: www.rolconvenix.com
SIC: 3535 3561 Conveyors & conveying equipment; cylinders, pump
PA: Rolcon, Inc
134 Carthage Ave
Cincinnati OH 45215
513 821-7259

(G-4282)
ROTEX GLOBAL LLC
Also Called: Gundlach
1230 Knowlton St (45223-1800)
P.O. Box 630317 (45263-0317)
PHONE................................513 541-1236
William J Herkamp, *President*
Gary Armstrong, *Vice Pres*
Bob Dieckman, *Vice Pres*
Mark J Moore, *Vice Pres*
Mark Moore, *Vice Pres*
◆ **EMP:** 165 **EST:** 1844
SQ FT: 150,000
SALES (est): 70.9MM **Publicly Held**
SIC: 3569 3826 Sifting & screening machines; particle size analyzers
PA: Hillenbrand, Inc.
1 Batesvile Blvd
Batesville IN 47006

(G-4283)
ROUGH BROTHERS MFG INC
5513 Vine St Ste 1 (45217-1022)
PHONE................................513 242-0310
Richard Reilly, *President*
James Parris, *General Mgr*
Nick Workman, *Superintendent*
Kevin Caron, *Vice Pres*
James Gross, *Safety Mgr*
◆ **EMP:** 90
SQ FT: 100,000
SALES (est): 96.7MM
SALES (corp-wide): 1B **Publicly Held**
SIC: 1542 3448 Greenhouse construction; greenhouses: prefabricated metal
HQ: Rough Brothers Holding Co., Inc
3556 Lake Shore Rd # 100
Buffalo NY 14219
716 826-6500

(G-4284)
ROYAL SPECIALTY PRODUCTS INC
4114 Montgomery Rd (45212-3651)
PHONE................................513 841-1267
Herbert C Brandenburg Jr, *President*
EMP: 5 **EST:** 1999
SALES (est): 458.5K **Privately Held**
SIC: 3577 Printers & plotters

(G-4285)
RPI COLOR SERVICE INC
Also Called: RPI Graphic Data Solutions
1950 Radcliff Dr (45204-1823)
PHONE................................513 471-4040
Patricia A Raker, *President*
Denise L Rellar, *Exec VP*
Denise Rellar, *Exec VP*
Karen E Rellar, *Exec VP*
William Rellar, *Vice Pres*
EMP: 70 **EST:** 1980
SQ FT: 65,000
SALES: 10MM **Privately Held**
SIC: 2752 Commercial printing, lithographic

(G-4286)
RS PRO SALES LLC
1512 Eastern Ave (45202)
PHONE................................513 699-5329
Taft Stricklind, *Mng Member*
Dee Jones, *Manager*
EMP: 5
SALES (est): 660.5K **Privately Held**
SIC: 3651 3585 Household audio & video equipment; air conditioning equipment, complete

(G-4287)
RUDD EQUIPMENT COMPANY INC
11807 Enterprise Dr (45241-1511)
PHONE................................513 321-7833
EMP: 22
SALES (corp-wide): 50.9MM **Privately Held**
SIC: 3462 Construction or mining equipment forgings, ferrous
PA: Rudd Equipment Company, Inc.
4344 Poplar Level Rd
Louisville KY 40213
502 456-4050

(G-4288)
RUMPKE TRANSPORTATION CO LLC (HQ)
10795 Hughes Rd (45251-4598)
PHONE................................513 851-0122
William J Rumpke, *President*
Phil Wehrman, *CFO*
EMP: 10 **EST:** 1999
SQ FT: 10,000
SALES (est): 106.3MM **Privately Held**
SIC: 3561 5084 7537 4953 Pumps & pumping equipment; hydraulic systems equipment & supplies; automotive transmission repair shops; refuse systems

(G-4289)
RUMPKE TRANSPORTATION CO LLC
Also Called: Rumpke Container Service
553 Vine St (45202-3105)
PHONE................................513 242-4600
Jeff Rumpke, *Manager*
EMP: 150 **Privately Held**
SIC: 4953 3341 3231 2611 Recycling, waste materials; secondary nonferrous metals; products of purchased glass; pulp mills
HQ: Rumpke Transportation Company, Llc
10795 Hughes Rd
Cincinnati OH 45251
513 851-0122

(G-4290)
RUSSMENTS INC
3714 Church St (45244-3005)
PHONE................................513 602-5035
Russell Mc Murry, *President*
Kyndle Mc Murry, *Vice Pres*
Shirley Mc Murry, *Treasurer*
EMP: 1

▲ = Import ▼ = Export
◆ = Import/Export

GEOGRAPHIC SECTION

Cincinnati - Hamilton County (G-4318)

SALES: 2MM **Privately Held**
SIC: **5084** 3491 Controlling instruments & accessories; industrial valves

(G-4291)
RUTHMAN PUMP AND ENGINEERING (PA)
Also Called: Fulflo Specialties Company
1212 Streng St (45223-2643)
PHONE.................................513 559-1901
Thomas R Ruthman, *President*
Tom Day, *Sales Associate*
▲ EMP: 5
SQ FT: 45,000
SALES (est): 45.4MM **Privately Held**
WEB: www.ruthmannpumpen.de
SIC: **3561** 3492 Industrial pumps & parts; control valves, fluid power: hydraulic & pneumatic

(G-4292)
RX FRAMES N LENSES LTD
4270 Boomer Rd (45247-7912)
PHONE.................................513 557-2970
Daniel Louallen, *Principal*
EMP: 3
SALES (est): 291.7K **Privately Held**
SIC: **3851** Ophthalmic goods

(G-4293)
RYKRISP LLC
4342 Centennial Dr Apt 33 (45227-2579)
PHONE.................................843 338-0750
William Leavitt, *CEO*
Robert Holden, *Principal*
Edward Slanga, *Principal*
EMP: 4
SALES: 2MM **Privately Held**
SIC: **2052** Cookies & crackers

(G-4294)
S C JOHNSON & SON INC
36 E 7th St Ste 2450 (45202-4400)
PHONE.................................513 665-3600
Jeff Johnson, *Manager*
EMP: 20
SALES (corp-wide): 3.6B **Privately Held**
WEB: www.scjohnson.com
SIC: **2842** Floor waxes; furniture polish or wax; stain removers; disinfectants, household or industrial plant
PA: S. C. Johnson & Son, Inc.
   1525 Howe St
   Racine WI 53403
   262 260-2000

(G-4295)
S E ANNING COMPANY
822 Delta Ave Ste 2 (45226-1297)
PHONE.................................513 702-4417
George Koesterman, *President*
Steven A Koesterman, *Vice Pres*
EMP: 4
SALES (est): 450.2K **Privately Held**
SIC: **8743** 3498 Sales promotion; tube fabricating (contract bending & shaping)

(G-4296)
S J ROTH ENTERPRISES INC
Also Called: Roth Ready Mix Concrete Co
900 Kieley Pl (45217-1153)
PHONE.................................513 242-8400
Steven Roth, *President*
Darlene Roy, *Executive*
Frank J Roth, *Admin Sec*
EMP: 40
SQ FT: 1,200
SALES (est): 6.3MM **Privately Held**
SIC: **3273** Ready-mixed concrete

(G-4297)
S L C SOFTWARE SERVICES
1958 Anderson Ferry Rd (45238-3324)
PHONE.................................513 922-4303
Sandra L Gerhardt, *Owner*
EMP: 3
SQ FT: 1,000
SALES: 100K **Privately Held**
WEB: www.slcsoftware.com
SIC: **7379** 7372 5063 Computer related consulting services; prepackaged software; electrical apparatus & equipment

(G-4298)
S T CUSTOM SIGNS
9493 Reading Rd (45215-3520)
PHONE.................................513 733-4227
Thomas F Harsch, *Partner*
Sandra L Pierce-Harsch, *Partner*
EMP: 3
SALES (est): 180.5K **Privately Held**
SIC: **8999** 3993 Communication services; signs & advertising specialties

(G-4299)
SAKRETE INC (PA)
5155 Fischer Ave (45217-1157)
PHONE.................................513 242-3644
John G Avril, *Ch of Bd*
J Craig Avril, *President*
EMP: 20 EST: 1936
SQ FT: 35,000
SALES (est): 2.4MM **Privately Held**
SIC: **3273** 6794 Ready-mixed concrete; patent buying, licensing, leasing

(G-4300)
SATURDAY KNIGHT LTD (PA)
4330 Winton Rd (45232-1827)
PHONE.................................513 641-1400
Frank Kling, *Ch of Bd*
Jim Lewis, *President*
Julie Copenhaver, *General Mgr*
Carol Ferguson, *General Mgr*
Dianne Weidman, *Vice Pres*
◆ EMP: 52
SQ FT: 450,000
SALES (est): 13.1MM **Privately Held**
WEB: www.skltd.com
SIC: **2392** Towels, fabric & nonwoven: made from purchased materials; shower curtains: made from purchased materials

(G-4301)
SAUERWEIN WELDING
605 Wayne Park Dr (45215-2848)
P.O. Box 15033 (45215-0033)
PHONE.................................513 563-2979
Donald Sauerwein, *President*
EMP: 7
SQ FT: 5,000
SALES (est): 430K **Privately Held**
SIC: **7692** Welding repair

(G-4302)
SAWBROOK STEEL CASTINGS CO (PA)
Also Called: Cushman Foundry Div
425 Shepherd Ave (45215-3114)
P.O. Box 15527 (45215-0527)
PHONE.................................513 554-1700
John C Beyersdorfer Sr, *Ch of Bd*
Michael Beyersdorfer, *President*
John C Beyersdorfer Jr, *Vice Pres*
Don Thatcher, *Engineer*
Hugh Kelly, *Controller*
▲ EMP: 90 EST: 1923
SQ FT: 523,000
SALES (est): 16.3MM **Privately Held**
WEB: www.sawbrooksteel.com
SIC: **3365** 3325 3369 3341 Aluminum & aluminum-based alloy castings; alloy steel castings, except investment; nonferrous foundries; secondary nonferrous metals

(G-4303)
SCALLYWAG TAG
5055 Glencrossing Way (45238-3362)
PHONE.................................513 922-4999
James Leopold, *Owner*
EMP: 6 EST: 2008
SALES (est): 449.5K **Privately Held**
SIC: **3845** Laser systems & equipment, medical

(G-4304)
SCHAAF CO INC
2440 Spring Grove Ave (45214-1755)
PHONE.................................513 241-7044
Walter A Smith, *President*
Chuck Smith, *Vice Pres*
Barb Meeks, *Admin Sec*
EMP: 9
SQ FT: 6,500
SALES (est): 1.2MM **Privately Held**
WEB: www.schaaf.com
SIC: **2394** Awnings, fabric: made from purchased materials

(G-4305)
SCHAERER MEDICAL USA INC
675 Wilmer Ave (45226-1802)
P.O. Box 645110 (45264-0301)
PHONE.................................513 561-2241
Michal Palazzola, *CEO*
Mark D Budde, *CEO*
Hans Rudolf Saegesser, *Ch of Bd*
Ted Melton, *Principal*
Jan Osborne, *Principal*
▲ EMP: 11 EST: 1965
SQ FT: 100,000
SALES (est): 2.3MM **Privately Held**
WEB: www.schaerermayfieldusa.com
SIC: **5999** 3842 Medical apparatus & supplies; surgical appliances & supplies

(G-4306)
SCHENZ THEATRICAL SUPPLY INC
2959 Colerain Ave (45225-2103)
PHONE.................................513 542-6100
John J Schenz, *President*
EMP: 13
SQ FT: 15,000
SALES: 350K **Privately Held**
WEB: www.schenz.com
SIC: **2389** 5999 7922 Theatrical costumes; theatrical equipment & supplies; equipment rental, theatrical

(G-4307)
SCHOMAKER NATURAL RESOURCE
2741 Blue Rock Rd (45239-6332)
PHONE.................................513 741-1370
Joseph E Schomaker, *Owner*
EMP: 4
SALES: 130K **Privately Held**
SIC: **3524** Lawn & garden equipment

(G-4308)
SCHWAB WELDING INC
7046 Harrison Ave (45247-3208)
PHONE.................................513 353-4262
Wilbur J Schwab, *President*
EMP: 3
SQ FT: 1,800
SALES: 300K **Privately Held**
SIC: **7692** 3446 Welding repair; architectural metalwork

(G-4309)
SCOTT MODELS INC
607 Redna Ter Ste 400 (45215-1183)
PHONE.................................513 771-8005
Thomas Scott, *President*
EMP: 15
SQ FT: 10,000
SALES (est): 1.4MM **Privately Held**
WEB: www.scottmodels.com
SIC: **3999** Models, except toy

(G-4310)
SCRIPPS MEDIA INC
312 Walnut St Fl 28 (45202-4024)
PHONE.................................513 977-3000
Ray Thurber, *President*
William Appleton, *Vice Pres*
Jim Gilles, *Creative Dir*
EMP: 100
SALES (est): 11.8MM
SALES (corp-wide): 2.9B **Publicly Held**
SIC: **2711** Newspapers, publishing & printing
HQ: Journal Media Group, Inc.
   333 W State St
   Milwaukee WI 53203
   414 224-2000

(G-4311)
SCS CONSTRUCTION SERVICES INC
2130 Western Ave (45214-1744)
PHONE.................................513 929-0260
Jerry Back, *President*
Larry Back, *Vice Pres*
John Freibert, *Foreman/Supr*
Charlie Hull, *CFO*
Dave Roark, *Technology*
EMP: 45 EST: 2000
SQ FT: 8,000

SALES (est): 8.7MM **Privately Held**
SIC: **1542** 3231 1761 3449 Commercial & office building, new construction; doors, glass: made from purchased glass; skylight installation; curtain walls for buildings, steel; metalware

(G-4312)
SDH FLOW CONTROLS LLC
7437 Wallingford Dr (45244-3635)
PHONE.................................513 624-7001
Steven Hendricks, *Principal*
EMP: 3
SALES (est): 342.9K **Privately Held**
SIC: **3491** Industrial valves

(G-4313)
SDI INDUSTRIES
8561 New England Ct (45236-2093)
PHONE.................................513 561-4032
Edward Boll, *Principal*
EMP: 3 EST: 2010
SALES (est): 178.8K **Privately Held**
SIC: **3999** Manufacturing industries

(G-4314)
SECURITY FENCE GROUP INC (PA)
4260 Dane Ave (45223-1855)
PHONE.................................513 681-3700
Christine Frankenstein, *President*
Angela Case, *Corp Secy*
George Frankenstein, *Vice Pres*
EMP: 49
SQ FT: 140,000
SALES (est): 12.1MM **Privately Held**
SIC: **1611** 1799 5039 1731 Guardrail construction, highways; highway & street sign installation; fence construction; wire fence, gates & accessories; general electrical contractor; traffic signals, electric

(G-4315)
SEEMLESS DESIGN & PRINTING LLC
717 Linn St (45203-1703)
PHONE.................................513 871-2366
Christian Wilhelmy,
EMP: 6
SALES (est): 926.4K **Privately Held**
SIC: **2752** Commercial printing, offset

(G-4316)
SEILKOP INDUSTRIES INC (PA)
Also Called: Epcor Foundries
425 W North Bend Rd (45216-1731)
PHONE.................................513 761-1035
Ken Seilkop, *President*
Dave Seilkop, *Vice Pres*
Julie Hammons, *Purch Mgr*
Robin Vogel, *CFO*
EMP: 50
SQ FT: 35,000
SALES (est): 24.1MM **Privately Held**
WEB: www.epcorfoundry.com
SIC: **3363** 3544 3553 3469 Aluminum die-castings; special dies & tools; pattern makers' machinery, woodworking; patterns on metal; industrial tool grinding

(G-4317)
SEILKOP INDUSTRIES INC
Also Called: Hitech Shapes & Designs
7211 Market Pl (45216-2020)
PHONE.................................513 679-5680
Ken Seilkop, *Owner*
EMP: 12
SALES (est): 1.7MM
SALES (corp-wide): 24.1MM **Privately Held**
WEB: www.epcorfoundry.com
SIC: **3543** 3369 3365 3363 Foundry patternmaking; nonferrous foundries; aluminum foundries; aluminum die-castings
PA: Seilkop Industries, Inc.
   425 W North Bend Rd
   Cincinnati OH 45216
   513 761-1035

(G-4318)
SELBY SERVICE/ROXY PRESS INC
2020 Elm St (45202-4911)
PHONE.................................513 241-3445
Clarence Stricker, *Ch of Bd*

Cincinnati - Hamilton County (G-4319)

Robert Stricker, *President*
Bob Furnish, *Vice Pres*
Loretta Stricker, *Treasurer*
Jeanne Meinzen, *Admin Sec*
EMP: 6
SALES (est): 698.7K **Privately Held**
SIC: 2752 7331 2759 Commercial printing, offset; addressographing service; mailing service; letterpress printing

(G-4319)
SELECT WOODWORKING INC
427c W Seymour Ave (45216)
PHONE................................513 948-9901
EMP: 7
SALES (est): 690K **Privately Held**
SIC: 2431 Mfg Millwork

(G-4320)
SENCO BRANDS INC
8450 Broadwell Rd (45244-1612)
PHONE................................513 388-2833
Arthur West, *Branch Mgr*
EMP: 23
SALES (corp-wide): 14.8B **Publicly Held**
SIC: 3546 Power-driven handtools
HQ: Senco Brands, Inc.
    4270 Ivy Pointe Blvd
    Cincinnati OH 45245

(G-4321)
SENIOR IMPACT PUBLICATION
5980 Kugler Mill Rd (45236-2075)
PHONE................................513 791-8800
Robert Jutze, *President*
EMP: 10
SALES (est): 450K **Privately Held**
WEB: www.seniorimpact.net
SIC: 2741 Guides: publishing only, not printed on site

(G-4322)
SENNECA HOLDINGS INC (HQ)
11502 Century Blvd (45246-3305)
PHONE................................800 543-4455
Robert G Isaman, *CEO*
Jeffrey Stark, *Ch of Bd*
Karl Adrian, *COO*
Lisa Botz, *Vice Pres*
Pat McMullen, *CFO*
EMP: 52
SALES (est): 98.1MM
SALES (corp-wide): 6.3B **Privately Held**
SIC: 3442 Metal doors, sash & trim
PA: Kohlberg & Co., L.L.C.
    111 Radio Circle Dr
    Mount Kisco NY 10549
    914 241-7430

(G-4323)
SENSE DIAGNOSTICS INC
1776 Mentor Ave Ste 178 (45212-3596)
PHONE................................513 515-3853
Daniel Kincaid, *CEO*
Opeolu Adeoye, *Owner*
Joseph Clark,
Matthew Flaherty,
George Shaw,
EMP: 5
SALES (est): 590.8K **Privately Held**
SIC: 3841 Diagnostic apparatus, medical

(G-4324)
SERVATII INC
7161 Beechmont Ave (45230-4111)
PHONE................................513 231-4455
Wilhelm Gottenbusch, *Owner*
EMP: 10
SALES (corp-wide): 35.5MM **Privately Held**
WEB: www.servati.com
SIC: 2051 Doughnuts, except frozen
PA: Servatii, Inc.
    3888 Virginia Ave
    Cincinnati OH 45227
    513 271-5040

(G-4325)
SERVATII INC
3774 Paxton Ave (45209-2306)
PHONE................................513 271-5040
Becky Free, *Manager*
EMP: 13
SALES (corp-wide): 35.5MM **Privately Held**
WEB: www.servati.com
SIC: 2051 Bread, cake & related products
PA: Servatii, Inc.
    3888 Virginia Ave
    Cincinnati OH 45227
    513 271-5040

(G-4326)
SESH COMMUNICATIONS
Also Called: N J E M A Magazine
3440 Burnet Ave Ste 130 (45229-2857)
PHONE................................513 851-1693
Eric Kearney, *President*
Wilton Blake, *Vice Pres*
Ronda Gooden, *Vice Pres*
Jan-Michele Kearney, *Vice Pres*
EMP: 13
SALES (est): 804.4K **Privately Held**
SIC: 2711 2721 Newspapers, publishing & printing; periodicals

(G-4327)
SETCO INDUSTRIES INC
5880 Hillside Ave (45233-1599)
PHONE................................513 941-5110
Jeff Clark, *CEO*
Ryan Toebe, *Manager*
EMP: 3 **EST:** 2017
SALES (est): 183K **Privately Held**
SIC: 3999 Manufacturing industries

(G-4328)
SETCO SALES COMPANY (HQ)
5880 Hillside Ave (45233-1599)
PHONE................................513 941-5110
Jeffrey J Clark, *President*
Joseph S Haas, *Vice Pres*
Jerry Abbott, *Purch Mgr*
Philip Sauerbeck, *Engineer*
William Schroer, *Engineer*
▲ **EMP:** 80 **EST:** 1986
SQ FT: 55,000
SALES: 30MM
SALES (corp-wide): 322.3MM **Privately Held**
SIC: 3545 7694 Machine tool accessories; armature rewinding shops
PA: Holden Industries, Inc.
    500 Lake Cook Rd Ste 400
    Deerfield IL 60015
    847 940-1500

(G-4329)
SHANNON TOOL INC
3355 Hill St (45241-1934)
PHONE................................513 563-2300
William Price, *President*
EMP: 4 **EST:** 1931
SQ FT: 10,000
SALES (est): 380K **Privately Held**
SIC: 3599 Machine shop, jobbing & repair

(G-4330)
SHAWNEE SYSTEMS INC
3616 Church St (45244-3004)
PHONE................................513 561-9932
Richard Rogers, *President*
Mark Braun, *Vice Pres*
Warren Hensel Jr, *Vice Pres*
Richard Rogers II, *Vice Pres*
Veronica Dickerson, *Receptionist*
▲ **EMP:** 57
SQ FT: 40,000
SALES (est): 5.7MM **Privately Held**
WEB: www.shawneesystems.com
SIC: 2761 2752 Manifold business forms; commercial printing, lithographic

(G-4331)
SHEPHERD CHEMICAL COMPANY
2825 Highland Ave (45212-2409)
PHONE................................513 200-6987
Aaron Mehan, *Manager*
EMP: 15
SQ FT: 39,516
SALES (corp-wide): 90MM **Privately Held**
SIC: 2819 2869 Industrial inorganic chemicals; industrial organic chemicals
HQ: The Shepherd Chemical Company
    4900 Beech St
    Norwood OH 45212
    513 731-1110

(G-4332)
SHEPHERD CHEMICAL COMPANY
2803 Highland Ave (45219-2311)
PHONE................................513 731-1110
Thomas Shepherd, *CEO*
EMP: 15
SALES (corp-wide): 90MM **Privately Held**
SIC: 2819 Metal salts & compounds, except sodium, potassium, aluminum
HQ: The Shepherd Chemical Company
    4900 Beech St
    Norwood OH 45212
    513 731-1110

(G-4333)
SIDNEY PRINTING WORKS INC
2611 Colerain Ave (45214-1777)
PHONE................................513 542-4000
Josh Deutch, *President*
Tim King, *Plant Mgr*
EMP: 4
SQ FT: 11,439
SALES (est): 395.8K **Privately Held**
SIC: 2752 Commercial printing, offset

(G-4334)
SIEMENS INDUSTRY INC
Also Called: Motors & Drives Division
4620 Forest Ave (45212-3306)
PHONE................................513 841-3100
Susan Macdonald, *Buyer*
Bill Perry, *Engineer*
Ryan Queen, *Engineer*
Rustin Reitinger, *Engineer*
Joerg Ernst, *Manager*
EMP: 200
SQ FT: 550,000
SALES (corp-wide): 95B **Privately Held**
WEB: www.sea.siemens.com
SIC: 3621 Motors, electric; generators & sets, electric
HQ: Siemens Industry, Inc.
    1000 Deerfield Pkwy
    Buffalo Grove IL 60089
    800 743-6367

(G-4335)
SIGMATEK SYSTEMS LLC (PA)
Also Called: Sigma T E K
1445 Kemper Meadow Dr (45240-1637)
PHONE................................513 674-0005
Ben Terreblanche, *CEO*
Chris Eldridge, *Controller*
Chris Cooper,
Joseph Keblesh,
John Leuzinger,
EMP: 65
SQ FT: 23,000
SALES (est): 17MM **Privately Held**
WEB: www.sigmanest.com
SIC: 7372 Prepackaged software

(G-4336)
SIGN A RAMA INC
Also Called: Sign-A-Rama
2519 Crescentville Rd (45241-1575)
PHONE................................513 671-2213
Vlad Shmulevich, *Manager*
EMP: 4
SALES (corp-wide): 92.3MM **Privately Held**
WEB: www.franchisemart.com
SIC: 3993 Signs & advertising specialties
HQ: Sign A Rama Inc.
    2121 Vista Pkwy
    West Palm Beach FL 33411
    561 640-5570

(G-4337)
SIGNALYSIS INC
539 Glenrose Ln (45244-1509)
PHONE................................513 528-6164
Robert Neil Coleman, *President*
Kyle Coleman, *Vice Pres*
Phil Wilkin, *Shareholder*
EMP: 12
SALES (est): 2.1MM **Privately Held**
WEB: www.signalysis.com
SIC: 8711 7371 3695 7389 Consulting engineer; computer software development & applications; computer software tape & disks: blank, rigid & floppy;

(G-4338)
SIMPLE VMS LLC
7373 Beechmont Ave # 130 (45230-4100)
PHONE................................888 255-8918
Joseph Clancy, *President*
Jaime Frost, *Accounts Mgr*
Karen Oswald, *Manager*
EMP: 7 **EST:** 2011
SALES (est): 891.9K **Privately Held**
SIC: 7372 7371 8742 8748 Business oriented computer software; computer software development & applications; human resource consulting services; business consulting

(G-4339)
SIMPLY UNIQUE SNACKS LLC
4420 Haight Ave (45223-1705)
PHONE................................513 223-7736
Steve Hofford, *President*
EMP: 6
SALES (est): 526.7K
SALES (corp-wide): 1.1MM **Privately Held**
SIC: 2013 2037 2068 7389 Snack sticks, including jerky: from purchased meat; fruit juices, frozen; salted & roasted nuts & seeds;
PA: United Snacks Of America Llc

    Plainview NY 11803
    516 319-9448

(G-4340)
SIMS-LOHMAN INC (PA)
Also Called: Sims-Lohman Fine Kitchens Gran
6325 Este Ave (45232-1458)
PHONE................................513 651-3510
Steve Steinman, *CEO*
John Beiersdorfer, *President*
Dan Sullivan, *Opers Mgr*
James Mitchell, *Opers Staff*
▲ **EMP:** 50 **EST:** 1974
SQ FT: 153,000
SALES (est): 127.4MM **Privately Held**
WEB: www.moelleringindustries.com
SIC: 5031 2435 Kitchen cabinets; hardwood veneer & plywood

(G-4341)
SK TEXTILE INC
1 Knollcrest Dr (45237-1608)
PHONE................................323 581-8986
Kim Morris Heiman, *President*
▲ **EMP:** 105
SALES (est): 12.9MM **Privately Held**
WEB: www.sktextile.com
SIC: 2391 2211 Curtains & draperies; bedspreads, cotton

(G-4342)
SKINNY PIGGY KOMBUCHA LLC
5510 Glengate Ln (45212-2429)
PHONE................................513 646-5753
Algirdas Aukstuolis, *Mng Member*
EMP: 3
SALES: 100K **Privately Held**
SIC: 2086 Soft drinks: packaged in cans, bottles, etc.

(G-4343)
SKYLINE EXHIBITS GRTR CNCNT
9850 Prncton Glndle Rd Ste (45246)
PHONE................................513 671-4460
Lee Sjoquist, *President*
Kenda Sjoquist, *Vice Pres*
EMP: 5
SQ FT: 10,000
SALES (est): 1.5MM **Privately Held**
WEB: www.skylinecinti.com
SIC: 3993 Displays & cutouts, window & lobby; displays, paint process

(G-4344)
SMALL BUSINESS PRODUCTS
8603 Winton Rd (45231-4816)
P.O. Box 297257, Hollywood FL (33029-7257)
PHONE................................800 553-6485
Brandi Pedersen, *Principal*
EMP: 5
SALES (est): 604.7K **Privately Held**
SIC: 3577 Printers & plotters

GEOGRAPHIC SECTION
Cincinnati - Hamilton County (G-4371)

(G-4345)
SMITH & NEPHEW INC
5005 Barrow Ave Ste 100 (45209-1045)
PHONE....................513 821-5888
Patrick Henrey, *Branch Mgr*
Trevor Wall, *Executive*
EMP: 50
SALES (corp-wide): 4.7B **Privately Held**
SIC: 3842 Surgical appliances & supplies
HQ: Smith & Nephew, Inc.
 1450 E Brooks Rd
 Memphis TN 38116
 901 396-2121

(G-4346)
SMITH ELECTRO CHEMICAL CO
5936 Carthage Ct (45212-1103)
PHONE....................513 351-7227
Donald W Kifer, *President*
Robert Kifer, *Vice Pres*
EMP: 30 **EST:** 1948
SQ FT: 25,000
SALES (est): 3.6MM **Privately Held**
WEB: www.smithelectrochemical.com
SIC: 3471 Electroplating of metals or formed products; anodizing (plating) of metals or formed products

(G-4347)
SMITHFIELD BIOSCIENCE INC
Also Called: Celsus
12150 Best Pl (45241-1569)
PHONE....................513 772-8130
Cornelius L Van Gorp, *President*
Cornelius Van, *General Mgr*
Raymond A Stefanski, *Vice Pres*
Isabelle B Van Gorp, *Vice Pres*
Robert A Van Gorp, *Vice Pres*
◆ **EMP:** 20
SQ FT: 16,000
SALES (est): 5.6MM **Privately Held**
WEB: www.celsuslaboratories.com
SIC: 2899 Chemical preparations

(G-4348)
SMITHFIELD PACKAGED MEATS CORP (DH)
805 E Kemper Rd (45246-2515)
P.O. Box 405020 (45240-5020)
PHONE....................513 782-3800
Joseph B Sebring, *President*
Mark Dorsey, *Principal*
Paul Landwehr, *Engineer*
Kent Hilbrands, *Controller*
Eric O'Brien, *Marketing Staff*
◆ **EMP:** 125 **EST:** 1957
SQ FT: 10,000
SALES (est): 1.7B **Privately Held**
WEB: www.johnmorrell.com
SIC: 2011 Pork products from pork slaughtered on site
HQ: Smithfield Foods, Inc.
 200 Commerce St
 Smithfield VA 23430
 757 365-3000

(G-4349)
SMITHFIELD PACKAGED MEATS CORP
801 E Kemper Rd (45246-2515)
PHONE....................513 782-3805
Daneil Yher, *Manager*
EMP: 350 **Privately Held**
WEB: www.johnmorrell.com
SIC: 2011 Meat packing plants
HQ: Smithfield Packaged Meats Corp.
 805 E Kemper Rd
 Cincinnati OH 45246
 513 782-3800

(G-4350)
SO-LOW ENVIRONMENTAL EQP CO
10310 Spartan Dr (45215-1279)
PHONE....................513 772-9410
Walter Schum, *President*
Aaron Snyder, *General Mgr*
James Schum, *Vice Pres*
Kevin Harpen, *Traffic Mgr*
Dan Hensler, *Marketing Mgr*
EMP: 48
SQ FT: 66,000
SALES (est): 13.5MM **Privately Held**
WEB: www.so-low.com
SIC: 3821 3585 Laboratory apparatus & furniture; refrigeration equipment, complete

(G-4351)
SOFTWARE MANAGEMENT GROUP
1128 Main St Fl 6 (45202-7276)
PHONE....................513 618-2165
Dave Nolnan, *President*
EMP: 25
SALES (est): 878.2K **Privately Held**
SIC: 7372 Prepackaged software

(G-4352)
SOLO PRODUCTS INC
838 Reedy St (45202-2216)
PHONE....................513 321-7884
Steve Kunkemoeller, *CEO*
Doug Hearn, *CFO*
EMP: 12
SALES (est): 4.3MM **Privately Held**
SIC: 5085 3086 Rubber goods, mechanical; carpet & rug cushions, foamed plastic

(G-4353)
SOLVAY USA INC
4775 Paddock Rd (45229-1003)
P.O. Box 29075 (45229-0075)
PHONE....................513 482-5700
Todd Wisener, *General Mgr*
EMP: 49
SALES (corp-wide): 10MM **Privately Held**
WEB: www.food.us.rhodia.com
SIC: 2819 2899 Catalysts, chemical; chemical preparations
HQ: Solvay Usa Inc.
 504 Carnegie Ctr
 Princeton NJ 08540
 609 860-4000

(G-4354)
SOTTO
118 E 6th St (45202-3202)
PHONE....................513 977-6886
EMP: 4 **EST:** 2013
SALES (est): 13.2K **Privately Held**
SIC: 2599 Carts, restaurant equipment

(G-4355)
SOUTHERN ADHESIVE COATINGS
Also Called: Mirror-Coat
8121 Camargo Rd (45243-2203)
P.O. Box 43250 (45243-0250)
PHONE....................513 561-8440
Richard Williams, *President*
Muriel Williams, *Corp Secy*
Robert M Williams, *Vice Pres*
EMP: 4
SQ FT: 10,000
SALES (est): 2MM **Privately Held**
SIC: 2891 2269 Adhesives; sealants; chemical coating or treating of narrow fabrics

(G-4356)
SPARK LLC
Also Called: Kinetic Dsign Group - Columbus
10760 Chester Rd (45246-4732)
PHONE....................513 924-1559
Wendell Beachy, *Principal*
EMP: 3
SALES (est): 214.7K **Privately Held**
SIC: 3599 8711 Custom machinery; industrial engineers

(G-4357)
SPECIALTY LITHOGRAPHING CO
1035 W 7th St (45203-1285)
PHONE....................513 621-0222
Elmer A Babey, *CEO*
Mark Babey, *President*
James Babey, *Vice Pres*
Carol Evans, *Admin Sec*
EMP: 17
SQ FT: 20,000
SALES (est): 2.4MM **Privately Held**
WEB: www.specialtylitho.com
SIC: 2752 Commercial printing, offset

(G-4358)
SPEEDWAY LLC
Also Called: Speedway Superamerica 5110
12184 Mason Rd (45249-1336)
PHONE....................513 683-2034
Tom Giovis, *Branch Mgr*
EMP: 10 **Publicly Held**
WEB: www.speedwaynet.com
SIC: 1311 Crude petroleum production
HQ: Speedway Llc
 500 Speedway Dr
 Enon OH 45323
 937 864-3000

(G-4359)
SPICY OLIVE LLC
2736 Erie Ave (45208-2104)
PHONE....................513 376-9061
EMP: 3
SALES (corp-wide): 22.4MM **Privately Held**
SIC: 2079 Olive oil
PA: Spicy Olive Llc
 7671 Cox Ln
 West Chester OH 45069
 513 847-4397

(G-4360)
SPORTSCO IMPRINTING
8277 Wicklow Ave (45236-1613)
PHONE....................513 641-5111
Joe Eigel, *Partner*
Eric Kattus, *Partner*
EMP: 8
SQ FT: 1,800
SALES (est): 641.2K **Privately Held**
SIC: 2262 2395 Screen printing: man-made fiber & silk broadwoven fabrics; emblems, embroidered

(G-4361)
SPRING GROVE MANUFACTURING
2838 Spring Grove Ave (45225-2268)
PHONE....................513 542-0185
Jeffrey S Best, *President*
Todd M Johnson, *Vice Pres*
EMP: 10 **EST:** 2001
SQ FT: 30,000
SALES (est): 998K **Privately Held**
SIC: 3083 Plastic finished products, laminated

(G-4362)
SPRING GROVE MANUFACTURING
Also Called: Cinncinati Bindery
2838 Spring Grove Ave (45225-2268)
PHONE....................513 542-6900
Jeff Best, *President*
EMP: 15
SALES (est): 1.2MM **Privately Held**
SIC: 2789 Binding only: books, pamphlets, magazines, etc.

(G-4363)
SPRINGDALE BINDERY LLC
11411 Landan Ln (45246-3611)
PHONE....................513 772-8500
Steve Dehamer, *Manager*
EMP: 5
SALES (est): 645K **Privately Held**
SIC: 2789 Binding only: books, pamphlets, magazines, etc.

(G-4364)
SPRINGDALE ICE CREAM BEVERAGE
11801 Chesterdale Rd (45246-3407)
PHONE....................513 699-4984
Fax: 513 671-2864
EMP: 35
SALES (est): 5.8MM **Privately Held**
SIC: 2024 0241 Mfg Ice Cream/Frozen Desert Dairy Farm

(G-4365)
SPRINGDOT INC
2611 Colerain Ave (45214-1711)
PHONE....................513 542-4000
Jeff Deutsch, *Ch of Bd*
Josh Deutsch, *President*
John Brenner, *Vice Pres*
Craig Miller, *Vice Pres*
Bill Fultz, *Traffic Mgr*
EMP: 65 **EST:** 1904
SQ FT: 70,000
SALES (est): 13.5MM **Privately Held**
WEB: www.springdot.com
SIC: 2752 4899 2759 2675 Commercial printing, offset; color lithography; data communication services; commercial printing; die-cut paper & board; packaging paper & plastics film, coated & laminated

(G-4366)
SRO PRINTS LLC
4430 Yakima Ct (45236-3720)
PHONE....................865 604-0420
Brandon Swinehart, *Principal*
EMP: 4
SALES (est): 135.1K **Privately Held**
SIC: 2752 2759 7389 Commercial printing, lithographic; promotional printing; screen printing;

(G-4367)
ST BERNARD INSULATION LLC
8703 Pippin Rd (45251-3130)
PHONE....................513 266-2158
Janice Ruiz, *Mng Member*
EMP: 18 **EST:** 2014
SALES (est): 1MM **Privately Held**
SIC: 2899 5211 Insulating compounds; insulation material, building

(G-4368)
ST BERNARD SOAP COMPANY
5177 Spring Grove Ave (45217-1050)
PHONE....................513 242-2227
William Biedenharm, *President*
▲ **EMP:** 301
SALES (est): 196.4MM
SALES (corp-wide): 2.7B **Privately Held**
WEB: www.trilliumhealthcare.com
SIC: 2841 Soap & other toiletries
HQ: Trillium Health Care Products Inc
 2337 Parkdale Ave E
 Brockville ON K6V 5
 613 342-4436

(G-4369)
STAGECRAFT COSTUMING INC
Also Called: Stagecraft Theatrical
3950 Spring Grove Ave (45223-2639)
PHONE....................513 541-7150
Randy Kent, *President*
EMP: 10 **EST:** 1975
SQ FT: 20,000
SALES (est): 1MM **Privately Held**
WEB: www.stagecraftinc.com
SIC: 2389 7299 Theatrical costumes; costume rental

(G-4370)
STAN RILEYS CUSTOM DRAPERIES
7041 Vine St (45216-2031)
PHONE....................513 821-3732
Stanton J Riley Jr, *Owner*
EMP: 7 **EST:** 1971
SALES: 250K **Privately Held**
SIC: 2391 2392 2394 Draperies, plastic & textile: from purchased materials; household furnishings; pillows, bed: made from purchased materials; bedspreads & bed sets: made from purchased materials; canvas & related products

(G-4371)
STANDARD PUBLISHING LLC
8805 Governors Hill Dr # 400 (45249-3319)
PHONE....................513 931-4050
Peter M Esposito, *CEO*
Matthew Thibeau, *General Ptnr*
Mark Rosenbaun, *CFO*
▲ **EMP:** 200
SALES (est): 27.6MM **Privately Held**
SIC: 2721 Magazines: publishing only, not printed on site
PA: Cfm Religion Publishing Group Llc
 8805 Governors Hill Dr # 400
 Cincinnati OH 45249

Cincinnati - Hamilton County (G-4372)

(G-4372)
STANDARD TEXTILE CO INC (PA)
Also Called: Pridecraft Enterprises
1 Knollcrest Dr (45237-1608)
P.O. Box 371805 (45222-1805)
PHONE.................................513 761-9256
Gary Heiman, *President*
Chris Bopp, *Senior VP*
Norman Frankel, *Senior VP*
Kim Heiman, *Senior VP*
Steve Tracey, *Senior VP*
◆ **EMP:** 300
SQ FT: 150,000
SALES (est): 906.9MM **Privately Held**
WEB: www.standardtextile.com
SIC: 2389 2326 2337 2211 Hospital gowns; medical & hospital uniforms, men's; uniforms, except athletic: women's, misses' & juniors'; bandages, gauzes & surgical fabrics, cotton; surgical fabrics, cotton; draperies, plastic & textile; from purchased materials; uniforms, men's & boys'

(G-4373)
STARCHEM INC (PA)
3000 Disney St (45209-5028)
PHONE.................................513 458-8262
Ronald Smith, *President*
Michael Tabor, *Vice Pres*
Henry Turchin, *Vice Pres*
Mark Williams, *Vice Pres*
EMP: 6
SQ FT: 12,000
SALES (est): 901K **Privately Held**
WEB: www.starchem.net
SIC: 2992 Cutting oils, blending: made from purchased materials

(G-4374)
STARKS PLASTICS LLC
11236 Sebring Dr (45240-2715)
PHONE.................................513 541-4591
Larry Clark, *Mng Member*
Kim Clark,
EMP: 5
SQ FT: 1,400
SALES (est): 450K **Privately Held**
SIC: 3089 5046 Plastic processing; store fixtures

(G-4375)
STARR PRINTING SERVICES INC
3625 Spring Grove Ave (45223-2458)
PHONE.................................513 241-7708
Robert Meade, *President*
EMP: 7
SQ FT: 5,000
SALES (est): 948.8K **Privately Held**
SIC: 2752 2759 Commercial printing, offset; letterpress printing

(G-4376)
STEAM ENGINE WORKS LLC
2364 Heather Hill Blvd N (45244-2667)
PHONE.................................513 813-3690
David Pommert, *Owner*
EMP: 3
SALES (est): 118.7K **Privately Held**
SIC: 3511 Steam engines

(G-4377)
STEEL QUEST INC
8180 Corp Pk Dr Ste 250 (45242)
PHONE.................................513 772-5030
Matthew S Kuhnell, *President*
EMP: 9
SQ FT: 3,500
SALES (est): 2.7MM **Privately Held**
WEB: www.steelquest.com
SIC: 3441 Fabricated structural metal

(G-4378)
STEGEMEYER MACHINE
212 Mccullough St (45226-2120)
PHONE.................................513 321-5651
Richard Stegemeyer, *President*
Deanna Stegemeyer, *Admin Sec*
EMP: 7
SQ FT: 4,500
SALES: 375K **Privately Held**
SIC: 3599 Machine shop, jobbing & repair

(G-4379)
STELLAR SYSTEMS INC
1944 Harrison Ave (45214-1176)
PHONE.................................513 921-8748
William L Spetz, *President*
EMP: 7
SQ FT: 8,000
SALES (est): 470K **Privately Held**
WEB: www.stellarsystemsinc.com
SIC: 7371 3577 Computer software development; computer peripheral equipment

(G-4380)
STEVE SCHAEFER
Also Called: Mis Micro Information Services
9200 Montgomery Rd 23a (45242-7797)
P.O. Box 42377 (45242-0377)
PHONE.................................513 792-9911
Steve Schaefer, *Owner*
Karen Schaefer, *Manager*
EMP: 4
SALES (est): 210K **Privately Held**
WEB: www.mismicro.com
SIC: 7372 Prepackaged software

(G-4381)
STEVENSON COLOR INC
535 Wilmer Ave (45226-1828)
PHONE.................................513 321-7500
Thomas Stevenson, *President*
Kris Krause, *General Mgr*
Mark Smith, *Facilities Mgr*
Tina Carter, *Production*
Jeff Egbert, *Production*
EMP: 190 **EST:** 1926
SQ FT: 116,800
SALES (est): 31.2MM
SALES (corp-wide): 272.7MM **Privately Held**
WEB: www.stevensoncolor.com
SIC: 2796 2752 Color separations for printing; commercial printing, lithographic
HQ: Southern Graphic Systems, Llc
626 W Main St Ste 500
Louisville KY 40202
502 637-5443

(G-4382)
STEVENSON MACHINE INC
7666 Production Dr (45237-3209)
PHONE.................................513 761-4121
Donald Goepper, *President*
EMP: 11 **EST:** 1927
SQ FT: 15,000
SALES (est): 2MM **Privately Held**
WEB: www.stevensonmachine.com
SIC: 3599 3568 5085 Machine shop, jobbing & repair; power transmission equipment; power transmission equipment & apparatus

(G-4383)
STINE CONSULTING INC
Also Called: Fastsigns
120 W 7th St (45202-2328)
PHONE.................................513 723-4800
Stephen Stine, *President*
EMP: 5
SQ FT: 3,500
SALES (est): 823K **Privately Held**
SIC: 3993 Signs & advertising specialties

(G-4384)
STONE STATEMENTS INCORPORATED
7451 Fields Ertel Rd (45241-6083)
PHONE.................................513 489-7866
Douglas R Beyersdoerfer, *President*
Tom Beyersdoerfer, *Vice Pres*
Kathy Smith, *Admin Asst*
▲ **EMP:** 8
SALES (est): 1.8MM **Privately Held**
WEB: www.stonestatements.com
SIC: 1411 1799 Granite dimension stone; counter top installation

(G-4385)
STRONGHOLD COATING LTD
Also Called: Stronghold Coating Systems
3495 Mustafa Dr (45241-1668)
PHONE.................................937 704-4020
Larry F Grimenstein, *President*
EMP: 4
SALES: 300K **Privately Held**
SIC: 2851 7389 Polyurethane coatings;

(G-4386)
STUART COMPANY
2160 Patterson St (45214-1844)
PHONE.................................513 621-9462
Philip G Gossard, *CEO*
EMP: 15
SQ FT: 50,000
SALES: 1.1MM **Privately Held**
SIC: 2675 Die-cut paper & board

(G-4387)
STUDIO VERTU INC
1208 Central Pkwy 1 (45202-7509)
PHONE.................................513 241-9038
Mark Schmidt, *President*
Heather Schmidt, *Vice Pres*
▲ **EMP:** 35
SQ FT: 18,000
SALES (est): 3.3MM **Privately Held**
WEB: www.studiovertu.com
SIC: 3253 3281 Ceramic wall & floor tile; cut stone & stone products

(G-4388)
STUEBING AUTOMATIC MACHINE CO
2518 Leslie Ave (45212-4206)
PHONE.................................513 771-8028
EMP: 21 **EST:** 1892
SQ FT: 30,000
SALES (est): 3.7MM **Privately Held**
SIC: 3469 5084 Mfg Metal Stampings Whol Industrial Equipment

(G-4389)
SUMMIT DIAGNOSTIC IMAGING LLC
Also Called: Medical Imaging
7755 5 Mile Rd (45230-2355)
PHONE.................................513 233-3320
John Mattes, *General Mgr*
Patty Noll, *Administration*
EMP: 20 **EST:** 2000
SQ FT: 2,500
SALES (est): 2.4MM **Privately Held**
SIC: 3826 Magnetic resonance imaging apparatus

(G-4390)
SUN CHEMICAL CORPORATION
General Printing Ink Division
12049 Centron Pl (45246-1789)
PHONE.................................513 671-0407
Pat Myers, *Branch Mgr*
EMP: 60
SQ FT: 11,000
SALES (corp-wide): 7.1B **Privately Held**
WEB: www.sunchemical.com
SIC: 2893 2899 Printing ink; ink or writing fluids
HQ: Sun Chemical Corporation
35 Waterview Blvd Ste 100
Parsippany NJ 07054
973 404-6000

(G-4391)
SUN CHEMICAL CORPORATION
Also Called: Pigments Division
4526 Chickering Ave (45232-1935)
PHONE.................................513 681-5950
Dennis Keyes, *Buyer*
Ryan Fulkerson, *Project Engr*
Brian Leen, *Branch Mgr*
Greg Ervin, *Manager*
Paul Merchak, *Manager*
EMP: 210
SQ FT: 91,671
SALES (corp-wide): 7.1B **Privately Held**
WEB: www.sunchemical.com
SIC: 2816 2865 Inorganic pigments; cyclic crudes & intermediates
HQ: Sun Chemical Corporation
35 Waterview Blvd Ste 100
Parsippany NJ 07054
973 404-6000

(G-4392)
SUN CHEMICAL CORPORATION
Kohl & Madden Printing Ink Div
5020 Spring Grove Ave (45232-1988)
P.O. Box 32040 (45232-0040)
PHONE.................................513 681-5950
Russ Henke, *Vice Pres*
Ralph Steinmetz, *Materials Mgr*
Orly Janssen, *QC Dir*
Mike Willis, *Technical Mgr*
Deborah Charlson, *Research*
EMP: 39
SALES (corp-wide): 7.1B **Privately Held**
SIC: 2893 Printing ink
HQ: Sun Chemical Corporation
35 Waterview Blvd Ste 100
Parsippany NJ 07054
973 404-6000

(G-4393)
SUN CHEMICAL CORPORATION
600 Redna Ter (45215-1108)
PHONE.................................513 771-4030
Steve Cornwell, *Plant Mgr*
Gloria Rutledge, *Manager*
EMP: 44
SALES (corp-wide): 7.1B **Privately Held**
SIC: 2893 Lithographic ink
HQ: Sun Chemical Corporation
35 Waterview Blvd Ste 100
Parsippany NJ 07054
973 404-6000

(G-4394)
SUN CHEMICAL CORPORATION
Sun Chmcal Corp Prfmce Pgments
5020 Spring Grove Ave (45232-1988)
P.O. Box 16096 (45216-0096)
PHONE.................................513 681-5950
Brian Leen, *Vice Pres*
W E Breagy, *Marketing Staff*
EMP: 300
SALES (corp-wide): 7.1B **Privately Held**
WEB: www.sunchemical.com
SIC: 2893 Printing ink
HQ: Sun Chemical Corporation
35 Waterview Blvd Ste 100
Parsippany NJ 07054
973 404-6000

(G-4395)
SUN CHEMICAL CORPORATION
5000 Spring Grove Ave (45232-1926)
PHONE.................................513 830-8667
Thad Karbowsky, *Controller*
Milt Barnes, *Branch Mgr*
EMP: 39
SALES (corp-wide): 7.1B **Privately Held**
SIC: 2893 2865 Printing ink; dyes & pigments
HQ: Sun Chemical Corporation
35 Waterview Blvd Ste 100
Parsippany NJ 07054
973 404-6000

(G-4396)
SUNNY OLIVE LLC
9901 Montgomery Rd (45242-5311)
PHONE.................................513 996-4091
EMP: 3
SALES (est): 144.1K **Privately Held**
SIC: 2079 Olive oil

(G-4397)
SUPER SYSTEMS INC (PA)
7205 Edington Dr (45249-1064)
PHONE.................................513 772-0060
Stephen Thompson, *President*
Jim Oakes, *President*
Scott Johnstone, *Vice Pres*
Bill Heckman, *Project Mgr*
Haoxiang Wang, *Engineer*
EMP: 45
SQ FT: 5,000
SALES (est): 6.9MM **Privately Held**
SIC: 3829 5084 Measuring & controlling devices; industrial machinery & equipment

(G-4398)
SUR-SEAL LLC (HQ)
Also Called: Sur-Seal Gasket & Packing
6156 Wesselman Rd (45248-1204)
PHONE.................................513 574-8500
Larry Faist, *CEO*
▲ **EMP:** 135
SQ FT: 67,000
SALES: 40MM **Privately Held**
WEB: www.sur-seal.com
SIC: 3053 3069 Gaskets, all materials; packing, rubber; molded rubber products
PA: Sur-Seal Holding, Llc
301 Merritt 7
Norwalk CT 06851
203 625-0770

GEOGRAPHIC SECTION
Cincinnati - Hamilton County (G-4425)

(G-4399)
SURFACE DYNAMICS INC
231 Northland Blvd (45246-3603)
PHONE.................513 772-6635
Leo Glass, *Branch Mgr*
EMP: 3
SALES (corp-wide): 45.6MM **Privately Held**
SIC: 3086 Insulation or cushioning material, foamed plastic
HQ: Surface Dynamics, Inc
231 Northland Blvd
Cincinnati OH 45246

(G-4400)
SURFACE ENHANCEMENT TECH LLC
3929 Virginia Ave (45227-3411)
PHONE.................513 561-1520
Paul Prevey,
Jacqueline Pervey,
EMP: 17
SQ FT: 28,000
SALES (est): 4.1MM **Privately Held**
WEB: www.surfaceenhancement.com
SIC: 3398 Brazing (hardening) of metal

(G-4401)
SURGICAL APPLIANCE INDS INC (PA)
3960 Rosslyn Dr (45209-1195)
PHONE.................513 271-4594
L Thomas Applegate, *Ch of Bd*
Steve McSherry, *Business Mgr*
Ginny Faught, *VP Opers*
Tim Donovan, *Controller*
Dave Perry, *Accountant*
▲ **EMP:** 200 **EST:** 1893
SQ FT: 225,000
SALES (est): 64.5MM **Privately Held**
WEB: www.surgicalappliance.com
SIC: 3842 Surgical appliances & supplies; orthopedic appliances; braces, elastic

(G-4402)
SWEATY BANDS LLC
3802 Ford Cir (45227-3403)
PHONE.................513 871-1222
Douglas Browning, *Managing Prtnr*
Donna Browning, *Managing Prtnr*
Lisa Fleming, *Finance Dir*
Carla Caruso, *Sales Staff*
Lindsey Paulin, *Director*
EMP: 20 **EST:** 2008
SALES: 5MM **Privately Held**
SIC: 2396 Sweat bands, hat & cap: made from purchased materials

(G-4403)
T P F INC
313 S Wayne Ave (45215-4522)
P.O. Box 15171 (45215-0171)
PHONE.................513 761-9968
Charles Stiens, *President*
Robert Stiens, *Chairman*
Charlotte Stiens, *Corp Secy*
Kenneth Stiens, *Vice Pres*
EMP: 8
SQ FT: 2,400
SALES (est): 1.5MM **Privately Held**
WEB: www.tpftherm.com
SIC: 3823 7699 Thermometers, filled system: industrial process type; pressure measurement instruments, industrial; industrial machinery & equipment repair

(G-4404)
TAMARRON TECHNOLOGY INC
8044 Montgomery Rd (45236-2919)
PHONE.................800 277-3207
John Gill, *Vice Pres*
EMP: 10
SQ FT: 4,000
SALES (est): 271.7K **Privately Held**
SIC: 3272 5032 Building materials, except block or brick: concrete; concrete building products

(G-4405)
TAMBRANDS SALES CORP (HQ)
Also Called: Tampax
1 Procter And Gamble Plz (45202-3315)
PHONE.................513 983-1100
Wolfgang C Berndt, *President*
Erik G Nelson, *Vice Pres*
▲ **EMP:** 130 **EST:** 1936
SQ FT: 100,000
SALES (est): 168.3MM
SALES (corp-wide): 66.8B **Publicly Held**
WEB: www.tampax.com
SIC: 2676 Tampons, sanitary: made from purchased paper
PA: The Procter & Gamble Company
1 Procter And Gamble Plz
Cincinnati OH 45202
513 983-1100

(G-4406)
TASTE OF BELGIUM LLC
1801 Race St Ste 30 (45202-5917)
PHONE.................513 381-3280
Brendon Fox, *General Mgr*
Phil Leisure, *General Mgr*
Zach Bihlman, *Controller*
Bobbi Steberl, *Marketing Staff*
Chorrinda Bausman, *Manager*
▲ **EMP:** 4 **EST:** 2008
SALES (est): 481.1K **Privately Held**
SIC: 2051 Bread, cake & related products

(G-4407)
TAYLOR & MOORE CO
807 Wachendorf St (45215-4743)
PHONE.................513 733-5530
George R Taylor, *President*
EMP: 12
SQ FT: 11,898
SALES (est): 1.7MM **Privately Held**
SIC: 3585 Air conditioning units, complete: domestic or industrial; heating & air conditioning combination units

(G-4408)
TAYLOR COMPANY (PA)
5721 Dragon Way Ste 117 (45227-4518)
PHONE.................513 271-2550
Paul Roberts, *Principal*
EMP: 2
SQ FT: 900
SALES (est): 12.6MM **Privately Held**
SIC: 6799 2656 Investors; plates, paper: made from purchased material

(G-4409)
TECH/III INC (PA)
Also Called: Printing Plant
1330 Tennessee Ave (45229-1045)
PHONE.................513 482-7500
James E Oconnor, *President*
Carol S Horan, *Principal*
Sean Nevin, *Sales Staff*
EMP: 42 **EST:** 1970
SQ FT: 38,000
SALES (est): 10MM **Privately Held**
SIC: 2671 2759 Packaging paper & plastics film, coated & laminated; labels & seals: printing

(G-4410)
TECHBRITE LLC
1000 Kieley Pl (45217-1118)
PHONE.................800 246-9977
Brett Heekin, *President*
David Brown, *Vice Pres*
▲ **EMP:** 22
SQ FT: 15,000
SALES (est): 5.8MM **Privately Held**
WEB: www.techbrite.com
SIC: 3646 Fluorescent lighting fixtures, commercial

(G-4411)
TEGRATEK
500 Northland Blvd (45240-3213)
PHONE.................513 742-5100
Thomas Mohring, *Owner*
Cliff Mohring, *Mfg Mgr*
EMP: 4 **EST:** 1976
SQ FT: 5,000
SALES (est): 480.5K **Privately Held**
SIC: 3559 3567 3599 Concrete products machinery; heating units & devices, industrial: electric; water leak detectors

(G-4412)
TEMA ISENMANN INC (DH)
7806 Redsky Dr (45249-1632)
PHONE.................859 252-0613
Tammy K Runyan, *Treasurer*
▲ **EMP:** 4
SQ FT: 15,000
SALES (est): 16.1MM
SALES (corp-wide): 351.5MM **Privately Held**
WEB: www.temaisenmann.com
SIC: 3089 7389 Panels, building: plastic; personal service agents, brokers & bureaus
HQ: Steinhaus Gesellschaft Mit Beschrankter Haftung
Platanenallee 46
Mulheim An Der Ruhr 45478
208 580-101

(G-4413)
TEMA SYSTEMS INC
7806 Redsky Dr (45249-1632)
PHONE.................513 489-7811
Mike Mullins, *President*
Chad Mendelsohn, *Sales Mgr*
Gary Helsley, *Manager*
Jeff Sullivan, *Technology*
J Neal Gardner, *Admin Sec*
◆ **EMP:** 25
SQ FT: 15,000
SALES (est): 6.8MM
SALES (corp-wide): 351.5MM **Privately Held**
WEB: www.tema.net
SIC: 3532 3599 3589 Cages, mine shaft; mineral beneficiation equipment; custom machinery; commercial cooking & food-warming equipment
HQ: Siebtechnik Gmbh
Platanenallee 46
Mulheim An Der Ruhr 45478
208 580-100

(G-4414)
TESTLINK USA
11445 Century Cir W (45246-3303)
PHONE.................513 272-1081
Paula Walker, *Principal*
EMP: 13 **EST:** 2013
SALES (est): 2.4MM **Privately Held**
SIC: 3578 Automatic teller machines (ATM)

(G-4415)
TEVA PHARMACEUTICALS INC
5040 Duramed Rd (45213-2520)
PHONE.................800 225-6878
Gene Lawrence, *Principal*
Timothy Heyd, *Manager*
Dipti Joshi, *Consultant*
Wiltrud Lopez, *Technical Staff*
Laura Cannon, *Director*
EMP: 7
SALES (est): 1.8MM **Privately Held**
SIC: 2834 Pharmaceutical preparations

(G-4416)
TEVA WOMENS HEALTH INC (DH)
5040 Duramed Rd (45213-2520)
PHONE.................513 731-9900
Bruce L Downey, *Principal*
Timothy J Holt, *Principal*
Lawrence A Glassman, *Senior VP*
EMP: 250 **EST:** 1982
SQ FT: 28,200
SALES: 125.7MM
SALES (corp-wide): 18.8B **Privately Held**
WEB: www.barrlabs.com
SIC: 5122 2834 7389 Patent medicines; pharmaceutical preparations; tablets, pharmaceutical; medicines, capsuled or ampuled; solutions, pharmaceutical; packaging & labeling services
HQ: Teva Pharmaceuticals Usa, Inc.
1090 Horsham Rd
North Wales PA 19454
215 591-3000

(G-4417)
TH MAGNESIUM INC
9435 Waterstone Blvd (45249-8226)
PHONE.................513 285-7568
Stephen Norris, *President*
Oliver Haun, *VP Sales*
Steve Norris, *Executive*
EMP: 6 **EST:** 2015
SALES (est): 531.3K **Privately Held**
SIC: 3356 Magnesium

(G-4418)
THERMOGENICS CORP
300 E Bus Way Ste 200 (45241)
PHONE.................513 247-7963
Mark H Ingham, *Principal*
EMP: 5
SALES (est): 531.2K **Privately Held**
SIC: 3443 Fabricated plate work (boiler shop)

(G-4419)
THINKWARE INCORPORATED
7611 Cheviot Rd Ste 2 (45247-4015)
PHONE.................513 598-3300
Kevin Eickmann, *President*
Jack Dossou, *Software Engr*
EMP: 28
SQ FT: 7,500
SALES: 5.4MM **Privately Held**
WEB: www.thinkwareinc.com
SIC: 7371 7374 7372 Computer software development; data processing & preparation; prepackaged software

(G-4420)
THOMAS PRODUCTS CO INC (PA)
3625 Spring Grove Ave (45223-2458)
PHONE.................513 756-9009
Joseph Thomas, *CEO*
Paul Green, *President*
EMP: 25
SQ FT: 25,000
SALES (est): 4.6MM **Privately Held**
WEB: www.tpclabels.com
SIC: 2759 3842 2761 2672 Flexographic printing; surgical appliances & supplies; manifold business forms; coated & laminated paper; packaging paper & plastics film, coated & laminated

(G-4421)
TIA MARIE & COMPANY
8694 Long Ln (45231-5019)
PHONE.................513 521-8694
Alice Huff, *Principal*
David Alford, *Principal*
▲ **EMP:** 4
SALES (est): 160K **Privately Held**
SIC: 3161 5948 Luggage; luggage & leather goods stores

(G-4422)
TITANIUM CONTRACTORS LTD
9400 Reading Rd (45215-3401)
PHONE.................513 256-2152
Michael Postell, *Principal*
EMP: 3 **EST:** 2011
SALES (est): 223.9K **Privately Held**
SIC: 3356 Titanium

(G-4423)
TKF CONVEYOR SYSTEMS LLC
5298 River Rd (45233-1643)
PHONE.................513 621-5260
Ron Eubanks,
EMP: 110
SALES (est): 14.4MM **Privately Held**
SIC: 3535 Conveyors & conveying equipment

(G-4424)
TL KRIEG OFFSET INC
10600 Chester Rd (45215-1206)
PHONE.................513 542-1522
Terry L Krieg, *President*
Tom Schaefer, *General Mgr*
Rob Murphy, *Production*
EMP: 29
SQ FT: 30,000
SALES (est): 5.2MM **Privately Held**
WEB: www.tlkriegoffset.com
SIC: 2752 2789 Commercial printing, offset; bookbinding & related work

(G-4425)
TOM BAD BREWING LLC
4720 Eastern Ave (45226-1893)
PHONE.................513 871-4677
John Vojtush,
Sheryl Gittins,
EMP: 10
SQ FT: 2,000

(PA)=Parent Co (HQ)=Headquarters (DH)=Div Headquarters
✿ = New Business established in last 2 years

Cincinnati - Hamilton County (G-4426)

SALES (est): 519.4K **Privately Held**
SIC: 5813 2082 Bars & lounges; ale (alcoholic beverage)

(G-4426)
TORMAXX CO
1150 W 8th St Ste 111 (45203-1245)
PHONE..................................513 721-6299
Gregg Sample, *President*
Ronald E Heithaus, *Principal*
EMP: 6
SQ FT: 8,000
SALES (est): 1.1MM **Privately Held**
SIC: 3545 Machine tool accessories

(G-4427)
TOYOBO KUREHA AMERICA CO LTD
Also Called: Tk America
11630 Mosteller Rd (45241-1521)
PHONE..................................513 771-6788
Morley Thompson Jr, *Exec VP*
Mark Welch, *Opers Mgr*
Angelia Settles, *QC Mgr*
Angelia Winters, *QC Mgr*
Zoe Enright, *Manager*
▲ EMP: 38
SQ FT: 120,000
SALES: 10MM
SALES (corp-wide): 3.1B **Privately Held**
SIC: 2297 Nonwoven fabrics
HQ: Kureha Ltd.
255, Oka
Ritto SGA 520-3
775 535-660

(G-4428)
TRACK-IT SYSTEMS
1776 Mentor Ave Ste 560 (45212-3583)
PHONE..................................513 522-0083
Natalie Graves, *Principal*
EMP: 5
SALES: 950K **Privately Held**
SIC: 3663 Radio & TV communications equipment

(G-4429)
TRANE US INC
10300 Springfield Pike (45215-1118)
PHONE..................................513 771-8884
Al Fullerton, *Manager*
EMP: 50 **Privately Held**
SIC: 3585 Refrigeration & heating equipment
HQ: Trane U.S. Inc.
3600 Pammel Creek Rd
La Crosse WI 54601
608 787-2000

(G-4430)
TRANS ASH INC
Also Called: Gibbco
360 S Wayne Ave (45215-4523)
PHONE..................................859 341-1528
Brian Keplinger, *Manager*
EMP: 10
SALES (corp-wide): 55.7MM **Privately Held**
WEB: www.transash.com
SIC: 3295 Slag, crushed or ground
PA: Trans Ash, Inc.
617 Shepherd Dr
Cincinnati OH 45215
513 733-4770

(G-4431)
TRANSDUCERS DIRECT LLC
12115 Ellington Ct (45249-1000)
PHONE..................................513 247-0601
Robert W Matthes, *President*
▲ EMP: 16
SALES: 3.5MM **Privately Held**
WEB: www.transducersdirect.com
SIC: 3543 5084 Industrial patterns; industrial machine parts

(G-4432)
TREVED EXTERIORS
10235 Spartan Dr Ste T (45215-1243)
PHONE..................................513 771-3888
Eddie Oblinger, *Principal*
EMP: 7
SALES (est): 1.1MM **Privately Held**
SIC: 2851 Paint removers

(G-4433)
TRI-STATE BEEF CO INC
2124 Baymiller St (45214-2208)
PHONE..................................513 579-1722
Yong Woo Koo, *President*
EMP: 30
SALES (est): 6MM **Privately Held**
SIC: 2011 2013 5147 Meat packing plants; sausages & other prepared meats; meats & meat products

(G-4434)
TRI-STATE BELTING LTD
Also Called: Greeno Company
5525 Vine St (45217-1003)
PHONE..................................800 330-2358
Jeffrey Stagnaro, *Partner*
EMP: 5
SALES (est): 380K **Privately Held**
SIC: 3496 Conveyor belts

(G-4435)
TRI-STATE SPECIAL EVENTS INC
614 Tafel St (45225-2366)
PHONE..................................513 221-2962
Gary Robinson, *Vice Pres*
EMP: 4
SALES: 42.1K **Privately Held**
WEB: www.tristate-events.com
SIC: 2037 Frozen fruits & vegetables

(G-4436)
TRI-STATE TOOL GRINDING INC
5311 Robert Ave Ste A (45248-7200)
PHONE..................................513 347-0100
Michael L Dinkelacker, *President*
James C Dinkelacker, *Vice Pres*
Betty Dinkelacker, *Office Mgr*
EMP: 22
SQ FT: 12,000
SALES (est): 2MM **Privately Held**
SIC: 3541 Boring mills

(G-4437)
TRI-STATE WIRE ROPE SUPPLY INC (HQ)
5246 Wooster Pike (45226-2229)
PHONE..................................513 871-8623
Mel Fireovid, *President*
Patricia Fireovid, *Corp Secy*
Pat Fireovid, *Executive*
Susan Busch, *Clerk*
▲ EMP: 11
SQ FT: 6,500
SALES (est): 4.6MM **Privately Held**
WEB: www.tswr.com
SIC: 5051 3496 Metals Service Center Mfg Misc Fabricated Wire Products
PA: Fulcrum Lifting, Llc
5246 Wooster Pike
Cincinnati OH 45226
513 871-8623

(G-4438)
TRILLIUM HEALTH CARE PRODUCTS
5177 Spring Grove Ave (45217-1050)
PHONE..................................513 242-2227
Alan Gropp, *Branch Mgr*
EMP: 7
SALES (corp-wide): 2.7B **Privately Held**
WEB: www.trillium.cc
SIC: 2841 Soap: granulated, liquid, cake, flaked or chip
HQ: Trillium Health Care Products Inc
2337 Parkdale Ave E
Brockville ON K6V 5
613 342-4536

(G-4439)
TRINITY PRINTING CO
2300 E Kemper Rd Ste A19 (45241-6501)
P.O. Box 42786 (45242-0786)
PHONE..................................513 469-1000
Thomas Schroeder, *Owner*
EMP: 12
SALES: 652.6K **Privately Held**
SIC: 2759 Commercial printing

(G-4440)
TRIPOINT INSTRUMENTS INC
7513 Hamilton Ave (45231-4307)
PHONE..................................513 702-9217
Jeff Hering, *President*
Donald Hering, *Vice Pres*
Ginger Hering, *Admin Sec*
EMP: 3
SALES (est): 384.5K **Privately Held**
WEB: www.tripointinstruments.com
SIC: 3829 Fire detector systems, non-electric

(G-4441)
TROYKE MANUFACTURING COMPANY
11294 Orchard St (45241-1996)
PHONE..................................513 769-4242
Bernard R Froehlich, *President*
Eric N Froehlich, *Vice Pres*
Gary Edmondson, *Prdtn Mgr*
August Foehlich, *Manager*
EMP: 12 EST: 1952
SQ FT: 40,000
SALES (est): 2.4MM **Privately Held**
SIC: 3545 Rotary tables

(G-4442)
TRU-TEX INTERNATIONAL CORP
11050 Southland Rd (45240-3713)
P.O. Box 40107 (45240-0107)
PHONE..................................513 825-8844
Ruth Henn, *CEO*
Harry G Henn, *President*
Chris Henn, *Vice Pres*
Chrisopher Henn, *Vice Pres*
EMP: 21
SQ FT: 8,000
SALES (est): 2.6MM **Privately Held**
SIC: 3544 Dies & die holders for metal cutting, forming, die casting; punches, forming & stamping

(G-4443)
TRUE DINERO RECORDS & TECH LLC
2611 Kemper Ln Uppr Lv1 (45206-1220)
PHONE..................................513 428-4610
Aaron Savage, *President*
Tracy Savage, *Principal*
David Thompson, *Principal*
EMP: 8
SALES (est): 162.4K **Privately Held**
SIC: 5735 7336 2759 2752 Records; commercial art & graphic design; laser printing; commercial printing, offset; application computer software

(G-4444)
TSS ACQUISITION COMPANY
1201 Hill Smith Dr (45215-1228)
PHONE..................................513 772-7000
Bob Queen, *Manager*
EMP: 6
SALES (corp-wide): 226.8MM **Privately Held**
SIC: 3599 Machine shop, jobbing & repair
HQ: Tss Acquisition Company
25101 Chagrin Blvd D
Cleveland OH 44122
513 772-7000

(G-4445)
U S TERMINALS INC
7504 Camargo Rd (45243-3147)
PHONE..................................513 561-8145
Fax: 513 561-8755
EMP: 8
SQ FT: 16,000
SALES (est): 790K **Privately Held**
SIC: 3679 3678 Mfg Electronic Terminals & Connectors

(G-4446)
UNDERGROUND SPORT SHOP INC
1233 Findlay St Ste Frnt (45214-2012)
PHONE..................................513 751-1662
Sean Mason, *President*
Andy Wolterman, *Vice Pres*
Jim Hebert, *Admin Sec*
▲ EMP: 10
SQ FT: 12,000
SALES: 1MM **Privately Held**
WEB: www.undergroundsportsshop.com
SIC: 2759 7389 5199 Screen printing; embroidering of advertising on shirts, etc.; advertising specialties

(G-4447)
UNITED DAIRY FARMERS INC (PA)
Also Called: U D F
3955 Montgomery Rd (45212-3798)
PHONE..................................513 396-8700
Brad Lindner, *President*
Frank Cogliano, *Vice Pres*
Ronald Anderson, *Opers Mgr*
Angelos Christon, *Opers Staff*
Daniel May, *Production*
EMP: 200
SALES (est): 614.2MM **Privately Held**
SIC: 5411 5143 2026 2024 Convenience stores, chain; ice cream & ices; frozen dairy desserts; milk processing (pasteurizing, homogenizing, bottling); ice cream & ice milk; filling stations, gasoline; dairy products stores

(G-4448)
UNITED ENVELOPE LLC
4890 Spring Grove Ave (45232-1933)
PHONE..................................513 542-4700
Stuart Grover, *Branch Mgr*
EMP: 280
SALES (corp-wide): 30.2MM **Privately Held**
WEB: www.specialtyenvelope.com
SIC: 2677 Envelopes
HQ: United Envelope, Llc
65 Railroad Ave
Ridgefield NJ 07657

(G-4449)
UNITED PRECISION SERVICES INC
Also Called: Union America
11180 Southland Rd (45240-3202)
PHONE..................................513 851-6900
Paul Kramer, *President*
Bob Conners, *VP Sales*
▲ EMP: 9
SQ FT: 10,000
SALES (est): 1MM **Privately Held**
SIC: 3599 Machine shop, jobbing & repair

(G-4450)
UNITED STATES DRILL HEAD CO
5298 River Rd (45233-1688)
PHONE..................................513 941-0300
J H Nymberg Jr, *President*
Joseph E Bashor, *Treasurer*
EMP: 30
SQ FT: 47,772
SALES (est): 4MM **Privately Held**
SIC: 3545 3363 3543 Cutting tools for machine tools; aluminum die-castings; industrial patterns

(G-4451)
UNITED-MAIER SIGNS INC
1030 Straight St (45214-1734)
PHONE..................................513 681-6600
Antony E Maier, *President*
Elvera Maier, *Vice Pres*
Chris Maier, *Opers Mgr*
Michele Wocher, *Human Resources*
EMP: 54 EST: 1964
SQ FT: 18,000
SALES (est): 7.9MM **Privately Held**
WEB: www.united-maier.com
SIC: 3993 1799 Electric signs; sign installation & maintenance

(G-4452)
UNIVERSAL PACKG SYSTEMS INC
Also Called: Paklab
470 Northland Blvd (45240-3211)
PHONE..................................513 674-9400
Jeff Topits, *Branch Mgr*
EMP: 388
SALES (corp-wide): 399.6MM **Privately Held**
SIC: 2844 3565 7389 2671 Cosmetic preparations; bottling machinery: filling, capping, labeling; packaging & labeling services; plastic film, coated or laminated for packaging
PA: Universal Packaging Systems, Inc.
380 Townline Rd Ste 130
Hauppauge NY 11788
631 543-2277

GEOGRAPHIC SECTION
Cincinnati - Hamilton County (G-4477)

(G-4453)
UNIVERSITY OF CINCINNATI
Also Called: Hoxworth Blood Center
3130 Highland Ave Fl 3 (45219-2399)
PHONE..................513 558-1243
Christine Ackerman, *Assoc VP*
EMP: 17
SALES (corp-wide): 1.2B **Privately Held**
SIC: 2899
PA: University Of Cincinnati
2600 Clifton Ave
Cincinnati OH 45220
513 556-6000

(G-4454)
UNIVERSITY OF CINCINNATI
Also Called: U C Printing Service
5121 Fishwick Dr Ste 120 (45216-2215)
P.O. Box 210027 (45221-0027)
PHONE..................513 556-5042
Karen Kappen, *Manager*
EMP: 5
SALES (corp-wide): 1.2B **Privately Held**
SIC: 2752 8221 Commercial printing, lithographic; university
PA: University Of Cincinnati
2600 Clifton Ave
Cincinnati OH 45220
513 556-6000

(G-4455)
UPPER ECHELON BAR LLC
1747 Avonlea Ave (45237-6109)
PHONE..................513 531-2814
EMP: 3 EST: 2013
SALES (est): 184.5K **Privately Held**
SIC: 3131 Mfg Footwear Cut Stock

(G-4456)
US FOAM CORPORATION (PA)
7412 Jager Ct (45230-4344)
PHONE..................513 528-9800
Jerry Schoch, *President*
EMP: 3
SALES (est): 1.6MM **Privately Held**
SIC: 3086 Packaging & shipping materials, foamed plastic; padding, foamed plastic

(G-4457)
US GREENTECH
3607 Church St (45244-3096)
PHONE..................513 371-5520
Joe Motz, *Principal*
Brad Borgman, *Natl Sales Mgr*
EMP: 6
SALES (est): 714.4K **Privately Held**
SIC: 2282 Manmade & synthetic fiber yarns: twisting, winding, etc.

(G-4458)
US INDUSTRIAL LUBRICANTS INC
Also Called: Oil Kraft Div
3330 Beekman St (45223-2424)
PHONE..................513 541-2225
Donald L Mattcheck, *President*
Adam Freeman, *Vice Pres*
David E Ziegler, *Vice Pres*
Jenny Anderson, *Admin Sec*
EMP: 20
SQ FT: 45,000
SALES: 8MM **Privately Held**
WEB: www.usindustriallubricants.com
SIC: 2842 2992 2841 Specialty cleaning preparations; sanitation preparations; oils & greases, blending & compounding; soap & other detergents

(G-4459)
USUI INTERNATIONAL CORPORATION
88 Partnership Way (45241-1507)
PHONE..................513 448-0410
Joseph Tacinelli, *Manager*
EMP: 25
SALES (corp-wide): 776.2MM **Privately Held**
SIC: 3069 3564 Tubes, hard rubber; tubing, rubber; ventilating fans: industrial or commercial
HQ: Usui International Corporation
44780 Helm St
Plymouth MI 48170
734 354-3626

(G-4460)
UTC FIRE SEC AMERICAS CORP INC
14 Knollcrest Dr (45237-1635)
PHONE..................513 821-7945
Karen Lamhem, *Branch Mgr*
EMP: 3
SALES (corp-wide): 66.5B **Publicly Held**
SIC: 3669 Emergency alarms
HQ: Utc Fire & Security Americas Corporation, Inc.
8985 Town Center Pkwy
Lakewood Ranch FL 34202

(G-4461)
V&P GROUP INTERNATIONAL LLC
1931 Lawn Ave (45237-6125)
PHONE..................703 349-6432
Leslie Glosby, *Manager*
EMP: 16
SALES: 455.9K **Privately Held**
SIC: 6531 3731 6552 8711 Real estate agents & managers; shipbuilding & repairing; subdividers & developers; engineering services; home furnishings

(G-4462)
VALLEY ASPHALT CORPORATION
7940 Main St (45244)
PHONE..................513 561-1551
Kyle Napier, *Manager*
EMP: 3
SQ FT: 800
SALES (corp-wide): 84MM **Privately Held**
SIC: 1611 2951 General contractor, highway & street construction; asphalt & asphaltic paving mixtures (not from refineries)
HQ: Valley Asphalt Corporation
11641 Mosteller Rd
Cincinnati OH 45241
513 771-0820

(G-4463)
VALLEY ASPHALT CORPORATION
612 W Mehring Way (45202-3422)
PHONE..................513 784-1476
Buddy Cryfield, *Manager*
EMP: 3
SALES (corp-wide): 84MM **Privately Held**
SIC: 2951 Asphalt & asphaltic paving mixtures (not from refineries)
HQ: Valley Asphalt Corporation
11641 Mosteller Rd
Cincinnati OH 45241
513 771-0820

(G-4464)
VALLEY METAL WORKS INC
698 W Columbia Ave (45215-3184)
PHONE..................513 554-1022
James Steinbeck, *President*
Kevin Graham, *President*
Joe R Rings, *COO*
Fred Horst, *Vice Pres*
James Stiebeck, *Vice Pres*
EMP: 25 EST: 1934
SQ FT: 19,000
SALES (est): 6.4MM **Privately Held**
WEB: www.valleymetalworks.com
SIC: 3444 Sheet metal specialties, not stamped

(G-4465)
VAN-GRINER LLC
1009 Delta Ave (45208-3103)
PHONE..................419 733-7951
Michael Griner,
Dreis Van Landuyg,
EMP: 4
SALES: 100K **Privately Held**
SIC: 2741 Miscellaneous publishing

(G-4466)
VAPOR VAULT
2601 1/2 Short Vine St (45219-2016)
PHONE..................513 400-8789
EMP: 3

SALES (est): 147.7K **Privately Held**
SIC: 3272 Burial vaults, concrete or precast terrazzo

(G-4467)
VARIFLOW EQUIPMENT INC
3834 Ridgedale Dr (45247-6947)
PHONE..................513 245-0420
Steve Weddendorf, *President*
EMP: 2
SQ FT: 1,000
SALES: 1.5MM **Privately Held**
WEB: www.variflow.com
SIC: 3585 Refrigeration & heating equipment

(G-4468)
VEEDERS MAILBOX INC
10050 Montgomery Rd # 324 (45242)
PHONE..................513 984-8749
Jenny Lamson Magro, *President*
Jonathon Margo, *Vice Pres*
EMP: 3
SQ FT: 6,386
SALES (est): 260K **Privately Held**
SIC: 3469 Boxes: tool, lunch, mail, etc.: stamped metal

(G-4469)
VEELO TECHNOLOGIES LLC
Also Called: General Nano
10340 Julian Dr (45215-1131)
PHONE..................513 309-5947
Larry Christy, *Engineer*
Mark Schulz, *Engineer*
Joseph E Sprengard,
EMP: 14
SALES (est): 997.1K **Privately Held**
SIC: 3399 Metal powders, pastes & flakes

(G-4470)
VEGA AMERICAS INC (HQ)
Also Called: Ohmart Vega
4170 Rosslyn Dr Ste A (45209-1193)
PHONE..................513 272-0131
Cesar Malpica, *Regional Mgr*
Dan Stigler, *Regional Mgr*
Carol Ritter, *VP Admin*
Shawn Little, *Vice Pres*
Brian Oeder, *Vice Pres*
◆ EMP: 200
SQ FT: 100,000
SALES: 134.5MM
SALES (corp-wide): 261.7MM **Privately Held**
WEB: www.ohmartvega.com
SIC: 3823 Industrial instrmnts msrmnt display/control process variable
PA: Vega Grieshaber Kg
Am Hohenstein 113
Schiltach 77761
783 650-0

(G-4471)
VEMURI INTERNATIONAL LLC (PA)
Also Called: Queen City Paper
10600 Evendale Dr (45241-2518)
PHONE..................513 483-6300
Janet Bain, *Human Res Mgr*
Phil Holt, *Sales Staff*
Frank Horvat, *Marketing Staff*
Kevin Bain, *Manager*
Kusuma Vemuri,
▲ EMP: 8
SQ FT: 100,000
SALES (est): 9.1MM **Privately Held**
WEB: www.queencitypaper.com
SIC: 2679 Paperboard products, converted

(G-4472)
VENCO MANUFACTURING INC (HQ)
Also Called: Collins & Venco Venturo
12110 Best Pl (45241-1569)
PHONE..................513 772-8448
Larry R Collins, *President*
Ronald A Collins, *Vice Pres*
Mike Stritthott, *Treasurer*
Barbara Duke, *Admin Sec*
▲ EMP: 66
SQ FT: 35,000

SALES (est): 12.1MM
SALES (corp-wide): 18.3MM **Privately Held**
SIC: 3714 Motor vehicle parts & accessories
PA: Venco Venturo Industries Llc
12110 Best Pl
Cincinnati OH 45241
513 772-8448

(G-4473)
VENCO VENTURO INDUSTRIES LLC (PA)
Also Called: Venco/Venturo Div
12110 Best Pl (45241-1569)
PHONE..................513 772-8448
Brett Collins, *President*
Dave Foster, *Vice Pres*
Mike Stritthott, *CFO*
▲ EMP: 41
SQ FT: 100,000
SALES (est): 18.3MM **Privately Held**
WEB: www.venturo.com
SIC: 3713 5012 3714 5084 Truck bodies (motor vehicles); truck bodies; motor vehicle parts & accessories; cranes, industrial

(G-4474)
VENTURO MANUFACTURING INC
12110 Best Pl (45241-1569)
PHONE..................513 772-8448
Larry Collins, *President*
Ronald A Collins, *Vice Pres*
Jeremy Sapp, *Purchasing*
Joe Dirr, *QC Mgr*
Stuart Phipps, *Design Engr*
EMP: 32 EST: 1952
SQ FT: 5,000
SALES (est): 9MM
SALES (corp-wide): 18.3MM **Privately Held**
WEB: www.venturo.com
SIC: 3537 5084 Cranes, industrial truck; industrial machinery & equipment
PA: Venco Venturo Industries Llc
12110 Best Pl
Cincinnati OH 45241
513 772-8448

(G-4475)
VENUE LIFESTYLE & EVENT GUIDE
11959 Tramway Dr (45241-1666)
PHONE..................513 405-6822
Kim Wanamaker, *President*
Steve Wanamaker, *Vice Pres*
EMP: 15 EST: 2010
SALES (est): 1MM **Privately Held**
SIC: 2721 Magazines: publishing & printing

(G-4476)
VERO SECURITY GROUP LTD
5296 Montgomery Rd (45212-1656)
PHONE..................513 731-8376
Al Overson, *CEO*
Leonard M Watson, *President*
Kumar Chattoraj, *COO*
EMP: 6
SALES (est): 608.4K **Privately Held**
WEB: www.verosecurity.com
SIC: 3699 Security control equipment & systems

(G-4477)
VERTEX COMPUTER SYSTEMS INC
11260 Chester Rd Ste 300 (45246-4051)
PHONE..................513 662-6888
Murali Swamy, *Branch Mgr*
Ramam Gadela, *Manager*
Robert Harris, *Manager*
EMP: 15
SALES (corp-wide): 25.6MM **Privately Held**
WEB: www.vertexcs.com
SIC: 7372 Business oriented computer software
PA: Vertex Computer Systems, Inc.
2245 E Enterprise Pkwy
Twinsburg OH 44087
330 963-0044

Cincinnati - Hamilton County (G-4478)

(G-4478)
VERTIFLO PUMP COMPANY
7807 Redsky Dr (45249-1636)
PHONE.................513 530-0888
Mark Werner, *President*
EMP: 17
SQ FT: 18,000
SALES (est): 4.1MM **Privately Held**
WEB: www.vertiflopump.com
SIC: 3594 3561 Fluid power pumps; pumps & pumping equipment

(G-4479)
VESI INCORPORATED
16 Techview Dr (45215-1985)
PHONE.................513 563-6002
Greg Visconti, *CEO*
Dale Davidson, *COO*
Susan Litster, *Vice Pres*
Natasha Rook, *Purchasing*
Melinda Cramer, *Human Res Dir*
▲ **EMP:** 45
SQ FT: 44,500
SALES (est): 6.5MM **Privately Held**
WEB: www.vesiinc.com
SIC: 2329 2339 Men's & boys' sportswear & athletic clothing; sportswear, women's

(G-4480)
VICAS MANUFACTURING CO INC
8407 Monroe Ave (45236-1909)
P.O. Box 36310 (45236-0310)
PHONE.................513 791-7741
Virginia Willoughby, *President*
Pon May, *Vice Pres*
EMP: 47
SQ FT: 25,600
SALES (est): 8.4MM **Privately Held**
SIC: 3089 3599 Injection molding of plastics; casting of plastic; machine shop, jobbing & repair

(G-4481)
VILLAGE CABINET SHOP INC
Also Called: Reynolds Cabinetry & Millwork
1820 Loisview Ln (45255-2617)
PHONE.................704 966-0801
Derrick A Reynolds, *Branch Mgr*
EMP: 6
SALES (est): 578.6K **Privately Held**
SIC: 2541 Cabinets, except refrigerated: show, display, etc.: wood
PA: The Village Cabinet Shop Inc
17746 93rd Pl N
Osseo MN 55311

(G-4482)
VIVID WRAPS LLC
12130 Royal Point Dr (45249-3306)
PHONE.................513 515-8386
Nick Durante, *Owner*
EMP: 3
SALES (est): 94K **Privately Held**
SIC: 7336 3714 Graphic arts & related design; motor vehicle body components & frame

(G-4483)
VOLK CORPORATION
Also Called: Hathaway
635 Main St Ste 1 (45202-2524)
PHONE.................513 621-1052
Larry Schultz, *Branch Mgr*
EMP: 8
SALES (corp-wide): 30.7MM **Privately Held**
WEB: www.volkcorp.com
SIC: 3953 Marking devices
PA: Volk Corporation
23936 Indl Pk Dr
Farmington Hills MI 48335
248 477-6700

(G-4484)
VULCAN INTERNATIONAL CORP
30 Garfield Pl Ste 1000 (45202-4308)
PHONE.................513 621-2850
Benjamin Gattler, *Branch Mgr*
EMP: 9
SALES (corp-wide): 9.7MM **Publicly Held**
SIC: 3069 Medical & laboratory rubber sundries & related products

PA: Vulcan International Corporation
300 Delaware Ave Ste 1704
Wilmington DE 19801
302 428-3181

(G-4485)
VYA INC
Also Called: Docustar
1325 Glendale Milford Rd (45215-1210)
P.O. Box 634015 (45263-4015)
PHONE.................513 772-5400
Jay Brokamp, *President*
Terry Brokamp, *Vice Pres*
Michael Rice, *Manager*
Liz Schaefer, *Director*
EMP: 41
SQ FT: 56,000
SALES (est): 9.6MM **Privately Held**
WEB: www.docustar.com
SIC: 2759 2675 2752 Commercial printing; die-cut paper & board; commercial printing, lithographic

(G-4486)
WAITS INSTRUMENTS LLC
1337 Karahill Dr (45240-2253)
PHONE.................513 600-5996
Matthew Waits, *CEO*
Brandy Waits, *President*
Gary Waits, *Vice Pres*
EMP: 3 EST: 2016
SALES (est): 125.4K **Privately Held**
SIC: 3931 Fretted instruments & parts

(G-4487)
WALL COLMONOY CORPORATION
940 Redna Ter (45215-1113)
P.O. Box Na Ter (45215)
PHONE.................937 278-9111
Don Hainley, *General Mgr*
Amy Lewis, *Manager*
EMP: 18
SQ FT: 3,200
SALES (corp-wide): 71.7MM **Privately Held**
WEB: www.wallcolmonoy.com
SIC: 3398 3341 Brazing (hardening) of metal; secondary nonferrous metals
HQ: Wall Colmonoy Corporation
101 W Girard Ave
Madison Heights MI 48071
248 585-6400

(G-4488)
WALL COLMONOY CORPORATION
Aerobraze Division
940 Redna Ter (45215-1113)
PHONE.................513 842-4200
Ken Coldfelter, *Branch Mgr*
EMP: 55
SALES (corp-wide): 71.7MM **Privately Held**
WEB: www.wallcolmonoy.com
SIC: 3812 Search & navigation equipment
HQ: Wall Colmonoy Corporation
101 W Girard Ave
Madison Heights MI 48071
248 585-6400

(G-4489)
WALLINGFORD COFFEE MILLS INC (PA)
11401 Rockfield Ct (45241-1971)
PHONE.................513 771-3131
Gary Weber Sr, *President*
▼ **EMP:** 80
SQ FT: 38,000
SALES (est): 14.9MM **Privately Held**
WEB: www.wallingfordcoffee.com
SIC: 2095 2099 Coffee roasting (except by wholesale grocers); tea blending

(G-4490)
WARNER CHLCOTT PHRMCTICALS INC (PA)
1 Procter And Gamble Plz (45202-3315)
PHONE.................513 983-1100
EMP: 11
SQ FT: 1,600,000
SALES (est): 259.8MM **Privately Held**
SIC: 2834 Mfg Pharmaceutical Preparations

(G-4491)
WATER WARRIORS INC
1776 Mentor Ave Ste 400f (45212-3573)
PHONE.................513 288-5669
John Gradek, *CEO*
EMP: 3
SALES (est): 200.8K **Privately Held**
SIC: 2899 Waterproofing compounds

(G-4492)
WAYNE SIGNER ENTERPRISES INC
Also Called: E-Z Pack
6545 Wiehe Rd (45237-4217)
PHONE.................513 841-1351
Wayne A Signer, *CEO*
Barry Schwartz, *President*
Barbara Signer, *Vice Pres*
Teri Junker, *VP Sales*
EMP: 35
SQ FT: 38,000
SALES (est): 4MM **Privately Held**
WEB: www.ezpack.com
SIC: 2631 Container, packaging & boxboard

(G-4493)
WCM HOLDINGS INC
11500 Canal Rd (45241-1862)
PHONE.................513 705-2100
David Herche, *CEO*
Tim Fogarty, *President*
Melvyn Fisher, *Chairman*
▲ **EMP:** 6
SALES (est): 59.2MM **Privately Held**
SIC: 5099 2381 3842 Safety equipment & supplies; gloves, work: woven or knit, made from purchased materials; clothing, fire resistant & protective

(G-4494)
WEEKLY JUICERY
2727 Erie Ave (45208-2164)
PHONE.................513 321-0680
EMP: 3
SALES (est): 121.2K **Privately Held**
SIC: 2711 Newspapers

(G-4495)
WELAGE CORPORATION
1925 Powers St (45223-2373)
PHONE.................513 681-2300
David Welage, *President*
Brad Ruter, *Vice Pres*
Sean Munyon, *Project Mgr*
Steve Thompson, *Sales Mgr*
Stephanie Kramer, *Technology*
EMP: 15 EST: 1937
SQ FT: 15,000
SALES (est): 4MM **Privately Held**
WEB: www.welagecorp.com
SIC: 3441 3469 3544 Fabricated structural metal; metal stampings; special dies, tools, jigs & fixtures

(G-4496)
WELCH FOODS INC A COOPERATIVE
720 E Pete Rose Way (45202-3579)
PHONE.................513 632-5610
EMP: 3
SALES (corp-wide): 608.4MM **Privately Held**
SIC: 2033 Canned fruits & specialties
HQ: Welch Foods Inc., A Cooperative
300 Baker Ave Ste 101
Concord MA 01742
978 371-1000

(G-4497)
WELCH HOLDINGS INC
8953 E Miami River Rd (45247-2232)
PHONE.................513 353-3220
James R Welch, *President*
Ronnie L Welch, *Treasurer*
EMP: 45
SQ FT: 3,400
SALES (est): 4.4MM **Privately Held**
WEB: www.welchsand.com
SIC: 1442 Common sand mining; gravel mining

(G-4498)
WELSH FARMS LLC
221 E 4th St Ste 2000 (45202-4194)
PHONE.................513 723-4487
Rosemary Welsh, *Principal*
EMP: 3
SALES (est): 140.7K **Privately Held**
SIC: 2024 Ice cream & frozen desserts

(G-4499)
WEST CHESTER HOLDINGS LLC
Also Called: West Chester Protective Gear
11500 Canal Rd (45241-1862)
PHONE.................800 647-1900
Tim Fogarty, *CEO*
Mark J Jahnke, *President*
Ken Meyer, *President*
Robert W Fisher, *Corp Secy*
Mike Derge, *Vice Pres*
▲ **EMP:** 110
SQ FT: 200,000
SALES (est): 48MM
SALES (corp-wide): 1.9B **Privately Held**
SIC: 3842 2381 5136 5137 Clothing, fire resistant & protective; gloves, work: woven or knit, made from purchased materials; men's & boys' clothing; women's & children's clothing; safety equipment & supplies
HQ: Protective Industrial Products, Inc.
968 Albany Shaker Rd
Latham NY 12110
518 861-0133

(G-4500)
WEST PHARMACEUTICAL SVCS INC
3309 Wheatcroft Dr (45239-6158)
PHONE.................513 741-3004
Karen Beck, *Principal*
EMP: 4
SALES (corp-wide): 1.7B **Publicly Held**
SIC: 2834 Pharmaceutical preparations
PA: West Pharmaceutical Services, Inc.
530 Herman O West Dr
Exton PA 19341
610 594-2900

(G-4501)
WESTEND BREWING LLC
5091 Orangelawn Dr (45238-5721)
PHONE.................513 922-0289
Barbara Bain, *Principal*
EMP: 3
SALES (est): 113.7K **Privately Held**
SIC: 2082 Malt beverages

(G-4502)
WESTERHAUS METALS LLC
3965 Delmar Ave (45211-3531)
PHONE.................513 240-9441
David Westerhaus, *Principal*
EMP: 4
SALES (est): 408.1K **Privately Held**
SIC: 3441 Fabricated structural metal

(G-4503)
WESTERN & SOUTHERN LF INSUR CO (DH)
Also Called: Western-Southern Life
400 Broadway St (45202-3341)
P.O. Box 1119 (45201-1119)
PHONE.................513 629-1800
John F Barrett, *President*
Marilyn Cobb, *President*
Dennis Dietz, *President*
David Dimartino, *President*
Donna Parobek, *President*
EMP: 982 EST: 1888
SQ FT: 600,000
SALES (est): 1.6B **Privately Held**
SIC: 6211 6311 2511 Investment firm, general brokerage; life insurance; play pens, children's: wood
HQ: Western & Southern Financial Group, Inc.
400 Broadway St
Cincinnati OH 45202
866 832-7719

GEOGRAPHIC SECTION

Cincinnati - Hamilton County (G-4530)

(G-4504)
WESTROCK CP LLC
Also Called: Smurfit Stone
414 S Cooper Ave (45215-4555)
PHONE.................513 745-2586
Rich Branson, *Manager*
EMP: 310
SALES (corp-wide): 16.2B **Publicly Held**
SIC: 2621 Wrapping & packaging papers
HQ: Westrock Cp, Llc
1000 Abernathy Rd
Atlanta GA 30328

(G-4505)
WHEATLEY ELECTRIC SERVICE CO
2046 Ross Ave (45212-2040)
PHONE.................513 531-4951
Dorothy Elsbrock, *President*
Jim Elsbrock, *Vice Pres*
EMP: 7 **EST:** 1934
SQ FT: 5,000
SALES (est): 1.6MM **Privately Held**
WEB: www.wheatleyelectric.com
SIC: 7694 5999 5063 Electric motor repair; motors, electric; motors, electric

(G-4506)
WHITE CASTLE SYSTEM INC
3126 Exon Ave (45241-2548)
PHONE.................513 563-2290
Jarrett Cook, *Plant Mgr*
Scott Hacker, *Manager*
Cindy Merritt, *Maintence Staff*
EMP: 28
SALES (corp-wide): 613.7MM **Privately Held**
WEB: www.whitecastle.com
SIC: 5812 2099 Fast-food restaurant, chain; sandwiches, assembled & packaged: for wholesale market
PA: White Castle System, Inc.
555 W Goodale St
Columbus OH 43215
614 228-5781

(G-4507)
WHITWORTH KNIFE COMPANY
508 Missouri Ave (45226-1121)
PHONE.................513 321-9177
Raymond Whitworth, *Owner*
EMP: 3
SALES: 150K **Privately Held**
SIC: 3545 Shear knives

(G-4508)
WILD JOES INC
Also Called: Wild Joe's Beef Jerky
2905 Jessamine St (45225-2147)
P.O. Box 14154 (45250-0154)
PHONE.................513 681-9200
Micah Gaunt, *Principal*
Joe Lachenman, *Admin Sec*
▲ **EMP:** 4
SQ FT: 5,800
SALES: 28K **Privately Held**
WEB: www.wildjoesbeefjerky.com
SIC: 2013 Prepared beef products from purchased beef

(G-4509)
WILD OAK LLC
35 Lenore Dr (45215-4024)
PHONE.................513 769-0526
Rich Theil,
EMP: 4
SALES: 100K **Privately Held**
SIC: 7372 8742 7389 Application computer software; management consulting services;

(G-4510)
WILLIAM POWELL COMPANY (PA)
Also Called: Powell Valve
2503 Spring Grove Ave (45214-1729)
PHONE.................513 852-2000
David R Cowart, *President*
Steve Flynn, *Regional Mgr*
Brandy Cowart, *Exec VP*
Tim Fries, *Vice Pres*
Jeff Thompson, *Vice Pres*
▲ **EMP:** 70 **EST:** 1846

SALES (est): 94.2MM **Privately Held**
WEB: www.powellvalves.com
SIC: 3491 3494 Pressure valves & regulators, industrial; valves & pipe fittings

(G-4511)
WILLIS MUSIC COMPANY
11700 Princeton Pike E209 (45246-2535)
PHONE.................513 671-3288
Robert Mooney, *Manager*
EMP: 10
SALES (corp-wide): 7.2MM **Privately Held**
WEB: www.willismusic.com
SIC: 2741 5736 Music, sheet: publishing & printing; musical instrument stores
PA: Willis Music Company
7567 Mall Rd
Florence KY 41042
859 283-2050

(G-4512)
WILLOW FROG LLC
9 Briarwood Ln (45218-1313)
PHONE.................513 861-4834
David Otting,
Jarrod Becker,
Jennifer Bucheit,
EMP: 3 **EST:** 2012
SALES (est): 102.2K **Privately Held**
SIC: 7372 Application computer software

(G-4513)
WINE CELLAR INNOVATIONS LLC
Also Called: Honeywell Authorized Dealer
4575 Eastern Ave (45226-1805)
PHONE.................513 321-3733
James L Deckebach, *Owner*
◆ **EMP:** 157 **EST:** 1978
SQ FT: 350,000
SALES (est): 22.9MM **Privately Held**
SIC: 2511 2541 Wood household furniture; wood partitions & fixtures

(G-4514)
WJF ENTERPRISES LLC
Also Called: Specialty Wood Products
1347 Custer Ave (45208-2556)
PHONE.................513 871-7320
William Funk,
EMP: 15
SQ FT: 32,000
SALES: 2MM **Privately Held**
SIC: 2448 Wood pallets & skids

(G-4515)
WM LANG & SONS COMPANY
3280 Beekman St (45223-2423)
PHONE.................513 541-3304
Robert Schutte, *President*
Howard Schutte Jr, *Vice Pres*
Jeffrey Tuttle, *Vice Pres*
Joseph Schutte, *Admin Sec*
EMP: 18 **EST:** 1892
SQ FT: 16,800
SALES (est): 4.1MM **Privately Held**
SIC: 3441 Building components, structural steel

(G-4516)
WOOD GRAPHICS INC (HQ)
Also Called: United Engraving
8075 Reading Rd Ste 301 (45237-1416)
PHONE.................513 771-6300
Mark Richler, *President*
Gaylord H Fill, *Corp Secy*
◆ **EMP:** 30 **EST:** 1972
SQ FT: 21,500
SALES (est): 2.7MM
SALES (corp-wide): 164.4MM **Privately Held**
SIC: 3555 7699 2796 Printing trades machinery; industrial machinery & equipment repair; platemaking services
PA: Rotation Dynamics Corporation
1101 Windham Pkwy
Romeoville IL 60446
630 769-9255

(G-4517)
WORKFLEX SOLUTIONS LLC (DH)
7872 Cooper Rd (45242-7612)
PHONE.................513 257-0215
Larry Schwartz, *CEO*

Mitesh Desai, *COO*
EMP: 8
SALES (est): 3.4MM
SALES (corp-wide): 1.3B **Privately Held**
SIC: 7372 Business oriented computer software
HQ: Nice Systems, Inc.
221 River St Ste 10
Hoboken NJ 07030
551 256-5000

(G-4518)
WORKS INTERNATIONAL INC
Also Called: Public School Works
3825 Edwards Rd Ste 400 (45209-1288)
PHONE.................513 631-6111
Stephen J Temming, *President*
Jeff Blain, *Vice Pres*
Carrie Mockler, *Vice Pres*
Tom Strasburger, *Vice Pres*
EMP: 4
SALES (est): 119.5K **Privately Held**
SIC: 7372 Business oriented computer software; educational computer software

(G-4519)
WORTHMORE FOOD PRODUCTS CO
1021 Ludlow Ave (45223-2621)
PHONE.................513 559-1473
Phil Hock III, *President*
Richard Hock, *Admin Sec*
EMP: 12 **EST:** 1924
SQ FT: 15,000
SALES: 4MM **Privately Held**
SIC: 2032 2033 Soups, except seafood: packaged in cans, jars, etc.; chili with or without meat: packaged in cans, jars, etc.; spaghetti: packaged in cans, jars, etc.; Italian foods: packaged in cans, jars, etc.; pizza sauce: packaged in cans, jars, etc.; spaghetti & other pasta sauce: packaged in cans, jars, etc.

(G-4520)
WRIGHT BROTHERS INC (PA)
1930 Losantiville Ave (45237-4106)
PHONE.................513 731-2222
Charles Wright, *President*
Josh Gerdes, *General Mgr*
Dee Wright, *Purchasing*
Tim Mooney, *Treasurer*
Ashley Werthaiser, *Marketing Mgr*
EMP: 35
SQ FT: 15,000
SALES (est): 8.7MM **Privately Held**
WEB: www.expectthebest.com
SIC: 2813 3446 5084 Industrial gases; architectural metalwork; welding machinery & equipment

(G-4521)
WRIGHT BROTHERS GLOBAL GAS LLC
7825 Cooper Rd (45242-7605)
PHONE.................513 731-2222
Ashley Werthaiser, *President*
Neal O Willmann, *Principal*
Cyndi Blalock, *COO*
EMP: 7
SALES (est): 1.2MM **Privately Held**
SIC: 2813 Industrial gases

(G-4522)
WRIGHT WAY PATTERNS
6109 W Fork Rd (45247-5765)
PHONE.................513 574-5776
Robert Wright, *Owner*
EMP: 4
SQ FT: 9,500
SALES (est): 264K **Privately Held**
SIC: 3543 Foundry patternmaking

(G-4523)
WRITELY SEW LLC
3862 Race Rd (45211)
PHONE.................513 728-2682
Lee Schaefer, *Vice Pres*
Raymond G Hollenkamp Jr,
EMP: 4
SALES: 250K **Privately Held**
SIC: 2395 Embroidery & art needlework

(G-4524)
WULCO INC
Also Called: Jet Machine
6900 Steger Dr (45237-3096)
PHONE.................513 679-2600
Adam Wulfeck, *Vice Pres*
EMP: 99
SQ FT: 80,000 **Privately Held**
SIC: 3599 Machine shop, jobbing & repair
PA: Wulco, Inc.
6899 Steger Dr Ste A
Cincinnati OH 45237

(G-4525)
WULCO INC (PA)
Also Called: Jet Machine & Manufacturing
6899 Steger Dr Ste A (45237-3059)
PHONE.................513 679-2600
Richard G Wulfeck, *President*
Adam Wulfeck, *Vice Pres*
Chris Wulfeck, *Safety Dir*
Jeff Wulfeck, *Opers Mgr*
Zach Stoeppel, *Mfg Mgr*
▲ **EMP:** 100
SQ FT: 100,000
SALES (est): 145.3MM **Privately Held**
WEB: www.wulco.com
SIC: 5085 3599 Industrial supplies; machine shop, jobbing & repair

(G-4526)
X-3-5 LLC
Also Called: Solstreme
7621 E Kemper Rd (45249-1609)
PHONE.................513 489-5477
Randal Sadler, *Partner*
David Necamp, *Partner*
EMP: 5
SQ FT: 7,400
SALES (est): 345.3K **Privately Held**
SIC: 3589 5084 9511 Sewage & water treatment equipment; pollution control equipment, water (environmental); air, water & solid waste management

(G-4527)
XOMOX CORPORATION
Also Called: Crane Chempharma & Energy
4444 Cooper Rd (45242-5686)
PHONE.................936 271-6500
Dale Friemoth, *Vice Pres*
Bill Hayes, *Vice Pres*
Steve Garrett, *Sales Staff*
Ron Mathis, *Director*
Aneta Stephens, *Director*
EMP: 33
SALES (corp-wide): 3.3B **Publicly Held**
SIC: 3491 3593 3494 Boiler gauge cocks; fluid power actuators, hydraulic or pneumatic; plumbing & heating valves
HQ: Xomox Corporation
4526 Res Frest Dr Ste 400
The Woodlands TX 77381
936 271-6500

(G-4528)
XRAY MEDIA LTD
445 Mcgregor Ave (45206-2365)
PHONE.................513 751-9641
Arie Vandenberg, *Principal*
EMP: 4
SALES (est): 271.6K **Privately Held**
SIC: 2721 Magazines: publishing only, not printed on site

(G-4529)
XS SMITH INC (PA)
5513 Vine St Ste 1 (45217-1022)
PHONE.................252 940-5060
Richard W Smith Jr, *President*
Scott Thompson, *Exec VP*
Cheryl Difiore, *Treasurer*
EMP: 20 **EST:** 1946
SQ FT: 40,000
SALES (est): 8.4MM **Privately Held**
WEB: www.xssmith.com
SIC: 5191 3448 3231 Greenhouse equipment & supplies; greenhouses: prefabricated metal; products of purchased glass

(G-4530)
XTEK INC (PA)
11451 Reading Rd (45241-2283)
PHONE.................513 733-7800
James E Schwab, *President*
Frank P Petrek, *Vice Pres*

(PA)=Parent Co (HQ)=Headquarters (DH)=Div Headquarters
✪ = New Business established in last 2 years

2019 Harris Ohio Industrial Directory

Cincinnati - Hamilton County (G-4531)

GEOGRAPHIC SECTION

Frank Petrek, *Vice Pres*
James J Raible, *Vice Pres*
Albert Schreiver IV, *Vice Pres*
◆ **EMP:** 336 **EST:** 1909
SQ FT: 363,440
SALES (est): 151.5MM **Privately Held**
WEB: www.xtek.com
SIC: 3568 3547 3398 3312 Power transmission equipment; rolling mill machinery; metal heat treating; wheels, locomotive & car: iron & steel

(G-4531)
YAGOOT
7875 Montgomery Rd # 1241 (45236-4606)
PHONE 513 791-6600
EMP: 3
SALES (est): 161.1K **Privately Held**
SIC: 2024 Mfg Ice Cream/Frozen Desert

(G-4532)
ZECH PRINTING INDUSTRIES INC
6310 Este Ave (45232-1450)
PHONE 937 748-2776
Kip R Zech, *President*
EMP: 22
SALES (est): 1.6MM **Privately Held**
SIC: 2759 2671 Letterpress printing; packaging paper & plastics film, coated & laminated

(G-4533)
ZIPSCENE LLC
615 Main St Fl 5 (45202-2538)
PHONE 513 201-5174
Sameer Mungur, *CEO*
Mohamed Berete, *Director*
Rick Lamy, *Officer*
EMP: 62
SQ FT: 2,000
SALES (est): 10.8MM **Privately Held**
SIC: 7372 Business oriented computer software

(G-4534)
ZTS INC
5628 Wooster Pike (45227-4121)
PHONE 513 271-2557
Dave Zimmerman, *President*
Philip D Zimmerman, *President*
Phil Zimmerman, *Principal*
Marge Zimmerman, *Corp Secy*
▲ **EMP:** 10 **EST:** 1970
SQ FT: 8,000
SALES (est): 1.7MM **Privately Held**
SIC: 3825 Battery testers, electrical

(G-4535)
ZYGO INC
Also Called: Cincy Deli & Carryout
2832 Jefferson Ave (45219-1920)
P.O. Box 19311 (45219-0311)
PHONE 513 281-0888
Jim Powers, *CEO*
EMP: 8
SQ FT: 1,500
SALES (est): 1MM **Privately Held**
SIC: 5411 2097 Delicatessens; supermarkets, hypermarket; ice cubes

Circleville
Pickaway County

(G-4536)
ALL DO WELD & FAB LLC
28155 River Dr (43113-9726)
PHONE 740 477-2133
Sheng Stack, *Opers Mgr*
Dustin Picklesimer,
Troy S Brady,
EMP: 6
SALES: 250K **Privately Held**
SIC: 7692 Welding repair

(G-4537)
AMERICAN WOOD FIBERS INC
2500 Owens Rd (43113-8963)
PHONE 740 420-3233
Mark Roth, *Manager*
EMP: 32 **Privately Held**
WEB: www.awf.com
SIC: 2499 Mulch or sawdust products, wood; wood flour
PA: American Wood Fibers, Inc.
9740 Patuxent
Columbia MD 21046

(G-4538)
CENTRAL COCA-COLA BTLG CO INC
387 Walnut St (43113-2225)
PHONE 740 474-2180
EMP: 5
SALES (corp-wide): 35.4B **Publicly Held**
SIC: 5149 2086 8741 Soft drinks; soft drinks: packaged in cans, bottles, etc.; management services
HQ: Central Coca-Cola Bottling Company, Inc.
555 Taxter Rd Ste 550
Elmsford NY 10523
914 789-1100

(G-4539)
CIRCLEVILLE OIL CO
Also Called: Subway
224 Lancaster Pike (43113-1507)
P.O. Box 189 (43113-0189)
PHONE 740 477-3341
Lori Whited, *Manager*
EMP: 8
SALES (corp-wide): 43.7MM **Privately Held**
WEB: www.circlevilleoil.com
SIC: 1389 7539 5812 Construction, repair & dismantling services; brake services; sandwiches & submarines shop
PA: Circleville Oil Co (Inc)
315 Town St
Circleville OH 43113
740 474-7544

(G-4540)
COLONELS QUARTERS
131 Park Pl (43113-1211)
PHONE 740 385-3374
Amanda Aquino, *Owner*
EMP: 4
SALES (est): 65.4K **Privately Held**
SIC: 3131 Mfg Footwear Cut Stock

(G-4541)
CROWN PRINTING INC
118 S Scioto St (43113-1638)
PHONE 740 477-2511
Ronald Snyder, *President*
Kristy June, *Office Mgr*
EMP: 4 **EST:** 1976
SQ FT: 3,800
SALES (est): 482.7K **Privately Held**
WEB: www.crownprintingcorp.com
SIC: 2752 Commercial printing, offset

(G-4542)
DAN PATRICK ENTERPRISES INC
8564 Zane Trail Rd (43113-9745)
PHONE 740 477-1006
Daniel E Patrick, *President*
Christine Patrick, *Corp Secy*
EMP: 6
SQ FT: 3,500
SALES: 1MM **Privately Held**
WEB: www.samson4x4.com
SIC: 3713 5013 7538 Truck bodies & parts; truck parts & accessories; general truck repair

(G-4543)
DUPONT SPECIALTY PDTS USA LLC
S Dupont Rd Rr 23 (43113)
PHONE 740 474-0220
John Roberts, *Safety Mgr*
Tony Eichstadt, *Manager*
EMP: 50
SALES (corp-wide): 85.9B **Publicly Held**
WEB: www.dupont.com
SIC: 2821 3861 3081 Polyesters; polytrafluoroethylene resins (teflon); photographic equipment & supplies; unsupported plastics film & sheet
HQ: Dupont Specialty Products Usa, Llc
2030 Dow Ctr
Midland MI 48674
989 636-1000

(G-4544)
DUPONT SPECIALTY PDTS USA LLC
Also Called: Dupont Vespel Parts and Shapes
800 Dupont Rd (43113)
PHONE 740 474-0635
Wayne Macdonald, *Manager*
EMP: 75
SALES (corp-wide): 85.9B **Publicly Held**
WEB: www.dupont.com
SIC: 2821 Plastics materials & resins
HQ: Dupont Specialty Products Usa, Llc
2030 Dow Ctr
Midland MI 48674
989 636-1000

(G-4545)
FLORIDA PRODUCTION ENGRG INC
Also Called: Eg Industries
30627 Orr Rd (43113-9731)
PHONE 740 420-5252
Chuck Reisinger, *Manager*
EMP: 160
SALES (corp-wide): 582.7MM **Privately Held**
SIC: 3089 Injection molding of plastics
HQ: Florida Production Engineering, Inc.
2 E Tower Cir
Ormond Beach FL 32174
386 677-2566

(G-4546)
GEORGIA-PACIFIC LLC
2850 Owens Rd (43113-9079)
P.O. Box 379 (43113-0379)
PHONE 740 477-3347
Terry Gaffney, *Manager*
EMP: 130
SALES (corp-wide): 42.4B **Privately Held**
WEB: www.gp.com
SIC: 2653 3412 2675 2671 Boxes, corrugated: made from purchased materials; metal barrels, drums & pails; die-cut paper & board; packaging paper & plastics film, coated & laminated; paperboard mills
HQ: Georgia-Pacific Llc
133 Peachtree St Nw
Atlanta GA 30303
404 652-4000

(G-4547)
JM PRINTING
134 W Main St (43113-1620)
PHONE 740 412-8666
EMP: 4
SALES (est): 393.3K **Privately Held**
SIC: 2752 Commercial printing, lithographic

(G-4548)
MES MATERIAL HDLG SYSTEMS LLC
28196 Scippo Creek Rd (43113-9796)
P.O. Box 370 (43113-0370)
PHONE 740 477-8920
Nancy Picklesimer,
EMP: 4
SALES (est): 226.2K **Privately Held**
SIC: 3599 5084 Industrial machinery; materials handling machinery

(G-4549)
NANOMELD LLC
18646 Us Rte 23 N (43113)
PHONE 740 477-5900
Michael Rhodes, *General Mgr*
EMP: 4
SALES (est): 584.9K **Privately Held**
SIC: 2299 Yarn, metallic, ceramic or paper fibers

(G-4550)
NANOSTATICS CORPORATION
18646 Us Rte 23 (43113)
PHONE 740 477-5900
Mark Schweizer, *President*
Dr John Robertson, *Founder*
Dr Ashley Scott, *CFO*
EMP: 10
SQ FT: 5,000
SALES (est): 1.1MM **Privately Held**
SIC: 3823 Industrial process control instruments

(G-4551)
PHIL D DE MINT
Also Called: Phil's Custom Cabinets
6345 State Route 56 E (43113-9449)
PHONE 740 474-7777
Phil De Mint, *Owner*
EMP: 4
SALES: 150K **Privately Held**
SIC: 2434 Wood kitchen cabinets

(G-4552)
PICKAWAY NEWS JOURNAL
375 Edwards Rd (43113-1314)
PHONE 740 851-3072
Patricia L Bennett, *Administration*
EMP: 3
SALES (est): 92.2K **Privately Held**
SIC: 2711 Newspapers, publishing & printing

(G-4553)
PPG INDUSTRIES INC
559 Pittsburgh Rd (43113-9436)
PHONE 740 474-3161
Dave Moss, *Branch Mgr*
EMP: 210
SALES (corp-wide): 15.3B **Publicly Held**
SIC: 2851 Paints & allied products
PA: Ppg Industries, Inc.
1 Ppg Pl
Pittsburgh PA 15272
412 434-3131

(G-4554)
PPG INDUSTRIES INC
Also Called: PPG 5412
221 E Main St (43113-1727)
PHONE 740 474-3945
Sandy Carnein, *Manager*
EMP: 24
SALES (corp-wide): 15.3B **Publicly Held**
WEB: www.ppg.com
SIC: 2851 Paints & allied products
PA: Ppg Industries, Inc.
1 Ppg Pl
Pittsburgh PA 15272
412 434-3131

(G-4555)
QUALITY CRAFTSMAN INC
28155 River Dr (43113-9726)
PHONE 740 474-9685
EMP: 10
SQ FT: 10,000
SALES: 1.8MM **Privately Held**
SIC: 3444 Mfg Sheet Metalwork

(G-4556)
RED BARN SCREEN PRINTING & EMB
Also Called: Red Barn, The
1144 Northridge Rd (43113-9396)
PHONE 740 474-6657
Raymond Larry, *President*
Jerrilyn Stevens, *President*
EMP: 15
SALES (est): 1.1MM **Privately Held**
WEB: www.redbarntshirts.com
SIC: 2395 7336 Embroidery & art needlework; silk screen design

(G-4557)
SHELLY COMPANY
24537 Canal Rd (43113-9691)
PHONE 740 474-6255
Dave McCay, *Superintendent*
EMP: 3
SALES (corp-wide): 29.7B **Privately Held**
SIC: 1611 2951 Highway & street paving contractor; concrete, bituminous
HQ: Shelly Company
80 Park Dr
Thornville OH 43076
740 246-6315

(G-4558)
SIGN SHOP
Also Called: Lighted House Numbers
3269 State Route 361 (43113-9728)
PHONE 740 474-1499
Tony McCammon, *Owner*
Garnet McCammon, *Co-Owner*
EMP: 4
SALES (est): 182.6K **Privately Held**
SIC: 3993 Signs & advertising specialties

GEOGRAPHIC SECTION

Cleveland - Cuyahoga County (G-4584)

(G-4559)
SUBURBAN METAL PRODUCTS INC
1050 Tarlton Rd (43113-9132)
PHONE.................................740 474-4237
Linda Kempton, *Corp Secy*
Joe Cline, *Director*
EMP: 18
SQ FT: 12,000
SALES (est): 3.6MM **Privately Held**
SIC: 3599 3441 7692 3544 Machine shop, jobbing & repair; fabricated structural metal; welding repair; special dies, tools, jigs & fixtures; sheet metalwork

(G-4560)
TANGENT AIR INC
127 Edison Ave (43113-2117)
PHONE.................................740 474-1114
John Morehead, *President*
Susan Potter, *Sales Staff*
Jerry Jones, *Admin Sec*
EMP: 38
SQ FT: 17,000
SALES (est): 6.9MM **Privately Held**
WEB: www.tangentairinc.com
SIC: 3321 3444 Cast iron pipe & fittings; sheet metalwork

(G-4561)
TECHNICOLOR USA INC
Also Called: Circleville Glass Operations
155 E Circle Ln (43113-7566)
PHONE.................................614 474-8821
Chet Kucinski, *Manager*
EMP: 925
SQ FT: 325,000
SALES (corp-wide): 62.9MM **Privately Held**
SIC: 3651 3231 Household audio & video equipment; products of purchased glass
HQ: Technicolor Usa, Inc.
  101 W 103rd St
  Indianapolis IN 46290
  317 587-4287

(G-4562)
TELESIS TECHNOLOGIES INC (DH)
Also Called: Telesis Marking Systems
28181 River Dr (43113-9726)
P.O. Box 1000 (43113-7000)
PHONE.................................740 477-5000
Steve Sheng, *President*
Warren R Knipple, *Vice Pres*
▲ EMP: 135
SQ FT: 39,900
SALES (est): 40.5MM
SALES (corp-wide): 448.5MM **Privately Held**
SIC: 3953 Cancelling stamps, hand: rubber or metal
HQ: Tyden Group Holdings Corp.
  409 Hoosier Dr
  Angola IN 46703
  740 420-6777

(G-4563)
TRIMOLD LLC
200 Pittsburgh Rd (43113-9288)
PHONE.................................740 474-7591
Yoshimasa Okada, *Mng Member*
Katsuya Kanda,
EMP: 360
SALES (est): 66.1MM
SALES (corp-wide): 4.5B **Privately Held**
WEB: www.tstrim.com
SIC: 3089 Injection molding of plastics
HQ: Ts Trim Industries Inc.
  6380 Canal St
  Canal Winchester OH 43110
  614 837-4114

(G-4564)
WITTICHS CANDIES INC
Also Called: Wittich's Candy Shop
117 W High St (43113-1615)
PHONE.................................740 474-3313
Fred Wittich, *President*
EMP: 5
SQ FT: 5,000
SALES (est): 495.2K **Privately Held**
SIC: 5441 2064 Candy; candy & other confectionery products

(G-4565)
WYATT SPECIALTIES INC
4761 State Route 361 (43113-9736)
PHONE.................................614 989-5362
James Wyatt, *Principal*
Deborah Wyatt, *Admin Sec*
EMP: 3
SALES: 130K **Privately Held**
SIC: 3711 Automobile assembly, including specialty automobiles

Clarington
Monroe County

(G-4566)
AMERICAN HVY PLATE SLTIONS LLC
42722 State Route 7 Ste 1 (43915-9583)
PHONE.................................740 331-4620
Rebecca A Znidarsich,
EMP: 5 EST: 2017
SALES (est): 154.1K **Privately Held**
SIC: 2796 Plates & cylinders for rotogravure printing

(G-4567)
DIVERSIFD OH VLLY EQPT & SRVCS
Also Called: D.O.V.E.S.
50817 State Route 556 (43915-9632)
P.O. Box 73 (43915-0073)
PHONE.................................740 458-9881
Mary Rankin,
▲ EMP: 10
SALES: 1MM **Privately Held**
WEB: www.doves.com
SIC: 3441 8611 3312 5012 Fabricated structural metal; business associations; blast furnaces & steel mills; automobiles & other motor vehicles; equipment rental & leasing; industrial buildings & warehouses

Clarksville
Clinton County

(G-4568)
SHATZELS BACKHOE SERVICE LLC
4044 Pansy Rd (45113-8667)
PHONE.................................937 289-9630
Richard Schatzel, *Principal*
EMP: 4
SALES (est): 404K **Privately Held**
SIC: 3531 Backhoes

Clay Center
Ottawa County

(G-4569)
TIGER MIRROR CORPORATION
465 Main St (43408-7718)
PHONE.................................419 855-3146
Joan Pietrowski, *President*
EMP: 5 EST: 1997
SALES (est): 196K **Privately Held**
SIC: 3231 Mirrors, truck & automobile: made from purchased glass

(G-4570)
WHITE ROCK QUARRY L P
3800 Bolander Rd (43408-7713)
PHONE.................................419 855-8388
Ray Advnia, *Principal*
U S Aggregates, *General Ptnr*
Robert Simpson, *General Ptnr*
Jim Fehsenseld, *Ltd Ptnr*
Heritage Group, *Ltd Ptnr*
EMP: 590
SALES (est): 13.6MM
SALES (corp-wide): 248.2MM **Privately Held**
SIC: 1422 Crushed & broken limestone
PA: Asphalt Materials, Inc.
  5400 W 86th St
  Indianapolis IN 46268
  317 872-6010

Clayton
Montgomery County

(G-4571)
ANCHOR FABRICATORS INC
386 Talmadge Rd (45315-9621)
P.O. Box 99 (45315-0099)
PHONE.................................937 836-5117
Tom Saldoff, *President*
Randee Saldoff, *Shareholder*
Marshall Ruchman, *Admin Sec*
EMP: 43
SQ FT: 60,000
SALES (est): 8.1MM **Privately Held**
WEB: www.anchorfab.com
SIC: 3471 3599 3469 Buffing for the trade; polishing, metals or formed products; machine shop, jobbing & repair; metal stampings

(G-4572)
BLACKTHORN LLC
6113 Brookville Salem Rd (45315-9701)
PHONE.................................937 836-9296
Greg Benedict, *General Mgr*
Sharon Yoakum, *Vice Pres*
Nate Benedict, *Manager*
Sharon Buehler, *Admin Sec*
EMP: 10 EST: 1985
SQ FT: 20,000
SALES (est): 2MM **Privately Held**
WEB: www.blackthorn-inc.com
SIC: 3053 2899 3089 3296 Gaskets, all materials; concrete curing & hardening compounds; plastic hardware & building products; fiberglass insulation

(G-4573)
FCA LLC
6611 Hoke Rd (45315-9008)
PHONE.................................309 644-2424
Earnest Reed, *Branch Mgr*
EMP: 18 **Privately Held**
SIC: 2441 Cases, wood
PA: Fca, Llc
  7601 John Deere Pkwy
  Moline IL 61265

(G-4574)
HOFACKER PRCSION MACHINING LLC
7560 Jacks Ln (45315-8779)
PHONE.................................937 832-7712
Fredrick Hofacker,
Stacy Hofacker, *Admin Asst*
Jerry Henshaw,
EMP: 18 EST: 1997
SQ FT: 2,500
SALES (est): 3.1MM **Privately Held**
WEB: www.hofackerprecision.com
SIC: 3599 3544 Machine shop, jobbing & repair; special dies & tools; jigs & fixtures

(G-4575)
IMAGE INDUSTRIES INC
Also Called: Secret Image Promotion
5700 Swan Dr (45315-9614)
PHONE.................................937 832-7969
Bill Michael, *President*
EMP: 7
SALES (est): 767.5K **Privately Held**
WEB: www.secretimage.com
SIC: 2791 7336 Typesetting; silk screen design

(G-4576)
KITTO KATSU INC
7445 Lockwood St (45315)
PHONE.................................818 256-6997
Hiran Jayasinghe, *President*
EMP: 7
SALES (est): 210.3K **Privately Held**
SIC: 3999 8742 Manufacturing industries; marketing consulting services

(G-4577)
NORTHMONT TOOL AND GAGE INC
8741 Kimmel Rd (45315-8900)
P.O. Box 163 (45315-0163)
PHONE.................................937 836-9879
Lawrence R Cordell, *President*
EMP: 8
SQ FT: 15,200
SALES: 869K **Privately Held**
SIC: 3599 Machine shop, jobbing & repair

(G-4578)
SLUTERBECK TOOL & DIE INC
Also Called: Sluterbeck Tool Co
7540 Jacks Ln (45315-8779)
P.O. Box 87 (45315-0087)
PHONE.................................937 836-5736
Ronald Sluterbeck, *President*
Anne Goss, *Corp Secy*
Greg Sluterbeck, *Vice Pres*
Steve Sluterbeck, *Vice Pres*
EMP: 10
SQ FT: 6,000
SALES: 500K **Privately Held**
SIC: 3599 Machine shop, jobbing & repair

Cleveland
Cuyahoga County

(G-4579)
1923 W 25TH ST INC
1923 W 25th St (44113-3418)
PHONE.................................216 696-7529
Richard Brown, *Principal*
EMP: 6
SALES (est): 538.8K **Privately Held**
SIC: 2653 Corrugated & solid fiber boxes

(G-4580)
3D SYSTEMS INC
7100 Euclid Ave (44103-4036)
PHONE.................................216 229-2040
Robert Heinlein, *Business Mgr*
William Lewandowski, *Vice Pres*
EMP: 99
SALES (est): 4.3MM **Privately Held**
SIC: 3841 Instruments, microsurgical: except electromedical

(G-4581)
4 WALLS COM LLC
4700 Lakeside Ave E 173a (44114-3863)
PHONE.................................216 432-1400
Gale Flanagan, *VP Opers*
Gretchen Ciccotti, *Marketing Staff*
Ronald Soeder,
EMP: 10
SALES (est): 1.1MM **Privately Held**
SIC: 2679 Wallpaper

(G-4582)
A & W TABLE PAD CO
Also Called: Pioneer Table Pad
6520 Carnegie Ave (44103-4697)
PHONE.................................800 541-0271
Tamara Christman, *President*
EMP: 10
SQ FT: 12,000
SALES (est): 1MM **Privately Held**
WEB: www.pioneertablepads.com
SIC: 2392 Table mats, plastic & textile

(G-4583)
A AABACO PLASTICS INC
9520 Midwest Ave (44125-2463)
PHONE.................................216 663-9494
Daniel R Lee, *President*
David Lee, *Corp Secy*
Jonathan Lee, *Vice Pres*
EMP: 11
SQ FT: 25,000
SALES (est): 2.1MM **Privately Held**
WEB: www.aabacoplastics.com
SIC: 3089 Blister or bubble formed packaging, plastic; closures, plastic

(G-4584)
A C SHUTTERS INC
8119 Mansfield Ave (44105-1549)
PHONE.................................216 429-2424
Frank Was, *CEO*
Stefan Was, *President*
Mark Krejsa, *Vice Pres*
Barbara Was, *CFO*
EMP: 5
SQ FT: 10,000

Cleveland - Cuyahoga County (G-4585)

SALES (est): 460K **Privately Held**
WEB: www.acshutters.com
SIC: 3442 3089 3444 2431 Shutters, door or window: metal; shutters, plastic; sheet metalwork; millwork

(G-4585)
A E F INC
Also Called: American Electric Furnace Co
24050 Commerce Park Fl 2 (44122-5833)
PHONE..............................216 360-9800
Robert Sords, *President*
Virginia Sords, *Admin Sec*
EMP: 75 EST: 1920
SQ FT: 33,000
SALES (est): 7.5MM **Privately Held**
SIC: 3567 Electrical furnaces, ovens & heating devices, exc. induction

(G-4586)
A F KRAINZ CO
1364 E 47th St (44103-1220)
PHONE..............................216 431-4341
Andrew F Krainz Jr, *Owner*
EMP: 8
SALES (est): 824.1K **Privately Held**
SIC: 2752 Commercial printing, offset

(G-4587)
A GRAPHIC SOLUTION
Also Called: Advanced Graphic Solutions
14900 Detroit Ave Ste 205 (44107-3922)
PHONE..............................216 228-7223
James Clark O'Bryan, *Owner*
EMP: 10
SALES: 175K **Privately Held**
WEB: www.motorsportsguide.com
SIC: 7336 8748 8243 5045 Graphic arts & related design; systems engineering consultant, ex. computer or professional; software training, computer; computer software; software, business & non-game; pleating & stitching

(G-4588)
A H MARTY CO LTD
6900 Union Ave (44105-1383)
PHONE..............................216 641-8950
Diane Champion, *President*
Tom Champion, *Vice Pres*
Albert Chamoion, *Prdtn Mgr*
Kathy Curry, *Sales Mgr*
EMP: 12 EST: 1910
SQ FT: 15,000
SALES: 468K **Privately Held**
SIC: 3443 Weldments

(G-4589)
A H PELZ CO
2498 Superior Ave E (44114-4227)
PHONE..............................216 861-1882
EMP: 8
SQ FT: 6,500
SALES (est): 941.2K **Privately Held**
SIC: 2782 2675 Mfg Blankbooks/Binders Mfg Die-Cut Paper/Paperboard

(G-4590)
A J ROSE MFGCO
3115 W 38th St (44109-1205)
PHONE..............................216 631-4645
James Hoffman, *Plant Mgr*
Chad Barton, *Opers Mgr*
Steve Wilson, *Project Engr*
H John Warnkey, *Branch Mgr*
Dan Boggs, *Manager*
EMP: 183
SALES (corp-wide): 99.5MM **Privately Held**
WEB: www.ajrose.com
SIC: 3465 3568 3469 Automotive stampings; pulleys, power transmission; metal stampings
PA: A. J. Rose Mfg. Co.
38000 Chester Rd
Avon OH 44011
216 631-4645

(G-4591)
A JACKS MANUFACTURING CO
1441 Chardon Rd (44117-1510)
PHONE..............................216 531-1010
Charlie Crout, *President*
Jim Eason, *Engineer*
▲ EMP: 21
SALES (est): 3.1MM
SALES (corp-wide): 1.6B **Publicly Held**
WEB: www.pkoh.com.cn
SIC: 3567 Industrial furnaces & ovens
HQ: Park-Ohio Industries, Inc.
6065 Parkland Blvd Ste 1
Cleveland OH 44124
440 947-2000

(G-4592)
A S MANUFACTURING INC
4412 W 130th St (44135-3004)
P.O. Box 31388 (44131-0388)
PHONE..............................216 476-0656
David Ptacek, *President*
Karen Cesa, *Shareholder*
EMP: 3
SQ FT: 2,000
SALES (est): 454.1K **Privately Held**
WEB: www.asmfg.net
SIC: 3569 Lubricating equipment

(G-4593)
A SIGN FOR THE TIMES INC
Also Called: Signs of The Times
4100 Mayfield Rd (44121-3006)
PHONE..............................216 297-2977
Ray Bayless, *President*
EMP: 5
SALES: 100K **Privately Held**
WEB: www.asignforthetimes.com
SIC: 3993 2759 Signs, not made in custom sign painting shops; commercial printing

(G-4594)
A-BRITE LP
3000 W 121st St (44111-1639)
PHONE..............................216 252-2995
Hal Leitch, *President*
Kathy Mariner, *Hum Res Coord*
EMP: 64 EST: 1992
SQ FT: 58,000
SALES (est): 11.3MM **Privately Held**
WEB: www.abriteplating.com
SIC: 3471 Plating & polishing
PA: App Holdings Lp
5245 Burke St
Windsor ON N9A 6
519 737-6984

(G-4595)
AA PALLETS LLC
4326 W 48th St (44144-1934)
PHONE..............................216 856-2614
Areli Arreaga, *Principal*
EMP: 5
SALES (est): 159.6K **Privately Held**
SIC: 2448 Wood pallets & skids

(G-4596)
AAA STAMPING INC
4001 Pearl Rd Uppr (44109-3198)
PHONE..............................216 749-4494
Stan Gawor, *President*
EMP: 22
SQ FT: 25,000
SALES (est): 4.5MM **Privately Held**
SIC: 3469 Stamping metal for the trade

(G-4597)
ABEL METAL PROCESSING INC
2105 E 77th St (44103-4990)
PHONE..............................216 881-4156
Eugene Schoenemeyer, *President*
Joan Kern, *Vice Pres*
Bob Roth, *Sales Staff*
Jo Ann Kern, *Office Mgr*
EMP: 12 EST: 1975
SQ FT: 8,000
SALES (est): 1.5MM **Privately Held**
WEB: www.abelmetal.com
SIC: 3471 Electroplating of metals or formed products

(G-4598)
ABL PRODUCTS INC
3726 Ridge Rd (44144-1182)
PHONE..............................216 281-2400
Athel Gicei, *President*
Leslie Gicei, *Vice Pres*
EMP: 13
SALES (est): 2MM **Privately Held**
WEB: www.ablproducts.com
SIC: 3469 3568 Stamping metal for the trade; sprockets (power transmission equipment)

(G-4599)
ABLE ALLOY INC
3500 W 140th St (44111-2410)
PHONE..............................216 251-6110
Ken Cohen, *President*
EMP: 15 EST: 1981
SQ FT: 12,000
SALES (est): 2.2MM **Privately Held**
SIC: 3341 Recovery & refining of nonferrous metals

(G-4600)
ABLE GRINDING CO INC
10015 Walford Ave (44102-4697)
PHONE..............................216 961-6555
Robert Urban, *President*
Martha Urban, *Treasurer*
EMP: 4
SQ FT: 6,000
SALES (est): 1.1MM **Privately Held**
SIC: 3599 Grinding castings for the trade

(G-4601)
ABRAXUS SALT INC
5595 Ridge Rd (44129-2601)
PHONE..............................440 743-7669
John Klejka, *Principal*
EMP: 9
SALES (est): 916.7K **Privately Held**
SIC: 2899 Salt

(G-4602)
ABSOLUTELY PAPER ESTABLISHED
14000 Mont Ave (44118-1022)
PHONE..............................216 932-4822
Jermaine Golphin, *Principal*
EMP: 5
SALES (est): 208.8K **Privately Held**
SIC: 2531 Public building & related furniture

(G-4603)
ACADEMY GRAPHIC COMM INC
1000 Brookpark Rd (44109-5824)
PHONE..............................216 661-2550
James M Champion, *President*
Erik Eichenberger, *General Mgr*
Elaine Champion, *Vice Pres*
Courtney Dolinar, *VP Sales*
Courtney Champion, *Mktg Dir*
EMP: 27
SQ FT: 1,400
SALES (est): 4.7MM **Privately Held**
WEB: www.visitagc.com
SIC: 2752 7336 Commercial printing, offset; graphic arts & related design

(G-4604)
ACE RUBBER STAMP & OFF SUP CO
Also Called: Royal Acme
3110 Payne Ave (44114-4504)
PHONE..............................216 771-8483
Ted Cutts, *President*
EMP: 35 EST: 1935
SALES (est): 2.3MM **Privately Held**
WEB: www.acerubberstamps.com
SIC: 3953 5943 Embossing seals & hand stamps; office forms & supplies

(G-4605)
ACME BOILER CO INC
Also Called: Acme Lead Burning Company
3718 Ridge Rd (44144-1183)
PHONE..............................216 961-2471
Dawn Hammerle, *President*
Hedy Hammerle, *Vice Pres*
Ewald Hammerle, *Treasurer*
EMP: 5
SQ FT: 3,200
SALES (est): 552.8K **Privately Held**
SIC: 7699 3443 Boiler repair shop; fabricated plate work (boiler shop)

(G-4606)
ACME LIFTING PRODUCTS INC
Also Called: Universal Cargo
6892 W Snowville Rd Ste 2 (44141-3288)
PHONE..............................440 838-4430
Laura Davis, *President*
Arnold Davis, *Vice Pres*
EMP: 8
SQ FT: 6,000
SALES (est): 880K **Privately Held**
WEB: www.universalcargo.com
SIC: 3536 Hoisting slings

(G-4607)
ACME SPIRALLY WOUND PAPER PDTS
Also Called: Acme Paper Tube
4810 W 139th St (44135-5036)
P.O. Box 35320 (44135-0320)
PHONE..............................216 267-2950
Dan Kobrak, *CEO*
Donald H Kobak Jr, *CEO*
EMP: 17
SQ FT: 36,000
SALES (est): 8.6MM **Privately Held**
WEB: www.acmespiral.com
SIC: 2655 Tubes, fiber or paper: made from purchased material

(G-4608)
ACOR ORTHOPAEDIC INC
18530 S Miles Rd (44128-4200)
PHONE..............................216 662-4500
Greg Alaimo, *CEO*
Jeff Alaimo, *President*
▲ EMP: 100
SQ FT: 35,000
SALES (est): 19.1MM **Privately Held**
WEB: www.acor.com
SIC: 3842 3144 3143 Orthopedic appliances; prosthetic appliances; foot appliances, orthopedic; women's footwear, except athletic; men's footwear, except athletic

(G-4609)
ACOR ORTHOPAEDIC INC
Also Called: Cleveland Prosthetic Center
18700 S Miles Rd (44128-4242)
PHONE..............................440 532-0117
Frank Zingales, *President*
EMP: 3
SALES (est): 228.8K **Privately Held**
SIC: 3842 Orthopedic appliances

(G-4610)
ACORN TECHNOLOGY CORPORATION
23103 Miles Rd (44128-5475)
PHONE..............................216 663-1244
Lalana Green, *President*
Dick Smith, *President*
Richard Smith, *Exec VP*
Robert Green, *Vice Pres*
Barbara Goode, *Controller*
EMP: 20
SQ FT: 150,000
SALES (est): 4.8MM **Privately Held**
WEB: www.acorntechnology.com
SIC: 3613 5063 3634 3429 Panel & distribution boards & other related apparatus; electrical apparatus & equipment; ceiling fans; aircraft & marine hardware, inc. pulleys & similar items

(G-4611)
ACTION DEFENSE LLC
6518 Denison Blvd (44130-4103)
PHONE..............................440 503-7886
Doug Murillo, *Principal*
EMP: 3
SALES (est): 180.4K **Privately Held**
SIC: 3812 Defense systems & equipment

(G-4612)
AD PISTON RING COMPANY LLC
3145 Superior Ave E (44114-4342)
PHONE..............................216 781-5200
Craig Duber, *General Mgr*
Bob Lee, *Mng Member*
EMP: 10 EST: 1921
SQ FT: 12,000
SALES: 980K **Privately Held**
SIC: 3592 Pistons & piston rings

GEOGRAPHIC SECTION
Cleveland - Cuyahoga County (G-4641)

(G-4613)
ADAMS MANUFACTURING COMPANY (PA)
Also Called: Dornback Furnace Division
9790 Midwest Ave (44125-2497)
PHONE..................216 662-1600
Marty Schonberger Jr, *President*
Ruth Schonberger, *Vice Pres*
▲ EMP: 25 EST: 1945
SQ FT: 80,000
SALES (est): 4.4MM **Privately Held**
WEB: www.adamsmanufacturing.com
SIC: 3585 Heating equipment, complete

(G-4614)
ADCHEM ADHESIVES INC
4111 E Royalton Rd (44147-2931)
PHONE..................440 526-1976
Claude Dandurande, *President*
Brett Joint, *Manager*
▲ EMP: 10
SQ FT: 15,000
SALES: 1MM **Privately Held**
WEB: www.adchemadhesives.com
SIC: 2891 Adhesives

(G-4615)
ADCRAFT DECALS INC
7708 Commerce Park Oval (44131-2394)
PHONE..................216 524-2934
Robert W Talion, *President*
Ciliox Rendina, *Vice Pres*
Tim Talion, *Vice Pres*
Bill Talion, *VP Prdtn*
Bruce Turner, *Purch Agent*
EMP: 31 EST: 1961
SQ FT: 21,200
SALES (est): 4MM **Privately Held**
WEB: www.adcraftdecals.com
SIC: 2759 3993 2752 2672 Screen printing; decals: printing; signs & advertising specialties; commercial printing, lithographic; coated & laminated paper; automotive & apparel trimmings

(G-4616)
ADDED EDGE ASSEMBLY INC
26800 Fargo Ave Ste A (44146-1341)
PHONE..................216 464-4305
Kurt Kodrich, *President*
Janet Kodrich, *Admin Sec*
EMP: 11
SQ FT: 3,000
SALES (est): 1.6MM **Privately Held**
WEB: www.addedge.com
SIC: 3549 Assembly machines, including robotic

(G-4617)
ADKINS MARLENA
Also Called: Tolento's Family Restaurant
4729 W 157th St (44135-2737)
PHONE..................216 704-2751
Marlena Adkins, *Owner*
EMP: 4 EST: 2014
SALES (est): 141.7K **Privately Held**
SIC: 2599 Bar, restaurant & cafeteria furniture

(G-4618)
ADKINS & CO INC
Also Called: Adkins Printing
14541 Madison Ave (44107-4325)
PHONE..................216 521-6323
Charles Davis, *President*
EMP: 3
SQ FT: 3,600
SALES (est): 424.6K **Privately Held**
WEB: www.adkinsprinting.com
SIC: 2752 Commercial printing, offset

(G-4619)
ADMIRAL PRODUCTS COMPANY INC
4101 W 150th St (44135-1303)
PHONE..................216 671-0600
Vincent C Hvizda, *CEO*
Paul Hvizda, *Vice Pres*
Margaret Schroeder Hvizda, *Admin Sec*
EMP: 37 EST: 1948
SQ FT: 39,000
SALES (est): 10.3MM **Privately Held**
WEB: www.admiralproducts.com
SIC: 2752 2759 2754 2672 Commercial printing, offset; flexographic printing; labels: gravure printing; coated & laminated paper

(G-4620)
ADVAL TECH US INC
12200 Brookpark Rd (44130-1146)
PHONE..................216 362-1850
Rene Rothen, *President*
EMP: 3
SALES (est): 271.2K
SALES (corp-wide): 210.2MM **Privately Held**
SIC: 3465 3544 Automotive stampings; special dies, tools, jigs & fixtures
PA: Adval Tech Holding Ag
Freiburgstrasse 556
Niederwangen Bei Bern BE 3172
319 808-444

(G-4621)
ADVANCE INDUSTRIES GROUP LLC
3636 W 58th St (44102-5641)
PHONE..................216 741-1800
Jim Williams,
Jeff Stein,
EMP: 20
SQ FT: 35,000
SALES (est): 5.4MM **Privately Held**
WEB: www.advanceindustriesgroup.com
SIC: 3441 3315 Fabricated structural metal; wire & fabricated wire products

(G-4622)
ADVANCE MANUFACTURING CORP
6800 Madison Ave (44102-4099)
PHONE..................216 333-1684
Herman Bredenbeck, *President*
Jon Bredenbeck, *President*
Kenneth Bailey, *Vice Pres*
Doug Carlson, *Admin Sec*
EMP: 48 EST: 1936
SQ FT: 64,000
SALES (est): 10.8MM **Privately Held**
WEB: www.advancemanuf.com
SIC: 3599 3549 Machine shop, jobbing & repair; metalworking machinery

(G-4623)
ADVANCE METAL PRODUCTS INC
3636 W 58th St (44102-5641)
PHONE..................216 741-1800
James Williams, *President*
EMP: 18
SQ FT: 30,000
SALES: 1.5MM **Privately Held**
SIC: 3444 Sheet metalwork

(G-4624)
ADVANCE WIRE FORMING INC
3636 W 58th St (44102-5641)
PHONE..................216 432-3250
Jeff Stein, *President*
Frank Stupka, *Foreman/Supr*
EMP: 10 EST: 2000
SQ FT: 30,000
SALES (est): 1.9MM **Privately Held**
WEB: www.advancewireforming.com
SIC: 3315 Steel wire & related products

(G-4625)
ADVANCED FLAME HARDENING INC
1209 Marquette St (44114-3919)
PHONE..................216 431-0370
Eleanor Syms, *Principal*
EMP: 5
SALES (est): 455.3K **Privately Held**
SIC: 3398 Brazing (hardening) of metal

(G-4626)
ADVANCED FLUIDS INC
18127 Roseland Rd (44112-1001)
PHONE..................216 692-3050
Emil T Rosul, *President*
EMP: 7
SQ FT: 12,800
SALES (est): 1.7MM **Privately Held**
WEB: www.advancedfluids.com
SIC: 2992 Lubricating oils

(G-4627)
ADVANCED KIFFER SYSTEMS INC
4905 Rocky River Dr (44135-3245)
PHONE..................216 267-8181
Dale C Phillip, *President*
Lars Eriksson, *Vice Pres*
Susan Phillip, *Admin Sec*
EMP: 16
SQ FT: 85,000
SALES (est): 2.9MM
SALES (corp-wide): 10.8MM **Privately Held**
WEB: www.aks-inc.com
SIC: 3825 Test equipment for electronic & electric measurement
PA: Kiffer Industries, Inc.
4905 Rocky River Dr
Cleveland OH 44135
216 267-1818

(G-4628)
ADVANCED LIVESCAN TECHNOLOGIES
3575 W 132nd St (44111-3418)
PHONE..................440 759-7028
Kevin Burke, *CEO*
EMP: 4
SALES: 500K **Privately Held**
SIC: 3999 Fingerprint equipment

(G-4629)
ADVANCED MEDIA CORPORATION
Also Called: 48hourprint.com
6410 Eastland Rd Ste F (44142-1306)
PHONE..................440 260-9910
EMP: 10
SALES (corp-wide): 14.5MM **Privately Held**
SIC: 2721 Printing Company
PA: Advanced Media Corporation
159 Thomas Burgin Pkwy
Quincy MA 02169
800 844-0599

(G-4630)
ADVANCED PAPER TUBE INC
1951 W 90th St (44102-2742)
PHONE..................216 281-5691
Leon Lasky, *President*
Dorothy Lasky, *Vice Pres*
EMP: 12
SQ FT: 27,000
SALES (est): 2.3MM **Privately Held**
WEB: www.advancedpapertube.com
SIC: 2655 Tubes, fiber or paper: made from purchased material

(G-4631)
AERO-MED INDUSTRIES INC
1205 Brookpark Rd (44109-5827)
P.O. Box 1053, Brunswick (44212-8553)
PHONE..................216 459-0004
Guy Weaver III, *President*
Donna Weaver, *Treasurer*
EMP: 3
SQ FT: 1,000
SALES: 350K **Privately Held**
SIC: 3599 Machine shop, jobbing & repair

(G-4632)
AEROLL ENGINEERING CORP
18511 Euclid Ave Rear (44112-1018)
PHONE..................216 481-2266
Carl E Weaver III, *President*
Sherri Weaver, *Corp Secy*
EMP: 7
SQ FT: 8,000
SALES: 750K **Privately Held**
SIC: 3545 Thread cutting dies

(G-4633)
AEROQUIP-VICKERS INC (DH)
1111 Superior Ave E (44114-2522)
PHONE..................216 523-5000
A M Cutler, *President*
A T Dillon, *CFO*
Mark Ward, *Sales Mgr*
EMP: 9
SQ FT: 21,000
SALES (est): 1.1B **Privately Held**
SIC: 3052 3492 3429 3069 Rubber hose; plastic hose; hose & tube fittings & assemblies, hydraulic/pneumatic; clamps & couplings; hose; keys & key blanks; molded rubber products; parts for heating, cooling & refrigerating equipment; aircraft parts & equipment
HQ: Eaton Corporation
1000 Eaton Blvd
Cleveland OH 44122
440 523-5000

(G-4634)
AEROSCENA LLC
Also Called: Ascents
10000 Cedar Ave (44106-2119)
PHONE..................800 671-1890
Mark Kohoot, *CEO*
EMP: 16 EST: 2010
SALES (est): 2.5MM **Privately Held**
SIC: 2844 Perfumes, natural or synthetic

(G-4635)
AEROSPACE CO INC
600 Superior Ave E (44114-2614)
PHONE..................413 998-1637
Kent Rosenthal, *President*
EMP: 99 EST: 1961
SALES (est): 3.6MM **Privately Held**
SIC: 3724 Research & development on aircraft engines & parts

(G-4636)
AEROTECH INDUSTRIES INC
1435 E 49th St (44103-1225)
PHONE..................216 881-6660
Nicolas Tadic, *President*
EMP: 3
SQ FT: 8,000
SALES (est): 365.3K **Privately Held**
SIC: 3399 Metal fasteners

(G-4637)
AETNA PLATING CO
6511 Morgan Ave (44127-1947)
PHONE..................216 341-9111
Peter Sobey, *President*
Joel Newman, *Admin Sec*
EMP: 15 EST: 1934
SQ FT: 55,000
SALES: 1MM **Privately Held**
SIC: 3471 Electroplating of metals or formed products; plating of metals or formed products; anodizing (plating) of metals or formed products

(G-4638)
AETNA WELDING CO INC
4613 Broadway Ave (44127-1098)
PHONE..................216 883-1801
William Sharp, *President*
EMP: 5
SQ FT: 7,000
SALES: 300K **Privately Held**
SIC: 7692 Welding repair

(G-4639)
AFFINITY THERAPEUTICS LLC
11000 Cedar Ave (44106-3069)
P.O. Box 606044 (44106-0544)
PHONE..................216 224-9364
Tacarra Bowens, *General Mgr*
Sean Zuckerman, *Research*
Julius Korley,
EMP: 5
SALES (est): 574.5K **Privately Held**
SIC: 2834 Pharmaceutical preparations

(G-4640)
AFFYMETRIX INC
26309 Miles Rd (44128-5960)
PHONE..................216 765-5000
Kristin Yakimow, *Branch Mgr*
EMP: 103
SALES (corp-wide): 24.3B **Publicly Held**
SIC: 3826 Analytical instruments
HQ: Affymetrix, Inc.
3380 Central Expy
Santa Clara CA 95051

(G-4641)
AGMET LLC
5533 Dunham Rd (44137-3645)
PHONE..................216 663-8200
Dave Crose, *Branch Mgr*

Cleveland - Cuyahoga County (G-4642)

EMP: 10
SALES (corp-wide): 21.8MM **Privately Held**
SIC: 5093 3341 Ferrous metal scrap & waste; nonferrous metals scrap; secondary nonferrous metals
PA: Agmet Llc
7800 Medusa Rd
Cleveland OH 44146
440 439-7400

(G-4642)
AGRI-PRODUCTS INC
29326 Bolingbrook Rd (44124-5330)
P.O. Box 22032 (44122-0032)
PHONE..................................216 831-5890
Paul F Dickey, *President*
Kevin Dickey, *Vice Pres*
Harry Valley, *Treasurer*
W Dean Hopkins, *Admin Sec*
EMP: 3 EST: 1962
SALES (est): 220.1K **Privately Held**
SIC: 2048 Feed supplements

(G-4643)
AIN INDUSTRIES INC
13901 Aspinwall Ave (44110-2210)
P.O. Box 464, Avon (44011-0464)
PHONE..................................440 781-0950
Bill Kavila, *President*
Ted Black, *Corp Secy*
Steve Misch, *Vice Pres*
EMP: 6
SQ FT: 6,500
SALES (est): 945.1K **Privately Held**
SIC: 2841 5169 5087 Soap & other detergents; chemicals & allied products; service establishment equipment

(G-4644)
AIR PRODUCTS AND CHEMICALS INC
2820 Quigley Rd (44113-4598)
PHONE..................................216 781-2801
Charles Dawson, *Branch Mgr*
EMP: 15
SALES (corp-wide): 8.9B **Publicly Held**
WEB: www.airproducts.com
SIC: 2813 Industrial gases
PA: Air Products And Chemicals, Inc.
7201 Hamilton Blvd
Allentown PA 18195
610 481-4911

(G-4645)
AIR-RITE INC
Also Called: AIR RITE SERVICE SUPPLY
1290 W 117th St (44107-3096)
PHONE..................................216 228-8200
David Harris, *President*
Marilyn Harris, *Treasurer*
▼ EMP: 24
SQ FT: 28,000
SALES: 3.9MM **Privately Held**
WEB: www.airrite-supply.com
SIC: 7623 7699 5075 3564 Air conditioning repair; boiler & heating repair services; warm air heating equipment & supplies; blowers & fans

(G-4646)
AIRCRAFT AND AUTO FITTINGS CO
17120 Saint Clair Ave (44110-2531)
PHONE..................................216 486-0047
Martin Sexton, *President*
John Markulin, *Corp Secy*
EMP: 8
SQ FT: 4,800
SALES: 450K **Privately Held**
SIC: 3599 Machine shop, jobbing & repair

(G-4647)
AK-ISG STEEL COATING COMPANY
3531 Campbell Rd (44105-1017)
PHONE..................................216 429-6901
Wilbur Ross-Chb, *Principal*
Gene Wimmer, *Controller*
EMP: 93
SQ FT: 500,000
SALES (est): 6.6MM **Privately Held**
SIC: 3479 3471 Galvanizing of iron, steel or end-formed products; plating & polishing

(G-4648)
AKRON REBAR CO
16216 Brookpark Rd (44135-3341)
PHONE..................................216 433-0000
Tara Lopez, *Sales Staff*
Bill Cooper, *Branch Mgr*
EMP: 15
SALES (corp-wide): 10.1MM **Privately Held**
WEB: www.akronrebar.com
SIC: 3441 Fabricated structural metal
PA: Akron Rebar Co.
809 W Waterloo Rd
Akron OH 44314
330 745-7100

(G-4649)
ALABAMA SLING CENTER INC
21000 Aerospace Pkwy (44142-1072)
PHONE..................................440 239-7000
Tony Mazzela, *Principal*
EMP: 12
SALES (est): 2.7MM **Privately Held**
SIC: 3496 Miscellaneous fabricated wire products

(G-4650)
ALCAN CORPORATION (HQ)
6060 Parkland Blvd (44124-4225)
PHONE..................................440 460-3307
Tom Albanese, *President*
Timothy Guerra, *President*
William J Adams, *Vice Pres*
Eileen Burns Lerum, *Vice Pres*
Donald P Seberger, *Vice Pres*
◆ EMP: 22
SQ FT: 11,000
SALES (est): 848.8MM
SALES (corp-wide): 40.5B **Privately Held**
WEB: www.alcan.com
SIC: 3351 3355 3496 3357 Wire, copper & copper alloy; wire, aluminum: made in rolling mills; miscellaneous fabricated wire products; nonferrous wiredrawing & insulating
PA: Rio Tinto Plc
6 St James's Square
London SW1Y
207 781-1900

(G-4651)
ALCHEMICAL TRANSMUTATION
314 E 195th St (44119-1118)
PHONE..................................216 313-8674
James Stuart Koch, *Owner*
EMP: 101
SALES (est): 4.2MM **Privately Held**
SIC: 3499 Fire- or burglary-resistive products

(G-4652)
ALCOHOL & DRUG ADDICTION SVCS
2012 W 25th St Ste 600 (44113-4119)
PHONE..................................216 348-4830
Russell Kaye, *Exec Dir*
EMP: 30
SALES: 21.4MM **Privately Held**
WEB: www.adasbcc.org
SIC: 2721 Periodicals

(G-4653)
ALCON INDUSTRIES INC
7990 Baker Ave (44102-1900)
PHONE..................................216 961-1100
Richard J Chalet, *Ch of Bd*
Ralph Kacik, *Production*
Brian Gill, *CFO*
Denise McKenna, *Finance Mgr*
▲ EMP: 100 EST: 1977
SQ FT: 130,000
SALES (est): 28.8MM **Privately Held**
WEB: www.alconalloys.com
SIC: 3325 3441 3369 Alloy steel castings, except investment; fabricated structural metal; nonferrous foundries

(G-4654)
ALERIS CORPORATION (PA)
25825 Science Park Dr # 400 (44122-7392)
PHONE..................................216 910-3400
Sean M Stack, *Ch of Bd*
Christopher R Clegg, *Exec VP*
Jacobus Aj Govers, *Exec VP*
Michael T Keown, *Exec VP*

Chris Tiller, *Vice Pres*
EMP: 3
SALES: 3.4B **Privately Held**
SIC: 3355 3354 Bars, rolled, aluminum; aluminum extruded products

(G-4655)
ALERIS OHIO MANAGEMENT INC (DH)
25825 Science Park Dr # 400 (44122-7323)
PHONE..................................216 910-3400
Sean M Stack, *CEO*
K Alan Di CK, *CEO*
Christopher R Clegg, *Exec VP*
Roeland Baan, *Vice Pres*
Scott A McKinley, *Vice Pres*
EMP: 16
SALES (est): 3.9MM **Privately Held**
SIC: 3555 Printing trades machinery

(G-4656)
ALERIS ROLLED PDTS SLS CORP
25825 Science Park Dr (44122-7323)
PHONE..................................216 910-3400
Sean M Stack, *CEO*
EMP: 1 EST: 2013
SALES (est): 9.6MM **Privately Held**
SIC: 3341 Secondary nonferrous metals
HQ: Aleris Rolled Products, Inc.
25825 Science Park Dr # 400
Beachwood OH 44122
216 910-3400

(G-4657)
ALERIS ROLLED PRODUCTS LLC (DH)
25825 Science Park Dr # 400 (44122-7323)
PHONE..................................216 910-3400
Sean M Stack, *CEO*
▲ EMP: 21
SALES (est): 146.9MM **Privately Held**
SIC: 3355 Aluminum rolling & drawing
HQ: Aleris Rolled Products, Inc.
25825 Science Park Dr # 400
Beachwood OH 44122
216 910-3400

(G-4658)
ALERT SAFETY LITE PRODUCTS CO
24500 Solon Rd (44146-4716)
PHONE..................................440 232-5020
Alan Kovacik, *President*
Paul S Blanch, *Corp Secy*
EMP: 15
SQ FT: 40,000
SALES (est): 2.3MM **Privately Held**
SIC: 3699 3643 Trouble lights; outlets, electric: convenience

(G-4659)
ALFACOMP INC
Also Called: Digital Graphics
4485 Broadview Rd (44109-4373)
PHONE..................................216 459-1790
Jennifer Tripoli, *President*
Russ Tripoli, *Treasurer*
EMP: 5
SQ FT: 1,700
SALES (est): 661.9K **Privately Held**
SIC: 7336 2791 2759 Graphic arts & related design; typesetting; commercial printing

(G-4660)
ALFRED J BUESCHER JR
17001 Shaker Blvd (44120-1633)
PHONE..................................216 752-3676
Alfred J Buescher Jr, *Owner*
EMP: 3 EST: 2001
SALES (est): 163.5K **Privately Held**
SIC: 3612 Ignition transformers, for use on domestic fuel burners

(G-4661)
ALFRED MACHINE CO (HQ)
29500 Solon Rd (44139-3449)
PHONE..................................440 248-4600
Art Anton, *CEO*
EMP: 85 EST: 1964
SQ FT: 100,000

SALES (est): 6.4MM
SALES (corp-wide): 940.1MM **Privately Held**
SIC: 3599 Machine shop, jobbing & repair
PA: Swagelok Company
29500 Solon Rd
Solon OH 44139
440 248-4600

(G-4662)
ALKID CORPORATION
6035 Parkland Blvd (44124-4186)
PHONE..................................216 896-3000
Jon P Marten, *CEO*
EMP: 4
SALES (est): 201.5K
SALES (corp-wide): 12B **Publicly Held**
SIC: 3594 Fluid power pumps
PA: Parker-Hannifin Corporation
6035 Parkland Blvd
Cleveland OH 44124
216 896-3000

(G-4663)
ALL METAL FABRICATORS INC
15400 Commerce Park Dr (44142-2011)
PHONE..................................216 267-0033
William Yankovich, *President*
Carol Yankovich, *Corp Secy*
Mike Yankovich, *Vice Pres*
EMP: 15
SQ FT: 14,000
SALES (est): 2.7MM **Privately Held**
SIC: 3444 Sheet metal specialties, not stamped

(G-4664)
ALL OHIO COMPANIES INC
2735 Scranton Rd (44113-5181)
PHONE..................................216 420-9274
Paul Colletti, *Principal*
EMP: 17
SQ FT: 5,088
SALES (est): 2.5MM **Privately Held**
SIC: 3446 1721 1799 Gates, ornamental metal; exterior residential painting contractor; industrial painting; exterior cleaning, including sandblasting; steam cleaning of building exteriors

(G-4665)
ALL OHIO THREADED ROD CO INC
5349 Saint Clair Ave (44103-1311)
PHONE..................................216 426-1800
James Wolford, *CEO*
Rick Fien, *President*
Brian Wolford, *Vice Pres*
Raechel Sanichar, *Office Mgr*
▲ EMP: 28
SQ FT: 40,000
SALES (est): 7.6MM **Privately Held**
SIC: 3312 5085 3316 Bar, rod & wire products; industrial supplies; cold finishing of steel shapes

(G-4666)
ALL SIGNS AND DESIGNS LLC
5101 W 161st St (44142-1604)
PHONE..................................216 267-8588
Skip Collins, *President*
Carol Collins, *Vice Pres*
Melanie Collins, *Vice Pres*
EMP: 6
SQ FT: 2,500
SALES: 800K **Privately Held**
SIC: 7389 3993 Sign painting & lettering shop; signs & advertising specialties; electric signs

(G-4667)
ALL SPORT SERVICES CORPORATION
3635 Perkins Ave Ste 1e (44114-4605)
PHONE..................................216 361-1965
EMP: 5
SQ FT: 11,400
SALES: 250K **Privately Held**
SIC: 3949 Reconditions Athletic Equipment

(G-4668)
ALL-SEASONS PAPER COMPANY
6346 Eastland Rd (44142-1300)
PHONE..................................440 826-1700

GEOGRAPHIC SECTION
Cleveland - Cuyahoga County (G-4691)

Wayne Buffington, *President*
Randall Buffington, *Treasurer*
EMP: 20
SQ FT: 32,000
SALES (est): 5.4MM **Privately Held**
WEB: www.allseasonspaper.com
SIC: 2672 Coated & laminated paper

(G-4669)
ALL-TYPE WELDING & FABRICATION
7690 Bond St (44139-5351)
PHONE 440 439-3990
Mike Distaulo, *President*
William Jones, *Vice Pres*
Dennis Whitaker, *Vice Pres*
Anton Wingren, *Plant Supt*
EMP: 40
SQ FT: 34,000
SALES (est): 8.1MM **Privately Held**
WEB: www.atwf-inc.com
SIC: 3599 7692 1761 Machine & other job shop work; welding repair; sheet metalwork

(G-4670)
ALLEGA CONCRETE CORP
5585 Canal Rd (44125-4874)
PHONE 216 447-0814
John Allega, *President*
Jim Allega, *Vice Pres*
Joe Allega, *Vice Pres*
Dennis Kramer, *Project Mgr*
Gary Thomas, *Facilities Mgr*
EMP: 35
SQ FT: 5,000
SALES (est): 8.2MM **Privately Held**
SIC: 3273 Ready-mixed concrete

(G-4671)
ALLIED CONSTRUCTION PDTS LLC (HQ)
3900 Kelley Ave (44114-4536)
PHONE 216 431-2600
Eileen Johnson, *President*
Rich Steinbrenner, *District Mgr*
Bernedy Munoz, *Buyer*
Leo Matthews, *Mng Member*
Joe Calabrese, *Manager*
▲ **EMP:** 47
SQ FT: 110,000
SALES (est): 11.4MM
SALES (corp-wide): 96.4MM **Privately Held**
WEB: www.alliedcp.com
SIC: 3531 Bituminous batching plants
PA: Pubco Corporation
 3830 Kelley Ave
 Cleveland OH 44114
 216 881-5300

(G-4672)
ALLIED CONSTRUCTION PDTS LLC
1840 E 40th St (44103-3504)
PHONE 216 431-2600
Leo Matthews, *Manager*
EMP: 25
SALES (corp-wide): 96.4MM **Privately Held**
SIC: 3531 Construction machinery
HQ: Allied Construction Products Llc
 3900 Kelley Ave
 Cleveland OH 44114
 216 431-2600

(G-4673)
ALLIED TOOL & DIE INC
16146 Puritas Ave (44135-2691)
PHONE 216 941-6196
Fred Montag, *President*
Edward Kern, *Engineer*
Dana Mack, *Office Mgr*
Walter Montag, *Shareholder*
EMP: 19 **EST:** 1946
SALES (est): 3.7MM **Privately Held**
SIC: 3469 3544 Stamping metal for the trade; special dies & tools; jigs & fixtures

(G-4674)
ALLOY BLLOWS PRCISION WLDG INC (PA)
653 Miner Rd (44143-2115)
PHONE 440 684-3000
Michael Canty, *President*

Frank Loucka, *General Mgr*
Jason Cole, *Business Mgr*
Doug Isham, *Business Mgr*
Carl Ondraka, *Mfg Staff*
◆ **EMP:** 63 **EST:** 1935
SQ FT: 45,000
SALES (est): 34.7MM **Privately Held**
WEB: www.alloybellows.com
SIC: 3599 3498 3494 Bellows, industrial: metal; machine & other job shop work; fabricated pipe & fittings; valves & pipe fittings

(G-4675)
ALPHA PACKAGING HOLDINGS INC
Also Called: Progressive Plastics
14801 Emery Ave (44135-1476)
PHONE 216 252-5595
A J Busa, *Manager*
EMP: 275 **Privately Held**
SIC: 3089 3085 Molding primary plastic; plastics bottles
PA: Alpha Packaging Holdings, Inc.
 1555 Page Industrial Blvd
 Saint Louis MO 63132

(G-4676)
ALPHA TOOL & MOLD INC
83 Alpha Park (44143-2265)
PHONE 440 473-2343
Robert Pischel, *President*
William M Fumich, *Principal*
Alfred Pischel, *Principal*
Helen Pischel, *Principal*
Al Pischel, *Corp Secy*
▲ **EMP:** 12
SQ FT: 8,500
SALES (est): 2.3MM **Privately Held**
SIC: 3544 Industrial molds; special dies & tools

(G-4677)
ALPHA ZETA HOLDINGS INC (PA)
2981 Independence Rd (44115-3615)
PHONE 216 271-1601
Joseph T Turgeon, *CEO*
James B Krimmel, *President*
EMP: 8
SALES (est): 6.5MM **Privately Held**
SIC: 2819 2869 6799 Industrial inorganic chemicals; industrial organic chemicals; investors

(G-4678)
ALTERNATIVE PRESS MAGAZINE INC
1305 W 80th St Ste 21 (44102-6214)
PHONE 216 631-1510
Michael P Shea, *President*
Joe Scarpelli, *General Mgr*
Amber Funk, *Merchandise Mgr*
EMP: 20
SQ FT: 2,500
SALES (est): 3MM **Privately Held**
WEB: www.altpress.com
SIC: 2721 Magazines: publishing only, not printed on site

(G-4679)
ALUMINUM BEARING CO OF AMERICA
Also Called: Albeco
4775 W 139th St (44135-5033)
PHONE 216 267-8560
Jane Beyer, *President*
EMP: 9 **EST:** 1956
SQ FT: 3,000
SALES (est): 3.4MM **Privately Held**
SIC: 5051 3429 Aluminum bars, rods, ingots, sheets, pipes, plates, etc.; manufactured hardware (general)

(G-4680)
ALUMINUM COATING MANUFACTURERS
Also Called: Alcm
7301 Bessemer Ave (44127-1817)
PHONE 216 341-2000
Richard Kaplan, *President*
EMP: 23
SQ FT: 50,000

SALES (est): 3.7MM **Privately Held**
WEB: www.alcm.com
SIC: 2891 2851 2952 2951 Sealants; paints & paint additives; asphalt felts & coatings; asphalt paving mixtures & blocks

(G-4681)
AMAC ENTERPRISES INC
5925 W 130th St (44130-1076)
PHONE 216 362-1880
Dean Caimples, *Manager*
EMP: 100
SQ FT: 160,000
SALES (corp-wide): 16.2MM **Privately Held**
WEB: www.amacent.com
SIC: 3471 Anodizing (plating) of metals or formed products
PA: Amac Enterprises, Inc.
 5909 W 130th St
 Parma OH 44130
 216 362-1880

(G-4682)
AMECO USA METAL FABRICATION
4600 W 160th St (44135-2630)
PHONE 440 899-9400
David Perkins, *General Mgr*
Thomas M McLaughlin, *Vice Pres*
Dave Kloss, *Mktg Dir*
Michael Perkins,
EMP: 7 **EST:** 2010
SALES (est): 584K **Privately Held**
SIC: 3441 Fabricated structural metal
PA: American Manufacturing And Engineering Company
 4600 W 160th St
 Cleveland OH 44135

(G-4683)
AMERICAN BRASS MANUFACTURING
5000 Superior Ave (44103-1299)
PHONE 216 431-6565
Robert Mc Conville Jr, *Chairman*
▲ **EMP:** 30 **EST:** 1894
SQ FT: 40,000
SALES (est): 5.6MM **Privately Held**
WEB: www.americanbrass.com
SIC: 3432 Plumbers' brass goods: drain cocks, faucets, spigots, etc.

(G-4684)
AMERICAN BRONZE CORPORATION
2941 Broadway Ave (44115-3692)
PHONE 216 341-7800
Gerald Goldstein, *President*
Joshua Goldstein, *Vice Pres*
EMP: 25 **EST:** 1924
SQ FT: 50,000
SALES: 10MM **Privately Held**
WEB: www.americanbronzecorp.com
SIC: 3366 Copper foundries

(G-4685)
AMERICAN CHEMICAL PRODUCTS
5041 W 161st St (44142-1602)
PHONE 216 267-7722
Don Manak, *President*
Tom McCormick, *General Mgr*
Janet Metro, *Corp Secy*
Thomas McCormick, *Vice Pres*
Steve Alexander, *Engineer*
EMP: 10
SQ FT: 10,000
SALES (est): 2.2MM **Privately Held**
SIC: 2842 Cleaning or polishing preparations

(G-4686)
AMERICAN CRAFT HARDWARE LLC
4025 Riveredge Rd (44111-5626)
PHONE 440 746-0098
James Immke, *Vice Pres*
EMP: 5
SQ FT: 5,000

SALES (est): 195.3K **Privately Held**
SIC: 3444 3469 3589 5712 Restaurant sheet metalwork; household cooking & kitchen utensils, metal; coffee brewing equipment; cabinets, except custom made: kitchen

(G-4687)
AMERICAN FRICTION TECH LLC
9300 Midwest Ave (44125-2418)
PHONE 216 823-0861
Raven Soukup, *Materials Mgr*
Mark Havir, *QA Dir*
Alexander Djordjevich, *Engineer*
Gregory C Soukup, *Mng Member*
Teresa Berki, *Manager*
▲ **EMP:** 65
SQ FT: 54,000
SALES: 15MM **Privately Held**
SIC: 3339 Primary nonferrous metals

(G-4688)
AMERICAN GREETINGS CORPORATION (HQ)
1 American Way (44145-8151)
PHONE 216 252-7300
John W Beeder, *President*
Jeffrey Weiss, *Co-CEO*
Zev Weiss, *Co-CEO*
Erwin Weiss, *Senior VP*
Joseph Cipollone, *Vice Pres*
◆ **EMP:** 1700 **EST:** 1906
SQ FT: 1,194,414
SALES (est): 2B
SALES (corp-wide): 7.2B **Privately Held**
WEB: www.americangreetings.com
SIC: 2771 2679 2656 2678 Greeting cards; gift wrap, paper: made from purchased material; cups, paper: made from purchased material; plates, paper: made from purchased material; stationery: made from purchased materials
PA: Clayton, Dubilier & Rice, Inc.
 375 Park Ave Fl 18
 New York NY 10152
 212 407-5200

(G-4689)
AMERICAN INTERIOR DESIGN INC
19561 Miles Rd (44128-4111)
PHONE 216 663-0606
Frank Zorman Jr, *President*
Ed Zorman, *Vice Pres*
EMP: 15
SQ FT: 10,000
SALES (est): 1.5MM **Privately Held**
WEB: www.americaninterior.com
SIC: 2541 Cabinets, lockers & shelving

(G-4690)
AMERICAN IR MET CLEVELAND LLC
1240 Marquette St (44114-3920)
PHONE 216 266-0509
Michael Simms,
Tim Wilson,
▼ **EMP:** 20
SQ FT: 70,000
SALES (est): 16.2MM
SALES (corp-wide): 814.3MM **Privately Held**
WEB: www.conversionresources.com
SIC: 5051 3441 Metals service centers & offices; fabricated structural metal
HQ: American Iron & Metal (U.S.A.), Inc.
 25 Kenney Dr
 Cranston RI 02920
 401 463-5605

(G-4691)
AMERICAN LITHUANIAN PRESS
Also Called: DIRVA LITHUANIAN NEWSPAPER
19807 Cherokee Ave (44119-2825)
P.O. Box 19010 (44119-0010)
PHONE 216 531-8150
Algirdas V Matulionis, *President*
EMP: 3
SQ FT: 4,000
SALES: 51.3K **Privately Held**
SIC: 2711 Newspapers: publishing only, not printed on site

(PA)=Parent Co (HQ)=Headquarters (DH)=Div Headquarters
✿ = New Business established in last 2 years

Cleveland - Cuyahoga County (G-4692)

(G-4692)
AMERICAN METAL TREATING CO
1043 E 62nd St (44103-1094)
PHONE...........................216 431-4492
Richard Roenn, *President*
Carol Roenn, *Corp Secy*
▲ **EMP:** 22 **EST:** 1926
SQ FT: 15,830
SALES (est): 5.4MM **Privately Held**
WEB: www.americanmetaltreating.com
SIC: 3398 Brazing (hardening) of metal

(G-4693)
AMERICAN MFG & ENGRG CO
7500 Grand Division Ave (44125-1282)
PHONE...........................440 899-9400
Michael Perkins, *Manager*
EMP: 3 **Privately Held**
WEB: www.ameco-usa.com
SIC: 3441 Fabricated structural metal
PA: American Manufacturing And Engineering Company
4600 W 160th St
Cleveland OH 44135

(G-4694)
AMERICAN PRECISION SPINDLES
Also Called: SKF Machine Tools Service
670 Alpha Dr (44143-2123)
PHONE...........................267 436-6000
Phillip J Wykoff,
Rosemary A Wykoff,
EMP: 8
SQ FT: 10,000
SALES (est): 1.3MM
SALES (corp-wide): 9.2B **Privately Held**
SIC: 3552 Spindles, textile
HQ: Skf Usa Inc.
890 Forty Foot Rd
Lansdale PA 19446
267 436-6000

(G-4695)
AMERICAN PROCESSING LLC
17001 Saranac Rd (44110-2534)
PHONE...........................216 486-4600
Chuck Shepard, *Manager*
EMP: 26
SALES (est): 4.7MM **Privately Held**
SIC: 3312 Sheet or strip, steel, cold-rolled: own hot-rolled

(G-4696)
AMERICAN RIDE WHEELCHAIR COACH
1368 W 65th St (44102-2160)
PHONE...........................216 276-1700
C Patricia Augustine, *Principal*
EMP: 3
SALES (est): 177.4K **Privately Held**
SIC: 3842 Wheelchairs

(G-4697)
AMERICAN SCAFFOLDING INC
7600 Wall St Ste 200 (44125-3358)
PHONE...........................216 524-7733
Mike Tabar, *Branch Mgr*
EMP: 3
SALES (est): 218.3K **Privately Held**
SIC: 3499 5082 5999 Metal ladders; ladders; alarm & safety equipment stores
PA: American Scaffolding, Inc.
7161 Eagle Creek Rd
Cincinnati OH

(G-4698)
AMERICAN TANK & FABRICATING CO (PA)
Also Called: A T & F Co
12314 Elmwood Ave (44111-5991)
PHONE...........................216 252-1500
Terry Ripich, *Ch of Bd*
Bob Ripich, *President*
Michael Ripich, *President*
Kevin Cantrell, *Vice Pres*
Michael Puleo, *Vice Pres*
▲ **EMP:** 190 **EST:** 1940
SQ FT: 300,000
SALES (est): 183.4MM **Privately Held**
WEB: www.amtank.com
SIC: 5051 3443 Metals service centers & offices; iron & steel (ferrous) products; weldments

(G-4699)
AMERICAN TRUCK EQUIPMENT INC
5021 W 161st St (44142-1602)
PHONE...........................216 362-0400
Mark Winter, *President*
EMP: 5
SQ FT: 8,200
SALES (est): 868.5K **Privately Held**
WEB: www.goamericantruck.com
SIC: 3537 3545 2542 3792 Pallets, metal; tool holders; shelving angles or slotted bars: except wood; pickup covers, canopies or caps; metal stampings; sheet metalwork

(G-4700)
AMERILAM LAMINATING
4651 W 130th St (44135-3758)
P.O. Box 35286 (44135-0286)
PHONE...........................440 235-4687
Dan Wyman, *Owner*
EMP: 3
SQ FT: 3,500
SALES (est): 200K **Privately Held**
SIC: 2493 2732 Particleboard, plastic laminated; textbooks: printing & binding, not publishing

(G-4701)
AMRESCO LLC
29999 Solon Indus Pkwy (44139-4317)
P.O. Box 39098, Solon (44139-0098)
PHONE...........................440 349-2805
EMP: 162 **Privately Held**
SIC: 2833 2899 2819 Mfg Medicinal/Botanical Products Mfg Chemical Preparations Mfg Industrial Inorganic Chemicals
HQ: Amresco, Llc
28600 Fountain Pkwy
Solon OH 44139
440 349-1199

(G-4702)
AMROS INDUSTRIES INC
14701 Industrial Pkwy (44135-4547)
PHONE...........................216 433-0010
Gregory Shteyngarts, *President*
EMP: 22
SQ FT: 65,000
SALES (est): 4.5MM **Privately Held**
SIC: 7389 2821 Packaging & labeling services; thermoplastic materials

(G-4703)
AMTANK ARMOR LLC
12314 Elmwood Ave (44111-5906)
PHONE...........................216 252-1500
John Mayles,
EMP: 4
SQ FT: 3,600
SALES (est): 429.1K **Privately Held**
SIC: 3441 Fabricated structural metal

(G-4704)
ANALIZA INC (PA)
3615 Superior Ave E 4407b (44114-4139)
PHONE...........................216 432-9050
Arnon Chait, *President*
EMP: 10
SQ FT: 5,000
SALES (est): 350K **Privately Held**
SIC: 2834 Pharmaceutical preparations

(G-4705)
ANCHOR BRONZE AND METALS INC
11470 Euclid Ave Ste 509 (44106-3934)
PHONE...........................440 549-5653
Roger Moore, *President*
EMP: 32
SQ FT: 42,000
SALES (est): 5.4MM **Privately Held**
SIC: 5051 3366 Copper; copper products; miscellaneous nonferrous products; castings, rough: iron or steel; brass foundry

(G-4706)
ANCHOR INDUSTRIES INCORPORATED
30775 Solon Indus Pkwy (44139-4338)
PHONE...........................440 473-1414
Doug Kaufman, *President*
▲ **EMP:** 47
SALES (est): 8MM **Privately Held**
SIC: 3462 Automotive forgings, ferrous: crankshaft, engine, axle, etc.

(G-4707)
ANCHOR METAL PROCESSING INC
12200 Brookpark Rd (44130-1146)
PHONE...........................216 362-6463
Fred Pfaff, *Branch Mgr*
EMP: 15 **Privately Held**
SIC: 3599 1761 3444 Machine shop, jobbing & repair; sheet metalwork; sheet metalwork
PA: Anchor Metal Processing, Inc.
11830 Brookpark Rd
Cleveland OH 44130

(G-4708)
ANCHOR METAL PROCESSING INC (PA)
11830 Brookpark Rd (44130-1103)
PHONE...........................216 362-1850
Edward Pfaff, *Ch of Bd*
Frederick Pfaff, *President*
Jeff Pfaff, *Vice Pres*
Dave Pippert, *Purchasing*
Robert Pfaff, *Admin Sec*
EMP: 30
SQ FT: 46,000
SALES (est): 9MM **Privately Held**
SIC: 3599 1761 3444 Machine shop, jobbing & repair; sheet metalwork; sheet metalwork

(G-4709)
ANCHOR TOOL & DIE CO (PA)
Also Called: Anchor Manufacturing Group Inc
12200 Brookpark Rd (44130-1177)
PHONE...........................216 362-1850
Frederick A Pfaff, *President*
Edward Pfaff, *Chairman*
Jeff Wilson, *Business Mgr*
Rick Gratzer, *Plant Mgr*
Barb Murawski, *Project Mgr*
▲ **EMP:** 275 **EST:** 1970
SQ FT: 350,000
SALES (est): 102.9MM **Privately Held**
WEB: www.anchor-mfg.com
SIC: 3465 3544 3469 Automotive stampings; special dies, tools, jigs & fixtures; metal stampings

(G-4710)
ANCHOR TOOL & DIE CO
Also Called: Anchor Manufacturing Group
12200 Brookpark Rd (44130-1177)
PHONE...........................216 362-1850
Fred Pfaff, *Manager*
EMP: 100
SALES (corp-wide): 102.9MM **Privately Held**
WEB: www.anchor-mfg.com
SIC: 3469 Metal stampings
PA: Anchor Tool & Die Co.
12200 Brookpark Rd
Cleveland OH 44130
216 362-1850

(G-4711)
ANDEEN-HAGERLING INC
31200 Bainbridge Rd Ste 2 (44139-2298)
PHONE...........................440 349-0370
Carl W Hagerling, *President*
Carl G Andeen, *Treasurer*
Paul Sauerland, *Sales Dir*
Ted Seman, *Director*
John Keppler, *Executive*
EMP: 14
SQ FT: 7,600
SALES (est): 2.4MM **Privately Held**
WEB: www.andeen-hagerling.com
SIC: 3825 Bridges: kelvin, wheatstone, vacuum tube, megohm, etc.; test equipment for electronic & electric measurement; standards & calibration equipment for electrical measuring

(G-4712)
ANDERSON DOOR CO
18090 Miles Rd (44128-3435)
PHONE...........................216 475-5700
James B Anderson Jr, *President*
Virginia Anderson, *Corp Secy*
James B Anderson III, *Vice Pres*
EMP: 30
SQ FT: 30,000
SALES (est): 4.2MM **Privately Held**
SIC: 2431 3442 Garage doors, overhead: wood; garage doors, overhead: metal

(G-4713)
ANDERSOUND PA SERVICE
15911 Harvard Ave (44128-2049)
PHONE...........................216 561-2636
Clarence Anderson Jr, *Owner*
EMP: 6
SALES (est): 398.5K **Privately Held**
SIC: 3651 Audio electronic systems

(G-4714)
ANGEL PRTG & REPRODUCTION CO
1400 W 57th St (44102-3044)
PHONE...........................216 631-5225
Frank Petkovsek, *President*
Mary Louise Petkovsek, *Vice Pres*
EMP: 10
SQ FT: 16,000
SALES (est): 1.1MM **Privately Held**
WEB: www.angelprinting.com
SIC: 2752 Commercial printing, offset

(G-4715)
ANGRY CUPCAKES PRODUCTIONS LLC
2300 E 95th St (44106-3452)
PHONE...........................216 229-2394
Doris Horn, *Owner*
EMP: 4
SALES (est): 152.2K **Privately Held**
SIC: 2051 Bread, cake & related products

(G-4716)
ANGSTROM GRAPHICS INC (PA)
4437 E 49th St (44125-1005)
PHONE...........................216 271-5300
Wayne R Angstrom, *CEO*
Jaime Caraballo, *Opers Mgr*
Matt Moehring, *Purch Dir*
Rachel Malakoff, *CFO*
Timothy Gailey, *Accounting Mgr*
▼ **EMP:** 250
SQ FT: 225,000
SALES (est): 272.1MM **Privately Held**
SIC: 2721 2754 2752 Magazines: publishing & printing; commercial printing, gravure; commercial printing, lithographic

(G-4717)
ANGSTROM GRAPHICS INC MIDWEST (HQ)
4437 E 49th St (44125-1005)
PHONE...........................216 271-5300
Wayne R Angstrom, *Ch of Bd*
Bruce Macdonald, *Vice Pres*
Rachel Malakoff, *CFO*
Tim Gailey, *Accounting Mgr*
Kathy Lazar, *Credit Mgr*
EMP: 295
SQ FT: 230,000
SALES: 56.9MM
SALES (corp-wide): 288.8MM **Privately Held**
SIC: 2752 7331 Commercial printing, offset; direct mail advertising services
PA: Angstrom Graphics Inc
4437 E 49th St
Cleveland OH 44125
216 271-5300

(G-4718)
ANGSTROM GRAPHICS SOUTHEAST (HQ)
4437 E 49th St (44125-1005)
PHONE...........................216 271-5300
Wayne R Angstrom, *Ch of Bd*
Mark Berkey, *President*
Rachel L Malakoff, *CFO*
◆ **EMP:** 4
SQ FT: 225,000
SALES (est): 37MM
SALES (corp-wide): 272.1MM **Privately Held**
WEB: www.st-ives.com
SIC: 2752 Commercial printing, offset
PA: Angstrom Graphics Inc
4437 E 49th St
Cleveland OH 44125
216 271-5300

GEOGRAPHIC SECTION

Cleveland - Cuyahoga County (G-4746)

(G-4719)
ANVIL PRODUCTS CO
4535 E 71st St (44105-5603)
PHONE..................216 883-3740
Alex Berkes Jr, *Owner*
Aaron J Johnson, *Manager*
EMP: 3
SQ FT: 7,400
SALES: 130K **Privately Held**
SIC: 3599 Machine shop, jobbing & repair

(G-4720)
APEX ADVANCED TECHNOLOGIES LLC
4857a W 130th St (44135-5137)
PHONE..................216 898-1595
Dennis Hammond, *Mng Member*
▲ **EMP:** 6
SQ FT: 12,000
SALES: 700K **Privately Held**
WEB: www.apexadvancedtechnologies.com
SIC: 2899 Corrosion preventive lubricant

(G-4721)
APOLLO MEDICAL DEVICES LLC
11000 Cedar Ave Ste 146 (44106-3067)
PHONE..................440 935-5027
Patrick Leimkuehler, *CEO*
Punkaj Ahuja,
EMP: 4
SQ FT: 500
SALES (est): 288.4K **Privately Held**
SIC: 2835 In vitro diagnostics

(G-4722)
APPROVED PLUMBING CO
Also Called: Approved Plbg & Sewer Clg Co
770 Ken Mar Indus Pkwy (44147-2920)
PHONE..................216 663-5063
Dennis Schlekie, *President*
EMP: 10 **EST:** 1940
SALES (est): 1MM **Privately Held**
WEB: www.approvedplumbing.com
SIC: 1711 2434 Plumbing contractors; wood kitchen cabinets

(G-4723)
ARC DRILLING INC (PA)
9551 Corporate Cir (44125-4261)
PHONE..................216 525-0920
Lee Trem, *President*
Kevin Trem, *Vice Pres*
EMP: 16 **EST:** 1947
SQ FT: 5,000
SALES (est): 2.5MM **Privately Held**
WEB: www.arcdrilling.com
SIC: 3829 3599 Thermometers, including digital; clinical; machine & other job shop work

(G-4724)
ARC GAS & SUPPLY LLC
4560 Nicky Blvd Ste D (44125-1058)
PHONE..................216 341-5882
Sam Strazzanti, *President*
Jim Kinser, *Vice Pres*
Danny Strazzanti, *Opers Mgr*
Dan Trappe, *Store Mgr*
Gary Mroczka, *Controller*
EMP: 38
SALES (est): 7.4MM **Privately Held**
SIC: 7692 Welding repair

(G-4725)
ARCELORMITTAL CLEVELAND LLC (HQ)
3060 Eggers Ave (44105-1012)
PHONE..................216 429-6000
Micheal Rippey, *CEO*
Louis Schorsch, *CEO*
Philip Zeppo, *Division Mgr*
David Whitesmith, *Project Mgr*
Bob Kaletta, *Opers Mgr*
▲ **EMP:** 204
SQ FT: 40,000
SALES (est): 392.2MM
SALES (corp-wide): 9.1B **Privately Held**
SIC: 3312 Blast furnaces & steel mills
PA: Arcelormittal
Boulevard D'avranches 24-26
Luxembourg 1160
479 21 -

(G-4726)
ARCELORMITTAL CLEVELAND LLC
3060 Eggers Ave (44105-1012)
PHONE..................216 429-6000
Alexander Ivanov, *Engineer*
Shailesh Thakkar, *Engineer*
Mark Yahraus, *Engineer*
Terry Fedor, *Manager*
EMP: 30
SALES (corp-wide): 9.1B **Privately Held**
SIC: 3312 Blast furnaces & steel mills
HQ: Arcelormittal Cleveland Llc
3060 Eggers Ave
Cleveland OH 44105
216 429-6000

(G-4727)
ARCHITECTURAL FIBERGLASS INC
8300 Bessemer Ave (44127-1839)
PHONE..................216 641-8300
Michael Dobronos, *President*
Tanya Dobronos, *Vice Pres*
Steve Dobronos, *Sls & Mktg Exec*
▲ **EMP:** 30
SQ FT: 20,000
SALES (est): 5.7MM **Privately Held**
WEB: www.fiberglassafi.com
SIC: 2221 Glass & fiberglass broadwoven fabrics

(G-4728)
ARCHITECTURAL PRODUCTS DEV
6605 Clark Ave Rear 1 (44102-5330)
PHONE..................216 631-6260
Arthur Petrauskis, *President*
Maureen Petrauskis, *Vice Pres*
EMP: 5
SQ FT: 17,500
SALES (est): 828.6K **Privately Held**
WEB: www.apd-inc.com
SIC: 1791 3299 Elevator front installation, metal; architectural sculptures: gypsum, clay, papier mache, etc.

(G-4729)
ARCHITECTURAL SHEET METALS LLC
1457 E 39th St (44114-4120)
PHONE..................216 361-9952
Arthur A Petrauskis, *President*
EMP: 5
SALES (est): 639K **Privately Held**
SIC: 3444 Restaurant sheet metalwork

(G-4730)
ARCONIC INC
3960 S Marginal Rd (44114-3835)
PHONE..................216 391-3885
Andy Vasas, *Plant Mgr*
Klaus Kleinfeld, *Branch Mgr*
John Topeka, *Maintence Staff*
EMP: 8
SALES (corp-wide): 14B **Publicly Held**
SIC: 3334 Primary aluminum
PA: Arconic Inc.
390 Park Ave Fl 12
New York NY 10022
212 836-2758

(G-4731)
ARDAR CO INC
12955 York Delta Dr Ste A (44133-3550)
PHONE..................440 582-3371
Wally Marij, *President*
Irene Marij, *Corp Secy*
EMP: 5
SALES: 550K **Privately Held**
SIC: 3599 Machine shop, jobbing & repair

(G-4732)
ARISDYNE SYSTEMS INC
17909 Cleveland Pkwy Dr # 100 (44135-3236)
PHONE..................216 458-1991
Peter Reimers, *President*
Frederick W Clarke, *Exec VP*
Nick Berchtold, *CFO*
EMP: 15
SQ FT: 15,000
SALES (est): 3.8MM **Privately Held**
SIC: 3612 Saturable reactors

(G-4733)
ARKEN MANUFACTURING INC
3502 Beyerle Rd (44105-1016)
PHONE..................216 883-6628
Donald Dostie, *President*
Ken Dostie, *Vice Pres*
EMP: 5
SQ FT: 2,500
SALES (est): 795.8K **Privately Held**
WEB: www.arkenusa.com
SIC: 3544 Special dies & tools

(G-4734)
ARMATURE COIL EQUIPMENT INC
Also Called: Ace Equipment Company
4725 Manufacturing Ave (44135-2696)
PHONE..................216 267-6366
Robert F Heran, *President*
Jean Heran, *Admin Sec*
EMP: 12
SQ FT: 25,140
SALES (est): 2.5MM **Privately Held**
WEB: www.armaturecoil.com
SIC: 3549 3567 Coil winding machines for springs; industrial furnaces & ovens

(G-4735)
ARMOUR SPRAY SYSTEMS INC
210 Hayes Dr Ste I (44131-1056)
PHONE..................216 398-3838
Michael J Mihna Jr, *President*
Michael J Mihna III, *Vice Pres*
▲ **EMP:** 10 **EST:** 1976
SQ FT: 5,000
SALES (est): 1.9MM **Privately Held**
WEB: www.armourspray.com
SIC: 5084 3563 Pumps & pumping equipment; spraying outfits: metals, paints & chemicals (compressor)

(G-4736)
ARROW INTERNATIONAL INC (PA)
9900 Clinton Rd (44144-1097)
PHONE..................216 961-3500
John E Gallagher, *CEO*
Edward J Maher, *Principal*
Robert E Sweeney, *Principal*
Joel Horne, *Vice Pres*
Greg Pollock, *Vice Pres*
◆ **EMP:** 277
SALES (est): 235.9MM **Privately Held**
WEB: www.arrowgames.com
SIC: 3944 Board games, puzzles & models, except electronic

(G-4737)
ART GALVANIZING WORKS INC
3935 Valley Rd (44109-3092)
PHONE..................216 749-0020
James Klein, *President*
Adrienne Klein, *Vice Pres*
EMP: 15 **EST:** 1935
SQ FT: 9,775
SALES (est): 1.6MM **Privately Held**
WEB: www.artgalvanizing.com
SIC: 3479 Galvanizing of iron, steel or end-formed products

(G-4738)
ART-AMERICAN PRINTING PLATES
1138 W 9th St Fl 4 (44113-1007)
PHONE..................216 241-4420
John T Mc Sweeney, *President*
Lawrence Mc Sweeney, *Vice Pres*
EMP: 25
SQ FT: 11,000
SALES (est): 3.5MM **Privately Held**
WEB: www.art-american.com
SIC: 2796 7336 Platemaking services; graphic arts & related design

(G-4739)
ARTHUR W GUILFORD III INC
Also Called: G A Guilford & Sons
13515 Brookpark Rd (44142-1824)
PHONE..................216 362-1350
Arthur W Guilford III, *President*
EMP: 8
SQ FT: 5,000
SALES (est): 925.1K **Privately Held**
SIC: 3842 Braces, orthopedic

(G-4740)
ARTISAN TOOL & DIE CORP
4911 Grant Ave (44125-1027)
PHONE..................216 883-2769
James Berkes, *President*
David Dross, *Treasurer*
▼ **EMP:** 40
SQ FT: 65,000
SALES: 2.9MM **Privately Held**
SIC: 3469 3544 Metal stampings; special dies & tools

(G-4741)
ARTISTIC METAL SPINNING INC
Also Called: Zoia
4700 Lorain Ave (44102-3443)
PHONE..................216 961-3336
Lorraine Hangauer, *President*
Ronald W Hangauer, *Vice Pres*
Donald E Hangauer, *Admin Sec*
EMP: 6 **EST:** 1930
SQ FT: 12,000
SALES (est): 948.8K **Privately Held**
SIC: 3469 Spinning metal for the trade

(G-4742)
ARTISTIC ROCK LLC
3786 Fairoaks Rd (44121-1923)
PHONE..................216 291-8856
Ronan Basler, *Principal*
EMP: 3 **EST:** 2011
SALES (est): 123.5K **Privately Held**
SIC: 5999 3272 Concrete products, precast; art marble, concrete

(G-4743)
ARZEL TECHNOLOGY INC
Also Called: Arzel Zoning Technology
4801 Commerce Pkwy (44128-5905)
PHONE..................216 831-6068
Lenny Roth, *Senior VP*
Adam Bush, *Engineer*
Stephanie Lupica, *Mktg Coord*
Jessi Finley, *Manager*
Fred Martinez, *Manager*
▼ **EMP:** 29
SQ FT: 40,000
SALES (est): 7.3MM **Privately Held**
WEB: www.arzelzoning.com
SIC: 3823 Industrial instrmnts msrmnt display/control process variable

(G-4744)
ASCO POWER TECHNOLOGIES LP
Also Called: Avtron Loadbank
6255 Halle Dr (44125-4615)
PHONE..................216 573-7600
Bob Daniels, *General Mgr*
EMP: 106
SALES (corp-wide): 355.8K **Privately Held**
SIC: 3613 3625 Switchgear & switchboard apparatus; resistors & resistor units
HQ: Asco Power Technologies, L.P.
160 Park Ave
Florham Park NJ 07932

(G-4745)
ASCO POWER TECHNOLOGIES LP
8400 E Pleasant Valley Rd (44131-5519)
PHONE..................216 573-7600
Bob Daniels, *General Mgr*
EMP: 35
SALES (corp-wide): 355.8K **Privately Held**
SIC: 3613 3625 Switchgear & switchboard apparatus; resistors & resistor units
HQ: Asco Power Technologies, L.P.
160 Park Ave
Florham Park NJ 07932

(G-4746)
ASCO VALVE INC
26401 Emery Rd Ste 105 (44128-6210)
PHONE..................216 360-0366
EMP: 13
SALES (corp-wide): 24.5B **Publicly Held**
SIC: 3625 Mfg Relays/Industrial Controls
HQ: Asco Valve, Inc.
50-60 Hanover Rd
Florham Park NJ 07932
973 966-2000

(PA)=Parent Co (HQ)=Headquarters (DH)=Div Headquarters
✪ = New Business established in last 2 years

Cleveland - Cuyahoga County (G-4747)

(G-4747)
ASCON TECNOLOGIC N AMER LLC
1111 Brookpark Rd (44109-5825)
PHONE..................216 485-8350
Steven Craig, *General Mgr*
Lisa Foose, *Accountant*
Rick Pelton, *Sales Mgr*
EMP: 6 **EST:** 2012
SALES: 10MM **Privately Held**
SIC: 3823 Industrial instrmnts msrmnt display/control process variable

(G-4748)
ASG
15700 S Waterloo Rd (44110-3814)
PHONE..................216 486-6163
Bryon Schafer, *Manager*
EMP: 11
SALES (est): 1.5MM **Privately Held**
SIC: 3423 Hand & edge tools

(G-4749)
ASG DIVISION JERGENS INC
15700 S Waterloo Rd (44110-3814)
PHONE..................888 486-6163
Bryon Shafer, *General Mgr*
Charles Ohara, *Opers Mgr*
Chris Emanuele, *Manager*
EMP: 5
SALES (est): 75K **Privately Held**
SIC: 3423 3629 1731 Screw drivers, pliers, chisels, etc. (hand tools); battery chargers, rectifying or nonrotating; electric power systems contractors

(G-4750)
ASHTA FORGE & MACHINE INC
3001 W 121st St (44111-1638)
PHONE..................216 252-7000
Wayne Phelps, *President*
Karen Mason, *Corp Secy*
EMP: 20
SALES (est): 2MM **Privately Held**
SIC: 3599 Machine shop, jobbing & repair

(G-4751)
ASK CHEMICALS
2191 W 110th St (44102-3509)
PHONE..................216 961-4690
Cindy Detraz, *Purch Mgr*
Frank Blackwell, *Engineer*
Terri Green, *Engineer*
Marcus Leatherberry, *Engineer*
Susan Manhart, *Manager*
EMP: 14
SALES (est): 3.9MM **Privately Held**
SIC: 2899 Chemical preparations

(G-4752)
ASSEMBLY SPECIALTY PDTS INC
14700 Brookpark Rd (44135-5166)
PHONE..................216 676-5600
Erno Nagy, *President*
Steve Konig, *COO*
Attila Nagy, *Vice Pres*
Marian Stewart, *Purch Mgr*
Missy Main, *Sales Staff*
EMP: 22 **EST:** 1971
SQ FT: 33,500
SALES (est): 6.2MM **Privately Held**
WEB: www.assemblyspecialty.com
SIC: 3496 Cable, uninsulated wire: made from purchased wire

(G-4753)
ASSOCIATED PRESS REPAIR INC
5321 Saint Clair Ave (44103-1311)
PHONE..................216 881-2288
Anthony Grbavac, *President*
Steve Grbavac, *Vice Pres*
EMP: 8
SQ FT: 24,000
SALES (est): 1MM **Privately Held**
SIC: 3599 Machine shop, jobbing & repair

(G-4754)
ASTER ELEMENTS INC
7100 Euclid Ave (44103-4036)
PHONE..................440 942-2799
Joe Lopez, *CEO*
EMP: 22
SQ FT: 30,000
SALES (est): 4.9MM **Privately Held**
SIC: 3441 Fabricated structural metal

(G-4755)
AT HOLDINGS CORPORATION
23555 Euclid Ave (44117-1703)
PHONE..................216 692-6000
Michael S Lipscomb, *Ch of Bd*
David Scaife, *Vice Pres*
Frances S St Clair, *CFO*
Shawn Berry, *Accounts Exec*
Jeffrey Tomson, *Info Tech Mgr*
EMP: 736
SQ FT: 1,800,000
SALES (est): 42MM **Privately Held**
SIC: 3724 3728 6512 Pumps, aircraft engine; aircraft parts & equipment; commercial & industrial building operation
HQ: Eaton Corporation
1000 Eaton Blvd
Cleveland OH 44122
440 523-5000

(G-4756)
AT&F ADVANCED METALS LLC (PA)
12314 Elmwood Ave (44111-5906)
PHONE..................330 684-1122
John Deily,
Brian Spitz, *Pediatrics*
Terry Riplch,
▲ **EMP:** 35
SQ FT: 15,000
SALES (est): 6.4MM **Privately Held**
WEB: www.advmetals.com
SIC: 3446 3443 Railings, prefabricated metal; process vessels, industrial: metal plate

(G-4757)
AT&F NUCLEAR INC (HQ)
12314 Elmwood Ave (44111-5906)
PHONE..................216 252-1500
Michael Ripich, *CEO*
EMP: 5
SALES (est): 2.3MM
SALES (corp-wide): 183.4MM **Privately Held**
SIC: 5051 5999 3999 Steel; welding supplies; atomizers, toiletry
PA: The American Tank & Fabricating Co
12314 Elmwood Ave
Cleveland OH 44111
216 252-1500

(G-4758)
ATHENS FOODS INC
13600 Snow Rd (44142-2546)
PHONE..................216 676-8500
Eric Moscahlaidis, *Ch of Bd*
Scott Sumser, *President*
William Buckingham, *Vice Pres*
Jeff Swint, *Vice Pres*
Robert Tansing, *Vice Pres*
EMP: 180
SQ FT: 114,000
SALES (est): 27MM **Privately Held**
WEB: www.athensfoods.com
SIC: 2038 2045 Frozen specialties; prepared flour mixes & doughs

(G-4759)
ATHERSYS INC (PA)
3201 Carnegie Ave (44115-2634)
PHONE..................216 431-9900
Gil Van Bokkelen, *Ch of Bd*
William Lehmann Jr, *President*
John J Harrington, *Exec VP*
Laura K Campbell, *Senior VP*
Chris Bruns, *Mfg Staff*
EMP: 60
SQ FT: 45,000
SALES: 24.2MM **Publicly Held**
WEB: www.athersys.com
SIC: 2834 Pharmaceutical preparations

(G-4760)
ATLAS MACHINE PRODUCTS CO
Also Called: Atlas Portable Space Solutions
12507 Plover St (44107-5213)
PHONE..................216 228-3688
N Medley, *President*
Ed Medley, *Corp Secy*
William Slabe, *VP Mfg*
EMP: 7 **EST:** 1952
SQ FT: 3,000
SALES: 300K **Privately Held**
SIC: 3451 Screw machine products

(G-4761)
ATLAS PRINTING AND EMBROIDERY
Also Called: Brian Rengh
7632 Pleasant View Dr (44134-5817)
PHONE..................440 882-3537
Brian Rengh, *Owner*
EMP: 4 **EST:** 1999
SQ FT: 5,000
SALES: 280K **Privately Held**
WEB: www.atlas-printing.com
SIC: 2759 Commercial printing

(G-4762)
ATOTECH USA INC
1000 Harvard Ave (44109-3048)
PHONE..................216 398-0550
Steve Bellavita, *Branch Mgr*
Robin Taylor, *Manager*
EMP: 80
SALES (corp-wide): 8.4B **Publicly Held**
SIC: 2899 4225 Chemical supplies for foundries; general warehousing & storage
HQ: Atotech Usa, Llc
1750 Overview Dr
Rock Hill SC 29730

(G-4763)
ATTENTION DSASE DIAGNSTC GROUP
2944 E Derbyshire Rd (44118-2713)
PHONE..................216 577-3075
EMP: 3 **EST:** 2017
SALES (est): 275.6K **Privately Held**
SIC: 3841 Diagnostic apparatus, medical

(G-4764)
AUSTIN FINISHING CO INC
3805 E 91st St (44105-2196)
PHONE..................216 883-0326
Austin Smith, *President*
Nancy Smith, *Vice Pres*
EMP: 5
SQ FT: 7,200
SALES: 438K **Privately Held**
SIC: 3479 Painting of metal products

(G-4765)
AUSTIN POWDER COMPANY (DH)
25800 Science Park Dr # 300 (44122-7386)
PHONE..................216 464-2400
William Jack Davis, *Ch of Bd*
David M Gleason, *President*
Jason F Rawlings, *President*
Michael A Gleason, *Exec VP*
▲ **EMP:** 70
SQ FT: 25,000
SALES (est): 538.9MM
SALES (corp-wide): 567.4MM **Privately Held**
SIC: 2892 Explosives

(G-4766)
AUSTIN POWDER HOLDINGS COMPANY (HQ)
25800 Science Park Dr # 300 (44122-7311)
PHONE..................216 464-2400
William Jack Davis, *Ch of Bd*
David M Gleason, *President*
Michael Gleason, *COO*
◆ **EMP:** 60
SQ FT: 25,000
SALES (est): 567.4MM **Privately Held**
WEB: www.austinpowder.com
SIC: 2892 Explosives
PA: Davis Mining & Manufacturing, Inc.
613 Front St E
Coeburn VA 24230
276 395-3354

(G-4767)
AUTO BOLT COMPANY
Also Called: Auto Bolt and Nut Company, The
4740 Manufacturing Ave (44135-2640)
PHONE..................216 881-3913
Robert Kocian, *President*
Chuck Chapman, *Plant Supt*
John Rottenborn, *QC Mgr*
Matthew Baker, *Engineer*
Ricky Singh, *Engineer*
EMP: 60
SQ FT: 64,100
SALES (est): 10MM **Privately Held**
SIC: 3452 Bolts, metal

(G-4768)
AUTO EXPO USA OF CLEVELAND
3250 W 117th St (44111-1701)
PHONE..................216 889-3000
Mike Daniel, *Owner*
Majdulyn Assad,
EMP: 6
SALES (est): 187K **Privately Held**
SIC: 3711 Automobile assembly, including specialty automobiles

(G-4769)
AUTO-TAP INC
3317 W 140th St (44111-2428)
PHONE..................216 671-1043
Jim Sullivan, *President*
Mike Peteras, *Shareholder*
Frank Suarez, *Shareholder*
EMP: 9
SQ FT: 18,000
SALES (est): 3MM **Privately Held**
WEB: www.auto-tap.net
SIC: 3559 Degreasing machines, automotive & industrial

(G-4770)
AUTOMATED PACKG SYSTEMS INC
13555 Mccracken Rd (44125-1993)
PHONE..................216 663-2000
Yates Brad, *Opers-Prdtn-Mfg*
EMP: 120
SALES (corp-wide): 225.2MM **Privately Held**
WEB: www.autobag.com
SIC: 3081 2673 Packing materials, plastic sheet; bags: plastic, laminated & coated
PA: Automated Packaging Systems Inc.
10175 Philipp Pkwy
Streetsboro OH 44241
330 528-2000

(G-4771)
AUTOMATED WHEEL LLC
8525 Clinton Rd (44144-1014)
PHONE..................216 651-9022
Gregory S Hadgis,
◆ **EMP:** 99
SALES (est): 7.6MM **Privately Held**
WEB: www.automatedwheel.com
SIC: 3471 Plating of metals or formed products; cleaning, polishing & finishing

(G-4772)
AUTOMATIC SCREW PRODUCTS CO
2070 W 7th St (44113-3690)
PHONE..................216 241-7896
Bruce Bacik, *President*
Joanna Bacik, *Vice Pres*
▲ **EMP:** 8
SQ FT: 15,500
SALES (est): 650K **Privately Held**
SIC: 3451 Screw machine products

(G-4773)
AUTOMATIC STAMP PRODUCTS INC
1822 Columbus Rd (44113-2472)
PHONE..................216 781-7933
Raymond L Haserodt, *Vice Pres*
David McAndrews, *Vice Pres*
Chuck Horvath, *Manager*
Tony Lozar, *Executive*
EMP: 12 **EST:** 1946
SQ FT: 44,000
SALES (est): 3.7MM **Privately Held**
WEB: www.automaticstamp.com
SIC: 3469 Stamping metal for the trade

(G-4774)
AUTOMATION FINISHING INC
3206 W 121st St (44111-1720)
PHONE..................216 251-8805
Steve Star, *President*
EMP: 20

▲ = Import ▼ = Export
◆ = Import/Export

SALES (est): 1.3MM **Privately Held**
SIC: **3471** Electroplating & plating

(G-4775)
AVERY DENNISON CORPORATION
15939 Industrial Pkwy (44135-3321)
PHONE..................216 267-8700
Steve Horvath, *Production*
Michael Welch, *Engineer*
Jake Cowdrick, *Technical Staff*
EMP: 7
SALES (corp-wide): 7.1B **Publicly Held**
SIC: **2672** Adhesive papers, labels or tapes: from purchased material
PA: Avery Dennison Corporation
207 N Goode Ave Ste 500
Glendale CA 91203
626 304-2000

(G-4776)
AVIATION TECHNOLOGIES INC (DH)
1301 E 9th St Ste 3000 (44114-1871)
PHONE..................216 706-2960
W Nicholas Howley, *CEO*
Gregory Ruful, *CFO*
EMP: 2
SQ FT: 27,000
SALES (est): 43MM
SALES (corp-wide): 3.8B **Publicly Held**
SIC: **3643** 3678 3679 3728 Contacts, electrical; electronic connectors; liquid crystal displays (LCD); aircraft parts & equipment; search & navigation equipment; lighting equipment

(G-4777)
AVILES CONSTRUCTION COMPANY
7011 Clark Ave (44102-5316)
PHONE..................216 939-1084
Jose Aviles, *President*
Jose E Aviles, *President*
Alex Aviles, *Vice Pres*
Maria Aviles, *Treasurer*
Elisa E Velez, *Admin Sec*
EMP: 21
SALES (est): 4.1MM **Privately Held**
SIC: **2821** Cellulose acetate (plastics)

(G-4778)
AVTRON AEROSPACE INC (PA)
7900 E Pleasant Valley Rd (44131-5529)
PHONE..................216 750-5152
John Pesec, *President*
Joseph Flower, *Controller*
EMP: 113
SQ FT: 65,000
SALES (est): 31.6MM **Privately Held**
WEB: www.avtron.com
SIC: **3351** 3728 Bars & bar shapes, copper & copper alloy; aircraft parts & equipment

(G-4779)
AVTRON HOLDINGS LLC
7900 E Pleasant Valley Rd (44131-5529)
PHONE..................216 642-1230
Alfred Stanley,
James Ettamarna,
Theodore A Laufik,
Peter Taft,
Karen Tuleta,
EMP: 350
SQ FT: 47,707
SALES (est): 37.9MM **Privately Held**
SIC: **3625** 3825 Electric controls & control accessories, industrial; instruments to measure electricity; test equipment for electronic & electric measurement; test equipment for electronic & electrical circuits

(G-4780)
AW FABER-CASTELL USA INC
Also Called: Creativity For Kids
9450 Allen Dr Ste B (44125-4602)
PHONE..................216 643-4660
Jamie Gallagher, *CEO*
Phyllis Brody, *Vice Pres*
Don Fischer, *CFO*
Michael Smith, *Info Tech Dir*
▲ EMP: 100
SQ FT: 85,000
SALES (est): 37MM
SALES (corp-wide): 712.9MM **Privately Held**
WEB: www.faber-castell.com
SIC: **5092** 5112 3944 Arts & crafts equipment & supplies; stationery & office supplies; writing instruments & supplies; games, toys & children's vehicles; craft & hobby kits & sets
HQ: Faber-Castell Ag
Nurnberger Str. 2
Stein 90547
911 996-50

(G-4781)
AWNING FABRI CATERS INC
10237 Lorain Ave (44111-5435)
P.O. Box 182, Avon Lake (44012-0182)
PHONE..................216 476-4888
Todd Krupa, *President*
EMP: 7
SALES (est): 590K **Privately Held**
SIC: **2394** Awnings, fabric: made from purchased materials

(G-4782)
B & B PAPER CONVERTERS INC
12500 Elmwood Ave Frnt (44111-5987)
PHONE..................216 941-8100
Jerry Jazwa, *President*
Cindy Wagner, *CFO*
EMP: 12 EST: 1947
SQ FT: 120,000
SALES (est): 3MM **Privately Held**
SIC: **2621** Newsprint paper

(G-4783)
B & P SPRING PRODUCTION CO
19520 Nottingham Rd (44110-2730)
PHONE..................216 486-4260
Ken Godnavec, *President*
Justin Ray, *General Mgr*
Lorraine Ray, *Corp Secy*
EMP: 17 EST: 1952
SQ FT: 13,000
SALES: 1MM **Privately Held**
SIC: **3495** Precision springs

(G-4784)
B & R MACHINE CO INC
2216 W 65th St (44102-5302)
PHONE..................216 961-7370
William E Graham, *President*
Teala Graham, *Corp Secy*
William G Graham, *Manager*
EMP: 18
SQ FT: 12,000
SALES (est): 3.4MM **Privately Held**
SIC: **3545** 3599 Machine tool accessories; machine shop, jobbing & repair

(G-4785)
B Y G INDUSTRIES INC
Also Called: Guerin-Zimmerman Co
8003 Clinton Rd (44144-1004)
PHONE..................216 961-5436
James R Brasty, *President*
John Brasty Sr, *Vice Pres*
EMP: 6
SQ FT: 10,000
SALES (est): 764K **Privately Held**
SIC: **3444** 3599 Sheet metalwork; machine shop, jobbing & repair

(G-4786)
B-R-O-T INCORPORATED
4730 Briar Rd (44135-2595)
PHONE..................216 267-5335
Kenneth Ott, *President*
Robert Ott, *Vice Pres*
Daniel Plumb, *Prdtn Mgr*
Patricia Ott, *Treasurer*
▲ EMP: 25 EST: 1946
SQ FT: 22,000
SALES (est): 5.3MM **Privately Held**
WEB: www.brot-inc.com
SIC: **3444** 2542 Sheet metalwork; partitions & fixtures, except wood

(G-4787)
BACK DEVELOPMENT LLC
3700 Northfield Rd Ste 11 (44122-5240)
PHONE..................937 671-7896
Brian Back, *President*
Lauren Back, *Vice Pres*
EMP: 3
SQ FT: 2,500
SALES (est): 91.3K **Privately Held**
SIC: **2068** Salted & roasted nuts & seeds

(G-4788)
BAN-FAM INDUSTRIES INC
4740 Briar Rd (44135-5038)
PHONE..................216 265-9588
Gary Banyasz, *President*
Frank Banyasz, *President*
Jim Banyasz, *Vice Pres*
Alice Banyasz, *Treasurer*
Chris Staab, *Treasurer*
EMP: 8
SQ FT: 15,000
SALES: 500K **Privately Held**
SIC: **3599** 3594 3568 Machine shop, jobbing & repair; fluid power pumps & motors; power transmission equipment

(G-4789)
BAR 25 LLC
Also Called: Market Garden Brewery
1939 W 25th St (44113-3474)
PHONE..................216 621-4000
Adam Gullett,
Mark Priemer,
EMP: 4
SQ FT: 35,000
SALES (est): 387.3K **Privately Held**
SIC: **5813** 2082 Beer garden (drinking places); beer (alcoholic beverage)

(G-4790)
BARBS GRAFFITI INC (PA)
Also Called: Graffiti Co
3111 Carnegie Ave (44115-2632)
PHONE..................216 881-5550
Abe Miller, *President*
Barbara Miller, *Corp Secy*
Monica McKinley, *Controller*
Mike Struk, *Sales Associate*
▲ EMP: 40
SQ FT: 18,000
SALES (est): 6.3MM **Privately Held**
WEB: www.graffiticaps.com
SIC: **2353** 2395 5136 5137 Baseball caps; pleating & stitching; sportswear, men's & boys'; sportswear, women's & children's

(G-4791)
BARILE PRECISION GRINDING INC
12320 Plaza Dr (44130-1043)
PHONE..................216 267-6500
Michael Barile, *President*
EMP: 25
SALES: 1.4MM **Privately Held**
WEB: www.barilegrinding.com
SIC: **3599** Machine shop, jobbing & repair

(G-4792)
BARKER PRODUCTS COMPANY
1028 E 134th St (44110-2248)
P.O. Box 10845 (44110-0845)
PHONE..................216 249-0900
Hal Myers, *President*
Benjamin Dagley, *President*
Dr Dieter Myers, *Vice Pres*
Elba Wade, *Vice Pres*
Nora Myers, *Admin Sec*
▲ EMP: 30 EST: 1945
SALES (est): 4.4MM **Privately Held**
SIC: **3471** Plating/Polishing Service

(G-4793)
BARTH INDUSTRIES CO LP (PA)
12650 Brookpark Rd (44130-1154)
PHONE..................216 267-0531
Clark Neft, *President*
Richard Legan, *Exec VP*
Russ Lauer, *Vice Pres*
Anne Margaretha, *Asst Controller*
David Dragony, *Manager*
▲ EMP: 72
SQ FT: 120,700
SALES (est): 13.5MM **Privately Held**
WEB: www.barth-landis.com
SIC: **3541** 3542 3535 3699 Machine tools, metal cutting type; machine tools, metal forming type; conveyors & conveying equipment; electrical equipment & supplies; metalworking machinery

(G-4794)
BASF CATALYSTS LLC
23800 Mercantile Rd (44122-5908)
P.O. Box 22126 (44122-0126)
PHONE..................216 360-5005
John Ferek, *Branch Mgr*
EMP: 83
SALES (corp-wide): 71.7B **Privately Held**
SIC: **2819** 8731 Catalysts, chemical; commercial physical research
HQ: Basf Catalysts Llc
33 Wood Ave S
Iselin NJ 08830
732 205-5000

(G-4795)
BASIC CASES INC
19561 Miles Rd (44128-4111)
PHONE..................216 662-3900
Kenneth Wieder, *President*
Ruth Wieder, *Treasurer*
EMP: 8
SQ FT: 22,000
SALES (est): 939.5K **Privately Held**
WEB: www.basiccases.com
SIC: **2511** 2521 Wood household furniture; wood office furniture

(G-4796)
BDI INC (PA)
Also Called: Baring Distributors
8000 Hub Pkwy (44125-5731)
PHONE..................216 642-9100
Frank L Bystricky, *CEO*
Mike Fryz, *Principal*
Bud Thayer, *Vice Pres*
▲ EMP: 188
SALES (est): 346.5MM **Privately Held**
WEB: www.bdi.com
SIC: **1389** Oil sampling service for oil companies

(G-4797)
BEA-ECC APPARELS INC
1287 W 76th St (44102-2050)
PHONE..................216 650-6336
Siba Beavogui, *Principal*
EMP: 8
SALES (est): 487.9K **Privately Held**
SIC: **2311** Men's & boys' suits & coats

(G-4798)
BEACON METAL FABRICATORS INC
5425 Hamilton Ave Ste D (44114-3983)
PHONE..................216 391-7444
Kenneth Grobolsek, *President*
Robert Grobolssek, *Vice Pres*
EMP: 13
SQ FT: 11,000
SALES (est): 700K **Privately Held**
WEB: www.beaconmetalfab.com
SIC: **3599** 3444 3446 Machine & other job shop work; bins, prefabricated sheet metal; railings, prefabricated metal; ornamental metalwork

(G-4799)
BEAR DIVERSIFIED INC (PA)
4580 E 71st St (44125-1018)
PHONE..................216 883-5494
Matthew Friedman, *CEO*
Ian Hessel, *President*
Ronald Campbell, *COO*
EMP: 4
SALES (est): 453.1MM **Privately Held**
SIC: **3465** 5013 5051 Automotive stampings; automotive stampings; stampings, metal

(G-4800)
BECKERS BAKESHOP INC
13510 Miles Ave (44105-5526)
PHONE..................216 752-4161
Joe J Becker, *President*
Jaean Becker, *Assistant VP*
EMP: 12
SQ FT: 8,000
SALES (est): 1.5MM **Privately Held**
WEB: www.thebridalcafe.com
SIC: **2051** 2052 Cakes, bakery: except frozen; cookies

Cleveland - Cuyahoga County (G-4801) GEOGRAPHIC SECTION

(G-4801)
BECKWORTH INDUSTRIES INC
Also Called: Ridgewood Brake Co
14511 Saranac Rd (44110-2336)
PHONE..................216 268-5557
Richard K Strauss, *President*
Richard K Strauss, *President*
Richard Strauss Jr, *Vice Pres*
EMP: 4
SQ FT: 10,000
SALES: 85K **Privately Held**
SIC: 3625 Brakes, electromagnetic

(G-4802)
BEDFORD CABINET INC
21891 Forbes Rd Ste 102 (44146-5462)
PHONE..................440 439-4830
Bruce Smerglia, *President*
EMP: 5
SQ FT: 900
SALES (est): 1.5MM **Privately Held**
SIC: 2542 Cabinets: show, display or storage: except wood

(G-4803)
BELLISSIMO DISTRIBUTION LLC
Also Called: Sidaris Italian Foods
3820 Lakeside Ave E (44114-3848)
PHONE..................216 431-3344
Jim Debruzzi, *CFO*
EMP: 18
SALES (corp-wide): 35MM **Privately Held**
SIC: 2099 Packaged combination products: pasta, rice & potato
HQ: Bellissimo Distribution, Llc
1550 Hecht Dr
Bartlett IL 60103
630 837-9900

(G-4804)
BEREA HARDWOOD CO INC
18745 Sheldon Rd (44130-2472)
PHONE..................216 898-8956
James J Heusinger, *President*
▲ **EMP:** 5
SQ FT: 10,000
SALES (est): 1.2MM **Privately Held**
SIC: 5031 3951 5112 Lumber: rough, dressed & finished; ball point pens & parts; cartridges, refill: ball point pens; fountain pens & fountain pen desk sets; pens &/or pencils; stationery

(G-4805)
BERGSTROM COMPANY LTD PARTNR
Also Called: Weldon Pump
640 Golden Oak Pkwy (44146-6504)
PHONE..................440 232-2282
Tony Coletto, *CEO*
Barbara Bergstrom, *Partner*
Jon Bergstrom, *Partner*
Walter T Bergstrom, *Partner*
Kim Colegrove, *General Mgr*
EMP: 33
SQ FT: 13,600
SALES (est): 6.9MM **Privately Held**
WEB: www.weldonracing.com
SIC: 3714 3594 3586 3561 Fuel pumps, motor vehicle; lubrication systems & parts, motor vehicle; hydraulic fluid power pumps for auto steering mechanism; fluid power pumps & motors; measuring & dispensing pumps; pumps & pumping equipment

(G-4806)
BERNARD R DOYLES INC
Also Called: Fastsigns
2102 Saint Clair Ave Ne (44114-4047)
PHONE..................216 523-2288
Bernard R Doyle, *President*
Mary Doyle, *Vice Pres*
EMP: 5
SQ FT: 1,800
SALES (est): 709.5K **Privately Held**
SIC: 3993 7389 Signs & advertising specialties; sign painting & lettering shop

(G-4807)
BERNARD SPECIALTY CO
2800 E 55th St Frnt (44104-2861)
PHONE..................216 881-2200
Thomas K Dunkle, *President*
Dennis B Dunkle, *Vice Pres*
EMP: 5
SQ FT: 12,500
SALES (est): 553.2K **Privately Held**
WEB: www.bernardscycle.com
SIC: 2789 Binding only: books, pamphlets, magazines, etc.

(G-4808)
BESTEN INC
4416 Lee Rd (44128-2902)
PHONE..................216 910-2880
Fred Floyd, *Principal*
EMP: 4
SALES (est): 215.9K **Privately Held**
SIC: 3559 Special industry machinery

(G-4809)
BETA MACHINE COMPANY INC
17702 S Waterloo Rd (44119-3220)
PHONE..................216 383-0000
John Haymond, *President*
EMP: 14 **EST:** 1978
SQ FT: 8,000
SALES: 300K **Privately Held**
SIC: 3599 Machine shop, jobbing & repair

(G-4810)
BETLEY PRINTING CO
Also Called: American Book Screening
3816 Cullen Dr (44105-7201)
PHONE..................216 206-5600
William T Betley, *Owner*
EMP: 3
SQ FT: 3,200
SALES (est): 261.3K **Privately Held**
SIC: 2752 2759 Business forms, lithographed; letterpress printing

(G-4811)
BEVERAGE MACHINE & FABRICATORS
13301 Lakewood Hts Blvd (44107-6288)
PHONE..................216 252-5100
John D Geiger, *President*
Nancy Geiger, *Admin Sec*
EMP: 15
SQ FT: 15,000
SALES (est): 2.2MM **Privately Held**
SIC: 3599 Machine shop, jobbing & repair

(G-4812)
BIG GUS ONION RINGS INC
4500 Turney Rd (44105-6716)
PHONE..................216 883-9045
Peter George, *President*
Angela George, *Corp Secy*
Thomas George, *Vice Pres*
EMP: 20
SQ FT: 5,000
SALES (est): 3.5MM **Privately Held**
SIC: 2037 5148 2099 Vegetables, quick frozen & cold pack, excl. potato products; fruits, fresh; vegetables, fresh; food preparations

(G-4813)
BIGMOUTH DONUT COMPANY LLC
1361 E 55th St (44103-1301)
PHONE..................216 264-0250
EMP: 4 **Privately Held**
SIC: 2045 Doughnut mixes, prepared: from purchased flour
PA: Bigmouth Donut Company, Llc
1418 W 29th St
Cleveland OH 44113

(G-4814)
BIMBO BAKERIES USA CLEVELAND
4570 E 71st St (44105-5604)
PHONE..................216 641-5700
EMP: 12 **EST:** 2010
SALES (est): 1.5MM **Privately Held**
SIC: 2051 Bread, cake & related products

(G-4815)
BINDTECH LLC
Also Called: Finish Line Binderies
5344 Bragg Rd (44127-1274)
PHONE..................615 834-0404
EMP: 57
SALES (corp-wide): 21.6MM **Privately Held**
SIC: 2789 Binding only: books, pamphlets, magazines, etc.
HQ: Bindtech, Llc
1232 Antioch Pike
Nashville TN 37211
615 834-0404

(G-4816)
BLACK & DECKER CORPORATION
12100 Snow Rd Ste 1 (44130-9319)
PHONE..................440 842-9100
Mark Konecek, *Branch Mgr*
EMP: 33
SALES (corp-wide): 13.9B **Publicly Held**
WEB: www.blackanddecker.com
SIC: 3546 Power-driven handtools
HQ: The Black & Decker Corporation
701 E Joppa Rd
Towson MD 21286
410 716-3900

(G-4817)
BLAINS FOLDING SERVICE INC
4103 Detroit Ave (44113-2721)
PHONE..................216 631-4700
Edward Blain, *President*
Carol Blain, *Corp Secy*
EMP: 7
SALES: 700K **Privately Held**
SIC: 2789 Binding only: books, pamphlets, magazines, etc.

(G-4818)
BLASTER CHEMICAL CO INC
8500 Sweet Valley Dr (44125-4214)
PHONE..................216 901-5800
Tom Porter, *Chairman*
EMP: 3
SALES (est): 394.7K **Privately Held**
SIC: 2911 Petroleum refining

(G-4819)
BLASTER CORPORATION
8500 Sweet Valley Dr (44125-4214)
PHONE..................216 901-5800
Thomas Porter, *CEO*
Kurt Gabram, *CEO*
Randy Pindor, *President*
Paul Gardner, *General Mgr*
Randy M Pindor, *COO*
EMP: 42 **EST:** 1959
SQ FT: 20,000
SALES (est): 11.7MM **Privately Held**
WEB: www.pbblaster.com
SIC: 2911 2819 2842 2992 Fuel additives; catalysts, chemical; automobile polish; lubricating oils & greases; chemical preparations

(G-4820)
BLINK MARKETING INC
Also Called: Blink Marketing & Signs
1925 Saint Clair Ave Ne (44114-2028)
PHONE..................216 503-2568
Syed Nida, *Principal*
EMP: 4
SALES (est): 215.3K **Privately Held**
SIC: 3993 Signs & advertising specialties

(G-4821)
BLITZ TOOL & DIE INC
11941 Abbey Rd Ste I (44133-2663)
PHONE..................440 237-1177
Ralph Rehner, *President*
EMP: 6
SQ FT: 3,500
SALES: 300K **Privately Held**
SIC: 3544 Special dies & tools

(G-4822)
BLOOM LAKE IRON ORE MINE LTD
200 Public Sq (44114-2316)
PHONE..................216 694-5700
Joe Carrabba, *CEO*
Joseph A Carrabba, *President*
Laurie Brlas, *President*
Donald Gallagher, *President*
Clifford Smith, *Vice Pres*
EMP: 1 **EST:** 2012
SALES (est): 37.8MM
SALES (corp-wide): 2.3B **Publicly Held**
SIC: 1011 Iron ore mining
PA: Cleveland-Cliffs Inc.
200 Public Sq Ste 3300
Cleveland OH 44114
216 694-5700

(G-4823)
BLUE LINE PAINTING LLC
19520 Nottingham Rd (44110-2730)
PHONE..................440 951-2583
Sean Rogers, *Owner*
EMP: 4
SALES (est): 326.4K **Privately Held**
SIC: 2741 Miscellaneous publishing

(G-4824)
BLUE POINT CAPITL PARTNERS LLC (PA)
127 Public Sq Ste 5100 (44114-1312)
PHONE..................216 535-4700
David Given, *Managing Prtnr*
Thomas Cresante, *Partner*
Mike Kane, *Partner*
Douglas McGregor, *Partner*
Jason Xi, *Vice Pres*
EMP: 15
SQ FT: 7,000
SALES (est): 433.3MM **Privately Held**
WEB: www.bluepointcapital.com
SIC: 2099 2035 Seasonings & spices; pickles, sauces & salad dressings

(G-4825)
BLUE STREAK SERVICES INC
25001 Emery Rd Ste 410 (44128-5626)
PHONE..................216 223-3282
Carole Sanderson, *President*
Mike Crislip, *Vice Pres*
EMP: 3
SQ FT: 400
SALES: 395.5K **Privately Held**
SIC: 2752 7389 Commercial printing, lithographic; interior design services

(G-4826)
BOARD OF PARK COMMISSIONERS
4101 Fulton Pkwy (44144-1923)
PHONE..................216 635-3200
Dan T Moore, *Principal*
EMP: 4
SALES (est): 187.8K **Privately Held**
SIC: 3949 Shafts, golf club

(G-4827)
BODYCOTE THERMAL PROC INC
5475 Avion Park Dr (44143-1918)
PHONE..................440 473-2020
Anthony Sharaba, *Prdtn Mgr*
Ron Perkins, *Branch Mgr*
EMP: 18
SALES (corp-wide): 911.9MM **Privately Held**
SIC: 3398 Metal heat treating
HQ: Bodycote Thermal Processing, Inc.
12700 Park Central Dr # 700
Dallas TX 75251
214 904-2420

(G-4828)
BODYCOTE THERMAL PROC INC
14701 Industrial Ave (44137-3244)
PHONE..................216 475-0400
Bill Baxter, *Branch Mgr*
EMP: 30
SALES (corp-wide): 911.9MM **Privately Held**
SIC: 3398 Metal heat treating
HQ: Bodycote Thermal Processing, Inc.
12700 Park Central Dr # 700
Dallas TX 75251
214 904-2420

(G-4829)
BOMEN MARKING PRODUCTS INC
12905 York Delta Dr Ste A (44133-3551)
PHONE..................440 582-0053
Joseph Mendyka, *President*
EMP: 9
SQ FT: 3,800
SALES: 700K **Privately Held**
SIC: 2796 3599 Steel line engraving for the printing trade; custom machinery

▲ = Import ▼ = Export
◆ = Import/Export

GEOGRAPHIC SECTION

Cleveland - Cuyahoga County (G-4858)

(G-4830)
BOND DISTRIBUTING LLC
Also Called: One Time
701 Beta Dr Ste 8 (44143-2337)
PHONE.....................440 461-7920
Diana Pummel, *Sales Staff*
Scott Fishel, *Mng Member*
EMP: 6
SQ FT: 4,650
SALES: 832K **Privately Held**
WEB: www.onetimewood.com
SIC: 2899 Chemical preparations

(G-4831)
BONFOEY CO
1710 Euclid Ave (44115-2134)
PHONE.....................216 621-0178
Richard G Moore, *President*
Olga Merela, *Treasurer*
Diane Schaffstein, *Director*
Kate Zimmerer, *Executive Asst*
Mina V Moore, *Admin Sec*
EMP: 15 EST: 1893
SQ FT: 9,300
SALES (est): 2.5MM **Privately Held**
WEB: www.bonfoey.com
SIC: 2499 5719 8999 Picture & mirror frames, wood; pictures, wall; art restoration

(G-4832)
BORDEN DAIRY COMPANY OHIO LLC
Also Called: Dairymens
3068 W 106th St (44111-1801)
PHONE.....................216 671-2300
Gina Roganish, *Purch Mgr*
Kris Kubit, *Engineer*
F David Race, *Controller*
Russell Dzurec, *Mng Member*
David Race, *Surgery Dir*
EMP: 150 EST: 1999
SQ FT: 360,000
SALES (est): 34.9MM **Privately Held**
SIC: 2026 Milk processing (pasteurizing, homogenizing, bottling)
PA: Borden Dairy Company
    8750 N Central Expy # 400
    Dallas TX 75231

(G-4833)
BORMAN ENTERPRISES INC
Also Called: Cleveland Indus Training Ctr
1311 Brookpark Rd (44109-5829)
PHONE.....................216 459-9292
Donald Borman, *President*
Marybeth Borman, *Corp Secy*
Joseph Scheall, *Vice Pres*
EMP: 10 EST: 1975
SQ FT: 13,000
SALES (est): 1.6MM **Privately Held**
WEB: www.bormanenterprises.com
SIC: 3599 8222 Machine shop, jobbing & repair; technical institute

(G-4834)
BOXIT CORPORATION (HQ)
5555 Walworth Ave (44102-4430)
PHONE.....................216 631-6900
Donald Zaas, *Ch of Bd*
Joel Zaas, *President*
Mark Cassese, *COO*
John L Asimakopoulos, *CFO*
EMP: 55
SQ FT: 100,000
SALES (est): 37.3MM
SALES (corp-wide): 59.4MM **Privately Held**
SIC: 2652 2657 Setup paperboard boxes; folding paperboard boxes
PA: The Apex Paper Box Company
    5555 Walworth Ave
    Cleveland OH 44102
    216 631-4000

(G-4835)
BOXIT CORPORATION
3000 Quigley Rd B (44113-4591)
PHONE.....................216 416-9475
Mark Cassese, *Principal*
EMP: 9
SALES (corp-wide): 59.4MM **Privately Held**
SIC: 2657 2652 Folding paperboard boxes; setup paperboard boxes

HQ: Boxit Corporation
    5555 Walworth Ave
    Cleveland OH 44102
    216 631-6900

(G-4836)
BREITS INC
5218 Detroit Ave (44102-2225)
PHONE.....................216 651-5800
Robert Breitenbach, *President*
EMP: 3 EST: 1947
SQ FT: 10,000
SALES (est): 384K **Privately Held**
WEB: www.breits.com
SIC: 2434 Wood kitchen cabinets

(G-4837)
BRICK AND BARREL
1844 Columbus Rd (44113-2412)
PHONE.....................503 927-0629
Karl Spiesman, *President*
EMP: 7
SALES (est): 631.9K **Privately Held**
SIC: 2082 Malt beverages

(G-4838)
BRIGHT FOCUS SALES INC
2310 Superior Ave E # 225 (44114-4256)
PHONE.....................216 751-8384
Greg Shick, *President*
EMP: 15 EST: 2004
SALES (est): 2MM **Privately Held**
SIC: 3674 Light emitting diodes

(G-4839)
BROCO PRODUCTS INC
18624 Syracuse Ave (44110-2521)
PHONE.....................216 531-0880
Barry Brown, *President*
Joyce Brown, *Vice Pres*
Kevin Lovas, *Technical Staff*
Darrell Gorzelanczyk,
EMP: 9
SQ FT: 18,000
SALES (est): 1.8MM **Privately Held**
WEB: www.brocoproducts.com
SIC: 3559 2899 Metal finishing equipment for plating, etc.; metal treating compounds

(G-4840)
BROOKLYN MACHINE & MFG CO INC
5180 Grant Ave (44125-1065)
PHONE.....................216 341-1846
Walter Spann, *President*
Frederick Spann, *Corp Secy*
EMP: 7
SQ FT: 8,500
SALES (est): 968K **Privately Held**
SIC: 3599 Machine shop, jobbing & repair

(G-4841)
BROOKPARK LABORATORIES INC
4595 Manufacturing Ave (44135-2635)
PHONE.....................216 267-7140
Robin Ancell, *President*
Jean Roch, *General Mgr*
EMP: 5 EST: 1963
SQ FT: 1,500
SALES (est): 500K **Privately Held**
SIC: 3585 3812 Coolers, milk & water; electric; search & navigation equipment

(G-4842)
BROST FOUNDRY COMPANY (PA)
2934 E 55th St (44127-1207)
PHONE.....................216 641-1131
Tom Peretti, *President*
Carl Robards, *Department Mgr*
EMP: 28 EST: 1910
SQ FT: 45,000
SALES (est): 5.3MM **Privately Held**
WEB: www.brostfoundry.com
SIC: 3366 3365 3369 3325 Castings (except die); bronze; castings (except die); brass; aluminum & aluminum-based alloy castings; nonferrous foundries; steel foundries; steel investment foundries

(G-4843)
BROTHERS EQUIPMENT INC
Also Called: Ace
1335 E 171st St (44110-2525)
PHONE.....................216 458-0180
Tracy Jurek, *Admin Sec*
EMP: 9
SALES (est): 950K **Privately Held**
SIC: 3715 Truck trailers

(G-4844)
BROTHERS PRINTING CO INC
2000 Euclid Ave (44115-2276)
PHONE.....................216 621-6050
Dotty Kaufman, *CEO*
Jay Kaufman, *President*
David Kaufman, *Treasurer*
EMP: 14 EST: 1925
SQ FT: 36,000
SALES (est): 1.1MM **Privately Held**
SIC: 2752 2759 Commercial printing, offset; letterpress printing

(G-4845)
BROWN MACHINE CO
16151 Puritas Ave (44135-2617)
PHONE.....................216 631-1255
Robert Brown, *Owner*
EMP: 4
SQ FT: 6,000
SALES (est): 362.4K **Privately Held**
SIC: 3599 Machine shop, jobbing & repair

(G-4846)
BRUENING GLASS WORKS INC
Also Called: Konys, Mark Glass Design
20157 Lake Rd (44116-1514)
PHONE.....................440 333-4768
Marc Konys, *President*
Chris Konys, *Vice Pres*
EMP: 6 EST: 1945
SQ FT: 1,500
SALES: 290K **Privately Held**
WEB: www.brueningglass.com
SIC: 3231 5719 5712 Mirrored glass; furniture tops, glass: cut, beveled or polished; mirrors; furniture stores

(G-4847)
BRUSHES INC
5400 Smith Rd (44142-2025)
PHONE.....................216 267-8084
Mary Drews, *President*
EMP: 25 EST: 1958
SQ FT: 9,600
SALES (est): 2.1MM **Privately Held**
SIC: 3991 Brushes, household or industrial; shaving brushes

(G-4848)
BRUSHES INC
Also Called: Malin Company
5400 Smith Rd (44142-2025)
PHONE.....................216 267-8084
Leonard Defino, *President*
Jom Hauck, *Vice Pres*
▲ EMP: 31
SALES (est): 6MM **Privately Held**
WEB: www.brushescorp.com
SIC: 3315 Wire & fabricated wire products

(G-4849)
BUCKEYE METALS INDUSTRIES INC
3238 E 82nd St (44104-4338)
PHONE.....................216 663-4300
Bruce Ison, *President*
Lowy M Marty, *Plant Supt*
Perry Friedman, *Marketing Staff*
EMP: 10
SQ FT: 45,000
SALES (est): 2.8MM **Privately Held**
SIC: 3469 5051 Metal stampings; steel

(G-4850)
BUD MAY INC
Also Called: Maynard Company, The
16850 Hummel Rd (44142-2131)
PHONE.....................216 676-8850
John Maynard, *President*
Tom Maynard, *Vice Pres*
Joan Santoro, *Manager*
EMP: 10 EST: 1974
SQ FT: 18,000
SALES: 571K **Privately Held**
SIC: 3541 Grinding, polishing, buffing, lapping & honing machines; deburring machines

(G-4851)
BUFFEX METAL FINISHING INC
1935 W 96th St Ste L (44102-2600)
PHONE.....................216 631-2202
Orlando R Quintana, *President*
Louis Quintana, *Vice Pres*
EMP: 11
SQ FT: 10,000
SALES (est): 500K **Privately Held**
SIC: 3471 Buffing for the trade; polishing, metals or formed products

(G-4852)
BULA FORGE & MACHINE INC
Also Called: B F
3001 W 121st St (44111-1638)
PHONE.....................216 252-7600
Wayne Phelps, *President*
Karen Mason, *Vice Pres*
EMP: 22
SALES: 3MM **Privately Held**
WEB: www.bulaforge.com
SIC: 3462 Iron & steel forgings

(G-4853)
BUSCHMAN CORPORATION
4100 Payne Ave Ste 1 (44103-2340)
PHONE.....................216 431-6633
Tom Buschman, *CEO*
Ross Defelice, *President*
▲ EMP: 19
SQ FT: 90,000
SALES (est): 5.7MM **Privately Held**
WEB: www.buschmancorp.com
SIC: 3312 2679 2295 Rods, iron & steel: made in steel mills; paper products, converted; tape, varnished: plastic & other coated (except magnetic)

(G-4854)
BUSH INC
15901 Industrial Pkwy (44135-3321)
PHONE.....................216 362-6700
H Russell Bush, *President*
Kim Burgess, *Sales Staff*
Kathy Bush, *Sales Staff*
Martin King, *Sales Staff*
Tim Pluhar, *Sales Staff*
EMP: 21
SALES (est): 2.8MM **Privately Held**
SIC: 2759 Commercial printing

(G-4855)
BUTERA MANUFACTURING INDS
1068 E 134th St (44110-2248)
P.O. Box 349, Wickliffe (44092-0349)
PHONE.....................216 761-8800
Brian Butera, *President*
EMP: 6
SQ FT: 3,000
SALES (est): 716.1K **Privately Held**
SIC: 3429 Animal traps, iron or steel

(G-4856)
C D C AT CITYVIEW
6606 Carnegie Ave (44103-4622)
PHONE.....................216 426-2020
EMP: 35
SALES (est): 2.1MM **Privately Held**
SIC: 3826 Mfg Analytical Instruments

(G-4857)
C L S INC
3812 W 150th St (44111-5805)
PHONE.....................216 251-5011
Ron Anderson, *President*
EMP: 3 EST: 2008
SALES (est): 236.7K **Privately Held**
SIC: 3699 Laser welding, drilling & cutting equipment

(G-4858)
C P S ENTERPRISES INC
Also Called: Able One's Moving Company
9815 Reno Ave (44105-2723)
PHONE.....................216 441-7969
Charles P Stephens, *President*
EMP: 15

Cleveland - Cuyahoga County (G-4859)

SALES (est): 1.2MM **Privately Held**
SIC: 4212 2759 Moving services; commercial printing

(G-4859)
CA LITZLER CO INC
4800 W 160th St (44135-2689)
PHONE..........................216 267-8020
Matthew C Litzler, *President*
William J Urban, *COO*
Julia Mayer, *Vice Pres*
J H Rogers, *Vice Pres*
James Rogers, *Vice Pres*
◆ EMP: 42 EST: 1953
SQ FT: 32,000
SALES (est): 20.4MM
SALES (corp-wide): 36.1MM **Privately Held**
WEB: www.calitzler.com
SIC: 3567 3535 3552 3549 Industrial furnaces & ovens; conveyors & conveying equipment; textile machinery; metalworking machinery; fabricated plate work (boiler shop)
PA: C.A. Litzler Holding Company
4800 W 160th St
Cleveland OH 44135
216 267-8020

(G-4860)
CA LITZLER HOLDING COMPANY (PA)
4800 W 160th St (44135-2634)
PHONE..........................216 267-8020
Matthew C Litzler, *CEO*
Bill Urban, *COO*
William J Urban, *COO*
Juila L Mayer, *Vice Pres*
▲ EMP: 59 EST: 1999
SALES (est): 36.1MM **Privately Held**
SIC: 3567 Industrial furnaces & ovens

(G-4861)
CABINET SYSTEMS INC
9830 York Theta Dr (44133-3533)
PHONE..........................440 237-1924
John W Petrow Jr, *President*
EMP: 4
SQ FT: 10,000
SALES: 450K **Privately Held**
SIC: 2434 2521 2511 1521 Wood kitchen cabinets; cabinets, office: wood; wood household furniture; new construction, single-family houses; general remodeling, single-family houses

(G-4862)
CAILIN DEV LTD LBLTY CO
8960 70th St (44102)
PHONE..........................216 408-6261
Louis Finucane, *Mng Member*
EMP: 10
SALES (est): 2MM **Privately Held**
SIC: 3523 3532 3965 3462 Farm machinery & equipment; mining machinery; straight pins: steel or brass; iron & steel forgings

(G-4863)
CAM-LEM INC
1768 E 25th St (44114-4418)
PHONE..........................216 391-7750
Brian Mathewson, *CEO*
Terrell Pin, *COO*
EMP: 9
SQ FT: 1,100
SALES (est): 913.6K **Privately Held**
WEB: www.camlem.com
SIC: 3559 3544 3264 Robots, molding & forming plastics; special dies, tools, jigs & fixtures; porcelain electrical supplies

(G-4864)
CAMELOT TYPESETTING COMPANY
Also Called: Camelot Digital
2570 Superior Ave E # 201 (44114-4252)
PHONE..........................216 574-8973
Jack East, *Owner*
EMP: 6
SQ FT: 1,300
SALES (est): 522.5K **Privately Held**
SIC: 2791 Typesetting

(G-4865)
CANSTO COATINGS LTD
9320 Woodland Ave (44104-2410)
P.O. Box 241303 (44124-8303)
PHONE..........................216 231-6115
Sam P Cannata, *Managing Prtnr*
EMP: 10
SALES (est): 2MM **Privately Held**
SIC: 2851 Paints & allied products

(G-4866)
CANSTO PAINT AND VARNISH CO
9320 Woodland Ave (44104-2489)
PHONE..........................216 231-6115
Sam A Cannata Jr, *President*
Nancy G Glorioso, *Treasurer*
Katherine Wojtowicz, *Admin Sec*
EMP: 7 EST: 1932
SQ FT: 18,000
SALES (est): 1MM **Privately Held**
SIC: 2851 Paints & paint additives; enamels; lacquer: bases, dopes, thinner; varnishes

(G-4867)
CANVAS EXCHANGE INC
5777 Grant Ave (44105-5605)
PHONE..........................216 749-2233
William Morse, *President*
EMP: 5
SQ FT: 5,000
SALES (est): 659.9K **Privately Held**
SIC: 2394 Canvas & related products
PA: Ohio Awning & Manufacturing Co.
5777 Grant Ave
Cleveland OH 44105

(G-4868)
CANVAS SPECIALTY MFG CO
4045 Saint Clair Ave (44103-1117)
PHONE..........................216 881-0647
Carl E Heilman, *President*
EMP: 7
SQ FT: 8,500
SALES (est): 935K **Privately Held**
WEB: www.canvasspecialty.com
SIC: 2394 7699 Awnings, fabric: made from purchased materials; nautical repair services; recreational sporting equipment repair services; tent repair shop

(G-4869)
CAP DATA SUPPLY INC
15227 Triskett Rd (44111-3113)
PHONE..........................216 252-2280
James De Caprio, *President*
John Thompson, *Executive*
EMP: 5
SQ FT: 3,000
SALES: 350K **Privately Held**
SIC: 3579 Word processing equipment

(G-4870)
CAPITAL ENGRAVING COMPANY
11963 Abbey Rd (44133-2635)
PHONE..........................440 237-7760
Norman Andrysco, *Owner*
EMP: 4 EST: 1966
SALES: 200K **Privately Held**
SIC: 2796 Engraving on copper, steel, wood or rubber: printing plates

(G-4871)
CAPITAL TOOL COMPANY
1110 Brookpark Rd (44109-5871)
PHONE..........................216 661-5750
Richard Crane, *President*
EMP: 45 EST: 1962
SQ FT: 20,000
SALES (est): 7.4MM **Privately Held**
WEB: www.capitaltoolco.com
SIC: 3544 3545 3443 Special dies & tools; jigs & fixtures; machine tool accessories; fabricated plate work (boiler shop)

(G-4872)
CAPS
8300 Sweet Valley Dr # 301 (44125-4264)
PHONE..........................216 524-0418
Amy Piorkowski, *Manager*
EMP: 8 EST: 2010
SALES (est): 1.2MM **Privately Held**
SIC: 2834 Pharmaceutical preparations

(G-4873)
CARAUSTAR INDUSTRIES INC
Also Called: Cleveland Recycling Plant
3400 Vega Ave (44113-4954)
PHONE..........................216 961-5060
Richard Ryan, *Opers-Prdtn-Mfg*
EMP: 10
SALES (corp-wide): 3.8B **Publicly Held**
WEB: www.caraustar.com
SIC: 2679 2611 Paperboard products, converted; pulp mills
HQ: Caraustar Industries, Inc.
5000 Austell Powder Sprin
Austell GA 30106
770 948-3101

(G-4874)
CARAUSTAR INDUSTRIES INC
Also Called: Cleveland Digital Imaging Svcs
7960 Lorain Ave (44102-4256)
PHONE..........................216 939-3001
Petrelli Tony, *Vice Pres*
EMP: 15
SALES (corp-wide): 3.8B **Publicly Held**
WEB: www.caraustar.com
SIC: 2631 Paperboard mills
HQ: Caraustar Industries, Inc.
5000 Austell Powder Sprin
Austell GA 30106
770 948-3101

(G-4875)
CARAVAN PACKAGING INC (PA)
6427 Eastland Rd (44142-1305)
PHONE..........................440 243-4100
Fred Hitti, *President*
Chris Pisanelli, *Vice Pres*
Sue Hitti, *Treasurer*
Susan Hitti, *Treasurer*
Wesley Holcombs, *Mktg Dir*
EMP: 10 EST: 1962
SQ FT: 40,000
SALES (est): 2.1MM **Privately Held**
WEB: www.caravanpackaging.com
SIC: 4783 2441 6512 Packing goods for shipping; nailed wood boxes & shook; boxes, wood; commercial & industrial building operation

(G-4876)
CARDINAL CUSTOM CABINETS LTD
8201 Almira Ave Ste 10 (44102-5400)
PHONE..........................216 281-1570
Anthony Cardinal, *Partner*
James V Cardinal, *Partner*
EMP: 5
SQ FT: 9,000
SALES (est): 497.7K **Privately Held**
SIC: 2434 Wood kitchen cabinets

(G-4877)
CARGILL INCORPORATED
2400 Ships Channel (44113-2673)
P.O. Box 6920 (44101-1920)
PHONE..........................216 651-7200
Bob Soupko, *Branch Mgr*
EMP: 205
SALES (corp-wide): 114.7B **Privately Held**
WEB: www.cargill.com
SIC: 1479 2899 Salt (common) mining; chemical preparations
PA: Cargill, Incorporated
15407 Mcginty Rd W
Wayzata MN 55391
952 742-7575

(G-4878)
CARLTON NATCO
13020 Saint Clair Ave (44108-2033)
PHONE..........................216 451-5588
Eugene Sizelove, *General Ptnr*
Paul Gierosky, *General Ptnr*
EMP: 3
SQ FT: 3,500
SALES (est): 632.2K **Privately Held**
SIC: 3541 5084 7629 3545 Machine tools, metal cutting type; industrial machinery & equipment; electrical repair shops; machine tool accessories

(G-4879)
CARMENS INSTALLATION CO
2865 Mayfield Rd (44118-1633)
PHONE..........................216 321-4040
Carmen T Montello, *President*
Rose Marie Montello, *Corp Secy*
Salvatore Montello, *Vice Pres*
EMP: 15
SQ FT: 4,500
SALES (est): 1.7MM **Privately Held**
SIC: 1799 2211 Drapery track installation; draperies & drapery fabrics, cotton

(G-4880)
CARNEGIE PLAS CABINETRY INC
1755 Coit Ave (44112-2018)
PHONE..........................216 451-3300
Craig Warner, *President*
EMP: 8
SQ FT: 4,500
SALES: 1MM **Privately Held**
SIC: 2434 Wood kitchen cabinets

(G-4881)
CARNEGIE PROMOTIONS INC
697 Davidson Dr (44143-2052)
PHONE..........................440 442-2099
Carol Calta, *Owner*
EMP: 3
SALES (est): 238.7K **Privately Held**
SIC: 2759 Screen printing

(G-4882)
CARR BROS BLDRS SUP & COAL CO
7177 Northfield Rd (44146-5403)
PHONE..........................440 232-3700
Floyd E Carr Jr, *President*
Duane Carr, *Vice Pres*
Michael Carr, *Treasurer*
Amy Rickleman, *Admin Sec*
EMP: 35 EST: 1892
SQ FT: 3,000
SALES (est): 4.2MM **Privately Held**
WEB: www.carrbrothers.com
SIC: 3273 Ready-mixed concrete

(G-4883)
CARRERA HOLDINGS INC
101 W Prospect Ave (44115-1093)
PHONE..........................216 687-1311
James B Mooney, *Principal*
EMP: 4
SALES (est): 237.9K
SALES (corp-wide): 40.1MM **Privately Held**
SIC: 2329 2339 Knickers, dress (separate): men's & boys'; aprons, except rubber or plastic: women's, misses', juniors'
PA: Carrera Spa
Via Sant'irene 1
Caldiero VR 37042
045 613-9111

(G-4884)
CARROLL EXHIBIT AND PRINT SVCS
Also Called: Carroll Graphic
5150 Prospect Ave (44103-4324)
PHONE..........................216 361-2325
John A Carroll, *President*
EMP: 4
SQ FT: 4,000
SALES (est): 501.4K **Privately Held**
SIC: 2759 7389 Screen printing; sign painting & lettering shop

(G-4885)
CASE OHIO BURIAL CO (PA)
1720 Columbus Rd (44113-2410)
P.O. Box 26020 (44126-0020)
PHONE..........................440 779-1992
Grace Caffo, *President*
Ronald Caffo, *Treasurer*
Wanda Armburger, *Admin Sec*
EMP: 13
SQ FT: 70,000
SALES (est): 1.1MM **Privately Held**
SIC: 3995 5087 Burial caskets; caskets

(G-4886)
CASPA HOME PAGE INC
1501 N Marginal Rd # 166 (44114-3760)
PHONE..........................216 781-0748
Charles K Newcomb, *President*
EMP: 5 EST: 1998

SALES: 500K Privately Held
SIC: 3324 Aerospace investment castings, ferrous

(G-4887)
CASSELBERRY CLINIC INC
Also Called: Progressive Pain Relief
5555 Mayfield Rd (44124-2939)
PHONE..................................440 995-0555
Ronald Casselberry MD, *President*
Carol Cruise, *Exec Dir*
EMP: 5
SQ FT: 2,000
SALES (est): 636.3K Privately Held
SIC: 2834 Medicines, capsuled or ampuled

(G-4888)
CAST SPECIALTIES INC
26711 Miles Rd (44128-5927)
PHONE..................................216 292-7393
Martin Dragich, *President*
Benjamin G Ammons, *Chairman*
Michael Paskevich, *Vice Pres*
John Krisfalusy, *Controller*
Elaine Zelch, *Admin Sec*
EMP: 38 EST: 1960
SQ FT: 40,000
SALES (est): 10.1MM Privately Held
WEB: www.castspecialties.com
SIC: 3364 3363 Zinc & zinc-base alloy die-castings; aluminum die-castings

(G-4889)
CASTALLOY INC
7990 Baker Ave (44102-1903)
PHONE..................................216 961-7990
Michael Wood, *President*
Richard J Chalei, *Principal*
Thomas Waldin, *Treasurer*
Rudy Koishor, *Sales Mgr*
▲ EMP: 55
SQ FT: 40,000
SALES (est): 12.5MM Privately Held
WEB: www.castalloy.com
SIC: 3324 Steel investment foundries

(G-4890)
CASTELLI MARBLE INC (PA)
1521 E 47th St (44103-2437)
PHONE..................................216 361-2410
Carmelo Cario, *President*
Gina Vicio, *Admin Sec*
▲ EMP: 9
SQ FT: 10,000
SALES (est): 1.6MM Privately Held
SIC: 5032 3281 Marble building stone; granite building stone; cut stone & stone products

(G-4891)
CATHOLIC CHARITY HISPANIC OFF
2012 W 25th St Ste 507 (44113-4131)
PHONE..................................216 696-2197
Maureen Dee, *Owner*
EMP: 15 EST: 2001
SALES (est): 1.1MM Privately Held
SIC: 2869 Alcohols, non-beverage

(G-4892)
CATS PRINTING INC
3980 Mayfield Rd (44121-2223)
PHONE..................................216 381-8181
Gary Katz, *President*
Jonathon Kittredge, *Vice Pres*
Susanne Katz, *Treasurer*
EMP: 4
SQ FT: 1,000
SALES (est): 165K Privately Held
SIC: 2752 Commercial printing, offset

(G-4893)
CBL PRODUCTS
1661 Cumberland Rd (44118-1718)
PHONE..................................216 321-2599
Charlene Lynch, *Owner*
EMP: 3
SALES (est): 193.6K Privately Held
SIC: 2676 Tampons, sanitary: made from purchased paper

(G-4894)
CCL LABEL INC
15939 Industrial Pkwy (44135-3321)
PHONE..................................216 676-2703
Chief Anderson, *Manager*
EMP: 150
SALES (corp-wide): 3.7B Privately Held
WEB: www.avery.com
SIC: 2672 3081 3497 2678 Adhesive papers, labels & tapes: from purchased material; gummed paper: made from purchased materials; coated paper, except photographic, carbon or abrasive; unsupported plastics film & sheet; metal foil & leaf; stationery products; notebooks: made from purchased paper; labels, paper: made from purchased material; tags, paper (unprinted): made from purchased paper; paperboard products, converted
HQ: Ccl Label, Inc.
     161 Worcester Rd Ste 504
     Framingham MA 01701
     508 872-4511

(G-4895)
CDI INDUSTRIES INC
Also Called: Coaxial Dynamics
6800 Lake Abrams Dr (44130-3455)
PHONE..................................440 243-1100
Joseph D Kluha, *President*
EMP: 24
SQ FT: 16,000
SALES (est): 4MM Privately Held
WEB: www.coaxial.com
SIC: 3663 3825 3613 Receivers, radio communications; instruments to measure electricity; switchgear & switchboard apparatus

(G-4896)
CEJA PUBLISHING
3654 Atherstone Rd (44121-1358)
PHONE..................................216 319-0268
Celena Howard, *Principal*
EMP: 4
SALES (est): 145.3K Privately Held
SIC: 2741 Miscellaneous publishing

(G-4897)
CELCORE INC (PA)
7850 Freeway Cir Ste 100 (44130-6317)
PHONE..................................440 234-7888
William McDonald, *President*
Mark Bates, *President*
Vicky Anderson, *Treasurer*
EMP: 10
SQ FT: 8,500
SALES (est): 1MM Privately Held
WEB: www.celcoreinc.com
SIC: 2493 1761 Insulation & roofing material, reconstituted wood; roofing contractor

(G-4898)
CEMEX CONSTRUCTION MTLS INC
6525 Highland Rd (44143-2324)
PHONE..................................440 449-0872
Bruno Gianmichele, *President*
EMP: 5 Privately Held
SIC: 3273 Ready-mixed concrete
HQ: Cemex Construction Materials, Inc.
     3990 Concours Ste 200
     Ontario CA 91764
     909 974-5500

(G-4899)
CEN-TROL MACHINE CO
7601 Commerce Park Oval (44131-2303)
PHONE..................................216 524-1932
Henry J Kuska, *Principal*
Allen Straka, *Corp Secy*
Theresa Kuska, *Vice Pres*
EMP: 6 EST: 1964
SQ FT: 11,000
SALES: 435.3K Privately Held
SIC: 3599 Machine shop, jobbing & repair

(G-4900)
CENTERLESS GRINDING SERVICE
Also Called: C G S
19500 S Miles Rd (44128-4251)
PHONE..................................216 251-4100
Jim Daso, *President*
Terry Daso, *Treasurer*
EMP: 8
SQ FT: 3,632
SALES: 800K Privately Held
SIC: 3999 3599 Custom pulverizing & grinding of plastic materials; machine shop, jobbing & repair

(G-4901)
CENTRAL SYSTEMS & CONTROL
26933 Westwood Rd Ste 400 (44145-4690)
PHONE..................................440 835-0015
Thomas Ruffing, *President*
EMP: 3
SALES (est): 440.2K Privately Held
SIC: 3672 3625 Printed circuit boards; control equipment, electric

(G-4902)
CENTURY PLATING INC
18006 S Waterloo Rd (44119-3223)
PHONE..................................216 531-4131
Peter Mooney, *President*
EMP: 9 EST: 1950
SQ FT: 20,000
SALES (est): 1.4MM Privately Held
WEB: www.centuryplating.com
SIC: 3471 Polishing, metals or formed products; plating of metals or formed products

(G-4903)
CENTURY TOOL & STAMPING INC
1510 University Rd (44113-3585)
PHONE..................................216 241-2032
Todd Guist, *President*
William Guist Jr, *President*
William Guist Ll, *Treasurer*
James Vespoli, *Treasurer*
Cathy Hoy, *Admin Sec*
EMP: 13
SQ FT: 7,800
SALES: 1MM Privately Held
SIC: 3599 Machine shop, jobbing & repair

(G-4904)
CERTIFIED WELDING CO
9603 Clinton Rd (44144-1083)
PHONE..................................216 961-5410
John Salisbury, *President*
Doris Ann Salisbury, *Vice Pres*
EMP: 15
SALES (est): 1MM Privately Held
WEB: www.cwcionline.com
SIC: 7692 3599 Welding repair; machine shop, jobbing & repair

(G-4905)
CETEK LTD
6779 Engle Rd Ste A (44130-7926)
PHONE..................................216 362-3900
Derek Scott, *CEO*
EMP: 30
SALES (est): 2.1MM Privately Held
SIC: 2851 8711 Lacquers, varnishes, enamels & other coatings; heating & ventilation engineering
PA: Integrated Global Services, Inc.
     7600 Whitepine Rd
     North Chesterfield VA 23237

(G-4906)
CFRC WTR & ENRGY SOLUTIONS INC
850 Euclid Ave Ste 1314 (44114-3308)
P.O. Box 670482, Northfield (44067-0482)
PHONE..................................216 479-0290
Chuck Williams, *Chairman*
EMP: 5 EST: 2014
SQ FT: 400
SALES (est): 297.8K Privately Held
SIC: 3432 3491 3492 3088 Plumbing fixture fittings & trim; boiler gauge cocks; control valves, fluid power: hydraulic & pneumatic; shower stalls, fiberglass & plastic; liquid level controls, residential or commercial heating

(G-4907)
CHALFANT SEW FABRICATORS INC
Also Called: Chalfant Loading Dock Eqp
11525 Madison Ave (44102-2392)
PHONE..................................216 521-7922
Jeff Chalfant, *President*
Stephanie Chalfant, *Vice Pres*
▼ EMP: 41 EST: 1940
SQ FT: 50,000
SALES (est): 8.7MM Privately Held
WEB: www.chalfantusa.com
SIC: 3069 2394 Sponge rubber & sponge rubber products; canvas & related products

(G-4908)
CHALK OUTLINE PICTURES
4773 Hillary Ln (44143-2910)
PHONE..................................216 291-3944
Lena Chalk, *Principal*
EMP: 3
SALES (est): 132.8K Privately Held
SIC: 1422 Chalk mining, crushed & broken-quarrying

(G-4909)
CHARIZMA CORP
Also Called: National Screen Production
1400 E 30th St Ste 201 (44114-4050)
P.O. Box 33520, North Royalton (44133-0520)
PHONE..................................216 621-2220
Marcy Szabados, *President*
EMP: 7 EST: 1980
SQ FT: 5,000
SALES (est): 753.2K Privately Held
SIC: 2396 5199 Screen printing on fabric articles; advertising specialties

(G-4910)
CHARLES C LEWIS COMPANY
1 W Interstate St Ste 200 (44146-4256)
PHONE..................................440 439-3150
Steve McCoy, *Manager*
EMP: 16
SALES (corp-wide): 10.6MM Privately Held
WEB: www.charleslewis.com
SIC: 3312 Plate, steel
PA: The Charles C Lewis Company
     209 Page Blvd
     Springfield MA 01104
     413 733-2121

(G-4911)
CHARLES MESSINA
Also Called: Joseph Industries
16645 Granite Rd (44137-4301)
PHONE..................................216 663-3344
Charles Messina, *Owner*
EMP: 80
SQ FT: 170,000
SALES (est): 6.5MM Privately Held
SIC: 2653 Corrugated & solid fiber boxes

(G-4912)
CHARLOTTE M PETERS
3452 W 126th St (44111-3562)
PHONE..................................216 798-8997
Charlotte M Peters, *Principal*
EMP: 3
SALES (est): 220K Privately Held
SIC: 2721 Periodicals

(G-4913)
CHART ASIA INC
1 Infinity Corp Ctr Dr (44125-5369)
PHONE..................................440 753-1490
Samuel F Thomas, *President*
EMP: 94
SALES (est): 9.7MM Publicly Held
WEB: www.chart-ind.com
SIC: 3443 Heat exchangers, plate type
HQ: Chart Inc.
     407 7th St Nw
     New Prague MN 56071
     952 758-4484

(G-4914)
CHART INDUSTRIES INC
5885 Landerbrook Dr # 150 (44124-4045)
PHONE..................................440 753-1490
Samuel F Thomas, *President*
Sean Kharche, *Managing Dir*
Arthur S Holmes, *Principal*
Ed Kern, *Business Mgr*
Buzz Bies, *Vice Pres*
EMP: 377
SALES (est): 34.4MM Publicly Held
WEB: www.chart-ind.com
SIC: 3443 Heat exchangers, plate type

Cleveland - Cuyahoga County (G-4915) GEOGRAPHIC SECTION

HQ: Chart Inc.
407 7th St Nw
New Prague MN 56071
952 758-4484

(G-4915)
CHART INTERNATIONAL INC (HQ)
1 Infinity Corp Ctr Dr (44125-5369)
PHONE....................440 753-1490
Samuel F Thomas, *President*
Laddie Bohlmann, *Mfg Staff*
Charlie Svoboda, *Engineer*
Erich Wetzel, *Sales Engr*
Mark Gill, *Manager*
EMP: 50
SALES (est): 33.9MM **Publicly Held**
SIC: **3443** 3317 3559 3569 Heat exchangers, plate type; tanks for tank trucks, metal plate; vessels, process or storage (from another shops): metal plate; steel pipe & tubes; cryogenic machinery, industrial; separators for steam, gas, vapor or air (machinery)

(G-4916)
CHARTER MANUFACTURING CO INC
Charter Steel Division
4300 E 49th St (44125-1048)
PHONE....................216 883-3800
Kevin Burg, *Branch Mgr*
Parminder Shergill, *Administration*
EMP: 992
SALES (corp-wide): 754.3MM **Privately Held**
WEB: www.chartermfg.com
SIC: **3312** Rods, iron & steel: made in steel mills; wire products, steel or iron
PA: Charter Manufacturing Company, Inc.
1212 W Glen Oaks Ln
Mequon WI 53092
262 243-4700

(G-4917)
CHECKPOINT SURGICAL INC
22901 Millcreek Blvd # 110 (44122-5728)
PHONE....................216 378-9107
Leonard Cosentino, *President*
Terri Zmina, *Opers Staff*
Steven Galecki, *Engineer*
Laura Keck, *Finance*
Steve Gillespie, *Regl Sales Mgr*
EMP: 6
SALES (est): 803.9K **Privately Held**
SIC: **3845** Electromedical equipment

(G-4918)
CHEF 2 CHEF FOODS
1893 E 55th St (44103-3640)
PHONE....................216 696-0080
EMP: 5
SALES (est): 147.9K **Privately Held**
SIC: **2038** Frozen specialties

(G-4919)
CHEMICAL SOLVENTS INC (PA)
3751 Jennings Rd (44109-2889)
PHONE....................216 741-9310
Edward Pavlish, *Ch of Bd*
Thos A Mason, *Principal*
E H Pavlish, *Principal*
Patricia Pavlish, *Corp Secy*
Blaine Davidson, *Vice Pres*
▲ EMP: 45 EST: 1970
SQ FT: 30,000
SALES (est): 112.5MM **Privately Held**
WEB: www.chemicalsolvents.com
SIC: **5169** 7349 3471 2992 Detergents & soaps, except specialty cleaning; specialty cleaning & sanitation preparations; chemical cleaning services; cleaning & descaling metal products; oils & greases, blending & compounding

(G-4920)
CHI CORPORATION (PA)
5265 Naiman Pkwy Ste H (44139-1013)
PHONE....................440 498-2300
John Thome Jr, *President*
John R Thome Sr, *Chairman*
Lisa Dempsey, *Office Mgr*
EMP: 10

SALES (est): 3.7MM **Privately Held**
WEB: www.chicorporation.com
SIC: **7373** 3572 Systems software development services; computer tape drives & components

(G-4921)
CHIEFS MANUFACTURING & EQP CO
4325 Monticello Blvd (44121-2816)
PHONE....................216 291-3200
William Consolo, *President*
Keith Metzung, *Vice Pres*
EMP: 5
SALES (est): 390K **Privately Held**
SIC: **3589** Car washing machinery

(G-4922)
CHILCOTE COMPANY
Also Called: Tap Packaging Solutions
2160 Superior Ave E (44114-2184)
PHONE....................216 781-6000
Jay Anthony Hyland, *CEO*
David B Chilcote, *Chairman*
Matthew Moir, *Vice Pres*
Daniel Malloy, *Controller*
Nada Alempijevic, *Internal Med*
◆ EMP: 140
SQ FT: 190,000
SALES (est): 22MM **Privately Held**
WEB: www.tap-usa.com
SIC: **2652** 2657 2675 Setup paperboard boxes; folding paperboard boxes; die-cut paper & board

(G-4923)
CHOCOLATE PIG INC (PA)
Also Called: Fantasy Candies
5338 Mayfield Rd (44124-2479)
PHONE....................440 461-4511
Joel Fink, *President*
EMP: 30
SQ FT: 3,500
SALES (est): 3.7MM **Privately Held**
WEB: www.fantasycandies.com
SIC: **2064** 5441 2066 Candy & other confectionery products; candy, nut & confectionery stores; chocolate & cocoa products

(G-4924)
CHRISTOPHER TOOL & MFG CO
30500 Carter St Frnt (44139-3580)
PHONE....................440 248-8080
Patrick D Christopher, *President*
Craig Peck, *Vice Pres*
Larry Walker, *Vice Pres*
Kathy Kuzniakowski, *Opers Mgr*
Gene Ainsworth, *Engineer*
EMP: 104 EST: 1951
SQ FT: 48,500
SALES (est): 23.5MM **Privately Held**
WEB: www.christophertool.com
SIC: **3599** Machine shop, jobbing & repair

(G-4925)
CHROMACOVE LLC
9000 Bank St (44125-3437)
PHONE....................216 264-1104
EMP: 3
SALES (est): 279.4K **Privately Held**
SIC: **3648** Lighting equipment

(G-4926)
CHROMATIC INC
839 E 63rd St (44103-1018)
PHONE....................216 881-2228
Dennis L Paul, *President*
Dennis Paul, *President*
EMP: 10
SQ FT: 12,000
SALES (est): 900K **Privately Held**
WEB: www.chromatic.net
SIC: **3471** Chromium plating of metals or formed products; decorative plating & finishing of formed products

(G-4927)
CHROME INDUSTRIES INC
3041 Perkins Ave (44114-4626)
PHONE....................216 771-2266
Wolfgang Hein, *President*
Roland Hein, *Vice Pres*
EMP: 4
SQ FT: 12,000

SALES (est): 600K **Privately Held**
SIC: **3471** Chromium plating of metals or formed products

(G-4928)
CIMINO BOX INC
Also Called: Cimino Box & Pallet Company
8500 Clinton Rd Ste 6 (44144-1001)
PHONE....................216 961-7377
Frank Ritson, *President*
EMP: 4
SQ FT: 5,000
SALES (est): 731.8K **Privately Held**
SIC: **2448** Pallets, wood

(G-4929)
CITY GIRL MAGAZINE LLC
801 E 212th St (44119-2415)
PHONE....................216 481-4110
Anthony Swift, *Principal*
EMP: 3
SALES (est): 112.9K **Privately Held**
SIC: **2721** Periodicals

(G-4930)
CITY OF CLEVELAND
Also Called: Printing & Reproduction Div
1735 Lakeside Ave E (44114-1118)
PHONE....................216 664-3013
Michael Hewett, *Commissioner*
EMP: 15 **Privately Held**
SIC: **2752** 9199 Commercial printing, lithographic; general government administration;
PA: City Of Cleveland
601 Lakeside Ave E Rm 210
Cleveland OH 44114
216 664-2000

(G-4931)
CITY OF CLEVELAND
Also Called: Parking Facilities
500 Lakeside Ave E (44114-1019)
PHONE....................216 664-2711
Paul Bender, *Director*
EMP: 1
SALES (est): 43.1MM **Privately Held**
SIC: **3559** Parking facility equipment & supplies
PA: City Of Cleveland
601 Lakeside Ave E Rm 210
Cleveland OH 44114
216 664-2000

(G-4932)
CITY OF PARMA
Vital Statistics
6611 Ridge Rd Fl 2 (44129-5530)
PHONE....................440 885-8816
Dennis Kish, *Manager*
EMP: 7 **Privately Held**
WEB: www.parmajustice.net
SIC: **2721** Statistical reports (periodicals): publishing & printing
PA: Parma City Of (Inc)
6611 Ridge Rd
Cleveland OH 44129
440 885-8000

(G-4933)
CITY PLATING AND POLISHING LLC
4821 W 130th St (44135-5137)
PHONE....................216 267-8158
Randy Solganik, *Mng Member*
EMP: 7
SQ FT: 20,000
SALES (est): 890.8K **Privately Held**
WEB: www.cityplate.com
SIC: **3471** Electroplating of metals or formed products

(G-4934)
CITY VISITOR INC
Also Called: City Visitor Publications
5755 Granger Rd Ste 600 (44131-1458)
PHONE....................216 661-6666
Rocco Dilillo, *President*
Mark Timm, *Vice Pres*
Yvonne Pelino, *Sales Staff*
Sheila Lopez, *Marketing Staff*
EMP: 9
SQ FT: 1,500

SALES (est): 1MM **Privately Held**
WEB: www.cityvisitor.com
SIC: **2721** Magazines: publishing only, not printed on site

(G-4935)
CKM VENTURES LLC (PA)
Also Called: George R Klein News
2635 Payne Ave (44114-4432)
PHONE....................216 623-0370
Shawn Spindel, *Mng Member*
EMP: 7
SALES (est): 755.9K **Privately Held**
SIC: **2759** 5199 Newspapers: printing; directories (except telephone): printing; maps & charts

(G-4936)
CLARE SKY INC (HQ)
Also Called: Kichler Lighting
7711 E Pleasant Valley Rd (44131-5532)
P.O. Box 318010 (44131-8010)
PHONE....................866 558-5706
Tony Davidson, *CEO*
John Sznewajs,
◆ EMP: 500 EST: 1938
SQ FT: 630,000
SALES (est): 122.6MM
SALES (corp-wide): 8.3B **Publicly Held**
WEB: www.kichler.com
SIC: **3645** 3648 3641 Residential lighting fixtures; lighting equipment; electric lamps
PA: Masco Corporation
17450 College Pkwy
Livonia MI 48152
313 274-7400

(G-4937)
CLARK AUTO MACHINE SHOP
4607 Clark Ave (44102-4511)
PHONE....................216 939-0768
Douglas Strimpel, *Principal*
EMP: 4
SALES (est): 387.2K **Privately Held**
SIC: **3589** Service industry machinery

(G-4938)
CLARKE-BOXIT CORPORATION
5601 Walworth Ave (44102-4432)
PHONE....................716 487-1950
Donald Zaas, *Ch of Bd*
Joel Zaas, *President*
Mark Cassese, *COO*
John Asimakopoulos, *CFO*
EMP: 7
SALES (est): 245.9K
SALES (corp-wide): 59.4MM **Privately Held**
WEB: www.boxit.com
SIC: **2652** Setup paperboard boxes
PA: The Apex Paper Box Company
5555 Walworth Ave
Cleveland OH 44102
216 631-4000

(G-4939)
CLASSIC LAMINATIONS INC
7703 First Pl Ste B (44146-6730)
PHONE....................440 735-1333
James Tidd, *President*
Donna Tidd, *Admin Sec*
EMP: 25
SQ FT: 3,800
SALES (est): 2.5MM **Privately Held**
WEB: www.classiclaminations.com
SIC: **3089** 2789 Laminating of plastic; bookbinding & related work

(G-4940)
CLASSIC TOY COMPANY INC
12825 Taft Ave (44108-1635)
PHONE....................216 851-2000
Larry Feuer, *President*
Michael Abrams, *Vice Pres*
Ira Feuer, *Vice Pres*
▲ EMP: 3
SQ FT: 40,000
SALES (est): 230K **Privately Held**
WEB: www.classictoycompany.com
SIC: **3942** Stuffed toys, including animals

(G-4941)
CLEANLIFE ENERGY LLC
Also Called: Unibat
2400 Superior Ave E # 205 (44114-4258)
PHONE....................800 316-2532

GEOGRAPHIC SECTION

Justin Miller, *CEO*
Jonathan Koslo, *Vice Pres*
▲ EMP: 18
SQ FT: 10,000
SALES (est): 2.5MM **Privately Held**
SIC: 3679 3356 Liquid crystal displays (LCD); battery metal

(G-4942)
CLEAR FOLD DOOR INC
Also Called: C F Doors
7703 First Pl Ste A (44146-6730)
PHONE.....................440 735-1351
Donald E De Roia, *President*
Dan De Roia, *General Mgr*
Rosetta A De Roia, *Corp Secy*
EMP: 5
SQ FT: 2,700
SALES: 1MM **Privately Held**
WEB: www.cfdoors.com
SIC: 3089 5084 5211 Doors, folding: plastic or plastic coated fabric; machine tools & accessories; door & window products

(G-4943)
CLEARWATER ONE LLC
21400 Lorain Rd (44126-2125)
P.O. Box 1369, Minot ND (58702-1369)
PHONE.....................216 554-4747
David Niederst, *Mng Member*
EMP: 12
SALES: 5MM **Privately Held**
SIC: 2834 Chlorination tablets & kits (water purification)

(G-4944)
CLECORR INC
Also Called: Clecorr Packaging
10610 Berea Rd Rear (44102-2595)
PHONE.....................216 961-5500
Kevin L Smith, *President*
Christopher Dye, *Vice Pres*
EMP: 29
SQ FT: 67,000
SALES (est): 6MM **Privately Held**
SIC: 2653 Boxes, corrugated: made from purchased materials

(G-4945)
CLEVELAND AEC WEST LLC
14000 Keystone Pkwy (44135-5170)
PHONE.....................216 362-6000
Deepmala Agarwal, *Principal*
EMP: 3 EST: 2015
SALES (est): 90K **Privately Held**
SIC: 2835 Veterinary diagnostic substances

(G-4946)
CLEVELAND BAGEL COMPANY LLC
Also Called: Cleveland Bagel Company, The
4309 Larrain Ave (44113)
PHONE.....................216 385-7723
Geoffry Hardman, *Principal*
Dan Herbst, *Principal*
EMP: 3 EST: 2013
SALES (est): 125.1K **Privately Held**
SIC: 2053 Cakes, bakery: frozen

(G-4947)
CLEVELAND BEAN SPROUT INC
2675 E 40th St (44115-3508)
PHONE.....................216 881-2112
Casey Chiu, *President*
Judy Chiu, *Vice Pres*
EMP: 12
SQ FT: 12,000
SALES (est): 770K **Privately Held**
SIC: 0139 0161 2052 Alfalfa farm; pea & bean farms; cookies

(G-4948)
CLEVELAND CANVAS GOODS MFG CO
1960 E 57th St (44103-3804)
PHONE.....................216 361-4567
William J Morton III, *President*
Michael L Morton Jr, *Corp Secy*
Jack Morton, *Manager*
Mike Morton, *Manager*
EMP: 70 EST: 1922
SQ FT: 29,500
SALES (est): 10.4MM **Privately Held**
WEB: www.clevelandcanvas.com
SIC: 3161 2394 2393 2326 Luggage; canvas & related products; textile bags; men's & boys' work clothing; tire cord & fabrics; vacuum cleaner bags: made from purchased materials

(G-4949)
CLEVELAND CASTER LLC
19885 Detroit Rd 243 (44116-1815)
PHONE.....................440 333-1443
Ellen M Wittenbrook,
EMP: 4
SALES (est): 286.4K **Privately Held**
SIC: 3562 Casters

(G-4950)
CLEVELAND CIRCUITS CORP
Also Called: Instrumatics
15516 Industrial Pkwy (44135-3314)
PHONE.....................216 267-9020
Sumir Amin, *President*
Jay Amin, *Vice Pres*
Nirja Kapadia, *Admin Sec*
EMP: 25
SQ FT: 18,500
SALES: 1.9MM **Privately Held**
WEB: www.clevelandcircuits.com
SIC: 3679 Electronic circuits

(G-4951)
CLEVELAND CITIZEN PUBG CO
2012 W 25th St Ste 900 (44113-4124)
PHONE.....................216 861-4283
Loree K Soggs, *President*
John Banno, *Vice Pres*
EMP: 8
SQ FT: 2,214
SALES: 200K **Privately Held**
WEB: www.cbctc.org
SIC: 2711 Newspapers: publishing only, not printed on site
PA: Cleveland Building & Construction Trades Council
3250 Euclid Ave Ste 280
Cleveland OH 44115

(G-4952)
CLEVELAND CONTROLS INC
1111 Brookpark Rd (44109-5825)
PHONE.....................216 398-0330
Steve Craig, *President*
EMP: 60 EST: 1942
SQ FT: 10,000
SALES (est): 6.5MM **Privately Held**
WEB: www.clevelandcontrols.com
SIC: 3823 Combustion control instruments; differential pressure instruments, industrial process type

(G-4953)
CLEVELAND COPY & PRTG SVC LLC (PA)
1835 E 30th St Fl 3 (44114-4438)
PHONE.....................216 861-0324
James Koelpin,
EMP: 5 EST: 1961
SALES (est): 508.8K **Privately Held**
SIC: 2759 Commercial printing

(G-4954)
CLEVELAND CSTM PLLET CRATE INC
4201 Lakeside Ave E (44114-3814)
PHONE.....................216 881-1414
Gary Petric, *President*
Michael Broeckel, *Corp Secy*
Robert Mc Millan, *Vice Pres*
EMP: 38
SQ FT: 50,000
SALES (est): 6.1MM **Privately Held**
WEB: www.gmpallet.com
SIC: 2448 Pallets, wood & wood with metal; skids, wood & wood with metal

(G-4955)
CLEVELAND CUSTOM CABINETS LLC
19561 Miles Rd (44128-4111)
PHONE.....................213 663-0606
EMP: 5 EST: 2014
SALES (est): 172.2K **Privately Held**
SIC: 2434 Wood kitchen cabinets

(G-4956)
CLEVELAND DEBURRING MACHINE CO
Also Called: Cdmc
3370 W 140th St (44111-2433)
PHONE.....................216 472-0200
Adam Mutschler,
Chris Mutschler,
EMP: 4
SALES (est): 793.7K **Privately Held**
SIC: 3541 Deburring machines

(G-4957)
CLEVELAND DRAPERY STITCH INC
12890 Berea Rd (44111-1624)
PHONE.....................216 252-3857
George Beckmann, *President*
Wayne Monar, *Vice Pres*
EMP: 14
SQ FT: 7,200
SALES (est): 1.3MM **Privately Held**
SIC: 2211 2221 Draperies & drapery fabrics, cotton; draperies & drapery fabrics, manmade fiber & silk

(G-4958)
CLEVELAND EAST ED WNS JURNL
1663 Saint Charles Ave (44107-4312)
PHONE.....................216 228-1379
EMP: 3
SALES (est): 122.7K **Privately Held**
SIC: 2711 Newspapers

(G-4959)
CLEVELAND FP INC (PA)
12819 Coit Rd (44108-1614)
PHONE.....................216 249-4900
Michael Ivany, *President*
Bob Dragolic, *Plant Mgr*
Michael Ford, *Warehouse Mgr*
Earl Youngblood, *Production*
Rachel Tuck, *Purch Agent*
◆ EMP: 90
SQ FT: 103,000
SALES (est): 25.2MM **Privately Held**
SIC: 2865 Cyclic crudes & intermediates

(G-4960)
CLEVELAND GEAR COMPANY INC (DH)
3249 E 80th St (44104-4396)
P.O. Box 70100t (44190-0001)
PHONE.....................216 641-9000
Dana Lynch, *President*
John M Atkinson, *Vice Pres*
Russell Warner, *Vice Pres*
Robert Wightman, *Vice Pres*
Clark Wormer, *Vice Pres*
▲ EMP: 115
SALES (est): 23.2MM
SALES (corp-wide): 506.2MM **Privately Held**
WEB: www.clevelandgear.com
SIC: 3566 3569 Speed changers, drives & gears; gears, power transmission, except automotive; lubricating equipment
HQ: Industrial Manufacturing Company Llc
8223 Brecksville Rd Ste 1
Brecksville OH 44141
440 838-4700

(G-4961)
CLEVELAND GRANITE & MARBLE LLC
4121 Carnegie Ave (44103-4336)
PHONE.....................216 291-7637
Kimberly K Lisboa, *Mng Member*
Uwe Eibich,
Frank Gotthardt,
Christian B Teig,
▲ EMP: 33
SQ FT: 50,000
SALES (est): 3.9MM **Privately Held**
WEB: www.clevelandgranite.com
SIC: 3281 3291 Dimension stone for buildings; abrasive metal & steel products

(G-4962)
CLEVELAND HDWR & FORGING CO (PA)
Also Called: Fox Valley Forge
3270 E 79th St (44104-4306)
PHONE.....................216 641-5200
William E Hoban, *Ch of Bd*
James Socha, *CFO*
▲ EMP: 50
SQ FT: 175,000
SALES (est): 28.4MM **Privately Held**
WEB: www.clevelandhardware.com
SIC: 3463 3799 3462 3625 Nonferrous forgings; trailers & trailer equipment; towing bars & systems; iron & steel forgings; relays & industrial controls; truck & bus bodies; manufactured hardware (general)

(G-4963)
CLEVELAND HOLLOW BORING INC
Also Called: Coomercial Forg Heat Treatment
4501 Lakeside Ave E (44114-3818)
P.O. Box 605028 (44105-0028)
PHONE.....................216 883-1926
Walt Illingworgh, *Manager*
EMP: 3
SALES (corp-wide): 772.9K **Privately Held**
SIC: 3462 3398 3469 Iron & steel forgings; metal heat treating; machine parts, stamped or pressed metal
PA: Cleveland Hollow Boring, Inc
3714 E 93rd St
Cleveland OH 44105
216 883-1926

(G-4964)
CLEVELAND IGNITION CO INC
600 Golden Oak Pkwy (44146-6504)
PHONE.....................440 439-3688
Walt Lemonovith, *President*
Charles O'Toole, *Principal*
▲ EMP: 9 EST: 1917
SQ FT: 8,000
SALES (est): 1.7MM **Privately Held**
SIC: 3714 Motor vehicle parts & accessories

(G-4965)
CLEVELAND IRON WORKERS MEMBERS
2121 Euclid Ave Mm304 (44115-2214)
PHONE.....................216 687-2290
Sara Bartlett, *Opers Staff*
EMP: 3
SALES (est): 247.8K **Privately Held**
SIC: 3423 Hand & edge tools

(G-4966)
CLEVELAND JEWISH PUBL CO
Also Called: Cleveland Jewish News
23880 Commerce Park Ste 1 (44122-5830)
PHONE.....................216 454-8300
Rob Certner, *CEO*
Cynthia Dettelbach, *Exec VP*
Rebecca Fellenbaum, *Marketing Staff*
EMP: 38 EST: 1964
SQ FT: 9,000
SALES (est): 2.6MM **Privately Held**
WEB: www.clevelandjewishnews.com
SIC: 2711 Newspapers: publishing only, not printed on site

(G-4967)
CLEVELAND MENU PRINTING INC
1441 E 17th St (44114-2012)
PHONE.....................216 241-5256
Tom Ramella, *President*
Gerry Ramella, *Owner*
Homas A Grabien, *Principal*
George Maxwell, *Principal*
Daniel Payne, *Principal*
▼ EMP: 25
SQ FT: 15,000
SALES (est): 4.5MM **Privately Held**
WEB: www.clevelandmenu.com
SIC: 2759 Menus: printing

Cleveland - Cuyahoga County (G-4968)

(G-4968)
CLEVELAND METAL PROCESSING INC (PA)
20303 1st Ave (44130-2433)
P.O. Box 30249 (44130-0249)
PHONE....................440 243-3404
Juan Chahda, *President*
Liliana Chahda, *Vice Pres*
Marty Curry, *Sales Associate*
EMP: 114 EST: 1947
SQ FT: 119,000
SALES (est): 7MM Privately Held
SIC: 3465 3544 Automotive stampings; special dies & tools

(G-4969)
CLEVELAND PLATING
1028 E 134th St (44110-2248)
PHONE....................216 249-0300
EMP: 7
SALES (est): 688.2K Privately Held
SIC: 3471 Plating of metals or formed products

(G-4970)
CLEVELAND PRINTWEAR INC
13300 Madison Ave (44107-4894)
PHONE....................216 521-5500
Michael Cannon, *President*
Matt Cannon, *Sales Staff*
Karen Cannon, *Admin Sec*
EMP: 9
SQ FT: 8,000
SALES (est): 1.1MM Privately Held
WEB: www.clevelandprintwear.com
SIC: 2759 Screen printing

(G-4971)
CLEVELAND RANGE LLC
Also Called: Sub of Manitowoc Company
18901 Euclid Ave (44117-3351)
PHONE....................216 481-4900
▲ EMP: 4 EST: 2013
SALES (est): 426K
SALES (corp-wide): 3.4B Publicly Held
SIC: 3556 Mfg Food Products Machinery
PA: The Manitowoc Company Inc
    2400 S 44th St
    Manitowoc WI 53224
    920 684-4410

(G-4972)
CLEVELAND RANGE LLC (HQ)
Also Called: Manitwoc Ovens Advnced Cooking
18301 Saint Clair Ave (44110-2587)
PHONE....................216 481-4900
Robert Pritt, *Mng Member*
John Stevenson,
▲ EMP: 127
SQ FT: 150,000
SALES (est): 36MM
SALES (corp-wide): 1.5B Publicly Held
WEB: www.clevelandrange.com
SIC: 3589 3556 3634 Commercial cooking & foodwarming equipment; food products machinery; electric housewares & fans
PA: Welbilt, Inc.
    2227 Welbilt Blvd
    Trinity FL 34655
    727 375-7010

(G-4973)
CLEVELAND READY MIX
4860 Orchard Rd (44128-3130)
PHONE....................216 399-6688
EMP: 3
SALES (est): 210.1K Privately Held
SIC: 3273 Ready-mixed concrete

(G-4974)
CLEVELAND REBABBITTING SERVICE
15593 Brookpark Rd (44142-1618)
PHONE....................216 433-0123
Kenneth Roller, *President*
Bradford Roller, *Vice Pres*
EMP: 9
SQ FT: 15,000
SALES (est): 1.3MM Privately Held
WEB: www.rebabbit.com
SIC: 3568 Bearings, bushings & blocks

(G-4975)
CLEVELAND ROLL FORMING CO
3170 W 32nd St (44109-1529)
PHONE....................216 281-0202
Paul Ekey, *President*
Edward L Ekey, *Vice Pres*
EMP: 7
SQ FT: 11,700
SALES (est): 1.1MM Privately Held
WEB: www.clevelandrollforming.com
SIC: 3544 Special dies & tools

(G-4976)
CLEVELAND SMACNA
6060 Royalton Rd (44133-5104)
PHONE....................440 877-3500
Margaret Schultz, *Principal*
Dennis Clark, *Opers Mgr*
EMP: 3
SALES (est): 297.1K Privately Held
SIC: 3585 Air conditioning condensers & condensing units

(G-4977)
CLEVELAND SPECIALTY PDTS INC
2130 W 110th St (44102-3510)
PHONE....................216 281-8300
Manuel P Glynias, *President*
EMP: 32
SALES (est): 5.5MM Privately Held
SIC: 3089 Extruded finished plastic products

(G-4978)
CLEVELAND STEEL TOOL COMPANY
474 E 105th St (44108-1378)
PHONE....................216 681-7400
Mark Dawson, *President*
Wayne Haas, *Senior VP*
Charlie Balch, *Plant Mgr*
Kevin Zavodny, *Purchasing*
◆ EMP: 26 EST: 1908
SQ FT: 25,000
SALES (est): 4.7MM Privately Held
WEB: www.clevelandsteeltool.com
SIC: 3544 Punches, forming & stamping; special dies & tools

(G-4979)
CLEVELAND TOOL AND MACHINE INC (PA)
5240 Smith Rd Ste 3 (44142-1700)
PHONE....................216 267-6010
Victor Bota, *President*
Maria Bota, *Vice Pres*
Douglas Neece, *Vice Pres*
Laurentiu Taraboanta, *Engineer*
◆ EMP: 15
SQ FT: 30,000
SALES (est): 2.7MM Privately Held
WEB: www.clevtool.com
SIC: 3599 Machine shop, jobbing & repair

(G-4980)
CLEVELAND TRACK MATERIAL INC (HQ)
Also Called: Cylindrical Fabrications
6600 Bessemer Ave (44127-1804)
P.O. Box 603160 (44103-0160)
PHONE....................216 641-4000
Eliseo Bandala, *CEO*
Michael Carlo, *COO*
William F Willoughby, *VP Opers*
Martin Newmann, *CFO*
Mike Zatorsky, *CFO*
▲ EMP: 100
SALES (est): 45.6MM
SALES (corp-wide): 990.2MM Privately Held
WEB: www.clevelandtrack.com
SIC: 3312 Structural & rail mill products
PA: Vossloh Ag
    Vosslohstr. 4
    Werdohl 58791
    239 252-0

(G-4981)
CLEVELAND TRACK MATERIAL INC
6600 Bessemer Ave (44127-1804)
P.O. Box 603160 (44103-0160)
PHONE....................216 641-4000
William Willoughby, *Branch Mgr*
EMP: 11
SALES (corp-wide): 990.2MM Privately Held
WEB: www.clevelandtrack.com
SIC: 3312 3443 Structural & rail mill products; fabricated plate work (boiler shop)
HQ: Cleveland Track Material, Inc.
    6600 Bessemer Ave
    Cleveland OH 44127
    216 641-4000

(G-4982)
CLEVELAND VALVE & GAUGE CO LLC
4755 W 150th St Ste H (44135-3330)
PHONE....................216 362-1702
Shirley Trusso, *Owner*
Jerry Huttner, *Foreman/Supr*
Richard McCarthy,
EMP: 3
SALES (est): 606.8K Privately Held
WEB: www.clevelandvalve.com
SIC: 3491 Industrial valves

(G-4983)
CLEVELAND WELDING & FABG LLC
4410 Perkins Ave (44103-3544)
PHONE....................440 364-5137
Richard K Lehmann, *Mng Member*
EMP: 3
SQ FT: 3,000
SALES (est): 64.4K Privately Held
SIC: 7692 Welding repair

(G-4984)
CLEVELAND WHISKEY LLC
1768 E 25th St (44114-4418)
PHONE....................216 881-8481
Tom Lix,
EMP: 5
SALES (est): 577.6K Privately Held
SIC: 2085 Distilled & blended liquors

(G-4985)
CLEVELAND WIRE CLOTH & MFG CO
3573 E 78th St (44105-1517)
PHONE....................216 341-1832
Chester F Crone, *President*
George Karnavas, *Engineer*
Joseph Sarasa, *Treasurer*
Travis Clark, *Technical Staff*
Christine Berry, *Executive*
▲ EMP: 32
SQ FT: 100,000
SALES: 7.6MM Privately Held
WEB: www.wirecloth.com
SIC: 3496 Hardware cloth, woven wire

(G-4986)
CLEVELAND-CLIFFS INC (PA)
200 Public Sq Ste 3300 (44114-2315)
PHONE....................216 694-5700
Lourenco Goncalves, *Ch of Bd*
Clifford T Smith, *COO*
Terry G Fedor, *Exec VP*
Maurice D Harapiak, *Exec VP*
Terrence R Mee, *Exec VP*
EMP: 76
SALES: 2.3B Publicly Held
WEB: www.cliffsnaturalresources.com
SIC: 1011 Iron ore mining; iron ore pelletizing

(G-4987)
CLEVELANDCOM
1801 Superior Ave E (44114-2135)
PHONE....................216 862-7159
Andrew S Wolfe, *Principal*
Dennis Lehman, *Exec VP*
David Falk, *Treasurer*
James Levin, *Exec Dir*
EMP: 4
SALES (est): 205.4K Privately Held
SIC: 2711 Newspapers

(G-4988)
CLIFFS & ASSOCIATES LTD
1100 Superior Ave E # 1500 (44114-2530)
PHONE....................216 694-5700
W R Calfee, *President*
Rainald Von Bitter, *Vice Pres*
Jamie Bailey, *Electrical Engi*
EMP: 6
SQ FT: 65,000
SALES (est): 379.1K Privately Held
SIC: 1011 Iron ores

(G-4989)
CLIFFS LOGAN COUNTY COAL LLC
200 Public Sq Ste 3300 (44114-2315)
PHONE....................216 694-5700
Joseph Carrabba, *CEO*
▼ EMP: 1
SALES (est): 2.2MM
SALES (corp-wide): 2.3B Publicly Held
SIC: 5989 1221 Coal; coal preparation plant, bituminous or lignite
PA: Cleveland-Cliffs Inc.
    200 Public Sq Ste 3300
    Cleveland OH 44114
    216 694-5700

(G-4990)
CLIFFS MICHIGAN OPERATION
District 1072 Ste 1500 (44114)
PHONE....................216 694-5303
EMP: 24
SALES (est): 4.3MM Privately Held
SIC: 1011 Iron ores

(G-4991)
CLIFFS MINING COMPANY
200 Public Sq Ste 3300 (44114-2315)
PHONE....................216 694-5700
W R Calfee, *Vice Pres*
D J Gallagher, *Vice Pres*
Laurie Brlas, *CFO*
J A Carrabba, *Director*
EMP: 15
SQ FT: 40,000
SALES (est): 5.4MM
SALES (corp-wide): 2.3B Publicly Held
SIC: 1011 Iron ores
PA: Cleveland-Cliffs Inc.
    200 Public Sq Ste 3300
    Cleveland OH 44114
    216 694-5700

(G-4992)
CLIFFS MINNESOTA MINERALS CO
1100 Superior Ave E (44114-2530)
PHONE....................216 694-5700
W R Calfee, *President*
EMP: 511
SQ FT: 65,000
SALES (est): 9.1MM
SALES (corp-wide): 2.3B Publicly Held
SIC: 1011 4931 Iron ore mining; electric & other services combined
PA: Cleveland-Cliffs Inc.
    200 Public Sq Ste 3300
    Cleveland OH 44114
    216 694-5700

(G-4993)
CMC PHARMACEUTICALS INC (PA)
Also Called: CMC Consulting
7100 Euclid Ave Ste 152 (44103-4036)
PHONE....................216 600-9430
Mike Radomsky, *President*
EMP: 6
SQ FT: 1,000
SALES (est): 1.1MM Privately Held
SIC: 2834 Druggists' preparations (pharmaceuticals)

(G-4994)
CO PAC SERVICES INC
3113 W 110th St (44111-2753)
PHONE....................216 688-1780
Craig Jaworski, *President*
Mike Marfeka, *Vice Pres*
Tom Maggard, *Manager*
Phil Puhala, *Admin Sec*
▲ EMP: 15
SQ FT: 65,000

GEOGRAPHIC SECTION

Cleveland - Cuyahoga County (G-5017)

SALES (est): 2.1MM **Privately Held**
WEB: www.copac.com
SIC: **3993** Displays & cutouts, window & lobby

(G-4995)
CODONICS INC (PA)
17991 Englewood Dr Ste D (44130-3493)
PHONE...................................216 226-1066
Peter O Botten, *CEO*
Donna Botten, *President*
Mike Kohlberg, *General Mgr*
Minglin LI, *General Mgr*
Alan Desantis, *Vice Pres*
◆ EMP: 166
SALES (est): 31.7MM **Privately Held**
WEB: www.codonics.com
SIC: **3571** Electronic computers

(G-4996)
COLD HEADING CO
4444 Lee Rd (44128-2902)
PHONE...................................216 581-3000
Mark Ebersbacher, *Manager*
EMP: 100
SALES (corp-wide): 55.6MM **Privately Held**
WEB: www.spst.com
SIC: **3452** Bolts, metal
HQ: The Cold Heading Co
21777 Hoover Rd
Warren MI 48089
586 497-7000

(G-4997)
COLOR BAR PRINTING CENTERS INC
4576 Renaissance Pkwy (44128-5702)
PHONE...................................216 595-3939
Roger Perlmuter, *President*
Mary Ann Perlmuter, *Vice Pres*
EMP: 20
SQ FT: 16,248
SALES (est): 1.1MM **Privately Held**
SIC: **2752** Commercial printing, offset

(G-4998)
COLOR BRITE COMPANY INC
5209 Grant Ave (44125-1033)
PHONE...................................216 441-4117
Charles Pedro, *CEO*
EMP: 5
SQ FT: 10,000
SALES (est): 497.5K **Privately Held**
SIC: **2493** 1761 3444 Awning installation; siding contractor; awnings, sheet metal

(G-4999)
COM-CORP INDUSTRIES INC
7601 Bittern Ave (44103-1060)
PHONE...................................216 431-6266
Thomas Stanciu, *CEO*
William Beckwith, *Vice Pres*
Edison LI, *Purchasing*
Kimberly Watroba, *CFO*
Fred Chordas, *Manager*
◆ EMP: 100 EST: 1980
SQ FT: 150,000
SALES (est): 30.8MM **Privately Held**
SIC: **3469** Stamping metal for the trade

(G-5000)
COMCORP INC
Also Called: Sun Newspaper Div
1801 Superior Ave E (44114-2135)
PHONE...................................718 981-1234
John Urbancich, *President*
Douglas J Lightner, *CFO*
EMP: 310
SQ FT: 22,500
SALES (est): 638K
SALES (corp-wide): 5.5B **Privately Held**
SIC: **2711** Newspapers: publishing only, not printed on site
PA: Advance Publications, Inc.
1 World Trade Ctr Fl 43
New York NY 10007
718 981-1234

(G-5001)
COMEX NORTH AMERICA INC (HQ)
Also Called: Comex Group
101 W Prospect Ave # 1020 (44115-1093)
PHONE...................................303 307-2100
Christopher Connor, *CEO*

Leon Cohen, *President*
Julie Zamski, *City Mgr*
◆ EMP: 90
SQ FT: 2,900
SALES (est): 204.4MM
SALES (corp-wide): 17.5B **Publicly Held**
WEB: www.professionalpaintinc.com
SIC: **2851** 8742 5198 5231 Paints & paint additives; paints, waterproof; paints: oil or alkyd vehicle or water thinned; corporation organizing; paints; paint brushes, rollers, sprayers; wallcoverings; paint; paint brushes, rollers, sprayers & other supplies; wallcoverings
PA: The Sherwin-Williams Company
101 W Prospect Ave # 1020
Cleveland OH 44115
216 566-2000

(G-5002)
COMMERCIAL ELECTRIC PDTS CORP (PA)
1821 E 40th St (44103-3503)
PHONE...................................216 241-2886
Roger Meyer, *President*
Russ Arslanian, *General Mgr*
Kenneth Culp, *Vice Pres*
Char Page, *Sales Staff*
Scott Sacerich, *Sales Staff*
EMP: 44 EST: 1927
SQ FT: 15,000
SALES (est): 25.7MM **Privately Held**
WEB: www.commercialelectric.com
SIC: **5085** 3661 3824 1731 Power transmission equipment & apparatus; telephones & telephone apparatus; telegraph & related apparatus; mechanical & electromechanical counters & devices; general electrical contractor; industrial equipment services; electrical equipment & supplies

(G-5003)
COMMERCIAL INNOVATIONS INC
3812 E 91st St (44105-2103)
PHONE...................................216 641-7500
Matt Robinson, *CEO*
Matthew Robinson, *General Mgr*
Ron Casper, *Manager*
EMP: 5
SQ FT: 106,500
SALES (est): 870K **Privately Held**
WEB: www.com-innov.com
SIC: **2493** 2952 Insulation & roofing material, reconstituted wood; roofing materials

(G-5004)
COMMERCIAL STEEL TREATING CO
1394 E 39th St (44114-4119)
PHONE...................................216 431-8204
Jeff Seitz, *President*
Donna Seitz, *Corp Secy*
Lisa Seitz, *Admin Sec*
EMP: 10 EST: 1941
SQ FT: 36,000
SALES (est): 1.5MM **Privately Held**
SIC: **3398** 3471 Metal heat treating; plating & polishing

(G-5005)
COMMERCIAL TRANSPORTATION SVCS
12487 Plaza Dr (44130-1056)
PHONE...................................216 267-2000
Allan J Miner, *President*
Ralph Napletana, *Treasurer*
Patrick Cahill, *CPA*
Connie Roma, *Human Res Mgr*
Connie Romer, *Human Res Mgr*
EMP: 3
SQ FT: 15,000
SALES: 894.5K **Privately Held**
SIC: **7372** Prepackaged software

(G-5006)
COMMSCOPE TECHNOLOGIES LLC
1668 Sunview Rd (44124-2872)
PHONE...................................216 272-0055
Robert Andrews, *Branch Mgr*
EMP: 119 **Publicly Held**
WEB: www.andrew.com

SIC: **3663** Radio & TV communications equipment
HQ: Commscope Technologies Llc
4 Westbrook Corporate Ctr
Westchester IL 60154
708 236-6600

(G-5007)
COMMUNITY CARE NETWORK INC (PA)
4614 Prospect Ave Ste 240 (44103-4365)
PHONE...................................216 671-0977
David Lundeen, *President*
Christopher Cassidy, *CFO*
EMP: 50
SALES: 1.3MM **Privately Held**
WEB: www.ccnusa.com
SIC: **3825** Network analyzers

(G-5008)
COMPANIES OF NORTH COAST LLC (HQ)
4605 Spring Rd (44131-1021)
PHONE...................................216 398-8550
Richard Petrovich, *President*
EMP: 2
SQ FT: 38,500
SALES: 2.8MM
SALES (corp-wide): 30.5MM **Privately Held**
SIC: **2655** 3544 6719 Cans, composite: foil-fiber & other: from purchased fiber; special dies & tools; investment holding companies, except banks
PA: Unitech Holdings, Inc.
10413 N Aero Dr
Hayden ID 83835
208 772-0533

(G-5009)
COMPASS ENERGY LLC
17877 Saint Clair Ave # 1 (44110-2636)
PHONE...................................866 665-2225
Hendrik Hoeve, *Managing Dir*
Craig P Christ,
EMP: 60
SQ FT: 238,000
SALES (est): 3.7MM **Privately Held**
WEB: www.compassenergy.com
SIC: **2211** Broadwoven fabric mills, cotton

(G-5010)
COMPLIANT HEALTHCARE TECH LLC
7123 Pearl Rd Ste 305 (44130-4944)
PHONE...................................216 255-9607
Rick Ziegan, *Branch Mgr*
EMP: 15 **Privately Held**
WEB: www.chtechllc.com
SIC: **3826** Gas testing apparatus
PA: Compliant Healthcare Technologies, Llc
7123 Pearl Rd Ste 305
Cleveland OH 44130

(G-5011)
COMPLIANT HEALTHCARE TECH LLC (PA)
Also Called: C H T
7123 Pearl Rd Ste 305 (44130-4944)
PHONE...................................216 255-9607
John Zbozien, *Vice Pres*
Dave Boehne, *Accounts Mgr*
Keith Kassouf, *Sales Staff*
Jason Di Marco, *Mng Member*
Scot Wederquist,
EMP: 25
SQ FT: 8,200
SALES: 7.5MM **Privately Held**
SIC: **7389** 3826 Gas system conversion; gas testing apparatus

(G-5012)
COMPONENT SYSTEMS INC
Also Called: A-Wall
2245 W 114th St (44102-3517)
PHONE...................................216 252-9292
Tim Nelson, *President*
Thomas A Nelson, *Vice Pres*
Thomas Nelson, *VP Mfg*
Curtis Theriot, *Engineer*
Suzanne Reilly, *Controller*
EMP: 20
SQ FT: 26,000

SALES (est): 3.7MM **Privately Held**
WEB: www.comp-sys.com
SIC: **2542** Partitions & fixtures, except wood

(G-5013)
COMTURN MANUFACTURING LLC
13704 Enterprise Ave (44135-5114)
PHONE...................................219 267-6911
Mark A Trubiano,
EMP: 4
SALES (est): 103.6K **Privately Held**
SIC: **3599** Machine shop, jobbing & repair

(G-5014)
CONN-SELMER INC
Glaesel String Instuments
1440 E 36th St Ste 501 (44114-4117)
PHONE...................................216 391-7723
Fax: 216 391-5318
EMP: 32
SALES (corp-wide): 179.6MM **Privately Held**
SIC: **3931** Mfg Musical Instruments
HQ: Conn-Selmer, Inc.
600 Industrial Pkwy
Elkhart IN 46516
574 522-1675

(G-5015)
CONSOLIDATED GRAPHICS GROUP INC
Also Called: Consolidated Solutions
1614 E 40th St (44103-2319)
PHONE...................................216 881-9191
Terry Hartman, *CEO*
Kenneth A Lanci, *Ch of Bd*
Matt Reville, *COO*
Matthew Reville, *COO*
Stephen Henn, *Vice Pres*
▲ EMP: 140
SQ FT: 75,000
SALES: 25MM **Privately Held**
SIC: **2752** 2759 7331 2791 Commercial printing, offset; commercial printing; direct mail advertising services; typesetting; bookbinding & related work

(G-5016)
CONSOLDTED PRECISION PDTS CORP (HQ)
Also Called: Cpp Pomona
1621 Euclid Ave Ste 1850 (44115-2126)
PHONE...................................216 453-4800
James V Stewart, *CEO*
Steve Clodfelter, *President*
Debbie Comstock, *Vice Pres*
Ali Ghavami, *Vice Pres*
Ron Hamilton, *CFO*
▲ EMP: 250
SQ FT: 10,000
SALES (est): 555.5MM
SALES (corp-wide): 8.4B **Privately Held**
SIC: **3365** 3324 Aluminum foundries; steel investment foundries
PA: Warburg Pincus Llc
450 Lexington Ave Fl 32
New York NY 10017
212 878-0600

(G-5017)
CONSOLIDATED COATINGS CORP
3735 Green Rd (44122-5705)
PHONE...................................216 514-7596
Thomas C Sullivan, *Ch of Bd*
J K Milliken, *General Mgr*
Paul A Granzier, *Vice Pres*
EMP: 20
SQ FT: 4,000
SALES (est): 3.3MM
SALES (corp-wide): 5.3B **Publicly Held**
WEB: www.rpmrepublic.com
SIC: **5169** 2891 2851 2842 Adhesives & sealants; adhesives & sealants; paints & allied products; specialty cleaning, polishes & sanitation goods; roofing felts, cements or coatings
HQ: Republic Powdered Metals, Inc.
2628 Pearl Rd
Medina OH 44256
330 225-3192

(PA)=Parent Co (HQ)=Headquarters (DH)=Div Headquarters
✪ = New Business established in last 2 years

Cleveland - Cuyahoga County (G-5018) GEOGRAPHIC SECTION

(G-5018)
CONSOLIDATED WEB
Also Called: Consolidated Solutions
3831 Kelley Ave (44114-4537)
PHONE..................216 881-7816
Kenneth Lanci, *President*
Dave Wasielewski, *General Mgr*
EMP: 4
SALES (est): 226.6K **Privately Held**
SIC: 2759 Commercial printing

(G-5019)
CONSTRUCTION TECHNIQUES INC (HQ)
15887 Snow Rd Ste 100 (44142-2854)
PHONE..................216 267-7310
B J Akers, *President*
EMP: 15
SQ FT: 1,500
SALES (est): 1.1MM
SALES (corp-wide): 2.5MM **Privately Held**
WEB: www.fabriform1.com
SIC: 2299 6794 Jute & flax textile products; patent buying, licensing, leasing
PA: Intrusion-Prepakt Inc
   15910 Pearl Rd Ste 101
   Cleveland OH 44136
   440 238-6950

(G-5020)
CONTINENTAL BUSINESS ENTPS INC (PA)
Also Called: Ace Metal Stamping Company
7311 Northfield Rd (44146-6199)
PHONE..................440 439-4400
Louis P Trolli, *President*
Lynn Di Geronimo House, *Asst Sec*
Richard L Laribee, *Asst Sec*
EMP: 17 EST: 1966
SQ FT: 33,000
SALES (est): 1.4MM **Privately Held**
SIC: 3469 3544 Stamping metal for the trade; special dies, tools, jigs & fixtures

(G-5021)
CONTINENTAL METAL PROC CO (PA)
18711 Cleveland Ave (44110)
PHONE..................216 268-0000
Joseph Freund, *President*
Mike Freund, *Vice Pres*
Rubin Freund, *Vice Pres*
EMP: 19
SQ FT: 328,000
SALES (est): 3MM **Privately Held**
SIC: 3341 Aluminum smelting & refining (secondary); zinc smelting & refining (secondary)

(G-5022)
CONTINENTAL METAL PROC CO
14919 Saranac Rd (44110-2344)
PHONE..................216 268-0000
Michael Freund, *Vice Pres*
EMP: 22
SQ FT: 320,000
SALES (corp-wide): 3MM **Privately Held**
SIC: 3341 Aluminum smelting & refining (secondary)
PA: Continental Metal Processing Co Inc
   18711 Cleveland Ave
   Cleveland OH 44110
   216 268-0000

(G-5023)
CONTINENTAL PRODUCTS COMPANY (PA)
2926 Chester Ave (44114-4414)
PHONE..................216 383-3932
Miriam Strebeck, *Ch of Bd*
Emerson O McArthur III, *President*
Angela McArthur, *Administration*
EMP: 30 EST: 1916
SALES (est): 8.7MM **Privately Held**
WEB: www.paintdoc.com
SIC: 2851 Paints & paint additives; stains: varnish, oil or wax; putty

(G-5024)
CONTINENTAL PRODUCTS COMPANY
2926 Chester Ave (44114-4414)
PHONE..................216 531-0710
Mary Ann Strebeck, *CEO*
EMP: 26
SALES (est): 3.2MM
SALES (corp-wide): 8.7MM **Privately Held**
WEB: www.paintdoc.com
SIC: 2851 5198 2891 Paints & paint additives; stains: varnish, oil or wax; putty; paints, varnishes & supplies; adhesives & sealants
PA: The Continental Products Company
   2926 Chester Ave
   Cleveland OH 44114
   216 383-3932

(G-5025)
CONTROL LINE EQUIPMENT INC
14750 Industrial Pkwy (44135-4548)
PHONE..................216 433-7766
Mike Rotella, *CEO*
Robert May, *Vice Pres*
▲ EMP: 12
SQ FT: 12,000
SALES (est): 4.4MM **Privately Held**
WEB: www.control-line.com
SIC: 5084 3593 Hydraulic systems equipment & supplies; fluid power cylinders & actuators

(G-5026)
CONWAY GREENE CO INC
1400 E 30th St Ste 402 (44114-4050)
PHONE..................216 619-8091
Barry Conway, *President*
Evalyn Greene, *Principal*
Patrick Phillips, *Manager*
EMP: 7
SQ FT: 2,880
SALES (est): 967.4K **Privately Held**
WEB: www.conwaygreene.com
SIC: 2731 Book publishing

(G-5027)
COOK BONDING & MFG CO INC
701 W Schaaf Rd (44109-4638)
PHONE..................216 661-1698
Brian Reneker, *CEO*
David M Cook, *President*
Mary Jo Knapper, *Manager*
EMP: 5
SQ FT: 3,200
SALES (est): 914K **Privately Held**
WEB: www.cookbonding.com
SIC: 3568 Clutches, except vehicular

(G-5028)
COOPER INTERCONNECT INC
Also Called: Cooper - Eaton Center
1000 Eaton Blvd (44122-6058)
PHONE..................800 386-1911
Tony Dertouzos, *Program Mgr*
Michael Lemieux, *Manager*
Lawrence Mendoza, *Supervisor*
EMP: 7 **Privately Held**
SIC: 3643 3678 Electric connectors; electronic connectors
HQ: Cooper Interconnect, Inc.
   750 W Ventura Blvd
   Camarillo CA 93010
   805 484-0543

(G-5029)
COPERNICUS THERAPEUTICS INC
11000 Cedar Ave Ste 145 (44106-3060)
PHONE..................216 707-1776
Joseph Ashley, *Ch of Bd*
Robert C Moen, *President*
Mark Cooper, *Senior VP*
EMP: 14
SQ FT: 6,000
SALES (est): 2.3MM **Privately Held**
WEB: www.cgsys.com
SIC: 2836 8731 Mfg Biological Products Commercial Physical Research

(G-5030)
COPY CATS PRINTING LLC
6659 Pearl Rd Ste 101 (44130-3840)
PHONE..................440 345-5966
Nino Paglia, *Partner*
Donna Paglia, *Partner*
EMP: 3
SALES (est): 285.4K **Privately Held**
SIC: 2752 Commercial printing, lithographic

(G-5031)
CORRO-TECH EQUIPMENT CORP
4034 W 163rd St (44135-1202)
PHONE..................216 941-1552
Mark Burger, *President*
Mark Brown, *Corp Secy*
EMP: 4
SQ FT: 8,500
SALES (est): 515.9K **Privately Held**
SIC: 3823 1796 Industrial process control instruments; pollution control equipment installation

(G-5032)
COUNTRY PARLOUR ICE CREAM CO
12905 York Delta Dr Ste C (44133-3551)
PHONE..................440 237-4040
Jeri Hovanec, *Principal*
Craig Hovanec, *Corp Secy*
EMP: 14
SALES (est): 1.9MM **Privately Held**
SIC: 2024 2099 5143 Ice cream, bulk; food preparations; dairy products, except dried or canned

(G-5033)
COVENTRY STEEL SERVICES INC
4200 E 71st St Ste 1 (44105-5721)
P.O. Box 25077 (44125-0077)
PHONE..................216 883-4477
Brian Migchelbrink, *President*
Jeff Migchelbrink, *Corp Secy*
Joseph Hustosky, *Vice Pres*
EMP: 12
SQ FT: 35,000
SALES (est): 1MM **Privately Held**
WEB: www.coventrysteel.com
SIC: 3441 5051 Fabricated structural metal; steel

(G-5034)
COWELLS - ARROW BINGO COMPANY
9900 Clinton Rd (44144-1034)
PHONE..................216 961-3500
John E Gallagher Jr, *President*
James Cochran, *Corp Secy*
Bill Kay, *Manager*
Jason Fullington, *Administration*
EMP: 4
SALES (est): 200K **Privately Held**
SIC: 3944 Bingo boards (games)

(G-5035)
CPI GROUP LIMITED
Also Called: Puremonics
13858 Tinkers Creek Rd (44125-5661)
P.O. Box 25411 (44125-0411)
PHONE..................216 525-0046
Benjamin Rosolowski,
EMP: 9
SQ FT: 2,000
SALES (est): 1.1MM **Privately Held**
SIC: 3675 8711 Electronic capacitors; electrical or electronic engineering

(G-5036)
CR LAURENCE CO INC
31600 Carter St (44139-3551)
PHONE..................440 248-0003
Steve Newton, *Manager*
EMP: 8
SALES (corp-wide): 29.7B **Privately Held**
WEB: www.crlaurence.com
SIC: 5072 3714 Hand tools; sun roofs, motor vehicle
HQ: C.R. Laurence Co., Inc.
   2503 E Vernon Ave
   Vernon CA 90058
   323 588-1281

(G-5037)
CRAIN COMMUNICATIONS INC
Also Called: Crain's Cleveland Business
700 W Saint Clair Ave # 310 (44113-1230)
PHONE..................216 522-1383
Dawn Donegan, *Accounts Exec*
Michelle Sustar, *Marketing Staff*
Elizabeth McIntyre, *Manager*
EMP: 29
SALES (corp-wide): 225MM **Privately Held**
WEB: www.crainsnewyork.com
SIC: 2721 2711 Magazines: publishing only, not printed on site; newspapers
PA: Crain Communications, Inc.
   1155 Gratiot Ave
   Detroit MI 48207
   313 446-6000

(G-5038)
CRAWFORD ACQUISITION CORP
Also Called: Famous Kiss-N-Korn Shop
16130 Saint Clair Ave (44110-3029)
PHONE..................216 486-0702
Dan Crawford, *Owner*
Dave Crawford, *Vice Pres*
EMP: 15 EST: 1973
SQ FT: 8,000
SALES (est): 520K **Privately Held**
SIC: 2064 Popcorn balls or other treated popcorn products

(G-5039)
CROOKED RIVER COFFEE CO
761 Beta Dr Ste E (44143-2329)
PHONE..................440 442-8330
Howard Sobel, *President*
EMP: 3 EST: 1991
SQ FT: 8,000
SALES (est): 484.4K **Privately Held**
WEB: www.crookedrivercoffee.com
SIC: 5149 2095 Coffee, green or roasted; coffee roasting (except by wholesale grocers)

(G-5040)
CROWNE GROUP LLC (PA)
127 Public Sq Ste 5110 (44114-1313)
PHONE..................216 589-0198
Robert Henderson, *Mng Member*
EMP: 65
SALES (est): 830.8MM **Privately Held**
SIC: 3559 8711 Degreasing machines, automotive & industrial; industrial engineers

(G-5041)
CT FERRY SCREW PRODUCTS I
1660 Queen Annes Gate (44145-2640)
PHONE..................440 871-1617
EMP: 3 EST: 2001
SALES (est): 180K **Privately Held**
SIC: 3451 Mfg Screw Machine Products

(G-5042)
CUMMINS - ALLISON CORP
6777 Engle Rd Ste H (44130-7941)
PHONE..................440 824-5050
David Profera, *Manager*
EMP: 8
SALES (corp-wide): 383.8MM **Privately Held**
WEB: www.gsb.com
SIC: 5046 5087 5044 3519 Commercial equipment; shredders, industrial & commercial; check writing, signing & endorsing machines; internal combustion engines
PA: Cummins - Allison Corp.
   852 Feehanville Dr
   Mount Prospect IL 60056
   847 759-6403

(G-5043)
CURRENT LIGHTING SOLUTIONS LLC (HQ)
1975 Noble Rd Ste 338e (44112-1719)
P.O. Box 5000, Schenectady NY (12301-5000)
PHONE..................800 435-4448
Maryrose Sylvester, *President*
Agostino Renna, *President*
Steve Germain, *Engineer*
◆ EMP: 42
SQ FT: 20,890
SALES (est): 26.5MM
SALES (corp-wide): 78.3MM **Privately Held**
WEB: www.gelcore.com
SIC: 3648 5063 Lighting equipment; lighting fixtures

▲ = Import ▼= Export
◆ = Import/Export

GEOGRAPHIC SECTION
Cleveland - Cuyahoga County (G-5070)

PA: Current Lighting Holdco, Inc.
745 Atlantic Ave
Boston MA 02111
216 956-7734

(G-5044)
CURT HARLER INC
Also Called: Covered Bridge Press
12936 Falling Water Rd (44136-4307)
PHONE......................440 238-4556
Curt Harler, *Owner*
EMP: 5
SALES: 200K **Privately Held**
WEB: www.curtharler.com
SIC: 2721 7371 Magazines: publishing & printing; computer software writers, freelance

(G-5045)
CURTISS-WRIGHT FLOW CTRL CORP
Nova Machine Div
18001 Sheldon Rd (44130-2465)
PHONE......................216 267-3200
David Linton, *CEO*
Jackie Call, *Purchasing*
Jim Zubovic, *Controller*
Deane Beck, *Program Dir*
EMP: 84
SALES (corp-wide): 2.4B **Publicly Held**
SIC: 3452 3429 3369 3356 Bolts, metal; washers; nuts, metal; lock washers; manufactured hardware (general); nonferrous foundries; nonferrous rolling & drawing
HQ: Curtiss-Wright Flow Control Service, Llc
1966 Broadhollow Rd Ste E
Farmingdale NY 11735
631 293-3800

(G-5046)
CUSTOM CLTCH JINT HYDRLICS INC (PA)
3417 Saint Clair Ave Ne (44114-4186)
PHONE......................216 431-1630
David Ballantyne, *CEO*
Donald Meintel, *President*
Elmer T Elbrecht, *Principal*
John G Roberts, *Principal*
Mary Ann Tomasch, *Principal*
EMP: 11
SQ FT: 52,000
SALES: 5.9MM **Privately Held**
WEB: www.customclutch.com
SIC: 3714 3594 3561 3492 Motor vehicle transmissions, drive assemblies & parts; clutches, motor vehicle; fluid power pumps; cylinders, pump; hose & tube couplings, hydraulic/pneumatic; power transmission equipment; steel wire & related products

(G-5047)
CUSTOM INDUSTRIES INC
10701 Briggs Rd (44111-5330)
PHONE......................216 251-2804
Jacob Schaufele Jr, *President*
Harold Schaufele, *Vice Pres*
John Schaufele, *Vice Pres*
Irma Schaufele, *Treasurer*
EMP: 4
SQ FT: 3,900
SALES: 550K **Privately Held**
WEB: www.customindustries.net
SIC: 3364 3369 3363 Nonferrous diecastings except aluminum; zinc & zincbase alloy castings, except die-castings; aluminum die-castings

(G-5048)
CUSTOM RUBBER CORPORATION
1274 E 55th St (44103-1029)
PHONE......................216 391-2928
William Braun, *President*
Richard Torres, *Plant Supt*
John Bellett, *Engineer*
Patti Widmar, *Controller*
Tracy Mack, *Human Res Mgr*
◆ **EMP:** 75
SQ FT: 70,000
SALES: 10MM **Privately Held**
WEB: www.customrubbercorp.com
SIC: 3069 Molded rubber products

(G-5049)
CUSTOM STAMP MAKERS INC
4901 Brookpark Rd (44134-1017)
PHONE......................216 351-1470
Sherry Miller, *President*
Kenneth Jaeger, *Corp Secy*
Mark Miller, *Vice Pres*
EMP: 5
SQ FT: 1,200
SALES: 160K **Privately Held**
SIC: 3069 Stationers' rubber sundries

(G-5050)
CUTLER RICHARD DBA OHIO CONTRO
21506 Ellen Dr (44126-3008)
PHONE......................440 892-1858
Richard Cutler, *Principal*
EMP: 3 EST: 2010
SALES (est): 295.6K **Privately Held**
SIC: 3613 Control panels, electric

(G-5051)
CUTTING EDGE TECHNOLOGIES INC
Also Called: Telos Systems
1241 Superior Ave E (44114-3204)
PHONE......................216 574-4759
Steve Church, *CEO*
Frank J Foti, *Vice Pres*
Anthony Foti, *Admin Sec*
EMP: 50
SALES (est): 4.7MM **Privately Held**
SIC: 3679 3661 Electronic circuits; telephone & telegraph apparatus

(G-5052)
CUTTING SYSTEMS INC
15593 Brookpark Rd (44142-1618)
PHONE......................216 928-0500
Kris Asadorian, *President*
George Asadorian, *President*
Kevan Asadorian, *Vice Pres*
Sergey Edilyan, *Vice Pres*
Tim Bowen, *Prdtn Mgr*
▲ **EMP:** 16
SQ FT: 44,500
SALES (est): 4.2MM **Privately Held**
WEB: www.cuttingsystems.com
SIC: 3541 Plasma process metal cutting machines

(G-5053)
CUYAHOGA CO MED EXAMINERS OFF
11001 Cedar Ave (44106-3022)
PHONE......................216 721-5610
Dave Buehner, *Manager*
EMP: 4
SALES (est): 175.9K **Privately Held**
SIC: 2711 Newspapers, publishing & printing

(G-5054)
CUYAHOGA REBUILDERS INC
5111 Brookpark Rd (44134-1047)
PHONE......................440 846-0532
Reiner Mueller, *President*
Randolph Treudler, *Vice Pres*
EMP: 6
SQ FT: 2,500
SALES (est): 827.6K **Privately Held**
SIC: 3694 Alternators, automotive

(G-5055)
CYBERUTILITY LLC
1599 Maywood Rd (44121-4101)
PHONE......................216 291-8723
John Scott Minor, *Mng Member*
EMP: 8
SALES: 350K **Privately Held**
SIC: 2911 Petroleum refining

(G-5056)
D AND D BUSINESS EQUIPMENT INC
Also Called: Complete Business Machines
3298 Columbia Rd (44145-5525)
PHONE......................440 777-5441
David Wiechec, *President*
Diane Smith, *Vice Pres*
EMP: 4
SQ FT: 1,500

SALES: 150K **Privately Held**
SIC: 5044 7699 2789 Copying equipment; photocopy machine repair; paper cutting

(G-5057)
D M J F INC
Also Called: Swift Print
6571 Pearl Rd (44130-3826)
PHONE......................440 845-1155
David Fackelman, *President*
Martin Fackelman, *Vice Pres*
Yolanda Fackelman, *Vice Pres*
EMP: 4
SQ FT: 1,800
SALES: 125K **Privately Held**
SIC: 2752 Commercial printing, offset

(G-5058)
DAKOTA SOFTWARE CORPORATION (PA)
1375 Euclid Ave Ste 500 (44115-1808)
PHONE......................216 765-7100
Reginald C Shiverick, *President*
Darrin Fleming, *Partner*
Chuck Schmermund, *Business Mgr*
Larry Taylor, *Engineer*
Nick Lay, *Finance*
EMP: 61
SALES (est): 7.7MM **Privately Held**
WEB: www.dakotasoft.com
SIC: 7372 Prepackaged software

(G-5059)
DAL-LITTLE FABRICATING INC
Also Called: Megna Plastics
11707 Putnam Ave (44105-5416)
P.O. Box 44067 (44144-0067)
PHONE......................216 883-3323
Betty J Massielle, *President*
Joe Massielle, *President*
EMP: 8
SQ FT: 13,000
SALES (est): 580K **Privately Held**
SIC: 3229 3441 Glass fiber products; fabricated structural metal

(G-5060)
DALTON COMBUSTION SYSTEMS INC
9701 Stone Rd (44125-4730)
PHONE......................216 447-0647
David Dalton, *President*
EMP: 4
SALES: 500K **Privately Held**
SIC: 1711 3433 Boiler maintenance contractor; burners, furnaces, boilers & stokers

(G-5061)
DANAHER CORPORATION
6095 Parkland Blvd # 310 (44124-6140)
PHONE......................440 995-3003
Alexander Joseph, *Principal*
Richard Earley, *Manager*
Danielle Sauve, *Director*
Beverly Pinkney, *Admin Asst*
EMP: 173
SALES (corp-wide): 19.8B **Publicly Held**
SIC: 3823 Water quality monitoring & control systems
PA: Danaher Corporation
2200 Penn Ave Nw Ste 800w
Washington DC 20037
202 828-0850

(G-5062)
DANNY CABINET CO
11983 Abbey Rd Unit 1 (44133-2635)
PHONE......................440 667-6635
Danny Milovanovich, *Owner*
Vicki Milovanovich, *Co-Owner*
EMP: 7
SQ FT: 7,000
SALES (est): 304.6K **Privately Held**
SIC: 2434 Wood kitchen cabinets

(G-5063)
DANO JR LLC
6185 Ridgebury Blvd (44124-1751)
PHONE......................440 781-5774
Louis M Giordano,
EMP: 4
SALES (est): 240.2K **Privately Held**
SIC: 3999 Candles

(G-5064)
DANTE SOLUTIONS INC
7261 Engle Rd Ste 105 (44130-3479)
PHONE......................440 234-8477
Blake Lynn Ferguson, *President*
Andrew Freborg, *Vice Pres*
Zhichao LI, *Vice Pres*
EMP: 3
SQ FT: 900
SALES (est): 567K **Privately Held**
WEB: www.deformationcontrol.com
SIC: 8711 7372 Engineering services; application computer software

(G-5065)
DARLING INGREDIENTS INC
1002 Belt Line Ave (44109-2848)
PHONE......................216 351-3440
Howard Murray, *Manager*
EMP: 7
SALES (corp-wide): 3.3B **Publicly Held**
SIC: 2077 Animal & marine fats & oils
PA: Darling Ingredients Inc.
251 Oconnor Ridge Blvd
Irving TX 75038
972 717-0300

(G-5066)
DARLING INTERNATIONAL INC
1002 Peltnine Ave (44109)
PHONE......................216 651-9300
Lorie Shorvath, *Manager*
EMP: 18
SQ FT: 28,122
SALES (corp-wide): 3.3B **Publicly Held**
WEB: www.darlingii.com
SIC: 2077 5191 Animal & marine fats & oils; farm supplies
PA: Darling Ingredients Inc.
251 Oconnor Ridge Blvd
Irving TX 75038
972 717-0300

(G-5067)
DARRAH ELECTRIC COMPANY (PA)
5914 Merrill Ave (44102-5699)
PHONE......................216 631-0912
Robert J Darrah, *Ch of Bd*
David J Darrah, *President*
Neal A Darrah, *Corp Secy*
John A Darrah, *Vice Pres*
Diane Bednar, *Executive*
EMP: 20
SQ FT: 18,000
SALES (est): 14.5MM **Privately Held**
WEB: www.darrahelectric.com
SIC: 3679 3612 3674 Rectifiers, electronic; electronic circuits; power & distribution transformers; semiconductors & related devices

(G-5068)
DARRYL SMITH
Also Called: Targa Enterprises
3571 E 147th St (44120-4833)
PHONE......................216 991-5468
Darryl Smith, *Owner*
EMP: 4
SALES (est): 168.5K **Privately Held**
SIC: 3496 Cages, wire

(G-5069)
DATA GENOMIX INC
1215 W 10th St Ste B (44113-1273)
PHONE......................216 860-4770
Nicholas Martin, *CEO*
EMP: 11
SALES (est): 652.3K **Privately Held**
SIC: 7372 5045 7371 Business oriented computer software; computer software; computer software development & applications; custom computer programming services

(G-5070)
DATATEX MEDIA DOLLS
7027 Columbia Rd (44138-1527)
P.O. Box 38125 (44138-0125)
PHONE......................216 598-1000
Katherine Sanders, *President*
Denise Cefal0, *Vice Pres*
EMP: 5

Cleveland - Cuyahoga County (G-5071)

SALES (est): 148.9K **Privately Held**
WEB: www.spiritbeach.com
SIC: 7374 3942 Computer graphics service; dolls & stuffed toys

(G-5071)
DAVRO LTD
1200 E 152nd St (44110-3333)
PHONE..................................216 258-0057
Tom Bell, *Principal*
EMP: 5
SALES (est): 445.5K **Privately Held**
SIC: 3471 Finishing, metals or formed products

(G-5072)
DAWN ENTERPRISES INC (PA)
Also Called: Sportwing
9155 Sweet Valley Dr (44125-4223)
PHONE..................................216 642-5506
Robert Kovach, *President*
Lawrence De Laat, *COO*
Kim Knisely, *Sales Staff*
Keith Jak, *Officer*
Lori M Kovach, *Admin Sec*
▲ EMP: 40 EST: 1973
SQ FT: 69,900
SALES (est): 6.4MM **Privately Held**
WEB: www.sportwing.com
SIC: 3089 5521 Plastic processing; used car dealers

(G-5073)
DAY-GLO COLOR CORP (DH)
4515 Saint Clair Ave (44103-1268)
PHONE..................................216 391-7070
Phil Rozick, *Vice Pres*
Alice J Walker, *Incorporator*
Arthur A Sayre, *Incorporator*
John D Steele, *Incorporator*
▲ EMP: 140 EST: 1934
SQ FT: 36,000
SALES (est): 60MM
SALES (corp-wide): 5.3B **Publicly Held**
WEB: www.dayglo.com
SIC: 2816 2851 Inorganic pigments; lacquers, varnishes, enamels & other coatings
HQ: Republic Powdered Metals, Inc.
    2628 Pearl Rd
    Medina OH 44256
    330 225-3192

(G-5074)
DAY-GLO COLOR CORP
4518 Hamilton Ave (44114-3854)
PHONE..................................216 391-7070
Steven Jackson, *Branch Mgr*
EMP: 140
SALES (corp-wide): 5.3B **Publicly Held**
SIC: 2816 2851 Inorganic pigments; lacquers, varnishes, enamels & other coatings
HQ: Day-Glo Color Corp.
    4515 Saint Clair Ave
    Cleveland OH 44103
    216 391-7070

(G-5075)
DB REDIHEAT INC
Also Called: National Bios Fabric Company
4516 Saint Clair Ave (44103-1204)
PHONE..................................216 361-0530
David Breen, *President*
◆ EMP: 20 EST: 2011
SQ FT: 28,000
SALES (est): 1.7MM **Privately Held**
SIC: 2392 5131 2241 7389 Bags, garment storage: except paper or plastic film; textile converters; bindings, textile; sewing contractor

(G-5076)
DBHL INC (HQ)
4700 W 160th St (44135-2632)
PHONE..................................216 267-7100
Gary A Oatey, *President*
Pete Rogers,
▲ EMP: 13
SALES (est): 9.1MM
SALES (corp-wide): 470MM **Privately Held**
WEB: www.dbhl.com
SIC: 5999 3088 Plumbing & heating supplies; plastics plumbing fixtures

PA: Oatey Co.
    20600 Emerald Pkwy
    Cleveland OH 44135
    800 203-1155

(G-5077)
DCD TECHNOLOGIES INC
17920 S Waterloo Rd (44119-3222)
PHONE..................................216 481-0056
Dave Hodgson, *President*
Mike Palsha, *Engineer*
Art Adzema, *Director*
EMP: 20
SQ FT: 18,000
SALES (est): 4.5MM **Privately Held**
WEB: www.dcdtech.com
SIC: 3544 Dies & die holders for metal cutting, forming, die casting

(G-5078)
DCM MANUFACTURING INC (HQ)
4540 W 160th St (44135-2628)
PHONE..................................216 265-8006
Theodore Berger Jr, *President*
Theodore Berger, *Chairman*
Kevin J Berger, *Vice Pres*
Rob Knight, *VP Opers*
Donna Federer, *Purchasing*
◆ EMP: 50
SQ FT: 68,000
SALES (est): 15.1MM
SALES (corp-wide): 49.2MM **Privately Held**
SIC: 3621 3433 3714 Motors, electric; heating equipment, except electric; motor vehicle parts & accessories
PA: Dreison International, Inc.
    4540 W 160th St
    Cleveland OH 44135
    216 362-0755

(G-5079)
DCW ACQUISITION INC
Also Called: Regol-G Industries
10646 Leuer Ave (44108-1352)
P.O. Box 608957 (44108-0957)
PHONE..................................216 451-0666
Dan Waite, *President*
EMP: 15
SQ FT: 20,000
SALES: 850K **Privately Held**
SIC: 7389 2394 2393 2392 Sewing contractor; canvas & related products; textile bags; household furnishings; men's & boys' work clothing

(G-5080)
DECORATIVE VENEER INC (PA)
2121 Saint Clair Ave Ne (44114-4018)
PHONE..................................216 741-5511
Michael Knoblouch, *President*
EMP: 2
SQ FT: 7,000
SALES (est): 1.3MM **Privately Held**
WEB: www.decorativeveneer.com
SIC: 2499 Veneer work, inlaid

(G-5081)
DEFENSE CO INC
600 Superior Ave E (44114-2614)
PHONE..................................413 998-1637
Kent Rosenthal, *President*
EMP: 99
SALES (est): 3.1MM **Privately Held**
SIC: 3769 Guided missile & space vehicle parts & aux eqpt, rsch & dev

(G-5082)
DELORES E OBEIRN
Also Called: O'Beirn Printing Co
13022 Kingston Way (44133-5971)
P.O. Box 81224 (44181-0224)
PHONE..................................440 582-3610
Delores E O'Beirn, *Owner*
Delores E Obeirn, *Owner*
EMP: 3
SALES: 100K **Privately Held**
SIC: 2752 5112 5734 2761 Lithographing on metal; business forms; software, business & non-game; manifold business forms

(G-5083)
DELTA MACHINE & TOOL CO
7575 Wall St (44125-3384)
PHONE..................................216 524-2477
Jim Kafun, *President*
Thomas Kafun, *Vice Pres*
EMP: 10 EST: 1951
SQ FT: 12,500
SALES: 750K **Privately Held**
SIC: 3599 7692 3545 3544 Machine shop, jobbing & repair; welding repair; machine tool accessories; special dies, tools, jigs & fixtures

(G-5084)
DEPENDABLE STAMPING COMPANY
1160 E 222nd St (44117-1176)
PHONE..................................216 486-5522
Jeffrey N Beres, *President*
Michael Beres, *Vice Pres*
Roy Beres, *Vice Pres*
Curt Gasser, *QC Mgr*
Mike Beres, *Sales Executive*
EMP: 25
SQ FT: 20,000
SALES (est): 5.9MM **Privately Held**
WEB: www.dependablestamping.com
SIC: 3469 Stamping metal for the trade

(G-5085)
DESIGN SIGN INC
6380 Nelwood Rd (44130-3209)
PHONE..................................216 398-9900
Paul Sole, *President*
EMP: 8
SALES (est): 1.1MM **Privately Held**
WEB: www.designsign.com
SIC: 3993 Signs & advertising specialties

(G-5086)
DESMOND ENGRAVING CO INC
13410 Enterprise Ave D (44135-5162)
PHONE..................................216 265-8338
William Bozak, *President*
Brett J May, *Vice Pres*
EMP: 7 EST: 1968
SQ FT: 3,200
SALES: 350K **Privately Held**
SIC: 3953 Date stamps, hand: rubber or metal; figures (marking devices), metal; letters (marking devices), metal; time stamps, hand: rubber or metal

(G-5087)
DETREX CORPORATION (DH)
Also Called: Research Technologies Intl
1000 Belt Line Ave (44109-2848)
P.O. Box 5111, Southfield MI (48086-5111)
PHONE..................................216 749-2605
Thomas E Mark, *President*
Robert M Currie, *Vice Pres*
◆ EMP: 10 EST: 1920
SQ FT: 5,000
SALES (est): 65.9MM
SALES (corp-wide): 571K **Privately Held**
WEB: www.detrex.com
SIC: 2819 3589 Inorganic acids, except nitric & phosphoric; commercial cleaning equipment
HQ: Italmatch Chemicals Spa
    Via Magazzini Del Cotone 17 Modulo 4
    Genova GE 16128
    010 642-081

(G-5088)
DI LORIO SHEET METAL INC
5002 Clark Ave (44102-4552)
PHONE..................................216 961-3703
Anthony Di Lorio, *President*
Anna Di Lorio, *Corp Secy*
Antonio Di lorio, *Manager*
EMP: 12
SQ FT: 34,000
SALES (est): 1.7MM **Privately Held**
SIC: 3444 Sheet metalwork

(G-5089)
DIAMOND HARD CHROME CO INC
6110 Grand Ave (44104-3955)
PHONE..................................216 391-3618
John R Tankovich, *President*
Robert Tankovich, *President*
EMP: 13
SQ FT: 45,000
SALES (est): 1.2MM **Privately Held**
SIC: 3471 Chromium plating of metals or formed products

(G-5090)
DIAMOND WELDING CO INC
11030 Briggs Rd (44111-5334)
PHONE..................................216 251-1679
Michael D Janosko, *President*
EMP: 4
SQ FT: 6,000
SALES: 245K **Privately Held**
SIC: 7692 Welding repair

(G-5091)
DIASCOPIC LLC
16173 Clevidien Rd (44112-3601)
P.O. Box 20701, Columbus (43220-0701)
PHONE..................................312 282-1800
Cary Serif, *Chairman*
EMP: 3
SALES: 25K **Privately Held**
SIC: 3826 Analytical instruments

(G-5092)
DIASOME PHARMACEUTICALS INC
10000 Cedar Ave Ste 6 (44106-2119)
PHONE..................................216 444-7110
Robert Geho, *CEO*
EMP: 7
SALES (est): 762.9K **Privately Held**
SIC: 2834 Pharmaceutical preparations

(G-5093)
DIE SERVICES LTD
9200 Inman Ave (44105-2110)
PHONE..................................216 883-5800
Kenneth Raftery, *President*
EMP: 4
SALES (est): 568.8K **Privately Held**
SIC: 3312 Tool & die steel

(G-5094)
DIE-CUT PRODUCTS CO
Also Called: D C
1801 E 30th St (44114-4471)
PHONE..................................216 771-6994
Steve A Comet, *President*
Arlene R Comet, *Treasurer*
Beth Comet, *Human Resources*
EMP: 22
SQ FT: 10,600
SALES (est): 4MM **Privately Held**
WEB: www.diecut.com
SIC: 3069 3452 3053 3499 Washers, rubber; washers; gaskets, packing & sealing devices; gaskets & sealing devices; shims, metal; sheet metalwork

(G-5095)
DIETRICH INDUSTRIES INC
818 E 73rd St (44103-1708)
PHONE..................................216 472-1511
Libby Noce, *Manager*
EMP: 51
SALES (corp-wide): 3.5B **Publicly Held**
WEB: www.dietrichmetalframing.com
SIC: 3441 Building components, structural steel
HQ: Dietrich Industries, Inc.
    200 W Wlson Bridge Rd
    Worthington OH 43085
    800 873-2604

(G-5096)
DING PRODUCTS
Also Called: D'Ing Meeting Room Products
5695 Cherokee Dr (44124-3047)
PHONE..................................440 442-7777
John Selvaggio, *Owner*
Anna Selvaggio, *Owner*
EMP: 8
SALES: 250K **Privately Held**
SIC: 2521 3651 Wood office furniture; household audio & video equipment

(G-5097)
DIRECTCONNECTGROUP LTD
Also Called: D C G
5501 Cass Ave (44102-2121)
PHONE..................................216 281-2866
Robert A Durham, *Partner*
Brad Clarke, *Partner*

▲ = Import ▼ = Export
◆ = Import/Export

GEOGRAPHIC SECTION

Cleveland - Cuyahoga County (G-5125)

Scott L Durham, *Partner*
Tammy Peniston, *Partner*
James E Pinkin, *Partner*
EMP: 525
SALES (est): 34.2MM **Privately Held**
WEB: www.dcgrp.net
SIC: 2752 7331 Commercial printing, lithographic; mailing service

(G-5098)
DISTILLATA COMPANY (PA)
1608 E 24th St (44114-4212)
P.O. Box 93845 (44101-5845)
PHONE..................................216 771-2900
William E Schroeder, *President*
Dalphne Axline, *Principal*
R M Egan, *Principal*
J C Little, *Principal*
Herbert Buckman, *Corp Secy*
EMP: 70 **EST:** 1897
SQ FT: 100,000
SALES (est): 15.9MM **Privately Held**
WEB: www.distillata.com
SIC: 2899 5149 Distilled water; mineral or spring water bottling

(G-5099)
DISTRIBUTOR GRAPHICS INC
6909 Engle Rd Ste 13 (44130-3484)
PHONE..................................440 260-0024
Richard Doerr, *President*
James F Gottschalk, *Vice Pres*
Robert Wilson, *Treasurer*
EMP: 8
SQ FT: 8,500
SALES: 725K **Privately Held**
SIC: 2752 Commercial printing, offset

(G-5100)
DIVERSIFIED MOLD CASTINGS LLC
Also Called: Diversified Mold & Castings Co
19800 Miles Rd (44128-4118)
PHONE..................................216 663-1814
Vince Costello, *Principal*
Kenneth Dorsey, *Controller*
Jim Henry, *Sales Staff*
Tony Short, *Manager*
EMP: 37
SALES (est): 6.5MM **Privately Held**
SIC: 3544 Industrial molds

(G-5101)
DLA DOCUMENT SERVICES
1240 E 9th St Rm B31 (44199-9904)
PHONE..................................216 522-3535
Craig White, *Manager*
EMP: 5 **Publicly Held**
SIC: 2752 9711 Commercial printing, lithographic; national security
HQ: Dla Document Services
5450 Carlisle Pike Bldg 9
Mechanicsburg PA 17050
717 605-2362

(G-5102)
DOAN/PYRAMID SOLUTIONS LLC
5069 Corbin Dr (44128-5413)
PHONE..................................216 587-9510
Lenny Heiser,
Peter Appler,
EMP: 11
SALES (est): 2.3MM **Privately Held**
SIC: 3822 Auto controls regulating residntl & coml environmt & applncs

(G-5103)
DOG DAILY
1180 Blanchester Rd (44124-1360)
PHONE..................................216 624-0375
Talun Thomas, *Principal*
EMP: 3
SALES (est): 143K **Privately Held**
SIC: 2711 Newspapers, publishing & printing

(G-5104)
DOMESTIC OIL & GAS CO INC
19600 Rockside Rd (44146-2079)
PHONE..................................440 232-3150
Glenn Siegler, *President*
Randall Matheny, *Admin Sec*
EMP: 3
SQ FT: 2,000
SALES (est): 279.6K **Privately Held**
SIC: 1381 Drilling oil & gas wells

(G-5105)
DOMINION ENTERPRISES
26301 Curtiss Wright Pkwy (44143-4413)
PHONE..................................216 472-1870
Michelle Dubblestyne, *Principal*
EMP: 21 **Privately Held**
WEB: www.traderonline.com
SIC: 2721 Periodicals
HQ: Dominion Enterprises
150 Granby St
Norfolk VA 23510
757 351-7000

(G-5106)
DOMINO FOODS INC
Also Called: Domino Sugar
2075 E 65th St (44103-4630)
PHONE..................................216 432-3222
Darrell Lubinsky, *Vice Pres*
Jeffrey Bender, *Branch Mgr*
EMP: 70
SALES (corp-wide): 2B **Privately Held**
WEB: www.dominospecialtyingredients.com
SIC: 2099 7389 Sugar; packaging & labeling services
HQ: Domino Foods Inc.
99 Wood Ave S Ste 901
Iselin NJ 08830
732 590-1173

(G-5107)
DONE RIGHT ENGINE & MACHINE
12955 York Delta Dr Ste J (44133-3550)
PHONE..................................440 582-1366
Rita Yanus, *President*
Richard Yanus, *Vice Pres*
EMP: 4
SQ FT: 3,000
SALES: 400K **Privately Held**
SIC: 7538 3714 Engine rebuilding: automotive; cylinder heads, motor vehicle

(G-5108)
DONNELLEY FINANCIAL LLC
1300 E 9th St Ste 1200 (44114-1513)
PHONE..................................216 621-8384
Andrew Komer, *Manager*
EMP: 13
SALES (corp-wide): 963MM **Publicly Held**
SIC: 2752 Commercial printing, offset
HQ: Donnelley Financial, Llc
55 Water St Fl 11
New York NY 10041
212 425-0298

(G-5109)
DOVE DIE AND STAMPING COMPANY
15665 Brookpark Rd (44142-1668)
PHONE..................................216 267-3720
Gerald Wagner, *President*
Norma Wagner, *Corp Secy*
EMP: 45 **EST:** 1952
SQ FT: 42,000
SALES (est): 14.6MM **Privately Held**
WEB: www.dovedie.com
SIC: 3469 3544 Stamping metal for the trade; special dies & tools

(G-5110)
DOVE GRAPHICS INC
13500 Pearl Rd (44136-3400)
PHONE..................................440 238-1800
EMP: 4 **EST:** 1982
SQ FT: 800
SALES: 80K **Privately Held**
SIC: 2752 Lithographic Commercial Printing

(G-5111)
DOYLE SAILMAKER
805 E 185th St (44119-2701)
PHONE..................................216 486-5732
Greg Koski, *Owner*
Doyle Sailmaker, *Owner*
EMP: 5
SALES (est): 441.1K **Privately Held**
SIC: 3732 Sailboats, building & repairing

(G-5112)
DRABIK MANUFACTURING INC
15601 Commerce Park Dr (44142-2016)
PHONE..................................216 267-1616
James Drabik, *President*
Cathy Prest, *Purchasing*
Deb Arida, *QC Mgr*
Jim Drabik, *Finance*
EMP: 17
SQ FT: 13,000
SALES (est): 3MM **Privately Held**
WEB: www.drabikinc.com
SIC: 3599 7692 Machine shop, jobbing & repair; welding repair

(G-5113)
DREISON INTERNATIONAL INC (PA)
4540 W 160th St (44135-2628)
PHONE..................................216 362-0755
Theodore J Berger Sr, *Ch of Bd*
Theodore Berger Jr, *President*
Marilyn J Berger, *Corp Secy*
Joe Rivera, *QC Mgr*
Whitney Slaght, *CFO*
▲ **EMP:** 190
SQ FT: 210,000
SALES (est): 49.2MM **Privately Held**
WEB: www.dreison.com
SIC: 3714 3643 3621 3561 Mufflers (exhaust), motor vehicle; current-carrying wiring devices; motors, electric; pumps & pumping equipment; purification & dust collection equipment

(G-5114)
DRG HYDRAULICS INC
18200 S Miles Rd (44128-4232)
PHONE..................................216 663-9747
Don I Stetner, *President*
Mary Wise, *General Mgr*
Scott Payne, *Plant Mgr*
Tammy Johns, *Purch Mgr*
▲ **EMP:** 35
SQ FT: 35,000
SALES (est): 7.4MM **Privately Held**
SIC: 3542 3559 Presses: hydraulic & pneumatic, mechanical & manual; plastics working machinery

(G-5115)
DUBLIN PLASTICS INC
9202 Reno Ave (44105-2125)
PHONE..................................216 641-5904
Donald R Newman, *President*
James Newman, *Admin Sec*
EMP: 8
SALES: 2MM **Privately Held**
SIC: 3089 Injection molding of plastics

(G-5116)
DUCT FABRICATORS INC
Also Called: Fab3 Group
883 Addison Rd (44103-1607)
PHONE..................................216 391-2400
John Sickle, *Principal*
Steven Haydu, *Principal*
EMP: 8
SALES (est): 1.5MM **Privately Held**
SIC: 3444 Sheet metalwork

(G-5117)
DUCTS INC
883 Addison Rd (44103-1607)
PHONE..................................216 391-2400
Patricia Sickle Mc Elroy, *CEO*
John E Sickle Jr, *President*
Charlotte Sickle, *Chairman*
James Sickle, *Vice Pres*
EMP: 50
SQ FT: 30,000
SALES (est): 3.1MM **Privately Held**
SIC: 1761 3444 Sheet metalwork; sheet metalwork

(G-5118)
DULCELICIOUS CUPCAKES AND MORE
22368 Lorain Rd (44126-2208)
PHONE..................................440 385-7706
EMP: 4
SALES (est): 268.5K **Privately Held**
SIC: 2051 Mfg Bread/Related Products

(G-5119)
DUNECRAFT INC
19201 Cranwood Pkwy (44128-4043)
P.O. Box 808, Chagrin Falls (44022-0808)
PHONE..................................800 306-4168
Grant Cleveland, *President*
▲ **EMP:** 24
SALES (est): 5.6MM **Privately Held**
WEB: www.dunecraft.com
SIC: 3944 Science kits: microscopes, chemistry sets, etc.

(G-5120)
DUPONT SPECIALTY PDTS USA LLC
Also Called: Dupont Vespel Parts and Shapes
6200 Hillcrest Dr (44125-4624)
PHONE..................................216 901-3600
Anthony Adetayo, *Branch Mgr*
EMP: 118
SALES (corp-wide): 85.9B **Publicly Held**
WEB: www.dupont.com
SIC: 3366 3568 Bushings & bearings; power transmission equipment
HQ: Dupont Specialty Products Usa, Llc
2030 Dow Ctr
Midland MI 48674
989 636-1000

(G-5121)
DURABLE PLATING CO
4404 Saint Clair Ave (44103-1188)
PHONE..................................216 391-2132
Joe Akers, *President*
Tim Akers, *Vice Pres*
Shirley Akers, *Admin Sec*
EMP: 7 **EST:** 1935
SQ FT: 6,500
SALES: 850K **Privately Held**
SIC: 3471 Plating of metals or formed products

(G-5122)
DURAY PLATING COMPANY INC
13701 Triskett Rd (44111-1520)
PHONE..................................216 941-5540
Kenneth R Roth, *President*
Jeff Roth, *General Mgr*
Bruce G Roth, *Sales Mgr*
Bruce Roth, *Manager*
Ellie Yanky, *Director*
EMP: 25
SQ FT: 6,000
SALES (est): 1MM **Privately Held**
WEB: www.durayplatingco.com
SIC: 3471 Electroplating of metals or formed products; chromium plating of metals or formed products

(G-5123)
DURISEK ENTERPRISES INC
Also Called: Midwest Welding & Boiler Co
5200 Train Ave (44102-4525)
PHONE..................................216 281-3898
George R Durisek Sr, *President*
George R Durisek Jr, *Vice Pres*
Caroline Durisek, *Admin Sec*
EMP: 4
SQ FT: 2,800
SALES (est): 432.7K **Privately Held**
SIC: 7692 Welding repair

(G-5124)
DVUV LLC
4641 Hinckley Indus Pkwy (44109-6002)
PHONE..................................216 741-5511
Michael Knoblauch,
▼ **EMP:** 15
SQ FT: 20,000
SALES (est): 2.2MM **Privately Held**
SIC: 2521 Wood office furniture

(G-5125)
DYNAMIC TOOL & MOLD INC
12126 York Rd Unit N (44133-3688)
PHONE..................................440 237-8665
Dale English, *President*
John Getchell, *Vice Pres*
EMP: 7
SQ FT: 3,500
SALES (est): 1.1MM **Privately Held**
SIC: 3544 Industrial molds

Cleveland - Cuyahoga County (G-5126)

(G-5126)
E & E MOLD & DIE INC
4605 Manufacturing Ave (44135-2637)
PHONE 216 898-5853
Michael Saintz, *President*
Troy Beahr, *Vice Pres*
EMP: 6
SQ FT: 10,000
SALES (est): 693.1K **Privately Held**
SIC: 3544 Dies & die holders for metal cutting, forming, die casting; dies, plastics forming

(G-5127)
E & K PRODUCTS CO INC
3520 Cesko Ave (44109-1487)
PHONE 216 631-2510
Lee Klimek, *President*
David Klimek, *Vice Pres*
Joyce Klimek, *Admin Sec*
EMP: 8 EST: 1966
SQ FT: 25,000
SALES: 440K **Privately Held**
SIC: 3599 3444 Machine shop, jobbing & repair; sheet metalwork

(G-5128)
E B P INC
Also Called: Epic Steel
2041 W 17th St (44113-3579)
PHONE 216 241-2550
Dan Fremont, *President*
Arthur M Hemlock, *Principal*
Robert M Lustig, *Principal*
Neff Fremont, *Vice Pres*
Mark Fremont, *Admin Sec*
EMP: 29
SQ FT: 53,500
SALES: 6.5MM **Privately Held**
WEB: www.epicsteel.com
SIC: 3441 3446 3444 Fabricated structural metal; architectural metalwork; railings, bannisters, guards, etc.: made from metal pipe; stairs, staircases, stair treads: prefabricated metal; sheet metalwork

(G-5129)
E D M FASTAR INC
13410 Enterprise Ave (44135-5162)
PHONE 216 676-0100
Frank Star, *President*
EMP: 7 EST: 1999
SQ FT: 3,000
SALES (est): 906.5K **Privately Held**
SIC: 3544 Special dies & tools

(G-5130)
E POMPILI & SONS INC
Also Called: Pompili Precast Concrete
12307 Broadway Ave (44125-1847)
PHONE 216 581-8080
William Pompili, *President*
EMP: 8
SQ FT: 14,500
SALES (est): 810K **Privately Held**
WEB: www.pompiliprecastconcrete.com
SIC: 3272 Concrete products, precast

(G-5131)
E T & K INC
Also Called: American Speedy Printing
9809 Running Brook Dr (44130-8217)
PHONE 440 888-4780
Edward Scully, *President*
Theresa Scully, *Corp Secy*
EMP: 3
SALES (est): 153.1K **Privately Held**
SIC: 2752 Commercial printing, offset

(G-5132)
E-Z ELECTRIC MOTOR SVC CORP
8510 Bessemer Ave (44127-1843)
PHONE 216 581-8820
Demetrius Ledgyard, *President*
EMP: 13
SQ FT: 15,000
SALES (est): 746K **Privately Held**
SIC: 7694 Electric motor repair

(G-5133)
EADHERE SOLUTIONS LLC (PA)
6815 Euclid Ave (44103-3915)
PHONE 216 372-6009
Tasheika Johnson, *CEO*
EMP: 5
SALES: 100K **Privately Held**
SIC: 7372 Application computer software

(G-5134)
EAGLE ADVERTISING
4101 Commerce Ave (44103-3507)
PHONE 216 881-0800
Thomas M Baginski, *Owner*
EMP: 4
SALES (est): 240K **Privately Held**
SIC: 2752 5999 Offset & photolithographic printing; banners, flags, decals & posters

(G-5135)
EAGLE TOOL & DIE INC
10805 Briggs Rd (44111-5331)
PHONE 216 671-5055
Miroslaw Zebrowski, *President*
EMP: 3
SQ FT: 3,300
SALES: 200K **Privately Held**
SIC: 3544 Special dies & tools

(G-5136)
EAGLE WIRE WORKS INC
3173 E 66th St Fl 3 (44127-1404)
PHONE 216 341-8550
Fax: 216 341-6460
EMP: 10 EST: 1896
SQ FT: 30,000
SALES: 676.1K **Privately Held**
SIC: 3496 Mfg Misc Fabricated Wire Products

(G-5137)
EAST CLEVELAND RUBBER STAMP
16501 Euclid Ave (44112-1403)
PHONE 216 851-5050
Harold Stern, *President*
EMP: 3
SQ FT: 4,044
SALES (est): 330.7K **Privately Held**
SIC: 3953 Marking devices

(G-5138)
EAST WEST COPOLYMER & RBR LLC
28026 Gates Mills Blvd (44124-4730)
PHONE 225 267-3713
Gregory Nelson, *President*
Greg Nelson, *CEO*
Bob Baxter, *Vice Pres*
Dana Coody, *Vice Pres*
Bobby Rikhoff, *Vice Pres*
EMP: 10
SALES (est): 1.5MM **Privately Held**
SIC: 2822 Ethylene-propylene rubbers, EPDM polymers

(G-5139)
EAST WEST COPOLYMER LLC
28026 Gates Mills Blvd (44124-4730)
PHONE 225 267-3400
Patrick Bowers, *Vice Pres*
Dana Coody, *Vice Pres*
Bobby Rikhoff, *Vice Pres*
Celso Goncalves, *CFO*
Gregory Nelson,
▲ EMP: 153
SALES (est): 103.9MM **Privately Held**
SIC: 2822 Synthetic rubber

(G-5140)
EAST WOODWORKING COMPANY
2044 Random Rd (44106-2320)
P.O. Box 221185, Beachwood (44122-0995)
PHONE 216 791-5950
Zigmund T Hersh, *President*
Albert Hersh, *Vice Pres*
Coby Hersh, *Manager*
Ken Hersh, *Manager*
EMP: 8 EST: 1956
SQ FT: 12,400
SALES: 1.5MM **Privately Held**
WEB: www.eastwoodworking.com
SIC: 1751 2521 2522 3261 Cabinet building & installation; cabinets, office: wood; office cabinets & filing drawers: except wood; vitreous plumbing fixtures

(G-5141)
EASTWORD PUBLICATIONS DEV
Also Called: Lincoln Library Press
812 Huron Rd E Ste 401 (44115-1172)
PHONE 216 781-9594
Timothy Gall, *President*
Susan Bevan-Gall, *Vice Pres*
EMP: 5
SQ FT: 900
SALES (est): 23.8K **Privately Held**
WEB: www.thelincnlibrary.com
SIC: 2731 Book publishing

(G-5142)
EASY SIDE PUBLISHING CO INC
Also Called: Eastside Daily News
11400 Woodland Ave (44104-2636)
PHONE 216 721-1674
Ulysses Glenn, *President*
EMP: 5
SQ FT: 1,311
SALES: 150K **Privately Held**
SIC: 2711 Newspapers: publishing only, not printed on site

(G-5143)
EATON AEROQUIP LLC (DH)
Also Called: Eaton Global Hose
1000 Eaton Blvd (44122-6058)
PHONE 216 523-5000
Alexander M Cutler, *CEO*
Adam Bloch, *General Mgr*
E R Franklin, *Vice Pres*
Dan Roth, *Manager*
◆ EMP: 220 EST: 1940
SQ FT: 21,000
SALES (est): 1.1B **Privately Held**
SIC: 3052 3492 3429 3069 Rubber hose; plastic hose; hose & tube fittings & assemblies, hydraulic/pneumatic; clamps & couplings, hose; clamps, metal; molded rubber products; parts for heating, cooling & refrigerating equipment; aircraft parts & equipment
HQ: Aeroquip-Vickers, Inc.
  1111 Superior Ave E
  Cleveland OH 44114
  216 523-5000

(G-5144)
EATON AEROSPACE LLC (DH)
Also Called: E E M C O
1000 Eaton Blvd (44122-6058)
PHONE 216 523-5000
Alexander M Cutler, *CEO*
Seung OH, *Senior Buyer*
R H Fearon, *CFO*
Nathan Eldredge, *Manager*
▲ EMP: 10
SALES (est): 266.8MM **Privately Held**
SIC: 3812 Acceleration indicators & systems components, aerospace
HQ: Eaton Hydraulics Llc
  14615 Lone Oak Rd
  Eden Prairie MN 55344
  952 937-9800

(G-5145)
EATON AEROSPACE LLC
2000 Apollo Dr (44142-4102)
P.O. Box 818025 (44181-8025)
PHONE 216 523-5000
EMP: 25 **Privately Held**
SIC: 3812 Acceleration indicators & systems components, aerospace
HQ: Eaton Aerospace Llc
  1000 Eaton Blvd
  Cleveland OH 44122
  216 523-5000

(G-5146)
EATON CORPORATION (HQ)
1000 Eaton Blvd (44122-6058)
PHONE 440 523-5000
Craig Arnold, *Ch of Bd*
Nitin Chalke, *Managing Dir*
Revathi Advaithi, *COO*
Mark McGuire, *Exec VP*
Donald Bullock, *Senior VP*
◆ EMP: 450
SALES: 6.6B **Privately Held**
WEB: www.eaton.com
SIC: 3625 3714 3594 3559 Motor controls & accessories; motor starters & controllers, electric; actuators, industrial; motor vehicle engines & parts; motor vehicle transmissions, drive assemblies & parts; motor vehicle steering systems & parts; pumps, hydraulic power transfer; motors: hydraulic, fluid power or air; semiconductor manufacturing machinery; personal computers (microcomputers)

(G-5147)
EATON CORPORATION
Airflex Div
9919 Clinton Rd (44144-1077)
PHONE 216 281-2211
Greg Lutzweiler, *Mfg Staff*
Tim Gufreda, *Design Engr*
Jeff Fobes, *Marketing Staff*
James W Fisher, *Branch Mgr*
Bethany Bocan, *Manager*
EMP: 200 **Privately Held**
WEB: www.eaton.com
SIC: 3714 3625 3542 3568 Air brakes, motor vehicle; transmission housings or parts, motor vehicle; clutches, motor vehicle; electromagnetic clutches or brakes; brakes, metal forming; clutches, except vehicular
HQ: Eaton Corporation
  1000 Eaton Blvd
  Cleveland OH 44122
  440 523-5000

(G-5148)
EATON CORPORATION
6055 Rckside Woods Blvd N (44131-2301)
P.O. Box 818028 (44181-8028)
PHONE 888 328-6677
EMP: 217 **Privately Held**
WEB: www.eaton.com
SIC: 3625 Motor controls & accessories
HQ: Eaton Corporation
  1000 Eaton Blvd
  Cleveland OH 44122
  440 523-5000

(G-5149)
EATON CORPORATION
Eaton Family Credit Union
333 Babbitt Rd Ste 100 (44123-1636)
PHONE 216 920-2000
Michael Losneck, *Branch Mgr*
EMP: 260 **Privately Held**
WEB: www.eaton.com
SIC: 3714 5084 Hydraulic fluid power pumps for auto steering mechanism; hydraulic systems equipment & supplies
HQ: Eaton Corporation
  1000 Eaton Blvd
  Cleveland OH 44122
  440 523-5000

(G-5150)
EATON CORPORATION
Also Called: NA Financial Service Center
6055 Rckside Woods Blvd N (44131-2301)
P.O. Box 818035 (44181-8035)
PHONE 440 826-1115
A Valore, *Manager*
EMP: 217 **Privately Held**
WEB: www.eaton.com
SIC: 3625 Relays & industrial controls
HQ: Eaton Corporation
  1000 Eaton Blvd
  Cleveland OH 44122
  440 523-5000

(G-5151)
EATON ELECTRIC HOLDINGS LLC (HQ)
1000 Eaton Blvd (44122-6058)
PHONE 440 523-5000
Kirk Hachigian, *President*
Bruce M Taten, *Senior VP*
David Barta, *CFO*
Tyler Johnson, *Treasurer*
▲ EMP: 277

GEOGRAPHIC SECTION
Cleveland - Cuyahoga County (G-5176)

SALES (est): 3.7B Privately Held
WEB: www.cooperus.com
SIC: 3612 3613 3644 3536 Transformers, except electric; power & distribution transformers; power transformers, electric; voltage regulators, transmission & distribution; panel & distribution boards & other related apparatus; power circuit breakers; switches, electric power except snap, push button, etc.; fuses & fuse equipment; noncurrent-carrying wiring services; electric outlet, switch & fuse boxes; electric conduits & fittings; hoists, cranes & monorails; hoists; hand & edge tools; wrenches, hand tools; hammers (hand tools); soldering tools; ceiling systems, luminous

(G-5152)
EATON INDUSTRIAL CORPORATION (HQ)
23555 Euclid Ave (44117-1703)
PHONE.................................216 523-4205
Craig Arnold, *CEO*
Paul R Keen, *Exec VP*
Earl R Franklin, *Vice Pres*
John S Glover, *CFO*
Ryan Duran, *Technology*
EMP: 433
SQ FT: 1,800,000
SALES (est): 82.2MM Privately Held
WEB: www.atclabs.com
SIC: 3724 3728 Pumps, aircraft engine; aircraft parts & equipment

(G-5153)
EATON USEV HOLDING COMPANY (DH)
1111 Suprr Eatn Ctr 173 (44114)
PHONE.................................216 523-5000
Alexander M Cutler, *CEO*
EMP: 7
SALES (est): 94.5MM Privately Held
SIC: 3592 Valves, engine
HQ: Eaton Corporation
1000 Eaton Blvd
Cleveland OH 44122
440 523-5000

(G-5154)
EBONI CORNER
1780 S Belvoir Blvd (44121-3745)
P.O. Box 116, Venetia PA (15367-0116)
PHONE.................................724 518-3065
Gwen Hawkins, *President*
Arthur J Hawkins Jr, *Admin Sec*
EMP: 5
SALES: 250K Privately Held
SIC: 3942 Dolls, except stuffed toy animals

(G-5155)
ECONOMY STRAIGHTENING SERVICE
896 E 70th St (44103-1706)
PHONE.................................216 432-4410
Charles Triplett, *President*
Bob Solinski, *Vice Pres*
EMP: 5
SQ FT: 3,000
SALES (est): 510K Privately Held
SIC: 3356 Nonferrous rolling & drawing

(G-5156)
ECOWISE LLC
Also Called: Natgascar
17000 Saint Clair Ave (44110-2535)
PHONE.................................216 692-3700
Bradley Trembath, *President*
EMP: 5
SALES (est): 1.1MM Privately Held
SIC: 3563 Air & gas compressors

(G-5157)
EDGE-RITE TOOLS INC
7700 Exchange St (44125-3310)
PHONE.................................216 642-0966
John Kaput, *President*
EMP: 14
SQ FT: 3,000
SALES (est): 1.8MM Privately Held
SIC: 3544 3545 Special dies, tools, jigs & fixtures; cutting tools for machine tools

(G-5158)
EG ENTERPRISE SERVICES INC
5000 Euclid Ave Ste 100 (44103-3752)
P.O. Box 18029 (44118-0029)
PHONE.................................216 431-3300
Fax: 216 431-1050
EMP: 12 **EST:** 1993
SQ FT: 10,000
SALES (est): 950K Privately Held
SIC: 2752 7331 7334 Commercial Offset Printing

(G-5159)
EJ USA INC
4160 Glenridge Rd (44121-2802)
PHONE.................................216 692-3001
Richard Humkes Jr, *Manager*
EMP: 25
SQ FT: 11,397 Privately Held
WEB: www.ejiw.com
SIC: 3321 3322 Gray iron castings; malleable iron foundries
HQ: Ej Usa, Inc.
301 Spring St
East Jordan MI 49727
800 874-4100

(G-5160)
ELCO CORPORATION (DH)
1000 Belt Line Ave (44109-2800)
PHONE.................................800 321-0467
Dave Millin, *CEO*
Bob Lunoe, *Vice Pres*
▼ **EMP:** 61 **EST:** 1929
SQ FT: 72,000
SALES (est): 17.4MM
SALES (corp-wide): 571K Privately Held
WEB: www.elcocorp.com
SIC: 2869 Industrial organic chemicals
HQ: Detrex Corporation
1000 Belt Line Ave
Cleveland OH 44109
216 749-2605

(G-5161)
ELECTRIC CORD SETS INC (PA)
Also Called: Happy Trails Rv
4700 Manufacturing Ave (44135-2640)
PHONE.................................216 261-1000
Thomas Benbow, *Ch of Bd*
Edward Benbow, *Vice Pres*
Cathy Gilmour, *Treasurer*
▲ **EMP:** 6
SQ FT: 3,500
SALES (est): 14.8MM Privately Held
WEB: www.elecordset.com
SIC: 3643 Current-carrying wiring devices

(G-5162)
ELECTRIC CTRL & MTR REPR SVC
6717 Saint Clair Ave (44103-1743)
PHONE.................................216 881-3143
Leslie Imeli, *President*
Zoltan Imeli, *Vice Pres*
EMP: 4
SQ FT: 1,500
SALES: 115K Privately Held
SIC: 7694 1731 Electric motor repair; rebuilding motors, except automotive; electrical work

(G-5163)
ELECTRIC SPEED INDICATOR CO
12234 Triskett Rd (44111-2519)
PHONE.................................216 251-2540
Robert P Riley, *President*
EMP: 10 **EST:** 1934
SQ FT: 4,000
SALES (est): 1.3MM Privately Held
WEB: www.electricspeedindicator.com
SIC: 3829 7699 Geophysical & meteorological testing equipment; meteorological instruments; meteorological instrument repair

(G-5164)
ELECTRO-MAGWAVE INC
Also Called: E M Wave
6111 Carey Dr Ste 1 (44125-4274)
PHONE.................................216 453-1160
Frank Kim Goryance, *President*
Robert Truthan, *Vice Pres*
Anthony Zupancic, *Vice Pres*
Tony Zupancic, *Manager*
EMP: 7
SQ FT: 6,300
SALES (est): 1.1MM Privately Held
SIC: 3663 Antennas, transmitting & communications

(G-5165)
ELECTROLIZING CORPORATION OHIO (PA)
1325 E 152nd St (44112-2075)
P.O. Box 12007 (44112-0007)
PHONE.................................216 451-3153
Lawrence E Noble, *President*
Scott Noble, *Exec VP*
Todd Noble, *Vice Pres*
EMP: 20 **EST:** 1948
SQ FT: 20,000
SALES (est): 3.6MM Privately Held
WEB: www.electrohio.com
SIC: 3471 Anodizing (plating) of metals or formed products

(G-5166)
ELECTROLIZING CORPORATION OHIO
1655 Collamer Ave (44110-3201)
PHONE.................................216 451-8653
Daral Cook, *Manager*
EMP: 10
SQ FT: 12,342
SALES (corp-wide): 3.6MM Privately Held
WEB: www.electrohio.com
SIC: 3471 Anodizing (plating) of metals or formed products
PA: Electrolizing Corporation Of Ohio
1325 E 152nd St
Cleveland OH 44112
216 451-3153

(G-5167)
ELECTROLUX PROFESSIONAL INC (DH)
20445 Emerald Pkwy (44135-6009)
P.O. Box 35920 (44135-0920)
PHONE.................................216 898-1800
George C Weigand, *President*
Richard S Pietch, *Senior VP*
Ronald E Zajaczkowski, *Senior VP*
Mark W Russell, *Vice Pres*
Marie-Louise Wingard, *Treasurer*
◆ **EMP:** 25
SALES (est): 23.8MM
SALES (corp-wide): 14.4B Privately Held
WEB: www.electroluxprofessional.com
SIC: 3585 Air conditioning units, complete: domestic or industrial
HQ: Electrolux North America, Inc.
10200 David Taylor Dr
Charlotte NC 28262
980 236-2000

(G-5168)
ELGIN FASTENER GROUP LLC
Chandler Products
1491 Chardon Rd (44117-1510)
PHONE.................................216 481-4400
Gary Walston, *Manager*
EMP: 38
SALES (corp-wide): 70MM Privately Held
SIC: 3452 3451 3316 Bolts, nuts, rivets & washers; screw machine products; cold finishing of steel shapes
HQ: Elgin Fastener Group, Llc
10217 Brecksville Rd # 101
Brecksville OH 44141

(G-5169)
ELLWOOD GROUP INC
Also Called: Elwood Crankshaft Group
777 E 79th St (44103-1805)
PHONE.................................216 862-6341
EMP: 5
SALES (corp-wide): 775.5MM Privately Held
SIC: 3599 Crankshafts & camshafts, machining
PA: Ellwood Group, Inc.
600 Commercial Ave
Ellwood City PA 16117
724 752-3680

(G-5170)
EM ES BE COMPANY LLC
Also Called: M.S. Barkin Company
246 E 131st St Ste 2 (44108-1646)
PHONE.................................216 761-9500
Moshe R Barkin, *Mng Member*
EMP: 8
SQ FT: 2,500
SALES (est): 842.9K Privately Held
WEB: www.msbarkinco.com
SIC: 3911 5944 Jewelry, precious metal; jewelry, precious stones & precious metals

(G-5171)
EMBROID ME
4311 Ridge Rd (44144-2714)
PHONE.................................216 459-9250
Ken Grodek, *Owner*
EMP: 3
SALES (est): 284.1K Privately Held
SIC: 2395 Embroidery products, except schiffli machine; embroidery & art needlework

(G-5172)
EMMCO INC
4540 E 71st St (44105-5604)
PHONE.................................216 429-2020
Eugene Mitocky, *President*
Loreen Mitocky, *Treasurer*
EMP: 6
SQ FT: 7,500
SALES: 815K Privately Held
WEB: www.emmcoinc.net
SIC: 3593 Fluid power cylinders, hydraulic or pneumatic

(G-5173)
EMPIRE BRASS CO
Also Called: American Brass
5000 Superior Ave (44103-1238)
PHONE.................................216 431-6565
Robert Mc Connville, *President*
▲ **EMP:** 50
SALES (est): 6.8MM Privately Held
WEB: www.empirebrassfaucets.com
SIC: 5074 3432 3364 Plumbing fittings & supplies; plumbing fixture fittings & trim; nonferrous die-castings except aluminum

(G-5174)
EMPIRE IRON MINING PARTNERSHIP (PA)
1100 Superior Ave E Fl 15 (44114-2530)
PHONE.................................216 694-5700
David B Blake, *General Mgr*
The Cleveland-Cliffs Iron Comp, *General Ptnr*
Mittal Steel USA, *General Ptnr*
John Cotter, *Controller*
EMP: 1 **EST:** 1959
SALES (est): 84.4MM Privately Held
SIC: 1011 Iron ore mining; iron ore pelletizing; iron ore beneficiating

(G-5175)
EMPIRE PLOW COMPANY INC (DH)
3140 E 65th St (44127-1490)
PHONE.................................216 641-2290
David Pitt, *President*
EMP: 25 **EST:** 1840
SQ FT: 123,000
SALES (est): 19.9MM Privately Held
WEB: www.mckayempire.com
SIC: 3523 3423 Farm machinery & equipment; hand & edge tools
HQ: Ralph Mckay Industries Inc
130 Hodsman Rd
Regina SK S4N 5
306 721-9292

(G-5176)
EMX INDUSTRIES INC
4564 Johnston Pkwy (44128-2953)
PHONE.................................216 518-9888
Joseph Williams, *President*
Bob Hausch, *Vice Pres*
Jeannin Hausch, *Purch Mgr*
Robert Hausch, *Draft/Design*
Lewis David, *Accounts Exec*
▲ **EMP:** 35
SQ FT: 20,000

Cleveland - Cuyahoga County (G-5177)

SALES (est): 8.1MM **Privately Held**
WEB: www.emxinc.com
SIC: 3699 Security control equipment & systems
PA: Watervale Equity Partners Fund I G.P., Llc
    29525 Chagrin Blvd
    Beachwood OH 44122
    216 926-7219

(G-5177)
ENERCO GROUP INC (PA)
Also Called: Mr Heater
4560 W 160th St (44135-2628)
P.O. Box 6660 (44101-1660)
PHONE..................................216 916-3000
Allen Haire, *CEO*
Jeff Bush, *President*
John D Duross, *Vice Pres*
Mark Przypyfz, *Vice Pres*
Brian Vandrak, *Vice Pres*
▲ EMP: 101
SQ FT: 120,875
SALES (est): 36MM **Privately Held**
SIC: 3433 Gas infrared heating units

(G-5178)
ENERCO TECHNICAL PRODUCTS INC
Also Called: Mr. Heater
4560 W 160th St (44135-2628)
P.O. Box 6660 (44101-1660)
PHONE..................................216 916-3000
Allen L Haire, *CEO*
John D Duross, *President*
Carl Meermans, *Vice Pres*
Francis Verchick, *Vice Pres*
Al Haire, *Export Mgr*
▲ EMP: 180
SQ FT: 48,000
SALES (est): 17.8MM
SALES (corp-wide): 36MM **Privately Held**
SIC: 3433 Gas infrared heating units
PA: Enerco Group, Inc.
    4560 W 160th St
    Cleveland OH 44135
    216 916-3000

(G-5179)
ENPROTECH INDUSTRIAL TECH LLC (DH)
4259 E 49th St (44125-1001)
PHONE..................................216 883-3220
Pedro Garcia, *Mng Member*
Ben Handshue, *Sr Project Mgr*
▲ EMP: 210
SQ FT: 96,000
SALES: 75MM
SALES (corp-wide): 51.7B **Privately Held**
WEB: www.itochu.com
SIC: 3547 3365 3599 8711 Rolling mill machinery; machinery castings, aluminum; custom machinery; engineering services; electrical repair shops
HQ: Enprotech Corp.
    4259 E 49th St
    Cleveland OH 44125
    216 206-0080

(G-5180)
ENSIGN PRODUCT COMPANY INC
3528 E 76th St (44105-1510)
P.O. Box 27167 (44127-0167)
PHONE..................................216 341-5911
Birney R Walker III, *President*
Charles Snyder, *Corp Secy*
Christopher Walker, *Vice Pres*
EMP: 6 EST: 1920
SQ FT: 9,000
SALES (est): 1.2MM **Privately Held**
WEB: www.ensignproductsco.com
SIC: 2992 2899 Lubricating oils; chemical preparations

(G-5181)
ENTERPRISE TOOL & DIE COMPANY
4940 Schaaf Ln (44131-1008)
PHONE..................................216 351-1300
Robert C Schweikert, *President*
Todd Schweikert, *Corp Secy*
Richard W Schweikert, *Vice Pres*
EMP: 10 EST: 1954
SQ FT: 10,000
SALES (est): 1.4MM **Privately Held**
WEB: www.enterprisetoolanddie.com
SIC: 3544 Dies & die holders for metal cutting, forming, die casting; special dies & tools

(G-5182)
ENVIROFAB INC
7914 Lake Ave (44102-1992)
PHONE..................................216 651-1767
Thomas J Rusnak, *President*
Richard Rusnak, *Vice Pres*
EMP: 11
SQ FT: 42,000
SALES (est): 2.2MM **Privately Held**
WEB: www.envirofab.com
SIC: 3564 Dust or fume collecting equipment, industrial

(G-5183)
EOS TECHNOLOGY INC
8525 Clinton Rd (44144-1014)
PHONE..................................216 281-2999
John Hadgis, *President*
Gregory Hadgis, *Vice Pres*
EMP: 20
SALES (est): 2.5MM **Privately Held**
SIC: 3599 Machine & other job shop work

(G-5184)
EPD ENTERPRISES INC
9921 Clinton Rd (44144-1035)
PHONE..................................216 961-1200
Edward Durkin, *President*
Robert Myers, *Vice Pres*
EMP: 75
SQ FT: 92,000
SALES (est): 5.7MM **Privately Held**
WEB: www.plasticplaters.com
SIC: 3471 Electroplating of metals or formed products

(G-5185)
EQ TECHNOLOGIES LLC
11601 Wade Park Ave (44106-4403)
PHONE..................................216 548-3684
Michael Schaffer,
EMP: 6
SALES (est): 542.1K **Privately Held**
SIC: 3651 7389 Household audio & video equipment;

(G-5186)
EQUIPMENT MANUFACTURERS INTL
Also Called: E M I
16151 Puritas Ave (44135-2617)
P.O. Box 94725 (44101-4725)
PHONE..................................216 651-6700
Jerry Senk, *Principal*
John Zelli, *Engineer*
R T Mackin, *Treasurer*
Jim Mudri, *Finance Mgr*
Dave Bowman, *Sales Engr*
▲ EMP: 30
SQ FT: 65,000
SALES (est): 10MM **Privately Held**
WEB: www.emi-inc.com
SIC: 3559 5084 Foundry machinery & equipment; industrial machinery & equipment

(G-5187)
EQUIPSYNC LLC
4755 W 150th St (44135-3329)
PHONE..................................216 367-6640
John Kappus, *Partner*
William Cunningham, *Partner*
Fred Kappus, *Partner*
EMP: 3
SQ FT: 14,000
SALES (est): 113.4K **Privately Held**
SIC: 7372 Application computer software

(G-5188)
ERICHAR INC
2051 W Ridgewood Dr (44134-4305)
P.O. Box 311081 (44131-8181)
PHONE..................................216 402-2628
Dana Denallo, *President*
EMP: 3

SALES (est): 348.7K **Privately Held**
SIC: 2411 3999 3589 0851 Wood chips, produced in the field; custom pulverizing & grinding of plastic materials; service industry machinery; forestry services; local trucking, without storage

(G-5189)
ERIE LAKE PLASTIC INC
19940 Ingersoll Dr (44116-1820)
P.O. Box 16924, Rocky River (44116-0924)
PHONE..................................440 333-4880
John Derethik, *President*
EMP: 18
SALES (est): 2.9MM **Privately Held**
WEB: www.lakeerieplastics.com
SIC: 3089 Extruded finished plastic products

(G-5190)
ERIE SHORE MACHINE CO INC
18602 Syracuse Ave (44110-2521)
PHONE..................................216 692-1484
Lawrence G Pinter, *President*
James Pinter, *Vice Pres*
Sarah Pinter, *Admin Sec*
EMP: 6 EST: 1975
SQ FT: 5,000
SALES (est): 702.9K **Privately Held**
WEB: www.erieshoremachine.com
SIC: 3599 Job Machine Shop

(G-5191)
ERIEVIEW METAL TREATING CO
Also Called: Apex Metals
4465 Johnston Pkwy (44128-2998)
PHONE..................................216 663-1780
Alex Kappos, *President*
Dennis Kappos, *Vice Pres*
George Kappos Jr, *CFO*
Skip Harger, *Sales Staff*
Tom Kappos, *Supervisor*
EMP: 100 EST: 1961
SQ FT: 70,000
SALES (est): 14.7MM **Privately Held**
WEB: www.erieview.us
SIC: 3471 Electroplating of metals or formed products

(G-5192)
ESSI ACOUSTICAL PRODUCTS
11750 Berea Rd Ste 1 (44111-1603)
P.O. Box 643 (44107-0943)
PHONE..................................216 251-7888
Mark Essi, *President*
EMP: 10
SQ FT: 6,000
SALES (est): 120.1K **Privately Held**
WEB: www.essiacoustical.com
SIC: 3296 Acoustical board & tile, mineral wool

(G-5193)
EUCLID CHEMICAL COMPANY (DH)
Also Called: Epoxy Chemicals
19218 Redwood Rd (44110-2799)
PHONE..................................800 321-7628
Moorman L Scott Jr, *President*
Nick Adams, *General Mgr*
Carol Rode, *General Mgr*
Mike Cassell, *Regional Mgr*
Matt Hansen, *Regional Mgr*
◆ EMP: 20 EST: 1965
SQ FT: 5,000
SALES: 140.2MM
SALES (corp-wide): 5.3B **Publicly Held**
WEB: www.epoxychemicals.com
SIC: 2899 4213 Chemical preparations; trucking, except local
HQ: Tremco Incorporated
    3735 Green Rd
    Beachwood OH 44122
    216 292-5000

(G-5194)
EUCLID CHEMICAL COMPANY
19218 Redwood Rd (44110-2799)
PHONE..................................216 531-9222
Dave Spivak, *Foreman/Supr*
Wendy Oneal, *Office Mgr*
Glenn Strasshofer, *Branch Mgr*
Robert Scott, *Info Tech Mgr*
EMP: 100
SALES (corp-wide): 5.3B **Publicly Held**
SIC: 2899 Chemical preparations
HQ: The Euclid Chemical Company
    19218 Redwood Rd
    Cleveland OH 44110
    800 321-7628

(G-5195)
EUCLID COFFEE CO INC
17230 S Waterloo Rd (44110-3811)
PHONE..................................216 481-3330
M J Repak, *CEO*
James M Repak, *President*
EMP: 8 EST: 1935
SQ FT: 10,000
SALES (est): 693.7K **Privately Held**
SIC: 2095 Coffee roasting (except by wholesale grocers)

(G-5196)
EUCLID JALOUSIES INC
490 E 200th St (44119-1500)
PHONE..................................440 953-1112
Timothy Huquila, *President*
Bob Dunmire, *Vice Pres*
EMP: 7 EST: 1954
SQ FT: 2,400
SALES (est): 823.6K **Privately Held**
SIC: 3442 5211 Screen & storm doors & windows; windows, storm: wood or metal; doors, storm: wood or metal

(G-5197)
EUCLID MEDIA GROUP LLC (PA)
737 Bolivar Rd (44115-1246)
PHONE..................................216 241-7550
Daniel N Zelman, *Mng Member*
EMP: 29
SALES (est): 3.8MM **Privately Held**
SIC: 2711 Newspapers, publishing & printing

(G-5198)
EUREKA SCREW MACHINE PDTS CO
Also Called: Eureka Screw Machine Co
3960 E 91st St (44105-3964)
PHONE..................................216 883-1715
William Rubick, *President*
Irene Rubick, *Treasurer*
EMP: 6
SQ FT: 5,136
SALES (est): 657.9K **Privately Held**
SIC: 3451 Screw machine products

(G-5199)
EVANDY CO INC
5450 Dunham Rd (44137-3653)
PHONE..................................216 518-9713
Eva Dezsi, *President*
Andras Dezsi, *Vice Pres*
EMP: 5
SQ FT: 6,000
SALES: 400K **Privately Held**
SIC: 3545 Machine tool accessories

(G-5200)
EVEREADY PRINTING INC
Also Called: Weprintquick.com
20700 Miles Pkwy (44128-5506)
PHONE..................................216 587-2389
Roger Wolfson, *President*
Scott Wolfson, *Vice Pres*
EMP: 20 EST: 1905
SALES (est): 3.1MM **Privately Held**
WEB: www.evereadyprint.com
SIC: 2752 Commercial printing, offset

(G-5201)
EVEREADY PRODUCTS CORPORATION
1101 Belt Line Ave (44109-2849)
PHONE..................................216 661-2755
Samuel Vandivort, *Ch of Bd*
Daniel Harrington, *President*
EMP: 14 EST: 1951
SQ FT: 36,000
SALES (est): 4.2MM **Privately Held**
WEB: www.evereadyproducts.com
SIC: 2813 Aerosols

(G-5202)
EVERYKEY INC
12018 Mayfield Rd (44106-1922)
PHONE..................................855 666-5006
Christopher Wentz, *CEO*
EMP: 3

GEOGRAPHIC SECTION
Cleveland - Cuyahoga County (G-5231)

SALES (est): 117K **Privately Held**
SIC: 3699 7389 Security devices;

(G-5203)
EVERYTHING IN AMERICA
Also Called: Eia
4141 Stilmore Rd (44121-3129)
PHONE..................347 871-6872
Patrick Hadley, *Vice Pres*
EMP: 8
SALES (est): 633.8K **Privately Held**
SIC: 5211 2452 7389 Modular homes; modular homes, prefabricated, wood;

(G-5204)
EXACT-TOOL & DIE INC
5425 W 140th St (44142-1704)
PHONE..................216 676-9140
Frank K Chesek, *CEO*
Robert Hickerson, *Business Mgr*
Mark S Klepper, *Vice Pres*
Mark Klepper, *Vice Pres*
John J Melnik, *Vice Pres*
EMP: 35
SQ FT: 60,000
SALES (est): 9.4MM **Privately Held**
WEB: www.exact-tool.com
SIC: 3465 3469 3544 3694 Automotive stampings; metal stampings; special dies, tools, jigs & fixtures; engine electrical equipment

(G-5205)
EXCEL FLUID GROUP LLC
15939 Industrial Pkwy (44135-3321)
PHONE..................800 892-2009
Reginald Wyman, *Mng Member*
Rick Sykora,
EMP: 15
SALES: 6.7MM **Privately Held**
SIC: 3561 Pumps & pumping equipment

(G-5206)
EXCELLENT TOOL & DIE INC
10921 Briggs Rd (44111-5333)
PHONE..................216 671-9222
John Kinsch, *President*
Edith Burnside, *President*
EMP: 6
SQ FT: 4,800
SALES: 400K **Privately Held**
SIC: 3599 Machine shop, jobbing & repair

(G-5207)
EXIKON INDUSTRIES LLC
15215 Chatfield Ave (44111-4306)
PHONE..................216 485-2947
John T Kondilas, *Director*
EMP: 12 EST: 2009
SALES (est): 1.3MM **Privately Held**
SIC: 3999 Barber & beauty shop equipment

(G-5208)
EXPANSION PROGRAMS INTL
11115 Edgewater Dr (44102-6138)
PHONE..................216 631-8544
M C Richards, *Principal*
EMP: 3
SALES (est): 256.8K **Privately Held**
SIC: 3572 Computer storage devices

(G-5209)
EXPERT CRANE INC
5755 Grant Ave (44105-5605)
PHONE..................216 451-9900
James C Doty, *President*
Rebecca Doty, *Vice Pres*
Carl Dell, *VP Opers*
Brian Doles, *Purchasing*
Tempest Doty, *Manager*
EMP: 47
SQ FT: 15,000
SALES (est): 22.2MM **Privately Held**
WEB: www.expertcrane.com
SIC: 3536 7699 1796 5084 Hoists, cranes & monorails; industrial machinery & equipment repair; machinery installation; cranes, industrial

(G-5210)
EXPLORYS INC
1111 Superior Ave E # 2600 (44114-2560)
PHONE..................216 767-4700
Stephen McHale, *CEO*
Charles Lougheed, *President*

Thomas Chickerella, *COO*
Aaron Cornell, *CFO*
EMP: 54
SALES (est): 12.7MM
SALES (corp-wide): 79.5B **Publicly Held**
SIC: 7372 Prepackaged software
PA: International Business Machines Corporation
1 New Orchard Rd Ste 1 # 1
Armonk NY 10504
914 499-1900

(G-5211)
EZ BRITE BRANDS INC
806 Sharon Dr Ste C (44145-7701)
P.O. Box 40025 (44140-0025)
PHONE..................440 871-7817
Edmond Aghajanian, *President*
Marcia Meermans, *Vice Pres*
EMP: 15
SQ FT: 11,000
SALES (est): 3.7MM **Privately Held**
WEB: www.ezbritebrands.com
SIC: 2842 2841 Cleaning or polishing preparations; soap: granulated, liquid, cake, flaked or chip

(G-5212)
F L ENTERPRISES
Also Called: F L Distributors
4740 Briar Rd (44135-5038)
PHONE..................216 898-5551
Fred Loeffler, *President*
Jeff Loeffler, *Vice Pres*
EMP: 4 EST: 1971
SQ FT: 8,400
SALES: 500K **Privately Held**
WEB: www.fldistributors.com
SIC: 3549 Metalworking machinery

(G-5213)
FABRICATION GROUP LLC
3453 W 140th St (44111-2429)
PHONE..................216 251-1725
Patricia B Setlock, *President*
EMP: 20 EST: 2008
SALES (est): 6.2MM **Privately Held**
SIC: 3334 1799 3449 Primary aluminum; ornamental metal work; miscellaneous metalwork

(G-5214)
FAIRCHILD PRINTING CO
5807 Fleet Ave (44105-3495)
PHONE..................216 641-4192
Larry Hovater, *Owner*
Suzanne Hovater, *Co-Owner*
EMP: 4 EST: 1933
SQ FT: 2,128
SALES: 350K **Privately Held**
SIC: 2752 Commercial printing, offset

(G-5215)
FAIRCOSA LLC
4296 E 167th St (44128-3384)
PHONE..................216 577-9909
Matthew Fairfield,
EMP: 3
SALES (est): 127.1K **Privately Held**
SIC: 6799 3669 4213 4412 Real estate investors, except property operators; transportation signaling devices; trucking, except local; deep sea foreign transportation of freight; freight transportation arrangement

(G-5216)
FAIRMONT CREAMERY LLC
1720 Willey Ave (44113-4367)
PHONE..................216 357-2560
EMP: 3 EST: 2014
SALES (est): 145.8K **Privately Held**
SIC: 2021 Creamery butter

(G-5217)
FALCON INNOVATIONS INC
3316 W 118th St (44111-1723)
PHONE..................216 252-0676
Robert A Jewell Jr, *President*
Kenneth Jewell, *Partner*
Judith Jewell, *CFO*
EMP: 6 EST: 1964
SQ FT: 6,400
SALES: 250K **Privately Held**
SIC: 3599 Machine shop, jobbing & repair

(G-5218)
FALLS STAMPING & WELDING CO
Also Called: Plant Two
1720 Fall St (44113-2416)
PHONE..................216 771-9635
John Hall, *Foreman/Supr*
EMP: 13
SALES (corp-wide): 39.7MM **Privately Held**
WEB: www.falls-stamping.com
SIC: 3465 Automotive stampings
PA: Falls Stamping & Welding Company
2900 Vincent St
Cuyahoga Falls OH 44221
330 928-1191

(G-5219)
FARASEY STEEL FABRICATORS INC
4000 Iron Ct (44115-3582)
PHONE..................216 641-1853
Don J Henderson, *President*
George R Henderson, *Vice Pres*
Robert L Henderson, *Vice Pres*
EMP: 15 EST: 1859
SQ FT: 14,000
SALES: 1MM **Privately Held**
WEB: www.faraseysteelfab.com
SIC: 3441 Fabricated structural metal

(G-5220)
FAS MACHINERY LLC
9916 Broadway Ave (44125-1635)
PHONE..................216 472-3800
Marcia J Sadlowski, *Owner*
Robert J Sadlowski,
▼ EMP: 4
SQ FT: 20,000
SALES (est): 1.1MM **Privately Held**
SIC: 3599 Mfg & Repair Intensive Mixers And Replacement Parts For The Rubber Plastic & Composite Industries

(G-5221)
FASTENER INDUSTRIES INC
Buckeye Fasteners Company Div
5250 W 164th St (44142-1506)
PHONE..................216 267-2240
Doug Campbell, *General Mgr*
Tom Schindler, *Engineer*
Lawrence Kelly, *Sales Mgr*
Douglas Campbell, *Sales Staff*
Forest Franklin, *Manager*
EMP: 16
SALES (corp-wide): 42.3MM **Privately Held**
WEB: www.buckeyefasteners.com
SIC: 3496 5085 Wire fasteners; industrial supplies
PA: Fastener Industries, Inc.
1 Berea Cmns Ste 209
Berea OH 44017
440 243-0034

(G-5222)
FAW INDUSTRIES
14837 Detroit Ave 207 (44107-3909)
PHONE..................216 651-9595
Fred Walton, *Principal*
EMP: 3
SALES (est): 172.2K **Privately Held**
SIC: 3999 Manufacturing industries

(G-5223)
FBC CHEMICAL CORPORATION
7301 Bessemer Ave (44127-1817)
PHONE..................216 341-2000
EMP: 9
SALES (corp-wide): 60MM **Privately Held**
SIC: 3312 Chemicals & other products derived from coking
PA: Fbc Chemical Corporation
634 Route 228
Mars PA 16046
724 625-3116

(G-5224)
FCI INC
4661 Giles Rd (44135-3756)
PHONE..................216 251-5200
Kenneth Edgar, *President*
Irene Edgar, *Vice Pres*
EMP: 80 EST: 1958

SQ FT: 48,000
SALES (est): 13.7MM **Privately Held**
WEB: www.fci-usa.com
SIC: 3089 Injection molding of plastics

(G-5225)
FCS GRAPHICS INC
Also Called: Forest City Specialties
2169 Saint Clair Ave Ne (44114-4018)
PHONE..................216 771-5177
Anthony Gliozzi, *President*
EMP: 4
SQ FT: 1,600
SALES (est): 597.2K **Privately Held**
SIC: 2262 2395 Screen printing: manmade fiber & silk broadwoven fabrics; embroidery & art needlework

(G-5226)
FDI ENTERPRISES
17700 Saint Clair Ave (44110-2621)
PHONE..................440 269-8282
EMP: 6 EST: 2016
SALES (est): 760.5K **Privately Held**
SIC: 3089 Plastics products

(G-5227)
FEDERAL PROCESS CORPORATION (PA)
Also Called: Gasoila Thred-Taper
4520 Richmond Rd (44128-5757)
PHONE..................216 464-6440
Jon Outcalt Jr, *President*
Jon Outcalt Sr, *Chairman*
David Anderson, *Vice Pres*
Dave Johnson, *Vice Pres*
Bill Sickenberger, *Plant Mgr*
▲ EMP: 28
SQ FT: 4,000
SALES (est): 25.5MM **Privately Held**
WEB: www.federalprocess.com
SIC: 2891 Sealing compounds, synthetic rubber or plastic

(G-5228)
FEDEX OFFICE & PRINT SVCS INC
6901 Rockside Rd (44131-2379)
PHONE..................216 573-1511
EMP: 20
SALES (corp-wide): 65.4B **Publicly Held**
WEB: www.kinkos.com
SIC: 7334 2791 2789 Photocopying & duplicating services; typesetting; bookbinding & related work
HQ: Fedex Office And Print Services, Inc.
7900 Legacy Dr
Plano TX 75024
800 463-3339

(G-5229)
FENCE ONE INC
Also Called: Great Lake Fence
11111 Broadway Ave (44125-1659)
PHONE..................216 441-2600
Michael Ely, *President*
EMP: 14
SQ FT: 12,000
SALES (est): 2.7MM **Privately Held**
SIC: 1521 1799 3496 General remodeling, single-family houses; fence construction; miscellaneous fabricated wire products

(G-5230)
FERRALLOY INC
28001 Ranney Pkwy (44145-1159)
PHONE..................440 250-1900
William Habansky Jr, *President*
Sherri Habansky, *Corp Secy*
▲ EMP: 27
SQ FT: 15,000
SALES (est): 10.3MM **Privately Held**
WEB: www.ferralloy.com
SIC: 5051 3599 Castings, rough: iron or steel; machine shop, jobbing & repair

(G-5231)
FERRO CORPORATION
Ferro Crmic Glz Prclan Enmel
4150 E 56th St Ste 1 (44105-4890)
P.O. Box 6550 (44101-1550)
PHONE..................216 875-6178
John V Belcastro, *Principal*
EMP: 250

(PA)=Parent Co (HQ)=Headquarters (DH)=Div Headquarters
✪ = New Business established in last 2 years

Cleveland - Cuyahoga County (G-5232)

SALES (corp-wide): 1.6B **Publicly Held**
SIC: 2899 2851 3264 2893 Frit; lacquers, varnishes, enamels & other coatings; porcelain electrical supplies; printing ink; color lakes or toners; color pigments, organic
PA: Ferro Corporation
6060 Parkland Blvd # 250
Mayfield Heights OH 44124
216 875-5600

(G-5232)
FERRO CORPORATION
Also Called: Porcelain Enamels
6060 Parkland Blvd # 250 (44124-4225)
PHONE..................216 875-5600
Robert Szabo, *Manager*
EMP: 80
SALES (corp-wide): 1.6B **Publicly Held**
SIC: 2899 Chemical preparations
PA: Ferro Corporation
6060 Parkland Blvd # 250
Mayfield Heights OH 44124
216 875-5600

(G-5233)
FERROTHERM CORPORATION
4758 Warner Rd (44125-1117)
PHONE..................216 883-9350
Haakon Egeland, *CEO*
Thor Egeland, *Exec VP*
Ron Obrzut, *Vice Pres*
Alf Egeland, *Treasurer*
Dave Snyder, *Director*
▲ **EMP:** 105
SQ FT: 90,000
SALES (est): 22.8MM **Privately Held**
WEB: www.ferrotherm.com
SIC: 3462 3724 3812 3694 Turbine engine forgings, ferrous; aircraft engines & engine parts; turbines, aircraft type; search & navigation equipment; engine electrical equipment; gaskets, packing & sealing devices

(G-5234)
FERTILITY SOLUTIONS INC
11811 Shaker Blvd Ste 330 (44120-1927)
PHONE..................216 491-0030
Susan A Rothmann, *President*
Anne D Wold, *Med Doctor*
John Quigley, *Executive*
EMP: 9
SQ FT: 3,000
SALES: 3.1MM **Privately Held**
WEB: www.fertilitysolutions.com
SIC: 3826 8734 8731 Analytical instruments; biological research

(G-5235)
FGB INTERNATIONAL LLC (PA)
7670 First Pl (44146-6714)
PHONE..................440 359-0000
Joe Golombek
Fairmount Investors LLP,
Edward C Smith,
EMP: 3
SQ FT: 600
SALES (est): 200K **Privately Held**
WEB: www.oakwoodlabs.com
SIC: 1481 Mine exploration, nonmetallic minerals

(G-5236)
FIBERGLASS LINK INC
Also Called: Link's Auto
18607 Saint Clair Ave (44110-2617)
PHONE..................216 531-5515
Robert Linkous, *President*
Robert Hencie, *Principal*
EMP: 3 **EST:** 1979
SQ FT: 4,200
SALES (est): 316.6K **Privately Held**
SIC: 3465 Fenders, automobile: stamped or pressed metal

(G-5237)
FILLOUS & RUPPEL INC
7411 Cedar Ave (44103-4925)
PHONE..................216 431-0470
Robert V Fillous, *President*
Leonard Fillous, *Vice Pres*
Florence Fillous, *Admin Sec*
EMP: 4 **EST:** 1934
SALES (est): 210K **Privately Held**
SIC: 3299 Mica products

(G-5238)
FINAL TOUCH METAL FABRICATING
2290 Scranton Rd (44113-4310)
PHONE..................216 348-1750
Mark Koenig, *President*
Kathleen Koenig, *Vice Pres*
EMP: 3
SALES: 130K **Privately Held**
SIC: 3446 Gratings, tread: fabricated metal

(G-5239)
FINE POINTS INC
Also Called: Tekus, L Sweater Design
12620 Larchmere Blvd (44120-1110)
PHONE..................216 229-6644
Liz Tekus, *President*
Henry Roth, *Treasurer*
EMP: 12
SQ FT: 2,000
SALES (est): 1.3MM **Privately Held**
WEB: www.finepoints.com
SIC: 2253 5949 Sweaters & sweater coats, knit; sewing, needlework & piece goods

(G-5240)
FINELLI ORNAMENTAL IRON CO
Also Called: Finelli Architectural Iron Co
30815 Solon Rd (44139-3485)
PHONE..................440 248-0050
Frank Finelli, *President*
Angelo Finelli, *Vice Pres*
James Korosec, *Vice Pres*
EMP: 15
SQ FT: 15,000
SALES: 2MM **Privately Held**
WEB: www.finelliironworks.com
SIC: 3446 1751 Ornamental metalwork; railings, prefabricated metal; stairs, staircases, stair treads: prefabricated metal; gates, ornamental metal; carpentry work

(G-5241)
FINISHING TOUCH
22084 Lorain Rd (44126-3313)
PHONE..................440 263-9264
Carolyn R Ofiara, *Owner*
EMP: 15 **EST:** 2010
SALES (est): 972.9K **Privately Held**
SIC: 2335 Wedding gowns & dresses

(G-5242)
FIRST CATHOLC SLOVAK UNION U S (PA)
6611 Rockside Rd (44131-2365)
P.O. Box 318013 (44131-8013)
PHONE..................216 642-9406
Andrew M Rajec, *President*
Andrew Harcar, *Vice Pres*
George Matta, *Treasurer*
Ken Arendt, *Exec Sec*
EMP: 15
SQ FT: 7,000
SALES (est): 37.6MM **Privately Held**
WEB: www.fcsu.com
SIC: 6411 2711 Life insurance agents; job printing & newspaper publishing combined

(G-5243)
FIRSTFUELCELLSCOM LLC
11163 Blossom Ave (44130-4430)
PHONE..................440 884-2503
Diane L Sadowski, *Mng Member*
EMP: 6
SALES (est): 534.8K **Privately Held**
WEB: www.firstfuelcells.com
SIC: 3674 Fuel cells, solid state

(G-5244)
FIVES N AMERCN COMBUSTN INC (DH)
4455 E 71st St (44105-5601)
PHONE..................216 271-6000
Luigi Russo, *Ch of Bd*
Erik Paulhardt, *President*
Eric Pedaci, *Engineer*
Kathy E Ruekberg, *CFO*
Philippe Guerreau, *Admin Sec*
◆ **EMP:** 244
SQ FT: 400,000

SALES (est): 112.9MM
SALES (corp-wide): 4.5MM **Privately Held**
WEB: www.namfg.com
SIC: 3433 Heating equipment, except electric
HQ: Fives Inc.
23400 Halsted Rd
Farmington Hills MI 48335
248 477-0800

(G-5245)
FIVES N AMERCN COMBUSTN INC
4455 E 71st St (44105-5601)
PHONE..................734 207-7008
Sue Kren, *Manager*
EMP: 4
SALES (corp-wide): 4.5MM **Privately Held**
SIC: 3433 Heating equipment, except electric
HQ: Fives North American Combustion, Inc.
4455 E 71st St
Cleveland OH 44105
216 271-6000

(G-5246)
FIVES N AMERCN COMBUSTN INC
4455 E 71st St (44105-5601)
P.O. Box 160, East Lyme CT (06333-0160)
PHONE..................412 655-0101
Frederic Sanchez, *Branch Mgr*
EMP: 4
SALES (corp-wide): 4.5MM **Privately Held**
SIC: 3433 Heating equipment, except electric
HQ: Fives North American Combustion, Inc.
4455 E 71st St
Cleveland OH 44105
216 271-6000

(G-5247)
FLASH INDUSTRIAL TECH LTD
30 Industry Dr (44146-4414)
PHONE..................440 786-8979
Lawrence P Zajac, *Principal*
▲ **EMP:** 9
SQ FT: 18,000
SALES (est): 1.8MM **Privately Held**
SIC: 3451 Screw machine products

(G-5248)
FLEETLINE TOOL & DIE CO
7803 Harvard Ave (44105-3938)
PHONE..................216 441-4949
Zenobivsz Buckzkowski, *Owner*
EMP: 3 **EST:** 1965
SQ FT: 1,200
SALES (est): 200K **Privately Held**
SIC: 3599 Machine shop, jobbing & repair

(G-5249)
FLEIG ENTERPRISES INC
Also Called: Smith Facing and Supply Co
940 E 67th St (44103-1724)
PHONE..................216 361-8020
Daniel Fleig, *President*
Caroline Fleig, *Vice Pres*
EMP: 3
SQ FT: 25,000
SALES (est): 320K **Privately Held**
SIC: 3999 Custom pulverizing & grinding of plastic materials

(G-5250)
FLEXNOVA INC
6100 Oak Tree Blvd (44131-2544)
PHONE..................216 288-6961
Steve Rossi, *President*
EMP: 30
SQ FT: 1,000
SALES (est): 2MM **Privately Held**
SIC: 7372 Prepackaged software

(G-5251)
FLOCEL INC
4415 Euclid Ave Ste 421 (44103-3757)
PHONE..................216 619-5903
Edward Rapp, *President*
Robert N Schmidt, *Corp Secy*
Brian M Kolkowski, *Vice Pres*
EMP: 5
SQ FT: 500

SALES (est): 505.6K **Privately Held**
WEB: www.flocel.com
SIC: 3845 Ultrasonic scanning devices, medical

(G-5252)
FLOTBI INC
4415 Euclid Ave Ste 421 (44103-3757)
PHONE..................216 619-5928
Matthew Mahoney, *CFO*
EMP: 4
SALES (est): 160.5K **Privately Held**
SIC: 3841 Diagnostic apparatus, medical

(G-5253)
FLOWCRETE NORTH AMERICA INC
19218 Redwood Rd (44110-2736)
PHONE..................936 539-6700
Mark Greaves, *President*
Edward W Moore, *Admin Sec*
▲ **EMP:** 24
SALES (est): 12.2MM
SALES (corp-wide): 5.3B **Publicly Held**
SIC: 3996 Tile, floor: supported plastic
HQ: Flowcrete Group Limited
The Flooring Technology Centre
Sandbach CW11
127 075-3000

(G-5254)
FLUID SYSTEM SERVICE INC
13825 Triskett Rd (44111-1523)
P.O. Box 771414, Lakewood (44107-0057)
PHONE..................216 651-2450
John C Balliett, *President*
D Thomas George, *Corp Secy*
EMP: 8
SALES (est): 1.3MM **Privately Held**
SIC: 3511 7699 Hydraulic turbines; hydraulic equipment repair

(G-5255)
FLUKE BIOMEDICAL LLC
6045 Cochran Rd (44139-3303)
PHONE..................440 248-9300
James Lico, *President*
Mark Svajger, *Safety Mgr*
Ramon Rodriguez, *Info Tech Mgr*
▲ **EMP:** 150
SALES (est): 29.7MM
SALES (corp-wide): 6.4B **Publicly Held**
WEB: www.flukebiomedical.com
SIC: 3829 Nuclear radiation & testing apparatus
HQ: Fluke Electronics Corporation
6920 Seaway Blvd
Everett WA 98203
425 347-6100

(G-5256)
FOAM SEAL INC
5109 Hamilton Ave (44114-3907)
P.O. Box 951130 (44193-0005)
PHONE..................216 881-8111
Kenneth Dagg, *President*
Douglas Mackinzie, *President*
Michael S Sylvester, *Chairman*
EMP: 75 **EST:** 1971
SQ FT: 250,000
SALES (est): 11.3MM **Privately Held**
WEB: www.foam-seal.com
SIC: 3053 2891 2911 Gaskets, packing & sealing devices; sealing compounds, synthetic rubber or plastic; caulking compounds; greases, lubricating
PA: Novagard Solutions, Inc.
5109 Hamilton Ave
Cleveland OH 44114

(G-5257)
FOAM-TEX SOLUTIONS CORP
13981 W Parkway Rd (44135-4511)
PHONE..................216 889-2702
Donald Abshire, *CEO*
Alan Abshire, *Vice Pres*
▲ **EMP:** 6
SQ FT: 6,700
SALES: 300K **Privately Held**
WEB: www.foam-tex.com
SIC: 2841 Soap & other detergents

GEOGRAPHIC SECTION
Cleveland - Cuyahoga County (G-5282)

(G-5258)
FOLLOW PRINT CLUB ON FACEBOOK
11150 East Blvd (44106-1711)
PHONE..................................216 707-2579
EMP: 3
SALES: 135.5K Privately Held
SIC: 2752 Commercial printing, lithographic

(G-5259)
FOOD DESIGNS INC
Also Called: Ohio City Pasta
5299 Crayton Ave (44104-2829)
PHONE..................................216 651-9221
Gary W Thomas, *President*
EMP: 10
SALES (est): 996.1K Privately Held
WEB: www.ohiocitypasta.com
SIC: 2099 2032 Pasta, uncooked: packaged with other ingredients; ravioli: packaged in cans, jars, etc.

(G-5260)
FOOTE PRINTING COMPANY INC
Also Called: Audit Forms
2800 E 55th St (44104-2862)
PHONE..................................216 431-1757
Steven Duhrr, *CEO*
Michael Duhr, *President*
Karl-Heinz Duhr, *President*
Steven Duhr, *Vice Pres*
EMP: 12 EST: 1907
SQ FT: 16,000
SALES: 1.8MM Privately Held
WEB: www.auditforms.com
SIC: 2752 2759 Commercial printing, offset; business forms, lithographed; letterpress printing

(G-5261)
FOREST CITY COMPANIES INC
Also Called: Forest City Packaging
3607 W 56th St (44102-5739)
PHONE..................................216 586-5279
Anthony Galang, *President*
Ken Lewandowski, *General Mgr*
Dawn Galang, *Admin Sec*
EMP: 23
SQ FT: 42,000
SALES (est): 6.1MM Privately Held
WEB: www.forestcityco.com
SIC: 4783 2441 2394 Packing goods for shipping; boxes, wood; canvas & related products

(G-5262)
FORGE PRODUCTS CORPORATION
Also Called: Forged Products
9503 Woodland Ave (44104-2487)
PHONE..................................216 231-2600
Charles E Thayer II, *President*
Joann Notaro, *Finance*
Debbie McVaugh, *Admin Asst*
EMP: 56 EST: 1962
SQ FT: 31,600
SALES (est): 12.6MM Privately Held
WEB: www.forgeproducts.com
SIC: 3312 3463 3462 Forgings, iron & steel; nonferrous forgings; iron & steel forgings

(G-5263)
FORMTEK INC
Krasny Kaplan Division
4899 Commerce Pkwy (44128-5905)
PHONE..................................216 292-6300
Roger K Steel, *Division Pres*
EMP: 100
SALES (corp-wide): 678.1MM Privately Held
WEB: www.formtekcleveland.com
SIC: 3547 3535 Conveyors & conveying equipment; pipe & tube mills
HQ: Formtek, Inc.
4899 Commerce Pkwy
Cleveland OH 44128
216 292-4460

(G-5264)
FORMTEK INC (DH)
Also Called: Formtek International
4899 Commerce Pkwy (44128-5905)
PHONE..................................216 292-4460
Joe Mayer, *President*
Jack Pennuto, *Sales Engr*
▲ EMP: 60
SQ FT: 56,000
SALES: 34.7MM
SALES (corp-wide): 669.8MM Privately Held
WEB: www.formtekcleveland.com
SIC: 3547 3549 3535 Pipe & tube mills; coiling machinery; conveyors & conveying equipment
HQ: Formtek Inc
711 Ogden Ave
Lisle IL 60532
630 285-1500

(G-5265)
FOSBEL INC (HQ)
Also Called: Cetek
6779 Engle Rd Ste A (44130-7926)
PHONE..................................216 362-3900
Derek Scott, *President*
Kathlene Stevens, *CFO*
◆ EMP: 120
SALES (est): 25.4MM
SALES (corp-wide): 24.3MM Privately Held
SIC: 7629 7692 Electrical repair shops; welding repair
PA: Fosbel Holding, Inc.
20600 Sheldon Rd
Cleveland OH 44142
216 362-3900

(G-5266)
FOSBEL HOLDING INC (PA)
20600 Sheldon Rd (44142-1319)
PHONE..................................216 362-3900
Derek Scott, *President*
Kathleen Stevens, *CFO*
EMP: 30
SALES (est): 24.3MM Privately Held
SIC: 7692 Investment holding companies, except banks

(G-5267)
FOSECO INC (DH)
20200 Sheldon Rd (44142-1380)
P.O. Box 81227 (44181-0227)
PHONE..................................440 826-4548
Lee Plutshack, *Ch of Bd*
Sanjay Gandhi, *Business Mgr*
John S Rodgers Jr, *Vice Pres*
Roger P Stanbridge, *Vice Pres*
Nimrod Pooe, *Production*
▲ EMP: 5 EST: 1933
SQ FT: 380,000
SALES (est): 9.2MM
SALES (corp-wide): 2.2B Privately Held
WEB: www.foseco.com
SIC: 2899 3569 3547 Metal treating compounds; fluxes: brazing, soldering, galvanizing & welding; filters; rolling mill machinery
HQ: Vesuvius U S A Corporation
1404 Newton Dr
Champaign IL 61822
217 351-5000

(G-5268)
FOUNDRY ARTIST INC
Also Called: Studio Foundry
4404 Perkins Ave (44103-3544)
PHONE..................................216 391-9030
Mark Olitsky, *President*
Lisa Kenion, *Vice Pres*
Craig Horstman, *Treasurer*
John Ranally, *Admin Sec*
EMP: 7
SQ FT: 3,000
SALES (est): 981.6K Privately Held
WEB: www.studiofoundry.com
SIC: 3366 Bronze foundry

(G-5269)
FOUNT
2280 Bellfield Ave Apt 3 (44106-3160)
PHONE..................................540 810-0594
EMP: 4 EST: 2014
SALES (est): 404.4K Privately Held
SIC: 3172 Personal leather goods

(G-5270)
FPT CLEVELAND LLC (DH)
Also Called: Ferrous Processing and Trading
8550 Aetna Rd (44105-1607)
PHONE..................................216 441-3800
Andrew M Luntz, *President*
James Prokes, *Vice Pres*
Yale Levin,
▲ EMP: 115
SALES (est): 31.6MM
SALES (corp-wide): 1.8B Privately Held
SIC: 4953 5051 5093 3341 Recycling, waste materials; iron & steel (ferrous) products; ferrous metal scrap & waste; secondary nonferrous metals
HQ: Ferrous Processing And Trading Company
3400 E Lafayette St
Detroit MI 48207
313 567-9710

(G-5271)
FRANCK AND FRIC INCORPORATED
7919 Old Rockside Rd (44131-2300)
P.O. Box 31148 (44131-0148)
PHONE..................................216 524-4451
Donald R Skala Sr, *President*
Stacey Carson, *Assistant VP*
David R Skala, *Vice Pres*
Donald C Skala Jr, *Treasurer*
EMP: 51
SQ FT: 20,000
SALES (est): 7.2MM Privately Held
SIC: 1711 1761 3441 3444 Ventilation & duct work contractor; warm air heating & air conditioning contractor; sheet metalwork; fabricated structural metal; sheet metalwork

(G-5272)
FRANK J PRUCHA & ASSOCIATES
Also Called: Sir Speedy
6916 Daisy Ave (44131-3380)
PHONE..................................216 642-3838
Frank J Prucha Jr, *President*
Nancy H Prucha, *Vice Pres*
EMP: 4
SALES (est): 485K Privately Held
WEB: www.speedy77.com
SIC: 2752 2791 2789 Commercial printing, lithographic; typesetting; bookbinding & related work

(G-5273)
FRASERNET INC
2940 Noble Rd Ste 1 (44121-2242)
PHONE..................................216 691-6686
George Fraser, *President*
Gregory Williams, *Vice Pres*
EMP: 2
SQ FT: 2,000
SALES (est): 1.2MM Privately Held
WEB: www.frasernet.com
SIC: 2731 Book publishing

(G-5274)
FRED W HANKS COMPANY
25018 Lakeland Blvd (44132-2628)
PHONE..................................216 731-1774
Karen Bowen, *President*
Ernest Shandle, *Treasurer*
EMP: 4
SQ FT: 7,000
SALES (est): 417.9K Privately Held
SIC: 3824 3599 Water meters; machine & other job shop work

(G-5275)
FRIENDS ORNAMENTAL IRON CO
1593 E 41st St (44103-2303)
PHONE..................................216 431-6710
Jim Cahlik, *President*
EMP: 4
SQ FT: 7,200
SALES: 300K Privately Held
SIC: 5211 1799 3496 3446 Lumber & other building materials; ornamental metal work; miscellaneous fabricated wire products; architectural metalwork; metal doors, sash & trim

(G-5276)
FULL CIRCLE TECHNOLOGIES LLC
1175 Piermont Rd (44121-2936)
PHONE..................................216 650-0007
Hari Chandra, *CEO*
EMP: 3
SALES (est): 278.2K Privately Held
SIC: 2951 Asphalt & asphaltic paving mixtures (not from refineries)

(G-5277)
FUNNY TIMES INC
2176 Lee Rd (44118-2908)
P.O. Box 18530 (44118-0530)
PHONE..................................216 371-8600
Raymond Lesser, *President*
Susan Wolpert, *Corp Secy*
Sandee Beyerle, *Manager*
Amy Jenkins, *Associate*
EMP: 6
SALES (est): 510.8K Privately Held
WEB: www.funnytimes.com
SIC: 2711 Newspapers: publishing only, not printed on site

(G-5278)
FURNACE PARTS LLC
4755 W 150th St Ste C (44135-3330)
PHONE..................................216 916-9601
Fax: 216 676-5557
▲ EMP: 30
SQ FT: 15,000
SALES (est): 7.6MM Privately Held
SIC: 3823 Mfg Process Control Instruments

(G-5279)
FURNACE PARTS LLC
6133 Rockside Rd Ste 300 (44131-2243)
PHONE..................................800 321-0796
EMP: 3
SALES (est): 163.1K
SALES (corp-wide): 1B Privately Held
SIC: 3823 Temperature measurement instruments, industrial
PA: Ultra Electronics Holdings Plc
417 Bridport Road
Greenford MIDDX UB6 8
208 813-4321

(G-5280)
FURNITURE CONCEPTS INC
4925 Galaxy Pkwy Ste G (44128-5961)
PHONE..................................216 292-9100
Keith Voigt, *President*
Karyl Voigt-Walker, *Vice Pres*
Joann Ann, *Office Mgr*
Mike Weissman, *Admin Sec*
EMP: 10
SQ FT: 1,700
SALES: 4MM Privately Held
SIC: 2522 5021 7641 Office furniture, except wood; office furniture; furniture repair & maintenance

(G-5281)
FUTURE SCREEN INC
9009 Broadview Rd Unit B (44147-2598)
PHONE..................................440 838-5055
Eugene Gryskewich, *President*
EMP: 5
SQ FT: 2,100
SALES: 250K Privately Held
SIC: 2759 Screen printing

(G-5282)
FX DIGITAL MEDIA INC (PA)
1600 E 23rs St Rs (44114)
PHONE..................................216 241-4040
John Gadd, *CEO*
Columbus Woodruff, *President*
Nora Lane, *Marketing Staff*
Nikki Woodruff, *Shareholder*
EMP: 35
SQ FT: 15,000
SALES (est): 4MM Privately Held
WEB: www.hotcards.com
SIC: 7336 2754 Commercial art & graphic design; color printing, gravure

Cleveland - Cuyahoga County (G-5283)

(G-5283)
FX DIGITAL MEDIA INC
Also Called: Hot Cards.com
2400 Superior Ave E # 100 (44114-4237)
PHONE..................................216 241-4040
Columbus Woodruff, *President*
Karl Edward Singleton Jr, *Manager*
EMP: 40
SQ FT: 7,000
SALES (est): 6.1MM **Privately Held**
SIC: 2752 Commercial printing, offset

(G-5284)
G T METAL FABRICATORS INC
Also Called: Acromet Metal Fabricators
12126 York Rd Unit E (44133-3688)
PHONE..................................440 237-8745
Gary Callahan, *President*
Judy Callahan, *Vice Pres*
EMP: 12 **EST:** 1966
SQ FT: 9,000
SALES (est): 2.3MM **Privately Held**
WEB: www.acromet.com
SIC: 3444 Sheet metal specialties, not stamped

(G-5285)
G W COBB CO
3914 Broadway Ave 16 (44115-3694)
PHONE..................................216 341-0100
George W Cobb Jr, *President*
EMP: 12
SQ FT: 15,000
SALES (est): 2.5MM **Privately Held**
WEB: www.gwcobb.com
SIC: 3411 5084 Food containers, metal; industrial machinery & equipment

(G-5286)
GAIL ZEILMANN
Also Called: Ultra Graphics
3560 W 105th St (44111-3838)
PHONE..................................440 888-4858
Gail Zeilmann, *Owner*
EMP: 3 **EST:** 1976
SQ FT: 2,000
SALES (est): 315.8K **Privately Held**
SIC: 2759 2396 Screen printing; automotive & apparel trimmings

(G-5287)
GALAXY BALLOONS INCORPORATED
11750 Berea Rd Ste 3 (44111-1603)
P.O. Box 698, Lakewood (44107-0998)
PHONE..................................216 476-3360
Terry Brizz, *President*
Alex Kovarik, *Purch Mgr*
▲ **EMP:** 130
SQ FT: 50,000
SALES (est): 21.1MM **Privately Held**
WEB: www.galaxyballoon.com
SIC: 2752 7336 5092 5199 Commercial printing, offset; silk screen design; balloons, novelty; advertising specialties; signs & advertising specialties; sporting & athletic goods

(G-5288)
GALLO DISPLAYS INC (PA)
4922 E 49th St (44125-1016)
P.O. Box 788, Twinsburg (44087-0788)
PHONE..................................216 431-9500
Don Lockwood, *President*
Phil Ridolfi, *CFO*
◆ **EMP:** 37 **EST:** 1928
SQ FT: 300,000
SALES (est): 18.9MM **Privately Held**
WEB: www.galloinspires.com/
SIC: 2542 3993 Partitions & fixtures, except wood; signs & advertising specialties

(G-5289)
GANNONS DISCOUNT BLINDS
2725 Ralph Ave (44109-5413)
PHONE..................................216 398-2761
Ray Gannon, *Owner*
EMP: 4
SALES (est): 210K **Privately Held**
SIC: 2591 5999 Drapery hardware & blinds & shades; miscellaneous retail stores

(G-5290)
GARDEN OF FLAVOR LLC
7501 Carnegie Ave (44103-4809)
PHONE..................................216 702-7991
Lisa Reed,
Keith Kress,
EMP: 4
SQ FT: 3,000
SALES (est): 466.3K **Privately Held**
SIC: 2033 Vegetable juices: packaged in cans, jars, etc.

(G-5291)
GARDNER DENVER NASH LLC
Also Called: Gardener
7420 Pine River Ct (44130-5519)
PHONE..................................440 871-9505
Marshall Heller, *Sales/Mktg Mgr*
Amanda Davis, *Regl Sales Mgr*
EMP: 12
SALES (corp-wide): 2.6B **Publicly Held**
WEB: www.nasheng.com
SIC: 3563 Air & gas compressors
HQ: Gardner Denver Nash Llc
2 Trefoil Dr
Trumbull CT 06611
203 459-3923

(G-5292)
GARFIELD ALLOYS INC (PA)
4878 Chaincraft Rd (44125)
PHONE..................................216 587-4843
Chuck Slovich, *President*
Mike Slovich Jr, *Corp Secy*
▼ **EMP:** 12 **EST:** 1950
SQ FT: 60,000
SALES (est): 11.7MM **Privately Held**
WEB: www.magretechinc.com
SIC: 3369 Magnesium & magnes.-base alloy castings, exc. die-casting

(G-5293)
GARICK LLC (PA)
Also Called: Ogg Garick
13600 Broadway Ave Ste 1 (44125-1999)
PHONE..................................216 581-0100
Holden McNeal, *Transportation*
Gary P Trinetti, *Mng Member*
Cristian Croitoru, *Manager*
James Kwiatkowski, *Manager*
Richard Coan,
EMP: 20 **EST:** 1980
SQ FT: 3,500
SALES (est): 52.5MM **Privately Held**
WEB: www.garick.com
SIC: 2875 0711 2499 5091 Potting soil, mixed; soil preparation services; mulch or sawdust products, wood; athletic goods; lumber scrap

(G-5294)
GARLAND INDUSTRIES INC (PA)
3800 E 91st St (44105-2103)
PHONE..................................216 641-7500
David Sokol, *President*
Melvin Chrostowski, *Vice Pres*
Richard Debacco, *Vice Pres*
William Oley, *Vice Pres*
G Richard Olivier, *Vice Pres*
EMP: 8
SQ FT: 150,000
SALES (est): 378.6MM **Privately Held**
SIC: 2952 6512 8712 Roofing materials; roofing felts, cements or coatings; coating compounds, tar; commercial & industrial building operation; architectural services

(G-5295)
GARLAND/DBS INC
3800 E 91st St (44105-2103)
PHONE..................................216 641-7500
Dave Sokol, *President*
Melvin Chrostowski, *Vice Pres*
Richard Debacco, *Vice Pres*
Dan Healy, *Plant Mgr*
Chuck Ripepi, *CFO*
EMP: 250
SALES: 157.1MM
SALES (corp-wide): 378.6MM **Privately Held**
WEB: www.garlandco.com
SIC: 2952 6512 8712 Roofing materials; roofing felts, cements or coatings; coating compounds, tar; commercial & industrial building operation; architectural services
HQ: The Garland Company Inc
3800 E 91st St
Cleveland OH 44105
216 641-7500

(G-5296)
GATEWAY METAL FINISHING INC
5310 W 161st St Ste J (44142-1627)
PHONE..................................216 267-2580
Edward F Eibel III, *CEO*
Ed Steele, *President*
EMP: 27
SALES (est): 800K **Privately Held**
SIC: 3471 Finishing, metals or formed products; plating of metals or formed products

(G-5297)
GDIC GROUP LLC (PA)
1300 E 9th St Fl 20 (44114-1501)
PHONE..................................330 468-0700
Steve White, *President*
George Anthony,
Ed Heil,
EMP: 0
SALES (est): 61.2MM **Privately Held**
SIC: 6719 3354 Personal holding companies, except banks; aluminum extruded products

(G-5298)
GEAR COMPANY OF AMERICA INC
14300 Lorain Ave (44111-2297)
PHONE..................................216 671-5400
Edward Morel, *President*
Scott Britvec, *General Mgr*
Joel Wauthier, *Engineer*
EMP: 60 **EST:** 1946
SQ FT: 96,000
SALES (est): 13.2MM **Privately Held**
WEB: www.gearcoa.com
SIC: 3714 3566 3462 Gears, motor vehicle; gears, power transmission, except automotive; gears, forged steel

(G-5299)
GEBAUER COMPANY
4444 E 153rd St (44128-2955)
PHONE..................................216 581-3030
John Giltinan, *Ch of Bd*
David O'Halloran, *President*
Jeff Laturell, *Vice Pres*
Skip Schmies, *Mfg Staff*
Nick Popov, *Engineer*
▲ **EMP:** 34 **EST:** 1957
SQ FT: 16,000
SALES (est): 11.8MM **Privately Held**
WEB: www.gebauerco.com
SIC: 2834 Pharmaceutical preparations

(G-5300)
GEIST CO INC
1814 W 30th St (44113-3026)
PHONE..................................216 771-2200
Thom Geist, *President*
Sarah Gorman, *Admin Sec*
EMP: 16
SQ FT: 19,000
SALES (est): 1.6MM **Privately Held**
WEB: www.geistco.com
SIC: 3446 3444 Architectural metalwork; canopies, sheet metal

(G-5301)
GELLNER ENGINEERING INC
2827 Brookpark Rd (44134-1308)
PHONE..................................216 398-8500
Dean Gellner, *President*
Carol Gellner, *Vice Pres*
EMP: 4
SQ FT: 3,300
SALES (est): 275K **Privately Held**
WEB: www.gellnerengineering.com
SIC: 5531 7539 3714 3519 Automotive parts; machine shop, automotive; motor vehicle parts & accessories; internal combustion engines

(G-5302)
GEM ORNAMENTAL IRON CO
4681 Broadview Rd (44109-4619)
PHONE..................................216 661-6965
John J Klimo, *President*
Roberta Klimo, *Admin Sec*
EMP: 3 **EST:** 1959
SQ FT: 4,000
SALES (est): 420.1K **Privately Held**
SIC: 3446 Stairs, staircases, stair treads: prefabricated metal

(G-5303)
GEM TOOL LLC
127 Public Sq (44114-1217)
PHONE..................................216 771-8444
Nick Carlozzi, *Principal*
EMP: 8
SALES (est): 880.4K **Privately Held**
SIC: 3545 Cutting tools for machine tools

(G-5304)
GENERAL ALUMINUM MFG COMPANY (DH)
Also Called: Gamco
6065 Parkland Blvd (44124-6119)
PHONE..................................330 297-1225
Bob Paulenske, *President*
Rick Steffenson, *General Mgr*
Douglas Stoops, *General Mgr*
Richard Burcham, *QC Mgr*
Rick White, *Engineer*
▲ **EMP:** 277
SQ FT: 2,000
SALES (est): 208.6MM
SALES (corp-wide): 1.6B **Publicly Held**
WEB: www.generalaluminum.com
SIC: 3365 3369 Aluminum & aluminum-based alloy castings; nonferrous foundries
HQ: Park-Ohio Industries, Inc.
6065 Parkland Blvd Ste 1
Cleveland OH 44124
440 947-2000

(G-5305)
GENERAL AWNING COMPANY INC
1350 E Granger Rd (44131-1206)
PHONE..................................216 749-0110
Paul Gall, *President*
EMP: 15
SQ FT: 10,000
SALES (est): 2.5MM **Privately Held**
WEB: www.genawning.com
SIC: 3444 1751 1761 Awnings, sheet metal; window & door (prefabricated) installation; siding contractor

(G-5306)
GENERAL ELECTRIC COMPANY
4477 E 49th St (44125-1097)
PHONE..................................216 883-1000
Donald Mysliwiec, *Enginr/R&D Mgr*
EMP: 100
SQ FT: 12,000
SALES (corp-wide): 121.6B **Publicly Held**
SIC: 7629 3621 3613 3612 Electrical repair shops; motors & generators; switchgear & switchboard apparatus; transformers, except electric; power transmission equipment; pumps & pumping equipment
PA: General Electric Company
41 Farnsworth St
Boston MA 02210
617 443-3000

(G-5307)
GENERAL ELECTRIC COMPANY
1975 Noble Rd (44112-1719)
PHONE..................................216 266-2121
Thomas Haunert, *Manager*
Michael Sabat, *Manager*
Steven Melfi, *Senior Mgr*
Philip Carino, *Director*
Jennifer House, *Executive Asst*
EMP: 800
SALES (corp-wide): 121.6B **Publicly Held**
SIC: 3646 Commercial indusl & institutional electric lighting fixtures
PA: General Electric Company
41 Farnsworth St
Boston MA 02210
617 443-3000

(G-5308)
GENERAL ELECTRIC COMPANY
18683 S Miles Rd (44128-4297)
PHONE..................................216 663-2110
John Favaloro, *Opers Mgr*

GEOGRAPHIC SECTION

Cleveland - Cuyahoga County (G-5334)

Pei Chan, *Engineer*
Michael Clark, *Engineer*
Jarrod Deangelo, *Engineer*
Eric Dolence, *Engineer*
EMP: 70
SQ FT: 53,462
SALES (corp-wide): 121.6B **Publicly Held**
SIC: 3844 Radiographic X-ray apparatus & tubes
PA: General Electric Company
41 Farnsworth St
Boston MA 02210
617 443-3000

(G-5309)
GENERAL ELECTRIC COMPANY
1814 E 45th St (44103-2321)
PHONE.................................216 391-8741
Mike Kridle, *Manager*
Jim Thompson, *Manager*
EMP: 300
SALES (corp-wide): 121.6B **Publicly Held**
SIC: 3641 Lamps, incandescent filament, electric
PA: General Electric Company
41 Farnsworth St
Boston MA 02210
617 443-3000

(G-5310)
GENERAL ELECTRIC COMPANY
1099 Ivanhoe Rd (44110-3293)
PHONE.................................216 268-3846
James C Wiester, *Branch Mgr*
EMP: 100
SALES (corp-wide): 121.6B **Publicly Held**
SIC: 2819 2899 2851 Industrial inorganic chemicals; chemical preparations; paints & allied products
PA: General Electric Company
41 Farnsworth St
Boston MA 02210
617 443-3000

(G-5311)
GENERAL ELECTRIC COMPANY
21800 Tungsten Rd (44117-1195)
PHONE.................................216 266-2357
Mike Credell, *Manager*
EMP: 180
SALES (corp-wide): 121.6B **Publicly Held**
SIC: 3699 Electrical work
PA: General Electric Company
41 Farnsworth St
Boston MA 02210
617 443-3000

(G-5312)
GENERAL MOTORS LLC
5400 Chevrolet Blvd (44130-1451)
PHONE.................................216 265-5000
Al Maclauhlin, *Opers-Prdtn-Mfg*
Scott Buddie, *Engineer*
John Toth, *Engineer*
John Martinis, *Manager*
Barry Kostura, *Maintence Staff*
EMP: 2028 **Publicly Held**
SIC: 3711 3465 3714 2531 Motor vehicles & car bodies; body parts, automobile: stamped metal; motor vehicle parts & accessories; public building & related furniture
HQ: General Motors Llc
300 Renaissance Ctr L1
Detroit MI 48243

(G-5313)
GENERAL SHEAVE COMPANY INC
1335 Main Ave (44113-2389)
PHONE.................................216 781-8120
Antun Bunjevac, *President*
EMP: 9 **EST:** 1951
SQ FT: 7,500
SALES (est): 1.1MM **Privately Held**
WEB: www.generalsheave.com
SIC: 3599 Machine shop, jobbing & repair

(G-5314)
GENERAL STEEL CORPORATION
3344 E 80th St (44127-1851)
PHONE.................................216 883-4200
James Lamantia, *President*
Jay E Irvin, *Exec VP*
Andy Tomc, *Sales Staff*
EMP: 18
SQ FT: 60,000
SALES (est): 12.7MM **Privately Held**
WEB: www.generalsteelcorporation.com
SIC: 5051 3398 3441 Steel; metal heat treating; fabricated structural metal

(G-5315)
GENIE REPROS INC
2211 Hamilton Ave (44114-1154)
PHONE.................................216 965-0213
Barry Bishop, *President*
Don Mc Quilkin, *CPA*
Michelle Toivonen, *Sales Staff*
Bob Paukst, *CIO*
EMP: 20
SQ FT: 7,900
SALES (est): 4.1MM **Privately Held**
WEB: www.genierepros.com
SIC: 2752 Lithographing on metal

(G-5316)
GENT MACHINE COMPANY
12315 Kirby Ave (44108-1616)
PHONE.................................216 481-2334
Richard W Gent Jr, *President*
Diane Gent, *Vice Pres*
Richard W Gent IV, *Vice Pres*
Lori Smith, *Office Admin*
EMP: 50 **EST:** 1927
SALES (est): 5.6MM **Privately Held**
WEB: www.gentmachine.com
SIC: 3451 Screw machine products

(G-5317)
GENVAC AEROSPACE CORP (PA)
110 Alpha Park (44143-2215)
P.O. Box 12105, Birmingham AL (35202-2105)
PHONE.................................440 646-9986
Gerald T Mearini, *CEO*
Carol Kory, *Vice Pres*
David Vance, *Info Tech Mgr*
EMP: 12 **EST:** 2000
SQ FT: 18,000
SALES (est): 3.2MM **Privately Held**
WEB: www.genvacaerospace.com
SIC: 3827 2851 Optical instruments & lenses; paints & allied products

(G-5318)
GERGEL-KELLEM COMPANY INC
Also Called: Watt Printers
4544 Hinckley Indus Pkwy (44109-6010)
PHONE.................................216 398-2000
John Gergel, *President*
Mike Nakonek, *Vice Pres*
EMP: 60
SQ FT: 60,000
SALES (est): 14.8MM **Privately Held**
WEB: www.wattprinters.com
SIC: 2752 Commercial printing, offset

(G-5319)
GEROW EQUIPMENT COMPANY INC
706 E 163rd St (44110-2453)
PHONE.................................216 383-8800
Robert L Gerow, *CEO*
EMP: 7 **EST:** 1943
SQ FT: 1,500
SALES (est): 1.3MM **Privately Held**
SIC: 3561 5084 Industrial pumps & parts; heat exchange equipment, industrial

(G-5320)
GEW INC
11941 Abbey Rd Ste X (44133-2663)
PHONE.................................440 237-4439
Brian Wenger, *President*
Malcolm Rae, *Managing Dir*
Billy Adams, *Cust Mgr*
▲ **EMP:** 9

SALES (est): 1.6MM **Privately Held**
WEB: www.gewuv.com
SIC: 3555 Printing trades machinery

(G-5321)
GIBSON MACHINERY LLC
181 Oak Leaf Oval (44146-6156)
PHONE.................................440 439-4000
M Lee Gibson, *Mng Member*
Larysa Gibson,
EMP: 30
SALES (est): 10MM **Privately Held**
WEB: www.gibsonmachinery.com
SIC: 3531 Construction machinery

(G-5322)
GIE MEDIA INC (PA)
5811 Canal Rd (44125-3430)
PHONE.................................800 456-0707
Richard J W Foster, *CEO*
Chris Foster, *President*
Dan Moreland, *Exec VP*
EMP: 35
SQ FT: 6,500
SALES (est): 13.2MM **Privately Held**
WEB: www.giemedia.com
SIC: 2721 2731 Magazines: publishing only, not printed on site; books: publishing only

(G-5323)
GLAUNERS WHOLESALE INC
Also Called: G & G Originals
5011 Brookpark Rd (44134-1049)
PHONE.................................216 398-7088
Gregory Glauner, *President*
Monica Glauner, *Principal*
Sandy Phillips, *Principal*
EMP: 4
SQ FT: 4,000
SALES (est): 220K **Privately Held**
SIC: 2759 Screen printing

(G-5324)
GLF INTERNATIONAL INC (PA)
3690 Orange Pl Ste 495 (44122-4465)
PHONE.................................216 621-6901
James McClurg, *President*
Gary McClurg, *Admin Sec*
EMP: 10
SQ FT: 20,000
SALES (est): 1.7MM **Privately Held**
SIC: 1479 Fluorspar mining

(G-5325)
GLOBAL FURNISHINGS INC
1621 E 41st St (44103-2305)
PHONE.................................216 595-0901
Colleen Porche, *President*
EMP: 3
SALES (est): 678.6K **Privately Held**
SIC: 2531 Public building & related furniture

(G-5326)
GLOBE PIPE HANGER PRODUCTS INC
14601 Industrial Pkwy (44135-4545)
PHONE.................................216 362-6300
E Scot Kennedy, *Ch of Bd*
Gary Horvath, *COO*
Dale Zeleznik, *Vice Pres*
Dan Collins, *VP Sls/Mktg*
▲ **EMP:** 20
SQ FT: 30,000
SALES (est): 3.2MM **Privately Held**
WEB: www.wireproducts.com
SIC: 3569 Firefighting apparatus & related equipment

(G-5327)
GOLD PRO INC
850 Euclid Ave Ste 518 (44114-3304)
PHONE.................................216 241-5143
Matthew Elkanick, *President*
Frank Schaefer, *Manager*
EMP: 3
SALES: 150K **Privately Held**
SIC: 3911 Jewelry, precious metal

(G-5328)
GOLDA INC (PA)
24050 Commerce Park (44122-5833)
PHONE.................................216 464-5490
Alfred G Corrado, *President*
◆ **EMP:** 350 **EST:** 1970

SQ FT: 10,000
SALES (est): 20.4MM **Privately Held**
SIC: 2342 2389 Maternity bras & corsets; garter belts

(G-5329)
GOLUBITSKY CORPORATION
Also Called: Alvio
4364 Cranwood Pkwy (44128-4002)
PHONE.................................800 552-4204
Leo Golubitsky, *President*
Alex Fonis, *Shareholder*
▲ **EMP:** 5
SQ FT: 6,000
SALES (est): 798.7K **Privately Held**
WEB: www.alvio.com
SIC: 5734 5999 3571 Computer peripheral equipment; typewriters & business machines; electronic computers

(G-5330)
GOOCH & HOUSEGO (FLORIDA) LLC (HQ)
676 Alpha Dr (44143-2123)
PHONE.................................321 242-7818
Pat Shannonhouse, *General Mgr*
Huey Ho, *Vice Pres*
Gary Catella, *VP Opers*
Jeff Luken, *Plant Mgr*
Harry Mason, *QC Mgr*
EMP: 58
SQ FT: 20,000
SALES (est): 16MM
SALES (corp-wide): 159.2MM **Privately Held**
WEB: www.neostech.com
SIC: 3827 Optical instruments & lenses
PA: Gooch & Housego Plc
Dowlish Ford
Ilminster TA19
146 025-6440

(G-5331)
GOODRICH CORPORATION
8000 Marble Ave (44105-2060)
P.O. Box 73536 (44193-0002)
PHONE.................................216 706-2530
Steve Rahija, *Project Engr*
Kevin Young, *Marketing Staff*
Greg Marchak, *Director*
EMP: 7
SALES (corp-wide): 66.5B **Publicly Held**
SIC: 3728 Aircraft parts & equipment
HQ: Goodrich Corporation
2730 W Tyvola Rd
Charlotte NC 28217
704 423-7000

(G-5332)
GOODYEAR TIRE & RUBBER COMPANY
18901 Snow Rd (44142-1465)
PHONE.................................216 265-1800
Ken Dombrowski, *General Mgr*
EMP: 200
SALES (corp-wide): 15.4B **Publicly Held**
WEB: www.goodyear.com
SIC: 5531 3011 Automotive tires; tires & inner tubes
PA: The Goodyear Tire & Rubber Company
200 E Innovation Way
Akron OH 44316
330 796-2121

(G-5333)
GORTONS INC
Also Called: Specialty Products
13525 Hummel Rd (44142-2519)
PHONE.................................216 362-1050
Louis Granja, *Opers-Prdtn-Mfg*
EMP: 36
SQ FT: 15,000
SALES (corp-wide): 6.4B **Privately Held**
WEB: www.gortons.com
SIC: 2011 Meat packing plants
HQ: Gorton's Inc.
128 Rogers St
Gloucester MA 01930
978 283-3000

(G-5334)
GOTTA GROOVE RECORDS INC
3615 Superior Ave E 4201a (44114-4185)
PHONE.................................216 431-7373
Vince Slusarz, *President*
Chris Smith, *Manager*

Cleveland - Cuyahoga County (G-5335)

EMP: 40
SALES (est): 5.1MM Privately Held
SIC: 2782 Account books

(G-5335)
GRABO INTERIORS INC
3605 Perkins Ave (44114-4632)
PHONE..................216 391-6677
Joseph Grabo, *President*
Paul Grabo, *Vice Pres*
EMP: 6
SQ FT: 4,400
SALES: 500K Privately Held
SIC: 2511 Wood household furniture

(G-5336)
GRAFTECH GLOBAL ENTPS INC
12900 Snow Rd (44130-1012)
PHONE..................216 676-2000
Joel Hawthorne, *President*
EMP: 3 **EST:** 2016
SALES (est): 106.9K
SALES (corp-wide): 8.5B Publicly Held
SIC: 3629 Electrical industrial apparatus
HQ: Graftech International Ltd.
  982 Keynote Cir Ste 6
  Brooklyn Heights OH 44131

(G-5337)
GRAFTECH INTL HOLDINGS INC
11709 Madison Ave (44107-5230)
PHONE..................216 529-3777
Ryan Weiss, *Tax Mgr*
Dennis Robinson, *Human Res Mgr*
Matthew Smith, *Manager*
EMP: 101
SALES (corp-wide): 8.5B Publicly Held
SIC: 3624 Carbon & graphite products
HQ: Graftech International Holdings Inc.
  982 Keynote Cir
  Brooklyn Heights OH 44131
  216 676-2000

(G-5338)
GRAIN CRAFT INC
1635 Merwin Ave (44113-2421)
PHONE..................216 621-3206
Joe E Blanton, *General Mgr*
EMP: 27
SQ FT: 20,000
SALES (corp-wide): 320.5MM Privately Held
WEB: www.cerealfood.com
SIC: 2041 Flour mills, cereal (except rice)
PA: Grain Craft, Inc.
  201 W Main St Ste 203
  Chattanooga TN 37408
  423 265-2313

(G-5339)
GRAND HARBOR YACHT SALES & SVC
Also Called: Sneller Machine Tool Division
706 Alpha Dr (44143-2125)
PHONE..................440 442-2919
John Bennington, *President*
EMP: 6 **EST:** 1973
SQ FT: 7,000
SALES (est): 846.3K Privately Held
WEB: www.snellermachine.com
SIC: 3599 5084 3537 3531 Machine shop, jobbing & repair; industrial machinery & equipment; industrial trucks & tractors; construction machinery

(G-5340)
GRANITE FABRICATORS INC
1250 Marquette St (44114)
PHONE..................216 228-3669
Paul Bussert, *President*
▲ **EMP:** 6
SQ FT: 25,000
SALES (est): 889.8K Privately Held
WEB: www.granitefabricators.com
SIC: 3281 Mfg Cut Stone/Products

(G-5341)
GRAPHIC ART SYSTEMS INC
Also Called: Grafix
5800 Pennsylvania Ave (44137-4331)
PHONE..................216 581-9050
Jordan Katz, *President*
Hayley Ann Prendergast, *President*
Karl Szelpal, *Sales Mgr*
Katelyn Boothby, *Marketing Staff*
Doris Morton, *Technology*
▲ **EMP:** 27 **EST:** 1963
SQ FT: 45,000
SALES: 10MM Privately Held
WEB: www.grafixplastics.com
SIC: 3081 Plastic film & sheet

(G-5342)
GRAPHTECH COMMUNICATIONS INC
4724 W 150th St (44135-3464)
PHONE..................216 676-1020
Stephen L Adamson, *President*
William Kall, *Vice Pres*
EMP: 10
SQ FT: 13,500
SALES: 1MM Privately Held
WEB: www.graphtechcommunications.com
SIC: 2752 Commercial printing, offset

(G-5343)
GRAY & COMPANY PUBLISHERS
1588 E 40th St Ste 1b (44103-2386)
PHONE..................216 431-2665
David Gray, *President*
EMP: 6
SALES (est): 623.5K Privately Held
WEB: www.grayco.com
SIC: 2741 Miscellaneous publishing

(G-5344)
GREAT LAKES ETCHING FINSHG CO
7010 Krick Rd Ste 3 (44146-4483)
PHONE..................440 439-3624
Ronald Pool Sr, *President*
Ronald Pool, *Owner*
Joanne Marold, *Vice Pres*
Ronald Pool III, *Vice Pres*
Lisa Schechterman, *Sales Staff*
EMP: 11 **EST:** 1962
SALES: 1MM Privately Held
SIC: 3479 Etching on metals

(G-5345)
GREAT LAKES GRAPHICS INC
3354 Superior Ave E (44114-4123)
PHONE..................216 391-0077
Anthony R Lux, *President*
EMP: 20
SQ FT: 15,000
SALES (est): 3.2MM Privately Held
WEB: www.greatlakesgraphicsinc.com
SIC: 3555 7336 Plates, offset; graphic arts & related design

(G-5346)
GREAT LAKES GROUP
Also Called: Great Lakes Towing
4500 Division Ave (44102-2228)
PHONE..................216 621-4854
Sheldon Guren, *Ch of Bd*
Ronald Rasmus, *President*
George Sogar, *Vice Pres*
EMP: 120
SQ FT: 6,000
SALES (est): 21.3MM Privately Held
SIC: 3731 4492 Shipbuilding & repairing; marine towing services

(G-5347)
GREAT LAKES INTEGRATED INC (PA)
Also Called: Gli
4005 Clark Ave (44109-1128)
PHONE..................216 651-1500
James R Schultz, *President*
Scot D Adkins, *President*
Carrie Spence, *President*
Anthony Sanson, *Vice Pres*
Robert J Schultz, *Vice Pres*
▲ **EMP:** 90 **EST:** 1931
SQ FT: 75,000
SALES (est): 29.1MM Privately Held
SIC: 2752 2796 2789 Commercial printing, offset; lithographic plates, positives or negatives; bookbinding & related work

(G-5348)
GREAT LAKES LITHOGRAPH
4005 Clark Ave (44109-1186)
PHONE..................216 651-1500
Chris Donnelly, *Principal*
EMP: 11
SQ FT: 45,469
SALES (est): 1.1MM Privately Held
SIC: 2752 Commercial printing, offset

(G-5349)
GREAT LAKES MANAGEMENT INC (PA)
2700 E 40th St Ste 1 (44115-3501)
PHONE..................216 883-6500
Margaret Ruebensaal, *President*
Charles M Ruebensaal Jr, *Treasurer*
David Biasio, *Admin Sec*
David Di Biasio, *Admin Sec*
EMP: 35
SALES (est): 2.3MM Privately Held
SIC: 6512 3822 Nonresidential building operators; switches, thermostatic

(G-5350)
GREAT LAKES PUBLISHING COMPANY (PA)
Also Called: Cleveland Magazine
1422 Euclid Ave Ste 730 (44115-2001)
PHONE..................216 771-2833
Lute Harmon Jr, *Ch of Bd*
Steve Gleydura, *Vice Pres*
Susan Harmon, *Vice Pres*
George Sedlak, *CFO*
Sarah Desmond, *Director*
EMP: 75
SQ FT: 19,000
SALES (est): 9.2MM Privately Held
WEB: www.clevelandmagazine.com
SIC: 2721 7374 Magazines: publishing only, not printed on site; computer graphics service

(G-5351)
GREAT LKES NROTECHNOLOGIES INC
6100 Rockside Woods # 415 (44131-2339)
PHONE..................855 456-3876
Robert N Schmidt, *Ch of Bd*
Joseph P Giuffrida, *President*
Brian M Kolkowski, *President*
Chad Gerbick, *QC Mgr*
Stephan Kruger, *Engineer*
EMP: 20
SALES (est): 3.5MM Privately Held
WEB: www.glneurotech.com
SIC: 3845 Electromedical apparatus

(G-5352)
GREAT WESTERN JUICE COMPANY
Also Called: Perfection Fine Products
16153 Libby Rd (44137-1219)
PHONE..................216 475-5770
Jack M Goldberg, *President*
William Overton, *Vice Pres*
EMP: 18
SQ FT: 30,000
SALES (est): 3.3MM Privately Held
SIC: 2033 2087 Fruit juices: fresh; cocktail mixes, nonalcoholic

(G-5353)
GREATER CLEVE PIPE FTTING FUND
6305 Halle Dr (44125-4617)
PHONE..................216 524-8334
Niel Ginley, *President*
EMP: 10
SALES (est): 1.1MM Privately Held
SIC: 3494 Pipe fittings

(G-5354)
GROFF INDUSTRIES
2201 W 110th St (44102-3511)
PHONE..................216 634-9100
John Rusnak, *Mng Member*
EMP: 15
SALES (est): 877.9K Privately Held
WEB: www.groffeng.com
SIC: 3999 7389 Manufacturing industries; packaging & labeling services

(G-5355)
GROUP INDUSTRIES INC (PA)
Also Called: Drum Parts
7580 Garfield Blvd (44125-1216)
P.O. Box 25409 (44125-0409)
PHONE..................216 271-0702
Martin Tiernan, *Ch of Bd*
Lane A Zamin, *President*
Curtis Crowder, *Vice Pres*
Dale Zeleznik, *Vice Pres*
▲ **EMP:** 32
SQ FT: 24,000
SALES (est): 10.5MM Privately Held
WEB: www.drumpartsinc.com
SIC: 3429 3592 3452 Manufactured hardware (general); carburetors, pistons, rings, valves; bolts, nuts, rivets & washers

(G-5356)
GROVER MUSICAL PRODUCTS INC (PA)
Also Called: Grover Trophy Musical Products
9287 Midwest Ave (44125-2415)
PHONE..................216 391-1188
Richard I Berger, *President*
Dann Skutt, *Vice Pres*
Dan Greene, *Controller*
Chuck Kirschling, *Sales Mgr*
Cory Berger, *Adv Mgr*
▲ **EMP:** 25
SQ FT: 60,000
SALES (est): 3.6MM Privately Held
SIC: 3931 Musical instruments

(G-5357)
GSR INDUSTRIES LLC
Also Called: Roto-Rooter
21648 N Park Dr (44126-2326)
PHONE..................440 934-0201
Geoff S Ristagno, *Principal*
EMP: 3
SALES (est): 263.5K Privately Held
SIC: 3999 Manufacturing industries

(G-5358)
GUARANTEED FNSHG UNLIMITED INC
3200 W 121st St (44111-1720)
PHONE..................216 252-8200
William Kozak Jr, *CEO*
Joseph Janke, *President*
▲ **EMP:** 35
SQ FT: 50,000
SALES (est): 4.8MM Privately Held
SIC: 3471 Electroplating of metals or formed products

(G-5359)
GUARDIAN CO INC
2754 Woodhill Rd (44104-3661)
PHONE..................216 721-2262
Herbert K Kubach, *President*
Kenneth Kubach, *Vice Pres*
EMP: 5
SQ FT: 15,000
SALES (est): 460K Privately Held
SIC: 2842 2841 2392 Waxes for wood, leather & other materials; degreasing solvent; detergents, synthetic organic or inorganic alkaline; soap: granulated, liquid, cake, flaked or chip; mops, floor & dust

(G-5360)
GUSTAVE JULIAN JEWELERS INC
7432 State Rd (44134-5858)
PHONE..................440 888-1100
Jim Julian, *President*
Jayne Julian, *Corp Secy*
Edward Julian, *Vice Pres*
EMP: 7 **EST:** 1948
SQ FT: 2,400
SALES (est): 789.6K Privately Held
SIC: 5944 7631 3911 Silverware; jewelry repair services; watch repair; jewelry, precious metal

(G-5361)
H & B MACHINE & TOOL INC
1390 E 40th St (44103-1102)
PHONE..................216 431-3254
Frank Spisich, *President*
Geraldine Spisich, *Vice Pres*
EMP: 12 **EST:** 1962
SQ FT: 8,000
SALES (est): 1.8MM Privately Held
WEB: www.hb-machine.com
SIC: 3599 Machine shop, jobbing & repair

(G-5362)
H & H TRUCK PARTS LLC
5500s Cloverleaf Pkwy (44125-4815)
PHONE..................216 642-4540
Mark Harris,

GEOGRAPHIC SECTION
Cleveland - Cuyahoga County (G-5390)

Jeff Heater,
EMP: 5
SQ FT: 12,000
SALES: 1MM **Privately Held**
WEB: www.hhtruckparts.com
SIC: 3713 5531 Truck bodies & parts; truck equipment & parts

(G-5363)
H P MANUFACTURING CO
3740 Prospect Ave E (44115-2706)
PHONE..................216 361-6500
EMP: 63 **EST:** 2015
SALES (est): 4.4MM **Privately Held**
SIC: 3089 Plastic processing

(G-5364)
H S PROCESSING LP
4600 Heidtman Pkwy (44105-1023)
PHONE..................216 641-6995
Greg Glenn, *Principal*
EMP: 3
SALES (est): 167K **Privately Held**
SIC: 3316 Strip steel, cold-rolled: from purchased hot-rolled

(G-5365)
HAFCO-CASE INC
12212 Sprecher Ave (44135-5122)
PHONE..................216 267-4644
Phyllis Tarnawsky, *President*
Natalie Tarnawsky, *Corp Secy*
Bohdan Tarnawsky, *Vice Pres*
EMP: 8 **EST:** 1951
SQ FT: 8,000
SALES (est): 934.7K **Privately Held**
SIC: 3599 Machine shop, jobbing & repair

(G-5366)
HAHN MANUFACTURING COMPANY
5332 Hamilton Ave (44114-3984)
PHONE..................216 391-9300
Robert E Hahn, *President*
Greg Hahn, *Vice Pres*
Laura L Hahn, *Vice Pres*
EMP: 45 **EST:** 1916
SQ FT: 17,000
SALES (est): 7MM **Privately Held**
WEB: www.hahnmfg.com
SIC: 3549 3599 Metalworking machinery; machine shop, jobbing & repair

(G-5367)
HALVORSEN COMPANY
7500 Grand Division Ave # 1 (44125-1282)
P.O. Box 25625 (44125-0625)
PHONE..................216 341-7500
Ross C Frick, *President*
William Patrick Clyne, *Principal*
John F Ray Jr, *Principal*
Francis J Talty, *Principal*
▲ **EMP:** 32 **EST:** 1954
SQ FT: 68,000
SALES (est): 9.8MM **Privately Held**
WEB: www.halvorsenusa.com
SIC: 3441 3444 3443 Fabricated structural metal; sheet metalwork; fabricated plate work (boiler shop)

(G-5368)
HAMILTON MOLD & MACHINE CO
25016 Lakeland Blvd (44132-2685)
PHONE..................216 732-8200
Dale Fleming, *President*
Mark Fleming, *Treasurer*
John Fleming, *Admin Sec*
EMP: 39 **EST:** 1917
SQ FT: 20,000
SALES (est): 5.8MM **Privately Held**
SIC: 3544 Forms (molds), for foundry & plastics working machinery

(G-5369)
HANG TIME GROUP INC
5340 Hamilton Ave Ste 107 (44114-3954)
PHONE..................216 771-5885
Dave Stilson, *President*
David Stilson, *President*
Sharon Furey, *Officer*
David Stine, *Admin Sec*
EMP: 4 **EST:** 1997
SQ FT: 800
SALES (est): 304.9K **Privately Held**
SIC: 2395 Embroidery & art needlework

(G-5370)
HANINI SEVEN OIL
6501 Denison Ave (44102-5434)
PHONE..................216 857-0172
Amal Ajjar, *Principal*
EMP: 3
SALES (est): 258.7K **Privately Held**
SIC: 1311 Crude petroleum & natural gas

(G-5371)
HANLON INDUSTRIES INC
Also Called: Fiberglass Engineering Co
1280 E 286th St (44132-2195)
PHONE..................216 261-7056
Bernard M Hanlon, *President*
EMP: 10
SALES (est): 665.5K **Privately Held**
SIC: 3089 Plastic processing

(G-5372)
HANSA BEWERY LLC
2717 Lorain Ave (44113-3414)
PHONE..................216 631-6585
Boris Music,
EMP: 4 **EST:** 2012
SALES (est): 75.4K **Privately Held**
SIC: 2082 Brewers' grain

(G-5373)
HARBISONWALKER INTL INC
6950 Engle Rd (44130-3445)
PHONE..................440 234-8002
Graham Roberts, *Branch Mgr*
EMP: 4
SALES (corp-wide): 703.8MM **Privately Held**
SIC: 3255 Clay refractories
HQ: Harbisonwalker International, Inc.
1305 Cherrington Pkwy # 100
Moon Township PA 15108

(G-5374)
HARD CHROME PLATING CONSULTANT
2196 W 59th St (44102-4470)
P.O. Box 44082 (44144-0082)
PHONE..................216 631-9090
Clarence Peger Jr, *President*
Denise Ward, *Corp Secy*
Christine Peger, *Vice Pres*
EMP: 3
SQ FT: 4,000
SALES (est): 810K **Privately Held**
WEB: www.hard-chromesystems.com
SIC: 8742 8331 3443 Training & development consultant; vocational training agency; plate work for the metalworking trade

(G-5375)
HARRIS CALORIFIC INC
22801 Saint Clair Ave (44117-2524)
PHONE..................216 383-4107
EMP: 7
SALES (est): 803.4K **Privately Held**
SIC: 3548 Welding apparatus

(G-5376)
HARSCO CORPORATION
Sherwood Divisions of Harsco
7900 Hub Pkwy (44125-5713)
PHONE..................216 961-1570
Tom Hensley, *Manager*
EMP: 30
SALES (corp-wide): 1.6B **Publicly Held**
WEB: www.harsco.com
SIC: 3443 Industrial vessels, tanks & containers
PA: Harsco Corporation
350 Poplar Church Rd
Camp Hill PA 17011
717 763-7064

(G-5377)
HARTLINE PRODUCTS COINC (PA)
4568 Mayfield Rd Ste 202 (44121-4050)
PHONE..................216 291-2303
Christopher J Hart, *President*
Rebecca F Hart, *Treasurer*
EMP: 5
SQ FT: 1,000
SALES (est): 2.8MM **Privately Held**
SIC: 2891 Cement, except linoleum & tile

(G-5378)
HARTLINE PRODUCTS COINC
15035 Woodworth Rd Ste 3 (44110-3345)
PHONE..................216 851-7189
Becky Hart, *Plant Mgr*
EMP: 9
SALES (corp-wide): 2.8MM **Privately Held**
SIC: 2891 3241 Cement, except linoleum & tile; cement, hydraulic
PA: Hartline Products Co.Inc.
4568 Mayfield Rd Ste 202
Cleveland OH 44121
216 291-2303

(G-5379)
HARVARD COIL PROCESSING INC
5400 Harvard Ave (44105-4828)
PHONE..................216 883-6366
Eileen Jacobs, *President*
Cindi Disiena, *QC Mgr*
EMP: 20
SQ FT: 2,000
SALES (est): 3.9MM **Privately Held**
WEB: www.harvardcoilprocessing.com
SIC: 3312 Blast furnaces & steel mills

(G-5380)
HATTENBACH COMPANY (PA)
5309 Hamilton Ave (44114-3909)
PHONE..................216 881-5200
Cathy Hattenbach, *President*
Joseph G Berick, *Principal*
Dennis Bruckman, *Vice Pres*
John Heinert, *CFO*
EMP: 65 **EST:** 1944
SQ FT: 50,000
SALES (est): 15MM **Privately Held**
WEB: www.hattenbach.com
SIC: 1711 5078 2541 2434 Refrigeration contractor; commercial refrigeration equipment; cabinets, except refrigerated: show, display, etc.: wood; wood kitchen cabinets

(G-5381)
HBB PRO SALES (PA)
9700 Rockside Rd Ste 120 (44125-6264)
PHONE..................216 901-7900
Jeff Hutton, *Principal*
EMP: 9 **EST:** 2011
SALES (est): 1.9MM **Privately Held**
SIC: 3585 Heating equipment, complete

(G-5382)
HC STARCK INC
21801 Tungsten Rd (44117-1117)
PHONE..................216 692-3990
Larry McHugh, *CEO*
Joel Hoffman, *COO*
Pete Calfo, *Senior VP*
John Durham, *Senior VP*
EMP: 500
SQ FT: 150,000
SALES (est): 45.6MM **Privately Held**
SIC: 3341 Secondary nonferrous metals

(G-5383)
HCC HOLDINGS INC
4700 W 160th St (44135-2632)
PHONE..................800 203-1155
EMP: 5
SALES (est): 343.6K
SALES (corp-wide): 470MM **Privately Held**
SIC: 3444 Metal roofing & roof drainage equipment
PA: Oatey Co.
20600 Emerald Pkwy
Cleveland OH 44135
800 203-1155

(G-5384)
HEALTH NUTS MEDIA LLC
4225 W 229th St (44126-1834)
PHONE..................818 802-5222
Timothy Jones,
EMP: 6 **EST:** 2012
SALES (est): 342.5K **Privately Held**
SIC: 7371 5999 7389 7372 Computer software writing services; computer software systems analysis & design, custom; educational aids & electronic training materials; ; educational computer software

(G-5385)
HEAT EXCHANGE INSTITUTE INC
1300 Sumner Ave (44115-2851)
PHONE..................216 241-7333
John Addington, *Director*
EMP: 4
SQ FT: 5,200
SALES: 281.9K **Privately Held**
SIC: 8611 3699 Contractors' association; electrical equipment & supplies

(G-5386)
HEAT SEAL LLC
Also Called: Ampak
4922 E 49th St (44125-1016)
PHONE..................216 341-2022
Bryan Rakovec, *Principal*
James Sovacool, *Vice Pres*
Karie Casper, *Marketing Mgr*
Rick Price, *Manager*
Thomas Dougherty,
◆ **EMP:** 110
SQ FT: 80,000
SALES (est): 26.6MM **Privately Held**
WEB: www.heatsealco.com
SIC: 2542 3565 Fixtures, store: except wood; wrapping machines

(G-5387)
HEATHER B MOORE INC
4502 Prospect Ave (44103-4312)
PHONE..................216 932-5430
Heather Moore, *President*
Kate Miranda, *Representative*
EMP: 5
SQ FT: 1,000
SALES (est): 1MM **Privately Held**
WEB: www.heatherbmoore.com
SIC: 7389 3911 Apparel designers, commercial; jewelry, precious metal

(G-5388)
HEDALLOY DIE CORP
3266 E 49th St (44127-1092)
PHONE..................216 341-3768
John Susa Jr, *President*
Joseph Susa, *General Mgr*
EMP: 12
SQ FT: 10,000
SALES: 1MM **Privately Held**
SIC: 3544 Dies, steel rule; die sets for metal stamping (presses); jigs & fixtures; industrial molds

(G-5389)
HELLAN STRAINER COMPANY
3249 E 80th St (44104-4341)
PHONE..................216 206-4200
Jon Crowley, *President*
William Hupp, *Engineer*
Patrick Barrett, *Sales Mgr*
▲ **EMP:** 9
SALES (est): 2.4MM
SALES (corp-wide): 506.2MM **Privately Held**
WEB: www.hellanstrainer.com
SIC: 3569 Filters & strainers, pipeline
HQ: Industrial Manufacturing Company Llc
8223 Brecksville Rd Ste 1
Brecksville OH 44141
440 838-4700

(G-5390)
HELLER MACHINE PRODUCTS INC
1971 W 90th St (44102-2742)
PHONE..................216 281-2951
Jeff Evin, *President*
David Heller, *Vice Pres*
Mary Heller, *Vice Pres*
Joyce Evin, *Director*
Eda Heller, *Director*
EMP: 8 **EST:** 1953
SQ FT: 10,000
SALES (est): 945.4K **Privately Held**
SIC: 3451 3812 3728 3429 Screw machine products; search & navigation equipment; aircraft parts & equipment; manufactured hardware (general)

(PA)=Parent Co (HQ)=Headquarters (DH)=Div Headquarters
⊙ = New Business established in last 2 years

Cleveland - Cuyahoga County (G-5391)

(G-5391)
HENDERSON FABRICATING CO INC
6217 Central Ave (44104-1756)
PHONE..................216 432-0404
John Henderson, *President*
Karen Henderson, *Admin Sec*
EMP: 12
SQ FT: 8,000
SALES (est): 1.2MM **Privately Held**
SIC: 1791 3599 Structural steel erection; machine shop, jobbing & repair

(G-5392)
HENKEL CORPORATION
Cleveland Manufacturing Fcilty
18731 Cranwood Pkwy (44128-4037)
PHONE..................216 475-3600
Jean Bolling, *Production*
Rick Marrero, *Buyer*
Keith Laughlin, *Engineer*
Seth Meyers, *Sales Mgr*
Doug Karns, *Manager*
EMP: 250
SALES (corp-wide): 22.7B **Privately Held**
SIC: 2891 2851 2842 Adhesives; sealants; paints & allied products; specialty cleaning, polishes & sanitation goods
HQ: Henkel Us Operations Corporation
1 Henkel Way
Rocky Hill CT 06067
860 571-5100

(G-5393)
HENNINGS QUALITY SERVICE INC
3115 Berea Rd (44111-1503)
PHONE..................216 941-9120
Herbert Morrow, *President*
James Brinker, *Vice Pres*
EMP: 17
SQ FT: 20,000
SALES: 1.6MM **Privately Held**
SIC: 7694 Electric motor repair

(G-5394)
HENRY & WRIGHT CORPORATION
739 E 140th St Ste 1 (44110-2182)
PHONE..................216 851-3750
Austin W Moore, *President*
Jonathan Moore, *Vice Pres*
Chuck Fetheroff, *Manager*
Tammy Moore, *Assistant*
EMP: 13
SQ FT: 55,000
SALES (est): 3.5MM **Privately Held**
WEB: www.henrywright.com
SIC: 3542 3829 3823 Presses: hydraulic & pneumatic, mechanical & manual; measuring & controlling devices; industrial instrmnts msrmnt display/control process variable

(G-5395)
HENRY TOOLS INC
498 S Belvoir Blvd (44121-2351)
PHONE..................216 291-1011
Clara Henry, *Ch of Bd*
Richard Henry Sr, *President*
David Henry, *Vice Pres*
▲ **EMP:** 9
SALES (est): 1.3MM **Privately Held**
WEB: www.henrytools.com
SIC: 3724 Aircraft engines & engine parts

(G-5396)
HEPHAESTUS TECHNOLOGIES LLC
Also Called: Gray Tech International
3811 W 150th St (44111-5806)
PHONE..................216 252-0430
Helun Chahda, *CEO*
Helun Bachour Chahda, *CEO*
Eric Attel, *President*
Mario Chahda, *Vice Pres*
Doug Murillo, *Engineer*
EMP: 24 **EST:** 1987
SQ FT: 20,000
SALES (est): 5MM **Privately Held**
WEB: www.graytechintl.com
SIC: 3599 Machine shop, jobbing & repair

(G-5397)
HERD MANUFACTURING INC
9227 Clinton Rd (44144-1088)
PHONE..................216 651-4221
Erich J Rock, *President*
Rita Laurenzi, *Treasurer*
Verne Campbell, *Manager*
James Knauss, *MIS Staff*
Rita Laurenci, *Admin Sec*
EMP: 40
SQ FT: 25,000
SALES (est): 7.1MM **Privately Held**
WEB: www.herdmfg.com
SIC: 3469 3544 3599 Stamping metal for the trade; special dies & tools; custom machinery

(G-5398)
HERMAN MANUFACTURING LLC
Also Called: Walsh Manufacturing
13825 Triskett Rd (44111-1523)
PHONE..................216 251-6400
Art Blanc, *Engineer*
Martin Herman, *Mng Member*
Michael Herman,
EMP: 16
SQ FT: 25,000
SALES (est): 4.7MM **Privately Held**
WEB: www.walshmfg.com
SIC: 3564 3441 Dust or fume collecting equipment, industrial; fabricated structural metal

(G-5399)
HEROLD SALADS INC
17512 Miles Ave (44128-3404)
PHONE..................216 991-7500
Cathy L Herold, *President*
Peggy Waugh, *Office Mgr*
EMP: 25
SQ FT: 20,000
SALES (est): 3.8MM **Privately Held**
SIC: 2099 Salads, fresh or refrigerated; desserts, ready-to-mix

(G-5400)
HEXAGON INDUSTRIES INC
1135 Ivanhoe Rd (44110-3249)
PHONE..................216 249-0200
Stephen R Jackson, *President*
Peter M Jackson, *Vice Pres*
Peter Jackson, *Vice Pres*
Robin Burlinski, *Purchasing*
Bonita Thompson, *Human Res Dir*
▲ **EMP:** 50
SQ FT: 270,000
SALES (est): 11.8MM **Privately Held**
SIC: 3452 Screws, metal

(G-5401)
HI CARB CORP
23610 Saint Clair Ave (44117-2591)
PHONE..................216 486-5000
John R Sonnie, *President*
EMP: 17
SQ FT: 10,000
SALES (est): 2.9MM **Privately Held**
WEB: www.hicarb.com
SIC: 3545 Tools & accessories for machine tools

(G-5402)
HI TECMETAL GROUP INC (PA)
Also Called: Hydro-Vac
1101 E 55th St (44103-1026)
PHONE..................216 881-8100
Terence Profughi, *President*
Harold Baron, *Principal*
Mary Finley, *Principal*
N M Salkover, *Principal*
Cole Coe, *Vice Pres*
EMP: 20 **EST:** 1943
SQ FT: 398,700
SALES: 9.4MM **Privately Held**
SIC: 3398 7692 Brazing (hardening) of metal; annealing of metal; tempering of metal; welding repair

(G-5403)
HI TECMETAL GROUP INC
Walker Heat Treating
10601 Briggs Rd (44111-5329)
PHONE..................216 941-0440
Terence Profughi, *CEO*
EMP: 15
SALES (corp-wide): 25.2MM **Privately Held**
SIC: 3398 Metal heat treating
PA: Hi Tecmetal Group Inc
1101 E 55th St
Cleveland OH 44103
216 881-8100

(G-5404)
HI TECMETAL GROUP INC
1432 E 47th St (44103-1222)
PHONE..................216 881-8100
Greg Hercik, *Manager*
EMP: 11
SALES (corp-wide): 25.2MM **Privately Held**
SIC: 3398 Metal heat treating
PA: Hi Tecmetal Group Inc
1101 E 55th St
Cleveland OH 44103
216 881-8100

(G-5405)
HI-TECH SOLUTIONS LLC
510 Karl Dr (44143-2544)
PHONE..................216 331-3050
Scott Bennett, *President*
EMP: 3 **EST:** 2015
SALES (est): 176K **Privately Held**
SIC: 3451 3489 Screw machine products; ordnance & accessories; artillery or artillery parts, over 30 mm.; guns or gun parts, over 30 mm.

(G-5406)
HIBBING TACONITE A JOINT VENTR (DH)
200 Public Sq Ste 3300 (44114-2315)
PHONE..................216 694-5700
Joseph A Carrabba, *CEO*
Laurie Brlas, *Exec VP*
Donald Gallagher, *Exec VP*
Edward M Latendresse,
Mittal S US,
▲ **EMP:** 1
SALES (est): 948.7MM
SALES (corp-wide): 9.1B **Privately Held**
SIC: 1011 Iron ore mining; iron ore pelletizing; iron ore beneficiating
HQ: Arcelormittal Usa Llc
1 S Dearborn St Ste 1800
Chicago IL 60603
312 346-0300

(G-5407)
HICKOK INCORPORATED (PA)
10514 Dupont Ave (44108-1348)
PHONE..................216 541-8060
Brian E Powers, *Ch of Bd*
Kelly J Marek, *CFO*
Gregory M Zoloty, *CFO*
John Dzuroff, *Creative Dir*
EMP: 95 **EST:** 1910
SQ FT: 37,000
SALES: 66.3MM **Publicly Held**
WEB: www.hickok-inc.com
SIC: 3823 3829 Industrial process measurement equipment; measuring & controlling devices; aircraft & motor vehicle measurement equipment

(G-5408)
HICKOK WAEKON LLC
10514 Dupont Ave (44108-1348)
PHONE..................216 541-8060
Robert Bauman,
EMP: 55
SQ FT: 7,200
SALES: 6MM **Privately Held**
SIC: 3841 Diagnostic apparatus, medical

(G-5409)
HILLMAN GROUP INC
American Consumer Products Div
31100 Solon Rd (44139-3462)
PHONE..................440 248-7000
EMP: 4
SALES (corp-wide): 484.2MM **Privately Held**
SIC: 2381 3151 3842 3949 Fabric dress & work gloves; leather gloves & mittens; gloves, safety; gloves, sport & athletic: boxing, handball, etc.; keys & key blanks; letters for signs, metal; signs, not made in custom sign painting shops
HQ: The Hillman Group Inc
10590 Hamilton Av
Cincinnati OH 45231
513 851-4900

(G-5410)
HITTI ENTERPRISES INC
6427 Eastland Rd (44142-1305)
PHONE..................440 243-4100
Fred Hitti, *President*
EMP: 10
SQ FT: 40,000
SALES (est): 1MM **Privately Held**
SIC: 3086 6531 Packaging & shipping materials, foamed plastic; real estate agents & managers

(G-5411)
HK TECHNOLOGIES
2828 Clinton Ave (44113-2939)
PHONE..................330 337-9710
Micheal A Valore, *Principal*
EMP: 3
SALES (est): 193.4K **Privately Held**
SIC: 3999 Vibrators, electric: designed for barber & beauty shops

(G-5412)
HKM DRECT MKT CMMNICATIONS INC (PA)
Also Called: H K M
5501 Cass Ave (44102-2121)
PHONE..................216 651-9500
Rob Durham, *President*
Scott Durham, *COO*
EMP: 135
SQ FT: 86,000
SALES (est): 55.8MM **Privately Held**
WEB: www.hkmdirectmarket.com
SIC: 2752 7375 2791 2759 Commercial printing, lithographic; information retrieval services; typesetting; commercial printing; mailing service

(G-5413)
HOME RESOLVER
11121 Magdala Dr (44130-1547)
PHONE..................440 886-6758
Kevin Sheridan, *Principal*
EMP: 4
SALES (est): 338.9K **Privately Held**
SIC: 3621 Resolvers

(G-5414)
HOME STOR & OFF SOLUTIONS INC
Also Called: Closet Factory, The
5305 Commerce Pkwy W (44130-1274)
PHONE..................216 362-4660
Kathy Pietrick, *President*
Robert J Pietrick Jr, *Vice Pres*
EMP: 16
SQ FT: 5,000
SALES (est): 3.1MM **Privately Held**
SIC: 5211 5712 2541 Closets, interiors & accessories; furniture stores; wood partitions & fixtures

(G-5415)
HOMELAND AG FUELS LLC
25700 Science Park Dr # 210 (44122-7319)
PHONE..................216 763-1004
Anthony Senagore, *CEO*
J Kieran Jennings, *COO*
EMP: 3
SALES (est): 1,000K **Privately Held**
SIC: 2869 Fuels

(G-5416)
HORIZONS INC CAMCODE DIVISION
18531 S Miles Rd (44128-4237)
PHONE..................216 714-0020
Nicole Pontius, *Principal*
Brad Davey, *Project Mgr*
Alan Cunningham, *Opers Mgr*
Dan Fitzwater, *Prdtn Mgr*
Chris Knarr, *Mfg Staff*
EMP: 20
SQ FT: 20,000

GEOGRAPHIC SECTION

Cleveland - Cuyahoga County (G-5442)

SALES (est): 1.7MM
SALES (corp-wide): 30.4MM **Privately Held**
SIC: 3861 Photographic equipment & supplies
PA: Horizons Incorporated
    18531 S Miles Rd
    Cleveland OH 44128
    216 475-0555

(G-5417)
HORIZONS INCORPORATED (PA)
Also Called: Panam Imaging Systems
18531 S Miles Rd (44128-4237)
PHONE.................................216 475-0555
  Herbert A Wainer, *President*
  Joe Lough, *General Mgr*
  David Kesic, *Business Mgr*
  Trey Hooper, *Vice Pres*
  Robert Miller, *Vice Pres*
◆ EMP: 115 EST: 1967
SQ FT: 51,000
SALES (est): 30.4MM **Privately Held**
WEB: www.horizonsisg.com
SIC: 3861 Plates, photographic (sensitized)

(G-5418)
HORSBURGH & SCOTT CO (PA)
5114 Hamilton Ave (44114-3985)
PHONE.................................216 432-5858
  Randy Burdick, *CEO*
  Lloyd G Trotter, *Ch of Bd*
  Phil Griffith, *COO*
  Doug Thomson, *Opers Staff*
  Jadran Golem, *Buyer*
▲ EMP: 180
SQ FT: 240,000
SALES (est): 60.3MM **Privately Held**
WEB: www.horsburgh-scott.com
SIC: 3566 Gears, power transmission, except automotive; speed changers (power transmission equipment), except auto

(G-5419)
HORSBURGH & SCOTT CO
1441 Chardon Rd (44117-1510)
PHONE.................................216 383-2909
  Felix Tarorick, *Branch Mgr*
EMP: 8
SALES (corp-wide): 60.3MM **Privately Held**
SIC: 3566 Gears, power transmission, except automotive; speed changers (power transmission equipment), except auto
PA: The Horsburgh & Scott Co
    5114 Hamilton Ave
    Cleveland OH 44114
    216 432-5858

(G-5420)
HOUSE OF DELARA FRAGRANCES
1810 W 47th St (44102-3412)
PHONE.................................216 651-5803
  Fay M Harris, *Owner*
EMP: 3 EST: 1987
SALES (est): 184.7K **Privately Held**
SIC: 2844 Cosmetic preparations

(G-5421)
HP MANUFACTURING COMPANY INC (PA)
Also Called: House of Plastics
3705 Carnegie Ave (44115-2750)
PHONE.................................216 361-6500
  John R Melchiorre, *President*
  Elmer Krizek, *Principal*
  Paul Glozer, *QC Mgr*
EMP: 63
SQ FT: 110,000
SALES (est): 10.2MM **Privately Held**
WEB: www.hpmanufacturing.com
SIC: 3089 5162 3993 3082 Plastic processing; plastics sheets & rods; signs & advertising specialties; unsupported plastics profile shapes; partitions & fixtures, except wood

(G-5422)
HPM BUSINESS SYSTEMS INC
21887 Lorain Rd 300 (44126-3330)
PHONE.................................216 520-1330
  Harry P Miller, *President*
  Kevin Skelly, *General Mgr*
EMP: 5

SQ FT: 1,500
SALES (est): 546.8K **Privately Held**
WEB: www.hpmweb.com
SIC: 7389 3993 Advertising, promotional & trade show services; balloons, novelty & toy; child restraint seat, automotive: rental; signs & advertising specialties; advertising novelties

(G-5423)
HUBBELL MACHINE TOOLING INC
7507 Exchange St (44125-3305)
PHONE.................................216 524-1797
  Claude Petek, *CEO*
EMP: 12
SQ FT: 16,000
SALES (est): 1.1MM **Privately Held**
SIC: 3599 Machine shop, jobbing & repair

(G-5424)
HUDSON SUPPLY COMPANY INC
4500 Lee Rd Ste 120 (44128-2959)
PHONE.................................216 518-3000
  Richard Kopittke, *President*
▲ EMP: 6
SALES (est): 964.6K **Privately Held**
SIC: 3545 Machine tool accessories

(G-5425)
HUGO BOSS USA INC
4600 Piderman Rd (44144)
PHONE.................................216 671-8100
  Bill Scott, *Manager*
EMP: 400
SALES (corp-wide): 3.2B **Privately Held**
WEB: www.hugobossusa.com
SIC: 2311 Suits, men's & boys': made from purchased materials; tailored dress & sport coats: men's & boys'; topcoats, men's & boys': made from purchased materials
HQ: Hugo Boss Usa, Inc.
    55 Water St Fl 48
    New York NY 10041
    212 940-0600

(G-5426)
HURST AUTO-TRUCK ELECTRIC
Also Called: Tuff Stuff Performance
9004 Madison Ave (44102-2715)
PHONE.................................216 961-1800
  Frank Hurst, *President*
  Thomas Hurst, *President*
▲ EMP: 4
SALES (est): 968.3K **Privately Held**
WEB: www.tuffstuffperformance.com
SIC: 3714 3694 3625 3621 Motor vehicle parts & accessories; engine electrical equipment; relays & industrial controls; motors & generators; pumps & pumping equipment; alternators & generators, rebuilding & repair

(G-5427)
HUSQVARNA US HOLDING INC (HQ)
Also Called: Husqvarna Construction Pdts
20445 Emerald Pkwy (44135-6009)
PHONE.................................216 898-1800
  Richard Pietch, *Senior VP*
  Ronald Zajaczkowski, *Senior VP*
  George Weigand, *CFO*
  Marie-Louise Wingard, *Treasurer*
▲ EMP: 70
SQ FT: 18,000
SALES (est): 159.9MM
SALES (corp-wide): 4.6B **Privately Held**
SIC: 3582 Dryers, laundry: commercial, including coin-operated
PA: Husqvarna Ab
    Drottninggatan 2
    Huskvarna 561 3
    361 465-00

(G-5428)
HUTCHINSON-STEVENS INC
Also Called: Bradshaw Manufacturing
9627 Clinton Rd (44144-1029)
PHONE.................................216 281-8785
  Andrew Milgram, *President*
  Cara Cuddy, *Vice Pres*
EMP: 5
SQ FT: 600

SALES (est): 746.6K **Privately Held**
SIC: 3423 Soldering guns or tools, hand: electric

(G-5429)
HY-GRADE CORPORATION (PA)
3993 E 93rd St (44105-4052)
PHONE.................................216 341-7711
  Michael Pemberton, *President*
EMP: 35
SQ FT: 25,000
SALES (est): 9.1MM **Privately Held**
WEB: www.upm.com
SIC: 5032 2952 2951 Asphalt mixture; asphalt felts & coatings; asphalt paving mixtures & blocks

(G-5430)
HYDROGEN 411 TECHNOLOGY LLC
7777 W 130th St (44130-7161)
PHONE.................................440 941-6760
  Arnold Rusch,
EMP: 5 EST: 2012
SALES (est): 465.4K **Privately Held**
SIC: 3674 Fuel cells, solid state

(G-5431)
HYGIENT CORPORATION
5815 Landerbrook Dr # 24702 (44124-7900)
PHONE.................................440 796-7964
  Nailesh Sangani, *President*
EMP: 5
SALES (est): 477K **Privately Held**
SIC: 2671 2676 Packaging paper & plastics film, coated & laminated; infant & baby paper products

(G-5432)
HYSTER-YALE MATERIALS HDLG INC (PA)
5875 Landerbrook Dr # 300 (44124-6511)
PHONE.................................440 449-9600
  Alfred M Rankin Jr, *Ch of Bd*
  Jerry Dyer, *Business Mgr*
  Charles A Bittenbender, *Senior VP*
  Greg Breier, *Vice Pres*
  Joe Bugica, *Vice Pres*
EMP: 120
SALES: 3.1B **Publicly Held**
SIC: 3537 Lift trucks, industrial: fork, platform, straddle, etc.

(G-5433)
I L R INC
5240 Greenhurst Ext (44137-1128)
P.O. Box 31336 (44131-0336)
PHONE.................................216 587-2212
  Robert E Gazdak, *President*
  Lisa Joy Kemenyes, *Treasurer*
  Duane Kemenyes, *Executive*
EMP: 5 EST: 1977
SQ FT: 4,000
SALES (est): 931.9K **Privately Held**
SIC: 3443 Fabricated plate work (boiler shop)

(G-5434)
I P SPECRETE INC
10703 Quebec Ave (44106-4251)
PHONE.................................216 721-2050
  John Anderson, *President*
▲ EMP: 5
SQ FT: 30,000
SALES (est): 1MM **Privately Held**
WEB: www.specrete.com
SIC: 2899 Concrete curing & hardening compounds

(G-5435)
IDENTITY HOLDING COMPANY LLC
Also Called: Business Stationery
4944 Commerce Pkwy (44128-5908)
PHONE.................................216 514-1277
EMP: 100 **Privately Held**
SIC: 3953 Marking devices
PA: Identity Holding Company, Llc
    1480 Gould Dr
    Cookeville TN 38506

(G-5436)
IHOD USA LLC
127 Public Sq Ste 4120 (44114-1312)
PHONE.................................216 459-7179
  Mark Collins,
  Chris Baker,
EMP: 2
SQ FT: 2,500
SALES: 5MM
SALES (corp-wide): 725.3K **Privately Held**
SIC: 2813 Hydrogen
PA: Ihod Limited
    Suite 29 Forum House
    Chichester W SUSSEX PO19

(G-5437)
IMAGE CONCEPTS INC
Also Called: AlphaGraphics Valley View
8200 Sweet Valley Dr # 107 (44125-4267)
PHONE.................................216 524-9000
  Karey Zorv, *President*
  Patrick Delahunty, *Vice Pres*
EMP: 10
SQ FT: 8,000
SALES (est): 2MM **Privately Held**
WEB: www.imageconceptsprint.com
SIC: 2752 Commercial printing, offset; business form & card printing, lithographic

(G-5438)
IMAGEIQ INC
26801 Miles Rd Ste 103 (44128-5977)
PHONE.................................855 462-4347
  Timothy Kulbago, *CEO*
EMP: 10
SQ FT: 1,150
SALES (est): 1.7MM **Privately Held**
SIC: 3845 CAT scanner (Computerized Axial Tomography) apparatus
PA: Ert, Inc.
    1818 Market St Ste 1000
    Philadelphia PA 19103

(G-5439)
IMAGEMART INC
17320 Saint Clair Ave (44110-2537)
PHONE.................................216 486-4767
  Joseph Bruzas, *President*
EMP: 3
SALES (est): 379.4K **Privately Held**
SIC: 2759 Screen printing

(G-5440)
IMALUX CORPORATION
11000 Cedar Ave Ste 250 (44106-3056)
PHONE.................................216 502-0755
  Michael Burke, *President*
  Bill R Sanford, *Chairman*
  Paul G Amazeen, *Exec VP*
  Thomas F Barnish, *CFO*
  Nancy J Tresser, *Chief Mktg Ofcr*
EMP: 10
SQ FT: 1,000
SALES (est): 1.6MM **Privately Held**
WEB: www.imalux.com
SIC: 3845 Electromedical apparatus

(G-5441)
IMET CORPORATION
13400 Glenside Rd (44110-3528)
P.O. Box 470812 (44147-0812)
PHONE.................................440 799-3135
  Mehmet Gencer, *CEO*
  Paul Zakriski, *President*
  Carol Mills, *Treasurer*
EMP: 7
SQ FT: 700
SALES (est): 1.3MM **Privately Held**
SIC: 3589 Water treatment equipment, industrial

(G-5442)
IMPACT ARMOR TECHNOLOGIES LLC
17000 Saint Clair Ave (44110-2535)
PHONE.................................216 706-2024
  Dan T Moore,
  Randi Deluga,
EMP: 10
SALES (est): 918K **Privately Held**
SIC: 3297 Nonclay refractories

Cleveland - Cuyahoga County (G-5443)

(G-5443)
IMPERIAL COUNTERTOPS
10646 Leuer Ave (44108-1352)
P.O. Box 656, Eustis FL (32727-0656)
PHONE..................................216 851-0888
EMP: 15 **EST:** 1989
SQ FT: 12,000
SALES: 1.6MM **Privately Held**
SIC: 5211 2541 1799 Mfg Ret And Install Counter Tops

(G-5444)
IMPERIAL METAL SOLUTIONS LLC
2284 Scranton Rd (44113-4310)
PHONE..................................216 781-4094
Paul Libby,
EMP: 18
SQ FT: 23,000
SALES (est): 2MM **Privately Held**
SIC: 3479 Coating or wrapping steel pipe

(G-5445)
IMPERIAL METAL SPINNING CO
7600 Exchange St (44125-3308)
PHONE..................................216 524-5020
Christopher Bindel, *President*
Timothy Bindel, *Vice Pres*
EMP: 8 **EST:** 1954
SQ FT: 7,000
SALES (est): 1.5MM **Privately Held**
SIC: 3469 Spinning metal for the trade

(G-5446)
IMPRESSIONS - A PRINT SHOP
370 Alpha Park (44143-2221)
PHONE..................................440 449-6966
Mike Myers, *President*
Brenda Myers, *Admin Sec*
EMP: 3
SQ FT: 1,800
SALES (est): 180K **Privately Held**
SIC: 2759 Commercial printing

(G-5447)
IN-TOUCH CORP
Also Called: Proforma Joe Thomas Group
13500 Pearl Rd Ste 139 (44136-3428)
PHONE..................................440 268-0881
Joseph Thomas, *President*
◆ **EMP:** 3
SQ FT: 1,100
SALES (est): 346.9K **Privately Held**
SIC: 2752 5199 Commercial printing, offset; advertising specialties; packaging materials

(G-5448)
INCORPORATED TRST GSPL WK SCTY
Also Called: Union Gospel Press Division
2000 Brookpark Rd (44109-5812)
P.O. Box 6059 (44101-1059)
PHONE..................................216 749-2100
Beryl C Bidlen, *President*
Robert Andrews, *Corp Secy*
Rev Lanny C Akers, *Vice Pres*
Vera Mc Kinney, *Asst Treas*
EMP: 90 **EST:** 1902
SQ FT: 60,000
SALES (est): 12.6MM **Privately Held**
WEB: www.uniongospelpress.com
SIC: 2721 5942 5999 8661 Periodicals: publishing & printing; books, religious; religious goods; non-church religious organizations

(G-5449)
INCORPORATED TRUSTEES GOSPEL W
1980 Brookpark Rd (44109-5810)
P.O. Box 6059 (44101-1059)
PHONE..................................216 749-1428
Beryl Bidlen, *President*
EMP: 65
SALES (est): 5.4MM **Privately Held**
SIC: 3555 2741 Printing presses; miscellaneous publishing

(G-5450)
INDEPENDENT DIE & MFG CO
5161 W 161st St (44142-1604)
PHONE..................................216 362-6778
John Quallich, *President*
Douglas Quallich, *Treasurer*
EMP: 5
SQ FT: 2,500
SALES (est): 595.9K **Privately Held**
SIC: 3545 Cutting tools for machine tools

(G-5451)
INDEPENDENT STAMPING INC
12025 Zelis Rd (44135-4699)
PHONE..................................216 251-3500
William Nester, *President*
EMP: 25
SQ FT: 11,000
SALES (est): 4.3MM **Privately Held**
SIC: 3469 3544 Stamping metal for the trade; special dies & tools

(G-5452)
INDUSTRIAL MACHINE TOOL SVC
3560 Ridge Rd (44102-5444)
PHONE..................................216 651-1122
Ron Badovick, *President*
Roberta Badovick, *Vice Pres*
EMP: 5
SQ FT: 40,000
SALES (est): 1MM **Privately Held**
WEB: www.industrialmachinetool.com
SIC: 5084 3542 Industrial machinery & equipment; rebuilt machine tools, metal forming types

(G-5453)
INDUSTRIAL MASUREMENT CTRL INC
9901 Beechwood Dr (44133-1317)
PHONE..................................440 877-1140
Guy Baetjer, *President*
EMP: 7
SALES (est): 920.8K **Privately Held**
SIC: 3829 Measuring & controlling devices

(G-5454)
INDUSTRIAL PACKAGING PRODUCTS
22259 Spencer Ln (44126-2523)
P.O. Box 26332 (44126-0332)
PHONE..................................440 734-2663
Charles Gantzler, *Owner*
EMP: 3
SALES (est): 256.9K **Privately Held**
SIC: 2011 Meat packing plants

(G-5455)
INDUSTRIAL WIRE CO INC (PA)
2805 Superior Ave E (44114-4201)
PHONE..................................216 781-2230
David Ehrmann, *President*
EMP: 4 **EST:** 1973
SQ FT: 2,500
SALES (est): 570.3K **Privately Held**
WEB: www.ind-wire.com
SIC: 3496 Miscellaneous fabricated wire products

(G-5456)
INFOACCESSNET LLC
8801 E Pleasant Valley Rd (44131-5510)
PHONE..................................216 328-0100
Daniel Andrew, *Mng Member*
EMP: 31
SQ FT: 25,000
SALES (est): 3.1MM
SALES (corp-wide): 90MM **Privately Held**
WEB: www.infoaccess.net
SIC: 7372 Business oriented computer software
HQ: Corcentric Collective Business System Corp.
7927 Jones Branch Dr # 3200
Mc Lean VA 22102
703 790-7272

(G-5457)
INFORMA MEDIA INC
1300 E 9th St (44114-1501)
PHONE..................................216 696-7000
Frank Craven, *Publisher*
Steve Minter, *Publisher*
David Blanchard, *Editor*
Michael Buzalka, *Editor*
Don Cuppett, *Editor*
EMP: 650
SALES (corp-wide): 2.3B **Privately Held**
SIC: 2759 Publication printing
HQ: Informa Media, Inc.
605 3rd Ave Fl 22
New York NY 10158
212 204-4200

(G-5458)
INK TECHNOLOGY CORPORATION (PA)
18320 Lanken Ave (44119-3216)
PHONE..................................216 486-6720
Ian Walker, *President*
David Ringler, *President*
Ethel R Haff, *Principal*
Robert Jenson, *Principal*
Ernest Walker, *Principal*
▲ **EMP:** 20 **EST:** 1980
SQ FT: 20,000
SALES (est): 3MM **Privately Held**
WEB: www.inktechnology.com
SIC: 2893 Printing ink

(G-5459)
INNER CITY ABRASIVES LLC
7209 Saint Clair Ave 101b (44103-1769)
P.O. Box 603050 (44103-0050)
PHONE..................................216 391-4402
Yuri Abramovich,
EMP: 3
SALES (est): 250K **Privately Held**
WEB: www.icabrasives.com
SIC: 3291 Abrasive products

(G-5460)
INNOVATIONS IN PLASTIC INC
1643 Eddy Rd (44112-4207)
PHONE..................................216 541-6060
Charles Hazle, *President*
Mary Ann Hazle, *Corp Secy*
EMP: 7
SQ FT: 13,000
SALES (est): 1MM **Privately Held**
SIC: 3089 Injection molding of plastics

(G-5461)
INSTA-PRINT INC
3101 Brookpark Rd (44134-1314)
PHONE..................................216 741-6500
Vincent Calo, *President*
Vincent J Calo Jr, *President*
Karen M Calo, *Vice Pres*
EMP: 5
SQ FT: 6,700
SALES (est): 653.8K **Privately Held**
SIC: 2752 Commercial printing, offset

(G-5462)
INTEGRAL DESIGN INC
7670 Hub Pkwy (44125-5707)
P.O. Box 25553 (44125-0553)
PHONE..................................216 524-0555
Robert S Liptak, *President*
Richard M Liptak, *Corp Secy*
EMP: 16
SQ FT: 8,000
SALES (est): 1.1MM **Privately Held**
WEB: www.integraldesigninc.com
SIC: 3089 3993 2542 2511 Thermoformed finished plastic products; signs & advertising specialties; partitions & fixtures, except wood; wood household furniture

(G-5463)
INTEGRATED POWER SERVICES LLC
Also Called: Monarch
5325 W 130th St (44130-1034)
PHONE..................................216 433-7808
Bridgette Gullatta, *President*
EMP: 27
SALES (corp-wide): 924.8MM **Privately Held**
SIC: 7694 Armature rewinding shops
HQ: Integrated Power Services Llc
3 Independence Pt Ste 100
Greenville SC 29615

(G-5464)
INTER CAB CORPORATION
8551 Brookpark Rd (44129-6805)
PHONE..................................216 351-0770
Jamie Nagel, *President*
Stacey Rannigan, *Corp Secy*
EMP: 5
SQ FT: 12,000
SALES (est): 635.5K **Privately Held**
SIC: 2434 2431 Wood kitchen cabinets; millwork

(G-5465)
INTERFAST INC
4444 Lee Rd (44128-2902)
PHONE..................................216 581-3000
EMP: 4 **Publicly Held**
SIC: 3965 Fasteners
HQ: Interfast Inc
22 Worcester Rd
Toronto ON M9W 5
416 674-0770

(G-5466)
INTERIOR PRODUCTS CO INC
3615 Superior Ave E 3104f (44114-4138)
PHONE..................................216 641-1919
Joseph J Frisse, *President*
EMP: 12
SQ FT: 14,000
SALES (est): 1.9MM **Privately Held**
SIC: 2521 Cabinets, office: wood

(G-5467)
INTERNATIONAL ADVG CONCEPTS
4285 W 217th St (44126-1839)
PHONE..................................440 331-4733
Jerome Leslie, *Owner*
EMP: 3 **EST:** 1980
SALES (est): 240K **Privately Held**
WEB: www.iaauae.org
SIC: 7311 8742 2759 Advertising agencies; marketing consulting services; commercial printing

(G-5468)
INTERNATIONAL CONT SYSTEMS LLC
Also Called: Elsons International
16601 Saint Clair Ave (44110-2951)
PHONE..................................216 481-8219
Steven J Williams,
EMP: 15
SALES (est): 4.2MM **Privately Held**
SIC: 2631 Container, packaging & boxboard

(G-5469)
INTERSOFT GROUP INC
26380 Curtiss Wright Pkwy # 303 (44143-1442)
PHONE..................................216 765-7351
Louis Muttillo, *President*
Ursula Muttillo, *Vice Pres*
Angela Iacofano, *Project Mgr*
Lou Muttillo, *Human Res Mgr*
Joseph Muttillo, *Manager*
EMP: 10
SALES (est): 1MM **Privately Held**
SIC: 7372 Prepackaged software

(G-5470)
INTERSTATE DIESEL SERVICE INC (PA)
Also Called: American Diesel, Inc.
5300 Lakeside Ave E (44114-3916)
PHONE..................................216 881-0015
Alfred J Buescher, *CEO*
Ann Buescher, *President*
Brad Buescher, *COO*
◆ **EMP:** 325 **EST:** 1947
SQ FT: 70,000
SALES (est): 62.6MM **Privately Held**
WEB: www.interstate-mcbee.com
SIC: 5013 3714 Automotive engines & engine parts; fuel systems & parts, motor vehicle; fuel pumps, motor vehicle

(G-5471)
INTERSTATE TOOL CORPORATION
4538 W 130th St (44135-3574)
PHONE..................................216 671-1077
Warren Thompson, *President*
Kevin Lavelle, *Manager*
Joseph Szabo, *Manager*
EMP: 20 **EST:** 1962
SQ FT: 22,000
SALES (est): 6.4MM **Privately Held**
SIC: 5084 3545 3541 Machine tools & accessories; cutting tools for machine tools; machine tools, metal cutting type

GEOGRAPHIC SECTION

Cleveland - Cuyahoga County (G-5500)

(G-5472)
INTRUSION-PREPAKT INC (PA)
15910 Pearl Rd Ste 101 (44136-6032)
PHONE..................................440 238-6950
B J Akers, *President*
George Bergemann, *Vice Pres*
Donald S Daczko, *Admin Sec*
EMP: 2
SALES (est): 2.5MM Privately Held
SIC: 1629 1771 2297 Land preparation construction; foundation & footing contractor; concrete repair; nonwoven fabrics

(G-5473)
INX INTERNATIONAL INK CO
18001 Englewood Dr Unit P (44130-3422)
PHONE..................................440 239-1766
Kyle Hurrle, *Manager*
EMP: 12
SALES (corp-wide): 1.4B Privately Held
SIC: 2893 Printing ink
HQ: Inx International Ink Co.
150 N Martingale Rd # 700
Schaumburg IL 60173
630 382-1800

(G-5474)
IONBOND LLC
24700 Highpoint Rd (44122-6005)
PHONE..................................216 831-0880
Alan Whittaker, *Opers Mgr*
Heidi Froelich, *Branch Mgr*
EMP: 15
SALES (corp-wide): 14.9B Privately Held
SIC: 3479 Coating of metals & formed products
HQ: Ionbond Llc
1823 E Whitcomb Ave
Madison Heights MI 48071

(G-5475)
IROCK CRUSHERS LLC
5531 Canal Rd (44125-4874)
PHONE..................................866 240-0201
Nancy Frognowski, *Principal*
Kenneth E Taylor, *Principal*
Sean Donaghy, *Sales Executive*
Dan Davis, *Manager*
John Reynolds,
◆ EMP: 5
SALES (est): 2MM Privately Held
WEB: www.irockcrushers.com
SIC: 3532 Rock crushing machinery, stationary

(G-5476)
IRVIN OSLIN INC
Also Called: Abbot Bindery
2800 E 55th St Frnt (44104-2861)
PHONE..................................216 361-7555
Fax: 216 361-1354
EMP: 7 EST: 1953
SQ FT: 10,000
SALES: 590K Privately Held
SIC: 2789 Bookbinding

(G-5477)
IRWIN ENGRAVING & PRINTING CO
5318 Saint Clair Ave # 1 (44103-1355)
PHONE..................................216 391-7300
Milan L Nass, *President*
Martha Ness, *Admin Sec*
EMP: 9 EST: 1922
SQ FT: 16,000
SALES (est): 1.1MM Privately Held
SIC: 2759 2752 Engraving; commercial printing, offset

(G-5478)
ITL CORP (DH)
Also Called: Industrial Timber & Lumber Co
23925 Commerce Park (44122-5821)
PHONE..................................216 831-3140
Larry Evans, *President*
Paul Kephart, *Sales Staff*
▼ EMP: 30 EST: 1957
SQ FT: 10,000
SALES (est): 80.1MM Privately Held
WEB: www.itlcorp.com
SIC: 2421 2426 Kiln drying of lumber; custom sawmill; hardwood dimension & flooring mills

(G-5479)
IVAC TECHNOLOGIES CORP
Also Called: Ion Vacuum Technologies
18678 Cranwood Pkwy (44128-4036)
PHONE..................................216 662-4987
EMP: 12
SQ FT: 4,000
SALES (est): 1.4MM Privately Held
SIC: 3479 8731 Coating Of Tools & Commercial Research & Development

(G-5480)
J & C INDUSTRIES INC
4808 W 130th St (44135-5138)
PHONE..................................216 362-8867
Bruce Jasen, *President*
EMP: 11
SQ FT: 16,000
SALES (est): 1.7MM Privately Held
SIC: 3599 Machine shop, jobbing & repair

(G-5481)
J AND L JEWELRY MANUFACTURING
Also Called: Bookman & Son Fine Jewelry
8803 Brecksville Rd # 6 (44141-1932)
PHONE..................................440 546-9988
Jeff Bookman, *President*
EMP: 7
SALES (est): 1MM Privately Held
SIC: 3911 Jewelry, precious metal

(G-5482)
J AND S TOOL INCORPORATED
15330 Brookpark Rd (44135-3355)
PHONE..................................216 676-8330
Vernon Justice, *President*
Donald Justice, *Vice Pres*
EMP: 36
SQ FT: 10,000
SALES: 2MM Privately Held
SIC: 3542 5084 3544 3541 Machine tools, metal forming type; machine tools & accessories; special dies, tools, jigs & fixtures; machine tools, metal cutting type; saw blades & handsaws; hand & edge tools

(G-5483)
J B M MACHINE CO INC
Also Called: Custom Brackets
32 Alpha Park (44143-2208)
PHONE..................................440 446-0819
Michael Muzila, *President*
Patricia Muzila, *Vice Pres*
EMP: 3
SALES (est): 489.6K Privately Held
SIC: 3599 Machine shop, jobbing & repair

(G-5484)
J B STAMPING INC
7413 Associate Ave (44144-1190)
PHONE..................................216 631-0013
James P Bailey, *President*
Richard B Ginley, *Principal*
Linda G Glover, *Principal*
George Gibson, *Vice Pres*
Paul Dobos, *Sales Staff*
EMP: 35
SQ FT: 35,000
SALES (est): 7.6MM Privately Held
WEB: www.jbstamping.com
SIC: 3469 Stamping metal for the trade

(G-5485)
J P QUALITY PRINTING INC
12614 Larchmere Blvd (44120-1110)
PHONE..................................216 791-6303
John Pathko, *President*
EMP: 5
SALES (est): 594.4K Privately Held
SIC: 2752 2759 Commercial printing, offset; letterpress printing

(G-5486)
J P SUGGINS MOBILE WELDING
2020 Saint Clair Ave Ne (44114-2013)
PHONE..................................216 566-7131
Jeffrey Hulligan, *President*
EMP: 20
SQ FT: 3,500
SALES (est): 3.5MM Privately Held
SIC: 3441 7692 Fabricated structural metal; welding repair

(G-5487)
J R M CHEMICAL INC
4881 Neo Pkwy (44128-3101)
PHONE..................................216 475-8488
Dave Czehut, *Vice Pres*
Scott Wiesler, *Vice Pres*
▲ EMP: 12
SQ FT: 12,000
SALES (est): 3.5MM Privately Held
WEB: www.soilmoist.com
SIC: 2869 Industrial inorganic chemicals

(G-5488)
J SCHRADER CO
4603 Fenwick Ave (44102-4597)
PHONE..................................216 961-2890
Len Gagnon, *President*
EMP: 13 EST: 1922
SQ FT: 34,000
SALES (est): 2.2MM Privately Held
SIC: 3469 3645 3646 Spinning metal for the trade; table lamps; wall lamps; commercial indusl & institutional electric lighting fixtures

(G-5489)
J W HARWOOD CO (PA)
18001 Roseland Rd (44112-1109)
PHONE..................................216 531-6230
Walter B Harwood, *President*
Madeleine Harwood, *Vice Pres*
Marilyn Harwood, *Admin Sec*
EMP: 12 EST: 1934
SQ FT: 12,000
SALES (est): 2.2MM Privately Held
SIC: 3544 Special dies & tools

(G-5490)
JAB SALES INC (PA)
39 Alpha Park (44143-2202)
PHONE..................................440 446-0606
Bruce Beeth, *President*
EMP: 3
SALES (est): 314.2K Privately Held
SIC: 3441 Fabricated structural metal

(G-5491)
JACKPOT FESTIVAL & GAMING
650a E 185th St (44119-1767)
PHONE..................................216 531-3500
John Copic Jr, *President*
EMP: 5
SALES (est): 659.8K Privately Held
WEB: www.jackpotgames.biz
SIC: 3944 5199 Games, toys & children's vehicles; carnival supplies

(G-5492)
JALO INC
Also Called: Signs By Tomorrow
7619 Brookpark Rd (44129-1107)
PHONE..................................216 661-2222
Jaqueline Golonka, *President*
Lori Crosby, *Vice Pres*
EMP: 3
SQ FT: 2,250
SALES: 188.6K Privately Held
SIC: 3993 Signs & advertising specialties

(G-5493)
JAMESTOWN CONT CLEVELAND INC
4500 Renaissance Pkwy (44128-5702)
PHONE..................................216 831-3700
Glen Jenowsky, *Ch of Bd*
Bruce Janowsky, *Treasurer*
Larry Hudson, *VP Sales*
Josh Sobel, *Accounts Mgr*
Dick Weimer, *Admin Sec*
EMP: 350
SQ FT: 100,000
SALES: 41.8MM
SALES (corp-wide): 148.3MM Privately Held
WEB: www.jamestowncontainer.com
SIC: 2653 Corrugated boxes, partitions, display items, sheets & pad
PA: Jamestown Container Corp
14 Deming Dr
Falconer NY 14733
716 665-4623

(G-5494)
JASMINE DISTRIBUTING LTD
12117 Berea Rd (44111-1600)
PHONE..................................216 251-9420
Fady Chamoun, *Owner*
Alisha Foley, *Opers Staff*
▲ EMP: 20
SALES (est): 2.2MM Privately Held
SIC: 2051 Breads, rolls & buns; bakery: wholesale or wholesale/retail combined

(G-5495)
JERGENS INC (PA)
Also Called: Tooling Components Division
15700 S Waterloo Rd (44110-3898)
PHONE..................................216 486-5540
Jack H Schron Jr, *President*
W Wesley Howard III, *CFO*
Tim Easton, *Natl Sales Mgr*
Mary Delaney, *Marketing Mgr*
Mark Kish, *Manager*
▲ EMP: 195 EST: 1942
SQ FT: 104,000
SALES (est): 63MM Privately Held
WEB: www.jergensinc.com
SIC: 3443 3452 5084 3545 Fabricated plate work (boiler shop); bolts, nuts, rivets & washers; machine tools & accessories; drill bushings (drilling jig); precision measuring tools; jigs & fixtures

(G-5496)
JEROLD OPTICAL INC
800 Huron Rd E (44115-1121)
PHONE..................................216 781-4279
Jerold Rabnick, *CEO*
Loren Rabnick, *President*
Lisa Rabnick, *Assistant VP*
Beverly Rabnick, *Admin Sec*
EMP: 5
SQ FT: 2,000
SALES: 450K Privately Held
WEB: www.jeroldoptical.com
SIC: 3851 5995 Ophthalmic goods; eyeglasses, prescription

(G-5497)
JET DOCK SYSTEMS INC
9601 Corporate Cir (44125-4261)
PHONE..................................216 750-2264
David Faber, *President*
W A Eva III, *Vice Pres*
Dan Burman, *Sales Staff*
Jeremy Clickner, *Sales Staff*
Beverly Frollo, *Info Tech Mgr*
▼ EMP: 30
SQ FT: 30,000
SALES (est): 7.5MM Privately Held
WEB: www.jetdock.com
SIC: 3448 Docks: prefabricated metal

(G-5498)
JEWELS BY IMG INC
5470 Mayfield Rd (44124-2986)
PHONE..................................440 461-4464
Steven Greenberg, *President*
EMP: 12
SQ FT: 5,500
SALES (est): 800K Privately Held
SIC: 3911 7631 Jewelry, precious metal; diamond setter

(G-5499)
JIM DENIGRIS & SONS LDSCPG
1520 Longwood Dr (44124-3006)
PHONE..................................440 449-5548
Anthony Denigris, *President*
EMP: 4
SALES (est): 364.2K Privately Held
SIC: 3446 0782 Architectural metalwork; lawn & garden services

(G-5500)
JOB ONE CONTROL SERVICES
6893 Lantern Ln (44130-4532)
PHONE..................................216 347-0133
Ann O'Brien, *President*
EMP: 3
SALES: 15K Privately Held
SIC: 3625 Relays & industrial controls

Cleveland - Cuyahoga County (G-5501)

GEOGRAPHIC SECTION

(G-5501)
JOHN KOLESAR AND SONS INC
Also Called: Printing Partner
13437 Detroit Ave (44107-4608)
P.O. Box 30668 (44130-0668)
PHONE..................216 221-7117
James Kolesar, *President*
John E Kolesar Jr, *Vice Pres*
EMP: 4
SQ FT: 1,600
SALES (est): 480.4K **Privately Held**
SIC: 2752 Commercial printing, offset

(G-5502)
JOHN KRUSINSKI
Also Called: Krusinski's Meat Market
6300 Heisley Ave (44105-1226)
PHONE..................216 441-0100
John Krusinski, *Owner*
EMP: 10
SQ FT: 10,000
SALES (est): 1.2MM **Privately Held**
SIC: 5147 5421 2099 2013 Meats, fresh; meat markets, including freezer provisioners; food preparations; sausages & other prepared meats

(G-5503)
JOHN P ELLIS CLINIC PODIATRY
730 Som Center Rd Ste 350 (44143-2362)
PHONE..................440 460-0444
John P Ellis, *Owner*
EMP: 4 **EST:** 2015
SALES (est): 288.7K **Privately Held**
SIC: 2835 8071 0783 In vitro & in vivo diagnostic substances; ultrasound laboratory; surgery services, ornamental bush

(G-5504)
JOHNSON CONTROLS INC
9797 Midwest Ave (44125-2498)
PHONE..................216 587-0100
Todd Van Denbusche, *Principal*
EMP: 60 **Privately Held**
SIC: 2531 Seats, automobile
HQ: Johnson Controls, Inc.
5757 N Green Bay Ave
Milwaukee WI 53209
414 524-1200

(G-5505)
JORDON AUTO SERVICE & TIRE INC
5201 Carnegie Ave (44103-4357)
PHONE..................216 214-6528
Jordan Kaminsky, *Owner*
EMP: 7 **EST:** 2011
SALES (est): 475.9K **Privately Held**
SIC: 2653 7539 Pallets, corrugated: made from purchased materials; automotive repair shops

(G-5506)
JOSEPH T SNYDER INDUSTRIES
9210 Loren Ave (44105-2133)
PHONE..................216 883-6900
Gregory Snyder, *President*
Robert Snyder, *Vice Pres*
EMP: 9
SQ FT: 12,000
SALES: 2.5MM **Privately Held**
SIC: 7389 2671 2653 Packaging & labeling services; packaging paper & plastics film, coated & laminated; corrugated & solid fiber boxes

(G-5507)
JOY GLOBAL UNDERGROUND MIN LLC
6160 Cochran Rd (44139-3306)
PHONE..................440 248-7970
Mark Sanders, *Branch Mgr*
EMP: 15
SALES (corp-wide): 23.4B **Privately Held**
SIC: 3535 Bucket type conveyor systems
HQ: Joy Global Underground Mining Llc
40 Pennwood Pl Ste 100
Warrendale PA 15086
724 779-4500

(G-5508)
JRG PERFORMANCE TECHNOLOGIES
340 Balmoral Dr (44143-1759)
PHONE..................216 408-5974
Raymond Glumm, *Principal*
EMP: 4
SALES: 65K **Privately Held**
SIC: 3599 7389 Machine shop, jobbing & repair; business services

(G-5509)
JT PREMIER PRINTING CORP
18780 Cranwood Pkwy (44128-4038)
PHONE..................216 831-8785
James Trombo, *President*
EMP: 3
SALES (est): 463K **Privately Held**
SIC: 2752 Commercial printing, offset

(G-5510)
JUST NATURAL PROVISION COMPANY
4800 Crayton Ave (44104-2822)
PHONE..................216 431-7922
Dennis Parker, *President*
EMP: 6
SALES (est): 810K **Privately Held**
SIC: 2015 5144 Poultry slaughtering & processing; poultry & poultry products

(G-5511)
K & E CHEMICAL CO INC
3960 E 93rd St (44105-4050)
PHONE..................216 341-0500
Edgar Bleick Jr, *President*
Carl Bleick, *VP Opers*
EMP: 10 **EST:** 1954
SQ FT: 11,000
SALES (est): 1MM **Privately Held**
WEB: www.klenztone.com
SIC: 2869 Industrial organic chemicals

(G-5512)
K & G MACHINE CO
26981 Tungsten Rd (44132-2992)
PHONE..................216 732-7115
Monte Curtis, *President*
Kathy Sentill, *Manager*
EMP: 23 **EST:** 1953
SQ FT: 24,000
SALES (est): 3.8MM **Privately Held**
WEB: www.kandgmachine.com
SIC: 3599 3743 Machine shop, jobbing & repair; railroad equipment

(G-5513)
K S MACHINE INC
3215 Superior Ave E (44114-4344)
PHONE..................216 687-0459
Thomas Wallace, *President*
EMP: 15
SALES (est): 2.1MM **Privately Held**
WEB: www.ksmachineinc.com
SIC: 3599 Machine shop, jobbing & repair

(G-5514)
K-B PLATING INC
3685 E 78th St (44105-2048)
PHONE..................216 341-1115
David Kopea, *President*
Thomas Thome, *Vice Pres*
Doris Kopea, *Treasurer*
Gordon Loux, *Admin Sec*
EMP: 10 **EST:** 1961
SQ FT: 21,000
SALES: 1.3MM **Privately Held**
SIC: 3471 Anodizing (plating) of metals or formed products

(G-5515)
KALEIDOSCOPE MAGAZINE LLC
1677 E 40th St (44103-2304)
PHONE..................216 566-5500
Richard A Johnson, *CEO*
EMP: 20
SALES (est): 1.6MM **Privately Held**
WEB: www.kaleidoscopemagazine.net
SIC: 2721 Periodicals

(G-5516)
KARYALL-TELDAY INC
8221 Clinton Rd (44144-1008)
PHONE..................216 281-4063
James Mindek, *President*
EMP: 20 **EST:** 1947
SQ FT: 43,000
SALES (est): 2.9MM **Privately Held**
SIC: 2851 3499 Paints & paint additives; boxes for packing & shipping, metal

(G-5517)
KASE EQUIPMENT
7400 Hub Pkwy (44125-5735)
PHONE..................216 642-9040
Edward Hawkins, *Ch of Bd*
Partick Hawkins, *President*
Dave Hodgson, *Vice Pres*
Ed Krane, *Purch Mgr*
Bruce Longenecker, *Engineer*
▲ **EMP:** 100
SQ FT: 68,360
SALES (est): 20.4MM **Privately Held**
WEB: www.kaseequip.com
SIC: 3555 Printing trades machinery

(G-5518)
KATHY SIMECEK
Also Called: Celebrations Monogramming
8506 Pin Oak Dr (44130-7651)
PHONE..................440 886-2468
Kathy Simecek, *Owner*
Kethy Simecek, *Owner*
EMP: 3
SALES: 40K **Privately Held**
SIC: 2395 Embroidery & art needlework

(G-5519)
KAUFMAN CONTAINER COMPANY (PA)
1000 Keystone Pkwy # 100 (44135-5119)
P.O. Box 35902 (44135-0902)
PHONE..................216 898-2000
Roger Seid, *CEO*
Ken Slater, *President*
Charles Borowiak, *Vice Pres*
Roderick Cywinski, *Vice Pres*
Jeffery Gross, *Vice Pres*
▲ **EMP:** 128 **EST:** 1910
SQ FT: 180,000
SALES (est): 81.9MM **Privately Held**
SIC: 5085 2759 Commercial containers; plastic bottles; glass bottles; screen printing; labels & seals: printing

(G-5520)
KAWNEER COMPANY INC
4536 Industrial Pkwy (44135-4593)
PHONE..................216 252-3203
Janice Gibson, *General Mgr*
EMP: 14
SALES (corp-wide): 14B **Publicly Held**
WEB: www.kawneer.com
SIC: 3442 Metal doors
HQ: Kawneer Company, Inc.
555 Guthridge Ct
Norcross GA 30092
770 449-5555

(G-5521)
KAY CAPITAL COMPANY (DH)
Also Called: Advanced Vehicles
1441 Chardon Rd (44117-1510)
PHONE..................216 531-1010
Felix Tarorick, *Vice Ch Bd*
Tim Dunagan, *President*
▲ **EMP:** 5 **EST:** 1875
SQ FT: 160,000
SALES: 6.5MM
SALES (corp-wide): 1.6B **Publicly Held**
WEB: www.ajaxtech.com
SIC: 3542 3537 3549 3541 Machine tools, metal forming type; lift trucks, industrial: fork, platform, straddle, etc.; metalworking machinery; machine tools, metal cutting type
HQ: Park-Ohio Industries, Inc.
6065 Parkland Blvd Ste 1
Cleveland OH 44124
440 947-2000

(G-5522)
KEBAN INDUSTRIES INC
Also Called: Stefan Restoration
7500 Wall St Ste 100 (44125-3357)
PHONE..................216 446-0159
Ken Stefan, *Principal*
Kenneth Stefan, *Principal*
EMP: 7
SALES (est): 776.4K **Privately Held**
SIC: 3599 Custom machinery

(G-5523)
KEENER PRINTING INC
401 E 200th St (44119-1594)
PHONE..................216 531-7595
Duane Pecjak, *President*
EMP: 12 **EST:** 1976
SQ FT: 3,600
SALES (est): 1.9MM **Privately Held**
WEB: www.keenerprinting.com
SIC: 2752 2791 Commercial printing, offset; typesetting

(G-5524)
KEHOE BROTHERS PRINTING INC
910 W Schaaf Rd (44109-4643)
PHONE..................216 351-4100
Thomas Kehoe Sr, *President*
Tom Kehle, *Managing Dir*
Elizabeth Kehoe, *Treasurer*
EMP: 4
SALES (est): 466.5K **Privately Held**
SIC: 2752 2759 Commercial printing, offset; letterpress printing

(G-5525)
KEITHLEY INSTRUMENTS INTL CORP
28775 Aurora Rd (44139-1891)
PHONE..................440 248-0400
Joseph P Keithley, *President*
Ron Molder, *Treasurer*
EMP: 450
SQ FT: 200,000
SALES (est): 38.8MM
SALES (corp-wide): 6.4B **Publicly Held**
WEB: www.keithley.com
SIC: 5065 3825 Electronic parts & equipment; test equipment for electronic & electric measurement
HQ: Keithley Instruments, Llc
28775 Aurora Rd
Solon OH 44139
440 248-0400

(G-5526)
KELLY PLATING CO
10316 Madison Ave (44102-3594)
PHONE..................216 961-1080
Donald J Kelly, *President*
James Kelly, *Vice Pres*
Lauralee Paukert, *Admin Sec*
EMP: 37 **EST:** 1932
SQ FT: 20,000
SALES (est): 5.3MM **Privately Held**
SIC: 3471 Electroplating of metals or formed products

(G-5527)
KENNAMETAL INC
18105 Cleveland Pkwy Dr (44135-3251)
PHONE..................216 898-6120
Tom McNamara, *Manager*
Andy Moler, *Executive*
EMP: 80
SALES (corp-wide): 2.3B **Publicly Held**
WEB: www.kennametal.com
SIC: 3545 Machine tool accessories
PA: Kennametal Inc.
600 Grant St Ste 5100
Pittsburgh PA 15219
412 248-8000

(G-5528)
KENNEDY MINT INC
Also Called: Kennedy Graphics
12102 Pearl Rd Rear (44136-3398)
PHONE..................440 572-3222
Renato Montorsi, *President*
Theresa Montorsi, *Vice Pres*
George Berk, *Director*
EMP: 55
SQ FT: 60,000
SALES (est): 8.4MM **Privately Held**
WEB: www.kennedysg.com
SIC: 2653 2752 7538 Corrugated boxes, partitions, display items, sheets & pad; offset & photolithographic printing; general automotive repair shops

(G-5529)
KENNICK MOLD & DIE INC
3601 Detroit Ave (44113-2791)
PHONE..................216 631-3535
Bob Hotujac, *President*
Florence Hotujac, *Admin Sec*
EMP: 5
SQ FT: 2,400

GEOGRAPHIC SECTION
Cleveland - Cuyahoga County (G-5556)

SALES (est): 331.2K **Privately Held**
WEB: www.kennickmold.com
SIC: 3089 Injection molded finished plastic products

(G-5530)
KEREK INDUSTRIES LTD LBLTY CO
750 Beta Dr Ste A (44143-2333)
PHONE..................440 461-1450
Tom Linsenmeier, *Prdtn Mgr*
Richard Kerek,
John Kerek,
EMP: 13
SQ FT: 22,000
SALES (est): 1.9MM **Privately Held**
WEB: www.kerekindustries.com
SIC: 3599 Machine shop, jobbing & repair

(G-5531)
KERN INC
755 Alpha Dr (44143-2124)
PHONE..................440 930-7315
Thomas Brock, *President*
EMP: 3
SALES (corp-wide): 134.3MM **Privately Held**
SIC: 3579 3577 Envelope stuffing, sealing & addressing machines; computer peripheral equipment
HQ: Kern, Inc.
3940 Gantz Rd Ste A
Grove City OH 43123
614 317-2600

(G-5532)
KEYSTONE BOLT & NUT COMPANY
Also Called: Keystone Threaded Products
7600 Hub Pkwy (44125-5707)
P.O. Box 31059 (44131-0059)
PHONE..................216 524-9626
James W Krejci, *President*
Betsy Mitchell, *Vice Pres*
Dean Mitchell, *Opers Mgr*
▲ **EMP:** 60 **EST:** 1919
SQ FT: 30,000
SALES (est): 12.9MM **Privately Held**
WEB: www.keystonethreaded.com
SIC: 3452 Bolts, metal

(G-5533)
KG63 LLC
Also Called: Multiple Products Company
15501 Chatfield Ave (44111-4311)
PHONE..................216 941-7766
William F Anderson, *President*
Joseph Anderson, *Vice Pres*
Joseph T Anderson, *Treasurer*
Joel Newman, *Admin Sec*
◆ **EMP:** 11 **EST:** 1945
SQ FT: 22,000
SALES (est): 2.6MM **Privately Held**
WEB: www.greenssweep.com
SIC: 3469 3861 Stamping metal for the trade; photographic equipment & supplies

(G-5534)
KIEFER TOOL & MOLD INC
3855 W 150th St (44111-5806)
PHONE..................216 251-0076
John Kiefer Jr, *President*
Thomas Kiefer, *Corp Secy*
Jim Kiefer, *Vice Pres*
EMP: 15 **EST:** 1966
SQ FT: 12,000
SALES: 1MM **Privately Held**
SIC: 3599 Machine shop, jobbing & repair

(G-5535)
KING MEDIA ENTERPRISES INC
Also Called: Call & Post
11800 Shaker Blvd (44120-1919)
P.O. Box 6237 (44101-1237)
PHONE..................216 588-6700
Don King, *President*
Constance Harper, *Exec Dir*
EMP: 35
SALES (est): 2.3MM **Privately Held**
SIC: 2711 Commercial printing & newspaper publishing combined

(G-5536)
KINZUA ENVIRONMENTAL INC
1176 E 38th St Ste 1 (44114-3898)
PHONE..................216 881-4040
Bradley R Waxman, *President*
Matt Waxman, *Regl Sales Mgr*
EMP: 20
SQ FT: 20,000
SALES (est): 4.6MM **Privately Held**
WEB: www.kinzuachem.com
SIC: 2842 Specialty cleaning preparations

(G-5537)
KIP-CRAFT INCORPORATED (PA)
Also Called: Schoolbelles
4747 W 160th St (44135-2631)
PHONE..................216 898-5500
Bruce J Carroll, *President*
Mary Carroll, *Corp Secy*
Elaine Stephens, *Vice Pres*
Kathleen Luchansky, *CFO*
Jennifer Samuel, *Accountant*
EMP: 60
SALES (est): 11.6MM **Privately Held**
WEB: www.schoolbells.com
SIC: 5699 2339 2326 Uniforms; women's & misses' outerwear; men's & boys' work clothing

(G-5538)
KIRK WELDING & FABRICATING
10410 Madison Ave (44102-3547)
PHONE..................216 961-6403
James A Baronak, *President*
George Baronak, *Corp Secy*
Rick Baronak, *Vice Pres*
EMP: 3
SQ FT: 1,800
SALES: 170K **Privately Held**
SIC: 7692 3441 Welding repair; fabricated structural metal

(G-5539)
KIRKWOOD HOLDING INC (PA)
1239 Rockside Rd (44134-2772)
PHONE..................216 267-6200
L Thomas Koechley, *CEO*
Paul Hensen, *Vice Pres*
Donna Ross, *CFO*
Steve McNutt, *Technology*
Frederick Assini, *Admin Sec*
EMP: 200
SQ FT: 3,500
SALES (est): 29.7MM **Privately Held**
SIC: 3621 Commutators, electric motor; collector rings, for electric motors or generators

(G-5540)
KNITTING MACHINERY CORP (PA)
Also Called: K M C
15625 Saranac Rd (44110-2427)
PHONE..................216 851-9900
Edward F Crawford, *President*
EMP: 5
SQ FT: 6,600
SALES (est): 7.2MM **Privately Held**
SIC: 3552 Knitting machines

(G-5541)
KOEHLER RUBBER & SUPPLY CO
800 W Resource Dr (44131-1837)
PHONE..................216 749-5100
Bernard Green, *President*
Betty Parsell, *Corp Secy*
Michael Ticchione, *Vice Pres*
▲ **EMP:** 17 **EST:** 1917
SQ FT: 27,000
SALES: 5.5MM **Privately Held**
WEB: www.koehlerrubber.com
SIC: 3569 Lubrication equipment, industrial

(G-5542)
KOVACEVIC PRINTING INC
Also Called: Minuteman Press
13367 Smith Rd (44130-7810)
PHONE..................440 887-1000
Robert Kovacevic, *President*
EMP: 4
SALES (est): 423.5K **Privately Held**
SIC: 2752 Commercial printing, lithographic

(G-5543)
KOWALSKI HEAT TREATING CO
3611 Detroit Ave (44113-2790)
PHONE..................216 631-4411
Robert Kowalski, *President*
Stephen Kowalski, *Vice Pres*
Carole Kowalski, *Treasurer*
Nancy Vermilye, *Admin Sec*
EMP: 13 **EST:** 1975
SQ FT: 11,000
SALES (est): 3.4MM **Privately Held**
WEB: www.khtheat.com
SIC: 3398 Metal heat treating

(G-5544)
KROY LLC (HQ)
Also Called: Buckeye Business Products
3830 Kelley Ave (44114-4534)
PHONE..................216 426-5600
Kevin Devers, *Exec VP*
Benny Bonanno, *Vice Pres*
Elenora Grmek, *Vice Pres*
Stephen Rawlings, *Purch Mgr*
Mike Knack, *Purchasing*
▲ **EMP:** 125 **EST:** 1997
SQ FT: 110,000
SALES (est): 81.9MM
SALES (corp-wide): 94.9MM **Privately Held**
SIC: 2671 3955 2761 Packaging paper & plastics film, coated & laminated; carbon paper & inked ribbons; manifold business forms
PA: Pubco Corporation
3830 Kelley Ave
Cleveland OH 44114
216 881-5300

(G-5545)
KRUMOR INC
7655 Hub Pkwy Ste 206 (44125-5739)
PHONE..................216 328-9802
Robert Mikals, *President*
Herbert H Sher, *Vice Pres*
Lisa Mikals, *Manager*
EMP: 10 **EST:** 1972
SALES (est): 2.5MM **Privately Held**
WEB: www.krumor.com
SIC: 3829 Temperature sensors, except industrial process & aircraft

(G-5546)
KTRI HOLDINGS INC (PA)
127 Public Sq Ste 5110 (44114-1313)
PHONE..................216 371-1700
Patrick James, *President*
Stephen Graham, *CFO*
EMP: 5
SALES (est): 344.8MM **Privately Held**
SIC: 3714 Motor vehicle parts & accessories

(G-5547)
KUSAKABE AMERICA CORPORATION
Also Called: Xth Industries
6116 W Creek Rd (44131-6816)
PHONE..................216 524-2485
Terry Sakapine, *President*
EMP: 3
SALES (est): 322.1K **Privately Held**
SIC: 3547 Pipe & tube mills

(G-5548)
KYRON PLATING CORP
Also Called: Miracle Metal Finishing
1336 W 114th St (44102-1397)
P.O. Box 728 (44107-0728)
PHONE..................216 221-7275
Ken O'Bloy, *President*
Ken Obloy, *President*
EMP: 12 **EST:** 1960
SQ FT: 9,000
SALES: 700K **Privately Held**
SIC: 3471 Plating of metals or formed products; electroplating of metals or formed products

(G-5549)
L A MACHINE
3818 Trent Ave (44109)
PHONE..................216 651-1712
Leonard Andreasik, *Owner*
EMP: 3
SQ FT: 7,275

SALES: 300K **Privately Held**
SIC: 3599 2893 Machine shop, jobbing & repair; printing ink

(G-5550)
L J MINOR CORP
2621 W 25th St (44113-4794)
PHONE..................216 861-8350
Engas Nitch, *Principal*
EMP: 5
SALES (est): 437.5K **Privately Held**
SIC: 2032 Canned specialties

(G-5551)
L-MOR INC
Also Called: Carhoff
13404 Saint Clair Ave (44110-3543)
P.O. Box 10876 (44110-0876)
PHONE..................216 541-2224
Lisa Morell, *President*
EMP: 10
SQ FT: 14,000
SALES (est): 2.1MM **Privately Held**
WEB: www.darlingfiresafety.com
SIC: 2842 7389 5099 Sanitation preparations; fire extinguisher servicing; safety equipment & supplies; fire extinguishers

(G-5552)
LACHINA CREATIVE INC
3791 Green Rd (44122-5705)
PHONE..................216 292-7959
Jeff Lachina, *President*
Bonnie Briggle, *Editor*
Mandy Walden, *Accounts Mgr*
Lee Mejia, *Technology*
EMP: 65
SALES (est): 8.1MM **Privately Held**
WEB: www.lachina.com
SIC: 2731 Book publishing

(G-5553)
LAFARGE NORTH AMERICA INC
Also Called: Lafargeholcim
2500 Elm St (44113-1114)
PHONE..................216 781-9330
Thomas Peck, *Branch Mgr*
EMP: 7
SALES (corp-wide): 26.4B **Privately Held**
WEB: www.lafargenorthamerica.com
SIC: 3241 Cement, hydraulic
HQ: Lafarge North America Inc.
8700 W Bryn Mawr Ave
Chicago IL 60631
773 372-1000

(G-5554)
LAIRD TECHNOLOGIES INC
4707 Detroit Ave (44102-2216)
PHONE..................216 939-2300
Martin Rapp, *President*
EMP: 75
SALES (corp-wide): 1.2B **Privately Held**
SIC: 2891 Adhesives & sealants
HQ: Laird Technologies, Inc.
16401 Swingley
Chesterfield MO 63017
636 898-6000

(G-5555)
LAKESHORE FEED & SEED INC
5116 Clark Ave (44102-4553)
PHONE..................216 961-5729
Marilyn Brown, *Owner*
Darnelle Brown, *Vice Pres*
EMP: 4
SALES: 330K **Privately Held**
SIC: 2047 2048 Dog food; bird food, prepared

(G-5556)
LAM PRO INC
4701 Crayton Ave Ste A (44104-2819)
PHONE..................216 426-0661
Kerry Stewart, *President*
Pam Moore, *Sales Staff*
Debbie Dragar, *Admin Sec*
EMP: 13
SQ FT: 33,000
SALES (est): 1.9MM **Privately Held**
WEB: www.lampro.com
SIC: 3089 2789 2675 2672 Laminating of plastic; bookbinding & related work; die-cut paper & board; coated & laminated paper

Cleveland - Cuyahoga County (G-5557)

(G-5557)
LAMPORTS FILTER MEDIA INC
837 E 79th St (44103-1807)
PHONE..................................216 881-2050
Walter Senney, *President*
Joyce Senney, *Vice Pres*
EMP: 15
SQ FT: 25,000
SALES (est): 155.4K **Privately Held**
WEB: www.lamports.com
SIC: 2393 Textile bags

(G-5558)
LANGENAU MANUFACTURING COMPANY
7306 Madison Ave (44102-4094)
PHONE..................................216 651-3400
W C Strangward, *President*
Mark Schwartz, *Plant Mgr*
Dan Masterson, *Mfg Staff*
Katie Loeser, *Controller*
Katie Weddle-Loeser, *Controller*
EMP: 15
SQ FT: 40,000
SALES (est): 2.7MM **Privately Held**
WEB: www.langenau.com
SIC: 3432 3465 3469 3544 Plastic plumbing fixture fittings, assembly; automotive stampings; metal stampings; special dies, tools, jigs & fixtures; casket hardware

(G-5559)
LANIER & ASSOCIATES INC
Also Called: Cleveland Black Pages
1814 E 40th St Ste 1c (44103-3500)
PHONE..................................216 391-7735
Bob Lanier, *President*
Linda Lanier, *Vice Pres*
EMP: 6
SALES: 450K **Privately Held**
WEB: www.blackpagesohio.com
SIC: 2741 Directories, telephone: publishing only, not printed on site

(G-5560)
LANLY COMPANY
26201 Tungsten Rd (44132-2922)
PHONE..................................216 731-1115
Dennis W Hill, *President*
David Fowle, *Vice Pres*
Dominic Mazza, *Purch Mgr*
Kyle Martinac, *Engineer*
Stanley Wauthier, *Engineer*
EMP: 44 **EST:** 1938
SQ FT: 68,000
SALES (est): 13.6MM **Privately Held**
WEB: www.lanly.com
SIC: 3567 Heating units & devices, industrial: electric; driers & redriers, industrial process

(G-5561)
LAPCHI LLC
23533 Mercantile Rd # 103 (44122-5958)
PHONE..................................216 360-0104
Colleen Joyce, *Owner*
EMP: 6
SALES (est): 396.6K
SALES (corp-wide): 315.8K **Privately Held**
SIC: 2273 Carpets & rugs
PA: Lapchi Llc
821 Nw Flanders St # 335
Portland OR 97209
503 239-0080

(G-5562)
LARMCO WINDOWS INC (PA)
8400 Sweet Valley Dr # 404 (44125-4243)
PHONE..................................216 502-2832
William Simon, *Ch of Bd*
Joe Talmon, *President*
EMP: 30
SALES (est): 5.6MM **Privately Held**
WEB: www.larmco.com
SIC: 3089 Windows, plastic; siding, plastic; doors, folding: plastic or plastic coated fabric

(G-5563)
LASER PRINTING SOLUTIONS INC
Also Called: L P S I
6040 Hillcrest Dr (44125-4620)
PHONE..................................216 351-4444
Bob Lasser, *Ch of Bd*
Mike Piaser, *President*
James G Skimin, *Opers Staff*
EMP: 14
SQ FT: 5,000
SALES (est): 1.9MM **Privately Held**
WEB: www.laserprintingsolutions.com
SIC: 2759 Laser printing

(G-5564)
LATTE LIVING
11005 Johnson Dr (44130-7352)
PHONE..................................440 364-2201
Lisa Timko, *Owner*
EMP: 4
SALES (est): 196.9K **Privately Held**
SIC: 2741

(G-5565)
LAUNCHVECTOR IDENTITY LLC
3635 Perkins Ave Ste 6a (44114-4605)
PHONE..................................216 333-1815
EMP: 11
SALES: 2.9K
SALES (corp-wide): 1.4MM **Privately Held**
SIC: 7372 Prepackaged Software Services
PA: Launchvector Llc
3635 Perkins Ave Ste 6a
Cleveland OH 44114
216 333-1815

(G-5566)
LAWRENCE INDUSTRIES INC (PA)
4500 Lee Rd Ste 120 (44128-2959)
PHONE..................................216 518-7000
Lawrence A Kopittke Sr, *President*
Arthur Kopittke, *Vice Pres*
Richard L Kopittke, *Vice Pres*
◆ **EMP:** 151
SQ FT: 160,000
SALES (est): 17.2MM **Privately Held**
WEB: www.hudsonsupply.com
SIC: 3599 3541 7699 5084 Machine shop, jobbing & repair; sawing & cutoff machines (metalworking machinery); tool repair services; metalworking tools (such as drills, taps, dies, files); machine tools & metalworking machinery; industrial supplies; abrasive products

(G-5567)
LAWRENCE INDUSTRIES INC
Also Called: Arte Limited
4500 Lee Rd Ste 120 (44128-2959)
PHONE..................................216 518-1400
Robert Kopittke, *Branch Mgr*
EMP: 100
SALES (corp-wide): 17.2MM **Privately Held**
WEB: www.hudsonsupply.com
SIC: 3599 3541 Machine shop, jobbing & repair; sawing & cutoff machines (metalworking machinery)
PA: Lawrence Industries, Inc.
4500 Lee Rd Ste 120
Cleveland OH 44128
216 518-7000

(G-5568)
LAWSONS TOWING & AUTO WRCKG
14114 Miles Ave (44128-2329)
PHONE..................................216 883-9050
EMP: 10
SALES (est): 920K **Privately Held**
SIC: 5093 3711 Whol Scrap/Waste Material Mfg Motor Vehicle/Car Bodies

(G-5569)
LAZARUS STEEL LLC
901 Addison Rd (44103-1607)
PHONE..................................216 391-3245
Timothy Harlan,
EMP: 3
SQ FT: 23,500
SALES (est): 2.2MM **Privately Held**
SIC: 3441 Fabricated structural metal

(G-5570)
LEDGE HILL SIGNS LIMITED
Also Called: Fastsigns
5369 Mayfield Rd (44124-2456)
PHONE..................................440 461-4445
Ed Davis, *Owner*
EMP: 3
SALES (est): 315.2K **Privately Held**
SIC: 3993 Signs & advertising specialties

(G-5571)
LEFCO WORTHINGTON LLC
18451 Euclid Ave (44112-1016)
PHONE..................................216 432-4422
Larry E Fulton,
EMP: 31
SQ FT: 30,000
SALES (est): 6.2MM **Privately Held**
WEB: www.lefcoindustries.com
SIC: 4783 2441 4226 Packing & crating; boxes, wood; special warehousing & storage

(G-5572)
LEGAL NEWS PUBLISHING CO
Also Called: Daily Legal News
2935 Prospect Ave E (44115-2607)
PHONE..................................216 696-3322
Lucien B Karlovec Jr, *President*
Lisa Cech, *Editor*
Jeffrey Karlovec, *Exec VP*
Charles E Bergstresser, *Treasurer*
John Karlovec, *Admin Sec*
EMP: 28
SQ FT: 14,238
SALES (est): 3.7MM **Privately Held**
WEB: www.dln.com
SIC: 2791 2711 2752 2789 Typesetting; newspapers, publishing & printing; commercial printing, offset; bookbinding & related work; periodicals

(G-5573)
LEIMKUEHLER INC (PA)
4625 Detroit Ave (44102-2295)
PHONE..................................440 899-7842
Robert Leimkuehler, *President*
EMP: 21 **EST:** 1948
SQ FT: 10,000
SALES (est): 2.6MM **Privately Held**
SIC: 5999 3842 Orthopedic & prosthesis applications; surgical appliances & supplies

(G-5574)
LEXTECH INDUSTRIES LTD
6800 Union Ave (44105-1326)
PHONE..................................216 883-7900
David N Bortz, *President*
EMP: 6 **EST:** 1998
SQ FT: 143,000
SALES (est): 883.4K **Privately Held**
WEB: www.lextechindustries.com
SIC: 3469 3568 3462 Stamping metal for the trade; power transmission equipment; iron & steel forgings

(G-5575)
LINCOLN ELECTRIC COMPANY (HQ)
22801 Saint Clair Ave (44117-1199)
PHONE..................................216 481-8100
Steven B Hedlund, *President*
Christopher L Mapes, *Chairman*
Frederick G Stueber, *Exec VP*
Geoffrey P Allman, *Senior VP*
Anthony Battle, *Senior VP*
◆ **EMP:** 3200
SQ FT: 2,658,410
SALES (est): 1.1B
SALES (corp-wide): 3B **Publicly Held**
WEB: www.subarc-welding.com
SIC: 3548 Arc welding generators, alternating current & direct current; electrodes, electric welding
PA: Lincoln Electric Holdings, Inc.
22801 Saint Clair Ave
Cleveland OH 44117
216 481-8100

(G-5576)
LINCOLN ELECTRIC COMPANY
7550 Hub Pkwy (44125-5705)
PHONE..................................216 524-8800
EMP: 230

SALES (corp-wide): 3B **Publicly Held**
SIC: 3625 3823 3566 Controls for adjustable speed drives; numerical controls; industrial instrmnts msrmnt display/control process variable; speed changers, drives & gears
HQ: Lincoln Electric Company
22801 Saint Clair Ave
Cleveland OH 44117
216 481-8100

(G-5577)
LINCOLN ELECTRIC HOLDINGS INC (PA)
22801 Saint Clair Ave (44117-2524)
PHONE..................................216 481-8100
Christopher L Mapes, *Ch of Bd*
George D Blankenship, *President*
Thomas A Flohn, *President*
Steven B Hedlund, *President*
Doug Lance, *President*
EMP: 204 **EST:** 1895
SQ FT: 3,017,090
SALES: 3B **Publicly Held**
WEB: www.lincolnelectric.com
SIC: 3548 Welding & cutting apparatus & accessories

(G-5578)
LINESTREAM TECHNOLOGIES
1468 W 9th St Ste 435 (44113-1316)
PHONE..................................216 862-7874
Dave Neundorfer, *CEO*
James G Dawson, *Principal*
David Stopher, *Opers Staff*
Gang Tian, *CTO*
EMP: 7
SALES (est): 872.8K **Privately Held**
SIC: 7372 Business oriented computer software

(G-5579)
LINSALATA CAPITAL PARTNERS FUN
5900 Landerbrook Dr # 280 (44124-4020)
PHONE..................................440 684-1400
Frank Linsalata, *Partner*
James V Guddy, *Vice Pres*
EMP: 9
SALES (est): 2.1MM **Privately Held**
WEB: www.lincap3.com
SIC: 6282 6799 3499 2676 Investment advisory service; investment research; venture capital companies; safes & vaults, metal; sanitary paper products; napkins, sanitary: made from purchased paper; tampons, sanitary: made from purchased paper; diapers, paper (disposable): made from purchased paper; scrub cloths; work garments, except raincoats: waterproof

(G-5580)
LIQUID IMAGE CORP OF AMERICA
3700 Prospect Ave E (44115-2706)
PHONE..................................216 458-9800
Lea Wiertel, *President*
Michael Wiertel, *Vice Pres*
EMP: 7
SQ FT: 2,500
SALES (est): 1.3MM **Privately Held**
WEB: www.liquid-image.com
SIC: 3663 Digital encoders

(G-5581)
LISA MODEM
4195 Zalley Rd (44109)
PHONE..................................216 551-3365
Lynn Westfall, *Owner*
EMP: 3
SALES (est): 176.1K **Privately Held**
SIC: 3661 Modems

(G-5582)
LOGAN CLUTCH CORPORATION
Also Called: Lc
28855 Ranney Pkwy (44145-1173)
PHONE..................................440 808-4258
Madelon Logan, *CEO*
William A Logan, *President*
Elyse Logan, *Vice Pres*
▲ **EMP:** 30
SQ FT: 33,000

GEOGRAPHIC SECTION

Cleveland - Cuyahoga County (G-5611)

SALES (est): 8.1MM **Privately Held**
WEB: www.loganclutch.com
SIC: **3568** 5085 Clutches, except vehicular; industrial supplies

(G-5583)
LOGOS ON LEE
3105 Mayfield Rd (44118-1713)
PHONE..................................216 862-5226
Todd Guenther, *Principal*
EMP: 6
SALES (est): 529.3K **Privately Held**
SIC: **2759** Screen printing

(G-5584)
LOREAL USA INC
30601 Carter St (44139-3513)
P.O. Box 39608 (44139-0608)
PHONE..................................440 248-3700
Rex Mason, *Principal*
EMP: 650
SALES (corp-wide): 4.4B **Privately Held**
WEB: www.lorealparisusa.com
SIC: **2844** Hair preparations, including shampoos; cosmetic preparations; perfumes & colognes
HQ: L'oreal Usa, Inc.
10 Hudson Yards
New York NY 10001
212 818-1500

(G-5585)
LOUS SAUSAGE LTD
14723 Miles Ave (44128-2397)
PHONE..................................216 752-5060
Joseph Vinciguerra,
Frank Vinciguerra,
EMP: 17
SQ FT: 7,500
SALES: 1.7MM **Privately Held**
SIC: **2013** Sausages from purchased meat

(G-5586)
LPC PUBLISHING CO
2026 Murray Hill Rd # 10 (44106-5958)
PHONE..................................216 721-1800
Gail Smith, *Principal*
EMP: 4
SALES (est): 275.7K **Privately Held**
SIC: **2741** Miscellaneous publishing

(G-5587)
LUCKY THIRTEEN INC
Also Called: Lucky Thirteen Laser
7413 Associate Ave (44144-1104)
PHONE..................................216 631-0013
James Bailey, *President*
James P Bailey, *Principal*
Francis J Dempsey, *Principal*
Thomas G Scheiman, *Principal*
EMP: 8
SALES (est): 1.3MM **Privately Held**
SIC: **3699** Laser welding, drilling & cutting equipment

(G-5588)
LUXCO INC
Also Called: Paramount Distillers
3116 Berea Rd (44111-1501)
PHONE..................................216 671-6300
Paul A Lux, *Branch Mgr*
EMP: 40
SALES (corp-wide): 61.9MM **Privately Held**
SIC: **2085** Bourbon whiskey
PA: Luxco, Inc.
5050 Kemper Ave
Saint Louis MO 63139
314 772-2626

(G-5589)
LYNNS LOGOS INC
386 Broadway Ave (44146-2604)
PHONE..................................440 786-1156
Linda Overholt, *President*
EMP: 4
SALES (est): 236.2K **Privately Held**
SIC: **2395** Embroidery products, except schiffli machine

(G-5590)
M & M DIES INC
3502 Beyerle Rd (44105-1016)
PHONE..................................216 883-6628
Donald Dostie, *President*
Ken Dostie, *Purchasing*
EMP: 7
SQ FT: 2,940
SALES (est): 726.9K **Privately Held**
SIC: **3364** 3544 Nonferrous die-castings except aluminum; special dies & tools

(G-5591)
M & M ENGRAVING
5411 State Rd (44134-1248)
PHONE..................................216 749-7166
Tom May, *Partner*
Frank Mamone, *Partner*
EMP: 3 EST: 2007
SALES: 499K **Privately Held**
SIC: **3479** 5999 Etching & engraving; trophies & plaques

(G-5592)
M B SAXON CO INC
Also Called: Saxon Jewelers
47 Alpha Park (44143-2219)
PHONE..................................440 229-5006
Michael B Saxon, *President*
EMP: 15
SQ FT: 3,200
SALES (est): 2.3MM **Privately Held**
WEB: www.saxonjewelers.com
SIC: **3911** 5944 5094 Jewelry, precious metal; jewelry, precious stones & precious metals; jewelry

(G-5593)
M MAZZONE & SONS BAKERY INC
Also Called: Mazzone Bakery
3519 Clark Ave (44109-1137)
PHONE..................................216 631-6511
Luigi Mazzone, *President*
Frank B Mazzone, *Admin Sec*
EMP: 9
SQ FT: 6,650
SALES (est): 1.3MM **Privately Held**
SIC: **2051** Bread, cake & related products

(G-5594)
M-BOSS INC
4510 E 71st St Ste 2 (44105-5638)
PHONE..................................216 441-6080
William Perk, *President*
EMP: 20
SQ FT: 6,000
SALES (est): 4.3MM **Privately Held**
WEB: www.mbossinc.com
SIC: **3646** Ceiling systems, luminous

(G-5595)
M2M IMAGING CORPORATION
5427 Wilson Mills Rd (44143)
PHONE..................................440 684-9690
Joe Flicek, *CEO*
Jon T Devries, *President*
EMP: 13
SQ FT: 2,500
SALES (est): 1.6MM **Privately Held**
SIC: **3677** Coil windings, electronic

(G-5596)
M3 TECHNOLOGIES INC
13910 Enterprise Ave (44135-5118)
PHONE..................................216 898-9736
Roger May, *President*
Barry May, *Treasurer*
Danny May, *Admin Sec*
EMP: 10
SALES (est): 1.7MM **Privately Held**
WEB: www.m3technologies.com
SIC: **3444** Sheet metal specialties, not stamped

(G-5597)
MACE PERSONAL DEF & SEC INC (HQ)
4400 Carnegie Ave (44103-4342)
PHONE..................................440 424-5321
Carl Smith, *CFO*
◆ EMP: 30
SQ FT: 30,000
SALES (est): 5.1MM
SALES (corp-wide): 28.3MM **Publicly Held**
SIC: **3999** 5065 Self-defense sprays; security control equipment & systems
PA: Mace Security International, Inc.
4400 Carnegie Ave
Cleveland OH 44103
440 424-5321

(G-5598)
MACE SECURITY INTL INC (PA)
4400 Carnegie Ave (44103-4342)
PHONE..................................440 424-5321
Gary Medved, *President*
Paul Hughes, *Exec VP*
Carl R Smith, *Senior VP*
Eric Crawford, *Vice Pres*
Garnett Meador, *Vice Pres*
◆ EMP: 81
SQ FT: 5,000
SALES (est): 28.3MM **Publicly Held**
WEB: www.securityandmore.com
SIC: **3699** 3999 Security devices; self-defense sprays

(G-5599)
MACHINE INDUSTRIES INC (PA)
5200 Perkins Ave (44103-3524)
P.O. Box 603773 (44103-0773)
PHONE..................................216 881-8555
Jerry Mandell, *President*
EMP: 3
SQ FT: 4,000
SALES (est): 528K **Privately Held**
SIC: **3599** Machine shop, jobbing & repair

(G-5600)
MACHINE PARTS INTERNATIONAL
10925 Briggs Rd (44111-5333)
PHONE..................................216 251-4334
Greg Chlastosz, *President*
Kenneth Seiter, *Vice Pres*
EMP: 5
SQ FT: 3,500
SALES: 300K **Privately Held**
SIC: **3599** Machine & other job shop work

(G-5601)
MADISON GRAPHICS
13130 Detroit Ave (44107-2840)
PHONE..................................216 226-5770
Sam Salim, *Owner*
EMP: 5
SQ FT: 3,500
SALES (est): 541.9K **Privately Held**
SIC: **7336** 2759 Silk screen design; commercial printing

(G-5602)
MADISON GROUP INC
Also Called: Logotec
15919 Industrial Pkwy (44135-3353)
PHONE..................................216 362-9000
Robert Stein, *CEO*
Matthew Stein, *President*
Gayle Stein, *Vice Pres*
EMP: 7
SQ FT: 5,000
SALES (est): 521.6K **Privately Held**
WEB: www.logotec.com
SIC: **7389** 2396 5199 Embroidering of advertising on shirts, etc.; screen printing on fabric articles; advertising specialties

(G-5603)
MAGENTA INCORPORATED
3185a W 33rd St (44109-1524)
PHONE..................................216 571-4094
Virginia Benson, *President*
EMP: 22
SALES (est): 1.4MM **Privately Held**
SIC: **3641** Electric lamps & parts for specialized applications

(G-5604)
MAGNESIUM REFINING TECH INC (PA)
29695 Pettibone Rd (44139-5462)
PHONE..................................419 483-9199
Mike Slovich, *President*
▲ EMP: 40
SALES (est): 12.1MM **Privately Held**
SIC: **3339** Magnesium refining (primary)

(G-5605)
MAGNUM COMPUTERS INC
868 Montford Rd (44121-2012)
PHONE..................................216 781-1757
Dan Hanson, *President*
EMP: 10
SQ FT: 3,000
SALES (est): 1.3MM **Privately Held**
WEB: www.magnuminc.com
SIC: **5045** 1731 8748 7378 Computers, peripherals & software; general electrical contractor; business consulting; computer maintenance & repair; electronic computers

(G-5606)
MAHAR SPAR INDUSTRIES INC
341 E 131st St (44108-1607)
PHONE..................................216 249-7143
Michael Mahar, *President*
Robert Schilling, *Vice Pres*
Alvin Hensel, *Treasurer*
▲ EMP: 6
SQ FT: 22,000
SALES: 700K **Privately Held**
SIC: **3089** Injection molding of plastics

(G-5607)
MALIN WIRE CO (HQ)
5400 Smith Rd (44142-2081)
PHONE..................................216 267-9080
Leonard Defino, *President*
Mary Defino, *Corp Secy*
Frank Defino, *Vice Pres*
▲ EMP: 2
SQ FT: 56,000
SALES (est): 2.4MM **Privately Held**
WEB: www.malinco.com
SIC: **3496** 3469 Miscellaneous fabricated wire products; metal stampings

(G-5608)
MALIN WIRE CO
Also Called: Malin Co
5400 Smith Rd (44142-2081)
PHONE..................................216 267-9080
Leonard De Find, *Principal*
EMP: 25 **Privately Held**
WEB: www.malinco.com
SIC: **3469** Metal stampings
HQ: Malin Wire Co
5400 Smith Rd
Cleveland OH 44142
216 267-9080

(G-5609)
MALLEYS CANDIES INC
Also Called: Malley's Chocolates
13400 Brookpark Rd (44135-5145)
PHONE..................................216 529-6262
Patrick Malley, *Manager*
EMP: 25
SQ FT: 1,960
SALES (corp-wide): 53.5MM **Privately Held**
WEB: www.malleys.com
SIC: **2066** 4225 5441 2064 Chocolate & cocoa products; general warehousing & storage; candy, nut & confectionery stores; candy & other confectionery products
PA: Malley's Candies
1685 Victoria Ave
Lakewood OH 44107
216 362-8700

(G-5610)
MAMA MIAS FOODS INC
Also Called: M & M Foods
3270 W 67th Pl (44102-5295)
PHONE..................................216 281-2188
Joseph Carrino, *President*
EMP: 3
SQ FT: 12,000
SALES (est): 259K **Privately Held**
SIC: **2013** 5147 Sausages from purchased meat; meats, cured or smoked

(G-5611)
MAMECO INTERNATIONAL INC
4475 E 175th St (44128-3599)
PHONE..................................216 752-4400
Jeff Korach, *Principal*
EMP: 12
SQ FT: 77,000
SALES: 2.2MM
SALES (corp-wide): 5.3B **Publicly Held**
WEB: www.rpminc.com
SIC: **2891** 2851 3069 Adhesives & sealants; paints & allied products; floor coverings, rubber

Cleveland - Cuyahoga County (G-5612)

PA: Rpm International Inc.
2628 Pearl Rd
Medina OH 44256
330 273-5090

(G-5612)
MANITOWOC COMPANY INC
Also Called: Cleveland Shiprepair Company
1847 Columbus Rd (44113-2411)
PHONE.................................920 746-3332
Steve Konzel, *Manager*
EMP: 4
SALES (corp-wide): 1.8B **Publicly Held**
WEB: www.manitowoc.com
SIC: 3731 7699 3441 3599 Cargo vessels, building & repairing; boiler repair shop; fabricated structural metal; machine shop, jobbing & repair
PA: The Manitowoc Company Inc
11270 W Park Pl Ste 1000
Milwaukee WI 53224
414 760-4600

(G-5613)
MANUFACTURING FUTURES INC (PA)
40 Haskell Dr (44108-1169)
PHONE.................................216 903-7993
David O'Halloran, *President*
EMP: 1
SALES: 5MM **Privately Held**
SIC: 3499 Fountains (except drinking), metal

(G-5614)
MAR MOR INC
Also Called: Mealey Industrial Lubricants
3591 W 56th St (44102-5737)
PHONE.................................216 961-6900
Mario Pisano, *President*
EMP: 6
SQ FT: 8,500
SALES (est): 1.3MM **Privately Held**
SIC: 2992 Lubricating oils & greases

(G-5615)
MARBLE WORKS
Also Called: Outdoorwarehouse
17827 Roseland Rd (44112-1230)
PHONE.................................216 496-7745
Rich Duleba, *Owner*
EMP: 5
SQ FT: 6,500
SALES: 1.7MM **Privately Held**
WEB: www.polarhood.com
SIC: 3281 5149 Cut stone & stone products; baking supplies

(G-5616)
MARCUS UPPE INC
Also Called: Clicks Document Management
815 Superior Ave E # 714 (44114-2706)
PHONE.................................216 263-4000
Mark Sukie, *Branch Mgr*
EMP: 60 **Privately Held**
SIC: 2759 Commercial printing
PA: Marcus Uppe Inc.
320 Fort Duquesne Blvd # 300
Pittsburgh PA 15222

(G-5617)
MARICH MACHINE & TOOL CO INC
3815 Lakeside Ave E (44114-3843)
PHONE.................................216 391-5502
Andrew Marich, *President*
EMP: 9
SQ FT: 10,000
SALES (est): 1.2MM **Privately Held**
SIC: 3599 Machine shop, jobbing & repair

(G-5618)
MARK DENTAL LABORATORY
24300 Chagrin Blvd # 310 (44122-5639)
PHONE.................................216 464-6424
EMP: 8
SQ FT: 3,000
SALES (est): 470K **Privately Held**
SIC: 8072 3843 Dental Laboratory Mfg Dental Equipment/Supplies

(G-5619)
MARK TRUE ENGRAVING CO
1250 W 76th St (44102)
PHONE.................................216 651-7700
Thomas Timura, *President*
EMP: 5
SQ FT: 40,000
SALES (est): 628.7K **Privately Held**
SIC: 3469 Stamping metal for the trade

(G-5620)
MARK TRUE ENGRAVING COMPANY
3264 W 105th St (44111-2865)
PHONE.................................216 252-7422
David Timura, *Owner*
EMP: 5
SALES (est): 527K **Privately Held**
SIC: 3479 Etching & engraving

(G-5621)
MARKETING DIRECTIONS INC
Also Called: Trend Curve, The
28005 Clemens Rd (44145-1139)
P.O. Box 60696, Irvine CA (92602-6023)
PHONE.................................440 835-5550
Steven Borsch, *Managing Prtnr*
Michelle Lamb, *Chairman*
EMP: 5
SALES (est): 395.6K **Privately Held**
SIC: 2721 Periodicals

(G-5622)
MARKING DEVICES INC
3110 Payne Ave (44114-4504)
PHONE.................................216 861-4498
Theodore Cutts, *President*
Margaret Hamge, *Relations*
EMP: 30
SALES (est): 1.7MM
SALES (corp-wide): 3.4MM **Privately Held**
WEB: www.royalacme.com
SIC: 3953 Embossing seals & hand stamps
PA: Royal Acme Corporation
3110 Payne Ave
Cleveland OH 44114
216 241-1477

(G-5623)
MARLIN MANUFACTURING CORP (PA)
12800 Corporate Dr (44130-9311)
PHONE.................................216 676-1340
John Tymkewicz, *Principal*
John H Breisch, *Principal*
Wallace B Heiser, *Principal*
Joe Bondra, *Engineer*
Dan Nerad, *Sales Staff*
▲ **EMP:** 70 **EST:** 1952
SQ FT: 42,000
SALES (est): 10.1MM **Privately Held**
WEB: www.marlinmfg.com
SIC: 3823 Pyrometers, industrial process type; thermocouples, industrial process type

(G-5624)
MARLIN THERMOCOUPLE WIRE INC
Also Called: Miller Wire & Cable
12800 Corporate Dr (44130-9311)
PHONE.................................440 835-1950
Ronald A Miller, *President*
David A Miller, *Vice Pres*
Patrick Gillis, *Sales Staff*
▲ **EMP:** 24
SQ FT: 46,000
SALES (est): 6.2MM **Privately Held**
SIC: 3315 Wire, steel: insulated or armored

(G-5625)
MARLOW-2000 INC
Also Called: Martin Industrial Truck
13811 Enterprise Ave (44135-5115)
PHONE.................................216 362-8500
Danny E Martin, *President*
Tom Nelson, *Vice Pres*
Sandra Martin, *Treasurer*
Bill Ranke, *Manager*
EMP: 13
SQ FT: 22,000
SALES: 1MM **Privately Held**
WEB: www.mit1976.com
SIC: 5531 3537 7513 Truck equipment & parts; forklift trucks; truck rental & leasing, no drivers

(G-5626)
MARTIN PULTRUSION GROUP INC
20801 Miles Rd Ste B (44128-4530)
PHONE.................................440 439-9130
Jeff Martin, *President*
William Ard, *Vice Pres*
Chris Mrugacz, *Engineer*
▼ **EMP:** 6 **EST:** 1993
SQ FT: 7,360
SALES (est): 1.2MM **Privately Held**
WEB: www.martinpultrusion.com
SIC: 3544 Special dies, tools, jigs & fixtures

(G-5627)
MARTIN SHEET METAL INC
Also Called: Martin Cab Div
7108 Madison Ave (44102-4093)
PHONE.................................216 377-8200
Robert P Martin Sr, *CEO*
Pauline Martin, *Ch of Bd*
Frank Bendyck, *Principal*
George F Voinovich, *CFO*
EMP: 80 **EST:** 1920
SQ FT: 100,000
SALES (est): 18.3MM **Privately Held**
WEB: www.martincab.com
SIC: 3537 3713 Cabs, for industrial trucks & tractors; truck & bus bodies

(G-5628)
MARTINDALE ELECTRIC COMPANY
1375 Hird Ave (44107-3008)
P.O. Box 72419 (44192-0002)
PHONE.................................216 521-8567
Jim Satterthwaite, *President*
F Z Marty, *Principal*
Jeffrey Snyder, *Vice Pres*
EMP: 48
SQ FT: 33,000
SALES (est): 10.1MM **Privately Held**
SIC: 3425 3541 Saw blades & handsaws; machine tools, metal cutting type

(G-5629)
MARXWARE COMPUTING SERVICES
4963 Schaaf Ln (44131-1034)
PHONE.................................216 661-5263
Mark Butler, *President*
EMP: 10
SALES (est): 764.6K **Privately Held**
SIC: 7372 Prepackaged software

(G-5630)
MASTER CHROME SERVICE INC
5709 Herman Ave (44102-2195)
PHONE.................................216 961-2012
Gerald J Garver, *President*
Micheal J Rowe, *Vice Pres*
Charloes Rowe, *Admin Sec*
EMP: 33
SQ FT: 10,000
SALES (est): 3.1MM **Privately Held**
SIC: 3471 Chromium plating of metals or formed products

(G-5631)
MASTER CRAFT PRODUCTS INC
10621 Briggs Rd (44111-5329)
PHONE.................................216 281-5910
Jim Szente Jr, *President*
Cyndi Szente, *Treasurer*
EMP: 12
SQ FT: 4,400
SALES (est): 1.5MM **Privately Held**
WEB: www.mastercraftdies.com
SIC: 3544 Special dies & tools

(G-5632)
MASTER MFG CO INC
Also Called: Master Caster Company
9200 Inman Ave (44105-2110)
PHONE.................................216 641-0500
Iris Rubinfield, *President*
Bob Ptacek, *Vice Pres*
Penny Heinzmann, *Treasurer*
Tiffany Goodwin, *Office Mgr*
Pamela Vestal, *Admin Sec*
▲ **EMP:** 34
SQ FT: 10,000
SALES (est): 5.8MM **Privately Held**
SIC: 3429 2599 2392 3069 Furniture builders' & other household hardware; factory furniture & fixtures; household furnishings; hard rubber & molded rubber products

(G-5633)
MASTER PRINTING COMPANY
3112 Broadview Rd (44109-3390)
PHONE.................................216 351-2246
Donald Dobos, *President*
Russell Dobos, *Vice Pres*
David Dobos, *Treasurer*
Pam Sloat, *Office Mgr*
Ed Kulavick, *CIO*
EMP: 23 **EST:** 1928
SQ FT: 20,000
SALES (est): 4MM **Privately Held**
WEB: www.mprinting.com
SIC: 2752 Commercial printing, offset

(G-5634)
MASTER PRODUCTS COMPANY
6400 Park Ave (44105-4991)
PHONE.................................216 341-1740
R Jeffrey Walters, *President*
Greg Walters, *Vice Pres*
David Mitskavich, *Treasurer*
EMP: 57
SQ FT: 70,000
SALES: 8MM **Privately Held**
SIC: 3452 3469 3568 Washers, metal; stamping metal for the trade; power transmission equipment

(G-5635)
MATERION TECHNICAL MTLS INC
6070 Parkland Blvd (44124-4191)
PHONE.................................216 486-4200
EMP: 85
SALES (est): 18.8MM **Privately Held**
SIC: 3399 Mfg Primary Metal Products

(G-5636)
MAYFAIR GRANITE CO INC
Also Called: Mayfair Memorial
4202 Mayfield Rd (44121-3008)
PHONE.................................216 382-8150
Michael J Johns Sr, *President*
Nicolette L Johns, *Corp Secy*
Michael N Johns, *Vice Pres*
Monica Johns, *Vice Pres*
Michael Johns, *Bd of Directors*
EMP: 7 **EST:** 1937
SALES (est): 969K **Privately Held**
SIC: 5999 5032 3993 Monuments, finished to custom order; granite building stone; signs & advertising specialties

(G-5637)
MAYFRAN INTERNATIONAL INC (HQ)
6650 Beta Dr (44143-2352)
PHONE.................................440 461-4100
Naoshige Sakai, *President*
Frank Sraj, *COO*
Ed McManus, *Vice Pres*
Steve Queen, *Maint Spvr*
Robert Clinton, *QC Mgr*
▲ **EMP:** 228
SQ FT: 154,000
SALES: 60.8MM
SALES (corp-wide): 2B **Privately Held**
WEB: www.mayfran.com
SIC: 3535 Belt conveyor systems, general industrial use
PA: Tsubakimoto Chain Co.
3-3-3, Nakanoshima, Kita-Ku
Osaka OSK 530-0
664 410-011

(G-5638)
MAZZELLA LIFTING TECH INC (HQ)
21000 Aerospace Pkwy (44142-1072)
PHONE.................................440 239-7000
Anthony Mazzella, *CEO*
James J Mazzella, *Vice Pres*
Steve Thur, *Opers Staff*
Stephanie Whitney, *Purch Agent*
Richard Mikut, *Engineer*
▲ **EMP:** 80 **EST:** 1959
SQ FT: 50,000

GEOGRAPHIC SECTION
Cleveland - Cuyahoga County (G-5665)

SALES (est): 51.5MM **Privately Held**
WEB: www.mazzellalifting.com
SIC: 3496 Miscellaneous fabricated wire products

(G-5639)
MAZZELLA LIFTING TECH INC
21000 Aerospace Pkwy (44142-1072)
PHONE..................440 239-5700
Tony Mazzella, *President*
Eric Parkerson, *Vice Pres*
Terry Pipik, *Plant Mgr*
EMP: 60 **Privately Held**
WEB: www.mazzellalifting.com
SIC: 3531 Backhoes, tractors, cranes, plows & similar equipment; cranes
HQ: Mazzella Lifting Technologies, Inc.
21000 Aerospace Pkwy
Cleveland OH 44142
440 239-7000

(G-5640)
MAZZOLINI ARTCRAFT CO INC
1607 E 41st St (44103-2396)
PHONE..................216 431-7529
John Mazzolini, *President*
▲ EMP: 11
SQ FT: 4,800
SALES (est): 1.5MM **Privately Held**
WEB: www.mazzart.com
SIC: 3299 5199 Statuary: gypsum, clay, papier mache, metal, etc.; statuary

(G-5641)
MB DYNAMICS INC
25865 Richmond Rd (44146-1431)
PHONE..................216 292-5850
Richard E Mc Cormick, *CEO*
Phillip Lehmann, *Design Engr*
Dick Deemer, *Human Resources*
Mike Priebe, *Director*
▼ EMP: 34
SQ FT: 25,000
SALES (est): 10MM **Privately Held**
WEB: www.mbdynamics.com
SIC: 3829 Testing equipment: abrasion, shearing strength, etc.

(G-5642)
MCHAEL D GORONOK STRING INSTRS
10823 Magnolia Dr (44106-1807)
PHONE..................216 421-4227
Michael D Goronok, *Owner*
EMP: 9
SQ FT: 8,000
SALES (est): 145K **Privately Held**
SIC: 3931 5099 String instruments & parts; musical instruments

(G-5643)
MCI INC (HQ)
22901 Millcreek Blvd (44122-5728)
PHONE..................216 292-3800
Richard T Marabito, *CEO*
EMP: 40
SALES (est): 1.7MM
SALES (corp-wide): 1.3B **Publicly Held**
SIC: 3537 Hoppers, end dump
PA: Olympic Steel, Inc.
22901 Millcreek Blvd # 650
Cleveland OH 44122
216 292-3800

(G-5644)
MCM IND CO INC (PA)
Also Called: McM Industries
22901 Millcreek Blvd (44122-5728)
PHONE..................216 292-3800
Gloria Reljanovic, *CEO*
Michael Reljanovic, *President*
◆ EMP: 12
SQ FT: 1,000
SALES (est): 6.7MM **Privately Held**
SIC: 3496 Miscellaneous fabricated wire products

(G-5645)
MCM IND CO INC
7800 Finney Ave (44105-5125)
PHONE..................216 641-9700
Mike Zlojutro, *Branch Mgr*
EMP: 30
SQ FT: 51,055
SALES (corp-wide): 6.7MM **Privately Held**
SIC: 3496 Miscellaneous fabricated wire products
PA: Mcm Ind. Co., Inc.
22901 Millcreek Blvd
Cleveland OH 44122
216 292-4506

(G-5646)
MCMATH & SHEETS UNLIMITED INC
Also Called: Offset Theory
4427 Mayfield Rd (44121-3633)
PHONE..................216 381-0010
David Thompson, *President*
EMP: 3
SQ FT: 2,000
SALES (est): 450K **Privately Held**
SIC: 2752 Commercial printing, offset

(G-5647)
MCNAMARAS PUB INC
3498 W 146th St (44111-2209)
PHONE..................216 671-8820
Gary McNamara, *CEO*
EMP: 4
SALES (est): 236.8K **Privately Held**
SIC: 2731 Book publishing

(G-5648)
MCO INC (PA)
7555 Bessemer Ave (44127-1821)
PHONE..................216 341-8914
Tom Mesterhazy, *President*
EMP: 35
SQ FT: 18,000
SALES (est): 3.6MM **Privately Held**
SIC: 2992 Lubricating oils & greases

(G-5649)
MCTECH CORP
5000 Crayton Ave (44104-2826)
PHONE..................216 391-7700
Linda Frazier, *Exec VP*
EMP: 12
SALES (corp-wide): 32.7MM **Privately Held**
SIC: 3531 Concrete plants
PA: Mctech Corp
8100 Grand Ave Ste 100
Cleveland OH 44104
216 391-7700

(G-5650)
MEASUREMENT COMPUTING CORP (HQ)
Also Called: Iotech
25971 Cannon Rd (44146-1833)
PHONE..................440 439-4091
Mark Marini, *President*
Pat McCoy, *Controller*
EMP: 22
SQ FT: 30,000
SALES (est): 4.3MM
SALES (corp-wide): 1.3B **Publicly Held**
WEB: www.iotech.com
SIC: 3823 Computer interface equipment for industrial process control
PA: National Instruments Corporation
11500 N Mopac Expy
Austin TX 78759
512 683-0100

(G-5651)
MEDCO LABS INC
Also Called: Medco Adhesive Coated Products
5156 Richmond Rd (44146-1331)
PHONE..................216 292-7546
Gary Fenton, *President*
Marvin Magar, *Vice Pres*
EMP: 15
SQ FT: 15,000
SALES (est): 2.7MM
SALES (corp-wide): 6.1MM **Privately Held**
WEB: www.medcocoatedproducts.com
SIC: 3842 Adhesive tape & plasters, medicated or non-medicated
PA: Marlen Manufacturing And Development Co.
5150 Richmond Rd
Bedford OH 44146
216 292-7060

(G-5652)
MEDTRONIC INC
5005 Rockside Rd Ste 1160 (44131-6801)
PHONE..................216 642-1977
Larry Saunders, *Branch Mgr*
EMP: 17 **Privately Held**
SIC: 3841 Surgical & medical instruments
HQ: Medtronic, Inc.
710 Medtronic Pkwy
Minneapolis MN 55432
763 514-4000

(G-5653)
MEGA BRIGHT LLC
4979 W 130th St (44135-5139)
PHONE..................216 712-4689
Brad Du, *Principal*
EMP: 7
SALES (est): 657.6K **Privately Held**
SIC: 3646 Commercial indusl & institutional electric lighting fixtures

(G-5654)
MELIN TOOL COMPANY INC
5565 Venture Dr Ste C (44130-9302)
PHONE..................216 362-4200
Mildred Rathberger, *Ch of Bd*
Mike Wochna, *President*
Michael Wochna, *Exec VP*
Jack Dean, *Plant Supt*
Sue Dimassa, *Accountant*
EMP: 70
SQ FT: 25,000
SALES (est): 16.2MM **Privately Held**
WEB: www.endmill.com
SIC: 3545 3541 Cutting tools for machine tools; machine tools, metal cutting type

(G-5655)
MERCURY BIOMED LLC
29001 Cedar Rd Ste 326 (44124-6501)
PHONE..................216 777-1492
Brad Pulver, *CEO*
Brian Patrick, *Vice Pres*
EMP: 3 EST: 2015
SQ FT: 3,000
SALES (est): 211.3K **Privately Held**
SIC: 3845 Electromedical equipment

(G-5656)
MERIT FOUNDRY CO INC
2289 N Saint James Pkwy (44106-3657)
PHONE..................216 741-4282
George R Mroz Jr, *President*
EMP: 4
SQ FT: 8,000
SALES (est): 572.5K **Privately Held**
SIC: 3365 Aluminum & aluminum-based alloy castings

(G-5657)
MESSER LLC
6300 Halle Dr (44125-4618)
PHONE..................216 533-7256
Jim Hansen, *Project Mgr*
EMP: 24
SALES (corp-wide): 1.4B **Privately Held**
SIC: 2813 Oxygen, compressed or liquefied
HQ: Messer Llc
200 Somerset Corporate
Bridgewater NJ 08807
908 464-8100

(G-5658)
METAL FABRICATING CORPORATION
10408 Berea Rd (44102-2506)
PHONE..................216 631-8121
Judy Kalski, *President*
Bernard Golias Sr, *Chairman*
Joseph Golias, *Vice Pres*
Robert Golias, *Vice Pres*
Tom Hammond, *Production*
EMP: 87 EST: 1932
SQ FT: 150,000
SALES (est): 17.8MM **Privately Held**
WEB: www.metalfabricatingcorp.com
SIC: 2542 3444 3469 3443 Cabinets: show, display or storage: except wood; bins, prefabricated sheet metal; stamping metal for the trade; fabricated plate work (boiler shop); office furniture, except wood; metal household furniture

(G-5659)
METAL FINISHING NEEDS LTD
16025 Van Aken Blvd (44120-5349)
PHONE..................216 561-6334
Thomas J Foley, *Principal*
EMP: 3
SALES (est): 136.1K **Privately Held**
SIC: 3471 Cleaning, polishing & finishing

(G-5660)
METAL-MATION INC
2391 W 38th St (44113-3838)
PHONE..................216 651-1083
Robert Nagel, *President*
Jerry Walker, *Vice Pres*
EMP: 16
SQ FT: 2,500
SALES (est): 1.6MM **Privately Held**
WEB: www.wellwalker.com
SIC: 8748 3365 Business consulting; aluminum foundries

(G-5661)
METALS CRANKSHAFT GRINDING
1435 E 45th St (44103-1115)
PHONE..................216 431-5778
Patrick Obermayer, *President*
EMP: 4
SQ FT: 6,000
SALES: 300K **Privately Held**
SIC: 3599 Machine shop, jobbing & repair

(G-5662)
METRO MECH INC
Also Called: Metalsmiths
3599 E 49th St (44105-1151)
PHONE..................216 641-6262
Larry Zebrasky, *President*
Tom Zebrasky, *Vice Pres*
EMP: 4 EST: 1964
SQ FT: 4,000
SALES: 200K **Privately Held**
SIC: 3714 3724 3568 3544 Motor vehicle transmissions, drive assemblies & parts; aircraft engines & engine parts; power transmission equipment; special dies, tools, jigs & fixtures; construction machinery; concrete products

(G-5663)
MEYER COMPANY (PA)
Also Called: Tomlinson Industries
13700 Broadway Ave (44125-1945)
PHONE..................216 587-3400
H F Meyer, *President*
Heidi Figas, *Corp Secy*
Donald Calkins, *Vice Pres*
Michael E Figas, *Vice Pres*
H F Meyer III, *Vice Pres*
▲ EMP: 170
SQ FT: 100,000
SALES (est): 30.9MM **Privately Held**
WEB: www.tomlinsonind.com
SIC: 3556 Food products machinery

(G-5664)
MFH PARTNERS INC (PA)
6650 Beta Dr (44143-2352)
P.O. Box 43038 (44143-0045)
PHONE..................440 461-4100
J D Sullivan, *Ch of Bd*
Kevin Hatridge, *Info Tech Dir*
Carron Redena, *Exec Sec*
EMP: 10
SQ FT: 4,000
SALES (est): 59.2MM **Privately Held**
SIC: 5084 3535 3568 2296 Industrial machinery & equipment; belt conveyor systems, general industrial use; power transmission equipment; tire cord & fabrics

(G-5665)
MIC-RAY METAL PRODUCTS INC
9016 Manor Ave (44104-4524)
PHONE..................216 791-2206
Michael Konicky Jr, *President*
Raymond Konicky, *Treasurer*
EMP: 10 EST: 1947
SQ FT: 5,000
SALES (est): 960K **Privately Held**
SIC: 3469 Metal stampings

Cleveland - Cuyahoga County (G-5666)

(G-5666)
MICELI DAIRY PRODUCTS CO (PA)
2721 E 90th St (44104-3396)
PHONE....................216 791-6222
Joseph D Miceli, *CEO*
John J Miceli Jr, *Exec VP*
Joseph Lograsso, *Vice Pres*
Charles Surace, *Vice Pres*
Rosemary Surace, *Treasurer*
▲ **EMP:** 90
SQ FT: 25,000
SALES (est): 74.4MM **Privately Held**
SIC: 2022 0241 Natural cheese; milk production

(G-5667)
MICRO LAPPING & GRINDING CO
12320 Plaza Dr (44130-1060)
PHONE....................216 267-6500
Ray Robaugh, *President*
John Dunmire, *Vice Pres*
EMP: 40
SQ FT: 25,000
SALES (est): 4.4MM **Privately Held**
SIC: 3599 3471 Grinding castings for the trade; plating & polishing

(G-5668)
MICROFORM INC
29529 Goulders Grn (44140-1271)
PHONE....................440 899-6339
N A Shanks, *President*
EMP: 5
SQ FT: 500
SALES (est): 265.4K **Privately Held**
SIC: 3452 Bolts, nuts, rivets & washers

(G-5669)
MICROPURE FILTRATION INC
Also Called: Wfs Filter Co
837 E 79th St (44103-1807)
PHONE....................952 472-2323
Trey Senney, *CEO*
Robert Pollmann, *President*
Marcy Pollmann, *Corp Secy*
▲ **EMP:** 16
SQ FT: 10,000
SALES (est): 750K **Privately Held**
WEB: www.micropure.com
SIC: 3677 Filtration devices, electronic

(G-5670)
MICROSHEEN CORPORATION
1100 E 222nd St Ste 1 (44117-1127)
PHONE....................216 481-5610
Lisa Habe, *Owner*
Mark Scanlon, *General Mgr*
Dan Roe, *Supervisor*
EMP: 10 **EST:** 1960
SQ FT: 30,000
SALES (est): 943.3K
SALES (corp-wide): 23.4MM **Privately Held**
WEB: www.microsheencorporation.com
SIC: 3471 Polishing, metals or formed products; anodizing (plating) of metals or formed products
PA: Interlake Industries, Inc.
  4732 E 355th St
  Willoughby OH 44094
  440 942-0800

(G-5671)
MICROSOFT CORPORATION
6050 Oak Tree Blvd # 300 (44131-6929)
PHONE....................216 986-1440
Kerry Duncan, *Accounts Mgr*
Chris Caster, *Manager*
EMP: 50
SALES (corp-wide): 110.3B **Publicly Held**
WEB: www.microsoft.com
SIC: 7372 Application computer software
PA: Microsoft Corporation
  1 Microsoft Way
  Redmond WA 98052
  425 882-8080

(G-5672)
MID AMERICA CHEMICAL CORP
4701 Spring Rd (44131-1025)
PHONE....................216 749-0100
Frank J Martinek Jr, *President*
Julienne C Martinek, *Vice Pres*
Debra Matrinek, *Vice Pres*
Doris Hallaman, *Admin Sec*
EMP: 9
SQ FT: 19,000
SALES (est): 825K **Privately Held**
SIC: 2851 2869 Paints & allied products; varnishes; removers & cleaners; solvents, organic

(G-5673)
MID AMERICAN VENTURES INC
Also Called: Cookie Cupboard
7600 Wall St Ste 205 (44125-3358)
PHONE....................216 524-0974
Richard A Pignatiello, *President*
Ellen Pignatiello, *Vice Pres*
EMP: 10
SALES (est): 1.2MM **Privately Held**
SIC: 2045 2099 Doughs, frozen or refrigerated: from purchased flour; food preparations

(G-5674)
MID-AMERICA STEEL CORP
Also Called: Mid-America Stainless
20900 Saint Clair Ave (44117-1020)
PHONE....................800 282-3466
John Ratica, *Sales Staff*
Jim Cash, *Pub Rel Dir*
Elliot M Kaufman, *Incorporator*
EMP: 50
SQ FT: 120,000
SALES (est): 58.4MM **Privately Held**
SIC: 5051 3469 3316 3312 Steel; sheets, metal; metal stampings; cold finishing of steel shapes; blast furnaces & steel mills

(G-5675)
MID-CONTINENT COAL AND COKE CO
Also Called: Mid-Continent River Dock
761 Stones Levee (44113-2573)
PHONE....................216 283-5700
John Kowalewski, *Principal*
EMP: 6
SQ FT: 10,136
SALES (corp-wide): 51.5MM **Privately Held**
WEB: www.midcontinentcoke.com
SIC: 3312 Blast furnaces & steel mills
HQ: Mid-Continent Coal And Coke Company
  20600 Chagrin Blvd # 850
  Cleveland OH 44122
  216 283-5700

(G-5676)
MID-CONTINENT MINERALS CORP (PA)
20600 Chagrin Blvd # 850 (44122-5374)
PHONE....................216 283-5700
Thomas G Gibbs, *President*
Mike Bakonyi, *CFO*
Harold Geiss, *Treasurer*
◆ **EMP:** 10
SALES (est): 51.5MM **Privately Held**
SIC: 3296 Insulation: rock wool, slag & silica minerals

(G-5677)
MID-WEST FORGE CORPORATION (PA)
17301 Saint Clair Ave (44110-2508)
PHONE....................216 481-3030
Robert I Gale III, *Ch of Bd*
Michael Sherwin, *Vice Ch Bd*
Paul C Gum, *President*
John T Webster, *Vice Pres*
Robert W Dems, *Treasurer*
EMP: 150
SQ FT: 165,000
SALES (est): 36.3MM **Privately Held**
WEB: www.mid-westforge.com
SIC: 3462 Iron & steel forgings

(G-5678)
MIDWEST BOX COMPANY
9801 Walford Ave Ste C (44102-4788)
PHONE....................216 281-9021
Susan Hecht Remer, *CEO*
Simon Tucker, *Plant Mgr*
EMP: 20 **EST:** 1964
SQ FT: 150,000

SALES (est): 7MM **Privately Held**
WEB: www.midwestbox.com
SIC: 2653 Boxes, corrugated: made from purchased materials

(G-5679)
MIDWEST COMPRESSOR CO INC (PA)
12901 Elmwood Ave (44111-5916)
PHONE....................216 941-9200
Alex Syntax, *President*
EMP: 4
SALES (est): 638.9K **Privately Held**
WEB: www.midwestcompressor.com
SIC: 3585 1711 Compressors for refrigeration & air conditioning equipment; plumbing, heating, air-conditioning contractors

(G-5680)
MIDWEST CURTAINWALLS INC
5171 Grant Ave (44125-1031)
PHONE....................216 641-7900
Donald F Kelly Jr, *President*
Lisa Smith, *Mktg Dir*
EMP: 80
SQ FT: 55,000
SALES (est): 18.5MM
SALES (corp-wide): 11.6MM **Privately Held**
WEB: www.midwestcurtainwalls.com
SIC: 3449 3442 1751 Curtain wall, metal; curtain walls for buildings, steel; window & door frames; window & door (prefabricated) installation
PA: Innovest Global, Inc.
  8834 Mayfield Rd Ste A
  Chesterland OH 44026
  216 815-1122

(G-5681)
MIDWEST INDUSTRIAL PRODUCTS
7424 Bessemer Ave (44127-1820)
PHONE....................216 771-8555
Michael Dunn, *President*
EMP: 4
SALES (est): 300K **Privately Held**
WEB: www.mipco.com
SIC: 2952 5033 Asphalt felts & coatings; roofing & siding materials

(G-5682)
MIDWEST MACHINE SERVICE INC
4700 Train Ave Ste 1 (44102-4591)
PHONE....................216 631-8151
Kevin Klapcic, *President*
EMP: 7
SQ FT: 6,000
SALES (est): 1.2MM **Privately Held**
SIC: 3599 Machine shop, jobbing & repair

(G-5683)
MIDWEST PRECISION PRODUCTS
9940 York Alpha Dr (44133-3510)
PHONE....................440 237-9500
Jim Diamond, *President*
EMP: 10
SQ FT: 25,000
SALES (est): 1MM **Privately Held**
WEB: www.midwestprecision.com
SIC: 2296 Fabric for reinforcing industrial belting

(G-5684)
MIKAN DIE AND TOOL LLC
13410 Enterprise Ave (44135-5162)
PHONE....................216 265-2811
Mike Pillar, *Mng Member*
Andrew McInnes,
EMP: 5 **EST:** 2007
SALES: 400K **Privately Held**
SIC: 3544 3545 Special dies & tools; machine tool accessories

(G-5685)
MILAN TOOL CORP
8989 Brookpark Rd (44129-6819)
P.O. Box 29336 (44129-0336)
PHONE....................216 661-1078
Mark Milan, *President*
▲ **EMP:** 30 **EST:** 1946
SQ FT: 20,000

SALES (est): 8.3MM **Privately Held**
SIC: 3728 3541 Aircraft body assemblies & parts; grinding machines, metalworking; machine tool replacement & repair parts, metal cutting types

(G-5686)
MILETI OPTICAL INC
Also Called: Mileti Optical & Hearing Ctr
5957 State Rd Ste 1 (44134-2872)
PHONE....................440 884-6333
Mark Mileti, *President*
Victor Mileti, *Vice Pres*
EMP: 3 **EST:** 1962
SQ FT: 1,500
SALES (est): 540.6K **Privately Held**
SIC: 3851 5995 Ophthalmic goods; optical goods stores

(G-5687)
MILKMEN DESIGN LLC
2332 Prospect Ave E (44115-2603)
PHONE....................440 590-5788
Tony Lahood,
EMP: 3
SALES (est): 123.8K **Privately Held**
SIC: 3089 Automotive parts, plastic

(G-5688)
MILL & MOTION INC
5415 E Schaaf Rd Ste 101 (44131-1335)
PHONE....................216 524-4000
Daniel A Hala, *President*
Albert E Hala, *Chairman*
Bruce Sidaway, *Vice Pres*
EMP: 12
SQ FT: 18,000
SALES (est): 2.8MM **Privately Held**
WEB: www.millmotion.com
SIC: 3599 8711 Machine shop, jobbing & repair; designing: ship, boat, machine & product

(G-5689)
MILLCRAFT GROUP LLC (PA)
Also Called: Deltacraft
6800 Grant Ave (44105-5628)
PHONE....................216 441-5500
Kay Mlakar, *Ch of Bd*
Katherine Mlakar, *Ch of Bd*
Travis Mlakar, *President*
Frank Kohl, *Division Mgr*
Lisa Pryor, *Division Mgr*
▲ **EMP:** 75
SQ FT: 90,000
SALES (est): 430.1MM **Privately Held**
WEB: www.deltacraft.com
SIC: 5111 5113 2679 Printing paper; industrial & personal service paper; paper products, converted

(G-5690)
MILLCRAFT PAPER COMPANY
4640 Hinckley Indus Pkwy (44109-6017)
PHONE....................216 429-9860
Barb Elish, *Sales Staff*
EMP: 6 **Privately Held**
SIC: 5943 5113 2621 Office forms & supplies; paper & products, wrapping or coarse; paper mills
HQ: The Millcraft Paper Company
  6800 Grant Ave
  Cleveland OH 44105
  216 441-5505

(G-5691)
MILLS CUSTOMS WOODWORKS
3950 Prospect Ave E (44115-2710)
PHONE....................216 407-3600
Paul Mills, *Principal*
EMP: 4 **EST:** 2008
SALES (est): 491.7K **Privately Held**
SIC: 2431 Millwork

(G-5692)
MINDCRAFTED SYSTEMS INC
1969 Newbury Dr (44145-3334)
PHONE....................440 821-2245
Frank Shoemaker, *President*
EMP: 4
SALES (est): 288.4K **Privately Held**
WEB: www.mindcrafted.com
SIC: 7372 Prepackaged software

GEOGRAPHIC SECTION
Cleveland - Cuyahoga County (G-5720)

(G-5693)
MINGS HEATING & AC
11902 Larchmere Blvd (44120-1135)
PHONE..................................216 721-2007
Ming Sing Gum, *President*
EMP: 4
SQ FT: 1,340
SALES (corp-wide): 634.9K **Privately Held**
SIC: 3444 1711 Plumbing, heating, air-conditioning contractors; furnace casings, sheet metal
PA: Ming's Heating & Air Conditioning Inc
2469 S Taylor Rd
Cleveland Heights OH 44118
216 321-0578

(G-5694)
MINNIE HANMONS CATERING INC
1738 Coit Ave (44112-2059)
PHONE..................................216 815-7744
Isaiah Medley, *Vice Pres*
EMP: 3 **EST:** 2017
SALES (est): 157.4K **Privately Held**
SIC: 2099 7389 Food preparations;

(G-5695)
MINOR CORPORATION
1599 Maywood Rd (44121-4101)
PHONE..................................216 291-8723
John Scott Minor, *President*
EMP: 5
SALES (est): 323.9K **Privately Held**
WEB: www.bailey.com
SIC: 3661 8742 Telephone sets, all types except cellular radio; marketing consulting services

(G-5696)
MINOTAS TROPHIES & AWARDS
40 Alpha Park (44143-2208)
PHONE..................................440 720-1288
Jacqueline Minotas, *President*
Greg Minotas, *Principal*
EMP: 4
SALES (est): 300K **Privately Held**
SIC: 5999 5094 2499 3089 Trophies & plaques; coins, medals & trophies; engraved wood products; engraving of plastic; advertising, promotional & trade show services; engraving service

(G-5697)
MITCHELL BROS ICE CREAM INC
1867 W 25th St (44113-3406)
PHONE..................................216 861-2799
Michael Mitchell, *President*
EMP: 15
SALES (est): 1.5MM **Privately Held**
SIC: 2024 Ice cream, bulk

(G-5698)
MODERN DESIGN STAMPING DIV
Also Called: R L Corbett Co, The
1618 Maple Rd (44121-1732)
PHONE..................................216 382-6318
R L Corbertt, *President*
James P Corbett, *President*
Robert Corbett, *Vice Pres*
Paul Reik, *Admin Sec*
EMP: 4 **EST:** 1958
SALES: 250K **Privately Held**
SIC: 3599 5084 Custom machinery; hydraulic systems equipment & supplies

(G-5699)
MODERN INDUSTRIES INC
6610 Metta Ave (44103-1678)
PHONE..................................216 432-2855
Steve Seredick, *Ch of Bd*
Gregory Senn, *President*
EMP: 7 **EST:** 1966
SQ FT: 22,000
SALES (est): 3.1MM **Privately Held**
SIC: 3599 Mfg Industrial Machinery

(G-5700)
MODERN PIPE SUPPORTS CORP
4734 Commerce Ave (44103-3520)
P.O. Box 603544 (44103-0541)
PHONE..................................216 361-1666
Albert J Laufer, *President*
Cheryl A Laufer, *Corp Secy*
EMP: 25
SQ FT: 26,000
SALES (est): 3.4MM **Privately Held**
SIC: 3469 Metal stampings

(G-5701)
MOLECULAR THERANOSTICS LLC
1768 E 25th St Ste 208 (44114-4418)
PHONE..................................216 595-1968
Zheng-Rong Lu, *Partner*
Hui Zhu, *Partner*
Todd Kaneshiro, *Principal*
EMP: 3
SALES (est): 217.9K **Privately Held**
SIC: 2835 In vitro diagnostics; in vivo diagnostics

(G-5702)
MOM TOOLS LLC
3659 Green Rd Ste 304 (44122-5715)
PHONE..................................216 283-4014
John Collier, *Mng Member*
Anthony Lockhart, *Mng Member*
EMP: 4
SALES: 50K **Privately Held**
SIC: 3544 Special dies & tools

(G-5703)
MONARCH STEEL COMPANY INC
4650 Johnston Pkwy (44128-3219)
PHONE..................................216 587-8000
Josh Kaufman, *CEO*
Robert L Meyer, *President*
Phil Stidham, *Plant Mgr*
Nino Frostino, *Materials Mgr*
Otis Friday, *Transportation*
▲ **EMP:** 40 **EST:** 1934
SQ FT: 118,000
SALES (est): 43.6MM
SALES (corp-wide): 24.9MM **Privately Held**
WEB: www.monarchsteel.com
SIC: 5051 5049 3353 Steel; precision tools; coils, sheet aluminum
PA: American Consolidated Industries, Inc.
4650 Johnston Pkwy
Cleveland OH 44128
216 587-8000

(G-5704)
MONROE TOOL AND MFG CO
3900 E 93rd St (44105-4094)
PHONE..................................216 883-7360
Herbert C Brosnan Jr, *President*
Herbert Brosnan III, *Vice Pres*
Anne Brosnan, *CFO*
EMP: 15 **EST:** 1940
SQ FT: 7,200
SALES (est): 2.8MM **Privately Held**
SIC: 3599 Machine shop, jobbing & repair

(G-5705)
MOONLIGHT SPECIALTIES
4555 Renaissance Pkwy # 105 (44128-5762)
PHONE..................................216 464-6444
Ronald Rivchun, *President*
EMP: 3
SALES (est): 604.7K **Privately Held**
SIC: 7389 3993 Advertising, promotional & trade show services; signs & advertising specialties

(G-5706)
MORRISON MEDIA GROUP-CMJ LLP
11800 Shaker Blvd (44120-1919)
PHONE..................................216 973-4005
Paula D Morrsion, *Managing Prtnr*
Paula D Morrison, *Partner*
EMP: 3
SALES (est): 183.9K **Privately Held**
WEB: www.morrisonmediagroup.com
SIC: 2721 Magazines: publishing & printing

(G-5707)
MPC INC
5350 Tradex Pkwy (44102-5887)
PHONE..................................440 835-1405
John Beverstock, *President*
EMP: 15

SQ FT: 14,000
SALES (est): 1.8MM
SALES (corp-wide): 337.3MM **Publicly Held**
WEB: www.mpcsilentwall.com
SIC: 3296 5044 2493 Acoustical board & tile, mineral wool; office equipment; bulletin boards, cork; bulletin boards, wood
PA: Ceco Environmental Corp.
14651 Dallas Pkwy
Dallas TX 75254
513 458-2600

(G-5708)
MPC PLASTICS INC
1859 E 63rd St (44103-3832)
PHONE..................................216 881-7220
Albert Walcutt, *President*
EMP: 60
SQ FT: 26,000
SALES (est): 6.1MM **Privately Held**
WEB: www.mpcplastics.com
SIC: 3471 Electroplating of metals or formed products

(G-5709)
MPC PLATING LLC (PA)
1859 E 63rd St (44103-3832)
PHONE..................................216 881-7220
Albert N Walcutt, *President*
Rose Ann Walcutt, *Corp Secy*
▲ **EMP:** 40
SQ FT: 26,000
SALES (est): 13.2MM **Privately Held**
WEB: www.mpcplating.com
SIC: 3471 Electroplating of metals or formed products; anodizing (plating) of metals or formed products; buffing for the trade

(G-5710)
MPC PLATING LLC
1859 E 63rd St (44103-3832)
PHONE..................................216 881-7220
Albert N Walcutt, *President*
EMP: 50
SALES (corp-wide): 13.2MM **Privately Held**
WEB: www.mpcplating.com
SIC: 3471 Chromium plating of metals or formed products
PA: M.P.C. Plating, Llc
1859 E 63rd St
Cleveland OH 44103
216 881-7220

(G-5711)
MR HEATER INC
Also Called: Heatstar
4560 W 160th St (44135-2628)
P.O. Box 44101 (44144-0101)
PHONE..................................216 916-3000
Allen L Haire, *Ch of Bd*
Jeff Mack, *President*
Kevin McDonough, *Vice Pres*
▲ **EMP:** 40
SQ FT: 100,000
SALES (est): 6MM
SALES (corp-wide): 36MM **Privately Held**
SIC: 3433 Gas infrared heating units
PA: Enerco Group, Inc.
4560 W 160th St
Cleveland OH 44135
216 916-3000

(G-5712)
MRPICKER
595 Miner Rd (44143-2131)
PHONE..................................440 354-6497
Robert Blankenship, *CFO*
EMP: 3 **EST:** 2017
SALES (est): 95.3K **Privately Held**
SIC: 3845 Electromedical equipment

(G-5713)
MURRAY FABRICS INC (PA)
837 E 79th St (44103-1807)
PHONE..................................216 881-4041
Walter Senney, *President*
Joyce Senney, *Admin Sec*
EMP: 10
SALES (est): 1.9MM **Privately Held**
WEB: www.murrayfabrics.com
SIC: 2258 Net & netting products

(G-5714)
MURRAY MACHINE & TOOL INC
17801 Sheldon Rd Side (44130-7992)
PHONE..................................216 267-1126
Frank P Ondercik Jr, *President*
EMP: 7 **EST:** 1927
SQ FT: 8,500
SALES (est): 926.5K **Privately Held**
SIC: 3599 3451 Machine shop, jobbing & repair; screw machine products

(G-5715)
MV DESIGNLABS LLC
17138 Lorain Ave Ste 201 (44111-5538)
PHONE..................................724 355-7986
Brad Hughes, *Mng Member*
Timothy Cochrane,
Jonathan Hall,
EMP: 3
SALES (est): 100K **Privately Held**
SIC: 8748 3621 Systems engineering consultant, ex. computer or professional; electric motor & generator auxillary parts

(G-5716)
MYERS AND LASCH INC
8026 Columbia Rd (44138-2022)
PHONE..................................440 235-2050
Phil Puhala, *Owner*
Mike Marhefka, *Vice Pres*
EMP: 6 **EST:** 1962
SQ FT: 2,500
SALES (est): 824.3K **Privately Held**
WEB: www.myers-lasch.com
SIC: 3993 Displays & cutouts, window & lobby

(G-5717)
MYKO INDUSTRIES
896 E 70th St (44103-1706)
PHONE..................................216 431-0900
Richard Peterson, *Manager*
EMP: 3
SALES (corp-wide): 999.4K **Privately Held**
SIC: 1752 3241 2851 5032 Floor laying & floor work; cement, hydraulic; paints & allied products; brick, stone & related material; paints, varnishes & supplies
PA: Myko Industries
14676 Rapids Rd
Burton OH 44021
216 459-9606

(G-5718)
MYSTIC CHEMICAL PRODUCTS CO
Also Called: Susan Products
3561 W 105th St (44111-3836)
PHONE..................................216 251-4416
John Gedeon Jr, *President*
John H Gedeon Sr, *Principal*
R M Gedeon, *Principal*
EMP: 9
SQ FT: 4,000
SALES (est): 1.2MM **Privately Held**
WEB: www.susanproducts.com
SIC: 2879 Pesticides, agricultural or household

(G-5719)
NACCO INDUSTRIES INC (PA)
5875 Landerbrook Dr # 220 (44124-6511)
PHONE..................................440 229-5151
Alfred M Rankin Jr, *Ch of Bd*
J C Butler Jr, *President*
Fernando Urquidi, *Business Mgr*
Elizabeth I Loveman, *Vice Pres*
John D Neumann, *Vice Pres*
EMP: 39
SALES: 104.7MM **Publicly Held**
SIC: 3634 1221 5719 3631 Electric household cooking appliances; toasters, electric; household; irons, electric: household; coffee makers, electric: household; surface mining, lignite; kitchenware; cookware, except aluminum; household cooking equipment; microwave ovens, including portable: household

(G-5720)
NANO MARK LLC
4415 Euclid Ave (44103-3759)
PHONE..................................216 409-3104
Colin Drummond, *Partner*
EMP: 3

Cleveland - Cuyahoga County (G-5721)

SALES: 25K **Privately Held**
SIC: 3845 Electromedical equipment

(G-5721)
NATIONAL BANK NOTE COMPANY (PA)
9800 Detroit Ave Ste 1 (44102-1799)
PHONE.................................216 281-7792
Daniel L Roberts, *President*
E L Roberts, *Corp Secy*
Debbie Luster, *Vice Pres*
EMP: 5 EST: 1909
SQ FT: 3,000
SALES (est): 250K **Privately Held**
SIC: 2752 Commercial printing, offset

(G-5722)
NATIONAL BIAS FABRIC CO
4516 Saint Clair Ave (44103-1288)
PHONE.................................216 361-0530
James R Engelbert, *President*
Keith Engelbert, *Vice Pres*
Carol Ann Engelbert, *Admin Sec*
EMP: 35 EST: 1902
SQ FT: 33,000
SALES (est): 3.5MM **Privately Held**
WEB: www.nationalbias.com
SIC: 2396 2631 2394 Bindings, bias: made from purchased materials; waistbands, trouser; trimming, fabric; paperboard mills; canvas & related products

(G-5723)
NATIONAL BRASS COMPANY INC
3179 W 33rd St (44109-1524)
PHONE.................................216 651-8530
Mirna Maalouf, *President*
EMP: 4
SQ FT: 5,000
SALES: 900K **Privately Held**
SIC: 3366 3432 Brass foundry; plumbers' brass goods: drain cocks, faucets, spigots, etc.

(G-5724)
NATIONAL ELECTRO-COATINGS INC
Also Called: National Office
15655 Brookpark Rd (44142-1619)
PHONE.................................216 898-0080
Gregory R Schneider, *CEO*
Richard Corl, *President*
Robert W Schneider, *Chairman*
Greg Hurst, *Plant Mgr*
Katie Saliba, *Accounts Mgr*
▲ EMP: 90
SQ FT: 175,000
SALES (est): 20MM **Privately Held**
WEB: www.natoffice.com
SIC: 2522 2521 1721 Office furniture, except wood; wood office furniture; painting & paper hanging

(G-5725)
NATIONAL FOODS PACKAGING INC
8200 Madison Ave (44102-2727)
PHONE.................................216 415-7102
John Pallas, *President*
▲ EMP: 15
SQ FT: 10,000
SALES (est): 4.6MM **Privately Held**
SIC: 2099 Seasonings & spices; pickles, sauces & salad dressings; bread & bread type roll mixes: from purchased flour; cake mixes, prepared: from purchased flour; breakfast cereals

(G-5726)
NATIONAL LIME AND STONE CO
4200 E 71st St (44105-5719)
PHONE.................................216 883-9840
EMP: 3
SALES (corp-wide): 3.2B **Privately Held**
SIC: 1422 1442 3273 1423 Crushed & broken limestone; sand mining; gravel mining; ready-mixed concrete; crushed & broken granite; asphalt (native) mining
PA: The National Lime And Stone Company
551 Lake Cascade Pkwy
Findlay OH 45840
419 422-4341

(G-5727)
NATIONAL PLATING CORPORATION
6701 Hubbard Ave Ste 1 (44127-1479)
PHONE.................................216 341-6707
Mark Palik, *President*
Sherrie Jezerinac, *Admin Sec*
Greg Pramik, *Maintence Staff*
EMP: 48 EST: 1946
SQ FT: 100,000
SALES (est): 7.2MM **Privately Held**
SIC: 3471 Electroplating of metals or formed products

(G-5728)
NATIONAL ROLLED THREAD DIE CO
7051 Krick Rd (44146-4497)
PHONE.................................440 232-8101
Paula Mau, *President*
Ronald D Mau, *VP Mfg*
Goetz Arndt, *Admin Sec*
EMP: 15
SQ FT: 18,000
SALES (est): 2.1MM **Privately Held**
WEB: www.nationaldie.com
SIC: 3545 Thread cutting dies

(G-5729)
NATIONAL SECURITY PRODUCTS
Also Called: Cleveland Safe Co
1636 Saint Clair Ave Ne (44114-2006)
PHONE.................................216 566-9962
Mark Brajdich, *President*
EMP: 3 EST: 1978
SQ FT: 4,000
SALES: 325K **Privately Held**
WEB: www.clevelandsafe.com
SIC: 5044 5999 3499 Vaults & safes; vaults & safes; locks, safe & vault: metal; safe deposit boxes or chests, metal

(G-5730)
NATURE FRIENDLY PRODUCTS LLC
24050 Commerce Park # 101 (44122-5833)
PHONE.................................216 464-5490
Bill Biggar,
▲ EMP: 5
SALES (est): 508.7K **Privately Held**
SIC: 2678 Stationery products

(G-5731)
NBC INDUSTRIES INC
4700 Train Ave Ste 3 (44102-4591)
PHONE.................................216 651-9800
EMP: 10
SQ FT: 10,000
SALES (est): 1.1MM **Privately Held**
SIC: 3089 3544 Manufactures Plastic Products Dies Tools Jigs & Fixtures

(G-5732)
NBW INC
4556 Industrial Pkwy (44135-4542)
PHONE.................................216 377-1700
Burgess J Holt, *Chairman*
Thomas Graves, *Vice Pres*
Buck L Holt, *Treasurer*
Todd Holt, *Admin Sec*
EMP: 48
SQ FT: 25,000
SALES (est): 15MM **Privately Held**
WEB: www.nbwinc.com
SIC: 1711 1796 7699 3443 Boiler setting contractor; installing building equipment; boiler & heating repair services; fabricated plate work (boiler shop)

(G-5733)
NDI MEDICAL LLC (PA)
22901 Millcreek Blvd # 110 (44122-5724)
PHONE.................................216 378-9106
Geoff Thrope, *CEO*
Leonard Cosentino, *President*
Geoffrey Thrope,
◆ EMP: 26
SALES (est): 4.2MM **Privately Held**
WEB: www.ndimedical.com
SIC: 3845 Electromedical equipment

(G-5734)
NEIGHBORHOOD NEWS PUBG CO
8613 Garfield Blvd (44125-1317)
P.O. Box 25400 (44125-0400)
PHONE.................................216 441-2141
Ellen Psenicka, *Owner*
James Psenicka, *Owner*
Michael Psenicka, *Manager*
EMP: 5
SALES (est): 263.9K **Privately Held**
SIC: 2711 Newspapers, publishing & printing

(G-5735)
NEON
15201 Euclid Ave (44112-2803)
PHONE.................................216 761-4782
EMP: 3 EST: 2010
SALES (est): 197.3K **Privately Held**
SIC: 2813 Neon

(G-5736)
NEON BY DEON LLC
7801 Day Dr Unit 29522 (44129-5685)
PHONE.................................440 292-5626
Shireen Nassar, *Owner*
EMP: 3
SALES (est): 102.5K **Privately Held**
SIC: 2813 Neon

(G-5737)
NEON CITY
11500 Madison Ave (44102-2326)
PHONE.................................440 301-2000
EMP: 3 EST: 2017
SALES (est): 123.2K **Privately Held**
SIC: 2813 Neon

(G-5738)
NEON HEALTH SERVICES INC
4800 Payne Ave (44103-2443)
PHONE.................................216 231-7700
Willie Austin, *Principal*
Lynn Johnson, *Opers Staff*
Cynthia Penny, *Manager*
Gwendolyn Solomon, *Supervisor*
Lee Jackson, *Director*
EMP: 50 EST: 2010
SALES (est): 7.9MM **Privately Held**
SIC: 2813 Neon

(G-5739)
NEON LIGHT MANUFACTURING CO
12655 Coit Rd (44108-1610)
PHONE.................................216 851-1000
Michael Holsman, *Principal*
EMP: 3 EST: 2010
SALES (est): 169.5K **Privately Held**
SIC: 3993 Signs & advertising specialties

(G-5740)
NERVIVE INC
5900 Landerbrook Dr # 350 (44124-4020)
PHONE.................................847 274-1790
Mark K Borsody, *Principal*
Dagmar Nikles, *Principal*
EMP: 10
SALES (est): 477.2K **Privately Held**
SIC: 3841 Medical instruments & equipment, blood & bone work

(G-5741)
NESCO INC (PA)
Also Called: Nesco Resource
6140 Parkland Blvd # 110 (44124-6106)
PHONE.................................440 461-6000
Robert Tomsich, *President*
Christopher Sherron, *Area Mgr*
Cristopher Chacon, *Business Mgr*
Donna Irvin-Lockhart, *Business Mgr*
Jessica Jeffries-Lewell, *Business Mgr*
◆ EMP: 20
SQ FT: 55,000
SALES (est): 699.1MM **Privately Held**
SIC: 3535 3541 3544 8711 Conveyors & conveying equipment; machine tools, metal cutting type; special dies, tools, jigs & fixtures; engineering services; real estate managers

(G-5742)
NESTLE USA INC
7645 Granger Rd (44125-4820)
PHONE.................................216 524-7738
EMP: 135
SALES (corp-wide): 90.8B **Privately Held**
SIC: 2023 Evaporated milk
HQ: Nestle Usa, Inc.
1812 N Moore St
Rosslyn VA 22209
818 549-6000

(G-5743)
NESTLE USA INC
7605 Granger Rd (44125-4820)
PHONE.................................216 524-3397
EMP: 135
SALES (corp-wide): 90.8B **Privately Held**
SIC: 2023 Evaporated milk
HQ: Nestle Usa, Inc.
1812 N Moore St
Rosslyn VA 22209
818 549-6000

(G-5744)
NESTLE USA INC
Also Called: Nestle Food Service Factory
2621 W 25th St (44113-4708)
PHONE.................................216 861-8350
Ingolf Nitsch, *Branch Mgr*
EMP: 100
SALES (corp-wide): 90.8B **Privately Held**
WEB: www.nestleusa.com
SIC: 5499 2023 Health foods; dry, condensed, evaporated dairy products
HQ: Nestle Usa, Inc.
1812 N Moore St
Rosslyn VA 22209
818 549-6000

(G-5745)
NEUROWAVE SYSTEMS INC
2490 Lee Blvd Ste 300 (44118-1271)
PHONE.................................216 361-1591
Robert N Schmidt, *CEO*
MO Modarres, *President*
Sladjana Krstic, *Purchasing*
Stephane Bibian, *VP Engrg*
Sankar Barua, *Engineer*
EMP: 7
SQ FT: 10,000
SALES (est): 1.9MM **Privately Held**
SIC: 5047 3845 Patient monitoring equipment; ultrasonic scanning devices, medical

(G-5746)
NEW CLEVELAND GROUP INC
2917 Mayfield Rd (44118-1604)
PHONE.................................216 932-9310
Michael Goronok, *President*
Yangbing Chen, *Vice Pres*
▲ EMP: 9
SALES (est): 972.8K **Privately Held**
SIC: 3931 Musical instruments

(G-5747)
NEW ERA CONTROLS INC
11002 Edgepark Dr (44125-2240)
PHONE.................................216 641-8683
Martin F Marincic, *President*
Frank Lembo, *Corp Secy*
Bob Pasquale, *Vice Pres*
EMP: 5
SQ FT: 1,000
SALES (est): 510K **Privately Held**
SIC: 3625 7373 Industrial controls: push button, selector switches, pilot; computer integrated systems design

(G-5748)
NEW LEAF MEDICAL INC
1768 E 25th St (44114-4418)
PHONE.................................216 391-7749
Richard T Nock, *President*
EMP: 3
SALES (est): 292K **Privately Held**
SIC: 3841 Surgical & medical instruments

(G-5749)
NEW URBAN DISTRIBUTORS LLC
13940 Cedar Rd Ste 224 (44118-3204)
PHONE.................................216 373-2349
Angela Underwood, *Principal*

GEOGRAPHIC SECTION
Cleveland - Cuyahoga County (G-5774)

EMP: 4
SALES (est): 201.1K **Privately Held**
SIC: **2711** Commercial printing & newspaper publishing combined

(G-5750)
NEWKOR INC
10410 Berea Rd (44102-2587)
PHONE.................................216 631-7800
Gordon Barr, *President*
Annette Kinder, *Software Engr*
EMP: 20
SQ FT: 23,000
SALES (est): 5MM **Privately Held**
WEB: www.newkor.com
SIC: **2655** Tubes, for chemical or electrical uses: paper or fiber

(G-5751)
NEXTANT AEROSPACE LLC
18601 Cleveland Pkwy Dr (44135-3231)
PHONE.................................216 898-4800
Stephen Maiden,
Jacqueline Disanto, *Administration*
EMP: 30 EST: 2012
SALES (est): 4.7MM **Privately Held**
SIC: **3728** Aircraft parts & equipment

(G-5752)
NEXTANT AEROSPACE HOLDINGS LLC
355 Richmond Rd Ste 8 (44143-4404)
PHONE.................................216 261-9000
Kenneth C Ricci, *CEO*
Sean McGeough, *President*
Jim Miller, *President*
Jay Heublein, *Exec VP*
James Immke, *Vice Pres*
EMP: 75
SQ FT: 3,000
SALES (est): 14.4MM
SALES (corp-wide): 61.7MM **Privately Held**
WEB: www.nextantaerospace.com
SIC: **3721** Aircraft
HQ: Flight Options International, Inc.
 355 Richmond Rd
 Richmond Heights OH 44143
 216 261-3500

(G-5753)
NIDEC INDUS AUTOMTN USA LLC
7800 Hub Pkwy (44125-5711)
PHONE.................................216 901-2400
EMP: 20
SALES (corp-wide): 13.9B **Privately Held**
SIC: **3566** 3823 Mfg Indstrl Machinery & Equip Process Control Instrmnts
HQ: Nidec Industrial Automation Usa, Llc
 7078 Shady Oak Rd
 Eden Prairie MN 55344
 952 995-8000

(G-5754)
NOCK AND SON COMPANY (PA)
27320 W Oviatt Rd (44140-2195)
P.O. Box 40368 (44140-0368)
PHONE.................................440 871-5525
Charles J Nock, *President*
Stephen Nock, *Vice Pres*
Michael C Nock, *Treasurer*
Patricia P Nock, *Admin Sec*
Patricia Nock, *Admin Sec*
▲ EMP: 19
SQ FT: 1,200
SALES (est): 3.6MM **Privately Held**
WEB: www.nockandson.com
SIC: **3255** 3297 Clay refractories; nonclay refractories

(G-5755)
NOGGIN LLC
3500 Lorain Ave Ste 300 (44113-3726)
PHONE.................................440 305-6188
EMP: 7
SQ FT: 1,500
SALES (est): 144K **Privately Held**
SIC: **7372** 8731 Prepackaged Software Services Commercial Physical Research

(G-5756)
NOOK INDUSTRIES INC (PA)
4950 E 49th St (44125-1016)
PHONE.................................216 271-7900
Chirstopher Nook, *CEO*

Ronald Domeck, *President*
Joseph H Nook Jr, *Chairman*
Joseph H Nook III, *COO*
Jim Rowell, *COO*
▲ EMP: 160
SQ FT: 110,000
SALES (est): 35.9MM **Privately Held**
WEB: www.nookind.com
SIC: **3451** 3699 3593 3568 Screw machine products

(G-5757)
NORMAN NOBLE INC
Also Called: N N I
5507 Avion Park Dr (44143-1921)
PHONE.................................216 761-5387
Kevin Noble, *Principal*
Dan Foust, *Opers Staff*
Thomas Lowe, *Purchasing*
Dave Saletrik, *QC Dir*
Lindsay Hart, *Sales Mgr*
EMP: 85
SALES (corp-wide): 125.3MM **Privately Held**
WEB: www.nnoble.com
SIC: **3599** Machine shop, jobbing & repair
PA: Norman Noble, Inc.
 5507 Avion Park Dr
 Highland Heights OH 44143
 216 761-5387

(G-5758)
NORMAN NOBLE INC
6120 Parkland Blvd # 306 (44124-6129)
PHONE.................................216 761-2133
Daniel Haddock, *Branch Mgr*
EMP: 190
SALES (corp-wide): 125.3MM **Privately Held**
WEB: www.nnoble.com
SIC: **3599** 7692 Machine shop, jobbing & repair; welding repair
PA: Norman Noble, Inc.
 5507 Avion Park Dr
 Highland Heights OH 44143
 216 761-5387

(G-5759)
NORTH AMERICAN STEEL COMPANY
18300 Miles Rd (44128-3441)
P.O. Box 28335 (44128-0335)
PHONE.................................216 475-7300
Theodore Cohen Jr, *Owner*
EMP: 20
SQ FT: 48,000
SALES (est): 2.7MM **Privately Held**
WEB: www.northamerican-steel.com
SIC: **5051** 3499 3312 Steel; aerosol valves, metal; stainless steel

(G-5760)
NORTH CENTRAL PROCESSING INC (PA)
761 Stones Levee (44113-2541)
P.O. Box 93941 (44101-5941)
PHONE.................................216 623-1090
Jack Joyce, *President*
EMP: 5
SALES (est): 4MM **Privately Held**
SIC: **2895** Carbon black

(G-5761)
NORTH COAST CAMSHAFT INC
10910 Briggs Rd (44111-5332)
PHONE.................................216 671-3700
David Schultheis, *President*
EMP: 5
SQ FT: 2,000
SALES (est): 941.8K **Privately Held**
SIC: **3714** Camshafts, motor vehicle

(G-5762)
NORTH COAST COMPOSITES INC
4605 Spring Rd (44131-1021)
PHONE.................................216 398-8550
Richard L Petrovich, *President*
▲ EMP: 8
SALES (est): 1.8MM
SALES (corp-wide): 30.5MM **Privately Held**
SIC: **2655** Cans, composite: foil-fiber & other: from purchased fiber

HQ: The Companies Of North Coast Llc
 4605 Spring Rd
 Cleveland OH 44131
 216 398-8550

(G-5763)
NORTH COAST CONTAINER CORP (PA)
Also Called: Ncc
8806 Crane Ave (44105-1622)
PHONE.................................216 441-6214
Jim Beardsley, *CEO*
Don Kish, *President*
Kevin Outrich, *Superintendent*
James Drozdowski, *COO*
Bill Syvuk, *COO*
EMP: 82
SQ FT: 120,000
SALES (est): 44.9MM **Privately Held**
WEB: www.ncc-corp.com
SIC: **3412** Drums, shipping: metal

(G-5764)
NORTH COAST DUMPSTER SVCS LLC
3740 Carnegie Ave (44115-2755)
PHONE.................................216 644-5647
Gary Huddleston, *Principal*
EMP: 4 EST: 2016
SALES (est): 408K **Privately Held**
SIC: **3443** Dumpsters, garbage

(G-5765)
NORTH COAST EXOTICS INC
3159 W 68th St (44102-5305)
PHONE.................................216 651-5512
Earl Gibbs Jr, *President*
EMP: 6
SQ FT: 15,000
SALES (est): 492.9K **Privately Held**
SIC: **7699** 3714 Miscellaneous automotive repair services; motor vehicle parts & accessories

(G-5766)
NORTH COAST INSTRUMENTS INC
14615 Lorain Ave (44111-3166)
PHONE.................................216 251-2353
James Irwin, *President*
Julia W Irwin, *Treasurer*
Charlotte G Irwin, *Admin Sec*
EMP: 20
SQ FT: 20,000
SALES: 8MM **Privately Held**
SIC: **3593** Fluid power cylinders & actuators
PA: Ohio Pipe & Supply Company Incorporated
 14615 Lorain Ave
 Cleveland OH
 216 251-2345

(G-5767)
NORTH COAST LITHO INC
4701 Manufacturing Ave (44135-2639)
PHONE.................................216 881-1952
Keith P Jaworski, *President*
Stephen Davis, *Sales Staff*
EMP: 20
SQ FT: 12,000
SALES (est): 4.5MM **Privately Held**
WEB: www.northcoastlitho.com
SIC: **2752** Commercial printing, lithographic

(G-5768)
NORTH COAST MEDIA LLC
Also Called: NCM
1360 E 9th St Ste 1070 (44114-1754)
PHONE.................................216 706-3700
Kevin Stoltman, *President*
Brian Kanaba, *Publisher*
Steve Galperin, *Vice Pres*
Deborah Pipik, *Human Res Dir*
Chloe Scoular, *Sales Staff*
EMP: 39
SALES (est): 7.2MM **Privately Held**
SIC: **2731** Book publishing

(G-5769)
NORTH COAST MINORITY MEDIA LLC
Also Called: North Coast Publications
1360 E 9th St (44114-1737)
PHONE.................................216 407-4327
Louis A Acosta, *Managing Dir*
EMP: 30
SALES (est): 1.2MM **Privately Held**
SIC: **2721** Magazines: publishing & printing; periodicals: publishing only

(G-5770)
NORTH SHORE STRAPPING INC
9401 Maywood Ave (44102-4852)
PHONE.................................216 661-5200
Sean Leneghan, *CFO*
Kevin Leneghan, *Manager*
EMP: 53
SALES (corp-wide): 15.2MM **Privately Held**
SIC: **3081** Unsupported plastics film & sheet
PA: North Shore Strapping Inc
 1400 Valley Belt Rd
 Brooklyn Heights OH 44131
 216 661-5200

(G-5771)
NORTHCOAST PROCESS CONTROLS
6283 Sunnywood Dr (44139-3054)
P.O. Box 39071 (44139-0071)
PHONE.................................440 498-0542
Nevio E Bais, *President*
Micheal Bais, *Vice Pres*
EMP: 3
SQ FT: 2,000
SALES (est): 450.9K **Privately Held**
SIC: **3625** 5074 3592 3593 Industrial controls: push button, selector switches, pilot; plumbing & heating valves; valves; fluid power cylinders & actuators

(G-5772)
NORTHCOAST TAPE & LABEL INC
24300 Solon Rd Ste 7 (44146-4794)
PHONE.................................440 439-3200
Paul Bukas, *President*
▲ EMP: 5
SQ FT: 5,000
SALES (est): 1MM **Privately Held**
WEB: www.nclabel.com
SIC: **2672** Labels (unprinted), gummed: made from purchased materials; tape, pressure sensitive: made from purchased materials

(G-5773)
NORTHEAST BLUEPRINT & SUP CO
1230 E 286th St (44132-2138)
PHONE.................................216 261-7500
James Yurick, *President*
Mike Rogazione, *Info Tech Mgr*
EMP: 7
SQ FT: 7,000
SALES (est): 1MM **Privately Held**
WEB: www.northeastblueprint.com
SIC: **7334** 2752 Blueprinting service; commercial printing, lithographic; color lithography

(G-5774)
NORTHEAST OH NEIGHBORHOOD HEAL
Also Called: Southeast Health Center
13301 Miles Ave (44105-5521)
PHONE.................................216 751-3100
Benjamin Clark, *Exec Dir*
Prabhleen Bhatia, *Fmly & Gen Dent*
EMP: 58
SALES (corp-wide): 25.8MM **Privately Held**
SIC: **2813** Neon
PA: Northeast Ohio Neighborhood Health Services, Inc.
 4800 Payne Ave
 Cleveland OH 44103
 216 231-7700

Cleveland - Cuyahoga County (G-5775) GEOGRAPHIC SECTION

(G-5775)
NORTHEAST OHIO CONTRACTORS LLC
3555 W 69th St (44102-5419)
PHONE.................................216 269-7881
Brian Petruccelli, Mng Member
EMP: 3
SQ FT: 1,000
SALES: 200K Privately Held
SIC: 3441 1711 Building components, structural steel; plumbing contractors

(G-5776)
NORTHEAST SCENE INC
Also Called: Scene Magazine
737 Bolivar Rd (44115-1246)
PHONE.................................216 241-7550
Richard Kabat, President
Desiree Bourgeois, Publisher
Keith Rathbun, Corp Secy
EMP: 48
SQ FT: 5,300
SALES (est): 4.3MM Privately Held
SIC: 2721 7336 2711 Periodicals: publishing only; graphic arts & related design; newspapers

(G-5777)
NORTHERN BOILER COMPANY
Also Called: Northern Fabricator
3453 W 86th St (44102-4999)
PHONE.................................216 961-3033
Edward Kosman, President
Robert Kosman, Vice Pres
EMP: 10 EST: 1906
SQ FT: 50,000
SALES: 890K Privately Held
WEB: www.northernboiler.com
SIC: 3441 Fabricated structural metal

(G-5778)
NORTHERN CHEM BLNDING CORP INC
360 Literary Rd (44113-4560)
PHONE.................................216 781-7799
John Zemaitis, President
▲ EMP: 9
SQ FT: 35,000
SALES (est): 1.9MM Privately Held
SIC: 2899 Metal treating compounds; water treating compounds

(G-5779)
NORTHERN INSTRUMENTS CORP LLC
23205 Mercantile Rd (44122-5911)
PHONE.................................216 450-5073
James Henderson, President
Tiffany Swann, Vice Pres
EMP: 3
SALES: 400K
SALES (corp-wide): 51.4MM Publicly Held
SIC: 3823 Industrial process measurement equipment
PA: Northern Technologies International Corporation
 4201 Woodland Rd
 Circle Pines MN 55014
 763 225-6600

(G-5780)
NORTHERN MACHINE TOOL CO
3453 W 86th St (44102-4917)
PHONE.................................216 961-0444
Edward Kosman, President
Robert Kosman, Vice Pres
EMP: 5 EST: 1968
SQ FT: 50,000
SALES (est): 710K Privately Held
SIC: 5084 3599 Machine tools & metalworking machinery; machine & other job shop work

(G-5781)
NORTHERN OHIO PRINTING INC
4721 Hinckley Indus Pkwy (44109-6004)
PHONE.................................216 398-0000
Gary Chmielewski, President
John Loprich, Sales Staff
Lisa Albergo, Office Mgr
EMP: 30
SQ FT: 5,000
SALES (est): 10.6MM Privately Held
WEB: www.nohioprint.com
SIC: 2752 Commercial printing, offset

(G-5782)
NORTHERN STAMPING CO
5900 Harvard Ave (44105-4850)
PHONE.................................216 883-8888
Mike Ford, Manager
EMP: 10
SALES (corp-wide): 453.1MM Privately Held
SIC: 3465 3469 Automotive stampings; metal stampings
HQ: Northern Stamping Co.
 6600 Chapek Pkwy
 Cleveland OH 44125
 216 883-8888

(G-5783)
NORTHERN STAMPING CO (HQ)
Also Called: Northern Stamping, Inc.
6600 Chapek Pkwy (44125-1049)
PHONE.................................216 883-8888
Matthew S Friedman, Ch of Bd
Ron Campbell, COO
Scott Sheffield, Vice Pres
Valerie Pitts, Project Mgr
Ian Hessel, CFO
▲ EMP: 120
SQ FT: 118,000
SALES (est): 390.4MM
SALES (corp-wide): 453.1MM Privately Held
WEB: www.hilite.com
SIC: 3465 3469 Automotive stampings; metal stampings
PA: Bear Diversified, Inc.
 4580 E 71st St
 Cleveland OH 44125
 216 883-5494

(G-5784)
NORTHERN STAMPING CO
Also Called: Northern Stamping Plant 2
7750 Hub Pkwy (44125-5709)
PHONE.................................216 642-8081
Scott Sheffield, Production
EMP: 200
SALES (corp-wide): 453.1MM Privately Held
WEB: www.hilite.com
SIC: 3465 3714 Automotive stampings; motor vehicle parts & accessories
HQ: Northern Stamping Co.
 6600 Chapek Pkwy
 Cleveland OH 44125
 216 883-8888

(G-5785)
NORTHSHORE MINING COMPANY (HQ)
Also Called: Cliffs
200 Public Sq (44114-2316)
PHONE.................................216 694-5700
Donald R Prahl, Vice Pres
Ngoc Nguyen, Engineer
David Toler, Human Res Mgr
Jill Baumann, Manager
Don Morrison, Technology
▼ EMP: 1
SALES (est): 377.6MM
SALES (corp-wide): 2.3B Publicly Held
WEB: www.cci-northshore.com
SIC: 1011 4931 Iron ore mining; iron ore preparation; electric & other services combined
PA: Cleveland-Cliffs Inc.
 200 Public Sq Ste 3300
 Cleveland OH 44114
 216 694-5700

(G-5786)
NORTHSHORE MOLD INC
2861 E Royalton Rd (44147-2827)
PHONE.................................440 838-8212
Joseph E Pajestka Jr, President
Vivian Pajestka, Vice Pres
EMP: 7
SQ FT: 6,000
SALES (est): 676.1K Privately Held
SIC: 3599 3089 Machine & other job shop work; injection molding of plastics

(G-5787)
NORTHWIND INDUSTRIES INC
15500 Commerce Park Dr (44142-2013)
PHONE.................................216 433-0666
Garry Patla, President
Christine Klukan, Vice Pres
EMP: 27
SQ FT: 2,000
SALES (est): 3.4MM Privately Held
SIC: 3599 7692 3469 3444 Machine shop, jobbing & repair; grinding castings for the trade; welding repair; metal stampings; sheet metalwork; fabricated structural metal; metal heat treating

(G-5788)
NOVA STRUCTURAL STEEL INC
900 E 69th St (44103-1736)
PHONE.................................216 938-7476
Mariella Kaufman, CEO
Michael Ciofani, President
Robert Rottinger, General Mgr
EMP: 15
SALES: 3.8MM Privately Held
SIC: 3312 1531 3441 Structural shapes & pilings, steel; ; building components, structural steel

(G-5789)
NOVAGARD SOLUTIONS INC (PA)
Also Called: Soam Seal
5109 Hamilton Ave (44114-3907)
PHONE.................................216 881-3890
Michael S Sylvester, CEO
George Buzzy, President
Larry Webb, VP Opers
Ron Moeller, CFO
Michael Griffin, Controller
EMP: 13
SALES: 20MM Privately Held
SIC: 3053 2911 2891 Gaskets, packing & sealing devices; oils, lubricating; sealing compounds, synthetic rubber or plastic; caulking compounds

(G-5790)
NOVAK J F MANUFACTURING CO LLC
Also Called: Cleveland Church Supply
2701 Meyer Ave (44109-1532)
PHONE.................................216 741-5112
Sharon Campbell, Manager
Eleanor Rusnak,
James Rusnak,
EMP: 6 EST: 1932
SQ FT: 7,000
SALES (est): 380K Privately Held
WEB: www.jfnovakcompany.com
SIC: 2395 5049 Emblems, embroidered; religious supplies

(G-5791)
NOVAK SUPPLY LLC
2701 Meyer Ave (44109-1532)
PHONE.................................216 741-5112
John Hunt, Mng Member
EMP: 4
SALES: 600K Privately Held
SIC: 2389 Uniforms & vestments

(G-5792)
NPA COATINGS INC
11100 Berea Rd Ste 1 (44102-2540)
PHONE.................................216 651-5900
Hidefumi Morita, CEO
Takeshi Makano, President
Joan Daniels, Corp Secy
Gary Rizzardi, Exec VP
Christopher Szoly, Senior Buyer
▲ EMP: 180
SQ FT: 235,000
SALES: 82MM
SALES (corp-wide): 5.5B Privately Held
SIC: 2851 Paints & allied products
HQ: Nippon Paint (Usa) Inc.
 400 Frank W Burr Blvd # 10
 Teaneck NJ 07666

(G-5793)
NU-DI PRODUCTS CO INC
Also Called: Nu-Di Corporation
12730 Triskett Rd (44111-2529)
PHONE.................................216 251-9070
Kenneth Bihn, President
Tim Bihn, Vice Pres
Michael Cupach, Buyer
Charles Novicky, Maintence Staff
EMP: 85
SQ FT: 38,000
SALES (est): 15.7MM Privately Held
WEB: www.nu-di.com
SIC: 3825 5013 Engine electrical test equipment; testing equipment, electrical: automotive

(G-5794)
OASIS CONSUMER HEALTHCARE LLC
Also Called: Ochc
737 Bolivar Rd Ste 4500 (44115-1233)
PHONE.................................216 394-0544
Brian Sokol,
Kathy Dise,
Afif Ghannoum,
EMP: 6
SQ FT: 1,500
SALES: 1.5MM Privately Held
WEB: www.oasisdrymouth.com
SIC: 2844 Mouthwashes

(G-5795)
OATEY SUPPLY CHAIN SVCS INC (HQ)
Also Called: Oatey Company
20600 Emerald Pkwy (44135-6022)
PHONE.................................216 267-7100
John H McMillan, CEO
Gary Oatey, Ch of Bd
Eric Hull, Director
▲ EMP: 200
SQ FT: 165,000
SALES (est): 99.6MM
SALES (corp-wide): 470MM Privately Held
WEB: www.oateyscs.com
SIC: 3444 5074 Metal roofing & roof drainage equipment; plumbing & hydronic heating supplies
PA: Oatey Co.
 20600 Emerald Pkwy
 Cleveland OH 44135
 800 203-1155

(G-5796)
OBRIEN CUT STONE COMPANY (PA)
19100 Miles Rd (44128-4104)
PHONE.................................216 663-7800
John O'Brien, President
Jerry Muchewicz, General Mgr
Margaret Kingsmill, Corp Secy
Robert O'Brien, Vice Pres
Russ Austin, Accounts Mgr
▲ EMP: 30
SQ FT: 20,000
SALES (est): 3.9MM Privately Held
WEB: www.obriencutstone.net
SIC: 3281 Cut stone & stone products

(G-5797)
OBRIEN CUT STONE COMPANY
19100 Miles Rd (44128-4104)
PHONE.................................216 663-7800
John P O'Brien, President
EMP: 30
SALES (corp-wide): 3.9MM Privately Held
WEB: www.obriencutstone.net
SIC: 3281 Cut stone & stone products
PA: The O'brien Cut Stone Company
 19100 Miles Rd
 Cleveland OH 44128
 216 663-7800

(G-5798)
OHIO ALUMINUM INDUSTRIES INC
4840 Warner Rd (44125-1193)
PHONE.................................216 641-8865
John Blemaster, CEO
Kurt Blemaster, President
Willem Der Velde, COO
James E Herkner, Treasurer
Stacy George, Manager
▲ EMP: 152
SQ FT: 78,000
SALES: 17.7MM Privately Held
WEB: www.ohioaluminum.com
SIC: 3363 Aluminum die-castings

▲ = Import ▼=Export
◆ =Import/Export

GEOGRAPHIC SECTION

Cleveland - Cuyahoga County (G-5826)

(G-5799)
OHIO AWNING & MANUFACTURING CO (PA)
5777 Grant Ave (44105-5605)
PHONE..................216 861-2400
Andrew Morse, *President*
Anne L Morse, *Vice Pres*
▲ **EMP:** 29
SQ FT: 80,000
SALES (est): 3.9MM **Privately Held**
WEB: www.ohioawning.com
SIC: 2394 3993 Awnings, fabric: made from purchased materials; electric signs

(G-5800)
OHIO BEVERAGE SYSTEMS INC
9200 Midwest Ave (44125-2416)
PHONE..................216 475-3900
James Rickon, *President*
EMP: 15
SQ FT: 28,000
SALES (est): 2.4MM **Privately Held**
SIC: 2086 Fruit drinks (less than 100% juice): packaged in cans, etc.

(G-5801)
OHIO BLOW PIPE COMPANY (PA)
446 E 131st St (44108-1684)
PHONE..................216 681-7379
Edward Fakeris, *President*
William Roberts, *Vice Pres*
Lisa Kern, *CFO*
EMP: 33
SQ FT: 45,000
SALES (est): 24.2MM **Privately Held**
WEB: www.obpairsystems.com
SIC: 8711 3564 3444 Engineering services; blowers & fans; sheet metalwork

(G-5802)
OHIO BRUSH COMPANY
2680 Lisbon Rd (44104-3188)
PHONE..................216 791-3265
EMP: 19 **EST:** 1879
SQ FT: 14,000
SALES (est): 2.2MM **Privately Held**
SIC: 3991 Mfg Brooms/Brushes

(G-5803)
OHIO CAM & TOOL CO
23572 Saint Clair Ave (44117-2513)
PHONE..................216 531-7900
Steve J Raab, *President*
EMP: 5 **EST:** 1957
SQ FT: 4,000
SALES: 325K **Privately Held**
SIC: 3541 Screw machines, automatic

(G-5804)
OHIO CITY POWER
4427 Franklin Blvd (44113-2845)
PHONE..................216 651-6250
Lisa Braun, *Exec Dir*
EMP: 3
SALES (est): 130.3K **Privately Held**
SIC: 2711 Newspapers

(G-5805)
OHIO ENVELOPE MANUFACTURING CO
5161 W 164th St (44142-1592)
PHONE..................216 267-2920
David Gould III, *President*
David Gould III, *President*
Carol J Gould, *Corp Secy*
EMP: 35 **EST:** 1936
SQ FT: 35,000
SALES (est): 4.8MM **Privately Held**
WEB: www.ohioenvelope.com
SIC: 2759 2754 2677 Envelopes: printing; envelopes: gravure printing; envelopes

(G-5806)
OHIO LEGAL BLANK CO
9800 Detroit Ave Ste 1 (44102-6510)
PHONE..................216 281-7792
Daniel L Roberts, *President*
EMP: 4
SQ FT: 3,000
SALES (est): 388.1K **Privately Held**
WEB: www.ohiolegalblank.com
SIC: 2759 Commercial printing

(G-5807)
OHIO MILLS CORPORATION (PA)
Also Called: Ohio Mill Supply
1719 E 39th St (44114-4530)
PHONE..................216 431-3979
Ronald Katz, *President*
EMP: 8 **EST:** 1983
SQ FT: 15,000
SALES (est): 1.5MM **Privately Held**
SIC: 5651 2842 Unisex clothing stores; dusting cloths, chemically treated

(G-5808)
OKM LLC
Also Called: Ohio Knitting Mills
4701 Perkins Ave Ste 1 (44103-3525)
PHONE..................216 272-6375
Steven Tatar, *President*
EMP: 7
SQ FT: 4,000
SALES: 100K **Privately Held**
SIC: 2253 Knit outerwear mills

(G-5809)
OLD COUNTRY SAUSAGE KITCHEN
15711 Libby Rd (44137-1212)
PHONE..................216 662-5988
George S Neiden, *President*
Maria Neiden, *Corp Secy*
EMP: 3
SQ FT: 4,555
SALES (est): 254.1K **Privately Held**
SIC: 2013 5421 Sausages from purchased meat; meat markets, including freezer provisioners

(G-5810)
OLD WORLD FOODS INC
3545 E 76th St (44105-1509)
P.O. Box 27382 (44127-0382)
PHONE..................216 341-5665
Andy Emrisko, *President*
EMP: 5 **EST:** 1994
SALES (est): 495.2K **Privately Held**
WEB: www.oldworldfoods.com
SIC: 2037 5812 Potato products, quick frozen & cold pack; eating places

(G-5811)
OLFACTORIUM CORP INC
Also Called: Kristine Marie's Olfactorium
12395 Mccracken Rd (44125-2967)
PHONE..................216 663-8831
Henry Drewes, *President*
Gregory Page, *Vice Pres*
Mary Ellen Drewes, *Treasurer*
Christine Page, *Admin Sec*
EMP: 6 **EST:** 1980
SALES: 337.1K **Privately Held**
WEB: www.aromadeterra.com
SIC: 5999 5122 2844 Toiletries, cosmetics & perfumes; cosmetics, perfumes & hair products; toilet preparations

(G-5812)
OLYMPIC FOREST PRODUCTS CO
2200 Carnegie Ave (44115-2621)
PHONE..................216 421-2775
Daniel Andrews, *President*
Howard A Steindler, *Principal*
Kaitlin Kuharik, *Human Resources*
Bill Andrews, *Sales Staff*
Gary Sindelar, *Sales Staff*
EMP: 18
SQ FT: 6,300
SALES (est): 4.1MM **Privately Held**
WEB: www.olyforest.com
SIC: 2448 Pallets, wood

(G-5813)
OMNI MEDIA
1375 E 9th St Fl 10 (44114-1788)
PHONE..................216 687-0077
Simon Badinter, *CEO*
Solomon Evans, *Graphic Designe*
EMP: 3
SALES (est): 257K **Privately Held**
WEB: www.mediasregies.com
SIC: 3993 Signs & advertising specialties

(G-5814)
OMNI TECHNICAL PRODUCTS INC
Also Called: Wire Lab Company
15300 Industrial Pkwy (44135-3310)
PHONE..................216 433-1970
Robert J Fulop, *President*
Robert L Fulop, *Vice Pres*
EMP: 11
SQ FT: 20,000
SALES (est): 2MM **Privately Held**
WEB: www.wirelab.com
SIC: 3542 Mechanical (pneumatic or hydraulic) metal forming machines

(G-5815)
ONX USA LLC (DH)
5910 Landerbrook Dr # 250 (44124-6508)
PHONE..................440 569-2300
Mike Cox, *CEO*
Bart Foster, *Ch of Bd*
Paul Khawaja, *President*
Wayne Kiphart, *President*
Andrew Tweedie, *Mfg Mgr*
EMP: 75
SQ FT: 20,000
SALES (est): 78.4MM
SALES (corp-wide): 1.3B **Publicly Held**
SIC: 7379 7372 Computer related consulting services; business oriented computer software
HQ: Onx Holdings Llc
221 E 4th St
Cincinnati OH 45202
866 587-2287

(G-5816)
OPTOQUEST CORPORATION
10000 Cedar Ave (44106-2119)
PHONE..................216 445-3637
William J Dupps Jr, *Principal*
EMP: 9 **EST:** 2015
SALES (est): 132.5K **Privately Held**
SIC: 8062 3841 General medical & surgical hospitals; surgical & medical instruments

(G-5817)
ORACLE CORPORATION
30500 Bruce Indus Pkwy (44139-3969)
PHONE..................440 264-1620
EMP: 5
SALES (est): 179.6K **Privately Held**
SIC: 7372 Prepackaged software

(G-5818)
ORBYTEL PRINT AND PACKG INC
4901 Johnston Pkwy (44128-3201)
PHONE..................216 267-8734
Albert Uvlin, *President*
James R Bingham, *Principal*
Clarence D Finke, *Principal*
Cynthia Uvlin, *Corp Secy*
Mark Uvlin, *COO*
EMP: 8
SQ FT: 12,300
SALES (est): 2.8MM **Privately Held**
WEB: www.diagraphohio.com
SIC: 2679 5085 Tags & labels, paper; industrial supplies

(G-5819)
ORIGINAL MATTRESS FACTORY INC (PA)
4930 State Rd (44134-1214)
PHONE..................216 661-8388
Ron Trzcinski, *President*
Lawrence S Carlson, *Vice Pres*
Douglas B Stroup, *Vice Pres*
Perry Doermann, *Treasurer*
EMP: 4
SQ FT: 33,000
SALES (est): 26.6MM **Privately Held**
WEB: www.originalmattress.com
SIC: 2515 5712 Mattresses & foundations; furniture springs; bedding & bedsprings; mattresses

(G-5820)
ORLANDO BAKING COMPANY (PA)
7777 Grand Ave (44104-3061)
PHONE..................216 361-1872
Chester Orlando, *President*

Glenn W Eckert, *Principal*
Edna Rosenblum, *Principal*
Hattie Wagner, *Principal*
Joseph Orlando, *Vice Pres*
▲ **EMP:** 215
SQ FT: 80,000
SALES (est): 99.4MM **Privately Held**
WEB: www.orlandobaking.com
SIC: 2051 Bread, all types (white, wheat, rye, etc): fresh or frozen; rolls, bread type: fresh or frozen

(G-5821)
OSBORNE INC
Also Called: Cuyahoga Concrete Products
2100 Central Furnace Ct (44115-3621)
P.O. Box 91836 (44101-3836)
PHONE..................216 771-0010
Bill Tagalmonte, *Manager*
EMP: 29
SALES (corp-wide): 15MM **Privately Held**
SIC: 5211 3273 Concrete & cinder block; ready-mixed concrete
PA: Osborne, Inc.
7954 Reynolds Rd
Mentor OH 44060
440 942-7000

(G-5822)
OSBORNE INC
26481 Cannon Rd (44146-1843)
PHONE..................440 232-1440
Patrick Donnelly, *General Mgr*
EMP: 10
SQ FT: 6,000
SALES (corp-wide): 15MM **Privately Held**
SIC: 3273 Ready-mixed concrete
PA: Osborne, Inc.
7954 Reynolds Rd
Mentor OH 44060
440 942-7000

(G-5823)
OSISOFT LLC
Also Called: OSI Software
5885 Landerbrook Dr # 310 (44124-4045)
PHONE..................440 442-2000
Renee Villnave, *Opers Staff*
Phil Ryder, *Manager*
EMP: 6
SALES (corp-wide): 315.7MM **Privately Held**
SIC: 7372 Application computer software
PA: Osisoft, Llc
1600 Alvarado St
San Leandro CA 94577
510 297-5800

(G-5824)
OSTEOSYMBIONICS LLC
1768 E 25th St Ste 316 (44114-4418)
P.O. Box 128, Aurora (44202-0128)
PHONE..................216 881-8500
Cynthia Brogan, *Mng Member*
EMP: 10
SALES: 2.6MM **Privately Held**
WEB: www.osteosymbionics.com
SIC: 3842 Implants, surgical

(G-5825)
OTIS ELEVATOR COMPANY
9800 Rockside Rd Ste 1200 (44125-6270)
PHONE..................216 573-2333
Gordy Sell, *Manager*
EMP: 73
SALES (corp-wide): 66.5B **Publicly Held**
WEB: www.otis.com
SIC: 7699 1796 3534 Elevators: inspection, service & repair; elevator installation & conversion; elevators & equipment
HQ: Otis Elevator Company
1 Carrier Pl
Farmington CT 06032
860 674-3000

(G-5826)
OTTO KONIGSLOW MFG CO
13300 Coit Rd (44110-2285)
PHONE..................216 851-7900
Cofer McIntosh, *CEO*
J P Lawson, *President*
JP Lawson, *General Mgr*
EMP: 15
SQ FT: 72,500

Cleveland - Cuyahoga County (G-5827)

SALES: 2MM **Privately Held**
SIC: **3724** 3548 Aircraft engines & engine parts; welding & cutting apparatus & accessories

(G-5827)
OUR FAMILY MALL
Also Called: Kraftee Kreations
13400 6th Ave (44112-3142)
P.O. Box 20915 (44120-7915)
PHONE..................................216 761-8669
Tiffany Mc Daniel, *Owner*
EMP: 5
SALES: 26K **Privately Held**
WEB: www.krafteekreations.com
SIC: **5945** 2395 Arts & crafts supplies; embroidery & art needlework

(G-5828)
P & P MACHINE TOOL INC
26189 Broadway Ave (44146-6512)
PHONE..................................440 232-7404
Wayne Pelcarsky, *President*
Thomas Pelcarsky, *Vice Pres*
EMP: 6 EST: 1980
SQ FT: 4,000
SALES (est): 936.7K **Privately Held**
SIC: **3599** Machine shop, jobbing & repair

(G-5829)
P F S INCORPORATED
9861 York Alpha Dr (44133-3507)
PHONE..................................440 582-1620
Ronald Miller, *President*
Robert Miller, *Vice Pres*
EMP: 4 EST: 1976
SQ FT: 4,800
SALES: 350K **Privately Held**
SIC: **3599** 3545 Machine shop, jobbing & repair; cutting tools for machine tools

(G-5830)
P G M DIVERSIFIED INDUSTRIES
6514 Alexandria Dr (44130-2850)
PHONE..................................440 885-3500
Mark Podany, *President*
George Rowley, *Vice Pres*
Frances L Merat, *Treasurer*
EMP: 5
SALES: 260K **Privately Held**
WEB: www.pgmdi.com
SIC: **8711** 3825 Consulting engineer; measuring instruments & meters, electric

(G-5831)
P L M CORPORATION
7424 Bessemer Ave (44127-1820)
PHONE..................................216 341-8008
Michael Dunn, *President*
EMP: 9
SQ FT: 25,000
SALES (est): 1.3MM **Privately Held**
SIC: **3272** Paving materials, prefabricated concrete

(G-5832)
P S C INC
21761 Tungsten Rd (44117-1116)
PHONE..................................216 531-3375
Matthew C Litzler, *President*
Sue Glass, *General Mgr*
William J Urban, *COO*
Michael London, *Engineer*
▲ EMP: 8
SQ FT: 12,000
SALES (est): 1.7MM
SALES (corp-wide): 36.1MM **Privately Held**
WEB: www.pscrfheat.com
SIC: **3567** 1731 Dielectric heating equipment; general electrical contractor
PA: C.A. Litzler Holding Company
    4800 W 160th St
    Cleveland OH 44135
    216 267-8020

(G-5833)
P S SUPERIOR INC
Also Called: P S Awards
9257 Midwest Ave (44125-2415)
PHONE..................................216 587-1000
Elizabeth Sudyk, *President*
Joanne Sudyk, *Treasurer*
EMP: 11
SQ FT: 10,000
SALES (est): 825K **Privately Held**
SIC: **3499** 7389 5199 Trophies, metal, except silver; lettering service; advertising specialties

(G-5834)
PACE CONVERTING EQP CO INC
8500 Lake Ave (44102-1912)
PHONE..................................216 631-4555
Michael Chrystyna, *CEO*
Dave Westerfield, *General Mgr*
EMP: 14
SQ FT: 15,000
SALES: 1.2MM **Privately Held**
WEB: www.pace-equipment.com
SIC: **3621** Phase or rotary converters (electrical equipment)

(G-5835)
PACK LINE CORP
22900 Miles Rd (44128-5445)
PHONE..................................212 564-0664
Michael Beilinson, *Principal*
▲ EMP: 15
SALES (est): 3.4MM
SALES (corp-wide): 8MM **Privately Held**
SIC: **3565** Packaging machinery
PA: Packline Ltd
    59 Prof. Shor
    Holon 58811
    355 815-34

(G-5836)
PACKAGING TECH LLC
17325 Euclid Ave Ste 3045 (44112-1276)
PHONE..................................216 374-7308
Steven Williams,
EMP: 20 EST: 2017
SALES (est): 1.2MM **Privately Held**
SIC: **2671** 2653 Packaging paper & plastics film, coated & laminated; corrugated & solid fiber boxes

(G-5837)
PARADISE MOLD & DIE LLC
10815 Briggs Rd (44111-5331)
PHONE..................................216 362-1945
Tom Edgehouse,
EMP: 3
SALES (est): 590.4K **Privately Held**
SIC: **3544** Industrial molds

(G-5838)
PARALLEL SOLUTIONS
5380 Naiman Pkwy Ste B (44139-1032)
PHONE..................................440 498-9920
Keith Sherwin, *Principal*
EMP: 3
SALES (est): 233.1K **Privately Held**
SIC: **3579** Time clocks & time recording devices

(G-5839)
PARAMELT ARGUESO KINDT INC
12651 Elmwood Ave (44111-5911)
PHONE..................................216 252-4122
David P Kindt, *President*
Kathy Louney, *Manager*
Scott Pagel, *Maintence Staff*
▲ EMP: 7 EST: 2010
SALES (est): 184.9K **Privately Held**
SIC: **2891** Adhesives

(G-5840)
PARAMOUNT STAMPING & WLDG CO
Also Called: Anchor Template Die Div
1200 W 58th St (44102-2118)
PHONE..................................216 631-1755
Peter Kole, *President*
Lisa Smith, *Purchasing*
Kathy Lindsay, *Cust Mgr*
EMP: 100
SQ FT: 300,000
SALES (est): 15.4MM **Privately Held**
WEB: www.metalstamping99.com
SIC: **3469** 3544 Stamping metal for the trade; special dies & tools

(G-5841)
PARK CORPORATION (PA)
6200 Riverside Dr (44135-3132)
P.O. Box 8678, South Charleston WV (25303-0678)
PHONE..................................216 267-4870
Raymond P Park, *Ch of Bd*
Daniel K Park, *President*
Ricky L Bertrem, *Vice Pres*
Shelva J Davis, *Vice Pres*
Kelly C Park, *Vice Pres*
◆ EMP: 300
SQ FT: 2,500,000
SALES (est): 568.1MM **Privately Held**
WEB: www.parkcorp.com
SIC: **3547** 1711 3443 5084 Rolling mill machinery; boiler maintenance contractor; mechanical contractor; boilers: industrial, power, or marine; industrial machinery & equipment; commercial & industrial building operation; exposition operation

(G-5842)
PARK-OHIO HOLDINGS CORP (PA)
6065 Parkland Blvd Ste 1 (44124-6145)
PHONE..................................440 947-2000
Matthew V Crawford, *CEO*
Edward F Crawford, *President*
Darryl Niven, *VP Mfg*
James Nicoulin, *Materials Mgr*
Douglas Marting, *Purch Mgr*
◆ EMP: 18
SQ FT: 20,150
SALES: 1.6B **Publicly Held**
SIC: **3069** 3567 3363 3524 Molded rubber products; roll coverings, rubber; rubber hardware; rubber automotive products; induction heating equipment; aluminum die-castings; lawn & garden tractors & equipment; internal combustion engine forgings, ferrous

(G-5843)
PARK-OHIO INDUSTRIES INC (HQ)
6065 Parkland Blvd Ste 1 (44124-6145)
PHONE..................................440 947-2000
Matthew V Crawford, *President*
Brian Murkey, *Vice Pres*
Darryl Niven, *VP Mfg*
Patrick W Fogarty, *CFO*
Steve White, *Controller*
EMP: 227
SQ FT: 60,450
SALES: 1.6B **Publicly Held**
WEB: www.pkoh.com.cn
SIC: **3462** 3069 3567 3363 Iron & steel forgings; internal combustion engine forgings, ferrous; aircraft forgings, ferrous; ordnance forgings, ferrous; molded rubber products; roll coverings, rubber; rubber hardware; rubber automotive products; induction heating equipment; aluminum die-castings; lawn & garden tractors & equipment
PA: Park-Ohio Holdings Corp.
    6065 Parkland Blvd Ste 1
    Cleveland OH 44124
    440 947-2000

(G-5844)
PARK-OHIO PRODUCTS INC
7000 Denison Ave (44102-5247)
PHONE..................................216 961-7200
Craig Cowan, *President*
Richard Paul Elliott, *Vice Pres*
Anthony Hall, *Vice Pres*
Robert Poeppleman, *Vice Pres*
Robert Vilsack, *Vice Pres*
▲ EMP: 100
SQ FT: 40,000
SALES (est): 28MM
SALES (corp-wide): 1.6B **Publicly Held**
WEB: www.pkoh.com.cn
SIC: **3069** Molded rubber products
HQ: Park-Ohio Industries, Inc.
    6065 Parkland Blvd Ste 1
    Cleveland OH 44124
    440 947-2000

(G-5845)
PARKER HANNIFIN PARTNER B LLC
6035 Parkland Blvd (44124-4186)
PHONE..................................216 896-3000
David Noseworthy, *Technology*
EMP: 7
SALES (est): 821.7K
SALES (corp-wide): 14.3B **Publicly Held**
SIC: **3594** Fluid power pumps & motors
PA: Parker-Hannifin Corporation
    6035 Parkland Blvd
    Cleveland OH 44124
    216 896-3000

(G-5846)
PARKER ROYALTY PARTNERSHIP
6035 Parkland Blvd (44124-4186)
PHONE..................................216 896-3000
John Hollandsworth, *QC Mgr*
Ryne Kawabata, *Engineer*
Patrick Toops, *Engineer*
Jeff Walukas, *Sales Mgr*
Juan Carrasco, *Sales Associate*
EMP: 55
SALES (est): 6.8MM
SALES (corp-wide): 12B **Publicly Held**
SIC: **3594** Fluid power pumps & motors
PA: Parker-Hannifin Corporation
    6035 Parkland Blvd
    Cleveland OH 44124
    216 896-3000

(G-5847)
PARKER RST-PROOF CLEVELAND INC
1688 Arabella Rd (44112-1418)
PHONE..................................216 481-6680
Frederick A Fruscella, *Ch of Bd*
Sharon Bodine, *Vice Pres*
EMP: 37 EST: 1935
SQ FT: 75,000
SALES (est): 5.5MM **Privately Held**
SIC: **3479** 3471 Rust proofing (hot dipping) of metals & formed products; plating & polishing

(G-5848)
PARKER-HANNIFIN CORPORATION (PA)
6035 Parkland Blvd (44124-4186)
PHONE..................................216 896-3000
Thomas L Williams, *Ch of Bd*
Lee C Banks, *President*
Mark J Hart, *Exec VP*
John Connors, *Vice Pres*
Todd M Leombruno, *Vice Pres*
▲ EMP: 500
SALES: 14.3B **Publicly Held**
WEB: www.parker.com
SIC: **3593** 3492 3569 3053 Fluid power cylinders & actuators; fluid power actuators, hydraulic or pneumatic; fluid power cylinders, hydraulic or pneumatic; control valves, fluid power: hydraulic & pneumatic; hose & tube fittings & assemblies, hydraulic/pneumatic; control valves, aircraft: hydraulic & pneumatic; valves, hydraulic, aircraft; filter elements, fluid, hydraulic line; gaskets & sealing devices; aircraft & motor vehicle measurement equipment; fluid power pumps

(G-5849)
PARKER-HANNIFIN CORPORATION
Motion & Control Training Div
6035 Parkland Blvd (44124-4186)
PHONE..................................216 531-3000
Joe Bocian, *Branch Mgr*
EMP: 600
SALES (corp-wide): 12B **Publicly Held**
WEB: www.parker.com
SIC: **4225** 3823 3714 General Warehouse/Storage Mfg Process Control Instruments Mfg Motor Vehicle Parts/Accessories
PA: Parker-Hannifin Corporation
    6035 Parkland Blvd
    Cleveland OH 44124
    216 896-3000

Cleveland - Cuyahoga County (G-5875)

(G-5850)
PARKER-HANNIFIN CORPORATION
Export Division
6035 Parkland Blvd (44124-4186)
P.O. Box 92613 (44190-0002)
PHONE..................216 896-3000
Melissa McLaughlin, *General Mgr*
EMP: 12
SALES (corp-wide): 12B **Publicly Held**
SIC: 3594 3593 3492 3569 Fluid power pumps; fluid power motors; fluid power cylinders, hydraulic or pneumatic; fluid power actuators, hydraulic or pneumatic; control valves, fluid power: hydraulic & pneumatic; hose & tube fittings & assemblies, hydraulic/pneumatic; control valves, aircraft: hydraulic & pneumatic; valves, hydraulic, aircraft; filter elements, fluid, hydraulic line; gaskets & sealing devices; aircraft & motor vehicle measurement equipment
PA: Parker-Hannifin Corporation
  6035 Parkland Blvd
  Cleveland OH 44124
  216 896-3000

(G-5851)
PARKING & TRAFFIC CONTROL SEC
Also Called: Ptc Industries
13651 Newton Rd (44130-2735)
PHONE..................440 243-7565
Donald Shorts, *CEO*
Lee Shorts, *President*
EMP: 15
SQ FT: 20,000
SALES (est): 3MM **Privately Held**
WEB: www.ptcind.com
SIC: 3824 1799 8711 Parking meters; parking facility equipment & maintenance; designing: ship, boat, machine & product

(G-5852)
PARMA HEIGHTS LICENSE BUREAU
6339 Olde York Rd (44130-3059)
PHONE..................440 888-0388
Dan Hughes, *Owner*
EMP: 7
SALES (est): 581.5K **Privately Held**
SIC: 3469 Automobile license tags, stamped metal

(G-5853)
PARTHENON GLOBAL LLC
Also Called: Parthenon Globalsystems, LLC
3615 Superior Ave E (44114-4138)
PHONE..................888 332-5303
Ademola Solaru, *CEO*
Tyler Virgin, *CFO*
EMP: 4
SALES (est): 98.3K **Privately Held**
SIC: 7372 Application computer software

(G-5854)
PATS NU-STYLE CLEANERS INC
Also Called: Pat's Cleaners
5851 Smith Rd (44142-2005)
PHONE..................216 676-4855
Pat Mahoney, *President*
EMP: 3
SALES (corp-wide): 451.8K **Privately Held**
SIC: 2842 Drycleaning preparations
PA: Pat's Nu-Style Cleaners Inc
  21420 Lorain Rd
  Cleveland OH 44126
  440 331-7300

(G-5855)
PATTERSON-BRITTON PRINTING
2165 Lakeside Ave E (44114-1124)
PHONE..................216 781-7997
Harry Britton, *President*
John Britton, *Vice Pres*
EMP: 8
SQ FT: 15,000
SALES: 1.7MM **Privately Held**
SIC: 2752 Commercial printing, offset

(G-5856)
PCC AIRFOILS LLC (DH)
3401 Entp Pkwy Ste 200 (44122)
PHONE..................216 831-3590
Peter Waite,
William D Larsson,
William Mc Cormick,
John O Neill,
◆ **EMP:** 29
SQ FT: 14,000
SALES (est): 705.6MM
SALES (corp-wide): 225.3B **Publicly Held**
WEB: www.pccairfoils.com
SIC: 3369 Nonferrous foundries
HQ: Precision Castparts Corp.
  4650 Sw Mcdam Ave Ste 300
  Portland OR 97239
  503 946-4800

(G-5857)
PCC AIRFOILS LLC
Also Called: Sherwood Refractores
1781 Octavia Rd (44112-1410)
PHONE..................216 692-7900
Thomas Lenard, *General Mgr*
EMP: 150
SALES (corp-wide): 225.3B **Publicly Held**
WEB: www.pccairfoils.com
SIC: 3369 3812 3677 3543 Castings, except die-castings, precision; search & navigation equipment; electronic coils, transformers & other inductors; foundry cores
HQ: Pcc Airfoils Llc
  3401 Entp Pkwy Ste 200
  Cleveland OH 44122
  216 831-3590

(G-5858)
PDQ PRINTING SERVICE
1914 Clark Ave (44109-1156)
PHONE..................216 241-5443
Dorry Smotzer, *Owner*
EMP: 10
SQ FT: 3,000
SALES (est): 1.2MM **Privately Held**
SIC: 2752 Commercial printing, offset

(G-5859)
PEARL HEALTHWEAR INC (PA)
5900 Maurice Ave (44127-1289)
PHONE..................440 446-0265
Kevin Goldsmith, *President*
Alice Goldsmith, *Admin Sec*
EMP: 5
SQ FT: 5,000 **Privately Held**
SIC: 2326 2337 Medical & hospital uniforms, men's; uniforms, except athletic: women's, misses' & juniors'

(G-5860)
PECK ENGRAVING CO
14398 Detroit Ave (44107-4408)
PHONE..................216 221-1556
Richard D Zaletel Jr, *President*
Laura Zaletel, *Corp Secy*
EMP: 20 **EST:** 1912
SQ FT: 13,536
SALES (est): 1.9MM **Privately Held**
WEB: www.peckengraving.com
SIC: 2796 2752 Engraving on copper, steel, wood or rubber: printing plates; commercial printing, lithographic

(G-5861)
PEERLESS METAL PRODUCTS INC
6017 Superior Ave (44103-1447)
PHONE..................216 431-6905
Thomas Banyas, *President*
Judy Szabo, *CFO*
EMP: 22
SQ FT: 32,000
SALES (est): 2MM **Privately Held**
WEB: www.peerlessmetalproducts.com
SIC: 3469 Stamping metal for the trade

(G-5862)
PEMCO INC
5663 Brecksville Rd (44131-1593)
PHONE..................216 524-2990
William John Koteles, *President*
Bob Socheck, *General Mgr*
Matt Koteles, *Vice Pres*
Ivan Kovacs, *VP Mfg*
Charles Fruscella, *Human Res Mgr*
EMP: 43 **EST:** 1942
SQ FT: 25,000
SALES (est): 1.2MM **Privately Held**
WEB: www.pemcomed.com
SIC: 3841 3599 3845 3545 Surgical & medical instruments; machine shop, jobbing & repair; electromedical equipment; machine tool accessories

(G-5863)
PEMRO CORPORATION
Also Called: Pemro Distribution
125 Alpha Park (44143-2224)
PHONE..................800 440-5441
Jon C Raney, *President*
Matt Raney, *General Mgr*
Gregory J Dziak, *Principal*
Todd Chaston, *Sales Mgr*
Jeff Shirley, *Sales Mgr*
EMP: 10
SQ FT: 3,500
SALES (est): 4.9MM **Privately Held**
WEB: www.pemro.com
SIC: 5065 2899 5045 Electronic parts; fluxes: brazing, soldering, galvanizing & welding; anti-static equipment & devices

(G-5864)
PERFUSION SOLUTIONS INC
4320 Mayfield Rd Ste 108 (44121-3601)
PHONE..................216 848-1610
Sam Kiderman, *Principal*
EMP: 3
SALES (est): 257.3K **Privately Held**
SIC: 3841 Surgical & medical instruments

(G-5865)
PERSONNEL SELECTION SERVICES
31517 Walker Rd (44140-1415)
PHONE..................440 835-3255
Paul Michalko, *President*
EMP: 10
SALES (est): 418.2K **Privately Held**
SIC: 1389 8071 Testing, measuring, surveying & analysis services; testing laboratories

(G-5866)
PETFIBER LLC
17000 Saint Clair Ave # 1 (44110-2535)
PHONE..................216 767-4482
Daniel T Moore, *Mng Member*
EMP: 3
SALES (est): 396.4K **Privately Held**
SIC: 2295 Resin or plastic coated fabrics

(G-5867)
PETNET SOLUTIONS INC
11100 Euclid Ave (44106-1716)
PHONE..................865 218-2000
Danny Bingham, *Manager*
EMP: 4
SALES (corp-wide): 95B **Privately Held**
SIC: 2835 Radioactive diagnostic substances
HQ: Petnet Solutions, Inc.
  810 Innovation Dr
  Knoxville TN 37932
  865 218-2000

(G-5868)
PETRO GEAR CORPORATION (PA)
3901 Hamilton Ave (44114-3831)
PHONE..................216 431-2820
Herman Bronstein, *President*
Joel Bronstein, *Vice Pres*
EMP: 10
SQ FT: 40,000
SALES (est): 2MM **Privately Held**
SIC: 3566 Gears, power transmission, except automotive

(G-5869)
PETROLIANCE LLC
8500 Clinton Rd Ste 11 (44144-1001)
PHONE..................216 441-7200
Kevin McCarter, *CEO*
EMP: 102
SALES (est): 2.6MM
SALES (corp-wide): 307.8MM **Privately Held**
SIC: 2992 Lubricating oils & greases
HQ: Petroliance Llc
  1009 Schieffelin Rd
  Apex NC 27502

(G-5870)
PHIL VEDDA & SONS INC
Also Called: Vedda Printing
12000 Berea Rd (44111-1608)
PHONE..................216 671-2222
Phillip Vedda, *President*
James Vedda, *Vice Pres*
Eric Moss, *Accounts Exec*
Michelle Black, *Manager*
William Maglosky, *Director*
EMP: 8 **EST:** 1956
SQ FT: 20,000
SALES (est): 3MM **Privately Held**
SIC: 2752 Commercial printing, offset

(G-5871)
PHILIPS MEDICAL SYSTEMS CLEVEL (HQ)
Also Called: Medical Imaging Equipment
595 Miner Rd (44143-2131)
PHONE..................440 247-2652
David A Dripchak, *CEO*
Jerry C Cirino, *Exec VP*
William J Cull Sr, *Vice Pres*
Robert Blankenship, *CFO*
◆ **EMP:** 500
SQ FT: 495,000
SALES (est): 739.7MM
SALES (corp-wide): 20.9B **Privately Held**
SIC: 3844 5047 5137 3842 X-ray apparatus & tubes; X-ray film & supplies; instruments, surgical & medical; hospital gowns, women's & children's; surgical appliances & supplies; laboratory apparatus & furniture; electrical equipment & supplies
PA: Koninklijke Philips N.V.
  High Tech Campus 5
  Eindhoven 5656
  402 791-111

(G-5872)
PHILLIPS CONTRACTORS SUP LLC
Also Called: Colony Hardware
1800 E 30th St (44114-4410)
PHONE..................216 861-5730
Gary Yarina, *Technology*
James D Beckett,
Ian Greenhill, *Admin Sec*
Jeffrey Williams,
EMP: 15
SQ FT: 40,000
SALES (est): 3.8MM **Privately Held**
WEB: www.pcscleveland.com
SIC: 3965 Fasteners

(G-5873)
PHILLIPS ELECTRIC CO
Also Called: Redmond Waltz Electric
4126 Saint Clair Ave (44103-1120)
PHONE..................216 361-0014
Jennifer Marriott, *President*
EMP: 15
SQ FT: 40,000
SALES (est): 2.3MM **Privately Held**
WEB: www.phillipselectric.com
SIC: 7694 5063 Electric motor repair; motors, electric

(G-5874)
PHOENIX TOOL & THREAD GRINDNG
4760 Briar Rd (44135-5038)
PHONE..................216 433-7008
John Bilboaca, *Owner*
EMP: 3
SALES: 250K **Privately Held**
WEB: www.phoenixthreadgrinding.com
SIC: 3599 Machine shop, jobbing & repair

(G-5875)
PIERCE-WRIGHT PRECISION INC
13606 Enterprise Ave (44135-5112)
PHONE..................216 362-2870
David B Pierce, *President*
EMP: 7 **EST:** 1978
SQ FT: 10,000
SALES (est): 792K **Privately Held**
SIC: 3599 Machine shop, jobbing & repair

Cleveland - Cuyahoga County (G-5876)

(G-5876)
PIERRES FRENCH ICE CREAM INC
6519 Carnegie Ave (44103)
PHONE..................................216 431-2555
Sol Roth, *President*
Elliot Kaminsky, *Vice Pres*
Shelly Roth, *Vice Pres*
Harriet Roth, *Admin Sec*
▲ **EMP:** 25 **EST:** 1937
SQ FT: 75,000
SALES (est): 3.4MM **Privately Held**
SIC: 2024 Ice cream, bulk

(G-5877)
PILE DYNAMICS INC
Also Called: Pdi
30725 Aurora Rd (44139-2735)
PHONE..................................216 831-6131
Garland Likins, *President*
George Piscsalko, *Vice Pres*
Robert Sprenger, *Prdtn Mgr*
Laura Klein, *Purch Mgr*
Michael Ference, *Engineer*
▲ **EMP:** 35 **EST:** 1972
SQ FT: 12,000
SALES (est): 11.9MM **Privately Held**
WEB: www.pile.com
SIC: 3825 Test equipment for electronic & electrical circuits

(G-5878)
PINNACLE GRAPHICS & IMAGING
Also Called: P G I
1138 W 9th St Ste LI (44113-1046)
PHONE..................................216 781-1800
Dan J Nugent, *President*
EMP: 11
SQ FT: 3,000
SALES (est): 1.1MM **Privately Held**
SIC: 2796 Color separations for printing

(G-5879)
PIONEER CLDDING GLZING SYSTEMS
2550 Brookpark Rd (44134-1407)
PHONE..................................216 816-4242
Michael Robinson, *Branch Mgr*
EMP: 35
SALES (corp-wide): 56.9MM **Privately Held**
SIC: 1793 1741 3448 Glass & glazing work; masonry & other stonework; prefabricated metal components
PA: Pioneer Cladding And Glazing Systems
    4074 Bethany Rd
    Mason OH 45040
    513 583-5925

(G-5880)
PITNEY BOWES INC
4640 Hnckley Indus Prkway (44109)
PHONE..................................216 351-2598
Steven Shamblin, *Branch Mgr*
EMP: 3
SALES (corp-wide): 3.5B **Publicly Held**
SIC: 3579 7359 Mailing machines; business machine & electronic equipment rental services
PA: Pitney Bowes Inc.
    3001 Summer St Ste 3
    Stamford CT 06905
    203 356-5000

(G-5881)
PJ BUSH ASSOCIATES INC
Also Called: Bush Integrated
15901 Industrial Pkwy (44135-3321)
PHONE..................................216 362-6700
Kathleen Bush, *President*
Patrick J Bush, *Principal*
EMP: 21
SQ FT: 40,000
SALES (est): 3.6MM **Privately Held**
WEB: www.bushprinting.com
SIC: 2759 Business forms; printing; promotional printing; screen printing

(G-5882)
PLAIN DEALER PUBLISHING CO (HQ)
Also Called: Plain Dealer, The
4800 Tiedeman Rd (44144-2336)
P.O. Box 630504, Cincinnati (45263-0504)
PHONE..................................216 999-5000
Terrance C Z Egger, *President*
Daryl Kannberg, *Editor*
John Kappes, *Editor*
Chris Quinn, *Editor*
Clara Roberts, *Editor*
EMP: 15 **EST:** 1932
SQ FT: 210,000
SALES (est): 150.5MM
SALES (corp-wide): 1.4B **Privately Held**
WEB: www.plaind.com
SIC: 2711 Newspapers, publishing & printing
PA: Advance Digital Inc.
    3100 Harborside Fincl 3
    Jersey City NJ 07311
    201 459-2808

(G-5883)
PLAIN DEALER PUBLISHING CO
4800 Tiedeman Rd (44144-2336)
PHONE..................................216 999-5000
Steve Chalabian, *Manager*
EMP: 900
SALES (corp-wide): 1.4B **Privately Held**
WEB: www.plaind.com
SIC: 2711 2752 Newspapers; commercial printing, lithographic
HQ: Plain Dealer Publishing Co.
    4800 Tiedeman Rd
    Cleveland OH 44144
    216 999-5000

(G-5884)
PLANET DISPLAY & PACKAGING INC
12500 Berea Rd (44111-1618)
PHONE..................................216 251-9641
Jason Berns, *President*
EMP: 5 **EST:** 2016
SALES (est): 120.7K **Privately Held**
SIC: 2631 Container, packaging & boxboard

(G-5885)
PLASTER PROCESS CASTINGS CO
Also Called: Diversified Mold and Castings
19800 Miles Rd (44128-4118)
PHONE..................................216 663-1814
Vince Costello, *President*
EMP: 30 **EST:** 1939
SQ FT: 7,500
SALES: 7.6MM **Privately Held**
WEB: www.plasterprocesscastings.com
SIC: 3363 3364 Aluminum die-castings; zinc & zinc-base alloy die-castings

(G-5886)
PLASTIC PLATERS LLC
Also Called: Ppi
9921 Clinton Rd (44144-1086)
PHONE..................................216 961-1200
Brad Gotts, *President*
Derrick Redding, *COO*
EMP: 150
SQ FT: 92,000
SALES (est): 21.3MM
SALES (corp-wide): 580.4MM **Privately Held**
WEB: www.egreeninc.com
SIC: 3471 Electroplating of metals or formed products
PA: Ernie Green Industries, Inc.
    2030 Dividend Dr
    Columbus OH 43228
    614 219-1423

(G-5887)
PLASTIC WORKS INC
19851 Ingersoll Dr (44116-1817)
P.O. Box 369, Huron (44839-0369)
PHONE..................................440 331-5575
Eric Kvame, *Manager*
EMP: 12
SALES (corp-wide): 1.7MM **Privately Held**
SIC: 3086 2671 Packaging & shipping materials, foamed plastic; packaging paper & plastics film, coated & laminated
PA: The Plastic Works Inc
    10502 Mudbrook Rd
    Huron OH 44839
    419 433-6576

(G-5888)
PLASTRAN INC
Also Called: P T X
9841 York Alpha Dr Ste N (44133-3554)
PHONE..................................440 237-8404
Charles Frishe, *President*
EMP: 4
SQ FT: 2,500
SALES (est): 615.3K **Privately Held**
SIC: 3443 5084 Metal parts; industrial machinery & equipment

(G-5889)
PLATFORM BEERS LLC
4125 Lorain Ave (44113-3718)
PHONE..................................440 539-3245
Amy Cain, *VP Sales*
Paul Benner, *Mng Member*
Justin Carson, *Mng Member*
EMP: 12
SQ FT: 5,000
SALES: 700K **Privately Held**
SIC: 2082 Near beer

(G-5890)
PLATING TEST CELL SUPPLY CO
948 Wayside Rd B (44110-2957)
PHONE..................................216 486-8400
David E Geduld, *Owner*
EMP: 3
SQ FT: 1,000
SALES: 200K **Privately Held**
SIC: 3829 Physical property testing equipment

(G-5891)
PLUS MARK LLC
1 American Rd (44144-2354)
PHONE..................................216 252-6770
Kurt Schoen, *President*
Dick Gygi, *Vice Pres*
Gui De Mello, *Treasurer*
Stephen J Smith, *Treasurer*
Jim Kaiser, *Asst Treas*
▲ **EMP:** 35 **EST:** 1977
SQ FT: 1,600,000
SALES (est): 16.7MM
SALES (corp-wide): 7.2B **Privately Held**
SIC: 2621 2396 2771 Wrapping paper; automotive & apparel trimmings; greeting cards
HQ: American Greetings Corporation
    1 American Way
    Cleveland OH 44145
    216 252-7300

(G-5892)
POLGENIX INC
11000 Cedar Ave Ste 100 (44106-3056)
PHONE..................................440 537-9691
Joseph Jankowski, *President*
Vida M Tripodo, *Finance*
Grazyna Palczewska, *Director*
EMP: 3
SALES (est): 423K **Privately Held**
WEB: www.polgenixinc.com
SIC: 2834 Pharmaceutical preparations

(G-5893)
POLY PRODUCTS INC
837 E 79th St (44103-1807)
PHONE..................................216 391-7659
Walter Senney, *President*
Joyce Senney, *Vice Pres*
EMP: 6
SQ FT: 12,000
SALES (est): 103.8K **Privately Held**
WEB: www.poly-products.com
SIC: 3559 3568 Refinery, chemical processing & similar machinery; bearings, bushings & blocks

(G-5894)
POLYMER ADDITIVES INC
1636 Wayside Rd (44112-1233)
PHONE..................................216 875-7273
EMP: 3 **EST:** 2017
SALES (est): 192.6K **Privately Held**
SIC: 2869 Industrial organic chemicals

(G-5895)
POLYMER ADDITIVES INC
Also Called: Valtris Specialty Chemical
1636 Wayside Rd (44112-1233)
PHONE..................................216 875-5840
EMP: 6
SALES (corp-wide): 727.7MM **Privately Held**
SIC: 2899 Fire retardant chemicals
HQ: Polymer Additives, Inc.
    7500 E Pleasant Valley Rd
    Independence OH 44131
    216 875-7200

(G-5896)
PORATH BUSINESS SERVICES INC
Also Called: Porath Printing
21000 Miles Pkwy (44128-5515)
PHONE..................................216 626-0060
Gerald A Engelhart, *President*
Mindy Lapine, *Controller*
Annjoy Pickholtz, *Sales Staff*
Erich Kerstetter, *Graphic Designe*
Tiffany Stuewe, *Graphic Designe*
EMP: 17
SQ FT: 5,000
SALES (est): 2.9MM **Privately Held**
SIC: 2752 7331 Commercial printing, offset; mailing service

(G-5897)
POSTLE INDUSTRIES INC
Also Called: Cermet Technologies
5500 W 164th St (44142-1512)
P.O. Box 42037 (44142-0037)
PHONE..................................216 265-9000
John G Postle, *President*
Chris J Postle, *Vice Pres*
▲ **EMP:** 25 **EST:** 1968
SQ FT: 15,000
SALES (est): 6.1MM **Privately Held**
WEB: www.postle.com
SIC: 3548 2851 Welding & cutting apparatus & accessories; epoxy coatings

(G-5898)
POTTERS INDUSTRIES LLC
2380 W 3rd St (44113-2509)
PHONE..................................216 621-0840
Mark Nicholson, *Regl Sales Mgr*
Bob Hooper, *Manager*
Billy Boler, *Manager*
Kevin Goforth, *Manager*
Patrick U Brady, *Executive*
EMP: 30
SALES (corp-wide): 1.6B **Publicly Held**
WEB: www.flexolite.com
SIC: 3231 Reflector glass beads, for highway signs or reflectors
HQ: Potters Industries, Llc
    300 Lindenwood Dr
    Malvern PA 19355
    610 651-4700

(G-5899)
POWER METRICS INC
17 Alpha Park (44143-2202)
PHONE..................................440 461-9352
Jeffrey Thornberry, *President*
John Unterwagner, *General Mgr*
EMP: 3
SQ FT: 1,800
SALES (est): 478.2K **Privately Held**
WEB: www.powermetrics.com
SIC: 3679 Power supplies, all types: static

(G-5900)
PPG INDUSTRIES INC
14800 Emery Ave (44135-1477)
PHONE..................................216 671-7793
Dian Lind, *Branch Mgr*
EMP: 24
SALES (corp-wide): 15.3B **Publicly Held**
SIC: 2851 Paints & allied products

GEOGRAPHIC SECTION

Cleveland - Cuyahoga County (G-5927)

PA: Ppg Industries, Inc.
1 Ppg Pl
Pittsburgh PA 15272
412 434-3131

(G-5901)
PPG INDUSTRIES OHIO INC (HQ)
Also Called: PPG Oak Creek
3800 W 143rd St (44111-4997)
PHONE..................216 671-0050
Charles E Bunch, *CEO*
Bill Silvestri, *President*
J Rich Alexander, *Vice Pres*
Matt Lynch, *Manager*
Dennis N Taljan, *Admin Sec*
◆ EMP: 602 EST: 1999
SQ FT: 439,551
SALES (est): 301.9MM
SALES (corp-wide): 15.3B **Publicly Held**
WEB: www.ppgglass.com
SIC: 2851 Paints & paint additives
PA: Ppg Industries, Inc.
1 Ppg Pl
Pittsburgh PA 15272
412 434-3131

(G-5902)
PPL HOLDING COMPANY
25201 Chagrin Blvd # 360 (44122-5600)
PHONE..................216 514-1840
Mark Mansour, *Bd of Directors*
EMP: 50
SALES (est): 2.3MM **Privately Held**
SIC: 2821 Thermoplastic materials

(G-5903)
PRAXAIR INC
2500 Metrohealth Dr (44109-1900)
PHONE..................216 778-5555
Ken Papa, *Manager*
EMP: 20 **Privately Held**
SIC: 2813 Industrial gases
HQ: Praxair, Inc.
10 Riverview Dr
Danbury CT 06810
203 837-2000

(G-5904)
PRAXAIR INC
14788 York Rd (44133-4508)
PHONE..................440 237-8690
Brian Pasquerlo, *Superintendent*
EMP: 30 **Privately Held**
SIC: 2813 Industrial gases
HQ: Praxair, Inc.
10 Riverview Dr
Danbury CT 06810
203 837-2000

(G-5905)
PRAXAIR INC
5480 Cloverleaf Pkwy # 6 (44125-4804)
PHONE..................419 652-3562
Mike Barr, *Principal*
EMP: 20 **Privately Held**
SIC: 2813 Industrial gases
HQ: Praxair, Inc.
10 Riverview Dr
Danbury CT 06810
203 837-2000

(G-5906)
PRAXAIR INC
5324 Grant Ave (44125-1036)
PHONE..................440 944-8844
Don Mocarski, *Manager*
EMP: 6 **Privately Held**
SIC: 2813 Industrial gases
HQ: Praxair, Inc.
10 Riverview Dr
Danbury CT 06810
203 837-2000

(G-5907)
PRECISE TOOL & MFG CORP
5755 Canal Rd (44125-3429)
PHONE..................216 524-1500
Ronald Volandt, *President*
EMP: 10 EST: 1950
SQ FT: 5,200
SALES (est): 644.2K **Privately Held**
SIC: 3545 Cutting tools for machine tools

(G-5908)
PRECISION COATINGS INC
Also Called: Precison Coating Technology
3289 E 80th St (44104-4341)
PHONE..................216 441-0805
Dale Palik, *President*
Mike Palik, *Vice Pres*
John Gale, *Finance*
Lucille Palik, *Admin Sec*
EMP: 12 EST: 1981
SQ FT: 22,000
SALES (est): 1.3MM **Privately Held**
WEB: www.precisioncoatingsinc.org
SIC: 3479 Coating of metals & formed products; coating of metals with plastic or resins

(G-5909)
PRECISION GRINDING CORPORATION
6717 Saint Clair Ave (44103-1743)
PHONE..................216 391-7294
John V Semen, *President*
EMP: 3 EST: 1951
SQ FT: 3,000
SALES: 150K **Privately Held**
SIC: 3599 Machine shop, jobbing & repair

(G-5910)
PRECISION MCHNING SRFACING INC
5435 Perkins Rd (44146-1856)
PHONE..................440 439-9850
David Slifka, *President*
EMP: 6
SALES (est): 734.7K **Privately Held**
WEB: www.pre-machining.com
SIC: 3599 Machine shop, jobbing & repair

(G-5911)
PRECISION METAL PRODUCTS INC
7641 Commerce Park Oval (44131-2303)
PHONE..................216 447-1900
Thomas Jacin, *CEO*
George A Jacin, *President*
Robert Weisert, *QC Mgr*
Janet Breneman, *Human Res Dir*
Mark Spilker, *Administration*
EMP: 17 EST: 1961
SQ FT: 16,000
SALES: 7MM **Privately Held**
WEB: www.pmpstamping.com
SIC: 3469 3549 Stamping metal for the trade; assembly machines, including robotic

(G-5912)
PRECISION WELDING CORPORATION
7900 Exchange St (44125-3334)
P.O. Box 25548 (44125-0548)
PHONE..................216 524-6110
Dennis Nader, *President*
Randy Nader, *Vice Pres*
EMP: 32
SQ FT: 26,000
SALES (est): 4.5MM **Privately Held**
SIC: 7692 3444 3441 Welding repair; sheet metalwork; fabricated structural metal

(G-5913)
PRECISION WIRE PRODUCTS INC (PA)
Also Called: Cages By Jim
4791 W 139th St (44135-5033)
PHONE..................216 265-7580
Jim Damian Jr, *President*
EMP: 4
SQ FT: 4,500
SALES (est): 200K **Privately Held**
SIC: 3496 Cages, wire

(G-5914)
PREDICT INC
9555 Rockside Rd Ste 350 (44125-6283)
PHONE..................216 642-3223
Robert Jung, *CEO*
Nicholas Kroll, *President*
EMP: 18
SQ FT: 20,000
SALES: 3.9MM
SALES (corp-wide): 10.9MM **Privately Held**
SIC: 1389 Oil sampling service for oil companies
PA: Trico Corporation
1235 Hickory St
Pewaukee WI 53072
262 691-9336

(G-5915)
PREEMPTIVE SOLUTIONS LLC
767 Beta Dr (44143-2379)
PHONE..................440 443-7200
Gabriel Torok, *CEO*
Paul Ruflin, *President*
Andy Forsyth, *Vice Pres*
Mark Fagerholm, *CFO*
EMP: 30
SQ FT: 4,000
SALES (est): 3.8MM **Privately Held**
WEB: www.preemptive.com
SIC: 7372 Application computer software

(G-5916)
PREMIER MANUFACTURING CORP (HQ)
3003 Priscilla Ave (44134-4230)
PHONE..................216 941-9700
Paul Kara, *President*
Donald C Dawson, *President*
Bill Rush, *General Mgr*
John Petro, *Engineer*
Steve Koss, *CFO*
◆ EMP: 63 EST: 1962
SALES (est): 23.2MM
SALES (corp-wide): 483.8MM **Privately Held**
WEB: www.premiermfg.com
SIC: 3496 3296 Miscellaneous fabricated wire products; mineral wool
PA: Ssw Holding Company, Llc
3501 Tulsa St
Fort Smith AR 72903
479 646-1651

(G-5917)
PREMIER PRINTING CORPORATION
18780 Cranwood Pkwy (44128-4038)
PHONE..................216 478-9720
James Trombo, *President*
Jeffrey Trombo, *Vice Pres*
Coleen Keefer, *Manager*
Aldo Liberatore, *Manager*
EMP: 12
SQ FT: 10,000
SALES (est): 2.3MM **Privately Held**
WEB: www.premierprintingcorp.com
SIC: 2752 Commercial printing, offset

(G-5918)
PRESRITE CORPORATION (PA)
3665 E 78th St (44105-2048)
PHONE..................216 441-5990
Donald J Diemer, *Ch of Bd*
Chris Carman, *President*
William Berglund, *Exec VP*
George Longhour, *Vice Pres*
Keith Vanderburg, *Admin Sec*
EMP: 425
SQ FT: 180,000
SALES (est): 187.6MM **Privately Held**
WEB: www.presrite.com
SIC: 3462 Automotive & internal combustion engine forgings

(G-5919)
PRESSCO TECHNOLOGY INC (PA)
29200 Aurora Rd (44139-1847)
PHONE..................440 498-2600
Don W Cochran, *President*
James R Bridgeland Jr, *Principal*
William C Holmes, *COO*
Jon Katz, *Vice Pres*
Ed Morgan, *Vice Pres*
▲ EMP: 90
SQ FT: 60,000
SALES (est): 15.6MM **Privately Held**
SIC: 3829 3825 Physical property testing equipment; instruments to measure electricity

(G-5920)
PRESSURE WASHER MFRS ASSN
1300 Sumner Ave (44115-2851)
PHONE..................216 241-7333
John H Addington, *Principal*
EMP: 4 EST: 2008
SALES: 36K **Privately Held**
SIC: 3452 Washers

(G-5921)
PRIME INSTRUMENTS INC
9805 Walford Ave (44102-4734)
PHONE..................216 651-0400
James R Moran, *President*
▲ EMP: 75 EST: 1970
SQ FT: 37,000
SALES (est): 15.6MM **Privately Held**
WEB: www.primeinstruments.com
SIC: 3823 Industrial instrmnts msrmnt display/control process variable

(G-5922)
PRINCE PLATING INC
1530 E 40th St (44103-2302)
PHONE..................216 881-7523
Mark Stover, *President*
EMP: 62
SALES (est): 6.4MM **Privately Held**
SIC: 3471 Rechroming auto bumpers

(G-5923)
PRIORITY VENDING INC
3425 Prospect Ave E (44115-2617)
PHONE..................216 361-4100
Joseph N Abraham, *President*
EMP: 5
SQ FT: 10,000
SALES (est): 774.4K **Privately Held**
WEB: www.priorityvending.com
SIC: 5962 3999 Cigarettes vending machines; cigarette & cigar products & accessories

(G-5924)
PRO ROOF WASHERS
1403 Ford Rd (44124-1432)
PHONE..................440 521-2622
Frank Sciaulino, *Principal*
EMP: 4
SALES (est): 339.1K **Privately Held**
SIC: 3452 Washers

(G-5925)
PRODUCE PACKAGING INC
7501 Carnegie Ave (44103-4809)
PHONE..................216 391-6129
Greg Fritz, *President*
Jerome Fritz, *Vice Pres*
Gerald Lewis, *Materials Mgr*
Jason Mishler, *Buyer*
Hira Devito, *Office Mgr*
EMP: 150
SQ FT: 35,000
SALES (est): 47.8MM **Privately Held**
WEB: www.producepackagingltd.com
SIC: 3053 Packing materials

(G-5926)
PRODUCTS INNOVATORS
2567 Lafayette Dr (44118-4607)
PHONE..................216 932-5269
Harold Isaacs, *President*
EMP: 20
SQ FT: 16,000
SALES (est): 1.2MM **Privately Held**
SIC: 3537 Trucks, tractors, loaders, carriers & similar equipment

(G-5927)
PROFESSIONAL FABRICATORS INC
Also Called: Pro Fab
15708 Brookpark Rd (44135-3336)
PHONE..................216 362-1208
Paul Sutton, *President*
Louis R Sutton, *Vice Pres*
EMP: 3
SQ FT: 2,500
SALES: 252.2K **Privately Held**
SIC: 3441 Fabricated structural metal

Cleveland - Cuyahoga County (G-5928)

(G-5928)
PROFILE GRINDING INC
4593 Spring Rd (44131-1023)
PHONE.................................216 351-0600
Karen Homer, *President*
W Robert Benton, *General Mgr*
EMP: 29 **EST:** 1945
SQ FT: 20,000
SALES: 1.8MM **Privately Held**
WEB: www.profilegrinding.com
SIC: 3451 3599 Screw machine products; machine shop, jobbing & repair

(G-5929)
PROPRESS INC
3135 Berea Rd Ste 1 (44111-1513)
PHONE.................................216 631-8200
Steve Forster, *President*
James Branagan, *Partner*
Teresa Tarantino, *Partner*
Robert Sweet, *Engineer*
Barbara Brucker, *Manager*
EMP: 10
SQ FT: 3,000
SALES (est): 1.1MM **Privately Held**
WEB: www.propressinc.com
SIC: 2741 7311 Telephone & other directory publishing; advertising agencies

(G-5930)
PROSPERITY ON PAYNE INC
1814 E 40th St Ste 5e (44103-3528)
PHONE.................................216 431-7677
Catherine Zurchin, *President*
Laura Bosse, *Vice Pres*
EMP: 3
SQ FT: 4,500
SALES: 80K **Privately Held**
WEB: www.prosperity.com
SIC: 3961 Jewelry apparel, non-precious metals

(G-5931)
PROTOTYPE FABRICATORS COMPANY
10911 Briggs Rd (44111-5300)
PHONE.................................216 252-0080
Richard Poddubny, *President*
EMP: 10
SQ FT: 7,200
SALES: 1.3MM **Privately Held**
SIC: 3444 Sheet metalwork

(G-5932)
PUBCO CORPORATION (PA)
3830 Kelley Ave (44114-4534)
PHONE.................................216 881-5300
William Dillingham, *President*
Stephen R Kalette, *Vice Pres*
Robert Turnbull, *Vice Pres*
Maria Szubski, *CFO*
◆ **EMP:** 85
SQ FT: 312,000
SALES (est): 94.9MM **Privately Held**
SIC: 3531 6512 3955 Construction machinery; nonresidential building operators; carbon paper & inked ribbons

(G-5933)
PUCEL ENTERPRISES INC
1440 E 36th St (44114-4117)
PHONE.................................216 881-4604
Robert A Mlakar, *President*
Kathleen Cook, *Vice Pres*
Ann Mlakar, *Vice Pres*
Anthony F Mlakar, *Vice Pres*
Kathleen M Mlakar-Cook, *Vice Pres*
EMP: 55 **EST:** 1949
SQ FT: 105,000
SALES (est): 11.9MM **Privately Held**
WEB: www.pucelenterprises.com
SIC: 3499 3441 3537 3443 Furniture parts, metal; fabricated structural metal; industrial trucks & tractors; fabricated plate work (boiler shop); partitions & fixtures, except wood; office furniture, except wood

(G-5934)
PUEHLER TOOL CO
7670 Hub Pkwy (44125-5707)
PHONE.................................216 447-0101
William Puehler, *President*
EMP: 4
SQ FT: 9,200
SALES (est): 588.8K **Privately Held**
SIC: 3544 Special dies & tools; industrial molds

(G-5935)
PUPPY PAWS INC
6763 Stafford Dr (44124-3612)
PHONE.................................440 461-9667
Pamela Meltzer, *President*
James Meltzer, *CFO*
EMP: 3
SQ FT: 641
SALES: 150K **Privately Held**
SIC: 3911 Collar/cuff buttons, precious/semiprecious metal or stone

(G-5936)
PYRAMID PLASTICS INC
9202 Reno Ave (44105-2187)
PHONE.................................216 641-5904
Donald Newman, *Ch of Bd*
Mike Dezort, *President*
James E Newman, *Vice Pres*
Theresa Martin, *Finance Mgr*
Rosalyn Slade, *Receptionist*
EMP: 30 **EST:** 1931
SQ FT: 10,000
SALES (est): 4.9MM **Privately Held**
SIC: 3089 Injection molded finished plastic products

(G-5937)
QCSM LLC
Also Called: Columbia Industries
9335 Mccracken Blvd (44125-2311)
PHONE.................................216 531-5960
John Quigley,
EMP: 5
SALES (est): 307.1K **Privately Held**
SIC: 3451 8711 3599 3593 Screw machine products; mechanical engineering; machine & other job shop work; fluid power cylinders, hydraulic or pneumatic

(G-5938)
QUALICO INC
3201 E 66th St (44127-1403)
PHONE.................................216 271-2550
John Fry, *President*
Arlan Knopple, *Vice Pres*
Jeff Mignus, *Vice Pres*
EMP: 4
SQ FT: 10,000
SALES (est): 676.7K **Privately Held**
SIC: 2899 2952 Metal treating compounds; rust resisting compounds; waterproofing compounds; asphalt felts & coatings; roofing felts, cements or coatings

(G-5939)
QUALITECH ASSOCIATES INC
11324 Brookpark Rd (44130-1129)
PHONE.................................216 265-8702
Phil Kovach, *Treasurer*
EMP: 3 **EST:** 1982
SQ FT: 1,110
SALES (est): 500.7K **Privately Held**
SIC: 3821 Calibration tapes for physical testing machines

(G-5940)
QUALITY BORATE CO LLC
3690 Orange Pl Ste 495 (44122-4465)
PHONE.................................216 896-1949
Vincent Opaskar, *Technical Mgr*
Gary McClurg,
▲ **EMP:** 10
SQ FT: 3,500
SALES (est): 1.7MM **Privately Held**
SIC: 5169 2879 Chemicals & allied products; agricultural chemicals

(G-5941)
QUALITY CUTTER GRINDING CO
15501 Commerce Park Dr (44142-2014)
PHONE.................................216 362-6444
Carl Scafuro, *President*
Debbie Ebert, *Treasurer*
EMP: 11
SQ FT: 13,500
SALES (est): 1.5MM **Privately Held**
SIC: 3545 7699 Cutting tools for machine tools; knife, saw & tool sharpening & repair

(G-5942)
QUALITY PLATING CO
1443 E 40th St (44103-1182)
P.O. Box 603247 (44103-0247)
PHONE.................................216 361-0151
Daniel Miller, *President*
▲ **EMP:** 9 **EST:** 1944
SQ FT: 11,895
SALES: 865K **Privately Held**
WEB: www.qualityplatinginc.com
SIC: 3471 8711 Chromium plating of metals or formed products; electroplating of metals or formed products; polishing, metals or formed products; engineering services

(G-5943)
QUALITY REPLACEMENT PARTS INC
9099 Bank St Ste 2 (44125-3435)
PHONE.................................216 674-0200
Patricia Kuntz, *President*
Allan Kuntz, *Vice Pres*
▲ **EMP:** 4
SQ FT: 4,000
SALES (est): 270K **Privately Held**
WEB: www.qualityreplacementparts.com
SIC: 3484 Shotguns or shotgun parts, 30 mm. & below

(G-5944)
QUALITY SEWING INC
5656 Dunham Rd (44137-3655)
PHONE.................................216 475-0411
Domonic Armani, *President*
EMP: 3
SALES (est): 213.5K **Privately Held**
SIC: 2329 2331 2335 7219 Shirt & slack suits: men's, youths' & boys'; women's & misses' blouses & shirts; women's, juniors' & misses' dresses; garment alteration & repair shop

(G-5945)
QUALITY STAMPING PRODUCTS CO (PA)
5322 Bragg Rd (44127-1283)
PHONE.................................216 441-2700
Alan Nayman, *President*
Kenneth Nayman, *Vice Pres*
Nan Nayman, *Vice Pres*
Dorothy Nayman, *Admin Sec*
EMP: 16 **EST:** 1951
SQ FT: 20,000
SALES (est): 3.1MM **Privately Held**
SIC: 3469 Stamping metal for the trade

(G-5946)
QUES INDUSTRIES INC
5420 W 140th St (44142-1703)
PHONE.................................216 267-8989
Quentin Meng, *President*
▲ **EMP:** 16
SQ FT: 50,000
SALES (est): 5MM **Privately Held**
WEB: www.quesinc.com
SIC: 2899 Water treating compounds

(G-5947)
R & R COMFORT EXPERTS LLC
13370 Hathaway Rd (44125-5218)
PHONE.................................216 475-3995
Robert Maglionico,
EMP: 3
SALES (est): 243.1K **Privately Held**
SIC: 3585 Heating & air conditioning combination units

(G-5948)
R & R MACHINE & TOOL CO
3148 W 32nd St Ste 3 (44109-1549)
PHONE.................................216 281-7609
Richard Rauske, *President*
Michelle Rauske, *Corp Secy*
EMP: 3 **EST:** 1969
SALES: 140K **Privately Held**
WEB: www.reinersranch.com
SIC: 3544 Special dies & tools

(G-5949)
R A K MACHINE INC
5900 Walworth Ave (44102-4461)
PHONE.................................216 631-7750
Tim Bragg, *President*
EMP: 15
SQ FT: 5,500
SALES (est): 2.6MM **Privately Held**
SIC: 3559 Rubber working machinery, including tires

(G-5950)
R E MAY INC
1401 E 24th St (44114-2176)
PHONE.................................216 771-6332
Betty D Pangrace, *President*
John E Pangrace, *Vice Pres*
Fwzimmer Zimmer, *Sales Staff*
EMP: 16
SQ FT: 5,000
SALES (est): 1.6MM **Privately Held**
WEB: www.remay.com
SIC: 2796 Lithographic plates, positives or negatives

(G-5951)
R F W HOLDINGS INC
1200 Smith Ct (44116-1520)
PHONE.................................440 331-8300
Richard Wilber, *President*
EMP: 8
SALES (est): 718.8K **Privately Held**
SIC: 2394 Sails: made from purchased materials

(G-5952)
R H INDUSTRIES INC
3155 W 33rd St (44109-1524)
PHONE.................................216 281-5210
Tina Haddad, *President*
Celia Santiago, *Manager*
EMP: 21 **EST:** 1972
SQ FT: 10,000
SALES (est): 3.7MM **Privately Held**
SIC: 3429 3599 3511 Motor vehicle hardware; machine shop, jobbing & repair; turbines & turbine generator sets

(G-5953)
R M YATES CO INC
Also Called: American Carved Crystal
4452 Warner Rd (44105-5958)
PHONE.................................216 441-0900
Robert M Yates Jr, *President*
Diane Yates, *Vice Pres*
EMP: 4
SQ FT: 3,500
SALES (est): 395.9K **Privately Held**
WEB: www.americancarvedcrystal.com
SIC: 3231 Products of purchased glass

(G-5954)
RADDELLS SAUSAGE
478 E 152nd St (44110-1762)
PHONE.................................216 486-1944
Thomas Raddell, *Owner*
Jacob Raddell, *Manager*
EMP: 5 **EST:** 1958
SQ FT: 2,973
SALES (est): 280K **Privately Held**
SIC: 2013 Sausages from purchased meat

(G-5955)
RADIX WIRE & CABLE LLC
26000 Lakeland Blvd (44132-2638)
PHONE.................................216 731-9191
Steve Demko, *CFO*
EMP: 9 **EST:** 2013
SALES (est): 1.4MM **Privately Held**
SIC: 2298 3312 3315 Ropes & fiber cables; cable, fiber; wire products, steel or iron; wire & fabricated wire products

(G-5956)
RADIX WIRE CO (PA)
Also Called: Radix Wire Company, The
26000 Lakeland Blvd (44132-2638)
PHONE.................................216 731-9191
Keith D Nootbaar, *President*
Jim Schaefer, *President*
Marylou Vermerris, *Chairman*
Brain Bukovec, *Vice Pres*
EMP: 60 **EST:** 1944
SQ FT: 14,000
SALES (est): 21.5MM **Privately Held**
WEB: www.radix-wire.com
SIC: 3357 5051 Nonferrous wiredrawing & insulating; cable, wire

GEOGRAPHIC SECTION
Cleveland - Cuyahoga County (G-5983)

(G-5957)
RADIX WIRE CO
26260 Lakeland Blvd (44132-2640)
PHONE...................216 731-9191
Bill Toll, *Manager*
EMP: 85
SALES (est): 10.5MM
SALES (corp-wide): 21.5MM **Privately Held**
WEB: www.radix-wire.com
SIC: 3357 Nonferrous wiredrawing & insulating
PA: Radix Wire Co
  26000 Lakeland Blvd
  Cleveland OH 44132
  216 731-9191

(G-5958)
RAGEON INC
Also Called: Let's Rage
1163 E 40th St Ste 2 (44114-3866)
PHONE...................617 633-0544
Juan Caminero, *Advt Staff*
Faisal Ali, *Sr Software Eng*
Mike Krilivsky,
EMP: 22
SALES (est): 2MM **Privately Held**
SIC: 2389 7389 Apparel & accessories;

(G-5959)
RAM SENSORS INC (PA)
875 Canterbury Rd (44145-1488)
PHONE...................440 835-3540
Ron Miller, *President*
Caroline J Miller, *Corp Secy*
EMP: 17 **EST:** 1981
SQ FT: 16,000
SALES: 1.4MM **Privately Held**
WEB: www.ramsensors.com
SIC: 3823 3315 Temperature instruments: industrial process type; wire, steel: insulated or armored

(G-5960)
RANDYS PICKLES LLC
2203 Superior Ave E (44114-4222)
PHONE...................440 864-6611
Andrew Rainey, *CEO*
EMP: 8 **EST:** 2013
SQ FT: 3,000
SALES (est): 235.3K **Privately Held**
SIC: 2035 Pickles, sauces & salad dressings

(G-5961)
RASCAL HOUSE INC
1836 Euclid Ave Ste 800 (44115-2234)
PHONE...................216 781-0904
Niko Frangos, *President*
EMP: 7
SALES: 109.1K **Privately Held**
SIC: 6794 7372 Franchises, selling or licensing; application computer software

(G-5962)
RAY FOGG CONSTRUCTION INC
981 Keynote Cir Ste 15 (44131-1842)
PHONE...................216 351-7976
Raymon B Fogg Sr, *President*
Raymon B Fogg Jr, *Exec VP*
Michael J Merle, *Exec VP*
Richard Neiden, *Vice Pres*
Virginia Fogg, *Admin Sec*
EMP: 15
SQ FT: 5,760
SALES: 15MM **Privately Held**
SIC: 2821 Plastics materials & resins

(G-5963)
RAYS SAUSAGE INC
3146 E 123rd St (44120-3179)
PHONE...................216 921-8782
Renee Cash, *President*
Raymond Cash, *Vice Pres*
Leslie Lester, *CFO*
Lesile Cash Lester, *Manager*
EMP: 8
SQ FT: 660
SALES: 800K **Privately Held**
SIC: 2013 Sausages from purchased meat; pork, cured: from purchased meat; beef, dried: from purchased meat

(G-5964)
READY TO GO LLC
17325 Euclid Ave (44112-1247)
PHONE...................216 862-8572
Antonio Lee, *Principal*
EMP: 3
SALES (est): 158.7K **Privately Held**
SIC: 3273 Ready-mixed concrete

(G-5965)
REBIZ LLC
1925 Saint Clair Ave Ne (44114-2028)
PHONE...................844 467-3249
Jumaid Hasan, *Mng Member*
EMP: 50 **EST:** 2014
SALES (est): 55.4K **Privately Held**
SIC: 7372 7374 Business oriented computer software; optical scanning data service

(G-5966)
RECOB GREAT LAKES EXPRESS INC
20600 Sheldon Rd (44142-1319)
PHONE...................216 265-7940
Daniel S Recob, *President*
EMP: 5
SALES (est): 334K **Privately Held**
WEB: www.rglexpress.com
SIC: 2741 Miscellaneous publishing

(G-5967)
RED SEAL ELECTRIC CO
3835 W 150th St (44111-5891)
PHONE...................216 941-3900
Samuel Stryffeler, *President*
Daniel T Stryffeler, *President*
Robbie Gray, *Facilities Mgr*
Jeff Stryffeler, *Treasurer*
Sandy Hopkins, *Bookkeeper*
▲ **EMP:** 38 **EST:** 1946
SQ FT: 28,000
SALES (est): 10.2MM **Privately Held**
WEB: www.redseal.com
SIC: 3644 Insulators & insulation materials, electrical

(G-5968)
RED TIE GROUP INC (HQ)
Also Called: Braden-Sutphin Ink Company
3650 E 93rd St (44105-1620)
PHONE...................216 271-2300
Jim Leitch, *CEO*
Ted Zelek, *Ch of Bd*
Albert C Sutphin Jr, *President*
Maurice Parker, *Prdtn Mgr*
Rainer Wiewel, *Purch Mgr*
▲ **EMP:** 118
SQ FT: 98,000
SALES (est): 33.9MM
SALES (corp-wide): 155.8MM **Privately Held**
WEB: www.bsink.com
SIC: 2893 Printing ink
PA: Wikoff Color Corporation
  1886 Merritt Rd
  Fort Mill SC 29715
  803 548-2210

(G-5969)
REDCO INSTRUMENT
659 Broadway Ave (44146-3504)
PHONE...................440 232-2132
Steve Radecky, *Owner*
EMP: 5
SQ FT: 1,500
SALES (est): 551.7K **Privately Held**
SIC: 3812 Search & navigation equipment

(G-5970)
REID ASSET MANAGEMENT COMPANY (PA)
Also Called: Magnus Equipment
9555 Rockside Rd Ste 350 (44125-6283)
PHONE...................216 642-3223
Pete Breeden, *Vice Pres*
Helen Stois, *Incorporator*
Norman K Austad, *Incorporator*
Norman Tischler, *Incorporator*
EMP: 1
SQ FT: 40,000
SALES (est): 9.9MM **Privately Held**
WEB: www.magnusequipment.com
SIC: 3589 Commercial cleaning equipment

(G-5971)
REID ASSET MANAGEMENT COMPANY
Also Called: Predict Technologies Div
9555 Rockside Rd Ste 350 (44125-6283)
PHONE...................216 642-3223
Donald F Kautzman, *Principal*
EMP: 40
SALES (est): 1.6MM
SALES (corp-wide): 9.9MM **Privately Held**
WEB: www.magnusequipment.com
SIC: 7389 8734 3826 5084 Industrial & commercial equipment inspection service; testing laboratories; analytical instruments; industrial machinery & equipment
PA: Reid Asset Management Company
  9555 Rockside Rd Ste 350
  Cleveland OH 44125
  216 642-3223

(G-5972)
RELIABLE PATTERN WORKS INC
590 Golden Oak Pkwy (44146-6502)
PHONE...................440 232-8820
Stephanie Kapcio, *President*
Stephanie Kacio, *Corp Secy*
EMP: 7 **EST:** 1913
SQ FT: 7,500
SALES (est): 1.1MM **Privately Held**
WEB: www.reliablepattern.com
SIC: 3543 Industrial patterns

(G-5973)
RENCO PRINTING INC
5261 W 161st St (44142-1640)
PHONE...................216 267-5585
Betty Marquard, *President*
Jim Marquard, *Vice Pres*
Jeff Marquard, *Admin Sec*
EMP: 3
SQ FT: 4,500
SALES (est): 200K **Privately Held**
SIC: 2752 Commercial printing, offset

(G-5974)
RENEGADE BRANDS LLC
3201 Enterprise Pkwy # 490 (44122-7320)
PHONE...................216 342-4347
Cathy Horton, *CEO*
Adam Short, *VP Sales*
Hannah Griffin, *Sales Staff*
Michael Hurley, *Sales Staff*
Dick Miller, *Sales Staff*
EMP: 7
SQ FT: 5,000
SALES: 4MM **Privately Held**
SIC: 2841 Soap: granulated, liquid, cake, flaked or chip

(G-5975)
REPKO MACHINE INC
5081 W 164th St (44142-1599)
PHONE...................216 267-1144
John Palmer III, *President*
Valentyna Palmer, *Admin Sec*
EMP: 9 **EST:** 1951
SQ FT: 16,000
SALES (est): 1.3MM **Privately Held**
WEB: www.repko.com
SIC: 3599 Machine shop, jobbing & repair

(G-5976)
REPLICA ENGINEERING INC
3483 W 140th St (44111-2418)
PHONE...................216 252-2204
Elwyn J Price, *President*
Glyn Price, *Vice Pres*
Brian Downs, *Manager*
▲ **EMP:** 17
SQ FT: 9,000
SALES (est): 2MM **Privately Held**
WEB: www.replicaeng.com
SIC: 3561 Industrial pumps & parts

(G-5977)
REPRO ACQUISITION COMPANY LLC
Also Called: Reprocenter, The
25001 Rockwell Dr (44117-1239)
PHONE...................216 738-3800
Ronald Smith, *Sales Executive*
▲ **EMP:** 40
SQ FT: 32,000
SALES (est): 4.7MM **Privately Held**
WEB: www.reprocntr.com
SIC: 2752 7375 2789 Commercial printing, offset; information retrieval services; bookbinding & related work

(G-5978)
RESEARCH ORGANICS LLC
Also Called: Safc Cleveland
4353 E 49th St (44125-1083)
PHONE...................216 883-8025
Rob Sternfeld, *President*
Fred Sternfeld, *Vice Pres*
John Hart, *MIS Dir*
Becca Traggiai, *Technology*
▲ **EMP:** 75 **EST:** 1966
SQ FT: 100,000
SALES (est): 30.6MM
SALES (corp-wide): 16.9B **Privately Held**
WEB: www.resorg.com
SIC: 2899 2869 Chemical preparations; industrial organic chemicals
HQ: Sigma-Aldrich Corporation
  3050 Spruce St
  Saint Louis MO 63103
  314 771-5765

(G-5979)
RESILIENCE FUND III LP (PA)
25101 Chagrin Blvd (44122-5643)
PHONE...................216 292-0200
Michael Cavanaugh, *Partner*
Ki Mixon, *Partner*
Ted Laufik, *CFO*
Bassem Mansour, *Mng Member*
EMP: 12
SALES (est): 95.3MM **Privately Held**
SIC: 6799 3567 Investors; industrial furnaces & ovens

(G-5980)
RESOLUTE FP US INC
Also Called: Recycling Div
3400 Vega Ave (44113-4954)
PHONE...................216 961-3900
Rich Ryan, *Principal*
EMP: 481
SALES (corp-wide): 3.5B **Privately Held**
WEB: www.bowater.com
SIC: 2621 Paper mills
HQ: Resolute Fp Us Inc.
  5300 Cureton Ferry Rd
  Catawba SC 29704
  803 981-8000

(G-5981)
REXON COMPONENTS INC
24500 Highpoint Rd (44122-6002)
PHONE...................440 585-7086
Steve Fink, *Branch Mgr*
EMP: 17
SALES (corp-wide): 3.6MM **Privately Held**
WEB: www.rexon.com
SIC: 3674 Nuclear detectors, solid state
PA: Rexon Components, Inc.
  24500 Highpoint Rd
  Beachwood OH 44122
  216 292-7373

(G-5982)
REZMANN KAROLY
Also Called: Quality Metal Works
7216 Bessemer Ave (44127-1816)
PHONE...................216 441-4357
Karoly Rezmann, *Owner*
EMP: 3 **EST:** 1965
SQ FT: 12,000
SALES (est): 257.4K **Privately Held**
SIC: 3443 3599 3469 3446 Plate work for the metalworking trade; machine shop, jobbing & repair; metal stampings; architectural metalwork; sheet metalwork; fabricated structural metal

(G-5983)
RICHARD STEEL COMPANY INC
11110 Avon Ave (44105-4223)
P.O. Box 31516 (44131-0516)
PHONE...................216 520-6390
Richard Jereb, *President*
EMP: 9
SQ FT: 5,000
SALES (est): 1.2MM **Privately Held**
SIC: 3441 Fabricated structural metal

Cleveland - Cuyahoga County (G-5984)

(G-5984)
RICHARDS GRINDING CO INC
4914 Walworth Ave (44102-4592)
PHONE..................216 631-7675
Richard A Oliver Sr, *President*
Betty Oliver, *Corp Secy*
Deb Luber, *Vice Pres*
Jeff Yates, *Plant Mgr*
EMP: 14
SQ FT: 6,400
SALES (est): 1.4MM **Privately Held**
SIC: 3599 Machine shop, jobbing & repair; grinding castings for the trade

(G-5985)
RITE MACHINE INC
13704 Enterprise Ave (44135-5114)
PHONE..................216 267-6911
Jay Kalchoff, *President*
Adrian Kalchoff, *Corp Secy*
Dana Kalchoff, *Vice Pres*
EMP: 3 **EST:** 1943
SQ FT: 5,000
SALES (est): 386.8K **Privately Held**
SIC: 3599 Machine shop, jobbing & repair

(G-5986)
RITIME INCORPORATED
6363 York Rd Ste 104 (44130-3031)
PHONE..................330 273-3443
William E Avis, *President*
EMP: 17
SQ FT: 10,000
SALES (est): 1.2MM **Privately Held**
WEB: www.alternativesurfacegrind.com
SIC: 3599 3542 Machine shop, jobbing & repair; machine tools, metal forming type

(G-5987)
RIVER SMELTING & REF MFG CO
Also Called: River Foundry Supply
4195 Bradley Rd (44109-3779)
PHONE..................216 459-2100
William A Grodin, *President*
James A Grodin, *Vice Pres*
EMP: 25
SQ FT: 70,000
SALES (est): 4.5MM
SALES (corp-wide): 45MM **Privately Held**
WEB: www.rivershell.com
SIC: 3341 Copper smelting & refining (secondary)
PA: River Recycling Enterprises, Ltd.
4195 Bradley Rd
Cleveland OH 44109
216 459-2100

(G-5988)
RIVERSIDE DRIVES INC
Also Called: Riverside Drives Disc
4509 W 160th St (44135-2627)
P.O. Box 35166 (44135-0166)
PHONE..................216 362-1211
Bernard Dillemuth, *President*
Kathleen Dillemuth, *Corp Secy*
David Dillemuth, *Vice Pres*
Kathy Straka, *Purchasing*
Vic Pringle, *Sales Engr*
▼**EMP:** 28
SQ FT: 7,500
SALES (est): 19.8MM **Privately Held**
WEB: www.riversidedrives.com
SIC: 5063 3699 Power transmission equipment, electric; electrical equipment & supplies

(G-5989)
RIVERSIDE MFG ACQUISITION LLC
5344 Bragg Rd (44127-1274)
PHONE..................585 458-2090
Mike Hill, *President*
Gerard Shafer, *Vice Pres*
EMP: 110 **EST:** 1973
SQ FT: 120,000
SALES (est): 14.4MM **Privately Held**
SIC: 2789 Binding only: books, pamphlets, magazines, etc.; bookbinding & repairing: trade, edition, library, etc.; paper cutting; display mounting

(G-5990)
RJR SURGICAL INC
2530 Superior Ave E # 703 (44114-4230)
PHONE..................216 241-2804
John Redmond, *President*
Lisa Hower, *Vice Pres*
Mark Whiteaker, *Vice Pres*
EMP: 3
SQ FT: 4,000
SALES (est): 235.6K **Privately Held**
SIC: 3841 Surgical & medical instruments

(G-5991)
RML TOOL INC
15115 Chatfield Ave B (44111-4304)
PHONE..................216 941-1615
Rick Silvaggio, *President*
EMP: 4
SALES (est): 450K **Privately Held**
SIC: 3339 Primary nonferrous metals

(G-5992)
ROBERTS DEMAND NO 3 CORP
Also Called: Electro-Plating & Fabricating
4008 E 89th St (44105-3919)
PHONE..................216 641-0660
Les Demand, *President*
William Demand, *Vice Pres*
Don Paukert, *Shareholder*
EMP: 15 **EST:** 1939
SQ FT: 13,500
SALES: 1.7MM **Privately Held**
WEB: www.molectrics.com
SIC: 3471 Cleaning & descaling metal products; polishing, metals or formed products

(G-5993)
ROBERTS-DEMAND CORP
Also Called: Keco Plating
17401 S Miles Rd (44128-3946)
P.O. Box 1012, Burton (44021-1012)
PHONE..................216 581-1300
Rex Roberts, *President*
Brenda Roberts, *Vice Pres*
Albert Roberts, *Admin Sec*
EMP: 5 **EST:** 1946
SQ FT: 5,000
SALES (est): 430.2K **Privately Held**
SIC: 3471 Electroplating of metals or formed products; plating of metals or formed products; polishing, metals or formed products; anodizing (plating) of metals or formed products

(G-5994)
ROBERTSON MANUFACTURING CO
17917 Roseland Rd (44112-1284)
PHONE..................216 531-8222
John S Green, *President*
Sandra Essick, *Treasurer*
Shannon Catalano, *Director*
EMP: 10
SQ FT: 10,000
SALES (est): 4.3MM **Privately Held**
SIC: 3568 3566 Sprockets (power transmission equipment); gears, power transmission, except automotive

(G-5995)
ROBIN INDUSTRIES INC
Also Called: Niagara Stamping Co
4780 W 139th St (44135-5034)
PHONE..................216 267-3554
Jack Browning, *Branch Mgr*
EMP: 4
SALES (corp-wide): 81.6MM **Privately Held**
WEB: www.robin-industries.com
SIC: 3469 Metal stampings
PA: Robin Industries, Inc.
6500 Rockside Rd Ste 230
Independence OH 44131
216 631-7000

(G-5996)
ROCHLING GLASTIC COMPOSITES LP (DH)
4321 Glenridge Rd (44121-2805)
PHONE..................216 486-0100
Georg Duffner, *CEO*
Mark Digiampietro, *General Mgr*
Ludger Bartels, *Chairman*
Kevin Streussnig, *Business Mgr*
Michelle Prince, *Vice Pres*
◆ **EMP:** 200
SQ FT: 127,000
SALES (est): 51.6MM
SALES (corp-wide): 2.1B **Privately Held**
WEB: www.glastic.com
SIC: 3089 2821 3083 3644 Thermoformed finished plastic products; molding compounds, plastics; laminated plastic sheets; noncurrent-carrying wiring services
HQ: Rochling Engineering Plastics Se & Co. Kg
Rochlingstr. 1
Haren (Ems) 49733
593 470-10

(G-5997)
ROCKPORT CNSTR & MTLS INC
Also Called: Rockport Ready Mix
3092 Rockefeller Ave (44115-3612)
PHONE..................216 432-9465
Ann Nock, *President*
EMP: 25
SALES (est): 4.4MM **Privately Held**
SIC: 3273 Ready-mixed concrete

(G-5998)
ROCKWELL AUTOMATION INC
760 Beta Dr Ste A (44143-2334)
PHONE..................440 604-8410
Ron Fruh, *Branch Mgr*
EMP: 40 **Publicly Held**
SIC: 3625 Relays & industrial controls
PA: Rockwell Automation, Inc.
1201 S 2nd St
Milwaukee WI 53204

(G-5999)
ROCKWELL AUTOMATION INC
1 Allen Bradley Dr (44124-6118)
PHONE..................440 646-5000
Rich Novak, *Business Mgr*
Frank Watkins, *Business Mgr*
Edward Blakemore, *Counsel*
Joseph Rosing, *Plant Mgr*
Shelley Miller, *Project Mgr*
EMP: 99
SQ FT: 156,653 **Publicly Held**
SIC: 3625 Electric controls & control accessories, industrial
PA: Rockwell Automation, Inc.
1201 S 2nd St
Milwaukee WI 53204

(G-6000)
ROCKWELL AUTOMATION INC
6680 Beta Dr (44143-2352)
PHONE..................440 646-7900
Wayne Foster, *Engineer*
Walter Fuchs, *Engineer*
Maureen Garnett, *Engineer*
Chris Sethman, *Marketing Staff*
Michael Bless, *Branch Mgr*
EMP: 10 **Publicly Held**
SIC: 3625 Relays & industrial controls
PA: Rockwell Automation, Inc.
1201 S 2nd St
Milwaukee WI 53204

(G-6001)
ROL- FAB INC
4949 Johnston Pkwy (44128-3201)
PHONE..................216 662-2500
Robert Hansen, *President*
▼**EMP:** 32
SQ FT: 70,000
SALES: 4.8MM **Privately Held**
WEB: www.rol-fab.com
SIC: 3441 Building components, structural steel

(G-6002)
ROSE METAL INDUSTRIES LLC (PA)
1536 E 43rd St (44103-2310)
PHONE..................216 881-3355
Robert B Rose, *Mng Member*
EMP: 11 **EST:** 1904
SQ FT: 10,000
SALES (est): 5.2MM **Privately Held**
WEB: www.rosemetal.com
SIC: 3441 7692 3462 3443 Fabricated structural metal; welding repair; iron & steel forgings; ladles, metal plate

(G-6003)
ROSE METAL INDUSTRIES LLC
1155 Marquette St (44114-3919)
PHONE..................216 426-8615
Robert Rose, *President*
EMP: 20
SALES (corp-wide): 5.6MM **Privately Held**
WEB: www.rosemetal.com
SIC: 3441 Fabricated structural metal
PA: Rose Metal Industries, Llc
1536 E 43rd St
Cleveland OH 44103
216 881-3355

(G-6004)
ROSENFELD JEWELRY INC
5668 Mayfield Rd (44124-2916)
PHONE..................440 446-0099
Henry Rosenfeld, *President*
Ruth Rosenfeld, *Vice Pres*
Arthur Rosenfeld, *Treasurer*
EMP: 8
SQ FT: 1,350
SALES (est): 1.1MM **Privately Held**
WEB: www.rosenfeld-jewelry.com
SIC: 3911 5944 Jewelry, precious metal; jewelry stores

(G-6005)
ROSSBOROUGH SUPPLY CO
3425 Service Rd (44111-2421)
PHONE..................216 941-6115
EMP: 4
SALES (est): 177.3K **Privately Held**
SIC: 3369 Machinery castings, nonferrous: ex. alum., copper, die, etc.

(G-6006)
ROTECH PRODUCTS INCORPORATED
16901 Albers Ave (44111-4241)
PHONE..................216 476-3722
Michael Maloney, *Principal*
Mary Maloney, *Corp Secy*
EMP: 3 **EST:** 1980
SQ FT: 2,000
SALES: 500K **Privately Held**
SIC: 5169 2899 Industrial chemicals; plating compounds; metal treating compounds

(G-6007)
ROTO-DIE INC
21751 Tungsten Rd (44117-1116)
P.O. Box 17503 (44117-0503)
PHONE..................216 531-4800
Gary Medved, *President*
EMP: 5
SQ FT: 7,500
SALES (est): 43K **Privately Held**
WEB: www.roto-die.com
SIC: 3545 Tools & accessories for machine tools

(G-6008)
ROTOPOLYMERS
26210 Emery Rd Ste 202 (44128-5770)
PHONE..................216 645-0333
Jose A Gomez Godoy, *Principal*
EMP: 3 **EST:** 2016
SALES (est): 141.3K **Privately Held**
SIC: 2821 Plastics materials & resins

(G-6009)
ROYAL ACME CORPORATION (PA)
Also Called: Adsetting Service
3110 Payne Ave (44114-4504)
PHONE..................216 241-1477
Theodore D Cutts, *President*
Sandy Wengstrom, *Office Mgr*
▲**EMP:** 30 **EST:** 1932
SALES (est): 3.4MM **Privately Held**
WEB: www.royalacme.com
SIC: 3953 2791 3993 3053 Embossing seals & hand stamps; figures (marking devices), metal; stencils, painting & marking; seal presses, notary & hand; typesetting; signs & advertising specialties; gaskets, packing & sealing devices

GEOGRAPHIC SECTION
Cleveland - Cuyahoga County (G-6035)

(G-6010)
ROYAL CABINET DESIGN CO INC
15800 Commerce Park Dr (44142-2019)
PHONE 216 267-5330
Joseph Estephan, *President*
Georgette Estephan, *Corp Secy*
Elie Estephan, *Vice Pres*
EMP: 12
SALES (est): 2MM **Privately Held**
SIC: 2434 Wood kitchen cabinets

(G-6011)
ROYAL GATEAU
4276 Pearl Rd (44109-4235)
P.O. Box 609225 (44109-0225)
PHONE 216 351-3553
Michel Kahwagi, *Owner*
EMP: 3
SQ FT: 1,500
SALES (est): 186.3K **Privately Held**
SIC: 2051 Pastries, e.g. danish: except frozen

(G-6012)
ROYAL ICE CREAM CO
Also Called: Pierre's Ice Cream Company
6200 Euclid Ave (44103-3724)
PHONE 216 432-1144
Rochelle Roth, *President*
Lawrence Bloomenthal, *Principal*
Helen Dorman, *Principal*
Jerome Ellerin, *Principal*
Frank Elliott, *Vice Pres*
◆ **EMP:** 85 **EST:** 1932
SQ FT: 16,500
SALES (est): 32MM **Privately Held**
WEB: www.pierres.com
SIC: 2024 Ice cream, bulk

(G-6013)
ROYAL POWDER CORPORATION
4800 Briar Rd (44135-5040)
PHONE 216 898-0074
Kirit Patel, *President*
EMP: 6
SQ FT: 1,300
SALES (est): 1.3MM **Privately Held**
SIC: 3399 Metal powders, pastes & flakes

(G-6014)
RSB SPINE LLC
2530 Superior Ave E # 703 (44114-4200)
PHONE 216 241-2804
James Moran, *President*
John Redmond, *Mng Member*
Lisa Hower, *Manager*
EMP: 13
SALES (est): 1.8MM **Privately Held**
WEB: www.rsbspine.com
SIC: 3841 Surgical instruments & apparatus

(G-6015)
RUBBERSET COMPANY
101 W Prospect Ave (44115-1093)
PHONE 800 345-4939
EMP: 3
SALES (est): 232.5K **Privately Held**
SIC: 3563 Robots for industrial spraying, painting, etc.

(G-6016)
RUDYS STRUDEL SHOP
Also Called: Rudy's Strudel & Bakery
5580 Ridge Rd (44129-2396)
PHONE 440 886-4430
Eugenia Polatajko, *Owner*
EMP: 6 **EST:** 1948
SQ FT: 7,900
SALES (est): 300K **Privately Held**
SIC: 2051 2052 Bakery: wholesale or wholesale/retail combined; cookies & crackers

(G-6017)
RULTRACT INC
5663 Brecksville Rd (44131-1510)
PHONE 216 524-2990
Janice Schilt, *President*
Dr Reiss Beg, *Vice Pres*
Phillip M Rullo Jr, *Sales Staff*
EMP: 5
SQ FT: 20,000
SALES (est): 1.1MM **Privately Held**
WEB: www.rultract.net
SIC: 5047 3841 Instruments, surgical & medical; surgical instruments & apparatus

(G-6018)
S & H INDUSTRIES INC
Also Called: Keysco Tools
5200 Richmond Rd (44146-1387)
PHONE 216 831-0550
John Turk, *President*
Edward Clancy, *General Mgr*
Steven Perney, *Treasurer*
▲ **EMP:** 30 **EST:** 1952
SQ FT: 23,000
SALES: 5MM **Privately Held**
WEB: www.shindustries.com
SIC: 3423 Mechanics' hand tools; jacks: lifting, screw or ratchet (hand tools)
PA: S & H Industries Inc
5200 Richmond Rd
Bedford OH 44146
216 831-0550

(G-6019)
S & H INDUSTRIES INC
14577 Lorain Ave (44111-3156)
PHONE 216 831-0550
Sharon M Conrad, *Principal*
▲ **EMP:** 7 **EST:** 2010
SALES (est): 999.8K **Privately Held**
SIC: 3999 Manufacturing industries

(G-6020)
S & N ENGINEERING SVCS CORP
Also Called: S & N Engineering and Supply
2901 Henninger Rd (44109-3324)
PHONE 216 433-1700
Nancy Novinc, *President*
EMP: 4
SQ FT: 2,400
SALES (est): 556.6K **Privately Held**
SIC: 5085 3599 Industrial supplies; machine & other job shop work

(G-6021)
S A LANGMACK COMPANY
Also Called: Niagara Custombilt Mfg
13400 Glenside Rd (44110-3528)
PHONE 216 541-0500
Chris Langmack, *President*
John C Langmack, *Principal*
Virginia Langmack, *Corp Secy*
Clark B Langmack, *Vice Pres*
EMP: 15
SQ FT: 25,000
SALES (est): 3.9MM **Privately Held**
WEB: www.niagaracustom.com
SIC: 3565 3569 Bottle washing & sterilizing machines; filters, general line: industrial

(G-6022)
S L M INC
3148 W 32nd St Ste 3 (44109-1549)
PHONE 216 651-0666
Fax: 216 651-0811
EMP: 6
SALES (est): 456.7K **Privately Held**
SIC: 1711 3444 Plumbing/Heating/Air Cond Contractor Mfg Sheet Metalwork

(G-6023)
S R P M INC
30300 Bruce Industrial Pk (44139-3921)
PHONE 440 248-8440
Mark Steinmeyer, *President*
Craig Steinmeyer, *Vice Pres*
Gary Rivett, *Mfg Mgr*
Thomas Jackson, *Engineer*
EMP: 30
SQ FT: 15,000
SALES (est): 6.5MM **Privately Held**
WEB: www.srpm.com
SIC: 3599 Custom machinery

(G-6024)
SAFE SYSTEMS INC
Also Called: Ramzi
5401 Brookpark Rd (44129-1201)
PHONE 216 661-1166
Christy Farhat, *President*
Kamal Farhat, *Treasurer*
EMP: 3

(G-6025)
SAGITTA INC
1048 Literary Rd (44113-4443)
P.O. Box 381731, Miami FL (33238-1731)
PHONE 440 570-5393
David Purpera, *CEO*
Henry Butler, *Senior VP*
Steve Rawlings, *Vice Pres*
EMP: 5
SALES: 100K **Privately Held**
SIC: 8742 3841 Marketing consulting services; surgical & medical instruments

(G-6026)
SAINT CTHERINES METALWORKS INC (PA)
1985 W 68th St (44102-3906)
PHONE 216 409-0576
Van Peplin, *President*
EMP: 8 **EST:** 2001
SQ FT: 20,000
SALES: 500K **Privately Held**
WEB: www.scmetalworking.com
SIC: 2842 8661 Metal polish; religious organizations

(G-6027)
SAINT-GOBAIN HYCOMP LLC
17960 Englewood Dr (44130-3438)
PHONE 440 234-2002
Andrew Boisvert, *COO*
Bill Hanna, *Mfg Mgr*
Todd Devorace, *Controller*
Brian Bosworth, *Sales Mgr*
Patrick McSweeney, *Sales Staff*
EMP: 120
SQ FT: 48,600
SALES (est): 23.3MM
SALES (corp-wide): 215.9MM **Privately Held**
WEB: www.hycompinc.com
SIC: 3089 Injection molding of plastics
HQ: Saint Gobain Performance Plastics France
34 Rue Du Moulin Des Aulnaies
Charny Oree De Puisaye 89120
386 637-878

(G-6028)
SAMSCO CORP
837 E 79th St (44103-1807)
PHONE 216 400-8207
Walter F Senney, *President*
Jason Verderber, *CFO*
EMP: 10
SQ FT: 100,000
SALES: 4MM **Privately Held**
SIC: 5084 3589 Pollution control equipment, water (environmental); water treatment equipment, industrial

(G-6029)
SAMSEL ROPE & MARINE SUPPLY CO (PA)
Also Called: Samsel Supply Company
1285 Old River Rd Uppr (44113-1279)
PHONE 216 241-0333
Kathleen A Petrick, *President*
Larry E Nauth, *Principal*
Grace F Wilcox, *Principal*
Rosemary Woidke, *Principal*
F Michael Samsel, *Exec VP*
▲ **EMP:** 33
SQ FT: 100,000
SALES (est): 4.4MM **Privately Held**
WEB: www.samselsupply.com
SIC: 2394 5051 4959 5085 Canvas & related products; rope, wire (not insulated); miscellaneous nonferrous products; environmental cleanup services; industrial supplies; industrial tools; manufactured hardware (general); narrow fabric mills

(G-6030)
SANSEI SHOWA CO LTD
31000 Bainbridge Rd (44139-2227)
PHONE 440 248-4440
Michihiko Kobayashi, *President*
Paul Biddlestone, *Vice Pres*
John Leitz, *Engineer*
Nancy Harp, *Human Res Dir*
EMP: 21
SQ FT: 12,500
SALES (est): 3.5MM
SALES (corp-wide): 59.4MM **Privately Held**
WEB: www.sanseishowa.com
SIC: 3823 Industrial instrmnts msrmnt display/control process variable
PA: Sansei Denshi Co., Ltd.
1-11-8, Iwadokita
Komae TKY 201-0
334 894-131

(G-6031)
SARCOKINETICS LLC
11000 Cedar Ave Ste 265 (44106-3021)
PHONE 414 477-9585
Julian Stelzer,
Mark Pelletier,
EMP: 3
SALES (est): 193.8K **Privately Held**
SIC: 2835 In vitro & in vivo diagnostic substances

(G-6032)
SARK TECHNOLOGIES LLC
Also Called: Super Inn.com
2270 Tudor Dr (44106-3210)
PHONE 216 932-3171
Sagi Shilo, *Mng Member*
Kirk Dietrich,
Richard Dietrich,
Aviv Sack,
EMP: 4
SALES: 350K **Privately Held**
WEB: www.sarktech.com
SIC: 7372 Utility computer software

(G-6033)
SCHUMANN ENTERPRISES INC
Also Called: E.C. Kitzel & Sons
12340 Plaza Dr (44130-1043)
PHONE 216 267-6850
Thomas Schumann, *President*
Meredith Schumann, *Admin Sec*
EMP: 30 **EST:** 1927
SALES (est): 5MM **Privately Held**
WEB: www.kitzel.com
SIC: 3545 3291 Diamond cutting tools for turning, boring, burnishing, etc.; abrasive wheels & grindstones, not artificial; diamond powder

(G-6034)
SCHWEIZER DIPPLE INC
7227 Division St (44146-5405)
PHONE 440 786-8090
Michael J Kelley, *President*
Dennis Clark, *Exec VP*
Dennis J Clark, *Vice Pres*
James G Dwyer, *Vice Pres*
Peter A McGrogan, *Vice Pres*
EMP: 55
SQ FT: 27,000
SALES (est): 11.7MM
SALES (corp-wide): 38.4MM **Privately Held**
WEB: www.schweizer-dipple.com
SIC: 1711 3496 3444 3443 Mechanical contractor; process piping contractor; plumbing contractors; warm air heating & air conditioning contractor; miscellaneous fabricated wire products; sheet metalwork; fabricated plate work (boiler shop)
PA: Kelley Steel Erectors, Inc.
7220 Division St
Cleveland OH 44146
440 232-1573

(G-6035)
SCOTT FETZER COMPANY
Adalet
4801 W 150th St (44135-3301)
PHONE 216 267-9000
Fred Lemke, *Sales Staff*
EMP: 150
SALES (corp-wide): 225.3B **Publicly Held**
WEB: www.adalet.com
SIC: 5063 3469 3357 3613 Wire & cable; metal stampings; nonferrous wiredrawing & insulating; control panels, electric; metal housings, enclosures, casings & other containers

Cleveland - Cuyahoga County (G-6036)   GEOGRAPHIC SECTION

HQ: The Scott Fetzer Company
28800 Clemens Rd
Westlake OH 44145
440 892-3000

(G-6036)
SCOTT FETZER COMPANY
Kirby Vacuum Cleaner
1920 W 114th St (44102-2391)
PHONE..................216 228-2403
Robert McBride, *President*
EMP: 350
SALES (corp-wide): 225.3B **Publicly Held**
SIC: 3635 Household vacuum cleaners
HQ: The Scott Fetzer Company
28800 Clemens Rd
Westlake OH 44145
440 892-3000

(G-6037)
SCOTT FETZER COMPANY
Cleveland Wood Products
3881 W 150th St (44111-5806)
PHONE..................216 252-1190
Ryan Pereira, *General Mgr*
EMP: 45
SQ FT: 15,280
SALES (corp-wide): 225.3B **Publicly Held**
SIC: 3635 Household vacuum cleaners
HQ: The Scott Fetzer Company
28800 Clemens Rd
Westlake OH 44145
440 892-3000

(G-6038)
SCOTT FETZER COMPANY
875 Bassett Rd (44145-1142)
PHONE..................440 871-2160
Byron Crampton, *Manager*
EMP: 450
SALES (corp-wide): 225.3B **Publicly Held**
SIC: 3635 Household vacuum cleaners
HQ: The Scott Fetzer Company
28800 Clemens Rd
Westlake OH 44145
440 892-3000

(G-6039)
SCOTT FETZER COMPANY
Meriam Process Technologies
10920 Madison Ave (44102-2526)
PHONE..................216 281-1100
Bryan Telepak, *General Mgr*
EMP: 90
SQ FT: 30,768
SALES (corp-wide): 225.3B **Publicly Held**
SIC: 3635 Household vacuum cleaners
HQ: The Scott Fetzer Company
28800 Clemens Rd
Westlake OH 44145
440 892-3000

(G-6040)
SCOTT FETZER COMPANY
Also Called: Kirby Customer Service Center
4750 W 160th St (44135-2632)
PHONE..................216 433-7797
Lou Verarvi, *Manager*
EMP: 60
SALES (corp-wide): 225.3B **Publicly Held**
SIC: 3635 Household vacuum cleaners
HQ: The Scott Fetzer Company
28800 Clemens Rd
Westlake OH 44145
440 892-3000

(G-6041)
SCOTTCARE CORPORATION (DH)
4791 W 150th St (44135-3301)
PHONE..................216 362-0550
Deepak Malhotra, *General Mgr*
EMP: 31
SALES (est): 5.3MM
SALES (corp-wide): 225.3B **Publicly Held**
SIC: 3841 Surgical instruments & apparatus

HQ: The Scott Fetzer Company
28800 Clemens Rd
Westlake OH 44145
440 892-3000

(G-6042)
SEAFORTH MINERAL & ORE CO INC (PA)
3690 Orange Pl Ste 495 (44122-4465)
PHONE..................216 292-5820
Gary McClurg, *Ch of Bd*
James McClurg, *President*
Vince Opaskar, *Technical Mgr*
James Temple, *CFO*
Mary Ellen Sennet, *Manager*
▲ EMP: 15
SQ FT: 3,500
SALES (est): 22.9MM **Privately Held**
WEB: www.seaforthinc.com
SIC: 5052 3295 Nonmetallic minerals & concentrate; minerals, ground or treated

(G-6043)
SECURE MEDICAL MAIL LLC
3257 Mayfield Rd Apt 21 (44118-1864)
PHONE..................216 269-1971
Sachin Doshi, *Co-Owner*
Ravi Patel,
Vipul Sheth,
EMP: 3
SALES (est): 152.3K **Privately Held**
SIC: 7372 Application computer software

(G-6044)
SENECA LABEL INC
13821 Progress Pkwy (44133-4303)
PHONE..................440 237-1600
Michael Hoopingarner, *President*
Terry Richissin, *Prdtn Mgr*
Kyle D Hoopingarner, *Sales Mgr*
Karen Stahlnecker, *Supervisor*
Diane Tawney, *Director*
EMP: 35
SQ FT: 31,000
SALES (est): 5.6MM **Privately Held**
WEB: www.senecalabel.com
SIC: 2759 Flexographic printing

(G-6045)
SERVICE STATION EQUIPMENT CO (PA)
Also Called: Sseco Solutions
1294 E 55th St (44103-1029)
PHONE..................216 431-6100
David Chrien, *President*
Diana Chrien, *Vice Pres*
Donna Russell,
EMP: 10 EST: 1960
SQ FT: 45,000
SALES: 3.5MM **Privately Held**
WEB: www.sseqco.com
SIC: 5087 3559 Carwash equipment & supplies; petroleum refinery equipment

(G-6046)
SHAKER VALLEY FOODS INC
3304 W 67th Pl (44102-5243)
PHONE..................216 961-8600
Dean Comber, *President*
Jeff Koutris, *Purch Mgr*
Jim Comber, *Technology*
EMP: 40
SQ FT: 30,000
SALES (est): 21.6MM **Privately Held**
WEB: www.shakervalleyfoods.com
SIC: 5141 2011 Food brokers; meat packing plants

(G-6047)
SHALIX INC
10910 Briggs Rd (44111-5332)
PHONE..................216 941-3546
David Schultheis, *President*
EMP: 10 EST: 1996
SALES (est): 1.1MM **Privately Held**
WEB: www.shalix.com
SIC: 3544 Special dies, tools, jigs & fixtures

(G-6048)
SHARP TOOL SERVICE INC
4735 W 150th St Frnt B (44135-3350)
PHONE..................330 273-4144
Richard Schirripa, *CEO*
Jeff Schirripa, *President*
Laura Schirripa, *Corp Secy*

Joe Schirripa, *Shareholder*
Rick Schirripa, *Shareholder*
EMP: 25
SQ FT: 22,000
SALES (est): 4.2MM **Privately Held**
WEB: www.sharptoolservice.com
SIC: 3545 Cutting tools for machine tools

(G-6049)
SHEAR SERVICE INC
Also Called: Shear Service, The
3175 E 81st St (44104-4386)
PHONE..................216 341-2700
Kim Curtis, *President*
EMP: 8
SALES: 370K **Privately Held**
SIC: 7389 3312 Metal slitting & shearing; blast furnaces & steel mills

(G-6050)
SHEFFIELD BRONZE PAINT CORP
17814 S Waterloo Rd (44119-3295)
P.O. Box 19206 (44119-0206)
PHONE..................216 481-8330
Mel Hart, *President*
Morton Gross, *Chairman*
EMP: 20 EST: 1925
SQ FT: 100,000
SALES (est): 3.1MM **Privately Held**
WEB: www.sheffieldbronze.com
SIC: 2851 Paints & paint additives

(G-6051)
SHELLY LIQUID DIVISION
101 Mahoning Ave (44113-2500)
PHONE..................216 781-9264
Thomas Hill, *Principal*
EMP: 6
SALES (est): 332K **Privately Held**
SIC: 1499 Asphalt mining & bituminous stone quarrying

(G-6052)
SHERIDAN WOODWORKS INC
17801 S Miles Rd (44128-4249)
PHONE..................216 663-9333
Edward Sheridan, *President*
EMP: 11
SQ FT: 16,000
SALES (est): 1.8MM **Privately Held**
WEB: www.sheridanwoodworks.com
SIC: 2431 1751 Millwork; cabinet building & installation

(G-6053)
SHERWIN-WILLIAMS COMPANY (PA)
101 W Prospect Ave # 1020 (44115-1027)
PHONE..................216 566-2000
John G Morikis, *Ch of Bd*
Aaron M Erter, *President*
Peter J Ippolito, *President*
David B Sewell, *President*
Justin Jense, *District Mgr*
EMP: 1200
SALES: 17.5B **Publicly Held**
WEB: www.sherwin.com
SIC: 2851 5231 Paints & allied products; paint & painting supplies; wallcoverings

(G-6054)
SHERWIN-WILLIAMS COMPANY
5020 Turney Rd (44125-2503)
PHONE..................216 662-3300
Shannon Zipf, *Manager*
EMP: 4
SALES (corp-wide): 17.5B **Publicly Held**
WEB: www.sherwin.com
SIC: 5231 2851 Paint; wallcoverings; paints & allied products; varnishes; lacquer: bases, dopes, thinner
PA: The Sherwin-Williams Company
101 W Prospect Ave # 1020
Cleveland OH 44115
216 566-2000

(G-6055)
SHERWIN-WILLIAMS MFG CO
101 W Prospect Ave # 1020 (44115-1027)
PHONE..................216 566-2000
John G Morikis, *President*
Joel D Baxter, *Vice Pres*
David J Biondo, *Vice Pres*
Lawrence J Boron, *Vice Pres*
Mary L Garceau, *Vice Pres*

EMP: 10
SALES (est): 559.6K
SALES (corp-wide): 17.5B **Publicly Held**
SIC: 2851 5198 Paints & allied products; paint or varnish thinner
PA: The Sherwin-Williams Company
101 W Prospect Ave # 1020
Cleveland OH 44115
216 566-2000

(G-6056)
SHERWN-WLLAMS AUTO FNSHES CORP (HQ)
4440 Warrensville Ctr Rd (44128-2837)
PHONE..................216 332-8330
Christopher Connor, *CEO*
Thomas Havlitzel, *President*
Terrence A Kacik, *Research*
Karen Webb, *Research*
Willie Harris, *Human Resources*
◆ EMP: 129
SALES (est): 262.8MM
SALES (corp-wide): 17.5B **Publicly Held**
WEB: www.sherwin-automotive.com
SIC: 5231 2851 Paint; paints & allied products
PA: The Sherwin-Williams Company
101 W Prospect Ave # 1020
Cleveland OH 44115
216 566-2000

(G-6057)
SHERWOOD VALVE LLC
7900 Hub Pkwy (44125-5713)
PHONE..................216 264-5023
Richard Gravagna, *Branch Mgr*
Tom Hensley, *Manager*
EMP: 22
SALES (corp-wide): 2.5B **Publicly Held**
SIC: 3491 Industrial valves
HQ: Sherwood Valve Llc
100 Business Center Dr # 400
Pittsburgh PA 15205

(G-6058)
SHERWOOD VALVE LLC
7900 Hub Pkwy (44125-5713)
PHONE..................216 264-5028
Tom Hensley, *Manager*
EMP: 61
SALES (corp-wide): 2.5B **Publicly Held**
SIC: 3491 Automatic regulating & control valves; compressed gas cylinder valves; gas valves & parts, industrial; pressure valves & regulators, industrial
HQ: Sherwood Valve Llc
100 Business Center Dr # 400
Pittsburgh PA 15205

(G-6059)
SHIPPING ROOM PRODUCTS INC
19400 Saint Clair Ave (44117-1006)
P.O. Box 17120 (44117-0120)
PHONE..................216 531-4422
Doug Painting, *President*
EMP: 4
SQ FT: 7,500
SALES (est): 612.3K **Privately Held**
SIC: 3499 Strapping, metal

(G-6060)
SHORELINE MACHINE PRODUCTS CO (PA)
19301 Saint Clair Ave (44117-1087)
PHONE..................216 481-8033
Robert Arth, *President*
John J Ewers, *Principal*
Richard Kaufman, *Principal*
Joseph Frank Tekavic, *Principal*
Larry Arth, *Vice Pres*
EMP: 11 EST: 1967
SQ FT: 15,000
SALES (est): 3MM **Privately Held**
SIC: 3599 Machine shop, jobbing & repair

(G-6061)
SIETINS PLASTICS INC
Also Called: Sietins Precision
380 Solon Rd Ste 4 (44146-3809)
PHONE..................440 232-8515
Rhonda Caldwell, *President*
Hugh Caldwell, *Vice Pres*
EMP: 4
SQ FT: 3,960

SALES: 200K **Privately Held**
SIC: 3599 Machine shop, jobbing & repair

(G-6062)
SIFCO APPLIED SRFC CNCEPTS LLC (PA)
Also Called: Sifco ASC
5708 E Schaaf Rd (44131-1308)
PHONE..............................216 524-0099
Danijela Milosevic, *Research*
Alli Stockdale, *Mktg Coord*
Charles Allen, *Mng Member*
Kristi Baker, *Manager*
Sherri Beedles, *Manager*
EMP: 34 **EST:** 2012
SQ FT: 18,000
SALES (est): 7.6MM **Privately Held**
SIC: 3471 Electroplating & plating

(G-6063)
SIFCO INDUSTRIES INC (PA)
970 E 64th St (44103-1694)
PHONE..............................216 881-8600
Norman E Wells Jr, *Ch of Bd*
Peter W Knapper, *President*
Michael Candow, *Plant Mgr*
Thomas R Kubera, *CFO*
Robert Saintz, *Manager*
◆ **EMP:** 268 **EST:** 1916
SQ FT: 240,000
SALES: 111.2MM **Publicly Held**
WEB: www.sifco.com
SIC: 3724 3462 3471 Aircraft engines & engine parts; aircraft forgings, ferrous; anodizing (plating) of metals or formed products

(G-6064)
SIGN A RAMA INC
Also Called: Sign-A-Rama
731 Beta Dr Ste D (44143-2358)
P.O. Box 24272 (44124-0272)
PHONE..............................440 442-5002
Victor Baskins, *Principal*
EMP: 3
SALES (est): 228K **Privately Held**
SIC: 3993 Signs & advertising specialties

(G-6065)
SIGNATURE SIGN CO INC
1776 E 43rd St (44103-2314)
PHONE..............................216 426-1234
Bruce Farkas, *President*
EMP: 15
SQ FT: 10,000
SALES (est): 1MM **Privately Held**
SIC: 1799 2499 Sign installation & maintenance; signboards, wood

(G-6066)
SINGLETON CORPORATION
3280 W 67th Pl (44102-5241)
PHONE..............................216 651-7800
Raymund Singleton, *President*
Eric Singleton, *Vice Pres*
Laura Singleton, *Treasurer*
Carol Singleton, *Admin Sec*
▼ **EMP:** 17 **EST:** 1947
SQ FT: 30,000
SALES (est): 4.6MM **Privately Held**
WEB: www.singletoncorp.com
SIC: 3559 5169 Anodizing equipment; electroplating machinery & equipment; anti-corrosion products

(G-6067)
SINICO MTM US INC
8001 Sweet Valley Dr # 6 (44125-4218)
PHONE..............................216 264-8344
Marco Barban, *President*
EMP: 7
SALES (est): 585.8K **Privately Held**
SIC: 3541 Machine tools, metal cutting type

(G-6068)
SKF USA INC
Also Called: Machined Seals
670 Alpha Dr (44143-2123)
PHONE..............................800 589-5563
Ajay Naik, *General Mgr*
Jim Dwyer, *Principal*
Fabrice Drommi, *Project Mgr*
Jason Mais, *Project Mgr*
Domenico Bosco, *Engineer*
▲ **EMP:** 12
SQ FT: 12,000
SALES (est): 2.1MM
SALES (corp-wide): 9.2B **Privately Held**
WEB: www.ecosealtech.com
SIC: 3053 Gaskets & sealing devices
HQ: Skf Usa Inc.
890 Forty Foot Rd
Lansdale PA 19446
267 436-6000

(G-6069)
SKINNER MACHINING CO
23574 Saint Clair Ave (44117-2513)
PHONE..............................216 486-6636
Walter B Harwood, *President*
EMP: 8
SALES (est): 1.3MM
SALES (corp-wide): 2.2MM **Privately Held**
SIC: 3599 Electrical discharge machining (EDM)
PA: J W Harwood Co
18001 Roseland Rd
Cleveland OH 44112
216 531-6230

(G-6070)
SKYBRYTE COMPANY INC
3125 Perkins Ave (44114-4627)
PHONE..............................216 771-1590
Cecil Stanley, *President*
Terry Wise, *Vice Pres*
EMP: 7 **EST:** 1915
SQ FT: 7,500
SALES: 1MM **Privately Held**
SIC: 2842 Rust removers

(G-6071)
SMART BUSINESS NETWORK INC (PA)
Also Called: Smart Business Magazine
835 Sharon Dr Ste 200 (44145-7703)
PHONE..............................440 250-7000
Fred Koury, *CEO*
David W Fazekas, *Vice Pres*
EMP: 37
SQ FT: 10,000
SALES (est): 6.7MM **Privately Held**
SIC: 2711 Newspapers: publishing only, not printed on site

(G-6072)
SMART SONIC CORPORATION
837 E 79th St (44103-1807)
PHONE..............................818 610-7900
William C Schreiber, *President*
EMP: 8
SQ FT: 4,400
SALES (est): 1.7MM **Privately Held**
WEB: www.smartsonic.com
SIC: 3699 2842 3589 Cleaning equipment, ultrasonic, except medical & dental; specialty cleaning, polishes & sanitation goods; sewage & water treatment equipment

(G-6073)
SMEDLEYS BAR AND GRILL
17004 Lorain Ave (44111-5513)
PHONE..............................216 941-0124
Sean Mettler, *Principal*
EMP: 4
SALES (est): 321.3K **Privately Held**
SIC: 2085 Distilled & blended liquors

(G-6074)
SMOKEHEAL INC
5247 Wilson Mills Rd # 421 (44143-3016)
PHONE..............................216 255-5119
Yuriy Krasnov, *President*
EMP: 3 **EST:** 2015
SALES (est): 149K **Privately Held**
SIC: 3911 8732 Cigar & cigarette accessories; business research service

(G-6075)
SNAP RITE MANUFACTURING INC
14300 Darley Ave (44110-2172)
PHONE..............................910 897-4080
Bill Gray, *Branch Mgr*
Valeria Nunez, *Admin Asst*
EMP: 28
SALES (corp-wide): 18MM **Privately Held**
SIC: 3585 Air conditioning equipment, complete
PA: Snap Rite Manufacturing, Inc.
232 N Ida St
Coats NC 27521
910 897-4080

(G-6076)
SNYDER INTL BREWING GROUP LLC (PA)
Also Called: Sibg
1940 E 6th St Ste 200 (44114-2239)
PHONE..............................216 619-7424
Dave Snyder, *Partner*
Christopher Livingston, *Partner*
EMP: 25
SALES (est): 10.2MM **Privately Held**
SIC: 2082 Beer (alcoholic beverage)

(G-6077)
SOFTWARE AUTHORITY INC
6001 W Creek Rd (44131-2127)
PHONE..............................216 236-0200
George Gates, *President*
Daniel Bays, *President*
Jeff Gates, *Vice Pres*
EMP: 3
SALES (est): 197.3K **Privately Held**
WEB: www.softwareauthority.com
SIC: 7372 Application computer software

(G-6078)
SOLON GLASS CENTER INC
Also Called: Solon Glass Ctr
33001 Station St (44139-2935)
PHONE..............................440 248-5018
Roy Kucia, *President*
EMP: 10
SALES (est): 1.4MM **Privately Held**
WEB: www.solonglasscenter.com
SIC: 1793 3231 Glass & glazing work; products of purchased glass

(G-6079)
SONOGAGE INC
26650 Rnohance Pkwy Ste 3 (44128)
PHONE..............................216 464-1119
Alex Dybbs, *President*
EMP: 10
SALES (est): 1.8MM **Privately Held**
WEB: www.sonogage.com
SIC: 3841 Diagnostic apparatus, medical

(G-6080)
SOUNDWICH INC (PA)
881 Wayside Rd (44110-2961)
PHONE..............................216 486-2666
Perry Peck, *CEO*
Kevin Cleary, *President*
J Patrick Morris, *Principal*
Steve Tomoba, *Vice Pres*
Michael Ortman, *Buyer*
EMP: 80
SQ FT: 46,974
SALES (est): 31.4MM **Privately Held**
WEB: www.soundwich.com
SIC: 3714 Motor vehicle engines & parts

(G-6081)
SOUTH END PRINTING CO
3558 E 80th St (44105-1522)
P.O. Box 605593 (44105-0593)
PHONE..............................216 341-0669
Anthony D Dardy, *Owner*
Pat Dardy, *Co-Owner*
EMP: 3 **EST:** 1968
SQ FT: 2,400
SALES (est): 330.9K **Privately Held**
SIC: 2752 2796 2759 2791 Commercial printing, offset; lithographic plates, positives or negatives; letterpress printing; typesetting

(G-6082)
SP MOUNT PRINTING COMPANY
1306 E 55th St (44103-1302)
PHONE..............................216 881-3316
Gerald Mc Gill Sr, *Ch of Bd*
Scott C Mc Gill, *President*
Gerald McGill Jr, *Vice Pres*
Ron Reebel, *Opers Mgr*
Jerry McGill, *Sales Executive*
EMP: 25 **EST:** 1867
SQ FT: 45,000
SALES (est): 3.6MM **Privately Held**
WEB: www.spmount.com
SIC: 2752 Color lithography

(G-6083)
SPARKS BELTING COMPANY INC
4653 Spring Rd (44131-1078)
PHONE..............................216 398-7774
Andy Balog, *Regional Mgr*
EMP: 6
SQ FT: 13,800
SALES (corp-wide): 541.6MM **Privately Held**
SIC: 3535 Conveyors & conveying equipment
HQ: Sparks Belting Company, Inc.
3800 Stahl Dr Se
Grand Rapids MI 49546

(G-6084)
SPECIALTY GAS PUBLISHING INC
Also Called: Specialty Gas Report
12550 Lake Ave Apt 1312 (44107-1570)
PHONE..............................216 226-3796
Henry Grieco, *Owner*
Mike Vasilakes, *Vice Pres*
EMP: 3
SALES: 35K **Privately Held**
WEB: www.specgasreport.com
SIC: 2741 Miscellaneous publishing

(G-6085)
SPERZEL INC
Also Called: Sperco
15728 Industrial Pkwy (44135-3318)
PHONE..............................216 281-6868
Ronald Sperzel, *Vice Pres*
EMP: 20 **EST:** 1951
SQ FT: 5,000
SALES: 750K **Privately Held**
WEB: www.sperzel.com
SIC: 3931 String instruments & parts

(G-6086)
SPORTS CARE PRODUCTS INC
Also Called: Chemical Systems
4310 Cranwood Pkwy (44128-4002)
PHONE..............................216 663-8110
David Komocki, *Vice Pres*
EMP: 4
SALES (est): 623.2K **Privately Held**
WEB: www.chemicalsys.com
SIC: 2899 2911 Rifle bore cleaning compounds; oils, lubricating

(G-6087)
SPRINGCO METAL COATINGS INC (PA)
12500 Elmwood Ave (44111-5910)
PHONE..............................216 941-0020
Paul W Springer, *President*
Jason Conn, *Vice Pres*
David Starn, *Vice Pres*
EMP: 160
SQ FT: 140,000
SALES (est): 34.6MM **Privately Held**
WEB: www.springco-coatings.com
SIC: 3479 3471 Painting of metal products; coating of metals & formed products; plating & polishing

(G-6088)
SRC WORLDWIDE INC (HQ)
3425 Service Rd (44111-2421)
PHONE..............................216 941-6115
Marc Pignataro, *CEO*
Cary Nordan, *President*
Brian Kucia, *COO*
Jonathan Ward, *Admin Sec*
▲ **EMP:** 15
SQ FT: 70,000
SALES (est): 3.6MM **Publicly Held**
SIC: 2899 Fluxes: brazing, soldering, galvanizing & welding

(G-6089)
STAHL GEAR & MACHINE CO
3901 Hamilton Ave (44114-3831)
PHONE..............................216 431-2820
Herman Bronstein, *President*
Joel Bronstein, *Vice Pres*
Mike Kramer, *Vice Pres*
Nikiel Walley, *Vice Pres*

Cleveland - Cuyahoga County (G-6090)

Mark Bronstein, *Manager*
EMP: 50
SQ FT: 40,000
SALES: 5MM **Privately Held**
SIC: 3566 3561 3462 Gears, power transmission, except automotive; pumps & pumping equipment; iron & steel forgings

(G-6090)
STAINLESS AUTOMATION
1978 W 74th St (44102-2987)
PHONE..................................216 961-4550
Lois Martin, *Owner*
EMP: 7
SQ FT: 3,000
SALES: 1MM **Privately Held**
WEB: www.stainlessautomation.com
SIC: 3549 3559 Metalworking machinery;

(G-6091)
STAMCO INDUSTRIES INC
26650 Lakeland Blvd (44132-2644)
PHONE..................................216 731-9333
William Sopko, *President*
John Pyle, *General Mgr*
Dave Seward, *QC Mgr*
Kurt Weisbarth, *Supervisor*
▲ **EMP:** 38
SQ FT: 130,000
SALES (est): 9.5MM **Privately Held**
WEB: www.stamcoind.com
SIC: 3465 Automotive stampings

(G-6092)
STANDARD MACHINE INC
1952 W 93rd St (44102-2790)
PHONE..................................216 631-4440
Jim Dopoulos, *President*
Marion R Herringson, *Principal*
Linda S Kratky, *Principal*
Eli Manos, *Principal*
Joe Nelson, *Sales Mgr*
EMP: 32
SQ FT: 31,000
SALES (est): 5.9MM **Privately Held**
WEB: www.standardmachineinc.com
SIC: 3599 Machine shop, jobbing & repair

(G-6093)
STANLEY ACCESS TECH LLC
Stanley Assembly Technologies
5335 Avion Park Dr (44143-1916)
P.O. Box 50400, Indianapolis IN (46250-0400)
PHONE..................................440 461-5500
John E Turpin, *Branch Mgr*
EMP: 200
SQ FT: 40,000
SALES (corp-wide): 13.9B **Publicly Held**
WEB: www.stanleyworks.com
SIC: 3423 3546 Hand & edge tools; power-driven handtools
HQ: Stanley Access Technologies Llc
65 Scott Swamp Rd
Farmington CT 06032

(G-6094)
STANLEY INDUSTRIES INC
19120 Cranwood Pkwy (44128-4088)
PHONE..................................216 475-4000
Jay Cusick, *President*
Winng Markovitz, *QC Mgr*
Roger Asbury, *Office Mgr*
▼ **EMP:** 20 EST: 1946
SQ FT: 20,000
SALES (est): 3.3MM **Privately Held**
WEB: www.stanley-industries.com
SIC: 3599 5084 Machine shop, jobbing & repair; metal refining machinery & equipment

(G-6095)
STAR CALENDAR & PRINTING CO
4354 Pearl Rd (44109-4211)
PHONE..................................216 741-3223
Robert Cortelezzi, *President*
EMP: 6 EST: 1946
SQ FT: 4,000
SALES (est): 570K **Privately Held**
SIC: 2752 5199 2759 Commercial printing, offset; advertising specialties; calendars; letterpress printing

(G-6096)
STAR SCREW MACHINE PRODUCTS
1531 E 41st St (44103-2303)
PHONE..................................216 361-0307
James Sanker, *President*
Pete Anastasakis, *Treasurer*
EMP: 4
SQ FT: 1,600
SALES (est): 492.5K **Privately Held**
SIC: 3451 Screw machine products

(G-6097)
STATE INDUSTRIAL PRODUCTS CORP (PA)
Also Called: State Chemical Manufacturing
5915 Landerbrook Dr # 300 (44124-4039)
PHONE..................................877 747-6986
Harold Uhrman, *President*
Robert M San Julian, *President*
William Barnett, *Corp Secy*
Brian Limbert, *COO*
Dan Prugar, *CFO*
▼ **EMP:** 300 EST: 1911
SQ FT: 240,000
SALES: 107.9MM **Privately Held**
WEB: www.stateindustrial.com
SIC: 2841 5072 2842 2992 Soap: granulated, liquid, cake, flaked or chip; bolts, nuts & screws; specialty cleaning, polishes & sanitation goods; degreasing solvent; disinfectants, household or industrial plant; lubricating oils & greases; asphalt felts & coatings; chemical preparations

(G-6098)
STATE MACHINE CO INC
30400 Solon Indus Pkwy (44139-4328)
PHONE..................................440 248-1050
Christopher Catanese Jr, *President*
EMP: 7 EST: 1951
SQ FT: 6,000
SALES (est): 740K **Privately Held**
SIC: 3451 Screw machine products

(G-6099)
STATE TOOL AND DIE INC
Also Called: State Molded Plastics Division
4780 Briar Rd (44135-5038)
PHONE..................................216 267-6030
Emil J Orenick, *President*
EMP: 5 EST: 1945
SQ FT: 14,500
SALES (est): 1MM **Privately Held**
SIC: 3089 Injection molding of plastics

(G-6100)
STATUS MENS ACCESSORIES
7781 First Pl (44146-6705)
PHONE..................................440 232-6700
Scott Weger, *President*
Lee Schloss, *Vice Pres*
Mark Schloss, *Vice Pres*
▲ **EMP:** 6
SALES: 1.2MM **Privately Held**
WEB: www.statusmens.com
SIC: 2389 Men's miscellaneous accessories

(G-6101)
STD SPECIALTY FILTERS INC
837 E 79th St (44103-1807)
PHONE..................................216 881-3727
Walter Senney, *President*
Joyce P Senney, *Admin Sec*
EMP: 10
SQ FT: 25,000
SALES (est): 220K **Privately Held**
WEB: www.std-filters.com
SIC: 3564 3714 Filters, air: furnaces, air conditioning equipment, etc.; motor vehicle parts & accessories

(G-6102)
STEEL SERVICE PLUS LTD
6515 Juniata Ave (44103-1613)
PHONE..................................216 391-9000
Robert A Barrett, *President*
EMP: 13
SQ FT: 45,000
SALES (est): 2.2MM **Privately Held**
SIC: 3325 Steel foundries

(G-6103)
STEELTEC PRODUCTS LLC
13000 Saint Clair Ave (44108-2033)
PHONE..................................216 681-1114
David Bargar, *CFO*
John Bargar, *Mng Member*
Brian Bargar,
EMP: 23
SQ FT: 100,000
SALES (est): 4.7MM **Privately Held**
WEB: www.steeltecproducts.com
SIC: 3444 Sheet metalwork

(G-6104)
STEIN INC (PA)
1929 E Royalton Rd Ste C (44147-2868)
P.O. Box 470548, Broadview Heights (44147-0548)
PHONE..................................440 526-9301
Donald Ries, *CEO*
Gary Grantham, *Superintendent*
Doug Huffnagel, *Superintendent*
Marc Glasgow, *Principal*
Joe Russo, *Vice Pres*
▲ **EMP:** 15
SQ FT: 17,000
SALES (est): 83.5MM **Privately Held**
WEB: www.stein.com
SIC: 3399 7699 7629 Iron ore recovery from open hearth slag; cleaning services; electrical repair shops

(G-6105)
STEIN INC
2032 Campbell Rd (44105-1059)
P.O. Box 470548 (44147-0548)
PHONE..................................216 883-7444
Dave Bilek, *Branch Mgr*
EMP: 75
SALES (corp-wide): 83.5MM **Privately Held**
WEB: www.stein.com
SIC: 3399 3549 Iron ore recovery from open hearth slag; metalworking machinery
PA: Stein, Inc.
1929 E Royalton Rd Ste C
Cleveland OH 44147
440 526-9301

(G-6106)
STOFIEL AEROSPACE LLC
11115 Lake Ave Apt 309 (44102-1101)
PHONE..................................216 389-0084
Ronald Wilkinson, *COO*
Jason Beeman, *CFO*
Brian Stofiel,
EMP: 5 EST: 2015
SALES (est): 251K **Privately Held**
SIC: 3724 Rocket motors, aircraft

(G-6107)
STRETCHTAPE INC
3100 Hamilton Ave (44114-3701)
PHONE..................................216 486-9400
Alex F Mc Donald, *CEO*
Harry Mc Donald, *Treasurer*
Vonna Mc Donald, *Admin Sec*
▲ **EMP:** 40
SQ FT: 55,000
SALES (est): 10.2MM **Privately Held**
WEB: www.stretchtape.com
SIC: 2672 2671 3861 Adhesive papers, labels or tapes: from purchased material; packaging paper & plastics film, coated & laminated; sensitized film, cloth & paper

(G-6108)
STRIB INDUSTRIES INC
Also Called: Products Chemical
6400 Herman Ave (44102-2116)
PHONE..................................216 281-1155
John J Stibrick, *President*
▼ **EMP:** 25 EST: 1982
SALES (est): 5.4MM **Privately Held**
WEB: www.prod-chem.com
SIC: 2842 Mfg Polish/Sanitation Goods

(G-6109)
STRICKER REFINISHING INC
2060 Hamilton Ave (44114-1115)
PHONE..................................216 696-2906
Tom Stricker, *President*
Beth Stricker, *Treasurer*
Greg Stricker, *Treasurer*
EMP: 7

SQ FT: 4,000
SALES (est): 1MM **Privately Held**
WEB: www.strickerrefinishing.com
SIC: 3471 Finishing, metals or formed products; plating of metals or formed products

(G-6110)
STRICTLY STITCHERY INC
Also Called: In Sttches Ctr For Ltrgcal Art
13801 Shaker Blvd Apt 4a (44120-5628)
PHONE..................................440 543-7128
Brenda Grauer, *President*
EMP: 10
SQ FT: 800
SALES: 175K **Privately Held**
SIC: 3269 5999 Art & ornamental ware, pottery; religious goods

(G-6111)
STRIPMATIC PRODUCTS INC
5301 Grant Ave Ste 200 (44125-1053)
PHONE..................................216 241-7143
William J Adler Jr, *President*
Elizabeth R Adler, *Vice Pres*
Liz Adler, *Vice Pres*
Thomas Stanford, *Controller*
Arnold Mayher, *Sales Mgr*
▲ **EMP:** 29 EST: 1946
SQ FT: 42,000
SALES: 5.7MM **Privately Held**
WEB: www.stripmatic.com
SIC: 3469 3465 3568 3498 Metal stampings; automotive stampings; power transmission equipment; fabricated pipe & fittings; copper foundries; aluminum foundries

(G-6112)
STRONG BINDERY
13015 Larchmere Blvd (44120-1147)
PHONE..................................216 231-0001
Ellen Strong, *President*
EMP: 9
SALES (est): 760.6K **Privately Held**
SIC: 2789 Bookbinding & related work

(G-6113)
SUBURBAN MARBLE AND GRANITE CO
7818 Lake Ave (44102-1931)
PHONE..................................216 281-5557
Greg Gianvito, *Manager*
EMP: 6
SQ FT: 6,904
SALES (corp-wide): 750.1K **Privately Held**
SIC: 3281 Marble, building: cut & shaped
PA: Suburban Marble And Granite Co
26940 Bagley Rd
Olmsted Twp OH
440 235-0810

(G-6114)
SUBURBAN PRESS INC
3818 Lorain Ave (44113-3785)
PHONE..................................216 961-0766
William C Mueller, *President*
Ellen Mueller, *Corp Secy*
Paul R Mueller, *Vice Pres*
Richard M Mueller, *Vice Pres*
EMP: 24 EST: 1955
SALES (est): 3.9MM **Privately Held**
WEB: www.suburbanpressinc.com
SIC: 2752 2791 2789 2759 Commercial printing, offset; typesetting; bookbinding & related work; commercial printing

(G-6115)
SUGAR MEMORIES LLC
Also Called: Www.groovycandies.com
6770 Brookpark Rd (44129-1225)
PHONE..................................216 472-0206
Kevin Freese, *CEO*
Nicholas Marra, *President*
Joseph Martin, *Marketing Staff*
EMP: 5
SQ FT: 40,000
SALES (est): 507.9K **Privately Held**
WEB: www.groovycandies.com
SIC: 2064 Candy & other confectionery products

GEOGRAPHIC SECTION
Cleveland - Cuyahoga County (G-6140)

(G-6116)
SUMMA HOLDINGS INC (PA)
8223 Brecksville Rd # 100 (44141-1361)
PHONE..................440 838-4700
James Benenson Jr, *Ch of Bd*
Clement C Benenson, *Co-President*
James Benenson III, *Co-President*
John E Cvetic, *CFO*
Nancy Lenhart, *Admin Sec*
◆ EMP: 4
SQ FT: 4,700
SALES (est): 506.2MM **Privately Held**
SIC: 2542 3462 3569 7359 Lockers (not refrigerated): except wood; cabinets: show, display or storage: except wood; shelving, office & store: except wood; gears, forged steel; lubricating systems, centralized; equipment rental & leasing; aircraft assemblies, subassemblies & parts

(G-6117)
SUMMERS ACQUISITION CORP (DH)
Also Called: Summers Rubber Company
12555 Berea Rd (44111-1619)
PHONE..................216 941-7700
Mike Summers, *President*
William M Summers, *Chairman*
Eugene Mayo, *Vice Pres*
Gene Mayo, *Vice Pres*
Sam Petillo, *Vice Pres*
▲ EMP: 26
SQ FT: 63,000
SALES (est): 22.3MM
SALES (corp-wide): 3.1B **Privately Held**
WEB: www.summersrubber.com
SIC: 5085 3429 Rubber goods, mechanical; manufactured hardware (general)
HQ: Hampton Rubber Company
1669 W Pembroke Ave
Hampton VA 23661
757 722-9818

(G-6118)
SUN POLISHING CORP
13800 Progress Pkwy Ste E (44133-4354)
PHONE..................440 237-5525
Frank Schumacher, *President*
EMP: 8
SQ FT: 3,160
SALES: 500K **Privately Held**
SIC: 3471 Polishing, metals or formed products

(G-6119)
SUP-R-DIE INC (PA)
10003 Memphis Ave (44144-2097)
PHONE..................216 252-3930
David L Palisin, *President*
Marilyn J Palisin, *Vice Pres*
EMP: 22 EST: 1956
SQ FT: 11,000
SALES (est): 3.9MM **Privately Held**
WEB: www.suprdie.com
SIC: 3544 Special dies & tools

(G-6120)
SUPERIOR FLUX & MFG CO
6615 Parkland Blvd (44139-4345)
PHONE..................440 349-3000
Yehuda Baskin, *President*
Barbara Baskin, *Vice Pres*
John Dunn, *Admin Sec*
◆ EMP: 13 EST: 1932
SQ FT: 16,500
SALES (est): 3.7MM **Privately Held**
WEB: www.superiorflux.com
SIC: 2899 Fluxes: brazing, soldering, galvanizing & welding

(G-6121)
SUPERIOR HOLDING LLC (DH)
3786 Ridge Rd (44144-1127)
PHONE..................216 651-9400
Thomas Farrel, *President*
EMP: 7
SALES (est): 600.1K
SALES (corp-wide): 145.8MM **Privately Held**
SIC: 3494 5085 3492 Valves & pipe fittings; industrial supplies; fluid power valves & hose fittings

(G-6122)
SUPERIOR PNEUMATIC & MFG INC
855 Canterbury Rd (44145-1420)
P.O. Box 40420 (44140-0420)
PHONE..................440 871-8780
Walter I Krewson Jr, *CEO*
Bradley Krewson, *President*
Robert Janusky, *Exec VP*
EMP: 19 EST: 1945
SQ FT: 10,000
SALES (est): 2.8MM **Privately Held**
WEB: www.superiorpneumatic.com
SIC: 3546 Power-driven handtools

(G-6123)
SUPERIOR PRECISION PRODUCTS
968 E 69th Pl (44103-1760)
PHONE..................216 881-3696
Zeljko Tokic, *President*
EMP: 6
SQ FT: 16,000
SALES (est): 610K **Privately Held**
SIC: 3599 Machine shop, jobbing & repair

(G-6124)
SUPERIOR PRINTING INK CO INC
7655 Hub Pkwy Ste 205 (44125-5739)
PHONE..................216 328-1720
Scott Allen, *Manager*
EMP: 7
SALES (corp-wide): 125.3MM **Privately Held**
SIC: 2851 2893 Varnishes; gravure ink
PA: Superior Printing Ink Co Inc
100 North St
Teterboro NJ 07608
201 478-5600

(G-6125)
SUPERIOR PRODUCTS LLC
Also Called: Sp Medical
3786 Ridge Rd (44144-1127)
PHONE..................216 651-9400
Tomas Sarrel, *President*
Donald L Mottinger, *President*
Tim Austin, *Managing Dir*
Louise Egofske, *CFO*
Tim Giesse, *Admin Sec*
◆ EMP: 80 EST: 1961
SALES (est): 17.8MM **Privately Held**
WEB: www.superiorprod.com
SIC: 3451 3494 5085 3492 Screw machine products; valves & pipe fittings; industrial fittings; fluid power valves & hose fittings

(G-6126)
SUPERIOR PRODUCTS LLC
3786 Ridge Rd (44144-1127)
PHONE..................216 651-9400
Donald L Mottinger, *President*
Tim Austin, *Managing Dir*
Gregory K Gens, *CFO*
Tim Giesse, *Admin Sec*
EMP: 65
SQ FT: 75,000
SALES (est): 8.5MM
SALES (corp-wide): 145.8MM **Privately Held**
SIC: 3494 5085 3492 Valves & pipe fittings; industrial fittings; fluid power valves & hose fittings
HQ: Superior Holding, Llc
3786 Ridge Rd
Cleveland OH 44144
216 651-9400

(G-6127)
SUPERIOR STEEL STAMP CO
3200 Lakeside Ave E (44114-3750)
PHONE..................216 431-6460
Ramzi Jammal, *President*
EMP: 4 EST: 1914
SALES (est): 551.8K **Privately Held**
SIC: 3469 3953 Stamping metal for the trade; marking devices

(G-6128)
SUPERIOR WELD AND FABG CO INC
15002 Woodworth Rd (44110-3310)
PHONE..................216 249-5122
Howard Holmes, *President*
Joanne Holmes, *Manager*
EMP: 6
SQ FT: 7,000
SALES (est): 943.1K **Privately Held**
SIC: 3442 7692 Metal doors, sash & trim; welding repair

(G-6129)
SUPERTRAPP INDUSTRIES INC
4540 W 160th St (44135-2628)
PHONE..................216 265-8400
Kevin Berger, *President*
James M Smith, *Principal*
Theodore Berger, *Vice Pres*
Jean Foraker, *Manager*
Whitney Slaght III, *Admin Sec*
▲ EMP: 83
SQ FT: 210,000
SALES (est): 21.5MM
SALES (corp-wide): 49.2MM **Privately Held**
WEB: www.supertrapp.com
SIC: 3714 Mufflers (exhaust), motor vehicle
PA: Dreison International, Inc.
4540 W 160th St
Cleveland OH 44135
216 362-0755

(G-6130)
SUPPLY TECHNOLOGIES LLC (HQ)
Also Called: I L S
6065 Parkland Blvd Ste 2 (44124-6146)
P.O. Box 248199 (44124-8199)
PHONE..................440 947-2100
Michael L Justice, *President*
Brad Hudson, *Vice Pres*
Tom Blevins, *Opers Mgr*
Mike Nixon, *Opers Mgr*
Jim Rabb, *Opers Staff*
▲ EMP: 150 EST: 1998
SQ FT: 7,000
SALES (est): 43.2MM
SALES (corp-wide): 1.6B **Publicly Held**
WEB: www.deloscrew.com
SIC: 5085 3452 3469 Fasteners, industrial: nuts, bolts, screws, etc.; bolts, nuts, rivets & washers; screws, metal; nuts, metal; stamping metal for the trade
PA: Park-Ohio Holdings Corp.
6065 Parkland Blvd Ste 1
Cleveland OH 44124
440 947-2000

(G-6131)
SURE-FOOT INDUSTRIES CORP
Also Called: Skid Guard
20260 1st Ave (44130-2430)
P.O. Box 707, Berea (44017-0707)
PHONE..................440 234-4446
Clarence Haas, *President*
Shirley Haas, *Corp Secy*
Raymond Buckley, *Vice Pres*
Bill Campbell, *Sales Staff*
Brian Haas, *Sales Executive*
▲ EMP: 32
SQ FT: 65,000
SALES (est): 5.9MM **Privately Held**
WEB: www.surefootcorp.com
SIC: 3291 Abrasive products

(G-6132)
SURGICAL THEATER LLC
4541 Greenwold Rd (44121-4233)
PHONE..................216 496-7884
Morvechai Avisar,
EMP: 4
SALES: 500K **Privately Held**
SIC: 3841 Surgical & medical instruments

(G-6133)
SWAGELOK COMPANY
Also Called: Flight Operations
328 Bishop Rd (44143-1446)
PHONE..................440 442-6611
Bob Parmelee, *Manager*
EMP: 10
SALES (corp-wide): 940.1MM **Privately Held**
WEB: www.swagelok.com
SIC: 4581 3494 Hangar operation; valves & pipe fittings

PA: Swagelok Company
29500 Solon Rd
Solon OH 44139
440 248-4600

(G-6134)
SWAGELOK COMPANY
318 Bishop Rd (44143-1446)
PHONE..................440 473-1050
Jeremy Kohlmorgan, *Engineer*
Mike Rossiter, *Design Engr*
William Cosgrove, *Manager*
Ken Croy, *Technical Staff*
Joel Feldman, *Director*
EMP: 35
SALES (corp-wide): 940.1MM **Privately Held**
WEB: www.swagelok.com
SIC: 3494 Pipe fittings
PA: Swagelok Company
29500 Solon Rd
Solon OH 44139
440 248-4600

(G-6135)
SWAGELOK COMPANY
358 Bishop Rd (44143-1446)
PHONE..................440 461-7714
Robin Lavigne, *Manager*
EMP: 200
SALES (corp-wide): 940.1MM **Privately Held**
WEB: www.swagelok.com
SIC: 3599 Machine shop, jobbing & repair
PA: Swagelok Company
29500 Solon Rd
Solon OH 44139
440 248-4600

(G-6136)
SWAROVSKI NORTH AMERICA LTD
26300 Cedar Rd (44122-1158)
PHONE..................216 292-9737
Rima Daoudi, *Manager*
EMP: 5
SALES (corp-wide): 3.7B **Privately Held**
SIC: 3961 Costume jewelry
HQ: Swarovski North America Limited
1 Kenney Dr
Cranston RI 02920
401 463-6400

(G-6137)
SWIGER COIL SYSTEMS LTD
4677 Manufacturing Ave (44135-2673)
PHONE..................216 362-7500
Michael Aladjem, *Mng Member*
▲ EMP: 190
SALES (est): 88.4MM **Privately Held**
WEB: www.swigercoil.com
SIC: 3621 3677 Electric motor & generator parts; coils, for electric motors or generators; electronic coils, transformers & other inductors

(G-6138)
SWIMMER PRINTING INC
Also Called: AlphaGraphics
1701 E 12th St (44114-3236)
PHONE..................216 623-1005
Judith Swimmer, *President*
Brad Swimmer, *Vice Pres*
EMP: 8
SQ FT: 3,900
SALES (est): 1.7MM **Privately Held**
SIC: 2752 Commercial printing, lithographic

(G-6139)
SYSTEM CONTROLS INC
4549 State Rd (44109-4786)
PHONE..................216 351-9121
Fax: 216 351-0002
EMP: 6
SQ FT: 4,500
SALES (est): 944.4K **Privately Held**
SIC: 3613 Mfg Electric Control Panels

(G-6140)
SYSTEM SEALS INC (HQ)
9505 Midwest Ave (44125-2421)
PHONE..................440 735-0200
Arnold V Engelbrechten, *President*
▲ EMP: 60
SQ FT: 10,000

Cleveland - Cuyahoga County (G-6141)

SALES (est): 8.4MM
SALES (corp-wide): 319.4K Privately Held
WEB: www.systemseals.com
SIC: 3953 5084 Embossing seals & hand stamps; hydraulic systems equipment & supplies

(G-6141)
T & B FOUNDRY COMPANY
2469 E 71st St (44104-1967)
PHONE..................................216 391-4200
Edward Pruc, *President*
Ted Pruc, *Exec VP*
EMP: 80 EST: 1992
SQ FT: 275,000
SALES (est): 1.4MM Privately Held
WEB: www.tbfoundry.com
SIC: 3321 3369 3322 Gray iron castings; ductile iron castings; nonferrous foundries; malleable iron foundries

(G-6142)
T & K WELDING CO INC
1405 E 39th St (44114-4164)
PHONE..................................216 432-0221
Bruce Komandt, *President*
Susan Komandt, *Vice Pres*
EMP: 3 EST: 1951
SQ FT: 9,000
SALES (est): 365.4K Privately Held
SIC: 3599 3441 Machine shop, jobbing & repair; fabricated structural metal

(G-6143)
T D DYNAMICS INC
Also Called: Morgan Litho
4101 Commerce Ave (44103-3507)
PHONE..................................216 881-0800
Dale Fellows, *President*
Thomas M Baginski, *Vice Pres*
EMP: 10
SQ FT: 19,800
SALES (est): 880K Privately Held
WEB: www.morganlitho.com
SIC: 2752 Commercial printing, offset

(G-6144)
T D GROUP HOLDINGS LLC
1301 E 9th St Ste 3710 (44114-1838)
PHONE..................................216 706-2939
Kenneth Kates, *Director*
Kevin Kruse, *Bd of Directors*
W Nicholas Howley,
David A Barr,
Michael Graff,
EMP: 3
SALES (est): 234.9K Privately Held
SIC: 3561 3563 3625 3492 Pumps & pumping equipment; air & gas compressors; relays & industrial controls; fluid power valves & hose fittings

(G-6145)
T H E B INC
Also Called: A Quick Copy Center
3700 Kelley Ave (44114-4533)
PHONE..................................216 391-4800
Rhonda Garcia, *President*
Tom Garcia, *Admin Sec*
EMP: 7
SQ FT: 4,000
SALES (est): 717.2K Privately Held
SIC: 2752 Commercial printing, offset

(G-6146)
T&M PLASTICS CO INC
1249 W 78th St (44102-1913)
P.O. Box 602500 (44102-0500)
PHONE..................................216 651-7700
Tom Timura, *President*
EMP: 5
SALES (est): 570K Privately Held
SIC: 3089 Injection molded finished plastic products; injection molding of plastics

(G-6147)
TALAN PRODUCTS INC
18800 Cochran Ave (44110-2700)
PHONE..................................216 458-0170
Steve Peplin, *CEO*
Peter Accorti, *President*
Miguel Lugo, *Plant Mgr*
Jeff Millis, *Inv Control Mgr*
Nancy Oates, *Senior Buyer*
▲ EMP: 60

SQ FT: 100,000
SALES (est): 19.3MM Privately Held
WEB: www.talanproducts.com
SIC: 3469 Stamping metal for the trade

(G-6148)
TALBOT DRAKE INCORPORATED
Also Called: Talbot Drake & Co
5808 Grant Ave (44105-5608)
PHONE..................................216 441-5600
Mary Morvan, *President*
EMP: 4
SQ FT: 2,034
SALES (est): 260K Privately Held
WEB: www.talbotdrake.com
SIC: 2731 Book publishing

(G-6149)
TATHAM SCHULZ INCORPORATED
Also Called: Cleveland Black Oxide
836 Broadway Ave (44115-2813)
PHONE..................................216 861-4431
David Tatham, *President*
Ken Schulz, *Vice Pres*
Richard Tatham, *Vice Pres*
Walter Johnston, *Purchasing*
Loreen Crawford, *Human Res Mgr*
EMP: 35
SQ FT: 21,000
SALES (est): 4MM Privately Held
WEB: www.clevelandblackoxide.com
SIC: 3471 Finishing, metals or formed products

(G-6150)
TEAM PLASTICS INC
3901 W 150th St (44111-5810)
PHONE..................................216 251-8270
Ed Busch, *President*
Robert Timko, *CFO*
William Madar, *Treasurer*
EMP: 10
SQ FT: 14,000
SALES (est): 2.1MM Privately Held
SIC: 3081 Unsupported plastics film & sheet

(G-6151)
TEAM WENDY LLC
17000 Saint Clair Ave # 5 (44110-2539)
PHONE..................................216 738-2518
Thomas J Prodouz, *President*
Dan T Moore III, *Chairman*
Amy Carpenter, *Opers Dir*
Robert James, *Prdtn Mgr*
Amanda Grandt, *Purchasing*
▲ EMP: 60
SQ FT: 40,000
SALES (est): 12.7MM Privately Held
WEB: www.teamwendy.com
SIC: 3086 Padding, foamed plastic

(G-6152)
TEC DESIGN AND MFG LLC
5240 Smith Rd Ste 4 (44142-1700)
PHONE..................................216 362-8962
Zoltan TEC, *Mng Member*
John Adam, *Mng Member*
Silvia Tcec, *Mng Member*
EMP: 3 EST: 2006
SALES (est): 364.4K Privately Held
SIC: 3533 3569 Oil field machinery & equipment; assembly machines, non-metalworking

(G-6153)
TECH INDUSTRIES INC
1313 Washington Ave (44113-2332)
PHONE..................................216 861-7337
Bruno Aldons, *President*
James Weiskittel, *Vice Pres*
Arnold Lowe, *Treasurer*
EMP: 27 EST: 1953
SQ FT: 10,000
SALES (est): 3.3MM Privately Held
WEB: www.tech-ind.com
SIC: 3544 Special dies & tools; jigs & fixtures

(G-6154)
TECH READY MIX INC
5000 Crayton Ave (44104-2826)
P.O. Box 5270 (44101-0270)
PHONE..................................216 361-5000

Mark F Perkins, *President*
Janice Knight, *Principal*
EMP: 45 EST: 2008
SALES (est): 7.3MM Privately Held
SIC: 3273 Ready-mixed concrete

(G-6155)
TECHNIPLATE INC
700 E 163rd St (44110-2493)
PHONE..................................216 486-8825
Allan Stickler, *CEO*
Don Perry, *President*
EMP: 13
SQ FT: 13,200
SALES (est): 1.3MM Privately Held
WEB: www.techniplate.com
SIC: 3471 Electroplating of metals or formed products

(G-6156)
TECHNLOGY INSTALL PARTNERS LLC
Also Called: Security Designs
13701 Enterprise Ave (44135-5113)
PHONE..................................888 586-7040
Erica Temple, *President*
Ryan Temple, *Vice Pres*
EMP: 25
SALES (est): 2.4MM Privately Held
SIC: 3699 Security control equipment & systems

(G-6157)
TEMPCRAFT CORPORATION
3960 S Marginal Rd (44114-3835)
PHONE..................................216 391-3885
John Plant, *Ch of Bd*
EMP: 225 EST: 1960
SQ FT: 100,000
SALES (est): 19.4MM
SALES (corp-wide): 14B Publicly Held
SIC: 3544 3543 Industrial molds; industrial patterns
HQ: Howmet Corporation
1616 Harvard Ave
Newburgh Heights OH 44105
757 825-7086

(G-6158)
TEMPEST INC
12750 Berea Rd (44111-1622)
PHONE..................................216 883-6500
Charles M Ruebensaal, *President*
Tracy Cherotti, *Manager*
◆ EMP: 25
SQ FT: 65,000
SALES: 10MM
SALES (corp-wide): 2.3MM Privately Held
WEB: www.tempest-eng.com
SIC: 3585 Refrigeration & heating equipment
PA: Great Lakes Management, Inc.
2700 E 40th St Ste 1
Cleveland OH 44115
216 883-6500

(G-6159)
TENDON MANUFACTURING INC
20805 Aurora Rd (44146-1005)
PHONE..................................216 663-3200
Gregory F Tench, *President*
Michael J Gordon, *Corp Secy*
Thomas Tench, *Sls & Mktg Exec*
Nancy Ryzner, *Finance Mgr*
Kathy Thomas, *Office Mgr*
EMP: 46
SQ FT: 36,000
SALES (est): 9.4MM Privately Held
WEB: www.tendon.com
SIC: 3599 3479 1761 7692 Machine shop, jobbing & repair; painting of metal products; sheet metalwork; welding repair; sheet metalwork; automotive & apparel trimmings

(G-6160)
TEREWELL INC
2683 W 14th St (44113-5215)
PHONE..................................216 334-6897
Terewell Harmon, *CEO*
EMP: 3

SALES (est): 65.7K Privately Held
SIC: 8082 2741 8748 8999 Home health care services; music book & sheet music publishing; testing service, educational or personnel; artists & artists' studios

(G-6161)
TERNION INC (PA)
Also Called: Skyline Trisource Exhibits
7635 Hub Pkwy Ste A (44125-5741)
PHONE..................................216 642-6180
Wendy Ressing-Seitz, *President*
Tammy Scordo, *Marketing Staff*
Kristie Jones-Damalas, *Admin Sec*
◆ EMP: 23
SQ FT: 23,000
SALES (est): 6.6MM Privately Held
WEB: www.skylinees.com
SIC: 5046 3993 2542 Display equipment, except refrigerated; signs & advertising specialties; partitions & fixtures, except wood

(G-6162)
THE CLEVELAND-CLIFFS IRON CO
1100 Superior Ave E # 1500 (44114-2530)
PHONE..................................216 694-5700
J A Carrabba, *CEO*
D S Gallagher, *President*
W R Calfee, *Exec VP*
Laurie Brlas, *CFO*
EMP: 176
SQ FT: 40,000
SALES (est): 14.1MM
SALES (corp-wide): 2.3B Publicly Held
SIC: 1011 Iron ore mining; iron ore beneficiating
PA: Cleveland-Cliffs Inc.
200 Public Sq Ste 3300
Cleveland OH 44114
216 694-5700

(G-6163)
THE FISCHER & JIROUCH COMPANY
4821 Superior Ave (44103-1233)
PHONE..................................216 361-3840
Robert Mattei, *President*
Salvatore Grandinetti, *Corp Secy*
Carloina Cretoni, *Shareholder*
EMP: 8
SQ FT: 30,000
SALES: 760K Privately Held
SIC: 3299 Architectural sculptures: gypsum, clay, papier mache, etc.

(G-6164)
THE GREAT LAKES BREWING CO
2516 Market Ave (44113-3434)
PHONE..................................216 771-4404
Patrick F Conway, *President*
Daniel J Conway, *Corp Secy*
▲ EMP: 85
SQ FT: 20,000
SALES (est): 29MM Privately Held
WEB: www.greatlakesbrewing.com
SIC: 2082 5813 5812 Beer (alcoholic beverage); bar (drinking places); American restaurant

(G-6165)
THE HOLTKAMP ORGAN CO
2909 Meyer Ave (44109-1584)
PHONE..................................216 741-5180
F Christian Holtkamp, *President*
Michal Leutsch, *Design Engr*
Thomas Lucchesi, *Admin Sec*
EMP: 12 EST: 1855
SQ FT: 15,700
SALES (est): 1.7MM Privately Held
WEB: www.holtkamporgan.com
SIC: 3931 Pipes, organ

(G-6166)
THERMAL INDUSTRIES INC
4920 Commerce Pkwy Ste 4 (44128-5943)
PHONE..................................216 464-0674
Ron Berna, *Manager*
EMP: 5
SALES (corp-wide): 2B Publicly Held
WEB: www.thermalindustries.com
SIC: 3442 Screens, window, metal

GEOGRAPHIC SECTION

Cleveland - Cuyahoga County (G-6192)

HQ: Thermal Industries, Inc.
3700 Haney Ct
Murrysville PA 15668
724 325-6100

(G-6167)
THERMAL TREATMENT CENTER INC (HQ)
Also Called: Nettleton Steel Treating Div
1101 E 55th St (44103-1026)
PHONE..................216 881-8100
Carmen Paponitti, *President*
Jack Luck, *Vice Pres*
Louise Profughi, *Treasurer*
EMP: 35 **EST:** 1945
SQ FT: 85,000
SALES (est): 7.1MM
SALES (corp-wide): 9.4MM **Privately Held**
WEB: www.htg.cc
SIC: 3398 8711 Metal heat treating; engineering services
PA: Hi Tecmetal Group, Inc.
1101 E 55th St
Cleveland OH 44103
216 881-8100

(G-6168)
THERMAL TREATMENT CENTER INC
Commercial Induction Division
11116 Avon Ave (44105-4257)
PHONE..................216 883-4820
Chip Gench, *Manager*
EMP: 5
SALES (corp-wide): 25.2MM **Privately Held**
WEB: www.htg.cc
SIC: 3398 Metal heat treating
HQ: Thermal Treatment Center Inc
1101 E 55th St
Cleveland OH 44103
216 881-8100

(G-6169)
THERMAL TREATMENT CENTER INC
Walker Steel Treating Division
10601 Briggs Rd (44111-5329)
PHONE..................216 941-0440
Will Helber, *Manager*
EMP: 15
SALES (corp-wide): 25.2MM **Privately Held**
WEB: www.htg.cc
SIC: 3398 Metal heat treating
HQ: Thermal Treatment Center Inc
1101 E 55th St
Cleveland OH 44103
216 881-8100

(G-6170)
THERMO SYSTEMS TECHNOLOGY
2000 Auburn Dr Ste 200 (44122-4328)
PHONE..................216 292-8250
Henry A Becker, *President*
EMP: 50
SALES (est): 7.9MM **Privately Held**
WEB: www.thermosys.com
SIC: 3567 3433 Heating units & devices, industrial: electric; heating equipment, except electric

(G-6171)
THOMPSON ALUMINUM CASTING CO
Also Called: Thompson Castings
5161 Canal Rd (44125-1143)
PHONE..................216 206-2781
Dave Oberg, *Principal*
Rick D'Amico, *QC Mgr*
Paul Deininger, *Human Res Mgr*
Pat Cassell, *Manager*
Brian Thomas, *CIO*
▲ **EMP:** 71
SQ FT: 60,000
SALES (est): 19.2MM **Privately Held**
WEB: www.thompsoncasting.com
SIC: 3364 3369 3363 3365 Magnesium & magnesium-base alloy die-castings; magnesium & magnes.-base alloy castings, exc. die-casting; aluminum die-castings; aluminum foundries

(G-6172)
THOSE CHARC FROM CLEVE INC
Also Called: T C F C
1 American Rd (44144-2354)
PHONE..................216 252-7300
Ed Fructembaum, *President*
William Meyer, *Vice Pres*
Thomas Schneider, *Vice Pres*
Howard Weinshenker, *Vice Pres*
Dale A Cable, *Treasurer*
EMP: 14
SQ FT: 5,000
SALES (est): 346K
SALES (corp-wide): 7.2B **Privately Held**
SIC: 8999 2771 Art related services; greeting cards
HQ: American Greetings Corporation
1 American Way
Cleveland OH 44145
216 252-7300

(G-6173)
THREE PEAKS WELLNESS LLC
818 E 185th St (44119-2702)
P.O. Box 19092 (44119-0092)
PHONE..................216 438-3334
EMP: 3 **EST:** 2015
SALES (est): 320.5K **Privately Held**
SIC: 2099 Packaged combination products: pasta, rice & potato

(G-6174)
TIG WELDING SPECIALTIES INC
13616 Enterprise Ave (44135-5112)
PHONE..................216 621-1763
Fred Backus, *President*
Scott Backus, *Vice Pres*
EMP: 5
SQ FT: 2,000
SALES (est): 350K **Privately Held**
SIC: 7692 3599 Welding repair; ties, form: metal

(G-6175)
TILDEN MINING COMPANY LC (HQ)
200 Public Sq Ste 3300 (44114-2315)
PHONE..................216 694-5700
Lourenco Goncalves, *President*
P Kelly Tompkins, *COO*
Terry Fedor, *Exec VP*
Maurice Harapiak, *Exec VP*
Terrence Mee, *Exec VP*
EMP: 580
SALES (est): 346.6MM
SALES (corp-wide): 2.3B **Publicly Held**
SIC: 1011 Iron ore mining; iron ore pelletizing; iron ore beneficiating
PA: Cleveland-Cliffs Inc.
200 Public Sq Ste 3300
Cleveland OH 44114
216 694-5700

(G-6176)
TIP PRODUCTS INC
15411 Chatfield Ave Ste 5 (44111-4300)
PHONE..................216 252-2535
Wayne T Gielow, *President*
Rhonda Gielow, *Corp Secy*
EMP: 23 **EST:** 1965
SQ FT: 10,000
SALES (est): 4.1MM **Privately Held**
WEB: www.tipproducts.com
SIC: 3643 3699 Connectors, electric cord; plugs, electric; electrical equipment & supplies

(G-6177)
TLS CORP (PA)
Also Called: Telos Alliance, The
1241 Superior Ave E (44114-3204)
PHONE..................216 574-4759
Frank Foti, *CEO*
Timothy Carroll, *President*
Steve Church, *Principal*
Scott Stiefel, *COO*
Martin Sacks, *Vice Pres*
▲ **EMP:** 48
SQ FT: 10,500

SALES (est): 7.8MM **Privately Held**
WEB: www.axiaaudio.com
SIC: 3663 3679 3823 3661 Radio & TV communications equipment; electronic circuits; industrial instrmnts msrmnt display/control process variable; telephone & telegraph apparatus; household audio & video equipment

(G-6178)
TMS INTERNATIONAL LLC
4300 E 49th St (44125-1048)
PHONE..................216 441-9702
Keith Kelley, *Principal*
EMP: 19 **Privately Held**
SIC: 3312 Blast furnaces & steel mills
HQ: Tms International, Llc
12 Monongahela Ave
Glassport PA 15045
412 678-6141

(G-6179)
TMW SYSTEMS INC
6085 Parkland Blvd (44124-4184)
PHONE..................615 986-1900
Leigh Anderson, *Human Res Mgr*
Frank Dorenkamp, *Manager*
EMP: 13
SALES (corp-wide): 3.1B **Publicly Held**
SIC: 3829 3812 Measuring & controlling devices; navigational systems & instruments
HQ: Tmw Systems, Inc.
6085 Parkland Blvd
Mayfield Heights OH 44124
216 831-6606

(G-6180)
TOMAHAWK ENTERTAINMENT GROUP
6501 Marsol Rd Apt 108 (44124-3563)
PHONE..................216 505-0548
Javon Bates, *Principal*
EMP: 3 **EST:** 2015
SALES (est): 39.2K **Privately Held**
SIC: 7929 4832 2731 7389 Entertainers & entertainment groups; radio broadcasting stations, music format; radio broadcasting stations, except music format; book publishing; music recording producer; marketing consulting services

(G-6181)
TOMLINSON INDUSTRIES LLC
13700 Brdwy Ave (44125)
PHONE..................216 587-3400
Michael E Figas, *President*
▲ **EMP:** 170
SALES (est): 4.6MM
SALES (corp-wide): 32.9MM **Privately Held**
SIC: 3556 Food products machinery
PA: Crown Brands Llc
300 Knightsbridge Pkwy
Lincolnshire IL 60069
224 513-2917

(G-6182)
TOOL SYSTEMS INC
71 Alpha Park (44143-2202)
PHONE..................440 461-6363
Joseph Fortunato, *President*
Lillian A Fortunato, *Corp Secy*
EMP: 11
SQ FT: 1,300
SALES (est): 2.8MM **Privately Held**
WEB: www.toolsystemsinc.com
SIC: 5084 3545 Machine tools & accessories; cutting tools for machine tools

(G-6183)
TOOLBOLD CORPORATION (PA)
5330 Commerce Pkwy W (44130-1273)
PHONE..................216 676-9840
Harry Eisengrein, *CEO*
Barbara Blech, *President*
EMP: 6
SQ FT: 14,000
SALES (est): 5.2MM **Privately Held**
SIC: 3599 Machine shop, jobbing & repair

(G-6184)
TOOLBOLD CORPORATION
Leadfree Faucets Division
5330 Commerce Pkwy W (44130-1273)
PHONE..................440 543-1660

Harry Eisengrein, *Branch Mgr*
EMP: 24
SALES (corp-wide): 5.2MM **Privately Held**
SIC: 3432 Faucets & spigots, metal & plastic
PA: Toolbold Corporation
5330 Commerce Pkwy W
Cleveland OH 44130
216 676-9840

(G-6185)
TOOLOVATION LLC
Also Called: Igo Home Products
23980 Mercantile Rd Uppr (44122-5944)
PHONE..................216 514-3022
Russelll D Owens,
David Levine,
EMP: 3
SQ FT: 300
SALES (est): 366.5K **Privately Held**
WEB: www.igohomeproducts.com
SIC: 3423 Hand & edge tools

(G-6186)
TOP KNOTCH PRODUCTS INC
819 Colonel Dr (44109-3768)
PHONE..................419 543-2266
Lance E Larson, *President*
EMP: 8
SQ FT: 5,000
SALES (est): 1.4MM **Privately Held**
WEB: www.topnotchproduct.com
SIC: 3496 Miscellaneous fabricated wire products

(G-6187)
TOP TOOL & DIE INC
15500 Brookpark Rd (44135-3334)
PHONE..................216 267-5878
Anton Schiro, *President*
Bob Schiro, *Vice Pres*
Irma Schiro, *Treasurer*
EMP: 11 **EST:** 1979
SQ FT: 12,000
SALES (est): 1.2MM **Privately Held**
SIC: 3544 Special dies & tools

(G-6188)
TOPPS PRODUCTS INC
3201 E 66th St (44127-1403)
P.O. Box 1632, Canton MS (39046-1632)
PHONE..................216 271-2550
Thomas Tamulewicz, *Branch Mgr*
EMP: 6 **Privately Held**
SIC: 2952 Roofing materials
PA: Topps Products, Inc.
20105 Metcalf Ave
Bucyrus KS 66013

(G-6189)
TORR METAL PRODUCTS INC
12125 Bennington Ave (44135-3729)
PHONE..................216 671-1616
Pat Sheehan, *President*
EMP: 21 **EST:** 1992
SQ FT: 25,000
SALES (est): 4.8MM **Privately Held**
WEB: www.torrmetal.com
SIC: 3469 3544 Stamping metal for the trade; special dies, tools, jigs & fixtures

(G-6190)
TORTILLERIA LA BAMBA LLC
1849 W 24th St (44113-3513)
PHONE..................216 469-0410
Leticia Ortiz, *Principal*
▼ **EMP:** 6
SALES (est): 622.4K **Privately Held**
SIC: 2099 Tortillas, fresh or refrigerated

(G-6191)
TORTILLERIA LA BAMBA LLC
12119 Bennington Ave (44135-3729)
PHONE..................216 515-1600
Leticia Ortiz, *Mng Member*
EMP: 20
SALES (est): 590.8K **Privately Held**
SIC: 2099 Tortillas, fresh or refrigerated

(G-6192)
TOTAL PLASTICS RESOURCES LLC
17851 Englewood Dr Ste A (44130-3489)
PHONE..................440 891-1140
Toll Free..................877 -

Cleveland - Cuyahoga County (G-6193)

David Gabay, *Branch Mgr*
EMP: 6
SALES (corp-wide): 869.1MM **Privately Held**
WEB: www.totalplastics.com
SIC: 3089 5162 Plastic processing; plastics sheets & rods
HQ: Total Plastics Resources Llc
2810 N Burdick St Ste A
Kalamazoo MI 49004
269 344-0009

(G-6193)
TOTH MOLD & DIE INC
380 Solon Rd Ste 7 (44146-3809)
PHONE 440 232-8530
Timothy Toth, *President*
Thomas Toth, *Corp Secy*
EMP: 10
SQ FT: 6,400
SALES (est): 1.2MM **Privately Held**
WEB: www.tothmold.net
SIC: 3089 Injection molded finished plastic products; injection molding of plastics

(G-6194)
TRACER SPECIALTIES INC
1842 Columbus Rd (44113-2412)
PHONE 216 696-2363
Tejinder Singh, *President*
EMP: 8
SQ FT: 7,500
SALES (est): 970.6K **Privately Held**
SIC: 3599 Machine shop, jobbing & repair

(G-6195)
TRANSDIGM INC
Also Called: Aerocontrolex
4223 Monticello Blvd (44121-2814)
PHONE 216 291-6025
Roger Jones, *President*
Cathy Leak, *Principal*
EMP: 12
SALES (corp-wide): 3.8B **Publicly Held**
WEB: www.electromotion.com
SIC: 3561 3492 3563 3625 Pumps & pumping equipment; fluid power valves & hose fittings; air & gas compressors; relays & industrial controls; alkaline cell storage batteries; batteries, rechargeable; lead acid batteries (storage batteries); nickel cadmium storage batteries
HQ: Transdigm, Inc.
4223 Monticello Blvd
Cleveland OH 44121

(G-6196)
TRANSDIGM INC (HQ)
Also Called: Aerocontrolex
4223 Monticello Blvd (44121-2814)
P.O. Box 932066 (44193-0007)
PHONE 216 706-2939
Raymond Laubenthal, *President*
Robert Henderson, *Exec VP*
Albert Rodriguez, *Exec VP*
Gregory Rufus, *CFO*
EMP: 8
SALES (est): 827.5MM
SALES (corp-wide): 3.8B **Publicly Held**
WEB: www.electromotion.com
SIC: 5088 3563 3625 3492 Aircraft equipment & supplies; air & gas compressors; relays & industrial controls; fluid power fittings & hose fittings; alkaline cell storage batteries; batteries, rechargeable; lead acid batteries (storage batteries); nickel cadmium storage batteries; industrial valves
PA: Transdigm Group Incorporated
1301 E 9th St Ste 3000
Cleveland OH 44114
216 706-2960

(G-6197)
TRANSDIGM GROUP INCORPORATED (PA)
1301 E 9th St Ste 3000 (44114-1871)
PHONE 216 706-2960
W Nicholas Howley, *Ch of Bd*
Kevin Stein, *President*
Jorge L Valladares III, *COO*
Bernt G Iversen II, *Exec VP*
Jorge Valladares, *Exec VP*
EMP: 136
SQ FT: 20,100
SALES: 3.8B **Publicly Held**
WEB: www.transdigm.com
SIC: 3728 5088 Aircraft parts & equipment; aircraft equipment & supplies

(G-6198)
TRANZONIC COMPANIES
26301 Curtiss Wright Pkwy # 200 (44143-1454)
PHONE 440 446-0643
Ken F Vuylsteke, *President*
Frank Gancedo, *Purchasing*
Nae Walker, *Human Resources*
Melissa Bales, *Manager*
Milan Ghosh, *Manager*
EMP: 233
SALES (corp-wide): 295.9MM **Privately Held**
SIC: 2211 2326 2842 2273 Scrub cloths; work garments, except raincoats: waterproof; sanitation preparations, disinfectants & deodorants; industrial plant disinfectants or deodorants; mats & matting; napping; manmade fiber & silk broadwoven fabrics; napkins, sanitary: made from purchased paper
PA: The Tranzonic Companies
26301 Curtiss Wright Pkwy # 200
Richmond Heights OH 44143
216 535-4300

(G-6199)
TRAVELERS CUSTOM CASE INC
2261 E 14th St (44115-2396)
PHONE 216 621-8447
Kenneth Nosse, *President*
Betsy Nosse, *Executive*
Elizabeth Nosse, *Admin Sec*
EMP: 10 **EST:** 1946
SQ FT: 18,000
SALES (est): 1.4MM **Privately Held**
WEB: www.travelerscustomcase.com
SIC: 3161 Cases, carrying

(G-6200)
TRD LEATHERS
6321 Detroit Ave (44102-3009)
PHONE 216 631-6233
Chuck Perez, *Owner*
▼ **EMP:** 4
SALES: 200K **Privately Held**
WEB: www.trdleather.com
SIC: 3199 5699 Leggings or chaps, canvas or leather; sports apparel

(G-6201)
TREC INDUSTRIES INC
4713 Spring Rd (44131-1025)
PHONE 216 741-4114
James M Trecokas, *President*
Laurel Trecokas, *Corp Secy*
Tom Erhard, *Plant Supt*
EMP: 22
SQ FT: 10,000
SALES (est): 4MM **Privately Held**
WEB: www.trecindustries.com
SIC: 3599 Machine shop, jobbing & repair

(G-6202)
TREMCO INCORPORATED
4475 E 175th St (44128-3411)
PHONE 216 752-4401
Igor Mijic, *Maint Spvr*
John Kadlec, *Manager*
Mary Kuehn, *Administration*
EMP: 110
SALES (corp-wide): 5.3B **Publicly Held**
WEB: www.tremcoinc.com
SIC: 2891 Sealants
HQ: Tremco Incorporated
3735 Green Rd
Beachwood OH 44122
216 292-5000

(G-6203)
TREMONT ELECTRIC INCORPORATED
Also Called: Delaware Company
2112 W 7th St (44113-3622)
PHONE 888 214-3137
Aaron Lemieux, *CEO*
Charles Ames, *President*
Aaron Lemieux, *Principal*
Jill Lemieux, *Vice Pres*
Benjamin Brooks, *Director*
EMP: 9
SALES (est): 1.3K **Privately Held**
WEB: www.npowerpeg.com
SIC: 3621 Motors & generators

(G-6204)
TRENT MANUFACTURING COMPANY
6212 Carnegie Ave (44103-4614)
PHONE 216 391-1551
Lynn Gallatin, *President*
EMP: 11 **EST:** 1958
SQ FT: 12,000
SALES (est): 1.4MM **Privately Held**
SIC: 3991 5085 Brushes, household or industrial; brushes, industrial

(G-6205)
TRI COUNTY CONCRETE INC
Also Called: Tri County Ready Mixed Con Co
10155 Royalton Rd (44133-4426)
P.O. Box 665, Twinsburg (44087-0665)
PHONE 330 425-4464
Tony Farinacci, *President*
EMP: 19
SQ FT: 23,282
SALES (est): 4.8MM **Privately Held**
SIC: 3273 Ready-mixed concrete
PA: Tri County Concrete Inc
9423 Darrow Rd
Twinsburg OH 44087
330 425-4464

(G-6206)
TRI-CRAFT INC
17941 Englewood Dr (44130-3488)
PHONE 440 826-1050
Kathleen Byrnes, *President*
Stephen Pilhartz, *Principal*
Josef Schuessler, *Principal*
Monica Hargis, *Vice Pres*
Brian Rosenstock, *Buyer*
EMP: 28
SQ FT: 30,000
SALES (est): 7.6MM **Privately Held**
SIC: 3089 3544 Injection molded finished plastic products; special dies, tools, jigs & fixtures

(G-6207)
TRI-WELD INC
4411 Detroit Ave (44113-2761)
PHONE 216 281-6009
George Calogar, *President*
Betty Calogar, *Treasurer*
EMP: 15
SQ FT: 5,800
SALES (est): 2.5MM **Privately Held**
SIC: 3599 Machine shop, jobbing & repair

(G-6208)
TRIANGLE MACHINE PRODUCTS CO
6055 Hillcrest Dr (44125-4687)
PHONE 216 524-5872
Raymond Scherler, *Ch of Bd*
Robb Scherler, *President*
Don Lagoni, *Vice Pres*
Randy Scherler, *Vice Pres*
Roy Scherler, *Vice Pres*
EMP: 35 **EST:** 1950
SQ FT: 42,000
SALES: 6.9MM
SALES (corp-wide): 51.5MM **Privately Held**
WEB: www.trianglemachprod.com
SIC: 3451 Screw machine products
PA: Freeway Corporation
9301 Allen Dr
Cleveland OH 44125
216 524-9700

(G-6209)
TRIBCO INCORPORATED
18901 Cranwood Pkwy (44128-4041)
P.O. Box 202148 (44120-8119)
PHONE 216 486-2000
David N Bortz, *President*
Rick Boruszkowski, *Plant Mgr*
Dave Bortz, *VP Engrg*
Dorothy Werblow, *Administration*
EMP: 40
SALES (est): 7.4MM **Privately Held**
WEB: www.tribco.com
SIC: 3499 Friction material, made from powdered metal

(G-6210)
TRIBOTECH COMPOSITES INC
7800 Exchange St (44125-3332)
PHONE 216 901-1300
Arnold Von, *President*
EMP: 9
SALES (est): 1.4MM
SALES (corp-wide): 319.4K **Privately Held**
SIC: 2821 Plastics materials & resins
HQ: System Seals, Inc.
9505 Midwest Ave
Cleveland OH 44125

(G-6211)
TRICO CORPORATION
9700 Rockside Rd Ste 430 (44125-6285)
PHONE 216 642-3223
Bob Young, *Branch Mgr*
EMP: 20
SALES (corp-wide): 10.9MM **Privately Held**
SIC: 1389 Oil field services
PA: Trico Corporation
1235 Hickory St
Pewaukee WI 53072
262 691-9336

(G-6212)
TRICO GROUP LLC (HQ)
127 Public Sq Ste 5110 (44114-1313)
PHONE 216 589-0198
Patrick James, *CEO*
EMP: 8
SALES (est): 207.4MM **Privately Held**
SIC: 3069 Tubing, rubber
PA: Trico Group Holdings, Llc
127 Public Sq Ste 5110
Cleveland OH 44114
216 274-9027

(G-6213)
TRICO GROUP HOLDINGS LLC (PA)
127 Public Sq Ste 5110 (44114-1313)
PHONE 216 274-9027
Patrick James, *Mng Member*
EMP: 9
SALES (est): 207.4MM **Privately Held**
SIC: 3069 Mfg Fabricated Rubber Products

(G-6214)
TRICO MACHINE PRODUCTS CORP
5081 Corbin Dr (44128-5413)
PHONE 216 662-4194
Julius Szorady Jr, *President*
James Szorady, *Vice Pres*
Mark Szorady, *Treasurer*
EMP: 10
SQ FT: 8,000
SALES (est): 1.5MM **Privately Held**
WEB: www.tricomachine.com
SIC: 3544 Dies, plastics forming

(G-6215)
TRIM TOOL & MACHINE INC
3431 Service Rd (44111-2421)
PHONE 216 889-1916
Dane Willis, *President*
Lisa Willis, *Office Mgr*
EMP: 20
SALES (est): 1.6MM **Privately Held**
SIC: 3544 Special dies & tools

(G-6216)
TRINEL INC
5251 W 137th St (44142-1800)
PHONE 216 265-9190
Jimmy M Martella, *President*
Rose Martella, *Corp Secy*
Thomas A Martella, *Assistant VP*
EMP: 12 **EST:** 1986
SQ FT: 22,000
SALES: 2.5MM **Privately Held**
WEB: www.trinelinc.com
SIC: 3599 Grinding castings for the trade

GEOGRAPHIC SECTION — Cleveland - Cuyahoga County (G-6242)

(G-6217)
TRU FORM METAL PRODUCTS INC
12305 Grimsby Ave (44135-4843)
PHONE..................216 252-3700
Ron Seith, *President*
EMP: 8 EST: 2001
SALES (est): 1.4MM **Privately Held**
SIC: 3444 Sheet metalwork

(G-6218)
TRUCK FAX INC
17700 S Woodland Rd (44120-1767)
PHONE..................216 921-8866
Brian Luntz, *President*
Melissa Beesley, *Treasurer*
◆ **EMP:** 8
SALES (est): 1MM **Privately Held**
SIC: 3399 7371 3999 Iron, powdered; computer software development; atomizers, toiletry

(G-6219)
TRUCO INC
3033 W 44th St (44113-4817)
PHONE..................216 631-1000
Christopher S Hoskins, *President*
Richard P Hoskins, *Chairman*
Ellen Hoskins, *Human Res Dir*
Elisa Adams, *Cust Mgr*
Ellen Deangelis, *Marketing Mgr*
EMP: 300 EST: 1978
SQ FT: 10,000
SALES (est): 54.5MM **Privately Held**
WEB: www.truco-inc.com
SIC: 2899 2952 Waterproofing compounds; rust resisting compounds; metal treating compounds; roofing felts, cements or coatings

(G-6220)
TRW AUTOMOTIVE INC
Also Called: TRW Shared Services
8333 Rockside Rd (44125-6134)
P.O. Box 318076, Independence (44131-8076)
PHONE..................216 750-2400
Shelly Peet, *Principal*
EMP: 30
SALES (corp-wide): 144.2K **Privately Held**
SIC: 3714 Mfg Motor Vehicle Parts
HQ: Trw Automotive Inc.
   12001 Tech Center Dr
   Livonia MI 48150
   734 855-2600

(G-6221)
TUNGSTEN CAPITAL PARTNERS LLC
Also Called: Skidmore-Wilhelm Manufacturing
30340 Solon Industrial Pk (44139-4358)
PHONE..................216 481-4774
John O'Brien,
Scott M Lewis,
EMP: 3
SALES (est): 325K **Privately Held**
SIC: 8734 3569 3429 Calibration & certification; filters, general line: industrial; clamps, couplings, nozzles & other metal hose fittings

(G-6222)
TURBINE ENG CMPNENTS TECH CORP
23555 Euclid Ave (44117-1703)
PHONE..................216 692-6173
Ken Salacienski, *Mfg Mgr*
Robert S Cohen, *Branch Mgr*
EMP: 24 Privately Held
WEB: www.tectcorp.com
SIC: 3724 3728 3463 Airfoils, aircraft engine; aircraft parts & equipment; nonferrous forgings
HQ: Turbine Engine Components Technologies Corporation
   1211 Old Albany Rd
   Thomasville GA 31792
   229 228-2600

(G-6223)
TURBO MACHINE & TOOL INC
2151 W 117th St (44111-1642)
PHONE..................216 651-1940
Nick Stipanovich, *President*
Mary Stipanovich, *Exec VP*
EMP: 6
SQ FT: 8,000
SALES (est): 902.5K **Privately Held**
WEB: www.turbomachineandtool.com
SIC: 3089 3599 3544 Injection molding of plastics; machine shop, jobbing & repair; special dies, tools, jigs & fixtures

(G-6224)
TWINSBURG DEVELOPMENT CORP (PA)
20389 1st Ave (44130-2433)
PHONE..................440 357-5562
Harold T Larned, *President*
Jerome T Osborne, *Principal*
Michael E Osborne, *Principal*
EMP: 1
SQ FT: 2,500
SALES: 1MM **Privately Held**
SIC: 1442 Sand mining; gravel mining

(G-6225)
TYLOK INTERNATIONAL INC
1061 E 260th St (44132-2877)
PHONE..................216 261-7310
Carole Hahl, *President*
Scott Hahl, *General Mgr*
Sandy Carroll, *Vice Pres*
Vince Traina, *VP Opers*
Matthew Muffet, *Opers Mgr*
▲ **EMP: 55 EST:** 1955
SQ FT: 72,000
SALES (est): 15.6MM **Privately Held**
SIC: 3491 3494 3492 Pressure valves & regulators, industrial; valves & pipe fittings; hose & tube fittings & assemblies, hydraulic/pneumatic

(G-6226)
TYMEX PLASTICS INC
5300 Harvard Ave (44105-4826)
PHONE..................216 429-8950
Michael Turkovich, *President*
EMP: 45
SQ FT: 160,000
SALES: 5.6MM **Privately Held**
WEB: www.tymexplastics.com
SIC: 3087 Custom compound purchased resins

(G-6227)
U S ALLOY DIE CORP
4007 Brookpark Rd (44134-1131)
PHONE..................216 749-9700
Anthony Corrao Sr, *President*
Anthony Corrao Jr, *Vice Pres*
Rachelle Corrao, *Vice Pres*
Dyann Corrao, *Treasurer*
EMP: 17 EST: 1955
SQ FT: 12,000
SALES: 1.5MM **Privately Held**
SIC: 3544 3599 3541 Special dies & tools; electrical discharge machining (EDM); machine tools, metal cutting type

(G-6228)
ULTRA PRINTING & DESIGN INC
707 Brookpark Rd Ste 3 (44109-5834)
P.O. Box 31027, Independence (44131-0027)
PHONE..................440 887-0393
Judith Juhasz, *President*
EMP: 3
SQ FT: 2,800
SALES (est): 477.8K **Privately Held**
SIC: 2752 7336 Commercial printing, offset; graphic arts & related design

(G-6229)
UNDERCAR EXPRESS LLC
Also Called: U C X
18451 Euclid Ave (44112-1016)
PHONE..................216 531-7004
Joe Zorko, *Controller*
Rob Wright, *Sales Staff*
David A Wright, *Mng Member*
Paul Schuck,
Robert P Wright,
▲ **EMP: 50 EST:** 1997
SQ FT: 30,000
SALES (est): 10.7MM **Privately Held**
WEB: www.ucx.com
SIC: 3714 Motor vehicle brake systems & parts

(G-6230)
UNICONTROL INC (PA)
Also Called: Hays Cleveland
1111 Brookpark Rd (44109-5825)
PHONE..................216 398-0330
Steve Craig, *President*
Charles M Rowan, *Vice Pres*
Valerie Roth, *Administration*
▲ **EMP:** 73
SQ FT: 50,000
SALES (est): 26.9MM **Privately Held**
WEB: www.unicontrolinc.com
SIC: 3823 Combustion control instruments

(G-6231)
UNION CARBIDE CORPORATION
11709 Madison Ave (44107-5230)
P.O. Box 1153, Lorain (44055-0153)
PHONE..................216 529-3784
Al Miller, *Principal*
EMP: 56
SALES (corp-wide): 85.9B **Publicly Held**
SIC: 2869 Industrial organic chemicals
HQ: Union Carbide Corporation
   1254 Enclave Pkwy
   Houston TX 77077
   281 966-2727

(G-6232)
UNIQUE PAVING MATERIALS CORP
3993 E 93rd St (44105-4096)
PHONE..................216 341-7711
Jeffrey J Higerd, *Ch of Bd*
Michael Pemberton, *President*
Donna Letizia, *Exec VP*
Don Kautzman, *Treasurer*
EMP: 41
SQ FT: 25,000
SALES (est): 13.6MM **Privately Held**
WEB: www.UniquePavingMaterials.com
SIC: 2951 Asphalt & asphaltic paving mixtures (not from refineries)

(G-6233)
UNITED FINSHG & DIE CUTNG INC
3875 King Ave (44114-3727)
PHONE..................216 881-0239
Laurie Jacbec, *President*
Aaron Jacbec, *VP Admin*
EMP: 16
SALES (est): 2.3MM **Privately Held**
WEB: www.unitedfdc.com
SIC: 3544 Special dies & tools

(G-6234)
UNITED IGNITION WIRE CORP
15620 Industrial Pkwy (44135-3316)
PHONE..................216 898-1112
Richard L Maxwell, *President*
Marie Maxwell, *Admin Sec*
▲ **EMP:** 8
SQ FT: 20,000
SALES: 3MM **Privately Held**
WEB: www.united-wire.com
SIC: 3694 5521 Ignition apparatus, internal combustion engines; used car dealers

(G-6235)
UNITED PRTRS & LITHOGRAPHERS
1045 French St (44113-2441)
PHONE..................216 771-2759
Barbara Scott, *President*
Greg Scott, *Vice Pres*
EMP: 4 EST: 1952
SQ FT: 7,500
SALES: 250K **Privately Held**
SIC: 2752 Commercial printing, offset

(G-6236)
UNITED READY MIX INC
7820 Carnegie Ave (44103-4904)
PHONE..................216 696-1600
Harvey J Newsom, *President*
Alvin Robinson, *Vice Pres*
EMP: 20
SQ FT: 4,000
SALES (est): 2.3MM **Privately Held**
WEB: www.unitedreadymix.com
SIC: 3273 Ready-mixed concrete

(G-6237)
UNITED TACONITE LLC (HQ)
Also Called: UTAC
1100 Superior Ave E # 1500 (44114-2544)
PHONE..................218 744-7800
David H Gunning, *Vice Pres*
J A Carrabba,
Donald J Gallagher,
George W Hawk,
R J Leroux,
▼ **EMP:** 4
SALES (est): 403.4MM
SALES (corp-wide): 2.3B **Publicly Held**
SIC: 1011 Iron ore pelletizing
PA: Cleveland-Cliffs Inc.
   200 Public Sq Ste 3300
   Cleveland OH 44114
   216 694-5700

(G-6238)
UNIVERSAL HEAT TREATING INC
Also Called: Universal Black Oxiding
3878 E 93rd St (44105-2148)
PHONE..................216 641-2000
Ernie D'Amato, *CEO*
Michael D Amato, *President*
Kevin D'Amato, *Vice Pres*
EMP: 32 EST: 1965
SQ FT: 30,000
SALES: 3.6MM **Privately Held**
SIC: 3398 Metal heat treating

(G-6239)
UNIVERSAL OIL INC
265 Jefferson Ave (44113-2594)
PHONE..................216 771-4300
John J Purcell, *President*
Scott Fox, *COO*
Steven Cala, *Controller*
EMP: 30
SQ FT: 25,000
SALES (est): 30.9MM **Privately Held**
WEB: www.universaloil.com
SIC: 5171 2992 Petroleum bulk stations; lubricating oils

(G-6240)
UNIVERSAL STEEL COMPANY
6600 Grant Ave (44105-5692)
PHONE..................216 883-4972
Richard W Williams, *President*
David P Miller, *Chairman*
Tom Vinci, *COO*
William B Bourne, *Treasurer*
Stephen F Ruscher, *Treasurer*
▲ **EMP:** 100
SQ FT: 200,000
SALES (est): 28MM
SALES (corp-wide): 78.3MM **Privately Held**
WEB: www.univsteel.com
SIC: 3444 5051 Sheet metalwork; steel
PA: Columbia National Group, Inc.
   6600 Grant Ave
   Cleveland OH 44105
   216 883-4972

(G-6241)
UPDEGRAFF INC
1335 Main Ave (44113-2312)
PHONE..................216 621-7600
David Updegraff, *President*
EMP: 3
SQ FT: 8,000
SALES (est): 250K **Privately Held**
SIC: 3599 3441 8711 Machine shop, jobbing & repair; fabricated structural metal; engineering services

(G-6242)
UPRIGHT STEEL LLC
1335 E 171st St (44110-2525)
PHONE..................216 923-0852
Gerald Quinn, *Manager*
EMP: 20
SALES (est): 6.2MM **Privately Held**
SIC: 3441 3446 1791 Fabricated structural metal; building components, structural steel; stairs, fire escapes, balconies, railings & ladders; balconies, metal; concrete reinforcement, placing of

Cleveland - Cuyahoga County (G-6243) GEOGRAPHIC SECTION

(G-6243)
US 261 CORP
341 E 131st St (44108-1607)
PHONE..................................216 531-7143
Mike Mahar, *President*
Bob Schilling, *Corp Secy*
EMP: 5
SALES: 100K **Privately Held**
SIC: 3069 Grips or handles, rubber

(G-6244)
US COTTON LLC
15501 Industrial Pkwy (44135-3313)
PHONE..................................216 676-6400
John Levinsky, *Owner*
Andrew York, *Manager*
EMP: 500
SALES (corp-wide): 1.4B **Privately Held**
WEB: www.uscotton.com
SIC: 2844 2241 Toilet preparations; cotton narrow fabrics
HQ: U.S. Cotton, Llc
531 Cotton Blossom Cir
Gastonia NC 28054
216 676-6400

(G-6245)
USA HEAT TREATING INC
4500 Lee Rd Ste B (44128-2959)
PHONE..................................216 587-4700
Forest Delaine, *President*
Norman R Fisher Jr, *President*
Ray Keller, *Engineer*
EMP: 26
SQ FT: 50,000
SALES (est): 5MM **Privately Held**
SIC: 3398 Metal heat treating

(G-6246)
USB CORPORATION
26111 Miles Rd (44128-5933)
P.O. Box 68, Carlsbad CA (92018-0068)
PHONE..................................216 765-5000
Michael Lachman, *President*
Kathy Fortney, *Vice Pres*
Fred Leffler, *Vice Pres*
Frank Maenpa, *Vice Pres*
EMP: 84
SQ FT: 60,000
SALES (est): 12.5MM
SALES (corp-wide): 24.3B **Publicly Held**
WEB: www.usbweb.com
SIC: 2833 2834 2835 Medicinals & botanicals; pharmaceutical preparations; radioactive diagnostic substances
HQ: Affymetrix, Inc.
3380 Central Expy
Santa Clara CA 95051

(G-6247)
UTILITY WIRE PRODUCTS INC
3302 E 87th St (44127-1849)
PHONE..................................216 441-2180
Ronald F Anzells, *President*
Donald J Anzells, *Treasurer*
Marcia Anzells, *Admin Sec*
EMP: 15
SQ FT: 48,000
SALES: 1.2MM **Privately Held**
WEB: www.utilitywire.com
SIC: 3496 Woven wire products

(G-6248)
V M MACHINE CO INC
9607 Clinton Rd (44144-1029)
P.O. Box 44510 (44144-0510)
PHONE..................................216 281-4569
Victor Mustapic, *President*
Carol Sheperd, *Admin Sec*
EMP: 4
SALES: 50K **Privately Held**
SIC: 3599 Grinding castings for the trade

(G-6249)
VACONO AMERICA LLC
1163 E 40th St Ste 301 (44114-3869)
P.O. Box 307, Hudson (44236-0307)
PHONE..................................216 938-7428
Chad Derringer, *President*
▲ **EMP:** 29 **EST:** 2011
SALES (est): 4.6MM **Privately Held**
SIC: 3479 Aluminum coating of metal products

(G-6250)
VARBROS LLC
16025 Brookpark Rd (44142-1623)
PHONE..................................216 267-5200
Joseph Dunn, *CEO*
Dave Gido, *President*
Rick Vargo, *President*
Robert Jester, *Vice Pres*
Tim Bailey, *VP Mfg*
▼ **EMP:** 110 **EST:** 1951
SQ FT: 113,000
SALES (est): 37MM **Privately Held**
WEB: www.varbroscorp.com
SIC: 3469 3714 Stamping metal for the trade; motor vehicle parts & accessories

(G-6251)
VARMLAND INC
Also Called: All Cstom Fabricators Erectors
1200 Brookpark Rd (44109-5828)
PHONE..................................216 741-1510
Erik V Schneider, *President*
Deborah Schneider, *Corp Secy*
Karl M Schneider, *Vice Pres*
Karl Schneider, *Engineer*
EMP: 12 **EST:** 1943
SQ FT: 20,000
SALES (est): 1.4MM **Privately Held**
SIC: 3444 Sheet metal specialties, not stamped

(G-6252)
VE GLOBAL VENDING INC
Also Called: Vegv
8700 Brookpark Rd (44129-6810)
PHONE..................................216 785-2611
Aviel Dafna, *President*
Nate Stansell, *COO*
▲ **EMP:** 18
SALES (est): 2.7MM **Privately Held**
SIC: 3581 Automatic vending machines

(G-6253)
VERTIV GROUP CORPORATION
5900 Landerbrook Dr # 300 (44124-4020)
PHONE..................................440 460-3600
David Marsden, *Vice Pres*
Steven M Barto, *CFO*
Ron Baker, *Treasurer*
William R Calise, *Director*
James H Greene, *Director*
EMP: 11
SALES (corp-wide): 322.9MM **Privately Held**
SIC: 3661 1731 Telephone & telegraph apparatus; communications specialization
HQ: Vertiv Group Corporation
1050 Dearborn Dr
Columbus OH 43085
614 888-0246

(G-6254)
VESUVIUS U S A CORPORATION
Foseco Metallurgical
20200 Sheldon Rd (44142-1315)
PHONE..................................440 816-3051
Dave Smith, *Technical Mgr*
William Kelly, *Manager*
Don Zacharias, *Manager*
Mike Brausch, *Director*
EMP: 36
SALES (corp-wide): 2.2B **Privately Held**
WEB: www.vesuvius.com
SIC: 2899 Chemical preparations
HQ: Vesuvius U S A Corporation
1404 Newton Dr
Champaign IL 61822
217 351-5000

(G-6255)
VETERANS STEEL INC
900 E 69th St (44103-1736)
PHONE..................................216 938-7476
EMP: 13 **EST:** 2014
SALES (est): 779.5K **Privately Held**
SIC: 3449 Mfg Misc Structural Metalwork

(G-6256)
VGS INC
2239 E 55th St (44103-4451)
PHONE..................................216 431-7800
Robert Comben Jr, *President*
James Huduk, *Vice Pres*
Mick Latkovich, *Vice Pres*
Donald E Carlton, *CFO*
James Hudak, *Sales Staff*
EMP: 200
SQ FT: 36,000
SALES: 5MM **Privately Held**
SIC: 8331 2326 2311 Job training & vocational rehabilitation services; work uniforms; military uniforms, men's & youths': purchased materials

(G-6257)
VGU INDUSTRIES INC
Also Called: Vinyl Graphics
4747 Manufacturing Ave (44135-2639)
PHONE..................................216 676-9093
Brian Stransky, *President*
Jerry Lubich, *VP Sales*
Troy Lightfoot, *Manager*
▲ **EMP:** 35
SQ FT: 40,000
SALES (est): 5.1MM **Privately Held**
SIC: 3993 2759 2396 Signs, not made in custom sign painting shops; screen printing; automotive & apparel trimmings

(G-6258)
VICS TURNING CO INC
16911 Saint Clair Ave (44110-2536)
PHONE..................................216 531-5016
John Lamovec, *President*
Ann Maher, *Corp Secy*
EMP: 6
SQ FT: 16,500
SALES (est): 260K **Privately Held**
WEB: www.vicsturning.com
SIC: 3599 Machine shop, jobbing & repair

(G-6259)
VICTORY WHITE METAL COMPANY
Also Called: Vwm Republic Metals
7930 Jones Rd (44105-3908)
P.O. Box 605217 (44105-0217)
PHONE..................................216 641-2575
Lynn Carlson, *Manager*
EMP: 13
SALES (corp-wide): 30.8MM **Privately Held**
WEB: www.vwmc.com
SIC: 5051 3356 Lead; lead & zinc
PA: The Victory White Metal Company
6100 Roland Ave
Cleveland OH 44127
216 271-1400

(G-6260)
VICTORY WHITE METAL COMPANY (PA)
6100 Roland Ave (44127-1399)
PHONE..................................216 271-1400
Alex J Stanwick, *President*
Jennifer Sturman, *Admin Sec*
▲ **EMP:** 60 **EST:** 1920
SQ FT: 60,000
SALES (est): 30.8MM **Privately Held**
WEB: www.vwmc.com
SIC: 5085 3356 Valves & fittings; solder: wire, bar, acid core, & rosin core; lead & zinc; tin

(G-6261)
VICTORY WHITE METAL COMPANY
3027 E 55th St (44127-1275)
PHONE..................................216 271-1400
Tim Hess, *Manager*
EMP: 25
SQ FT: 50,000
SALES (corp-wide): 30.8MM **Privately Held**
WEB: www.vwmc.com
SIC: 3341 4941 4225 Lead smelting & refining (secondary); water supply; general warehousing & storage
PA: The Victory White Metal Company
6100 Roland Ave
Cleveland OH 44127
216 271-1400

(G-6262)
VIKING EXPLOSIVES LLC
25800 Science Park Dr (44122-7339)
PHONE..................................218 263-8845
Bob Prittinen, *Manager*
EMP: 28

SALES (corp-wide): 22.6MM **Privately Held**
SIC: 5169 2892 Explosives; explosives
HQ: Viking Explosives Llc
25800 Science Park Dr # 300
Cleveland OH
216 464-2400

(G-6263)
VINCO MACHINE PRODUCTS INC
17601 Pennsylvania Ave (44137-4308)
PHONE..................................216 475-6708
EMP: 5 **EST:** 1975
SQ FT: 10,000
SALES (est): 390K **Privately Held**
SIC: 3451 Mfg Machine Products

(G-6264)
VISI-TRAK WORLDWIDE LLC (PA)
8400 Sweet Valley Dr # 406 (44125-4244)
PHONE..................................216 524-2363
Jack Vann, *President*
Sue Thayer, *Accountant*
Arick Kaschalk, *Sales Mgr*
Mark Vann, *Sales Staff*
Tony Senyitko, *Manager*
EMP: 13
SQ FT: 8,050
SALES (est): 2.4MM **Privately Held**
WEB: www.visi-trakworldwide.com
SIC: 3823 Industrial instrmnts msrmnt display/control process variable

(G-6265)
VISUALLY IMP EXP WM ISUES FR GR
Also Called: V I E W I N G
3041 E 121st St (44120-2965)
PHONE..................................216 561-6864
Thelia Turner, *Director*
EMP: 4
SALES (est): 308.4K **Privately Held**
WEB: www.viewing.com
SIC: 3842 Technical aids for the handicapped

(G-6266)
VITEX CORPORATION
2960 Broadway Ave (44115-3606)
PHONE..................................216 883-0920
Robert Vitek Sr, *President*
Marie Vitek, *Corp Secy*
Robert Vitek Jr, *Vice Pres*
EMP: 15 **EST:** 1970
SQ FT: 60,000
SALES (est): 3.9MM **Privately Held**
WEB: www.vitexcorporation.com
SIC: 2842 Cleaning or polishing preparations

(G-6267)
VOCATIONAL SERVICES INC
2239 E 55th St (44103-4451)
PHONE..................................216 431-8085
Robert Comben, *President*
Donald E Carlson, *CFO*
Donald Carlson, *Treasurer*
EMP: 150
SQ FT: 17,541
SALES: 1.2MM **Privately Held**
SIC: 2391 2511 8331 Curtains & draperies; wood household furniture; job training & vocational rehabilitation services

(G-6268)
VOICE MEDIA GROUP INC
Also Called: Cleveland Scene
1468 W 9th St Ste 805 (44113-1299)
PHONE..................................216 241-7550
Pete Kotz, *Manager*
EMP: 70
SALES (corp-wide): 269.2MM **Privately Held**
WEB: www.ruxton.com
SIC: 2711 Newspapers: publishing only, not printed on site
PA: Voice Media Group, Inc.
969 N Broadway
Denver CO 80203
303 296-7744

GEOGRAPHIC SECTION
Cleveland - Cuyahoga County (G-6296)

(G-6269)
VOICE PRODUCTS INC
23715 Merc Rd Ste A200 (44122)
PHONE.................................216 360-0433
Michael Kaufman, *President*
EMP: 10
SALES (est): 710K Privately Held
WEB: www.vproducts.com
SIC: 3669 Smoke detectors

(G-6270)
VOLPE MILLWORK INC
4500 Lee Rd (44128-2963)
PHONE.................................216 581-0200
John Volpe, *President*
Christine Vegh, *Office Mgr*
William Roy Laubscher, *Shareholder*
Mary Ellen Volpe, *Shareholder*
Salvatore Volpe, *Admin Sec*
EMP: 7
SQ FT: 9,000
SALES (est): 900K Privately Held
SIC: 1521 2431 Single-family housing construction; millwork

(G-6271)
VON ROLL USA INC
Also Called: Von Roll Isola
4853 W 130th St (44135-5137)
PHONE.................................216 433-7474
Larry Schwener, *Branch Mgr*
EMP: 33
SALES (corp-wide): 323.3MM Privately Held
SIC: 3644 Insulators & insulation materials, electrical
HQ: Von Roll Usa, Inc.
   200 Von Roll Dr
   Schenectady NY 12306
   518 344-7100

(G-6272)
VOSS INDUSTRIES INC
Also Called: Voss Clamp Technology Division
2168 W 25th St (44113-4172)
PHONE.................................216 771-7655
Daniel W Sedor Sr, *President*
John Fritskey, *President*
Barbara Clark, *COO*
Mark Schodowski, *VP Opers*
Rick Baker, *Plant Mgr*
EMP: 75
SALES (corp-wide): 167.6MM Privately Held
SIC: 3429 Clamps & couplings, hose
HQ: Voss Industries, Llc
   2168 W 25th St
   Cleveland OH 44113
   216 771-7655

(G-6273)
VOSS INDUSTRIES LLC (HQ)
2168 W 25th St (44113-4172)
PHONE.................................216 771-7655
Daniel W Sedor Sr, *President*
Nicola Antonelli, *Vice Pres*
John F Fritskey, *Vice Pres*
Mark Schodowski, *VP Mfg*
Gerald Kaminski, *Engineer*
▲ EMP: 181 EST: 1957
SQ FT: 240,000
SALES (est): 71.3MM
SALES (corp-wide): 167.6MM Privately Held
WEB: www.vossind.com
SIC: 3429 3469 3369 3499 Clamps & couplings, hose; machine parts, stamped or pressed metal; aerospace castings, nonferrous: except aluminum; strapping, metal
PA: Consolidated Aerospace Manufacturing, Llc
   1425 S Acacia Ave
   Fullerton CA 92831
   714 989-2797

(G-6274)
VOYALE MINORITY ENTERPRISE LLC
5855 Grant Ave (44105-5607)
PHONE.................................216 271-3661
Jim Vojtech, *Sales Executive*
Paula S Corcoran,
EMP: 20
SQ FT: 116,000
SALES (est): 4.7MM Privately Held
WEB: www.vmellc.com
SIC: 3499 Metal household articles

(G-6275)
VTI INSTRUMENTS CORPORATION
7525 Granger Rd Ste 7 (44125-4859)
PHONE.................................216 447-8950
Tom Sarfi, *Branch Mgr*
EMP: 4
SALES (corp-wide): 4.8B Publicly Held
WEB: www.vxitech.com
SIC: 3699 Electrical equipment & supplies
HQ: Vti Instruments Corporation
   2031 Main St
   Irvine CA 92614
   949 955-1894

(G-6276)
VWM-REPUBLIC INC
Also Called: Republic Metals
6100 Roland Ave (44127-1353)
P.O. Box 605217 (44105-0217)
PHONE.................................216 271-1400
Lynn Carlson, *Manager*
EMP: 15
SALES (est): 2.6MM Privately Held
SIC: 2816 Lead pigments: white lead, lead oxides, lead sulfate

(G-6277)
W B MASON CO INC
12985 Snow Rd (44130-1006)
PHONE.................................888 926-2766
EMP: 40
SALES (corp-wide): 773MM Privately Held
SIC: 5943 5712 2752 Office forms & supplies; office furniture; commercial printing, lithographic
PA: W. B. Mason Co., Inc.
   59 Center St
   Brockton MA 02301
   781 794-8800

(G-6278)
W N ALBUMS AND FRAMES INC
2160 Superior Ave E (44114-2102)
PHONE.................................800 325-5179
Steven Gregory, *Principal*
EMP: 4
SALES (est): 338.3K Privately Held
SIC: 2782 Albums

(G-6279)
W R G INC
Also Called: Buckeye Metals
3961 Pearl Rd (44109-3103)
PHONE.................................216 351-8494
Mike Rauch, *President*
Mildred Neumann, *Principal*
Nathan R Simon, *Principal*
Sandra L Sotos, *Principal*
Robert Rauch, *Vice Pres*
EMP: 25
SQ FT: 121,500
SALES (est): 12.3MM Privately Held
SIC: 5093 3341 Nonferrous metals scrap; secondary nonferrous metals

(G-6280)
WABTEC CORPORATION
4677 Manufacturing Ave (44135-2637)
PHONE.................................216 362-7500
EMP: 5
SALES (corp-wide): 4.3B Publicly Held
SIC: 3621 3677 Electric motor & generator parts; electronic coils, transformers & other inductors
HQ: Wabtec Corporation
   1001 Airbrake Ave
   Wilmerding PA 15148

(G-6281)
WABUSH MINES CLIFFS MINING CO
200 Public Sq Ste 3300 (44114-2315)
PHONE.................................216 694-5700
Terrance Taridei, *CFO*
John Tuomi, *Mng Member*
EMP: 800
SALES (est): 15.8MM
SALES (corp-wide): 2.3B Publicly Held
SIC: 1011 Iron ore mining; iron ore pelletizing; iron ore beneficiating

PA: Cleveland-Cliffs Inc.
   200 Public Sq Ste 3300
   Cleveland OH 44114
   216 694-5700

(G-6282)
WADE DYNAMICS INC
1411 E 39th St (44114-4120)
PHONE.................................216 431-8484
Dennis Wade, *President*
Peter Wade, *Vice Pres*
Denise Wade, *Treasurer*
EMP: 9 EST: 1963
SQ FT: 6,000
SALES (est): 1.3MM Privately Held
WEB: www.wadedynamics.net
SIC: 3599 Machine shop, jobbing & repair

(G-6283)
WAGNER RUSTPROOFING CO INC
7708 Quincy Ave (44104-2099)
P.O. Box 31156 (44131-0156)
PHONE.................................216 361-4930
Gregory Spann, *President*
Mark Spann, *Vice Pres*
EMP: 15 EST: 1919
SQ FT: 15,000
SALES (est): 1.6MM Privately Held
SIC: 3334 Primary aluminum

(G-6284)
WAHCONAH GROUP INC
2930 Euclid Ave (44115-2416)
P.O. Box 141136 (44114-6136)
PHONE.................................216 923-0570
Isaac Crawford, *CEO*
Robert Carlston, *Vice Pres*
EMP: 15
SQ FT: 82,000
SALES (est): 123.1K Privately Held
SIC: 2311 Men's & boys' suits & coats

(G-6285)
WAKE ROBIN FERMENTED FOODS LLC
1303 W 103rd St (44102-1622)
PHONE.................................216 961-9944
Patrick Murray, *Principal*
EMP: 3
SALES (est): 249.6K Privately Held
SIC: 2099 Food preparations

(G-6286)
WALEST INCORPORATED
Also Called: Kol-Cap Manufacturing Co
15500 Commerce Park Dr (44142-2013)
PHONE.................................216 362-8110
Mike Gorbulja, *President*
EMP: 8
SQ FT: 14,000
SALES (est): 870K Privately Held
WEB: www.walest.com
SIC: 3544 3599 Special dies & tools; jigs & fixtures; machine shop, jobbing & repair

(G-6287)
WALLSEYE CONCRETE CORP (PA)
Also Called: Avon
26000 Sprague Rd (44138-2743)
P.O. Box 38159 (44138-0159)
PHONE.................................440 235-1800
Sandra Hill, *Corp Secy*
Brock Walls, *Vice Pres*
EMP: 11
SQ FT: 3,400
SALES (est): 833.3K Privately Held
SIC: 3241 Portland cement

(G-6288)
WANASHAB INC
1768 E 25th St Ste 308 (44114-4418)
PHONE.................................330 606-6675
EMP: 5 EST: 2016
SQ FT: 20,000
SALES (est): 210.6K Privately Held
SIC: 3721 Aircraft, Nsk

(G-6289)
WARREN CASTINGS INC
2934 E 55th St (44127-1207)
PHONE.................................216 883-2520
Willie Warren, *President*
EMP: 14

SALES (est): 1.5MM Privately Held
SIC: 3369 Castings, except die-castings, precision

(G-6290)
WARRENTON COPPER LLC
1240 Marquette St (44114-3920)
PHONE.................................636 456-3488
◆ EMP: 50
SQ FT: 100,000
SALES (est): 3.5MM Privately Held
SIC: 1021 Copper Ore Mining
PA: Compagnie Americaine De Fer & Metaux Inc, La
   9100 Boul Henri-Bourassa E
   Montreal-Est QC H1E 2
   514 494-2000

(G-6291)
WARWICK PRODUCTS COMPANY
5350 Tradex Pkwy (44102-5887)
PHONE.................................216 334-1200
Matthew Beverstock, *President*
Tom Kunes, *Top Exec*
Susan Beverstock, *Corp Secy*
Betty Perry, *Project Mgr*
Matt Beverstock, *Human Res Dir*
▼ EMP: 50
SQ FT: 17,000
SALES (est): 14.8MM Privately Held
WEB: www.warwickproducts.com
SIC: 2653 3089 Solid fiber boxes, partitions, display items & sheets; cases, plastic

(G-6292)
WATERLOO INDUSTRIES INC
12487 Plaza Dr (44130-1056)
P.O. Box 30382 (44130-0382)
PHONE.................................800 833-8851
EMP: 3
SALES (est): 223.6K Privately Held
SIC: 3999 Manufacturing industries

(G-6293)
WATERLOX COATINGS CORPORATION
9808 Meech Ave (44105-4191)
PHONE.................................216 641-4877
John Wilson Hawkins, *President*
Kellie Hawkins Schaffner, *Vice Pres*
▼ EMP: 13 EST: 1910
SQ FT: 40,000
SALES (est): 5.1MM Privately Held
WEB: www.waterlox.com
SIC: 2851 Paints: oil or alkyd vehicle or water thinned; varnishes; enamels; wood stains

(G-6294)
WATTERS MANUFACTURING CO INC
1931 W 47th St (44102-3413)
PHONE.................................216 281-8600
Charles D Watters, *President*
Keith Williams, *Personnel*
EMP: 6
SQ FT: 2,500
SALES (est): 840.7K Privately Held
SIC: 3451 Screw machine products

(G-6295)
WAXMAN INDUSTRIES INC (PA)
24460 Aurora Rd (44146-1794)
PHONE.................................440 439-1830
Armond Waxman, *Ch of Bd*
Melvin Waxman, *Ch of Bd*
Larry Waxman, *President*
Laurence Waxman, *President*
Robert Feldman, *Senior VP*
◆ EMP: 110 EST: 1962
SQ FT: 21,000
SALES (est): 100MM Privately Held
WEB: www.waxmanind.com
SIC: 5072 5074 3494 3491 Hardware; plumbing & hydronic heating supplies; valves & pipe fittings; industrial valves; plumbing fixture fittings & trim

(G-6296)
WEDGEWORKS MCH TL & BORING CO
3169 E 80th St (44104-4343)
PHONE.................................216 441-1200

Cleveland - Cuyahoga County (G-6297)

Bradford Braude, *President*
Sherry Braude, *Treasurer*
EMP: 6
SQ FT: 20,000
SALES (est): 759.9K **Privately Held**
SIC: 3599 Machine shop, jobbing & repair

(G-6297)
WEISKOPF INDUSTRIES CORP
54 Alpha Park (44143-2208)
P.O. Box 24390 (44124-0390)
PHONE..................440 442-4400
Edward A Weiskopf, *President*
Geoffrey Weiskopf, *Exec VP*
Weiskopf Industries, *E-Business*
Pam Keidel, *Admin Sec*
EMP: 25
SALES (est): 3MM **Privately Held**
WEB: www.wicwipers.com
SIC: 2211 Tracing cloth, cotton

(G-6298)
WELDED RING PRODUCTS CO (PA)
2180 W 114th St (44102-3582)
PHONE..................216 961-3800
James C Janosek, *President*
Gary Horvath, *Exec VP*
▲ **EMP:** 80 **EST:** 1960
SQ FT: 250,000
SALES (est): 11.8MM **Privately Held**
WEB: www.weldedring.com
SIC: 3724 Aircraft engines & engine parts

(G-6299)
WELDERS SUPPLY INC (HQ)
Also Called: Lake Erie Iron and Metal
2020 Train Ave (44113-4282)
PHONE..................216 241-1696
Richard Osborne, *President*
Martin Hathy, *Vice Pres*
Stanley Brock, *Manager*
Tom Kall, *Manager*
EMP: 12 **EST:** 1946
SQ FT: 8,000
SALES (est): 3.5MM
SALES (corp-wide): 15.5MM **Privately Held**
SIC: 2813 5084 5999 Oxygen, compressed or liquefied; acetylene; welding machinery & equipment; welding supplies
PA: Osair, Inc.
    7001 Center St
    Mentor OH 44060
    440 974-6500

(G-6300)
WELKER MACHINE & GRINDING CO
718 E 163rd St (44110-2453)
PHONE..................216 481-1360
Andy Spiranovich, *Partner*
Mark Spiranovich, *Partner*
EMP: 3 **EST:** 1966
SALES: 300K **Privately Held**
SIC: 3599 Machine shop, jobbing & repair

(G-6301)
WEST-CAMP PRESS INC
1538 E 41st St (44103-2337)
PHONE..................216 426-2660
EMP: 53
SALES (corp-wide): 26.9MM **Privately Held**
SIC: 2261 Screen printing of cotton broad-woven fabrics
PA: West-Camp Press, Inc.
    39 Collegeview Rd
    Westerville OH 43081
    614 882-2378

(G-6302)
WESTERN DIGITAL CORPORATION
2635 Butternut Ln (44124-4208)
PHONE..................440 684-1331
Scott Schechtman, *Manager*
EMP: 6
SALES (corp-wide): 20.6B **Publicly Held**
WEB: www.wdc.com
SIC: 3572 Disk drives, computer
PA: Western Digital Corporation
    5601 Great Oaks Pkwy
    San Jose CA 95119
    408 717-6000

(G-6303)
WESTERN RESERVE MFG CO
9200 Inman Ave (44105-2110)
PHONE..................216 641-0500
Iris R Rubinfield, *Partner*
Penny Heinzmann, *Partner*
Pamela Vestal, *Partner*
EMP: 3 **EST:** 1943
SQ FT: 10,000
SALES (est): 250K **Privately Held**
SIC: 3462 3562 Flange, valve & pipe fitting forgings, ferrous; casters

(G-6304)
WHIP APPEAL INC
13405 Graham Rd (44112-3131)
PHONE..................216 288-6201
Fred Neal, *President*
Martha Neal, *Admin Sec*
EMP: 4
SALES (est): 416.3K **Privately Held**
SIC: 5948 2339 2326 2329 Luggage & leather goods stores; sportswear, women's; jeans: women's, misses' & juniors'; work uniforms; men's & boys' sportswear & athletic clothing; jeans: men's, youths' & boys'

(G-6305)
WHITEROCK PIGMENTS INC
1768 E 25th St (44114-4418)
PHONE..................216 391-7765
Robert L Meyer, *CEO*
Thomas M Forman, *Chairman*
EMP: 5
SALES (est): 611.6K **Privately Held**
SIC: 2816 Titanium dioxide, anatase or rutile (pigments)

(G-6306)
WHITNEY STAINED GLASS STUDIO
5939 Broadway Ave (44127-1718)
PHONE..................216 348-1616
Peter Billington, *President*
Glenn Billington, *Vice Pres*
Janet Lipstreu, *Director*
EMP: 9
SQ FT: 12,000
SALES (est): 276.9K **Privately Held**
WEB: www.whitneystainedglass.com
SIC: 8999 3231 Stained glass art; stained glass: made from purchased glass

(G-6307)
WIKOFF COLOR CORPORATION
Also Called: Braden-Sutphin Ink
3650 E 93rd St (44105-1620)
PHONE..................216 271-2300
EMP: 60
SALES (corp-wide): 150MM **Privately Held**
SIC: 2893 Printing ink
PA: Wikoff Color Corporation
    1886 Merritt Rd
    Fort Mill SC 29715
    803 548-2210

(G-6308)
WILD FIRE SYSTEMS
535 Ransome Rd (44143-1993)
PHONE..................440 442-8999
James Berilla, *Owner*
Mark Andrews, *Sales Dir*
EMP: 6 **EST:** 1975
SALES (est): 566.6K **Privately Held**
SIC: 3823 7379 Computer interface equipment for industrial process control; computer related consulting services

(G-6309)
WILLIAM EXLINE INC
12301 Bennington Ave (44135-3796)
PHONE..................216 941-0800
William B Exline, *President*
Michael P Exline, *Vice Pres*
August Tischer, *Vice Pres*
Sharon Forke, *Graphic Designe*
EMP: 24 **EST:** 1929
SQ FT: 35,000
SALES (est): 3.7MM **Privately Held**
WEB: www.williamexlineinc.com
SIC: 2782 Passbooks: bank, etc.; checkbooks; ledgers & ledger sheets

(G-6310)
WILLIAMS EXECUTIVE ENTPS INC
Also Called: Minuteman Press
13367 Smith Rd (44130-7810)
PHONE..................440 887-1000
Christopher Williams, *President*
EMP: 3 **EST:** 2016
SALES (est): 153.2K **Privately Held**
SIC: 2752 Commercial printing, lithographic

(G-6311)
WILLIAMS STEEL RULE DIE CO
1633 E 40th St (44103-2304)
PHONE..................216 431-3232
Jeff Jazbec, *President*
EMP: 14 **EST:** 1961
SQ FT: 52,000
SALES (est): 1.6MM **Privately Held**
WEB: www.wsrdc.com
SIC: 3544 3953 2675 3993 Paper cutting dies; embossing seals, corporate & official; paper die-cutting; signs & advertising specialties; platemaking services; commercial printing

(G-6312)
WILSON MOBILITY LLC
17602 Deforest Ave (44128-2606)
PHONE..................216 921-9457
Rodney Wilson, *Principal*
EMP: 3
SALES (est): 264.6K **Privately Held**
SIC: 3842 Wheelchairs

(G-6313)
WINDSOR TOOL INC
10714 Bellaire Rd (44111-5324)
PHONE..................216 671-1900
Marc Ravas, *President*
EMP: 10 **EST:** 1946
SQ FT: 5,000
SALES (est): 710K **Privately Held**
WEB: www.windsortool.com
SIC: 3544 Special dies & tools

(G-6314)
WINSTON PRODUCTS LLC
30339 Diamond Pkwy # 105 (44139-5473)
PHONE..................440 478-1418
Winston Breeden, *CEO*
Scott Jared, *President*
Bob Schmidt, *General Mgr*
Melissa Mirt, *Purch Mgr*
Kris Ramer, *VP Sales*
▲ **EMP:** 100
SQ FT: 115,000
SALES (est): 36.5MM **Privately Held**
SIC: 3556 5013 Food products machinery; automotive supplies

(G-6315)
WIRE PRODUCTS COMPANY INC (PA)
Also Called: Universal Fabrication Assembly
14601 Industrial Pkwy (44135-4595)
PHONE..................216 267-0777
E Scot Kennedy, *President*
Winston Breeden Jr, *Exec VP*
Steve Adcock, *Vice Pres*
Dan Collins, *Vice Pres*
Gary Horvath, *Vice Pres*
EMP: 100 **EST:** 1951
SQ FT: 43,000
SALES (est): 22.3MM **Privately Held**
WEB: www.wire-products.com
SIC: 3496 Miscellaneous fabricated wire products

(G-6316)
WIRE PRODUCTS COMPANY INC
14700 Industrial Pkwy (44135-4548)
PHONE..................216 267-0777
Dale Zeleznik, *Manager*
EMP: 225
SQ FT: 56,625
SALES (corp-wide): 22.3MM **Privately Held**
WEB: www.wire-products.com
SIC: 3495 3315 3469 Mechanical springs, precision; hangers (garment); wire; metal stampings
PA: Wire Products Company, Inc.
    14601 Industrial Pkwy
    Cleveland OH 44135
    216 267-0777

(G-6317)
WLS FABRICATING CO
5405 Avion Park Dr (44143-1918)
PHONE..................440 449-0543
Craig Kotnik, *Vice Pres*
▲ **EMP:** 30
SALES (est): 4.7MM
SALES (corp-wide): 18MM **Privately Held**
WEB: www.wlsstamping.com
SIC: 3469 Stamping metal for the trade
PA: W.L.S. Stamping Co.
    3292 E 80th St
    Cleveland OH 44104
    216 271-5100

(G-6318)
WLS STAMPING CO (PA)
3292 E 80th St (44104-4392)
PHONE..................216 271-5100
Daniel C Cronin, *Ch of Bd*
Craig Kotnik, *Vice Pres*
Mike Deckert, *Plant Mgr*
Michelle Miarka, *Purch Agent*
Kathy Sinkiewicz, *Purch Agent*
▲ **EMP:** 74 **EST:** 1944
SQ FT: 30,000
SALES (est): 18MM **Privately Held**
WEB: www.wlsstamping.com
SIC: 3469 3544 Stamping metal for the trade; special dies & tools

(G-6319)
WM PLOTZ MACHINE AND FORGE CO
Also Called: Peerless Pump Clveland Svc Ctr
2514 Center St (44113-1111)
PHONE..................216 861-0441
James W Plotz, *President*
Thomas D Plotz, *Corp Secy*
EMP: 11 **EST:** 1888
SQ FT: 21,000
SALES (est): 1.7MM **Privately Held**
SIC: 3599 7699 Machine shop, jobbing & repair; pumps & pumping equipment repair

(G-6320)
WODIN INC
5441 Perkins Rd (44146-1891)
PHONE..................440 439-4222
R Grant Murphy, *Ch of Bd*
EMP: 35
SQ FT: 30,000
SALES (est): 8.2MM **Privately Held**
WEB: www.wodin.com
SIC: 3462 3463 3599 3965 Machinery forgings, ferrous; nonferrous forgings; machine shop, jobbing & repair; fasteners; bolts, nuts, rivets & washers; blast furnaces & steel mills

(G-6321)
WOOD-SEBRING CORPORATION
13800 Enterprise Ave (44135-5116)
PHONE..................216 267-3191
Joseph Kronander, *President*
Mary Kronander, *Admin Sec*
EMP: 7 **EST:** 1944
SQ FT: 10,000
SALES (est): 918.4K **Privately Held**
SIC: 3451 Screw machine products

(G-6322)
WOODHILL PLATING WORKS COMPANY
9114 Reno Ave (44105-2186)
PHONE..................216 883-1344
John W Sparano Sr, *President*
Robt Friel, *Principal*
Thomas Friel, *Principal*
James Sparano, *Vice Pres*
Jeff Sparano, *Vice Pres*
EMP: 25
SQ FT: 25,000
SALES (est): 2.8MM **Privately Held**
WEB: www.woodhillplating.com
SIC: 3471 Plating of metals or formed products

GEOGRAPHIC SECTION

Cleveland Heights - Cuyahoga County (G-6350)

(G-6323)
WOODSTOCK PRODUCTS INC
2914 Broadway Ave (44115-3606)
PHONE..................................216 641-3811
Terry Dunay, *President*
Clara Dunay, *Corp Secy*
EMP: 6
SQ FT: 5,000
SALES (est): 750.4K **Privately Held**
SIC: 2048 Feed concentrates

(G-6324)
WORLD EXPRESS PACKAGING CORP
3607 W 56th St (44102-5739)
PHONE..................................216 634-9000
Tony Galang, *President*
Mike Lewandowski, *Corp Secy*
Ken Lewandowski, *Vice Pres*
EMP: 3
SQ FT: 14,000
SALES (est): 363.6K **Privately Held**
SIC: 4783 2441 Packing goods for shipping; boxes, wood; cases, wood

(G-6325)
WORLD JOURNAL
1735 E 36th St (44114-4521)
PHONE..................................216 458-0988
Yu-Chen Hsiao, *Principal*
EMP: 5
SQ FT: 36,000
SALES (est): 265.9K **Privately Held**
SIC: 2711 Newspapers, publishing & printing

(G-6326)
WORTHINGTON CNSTR GROUP INC
3100 E 45th St Ste 400 (44127-1095)
PHONE..................................216 472-1511
Anna Unwin, *Principal*
EMP: 1 **EST:** 2013
SALES (est): 1.4MM
SALES (corp-wide): 3.5B **Publicly Held**
SIC: 3446 Purlins, light gauge steel
HQ: Worthington Mid-Rise Construction Inc.
3100 E 45th St Ste 400
Cleveland OH 44127
216 472-1511

(G-6327)
WORTHINGTON MID-RISE CNSTR INC (HQ)
Also Called: Worthington Industries
3100 E 45th St Ste 400 (44127-1095)
PHONE..................................216 472-1511
Marybeth Bosko, *President*
Michael Whitticar, *President*
EMP: 40
SQ FT: 14,000
SALES (est): 4.7MM
SALES (corp-wide): 3.5B **Publicly Held**
SIC: 3446 Purlins, light gauge steel
PA: Worthington Industries, Inc.
200 W Old Wlson Bridge Rd
Worthington OH 43085
614 438-3210

(G-6328)
WORTHINGTON STEEL COMPANY
4310 E 49th St (44125-1004)
PHONE..................................216 441-8300
Pauline Glomski, *Human Res Mgr*
Brittany Thomas, *Branch Mgr*
EMP: 175
SALES (corp-wide): 3.5B **Publicly Held**
SIC: 3316 Strip steel, cold-rolled: from purchased hot-rolled
HQ: The Worthington Steel Company
200 W Old Wlson Bridge Rd
Worthington OH 43085
614 438-3210

(G-6329)
WRIGHT DESIGNS INC (PA)
5099 Valley Woods Dr (44131-5253)
P.O. Box 31482 (44131-0482)
PHONE..................................216 524-6662
Robert A Wright, *President*
EMP: 3
SQ FT: 1,500

SALES (est): 454.7K **Privately Held**
WEB: www.brewkeeper.com
SIC: 1521 7389 2082 New construction, single-family houses; interior designer; malt beverages

(G-6330)
WYMAN-GORDON COMPANY
Also Called: Wyman Gordon
3097 E 61st St (44127-1312)
PHONE..................................216 341-0085
Tim Herron, *Branch Mgr*
EMP: 48
SALES (corp-wide): 225.3B **Publicly Held**
WEB: www.dropdies.com
SIC: 3462 Iron & steel forgings
HQ: Wyman-Gordon Company
244 Worcester St
North Grafton MA 01536
508 839-8252

(G-6331)
XAPC CO (PA)
Also Called: Avalon
15583 Brookpark Rd (44142-1618)
PHONE..................................216 362-4100
Doug Ciabotti, *CEO*
Lindsey Krauth, *Human Res Mgr*
Tom Ward, *VP Sales*
▲ **EMP:** 85 **EST:** 1982
SQ FT: 36,000
SALES (est): 51.3MM **Privately Held**
SIC: 3324 Steel investment foundries

(G-6332)
XXX INTRNTIONAL AMUSEMENTS INC (PA)
3313 W 140th St Ste D (44111-2444)
PHONE..................................216 671-6900
Scott Moore, *President*
EMP: 22
SQ FT: 10,000
SALES (est): 4.7MM **Privately Held**
WEB: www.vgrsystems.com
SIC: 1731 2541 2517 2434 Cable television installation; wood partitions & fixtures; wood television & radio cabinets; wood kitchen cabinets

(G-6333)
YOUR CARPENTER INC
2403 Saint Clair Ave Ne (44114-4020)
P.O. Box 14519 (44114-0519)
PHONE..................................216 241-6434
Matt Howells, *Principal*
EMP: 8
SALES (est): 1.3MM **Privately Held**
SIC: 3423 Carpenters' hand tools, except saws: levels, chisels, etc.

(G-6334)
YUCKON INTERNATIONAL CORP
Also Called: Ross Printing Co.
1400 E 34th St (44114-4113)
PHONE..................................216 361-2103
EMP: 9 **EST:** 1947
SQ FT: 3,000
SALES: 900K **Privately Held**
SIC: 2752 2657 Lithographic Coml Print Mfg Folding Paperbrd Box

(G-6335)
ZACLON LLC
2981 Independence Rd (44115-3699)
PHONE..................................216 271-1601
James B Krimmel, *President*
▲ **EMP:** 22
SALES (est): 5.9MM
SALES (corp-wide): 6.5MM **Privately Held**
SIC: 2819 2869 Industrial inorganic chemicals; industrial organic chemicals
PA: Alpha Zeta Holdings, Inc.
2981 Independence Rd
Cleveland OH 44115
216 271-1601

(G-6336)
ZAGAR INC
24000 Lakeland Blvd (44132-2618)
PHONE..................................216 731-0500
John F Zagar, *President*
George Zagar, *Vice Pres*
Bill Schimke, *Engineer*
David Arnold, *Admin Sec*

◆ **EMP:** 25 **EST:** 1941
SQ FT: 50,000
SALES (est): 6.6MM **Privately Held**
WEB: www.zagar.com
SIC: 3546 3541 Power-driven handtools; machine tools, metal cutting type

(G-6337)
ZAK BOX CO INC
7100 Clark Ave (44102-5225)
P.O. Box 602697 (44102-0697)
PHONE..................................216 961-5636
Richard Helbig, *President*
EMP: 5
SQ FT: 10,400
SALES: 400K **Privately Held**
SIC: 2441 2542 2448 Boxes, wood; shipping cases, wood: nailed or lock corner; racks, merchandise display or storage: except wood; wood pallets & skids

(G-6338)
ZAL AIR PRODUCTS INC
Also Called: Zap
1687 W Royalton Rd (44147-2413)
PHONE..................................440 237-7155
Ed Zalar, *President*
Michele M Zalar, *Vice Pres*
Edward H Zalar III, *Admin Sec*
EMP: 4
SQ FT: 400
SALES (est): 293.8K **Privately Held**
SIC: 3491 5085 5084 Water works valves; industrial supplies; industrial machinery & equipment

(G-6339)
ZEN INDUSTRIES INC
Also Called: American Mine Door
6200 Harvard Ave (44105-4861)
PHONE..................................216 432-3240
Kim Zenisek, *President*
Ed Ebner, *Vice Pres*
Adam Defrank, *Project Mgr*
Drew McCaffrey, *Sales Staff*
EMP: 35
SQ FT: 70,000
SALES (est): 10.9MM **Privately Held**
WEB: www.minedoor.com
SIC: 3532 Mining machinery

(G-6340)
ZF NORTH AMERICA INC
8333 Rockside Rd (44125-6134)
PHONE..................................216 750-2400
Richard Rowan, *Manager*
EMP: 50
SALES (corp-wide): 144.2K **Privately Held**
WEB: www.trw.mediaroom.com
SIC: 3469 Metal stampings
HQ: Trw Automotive U.S. Llc
12001 Tech Center Dr
Livonia MI 48150
734 855-2600

(G-6341)
ZF NORTH AMERICA INC
19501 Emery Rd (44128-4162)
PHONE..................................216 332-7100
Bernd Blankenstein, *Branch Mgr*
EMP: 405
SALES (corp-wide): 144.2K **Privately Held**
SIC: 3469 Metal stampings
HQ: Trw Automotive U.S. Llc
12001 Tech Center Dr
Livonia MI 48150
734 855-2600

(G-6342)
ZING PAC INC
30300 Solon Indus Pkwy (44139-4378)
PHONE..................................440 248-7997
Daniel McBride, *Principal*
EMP: 3
SALES (est): 256.7K **Privately Held**
SIC: 3086 Packaging & shipping materials, foamed plastic

(G-6343)
ZIP TOOL & DIE INC
12200 Sprecher Ave (44135-5122)
PHONE..................................216 267-1117
Victor De Leon, *CEO*
EMP: 19 **EST:** 1967

SQ FT: 12,000
SALES (est): 2.8MM **Privately Held**
WEB: www.ziptool.com
SIC: 3465 3469 Automotive stampings; metal stampings

(G-6344)
ZIPPITYCOM PRINT LLC
1600 E 23rd St (44114-4208)
PHONE..................................216 438-0001
Dennis Dimitrov, *COO*
J P Dell'aquila, *Mng Member*
EMP: 12 **EST:** 2017
SALES (est): 268.6K **Privately Held**
SIC: 2752 Commercial printing, offset

(G-6345)
ZIRCOA INC (PA)
31501 Solon Rd (44139-3526)
PHONE..................................440 248-0500
John Kaniuk, *President*
Sherry Just, *President*
Gala Shuk, *Research*
Elaine Myrick-Bey, *Human Res Mgr*
▲ **EMP:** 130
SQ FT: 120,000
SALES (est): 27.1MM **Privately Held**
WEB: www.zircoa.com
SIC: 3339 3297 2851 Zirconium metal, sponge & granules; nonclay refractories; paints & allied products

(G-6346)
ZIRCON INDUSTRIES INC
4920 Commerce Pkwy Ste 9 (44128-5943)
PHONE..................................216 595-0200
Robert Zinamon, *President*
Sidney A Zinamon, *Vice Pres*
Marlene Zinamon, *Treasurer*
EMP: 5 **EST:** 1973
SALES (est): 1MM **Privately Held**
WEB: www.greenchem.com
SIC: 5087 2899 Janitors' supplies; deicing or defrosting fluid

---

Cleveland Heights
Cuyahoga County

(G-6347)
DATA COOLING TECHNOLOGIES LLC
3092 Euclid Heights Blvd (44118-2026)
PHONE..................................330 954-3800
Gregory Gyllstrom, *CEO*
William M Weber, *CEO*
EMP: 130
SQ FT: 100,000
SALES (est): 47.6MM **Privately Held**
SIC: 3433 Heating equipment, except electric

(G-6348)
FOUR ELEMENTS INTEGRATVE CNSEL
1083 Selwyn Rd (44112-3050)
PHONE..................................216 381-8584
Siobhan Malave, *Principal*
EMP: 3
SALES (est): 99K **Privately Held**
SIC: 2819 Mfg Industrial Inorganic Chemicals

(G-6349)
KINGSFORD INK LLC
2663 Noble Rd Apt 4 (44121-2119)
PHONE..................................216 507-4032
Ronnie Townsend, *Principal*
EMP: 3
SALES (est): 88K **Privately Held**
SIC: 2861 Charcoal, except activated

(G-6350)
PHO & RICE LLC
1780 Coventry Rd (44118-1630)
PHONE..................................216 563-1122
Wansiri Kulsaree, *Principal*
EMP: 4 **EST:** 2013
SALES (est): 329K **Privately Held**
SIC: 2098 Noodles (e.g. egg, plain & water), dry

Cleveland Heights - Cuyahoga County (G-6351)

(G-6351)
ROBERT RAACK
2943 Berkshire Rd (44118-2443)
PHONE 216 932-6127
Robert Raack, *Principal*
EMP: 3
SALES (est): 246.2K **Privately Held**
SIC: 2851 Colors in oil, except artists'

(G-6352)
UNGER KOSHER BAKERY INC
Also Called: Ungers Bakery
1831 S Taylor Rd (44118-2101)
PHONE 216 321-7176
Marek Rosenberg, *President*
Magdalena Rosenberg, *Admin Sec*
EMP: 20
SQ FT: 12,000
SALES (est): 906.2K **Privately Held**
SIC: 5461 5411 5149 2099 Bread; grocery stores, independent; bakery products; food preparations; bread, cake & related products

Cleves
Hamilton County

(G-6353)
4D SCREENPRINTING LTD
5833 Hamilton Cleves Rd (45002-9529)
PHONE 513 353-1070
Chris Drew, *Principal*
EMP: 4
SALES (est): 455.9K **Privately Held**
SIC: 2759 Screen printing

(G-6354)
AADCO INSTRUMENTS INC
145 S Miami Ave (45002-1250)
PHONE 513 467-1477
Fred Taphorn, *President*
Diane Tisch, *Vice Pres*
James P Tisch, *Vice Pres*
Wilbur John Tisch, *Vice Pres*
Shawn Hines, *Manager*
EMP: 3 EST: 1971
SQ FT: 7,500
SALES (est): 431.2K **Privately Held**
WEB: www.aadcoinst.com
SIC: 3621 Motors & generators

(G-6355)
BRUEWER WOODWORK MFG CO
10000 Cilley Rd (45002-9735)
PHONE 513 353-3505
August Bruewer, *Ch of Bd*
Ralph H Bruewer, *President*
Gary Bruewer, *General Mgr*
Gary A Bruewer, *Vice Pres*
Richard M Ruffing, *Vice Pres*
▲ EMP: 55
SQ FT: 155,000
SALES (est): 10.3MM **Privately Held**
WEB: www.bruewerwoodwork.com
SIC: 3083 2541 2435 2434 Plastic finished products, laminated; office fixtures, wood; counters or counter display cases, wood; hardwood veneer & plywood; wood kitchen cabinets; millwork; sawmills & planing mills, general

(G-6356)
CENTRAL READY MIX LLC
7340 Dry Fork Rd (45002-9431)
PHONE 513 367-1939
Dick England, *Manager*
EMP: 8
SALES (corp-wide): 11.1MM **Privately Held**
WEB: www.morainematerials.com
SIC: 3273 Ready-mixed concrete
PA: Central Ready Mix, Llc
6310 E Kemper Rd Ste 125
Cincinnati OH 45241
513 402-5001

(G-6357)
CINCY-DUMPSTER INC
50 Timea Ave (45002-1242)
PHONE 513 941-3063
Kevin Richardson, *Principal*
EMP: 3
SALES (est): 198.9K **Privately Held**
SIC: 3443 Dumpsters, garbage

(G-6358)
COMPLIANT ACCESS PRODUCTS LLC
5885 Hamilton Cleves Rd (45002-9529)
P.O. Box 58203, Cincinnati (45258-0203)
PHONE 513 518-4525
Tom Reilly, *Mng Member*
EMP: 5
SALES (est): 643.7K **Privately Held**
SIC: 3354 Aluminum extruded products

(G-6359)
CONSOLIDATD ANALYTICAL SYS INC
Also Called: Cas
201 S Miami Ave (45002-1220)
PHONE 513 542-1200
Seth Cloran, *President*
John Tish, *Corp Secy*
Jim Tish, *Vice Pres*
EMP: 14
SQ FT: 25,000
SALES: 1MM **Privately Held**
SIC: 8711 2452 3448 3823 Consulting engineer; prefabricated buildings, wood; prefabricated metal buildings; chromatographs, industrial process type; analytical instruments; analytical instruments

(G-6360)
CONVEYOR SOLUTIONS LLC
6705 Dry Fork Rd (45002-9732)
PHONE 513 367-4845
Aaron Doerflein,
Robert Brinck,
James Hillgrove,
EMP: 7
SQ FT: 6,200
SALES (est): 1.7MM **Privately Held**
WEB: www.conveyorsolutionsllc.com
SIC: 3535 Belt conveyor systems, general industrial use

(G-6361)
EPOXY SYSTEMS BLSTG CATING INC
5640 Morgan Rd (45002-8720)
PHONE 513 924-1800
Barbara Ferneding, *President*
EMP: 5 EST: 2011
SALES (est): 629.7K **Privately Held**
SIC: 2851 Epoxy coatings

(G-6362)
FDI CABINETRY LLC
5555 Dry Fork Rd (45002-9733)
P.O. Box 16, Ross (45061-0016)
PHONE 513 353-4500
Diane Hart, *Mng Member*
EMP: 9
SQ FT: 12,000
SALES (est): 1.1MM **Privately Held**
SIC: 2434 3993 1799 3083 Wood kitchen cabinets; signs & advertising specialties; home/office interiors finishing, furnishing & remodeling; plastic finished products, laminated; millwork

(G-6363)
HANSON AGGREGATES EAST
7000 Dry Fork Rd (45002-9732)
PHONE 513 353-1100
Tom Rodurbush, *Principal*
EMP: 6
SALES (est): 280K **Privately Held**
SIC: 1442 Construction sand & gravel

(G-6364)
HEALTHWARES MANUFACTURING
5838b Hamilton Cleves Rd (45002-9529)
PHONE 513 353-3691
Greg Overman, *President*
Joe Overman, *Vice Pres*
Katie Wood, *Info Tech Mgr*
EMP: 12
SALES (est): 1.4MM **Privately Held**
WEB: www.healthwares.com
SIC: 3842 Wheelchairs

(G-6365)
JAMES BUNNELL INC
7000 Dry Fork Rd (45002-9732)
PHONE 513 353-1100
Jack Ernest, *President*
Vicki Earnst, *Corp Secy*
EMP: 10
SQ FT: 1,160
SALES (est): 890K **Privately Held**
SIC: 1442 Construction sand & gravel

(G-6366)
JOHNSON PRECISION MACHINING
5919 Hamilton Cleves Rd (45002-9051)
PHONE 513 353-4252
Mary C Hubbard, *President*
Ellis Hubbard, *Vice Pres*
EMP: 8
SQ FT: 7,500
SALES: 1MM **Privately Held**
SIC: 3599 Machine shop, jobbing & repair

(G-6367)
KINNEMYERS CORNERSTONE CAB INC
Also Called: Kinnemyers Cornerstone Cab Co
6000 Hamilton Cleves Rd (45002-9530)
PHONE 513 353-3030
Ken Kinnemeyer, *President*
EMP: 6
SALES: 600K **Privately Held**
SIC: 2599 2434 Cabinets, factory; wood kitchen cabinets

(G-6368)
KOHL PATTERNS
7983 Morgan Rd (45002-9709)
PHONE 513 353-3831
Gregory A Kohl, *Partner*
William F Kohl, *Partner*
EMP: 3
SALES (est): 418K **Privately Held**
SIC: 3543 Industrial patterns

(G-6369)
L & L ORNAMENTAL IRON CO
Also Called: L & L Railings
6024 Hamilton Cleves Rd (45002-9530)
PHONE 513 353-1930
Randy Seiler, *President*
Dean Seiler, *Vice Pres*
EMP: 15
SQ FT: 8,000
SALES: 500K **Privately Held**
SIC: 2431 3446 3354 Stair railings, wood; ornamental metalwork; aluminum extruded products

(G-6370)
METAL MAINTENANCE INC
Also Called: Architectural Metal Maint
322 N Finley St (45002-1005)
P.O. Box 41, Addyston (45001-0041)
PHONE 513 661-3300
Steve Campbell, *President*
EMP: 10
SALES (est): 1.1MM **Privately Held**
WEB: www.metal-maintenance.com
SIC: 3446 Architectural metalwork

(G-6371)
MINI MIX INC
5852 Hamilton Cleves Rd (45002-9529)
PHONE 513 353-3811
Ken Warby, *President*
Pete Warby, *Vice Pres*
▲ EMP: 12
SQ FT: 900
SALES (est): 156.5K **Privately Held**
WEB: www.minimix.com
SIC: 3273 5082 Ready-mixed concrete; concrete processing equipment

(G-6372)
POHL MACHINING INC (PA)
Also Called: Miami Machine
4901 Hamilton Cleves Rd (45002-9753)
P.O. Box 10 (45002-0010)
PHONE 513 353-2929
Shawna Vanderpohl, *President*
Irvin Vanderpohl, *Vice Pres*
EMP: 48
SALES (est): 5.7MM **Privately Held**
SIC: 3599 Machine & other job shop work

(G-6373)
POLYCRAFT PRODUCTS INC
5511 Hamilton Cleves Rd (45002-9501)
PHONE 513 353-3334
Scott Fisher, *QC Mgr*
Kay Landers, *CFO*
Shawn Walker, *Branch Mgr*
EMP: 5
SALES (corp-wide): 6.4MM **Privately Held**
SIC: 3724 3061 Aircraft engines & engine parts; mechanical rubber goods
PA: Polycraft Products, Inc.
897 Rudolph Way
Greendale IN 47025
812 577-3400

(G-6374)
POWERCLEAN EQUIPMENT COMPANY
5945 Dry Fork Rd (45002-9794)
PHONE 513 202-0001
Tom Ossege, *President*
Gary Ossege, *Vice Pres*
EMP: 16
SALES (est): 735.3K **Privately Held**
WEB: www.powercleanequipment.com
SIC: 7359 3635 5084 Equipment rental & leasing; household vacuum cleaners; cleaning equipment, high pressure, sand or steam

(G-6375)
SPECIALTY ADHESIVE FILM CO
5838 Hamilton Cleves Rd (45002-9529)
P.O. Box 150, Aurora IN (47001-0150)
PHONE 513 353-1885
Jack Morline, *Manager*
EMP: 3
SALES (corp-wide): 6.8MM **Privately Held**
WEB: www.specialtyadhesive.com
SIC: 2672 2891 3083 Adhesive backed films, foams & foils; laminating compounds; laminated plastics plate & sheet
PA: Specialty Adhesive Film Co
10510 Randall Ave
Aurora IN 47001
812 926-0156

(G-6376)
SPURLINO MATERIALS LLC
6600 Dry Fork Rd (45002-9392)
PHONE 513 202-1111
Allan Roelle, *Manager*
EMP: 9
SALES (corp-wide): 27MM **Privately Held**
WEB: www.spurlino.net
SIC: 3273 Ready-mixed concrete
PA: Spurlino Materials, Llc
4000 Oxford State Rd
Middletown OH 45044
513 705-0111

(G-6377)
STOCK MFG & DESIGN CO INC (PA)
Also Called: Q M P
10040 Cilley Rd (45002-9735)
P.O. Box 68 (45002-0068)
PHONE 513 353-3600
William H Reyering, *President*
Jeremy Stock, *Managing Prtnr*
Anthony Stock, *Corp Secy*
Dennis K Stock, *Vice Pres*
Dennis Stock, *Vice Pres*
EMP: 65
SQ FT: 80,000
SALES (est): 12.3MM **Privately Held**
WEB: www.stockmfg.com
SIC: 3441 Fabricated structural metal

(G-6378)
TAKK INDUSTRIES INC
5838a Hamilton Cleves Rd (45002-9529)
PHONE 513 353-4306
Joseph Overman, *President*
Gregory Overman, *Exec VP*
Terrance Clark, *Sales Mgr*
▲ EMP: 16

GEOGRAPHIC SECTION

Coldwater - Mercer County (G-6405)

SALES (est): 3MM **Privately Held**
WEB: www.takk.com
SIC: 3629 3469 Static elimination equipment, industrial; metal stampings

(G-6379)
TISCH ENVIRONMENTAL INC
145 S Miami Ave (45002-1250)
PHONE..................513 467-9000
W John Tisch, *President*
John W Tisch, *President*
James P Tisch, *Vice Pres*
Brad Liggett, *Opers Staff*
Rick Bollinger, *Controller*
▲ **EMP:** 18 **EST:** 1998
SQ FT: 12,000
SALES (est): 5.2MM **Privately Held**
WEB: www.tisch-env.com
SIC: 3564 Blowers & fans

(G-6380)
TRI-STATE MACHINING LLC
6088 Hamilton Cleves Rd # 2 (45002-9530)
PHONE..................513 257-9442
Shane Williams,
EMP: 3
SALES (est): 232.1K **Privately Held**
SIC: 3599 Machine & other job shop work

(G-6381)
VALLEY ASPHALT CORPORATION
5073 Kilby Rd (45002)
PHONE..................513 353-2171
Bud Crihfield, *Manager*
EMP: 3
SALES (corp-wide): 84MM **Privately Held**
SIC: 2951 Asphalt & asphaltic paving mixtures (not from refineries)
HQ: Valley Asphalt Corporation
11641 Mosteller Rd
Cincinnati OH 45241
513 771-0820

(G-6382)
W & W CUSTOM FABRICATION INC
4801 Hamilton Cleves Rd (45002-9752)
P.O. Box 288 (45002-0288)
PHONE..................513 353-4617
Steve Webb, *President*
Mike Hutchison, *General Mgr*
EMP: 6
SALES (est): 1MM **Privately Held**
SIC: 3441 Fabricated structural metal

Clinton
Summit County

(G-6383)
ANGER PATTERN COMPANY INC
2999 S 1st St (44216-9157)
PHONE..................330 882-6519
Richard Anger Jr, *President*
EMP: 5
SQ FT: 2,500
SALES: 500K **Privately Held**
SIC: 3543 Industrial patterns

(G-6384)
CLARK WOOD SPECIALTIES INC
9235 Shadybrook St Nw (44216-9546)
PHONE..................330 499-8711
EMP: 8
SQ FT: 12,500
SALES (est): 1MM **Privately Held**
SIC: 2431 5031 Mfg Millwork Whol Lumber/Plywood/Millwork

(G-6385)
COMMUNITY CARE ON WHEELS
2 Kauffmans Crk (44216)
PHONE..................330 882-5506
Cathy Jacobs, *President*
EMP: 12
SALES (est): 1.4MM **Privately Held**
SIC: 3312 Blast furnaces & steel mills

Cloverdale
Putnam County

(G-6386)
JONASHTONS
12485 State Route 634 (45827-9723)
PHONE..................419 488-2363
Susan Knippen, *Owner*
EMP: 7
SALES (est): 310K **Privately Held**
SIC: 3599 Machine shop, jobbing & repair

Clyde
Sandusky County

(G-6387)
CLYDE TOOL & DIE INC (PA)
Also Called: Clyde Foam
524 S Church St (43410-2100)
PHONE..................419 547-9574
Bruce G Schrader, *President*
Janice Smith, *Office Mgr*
EMP: 18
SQ FT: 30,000
SALES (est): 2.7MM **Privately Held**
WEB: www.clydetool.com
SIC: 3544 2821 Special dies & tools; molding compounds, plastics

(G-6388)
CUTTING EDGE MANUFACTURING LLC
1744 W Mcpherson Hwy B (43410-1011)
PHONE..................419 547-9204
Joseph Fisher, *Principal*
EMP: 6 **EST:** 2016
SALES (est): 280.4K **Privately Held**
SIC: 3599 Machine shop, jobbing & repair

(G-6389)
HOFFMAN MACHINING & REPAIR LLC
1744 W Mcpherson Hwy (43410-1052)
PHONE..................419 547-9204
William D Hoffman,
EMP: 3
SQ FT: 16,000
SALES: 300K **Privately Held**
SIC: 3499 3444 3599 7692 Metal household articles; sheet metalwork; machine shop, jobbing & repair; welding repair

(G-6390)
J TEK TOOL & MOLD INC
304 Elm St (43410-2124)
PHONE..................419 547-9476
John Cattano, *President*
EMP: 10
SQ FT: 10,000
SALES (est): 1.4MM **Privately Held**
WEB: www.jtektool.com
SIC: 3599 Machine shop, jobbing & repair

(G-6391)
MIDWEST COMPOST INC
7250 State Route 101 E (43410-8519)
PHONE..................419 547-7979
Eugene F Windau, *President*
John Steager, *Corp Secy*
Joseph Tauch, *Vice Pres*
EMP: 15
SQ FT: 2,432
SALES: 2MM **Privately Held**
SIC: 2875 Compost

(G-6392)
POLYCHEM CORPORATION
Also Called: Evergreen Plastics
202 Watertower Dr (43410-2154)
PHONE..................419 547-1400
Mark Jeckering, *General Mgr*
EMP: 75 **Privately Held**
SIC: 3052 4953 Plastic belting; recycling, waste materials
HQ: Polychem Corporation
6277 Heisley Rd
Mentor OH 44060
440 357-1500

(G-6393)
REVERE PLAS SYSTEMS GROUP LLC (HQ)
401 Elm St (43410-2148)
PHONE..................419 547-6918
Rustin Shields,
EMP: 450
SALES (est): 61.3MM **Privately Held**
SIC: 3089 Injection molded finished plastic products

(G-6394)
REVERE PLASTICS SYSTEMS LLC (HQ)
401 Elm St (43410-2148)
PHONE..................419 547-6918
Rustin Shields, *General Mgr*
Kenneth Bowers, *General Mgr*
Jeff Grames, *General Mgr*
Brian Kinnie, *Vice Pres*
Kim Toombs, *Materials Mgr*
▲ **EMP:** 277
SALES (est): 165.6MM **Privately Held**
SIC: 3089 Injection molding of plastics

(G-6395)
RFS FABRICATION
Also Called: Richard Farm Shop
2515 County Road 213 (43410-9517)
PHONE..................419 547-0650
Richard L Dickman, *Owner*
EMP: 3
SALES (est): 279K **Privately Held**
SIC: 3496 Miscellaneous fabricated wire products

(G-6396)
SLICE OF HEAVEN BAKERY
463 N County Road 268 (43410-9759)
PHONE..................419 656-6606
Meredith Hinds, *Principal*
EMP: 4
SALES (est): 265.3K **Privately Held**
SIC: 2051 Bakery: wholesale or wholesale/retail combined

(G-6397)
WHIRLPOOL CORPORATION
119 Birdseye St (43410-1397)
PHONE..................419 547-7711
Casey Drabik, *Vice Pres*
Tom Grothouse, *Opers Staff*
William Schieferstein, *Engineer*
Jason Schoch, *Engineer*
Jim Risner, *Plant Engr*
EMP: 300
SQ FT: 1,500,000
SALES (corp-wide): 21B **Publicly Held**
WEB: www.whirlpoolcorp.com
SIC: 3632 3639 3582 3633 Freezers, home & farm; refrigerators, mechanical & absorption: household; dishwashing machines, household; commercial laundry equipment; washing machines, household: including coin-operated
PA: Whirlpool Corporation
2000 N M 63
Benton Harbor MI 49022
269 923-5000

Coldwater
Mercer County

(G-6398)
ACCUTECH FILMS INC (DH)
Also Called: Novolex
620 Hardin St (45828-8738)
P.O. Box 115 (45828-0115)
PHONE..................419 678-8700
Fred Wampnar, *CEO*
George Thomas, *President*
Richard Bornhorst, *VP Sales*
EMP: 18 **EST:** 1997
SQ FT: 66,000
SALES: 18.1MM
SALES (corp-wide): 3B **Privately Held**
WEB: www.accutechfilms.com
SIC: 2673 Food storage & trash bags (plastic); plastic bags: made from purchased materials
HQ: Hilex Poly Co. Llc
101 E Carolina Ave
Hartsville SC 29550
843 857-4800

(G-6399)
ALUMETAL MANUFACTURING COMPANY
4555 Sr 127 (45828)
P.O. Box 166 (45828-0166)
PHONE..................419 268-2311
Lavern W Gross, *President*
Oliver Giere, *Corp Secy*
EMP: 21
SQ FT: 25,000
SALES: 1.5MM **Privately Held**
SIC: 3444 Awnings, sheet metal; canopies, sheet metal

(G-6400)
BARNSTORM BREWING COMPANY LLC
706 N 2nd St (45828-9779)
PHONE..................419 852-9366
Teresa Waite, *Principal*
EMP: 6
SALES (est): 110.5K **Privately Held**
SIC: 2082 Malt beverages

(G-6401)
BASIC GRAIN PRODUCTS INC
Tastemorr Snack
300 E Vine St (45828-1354)
PHONE..................614 408-3091
EMP: 32 **Privately Held**
SIC: 2096 Mfg Potato Chips/Snacks
PA: Basic Grain Products, Inc
300310 E Vine St
Coldwater OH 45828

(G-6402)
BASIC GRAIN PRODUCTS INC
Also Called: Tastemorr Snacks
300-310 E Vine St (45828)
PHONE..................419 678-2304
Carol Knapke, *President*
Amy Day, *Principal*
Ralph F Keister, *Principal*
Jim Wilsky, *Natl Sales Mgr*
Andrew Bierer, *Accounts Mgr*
EMP: 100
SQ FT: 100,000
SALES (est): 22.9MM **Privately Held**
WEB: www.tastemorr.com
SIC: 2052 2099 2096 Rice cakes; food preparations; potato chips & similar snacks

(G-6403)
CAMELOT MANUFACTURING INC
210 Butler St (45828-1103)
P.O. Box 44 (45828-0044)
PHONE..................419 678-2603
Charles A Froning, *President*
EMP: 15 **EST:** 1981
SQ FT: 14,000
SALES (est): 2.7MM **Privately Held**
WEB: www.camelotmanufacturing.com
SIC: 3441 7692 3469 Fabricated structural metal; welding repair; metal stampings

(G-6404)
CASAD COMPANY INC
Also Called: Totally Promotional
450 S 2nd St (45828-1803)
PHONE..................419 586-9457
Thomas R Casad, *President*
Jennifer Kremer, *Sales Staff*
Lisa Reinhart, *Sales Staff*
Natalie Bellando, *Representative*
Krista Kremer, *Representative*
▲ **EMP:** 15
SQ FT: 7,000
SALES (est): 3.1MM **Privately Held**
WEB: www.casad.com
SIC: 2759 3993 Screen printing; signs & advertising specialties

(G-6405)
DERUIJTER INTL USA INC
120 Harvest Dr (45828-8733)
P.O. Box 90 (45828-0090)
PHONE..................419 678-3909

Coldwater - Mercer County (G-6406)

Hubert Deruijter, *CEO*
Roger Deruijter, *President*
◆ **EMP:** 10
SQ FT: 35,000
SALES (est): 2.2MM **Privately Held**
WEB: www.deruijterusa.com
SIC: 3069 Plumbers' rubber goods
HQ: De Ruijter International B.V.
Prof. Minckelersweg 1
Waalwijk 5144
416 674-000

(G-6406)
DUES JERSEY FARM
Also Called: Dues Lumbermill
4131 Philothea Rd (45828-9756)
PHONE 419 678-2102
Ken Dues, *Partner*
EMP: 5
SALES (est): 616.1K **Privately Held**
SIC: 2421 0241 0119 Sawmills & planing mills, general; milk production; feeder grains

(G-6407)
EMBEDEE LLC
Also Called: Imperial Tent Company
625 Cron St (45828-8730)
PHONE 419 678-7007
Mary Doll, *President*
EMP: 5
SALES (est): 600.2K **Privately Held**
WEB: www.imperialtent.com
SIC: 2394 Tents: made from purchased materials

(G-6408)
EXCEL MACHINE & TOOL INC
212 Butler St (45828 1103)
PHONE 419 678-3318
Timothy Moorman, *President*
Dale Kahlig, *Vice Pres*
EMP: 10
SALES: 1.6MM **Privately Held**
WEB: www.tubebenders.com
SIC: 3599 Machine shop, jobbing & repair

(G-6409)
FORTY NINE DEGREES LLC
149 Harvest Dr (45828-8748)
PHONE 419 678-0100
Michael McClurg, *President*
Brad Meyer, *Exec VP*
Paul Niekamp, *Senior VP*
EMP: 11
SALES (est): 2.4MM **Privately Held**
WEB: www.fortyninedegrees.com
SIC: 3993 Signs & advertising specialties

(G-6410)
HARDIN CREEK MACHINE & TOOL
200 Hardin St (45828-9794)
PHONE 419 678-4913
Joseph Wenning, *President*
Randy Schmitz, *Vice Pres*
EMP: 10
SQ FT: 6,000
SALES (est): 3MM **Privately Held**
SIC: 3544 3599 Special dies & tools; machine & other job shop work

(G-6411)
HEALTH CARE PRODUCTS INC
410 Nisco St (45828-8750)
P.O. Box 116 (45828-0116)
PHONE 419 678-9620
Michael Bruns, *President*
▲ **EMP:** 38
SQ FT: 50,000
SALES (est): 10.1MM **Privately Held**
WEB: www.healthcareproducts.net
SIC: 2676 Napkins, sanitary: made from purchased paper

(G-6412)
HEMMELGARN & SONS INC
3763 Philothea Rd (45828-8710)
P.O. Box 169 (45828-0169)
PHONE 419 678-2351
Ronald Gross, *President*
David Koesters, *Principal*
EMP: 95 **EST:** 1930
SQ FT: 40,000
SALES (est): 13.1MM **Privately Held**
SIC: 2015 Egg processing

(G-6413)
HOME BAKERY
109 W Main St (45828-1702)
PHONE 419 678-3018
Carl Brunson, *Owner*
Bruce A Fox, *Owner*
EMP: 10
SQ FT: 3,000
SALES: 120K **Privately Held**
SIC: 2051 Bakery: wholesale or wholesale/retail combined

(G-6414)
HOME SERVICE STATION INC
116 S 1st St (45828-1740)
PHONE 419 678-2612
Larry Hausfeld, *President*
EMP: 3
SALES (est): 300K **Privately Held**
SIC: 7694 Motor repair services

(G-6415)
K VENTURES INC
Also Called: EMB Designs
211 E Main St (45828-1720)
P.O. Box 112 (45828-0112)
PHONE 419 678-2308
Michelle Ebbing, *President*
Mike Knapschaefer, *Corp Secy*
EMP: 10
SQ FT: 24,000
SALES (est): 950K **Privately Held**
WEB: www.designsemb.com
SIC: 5099 5137 5699 2395 Signs, except electric; women's & children's sportswear & swimsuits; uniforms; embroidery & art needlework

(G-6416)
LEFELD WELDING & STL SUPS INC (PA)
Also Called: Lefeld Supplies Rental
600 N 2nd St (45828-9777)
PHONE 419 678-2397
Stanley E Lefeld, *CEO*
Gary Lefeld, *President*
Stan Lefeld, *General Mgr*
Roy Kremer, *Purchasing*
Marge Lefeld, *Controller*
▲ **EMP:** 43 **EST:** 1953
SQ FT: 10,400
SALES (est): 25.1MM **Privately Held**
WEB: www.lefeld.com
SIC: 5084 7353 1799 3441 Welding machinery & equipment; heavy construction equipment rental; welding on site; fabricated structural metal

(G-6417)
MERCER COLOR CORPORATION
425 Hardin St (45828-8742)
P.O. Box 113 (45828-0113)
PHONE 419 678-8273
Mark A Baumer, *President*
Patrick J Berger, *Vice Pres*
EMP: 9
SQ FT: 12,000
SALES (est): 1.5MM **Privately Held**
SIC: 2752 Commercial printing, offset

(G-6418)
POLY WORKS
4830 State Route 219 (45828-8716)
PHONE 419 678-3758
Michael Buschur, *Owner*
▲ **EMP:** 3
SQ FT: 12,000
SALES (est): 475K **Privately Held**
SIC: 2673 Plastic bags: made from purchased materials

(G-6419)
RANDALL BEARINGS INC
821 Weis St (45828-9612)
PHONE 419 678-2486
Jeff Hager, *Branch Mgr*
EMP: 12
SALES (corp-wide): 29.3MM **Privately Held**
WEB: www.randallbearings.com
SIC: 3568 3624 3366 Bearings, bushings & blocks; carbon & graphite products; copper foundries
PA: Randall Bearings, Inc.
1046 S Greenlawn Ave
Lima OH 45804
419 223-1075

(G-6420)
SIGNATURE PARTNERS INC
Also Called: Signature 4 Image
149 Harvest Dr (45828-8748)
PHONE 419 678-1400
Bradley Meyer, *President*
Doug Klosterman, *Vice Pres*
Paul Meikemp, *Vice Pres*
Scott Wolford, *Vice Pres*
Josh Wuebker, *Engineer*
▲ **EMP:** 65
SALES (est): 10MM **Privately Held**
SIC: 3479 Name plates: engraved, etched, etc.

(G-6421)
TAILSPIN BREWING COMPANY
626 S 2nd St (45828-9603)
PHONE 419 852-9366
EMP: 3 **EST:** 2016
SALES (est): 75.4K **Privately Held**
SIC: 2082 Malt beverages

(G-6422)
TAYLOR COMMUNICATIONS INC
Also Called: Standard Register
515 W Sycamore St (45828-1663)
P.O. Box 109 (45828-0109)
PHONE 419 678-6000
Barry Paynter, *Branch Mgr*
EMP: 158
SALES (corp-wide): 3.2B **Privately Held**
SIC: 2759 Commercial printing
HQ: Taylor Communications, Inc.
1725 Roe Crest Dr
North Mankato MN 56003
507 625-2828

(G-6423)
VAL-CO PAX INC (DH)
Also Called: Val Products
210 E Main St (45828-1751)
P.O. Box 117 (45828-0117)
PHONE 717 354-4586
Frederick Steudler, *CEO*
Steve Hough, *Vice Pres*
William Kramer, *Vice Pres*
Vincent Lefeld, *Production*
Mike Kramer, *Purch Mgr*
▲ **EMP:** 67 **EST:** 1935
SQ FT: 130,000
SALES (est): 13.8MM
SALES (corp-wide): 72.5MM **Privately Held**
SIC: 3523 3443 Hog feeding, handling & watering equipment; poultry brooders, feeders & waterers; fabricated plate work (boiler shop)
HQ: Val Products, Inc.
2599 Old Phladelphia Pike
Bird In Hand PA 17505
717 392-3978

(G-6424)
WILMER
515 W Sycamore St (45828-1663)
PHONE 419 678-6000
EMP: 6
SALES (est): 804.4K **Privately Held**
SIC: 2754 Gravure Commercial Printing

Collins
Huron County

(G-6425)
PA STRATTON & CO INC
3768 State Route 20 (44826-9514)
P.O. Box 61 (44826-0061)
PHONE 419 660-9979
Paul Stratton, *President*
Sally Stratton, *Corp Secy*
EMP: 3
SALES: 17K **Privately Held**
SIC: 3429 Furniture builders' & other household hardware

Columbia Station
Lorain County

(G-6426)
252 TATTOO (PA)
24525 Sprague Rd (44028-9601)
PHONE 440 235-6699
James Bulloch, *Owner*
EMP: 4
SALES (est): 259.9K **Privately Held**
SIC: 7299 7372 Tattoo parlor; prepackaged software

(G-6427)
ANDY PAC INC
11600 Hawke Rd (44028-9192)
P.O. Box 546 (44028-0546)
PHONE 440 748-8800
Robert A Anderson, *CEO*
Eric Anderson, *President*
EMP: 4
SQ FT: 4,000
SALES: 1MM **Privately Held**
SIC: 3565 Packaging machinery

(G-6428)
AQUATIC TECHNOLOGY
26966 Royalton Rd (44028-9758)
PHONE 440 236-8330
Greg Smith, *Owner*
◆ **EMP:** 10
SQ FT: 4,300
SALES: 1.5MM **Privately Held**
WEB: www.aquatictech.com
SIC: 5999 5199 3999 Aquarium supplies; pets & pet supplies; pet supplies

(G-6429)
ATOM BLASTING & FINISHING INC
24933 Sprague Rd (44028-9671)
PHONE 440 235-4765
Richard Ferry, *President*
Karen Widener, *Vice Pres*
▲ **EMP:** 6
SALES (est): 550K **Privately Held**
SIC: 3471 Finishing, metals or formed products; sand blasting of metal parts

(G-6430)
BOWES MILL AND CABINET LLC
33549 E Royalton Rd # 7 (44028-9307)
PHONE 440 236-3255
Tom Bowes,
EMP: 3
SALES: 100K **Privately Held**
SIC: 2434 Wood kitchen cabinets

(G-6431)
CAL SALES EMBROIDERY
13975 Station Rd (44028-9401)
PHONE 440 236-3820
Edward L Pete Houston, *Owner*
Edward L Houston, *Owner*
EMP: 6
SQ FT: 1,800
SALES (est): 431.8K **Privately Held**
SIC: 2395 2396 5199 Embroidery products, except schiffli machine; screen printing on fabric articles; advertising specialties

(G-6432)
COLUMBIA CABINETS INC
33549 E Royalton Rd 4-5 (44028-9306)
PHONE 440 748-1010
Charles Dunn, *President*
EMP: 3
SQ FT: 4,000
SALES: 200K **Privately Held**
SIC: 2599 1799 Cabinets, factory; counter top installation

(G-6433)
COLUMBIA STAMPING INC
Also Called: Total Automation
13676 Station Rd (44028-9538)
PHONE 440 236-6677
James D Galvin, *President*
Ken Dillinger, *Corp Secy*
EMP: 15
SQ FT: 37,000

SALES (est): 3MM Privately Held
SIC: 3544 3542 Die sets for metal stamping (presses); die casting machines

(G-6434)
CONTROL ELECTRIC CO
12130 Eaton Commerce Pkwy (44028-9208)
PHONE.....................216 671-8010
Mike Vogt, *President*
Rob Horvath, *Engineer*
Adam Lenhoff, *Sales Staff*
Nancy Dennler, *Office Mgr*
EMP: 23 EST: 1963
SQ FT: 6,800
SALES (est): 6.4MM Privately Held
WEB: www.controlelectric.com
SIC: 3625 8711 2542 Industrial electrical relays & switches; engineering services; partitions & fixtures, except wood

(G-6435)
DIMENSION INDUSTRIES INC
27335 Royalton Rd (44028-9159)
P.O. Box 1130 (44028-1130)
PHONE.....................440 236-3265
William Biljes, *President*
EMP: 12
SQ FT: 7,200
SALES (est): 1MM Privately Held
SIC: 3599 Machine & other job shop work

(G-6436)
DJ PALLETS
23845 Royalton Rd (44028-9458)
PHONE.....................216 701-9183
James Violi, *Principal*
EMP: 4
SALES (est): 393.4K Privately Held
SIC: 2448 Pallets, wood & wood with metal

(G-6437)
DOVE MACHINE INC
27100 Royalton Rd (44028-9048)
P.O. Box 1003 (44028-1003)
PHONE.....................440 864-2645
James Dove, *President*
Anna Dove, *Vice Pres*
EMP: 15
SQ FT: 37,000
SALES (est): 2MM Privately Held
SIC: 3451 3714 Screw machine products; motor vehicle parts & accessories

(G-6438)
HOTEND WORKS INC
11470 Hawke Rd Unit 9 (44028-9805)
PHONE.....................440 787-3181
Benjamin Becker, *Administration*
EMP: 3
SALES (est): 198.2K Privately Held
SIC: 3555 Printing trades machinery

(G-6439)
LA GANKE & SONS STAMPING CO
13676 Station Rd (44028-9538)
PHONE.....................216 451-0278
Charles Laganke, *President*
Kim Lorris, *Admin Sec*
EMP: 10 EST: 1961
SQ FT: 18,500
SALES (est): 1.4MM Privately Held
SIC: 3469 3544 Stamping metal for the trade; special dies & tools; jigs & fixtures

(G-6440)
MODERN MOLD CORPORATION
27684 Royalton Rd (44028-9073)
PHONE.....................440 236-9600
David Bowes, *President*
EMP: 7
SALES (est): 856.6K Privately Held
WEB: www.modernmoldandtool.com
SIC: 3089 Injection molding of plastics

(G-6441)
NOBAL ENTERPRISES INC
11470 Hawke Rd Unit 3 (44028-9805)
PHONE.....................440 748-0522
Paul J Novak, *President*
EMP: 5
SQ FT: 2,500
SALES: 92K Privately Held
SIC: 3599 Machine shop, jobbing & repair

(G-6442)
PERRONS PRINTING COMPANY
Also Called: Image Graphics
27500 Royalton Rd Ste D (44028-9713)
P.O. Box 669 (44028-0669)
PHONE.....................440 236-8870
Edward Perron Sr, *President*
George D Maurer Sr, *Principal*
Linda Perron, *Vice Pres*
EMP: 20
SQ FT: 10,000
SALES (est): 4.1MM Privately Held
SIC: 2752 7336 Commercial printing, offset; graphic arts & related design

(G-6443)
PIER TOOL & DIE INC
27369 Royalton Rd (44028-9159)
P.O. Box 452 (44028-0452)
PHONE.....................440 236-3188
Mario J Pierzchala, *President*
Karen Pierzchala, *Vice Pres*
Randy Pierzchala, *Plant Mgr*
EMP: 13
SQ FT: 15,000
SALES: 1.5MM Privately Held
SIC: 3544 Special dies & tools

(G-6444)
PRINT DIRECT FOR LESS 2 INC
27500 Royalton Rd (44028-9713)
P.O. Box 669 (44028-0669)
PHONE.....................440 236-8870
Linda Perron, *President*
Nellie Akalp, *Principal*
Edward M Perron Jr, *Vice Pres*
Pam Morris, *Manager*
Jeff Dickey, *Graphic Designe*
▼ EMP: 22
SALES (est): 4.3MM Privately Held
WEB: www.printdirectforless.com
SIC: 2752 Commercial printing, offset

(G-6445)
ROLLER SOURCE INC
34100 E Royalton Rd (44028-9759)
PHONE.....................440 748-4033
Steve Leuschel, *President*
George Novak, *Vice Pres*
EMP: 10
SALES: 600K Privately Held
WEB: www.therollersource.com
SIC: 3052 Rubber & plastics hose & beltings

(G-6446)
ROYALTON INDUSTRIES INC
12450 Eaton Commerce Pkwy (44028-9213)
PHONE.....................440 748-9900
William A Baltes Sr, *Ch of Bd*
William A Baltes Jr, *Treasurer*
Len Steinmeyer, *VP Sales*
EMP: 10 EST: 1979
SQ FT: 10,000
SALES (est): 1.8MM Privately Held
WEB: www.royaltonindustries.com
SIC: 3599 Custom machinery

(G-6447)
RURAL URBAN RECORD INC
24487 Squire Rd (44028-9648)
P.O. Box 966 (44028-0966)
PHONE.....................440 236-8982
Leonard Boise, *President*
Lee Boise, *Vice Pres*
EMP: 6
SQ FT: 1,966
SALES (est): 492.1K Privately Held
SIC: 2711 Newspapers: publishing only, not printed on site

(G-6448)
SHARC INDUSTRIES
10600 Bridle Path (44028-9699)
PHONE.....................216 272-0668
Scott Thomas, *Principal*
EMP: 9
SALES (est): 909.5K Privately Held
SIC: 3999 Manufacturing industries

(G-6449)
SUPERIOR ENERGY SYSTEMS LLC
13660 Station Rd (44028-9538)
PHONE.....................440 236-6009
Donald Fernald, *CEO*
Philip J Lombardo, *Principal*
Derek Rimko, *Vice Pres*
Mike Walters, *Vice Pres*
William J Young, *Vice Pres*
▼ EMP: 17
SQ FT: 14,000
SALES (est): 5.4MM Privately Held
WEB: www.superiorenergysystems.com
SIC: 3714 Propane conversion equipment, motor vehicle

(G-6450)
SZPAK MANUFACTURING CO INC
27500 Royalton Rd Unit 5 (44028-9713)
P.O. Box 543 (44028-0543)
PHONE.....................440 236-5233
Joseph Szpak Jr, *President*
Tony Szpak, *Vice Pres*
EMP: 7
SQ FT: 2,500
SALES (est): 450K Privately Held
WEB: www.szpakmfg.com
SIC: 3599 Machine shop, jobbing & repair

(G-6451)
TRIAD CAPITAL AAT LLC
Also Called: American Assembly Tools
13676 Station Rd (44028-9538)
PHONE.....................440 236-4163
EMP: 4
SQ FT: 27,500
SALES (est): 321K Privately Held
SIC: 3546 Mfg Power-Driven Handtools

Columbiana
Columbiana County

(G-6452)
A PLUS POWDER COATERS INC
1384 Kauffman Ave (44408-9750)
PHONE.....................330 482-4389
Robert Bertelsen, *President*
EMP: 12
SQ FT: 20,250
SALES (est): 1.3MM Privately Held
WEB: www.apluspowder.com
SIC: 3479 Coating of metals & formed products

(G-6453)
ALLOY MACHINING AND FABG
1028 Lower Elkton Rd (44408-8427)
P.O. Box 49 (44408-0049)
PHONE.....................330 482-5543
Ed Keating, *President*
EMP: 23
SALES (est): 4.1MM Privately Held
SIC: 3599 Machine shop, jobbing & repair

(G-6454)
BIRDFISH BREWING COMPANY LLC
16 S Main St (44408-1348)
PHONE.....................330 397-4010
Joshua Dunn, *CEO*
Jared Channell, *President*
Gregory Snyder, *Vice Pres*
EMP: 7 EST: 2014
SQ FT: 1,250
SALES (est): 220.3K Privately Held
SIC: 2082 Beer (alcoholic beverage)

(G-6455)
BOARDMAN STEEL INC
156 Nulf Dr (44408-9720)
PHONE.....................330 758-0951
Dave Deibel, *President*
Holly Baker, *Admin Asst*
EMP: 55 EST: 1963
SQ FT: 49,000
SALES (est): 12.2MM Privately Held
WEB: www.boardmansteel.com
SIC: 3441 Building components, structural steel

(G-6456)
BUCKEYE COMPONENTS LLC
1340 State Route 14 (44408-9648)
PHONE.....................330 482-5163
Robert Holmes,
EMP: 30
SQ FT: 8,000
SALES (est): 2.8MM Privately Held
SIC: 5031 2439 Lumber, plywood & millwork; trusses, wooden roof

(G-6457)
CENTURY CONTAINER LLC
32 W Railroad St (44408-1203)
PHONE.....................330 457-2367
Don R BR, *CEO*
EMP: 8
SALES (corp-wide): 89.9MM Privately Held
SIC: 3089 Plastic containers, except foam
HQ: Century Container, Llc
    5331 State Route 7
    New Waterford OH 44445
    330 457-2367

(G-6458)
COBBLERS CORNER LLC
1115 Village Plz (44408-8480)
PHONE.....................330 482-4005
Terry Thompson,
Jennifer Balint,
EMP: 13 EST: 1975
SQ FT: 8,000
SALES: 850K Privately Held
SIC: 5661 3021 7251 Men's boots; women's boots; rubber & plastics footwear; shoes, rubber or rubber soled fabric uppers; footwear, custom made; shoe repair shop

(G-6459)
COL-PUMP COMPANY INC
131 E Railroad St (44408-1318)
PHONE.....................330 482-1029
Thomas Bowker, *President*
Paul Rance, *Vice Pres*
EMP: 60
SQ FT: 100,000
SALES (est): 12.9MM Privately Held
WEB: www.col-pump.net
SIC: 3321 Gray iron castings

(G-6460)
COLUMBIANA BOILER COMPANY LLC
200 W Railroad St (44408-1281)
PHONE.....................330 482-3373
Michael J Sherwin, *President*
Wayne Good, *Vice Pres*
Chuck Gorby, *Vice Pres*
Gerianne Klepfer, *CFO*
Tina Cousins, *Asst Mgr*
◆ EMP: 45 EST: 1894
SQ FT: 50,000
SALES: 9.5MM
SALES (corp-wide): 4.3MM Privately Held
SIC: 1791 3443 Storage tanks, metal: erection; process vessels, industrial: metal plate
PA: Columbiana Holding Co Inc
    200 W Railroad St
    Columbiana OH 44408
    330 482-3373

(G-6461)
COLUMBIANA HOLDING CO INC (PA)
200 W Railroad St (44408-1281)
PHONE.....................330 482-3373
Thomas F Dougherty, *Ch of Bd*
John J Barrow, *Ch of Bd*
Gerianne Klepfer, *CFO*
Michael Sherwin, *Director*
▲ EMP: 54
SALES (est): 4.3MM Privately Held
SIC: 3443 Process vessels, industrial: metal plate

(G-6462)
COMPCO COLUMBIANA COMPANY (PA)
Also Called: Compco Industries
400 W Railroad St Ste 1 (44408-1213)
PHONE.....................330 482-0200

Columbiana - Columbiana County (G-6463)

Clarence Smith Sr, *Principal*
Martin Poschner, *Principal*
EMP: 6
SALES (est): 10.4MM **Privately Held**
SIC: 3469 Household cooking & kitchen utensils, metal

(G-6463)
COMPCO INDUSTRIES INC (HQ)
400 W Railroad St Ste 1 (44408-1213)
PHONE..................330 482-6488
Clarence R Smith Jr, *Ch of Bd*
Gregory B Smith Sr, *President*
Russ Werner, *Opers Mgr*
Brian McLemore, *Warehouse Mgr*
Shaun Reed, *Foreman/Supr*
EMP: 63 **EST:** 1952
SQ FT: 200,000
SALES (est): 23.3MM
SALES (corp-wide): 22.9MM **Privately Held**
WEB: www.compcoind.com
SIC: 3443 3469 3444 Tanks, standard or custom fabricated: metal plate; metal stampings; sheet metalwork
PA: S-P Company, Inc
400 W Railroad St Ste 1
Columbiana OH 44408
330 482-0200

(G-6464)
ENVELOPE 1 INC (PA)
41969 State Route 344 (44408-9421)
PHONE..................330 482-3900
Tarry Pidgeon, *CEO*
▲ **EMP:** 96
SALES (est): 105.1MM **Privately Held**
SIC: 2677 Envelopes

(G-6465)
FEDERAL IRON WORKS COMPANY
42082 State Route 344 (44408-9421)
P.O. Box 150 (44408-0150)
PHONE..................330 482-5910
Edward M Sferra Jr, *President*
Marcella A Sferra, *Vice Pres*
EMP: 20
SALES (est): 3.7MM **Privately Held**
SIC: 3446 1761 Architectural metalwork; architectural sheet metal work

(G-6466)
FOSTER PATTERN WORKS INC
1371 Kauffman Ave (44408)
P.O. Box 14 (44408-0014)
PHONE..................330 482-3612
William Huffman, *President*
Louis Huffman, *Vice Pres*
EMP: 4
SQ FT: 5,000
SALES: 280K **Privately Held**
SIC: 3543 Industrial patterns

(G-6467)
GREEN HARVEST ENERGY LLC
1340 State Route 14 (44408-9648)
P.O. Box 82, Greenford (44422-0082)
PHONE..................330 716-3068
John J Monroe, *President*
Jean Holt, *Principal*
Robert J Holmes, *Chairman*
EMP: 16 **EST:** 2009
SALES: 0 **Privately Held**
SIC: 2869 Industrial organic chemicals

(G-6468)
HAYS ORCHARD & CIDER MILL LLC
3622 Middleton Rd (44408-9596)
PHONE..................330 482-2924
Todd Valendza, *Mng Member*
EMP: 15
SALES: 3MM **Privately Held**
SIC: 2099 Cider, nonalcoholic

(G-6469)
HORST PACKING INC
3535 Renkenberger Rd (44408-9763)
PHONE..................330 482-2997
David Horst, *President*
Debra Horst, *Admin Sec*
EMP: 6
SQ FT: 1,500
SALES (est): 630.6K **Privately Held**
SIC: 2011 Meat packing plants

(G-6470)
HUMTOWN PATTERN COMPANY
Also Called: Humtown Products
44708 Clmbana Wterford Rd (44408-9605)
P.O. Box 367 (44408-0367)
PHONE..................330 482-5555
Mark Lamoncha, *President*
Brandon Lamoncha, *Principal*
Bronson Lamoncha, *Principal*
Sheri Lamoncha, *Principal*
Terrie Marshall, *Principal*
EMP: 60 **EST:** 1959
SQ FT: 55,000
SALES: 10MM **Privately Held**
WEB: www.humtown.com
SIC: 2759 3543 Commercial printing; foundry cores

(G-6471)
J & H MANUFACTURING LLC
1652 Columbiana Lisbon Rd (44408-9443)
P.O. Box 12 (44408-0012)
PHONE..................330 482-2636
John Kephart, *Mng Member*
▲ **EMP:** 11
SQ FT: 41,000
SALES (est): 2.3MM **Privately Held**
SIC: 3462 Iron & steel forgings

(G-6472)
J&J PRECISION FABRICATORS
1341 Heck Rd (44408-9599)
PHONE..................330 482-4964
Hans Leitner, *Managing Prtnr*
EMP: 17
SQ FT: 11,500
SALES (est): 3.4MM **Privately Held**
SIC: 3441 Fabricated structural metal

(G-6473)
MILLER CASTING INC
1634 Lower Elkton Rd (44408-9404)
P.O. Box 440 (44408-0440)
PHONE..................330 482-2923
Mike Miller, *President*
EMP: 15
SALES (est): 2MM **Privately Held**
SIC: 3365 Aluminum foundries

(G-6474)
MUNICIPAL SIGNS AND SALES INC
1219 Mcclosky Rd (44408-9510)
PHONE..................330 457-2421
Jay Strohecker, *President*
Jean Gernert, *Vice Pres*
EMP: 5
SQ FT: 1,260
SALES: 410K **Privately Held**
SIC: 3993 5099 Signs, not made in custom sign painting shops; safety equipment & supplies

(G-6475)
OAKS WELDING INC
201 Prospect St (44408)
PHONE..................330 482-4216
Jack Guy, *President*
Jeff Guy, *President*
Geri Rubicky, *Treasurer*
Maribell Guy, *Admin Sec*
EMP: 8
SQ FT: 11,025
SALES (est): 1.1MM **Privately Held**
SIC: 3599 7692 7629 Machine shop, jobbing & repair; welding repair; electrical repair shops

(G-6476)
PHD MANUFACTURING INC
44018 Clmbana Wterford Rd (44408-9481)
PHONE..................330 482-9256
Anthony A Kopatich, *President*
Joseph J Corvino, *President*
Gene Hancock, *Natl Sales Mgr*
Harry Forbes, *Sales Staff*
Anthony Kopatich, *CTO*
EMP: 110
SQ FT: 131,000
SALES (est): 48.5MM **Privately Held**
WEB: www.phd-mfg.com
SIC: 3494 Pipe fittings

(G-6477)
RANCE INDUSTRIES INC
1361 Heck Rd (44408-9599)
P.O. Box 325 (44408-0325)
PHONE..................330 482-1745
John Rance, *President*
Karen Rance, *Treasurer*
Danny Ferry, *Manager*
EMP: 15
SQ FT: 20,000
SALES (est): 2.4MM **Privately Held**
WEB: www.ranceindustries.com
SIC: 3441 Fabricated structural metal

(G-6478)
REICHARD INDUSTRIES LLC (PA)
338 S Main St (44408-1500)
PHONE..................330 482-5511
Keith A Reichard, *President*
Duane E Reichard, *Vice Pres*
James Hawkins, *Controller*
EMP: 2
SQ FT: 57,000
SALES: 13MM **Privately Held**
SIC: 3599 Custom machinery

(G-6479)
S-P COMPANY INC (PA)
400 W Railroad St Ste 1 (44408-1294)
PHONE..................330 482-0200
Clarence R Smith Jr, *Ch of Bd*
Gregory B Smith, *President*
Douglas Hagy, *CFO*
EMP: 13
SQ FT: 44,000
SALES (est): 22.9MM **Privately Held**
SIC: 3469 3443 3498 6512 Metal stampings, tanks, standard or custom fabricated: metal plate; tube fabricating (contract bending & shaping); commercial & industrial building operation; gift shop; custom machinery

(G-6480)
SITLER PRINTER INC
707 E Park Ave (44408-1447)
PHONE..................330 482-4463
Christine R Davis, *President*
Lee Davis, *Vice Pres*
EMP: 8 **EST:** 1909
SQ FT: 2,000
SALES (est): 1.3MM **Privately Held**
WEB: www.sitlertheprinter.com
SIC: 2752 2759 Commercial printing, offset; letterpress printing

(G-6481)
SPECIALTY CERAMICS INC
41995 State Route 344 (44408-9421)
PHONE..................330 482-0800
Richard Ludwig, *President*
Richard F Wilk, *Corp Secy*
EMP: 100
SQ FT: 47,000
SALES (est): 27.8MM **Privately Held**
WEB: www.scilogs.com
SIC: 3433 3255 Logs, gas fireplace; clay refractories

(G-6482)
STAR FAB INC
400 W Railroad St Ste 8 (44408-1294)
P.O. Box 553, Canfield (44406-0553)
PHONE..................330 482-1601
John Zepernick, *Branch Mgr*
EMP: 50
SALES (corp-wide): 24.2MM **Privately Held**
WEB: www.starext.com
SIC: 3354 3711 Aluminum extruded products; automobile assembly, including specialty automobiles
PA: Star Fab, Inc.
7055 Herbert Rd
Canfield OH 44406
330 533-9863

(G-6483)
TRACKER MACHINE INC
1370 Kauffman Ave (44408-9750)
PHONE..................330 482-4086
William Niemi, *President*
EMP: 5
SALES: 250K **Privately Held**
SIC: 3544 Industrial molds

(G-6484)
UNIVERSAL PERCUSSION INC
1431 Heck Rd (44408-9599)
PHONE..................330 482-5750
Howert Rubenstein, *President*
▲ **EMP:** 10
SALES (est): 760K **Privately Held**
WEB: www.universalpercussion.com
SIC: 3931 5736 Percussion instruments & parts; musical instrument stores

(G-6485)
VARI-WALL TUBE SPECIALISTS INC
1350 Wardingsley Ave (44408-9727)
P.O. Box 340 (44408-0340)
PHONE..................330 482-0000
Randall Alexoff, *President*
Peter Alexoff, *Exec VP*
Katelynn Alexoff, *Opers Mgr*
Joe Mortellaro, *Controller*
Thomas Lodge, *Admin Sec*
▲ **EMP:** 100
SQ FT: 60,000
SALES (est): 20.3MM **Privately Held**
WEB: www.vari-wall.com
SIC: 3354 3751 3714 Shapes, extruded aluminum; motorcycles, bicycles & parts; motor vehicle parts & accessories

(G-6486)
YES MANAGEMENT INC (PA)
Also Called: Youngstown Electric Supply
44612 State Route 14 (44408-9540)
PHONE..................330 747-8593
Lee De Rose, *President*
James Hunt, *Human Res Dir*
Bill Farmer, *Sales Staff*
Carle Robeson, *Sales Staff*
Lee J Derose, *Manager*
EMP: 2
SQ FT: 22,000
SALES (est): 63.5MM **Privately Held**
WEB: www.yeselectric.com
SIC: 5063 3993 Electrical supplies; signs & advertising specialties

(G-6487)
ZARBANA ALUM EXTRUSIONS LLC
41738 Esterly Dr (44408-9448)
P.O. Box 46 (44408-0046)
PHONE..................330 482-5092
Billy Joe Miller, *Manager*
EMP: 37 **EST:** 2005
SALES: 11.5MM
SALES (corp-wide): 425.9K **Privately Held**
SIC: 3354 Aluminum extruded products
HQ: Roccafranca Spa
Via Rudiana 4
Roccafranca BS 25030
030 709-1181

(G-6488)
ZORICH INDUSTRIES INC
1400 Wardingsley Ave (44408-9727)
PHONE..................330 482-9803
Frank Phillips, *Principal*
EMP: 16
SALES (est): 1.9MM **Privately Held**
SIC: 3999 Atomizers, toiletry

Columbus
Delaware County

(G-6489)
BRISTOL-MYERS SQUIBB COMPANY
999 Polaris Pkwy Ste 100 (43240-2051)
PHONE..................800 321-1335
Steve Betulius, *Branch Mgr*
EMP: 40
SALES (corp-wide): 22.5B **Publicly Held**
WEB: www.bms.com
SIC: 2834 Druggists' preparations (pharmaceuticals); drugs acting on the central nervous system & sense organs
PA: Bristol-Myers Squibb Company
430 E 29th St Fl 14
New York NY 10016
212 546-4000

▲ = Import ▼ = Export
◆ = Import/Export

Columbus — Franklin County

(G-6490)
EMERSON PROCESS MGT LLLP
8460 Orion Pl Ste 110 (43240)
PHONE...............................877 468-6384
Chris Village, *Manager*
EMP: 50
SALES (corp-wide): 17.4B **Publicly Held**
SIC: 3823 Industrial instrmnts msrmnt display/control process variable
HQ: Emerson Process Management Lllp
1100 W Louis Henna Blvd
Round Rock TX 78681

(G-6491)
EXACT EQUIPMENT CORPORATION (HQ)
1900 Polaris Pkwy (43240-4035)
PHONE...............................215 295-2000
Robert C Enichan, *President*
EMP: 10
SQ FT: 9,000
SALES (est): 1.6MM
SALES (corp-wide): 2.9B **Publicly Held**
WEB: www.exactequipment.com
SIC: 3565 3596 3824 Packaging machinery; industrial scales; fluid meters & counting devices
PA: Mettler-Toledo International Inc.
1900 Polaris Pkwy Fl 6
Columbus OH 43240
614 438-4511

(G-6492)
FARAH JEWELERS INC
1500 Polaris Pkwy # 2156 (43240-2133)
PHONE...............................614 438-6140
Eli Hannoush, *President*
EMP: 18
SQ FT: 1,500
SALES (est): 2.5MM **Privately Held**
SIC: 3911 5944 Jewelry mountings & trimmings; jewelry stores

(G-6493)
FIDELUX LIGHTING LLC
8415 Pulsar Pl Ste 300 (43240-4032)
PHONE...............................404 941-4182
EMP: 3
SALES (est): 212.5K **Privately Held**
SIC: 3674 Solar cells

(G-6494)
FUSIONSTORM
Also Called: Adexis
1900 Polaris Pkwy Ste 385 (43240-4035)
PHONE...............................614 431-8000
EMP: 9
SALES (corp-wide): 5B **Privately Held**
SIC: 7372 Prepackaged software
HQ: Computacenter Fusionstorm Inc.
124 Grove St Ste 311
Franklin MA 02038
508 520-5000

(G-6495)
GLOBAL BIOPROTECT LLC
8720 Orion Pl Ste 110 (43240-2111)
PHONE...............................336 861-0162
Gary Willet,
EMP: 10 **EST:** 2016
SALES (est): 545K **Privately Held**
SIC: 2899 Chemical preparations

(G-6496)
HEADLEE ENTERPRISES LTD
Also Called: AlphaGraphics
9015 Antares Ave (43240-2012)
PHONE...............................614 785-0011
Chad M Headlee, *Partner*
Murray A Headlee, *Partner*
EMP: 8
SQ FT: 4,200
SALES (est): 1.5MM **Privately Held**
SIC: 2752 Commercial printing, offset

(G-6497)
HYPE SOCKS LLC
8836 Commerce Loop Dr (43240-2121)
PHONE...............................855 497-3769
Josh M Wintermantel, *Mng Member*
Tony Garber,
EMP: 15
SALES (est): 143K **Privately Held**
SIC: 2252 Socks

(G-6498)
LEAF & THORN PRESS
1080 Pebble Brook Dr (43240-6040)
PHONE...............................614 396-6055
Kathleen Groger, *Principal*
EMP: 3
SALES (est): 76.2K **Privately Held**
SIC: 2711 Newspapers

(G-6499)
MCGRAW-HILL SCHOOL EDUCATION H
8787 Orion Pl (43240-4027)
PHONE...............................614 430-4000
Chris Wiggens, *Principal*
Rukmini Nanduri, *QC Mgr*
Renata Harris, *Cust Mgr*
EMP: 500
SALES (corp-wide): 158MM **Privately Held**
WEB: www.mcgraw-hill.com
SIC: 2731 Book publishing
HQ: Mcgraw-Hill School Education Holdings, Llc
2 Penn Plz Fl 20
New York NY 10121
646 766-2000

(G-6500)
METTLER-TOLEDO INTL FIN INC (DH)
1900 Polaris Pkwy Fl 6 (43240-4055)
PHONE...............................614 438-4511
Olivier Filliol, *CEO*
EMP: 6
SALES (est): 340.2K
SALES (corp-wide): 2.9B **Publicly Held**
SIC: 3596 5049 7699 3821 Industrial scales; weighing machines & apparatus; analytical instruments; professional instrument repair services; pipettes, hemocytometer; balances, laboratory; electrodes used in industrial process measurement; refractometers, except industrial process type; liquid chromatographic instruments; moisture analyzers; pH meters, except industrial process type
HQ: Mettler-Toledo, Llc
1900 Polaris Pkwy Fl 6
Columbus OH 43240
614 438-4511

(G-6501)
METTLER-TOLEDO INTL INC (PA)
1900 Polaris Pkwy Fl 6 (43240-4055)
PHONE...............................614 438-4511
Robert F Spoerry, *Ch of Bd*
Olivier A Filliol, *President*
Gary Wilkins, *Regional Mgr*
William P Donnelly, *Exec VP*
Michael Heidingsfelder, *Indstl Engineer*
◆ **EMP:** 277
SALES: 2.9B **Publicly Held**
WEB: www.mt.com
SIC: 3596 3821 3826 3823 Industrial scales; laboratory measuring apparatus; balances, laboratory; analytical instruments; industrial instrmnts msrmnt display/control process variable

(G-6502)
METTLR-TLEDO GLOBL HLDINGS LLC (HQ)
1900 Polaris Pkwy (43240-4035)
PHONE...............................614 438-4511
Mary T Finnegan, *Treasurer*
EMP: 10 **EST:** 2010
SALES (est): 9.2MM
SALES (corp-wide): 2.9B **Publicly Held**
SIC: 3451 3826 Screw machine products; analytical instruments
PA: Mettler-Toledo International Inc.
1900 Polaris Pkwy Fl 6
Columbus OH 43240
614 438-4511

(G-6503)
MICROSOFT CORPORATION
8800 Lyra Dr Ste 400 (43240-2100)
PHONE...............................614 719-5900
Marrida Davis, *General Mgr*
EMP: 45
SALES (corp-wide): 110.3B **Publicly Held**
WEB: www.microsoft.com
SIC: 7372 Application computer software
PA: Microsoft Corporation
1 Microsoft Way
Redmond WA 98052
425 882-8080

(G-6504)
OIL BAR LLC
1500 Polaris Pkwy # 2072 (43240-2132)
PHONE...............................614 880-3950
Jamie Dennis, *Branch Mgr*
EMP: 14
SALES: 770K **Privately Held**
SIC: 2844 7299 Toilet preparations; massage parlor

(G-6505)
RAININ INSTRUMENT LLC
1900 Polaris Pkwy (43240-4035)
PHONE...............................510 564-1600
Ruben Rosso, *Principal*
EMP: 5 **EST:** 2008
SALES (est): 907.1K **Privately Held**
SIC: 3823 Industrial instrmnts msrmnt display/control process variable

(G-6506)
RENEWAL BY ANDERSEN LLC
400 Lazelle Rd Ste 1 (43240-2077)
PHONE...............................614 781-9600
Jake Zahnow, *Principal*
EMP: 7
SALES (corp-wide): 2.9B **Privately Held**
SIC: 3442 2431 Screens, window, metal; millwork
HQ: Renewal By Andersen Llc
9900 Jamaica Ave S
Cottage Grove MN 55016
855 871-7377

(G-6507)
UNITED CONTROLS GROUP INC
400 Lazelle Rd Ste 14 (43240-2077)
PHONE...............................740 936-0005
Elliott Allison, *Principal*
Paul Mayhan, *Chief Engr*
EMP: 6 **Privately Held**
SIC: 3694 Engine electrical equipment
PA: United Controls Group, Inc.
4725 121st St
Urbandale IA 50323

(G-6508)
VEEAM SOFTWARE CORPORATION (PA)
8800 Lyra Dr Ste 350 (43240-2151)
PHONE...............................614 339-8200
Ratmir Timashev, *President*
David Berney, *Partner*
Jessica Degenhardt, *Partner*
Justin Hollmann, *Partner*
Josh Plumley, *Partner*
EMP: 13
SALES: 90.1K **Privately Held**
SIC: 7372 Business oriented computer software

(G-6509)
ZNODE INC
8415 Pulsar Pl Ste 200 (43240-4032)
P.O. Box 3162, Cedar Rapids IA (52406-3162)
PHONE...............................888 755-5541
Vish Vishwanathan, *CEO*
David Chu, *CTO*
EMP: 16
SALES (est): 1.3MM **Privately Held**
WEB: www.znode.com
SIC: 7372 Business oriented computer software
PA: Woodpro Software Inc
2680 Shell Rd Suite 208
Richmond BC V6X 4
604 270-2595

Columbus
Franklin County

(G-6510)
1803 BACON LTD
1081 Norris Dr (43224-2732)
PHONE...............................740 398-7644
Tony Terrell, *Principal*
EMP: 3 **EST:** 2015
SALES (est): 231.6K **Privately Held**
SIC: 2869 Industrial organic chemicals

(G-6511)
360WATER INC
965 W 3rd Ave (43212-3109)
PHONE...............................614 294-3600
Laura Tegethoff, *President*
Todd Raish, *Vice Pres*
EMP: 5
SQ FT: 2,000
SALES (est): 210K **Privately Held**
WEB: www.360water.com
SIC: 8299 8742 7372 Educational service, nondegree granting: continuing educ.; human resource consulting services; educational computer software

(G-6512)
3D SYSTEMS INC
950 Taylor Station Rd K (43230-6670)
PHONE...............................215 757-9611
EMP: 192 **Publicly Held**
SIC: 3571 Mfg Electronic Computers
HQ: 3d Systems, Inc.
333 Three D Systems Cir
Rock Hill SC 29730
803 326-3900

(G-6513)
614 MEDIA GROUP LLC
Also Called: 614 Magazine
458 E Main St (43215-5344)
PHONE...............................614 488-4400
Meggin Weimerskirch, *VP Sales*
Liza Worthington, *Accounts Exec*
Lindsay Arnett, *Mktg Dir*
Wayne T Lewis, *Mng Member*
Clark Gaines,
EMP: 60
SALES (est): 9.3MM **Privately Held**
SIC: 2721 Magazines: publishing & printing

(G-6514)
A & H AUTOMOTIVE INDUSTRIES
Also Called: A & H Truck Parts
701 Hadley Dr (43228-1029)
P.O. Box 91256 (43209-7256)
PHONE...............................614 235-1759
Alex B Rosen, *President*
Susan Rosen, *General Mgr*
Susan K Rosen, *Vice Pres*
EMP: 5 **EST:** 1979
SALES (est): 752.7K **Privately Held**
WEB: www.ahautomotive.com
SIC: 5013 3714 3366 Automotive supplies & parts; motor vehicle transmissions, drive assemblies & parts; bushings & bearings, brass (nonmachined)

(G-6515)
A B SIEMER INC
150 E Campus View Blvd # 250 (43235-4648)
PHONE...............................614 888-8855
Arnold B Siemer, *President*
EMP: 251
SALES (est): 15.9MM
SALES (corp-wide): 180.1MM **Privately Held**
WEB: www.descoventurecapital.com
SIC: 3442 Window & door frames
PA: Desco Corporation
7795 Walton Pkwy Ste 175
New Albany OH 43054
614 888-8855

(G-6516)
A R HARDING PUBLISHING CO
Also Called: Fur-Fish-Game
2878 E Main St (43209-2613)
PHONE...............................614 231-5735
Jeffrey A Kirn, *President*

Columbus - Franklin County (G-6517)   GEOGRAPHIC SECTION

Jeffrey A Kim, *President*
Vic Attardo, *Editor*
Mitch Cox, *Editor*
Jeffrey Kirn, *Exec VP*
EMP: 10 **EST:** 1987
SQ FT: 1,500
SALES (est): 1.4MM **Privately Held**
WEB: www.furfishgame.com
SIC: 2721 Periodicals-Publishing/Printing

(G-6517)
A-DISPLAY SERVICE CORP
Also Called: Signature Store Fixtures
541 Dana Ave (43223-5202)
PHONE.................................614 469-1230
Mario Grilli, *CEO*
Anthony Grilli, *President*
Nancy Grilli, *Corp Secy*
EMP: 10
SQ FT: 8,500
SALES (est): 1.7MM **Privately Held**
WEB: www.blueshore.com
SIC: 2541 Display fixtures, wood; showcases, except refrigerated: wood; store fixtures, wood

(G-6518)
A-Z PACKAGING COMPANY
1221 Harmon Ave (43223-3306)
PHONE.................................614 444-8441
Charles Ellyson Jr, *CEO*
Jo Ann Ellyson, *President*
Charles Ellyson Sr, *Vice Pres*
Gloria Ellyson, *Treasurer*
EMP: 14 **EST:** 1974
SQ FT: 12,000
SALES (est): 1.3MM **Privately Held**
SIC: 7389 2449 2448 Commercial Packaging

(G-6519)
ABBOTT LABORATORIES
Also Called: Abbott Nutrition
585 Cleveland Ave (43215-1755)
P.O. Box 16546 (43216-6546)
PHONE.................................614 624-3191
Chuck Mundy, *Principal*
Ed Govekar, *Manager*
EMP: 550
SQ FT: 378,500
SALES (corp-wide): 30.5B **Publicly Held**
WEB: www.abbott.com
SIC: 8099 2834 2087 2086 Nutrition services; pharmaceutical preparations; flavoring extracts & syrups; bottled & canned soft drinks; canned specialties
PA: Abbott Laboratories
100 Abbott Park Rd
Abbott Park IL 60064
224 667-6100

(G-6520)
ABBOTT LABORATORIES
350 N 5th St (43215-2103)
PHONE.................................614 624-3192
EMP: 15
SALES (corp-wide): 30.5B **Publicly Held**
SIC: 2834 Pharmaceutical preparations
PA: Abbott Laboratories
100 Abbott Park Rd
Abbott Park IL 60064
224 667-6100

(G-6521)
ABBOTT LABORATORIES
Abbott Nutrition
3300 Stelzer Rd (43219-3034)
PHONE.................................614 624-7677
Don Paton, *Branch Mgr*
EMP: 3000
SALES (corp-wide): 30.5B **Publicly Held**
WEB: www.abbott.com
SIC: 2834 Druggists' preparations (pharmaceuticals)
PA: Abbott Laboratories
100 Abbott Park Rd
Abbott Park IL 60064
224 667-6100

(G-6522)
ABBOTT LABORATORIES
Also Called: Ross Products Division
1033 Kingsmill Pkwy (43229-1129)
P.O. Box 16546 (43216)
PHONE.................................614 624-6627
Marlene Hernandez, *Manager*
EMP: 75
SALES (corp-wide): 30.5B **Publicly Held**
WEB: www.abbott.com
SIC: 2834 Druggists' preparations (pharmaceuticals)
PA: Abbott Laboratories
100 Abbott Park Rd
Abbott Park IL 60064
224 667-6100

(G-6523)
ABBOTT LABORATORIES
6550 Singletree Dr (43229-1119)
PHONE.................................614 624-6627
EMP: 617
SALES (corp-wide): 30.5B **Publicly Held**
WEB: www.abbott.com
SIC: 2834 Druggists' preparations (pharmaceuticals)
PA: Abbott Laboratories
100 Abbott Park Rd
Abbott Park IL 60064
224 667-6100

(G-6524)
ABBOTT LABORATORIES
625 Cleveland Ave (43215-1754)
P.O. Box 16718 (43216-6718)
PHONE.................................800 551-5838
EMP: 51
SALES (corp-wide): 30.5B **Publicly Held**
SIC: 2834 Pharmaceutical preparations
PA: Abbott Laboratories
100 Abbott Park Rd
Abbott Park IL 60064
224 667-6100

(G-6525)
ABBOTT LABORATORIES
Also Called: Ross Products Division
6 Cleveland Ave (43215)
PHONE.................................614 624-6088
David Hill, *Branch Mgr*
EMP: 2500
SALES (corp-wide): 30.5B **Publicly Held**
WEB: www.abbott.com
SIC: 2834 Druggists' preparations (pharmaceuticals)
PA: Abbott Laboratories
100 Abbott Park Rd
Abbott Park IL 60064
224 667-6100

(G-6526)
ABBOTT NUTRITION MFG INC
625 Cleveland Ave (43215-1754)
PHONE.................................614 624-7485
EMP: 10
SALES (corp-wide): 20.8B **Publicly Held**
SIC: 2834 Mfg Pharmaceutical Preparations
HQ: Abbott Nutrition Manufacturing Inc.
2351 N Watney Way Ste C
Fairfield CA 94533
707 399-1100

(G-6527)
ABITEC CORPORATION (HQ)
501 W 1st Ave (43215-1101)
PHONE.................................614 429-6464
Jeff Walton, *CEO*
Susan Taylor, *CFO*
◆ **EMP:** 20
SQ FT: 12,000
SALES (est): 44.7MM
SALES (corp-wide): 19.9B **Privately Held**
WEB: www.abiteccorp.com
SIC: 2844 2834 2869 2045 Toilet preparations; pharmaceutical preparations; industrial organic chemicals; prepared flour mixes & doughs
PA: Wittington Investments Limited
Weston Centre
London W1K 4
207 399-6565

(G-6528)
ABLE INDUSTRIES INC
Also Called: Able Manufacturing
870 N 20th St (43219-2421)
P.O. Box 426, Wooster (44691-0426)
PHONE.................................614 252-1050
Tim Dye, *President*
EMP: 5
SQ FT: 20,000
SALES (est): 1MM **Privately Held**
WEB: www.ableindustries.net
SIC: 1611 3713 Highway & street paving contractor; truck beds

(G-6529)
ABLE PALLET MFG & REPR
1271 Harmon Ave (43223-3306)
P.O. Box 23083 (43223-0083)
PHONE.................................614 444-2115
Charles O'Hara, *President*
EMP: 11
SQ FT: 5,089
SALES (est): 986.2K **Privately Held**
SIC: 7699 2448 Pallet repair; wood pallets & skids

(G-6530)
ABLE PRINTING COMPANY
1325 Holly Ave (43212-3116)
PHONE.................................614 294-4547
Patrick Davis, *President*
EMP: 5 **EST:** 1954
SQ FT: 13,000
SALES (est): 615.5K **Privately Held**
WEB: www.ableprintingco.com
SIC: 2752 Commercial printing, offset

(G-6531)
ACCENT DRAPERY CO INC
Also Called: Accent Drapery Supply Co
1180 Goodale Blvd (43212-3793)
PHONE.................................614 488-0741
Patrick Casbarro, *President*
Brian Whiteside, *Vice Pres*
Pat Casbarro, *Info Tech Mgr*
EMP: 27
SQ FT: 19,500
SALES (est): 4.1MM **Privately Held**
SIC: 5714 5023 2391 Draperies; draperies; curtains & draperies

(G-6532)
ACCLAIMD INC
1275 Kinnear Rd (43212-1180)
PHONE.................................614 219-9519
David Lyons, *President*
EMP: 4
SALES (est): 181.7K **Privately Held**
SIC: 7372 Application computer software
PA: Eboss Online Recruitment Solutions (Eboss) Limited
612 - 616 Wimborne Road
Bournemouth
207 183-0675

(G-6533)
ACCURATE INSULLATION LLC
495 S High St Ste 50 (43215-5689)
PHONE.................................302 241-0940
EMP: 3
SALES (est): 94.5K **Privately Held**
SIC: 3571 Personal computers (microputers)

(G-6534)
ACCURATE MANUFACTURING COMPANY
1940 Lone Eagle St (43228-3626)
P.O. Box 28666 (43228-0666)
PHONE.................................614 878-6510
Tom Lindblom, *CEO*
Angela Merrill, *Vice Pres*
EMP: 20
SQ FT: 10,000
SALES (est): 3.1MM **Privately Held**
SIC: 3542 3599 3548 Presses: hydraulic & pneumatic, mechanical & manual; machine shop, jobbing & repair; welding apparatus

(G-6535)
ACCUSCAN INSTRUMENTS INC
Also Called: Omni Tech Electronics
5098 Trabue Rd (43228-9391)
PHONE.................................614 878-6644
R H Mandalaywala, *President*
Myrna Ocasio, *Sales/Mktg Dir*
Myrna Mandalaywala, *Manager*
EMP: 10
SQ FT: 10,000
SALES (est): 2.1MM **Privately Held**
WEB: www.accuscan-usa.com
SIC: 3821 Laboratory apparatus, except heating & measuring

(G-6536)
ACE PROSTHETICS INC
4971 Arlngton Centre Blvd (43220-2910)
PHONE.................................614 291-8325
John Alan Hays, *President*
EMP: 2
SALES: 1MM **Privately Held**
SIC: 3842 Prosthetic appliances

(G-6537)
ACER CONTRACTING LLC
3840 N High St Ste B (43214-3780)
PHONE.................................702 236-5917
Christopher Garcia, *President*
EMP: 3
SALES (est): 99.8K **Privately Held**
SIC: 1389 8742 Construction, repair & dismantling services; real estate consultant

(G-6538)
ACRODYNE MFG CO
41 Kingston Ave (43207-2438)
PHONE.................................614 443-5517
Tim Burris, *President*
David Bals, *Vice Pres*
Michael R Bals, *Treasurer*
EMP: 3
SQ FT: 4,500
SALES: 400K **Privately Held**
SIC: 3599 Machine shop, jobbing & repair

(G-6539)
ACRYLICON INC
1976 Britains Ln (43224-5611)
PHONE.................................614 263-2086
Greg Gruff, *President*
EMP: 3
SQ FT: 2,400
SALES (est): 450K **Privately Held**
WEB: www.acrylicon.com
SIC: 2542 2653 Fixtures, office: except wood; display items, solid fiber: made from purchased materials

(G-6540)
ACTUAL BREWING COMPANY LLC
655 N James Rd (43219-1837)
PHONE.................................614 636-3825
Jonathan Carroll, *CEO*
Nicole Felter,
EMP: 12
SALES (est): 1.2MM **Privately Held**
SIC: 2082 Beer (alcoholic beverage); malt beverage products; ale (alcoholic beverage); stout (alcoholic beverage)

(G-6541)
ACTUAL INDUSTRIES LLC
655 N James Rd (43219-1837)
PHONE.................................614 379-2739
Fredrick Lee, *Principal*
EMP: 3
SALES (est): 257.3K **Privately Held**
SIC: 3999 Manufacturing industries

(G-6542)
ADB SAFEGATE AMERICAS LLC
977 Gahanna Pkwy (43230-6610)
P.O. Box 30829 (43230-0829)
PHONE.................................614 861-1304
Dan Hammond, *Project Mgr*
Fabiola P Le N, *Project Mgr*
Rosario Beltran, *Export Mgr*
Paul Kaser, *Buyer*
Joe Reichert, *Engineer*
◆ **EMP:** 300
SALES (est): 134.8MM **Privately Held**
WEB: www.sea.siemens.com
SIC: 3648 3812 Airport lighting fixtures: runway approach, taxi or ramp; search & navigation equipment
HQ: Adb Safegate
Leuvensesteenweg 585
Zaventem (Brucargo) 1930
272 217-11

(G-6543)
ADVANATAGE PRINT SOLUT
79 Acton Rd (43214-3301)
PHONE.................................614 519-2392
Debbie Smith, *Principal*
EMP: 6 **EST:** 2009
SALES (est): 801.6K **Privately Held**
SIC: 2752 Commercial printing, offset

▲ = Import ▼ = Export
◆ = Import/Export

GEOGRAPHIC SECTION

Columbus - Franklin County (G-6572)

(G-6544)
ADVANCE SIGN GROUP LLC
5150 Walcutt Ct (43228-9641)
PHONE.................614 429-2111
Ron Van Horn, *Project Mgr*
Craig Reynolds, *Purchasing*
Karen Etnyre, *Accounting Mgr*
Nancy Wasserstrom, *Sales Associate*
James Wafferftrom,
EMP: 50 **EST:** 2001
SALES (est): 8.4MM **Privately Held**
WEB: www.advancesigngroup.com
SIC: 3993 Electric signs

(G-6545)
ADVANCED FUEL SYSTEMS INC
841 Alton Ave (43219-3710)
PHONE.................614 252-8422
Timothy L Thickstun, *President*
Steve Thickstun, *Vice Pres*
Joanne Thickstun, *Admin Sec*
▼ **EMP:** 8 **EST:** 1998
SQ FT: 8,500
SALES (est): 2.1MM **Privately Held**
WEB: www.advfuel.com
SIC: 3561 3728 Pumps & pumping equipment; aircraft parts & equipment

(G-6546)
ADVANTAGE PRINTING INC
1369 Royston Dr (43204-1532)
PHONE.................614 272-8259
EMP: 2
SALES: 1MM **Privately Held**
SIC: 2752 Offset Printing

(G-6547)
AEIOU SCIENTIFIC LLC
Also Called: Aeiou Diagnostics
311 Kendall Pl (43205-2016)
PHONE.................614 325-2103
Jeffrey Spitzner, *President*
Lyn Bowman, *Chief Engr*
Brian Clark, *Director*
Anne Loucks, *Director*
EMP: 5
SALES (est): 198.4K **Privately Held**
SIC: 3841 8731 Diagnostic apparatus, medical; biological research; medical research, commercial

(G-6548)
AEP RESOURCES INC
Also Called: American Electric Power
1 Riverside Plz (43215-2355)
PHONE.................614 716-1000
John M Adams Jr, *Principal*
Darren Kelsey, *Business Mgr*
Bradford Signet, *Counsel*
Venita Cellon, *Exec VP*
Ed Bradley, *Vice Pres*
EMP: 18
SALES (est): 8.5MM **Privately Held**
SIC: 3621 Power generators

(G-6549)
AEROSPACE LUBRICANTS INC
1600 Georgesville Rd (43228-3616)
PHONE.................614 878-3600
Steven Gates, *President*
▲ **EMP:** 15
SQ FT: 25,000
SALES: 5.3MM **Privately Held**
WEB: www.aerospacelubricants.com
SIC: 2992 Lubricating oils

(G-6550)
AGILE SOCKS LLC
168 E Frankfort St (43206-2169)
PHONE.................614 440-2812
EMP: 3
SALES (est): 138.6K **Privately Held**
SIC: 2252 Socks

(G-6551)
AGRI COMMUNICATORS INC
Also Called: Ohio's Country Journal
1625 Bethel Rd Ste 203 (43220-2071)
PHONE.................614 273-0465
Bart Johnson, *President*
Marilyn Johnson, *Corp Secy*
EMP: 25
SQ FT: 4,000
SALES (est): 2.2MM **Privately Held**
WEB: www.ocj.com
SIC: 7313 2721 Radio, television, publisher representatives; periodicals: publishing only

(G-6552)
AGRIUM ADVANCED TECH US INC
701 Kaderly Dr (43228-1031)
PHONE.................614 276-5103
Karl Creighton, *Branch Mgr*
EMP: 7
SALES (corp-wide): 8.8B **Privately Held**
WEB: www.cropproductionservices.com
SIC: 2873 Nitrogenous fertilizers
HQ: Agrium Advanced Technologies (U.S.) Inc.
2915 Rocky Mountain Ave # 400
Loveland CO 80538

(G-6553)
AHMF INC (PA)
Also Called: Original Mattress Factory
2245 Wilson Rd (43228-9594)
PHONE.................614 921-1223
Ronald E Trzcinski, *Ch of Bd*
Perry Doermann, *Corp Secy*
Lawrence S Carlson, *Vice Pres*
Tony Dempsey, *Vice Pres*
Jeffrey C Merill, *Vice Pres*
EMP: 20
SQ FT: 22,000
SALES (est): 5.1MM **Privately Held**
WEB: www.originalmattress.com
SIC: 2515 5712 5021 Mattresses & foundations; furniture springs; bedding & bedsprings; mattresses; mattresses

(G-6554)
AIRGAS USA LLC
858 Distribution Dr (43228-1004)
PHONE.................614 308-3730
EMP: 3
SALES (corp-wide): 125.9MM **Privately Held**
SIC: 7692 5169 Welding repair; chemicals & allied products
HQ: Airgas Usa, Llc
259 N Radnor Chester Rd # 100
Radnor PA 19087
610 687-5253

(G-6555)
AJ STINEBURG WDWKG STUDIO LLC
4651 Tatersall Ct (43230-8327)
PHONE.................614 526-9480
Anthony Stineburg, *Principal*
EMP: 4 **EST:** 2012
SALES (est): 343.1K **Privately Held**
SIC: 2431 Millwork

(G-6556)
AJAX INDUSTRIES INC
Also Called: Ajax Jaws
575 N Hague Ave (43204-1420)
PHONE.................614 272-6944
David P De Matteo, *President*
Rocco De Matteo, *Principal*
Tony De Matteo, *Vice Pres*
▲ **EMP:** 20
SQ FT: 10,000
SALES (est): 3.2MM **Privately Held**
WEB: www.ajaxjaws.com
SIC: 3545 Chucks: drill, lathe or magnetic (machine tool accessories)

(G-6557)
AKRON BRASS COMPANY
Also Called: Weldon Technologies
3656 Paragon Dr (43228-9750)
PHONE.................614 529-7230
Sean Tillinghast, *Principal*
Kent Clasen, *Marketing Staff*
Peter Luhrs, *Director*
EMP: 46
SALES (corp-wide): 2.4B **Publicly Held**
WEB: www.v-mux.com
SIC: 3647 3699 3648 Vehicular lighting equipment; electrical equipment & supplies; lighting equipment
HQ: Akron Brass Company
343 Venture Blvd
Wooster OH 44691

(G-6558)
AKZO NOBEL COATINGS INC
1313 Windsor Ave Ste 1313 # 1313 (43211-2851)
PHONE.................614 294-3361
Paul Hoelzer, *General Mgr*
EMP: 200
SALES (corp-wide): 11.3B **Privately Held**
WEB: www.nam.sikkens.com
SIC: 2851 Paints & allied products
HQ: Akzo Nobel Coatings Inc.
8220 Mohawk Dr
Strongsville OH 44136
440 297-5100

(G-6559)
AKZO NOBEL COATINGS INC
1313 Windsor Ave (43211-2851)
P.O. Box 489 (43216-0489)
PHONE.................614 294-3361
John Wolff, *Manager*
EMP: 200
SALES (corp-wide): 11.3B **Privately Held**
WEB: www.nam.sikkens.com
SIC: 2851 8734 Paints & allied products; testing laboratories
HQ: Akzo Nobel Coatings Inc.
8220 Mohawk Dr
Strongsville OH 44136
440 297-5100

(G-6560)
AKZO NOBEL INC
Also Called: ICI Paints Store
1313 Windsor Ave (43211-2851)
PHONE.................614 294-3361
Jim Penikas, *Engineer*
John Carson, *Accounts Exec*
Phil Boutron, *Branch Mgr*
Kevin Martin, *Manager*
Tom Starcher, *Manager*
EMP: 34
SALES (corp-wide): 11.3B **Privately Held**
SIC: 2851 Paints & allied products
HQ: Akzo Nobel Inc.
525 W Van Buren St Fl 16
Chicago IL 60607
312 544-7000

(G-6561)
ALACWIN NUTRITION CORPORATION
3706 Kimberly Pkwy N (43232-8481)
PHONE.................614 961-6479
Mary E Knight, *CEO*
EMP: 4
SALES (est): 154.6K **Privately Held**
SIC: 2099 5149 Food preparations; juices

(G-6562)
ALD PRECAST CORP (PA)
400 Frank Rd (43207-2423)
PHONE.................614 449-3366
William E Anderson, *Principal*
EMP: 7
SALES (est): 1.7MM **Privately Held**
SIC: 3272 Concrete products, precast

(G-6563)
ALIGN ASSESS ACHIEVE LLC
900 Michigan Ave (43215-1165)
PHONE.................614 505-6820
K M Bainbridge, *Mng Member*
Kathleen M Bainbridge, *Mng Member*
Morris Holman,
EMP: 4
SALES: 1MM **Privately Held**
SIC: 8748 2741 Educational consultant; miscellaneous publishing

(G-6564)
ALL ABOUT HOUSE
1071 Afton Rd (43221-1603)
PHONE.................614 725-3595
Margaret Vickers, *Principal*
EMP: 5
SALES (est): 351.9K **Privately Held**
SIC: 3585 Room coolers, portable

(G-6565)
ALL AMERICAN TROPHY
3055 Templeton Rd Ste M (43209-2589)
PHONE.................614 231-8824
Brian Strickler,
Randy Laymon,
EMP: 3
SALES: 200K **Privately Held**
SIC: 3914 Trophies

(G-6566)
ALL AMERICAN WELDING CO
185 Mcdowell St (43215-4011)
P.O. Box 547, Grove City (43123-0547)
PHONE.................614 224-7752
Ken Radich, *President*
Charles Radich, *Vice Pres*
EMP: 5
SQ FT: 60,000
SALES (est): 370K **Privately Held**
SIC: 7692 3443 Welding repair; weldments

(G-6567)
ALL PRO OVRHD DOOR SYSTEMS LLC
1985 Oakland Park Ave (43224-3636)
PHONE.................614 444-3667
Joseph Miller,
EMP: 8
SALES (est): 790K **Privately Held**
SIC: 3442 2431 Metal doors, sash & trim; door frames, wood; doors, wood

(G-6568)
ALL STAR SIGN COMPANY
112 S Glenwood Ave (43222-1406)
P.O. Box 23071 (43223-0071)
PHONE.................614 461-9052
James E Waller, *President*
Howard Berridge, *Vice Pres*
EMP: 32
SQ FT: 7,600
SALES (est): 4.1MM **Privately Held**
SIC: 3993 Electric signs

(G-6569)
ALL-STATE BELTING LLC
6951 Alan Schwrzwalder St (43217-1118)
PHONE.................614 497-4281
EMP: 7
SALES (corp-wide): 70.7B **Privately Held**
SIC: 3496 Barbed wire, made from purchased wire
HQ: All-State Belting, Llc
520 S 18th St
West Des Moines IA 50265
515 645-6959

(G-6570)
ALLFAB INC
2273 Williams Rd (43207-5121)
PHONE.................614 491-4944
Lise S Roth, *President*
Lise Roth, *Chairman*
Russell W Roth, *Vice Pres*
Russell Roth, *VP Engrg*
EMP: 15
SQ FT: 15,000
SALES (est): 3.2MM **Privately Held**
WEB: www.allfabinc.com
SIC: 3444 Sheet metalwork

(G-6571)
ALLIED CUSTOM MOLDED PRODUCTS
1240 Essex Ave (43201-2928)
PHONE.................614 291-0629
Kenneth Palmer, *President*
Donald O Palmer, *Vice Pres*
Linda Palmer, *Admin Sec*
EMP: 3
SQ FT: 4,500
SALES (est): 185K **Privately Held**
SIC: 3089 Injection molding of plastics

(G-6572)
ALLIED FABRICATING & WLDG CO
5699 Chantry Dr (43232-4799)
PHONE.................614 751-6664
Thomas Caminiti, *CEO*
Jack Burgoon, *President*
Joseph Caminiti, *President*
Raymond Cunningham, *Vice Pres*
Gary Arthurs, *Plant Mgr*
EMP: 34
SQ FT: 30,000

Columbus - Franklin County (G-6573)   GEOGRAPHIC SECTION

SALES (est): 7.4MM **Privately Held**
WEB: www.afaw.net
SIC: 3444 7692 3535 3441 Sheet metal specialties, not stamped; welding repair; conveyors & conveying equipment; fabricated structural metal; rubber & plastics hose & beltings

(G-6573)
ALLIED MINERAL PRODUCTS INC (PA)
2700 Scioto Pkwy (43221-4660)
PHONE..................614 876-0244
Jon R Tabor, *President*
Ben GE, *General Mgr*
Brian Huang, *General Mgr*
Koos Heijboer, *Managing Dir*
Jim Bade, *Business Mgr*
◆ EMP: 290
SQ FT: 450,000
SALES (est): 149.2MM **Privately Held**
WEB: www.alliedmin.com
SIC: 3297 Nonclay refractories

(G-6574)
ALLIED SIGN COMPANY INC
818 Marion Rd (43207-2553)
PHONE..................614 443-9656
Richard L Frost, *President*
EMP: 12 EST: 1955
SQ FT: 8,000
SALES (est): 1.6MM **Privately Held**
SIC: 3993 Signs & advertising specialties

(G-6575)
ALLYN CORP (PA)
1491 Clairmonte Rd (43221)
P.O. Box 21162 (43221-0162)
PHONE..................614 442-3900
Larry B Anderson, *President*
EMP: 3
SALES (est): 456.5K **Privately Held**
SIC: 2819 2899 Industrial inorganic chemicals; chemical preparations

(G-6576)
ALMA MATER SPORTSWEAR LLC
Also Called: Alma Mater Wear
3029 Silver Dr (43224-3945)
PHONE..................614 260-8222
Amanda Sima, *Principal*
EMP: 4
SALES (est): 254.1K **Privately Held**
SIC: 2389 Uniforms & vestments

(G-6577)
ALPHA OMEGA BIOREMEDIATION LLC
2824 Fisher Rd Ste E (43204-3553)
PHONE..................614 287-2600
John Chabray, *Partner*
Rita Lang, *Partner*
Lynn Marshall, *Partner*
EMP: 11
SALES (est): 394.9K **Privately Held**
SIC: 4959 8744 8748 2873 Environmental cleanup services; ; environmental consultant; fertilizers: natural (organic), except compost

(G-6578)
ALRO STEEL CORPORATION
555 Hilliard Rome Rd (43228-9265)
PHONE..................614 878-7271
Steve White, *Manager*
Tim Castle, *Manager*
EMP: 40
SALES (corp-wide): 1.9B **Privately Held**
WEB: www.alro.com
SIC: 5051 5085 5162 3444 Steel; aluminum bars, rods, ingots, sheets, pipes, plates, etc.; nonferrous metal sheets, bars, rods, etc.; industrial supplies; plastics materials; sheet metalwork
PA: Alro Steel Corporation
3100 E High St
Jackson MI 49203
517 787-5500

(G-6579)
AMATECH INC
1633 Woodland Ave (43219-1135)
PHONE..................614 252-2506
Rick Bittner, *Branch Mgr*

EMP: 20 **Privately Held**
SIC: 3086 7336 2671 Plastics foam products; package design; plastic film, coated or laminated for packaging
PA: Amatech, Inc.
1460 Grimm Dr
Erie PA 16501

(G-6580)
AMERICAN BOTTLING COMPANY
Also Called: Dr. Pepper 7 Up Columbus
960 Stelzer Rd (43219-3740)
PHONE..................614 237-4201
Dan Grassbaugh, *Branch Mgr*
EMP: 100 **Publicly Held**
WEB: www.cs-americas.com
SIC: 2086 Soft drinks: packaged in cans, bottles, etc.
HQ: The American Bottling Company
5301 Legacy Dr
Plano TX 75024

(G-6581)
AMERICAN BOTTLING COMPANY
Also Called: 7 Up / R C/Canada Dry Btlg Co
950 Stelzer Rd (43219-3740)
PHONE..................614 237-4201
Mike Stall, *Branch Mgr*
EMP: 100 **Publicly Held**
WEB: www.cs-americas.com
SIC: 2086 5149 Soft drinks: packaged in cans, bottles, etc.; groceries & related products
HQ: The American Bottling Company
5301 Legacy Dr
Plano TX 75024

(G-6582)
AMERICAN COMMUNITY NEWSPAPERS
5255 Sinclair Rd (43229-5042)
PHONE..................614 888-4567
Leanne Brandell, *Principal*
EMP: 5
SALES (est): 50.4K **Privately Held**
SIC: 2711 Newspapers

(G-6583)
AMERICAN ISOSTATIC PRESSES INC
Also Called: A I P
1205 S Columbus Arprt Rd (43207-4304)
PHONE..................614 497-3148
Rajendra Persaud, *President*
Carol Sprang, *Principal*
Cliff Orcutt, *Vice Pres*
Lisa Persaud, *Admin Sec*
◆ EMP: 16
SQ FT: 14,000
SALES (est): 4.4MM **Privately Held**
WEB: www.aiphip.com
SIC: 3821 Furnaces, laboratory

(G-6584)
AMERICAN LED-GIBLE INC
Also Called: LED-ANDON
1776 Lone Eagle St (43228-3655)
PHONE..................614 851-1100
Charles R Morrison, *President*
Robin L Morrison, *CFO*
▲ EMP: 10
SQ FT: 7,000
SALES: 1.4MM **Privately Held**
WEB: www.ledgible.com
SIC: 3993 Electric signs

(G-6585)
AMERICAN ORTHOPEDICS INC (PA)
1151 W 5th Ave (43212-2529)
PHONE..................614 291-6454
Richard F Nitsch, *President*
Ronald Kidd, *President*
Zachary Ruhl, *Vice Pres*
Barbara Berndt, *Manager*
Loretta Kidd, *Admin Sec*
EMP: 22
SQ FT: 7,000
SALES: 4MM **Privately Held**
SIC: 3842 Prosthetic appliances; limbs, artificial; braces, orthopedic

(G-6586)
AMERICAN REGENT INC
960 Crupper Ave (43229-1109)
PHONE..................614 436-2222
Joseph Kenneth Keller, *CEO*
Robert Vultaggio, *Controller*
Linda Romaine, *Manager*
EMP: 100 **Privately Held**
SIC: 2834 Adrenal pharmaceutical preparations
HQ: American Regent, Inc.
5 Ramsey Rd
Shirley NY 11967
631 924-4000

(G-6587)
AMERICAN WHISTLE CORPORATION
6540 Huntley Rd Ste B (43229-1088)
PHONE..................614 846-2918
Kelly Davirro, *President*
Amber Robertson, *Accounts Mgr*
▲ EMP: 14 EST: 1957
SQ FT: 5,000
SALES (est): 1.4MM **Privately Held**
WEB: www.americanwhistle.com
SIC: 3949 Sporting & athletic goods

(G-6588)
AMERICANHORT SERVICES INC
2130 Stella Ct Ste 200 (43215-1011)
PHONE..................614 884-1203
Doug Cole, *President*
Bobby Barnitz, *Vice Pres*
David Saboia, *Treasurer*
EMP: 12
SQ FT: 3,700
SALES (est): 754.6K **Privately Held**
SIC: 2731 6733 8611 Books: publishing only; trusts, except educational, religious, charity: management; business associations

(G-6589)
AMERIGRAPH LLC
2727 Harrison Rd (43204-3514)
PHONE..................614 278-8000
Dirk C Grizzle, *Principal*
EMP: 6
SALES (est): 527.4K **Privately Held**
SIC: 2759 Commercial printing

(G-6590)
AMERISOURCE HEALTH SVCS LLC
Also Called: American Health Packaging
2550 John Glenn Ave Ste A (43217-1188)
PHONE..................614 492-8177
Rick Knight, *President*
Greg Hamilton, *Vice Pres*
Bob Kavanaugh, *Vice Pres*
Robert Kavanaugh, *Vice Pres*
John Swartz, *Vice Pres*
EMP: 89
SQ FT: 153,000
SALES (est): 22.3MM
SALES (corp-wide): 167.9B **Publicly Held**
WEB: www.healthpack.com
SIC: 2064 4783 Cough drops, except pharmaceutical preparations; packing goods for shipping
HQ: Amerisourcebergen Drug Corporation
1300 Morris Dr Ste 100
Chesterbrook PA 19087
610 727-7000

(G-6591)
AMERITECH PUBLISHING INC
Also Called: SBC
2550 Corp Exchange Dr # 310 (43231-7659)
PHONE..................614 895-6123
David Lobdell, *Manager*
EMP: 75
SALES (corp-wide): 170.7B **Publicly Held**
SIC: 2741 Directories, telephone: publishing only, not printed on site
HQ: Ameritech Publishing, Inc.
23500 Northwestern Hwy
Southfield MI 48075
800 996-4609

(G-6592)
AMPSCO DIVISION
2301 Fairwood Ave (43207-2768)
PHONE..................614 444-2181
Dennis J Leukart, *President*
Mike Morrison, *Foreman/Supr*
Phillip Ecos, *Purch Mgr*
Matthew Leukart, *CFO*
Marisa Solis, *Human Res Mgr*
EMP: 19 EST: 1960
SQ FT: 250,000
SALES: 1.2MM
SALES (corp-wide): 76.1MM **Privately Held**
WEB: www.superior-dietool.com
SIC: 3599 Machine shop, jobbing & repair
PA: Superior Production Llc
2301 Fairwood Ave
Columbus OH 43207
614 444-2181

(G-6593)
AMSOIL INC
707 Hadley Dr (43228-1029)
PHONE..................614 274-9851
Scott Davis, *Manager*
EMP: 8
SALES (corp-wide): 121.4MM **Privately Held**
WEB: www.amsoil.com
SIC: 2992 3589 2873 3714 Lubricating oils & greases; water filters & softeners, household type; fertilizers: natural (organic), except compost; motor vehicle parts & accessories
PA: Amsoil Inc.
925 Tower Ave
Superior WI 54880
715 392-7101

(G-6594)
AMT MACHINE SYSTEMS LIMITED
1760 Zollinger Rd Ste 2 (43221-2848)
PHONE..................740 965-2693
Gregory Knight, *Partner*
Eric Ribble, *Partner*
Howard Ubert, *Partner*
Dennis R Pugh,
EMP: 10
SQ FT: 2,000
SALES (est): 1.1MM **Privately Held**
WEB: www.amtmachinesystems.com
SIC: 3451 Screw machine products

(G-6595)
AMT MACHINE SYSTEMS LTD
50 W Broad St Ste 1200 (43215-3301)
PHONE..................614 635-8050
Dennis R Pugh, *CEO*
Howard Ubert, *Principal*
▲ EMP: 12 EST: 2009
SALES (est): 1.2MM **Privately Held**
SIC: 3599 Custom machinery

(G-6596)
AMTEKCO INDUSTRIES LLC (HQ)
2300 Lockbourne Rd (43207-2167)
PHONE..................614 228-6590
Earl B Sisson, *President*
Hugh E Kirkwood Jr, *President*
John McCormick, *President*
Ollie Rossman, *President*
Bruce Wasserstrom, *Vice Pres*
EMP: 100
SALES: 25.5MM
SALES (corp-wide): 824.5MM **Privately Held**
WEB: www.amtekco.com
SIC: 3469 2541 Kitchen fixtures & equipment: metal, except cast aluminum; cabinets, except refrigerated: show, display, etc.: wood
PA: The Wasserstrom Company
4500 E Broad St
Columbus OH 43213
614 228-6525

(G-6597)
AMTEKCO INDUSTRIES INC
33 W Hinman Ave (43207-1809)
PHONE..................614 228-6525
Ron Bower, *President*
EMP: 6

GEOGRAPHIC SECTION

Columbus - Franklin County (G-6622)

SALES (corp-wide): 824.5MM **Privately Held**
WEB: www.amtekco.com
SIC: 2541 3469 Wood partitions & fixtures; metal stampings
HQ: Amtekco Industries, Llc
1205 Refugee Rd
Columbus OH 43207
614 228-6590

(G-6598)
ANADEM INC
3620 N High St Ste 201 (43214-3643)
PHONE..................................614 262-2539
Will Kuhlmann, *CEO*
Mike Cheadle, *Vice Pres*
EMP: 7
SALES (est): 590.4K **Privately Held**
SIC: 2741 Miscellaneous publishing

(G-6599)
ANALYNK WIRELESS LLC
790 Cross Pointe Rd (43230-6685)
PHONE..................................614 755-5091
Tom Mackessy, *President*
John Robbins, *Prdtn Mgr*
Robert Longest, *VP Engrg*
Rick Catlett, *Engineer*
◆ EMP: 5
SQ FT: 5,000
SALES: 700K **Privately Held**
WEB: www.analynk.com
SIC: 3663 Radio receiver networks; receiver-transmitter units (transceiver); receivers, radio communications; antennas, transmitting & communications

(G-6600)
ANCHOR CORPORATION
2160 Cloverleaf St E (43232-4166)
P.O. Box 294, Groveport (43125-0294)
PHONE..................................614 836-9590
Michael W Brumm, *President*
EMP: 3
SQ FT: 2,000
SALES (est): 265K **Privately Held**
SIC: 2899 1711 Water treating compounds; plumbing, heating, air-conditioning contractors

(G-6601)
ANCHOR PATTERN COMPANY
748 Frebis Ave (43206-3709)
PHONE..................................614 443-2221
Wilbur S Smith III, *President*
Barbara L Smith, *Corp Secy*
Will Smith, *Vice Pres*
EMP: 6
SQ FT: 4,000
SALES: 1.2MM **Privately Held**
SIC: 3543 Industrial patterns

(G-6602)
ANDERSON CONCRETE CORP (PA)
Also Called: Buckeye Ready Mix
400 Frank Rd (43207-2456)
P.O. Box 398 (43216-0398)
PHONE..................................614 443-0123
Douglas Anderson, *President*
Richard D Anderson, *Exec VP*
William Feltz, *Vice Pres*
John Mynes, *Treasurer*
William S Dunn, *Admin Sec*
EMP: 130
SALES (est): 15.4MM **Privately Held**
WEB: www.andersonconcrete.com
SIC: 3273 Ready-mixed concrete

(G-6603)
ANDERSON GLASS CO INC
2816 Morse Rd (43231-6094)
PHONE..................................614 476-4877
Bradley Anderson, *President*
Helena Anderson, *Vice Pres*
Judy Mullen, *Office Mgr*
EMP: 30 EST: 1949
SQ FT: 32,000
SALES: 4MM **Privately Held**
WEB: www.andersonglassco.com
SIC: 5039 3231 3229 Exterior flat glass: plate or window; interior flat glass: plate or window; products of purchased glass; pressed & blown glass

(G-6604)
ANHEUSER-BUSCH LLC
700 Schrock Rd (43229-1159)
PHONE..................................614 847-6213
Kevin Lee, *General Mgr*
Susan Robinson, *QC Dir*
Dave Dunn, *Engineer*
Laurence Lenoir, *Engineer*
Matthew Schlemmer, *Engineer*
EMP: 500
SALES (corp-wide): 1.9B **Privately Held**
WEB: www.hispanicbud.com
SIC: 2082 Beer (alcoholic beverage)
HQ: Anheuser-Busch, Llc
1 Busch Pl
Saint Louis MO 63118
314 632-6777

(G-6605)
ANNES AUNTIE PRETZELS
125 Easton Town Ctr (43219-6075)
PHONE..................................614 418-7021
Marty Pete, *Owner*
Sharron Wheeler, *Owner*
EMP: 22
SALES (est): 413.6K **Privately Held**
SIC: 5461 2052 Pretzels; pretzels

(G-6606)
ANTHONY-THOMAS CANDY COMPANY (PA)
Also Called: Anthony-Thomas Candy Shoppes
1777 Arlingate Ln (43228-4114)
P.O. Box 21865 (43221-0865)
PHONE..................................614 274-8405
Tom Zanetos, *CEO*
Joseph Zanetos, *President*
Gregory Zanetos, *General Mgr*
Agnes Zanetos, *Corp Secy*
Greg Zanetos, *Exec VP*
▲ EMP: 125 EST: 1907
SQ FT: 152,000
SALES (est): 60.7MM **Privately Held**
WEB: www.anthony-thomas.com
SIC: 2064 5441 2068 2066 Candy & other confectionery products; candy, nut & confectionery stores; salted & roasted nuts & seeds; chocolate & cocoa products

(G-6607)
ANTHONY-THOMAS CANDY COMPANY
Also Called: Anthony Thomas Candy Shoppes
4636 W Broad St (43228-1611)
PHONE..................................614 870-8899
Joe Zanetos, *Branch Mgr*
EMP: 4
SALES (corp-wide): 60.7MM **Privately Held**
WEB: www.anthony-thomas.com
SIC: 2064 5441 Candy & other confectionery products; candy, nut & confectionery stores
PA: Anthony-Thomas Candy Company
1777 Arlingate Ln
Columbus OH 43228
614 274-8405

(G-6608)
APPIAN MANUFACTURING CORP
Also Called: Necco American
2025 Camaro Ave (43207-1716)
PHONE..................................614 445-2230
Fran A Vendetta, *President*
Eric Schmidt, *VP Opers*
Ryan Lauer, *Engineer*
Jean Lewis, *Admin Mgr*
Amber Wilson, *Administration*
▲ EMP: 30
SQ FT: 40,000
SALES (est): 7.8MM **Privately Held**
WEB: www.appian.com
SIC: 3441 3498 Fabricated structural metal; fabricated pipe & fittings

(G-6609)
APPLICATION LINK INC
4449 Easton Way Fl 2 (43219-7005)
PHONE..................................614 934-1735
Michael Reed, *President*
EMP: 15
SQ FT: 2,000

SALES (est): 1.5MM **Privately Held**
WEB: www.applicationlink.com
SIC: 7372 5045 7371 Business oriented computer software; computers, peripherals & software; custom computer programming services

(G-6610)
APPLIED EXPERIENCE LLC
1003 Kinnear Rd (43212-1150)
PHONE..................................614 943-2970
Christopher Brandon, *Principal*
George Catlin, *Principal*
Kedar Kapoor, *Principal*
Michael Krull, *Principal*
Matthew Schrader, *Principal*
EMP: 7
SALES (est): 150.1K **Privately Held**
SIC: 7389 7373 8711 3599 Drafting service, except temporary help; computer integrated systems design; engineering services; machine & other job shop work

(G-6611)
AQUA SCIENCE INC
1877 E 17th Ave (43219-1006)
PHONE..................................614 252-5000
Dan L Smucker, *President*
Darrell L Miller Jr, *Vice Pres*
John Miller, *Technical Staff*
EMP: 34
SQ FT: 28,000
SALES (est): 10.4MM **Privately Held**
SIC: 2899 Water treating compounds

(G-6612)
AQUACALC LLC
Also Called: Jbs Instruments
1700 Joyce Ave (43219-1026)
PHONE..................................916 372-0534
Greg Ruszovan, *President*
EMP: 3 EST: 2016
SQ FT: 3,500
SALES (est): 140.9K **Privately Held**
SIC: 3823 Flow instruments, industrial process type

(G-6613)
ARCELORMITTAL COLUMBUS LLC
1800 Watkins Rd (43207-3440)
PHONE..................................614 492-6800
Chad Ousley, *Plant Mgr*
Michael Boylan, *Engineer*
Scott Richardson, *Engineer*
Michael Rippey, *Mng Member*
Rebecca Feltz, *Manager*
▲ EMP: 113
SQ FT: 350,000
SALES (corp-wide): 15.2MM
SALES (corp-wide): 9.1B **Privately Held**
SIC: 3479 3471 3398 Galvanizing of iron, steel or end-formed products; plating & polishing; metal heat treating
HQ: Arcelormittal Usa Llc
1 S Dearborn St Ste 1800
Chicago IL 60603
312 346-0300

(G-6614)
ARCELORMITTAL OBETZ LLC
4300 Alum Creek Dr (43207-4519)
PHONE..................................614 492-8287
Rodney Mott, *President*
Robert Dalrymple, *Vice Pres*
John Goodwin, *Vice Pres*
Brian Pole, *Vice Pres*
Brian Stack, *Vice Pres*
EMP: 25
SQ FT: 83,600
SALES (est): 3.3MM
SALES (corp-wide): 9.1B **Privately Held**
SIC: 3312 Iron & steel: galvanized, pipes, plates, sheets, etc.
HQ: Arcelormittal Usa Llc
1 S Dearborn St Ste 1800
Chicago IL 60603
312 346-0300

(G-6615)
ARMADA POWER LLC
230 West St Ste 150 (43215-2785)
PHONE..................................614 204-9341
Kathyayani Mahadevan, *Principal*
EMP: 8 EST: 2014
SQ FT: 2,000

SALES (est): 478.6K **Privately Held**
SIC: 7371 3663 Computer software systems analysis & design, custom; light communications equipment; telemetering equipment, electronic

(G-6616)
ART COLUMBUS MEMORIAL INC
606 W Broad St (43215-2712)
PHONE..................................614 221-9333
Mel Lee, *Manager*
EMP: 8
SQ FT: 5,000
SALES (corp-wide): 2.5MM **Privately Held**
SIC: 3272 Monuments, concrete
PA: Art Columbus Memorial Inc
766 Greenlawn Ave
Columbus OH 43223
614 443-5778

(G-6617)
ART TEES INC
39 S Yearling Rd (43213-1823)
PHONE..................................614 338-8337
Mitchell Hirsch, *CEO*
David Hirsch, *President*
Zelda Hirsch, *Corp Secy*
EMP: 4
SQ FT: 20,000
SALES: 480K **Privately Held**
SIC: 2759 5941 3993 2791 Screen printing; sporting goods & bicycle shops; signs & advertising specialties; typesetting; automotive & apparel trimmings

(G-6618)
ASHLAND LLC
1979 Atlas St (43228-9645)
PHONE..................................614 529-3318
Timothy E Castle, *Branch Mgr*
EMP: 219
SALES (corp-wide): 3.7B **Publicly Held**
WEB: www.ispcorp.com
SIC: 2869 Amines, acids, salts, esters
HQ: Ashland Llc
50 E Rivercenter Blvd # 1600
Covington KY 41011
859 815-3333

(G-6619)
ASHLAND SPECIALTY INGREDIENTS
1979 Atlas St (43228-9645)
PHONE..................................614 529-3311
EMP: 54
SALES (corp-wide): 20.4MM **Privately Held**
SIC: 2844 Bath salts
PA: Ashland Specialty Ingredients
5200 Laser Pkwy
Dublin OH 43017
302 594-5000

(G-6620)
ASIST TRANSLATION SERVICES
4891 Sawmill Rd Ste 200 (43235-7266)
PHONE..................................614 451-6744
Elena Tsinman, *President*
EMP: 12
SQ FT: 8,000
SALES: 3.5K **Privately Held**
WEB: www.asisttranslations.com
SIC: 7389 2791 Translation services; typesetting

(G-6621)
ASPHALT SERVICES OHIO INC
4579 Poth Rd (43213-1327)
PHONE..................................614 864-4600
Edward Minhinnick, *President*
EMP: 5
SALES (est): 615.8K **Privately Held**
SIC: 1771 3241 Blacktop (asphalt) work; cement, hydraulic

(G-6622)
ASSEMBLY MACHINING WIRE PDTS
Also Called: A M W
2375 Refugee Park (43207-2173)
PHONE..................................614 443-1110
Gregory Allan Donovan, *President*
EMP: 7
SQ FT: 10,000

Columbus - Franklin County (G-6623) — GEOGRAPHIC SECTION

SALES: 350K **Privately Held**
SIC: 3599 Machine shop, jobbing & repair

(G-6623)
AT&T CORP
150 E Gay St Ste 4a (43215-3130)
PHONE..................614 223-8236
Connie Browning, *President*
Cari Walters, *Assistant VP*
Dustin Howell, *Sales Associate*
Jaymee Nemec, *Sales Executive*
Lois Gardner, *Manager*
EMP: 1000
SALES (corp-wide): 170.7B **Publicly Held**
WEB: www.att.com
SIC: 7629 4813 2741 Telecommunication equipment repair (except telephones); telephone communication, except radio; miscellaneous publishing
HQ: At&T Corp.
  1 At&T Way
  Bedminster NJ 07921
  800 403-3302

(G-6624)
ATCHLEY SIGNS & GRAPHICS
1616 Transamerica Ct (43228-9332)
PHONE..................614 421-7446
Derek Atchley, *Co-Owner*
Christine Atchley, *Co-Owner*
EMP: 9
SALES: 750K **Privately Held**
SIC: 3993 7389 Signs, not made in custom sign painting shops; printed circuitry graphic layout

(G-6625)
ATLAPAC CORP
2901 E 4th Ave Ste 5 (43219-2896)
PHONE..................614 252-2121
James R Staeck, *President*
Mike Mc Coy, *CFO*
▲ **EMP:** 70 **EST:** 1964
SQ FT: 50,000
SALES (est): 12.1MM **Privately Held**
WEB: www.atlapaccorp.com
SIC: 2673 5113 Plastic bags: made from purchased materials; cellophane bags, unprinted: made from purchased materials; bags, paper & disposable plastic

(G-6626)
ATLAS GEAR AND MACHINE CO
Also Called: A Jack'S Industries
575 N Hague Ave (43204-1420)
PHONE..................614 272-6944
David P De Matteo, *President*
Rocco D Matteo, *Manager*
EMP: 5
SQ FT: 10,000
SALES (est): 509.1K **Privately Held**
SIC: 3599 Machine shop, jobbing & repair

(G-6627)
ATLAS INDUSTRIAL CONTRS LLC (HQ)
5275 Sinclair Rd (43229-5042)
PHONE..................614 841-4500
George Ghanem, *President*
Jeff Forgey, *Division Mgr*
Dallas Gerwig, *Division Mgr*
Rich Wine, *Division Mgr*
Blue McDonald, *Vice Pres*
EMP: 300 **EST:** 1923
SQ FT: 20,000
SALES: 140.1MM **Privately Held**
WEB: www.atlascos.com
SIC: 1731 3498 1796 Electrical work; fabricated pipe & fittings; machine moving & rigging

(G-6628)
AUBURN DAIRY PRODUCTS INC
2200 Cardigan Ave (43215-1092)
PHONE..................614 488-2536
Douglas A Smith, *President*
Martin Lavine, *Vice Pres*
Thomas G Michaelides, *Treasurer*
G Frederick Smith, *Admin Sec*
EMP: 31
SQ FT: 10,300

SALES (est): 3.8MM
SALES (corp-wide): 47.5MM **Privately Held**
SIC: 2026 5143 Whipped topping, except frozen or dry mix; dairy products, except dried or canned
PA: Instantwhip Foods, Inc.
  2200 Cardigan Ave
  Columbus OH 43215
  614 488-2536

(G-6629)
AULD COMPANY
1003 Kinnear Rd (43212-1150)
PHONE..................614 454-1010
Daniel Auld, *President*
Douglas Auld, *Vice Pres*
EMP: 40
SQ FT: 9,000
SALES (est): 3.9MM **Privately Held**
WEB: www.theauldcompany.com
SIC: 3993 3479 3089 3369 Name plates: except engraved, etched, etc.: metal; name plates: engraved, etched, etc.; injection molding of plastics; white metal castings (lead, tin, antimony), except die

(G-6630)
AULD CRAFTERS INC
175 Cleveland Ave Rear (43215-1926)
PHONE..................614 221-6825
Linda Weltlich, *President*
Chris Carioti, *Vice Pres*
John Carioti, *Vice Pres*
Gary Weltlich, *Vice Pres*
EMP: 3 **EST:** 1935
SQ FT: 7,500
SALES: 450K **Privately Held**
SIC: 5999 3911 5947 Trophies & plaques; pearl jewelry, natural or cultured; gift, novelty & souvenir shop

(G-6631)
AULD TECHNOLOGIES LLC
2030 Dividend Dr (43228-3847)
PHONE..................614 755-2853
Elizabeth Jutte-Kill,
EMP: 17
SALES (est): 3.3MM **Privately Held**
SIC: 3993 Signs & advertising specialties

(G-6632)
AUSTIN FOAM PLASTICS INC
Also Called: A F P Ohio
2200 International St (43228-4630)
PHONE..................614 921-0824
Dan Berona, *Manager*
EMP: 25
SALES (corp-wide): 4.7B **Publicly Held**
WEB: www.austinfoam.com
SIC: 3086 7336 Insulation or cushioning material, foamed plastic; package design
HQ: Austin Foam Plastics, Inc.
  2933 A W Grimes Blvd
  Pflugerville TX 78660
  512 251-6300

(G-6633)
AUTOMATION SOLUTIONS INC
505 S Parkview Ave # 206 (43209-1676)
PHONE..................614 235-4060
Rolf Kates, *President*
Ellen Kates, *Vice Pres*
EMP: 2
SALES: 1MM **Privately Held**
SIC: 3565 5084 Packaging machinery; industrial machinery & equipment

(G-6634)
AUTOMTIQ MSUREMENT SYSTEMS LLC
797 Gatehouse Ln (43235-1731)
PHONE..................614 431-2667
Vincent Phillips, *Mng Member*
C Vincent Phillips, *Mng Member*
Gary W James,
EMP: 3 **EST:** 2000
SALES (est): 363K **Privately Held**
SIC: 3825 Test equipment for electronic & electric measurement

(G-6635)
AVER INC
41 S High St Ste 1400 (43215-3406)
PHONE..................877 841-2775
Bill Nordmark, *President*

Nick Augustinos, *Chairman*
Carol Wesolik, *Vice Pres*
Susan Dora, *Manager*
Kurt Brenkus, *Director*
EMP: 3
SALES: 110K **Privately Held**
SIC: 7372 Application computer software; business oriented computer software

(G-6636)
AVOTRONICS POWERTRAIN INC
4200 Regent St (43219-6229)
PHONE..................614 537-0261
Ugo Nwoke, *CEO*
EMP: 4
SALES (est): 335.8K **Privately Held**
SIC: 3566 Speed changers, drives & gears

(G-6637)
AVURE AUTOCLAVE SYSTEMS INC (DH)
Also Called: ABB Autoclave Systems
3721 Corp Dr (43231)
PHONE..................614 891-2732
Jerry Toops, *President*
◆ **EMP:** 20
SQ FT: 20,000
SALES (est): 2MM
SALES (corp-wide): 147.9MM **Privately Held**
WEB: www.avureae.com
SIC: 3823 5084 Pressure measurement instruments, industrial; industrial machinery & equipment
HQ: Flow International Corporation
  23500 64th Ave S
  Kent WA 98032
  253 850-3500

(G-6638)
AXIOM TOOL GROUP INC
1181 Claycraft Rd (43230-6639)
PHONE..................844 642-4902
Todd Damon, *President*
EMP: 5 **EST:** 2015
SALES (est): 275.9K **Privately Held**
SIC: 3553 Woodworking machinery

(G-6639)
B & A HOLISTIC FD & HERBS LLC
Also Called: Holistic Foods Herbs and Books
4550 Heaton Rd Ste B7 (43229-6611)
PHONE..................614 747-2200
Sonya Robinson, *Mng Member*
John Berry,
Ahrayah Robinson,
John Robinson,
EMP: 10
SALES: 200K **Privately Held**
SIC: 2833 Drugs & herbs: grading, grinding & milling

(G-6640)
B & G TOOL COMPANY
4832 Kenny Rd (43220-2793)
PHONE..................614 451-2538
Francis Plahuta, *President*
Francis Bud Plahuta, *President*
James Plahuta, *Vice Pres*
Steve Plahuta, *Admin Sec*
EMP: 9 **EST:** 1965
SQ FT: 8,800
SALES: 1.2MM **Privately Held**
SIC: 3599 3312 Machine shop, jobbing & repair; tool & die steel

(G-6641)
B B BRADLEY COMPANY INC
2699 Scioto Pkwy (43221-4658)
PHONE..................614 777-5600
Bruce Beaty, *President*
EMP: 7
SALES (corp-wide): 9.9MM **Privately Held**
WEB: www.bbbradley.com
SIC: 3086 5199 Packaging & shipping materials, foamed plastic; packaging materials
PA: The B B Bradley Company Inc
  7755 Crile Rd
  Painesville OH 44077
  440 354-2005

(G-6642)
BAISE ENTERPRISES INC
Also Called: Baise Quality Printing
695 Koebel Ave Frnt (43207-7103)
PHONE..................614 444-3171
Troy Baise, *President*
EMP: 5
SQ FT: 10,000
SALES (est): 533.5K **Privately Held**
WEB: www.baisequalityprinting.com
SIC: 2759 2791 2789 2752 Commercial printing; typesetting; bookbinding & related work; commercial printing, lithographic

(G-6643)
BAKE ME HAPPY LLC
116 E Moler St (43207)
PHONE..................614 477-3642
Letha Pugh, *Mng Member*
Wendy Miller Pugh,
EMP: 3 **EST:** 2013
SQ FT: 2,800
SALES (est): 754.9K **Privately Held**
SIC: 5142 5149 2051 Bakery products, frozen; crackers, cookies & bakery products; pies, bakery: except frozen

(G-6644)
BAKER WELDING LLC
2901 Eastport Ave Bldg 95 (43219)
PHONE..................614 252-6100
Ray Baker, *Owner*
EMP: 4
SQ FT: 10,060
SALES: 675K **Privately Held**
SIC: 7692 Welding repair

(G-6645)
BALL CORPORATION
2690 Charter St (43228-4600)
PHONE..................614 771-9112
Dan Griffit, *Plant Mgr*
Carol Stockett, *Purchasing*
Ralph Ciavarro, *Engineer*
John Ficek, *Engineer*
Raymond Sprungle, *Senior Engr*
EMP: 65
SALES (corp-wide): 11.6B **Publicly Held**
WEB: www.ball.com
SIC: 3411 Metal cans
PA: Ball Corporation
  10 Longs Peak Dr
  Broomfield CO 80021
  303 469-3131

(G-6646)
BANNER METALS GROUP INC
1308 Holly Ave (43212-3115)
PHONE..................614 291-3105
John E O'Brien III, *CEO*
Wm Seidensticker Et Al, *Principal*
F M Jaeger, *Principal*
James H Kennedy, *Principal*
C Bronson Jones, *Vice Pres*
EMP: 70 **EST:** 1921
SQ FT: 70,000
SALES (est): 15.2MM **Privately Held**
WEB: www.bannerstamping.com
SIC: 3469 3544 Stamping metal for the trade; special dies & tools; jigs & fixtures; jigs: inspection, gauging & checking

(G-6647)
BARBARA A EISENHARDT
7726 Cloister Dr (43235-1461)
PHONE..................614 436-9690
Barbara A Eisenhardt, *Principal*
EMP: 3
SALES (est): 133K **Privately Held**
SIC: 2711 Newspapers, publishing & printing

(G-6648)
BARNETT & RAMEL OPTICAL CO NEB
6510 Huntley Rd (43229-1012)
P.O. Box 3488, Omaha NE (68103-0488)
PHONE..................402 453-4900
Keith Besch, *Ch of Bd*
Frank J Besch, *President*
Janice A Besch, *Corp Secy*
Douglas Day, *Vice Pres*
Teri Miller, *Human Resources*
EMP: 45

GEOGRAPHIC SECTION

Columbus - Franklin County (G-6677)

SALES (est): 6.3MM
SALES (corp-wide): 283.5MM **Privately Held**
WEB: www.broptical.com
SIC: 3851 Lenses, ophthalmic; frames & parts, eyeglass & spectacle
HQ: Essilor Laboratories Of America, Inc.
13515 N Stemmons Fwy
Dallas TX 75234
972 241-4141

(G-6649)
BARR ENGINEERING INCORPORATED
Also Called: National Engrg Archtctral Svcs
5710 Westbourne Ave (43213-1400)
PHONE.................................614 892-0162
Enoch Chipukaizer, *CEO*
Margaret Henry, *Consultant*
EMP: 15 **Privately Held**
SIC: 8711 8734 8748 1799 Construction & civil engineering; civil engineering; structural engineering; testing laboratories; traffic consultant; lighting consultant; core drilling & cutting; nonmetallic minerals development & test boring; architectural services; architectural engineering
PA: Barr Engineering Incorporated
2800 Corp Exchange Dr # 240
Columbus OH 43231

(G-6650)
BARR ENGINEERING INCORPORATED (PA)
Also Called: National Engrg Archtctral Svcs
2800 Corp Exchange Dr # 240 (43231-7628)
PHONE.................................614 714-0299
Jawdat Siddiqi, *President*
Enoch Chipukaizer, *Principal*
Robin Lamb, *Principal*
Jessica Cave, *Accountant*
EMP: 35
SQ FT: 1,500
SALES (est): 9.4MM **Privately Held**
SIC: 8711 8713 8734 1799 Civil engineering; surveying services; testing laboratories; core drilling & cutting; nonmetallic minerals development & test boring

(G-6651)
BARRY BROTHERS ELECTRIC
1100 Leona Ave (43201-3039)
PHONE.................................614 299-8187
Boyce A Barry, *Owner*
EMP: 4
SQ FT: 1,000
SALES (est): 266.8K **Privately Held**
SIC: 7694 3625 Electric motor repair; electric controls & control accessories, industrial

(G-6652)
BARTEK SYSTEMS
6155 Chinaberry Dr (43213-3323)
PHONE.................................614 759-6014
Heywood Hampton, *Principal*
EMP: 5
SALES (est): 527.5K **Privately Held**
SIC: 3578 Cash registers

(G-6653)
BARTLEY OFFIE
Also Called: Capital Tool Grinding Co
3760 E 5th Ave (43219-1807)
PHONE.................................614 235-9050
Offie Bartley, *Owner*
EMP: 4
SQ FT: 10,500
SALES (est): 297.6K **Privately Held**
SIC: 3599 Machine shop, jobbing & repair

(G-6654)
BASINGER INC
2222 Wilson Rd (43228-9386)
PHONE.................................614 771-8300
EMP: 2
SALES: 2.7MM **Privately Held**
SIC: 2759 Commercial Printing

(G-6655)
BEAM TECHNOLOGIES INC
266 N 4th St Ste 200 (43215-2565)
PHONE.................................800 648-1179
Alex Frommeyer, *CEO*
Alexander Curry, *COO*
Dan Dykes, *CTO*
Daniel Dykes, *CTO*
EMP: 9
SALES (est): 1.1MM **Privately Held**
SIC: 3841 Surgical & medical instruments

(G-6656)
BECK & ORR INC
3097 W Broad St (43204-1306)
PHONE.................................614 276-8809
Roland L Bowman, *President*
EMP: 3 **EST:** 1888
SQ FT: 2,700
SALES: 175K **Privately Held**
SIC: 2789 Bookbinding & related work

(G-6657)
BECKENHORST PRESS INC
960 Old Henderson Rd (43220-3723)
P.O. Box 14273 (43214-0273)
PHONE.................................614 451-6461
Jeffrey D Hamm, *President*
Bryan Babcock, *Sales Staff*
Jeffrey Hamm, *Sales Staff*
Craig Courtney, *Director*
EMP: 4
SQ FT: 8,500
SALES (est): 510.3K **Privately Held**
WEB: www.beckenhorstpress.com
SIC: 2741 Music, sheet: publishing only, not printed on site

(G-6658)
BECKMAN XMO
376 Morrison Rd Ste D (43213-1447)
PHONE.................................614 864-2232
Tracy Beckman, *Principal*
Pam Taylor, *Office Mgr*
EMP: 13
SALES (est): 2MM **Privately Held**
SIC: 2752 Commercial printing, offset

(G-6659)
BECKY BRISKER
2260 E Main St (43209-2319)
PHONE.................................614 266-6575
Becky Brisker, *Principal*
EMP: 3
SALES (est): 148.9K **Privately Held**
SIC: 2711 Newspapers, publishing & printing

(G-6660)
BEEHEX INC
1130 Gahanna Pkwy (43230-6615)
PHONE.................................512 633-5304
Benjamin Felnter, *COO*
EMP: 7
SALES (est): 314.6K **Privately Held**
SIC: 3555 Printing trades machinery

(G-6661)
BELLO VERDE LLC
464 E Main St Ste 100 (43215-5364)
PHONE.................................614 365-3000
Joe Chay, *President*
EMP: 3
SALES (est): 165.1K **Privately Held**
SIC: 2326 Men's & boys' work clothing

(G-6662)
BENCHMARK ARCHTECTURAL SYSTEMS
Also Called: Kingspan Benchmark
720 Marion St (43207-2553)
PHONE.................................614 444-0110
Russel Shiels, *President*
Patrick Johnson, *Business Mgr*
Ilhan Eser, *Vice Pres*
▲ **EMP:** 40
SQ FT: 96,000
SALES (est): 10.3MM **Privately Held**
WEB: www.kingspanpanels.us
SIC: 3448 Prefabricated metal buildings
HQ: Kingspan Insulated Panels Inc.
726 Summerhill Dr
Deland FL 32724
386 626-6789

(G-6663)
BESTTRANSPORTCOM INC
1103 Schrock Rd Ste 100 (43229-1179)
PHONE.................................614 888-2378
Michael Dolan, *President*
Scott Cummans, *Vice Pres*
Denisa Cellar, *Engineer*
Pete Scolieri, *Sales Staff*
Randy Combs, *Manager*
EMP: 30
SALES (est): 4.7MM **Privately Held**
WEB: www.besttransport.com
SIC: 7372 Prepackaged software

(G-6664)
BETTER THAN SEX ICE CREAM LLC
Also Called: BTS Ice Cream
1352 Parsons Ave (43206-3643)
PHONE.................................614 444-5505
Troy Harris, *President*
EMP: 5
SQ FT: 800
SALES (est): 200K **Privately Held**
SIC: 2024 Ice cream & frozen desserts

(G-6665)
BEVERLY SNIDER
Also Called: Wedding Plantation
3900 Noe Bixby Rd (43232-6164)
PHONE.................................614 837-5817
Beverly Snider, *Owner*
EMP: 6
SQ FT: 2,400
SALES (est): 313.5K **Privately Held**
SIC: 5621 3652 Bridal shops; dress shops; pre-recorded records & tapes

(G-6666)
BEXLEY FABRICS INC
2476 E Main St (43209-2441)
P.O. Box 124, Galloway (43119-0124)
PHONE.................................614 231-7272
Edward E Goldin, *Owner*
EMP: 8
SALES (est): 555.3K **Privately Held**
SIC: 2295 Sleeving, textile: saturated

(G-6667)
BEXLEY PEN COMPANY INC
2840 Fisher Rd Ste B (43204-3551)
PHONE.................................614 351-9988
Howard Levy, *President*
Steven Vandyke, *Vice Pres*
Karen Dobis, *Manager*
▲ **EMP:** 5
SQ FT: 2,200
SALES (est): 588.8K **Privately Held**
WEB: www.bexleypen.com
SIC: 3951 3599 Pens & mechanical pencils; machine shop, jobbing & repair

(G-6668)
BIG NOODLE LLC
687 Kenwick Rd (43209-2592)
PHONE.................................614 558-7170
Christina Providence, *Principal*
EMP: 3
SALES (est): 201.1K **Privately Held**
SIC: 2098 Noodles (e.g. egg, plain & water), dry

(G-6669)
BIO-BLOOD COMPONENTS INC
1393 N High St (43201-2459)
PHONE.................................614 294-3183
Jane Hancock, *Manager*
EMP: 30
SALES (corp-wide): 18.6MM **Privately Held**
SIC: 8099 2836 Blood bank; biological products, except diagnostic
PA: Bio-Blood Components, Inc.
5700 Pleasant View Rd
Memphis TN 38134
901 384-6250

(G-6670)
BIOBENT HOLDINGS LLC
Also Called: Biobent Polymers
1275 Kinnear Rd Ste 239 (43212-1180)
PHONE.................................513 658-5560
Keith Masavage, *CEO*
Michele Cole, *Principal*
Curtis Crocker,
Ross Youngs,
EMP: 6 **EST:** 2012
SALES (est): 540.1K **Privately Held**
SIC: 2821 Plastics materials & resins

(G-6671)
BIOCARE ORTHOPEDIC PROSTHETICS
2976 E Broad St (43209-1965)
PHONE.................................614 754-7514
Sandra J Tomsic, *President*
EMP: 5
SQ FT: 2,000
SALES (est): 253.2K
SALES (corp-wide): 321.5K **Privately Held**
SIC: 5999 3842 Orthopedic & prosthesis appliances; canes, orthopedic
PA: Biocare Orthopedic Prosthetics & Orthotics, Inc.
8889 Basil Western Rd Nw
Canal Winchester OH 43110
614 920-2811

(G-6672)
BIZZY BEE PRINTING INC
Also Called: Innovative Computer Forms
1500 W 3rd Ave Ste 106 (43212-2887)
PHONE.................................614 771-1222
Chris Schmelzer, *President*
Rick Schmelzer, *Treasurer*
Rosemary Schmelzer, *Admin Sec*
EMP: 6
SALES (est): 753.5K **Privately Held**
SIC: 2752 Commercial printing, lithographic

(G-6673)
BJ EQUIPMENT LTD
Also Called: Rent-A-John
4522 Lockbourne Rd (43207-4231)
P.O. Box 753 (43216-0753)
PHONE.................................614 497-1776
William Reynolds Jr, *President*
Bonnie Jean Reynolds, *Corp Secy*
EMP: 15
SALES (est): 1.8MM **Privately Held**
SIC: 7359 3444 3443 3431 Portable toilet rental; sheet metalwork; fabricated plate work (boiler shop); metal sanitary ware

(G-6674)
BJOND INC
1463 Briarmeadow Dr (43235-1612)
PHONE.................................614 537-7246
Kenneth Leachman, *CEO*
EMP: 8
SALES (est): 328.2K **Privately Held**
SIC: 7372 7389 Business oriented computer software;

(G-6675)
BLACCO SPLCING RGGING LOFT INC (PA)
1976 Alum Creek Dr (43207-1711)
PHONE.................................614 444-2888
Boyd C Black, *CEO*
Bart Black, *President*
EMP: 3 **EST:** 1956
SQ FT: 22,500
SALES (est): 2.9MM **Privately Held**
SIC: 3496 Slings, lifting: made from purchased wire

(G-6676)
BLACK & DECKER (US) INC
1948 Schrock Rd (43229-1563)
PHONE.................................614 895-3112
Dave Burica, *Manager*
Diana Walker, *Supervisor*
EMP: 7
SALES (corp-wide): 13.9B **Publicly Held**
WEB: www.dewalt.com
SIC: 3546 Power-driven handtools
HQ: Black & Decker (U.S.) Inc.
1000 Stanley Dr
New Britain CT 06053
860 225-5111

(G-6677)
BLACKBURNS FABRICATION INC
2467 Jackson Pike (43223-3846)
PHONE.................................614 875-0784
Mark A Blackburn, *President*
Edsel L Blackburn Sr, *Vice Pres*
Steve Bosak, *Sales Associate*
Carolyn Blackburn, *Admin Sec*
Kim Green, *Admin Sec*

Columbus - Franklin County (G-6678)

EMP: 30
SQ FT: 50,000
SALES (est): 9.2MM **Privately Held**
WEB: www.blackburnsfab.com
SIC: 3441 5051 Fabricated structural metal; structural shapes, iron or steel

(G-6678)
BLACKWOOD SHEET METAL INC
844 Kerr St (43215-1499)
PHONE.................................614 291-3115
Diana Blackwood Newby, *President*
Charles Newby, *Vice Pres*
EMP: 8
SQ FT: 10,000
SALES: 550K **Privately Held**
SIC: 7692 3443 Welding repair; fabricated plate work (boiler shop)

(G-6679)
BLADE MANUFACTURING CO INC
915 Distribution Dr Ste A (43228-1009)
PHONE.................................614 294-1649
Michael F Callahan, *President*
Thomas J Callahan, *Corp Secy*
Michelle M Callahan, *Vice Pres*
Marc Callahan, *VP Sales*
▲ **EMP:** 10 EST: 1946
SQ FT: 10,000
SALES (est): 931.7K **Privately Held**
WEB: www.blademfg.com
SIC: 7389 3425 Grinding, precision: commercial or industrial; saw blades for hand or power saws

(G-6680)
BLOCKAMERICA CORPORATION
Also Called: Glass Block Warehouse, The
750 Kaderly Dr (43228-1032)
PHONE.................................614 274-0700
John Heisler II, *President*
Carol Heisler, *Vice Pres*
EMP: 6
SQ FT: 2,500
SALES: 500K **Privately Held**
SIC: 3229 5031 5231 Blocks & bricks, glass; windows; glass

(G-6681)
BMD BLASTING
1840 Federal Pkwy (43207-5709)
PHONE.................................614 580-9468
Michael Bradford, *Owner*
EMP: 4
SQ FT: 4,000
SALES (est): 186K **Privately Held**
SIC: 3471 Plating & polishing

(G-6682)
BMI MACHINE INC
Also Called: Butler Machine
8354 Fairway Dr (43235-1155)
PHONE.................................614 785-7020
Robert I Davidson, *President*
EMP: 3
SALES (est): 328.8K **Privately Held**
SIC: 3599 Machine shop, jobbing & repair

(G-6683)
BODYCOTE THERMAL PROC INC
Columbus Div
1515 Universal Rd (43207-1770)
PHONE.................................614 444-1181
Gregory Barezinsky, *General Mgr*
Chad Beamer, *Technical Mgr*
Lutz Paula, *Office Mgr*
Marc Walters, *Branch Mgr*
EMP: 45
SQ FT: 26,000
SALES (corp-wide): 911.9MM **Privately Held**
WEB: www.mic-houston.com
SIC: 3398 Metal heat treating
HQ: Bodycote Thermal Processing, Inc.
12700 Park Central Dr # 700
Dallas TX 75251
214 904-2420

(G-6684)
BOGGS & ASSOCIATES INC
3555 E Fulton St (43227-1195)
P.O. Box 9554 (43209-0554)
PHONE.................................614 237-0600
Stephan Boggs, *President*
Vicki Boggs, *Corp Secy*
EMP: 6
SQ FT: 5,000
SALES (est): 1.1MM **Privately Held**
SIC: 3599 Machine shop, jobbing & repair

(G-6685)
BOICH COMPANIES LLC
41 S High St Ste 3750s (43215-3406)
PHONE.................................614 221-0101
Brian T Murphy, *CFO*
Wayne M Boich, *Mng Member*
EMP: 7
SALES (est): 367.1K **Privately Held**
SIC: 1241 Coal mining services

(G-6686)
BOOKCOLOR BINDERY SERVICES
1685 Woodland Ave (43219-1135)
PHONE.................................614 252-2941
Glenn Morrow, *CEO*
Norris Joe, *Treasurer*
EMP: 20
SQ FT: 11,000
SALES: 950K **Privately Held**
WEB: www.bookcolorbindery.com
SIC: 2789 Binding only: books, pamphlets, magazines, etc.

(G-6687)
BORDEN BAKERS INC
4723 Reed Rd (43220-3051)
PHONE.................................614 457-9800
Michael Borden, *Principal*
EMP: 4
SALES (est): 150K **Privately Held**
SIC: 2051 Bakery: wholesale or wholesale/retail combined

(G-6688)
BOSE CORPORATION
Also Called: Bose Showcase Store
155 Easton Town Ctr Fl 1 (43219-6075)
PHONE.................................614 475-8565
Jim Pearsall, *Manager*
EMP: 9
SALES (corp-wide): 2.6B **Privately Held**
WEB: www.bose.com
SIC: 5731 3651 Ret Radio/Tv/Electronics Mfg Home Audio/Video Equipment
PA: Bose Corporation
100 The Mountain Rd
Framingham MA 01701
508 879-7330

(G-6689)
BOST & FILTREX INC (HQ)
Also Called: Robert C Bost Associates Inc
1783 Kenny Rd (43212-1311)
PHONE.................................301 206-9466
A Gregory Roberts, *President*
EMP: 11
SALES (est): 1.5MM
SALES (corp-wide): 8.4MM **Privately Held**
SIC: 3625 Noise control equipment
PA: Ketchum & Walton Co.
1783 Kenny Rd
Columbus OH
614 486-5961

(G-6690)
BOYCE LTD
2173 S James Rd (43232-3850)
PHONE.................................614 236-8901
Troy M Boyce, *Principal*
EMP: 3
SALES (est): 253.4K **Privately Held**
SIC: 1799 1521 7532 0782 Home/office interiors finishing, furnishing & remodeling; single-family home remodeling, additions & repairs; interior repair services; lawn services; construction, repair & dismantling services; roof repair

(G-6691)
BOYER SIGNS & GRAPHICS INC
3200 Valleyview Dr (43204-2080)
PHONE.................................216 383-7242
Clyde Boyer, *CEO*
Mike Boyer, *President*
EMP: 24
SQ FT: 22,000
SALES (est): 2.1MM **Privately Held**
WEB: www.boyersigns.com
SIC: 3993 1799 Electric signs; sign installation & maintenance

(G-6692)
BPM REALTY INC
195 N Grant Ave Fl 2a (43215-2855)
PHONE.................................614 221-6811
Frederick W Ziegler, *Ch of Bd*
John M Ziegler, *President*
EMP: 27
SQ FT: 43,000
SALES (est): 3MM **Privately Held**
WEB: www.buckeyepm.com
SIC: 7331 2752 Mailing service; commercial printing, offset

(G-6693)
BRENDONS FIBER WORKS
306 E Jeffrey Pl (43214-1714)
PHONE.................................614 353-6599
Laura K Brendon, *Principal*
EMP: 3
SALES (est): 172.9K **Privately Held**
SIC: 3296 Mineral wool

(G-6694)
BREWER COMPANY
472 Brehl Ave (43223-1973)
P.O. Box 23054 (43223-0054)
PHONE.................................614 279-8688
Bill Ison, *Manager*
EMP: 20
SQ FT: 55,000
SALES (corp-wide): 50MM **Privately Held**
WEB: www.thebrewerco.com
SIC: 2952 2951 2891 Asphalt felts & coatings; asphalt paving mixtures & blocks; adhesives & sealants
PA: The Brewer Company
1354 Us Route 50
Milford OH 45150
800 394-0017

(G-6695)
BREWERY REAL ESTATE PARTNR
467 N High St (43215-2007)
PHONE.................................614 224-9023
EMP: 4
SALES (est): 196.7K **Privately Held**
SIC: 2082 Beer (alcoholic beverage)

(G-6696)
BREWPUB RESTAURANT CORP
Also Called: Barley's Brewing Company
467 N High St (43215-2007)
PHONE.................................614 228-2537
Tiffany Jezerinac, *President*
Joe Colburn, *Opers Mgr*
EMP: 60
SALES: 3.3MM **Privately Held**
SIC: 5812 2082 American restaurant; malt beverages

(G-6697)
BRIDGE COMPONENTS INCORPORATED
3476 Millikin Ct (43228-9765)
P.O. Box 1228, Dublin (43017-6228)
PHONE.................................614 873-0777
Neil Spears, *President*
EMP: 7
SALES (est): 1.1MM **Privately Held**
WEB: www.bridgecomponentsinc.com
SIC: 2824 3449 Elastomeric fibers; bars, concrete reinforcing: fabricated steel

(G-6698)
BRIDGE COMPONENTS INDS INC
3476 Millikin Ct (43228-9765)
PHONE.................................614 873-0777
Tyler Spears, *President*
EMP: 6

SALES (est): 794K **Privately Held**
SIC: 3312 Railroad crossings, steel or iron

(G-6699)
BRIGHTON COLLECTIBLES LLC
217 Easton Town Ctr (43219-6077)
PHONE.................................614 418-7561
Jerry Kohl, *Branch Mgr*
EMP: 34
SALES (corp-wide): 326.5MM **Privately Held**
SIC: 3199 Corners, luggage: leather
PA: Brighton Collectibles, Llc
14022 Nelson Ave
City Of Industry CA 91746
626 961-9381

(G-6700)
BRILISTA FOODS COMPANY INC (PA)
Also Called: Krema Nut Co
1000 Goodale Blvd (43212-3827)
PHONE.................................614 299-4132
Michael Giunta, *President*
Brian Giunta, *Senior VP*
David Block, *Vice Pres*
Peggy Giunta, *Vice Pres*
EMP: 9
SQ FT: 8,500
SALES (est): 1.3MM **Privately Held**
WEB: www.krema.com
SIC: 2038 Snacks, including onion rings, cheese sticks, etc.

(G-6701)
BRILLIANT COLORWORKS LLC
2940 E 14th Ave (43219-2304)
PHONE.................................800 566-4162
Jim Kaminiski, *Principal*
EMP: 4
SALES (est): 345.7K **Privately Held**
SIC: 3479 Painting of metal products

(G-6702)
BRISKHEAT CORPORATION (PA)
4800 Hilton Corporate Dr (43232-4150)
PHONE.................................614 294-3376
Domenic Federico, *CEO*
James Zins, *Corp Secy*
Eric McIntyre, *Vice Pres*
Sorina Sok, *Purch Mgr*
Chee Ngeh, *Engineer*
▲ **EMP:** 159 EST: 1949
SQ FT: 40,000
SALES (est): 59.4MM **Privately Held**
WEB: www.bhthermal.com
SIC: 3585 Heating equipment, complete

(G-6703)
BRISKHEAT CORPORATION
460 E Starr Ave (43201-3695)
PHONE.................................614 429-3232
John Vanvleet, *President*
EMP: 23
SALES (corp-wide): 59.4MM **Privately Held**
SIC: 3567 Heating units & devices, industrial: electric
PA: Briskheat Corporation
4800 Hilton Corporate Dr
Columbus OH 43232
614 294-3376

(G-6704)
BROAD STREET FINANCIAL COMPANY (PA)
Also Called: Broadstreet Energy Company
1515 Lake Shore Dr # 225 (43204-4939)
PHONE.................................614 228-0326
William E Arthur, *Ch of Bd*
Geoff Arthur, *Exec VP*
Dan Kosikowski, *Comptroller*
EMP: 5
SQ FT: 3,100
SALES (est): 3.8MM **Privately Held**
SIC: 1311 1799 6722 Crude petroleum & natural gas production; real estate investors, except property operators; management investment, open-end

(G-6705)
BROWNIE POINTS INC
5712 Westbourne Ave (43213-1400)
PHONE.................................614 860-8470
Lisa King, *President*
EMP: 5

▲ = Import ▼ = Export
♦ = Import/Export

SQ FT: 1,326
SALES (est): 609.5K **Privately Held**
WEB: www.browniepointsinc.com
SIC: **2066** 5149 Chocolate & cocoa products; bakery products

(G-6706)
BSA INDUSTRIES INC
Also Called: Select Optical
6510 Huntley Rd (43229-1012)
PHONE.................................614 846-5515
Delbert M Lothes, *CFO*
Mike Downin, *Sales Staff*
EMP: 70
SQ FT: 20,000
SALES (est): 11MM
SALES (corp-wide): 283.5MM **Privately Held**
SIC: **3827** 3851 Lenses, optical: all types except ophthalmic; ophthalmic goods
HQ: Essilor Laboratories Of America, Inc.
  13515 N Stemmons Fwy
  Dallas TX 75234
  972 241-4141

(G-6707)
BUCKEYE BOXES INC (PA)
601 N Hague Ave (43204-1498)
PHONE.................................614 274-8484
Craig Hoyt, *President*
Ken Churchill, *Vice Pres*
Judd Hauenstein, *Vice Pres*
Douglas Goode, *Technology*
▲ EMP: 150 EST: 1966
SQ FT: 100,000
SALES (est): 56.9MM **Privately Held**
SIC: **2653** 3993 2675 2631 Boxes, corrugated: made from purchased materials; signs & advertising specialties; die-cut paper & board; paperboard mills; cellophane bags, unprinted: made from purchased materials

(G-6708)
BUCKEYE BOXES INC
601 N Hague Ave (43204-1498)
PHONE.................................614 274-8484
EMP: 30
SALES (est): 1.8MM
SALES (corp-wide): 56.9MM **Privately Held**
SIC: **5113** 2653 Industrial & personal service paper; corrugated & solid fiber boxes
PA: Buckeye Boxes, Inc.
  601 N Hague Ave
  Columbus OH 43204
  614 274-8484

(G-6709)
BUCKEYE CSTM SCREEN PRINT EMB
Also Called: Seymour, Lloyd
3822 Elbern Ave (43213-1723)
PHONE.................................614 237-0196
Lloyd Seymour, *Owner*
EMP: 10
SQ FT: 1,800
SALES (est): 443.2K **Privately Held**
SIC: **2759** 2752 Screen printing; commercial printing, lithographic

(G-6710)
BUCKEYE METAL WORKS INC
3240 Petzinger Rd (43232-3912)
PHONE.................................614 239-8000
Denny Arthurs, *President*
Walt Daniel, *Vice Pres*
Matt Daniel, *Project Mgr*
EMP: 17
SQ FT: 15,000
SALES (est): 3.5MM **Privately Held**
SIC: **3444** Sheet metal specialties, not stamped

(G-6711)
BUCKEYE RACEWAY LLC
4050 W Broad St (43228-1449)
PHONE.................................614 272-7888
EMP: 7
SALES (est): 489.7K **Privately Held**
SIC: **3644** Raceways

(G-6712)
BUCKEYE STAMPING COMPANY
Also Called: Buckeye Shapeform
555 Marion Rd (43207-2501)
PHONE.................................614 445-0059
Jon Hettinger, *Ch of Bd*
C A Morningstar, *President*
Ken Tumblison, *President*
Larry Doza, *Corp Secy*
Percy Hodge, *Regl Sales Mgr*
EMP: 60
SQ FT: 80,000
SALES (est): 17MM **Privately Held**
SIC: **3469** 3443 3089 3449 Electronic enclosures, stamped or pressed metal; containers, shipping (bombs, etc.): metal plate; plastic hardware & building products; miscellaneous metalwork; metal cans; luggage

(G-6713)
BURTON METAL FINISHING INC
Also Called: Burton Metal Finishing, Inc. &
1711 Woodland Ave (43219-1137)
PHONE.................................614 252-9523
Daniel Burton, *President*
Victoria Burton, *Corp Secy*
Scott Burton, *Vice Pres*
EMP: 25
SQ FT: 5,000
SALES (est): 6.1MM **Privately Held**
WEB: www.burton-metal-finishing.com
SIC: **3559** Metal finishing equipment for plating, etc.

(G-6714)
BUSCH PROPERTIES INC
1103 Schrock Rd Ste 200 (43229-1179)
P.O. Box 29229 (43229-0229)
PHONE.................................614 888-0946
Sherral Butler, *Director*
EMP: 6
SALES (corp-wide): 6.8B **Publicly Held**
WEB: www.abconference.com
SIC: **3411** Aluminum cans
HQ: Busch Properties, Inc.
  1 Busch Pl
  Saint Louis MO
  757 253-3943

(G-6715)
BUSINESS FIRST COLUMBUS INC (DH)
300 Marconi Blvd Ste 105 (43215-2395)
PHONE.................................614 461-4040
George N Corey, *CEO*
Sue Ellen Gabel, *Business Mgr*
Nick Fortine, *Adv Dir*
John Lauer, *Manager*
EMP: 20
SQ FT: 7,300
SALES (est): 2.4MM
SALES (corp-wide): 1.4B **Privately Held**
WEB: www.businessfirstofcolumbus.com
SIC: **2711** Newspapers, publishing & printing
HQ: American City Business Journals, Inc.
  120 W Morehead St Ste 400
  Charlotte NC 28202
  704 973-1000

(G-6716)
BUSINESS IDNTIFICATION SYSTEMS
Also Called: Sign-A-Rama
6185 Huntley Rd Ste M (43229-1094)
PHONE.................................614 841-1255
Stephen M Thompson, *President*
EMP: 6
SQ FT: 5,200
SALES (est): 656.6K **Privately Held**
SIC: **3993** 5999 Signs & advertising specialties; banners, flags, decals & posters

(G-6717)
BYERS SIGN CO
2940 E 14th Ave (43219-2304)
PHONE.................................614 561-1224
Ted Byers, *Owner*
EMP: 4
SALES (est): 277.4K **Privately Held**
SIC: **3993** Electric signs

(G-6718)
C AND O ELECTRIC MOTOR SERVICE
3105 Hillgate Rd (43207-3720)
PHONE.................................614 491-6387
EMP: 5
SQ FT: 3,000
SALES: 400K **Privately Held**
SIC: **5999** 7694 Retails And Repairs Electric Motors

(G-6719)
C J SMITH MACHINERY SERVICE
3000 E Main St Ste B (43209-3717)
PHONE.................................614 348-1376
Tim Gallen, *President*
EMP: 3
SALES (est): 223.1K **Privately Held**
SIC: **3589** Service industry machinery

(G-6720)
C SOLTESZ CO
4374 Dublin Rd (43221-5001)
PHONE.................................614 529-5494
Mary Soltesz, *Principal*
EMP: 4
SALES (est): 341K **Privately Held**
SIC: **2819** Nuclear fuel scrap, reprocessing

(G-6721)
CABINTPAK KITCHENS OF COLUMBUS
Also Called: Cabinet Works
899 King Ave (43212-2646)
PHONE.................................614 294-4646
Linda Owens, *President*
C Joseph Call, *President*
Christopher Morley, *Vice Pres*
James Owens, *Vice Pres*
EMP: 5
SQ FT: 3,600
SALES: 500K **Privately Held**
SIC: **2514** 1751 Kitchen cabinets: metal; cabinet & finish carpentry

(G-6722)
CADBURY SCHWEPPES BOTTLING
950 Stelzer Rd (43219-3740)
PHONE.................................614 238-0469
John Ferrante, *Principal*
EMP: 4 EST: 2007
SALES (est): 237.5K **Privately Held**
SIC: **2086** Bottled & canned soft drinks

(G-6723)
CALGON CARBON CORPORATION
835 N Cassady Ave (43219-2203)
PHONE.................................614 258-9501
Chuck Hegenberger, *QA Dir*
Maria D'Amico, *Branch Mgr*
Igor Rapovski, *Manager*
EMP: 110
SALES (corp-wide): 5.3B **Privately Held**
SIC: **2819** Charcoal (carbon), activated
HQ: Calgon Carbon Corporation
  3000 Gsk Dr
  Moon Township PA 15108
  412 787-6700

(G-6724)
CALLAHAN CUTTING TOOLS INC
Also Called: Blade Manufacturing Co, The
915 Distribution Dr Ste A (43228-1009)
PHONE.................................614 294-1649
Marc A Callahan, *Principal*
◆ EMP: 7
SQ FT: 10,000
SALES (est): 772.1K **Privately Held**
SIC: **3541** 3425 Machine tools, metal cutting type; saw blades & handsaws

(G-6725)
CALLCOPY INC (DH)
Also Called: Uptivity
555 S Front St (43215-5668)
PHONE.................................614 340-3346
Jeff Canter, *CEO*
Jonathan Dunham, *Exec VP*
Mark Studer CPA, *CFO*
Partick Hall, *Chief Mktg Ofcr*
Kevin Seeley, *Director*
EMP: 8
SQ FT: 12,000
SALES (est): 10.5MM
SALES (corp-wide): 1.3B **Privately Held**
WEB: www.callcopy.com
SIC: **7371** 7372 5045 Computer software development & applications; prepackaged software; computer software
HQ: Incontact, Inc.
  75 W Towne Ridge Pkwy # 1
  Sandy UT 84070
  801 320-3200

(G-6726)
CAMELOT CELLARS WINERY
901 Oak St (43205-1204)
PHONE.................................614 441-8860
Charles Frobose, *Principal*
EMP: 6
SALES (est): 490.8K **Privately Held**
WEB: www.camelotcellars.com
SIC: **2084** Wines

(G-6727)
CAMTON MECHANICAL INC
4531 Ellery Dr (43227-2541)
PHONE.................................614 864-7620
Frank Cardinale, *President*
Anthony Cardinale, *Vice Pres*
Dorothy J Cardinale, *Treasurer*
EMP: 3
SALES (est): 235.7K **Privately Held**
SIC: **3559** 1796 Automotive maintenance equipment; machinery installation

(G-6728)
CAP & ASSOCIATES INCORPORATED
445 Mccormick Blvd (43213-1526)
PHONE.................................614 863-3363
Charlene A Prosnik, *CEO*
Randy Griffith, *President*
Jason Prosnik, *President*
Joseph Chaulk, *Exec VP*
Ken Louis, *Opers Mgr*
▲ EMP: 170
SQ FT: 110,000
SALES: 74MM **Privately Held**
WEB: www.cap-associates.com
SIC: **2541** 2542 Store fixtures, wood; shelving, office & store, wood; fixtures, store: except wood

(G-6729)
CAP CITY DIRECT LLC
3203 E 11th Ave (43219-3735)
PHONE.................................614 252-6245
EMP: 17
SQ FT: 5,000
SALES (est): 2.6MM **Privately Held**
SIC: **2759** 7331 Commercial Printing Direct Mail Advertising Services

(G-6730)
CAPEHART ENTERPRISES LLC
Also Called: Minuteman Press
1724 Northwest Blvd B1 (43212-2246)
PHONE.................................614 769-7746
Gerald C Capehart, *Mng Member*
EMP: 15
SQ FT: 1,500
SALES (est): 77.9K **Privately Held**
SIC: **2752** 5199 8742 Commercial printing, offset; advertising specialties; marketing consulting services

(G-6731)
CAPITAL CITY AWNING COMPANY
577 N 4th St (43215-2183)
PHONE.................................614 221-5404
Timothy Kellogg, *President*
Michael Mc Connell, *Vice Pres*
Frank Collette, *Project Mgr*
Kisha Moldovan, *Treasurer*
Thomas Salser, *Finance Mgr*
EMP: 50 EST: 1944
SQ FT: 25,600
SALES (est): 5.6MM **Privately Held**
WEB: www.capitalcityawning.com
SIC: **2394** 2393 Awnings, fabric: made from purchased materials; canvas bags; cushions, except spring & carpet: purchased materials

Columbus - Franklin County (G-6732)

(G-6732)
CAPITAL PROSTHETIC & (PA)
4678 Larwell Dr (43220-3621)
PHONE.................................614 451-0446
David J Kozersky, *President*
Patricia W Kozersky, *Corp Secy*
EMP: 12
SQ FT: 3,200
SALES (est): 2.9MM **Privately Held**
SIC: 3842 Limbs, artificial; braces, orthopedic

(G-6733)
CAPITAL RESIN CORPORATION
324 Dering Ave (43207-2956)
PHONE.................................614 445-7177
Judithe Wensinger, *CEO*
Jon Gehman, *Project Mgr*
Matt Ducay, *Opers Staff*
David Bandy, *Research*
Steve Muryn, *Engineer*
▲ EMP: 76
SQ FT: 6,000
SALES (est): 34.2MM **Privately Held**
WEB: www.capitalresin.com
SIC: 2819 2821 Inorganic acids, except nitric & phosphoric; acrylic resins

(G-6734)
CAPITAL TRACK COMPANY INC
1364 Cardwell Sq S (43229-9022)
PHONE.................................614 595-5088
Matt Caldwell, *President*
EMP: 4
SQ FT: 16,000
SALES (est): 530K **Privately Held**
WEB: www.capitaltrack.com
SIC: 3555 Printing trades machinery

(G-6735)
CAPITOL CITICOM INC
2225 Citygate Dr Ste A (43219-3651)
PHONE.................................614 472-2679
Daniel J Oakes, *President*
Gail E Oakes, *Vice Pres*
Kelly Koons, *Accounts Mgr*
Lisa Young, *Marketing Staff*
Kevin Oakes, *Shareholder*
EMP: 20
SQ FT: 11,500
SALES (est): 3.2MM **Privately Held**
WEB: www.citicomprint.com
SIC: 7374 7372 7389 7334 Data processing service; publishers' computer software; printers' services: folding, collating; photocopying & duplicating services

(G-6736)
CAPITOL SQUARE PRINTING INC
59 E Gay St (43215-3103)
PHONE.................................614 221-2850
Marilyn S Smith, *President*
Craig Poland, *Vice Pres*
EMP: 7
SQ FT: 4,500
SALES (est): 1MM **Privately Held**
SIC: 2752 Commercial printing, offset

(G-6737)
CARAUSTAR INDUSTRIES INC
Also Called: Newark Recovery & Recycling
3024 Charter St (43228-4606)
PHONE.................................614 529-5535
Bill Theado, *Vice Pres*
EMP: 20
SALES (corp-wide): 3.8B **Publicly Held**
SIC: 2631 Paperboard mills
HQ: Caraustar Industries, Inc.
5000 Austell Powder Sprin
Austell GA 30106
770 948-3101

(G-6738)
CARBOGENE USA LLC
2252 Sedgwick Dr (43220-5430)
PHONE.................................215 378-4306
Qingjia Jeff Yao,
EMP: 3
SALES (est): 150K **Privately Held**
SIC: 2836 Biological products, except diagnostic

(G-6739)
CARDINAL BUILDERS INC
4409 E Main St (43213-3061)
PHONE.................................614 237-1000
Tim Coady, *President*
Tim Kane, *Shareholder*
EMP: 25 EST: 1965
SQ FT: 22,000
SALES (est): 6.5MM **Privately Held**
WEB: www.cardinalbuilders.com
SIC: 3541 1521 1522 1799 Machine tool replacement & repair parts, metal cutting types; general remodeling, single-family houses; patio & deck construction & repair; hotel/motel & multi-family home renovation & remodeling; kitchen & bathroom remodeling; siding contractor; roofing contractor

(G-6740)
CARDINAL BUILDING SUPPLY LLC
1000 Edgehill Rd Ste B (43212-3646)
PHONE.................................614 706-4499
Mark Hostettler, *CFO*
Mark Gundling, *Mng Member*
EMP: 7
SALES (est): 147.2K **Privately Held**
SIC: 5211 2426 5031 Flooring, wood; lumber, hardwood dimension; lumber, plywood & millwork

(G-6741)
CARDINAL CONTAINER CORPORATION
3700 Lockbourne Rd (43207-5133)
PHONE.................................614 497-3033
Charles Marcum, *President*
Mike Marcum, *Vice Pres*
EMP: 50
SQ FT: 29,000
SALES (est): 15MM **Privately Held**
SIC: 2653 Boxes, corrugated: made from purchased materials

(G-6742)
CARDINAL HEALTH 414 LLC
2215 Citygate Dr Ste D (43219-3589)
PHONE.................................614 473-0786
EMP: 9
SALES (corp-wide): 129.9B **Publicly Held**
SIC: 2835 2834 Mfg Diagnostic Substances Mfg Pharmaceutical Preparations
HQ: Cardinal Health 414, Llc
7000 Cardinal Pl
Dublin OH 43017
614 757-5000

(G-6743)
CARENECTION LLC
1103 Schrock Rd Ste 205 (43229-1179)
PHONE.................................614 468-6045
William Hannan, *CFO*
EMP: 3
SALES (est): 126K **Privately Held**
SIC: 7372 Prepackaged software

(G-6744)
CARING THINGS INC
435 W State St (43215-4010)
P.O. Box 693, Grove City (43123-0693)
PHONE.................................614 749-9084
Ryan McManus, *CEO*
Shaun Young, *COO*
Lee Wang, *Chief Engr*
Andi Sie, *Product Mgr*
EMP: 4
SQ FT: 300
SALES (est): 130.9K **Privately Held**
SIC: 7372 Prepackaged software

(G-6745)
CAROL J GUILER
Also Called: A-1 Welding & Sandblasting
1359 E 5th Ave (43219-2458)
PHONE.................................614 252-6920
Carol Guiler, *Owner*
EMP: 5
SQ FT: 5,500
SALES (est): 170K **Privately Held**
SIC: 7692 Welding repair

(G-6746)
CAROLYN CHEMICAL COMPANY
1601 Woodland Ave (43219-1135)
PHONE.................................614 252-5000
Dan Smucker, *President*
EMP: 13
SALES (est): 1.4MM **Privately Held**
SIC: 2842 Rug, upholstery, or dry cleaning detergents or spotters

(G-6747)
CARROLL DISTRG & CNSTR SUP INC
2929 E 14th Ave (43219-2303)
PHONE.................................614 564-9799
Chris Kreuzer, *Branch Mgr*
EMP: 6
SALES (corp-wide): 116.5MM **Privately Held**
SIC: 5082 3444 Contractors' materials; concrete forms, sheet metal
PA: Carroll Distributing & Construction Supply, Inc.
1502 E Main St
Ottumwa IA 52501
641 683-1888

(G-6748)
CARRY GRANDVIEW OUT
710 Neil Ave (43215-1612)
PHONE.................................614 487-0305
Jeffery Norris, *Owner*
EMP: 4 EST: 2008
SALES (est): 213.1K **Privately Held**
SIC: 2082 Beer (alcoholic beverage)

(G-6749)
CARYNS CUISINE
155 N Remington Rd (43209-1444)
PHONE.................................614 237-4143
Caryn Shapiro, *Principal*
EMP: 4 EST: 2010
SALES (est): 195.2K **Privately Held**
SIC: 2051 Cakes, bakery: except frozen

(G-6750)
CATHOLIC DIOCESE OF COLUMBUS
Also Called: Catholic Times
197 E Gay St Ste 4 (43215-3229)
PHONE.................................614 224-5195
Teresa Ianaggi, *Manager*
EMP: 9
SALES (corp-wide): 6.3MM **Privately Held**
WEB: www.colscss.org
SIC: 2711 Newspapers
PA: Catholic Diocese Of Columbus
198 E Broad St
Columbus OH 43215
614 224-2251

(G-6751)
CENTRAL COCA-COLA BTLG CO INC
4500 Groves Rd (43232-4106)
PHONE.................................614 863-7200
Doug Davis, *Manager*
EMP: 85
SQ FT: 150,000
SALES (corp-wide): 35.4B **Publicly Held**
WEB: www.colasic.net
SIC: 2086 Bottled & canned soft drinks
HQ: Central Coca-Cola Bottling Company, Inc.
555 Taxter Rd Ste 550
Elmsford NY 10523
914 789-1100

(G-6752)
CENTRAL OHIO DEFENSE LLC
292 E Weisheimer Rd (43214-2150)
PHONE.................................614 668-6527
Mark Basinger, *Principal*
EMP: 3
SALES (est): 178.9K **Privately Held**
SIC: 3812 Defense systems & equipment

(G-6753)
CENTRAL OHIO METAL STAMPI
1055 Claycraft Rd (43230-6637)
P.O. Box 307776 (43230-7776)
PHONE.................................614 861-3332
John Davidson, *President*
Pennie Davidson, *Corp Secy*
Lawrence Davidson, *Vice Pres*
EMP: 25
SQ FT: 25,000
SALES (est): 5.8MM **Privately Held**
WEB: www.centralohiometalstamping.com
SIC: 3469 Stamping metal for the trade

(G-6754)
CENTRAL OIL ASPHALT CORP (PA)
8 E Long St Ste 400 (43215-2914)
PHONE.................................614 224-8111
F L Shafer, *President*
EMP: 7
SQ FT: 4,600
SALES (est): 6.2MM **Privately Held**
SIC: 2951 Asphalt & asphaltic paving mixtures (not from refineries)

(G-6755)
CERTIFIED OIL COMPANY INC
949 King Ave (43212-2662)
PHONE.................................614 421-7500
Peter Lacaillade, *Ch of Bd*
David Hogan, *COO*
EMP: 107
SQ FT: 24,500
SALES (est): 17.3MM
SALES (corp-wide): 51.5MM **Privately Held**
SIC: 2911 Gasoline blending plants
PA: Certified Oil Corporation
949 King Ave
Columbus OH 43212
614 421-7500

(G-6756)
CERTIFIED WALK IN TUBS
Also Called: Home Pro
926 Freeway Dr N (43229-5424)
PHONE.................................614 436-4848
Skyler Alexander, *Partner*
EMP: 17
SALES (est): 772K **Privately Held**
SIC: 5999 3088 Plumbing & heating supplies; plastics plumbing fixtures

(G-6757)
CHARACTERISTIC SOLUTIONS LLC
Also Called: Discus Sofware
829 Bethel Rd Ste 105 (43214-1903)
PHONE.................................614 360-2424
Scot Morris, *Accounts Mgr*
Jake Hart, *Marketing Mgr*
Dan Sokol, *Mng Member*
Erol Yalaz, *Manager*
Randall Strobel, *Sr Software Eng*
EMP: 3
SQ FT: 1,500
SALES: 300K **Privately Held**
SIC: 3695 Computer software tape & disks: blank, rigid & floppy

(G-6758)
CHARLES RAY EVANS
Also Called: Penny Fab
1055 Gibbard Ave (43201-3052)
PHONE.................................740 967-3669
Charles Ray Evans, *Owner*
EMP: 12
SQ FT: 50,000
SALES (est): 1.6MM **Privately Held**
WEB: www.pennyfab.com
SIC: 3441 Fabricated structural metal

(G-6759)
CHC MANUFACTURING INC
2343 Westbrooke Dr (43228-9557)
PHONE.................................614 527-1606
Dan Blank, *Branch Mgr*
EMP: 4
SALES (corp-wide): 8MM **Privately Held**
SIC: 3446 3441 Stairs, staircases, stair treads: prefabricated metal; fabricated structural metal
PA: Chc Manufacturing, Inc.
10270 Wayne Ave
Cincinnati OH 45215
513 821-7757

(G-6760)
CHEAP DUMPSTERS LLC
5042 Astoria Ave (43207-4924)
PHONE.................................614 285-5865
Vanessa Nakanishi, *Principal*

GEOGRAPHIC SECTION

Columbus - Franklin County (G-6790)

EMP: 3
SALES (est): 251.2K **Privately Held**
SIC: 3443 Dumpsters, garbage

(G-6761)
CHEP (USA) INC
2130 New World Dr (43207-3433)
PHONE.................................614 497-9448
Matt Mallory, *Manager*
EMP: 50 **Privately Held**
HQ: Chep (U.S.A.) Inc.
5897 Windward Pkwy
Alpharetta GA 30005
SIC: 2448 Wood pallets & skids

(G-6762)
CHERYL A LUCAS
Also Called: It's Sew Much More
388 Morrison Rd (43213-1430)
PHONE.................................614 755-2100
Cheryl A Lucas, *Owner*
Greg Brown, *Owner*
EMP: 4 EST: 1998
SQ FT: 2,400
SALES: 150K **Privately Held**
SIC: 2395 Embroidery & art needlework

(G-6763)
CHEZ RAMA RESTAURANT
3669 E Livingston Ave (43227-2243)
PHONE.................................614 237-9315
Mouhamadou Toure, *Owner*
EMP: 4
SALES: 350K **Privately Held**
SIC: 2099 Food preparations

(G-6764)
CHRIS NCKEL CSTM LTHERWORK LLC
80 E Kelso Rd (43202-2312)
PHONE.................................614 262-2672
Paul Nickel, *Principal*
EMP: 3
SALES (est): 183K **Privately Held**
SIC: 3356 Nickel

(G-6765)
CHRONICLE YOUR LIFE STORY
123 S Virginialee Rd (43209-2051)
PHONE.................................614 456-7576
Naomi Kayne, *Principal*
EMP: 3
SALES (est): 159.8K **Privately Held**
SIC: 2711 Newspapers

(G-6766)
CITI 2 CITI LOGISTICS
Also Called: Abacus Biodiesel Complex
6031 E Main St (43213-3356)
PHONE.................................614 306-4109
Kenneth Turner, *Principal*
EMP: 50
SALES: 950K **Privately Held**
SIC: 2999 Petroleum & coal products

(G-6767)
CITY DOG
510 E Main St (43215-5311)
PHONE.................................614 228-3647
Becky S Hinga, *Principal*
EMP: 4
SALES (est): 497K **Privately Held**
SIC: 3999 Pet supplies

(G-6768)
CITYNET OHIO LLC
343 N Front St Ste 400 (43215-2266)
PHONE.................................614 364-7881
James Martin, *Mng Member*
EMP: 30
SALES (est): 1.4MM **Privately Held**
SIC: 7372 Prepackaged software

(G-6769)
CLARK GRAVE VAULT COMPANY (PA)
Also Called: C.T.L. Steel Division
375 E 5th Ave (43201-2819)
P.O. Box 8250 (43201-0250)
PHONE.................................614 294-3761
David Beck, *President*
David A Beck II, *Vice Pres*
Douglas A Beck, *Vice Pres*
Mark Beck, *Vice Pres*
Darrell Kovacs, *Purch Agent*
EMP: 140
SQ FT: 300,000
SALES (est): 48.4MM **Privately Held**
SIC: 3995 3316 Grave vaults, metal; strip steel, flat bright, cold-rolled: purchased hot-rolled; sheet, steel, cold-rolled: from purchased hot-rolled

(G-6770)
CLASSIC STONE COMPANY INC
4090 Janitrol Rd (43228-1396)
PHONE.................................614 833-3946
R G Reitter, *President*
Steven Waits, *CFO*
EMP: 10
SQ FT: 20,000
SALES (est): 1MM **Privately Held**
WEB: www.classicstonecompany.com
SIC: 3281 Cut stone & stone products

(G-6771)
CLEAN WATER CONDITIONING
305 Sumption Dr (43230-1639)
PHONE.................................614 475-4532
Frank Moeckel, *Owner*
EMP: 3
SALES: 75K **Privately Held**
SIC: 3589 5074 Swimming pool filter & water conditioning systems; plumbing & hydronic heating supplies

(G-6772)
CLEAR ONE LLC
99 S Remington Rd (43209-1855)
P.O. Box 9268 (43209-0268)
PHONE.................................800 279-3724
EMP: 3
SALES (est): 171.3K **Privately Held**
SIC: 3089 Plastics products

(G-6773)
CLEVELAND PLANT AND FLOWER CO
2370 Marilyn Ln (43219-1792)
P.O. Box 30837, Gahanna (43230-0837)
PHONE.................................614 478-9900
Brian Davis, *Manager*
EMP: 20
SQ FT: 3,000
SALES (corp-wide): 53.3MM **Privately Held**
WEB: www.cpfco.com
SIC: 5193 5992 3999 Flowers, fresh; florists' supplies; flowers, fresh; candles
PA: The Cleveland Plant And Flower Company
12920 Corporate Dr
Cleveland OH 44130
216 898-3500

(G-6774)
CLEVEX INC (PA)
1275 Kinnear Rd Ste 223 (43212-0017)
PHONE.................................614 675-3757
Doug Myers, *President*
EMP: 4
SALES (est): 550.4K **Privately Held**
SIC: 3841 Surgical & medical instruments

(G-6775)
CLIMATERIGHT LLC
Also Called: Climateright Air
777 Manor Park Dr (43228-9522)
PHONE.................................800 725-4628
Todd Arend, *CEO*
EMP: 5
SALES (est): 255.2K **Privately Held**
SIC: 3585 Room coolers, portable

(G-6776)
CLUSTER SOFTWARE INC
2674 Billingsley Rd (43235-1924)
PHONE.................................614 760-9380
Kailasnath Murthy, *President*
Vishwa Vedula, *Vice Pres*
EMP: 11
SALES (est): 1.7MM **Privately Held**
WEB: www.clustersoft.com
SIC: 7372 Business oriented computer software

(G-6777)
CMD MEDTECH LLC
3585 Interchange Rd (43204-1400)
PHONE.................................614 364-4243
EMP: 3
SALES (est): 242.9K **Privately Held**
SIC: 3841 Surgical & medical instruments

(G-6778)
COALESCENCE LLC
3455 Millennium Ct (43219-5550)
PHONE.................................614 861-3639
Angela N Cauley, *CEO*
Ian Blount,
▲ EMP: 39
SQ FT: 35,000
SALES: 26MM **Privately Held**
WEB: www.coalescencellc.com
SIC: 2099 Baking powder & soda, yeast & other leavening agents; seasonings & spices; sauces: gravy, dressing & dip mixes; sugar

(G-6779)
COCA-COLA COMPANY
2455 Watkins Rd (43207-3488)
PHONE.................................614 491-6305
Willi Pete, *Opers-Prdtn-Mfg*
EMP: 120
SALES (corp-wide): 35.4B **Publicly Held**
WEB: www.cocacola.com
SIC: 2086 Bottled & canned soft drinks
PA: The Coca-Cola Company
1 Coca Cola Plz Nw
Atlanta GA 30313
404 676-2121

(G-6780)
COLORTECH GRAPHICS & PRINTING (PA)
4000 Business Park Dr (43204-5023)
PHONE.................................614 766-2400
C Wayne Booker, *President*
EMP: 19
SQ FT: 1,600
SALES (est): 1.9MM **Privately Held**
WEB: www.colortechdesign.com
SIC: 7334 2791 Photocopying & duplicating services; typesetting

(G-6781)
COLUMBIA ENERGY GROUP
200 Civic Center Dr (43215-7510)
PHONE.................................614 460-4683
Robert Skaggs Jr, *President*
Robert Skaggs, *President*
Gary W Pottorff, *Vice Pres*
EMP: 2100
SALES (est): 341.3MM
SALES (corp-wide): 5.1B **Publicly Held**
WEB: www.nisource.com
SIC: 4922 1311 1731 Natural gas transmission; crude petroleum production; electric power systems contractors
PA: Nisource Inc.
801 E 86th Ave
Merrillville IN 46410
877 647-5990

(G-6782)
COLUMBIA GAS METER SHOP
5315 Fisher Rd (43228-9511)
PHONE.................................614 460-5519
Patrick Donnelly, *Principal*
EMP: 12
SALES (est): 588.2K **Privately Held**
SIC: 1311 Crude petroleum & natural gas

(G-6783)
COLUMBUS ALIVE INC
34 S 3rd St (43215-4201)
PHONE.................................614 221-2449
Sarah Sally Crane, *President*
Andy Downing, *Editor*
Greg Glasser, *Accounts Exec*
Joel Oliphint, *Assoc Editor*
EMP: 15
SALES (est): 719.1K
SALES (corp-wide): 651.9MM **Privately Held**
WEB: www.columbusdispatch.com
SIC: 2711 Newspapers, publishing & printing
PA: The Dispatch Printing Company
62 E Broad St
Columbus OH 43215
614 461-5000

(G-6784)
COLUMBUS BRIDE
34 S 3rd St (43215-4201)
PHONE.................................614 888-4567
Ray Tatrocki, *General Mgr*
Randy Beyer, *Controller*
EMP: 60
SQ FT: 1,000
SALES (est): 4.4MM **Privately Held**
WEB: www.columbusalive.com
SIC: 2721 7389 Magazines: publishing only, not printed on site; convention & show services

(G-6785)
COLUMBUS CANVAS PRODUCTS INC
577 N 4th St (43215-2101)
PHONE.................................614 375-1397
Janet M Kellogg, *President*
Timothy Kellogg, *Vice Pres*
Eugene E McConnell Jr, *Vice Pres*
Michael McConnell, *Vice Pres*
EMP: 10 EST: 1958
SQ FT: 10,000
SALES (est): 92.3K **Privately Held**
SIC: 2394 2393 3949 2392 Canvas & related products; cushions, except spring & carpet: purchased materials; sporting & athletic goods; household furnishings

(G-6786)
COLUMBUS COATINGS COMPANY
1800 Watkins Rd (43207-3440)
PHONE.................................614 492-6800
Brian R Stack, *General Mgr*
EMP: 100
SQ FT: 350,000
SALES (est): 10.6MM **Privately Held**
SIC: 3479 3398 3471 Galvanizing of iron, steel or end-formed products; metal heat treating; plating & polishing

(G-6787)
COLUMBUS ELECTRICAL WORKS CO
777 N 4th St (43215-1596)
PHONE.................................614 294-4651
Lon Johnson, *President*
Joe Johnson, *Vice Pres*
EMP: 11
SQ FT: 28,000
SALES (est): 1.6MM **Privately Held**
SIC: 5063 7694 Motors, electric; electric motor repair

(G-6788)
COLUMBUS FIRE FIGHTERS UNION
379 W Broad St (43215-2756)
PHONE.................................614 481-8900
Scott Main, *Principal*
EMP: 5
SALES: 150.7K **Privately Held**
SIC: 3711 Fire department vehicles (motor vehicles), assembly of

(G-6789)
COLUMBUS GASKET CO INC
Also Called: Columbus Gasket & Supply
1875 Lone Eagle St (43228-3692)
PHONE.................................614 878-6041
James K Green, *President*
▲ EMP: 9
SQ FT: 14,000
SALES: 1.2MM **Privately Held**
WEB: www.columbusgaskets.com
SIC: 3053 3069 Gaskets, all materials; molded rubber products

(G-6790)
COLUMBUS HEATING & VENT CO
182 N Yale Ave (43222-1127)
PHONE.................................614 274-1177
Charles R Gulley, *President*
Greogry Yoak, *President*
Michael Blythe, *Corp Secy*
Mikel Plythe, *Admin Sec*
EMP: 135 EST: 1874

Columbus - Franklin County (G-6791)

SALES (est): 23.6MM **Privately Held**
WEB: www.columbusheat.com
SIC: 1711 3585 Warm air heating & air conditioning contractor; ventilation & duct work contractor; furnaces, warm air: electric

(G-6791)
COLUMBUS HUMUNGOUS APPAREL LLC
Also Called: Hc Apparel
2913 Manola Dr Ste 100 (43209-3261)
PHONE 614 824-2657
Jamal Moore,
EMP: 4
SALES (est): 300K **Privately Held**
SIC: 2759 Screen printing

(G-6792)
COLUMBUS INCONTACT
555 S Front St (43215-5668)
PHONE 801 245-8369
EMP: 3
SALES (est): 149.2K **Privately Held**
SIC: 7372 Prepackaged software

(G-6793)
COLUMBUS INSTRUMENTS INTL CORP
950 N Hague Ave (43204-2121)
PHONE 614 276-0593
Jan A Czekajewski, *President*
Laura Damas, *Vice Pres*
◆ EMP: 48 EST: 1970
SQ FT: 19,460
SALES (est): 9.9MM **Privately Held**
WEB: www.colinst.com
SIC: 3826 Analytical instruments

(G-6794)
COLUMBUS INTERNATIONAL CORP
200 E Campus View Blvd # 200 (43235-4678)
PHONE 614 323-1086
Rajeev Kumar, *President*
EMP: 18
SQ FT: 2,000
SALES (est): 2MM **Privately Held**
WEB: www.americanbusiness.com
SIC: 7372 Business oriented computer software

(G-6795)
COLUMBUS KOMBUCHA COMPANY LLC
930 Freeway Dr N (43229-5424)
PHONE 614 262-0000
Michael Iannarino,
EMP: 8
SQ FT: 5,000
SALES (est): 1.5MM **Privately Held**
SIC: 2082 Malt beverages

(G-6796)
COLUMBUS MACHINE WORKS INC
2491 Fairwood Ave (43207-2709)
PHONE 614 409-0244
Michael Stacey, *President*
John Harm, *Project Engr*
Diana Stacey, *Treasurer*
Ken McMullen, *Sales Staff*
EMP: 11
SQ FT: 3,729
SALES (est): 1.7MM **Privately Held**
WEB: www.columbusmachine.com
SIC: 3599 Machine shop, jobbing & repair

(G-6797)
COLUMBUS MESSENGER COMPANY (PA)
Also Called: Madison Messenger
3500 Sullivant Ave (43204-1887)
PHONE 614 272-5422
Phillip Daubel, *Owner*
EMP: 25
SQ FT: 4,000
SALES (est): 2MM **Privately Held**
SIC: 2711 Newspapers: publishing only, not printed on site

(G-6798)
COLUMBUS PIPE AND EQUIPMENT CO
Also Called: Steel Warehouse Division
763 E Markison Ave (43207-1390)
P.O. Box 7843 (43207-0843)
PHONE 614 444-7871
Bruce Jay Silberstein, *President*
Jon Silberstein, *Vice Pres*
Jonathan Silberstein, *Vice Pres*
Mike Denoewer, *CFO*
Franklin Silberstein, *Shareholder*
EMP: 15
SQ FT: 50,000
SALES (est): 7.5MM **Privately Held**
SIC: 5082 7692 5074 Construction & mining machinery; welding repair; plumbing fittings & supplies

(G-6799)
COLUMBUS PROCESSING CO LLC
4300 Alum Creek Dr (43207-4519)
PHONE 614 492-8287
Roger Wolf, *President*
Roger A Wolf, *Manager*
EMP: 4
SALES (est): 401K **Privately Held**
SIC: 3312 Iron & steel: galvanized, pipes, plates, sheets, etc.

(G-6800)
COLUMBUS ROOF TRUSSES INC (PA)
2525 Fisher Rd (43204-3588)
PHONE 614 272-6464
Tony Iacovetta, *President*
Rose A Pritchard, *Corp Secy*
Eugene R Iacovetta, *Vice Pres*
EMP: 30
SQ FT: 51,000
SALES (est): 4.1MM **Privately Held**
SIC: 2439 Trusses, wooden roof; trusses, except roof: laminated lumber

(G-6801)
COLUMBUS SERUM CO
7570 Donora Ln (43235-1920)
PHONE 614 793-0615
EMP: 3
SALES (est): 151.9K **Privately Held**
SIC: 2836 Mfg Biological Products

(G-6802)
COLUMBUS SIGN COMPANY (PA)
1515 E 5th Ave (43219-2483)
PHONE 614 252-3133
Michael Hoy, *President*
Michael S Hoy, *President*
EMP: 30 EST: 1911
SQ FT: 15,000
SALES (est): 4.1MM **Privately Held**
WEB: www.columbussign.com
SIC: 3993 Neon signs; signs, not made in custom sign painting shops

(G-6803)
COLUMBUS STEELMASTERS INC
660 Concrea Rd (43219-1822)
PHONE 614 231-2141
Brenda Neale, *CEO*
Steven Neale, *President*
EMP: 12
SQ FT: 17,000
SALES (est): 1MM **Privately Held**
SIC: 3444 Sheet metal specialties, not stamped

(G-6804)
COLUMBUS-SPORTS PUBLICATIONS
Also Called: Buckeye Sports Bulletin
1350 W 5th Ave Ste 30 (43212-2907)
P.O. Box 12453 (43212-0453)
PHONE 614 486-2202
Frank L Moskowitz, *President*
EMP: 13
SQ FT: 1,250
SALES (est): 843.2K **Privately Held**
WEB: www.buckeyesports.com
SIC: 2711 Newspapers: publishing only, not printed on site

(G-6805)
COMDOC INC
330 W Spring St Ste 100 (43215-2346)
PHONE 330 899-8000
Paul Dipronio, *Director*
EMP: 3
SALES (corp-wide): 9.8B **Publicly Held**
SIC: 2759 Commercial printing
HQ: Comdoc, Inc.
3458 Massillon Rd
Uniontown OH 44685
330 896-2346

(G-6806)
COMMERCIAL LUBRICANTS INC
2854 Johnstown Rd (43219-1772)
PHONE 614 475-5952
Jim Vannett, *Branch Mgr*
EMP: 5 **Privately Held**
SIC: 2992 5172 Lubricating oils & greases; lubricating oils & greases
PA: Commercial Lubricants Inc.
2846 E 37th St
Cleveland OH 44115

(G-6807)
COMMISSARY BREWING
1400 Dublin Rd (43215-1009)
PHONE 614 636-3164
EMP: 6 EST: 2015
SALES (est): 110.5K **Privately Held**
SIC: 2082 Malt beverages

(G-6808)
COMPUTER ALLIED TECHNOLOGY CO
3385 Somerford Rd (43221-1438)
PHONE 614 457-2292
Mark Taylor, *President*
Pat Taylor, *Treasurer*
EMP: 7
SALES (est): 630K **Privately Held**
SIC: 7371 3569 Computer software development & applications; robots, assembly line: industrial & commercial

(G-6809)
COMPUTERCRAFTS
2936 Brownlee Ave (43209-3060)
PHONE 614 231-7559
EMP: 4
SALES (est): 154.9K **Privately Held**
SIC: 2741 Misc Publishing

(G-6810)
CONQUEST MAPS
5696 Westbourne Ave (43213-1487)
PHONE 614 654-1627
Ross Worden, *President*
EMP: 4
SALES (est): 217.8K **Privately Held**
SIC: 2741 Miscellaneous publishing

(G-6811)
CONSUMERS NEWS SERVICES INC (HQ)
Also Called: This Week
5300 Crosswind Dr (43228-3600)
PHONE 740 888-6000
Floyd V Jones, *President*
Marcus Uhl, *Executive*
EMP: 150
SALES (est): 15.7MM
SALES (corp-wide): 651.9MM **Privately Held**
SIC: 2711 Newspapers, publishing & printing
PA: The Dispatch Printing Company
62 E Broad St
Columbus OH 43215
614 461-5000

(G-6812)
CONTECH ENGNERED SOLUTIONS LLC
1103 Schrock Rd Ste 105 (43229-1179)
PHONE 614 477-1171
EMP: 3 **Privately Held**
SIC: 3443 Fabricated plate work (boiler shop)
HQ: Contech Engineered Solutions Llc
9025 Centre Pointe Dr # 400
West Chester OH 45069
513 645-7000

(G-6813)
CONTRACT LIGHTING INC
1207 Grandview Ave (43212-3449)
PHONE 614 746-7022
Andrew Brooks, *Principal*
EMP: 4
SALES (est): 555.2K **Privately Held**
SIC: 3645 5063 Residential lighting fixtures; lighting fixtures

(G-6814)
CONTRACT LUMBER INC
200 Schofield Dr (43213-3803)
PHONE 614 751-1109
EMP: 60
SALES (corp-wide): 76.6MM **Privately Held**
SIC: 7349 5211 5031 2421 Building maintenance services; lumber & other building materials; lumber: rough, dressed & finished; lumber: rough, sawed or planed
PA: Contract Lumber, Inc.
3245 Hazelton Etna Rd Sw
Pataskala OH 43062
740 964-3147

(G-6815)
CONTROL-X INC
2289 Westbrooke Dr (43228-9644)
PHONE 614 777-9729
Zsigmond Kovacs, *Principal*
EMP: 3
SALES (est): 359.7K **Privately Held**
SIC: 3844 X-ray apparatus & tubes

(G-6816)
CONVAULT OF OHIO INC
841 Alton Ave (43219-3710)
P.O. Box 89, Reynoldsburg (43068-0089)
PHONE 614 252-8422
Tim Thickstun, *President*
Steven Thickstun, *Corp Secy*
Joanne Thickstun, *Vice Pres*
EMP: 9
SALES: 1.5MM **Privately Held**
SIC: 3443 Fuel tanks (oil, gas, etc.): metal plate

(G-6817)
COOKIE BOUQUETS INC
6665 Huntley Rd Ste F (43229-1045)
PHONE 614 888-2171
Christian McCoy, *President*
EMP: 7
SQ FT: 4,500
SALES (est): 380K **Privately Held**
WEB: www.cookiebouquets.com
SIC: 5461 5947 2052 Cookies; gift baskets; cookies & crackers

(G-6818)
COPIER RESOURCES INC
Also Called: Cri Digital
4800 Evanswood Dr (43229-6207)
P.O. Box 14824 (43214-0824)
PHONE 614 268 1100
Scott Di Francesco, *President*
EMP: 6
SQ FT: 4,000
SALES (est): 1.5MM **Privately Held**
WEB: www.cridigital.net
SIC: 7629 7359 5734 3575 Electrical repair shops; office machine rental, except computers; computer & software stores; cathode ray tube (CRT), computer terminal; mailing machines; photocopy machines

(G-6819)
CORE AUTOMOTIVE TECH LLC (HQ)
800 Manor Park Dr (43228-9762)
PHONE 614 870-5000
Alan Golding,
Terrence O'Donovan,
EMP: 1
SQ FT: 15,000
SALES: 130.5MM **Publicly Held**
SIC: 3714 5521 Motor vehicle body components & frame; used car dealers

GEOGRAPHIC SECTION

(G-6820)
CORE MOLDING TECHNOLOGIES INC (PA)
800 Manor Park Dr (43228-9762)
PHONE..................614 870-5000
James L Simonton, *Ch of Bd*
Tom Cellitti, *Vice Ch Bd*
David L Duvall, *President*
Renee Anderson, *Exec VP*
Eric L Palomaki, *Vice Pres*
EMP: 372
SQ FT: 338,000
SALES: 269.4MM **Publicly Held**
SIC: 3089 Molding primary plastic

(G-6821)
CORE QUANTUM TECHNOLOGIES INC
1275 Kinnear Rd (43212-1180)
PHONE..................614 214-7210
Ted Greene, *CEO*
Kristie Melnik, *COO*
EMP: 4
SALES (est): 400.6K **Privately Held**
SIC: 2835 In vitro & in vivo diagnostic substances

(G-6822)
CORPORATE ELEVATOR LLC
35 E Gay St Ste 218 (43215-8128)
PHONE..................614 288-1847
Ivan Isreal, *Principal*
EMP: 15
SALES (est): 581.4K **Privately Held**
SIC: 8243 7372 7371 Repair training, computer; application computer software; educational computer software; custom computer programming services

(G-6823)
CORPORATE ID INC
Also Called: Signarama Worthington
6185 Huntley Rd Ste M (43229-1094)
PHONE..................614 841-1255
David Mayer, *President*
EMP: 4
SQ FT: 5,000
SALES: 360K **Privately Held**
SIC: 3993 Signs & advertising specialties

(G-6824)
CORPORATE SUPPLY LLC
Also Called: Golfpremiums.com
3608 Sugar Loaf Ct (43221-5255)
P.O. Box 3784, Dublin (43016-0403)
PHONE..................614 876-8400
James Lemmon, *Mng Member*
Jeff Minor, *Consultant*
EMP: 3
SALES: 200K **Privately Held**
WEB: www.corporatesupply.com
SIC: 2759 5112 Promotional printing; office filing supplies

(G-6825)
COSTUME SPECIALISTS INC (PA)
211 N 5th St Ste 100 (43215-2603)
PHONE..................614 464-2115
Wendy C Goldstein, *President*
Greg Manger, *Sales Staff*
Tracy Liberatore, *Admin Asst*
EMP: 36
SQ FT: 34,500
SALES (est): 3.1MM **Privately Held**
WEB: www.cospec.com
SIC: 2389 7299 Theatrical costumes; costume rental

(G-6826)
COSTUME SPECIALISTS INC
211 N 5th St Ste 100 (43215-2603)
PHONE..................614 464-2115
Vickie Little, *Manager*
EMP: 5
SALES (corp-wide): 3.1MM **Privately Held**
WEB: www.cospec.com
SIC: 2389 7299 5699 Theatrical costumes; costume rental; costumes, masquerade or theatrical
PA: Costume Specialists, Inc.
211 N 5th St Ste 100
Columbus OH 43215
614 464-2115

(G-6827)
COTT SYSTEMS INC
2800 Corp Exchange Dr # 300 (43231-1678)
PHONE..................614 847-4405
Deborah A Ball, *CEO*
Karen L Bailey, *Exec VP*
Jodie Bare, *Vice Pres*
Drew Sheppared, *Vice Pres*
Ron Swords, *Facilities Mgr*
EMP: 77
SQ FT: 20,000
SALES (est): 16.4MM **Privately Held**
WEB: www.cottsystems.com
SIC: 7373 7372 2789 Computer integrated systems design; computer software development & applications; beveling of cards

(G-6828)
COULTER VENTURES LLC (PA)
Also Called: Rogue Fitness
545 E 5th Ave (43201-2964)
PHONE..................614 358-6190
Steve South, *Opers Mgr*
Eddie Sanchez, *Production*
Christian Hermosilla, *Engineer*
Caleb Heitman, *Controller*
Jeff Halaparda, *Asst Controller*
▼ EMP: 48
SQ FT: 25,000
SALES (est): 17.7MM **Privately Held**
SIC: 3949 Sporting & athletic goods

(G-6829)
COUNTER RHYTHM GROUP
441 E Redbud Aly (43206-3570)
PHONE..................513 379-6587
EMP: 3
SALES (est): 278.9K **Privately Held**
SIC: 3131 Counters

(G-6830)
COUNTERTOP SALES
5767 Westbourne Ave (43213-1488)
PHONE..................614 626-4476
Phillip Holbrook, *President*
EMP: 11
SALES (est): 1.1MM **Privately Held**
SIC: 2541 Counter & sink tops

(G-6831)
COW INDUSTRIES INC (PA)
Also Called: Central Ohio Welding
1875 Progress Ave (43207-1781)
PHONE..................614 443-6537
John Burns, *President*
Michael Netto, *Vice Pres*
Craig Delong, *Prdtn Mgr*
Matthew Nicol, *Purch Mgr*
Christina Bradford, *Controller*
EMP: 40
SQ FT: 80,000
SALES (est): 6.4MM **Privately Held**
WEB: www.cowind.com
SIC: 3499 3444 Machine bases, metal; sheet metalwork

(G-6832)
COZMYK ENTERPRISES INC
3757 Courtright Ct (43227-2250)
PHONE..................614 231-1370
Alan L Cozmyk, *President*
Christopher J Minnillo, *Principal*
Cheryl Dutiel, *Finance Mgr*
Lance Shook, *Data Proc Dir*
EMP: 15
SQ FT: 20,000
SALES (est): 3.7MM **Privately Held**
WEB: www.cozmyk.com
SIC: 3446 Ornamental metalwork

(G-6833)
CPI INDUSTRIAL CO
2300 Parsons Ave (43207-2467)
P.O. Box 7867 (43207-0867)
PHONE..................614 445-0800
Mark T Owens, *President*
Mark Wolf, *General Mgr*
Susan Flannigan, *Corp Secy*
John Lawler, *Vice Pres*
Vince Paul, *Treasurer*
EMP: 22
SALES (est): 5.7MM **Privately Held**
SIC: 2851 Epoxy coatings

(G-6834)
CPMM SERVICES GROUP INC
3785 Indianola Ave (43214-3754)
PHONE..................614 447-0165
Dan Dimitroff, *President*
EMP: 15
SQ FT: 12,500
SALES (est): 1.6MM **Privately Held**
WEB: www.cpmmservices.com
SIC: 7331 2752 7374 Mailing list compilers; mailing service; commercial printing, offset; data processing service

(G-6835)
CRANE BLENDING CENTER
2141 Fairwood Ave (43207-1753)
P.O. Box 1058 (43216-1058)
PHONE..................614 542-1199
Phil Stobart, *President*
EMP: 40
SALES (est): 2.6MM **Privately Held**
SIC: 2821 Polyvinyl chloride resins (PVC)

(G-6836)
CRANE PLASTICS MFG LTD
2141 Fairwood Ave (43207-1779)
PHONE..................614 754-3700
Tim Tait, *Principal*
Linda Deworth, *Manager*
Gregory Scott Evans, *Technical Staff*
Debbie Adkins, *Administration*
EMP: 5
SALES (est): 1.2MM **Privately Held**
SIC: 2821 Plastics materials & resins

(G-6837)
CRAWFORD PRODUCTS INC
3637 Corporate Dr (43231-7997)
PHONE..................614 890-1822
William A Crawford, *CEO*
Kevin P Crawford, *President*
Scott Stauch, *Vice Pres*
▲ EMP: 21
SQ FT: 12,500
SALES (est): 15MM **Privately Held**
WEB: www.crawfordproducts.com
SIC: 5085 3452 Fasteners, industrial: nuts, bolts, screws, etc.; bolts, nuts, rivets & washers

(G-6838)
CRITICALAIRE LLC
6155 Huntley Rd Ste A (43229-1096)
PHONE..................513 475-3800
EMP: 14 **Privately Held**
SIC: 3564 Exhaust fans: industrial or commercial
PA: Criticalaire, Llc
11325 R Hartman Hwy 100
Cincinnati OH 45241

(G-6839)
CROWN DIELECTRIC INDS INC
Also Called: Crown Auto Top Mfg Co
830 W Broad St (43222-1421)
PHONE..................614 224-5161
Anthony Gurvis, *President*
Andrew M Kauffman, *Principal*
EMP: 105 EST: 1931
SQ FT: 2,000
SALES (est): 6.9MM **Privately Held**
SIC: 2394 2399 2273 5013 Convertible tops, canvas or boat: from purchased materials; seat covers, automobile; automobile floor coverings, except rubber or plastic; automotive supplies & parts; automotive parts

(G-6840)
CRYSTAL ART IMPORTS INC (PA)
Also Called: Crystal Classics
6185 Huntley Rd Ste K (43229-1094)
PHONE..................614 430-8180
Bruno Bergman, *President*
▲ EMP: 18
SALES (est): 3.4MM **Privately Held**
SIC: 5719 5947 3231 Kitchenware; gift shop; ornamental glass: cut, engraved or otherwise decorated

(G-6841)
CUMMINS - ALLISON CORP
Also Called: Cummins-Allison
2222 Wilson Rd (43228-9386)
PHONE..................614 529-1940
Darcy Devore, *Manager*
EMP: 3
SALES (corp-wide): 383.8MM **Privately Held**
WEB: www.gsb.com
SIC: 5046 3519 Commercial equipment; internal combustion engines
PA: Cummins - Allison Corp.
852 Feehanville Dr
Mount Prospect IL 60056
847 759-6403

(G-6842)
CURVES AND MORE WOODWORKING
2002 Zettler Rd (43232-3834)
PHONE..................614 239-7837
Steven Blake, *Principal*
EMP: 5 EST: 2007
SALES (est): 633.8K **Privately Held**
SIC: 2431 Millwork

(G-6843)
CUSTOM RETAIL GROUP LLC
Also Called: Crg Worldwide
6311 Busch Blvd (43229-1802)
PHONE..................614 409-9720
Colin Leveque, *Mng Member*
EMP: 9 EST: 2013
SQ FT: 25,000
SALES (est): 1.7MM **Privately Held**
SIC: 3993 Displays, paint process

(G-6844)
CUSTOM SIGN CENTER INC
3200 Valleyview Dr (43204-2080)
PHONE..................614 279-6700
Tim W Sheehy, *President*
Judy Ramsburg, *Vice Pres*
Michael Anderson, *Project Mgr*
James Brooks, *Project Mgr*
Sam Petee, *Purchasing*
EMP: 50
SQ FT: 40,000
SALES (est): 9.2MM **Privately Held**
WEB: www.customsigncenter.com
SIC: 3993 Electric signs

(G-6845)
D M PALLET SERVICE INC
2019 Rathmell Rd (43207-5012)
PHONE..................614 491-0881
Dexter Mounts II, *President*
Dexter Mounts Sr, *Corp Secy*
EMP: 16
SQ FT: 800
SALES (est): 2MM **Privately Held**
SIC: 2448 Pallets, wood

(G-6846)
DAILY REPORTER
580 S High St Ste 316 (43215-5659)
PHONE..................614 224-4835
Ed Frederickson, *President*
Dan Shillingburg, *Vice Pres*
EMP: 25 EST: 1896
SQ FT: 5,500
SALES (est): 2.1MM
SALES (corp-wide): 13.4MM **Privately Held**
WEB: www.sourcenews.com
SIC: 2711 Newspapers, publishing & printing
PA: Calcomco, Inc.
5544 S Red Pine Cir
Kalamazoo MI 49009
313 885-9228

(G-6847)
DALLAS INSTANTWHIP INC
Also Called: Instantwhip National Office
2200 Cardigan Ave (43215-1092)
PHONE..................614 488-2536
EMP: 18
SQ FT: 10,300
SALES (est): 1.9MM **Privately Held**
SIC: 2026 5143 Mfg & Whol Refrigerated Dairy Products

Columbus - Franklin County (G-6848)

(G-6848)
DAN WILZYNSKI
Also Called: Edge Makers
2000 Fairwood Ave (43207-1607)
PHONE..................................800 531-3343
Dan Wilzynski, *Partner*
Lisa Wilzynski, *Partner*
Mari Sander, *Facilities Mgr*
EMP: 3
SQ FT: 6,400
SALES: 350K **Privately Held**
SIC: 3421 5085 3541 Cutlery; industrial supplies; machine tools, metal cutting type

(G-6849)
DANITE HOLDINGS LTD
Also Called: Danite Sign Co
1640 Harmon Ave (43223-3321)
PHONE..................................614 444-3333
Tim McCord, *President*
C William Klausman, *Partner*
James Detty, *Project Mgr*
Jill Waddell, *Sales Executive*
Noah Brown, *Manager*
EMP: 50
SQ FT: 33,500
SALES (est): 8.1MM **Privately Held**
WEB: www.danitesign.com
SIC: 3993 1799 Electric signs; neon signs; sign installation & maintenance

(G-6850)
DASKAL ENTERPRISE LLC (PA)
Also Called: Laser Cutting Shapes
6522 Singletree Dr (43229-1119)
PHONE..................................614 848-5700
Vadim Daskal, *Mng Member*
EMP: 8 EST: 2008
SQ FT: 3,000
SALES: 1MM **Privately Held**
SIC: 3699 Laser systems & equipment

(G-6851)
DATA POWER SOLUTIONS
Also Called: Current Technology
804 Hedley Pl (43230-1617)
P.O. Box 30842 (43230-0842)
PHONE..................................614 471-1911
David Michael Beck, *Owner*
EMP: 3
SALES (est): 240K **Privately Held**
SIC: 3825 1731 5045 Instruments to measure electricity; computer installation; computers, peripherals & software

(G-6852)
DAVID BOSWELL
Also Called: Noun Research and Dev Svcs
1777 Franklin Park S (43205-2217)
PHONE..................................614 441-2497
David Boswell, *Owner*
EMP: 50
SALES (est): 1.6MM **Privately Held**
SIC: 3714 3669 3829 3812 Motor vehicle body components & frame; burglar alarm apparatus, electric; measuring & controlling devices; search & navigation equipment

(G-6853)
DAVIS LASER PRODUCTS
2700 E 6th Ave (43219-2754)
PHONE..................................614 252-7711
John Davis, *Owner*
EMP: 4
SALES: 107K **Privately Held**
SIC: 3571 7378 Electronic computers; computer maintenance & repair

(G-6854)
DC REPROGRAPHICS CO
Also Called: AlphaGraphics
1254 Courtland Ave (43201-2829)
PHONE..................................614 297-1200
Daniel R Cannell, *President*
Patrick Stroh, *Prdtn Mgr*
Robert Morris, *Production*
EMP: 3
SALES (est): 132.2K **Privately Held**
SIC: 2752 Commercial printing, offset

(G-6855)
DEADBOLT SOFTWARE
43 Amazon Pl (43214-3501)
PHONE..................................614 679-2093
Todd Cooperider, *President*
EMP: 4
SALES (est): 330K **Privately Held**
SIC: 7372 Prepackaged software

(G-6856)
DEE PRINTING INC
4999 Transamerica Dr (43228-9381)
P.O. Box 132 (43216-0132)
PHONE..................................614 777-8700
Dorothy J Murnane, *President*
EMP: 14
SQ FT: 4,000
SALES (est): 1.9MM **Privately Held**
SIC: 2759 7311 Letterpress printing; advertising agencies

(G-6857)
DELILLE OXYGEN COMPANY (PA)
772 Marion Rd (43207-2595)
P.O. Box 7809 (43207-0809)
PHONE..................................614 444-1177
Joseph R Smith, *Ch of Bd*
Tom Smith, *President*
Richard F Carlile, *Principal*
Jim Smith, *Vice Pres*
Tim Hefner, *Sales Staff*
EMP: 30
SQ FT: 20,000
SALES (est): 19.8MM **Privately Held**
WEB: www.delille.com
SIC: 2813 5085 Acetylene; welding supplies

(G-6858)
DELITE FRUIT JUICES
185 N Yale Ave (43222-1146)
PHONE..................................614 470-4333
Chad Carney, *Owner*
EMP: 4
SALES (est): 327K **Privately Held**
SIC: 2086 Bottled & canned soft drinks

(G-6859)
DELL FIXTURES INC
321 Dering Ave (43207-2955)
PHONE..................................614 449-1750
Donald C Koch, *President*
Rich Clemons, *Vice Pres*
Thomas M Koch, *Treasurer*
Julie Clemons, *Admin Sec*
▲ EMP: 20
SQ FT: 64,000
SALES (est): 2.9MM **Privately Held**
WEB: www.dellfixtures.com
SIC: 2541 1799 2542 Store & office display cases & fixtures; counter top installation; fixtures, store: except wood

(G-6860)
DELPHIA CONSULTING LLC
250 E Broad St Ste 1150 (43215-3773)
PHONE..................................614 421-2000
Brian Delphia, *CEO*
Alexander Main, *Vice Pres*
Jayma Duchene, *Opers Staff*
Kimberly Stewart CPA, *Consultant*
Jeff Olsen, *Director*
EMP: 4
SALES (est): 660.5K **Privately Held**
SIC: 8742 7372 Human resource consulting services; business oriented computer software

(G-6861)
DESTINATION DONUTS LLC
59 Spruce St (43215-1622)
PHONE..................................614 370-0754
Heather Morris, *President*
EMP: 4
SQ FT: 364
SALES (est): 197.7K **Privately Held**
SIC: 2051 Cakes, bakery: except frozen

(G-6862)
DEWITT GROUP INC
Also Called: Capital Office Supply
777 Dearborn Park Ln E (43085-5716)
PHONE..................................614 847-5919
Bill Dewitt, *Ch of Bd*
Jory Dewitt, *Corp Secy*
EMP: 10
SQ FT: 9,000
SALES (est): 3.3MM **Privately Held**
SIC: 5112 2752 Office supplies; commercial printing, offset

(G-6863)
DIAMOND INNOVATIONS INC (PA)
Also Called: Hyperion
6325 Huntley Rd (43229-1007)
P.O. Box 568, Worthington (43085-0568)
PHONE..................................614 438-2000
Ron Voigt, *CEO*
Larry Dues, *Engineer*
William English, *Sales Mgr*
Matt Smith, *Senior Mgr*
Andrew Furnas, *Technology*
▲ EMP: 406
SALES (est): 120.4MM **Privately Held**
WEB: www.diamondinnovations.com
SIC: 3291 Abrasive products

(G-6864)
DIRAMED LLC
5000 Arlington Centre 2 (43220-3083)
PHONE..................................614 487-3660
William Shane, *President*
Robert Schlegall, *Chairman*
EMP: 10
SALES (est): 700K **Privately Held**
SIC: 2835 In vitro & in vivo diagnostic substances

(G-6865)
DIRCKSEN AND ASSOCIATES INC
743 S Front St (43206-1905)
P.O. Box 13662 (43213-0662)
PHONE..................................614 238-0413
Daniel W Dircksen, *President*
Dan Dircksen, *Vice Pres*
EMP: 6
SALES (est): 1MM **Privately Held**
SIC: 3728 5088 Military aircraft equipment & armament; transportation equipment & supplies

(G-6866)
DISANTE SOCKS
1540 Westwood Ave (43212-2767)
PHONE..................................614 481-3243
EMP: 4
SALES (est): 355.8K **Privately Held**
SIC: 2252 Mfg Hosiery

(G-6867)
DISCOVER PUBLICATIONS
6425 Busch Blvd (43229-1862)
PHONE..................................614 785-1111
Tony Sylvester, *General Mgr*
Leo Zupam, *Principal*
Catherine Zupan, *Opers Staff*
Ally Newsome, *Sales Dir*
John Peck, *Marketing Staff*
EMP: 9
SALES (est): 766.9K **Privately Held**
SIC: 2741 Miscellaneous publishing

(G-6868)
DISPATCH PRINTING COMPANY
Also Called: CM Printing
5253 Sinclair Rd (43229-5042)
PHONE..................................614 885-6020
Roy Gray, *Manager*
EMP: 50
SALES (corp-wide): 651.9MM **Privately Held**
WEB: www.columbusmonthly.com
SIC: 2711 2752 2721 Commercial printing & newspaper publishing combined; commercial printing, lithographic; periodicals
PA: The Dispatch Printing Company
62 E Broad St
Columbus OH 43215
614 461-5000

(G-6869)
DISTINCTIVE SURFACES LLC
5158 Sinclair Rd (43229-5415)
PHONE..................................614 431-0898
Jonathan Ruper, *Mng Member*
EMP: 18
SALES (est): 1.9MM **Privately Held**
SIC: 2434 Wood kitchen cabinets

(G-6870)
DISTRICT BREWING CO INC
Also Called: Columbus Brewing Co
2555 Harrison Rd (43204-3511)
PHONE..................................614 224-3626
Susie Edwards, *President*
Ben Pridgeon, *Vice Pres*
▲ EMP: 5
SQ FT: 6,000
SALES: 500K **Privately Held**
SIC: 2082 Beer (alcoholic beverage)

(G-6871)
DLZ OHIO INC (HQ)
6121 Huntley Rd (43229-1003)
PHONE..................................614 888-0040
A James Siebert, *President*
Vikram Rajadhyaksha, *Chairman*
P V Rajadhyaksha, *COO*
David Cutlip, *Vice Pres*
John Sprouse, *Engineer*
EMP: 200
SQ FT: 45,000
SALES (est): 24.6MM
SALES (corp-wide): 93MM **Privately Held**
SIC: 8711 1382 8712 8713 Consulting engineer; civil engineering; geophysical exploration, oil & gas field; architectural services; surveying services
PA: Dlz Corporation
6121 Huntley Rd
Columbus OH 43229
614 888-0040

(G-6872)
DNO INC
3650 E 5th Ave (43219-1805)
PHONE..................................614 231-3601
Anthony Dinovo, *President*
Carol Dinovo, *Vice Pres*
EMP: 80
SQ FT: 10,000
SALES: 24MM **Privately Held**
WEB: www.dnoinc.com
SIC: 2099 5148 Salads, fresh or refrigerated; fruits, fresh

(G-6873)
DRAGON BEVERAGE INC
1945 Judwick Dr (43229-5305)
PHONE..................................614 506-5592
Igor Svishevskiy, *Principal*
EMP: 3
SALES: 124.2K **Privately Held**
SIC: 2086 Bottled & canned soft drinks

(G-6874)
DRAKE BROTHERS LTD
1215 Forsythe Ave (43201-3202)
PHONE..................................415 819-4941
EMP: 7
SALES (est): 488.1K **Privately Held**
SIC: 2084 Wines

(G-6875)
DRIVELINE 1 INC
1369 Frank Rd (43223-3729)
PHONE..................................614 279-7734
Bruce Hickman, *President*
EMP: 9
SQ FT: 7,500
SALES (est): 1.6MM **Privately Held**
WEB: www.driveline1.com
SIC: 3714 Motor vehicle parts & accessories

(G-6876)
DURR MEGTEC LLC
835 N Cassady Ave (43219-2203)
PHONE..................................614 258-9501
Mike Hunter, *Manager*
EMP: 110
SALES (corp-wide): 4.4B **Privately Held**
WEB: www.megtec.com
SIC: 2899 3674 3624 2842 Chemical preparations; bay oil; semiconductors & related devices; carbon & graphite products; specialty cleaning, polishes & sanitation goods; air purification equipment
HQ: Durr Megtec, Llc
830 Prosper St
De Pere WI 54115
920 336-5715

GEOGRAPHIC SECTION — Columbus - Franklin County (G-6904)

(G-6877)
DURR MEGTEC LLC
Also Called: Solvent Recovery Division
2120 Citygate Dr (43219-3566)
PHONE..................614 340-4154
David Evan, *Manager*
EMP: 7
SALES (corp-wide): 4.4B **Privately Held**
SIC: 2911 Solvents
HQ: Durr Megtec, Llc
  830 Prosper St
  De Pere WI 54115
  920 336-5715

(G-6878)
E & E SCREEN PRTG & CSTM EMB
901 Robinwood Ave Ste G (43213-1781)
PHONE..................614 235-2177
EMP: 4
SALES (est): 210K **Privately Held**
SIC: 2262 Screen Printing Embroidery

(G-6879)
E BEE PRINTING INC
70 S 4th St (43215-4315)
PHONE..................614 224-0416
Debbi Bussman, *Principal*
EMP: 3
SALES (est): 223.8K **Privately Held**
SIC: 2752 Commercial printing, offset

(G-6880)
E RETAILING ASSOCIATES LLC
Also Called: Customized Girl
2282 Westbrooke Dr (43228-9416)
PHONE..................614 300-5785
Cindy Terapak, *Cust Mgr*
Taj Schaffnit, *Mng Member*
Marty Laroche, *CTO*
Jeff Benzenberg, *Director*
Kurt J Schmalz,
EMP: 64
SALES (est): 8.6MM **Privately Held**
WEB: www.customisegirl.com
SIC: 8748 5961 2253 Business consulting; ; T-shirts & tops, knit

(G-6881)
E-WASTE SYSTEMS (OHIO) INC
1033 Brentnell Ave # 300 (43219-2186)
PHONE..................614 824-3057
George Pardos, *CEO*
Steve Hollinshead, *CFO*
EMP: 5
SALES (est): 609.4K **Privately Held**
SIC: 3861 Photocopy machines

(G-6882)
EANYTIME CORPORATION
833 Grandview Ave Ste B (43215-1123)
P.O. Box 5100, Huntington Beach CA (92615-5100)
PHONE..................714 969-7000
Laurence Cohn, *President*
EMP: 3
SALES (corp-wide): 7.8MM **Privately Held**
SIC: 3821 Laboratory apparatus & furniture
PA: Eanytime Corporation
  9151 Atlanta Ave # 5100
  Huntington Beach CA 92615
  714 969-7000

(G-6883)
EASTERN RESERVE DEVELOPMENT
3888 Stonewater Dr (43221-5931)
PHONE..................614 319-3179
Bruce Smith, *CEO*
Gerald Picker, *President*
EMP: 3
SALES: 2MM **Privately Held**
SIC: 1382 Oil & gas exploration services

(G-6884)
EDUCATIONAL PUBLISHER INC
1091 W 1st Ave (43212-3601)
PHONE..................614 485-0721
Robert Sims, *President*
EMP: 5
SALES (est): 66.9K **Privately Held**
SIC: 2741 Miscellaneous publishing

(G-6885)
EDWARDS ELECTRICAL & MECH
685 Grandview Ave (43215-1119)
PHONE..................614 485-2003
Matt Snyder, *Branch Mgr*
EMP: 40 **Privately Held**
WEB: www.edwards-elec.com
SIC: 2752 1711 Commercial printing, lithographic; mechanical contractor
HQ: Edwards Electrical & Mechanical Inc
  2350 N Shadeland Ave
  Indianapolis IN 46219
  317 543-3460

(G-6886)
EFCO CORP
Also Called: Economy Forms
3900 Zane Trace Dr (43228-3833)
PHONE..................614 876-1226
Jim Davis, *Manager*
Jim Grubb, *Manager*
EMP: 26
SALES (corp-wide): 256.4MM **Privately Held**
SIC: 5051 7353 4225 3444 Steel; heavy construction equipment rental; general warehousing; concrete forms, sheet metal; miscellaneous fabricated wire products; fabricated plate work (boiler shop)
HQ: Efco Corp
  1800 Ne Broadway Ave
  Des Moines IA 50313
  515 266-1141

(G-6887)
ELASTANCE IMAGING LLC
226 E Beechwold Blvd (43214-2120)
PHONE..................614 579-9520
William Timmons, *President*
EMP: 4
SALES (est): 178.6K **Privately Held**
SIC: 3845 8731 Magnetic resonance imaging device, nuclear; ultrasonic medical equipment, except cleaning; ultrasonic scanning devices, medical; biotechnical research, commercial; medical research, commercial

(G-6888)
ELASTOSTAR RUBBER CORP
7030 Huntley Rd Ste B (43229-1053)
PHONE..................614 841-4400
Ghanshyam Dungarani, *President*
Hiren Jetani, *Vice Pres*
EMP: 20
SALES (est): 3.1MM **Privately Held**
SIC: 3069 Medical & laboratory rubber sundries & related products

(G-6889)
ELBERN PUBLICATIONS
3120 Elbern Ave (43209-2075)
P.O. Box 9497 (43209-0497)
PHONE..................614 235-2643
Evelyn Becker, *Vice Pres*
EMP: 3
SALES (est): 137.8K **Privately Held**
SIC: 2741 Miscellaneous publishing

(G-6890)
ELECTRO TORQUE
Also Called: American Electric Motor Svc
900 Gray St (43201-3075)
P.O. Box 233, Corunna MI (48817-0233)
PHONE..................614 297-1600
Steve Omestead, *Owner*
Alice M Stout, *Corp Secy*
EMP: 4
SALES (est): 450K **Privately Held**
SIC: 5063 7694 Motors, electric; electric motor repair

(G-6891)
ELITE FIRE SERVICES LLC
1520 Harmon Ave Ste 667 (43223-3361)
PHONE..................614 586-4255
Sean Overbeck,
Rod Bishop,
Rob Callihan,
Doug Patterson,
EMP: 12
SQ FT: 850
SALES (est): 2.8MM **Privately Held**
SIC: 3569 Firefighting apparatus & related equipment

(G-6892)
ELMER S INC
180 E Broad St Fl 4 (43215-3763)
PHONE..................614 225-4000
Michael Endres, *Manager*
EMP: 3 EST: 2010
SALES (est): 255.8K **Privately Held**
SIC: 2891 Adhesives & sealants

(G-6893)
ELYTUS LTD
601 S High St (43215-5678)
PHONE..................614 824-4985
Drew Clauson, *Opers Mgr*
Paul Organ, *Technology*
Matthew Hollis,
Alan Dillman,
EMP: 11 EST: 2007
SALES (est): 1.6MM **Privately Held**
SIC: 7372 Utility computer software

(G-6894)
EMBROIDERY DESIGN GROUP LLC
2564 Billingsley Rd (43235-1990)
PHONE..................614 798-8152
Mary Bandeen, *Mng Member*
EMP: 13
SALES (est): 937.8K **Privately Held**
WEB: www.embroiderydesigngroup.com
SIC: 2395 Embroidery products, except schiffli machine; embroidery & art needlework

(G-6895)
ENGINEERED MARBLE INC
4064 Fisher Rd (43228-1020)
PHONE..................614 308-0041
Jeff Schmidt, *President*
Jeff Klein, *Vice Pres*
EMP: 6
SQ FT: 6,100
SALES (est): 400K **Privately Held**
WEB: www.engineeredstone.com
SIC: 3281 Marble, building; cut & shaped

(G-6896)
ENGINEERED PROFILES LLC
Also Called: Crane Plastics
2141 Fairwood Ave (43207-1753)
PHONE..................614 754-3700
Timothy T Miller, *Principal*
Mike Davis, *COO*
Brian Davis, *Vice Pres*
Erich Widmer, *Engineer*
Adam Wachter, *CFO*
EMP: 200
SQ FT: 300,000
SALES (est): 61.1MM **Privately Held**
WEB: www.craneplasticsmfg.com
SIC: 3089 Extruded finished plastic products
HQ: The Crane Group Companies Limited
  330 W Spring St Ste 200
  Columbus OH 43215
  614 754-3000

(G-6897)
ENLYTON LTD
1216 Kinnear Rd (43212-1154)
PHONE..................614 888-9220
Jeffrey R Bergen, *CEO*
EMP: 5
SALES (est): 572K **Privately Held**
SIC: 2835 In vitro & in vivo diagnostic substances

(G-6898)
ENNOVEA LLC
2030 Dividend Dr (43228-3847)
PHONE..................814 838-6664
Charles F Hertlein, *Principal*
EMP: 25
SALES (est): 6.1MM
SALES (corp-wide): 580.4MM **Privately Held**
SIC: 2834 Mfg Pharmaceutical Preparations
PA: Ernie Green Industries, Inc.
  2030 Dividend Dr
  Columbus OH 43228
  614 219-1423

(G-6899)
ENNOVEA MEDICAL LLC
2030 Dividend Dr (43228-3847)
PHONE..................855 997-2273
Vinc Ellerbrock, *CFO*
Larry Jutte, *Mng Member*
Robert Deans,
EMP: 3
SALES: 150K
SALES (corp-wide): 580.4MM **Privately Held**
SIC: 3841 Diagnostic apparatus, medical
PA: Ernie Green Industries, Inc.
  2030 Dividend Dr
  Columbus OH 43228
  614 219-1423

(G-6900)
ENTROCHEM INC
1245 Kinnear Rd (43212-1155)
PHONE..................614 946-7602
Jim McGuire, *President*
John Linkinhoker, *Planning*
EMP: 10
SALES (est): 1.8MM **Privately Held**
SIC: 2891 Adhesives

(G-6901)
ENTROTECH INC
1245 Kinnear Rd (43212-1155)
PHONE..................614 946-7602
James E McGuire Jr, *President*
Elizebeth Maag, *Principal*
Dave Bragg, *Vice Pres*
Jim Koch, *Vice Pres*
Doug Davis, *Controller*
▲ EMP: 18
SQ FT: 6,000
SALES (est): 7MM **Privately Held**
WEB: www.entrotech.com
SIC: 3081 Plastic film & sheet

(G-6902)
EP FERRIS & ASSOCIATES INC
880 King Ave (43212-2654)
PHONE..................614 299-2999
Edward P Ferris, *Ch of Bd*
Michael Peecook, *Chief*
Heather Mackling, *Senior Engr*
Timothy Bester, *Senior Mgr*
Matthew Ferris, *Director*
EMP: 3 EST: 1987
SALES (est): 144.6K **Privately Held**
SIC: 8742 8711 Management consulting services; construction & civil engineering; testing, measuring, surveying & analysis services

(G-6903)
ERNIE GREEN INDUSTRIES INC (PA)
Also Called: Eg Industries
2030 Dividend Dr (43228-3847)
PHONE..................614 219-1423
Ernie Green, *President*
Samuel Morgan, *Exec VP*
▲ EMP: 4
SQ FT: 7,000
SALES (est): 582.7MM **Privately Held**
WEB: www.egreeninc.com
SIC: 3714 3089 3471 3469 Motor vehicle wheels & parts; motor vehicle body components & frame; motor vehicle engines & parts; motor vehicle transmissions, drive assemblies & parts; injection molded finished plastic products; automotive parts, plastic; chromium plating of metals or formed products; metal stampings; medical & hospital equipment

(G-6904)
ERNST ENTERPRISES INC
711 Stimmel Rd (43223-2905)
PHONE..................614 443-9456
John C Ernst Jr, *Branch Mgr*
EMP: 25
SALES (corp-wide): 227.2MM **Privately Held**
SIC: 5211 3273 Cement; ready-mixed concrete
PA: Ernst Enterprises, Inc.
  3361 Successful Way
  Dayton OH 45414
  937 233-5555

Columbus - Franklin County (G-6905)

(G-6905)
ERNST ENTERPRISES INC
569 N Wilson Rd (43204-1459)
PHONE.................................614 308-0063
EMP: 7
SALES (corp-wide): 227.2MM **Privately Held**
SIC: 3273 Ready-mixed concrete
PA: Ernst Enterprises, Inc.
    3361 Successful Way
    Dayton OH 45414
    937 233-5555

(G-6906)
ESSILOR LABORATORIES AMER INC
Also Called: Top Network
3671 Interchange Rd (43204-1499)
PHONE.................................614 274-0840
Don Lepore, *Manager*
EMP: 50
SALES (corp-wide): 283.5MM **Privately Held**
WEB: www.crizal.com
SIC: 3851 5049 Eyeglasses, lenses & frames; optical goods
HQ: Essilor Laboratories Of America, Inc.
    13515 N Stemmons Fwy
    Dallas TX 75234
    972 241-4141

(G-6907)
ETHERIUM LIGHTING LLC
6969 Alum Creek Dr (43217-1244)
PHONE.................................310 800-8837
EMP: 5
SALES (est): 560K **Privately Held**
SIC: 3646 Commercial indusl & institutional electric lighting fixtures

(G-6908)
EVANS ADHESIVE CORPORATION (HQ)
925 Old Henderson Rd (43220-3779)
PHONE.................................614 451-2665
C Russell Thompson, *President*
Wilbur J Liddil, *Senior VP*
Gene Hollo, *Vice Pres*
Steve Overby, *Plant Mgr*
David Jarvis, *Opers Staff*
EMP: 27
SALES: 24MM
SALES (corp-wide): 42.1MM **Privately Held**
SIC: 2891 5085 Adhesives; abrasives & adhesives
PA: Meridian Adhesives Group Llc
    100 Park Ave Fl 31
    New York NY 10017
    212 771-1717

(G-6909)
EVANS CREATIVE GROUP LLC
Also Called: Columbus Underground
11 E Gay St (43215-3125)
PHONE.................................614 657-9439
Anne Evans,
Walker Evans,
EMP: 9
SQ FT: 2,600
SALES (est): 423.6K **Privately Held**
SIC: 2741

(G-6910)
EXONANORNA LLC
1507 Chambers Rd Ste 301 (43212-1568)
PHONE.................................614 928-3512
Mario Vieweger,
EMP: 6
SALES (est): 267.4K **Privately Held**
SIC: 2834 Tablets, pharmaceutical

(G-6911)
EXPONENTIA US INC
424 Beecher Rd Ste A (43230-3510)
PHONE.................................614 944-5103
Giri Suvramani, *President*
Gira Suvramani, *President*
EMP: 30
SQ FT: 5,200
SALES: 4.8MM **Privately Held**
SIC: 7372 Publishers' computer software

(G-6912)
EYE SURGERY CENTER OHIO INC (PA)
Also Called: Arena Eye Surgeons
262 Neil Ave Ste 320 (43215-4624)
PHONE.................................614 228-3937
Peter Utrata, *Principal*
Lisa Russell, *Corp Comm Staff*
Robert P Bennett, *Med Doctor*
Mary Delong, *Administration*
Kelly Kidd, *Ophthalmic Tech*
EMP: 25
SQ FT: 2,200
SALES (est): 4.7MM **Privately Held**
WEB: www.eyesurgerycenterofohio.com
SIC: 3841 8011 Eye examining instruments & apparatus; offices & clinics of medical doctors

(G-6913)
FACILITIES MANAGEMENT EX LLC
Also Called: Fmx
800 Yard St Ste 115 (43212-3866)
PHONE.................................844 664-4400
Jeffery Wilkins, *CEO*
Brian Gregory, *COO*
Katie Dye, *Cust Mgr*
Pat Rigsby, *Accounts Exec*
Marianella Mace, *Sales Staff*
EMP: 11 EST: 2014
SQ FT: 3,200
SALES (est): 547.2K **Privately Held**
SIC: 7372 Application computer software; business oriented computer software

(G-6914)
FBG BOTTLING GROUP LLC
Also Called: Frostop
1523 Alum Creek Dr (43209-2712)
P.O. Box 9841 (43209-0841)
PHONE.................................614 554-4646
Mike Gutter, *President*
EMP: 12
SALES (est): 2.2MM **Privately Held**
SIC: 2086 Bottled & canned soft drinks

(G-6915)
FCBDD
2879 Johnstown Rd (43219-1719)
PHONE.................................614 475-6440
Maggie Hart, *Manager*
EMP: 3
SALES (est): 178.9K **Privately Held**
SIC: 3999

(G-6916)
FCX PERFORMANCE INC (HQ)
Also Called: Jh Instruments
3000 E 14th Ave (43219-2355)
PHONE.................................614 324-6050
Thomas Cox, *CEO*
Jeff Caswell, *President*
Russell S Frazee, *COO*
Tim Cancila, *Division VP*
Chris Hill, *Exec VP*
▲ EMP: 40
SQ FT: 44,000
SALES (est): 338MM
SALES (corp-wide): 3B **Publicly Held**
WEB: www.fcxperformance.com
SIC: 5084 5085 3494 Instruments & control equipment; industrial supplies; valves & fittings; valves & pipe fittings
PA: Applied Industrial Technologies, Inc.
    1 Applied Plz
    Cleveland OH 44115
    216 426-4000

(G-6917)
FEDEX OFFICE & PRINT SVCS INC
180 N High St (43215-2403)
PHONE.................................614 621-1100
EMP: 32
SALES (corp-wide): 65.4B **Publicly Held**
WEB: www.kinkos.com
SIC: 7334 2791 Photocopying & duplicating services; typesetting
HQ: Fedex Office And Print Services, Inc.
    7900 Legacy Dr
    Plano TX 75024
    800 463-3339

(G-6918)
FERGUSON FIRE FABRICATION INC
1640 Clara St (43211-2628)
PHONE.................................614 299-2070
Dan Tober, *Branch Mgr*
EMP: 11
SALES (corp-wide): 20.7B **Privately Held**
SIC: 3312 3999 5074 Wheels; atomizers, toiletry; plumbing fittings & supplies
HQ: Ferguson Fire & Fabrication, Inc.
    2750 S Towne Ave
    Pomona CA 91766
    909 517-3085

(G-6919)
FIDELUX LIGHTING LLC
3000 Corp Exchange Dr # 600 (43231-7689)
PHONE.................................614 839-0250
EMP: 6
SALES (corp-wide): 5.1MM **Privately Held**
SIC: 3674 3648 Solar cells; lighting equipment
HQ: Fidelux Lighting Llc
    100 Great Meadow Rd # 600
    Hartford CT 06109
    860 436-5000

(G-6920)
FIFTH AVENUE FRET SHOP LLC
1597 W 5th Ave (43212-2310)
PHONE.................................614 481-8300
Phil Maneri, *Owner*
Olive Smith, *Treasurer*
EMP: 3
SQ FT: 900
SALES (est): 279.7K **Privately Held**
WEB: www.fretshop.com
SIC: 3931 5736 5932 7699 Guitars & parts, electric & nonelectric; string instruments; musical instruments, secondhand; musical instrument repair services

(G-6921)
FILAMENT LLC
1507 Chambers Rd Fl 1 (43212-1568)
PHONE.................................614 732-0754
Arfaan Rampersaud,
Cynthia Rampersaud,
EMP: 5 EST: 2014
SALES (est): 376.7K **Privately Held**
SIC: 2835 2851 3826 3841 In vitro diagnostics; paints & paint additives; ultraviolet analytical instruments; laser scientific & engineering instruments; diagnostic apparatus, medical

(G-6922)
FIMM USA INC
5454 Alkire Rd (43228-3606)
PHONE.................................253 243-1522
Enrico Spinelli, *President*
◆ EMP: 19
SQ FT: 120,000
SALES (est): 3.4MM **Privately Held**
SIC: 3991 Brooms & brushes

(G-6923)
FINE LINE GRAPHICS CORP (PA)
1481 Goodale Blvd (43212-3402)
P.O. Box 163370 (43216-3370)
PHONE.................................614 486-0276
James Basch, *President*
Mark Carro, *Principal*
Gregory Davis, *Vice Pres*
Allie Davis, *VP Human Res*
Greg Davis, *VP Sales*
▲ EMP: 151
SQ FT: 42,000
SALES (est): 39MM **Privately Held**
SIC: 2752 7331 Lithographic Commercial Printing Direct Mail Advertising Services

(G-6924)
FINISHMASTER INC
Also Called: Autobody Supply Company
212 N Grant Ave (43215-2642)
PHONE.................................614 228-4328
James Volpe, *Branch Mgr*
EMP: 68
SALES (corp-wide): 1.4B **Privately Held**
SIC: 3563 5013 5198 Air & gas compressors including vacuum pumps; automotive supplies; paints, varnishes & supplies; paints; lacquers; enamels
HQ: Finishmaster, Inc.
    115 W Washington St Fl 7
    Indianapolis IN 46204
    317 237-3678

(G-6925)
FIRE BALL PRESS
27 E 5th Ave (43201-4510)
PHONE.................................614 280-0100
Dough Holmes, *Owner*
EMP: 4 EST: 2013
SALES (est): 234.9K **Privately Held**
SIC: 2741 7336 Miscellaneous publishing; commercial art & graphic design

(G-6926)
FISHEL COMPANY
Johnson Brothers Construction
1600 Walcutt Rd (43228-9394)
PHONE.................................614 850-4400
Jason Montgomery, *Engineer*
Ed Evans, *Manager*
EMP: 65
SALES (corp-wide): 434.8MM **Privately Held**
WEB: www.fishelco.com
SIC: 1623 8711 1731 3612 Telephone & communication line construction; electric power line construction; cable television line construction; gas main construction; engineering services; electrical work; transformers, except electric
PA: The Fishel Company
    1366 Dublin Rd
    Columbus OH 43215
    614 274-8100

(G-6927)
FLAG LADY INC
Also Called: Flag Lady's Flag Store, The
4567 N High St (43214-2042)
PHONE.................................614 263-1776
Mary Leavitt, *President*
Lori Leavitt Watson, *Treasurer*
EMP: 9
SQ FT: 5,000
SALES (est): 1.7MM **Privately Held**
WEB: www.flagladyinc.com
SIC: 5999 2399 Flags; flags, fabric

(G-6928)
FLORIDA TILE INC
Florida Tile 59
7029 Huntley Rd Ste B (43229-1059)
PHONE.................................614 436-2511
Brian Cotterman, *Sales Staff*
Jason Tackett, *Branch Mgr*
Jason Reikowsky, *Asst Mgr*
EMP: 8
SALES (corp-wide): 147.6MM **Privately Held**
WEB: www.floridatile.com
SIC: 3253 Wall tile, ceramic
PA: Florida Tile, Inc.
    998 Governors Ln Ste 300
    Lexington KY 40513
    859 219-5200

(G-6929)
FORD PIPING AND BREWRY SVC LLC
1742 Kenny Rd (43212-1384)
PHONE.................................614 284-2409
Bryant Ford,
EMP: 3
SALES (est): 182.4K **Privately Held**
SIC: 3556 Brewers' & maltsters' machinery

(G-6930)
FORMWARE INC
3441 Winchester Pike (43232-5566)
PHONE.................................614 231-9387
James J Vatter, *President*
Margaret Kessler, *Corp Secy*
EMP: 9
SQ FT: 5,200
SALES (est): 730K **Privately Held**
SIC: 2434 2541 Wood kitchen cabinets; table or counter tops, plastic laminated; cabinets, except refrigerated: show, display, etc.: wood

▲ = Import ▼ = Export
◆ = Import/Export

GEOGRAPHIC SECTION

Columbus - Franklin County (G-6957)

(G-6931)
FORTERRA PIPE & PRECAST LLC
1500 Haul Rd (43207-1888)
PHONE....................614 445-3830
Wayne Greene, *President*
EMP: 11
SALES (est): 1.7MM **Privately Held**
SIC: 3272 Concrete products

(G-6932)
FORTIN WELDING & MFG INC
Also Called: Fortin Ironworks
944 W 5th Ave (43212-2657)
PHONE....................614 291-4342
Dan Fortin, *President*
Margaret V Gundy, *Corp Secy*
Fred Fortin, *Vice Pres*
John Fortin, *Vice Pres*
Robert Fortin, *Vice Pres*
EMP: 39 **EST:** 1946
SQ FT: 60,000
SALES (est): 10.6MM **Privately Held**
WEB: www.fortinironworks.com
SIC: 3449 3446 Miscellaneous metalwork; ornamental metalwork

(G-6933)
FORTNER UPHOLSTERING INC
2050 S High St (43207-2425)
PHONE....................614 475-8282
David F Fortner Jr, *President*
Glen McAllister, *President*
Wanda L Fortner, *Principal*
E J Silberman, *Principal*
Diana Orum, *Corp Secy*
▲ **EMP:** 16 **EST:** 1967
SQ FT: 7,000
SALES (est): 3.6MM **Privately Held**
WEB: www.fortnerinc.com
SIC: 5712 2512 7641 3429 Furniture stores; upholstered household furniture; reupholstery & furniture repair; reupholstery; furniture builders' & other household hardware

(G-6934)
FRANKIE TATUM
Also Called: Tatum Landscaping & Lawncare
56 Winner Ave (43203-1954)
P.O. Box 91293 (43209-7293)
PHONE....................614 216-1556
Frankie Tatum, *Owner*
EMP: 3
SALES: 40K **Privately Held**
SIC: 0783 3271 0782 Spraying services, ornamental tree; blocks, concrete: landscape or retaining wall; garden planting services

(G-6935)
FRANKLIN ART GLASS STUDIOS
222 E Sycamore St (43206-2198)
PHONE....................614 221-2972
Gary L Helf, *Ch of Bd*
Andrea Reid, *Vice Pres*
▲ **EMP:** 30 **EST:** 1900
SQ FT: 55,000
SALES (est): 3.6MM **Privately Held**
WEB: www.franklinartglass.com
SIC: 3231 5231 5945 Stained glass: made from purchased glass; glass, leaded or stained; hobby, toy & game shops

(G-6936)
FRANKLIN COMMUNICATIONS INC
Also Called: Wsny FM
4401 Carriage Hill Ln (43220-3837)
PHONE....................614 459-9769
Edward K Christian, *CEO*
Alan Goodman, *President*
EMP: 65
SQ FT: 10,000
SALES (est): 2.1MM **Publicly Held**
WEB: www.sagacommunications.com
SIC: 4832 2711 Radio broadcasting stations; newspapers
HQ: Saga Communications Of New England, Inc.
73 Kercheval Ave Ste 201
Grosse Pointe Farms MI 48236
313 886-7070

(G-6937)
FRANKLIN FIELD SERVICE
7065 Huntley Rd (43229-1055)
PHONE....................614 885-1779
David Nunez, *President*
EMP: 3
SALES (est): 187.5K **Privately Held**
SIC: 3398 Metal heat treating

(G-6938)
FRED D PFENING COMPANY (PA)
1075 W 5th Ave (43212-2691)
PHONE....................614 294-5361
Fred D Pfening Jr, *CEO*
Fred D Pfening III, *President*
Ed Brackman, *Vice Pres*
William F Kearns, *Vice Pres*
Patrick Inskeep, *VP Prdtn*
EMP: 41 **EST:** 1919
SQ FT: 55,000
SALES (est): 9.3MM **Privately Held**
WEB: www.pfening.com
SIC: 3535 3585 3556 Pneumatic tube conveyor systems; air conditioning units, complete: domestic or industrial; mixers, commercial, food

(G-6939)
FRED D PFENING COMPANY
Also Called: Plant 2
1075 W 5th Ave (43212-2691)
PHONE....................614 294-5361
John Legg, *Branch Mgr*
EMP: 7
SALES (corp-wide): 9.3MM **Privately Held**
WEB: www.pfening.com
SIC: 3556 Bakery machinery
PA: The Fred D Pfening Company
1075 W 5th Ave
Columbus OH 43212
614 294-5361

(G-6940)
FRITO-LAY NORTH AMERICA INC
6611 Broughton Ave (43213-1523)
PHONE....................614 508-3004
Don Jacklich, *Sales/Mktg Mgr*
EMP: 165
SALES (corp-wide): 64.6B **Publicly Held**
WEB: www.fritolay.com
SIC: 2096 Potato chips & similar snacks
HQ: Frito-Lay North America, Inc.
7701 Legacy Dr
Plano TX 75024

(G-6941)
FULL GOSPEL BAPTIST TIMES
Also Called: Oakley Full Gospel Baptist Ch
3415 El Paso Dr (43204-1448)
PHONE....................614 279-3307
Laverne Palmore, *Administration*
EMP: 4
SALES (est): 273.7K **Privately Held**
SIC: 2711 Newspapers

(G-6942)
G & J PEPSI-COLA BOTTLERS INC
Also Called: Pepsico
1241 Gibbard Ave (43219-2438)
PHONE....................614 253-8771
Tom Anderson, *Warehouse Mgr*
Thomas Pendrey, *Branch Mgr*
Dan Satterfield, *Supervisor*
EMP: 550
SQ FT: 200,000
SALES (corp-wide): 418.3MM **Privately Held**
WEB: www.gjpepsi.com
SIC: 2086 Soft drinks: packaged in cans, bottles, etc.
PA: G & J Pepsi-Cola Bottlers Inc
9435 Waterstone Blvd # 390
Cincinnati OH 45249
513 785-6060

(G-6943)
G2 PRINT PLUS
3787 Interchange Rd (43204-1485)
PHONE....................614 276-0500
George Wallace, *General Ptnr*
EMP: 10
SALES (est): 2.1MM **Privately Held**
WEB: www.g2printplus.com
SIC: 2759 Commercial printing

(G-6944)
GEN III
2300 Lockbourne Rd (43207-2167)
PHONE....................614 737-8744
John McCormick, *President*
Eric Wasserstrom, *President*
EMP: 6
SALES (est): 1.2MM **Privately Held**
SIC: 3441 Fabricated structural metal

(G-6945)
GENERAL THEMING CONTRS LLC
Also Called: GTC Artist With Machines
3750 Courtright Ct (43227-2253)
PHONE....................614 252-6342
Richard D Rogovin, *Principal*
April Andrick, *Director*
Kim Schanzenbach
Rich Witherspoon,
EMP: 105
SQ FT: 60,000
SALES (est): 17.9MM **Privately Held**
WEB: www.theming.net
SIC: 7389 7336 2759 2396 Sign painting & lettering shop; commercial art & graphic design; commercial printing; automotive & apparel trimmings

(G-6946)
GENERALS BOOKS
Also Called: The General's Books
522 Norton Rd (43228-2617)
P.O. Box 28685 (43228-0685)
PHONE....................614 870-1861
David Roth, *President*
Robin Patricia Roth, *President*
EMP: 8
SQ FT: 1,980
SALES (est): 1MM **Privately Held**
WEB: www.bluegraymagazine.com
SIC: 2721 Magazines: publishing only, not printed on site

(G-6947)
GENPAK LLC
845 Kaderly Dr (43228-1033)
PHONE....................614 276-5156
Scott Wilson, *Plant Mgr*
Lori Kear, *Manager*
Clarence Barnard, *Maintence Staff*
EMP: 50
SALES (corp-wide): 19B **Privately Held**
WEB: www.genpak.com
SIC: 3089 Plastic containers, except foam
HQ: Genpak Llc
10601 Westlake Dr
Charlotte NC 28273
980 256-7729

(G-6948)
GEORGE WESTON CO
1020 Claycraft Rd Ste D (43230-6684)
PHONE....................614 868-7565
Jeff Clark, *Principal*
EMP: 4
SALES (est): 221.2K **Privately Held**
SIC: 2051 Cakes, bakery: except frozen

(G-6949)
GEORGIA-PACIFIC LLC
1975 Watkins Rd (43207-3443)
PHONE....................614 491-9100
Kurt Miller, *Manager*
EMP: 40
SALES (corp-wide): 42.4B **Privately Held**
WEB: www.gp.com
SIC: 2621 Paper mills
HQ: Georgia-Pacific Llc
133 Peachtree St Nw
Atlanta GA 30303
404 652-4000

(G-6950)
GFS CHEMICALS INC
851 Mckinley Ave (43222-1148)
P.O. Box 245, Powell (43065-0245)
PHONE....................614 224-5345
Jay West, *Opers Mgr*
Theodore Elliott, *Engineer*
Robert Pierro, *Branch Mgr*
Vince Consoli, *IT/INT Sup*
EMP: 60
SALES (corp-wide): 23.6MM **Privately Held**
WEB: www.gfschemicals.com
SIC: 2819 2899 2869 Chemicals, reagent grade: refined from technical grade; chemical preparations; industrial organic chemicals
PA: Gfs Chemicals, Inc.
3041 Home Rd
Powell OH 43065
740 881-5501

(G-6951)
GFS CHEMICALS INC
800 Kaderly Dr (43228-1034)
PHONE....................614 351-5347
John Pringle, *Manager*
EMP: 60
SALES (corp-wide): 23.6MM **Privately Held**
SIC: 2819 Chemicals, reagent grade: refined from technical grade
PA: Gfs Chemicals, Inc.
3041 Home Rd
Powell OH 43065
740 881-5501

(G-6952)
GLASS AXIS
610 W Town St (43215-4446)
PHONE....................614 291-4250
Shawn Everette, *Facilities Mgr*
Rex Brown, *Exec Dir*
EMP: 5
SQ FT: 12,700
SALES: 495.8K **Privately Held**
WEB: www.glassaxis.org
SIC: 3229 Glassware, art or decorative

(G-6953)
GLAXOSMITHKLINE LLC
741 Chaffin Rdg (43214-2905)
PHONE....................937 623-2680
EMP: 26
SALES (corp-wide): 39.8B **Privately Held**
SIC: 2834 Pharmaceutical preparations
HQ: Glaxosmithkline Llc
5 Crescent Dr
Philadelphia PA 19112
215 751-4000

(G-6954)
GLAXOSMITHKLINE LLC
359 Garden Rd (43214-2133)
PHONE....................614 570-5970
EMP: 26
SALES (corp-wide): 39.8B **Privately Held**
SIC: 2834 Pharmaceutical preparations
HQ: Glaxosmithkline Llc
5 Crescent Dr
Philadelphia PA 19112
215 751-4000

(G-6955)
GLISTER INC
Also Called: Kingswood Company, The
3065 Switzer Ave (43219-2369)
PHONE....................614 252-6400
Kristie Nicolosi, *President*
EMP: 6
SALES (est): 1MM **Privately Held**
SIC: 2842 Specialty cleaning, polishes & sanitation goods

(G-6956)
GLOBAL COAL SALES GROUP LLC (HQ)
41 S High St Ste 3750s (43215-3406)
PHONE....................614 221-0101
Wayne M Boich, *Mng Member*
▼ **EMP:** 9
SALES (est): 18.6MM
SALES (corp-wide): 19.5MM **Privately Held**
SIC: 1241 Coal mining services
PA: Global Mining Holding Company, Llc
41 S High St
Columbus OH 43215
614 221-0101

(G-6957)
GLOBAL MINING HOLDING CO LLC (PA)
41 S High St (43215-6170)
PHONE....................614 221-0101

Columbus - Franklin County (G-6958)

Brian Murphy, *Mng Member*
EMP: 4
SALES (est): 19.5MM **Privately Held**
SIC: 1241 Coal mining services; investment holding companies, except banks

(G-6958)
GLOBAL TRUCKING LLC
3723 Ellerdale Dr (43230-4086)
PHONE.................614 598-6264
Ayan Abdirizak, *Mng Member*
Ayan Hassan Abdinizak, *Administration*
EMP: 10
SALES (est): 583.3K **Privately Held**
SIC: 3537 Trucks, tractors, loaders, carriers & similar equipment

(G-6959)
GOLDEN DYNAMIC INC
950 Taylor Station Rd M (43230-6670)
PHONE.................614 575-1222
Judy Sheu, *President*
▲ **EMP:** 7
SALES (est): 932K **Privately Held**
WEB: www.goldendynamic.com
SIC: 3291 Abrasive grains

(G-6960)
GONGWER NEWS SERVICE INC (PA)
Also Called: Michigan Report
17 S High St Ste 630 (43215-3413)
PHONE.................614 221-1992
Alan A Miller, *President*
Katie Colgan, *President*
Scott Miller, *Assistant VP*
Melissa Dilley, *Relations*
EMP: 11
SQ FT: 3,200
SALES (est): 1.5MM **Privately Held**
WEB: www.gongwer-oh.com
SIC: 2721 8111 Periodicals: publishing only; legal services

(G-6961)
GONGWER NEWS SERVICE INC (HQ)
17 S High St Ste 630 (43215-3413)
PHONE.................614 221-1992
Alan Miller, *President*
EMP: 5
SQ FT: 2,100
SALES (est): 848.3K
SALES (corp-wide): 1.5MM **Privately Held**
WEB: www.gongwer.com
SIC: 2721 Periodicals: publishing only
PA: Gongwer News Service Inc
 17 S High St Ste 630
 Columbus OH 43215
 614 221-1992

(G-6962)
GOODALE AUTO-TRUCK PARTS INC
1100 E 5th Ave (43201-3000)
PHONE.................614 294-4777
Jason Comer, *President*
James N Miller, *Principal*
Herbert S Peterson, *Principal*
Earle E Weimer, *Principal*
Nick Comer, *Vice Pres*
EMP: 25 **EST:** 1931
SQ FT: 36,000
SALES (est): 3.6MM **Privately Held**
WEB: www.goodale1.com
SIC: 3714 Transmissions, motor vehicle

(G-6963)
GRAFFITI FOODS LIMITED
333 Outerbelt St (43213-1529)
PHONE.................614 759-1921
Philip E Griesinger,
EMP: 13
SQ FT: 7,600
SALES (est): 2.4MM **Privately Held**
SIC: 2099 Food preparations

(G-6964)
GRAHAM ELECTRIC
2855 Banwick Rd (43232-3821)
PHONE.................614 231-8500
EMP: 4

SALES (est): 144.1K **Privately Held**
SIC: 3699 1731 Electrical equipment & supplies; electrical work

(G-6965)
GRAHAM FORD POWER PRODUCTS
850 Harmon Ave (43223-2410)
PHONE.................614 801-0049
EMP: 5
SQ FT: 3,200
SALES (est): 450K **Privately Held**
SIC: 3519 5084 Mfg Internal Combustion Engines Whol Industrial Equipment

(G-6966)
GRANDON MFG CO INC
530 Dow Ave (43211-2674)
PHONE.................614 294-2694
Bonnie May, *President*
Brian May, *General Mgr*
EMP: 3 **EST:** 1956
SQ FT: 4,000
SALES (est): 200K **Privately Held**
SIC: 3544 Special dies & tools

(G-6967)
GRANDVIEW GRIND
1423 Grandview Ave (43212-2853)
PHONE.................614 485-9005
Samantha J Demint, *Principal*
EMP: 3
SALES (est): 319.5K **Privately Held**
SIC: 3599 Grinding castings for the trade

(G-6968)
GREAT IMPRESSIONS SIGNS DESIGN
3800 Agler Rd (43219-3607)
PHONE.................614 428-8250
Gregory L Kitzmiller, *CEO*
EMP: 5
SQ FT: 4,000
SALES (est): 300K **Privately Held**
WEB: www.greatimpressions.org
SIC: 3993 Signs & advertising specialties

(G-6969)
GREAT OPPURTUNITIES INC
Also Called: Sportsales
1750 Idlewild Dr (43232-2917)
PHONE.................614 868-1899
Raymond Pribish, *President*
EMP: 4
SQ FT: 6,000
SALES (est): 500K **Privately Held**
SIC: 2262 5091 2395 Screen printing: manmade fiber & silk broadwoven fabrics; sporting & recreation goods; embroidery products, except schiffli machine

(G-6970)
GREEN ROOM BREWING LLC
1101 N 4th St (43201-3683)
PHONE.................614 596-3655
Jim W Baldrick,
David Spencer,
EMP: 7
SALES (est): 301.8K **Privately Held**
SIC: 5813 2082 Bars & lounges; near beer

(G-6971)
GURINA COMPANY
1379 River St (43222-1120)
PHONE.................614 279-3891
Burton L Smith, *Principal*
Donald L Smith, *Vice Pres*
Donald Smith, *Vice Pres*
EMP: 3
SQ FT: 9,300
SALES: 760.2K **Privately Held**
SIC: 1711 7699 7692 Boiler setting contractor; boiler repair shop; welding repair

(G-6972)
H & E MACHINE COMPANY
1646 Fairwood Ave (43206-3711)
PHONE.................614 443-7635
John Hanna, *President*
Janice A Hanna, *Admin Sec*
EMP: 10
SQ FT: 8,000
SALES (est): 1.5MM **Privately Held**
SIC: 3451 Screw machine products

(G-6973)
H ROSEN USA LLC
1195 Technology Dr (43230-6606)
PHONE.................614 354-6707
EMP: 200 **Privately Held**
SIC: 3999 Atomizers, toiletry
PA: H. Rosen Usa, Llc
 14120 Interdrive E
 Houston TX 77032

(G-6974)
H Y O INC
Also Called: Pengywn
2550 W 5th Ave (43204-3815)
PHONE.................614 488-2861
Jim Kime, *President*
Sheila Kime, *Corp Secy*
Nathan Bishop, *Prdtn Mgr*
Charles Hoskins, *Supervisor*
EMP: 11
SQ FT: 20,000
SALES (est): 1.3MM **Privately Held**
WEB: www.pengwyn.com
SIC: 3531 3594 Snow plow attachments; fluid power pumps & motors

(G-6975)
HACKMAN FRAMES LLC
502 Schrock Rd (43229-1028)
PHONE.................614 841-0007
Craig Hackman,
EMP: 15
SQ FT: 14,000
SALES (est): 1.4MM **Privately Held**
WEB: www.hackmanframes.com
SIC: 2499 Picture frame molding, finished; picture & mirror frames, wood

(G-6976)
HAKE HEAD LLC
Also Called: Maramor Chocolates
1855 E 17th Ave (43219-1006)
PHONE.................614 291-2244
Michael Ryan, *Mng Member*
Ben Spicer,
▲ **EMP:** 25
SQ FT: 30,000
SALES (est): 6.1MM **Privately Held**
WEB: www.maramor.com
SIC: 2064 Candy & other confectionery products

(G-6977)
HAMILTON TANKS LLC
2200 Refugee Rd (43207-2898)
PHONE.................614 445-8446
Stephen Meeker, *President*
Jeffrey Meeker,
EMP: 17
SQ FT: 30,000
SALES (est): 7.9MM **Privately Held**
WEB: www.hamiltontanks.com
SIC: 3443 Tanks, lined: metal plate
PA: Meeker Equipment Co., Inc.
 4381 Front Mountain Rd
 Belleville PA 17004
 717 667-6000

(G-6978)
HANG-UPS INSTLLATION GROUP INC
3751 April Ln (43227-3371)
P.O. Box 9811 (43209-0811)
PHONE.................614 239-7004
Mark Russell, *President*
Christine Russell, *Corp Secy*
EMP: 3
SQ FT: 3,000
SALES (est): 500K **Privately Held**
SIC: 7389 2591 Interior decorating; drapery hardware & blinds & shades

(G-6979)
HANGER PRSTHETCS & ORTHO INC
1357 Dublin Rd (43215-7046)
PHONE.................614 481-8338
Tim Riedinger, *Manager*
EMP: 16
SALES (corp-wide): 1B **Publicly Held**
SIC: 3842 Surgical appliances & supplies
HQ: Hanger Prosthetics & Orthotics, Inc.
 10910 Domain Dr Ste 300
 Austin TX 78758
 512 777-3800

(G-6980)
HANSON CONCRETE PRODUCTS OHIO
Also Called: Hanson Pipe & Products
1500 Haul Rd (43207-1888)
PHONE.................614 443-4846
Terry Feather, *Manager*
EMP: 35 **Privately Held**
SIC: 1771 3441 3272 Concrete Contractor Structural Metal Fabrication Mfg Concrete Products

(G-6981)
HANSON READY MIX INC
816 Mckinley Ave (43222-1107)
PHONE.................614 221-5345
Courtney Clewell, *Manager*
EMP: 60
SALES (corp-wide): 20.6B **Privately Held**
SIC: 3273 Mfg Ready-Mixed Concrete
HQ: Hanson Ready Mix, Inc.
 3251 Bath Pike
 Nazareth PA 18064

(G-6982)
HARPER ENGRAVING & PRINTING CO (PA)
2626 Fisher Rd (43204-3561)
P.O. Box 426 (43216-0426)
PHONE.................614 276-0700
Donald Mueller, *President*
Brian Regenye, *Natl Sales Mgr*
Jeffrey Lamter, *Info Tech Mgr*
Chad Johnson, *Executive*
Vincent Mueller, *Executive*
EMP: 73
SQ FT: 40,000
SALES (est): 12.7MM **Privately Held**
WEB: www.harperengraving.com
SIC: 2759 2752 Commercial printing; commercial printing, offset

(G-6983)
HARRIS PAPER CRAFTS INC
266 E 5th Ave (43201-2818)
PHONE.................614 299-2141
Richard Potts, *President*
EMP: 10
SALES (est): 1MM **Privately Held**
SIC: 2679 2796 2789 2675 Paper products, converted; platemaking services; bookbinding & related work; die-cut paper & board

(G-6984)
HAZELBAKER INDUSTRIES LTD
Also Called: Wellnitz
1661 Old Henderson Rd (43220-3644)
PHONE.................614 276-2631
David Buell, *President*
Donald Crites, *Vice Pres*
Joseph Hazelbaker, *Vice Pres*
K Robert Evenson Jr, *Treasurer*
EMP: 45
SQ FT: 2,500
SALES (est): 5.7MM **Privately Held**
WEB: www.wellnitz.com
SIC: 3271 5211 3272 Blocks, concrete or cinder: standard; masonry materials & supplies; concrete products

(G-6985)
HEARTLAND GROUP HOLDINGS LLC (HQ)
4001 E 5th Ave (43219-1812)
PHONE.................614 441-4001
EMP: 30
SALES (est): 19.5MM
SALES (corp-wide): 407.4MM **Privately Held**
SIC: 3559 Oil Refinery That Recycles Used Motor Oils Into Recycled Base Oils
PA: Warren Distribution, Inc.
 727 S 13th St
 Omaha NE 68108
 402 341-9397

(G-6986)
HELENA AGRI-ENTERPRISES LLC
800 Distribution Dr (43228-1004)
PHONE.................614 275-4200
Helena Cwu, *Branch Mgr*
EMP: 9

GEOGRAPHIC SECTION — Columbus - Franklin County (G-7012)

SALES (corp-wide): 70.7B **Privately Held**
WEB: www.helenachemical.com
SIC: 5191 2819 Chemicals, agricultural; seeds & bulbs; chemicals, high purity: refined from technical grade
HQ: Helena Agri-Enterprises, Llc
255 Schilling Blvd # 300
Collierville TN 38017
901 761-0050

(G-6987)
HENDERSON PARTNERS LLC
4424 N High St (43214)
PHONE 614 883-1310
Timothy Rollins, *Principal*
EMP: 5
SALES (est): 470K **Privately Held**
SIC: 6411 3699 Patrol services, insurance; security control equipment & systems

(G-6988)
HENRY BUSSMAN
Also Called: Minuteman Press
70 S 4th St (43215-4315)
PHONE 614 224-0417
Henry Bussman, *Owner*
EMP: 4
SQ FT: 950
SALES: 500K **Privately Held**
SIC: 2752 7334 2789 Photo-offset printing; photocopying & duplicating services; bookbinding & related work

(G-6989)
HENSEL READY MIX INC
477 Claycraft Rd (43230-5339)
PHONE 614 755-6365
EMP: 6
SALES (est): 425.8K
SALES (corp-wide): 1.7MM **Privately Held**
SIC: 5211 3273 Ret Lumber/Building Materials Mfg Ready-Mixed Concrete
PA: Hensel Ready Mix, Inc.
9925 County Road 265
Kenton OH 43326
419 675-1808

(G-6990)
HERITAGE MARBLE OF OHIO INC
Also Called: Heritage Marbles
7086 Huntley Rd (43229-1022)
PHONE 614 436-1464
Gene Daniels, *President*
EMP: 25
SQ FT: 22,000
SALES (est): 1.9MM **Privately Held**
WEB: www.heritagemarble.com
SIC: 3281 1411 Marble, building: cut & shaped; dimension stone

(G-6991)
HERO PAY LLC
341 S 3rd St Ste 107 (43215-5463)
PHONE 419 771-0515
Dylan Worden, *Mng Member*
EMP: 8
SALES (est): 186.1K **Privately Held**
SIC: 7372 Application computer software

(G-6992)
HEXION INC (DH)
180 E Broad St Fl 26 (43215-3707)
PHONE 614 225-4000
Craig A Rogerson, *Ch of Bd*
John P Auletto, *Exec VP*
Douglas A Johns, *Exec VP*
George F Knight, *CFO*
Matt Sokol, *Officer*
EMP: 277
SALES: 3.5B **Privately Held**
WEB: www.hexion.com
SIC: 2821 Thermosetting materials; acrylic resins; epoxy resins; melamine resins, melamine-formaldehyde
HQ: Hexion Llc
180 E Broad St Fl 26
Columbus OH 43215
614 225-4000

(G-6993)
HEXION LLC (HQ)
180 E Broad St Fl 26 (43215-3707)
PHONE 614 225-4000
William H Carter, *Exec VP*
William Hoffman, *Vice Pres*
Steve Prue, *Vice Pres*
David Rusinko, *Marketing Staff*
Jeff Rohde, *Manager*
◆ **EMP:** 100
SQ FT: 200,000
SALES (est): 3.5B **Privately Held**
SIC: 2821 2899 Thermosetting materials; chemical preparations

(G-6994)
HEXION US FINANCE CORP
180 E Broad St (43215-3707)
PHONE 614 225-4000
Jon Cremers, *Site Mgr*
Kathy Padova, *Chf Purch Ofc*
Anne McSweeney, *Engineer*
Daniel Rentz, *Plant Engr*
Vladimir Mika, *Finance Mgr*
▼ **EMP:** 17
SALES (est): 3.9MM **Privately Held**
SIC: 2821 Plastics materials & resins
HQ: Hexion Inc.
180 E Broad St Fl 26
Columbus OH 43215
614 225-4000

(G-6995)
HFI LLC (PA)
59 Gender Rd (43215)
PHONE 614 491-0700
Walter Dennis Jr, *CEO*
Takao Okamoto, *Vice Pres*
Todd Sousa, *Vice Pres*
Kurt Stuckenbrock, *Vice Pres*
Neil Fillman, *CFO*
▲ **EMP:** 350 **EST:** 1969
SQ FT: 140,000
SALES (est): 240MM **Privately Held**
WEB: www.hfi-inc.com
SIC: 2396 2821 3714 3429 Automotive trimmings, fabric; polyurethane resins; motor vehicle parts & accessories; manufactured hardware (general); plastics foam products

(G-6996)
HI LITE PLASTIC PRODUCTS
Also Called: Capital Toe Grinding
3760 E 5th Ave (43219-1807)
PHONE 614 235-9050
Offie Bartley, *Owner*
EMP: 6
SALES (est): 565.9K **Privately Held**
SIC: 3089 Kitchenware, plastic; plastic processing

(G-6997)
HIGHCOM GLOBAL SECURITY INC (HQ)
Also Called: BLASTWRAP
2901 E 4th Ave Unit J (43219-2896)
PHONE 727 592-9400
Francis Michaud, *Ch of Bd*
Michael L Bundy, *COO*
EMP: 19 **EST:** 1999
SQ FT: 32,155
SALES: 7.4MM **Publicly Held**
WEB: www.blastgardintl.com
SIC: 3699 Fire control or bombing equipment, electronic

(G-6998)
HIGHLIGHTS PRESS INC
1800 Watermark Dr (43215-1048)
P.O. Box 18360 (43218-0360)
PHONE 614 487-2767
Cheri Routzahn, *Treasurer*
Sherry Routzahn, *Controller*
EMP: 3
SQ FT: 1,000
SALES (est): 327.8K **Privately Held**
SIC: 2731 Books: publishing only

(G-6999)
HIKMA LABS INC
Also Called: Roxane Laboratories, Inc.
1809 Wilson Rd (43228-9579)
P.O. Box 16532 (43216-6532)
PHONE 614 276-4000
Michael Raya, *CEO*
Brian Hoffmann, *President*
Glenn Marina, *Vice Pres*
Mohammed Obeidat, *CFO*
George J Muench III, *Treasurer*
▲ **EMP:** 127
SALES: 500MM
SALES (corp-wide): 1.9B **Privately Held**
SIC: 2834 Druggists' preparations (pharmaceuticals)
HQ: West-Ward Holdings Limited
1 New Burlington Place
London

(G-7000)
HIKMA PHARMACEUTICALS USA INC
Also Called: Non-Injectable Manufacturing
1809 Wilson Rd (43228-9579)
PHONE 614 276-4000
Debbie Gray, *Opers Mgr*
Dennis Conkins, *Research*
Tod Gundrum, *Research*
Lester Fischer, *Engineer*
Jerry Woodruff, *Supervisor*
EMP: 41
SALES (corp-wide): 1.9B **Privately Held**
SIC: 2834 Chlorination tablets & kits (water purification)
HQ: Hikma Pharmaceuticals Usa Inc.
246 Industrial Way W # 7
Eatontown NJ 07724
732 542-1191

(G-7001)
HILLEARY-WHITAKER INC
Also Called: Kwik Kopy Printing
2646 Billingsley Rd (43235-1924)
PHONE 614 766-4694
Stephen Whitaker, *President*
EMP: 3
SALES (est): 454.5K **Privately Held**
SIC: 2752 2791 7334 Commercial printing, offset; typesetting; photocopying & duplicating services

(G-7002)
HIRSCHVOGEL INCORPORATED
2230 S 3rd St (43207-2431)
PHONE 614 340-5657
Felix Schmieder, *President*
Robert Hartwell, *VP Mfg*
Michael Gruskiewicz, *Opers Mgr*
Lisa Davis, *Safety Mgr*
Bob Sonntag, *Maint Spvr*
◆ **EMP:** 150
SQ FT: 155,000
SALES (est): 44.9MM
SALES (corp-wide): 1.3B **Privately Held**
WEB: www.hirschvogel.com
SIC: 3714 Motor vehicle parts & accessories
PA: Hirschvogel Holding Gmbh
Dr.-Manfred-Hirschvogel-Str. 6
Denklingen 86920
824 329-10

(G-7003)
HITE PARTS EXCHANGE INC
2235 Mckinley Ave (43204-3400)
PHONE 614 272-5115
Thomas A Blake, *President*
Chris Allred, *Sales Staff*
Dona Blake, *Admin Sec*
EMP: 30
SQ FT: 14,000
SALES (est): 4.7MM **Privately Held**
WEB: www.hiteparts.com
SIC: 5013 3714 3625 3594 Automotive supplies & parts; pumps, oil & gas; clutches; motor vehicle engines & parts; clutches, motor vehicle; relays & industrial controls; fluid power pumps & motors; carburetors, pistons, rings, valves; power transmission equipment

(G-7004)
HJ SYSTEMS INC
230 N Central Ave (43222-1001)
PHONE 614 351-9777
James E Stang, *President*
EMP: 10
SQ FT: 20,000
SALES (est): 800K **Privately Held**
WEB: www.hjsystemsinc.com
SIC: 2431 Millwork

(G-7005)
HONEYWELL
2199 Dividend Dr (43228-3805)
PHONE 614 850-8228
Matthew Chretien, *Principal*
EMP: 3
SALES (est): 295.6K **Privately Held**
SIC: 3724 Aircraft engines & engine parts

(G-7006)
HONEYWELL LEBOW PRODUCTS
Also Called: Honeywell Senfopec
2080 Arlingate Ln (43228-4112)
PHONE 614 850-5000
Phil Geraffo, *Vice Pres*
▲ **EMP:** 200
SALES (est): 13.1MM
SALES (corp-wide): 41.8B **Publicly Held**
WEB: www.honeywell.com
SIC: 3829 Measuring & controlling devices
PA: Honeywell International Inc.
115 Tabor Rd
Morris Plains NJ 07950
973 455-2000

(G-7007)
HOOKAH RUSH
2422 N High St (43202-2924)
PHONE 614 267-6463
EMP: 4 **EST:** 2009
SALES (est): 401.8K **Privately Held**
SIC: 2131 Smoking tobacco

(G-7008)
HOPCO RESOURCES INC
2829 E Dblin Granville Rd (43231-4037)
PHONE 614 882-8533
Gary Hopkins, *President*
Gary W Hopkins, *President*
Kenneth Hopkins, *Vice Pres*
EMP: 5
SQ FT: 1,800
SALES (est): 693.1K **Privately Held**
SIC: 1311 Crude petroleum production; natural gas production

(G-7009)
HOSTER GRAPHICS COMPANY INC
Also Called: Advance Graphics
1349 Delashmut Ave (43212-3103)
PHONE 614 299-9770
Frank Hoster, *President*
EMP: 13
SQ FT: 10,000
SALES (est): 2.6MM **Privately Held**
WEB: www.advancecolumbus.com
SIC: 2752 7334 Commercial printing, offset; photocopying & duplicating services

(G-7010)
HUMBLE CONSTRUCTION CO
3441 Morse Rd (43231-6183)
PHONE 614 888-8960
EMP: 22
SALES (corp-wide): 18.8MM **Privately Held**
SIC: 3499 3312 1521 Aerosol valves, metal; blast furnaces & steel mills; single-family housing construction
PA: Humble Construction Co.
1180 Carlisle Ave
Bellefontaine OH 43311
937 465-6035

(G-7011)
HUNG PHAM
5291 Westpointe Plaza Dr (43228-9131)
PHONE 614 850-9695
Pham Hung, *Owner*
EMP: 5
SALES (est): 317.8K **Privately Held**
SIC: 3999 Fingernails, artificial

(G-7012)
HUNTERS HIGHTECH ENERGY SYSTM
2059 Big Tree Dr (43223-3292)
PHONE 614 275-4777
James E Hunter,
EMP: 3
SALES: 150K **Privately Held**
SIC: 1711 5074 3674 Solar energy contractor; heating equipment & panels, solar; photovoltaic devices, solid state

---

(PA)=Parent Co (HQ)=Headquarters (DH)=Div Headquarters
✪ = New Business established in last 2 years

Columbus - Franklin County (G-7013) — GEOGRAPHIC SECTION

(G-7013)
HYPER TECH RESEARCH INC
539 Industrial Mile Rd (43228-2412)
PHONE..................................614 481-8050
Michael Tomsic, *President*
David Doll, *Principal*
Lawrence Walley, *CFO*
Sherrie Cantu, *Shareholder*
Sarah Tomsic, *Shareholder*
EMP: 16
SQ FT: 50,000
SALES (est): 3.6MM **Privately Held**
WEB: www.hypertechresearch.com
SIC: 3674 Semiconductors & related devices

(G-7014)
HYTEC AUTOMOTIVE IND LLC
4419 Equity Dr (43228-3856)
PHONE..................................614 527-9370
◆ EMP: 10
SQ FT: 40,000
SALES (est): 1.2MM **Privately Held**
SIC: 3714 Mfg Motor Vehicle Parts/Accessories

(G-7015)
HYTEC-DEBARTOLO LLC
Also Called: Hytec Automotive
4419 Equity Dr (43228-3856)
PHONE..................................614 527-9370
Denis Bruncak,
▲ EMP: 17
SQ FT: 34,600
SALES (est): 2.9MM
SALES (corp-wide): 30.8MM **Privately Held**
WEB: www.debartoloholdings.com
SIC: 3714 Water pump, motor vehicle
PA: Debartolo Holdings, Llc
15436 N Florida Ave # 200
Tampa FL 33613
813 908-8200

(G-7016)
I H SCHLEZINGER INC
Also Called: Schlezinger Metals
1041 Joyce Ave (43219-2448)
P.O. Box 83624 (43203-0624)
PHONE..................................614 252-1188
Kenneth Cohen, *President*
Jack Joseph, *Vice Pres*
John Miller, *Vice Pres*
Donald Zulanch, *Vice Pres*
Robert Joseph, *Treasurer*
EMP: 42
SQ FT: 9,000
SALES (est): 13.6MM **Privately Held**
WEB: www.ihschlezinger.com
SIC: 3341 5093 Secondary nonferrous metals; ferrous metal scrap & waste

(G-7017)
I HEART CUPCAKES
372 Hanton Way (43213-4435)
PHONE..................................614 787-3896
Stacee Streifel, *Principal*
EMP: 4 EST: 2014
SALES (est): 158.9K **Privately Held**
SIC: 2051 Bread, cake & related products

(G-7018)
IABF INC
Also Called: Industrial Aluminum Foundry
1890 Mckinley Ave (43222-1004)
PHONE..................................614 279-4498
Andrew B Kientz, *President*
EMP: 8 EST: 1966
SQ FT: 7,500
SALES (est): 732K **Privately Held**
SIC: 3365 3369 Aluminum & aluminum-based alloy castings; nonferrous foundries

(G-7019)
IC3D INC
Also Called: Ic3d Printers
1697 Westbelt Dr (43228-3809)
PHONE..................................614 344-0414
Michael Cao, *Principal*
EMP: 5
SALES (est): 562.9K **Privately Held**
SIC: 8731 2821 Computer (hardware) development; plastics materials & resins

(G-7020)
ICC SAFETY SERVICE INC
1070 Leona Ave (43201-3039)
PHONE..................................614 261-4557
Tiffany Adair, *President*
Christopher Duger, *Vice Pres*
EMP: 6
SQ FT: 3,900
SALES (est): 888.6K **Privately Held**
SIC: 3271 Blocks, concrete: insulating

(G-7021)
IMAGE PRINT INC
6417 Busch Blvd (43229-1862)
PHONE..................................614 430-8470
Bill Lang, *President*
EMP: 3
SQ FT: 1,700
SALES (est): 203.8K **Privately Held**
SIC: 2752 Commercial printing, offset

(G-7022)
IMAGING CENTER EAST MAIN
500 E Main St 2nd (43215-5369)
PHONE..................................614 566-8120
Shawn Sharp, *Manager*
EMP: 4
SALES (est): 344K **Privately Held**
SIC: 3845 Ultrasonic scanning devices, medical

(G-7023)
IMMIGRATION LAW SYSTEMS INC
1620 E Broad St Ste 107 (43203-2012)
PHONE..................................614 252-3078
Bernard Boiston, *President*
EMP: 3
SALES (est): 218.3K **Privately Held**
WEB: www.ilssys.com
SIC: 2741 7371 Miscellaneous publishing; custom computer programming services

(G-7024)
INDUSTRIAL PATTERN & MFG CO
899 N 20th St (43219-2420)
PHONE..................................614 252-0934
Thomas C Birkefeld, *President*
Charles J Birkefeld, *Vice Pres*
Jay Hrun, *Vice Pres*
Jay Thrun, *Engineer*
Donna Birkefeld, *Executive*
EMP: 12 EST: 1947
SQ FT: 5,000
SALES (est): 2.1MM **Privately Held**
WEB: www.industrialpattern.com
SIC: 3543 Industrial patterns

(G-7025)
INFANT FOOD PROJECT INC
638 S Hampton Rd (43213-2728)
P.O. Box 91169 (43209-7169)
PHONE..................................614 239-5763
Victor Alexander, *Principal*
EMP: 3
SALES (est): 184.4K **Privately Held**
SIC: 2099 Food preparations

(G-7026)
INHANCE TECHNOLOGIES LLC
6575 Huntley Rd Ste D (43229-1039)
PHONE..................................614 846-6400
Tom Gardener, *Opers-Prdtn-Mfg*
EMP: 18
SQ FT: 7,500
SALES (corp-wide): 11.1MM **Privately Held**
WEB: www.fluoroseal.com
SIC: 3089 Plastic processing
HQ: Inhance Technologies Llc
16223 Park Row Ste 100
Houston TX 77084
800 929-1743

(G-7027)
INLAND PRODUCTS INC (PA)
599 Frank Rd (43223-3813)
PHONE..................................614 443-3425
Gary H Baas, *President*
Jerry Phillips, *Vice Pres*
EMP: 25
SQ FT: 40,000
SALES (est): 5.5MM **Privately Held**
SIC: 2077 5159 Grease rendering, inedible; tallow rendering, inedible; bone meal, except as animal feed; meat meal & tankage, except as animal feed; hides

(G-7028)
INSKEEP BROTHERS INC
Also Called: Inskeep Brothers Printers
3193 E Dblin Granville Rd (43231-4035)
PHONE..................................614 898-6620
Jeff Inskeep, *President*
Paula Inskeep, *Vice Pres*
EMP: 15 EST: 1888
SQ FT: 11,000
SALES (est): 2MM **Privately Held**
WEB: www.inskeepbrothers.com
SIC: 2752 Commercial printing, offset

(G-7029)
INSTALLED BUILDING PDTS LLC
Swan Freedom
1320 Mckinley Ave Ste A (43222-1155)
PHONE..................................614 308-9900
Jeff Phipps, *Purchasing*
Mark Lomax, *Branch Mgr*
Todd Hite, *Director*
Michelle Gyurko, *Executive*
EMP: 35
SALES (corp-wide): 1.3B **Publicly Held**
SIC: 2511 2514 3231 3442 Whatnot shelves: wood; medicine cabinets & vanities: metal; mirrored glass; shutters, door or window: metal
HQ: Installed Building Products Llc
495 S High St Ste 50
Columbus OH 43215
614 221-3399

(G-7030)
INSTANT IMPRESSIONS INC
Also Called: Elektro Kopy
4499 Kenny Rd (43220-4034)
P.O. Box 20788 (43220-0788)
PHONE..................................614 538-9844
Chris Donnelly, *Director*
EMP: 3
SALES (corp-wide): 2.5MM **Privately Held**
WEB: www.instantimpressions.com
SIC: 7334 2759 Blueprinting service; commercial printing
PA: Instant Impressions, Inc.
4078 Anson Dr
Hilliard OH 43026
614 527-6925

(G-7031)
INSTANTWHIP CONNECTICUT INC (PA)
2200 Cardigan Ave (43215-1092)
PHONE..................................614 488-2536
Clifton J Smith, *Ch of Bd*
Douglas A Smith, *President*
Robert Pavlick, *Vice Pres*
Thomas G Michaelides, *Treasurer*
G Frederick Smith, *Admin Sec*
EMP: 18 EST: 1946
SQ FT: 10,300
SALES (est): 3.1MM **Privately Held**
SIC: 2026 5143 Whipped topping, except frozen or dry mix; dairy products, except dried or canned

(G-7032)
INSTANTWHIP DETROIT INC (PA)
2200 Cardigan Ave (43215-1092)
PHONE..................................614 488-2536
Clifton J Smith, *Ch of Bd*
Douglas A Smith, *President*
Fred Smith, *Vice Pres*
Thomas G Michaelides, *Treasurer*
G Fredrick Smith, *Admin Sec*
EMP: 18 EST: 1936
SALES (est): 2.8MM **Privately Held**
SIC: 2026 Whipped topping, except frozen or dry mix

(G-7033)
INSTANTWHIP DETROIT INC
Also Called: Instant Whip Detroit
2200 Cardigan Ave (43215-1092)
PHONE..................................800 544-9447
Ken Parks, *Manager*
EMP: 15
SALES (corp-wide): 2.8MM **Privately Held**
SIC: 2026 5143 Cream, whipped; dairy products, except dried or canned
PA: Instantwhip Detroit Inc
2200 Cardigan Ave
Columbus OH 43215
614 488-2536

(G-7034)
INSTANTWHIP FOODS INC (PA)
2200 Cardigan Ave (43215-1092)
PHONE..................................614 488-2536
Douglas A Smith, *President*
Thomas G Michaelides, *Treasurer*
EMP: 18 EST: 1934
SQ FT: 10,300
SALES (est): 47.5MM **Privately Held**
WEB: www.instantwhip.com
SIC: 6794 8741 2026 5143 Franchises, selling or licensing; administrative management; fluid milk; whipped topping, except frozen or dry mix; dairy products, except dried or canned

(G-7035)
INSTANTWHIP OF BUFFALO INC (HQ)
2200 Cardigan Ave (43215-1092)
PHONE..................................614 488-2536
Douglas A Smith, *President*
John Beck, *Vice Pres*
Thomas G Michaelides, *Treasurer*
G Frederick Smith, *Admin Sec*
EMP: 10
SQ FT: 10,300
SALES (est): 1.9MM
SALES (corp-wide): 47.5MM **Privately Held**
SIC: 2026 5143 Whipped topping, except frozen or dry mix; dairy products, except dried or canned
PA: Instantwhip Foods, Inc.
2200 Cardigan Ave
Columbus OH 43215
614 488-2536

(G-7036)
INSTANTWHIP PRODUCTS CO PA (HQ)
Also Called: Instantwhip of Pennsylvania
2200 Cardigan Ave (43215-1092)
PHONE..................................614 488-2536
Douglas A Smith, *President*
EMP: 18
SQ FT: 20,300
SALES (est): 1.3MM
SALES (corp-wide): 47.5MM **Privately Held**
SIC: 2026 5143 Whipped topping, except frozen or dry mix; dairy products, except dried or canned
PA: Instantwhip Foods, Inc.
2200 Cardigan Ave
Columbus OH 43215
614 488-2536

(G-7037)
INSTANTWHIP-CHICAGO INC (PA)
2200 Cardigan Ave (43215-1092)
PHONE..................................614 488-2536
Clifton J Smith, *Ch of Bd*
Douglas A Smith, *President*
Jim Ring, *Vice Pres*
Thomas G Michaelides, *Treasurer*
G Frederick Smith, *Admin Sec*
EMP: 36
SQ FT: 10,300
SALES (est): 5.5MM **Privately Held**
SIC: 2026 Cream, whipped

(G-7038)
INSTANTWHIP-SYRACUSE INC (PA)
2200 Cardigan Ave (43215-1092)
PHONE..................................614 488-2536
Clifton J Smith, *Ch of Bd*
Douglas A Smith, *President*
Raymond Winslow, *Vice Pres*
Thomas G Michaelides, *Treasurer*
G Frederick Smith, *Admin Sec*
EMP: 17
SQ FT: 10,300

GEOGRAPHIC SECTION
Columbus - Franklin County (G-7067)

SALES (est): 1.8MM **Privately Held**
SIC: 2026 Whipped topping, except frozen or dry mix

(G-7039)
INSULPRO INC
4650 Indianola Ave (43214-1884)
PHONE..................614 262-3768
Greg Freed, *President*
EMP: 10
SALES (est): 1.4MM **Privately Held**
SIC: 3494 Line strainers, for use in piping systems

(G-7040)
INTELLINETICS INC (PA)
2190 Dividend Dr (43228-3806)
PHONE..................614 388-8909
Robert C Schroeder, *Ch of Bd*
James F Desocio, *President*
Joseph D Spain, *CFO*
Matthew L Chretien, *Security Dir*
EMP: 12 EST: 1996
SQ FT: 6,000
SALES: 2.6MM **Privately Held**
SIC: 7372 Prepackaged software

(G-7041)
INTERFACE LOGIC SYSTEMS INC
Also Called: Weighing Division
3311 E Livingston Ave (43227-1923)
PHONE..................614 236-8388
Eli Sneward, *President*
EMP: 9
SQ FT: 3,500
SALES (est): 1MM **Privately Held**
WEB: www.interfacelogic.com
SIC: 7629 3596 Electrical measuring instrument repair & calibration; scales & balances, except laboratory

(G-7042)
INTERIOR DNNAGE SPCIALITES INC
470 E Starr Ave (43201-3695)
PHONE..................614 291-0900
Georgina Stevenson, *President*
Scott Stevenson, *Vice Pres*
EMP: 14
SQ FT: 35,000
SALES (est): 1.7MM **Privately Held**
WEB: www.idsinc-columbus.com
SIC: 3086 Plastics foam products

(G-7043)
INTERNATIONAL BEVERAGE WORKS
5636 Moorgate Dr (43235-2506)
P.O. Box 531331, Cincinnati (45253-1331)
PHONE..................614 798-5398
June M Slater, *President*
Jeff Slater, *Vice Pres*
Robert B Slater Jr, *Vice Pres*
EMP: 3
SALES (est): 437.9K **Privately Held**
SIC: 3585 5046 5078 Soda fountain & beverage dispensing equipment & parts; restaurant equipment & supplies; refrigerated beverage dispensers

(G-7044)
INTERNATIONAL PRODUCTS
Also Called: Ipsg
2701 Charter St Ste A (43228-4639)
PHONE..................614 334-1500
EMP: 3
SALES (corp-wide): 3.6B **Privately Held**
SIC: 3571 Electronic computers
HQ: International Products Sourcing Group, Inc.
4119 Leap Rd
Hilliard OH 43026
614 850-3000

(G-7045)
INTERNATIONAL TRADE GROUP INC
2920 North Star Rd (43221-2961)
P.O. Box 800, Oxford (45056-0800)
PHONE..................614 486-4634
James E Reider, *CEO*
EMP: 5

SALES (est): 591.1K **Privately Held**
SIC: 8742 5084 3469 3672 Management consulting services; industrial machinery & equipment; metal stampings; printed circuit boards

(G-7046)
INTERNTNAL TCHNCAL CATINGS INC
Also Called: Itc Manufacturing
845 E Markison Ave (43207-1388)
PHONE..................614 449-6669
Judith Fernandez, *Branch Mgr*
EMP: 75 **Privately Held**
SIC: 3496 3479 Shelving, made from purchased wire; painting, coating & hot dipping
PA: International Technical Coatings, Inc.
110 S 41st Ave
Phoenix AZ 85009

(G-7047)
INTERSTATE TRUCKWAY INC
5440 Renner Rd (43228-8941)
PHONE..................614 771-1220
Willy Walraven, *Branch Mgr*
EMP: 32 **Privately Held**
WEB: www.itdsdedicated.com
SIC: 3799 5012 Trailers & trailer equipment; automobiles & other motor vehicles
PA: Interstate Truckway Inc
1755 Dreman Ave
Cincinnati OH 45223

(G-7048)
IPA LTD
Also Called: Zed Digital
199 Mckenna Creek Dr (43230-6127)
PHONE..................614 523-3974
EMP: 13 EST: 2014
SQ FT: 1,500
SALES (est): 356K **Privately Held**
SIC: 7371 7373 2741 7374 Computer Programming Svc Computer Systems Design Internet Pub & Broad Data Processing/Prep

(G-7049)
IRONFAB LLC
1771 Progress Ave (43207-1749)
PHONE..................614 443-3900
Joey Stepleton, *President*
Laef Fox, *Prdtn Mgr*
EMP: 13
SALES (est): 3.3MM **Privately Held**
SIC: 3441 Fabricated structural metal

(G-7050)
ISCO INC
6360 Fiesta Dr (43235-5205)
PHONE..................614 792-2206
Brian D Amerine, *President*
Ivan R Amerine, *Chairman*
EMP: 10 EST: 1969
SQ FT: 19,000
SALES (est): 1.6MM **Privately Held**
WEB: www.iscoinc.com
SIC: 3599 Machine shop, jobbing & repair

(G-7051)
ISOSTATIC PRESSING SVCS LLC
1205 S Columbus Arprt Rd (43207-4304)
PHONE..................614 370-2140
Kenneth A Sprang,
EMP: 5
SALES (est): 456.9K **Privately Held**
SIC: 3398 Metal heat treating

(G-7052)
ISP CHEMICALS LLC
1979 Atlas St (43228-9645)
PHONE..................614 876-3637
Dr Paul Taylor, *Director*
EMP: 70 **Privately Held**
SIC: 2834 Pharmaceutical preparations
HQ: Isp Chemicals Llc
455 N Main St
Calvert City KY 42029
270 395-4165

(G-7053)
ITG BRANDS LLC
6740 Huntley Rd (43229-1064)
PHONE..................614 431-0044

Andrew Tish, *Branch Mgr*
EMP: 5
SALES (corp-wide): 38.9B **Privately Held**
SIC: 2111 Cigarettes
HQ: Itg Brands, Llc
714 Green Valley Rd
Greensboro NC 27408
336 335-7000

(G-7054)
J AMERICA LLC
580 N 4th St Ste 620 (43215-2125)
PHONE..................614 914-2091
EMP: 5
SALES (est): 364.8K
SALES (corp-wide): 50.1MM **Privately Held**
SIC: 2329 2396 2395 Men's & boys' sportswear & athletic clothing; automotive & apparel trimmings; screen printing on fabric articles; embroidery products, except schiffli machine
HQ: J. America, Llc
1200 Mason Ct
Webberville MI 48892

(G-7055)
J E JOHNSON PALLETT INC
1465 E 17th Ave (43219-1082)
P.O. Box 11623 (43211-0623)
PHONE..................614 424-9663
Fax: 614 424-9665
EMP: 8 EST: 1991
SQ FT: 20,000
SALES (est): 730K **Privately Held**
SIC: 2448 5999 Rebuilds & Recycles Wood Pallets

(G-7056)
J S C PUBLISHING
958 King Ave (43212-2655)
PHONE..................614 424-6911
Joe Paxton, *Owner*
EMP: 6
SALES (est): 225K **Privately Held**
SIC: 2731 Pamphlets: publishing & printing

(G-7057)
JACOBI CARBONS INC
432 Mccormick Blvd (43213-1525)
PHONE..................215 546-3900
Bill Eubanks, *President*
◆ EMP: 35
SALES (est): 13.5MM
SALES (corp-wide): 12.1B **Privately Held**
SIC: 2895 Carbon black
HQ: Jacobi Carbons Ab
Slojdaregatan 1
Kalmar 393 5
480 417-550

(G-7058)
JAIN AMERICA FOODS INC (HQ)
Also Called: Jain Americas
1819 Walcutt Rd Ste 1 (43228-0010)
PHONE..................614 850-9400
Anil Jain, *CEO*
Nerinder Gupta, *COO*
John Donovan, *CFO*
▲ EMP: 7
SQ FT: 30,000
SALES (est): 17.8MM **Privately Held**
SIC: 3086 2821 3081 Plastics foam products; molding compounds, plastics; polyvinyl film & sheet

(G-7059)
JAIN AMERICA HOLDINGS INC
1819 Walcutt Rd Ste 1 (43228-0010)
PHONE..................614 850-9400
Anil Jain, *CEO*
Nerinder Gupta, *COO*
◆ EMP: 100 EST: 2016
SQ FT: 30,000
SALES (est): 13.1MM
SALES (corp-wide): 651.2MM **Privately Held**
SIC: 3086 2821 3081 Plastics foam products; molding compounds, plastics; polyvinyl film & sheet
PA: Jain Irrigation Systems Limited
Jain Plastic Park,
Jalgaon MH 42500
257 225-8011

(G-7060)
JAMES EASTWOOD
663 Harmon Plz (43223-3341)
PHONE..................614 444-1340
James Eastwood, *Owner*
EMP: 4
SQ FT: 3,000
SALES (est): 291.7K **Privately Held**
SIC: 3599 Machine shop, jobbing & repair

(G-7061)
JAMES MCGUIRE
190 Ziegler Ave (43207-3752)
PHONE..................614 483-9825
James McGuire, *Principal*
EMP: 3
SALES (est): 210.1K **Privately Held**
SIC: 3081 Unsupported plastics film & sheet

(G-7062)
JAMES OSHEA
326 Richards Rd (43214-3740)
PHONE..................614 262-3188
James Oshea, *Principal*
EMP: 3
SALES (est): 161K **Privately Held**
SIC: 2711 Newspapers

(G-7063)
JANSZEN LOUDSPEAKER LTD
480 Trade Rd (43204-6241)
PHONE..................614 448-1811
Sungok Yoon, *President*
David A Janszen, *Mng Member*
EMP: 3
SALES (est): 150K **Privately Held**
WEB: www.janszenloudspeaker.com
SIC: 3651 Speaker systems; household audio equipment

(G-7064)
JAX WAX INC
3145 E 17th Ave (43219-2329)
PHONE..................614 476-6769
Jack Minor, *President*
EMP: 10 EST: 1993
SQ FT: 5,600
SALES (est): 1.8MM **Privately Held**
WEB: www.jaxwax.com
SIC: 2842 Automobile polish

(G-7065)
JE GROTE COMPANY INC (PA)
1160 Gahanna Pkwy (43230-6615)
PHONE..................614 868-8414
James E Grote, *Ch of Bd*
Bob Grote, *President*
Mike Melaragno, *Purchasing*
Matt Adams, *Engineer*
John Gorun, *Engineer*
◆ EMP: 100
SQ FT: 73,500
SALES (est): 32.1MM **Privately Held**
WEB: www.grotecompany.com
SIC: 3589 3556 Cooking equipment, commercial; food products machinery

(G-7066)
JET CONTAINER COMPANY
1033 Brentnell Ave # 100 (43219-2190)
PHONE..................614 444-2133
Stephen J Schmitt, *Vice Pres*
Mike Schmitt, *CFO*
Richard Prohl, *Mng Member*
EMP: 47
SQ FT: 175,000
SALES (est): 13MM **Privately Held**
WEB: www.jetcontainer.com
SIC: 2653 Boxes, corrugated: made from purchased materials

(G-7067)
JETCOAT LLC
472 Brehl Ave (43223-1973)
P.O. Box 23054 (43223-0054)
PHONE..................800 394-0047
David L Thorson, *Mng Member*
EMP: 20
SQ FT: 5,000
SALES (est): 4.9MM
SALES (corp-wide): 89.9MM **Privately Held**
WEB: www.sealmaster.net
SIC: 2891 Sealants

Columbus - Franklin County (G-7068)

PA: Thorworks Industries, Inc.
2520 Campbell St
Sandusky OH 44870
419 626-4375

(G-7068)
JLS FUNERAL HOME
2322 Randy Ct (43232-8470)
PHONE..........................614 625-1220
Jimmie Spurlock, *Principal*
EMP: 10
SALES (est): 420K **Privately Held**
SIC: 2396 5087 7389 Veils & veiling: bridal, funeral, etc.; cemetery & funeral directors' equipment & supplies;

(G-7069)
JMAC INC (PA)
200 W Nationwide Blvd # 1 (43215-2561)
PHONE..........................614 436-2418
John P McConnell, *Ch of Bd*
Michael A Priest, *President*
George N Corey, *Principal*
Michael Priest, *Manager*
▲ **EMP:** 20
SQ FT: 6,000
SALES (est): 105.6MM **Privately Held**
WEB: www.j-mac.com
SIC: 3325 5198 7999 5511 Steel foundries; paints; ice skating rink operation; automobiles, new & used; financial management for business

(G-7070)
JOB NEWS USA
150 E Campus View Blvd # 120 (43235-6602)
PHONE..........................614 310-1700
Marsha Olivieri, *Principal*
EMP: 12
SALES (est): 496.7K **Privately Held**
SIC: 2711 Newspapers, publishing & printing

(G-7071)
JOE PAXTON
Also Called: Graphic Awards
960 King Ave (43212-2655)
PHONE..........................614 424-9000
Joe Paxton, *Owner*
Dawn Blessing, *Sales Staff*
Steve Baden, *Graphic Designe*
EMP: 5
SQ FT: 5,100
SALES (est): 900K **Privately Held**
WEB: www.graphicawards.net
SIC: 2759 5999 3993 Screen printing; trophies & plaques; signs & advertising specialties

(G-7072)
JOHN B ALLEN
2346 Brandon Rd (43221-3803)
PHONE..........................614 488-7122
John B Allen, *Owner*
EMP: 5
SALES (est): 440.3K **Privately Held**
WEB: www.allen-systems.com
SIC: 3679 3674 7371 Electronic circuits; computer logic modules; computer software development

(G-7073)
JOHNSON BROTHERS HOLDINGS LLC
Also Called: Qkardz.com
717 Oak St (43205-1011)
P.O. Box 83282 (43203-0282)
PHONE..........................614 868-5273
Nathan Johnson Sr, *Mng Member*
Nathan K Johnson Sr, *Mng Member*
Beaux Johnson,
EMP: 4 **EST:** 2007
SALES (est): 100K **Privately Held**
SIC: 7336 1731 5131 2396 Commercial art & graphic design; telephone & telephone equipment installation; flags & banners; fabric printing & stamping

(G-7074)
JOHNSONS REAL ICE CREAM CO
Also Called: Wilcoxon, James H Jr
2728 E Main St (43209-2534)
PHONE..........................614 231-0014
James H Wilcoxon Jr, *President*
EMP: 20
SQ FT: 4,600
SALES (est): 1.1MM **Privately Held**
SIC: 5812 5143 2024 Ice cream stands or dairy bars; dairy products, except dried or canned; ice cream & frozen desserts

(G-7075)
JOHNSTON-MOREHOUSE-DICKEY CO
4647 Poth Rd (43213-1396)
PHONE..........................614 866-0452
Glenn Dupilka Jr, *Manager*
EMP: 5
SALES (corp-wide): 33.8MM **Privately Held**
SIC: 2299 3089 5082 Narrow woven fabrics: linen, jute, hemp & ramie; plastic hardware & building products; contractors' materials
PA: Johnston-Morehouse-Dickey Co Inc
5401 Progress Blvd
Bethel Park PA 15102
412 833-7100

(G-7076)
JORDAN REED LLC
5855 Parliament Dr (43213-3372)
PHONE..........................678 956-1222
Jordan Reed, *Mng Member*
EMP: 8
SALES: 128K **Privately Held**
SIC: 3571 7319 Computers, digital, analog or hybrid; display advertising service

(G-7077)
JOSEPH A PANICO & SONS INC (PA)
4605 E 5th Ave (43219-1819)
PHONE..........................614 235-3188
John E Panico, *President*
Joe Panico, *Vice Pres*
EMP: 4
SALES (est): 450.1K **Privately Held**
WEB: www.panico.org
SIC: 3993 Advertising novelties

(G-7078)
JPS PRINT
1014 Parsons Ave (43206-2741)
PHONE..........................614 235-8947
Zaridania Carmona, *Owner*
EMP: 4
SALES (est): 410.6K **Privately Held**
SIC: 2752 Commercial printing, lithographic

(G-7079)
JRS HYDRAULIC & WELDING
Also Called: J R S Hydraulic Welding
2774 Groveport Rd (43207-3149)
PHONE..........................614 497-1100
J R Stansell, *Owner*
EMP: 3
SQ FT: 1,500
SALES (est): 120K **Privately Held**
SIC: 7692 7699 3599 Welding repair; hydraulic equipment repair; machine shop, jobbing & repair

(G-7080)
JUDITH LEIBER LLC (PA)
4300 E 5th Ave (43219-1816)
PHONE..........................614 449-4217
Mary Gleason,
EMP: 82 **EST:** 2000
SALES (est): 19MM **Privately Held**
SIC: 3171 Women's handbags & purses

(G-7081)
K B PRINTING
Also Called: Bizzy Bee
1199 Goodale Blvd (43212-3730)
PHONE..........................614 771-1222
Chris Schmelzer, *Principal*
EMP: 5 **EST:** 2010
SALES (est): 306.1K **Privately Held**
SIC: 2752 Commercial printing, lithographic

(G-7082)
K EFFS INC
2117 S High St (43207-2428)
PHONE..........................614 443-0586
K R Gay, *President*
Kenneth Robert Gay, *President*
Elizabeth Sue Gay, *Vice Pres*
Kenneth Gay, *CFO*
EMP: 15 **EST:** 1962
SQ FT: 35,000
SALES (est): 2.9MM **Privately Held**
WEB: www.keffs.net
SIC: 3496 Shelving, made from purchased wire

(G-7083)
KARN MEATS INC
Also Called: Central Market Specialty Meats
922 Taylor Ave (43219-2558)
PHONE..........................614 252-3712
Richard Karn, *President*
EMP: 50
SQ FT: 50,000
SALES (est): 7.7MM **Privately Held**
SIC: 2011 2013 Meat packing plants; sausages & other prepared meats

(G-7084)
KCG INC
Also Called: Magnum Products
3939 E 5th Ave (43219-1810)
PHONE..........................614 238-9450
Todd Wellman, *Sales Executive*
Ed Hook, *Manager*
EMP: 5
SALES (corp-wide): 325.2MM **Privately Held**
WEB: www.kcg-inc.com
SIC: 3272 5032 2891 Building materials, except block or brick: concrete; drywall materials; adhesives & sealants
PA: Kcg, Inc.
15720 W 108th St Ste 100
Lenexa KS 66219
913 438-4142

(G-7085)
KENAN ADVANTAGE GROUP INC
Also Called: Advantage Truck Trailers
500 Manor Park Dr (43228-9396)
PHONE..........................614 878-4050
Dan Peckinpaugh, *Manager*
EMP: 34
SALES (corp-wide): 2.4B **Privately Held**
SIC: 3715 Truck trailers
PA: The Kenan Advantage Group Inc
4366 Mount Pleasant St Nw
North Canton OH 44720
800 969-5419

(G-7086)
KENDALL HOLDINGS LTD (PA)
Also Called: Phpk Technologies
2111 Builders Pl (43204-4886)
PHONE..........................614 486-4750
Richard Coleman, *Partner*
Ken Krienbrink, *Vice Pres*
Terry Deerfoot, *Mfg Mgr*
Steve Willming, *Design Engr*
Tim Savely, *Marketing Mgr*
▲ **EMP:** 45
SQ FT: 60,000
SALES (est): 10.8MM **Privately Held**
SIC: 3443 8711 Fabricated plate work (boiler shop); engineering services

(G-7087)
KENOSHA BEEF INTERNATIONAL LTD
Birchwood Meats & Provisions
1821 Dividend Dr (43228-3848)
PHONE..........................614 771-1330
Ken Fudy, *Principal*
Daniel Kesicki, *Plant Mgr*
Troy Maynard, *Opers Staff*
Marty Roberts, *Chief Mktg Ofcr*
Koenia Siebers, *Manager*
EMP: 107
SQ FT: 10,000
SALES (est): 16.1MM
SALES (corp-wide): 187.4MM **Privately Held**
WEB: www.bwfoods.com
SIC: 5147 2013 Meats, fresh; sausages & other prepared meats
PA: Kenosha Beef International, Ltd.
3111 152nd Ave
Kenosha WI 53144
800 541-1684

(G-7088)
KENWEL PRINTERS INC
4272 Indianola Ave (43214-2891)
PHONE..........................614 261-1011
David G Starner, *President*
Mike Fisher, *Vice Pres*
EMP: 36 **EST:** 1969
SQ FT: 15,000
SALES (est): 7.5MM **Privately Held**
WEB: www.kenwel.com
SIC: 2752 2789 2759 Commercial printing, offset; bookbinding & related work; commercial printing

(G-7089)
KEURIG DR PEPPER INC
950 Stelzer Rd (43219-3740)
PHONE..........................614 237-4201
Andy Bayfield, *Vice Pres*
Carolyn Ross, *Vice Pres*
Elizabeth Trilikis, *Buyer*
Laura Tzanavaris, *Controller*
Terrie Gregory, *Finance*
EMP: 100 **Publicly Held**
SIC: 2086 Soft drinks: packaged in cans, bottles, etc.
PA: Keurig Dr Pepper Inc.
53 South Ave
Burlington MA 01803

(G-7090)
KEURIG DR PEPPER INC
960 Stelzer Rd (43219-3740)
PHONE..........................614 237-4201
Dan Grassbaugh, *Branch Mgr*
EMP: 100 **Publicly Held**
SIC: 2086 Soft drinks: packaged in cans, bottles, etc.; carbonated beverages, non-alcoholic: bottled & canned
PA: Keurig Dr Pepper Inc.
53 South Ave
Burlington MA 01803

(G-7091)
KEVER INCORPORATED
Also Called: Kever Printing & Promotions
4581 Poth Rd (43213-1327)
PHONE..........................614 552-9000
Maureen Egan-Simons, *President*
Roger Simons, *Corp Secy*
EMP: 5
SQ FT: 6,000
SALES: 500K **Privately Held**
WEB: www.keverinc.com
SIC: 2752 Commercial printing, offset

(G-7092)
KEY BLUE PRINTS INC
1920 Schrock Rd (43229-1563)
PHONE..........................614 899-6180
Kristin Kinney, *Branch Mgr*
EMP: 3
SALES (corp-wide): 30.9MM **Privately Held**
SIC: 3555 Printing presses
PA: Key Blue Prints, Inc.
195 E Livingston Ave
Columbus OH 43215
614 228-3285

(G-7093)
KEY FINISHES LLC
727 Harrison Dr (43204-3507)
PHONE..........................614 351-8393
James H McCurdy, *CFO*
Tod Powers,
Robert Johnson,
▲ **EMP:** 9
SALES (est): 1.4MM **Privately Held**
SIC: 3399 Powder, metal

(G-7094)
KICK SALSA LLC
5281 Spring Beauty Ct (43230-1042)
PHONE..........................614 330-2499
Jose Martinez,
EMP: 4
SALES: 1K **Privately Held**
SIC: 2032 7372 7389 Mexican foods: packaged in cans, jars, etc.; application computer software;

GEOGRAPHIC SECTION — Columbus - Franklin County

(G-7095)
KIRK EXCAVATING & CONSTRUCTION
821 Stimmel Rd (43223-2907)
P.O. Box 8, Grove City (43123-0008)
PHONE..................614 444-4008
Charles Kirk, *President*
Tamara Pleskach, *Vice Pres*
EMP: 20
SALES (est): 6.3MM **Privately Held**
SIC: 1794 1381 Excavation & grading, building construction; directional drilling oil & gas wells

(G-7096)
KISSICAKES - N-SWEETS LLC
7660 Silver Fox Dr (43235-1835)
PHONE..................614 940-2779
George T Kissi, *Principal*
EMP: 6
SALES (est): 439.5K **Privately Held**
SIC: 2053 Cakes, bakery: frozen

(G-7097)
KLOSTERMAN BAKING CO
2655 Courtright Rd (43232-4838)
PHONE..................614 338-8111
Ron Hostelley, *Manager*
EMP: 6
SALES (corp-wide): 207.2MM **Privately Held**
SIC: 2051 Breads, rolls & buns
PA: Klosterman Baking Co.
    4760 Paddock Rd
    Cincinnati OH 45229
    513 242-5667

(G-7098)
KOKOSING MATERIALS INC
4755 S High St (43207-4028)
P.O. Box 334, Fredericktown (43019-0334)
PHONE..................614 491-1199
Bill Burgett, *President*
Bob Bailey, *Vice Pres*
EMP: 50
SALES (est): 5.7MM **Privately Held**
SIC: 2951 Asphalt & asphaltic paving mixtures (not from refineries)

(G-7099)
KONECRANES INC
1110 Claycraft Rd Ste C (43230-6630)
PHONE..................937 328-5123
EMP: 11
SALES (corp-wide): 3.7B **Privately Held**
SIC: 3625 Crane & hoist controls, including metal mill
HQ: Konecranes, Inc.
    4401 Gateway Blvd
    Springfield OH 45502

(G-7100)
KRAFT OF WRITING
46 Webster Park Ave (43214-3513)
PHONE..................614 620-2476
EMP: 6
SALES (est): 489.5K **Privately Held**
SIC: 2022 Mfg Cheese

(G-7101)
KRISPY KREME DOUGHNUT CORP
Also Called: Krispy Kreme 322
3690 W Dblin Granville Rd (43235-7987)
PHONE..................614 798-0812
James Lewis, *Manager*
EMP: 12
SQ FT: 2,158
SALES (corp-wide): 838.1MM **Privately Held**
WEB: www.kkreme.com
SIC: 5461 2051 Doughnuts; pastries, e.g. danish: except frozen
HQ: Krispy Kreme Doughnut Corp
    259 S Stratford Rd
    Winston Salem NC 27103
    336 725-2981

(G-7102)
KROEHLER FURNITURE MFG CO INC
4300 E 5th Ave (43219-1816)
P.O. Box 1178, Conover NC (28613-1178)
PHONE..................828 459-9865
Jay Schottenstein, *Ch of Bd*

David Sadlowski, *Vice Pres*
Mitch Howze, *QC Mgr*
Ed Cornell, *CFO*
Thomas Ketteler, *Treasurer*
▲ **EMP:** 400
SQ FT: 300,000
SALES (est): 58MM **Privately Held**
SIC: 2512 Upholstered household furniture

(G-7103)
KROGER CO
3417 N High St (43214-4051)
PHONE..................614 263-1766
John Ettenhofer, *Branch Mgr*
EMP: 180
SALES (corp-wide): 121.1B **Publicly Held**
WEB: www.kroger.com
SIC: 5411 5912 2051 Supermarkets, chain; drug stores & proprietary stores; bread, cake & related products
PA: The Kroger Co
    1014 Vine St Ste 1000
    Cincinnati OH 45202
    513 762-4000

(G-7104)
KROGER CO
7000 E Broad St (43213-1519)
PHONE..................614 575-3742
Denise Maynard, *Branch Mgr*
EMP: 250
SALES (corp-wide): 121.1B **Publicly Held**
WEB: www.kroger.com
SIC: 5411 5912 2051 Supermarkets, chain; drug stores & proprietary stores; bread, cake & related products
PA: The Kroger Co
    1014 Vine St Ste 1000
    Cincinnati OH 45202
    513 762-4000

(G-7105)
KYRON TOOL AND MACHINE CO INC
2900 Banwick Rd (43232-3838)
PHONE..................614 231-6000
Charles P Hauesein, *President*
Randal Hauesein, *Vice Pres*
Rosemary Hauesein, *Treasurer*
EMP: 10 **EST:** 1949
SQ FT: 50,000
SALES (est): 1.7MM **Privately Held**
SIC: 3599 Machine shop, jobbing & repair

(G-7106)
L BRANDS INC
Limited
3 Limited Pkwy (43230-1467)
P.O. Box 182145 (43218-2145)
PHONE..................614 479-2000
Fax: 614 224-4002
EMP: 117
SALES (corp-wide): 12.1B **Publicly Held**
SIC: 5641 2389 Ret Child's/Infant's Wear Mfg Apparel/Accessories
PA: L Brands, Inc.
    3 Limited Pkwy
    Columbus OH 43230
    614 415-7000

(G-7107)
L C G MACHINE & TOOL INC
2923 Grasmere Ave (43224-4155)
PHONE..................614 261-1651
Lowell C Garrett, *CEO*
▼ **EMP:** 3
SALES (est): 96.8K **Privately Held**
SIC: 3544 Special dies & tools

(G-7108)
L3 AVIATION PRODUCTS INC
Also Called: Goodrich Avionics
1105 Schrock Rd Ste 800 (43229-1154)
PHONE..................614 825-2001
Billie Stevens, *Manager*
EMP: 60
SALES (corp-wide): 10.2B **Publicly Held**
SIC: 3812 8711 Aircraft flight instruments; gyroscopes; automatic pilots, aircraft; radar systems & equipment; engineering services

HQ: L3 Aviation Products, Inc.
    5353 52nd St Se
    Grand Rapids MI 49512
    616 949-6600

(G-7109)
LA VOZ HISPANIA NEWSPAPER
3552 Sullivant Ave (43204-1106)
PHONE..................614 274-5505
Alex Flores, *President*
EMP: 5
SQ FT: 960
SALES (est): 253.7K **Privately Held**
SIC: 2711 Newspapers, publishing & printing

(G-7110)
LAIRD PLASTICS INC
Also Called: Branch 49
2220 International St (43228-4630)
PHONE..................614 272-0777
Roger Plizga, *Manager*
EMP: 10
SALES (corp-wide): 387.6MM **Privately Held**
SIC: 5162 3089 Plastics materials; plastics sheets & rods; plastics film; windows, plastic
PA: Laird Plastics, Inc.
    5800 Campus Circle Dr E # 1508
    Irving TX 75063
    469 299-7000

(G-7111)
LAMBERT SHEET METAL INC
Also Called: Lsmi
3776 E 5th Ave (43219-1807)
PHONE..................614 237-0384
Carl Lambert, *President*
Betty Lambert, *Vice Pres*
EMP: 15
SQ FT: 10,000
SALES (est): 3.4MM **Privately Held**
WEB: www.smcco.org
SIC: 3444 Sheet metal specialties, not stamped

(G-7112)
LANCASTER COMMERCIAL PDTS LLC
2353 Westbrooke Dr (43228-9557)
P.O. Box 870, Worthington (43085-0870)
PHONE..................740 286-5081
Kenneth Evans, *President*
◆ **EMP:** 34
SALES (est): 15.7MM **Privately Held**
SIC: 5085 3089 Whol Industrial Supplies Mfg Plastic Products

(G-7113)
LANDON VAULT COMPANY
1477 Frebis Ave (43206-3763)
PHONE..................614 443-5505
Martin Pehrson, *President*
Autumn Epperson, *Admin Sec*
EMP: 15 **EST:** 1920
SQ FT: 3,600
SALES (est): 1.2MM **Privately Held**
SIC: 3272 Burial vaults, concrete or precast terrazzo

(G-7114)
LANG STONE COMPANY INC (PA)
4099 E 5th Ave (43219-1812)
P.O. Box 360747 (43236-0747)
PHONE..................614 235-4099
E Dean Coffman, *President*
Joan First, *VP Admin*
Joann Coffman, *Vice Pres*
▲ **EMP:** 55 **EST:** 1856
SQ FT: 10,000
SALES (est): 20.3MM **Privately Held**
WEB: www.langstone.com
SIC: 5032 5211 3281 3272 Building stone; marble building stone; granite building stone; lumber & other building materials; masonry materials & supplies; cut stone & stone products; concrete products; crushed & broken limestone

(G-7115)
LANZ PRINTING CO INC
257 Cleveland Ave (43215-2107)
PHONE..................614 221-1724
Michael Llaneza, *President*

Mary Llaneza, *Vice Pres*
EMP: 3 **EST:** 1968
SQ FT: 10,000
SALES (est): 450K **Privately Held**
SIC: 2752 Commercial printing, offset

(G-7116)
LAPHAM-HICKEY STEEL CORP
753 Marion Rd (43207-2554)
PHONE..................614 443-4881
Mike Salmons, *Plant Mgr*
George Keel, *Safety Mgr*
Joni Fritz, *Sales Staff*
Eric Sattler, *Manager*
EMP: 25
SQ FT: 110,000
SALES (est): 279.5MM **Privately Held**
WEB: www.lapham-hickey.com
SIC: 5051 3443 3441 3398 Steel; fabricated plate work (boiler shop); fabricated structural metal; metal heat treating; blast furnaces & steel mills
PA: Lapham-Hickey Steel Corp.
    5500 W 73rd St
    Chicago IL 60638
    708 496-6111

(G-7117)
LASTING IMPRESSION LLC
4415 Berthstone Dr (43231-8722)
PHONE..................614 806-1186
Kayla Davila,
EMP: 5
SALES (est): 390.1K **Privately Held**
SIC: 2599 Bar furniture

(G-7118)
LEAR CORP
2181 International St (43228-4631)
P.O. Box 182104 (43218-2104)
PHONE..................614 850-8630
Joe Mauri, *Owner*
▼ **EMP:** 6
SALES (est): 3.2MM **Privately Held**
SIC: 3714 Motor vehicle parts & accessories

(G-7119)
LEAR CORPORATION
2181 International St (43228-4631)
PHONE..................614 850-8630
Joe Mauri, *Manager*
EMP: 15
SALES (corp-wide): 21.1B **Publicly Held**
WEB: www.lear.com
SIC: 3714 Motor vehicle parts & accessories
PA: Lear Corporation
    21557 Telegraph Rd
    Southfield MI 48033
    248 447-1500

(G-7120)
LEGENDARY INK INC
1559 Granville St (43203-1719)
PHONE..................614 766-5101
Steve Wolever, *President*
EMP: 3
SALES (est): 302.1K **Privately Held**
SIC: 2759 Screen printing

(G-7121)
LEHIGH HANSON ECC INC
1550 Williams Rd (43207-5108)
PHONE..................614 497-2001
Larry Moore, *Branch Mgr*
EMP: 3
SALES (corp-wide): 20.6B **Privately Held**
WEB: www.essroc.com
SIC: 3241 5032 Portland cement; cement
HQ: Lehigh Hanson Ecc, Inc.
    3251 Bath Pike
    Nazareth PA 18064
    610 837-6725

(G-7122)
LEHNER SIGNS INC
2983 Switzer Ave (43219-2315)
PHONE..................614 258-0500
Robin Owens, *President*
EMP: 7
SQ FT: 2,400
SALES (est): 530K **Privately Held**
WEB: www.lehnersigns.com
SIC: 2499 Signboards, wood

(PA)=Parent Co (HQ)=Headquarters (DH)=Div Headquarters
✪ = New Business established in last 2 years

Columbus - Franklin County (G-7123)

(G-7123)
LEVCOAT POWDER COATING
2773 Westbelt Dr (43228-3862)
PHONE..................614 802-7505
EMP: 6
SALES (est): 696.6K Privately Held
SIC: 3479 Painting, coating & hot dipping

(G-7124)
LH MARSHALL COMPANY
1601 Woodland Ave (43219-1135)
PHONE..................614 294-6433
Dorothy B Roberts, President
Courtney Roberts, Vice Pres
Chris Dale, Opers Mgr
Janet Forgue, Treasurer
Cynthia R Padilla, Admin Sec
EMP: 18
SALES (est): 3.8MM Privately Held
WEB: www.lhmarshall.com
SIC: 3829 Measuring & controlling devices

(G-7125)
LIEBERT NORTH AMERICA INC (DH)
Also Called: Vertiv
1050 Dearborn Dr (43085-4709)
P.O. Box 29186 (43229-0186)
PHONE..................614 888-0246
Robert P Bauer, President
Don Morris, Credit Staff
EMP: 22
SQ FT: 22,000
SALES (est): 173.2MM
SALES (corp-wide): 2.1B Privately Held
WEB: www.gotoemerson.com
SIC: 3699 3585 Electrical equipment & supplies; refrigeration & heating equipment
HQ: Vertiv Corporation
    1050 Dearborn Dr
    Columbus OH 43085
    614 888-0246

(G-7126)
LIFE SUPPORT DEVELOPMENT LTD
777 Dearborn Park Ln R (43085-5746)
PHONE..................614 221-1765
Cheryl Krueger, President
David Zamore, Treasurer
Chris Ellis, Finance Dir
Brad McKean, Sales Staff
Shannon Oshields, Marketing Staff
EMP: 8
SALES (est): 1MM Privately Held
SIC: 2086 Fruit drinks (less than 100% juice): packaged in cans, etc.

(G-7127)
LIGHTING SOLUTIONS GROUP LLC
Also Called: Specgrade Led
153 Outerbelt St (43213-1548)
PHONE..................614 868-5337
Doug Lauck, Mng Member
Rick Nathans,
▲ EMP: 10
SALES (est): 844.4K Privately Held
SIC: 3648 Lighting equipment

(G-7128)
LIND STONEWORKS LTD
175 Oberlin Ct N (43230-2872)
PHONE..................614 866-9733
James E Lind, Partner
Vincent Lind, Partner
▲ EMP: 12
SQ FT: 17,000
SALES: 1.6MM Privately Held
SIC: 3281 Mfg Cut Stone/Products

(G-7129)
LINDE GAS NORTH AMERICA LLC
Also Called: Lifegas
7029 Huntley Rd (43229-1099)
PHONE..................614 846-7048
Cindy Fenton, Branch Mgr
EMP: 19 Privately Held
SIC: 2813 Nitrogen; oxygen, compressed or liquefied
PA: Linde Gas North America Llc
    200 Somerset Corp Blvd # 7000
    Bridgewater NJ 08807

(G-7130)
LINEBACKER INC
1275 Kinnear Rd (43212-1180)
PHONE..................614 340-1446
David A Sybert MD, CEO
Curt Sybert, Director
EMP: 4
SALES (est): 215.1K Privately Held
SIC: 3999 Manufacturing industries

(G-7131)
LINEN CARE PLUS INC
84 N Glenwood Ave (43222-1241)
PHONE..................614 224-1791
Lindsey Hayman, Owner
Pam Conruly, Owner
EMP: 10 EST: 1979
SALES (est): 854.4K Privately Held
SIC: 3582 7218 7213 Dryers, laundry: commercial, including coin-operated; industrial launderers; linen supply

(G-7132)
LITTLE GHOST ROASTERS
247 1/2 King Ave (43201)
PHONE..................614 325-2065
Wyatt Burk, Principal
EMP: 4
SQ FT: 750
SALES (est): 116.1K Privately Held
SIC: 2095 5812 Roasted coffee; American restaurant

(G-7133)
LOCKHEED MARTIN CORPORATION
2720 Airport Dr Ste 100 (43219-2219)
PHONE..................614 418-1930
Michael Shimniok, General Mgr
Joseph Bitonti, Human Res Mgr
Stephen Callaghan, Sales Staff
Frank Andor, Marketing Staff
William Carithers, Marketing Staff
EMP: 6 Publicly Held
WEB: www.lockheedmartin.com
SIC: 7372 7371 Application computer software; computer software systems analysis & design, custom
PA: Lockheed Martin Corporation
    6801 Rockledge Dr
    Bethesda MD 20817

(G-7134)
LOCKHEED MARTIN CORPORATION
2740 Airport Dr Ste 150 (43219-2297)
P.O. Box 369016 (43236-9016)
PHONE..................866 562-2363
Brandi Crouch, Info Tech Mgr
EMP: 27 Publicly Held
WEB: www.lockheedmartin.com
SIC: 3812 Search & navigation equipment
PA: Lockheed Martin Corporation
    6801 Rockledge Dr
    Bethesda MD 20817

(G-7135)
LOFT VIOLIN SHOP
4604 N High St (43214-2002)
PHONE..................614 267-7221
David Schlub, Owner
Richard C Schlub, Partner
Jennifer Short, General Mgr
EMP: 14
SALES: 2MM Privately Held
WEB: www.theloftviolinshop.com
SIC: 7699 5736 3931 7359 Musical instrument repair services; musical instrument stores; string instruments; musical instruments; musical instrument rental services

(G-7136)
LONG SIGN CO
979 E 5th Ave (43201-3064)
PHONE..................614 294-1057
John Long, Owner
EMP: 3
SALES (est): 280.3K Privately Held
SIC: 3993 Signs & advertising specialties

(G-7137)
LOPAUS POINT INC
250 W Dodridge St (43202-1593)
PHONE..................614 302-7242
Stacie Skinner,
EMP: 4
SALES (est): 201.8K Privately Held
SIC: 2038 Ethnic foods, frozen

(G-7138)
LOUIS INSTANTWHIP-ST INC (PA)
2200 Cardigan Ave (43215-1092)
P.O. Box 333 (43216-0333)
PHONE..................614 488-2536
Douglas A Smith, President
Thomas G Michaelides, Treasurer
G Frederick Smith, Admin Sec
EMP: 18
SQ FT: 10,300
SALES (est): 1MM Privately Held
SIC: 2026 5143 Whipped topping, except frozen or dry mix; dairy products, except dried or canned

(G-7139)
M & W WELDING INC
72 N Glenwood Ave (43222-1241)
PHONE..................614 224-0501
Ernest D Whitehead Jr, President
EMP: 5
SQ FT: 6,000
SALES (est): 194.7K Privately Held
SIC: 7692 3441 Welding repair; fabricated structural metal

(G-7140)
M G 3D
320 E Weber Rd (43202-1452)
PHONE..................614 262-0956
Mike Grigsby, Owner
EMP: 12
SALES (est): 544.6K Privately Held
WEB: www.mg-3d.com
SIC: 3944 Science kits: microscopes, chemistry sets, etc.

(G-7141)
M WEB TYPE INC
3500 Sullivant Ave (43204-1105)
PHONE..................614 272-8973
Phil Daubel, President
EMP: 3 EST: 1971
SQ FT: 16,000
SALES (est): 281.5K
SALES (corp-wide): 2MM Privately Held
WEB: www.columbusmessenger.com
SIC: 2791 Typesetting
PA: The Columbus Messenger Company
    3500 Sullivant Ave
    Columbus OH 43204
    614 272-5422

(G-7142)
MACHINE TOOL REBUILDERS INC
2042 Leonard Ave (43219-2105)
PHONE..................614 228-1070
Mark Coleman, CEO
Janis Bowling, Principal
▲ EMP: 3
SQ FT: 6,400
SALES (est): 463.2K Privately Held
SIC: 3542 7699 Rebuilt machine tools, metal forming types; industrial machinery & equipment repair

(G-7143)
MACWOOD INC
Also Called: Macwood Custom Woodworking
397 Martha Ave (43223-1984)
PHONE..................614 279-7676
Mike McDonald, President
EMP: 3
SQ FT: 2,800
SALES: 250K Privately Held
WEB: www.macwood.com
SIC: 2521 2541 Cabinets, office: wood; cabinets, except refrigerated: show, display, etc.: wood

(G-7144)
MAD METAL WLDG FABRICATION LLC
3435 Polley Rd (43221-4705)
PHONE..................614 256-4163
Timothy Heer, Principal
EMP: 4
SALES (est): 239.1K Privately Held
SIC: 7692 Welding repair

(G-7145)
MAGNEXT LTD
7100 Huntley Rd (43229-1076)
PHONE..................614 433-0011
Alex Mindlin, Chief Engr
Dmitri Troianovski, Mng Member
Ilya Mindlin,
Zoey Fornof, Assistant
EMP: 19 EST: 2005
SQ FT: 28,000
SALES (est): 1.6MM Privately Held
SIC: 3572 Computer storage devices

(G-7146)
MAGSTOR INC
7100 Huntley Rd (43229-1076)
PHONE..................614 433-0011
Aleksandr Mindlin, President
▼ EMP: 5 EST: 2017
SQ FT: 2,400
SALES: 7K Privately Held
SIC: 3652 Pre-recorded records & tapes

(G-7147)
MANIFEST PRODUCTIONS LLC
272 S Front St Apt 601 (43215-5645)
PHONE..................614 806-3054
Karl Mechem,
EMP: 3
SALES: 90K Privately Held
SIC: 2731 7389 Books: publishing & printing;

(G-7148)
MAPSYS INC (PA)
Also Called: MAP SYSTEMS AND SOLUTIONS
920 Michigan Ave (43215-1165)
PHONE..................614 255-7258
Steve Bernard, President
Paul Neal, Corp Secy
Jim Heiberger, Vice Pres
Terry Payne, Vice Pres
Scott Abrams, Engineer
EMP: 40
SQ FT: 6,000
SALES: 19.3MM Privately Held
WEB: www.mapsysinc.com
SIC: 7372 7371 5045 Business oriented computer software; custom computer programming services; computers, peripherals & software

(G-7149)
MARATHON AT SAWMILL
Also Called: Sawmill Marathon
7200 Sawmill Rd (43235-5964)
PHONE..................614 734-0836
Donald Spangler, Owner
EMP: 10
SALES (est): 808.9K Privately Held
SIC: 2421 Sawmills & planing mills, general

(G-7150)
MARFO COMPANY (PA)
Also Called: Trading Corp of America
799 N Hague Ave (43204-1424)
PHONE..................614 276-3352
Bill Giovanello, CEO
Cheryl Beery, President
Crystal Kordes, Traffic Mgr
Carla Jay, Buyer
Alan Johnson, CFO
EMP: 100
SQ FT: 41,000
SALES (est): 21.9MM Privately Held
WEB: www.marsala.com
SIC: 5094 3911 Jewelry; jewelry apparel

(G-7151)
MARION SIGNS & LIGHTING LLC
3200 Valleyview Dr (43204-2080)
PHONE..................352 236-0936
Timothy Sheehy, Principal
EMP: 6
SALES (est): 605.3K
SALES (corp-wide): 913.8K Privately Held
SIC: 3993 Signs & advertising specialties

GEOGRAPHIC SECTION

Columbus - Franklin County (G-7179)

PA: Marion Signs & Lighting Llc
3175 Grissom Pkwy
Cocoa FL 32926
352 236-0936

(G-7152)
MARNE PLASTICS LLC
808 Distribution Dr (43228-1004)
PHONE..................614 732-4666
Marne Mavina,
EMP: 6 EST: 2013
SALES (est): 553.3K Privately Held
SIC: 3089 Injection molded finished plastic products

(G-7153)
MARS PETCARE US INC
Also Called: Masterfoods USA
5115 Fisher Rd (43228-9146)
PHONE..................614 878-7242
Goodwyn Morgan, Principal
EMP: 25
SQ FT: 175,000
SALES (corp-wide): 34.2B Privately Held
SIC: 2047 Dog food
HQ: Mars Petcare Us, Inc.
315 Cool Springs Blvd
Franklin TN 37067
615 807-4626

(G-7154)
MARSHALLTOWN PACKAGING INC
601 N Hague Ave (43204-1422)
PHONE..................641 753-5272
Gary Bolar, President
▲ EMP: 9
SQ FT: 54,000
SALES (est): 1.3MM
SALES (corp-wide): 56.9MM Privately Held
SIC: 2653 Corrugated & solid fiber boxes
PA: Buckeye Boxes, Inc.
601 N Hague Ave
Columbus OH 43204
614 274-8484

(G-7155)
MARTINA METAL LLC
1575 Shawnee Ave (43211-2643)
PHONE..................614 291-9700
Terry Kiliany, CFO
Greg Stewart, Mng Member
EMP: 20 EST: 1962
SQ FT: 12,500
SALES (est): 1.9MM
SALES (corp-wide): 126.4MM Privately Held
WEB: www.martinametal.com
SIC: 1761 3444 3441 3364 Sheet metalwork; sheet metalwork; fabricated structural metal; nonferrous die-castings except aluminum
PA: Sauer Holdings, Inc.
30 51st St
Pittsburgh PA 15201
412 687-4100

(G-7156)
MARVIN MIX
3113 Kentwood Pl (43227-3444)
P.O. Box 24851 (43224-0851)
PHONE..................614 774-9337
EMP: 3
SALES (est): 187.4K Privately Held
SIC: 3273 Mfg Ready-Mixed Concrete

(G-7157)
MATERIALS SCIENCE INTL INC
1660 Georgesville Rd (43228-3613)
PHONE..................614 870-0400
Neil Crabbe, President
William F Bailey, Vice Pres
John Davis, Financial Exec
Joe Kupisch, Executive
▲ EMP: 30
SQ FT: 12,500
SALES: 3.9MM Privately Held
SIC: 3599 Machine shop, jobbing & repair

(G-7158)
MATHEWS PRINTING COMPANY
1250 S Front St (43206-3437)
P.O. Box 188 (43216-0188)
PHONE..................614 444-1010
Robert Mathews, President
EMP: 16
SQ FT: 15,000
SALES (est): 3.1MM Privately Held
WEB: www.mathewsprintingcompany.com
SIC: 2752 Commercial printing, offset

(G-7159)
MATTHEW R COPP (PA)
2291 Scioto Harper Dr (43204-3495)
PHONE..................614 276-8959
Matthew R Copp, Principal
EMP: 5 EST: 2010
SALES (est): 508.8K Privately Held
SIC: 2741 Miscellaneous publishing

(G-7160)
MATTHEW WARREN INC
Also Called: Capital Spring
2000 Jetway Blvd (43219-1673)
PHONE..................614 418-0250
William Hunsucker, Principal
Hoyt Lolla, Business Mgr
EMP: 47
SALES (corp-wide): 169MM Privately Held
SIC: 3493 3495 Steel springs, except wire; wire springs
HQ: Matthew Warren, Inc.
9501 Tech Blvd Ste 401
Rosemont IL 60018
847 349-5760

(G-7161)
MATVEST INC
Also Called: Bermex
1380 Dublin Rd Ste 200 (43215-1025)
PHONE..................614 487-8720
Mark Everly, General Mgr
Chris Covey, Branch Mgr
Raymond Tackett, Manager
EMP: 30
SALES (corp-wide): 12MM Privately Held
WEB: www.bermexinc.com
SIC: 3545 7389 Machine tool accessories; meter readers, remote
PA: Matvest, Inc.
37244 S Groesbeck Hwy A
Clinton Township MI 48036
586 461-2051

(G-7162)
MCCLELLAN RAND L
65 E State St (43215-4213)
PHONE..................614 462-4782
Rand L McClellan, Principal
EMP: 3 EST: 2010
SALES (est): 182.3K Privately Held
SIC: 3131 Rands

(G-7163)
MCGILL AIRCLEAN LLC
1777 Refugee Rd (43207-2119)
PHONE..................614 829-1200
James D McGill, President
Paul R Hess, Mng Member
Jerry Childress,
◆ EMP: 70 EST: 2004
SQ FT: 15,000
SALES (est): 18.2MM
SALES (corp-wide): 67.7MM Privately Held
WEB: www.mcgillairclean.com
SIC: 3564 1796 Precipitators, electrostatic; pollution control equipment installation
HQ: United Mcgill Corporation
1 Mission Park
Groveport OH 43125
614 829-1200

(G-7164)
MCGILL AIRFLOW LLC
2400 Fairwood Ave (43207-2708)
PHONE..................614 829-1200
Ed Kromer, Manager
EMP: 15
SALES (corp-wide): 67.7MM Privately Held
WEB: www.mcgillairflow.com
SIC: 3444 Ducts, sheet metal
HQ: Mcgill Airflow Llc
1 Mission Park
Groveport OH 43125
614 829-1200

(G-7165)
MCGLAUGHLN OIL COMPNY/FAS LUBE (PA)
3750 E Livingston Ave (43227-2246)
PHONE..................614 231-2518
Steve Theodor, President
Teresa Mc Cormick, Admin Sec
EMP: 20
SQ FT: 4,000
SALES (est): 18.8MM Privately Held
SIC: 2992 Lubricating oils & greases

(G-7166)
MCGLENNON METAL PRODUCTS INC
940 N 20th St (43219-2423)
PHONE..................614 252-7114
Thomas Saldoff, President
EMP: 15
SQ FT: 22,000
SALES (est): 2.9MM Privately Held
WEB: www.mcglennonmetal.com
SIC: 3469 Spinning metal for the trade

(G-7167)
MCL INC
Also Called: McL Whitehall
5240 E Main St (43213-2501)
PHONE..................614 861-6259
Jim Bell, Manager
EMP: 60
SALES (corp-wide): 53.9MM Privately Held
WEB: www.mclcafe.com
SIC: 2051 Bakery: wholesale or wholesale/retail combined
PA: Mcl, Inc.
2730 E 62nd St
Indianapolis IN 46220
317 257-5425

(G-7168)
MCLEOD BAR GROUP LLC
234 King Ave (43201-2776)
PHONE..................614 299-2099
Matthew McLeod,
EMP: 15
SALES (est): 574.8K Privately Held
SIC: 2599 Bar, restaurant & cafeteria furniture

(G-7169)
MCNEIL GROUP INC
Also Called: Pinnacle Metal Products
1701 Woodland Ave (43219-1137)
PHONE..................614 298-0300
Susan McNeil, President
Michael McNeil, Vice Pres
EMP: 32
SQ FT: 41,000
SALES (est): 9.8MM Privately Held
SIC: 3441 Fabricated structural metal

(G-7170)
MCNEIL HOLDINGS LLC
1701 Woodland Ave (43219-1137)
PHONE..................614 298-0300
Michael R McNeil,
EMP: 6 EST: 1998
SALES (est): 670K Privately Held
SIC: 3441 Fabricated structural metal

(G-7171)
MEDFORALL LLC
1500 W 3rd Ave Ste 111 (43212-2890)
PHONE..................614 947-0791
Ali Rahimi, President
EMP: 4
SALES (est): 311.2K Privately Held
SIC: 7373 3845 Systems software development services; patient monitoring apparatus

(G-7172)
MEDRANO USA INC
4311 Janitrol Rd Ste 500 (43228-1390)
PHONE..................614 272-5856
Gerardo Fernandez, CEO
EMP: 125 EST: 2016
SQ FT: 700
SALES: 1.3MM Privately Held
SIC: 3537 Platforms, stands, tables, pallets & similar equipment

(G-7173)
METALS RECOVERY SERVICES LLC
1400 Norton Rd (43228-3631)
PHONE..................614 870-0364
Bill Bailey, Manager
EMP: 3
SALES (corp-wide): 303K Privately Held
SIC: 3341 4924 Silver recovery from used photographic film;
PA: Metals Recovery Services Llc
1660 Georgesville Rd
Columbus OH 43228
614 888-9272

(G-7174)
METTLER-TOLEDO LLC
Toledo Scales & Systems
6600 Huntley Rd (43229-1048)
PHONE..................614 841-7300
Al Hill, General Mgr
Wade Long, General Mgr
Alan L Purvis, Managing Dir
Dave Tatman, Opers Mgr
Sheri Dearth, Opers Staff
EMP: 170
SQ FT: 71,000
SALES (corp-wide): 2.9B Publicly Held
WEB: www.mtnw.com
SIC: 3596 Industrial scales
HQ: Mettler-Toledo, Llc
1900 Polaris Pkwy Fl 6
Columbus OH 43240
614 438-4511

(G-7175)
METZ DENTAL LABORATORY INC
Also Called: Metz Dental Laboratory, The
1271 E Broad St (43205-1429)
PHONE..................614 252-4444
James Metz, CEO
Mickey Harrison, President
Angie Rock, Business Mgr
EMP: 3
SQ FT: 700
SALES (est): 117.4K Privately Held
SIC: 3843 Dental equipment

(G-7176)
MEYER MACHINE TOOL COMPANY
3434 E 7th Ave (43219-1735)
PHONE..................614 235-0039
Richard A Meyer, Owner
Sheryl Meyer, Principal
EMP: 5
SQ FT: 5,500
SALES: 350K Privately Held
SIC: 3542 3544 Machine tools, metal forming type; special dies & tools

(G-7177)
MICKES QUALITY MACHINING
488 Trade Rd (43204-6241)
PHONE..................614 746-6639
Mickes Frank Jr, Principal
EMP: 3
SALES (est): 253.3K Privately Held
SIC: 3599 Machine shop, jobbing & repair

(G-7178)
MID-OHIO ELECTRIC CO
1170 Mckinley Ave (43222-1113)
PHONE..................614 274-8000
Cynthia Langhirt, President
Bruce A Langhirt, Vice Pres
Vince Langhirt, Vice Pres
Bret Law, Accountant
Bob Calkins, Sales Staff
EMP: 26
SQ FT: 13,800
SALES (est): 5.8MM Privately Held
WEB: www.mid-ohioelectric.com
SIC: 7694 5063 7629 8711 Electric motor repair; motors, electric; circuit board repair; generator repair; electrical or electronic engineering

(G-7179)
MID-OHIO REGIONAL PLG COMM
501 Industry Dr (43204-6242)
PHONE..................614 351-9210
Jim Fout, Assistant VP

(PA)=Parent Co (HQ)=Headquarters (DH)=Div Headquarters
✪ = New Business established in last 2 years

Columbus - Franklin County (G-7180)   GEOGRAPHIC SECTION

EMP: 36
SALES (corp-wide): 10.2MM **Privately Held**
SIC: 3433 Mfg Heating Equipment-Non-electric
PA: Mid-Ohio Regional Planning Commission
111 Liberty St Ste 100
Columbus OH 43215
614 228-2663

(G-7180)
MIDDLETON LEE ORIGINAL DOLLS (HQ)
2400 Corporate Exch Dr (43231-7605)
Fax: 614 901-0517
▲ **EMP:** 17
SQ FT: 18,000
SALES (est): 1.3MM
SALES (corp-wide): 8.2MM **Privately Held**
SIC: 3942 5945 5947 Mfg Dolls/Stuffed Toys Ret Hobbies/Toys/Games Ret Gifts/Novelties
PA: First Time Design Limited
2350 S 170th St
New Berlin WI 53151
262 364-5200

(G-7181)
MIDWEST MOTOR SUPPLY CO (PA)
Also Called: Kimball Midwest
4800 Roberts Rd (43228-9791)
P.O. Box 2470 (43216-2470)
PHONE 800 233-1294
Patrick J McCurdy Jr, *President*
A Glenn McClelland, *Principal*
Charles McCurdy, *Vice Pres*
David McCurdy, *Vice Pres*
Ed McCurdy, *Vice Pres*
▲ **EMP:** 200
SQ FT: 85,000
SALES (est): 147.9MM **Privately Held**
WEB: www.kimballmidwest.com
SIC: 3965 3399 8742 Fasteners; metal fasteners; materials mgmt. (purchasing, handling, inventory) consultant

(G-7182)
MIDWEST QUALITY BEDDING INC
3860 Morse Rd (43219-3014)
PHONE 614 504-5971
EMP: 3
SALES (est): 135.5K **Privately Held**
SIC: 2515 Mattresses & bedsprings

(G-7183)
MILLS LED LLC (PA)
81 S 5th St Ste 201 (43215-4323)
PHONE 800 690-6403
Rodney Nespeca,
EMP: 5
SALES: 1MM **Privately Held**
SIC: 3646 Commercial indusl & institutional electric lighting fixtures

(G-7184)
MINIMALLY INVASIVE DEVICES INC
Also Called: Mid
1275 Kinnear Rd (43212-1180)
PHONE 614 484-5036
Wayne Poll, *CEO*
Caroline Crisafulli, *Vice Pres*
Kenneth Jones, *CFO*
EMP: 25
SALES (est): 4.1MM **Privately Held**
SIC: 3841 Surgical & medical instruments

(G-7185)
MINUTEMAN PRESS
265 Lincoln Cir Ste C (43230-3084)
PHONE 614 337-2334
Jeff Remy, *Owner*
EMP: 3
SALES (est): 277K **Privately Held**
SIC: 2752 Commercial printing, offset

(G-7186)
MMF INC (PA)
Also Called: Mills Metal Finishing
1977 Mcallister Ave (43205-1614)
PHONE 614 252-0078
Brian L Mills, *President*
Cheryl Camp, *Vice Pres*
Foster Mills, *Director*
Steven Mills, *Shareholder*
EMP: 11
SQ FT: 9,400
SALES: 2.3MM **Privately Held**
SIC: 3479 Coating of metals & formed products; coating or wrapping steel pipe

(G-7187)
MMF INCORPORATED
Rainbow Custom Powder Coaters
1977 Mcallister Ave (43205-1614)
PHONE 614 252-2522
Brian Mills, *Manager*
EMP: 14
SALES (est): 822.8K
SALES (corp-wide): 2.3MM **Privately Held**
SIC: 3471 Plating of metals or formed products; polishing, metals or formed products
PA: Mmf, Inc
1977 Mcallister Ave
Columbus OH 43205
614 252-0078

(G-7188)
MOBILE MINI INC
871 Buckeye Park Rd (43207-2586)
PHONE 614 449-8655
Sean Roche, *Manager*
EMP: 12
SALES (corp-wide): 593.2MM **Publicly Held**
WEB: www.mobilemini.com
SIC: 3448 3441 3412 7359 Buildings, portable: prefabricated metal; fabricated structural metal; metal barrels, drums & pails; equipment rental & leasing
PA: Mobile Mini, Inc.
4646 E Van Buren St # 400
Phoenix AZ 85008
480 894-6311

(G-7189)
MOBILE SOLUTIONS LLC
149 N Hamilton Rd (43213-1308)
PHONE 614 286-3944
Darryl Crockett,
EMP: 10
SQ FT: 2,500
SALES (est): 453.4K **Privately Held**
SIC: 3711 Cars, electric, assembly of

(G-7190)
MODERN DEFENSE
2394 N High St (43202-2924)
PHONE 614 505-9338
EMP: 3
SALES (est): 256.7K **Privately Held**
SIC: 3812 Defense systems & equipment

(G-7191)
MOK INDUSTRIES LLC
4449 Easton Way (43219-6093)
PHONE 614 934-1734
William Mook,
EMP: 4
SQ FT: 3,000
SALES (est): 360.3K **Privately Held**
WEB: www.mokindustries.fuzing.com
SIC: 3674 Solar cells

(G-7192)
MOMENTIVE PERFORMANCE
180 E Broad St (43215-3707)
PHONE 281 325-3536
Thanos Yiagopoulos, *CTO*
Daniel Kirby, *Technical Staff*
EMP: 6
SALES (corp-wide): 2.7B **Publicly Held**
SIC: 2899 Chemical preparations
HQ: Momentive Performance Materials Worldwide Llc
260 Hudson River Rd
Waterford NY 12188
281 325-3536

(G-7193)
MOMENTIVE PERFORMANCE MTLS INC
180 E Broad St (43215-3707)
PHONE 614 986-2495
George Knight, *Exec VP*
Judith J Sonnett, *Exec VP*
EMP: 3 **EST:** 2016
SALES (est): 81.8K **Privately Held**
SIC: 2821 2899 2869 Thermosetting materials; chemical preparations; silicones

(G-7194)
MONITORTECH CORP
661 N James Rd (43219-1837)
PHONE 614 231-0500
Jeff York, *Principal*
Daniel Jurcich, *CFO*
Sarah Gunther, *Office Mgr*
Tom Mundy, *Software Engr*
EMP: 5
SALES (est): 1.4MM **Privately Held**
SIC: 3823 Industrial process control instruments

(G-7195)
MORCAST PRECISION INC
1615 Woodland Ave (43219-1135)
PHONE 614 258-5071
Doug Moran, *President*
Donald Young, *Vice Pres*
EMP: 5
SQ FT: 20,000
SALES (est): 581.3K **Privately Held**
SIC: 3543 Foundry patternmaking

(G-7196)
MORI SHUJI
Also Called: Geodyne One
3755 Mountview Rd (43220-4801)
PHONE 614 459-1296
Shuji Mori, *Owner*
EMP: 7
SALES (est): 381.4K **Privately Held**
WEB: www.geodyneone.com
SIC: 1382 Oil & gas exploration services

(G-7197)
MORRISON MEDICAL
3735 Paragon Dr (43228-9751)
PHONE 614 461-4400
Marshall Witzel, *Partner*
Donald Evans, *Principal*
EMP: 24
SQ FT: 4,700
SALES (est): 3.7MM **Privately Held**
WEB: www.morrisonmed.com
SIC: 3841 Probes, surgical

(G-7198)
MORRISON SIGN COMPANY INC
2757 Scioto Pkwy (43221-4658)
PHONE 614 276-1181
David Morrison, *President*
Helen Morrison, *Corp Secy*
EMP: 27
SQ FT: 18,000
SALES (est): 4.2MM **Privately Held**
WEB: www.morrisonsigns.com
SIC: 3993 2759 Signs, not made in custom sign painting shops; screen printing

(G-7199)
MRS INDUSTRIAL INC
Also Called: M R S
2583 Harrison St (43204-3511)
PHONE 614 308-1070
Scott J Cosgrove, *President*
Scott Cosgrove, *President*
Ronald L Belford, *Vice Pres*
Kenneth Michael Cosgrove, *Vice Pres*
▲ **EMP:** 24
SQ FT: 60,000
SALES (est): 5.4MM **Privately Held**
SIC: 3444 Sheet metalwork

(G-7200)
MULTIPRESS INC
1250 Refugee Ln (43207-2112)
PHONE 614 228-0185
Michael Pfister, *Principal*
EMP: 4
SALES (est): 547.3K **Privately Held**
SIC: 3542 Presses: hydraulic & pneumatic, mechanical & manual

(G-7201)
MURPHY TRACTOR & EQP CO INC
Also Called: John Deere Authorized Dealer
2121 Walcutt Rd (43228-9575)
PHONE 614 876-1141
Mike Slinger, *Manager*
EMP: 8 **Privately Held**
SIC: 3531 5082 Construction machinery; construction & mining machinery
HQ: Murphy Tractor & Equipment Co., Inc.
5375 N Deere Rd
Park City KS 67219
855 246-9124

(G-7202)
MUSICMAX INC
Also Called: R. Joseph Group
1517 Hess St Ste 200 (43212-2813)
PHONE 614 732-0777
Rob Joseph, *President*
EMP: 10
SALES (est): 1.4MM **Privately Held**
WEB: www.rjosephgroup.com
SIC: 3651 Music distribution apparatus

(G-7203)
MUSICOL INC
780 Oakland Park Ave (43224-3295)
PHONE 614 267-3133
John W Hull, *President*
Claud Ferguson, *Principal*
Jonathan Hull, *Principal*
Charlene Hull, *Vice Pres*
Boyd Niederlander, *Shareholder*
EMP: 5 **EST:** 1962
SQ FT: 6,000
SALES: 500K **Privately Held**
WEB: www.musicolrecording.com
SIC: 7389 7812 3652 Recording studio, noncommercial records; motion picture & video production; phonograph record blanks

(G-7204)
MVP PHARMACY
1931 Parsons Ave (43207-2364)
PHONE 614 449-8000
EMP: 4
SALES (est): 270.9K **Privately Held**
SIC: 2834 Pharmaceutical preparations

(G-7205)
MY CATERED TABLE LLC
1871 N High St (43210-1105)
PHONE 614 882-7323
Kimberly Scaggs, *Partner*
EMP: 7
SALES (est): 447.5K **Privately Held**
SIC: 3541 Milling machines

(G-7206)
N WASSERSTROM & SONS INC (HQ)
Also Called: Wasserstrom Marketing Division
2300 Lockbourne Rd (43207-6111)
PHONE 614 228-5550
William Wasserstrom, *President*
John H Mc Cormick, *Senior VP*
Reid Wasserstrom, *Admin Sec*
◆ **EMP:** 250
SQ FT: 175,000
SALES (est): 119.1MM
SALES (corp-wide): 824.5MM **Privately Held**
SIC: 3556 5046 3444 Food products machinery; restaurant equipment & supplies; sheet metalwork
PA: The Wasserstrom Company
4500 E Broad St
Columbus OH 43213
614 228-6525

(G-7207)
N WASSERSTROM & SONS INC
Also Called: Select Seating
862 E Jenkins Ave (43207-1317)
PHONE 614 737-5410
Greg Pell, *Manager*
EMP: 100
SALES (corp-wide): 824.5MM **Privately Held**
SIC: 2511 2531 Wood household furniture; public building & related furniture
HQ: N. Wasserstrom & Sons, Inc.
2300 Lockbourne Rd
Columbus OH 43207
614 228-5550

GEOGRAPHIC SECTION
Columbus - Franklin County (G-7235)

(G-7208)
NANO INNOVATIONS LLC
Also Called: Nano Fabrix
2121 Riverside Dr (43221-4052)
PHONE.................614 203-5706
Andy Dickson,
EMP: 5 **EST:** 2012
SALES (est): 368.8K **Privately Held**
SIC: 2821 Plastics materials & resins

(G-7209)
NATIONAL ELECTRIC COIL INC (PA)
Also Called: N E C Columbus
800 King Ave (43212-2644)
P.O. Box 370 (43216-0370)
PHONE.................614 488-1151
Robert Barton, *CEO*
Athena Amaxas, *Principal*
Danial Bucklew, *Vice Pres*
Stephen I Jeney, *Vice Pres*
Steve McMahon, *Plant Mgr*
◆ **EMP:** 300
SQ FT: 500,000
SALES (est): 77.4MM **Privately Held**
WEB: www.national-electric-coil.com
SIC: 7694 Electric motor repair

(G-7210)
NATIONAL FRUIT VEGETABLE TECH
Also Called: Fresh Vegetable Technology
250 Civic Center Dr (43215-5086)
PHONE.................740 400-4055
Daniel Cashman, *CEO*
Mitch Adams, *Ch of Bd*
Keith Stoll, *VP Mfg*
Richard Cashman, *Shareholder*
EMP: 50
SQ FT: 150,000
SALES (est): 6.3MM **Privately Held**
SIC: 2037 Fruits, quick frozen & cold pack (frozen); vegetables, quick frozen & cold pack, excl. potato products; potato products, quick frozen & cold pack

(G-7211)
NATIONAL MOLD REMEDIATION
3923 E Main St (43213-2948)
PHONE.................614 231-6653
Lynn Edelman, *President*
EMP: 5
SALES (est): 374.4K **Privately Held**
SIC: 3544 Industrial molds

(G-7212)
NBBI
1055 Crupper Ave (43229-1108)
PHONE.................614 888-8320
Brandon Sofsky, *Publications*
David Trent, *Analyst*
EMP: 3
SALES (est): 326.1K **Privately Held**
SIC: 3433 Boilers, low-pressure heating: steam or hot water

(G-7213)
NEON HUSSY LLC
237 E 12th Ave (43201-2216)
PHONE.................513 374-7644
Jess Mishos, *Principal*
EMP: 3
SALES (est): 123.2K **Privately Held**
SIC: 2813 Neon

(G-7214)
NETWORK PRINTING & GRAPHICS
443 Crestview Rd (43202-2244)
PHONE.................614 230-2084
Cathy Ann Dawson, *President*
EMP: 10
SQ FT: 7,500
SALES (est): 1.1MM **Privately Held**
SIC: 2752 7331 2791 2789 Commercial printing, lithographic; direct mail advertising services; typesetting; bookbinding & related work; commercial printing

(G-7215)
NEW AQUA LLC
3707 Interchange Rd (43204-1435)
PHONE.................614 265-9000
EMP: 9
SALES (est): 79.9K
SALES (corp-wide): 18.7MM **Privately Held**
SIC: 3589 Water filters & softeners, household type
PA: New Aqua Llc
7785 E Us Highway 36
Avon IN 46123
317 272-3000

(G-7216)
NEWALL ELECTRONICS INC
1803 Obrien Rd (43228-3866)
PHONE.................614 771-0213
Martha Sullivan, *President*
Paul Vasington, *CFO*
Jeffrey Cote, *Director*
▲ **EMP:** 14
SQ FT: 7,000
SALES (est): 2.1MM
SALES (corp-wide): 2.7MM **Privately Held**
WEB: www.newall.com
SIC: 3829 Measuring & controlling devices
HQ: Custom Sensors & Technologies, Inc.
1461 Lawrence Dr
Thousand Oaks CA 91320
805 716-0322

(G-7217)
NEWMAST MKTG & COMMUNICATIONS
Also Called: Printing Company, The
2060 Integrity Dr N (43209-2726)
PHONE.................614 837-1200
Terry L Wike, *President*
EMP: 20 **EST:** 1898
SQ FT: 15,000
SALES (est): 1.2MM **Privately Held**
SIC: 7336 2752 Silk screen design; commercial printing, offset

(G-7218)
NEWS REEL INC
Also Called: News Reel Mag By & For Blind
5 E Long St Ste 1001 (43215-2915)
PHONE.................614 469-0700
Kate Sniderman, *President*
Ed Eames, *President*
Tom Lykins, *Vice Pres*
Patty Silver, *Vice Pres*
Jeffrey Gardner, *Treasurer*
EMP: 3
SALES: 61.2K **Privately Held**
SIC: 3652 8399 Magnetic tape (audio): prerecorded; community development groups

(G-7219)
NEXT DAY SIGNS LLC
6403 Nicholas Dr (43235-5204)
PHONE.................614 764-7446
Cheryl A Raudabaugh, *Managing Prtnr*
Cheryl Raudabaugh, *Managing Prtnr*
Amanda B Martin, *Marketing Staff*
EMP: 3
SALES (est): 300K **Privately Held**
WEB: www.nextdaysignscols.com
SIC: 3993 Signs & advertising specialties

(G-7220)
NICHOLS INDUSTRIES
4555 Groves Rd Ste 16 (43232-4135)
PHONE.................614 866-8451
EMP: 3
SALES (est): 136.5K **Privately Held**
SIC: 3999 Mfg Misc Products

(G-7221)
NOISE SUPPRESSION TECHNOLOGIES
Also Called: Nsti
4182 Fisher Rd (43228-1024)
PHONE.................614 275-1818
Daniel F Belcher, *CEO*
EMP: 10
SQ FT: 5,000
SALES (est): 1.5MM **Privately Held**
WEB: www.noisesuppression.com
SIC: 3625 Noise control equipment

(G-7222)
NOM NOM NOM
2818 Banwick Rd (43232-3805)
PHONE.................614 302-4815
Johnna McDonald, *Owner*
EMP: 4 **EST:** 2013
SALES (est): 119.7K **Privately Held**
SIC: 2047 Dog food

(G-7223)
NORDIC LIGHT AMERICA INC
426 Mccormick Blvd (43213-1525)
PHONE.................614 981-9497
Kenneth Johansson, *President*
◆ **EMP:** 10
SQ FT: 96,000
SALES (est): 1.5MM
SALES (corp-wide): 756.1MM **Privately Held**
SIC: 7389 3646 Interior design services; ceiling systems, luminous
HQ: Nordic Light Ab
Servicegatan 13
Skelleftea 931 7
910 733-790

(G-7224)
NORSE DAIRY SYSTEMS INC
1700 E 17th Ave (43219-1005)
P.O. Box 1869 (43216-1869)
PHONE.................614 294-4931
Ralph Denisco, *President*
Randy Harvey, *Vice Pres*
EMP: 201
SQ FT: 850
SALES (corp-wide): 37.8B **Privately Held**
SIC: 6719 3565 3556 2671 Investment holding companies, except banks; packaging machinery; food products machinery; ice cream manufacturing machinery; packaging paper & plastics film, coated & laminated; paperboard mills
PA: George Weston Limited
22 St Clair Ave E Suite 1901
Toronto ON M4T 2
416 922-2500

(G-7225)
NORSE DAIRY SYSTEMS LP
1740 Joyce Ave (43219-1026)
P.O. Box 1869 (43216-1869)
PHONE.................614 421-5297
Scott Fullbright, *Partner*
◆ **EMP:** 340
SALES (est): 57.5MM
SALES (corp-wide): 37.8B **Privately Held**
WEB: www.norse.com
SIC: 3556 2052 2656 Ice cream manufacturing machinery; cones, ice cream; ice cream containers: made from purchased material
HQ: Interbake Foods Llc
3951 Westerre Pkwy # 200
Henrico VA 23233
804 755-7107

(G-7226)
NORTH COAST SECURITY GROUP LLC
750 E Long St Ste 3000 (43203-1874)
PHONE.................614 887-7255
Micheal Cudgel, *Co-Owner*
Malik Abdul-Zahir, *Co-Owner*
EMP: 4
SALES (est): 192.1K **Privately Held**
SIC: 8748 7372 7371 7373 Systems engineering consultant, ex. computer or professional; operating systems computer software; custom computer programming services; systems engineering, computer related; value-added resellers, computer systems

(G-7227)
NORTH HIGH BREWING LLC
1125 Cleveland Ave (43201-2900)
PHONE.................614 407-5278
Timothy Ward,
Gavin Meyers,
▲ **EMP:** 10 **EST:** 2011
SALES (est): 1.3MM **Privately Held**
SIC: 2082 Near beer

(G-7228)
NORTH SHORE STONE INC
915 Manor Park Dr (43228-9522)
PHONE.................614 870-7531
Denny Hamond, *President*
Cliff Hammond, *Vice Pres*
Willard Jakeway, *Treasurer*
EMP: 15
SQ FT: 1,280
SALES (est): 1.7MM **Privately Held**
WEB: www.northshorestone.com
SIC: 1411 Limestone & marble dimension stone

(G-7229)
NORTHEAST CABINET CO LLC
6063 Taylor Rd (43230-3211)
PHONE.................614 759-0800
James P Yankle, *Principal*
EMP: 8
SALES (est): 1MM **Privately Held**
SIC: 2434 Wood kitchen cabinets

(G-7230)
NORTHWOOD ENERGY CORPORATION
941 Chatham Ln Ste 100 (43221-2471)
PHONE.................614 457-1024
Ralph W Talmage, *President*
Tyna A Anderson, *Managing Dir*
Frederick H Kennedy, *Principal*
Joan S Talmage, *Principal*
Dave Haid, *Vice Pres*
EMP: 20
SQ FT: 5,000
SALES: 31.4MM **Privately Held**
SIC: 1311 Crude petroleum production; natural gas production

(G-7231)
NOXGEAR LLC
2264 Green Island Dr (43228-9432)
PHONE.................937 248-1860
Tom Walters, *CEO*
EMP: 3
SALES (est): 297.6K **Privately Held**
SIC: 2329 Mfg Men's/Boy's Clothing

(G-7232)
NUCON INTERNATIONAL INC (PA)
7000 Huntley Rd (43229-1035)
P.O. Box 29151 (43229-0151)
PHONE.................614 846-5710
J Louis Kovach, *President*
Joseph C Enneking, *Vice Pres*
Larry Shaffer, *Project Mgr*
Paul E Kovach, *Admin Sec*
▲ **EMP:** 11
SQ FT: 22,000
SALES (est): 9.1MM **Privately Held**
WEB: www.nucon-int.com
SIC: 5199 8711 8734 3829 Charcoal; pollution control engineering; pollution testing; nuclear radiation & testing apparatus; earth science services

(G-7233)
NUTS ARE GOOD INC (PA)
Also Called: Buffalo Peanuts
Busch Blvd (43229)
PHONE.................586 619-2400
Daniel B Levy, *President*
EMP: 12
SQ FT: 10,000
SALES: 3MM **Privately Held**
SIC: 2068 5145 Salted & roasted nuts & seeds; nuts, salted or roasted

(G-7234)
NUVOX
111 N 4th St (43215-3116)
PHONE.................614 232-9115
Andrea Kelly, *Principal*
EMP: 3
SALES (est): 190.7K **Privately Held**
SIC: 3355 Aluminum rolling & drawing

(G-7235)
OASIS EMBROIDERY
6663 Huntley Rd Ste R (43229-1040)
PHONE.................614 785-7266
Scott Wise, *Owner*
EMP: 3
SALES (est): 171.8K **Privately Held**
SIC: 2395 Embroidery products, except schiffli machine; embroidery & art needlework

Columbus - Franklin County (G-7236)   GEOGRAPHIC SECTION

(G-7236)
OBERFIELDS LLC
Also Called: Marble Cliff Block & Bldrs Sup
4033 Alum Creek Dr (43207-5138)
PHONE..................................614 491-7643
EMP: 50
SALES (est): 4.9MM
SALES (corp-wide): 1.1MM **Privately Held**
SIC: 3271 5211 3272 Mfg Concrete Block/Brick Ret Lumber/Building Materials Mfg Concrete Products
HQ: Oberfield's, Llc
528 London Rd
Delaware OH 43015
740 369-7644

(G-7237)
OBERFIELDS LLC
1165 Alum Creek Dr (43209-2719)
PHONE..................................614 252-0955
Chris Buttke, *Sales/Mktg Mgr*
EMP: 15
SALES (corp-wide): 1.2MM **Privately Held**
SIC: 3272 3271 2531 Concrete products; concrete block & brick; public building & related furniture
HQ: Oberfield's, Llc
528 London Rd
Delaware OH 43015
740 369-7644

(G-7238)
OCEAN PROVIDENCE COLUMBUS LLC
3699 Interchange Rd (43204-1499)
PHONE..................................614 272-5973
Kiwao Hayasaka, *President*
EMP: 3
SALES (est): 333.7K **Privately Held**
SIC: 2048 0913 Fish food; shellfish

(G-7239)
OCTSYS SECURITY CORP (PA)
Also Called: O S C
341 S 3rd St Ste 100-42 (43215-5463)
P.O. Box 1071 (43216-1071)
PHONE..................................614 470-4510
Vincent King, *Ch of Bd*
EMP: 6
SALES (est): 882.9K **Privately Held**
SIC: 3089 3999 Identification cards, plastic; stereographs, photographic

(G-7240)
OHIO ANODIZING COMPANY INC
915 N 20th St (43219-2422)
PHONE..................................614 252-7855
Jim Hoyle, *President*
Keith Willike, *Treasurer*
EMP: 16
SQ FT: 50,000
SALES: 2MM **Privately Held**
SIC: 3471 Plating/Polishing Service

(G-7241)
OHIO ASSOCIATION REALTORS INC
200 E Town St (43215-4608)
PHONE..................................614 228-6675
Robert E Fletcher, *CEO*
Robin Jennings, *VP Opers*
Denis Nowacki, *Treasurer*
Cherie Murray, *CTO*
Sample Sharon, *Director*
EMP: 25 **EST:** 1911
SQ FT: 15,168
SALES: 5.3MM **Privately Held**
WEB: www.ohiorealtor.com
SIC: 8611 2721 Trade associations; trade journals; publishing & printing

(G-7242)
OHIO CAST STONE CO LLC
45 W Barthman Ave (43207-1887)
P.O. Box 7852 (43207-0852)
PHONE..................................614 444-2278
Alan Cleary, *Principal*
EMP: 5
SALES (est): 360K **Privately Held**
SIC: 3272 Concrete products

(G-7243)
OHIO CHEMICAL TWO
8132 Linden Leaf Cir (43235-4617)
PHONE..................................614 482-8073
Megan E Horvath, *Principal*
EMP: 3
SALES (est): 298.8K **Privately Held**
SIC: 2869 Laboratory chemicals, organic

(G-7244)
OHIO DEPARTMENT TRANSPORTATION
1606 W Broad St (43223-1202)
PHONE..................................614 351-2898
Paul A Trapasso, *Branch Mgr*
EMP: 20 **Privately Held**
SIC: 3669 9621 Transportation signaling devices;
HQ: Ohio Department Of Transportation
1980 W Broad St
Columbus OH 43223

(G-7245)
OHIO DESIGNER CRAFTSMEN ENTPS (HQ)
Also Called: OHIO CRAFT MUSEUM
1665 W 5th Ave (43212-2315)
PHONE..................................614 486-7119
Sharon Kokot, *Director*
EMP: 12 **EST:** 1963
SQ FT: 2,000
SALES: 899.9K **Privately Held**
SIC: 5947 8741 2721 Artcraft & carvings; management services; periodicals: publishing only

(G-7246)
OHIO DISTINCTIVE ENTERPRISES
Also Called: Ohio Distinctive Software
6500 Fiesta Dr (43235-5201)
PHONE..................................614 459-0453
Stanford Apseloff, *President*
Timothy M Clark, *Corp Secy*
Glen Apseloff, *Vice Pres*
EMP: 20
SQ FT: 12,000
SALES (est): 2.7MM **Privately Held**
WEB: www.ohio-distinctive.com
SIC: 7372 Prepackaged software

(G-7247)
OHIO ELECTRIC MOTOR SVC LLC (PA)
1909 E Livingston Ave (43209-2733)
PHONE..................................614 444-1451
Gary Stroup, *Prdtn Mgr*
Harry Litton, *Consultant*
Mike Moshier, *Consultant*
Michael Moshier,
EMP: 11
SALES (est): 1.9MM **Privately Held**
SIC: 7694 Electric motor repair

(G-7248)
OHIO FOAM CORPORATION
1513 Alum Creek Dr (43209-2712)
PHONE..................................614 252-4877
Phil Johnson, *Branch Mgr*
EMP: 8
SALES (corp-wide): 11.7MM **Privately Held**
WEB: www.ohiofoam.com
SIC: 3069 3086 Foam rubber; plastics foam products
PA: Ohio Foam Corporation
820 Plymouth St
Bucyrus OH 44820
419 563-0399

(G-7249)
OHIO LABEL INC
5005 Transamerica Dr (43228-9381)
PHONE..................................614 777-0180
Stacy Graham, *CEO*
Matthew Renner, *Finance Mgr*
Wayne Fisher, *Manager*
EMP: 11 **EST:** 1990
SQ FT: 12,000
SALES: 1.8MM **Privately Held**
WEB: www.ohiolabel.com
SIC: 2672 Labels (unprinted), gummed: made from purchased materials

(G-7250)
OHIO MANUFACTURING EXT PARTNR
Also Called: Ohmep
77 S High St (43215-6108)
PHONE..................................614 644-8788
Beth Colbert, *Partner*
EMP: 3
SALES: 950K **Privately Held**
SIC: 3999 Manufacturing industries

(G-7251)
OHIO NEWS NETWORK
Also Called: Ohio News Network, The
770 Twin Rivers Dr (43215-1127)
PHONE..................................614 460-3700
Tom Greidorn, *General Mgr*
EMP: 80
SALES (est): 3.7MM **Privately Held**
WEB: www.onnnews.com
SIC: 7383 2711 4841 News syndicates; newspapers; cable & other pay television services

(G-7252)
OHIO NEWSPAPER SERVICES INC
Also Called: Adohio
1335 Dublin Rd Ste 216b (43215-1000)
PHONE..................................614 486-6677
Chris Dixon, *Advt Staff*
Sue Bazzoli, *Manager*
Frank Deaner, *Exec Dir*
EMP: 8 **EST:** 1933
SALES: 370.3K **Privately Held**
WEB: www.classifiedsohio.com
SIC: 7313 2711 Newspaper advertising representative; newspapers, publishing & printing
PA: Ohio News Media Association Ad Ohio
1335 Dublin Rd Ste 216b
Columbus OH 43215
614 486-6677

(G-7253)
OHIO NEWSPAPERS FOUNDATION
1335 Dublin Rd Ste 216b (43215-1000)
PHONE..................................614 486-6677
Al Sahafa, *Principal*
EMP: 4
SALES (est): 213.6K **Privately Held**
SIC: 2711 Newspapers, publishing & printing

(G-7254)
OHIO PACKING COMPANY (PA)
1306 Harmon Ave (43223-3365)
PHONE..................................614 445-0627
Walter Wilke Jr, *President*
Carla Jones, *Vice Pres*
James Wilke, *Treasurer*
Edward Wilke Jr, *Admin Sec*
EMP: 90 **EST:** 1907
SQ FT: 70,000
SALES (est): 15.2MM **Privately Held**
SIC: 2011 Pork products from pork slaughtered on site

(G-7255)
OHIO PROCESSORS INC (HQ)
2200 Cardigan Ave (43215-1092)
PHONE..................................740 852-9243
Clifton J Smith, *Ch of Bd*
Douglas A Smith, *President*
Thomas G Michaelides, *Treasurer*
G Frederick Smith, *Admin Sec*
EMP: 4 **EST:** 1974
SQ FT: 10,300
SALES (est): 3.5MM
SALES (corp-wide): 47.5MM **Privately Held**
SIC: 2026 5143 Whipped topping, except frozen or dry mix; dairy products, except dried or canned
PA: Instantwhip Foods, Inc.
2200 Cardigan Ave
Columbus OH 43215
614 488-2536

(G-7256)
OHIO PSYCHLOGY PBLICATIONS INC
Also Called: National Psychologist, The
620 Taylor Station Rd F (43230-6699)
PHONE..................................614 861-1999
Martin Saeman, *President*
Marilyn L Saeman, *Treasurer*
EMP: 5
SALES: 300K **Privately Held**
WEB: www.nationalpsychologist.com
SIC: 2731 Book publishing

(G-7257)
OHIO RIGHTS GROUP
1021 E Broad St (43205-1357)
PHONE..................................614 300-0529
Chad Callender, *Principal*
EMP: 4
SALES (est): 205.9K **Privately Held**
SIC: 2711 Newspapers, publishing & printing

(G-7258)
OHIO STATE PLASTICS
1917 Joyce Ave (43219-1029)
PHONE..................................614 299-5618
Dwayne Margin, *Manager*
EMP: 17
SALES (est): 198.9K
SALES (corp-wide): 14B **Publicly Held**
WEB: www.cccllc.com
SIC: 2656 Food containers (liquid tight), including milk cartons
HQ: Consolidated Container Company, Llc
2500 Windy Ridge Pkwy Se # 1400
Atlanta GA 30339
678 742-4600

(G-7259)
OHIO STATE UNIVERSITY
Also Called: Osu Arabidopsis Resource
1060 Carmack Rd Rm 39 (43210-1002)
PHONE..................................614 292-7656
Robert Tabita, *Director*
EMP: 40
SALES (corp-wide): 5.8B **Privately Held**
WEB: www.ohio-state.edu
SIC: 2869 8221 Laboratory chemicals, organic; university
PA: The Ohio State University
Student Acade Servi Bldg
Columbus OH 43210
614 292-6446

(G-7260)
OHIO STATE UNIVERSITY
Also Called: Osu Industrial Welding Sy
1248 Arthur E Adams Dr (43221-3560)
PHONE..................................614 292-4139
Richard A Miller, *Chairman*
EMP: 32
SALES (corp-wide): 5.8B **Privately Held**
WEB: www.ohio-state.edu
SIC: 7692 8221 Welding repair; university
PA: The Ohio State University
Student Acade Servi Bldg
Columbus OH 43210
614 292-6446

(G-7261)
OHIO STATE UNIVERSITY
Also Called: Assistive Technology of Ohio
2050 Kenny Rd Fl 9 (43221-3502)
PHONE..................................614 293-3600
Dena Truman, *Manager*
EMP: 7
SALES (corp-wide): 5.8B **Privately Held**
WEB: www.ohio-state.edu
SIC: 3842 8322 Technical aids for the handicapped; individual & family services
PA: The Ohio State University
Student Acade Servi Bldg
Columbus OH 43210
614 292-6446

(G-7262)
OHIO STATE UNIVERSITY
Also Called: Ohio State University Press
1070 Carmack Rd Rm 180 (43210-1002)
PHONE..................................614 292-1462
Tony Sanfilippo, *Director*
EMP: 13

SALES (corp-wide): 5.8B **Privately Held**
WEB: www.ohio-state.edu
SIC: **8221** 2721 University; periodicals; trade journals: publishing & printing
PA: The Ohio State University
   Student Acade Servi Bldg
   Columbus OH 43210
   614 292-6446

(G-7263)
OHIO TRAILER SUPPLY INC
Also Called: Ots
2966 Westerville Rd (43224-4563)
PHONE 614 471-9121
Jet Chrysler, *President*
EMP: 7
SQ FT: 8,000
SALES (est): 912.6K **Privately Held**
WEB: www.ohiotrailer.com
SIC: **7692** 5013 Welding repair; trailer parts & accessories

(G-7264)
OHIO WIRE FORM & SPRING CO
2270 S High St (43207-2432)
PHONE 614 444-3676
Stephen A Van Horn, *President*
P E Van Horn Jr, *Chairman*
Samuel E Van Horn, *Vice Pres*
Sharon Ward, *Safety Mgr*
EMP: 17 EST: 1947
SQ FT: 43,800
SALES (est): 4.2MM **Privately Held**
WEB: www.ohiowireform.com
SIC: **3496** 3495 Miscellaneous fabricated wire products; wire springs

(G-7265)
OHIO WOOD RECYCLING INC
Also Called: Dm Pallet Service
2019 Rathmell Rd (43207-5012)
PHONE 614 491-0881
Dexter Mounts, *President*
EMP: 20
SALES (est): 1.3MM **Privately Held**
SIC: **2448** Pallets, wood

(G-7266)
OHLHEISER CORP
1900 Jetway Blvd (43219-1681)
PHONE 860 953-7632
Robert Pellettier, *Owner*
EMP: 3 EST: 2017
SALES (est): 118.1K **Privately Held**
SIC: **3569** General industrial machinery

(G-7267)
OHLINGER PUBLISHING SVCS INC
28 W Henderson Rd (43214-2628)
PHONE 614 261-5360
Monica Ohlinger, *President*
Donna Petersch, *Principal*
EMP: 10
SALES (est): 725.7K **Privately Held**
SIC: **2741** Miscellaneous publishing

(G-7268)
OIL BAR LLC (PA)
2740 Eastland Mall (43232-4960)
PHONE 614 501-9815
Ernest E Dennis Jr,
EMP: 4
SALES: 250K **Privately Held**
SIC: **2899** Oils & essential oils

(G-7269)
OLD TRAIL PRINTING COMPANY
100 Fornoff Rd (43207-2475)
PHONE 614 443-4852
Mary Held, *Owner*
Jeff Lampert, *Sales Mgr*
Dave Held, *Shareholder*
Michael Held, *Shareholder*
Susan Horn, *Shareholder*
EMP: 125 EST: 1924
SQ FT: 55,000
SALES (est): 24.8MM **Privately Held**
WEB: www.oldtrailprinting.com
SIC: **2752** 2791 2789 2759 Commercial printing, offset; letters, circular or form: lithographed; typesetting; bookbinding & related work; commercial printing

(G-7270)
OLENTANGY EYE AND LASER A
3525 Olentngy Rvr Rd # 5310 (43214-3938)
PHONE 614 267-4122
Debbie Riegel, *Office Mgr*
EMP: 4
SALES (est): 436.1K **Privately Held**
SIC: **3841** Surgical lasers

(G-7271)
OMNITECH ELECTRONICS INC
5090 Trabue Rd (43228-9391)
PHONE 800 822-1344
Bogdan Zaleski, *President*
Paul Zaleski, *Managing Dir*
EMP: 12
SQ FT: 22,500
SALES (est): 880K **Privately Held**
SIC: **3826** Analytical instruments

(G-7272)
OPEN HOUSE MAGAZINE INC
1537 Guilford Rd (43221-3850)
PHONE 614 523-7775
Michael A Schadek, *President*
EMP: 3 EST: 1994
SALES (est): 300.9K **Privately Held**
WEB: www.openhousemag.com
SIC: **2721** 6531 Magazines: publishing & printing; real estate agents & managers

(G-7273)
OPTICAL DISTRIBUTION CORP
401 N Front St Ste 350 (43215-2249)
PHONE 937 405-7280
Dave Delle Donne, *President*
Michael R Morosky, *Vice Pres*
Timothy O Neal, *Admin Sec*
▲ EMP: 16
SQ FT: 11,500
SALES: 3.6MM **Privately Held**
WEB: www.rodenstockusa.com
SIC: **3851** Eyeglasses, lenses & frames

(G-7274)
OPTIMUS LLC
Also Called: Optimus Prosthetics
975 Bethel Rd (43214-1905)
PHONE 614 263-5462
John Brandt, *Branch Mgr*
Scott Schall,
EMP: 6
SALES (est): 664.8K **Privately Held**
SIC: **3842** Prosthetic appliances
PA: Optimus Llc
   8517 N Dixie Dr
   Dayton OH 45414

(G-7275)
ORANGE BARREL MEDIA LLC
250 N Hartford Ave (43222-1100)
PHONE 614 294-4898
Peter Scantland, *Principal*
Adam Borchers, *CFO*
Chad Truitt, *Asst Controller*
Lauren Stephens, *Executive*
Danielle Williamson, *Executive*
EMP: 25
SALES (est): 2.5MM **Privately Held**
WEB: www.orangebarrelmedia.com
SIC: **3993** 7312 Signs & advertising specialties; outdoor advertising services

(G-7276)
ORBIS RPM LLC
592 Claycraft Rd (43230-5319)
PHONE 419 307-8511
Chad Goodwin, *Branch Mgr*
EMP: 8
SALES (corp-wide): 1.7B **Privately Held**
SIC: **3081** Unsupported plastics film & sheet
HQ: Orbis Rpm, Llc
   1055 Corporate Center Dr
   Oconomowoc WI 53066
   262 560-5000

(G-7277)
OSI GLOBAL SOURCING LLC
2575 Ferris Rd (43224-2540)
PHONE 614 471-4800
Tom Martini, *President*
▲ EMP: 130 EST: 2008
SALES (est): 4.8MM **Privately Held**
SIC: **2821** Plastics materials & resins

(G-7278)
OSU LABANLENS ✪
1813 N High St (43210-1307)
PHONE 614 688-2356
Michael Kaylor, *Director*
EMP: 4 EST: 2018
SALES (est): 98.3K **Privately Held**
SIC: **7372** Application computer software

(G-7279)
OUR HEART HEALTH CARE SVCS LLC
1336 E Main St (43205-2081)
PHONE 614 943-5216
Erica Coit,
Leroy Kendrick,
Jackie Tunrbo,
EMP: 3 EST: 2010
SALES (est): 107.9K **Privately Held**
SIC: **2086** Fruit drinks (less than 100% juice): packaged in cans, etc.

(G-7280)
OUR NINE LLC
Also Called: Midwest Graphics
6740 Huntley Rd Ste F (43229-1037)
PHONE 614 844-6655
Gayle May,
EMP: 4
SQ FT: 2,032
SALES (est): 541.5K **Privately Held**
SIC: **2752** Commercial printing, lithographic

(G-7281)
OWENS CORNING
2050 Integrity Dr S (43209-2728)
PHONE 614 754-4098
Stephen Brooks, *Manager*
EMP: 9 **Publicly Held**
SIC: **3296** Mineral wool
PA: Owens Corning
   1 Owens Corning Pkwy
   Toledo OH 43659

(G-7282)
P S PLASTICS INC
2020 Britains Ln (43224-5612)
PHONE 614 262-7070
John Pyers, *President*
Rob Sutliff, *Corp Secy*
EMP: 11
SQ FT: 6,700
SALES: 500K **Privately Held**
SIC: **3089** Injection molding of plastics; plastic processing

(G-7283)
P-AMERICAS LLC
Also Called: Pepsico
1241 Gibbard Ave (43219-2438)
PHONE 614 253-8771
Dale Watkins, *CFO*
EMP: 123
SALES (corp-wide): 64.6B **Publicly Held**
SIC: **2086** Carbonated soft drinks, bottled & canned
HQ: P-Americas Llc
   1 Pepsi Way
   Somers NY 10589
   336 896-5740

(G-7284)
PACTIV LLC
2120 Westbelt Dr (43228-3820)
PHONE 815 547-1200
EMP: 53
SQ FT: 104,000 **Privately Held**
SIC: **2656** Mfg Sanitary Food Containers
HQ: Pactiv Llc
   1900 W Field Ct
   Lake Forest IL 60045
   847 482-2000

(G-7285)
PACTIV LLC
2120 Westbelt Dr (43228-3820)
P.O. Box 28147 (43228)
PHONE 614 771-5400
Joe Deal, *Opers Mgr*
Lynn Morgan, *Purch Agent*
EMP: 240
SALES (corp-wide): 1MM **Privately Held**
WEB: www.pactiv.com
SIC: **2631** 7389 Paperboard mills; packaging & labeling services
HQ: Pactiv Llc
   1900 W Field Ct
   Lake Forest IL 60045
   847 482-2000

(G-7286)
PAKRA LLC
449 E Mound St (43215-5514)
PHONE 614 477-6965
Rini Das, *Mng Member*
Pamela Schmdt- Cavaliero,
Anne Claire France,
Ashish Shah,
Michelle Stewart,
EMP: 10
SQ FT: 900
SALES: 100K **Privately Held**
WEB: www.pakragames.com
SIC: **7372** 8331 8249 8742 Business oriented computer software; educational computer software; job training & vocational rehabilitation services; business training services; management consulting services

(G-7287)
PANACEA PRODUCTS CORPORATION (PA)
Also Called: J-Mak Industries
2711 International St (43228-4604)
PHONE 614 850-7000
Frank A Paniccia, *President*
Louis Calderone, *Principal*
Fred Pagura, *Principal*
Jim Fancelli, *Vice Pres*
Gregg Paniccia, *Vice Pres*
◆ EMP: 40
SALES (est): 45.2MM **Privately Held**
WEB: www.panac.com
SIC: **5051** 2542 3496 Metals service centers & offices; partitions & fixtures, except wood; shelving, office & store: except wood; miscellaneous fabricated wire products; shelving, made from purchased wire

(G-7288)
PANACEA PRODUCTS CORPORATION
1825 Joyce Ave (43219-1027)
PHONE 614 429-6320
Bob Carroll, *Engineer*
Frank Panancea, *Branch Mgr*
EMP: 54
SALES (corp-wide): 45.2MM **Privately Held**
WEB: www.panac.com
SIC: **3496** 3423 2542 Miscellaneous fabricated wire products; hand & edge tools; partitions & fixtures, except wood
PA: Panacea Products Corporation
   2711 International St
   Columbus OH 43228
   614 850-7000

(G-7289)
PANTAC USA LTD
6155 Huntley Rd Ste D (43229-1096)
PHONE 614 423-6743
Wallace Lau,
William Fred Valentine,
EMP: 3
SALES (est): 26.4K **Privately Held**
SIC: **2329** Field jackets, military

(G-7290)
PAPEL COUTURE
Also Called: PC
6522 Singletree Dr (43229-1119)
PHONE 614 848-5700
Vadim Daskal, *Owner*
Scott Vogel, *General Mgr*
EMP: 6
SQ FT: 600
SALES: 1MM **Privately Held**
SIC: **2759** Invitation & stationery printing & engraving
PA: Daskal Enterprise, Llc
   6522 Singletree Dr
   Columbus OH 43229
   614 848-5700

Columbus - Franklin County (G-7291)

(G-7291)
PAPER VAULT
869 Montrose Ave (43209-2451)
PHONE..................614 859-5538
Darci Bonnington, *Principal*
EMP: 3
SALES (est): 195.9K **Privately Held**
SIC: 3272 Burial vaults, concrete or pre-cast terrazzo

(G-7292)
PAPWORTH PRINTS
4355 Boulder Creek Dr (43230-6327)
PHONE..................614 428-6137
William Papworth, *Principal*
EMP: 6
SALES (est): 610.7K **Privately Held**
SIC: 2752 Commercial printing, lithographic

(G-7293)
PARAGON WOODWORKING LLC
800 Reynolds Ave (43201-3767)
PHONE..................614 402-1459
Larry Griggs,
EMP: 3
SALES: 300K **Privately Held**
SIC: 2431 Millwork

(G-7294)
PARKER-HANNIFIN CORPORATION
Also Called: Tube Fittings Division
3885 Gateway Blvd (43228-9723)
PHONE..................614 279-7070
Wendy Moore, *Safety Mgr*
Richard Gulley, *Sales Mgr*
William Bowman, *Branch Mgr*
Joe Pfister, *Manager*
Todd Ulshafer, *Technical Staff*
EMP: 120
SALES (corp-wide): 14.3B **Publicly Held**
WEB: www.parker.com
SIC: 3494 5074 Pipe fittings; plumbing fittings & supplies
PA: Parker-Hannifin Corporation
6035 Parkland Blvd
Cleveland OH 44124
216 896-3000

(G-7295)
PATIO PRINTING INC
Also Called: Patio Print & Promotions
6663 Huntley Rd Ste S (43229-1040)
PHONE..................614 785-9553
Dieter Thellman, *President*
Dieter Thellmann, *President*
Margit Thellmann, *Vice Pres*
EMP: 7
SQ FT: 1,400
SALES: 1MM **Privately Held**
WEB: www.patioprinting.com
SIC: 2752 2759 Commercial printing, offset; screen printing

(G-7296)
PATIO ROOM FACTORY INC
2659 Beulah Rd (43211-1012)
PHONE..................614 449-7900
Walter Renz, *President*
Mark Yates, *Treasurer*
EMP: 5
SALES (est): 500K **Privately Held**
SIC: 3444 Awnings & canopies

(G-7297)
PATRIOT CONSULTING LLC
Also Called: Patriot Distributing
20 E Frambes Ave (43201-1406)
PHONE..................614 554-6455
Robert Packey,
EMP: 3
SALES: 150K **Privately Held**
SIC: 3646 Commercial indusl & institutional electric lighting fixtures

(G-7298)
PATS DELICIOUS LLC
737 Parkwood Ave (43219-2517)
PHONE..................614 441-7047
Patricia Okoro, *CEO*
EMP: 4
SALES (est): 140.5K **Privately Held**
SIC: 2096 Potato chips & similar snacks

(G-7299)
PAUL PETERSON COMPANY (PA)
950 Dublin Rd (43215-1169)
P.O. Box 1510 (43216-1510)
PHONE..................614 486-4375
Paul Peterson Jr, *CEO*
Parr Peterson, *President*
Andrew J White Jr, *Principal*
Richard L Miller, *Principal*
Grant S Richards, *Principal*
EMP: 47
SALES (est): 13.7MM **Privately Held**
WEB: www.ppco.net
SIC: 1611 1799 3669 5084 Guardrail construction, highways; highway & street sign installation; waterproofing; traffic signals, electric; safety equipment; work zone traffic equipment (flags, cones, barrels, etc.)

(G-7300)
PAUL PETERSON SAFETY DIV INC
950 Dublin Rd (43215-1169)
P.O. Box 1510 (43216-1510)
PHONE..................614 486-4375
Paul Peterson Jr, *President*
Colette Peterson, *Corp Secy*
Gary Boylan, *Vice Pres*
Parr Peterson, *Vice Pres*
EMP: 30
SQ FT: 3,800
SALES (est): 180.7K
SALES (corp-wide): 13.7MM **Privately Held**
WEB: www.ppco.net
SIC: 3993 5999 7359 Signs, not made in custom sign painting shops; safety supplies & equipment; work zone traffic equipment (flags, cones, barrels, etc.)
PA: The Paul Peterson Company
950 Dublin Rd
Columbus OH 43215
614 486-4375

(G-7301)
PAULA AND JULIES COOKBOOKS LLC
6034 Mcnaughten Grove Ln (43213-5103)
PHONE..................614 863-1193
Paula Weinstein, *Principal*
EMP: 3
SALES (est): 167.5K **Privately Held**
SIC: 2741 Miscellaneous publishing

(G-7302)
PAULG CORPORATION
1601 W 5th Ave (43212-2310)
PHONE..................914 662-9837
EMP: 40
SALES (est): 1.3MM **Privately Held**
SIC: 3499 Mfg Misc Fabricated Metal Products

(G-7303)
PEARSON EDUCATION INC
4350 Equity Dr (43228-4801)
PHONE..................614 876-0371
Sheila Hickle, *Branch Mgr*
Jim Mocogni, *Director*
EMP: 14
SALES (corp-wide): 5.9B **Privately Held**
SIC: 2721 Periodicals
HQ: Pearson Education, Inc.
221 River St
Hoboken NJ 07030
201 236-7000

(G-7304)
PEARSON EDUCATION INC
445 Hutchinson Ave # 400 (43235-5677)
PHONE..................614 841-3700
Tim Richards, *Vice Pres*
Donna Giacomini, *Purch Mgr*
Bruce Johnson, *Manager*
EMP: 17
SALES (corp-wide): 5.9B **Privately Held**
WEB: www.phgenit.com
SIC: 2721 Periodicals
HQ: Pearson Education, Inc.
221 River St
Hoboken NJ 07030
201 236-7000

(G-7305)
PECO II INC
7060 Huntley Rd (43229-1082)
PHONE..................614 431-0694
Rich Powell, *Opers Mgr*
EMP: 55
SALES (corp-wide): 121.6B **Publicly Held**
WEB: www.peco2.com
SIC: 3661 8711 7372 3822 Telephone & telegraph apparatus; engineering services; prepackaged software; auto controls regulating residntl & coml environcmt & applncs; relays & industrial controls
HQ: Peco Ii, Inc.
601 Shiloh Rd
Plano TX 75074
972 284-8449

(G-7306)
PEEBLES - HERZOG INC
50 Hayden Ave (43222-1019)
PHONE..................614 279-2211
Michael B Herzog, *President*
Molly Herzog, *Corp Secy*
Michael Lauffer, *Vice Pres*
EMP: 7 **EST:** 1975
SQ FT: 6,500
SALES: 884K **Privately Held**
WEB: www.peeblesherzog.com
SIC: 3931 7699 Pipes, organ; organ tuning & repair

(G-7307)
PEGGYS PRIDE
183 E Rich St (43215-5218)
PHONE..................614 464-2511
Bill Welch, *President*
EMP: 3
SALES (est): 180K **Privately Held**
SIC: 2013 Sausages & other prepared meats

(G-7308)
PENNANT COMPANIES (PA)
2000 Bethel Rd Ste D (43220-5810)
P.O. Box 188, Sabina (45169-0188)
PHONE..................614 451-1782
Chuck Foster, *CEO*
Larry Martin, *CFO*
EMP: 365
SQ FT: 200
SALES (est): 63.6MM **Privately Held**
WEB: www.pennantcompanies.com
SIC: 3465 Moldings or trim, automobile: stamped metal

(G-7309)
PEPPERIDGE FARM INCORPORATED
Also Called: Pepperidge Farm Thrift Store
1174 Kenny Centre Mall (43220-4036)
PHONE..................614 457-4800
Randy Leonard, *Manager*
EMP: 3
SALES (corp-wide): 8.6B **Publicly Held**
WEB: www.pepperidgefarm.com
SIC: 5145 2052 2099 2053 Snack foods; cookies; bread crumbs, not made in bakeries; frozen bakery products, except bread
HQ: Pepperidge Farm, Incorporated
595 Westport Ave
Norwalk CT 06851
203 846-7000

(G-7310)
PEPSI-COLA METRO BTLG CO INC
Also Called: Pepsico
2553 N High St (43202-2555)
PHONE..................614 261-8193
Al Vogt, *Manager*
EMP: 115
SALES (corp-wide): 64.6B **Publicly Held**
WEB: www.pbg.com
SIC: 2086 Carbonated soft drinks, bottled & canned
HQ: Pepsi-Cola Metropolitan Bottling Company, Inc.
1111 Westchester Ave
White Plains NY 10604
914 767-6000

(G-7311)
PERCUVISION LLC
2030 Dividend Dr (43228-3847)
PHONE..................614 891-4800
Errol Singh, *CEO*
Earl Singh, *COO*
Rick Karr, *Vice Pres*
Allen Stock, *Vice Pres*
David Busick, *Commissioner*
EMP: 18
SQ FT: 7,500
SALES (est): 2.3MM **Privately Held**
SIC: 3841 Surgical & medical instruments

(G-7312)
PERFORMANCE RESEARCH INC
Also Called: PRI Marine
3328 Westerville Rd (43224-3700)
PHONE..................614 475-8300
Robert M Proffit, *President*
EMP: 7
SQ FT: 10,000
SALES (est): 993.7K **Privately Held**
SIC: 3519 Marine engines

(G-7313)
PETROLIANCE
2854 Johnstown Rd (43219-1772)
PHONE..................614 475-5952
EMP: 3 **EST:** 2010
SALES (est): 130K **Privately Held**
SIC: 2992 Mfg Lubricating Oils/Greases

(G-7314)
PHILADELPHIA INSTANTWHIP INC
2200 Cardigan Ave (43215-1092)
PHONE..................614 488-2536
Douglas A Smith, *President*
Tom Willard, *General Mgr*
Thomas G Michaelides, *Treasurer*
G Frederick Smith, *Admin Sec*
EMP: 4 **EST:** 1954
SALES (est): 846.8K
SALES (corp-wide): 47.5MM **Privately Held**
SIC: 2026 5143 Whipped topping, except frozen or dry mix; dairy products, except dried or canned
PA: Instantwhip Foods, Inc.
2200 Cardigan Ave
Columbus OH 43215
614 488-2536

(G-7315)
PHOTO-TYPE ENGRAVING COMPANY
2500 Harrison Rd (43204-3510)
PHONE..................614 308-1900
Corey Ammons, *Vice Pres*
Doug Rittenhouse, *Branch Mgr*
EMP: 15
SALES (corp-wide): 41.2MM **Privately Held**
SIC: 2791 Photocomposition, for the printing trade
PA: The Photo-Type Engraving Company
2141 Gilbert Ave
Cincinnati OH 45206
513 281-0999

(G-7316)
PHOTO-TYPE ENGRAVING COMPANY
2500 Harrison Rd (43204-3510)
PHONE..................614 308-7914
Dave Olberding, *Manager*
EMP: 15
SALES (corp-wide): 41.2MM **Privately Held**
WEB: www.phototype.com
SIC: 2791 Photocomposition, for the printing trade
PA: The Photo-Type Engraving Company
2141 Gilbert Ave
Cincinnati OH 45206
513 281-0999

(G-7317)
PITT PLASTICS INC (DH)
3980 Groves Rd Ste A (43232-4172)
PHONE..................614 868-8660
Terry Callow, *Treasurer*
EMP: 65 **EST:** 1972
SQ FT: 120,000

GEOGRAPHIC SECTION
Columbus - Franklin County (G-7346)

SALES (est): 47.2MM **Privately Held**
SIC: 2821 2673 Polyethylene resins; bags: plastic, laminated & coated
HQ: Pitt Plastics, Inc.
1400 E Atkinson Ave
Pittsburg KS 66762
620 231-4030

(G-7318)
PJS WHOLESALE INC
2551 Westbelt Dr (43228-3826)
PHONE 614 402-9363
Azmi Azzam Alhamouri, *Principal*
Mahmoud T Almahmoud, *Principal*
▲ **EMP:** 6 EST: 2009
SALES (est): 515.1K **Privately Held**
SIC: 2253 T-shirts & tops, knit

(G-7319)
PLAIN DEALER PUBLISHING CO
155 E Broad St Fl 23 (43215-3609)
PHONE 614 228-8200
Reginald Fields, *Manager*
EMP: 5
SALES (corp-wide): 1.4B **Privately Held**
WEB: www.plaind.com
SIC: 2711 7383 Newspapers, publishing & printing; news syndicates
HQ: Plain Dealer Publishing Co.
4800 Tiedeman Rd
Cleveland OH 44144
216 999-5000

(G-7320)
PLASKOLITE LLC (PA)
400 W Nationwide Blvd # 400 (43215-2394)
PHONE 614 294-3281
Mitchell P Grindley, *President*
Mark Grindley, *COO*
Jack G Black Jr, *Exec VP*
John Szlag, *Exec VP*
Jeff Bostic, *Vice Pres*
◆ **EMP:** 238 EST: 1950
SQ FT: 650,000
SALES (est): 243.4MM **Privately Held**
WEB: www.plaskolite.com
SIC: 2821 Plastics materials & resins

(G-7321)
PLASKOLITE LLC
Also Called: Retail Display Group
400 W Nationwide Blvd # 400 (43215-2394)
P.O. Box 1497 (43216-1497)
PHONE 614 294-3281
James R Dunn, *Branch Mgr*
EMP: 280
SALES (corp-wide): 243.4MM **Privately Held**
WEB: www.plaskolite.com
SIC: 2821 3083 Acrylic resins; laminated plastics plate & sheet
PA: Plaskolite, Llc
400 W Nationwide Blvd # 400
Columbus OH 43215
614 294-3281

(G-7322)
PLASTIC SELECTION GROUP INC (PA)
Also Called: Psg
692 N High St Ste 310 (43215-1581)
PHONE 614 464-2008
Frank William Dickinson, *President*
Dee Walker, *Opers Staff*
▼ **EMP:** 5
SQ FT: 1,500
SALES (est): 1.3MM **Privately Held**
WEB: www.go2psg.com
SIC: 2821 Plastics materials & resins

(G-7323)
PLASTIC SUPPLIERS INC (PA)
2400 Marilyn Ln (43219-1721)
PHONE 614 471-9100
Peter Driscoll, *Ch of Bd*
George L Thomas, *President*
Erich Emhuff, *Vice Pres*
Edward Tweed, *Research*
Steve H Dudley, *CFO*
◆ **EMP:** 29 EST: 1959
SQ FT: 7,500

SALES (est): 103.2MM **Privately Held**
WEB: www.plasticsuppliers.com
SIC: 3081 Unsupported plastics film & sheet

(G-7324)
PLASTIC SUPPLIERS INC
2400 Marilyn Ln (43219-1721)
PHONE 214 467-3700
Fax: 214 467-3714
EMP: 27
SALES (corp-wide): 103.2MM **Privately Held**
SIC: 3081 Mfg Unsupported Plastic Film/Sheet
PA: Plastic Suppliers, Inc.
2400 Marilyn Ln
Columbus OH 43219
614 471-9100

(G-7325)
PLASTIC SUPPLIERS INC
2400 Marilyn Ln (43219-1721)
P.O. Box 360478 (43236-0478)
PHONE 614 475-8010
Fax: 614 475-0264
EMP: 93
SALES (corp-wide): 93.3MM **Privately Held**
SIC: 3081 Mfg Unsupported Plastic Film/Sheet
PA: Plastic Suppliers, Inc.
2887 Johnstown Rd
Columbus OH 43219
614 471-9100

(G-7326)
PLAZA AT SAWMILL PL
6472 Sawmill Rd (43235)
PHONE 614 889-6121
EMP: 9
SALES (est): 561.8K **Privately Held**
SIC: 2421 Sawmill/Planing Mill

(G-7327)
PLC CONNECTIONS LLC
673 N Wilson Rd (43204-1461)
PHONE 614 279-1796
◆ **EMP:** 15
SQ FT: 7,000
SALES (est): 1.6MM **Privately Held**
SIC: 3229 Mfg Fiber-Optic Components

(G-7328)
PLCC2 LLC
Also Called: PLC Connections
673 N Wilson Rd (43204-1461)
PHONE 614 279-1796
Andy Spector, *General Mgr*
Tadashi Miyashita, *Mng Member*
Michael Obrian,
◆ **EMP:** 8 EST: 2014
SQ FT: 7,000
SALES (est): 608.8K **Privately Held**
SIC: 3678 8711 Electronic connectors; engineering services

(G-7329)
PLOTT GRAPHIC DIRECTIONS INC
859 Harmony Dr (43230-4390)
PHONE 614 475-0217
Elizabeth Plott, *President*
James Galliher, *Vice Pres*
EMP: 8 EST: 1978
SQ FT: 3,500
SALES (est): 500K **Privately Held**
WEB: www.gdi324.com
SIC: 2791 Typesetting, computer controlled

(G-7330)
PMJ PARTNERS LLC
Also Called: Bucktask
281 Lenappe Dr (43214-3171)
PHONE 201 360-1914
Paul Weiss,
EMP: 4
SALES: 50K **Privately Held**
SIC: 7372 7389 Application computer software;

(G-7331)
POLYCEL INCORPORATED
Also Called: Amatech Polycell
1633 Woodland Ave (43219-1135)
PHONE 614 252-2400

David Amatangelo, *Principal*
EMP: 22 EST: 1980
SALES (est): 3.2MM **Privately Held**
WEB: www.polycel-inc.com
SIC: 3086 Packaging & shipping materials, foamed plastic

(G-7332)
POPS PRINTED APPAREL LLC
1758 N High St Unit 2 (43201-4422)
PHONE 614 372-5651
Austin Pence, *Mng Member*
Chad Campagna,
EMP: 6
SQ FT: 2,000
SALES: 200K **Privately Held**
SIC: 2759 Screen printing

(G-7333)
POSM SOFTWARE LLC
4925 Sharon Hill Dr (43235-3451)
PHONE 859 274-0041
Robert Katter, *Principal*
EMP: 7
SALES (est): 463.2K **Privately Held**
SIC: 7372 Prepackaged software

(G-7334)
POWER DISTRIBUTORS LLC (PA)
Also Called: Central Power Systems
3700 Paragon Dr (43228-9750)
PHONE 614 876-3533
Matthew Finn, *President*
Tim Snell, *Manager*
▲ **EMP:** 20
SALES (est): 108.6MM **Privately Held**
SIC: 5084 3524 Engines & parts, air-cooled; lawn & garden equipment; lawn & garden tractors & equipment

(G-7335)
PPAFCO INC
1096 Ridge St (43215-1154)
PHONE 614 488-7259
Laura Bowman, *President*
EMP: 14
SQ FT: 15,000
SALES: 950K **Privately Held**
SIC: 3089 3069 5074 Fittings for pipe, plastic; nipples, rubber; pipes & fittings, plastic

(G-7336)
PPG INDUSTRIES INC
1380 E 5th Ave (43219-2412)
PHONE 614 252-6384
John Tluchowski, *Branch Mgr*
EMP: 6
SALES (corp-wide): 15.3B **Publicly Held**
SIC: 2851 Paints & allied products
PA: Ppg Industries, Inc.
1 Ppg Pl
Pittsburgh PA 15272
412 434-3131

(G-7337)
PPG INDUSTRIES INC
Also Called: PPG 5537
5548 N Hamilton Rd (43230-1322)
PHONE 614 939-2365
Donna Matthews, *Branch Mgr*
EMP: 24
SALES (corp-wide): 15.3B **Publicly Held**
WEB: www.ppg.com
SIC: 2851 Paints & allied products
PA: Ppg Industries, Inc.
1 Ppg Pl
Pittsburgh PA 15272
412 434-3131

(G-7338)
PPG INDUSTRIES INC
Also Called: PPG 5404
2840 N High St (43202-1102)
PHONE 614 268-2609
Robert Seagle, *Branch Mgr*
EMP: 24
SALES (corp-wide): 15.3B **Publicly Held**
WEB: www.ppg.com
SIC: 2851 Paints & allied products
PA: Ppg Industries, Inc.
1 Ppg Pl
Pittsburgh PA 15272
412 434-3131

(G-7339)
PPG INDUSTRIES INC
Also Called: P P G Refinishing Group
777 Dearborn Park Ln C (43085-5716)
PHONE 614 846-3128
John Sutherland, *Manager*
EMP: 3
SALES (corp-wide): 15.3B **Publicly Held**
SIC: 2851 Paints & allied products
PA: Ppg Industries, Inc.
1 Ppg Pl
Pittsburgh PA 15272
412 434-3131

(G-7340)
PR SIGNS & SERVICE
3049 E 14th Ave (43219-2356)
PHONE 614 252-7090
Philip Radke, *Principal*
EMP: 5
SALES (est): 443.9K **Privately Held**
SIC: 3993 Electric signs

(G-7341)
PRAXAIR DISTRIBUTION INC
450 Greenlawn Ave (43223-2611)
PHONE 614 443-7687
Pratt Thompson, *Manager*
EMP: 19 **Privately Held**
SIC: 2813 Industrial gases
HQ: Praxair Distribution, Inc.
10 Riverview Dr
Danbury CT 06810
203 837-2000

(G-7342)
PRECISION APPLIED COATINGS
3021 E 4th Ave Ste B (43219-2888)
PHONE 614 252-8711
Michael R Gramke,
Scott J Gramke,
Tadd D Gruenewald,
▲ **EMP:** 7
SALES (est): 605K **Privately Held**
SIC: 3479 Painting, coating & hot dipping

(G-7343)
PREFERRED SOFT SOLUTIONS LLC
2906 Kool Air Way (43231-7655)
PHONE 614 975-2750
William T Nixon,
EMP: 3
SALES (est): 137K **Privately Held**
SIC: 7372 Prepackaged software

(G-7344)
PREISSER INC
Also Called: PIP Printing
3560 Millikin Ct Ste A (43228-9765)
P.O. Box 827, Dublin (43017-6827)
PHONE 614 345-0199
Gail Preisser, *President*
Thomas Preisser, *Corp Secy*
Ellen Sax, *Vice Pres*
EMP: 20 EST: 1974
SALES (est): 4.6MM **Privately Held**
SIC: 2752 2791 Commercial printing, offset; typesetting

(G-7345)
PRESS CHEMICAL & PHRM LAB
2700 E Main St Ste 102 (43209-2536)
P.O. Box 9103 (43209-0103)
PHONE 614 863-2802
Pearson Press, *President*
Phea Press, *Corp Secy*
Paul Wherry, *Vice Pres*
EMP: 3
SQ FT: 600
SALES (est): 320K **Privately Held**
SIC: 2819 2833 Industrial inorganic chemicals; organic medicinal chemicals: bulk, uncompounded

(G-7346)
PRESTRESS SERVICES INDS LLC (PA)
2250 N Hartford Ave (43222)
P.O. Box 55436, Lexington KY (40555-5436)
PHONE 859 299-0461
Martin Cohen, *Mng Member*
Barry Barger,
Greg Harville,

Columbus - Franklin County (G-7347)

Richard Hudnall,
EMP: 250
SALES (est): 91.7MM **Privately Held**
SIC: 3272 Concrete products

(G-7347)
PRIME EQUIPMENT GROUP INC
Also Called: Diversfied Mch Pdts Gnsvlle GA
2000 E Fulton St (43205-2534)
PHONE 614 253-8590
Joseph Gasbarro, *President*
Kirk Reis, *Research*
Geoff Moss, *Engineer*
Martin Knowles, *Design Engr*
Carol Finch, *CFO*
◆ **EMP:** 100
SALES (est): 47MM **Privately Held**
WEB: www.primeequipmentgroup.com
SIC: 3556 Poultry processing machinery

(G-7348)
PRINT SYNDICATE INC
1275 Kinnear Rd (43212-1180)
PHONE 614 657-8318
EMP: 4
SALES (est): 398.9K **Privately Held**
SIC: 2752 Commercial printing, lithographic

(G-7349)
PRINT SYNDICATE LLC
901 W 3rd Ave Ste A (43212-3131)
PHONE 614 519-0341
Jarred Mullins, *Manager*
Richard Kim, *Officer*
EMP: 15
SALES (est): 2.6MM **Privately Held**
SIC: 2752 Commercial printing, lithographic

(G-7350)
PRINTED IMAGE
Also Called: The Printed Image
41 S Grant Ave (43215-3979)
PHONE 614 221-1412
Cathleen Siech, *President*
Vicki Hamer, *Vice Pres*
Karen Norton, *Marketing Staff*
EMP: 10
SALES (est): 1.4MM **Privately Held**
WEB: www.printedimage.com
SIC: 2752 2791 2789 Commercial printing, offset; typesetting; bookbinding & related work

(G-7351)
PRO PRINTING INC
4191 W Broad St (43228-1651)
PHONE 614 276-8366
Sherri Sykes, *President*
Danielle Slone, *Sales Associate*
EMP: 5
SALES (est): 706.1K **Privately Held**
SIC: 2752 Commercial printing, offset

(G-7352)
PROCESS MACHINERY INC
860 Kaderly Dr (43228-1034)
PHONE 614 278-1055
Rose Savage, *Branch Mgr*
EMP: 23
SALES (corp-wide): 29.9MM **Privately Held**
SIC: 3569 Filters
PA: Process Machinery, Inc.
1636 Isaac Shelby Dr
Shelbyville KY 40065
502 633-5665

(G-7353)
PROFILE IMAGING COLUMBUS LLC
Also Called: Profile Discovery
46 N High St Ste 200 (43215-3010)
PHONE 614 222-2888
Larry Kotterman, *President*
Linda F Wong, *Opers Staff*
Andrew Keck, *Info Tech Dir*
EMP: 3 **EST:** 2005
SALES (est): 462.1K **Privately Held**
SIC: 7372 Prepackaged software

(G-7354)
PROFORM GROUP INC
1715 Georgesville Rd (43228-3619)
PHONE 614 332-9654
Joe Vannata, *Branch Mgr*
EMP: 42
SALES (corp-wide): 57.6MM **Privately Held**
SIC: 3713 Truck bodies (motor vehicles)
PA: Proform Group, Inc.
4400 Don Cayo Dr
Muskogee OK 74403
918 682-8666

(G-7355)
PROVIDENCE REES INC
2111 Builders Pl (43204-4886)
P.O. Box 12535 (43212-0535)
PHONE 614 833-6231
Leo Steger, *Corp Secy*
Billy Parsley, *Corp Secy*
Lee Nichols, *Production*
EMP: 35
SQ FT: 36,000
SALES: 4.7MM **Privately Held**
SIC: 3496 8711 Wire winding; engineering services

(G-7356)
PUBLISHING GROUP LTD
781 Northwest Blvd # 202 (43212-3874)
PHONE 614 572-1240
Chuck Steie, *CEO*
Chuck Stein, *CEO*
Dave Prosser, *President*
Garth Bishop, *Editor*
Kathy Gillis, *Vice Pres*
EMP: 10
SALES: 1.5MM **Privately Held**
WEB: www.pubgroupltd.com
SIC: 2721 7389 2741 5199 Magazines: publishing & printing; trade journals: publishing & printing; trade show arrangement; art copy: publishing & printing; advertising specialties

(G-7357)
PUREBRED PUBLISHING INC
1224 Alton Darby Creek Rd C (43228-9813)
PHONE 614 339-5393
Douglas Granitz, *CEO*
John Mocier, *President*
Seph Johnson, *General Mgr*
Seth Spencer, *Vice Pres*
EMP: 5
SALES (est): 393.4K
SALES (corp-wide): 870.5K **Privately Held**
WEB: www.brownswissusa.com
SIC: 2741 Miscellaneous publishing
PA: American Guernsey Association
1224 Alton Darby Creek Rd
Columbus OH 43228
614 864-2409

(G-7358)
PYRAMID INDUSTRIES LLC
2825 Booty Dr (43207-4681)
PHONE 614 783-1543
Eric Joyner, *Principal*
EMP: 10
SALES (est): 613.6K **Privately Held**
SIC: 3999 Manufacturing industries

(G-7359)
Q T COLUMBUS LLC
1330 Stimmel Rd (43223-2917)
PHONE 800 758-2410
Daniel Root, *President*
Dave Root, *Treasurer*
EMP: 6
SALES (est): 636.1K **Privately Held**
WEB: www.qtequipment.com
SIC: 7532 5531 3713 Body shop, trucks; automotive tires; utility truck bodies
PA: Q.T. Equipment Company
151 W Dartmore Ave
Akron OH 44301

(G-7360)
QLEANAIR SCANDINAVIA INC
941 Medinah Ter (43235-5028)
PHONE 614 323-1756
Bradley Ballantine, *President*
▲ **EMP:** 5
SALES (est): 424.7K **Privately Held**
SIC: 3822 7389 Building services monitoring controls, automatic;

(G-7361)
QPI MULTIPRESS INC
370 S 5th St Ste 2 (43215-5433)
PHONE 614 228-0185
Richard Drexler, *CEO*
Theodore P Schwartz, *President*
TAC Kensler, *CFO*
EMP: 7
SQ FT: 55,000
SALES (est): 1.1MM
SALES (corp-wide): 24MM **Privately Held**
WEB: www.quality-products.com
SIC: 3542 Presses: hydraulic & pneumatic, mechanical & manual
PA: Quality Products, Inc.
1 Air Cargo Pkwy E
Swanton OH 43558
614 228-0185

(G-7362)
QUADRA - TECH INC
864 E Jenkins Ave (43207-1317)
PHONE 614 445-0690
Alan Wasserstrom, *CEO*
John H McCormick, *President*
Howard Hickman, *Data Proc Staff*
EMP: 85
SQ FT: 125,000
SALES (est): 13.7MM
SALES (corp-wide): 824.5MM **Privately Held**
WEB: www.quadra-techinc.com
SIC: 2599 Carts, restaurant equipment
PA: The Wasserstrom Company
4500 E Broad St
Columbus OH 43213
614 228-6525

(G-7363)
QUALCO LLC
2211 S James Rd (43232-3852)
PHONE 614 257-7408
Michael Gibbs,
EMP: 3 **EST:** 2004
SQ FT: 12,000
SALES (est): 410K **Privately Held**
SIC: 2542 Fixtures: display, office or store: except wood

(G-7364)
QUALITY BAKERY COMPANY INC
Also Called: Mountain Top Frozen Pies Div
50 N Glenwood Ave (43222-1206)
P.O. Box 453 (43216)
PHONE 614 224-1424
Jeff Waller, *Manager*
EMP: 50
SQ FT: 32,836
SALES (corp-wide): 1.2B **Publicly Held**
WEB: www.marzetti.com
SIC: 2051 Bread, cake & related products
HQ: The Quality Bakery Company Inc
380 Polaris Pkwy Ste 400
Westerville OH 43082
614 816 2232

(G-7365)
QUALITY RUBBER STAMP INC
3314 Refugee Rd (43232-4810)
PHONE 614 235-2700
John J Lawler, *President*
EMP: 8 **EST:** 1971
SQ FT: 4,000
SALES: 900K **Privately Held**
WEB: www.qualityrubberstamp.com
SIC: 3953 3083 2396 2395 Numbering stamps, hand: rubber or metal; plastic finished products, laminated; screen printing on fabric articles; embroidery & art needlework; emblems, embroidered; platemaking services

(G-7366)
QUALITY STITCH EMBROIDERY INC
4300 E Main St (43213-3033)
PHONE 614 237-0480
Steve Fowler, *President*
EMP: 5
SQ FT: 1,500
SALES: 250K **Privately Held**
WEB: www.quality-stitch.com
SIC: 2395 Embroidery products, except schiffli machine

(G-7367)
QUALITY-SERVICE PRODUCTS INC
528 E Hudson St (43202-2766)
PHONE 614 447-9522
Nelson N Jeck Sr, *CEO*
Nelson N Jeck Jr, *President*
Jo Ann Jeck, *Corp Secy*
EMP: 11
SQ FT: 8,200
SALES (est): 1.8MM **Privately Held**
SIC: 3085 Plastics bottles

(G-7368)
QUICKSTITCH PLUS LLC
124 Granville St (43230-3043)
PHONE 614 476-3186
Michele Uber, *Principal*
Scott Uber, *Sales Staff*
EMP: 4
SALES (est): 372.3K **Privately Held**
SIC: 2395 Embroidery products, except schiffli machine

(G-7369)
QUIKRETE COMPANIES INC
Also Called: THE QUIKRETE COMPANIES INC
6225 Huntley Rd (43229-1005)
PHONE 614 885-4406
Robert Miller, *Branch Mgr*
Wendy Henry, *Manager*
EMP: 35
SQ FT: 10,000 **Privately Held**
WEB: www.quikrete.com
SIC: 3272 3241 2899 Dry mixture concrete; cement, hydraulic; chemical preparations
HQ: The Quikrete Companies Llc
5 Concourse Pkwy Ste 1900
Atlanta GA 30328
404 634-9100

(G-7370)
R & J BARDON INC
4676 Larwell Dr (43220-3621)
PHONE 614 457-5500
Chris Swearingen, *President*
Leslie Swearingen, *Vice Pres*
EMP: 9
SQ FT: 3,000
SALES: 850K **Privately Held**
SIC: 2752 Commercial printing, offset

(G-7371)
R & S MONITIONS INC
181 Rosslyn Ave (43214-1474)
PHONE 614 846-0597
Ron Herman, *President*
Sherry Herman, *Vice Pres*
EMP: 6
SALES (oct): 544.4K **Privately Held**
SIC: 3482 5941 Small arms ammunition; firearms

(G-7372)
R D COOK COMPANY LLC
Also Called: Cook, R D Company
883 E Hudson St (43211-1163)
PHONE 614 262-0550
Robert Cook,
▲ **EMP:** 5
SQ FT: 10,000
SALES: 750K **Privately Held**
WEB: www.robmcook.com
SIC: 2541 2511 Cabinets, except refrigerated: show, display, etc.: wood; counters or counter display cases, wood; wood household furniture

(G-7373)
R D LUCKY LLC
Also Called: Cold Stone Creamery
5336 Shiloh Dr (43220-5920)
PHONE 614 570-8005
Qing Ye, *Mng Member*
EMP: 10
SALES (est): 283.4K **Privately Held**
SIC: 2024 Ice cream & frozen desserts

GEOGRAPHIC SECTION
Columbus - Franklin County (G-7404)

(G-7374)
R DESIGN & PRINTING CO
30 E 4th Ave (43201-3502)
PHONE..................614 299-1420
David Ramirez, *CEO*
Juli Rogers, *President*
EMP: 4
SALES (est): 656.6K **Privately Held**
SIC: 2752 Commercial printing, offset

(G-7375)
RADON BE GONE INC
4319 Indianola Ave (43214-2220)
PHONE..................614 268-4440
Bill Dzackowitz, *President*
EMP: 3
SALES (est): 262.7K **Privately Held**
SIC: 3564 Air cleaning systems

(G-7376)
RAIL ROAD CORPORATION
Also Called: North Fork Southern
4881 Trabue Rd (43228-9613)
PHONE..................614 771-2102
Ron Pauly, *Manager*
EMP: 5
SALES (est): 234.9K **Privately Held**
SIC: 3743 Train cars & equipment, freight or passenger

(G-7377)
RAM PRODUCTS INC
1091 Stimmel Rd (43223-2911)
PHONE..................614 443-4634
John Pelleriti, *President*
Richard Dawson, *Vice Pres*
Anne Pelleriti, *Treasurer*
EMP: 12
SQ FT: 8,000
SALES (est): 1.9MM **Privately Held**
SIC: 3542 Presses: hydraulic & pneumatic, mechanical & manual; presses: forming, stamping, punching, sizing (machine tools)

(G-7378)
RAPID MR INTERNATIONAL LLC
1500 Lake Shore Dr # 310 (43204-3936)
PHONE..................614 486-6300
Dania Parsons, *Manager*
Ulrike Haase,
EMP: 7
SALES (est): 550K **Privately Held**
WEB: www.rapidmri.com
SIC: 3677 Electronic coils, transformers & other inductors

(G-7379)
RAY RIESER TROPHY CO
3852 Sullivant Ave (43228-2125)
PHONE..................614 279-1128
Freddie Rieser, *Owner*
EMP: 4
SQ FT: 2,500
SALES (est): 250K **Privately Held**
SIC: 5999 3499 Trophies & plaques; trophies, metal, except silver

(G-7380)
RED BARAKUDA LLC
4439 Shoupmill Dr (43230-1489)
PHONE..................614 596-5432
Isaiah Wambari,
EMP: 7
SALES (est): 443.6K **Privately Held**
SIC: 3949 7389 Flies, fishing: artificial;

(G-7381)
RED TIE GROUP INC
2272 S High St (43207-2432)
PHONE..................614 443-9100
Kevin Preston, *Manager*
EMP: 6
SALES (corp-wide): 155.8MM **Privately Held**
WEB: www.bsink.com
SIC: 2893 5085 Printing ink; ink, printers'
HQ: Red Tie Group, Inc.
3650 E 93rd St
Cleveland OH 44105
216 271-2300

(G-7382)
REDI-QUIK SIGNS INC
123 E Spring St (43215-2516)
PHONE..................614 228-6641
Larry Rausch, *CEO*
Millard Draudt, *President*
Skip Rausch, *President*
David Rausch, *Treasurer*
EMP: 3
SALES (est): 360.8K **Privately Held**
WEB: www.rediquik.com
SIC: 3993 Signs, not made in custom sign painting shops

(G-7383)
REGAL SPRING CO
2140 Eakin Rd Ste J (43223-6258)
PHONE..................614 278-7761
Robert Forby, *Owner*
EMP: 5
SQ FT: 22,000
SALES (est): 379.1K **Privately Held**
SIC: 3495 Wire springs

(G-7384)
REGALIA PRODUCTS INC
2117 S High St (43207-2428)
PHONE..................614 579-8399
Kenneth Gay, *Principal*
Jeffery Ferguson, *Principal*
EMP: 4 **EST:** 2013
SALES (est): 311.2K **Privately Held**
SIC: 2541 Store & office display cases & fixtures

(G-7385)
RENITE COMPANY
Also Called: Renite Lubrication Engineers
2500 E 5th Ave (43219-2700)
P.O. Box 30830 (43230-0830)
PHONE..................800 883-7876
Stephen M Halliday, *Ch of Bd*
Eugene F Cook, *Vice Pres*
Leo L Harding, *VP Sales*
Francis E Cook, *Admin Sec*
EMP: 15
SALES (est): 3.7MM **Privately Held**
WEB: www.renite.com
SIC: 2992 3569 Oils & greases, blending & compounding; lubrication equipment, industrial

(G-7386)
RESEARCH AND DEVELOPMENT GROUP
Also Called: R & D Group
1208 E Hudson St (43211-1308)
PHONE..................614 261-0454
John Wells, *President*
Martha Wells, *Admin Sec*
EMP: 4
SQ FT: 3,200
SALES (est): 75K **Privately Held**
SIC: 2741 2759 Miscellaneous publishing; commercial printing

(G-7387)
RESILIENT HOLDINGS INC
Also Called: Magnum Press
6155 Huntley Rd Ste F (43229-1096)
PHONE..................614 847-5600
David G Umbreit, *Principal*
Douglas J Conley, *Principal*
EMP: 10
SALES (est): 1.5MM **Privately Held**
WEB: www.theinkwell-worthington.com
SIC: 2752 Commercial printing, lithographic

(G-7388)
RESOLUTE FP US INC
Also Called: Recycling Div
995 Marion Rd (43207-2557)
PHONE..................614 443-6300
Sylvain-Yves Longval, *Owner*
EMP: 434
SALES (corp-wide): 3.5B **Privately Held**
WEB: www.bowater.com
SIC: 2621 Paper mills
HQ: Resolute Fp Us Inc.
5300 Cureton Ferry Rd
Catawba SC 29704
803 981-5000

(G-7389)
RESOURCE FUELS LLC (PA)
41 S High St Ste 3750s (43215-3406)
PHONE..................614 221-0101
Brian Murphy, *CFO*
Donald J Drabant, *Mng Member*
EMP: 5 **EST:** 1998
SQ FT: 3,000
SALES (est): 1.3MM **Privately Held**
SIC: 1241 Coal mining services

(G-7390)
REWORK FURNISHINGS LLC
1271 Edgehill Rd Bldg B (43212-3123)
PHONE..................614 300-5021
Alex Remley,
EMP: 12
SALES (est): 750K **Privately Held**
SIC: 3499 2499 Fabricated metal products; wood products

(G-7391)
REX AUTOMATION INC
2211 Aspenwood Ln (43235-2756)
PHONE..................614 766-4672
John Rex, *President*
Merle Rex, *Admin Sec*
EMP: 4
SQ FT: 1,425
SALES (est): 430K **Privately Held**
SIC: 3625 Relays & industrial controls

(G-7392)
RICHARDS AND SIMMONS INC
33 W Schreyer Pl (43214-2615)
PHONE..................614 268-3909
Thomas Simmons, *President*
EMP: 3
SALES (est): 336.7K **Privately Held**
SIC: 2671 5999 Plastic film, coated or laminated for packaging; packaging materials: boxes, padding, etc.

(G-7393)
RICKLY HYDROLOGICAL CO
1700 Joyce Ave (43219-1026)
PHONE..................614 297-9877
Michael Rickly, *Owner*
Steve Clark, *Prgrmr*
Josh Fultz, *Prgrmr*
EMP: 24
SALES (est): 3.9MM **Privately Held**
SIC: 3823 Industrial process measurement equipment

(G-7394)
RICKLY HYDROLOGICAL COMPANY
1700 Joyce Ave (43219-1026)
PHONE..................614 297-9877
Michael Rickly, *President*
Jerry Morrison, *Sales Staff*
William H Rickly, *Admin Sec*
EMP: 6
SQ FT: 5,200
SALES (est): 600K **Privately Held**
WEB: www.rickly.com
SIC: 3829 Gauging instruments, thickness ultrasonic

(G-7395)
RIMROCK HOLDINGS CORPORATION (HQ)
1700 Jetway Blvd (43219-1675)
PHONE..................614 471-5926
Tom Dejong, *President*
EMP: 50
SALES (est): 15.3MM
SALES (corp-wide): 3B **Publicly Held**
SIC: 3563 3569 3443 3541 Spraying outfits: metals, paints & chemicals (compressor); robots, assembly line: industrial & commercial; ladles, metal plate; machine tools, metal cutting type
PA: Lincoln Electric Holdings, Inc.
22801 Saint Clair Ave
Cleveland OH 44117
216 481-8100

(G-7396)
RJM STAMPING CO
1641 Universal Rd (43207-1704)
PHONE..................614 443-1191
Laura L Lloyd, *President*
Floyd Lloyd, *Vice Pres*
EMP: 12
SQ FT: 9,016
SALES (est): 1MM **Privately Held**
WEB: www.rjmstamping.com
SIC: 3469 Stamping metal for the trade

(G-7397)
RNM HOLDINGS INC
2350 Refugee Park (43207-2173)
PHONE..................614 444-5556
Matt Milton, *President*
EMP: 11 **Privately Held**
SIC: 7353 5084 3536 Cranes & aerial lift equipment, rental or leasing; cranes, industrial; hoists; cranes, overhead traveling; cranes & monorail systems; cranes, industrial plant
PA: Rnm Holdings, Inc.
550 Conover Dr
Franklin OH 45005

(G-7398)
ROADSAFE TRAFFIC SYSTEMS INC
1350 Stimmel Rd (43223-2917)
PHONE..................614 274-9782
Steve Fisher, *Manager*
EMP: 6 **Privately Held**
SIC: 3531 Construction machinery
PA: Roadsafe Traffic Systems, Inc.
8750 W Bryn Mawr Ave
Chicago IL 60631

(G-7399)
ROBEY TOOL & MACHINE
1593 E 5th Ave (43219-2572)
PHONE..................614 251-0412
Wilbur N Robey, *Owner*
EMP: 5
SQ FT: 5,500
SALES (est): 7.2MM **Privately Held**
SIC: 3599 Machine shop, jobbing & repair; machine & other job shop work

(G-7400)
RONS TEXSTYLES LLC
457 Thorburn Pl (43230-6847)
PHONE..................513 936-9975
Ron Melser, *Owner*
EMP: 3
SQ FT: 400
SALES (est): 500K **Privately Held**
SIC: 2326 5023 Work uniforms; linens, table

(G-7401)
ROOF DIE TOOL & MACHINE INC
2000 S High St (43207-2425)
PHONE..................614 444-6253
Robert L Roof, *President*
Margaret Roof, *Treasurer*
EMP: 4
SQ FT: 6,000
SALES (est): 350K **Privately Held**
SIC: 3599 Machine shop, jobbing & repair

(G-7402)
ROSE PRODUCTS AND SERVICES INC
545 Stimmel Rd (43223-2901)
PHONE..................614 443-7647
Robert Roth, *President*
EMP: 50 **EST:** 1926
SQ FT: 50,000
SALES (est): 7.9MM **Privately Held**
SIC: 5087 2842 Janitors' supplies; specialty cleaning preparations

(G-7403)
ROXANE LABORATORIES
1900 Arlingate Ln (43228-4112)
PHONE..................614 276-4000
Chris Boneham, *Principal*
EMP: 8 **EST:** 2010
SALES (est): 775.9K **Privately Held**
SIC: 2834 Pharmaceutical preparations

(G-7404)
ROY L BAYES
Also Called: Bayes, Roy Products
1593 Harrisburg Pike (43223-3611)
PHONE..................614 274-6729
Roy L Bayes, *Owner*
EMP: 3
SQ FT: 8,000
SALES (est): 182.8K **Privately Held**
SIC: 2541 5091 Showcases, except refrigerated: wood; sporting & recreation goods

Columbus - Franklin County (G-7405)

(G-7405)
RTZ MANUFACTURING CO
6530 Huntley Rd (43229-1012)
P.O. Box 289, Worthington (43085-0289)
PHONE 614 848-8366
Zoe Rosser, *President*
Ty Rosser, *Vice Pres*
Ty R Rosser, *Manager*
EMP: 9
SQ FT: 3,000
SALES: 900K **Privately Held**
SIC: 3599 Custom machinery

(G-7406)
RUBBERITE CORP
Also Called: Rubberite Cypress Sponge
1575 Frebis Ln (43206-3319)
PHONE 832 457-0654
Russell Miller, *Manager*
EMP: 4
SALES (corp-wide): 2.1MM **Privately Held**
SIC: 3069 Molded rubber products
PA: Rubberite Corp.
301 Goetz Ave
Santa Ana CA 92707
714 546-6464

(G-7407)
RUTLAND PLASTIC TECH INC
777 Dearborn Park Ln N (43085-5716)
PHONE 614 846-3055
Guy Lewis, *Manager*
EMP: 5 **Publicly Held**
WEB: www.rutlandinc.com
SIC: 3087 3089 2759 Custom compound purchased resins; plastic processing; screen printing
HQ: Rutland Group, Inc.
10021 Rodney St
Pineville NC 28134

(G-7408)
RUTOBO INC
Also Called: Allegra Print & Imaging
4279 E Main St (43213-3032)
PHONE 614 236-2948
Tom Boder, *CEO*
Brad Alexander, *Manager*
EMP: 5
SQ FT: 2,800
SALES (est): 517.5K **Privately Held**
SIC: 2752 Commercial printing, offset

(G-7409)
RXPERT CONSULTANTS LLC
4719 Reed Rd Ste 250 (43220-3051)
PHONE 614 579-9384
EMP: 5
SALES (est): 204.5K **Privately Held**
SIC: 2011 8748 Meat Packing Plant Business Consulting Services

(G-7410)
S BECKMAN PRINT & G
Also Called: Beckman Xmo
376 Morrison Rd Ste D (43213-1447)
PHONE 614 864-2232
Tracy Beckman, *President*
EMP: 21
SQ FT: 4,100
SALES (est): 3.3MM **Privately Held**
WEB: www.sbeckmanprint.com
SIC: 2752 Commercial printing, offset

(G-7411)
S&S SIGN SERVICE
485 Ternstedt Ln (43228-2128)
PHONE 614 279-9722
Robert Sherry, *CEO*
EMP: 6
SALES (est): 651.7K **Privately Held**
SIC: 3993 Signs & advertising specialties

(G-7412)
SAFECOR HEALTH LLC (PA)
Also Called: R S C
4060 Business Park Dr B (43204-5046)
PHONE 781 933-8780
Hilary Schnieders, *Opers Spvr*
Susan Blatti, *QC Mgr*
Steve Schneider, *Info Tech Dir*
Stephen Fischbach,
Ryan O'Dell,
EMP: 10
SALES (est): 24.4MM **Privately Held**
SIC: 7389 2834 Packaging & labeling services; pharmaceutical preparations

(G-7413)
SAFELITE GROUP INC (HQ)
Also Called: Safelite Autoglass
7400 Safelite Way (43235-5086)
P.O. Box 182827 (43218-2827)
PHONE 614 210-9000
Thomas Feeney, *CEO*
Michelle Beiter, *President*
Paul Groves, *President*
Kerry Hurff, *President*
Brett Decker, *General Mgr*
▲ **EMP:** 1000
SALES (est): 930MM
SALES (corp-wide): 2.6MM **Privately Held**
WEB: www.safelitegroup.com
SIC: 7536 3231 6411 Automotive glass replacement shops; windshields, glass: made from purchased glass; insurance claim processing, except medical
PA: D'im Sa
Rue Guillaume Kroll 12
Luxembourg 1882
274 788-60

(G-7414)
SAFEWHITE INC
1275 Kinnear Rd Ste 237 (43212-1180)
PHONE 614 340-1450
Ray Shealy, *President*
Mark Shary, *Chairman*
Alan Fermier, *Vice Pres*
Ada Sierraalta, *Opers Staff*
Gary Musso, *Security Dir*
EMP: 5
SQ FT: 500
SALES (est): 928.7K **Privately Held**
SIC: 2836 Biological products, except diagnostic

(G-7415)
SALEM MANUFACTURING AND SALES
Also Called: Salem Industries
171 N Hamilton Rd (43213-1300)
PHONE 614 572-4242
W Thomas Goble, *President*
EMP: 6
SQ FT: 5,000
SALES (est): 864.9K **Privately Held**
SIC: 3599 Machine shop, jobbing & repair

(G-7416)
SALINDIA LLC
2756 Eastland Mall (43232-4901)
PHONE 614 501-4799
Afsal Koya, *Principal*
EMP: 7
SALES (est): 38.9K **Privately Held**
SIC: 2389 Men's miscellaneous accessories

(G-7417)
SALSBURY INDUSTRIES INC
2300 Rickenbacker Pkwy (43217-5001)
PHONE 614 409-1600
Jeff Blosser, *President*
EMP: 116
SALES (corp-wide): 73.9MM **Privately Held**
SIC: 3444 Mail (post office) collection or storage boxes, sheet metal
PA: Salsbury Industries, Inc.
18300 Central Ave
Carson CA 90746
323 846-6700

(G-7418)
SAMMY S AUTO DETAIL
3514 Cleveland Ave (43224-2908)
PHONE 614 263-2728
Sam Cavin, *CEO*
EMP: 10
SALES (est): 971.1K **Privately Held**
SIC: 3589 7538 Car washing machinery; general automotive repair shops

(G-7419)
SAMSON
772 N High St Ste 101 (43215-1457)
PHONE 614 504-8038
Nicholas Dwane Starns, *Principal*
EMP: 3 **EST:** 2015
SALES (est): 170.1K **Privately Held**
SIC: 2326 Men's & boys' work clothing

(G-7420)
SANDVIK INC
Also Called: Sandvik Hyperion
6325 Huntley Rd (43229-1007)
PHONE 614 438-6579
Brenton Way, *Editor*
Greg Knisley, *Engineer*
Steve Chadwick, *Manager*
EMP: 14
SALES (corp-wide): 10.7B **Privately Held**
SIC: 3316 Strip steel, cold-rolled: from purchased hot-rolled
HQ: Sandvik, Inc.
17-02 Nevins Rd
Fair Lawn NJ 07410
201 794-5000

(G-7421)
SAT WELDING LLC
308 N Burgess Ave (43204-3308)
PHONE 614 747-2641
Schtt Thompson, *Principal*
EMP: 3 **EST:** 2016
SALES (est): 30.3K **Privately Held**
SIC: 7692 Welding repair

(G-7422)
SAVKO PLASTIC PIPE & FITTINGS
Also Called: Bath & Brass Emporium The
683 E Lincoln Ave (43229-5021)
PHONE 614 885-8420
Chuck Savko, *President*
Andrew C Puskas, *President*
Lindo Spinosi, *Vice Pres*
EMP: 13
SQ FT: 9,000
SALES (est): 2.5MM **Privately Held**
WEB: www.savko.com
SIC: 3084 5719 5074 Plastics pipe; bath accessories; plumbing & hydronic heating supplies

(G-7423)
SAWMILL CROSSING
6700 Allister Way (43235-7913)
PHONE 614 766-1685
Jennifer Harrison, *Principal*
EMP: 3
SALES (est): 261.9K **Privately Held**
SIC: 2421 Sawmills & planing mills, general

(G-7424)
SAWMILL EYE ASSOCIATES INC
6500 Sawmill Rd (43235-4942)
PHONE 614 734-2685
Scott P Caleodis, *Principal*
EMP: 3
SALES (est): 277.5K **Privately Held**
SIC: 2421 Sawmills & planing mills, general

(G-7425)
SCHELL SCENIC STUDIO INC
841 S Front St 843 (43206-2578)
PHONE 614 444-9550
Gustav Schell, *President*
Philip G Schell, *Vice Pres*
Lance Jones, *Manager*
Ed Twynham, *Manager*
Don Burkey, *Technology*
EMP: 7
SQ FT: 20,000
SALES (est): 750K **Privately Held**
WEB: www.schellscenic.com
SIC: 3999 7922 Theatrical scenery; scenery rental, theatrical

(G-7426)
SCHODORF TRUCK BODY & EQP CO
885 Harmon Ave (43223-2411)
P.O. Box 23322 (43223-0322)
PHONE 614 228-6793
Joe Schodorf, *President*
Paul F Schodorf, *Vice Pres*
Mattday Schodorfwinches, *Parts Mgr*
Paul Schodorf, *VP Sales*
EMP: 40
SQ FT: 52,000
SALES (est): 10.3MM **Privately Held**
WEB: www.schodorftruck.com
SIC: 5012 3713 3211 Truck bodies; truck bodies (motor vehicles); flat glass

(G-7427)
SCHOLZ & EY ENGRAVERS INC
1558 Parsons Ave (43207-1252)
PHONE 614 444-8052
Kevin Scholz, *President*
Stephen Scholz, *Principal*
EMP: 13 **EST:** 1950
SQ FT: 3,100
SALES: 425K **Privately Held**
SIC: 3479 5947 5094 5199 Engraving jewelry silverware, or metal; name plates: engraved, etched, etc.; gift shop; jewelry; gifts & novelties

(G-7428)
SCHOOL PRIDE LIMITED
3511 Johnny Appleseed Ct (43231-4985)
PHONE 614 568-0697
Daren Brown, *President*
Christopher Blakely, *Production*
Damien Coakley, *Manager*
Phil Foreman, *Graphic Designe*
Janet Brown,
EMP: 30
SALES (est): 2.3MM **Privately Held**
WEB: www.schoolpride.com
SIC: 2399 Banners, pennants & flags

(G-7429)
SCI ENGINEERED MATERIALS INC
2839 Charter St (43228-4607)
PHONE 614 486-0261
Daniel Rooney, *Ch of Bd*
Michael K Barna, *Vice Pres*
Elizabeth Heaston, *Purchasing*
Gerald S Blaskie, *CFO*
Gerald Blaskie, *CFO*
EMP: 24
SQ FT: 32,000
SALES: 11.3MM **Privately Held**
WEB: www.superconductivecomp.com
SIC: 3674 Semiconductors & related devices

(G-7430)
SCIOTO CERAMIC PRODUCTS INC
854 Curleys Ct (43235-2161)
PHONE 614 436-0405
Patrick J Langdale, *President*
James D Roullard, *Vice Pres*
EMP: 45
SQ FT: 48,000
SALES (est): 3.6MM **Privately Held**
SIC: 3299 Ceramic fiber

(G-7431)
SCIOTO READYMIX CO
1500 Williams Rd (43207-5108)
PHONE 614 491-0773
Ken Bolen, *Principal*
EMP: 3
SALES (est): 316.1K **Privately Held**
SIC: 3273 Ready-mixed concrete

(G-7432)
SCORECARDS UNLIMITED LLC
Also Called: Golf Dsign Srecards Unlimited
6334 Huntley Rd (43229-1008)
PHONE 614 885-0796
Susan Siegrist, *Sales Mgr*
Paul Filing, *Mng Member*
Brian Miller, *Manager*
EMP: 8
SALES (est): 890K **Privately Held**
WEB: www.golfdesign.com
SIC: 2752 Commercial printing, offset

(G-7433)
SCREEN PRINTING SHOW HOUSE
853 N Nelson Rd (43219-2732)
PHONE 614 252-2202
Joseph A Call, *President*
James B Call, *Vice Pres*
EMP: 5 **EST:** 1967
SQ FT: 7,000
SALES: 663K **Privately Held**
SIC: 2759 Screen printing

GEOGRAPHIC SECTION
Columbus - Franklin County (G-7463)

(G-7434)
SCRIPTEL CORPORATION
2174 Dividend Dr (43228-3806)
PHONE.................614 276-8402
Wayne Barphel, *President*
Robert Kable, *Principal*
Kristal Scott, *Manager*
▲ **EMP:** 17
SALES (est): 4.1MM **Privately Held**
SIC: 3577 Computer peripheral equipment
PA: Sutisoft, Inc.
 4984 El Camino Real Ste 2
 Los Altos CA 94022
 650 969-7884

(G-7435)
SEALANT SOLUTIONS
947 E Johnstown Rd (43230-1851)
PHONE.................614 599-8000
Donald McDaniels, *Principal*
EMP: 4
SALES (est): 271.1K **Privately Held**
SIC: 2891 Sealants

(G-7436)
SEEKIRK INC
2420 Scioto Harper Dr (43204-3480)
PHONE.................614 278-9200
Douglas Seeley, *CEO*
George Stiffler, *Design Engr*
Pamela Seeley, *Treasurer*
EMP: 14 **EST:** 1982
SQ FT: 11,000
SALES (est): 2.6MM **Privately Held**
WEB: www.seekirk.com
SIC: 3823 Annunciators, relay & solid state types

(G-7437)
SELECTEON CORPORATION
2041 Arlingate Ln (43228-4113)
PHONE.................614 710-1132
Thomas J Ward, *President*
Cecil Robinson, *President*
EMP: 26
SQ FT: 20,000
SALES (est): 4.4MM **Privately Held**
SIC: 3569 Assembly machines, non-metal-working

(G-7438)
SENTEK CORPORATION
1300 Memory Ln N (43209-2736)
PHONE.................614 586-1123
Niklas Almstedt, *President*
Ann Almstedt, *Vice Pres*
EMP: 7
SQ FT: 9,000
SALES (est): 1.3MM **Privately Held**
WEB: www.sentekcorp.com
SIC: 3547 8748 Ferrous & nonferrous mill equipment, auxiliary; systems analysis & engineering consulting services

(G-7439)
SERMONIX PHARMACEUTICALS
142 S Remington Rd (43209-1868)
PHONE.................614 864-4919
David Portman, *CEO*
Elizabeth Attias, *President*
Miriam Portman, *COO*
EMP: 4 **EST:** 2016
SALES (est): 223.7K **Privately Held**
SIC: 2834 Pills, pharmaceutical

(G-7440)
SEVAN AT-NDUSTRIAL PNT ABR LTD
1555 Alum Creek Dr (43209-2712)
PHONE.................614 258-4747
Dan Birt, *Principal*
EMP: 3
SALES (est): 606.7K **Privately Held**
SIC: 5085 2842 5012 Abrasives; automobile polish; automobiles & other motor vehicles

(G-7441)
SEVELL + SEVELL INC
692 N High St Ste 306 (43215-1580)
PHONE.................614 341-9700
Steve Sevell, *President*
Beverly Sevell, *Admin Sec*
EMP: 5

SALES (est): 449.2K **Privately Held**
WEB: www.sevell.com
SIC: 2741 2759 7336 7374 Miscellaneous publishing; commercial printing; graphic arts & related design; computer graphics service; information retrieval services; direct mail advertising services

(G-7442)
SEVENTH SON BREWING CO
1101 N 4th St (43201-3683)
PHONE.................614 783-4217
EMP: 4
SALES (est): 390.7K **Privately Held**
SIC: 2082 Ale (alcoholic beverage)

(G-7443)
SHADETREE SYSTEMS LLC
6317 Busch Blvd (43229-1802)
PHONE.................614 844-5990
Deana Haight, *Sales Mgr*
Ursula Jones, *Sales Staff*
John Molnar, *Consultant*
Bill Shaw, *Consultant*
Shirley Garnham, *Info Tech Dir*
◆ **EMP:** 19
SQ FT: 19,000
SALES (est): 3.7MM **Privately Held**
WEB: www.shadetreesystems.com
SIC: 3444 Canopies, sheet metal

(G-7444)
SHELLI R MCMURRAY
1360 Louvaine Dr Rear (43223-3445)
PHONE.................614 275-4381
Shelli R McMurray, *Principal*
EMP: 4
SALES (est): 260.8K **Privately Held**
SIC: 2891 Adhesives

(G-7445)
SHENET LLC
50 W Broad St Ste 12000 (43215-3301)
PHONE.................614 563-9600
Sally Haimbaugh,
EMP: 25
SALES (est): 1.7MM **Privately Held**
SIC: 3663 Radio & TV communications equipment

(G-7446)
SHIP PRINT E SELL
3145 Kingsdale Ctr (43221)
PHONE.................614 459-1205
Mark Heimrich, *Partner*
Charles Groezinger, *Partner*
John Pugh, *Partner*
EMP: 3
SALES (est): 170K **Privately Held**
SIC: 2752 Commercial printing, lithographic

(G-7447)
SHOEMAKER ELECTRIC COMPANY
Also Called: Shoemaker Industrial Solutions
831 Bonham Ave (43211-2999)
PHONE.................614 294-5626
Fred N Kletrovets, *President*
Derrick Crowe, *Engineer*
Teri Richardson, *Treasurer*
Betty Kletrovets, *Admin Sec*
▲ **EMP:** 29 **EST:** 1935
SQ FT: 16,000
SALES (est): 8.1MM **Privately Held**
WEB: www.shoemakerindustrial.com
SIC: 7694 5063 Electric motor repair; motors, electric

(G-7448)
SIEMENS INDUSTRY INC
977 Gahanna Pkwy (43230-6610)
PHONE.................614 573-8212
Michael Morrow, *Branch Mgr*
EMP: 87
SALES (corp-wide): 95B **Privately Held**
SIC: 3822 Air conditioning & refrigeration controls
HQ: Siemens Industry, Inc.
 1000 Deerfield Pkwy
 Buffalo Grove IL 60089
 800 743-6367

(G-7449)
SIGNAGE CONSULTANTS INC
870 E 5th Ave (43201-2960)
PHONE.................614 297-7446
Elizabeth Navarro, *President*
Elizabeth Navagrro, *President*
EMP: 6
SQ FT: 8,000
SALES (est): 675.2K **Privately Held**
WEB: www.signageconsultants.com
SIC: 3993 7336 Signs, not made in custom sign painting shops; graphic arts & related design

(G-7450)
SIGNATURE CABINETRY INC
1285 Alum Creek Dr (43209-2721)
PHONE.................614 252-2227
Jack E Mc Vey, *President*
Carmen Artis, *Office Mgr*
Gregory D Hughes, *Manager*
EMP: 15
SALES (est): 3.8MM **Privately Held**
SIC: 2434 Wood kitchen cabinets

(G-7451)
SIGNCOM INCORPORATED
527 W Rich St (43215-4903)
PHONE.................614 228-9999
Jim Hartley, *President*
Bret Gilmore, *Controller*
Bruce M Sommerfelt, *Sales Mgr*
EMP: 25
SALES (est): 2.7MM **Privately Held**
WEB: www.signcom.cc
SIC: 3993 Neon signs

(G-7452)
SIMEX INC
181 Pleasants Indus Park (43224)
PHONE.................304 665-1104
Mark Savan, *President*
EMP: 5
SALES (est): 1MM **Privately Held**
SIC: 2591 Window shades

(G-7453)
SIMON & SCHUSTER INC
Also Called: Silver, Burdett & Ginn
4350 Equity Dr (43228-4801)
PHONE.................614 876-0371
Sheila Hickle, *Director*
EMP: 140
SALES (corp-wide): 14.5B **Publicly Held**
WEB: www.digonsite.com
SIC: 2731 2741 Books: publishing & printing; textbooks: publishing & printing; miscellaneous publishing
HQ: Simon & Schuster, Inc.
 1230 Ave Of The Americas
 New York NY 10020
 212 698-7000

(G-7454)
SIMPSON STRONG-TIE COMPANY INC
2600 International St (43228-4617)
PHONE.................614 876-8060
Shane Vilasineekul, *Engineer*
Sharon Bott, *Human Res Dir*
Rick Reid, *Sales Staff*
Dave Williams, *Branch Mgr*
Jerry Gridley, *Manager*
EMP: 120
SALES (corp-wide): 1B **Publicly Held**
SIC: 5082 3643 3452 Construction & mining machinery; current-carrying wiring devices; bolts, nuts, rivets & washers
HQ: Simpson Strong-Tie Company Inc.
 5956 W Las Positas Blvd
 Pleasanton CA 94588
 925 560-9000

(G-7455)
SINNERS N SAINTS LLC
1515 Alum Creek Dr (43209-2712)
PHONE.................614 231-7467
EMP: 3
SALES (est): 230K **Privately Held**
SIC: 3751 7699 Mfg Motorcycles/Bicycles Repair Services

(G-7456)
SIX-3
2514 Summit St (43202-2729)
PHONE.................614 260-5610
EMP: 4
SALES (est): 389K **Privately Held**
SIC: 2752 Commercial printing, lithographic

(G-7457)
SKEELES MANUFACTURING CORP
4040 Fondorf Dr (43228-1026)
PHONE.................614 274-4700
Fred Skeeles, *President*
Jonathan Skeeles, *Vice Pres*
EMP: 18
SQ FT: 15,000
SALES (est): 2.4MM **Privately Held**
WEB: www.skeelesinc.com
SIC: 2541 Counter & sink tops

(G-7458)
SODA PIG LLC
790 Kerr St (43215-1559)
PHONE.................646 241-7126
Mark Wise,
Robert Malko,
Brannan McGill,
EMP: 3
SALES (est): 92K **Privately Held**
SIC: 7372 Application computer software

(G-7459)
SOFTCHOICE CORPORATION
300 Marconi Blvd Ste 303 (43215-2329)
PHONE.................614 224-4123
Chandran Rajaratnam, *President*
EMP: 3 **Privately Held**
WEB: www.softchoice.com
SIC: 7372 Prepackaged software
HQ: Softchoice Corporation
 314 W Superior St Ste 400
 Chicago IL 60654

(G-7460)
SOFTURA LEGAL SOLUTIONS LLC
1555 Lake Shore Dr (43204-3825)
PHONE.................614 220-5611
Brian Deas,
EMP: 5 **EST:** 2016
SALES (est): 117.2K **Privately Held**
SIC: 7372 Business oriented computer software

(G-7461)
SOMERSET GALLERIES INC
Also Called: Mica Laminates
1144 S 4th St (43206-2686)
PHONE.................614 443-0003
Kenneth G Haas, *President*
Maxine Haas, *Corp Secy*
Aaron Haas, *Vice Pres*
Leonard Haas, *Vice Pres*
EMP: 3
SQ FT: 10,000
SALES: 100K **Privately Held**
SIC: 3083 Laminated plastics plate & sheet

(G-7462)
SONOCO PRODUCTS COMPANY
444 Mccormick Blvd (43213-1525)
PHONE.................614 759-8470
Greg Ickes, *Principal*
EMP: 30
SALES (corp-wide): 5.3B **Publicly Held**
WEB: www.sonoco.com
SIC: 2631 2671 2653 2655 Paperboard mills; packaging paper & plastics film, coated & laminated; corrugated & solid fiber boxes; fiber cans, drums & similar products; injection molded finished plastic products; extruded finished plastic products; reels, plywood
PA: Sonoco Products Company
 1 N 2nd St
 Hartsville SC 29550
 843 383-7000

(G-7463)
SOONDOOK LLC
6344 Nicholas Dr (43235-5206)
PHONE.................614 389-5757
Alexander Golikov,

Columbus - Franklin County (G-7464)

EMP: 20 Privately Held
SIC: 2752 Commercial printing, lithographic

(G-7464)
SOUTH SIDE AUDIO LLC
2501 S High St Frnt Frnt (43207-2998)
PHONE..................................614 453-0757
Donavin Gleaton,
Michael Cumpston,
EMP: 3
SALES (est): 240K Privately Held
SIC: 3651 Audio electronic systems

(G-7465)
SOUTHWEST GREENS OHIO LLC
1781 Westbelt Dr (43228-3811)
PHONE..................................614 389-6042
Rick Dodson,
Kate Dodson,
EMP: 10
SQ FT: 1,500
SALES (est): 1.9MM Privately Held
WEB: www.southwestgreensohio.com
SIC: 3299 Synthetic stones, for gem stones & industrial use

(G-7466)
SPECIAL DESIGN PRODUCTS INC
520 Industrial Mile Rd (43228-2413)
PHONE..................................614 272-6700
Nancy Evanichko, President
Stan Evanichko, Vice Pres
Suzette King, Shareholder
EMP: 45
SALES (est): 11.4MM Privately Held
WEB: www.specialdesignproducts.com
SIC: 3086 Packaging & shipping materials, foamed plastic

(G-7467)
SPECIALTY FILMS INC
2887 Johnstown Rd (43219-1719)
PHONE..................................614 471-9100
Howard Callaghan Jr, President
EMP: 35
SQ FT: 7,500
SALES (est): 3.2MM
SALES (corp-wide): 103.2MM Privately Held
WEB: www.plasticsuppliers.net
SIC: 3081 Plastic film & sheet
PA: Plastic Suppliers, Inc.
    2400 Marilyn Ln
    Columbus OH 43219
    614 471-9100

(G-7468)
SPECIALTY PRINTING AND PROC
4670 Groves Rd (43232-4164)
PHONE..................................614 322-9035
Frank Schreck, Owner
Kathy Entsminger, Marketing Staff
Doug Szllagyl, Marketing Staff
EMP: 17 EST: 2000
SALES (est): 3.4MM Privately Held
WEB: www.extendedresources.net
SIC: 2759 Screen printing

(G-7469)
SPECIALTY SERVICES INC
1382 Ohlen Ave (43211-2640)
PHONE..................................614 421-1599
Michael Melton, President
Joann Melton, Corp Secy
EMP: 8
SQ FT: 10,200
SALES: 700K Privately Held
SIC: 2521 2511 Cabinets, office: wood; wood household furniture

(G-7470)
SPECIALTY TECHNOLOGY & RES
Also Called: Star
1150 Milepost Dr (43228-9388)
PHONE..................................614 870-0744
Girish Dubey, President
▼ EMP: 6
SQ FT: 4,500

SALES (est): 1.8MM Privately Held
WEB: www.spiritavionics.com
SIC: 2951 8731 Paving mixtures; commercial physical research

(G-7471)
SPECTROGLASS CORP
1380 Holly Ave (43212-3115)
PHONE..................................614 297-0412
EMP: 3 EST: 2002
SALES (est): 230K Privately Held
SIC: 2295 Mfg Coated Fabrics

(G-7472)
SPECTRUM DYNAMICS INC
1951 Hampshire Rd (43221-4116)
PHONE..................................614 486-3223
Steven Caton, President
EMP: 4
SALES (est): 66.5K Privately Held
SIC: 3599 Machine & other job shop work

(G-7473)
SPECTRUM IMAGE LLC
374 Morrison Rd Ste F (43213-1446)
PHONE..................................614 954-0102
Craig Faist, Mng Member
Thomas Faist,
EMP: 3 EST: 2015
SQ FT: 2,000
SALES (est): 111.4K Privately Held
SIC: 7334 2752 Photocopying & duplicating services; commercial printing, lithographic

(G-7474)
SPECTRUM MFG & SLS INC (PA)
1951 Hampshire Rd (43221-4116)
PHONE..................................614 486-3223
Steven Caton, President
EMP: 2
SQ FT: 4,000
SALES (est): 1.3MM Privately Held
SIC: 5084 3599 Industrial machine parts; machine shop, jobbing & repair

(G-7475)
SPEEDWAY LLC
Also Called: Speedway Superamerica 2034
2875 Stelzer Rd (43219-3132)
PHONE..................................614 418-9325
Josh Dillinger, Branch Mgr
EMP: 10 Publicly Held
WEB: www.speedwaynet.com
SIC: 1311 Crude petroleum production
HQ: Speedway Llc
    500 Speedway Dr
    Enon OH 45323
    937 864-3000

(G-7476)
SPILLMAN COMPANY
1701 Moler Rd (43207-1684)
P.O. Box 7847 (43207-0847)
PHONE..................................614 444-2184
Ted Coons, CEO
Don McNutt, President
Theodore W Coons, Principal
Lynn Coons, Treasurer
◆ EMP: 34 EST: 1948
SQ FT: 37,000
SALES (est): 7.9MM Privately Held
WEB: www.spillmanform.com
SIC: 1771 5084 3446 Concrete work; cement making machinery; architectural metalwork

(G-7477)
SPIRIT AVIONICS LTD
Also Called: Spirit Aeronautics
4808 E 5th Ave (43219-1853)
PHONE..................................614 237-4271
Tony Bailey, President
Rick Ochs, Partner
Steve Wathen, Partner
Brian Jay, QC Mgr
John Williamson, CFO
EMP: 13
SQ FT: 15,000

SALES (est): 5MM Privately Held
WEB: www.spiritavionics.com
SIC: 7629 4581 2396 3629 Aircraft electrical equipment repair; aircraft servicing & repairing; automotive trimmings, fabric; electronic generation equipment; aircraft engines & engine parts; electronic parts & equipment

(G-7478)
SPLENDID LLC
1415 E Dubln Grnvl Rd 2 (43229)
PHONE..................................614 396-6481
Moe Lee, Principal
Shurki Mire, Mng Member
EMP: 14
SALES (est): 1.8MM Privately Held
SIC: 3531 Crane carriers

(G-7479)
SPORTS MONSTER CORP
1553 Parsons Ave (43207-1214)
PHONE..................................614 443-0190
Bartholomew Fitzpatrick, Principal
EMP: 11
SALES (est): 1.1MM Privately Held
SIC: 3949 Sporting & athletic goods
PA: Sports Monster Corp
    4237 N Western Ave Ste 2
    Chicago IL 60618

(G-7480)
SPRING WORKS INC
3201 Alberta St (43204-2029)
PHONE..................................614 351-9345
Edgar Weil, CEO
Tom Jayjohn, Prdtn Mgr
Art Neu, QC Mgr
EMP: 20 EST: 1981
SQ FT: 27,000
SALES (est): 3.5MM Privately Held
WEB: www.thespringworks.com
SIC: 3495 Mechanical springs, precision

(G-7481)
SRICO INC
2724 Sawbury Blvd (43235-4579)
PHONE..................................614 799-0664
SRI Sriram, President
Judith C Sriram, Vice Pres
EMP: 8
SQ FT: 3,600
SALES (est): 819.1K Privately Held
WEB: www.srico.com
SIC: 3229 8731 Fiber optics strands; electronic research

(G-7482)
SRM GRAPHICS INC
Also Called: Concept Wear
950 Oakland Park Ave (43224-3310)
PHONE..................................614 263-4433
Stephen Miller, President
Linda Saup, Admin Sec
EMP: 3
SQ FT: 2,400
SALES (est): 323.8K Privately Held
WEB: www.conceptwear.com
SIC: 2759 Screen printing

(G-7483)
SSP TENNESSEE LLC
Also Called: Solstice Sleep Products
2652 Fisher Rd Ste A (43204-3576)
PHONE..................................614 279-8850
EMP: 3
SALES (est): 160.9K Privately Held
SIC: 2515 Mattresses & bedsprings

(G-7484)
STANDARD ENERGY COMPANY
1105 Schrock Rd Ste 602 (43229-1174)
PHONE..................................614 885-1901
Gerald S Jacobs, President
Donna Sanger, Vice Pres
Denise Amspoker, Admin Sec
EMP: 4
SQ FT: 3,400
SALES (est): 344.7K Privately Held
SIC: 1382 1311 6798 Oil & gas exploration services; crude petroleum production; natural gas production; realty investment trusts

(G-7485)
STAR JET LLC
4130 E 5th Ave (43219-1802)
PHONE..................................614 338-4379
Harvey Mosher, Asst Director
Robert Austin,
EMP: 15
SALES (est): 1.8MM Privately Held
WEB: www.starjet.com
SIC: 3721 Aircraft

(G-7486)
STAR NEWSPAPER
1472 Dobson Sq N (43229-1366)
PHONE..................................614 622-5930
Joseph Owusu Ansah, Owner
EMP: 3
SALES: 0 Privately Held
SIC: 2711 7389 Newspapers, publishing & printing;

(G-7487)
STAR SEAL OF OHIO INC
1400 Walcutt Rd (43228-9194)
PHONE..................................614 870-1590
Dr Sudhir Dubey, President
Girish Dubey, Chairman
Darla Bushell, Opers Mgr
Dee Denney, Marketing Mgr
EMP: 6
SALES (est): 1.4MM Privately Held
SIC: 2951 Coal tar paving materials (not from refineries)

(G-7488)
STARECASING SYSTEMS INC
2822 Fisher Rd (43204-3538)
PHONE..................................312 203-5632
Ryan Otoole, President
EMP: 9
SALES (est): 1MM Privately Held
SIC: 2435 Hardwood plywood, prefinished

(G-7489)
STEER & GEAR INC
Also Called: Steer & Geer
1000 Barnett Rd (43227-1188)
PHONE..................................614 231-4064
Gerald Ries, President
Susan Ries, Vice Pres
EMP: 35
SALES (est): 5.1MM Privately Held
WEB: www.steerandgear.com
SIC: 3714 Power steering equipment, motor vehicle

(G-7490)
STEP IT UP LLC
580 N 4th St (43215-2106)
PHONE..................................720 289-1520
Bob Myers,
EMP: 5 EST: 2017
SALES (est): 155.6K Privately Held
SIC: 7372 Application computer software

(G-7491)
STOCKER & SITLER OIL COMPANY (HQ)
4770 Indianola Ave (43214-1862)
PHONE..................................614 888-9588
Judson K Byrd, President
EMP: 4
SALES (est): 656.2K
SALES (corp-wide): 21.8MM Privately Held
SIC: 1311 1389 Crude petroleum & natural gas production; pumping of oil & gas wells
PA: Cgas Inc
    110 E Wilson Bridge Rd # 250
    Worthington OH 43085
    614 975-4697

(G-7492)
STONEWARE PALACE LTD
3560 Mountshannon Rd (43221-5237)
PHONE..................................614 529-6974
Sherri Lynn, President
Ben Wingeier, Vice Pres
EMP: 3
SALES (est): 58.5K Privately Held
WEB: www.stonewarepalace.com
SIC: 3269 Stoneware pottery products

GEOGRAPHIC SECTION

Columbus - Franklin County (G-7524)

(G-7493)
STREAMSAVVY LLC
629 N High St Fl 4 (43215-2025)
PHONE.............................614 256-7955
Christopher Kessler, *CEO*
EMP: 4 **EST:** 2016
SALES (est): 98.3K **Privately Held**
SIC: 7372 Application computer software

(G-7494)
STRONG M LLC
2046 Leonard Ave (43219-2105)
PHONE.............................614 329-8025
Michael Paterson,
EMP: 17
SALES (est): 1.6MM **Privately Held**
SIC: 3825 Radio frequency measuring equipment

(G-7495)
STRONGBASICS LLC
35 E Gay St Ste 322 (43215-8128)
PHONE.............................716 903-6151
Narasimha Vyakaranamkan,
EMP: 5
SALES (est): 540K **Privately Held**
SIC: 7371 7372 7379 Computer software development; application computer software; computer related consulting services

(G-7496)
STUDS N HIP HOP
2032 E Hudson St (43211-2328)
PHONE.............................614 477-0786
Tiffany Herding, *Owner*
EMP: 5 **EST:** 2014
SALES (est): 93.8K **Privately Held**
SIC: 7221 2759 Photographer, still or video; screen printing

(G-7497)
STYLE-LINE INCORPORATED (PA)
Also Called: Chelsea House Fabrics
901 W 3rd Ave Ste A (43212-3131)
P.O. Box 2706 (43216-2706)
PHONE.............................614 291-0600
Laura R Prophater, *President*
William H Prophater, *Vice Pres*
EMP: 45
SQ FT: 54,000
SALES (est): 6MM **Privately Held**
SIC: 5023 5131 2391 1799 Venetian blinds; vertical blinds; window shades; window covering parts & accessories; drapery material, woven; curtains, window; made from purchased materials; drapery track installation

(G-7498)
SUBURBAN STL SUP CO LTD PARTNR
Also Called: Suburban Steel of Indiana
1900 Deffenbaugh Ct (43230-8604)
PHONE.............................317 783-6555
Mark Debellis, *President*
EMP: 8
SALES (corp-wide): 13MM **Privately Held**
WEB: www.suburbansteelsupply.com
SIC: 3441 Fabricated structural metal
PA: Suburban Steel Supply Co. Limited Partnership
1900 Deffenbaugh Ct
Gahanna OH 43230
614 737-5501

(G-7499)
SUCCESS PRO PUBLICATIONS
3137 Houston Dr (43207-3330)
PHONE.............................614 886-9922
Lori Whitmore, *Principal*
EMP: 4
SALES (est): 164.4K **Privately Held**
SIC: 2741 Miscellaneous publishing

(G-7500)
SUNRISE FOODS INC
2097 Corvair Blvd (43207-1701)
PHONE.............................614 276-2880
Mark Pl Sr, *President*
EMP: 48
SQ FT: 38,000
SALES (est): 10.3MM **Privately Held**
WEB: www.sunrisefoods.org
SIC: 2038 2013 2035 2099 Ethnic foods, frozen; frozen meats from purchased meat; pickles, sauces & salad dressings; food preparations

(G-7501)
SUPERIOR METAL WORX LLC
1239 Alum Creek Dr (43209-2721)
PHONE.............................614 879-9400
Brian Kimes,
EMP: 15
SALES (est): 3.8MM **Privately Held**
SIC: 3444 Sheet metalwork

(G-7502)
SUPERIOR TASTING PRODUCTS INC
Also Called: Graeter's Ice Cream
2555 Bethel Rd (43220-2224)
PHONE.............................614 442-0622
Maurice E Levine, *President*
Nick Whitney, *Manager*
EMP: 40
SALES (est): 4.5MM **Privately Held**
SIC: 2024 5451 Ice milk, bulk; ice cream (packaged)

(G-7503)
SUPERIOR WELDING CO
906 S Nelson Rd (43205-3098)
PHONE.............................614 252-8539
Steve Shipley, *President*
Sandra R Shipley, *Vice Pres*
EMP: 17
SQ FT: 22,000
SALES (est): 2.9MM **Privately Held**
WEB: www.superiorweldingcompany.com
SIC: 3441 Fabricated structural metal

(G-7504)
SUPPLY TECHNOLOGIES LLC
590 Claycraft Rd (43230-5319)
PHONE.............................614 759-9939
Thomas Gisczinski, *Manager*
Tom Gisczinski, *Manager*
EMP: 15
SALES (corp-wide): 1.6B **Publicly Held**
WEB: www.deloscrew.com
SIC: 3452 Bolts, nuts, rivets & washers
HQ: Supply Technologies Llc
6065 Parkland Blvd Ste 2
Cleveland OH 44124
440 947-2100

(G-7505)
SWEET GS CUPCAKERY LTD
3820 Turnock Gln (43230-3494)
PHONE.............................419 610-8507
Brittany Griffin, *Principal*
EMP: 4
SALES (est): 175.1K **Privately Held**
SIC: 2051 Bread, cake & related products

(G-7506)
SYSCOM ADVANCED MATERIALS INC
1305 Kinnear Rd (43212-1574)
PHONE.............................614 487-3626
Jar-Wha Lee, *President*
EMP: 12
SALES (est): 1.4MM **Privately Held**
SIC: 3357 Fiber optic cable (insulated)

(G-7507)
T E MARTINDALE ENTERPRISES
Also Called: A & M Ornamental Mfg Co
2840 E 5th Ave (43219-2849)
PHONE.............................614 253-6826
Troy Martindale, *President*
Linda Martindale, *Treasurer*
EMP: 4
SQ FT: 2,500
SALES: 140K **Privately Held**
SIC: 3599 3446 Machine & other job shop work; architectural metalwork

(G-7508)
TAG
2226 Wilson Rd (43228-9386)
PHONE.............................614 921-1732
Yon Deweese, *Owner*
EMP: 4 **EST:** 2011

SALES: 500K **Privately Held**
SIC: 2759 Screen printing

(G-7509)
TAKEYA USA CORPORATION
265 N Hamilton Rd (43213-1311)
PHONE.............................714 374-9900
EMP: 12
SALES (est): 1.6MM **Privately Held**
SIC: 3089 Bottle caps, molded plastic

(G-7510)
TAMARKIN COMPANY
4780 W Broad St (43228-1613)
PHONE.............................614 878-8942
Debra B Krasnow, *Principal*
EMP: 5
SALES (est): 334.6K **Privately Held**
SIC: 2836 Vaccines & other immunizing products

(G-7511)
TARAHILL INC
Also Called: Pet Goods Mfg
3985 Groves Rd (43232-4138)
PHONE.............................706 864-0808
Floyd E Seal, *President*
◆ **EMP:** 20
SALES (est): 2.8MM **Privately Held**
WEB: www.petgoodsmfg.com
SIC: 3199 Dog furnishings: collars, leashes, muzzles, etc.: leather

(G-7512)
TARIGMA CORPORATION
Also Called: Ooteksofpak
6161 Busch Blvd Ste 110 (43229-2553)
PHONE.............................614 436-3734
J Declan Smith, *President*
Keith Sarbaugh, *CFO*
Aaron Grant, *Software Engr*
Winthrop Worcester, *Admin Sec*
EMP: 10
SQ FT: 1,000
SALES (est): 1MM **Privately Held**
WEB: www.tarigma.com
SIC: 7372 Prepackaged software

(G-7513)
TARRIER FOODS CORP
2700 International St # 100 (43228-4640)
PHONE.............................614 876-8594
Timothy A Tarrier, *President*
Julia A Grooms, *Principal*
Ann Tarrier, *Principal*
EMP: 42
SQ FT: 54,000
SALES (est): 23.2MM **Privately Held**
WEB: www.tarrierfoods.com
SIC: 5149 5145 2099 Dried or canned foods; nuts, salted or roasted; candy; food preparations

(G-7514)
TARRIER STEEL COMPANY INC
1379 S 22nd St (43206-3083)
PHONE.............................614 444-4000
Todd Tarrier, *President*
Ben Tarrier, *Vice Pres*
Andrew Tarrier, *Project Mgr*
Chris Hatfield, *Controller*
EMP: 41 **EST:** 1920
SQ FT: 36,000
SALES (est): 18.6MM **Privately Held**
SIC: 3441 3446 Fabricated structural metal; ornamental metalwork

(G-7515)
TAYLOR COMMUNICATIONS INC
3950 Business Park Dr (43204-5008)
PHONE.............................614 351-6868
EMP: 3
SALES (corp-wide): 3.2B **Privately Held**
SIC: 2752 4225 Commercial printing, lithographic; general warehousing & storage
HQ: Taylor Communications, Inc.
1725 Roe Crest Dr
North Mankato MN 56003
507 625-2828

(G-7516)
TDS CUSTOM CABINETS LLC
1819 Walcutt Rd Ste A (43228-9149)
PHONE.............................614 517-2220
Paula Sauer, *Vice Pres*
Terry Sauer, *Mng Member*

EMP: 6
SQ FT: 36,000
SALES: 3.4MM **Privately Held**
SIC: 2434 Wood kitchen cabinets

(G-7517)
TEAM INC
Tsi Manufacturing
3005 Silver Dr (43224-3945)
PHONE.............................614 263-1808
Sam Dematteo, *Vice Pres*
EMP: 12
SALES (corp-wide): 1.2B **Publicly Held**
SIC: 3398 Metal heat treating
HQ: Team, Inc.
5095 Paris St
Denver CO 80239

(G-7518)
TEAM COOPERHEAT MQS
5764 Westbourne Ave (43213-1400)
PHONE.............................614 501-7304
Sam Dematteo, *Principal*
EMP: 3
SALES (est): 231.6K **Privately Held**
SIC: 3398 Metal heat treating

(G-7519)
TECH-SONIC INC
2710 Sawbury Blvd (43235-1821)
PHONE.............................614 792-3117
Byoung Ou, *President*
Hyun Ou, *Treasurer*
EMP: 14
SALES (est): 2.2MM **Privately Held**
SIC: 3548 3699 Electric welding equipment; generators, ultrasonic

(G-7520)
TECHNICAL ARTISTRY INC
Also Called: Tech Art Productions
1945 Corvair Ave (43207-1719)
P.O. Box 1239, Hilliard (43026-6239)
PHONE.............................614 299-7777
Tim McLaughlin, *CEO*
EMP: 6
SALES: 350K **Privately Held**
WEB: www.techartproductions.com
SIC: 5063 7929 5099 7359 Lighting fixtures; entertainment service; video & audio equipment; sound & lighting equipment rental; speaker systems

(G-7521)
TESLA INC
4005 The Strand W (43219-6128)
PHONE.............................614 532-5060
Tesla Tdej, *Principal*
EMP: 5
SALES (corp-wide): 21.4B **Publicly Held**
SIC: 3711 Motor vehicles & car bodies
PA: Tesla, Inc.
3500 Deer Creek Rd
Palo Alto CA 94304
650 681-5000

(G-7522)
TEX-VENT CO
6100 Huntley Rd (43229-1004)
PHONE.............................614 299-1902
Fax: 614 299-5488
EMP: 3 **EST:** 2010
SALES (est): 150K **Privately Held**
SIC: 3559 Mfg Misc Industry Machinery

(G-7523)
THATCHER ENTERPRISES CO LTD
Also Called: Fastsigns
205 E Broad St (43215-3701)
PHONE.............................614 228-2013
Michael Thatcher, *Owner*
Lynn Thatcher, *Co-Owner*
EMP: 5
SQ FT: 1,600
SALES (est): 710.4K **Privately Held**
SIC: 3993 Signs & advertising specialties

(G-7524)
THE GUARDTOWER INC
Also Called: Shield Laminating
3600 Trabue Rd (43204-3609)
PHONE.............................614 488-4311
Lynn Bartells, *President*
EMP: 10

Columbus - Franklin County (G-7525)

SALES (est): 1MM **Privately Held**
SIC: 3944 5945 Games, toys & children's vehicles; models, toy & hobby

(G-7525)
THE HARTMAN CORP
Also Called: Hartman Baseball Cards
3216 Morse Rd (43231-6132)
PHONE 614 475-5035
Larry Hartman, *President*
Gary Hartman, *Vice Pres*
Linda Hartman, *Admin Sec*
EMP: 6
SQ FT: 6,500
SALES (est): 874.1K **Privately Held**
SIC: 5999 5941 5947 3993 Trophies & plaques; bowling equipment & supplies; trading cards: baseball or other sports, entertainment, etc.; signs & advertising specialties

(G-7526)
THERMAL SOLUTIONS INC
3005 Silver Dr (43224-3945)
PHONE 614 263-1808
Mike Urban, *Principal*
EMP: 3
SALES (est): 194.6K **Privately Held**
SIC: 3398 Metal heat treating

(G-7527)
THURNS BAKERY & DELI
541 S 3rd St (43215-5721)
PHONE 614 221-9246
Marilyn Plank, *President*
Bill Plank, *Vice Pres*
Chris Plank, *Vice Pres*
Dan Plank, *Vice Pres*
EMP: 25 **EST:** 1972
SQ FT: 2,100
SALES (est): 1.1MM **Privately Held**
SIC: 5461 5149 2051 Bakeries; bakery products; bread, cake & related products

(G-7528)
TIBA LLC
Also Called: Signature Control Systems
2228 Citygate Dr (43219-3565)
PHONE 614 328-2040
Kon Dawsher, *Mng Member*
EMP: 30 **EST:** 1987
SALES: 6MM **Privately Held**
SIC: 3559 Parking facility equipment & supplies

(G-7529)
TIMBERTECH LIMITED
2141 Fairwood Ave (43207-1753)
PHONE 614 443-4891
EMP: 10
SALES (corp-wide): 1.2B **Publicly Held**
SIC: 3089 Mfg Plastic Products
HQ: Timbertech Limited
894 Prairie Rd
Wilmington OH 45177
937 655-8766

(G-7530)
TIME 4 YOU
5938 Sedgwick Rd (43235-3319)
PHONE 614 593-2695
Rae Beasley, *Principal*
EMP: 3
SALES (est): 149.1K **Privately Held**
SIC: 2711 Newspapers, publishing & printing

(G-7531)
TKS INDUSTRIAL COMPANY
1939 Refugee Rd (43207-1743)
PHONE 614 444-5602
Mark Swedni, *Branch Mgr*
EMP: 65
SALES (corp-wide): 2.1B **Privately Held**
WEB: www.tks-america.com
SIC: 3559 Metal finishing equipment for plating, etc.
HQ: Tks Industrial Company
901 Tower Dr Ste 300
Troy MI 48098
248 786-5000

(G-7532)
TMARZETTI COMPANY
Also Called: Allen Milk Division
1709 Frank Rd (43223-3726)
P.O. Box 453 (43216)
PHONE 614 279-8673
Tom Deschler, *Vice Pres*
Jeff Wallace, *Plant Mgr*
Tiffany Robb, *Manager*
Jim Weimerskirch, *Manager*
James Bachmann, *Director*
EMP: 133
SALES (corp-wide): 1.2B **Publicly Held**
SIC: 2024 2023 Yogurt desserts, frozen; canned cream
HQ: T.Marzetti Company
380 Polaris Pkwy Ste 400
Westerville OH 43082
614 846-2232

(G-7533)
TOM JAMES COMPANY
1156 Dublin Rd Ste 101 (43215-1095)
PHONE 614 488-8400
Bruce Bays, *Division VP*
EMP: 11
SALES (corp-wide): 631.4MM **Privately Held**
SIC: 2311 Suits, men's & boys': made from purchased materials
PA: Tom James Company
263 Seaboard Ln
Franklin TN 37067
615 771-1122

(G-7534)
TORSO
772 N High St Ste 100 (43215-1457)
PHONE 614 421-7663
Scott Rousku, *Owner*
EMP: 4
SALES (est): 433.7K **Privately Held**
WEB: www.torsoonline.com
SIC: 2329 Men's & boys' sportswear & athletic clothing

(G-7535)
TOTAL TENNIS INC
Also Called: TTI Sports Equipment
1733 Cardiff Rd (43221-3806)
PHONE 614 488-5004
James Lathrop, *President*
Sally Ann Lathrop, *Vice Pres*
EMP: 7
SALES: 1MM **Privately Held**
SIC: 3949 5091 Tennis equipment & supplies; sporting & recreation goods

(G-7536)
TRANE US INC
2300 Citygate Dr Ste 100 (43219-3664)
PHONE 614 473-3131
Al Fullerton, *District Mgr*
Becky Munn, *Human Res Mgr*
William Whitmeyer, *Sales Staff*
EMP: 150 **Privately Held**
SIC: 3585 Refrigeration & heating equipment
HQ: Trane U.S. Inc.
3600 Pammel Creek Rd
La Crosse WI 54601
608 787-2000

(G-7537)
TRANE US INC
Also Called: Trane National Account Service
2300 Citygate Dr Ste 250 (43219-3664)
PHONE 614 473-8701
EMP: 61 **Privately Held**
SIC: 3585 Refrigeration & heating equipment
HQ: Trane U.S. Inc.
3600 Pammel Creek Rd
La Crosse WI 54601
608 787-2000

(G-7538)
TRANSCONTINENTAL ELECTRIC LLC
3155 Wareham Rd (43221-2245)
PHONE 614 496-4379
Eric Odita, *Principal*
EMP: 4
SALES (est): 214.2K **Privately Held**
SIC: 3612 Power transformers, electric

(G-7539)
TRANSMET CORPORATION
4290 Perimeter Dr (43228-1036)
PHONE 614 276-5522
Douglas Shull, *President*
▼ **EMP:** 8
SQ FT: 17,000
SALES (est): 1.9MM **Privately Held**
WEB: www.transmet.com
SIC: 3399 Flakes, metal; powder, metal

(G-7540)
TRANSPORT CONTAINER CORP
950 Augusta Glen Dr (43235-5097)
PHONE 614 459-8140
Peter F Demarco, *President*
Cynthia Demarco, *Corp Secy*
EMP: 4
SALES: 500K **Privately Held**
SIC: 2655 Fiber cans, drums & containers

(G-7541)
TRAXLER PRINTING
3029 Silver Dr (43224-3945)
PHONE 614 593-1270
Zachary Traxler, *CEO*
EMP: 3
SALES (est): 122.4K **Privately Held**
SIC: 2752 Commercial printing, lithographic

(G-7542)
TREVI TECHNOLOGY INC
1029 Dublin Rd (43215-1199)
PHONE 614 754-7175
Brent Ludington, *Principal*
▲ **EMP:** 3
SALES (est): 371.3K **Privately Held**
SIC: 3827 Optical instruments & apparatus

(G-7543)
TRI-STATE SUPPLY CO INC
3840 Fisher Rd (43228-1016)
PHONE 614 272-6767
Jim Bruce, *Principal*
EMP: 10 **EST:** 1950
SQ FT: 10,000
SALES (est): 1.2MM **Privately Held**
SIC: 2493 5046 2531 Bulletin boards, wood; bulletin boards, cork; partitions; blackboards, wood

(G-7544)
TRIO INSULATED GLASS INC
1094 Mckinley Ave (43222-1111)
PHONE 614 276-1647
Timothy Marburger, *President*
Paul Marburger, *Corp Secy*
David Marburger, *Vice Pres*
Mark Marburger, *Vice Pres*
EMP: 5 **EST:** 1974
SQ FT: 8,500
SALES (est): 575.2K **Privately Held**
SIC: 3231 Insulating glass: made from purchased glass

(G-7545)
TRIP TRANSPORT LLC
2905 Sunbury Sq (43219-3409)
PHONE 773 969-1402
Alibashi Maalin, *Administration*
EMP: 3
SALES (est): 127.2K **Privately Held**
SIC: 3537 Trucks, tractors, loaders, carriers & similar equipment

(G-7546)
TROY FILTERS LTD
1680 Westbelt Dr (43228-3812)
P.O. Box 21295 (43221-0295)
PHONE 614 777-8222
Cory Elliott, *Mng Member*
Clay Elliott,
EMP: 20 **EST:** 1993
SQ FT: 16,000
SALES (est): 427.8K **Privately Held**
WEB: www.troyfilters.com
SIC: 3564 Filters, air: furnaces, air conditioning equipment, etc.

(G-7547)
TRU-CHEM COMPANY INC
6645 Singletree Dr (43229-1120)
PHONE 614 888-2436
William S Bartley Jr, *President*
EMP: 12

SALES (est): 1.5MM **Privately Held**
WEB: www.truchem.com
SIC: 2819 Industrial inorganic chemicals

(G-7548)
TRULITE GL ALUM SOLUTIONS LLC
Arch Ohio
2395 Setterlin Dr (43228-9499)
PHONE 614 876-1057
David Kruse, *President*
Leon Silverstein, *General Mgr*
EMP: 85
SQ FT: 135,000 **Privately Held**
SIC: 3449 Miscellaneous metalwork
PA: Trulite Glass & Aluminum Solutions, Llc
403 Westpark Ct Ste 201
Peachtree City GA 30269

(G-7549)
TRUTECH CABINETRY
2121 S James Rd (43232-3829)
PHONE 614 338-0680
Nick Willis, *Owner*
EMP: 8
SALES (est): 850K **Privately Held**
SIC: 2434 Wood kitchen cabinets

(G-7550)
TURBOS FBC LLC
Also Called: Mrs Turbos Cookies
1050 Beecher Xing N (43230-4567)
PHONE 614 245-4840
Holly Schaffner, *Mng Member*
Jeff Schaffner,
EMP: 9
SQ FT: 1,699
SALES: 150K **Privately Held**
SIC: 2051 Bakery: wholesale or wholesale/retail combined

(G-7551)
TURN-KEY INDUSTRIAL SVCS LLC
820 Distribution Dr (43228-1004)
PHONE 614 274-1128
Gregory Less, *Mng Member*
EMP: 52
SQ FT: 10,000
SALES (est): 7.6MM **Privately Held**
SIC: 7692 3441 Automotive welding; building components, structural steel

(G-7552)
TURN-KEY TUNNELING INC
1247 Stimmel Rd (43223-2915)
PHONE 614 275-4832
Christine Froehrlich, *President*
Deborah Tingler, *President*
Michael J Fusco, *Principal*
Brian Froehrlich, *Vice Pres*
Joel Froehlich, *Contractor*
EMP: 35
SALES (est): 9.6MM **Privately Held**
SIC: 3531 Tunnelling machinery

(G-7553)
U S FUEL DEVELOPMENT CO (PA)
Also Called: General Equipped Products
1445 Goodale Blvd (43212-3402)
PHONE 614 486-0614
Harold B Epler Jr, *President*
EMP: 1
SQ FT: 800
SALES (est): 1.2MM **Privately Held**
SIC: 6552 1311 1381 6792 Land Development Operates And Drills Oil & Gas Wells And Oil Royalties

(G-7554)
U S HAIR INC
3727 E Broad St (43213-1127)
PHONE 614 235-5190
Tom Jeon, *President*
EMP: 6
SALES (est): 483.4K **Privately Held**
WEB: www.ushairbeauty.com
SIC: 3999 Hair & hair-based products

(G-7555)
UMAMI SEASONINGS LLC
4996 Tamarack Blvd (43229-5241)
PHONE 614 687-0315
Katie D Neely, *Principal*

GEOGRAPHIC SECTION

Columbus - Franklin County (G-7584)

EMP: 3
SALES (est): 125.7K Privately Held
SIC: 2099 Food preparations

(G-7556)
UNITED CONVERTING INC
3960 Groves Rd Unit B (43232-4137)
PHONE 614 863-9972
Preecha Inthisarn, *President*
John Malaby, *Vice Pres*
▲ EMP: 3
SQ FT: 16,000
SALES: 1.4MM Privately Held
SIC: 3081 3083 Plastic film & sheet; laminated plastic sheets

(G-7557)
UNITED MCGILL
1777 Refugee Rd (43207-2119)
PHONE 614 829-1226
EMP: 6
SALES (est): 1.2MM Privately Held
SIC: 3589 Service Industry Machinery, Nec, Nsk

(G-7558)
UNITED SECURITY SEALS INC (PA)
Also Called: United Seal Company
2000 Fairwood Ave (43207-1607)
P.O. Box 7852 (43207-0852)
PHONE 614 443-7633
Herbert Cook, *President*
Daniel P Sander, *Principal*
Bryan Kern, *Opers Staff*
Mari Sander, *Marketing Mgr*
▲ EMP: 30 EST: 1900
SQ FT: 20,000
SALES (est): 2.6MM Privately Held
SIC: 3312 3089 Bar, rod & wire products; plastic processing

(G-7559)
UNITY ENTERPRISES INC
Also Called: Cozmyk Enterprises
3757 Courtright Ct (43227-2250)
PHONE 614 231-1370
Christopher J Minnillo, *Principal*
EMP: 3
SALES (est): 173.8K Privately Held
SIC: 3565 Packaging machinery

(G-7560)
UNIVERSAL EQUIPMENT MFG
2140 Advance Ave (43207-1722)
PHONE 614 586-1780
Pat Seymour, *Principal*
EMP: 4
SALES (est): 238.9K Privately Held
SIC: 3523 Farm machinery & equipment

(G-7561)
UNIVERSAL FABG CNSTR SVCS INC
Also Called: UNI-Facs
1241 Mckinley Ave (43222-1114)
PHONE 614 274-1128
Steve Finkel, *President*
Robert Watts, *Treasurer*
▲ EMP: 86
SQ FT: 120,000
SALES (est): 25.1MM Privately Held
WEB: www.unifacs.com
SIC: 1541 3441 3599 1799 Renovation, remodeling & repairs: industrial buildings; building components, structural steel; expansion joints (structural shapes), iron or steel; catapults; sandblasting of building exteriors

(G-7562)
UNIVERSAL PALLETS INC (PA)
659 Marion Rd (43207-2552)
P.O. Box 77455 (43207-7455)
PHONE 614 444-1095
Mike Afaghi, *President*
EMP: 3 EST: 2008
SALES (est): 1.8MM Privately Held
SIC: 2448 Pallets, wood & wood with metal

(G-7563)
UNIVERSAL PALLETS INC
611 Marion Rd (43207-2552)
PHONE 614 444-1095
Mike Afaghi, *Branch Mgr*

EMP: 20
SALES (corp-wide): 1.8MM Privately Held
SIC: 5031 2448 Pallets, wood; cargo containers, wood
PA: Universal Pallets Inc.
659 Marion Rd
Columbus OH 43207
614 444-1095

(G-7564)
UNIVERSITY SPORTS PUBLICATIONS
1265 Indianola Ave (43201-2838)
PHONE 614 291-6416
Michael Shavefels, *CEO*
EMP: 20
SALES (est): 522.1K Privately Held
SIC: 2711 2721 Newspapers; periodicals

(G-7565)
URBN TIMBER LLC
29 Kingston Ave (43207-2437)
PHONE 614 981-3043
Tyler Sirak, *Mng Member*
Tyler Hillyard, *Mng Member*
Treg Sherman, *Mng Member*
EMP: 6
SALES (est): 541.1K Privately Held
SIC: 2491 2426 5712 5021 Structural lumber & timber, treated wood; carvings, furniture: wood; custom made furniture, except cabinets; furniture

(G-7566)
US GOVERNMENT PUBLISHING OFF
Also Called: Book Store
200 N High St Rm 207 (43215-2408)
PHONE 614 469-5657
EMP: 3 Publicly Held
SIC: 2759 5942 9199 Commercial Printing Ret Books
HQ: Us Government Publishing Office
732 N Capitol St Nw
Washington DC 20401
202 512-0000

(G-7567)
USTEK INCORPORATED
4663 Executive Dr Ste 3 (43220-3627)
PHONE 614 538-8000
Robert M Simon, *President*
Wendy Simon, *Admin Sec*
▲ EMP: 10
SQ FT: 650
SALES: 3.8MM Privately Held
WEB: www.ustek.com
SIC: 3674 Semiconductors & related devices

(G-7568)
V & C ENTERPRISES CO
Also Called: Printed Image, The
41 S Grant Ave (43215-3979)
PHONE 614 221-1412
Cathleen Siech, *Principal*
Vicki Hamer, *Principal*
EMP: 7
SALES (est): 778.7K Privately Held
SIC: 2752 Commercial printing, lithographic

(G-7569)
V & S COLUMBUS GALANIZING LLC
987 Buckeye Park Rd (43207-2596)
PHONE 614 449-8281
Werner Niehaus, *President*
Brian Miller, *Vice Pres*
EMP: 90
SALES (est): 14.6MM Privately Held
WEB: www.hotdipgalv.com
SIC: 3479 Galvanizing of iron, steel or end-formed products

(G-7570)
VALLEY VITAMINS II INC
4449 Easton Way Fl 2 (43219-7005)
PHONE 330 533-0051
Adam Crouch, *CEO*
EMP: 26
SALES: 950K Privately Held
SIC: 2833 Medicinals & botanicals

(G-7571)
VAN DYKE CUSTOM IRON INC
311 Outerbelt St (43213-1529)
PHONE 614 860-9300
John Van Dyke, *President*
Darrell V Dyke, *Vice Pres*
Darrell Van Dyke, *Vice Pres*
Michael V Dyke, *VP Opers*
Michael Van Dyke, *VP Opers*
EMP: 6
SQ FT: 6,000
SALES (est): 620K Privately Held
SIC: 1521 3446 General remodeling, single-family houses; architectural metalwork

(G-7572)
VELLUS PRODUCTS INC
64906490 Fiesta Dr (43235)
PHONE 614 889-2391
Teryl Hotz, *President*
EMP: 5
SQ FT: 2,400
SALES (est): 722.3K Privately Held
WEB: www.vellus.com
SIC: 2844 Shampoos, rinses, conditioners: hair

(G-7573)
VERESSA MEDICAL INC
1375 Perry St (43201-3177)
PHONE 614 591-4201
Ben Tranchina, *CEO*
Kevin Wasserstein, *Chairman*
Chris Hobbs, *CFO*
EMP: 10
SQ FT: 2,500
SALES: 20MM Privately Held
SIC: 3845 Electromedical equipment

(G-7574)
VERTEX REFINING OH LLC
4001 E 5th Ave (43219-1812)
PHONE 614 441-4001
Kyle Senegar, *Plant Mgr*
EMP: 45 Publicly Held
SIC: 2911 Mineral oils, natural
HQ: Vertex Refining Oh Llc
4376 State Route 601
Norwalk OH 44857
281 486-4182

(G-7575)
VERTIV CORPORATION (DH)
1050 Dearborn Dr (43085-1544)
P.O. Box 29186 (43229-0186)
PHONE 614 888-0246
Rob Johnson, *CEO*
Jason Forcier, *Exec VP*
David Fallon, *CFO*
◆ EMP: 1300
SQ FT: 330,000
SALES (est): 1.4B
SALES (corp-wide): 2.1B Privately Held
WEB: www.liebert.com
SIC: 3585 3613 7629 Air conditioning equipment, complete; regulators, power; electronic equipment repair
HQ: Vertiv Group Corporation
1050 Dearborn Dr
Columbus OH 43085
614 888-0246

(G-7576)
VERTIV GROUP CORPORATION (DH)
Also Called: Vertiv Co.
1050 Dearborn Dr (43085-1544)
PHONE 614 888-0246
Rob Johnson, *President*
Giordano Albertazzi, *President*
Frank Bibens, *President*
John Hewitt, *President*
Stephen Liang, *President*
EMP: 1000
SALES (est): 1.9B
SALES (corp-wide): 322.9MM Privately Held
SIC: 3679 3585 Power supplies, all types: static; air conditioning units, complete: domestic or industrial
HQ: Vertiv Holdings, Llc
1050 Dearborn Dr
Columbus OH 43085
614 888-0246

(G-7577)
VERTIV HOLDINGS LLC (HQ)
1050 Dearborn Dr (43085-1544)
PHONE 614 888-0246
Eva M Kalawski, *Vice Pres*
EMP: 7
SALES (est): 1.9B
SALES (corp-wide): 2.1B Privately Held
SIC: 3679 3585 Power supplies, all types: static; air conditioning units, complete: domestic or industrial
PA: Vertiv Jv Holdings, Llc
360 N Crescent Dr
Beverly Hills CA 90210
310 712-1195

(G-7578)
VERTIV NORTH AMERICA INC
1050 Dearborn Dr (43085-1544)
PHONE 614 888-0246
Rob Johnson, *CEO*
Becky Blatt, *Executive Asst*
EMP: 20000
SALES (est): 228.8MM Privately Held
SIC: 3823 Computer interface equipment for industrial process control

(G-7579)
VERTIV SOLUTIONS INC (DH)
1050 Dearborn Dr (43085-1544)
PHONE 614 888-0246
EMP: 40 EST: 2012
SALES (est): 191.9MM
SALES (corp-wide): 242.6MM Privately Held
SIC: 3823 Manufactures Process Control Instruments
HQ: Vertiv Group Corporation
1050 Dearborn Dr
Columbus OH 43085
614 888-0246

(G-7580)
VESCO MEDICAL LLC
1039 Kingsmill Pkwy (43229-1129)
PHONE 614 914-5991
Tom Hancock, *Branch Mgr*
EMP: 11
SALES (corp-wide): 1.2MM Privately Held
SIC: 3841 Surgical & medical instruments
PA: Vesco Medical, Llc
4400 Chavenelle Rd
Dubuque IA 52002
614 914-5991

(G-7581)
VETERAN INDUSTRIES LLC
147 Lake Bluff Dr (43235-4642)
PHONE 937 751-2133
Charles Witt,
EMP: 3
SALES (est): 153.3K Privately Held
SIC: 3357 Nonferrous wiredrawing & insulating

(G-7582)
VF OUTDOOR LLC
4025 Gramercy St (43219-6078)
PHONE 614 337-1147
EMP: 5
SALES (corp-wide): 11.8B Publicly Held
SIC: 3949 Sporting & athletic goods
HQ: Vf Outdoor, Llc
2701 Harbor Bay Pkwy
Alameda CA 94502
510 618-3500

(G-7583)
VICTORY POSTCARDS INC
Also Called: Victory Postcards & Souvenirs
1005 Old Henderson Rd (43220-3701)
PHONE 614 764-8975
Scott Armstrong, *President*
Kimberly Armstrong, *Vice Pres*
EMP: 6
SALES: 400K Privately Held
SIC: 2759 5099 Post cards, picture: printing; souvenirs

(G-7584)
VIRGINIA AIR DISTRIBUTORS INC
2821 Silver Dr (43211-1052)
PHONE 614 262-1129

Columbus - Franklin County (G-7585)

Ken Baker, *CEO*
EMP: 8
SALES (corp-wide): 67.9MM **Privately Held**
SIC: 3585 Parts for heating, cooling & refrigerating equipment
PA: Virginia Air Distributors Inc
2501 Waterford Lake Dr
Midlothian VA 23112
804 608-3600

(G-7585)
VISIONARY SIGNS LLC
6155 Huntley Rd Ste C (43229-1096)
PHONE..................614 504-5899
Bill Hennessy, *Owner*
EMP: 3 **EST:** 2009
SALES (est): 353.1K **Privately Held**
SIC: 3993 Signs & advertising specialties

(G-7586)
VISTA INDUSTRIAL PACKAGING LLC
Also Called: Vista Packaging & Logistics
4700 Fisher Rd (43228-9752)
PHONE..................800 454-6117
Martha J Cahall,
J Matthew Cahall,
Kyle A Cahall,
Todd Hampton,
Jennifer Smith,
EMP: 65
SQ FT: 350,000
SALES (est): 25.5MM **Privately Held**
SIC: 4783 7389 4226 2679 Packing & crating; inspection & testing services; special warehousing & storage; pressed fiber & molded pulp products except food products

(G-7587)
VOIGT & SCHWEITZER LLC (HQ)
987 Buckeye Park Rd (43207-2596)
PHONE..................614 449-8281
Werner Niehaus, *President*
Gutkoski Steve, *COO*
Brian Miller, *Senior VP*
Mason Shiveley, *Plant Mgr*
John Roibu, *Opers Mgr*
▲ **EMP:** 12
SQ FT: 55,000
SALES (est): 100.3MM
SALES (corp-wide): 773.1MM **Privately Held**
WEB: www.hotdipgalvanizing.com
SIC: 3479 Galvanizing of iron, steel or endformed products; hot dip coating of metals or formed products
PA: Hill & Smith Holdings Plc
Westhaven House
Solihull W MIDLANDS B90 4
121 704-7430

(G-7588)
WALKER MAGNETICS GROUP INC
Also Called: Walker National
2195 Wright Brothers Ave (43217-1157)
PHONE..................614 492-1614
Larry Staats, *Manager*
EMP: 26
SALES (corp-wide): 116.9MM **Privately Held**
WEB: www.walkermagnet.com
SIC: 3499 Magnets, permanent: metallic
HQ: Walker Magnetics Group, Inc.
600 Day Hill Rd
Windsor CT 06095
508 853-3232

(G-7589)
WALKER NATIONAL INC
2195 Wright Brothers Ave (43217-1157)
PHONE..................614 492-1614
Richard Longo, *President*
Deborah Krikorian, *CFO*
◆ **EMP:** 30
SALES (est): 6.6MM
SALES (corp-wide): 116.9MM **Privately Held**
WEB: www.walkernational.com
SIC: 3499 7699 Magnets, permanent: metallic; industrial equipment services

HQ: Walker Magnetics Group, Inc.
600 Day Hill Rd
Windsor CT 06095
508 853-3232

(G-7590)
WARLOCK INC
Also Called: Custom Welding
2179 Citygate Dr (43219-3564)
PHONE..................614 471-4055
Scott Rogers, *President*
EMP: 5 **EST:** 1979
SQ FT: 3,500
SALES (est): 438K **Privately Held**
SIC: 7692 Welding repair

(G-7591)
WASSERSTROM COMPANY (PA)
Also Called: National Smallwares
4500 E Broad St (43213-1360)
PHONE..................614 228-6525
Rodney Wasserstrom, *President*
David A Tumen, *Principal*
Reid Wasserstrom, *Exec VP*
Dennis Blank, *CFO*
Alan Wasserstrom, *Treasurer*
◆ **EMP:** 395 **EST:** 1902
SQ FT: 250,000
SALES (est): 824.5MM **Privately Held**
WEB: www.wasserstrom.com
SIC: 5087 3566 5021 5046 Restaurant supplies; speed changers, drives & gears; office furniture; commercial cooking & food service equipment; office supplies; kitchenware

(G-7592)
WASSERSTROM COMPANY
National Office Warehouse Div
2777 Silver Dr (43211-1054)
PHONE..................614 228-2233
Mike Burroughs, *General Mgr*
EMP: 10
SQ FT: 70,000
SALES (corp-wide): 824.5MM **Privately Held**
WEB: www.wasserstrom.com
SIC: 5044 5112 5021 2752 Office equipment; office supplies; office furniture; commercial printing, offset
PA: The Wasserstrom Company
4500 E Broad St
Columbus OH 43213
614 228-6525

(G-7593)
WATKINS PRINTING COMPANY
1401 E 17th Ave (43211-2849)
PHONE..................614 297-8270
Tamara Watkins Green, *Co-Owner*
David Watkins, *Vice Pres*
Eric Watkins, *Vice Pres*
Debra Llewellyn, *Info Tech Dir*
EMP: 45 **EST:** 1949
SQ FT: 35,000
SALES (est): 9.7MM **Privately Held**
WEB: www.watkinsprinting.com
SIC: 2752 2791 2789 Commercial printing, offset; typesetting; bookbinding & related work

(G-7594)
WATSON ELECTRIC MOTOR SVC INC
536 Stockbridge Rd (43207-3965)
PHONE..................614 836-9904
Maria Swonger, *President*
Mike Watson, *Principal*
Helen Watson, *Admin Sec*
EMP: 10
SQ FT: 4,800
SALES (est): 690K **Privately Held**
SIC: 7694 5063 Electric motor repair; rebuilding motors, except automotive; motors, electric

(G-7595)
WE GRIND MUZIK
4000 Andrus Ct Apt D (43227-1296)
PHONE..................614 670-4142
Avery-El Grier, *Owner*
EMP: 4 **EST:** 2015
SALES (est): 72.6K **Privately Held**
SIC: 3599 Grinding castings for the trade

(G-7596)
WEENK LABS LLC
221 N 4th St (43215-2510)
PHONE..................614 448-0160
Stephan Smith,
EMP: 5
SALES (est): 356.1K **Privately Held**
SIC: 3944 Electronic games & toys

(G-7597)
WELCH PACKAGING GROUP INC
Also Called: Welch Packaging Columbus
4700 Alkire Rd (43228-3495)
PHONE..................614 870-2000
Tayler Darling, *Manager*
EMP: 110
SALES (corp-wide): 546.3MM **Privately Held**
SIC: 2621 7389 Wrapping & packaging papers; packaging & labeling services
PA: Welch Packaging Group, Inc.
1020 Herman St
Elkhart IN 46516
574 295-2460

(G-7598)
WELDING CONSULTANTS INC
889 N 22nd St (43219-2426)
PHONE..................614 258-7018
William A Svekric Sr, *President*
William Svekric Jr, *Vice Pres*
EMP: 6
SQ FT: 4,800
SALES (est): 975.6K **Privately Held**
SIC: 8742 8734 8711 7692 Management consulting services; testing laboratories; engineering services; welding repair; measuring & controlling devices

(G-7599)
WELDON
3834 Zane Trace Dr (43228-3831)
PHONE..................330 263-9533
John Wingo, *Manager*
EMP: 3
SALES (est): 241.7K **Privately Held**
SIC: 3679 Vehicular lighting equipment

(G-7600)
WEST-CAMP PRESS INC
Also Called: American Colorscans
5178 Sinclair Rd (43229-5437)
PHONE..................614 895-0233
EMP: 22
SALES (corp-wide): 26.9MM **Privately Held**
SIC: 2752 Color lithography
PA: West-Camp Press, Inc.
39 Collegeview Rd
Westerville OH 43081
614 882-2378

(G-7601)
WESTROCK CP LLC
1015 Marion Rd (43207-2558)
PHONE..................614 445-6050
Rich Simon, *General Mgr*
EMP: 34
SALES (corp-wide): 16.2B **Publicly Held**
WEB: www.sto.com
SIC: 2631 Paperboard mills
HQ: Westrock Cp, Llc
1000 Abernathy Rd
Atlanta GA 30328

(G-7602)
WHEEL GROUP HOLDINGS LLC
Also Called: Wheel One
2901 E 4th Ave Ste 3 (43219-2896)
PHONE..................614 253-6247
Joseph Nantle, *Office Mgr*
EMP: 6
SALES (corp-wide): 44MM **Privately Held**
SIC: 3714 3452 Wheel rims, motor vehicle; nuts, metal
PA: Wheel Group Holdings, Llc
1050 N Vineyard Ave
Ontario CA 91764
888 399-8885

(G-7603)
WHITE CASTLE SYSTEM INC (PA)
555 W Goodale St (43215-1104)
P.O. Box 1498 (43216-1498)
PHONE..................614 228-5781
Edgar W Ingram III, *Ch of Bd*
Bette Everson, *President*
Elizabeth Ingram, *President*
David Rife, *President*
Laura Franson, *General Mgr*
◆ **EMP:** 275
SQ FT: 143,000
SALES (est): 613.7MM **Privately Held**
WEB: www.whitecastle.com
SIC: 5812 5142 2051 2013 Fast-food restaurant, chain; meat, frozen: packaged; bread, cake & related products; sausages & other prepared meats

(G-7604)
WILLIAM DARLING COMPANY INC
615 Hilliard Rome Rd A (43228-9475)
PHONE..................614 878-0085
William J Darling, *President*
Kathy Moss, *Purchasing*
EMP: 6
SQ FT: 1,500
SALES (est): 1.4MM **Privately Held**
SIC: 5084 3545 Industrial machinery & equipment; cutting tools for machine tools

(G-7605)
WILSONART LLC
2500 International St (43228-4601)
PHONE..................614 876-1515
Buddy Mohler, *Engin/R&D Mgr*
EMP: 24
SALES (corp-wide): 14.7B **Publicly Held**
WEB: www.wilsonart.com
SIC: 2821 2541 Plastics materials & resins; table or counter tops, plastic laminated
HQ: Wilsonart Llc
2501 Wilsonart Dr
Temple TX 76504
254 207-7000

(G-7606)
WINSTON CAMPBELL LLC
1777 Mckinley Ave (43222-1050)
PHONE..................614 274-7015
Jonathan Edwards,
EMP: 3
SALES (est): 502K **Privately Held**
SIC: 3441 Fabricated structural metal

(G-7607)
WK BRICK COMPANY
Also Called: Ceramitec
970 Claycraft Rd (43230-6634)
P.O. Box 361034 (43236-1034)
PHONE..................614 416-6700
Luke Castilli, *Partner*
EMP: 4
SALES (est): 280K **Privately Held**
WEB: www.ceramitec.com
SIC: 3251 Ceramic glazed brick, clay

(G-7608)
WOLF METALS INC
1625 W Mound St (43223-1809)
PHONE..................614 461-6361
James Wolf, *President*
Donna Wolf, *Vice Pres*
Mike Wolf, *Plant Mgr*
Karen Gould, *Admin Sec*
EMP: 6 **EST:** 1974
SQ FT: 10,000
SALES (est): 1.3MM **Privately Held**
SIC: 3444 Sheet metal specialties, not stamped

(G-7609)
WOLFDEN PRODUCTS INC
Also Called: Wolf Composite Solutions
3991 Fondorf Dr (43228-1025)
PHONE..................614 219-6990
Alex Wolford, *President*
Bethany Wolford, *Office Mgr*
▼ **EMP:** 7
SQ FT: 53,000

GEOGRAPHIC SECTION

Columbus Grove - Putnam County (G-7634)

SALES: 1MM **Privately Held**
WEB: www.wolfdenproducts.com
SIC: 3624 Fibers, carbon & graphite

(G-7610)
WOLFE ASSOCIATES INC
Also Called: DISPATCH PRINTING
34 S 3rd St (43215-4201)
PHONE...................................614 461-5000
John F Wolfe, *President*
Nancy W Lane, *Vice Pres*
William C Wolfe Jr, *Vice Pres*
James H Gilmore, *CFO*
A K Pierce Jr, *Treasurer*
EMP: 4
SALES: 4MM **Privately Held**
SIC: 2759 Newspapers: printing

(G-7611)
WOODCOR AMERICA INC (PA)
Also Called: Cedar America
625 Crescent Rd (43204-2460)
P.O. Box 668, Grove City (43123-0668)
PHONE...................................614 277-2930
Ted Gawel, *President*
Thane Bock, *Corp Secy*
Kerry Lind, *Vice Pres*
Brian Kinn, *Controller*
▲ EMP: 5
SQ FT: 12,000
SALES (est): 1.7MM **Privately Held**
WEB: www.cedaramerica.com
SIC: 2499 Applicators, wood

(G-7612)
WORDCROSS ENTERPRISES INC
Also Called: Christian Happenings Magazine
735 Taylor Rd Ste 230 (43230-6546)
PHONE...................................614 410-4140
Edward J Novak, *President*
Cynthia Novak, *Shareholder*
EMP: 15
SQ FT: 3,300
SALES (est): 1.7MM **Privately Held**
WEB: www.christianhappenings.com
SIC: 2721 7336 Magazines: publishing only, not printed on site; graphic arts & related design

(G-7613)
WORLD WIDE RECYCLERS INC
3755 S High St (43207-4011)
PHONE...................................614 554-3296
Jeffery May Sr, *President*
EMP: 14
SALES (est): 1.2MM **Privately Held**
SIC: 2611 5064 Pulp mills, mechanical & recycling processing; electric household appliances

(G-7614)
WORTHINGTON CYLINDER CORP
1085 Dearborn Dr (43085-1542)
PHONE...................................614 438-7900
Jim Stegmayer, *Purchasing*
John McConnell, *Manager*
EMP: 196
SALES (corp-wide): 3.5B **Publicly Held**
SIC: 3443 Cylinders, pressure: metal plate
HQ: Worthington Cylinder Corporation
200 W Old Wlson Bridge Rd
Worthington OH 43085
614 840-3210

(G-7615)
WORTHINGTON INDUSTRIES INC
2170 West Case Rd (43235-7527)
PHONE...................................614 438-3113
Paul Spreng, *Manager*
EMP: 12
SALES (corp-wide): 3.5B **Publicly Held**
WEB: www.worthingtonindustries.com
SIC: 3316 Strip steel, cold-rolled: from purchased hot-rolled
PA: Worthington Industries, Inc.
200 W Old Wlson Bridge Rd
Worthington OH 43085
614 438-3210

(G-7616)
WORTHINGTON INDUSTRIES INC
Also Called: Worthington Steel Div
1127 Dearborn Dr (43085-4920)
PHONE...................................614 438-3190
Frank Roberto, *Principal*
Donald Burton, *Manager*
EMP: 12
SALES (corp-wide): 3.5B **Publicly Held**
WEB: www.worthingtonindustries.com
SIC: 3316 Cold finishing of steel shapes
PA: Worthington Industries, Inc.
200 W Old Wlson Bridge Rd
Worthington OH 43085
614 438-3210

(G-7617)
WORTHNGTON STELPAC SYSTEMS LLC (HQ)
1205 Dearborn Dr (43085-4769)
PHONE...................................614 438-3205
Mark Russell, *CEO*
EMP: 250
SALES (est): 47.5MM
SALES (corp-wide): 3.5B **Publicly Held**
SIC: 3325 5051 Steel foundries; metals service centers & offices
PA: Worthington Industries, Inc.
200 W Old Wlson Bridge Rd
Worthington OH 43085
614 438-3210

(G-7618)
WYANDOTTE WINE CELLAR INC
4640 Wyandotte Dr (43230-1258)
PHONE...................................614 476-3624
William Butler, *Principal*
Valerie Coolidge, *Manager*
Sarah Shroyer, *Manager*
Ryan Coolidge, *Assistant*
EMP: 5
SALES (est): 445.2K
SALES (corp-wide): 810.4K **Privately Held**
SIC: 2084 Wines
PA: Wyandotte Wine Cellar Inc
232 Overbrook Dr
Columbus OH 43214
614 784-0161

(G-7619)
WYMAN WOODWORKING
389 Robinwood Ave (43213-1752)
PHONE...................................614 338-0615
Marc Wyman, *Principal*
EMP: 4 EST: 2008
SALES (est): 446.4K **Privately Held**
SIC: 2431 Millwork

(G-7620)
YACHIYO OF AMERICA INC (DH)
2285 Walcutt Rd (43228-9575)
PHONE...................................614 876-3220
Poshio Yanada, *CEO*
Jason Armstrong, *Production*
Dale Pike, *Purchasing*
Kirk Bohanan, *Engineer*
Thomas Cahill, *Asst Mgr*
▲ EMP: 112
SALES (est): 137MM
SALES (corp-wide): 144.1B **Privately Held**
SIC: 3465 3714 3089 Automotive stampings; acceleration equipment, motor vehicle; novelties, plastic
HQ: Yachiyo Industry Co., Ltd.
393, Kashiwabara
Sayama STM 350-1
429 551-211

(G-7621)
YARN SHOP INC
1125 Kenny Centre Mall (43220-4036)
PHONE...................................614 457-7836
Joyce Lewis, *President*
EMP: 5 EST: 2007
SALES: 300K **Privately Held**
SIC: 2281 5949 Yarn spinning mills; knitting goods & supplies

(G-7622)
YEMANEH MUSIE
Also Called: Red Sea Truck Line
2734 Rosedale Ave (43204-2762)
PHONE...................................614 506-3687
Musie Yemaneh, *Owner*
EMP: 3
SQ FT: 625
SALES: 500K **Privately Held**
SIC: 4212 3537 4789 Animal transport; trucks: freight, baggage, etc.: industrial, except mining; car loading

(G-7623)
YI XING INC
850 Busch Ct (43229-1792)
PHONE...................................614 785-9631
EMP: 5
SALES: 100K **Privately Held**
SIC: 2759 2396 Commercial Printing Mfg Auto/Apparel Trimming

(G-7624)
ZANER-BLOSER INC (HQ)
Also Called: Superkids Reading Program
1400 Goodale Blvd Ste 200 (43212-3777)
P.O. Box 16764 (43216-6764)
PHONE...................................614 486-0221
Lisa Carmona, *President*
Dawn Danneman, *Office Mgr*
EMP: 61
SQ FT: 15,000
SALES (est): 88.5MM
SALES (corp-wide): 216.2MM **Privately Held**
WEB: www.zaner-bloser.com
SIC: 5192 5049 8249 2731 Books; school supplies; correspondence school; book publishing
PA: Highlights For Children, Inc.
1800 Watermark Dr
Columbus OH 43215
614 486-0631

(G-7625)
ZANER-BLOSER INC
1400 Goodale Blvd Ste 200 (43212-3777)
PHONE...................................608 441-5555
EMP: 4
SALES (corp-wide): 216.2MM **Privately Held**
SIC: 5192 5049 8249 2731 Books; school supplies; correspondence school; book publishing
HQ: Zaner-Bloser, Inc.
1400 Goodale Blvd Ste 200
Columbus OH 43212
614 486-0221

(G-7626)
ZENOS ACTIVEWEAR INC
1354 Parsons Ave (43206-3643)
PHONE...................................614 443-0070
Steve White, *President*
David White, *Corp Secy*
Ed White, *Senior VP*
Robert White, *Vice Pres*
EMP: 5
SALES: 400K **Privately Held**
WEB: www.zenosactivewear.com
SIC: 2261 2759 2396 Screen printing of cotton broadwoven fabrics; screen printing; automotive & apparel trimmings

(G-7627)
ZIMMER INC
6816 Lauffer Rd (43231-1623)
PHONE...................................614 508-6000
Scott Klebunde, *Branch Mgr*
EMP: 104
SALES (corp-wide): 7.9B **Publicly Held**
SIC: 3842 Orthopedic appliances
HQ: Zimmer, Inc.
1800 W Center St
Warsaw IN 46580
800 348-9500

(G-7628)
ZSHOT INC
6155 Huntley Rd Ste D (43229-1096)
PHONE...................................800 385-8581
Wallace Lau, *President*
▲ EMP: 5
SALES (est): 526.2K **Privately Held**
SIC: 3484 Rifles or rifle parts, 30 mm. & below

(G-7629)
ZYVEX PERFORMANCE MTLS INC (HQ)
Also Called: Zyvex Technologies
1255 Kinnear Rd Ste 100 (43212-1162)
PHONE...................................614 481-2222
Lance Criscuolo, *President*
EMP: 21
SALES (est): 2.5MM
SALES (corp-wide): 4.9MM **Privately Held**
WEB: www.zyvexpro.com
SIC: 3624 Carbon & graphite products
PA: Ocsial Llc
1804 Embarcadero Rd # 202
Palo Alto CA 94303
415 906-5271

Columbus Grove
Putnam County

(G-7630)
ANCIENT INFUSIONS LLC
10246 Road P (45830-9733)
PHONE...................................419 659-5110
Kevin Gavin,
EMP: 4 EST: 2016
SQ FT: 14,130
SALES: 334.1K **Privately Held**
WEB: www.sassafrastea.com
SIC: 2099 5149 2087 Tea blending; beverages, except coffee & tea; beverage concentrates; beverage bases, concentrates, syrups, powders & mixes

(G-7631)
BUCKEYE TRACTOR COMPANY CORP
11313 Slabtown Rd (45830-9302)
P.O. Box 97 (45830-0097)
PHONE...................................419 659-2162
Lynn Graham, *President*
▼ EMP: 8 EST: 1972
SQ FT: 11,200
SALES (est): 1.6MM **Privately Held**
WEB: www.buctraco.com
SIC: 3523 5261 Farm machinery & equipment; nurseries & garden centers

(G-7632)
CARPE DIEM INDUSTRIES LLC (PA)
Also Called: Colonial Surface Solutions
4599 Campbell Rd (45830-9403)
PHONE...................................419 659-5639
Patricia Langhals, *President*
Darren Langhals, *Corp Secy*
EMP: 55
SQ FT: 750
SALES (est): 18.1MM **Privately Held**
WEB: www.colonialsurfacesolutions.com
SIC: 3479 3471 3398 1799 Painting of metal products; cleaning & descaling metal products; sand blasting of metal parts; tumbling (cleaning & polishing) of machine parts; metal heat treating; tempering of metal; coating of metal structures at construction site

(G-7633)
CLAIR ZEITS
7896 N Cool Rd (45830-9426)
PHONE...................................419 643-8980
Clair Zeits, *Principal*
EMP: 3
SALES (est): 162.3K **Privately Held**
SIC: 2711 Newspapers, publishing & printing

(G-7634)
COAT ALL
4599 Campbell Rd (45830-9403)
PHONE...................................419 659-2757
Dennis Schroeder, *Owner*
EMP: 3
SALES (est): 161.5K **Privately Held**
WEB: www.calmcoat.com
SIC: 3479 Coating of metals & formed products

Columbus Grove - Putnam County (G-7635)

(G-7635)
GROVE ENGINEERED PRODUCTS INC
201 E Cross St (45830-1302)
PHONE..................................419 659-5939
Larry Clymer, *President*
▲ EMP: 6
SALES: 6MM Privately Held
WEB: www.groveengineeredproducts.com
SIC: 2241 3011 Spindle banding; tire & inner tube materials & related products

(G-7636)
NATIONAL LIME AND STONE CO
18264 State Route 189 (45830-9207)
PHONE..................................419 642-6690
Nick Morris, *Branch Mgr*
EMP: 3
SALES (corp-wide): 3.2B Privately Held
WEB: www.natlime.com
SIC: 1422 Crushed & broken limestone
PA: The National Lime And Stone Company
551 Lake Cascade Pkwy
Findlay OH 45840
419 422-4341

(G-7637)
PRODUCTION PRODUCTS INC
200 Sugar Grove Ln (45830-9627)
PHONE..................................734 241-7242
Sam Modica, *President*
Grace Viers, *Vice Pres*
◆ EMP: 76
SQ FT: 20,000
SALES (est): 21.6MM Privately Held
SIC: 3469 3548 Metal stampings; electric welding equipment; arc welders, transformer-rectifier; arc welding generators, alternating current & direct current
PA: Midway Products Group, Inc.
1 Lyman E Hoyt Dr
Monroe MI 48161

(G-7638)
TALON DEFENSE
408 S Main St (45830-1131)
PHONE..................................419 236-7695
Brad McCluer, *Principal*
EMP: 3
SALES (est): 150.8K Privately Held
SIC: 3812 Defense systems & equipment

(G-7639)
WITT-GOR INC
108 S High St 110 (45830-1241)
P.O. Box 125 (45830-0125)
PHONE..................................419 659-2151
Fax: 419 659-2154
EMP: 5
SQ FT: 8,000
SALES (est): 517K Privately Held
SIC: 2541 5713 2542 Mfg Wood Partitions/Fixtures Ret Floor Covering Mfg Partitions/Fixtures-Nonwood

Concord Township
Lake County

(G-7640)
NOVELIS
11815 Oakhurst Ave (44077-9365)
PHONE..................................440 392-6150
EMP: 3 EST: 2015
SALES (est): 197.8K Privately Held
SIC: 3353 Aluminum sheet, plate & foil

Conneaut
Ashtabula County

(G-7641)
B C MACHINING INC
502 E Main Rd (44030-8673)
PHONE..................................440 593-4763
Neil Burger, *President*
Terrance Crowe, *Vice Pres*
EMP: 3
SALES (est): 437.3K Privately Held
WEB: www.bcmachininginc.com
SIC: 3599 Machine shop, jobbing & repair

(G-7642)
CASCADE OHIO INC
Also Called: C W Ohio
1209 Maple Ave (44030-2120)
PHONE..................................440 593-5800
Nicholas N Noirot, *President*
Gary C Trapp, *Vice Pres*
Harlan Smith, *Maintence Staff*
▲ EMP: 282
SQ FT: 250,000
SALES (est): 83.9MM Privately Held
WEB: www.cwohio.com
SIC: 2431 3442 Windows & window parts & trim, wood; louver windows, glass, wood frame; windows, wood; metal doors, sash & trim

(G-7643)
CITY OF CONNEAUT
Also Called: Conneaut Township Park
480 Lake Rd (44030-1460)
PHONE..................................440 599-7071
Bruce Mitchell, *Superintendent*
EMP: 6 Privately Held
SIC: 2531 Picnic tables or benches, park
PA: City Of Conneaut
294 Main St
Conneaut OH 44030
440 593-7413

(G-7644)
CONTINENTAL STRL PLAS INC
333 Gore Rd (44030-2909)
PHONE..................................440 945-4800
David Murtha, *Opers Mgr*
Jessica Van Epps, *Materials Mgr*
Dave Murtha, *Branch Mgr*
Kim Zitny, *Director*
EMP: 246
SALES (corp-wide): 7.8B Privately Held
SIC: 3089 Injection molding of plastics; plastic processing
HQ: Continental Structural Plastics, Inc.
255 Rex Blvd
Auburn Hills MI 48326
248 237-7800

(G-7645)
GAMCO COMPONETS GROUP LLC
1370 Chamberlain Blvd (44030-1100)
PHONE..................................440 593-1500
EMP: 9
SALES (est): 1MM
SALES (corp-wide): 1.6B Publicly Held
WEB: www.pkoh.com.cn
SIC: 3465 Automotive stampings
HQ: Park-Ohio Industries, Inc.
6065 Parkland Blvd Ste 1
Cleveland OH 44124
440 947-2000

(G-7646)
GENERAL ALUMINUM MFG COMPANY
1370 Chamberlain Blvd (44030-1100)
PHONE..................................440 593-6225
Milt Gallmeyer, *President*
Jim Onders, *Vice Pres*
Kathleen Difiori, *Plant Mgr*
Jack Ehretsman, *Sales Staff*
Doug Stoops, *Branch Mgr*
EMP: 300
SALES (corp-wide): 1.6B Publicly Held
SIC: 3365 3369 Aluminum & aluminum-based alloy castings; nonferrous foundries
HQ: General Aluminum Mfg. Company
6065 Parkland Blvd
Cleveland OH 44124
330 297-1225

(G-7647)
HARBOR INDUSTRIAL CORP
859 W Jackson St (44030-2255)
PHONE..................................440 599-8366
Michael D Legeza, *President*
Dale Hoskins, *Admin Sec*
EMP: 18
SQ FT: 92,000
SALES (est): 3.2MM Privately Held
SIC: 3089 Plastic hardware & building products

(G-7648)
HMT INC (PA)
360 Commerce St (44030-2200)
P.O. Box 88 (44030-0088)
PHONE..................................440 599-7005
Darrell Maukonen, *President*
EMP: 8
SQ FT: 5,000
SALES (est): 931.7K Privately Held
WEB: www.hmt.com
SIC: 3398 Metal heat treating

(G-7649)
HRH DOOR CORP
Also Called: Wayne - Dalton Plastics
1001 Chamberlain Blvd (44030-1168)
PHONE..................................440 593-5226
EMP: 76
SALES (corp-wide): 621.6MM Privately Held
WEB: www.waynedalton.com
SIC: 2431 3089 3083 Millwork; extruded finished plastic products; laminated plastics plate & sheet
PA: Hrh Door Corp.
1 Door Dr
Mount Hope OH 44660
850 208-3400

(G-7650)
INDEPENDENT CAN COMPANY
1049 Chamberlain Blvd (44030-1168)
PHONE..................................440 593-5300
Bob McClelland, *Exec VP*
Kevin Clinton, *Opers Mgr*
Denise Gallion, *Sales Staff*
Nancy Kalinowski, *Branch Mgr*
Thomas Carter, *Assistant*
EMP: 32
SALES (corp-wide): 63.2MM Privately Held
WEB: www.independentcan.com
SIC: 3411 Tin cans
PA: Independent Can Company
1300 Brass Mill Rd
Belcamp MD 21017
410 272-0090

(G-7651)
KELLYS WELDING & FABRICATING
285 N Amboy Rd (44030-3098)
PHONE..................................440 593-6040
Herbert Kelly Jr, *President*
EMP: 8
SALES (est): 883.9K Privately Held
SIC: 7692 3441 1799 1542 Welding repair; fabricated structural metal; welding on site; nonresidential construction

(G-7652)
LAKESIDE CUSTOM PLATING INC
373 Commerce St (44030-2288)
PHONE..................................440 593-2035
Tracy McBride, *President*
Trevor McBride, *Vice Pres*
Betty McBride, *Admin Sec*
EMP: 5
SALES: 300K Privately Held
SIC: 3471 Plating of metals or formed products

(G-7653)
LIGHTNING MOLD & MACHINE INC
509 W Main Rd (44030-2975)
PHONE..................................440 593-6460
Ronald R Newhart, *President*
Loretta Newhart, *Corp Secy*
Erik Newhart, *Vice Pres*
EMP: 10
SQ FT: 2,700
SALES (est): 1.2MM Privately Held
SIC: 3544 3599 Industrial molds; custom machinery

(G-7654)
LUKJAN METAL PRODUCTS INC (PA)
645 Industry Rd (44030-3045)
P.O. Box 357 (44030-0357)
PHONE..................................440 599-8127
Anatol Lukjanczuk, *President*
Herb Gibson, *General Mgr*
Elena Kelly, *Vice Pres*
Chelsey Corbett, *Human Res Dir*
Brenda Sembower, *Human Res Dir*
EMP: 140 EST: 1964
SQ FT: 100,000
SALES (est): 39MM Privately Held
WEB: www.lukjan.com
SIC: 3312 3444 Blast furnaces & steel mills; ducts, sheet metal

(G-7655)
MARKKO VINEYARD
4500 S Ridge Rd W (44030-9712)
PHONE..................................440 593-3197
Arnulf Esterer, *Owner*
Thomas H Hubbard, *Partner*
EMP: 4
SQ FT: 4,000
SALES: 180K Privately Held
WEB: www.markko.com
SIC: 0172 2084 Grapes; wines

(G-7656)
MODERN ENGINEERING
527 W Adams St (44030-2272)
PHONE..................................440 593-5414
David Mc Laughin, *Owner*
David McLaughlin, *Plant Mgr*
EMP: 6
SALES: 500K Privately Held
SIC: 3469 3599 Machine parts, stamped or pressed metal; machine shop, jobbing & repair

(G-7657)
PRINTCRAFT INC
866 W Jackson St (44030-2256)
PHONE..................................440 599-8903
Richard Truran, *CEO*
Thomas Truran, *President*
EMP: 3 EST: 1943
SQ FT: 3,000
SALES (est): 884.9K Privately Held
SIC: 2752 Commercial printing, offset

(G-7658)
S AND S TOOL INC
576 Blair St (44030-1463)
P.O. Box 127 (44030-0127)
PHONE..................................440 593-4000
Paul Sedmak, *President*
Joe Sedmak, *Vice Pres*
EMP: 8
SQ FT: 5,000
SALES (est): 1.1MM Privately Held
SIC: 3599 Machine shop, jobbing & repair

(G-7659)
SECONDARY MACHINING SERVICES
539 Center Rd (44030-2308)
P.O. Box 296 (44030-0296)
PHONE..................................440 593-1272
Art Distelrath Jr, *President*
Amy Distelrath, *Vice Pres*
Madelon L Distelrath, *Treasurer*
EMP: 7
SALES: 100K Privately Held
SIC: 3599 Machine shop, jobbing & repair

(G-7660)
THE GAZETTE PRINTING CO INC
Also Called: Gazette Publishing
218 Washington St (44030-2605)
P.O. Box 212 (44030-0212)
PHONE..................................440 593-6030
John Lampson, *Principal*
EMP: 9
SALES (corp-wide): 10.7MM Privately Held
WEB: www.gazetteprinting.com
SIC: 2752 2711 Commercial printing, offset; newspapers
PA: The Gazette Printing Co Inc
46 W Jefferson St
Jefferson OH 44047
440 576-9125

(G-7661)
VESUVIUS U S A CORPORATION
Also Called: Foseco Metallurgical
1100 Maple Ave (44030-2119)
PHONE..................................440 593-1161
Jeremy Wilkinson, *Manager*
EMP: 22

▲ = Import ▼ = Export
◆ = Import/Export

SALES (corp-wide): 2.2B **Privately Held**
WEB: www.vesuvius.com
SIC: **2899** Chemical preparations
HQ: Vesuvius U S A Corporation
1404 Newton Dr
Champaign IL 61822
217 351-5000

Conover
Miami County

(G-7662)
CAVEN AND SONS MEAT PACKING CO
7850 E Us Rte 36 (45317)
P.O. Box 400 (45317-0400)
PHONE.................................937 368-3841
Howard Caven, *President*
Victor Caven, *Vice Pres*
Dean Caven, *Treasurer*
Helen Caven, *Admin Sec*
EMP: **15 EST:** 1951
SALES (est): 1.1MM **Privately Held**
SIC: **2011** 5147 5421 2013 Meat packing plants; meats, fresh; meat markets, including freezer provisioners; sausages & other prepared meats

(G-7663)
CONOVER LUMBER COMPANY INC
Also Called: Staely Custom Crating
7960 N Alcony Conover Rd (45317-9763)
P.O. Box 464 (45317-0464)
PHONE.................................937 368-3010
John D Staley, *President*
EMP: **14**
SQ FT: 3,584
SALES (est): 3.5MM **Privately Held**
SIC: **5211** 2421 Lumber products; flooring (dressed lumber), softwood

(G-7664)
LOGAN ENTERPRISES INC
12229 W State Route 29 (45317-9666)
PHONE.................................937 465-8170
Laurel M McCombs, *President*
EMP: **3**
SQ FT: 4,700
SALES (est): 538.7K **Privately Held**
WEB: www.loganent.com
SIC: **3823** Temperature instruments: industrial process type

(G-7665)
MAGNUM MOLDING INC
7435 N Bollinger Rd (45317-9738)
P.O. Box 459 (45317-0459)
PHONE.................................937 368-3040
Greg Gross, *President*
EMP: **9**
SQ FT: 7,000
SALES (est): 1.8MM **Privately Held**
SIC: **3089** 3544 Injection molding of plastics; industrial molds

Continental
Putnam County

(G-7666)
HELENA AGRI-ENTERPRISES LLC
200 N Main St (45831-9172)
PHONE.................................419 596-3806
Wayne Nossfinger, *Branch Mgr*
EMP: **6**
SALES (corp-wide): 70.7B **Privately Held**
SIC: **2819** 5191 Chemicals, high purity: refined from technical grade; fertilizers & agricultural chemicals; seeds & bulbs
HQ: Helena Agri-Enterprises, Llc
255 Schilling Blvd # 300
Collierville TN 38017
901 761-0050

(G-7667)
LIEBRECHT MANUFACTURING LLC
Also Called: Liebrecht Excavating
Rd H 13 (45831)
PHONE.................................419 596-3501
S Liebrecht Jr, *Mng Member*
Sylvester Liebrecht Jr, *Mng Member*
EMP: **13**
SALES: 1.5MM **Privately Held**
WEB: www.farmdrainage.com
SIC: **3523** 1794 Farm machinery & equipment; excavation work

(G-7668)
SOCAR OF OHIO INC (PA)
21739 Road E16 (45831-9003)
PHONE.................................419 596-3100
Ken Charles, *President*
Cary Andrews, *Vice Pres*
Donald G Smith, *Treasurer*
John Morris, *Asst Treas*
EMP: **89**
SQ FT: 90,000
SALES (est): 5.2MM **Privately Held**
SIC: **3441** 2439 Joists, open web steel: long-span series; structural wood members

(G-7669)
VERHOFF MACHINE & WELDING INC
7300 Road 18 (45831-8826)
PHONE.................................419 596-3202
Edward Verhoff, *President*
Leonard J Verhoff, *Principal*
Joseph Verhoff, *Vice Pres*
Travis Verhoff, *Plant Mgr*
Jeff Bellman, *Engineer*
EMP: **120 EST:** 1955
SQ FT: 150,000
SALES (est): 22.7MM **Privately Held**
WEB: www.verhoff.com
SIC: **3599** 3469 3444 3443 Machine shop, jobbing & repair; metal stampings; sheet metalwork; fabricated plate work (boiler shop); fabricated structural metal; manufactured hardware (general)

Convoy
Van Wert County

(G-7670)
LINCOLN CANDLE COMPANY INC
6588 Pollock Rd (45832-8834)
PHONE.................................419 749-4224
Jeffery Thomas, *President*
Cathy Thomas, *Vice Pres*
EMP: **4**
SQ FT: 7,000
SALES (est): 292.4K **Privately Held**
WEB: www.lincolncandleco.com
SIC: **3999** Candles

(G-7671)
SHELLY MATERIALS INC
2364 Richey Rd (45832-9643)
PHONE.................................419 622-2101
Gary Ferguson, *CEO*
EMP: **4**
SALES (corp-wide): 29.7B **Privately Held**
SIC: **2951** Asphalt paving mixtures & blocks
HQ: Shelly Materials, Inc.
80 Park Dr
Thornville OH 43076
740 246-6315

Coolville
Athens County

(G-7672)
AMERICAN DOLL ACCESSORIES
24924 Brimstone Rd (45723-9477)
PHONE.................................740 590-8458
Janice Middleton, *Principal*
EMP: **3**

SALES (est): 121.7K **Privately Held**
SIC: **3021** Rubber & plastics footwear

(G-7673)
M & G TRUSS RAFTERS
Also Called: Lock-N-Logs Log Homes
26077 Congrove St (45723-8112)
PHONE.................................740 667-3166
Richard N Gillian, *Owner*
EMP: **3**
SQ FT: 900
SALES: 300K **Privately Held**
SIC: **2439** Trusses, wooden roof

(G-7674)
MIDDLETON LLYD DOLLS INC (PA)
Also Called: Middlton Lloyd Doll Fctry Outl
23689 Mountain Bell Rd (45723-9463)
PHONE.................................740 989-2082
Janice Middleston, *Principal*
Lloyd Middleton, *President*
Janice Middleton, *Vice Pres*
EMP: **7**
SQ FT: 8,000
SALES (est): 1.6MM **Privately Held**
WEB: www.lloydmiddleton.com
SIC: **3942** 5945 5092 Dolls, except stuffed toy animals; doll parts; hobby, toy & game shops; dolls

(G-7675)
MURPHY JAMES CONSTRUCTION LLC
4146 N Torch Rd (45723-9730)
PHONE.................................740 667-3626
Linney Murphy,
James Murphy,
EMP: **20 EST:** 1976
SALES (est): 450K **Privately Held**
SIC: **3241** Masonry cement

Copley
Summit County

(G-7676)
AKRON DISPERSIONS INC
3291 Sawmill Rd (44321-1637)
P.O. Box 4195 (44321-0195)
PHONE.................................330 666-0045
Michael Giustino, *CEO*
James Finn, *President*
Diane Hunsicker, *Principal*
▲ EMP: **25**
SQ FT: 56,000
SALES (est): 8.5MM **Privately Held**
WEB: www.akrondispersions.com
SIC: **2819** 2899 Industrial inorganic chemicals; chemical preparations

(G-7677)
ALL FIRED UP PNT YOUR OWN POT
30 Rothrock Loop (44321-1331)
PHONE.................................330 865-5858
Janelle Wertz, *Owner*
Kristopher Wertz, *Co-Owner*
EMP: **6**
SALES (est): 487.2K **Privately Held**
SIC: **3269** 5719 Art & ornamental ware, pottery; pottery

(G-7678)
BLOCH PRINTING COMPANY
3569 Copley Rd (44321-1646)
PHONE.................................330 576-6760
David Bloch, *President*
Maria Bloch, *Vice Pres*
EMP: **6 EST:** 1977
SALES (est): 1.1MM **Privately Held**
WEB: www.blochprinting.com
SIC: **5112** 2752 Business forms; computer & photocopying supplies; commercial printing, lithographic

(G-7679)
CARAUSTAR INDUSTRIES INC
202 Montrose West Ave # 315 (44321-2923)
PHONE.................................330 665-7700
EMP: **37**

SALES (corp-wide): 3.8B **Publicly Held**
WEB: www.caraustar.com
SIC: **2679** 2655 3275 3089 Paperboard products, converted; tubes, fiber or paper: made from purchased material; cores, fiber: made from purchased material; gypsum products; wallboard, gypsum; injection molded finished plastic products; extruded finished plastic products; folding boxboard
HQ: Caraustar Industries, Inc.
5000 Austell Powder Sprin
Austell GA 30106
770 948-3101

(G-7680)
COMPETITIVE PRESS INC
144 Scenic View Dr (44321-1343)
PHONE.................................330 289-1968
▲ EMP: **4 EST:** 2010
SALES (est): 343.4K **Privately Held**
SIC: **2741** Miscellaneous publishing

(G-7681)
COPLEY FIRE & RESCUE ASSN
Also Called: COPLEY TOWNSHIP FIRE DEPT
1540 S Clvland Mssllon Rd (44321-1908)
PHONE.................................330 666-6464
Chief Joseph Ezzi, *Principal*
Joseph Ezzi, *Principal*
EMP: **24**
SALES: 36.9K **Privately Held**
SIC: **3711** Fire department vehicles (motor vehicles), assembly of

(G-7682)
DOW SILICONES CORPORATION
3835 Copley Rd (44321-1617)
PHONE.................................330 319-1127
Jeff Clapp, *Branch Mgr*
EMP: **125**
SALES (corp-wide): 85.9B **Publicly Held**
WEB: www.dowcorning.com
SIC: **2869** Silicones
HQ: Dow Silicones Corporation
2200 W Salzburg Rd
Auburn MI 48611
989 496-4000

(G-7683)
DOWNING ENTERPRISES INC
Also Called: Downing Exhibits
1287 Centerview Cir (44321-1632)
PHONE.................................330 666-3888
William Downing Jr, *CEO*
Michael Carano, *President*
Ross Haffey, *Corp Secy*
Karen Gallaher, *Exec VP*
▲ EMP: **100**
SQ FT: 144,000
SALES: 20MM **Privately Held**
WEB: www.downingexhibits.com
SIC: **3993** Displays & cutouts, window & lobby

(G-7684)
ERIK V LAMB
1638 S Clvland Mssllon Rd (44321-1910)
P.O. Box 5223, Akron (44334-0223)
PHONE.................................330 962-1540
Erik V Lamb, *Principal*
EMP: **3**
SALES: 35K **Privately Held**
SIC: **2844** 7389 Toilet preparations;

(G-7685)
GLAXOSMITHKLINE LLC
4273 Ridge Crest Dr (44321-3067)
PHONE.................................330 608-2365
EMP: **26**
SALES (corp-wide): 39.8B **Privately Held**
SIC: **2834** Pharmaceutical preparations
HQ: Glaxosmithkline Llc
5 Crescent Dr
Philadelphia PA 19112
215 751-4000

(G-7686)
J J MERLIN SYSTEMS INC
1245 S Cleveland Massillo (44321-1676)
PHONE.................................330 666-8609
Robert Stroupe, *President*
EMP: **7**
SALES (est): 880K **Privately Held**
SIC: **2992** Lubricating oils

Copley - Summit County (G-7687)

(G-7687)
JRF INDUSTRIES LTD
3675 Copley Rd (44321-1645)
PHONE...................................330 665-3130
Jim Ripley, *Principal*
EMP: 3
SALES (est): 246.4K **Privately Held**
SIC: 3999 Manufacturing industries

(G-7688)
MEECH STTIC ELMINATORS USA INC
1298 Centerview Cir (44321-1632)
PHONE...................................330 564-2000
Matt Fyffe, *General Mgr*
▲ **EMP:** 15
SALES (est): 3.2MM **Privately Held**
WEB: www.meech.com
SIC: 3823 Industrial process measurement equipment

(G-7689)
MULTIBASE INC
3835 Copley Rd (44321-1671)
PHONE...................................330 666-0505
Brian Schell, *President*
Gifford Shearer, *President*
Thomas G Tangney, *Vice Pres*
Joseph Rinaldi, *Treasurer*
Paul A Marcela, *Admin Sec*
◆ **EMP:** 85
SQ FT: 160,000
SALES (est): 25.6MM
SALES (corp-wide): 85.9B **Publicly Held**
WEB: www.multibase.com
SIC: 2821 Plastics materials & resins
HQ: Dow Silicones Corporation
2200 W Salzburg Rd
Auburn MI 48611
989 496-4000

(G-7690)
NEWTECH MATERIALS & ANALYTICAL
618 Tresham Ct (44321-1297)
PHONE...................................330 329-1080
Haiming Xiao, *Partner*
EMP: 3
SALES (est): 331K **Privately Held**
SIC: 3823 Industrial instrmnts msrmnt display/control process variable

(G-7691)
PRCC HOLDINGS INC
Also Called: Preferred Compounding
175 Montrose West Ave # 200
(44321-3122)
PHONE...................................330 798-4790
Kenneth Bloom, *President*
David Kantor, *CFO*
EMP: 238
SQ FT: 5,000
SALES: 205MM **Privately Held**
SIC: 3069 Custom compounding of rubber materials

(G-7692)
PREFERRED COMPOUNDING CORP (PA)
175 Montrose West Ave # 200
(44321-3122)
PHONE...................................330 798-4790
Ken Bloom, *President*
Andrew Chan, *Vice Pres*
Joe Hudson, *Vice Pres*
Scott Lieberman, *Vice Pres*
Randy Niedermier, *Vice Pres*
▲ **EMP:** 109
SQ FT: 70,000
SALES (est): 81MM **Privately Held**
WEB: www.preferredperforms.com
SIC: 3069 Custom compounding of rubber materials

(G-7693)
PVS CHEMICAL SOLUTIONS INC
3149 Copley Rd (44321-2127)
P.O. Box 4143 (44321-0143)
PHONE...................................330 666-0888
Wendy Mangold, *Sales Staff*
Bob Vorhees, *Manager*
EMP: 10
SQ FT: 27,596
SALES (corp-wide): 628.6MM **Privately Held**
SIC: 2819 5169 Sulfur chloride; chemicals & allied products
HQ: Pvs Chemical Solutions, Inc.
10900 Harper Ave
Detroit MI 48213

(G-7694)
SHELLS INC (PA)
1245 S Cleveland Massillo (44321-1680)
PHONE...................................330 808-5558
Henry C Bray Jr, *President*
Henry Bray Jr, *President*
John Edminister, *Vice Pres*
Julie Tremain, *Manager*
EMP: 75 EST: 1972
SQ FT: 85,000
SALES (est): 28.7MM **Privately Held**
WEB: www.shells.com
SIC: 5051 3543 Foundry products; industrial patterns

(G-7695)
SHELLY COMPANY
3350 Sawmill Rd (44321-1635)
PHONE...................................330 666-1125
Joe Casto, *Manager*
EMP: 3
SALES (corp-wide): 29.7B **Privately Held**
SIC: 3648 Miners' lamps
HQ: Shelly Company
80 Park Dr
Thornville OH 43076
740 246-6315

(G-7696)
SOFTPOINT INDUSTRIES
988 Traci Ln (44321-1466)
PHONE...................................330 668-2645
Richard Porter, *Principal*
EMP: 3 EST: 2008
SALES (est): 242.8K **Privately Held**
SIC: 3999 Manufacturing industries

(G-7697)
SPORTSARTCOM
939 Traci Ln (44321-1467)
PHONE...................................330 903-0895
Philip Ferguson, *Partner*
Jeff Ferguson, *Executive*
EMP: 8
SALES (est): 1MM **Privately Held**
WEB: www.sportsart.com
SIC: 2752 Lithographing on metal

(G-7698)
VISION GRAPHICS
Also Called: Signal Graphics Printing
3545 Copley Rd (44321-1608)
PHONE...................................330 665-4451
Eric Schultz, *President*
Patty Zucco, *Sales Staff*
Steve Hall, *Agent*
Todd Van, *Graphic Designe*
EMP: 5
SQ FT: 2,000
SALES (est): 736.5K **Privately Held**
SIC: 2752 Commercial printing, offset

Corning
Perry County

(G-7699)
ALTEIRS OIL INC
140 W Main St (43730-9588)
P.O. Box 415 (43730-0415)
PHONE...................................740 347-4335
Leo Altier, *President*
Pat Sikorski, *Treasurer*
EMP: 3
SALES (est): 231.2K **Privately Held**
SIC: 1382 Oil & gas exploration services

(G-7700)
ALTHEIRS OIL INC
140 E Main St (43730-9550)
P.O. Box 415 (43730-0415)
PHONE...................................740 347-4335
Leo Altier, *President*
EMP: 7 EST: 2010
SALES (est): 481K **Privately Held**
SIC: 1389 Oil & gas field services

(G-7701)
ALTIER BROTHERS INC
155 Walnut St (43730)
P.O. Box 430 (43730-0430)
PHONE...................................740 347-4329
Louis Altier, *President*
EMP: 17
SQ FT: 5,000
SALES (est): 1.6MM **Privately Held**
SIC: 1389 Oil field services

(G-7702)
SERGEANT STONE INC
1425 State Route 555 Ne (43730-9532)
P.O. Box 2086, Zanesville (43702-2086)
PHONE...................................740 452-7434
Claude Imler, *President*
EMP: 5 EST: 2014
SALES (est): 290.8K **Privately Held**
SIC: 1422 Crushed & broken limestone

Cortland
Trumbull County

(G-7703)
BACCONIS LICKETY SPLIT
4194 Greenville Rd (44410-9750)
PHONE...................................330 924-0418
Abbey L Bacconi, *Principal*
EMP: 3
SALES (est): 206.6K **Privately Held**
SIC: 2024 Ice cream, bulk

(G-7704)
BORTNICK TRACTOR SALES INC
6192 Warren Rd (44410-9736)
PHONE...................................330 924-2555
Dana W Harju, *Principal*
EMP: 17
SALES (est): 2.5MM **Privately Held**
SIC: 3524 5261 3541 Grass catchers, lawn mower; lawn & garden equipment; saws & sawing machines

(G-7705)
CONCRETE CNSTR MCHY CO LLC
5210 State Route 46 (44410-9607)
PHONE...................................330 638-1515
Doug Roper,
Ward Roper,
John Thellman,
EMP: 4
SALES (est): 701.9K **Privately Held**
SIC: 3531 Construction machinery

(G-7706)
CONTROL TRANSFORMER INC
Also Called: Geneva Rubber Company
3701 Warren Meadville Rd (44410-9423)
PHONE...................................330 637-6015
William J Martin, *President*
▲ **EMP:** 45 EST: 2002
SQ FT: 30,000
SALES: 18MM
SALES (corp-wide): 1.6B **Publicly Held**
WEB: www.control-transformer.com
SIC: 3612 Power transformers, electric
HQ: Ajax Tocco Magnethermic Corporation
1745 Overland Ave Ne
Warren OH 44483
330 372-8511

(G-7707)
CORTLAND HARDWOOD PRODUCTS LLC
124 Pearl St (44410-1049)
PHONE...................................330 638-3232
Dave Denman, *Mng Member*
Dorothy Denman,
EMP: 25
SQ FT: 20,000
SALES (est): 3.4MM **Privately Held**
SIC: 2431 Doors & door parts & trim, wood

(G-7708)
CUBIC BLUE INC
2934 Warren Meadville Rd (44410-9321)
PHONE...................................330 638-2999
Joseph Teffner, *President*
Donna Meadows, *Vice Pres*
EMP: 3
SQ FT: 1,800
SALES: 400K **Privately Held**
SIC: 3544 Industrial molds

(G-7709)
CUSTOM COUNTER TOPS & SPC CO
161 W Main St (44410-1482)
PHONE...................................330 637-4856
Amil Roscoe, *President*
Ronald Roscoe, *Vice Pres*
Patty Roscoe, *Treasurer*
Margaret M Roscoe, *Admin Sec*
EMP: 4
SQ FT: 10,000
SALES (est): 470K **Privately Held**
WEB: www.mainstvideo.com
SIC: 5211 2541 Cabinets, kitchen; counters or counter display cases, wood

(G-7710)
HOWLAND PRINTING INC
Also Called: Proforma
3117 Niles Cortland Rd Ne (44410-1737)
PHONE...................................330 637-8255
Norma Harned, *President*
EMP: 7
SQ FT: 1,500
SALES (est): 797.8K **Privately Held**
SIC: 2752 Commercial printing, offset

(G-7711)
LAKESIDE SPORT SHOP INC
2115 Wlson Sharpsville Rd (44410-9384)
PHONE...................................330 637-2862
John C Wallace, *President*
J W Wallace, *Vice Pres*
EMP: 5
SQ FT: 2,048
SALES (est): 413.3K **Privately Held**
SIC: 1389 5941 Fishing for tools, oil & gas field; sporting goods & bicycle shops; fishing equipment

(G-7712)
LAWBRE CO
Also Called: Architechual Etc
3311 Warren Meadville Rd (44410-8808)
PHONE...................................330 637-3363
Christopher Riekert, *President*
EMP: 6
SQ FT: 5,000
SALES (est): 500.6K **Privately Held**
WEB: www.lawbre.com
SIC: 3944 Dollhouses & furniture

(G-7713)
NUFLUX LLC
2395 State Route 5 (44410-9217)
PHONE...................................330 399-1122
Robert White, *President*
William M West, *Mng Member*
EMP: 7
SALES (est): 3.1MM **Privately Held**
SIC: 3399 3312 Metal powders, pastes & flakes; electrometallurgical steel

(G-7714)
PARROT ENERGY COMPANY
180 Portal Dr (44410-1521)
P.O. Box 92 (44410-0092)
PHONE...................................330 637-0151
Natale Pestalozzi, *Owner*
EMP: 4
SALES (est): 230K **Privately Held**
SIC: 1381 Drilling oil & gas wells

(G-7715)
QUANTUM INTEGRATION LLC
1980 Niles Cortland Rd Ne (44410-9405)
PHONE...................................330 609-0355
Andre Camelli, *Principal*
EMP: 3
SALES (est): 188.5K **Privately Held**
SIC: 3572 Computer storage devices

(G-7716)
VENOM EXTERMINATING LLC
40 Monte Ln (44410-2010)
P.O. Box 321 (44410-0321)
PHONE...................................330 637-3366
Paul Antonchak, *Principal*
EMP: 3
SALES (est): 196.4K **Privately Held**
SIC: 2836 Venoms

▲ = Import ▼ = Export
◆ = Import/Export

GEOGRAPHIC SECTION   Coshocton - Coshocton County (G-7742)

Coshocton
Coshocton County

(G-7717)
AK STEEL CORPORATION
Also Called: Coshocton Stainless
17400 State Route 16 (43812-9268)
PHONE..................................740 829-2206
Mike Frankland, *Marketing Staff*
Walt Beringer, *Branch Mgr*
Donald Pepper, *Supervisor*
Jerry Sturtz, *Supervisor*
Jerry Bailey, *Business Dir*
EMP: 584 **Publicly Held**
WEB: www.ketnar.org
SIC: 3312 3316 Stainless steel; cold finishing of steel shapes
HQ: Ak Steel Corporation
9227 Centre Pointe Dr
West Chester OH 45069
513 425-4200

(G-7718)
ANNIN & CO
700 S 3rd St (43812-2062)
PHONE..................................740 622-4447
Vane Scott III, *Production*
Rick Payne, *Manager*
EMP: 100
SQ FT: 15,000
SALES (corp-wide): 165.1MM **Privately Held**
WEB: www.annin.com
SIC: 2399 5999 3446 3429 Flags, fabric; banners, flags, decals & posters; architectural metalwork; manufactured hardware (general)
PA: Annin & Co.
105 Eisenhower Pkwy # 203
Roseland NJ 07068
973 228-9400

(G-7719)
ANSELL HEALTHCARE PRODUCTS LLC
925 Chestnut St (43812-1302)
PHONE..................................740 622-4311
D R Scholfield, *Marketing Staff*
Allan Roman, *Manager*
EMP: 70 **Privately Held**
WEB: www.ansellpro.com
SIC: 3842 3069 Gloves, safety; rubber coated fabrics & clothing; aprons, vulcanized rubbed or rubberized fabric
HQ: Ansell Healthcare Products Llc
111 Wood Ave S Ste 210
Iselin NJ 08830
732 345-5400

(G-7720)
ANSELL HEALTHCARE PRODUCTS LLC
Also Called: Cpp
925 Chestnut St (43812-1302)
PHONE..................................740 295-5414
EMP: 160
SALES (corp-wide): 1.6B **Privately Held**
SIC: 3842 2326 3069 Mfg Surgical Appliances Mfg Men/Boy Work Clothng Mfg Fabrcatd Rubber Prdt
HQ: Ansell Healthcare Products Llc
111 Wood Ave S Ste 210
Iselin NJ 08830
732 345-5400

(G-7721)
BAIRD CONCRETE PRODUCTS INC
15 Locust St (43812-1136)
P.O. Box 1028 (43812-5028)
PHONE..................................740 623-8600
John Baird, *President*
Cynthia Albertson, *Corp Secy*
Tom Albertson, *Vice Pres*
Margie Baird, *Vice Pres*
EMP: 10
SQ FT: 13,700
SALES: 1.6MM **Privately Held**
SIC: 3273 Ready-mixed concrete

(G-7722)
BEACH COMPANY
Also Called: Standard Advertising Co
240 Browns Ln (43812-2067)
P.O. Box 518 (43812-0518)
PHONE..................................740 622-0905
James M Beach, *President*
Esward Beach, *Vice Pres*
Dan Doyle, *Vice Pres*
Beverly M Beach, *Treasurer*
Margret Beach, *Admin Sec*
EMP: 14
SQ FT: 24,000
SALES (est): 2.1MM **Privately Held**
WEB: www.thebeachcompany.com
SIC: 2752 Calendars, lithographed

(G-7723)
BRYDET DEVELOPMENT CORPORATION
16867 State Route 83 (43812-9460)
P.O. Box 199, Conesville (43811-0199)
PHONE..................................740 623-0455
Paul E Bryant, *President*
Ron Deeter, *Principal*
▼ **EMP:** 50
SQ FT: 4,500
SALES (est): 10.2MM **Privately Held**
WEB: www.brydet.com
SIC: 3532 Auger mining equipment

(G-7724)
BUCKEYE BRINE LLC
23986 Airport Rd (43812-1562)
P.O. Box 425 (43812-0425)
PHONE..................................740 575-4482
Laura Sabine, *Accountant*
Todd Schlauch, *Maintence Staff*
EMP: 15 **EST:** 2013
SALES (est): 1.3MM **Privately Held**
SIC: 1389 Oil & gas field services

(G-7725)
COSHOCTON COMMUNITY CHOIR
142 N 4th St (43812-1504)
PHONE..................................740 623-0554
EMP: 3
SALES (est): 162.2K **Privately Held**
SIC: 2711 Newspapers: publishing only, not printed on site

(G-7726)
COSHOCTON COMMUNITY CHOIR INC
530 Cambridge Rd (43812-2254)
PHONE..................................740 622-8571
Beth Nelson, *President*
EMP: 3
SALES: 43.9K **Privately Held**
SIC: 2711 Newspapers, publishing & printing

(G-7727)
COSHOCTON ETHANOL LLC
18137 County Road 271 (43812-9465)
PHONE..................................740 623-3046
Mike Fedor, *Mng Member*
EMP: 42
SALES (est): 5.6MM **Privately Held**
SIC: 2869 Ethyl alcohol, ethanol

(G-7728)
COSHOCTON INDUSTRIES INC (PA)
605 N 15th St (43812-1496)
PHONE..................................740 622-4734
James R Harris, *President*
EMP: 4 **EST:** 1971
SQ FT: 17,500
SALES (est): 2MM **Privately Held**
WEB: www.jnindustries.com
SIC: 3599 Machine shop, jobbing & repair

(G-7729)
COSHOCTON PALLET & DOOR BLDG
23222 County Road 621 (43812-9766)
PHONE..................................740 622-9766
Brad Williams, *Owner*
EMP: 3
SALES (est): 119.9K **Privately Held**
SIC: 2448 Wood pallets & skids

(G-7730)
CRABAR/GBF INC
Also Called: Ennis Business Forms of Ohio
24170 Hangar Ct (43812-9225)
P.O. Box 730 (43812-0730)
PHONE..................................740 622-0222
Joe Fyte, *Manager*
EMP: 29
SALES (corp-wide): 370.1MM **Publicly Held**
WEB: www.ennis.com
SIC: 2752 Business form & card printing, lithographic
HQ: Crabar/Gbf, Inc.
68 Vine St
Leipsic OH 45856
419 943-2141

(G-7731)
DJ & WOODIES VINYL FRONTIER
2339 County Road 16 (43812-9454)
PHONE..................................740 623-2818
Donna Woodie, *Co-Owner*
Kevin Woodie, *Co-Owner*
EMP: 5 **EST:** 1999
SQ FT: 3,200
SALES (est): 424.8K **Privately Held**
SIC: 3442 5211 5033 5031 Window & door frames; siding; roofing, siding & insulation; lumber, plywood & millwork

(G-7732)
EXCELLO FABRIC FINISHERS INC
802 S 2nd St (43812-1916)
PHONE..................................740 622-7444
Edward L Lee, *Ch of Bd*
Kevin Lee, *President*
Lawrence Burns, *Principal*
Charles Milligan, *Principal*
Eugene Weir, *Principal*
EMP: 6 **EST:** 1966
SQ FT: 1,000
SALES (est): 1.5MM **Privately Held**
WEB: www.excellofabric.com
SIC: 2295 Waterproofing fabrics, except rubberizing

(G-7733)
FESLERS REFINISHING
315 Main St (43812-1510)
PHONE..................................740 622-4849
EMP: 4
SALES (est): 130K **Privately Held**
SIC: 7641 2511 Reupholstery/Furniture Repair Mfg Wood Household Furniture

(G-7734)
FRANCISCO JAUME
Also Called: Coshocton Orthopedic Center
311 S 15th St Ste 206 (43812-1875)
P.O. Box 490 (43812-0490)
PHONE..................................740 622-1200
Francisco Jaume, *Owner*
EMP: 6
SALES (est): 322.3K **Privately Held**
SIC: 3842 8011 Surgical appliances & supplies; offices & clinics of medical doctors

(G-7735)
GENERAL ELECTRIC COMPANY
1350 S 2nd St (43812-1980)
PHONE..................................740 623-5379
Bob Callahan, *Manager*
EMP: 70
SALES (corp-wide): 121.6B **Publicly Held**
SIC: 3083 Plastic finished products, laminated
PA: General Electric Company
41 Farnsworth St
Boston MA 02210
617 443-3000

(G-7736)
GRO2 BAGS & ACCESSORIES LLC
1760 Buena Vista Dr (43812-3005)
PHONE..................................740 622-0928
Laura Grogno,
EMP: 3

SALES (est): 203.9K **Privately Held**
SIC: 3171 7389 Women's handbags & purses;

(G-7737)
HOPEWELL INDUSTRIES INC (PA)
637 Chestnut St (43812-1212)
P.O. Box 4008, Newark (43058-4008)
PHONE..................................740 622-3563
Heather Kendall, *Principal*
Elaine Lipps, *Bookkeeper*
EMP: 70 **EST:** 1971
SQ FT: 14,000
SALES: 1.2MM **Privately Held**
WEB: www.hopewellind.org
SIC: 8331 7349 2789 0782 Sheltered workshop; building maintenance services; bookbinding & related work; lawn & garden services

(G-7738)
KRAFT HEINZ FOODS COMPANY
1660 S 2nd St (43812-1977)
PHONE..................................740 622-0523
Emil Pisch, *Engineer*
Carol Villa, *Manager*
EMP: 500
SQ FT: 120,000
SALES (corp-wide): 26.2B **Publicly Held**
WEB: www.kraftfoods.com
SIC: 2013 Sausages & other prepared meats
HQ: Kraft Heinz Foods Company
1 Ppg Pl Ste 3200
Pittsburgh PA 15222
412 456-5700

(G-7739)
MCWANE INC
Clow Water Systems Company
2266 S 6th St (43812-8906)
P.O. Box 6001 (43812-6001)
PHONE..................................740 622-6651
Frank Eschleman, *President*
Jeff Otterstedt, *Vice Pres*
Terry Crozier, *Foreman/Supr*
Brandy Albert, *Purch Agent*
Adam Welsh, *Engineer*
EMP: 400
SALES (corp-wide): 1.3B **Privately Held**
WEB: www.mcwane.com
SIC: 3321 5085 5051 3444 Cast iron pipe & fittings; industrial supplies; pipe & tubing, steel; sheet metalwork; fabricated structural metal; blast furnaces & steel mills
PA: Mcwane, Inc.
2900 Highway 280 S # 300
Birmingham AL 35223
205 414-3100

(G-7740)
MFC DRILLING INC
Also Called: Medina Fuel
46281 Us Highway 36 (43812-8707)
P.O. Box 715 (43812-0715)
PHONE..................................740 622-5600
James S Aslanides, *President*
Randy Matheny, *Vice Pres*
Jackie Wilkins, *Administration*
EMP: 10
SQ FT: 2,200
SALES (est): 1.4MM **Privately Held**
SIC: 1311 Crude petroleum production

(G-7741)
MUSKINGUM GRINDING & MCH CO
2155 Otsego Ave (43812-9401)
P.O. Box 396 (43812-0396)
PHONE..................................740 622-4741
Jeff Mulett, *President*
Janel Richards, *Corp Secy*
EMP: 10 **EST:** 1945
SQ FT: 14,000
SALES (est): 1.2MM **Privately Held**
SIC: 3599 Machine shop, jobbing & repair

(G-7742)
NEOLA INC
632 Main St (43812-1613)
PHONE..................................740 622-5341
Sam Kalbaugh, *Corp Comm Staff*
Richard Clapp, *Manager*
Melissa Chapman, *Manager*

Coshocton - Coshocton County (G-7743)

Tom Durbin, *Associate*
EMP: 14
SALES (corp-wide): 1.9MM **Privately Held**
WEB: www.neola.com
SIC: 2731 Books: publishing only
PA: Neola Inc.
3914 Clk Pnte Trl Ste 103
Stow OH 44224
330 926-0514

(G-7743)
NGO DEVELOPMENT CORPORATION
Also Called: Energy Corportive
504 N 3rd St (43812-1113)
P.O. Box 662 (43812-0662)
PHONE 740 622-9560
Scott Kees, *Manager*
EMP: 12
SALES (est): 754.6K
SALES (corp-wide): 18.8MM **Privately Held**
SIC: 1382 4923 5984 Oil & gas exploration services; gas transmission & distribution; propane gas, bottled
HQ: Ngo Development Corporation
1500 Granville Rd
Newark OH 43055
740 344-3790

(G-7744)
NORTH AMERICAN AUGER MINING
1816 Bayberry Ln (43812-3127)
PHONE 740 622-8782
David Glover, *President*
Chris Glover, *Corp Secy*
EMP: 4
SALES (est): 321K **Privately Held**
WEB: www.augermining.com
SIC: 1241 Coal mining services

(G-7745)
NOVELTY ADVERTISING CO INC
Also Called: Kenyon Co
1148 Walnut St (43812-1769)
P.O. Box 250 (43812-0250)
PHONE 740 622-3113
Gregory Coffman, *President*
James McConnel, *Vice Pres*
Casey Claxon, *Marketing Staff*
◆ **EMP:** 50 **EST:** 1895
SQ FT: 100,000
SALES (est): 9.6MM **Privately Held**
WEB: www.noveltyadv.com
SIC: 2752 5199 Calendars, lithographed; advertising specialties

(G-7746)
OFCO INC
Also Called: Ohio Fabricators
111 N 14th St (43812-1710)
P.O. Box 218 (43812-0218)
PHONE 740 622-5922
Marcia Bush, *CEO*
Harold R Shaw, *President*
▲ **EMP:** 65 **EST:** 1941
SQ FT: 50,000
SALES (est): 14.5MM **Privately Held**
WEB: www.ohfab.com
SIC: 3496 Wire cloth & woven wire products

(G-7747)
OXFORD MINING COMPANY INC (DH)
544 Chestnut St (43812-1209)
P.O. Box 427 (43812-0427)
PHONE 740 622-6302
Charles C Ungurean, *President*
Gregory J Honish, *Senior VP*
Daniel M Maher, *Senior VP*
Thomas T Ungurean, *Vice Pres*
Jeffrey M Gutman, *CFO*
EMP: 6
SQ FT: 3,200
SALES (est): 253.8MM
SALES (corp-wide): 1.3B **Privately Held**
SIC: 1241 Coal mining services

(G-7748)
OXFORD MINING COMPANY LLC (DH)
544 Chestnut St (43812-1209)
PHONE 740 622-6302
Samuel Hagreen,
EMP: 24
SALES (est): 20.4MM
SALES (corp-wide): 1.3B **Privately Held**
SIC: 1241 Coal mining services

(G-7749)
OXFORD MINING COMPANY - KY LLC
544 Chestnut St (43812-1209)
PHONE 740 622-6302
Samuel Hagreen,
EMP: 5
SALES (est): 4.9MM
SALES (corp-wide): 1.3B **Privately Held**
SIC: 1221 Strip mining, bituminous
HQ: Oxford Mining Company, Llc
544 Chestnut St
Coshocton OH 43812

(G-7750)
SANCAST INC
535 Clow Ln (43812-9782)
PHONE 740 622-8660
Don Hutchins, *Principal*
Nancy Foster, *Principal*
John Fox, *Principal*
Julie Starcher, *Principal*
Don Popernik, *Corp Secy*
EMP: 50
SQ FT: 56,000
SALES (est): 11.8MM
SALES (corp-wide): 4.3B **Publicly Held**
SIC: 3321 3322 Ductile iron castings; gray iron castings; malleable iron foundries
HQ: Standard Car Truck Company Inc
6400 Shafer Ct Ste 450
Rosemont IL 60018
847 692-6050

(G-7751)
SHAWNE SPRINGS WINERY
20093 County Road 6 (43812-9149)
PHONE 740 623-0744
Randy Hall, *Principal*
EMP: 4
SALES (est): 287.1K **Privately Held**
SIC: 2084 Wines

(G-7752)
SPRINT PRINT INC
Also Called: Market Media Creations
520 Main St (43812-1612)
PHONE 740 622-4429
Jeff Eikenberry, *President*
EMP: 9
SQ FT: 6,000
SALES (est): 1.1MM **Privately Held**
SIC: 2752 7319 Commercial printing, offset; poster advertising service, except outdoor

(G-7753)
STEVEN MERCER INC
Also Called: Signmaker Shop, The
801 Walnut St (43812-1623)
P.O. Box 26 (43812-0026)
PHONE 740 623-0033
Steven Mercer, *President*
EMP: 4
SQ FT: 5,500
SALES (est): 409.9K **Privately Held**
SIC: 7389 3993 Sign painting & lettering shop; signs & advertising specialties

(G-7754)
T JS OIL & GAS INC
Also Called: R & K Industrial Supply
23191 County Road 621 (43812-8903)
PHONE 740 623-0192
Rodney F Adams, *President*
Kathy A Adams, *Corp Secy*
Jeffrey D Adams, *Vice Pres*
EMP: 4
SQ FT: 5,600
SALES (est): 909.4K **Privately Held**
SIC: 1311 5084 5261 Crude petroleum production; natural gas production; petroleum industry machinery; lawnmowers & tractors

(G-7755)
THOMAS J WEAVER INC (PA)
Also Called: Coshocton Pallet & Door Co
1501 Kenilworth Ave (43812-2430)
P.O. Box 412 (43812-0412)
PHONE 740 622-2040
Thomas J Weaver, *President*
EMP: 12 **EST:** 1963
SALES (est): 3.1MM **Privately Held**
SIC: 1542 1541 1521 2448 Commercial & office building, new construction; industrial buildings, new construction; new construction, single-family houses; pallets, wood; boxes, wood; metal doors

(G-7756)
WESTMORELAND RESOURCES GP LLC
544 Chestnut St (43812-1209)
P.O. Box 427 (43812-0427)
PHONE 740 622-6302
Charles C Ungurean,
Charles Ungurean,
EMP: 15
SALES (est): 2.3MM
SALES (corp-wide): 1.3B **Privately Held**
SIC: 1221 Bituminous coal & lignite-surface mining
PA: Westmoreland Coal Company
9540 Maroon Cir Unit 200
Englewood CO 80112
855 922-6463

(G-7757)
WESTROCK CP LLC
Also Called: Smurfit-Stone Container
500 N 4th St (43812-1119)
PHONE 740 622-0581
M L Tripp, *Opers-Prdtn-Mfg*
Wes Enlow, *Manager*
EMP: 265
SALES (corp-wide): 16.2B **Publicly Held**
WEB: www.smurfit-stone.com
SIC: 2631 2621 Corrugating medium; paper mills
HQ: Westrock Cp, Llc
1000 Abernathy Rd
Atlanta GA 30328

(G-7758)
WILEY ORGANICS INC
Also Called: Organic Technologies
1245 S 6th St (43812-2809)
PHONE 740 622-0755
David Wiley, *Branch Mgr*
EMP: 200
SALES (corp-wide): 25.9MM **Privately Held**
SIC: 2087 Concentrates, flavoring (except drink)
PA: Wiley Organics, Inc.
545 Walnut St Frnt
Coshocton OH 43812
740 622-0755

(G-7759)
WILEYS FINEST LLC
545 Walnut St Ste B (43812-1656)
P.O. Box 1665 (43812-6665)
PHONE 740 622-1072
Shane Griffiths, *Principal*
Gretchen Rdn, *Nutritionist*
Sam Wiley, *Mng Member*
EMP: 200
SALES (est): 316.3K **Privately Held**
SIC: 2077 2079 2023 5499 Animal fats, oils & meals; fish oil; edible fats & oils; dietary supplements, dairy & non-dairy based; health foods

Coventry Township
Summit County

(G-7760)
ACCU-TECH MANUFACTURING CO
195 Olivet Ave (44319-2324)
PHONE 330 848-8100
Slyster Downs, *President*
John Ellis, *Vice Pres*
EMP: 13
SALES (est): 2.3MM **Privately Held**
SIC: 3441 Fabricated structural metal

(G-7761)
ADULT DAILY LIVING LLC
3603 Highspire Dr (44203-4409)
PHONE 330 612-7941
Michelle O'Connor, *Principal*
EMP: 3
SALES (est): 145.9K **Privately Held**
SIC: 2711 Newspapers, publishing & printing

(G-7762)
AKRON DESIGN & COSTUME CO
3425 Manchester Rd (44319-1412)
PHONE 330 644-4849
Debbie Meridith, *Owner*
EMP: 8
SALES (est): 720.3K **Privately Held**
WEB: www.akrondesign.com
SIC: 2389 7299 Costumes; costume rental

(G-7763)
AKRON EQUIPMENT COMPANY (PA)
3522 Manchester Rd Ste B (44319-1451)
P.O. Box 27027, Akron (44319-7027)
PHONE 330 645-3780
Edward L Mc Cartt, *Ch of Bd*
Gary A Hill, *President*
Andrea Friede, *Corp Secy*
▼ **EMP:** 6 **EST:** 1917
SQ FT: 2,000
SALES (est): 6.1MM **Privately Held**
WEB: www.marcomfg.com
SIC: 3599 Machine shop, jobbing & repair

(G-7764)
AKRON STEEL FABRICATORS CO
Also Called: Poling Group
3291 Manchester Rd (44319-1438)
PHONE 330 644-0616
David Poling Sr, *President*
Keith Kline, *Exec VP*
Leon Poole, *Exec VP*
Victor Flinner, *Engineer*
David Poling Jr, *CFO*
▼ **EMP:** 30
SQ FT: 28,000
SALES (est): 7.6MM **Privately Held**
WEB: www.akronsteel.com
SIC: 3491 Process control regulator valves

(G-7765)
AMERICAN CONFECTIONS CO LLC
90 Logan Pkwy (44319-1177)
PHONE 614 888-8838
Bill Wilson, *Director*
EMP: 8
SALES (est): 1MM **Privately Held**
SIC: 2026 2066 Yogurt; chocolate candy, solid

(G-7766)
CANVAS 123 INC
Also Called: Pixuru
277 Oak Grove Dr (44319-2366)
PHONE 312 805-0563
Adam Fried, *CEO*
EMP: 5 **EST:** 2012
SALES (est): 390K **Privately Held**
SIC: 2759 7389 Commercial printing;

(G-7767)
CHEMEQUIP SALES INC
Also Called: R & R Engine & Machine
1004 Swartz Rd (44319-1340)
PHONE 330 724-8300
Jeanie Menke, *President*
EMP: 30
SQ FT: 2,500
SALES (est): 7.9MM **Privately Held**
SIC: 3519 3621 Diesel engine rebuilding; motors & generators

(G-7768)
DORUM COLOR CO INC
2229 Stahl Rd (44319-1321)
PHONE 330 773-1900
Scott Dority, *President*
Ed Balash, *General Mgr*
EMP: 6
SQ FT: 7,000
SALES (est): 1.3MM **Privately Held**
SIC: 2865 Dyes & pigments

GEOGRAPHIC SECTION — Crestline - Crawford County (G-7795)

(G-7769)
EXCHANGE SIGNS
3152 Manchester Rd (44319-1439)
PHONE.................................330 644-4552
Frank Wingrove Sr, *Owner*
EMP: 4
SQ FT: 1,500
SALES (est): 210K **Privately Held**
SIC: 3993 7629 1799 Signs, not made in custom sign painting shops; electrical repair shops; sign installation & maintenance

(G-7770)
FRIESS WELDING INC
Also Called: Summit Trailer Sales & Svcs
3342 S Main St (44319-3099)
PHONE.................................330 644-8160
Russell C Friess, *CEO*
Jeff Friess, *President*
Betty Friess, *Corp Secy*
EMP: 11 **EST:** 1968
SQ FT: 7,000
SALES (est): 1.1MM **Privately Held**
WEB: www.summittrailers.com
SIC: 7692 7539 5511 Welding repair; radiator repair shop, automotive; trailer repair; trucks, tractors & trailers: new & used

(G-7771)
K F D INC
39 Alice Dr Unit B (44319-1163)
PHONE.................................330 773-4300
David K Friddle, *President*
EMP: 3
SQ FT: 10,000
SALES (est): 332.9K **Privately Held**
WEB: www.foamedge.com
SIC: 3069 Molded rubber products

(G-7772)
KEN-DAL CORPORATION
644 Killian Rd (44319-2599)
PHONE.................................330 644-7118
William Keasling, *President*
Alan Place, *Vice Pres*
▲ **EMP:** 10 **EST:** 1962
SQ FT: 12,000
SALES (est): 1.4MM **Privately Held**
SIC: 3599 Machine shop, jobbing & repair

(G-7773)
MODERN DESIGNS INC
310 Killian Rd (44319-2431)
P.O. Box 247, Green (44232-0247)
PHONE.................................330 644-1771
Greg Boyd, *President*
Mark Boyd, *Sales Mgr*
EMP: 5
SALES: 700K **Privately Held**
SIC: 2541 1751 Store fixtures, wood; cabinet & finish carpentry

(G-7774)
NAC PRODUCTS
3200 S Main St (44319-2435)
PHONE.................................330 644-3117
Nick Duve, *Principal*
EMP: 4
SALES (est): 408.9K **Privately Held**
SIC: 2891 Adhesives & sealants

(G-7775)
OHIO HICKORY HARVEST BRAND PRO
Also Called: Hickory Harvest Foods
90 Logan Pkwy (44319-1177)
PHONE.................................330 644-6266
Darlene Swiatkowski, *CEO*
Joseph Swiatkowski, *President*
Michael Swiatkowski, *Vice Pres*
EMP: 32 **EST:** 1972
SQ FT: 32,000
SALES: 17.7MM **Privately Held**
WEB: www.hickoryharvest.com
SIC: 5145 5149 2099 Nuts, salted or roasted; candy; fruits, dried; food preparations

(G-7776)
PACKAGING CORPORATION AMERICA
Also Called: PCA/Akron 312
708 Killian Rd Ste 1 (44319-2559)
PHONE.................................330 644-9542
Mike Washburn, *Plant Supt*
Ralph Snyder, *Manager*
Elaine Sinopoli, *Supervisor*
EMP: 44
SALES (corp-wide): 7B **Publicly Held**
WEB: www.packagingcorp.com
SIC: 2653 Boxes, corrugated: made from purchased materials
PA: Packaging Corporation Of America
1 N Field Ct
Lake Forest IL 60045
847 482-3000

(G-7777)
PACTIV LLC
708 Killian Rd (44319-2549)
PHONE.................................330 644-9542
Ralph Snyder, *Opers-Prdtn-Mfg*
EMP: 35
SALES (corp-wide): 1MM **Privately Held**
WEB: www.pactiv.com
SIC: 2653 Corrugated & solid fiber boxes
HQ: Pactiv Llc
1900 W Field Ct
Lake Forest IL 60045
847 482-2000

(G-7778)
PENNY PRINTING INC
2957 S Main St (44319-1857)
PHONE.................................330 645-2955
Robert Collier, *President*
Catherine Collier, *Corp Secy*
EMP: 3
SQ FT: 2,200
SALES: 175K **Privately Held**
SIC: 2752 Commercial printing, offset

Covington
Miami County

(G-7779)
AEROVENT INC
800 S High St (45318-1170)
PHONE.................................937 473-3789
Bob Day, *Principal*
EMP: 3
SALES (est): 327.2K **Privately Held**
SIC: 3999 5088 5099 Manufacturing industries; aircraft equipment & supplies; durable goods

(G-7780)
AIRAM PRESS CO LTD
2065 Industrial Ct (45318-1265)
P.O. Box 9 (45318-0009)
PHONE.................................937 473-5672
Fredrick J Ratermann, *President*
EMP: 24
SALES (est): 4.1MM **Privately Held**
SIC: 3542 Presses: hydraulic & pneumatic, mechanical & manual

(G-7781)
ARENS CORPORATION (PA)
395 S High St (45318-1121)
P.O. Box 69 (45318-0069)
PHONE.................................937 473-2028
Gary Godfrey, *President*
Ginger Godfrey, *Vice Pres*
Don Selanders, *Mktg Dir*
EMP: 22 **EST:** 1954
SQ FT: 2,000
SALES (est): 1.5MM **Privately Held**
WEB: www.arenspub.com
SIC: 2711 2721 2752 Newspapers: publishing only, not printed on site; magazines: publishing only, not printed on site; commercial printing, offset

(G-7782)
ARENS CORPORATION
Also Called: Arens Publications & Printing
22 N High St (45318-1306)
PHONE.................................937 473-2028
Connie Didier, *Manager*
EMP: 6
SALES (est): 313.3K
SALES (corp-wide): 1.5MM **Privately Held**
WEB: www.arenspub.com
SIC: 2711 2721 2752 Newspapers: publishing only, not printed on site; magazines: publishing only, not printed on site; commercial printing, offset
PA: The Arens Corporation
395 S High St
Covington OH 45318
937 473-2028

(G-7783)
B K PLASTICS INC
1400 Mote Dr (45318-1217)
P.O. Box 250 (45318-0250)
PHONE.................................937 473-2087
Robert Robbins, *President*
Karen Robbins, *Treasurer*
EMP: 6
SQ FT: 12,000
SALES (est): 1.1MM **Privately Held**
SIC: 2673 Plastic bags: made from purchased materials

(G-7784)
D & D CLASSIC AUTO RESTORATION
Also Called: D&D Classic Restoration
2300 Mote Dr (45318-1200)
PHONE.................................937 473-2229
Dale Sotsing, *President*
Rodger James, *Vice Pres*
Mark Kennison, *Admin Sec*
EMP: 22
SQ FT: 8,000
SALES (est): 1.3MM **Privately Held**
WEB: www.ddclassic.com
SIC: 7389 3711 5521 7532 Automobile recovery service; motor vehicles & car bodies; automobiles, used cars only; tops (canvas or plastic), installation or repair: automotive

(G-7785)
FAB-TECH MACHINE INC
Also Called: Fabtech Machine
2 W Spring St (45318-1324)
PHONE.................................937 473-5572
Randy Garber, *President*
EMP: 5
SALES: 250K **Privately Held**
SIC: 3599 7692 Machine shop, jobbing & repair; welding repair

(G-7786)
GENERAL FILMS INC
645 S High St (45318-1182)
PHONE.................................888 436-3456
Tim Weikert, *President*
Roy J Weikert, *Chairman*
Tom Granata, *Vice Pres*
Carla Steel, *Purchasing*
Nicole Hutson, *Human Res Dir*
EMP: 80
SQ FT: 55,000
SALES (est): 31.1MM **Privately Held**
WEB: www.generalfilms.com
SIC: 3081 2673 Polyethylene film; plastic & pliofilm bags

(G-7787)
HAROLD FLORY
Also Called: Flory Cabinetry
5225 W Myers Rd (45318-8714)
PHONE.................................937 473-3030
Harold Flory, *Owner*
EMP: 5
SQ FT: 2,500
SALES: 200K **Privately Held**
SIC: 2434 0119 Wood kitchen cabinets; feeder grains

(G-7788)
J&I DUCT FAB LLC
7502 W State Route 41 (45318-9746)
P.O. Box 190 (45318-0190)
PHONE.................................937 473-2121
Gerald Miller,
EMP: 12 **EST:** 2013
SALES (est): 80.9K **Privately Held**
SIC: 3585 Heating & air conditioning combination units

(G-7789)
L & C PLASTIC BAGS INC
500 Dick Minnich Dr (45318-1263)
P.O. Box 214 (45318-0214)
PHONE.................................937 473-2968
Rodney Sprenkel, *President*
Wesley Sprenkel, *QC Mgr*
EMP: 15 **EST:** 1967
SQ FT: 9,000
SALES: 500K **Privately Held**
WEB: www.lcplastics.com
SIC: 2673 Plastic bags: made from purchased materials

(G-7790)
MCMILLION LOCK & KEY
8822 N Rangeline Rd (45318-9638)
PHONE.................................937 473-5342
Jennifer McMillion, *Manager*
EMP: 9
SALES (est): 1MM **Privately Held**
SIC: 2421 4225 Sawdust & shavings; warehousing, self-storage

(G-7791)
PBM COVINGTON LLC
400 Hazel St (45318-1724)
PHONE.................................937 473-2050
Scott F Jamison, *Mng Member*
EMP: 15
SALES (est): 2.1MM **Privately Held**
SIC: 2834 Vitamin, nutrient & hematinic preparations for human use

(G-7792)
PERRIGO
400 Hazel St (45318-1724)
PHONE.................................937 473-2050
Chad Brown, *Opers Mgr*
Steve Frazier, *Buyer*
EMP: 9 **EST:** 2013
SALES (est): 1.3MM **Privately Held**
SIC: 2834 Pharmaceutical preparations

Crestline
Crawford County

(G-7793)
ANTHONY-LEE SCREEN PRTG INC
401 S Thoman St (44827-1849)
P.O. Box 292 (44827-0292)
PHONE.................................419 683-1861
Donald W Grady, *President*
Lisa Grady-Clerk, *Vice Pres*
Mike Grady, *Site Mgr*
Sandra J Grady, *Treasurer*
Lisa G Clark, *CPA*
EMP: 11
SQ FT: 20,000
SALES (est): 1.7MM **Privately Held**
SIC: 2759 Screen printing

(G-7794)
FOWLER PRODUCTS INC
810 Colby Rd (44827-1799)
PHONE.................................419 683-4057
Mark Fowler, *President*
Phyllis Fowler, *Chairman*
Larry Winch, *Manager*
Jean E Cole, *Shareholder*
Marcia A Dishon, *Shareholder*
▲ **EMP:** 18
SQ FT: 52,000
SALES (est): 3.7MM **Privately Held**
WEB: www.fowler-inc.com
SIC: 3089 3829 3084 3083 Extruded finished plastic products; measuring & controlling devices; plastics pipe; laminated plastics plate & sheet

(G-7795)
INTERSTATE SIGN PRODUCTS INC
432 E Main St (44827-1118)
P.O. Box 187 (44827-0187)
PHONE.................................419 683-1962
Robin Wittmer, *President*
EMP: 6
SQ FT: 4,000

Crestline - Crawford County (G-7796) **GEOGRAPHIC SECTION**

SALES (est): 990K Privately Held
WEB: www.interstate911.com
SIC: 5085 3993 Signmaker equipment & supplies; letters for signs, metal

(G-7796)
LINKS COUNTRY MEATS
7252 Leesville Rd (44827-9455)
PHONE.................................419 683-2195
Mike Link, *Owner*
Janice Link, *Co-Owner*
EMP: 5
SQ FT: 6,500
SALES (est): 220K Privately Held
SIC: 2011 5147 5421 Meat packing plants; meats, fresh; food & freezer plans, meat

(G-7797)
NIESE FARMS
7506 Cole Rd (44827-9742)
PHONE.................................419 347-1204
Patrick Niese, *Partner*
EMP: 7
SQ FT: 2,150
SALES (est): 487.8K Privately Held
SIC: 2043 Oatmeal: prepared as cereal breakfast food

(G-7798)
PITTSBURGH GLASS WORKS LLC
Also Called: Pgw
5064 Lincoln Hwy (44827-9605)
PHONE.................................419 569-7521
Praveen Vavaidya, *Plant Mgr*
EMP: 170 Privately Held
SIC: 3711 Automobile assembly, including specialty automobiles
HQ: Pittsburgh Glass Works, Llc
30 Isabella St Ste 500
Pittsburgh PA 15212

(G-7799)
PPG INDUSTRIES INC
Also Called: Satellite
5066 Lincoln Hwy (44827-9605)
P.O. Box 269 (44827-0269)
PHONE.................................419 683-2400
Dan Couch, *Site Mgr*
EMP: 24
SALES (corp-wide): 15.3B Publicly Held
WEB: www.ppg.com
SIC: 3211 3231 3229 2812 Flat glass; strengthened or reinforced glass; windshields, glass: made from purchased glass; glass fiber products; fiber optics strands; alkalies & chlorine; chlorine, compressed or liquefied; caustic soda, sodium hydroxide; plastics materials & resins; paints & paint additives
PA: Ppg Industries, Inc.
1 Ppg Pl
Pittsburgh PA 15272
412 434-3131

(G-7800)
ROCK IRON CORPORATION
1221 Warehouse Dr (44827)
PHONE.................................419 529-9411
Thomas Morehead, *President*
Gerald Morehead, *Vice Pres*
Brett Cole, *Accountant*
EMP: 7
SALES (est): 90K Privately Held
SIC: 3544 7389 Die sets for metal stamping (presses);

(G-7801)
SUNRISE COOPERATIVE INC
3000 W Bucyrus St (44827-1674)
P.O. Box 870, Fremont (43420-0870)
PHONE.................................419 683-4600
Steve Neise, *Branch Mgr*
EMP: 40
SALES (corp-wide): 56.3MM Privately Held
SIC: 3315 3465 2542 Baskets, steel wire; wire products, ferrous/iron: made in wire-drawing plants; automotive stampings; partitions & fixtures, except wood
PA: Sunrise Cooperative, Inc.
2025 W State St Ste A
Fremont OH 43420
419 332-6468

Creston
Wayne County

(G-7802)
ACCURATE AUTOMATIC MFG LTD
141 Factory St (44217-9236)
PHONE.................................330 435-4575
James Bush,
EMP: 4
SALES (est): 503.8K Privately Held
SIC: 3599 Machine shop, jobbing & repair

(G-7803)
ATLANTIC VEAL & LAMB LLC
2416 E West Salem Rd (44217-9650)
PHONE.................................330 435-6400
Phillip Peerless, *Mng Member*
EMP: 6
SALES (est): 59.5K
SALES (corp-wide): 111.6MM Privately Held
SIC: 2011 Veal from meat slaughtered on site
PA: Atlantic Veal And Lamb, Inc.
275 Morgan Ave
Brooklyn NY 11211
718 599-6400

(G-7804)
CANAAN COUNTRY MEATS
11970 Canaan Center Rd (44217-9767)
PHONE.................................330 435-4778
Ryan Lily, *Owner*
EMP: 4
SALES (est): 259.4K Privately Held
SIC: 2011 Meat packing plants

(G-7805)
FRANK CSAPO
Also Called: Frank Csapo Oil & Gas Producer
157 Myers St (44217-9704)
PHONE.................................330 435-4458
Frank Csapo, *Owner*
EMP: 6
SALES (est): 700.8K Privately Held
SIC: 1381 Drilling oil & gas wells

(G-7806)
LISA ARTERS
117 Maple Ave (44217-9691)
PHONE.................................330 435-1804
EMP: 3 EST: 2010
SALES (est): 116.7K Privately Held
SIC: 2711 Newspapers-Publishing/Printing

(G-7807)
MELLOTT BRONZE INC
4634 E Sterling Rd (44217-9241)
PHONE.................................330 435-6304
Ron Mellott, *President*
Ed Mellott, *Vice Pres*
Linda Mellott, *Admin Sec*
EMP: 13
SQ FT: 11,800
SALES (est): 2.3MM Privately Held
SIC: 3599 Machine shop, jobbing & repair

(G-7808)
OHIO FARMS PACKING CO LTD
2416 E West Salem Rd (44217-9650)
PHONE.................................330 435-6400
David Mullet, *Mng Member*
EMP: 4
SALES (est): 633.5K Privately Held
SIC: 2011 Veal from meat slaughtered on site

(G-7809)
SHRINER SHEET METAL INC
196 S Main St (44217-9799)
P.O. Box 3331 (44217-3331)
PHONE.................................330 435-6735
EMP: 16 EST: 1953
SQ FT: 1,800
SALES (est): 2.5MM Privately Held
SIC: 1711 3444 Plumbing/Heating/Air Cond Contractor Mfg Sheet Metalwork

Cridersville
Auglaize County

(G-7810)
HAWTHORNE-SEVING INC
320 W Main St (45806-2215)
PHONE.................................419 643-5531
Charles L Dale, *President*
EMP: 34 EST: 1950
SQ FT: 10,000
SALES (est): 7.2MM Privately Held
SIC: 3535 3556 Conveyors & conveying equipment; food products machinery
PA: E S Industries Inc
110 Brookview Ct
Lima OH 45801
419 643-2625

(G-7811)
KATIES LIGHT HOUSE LLC
300 Dupler Ave (45806-2304)
PHONE.................................419 645-5451
Richard Lavy,
EMP: 23
SALES (est): 2MM Privately Held
WEB: www.katieslighthouse.com
SIC: 3229 Bulbs for electric lights

(G-7812)
SS DEFENSE LLC
22160 State Route 198 (45806-9507)
PHONE.................................937 407-0659
Tyler Adam Shaffer, *Principal*
EMP: 3
SALES (est): 170.8K Privately Held
SIC: 3812 Defense systems & equipment

(G-7813)
UNITED FIRE APPARATUS CORP
204 S Gay St (45806-2312)
P.O. Box 2066 (45806-0066)
PHONE.................................419 645-4083
Darrel A Chapman, *President*
Sonja Chapman, *Admin Sec*
EMP: 5
SQ FT: 9,000
SALES: 867K Privately Held
SIC: 3711 3569 5012 5087 Fire department vehicles (motor vehicles), assembly of; firefighting apparatus; trucks, commercial; firefighting equipment

Crooksville
Perry County

(G-7814)
ALFMAN LOGGING LLC
4499 Township Road 448 Ne (43731-9740)
PHONE.................................740 982-6227
Jeff Hoffman, *President*
EMP: 8
SALES (est): 833.8K Privately Held
SIC: 2411 Logging camps & contractors

(G-7815)
BEAUMONT BROTHERS STONEWARE (PA)
Also Called: Beaumont Brothers Pottery
410 Keystone St (43731-1034)
PHONE.................................740 982-0055
Roger Beaumont, *President*
Margie Beaumont, *Vice Pres*
EMP: 2
SQ FT: 14,000
SALES (est): 1.4MM Privately Held
WEB: www.beaumontbrotherspottery.com
SIC: 3269 Stoneware pottery products

(G-7816)
I CERCO INC
416 Maple Ave (43731-1305)
P.O. Box 151 (43731-0151)
PHONE.................................740 982-2050
Gary Troyer, *Engineer*
Mick Pease, *Branch Mgr*
John Spung, *Supervisor*
Karen Burns, *CTO*
EMP: 75
SALES (corp-wide): 63.9MM Privately Held
WEB: www.cercollc.com
SIC: 3255 3567 3297 Clay refractories; industrial furnaces & ovens; nonclay refractories
PA: I Cerco Inc
453 W Mcconkey St
Shreve OH 44676
330 567-2145

(G-7817)
OLD MILL POWER EQUIPMENT
100 China St (43731-1112)
P.O. Box 28 (43731-0028)
PHONE.................................740 982-3246
Edward Gamble, *Owner*
EMP: 4
SALES (est): 322.7K Privately Held
SIC: 3751 Bicycles & related parts

(G-7818)
PCC AIRFOILS LLC
101 China St (43731-1111)
P.O. Box 206 (43731-0206)
PHONE.................................740 982-6025
Ryan Thrush, *Branch Mgr*
EMP: 300
SALES (corp-wide): 225.3B Publicly Held
WEB: www.pccairfoils.com
SIC: 3369 3728 Castings, except die-castings, precision; aircraft parts & equipment
HQ: Pcc Airfoils Llc
3401 Entp Pkwy Ste 200
Cleveland OH 44122
216 831-3590

(G-7819)
PETRO WARE INC
Also Called: Swingle Drilling
713 Keystone St (43731-1039)
P.O. Box 220 (43731-0220)
PHONE.................................740 982-1302
Mark B Swingle, *President*
James R Swingle, *Vice Pres*
EMP: 54
SQ FT: 2,000
SALES (est): 9.1MM Privately Held
SIC: 3569 3264 Filters, general line: industrial; porcelain electrical supplies

(G-7820)
TEMPLE OIL & GAS COMPANY
Also Called: Speed-O-Print
6626 Ceramic Rd Ne (43731-9419)
P.O. Box 70 (43731-0070)
PHONE.................................740 452-7878
Robert Swingle, *President*
Bob Swingle, *General Mgr*
Wendy Gorbi, *Office Mgr*
EMP: 8
SQ FT: 8,000
SALES (est): 1.6MM Privately Held
SIC: 1381 1311 Directional drilling oil & gas wells; natural gas production

Croton
Licking County

(G-7821)
MULLER PIPE ORGAN CO
Also Called: Muller Pipe Organ Company
122 N High St (43013-9007)
P.O. Box 353 (43013-0353)
PHONE.................................740 893-1700
John W Muller, *President*
Mary J Muller, *Corp Secy*
EMP: 10
SQ FT: 8,650
SALES (est): 1.2MM Privately Held
SIC: 3931 Musical instruments

(G-7822)
OHIO FRESH EGGS LLC (PA)
11212 Croton Rd (43013)
PHONE.................................740 893-7200
Gary Bethel, *Mng Member*
▲ EMP: 250
SQ FT: 5,000
SALES (est): 25.9MM Privately Held
SIC: 5144 2015 Eggs; egg processing

Cumberland
Guernsey County

(G-7823)
CUMBERLAND LIMESTONE LLC
53681 Spencer Rd (43732-9709)
PHONE..................740 638-3942
Bill Wheeler, *Superintendent*
Missy King, *Facilities Mgr*
Cris Sidwell, *Mng Member*
EMP: 19
SALES (est): 2.4MM **Privately Held**
SIC: 3281 Cut stone & stone products

(G-7824)
KING LIMESTONE INC
53681 Spencer Rd (43732-9709)
PHONE..................740 638-3942
Duane King, *President*
EMP: 19
SQ FT: 1,200
SALES (est): 1.9MM **Privately Held**
SIC: 1422 Crushed & broken limestone

Curtice
Ottawa County

(G-7825)
GREAT LAKES MACHINE AND TOOL
10705 Jerusalem Rd (43412-9419)
PHONE..................419 836-2346
EMP: 3 **EST:** 2005
SALES (est): 210K **Privately Held**
SIC: 3531 Mfg Construction Machinery

(G-7826)
OTTAWA PRODUCTS CO
Also Called: None
1602 N Curtice Rd Ste A (43412-9507)
PHONE..................419 836-5115
Jeffery Hepner, *President*
George F Wasmer, *Chairman*
Shawna Litten, *Manager*
Bruce Miller, *Director*
EMP: 20
SQ FT: 19,000
SALES (est): 1.7MM **Privately Held**
WEB: www.ottawaproducts.com
SIC: 3429 3469 Clamps, metal; spinning metal for the trade

(G-7827)
TAT MACHINE AND TOOL LTD
1313 S Cousino Rd (43412-9100)
P.O. Box 184 (43412-0184)
PHONE..................419 836-7706
Thomas A Truman, *Partner*
Joan C Truman, *Partner*
EMP: 8
SQ FT: 7,500
SALES (est): 637.5K **Privately Held**
SIC: 3599 Machine shop, jobbing & repair

Custar
Wood County

(G-7828)
232 DEFENSE LLC
5371 Otsego Pike (43511-9749)
PHONE..................419 348-4343
Michael Cortez,
EMP: 4 **EST:** 2017
SALES (est): 240.9K **Privately Held**
SIC: 3812 Defense systems & equipment

Cuyahoga Falls
Summit County

(G-7829)
4R ENTERPRISES INCORPORATED
Also Called: Radioshack
700 Portage Trl (44221-3057)
PHONE..................330 923-9799
EMP: 6
SQ FT: 2,000
SALES (est): 726.8K **Privately Held**
SIC: 5731 3826 3821 7389 Ret Radio/Tv/Electronics Mfg Analytical Instr Mfg Lab Apparatus/Furn Business Services Engineering Services

(G-7830)
ACU-SERVE CORP
2020 Front St Ste 205 (44221-3257)
PHONE..................330 923-5258
Angie Barone, *President*
Timothy Barone, *Vice Pres*
EMP: 9
SALES (est): 1.6MM **Privately Held**
SIC: 7372 6411 Prepackaged software; medical insurance claim processing, contract or fee basis

(G-7831)
ADVANCED HOLDING DESIGNS INC
Also Called: Ahd
3332 Cavalier Trl (44224-4906)
PHONE..................330 928-4456
Mark Smrekar, *President*
Anne Daugherty, *Manager*
Alastair L Crawford, *Exec Dir*
EMP: 13
SQ FT: 12,000
SALES (est): 1.8MM **Privately Held**
WEB: www.ahd-flex-e-on.com
SIC: 3545 Collets (machine tool accessories); chucks: drill, lathe or magnetic (machine tool accessories)

(G-7832)
ALDEN SAND & GRAVEL CO INC
Also Called: Alden Excavating
2486 Northampton Rd (44223-2712)
PHONE..................330 928-3249
Connie Ensign, *President*
Robert E Alden III, *Corp Secy*
EMP: 11 **EST:** 1963
SQ FT: 1,200
SALES (est): 980K **Privately Held**
WEB: www.aldenexcavating.com
SIC: 1442 1794 Sand mining; gravel & pebble mining; excavation work

(G-7833)
ALTEC INDUSTRIES INC
307 Munroe Falls Ave (44221-2827)
PHONE..................205 408-2341
Tim Smith, *Branch Mgr*
EMP: 10
SALES (corp-wide): 764.4MM **Privately Held**
SIC: 3531 3536 3713 Derricks, except oil & gas field; aerial work platforms: hydraulic/elec. truck/carrier mounted; cranes, overhead traveling; truck bodies (motor vehicles)
HQ: Altec Industries, Inc.
210 Inverness Center Dr
Birmingham AL 35242
205 991-7733

(G-7834)
AMERICHEM INC
155 E Steels Corners Rd (44224-4919)
PHONE..................330 926-3185
Ryan King, *COO*
Karen Jenior, *Buyer*
Rod Manfull, *Manager*
EMP: 50
SQ FT: 78,214
SALES (corp-wide): 228.8MM **Privately Held**
WEB: www.americhem.com
SIC: 2865 2816 Color pigments, organic; inorganic pigments
PA: Americhem, Inc.
2000 Americhem Way
Cuyahoga Falls OH 44221
330 929-4213

(G-7835)
AMERICHEM INC (PA)
2000 Americhem Way (44221-3303)
PHONE..................330 929-4213
Matthew Hellstern, *CEO*
Rick Allison, *General Mgr*
Thomas Weigl, *Managing Dir*
Matthew Miklos, *Vice Pres*
Matthew J Miklos, *Vice Pres*
▲ **EMP:** 620 **EST:** 1941
SQ FT: 83,000
SALES (est): 228.8MM **Privately Held**
WEB: www.americhem.com
SIC: 2865 2851 2819 2816 Color pigments, organic; paints & allied products; industrial inorganic chemicals; inorganic pigments

(G-7836)
AMH HOLDINGS LLC
3773 State Rd (44223-2603)
PHONE..................330 929-1811
Ira D Kleinman, *Ch of Bd*
Thomas N Chieffe, *President*
Warren J Arthur, *Senior VP*
Stephen E Graham, *CFO*
John F Haumesser, *VP Human Res*
EMP: 2400
SQ FT: 70,000
SALES (est): 192.9MM **Privately Held**
SIC: 3355 3444 Coils, wire aluminum: made in rolling mills; siding, sheet metal
PA: Associated Materials Group, Inc.
3773 State Rd
Cuyahoga Falls OH 44223

(G-7837)
AMH HOLDINGS II INC
3773 State Rd (44223-2603)
PHONE..................330 929-1811
Thomas N Chieffe, *CEO*
EMP: 500
SALES (est): 150.1MM **Privately Held**
SIC: 3355 Coils, wire aluminum: made in rolling mills

(G-7838)
APPLETON GRP LLC
4441 Hickory Trl (44224-3678)
PHONE..................330 689-1904
EMP: 108
SALES (corp-wide): 24.5B **Publicly Held**
SIC: 3823 Mfg Process Control Instruments
HQ: Appleton Grp Llc
9377 W Higgins Rd
Rosemont IL 60018
847 268-6024

(G-7839)
APPLIED VISION CORPORATION (PA)
2020 Vision Ln (44223-4706)
PHONE..................330 926-2222
Amir Novini, *CEO*
Jeff Hartung, *President*
Mike Kress, *President*
Amy Doll, *Vice Pres*
Robin Jackson, *Materials Mgr*
EMP: 62 **EST:** 1997
SQ FT: 80,000
SALES (est): 15.6MM **Privately Held**
WEB: www.applied1.com
SIC: 3577 Magnetic ink & optical scanning devices

(G-7840)
ASCOT VALLEY FOODS LLC (PA)
Also Called: Bunny B
205 Ascot Pkwy (44223-3701)
PHONE..................330 376-9411
Keith A Kropp, *CEO*
EMP: 8
SQ FT: 4,000
SALES (est): 2.7MM **Privately Held**
WEB: www.bunnyb.com
SIC: 2038 Snacks, including onion rings, cheese sticks, etc.

(G-7841)
ASSOCIATED MATERIALS LLC (DH)
3773 State Rd (44223-2603)
P.O. Box 2010, Akron (44309-2010)
PHONE..................330 929-1811
Erik D Ragatz, *Ch of Bd*
Brian C Strauss, *President*
William L Topper, *Exec VP*
Scott F Stephens, *CFO*
Dana A Schindler, *Chief Mktg Ofcr*
▲ **EMP:** 277
SQ FT: 63,000
SALES: 1.1B **Privately Held**
WEB: www.associatedmaterials.com
SIC: 3089 5033 5031 3442 Plastic hardware & building products; siding, plastic; windows, plastic; fences, gates & accessories: plastic; roofing & siding materials; siding, except wood; roofing, asphalt & sheet metal; insulation materials; windows; kitchen cabinets; metal doors, sash & trim

(G-7842)
ASSOCIATED MATERIALS GROUP INC (PA)
3773 State Rd (44223-2603)
PHONE..................330 929-1811
Brian C Strauss, *President*
EMP: 41
SALES (est): 1.5B **Privately Held**
SIC: 3089 5033 5031 3442 Plastic hardware & building products; siding, plastic; windows, plastic; fences, gates & accessories: plastic; roofing & siding materials; siding, except wood; roofing, asphalt & sheet metal; insulation materials; windows; kitchen cabinets; metal doors, sash & trim

(G-7843)
ASSOCIATED MTLS HOLDINGS LLC
3773 State Rd (44223-2603)
P.O. Box 2010, Akron (44309-2010)
PHONE..................330 929-1811
Ira D Kleinman, *Ch of Bd*
Alex Amerio, *Engineer*
Bob Schindler, *VP Mktg*
Abby Kujawski, *Director*
EMP: 2000
SALES (est): 132.3MM **Privately Held**
SIC: 3089 5033 5031 5063 Plastic hardware & building products; siding, plastic; windows, plastic; fences, gates & accessories: plastic; roofing & siding materials; siding, except wood; insulation materials; windows; kitchen cabinets; wire & cable; metal doors, sash & trim
PA: Associated Materials Group, Inc.
3773 State Rd
Cuyahoga Falls OH 44223

(G-7844)
ATA TOOLS INC
7 Ascot Pkwy (44223-3326)
PHONE..................330 928-7744
Tim Dunn, *Buyer*
Kim Scrogham, *Controller*
Heather Maddox, *Sales Staff*
Rick Tichon, *Supervisor*
EMP: 100
SALES (est): 23.9MM **Privately Held**
SIC: 3542 Brakes, metal forming

(G-7845)
BEECH ARMAMENT LLC
105 Marc Dr (44223-2629)
PHONE..................330 962-4694
Martin Beech,
EMP: 3
SALES (est): 120.5K **Privately Held**
SIC: 3484 Small arms

(G-7846)
CARTWRIGHT CONSTRUCTION INC
Also Called: Cartwright Cnstr H B A C
4898 Wild Lake Rd (44224)
PHONE..................330 929-3020
Darrell Cartwright, *President*
Margarett Cartwright, *Vice Pres*
EMP: 3
SALES (est): 350.1K **Privately Held**
SIC: 3585 1711 Heating & air conditioning combination units; heating & air conditioning contractors

(G-7847)
CENTRAL GRAPHICS INC
1658 State Rd (44223-1304)
PHONE..................330 928-7080
David Soulsby, *President*
Jeff Loofboro, *Manager*
EMP: 5

Cuyahoga Falls - Summit County (G-7848)

SALES (est): 681.4K **Privately Held**
WEB: www.sign-central.com
SIC: 3993 Electric signs

(G-7848)
CHAMPION WEBBING COMPANY INC
2748 2nd St (44221-2202)
PHONE..................................330 920-1007
Tong Choi, *President*
EMP: 4
SQ FT: 7,000
SALES (est): 400K **Privately Held**
SIC: 2241 Webbing, woven

(G-7849)
CHILD EVNGELISM FELLOWSHIP INC
641 Acorn Pl (44221-1001)
PHONE..................................440 218-4982
EMP: 41
SALES (corp-wide): 24.4MM **Privately Held**
SIC: 2752 Commercial printing, lithographic
PA: Child Evangelism Fellowship Incorporated
   17482 Highway M
   Warrenton MO 63383
   636 456-4321

(G-7850)
CIRCLE PRIME MANUFACTURING
2114 Front St (44221-3220)
P.O. Box 112 (44222-0112)
PHONE..................................330 923-0019
James Mothersbaugh, *President*
Robert Mothersbaugh, *Vice Pres*
EMP: 27
SQ FT: 50,000
SALES (est): 5.1MM **Privately Held**
WEB: www.circleprime.com
SIC: 8731 3672 3812 3663 Commercial physical research; printed circuit boards; antennas, radar or communications; electrical equipment & supplies; engineering services

(G-7851)
COLTENE/WHALEDENT INC (HQ)
235 Ascot Pkwy (44223-3701)
PHONE..................................330 916-8800
Nick Huber, *Ch of Bd*
Martin Schaufelberger, *Ch of Bd*
Jerry Sullivan, *President*
Joseph Fasano, *Vice Pres*
Craig Haueter, *Vice Pres*
◆ EMP: 222
SQ FT: 89,000
SALES (est): 49.9MM
SALES (corp-wide): 169.9MM **Privately Held**
SIC: 3843 Dental equipment
PA: Coltene Holding Ag
   Feldwiesenstrasse 20
   AltstAtten SG 9450
   717 575-472

(G-7852)
COMBUSTION PROCESS SYSTEM
2104 Front St (44221-3260)
PHONE..................................330 922-4161
EMP: 3
SALES (est): 196K **Privately Held**
SIC: 3823 Industrial instrmnts msrmnt display/control process variable

(G-7853)
CORTAPE INC
60 Marc Dr (44223-2628)
PHONE..................................330 929-6700
Erik W Akins, *Ch of Bd*
Matthew Mc Clellan, *President*
Matthew Balint, *Opers Mgr*
◆ EMP: 17
SQ FT: 25,000
SALES (est): 5.1MM **Privately Held**
WEB: www.cortape.com
SIC: 2672 Tape, pressure sensitive: made from purchased materials; labels (un-printed); gummed: made from purchased materials

(G-7854)
CREATIVE FUELS LLC
1093 Foxglove Cir (44223-2797)
PHONE..................................330 923-2222
Robert Dirgo,
Mary Dirgo, *Graphic Designe*
EMP: 10
SALES (est): 869.8K **Privately Held**
WEB: www.creativefuelsllc.com
SIC: 2869 Fuels

(G-7855)
CULT COUTURE LLC
1110 Munroe Falls Ave (44221-3448)
PHONE..................................330 801-9475
Royce Cleveland,
EMP: 3
SALES: 130K **Privately Held**
SIC: 3961 7389 Costume jewelry;

(G-7856)
CUSTOM CRAFT DRAP INC
1924 Portage Trl (44223-1743)
PHONE..................................330 929-5728
EMP: 4 EST: 1977
SQ FT: 800
SALES (est): 441.1K **Privately Held**
SIC: 2211 5714 Cotton Broadwoven Fabric Mill Ret Draperies/Upholstery

(G-7857)
D A STIRLING INC
2740 Hudson Dr (44221-1971)
PHONE..................................330 923-3195
Donald L Glenny, *President*
Dana Glenny, *Admin Sec*
Dana Shoff, *Admin Sec*
EMP: 5
SQ FT: 10,000
SALES (est): 584.7K **Privately Held**
WEB: www.dastirling.com
SIC: 3544 2675 Dies, steel rule; die-cut paper & board

(G-7858)
DANIEL MALEK
2315 21st St (44223-1548)
P.O. Box 1203 (44223-0203)
PHONE..................................330 701-5760
EMP: 3
SALES (est): 104.1K **Privately Held**
SIC: 3761 Guided missiles & space vehicles

(G-7859)
DBCR INC
Also Called: G.S. Steel Company
3400 Cavalier Trl (44224-4908)
PHONE..................................330 920-1900
Donald E Potoczek, *President*
Darla Gullatta, *Purch Mgr*
Beth Potoczek, *Treasurer*
EMP: 20
SALES (est): 4.9MM **Privately Held**
SIC: 3541 7389 7692 Plasma process metal cutting machines; metal cutting services; welding repair

(G-7860)
DENTRONIX INC
235 Ascot Pkwy (44223-3701)
PHONE..................................330 916-7300
Jerry Sullivan, *President*
Joseph Fasano, *Treasurer*
EMP: 50
SQ FT: 16,000
SALES: 5.5MM
SALES (corp-wide): 169.9MM **Privately Held**
WEB: www.dentronix.com
SIC: 3843 5047 3842 3841 Orthodontic appliances; dental equipment & supplies; surgical appliances & supplies; surgical & medical instruments; analytical instruments; laboratory apparatus & furniture
HQ: Coltene/Whaledent Inc.
   235 Ascot Pkwy
   Cuyahoga Falls OH 44223
   330 916-8800

(G-7861)
EBULENT TECHNOLOGIES CORP
Falls Town Ctr (44221)
PHONE..................................925 922-1448
Xiao-Yang Huang, *CEO*
Helen Zhang, *CFO*
EMP: 3
SALES (est): 267.2K **Privately Held**
SIC: 3679 Liquid crystal displays (LCD)

(G-7862)
ECONO PRODUCTS INC
Also Called: Graphic Arts Rubber
101 Ascot Pkwy (44223-3355)
PHONE..................................330 923-4101
Harry Millward, *Manager*
EMP: 12
SQ FT: 19,000
SALES (corp-wide): 5.9MM **Privately Held**
SIC: 3069 2891 2796 Reclaimed rubber & specialty rubber compounds; adhesives & sealants; platemaking services
PA: Econo Products, Inc.
   159 Huxley Way
   Victor NY 14564
   585 288-7550

(G-7863)
ESSENTIAL WONDERS INC
2926 State Rd Ste 202 (44223-1244)
PHONE..................................888 525-5282
Tom Osbourne, *President*
EMP: 6 EST: 2005
SQ FT: 50,000
SALES: 600K **Privately Held**
SIC: 2095 Roasted coffee

(G-7864)
EWART-OHLSON MACHINE COMPANY
1435 Main St (44221-4926)
P.O. Box 359 (44222-0359)
PHONE..................................330 928-2171
Brian L Ewart, *President*
David Achauer, *General Mgr*
David L Ewart, *Chairman*
Earl Norrod, *Vice Pres*
Karen Sims, *Office Mgr*
▲ EMP: 28
SQ FT: 39,000
SALES (est): 5MM **Privately Held**
WEB: www.ewart-ohlson.com
SIC: 3599 Machine shop, jobbing & repair

(G-7865)
EXACT PIPE TOOLS
141 Broad Blvd Ste 201 (44221-3817)
PHONE..................................330 922-8150
Mike Stone, *Owner*
EMP: 5 EST: 2014
SALES: 721.5K
SALES (corp-wide): 4.3MM **Privately Held**
SIC: 3429 Manufactured hardware (general)
PA: Exact Tools Oy
   Sarkiniementie 5d
   Helsinki 00210
   943 667-50

(G-7866)
FACTS INC
2737 Front St (44221-1904)
PHONE..................................330 928-2332
Albert H Curry, *President*
Thomas W Fisher III, *Vice Pres*
John Watts, *Engineer*
Wade Plymire, *Project Engr*
Wendell Watson, *Sales Engr*
EMP: 20
SQ FT: 10,000
SALES (est): 3.6MM **Privately Held**
WEB: www.facts-inc.com
SIC: 7371 3823 Computer software systems analysis & design, custom; industrial process control instruments

(G-7867)
FALLS STAMPING & WELDING CO (PA)
2900 Vincent St (44221-1954)
P.O. Box 153 (44222-0153)
PHONE..................................330 928-1191
David Cesar, *CEO*
Rick Boettner, *Chairman*
Charlie Williams, *Plant Mgr*
Mic Kempt, *QC Mgr*
Jason Taft, *CFO*
EMP: 125 EST: 1919
SQ FT: 95,000
SALES (est): 39.7MM **Privately Held**
WEB: www.falls-stamping.com
SIC: 3465 3469 3544 3711 Automotive stampings; stamping metal for the trade; special dies, tools, jigs & fixtures; chassis, motor vehicle; motor vehicle parts & accessories; welding repair

(G-7868)
FLEX-E-ON INC
3332 Cavalier Trl (44224-4906)
PHONE..................................330 928-4496
Mark Smrekar, *President*
EMP: 10
SQ FT: 12,000
SALES (est): 1.3MM **Privately Held**
WEB: www.flexeonrehabclinics.com
SIC: 3545 Chucks: drill, lathe or magnetic (machine tool accessories); mandrels

(G-7869)
FOX TOOL CO INC
1471 Main St (44221-4926)
PHONE..................................330 928-3402
Nathan Fox, *President*
EMP: 22
SQ FT: 5,120
SALES (est): 2.1MM **Privately Held**
SIC: 7699 3545 Knife, saw & tool sharpening & repair; cutting tools for machine tools

(G-7870)
FRONTLINE INTERNATIONAL INC
187 Ascot Pkwy (44223-3747)
PHONE..................................330 861-1100
John W Palazzo, *President*
Giovanni Brienza, *Vice Pres*
Zack Palazzo, *Sales Mgr*
▼ EMP: 15
SQ FT: 30,000
SALES (est): 4.2MM **Privately Held**
WEB: www.frontlineii.com
SIC: 3589 Cooking equipment, commercial

(G-7871)
FUSE CHICKEN LLC
2251 Front St Ste 200 (44221-2578)
PHONE..................................330 338-7108
Jon Fawcett, *Mng Member*
▼ EMP: 4 EST: 2012
SQ FT: 5,000
SALES (est): 508.8K **Privately Held**
SIC: 3625 Electric controls & control accessories, industrial

(G-7872)
GENTEK BUILDING PRODUCTS INC (DH)
Also Called: Revere Building Products
3773 State Rd (44223-2603)
PHONE..................................800 548-4542
Thomas Chieffe, *CEO*
Michael Caporale, *President*
D Keith Lavanway, *Vice Pres*
▲ EMP: 18
SQ FT: 8,000
SALES (est): 304.9MM **Privately Held**
WEB: www.gentekinc.com
SIC: 3444 3089 Siding, sheet metal; downspouts, sheet metal; siding, plastic
HQ: Associated Materials, Llc
   3773 State Rd
   Cuyahoga Falls OH 44223
   330 929-1811

(G-7873)
GOJO INDUSTRIES INC
Also Called: Production
3783 State Rd (44223-2698)
P.O. Box 991, Akron (44309-0991)
PHONE..................................330 255-6000
Bob Potvin, *Vice Pres*
Steven Zammarrelli, *Maint Spvr*
Cindy Simko, *Production*
Kevin Affeldt, *VP Sales*
Laura Huth, *Cust Mgr*
EMP: 50
SALES (corp-wide): 373.8MM **Privately Held**
WEB: www.gojo.com
SIC: 2842 Specialty cleaning, polishes & sanitation goods

GEOGRAPHIC SECTION

Cuyahoga Falls - Summit County (G-7900)

PA: Gojo Industries, Inc.
1 Gojo Plz Ste 500
Akron OH 44311
330 255-6000

(G-7874)
GOJO INDUSTRIES INC
3783 State Rd (44223-2698)
PHONE..................330 922-4522
Joe Drenik, *Vice Pres*
Sara Fusco, *Research*
Gregory Leonhard, *Engineer*
Mark Bullock, *Senior Engr*
Tawanda McCray, *Marketing Staff*
EMP: 125
SALES (corp-wide): 373.8MM **Privately Held**
SIC: 2842 3586 2844 Specialty cleaning, polishes & sanitation goods; measuring & dispensing pumps; toilet preparations
PA: Gojo Industries, Inc.
1 Gojo Plz Ste 500
Akron OH 44311
330 255-6000

(G-7875)
GOJO INDUSTRIES INC
200 W Steels Corners Rd (44223-2655)
PHONE..................800 321-9647
Jeffrey Vengrow, *Principal*
▼ **EMP:** 12
SALES (est): 1.2MM **Privately Held**
SIC: 3999 Manufacturing industries

(G-7876)
HALIFAX-FAN USA LLC
1474 Main St (44221-4927)
PHONE..................262 257-9779
Malcolm Staff, *Managing Dir*
Gareth Colley, *Chief Engr*
John Irons, *Chief Engr*
EMP: 3
SALES (est): 142.6K **Privately Held**
SIC: 3564 Blowing fans: industrial or commercial; exhaust fans: industrial or commercial; ventilating fans: industrial or commercial

(G-7877)
HARBOR CASTINGS INC (PA)
2508 Bailey Rd (44221-2585)
PHONE..................330 499-7178
C Richard Lynham, *CEO*
EMP: 45 **EST:** 1992
SQ FT: 13,000
SALES (est): 15MM **Privately Held**
WEB: www.harbor-castings.com
SIC: 3324 3369 3325 Steel investment foundries; nonferrous foundries; steel foundries

(G-7878)
HARWOOD RUBBER PRODUCTS INC
1365 Orlen Ave (44221-2957)
PHONE..................330 923-3256
Richard Harwood, *President*
Lundy Mills, *Corp Secy*
John H Eblen, *Vice Pres*
Donald R Harwood, *Shareholder*
EMP: 30 **EST:** 1952
SQ FT: 22,000
SALES (est): 4MM **Privately Held**
WEB: www.harwoodrubber.com
SIC: 3479 3061 Coating of metals with plastic or resins; mechanical rubber goods

(G-7879)
HEXACRAFTER LTD
2750 Northampton Rd (44223-2718)
PHONE..................330 929-0989
Andrew Rainers, *Principal*
EMP: 3
SALES: 100K **Privately Held**
SIC: 3721 Aircraft

(G-7880)
HOWARD B CLAFLIN CO
2475 2nd St (44221-2707)
PHONE..................330 928-1704
Howard B Claflin, *President*
Howard Claflin, *Owner*
Bruce Claflin, *Sales Mgr*
EMP: 6 **EST:** 1957
SQ FT: 3,600
SALES: 300K **Privately Held**
SIC: 2655 2599 Reels (fiber), textile; made from purchased material; boards: planning, display, notice

(G-7881)
INNOVATED HEALTH LLC
2241 Front St Fl 1 (44223-2501)
P.O. Box 963 (44223-0963)
PHONE..................330 858-0651
Fred Guerra, *Mng Member*
EMP: 9
SQ FT: 2,000
SALES (est): 650K **Privately Held**
SIC: 2023 Dietary supplements, dairy & non-dairy based

(G-7882)
INTER-ION INC
157 Ascot Pkwy (44223-3747)
PHONE..................330 928-9655
Adam Antonas, *President*
Panos Panayiotou, *Exec VP*
Ken Craft, *Project Mgr*
EMP: 25
SQ FT: 25,000
SALES (est): 3MM **Privately Held**
WEB: www.inter-ion.com
SIC: 3479 Coating of metals & formed products; painting, coating & hot dipping

(G-7883)
J&J PRECISION MACHINE LTD
1474 Main St (44221-4927)
PHONE..................330 923-5783
Hans R Leitner, *CEO*
Hans Leitner, *CEO*
EMP: 38
SALES (est): 7.1MM **Privately Held**
SIC: 3441 7699 Building components, structural steel; industrial machinery & equipment repair

(G-7884)
JAY-EM AEROSPACE CORPORATION
75 Marc Dr (44223-2627)
PHONE..................330 923-0333
Michael E Bell Sr, *CEO*
Michael Saltis, *General Mgr*
Brian Hodor, *Plant Mgr*
EMP: 25
SQ FT: 34,000
SALES (est): 8.2MM **Privately Held**
WEB: www.jay-em.com
SIC: 3728 3599 Wheels, aircraft; brakes, aircraft; machine shop, jobbing & repair

(G-7885)
JJB ENGINEER
2695 N Haven Blvd Ste 10 (44223-2123)
PHONE..................330 807-0671
Edward Sheehan, *President*
EMP: 5
SALES (est): 751.1K **Privately Held**
SIC: 3519 Internal combustion engines

(G-7886)
JULIUS ZORN INC
Also Called: Juzo
3690 Zorn Dr (44223-3580)
P.O. Box 1088 (44223-1088)
PHONE..................330 923-4999
Anne Rose Zorn, *President*
Petra Zorn, *Vice Pres*
Uwe Schettler, *Treasurer*
Ray Gornik LI, *Controller*
Thomas Gross, *Natl Sales Mgr*
▲ **EMP:** 75
SQ FT: 30,000
SALES (est): 31.2MM
SALES (corp-wide): 100.8MM **Privately Held**
WEB: www.juzousa.com
SIC: 5047 3842 Medical equipment & supplies; hosiery, support; supports: abdominal, ankle, arch, kneecap, etc.; socks, stump
PA: Julius Zorn Gmbh
Juliusplatz 1
Aichach 86551
825 190-10

(G-7887)
KENNETH J MOORE
3775 Wyoga Lake Rd (44224-4945)
PHONE..................330 923-8313
Kenneth Moore, *Principal*
EMP: 3
SALES (est): 144.5K **Privately Held**
SIC: 3993 Signs & advertising specialties

(G-7888)
KEUCHEL & ASSOCIATES INC
Also Called: Spunfab
175 Muffin Ln (44223-3359)
PHONE..................330 945-9455
Ken Keuchel, *President*
Herbert W Keuchel, *Principal*
Richard W Staehle, *Principal*
Herb Keuchel, *Shareholder*
◆ **EMP:** 50
SQ FT: 40,000
SALES (est): 7.8MM **Privately Held**
WEB: www.spunfab.com
SIC: 2241 8711 Narrow fabric mills; consulting engineer

(G-7889)
KOLPIN OUTDOORS CORPORATION
Also Called: Premier OEM
3479 State Rd (44223-2553)
PHONE..................330 328-0772
James Nagy, *President*
▲ **EMP:** 7
SALES (est): 152.4K **Privately Held**
SIC: 3799 All terrain vehicles (ATV); off-road automobiles, except recreational vehicles

(G-7890)
KYOCERA SGS PRECISION TOOLS
2824 2nd St (44221-1901)
PHONE..................330 688-6667
John Haag, *Branch Mgr*
EMP: 37
SQ FT: 29,973
SALES (corp-wide): 78.5MM **Privately Held**
WEB: www.sgstool.com
SIC: 3545 Cutting tools for machine tools
PA: Kyocera Sgs Precision Tools
55 S Main St
Munroe Falls OH 44262
330 688-6667

(G-7891)
KYOCERA SGS PRECISION TOOLS
150 Marc Dr (44223-2630)
PHONE..................330 686-4151
John A Haag, *Ch of Bd*
EMP: 114
SALES (corp-wide): 78.5MM **Privately Held**
WEB: www.sgstool.com
SIC: 3545 Cutting tools for machine tools
PA: Kyocera Sgs Precision Tools
55 S Main St
Munroe Falls OH 44262
330 688-6667

(G-7892)
KYOCERA SGS PRECISION TOOLS
238 Marc Dr (44223-2651)
PHONE..................330 922-1953
Richard G Tichon, *Branch Mgr*
EMP: 114
SALES (corp-wide): 78.5MM **Privately Held**
WEB: www.sgstool.com
SIC: 3545 Cutting tools for machine tools
PA: Kyocera Sgs Precision Tools
55 S Main St
Munroe Falls OH 44262
330 688-6667

(G-7893)
LINDEN INDUSTRIES INC
137 Ascot Pkwy (44223-3355)
PHONE..................330 928-4064
Peter Tilgner, *President*
Ken Erwin, *Vice Pres*
Mike Cice, *Engineer*
Bob Hughey, *CFO*
Robert Hughey, *Controller*
EMP: 42
SQ FT: 26,000
SALES (est): 9.9MM **Privately Held**
WEB: www.lindenindustries.com
SIC: 3559 5084 Plastics working machinery; robots, molding & forming plastics; industrial machinery & equipment

(G-7894)
MADAEN NATURAL PRODUCTS INC
Also Called: One With Nature
141 Broad Blvd Lowr (44223-3817)
PHONE..................800 600-1445
▲ **EMP:** 3
SALES (est): 250K **Privately Held**
SIC: 2844 Mfg Toilet Preparations

(G-7895)
MAIN STREET GOURMET LLC
Also Called: Main Street Cambritt Cookies
170 Muffin Ln (44223-3358)
PHONE..................330 929-0000
Marla Kuba, *Controller*
Robert Braun,
David Choe,
Steven Marks,
Harvey Nelson,
EMP: 108
SQ FT: 60,000
SALES (est): 67.6MM **Privately Held**
WEB: www.mainstreetgourmet.com
SIC: 2053 2099 2052 2051 Frozen bakery products, except bread; food preparations; cookies & crackers; bread, cake & related products

(G-7896)
MAJIC TOUCH
4133 State Rd (44223-2611)
PHONE..................330 923-8259
Keione Artite, *Owner*
EMP: 6
SALES (est): 563.7K **Privately Held**
SIC: 3589 Car washing machinery

(G-7897)
MARTZ MOLD & MACHINE INC
1365 Munroe Falls Ave (44221-3535)
PHONE..................330 928-2159
Dennis I Martz, *President*
M Dennis Martz, *Vice Pres*
William Martz, *Vice Pres*
EMP: 4 **EST:** 1944
SQ FT: 6,800
SALES (est): 521.4K **Privately Held**
SIC: 3544 Industrial molds

(G-7898)
MEGA BRIGHT LLC
2251 Front St (44221-2567)
PHONE..................330 577-8859
LI Coffee, *Managing Dir*
Bill Wang, *Director*
EMP: 10
SQ FT: 5,000
SALES (est): 966.1K **Privately Held**
SIC: 3645 3646 Residential lighting fixtures; commercial indusl & institutional electric lighting fixtures

(G-7899)
MOORE MC MILLEN HOLDINGS
1850 Front St (44221)
PHONE..................330 745-3075
Robert S Mc Millen, *President*
EMP: 85
SQ FT: 19,141
SALES (est): 7.2MM **Privately Held**
SIC: 3398 Metal heat treating

(G-7900)
NANOTRONICS IMAGING INC (PA)
2251 Front St Ste 109-111 (44221-2567)
P.O. Box 306 (44222-0306)
PHONE..................330 926-9809
Matthew Putnam, *CEO*
John Putman, *President*
EMP: 6
SALES (est): 2.4MM **Privately Held**
WEB: www.nanotronicsimaging.com
SIC: 3826 Analytical instruments

Cuyahoga Falls - Summit County (G-7901)

(G-7901)
NIKKICAKES
806 Myrtle Ave (44221-4104)
PHONE..................................330 606-5745
Nicole Longfellow, *Principal*
EMP: 4 EST: 2010
SALES (est): 242.5K **Privately Held**
SIC: 2051 Bakery: wholesale or wholesale/retail combined

(G-7902)
PARADISE INC
Also Called: ALCOHOLICS ANONYMOUS
1710 Front St (44221-4712)
PHONE..................................330 928-3789
Tim Crawford, *President*
EMP: 5 EST: 1951
SALES (est): 92.7K **Privately Held**
SIC: 2511 Club room furniture: wood

(G-7903)
PATRIOT ENERGY LLC
1574 Main St (44221-4937)
PHONE..................................330 923-4442
John A Shutsa,
EMP: 99
SALES (est): 10.7MM **Privately Held**
SIC: 2869 Fuels

(G-7904)
PNEUMATIC SCALE
4485 Allen Rd (44224-1033)
PHONE..................................330 923-0491
Mark Zaidan, *Parts Mgr*
Jim Foley, *CFO*
Lorne King, *Controller*
Jessica Morton, *Financial Analy*
Adam Brandt, *VP Sales*
EMP: 14
SALES (est): 2.2MM **Privately Held**
SIC: 3565 Packaging machinery

(G-7905)
PNEUMATIC SCALE CORPORATION (DH)
Also Called: Pneumatic Scale Angelus
10 Ascot Pkwy (44223-3325)
PHONE..................................330 923-0491
Timothy J Sulllivan, *CEO*
David Gianini, *President*
William J Morgan, *President*
Patty Fitzpatrick, *General Mgr*
Robert H Chapman, *Chairman*
▲ **EMP:** 225 EST: 1895
SQ FT: 102,000
SALES (est): 100.5MM
SALES (corp-wide): 2.4B **Privately Held**
WEB: www.pneumaticscale.com
SIC: 3535 3569 3565 Conveyors & conveying equipment; centrifuges, industrial; bottling machinery: filling, capping, labeling
HQ: Barry-Wehmiller Companies, Inc.
8020 Forsyth Blvd
Saint Louis MO 63105
314 862-8000

(G-7906)
POLYMERICS INC (PA)
2828 2nd St (44221-1953)
PHONE..................................330 434-6665
C Robert Samples, *Ch of Bd*
Joe Arhar, *President*
Tony Bisesi, *Accounting Mgr*
Brian Walters, *Maintence Staff*
▲ **EMP:** 50
SQ FT: 24,000
SALES (est): 15.3MM **Privately Held**
WEB: www.polymericsinc.com
SIC: 3069 2819 2891 2865 Custom compounding of rubber materials; industrial inorganic chemicals; adhesives & sealants; cyclic crudes & intermediates; paints & allied products; plastics materials & resins

(G-7907)
PREMIER UV PRODUCTS LLC
1738 Front St (44221-4712)
PHONE..................................330 715-2452
James R Nagy,
EMP: 4
SALES (est): 340K **Privately Held**
WEB: www.premieruv.com
SIC: 3799 All terrain vehicles (ATV)

(G-7908)
PREMIERE MEDICAL RESOURCES INC
2750 Front St (44221-1969)
PHONE..................................330 923-5899
Joseph Chase, *Principal*
EMP: 17
SALES (est): 2.6MM **Privately Held**
SIC: 3069 Hospital & health services consultant; accounting services, except auditing; computer related maintenance services

(G-7909)
PROSPECT MOLD & DIE COMPANY
1100 Main St (44221-4922)
PHONE..................................330 929-3311
Bruce W Wright, *CEO*
John D Wortman, *President*
Jeff Glick, *Vice Pres*
Walter Nagel, *Vice Pres*
▲ **EMP:** 100 EST: 1945
SQ FT: 100,000
SALES (est): 85.2MM **Privately Held**
WEB: www.prospectmold.com
SIC: 5084 3544 Industrial machinery & equipment; forms (molds), for foundry & plastics working machinery

(G-7910)
QUALITY CRAFT MACHINE INC
137 Ascot Pkwy (44223-3355)
PHONE..................................330 928-4064
Peter Tilgner, *President*
EMP: 15
SQ FT: 8,900
SALES (est): 1.9MM **Privately Held**
WEB: www.qcraft.com
SIC: 3599 Machine shop, jobbing & repair

(G-7911)
R T R SLOTTING & MACHINE INC
2742 2nd St (44221-2202)
PHONE..................................330 929-2608
Richard A Hamlet, *President*
Roland Steinlechner, *Corp Secy*
Timothy Hamlet, *Vice Pres*
EMP: 3
SQ FT: 4,500
SALES (est): 360.6K **Privately Held**
SIC: 3599 Machine shop, jobbing & repair

(G-7912)
RECYCLING EQP SOLUTIONS CORP
276 Remington Rd Ste C (44224-4900)
PHONE..................................330 920-1500
Gary Gaither, *President*
Mary Gaither, *Vice Pres*
▼ **EMP:** 8
SALES (est): 1.2MM **Privately Held**
SIC: 3542 Mechanical (pneumatic or hydraulic) metal forming machines

(G-7913)
REUTHER MOLD & MFG CO INC
Also Called: Reuther Mold & Manufacturing
1225 Munroe Falls Ave (44221-3598)
PHONE..................................330 923-5266
Karl A Reuther II, *President*
Dave Kolb, *Safety Mgr*
Bob Grigsby, *Engineer*
Karen Thompson, *Personnel*
Jessica Rhodes, *Admin Sec*
EMP: 60 EST: 1950
SQ FT: 61,000
SALES (est): 9.6MM **Privately Held**
WEB: www.reuthermold.com
SIC: 3544 3599 Industrial molds; machine shop, jobbing & repair

(G-7914)
RMS EQUIPMENT LLC
Also Called: RMS Equipment Company
1 Vision Ln (44221-4710)
PHONE..................................330 564-1360
Armand Massary, *President*
▲ **EMP:** 20
SQ FT: 50,000
SALES (est): 353K
SALES (corp-wide): 1.2B **Privately Held**
WEB: www.rmsequip.com
SIC: 3559 Rubber working machinery, including tires
HQ: Pettibone L.L.C.
27501 Bella Vista Pkwy
Warrenville IL 60555
630 353-5000

(G-7915)
SENNECO GLASS INC (PA)
1730 Newberry St (44221-4018)
PHONE..................................330 825-7717
Richard Sennebogen, *President*
EMP: 7
SQ FT: 4,000
SALES (est): 266K **Privately Held**
WEB: www.sennecoglass.com
SIC: 3714 Motor vehicle parts & accessories

(G-7916)
SILICON USA INC
1220 Orlen Ave (44221-2956)
P.O. Box 1079, Ravenna (44266-1079)
PHONE..................................330 928-6217
Walter Garot, *Principal*
▲ **EMP:** 4 EST: 2008
SALES (est): 451.6K **Privately Held**
SIC: 3965 Fasteners

(G-7917)
SILICONE SOLUTIONS INC
338 Remington Rd (44224-4916)
PHONE..................................330 920-3125
David M Brassard, *President*
Joe Iatonna, *Engineer*
Lorraine R Brassard, *Treasurer*
Laurie Brassard, *Manager*
EMP: 10 EST: 1996
SQ FT: 10,000
SALES (est): 1.4MM **Privately Held**
WEB: www.siliconesolutions.com
SIC: 2869 2891 Silicones; adhesives & sealants

(G-7918)
SIMON & SIMON BLUE POND INC
Also Called: Blue Pawn
2211 Harding Rd (44223-1131)
PHONE..................................330 928-2298
Frank T Simon, *President*
EMP: 3
SALES (est): 299.1K **Privately Held**
WEB: www.bluepawn.com
SIC: 3271 Blocks, concrete: landscape or retaining wall

(G-7919)
SMITH TRUCK CRANES & EQP CO
307 Munroe Falls Ave (44221-2827)
PHONE..................................330 929-3303
Fax: 330 929-9551
▲ **EMP:** 10
SQ FT: 14,000
SALES (est): 2MM **Privately Held**
SIC: 3441 Structural Metal Fabrication

(G-7920)
SNAKEBITE SNAPS
2642 Archwood Pl (44221-2453)
PHONE..................................520 227-5442
Michael Porter, *Owner*
EMP: 5 EST: 2016
SALES: 30K **Privately Held**
SIC: 3949 Fishing equipment

(G-7921)
SPECTRUM PLASTICS CORPORATION
99 E Ascot Ln (44223-3788)
PHONE..................................330 926-9766
Mohammad Malik, *President*
▲ **EMP:** 9
SQ FT: 25,000
SALES (est): 1.9MM **Privately Held**
SIC: 3089 Injection molding of plastics

(G-7922)
SPUNFAB LTD (PA)
175 Muffin Ln (44223-3359)
PHONE..................................330 945-9455
Kenneth Keuchel,
Herb Keuchel,
◆ **EMP:** 6
SALES (est): 1.5MM **Privately Held**
SIC: 2241 Manmade fiber narrow woven fabrics

(G-7923)
STEELASTIC COMPANY LLC
1 Vision Ln (44221-4710)
PHONE..................................330 633-0505
David Hull, *Engineer*
Harry Morton, *Engineer*
Bill Wise, *Engineer*
Victor Spinant, *Electrical Engi*
Matthew Abbey, *Regl Sales Mgr*
◆ **EMP:** 46 EST: 1970
SQ FT: 34,500
SALES (est): 23.4MM
SALES (corp-wide): 1.2B **Privately Held**
WEB: www.pettibone.com
SIC: 3559 Automotive related machinery
HQ: Pettibone L.L.C.
27501 Bella Vista Pkwy
Warrenville IL 60555
630 353-5000

(G-7924)
SUMMIT MILLWORK LLC
1619 Main St (44221-4047)
PHONE..................................330 920-4000
Dave Keenan, *Partner*
Keith Hall, *Sales Staff*
David Keenan,
EMP: 8
SQ FT: 30,000
SALES (est): 940K **Privately Held**
WEB: www.summitmillwork.com
SIC: 2431 Millwork

(G-7925)
SWIFT TOOL INC
1420 Ritchie St (44221-4931)
PHONE..................................330 945-6973
Doug Genova, *President*
EMP: 5
SQ FT: 3,500
SALES (est): 658.5K **Privately Held**
SIC: 3599 Custom machinery

(G-7926)
TECHNICOTE INC
70 Marc Dr (44223-2628)
PHONE..................................330 928-1476
Dave Bolanz, *Manager*
EMP: 45
SALES (corp-wide): 78.2MM **Privately Held**
WEB: www.technicote.com
SIC: 2891 Adhesives
PA: Technicote, Inc.
222 Mound Ave
Miamisburg OH 45342
800 358-4448

(G-7927)
TERRASOURCE GLOBAL CORPORATION
Also Called: Cuyahoga Falls Plant
601-607 Munroe Falls Ave (44221)
PHONE..................................330 923-5254
Fax: 330 923-7199
EMP: 60
SQ FT: 60,000
SALES (corp-wide): 1.6B **Publicly Held**
SIC: 3532 Mfg Mining Machinery
HQ: Terrasource Global Corporation
100 N Broadway Ste 1600
Saint Louis MO 63102
618 641-6966

(G-7928)
THICKEMZ ENTERTAINMENT LLC
Also Called: Amoney Train Music
1268 Wellingshire Cir (44221-5146)
PHONE..................................404 399-4255
Laurice Adams Simmons, *CEO*
Larenzo Adams, *Vice Pres*
Shantell M Florence, *Admin Sec*
EMP: 3
SALES (est): 53.8K **Privately Held**
SIC: 7922 7389 2741 Theatrical talent & booking agencies; theatrical production services; concert management service; artists' agents & brokers; ;

▲ = Import ▼=Export
◆ =Import/Export

GEOGRAPHIC SECTION

Danville - Knox County (G-7958)

(G-7929)
TRM MANUFACTURING INC
601 Munroe Falls Ave (44221-3437)
PHONE.................................330 769-2600
Yong-Chang Tang, *CEO*
EMP: 24 **EST:** 2011
SALES (est): 5.9MM **Privately Held**
SIC: 3462 Iron & steel forgings

(G-7930)
TUFFY MANUFACTURING
140 Ascot Pkwy (44223-3743)
PHONE.................................330 940-2356
Lewis Zimmerman, *President*
EMP: 4 **EST:** 2014
SALES (est): 194.9K **Privately Held**
SIC: 5521 5013 3999 Automobiles, used cars only; automotive servicing equipment; manufacturing industries

(G-7931)
ULTRA TECH MACHINERY INC
297 Ascot Pkwy (44223-3701)
PHONE.................................330 929-5544
Don Hagarty, *President*
Jim Hagarty, *Vice Pres*
Robert Hagarty, *Vice Pres*
Bruce Yuknavich, *Design Engr*
Debra Hoover, *Bookkeeper*
▲ **EMP:** 30
SQ FT: 11,000
SALES (est): 7.8MM **Privately Held**
WEB: www.utmachinery.com
SIC: 3599 7389 Machine shop, jobbing & repair; design, commercial & industrial

(G-7932)
ULTRATECH POLYMERS INC
280 Ascot Pkwy (44223-3346)
PHONE.................................330 945-9410
Anthony Kerkimis, *President*
John Herhold, *Vice Pres*
Vilie Kerkimis, *Office Mgr*
EMP: 15
SQ FT: 4,000
SALES (est): 2.6MM **Privately Held**
WEB: www.ultratechpolymers.com
SIC: 2821 Plastics materials & resins

(G-7933)
V-ASH MACHINE COMPANY
1220 Orlen Ave (44221-2956)
PHONE.................................216 267-3400
Vaden Ashley Jr, *President*
EMP: 4
SQ FT: 9,400
SALES (est): 160K **Privately Held**
SIC: 3599 Machine shop, jobbing & repair

(G-7934)
WIN CD INC
Also Called: Win Plex
3333 Win St (44223-3790)
PHONE.................................330 929-1999
David K Pulk, *President*
EMP: 18
SQ FT: 42,000
SALES (est): 5.9MM **Privately Held**
WEB: www.winplasticextrusions.com
SIC: 3089 Extruded finished plastic products

(G-7935)
YOUNGS SCREENPRINTING & EMBRO
1245 Munroe Falls Ave (44221-3533)
PHONE.................................330 922-5777
Penny Young, *Owner*
EMP: 4
SALES (est): 365.7K **Privately Held**
SIC: 2759 Screen printing

Dalton
Wayne County

(G-7936)
BUCKEYE DIMENSIONS LLC
1543 Zuercher Rd (44618-9776)
PHONE.................................330 857-0223
Leander Miller, *Principal*
EMP: 3
SALES (est): 89.7K **Privately Held**
SIC: 5999 2499 Alarm & safety equipment stores; decorative wood & woodwork

(G-7937)
C & D MANUFACTURING INC
374 Eckard Rd (44618-9160)
PHONE.................................330 828-8357
David Wengerd, *President*
Cheryl Wengerd, *Vice Pres*
EMP: 3
SQ FT: 5,000
SALES (est): 410K **Privately Held**
SIC: 3599 Machine shop, jobbing & repair

(G-7938)
CROSCO WOOD PRODUCTS
1543 Zuercher Rd (44618-9776)
PHONE.................................330 857-0228
Crist H Miller, *Owner*
EMP: 5
SALES (est): 220.2K **Privately Held**
SIC: 2499 5211 Carved & turned wood; lumber products

(G-7939)
DALTON VEAL
14978 Arnold Rd (44618-9228)
PHONE.................................330 828-8337
Lawrence Good, *President*
Andy Hershberger, *Manager*
EMP: 3
SALES (est): 159.8K **Privately Held**
SIC: 2011 0191 Veal from meat slaughtered on site; general farms, primarily crop

(G-7940)
DENDRATEC LTD
1417 Zuercher Rd (44618-9776)
PHONE.................................330 473-4878
Clarence Jennings, *Principal*
EMP: 6
SALES (est): 552.7K **Privately Held**
SIC: 2431 Millwork

(G-7941)
EGR PRODUCTS COMPANY INC (PA)
55 Eckard Rd (44618-9664)
PHONE.................................330 833-6554
Jeffery Daley, *President*
Jerome T Daley, *President*
Mary Ann Daley, *Vice Pres*
EMP: 13
SQ FT: 30,000
SALES (est): 2.4MM **Privately Held**
WEB: www.egrproducts.com
SIC: 3694 3714 Generators, automotive & aircraft; alternators, automotive; motors, starting; automotive & aircraft; motor vehicle parts & accessories

(G-7942)
GEDCO INC
Also Called: American Barricade
130 Briarwood Dr (44618-9789)
P.O. Box 202 (44618-0202)
PHONE.................................330 828-2044
Greg Donhue, *President*
EMP: 4
SALES (est): 225K **Privately Held**
SIC: 3993 Signs & advertising specialties

(G-7943)
HRH DOOR CORP
Also Called: Wayne - Dalton Rolling Doors
14512 Lincoln Way E (44618-9014)
PHONE.................................330 828-2291
Bill Hammer, *Manager*
Sandy Newman, *MIS Mgr*
Don Diglaw, *Executive*
EMP: 185
SALES (corp-wide): 621.6MM **Privately Held**
WEB: www.waynedalton.com
SIC: 3442 3446 Garage doors, overhead: metal; architectural metalwork
PA: Hrh Door Corp.
   1 Door Dr
   Mount Hope OH 44660
   850 208-3400

(G-7944)
J & L DOOR
13505 Bodine Rd (44618-9710)
PHONE.................................330 684-1496
Les Troyer, *Partner*
Joel Troyer, *Partner*
EMP: 3
SALES: 500K **Privately Held**
WEB: www.jldoor.com
SIC: 2434 Wood kitchen cabinets

(G-7945)
J HORST MANUFACTURING CO
Also Called: 2cravealloys
279 E Main St (44618-9601)
P.O. Box 507 (44618-0507)
PHONE.................................330 828-2216
Roland Horst, *President*
Mary Steiner, *Principal*
Richard Horst, *Vice Pres*
Kathleen Downs, *Human Res Mgr*
Don E Flath, *Incorporator*
EMP: 53
SQ FT: 78,000
SALES: 12MM **Privately Held**
WEB: www.jhorst.com
SIC: 3599 3441 3549 3547 Machine shop, jobbing & repair; fabricated structural metal; metalworking machinery; rolling mill machinery; plating & polishing

(G-7946)
LAKE REGION OIL INC
26 N Cochran St (44618-9808)
P.O. Box 1478, Massillon (44648-1478)
PHONE.................................330 828-8420
Robert Dervin II, *President*
EMP: 6
SQ FT: 2,500
SALES (est): 1.8MM **Privately Held**
SIC: 1311 Crude petroleum production; natural gas production

(G-7947)
MASSILLON MATERIALS INC (PA)
26 N Cochran St (44618-9808)
P.O. Box 499 (44618-0499)
PHONE.................................330 837-4767
Howard J Wenger, *President*
EMP: 22
SQ FT: 6,000
SALES (est): 2MM **Privately Held**
SIC: 1442 Sand mining; gravel mining

(G-7948)
NEISS BODY & EQUIPMENT CORP
17485 Old Lincoln Way (44618-9692)
PHONE.................................330 828-2409
John M Neiss, *President*
Marla Neiss, *Corp Secy*
Wendy Schumacher, *Data Proc Staff*
EMP: 7 **EST:** 1935
SQ FT: 12,000
SALES (est): 1.1MM **Privately Held**
WEB: www.neissbody.com
SIC: 3713 Truck bodies (motor vehicles)

(G-7949)
P GRAHAM DUNN INC (PA)
630 Henry St (44618-9280)
PHONE.................................330 828-2105
Paul Dunn, *President*
Joe Knutson, *President*
Robert Shetler, *Vice Pres*
Leanna Dunn, *Treasurer*
◆ **EMP:** 85
SQ FT: 100,000
SALES (est): 17.1MM **Privately Held**
SIC: 2511 Wood household furniture

(G-7950)
PETER GRAHAM DUNN INC
1417 Zuercher Rd (44618-9776)
PHONE.................................330 816-0035
Peter G Dunn, *President*
Leanna Dunn, *Corp Secy*
▲ **EMP:** 50
SQ FT: 36,000
SALES: 9.3MM **Privately Held**
WEB: www.pgrahamdunn.com
SIC: 3499 5199 Novelties & giftware, including trophies; advertising specialties

(G-7951)
PIONEER EQUIPMENT COMPANY
Also Called: Wengerd's Machine
16875 Jericho Rd (44618-9657)
PHONE.................................330 857-6340
Wayne H Wengerd, *President*
◆ **EMP:** 18
SALES (est): 3.7MM **Privately Held**
SIC: 3523 3312 Farm machinery & equipment; blast furnaces & steel mills

(G-7952)
R & S SHEET METAL LLC
5966 Mount Eaton Rd S (44618-8929)
PHONE.................................330 857-0225
Reuben Schlabach,
EMP: 4
SALES: 400K **Privately Held**
SIC: 3444 5075 Ventilators, sheet metal; dust collecting equipment

(G-7953)
WAYNEDALE TRUSS & PANEL CO
93 Lake Dr (44618-9720)
PHONE.................................330 683-4471
Dianne Fry, *Principal*
EMP: 4
SALES (est): 267.1K **Privately Held**
SIC: 2439 Trusses, wooden roof

(G-7954)
YOST CANDY CO
Also Called: Kiddi Pops
51 N Cochran St (44618)
PHONE.................................330 828-2777
Sofie Yost, *President*
Catherine S Farris, *Corp Secy*
Earl Yost, *Vice Pres*
Joseph Yost, *Vice Pres*
EMP: 35 **EST:** 1937
SQ FT: 45,000
SALES (est): 3.7MM **Privately Held**
WEB: www.yostcandy.com
SIC: 2064 Lollipops & other hard candy

(G-7955)
ZIMMERMAN STEEL & SUP CO LLC
18543 Davis Rd (44618-9697)
PHONE.................................330 828-1010
Nancy Zimmerman, *CFO*
David Zimmerman,
EMP: 10
SQ FT: 11,700
SALES (est): 2.3MM **Privately Held**
SIC: 3441 Fabricated structural metal

Danville
Knox County

(G-7956)
B & J DRILLING COMPANY INC
13911 Millersburg Rd (43014-9697)
PHONE.................................740 599-6700
William Samples, *President*
EMP: 3 **EST:** 1963
SQ FT: 3,200
SALES (est): 547.5K **Privately Held**
SIC: 1311 Natural gas production

(G-7957)
BESL SPECIALIZED CARRIER
Also Called: Gns
16559 Skyline Dr (43014-8620)
PHONE.................................740 599-6305
Glenn Nyharto, *Owner*
EMP: 3
SALES (est): 261.5K **Privately Held**
SIC: 3799 Transportation equipment

(G-7958)
BREEZEWAY SCREENS INC
513 Market St (43014)
P.O. Box A (43014-0601)
PHONE.................................740 599-5222
Larry J Grindle, *President*
Chris Bellow, *Admin Sec*
EMP: 5
SALES: 500K **Privately Held**
SIC: 3442 Screens, window, metal

Danville - Knox County (G-7959)

GEOGRAPHIC SECTION

(G-7959)
CAMPHIRE DRILLING INC
8 Ross St (43014)
P.O. Box 28 (43014-0028)
PHONE..................................740 599-6928
George E Camphire, *President*
Janet Camphire, *Vice Pres*
EMP: 4
SALES: 180K **Privately Held**
SIC: 1381 Directional drilling oil & gas wells

(G-7960)
CAROL MICKLEY (PA)
Also Called: Unocal
2 Richard St (43014)
P.O. Box J (43014-0610)
PHONE..................................740 599-7870
Carol Mickley, *President*
▲ **EMP:** 3
SALES (est): 947K **Privately Held**
SIC: 1311 7992 Crude petroleum production; public golf courses

(G-7961)
COUNTRY LANE CUSTOM BUILDINGS
Also Called: Countryside Construction
21318 Pealer Mill Rd (43014-9640)
PHONE..................................740 485-8481
Andrew C Nisley, *Owner*
Crist Nisley, *Co-Owner*
EMP: 9
SALES: 831K **Privately Held**
SIC: 3999 7389 Miniatures;

(G-7962)
DUNAGAN LOGGING
16844 Pritchard Rd (43014-8000)
PHONE..................................740 599-9368
Sue Dunagan, *Owner*
EMP: 3
SALES (est): 143.1K **Privately Held**
WEB: www.thesunlink.com
SIC: 2411 Logging camps & contractors

(G-7963)
ELECTROWARMTH PRODUCTS LLC
513 Market St (43014)
P.O. Box A (43014-0601)
PHONE..................................740 599-7222
Dan Grindle, *President*
Beulah Grindle, *Vice Pres*
▲ **EMP:** 4 **EST:** 1939
SQ FT: 6,500
SALES (est): 499.4K **Privately Held**
SIC: 3699 Heat emission operating apparatus

(G-7964)
MCFADDEN LOGGING
305 S Mickley St (43014)
PHONE..................................740 599-6902
Jim McFadden, *Owner*
EMP: 3
SALES (est): 225.5K **Privately Held**
SIC: 2411 5099 Logging; logs, hewn ties, posts & poles

(G-7965)
SHROCK PREFAB LLC
23403 College Hill Rd (43014-9634)
PHONE..................................740 599-9401
Russell Schaeffer, *President*
John Kauffman, *Manager*
Joseph Shrock,
EMP: 11
SALES: 950K **Privately Held**
SIC: 3448 Trusses & framing: prefabricated metal

(G-7966)
VALLEY VIEW PALLETS LLC
Also Called: Valley View Pallets Partners
22414 Hostetler Rd (43014-9638)
PHONE..................................740 599-0010
Ephraim Yoder, *Mng Member*
David Yoder,
Joseph Yoder,
Samuel Yoder,
EMP: 9
SALES: 2MM **Privately Held**
SIC: 2448 7389 Pallets, wood;

(G-7967)
YOUNGS LOCKER SERVICE INC
Also Called: Youngs Locker Serv & Meat Proc
16201 Nashville Rd (43014-9738)
P.O. Box Y (43014-0625)
PHONE..................................740 599-6833
Lawrence Payne, *President*
EMP: 10 **EST:** 1945
SQ FT: 10,000
SALES: 190K **Privately Held**
SIC: 2011 4222 2013 Meat packing plants; warehousing, cold storage or refrigerated; sausages & other prepared meats

Dayton
Greene County

(G-7968)
ADVANCED PROPELLER SYSTEMS
1297 Windsor Dr (45434-8019)
PHONE..................................937 409-1038
William Jeffrey, *Owner*
EMP: 3
SALES (est): 219.7K **Privately Held**
SIC: 3366 7389 Propellers; business services

(G-7969)
AIR FORCE US DEPT OF
4225 Logistics Ave (45433-5769)
PHONE..................................937 656-2354
EMP: 254 **Publicly Held**
SIC: 9711 7372 Air Force; business oriented computer software
HQ: United States Department Of The Air Force
1000 Air Force Pentagon
Washington DC 20330

(G-7970)
AMCO PRODUCTS INC
500 N Smithville Rd (45431-1069)
PHONE..................................937 433-7982
Joseph M Raby, *CEO*
Ronald J Raby, *President*
Karla Simmons, *Vice Pres*
EMP: 10 **EST:** 1966
SQ FT: 58,600
SALES (est): 1.6MM **Privately Held**
SIC: 3451 Screw machine products

(G-7971)
ANTHONY BUSINESS FORMS INC
3160 Plainfield Rd (45432-3713)
P.O. Box 24754 (45424-0754)
PHONE..................................937 253-0072
Katherine D Harrah, *President*
Kathy Harrah, *Sales Staff*
EMP: 12
SQ FT: 6,000
SALES (est): 2.4MM **Privately Held**
WEB: www.anthonybusinessforms.com
SIC: 5112 2754 2759 2791 Business forms; labels: gravure printing; envelopes: printing; typesetting; manifold business forms; commercial printing, lithographic

(G-7972)
CABLE AND CTRL SOLUTIONS LLC
4726 Springfield St (45431-1045)
PHONE..................................937 254-2227
Bob Day, *General Mgr*
EMP: 3
SALES (est): 422K **Privately Held**
SIC: 3496 3629 Cable, uninsulated wire: made from purchased wire; electronic generation equipment

(G-7973)
CAPITAL PRECISION MACHINE & TL
1865 Radio Rd (45431-1034)
PHONE..................................937 258-1176
Paul Powers Sr, *Owner*
Cliff Smith, *Owner*
EMP: 8
SQ FT: 10,000

SALES (est): 1.5MM **Privately Held**
WEB: www.cpmtool.com
SIC: 3544 Special dies & tools

(G-7974)
CASSADY WOODWORKS INC
446 N Smithville Rd (45431-1080)
PHONE..................................937 256-7948
Tom Joch, *President*
Dave Davis, *Vice Pres*
EMP: 25
SQ FT: 12,000
SALES: 6.3MM **Privately Held**
WEB: www.cassadywoodworks.com
SIC: 2431 2441 2541 Millwork; nailed wood boxes & shook; display fixtures, wood

(G-7975)
D & B INDUSTRIES INC
5031 Linden Ave Ste B (45432-1893)
PHONE..................................937 253-8658
Brent Gillott, *President*
Brent Grotegut, *Technology*
EMP: 7
SQ FT: 5,000
SALES (est): 972.2K **Privately Held**
WEB: www.d-bindustries.com
SIC: 3599 Machine shop, jobbing & repair

(G-7976)
DAILY SQUAWK LLC
3214 Bob White Pl (45431-3364)
PHONE..................................937 426-6247
Daniel W Ross, *Principal*
EMP: 3
SALES (est): 89.5K **Privately Held**
SIC: 2711 Newspapers, publishing & printing

(G-7977)
DAYTON INDUSTRIAL DRUM INC
1880 Radio Rd (45431-1035)
P.O. Box 172, Tipp City (45371-0172)
PHONE..................................937 253-8933
David Hussong, *President*
Ruth M Hussong, *Corp Secy*
Kylene Hussong, *Vice Pres*
EMP: 25
SQ FT: 25,000
SALES (est): 4.4MM **Privately Held**
WEB: www.daytonindustrialdrum.com
SIC: 7699 5085 5113 2673 Industrial equipment services; drums, new or reconditioned; industrial & personal service paper; bags: plastic, laminated & coated; fiber cans, drums & similar products

(G-7978)
DLA DOCUMENT SERVICES
4165 Communications Blvd (45433-5601)
PHONE..................................937 257-6014
Leonard Xavier, *Director*
EMP: 25 **Publicly Held**
SIC: 2752 9711 Commercial printing, lithographic; national security
HQ: Dla Document Services
5450 Carlisle Pike Bldg 9
Mechanicsburg PA 17050
717 605-2362

(G-7979)
G W SMITH AND SONS INC
1700 Spaulding Rd (45432-3728)
PHONE..................................937 253-5114
Victor W Smith Jr, *President*
Michael Fitzharris, *Vice Pres*
▲ **EMP:** 22 **EST:** 1939
SQ FT: 45,000
SALES (est): 6.4MM
SALES (corp-wide): 820MM **Publicly Held**
WEB: www.gwsmithandsons.com
SIC: 2992 Lubricating oils & greases
PA: Quaker Chemical Corporation
901 E Hector St
Conshohocken PA 19428
610 832-4000

(G-7980)
GREEN MACHINE TOOL INC
1865 Radio Rd (45431-1034)
PHONE..................................937 253-0771
Eugene Green, *President*
Mary Ann Green, *Vice Pres*

EMP: 12
SQ FT: 12,000
SALES: 1MM **Privately Held**
SIC: 3599 3544 Machine shop, jobbing & repair; forms (molds), for foundry & plastics working machinery

(G-7981)
GREENE COUNTY
Also Called: Green County Wtr Sup & Trtmnt
1122 Beaver Valley Rd (45434-7014)
PHONE..................................937 429-0127
Ken French, *Manager*
EMP: 8 **Privately Held**
WEB: www.greeneworks.com
SIC: 3589 4941 Sewage & water treatment equipment; water supply
PA: Greene County
35 Greene St
Xenia OH 45385
937 562-5006

(G-7982)
HEARTH PRODUCTS CONTROLS CO
3050 Plainfield Rd (45432-3711)
PHONE..................................937 436-9800
Greg Stech, *Vice Pres*
Jim Karns, *Purch Mgr*
John Wagner, *Natl Sales Mgr*
Jennifer Combs, *Accounts Mgr*
Keith Lambert, *Marketing Mgr*
▲ **EMP:** 18
SQ FT: 8,400
SALES (est): 4.8MM **Privately Held**
WEB: www.hearthproductscontrols.com
SIC: 3491 Process control regulator valves

(G-7983)
LAU INDUSTRIES INC (DH)
Also Called: Supreme Fan/Industrial Air
4509 Springfield St (45431-1042)
PHONE..................................937 476-6500
Damian Macaluso, *President*
Dan Disser, *Vice Pres*
Christopher Wampler, *Vice Pres*
▼ **EMP:** 131
SQ FT: 50,000
SALES (est): 286.9MM **Privately Held**
WEB: www.lauparts.com
SIC: 3564 Ventilating fans: industrial or commercial
HQ: Johnson Controls, Inc.
5757 N Green Bay Ave
Milwaukee WI 53209
414 524-1200

(G-7984)
MANTYCH METALWORKING INC
3175 Plainfield Rd (45432-3712)
PHONE..................................937 258-1373
Kathleen Mantych, *CEO*
Colleen Mantych, *President*
Cristy Mantych, *Vice Pres*
Dan Thieman, *Manager*
EMP: 24 **EST:** 1971
SQ FT: 24,000
SALES (est): 3.9MM **Privately Held**
WEB: www.mantych.net
SIC: 3599 3444 Machine shop, jobbing & repair; sheet metalwork

(G-7985)
MIAMI VALLEY LIGHTING LLC
1065 Woodman Dr (45432-1423)
PHONE..................................937 224-6000
Teresa Sloan, *General Mgr*
Joyce Reives, *Mng Member*
Dave Hinnan,
EMP: 7
SQ FT: 1,500
SALES: 9MM
SALES (corp-wide): 10.7B **Publicly Held**
WEB: www.dpl.com
SIC: 3648 Street lighting fixtures
HQ: Dpl Inc.
1065 Woodman Dr
Dayton OH 45432
937 331-4063

(G-7986)
MIAMI VLY MFG & ASSEMBLY INC
1889 Radio Rd (45431-1034)
PHONE..................................937 254-6665
Joseph S Rosenkranz, *President*

▲ = Import ▼ = Export
◆ = Import/Export

GEOGRAPHIC SECTION

Dayton - Montgomery County (G-8015)

EMP: 12
SQ FT: 5,000
SALES: 1MM **Privately Held**
SIC: 3599 Machine shop, jobbing & repair

(G-7987)
MULCH MAN
Also Called: Mulch Man Greenline Products
4595 Fairpark Ave (45431)
PHONE..................937 866-5370
John Randall, *Principal*
EMP: 20
SALES (est): 2MM **Privately Held**
SIC: 2499 Mulch, wood & bark

(G-7988)
POI HOLDINGS INC (HQ)
Also Called: Phase One
3203 Plainfield Rd (45432-3736)
PHONE..................937 253-7377
Frederick Ewing, *President*
John Schreiner, *Vice Pres*
EMP: 15 **EST:** 1975
SQ FT: 7,500
SALES (est): 1.9MM
SALES (corp-wide): 27.9MM **Privately Held**
SIC: 3821 3823 Laboratory apparatus & furniture; flow instruments, industrial process type
PA: Vacuum Instrument Corporation
2101 9th Ave Ste A
Ronkonkoma NY 11779
631 737-0900

(G-7989)
SALLEY TOOL & DIE CO
3180 Plainfield Rd Ste 1 (45432-3740)
PHONE..................937 258-3333
Stephen Salley, *Owner*
EMP: 13
SALES (est): 1.4MM **Privately Held**
SIC: 3728 3599 Military aircraft equipment & armament; machine shop, jobbing & repair

(G-7990)
STEINBARGER PRECISION CNC INC
3100 Plainfield Rd Ste A (45432-3725)
PHONE..................937 252-0322
EMP: 3 **EST:** 1998
SQ FT: 2,500
SALES: 300K **Privately Held**
SIC: 3599 Machine Shop

(G-7991)
TOASTMASTERS INTERNATIONAL
1854 Redleaf Ct (45432-4103)
PHONE..................937 429-2680
Dan Reeves, *Treasurer*
EMP: 10
SALES (corp-wide): 34.8MM **Privately Held**
WEB: www.d70toastmasters.org
SIC: 8299 2721 Educational service, non-degree granting: continuing educ.; magazines: publishing only, not printed on site
PA: Toastmasters International
9127 S Jamaica St 400
Englewood CO 80112
949 858-8255

(G-7992)
TOOL SERVICE CO INC
Also Called: Ohio Industrial Supply
4620 Tall Oaks Dr (45432-3241)
P.O. Box 292165 (45429-0165)
PHONE..................937 254-4000
Dwayne Jones, *President*
Shirley Jones, *Admin Sec*
EMP: 5
SQ FT: 6,400
SALES (est): 450K **Privately Held**
SIC: 3541 5084 Grinding, polishing, buffing, lapping & honing machines; machine tool replacement & repair parts, metal cutting types; machine tools & metalworking machinery

(G-7993)
TRACT INC
Also Called: Signs Now
3197 Beaver Vu Dr (45434-6366)
PHONE..................937 427-3431

Catherine Peters, *President*
Roger Peters, *Vice Pres*
EMP: 5
SALES: 750K **Privately Held**
SIC: 3993 Signs & advertising specialties

(G-7994)
UNISON INDUSTRIES LLC
2455 Dayton Xenia Rd (45434-7148)
PHONE..................904 667-9904
Belinda Kidwell, *Manager*
Allen Glaug, *Manager*
EMP: 400
SALES (corp-wide): 121.6B **Publicly Held**
WEB: www.unisonindustries.com
SIC: 3728 4581 3714 3498 Aircraft parts & equipment; aircraft servicing & repairing; motor vehicle parts & accessories; fabricated pipe & fittings; steel pipe & tubes
HQ: Unison Industries, Llc
7575 Baymeadows Way
Jacksonville FL 32256
904 739-4000

Dayton
Montgomery County

(G-7995)
4 OVER LLC
7801 Technology Blvd (45424-1574)
PHONE..................937 610-0629
Frank Johnston, *Vice Pres*
EMP: 13
SALES (corp-wide): 190.6MM **Privately Held**
SIC: 2759 Commercial printing
HQ: 4 Over, Llc
5900 San Fernando Rd D
Glendale CA 91202
818 246-1170

(G-7996)
5 AXIS GRINDING INC
86 Westpark Rd (45459-4813)
PHONE..................937 312-9797
Scott Ameduri, *President*
Barbara Ameduri, *Admin Sec*
EMP: 7
SALES (est): 1.1MM **Privately Held**
SIC: 3541 Machine tools, metal cutting type

(G-7997)
A & B IRON & METAL COMPANY
329 Washington St (45402-2541)
PHONE..................937 228-1561
Greg Thoma, *President*
Joseph Caperna, *President*
Rosalia Caperna, *Vice Pres*
EMP: 15
SQ FT: 500
SALES: 2MM **Privately Held**
SIC: 5093 4953 3341 3231 Metal scrap & waste materials; refuse systems; secondary nonferrous metals; products of purchased glass

(G-7998)
A & W SPRING CO INC
1000 E 2nd St Ste 8 (45402-1370)
PHONE..................937 222-7284
EMP: 4 **EST:** 1973
SQ FT: 1,800
SALES (est): 320K **Privately Held**
SIC: 3495 Mfg Wire Springs

(G-7999)
AABEL PLUMBING INC
440 Congress Park Dr (45459-4125)
PHONE..................937 434-4343
Charles Norman, *President*
EMP: 25
SQ FT: 16,000
SALES (est): 1.9MM **Privately Held**
SIC: 3261 Vitreous plumbing fixtures

(G-8000)
ABSOLUTE SMILE LLC
4469 Far Hills Ave (45429-2405)
PHONE..................937 293-9866
EMP: 4

SALES (est): 454.4K **Privately Held**
SIC: 3843 Mfg Dental Equipment/Supplies

(G-8001)
ACCRO-CAST CORPORATION
4147 Gardendale Ave (45417-9509)
PHONE..................937 228-0497
Fred Luther, *President*
EMP: 12 **EST:** 1964
SQ FT: 5,000
SALES (est): 163.3K **Privately Held**
SIC: 3365 Aluminum & aluminum-based alloy castings

(G-8002)
ACCU-GRIND & MFG CO INC
272 Leo St (45404-1006)
P.O. Box 117, Laura (45337-0117)
PHONE..................937 224-3303
Jeff Heisey, *President*
EMP: 43
SQ FT: 39,500
SALES (est): 5.8MM **Privately Held**
SIC: 3599 Machine shop, jobbing & repair

(G-8003)
ACCUMULUS SOFTWARE
6708 Innsbruck Dr (45459-1224)
P.O. Box 750171 (45475-0171)
PHONE..................937 435-0861
Eric Greenrose, *President*
EMP: 4
SALES (est): 176.5K **Privately Held**
SIC: 7372 Prepackaged software

(G-8004)
ACCUTECH PLASTIC MOLDING INC
5015 Kitridge Rd (45424-4433)
P.O. Box 24272 (45424-0272)
PHONE..................937 233-0017
William Stoddard Jr, *President*
EMP: 7 **EST:** 1977
SQ FT: 6,000
SALES: 1MM **Privately Held**
SIC: 3089 Injection molding of plastics

(G-8005)
ACTION RUBBER CO INC
601 Fame Rd (45449-2355)
PHONE..................937 866-5975
Ron Mc Croson, *President*
EMP: 10
SQ FT: 12,500
SALES (est): 770K **Privately Held**
WEB: www.actionrubber.com
SIC: 3069 Molded rubber products

(G-8006)
ACUREN INSPECTION INC
705 Albany St (45417-3460)
PHONE..................937 228-9729
Jim Bailey, *President*
EMP: 52
SALES (corp-wide): 1.6B **Privately Held**
SIC: 1389 Testing, measuring, surveying & analysis services
HQ: Acuren Inspection, Inc.
30 Main St Ste 402
Danbury CT 06810
203 702-8740

(G-8007)
ADAPTIVE DATA INC
8170 Washington Vlg Dr (45458-1848)
PHONE..................937 436-2343
Timothy Gribler, *President*
Jerry Gribler, *Office Mgr*
Mike Barker, *Manager*
Jevon Kennedy, *Technical Staff*
EMP: 10
SALES (est): 2.1MM **Privately Held**
WEB: www.adi-barcode.com
SIC: 2679 3955 3577 2671 Labels, paper: made from purchased material; carbon paper & inked ribbons; computer peripheral equipment; packaging paper & plastics film, coated & laminated

(G-8008)
ADCURA MFG
1314 Farr Dr (45404-2736)
PHONE..................937 222-3800
Russel Phie, *Owner*
EMP: 6

SALES (est): 793.1K **Privately Held**
SIC: 3679 Harness assemblies for electronic use: wire or cable

(G-8009)
ADEPT MANUFACTURING CORP
511 N Findlay St (45404-2205)
PHONE..................937 222-7110
Mike Mueller, *President*
Sandy Mueller, *Treasurer*
EMP: 10
SQ FT: 18,000
SALES (est): 1.4MM **Privately Held**
SIC: 3544 Special dies, tools, jigs & fixtures

(G-8010)
ADVANTIC LLC
4250 Display Ln (45429-5149)
PHONE..................937 490-4712
EMP: 5 **EST:** 2015
SALES (est): 198.4K **Privately Held**
SIC: 3272 Concrete stuctural support & building material

(G-8011)
AHLSTROM WEST CARROLLTON LLC
1 S Elm St (45449)
PHONE..................937 859-3621
Cameron Lonergar, *President*
Alan P Berens, *Vice Pres*
▲ **EMP:** 120
SQ FT: 100,000
SALES (est): 18.7MM
SALES (corp-wide): 2.3B **Privately Held**
WEB: www.wcparchment.com
SIC: 2621 2672 Parchment paper; coated & laminated paper
HQ: Ahlstrom-Munksjo Usa Inc.
2 Elm St
Windsor Locks CT 06096

(G-8012)
AIR CLEANING SOLUTIONS
8613 N Main St (45415-1329)
P.O. Box 13103 (45413-0103)
PHONE..................937 832-3600
Jim O'Bryan, *Owner*
Jim Obryan, *Owner*
EMP: 3
SALES (est): 325.2K **Privately Held**
SIC: 3564 Filters, air: furnaces, air conditioning equipment, etc.

(G-8013)
AIRGAS USA LLC
1223 Mccook Ave (45404-1011)
PHONE..................937 228-8594
Kevin Little, *Branch Mgr*
Julie Rengers, *Manager*
EMP: 21
SQ FT: 9,600
SALES (corp-wide): 125.9MM **Privately Held**
WEB: www.us.linde-gas.com
SIC: 5169 5084 5984 2813 Industrial gases; gases, compressed & liquefied; welding machinery & equipment; liquefied petroleum gas dealers; industrial gases
HQ: Airgas Usa, Llc
259 N Radnor Chester Rd # 100
Radnor PA 19087
610 687-5253

(G-8014)
AIRGAS USA LLC
3800 Dayton Park Dr (45414-4410)
PHONE..................937 237-0621
Dennis McCarten, *Branch Mgr*
Misti Wombold, *Admin Asst*
EMP: 5
SALES (corp-wide): 125.9MM **Privately Held**
WEB: www.us.linde-gas.com
SIC: 2813 Industrial gases
HQ: Airgas Usa, Llc
259 N Radnor Chester Rd # 100
Radnor PA 19087
610 687-5253

(G-8015)
ALFRED NICKLES BAKERY INC
201 Pritz Ave (45403-2521)
PHONE..................937 256-3762
Gary Huffman, *Manager*

(PA)=Parent Co (HQ)=Headquarters (DH)=Div Headquarters
✪ = New Business established in last 2 years

2019 Harris Ohio Industrial Directory

Dayton - Montgomery County (G-8016)   **GEOGRAPHIC SECTION**

EMP: 16
SALES (corp-wide): 205MM **Privately Held**
SIC: 2051 Bakery, for home service delivery
PA: Alfred Nickles Bakery, Inc.
26 Main St N
Navarre OH 44662
330 879-5635

(G-8016)
ALL SYSTEMS COLOUR INC
2032 S Alex Rd Ste A (45449-4023)
PHONE...................937 859-9701
George Dick, *President*
EMP: 4
SALES (est): 460.7K
SALES (corp-wide): 11MM **Privately Held**
WEB: www.allsystemscolour.com
SIC: 2732 2752 Books: printing & binding; commercial printing, lithographic
PA: Four Colour Imports, Ltd.
2410 Frankfort Ave Ste 1
Louisville KY 40206
502 896-9644

(G-8017)
ALLEY CAT DESIGNS INC
919 Senate Dr (45459-4017)
PHONE...................937 291-8803
Ron Dallessandris, *President*
Joyce Dallessandris, *Vice Pres*
Mariana Neal, *Vice Pres*
Patty Dallessandris, *Admin Sec*
EMP: 8
SQ FT: 2,800
SALES (est): 1.3MM **Privately Held**
WEB: www.alleycatworldwide.com
SIC: 3552 2395 Printing machinery, textile; embroidery products, except schiffli machine

(G-8018)
ALLIANCE INDUS MASKING INC
204 S Ludlow St Ste 201 (45402-2341)
PHONE...................937 681-5569
Donald Gray, *President*
EMP: 3
SALES (est): 179.2K **Privately Held**
SIC: 2675 Cutouts, cardboard, die-cut: from purchased materials

(G-8019)
ALLIANCE TORQUE CONVERTERS INC
Also Called: Alliance Manufacturing
5915 Wolf Creek Pike (45426-2439)
PHONE...................937 222-3394
Donald L Gray, *Principal*
Tiffany Stewart, *Manager*
EMP: 4
SALES: 500K **Privately Held**
SIC: 3621 Torque motors, electric

(G-8020)
ALLIED SILK SCREEN INC
2740 Thunderhawk Ct (45414-3464)
PHONE...................937 223-4921
Dennis Brzozowski, *President*
David Brzozowski, *Vice Pres*
EMP: 7
SQ FT: 10,000
SALES: 200K **Privately Held**
WEB: www.alliedsilkscreen.com
SIC: 2759 Screen printing

(G-8021)
ALRO STEEL CORPORATION
Also Called: Arlo Aluminum & Steel
821 Springfield St (45403-1252)
PHONE...................937 253-6121
Tim Elliott, *Manager*
EMP: 40
SQ FT: 120,000
SALES (corp-wide): 1.9B **Privately Held**
WEB: www.alro.com
SIC: 5051 3441 3317 3316 Steel; fabricated structural metal; steel pipe & tubes; cold finishing of steel shapes; blast furnaces & steel mills
PA: Alro Steel Corporation
3100 E High St
Jackson MI 49203
517 787-5500

(G-8022)
AMERICAN AERO COMPONENTS LLC
2601 W Stroop Rd Ste 62 (45439-2030)
PHONE...................937 367-5068
Ajitesh Kakade, *Info Tech Mgr*
EMP: 7
SQ FT: 50,000
SALES (est): 158.4K **Privately Held**
SIC: 3451 3599 3728 3724 Screw machine products; machine & other job shop work; aircraft parts & equipment; aircraft engines & engine parts

(G-8023)
AMERICAN BOTTLING COMPANY
7 Up Bottling Co of Dayton
3131 Transportation Rd (45404-2372)
PHONE...................937 236-0333
Christine Durr, *Train & Dev Mgr*
Michael Eichner, *Manager*
Mike Eichner, *Manager*
EMP: 100
SQ FT: 120,000
SALES (est): 100,000 **Publicly Held**
WEB: www.cs-americas.com
SIC: 2086 Bottled & canned soft drinks
HQ: The American Bottling Company
5301 Legacy Dr
Plano TX 75024

(G-8024)
AMERICAN CITY BUS JOURNALS INC
Also Called: Dayton Business Journal
40 N Main St Ste 800 (45423-1053)
PHONE...................937 528-4400
Caleb Stephens, *Editor*
Neil Arthur, *Manager*
Rick Titus, *Creative Dir*
EMP: 26
SALES (corp-wide): 1.4B **Privately Held**
SIC: 2711 7313 Newspapers: publishing only, not printed on site; newspaper advertising representative
HQ: American City Business Journals, Inc.
120 W Morehead St Ste 400
Charlotte NC 28202
704 973-1000

(G-8025)
AMERICAN CONCRETE PRODUCTS
Also Called: American Brick & Block
1433 S Euclid Ave (45417-3839)
PHONE...................937 224-1433
Lee Snyder, *President*
Lee E Snyder, *Treasurer*
EMP: 11
SQ FT: 10,000
SALES: 750K **Privately Held**
SIC: 3271 5211 Blocks, concrete or cinder: standard; brick

(G-8026)
AMERICAN INDUS MAINTANENCE
605 Springfield St (45403-1248)
PHONE...................937 254-3400
Marvin Price, *President*
Cari Price, *President*
EMP: 8
SQ FT: 19,000
SALES (est): 1.1MM **Privately Held**
SIC: 5231 3471 Paint & painting supplies; sand blasting of metal parts

(G-8027)
AMERICAN RESCUE TECHNOLOGY
2780 Culver Ave (45429-3724)
PHONE...................937 293-6240
Richard S Michalo, *President*
▲ **EMP:** 10
SQ FT: 11,000
SALES (est): 3.4MM **Privately Held**
WEB: www.genesisrescue.com
SIC: 5084 3569 Safety equipment; fire-fighting apparatus & related equipment

(G-8028)
AMERICAN WAY EXTERIORS LLC
3564 Intercity Dr (45424-5124)
PHONE...................855 766-3293
Stephen Moad, *President*
EMP: 4
SALES (est): 148K **Privately Held**
SIC: 3292 1761 1799 Roofing, asbestos felt roll; roofing, siding & sheet metal work; asbestos removal & encapsulation

(G-8029)
AMERICAN WOODWORK SPECIALTY CO
Also Called: A W S C O
4301 N James H Mcgee Blvd (45417-9537)
PHONE...................937 263-1053
Michael E Knapp, *President*
Janine A Knapp, *Treasurer*
EMP: 35
SQ FT: 120,000
SALES (est): 4.2MM **Privately Held**
WEB: www.awsco.com
SIC: 2431 3442 3231 Window frames, wood; louver windows, glass, wood frame; metal doors, sash & trim; products of purchased glass

(G-8030)
AMERIWATER LLC
3345 Stop 8 Rd (45414-3425)
PHONE...................937 461-8833
Diane Dolan, *CEO*
James Baker, *Vice Pres*
Brian Bowman, *Administration*
▲ **EMP:** 47
SQ FT: 48,000
SALES (est): 16.3MM
SALES (corp-wide): 94.7MM **Privately Held**
WEB: www.ameriwater.com
SIC: 3589 Water treatment equipment, industrial
HQ: Suez International
Tour Cb 21
Courbevoie 92400
146 256-000

(G-8031)
ANALYTICA USA INC (PA)
711 E Monu Ave Ste 309 (45402)
PHONE...................513 348-2333
Vikram Seshadri, *Owner*
EMP: 3 **EST:** 2006
SALES: 1.9MM **Privately Held**
SIC: 7371 3825 Software programming applications; radio apparatus analyzers

(G-8032)
ANGSTRON MATERIALS INC
1240 Mccook Ave (45404-1059)
PHONE...................937 331-9884
Meishio Jang, *President*
David Burton, *Exec VP*
Edward Chan, *Exec VP*
Bor Z Jang, *Vice Pres*
Nilo Joson, *Prdtn Mgr*
▲ **EMP:** 4
SALES (est): 1.1MM **Privately Held**
SIC: 3624 Carbon & graphite products

(G-8033)
APEX TOOL GROUP LLC
762 W Stewart St (45417-3971)
PHONE...................937 222-7871
Gary Alcorn, *Engineer*
Brian Smith, *Engineer*
Jerry Storts, *Engineer*
EMP: 200
SALES (corp-wide): 14.2B **Privately Held**
WEB: www.cooperhandtools.com
SIC: 3546 Power-driven handtools
HQ: Apex Tool Group, Llc
910 Ridgebrook Rd Ste 200
Sparks Glencoe MD 21152

(G-8034)
APS-MATERIALS INC (PA)
Also Called: A P S
4011 Riverside Dr (45405-2364)
P.O. Box 1106 (45401-1106)
PHONE...................937 278-6547
Michael C Wilson, *President*
Phil Chitty, *General Mgr*
Joseph T Cheng, *Chairman*
Robert Willson, *VP Opers*
Monty King, *Electrical Engi*
▲ **EMP:** 95 **EST:** 1975
SQ FT: 50,000
SALES (est): 16.7MM **Privately Held**
WEB: www.apsmaterials.com
SIC: 3479 2899 2851 Coating of metals & formed products; chemical preparations; paints & allied products

(G-8035)
APS-MATERIALS INC
Also Called: Ceranode Division
153 Walbrook Ave (45405-2343)
PHONE...................937 278-6547
Philip Chitty, *Manager*
EMP: 50
SALES (est): 4.6MM
SALES (corp-wide): 16.7MM **Privately Held**
WEB: www.apsmaterials.com
SIC: 3479 Coating of metals & formed products
PA: Aps-Materials, Inc.
4011 Riverside Dr
Dayton OH 45405
937 278-6547

(G-8036)
ARGROV BOX CO
6030 Webster St (45414-3434)
P.O. Box 305, Middletown (45042-0305)
PHONE...................937 898-1700
Kenneth Eppich, *President*
Dean Timmons, *COO*
Judith Eppich, *Vice Pres*
EMP: 14
SQ FT: 42,400
SALES (est): 1.9MM **Privately Held**
SIC: 2653 5113 Boxes, corrugated: made from purchased materials; boxes & containers

(G-8037)
ARMSTRONG S PRINTING EX LLC
8810 Grovecreek Ct (45458-3372)
PHONE...................937 276-7794
James A Armstrong, *Principal*
EMP: 4
SALES (est): 323.3K **Privately Held**
SIC: 2752 Commercial printing, lithographic

(G-8038)
ARTISAN GRINDING SERVICE INC
1300 Stanley Ave (45404-1092)
PHONE...................937 667-7383
Carolyn M Buechly, *President*
Teresa Landers, *Vice Pres*
Jeryl L Yantis, *Admin Sec*
EMP: 11 **EST:** 1977
SQ FT: 14,000
SALES (oct): 1.9MM **Privately Hold**
WEB: www.artisangrinding.com
SIC: 3599 Machine shop, jobbing & repair

(G-8039)
ASHTON PUMPMATIC INC
7670 Mcewen Rd (45459-3908)
P.O. Box 750783 (45475-0783)
PHONE...................937 424-1380
John Kelch, *President*
Jeanne E Kelch, *Vice Pres*
EMP: 4
SQ FT: 6,000
SALES: 400K **Privately Held**
WEB: www.pumpmatic.com
SIC: 5047 3821 Instruments, surgical & medical; clinical laboratory instruments, except medical & dental

(G-8040)
ASSOCIATED MATERIALS LLC
Also Called: Alside Supply Center
3361 Needmore Rd (45414-4311)
PHONE...................937 236-5679
Dough Singleton, *Manager*
EMP: 5 **Privately Held**
WEB: www.associatedmaterials.com
SIC: 3444 5031 5211 Metal flooring & siding; lumber, plywood & millwork; door & window products

GEOGRAPHIC SECTION

Dayton - Montgomery County (G-8066)

HQ: Associated Materials, Llc
3773 State Rd
Cuyahoga Falls OH 44223
330 929-1811

(G-8041)
ASTERENA CORPORATION
1413 Verna Ct (45458-9715)
PHONE..................937 605-6470
Sreeharshan Nambiar, *President*
Ponon Dileep Kumar, *Vice Pres*
Jayendran Moorkoth Arakkalath, *Admin Sec*
EMP: 3
SALES (est): 141K **Privately Held**
SIC: 7372 Utility computer software

(G-8042)
ATLAS PRODUCE LLC
104 Salem Ave (45406-5801)
P.O. Box 61091 (45406-9091)
PHONE..................937 223-1446
Sylvester Ballard,
EMP: 5
SALES (est): 227.8K **Privately Held**
WEB: www.sylresources.com
SIC: 2051 Bakery: wholesale or wholesale/retail combined

(G-8043)
AUTO-VALVE INC
1707 Guenther Rd (45417-9398)
PHONE..................937 854-3037
Raymond C Clark, *President*
Tim Claude, *Mfg Mgr*
Rob Williamson, *Controller*
Beth Seall, *Human Res Mgr*
Jeanette Monaghan, *Administration*
EMP: 50
SQ FT: 17,800
SALES (est): 7.4MM **Privately Held**
WEB: www.autovalve.com
SIC: 3592 Valves, aircraft

(G-8044)
AUTOMATION SYSTEMS DESIGNS INC
Also Called: A S D
6222 Webster St (45414-3438)
PHONE..................937 387-0351
Sunny Kullar, *Principal*
Joe Fife, *Opers Mgr*
Marc Molnar, *Engineer*
Sukhi Kullar, *CFO*
EMP: 20
SQ FT: 17,000
SALES (est): 9.1MM **Privately Held**
WEB: www.asddayton.com
SIC: 3535 Robotic conveyors

(G-8045)
AUTOMATION TECHNOLOGY INC
1900 Troy St (45404-2194)
PHONE..................937 233-6084
Robert Storar, *CEO*
Jeff Storar, *President*
N Chris Storar, *Corp Secy*
Christopher Hassan, *Project Engr*
EMP: 25
SQ FT: 20,000
SALES (est): 5.3MM **Privately Held**
SIC: 3625 3825 3829 3823 Actuators, industrial; test equipment for electronic & electrical circuits; measuring & controlling devices; industrial instrmnts msrmnt display/control process variable

(G-8046)
AVION TOOL CORPORATION
3620 Lenox Dr (45429-1516)
PHONE..................937 278-0779
Paul Molnar, *President*
EMP: 16 EST: 1947
SQ FT: 11,000
SALES (est): 2.4MM **Privately Held**
SIC: 3724 Aircraft engines & engine parts

(G-8047)
AWESOME YOGURT LLC
3337 Lenox Dr (45429-1509)
PHONE..................937 643-0879
Naomi Fogel, *Owner*
EMP: 5
SALES (est): 372.8K **Privately Held**
SIC: 2024 Yogurt desserts, frozen

(G-8048)
B & P COMPANY INC
97 Compark Rd (45459-4801)
P.O. Box 41184 (45441-0184)
PHONE..................937 298-0265
Margaret Wright, *President*
James Wright, *Manager*
EMP: 9
SQ FT: 13,000
SALES: 2MM **Privately Held**
WEB: www.frownies.com
SIC: 2844 Cosmetic preparations

(G-8049)
B C WILSON INC
85 Compark Rd (45459-4801)
PHONE..................937 439-1866
Fax: 937 439-1986
EMP: 5
SQ FT: 6,000
SALES (est): 682.7K **Privately Held**
SIC: 3544 7389 Mfg Dies/Tools/Jigs/Fixtures Business Services

(G-8050)
B S F INC (PA)
8895 N Dixie Dr (45414-1803)
P.O. Box 459, Vandalia (45377-0459)
PHONE..................937 890-6121
Kathryn Keel, *President*
Chris Bright, *Principal*
Jackie Frank, *Principal*
Eric Metzger, *Principal*
Sarah Gayman, *Editor*
EMP: 10
SQ FT: 2,000
SALES (est): 1.8MM **Privately Held**
SIC: 3498 3568 Couplings, pipe: fabricated from purchased pipe; couplings, shaft: rigid, flexible, universal joint, etc.

(G-8051)
BAR CODES UNLIMITED INC
683 Miamisburg Ctrvl 21 Ste (45459)
PHONE..................937 434-2633
Jay Dring, *President*
Karen Dring, *Vice Pres*
Anthony Scrimenti, *Vice Pres*
Craig Dring, *Treasurer*
EMP: 4
SALES (est): 908.5K **Privately Held**
WEB: www.bcuinc.com
SIC: 5046 2759 8742 Commercial equipment; labels & seals: printing; industry specialist consultants

(G-8052)
BELLBROOK TRANSPORT INC (HQ)
Also Called: Ernest Trucking
3361 Successful Way (45414-4317)
P.O. Box 13577 (45413-0577)
PHONE..................937 233-5555
John C Ernst Jr, *President*
Terry Killen, *Corp Secy*
David Ernst, *Vice Pres*
▼ EMP: 4
SQ FT: 10,000
SALES (est): 4.1MM
SALES (corp-wide): 227.2MM **Privately Held**
WEB: www.greentechohio.com
SIC: 3273 Ready-mixed concrete
PA: Ernst Enterprises, Inc.
3361 Successful Way
Dayton OH 45414
937 233-5555

(G-8053)
BELTON FOODS
2701 Thunderhawk Ct (45414-3445)
P.O. Box 13605 (45413-0605)
PHONE..................937 890-7768
David V Sipos, *President*
Ted Dorow, *Vice Pres*
Cindy Gillespie, *Vice Pres*
Eleanor Sipos, *Shareholder*
Barbara Berer, *Admin Sec*
EMP: 27 EST: 1949
SQ FT: 24,800
SALES (est): 10.2MM **Privately Held**
SIC: 2087 2086 2035 Concentrates, drink; syrups, flavoring (except drink); bottled & canned soft drinks; pickles, sauces & salad dressings

(G-8054)
BENCHWORKS JEWELERS INC
133 E Franklin St (45459-5915)
PHONE..................937 439-4243
George Steberl, *President*
EMP: 4
SQ FT: 1,462
SALES (est): 411K **Privately Held**
WEB: www.benchworksjewelers.com
SIC: 3911 5944 7631 Jewelry, precious metal; jewelry stores; jewelry repair services

(G-8055)
BENNETT & BENNETT INC (PA)
1744 Thomas Paine Pkwy (45459-2541)
PHONE..................937 324-1100
Bill Bennett, *President*
Tami Anderson, *General Mgr*
Michelle Bennett, *Treasurer*
John Denney, *Technology*
EMP: 11
SALES (est): 1.7MM **Privately Held**
WEB: www.bennettnbennett.com
SIC: 3679 Static power supply converters for electronic applications

(G-8056)
BETA INDUSTRIES INC (PA)
2860 Culver Ave (45429-3794)
PHONE..................937 299-7385
William B Walcott, *President*
Kenneth Walcott, *Vice Pres*
Linda Hepner, *Purchasing*
Wanda King, *Purchasing*
Carol Dayton, *VP Finance*
EMP: 22
SQ FT: 12,600
SALES (est): 3.4MM **Privately Held**
SIC: 3599 3699 Machine shop, jobbing & repair; custom machinery; electrical equipment & supplies

(G-8057)
BLAIRS CNC TURNING INC
245 Leo St (45404-1005)
P.O. Box 2840 (45401-2840)
PHONE..................937 461-1100
James Trochelman, *President*
Marina Trochelman, *Vice Pres*
EMP: 7
SQ FT: 13,100
SALES (est): 650K **Privately Held**
SIC: 3541 Lathes

(G-8058)
BLANG ACQUISITION LLC
Also Called: Kap Signs
1608 Kuntz Rd (45404-1234)
PHONE..................937 223-2155
Mark Thomas, *Supervisor*
John D Blang, *Vice Pres*
EMP: 15
SQ FT: 12,000
SALES (est): 2.6MM **Privately Held**
WEB: www.kapsigns.com
SIC: 2499 5199 5999 3993 Signboards, wood; letters, wood; decals; posters; banners; decals; signs & advertising specialties

(G-8059)
BOOKFACTORY LLC
2302 S Edwin C Moses Blvd (45417-4662)
PHONE..................937 226-7100
Jeff Erbes, *Vice Pres*
Ashley Myers, *Sales Executive*
Eleanor Gilmore, *Marketing Staff*
Judy Thaller, *Manager*
William Murray Jr,
▼ EMP: 30
SQ FT: 20,000
SALES (est): 4.9MM **Privately Held**
SIC: 5942 2678 2731 2789 Book stores; memorandum books, notebooks & looseleaf filler paper; book publishing; textbooks: publishing & printing; books: publishing & printing; bookbinding & related work

(G-8060)
BP PRODUCTS NORTH AMERICA INC
Also Called: B P Exploration
621 Brandt St (45404-2226)
PHONE..................937 461-3621
Allen Cook, *Manager*
EMP: 4
SALES (corp-wide): 240.2B **Privately Held**
WEB: www.bpproductsnorthamerica.com
SIC: 2911 Petroleum refining
HQ: Bp Products North America Inc.
501 Westlake Park Blvd
Houston TX 77079
281 366-2000

(G-8061)
BRIDGITS BATH LLC
1226 Pursell Ave (45420-1974)
PHONE..................937 259-1960
Joan Speicher,
Anne Ruhland,
Lawrence Speicher,
EMP: 7 EST: 2008
SALES (est): 466.7K **Privately Held**
SIC: 3261 7389 Soap dishes, vitreous china; bathroom accessories/fittings, vitreous china or earthenware;

(G-8062)
BRINKMAN TOOL & DIE INC
325 Kiser St (45404-1621)
PHONE..................937 222-1161
John Brinkman Sr, *President*
John C Brinkman Jr, *Vice Pres*
Charlene Brinkman, *Treasurer*
Charles L Brinkman Sr, *Shareholder*
▲ EMP: 30 EST: 1913
SQ FT: 24,000
SALES (est): 4.8MM **Privately Held**
WEB: www.brinkmantool.com
SIC: 3544 Special dies & tools; jigs & fixtures; industrial molds

(G-8063)
BROADWAY COMPANIES INC (PA)
6161 Ventnor Ave (45414-2651)
P.O. Box 13418 (45413-0418)
PHONE..................937 890-1888
Karin Gaiser, *President*
Debra Doyle, *Vice Pres*
EMP: 23
SQ FT: 5,000
SALES: 3MM **Privately Held**
SIC: 3544 Industrial molds

(G-8064)
BROCKMAN JIG GRINDING SERVICE
1535 Stanley Ave (45404-1112)
P.O. Box 71, Englewood (45322-0071)
PHONE..................937 220-9780
Rex Brockman, *Owner*
EMP: 3
SQ FT: 1,000
SALES: 100K **Privately Held**
SIC: 3599 7389 Grinding castings for the trade; grinding, precision: commercial or industrial

(G-8065)
BROWDER TOOL CO INC
Also Called: B T C
5924 Executive Blvd (45424-1419)
PHONE..................937 233-6731
Gerald Kozuh, *President*
Dave Kozuh, *Corp Secy*
Betty Kozuh, *Vice Pres*
EMP: 5
SQ FT: 2,600
SALES (est): 558.5K **Privately Held**
SIC: 3544 Special dies & tools

(G-8066)
BT INVESTMENTS II INC
Also Called: Farquhar Heating and Air
601 Congress Park Dr (45459-4007)
P.O. Box 751475 (45475-1475)
PHONE..................937 434-4321
William E O'Neill, *President*
Theresa Oneill, *Vice Pres*
EMP: 8
SALES (est): 515.5K **Privately Held**
SIC: 1711 4961 3444 1799 Heating & air conditioning contractors; warm air heating & air conditioning contractor; steam supply systems, including geothermal; elbows, for air ducts, stovepipes, etc.: sheet metal; insulation of pipes & boilers

---

(PA)=Parent Co (HQ)=Headquarters (DH)=Div Headquarters
✪ = New Business established in last 2 years

2019 Harris Ohio
Industrial Directory

Dayton - Montgomery County (G-8067)

GEOGRAPHIC SECTION

(G-8067)
BTA ENTERPRISES INC
4090 Little Richmond Rd (45417-9453)
PHONE....................937 277-0881
Billy T Atherton, *President*
Billy Atherton, *President*
Dusty Atherton, *Vice Pres*
EMP: 40 **EST:** 1984
SALES (est): 2.1MM **Privately Held**
SIC: 3089 Automotive parts, plastic; plastic processing

(G-8068)
BUDDE SHEET METAL WORKS INC (PA)
305 Leo St (45404-1083)
PHONE....................937 224-0868
Thomas Budde, *President*
William R Budde Jr, *Corp Secy*
Stephen L Budde, *Vice Pres*
Angie Budde-Obrien, *Manager*
EMP: 39
SQ FT: 20,000
SALES: 7.4MM **Privately Held**
WEB: www.buddesheetmetal.com
SIC: 1761 3444 1711 Sheet metalwork; sheet metalwork; plumbing, heating, air-conditioning contractors

(G-8069)
C & M RUBBER CO INC
414 Littell Ave (45419-3608)
PHONE....................937 299-2782
James McCloskey, *President*
Eric Weber, *Vice Pres*
EMP: 15 **EST:** 1964
SQ FT: 10,000
SALES: 1MM **Privately Held**
WEB: www.cmrubber.com
SIC: 3061 Mechanical rubber goods

(G-8070)
C G EGLI INC
515 Springfield St (45403-1246)
P.O. Box 82 (45404-0082)
PHONE....................937 254-8898
Christian G Egli, *President*
EMP: 5
SQ FT: 14,000
SALES (est): 816.1K **Privately Held**
SIC: 3599 Machine & other job shop work

(G-8071)
C-LINK ENTERPRISES LLC
Also Called: Southern Ohio Kitchens
1825 Webster St (45404-1147)
PHONE....................937 222-2829
Lisa J Buckner,
Lisa Buckner,
Nathan Buckner,
EMP: 10
SQ FT: 25,000
SALES: 1.2MM **Privately Held**
WEB: www.johnrgardner.com
SIC: 1521 2514 5722 General remodeling, single-family houses; kitchen cabinets: metal; kitchens, complete (sinks, cabinets, etc.)

(G-8072)
CAC ENERGY LTD
1025 N Main St (45405-4213)
PHONE....................937 867-5593
Ifeanyi Nwanoro, *CEO*
Chikere Umez-Eronini, *COO*
Charles Opoku Fordjour, *CFO*
EMP: 3 **EST:** 2015
SALES (est): 126.3K **Privately Held**
SIC: 1311 5172 6799 8742 Crude petroleum & natural gas; diesel fuel; engine fuels & oils; commodity contract trading companies; management consulting services

(G-8073)
CADENZA ENTERPRISES LLC
Also Called: Sgo Designer Glass
6533 Halberd Ct (45459-1308)
PHONE....................937 428-6058
EMP: 5
SALES: 100K **Privately Held**
SIC: 3231 Mfg Products-Purchased Glass

(G-8074)
CALVIN LANIER
4003 Foxboro Dr (45416-1624)
PHONE....................937 952-4221
Calvin Lanier, *Principal*
EMP: 25
SALES (est): 1MM **Privately Held**
SIC: 3423 7389 Plumbers' hand tools;

(G-8075)
CARGILL INCORPORATED
3201 Needmore Rd (45414-4321)
PHONE....................937 236-1971
Sheila Willhoite, *Branch Mgr*
EMP: 49
SALES (corp-wide): 114.7B **Privately Held**
WEB: www.cargill.com
SIC: 2046 2087 2041 Corn starch; corn syrup, dried or unmixed; flavoring extracts & syrups; flour & other grain mill products
PA: Cargill, Incorporated
15407 Mcginty Rd W
Wayzata MN 55391
952 742-7575

(G-8076)
CARR SUPPLY CO
4800 Webster St (45414-4850)
PHONE....................937 276-2555
Steve Shepherd, *Principal*
Steve Werling, *Manager*
EMP: 8
SALES (corp-wide): 4.9B **Privately Held**
SIC: 5999 5722 5074 3432 Plumbing & heating supplies; household appliance stores; plumbing & hydronic heating supplies; plumbing fixture fittings & trim
HQ: Carr Supply Co.
1415 Old Leonard Ave
Columbus OH 43219
614 252-7883

(G-8077)
CARRIER CORPORATION
6050 Milo Rd (45414-3418)
PHONE....................937 275-0645
Tim Spencer, *Project Mgr*
Dan Reekers, *Manager*
EMP: 24
SALES (corp-wide): 66.5B **Publicly Held**
WEB: www.carrier.com
SIC: 3585 1711 Refrigeration & heating equipment; heating & air conditioning contractors
HQ: Carrier Corporation
13995 Pasteur Blvd
Palm Beach Gardens FL 33418
800 379-6484

(G-8078)
CARSON-SAEKS INC (PA)
Also Called: Karen Carson Creations
2601 Timber Ln (45414-4733)
P.O. Box 13297 (45413-0297)
PHONE....................937 278-5311
William Smith, *Ch of Bd*
Terrence Mollaun, *President*
Jeff Smith, *Vice Pres*
▲ **EMP:** 60
SQ FT: 20,000
SALES (est): 11MM **Privately Held**
WEB: www.karencarson.com
SIC: 2869 Perfume materials, synthetic

(G-8079)
CB MANUFACTURING & SLS CO INC
American Cutting Edge
4475 Infirmary Rd (45449)
PHONE....................937 866-5986
Charles Biehn, *Manager*
EMP: 60
SALES (corp-wide): 35.8MM **Privately Held**
WEB: www.cbmfg.com
SIC: 3423 Hand & edge tools
PA: C. B. Manufacturing And Sales Company, Inc.
4455 Infirmary Rd
Miamisburg OH 45342
937 866-5986

(G-8080)
CELSTAR GROUP INC (PA)
40 N Main St Ste 1730 (45423-1002)
PHONE....................937 224-1730
Robert H Brethen, *President*
Jonas Gruenberg, *Admin Sec*
EMP: 2
SALES (est): 28.4MM **Privately Held**
SIC: 3229 Glass fiber products

(G-8081)
CEMEX MATERIALS LLC
1504 N Gettysburg Ave (45417-9518)
PHONE....................937 268-6706
Anthony Cox, *Manager*
EMP: 100 **Privately Held**
WEB: www.rinkermaterials.com
SIC: 3272 5211 Concrete products; masonry materials & supplies
HQ: Cemex Materials, Llc
1501 Belvedere Rd
West Palm Beach FL 33406
561 833-5555

(G-8082)
CEMEX MATERIALS LLC
4385 N James H Mcgee Blvd (45417-9537)
PHONE....................937 268-6706
Dennis Paulsgrove, *Branch Mgr*
EMP: 20 **Privately Held**
WEB: www.rinkermaterials.com
SIC: 3273 Ready-mixed concrete
HQ: Cemex Materials, Llc
1501 Belvedere Rd
West Palm Beach FL 33406
561 833-5555

(G-8083)
CENTERLINE TOOL & MACHINE
1330 E 2nd St (45403-1021)
PHONE....................937 222-3600
Michael A Gambrell, *Owner*
EMP: 5
SQ FT: 8,000
SALES: 700K **Privately Held**
SIC: 3544 3599 Forms (molds), for foundry & plastics working machinery; industrial molds; machine & other job shop work

(G-8084)
CERTIFIED HEAT TREATING INC (PA)
4475 Infirmary Rd (45449)
P.O. Box 354
PHONE....................937 866-0245
Joseph Biehn, *President*
EMP: 20 **EST:** 1970
SQ FT: 20,000
SALES (est): 2.4MM **Privately Held**
WEB: www.certifiedindustrialservices.com
SIC: 3398 Metal heat treating

(G-8085)
CERTIFIED SERVICE INC
2870 Culver Ave (45429-3720)
PHONE....................937 643-0393
Donald Groves, *President*
Mike Holmes, *General Mgr*
Mike Groves, *Vice Pres*
EMP: 5 **EST:** 1959
SQ FT: 15,000
SALES: 520K **Privately Held**
WEB: www.certifiedservice.com
SIC: 3585 Compressors for refrigeration & air conditioning equipment

(G-8086)
CHAOS ENTERTAINMENT
Also Called: CD / Dvd Distribution
7570 Mount Whitney St (45424-6944)
PHONE....................937 520-5260
Melvin Higgins,
EMP: 8
SALES: 10K **Privately Held**
SIC: 3561 Pumps & pumping equipment

(G-8087)
CHECKPOINT SYSTEMS INC
7620 Mcewen Rd (45459-3908)
PHONE....................937 281-1304
George Babich Jr, *Branch Mgr*
EMP: 128
SALES (corp-wide): 3.7B **Privately Held**
SIC: 3699 Security control equipment & systems
HQ: Checkpoint Systems, Inc.
101 Wolf Dr
West Deptford NJ 08086
800 257-5540

(G-8088)
CHEMCORE INC (PA)
20 Madison St (45402-2106)
P.O. Box 802 (45401-0802)
PHONE....................937 228-6118
Mike Klaus, *CEO*
Reiff Lorenz, *President*
Geoffrey Lorenz, *Vice Pres*
EMP: 10
SALES (est): 3.4MM **Privately Held**
SIC: 5169 2869 Chemical additives; industrial organic chemicals

(G-8089)
CINDERELLA
2700 Mmsburg Cntrville Rd (45459)
PHONE....................937 312-9969
James Paek, *Manager*
EMP: 3
SALES (est): 234.6K **Privately Held**
SIC: 2311 Tuxedos: made from purchased materials

(G-8090)
CINTAS CORPORATION NO 2
903 Brandt St Bldg A (45404-2231)
PHONE....................937 236-1506
James Lois, *Manager*
EMP: 4
SALES (corp-wide): 6.4B **Publicly Held**
WEB: www.cintas-corp.com
SIC: 3589 Shredders, industrial & commercial
HQ: Cintas Corporation No. 2
6800 Cintas Blvd
Mason OH 45040

(G-8091)
CIRCUIT CENTER
4738 Gateway Cir (45440-1724)
PHONE....................513 435-2131
Michael Kerr, *Principal*
EMP: 7
SALES (est): 664.6K **Privately Held**
SIC: 3672 Printed circuit boards

(G-8092)
CITIZENS USA
3651 Wright Way Rd (45424-5165)
PHONE....................937 280-2001
EMP: 3
SALES (est): 106.8K **Privately Held**
SIC: 2711 Newspapers, publishing & printing

(G-8093)
CLARK PRFMCE FABRICATION LLC
5647 Rowena Dr (45415-2400)
PHONE....................701 721-1378
Stephen Clark,
EMP: 3 **EST:** 2017
SALES (est): 97.8K **Privately Held**
SIC: 3089 Automotive parts, plastic

(G-8094)
CNR MARKETING LTD
Also Called: Proforma Cnr Marketing
7925 Paragon Rd 100 (45459-4019)
PHONE....................937 293-1030
Ron Muzechuk, *Mng Member*
EMP: 5
SQ FT: 775
SALES: 1.2MM **Privately Held**
SIC: 2759 5199 Commercial printing; advertising specialties

(G-8095)
COACH TOOL & DIE INC
5728 Webster St (45414-3521)
PHONE....................937 890-4716
Dave Hollon, *President*
Gregg Kopp, *Vice Pres*
EMP: 6
SALES: 900K **Privately Held**
SIC: 3544 Special dies & tools

GEOGRAPHIC SECTION
Dayton - Montgomery County (G-8123)

(G-8096)
COCA-COLA BOTTLING CO CNSLD
1000 Coca Cola Blvd (45424-6375)
PHONE................937 878-5000
Bob Tiootson, *Manager*
EMP: 95
SALES (corp-wide): 4.6B **Publicly Held**
WEB: www.colasic.net
SIC: 5149 2086 Soft drinks; carbonated beverages, nonalcoholic: bottled & canned
PA: Coca-Cola Consolidated, Inc.
4100 Coca Cola Plz # 100
Charlotte NC 28211
704 557-4400

(G-8097)
COLBY WOODWORKING INC
1912 Lucille Dr (45404-1109)
P.O. Box 138 (45404-0138)
PHONE................937 224-7676
Steven L Colby, *President*
EMP: 5
SALES (est): 288.3K **Privately Held**
SIC: 2499 1751 Decorative wood & woodwork; cabinet building & installation

(G-8098)
COMBINED TECH GROUP INC
6061 Milo Rd (45414-3417)
PHONE................937 274-4866
Kurtis Vanburen, *President*
Tina Vanburen, *Vice Pres*
Brian Greene, *Opers Mgr*
Chris Bautista, *Engineer*
Gary Steele, *Engineer*
EMP: 28
SQ FT: 50,000
SALES (est): 6.2MM **Privately Held**
WEB: www.comtechgrp.com
SIC: 3549 Assembly machines, including robotic

(G-8099)
COMMCONNECT
5747 Executive Blvd (45424-1448)
PHONE................937 414-0505
Scott Dilworth, *Principal*
EMP: 7
SALES (est): 853.7K **Privately Held**
SIC: 3351 Wire, copper & copper alloy

(G-8100)
COMMERCIAL MTAL FBRICATORS INC
150 Commerce Park Dr (45404-1273)
PHONE................937 233-4911
Patrick Dakin, *President*
James D Utrecht, *Principal*
Molly Dakin, *Controller*
Richard Oswald, *Sales Engr*
EMP: 40 **EST:** 1954
SALES (est): 11.5MM **Privately Held**
WEB: www.cmfweb.com
SIC: 3441 3444 3443 Fabricated structural metal; sheet metalwork; fabricated plate work (boiler shop)

(G-8101)
COMPOSITE TECHNOLOGIES CO LLC
401 N Keowee St (45404-1602)
PHONE................937 228-2880
Mike Dematto, *Mng Member*
Jay Binder,
EMP: 80
SQ FT: 100,000
SALES (est): 16.3MM
SALES (corp-wide): 132.5MM **Privately Held**
WEB: www.soinintemational.com
SIC: 3089 Plastic containers, except foam
PA: Soin International, Llc
1129 Miamsbg Ctrvl Rd 1 Ste
Dayton OH 45449
937 427-7646

(G-8102)
CONTAINER MANUFACTURING LTD
6450 Poe Ave Ste 511 (45414-2677)
P.O. Box 750455 (45475-0455)
PHONE................937 264-2370
Ralph P Stodd, *President*
James Wilkins, *Exec VP*
Jim Wilkins, *Exec VP*
EMP: 5
SQ FT: 2,100
SALES (est): 738K **Privately Held**
SIC: 3411 Beer cans, metal; beverage cans, metal: except beer

(G-8103)
CONTECH BRIDGE SOLUTIONS LLC
Also Called: Bridgetek
7941 New Carlisle Pike (45424-1507)
PHONE................937 878-2170
Jim Feltner, *Manager*
EMP: 12 **Privately Held**
SIC: 3272 Concrete products
HQ: Contech Bridge Solutions Llc
9025 Cntrpinte Dr Ste 400
West Chester OH 45069

(G-8104)
COUCH BUSINESS DEVELOPMENT INC
Also Called: Fordyce Custom Finishing
32 Bates Dr (45402-1326)
PHONE................937 253-1099
David Couch, *President*
EMP: 16
SQ FT: 49,250
SALES (est): 1MM **Privately Held**
SIC: 2541 2491 1751 Display fixtures, wood; store fixtures, wood; millwork, treated wood; store fixture installation

(G-8105)
COX MEDIA GROUP OHIO INC (DH)
1611 S Main St (45409-2547)
PHONE................937 225-2000
Dave Bennallack, *Managing Dir*
John Erickson, *Editor*
Mary Irby-Jones, *Editor*
Marc Pendleton, *Editor*
Karen Bennett, *Exec VP*
EMP: 550
SQ FT: 150,000
SALES (est): 136MM
SALES (corp-wide): 32.5B **Privately Held**
WEB: www.daytondailynews.com
SIC: 2711 Commercial printing & newspaper publishing combined; newspapers, publishing & printing

(G-8106)
COX MEDIA GROUP OHIO INC
1611 S Main St (45409-2547)
PHONE................937 743-6700
Barbara Parker, *Branch Mgr*
EMP: 3
SALES (corp-wide): 32.5B **Privately Held**
WEB: www.daytondailynews.com
SIC: 2711 Newspapers, publishing & printing
HQ: Cox Media Group Ohio, Inc.
1611 S Main St
Dayton OH 45409
937 225-2000

(G-8107)
COX NEWSPAPERS LLC
Also Called: Dayton Daily News
1611 S Main St (45409-2547)
PHONE................937 225-2000
John M Dyer, *Branch Mgr*
EMP: 60
SALES (corp-wide): 32.5B **Privately Held**
SIC: 2711 Newspapers, publishing & printing
HQ: Cox Newspapers, Inc.
6205 Peachtree Dunwoody
Atlanta GA 30328

(G-8108)
COX PUBLISHING HQ
1611 S Main St (45409-2547)
PHONE................937 225-2000
Michael Joseph, *Principal*
Ron Fowler, *Consultant*
Shelly Macduff, *Director*
EMP: 9
SALES (est): 643.3K **Privately Held**
SIC: 2741 Miscellaneous publishing

(G-8109)
CPCA MANUFACTURING LLC
Also Called: Composite Advantage
750 Rosedale Dr (45402-5758)
PHONE................937 723-9031
Shane Weyant, *President*
EMP: 85
SALES (est): 1.8MM
SALES (corp-wide): 773.1MM **Privately Held**
SIC: 3089 Plastic & fiberglass tanks
HQ: Creative Pultrusions, Inc.
214 Industrial Ln
Alum Bank PA 15521
814 839-4186

(G-8110)
CREATIVE DESIGN MARBLE INC
7901 S Suburban Rd (45458-2702)
PHONE................937 434-8892
Eric Maxel, *President*
Paul M Maxel, *Vice Pres*
Zelda Maxel, *Treasurer*
EMP: 5
SQ FT: 4,000
SALES (est): 410K **Privately Held**
SIC: 3281 Marble, building: cut & shaped

(G-8111)
CREATIVE FOAM DAYTON MOLD
3337 N Dixie Dr (45414-5645)
PHONE................937 279-9987
EMP: 5 **EST:** 2013
SALES (est): 295.2K **Privately Held**
SIC: 3086 Plastics foam products

(G-8112)
CREATIVE IMPRESSIONS INC
4611 Gateway Cir (45440-1713)
PHONE................937 435-5296
Dennis C Carter, *President*
Linda S Carter, *Vice Pres*
Ed Carter, *Director*
EMP: 10
SQ FT: 7,500
SALES (est): 1.8MM **Privately Held**
SIC: 2752 Commercial printing, offset

(G-8113)
CRG PLASTICS INC
2661 Culver Ave (45429-3721)
PHONE................937 298-2025
Jerry Wenzke, *President*
Nancy Wenzke, *Treasurer*
▲ **EMP:** 11
SQ FT: 8,000
SALES (est): 1.1MM **Privately Held**
SIC: 2821 3089 Polytetrafluoroethylene resins (teflon); molding primary plastic

(G-8114)
CRITICAL PATIENT CARE INC
4738 Gateway Cir Ste B (45440-1724)
PHONE................937 434-5455
Marie Cosgrove, *CEO*
▲ **EMP:** 3
SQ FT: 2,000
SALES (est): 431.6K **Privately Held**
SIC: 3845 Electromedical equipment

(G-8115)
CSV INC
Also Called: Beverage Dock
2080 E Rahn Rd (45440-2535)
PHONE................937 438-1142
Cosmo Savino, *President*
EMP: 11
SALES (est): 1.1MM **Privately Held**
SIC: 2086 5921 Bottled & canned soft drinks; beer (packaged)

(G-8116)
CTC PLASTICS (HQ)
401 N Keowee St (45404-1602)
PHONE................937 228-9184
Vishal Soin, *CEO*
Mike Dematto, *COO*
William R Senften, *CFO*
EMP: 306 **EST:** 2012
SALES (est): 28.9MM
SALES (corp-wide): 132.5MM **Privately Held**
SIC: 3089 Injection molding of plastics
PA: Soin International, Llc
1129 Miamsbg Ctrvl Rd 1 Ste
Dayton OH 45449
937 427-7646

(G-8117)
CUDA COMPOSITES LLC
1788 S Metro Pkwy (45459-2520)
PHONE................937 499-0360
David Havens, *President*
EMP: 5
SALES (est): 116.4K **Privately Held**
SIC: 3083 3728 Thermosetting laminates: rods, tubes, plates & sheet; aircraft parts & equipment

(G-8118)
CUSTOM DUCT & SUPPLY CO INC
912 Cincinnati St (45417-4098)
PHONE................937 228-2058
Jerry Sharp Sr, *President*
Martha Sharp, *Vice Pres*
EMP: 4
SQ FT: 6,000
SALES: 500K **Privately Held**
SIC: 5075 3444 Warm air heating & air conditioning; ducts, sheet metal

(G-8119)
CUSTOM MANUFACTURING SOLUTIONS (PA)
1129 Miamisburg Centervil (45449-4007)
PHONE................937 372-0777
Raj Soin, *CEO*
Mike Collinsworth, *President*
EMP: 125
SQ FT: 82,000
SALES (est): 20.1MM **Privately Held**
WEB: www.cusmfgsol.com
SIC: 3599 Machine shop, jobbing & repair

(G-8120)
CUSTOM METAL SHEARING INC
80 Commerce Park Dr (45404-1212)
PHONE................937 233-6950
Robert Colby, *President*
Marlene Colby, *Vice Pres*
Richard Colby, *Vice Pres*
EMP: 13
SQ FT: 20,000
SALES: 1MM **Privately Held**
WEB: www.custommetalshearing.com
SIC: 3444 7389 2819 Sheet metalwork; metal slitting & shearing; aluminum oxide

(G-8121)
CUSTOM NICKEL LLC
45 N Clinton St (45402-1346)
PHONE................937 222-1995
Kevin M McHugh,
EMP: 6
SALES (est): 772.5K **Privately Held**
SIC: 3471 Plating of metals or formed products; electroplating of metals or formed products

(G-8122)
CUSTOM POWDERCOATING LLC
2211 Bellefontaine Ave (45404-2289)
PHONE................937 972-3516
Curtis J Wise,
Jim Wise,
EMP: 5 **EST:** 2016
SALES (est): 381.4K **Privately Held**
SIC: 2851 3471 3479 3083 Undercoatings, paint; anodizing (plating) of metals or formed products; coating of metals & formed products; coating or wrapping steel pipe; coating, rust preventive; painting of metal products; thermosetting laminates: rods, tubes, plates & sheet; coating of concrete structures with plastic; sheet metalwork

(G-8123)
D & J MACHINE SHOP
442 Todd St (45403-2905)
PHONE................937 256-2730
Chuck Lehman, *Owner*
EMP: 6 **EST:** 1966
SQ FT: 2,200
SALES: 100K **Privately Held**
WEB: www.djmachineshop.com
SIC: 3599 Machine shop, jobbing & repair

Dayton - Montgomery County (G-8124)

GEOGRAPHIC SECTION

(G-8124)
D C M INDUSTRIES INC
1901 E 5th St (45403-2347)
P.O. Box 1942 (45401-1942)
PHONE.....................937 254-8500
Sam Nicolosi, *President*
EMP: 12
SQ FT: 10,000
SALES: 600K Privately Held
SIC: 3678 3679 Electronic connectors; transducers, electrical

(G-8125)
DAISYS PILLOWS LLC
Also Called: Manufacturing
4694 Free Pike (45416-1200)
PHONE.....................937 776-6968
Daisy Peterson,
EMP: 3
SALES (est): 179.9K Privately Held
SIC: 3949 Sporting & athletic goods

(G-8126)
DAVID ESRATI
Also Called: Next Wave Marketing Innovation
100 Bonner St (45410-1306)
PHONE.....................937 228-4433
David Esrati, *Owner*
Jennifer Selhorst, *Finance*
David Greenlee, *Manager*
EMP: 3
SQ FT: 1,700
SALES: 350K Privately Held
WEB: www.the-next-wave.com
SIC: 7311 7336 8742 3993 Advertising consultant; graphic arts & related design; marketing consulting services; signs & advertising specialties; commercial photography; motion picture & video production

(G-8127)
DAY-HIO PRODUCTS INC
709 Webster St (45404-1527)
PHONE.....................937 445-0782
John L Lenz, *President*
▲ EMP: 20
SQ FT: 15,000
SALES (est): 2.5MM Privately Held
SIC: 3451 Screw machine products

(G-8128)
DAYTON BAG & BURLAP CO
448 Huffman Ave (45403-2506)
PHONE.....................937 253-1722
Dave Barcus, *Branch Mgr*
EMP: 10
SALES (corp-wide): 41.2MM Privately Held
SIC: 4225 2299 General warehousing & storage; burlap, jute
PA: The Dayton Bag & Burlap Co
322 Davis Ave
Dayton OH 45403
937 258-8000

(G-8129)
DAYTON CITY PAPER NEW LLC
Also Called: Impact Weekly
126 N Main St Ste 240 (45402-1766)
P.O. Box 10065 (45402-7065)
PHONE.....................937 222-8855
Mehdi Adineh, *Mng Member*
EMP: 10
SALES (est): 689.4K Privately Held
WEB: www.impactweekly.com
SIC: 2711 Newspapers, publishing & printing

(G-8130)
DAYTON CLUTCH & JOINT INC (PA)
2005 Troy St 1 (45404-2936)
P.O. Box 163 (45404-0163)
PHONE.....................937 236-9770
Keith Knight, *President*
Nancy Knight, *Admin Sec*
EMP: 19 EST: 1956
SQ FT: 16,000
SALES: 3.4MM Privately Held
WEB: www.daytonclutch.com
SIC: 3714 Motor vehicle parts & accessories

(G-8131)
DAYTON COATING TECH LLC
1926 E Siebenthaler Ave (45414-5334)
PHONE.....................937 278-2060
George Korenyi-Both,
EMP: 6
SQ FT: 15,000
SALES (est): 1MM Privately Held
WEB: www.webdct.com
SIC: 3479 Etching & engraving; coating of metals & formed products

(G-8132)
DAYTON FORGING HEAT TREATING
215 N Findlay St (45403-1200)
P.O. Box 1629 (45401-1629)
PHONE.....................937 253-4126
Eric Wilson, *President*
Martha Todd Wilson, *Vice Pres*
Jason Wilson, *Foreman/Supr*
Joseph Carey, *Engineer*
Justin Moore, *Accounting Mgr*
EMP: 65
SQ FT: 100,000
SALES (est): 19.1MM Privately Held
WEB: www.daytonforging.com
SIC: 3398 3462 Metal heat treating; machinery forgings, ferrous

(G-8133)
DAYTON FRUIT TREE LABEL CO
Also Called: Dayton Garden Labels
1225 Ray St (45404-1656)
PHONE.....................937 223-4650
Richard Joyner, *President*
Bryan Rosencrance, *Accounts Exec*
▲ EMP: 2 EST: 1898
SQ FT: 8,000
SALES (est): 1MM Privately Held
WEB: www.daytongardenlabels.com
SIC: 2671 Packaging paper & plastics film, coated & laminated

(G-8134)
DAYTON GEAR & TOOL CO INC
500 Fame Rd (45449-2387)
PHONE.....................937 866-4327
Thomas R Baird, *President*
EMP: 20 EST: 1946
SQ FT: 3,000
SALES (est): 5.5MM Privately Held
WEB: www.daytongear.com
SIC: 3566 Gears, power transmission, except automotive

(G-8135)
DAYTON HAWKER CORPORATION
2844 Culver Ave (45429-3726)
PHONE.....................937 293-8147
William Darrow, *President*
▲ EMP: 10
SQ FT: 12,000
SALES (est): 1.8MM Privately Held
WEB: www.hawkermfg.com
SIC: 3553 3841 3915 Lathes, wood turning: including accessories; forceps, surgical; pin stems

(G-8136)
DAYTON LAMINA CORPORATION (DH)
Also Called: Anchor Lamina America
500 Progress Rd (45449-2326)
P.O. Box 39 (45449)
PHONE.....................937 859-5111
David Turpin, *President*
Melchor Cruz, *General Mgr*
Paul Coddington, *Project Mgr*
Roy King, *Mfg Spvr*
Cindy Schrock, *Senior Buyer*
EMP: 3
SALES (est): 218.6MM
SALES (corp-wide): 2.9B Privately Held
SIC: 3544 6719 Special dies & tools; investment holding companies, except banks
HQ: Misumi Investment Usa Corporation
500 Progress Rd
Dayton OH 45449
937 859-5111

(G-8137)
DAYTON LASER & AESTHETIC MEDIC
6611 Clyo Rd Ste E (45459-2785)
PHONE.....................937 208-8282
Lisa Smith, *Principal*
EMP: 8
SALES (est): 679.3K Privately Held
SIC: 2834 8011 Medicines, capsuled or ampuled; physicians' office, including specialists

(G-8138)
DAYTON MAILING SERVICES INC
100 S Keowee St (45402-2241)
P.O. Box 2436 (45401-2436)
PHONE.....................937 222-5056
Christine Soward, *President*
Mark Kuns, *Accounts Exec*
Tom Cooper, *Manager*
Jason Reid, *Supervisor*
Natalie Bisnow, *Info Tech Mgr*
EMP: 30
SQ FT: 100,000
SALES (est): 9MM Privately Held
WEB: www.daytonmailing.com
SIC: 7331 2759 Mailing service; commercial printing

(G-8139)
DAYTON MOLDED URETHANES LLC
Also Called: D M U
3337 N Dixie Dr (45414-5645)
PHONE.....................937 279-9987
William Palmer, *President*
EMP: 75 EST: 2001
SQ FT: 50,000
SALES (est): 11.1MM
SALES (corp-wide): 185.5MM Privately Held
WEB: www.daypp.com
SIC: 3086 Plastics foam products
PA: Creative Foam Corporation
300 N Alloy Dr
Fenton MI 48430
810 629-4149

(G-8140)
DAYTON PATTERN INC
5591 Wadsworth Rd (45414-3446)
P.O. Box 13779 (45413-0779)
PHONE.....................937 277-0761
Erik Zimmer, *President*
Janice Zimmer, *Corp Secy*
EMP: 6 EST: 1965
SQ FT: 7,000
SALES: 800K Privately Held
SIC: 3543 Industrial patterns

(G-8141)
DAYTON POLYMERIC PRODUCTS INC
3337 N Dixie Dr (45414-5645)
PHONE.....................937 279-9987
William Johnson, *Ch of Bd*
Loney Abney, *President*
Lisa S Pierce, *Principal*
EMP: 60
SQ FT: 55,000
SALES (est): 5.9MM Privately Held
SIC: 3086 Packaging & shipping materials, foamed plastic

(G-8142)
DAYTON PRECISION PUNCH
4900 Webster St (45414-4831)
PHONE.....................937 275-8700
Mike Casella, *Principal*
EMP: 5
SALES (est): 572.6K
SALES (corp-wide): 44.3MM Privately Held
SIC: 3545 Machine tool attachments & accessories
PA: Fc Industries, Inc.
4900 Webster St
Dayton OH 45414
937 275-8700

(G-8143)
DAYTON PROGRESS CORPORATION (DH)
500 Progress Rd (45449-2351)
P.O. Box 39 (45449)
PHONE.....................937 859-5111
David Turpin, *President*
John Vecore, *General Mgr*
Michael Purchase, *Vice Chairman*
Gary Wilson, *Regional Mgr*
Randy Wissinger, *Vice Pres*
▲ EMP: 525
SALES (est): 149.1MM
SALES (corp-wide): 2.9B Privately Held
WEB: www.daytonpunch.com
SIC: 3544 3545 3495 3493 Punches, forming & stamping; machine tool accessories; wire springs; steel springs, except wire
HQ: Dayton Lamina Corporation
500 Progress Rd
Dayton OH 45449
937 859-5111

(G-8144)
DAYTON PROGRESS INTL CORP
500 Progress Rd (45449-2326)
PHONE.....................937 859-5111
Alan Shaffer, *President*
Bill Mills, *Vice Pres*
David Turpin, *Vice Pres*
Randy S Wissinger, *Vice Pres*
EMP: 5
SALES (est): 446K
SALES (corp-wide): 2.9B Privately Held
WEB: www.daytonpunch.com
SIC: 3544 Special dies, tools, jigs & fixtures
HQ: Dayton Progress Corporation
500 Progress Rd
Dayton OH 45449
937 859-5111

(G-8145)
DAYTON STENCIL WORKS COMPANY
Also Called: Datono Products
113 E 2nd St (45402-1753)
P.O. Box 126 (45401-0126)
PHONE.....................937 223-3233
Edward Jauch, *President*
David Jauch, *General Mgr*
Larry Horwath, *Vice Pres*
Mike Bertke, *Purch Agent*
John Jauch, *Treasurer*
EMP: 20
SQ FT: 18,000
SALES: 2MM Privately Held
WEB: www.daytonstencil.com
SIC: 3949 3953 3544 5085 Golf equipment; marking devices; special dies, tools, jigs & fixtures; industrial supplies

(G-8146)
DAYTON TOOL CO INC
1825 E 1st St (45403-1129)
PHONE.....................937 222-5501
Larry Beam, *President*
Richard L Wiegand, *Vice Pres*
EMP: 44 EST: 1950
SQ FT: 28,500
SALES (est): 5.2MM Privately Held
SIC: 3544 3469 Special dies & tools; metal stampings

(G-8147)
DAYTON WEEKLY NEWS
Also Called: MWC Publishing Co
118 Salem Ave (45406-5803)
P.O. Box 17416 (45417-0416)
PHONE.....................937 223-8060
Donald Black, *President*
EMP: 4
SALES (est): 428.6K Privately Held
SIC: 8743 2711 Public relations & publicity; newspapers, publishing & printing

(G-8148)
DAYTON WHEEL CONCEPTS INC
Also Called: Dayton Wire Wheel
115 Compark Rd (45459-4803)
PHONE.....................937 438-0100
Brad Cruchleo, *General Mgr*
Charles Schroeder, *Principal*

GEOGRAPHIC SECTION

Dayton - Montgomery County (G-8175)

Pamela Good, *Accountant*
Rick King, *Manager*
▲ **EMP:** 30 **EST:** 1953
SQ FT: 150,000
SALES (est): 6.9MM **Privately Held**
WEB: www.dwpco.com
SIC: 3714 Wheels, motor vehicle

(G-8149)
DAYTON WIRE PRODUCTS INC
7 Dayton Wire Pkwy (45404-1282)
PHONE.................................937 236-8000
David Leiser, *President*
Brian Schissler, *Vice Pres*
Jimmy Fullen, *Opers Mgr*
Shawn Landis, *Safety Mgr*
Megan Dause, *Marketing Mgr*
EMP: 40
SQ FT: 62,500
SALES (est): 8MM **Privately Held**
WEB: www.daytonwireproducts.com
SIC: 3496 3993 Miscellaneous fabricated wire products; signs & advertising specialties

(G-8150)
DAYTON WRIGHT COMPOSITE
3251 Mccall St (45417-1907)
P.O. Box 69, Englewood (45322-0069)
PHONE.................................937 469-3962
John Prikkel, *President*
EMP: 3
SALES (est): 94.1K **Privately Held**
SIC: 3299 Mica products

(G-8151)
DAYTON-PHOENIX GROUP INC (PA)
1619 Kuntz Rd (45404-1240)
PHONE.................................937 496-3900
Gale Kooken, *President*
Roger Fleming, *Vice Pres*
John Murphy, *Vice Pres*
Gary Gaither, *Engineer*
Michael Mattingly, *Engineer*
◆ **EMP:** 240
SQ FT: 640,000
SALES (est): 144.5MM **Privately Held**
WEB: www.dayton-phoenix.com
SIC: 3621 3743 Motors & generators; railroad equipment; locomotives & parts

(G-8152)
DEBAN ENTERPRISES INC
611 Congress Park Dr (45459-4007)
PHONE.................................937 426-4235
Elias Aboujaoude, *President*
Hilda Aboujaoude, *Financial Exec*
EMP: 4
SQ FT: 1,250
SALES: 400K **Privately Held**
WEB: www.deban.com
SIC: 3823 Industrial instrmnts msrmnt display/control process variable

(G-8153)
DELMA CORP
Also Called: Dayton Manufacturing Company
3327 Elkton Ave (45403-1357)
PHONE.................................937 253-2142
Robert J Davis, *President*
Mary W Davis, *Principal*
Lisa D Houseman, *Principal*
Lisa Davis, *Corp Secy*
Robert Rouhier, *Vice Pres*
EMP: 65
SQ FT: 52,000
SALES (est): 14.8MM **Privately Held**
WEB: www.daytonmanufacturing.com
SIC: 3444 Metal housings, enclosures, casings & other containers; casings, sheet metal

(G-8154)
DELTA CONTROL INC (PA)
2532 Nordic Rd (45414-3422)
P.O. Box 13612 (45413-0612)
PHONE.................................937 277-3444
Michaela Grafton, *President*
Chris Carter, *Manager*
EMP: 5
SQ FT: 2,500

SALES (est): 1.2MM **Privately Held**
SIC: 7389 3625 8711 Water softener service; industrial controls: push button, selector switches, pilot; engineering services

(G-8155)
DEM TECHNOLOGY LLC
755 Albany St (45417-3460)
PHONE.................................937 223-1317
David M Morgan, *Mng Member*
Dave Morgan,
EMP: 4
SQ FT: 10,000
SALES (est): 523.4K **Privately Held**
SIC: 2842 Sanitation preparations, disinfectants & deodorants

(G-8156)
DENEB (PA)
Also Called: Deneb Software
270 Regency Ridge Dr # 200 (45459-4250)
PHONE.................................937 223-4849
David Coggins, *President*
Kenneth L Lykins, *Principal*
Jo Lykins, *Treasurer*
EMP: 4
SALES: 510K **Privately Held**
WEB: www.denebsoftware.com
SIC: 7372 Prepackaged software

(G-8157)
DESIGN PATTERN WORKS INC
2312 E 3rd St (45403-2015)
PHONE.................................937 252-0797
George Weckler, *President*
James Weckler, *Vice Pres*
EMP: 8 **EST:** 1977
SALES (est): 1MM **Privately Held**
SIC: 3543 Industrial patterns

(G-8158)
DESIGN TECH INC
1531 Keystone Ave (45403-3335)
PHONE.................................937 254-7000
Fax: 937 254-7720
EMP: 4
SQ FT: 12,000
SALES: 400K **Privately Held**
SIC: 3543 3599 Manufactures Industrial Patterns & Job Machine Shop

(G-8159)
DEUER MANUFACTURING INC
1100 S Smithville Rd (45403-3423)
P.O. Box 20254 (45420-0254)
PHONE.................................937 254-3812
Bruce Bennedict, *President*
▲ **EMP:** 4
SALES (est): 50.3K **Privately Held**
SIC: 3536 Hoists, cranes & monorails

(G-8160)
DIGITAL MEDIA INTEGRATION LLC
9090 State Route 48 B (45458-5125)
PHONE.................................937 305-5582
Philip R Lee,
EMP: 3
SQ FT: 1,100
SALES (est): 318.3K **Privately Held**
SIC: 3651 Audio electronic systems

(G-8161)
DIGITAL SHORTS INC
136 N Saint Clair St # 100 (45402-1774)
PHONE.................................937 228-1700
Edmund Grant, *President*
EMP: 3
SALES (est): 250.2K **Privately Held**
SIC: 2759 Screen printing

(G-8162)
DIK JAXON PRODUCTS CO
Also Called: Jaxon's
6195 Webster St (45414-3447)
PHONE.................................937 890-7350
Barry Jackson, *President*
EMP: 3
SQ FT: 5,400
SALES (est): 355.2K **Privately Held**
SIC: 2041 Flour & other grain mill products

(G-8163)
DISALVOS DELI & ITALIAN STORE
Also Called: Disalvo Deli & Italian Store
1383 E Stroop Rd (45429-4925)
PHONE.................................937 298-5053
Rinaldo S Disalvo, *Owner*
Matthew Booth, *Director*
EMP: 5
SALES (est): 433.8K **Privately Held**
WEB: www.disalvosdeli.com
SIC: 2032 5812 5499 Italian foods: packaged in cans, jars, etc.; caterers; gourmet food stores

(G-8164)
DOLING & ASSOCIATES DENTAL LAB
3318 Successful Way (45414-4318)
PHONE.................................937 254-0075
Ted Doling, *President*
Joe Wiener, *Vice Pres*
EMP: 25
SQ FT: 3,000
SALES (est): 2.4MM **Privately Held**
SIC: 3842 8072 Surgical appliances & supplies; crown & bridge production

(G-8165)
DONALD MARLO
Also Called: Mac Advertising Co
5003 Brock Ln (45415-3429)
PHONE.................................937 836-4880
Donald Marlo, *Owner*
EMP: 3
SALES (est): 192.1K **Privately Held**
SIC: 3993 Signs, not made in custom sign painting shops

(G-8166)
DOW CHEMICAL COMPANY
555 Gaddis Blvd (45403-1406)
PHONE.................................937 254-1550
EMP: 16
SALES (corp-wide): 57B **Publicly Held**
SIC: 2821 3081 3086 2879 Mfg Plastics Specialty Chemicals & Agricultural Products
PA: The Dow Chemical Company
2030 Dow Ctr
Midland MI 48642
989 636-1000

(G-8167)
DRAGOON TECHNOLOGIES INC (PA)
Also Called: Dragoonitcn
900 Senate Dr (45459-4017)
PHONE.................................937 439-9223
Kathy Appenzeller, *CEO*
EMP: 6
SQ FT: 51,000
SALES (est): 2MM **Privately Held**
WEB: www.dragoontech.com
SIC: 3812 Radar systems & equipment

(G-8168)
DRAWN METALS CORP
331 Congress Park Dr (45459-4127)
P.O. Box 750758 (45475-0758)
PHONE.................................937 433-6151
EMP: 12 **EST:** 1978
SQ FT: 10,000
SALES (est): 1.9MM **Privately Held**
SIC: 3499 Mfg Misc Fabricated Metal Products

(G-8169)
DRT HOLDINGS INC (PA)
618 Greenmount Blvd (45419-3271)
PHONE.................................937 298-7391
Gary Van Gundy, *President*
Sean McBermott, *Engineer*
John Penrod, *Engineer*
Joseph Zehenny, *CFO*
Greg Martin, *Admin Sec*
EMP: 60
SALES (est): 194.6MM **Privately Held**
SIC: 6719 3599 3728 Investment holding companies, except banks; machine shop, jobbing & repair; aircraft parts & equipment

(G-8170)
DRT MEDICAL LLC (HQ)
4201 Little York Rd (45414-2507)
PHONE.................................937 387-0880
Gary Van Gundy, *President*
EMP: 138
SALES (est): 20.3MM
SALES (corp-wide): 770.6MM **Publicly Held**
SIC: 3841 Surgical & medical instruments
PA: Nn, Inc.
6210 Ardrey Kell Rd
Charlotte NC 28277
980 264-4300

(G-8171)
DRT MFG CO (HQ)
618 Greenmount Blvd (45419-3271)
PHONE.................................937 297-6670
Gary L Van Gundy, *President*
Steven M Gagliardi, *Business Mgr*
Gregory S Martin, *Senior VP*
Tony Cornacchione, *Plant Mgr*
Brad Beasore, *Purch Mgr*
◆ **EMP:** 118 **EST:** 1949
SQ FT: 106,000
SALES (est): 31.5MM **Privately Held**
WEB: www.drtusa.com
SIC: 3544 3545 Special dies & tools; machine tool accessories

(G-8172)
DUPONT ELECTRONIC POLYMERS LP
1515 Nicholas Rd (45417-6712)
PHONE.................................937 268-3411
Ellen Kullman, *Ch of Bd*
Craig F Binetti, *President*
Charles Holiday, *Partner*
James C Borel, *Exec VP*
David G Bills, *Senior VP*
EMP: 65
SALES (est): 13.2MM
SALES (corp-wide): 85.9B **Publicly Held**
WEB: www.dupont.com
SIC: 3571 Electronic computers
HQ: E. I. Du Pont De Nemours And Company
974 Centre Rd
Wilmington DE 19805
302 774-1000

(G-8173)
DYNAPOINT TECHNOLOGIES INC
475 Progress Rd (45449-2323)
P.O. Box 1447, Springfield (45501-1447)
PHONE.................................937 859-5193
Jeffrey G Beatty, *President*
Jerry Frame, *Production*
Amanda Bafs, *Administration*
EMP: 23 **EST:** 1969
SQ FT: 14,000
SALES (est): 3.9MM **Privately Held**
WEB: www.dynapoint1.com
SIC: 3599 Machine shop, jobbing & repair

(G-8174)
E3 DIAGNOSTICS INC
Also Called: E3 Gordon Stowe
74 Marco Ln (45458-3817)
PHONE.................................937 435-2250
Alan Michelson, *Sales/Mktg Mgr*
EMP: 8
SALES (corp-wide): 1.2MM **Privately Held**
SIC: 3845 3651 Audiological equipment, electromedical; household audio & video equipment
HQ: E3 Diagnostics, Inc.
3333 N Kennicott Ave
Arlington Heights IL 60004
847 459-1770

(G-8175)
EASTMAN KODAK COMPANY
3000 Research Blvd (45420-4003)
PHONE.................................937 259-3000
Randy Vandagriff, *President*
Patty A Cord, *Branch Mgr*
EMP: 20

Dayton - Montgomery County (G-8176)   GEOGRAPHIC SECTION

SALES (corp-wide): 1.3B **Publicly Held**
SIC: **3355** 3577 5043 Aluminum rolling & drawing; computer peripheral equipment; projection apparatus, motion picture & slide
PA: Eastman Kodak Company
343 State St
Rochester NY 14650
585 724-4000

(G-8176)
ECO-GROUPE INC (PA)
6161 Ventnor Ave (45414-2651)
PHONE..................937 898-2603
William Gaiser, *CEO*
Karin Gaiser, *President*
Kelly Ferguson, *Vice Pres*
Steve Ferguson, *Manager*
EMP: 19
SALES (est): 36.5MM **Privately Held**
SIC: **3085** Plastics bottles

(G-8177)
EDGEWELL PER CARE BRANDS LLC
973 S Perry St (45402-2526)
P.O. Box 10488 (45402-7488)
PHONE..................937 228-0105
Kenneth Schriber, *Branch Mgr*
EMP: 100
SALES (corp-wide): 2.2B **Publicly Held**
SIC: **2844** Toilet preparations
HQ: Edgewell Personal Care Brands, Llc
6 Research Dr
Shelton CT 06484
203 944-5500

(G-8178)
EDWARD S EVELAND
6175 Falkland Dr (45424-3819)
PHONE..................937 233-6568
Ed Eveland, *Principal*
EMP: 3
SALES (est): 214.5K **Privately Held**
SIC: **3721** Aircraft

(G-8179)
ELECTRICAL CONTROL SYSTEMS
Also Called: E C S
3731 W Alex Bell Rd (45449-1920)
PHONE..................937 859-7136
Nicholas Vendel Jr, *President*
Kirk Vendel, *Vice Pres*
Jean Vendel, *Admin Sec*
EMP: 5
SQ FT: 15,000
SALES (est): 740K **Privately Held**
SIC: **3613** 3469 Control panels, electric; electronic enclosures, stamped or pressed metal

(G-8180)
ELECTRO POLISH COMPANY INC
332 Vermont Ave (45404-1597)
PHONE..................937 222-3611
Kent Kumbroch, *President*
Stuart Price, *Vice Pres*
Jen Haney, *Supervisor*
EMP: 28 EST: 1949
SQ FT: 8,000
SALES (est): 4.1MM **Privately Held**
WEB: www.electro-polish.com
SIC: **3471** Finishing, metals or formed products

(G-8181)
ELECTRO-LINE INC
118 S Terry St (45403-2312)
PHONE..................937 461-5683
Bruce Jump, *President*
Jeff Bucher, *Vice Pres*
Jeffrey J Bucher, *Vice Pres*
EMP: 15
SQ FT: 15,000
SALES: 1.8MM **Privately Held**
WEB: www.electroline.com
SIC: **3679** 5065 Electronic circuits; electronic parts & equipment

(G-8182)
ELLIOTT TOOL TECHNOLOGIES LTD (PA)
1760 Tuttle Ave (45403-3428)
PHONE..................937 253-6133
Joseph W Smith, *President*
Jason Triche, *Area Mgr*
Robert Columbus, *Vice Pres*
Tom Reynolds, *Mfg Mgr*
Dawn Luker, *Purchasing*
EMP: 68
SQ FT: 37,000
SALES (est): 16MM **Privately Held**
WEB: www.elliott-tool.com
SIC: **7359** 3542 5072 3541 Equipment rental & leasing; machine tools, metal forming type; hand tools; machine tools, metal cutting type; fabricated pipe & fittings

(G-8183)
ENERGY STORAGE TECHNOLOGIES
Also Called: Vacupanel
7610 Mcewen Rd (45459-3908)
PHONE..................937 312-0114
C William Swank, *President*
Michael Fisher, *CFO*
Robert Hussey, *Controller*
EMP: 50
SALES (est): 5.6MM **Privately Held**
SIC: **3086** Insulation or cushioning material, foamed plastic

(G-8184)
EPIX TUBE CO INC (PA)
5800 Wolf Creek Pike (45426-2438)
P.O. Box 187, West Alexandria (45381-0187)
PHONE..................937 529-4858
Paul Kasperski, *President*
Kevin Houlihan, *Vice Pres*
Angela Salazar, *CFO*
EMP: 53
SALES (est): 25.8MM **Privately Held**
SIC: **2599** 5531 Factory furniture & fixtures; automotive accessories

(G-8185)
EQUIPMENT SPCALISTS DAYTON LLC
5595 Webster St (45414-3516)
PHONE..................937 415-2151
Stephen Hart, *Partner*
Teresa Hart, *Partner*
EMP: 3
SQ FT: 2,000
SALES (est): 164K **Privately Held**
SIC: **2841** 7699 Soap & other detergents; industrial machinery & equipment repair; pumps & pumping equipment repair; agricultural equipment repair services

(G-8186)
ERNST ENTERPRISES INC (PA)
Also Called: Ernst Concrete
3361 Successful Way (45414-4317)
PHONE..................937 233-5555
John C Ernst Jr, *President*
Bob Hines, *Principal*
David Ernst, *Vice Pres*
Dan Ernst, *Shareholder*
EMP: 20
SQ FT: 6,300
SALES (est): 227.2MM **Privately Held**
WEB: www.ernstconcrete.com
SIC: **3273** Ready-mixed concrete

(G-8187)
EROCKETS LLC
2790 Thunderhawk Ct (45414-3464)
PHONE..................616 460-2678
Randy Boadway, *Mng Member*
EMP: 4 EST: 2015
SALES: 250K **Privately Held**
SIC: **3944** Airplane models, toy & hobby

(G-8188)
ESTEE MOLD & DIE INC
612 Linden Ave (45403-2513)
PHONE..................937 224-7853
Dan Rinehart, *President*
Gerhard Triftshouser, *Shareholder*
Werner Triftshouser, *Shareholder*
EMP: 20 EST: 1945
SQ FT: 28,000
SALES (est): 4.8MM **Privately Held**
WEB: www.esteemold.com
SIC: **3544** Industrial molds

(G-8189)
EUGENE STEWART
Also Called: Spectrum Printing & Design
5671 Webster St (45414-3518)
PHONE..................937 898-1117
Eugene Stewart, *Owner*
EMP: 8
SQ FT: 6,000
SALES: 987K **Privately Held**
SIC: **2791** 7336 2789 2752 Typesetting; art design services; bookbinding & related work; commercial printing, lithographic

(G-8190)
EVANS BAKERY INC
700 Troy St (45404-1851)
PHONE..................937 228-4151
Edward William Evans, *President*
Rose Mary Evans, *Vice Pres*
EMP: 8
SQ FT: 1,600
SALES (est): 858.4K **Privately Held**
SIC: **2051** 5461 Bakery: wholesale or wholesale/retail combined; doughnuts

(G-8191)
FAST FAB AND LASER LLC
401 Kiser St (45404-1639)
P.O. Box 327 (45409-0327)
PHONE..................937 224-3048
EMP: 13
SQ FT: 22,000
SALES (est): 1.2MM **Privately Held**
SIC: **3599** Laser Cutting Job Shop

(G-8192)
FEDEX OFFICE & PRINT SVCS INC
1189 Mmsburg Cntrville Rd (45459)
PHONE..................937 436-0677
EMP: 30
SALES (corp-wide): 47.4B **Publicly Held**
SIC: **7334** 2791 2789 Photocopying Services Typesetting Services Bookbinding/Related Work
HQ: Fedex Office And Print Services, Inc.
7900 Legacy Dr
Dallas TX 75024
214 550-7000

(G-8193)
FERNANDES ENTERPRISES LLC (PA)
Also Called: Fourjay Industries
2801 Ontario Ave (45414-5136)
PHONE..................937 890-6444
Vernon Fernandes, *President*
Jim Gamble, *Opers Mgr*
▲ EMP: 32
SQ FT: 9,600
SALES (est): 4.4MM **Privately Held**
SIC: **3699** Electric sound equipment

(G-8194)
FIDELITY ORTHOPEDIC INC
8514 N Main St (45415-1325)
PHONE..................937 228-0682
Hillmo Hodzic, *President*
Suzan Brandelik, *Supervisor*
Adam Murka, *Director*
Mark Murka, *Director*
EMP: 6 EST: 1929
SQ FT: 4,000
SALES (est): 994.4K **Privately Held**
WEB: www.fidelityorthopedic.com
SIC: **3842** Limbs, artificial; braces, orthopedic

(G-8195)
FIRST TOOL CORP (PA)
612 Linden Ave (45403-2589)
PHONE..................937 254-6197
Robert J Davis, *President*
Amy Howard, *General Mgr*
Pauline Miller, *Principal*
Seymour D Ramby, *Principal*
Rob Riber, *Foreman/Supr*
EMP: 50 EST: 1966
SQ FT: 60,000
SALES: 13.7MM **Privately Held**
WEB: www.firsttoolcorp.com
SIC: **3542** 3544 Machine tools, metal forming type: jigs & fixtures

(G-8196)
FISCHER ENGINEERING COMPANY
8220 Expansion Way (45424-6382)
PHONE..................937 754-1750
Glenn N Fischer, *President*
Justin Hartman, *General Mgr*
EMP: 4 EST: 1976
SQ FT: 14,400
SALES (est): 819.9K **Privately Held**
WEB: www.fischerengr.com
SIC: **3829** Tensile strength testing equipment

(G-8197)
FIVE POINTS DISTILLERY LLC
122 Van Buren St (45402-2934)
PHONE..................937 776-4634
Murphy Laselle, *Principal*
EMP: 4
SQ FT: 5,000
SALES (est): 195.7K **Privately Held**
SIC: **2085** Rye whiskey

(G-8198)
FLEET GRAPHICS INC
1701 Thomas Paine Pkwy (45459-2540)
PHONE..................937 252-2552
Scott Waggoner, *President*
Val R Waggoner, *Vice Pres*
Bob Brogan, *Accounts Exec*
Jane Mullins, *Office Mgr*
Rick Martin, *Art Dir*
EMP: 9
SQ FT: 6,000
SALES (est): 2.3MM **Privately Held**
WEB: www.fleetgraphicsinc.com
SIC: **3571** 2752 Computers, digital, analog or hybrid; commercial printing, lithographic

(G-8199)
FLOWERS & MONUMENTS R US
5858 N Main St (45415-3101)
PHONE..................937 813-8496
EMP: 3
SALES (est): 271.1K **Privately Held**
SIC: **3272** Monuments & grave markers, except terrazo

(G-8200)
FLOWSERVE CORPORATION
2200 E Monument Ave (45402-1362)
PHONE..................937 226-4000
John Carano, *Branch Mgr*
EMP: 55
SALES (corp-wide): 3.8B **Publicly Held**
SIC: **3561** Industrial pumps & parts
PA: Flowserve Corporation
5215 N Oconnor Blvd Connor
Irving TX 75039
972 443-6500

(G-8201)
FORM-A-CHIP INC
Also Called: Kneiss Saw & Tool Supply
2069 Webster St (45404-1143)
PHONE..................937 223-4135
Joe Tischler, *President*
EMP: 6
SQ FT: 4,600
SALES (est): 883.3K **Privately Held**
SIC: **5072** 3425 7699 Power tools & accessories; saw blades; saw blades & handsaws; professional instrument repair services

(G-8202)
FORSVARA ENGINEERING LLC
Also Called: Kerf Waterjet
313 E Helena St (45404-1031)
PHONE..................937 254-9711
Jon Wickersham, *Partner*
David Kleinfelder, *Mng Member*
EMP: 4
SQ FT: 3,500
SALES: 700K **Privately Held**
WEB: www.kerfwaterjet.com
SIC: **3599** 3993 1752 Machine & other job shop work; signs & advertising specialties; floor laying & floor work

▲ = Import ▼ = Export
◆ = Import/Export

GEOGRAPHIC SECTION

Dayton - Montgomery County (G-8228)

(G-8203)
FORTERRA PIPE & PRECAST LLC
Also Called: Hanson Pipe & Precast Hamburg
1504 N Gettysburg Ave (45417-9518)
PHONE..................937 268-6707
Kevin Sams, *Manager*
EMP: 3
SALES (corp-wide): 1.5B **Publicly Held**
SIC: 1771 5211 3272 Concrete work; masonry materials & supplies; concrete products
HQ: Forterra Pipe & Precast, Llc
511 E John Carpenter Fwy
Irving TX 75062
469 458-7973

(G-8204)
FORTERRA PIPE & PRECAST LLC
1504 N Gettysburg Ave (45417-9518)
PHONE..................937 268-6707
EMP: 20
SALES (corp-wide): 14.4B **Privately Held**
SIC: 3272 Mfg Concrete Products
HQ: Forterra Pipe & Precast, Llc
511 E John Carpenter Fwy
Irving TX 75062
469 458-7973

(G-8205)
FOUR AMBITION
2821 Kenmore Ave (45420-2231)
PHONE..................937 239-4479
Shannon Thomas, *Principal*
EMP: 3
SALES (est): 245.7K **Privately Held**
SIC: 2759 Commercial printing

(G-8206)
FRANKLIN IRON & METAL CORP
1939 E 1st St (45403-1131)
PHONE..................937 253-8184
Jack Edelman, *President*
Debra Edelman, *Treasurer*
▲ **EMP:** 105
SQ FT: 60,000
SALES (est): 50.7MM **Privately Held**
SIC: 5093 3341 3312 Ferrous metal scrap & waste; secondary nonferrous metals; blast furnaces & steel mills

(G-8207)
FRIED DADDY
Also Called: American Sports Center
448 N Union Rd (45417-7614)
PHONE..................937 854-4542
Fred Fry, *Owner*
Charles Roberts, *General Mgr*
EMP: 5
SALES (est): 100K **Privately Held**
SIC: 5941 5999 3993 2396 Sporting goods & bicycle shops; trophies & plaques; signs & advertising specialties; automotive & apparel trimmings

(G-8208)
FRIENDS SERVICE CO INC
4604 Salem Ave (45416-1712)
PHONE..................800 427-1704
Kenneth J Schroeder, *Branch Mgr*
EMP: 15 **Privately Held**
SIC: 5112 5021 5087 2752 Stationery & office supplies; furniture; service establishment equipment; commercial printing, lithographic; office equipment
PA: Friends Service Co., Inc.
2300 Bright Rd
Findlay OH 45840

(G-8209)
FRIES MACHINE & TOOL INC
5729 Webster St (45414-3520)
PHONE..................937 898-6432
Arland Fries, *CEO*
Tony E Fries, *President*
Lisa A Fries, *Corp Secy*
EMP: 12
SQ FT: 4,000
SALES: 1MM **Privately Held**
SIC: 3599 Machine shop, jobbing & repair

(G-8210)
FUKUVI USA INC
7631 Progress Ct (45424-6378)
PHONE..................937 236-7288
S Yagi, *President*
K Takagi, *Vice Pres*
▲ **EMP:** 65
SQ FT: 84,000
SALES (est): 13.7MM
SALES (corp-wide): 377.1MM **Privately Held**
WEB: www.fukuvi-usa.com
SIC: 3089 Plastic kitchenware, tableware & houseware; plastic processing
PA: Fukuvi Chemical Industry Co., Ltd.
33-66, Sanjuhasshacho
Fukui FKI 918-8
776 388-001

(G-8211)
FURNITURE BY OTMAR INC (PA)
301 Mmsburg Cnterville Rd (45459)
PHONE..................937 435-2039
Josef Otmar IV, *President*
Alberto Otmar, *Vice Pres*
EMP: 12 **EST:** 1960
SQ FT: 10,000
SALES (est): 1.1MM **Privately Held**
WEB: www.furniturebyotmar.com
SIC: 2511 5712 Wood household furniture; furniture stores

(G-8212)
FUYAO GLASS AMERICA INC (HQ)
2801 W Stroop Rd (45439)
PHONE..................937 496-5777
Frank Welling, *President*
EMP: 228 **EST:** 2014
SALES (est): 172.4MM
SALES (corp-wide): 2.9B **Privately Held**
SIC: 3231 5013 Products of purchased glass; automobile glass
PA: Fuyao Glass Industry Group Co., Ltd.
Fuyao Industry Area
Fuqing 35030
591 853-8377

(G-8213)
GALAPAGOS INC (PA)
Also Called: Biofocus Inc
3345 Old Salem Rd (45415-1232)
PHONE..................937 890-3068
Onno Van De Stolpe, *CEO*
EMP: 6
SALES (est): 16.4MM **Privately Held**
SIC: 2833 2899 Medicinals & botanicals; chemical preparations

(G-8214)
GAUNTLET AWARDS & ENGRAVING
9153 N Dixie Dr (45414-1859)
P.O. Box 267, Vandalia (45377-0267)
PHONE..................937 890-5811
Vickie Akers, *Owner*
EMP: 4
SQ FT: 4,000
SALES: 318K **Privately Held**
SIC: 5999 7389 5199 3993 Trophies & plaques; engraving service; advertising specialties; signs & advertising specialties; bolts, nuts, rivets & washers; packaging paper & plastics film, coated & laminated

(G-8215)
GCI METALS INC
7660 W 3rd St (45417-7539)
PHONE..................937 262-7500
Kimberly Smallwood, *President*
EMP: 8
SALES (est): 888.1K **Privately Held**
SIC: 3499 Fabricated metal products

(G-8216)
GDC INDUSTRIES LLC
49 Front St (45402-1328)
PHONE..................937 640-1212
EMP: 3
SALES (est): 111.2K **Privately Held**
SIC: 3999 Manufacturing industries

(G-8217)
GE AVIATION SYSTEMS LLC
6800 Poe Ave (45414-2530)
PHONE..................937 898-9600
Chuck Dipasquale, *Sales Staff*
EMP: 42
SALES (corp-wide): 121.6B **Publicly Held**
SIC: 3812 Aircraft control systems, electronic
HQ: Ge Aviation Systems Llc
1 Neumann Way
Cincinnati OH 45215
937 898-9600

(G-8218)
GEDICO INTERNATIONAL INC
Also Called: Largemachining.com
4050 Grafix Blvd (45417-9578)
PHONE..................937 274-2167
George E Dorin, *President*
Donald J Smith, *Vice Pres*
EMP: 7 **EST:** 1945
SQ FT: 20,000
SALES: 300K **Privately Held**
WEB: www.gedico.com
SIC: 3555 3599 Printing trades machinery; machine shop, jobbing & repair

(G-8219)
GEM CITY ENGINEERING CO (PA)
Also Called: Gem City Engineering & Mfg
401 Leo St (45404-1009)
PHONE..................937 223-5544
James Whalen, *CEO*
David D Harry, *President*
Greg Profitt, *Mfg Mgr*
Jeff Hankins, *Opers Staff*
John Castle, *Engineer*
EMP: 120
SQ FT: 250,000
SALES (est): 33.2MM **Privately Held**
WEB: www.gemcity.com
SIC: 3544 3549 3569 Special dies & tools; metalworking machinery; assembly machines, non-metalworking

(G-8220)
GEM CITY METAL TECH LLC
1825 E 1st St (45403-1129)
PHONE..................937 252-8998
Dennis Mc Wright, *CFO*
Dennis Nystrom, *Mng Member*
Don Nystron, *Mng Member*
Norb Overla,
EMP: 49
SQ FT: 53,000
SALES (est): 14.6MM **Privately Held**
SIC: 3356 3446 3444 3469 Nonferrous rolling & drawing; architectural metalwork; sheet metalwork; spinning metal for the trade; machine tools, metal forming type

(G-8221)
GENEVA GEAR & MACHINE INC
339 Progress Rd (45449-2321)
PHONE..................937 866-0318
Otto G Takacs Jr, *President*
EMP: 15
SQ FT: 12,700
SALES: 2MM **Privately Held**
SIC: 3568 3566 3462 Power transmission equipment; gears, power transmission, except automotive; iron & steel forgings

(G-8222)
GINKO VOTING SYSTEMS LLC (PA)
Also Called: Ginko Systems
600 Progress Rd (45449-2300)
PHONE..................937 291-4060
Franklin Dunkin, *CEO*
Lawrence Whitehead, *Vice Pres*
J R Dunkin, *Opers Staff*
EMP: 1
SQ FT: 12,000
SALES (est): 3.4MM **Privately Held**
SIC: 3578 3695 Automatic teller machines (ATM); computer software tape & disks; blank, rigid & floppy

(G-8223)
GLEASON METROLOGY SYSTEMS CORP (HQ)
Also Called: Gleason M & M Precision
300 Progress Rd (45449-2322)
PHONE..................937 384-8901
Douglas Beerck, *General Mgr*
Terry Turner, *Exec VP*
◆ **EMP:** 50
SQ FT: 68,000
SALES (est): 7.5MM
SALES (corp-wide): 919.1MM **Privately Held**
SIC: 3829 3823 3769 3621 Measuring & controlling devices; industrial instrmnts msrmnt display/control process variable; guided missile & space vehicle parts & auxiliary equipment; motors & generators; computer peripheral equipment; machine tool accessories
PA: Gleason Corporation
1000 University Ave
Rochester NY 14607
585 473-1000

(G-8224)
GLEN D LALA
Also Called: Innovative Creations
2610 Willowburn Ave (45417-9434)
P.O. Box 328, Springboro (45066-0328)
PHONE..................937 274-7770
Glen D Lala, *Owner*
EMP: 6
SQ FT: 12,000
SALES (est): 247.5K **Privately Held**
SIC: 2759 7699 Screen printing; printing trades machinery & equipment repair

(G-8225)
GLOBAL MANUFACTURING SOLUTIONS
2001 Kuntz Rd (45404-1221)
PHONE..................937 236-8315
Charles M Woods, *President*
William Bankes, *Vice Pres*
EMP: 13
SQ FT: 46,000
SALES (est): 1.7MM **Privately Held**
WEB: www.globalms.com
SIC: 3082 8734 5947 5199 Unsupported plastics profile shapes; product testing laboratory, safety or performance; gifts & novelties; foams & rubber

(G-8226)
GLOBE MOTORS INC (HQ)
2275 Stanley Ave (45404-1226)
PHONE..................334 983-3542
Steven McHenry, *CEO*
William Gillespie, *CFO*
▲ **EMP:** 150
SALES (est): 151MM
SALES (corp-wide): 252MM **Publicly Held**
WEB: www.globe-motors.com
SIC: 3621 Motors, electric
PA: Allied Motion Technologies Inc.
495 Commerce Way Ste 3
Amherst NY 14228
716 242-8634

(G-8227)
GLOBE MOTORS INC
1944 Troy St (45404-2159)
PHONE..................937 228-3171
Dick Peacock, *Manager*
EMP: 125
SALES (corp-wide): 252MM **Publicly Held**
WEB: www.globe-motors.com
SIC: 3621 3369 3365 Motors, electric; nonferrous foundries; aluminum foundries
HQ: Globe Motors, Inc.
2275 Stanley Ave
Dayton OH 45404
334 983-3542

(G-8228)
GLOBE MOTORS INC
2275 Stanley Ave (45404-1226)
PHONE..................937 228-3171
Steve McHenry, *Branch Mgr*
EMP: 100

Dayton - Montgomery County (G-8229)   **GEOGRAPHIC SECTION**

SALES (corp-wide): 252MM **Publicly Held**
WEB: www.globe-motors.com
SIC: 3621 Motors, electric
HQ: Globe Motors, Inc.
 2275 Stanley Ave
 Dayton OH 45404
 334 983-3542

(G-8229)
GLOBE PRODUCTS INC (PA)
5051 Kitridge Rd (45424-4433)
PHONE....................937 233-0233
James E Kroencke, CEO
Scott Kroencke, President
Don Knight, Plant Mgr
Joy Randolph, Finance Mgr
Sandy Sullenbarger, Marketing Staff
▲ **EMP:** 20 **EST:** 1919
SQ FT: 100,000
SALES (est): 2.5MM **Privately Held**
WEB: www.globe-usa.com
SIC: 3599 Custom machinery

(G-8230)
GLT INC (PA)
3341 Successful Way (45414-4317)
PHONE....................937 237-0055
Kevin Knight, CEO
Jeff Banford, Vice Pres
Vince Hinde, Vice Pres
Chris Knight, Vice Pres
Brad Labensky, Vice Pres
◆ **EMP:** 12
SQ FT: 75,000
SALES (est): 11.3MM **Privately Held**
WEB: www.gltonline.com
SIC: 3541 Machine tools, metal cutting type

(G-8231)
GMD INDUSTRIES LLC
Also Called: Production Screw Machine
1414 E 2nd St (45403-1023)
PHONE....................937 252-3643
Greg Macpherson, Business Mgr
Mark Michaels, Plant Mgr
Theresa Nichols, Human Res Dir
Mark Denlinger, Marketing Staff
Rick Mosteller, Info Tech Mgr
▼ **EMP:** 65
SQ FT: 35,000
SALES (est): 10.7MM **Privately Held**
WEB: www.psmco.com
SIC: 3599 Machine shop, jobbing & repair

(G-8232)
GO CUPCAKE
5017 Rolling Woods Trl (45429-1110)
PHONE....................937 299-4985
Jennifer Cox, Principal
EMP: 4
SALES (est): 234.6K **Privately Held**
SIC: 2051 Bread, cake & related products

(G-8233)
GOVERNMENT SPECIALTY PDTS LLC (PA)
9588 Quailwood Trl (45458-9630)
PHONE....................937 672-9473
John Hetzel,
EMP: 1
SALES: 3.2MM **Privately Held**
SIC: 2311 Military uniforms, men's & youths': purchased materials

(G-8234)
GRANT JOHN
Also Called: J & D Printing
2715 Culver Ave (45429-3723)
PHONE....................937 298-0633
John Grant, Owner
EMP: 3
SQ FT: 1,100
SALES: 200K **Privately Held**
SIC: 2752 2796 2789 2759 Lithographic Coml Print Platemaking Services Bookbinding/Related Work Commercial Printing

(G-8235)
GRB HOLDINGS INC
131 Janney Rd (45404-1225)
P.O. Box 173 (45404-0173)
PHONE....................937 236-3250
David Gitridge, President

David Gutridge, President
EMP: 80 **EST:** 1913
SQ FT: 50,000
SALES: 15MM **Privately Held**
WEB: www.behmquartz.com
SIC: 3295 3471 Minerals, ground or treated; plating & polishing

(G-8236)
GREEN LEAF PRINTING AND DESIGN
1001 E 2nd St Ste 2485 (45402-1498)
PHONE....................937 222-3634
Larry Blevins, Principal
EMP: 4
SALES (est): 407.7K **Privately Held**
SIC: 2752 Commercial printing, lithographic

(G-8237)
GREEN TOKAI CO LTD
3700 Inpark Dr (45414-4418)
PHONE....................937 237-1630
Charlie Sapp, Branch Mgr
EMP: 5
SALES (corp-wide): 1.6MM **Privately Held**
SIC: 3714 Motor vehicle parts & accessories
HQ: Green Tokai Co., Ltd.
 55 Robert Wright Dr
 Brookville OH 45309
 937 833-5444

(G-8238)
GREEN WILLOW INC
Also Called: Minuteman Press
90 Compark Rd Ste A (45459-4967)
PHONE....................937 436-5290
Jesse C Gaither, President
EMP: 4
SALES (est): 265K **Privately Held**
SIC: 2759 8742 Commercial Printing Management Consulting Services

(G-8239)
GREGORY STONE CO INC
1860 N Gettysburg Ave (45417-9585)
PHONE....................937 275-7455
Thomas L Call, President
Jackie K Call, Vice Pres
EMP: 9
SQ FT: 7,000
SALES (est): 1.9MM **Privately Held**
SIC: 5211 1411 Masonry materials & supplies; limestone, dimension-quarrying

(G-8240)
H & H SCREEN PROCESS INC
1220 Wyoming St (45410-1912)
PHONE....................937 253-7520
Robert Hess, President
Aileen Hess, Vice Pres
EMP: 4
SQ FT: 2,400
SALES: 200K **Privately Held**
SIC: 2396 2306 2759 Screen printing on fabric articles; embroidery & art needlework; screen printing

(G-8241)
H GERSTNER & SONS INC
Also Called: Gerstner International
20 Gerstner Way (45402-8408)
PHONE....................937 228-1662
John Campbell, President
John Scott Campbell Jr, Vice Pres
Nancy Campbell, Admin Sec
Vicki Campbell, Clerk
▲ **EMP:** 20 **EST:** 1906
SQ FT: 30,000
SALES (est): 1.5MM **Privately Held**
WEB: www.gerstnerusa.com
SIC: 2441 Tool chests, wood

(G-8242)
HAM SIGNS LLC
6020 N Dixie Dr (45414-4018)
PHONE....................937 454-9111
Larry Miller,
EMP: 5
SALES (est): 533.2K **Privately Held**
SIC: 3993 7532 Signs & advertising specialties; truck painting & lettering

(G-8243)
HANGER PRSTHETCS & ORTHO INC
Also Called: Orpro Prosthetics & Orthotics
1 Elizabeth Pl Ste 300 (45417-3445)
PHONE....................937 228-5462
Randy Daniel, Branch Mgr
EMP: 15
SALES (corp-wide): 1B **Publicly Held**
SIC: 3842 5999 Prosthetic appliances; orthopedic appliances; orthopedic & prosthesis applications
HQ: Hanger Prosthetics & Orthotics, Inc.
 10910 Domain Dr Ste 300
 Austin TX 78758
 512 777-3800

(G-8244)
HARBOR FREIGHT TOOLS USA INC
1941 Needmore Rd (45414-3807)
PHONE....................937 415-0770
Vance Moore, Manager
EMP: 20
SALES (corp-wide): 2.3B **Privately Held**
SIC: 7699 7389 5084 3423 Tool repair services; hand tool designers; compressors, except air conditioning; hand & edge tools
PA: Harbor Freight Tools Usa, Inc.
 26541 Agoura Rd
 Calabasas CA 91302
 818 836-5001

(G-8245)
HAYES METALFINISHING INC
Also Called: Quality Black Oxide
2617 Stanley Ave (45404-2732)
PHONE....................937 228-7550
Phillip Hayes, President
Kathy Hayes, Vice Pres
EMP: 5
SQ FT: 3,106
SALES (est): 494.3K **Privately Held**
SIC: 3471 Finishing, metals or formed products

(G-8246)
HAYES RECONDITIONING GROUP
Also Called: A R C of Dayton
1301 Robert Dickey Pkwy (45409-2122)
PHONE....................937 299-8013
Tim Hayes, CEO
EMP: 3
SALES: 120K **Privately Held**
SIC: 2396 Automotive & apparel trimmings

(G-8247)
HEC INVESTMENTS INC
4800 Wadsworth Rd (45414-4224)
PHONE....................937 278-9123
Lynne Henson, President
Shane Miller, Exec VP
John Cook, Vice Pres
Delma Overman, Prdtn Mgr
Carol Vician, Production
▲ **EMP:** 144 **EST:** 1975
SQ FT: 12,000
SALES (est): 24.8MM **Privately Held**
WEB: www.superiorabrasives.com
SIC: 3291 Abrasive products

(G-8248)
HESLER MACHINE TOOL
607 Brookfield Rd (45429-3321)
PHONE....................937 299-3833
Terry Hesler, Owner
Vicky Hesler, Co-Owner
EMP: 5
SQ FT: 8,000
SALES: 300K **Privately Held**
SIC: 3541 3599 Machine tools, metal cutting type; machine shop, jobbing & repair

(G-8249)
HESS ADVANCED SOLUTIONS LLC
7415 Chambersburg Rd (45424-3921)
P.O. Box 17669 (45417-0669)
PHONE....................937 829-4794
Frederick Edmonds, CEO
EMP: 8
SQ FT: 15,000

SALES (est): 351.6K **Privately Held**
SIC: 3699 1731 8711 1711 Electrical equipment & supplies; electrical work; heating & ventilation engineering; heating & air conditioning contractors; heating equipment & panels, solar

(G-8250)
HINKLE FINE FOODS INC
4800 Wadsworth Rd (45414-4224)
PHONE....................937 836-3665
Benny S Hinkle, President
Micheal Beller, Principal
Craig Frost, Principal
Marlene M Hinkle, Admin Sec
EMP: 8 **EST:** 1975
SQ FT: 8,200
SALES (est): 1.3MM **Privately Held**
SIC: 2035 Seasonings & sauces, except tomato & dry; dressings, salad: raw & cooked (except dry mixes)

(G-8251)
HOCKER TOOL AND DIE INC
5161 Webster St (45414-4227)
PHONE....................937 274-3443
Ronald S Hocker, President
William K Hocker, Vice Pres
EMP: 14
SQ FT: 12,000
SALES: 1.8MM **Privately Held**
WEB: www.hockertoolanddie.com
SIC: 3599 Machine shop, jobbing & repair

(G-8252)
HOME CITY ICE COMPANY
1020 Gateway Dr (45404-2281)
PHONE....................937 461-6028
Kyle Kenny, Sales Executive
Joel Heck, Manager
EMP: 25
SALES (corp-wide): 232.5MM **Privately Held**
WEB: www.homecityice.com
SIC: 2097 5999 Manufactured ice; ice
PA: The Home City Ice Company
 6045 Bridgetown Rd Ste 1
 Cincinnati OH 45248
 513 574-1800

(G-8253)
HOUSE OF 10000 PICTURE FRAMES
2210 Wilmington Pike (45420-1433)
PHONE....................937 254-5541
William Heath, Owner
EMP: 9
SQ FT: 4,000
SALES: 450K **Privately Held**
SIC: 5999 5719 2499 Picture frames, ready made; pictures, wall; picture frame molding, finished

(G-8254)
HOWMEDICA OSTEONICS CORP
474 Windsor Park Dr (45459-4111)
PHONE....................937 291-3900
Patrick Barnes, Branch Mgr
EMP: 13
SALES (corp-wide): 13.6B **Publicly Held**
SIC: 3841 Surgical & medical instruments
HQ: Howmedica Osteonics Corp.
 325 Corporate Dr
 Mahwah NJ 07430
 201 831-5000

(G-8255)
HTEC SYSTEMS INC
561 Congress Park Dr (45459-4036)
PHONE....................937 438-3010
Peter A Flaherty, President
Phillip Hayden, Chairman
Christopher Hayden, Corp Secy
EMP: 10
SQ FT: 4,000
SALES: 3MM **Privately Held**
WEB: www.htecsystems.com
SIC: 8711 7389 1629 3599 Engineering services; design services; industrial plant construction; custom machinery

(G-8256)
HUESTON INDUSTRIES INC
3020 Production Ct (45414-3514)
PHONE....................937 264-8163
Michael Parin, President

John Parin, *Manager*
EMP: 8
SQ FT: 5,100
SALES: 1.2MM **Privately Held**
SIC: 3625 Noise control equipment

(G-8257)
HUNTER TOOL AND DIE COMPANY
2104 E 1st St (45403-1207)
PHONE.....................937 256-9798
Mike Barok, *President*
Diane Barok, *Corp Secy*
EMP: 4
SALES: 450K **Privately Held**
SIC: 3544 Special dies & tools

(G-8258)
HYLAND MACHINE COMPANY
Also Called: Hyland Screw Machine Products
1900 Kuntz Rd (45404-1251)
P.O. Box 133 (45404-0133)
PHONE.....................937 233-8600
Forest Hyland, *President*
Dan Hyland, *Vice Pres*
Mitch Lambert, *Plant Mgr*
▲ **EMP:** 27 **EST:** 1928
SQ FT: 42,000
SALES (est): 7.1MM **Privately Held**
WEB: www.hylandmach.com
SIC: 3451 Screw machine products

(G-8259)
IDX CORPORATION
2875 Needmore Rd (45414-4301)
PHONE.....................937 401-3225
David Mueller, *General Mgr*
EMP: 150
SALES (corp-wide): 394.6MM **Privately Held**
SIC: 3083 2521 3999 2511 Plastic finished products, laminated; wood office furniture; plaques, picture, laminated; wood household furniture; wood kitchen cabinets; millwork
PA: Idx Corporation
1 Rider Trail Plaza Dr
Earth City MO 63045
314 739-4120

(G-8260)
IDX DAYTON LLC
Also Called: Universal Forest Products
2875 Needmore Rd (45414-4301)
PHONE.....................937 401-3460
Isaac Bokros, *Manager*
▲ **EMP:** 123
SALES (est): 18.2MM
SALES (corp-wide): 4.4B **Publicly Held**
SIC: 2542 2541 Partitions & fixtures, except wood; store & office display cases & fixtures; display fixtures, wood
PA: Universal Forest Products, Inc.
2801 E Beltline Ave Ne
Grand Rapids MI 49525
616 364-6161

(G-8261)
INDEPENDENT AWNING & CANVAS CO
324 Jones St (45410-1104)
PHONE.....................937 223-9661
Fred Utzinger III, *President*
Shirley Utzinger, *Corp Secy*
EMP: 7
SQ FT: 5,400
SALES: 575.2K **Privately Held**
SIC: 2394 Awnings, fabric: made from purchased materials

(G-8262)
INDOOR ENVMTL SPECIALISTS INC
Also Called: Environmental Doctor
438 Windsor Park Dr (45459-4111)
PHONE.....................937 433-5202
Brenden Gitzinger, *President*
Margie Gitzinger, *Vice Pres*
EMP: 12
SQ FT: 3,000
SALES: 950K **Privately Held**
SIC: 7349 5999 1799 3564 Air duct cleaning; air purification equipment; waterproofing; air purification equipment;

(G-8263)
INDUSTRIAL FIBERGLASS SPC INC
Also Called: Fiber Systems
521 Kiser St (45404-1641)
PHONE.....................937 222-9000
Theodore Morton, *Ch of Bd*
Diana Hall, *President*
Janice Morton, *Corp Secy*
Diana Partin, *Purchasing*
Rose Marie Wiliams, *Accounting Mgr*
EMP: 35 **EST:** 1978
SQ FT: 122,000
SALES (est): 5.9MM **Privately Held**
WEB: www.ifs-frp.com
SIC: 3229 1799 Glass fiber products; service station equipment installation, maintenance & repair

(G-8264)
INLAND MANUFACTURING LLC
6785 W 3rd St (45417-7837)
PHONE.....................937 835-0220
Ronald Norton,
EMP: 3
SALES (est): 215.7K **Privately Held**
SIC: 3484 Rifles or rifle parts, 30 mm. & below

(G-8265)
INNOVATIVE PLASTIC MOLDERS LLC
7438 Webster St (45414-5816)
PHONE.....................937 898-3775
Brian O' Leary, *Mng Member*
EMP: 50
SQ FT: 12,800
SALES (est): 10.7MM **Privately Held**
SIC: 3544 3089 Special dies, tools, jigs & fixtures; injection molding of plastics

(G-8266)
INNOVATIVE RETAIL DISPLAYS INC
2127 Troy St (45404-2162)
P.O. Box 156 (45404-0156)
PHONE.....................937 237-7708
Jackie Simpson, *CEO*
Michael Ely, *President*
Craig Simpson, *Vice Pres*
▲ **EMP:** 19
SQ FT: 12,000
SALES: 1.1MM **Privately Held**
SIC: 2541 Store & office display cases & fixtures; cabinets, lockers & shelving

(G-8267)
INNOVATIVE VEND SOLUTIONS LLC
2048 S Alex Rd (45449-4042)
PHONE.....................866 931-9413
Patrick McDonald, *Principal*
EMP: 24
SALES (est): 5.2MM **Privately Held**
SIC: 3581 Automatic vending machines

(G-8268)
INSIGNIA SIGNS INC
300 Gargrave Rd (45449-2464)
PHONE.....................937 866-2341
Rick Dobson, *President*
Dan McBride, *Principal*
Scott Warrick, *Graphic Designe*
EMP: 8
SALES (est): 1MM **Privately Held**
SIC: 3993 7336 Electric signs; graphic arts & related design

(G-8269)
INSTANTWHIP-DAYTON INC (PA)
Also Called: Tiller Foods
5820 Executive Blvd (45424-1451)
PHONE.....................937 235-5930
Donald Tiller Jr, *President*
William B Tiller, *Vice Pres*
David Yost, *Admin Sec*
▲ **EMP:** 15 **EST:** 1936
SQ FT: 15,000
SALES (est): 1.7MM **Privately Held**
SIC: 2026 2023 5143 Half & half; cream substitutes; dairy products, except dried or canned

(G-8270)
INSTANTWHIP-DAYTON INC
Also Called: Tiller Foods
967 Senate Dr (45459-4017)
PHONE.....................937 435-4371
David Yost, *General Mgr*
EMP: 6
SALES (corp-wide): 1.7MM **Privately Held**
SIC: 2026 2023 Half & half; cream substitutes
PA: Instantwhip-Dayton, Inc.
5820 Executive Blvd
Dayton OH 45424
937 235-5930

(G-8271)
INSTRUCTION & DESIGN CONCEPTS
441 Maple Springs Dr (45458-9232)
PHONE.....................937 439-2698
Fran Kick, *Owner*
EMP: 5
SALES: 156.7K **Privately Held**
WEB: www.kickitin.com
SIC: 8748 2731 8732 7336 Educational consultant; book publishing; educational research; commercial art & graphic design; management consulting services;

(G-8272)
INTEGRITY MANUFACTURING CORP
3723 Inpark Dr (45414-4417)
P.O. Box 312 (45404-0312)
PHONE.....................937 233-6792
Richard L Halderman, *President*
Gretchen Halderman, *Vice Pres*
EMP: 20
SQ FT: 11,950
SALES (est): 4.5MM **Privately Held**
WEB: www.integrity-mfg.com
SIC: 3451 3599 Screw machine products; machine shop, jobbing & repair

(G-8273)
INTERNATIONAL FINISHING LLC
2223 S Dixie Dr (45409-2014)
P.O. Box 290 (45409-0290)
PHONE.....................937 293-3340
Daniel J O'Connor, *President*
EMP: 5
SQ FT: 4,200
SALES (est): 1MM **Privately Held**
WEB: www.internationalfinishing.com
SIC: 3471 Plating & polishing

(G-8274)
INTERNATIONAL LAMINATING CORP
1712 Springfield St Ste 2 (45403-1447)
PHONE.....................937 254-8181
Raymond P Horan, *President*
Debbie Zengel, *General Mgr*
Debbie Burnett, *Mfg Staff*
Carolyn Leach, *Executive Asst*
EMP: 20
SQ FT: 25,000
SALES (est): 3.1MM **Privately Held**
WEB: www.intlam.com
SIC: 3083 Plastic finished products, laminated

(G-8275)
J T E CORP
5675 Webster St (45414-3518)
PHONE.....................937 454-1112
James Thorstenson, *President*
Jack Thornburg, *Vice Pres*
EMP: 4
SQ FT: 2,000
SALES (est): 549.3K **Privately Held**
WEB: www.jtecor.com
SIC: 3599 3548 Machine shop, jobbing & repair; welding & cutting apparatus & accessories

(G-8276)
JAFFE & GROSS JEWELRY COMPANY
3951 Far Hills Ave (45429-2438)
PHONE.....................937 461-9450
Lawrence Jaffe, *President*
Linda Matthews, *Corp Secy*
EMP: 3 **EST:** 1979
SALES: 1.6MM **Privately Held**
WEB: www.jaffejewelry.com
SIC: 5944 5094 7389 3911 Jewelry, precious stones & precious metals; jewelry & precious stones; appraisers, except real estate; jewelry, precious metal

(G-8277)
JAMES C FREE INC (PA)
Also Called: James Free Jewelers
3100 Far Hills Ave (45429-2512)
PHONE.....................937 298-0171
Michael S Karaman, *President*
Liz Mahoney, *General Mgr*
Joe Helm, *Sales Mgr*
Scott Hannig, *Sales Staff*
Dave Tellmann, *Mktg Dir*
▲ **EMP:** 20
SQ FT: 6,000
SALES (est): 3.4MM **Privately Held**
WEB: www.jamesfreejewelers.com
SIC: 3911 5944 Jewelry, precious metal; jewelry, precious stones & precious metals

(G-8278)
JAMES R EATON
535 Clareridge Ln (45458-2602)
PHONE.....................937 435-7767
EMP: 3
SALES (est): 285.8K **Privately Held**
SIC: 3625 Mfg Relays/Industrial Controls

(G-8279)
JANEWAY SIGNS INC
Also Called: Fastsigns
7825 Waynetowne Blvd (45424-2063)
PHONE.....................937 237-8433
Larry Miller, *President*
Wayne Beisner, *General Mgr*
EMP: 5
SQ FT: 1,500
SALES: 350K **Privately Held**
SIC: 3993 Signs & advertising specialties

(G-8280)
JBK MANUFACTURING LLC
Also Called: J B K Manufacturing & Dev
2127 Troy St (45404-2162)
PHONE.....................937 233-8300
Dave Freimuth, *General Mgr*
Mike Gearhardt, *General Mgr*
Jim Baxla, *Engineer*
Steve Cochran, *Engineer*
Jeremy Johnson, *Engineer*
▲ **EMP:** 44
SQ FT: 42,000
SALES (est): 7MM **Privately Held**
WEB: www.jbkmfg.com
SIC: 3599 Machine shop, jobbing & repair

(G-8281)
JC ROOFING SUPPLY (PA)
1535 Keystone Ave (45403-3335)
PHONE.....................937 258-9999
Gerald Jayne, *Owner*
EMP: 2
SQ FT: 2,000
SALES (est): 2.5MM **Privately Held**
SIC: 3531 Roofing equipment

(G-8282)
JEFF BONHAM ELECTRIC INC
3647 Wright Way Rd (45424-5165)
PHONE.....................937 233-7662
Jeff Bonham, *President*
Bryan Farlow, *Vice Pres*
EMP: 22
SQ FT: 1,500
SALES (est): 4.9MM **Privately Held**
WEB: www.jeffbonhamelectric.com
SIC: 1731 3613 General electrical contractor; panel & distribution boards & other related apparatus; fuses, electric

(G-8283)
JEFFREY L BECHT INC
Also Called: Sign Dynamics
2781 Thunderhawk Ct (45414-3445)
PHONE.....................937 264-2070
Jeffrey L Becht, *President*
Greg Alvarado, *Director*
EMP: 3
SQ FT: 6,000

Dayton - Montgomery County (G-8284)   GEOGRAPHIC SECTION

SALES (est): 692.5K **Privately Held**
WEB: www.signdynamics.com
SIC: 3993 Electric signs

(G-8284)
JEFFS BAKERY
210 Groveview Ave (45415-2305)
PHONE 937 890-9703
Jeff Morris, *Principal*
EMP: 6
SALES (est): 302.6K **Privately Held**
SIC: 2051 Bakery: wholesale or wholesale/retail combined

(G-8285)
JOYCE/DAYTON CORP (HQ)
3300 S Dixie Dr Ste 101 (45439-2318)
P.O. Box 635789, Cincinnati (45263-5789)
PHONE 937 294-6261
Michael Harris, *President*
Bradford Weiss, *Vice Pres*
Calvin Yadav, *Vice Pres*
Tim Hummel, *Opers Staff*
Matthew McAllister, *Engineer*
▲ EMP: 30 EST: 1893
SQ FT: 20,000
SALES: 26.6MM
SALES (corp-wide): 2.7B **Publicly Held**
SIC: 3569 Jacks, hydraulic
PA: Graham Holdings Company
   1300 17th St N Ste 1700
   Arlington VA 22209
   703 345-6300

(G-8286)
JULIE MAYNARD INC
Also Called: Consolidated Vehicle Converter
4991 Hempstead Station Dr (45429-5159)
PHONE 937 443-0408
Julie Maynard, *President*
Tim Prugh, *Corp Secy*
▲ EMP: 10
SQ FT: 20,000
SALES (est): 2.3MM **Privately Held**
SIC: 3714 3566 Motor vehicle parts & accessories; speed changers, drives & gears

(G-8287)
JUST BUSINESS INC
Also Called: Onstage Publications
1612 Prosser Ave Ste 100 (45409-2041)
PHONE 866 577-3303
Norman L Orlowski, *President*
Garett Orlowski, *Vice Pres*
Kyle Orlowski, *VP Sales*
Lee Mardis, *Accounts Mgr*
Pat Daley, *Accounts Exec*
EMP: 14 EST: 2001
SQ FT: 2,000
SALES: 2MM **Privately Held**
WEB: www.jusbiz.com
SIC: 8742 2731 7311 Marketing consulting services; book publishing; advertising consultant

(G-8288)
K & B ACQUISITIONS INC
Also Called: Mehaffie Pie Company
3013 Linden Ave (45410-3028)
PHONE 937 253-1163
Greg Hay, *President*
Jim Columbus, *Vice Pres*
Bruce Kouse, *Vice Pres*
Barb Columbus, *Treasurer*
EMP: 10 EST: 1930
SQ FT: 9,000
SALES: 650K **Privately Held**
SIC: 2051 5461 Pies, bakery: except frozen; pies

(G-8289)
K & R PRETZEL CO
1700 Flesher Ave (45420-3231)
PHONE 937 299-2231
Kathleen Glaze, *Owner*
EMP: 3 EST: 1967
SALES (est): 183.6K **Privately Held**
SIC: 2052 Pretzels

(G-8290)
KEITHLEY ENTERPRISES INC
Also Called: Bucher Printing
3425 Garianne Dr (45414-2221)
PHONE 937 890-1878
Randy Keithley, *President*
Sherry Keithley, *Admin Sec*
EMP: 9 EST: 1932
SQ FT: 5,000
SALES: 500K **Privately Held**
SIC: 2752 2759 2679 Commercial printing, offset; letterpress printing; labels, paper: made from purchased material

(G-8291)
KELLEY COMMUNICATION DEV
Also Called: Kelley Bible Books
2312 Candlewood Dr (45419-2825)
P.O. Box 292113 (45429-0113)
PHONE 937 298-6132
Robert Kelley, *Owner*
EMP: 7
SALES (est): 315.7K **Privately Held**
WEB: www.kcdev.com
SIC: 2731 Books: publishing only

(G-8292)
KENDALL & SONS COMPANY
Also Called: Kendall Printing
2800 E 3rd St (45403-2104)
PHONE 937 222-6996
Michael Kendall, *President*
Brian Kendall, *Principal*
Elma Kendall, *Corp Secy*
Susan Kendall, *Vice Pres*
EMP: 5
SQ FT: 3,800
SALES (est): 649.5K **Privately Held**
SIC: 2752 4731 Commercial printing, lithographic; freight transportation arrangement

(G-8293)
KENNEDY INK COMPANY INC
110 Vermont Ave (45404-1522)
PHONE 937 461-5600
James Bishop, *Manager*
EMP: 4
SALES (corp-wide): 2.5MM **Privately Held**
SIC: 2893 5085 Printing ink; ink, printers'
PA: Kennedy Ink Company, Inc.
   5230 Wooster Pike
   Cincinnati OH 45226
   513 871-2515

(G-8294)
KENWORTH OF DAYTON
7740 Center Point 70 Blvd (45424-6367)
PHONE 937 235-2589
Randy Pennington, *Principal*
Russell Jeffers, *Vice Pres*
Jim Buhrlage, *Store Mgr*
EMP: 16
SALES (est): 2.9MM **Privately Held**
SIC: 3519 Internal combustion engines

(G-8295)
KESSLER SIGN COMPANY
5804 Poe Ave (45414-3442)
PHONE 937 898-0633
Robert Kessler, *President*
Nichole Keylor, *Executive Asst*
EMP: 4
SALES (corp-wide): 7.4MM **Privately Held**
WEB: www.kesslersignco.com
SIC: 3993 7312 1799 Signs, not made in custom sign painting shops; outdoor advertising services; sign installation & maintenance
PA: Kessler Sign Company
   2669 National Rd
   Zanesville OH 43701
   740 453-0668

(G-8296)
KILLER BROWNIE LTD
6135 Far Hills Ave (45459-1925)
P.O. Box 751568 (45475-1568)
PHONE 937 535-5690
Norman C Mayne, *President*
EMP: 15
SALES (est): 1.4MM **Privately Held**
SIC: 2051 Bakery: wholesale or wholesale/retail combined

(G-8297)
KIMMATT CORP
Also Called: Best Glass
326 Troy St (45404-1856)
PHONE 937 228-3811
Susan Ballweg, *President*
Matthew Ballweg, *Vice Pres*
Larry Ballweg, *Treasurer*
EMP: 8
SQ FT: 5,000
SALES (est): 1MM **Privately Held**
SIC: 1793 3496 3231 Glass & glazing work; screening, woven wire: made from purchased wire; strengthened or reinforced glass; mirrored glass

(G-8298)
KISTLER INSTRUMENT CORP
3061 Dorf Dr (45439-7902)
PHONE 937 268-5920
Bob Hendricks, *Principal*
EMP: 3
SALES (est): 155.3K **Privately Held**
SIC: 1446 Molding sand mining

(G-8299)
KOLHFAB CSTM PLSTIC FBRICATION
2025 Webster St (45404-1143)
PHONE 937 237-2098
Bernie Kohlbarg, *CEO*
EMP: 6
SALES: 600K **Privately Held**
SIC: 2399 Emblems, badges & insignia

(G-8300)
KOMATEC TOOL & DIE INC
1415 E 2nd St (45403-1022)
PHONE 937 252-1133
Donald Koman, *President*
Kevin Stewart, *Admin Sec*
EMP: 4
SQ FT: 3,000
SALES: 250K **Privately Held**
SIC: 3599 Machine shop, jobbing & repair

(G-8301)
KRDC INC
Also Called: Martin-Palmer TI & Die Co Div
90 Vermont Ave (45404-1521)
PHONE 937 222-2332
Richie Blevins, *President*
Rick Syx, *Vice Pres*
EMP: 8
SQ FT: 12,500
SALES: 700K **Privately Held**
SIC: 3599 3544 Machine & other job shop work; special dies, tools, jigs & fixtures

(G-8302)
KROGER CO
1934 Needmore Rd (45414-3808)
PHONE 937 277-0950
Pete Gerger, *Manager*
EMP: 150
SALES (corp-wide): 121.1B **Publicly Held**
WEB: www.kroger.com
SIC: 5411 5992 5912 2052 Supermarkets, chain; florists; drug stores & proprietary stores; cookies & crackers; bread, cake & related products
PA: The Kroger Co
   1014 Vine St Ste 1000
   Cincinnati OH 45202
   513 762-4000

(G-8303)
KUSTOM CASES LLC
130 Oxford Ave (45402-6149)
PHONE 240 380-6275
Mike Smith, *CEO*
EMP: 4
SALES (est): 192.8K **Privately Held**
SIC: 2051 7389 Bakery: wholesale or wholesale/retail combined;

(G-8304)
LAB-PRO INC
11019 Cold Spring Dr (45458-4518)
PHONE 937 434-9600
Joseph Jobe, *President*
EMP: 9
SALES: 8MM **Privately Held**
SIC: 3448 5039 Prefabricated metal buildings; prefabricated buildings

(G-8305)
LAHM-TROSPER INC
Also Called: Lahm Tool
1030 Springfield St (45403-1350)
P.O. Box 336 (45401-0336)
PHONE 937 252-8791
James Trosper, *President*
EMP: 17
SQ FT: 10,000
SALES (est): 4.1MM **Privately Held**
SIC: 3541 3544 Machine tools, metal cutting type; special dies, tools, jigs & fixtures

(G-8306)
LASERMARK LLC
530 N Union Rd (45417-7615)
PHONE 513 312-9889
Charles Mark, *Agent*
Sherman McGill,
Ron Norton,
EMP: 3
SALES (est): 140.8K **Privately Held**
SIC: 5092 5734 3949 Video games; software, computer games; pigeons, clay (targets)

(G-8307)
LAVISH LYFE MAGAZINE
19 Colgate Ave (45417-8944)
PHONE 937 938-5816
Ryan Pope, *Principal*
EMP: 3
SALES (est): 167.4K **Privately Held**
SIC: 2721 Periodicals

(G-8308)
LAWRENCE TECHNOLOGIES INC
2571 Timber Ln (45414-4731)
PHONE 937 274-7771
Lawrence J Richards, *President*
Linda Heider, *Vice Pres*
▲ EMP: 8
SQ FT: 5,000
SALES (est): 1.5MM **Privately Held**
WEB: www.lawrencetechnologies.com
SIC: 3714 3728 3569 8711 Motor vehicle parts & accessories; aircraft parts & equipment; filters; professional engineer

(G-8309)
LEGRAND NORTH AMERICA LLC
Also Called: C2g
6500 Poe Ave (45414-2527)
PHONE 937 224-0639
Joe Cornwall, *Area Mgr*
Andrea McDermott, *Project Mgr*
April Mick, *Buyer*
Michael Leach, *Natl Sales Mgr*
Chad Studebaker, *Sales Mgr*
EMP: 420
SALES (corp-wide): 20.7MM **Privately Held**
SIC: 1731 5063 5045 3643 Communications specialization; cable conduit; computer peripheral equipment; current-carrying wiring devices; nonferrous wiredrawing & insulating
HQ: Legrand North America, Llc
   60 Woodlawn St
   West Hartford CT 06110
   860 233-6251

(G-8310)
LENCO INDUSTRIES INC
3301 Klepinger Rd (45406-1823)
PHONE 937 277-9364
John L Lenz, *President*
Robert Wagner, *Vice Pres*
EMP: 50 EST: 1955
SQ FT: 15,000
SALES (est): 4.9MM **Privately Held**
WEB: www.lenzinc.com
SIC: 3451 Screw machine products

(G-8311)
LENZ INC
Also Called: Lenz Company
3301 Klepinger Rd (45406-1823)
P.O. Box 1044 (45401-1044)
PHONE 937 277-9364
Robert Wagner, *President*
Grace Campbell, *Human Resources*

▲ = Import ▼=Export
◆ =Import/Export

Rick Brown, *Sales Staff*
Ken Whitson, *Sales Staff*
EMP: 50
SQ FT: 15,000
SALES (est): 6.5MM **Privately Held**
WEB: www.thelenz.com
SIC: 6531 3089 Real estate brokers & agents; fittings for pipe, plastic

(G-8312)
LEWARK METAL SPINNING INC
2746 Keenan Ave (45414-4912)
PHONE.............................937 275-3303
Larry W Lewark, *President*
Pete Hagenbuch, *President*
Gordon Vance, *Materials Mgr*
Esther Lewark, *Admin Asst*
Nancy Milstead, *Admin Asst*
EMP: 50
SQ FT: 35,000
SALES (est): 15MM **Privately Held**
WEB: www.lewarkmetalspinning.com
SIC: 3499 3469 Friction material, made from powdered metal; spinning metal for the trade

(G-8313)
LION APPAREL INC (DH)
7200 Poe Ave Ste 400 (45414-2798)
PHONE.............................937 898-1949
Steve Schwartz, *CEO*
Jeremy Blackburn, *General Mgr*
Mark Berliant, *Principal*
Mark Jahnke, *Principal*
Theodore Schwartz, *Principal*
◆ **EMP:** 150 **EST:** 1930
SQ FT: 37,000
SALES (est): 239.8MM **Privately Held**
WEB: www.lionprotectivesystems.com
SIC: 2311 Firemen's uniforms: made from purchased materials; military uniforms, men's & youths': purchased materials; policemen's uniforms: made from purchased materials
HQ: Lion Group, Inc.
7200 Poe Ave Ste 400
Dayton OH 45414
937 898-1949

(G-8314)
LITEFLEX LLC
3600 Maywood Ave (45417)
PHONE.............................937 836-7025
John Prikkel,
EMP: 10
SALES (corp-wide): 16.9MM **Privately Held**
SIC: 3493 Leaf springs: automobile, locomotive, etc.
PA: Liteflex Llc
100 Holiday Dr
Englewood OH 45322
937 836-7025

(G-8315)
LORD CORPORATION
Mechanical Products Division
4644 Wadsworth Rd (45414-4220)
PHONE.............................937 278-9431
Janet Eastep, *Manager*
EMP: 150
SQ FT: 30,000
SALES (corp-wide): 1B **Privately Held**
WEB: www.lordcorp.com
SIC: 3545 3769 Machine tool accessories; guided missile & space vehicle parts & auxiliary equipment
PA: Lord Corporation
111 Lord Dr
Cary NC 27511
919 468-5979

(G-8316)
LORENZ CORPORATION (PA)
Also Called: Show What You Know
501 E 3rd St (45402-2280)
P.O. Box 802 (45401-0802)
PHONE.............................937 228-6118
Reiff Lorenz, *Ch of Bd*
Tom Borchers, *Corp Secy*
▲ **EMP:** 78 **EST:** 1890
SQ FT: 55,000

SALES (est): 11.6MM **Privately Held**
WEB: www.lorenz.com
SIC: 2759 5049 2721 2741 Music sheet: printing; school supplies; periodicals: publishing only; music, sheet: publishing only, not printed on site

(G-8317)
M & R ELECTRIC MOTOR SVC INC
1516 E 5th St (45403-2397)
PHONE.............................937 222-6282
Charles Mader, *Corp Secy*
Ronald Mader, *Vice Pres*
Anthony Mader, *Vice Pres*
Craig Mader, *Treasurer*
EMP: 28 **EST:** 1949
SQ FT: 8,000
SALES: 4MM **Privately Held**
SIC: 5063 7694 Motors, electric; electric motor repair

(G-8318)
M J COATES CONSTRUCTION CO (PA)
Also Called: Mj Coates Homes
9809 Saddle Creek Trl (45458-9729)
P.O. Box 41231 (45441-0231)
PHONE.............................937 886-9546
Marty Coates, *President*
Toni Coates, *Admin Sec*
EMP: 3
SQ FT: 2,000
SALES: 4.5MM **Privately Held**
SIC: 1522 1442 Residential construction; gravel mining

(G-8319)
M21 INDUSTRIES LLC
Also Called: Module 21 Bldg Company
721 Springfield St (45403-1250)
P.O. Box 4044 (45401-4044)
PHONE.............................937 781-1377
Jeffrey Levine, *CEO*
Wolfgang Dalichau, *President*
David Allen, *Vice Pres*
Rusty Brown, *Vice Pres*
Don Carter, *Vice Pres*
EMP: 90
SQ FT: 230,000
SALES (est): 10.8MM **Privately Held**
WEB: www.m21industries.com
SIC: 2541 2431 Office fixtures, wood; windows, wood

(G-8320)
MACHINE PRODUCTS COMPANY
5660 Webster St (45414-3596)
PHONE.............................937 890-6600
Robert C Appenzeller, *President*
Rebecca A Cain, *Corp Secy*
David Mansfield, *Purchasing*
Jeff Hutchins, *Engineer*
Bob Neiswander, *Engineer*
EMP: 35 **EST:** 1956
SQ FT: 40,000
SALES (est): 5.6MM **Privately Held**
WEB: www.mpcdayton.com
SIC: 3599 3825 3694 Machine shop, jobbing & repair; instruments to measure electricity; engine electrical equipment

(G-8321)
MACHINEX OF DAYTON INC
2121 Old Vienna Dr (45459-1338)
PHONE.............................937 252-7021
William Brownsberger, *President*
Janet M Brownsberger, *Treasurer*
EMP: 4
SQ FT: 10,000
SALES: 125.1K **Privately Held**
SIC: 3599 Machine shop, jobbing & repair

(G-8322)
MADSEN WIRE PRODUCTS INC
101 Madison St (45402-1711)
P.O. Box 98, Orland IN (46776-0098)
PHONE.............................937 829-6561
Gary Stephens, *President*
▲ **EMP:** 50
SALES (est): 3.1MM **Privately Held**
SIC: 3315 Wire & fabricated wire products

(G-8323)
MAGNUM TOOL CORP
1407 Stanley Ave (45404-1110)
PHONE.............................937 228-0900
Christopher S Grooms, *President*
Gregory S Grooms, *Corp Secy*
◆ **EMP:** 8
SQ FT: 6,000
SALES: 720K **Privately Held**
SIC: 3544 Special dies & tools; jigs & fixtures; industrial molds

(G-8324)
MAHLE BEHR DAYTON LLC
1720 Webster St (45404-1128)
PHONE.............................937 369-2900
Rob Baker, *Branch Mgr*
EMP: 350
SALES (corp-wide): 336.4K **Privately Held**
SIC: 3714 Air conditioner parts, motor vehicle
HQ: Mahle Behr Dayton L.L.C.
1600 Webster St
Dayton OH 45404
937 369-2900

(G-8325)
MAHLE BEHR DAYTON LLC (DH)
1600 Webster St (45404-1144)
PHONE.............................937 369-2900
Willm Uhlenbecker, *CEO*
Ing Heinz K Junker, *Ch of Bd*
Wolf Hennig Scheider, *President*
Bruce Moorehouse, *Vice Pres*
Christopher Arkwright, *CFO*
◆ **EMP:** 93
SALES (est): 272.4MM
SALES (corp-wide): 336.4K **Privately Held**
SIC: 3714 Motor vehicle parts & accessories
HQ: Mahle Behr Gmbh & Co. Kg
Mauserstr. 3
Stuttgart
711 501-0

(G-8326)
MAHLE BEHR USA INC
1600 Webster St (45404-1144)
PHONE.............................937 369-2900
Joe Stewart, *Branch Mgr*
EMP: 9
SALES (corp-wide): 336.4K **Privately Held**
SIC: 3714 Motor vehicle parts & accessories
HQ: Mahle Behr Usa Inc.
2700 Daley Dr
Troy MI 48083
248 743-3700

(G-8327)
MAHLE BEHR USA INC
Also Called: Behr Dayton Thermal Products
1600 Webster St (45404-1144)
PHONE.............................937 369-2000
Wilhelm Baum, *Principal*
EMP: 2000
SALES (corp-wide): 336.4K **Privately Held**
SIC: 3443 3585 Heat exchangers, condensers & components; refrigeration & heating equipment
HQ: Mahle Behr Usa Inc.
2700 Daley Dr
Troy MI 48083
248 743-3700

(G-8328)
MAHLE INDUSTRIES INCORPORATED
Also Called: Delphi-T - Vandalia Ptc
1600 Webster St (45404-1144)
PHONE.............................937 890-2739
Samuel Cicatello, *Branch Mgr*
EMP: 30
SALES (corp-wide): 336.4K **Privately Held**
SIC: 3714 Motor vehicle parts & accessories
HQ: Mahle Industries, Incorporated
23030 Mahle Dr
Farmington Hills MI 48335
248 305-8200

(G-8329)
MANCOR OHIO INC (HQ)
1008 Leonhard St (45404-1666)
PHONE.............................937 228-6141
Art Church, *Ch of Bd*
Dale Harper, *President*
EMP: 50
SALES (est): 53.7MM
SALES (corp-wide): 156.6MM **Privately Held**
SIC: 3713 Truck bodies & parts
PA: Mancor Canada Inc
2485 Speers Rd
Oakville ON L6L 2
905 827-3737

(G-8330)
MANCOR OHIO INC
600 Kiser St (45404-1644)
PHONE.............................937 228-6141
George McNight, *General Mgr*
EMP: 55
SALES (corp-wide): 156.6MM **Privately Held**
SIC: 3713 Truck bodies & parts
HQ: Mancor Ohio Inc.
1008 Leonhard St
Dayton OH 45404

(G-8331)
MAR-VEL TOOL CO INC
858 Hall Ave (45404-1142)
PHONE.............................937 223-2137
John G Glaser, *President*
Brett R Glaser, *Vice Pres*
EMP: 25
SQ FT: 23,000
SALES (est): 2.7MM **Privately Held**
SIC: 3544 Special dies & tools; jigs & fixtures

(G-8332)
MARCO PRINTED PRODUCTS CO
Also Called: Marco's Papers
25 W Whipp Rd (45459-1811)
PHONE.............................937 433-7030
Gary Ihle, *President*
Margaret Ihle, *Treasurer*
Karen Ihle, *Manager*
David Ihle, *Admin Sec*
EMP: 20
SQ FT: 7,000
SALES (est): 1.9MM **Privately Held**
WEB: www.marcopaper.com
SIC: 2752 Commercial printing, offset

(G-8333)
MARCO PRINTED PRODUCTS CO INC (PA)
Also Called: Marco's Paper
14 Marco Ln (45458-3857)
PHONE.............................937 433-5680
R Gary Ihle, *President*
Margaret Ihle, *Treasurer*
David Ihle, *Admin Sec*
EMP: 5 **EST:** 1971
SQ FT: 3,200
SALES (est): 2.3MM **Privately Held**
SIC: 7331 2752 5111 Mailing service; commercial printing, offset; printing paper

(G-8334)
MAXTOOL COMPANY LIMITED
2946 Production Ct (45414-3537)
PHONE.............................937 415-5776
Mack Hufford, *President*
Chris Harlamert,
Herbert McClellan Hufford II,
EMP: 4
SQ FT: 1,000
SALES (est): 440K **Privately Held**
SIC: 3544 Special dies, tools, jigs & fixtures

(G-8335)
MCO SOLUTIONS INC
8820 Sugarcreek Pt (45458-2832)
PHONE.............................937 205-9512
Nympha Clark, *President*
EMP: 2
SALES: 2MM **Privately Held**
SIC: 3812 Defense systems & equipment

Dayton - Montgomery County (G-8336)

(G-8336)
MDF ENTERPRISES LLC
Also Called: Universal Tool Technology
821 Hall Ave (45404-1101)
PHONE..................937 640-3436
Marjorie Farmer, *CFO*
EMP: 5
SALES (est): 547.2K **Privately Held**
SIC: 3544 Special dies & tools

(G-8337)
MEASUREMENT SPECIALTIES INC
10522 Success Ln (45458-3561)
PHONE..................937 885-0800
Mike Campbell, *President*
Mitzi Keltz, *Vice Pres*
Sean Quinn, *Vice Pres*
Catherine Campbell, *Admin Sec*
EMP: 15
SQ FT: 13,500
SALES (est): 1.7MM **Privately Held**
SIC: 7699 8734 3559 Industrial machinery & equipment repair; calibration & certification; screening equipment, electric

(G-8338)
MEDICAL DEVICE BUS SVCS INC
2747 Armstrong Ln (45414-4225)
PHONE..................937 274-5850
David Smith, *Branch Mgr*
EMP: 28
SALES (corp-wide): 81.5B **Publicly Held**
SIC: 3842 Orthopedic appliances
HQ: Medical Device Business Services, Inc.
700 Orthopaedic Dr
Warsaw IN 46582

(G-8339)
MELS LIFE LIKE HAIR
Also Called: Mel's Lifelike Hair
6140 N Main St (45415-3174)
PHONE..................937 278-9486
Melvin P Garber, *Partner*
EMP: 3
SQ FT: 1,589
SALES (est): 181.5K **Privately Held**
SIC: 3999 7241 Hair & hair-based products; barber shop selling wigs; hair stylist, men

(G-8340)
MERIT MOLD & TOOL PRODUCTS
4648 Gateway Cir (45440-1714)
PHONE..................937 435-0932
James Reynolds, *President*
EMP: 8 EST: 1979
SQ FT: 10,000
SALES (est): 696.5K **Privately Held**
SIC: 3599 Machine shop, jobbing & repair

(G-8341)
MERRICK MANUFACTURING II LLC
836 Hall Ave (45404-1101)
PHONE..................937 222-7164
Stephen Smith, *Mng Member*
EMP: 4
SQ FT: 8,000
SALES: 500K **Privately Held**
SIC: 5087 3465 3469 Firefighting equipment; automotive stampings; metal stampings

(G-8342)
METAL BRITE POLISHING
2445 Neff Rd Unit 4 (45414-5067)
PHONE..................937 278-9739
Michael Barr, *Owner*
EMP: 12
SALES (est): 113.1K **Privately Held**
SIC: 3471 Plating of metals or formed products

(G-8343)
METOKOTE CORPORATION
8040 Center Point 70 Blvd (45424-6373)
PHONE..................937 235-2811
Frank Zack, *Branch Mgr*
EMP: 104
SALES (corp-wide): 15.3B **Publicly Held**
WEB: www.metokote.com
SIC: 3479 Coating of metals & formed products
HQ: Metokote Corporation
1340 Neubrecht Rd
Lima OH 45801
419 996-7800

(G-8344)
MEYERS PRINTING & DESIGN INC
254 Leo St (45404-1006)
PHONE..................937 461-6000
Gregory Meyers, *President*
EMP: 8 EST: 1999
SALES (est): 750K **Privately Held**
WEB: www.mpdink.com
SIC: 2759 Commercial printing

(G-8345)
MIAMI STEEL FABRICATORS INC
1525 Manchester Rd (45449-1933)
PHONE..................937 299-5550
Eugene Crase, *President*
Kevin Mc Coy, *Corp Secy*
EMP: 5
SQ FT: 1,800
SALES (est): 470K **Privately Held**
SIC: 3441 Structural Metal Fabrication

(G-8346)
MIAMI VALLEY GASKET CO INC
Also Called: Focke Rubber Products Div
1222 E 3rd St (45402-2255)
PHONE..................937 228-0781
Robin Cunningham, *President*
Jim Focke, *Vice Pres*
Elaine Cunningham, *Manager*
EMP: 25 EST: 1948
SQ FT: 29,000
SALES (est): 5MM **Privately Held**
WEB: www.miamivalleygasket.com
SIC: 3053 Gaskets, all materials

(G-8347)
MIAMI VALLEY PUNCH & MFG
3425 Successful Way (45414-4319)
PHONE..................937 237-0533
Kamlesh Trivedi, *President*
Sangita Trivedi, *Treasurer*
EMP: 20
SQ FT: 21,000
SALES (est): 3.8MM **Privately Held**
SIC: 3544 7699 Punches, forming & stamping; industrial equipment services

(G-8348)
MIAMI VLY PACKG SOLUTIONS INC
1752 Stanley Ave (45404-1117)
P.O. Box 296 (45404-0296)
PHONE..................937 224-1800
James Williams, *President*
Donald Chmiel, *Vice Pres*
Kenneth Phegley, *Vice Pres*
▲ EMP: 19
SQ FT: 6,000
SALES: 2.5MM **Privately Held**
SIC: 2653 Boxes, corrugated: made from purchased materials

(G-8349)
MICRO SYSTEMS DEVELOPMENT INC
419 E 6th St (45402-2927)
PHONE..................937 438-3567
EMP: 5
SQ FT: 1,250
SALES (est): 694.6K **Privately Held**
SIC: 3829 Manufacturer Of Measuring And Controlling Devices

(G-8350)
MICROCVD CORPORATION
10150 Meadow Woods Ln (45458-9712)
PHONE..................937 573-8984
Zhigang Xiao, *CEO*
Rebecca Steward, *CFO*
EMP: 3 EST: 2016
SALES: 468.6K **Privately Held**
SIC: 3559 Semiconductor manufacturing machinery

(G-8351)
MICROSUN LAMPS LLC
7890 Center Point 70 Blvd (45424-6369)
PHONE..................888 328-8701
Bob Conner, *CEO*
Greg Profitt, *Opers Mgr*
▲ EMP: 4
SALES (est): 194.6K **Privately Held**
SIC: 5719 3645 Lighting, lamps & accessories; desk lamps

(G-8352)
MIDWEST EXPOSURE MAGAZINE
1509 S Smithville Rd (45410-3243)
PHONE..................937 626-6738
Clois E Williams, *Owner*
◆ EMP: 3
SALES (est): 103.1K **Privately Held**
SIC: 2721 7389 Publishing & Printing Magazines

(G-8353)
MIDWEST IRON AND METAL CO
461 Homestead Ave (45417-3921)
P.O. Box 546 (45401-0546)
PHONE..................937 222-5992
Joel Frydman, *CEO*
Farley Frydman, *President*
Bert Appel, *Principal*
Judy Griffith, *Principal*
Miriam Jacobs, *Principal*
EMP: 65
SQ FT: 150,000
SALES (est): 18.5MM **Privately Held**
SIC: 3341 5093 Secondary nonferrous metals; scrap & waste materials

(G-8354)
MIDWEST SECURITY SERVICES
4050 Benfield Dr (45429-4651)
PHONE..................937 853-9000
Terry Rogers, *President*
Jeremy Filia, *Vice Pres*
EMP: 9
SALES (est): 1.3MM **Privately Held**
SIC: 3699 Security control equipment & systems

(G-8355)
MIDWEST SPRAY BOOTHS
7672 Mcewen Rd (45459-3908)
PHONE..................937 439-6600
Michael Fondy, *Owner*
EMP: 3
SALES (est): 339.9K **Privately Held**
SIC: 5013 3444 Body repair or paint shop supplies, automotive; booths, spray: prefabricated sheet metal

(G-8356)
MIDWEST TOOL & ENGINEERING CO
112 Webster St (45402-1388)
PHONE..................937 224-0756
JB McCarthy, *President*
Robert Cammerer, *President*
Dr Richard Cammerer, *Corp Secy*
EMP: 20 EST: 1920
SQ FT: 27,750
SALES (est): 3.7MM **Privately Held**
WEB: www.themidwesttool.com
SIC: 3544 3594 3545 Special dies & tools; jigs & fixtures; fluid power pumps & motors; machine tool accessories

(G-8357)
MIKE-SELLS POTATO CHIP CO (HQ)
333 Leo St (45404-1080)
P.O. Box 115 (45404-0115)
PHONE..................937 228-9400
D W Mikesell, *Principal*
Martha J Mikesell, *Principal*
Frank De Moss, *Mfg Staff*
Jennifer Terrell, *Purch Mgr*
Deanna Lewis, *Accountant*
EMP: 30
SQ FT: 95,000
SALES (est): 64MM
SALES (corp-wide): 65.7MM **Privately Held**
SIC: 2096 5145 Potato chips & other potato-based snacks; snack foods; pretzels; corn chips
PA: Mike-Sell's West Virginia, Inc.
333 Leo St
Dayton OH 45404
937 228-9400

(G-8358)
MIKES AUTOMOTIVE LLC
7581 Brandt Pike Unit B (45424-2337)
PHONE..................937 233-1433
Mike Leonard, *Mng Member*
EMP: 5
SQ FT: 45,000
SALES: 290K **Privately Held**
SIC: 7692 7539 Welding repair; automotive repair shops

(G-8359)
MILJA INC
Also Called: Serva Tool
1254 Stanley Ave (45404-1014)
PHONE..................937 223-1988
Kris Jackson, *President*
Randy Stites, *Foreman/Supr*
▲ EMP: 4
SQ FT: 5,000
SALES (est): 577.1K **Privately Held**
WEB: www.servatool.com
SIC: 3599 Machine shop, jobbing & repair

(G-8360)
MILLAT INDUSTRIES CORP (PA)
4901 Croftshire Dr (45440-1721)
P.O. Box 931188, Cleveland (44193-1449)
PHONE..................937 434-6666
Greg Millat, *President*
Robert Millat, *Chairman*
Keith Isaacs, *Manager*
Samuel Lawson, *IT/INT Sup*
▲ EMP: 100
SQ FT: 99,000
SALES: 56.5MM **Privately Held**
WEB: www.millatindustries.com
SIC: 3769 3599 3714 Guided missile & space vehicle parts & auxiliary equipment; machine shop, jobbing & repair; motor vehicle parts & accessories

(G-8361)
MILLAT INDUSTRIES CORP
7611 Center Pt I 70 Blvd (45424)
PHONE..................937 535-1500
Yogi Singhal, *Principal*
EMP: 32
SALES (corp-wide): 56.5MM **Privately Held**
SIC: 3714 Motor vehicle parts & accessories
PA: Millat Industries, Corp.
4901 Croftshire Dr
Dayton OH 45440
937 434-6666

(G-8362)
MILLER INDUSTRIES INC
139 Auto Club Dr (45402-2501)
PHONE..................937 293-2223
Douglas Thoma, *Branch Mgr*
EMP: 5
SALES (corp-wide): 615.1MM **Publicly Held**
WEB: www.swansenauctions.com
SIC: 3713 Automobile wrecker truck bodies
PA: Miller Industries, Inc.
8503 Hilltop Dr
Ooltewah TN 37363
423 238-4171

(G-8363)
MISUMI INVESTMENT USA CORP (HQ)
500 Progress Rd (45449-2326)
PHONE..................937 859-5111
Ryusei Ono, *President*
Sawato Hayashi, *Admin Sec*
EMP: 2
SALES: 106.2MM
SALES (corp-wide): 2.9B **Privately Held**
SIC: 6719 3544 Investment holding companies, except banks; die sets for metal stamping (presses)
PA: Misumi Group Inc.
2-5-1, Koraku
Bunkyo-Ku TKY 112-0
358 057-050

Dayton - Montgomery County (G-8390)

(G-8364)
MOLD CRAFTERS INC
1531 Keystone Ave (45403-3335)
PHONE..................937 426-3179
Tony E Carver, *President*
Ann L Carver, *Vice Pres*
EMP: 3
SALES: 372.5K **Privately Held**
SIC: 3544 Industrial molds

(G-8365)
MONAGHAN & ASSOCIATES INC
Also Called: Monaghan Tooling Group
30 N Clinton St (45402-1327)
PHONE..................937 253-7706
Scott Monaghan, *President*
Kelly Burns, *Engineer*
Mike Galloway, *Engineer*
Ken Macdonald, *Engineer*
Paul Hiltenbeitel, *Natl Sales Mgr*
EMP: 20
SALES (est): 4MM **Privately Held**
WEB: www.monaghaninc.com
SIC: 3545 5084 3541 Cutting tools for machine tools; industrial machinery & equipment; machine tools, metal cutting type

(G-8366)
MONCO ENTERPRISES INC (PA)
700 Liberty Ln (45449-2135)
PHONE..................937 461-0034
Phil Hartje, *General Mgr*
Dee Ann Yohe, *Vice Pres*
Alisha Hayes, *Manager*
Sarah Miller, *Manager*
Elvia Thomas, *Director*
EMP: 700
SQ FT: 50,000
SALES: 38.6K **Privately Held**
SIC: 8331 2789 Sheltered workshop; community service employment training program; bookbinding & related work

(G-8367)
MORNING PRIDE MFG LLC (HQ)
Also Called: Honeywell First Responder Pdts
1 Innovation Ct (45414-3967)
PHONE..................937 264-2662
William L Grilliot, *President*
Gary Mc Evoy, *Sls & Mktg Exec*
Mary I Grilliot,
▲ **EMP:** 521
SQ FT: 56,000
SALES (est): 272.8MM
SALES (corp-wide): 41.8B **Publicly Held**
WEB: www.morningpride.com
SIC: 3842 2326 Respirators; men's & boys' work clothing
PA: Honeywell International Inc.
115 Tabor Rd
Morris Plains NJ 07950
973 455-2000

(G-8368)
MORNING PRIDE MFG LLC
4978 Riverton Dr (45414-3964)
PHONE..................937 264-1726
Patrick Walls, *Supervisor*
EMP: 3
SALES (corp-wide): 41.8B **Publicly Held**
SIC: 3842 Respirators
HQ: Morning Pride Mfg Llc
1 Innovation Ct
Dayton OH 45414
937 264-2662

(G-8369)
MOSHER MACHINE & TOOL CO INC
1420 Springfield St (45403-1497)
PHONE..................937 258-8070
Kevin Mosher, *President*
Michael Mosher, *Vice Pres*
EMP: 25
SQ FT: 13,000
SALES (est): 4.6MM **Privately Held**
WEB: www.moshermachine.com
SIC: 3451 3599 Screw machine products; machine shop, jobbing & repair

(G-8370)
MOUND MANUFACTURING CENTER INC
33 Commerce Park Dr (45404-1211)
PHONE..................937 236-8387
Albert J Hodapp III, *President*
Steve Priser, *Vice Pres*
EMP: 12
SQ FT: 9,000
SALES (est): 1.6MM **Privately Held**
SIC: 8711 3599 Machine tool design; machine shop, jobbing & repair

(G-8371)
MRS ELECTRONIC INC
2149 Winners Cir (45404-1176)
PHONE..................937 660-6767
Franz Hoffmann, *CEO*
Guenther Doergeloh, *COO*
EMP: 12
SQ FT: 3,000
SALES (est): 222.3K **Privately Held**
SIC: 3714 Motor vehicle electrical equipment

(G-8372)
MULLINS RUBBER PRODUCTS INC
2949 Valley Pike (45404-2693)
P.O. Box 24830 (45424-0830)
PHONE..................937 233-4211
William D Mullins, *Principal*
Dennis Mullins, *Vice Pres*
William R Mullins Jr, *Vice Pres*
EMP: 52 **EST:** 1939
SQ FT: 75,000
SALES (est): 8.7MM **Privately Held**
WEB: www.mullinsrubber.com
SIC: 3069 Molded rubber products

(G-8373)
MV INNOVATIVE TECHNOLOGIES LLC
Also Called: Optonicus
711 E Monu Ave Ste 102 (45402)
PHONE..................301 661-0951
Rob Markovich, *CEO*
Mikhail Vorontsov, *CTO*
Jill Schalm,
EMP: 5
SALES (est): 709.4K **Privately Held**
SIC: 3699 Electrical equipment & supplies

(G-8374)
MY LADY MUFFINS LLC
2475 N Snyder Rd (45426-4429)
PHONE..................937 854-5317
EMP: 3
SQ FT: 350
SALES (est): 229.2K **Privately Held**
SIC: 2051 Mfg Bread/Related Products

(G-8375)
NAOMI KIGHT
Also Called: Kight Creations
132 Marson Dr (45405-2921)
PHONE..................937 278-0040
Naomi Kight, *Owner*
EMP: 3 **EST:** 2000
SALES (est): 46.5K **Privately Held**
SIC: 2732 Book printing

(G-8376)
NATIONAL OILWELL VARCO INC
Also Called: Chemineer
5870 Poe Ave (45414-3442)
PHONE..................978 687-0101
Daniel Margolien, *General Mgr*
Steve Canaley, *Manager*
EMP: 35
SALES (corp-wide): 8.4B **Publicly Held**
WEB: www.chemineer.com
SIC: 3569 3531 Liquid automation machinery & equipment; construction machinery
PA: National Oilwell Varco, Inc.
7909 Parkwood Circle Dr
Houston TX 77036
713 346-7500

(G-8377)
NATIONAL OILWELL VARCO LP
Also Called: Chemineer
5870 Poe Ave (45414-3442)
P.O. Box 1123 (45401-1123)
PHONE..................937 454-3200
EMP: 62
SALES (corp-wide): 7.3B **Publicly Held**
SIC: 3556 3554 Mfg Food Products Machinery Mfg Paper Industrial Machinery
HQ: National Oilwell Varco, L.P.
7909 Parkwood Circle Dr
Houston TX 77036
713 960-5100

(G-8378)
NATIONAL PALLET & MULCH LLC
3550 Intercity Dr (45424-5124)
PHONE..................937 237-1643
Gary Manson,
EMP: 10
SALES (est): 1.5MM **Privately Held**
SIC: 2499 Mulch or sawdust products, wood

(G-8379)
NDC TECHNOLOGIES INC
8001 Technology Blvd (45424-1568)
PHONE..................937 233-9935
Bromley Beadle, *President*
EMP: 115
SALES (corp-wide): 2B **Privately Held**
SIC: 3826 Analytical instruments
HQ: Ndc Technologies, Inc.
5314 Irwindale Ave
Irwindale CA 91706
626 960-3300

(G-8380)
NEVELS PRECISION MACHINING LLC
2770 Thunderhawk Ct (45414-3464)
PHONE..................937 387-6037
Ted J Nevels, *Mng Member*
EMP: 5
SALES (est): 500K **Privately Held**
SIC: 3599 Machine shop, jobbing & repair

(G-8381)
NOBLE TOOL CORP
1535 Stanley Ave (45404-1112)
PHONE..................937 461-4040
Thomas Biegel, *President*
Nick Rosenkranz, *Vice Pres*
Eddy Moorehouse, *Technical Staff*
EMP: 31
SQ FT: 7,500
SALES (est): 4.9MM **Privately Held**
WEB: www.nobletool.com
SIC: 3544 Special dies & tools

(G-8382)
NON-FERROUS CASTING CO
736 Albany St (45417-3486)
P.O. Box 364 (45409-0364)
PHONE..................937 228-1162
James D Claffey Jr, *Principal*
EMP: 6
SQ FT: 12,000
SALES (est): 1MM **Privately Held**
SIC: 3366 3365 Brass foundry; bronze foundry; masts, cast aluminum

(G-8383)
NORTH-WEST TOOL CO
2725 Kearns Ave (45414-5546)
P.O. Box 13115 (45413-0115)
PHONE..................937 278-7995
John Uhrig Jr, *President*
Joyce Uhrig, *Corp Secy*
EMP: 5
SQ FT: 13,000
SALES: 500K **Privately Held**
SIC: 3545 Cutting tools for machine tools; tool holders

(G-8384)
NORTHMONT SIGN CO INC
8400 N Main St (45415-1322)
PHONE..................937 890-0372
Lee Hodges, *President*
Vicki Walker, *Treasurer*
Judy Hodges, *Admin Sec*
EMP: 5
SQ FT: 5,000
SALES: 500K **Privately Held**
WEB: www.northmontsign.com
SIC: 2796 3993 5099 Engraving platemaking services; signs & advertising specialties; rubber stamps

(G-8385)
NORWOOD MEDICAL
2055 Winners Cir (45404-1182)
PHONE..................937 228-4101
EMP: 6
SALES (est): 118.3K **Privately Held**
SIC: 3469 3599 Metal stampings; air intake filters, internal combustion engine, except auto

(G-8386)
NORWOOD MEDICAL
2101 Winners Cir (45404-1176)
P.O. Box 3806 (45401-3806)
PHONE..................937 228-4101
Ken Hammelgarn, *Manager*
EMP: 125
SALES (corp-wide): 77.3MM **Privately Held**
WEB: www.norwoodtool.com
SIC: 3469 Metal stampings
PA: Norwood Tool Company
2122 Winners Cir
Dayton OH 45404
937 228-4101

(G-8387)
NORWOOD TOOL COMPANY (PA)
Also Called: Norwood Medical
2122 Winners Cir (45404-1148)
P.O. Box 3806 (45401-3806)
PHONE..................937 228-4101
Kenneth Hemmelgarn Sr, *President*
Kenneth J Hemmelgarn Jr, *President*
Brian Hemmelgarn, *Vice Pres*
Gary Smith, *Project Mgr*
Craig Lewis, *Opers Mgr*
EMP: 200
SQ FT: 65,000
SALES (est): 77.3MM **Privately Held**
WEB: www.norwoodtool.com
SIC: 3599 3469 Electromedical apparatus; surgical & medical instruments

(G-8388)
NOVA CREATIVE GROUP INC
7812 Mcewen Rd Ste 300 (45459-4069)
PHONE..................937 291-8653
Daniel Schlegel, *President*
J C King, *Vice Pres*
Larry Knapp, *Vice Pres*
Shannon Lipp, *Project Mgr*
Daniel Foley, *CFO*
EMP: 10
SQ FT: 5,000
SALES (est): 1.1MM **Privately Held**
WEB: www.novacreative.com
SIC: 7336 2752 Commercial Art/Graphic Design Lithographic Commercial Printing

(G-8389)
NTECH INDUSTRIES INC
5475 Kellenburger Rd (45424-1013)
PHONE..................707 467-3747
John Mayfield, *President*
EMP: 18
SQ FT: 1,600
SALES (est): 1.4MM
SALES (corp-wide): 3.1B **Publicly Held**
WEB: www.ntechindustries.com
SIC: 3523 Farm machinery & equipment
PA: Trimble Inc.
935 Stewart Dr
Sunnyvale CA 94085
408 481-8000

(G-8390)
NU STREAM FILTRATION INC
1257 Stanley Ave (45404-1013)
PHONE..................937 949-3174
James Baker, *President*
EMP: 4
SQ FT: 20,000
SALES (est): 198K **Privately Held**
SIC: 3677 Filtration devices, electronic

Dayton - Montgomery County (G-8391)

(G-8391)
NUFAB SHEET METAL
4750 Hempstead Station Dr
PHONE..................937 235-2030
Greg McAfee, *Owner*
Brad Frank, *Manager*
EMP: 3
SQ FT: 3,960
SALES (est): 294.6K **Privately Held**
WEB: www.nufabsheetmetal.com
SIC: 3444 Sheet metal specialties, not stamped

(G-8392)
OAKLEY INC
1421 Springfield St # 2 (45403-1435)
P.O. Box 8302, Mason (45040-5302)
PHONE..................949 672-6560
Sheila Oakley, *Branch Mgr*
EMP: 52
SALES (corp-wide): 283.5MM **Privately Held**
SIC: 3851 Ophthalmic goods
HQ: Oakley, Inc.
  1 Icon
  Foothill Ranch CA 92610
  949 951-0991

(G-8393)
OBERFIELDS LLC
10075 Sheehan Rd (45458-4301)
PHONE..................937 885-3711
Bruce Loris, *President*
EMP: 7
SALES (corp-wide): 1.2MM **Privately Held**
SIC: 3272 Concrete products, precast
HQ: Oberfield's, Llc
  528 London Rd
  Delaware OH 43015
  740 369-7644

(G-8394)
OERLIKON FRICTION SYSTEMS (HQ)
240 Detrick St (45404-1699)
P.O. Box 745 (45401-0745)
PHONE..................937 449-4000
Eric A Schueler, *President*
John Parker, *CFO*
Mark Szporka, *Director*
◆ **EMP:** 131
SQ FT: 115,000
SALES (est): 37.6MM
SALES (corp-wide): 2.6B **Privately Held**
WEB: www.johnston-pump.com
SIC: 3714 Transmission housings or parts, motor vehicle
PA: Oc Oerlikon Corporation Ag, Pfaffikon
  Churerstrasse 120
  PfAffikon SZ 8808
  583 609-696

(G-8395)
OERLIKON FRICTION SYSTEMS
Also Called: Plant 5
240 Detrick St (45404-1699)
PHONE..................937 233-9191
Joe Caffano, *Branch Mgr*
EMP: 20
SALES (corp-wide): 2.6B **Privately Held**
SIC: 3465 Automotive stampings
HQ: Oerlikon Friction Systems (Us) Inc.
  240 Detrick St
  Dayton OH 45404
  937 449-4000

(G-8396)
OHIO DEFENSE SERVICES INC
143 S Monmouth St (45403-2127)
PHONE..................937 608-2371
Michael Davis, *Principal*
EMP: 3
SALES (est): 223.1K **Privately Held**
SIC: 3812 Defense systems & equipment

(G-8397)
OHIO GRAPHIC SUPPLY INC
530 W Whipp Rd (45459-2947)
PHONE..................937 433-7537
Jo Ann Ruja, *President*
EMP: 3
SQ FT: 3,000
SALES (est): 370K **Privately Held**
SIC: 3555 5734 Printing trades machinery; computer tapes

(G-8398)
OHIO METAL FABRICATING INC
6057 Milo Rd (45414-3417)
PHONE..................937 233-2400
Gary Brandeberry, *President*
Leta Brandeberry, *Principal*
Jason Blood, *Plant Mgr*
Todd Back, *Mfg Mgr*
Misty Effler, *Info Tech Mgr*
EMP: 17
SQ FT: 18,000
SALES (est): 1.3MM **Privately Held**
WEB: www.gcmetalspinning.com
SIC: 3599 Machine shop, jobbing & repair

(G-8399)
OHIO METAL PRODUCTS COMPANY
35 Bates St (45402-1395)
PHONE..................937 228-6101
John D Moore, *President*
Janet A Simpson, *Corp Secy*
▲ **EMP:** 30 **EST:** 1909
SQ FT: 32,000
SALES (est): 5.6MM **Privately Held**
WEB: www.ohio-metal.com
SIC: 3451 3471 Screw machine products; plating & polishing

(G-8400)
OHIO TOOL & JIG GRIND INC
5724 Webster St (45414-3521)
PHONE..................937 415-0692
David A Brinker, *President*
Craig Price, *Mfg Mgr*
EMP: 35
SQ FT: 2,000
SALES: 1MM **Privately Held**
SIC: 3544 Special dies, tools, jigs & fixtures

(G-8401)
OLWIN METAL FABRICATION LLC
1933 Kuntz Rd (45404-1222)
PHONE..................937 277-4501
Derick Olwin, *Mng Member*
EMP: 4
SALES (est): 623.2K **Privately Held**
SIC: 3441 Fabricated structural metal

(G-8402)
OMEGA AUTOMATION INC
2850 Needmore Rd (45414-4300)
PHONE..................937 890-2350
Marybeth Krystofik, *President*
Alan King, *Chairman*
EMP: 55
SQ FT: 31,000
SALES (est): 11.9MM **Privately Held**
SIC: 3549 3569 3829 Assembly machines, including robotic; robots, assembly line: industrial & commercial; physical property testing equipment
HQ: Omega International, Inc
  6192 Webster St
  Dayton OH 45414
  937 890-2350

(G-8403)
OMEGA INTERNATIONAL INC (HQ)
6192 Webster St (45414-3436)
PHONE..................937 890-2350
Alan King, *Ch of Bd*
EMP: 50
SQ FT: 30,000
SALES (est): 17.4MM **Privately Held**
SIC: 3829 3599 3549 3569 Physical property testing equipment; machine shop, jobbing & repair; assembly machines, including robotic; robots, assembly line: industrial & commercial

(G-8404)
OMEGA TOOL & DIE INC
Also Called: Omega Tool and Die
2850 Needmore Rd (45414-4302)
PHONE..................937 890-2350
Geo Howdieshell, *President*
EMP: 45 **EST:** 1970
SQ FT: 30,000
SALES (est): 5.4MM **Privately Held**
WEB: www.omega-company.com
SIC: 3599 3544 Machine shop, jobbing & repair; special dies, tools, jigs & fixtures
HQ: Omega International, Inc
  6192 Webster St
  Dayton OH 45414
  937 890-2350

(G-8405)
OPTIMUS LLC (PA)
Also Called: Optimus Prosthetics
8517 N Dixie Dr (45414-2485)
PHONE..................937 454-1900
John Brandt,
Scott R Schall,
EMP: 3
SALES: 180K **Privately Held**
SIC: 3842 Orthopedic appliances

(G-8406)
ORCHEM CORPORATION
15 W 4th St Ste 450 (45402-1817)
PHONE..................513 874-9700
Oscar Robertson, *President*
Shana Robertson-Shaw, *Vice Pres*
Denise Ramey, *Sales Staff*
EMP: 26
SALES (est): 6.6MM **Privately Held**
WEB: www.orfoods.com
SIC: 2842 Specialty cleaning preparations; sanitation preparations

(G-8407)
OREGON VILLAGE PRINT SHOPPE
Also Called: Oregon Printing
29 N June St (45403-1015)
PHONE..................937 222-9418
Judd Plattenburg, *President*
EMP: 15 **EST:** 1974
SQ FT: 5,300
SALES (est): 2.3MM **Privately Held**
WEB: www.oregonprinting.com
SIC: 2752 Commercial printing, offset

(G-8408)
ORTRONICS INC
6500 Poe Ave (45414-2527)
PHONE..................937 224-0639
EMP: 3
SALES (corp-wide): 20.7MM **Privately Held**
SIC: 3678 Electronic connectors
HQ: Ortronics, Inc.
  125 Eugene Oneill Dr # 140
  New London CT 06320
  860 445-3900

(G-8409)
OSCAR HICKS
Also Called: Hobby Printing
9860 Atchison Rd (45458-9206)
PHONE..................937 435-4350
Oscar Hicks, *Owner*
EMP: 3
SALES (est): 124.4K **Privately Held**
SIC: 2752 Commercial printing, lithographic

(G-8410)
OTTER GROUP LLC
Also Called: Yale Industries
2725 Needmore Rd (45414-4207)
PHONE..................937 315-1199
EMP: 18
SALES: 2MM **Privately Held**
SIC: 3448 3442 5031 Mfg Mfg & Dist Windows Doors Awnings Patio Covers & Patio Rooms

(G-8411)
OUTLOOK TOOL INC
360 Fame Rd (45449-2313)
PHONE..................937 235-6330
Eric Staeuble, *President*
Ted Nevels, *Admin Sec*
EMP: 6 **EST:** 1997
SQ FT: 3,200
SALES (est): 605K **Privately Held**
SIC: 3599 Machine shop, jobbing & repair

(G-8412)
OUTTA BOX DISPENSERS LLC
Also Called: Otb
811 E 4th St (45402-2227)
PHONE..................937 221-7106
John Bongiorno, *Vice Pres*
Karen Anthony, *Research*
Michael J Emoff,
Mary J Miller,
EMP: 4
SALES (est): 373.3K **Privately Held**
WEB: www.outtathebox.com
SIC: 3578 Point-of-sale devices

(G-8413)
OVASE MANUFACTURING LLC
Also Called: Global Tool
1990 E Berwyck Ave (45414-5556)
P.O. Box 3, Springboro (45066-0003)
PHONE..................937 275-0617
Joe Kamil,
EMP: 28
SALES (est): 5.1MM **Privately Held**
WEB: www.globaltoolmfg.com
SIC: 3599 Machine shop, jobbing & repair

(G-8414)
P J TOOL COMPANY INC
1115 Springfield St (45403-1420)
PHONE..................937 254-2817
Paul Hedrick, *President*
Jim Fedor, *Corp Secy*
EMP: 6
SQ FT: 2,600
SALES (est): 889.3K **Privately Held**
SIC: 3599 3544 Machine shop, jobbing & repair; special dies, tools, jigs & fixtures

(G-8415)
P3 SECURE LLC
Also Called: 4everready
3535 Salem Ave (45406-2642)
PHONE..................937 610-5500
Felecia Greene, *Principal*
Jared Greene, *Principal*
Addie Keaton Harris, *Principal*
Marion Harris, *Principal*
Richard Harris,
EMP: 25
SALES (est): 1.8MM **Privately Held**
WEB: www.p3securellc.com
SIC: 2032 Canned specialties

(G-8416)
PARTS UNLIMITED
5221 Shiloh Springs Rd (45426-3905)
PHONE..................937 558-1527
Jack Daniel, *Owner*
EMP: 3
SALES: 200K **Privately Held**
SIC: 3599 Machine shop, jobbing & repair

(G-8417)
PAVE TECHNOLOGY CO
2751 Thunderhawk Ct (45414-3451)
PHONE..................937 890-1100
Walter D Wood, *Ch of Bd*
Brad Boomershine, *Vice Pres*
John Holloway, *QC Mgr*
Adam Habig, *Engineer*
Jennifer Young, *Accountant*
EMP: 45
SQ FT: 20,000
SALES (est): 9.1MM **Privately Held**
WEB: www.pavetechnology.com
SIC: 3643 3089 Current-carrying wiring devices; injection molding of plastics

(G-8418)
PAXAR CORPORATION
7801 Technology Blvd (45424-1574)
PHONE..................937 681-4541
Phil Warren, *Manager*
Kevin Parnell, *Technology*
EMP: 11
SALES (corp-wide): 7.1B **Publicly Held**
WEB: www.paxar.com
SIC: 2679 2752 2675 2672 Tags, paper (unprinted): made from purchased paper; commercial printing, lithographic; die-cut paper & board; coated & laminated paper; packaging paper & plastics film, coated & laminated; narrow fabric mills

GEOGRAPHIC SECTION
Dayton - Montgomery County (G-8446)

HQ: Paxar Corporation
8080 Norton Pkwy 22
Mentor OH 44060
845 398-3229

(G-8419)
PDQ TECHNOLOGIES INC
2608 Nordic Rd (45414-3424)
PHONE..................937 274-4958
Robert Adams, *Administration*
EMP: 13
SQ FT: 20,000
SALES (est): 2MM **Privately Held**
SIC: 3469 Machine parts, stamped or pressed metal

(G-8420)
PENTAGEAR PRODUCTS LLC
6161 Webster St (45414-3435)
PHONE..................937 660-8182
Marvin Nicholson,
EMP: 12
SALES (est): 1MM **Privately Held**
SIC: 3566 7389 Speed changers, drives & gears;

(G-8421)
PEPSI-COLA METRO BTLG CO INC
526 Milburn Ave (45404-1678)
PHONE..................937 461-4664
Tim Trant, *General Mgr*
Jon Amrozowicz, *Opers Mgr*
Phillip Beach, *Manager*
Michael Sidenstick, *Manager*
EMP: 300
SQ FT: 115,000
SALES (corp-wide): 64.6B **Publicly Held**
WEB: www.joy-of-cola.com
SIC: 2086 5149 Soft drinks: packaged in cans, bottles, etc.; groceries & related products
HQ: Pepsi-Cola Metropolitan Bottling Company, Inc.
1111 Westchester Ave
White Plains NY 10604
914 767-6000

(G-8422)
PERMA-FIX OF DAYTON INC
300 Cherokee Dr (45417-8113)
PHONE..................937 268-6501
Brad Malatesta, *President*
Richard Kelecy, *Vice Pres*
EMP: 13 **EST:** 1941
SQ FT: 25,000
SALES (est): 5.9MM **Privately Held**
SIC: 4953 2992 Recycling, waste materials; lubricating oils & greases

(G-8423)
PHILLIPS SHTMTL FABRICATIONS
1215 Ray St (45404-1656)
PHONE..................937 223-2722
Robert Holmes, *President*
▲ **EMP:** 5
SQ FT: 6,000
SALES (est): 290K **Privately Held**
SIC: 3444 Sheet metalwork

(G-8424)
PHOENIX METAL WORKS INC
Also Called: Phoenix Metal Fabricators
2528 Ashcraft Rd (45414-3402)
PHONE..................937 274-5555
Carl Abshire, *President*
Randy Abshire, *General Mgr*
EMP: 9
SQ FT: 10,000
SALES (est): 1.2MM **Privately Held**
WEB: www.phoenixdayton.com
SIC: 3441 Fabricated structural metal

(G-8425)
PICKETT ENTERPRISES INC
4643 Knollcroft Rd (45426-1938)
P.O. Box 552 (45405-0552)
PHONE..................937 428-6747
Don E Pickett, *President*
EMP: 7
SQ FT: 25,000
SALES (est): 116.7K **Privately Held**
SIC: 2819 Industrial inorganic chemicals

(G-8426)
PIEDMONT CHEMICAL CO INC
1516 Silver Lake Dr (45458-3529)
PHONE..................937 428-6640
Ed Kren, *Principal*
EMP: 3
SALES (est): 221.3K **Privately Held**
SIC: 3471 Cleaning, polishing & finishing

(G-8427)
PITCO PRODUCTS INC
120 N Terry St (45403-1029)
PHONE..................513 228-7245
Ralph Pippenger, *President*
EMP: 10 **EST:** 1958
SQ FT: 6,000
SALES (est): 1MM **Privately Held**
WEB: www.pitcoproducts.com
SIC: 3728 3544 Aircraft assemblies, sub-assemblies & parts; special dies & tools

(G-8428)
PLATING TECHNOLOGY INC (PA)
1525 W River Rd (45417-6740)
PHONE..................937 268-6882
Jody Pollack Blazar, *Owner*
▲ **EMP:** 70 **EST:** 1953
SQ FT: 190,000
SALES (est): 11.9MM **Privately Held**
WEB: www.platingtech.com
SIC: 3471 3469 Electroplating of metals or formed products; machine parts, stamped or pressed metal

(G-8429)
PLATING TECHNOLOGY INC
1525 W River Rd (45417-6740)
PHONE..................937 268-6788
Dana Hubbard, *Manager*
EMP: 15
SQ FT: 5,265
SALES (corp-wide): 11.9MM **Privately Held**
WEB: www.platingtech.com
SIC: 3471 Plating of metals or formed products
PA: Plating Technology, Inc.
1525 W River Rd
Dayton OH 45417
937 268-6882

(G-8430)
POWER MANAGEMENT INC (PA)
420 Davis Ave (45403-2912)
PHONE..................937 222-2909
Reece Powers, *President*
EMP: 28
SQ FT: 24,000
SALES (est): 2.8MM **Privately Held**
SIC: 6512 6513 2752 7331 Nonresidential building operators; apartment building operators; offset & photolithographic printing; mailing service; management consulting services; commercial nonphysical research

(G-8431)
PRECISION FINISHING SYSTEMS
6101 Webster St (45414-3435)
PHONE..................937 415-5794
Barbara Lipuma, *Owner*
EMP: 14
SALES (est): 2MM **Privately Held**
SIC: 3471 Cleaning, polishing & finishing

(G-8432)
PRECISION GAGE & TOOL COMPANY
375 Gargrave Rd (45449-2465)
PHONE..................937 866-9666
Gwen Waltz, *CEO*
Vicki Waltz, *President*
Leslie Heaton, *Vice Pres*
EMP: 20 **EST:** 1929
SQ FT: 16,000
SALES (est): 4MM **Privately Held**
WEB: www.pgtgage.com
SIC: 3545 7699 Gauges (machine tool accessories); caliper, gauge & other machinists' instrument repair

(G-8433)
PRECISION MANUFACTURING CO INC
2149 Valley Pike (45404-2542)
PHONE..................937 236-2170
Faye Ledwick, *CEO*
Catherine Hanlin, *General Mgr*
Bryan Camp, *Prdtn Mgr*
Ginger Webb, *Prdtn Mgr*
Lois Webb, *Prdtn Mgr*
EMP: 70
SQ FT: 30,000
SALES (est): 12.6MM **Privately Held**
WEB: www.precmfgco.com
SIC: 3679 Electronic circuits

(G-8434)
PRECISION MTAL FABRICATION INC (PA)
191 Heid Ave (45404-1217)
PHONE..................937 235-9261
Jim Hackenberger, *President*
John Limberg, *Corp Secy*
EMP: 52
SQ FT: 30,000
SALES (est): 7MM **Privately Held**
WEB: www.premetfab.com
SIC: 7692 3444 Welding repair; sheet metalwork

(G-8435)
PRECISION PRESSED POWDERED MET
1522 Manchester Rd (45449-1933)
PHONE..................937 433-6802
David Warner, *President*
Stephen G England, *Chairman*
EMP: 14 **EST:** 1983
SQ FT: 7,000
SALES (est): 2.5MM **Privately Held**
SIC: 3469 Machine parts, stamped or pressed metal

(G-8436)
PREMIER PRINTING AND PACKG INC
Also Called: Minuteman Press
90 Compark Rd Ste A (45459-4967)
PHONE..................937 436-5290
Frederic Polizzi, *President*
EMP: 5
SALES (est): 550K **Privately Held**
SIC: 2752 Commercial printing, lithographic

(G-8437)
PREMIERE FARNELL CORP
650 Congress Park Dr (45459-4000)
PHONE..................937 424-1204
Dale Bowman, *Principal*
Jen Patterson, *Pub Rel Mgr*
EMP: 4
SALES (est): 114.7K **Privately Held**
SIC: 3841 Surgical & medical instruments

(G-8438)
PRESTIGE PRINTING
5888 Executive Blvd (45424-1451)
PHONE..................937 236-8468
Jack Schaadt, *Owner*
EMP: 4
SQ FT: 2,440
SALES (est): 400K **Privately Held**
SIC: 2759 Commercial printing

(G-8439)
PRIDE INVESTMENTS LLC
Also Called: American Heat Treating
1346 Morris Ave (45417-3829)
PHONE..................937 461-1121
Lawrence Gray, *Owner*
Mike Gray, *QC Mgr*
Rick Young, *Sales Mgr*
Dale Barham, *Maintence Staff*
EMP: 15
SQ FT: 32,000
SALES (est): 2MM **Privately Held**
SIC: 3398 Metal heat treating

(G-8440)
PRIME CONTROLS INC
4528 Gateway Cir (45440-1712)
PHONE..................937 435-8659
Larry Tucker, *President*
Jim Michaud, *Treasurer*
EMP: 5
SQ FT: 9,000
SALES (est): 1.1MM **Privately Held**
WEB: www.primecontrols.com
SIC: 3625 5084 Relays & industrial controls; instruments & control equipment

(G-8441)
PRIME MANUFACTURING CORP (HQ)
1619 Kuntz Rd (45404-1240)
PHONE..................937 496-3900
Gale Kooken, *President*
Roger Fleming, *Vice Pres*
Jeff Mueller, *Vice Pres*
Christy Fox, *Treasurer*
John Murphy, *Admin Sec*
EMP: 7
SALES (est): 693.4K **Privately Held**
WEB: www.primemfg.com
SIC: 3743 3585 Railroad equipment; refrigeration & heating equipment

(G-8442)
PRIME PRINTING INC (PA)
8929 Kingsridge Dr (45458-1621)
P.O. Box 751591 (45475-1591)
PHONE..................937 438-3707
Gary Smith, *President*
Dan Cornelius, *Vice Pres*
Tim Cox, *Vice Pres*
EMP: 35
SQ FT: 12,000
SALES (est): 4.2MM **Privately Held**
WEB: www.primedigitalprinting.com
SIC: 2752 2796 2791 2789 Commercial printing, offset; platemaking services; typesetting; bookbinding & related work

(G-8443)
PRINTPOINT PRINTING INC
150 S Patterson Blvd (45402-2421)
PHONE..................937 223-9041
Mike Munch, *President*
Kathy Munch, *Manager*
EMP: 7
SQ FT: 13,000
SALES (est): 995.7K **Privately Held**
WEB: www.printpointprinting.com
SIC: 2752 Commercial printing, offset

(G-8444)
PRO LINE COLLISION AND PNT LLC (PA)
Also Called: Proline Finishing
1 Armor Pl (45417-3443)
PHONE..................937 223-7611
Les Butcher, *Sales Mgr*
Ronald E Burns,
Ana Burns,
EMP: 15
SQ FT: 44,000
SALES (est): 3MM **Privately Held**
SIC: 3471 Finishing, metals or formed products

(G-8445)
PROCESS DEVELOPMENT CORP
6060 Milo Rd (45414-3418)
PHONE..................937 890-3388
Cliff Blacke, *President*
EMP: 24
SQ FT: 42,000
SALES (est): 5.7MM **Privately Held**
WEB: www.processdev.com
SIC: 3559 3599 3582 3548 Automotive related machinery; machine & other job shop work; commercial laundry equipment; welding apparatus

(G-8446)
PRODUCTION DESIGN SERVICES INC (PA)
Also Called: Pdsi Technical Services
313 Mound St (45402-8370)
PHONE..................937 866-3377
John H Schultz, *President*
Jeffrey R Schultz, *Vice Pres*
Pat Moore, *Plant Mgr*
Jeff Schultz, *Chief Engr*
James A Schultz, *CFO*
EMP: 80
SQ FT: 48,000

Dayton - Montgomery County (G-8447)

SALES (est): 24.9MM **Privately Held**
WEB: www.p-d-s-i.com
SIC: 3569 8711 7363 3823 Robots, assembly line: industrial & commercial; industrial engineers; mechanical engineering; temporary help service; industrial instrmnts msrmnt display/control process variable; machine tool accessories; special dies, tools, jigs & fixtures

(G-8447)
PROFICIENT INFORMATION TECH
301 W 1st St (45402-3033)
PHONE...............................937 470-1300
Tina Bustillo, *President*
EMP: 8
SALES (est): 751.5K **Privately Held**
WEB: www.proficientinfotech.com
SIC: 7371 7372 7379 8742 Custom computer programming services; application computer software; computer related maintenance services; ; marketing consulting services; workmen's compensation office, government

(G-8448)
PROFILE DIGITAL PRINTING LLC
5449 Marina Dr (45449-1833)
PHONE...............................937 866-4241
Terry Harmeyer, *General Mgr*
Tom Helmers, *Principal*
June Helmers,
EMP: 25
SALES (est): 4.1MM **Privately Held**
WEB: www.profiledpi.com
SIC: 7334 2759 2752 Blueprinting service; commercial printing; commercial printing, lithographic

(G-8449)
PROFOUND LOGIC SOFTWARE INC
396 Congress Park Dr (45459-4149)
PHONE...............................937 439-7925
Alex Roytman, *President*
EMP: 9
SALES (est): 1MM **Privately Held**
SIC: 7372 Business oriented computer software

(G-8450)
PROGRESSIVE PRINTERS INC
6700 Homestretch Rd (45414-2516)
PHONE...............................937 222-1267
Dennis Livesay, *President*
Sharon L Staggs, *Vice Pres*
Traci Miller, *Accounts Exec*
Jeff Osborne, *Sales Staff*
Allen Haverkos, *Marketing Staff*
EMP: 55 EST: 2004
SQ FT: 26,000
SALES (est): 19.2MM **Privately Held**
WEB: www.progressiveprinters.com
SIC: 2752 2759 Commercial printing, offset; commercial printing

(G-8451)
PROSTAR MACHINE & TOOL CO
2039 Webster St (45404-1143)
PHONE...............................937 223-1997
Fax: 937 223-8805
EMP: 8
SQ FT: 3,000
SALES (est): 300K **Privately Held**
SIC: 3599 Machine Shop Jobbing And Repair

(G-8452)
PUTNAM PLASTICS INC
Also Called: Farm Products Division
255 S Alex Rd (45449-1910)
PHONE...............................937 866-6261
Gary Spacht, *General Mgr*
Sherry Miller, *Manager*
EMP: 8
SALES (est): 806K
SALES (corp-wide): 6.6MM **Privately Held**
WEB: www.putnamplasticsinc.com
SIC: 5199 5113 3081 Packaging materials; industrial & personal service paper; polyethylene film
PA: Putnam Plastics Inc
30 W Stardust Rd
Cloverdale IN 46120
765 795-6102

(G-8453)
PUTTCO INC
2613 Oakley Ave (45419-2351)
PHONE...............................937 299-1527
Frank Puthoff, *President*
EMP: 3
SALES (est): 181.3K **Privately Held**
SIC: 2396 Screen printing on fabric articles

(G-8454)
Q M C PLEASANTS INC
Also Called: Quality Machine
5648 Wadsworth Rd (45414-3412)
PHONE...............................937 278-7302
David Pleasant Jr, *President*
David K Pleasant Sr, *President*
Deborah Pleasant, *Admin Sec*
EMP: 3
SQ FT: 2,800
SALES (est): 350.1K **Privately Held**
SIC: 3599 Machine shop, jobbing & repair

(G-8455)
QUALITY QUARTZ ENGINEERING INC
131 Janney Rd (45404-1225)
PHONE...............................937 236-3250
William Cox, *QC Mgr*
Gary Zimmermen,
◆ EMP: 52
SQ FT: 55,000
SALES (est): 10.4MM **Privately Held**
SIC: 3679 Quartz crystals, for electronic application
PA: Quality Quartz Engineering, Incorporated
8484 Central Ave
Newark CA 94560

(G-8456)
QUEEN CITY POLYMERS INC
Also Called: Qc Plastics
365 Leo St (45404-1007)
PHONE...............................937 236-2710
Greg Hendon, *Manager*
EMP: 5
SALES (est): 531.9K
SALES (corp-wide): 11.2MM **Privately Held**
WEB: www.qcpinc.net
SIC: 5162 3089 Plastics products; plastic processing
PA: Queen City Polymers, Inc.
6101 Schumacher Park Dr
West Chester OH 45069
513 779-0990

(G-8457)
R & H SIGNS UNLIMITED INC
Also Called: Sign-A-Rama
3048 Wilmington Pike (45429-4002)
PHONE...............................937 293-3834
Brian Hodell, *Vice Pres*
Phyllis Ruber, *Treasurer*
Tami Hodell, *Admin Sec*
EMP: 5
SALES (est): 594.5K **Privately Held**
SIC: 3993 Signs & advertising specialties

(G-8458)
R D BAKER ENTERPRISES INC
Also Called: Alpha Water Conditioning Co
765 Liberty Ln (45449-2134)
PHONE...............................937 461-5225
Bill Miller, *Branch Mgr*
EMP: 6
SALES (corp-wide): 4.3MM **Privately Held**
WEB: www.daytonwatersystems.com
SIC: 3589 8734 5074 Water purification equipment, household type; water testing laboratory; water softeners
PA: R. D. Baker Enterprises, Inc.
765 Liberty Ln
Dayton OH 45449
937 461-5225

(G-8459)
R L TECHNOLOGIES INC (PA)
1711 Mccall St (45402-8036)
P.O. Box 17250 (45417-0250)
PHONE...............................937 321-5544
Tanya Epps, *President*
Harry Mayo, *Vice Pres*
EMP: 5
SALES (est): 699.2K **Privately Held**
SIC: 3965 Fasteners

(G-8460)
R S C SALES COMPANY
1347 E 4th St (45402-2235)
PHONE...............................423 581-4916
Richard Carper, *President*
Scott Carper, *Vice Pres*
▲ EMP: 20
SQ FT: 22,000
SALES (est): 1.9MM **Privately Held**
SIC: 2752 5013 7336 Commercial printing, offset; automotive supplies & parts; silk screen design

(G-8461)
R WEIR INC
Also Called: Fastsigns
978 Mmsburg Cnterville Rd (45459)
PHONE...............................937 438-5730
Ronald Weir, *President*
EMP: 5
SQ FT: 1,980
SALES (est): 300K **Privately Held**
WEB: www.rweir.com
SIC: 3993 5999 Signs & advertising specialties; banners, flags, decals & posters

(G-8462)
RAM PRECISION INDUSTRIES INC
Also Called: R A M Precision Tool
11125 Yankee St Ste A (45458-3698)
PHONE...............................937 885-7700
Richard Mount, *CEO*
▲ EMP: 85
SQ FT: 55,000
SALES (est): 16.8MM **Privately Held**
WEB: www.rampaintball.com
SIC: 3599 Machine shop, jobbing & repair

(G-8463)
RAM TOOL INC
1944 Neva Dr (45414-5525)
PHONE...............................937 277-0717
Robert Coblentz, *President*
Forrest Lemaster, *President*
EMP: 7
SQ FT: 4,000
SALES (est): 968.6K **Privately Held**
WEB: www.ramtoolohio.com
SIC: 3544 Special dies & tools

(G-8464)
RANDD ASSOC PRTG & PROMOTIONS
330 Progress Rd (45449-2322)
PHONE...............................937 204 1874
Rick Dobson, *President*
Pam Dobson, *Corp Secy*
EMP: 7
SQ FT: 3,200
SALES (est): 1.1MM **Privately Held**
WEB: www.randdassociates.com
SIC: 2752 5199 Commercial printing, offset; advertising specialties

(G-8465)
READY TECHNOLOGY INC
Also Called: Standard Die Supply
630 Kiser St (45404-1644)
PHONE...............................937 228-8181
Kelly Romer, *Branch Mgr*
EMP: 14 **Privately Held**
WEB: www.readytech.net
SIC: 3542 5084 Machine tools, metal forming type; tool & die makers' equipment
HQ: Ready Technology, Inc.
333 Progress Rd Unit A
Dayton OH 45449
937 866-7200

(G-8466)
READY TECHNOLOGY INC (HQ)
333 Progress Rd Unit A (45449-2490)
PHONE...............................937 866-7200
Michael Danly, *President*
Kelly Romer, *Plant Mgr*
Steve Thompson, *Plant Mgr*
Jim Pecqueux, *Controller*
Carleen Thompson, *Sales Executive*
▲ EMP: 14 EST: 1981
SQ FT: 10,000
SALES (est): 8.3MM **Privately Held**
WEB: www.readytech.net
SIC: 5084 3544 3542 Metalworking tools (such as drills, taps, dies, files); special dies, tools, jigs & fixtures; bending machines

(G-8467)
REECES LAS VEGAS SUPPLIES (PA)
5425 Fishburg Rd (45424-7500)
PHONE...............................937 274-5000
Reece Powers, *Partner*
Janice Powers, *Partner*
EMP: 4
SALES (est): 750K **Privately Held**
SIC: 3581 3599 Automatic vending machines; amusement park equipment

(G-8468)
REEL IMAGE
2520 Blackhawk Rd (45420-3902)
PHONE...............................937 296-9036
J Osborne, *Principal*
EMP: 5
SALES (est): 456.9K **Privately Held**
SIC: 2721 Periodicals

(G-8469)
REELFLYRODCOM
7635 Wilmington Pike D (45458-5425)
PHONE...............................937 434-8472
Todd Mikesell, *Owner*
EMP: 3 EST: 2009
SALES (est): 309.3K **Privately Held**
SIC: 3949 7999 Reels, fishing; outfitters, recreation

(G-8470)
RELY-ON MANUFACTURING INC
955 Springfield St (45403-1347)
PHONE...............................937 254-0118
Marsha Mosher, *President*
Peter T Mosher, *Vice Pres*
EMP: 6
SALES (est): 931.7K **Privately Held**
SIC: 3599 Machine shop, jobbing & repair

(G-8471)
REMNANT ROOM
1915 S Alex Rd (45449-4002)
PHONE...............................937 938-7350
Mike Daugherty, *Owner*
EMP: 3
SALES (est): 267.2K **Privately Held**
SIC: 2273 Carpets & rugs

(G-8472)
RENCO MOLD INC
2801 Ome Ave (45414-5118)
PHONE...............................937 233-3233
Marvin Evans, *President*
Glenn Renner, *Admin Sec*
EMP: 6
SQ FT: 3,000
SALES (est): 606.4K **Privately Held**
SIC: 3544 Special dies & tools

(G-8473)
REPUBLIC EDM SERVICES INC
5660 Wadsworth Rd (45414-3412)
PHONE...............................937 278-7070
Gary D Schinder, *President*
Kim S Schinder, *Corp Secy*
EMP: 3
SQ FT: 2,000
SALES (est): 250K **Privately Held**
SIC: 3541 Electron-discharge metal cutting machine tools

GEOGRAPHIC SECTION
Dayton - Montgomery County (G-8499)

(G-8474)
REX AMERICAN RESOURCES CORP (PA)
7720 Paragon Rd (45459-4050)
PHONE 937 276-3931
Stuart A Rose, *Ch of Bd*
Zafar Rizvi, *President*
Douglas L Bruggeman, *CFO*
Edward M Kress, *Admin Sec*
EMP: 102
SQ FT: 7,500
SALES: 486.6MM **Publicly Held**
WEB: www.rexstore.com
SIC: 2869 Fuels; ethyl alcohol, ethanol

(G-8475)
REYNOLDS AND REYNOLDS COMPANY
354 Mound St (45402-8325)
P.O. Box 2608 (45401-2608)
PHONE 937 485-4771
David R Holmes, *President*
Bill Thomas, *Branch Mgr*
EMP: 7
SQ FT: 1,575
SALES (corp-wide): 1.5B **Privately Held**
WEB: www.reyrey.com
SIC: 2759 5045 Business forms: printing; computers & accessories, personal & home entertainment
HQ: The Reynolds And Reynolds Company
1 Reynolds Way
Kettering OH 45430
937 485-2000

(G-8476)
REYNOLDS AND REYNOLDS COMPANY
115 S Ludlow St (45402-1812)
P.O. Box 2237 (45401-2237)
PHONE 937 449-4039
Melinda Vaughn, *Principal*
Austin Floyd, *Engineer*
Pat Freeman, *Manager*
EMP: 50
SALES (corp-wide): 1.5B **Privately Held**
WEB: www.reyrey.com
SIC: 2761 Manifold business forms
HQ: The Reynolds And Reynolds Company
1 Reynolds Way
Kettering OH 45430
937 485-2000

(G-8477)
RICHARD A SCOTT
8000 Allison Ave (45415-2205)
PHONE 937 898-1592
Richard A Scott, *Principal*
EMP: 3
SALES (est): 210.7K **Privately Held**
SIC: 3566 Speed changers, drives & gears

(G-8478)
RITE WAY BLACK & DEBURR INC
1138 E 2nd St (45403-1092)
PHONE 937 224-7762
Cecil W Parker, *President*
James Parker, *Vice Pres*
EMP: 5
SQ FT: 6,000
SALES (est): 548.3K **Privately Held**
SIC: 3471 3479 Finishing, metals or formed products; etching & engraving

(G-8479)
RIXAN ASSOCIATES INC
7560 Paragon Rd (45459-5317)
PHONE 937 438-3005
Stephen Harris, *President*
Aaron Harris, *Chairman*
Beatrice Harris, *Corp Secy*
David Ryan, *Vice Pres*
Jeff Conrad, *Engineer*
EMP: 20 EST: 1959
SQ FT: 14,000
SALES (est): 12.6MM **Privately Held**
WEB: www.rixan.com
SIC: 5084 5569 5065 Robots, industrial; robots, assembly line: industrial & commercial; electronic parts

(G-8480)
RLFSHOP LLC
Also Called: Shopsmith
6530 Poe Ave (45414-2527)
PHONE 937 898-6070
Robert L Folkerth,
▲ **EMP:** 3
SALES (est): 425.2K **Privately Held**
SIC: 3553 Woodworking machinery

(G-8481)
RMT CORPORATION
2552 Titus Ave (45414-4217)
PHONE 513 942-8308
Brent Shreiner, *President*
EMP: 10
SQ FT: 1,267
SALES (est): 1.9MM **Privately Held**
SIC: 3544 Special dies & tools

(G-8482)
ROBBINS & MYERS INC
5870 Poe Ave Ste A (45414-3442)
P.O. Box 1123 (45401-1123)
PHONE 937 454-3200
Kevin Brown, *Branch Mgr*
EMP: 17
SALES (corp-wide): 8.4B **Publicly Held**
SIC: 3533 Oil & gas field machinery
HQ: Robbins & Myers, Inc.
10586 N Highway 75
Willis TX 77378
936 890-1064

(G-8483)
ROBS WELDING TECHNOLOGIES LTD
2920 Production Ct (45414-3537)
PHONE 937 890-4963
Dean Shoup, *Partner*
Rob Shoup, *Partner*
Cheryl Shoup, *Office Mgr*
EMP: 9
SQ FT: 10,000
SALES: 1.5MM **Privately Held**
WEB: www.robsweldingtech.com
SIC: 3312 3441 1799 Tool & die steel; fabricated structural metal; welding on site

(G-8484)
RONALD T DODGE CO
Also Called: Dodge Company
55 Westpark Rd (45459-4812)
PHONE 937 439-4497
Ronald J Versic, *President*
Linda J Versic, *Treasurer*
EMP: 10
SQ FT: 8,000
SALES (est): 1.9MM **Privately Held**
WEB: www.rtdodge.com
SIC: 2869 8731 High purity grade chemicals, organic; commercial research laboratory

(G-8485)
ROTO TECH INC
351 Fame Rd Ste A (45449-2676)
PHONE 937 859-8503
David Millat, *President*
Natalie A Millat, *Vice Pres*
EMP: 30
SQ FT: 20,000
SALES (est): 132K **Privately Held**
SIC: 3545 3829 3823 3541 Rotary tables; gauges (machine tool accessories); measuring & controlling devices; industrial instrmnts msrmnt display/control process variable; machine tools, metal cutting type

(G-8486)
RPA ELECTRONIC DISTRIBUTORS
Also Called: R P A
122 S Terry St (45403-2340)
P.O. Box 1001 (45401-1001)
PHONE 937 223-7001
R Paul Perkins Jr, *Principal*
Sandy Strawser, *Treasurer*
Bajump Jump, *Info Tech Mgr*
EMP: 12
SQ FT: 9,000
SALES (est): 4.5MM **Privately Held**
SIC: 5065 3679 Electronic parts; electronic circuits

(G-8487)
RUBBER-TECH INC
5208 Wadsworth Rd (45414-3592)
PHONE 937 274-1114
Forest Back, *President*
L Irene Back, *Corp Secy*
Mike McElroy, *QC Mgr*
Penny Prechtl, *QC Mgr*
EMP: 17
SQ FT: 10,000
SALES (est): 3.2MM **Privately Held**
WEB: www.rubber-tech.com
SIC: 3069 3061 Molded rubber products; mechanical rubber goods

(G-8488)
RYANWORKS INC
Also Called: Woodcraft
175 E Alex Bell Rd # 264 (45459-2701)
PHONE 937 438-1282
Alan Ryan, *President*
EMP: 16
SALES: 1MM **Privately Held**
WEB: www.ryanworks.com
SIC: 5084 2499 Woodworking machinery; decorative wood & woodwork

(G-8489)
S & R SHEET METAL
320 Gargrave Rd (45449-2464)
P.O. Box 186, Miamisburg (45343-0186)
PHONE 937 865-9236
Jeffrey Cooper, *Partner*
Harold Urban, *Partner*
EMP: 5
SQ FT: 5,200
SALES: 500K **Privately Held**
SIC: 3444 Sheet metal specialties, not stamped

(G-8490)
S & S PRINTING SERVICE INC
Also Called: William A Selz
505 Hunter Ave (45404-1569)
PHONE 937 228-9411
Ken Selz, *President*
Betty Selz, *Treasurer*
EMP: 5
SQ FT: 3,600
SALES: 300K **Privately Held**
SIC: 2752 Commercial printing, offset

(G-8491)
S F MOCK & ASSOCIATES LLC
105 Westpark Rd (45459-4814)
PHONE 937 438-0196
Stephen F Mock,
EMP: 10
SALES (est): 430.4K **Privately Held**
SIC: 2761 5611 2759 Manifold business forms; men's & boys' clothing stores; business forms: printing

(G-8492)
SAMPLE MACHINING INC
Also Called: Bitec
220 N Jersey St (45403-1220)
PHONE 937 258-3338
Beverly Bleicher, *President*
Kevin Bleicher, *Vice Pres*
David Calmes, *Mfg Mgr*
Chris Bell, *QC Mgr*
Larry Mullett, *Engineer*
EMP: 45
SQ FT: 19,000
SALES: 7MM **Privately Held**
WEB: www.bitecsmi.com
SIC: 3599 8734 Custom machinery; testing laboratories

(G-8493)
SARA HUDSON
Also Called: Crime and Trauma Scene Clean
1632 Wayne Ave (45410-1710)
PHONE 850 890-1455
Sara Hudson, *Owner*
EMP: 4
SALES (est): 208.2K **Privately Held**
SIC: 7699 2842 4953 4212 Cleaning services; sanitation preparations, disinfectants & deodorants; hazardous waste collection & disposal; liquid waste, collection & disposal; medical waste disposal; hazardous waste transport

(G-8494)
SCENTSIBLE SCENTS LTD
2704 Parklawn Dr (45440-1537)
PHONE 937 572-6690
EMP: 3
SALES (est): 180.9K **Privately Held**
SIC: 5199 3999 Candles; manufacturing industries

(G-8495)
SCHNEIDER ELECTRIC USA INC
1875 Founders Dr (45420-4017)
PHONE 937 258-8426
Mike Edmiston, *Vice Pres*
Janet Filbrun, *Purchasing*
Mark Waggoner, *Engineer*
Marty Niehouse, *Branch Mgr*
EMP: 12
SALES (corp-wide): 355.8K **Privately Held**
WEB: www.squared.com
SIC: 3699 Electrical work
HQ: Schneider Electric Usa, Inc.
201 Wshington St Ste 2700
Boston MA 02108
978 975-9600

(G-8496)
SCHUERHOLZ PRINTING INC
3540 Marshall Rd (45429-4916)
PHONE 937 294-5218
Charles Schuerholz, *President*
Deb Brown, *Sales Staff*
EMP: 7
SQ FT: 4,500
SALES (est): 665.5K **Privately Held**
WEB: www.schuerholzgraphics.com
SIC: 2752 7336 Commercial printing, offset; graphic arts & related design

(G-8497)
SCIENCE/ELECTRONICS INC
Also Called: Earth and Atmospheric Sciences
521 Kiser St (45404-1641)
PHONE 937 224-4444
Ted Morton, *CEO*
Janice Morton, *CFO*
EMP: 15 EST: 1978
SQ FT: 90,000
SALES (est): 1.6MM **Privately Held**
SIC: 5049 3829 Scientific instruments; measuring & controlling devices

(G-8498)
SCOTTS COMPANY LLC
20 Innovation Ct (45414-3968)
PHONE 937 454-2782
Kevin Laughlin, *Manager*
EMP: 15
SALES (corp-wide): 2.6B **Publicly Held**
WEB: www.scottscompany.com
SIC: 2873 Fertilizers: natural (organic), except compost
HQ: The Scotts Company Llc
14111 Scottslawn Rd
Marysville OH 43040
937 644-0011

(G-8499)
SCREEN WORKS INC (PA)
3970 Image Dr (45414-2524)
PHONE 937 264-9111
Jeff Cottrell, *Principal*
EMP: 29
SQ FT: 42,000
SALES (est): 7MM **Privately Held**
WEB: www.screenworksinc.com
SIC: 7336 5199 7389 3993 Silk screen design; advertising specialties; embroidering of advertising on shirts, etc.; signs & advertising specialties; automotive & apparel trimmings

Dayton - Montgomery County (G-8500)

(G-8500)
SECURTEX INTERNATIONAL INC
Also Called: Sucurtex Digital
982 Senate Dr (45459-4017)
PHONE..................937 312-1414
Ted Humphrey, *President*
John McCallum, *Vice Pres*
Mindy Fernandez, *Manager*
EMP: 25
SQ FT: 12,500
SALES (est): 211.2K **Privately Held**
WEB: www.securtex.com
SIC: 3699 Security control equipment & systems

(G-8501)
SEEBACH INC
Also Called: Seebach Tools & Molds Mfg
2622 Keenan Ave (45414-4910)
PHONE..................937 275-3565
Mark Seebach, *CEO*
James Seebach, *President*
Carl Seebach, *Vice Pres*
EMP: 14
SQ FT: 9,600
SALES (est): 700K **Privately Held**
WEB: www.seebach.com
SIC: 3599 Machine shop, jobbing & repair

(G-8502)
SELECT INDUSTRIES CORPORATION
60 Heid Ave (45404-1216)
P.O. Box 887 (45401-0887)
PHONE..................937 233-9191
Mark Wogoman, *President*
Robert Whited, *Principal*
Kelly Wogoman, *Chairman*
◆ EMP: 200
SQ FT: 250,000
SALES (est): 64.9MM **Privately Held**
SIC: 3469 Capacitor or condenser cans & cases, stamped metal
PA: Select International Corp.
60 Heid Ave
Dayton OH 45404

(G-8503)
SELECT INTERNATIONAL CORP (PA)
60 Heid Ave (45404-1216)
P.O. Box 887 (45401-0887)
PHONE..................937 233-9191
Kelly Wogomanceo, *CEO*
Mark Wogoman, *Vice Pres*
Craig Puterbaugh, *Maint Spvr*
Karin Franklin, *Buyer*
Michael Dankworth, *Engineer*
EMP: 3
SALES (est): 64.9MM **Privately Held**
SIC: 3465 1799 Automotive stampings; welding on site

(G-8504)
SHILOH INDUSTRIES INC
5988 Executive Blvd Ste B (45424-1413)
PHONE..................937 236-5100
John Dixon, *President*
David W Dixon, *Vice Pres*
EMP: 18
SQ FT: 18,000
SALES (est): 3.6MM **Privately Held**
SIC: 3679 3089 Electronic circuits; injection molding of plastics

(G-8505)
SHORE TO SHORE INC (DH)
8170 Washington Vlg Dr (45458-1848)
PHONE..................937 866-1908
Howard Kurdin, *President*
John Lau, *Exec VP*
Chuck Rowland, *CFO*
▲ EMP: 100
SQ FT: 30,000
SALES (est): 115.8MM
SALES (corp-wide): 3.7B **Privately Held**
WEB: www.shr2shr.com
SIC: 2679 2241 Labels, paper: made from purchased material; labels, woven
HQ: Checkpoint Systems, Inc.
101 Wolf Dr
West Deptford NJ 08086
800 257-5540

(G-8506)
SIGN CONNECTION INC
90 Compark Rd Ste B (45459-4967)
PHONE..................937 435-4070
Jane Fiehrer, *President*
EMP: 4
SALES (est): 511.2K **Privately Held**
SIC: 3993 Signs, not made in custom sign painting shops

(G-8507)
SIGN TECHNOLOGIES LLC
Also Called: Signetics
2001 Kuntz Rd (45404-1221)
PHONE..................937 439-3970
Shari Brown, *Finance Mgr*
EMP: 6
SQ FT: 6,000
SALES (est): 796.7K **Privately Held**
WEB: www.signetics1.com
SIC: 3993 Signs & advertising specialties

(G-8508)
SIMON ELLIS SUPERABRASIVES
501 Progress Rd (45449-2325)
PHONE..................937 226-0683
David Rawson, *President*
Thomas Greene, *Vice Pres*
Theresa Tsmcatee, *Office Mgr*
Beverly Greene, *Admin Sec*
EMP: 9
SQ FT: 5,000
SALES (est): 1.1MM **Privately Held**
WEB: www.simonellis.com
SIC: 3423 Hand & edge tools

(G-8509)
SINEL COMPANY INC
4811 Pamela Sue Dr (45429-5349)
PHONE..................937 433-4772
Mitchell S Siler, *President*
EMP: 10 EST: 1934
SQ FT: 5,000
SALES (est): 1.3MM **Privately Held**
WEB: www.sinelcompany.com
SIC: 3543 Foundry cores

(G-8510)
SKIN
333 Wayne Ave (45410-1115)
PHONE..................937 222-0222
Iris Goldflies, *President*
Gary Golgflies, *Vice Pres*
EMP: 4
SALES: 260K **Privately Held**
SIC: 2844 Face creams or lotions

(G-8511)
SNYDER CONCRETE PRODUCTS INC
Also Called: Snyder Brick and Block
1433 S Euclid Ave (45417-3839)
PHONE..................937 224-1433
Chip Lytel, *Manager*
EMP: 6
SALES (corp-wide): 12.6MM **Privately Held**
WEB: www.snyderonline.com
SIC: 5032 3271 Brick, except refractory; concrete & cinder building products; blocks, concrete or cinder: standard
PA: Snyder Concrete Products, Inc.
2301 W Dorothy Ln
Moraine OH 45439
937 885-5176

(G-8512)
SOUTHERN ORNAMENTAL IRON CO (PA)
4267 Salem Ave (45416-1704)
PHONE..................937 278-4319
Steven Davis, *President*
EMP: 7 EST: 1961
SQ FT: 4,000
SALES (est): 739.8K **Privately Held**
WEB: www.mwdpc.com
SIC: 3446 Architectural metalwork

(G-8513)
SOUTHWESTERN OHIO INSTRUCTION
Also Called: S O I T A
1205 E 5th St (45402-2221)
PHONE..................937 746-6333
Dave Mc Williams, *Corp Secy*
Larry Pogue, *Exec Dir*
David Gibson, *Director*
EMP: 10
SQ FT: 2,000
SALES: 405.1K **Privately Held**
WEB: www.soita.org
SIC: 7372 Educational computer software

(G-8514)
SPACE AGE COATINGS LLC
Also Called: Space Age Concepts
4825 Wolf Creek Pike (45417-9439)
P.O. Box 26488 (45426-0488)
PHONE..................937 275-5117
Gerald Blessing, *CEO*
Dean Blessing,
EMP: 3
SQ FT: 4,000
SALES (est): 200.1K **Privately Held**
WEB: www.spaceagecoating.com
SIC: 7699 3544 Metal reshaping & replating services; special dies, tools, jigs & fixtures

(G-8515)
SPAOS INC (PA)
Also Called: Quality Office Products
6012 N Dixie Dr (45414-4018)
P.O. Box 13661 (45413-0661)
PHONE..................937 890-0783
Jack Roberts, *President*
Bonnie Roberts, *Corp Secy*
EMP: 11
SALES (est): 1.5MM **Privately Held**
SIC: 2752 Commercial printing, offset

(G-8516)
SPECTRACAM LTD
1112 E Race Dr (45404)
PHONE..................937 223-3805
Joseph Wendling, *Mng Member*
EMP: 7 EST: 1998
SQ FT: 6,300
SALES (est): 790K **Privately Held**
SIC: 3544 3543 Special dies, tools, jigs & fixtures; industrial patterns

(G-8517)
SPECTRON INC
132 S Terry St (45403-2340)
P.O. Box 3518 (45401-3518)
PHONE..................937 461-5590
Betty Burnett, *President*
Jeff Bucher, *President*
Linda Parr, *Manager*
EMP: 6 EST: 1966
SQ FT: 4,000
SALES (est): 737.3K **Privately Held**
WEB: www.spectroninc.com
SIC: 3679 Electronic circuits

(G-8518)
SPECTRUM EMBROIDERY INC
332 Gargrave Rd (45449-2464)
PHONE..................937 847-9905
Randy Russell, *President*
Donna Russell, *Vice Pres*
EMP: 3
SQ FT: 2,500
SALES (est): 338.9K **Privately Held**
SIC: 2759 2395 Promotional printing; embroidery products, except schiffli machine

(G-8519)
SPIEGLER BRAKE SYSTEMS USA LLC
1699 Thomas Paine Pkwy (45459-2538)
PHONE..................937 291-1735
Matthias Schaub, *Mng Member*
▲ EMP: 6
SQ FT: 3,500
SALES (est): 923.3K **Privately Held**
SIC: 3751 5571 Motorcycles, bicycles & parts; motorcycle parts & accessories

(G-8520)
SPITFIRE TECHNOLOGIES LLC
110 N Main St (45402-1795)
PHONE..................937 463-7729
Joseph Krebs, *CPA*
EMP: 4 EST: 2013
SQ FT: 2,500
SALES (est): 220K **Privately Held**
SIC: 7372 Application computer software

(G-8521)
SRC LIQUIDATION LLC (HQ)
600 Albany St (45417-3405)
P.O. Box 1167 (45401-1167)
PHONE..................937 221-1000
F David Clarke III, *Ch of Bd*
Landen Williams, *President*
Benjamin T Cutting, *CFO*
James M Vaughn, *Treasurer*
Diana Tullio, *CIO*
◆ EMP: 600
SALES (est): 826.9MM
SALES (corp-wide): 3.2B **Privately Held**
WEB: www.stdreg.com
SIC: 2761 2672 2677 2759 Manifold business forms; labels (unprinted), gummed: made from purchased materials; envelopes; promotional printing
PA: Taylor Corporation
1725 Roe Crest Dr
North Mankato MN 56003
507 625-2828

(G-8522)
SS METAL FABRICATORS INC
423 Rita St (45404-2716)
P.O. Box 157 (45404-0157)
PHONE..................937 226-9957
Jim Shanks, *President*
Tony Shanks, *Vice Pres*
EMP: 5
SQ FT: 10,000
SALES: 620K **Privately Held**
SIC: 3444 Sheet metalwork

(G-8523)
STAFFORD GAGE & TOOL INC
4606 Webster St (45414-4826)
PHONE..................937 277-9944
Jeff Stafford, *President*
Judy Stafford, *President*
Jean Stafford, *Vice Pres*
Teresa Stafford, *Vice Pres*
EMP: 9
SQ FT: 10,500
SALES: 500K **Privately Held**
WEB: www.sgandt.com
SIC: 3599 Machine shop, jobbing & repair

(G-8524)
STANCO PRECISION MANUFACTURING
Also Called: Ss Industries
1 Walbrook Ave (45405-2341)
PHONE..................937 274-1785
Stephen P Stanoikovich, *President*
Steve Strader, *General Mgr*
Rhonda Stanoikovich, *Manager*
▲ EMP: 9
SQ FT: 8,000
SALES (est): 1.1MM **Privately Held**
WEB: www.stancoprecision.com
SIC: 3599 3544 Machine shop, jobbing & repair; special dies & tools

(G-8525)
STARWIN INDUSTRIES LLC
Also Called: Starwin Industries, Inc.
3387 Woodman Dr (45429-4100)
PHONE..................937 293-8568
Rick Little, *President*
John Whitaker, *General Mgr*
Mark Belt, *Mfg Spvr*
John Gevedon, *Sales Dir*
Michael Little, *Sales Staff*
EMP: 40
SQ FT: 30,000
SALES (est): 7.4MM
SALES (corp-wide): 911.5K **Privately Held**
WEB: www.starwin-ind.com
SIC: 3599 7372 Machine shop, jobbing & repair; prepackaged software
PA: Eti Mission Controls, Llc
75 Holiday Dr
Englewood OH 45322
937 832-4200

(G-8526)
STATE OF OHIO DAYTON RACEWAY
777 Hollywood Blvd (45414-3698)
PHONE..................937 237-7802
EMP: 3 EST: 2015

▲ = Import ▼ = Export
◆ = Import/Export

GEOGRAPHIC SECTION
Dayton - Montgomery County (G-8552)

SALES (est): 209.9K Privately Held
SIC: 3644 Raceways

(G-8527)
STECK MANUFACTURING CO INC
1115 S Broadway St Ste 1 (45417-3940)
PHONE..................937 222-0062
John Brill, *President*
Rick Vogel, *Vice Pres*
▲ EMP: 16
SQ FT: 14,300
SALES: 4MM Privately Held
WEB: www.steckmfg.com
SIC: 3714 3599 Motor vehicle parts & accessories; machine shop, jobbing & repair

(G-8528)
SUGAR CREEK PACKING CO
1241 N Gettysburg Ave (45417-9513)
PHONE..................937 268-6601
Steve Shutte, *Opers-Prdtn-Mfg*
EMP: 350
SQ FT: 20,000
SALES (corp-wide): 700MM Privately Held
WEB: www.sugarcreek.com
SIC: 2013 2011 Bacon, side & sliced: from purchased meat; meat packing plants
PA: Sugar Creek Packing Co.
  2101 Kenskill Ave
  Wshngtn Ct Hs OH 43160
  740 335-3586

(G-8529)
SUPPLIER INSPECTION SVCS INC (PA)
2941 S Gettysburg Ave (45439-7912)
PHONE..................937 263-7097
Paul A Bowell, *President*
Steve Anklen, *Opers Mgr*
Ernest Henderson, *Opers Mgr*
Robert Austin, *Warehouse Mgr*
Rich Seeger, *Opers Staff*
EMP: 20
SQ FT: 50,000
SALES (est): 5.8MM Privately Held
WEB: www.sis-inspection.net
SIC: 3545 7389 Machine tool accessories; inspection & testing services

(G-8530)
SUPPLY TECHNOLOGIES LLC
4704 Wadsworth Rd (45414-4222)
PHONE..................937 898-5795
EMP: 6
SALES (corp-wide): 1.6B Publicly Held
SIC: 5085 3452 3469 Fasteners, industrial: nuts, bolts, screws, etc.; bolts, nuts, rivets & washers; nuts, metal; screws, metal; stamping metal for the trade
HQ: Supply Technologies Llc
  6065 Parkland Blvd Ste 2
  Cleveland OH 44124
  440 947-2100

(G-8531)
SURE TOOL & MANUFACTURING CO
429 Winston Ave (45403-1400)
PHONE..................937 253-9111
Jerrald Kuriger, *President*
Ruth Kuriger, *Corp Secy*
Russell B Kuriger, *Vice Pres*
EMP: 23
SQ FT: 14,000
SALES (est): 2.2MM Privately Held
WEB: www.suretool.com
SIC: 3544 Special dies & tools

(G-8532)
SYSTECH ENVIRONMENTAL CORP (DH)
3085 Woodman Dr Ste 300 (45420-1159)
PHONE..................800 888-8011
Thomas J Sponger, *Vice Ch Bd*
David Cheney, *President*
Rhonda Mc Ghee, *Engng Exec*
Zach Unruh, *Sales Mgr*
Wilma Davis, *Manager*
◆ EMP: 20
SQ FT: 10,000
SALES (est): 17.5MM
SALES (corp-wide): 26.4B Privately Held
WEB: www.sysenv.com
SIC: 2869 Fuels
HQ: Lafarge North America Inc.
  8700 W Bryn Mawr Ave
  Chicago IL 60631
  773 372-1000

(G-8533)
SYSTEMAX MANUFACTURING INC
6450 Poe Ave Ste 200 (45414-2655)
PHONE..................937 368-2300
Curt Rush, *Admin Sec*
▲ EMP: 200
SQ FT: 185,000
SALES (est): 21MM Publicly Held
WEB: www.systemax.com
SIC: 5961 7373 3577 3571 Computers & peripheral equipment, mail order; systems integration services; computer peripheral equipment; electronic computers; computer peripheral equipment
PA: Systemax Inc.
  11 Harbor Park Dr
  Port Washington NY 11050

(G-8534)
T & L CUSTOM SCREENING INC
3464 Successful Way (45414-4320)
PHONE..................937 237-3121
Louise Edwards, *President*
Tonya Snapp, *Corp Secy*
EMP: 7
SQ FT: 6,500
SALES (est): 390K Privately Held
SIC: 2759 5199 2395 2396 Screen printing; advertising specialties; embroidery products, except schiffli machine; automotive & apparel trimmings

(G-8535)
T & R WELDING SYSTEMS INC
1 Janney Rd (45404-1263)
PHONE..................937 228-7517
Mike Bozzo, *President*
▼ EMP: 15
SQ FT: 15,000
SALES (est): 3.4MM Privately Held
SIC: 3496 7692 Miscellaneous fabricated wire products; welding repair

(G-8536)
T AND D INDUSTRIES LLC
1325 Foxglen Cir (45429-5745)
PHONE..................937 321-3424
Trachelle Washington, *Administration*
EMP: 3 EST: 2016
SALES (est): 137K Privately Held
SIC: 3999 Manufacturing industries

(G-8537)
TABTRONICS INC
2153 Winners Cir (45404-1150)
PHONE..................937 222-9969
Thomas Biel, *President*
Cindy Biel, *Office Mgr*
Cheryl Faul, *Office Mgr*
Dave Noland, *Director*
EMP: 16
SQ FT: 9,000
SALES (est): 5.2MM Privately Held
WEB: www.pedtke.com
SIC: 3672 Printed circuit boards

(G-8538)
TANNING
7109 Taylorsville Rd (45424-3101)
PHONE..................937 233-4554
Tay Wazt, *Owner*
EMP: 3
SALES (est): 208.3K Privately Held
SIC: 2861 7299 Dyeing materials, natural; softwood distillates; miscellaneous personal service; tanning salon

(G-8539)
TARGET PRINTING & GRAPHICS
233 Leo St (45404-1005)
PHONE..................937 228-0170
Kris Willetts, *President*
Phyllis Swigart, *Corp Secy*
Kiela Willets, *Vice Pres*
EMP: 6
SQ FT: 12,000
SALES (est): 658K Privately Held
SIC: 2752 2791 2789 2721 Commercial printing, offset; typesetting; bookbinding & related work; periodicals

(G-8540)
TARK INC (PA)
420 Congress Park Dr (45459-4125)
PHONE..................937 434-6766
Joe McCarthy, *CEO*
Jim McCarthy, *President*
John Basnett, *Vice Pres*
Donna McCarthy, *Vice Pres*
John Koverman, *Treasurer*
EMP: 42
SQ FT: 600
SALES (est): 9.6MM Privately Held
WEB: www.tarkinc.com
SIC: 3561 Pumps & pumping equipment

(G-8541)
TATE LYLE INGRDNTS AMRICAS LLC
5600 Brentlinger Dr (45414-3512)
PHONE..................937 236-5906
Charles Kraft, *Branch Mgr*
Carlos Alvarez, *Maintence Staff*
Aaron Struewing, *Maintence Staff*
EMP: 75
SALES (corp-wide): 3.8B Privately Held
SIC: 2899 2819 2087 Chemical preparations; industrial inorganic chemicals; flavoring extracts & syrups
HQ: Tate & Lyle Ingredients Americas Llc
  2200 E Eldorado St
  Decatur IL 62521
  217 423-4411

(G-8542)
TATE LYLE INGRDNTS AMRICAS LLC
5584 Webster St (45414-3517)
PHONE..................937 235-4074
EMP: 86
SALES (corp-wide): 3.8B Privately Held
SIC: 2046 Wet corn milling
HQ: Tate & Lyle Ingredients Americas Llc
  2200 E Eldorado St
  Decatur IL 62521
  217 423-4411

(G-8543)
TAYLOR COMMUNICATIONS INC
600 Albany St (45417-3405)
PHONE..................937 221-1000
Joe Klenke, *Vice Pres*
Steve McDonell, *Vice Pres*
Keyton Weissinger, *Vice Pres*
William Leonard, *Project Mgr*
Georgeanne Howard, *Opers Staff*
EMP: 24
SALES (corp-wide): 3.2B Privately Held
WEB: www.stdreg.com
SIC: 2761 2759 2752 8744 Manifold business forms; commercial printing; commercial printing, lithographic; facilities support services
HQ: Taylor Communications, Inc.
  1725 Roe Crest Dr
  North Mankato MN 56003
  507 625-2828

(G-8544)
TAYLOR COMMUNICATIONS INC
7755 Paragon Rd Ste 101 (45459-4052)
PHONE..................732 356-0081
Brian Clark, *Manager*
EMP: 11
SALES (corp-wide): 3.2B Privately Held
WEB: www.stdreg.com
SIC: 2761 Manifold business forms
HQ: Taylor Communications, Inc.
  1725 Roe Crest Dr
  North Mankato MN 56003
  507 625-2828

(G-8545)
TAYLOR COMMUNICATIONS INC
220 E Monument Ave (45402-1287)
PHONE..................937 228-5800
Camille Palladino, *Principal*
EMP: 5
SALES (corp-wide): 3.2B Privately Held
SIC: 5112 2754 2789 2761 Business forms; commercial printing, gravure; bookbinding & related work; manifold business forms; commercial printing, lithographic
HQ: Taylor Communications, Inc.
  1725 Roe Crest Dr
  North Mankato MN 56003
  507 625-2828

(G-8546)
TAYLOR COMMUNICATIONS INC
2222 Philadelphia Dr (45406)
PHONE..................866 541-0937
EMP: 3
SALES (corp-wide): 3.2B Privately Held
SIC: 2754 Commercial printing, gravure
HQ: Taylor Communications, Inc.
  1725 Roe Crest Dr
  North Mankato MN 56003
  507 625-2828

(G-8547)
TC PRECISION MACHINE INC
2540 Ashcraft Rd (45414-3402)
PHONE..................937 278-3334
Thomas J Trick, *President*
Cheryl Herick, *Admin Sec*
EMP: 4
SQ FT: 4,800
SALES (est): 471K Privately Held
SIC: 3599 7389 Machine shop, jobbing & repair; grinding, precision: commercial or industrial

(G-8548)
TE BROWN LLC (PA)
1205 Lamar St (45404-1658)
P.O. Box 89 (45404)
PHONE..................937 223-2241
Teddy Brown, *President*
EMP: 5
SQ FT: 10,000
SALES (est): 1.1MM Privately Held
SIC: 7699 3823 Industrial equipment services; temperature measurement instruments, industrial

(G-8549)
TEC DESIGN & MANUFACTURING INC
4549 Gateway Cir (45440-1711)
PHONE..................937 435-2147
John A Hudock, *President*
EMP: 14
SQ FT: 13,000
SALES (est): 890K Privately Held
SIC: 3542 3469 Machine tools, metal forming type; machine parts, stamped or pressed metal

(G-8550)
TEKNOL INC (PA)
Also Called: Rubber Seal Products
5751 Webster St (45414-3520)
P.O. Box 13387 (45413-0387)
PHONE..................937 264-0190
Kent Von Behren, *President*
R Von Behren, *Shareholder*
▲ EMP: 57 EST: 1976
SQ FT: 60,000
SALES: 31MM Privately Held
WEB: www.rubber-seal.com
SIC: 2899 2891 5198 2851 Chemical preparations; sealants; paints, varnishes & supplies; paints & allied products

(G-8551)
TELEMECANIQUE SENSORS
1875 Founders Dr (45420-4017)
PHONE..................800 435-2121
Christopher Weir, *President*
Allan Hottovy, *Manager*
Scott Ezell, *Executive*
EMP: 5
SALES (est): 630.8K Privately Held
SIC: 3823 Industrial instrmnts msrmnt display/control process variable

(G-8552)
TESSEC LLC
5679 Webster St (45414-3518)
PHONE..................937 985-3552
David Evans, *President*
EMP: 21

Dayton - Montgomery County (G-8553)

SALES (est): 4.7MM **Privately Held**
SIC: 3364 3721 Nonferrous die-castings except aluminum; motorized aircraft

(G-8553)
TESSEC MANUFACTURING SVCS LLC
5679 Webster St (45414-3518)
PHONE...................937 985-3552
David Evans, *President*
Kathy North, *Sales Staff*
EMP: 21
SALES (est): 1.2MM **Privately Held**
SIC: 3452 3544 3721 3761 Bolts, nuts, rivets & washers; special dies, tools, jigs & fixtures; aircraft; guided missiles & space vehicles; tanks & tank components

(G-8554)
THOMAS CABINET SHOP INC
321 Gargrave Rd (45449-2465)
PHONE...................937 847-8239
Jon Thomas, *President*
Cherie Thomas, *Corp Secy*
Don Thomas, *Vice Pres*
EMP: 10
SQ FT: 11,800
SALES: 1.5MM **Privately Held**
SIC: 1542 1751 2541 2434 Commercial & office buildings, renovation & repair; cabinet building & installation; wood partitions & fixtures; wood kitchen cabinets

(G-8555)
THREAD-RITE TOOL & MFG INC
1200 E 1st St (45403-1008)
PHONE...................937 222-2836
Timothy D Turner, *President*
Joseph J Wilson, *Vice Pres*
EMP: 4
SQ FT: 10,000
SALES: 630K **Privately Held**
SIC: 7389 3599 Grinding, precision: commercial or industrial; machine shop, jobbing & repair

(G-8556)
THREE BOND INTERNATIONAL INC
101 Daruma Pkwy (45439-7908)
PHONE...................937 610-3000
EMP: 50 **Privately Held**
SIC: 2891 Adhesives; glue
HQ: Three Bond International, Inc.
6184 Schumacher Park Dr
West Chester OH 45069
513 779-7300

(G-8557)
THRIFT TOOL INC
5916 Milo Rd (45414-3416)
PHONE...................937 275-3600
Walter Jones, *President*
Jeff Jones, *Vice Pres*
EMP: 6
SQ FT: 8,000
SALES (est): 152.2K **Privately Held**
SIC: 3312 Tool & die steel & alloys

(G-8558)
THT PRESSES INC
Also Called: Tht Presses
7475 Webster St (45414-5817)
PHONE...................937 898-2012
Mike Thieman, *President*
Rick Kamm, *Engineer*
Larry Siefring, *Engineer*
Tim Yount, *Design Engr*
Lori Lawson, *Controller*
▲ EMP: 25 EST: 1977
SQ FT: 51,000
SALES (est): 6.1MM **Privately Held**
WEB: www.thtpresses.com
SIC: 3542 Die casting machines; pressing machines

(G-8559)
TIPP STONE INC
8172 Meeker Rd (45414)
PHONE...................937 890-4051
Thomas Eidemiller, *President*
EMP: 3 EST: 1966
SQ FT: 480
SALES (est): 307.2K **Privately Held**
SIC: 1442 Sand mining; gravel mining

(G-8560)
TOMCO MACHINING INC
4962 Riverton Dr (45414-3964)
PHONE...................937 264-1943
Kathy J Tomasiak, *Ch of Bd*
James W Tomasiak, *President*
Ellen McCusiton, *QC Mgr*
De Wayne Sutton, *Manager*
EMP: 20
SQ FT: 15,000
SALES: 2MM **Privately Held**
WEB: www.tomcoaero.com
SIC: 3498 Tube fabricating (contract bending & shaping)

(G-8561)
TOOLCRAFT PRODUCTS INC
1265 Mccook Ave (45404-2800)
P.O. Box 482 (45401-0482)
PHONE...................937 223-8271
Mark W Klug, *President*
Mark Newton, *General Mgr*
Thomas W Thompson, *Vice Pres*
Tom Thompson, *Vice Pres*
Cherilynn M O'Malley, *CFO*
EMP: 68 EST: 1939
SQ FT: 56,000
SALES (est): 12.5MM **Privately Held**
WEB: www.toolcraftproducts.com
SIC: 3544 Die sets for metal stamping (presses); special dies & tools

(G-8562)
TOOLRITE MANUFACTURING INC
5370 Wadsworth Rd (45414-3523)
PHONE...................937 278-1962
David Tangeman, *President*
Tim Ryan, *Vice Pres*
Cindy Loy, *Manager*
EMP: 12
SQ FT: 4,500
SALES: 2.2MM **Privately Held**
SIC: 3544 Special dies, tools, jigs & fixtures

(G-8563)
TORSION CONTROL PRODUCT
840 W Spring Valley Pike (45458-3251)
PHONE...................248 597-9997
Bob McLain, *Principal*
EMP: 4
SALES (est): 148.4K **Privately Held**
SIC: 3493 Steel springs, except wire

(G-8564)
TRIANGLE PRECISION INDUSTRIES
1650 Delco Park Dr (45420-1392)
PHONE...................937 299-6776
Gerald D Schriml, *President*
Paul S Holzinger, *Vice Pres*
EMP: 57
SQ FT: 23,400
SALES (est): 10.2MM **Privately Held**
WEB: www.triangleprecision.com
SIC: 3599 7692 3446 3444 Machine shop, jobbing & repair; welding repair; architectural metalwork; sheet metalwork; fabricated plate work (boiler shop); fabricated structural metal

(G-8565)
TRIFECTA TOOL & ENGRG LLC
4648 Gateway Cir (45440-1714)
PHONE...................937 291-0933
Yogi Ferstl, *Project Mgr*
Chris Nichols, *Project Mgr*
Bret West, *Engineer*
Cory Borrello,
▲ EMP: 9
SQ FT: 15,000
SALES (est): 1.2MM **Privately Held**
WEB: www.trifectatool.com
SIC: 3089 Automotive parts, plastic; injection molding of plastics

(G-8566)
TRIMBLE INC
Trimble Engineering
5475 Kellenburger Rd (45424-1013)
PHONE...................937 233-8921
Chris Shephard, *Branch Mgr*
EMP: 11

SALES (corp-wide): 3.1B **Publicly Held**
WEB: www.trimble.com
SIC: 3812 Navigational systems & instruments
PA: Trimble Inc.
935 Stewart Dr
Sunnyvale CA 94085
408 481-8000

(G-8567)
TRIUMPH TOOL LLC
229 Leo St (45404-1005)
PHONE...................937 222-6885
EMP: 3
SALES (est): 403.2K **Privately Held**
SIC: 3599 7699 Mfg Industrial Machinery Repair Services

(G-8568)
TROJON GEAR INC
418 San Jose St (45403-1419)
P.O. Box 1507 (45401-1507)
PHONE...................937 254-1737
Charles Trochelman, *President*
Candace Trochelman, *Vice Pres*
EMP: 18 EST: 1957
SQ FT: 18,000
SALES: 1.3MM **Privately Held**
WEB: www.trojon-gear.com
SIC: 3599 7389 3566 3724 Machine & other job shop work; machine shop, jobbing & repair; metal cutting services; grinding, precision: commercial or industrial; speed changers, drives & gears; gears, power transmission, except automotive; aircraft engines & engine parts; gears, motor vehicle; screw machine products

(G-8569)
TROY ENGINEERED COMPONENTS AND
Also Called: Teca
4900 Webster St (45414-4831)
PHONE...................937 335-8070
Marvin Sauner, *President*
Jack Spencer, *Vice Pres*
Tony Vukufich, *Vice Pres*
Larry Ishmael, *Admin Sec*
EMP: 8
SALES (est): 1.1MM **Privately Held**
WEB: www.ishmael-precision.com
SIC: 3011 Tire & inner tube materials & related products

(G-8570)
TROY VALLEY PETROLEUM
201 Valley St (45404-1864)
PHONE...................937 604-0012
Amarjid Singh, *Principal*
EMP: 3
SQ FT: 2,248
SALES (est): 401K **Privately Held**
SIC: 2911 Petroleum refining

(G-8571)
TRU-FAB INC
4751 Gateway Cir (45440-1787)
PHONE...................937 435-1733
Steven Dudley, *President*
Ed Parker, *Vice Pres*
EMP: 14
SQ FT: 13,000
SALES (est): 1.3MM **Privately Held**
SIC: 3441 Fabricated structural metal

(G-8572)
TWEEN BRANDS INC
Also Called: Limited Too 937
2700 Mmsburg Cntrville Rd (45459)
PHONE...................937 435-6928
EMP: 14
SALES (corp-wide): 4.7B **Publicly Held**
SIC: 2361 Mfg Girl/Youth Dresses/Blouses
HQ: Tween Brands, Inc.
8323 Walton Pkwy
New Albany OH 43054
614 775-3500

(G-8573)
TWIN DESIGN AP PROMOTIONS LTD
5785 Far Hills Ave (45429-2207)
PHONE...................937 732-6798
Dixie Scott, *Owner*
Nancy Honshell, *Owner*

EMP: 3
SALES (est): 170K **Privately Held**
SIC: 7389 2395 2211 Design services; embroidery & art needlework; apparel & outerwear fabrics, cotton

(G-8574)
TWIN TOOL LLC
4648 Gateway Cir (45440-1714)
PHONE...................937 435-8946
Cory Corello, *President*
Dan Miller, *Project Mgr*
EMP: 5 EST: 2000
SALES (est): 840.7K **Privately Held**
WEB: www.twintool.com
SIC: 3544 Special dies, tools, jigs & fixtures

(G-8575)
U S CHROME CORPORATION OHIO
Also Called: Production Plant
107 Westboro St (45417-4055)
PHONE...................877 872-7716
Greg Santo, *Branch Mgr*
EMP: 12
SQ FT: 8,000
SALES (corp-wide): 30.5MM **Privately Held**
SIC: 3471 Electroplating of metals or formed products
HQ: U.S. Chrome Corporation Of Ohio
175 Garfield Ave
Stratford CT
937 224-0548

(G-8576)
UNIVERSAL TOOL TECHNOLOGY LLC
3488 Stop 8 Rd (45414-3428)
P.O. Box 31249 (45437-0249)
PHONE...................937 222-4608
Debbie Toney, *CFO*
Michael Farmer,
Deborah Toney,
Walt Toney,
EMP: 45
SQ FT: 45,000
SALES (est): 3.2MM **Privately Held**
WEB: www.universal-systems.net
SIC: 3544 3599 Special dies & tools; die sets for metal stamping (presses); jigs & fixtures; industrial molds; machine shop, jobbing & repair

(G-8577)
US AEROTEAM INC
2601 W Stroop Rd Ste 60 (45439-2030)
PHONE...................937 458-0344
Suhas Kakde, *President*
Jim Zahora, *COO*
Jeff Maag, *Vice Pres*
Dennis Sparks, *VP Opers*
Kevin McGovern, *Mfg Mgr*
EMP: 48
SALES (est): 11.5MM **Privately Held**
WEB: www.usaeroteam.com
SIC: 3724 3728 3769 Aircraft engines & engine parts; aircraft parts & equipment; guided missile & space vehicle parts & auxiliary equipment

(G-8578)
VENU ON 3RD
905 E 3rd St (45402-2248)
PHONE...................937 222-2891
Jerry White, *Principal*
EMP: 4
SALES (est): 321.7K **Privately Held**
SIC: 2599 Bar, restaurant & cafeteria furniture

(G-8579)
VIBRONIC
5208 Wadsworth Rd (45414-3508)
PHONE...................937 274-1114
Leah Lach, *Branch Mgr*
EMP: 17
SALES (est): 1.7MM **Privately Held**
SIC: 2822 Synthetic rubber

(G-8580)
VIKING GROUP INC (PA)
2806 Wayne Ave (45420-1837)
PHONE...................937 443-0433
Todd Rodger, *President*

GEOGRAPHIC SECTION — Dayton - Montgomery County (G-8604)

EMP: 6
SQ FT: 1,200
SALES (est): 811K Privately Held
SIC: 3569 3491 3669 2899 Sprinkler systems, fire: automatic; automatic regulating & control valves; fire alarm apparatus, electric; fire retardant chemicals

(G-8581)
VULCAN TOOL COMPANY
730 Lorain Ave (45410-2400)
PHONE 937 253-6194
Gary Mertler, *General Mgr*
Dan Kuchenbuch, *Principal*
Matt Gonet, *Project Mgr*
Mary Martin, *Manager*
▲ **EMP:** 7 **EST:** 1916
SQ FT: 90,000
SALES (est): 1.2MM Privately Held
WEB: www.vulcancut.com
SIC: 3544 3542 3541 3643 Special dies & tools; jigs & fixtures; machine tools, metal forming type; machine tools, metal cutting type; current-carrying wiring devices

(G-8582)
WALTER NORTH
900 Pimlico Dr Apt 2a (45459-8265)
PHONE 937 204-6050
Walter North, *Owner*
EMP: 11
SALES (est): 483.1K Privately Held
SIC: 3571 7389 Electronic computers;

(G-8583)
WARPED WING BREWING CO LLC
26 Wyandot St (45402-2145)
P.O. Box 653 (45409-0653)
PHONE 937 222-7003
Nick Bowman, *VP Sales*
Annette Adams, *Office Mgr*
EMP: 11
SALES (est): 2.3MM Privately Held
SIC: 2082 Malt beverages

(G-8584)
WARRIOR TECHNOLOGIES INC
7320 Kings Run Rd (45459-3420)
PHONE 937 438-0279
Charles J Hardin, *President*
Stephanie McCabe, *Vice Pres*
EMP: 5
SQ FT: 26,000
SALES (est): 420K Privately Held
SIC: 3599 1799 Machine shop, jobbing & repair; welding on site

(G-8585)
WATSON HARAN & COMPANY INC
Also Called: Manoranjan Shaffer & Heidkamp
1500 Yankee Park Pl (45458-1878)
PHONE 937 436-1414
Angie Shaffer, *Manager*
EMP: 6
SALES (corp-wide): 807K Privately Held
WEB: www.hwcocpa.com
SIC: 8721 2759 Certified public accountant; financial note & certificate printing & engraving
PA: Watson Haran & Company Inc
445 Hutchinson Ave # 695
Columbus OH 43235
614 847-2333

(G-8586)
WAYNE SPORTING GOODS
7101 Taylorsville Rd (45424-3101)
PHONE 937 236-6665
Rick Breitfield, *Owner*
Marcia Breitfield, *Co-Owner*
EMP: 5 **EST:** 1976
SQ FT: 3,300
SALES (est): 400K Privately Held
SIC: 5941 3552 2262 Team sports equipment; embroidery machines; screen printing: manmade fiber & silk broadwoven fabrics

(G-8587)
WEBER JEWELERS INCORPORATED
Also Called: F & J Manufacturing
3155 Far Hills Ave (45429-2522)
PHONE 937 643-9200
Fred Weber, *Manager*
EMP: 3
SQ FT: 1,500
SALES (corp-wide): 1.4MM Privately Held
WEB: www.weberjewelers.com
SIC: 3911 Jewelry, precious metal
PA: Weber Jewelers Incorporated
3109 Far Hills Ave
Dayton OH
937 643-9600

(G-8588)
WELDMENTS INC
167 Heid Ave (45404-1217)
PHONE 937 235-9261
James Hackenberger, *President*
John Limberg, *Corp Secy*
Chuck Kraft, *Vice Pres*
EMP: 12
SQ FT: 10,000
SALES (est): 1.5MM
SALES (corp-wide): 7MM Privately Held
WEB: www.weldments.com
SIC: 7692 1799 Welding repair; welding on site
PA: Precision Metal Fabrication, Inc.
191 Heid Ave
Dayton OH 45404
937 235-9261

(G-8589)
WESTROCK CP LLC
7032 N Dixie Dr (45414-3126)
PHONE 937 898-2115
Julie Robinson, *Branch Mgr*
EMP: 213
SALES (corp-wide): 16.2B Publicly Held
WEB: www.smurfit-stone.com
SIC: 2621 2796 Wrapping & packaging papers; platemaking services
HQ: Westrock Cp, Llc
1000 Abernathy Rd
Atlanta GA 30328

(G-8590)
WESTROCK MWV LLC
Consumer & Office Products Div
10 W 2nd St (45402-1791)
PHONE 937 495-6323
Patricia B Robinson, *Manager*
EMP: 680
SALES (corp-wide): 16.2B Publicly Held
WEB: www.meadwestvaco.com
SIC: 2678 Stationery products
HQ: Westrock Mwv, Llc
501 S 5th St
Richmond VA 23219
804 444-1000

(G-8591)
WESTWOOD FVRICATION SHTMTL INC
1752 Stanley Ave (45404-1117)
PHONE 937 837-0494
Larry Highlander, *President*
EMP: 27
SQ FT: 25,000
SALES (est): 2.8MM Privately Held
WEB: www.westwoodfabrication.com
SIC: 3444 Sheet metalwork

(G-8592)
WFSR HOLDINGS LLC
220 E Monument Ave (45402-1287)
PHONE 877 735-4966
Tim Tatman, *President*
Tom Koenig, *CFO*
▲ **EMP:** 2000
SALES (est): 140.5MM
SALES (corp-wide): 3.2B Privately Held
SIC: 2752 2754 2759 2761 Commercial printing, lithographic; commercial printing, gravure; commercial printing; manifold business forms; bookbinding & related work; typesetting

(G-8593)
WILLIAM J MINNEMAN FAMILY LP
3370 Obco Ct (45414-3513)
P.O. Box 13117 (45413-0117)
PHONE 937 890-7461
Steve Minneman, *President*
Allen Minneman, *Vice Pres*
▼ **EMP:** 25 **EST:** 1966
SQ FT: 92,000
SALES (est): 6.5MM Privately Held
WEB: www.mtmmolded.com
SIC: 3089 Cases, plastic; molding primary plastic

(G-8594)
WILSON CONCRETE PRODUCTS INC (PA)
10075 Sheehan Rd (45458-4301)
PHONE 937 885-7965
Fax: 937 885-7984
EMP: 50 **EST:** 1946
SQ FT: 45,000
SALES (est): 6.2MM Privately Held
SIC: 3272 5211 Mfg Concrete Products Ret Lumber/Building Materials

(G-8595)
WILSON SIGN CO INC
Also Called: Wilson Electronic Displays
300 Hamilton Ave (45403-2450)
PHONE 937 253-2246
David Wilson, *President*
Lattie B Wilson, *CFO*
EMP: 11 **EST:** 1969
SQ FT: 17,000
SALES (est): 2.1MM Privately Held
SIC: 3993 7629 Electric signs; electrical equipment repair, high voltage

(G-8596)
WINKLER CO INC
Also Called: Oakwood Register, The
435 Patterson Rd (45419-4344)
P.O. Box 572 (45409-0572)
PHONE 937 294-2662
Dolores Winkler, *President*
Lance A Winkler, *Vice Pres*
Dana M Winkler, *Treasurer*
Vicky Holloway, *Accounts Exec*
Richard Brame, *Advt Staff*
EMP: 6 **EST:** 1960
SQ FT: 2,700
SALES (est): 430.1K Privately Held
WEB: www.oakwoodregister.com
SIC: 2711 2791 Newspapers: publishing only, not printed on site; typesetting

(G-8597)
WINSTON HEAT TREATING INC
711 E 2nd St (45402-1319)
P.O. Box 1551 (45401-1551)
PHONE 937 226-0110
John L Reger, *President*
Kirt Fourman, *Facilities Mgr*
Robert Cole, *Manager*
EMP: 33
SQ FT: 26,000
SALES (est): 8.3MM Privately Held
WEB: www.winstonht.com
SIC: 3398 Metal heat treating

(G-8598)
WISCO PRODUCTS INCORPORATED
109 Commercial St (45402-2297)
PHONE 937 228-2101
Mark Paxson, *President*
Kyle Paxson, *Opers Mgr*
Greg Lam, *Purch Mgr*
Derrick Maier, *Sales Mgr*
Jason Sorah, *Manager*
EMP: 30
SQ FT: 23,000
SALES (est): 5.8MM Privately Held
WEB: www.wiscoproducts.com
SIC: 3469 3089 Metal stampings; caps, plastic

(G-8599)
WOODBURN PRESS LLC
405 Littell Ave (45419-3609)
P.O. Box 329 (45409-0329)
PHONE 937 293-9245
John O'Brien, *President*
Linda O'Brien, *Owner*
Mike O'Brien, *Owner*
Brad Judy, *Sales Staff*
Chris Gooley, *Info Tech Mgr*
EMP: 6
SQ FT: 10,000
SALES (est): 721.3K Privately Held
WEB: www.woodburnpress.com
SIC: 2731 2741 Book publishing; posters: publishing & printing

(G-8600)
WRIGHT SOLUTIONS LLC
1085 Redbluff Dr (45449-3180)
PHONE 937 938-8745
Mario Duane Wright, *Principal*
EMP: 3 **EST:** 2016
SALES (est): 208.5K Privately Held
SIC: 3842 Surgical appliances & supplies

(G-8601)
WURTH ELECTRONICS ICS INC
Also Called: Wurth Elektronik
7496 Webster St (45414-5816)
PHONE 937 415-7700
Brad Weaver, *CEO*
Josh Shakeridge, *Sales Staff*
EMP: 27
SQ FT: 22,000
SALES (est): 3.5MM
SALES (corp-wide): 15B Privately Held
SIC: 3672 Printed circuit boards
HQ: Wurth Group Of North America Inc.
93 Grant St
Ramsey NJ 07446
201 818-8877

(G-8602)
YODER INDUSTRIES INC (PA)
2520 Needmore Rd (45414-4204)
PHONE 937 278-5769
Ron Zeverka, *President*
Janet E Roush, *Principal*
Ron Veverka, *Principal*
J B Yoder, *Principal*
Charles W Slicer, *Chairman*
EMP: 110 **EST:** 1956
SQ FT: 32,000
SALES (est): 13MM Privately Held
WEB: www.yoderindustries.com
SIC: 3369 3363 3365 3471 Nonferrous foundries; aluminum die-castings; aluminum foundries; plating & polishing; testing laboratories; nonferrous die-castings except aluminum

(G-8603)
YODER INDUSTRIES INC
3009 Production Ct (45414-3514)
PHONE 937 890-4322
John Ridder, *Manager*
EMP: 35
SALES (corp-wide): 13MM Privately Held
WEB: www.yoderindustries.com
SIC: 3364 3365 Nonferrous die-castings except aluminum; aluminum foundries
PA: Yoder Industries, Inc.
2520 Needmore Rd
Dayton OH 45414
937 278-5769

(G-8604)
ZIMMER ENTERPRISES INC (PA)
Also Called: Kettering Monogramming
911 Senate Dr (45459-4017)
PHONE 937 428-1057
Jeffrey Zimmer, *President*
Patricia M Zimmer, *Vice Pres*
▲ **EMP:** 25
SALES (est): 10.1MM Privately Held
WEB: www.pbj-sport.com
SIC: 5137 2395 Women's & children's clothing; embroidery products, except schiffli machine

De Graff - Logan County (G-8605)   GEOGRAPHIC SECTION

De Graff
Logan County

(G-8605)
PRECISION CUSTOM PRODUCTS INC
4590 County Road 35 (43318-9770)
PHONE 937 585-4011
James Kerg Jr, *CEO*
Dawn Beelman, *CFO*
Dan McMahon, *Sales Mgr*
Allison Prinkey, *Cust Svc*
Hazel Lambert, *Manager*
EMP: 26
SQ FT: 30,000
SALES: 4.8MM **Privately Held**
WEB: www.pcpiplastics.com
SIC: 3089 Injection molded finished plastic products; injection molding of plastics

(G-8606)
SUPERIOR MACHINE AND TOOL
7726 Crowl Rd (43318-9562)
PHONE 937 308-5771
Andrea Smith, *Owner*
EMP: 4
SQ FT: 2,500
SALES (est): 184.2K **Privately Held**
SIC: 3599 Machine shop, jobbing & repair

Deerfield
Portage County

(G-8607)
CHEVRON AE RESOURCES LLC
1823 State Route 14 (44411)
P.O. Box 160 (44411-0160)
PHONE 330 654-4343
EMP: 30
SALES (corp-wide): 129.9B **Publicly Held**
SIC: 1311 1382 Crude Petroleum/Natural Gas Production Oil/Gas Exploration Services
HQ: Chevron Ae Resources Llc
  1000 Commerce Dr Fl 4
  Pittsburgh PA 15275
  800 251-0171

(G-8608)
DEERFIELD FARMS SERVICE INC
9041 U S Route 224 (44411-8715)
PHONE 800 589-8606
EMP: 75 **EST:** 1959
SALES (est): 11.6MM **Privately Held**
SIC: 2873 Mfg Nitrogenous Fertilizers

(G-8609)
FOUNDER SERVICE & MFG CO
Also Called: Founder's Service Co
879 State Route 14 (44411-9777)
P.O. Box 56, North Benton (44449-0056)
PHONE 330 584-7759
Doug Stanley, *President*
Thad Stanley, *Admin Sec*
EMP: 13
SQ FT: 8,000
SALES (est): 1.9MM **Privately Held**
SIC: 3543 3544 Foundry cores; forms (molds), for foundry & plastics working machinery

(G-8610)
MIDWEST FIREWORKS MFG CO II
8550 State Route 224 (44411-8743)
PHONE 330 584-7000
EMP: 4
SALES (est): 304.2K **Privately Held**
SIC: 2899 Fireworks

Defiance
Defiance County

(G-8611)
ADVANTAGE POWDER COATING INC (PA)
2090 E 2nd St Ste 102 (43512-8648)
PHONE 419 782-2363
Joellen Hornish, *President*
Sam Hornish, *Vice Pres*
April P Hahn, *Office Mgr*
Mike Ketcham, *CIO*
EMP: 75
SQ FT: 51,000
SALES (est): 6.2MM **Privately Held**
SIC: 3479 Coating of metals & formed products; painting, coating & hot dipping

(G-8612)
AL-FE HEAT TREATING INC
Also Called: Al-Fe Heat Treating Defiance
2066 E 2nd St (43512-8654)
PHONE 419 782-7200
Andy Berg, *Business Anlyst*
Ernie Lackner, *Branch Mgr*
John Holifield, *Manager*
EMP: 27
SALES (corp-wide): 81.9MM **Privately Held**
WEB: www.al-fe.com
SIC: 3398 Metal heat treating
HQ: Al-Fe Heat Treating, Llc
  6920 Pointe Inverness Way # 140
  Fort Wayne IN 46804
  260 747-9422

(G-8613)
ARONIT MACHINE LLC
2018 Baltimore St (43512-1918)
PHONE 419 782-4740
John E Postema,
EMP: 10
SALES: 780K **Privately Held**
SIC: 3569 Filters

(G-8614)
B & B MOLDED PRODUCTS INC
1250 Ottawa Ave (43512-3004)
P.O. Box 213, Napoleon (43545-0213)
PHONE 419 592-8700
Donald V Gillett, *President*
▲ **EMP:** 40
SQ FT: 55,000
SALES (est): 10.6MM **Privately Held**
WEB: www.bbmolded.com
SIC: 3089 Injection molded finished plastic products; injection molding of plastics

(G-8615)
BAKER-SHINDLER CONTRACTING CO (PA)
Also Called: Baker-Shindler Builders Sup Co
525 Cleveland Ave (43512-3546)
P.O. Box 488 (43512-0400)
PHONE 419 782-5080
Douglas Shindler, *President*
EMP: 23 **EST:** 1921
SQ FT: 8,500
SALES (est): 6MM **Privately Held**
SIC: 1542 1541 3273 Specialized public building contractors; industrial buildings, new construction; ready-mixed concrete

(G-8616)
BARBS CUSTOM EMBROIDERY
14845 State Route 111 (43512-8616)
PHONE 419 393-2226
Barbara Brink, *Principal*
EMP: 3
SALES (est): 124K **Privately Held**
SIC: 2395 Embroidery & art needlework

(G-8617)
BRUNSWICK EYE & CONTACT LENS C
2011 S Clinton St (43512-3222)
PHONE 419 439-3381
EMP: 3
SALES (est): 180K **Privately Held**
SIC: 3851 Mfg Ophthalmic Goods

(G-8618)
CBS BORING AND MCH CO INC
2064 E 2nd St (43512-8654)
PHONE 419 784-9500
Todd Chupick, *Asst Controller*
Dave Hodell, *Manager*
David Oreilly, *Director*
EMP: 35
SALES (corp-wide): 20.5MM **Privately Held**
WEB: www.cbsboring.com
SIC: 3599 Machine shop, jobbing & repair
PA: C.B.S. Boring And Machine Company, Inc.
  33750 Riviera
  Fraser MI 48026
  586 294-7540

(G-8619)
DEFIANCE METAL PRODUCTS CO (HQ)
21 Seneca St (43512-2274)
P.O. Box 447 (43512-0447)
PHONE 419 784-5332
Stephen Mance, *CEO*
Sam Strausbaugh, *President*
Rick Creedmore, *Vice Pres*
Mark Koenen, *Vice Pres*
Jesse Horton, *Plant Mgr*
▲ **EMP:** 475
SQ FT: 165,000
SALES (est): 191.7MM
SALES (corp-wide): 499.1MM **Privately Held**
SIC: 3465 3443 3544 Fabricated plate work (boiler shop); special dies & tools
PA: Mayville Engineering Co Inc
  715 South St
  Mayville WI 53050
  920 387-4500

(G-8620)
DEFIANCE METAL PRODUCTS CO
6728 N State Route 66 (43512-6731)
PHONE 419 784-5332
Cecilia Montalvo-Silburn, *Manager*
EMP: 275
SALES (corp-wide): 499.1MM **Privately Held**
SIC: 3444 Sheet metalwork
HQ: Defiance Metal Products Co.
  21 Seneca St
  Defiance OH 43512
  419 784-5332

(G-8621)
DEFIANCE METAL PRODUCTS WI INC
Also Called: Medalist Laserfab
21 Seneca St (43512-2274)
PHONE 920 426-9207
Steve Mance, *CEO*
Ken Daiff, *CFO*
Michael Schoendorf, *Admin Sec*
EMP: 115
SQ FT: 36,000
SALES (est): 28.7MM
SALES (corp-wide): 499.1MM **Privately Held**
WEB: www.mlaserfab.com
SIC: 3441 3498 Fabricated structural metal; fabricated pipe & fittings; pipe fittings, fabricated from purchased pipe; pipe sections fabricated from purchased pipe
HQ: Defiance Metal Products Co.
  21 Seneca St
  Defiance OH 43512
  419 784-5332

(G-8622)
DOMINION LABELS & FORMS
232 Adams St (43512-1702)
P.O. Box 825 (43512-0825)
PHONE 419 784-1041
Bill Papenhagen, *Owner*
EMP: 3
SALES: 500K **Privately Held**
SIC: 2759 Commercial printing

(G-8623)
GENERAL MOTORS LLC
26427 State Route 281 (43512-6781)
PHONE 419 782-7010
Steve Brown, *Engineer*
Thomas Gallther, *Manager*
Sharon Griffith, *Telecom Exec*
EMP: 3600 **Publicly Held**
SIC: 3321 3322 3365 3369 Gray iron castings; malleable iron foundries; aluminum & aluminum-based alloy castings; nonferrous foundries
HQ: General Motors Llc
  300 Renaissance Ctr L1
  Detroit MI 48243

(G-8624)
GODFREY & WING INC
2066 E 2nd St (43512-8654)
PHONE 419 980-4616
John Horvath, *Branch Mgr*
EMP: 12
SALES (corp-wide): 19.3MM **Privately Held**
SIC: 3823 Absorption analyzers: infrared, X-ray, etc.: industrial
PA: Godfrey & Wing Inc.
  220 Campus Dr
  Aurora OH 44202
  330 562-1440

(G-8625)
GT TECHNOLOGIES INC
Also Called: Defiance Operations
1125 Precision Way (43512-1946)
PHONE 419 782-8955
Joe Molnar, *Plant Mgr*
EMP: 140
SALES (corp-wide): 101MM **Privately Held**
SIC: 3714 3562 3599 3398 Motor vehicle engines & parts; ball & roller bearings; machine shop, jobbing & repair; metal heat treating
PA: Gt Technologies, Inc.
  5859 E Executive Dr
  Westland MI 48185
  734 467-8371

(G-8626)
HILLTOP PRINTING
1815 Baltimore St (43512-1913)
PHONE 419 782-9898
Verle L Harner, *Owner*
EMP: 6
SQ FT: 5,000
SALES (est): 563.3K **Privately Held**
SIC: 2759 Commercial printing

(G-8627)
HUBBARD COMPANY
612 Clinton St (43512-2637)
P.O. Box 100 (43512-0100)
PHONE 419 784-4455
E Keith Hubbard, *Ch of Bd*
Thomas K Hubbard, *President*
Jean A Hubbard, *Treasurer*
Jean Hubbard, *Finance*
Dick Anderson, *Sales Staff*
EMP: 44
SQ FT: 20,000
SALES (est): 7.2MM **Privately Held**
WEB: www.hubbardcompany.com
SIC: 5943 5192 2752 2732 Office forms & supplies; books; commercial printing, offset; book printing; book publishing

(G-8628)
JOHNS MANVILLE CORPORATION
1410 Columbus Ave (43512-3181)
P.O. Box 7188 (43512-7188)
PHONE 419 782-0180
Randy Engel, *General Mgr*
Robert Belden, *Purchasing*
Joe Mota, *VP Sales*
Garry Caudill, *Sales Staff*
Frank Tressler, *IT/INT Sup*
EMP: 280
SALES (corp-wide): 225.3B **Publicly Held**
SIC: 3296 Mineral wool
HQ: Johns Manville Corporation
  717 17th St Ste 800
  Denver CO 80202
  303 978-2000

▲ = Import ▼=Export ◆ =Import/Export

GEOGRAPHIC SECTION

Delaware - Delaware County (G-8653)

(G-8629)
JOHNS MANVILLE CORPORATION
925 Carpenter Rd (43512-1765)
PHONE.................................419 784-7000
Jim Swift, *Plant Mgr*
Craig McKibben, *Facilities Mgr*
Brian Siler, *Warehouse Mgr*
David Morris, *Production*
Janet Spitnale, *Purch Agent*
EMP: 600
SALES (corp-wide): 225.3B **Publicly Held**
WEB: www.jm.com
SIC: 3296 Fiberglass insulation
HQ: Johns Manville Corporation
717 17th St Ste 800
Denver CO 80202
303 978-2000

(G-8630)
JOHNS MANVILLE CORPORATION
3rd And Perry (43512)
P.O. Box 158 (43512-0158)
PHONE.................................419 784-7000
Jerry Henry, *President*
EMP: 200
SALES (corp-wide): 225.3B **Publicly Held**
SIC: 3296 Fiberglass insulation
HQ: Johns Manville Corporation
717 17th St Ste 800
Denver CO 80202
303 978-2000

(G-8631)
JOHNS MANVILLE CORPORATION
408 Perry St Plant 02 2 Plant (43512)
PHONE.................................419 878-8111
Craig McKibben, *Manager*
EMP: 224
SALES (corp-wide): 225.3B **Publicly Held**
WEB: www.jm.com
SIC: 3296 Fiberglass insulation
HQ: Johns Manville Corporation
717 17th St Ste 800
Denver CO 80202
303 978-2000

(G-8632)
KOESTER MACHINED PRODUCTS CO
136 Fox Run Dr (43512-1394)
PHONE.................................419 782-0291
Michael Koester, *President*
William C Koester, *Director*
Jeanette Spiller, *Admin Sec*
EMP: 15
SQ FT: 21,000
SALES: 771K **Privately Held**
SIC: 3599 Machine shop, jobbing & repair

(G-8633)
M W SOLUTIONS LLC
1802 Baltimore St Ste B (43512-2081)
PHONE.................................419 782-1611
Matthew Winzeler, *Mng Member*
EMP: 10
SALES: 2MM **Privately Held**
SIC: 3089 3694 3559 Automotive parts, plastic; alternators, automotive; automotive electrical equipment; automotive related machinery

(G-8634)
M-FISCHER ENTERPRISES LLC
Also Called: Goin' Postal
925 S Clinton St Ste B (43512-2792)
PHONE.................................419 782-5309
Megan Fischer,
EMP: 3
SQ FT: 1,600
SALES: 350K **Privately Held**
SIC: 8611 2752 Shipping & steamship company association; commercial printing, lithographic

(G-8635)
MARC V CONCEPTS INC
Also Called: Figley Stamping Company
401 Agnes St (43512-3072)
PHONE.................................419 782-6505
Christopher Slee, *President*
Rick Behnfeldt, *Vice Pres*
▼ **EMP:** 10 **EST:** 1993
SQ FT: 23,000
SALES (est): 1MM **Privately Held**
WEB: www.figleystamping.com
SIC: 3469 Stamping metal for the trade

(G-8636)
MARTIN DIESEL INC
27809 County Road 424 (43512-8147)
P.O. Box 1000 (43512-1000)
PHONE.................................419 782-9911
James M Martin Jr, *President*
Cliff Martin, *Vice Pres*
Brian Martin, *Executive*
EMP: 21
SQ FT: 17,500
SALES (est): 3.8MM **Privately Held**
WEB: www.martindiesel.com
SIC: 3621 5013 5531 5084 Generators & sets, electric; automotive supplies & parts; truck equipment & parts; engines & parts, diesel

(G-8637)
MEEKS PASTRY SHOP
315 Clinton St (43512-2113)
PHONE.................................419 782-4871
William Meek, *Owner*
EMP: 6
SQ FT: 2,500
SALES (est): 512.5K **Privately Held**
SIC: 2051 5461 Bread, cake & related products; pastries

(G-8638)
MESSERMAN CORP
Also Called: Messerman Machine Co
407 Agnes St (43512-3072)
P.O. Box 116 (43512-0116)
PHONE.................................419 782-1136
Jeff Behlke, *President*
Jeffrey Pahl, *Vice Pres*
EMP: 5 **EST:** 1952
SQ FT: 5,000
SALES: 462.8K **Privately Held**
SIC: 3599 Custom machinery; machine shop, jobbing & repair

(G-8639)
MINUTEMAN PRESS
214 Clinton St (43512-0017)
P.O. Box 1010 (43512-1010)
PHONE.................................419 782-8002
EMP: 4
SQ FT: 1,000
SALES: 300K **Privately Held**
SIC: 2752 Lithographic Commercial Printing

(G-8640)
MOUNTAIN FILTRATION SYSTEMS
26705 Blanchard Rd (43512-8984)
PHONE.................................419 395-2526
Larry Moore, *Manager*
EMP: 3 **Privately Held**
SIC: 3589 5074 Water filters & softeners, household type; water heaters & purification equipment
PA: Mountain Filtration Systems Inc
907 Isaacs Creek Rd
Lost Creek WV

(G-8641)
NOSTALGIC IMAGES INC
26012 Nostalgic Rd (43512-7108)
PHONE.................................419 784-1728
William Westrick, *President*
Clay W Balyeat, *Principal*
Lynda Sue Westrick, *Principal*
Audrea Schindler, *Sales Staff*
Jason Westrick, *Marketing Staff*
▲ **EMP:** 24
SQ FT: 60,000
SALES (est): 6MM **Privately Held**
WEB: www.nostalgicimages.com
SIC: 3499 Picture frames, metal

(G-8642)
SENSORYEFFECTS FLAVOR COMPANY
Also Called: Sensory Effects
136 Fox Run Dr (43512-1394)
PHONE.................................419 782-5010
Brett Keezer, *Branch Mgr*
EMP: 26
SALES (corp-wide): 643.6MM **Publicly Held**
SIC: 2087 Extracts, flavoring
HQ: Sensoryeffects Flavor Company
231 Rock Indus Prk Dr
Bridgeton MO 63044
314 291-5444

(G-8643)
SENSORYFFCTS POWDR SYSTEMS INC
136 Fox Run Dr (43512-1394)
PHONE.................................419 783-5518
Charles A Nicolais, *CEO*
◆ **EMP:** 70
SQ FT: 160,000
SALES (est): 25.2MM
SALES (corp-wide): 643.6MM **Publicly Held**
WEB: www.diehlinc.com
SIC: 2099 Food preparations
HQ: Sensoryeffects, Inc.
13723 Rverport Dr Ste 201
Maryland Heights MO 63043

(G-8644)
SUPERIOR BAR PRODUCTS INC
1710 Spruce St (43512-2457)
PHONE.................................419 784-2590
Mark Crandall, *President*
Deb Wittenmyer, *Treasurer*
EMP: 6
SQ FT: 7,000
SALES: 600K **Privately Held**
SIC: 3451 Screw machine products

(G-8645)
THE DEFIANCE PUBLISHING CO
Also Called: Defiance Crescent News, The
624 W 2nd St (43512-2161)
P.O. Box 249 (43512-0249)
PHONE.................................419 784-5441
Mark Adams, *President*
Mark Froelich, *Editor*
Todd Helberg, *Editor*
Lisa Nicely, *Editor*
Brett Belew, *District Mgr*
EMP: 855 **EST:** 1888
SQ FT: 9,000
SALES (est): 41.1MM
SALES (corp-wide): 528.2MM **Privately Held**
WEB: www.crescent-news.com
SIC: 2711 Commercial printing & newspaper publishing combined; newspapers, publishing & printing
PA: Dix 1898, Inc.
212 E Liberty St
Wooster OH
330 264-3511

(G-8646)
TRESSLERS PLUMBING LLC
9170 State Route 15 (43512)
PHONE.................................419 784-2142
Doug Tressler,
Terry Tressler,
EMP: 7
SALES (est): 599.8K **Privately Held**
SIC: 1481 Pumping or draining, nonmetallic mineral mines

(G-8647)
WERLOR INC
Also Called: Werlor Waste Control
1420 Ralston Ave (43512-1380)
PHONE.................................419 784-4285
Gerald Wertz, *President*
Judy Wertz, *Corp Secy*
Mark Hageman, *Vice Pres*
Tom Taylor, *Vice Pres*
Casey Wertz, *Vice Pres*
EMP: 40
SQ FT: 8,000
SALES (est): 5.5MM **Privately Held**
WEB: www.werlor.com
SIC: 4212 2875 Garbage collection & transport, no disposal; compost

Delaware
Delaware County

(G-8648)
ACI INDUSTRIES LTD (PA)
970 Pittsburgh Dr (43015-3872)
PHONE.................................740 368-4160
Ralph Paglieri, *Partner*
Scott H Fischer, *Partner*
Helen Harper, *Partner*
Shreelal Bhatter, *Vice Pres*
Helen Hraper, *Vice Pres*
◆ **EMP:** 50
SQ FT: 225,000
SALES: 3.8MM **Privately Held**
WEB: www.aci-industries.com
SIC: 3341 5093 3339 Secondary nonferrous metals; scrap & waste materials; primary nonferrous metals

(G-8649)
ACI INDUSTRIES CONVERTING LTD (HQ)
Also Called: J and J Sales
970 Pittsburgh Dr (43015-3872)
PHONE.................................740 368-4160
Mike Paglieri, *General Ptnr*
◆ **EMP:** 33
SQ FT: 232,000
SALES (est): 2.7MM
SALES (corp-wide): 3.8MM **Privately Held**
SIC: 2676 5113 Towels, napkins & tissue paper products; towels, paper
PA: Aci Industries, Ltd.
970 Pittsburgh Dr
Delaware OH 43015
740 368-4160

(G-8650)
ADJUSTABLE KICKER LLC
45 River St (43015-2196)
PHONE.................................740 362-9170
Tim Colatruglio,
Ernest Massert,
EMP: 3
SALES (est): 474.1K **Privately Held**
WEB: www.adjustablekicker.com
SIC: 3444 Concrete forms, sheet metal

(G-8651)
AFTERMARKET PARTS COMPANY LLC
2338 Us Highway 42 S (43015-9502)
PHONE.................................740 369-1056
John Hankins, *Branch Mgr*
EMP: 302
SALES (corp-wide): 2.3B **Privately Held**
SIC: 3711 Buses, all types, assembly of
HQ: The Aftermarket Parts Company Llc
3229 Sawmill Pkwy
Delaware OH 43015
740 369-1056

(G-8652)
AG DESIGNS LLC
1165 Dunham Rd (43015-8689)
PHONE.................................614 506-2849
Matthew Ayers,
EMP: 4
SALES: 18K **Privately Held**
SIC: 3993 5999 7336 7389 Letters for signs, metal; banners, flags, decals & posters; commercial art & graphic design;

(G-8653)
AMERICAN FLANGE & MFG CO INC
425 Winter Rd (43015-8903)
PHONE.................................740 549-6073
David B Fischer, *Branch Mgr*
EMP: 7
SALES (corp-wide): 3.8B **Publicly Held**
SIC: 3466 Crowns & closures
HQ: American Flange & Manufacturing Co. Inc.
290 Fullerton Ave
Carol Stream IL 60188
630 665-7900

Delaware - Delaware County (G-8654)

(G-8654)
API MACHINING FABRICATION INC
377 London Rd (43015-2444)
P.O. Box 326 (43015-0326)
PHONE...................740 369-0455
Arthur Main, *President*
EMP: 4
SQ FT: 6,900
SALES: 350K **Privately Held**
SIC: 3356 3999 Nonferrous rolling & drawing; identification plates

(G-8655)
ASSOCIATED HYGIENIC PDTS LLC
2332 Us Highway 42 S (43015-9502)
PHONE...................770 497-9800
Dale Hanshaw, *Principal*
EMP: 375
SALES (corp-wide): 5.1B **Privately Held**
WEB: www.ahp-dsg.com
SIC: 2211 Diaper fabrics
HQ: Associated Hygienic Products Llc
1029 Old Creek Rd
Greenville NC 27834
770 476-3594

(G-8656)
ATTIA APPLIED SCIENCES INC
Also Called: Taasi
548 W Central Ave (43015-1421)
PHONE...................740 369-1891
Yosry Attia, *President*
Vera Attia, *Vice Pres*
EMP: 9 EST: 1985
SALES (est): 1.5MM **Privately Held**
SIC: 2899 Chemical preparations

(G-8657)
AUTO CORE SYSTEMS
2097 London Rd Unit A (43015-8485)
PHONE...................740 362-5599
Chuck Dodeci, *Principal*
EMP: 3
SALES (est): 198.4K **Privately Held**
SIC: 3471 Cleaning & descaling metal products

(G-8658)
BLACK WING SHOOTING CENTER LLC
3722 Marysville Rd (43015-9527)
PHONE...................740 363-7555
Rex Gore, *President*
EMP: 9
SALES (est): 1.2MM **Privately Held**
WEB: www.blackwingsc.com
SIC: 7999 3949 Shooting range operation; bases, baseball

(G-8659)
BUNS OF DELAWARE INC
Also Called: Buns Restaurant & Bakery
14 W Winter St (43015-1919)
PHONE...................740 363-2867
Vasili Konstantinidis, *President*
EMP: 40
SQ FT: 11,184
SALES (est): 1.1MM **Privately Held**
SIC: 5812 5461 7299 2051 Eating places; bakeries; banquet hall facilities; bread, cake & related products

(G-8660)
CAROLINA COLOR CORP OHIO
Also Called: Chroma Color
100 Colomet Dr (43015-3846)
P.O. Box 690 (43015-0690)
PHONE...................740 363-6622
J A Carter, *President*
Matt Barr, *Chairman*
Terry Jordon, *Treasurer*
EMP: 25
SQ FT: 35,000
SALES (est): 4.5MM **Privately Held**
WEB: www.carolinacolor.com
SIC: 2821 Plastics materials & resins

(G-8661)
CAST METALS TECHNOLOGY INC (PA)
Also Called: C M Tech
550 Liberty Rd (43015-8806)
PHONE...................740 363-1690
Jerome Harmeyer, *President*
Madelyn C Harmeyer, *Chairman*
Vera Maruli, *CFO*
EMP: 5
SQ FT (est): 7.9MM **Privately Held**
WEB: www.castmetalstec.com
SIC: 3365 Aluminum & aluminum-based alloy castings

(G-8662)
CEDEE CEDAR INC (PA)
Also Called: Cedar Woodworking
3903 Us Highway 42 S (43015-9517)
PHONE...................740 363-3148
Carl Reynolds, *CEO*
Kris Bargram, *Manager*
EMP: 10
SALES: 500K **Privately Held**
SIC: 2434 Wood kitchen cabinets

(G-8663)
CHARTER NEX FILMS - DEL OH INC
1188 S Houk Rd (43015-3857)
PHONE...................740 369-2770
Kathy Bolhous, *CEO*
David Timm, *President*
Thomas Ziolkowski, *CFO*
EMP: 45
SALES (est): 18.6MM **Privately Held**
WEB: www.optimumplastics.com
SIC: 3081 2673 Unsupported plastics film & sheet; plastic & pliofilm bags
HQ: Charter Nex Holding Company
1264 E High St
Milton WI 53563

(G-8664)
CHARTER NEX HOLDING COMPANY
1188 S Houk Rd (43015-3857)
PHONE...................740 369-2770
Kevin Keneally, *Branch Mgr*
EMP: 45 **Privately Held**
SIC: 3081 2673 Polyethylene film; plastic & pliofilm bags
HQ: Charter Nex Holding Company
1264 E High St
Milton WI 53563

(G-8665)
CHERHIRE CHOPPERS
4059 State Route 37 E A (43015-9461)
P.O. Box 843, Grove City (43123-0843)
PHONE...................740 362-0695
Scott Malenky, *Principal*
EMP: 4
SALES (est): 303K **Privately Held**
SIC: 3751 Motorcycles & related parts

(G-8666)
CHROMA COLOR CORPORATION
100 Colomet Dr (43015-3846)
P.O. Box 690 (43015-0690)
PHONE...................740 363-6622
Jeff Smik, *Branch Mgr*
EMP: 25
SALES (corp-wide): 16.1MM **Privately Held**
SIC: 2821 Plastics materials & resins
PA: Chroma Color Corporation
3900 W Dayton St
Mchenry IL 60050
877 385-8777

(G-8667)
CIRRUS LLC
120 Homestead Ln (43015-1310)
PHONE...................740 272-2012
Steven D Piroska, *Principal*
EMP: 3
SALES (est): 155.7K **Privately Held**
SIC: 3674 Semiconductors & related devices

(G-8668)
COLUMBUS ADVNCED MFG SFTWR INC
Also Called: Cams
105 Innovation Ct Ste J (43015-7538)
PHONE...................614 410-2300
Jeffrey Trevorrow, *President*
Brian Suchland, *Technology*
EMP: 5
SQ FT: 1,500
SALES (est): 1.3MM **Privately Held**
WEB: www.camsnet.com
SIC: 5045 3599 7374 Computer software; machine shop, jobbing & repair; computer graphics service

(G-8669)
DELA-GLASSWARE LTD LLC
130 N Liberty St (43015-1721)
PHONE...................740 369-6737
Fax: 614 369-3362
EMP: 7
SQ FT: 5,000
SALES (est): 530K **Privately Held**
SIC: 3211 6513 5211 Mfg Insulating Glass

(G-8670)
DELAWARE GAZETTE COMPANY
Also Called: Mid Ohio Net
40 N Sandusky St Ste 202 (43015-1973)
PHONE...................740 363-1161
Roy Brown, *President*
Walter D Thomson II, *President*
Art Ruth, *General Mgr*
Thomas T Thomson, *Treasurer*
Linzie Tope, *Finance*
EMP: 96 EST: 1818
SQ FT: 20,000
SALES (est): 4.1MM **Privately Held**
WEB: www.delgazette.com
SIC: 2711 Commercial printing & newspaper publishing combined; newspapers, publishing & printing

(G-8671)
DELOHIO TECH
2061 State Route 521 (43015-8754)
PHONE...................740 816-5628
Tom Davis, *President*
EMP: 12
SALES (est): 411.1K **Privately Held**
SIC: 3571 Electronic computers

(G-8672)
DIVERSE MFG SOLUTIONS LLC
970 Pittsburgh Dr Ste 22 (43015-3872)
PHONE...................740 363-3600
Carl Stover,
EMP: 10
SALES (est): 347K **Privately Held**
SIC: 3542 Sheet metalworking machines

(G-8673)
DOMESTIC CASTING COMPANY LLC
620 Liberty Rd (43015-9387)
PHONE...................717 532-6615
Jerry Harmeyer, *Mng Member*
Michael Heyne,
Tom James,
EMP: 115
SALES (est): 28.7MM **Privately Held**
WEB: www.domesticcasting.com
SIC: 3321 Gray iron castings; ductile iron castings

(G-8674)
EASYFIT PRODUCTS INC
320 London Rd Ste 302 (43015-6404)
P.O. Box 343 (43015-0343)
PHONE...................740 362-9900
Debra L Owens, *President*
Rodney L Owens, *Treasurer*
EMP: 6
SQ FT: 7,200
SALES (est): 1MM **Privately Held**
WEB: www.easyfitproductsinc.com
SIC: 2434 Wood kitchen cabinets

(G-8675)
ELECTRIMOTION INC
1484 Dale Ford Rd (43015-9633)
PHONE...................740 362-0251
David Leahy, *President*
EMP: 4 EST: 2000
SALES (est): 586.7K **Privately Held**
SIC: 3651 Home entertainment equipment, electronic

(G-8676)
ENGINEERED CONDUCTIVE MTL LLC
132 Johnson Dr (43015-8699)
PHONE...................740 362-4444
Chuck Feeny, *Principal*
Shirley Brown, *Accounts Mgr*
EMP: 4
SALES (est): 490.2K **Privately Held**
SIC: 2891 Adhesives & sealants

(G-8677)
ENGINEERED MTLS SYSTEMS INC
Also Called: E M S
100 Innovation Ct (43015-7532)
PHONE...................740 362-4444
Todd Irion, *President*
Lou Morris, *Corp Secy*
Kathy Clark, *Safety Mgr*
Teresa Peck, *Purchasing*
Alan Brown, *Research*
▲ EMP: 45
SQ FT: 20,000
SALES (est): 15.4MM **Privately Held**
SIC: 2891 Adhesives

(G-8678)
FEDERAL HEATH SIGN COMPANY LLC
1020 Pittsburgh Dr Ste B (43015-3878)
PHONE...................740 369-0999
Dave Rayburn, *Safety Mgr*
Ken Hermes, *Plt & Fclts Mgr*
Larry Yeats, *Sr Project Mgr*
Victoria Carr, *Program Mgr*
Pam Poore, *Program Mgr*
EMP: 70
SALES (corp-wide): 438.1MM **Privately Held**
WEB: www.zimsign.com
SIC: 3993 Electric signs
HQ: Federal Heath Sign Company, Llc
4602 North Ave
Oceanside CA 92056

(G-8679)
FOUR NATURES KEEPERS INC
4651 Marysville Rd (43015-9528)
PHONE...................740 363-8007
Willis J Whittaker, *President*
Nancy Pintavalli, *Admin Sec*
EMP: 10
SALES (est): 737.2K **Privately Held**
SIC: 2048 Bird food, prepared

(G-8680)
FRISCHCO INC
Also Called: Dairy Clean
715 Sunbury Rd (43015-9396)
PHONE...................740 363-7537
Jim Frisch, *Manager*
EMP: 3
SALES (est): 184.5K **Privately Held**
SIC: 2052 Cones, ice cream

(G-8681)
GREIF INC (PA)
425 Winter Rd (43015-8903)
P.O. Box 8014 (43015-8014)
PHONE...................740 549-6000
Michael J Gasser, *Ch of Bd*
Peter G Watson, *President*
Lawrence Hilsheimer, *Exec VP*
Gary R Martz, *Exec VP*
Mark N Mooney, *Vice Pres*
◆ EMP: 50 EST: 1877
SALES: 3.8B **Publicly Held**
WEB: www.greif.com
SIC: 2449 2655 3412 3089 Shipping cases & drums, wood: wirebound & plywood; barrels, wood: coopered; fiber cans, drums & similar products; drums, fiber: made from purchased material; fiber cans, drums & containers; drums, shipping: metal; plastic containers, except foam; paper bags: made from purchased materials; boxes, corrugated: made from purchased materials

(G-8682)
GREIF INC
Also Called: Grief Brothers
366 Greif Pkwy (43015-8260)
PHONE...................740 657-6500

GEOGRAPHIC SECTION

Delaware - Delaware County (G-8704)

Brian Hummell, *Vice Pres*
Kathy King, *Manager*
Mike Domansky, *Director*
Gina Filonenko, *Director*
Bruce Edwards, *Bd of Directors*
EMP: 46
SALES (corp-wide): 3.8B **Publicly Held**
WEB: www.greif.com
SIC: 2449 2655 3412 2653 Shipping cases & drums, wood: wirebound & plywood; barrels, wood: coopered; drums, fiber: made from purchased material; fiber cans, drums & containers; drums, shipping: metal; boxes, corrugated: made from purchased materials; paper bags: made from purchased materials; plastic containers, except foam
PA: Greif, Inc.
  425 Winter Rd
  Delaware OH 43015
  740 549-6000

(G-8683)
GREIF INC
Also Called: Independent Container
366 Greif Pkwy (43015-8260)
PHONE.................................740 657-6500
Max Marley, *General Mgr*
EMP: 90
SQ FT: 113,400
SALES (corp-wide): 3.8B **Publicly Held**
WEB: www.greif.com
SIC: 2655 Fiber cans, drums & similar products
PA: Greif, Inc.
  425 Winter Rd
  Delaware OH 43015
  740 549-6000

(G-8684)
GREIF INC
425 Winter Rd (43015-8903)
PHONE.................................740 549-6000
Ronald C Bogart, *Manager*
EMP: 15
SALES (corp-wide): 3.8B **Publicly Held**
WEB: www.greif.com
SIC: 2655 Fiber cans, drums & similar products
PA: Greif, Inc.
  425 Winter Rd
  Delaware OH 43015
  740 549-6000

(G-8685)
GREIF INC
425 Winter Rd (43015-8903)
PHONE.................................740 549-6000
EMP: 51
SALES (corp-wide): 3.8B **Publicly Held**
SIC: 2655 Fiber cans, drums & similar products
PA: Greif, Inc.
  425 Winter Rd
  Delaware OH 43015
  740 549-6000

(G-8686)
GREIF INC
366 Greif Pkwy (43015-8260)
PHONE.................................937 548-4111
Tony Perotin, *Branch Mgr*
EMP: 64
SALES (corp-wide): 3.8B **Publicly Held**
WEB: www.greif.com
SIC: 2655 Fiber cans, drums & similar products
PA: Greif, Inc.
  425 Winter Rd
  Delaware OH 43015
  740 549-6000

(G-8687)
GREIF BROS CORP OHIO INC
425 Winter Rd (43015-8903)
PHONE.................................740 549-6000
Ole Rosgaard, *Vice Pres*
Glenna Steck, *HR Admin*
William Neal, *Accounts Mgr*
Pamela Paul, *Business Anlyst*
Andy Pruzinsky, *Officer*
EMP: 13
SALES (est): 1.9MM
SALES (corp-wide): 3.8B **Publicly Held**
SIC: 2655 Ammunition cans or tubes, board laminated with metal foil
PA: Greif, Inc.
  425 Winter Rd
  Delaware OH 43015
  740 549-6000

(G-8688)
GREIF PACKAGING LLC (HQ)
366 Greif Pkwy (43015-8260)
PHONE.................................740 549-6000
Brian Dum, *CEO*
Michael J Gasser, *Chairman*
Tony Lutes, *Opers Mgr*
Christin Trocellier, *Human Res Dir*
Randall Siders, *Manager*
▲ **EMP:** 100
SALES (est): 180.1MM
SALES (corp-wide): 3.8B **Publicly Held**
SIC: 3086 Packaging & shipping materials, foamed plastic
PA: Greif, Inc.
  425 Winter Rd
  Delaware OH 43015
  740 549-6000

(G-8689)
GREIF PAPER PACKG & SVCS LLC
425 Winter Rd (43015-8903)
P.O. Box 675, Massillon (44648-0675)
PHONE.................................740 549-6000
Matt Patton,
EMP: 99
SALES (est): 19.5MM
SALES (corp-wide): 3.8B **Publicly Held**
SIC: 2631 Paperboard mills
PA: Greif, Inc.
  425 Winter Rd
  Delaware OH 43015
  740 549-6000

(G-8690)
GREIF USA LLC (DH)
366 Greif Pkwy (43015-8260)
PHONE.................................740 549-6000
Peter Watson, *CEO*
EMP: 8 **EST:** 2005
SALES (est): 175.1MM
SALES (corp-wide): 3.8B **Publicly Held**
SIC: 2655 Fiber cans, drums & similar products
HQ: Greif Packaging Llc
  366 Greif Pkwy
  Delaware OH 43015
  740 549-6000

(G-8691)
HALLIDAY TECHNOLOGIES INC
105 Innovation Ct Ste F (43015-7538)
PHONE.................................614 504-4150
Don Halliday, *President*
Patricia Halliday, *Vice Pres*
P Halliday, *Technology*
EMP: 5
SQ FT: 400
SALES: 1MM **Privately Held**
WEB: www.hallidaytech.com
SIC: 3829 8711 Measuring & controlling devices; consulting engineer

(G-8692)
HARRIS INSTRUMENT CORPORATION
155 Johnson Dr (43015-8500)
PHONE.................................740 369-3580
Cathy Harris, *President*
John Harris, *President*
David E Harris, *Owner*
Gary E Saum, *Shareholder*
EMP: 9 **EST:** 1979
SQ FT: 10,000
SALES: 1MM **Privately Held**
WEB: www.harris-instrument.com
SIC: 3829 3823 3625 Measuring & controlling devices; industrial instrmnts msrmnt display/control process variable; relays & industrial controls

(G-8693)
HENKEL CORPORATION
Also Called: Henkel Surface Technologies
421 London Rd (43015-2493)
P.O. Box 363 (43015-0363)
PHONE.................................740 363-1351
Michael V Biondolillo, *Senior VP*
Michael Craft, *Production*
Christopher Mayberry, *Production*

Elizabeth Taylor, *Buyer*
Keith Bishop, *Engineer*
EMP: 46
SQ FT: 1,634
SALES (corp-wide): 22.7B **Privately Held**
SIC: 2841 2842 Detergents, synthetic organic or inorganic alkaline; specialty cleaning, polishes & sanitation goods
HQ: Henkel Us Operations Corporation
  1 Henkel Way
  Rocky Hill CT 06067
  860 571-5100

(G-8694)
HOME CITY ICE COMPANY
150 Johnson Dr (43015-8699)
PHONE.................................419 562-4953
Bryan Stuckman, *Manager*
EMP: 10
SALES (corp-wide): 232.5MM **Privately Held**
WEB: www.homecityice.com
SIC: 2024 2097 Ice cream & frozen desserts; manufactured ice
PA: The Home City Ice Company
  6045 Bridgetown Rd Ste 1
  Cincinnati OH 45248
  513 574-1800

(G-8695)
INNO-PAK HOLDING INC
1932 Pittsburgh Dr (43015-3868)
PHONE.................................740 363-0090
Jonathan Sill, *President*
Gary Bechtold, *Vice Pres*
Christopher Sill, *Admin Sec*
▲ **EMP:** 5
SQ FT: 55,000
SALES (est): 1.3MM **Privately Held**
WEB: www.innopak.com
SIC: 2671 5162 Paper coated or laminated for packaging; plastics products

(G-8696)
INTERNATIONAL PAPER COMPANY
865 Pittsburgh Dr (43015-2860)
PHONE.................................740 363-9882
EMP: 147
SALES (corp-wide): 23.3B **Publicly Held**
SIC: 2653 2899 2671 2631 Boxes, corrugated: made from purchased materials; ink or writing fluids; packaging paper & plastics film, coated & laminated; paperboard mills
PA: International Paper Company
  6400 Poplar Ave
  Memphis TN 38197
  901 419-9000

(G-8697)
INTERNATIONAL PAPER COMPANY
875 Pittsburgh Dr (43015-2860)
P.O. Box 8005 (43015-8005)
PHONE.................................740 369-7691
Jason Belgya, *Design Engr*
David Harbaugh, *Manager*
EMP: 172
SALES (corp-wide): 23.3B **Publicly Held**
WEB: www.internationalpaper.com
SIC: 2653 Boxes, corrugated: made from purchased materials
PA: International Paper Company
  6400 Poplar Ave
  Memphis TN 38197
  901 419-9000

(G-8698)
J&B POSTAL AND PRINT SVCS LLC
Also Called: UPS Store 4862
175 S Sandusky St (43015-2621)
PHONE.................................740 363-7653
Javier Ramos, *Mng Member*
James Maurer, *Manager*
EMP: 3
SQ FT: 1,600
SALES: 320K **Privately Held**
SIC: 2752 Commercial printing, lithographic

(G-8699)
KELLOGG COMPANY
124 Hyatts Rd (43015-8961)
PHONE.................................614 855-3437
EMP: 703
SALES (corp-wide): 13.5B **Publicly Held**
SIC: 2043 Cereal breakfast foods
PA: Kellogg Company
  1 Kellogg Sq
  Battle Creek MI 49017
  269 961-2000

(G-8700)
KHEMPCO BLDG SUP CO LTD PARTNR (PA)
Also Called: Arlington-Blaine Lumber Co
130 Johnson Dr (43015-8699)
PHONE.................................740 549-0465
Donny Bowman, *Partner*
Richard Robinson, *Partner*
James D Klingbeil Jr, *General Ptnr*
EMP: 100
SALES (est): 22.5MM **Privately Held**
SIC: 5031 5211 2439 2431 Lumber: rough, dressed & finished; building materials, exterior; building materials, interior; lumber & other building materials; trusses, except roof: laminated lumber; trusses, wooden roof; doors, wood; hardware

(G-8701)
LARCOM & MITCHELL LLC
1800 Pittsburgh Dr (43015-3870)
PHONE.................................740 595-3750
Charles Mitchell, *Principal*
EMP: 13
SALES (est): 2.3MM **Privately Held**
SIC: 3599 Flexible metal hose, tubing & bellows

(G-8702)
LIBERTY CASTING COMPANY LLC (PA)
550 Liberty Rd (43015-8670)
PHONE.................................740 363-1941
Troy Fischer, *VP Mfg*
Melanie Rose, *Purch Agent*
Viera Maruli, *CFO*
Larry Jones, *Human Res Mgr*
William B Shearer, *Mng Member*
▲ **EMP:** 125
SQ FT: 400,000
SALES (est): 51.5MM **Privately Held**
SIC: 3321 Gray iron castings; ductile iron castings

(G-8703)
LIBERTY CASTING COMPANY LLC
407 Curtis St (43015-2439)
P.O. Box 1368 (43015-8368)
PHONE.................................740 363-1941
Lonnie Buckner, *Manager*
EMP: 31
SALES (corp-wide): 51.5MM **Privately Held**
SIC: 7699 7692 5085 Cleaning services; welding repair; industrial supplies
PA: Liberty Casting Company Llc
  550 Liberty Rd
  Delaware OH 43015
  740 363-1941

(G-8704)
LUVATA OHIO INC (HQ)
1376 Pittsburgh Dr (43015-3814)
PHONE.................................740 363-1981
Jyrki Vesaluona, *CEO*
Jussi Helavirta, *Ch of Bd*
Dirk Greywitt, *Vice Pres*
Carla Grispino, *Treasurer*
Paul Ruess, *Sales Mgr*
▲ **EMP:** 85
SQ FT: 60,000
SALES: 27MM
SALES (corp-wide): 15B **Privately Held**
WEB: www.luvata.com/ohio
SIC: 3548 Welding & cutting apparatus & accessories; electric welding equipment
PA: Mitsubishi Materials Corporation
  3-2-3, Marunouchi
  Chiyoda-Ku TKY 100-0
  352 525-200

Delaware - Delaware County (G-8705) — GEOGRAPHIC SECTION

(G-8705)
MIDWEST ACOUST-A-FIBER INC (PA)
Also Called: M. A. I.
759 Pittsburgh Dr (43015-2862)
P.O. Box 1279 (43015-8279)
PHONE 740 369-3624
Jerry M Wolf, *CEO*
Skip Allan, *President*
James E Hopple, *Principal*
Linda Wolf, *Vice Pres*
EMP: 124
SQ FT: 98,250
SALES (est): 53.8MM **Privately Held**
WEB: www.acoust-a-fiber.com
SIC: 3296 Mineral wool

(G-8706)
MIDWEST ACOUST-A-FIBER INC
487 London Rd (43015-3757)
PHONE 740 363-6247
Steve Pollock, *President*
EMP: 35
SALES (corp-wide): 53.8MM **Privately Held**
WEB: www.acoust-a-fiber.com
SIC: 3296 Mineral wool
PA: Midwest Acoust-A-Fiber, Inc.
759 Pittsburgh Dr
Delaware OH 43015
740 369-3624

(G-8707)
MULTICORR CORP
425 Winter Rd (43015-8903)
P.O. Box 8014 (43015-8014)
PHONE 502 935-1000
EMP: 4
SALES (corp-wide): 3.8B **Publicly Held**
SIC: 2679 Pressed fiber & molded pulp products except food products
HQ: Multicorr Corp.
5800 Cane Run Rd
Louisville KY 40258

(G-8708)
NATIONAL LIME AND STONE CO
Also Called: National Lime Stone Clmbus Reg
2406 S Section Line Rd (43015-9518)
P.O. Box 537 (43015-0537)
PHONE 740 548-4206
Carolyn Coder, *Office Mgr*
Chad Doll, *Manager*
EMP: 40
SALES (corp-wide): 3.2B **Privately Held**
WEB: www.natlime.com
SIC: 1422 Crushed & broken limestone
PA: The National Lime And Stone Company
551 Lake Cascade Pkwy
Findlay OH 45840
419 422-4341

(G-8709)
NATIONAL METAL SHAPES INC
425 S Sandusky St Ste 1 (43015-3604)
PHONE 740 363-9559
John Vogel, *President*
▲ **EMP:** 25
SQ FT: 85,000
SALES (est): 6.8MM **Privately Held**
SIC: 3354 Aluminum extruded products

(G-8710)
NEU PROSTHETICS & ORTHOTICS
2848 Jericho Pl (43015-3175)
PHONE 740 363-3522
William Neu, *Mng Member*
EMP: 3
SALES: 600K **Privately Held**
SIC: 3842 Prosthetic appliances

(G-8711)
NUTRIMIR LLC
Also Called: Nutrimir Personalized Wellness
408 Tipperary Loop (43015-7190)
PHONE 614 600-2478
Cameron Rink,
Savita Khanna,
Sashwati Roy,
Chandan Sen,
EMP: 4 EST: 2016

SALES (est): 172.3K **Privately Held**
SIC: 2834 Vitamin, nutrient & hematinic preparations for human use

(G-8712)
OBERFIELDS LLC (HQ)
528 London Rd (43015-2850)
P.O. Box 362 (43015-0362)
PHONE 740 369-7644
Bruce Loris, *President*
Todd Shepherd, *General Mgr*
Kellen Koenn, *Opers Mgr*
Mark Selhorst, *Opers Mgr*
Larry Gibbs, *Purchasing*
EMP: 70 EST: 1961
SQ FT: 52,000
SALES (est): 22.8MM
SALES (corp-wide): 1.2MM **Privately Held**
SIC: 3272 Concrete products, precast
PA: Oberfields Holdings Llc
528 London Rd
Delaware OH 43015
740 369-7644

(G-8713)
OBERFIELDS HOLDINGS LLC (PA)
528 London Rd (43015-2850)
PHONE 740 369-7644
Bruce Loris, *President*
EMP: 0 EST: 2017
SALES (est): 1.2MM **Privately Held**
SIC: 6719 3272 Investment holding companies, except banks; concrete products, precast

(G-8714)
OLD VILLAGE
2878 Jericho Pl (43015-3175)
PHONE 614 791-8467
EMP: 10
SALES (est): 948K **Privately Held**
SIC: 3911 5944 Mfg Precious Metal Jewelry Ret Jewelry

(G-8715)
PPG INDUSTRIES INC
Also Called: P P G Refinishing Group
760 Pittsburgh Dr (43015-3811)
PHONE 740 363-9610
Mike Tiehurst, *Manager*
EMP: 6
SALES (corp-wide): 15.3B **Publicly Held**
WEB: www.ppg.com
SIC: 2851 Paints & allied products
PA: Ppg Industries, Inc.
1 Ppg Pl
Pittsburgh PA 15272
412 434-3131

(G-8716)
PPG INDUSTRIES OHIO INC
760 Pittsburgh Dr (43015-3811)
PHONE 740 363-9610
Stoever Greg, *Finance Mgr*
James Boyd, *Branch Mgr*
EMP: 44
SALES (corp-wide): 15.3B **Publicly Held**
WEB: www.ppgglass.com
SIC: 2851 Paints & allied products
HQ: Ppg Industries Ohio, Inc.
3800 W 143rd St
Cleveland OH 44111
216 671-0050

(G-8717)
PRICE FARMS ORGANICS LTD
4838 Warrensburg Rd (43015-8589)
PHONE 740 369-1000
Tom Price, *Mng Member*
Tricia Kalmar,
EMP: 12
SQ FT: 1,000
SALES (est): 767.8K **Privately Held**
WEB: www.pricebarnes.org
SIC: 2875 Compost

(G-8718)
RB&W MANUFACTURING LLC
Also Called: Delo Screw Products
700 London Rd (43015-8637)
PHONE 740 363-1971
EMP: 4

SALES (corp-wide): 1.6B **Publicly Held**
WEB: www.pkoh.com.cn
SIC: 5085 3452 3469 Fasteners, industrial: nuts, bolts, screws, etc.; bolts, nuts, rivets & washers; screws, metal; nuts, metal; stamping metal for the trade
HQ: Rb&W Manufacturing Llc
10080 Wellman Rd
Streetsboro OH 44241

(G-8719)
REDBUILT LLC
200 Colomet Dr (43015-2873)
PHONE 740 363-0870
Peter Mellbolm, *General Mgr*
EMP: 20
SALES (corp-wide): 2.4B **Privately Held**
SIC: 2439 3441 Trusses, wooden roof; fabricated structural metal
HQ: Redbuilt Llc
200 E Mallard Dr
Boise ID 83706

(G-8720)
RJW TRUCKING COMPANY LTD
Also Called: Henderson Trucking
124 Henderson Ct (43015-8479)
PHONE 740 363-5343
Jack Henderson, *Mng Member*
Shaun Henderson,
EMP: 25
SALES (est): 1.6MM **Privately Held**
SIC: 1442 4212 Construction sand & gravel; local trucking, without storage; dump truck haulage

(G-8721)
SAM DONG OHIO INC
801 Pittsburgh Dr (43015-2860)
PHONE 740 363-1985
Jong, *General Mgr*
Randy Kaiser, *Vice Pres*
Mark Watkins, *QC Mgr*
Matt Johanson, *Engineer*
Michael Galyk, *Info Tech Mgr*
▲ **EMP:** 75
SALES (est): 25.1MM
SALES (corp-wide): 498.2MM **Privately Held**
SIC: 3331 Primary copper
PA: Sam Dong Co., Ltd.
816-41 Samyang-Ro, Daeso-Myeon
Eumseong 27673
438 794-075

(G-8722)
SANDRA WEDDINGTON
Also Called: Blend of Seven Winery
1400 Stratford Rd (43015-2922)
PHONE 740 417-4286
Sandra Weddington, *Owner*
EMP: 6
SALES (est): 550.2K **Privately Held**
SIC: 2084 5182 5921 Wines; wine; wine

(G-8723)
SAVARE SPECIALTY ADHESIVES LLC
1201 S Houk Rd (43015-3876)
P.O. Box 20344, Columbus (43220-0344)
PHONE 614 255-2648
Paolo Campitelli, *Marketing Staff*
Rick Schwieterman,
Tom Carr,
Biagio Savare,
◆ **EMP:** 45
SALES (est): 23.4MM
SALES (corp-wide): 467.6K **Privately Held**
SIC: 2891 Adhesives
HQ: Savare Corporation
230 West St Ste 700
Columbus OH 43215
614 255-2648

(G-8724)
SHRED AWAY
227 Rockmill St (43015-4288)
PHONE 740 363-6327
Kim Srail, *Principal*
EMP: 3
SALES (est): 251.5K **Privately Held**
SIC: 3559 Tire shredding machinery

(G-8725)
SKY CLIMBER LLC (PA)
Also Called: Sky Climber Wind Solutions
1800 Pittsburgh Dr (43015-3870)
PHONE 740 203-3900
George Anasis, *CEO*
Kelly Winkler, *President*
Donald Rice, *General Mgr*
Tom Warchol, *General Mgr*
Mike Dahlquist, *Business Mgr*
◆ **EMP:** 25
SQ FT: 55,000
SALES (est): 9.3MM **Privately Held**
WEB: www.skyclimber.com
SIC: 3446 Scaffolds, mobile or stationary: metal

(G-8726)
SKY CLIMBER FASTENERS LLC
1600 Pittsburgh Dr (43015-3884)
PHONE 740 816-9830
Kelly Winkler, *Vice Pres*
EMP: 3 EST: 2015
SQ FT: 100,000
SALES (est): 166.2K **Privately Held**
SIC: 3429 Metal fasteners

(G-8727)
SUPPLY TECHNOLOGIES LLC
Also Called: Delo Screw Products
700 London Rd (43015-8637)
PHONE 740 363-1971
Jane Scroggins, *Controller*
EMP: 70
SALES (corp-wide): 1.6B **Publicly Held**
WEB: www.deloscrew.com
SIC: 3451 Screw machine products
HQ: Supply Technologies Llc
6065 Parkland Blvd Ste 2
Cleveland OH 44124
440 947-2100

(G-8728)
THE DELO SCREW PRODUCTS CO
700 London Rd (43015-8638)
PHONE 740 363-1971
Mike Flora, *President*
Robi Dodadalltur, *President*
Jay Egelski, *Vice Pres*
EMP: 17
SALES (est): 1.9MM **Privately Held**
SIC: 3451 Screw machine products

(G-8729)
UTILITY SOLUTIONS INC
327 Curtis St (43015-2439)
PHONE 740 369-4300
Trent Hertzfeld, *President*
Mike Killian, *Vice Pres*
EMP: 3
SQ FT: 6,000
SALES (est): 561.3K **Privately Held**
SIC: 3084 Plastics pipe

(G-8730)
WANNER METAL WORX INC
525 London Rd (43015-2849)
P.O. Box 1004 (43015-7104)
PHONE 740 369-4034
Craig Wanner, *President*
Rick Wanner, *Exec VP*
Richard Wanner Jr, *Vice Pres*
Frank Lewis, *Plant Mgr*
Randy Archer, *VP Sales*
EMP: 50
SQ FT: 250,000
SALES (est): 13MM **Privately Held**
WEB: www.wannermetalworx.com
SIC: 3446 Stairs, staircases, stair treads: prefabricated metal; balconies, metal

(G-8731)
WATERFORD SIGNS INC
288 S Sandusky St Ste C (43015-2697)
PHONE 740 362-7446
Tim Moore, *President*
Debbie Moore, *Corp Secy*
EMP: 3
SALES: 500K **Privately Held**
SIC: 3993 Signs, not made in custom sign painting shops

GEOGRAPHIC SECTION

Delphos - Allen County (G-8757)

(G-8732)
WHITESIDE MANUFACTURING CO
309 Hayes St (43015-2189)
P.O. Box 322 (43015-0322)
PHONE..................................740 363-1179
Kirt Whiteside, *CEO*
Robert Whiteside, *President*
Terry Whiteside, *CFO*
Tenille Schoonover, *Human Res Mgr*
Kym Bell, *Sales Dir*
◆ **EMP:** 40
SQ FT: 75,000
SALES (est): 12.5MM **Privately Held**
WEB: www.whitesidemfg.com
SIC: 3537 3429 Platforms, stands, tables, pallets & similar equipment; manufactured hardware (general)

Dellroy
Carroll County

(G-8733)
BEUCLER BROTHERS INC
Also Called: Bbi Well Service
7237 Flint Rd Sw (44620-9648)
PHONE..................................330 735-2267
Louis Beucler, *President*
EMP: 4
SALES (est): 350K **Privately Held**
SIC: 1311 Crude petroleum production

Delphos
Allen County

(G-8734)
A & J WOODWORKING INC
808 Ohio St (45833-1824)
PHONE..................................419 695-5655
Arnold Mohler, *President*
Jill Mohler, *Corp Secy*
Jeff Mohler, *Vice Pres*
EMP: 8
SALES: 1.2MM **Privately Held**
SIC: 1751 2541 2434 2431 Cabinet building & installation; wood partitions & fixtures; wood kitchen cabinets; millwork

(G-8735)
AERO PRINTING INC
710 Elida Ave (45833-1737)
P.O. Box 68 (45833-0068)
PHONE..................................419 695-2931
Carl Core Jr, *President*
Dave Core, *Vice Pres*
EMP: 4
SQ FT: 2,100
SALES (est): 581.1K **Privately Held**
WEB: www.aeroprinting.com
SIC: 2752 Commercial printing, offset

(G-8736)
BABY LOVE PRENATAL IMAGING LLC
727 W 2nd St (45833-1614)
PHONE..................................419 905-7935
John Parent, *President*
Valerie Parent, *Co-Owner*
EMP: 4 **EST:** 2016
SALES (est): 154K **Privately Held**
SIC: 3841 Diagnostic apparatus, medical

(G-8737)
BETTER LIVING SUNROOMS NW OHIO
205 S Pierce St (45833-1924)
PHONE..................................419 692-4526
EMP: 4
SALES (est): 290K **Privately Held**
SIC: 3448 1521 Mfg Prefabricated Metal Buildings Single-Family House Construction

(G-8738)
DELPHOS HERALD INC (PA)
Also Called: Eagle Print
405 N Main St (45833-1598)
PHONE..................................419 695-0015
Murray Cohen, *Ch of Bd*
Ray Geary, *Treasurer*
EMP: 83 **EST:** 1962
SQ FT: 14,000
SALES: 1.1MM **Privately Held**
WEB: www.delphosherald.com
SIC: 2711 2752 Newspapers, publishing & printing; commercial printing, offset

(G-8739)
DELPHOS HERALD INC
Eagle Print
405 N Main St (45833-1598)
PHONE..................................419 695-0015
Murray Cohen, *Owner*
Denny Klausing, *Vice Pres*
EMP: 60
SALES (corp-wide): 1.1MM **Privately Held**
WEB: www.delphosherald.com
SIC: 2711 2789 2752 Newspapers, publishing & printing; bookbinding & related work; commercial printing, offset
PA: Herald Delphos Inc
 405 N Main St
 Delphos OH 45833
 419 695-0015

(G-8740)
DELPHOS TENT AND AWNING INC
1454 N Main St (45833-1150)
PHONE..................................419 692-5776
Andrew Wurst, *President*
Shellie Wurst, *Treasurer*
Charlie Gerdeman, *Director*
EMP: 24 **EST:** 1920
SQ FT: 5,000
SALES: 1MM **Privately Held**
WEB: www.delphostentawning.com
SIC: 2394 Canvas & related products

(G-8741)
DRAPERY STITCH OF DELPHOS
50 Summers Ln (45833-1791)
P.O. Box 307 (45833-0307)
PHONE..................................419 692-3921
Donald Beckman, *President*
Cheryl Beckman, *Vice Pres*
EMP: 25
SQ FT: 18,000
SALES: 1MM **Privately Held**
WEB: www.draperystitch.com
SIC: 2391 Draperies, plastic & textile: from purchased materials

(G-8742)
DTR EQUIPMENT INC
1430 N Main St (45833-1150)
P.O. Box 163, Kalida (45853-0163)
PHONE..................................419 692-3000
Robert T Horstman, *President*
Richard A Horstman, *Vice Pres*
▲ **EMP:** 12
SQ FT: 40,000
SALES: 267K **Privately Held**
WEB: www.rthprocessing.com
SIC: 3069 Mats or matting, rubber

(G-8743)
ETC ENTERPRISES LLC
330 Sunderland Rd S (45833-9768)
PHONE..................................417 262-6382
Tim Arheit,
EMP: 4
SALES (est): 310.8K **Privately Held**
SIC: 3822 5063 5065 Refrigeration controls (pressure); switches, thermostatic; refrigeration thermostats; switches, except electronic; transformers, electronic

(G-8744)
H G VIOLET INC
2103 N Main St (45833-1183)
PHONE..................................419 695-2000
G Howard, *Owner*
Clark Stoller, *Parts Mgr*
EMP: 6
SALES: 4.2MM **Privately Held**
SIC: 3523 Cabs, tractors & agricultural machinery

(G-8745)
HYDROFRESH LTD
1571 Gressel Dr (45833-9187)
PHONE..................................419 785-3221
Don Klausing, *President*
EMP: 7
SQ FT: 36,616
SALES: 2.5MM **Privately Held**
SIC: 2099 Food preparations
PA: Keller Logistics Group, Inc.
 24862 Elliott Rd Ste 101
 Defiance OH 43512

(G-8746)
KNIPPEN CHRYSLER DODGE JEEP
800 W 5th St (45833-9212)
PHONE..................................419 695-4976
Ronald Knippen, *President*
John Klausing, *Treasurer*
Tom Ring, *Sales Mgr*
Ronald Baumgarte, *Admin Sec*
▲ **EMP:** 22
SQ FT: 13,500
SALES (est): 8MM **Privately Held**
WEB: www.knippenchrysler.com
SIC: 5511 5521 3714 7513 Pickups, new & used; used car dealers; motor vehicle parts & accessories; truck rental & leasing, no drivers; automotive & home supply stores; general truck repair

(G-8747)
KRENDL MACHINE COMPANY
1201 Spencerville Rd (45833-2381)
PHONE..................................419 692-3060
Jack Krendl, *President*
Lori Presston, *COO*
Jeffrey Krendl, *Vice Pres*
Joseph Krendl, *Vice Pres*
Tara Krendl, *Plant Mgr*
▼ **EMP:** 70 **EST:** 1958
SQ FT: 55,000
SALES (est): 12.8MM **Privately Held**
WEB: www.krendlmachine.com
SIC: 3599 3827 3432 Machine shop, jobbing & repair; optical instruments & lenses; plumbing fixture fittings & trim

(G-8748)
LAKEVIEW FARMS INC
1700 Gressel Dr (45833-9152)
PHONE..................................419 695-9925
Mark Howell, *Purchasing*
Melissa Mc Clurg, *Human Res Mgr*
Noma Beining, *Cust Mgr*
Ernest Graves, *Manager*
EMP: 95
SALES (corp-wide): 103.2MM **Privately Held**
SIC: 2026 Cream, sour
PA: Lakeview Farms, Llc
 1600 Gressel Dr
 Delphos OH 45833
 419 695-9925

(G-8749)
LAKEVIEW FARMS LLC
1600 Gressel Dr (45833-9153)
P.O. Box 98 (45833-0098)
PHONE..................................419 695-9925
Pat Denor, *Branch Mgr*
EMP: 50
SALES (corp-wide): 103.2MM **Privately Held**
SIC: 2026 2022 Cream, sour; cheese spreads, dips, pastes & other cheese products

(G-8750)
LAKEVIEW FARMS LLC (PA)
1600 Gressel Dr (45833-9153)
P.O. Box 98 (45833-0098)
PHONE..................................419 695-9925
Tom Davis, *CEO*
John Kopilchack, *Vice Pres*
Justin Huffman, *Purchasing*
Chastity Dodson, *Research*
Nadege Mix, *Engineer*
EMP: 140
SQ FT: 36,250
SALES (est): 103.2MM **Privately Held**
SIC: 2099 2026 2022 Dips, except cheese & sour cream based; gelatin dessert preparations; cream, sour; dips, sour cream based; cheese, natural & processed

(G-8751)
LION CLOTHING INC
Also Called: Sports Loft
206 N Main St (45833-1767)
PHONE..................................419 692-9981
Carol Odenweller, *President*
John F Odenweller, *Corp Secy*
EMP: 4
SQ FT: 4,000
SALES (est): 641.9K **Privately Held**
WEB: www.lionsclothing.com
SIC: 5611 5941 7336 2395 Clothing, sportswear, men's & boys'; sporting goods & bicycle shops; silk screen design; emblems, embroidered

(G-8752)
NR LEE RESTORATION LTD
7470 Grone Rd (45833-9107)
PHONE..................................419 692-2233
Nathan R Lee, *President*
EMP: 6 **EST:** 2007
SALES (est): 925.3K **Privately Held**
SIC: 3259 1761 1741 Roofing tile, clay; roofing contractor; tuckpointing or restoration

(G-8753)
OSISTER JAMS & JELLIES
12198 Mddlpoint Wetzel Rd (45833-8808)
PHONE..................................419 968-2505
Patti Bonifas, *Principal*
EMP: 3
SALES (est): 119.7K **Privately Held**
SIC: 2033 Jams, jellies & preserves: packaged in cans, jars, etc.

(G-8754)
R T H PROCESSING INC
1430 N Main St (45833-1150)
P.O. Box 466 (45833-0466)
PHONE..................................419 692-3000
Ted Horstman, *President*
Rick Horstman, *Vice Pres*
◆ **EMP:** 100
SQ FT: 50,000
SALES (est): 15.4MM
SALES (corp-wide): 4.4B **Publicly Held**
WEB: www.rthprocessing.com
SIC: 3069 5941 Mats or matting, rubber; exercise equipment
HQ: Ultimate Rb, Inc.
 1430 N Main St
 Delphos OH 45833
 419 692-3000

(G-8755)
TECH-E-Z LLC
446 E Cleveland St (45833-1903)
PHONE..................................419 692-1700
EMP: 5 **EST:** 2006
SALES (est): 380K **Privately Held**
SIC: 5734 5045 7378 7372 Ret/Whol Tech Prod & Svcs

(G-8756)
TOLEDO MOLDING & DIE INC
900 Gressel Dr (45833-9154)
PHONE..................................419 692-6022
Jack Ruhe, *Manager*
EMP: 130
SALES (corp-wide): 309.9MM **Privately Held**
WEB: www.tmdinc.com
SIC: 3089 3714 Injection molding of plastics; motor vehicle parts & accessories
HQ: Toledo Molding & Die, Inc.
 1429 Coining Dr
 Toledo OH 43612
 419 470-3950

(G-8757)
TOLEDO MOLDING & DIE INC
Also Called: Delphos Plant 2
24086 State Route 697 (45833-9203)
P.O. Box 393 (45833-0393)
PHONE..................................419 692-6022
Craig Norbeck, *Plant Mgr*
Brian Hohenbrink, *Engineer*
Robert Whitney, *Engineer*
Keith Riegle, *Manager*
Kathy Vorst, *Admin Asst*
EMP: 85

Delphos - Allen County (G-8758)

SALES (corp-wide): 309.9MM **Privately Held**
WEB: www.tmdinc.com
SIC: 5031 3714 Molding, all materials; motor vehicle parts & accessories
HQ: Toledo Molding & Die, Inc.
 1429 Coining Dr
 Toledo OH 43612
 419 470-3950

(G-8758)
TRI-TECH MFG LLC
7404 State Route 66 (45833-9527)
PHONE.................................419 238-0140
William Evans, *Mng Member*
EMP: 3
SALES: 300K **Privately Held**
SIC: 3524 Lawn & garden mowers & accessories

(G-8759)
TWO TIN CANS LLC
21623 Lehman Rd (45833-8849)
PHONE.................................419 692-2027
Joe Vasquez, *Principal*
EMP: 3
SALES (est): 87.8K **Privately Held**
SIC: 3411 Tin cans

(G-8760)
ULTIMATE RB INC (DH)
1430 N Main St (45833-1150)
PHONE.................................419 692-3000
Marvin Wool, *President*
EMP: 24
SALES: 19.2MM
SALES (corp-wide): 4.4B **Publicly Held**
SIC: 3069 Mats or matting, rubber
HQ: Accella Performance Materials Inc.
 2500 Adie Rd
 Maryland Heights MO
 314 432-3200

(G-8761)
UNVERFERTH MFG CO INC
24325 State Route 697 (45833-9202)
PHONE.................................419 695-2060
Dave Unverferth, *Manager*
EMP: 55
SALES (corp-wide): 155.3MM **Privately Held**
WEB: www.unverferth.com
SIC: 3523 Farm machinery & equipment
PA: Unverferth Manufacturing Company, Inc.
 601 S Broad St
 Kalida OH 45853
 419 532-3121

(G-8762)
US METALCRAFT INC
101 S Franklin St (45833-1936)
P.O. Box 308 (45833-0308)
PHONE.................................419 692-4962
Joel Birkmeier, *President*
Steve Birkmeier, *Treasurer*
◆ EMP: 21
SQ FT: 20,000
SALES (est): 4.6MM **Privately Held**
WEB: www.usmetalcraft.com
SIC: 3365 Aluminum & aluminum-based alloy castings

(G-8763)
VAN WERT MACHINE INC
Also Called: Progressive Tool Division
210 E Cleveland St (45833-1941)
P.O. Box 40 (45833-0040)
PHONE.................................419 692-6836
Jesse F Hitchcock, *President*
Gloria Bechtol, *Corp Secy*
Donald E Bechtol, *Vice Pres*
EMP: 17 EST: 1961
SQ FT: 18,600
SALES (est): 2.3MM **Privately Held**
SIC: 3544 Special dies & tools

(G-8764)
VANAMATIC COMPANY
701 Ambrose Dr (45833-9179)
PHONE.................................419 692-6085
James N Wiltsie Jr, *Chairman*
Jeff Wiltsie, *Co-President*
Perry Wiltsie, *Co-President*
Patricia M Morris, *Officer*
EMP: 85 EST: 1954
SQ FT: 75,000
SALES: 13MM **Privately Held**
WEB: www.vanamatic.com
SIC: 3451 Screw machine products

Delta
Fulton County

(G-8765)
AXLE SURGEONS OF NW OHIO
811 Helvetia St (43515-1407)
PHONE.................................419 822-5775
Mike Irelan, *Owner*
EMP: 3
SALES (est): 548.7K **Privately Held**
SIC: 3714 Axles, motor vehicle

(G-8766)
BEAVERSON MACHINE INC
11600 County Road 10 2 (43515-9748)
PHONE.................................419 923-8064
Ralph Beaverson, *President*
James Beaverson, *Vice Pres*
EMP: 6
SQ FT: 3,000
SALES (est): 863.6K **Privately Held**
SIC: 3498 Tube fabricating (contract bending & shaping)

(G-8767)
DELTA TOOL & DIE STL BLOCK INC
5226 County Road 6 (43515-9648)
PHONE.................................419 822-5939
John Gilders, *President*
EMP: 13
SQ FT: 27,500
SALES (est): 2.1MM **Privately Held**
SIC: 3544 3469 Jigs & fixtures; metal stampings

(G-8768)
DESINGER WINDOW TREATMENT INC
302 Superior St (43515-1335)
P.O. Box 146 (43515-0146)
PHONE.................................419 822-4967
Leslie Zalecki, *President*
EMP: 8
SALES (est): 1MM **Privately Held**
SIC: 2591 Drapery hardware & blinds & shades

(G-8769)
EDW C LEVY CO
Also Called: Fultton Mill Services
6565 County Road 9 (43515-9449)
P.O. Box 86 (43515-0086)
PHONE.................................419 822-8286
Paul Ruffner, *Manager*
EMP: 30
SALES (corp-wide): 368.1MM **Privately Held**
WEB: www.edwclevy.com
SIC: 4212 3295 Dump truck haulage; minerals, ground or treated
PA: Edw. C. Levy Co.
 9300 Dix
 Dearborn MI 48120
 313 429-2200

(G-8770)
FORREST MACHINE SHOP
204 Main St (43515-1312)
PHONE.................................419 822-5847
Steve Forrest, *Owner*
EMP: 3
SALES (est): 329.9K **Privately Held**
SIC: 3599 Machine shop, jobbing & repair

(G-8771)
FULTON COUNTY PROCESSING LTD
7800 State Route 109 (43515-9335)
P.O. Box 67 (43515-0067)
PHONE.................................419 822-9266
James J Vanpoppel, *General Ptnr*
▲ EMP: 75
SALES: 36.4MM **Privately Held**
WEB: www.fcpltd.com
SIC: 3312 Stainless steel

(G-8772)
GB MANUFACTURING COMPANY (PA)
1120 E Main St (43515)
P.O. Box 8 (43515-0008)
PHONE.................................419 822-5323
Nelson U Reyes, *President*
Annette Y Petree, *Vice Pres*
Mark Ries, *Vice Pres*
Michael Pechette, *CFO*
▲ EMP: 53
SQ FT: 50,000
SALES (est): 55.5MM **Privately Held**
WEB: www.gbmfg.com
SIC: 3469 Machine parts, stamped or pressed metal

(G-8773)
GLENN HUNTER & ASSOCIATES INC
1222 County Road 6 (43515-9644)
PHONE.................................419 533-0925
James Clark, *Ch of Bd*
Glenn Hunter, *President*
Dean Daenens, *General Mgr*
Suzanne Hunter, *Admin Sec*
▼ EMP: 75
SQ FT: 2,500
SALES (est): 25MM **Privately Held**
SIC: 3559 Recycling machinery

(G-8774)
INDUSTRIAL REPAIR & MFG INC (PA)
1140 E Main St Ste A (43515-9406)
PHONE.................................419 822-4232
Toll Free:..........................877 -
William H Toedter, *President*
Peggy J Toedter, *Vice Pres*
▲ EMP: 65
SQ FT: 48,000
SALES (est): 8.7MM **Privately Held**
SIC: 7699 7363 3443 Industrial machinery & equipment repair; truck driver services; containers, shipping (bombs, etc.): metal plate

(G-8775)
LYNN JAMES CONTRACTING LLC
12490 County Road 5 (43515-9720)
PHONE.................................419 467-4505
EMP: 5
SALES: 200K **Privately Held**
SIC: 2951 1771 Mfg Asphalt Mixtures/Blocks Concrete Contractor

(G-8776)
MESSER LLC
6744 County Road 10 (43515)
PHONE.................................419 822-3909
Mike Murphy, *Manager*
EMP: 7
SALES (corp-wide): 1.4B **Privately Held**
SIC: 2813 Industrial gases
HQ: Messer Llc
 200 Somerset Corporate
 Bridgewater NJ 08807
 908 464-8100

(G-8777)
NORTH STAR BLUESCOPE STEEL LLC
6767 County Road 9 (43515-9449)
PHONE.................................419 822-2200
Miguel Alvarez, *President*
Mike Hanson, *Vice Pres*
Joe Budion, *VP Finance*
Jeremie Fisher, *Sales Staff*
Jamie Trzcinski, *Sales Staff*
◆ EMP: 345
SQ FT: 600,000
SALES (est): 192.1MM **Privately Held**
WEB: www.nsbhp.com
SIC: 3312 Hot-rolled iron & steel products
PA: Bluescope Steel Limited
 L 11 120 Collins St
 Melbourne VIC 3000

(G-8778)
TWIN POINT INC (PA)
Also Called: Workman Electronics
11955 County Road 10 2 (43515-9748)
PHONE.................................419 923-7525
Jerry Twining, *CEO*
▲ EMP: 13
SALES (est): 947.1K **Privately Held**
SIC: 3679 Electronic circuits

(G-8779)
WORKMAN ELECTRONIC PDTS INC
Also Called: Electrical Insulation Company
11955 County Road 10 2 (43515-9748)
PHONE.................................419 923-7525
Judy Eyer, *Ch of Bd*
Jerry Twining, *President*
Thomas A Yoder, *Principal*
James Twining, *Senior VP*
▲ EMP: 12 EST: 1936
SQ FT: 24,400
SALES (est): 258.5K
SALES (corp-wide): 2.2MM **Privately Held**
SIC: 3679 Electronic circuits
PA: Twin Point Inc
 11955 County Road 10 2
 Delta OH 43515
 419 923-7525

(G-8780)
WORTHINGTON INDUSTRIES INC
Worthington Steel Division
6303 County Road 10 (43515-9453)
PHONE.................................419 822-2500
Jeff Leeper, *Manager*
Don Siewertsen, *Executive*
EMP: 100
SALES (corp-wide): 3.5B **Publicly Held**
WEB: www.worthingtonindustries.com
SIC: 3312 Iron & steel: galvanized, pipes, plates, sheets, etc.
PA: Worthington Industries, Inc.
 200 W Old Wilson Bridge Rd
 Worthington OH 43085
 614 438-3210

Dennison
Tuscarawas County

(G-8781)
ALSCO METALS CORPORATION (DH)
1309 Deer Hill Rd (44621-9350)
PHONE.................................740 983-2571
Peter Ingermi, *Director*
◆ EMP: 30
SQ FT: 10,000
SALES (est): 41.7MM **Privately Held**
SIC: 3444 3089 3479 Siding, sheet metal; siding, plastic; painting of metal products

(G-8782)
BLOOMS PRINTING INC
Also Called: Blooming Services
4792 N 4th Street Ext Se (44621-8929)
PHONE.................................740 922-1765
Richard Bloom, *President*
Kay Bloom, *Admin Sec*
Christy Bloom, *Graphic Designe*
EMP: 11
SALES (est): 1.8MM **Privately Held**
SIC: 2752 Commercial printing, lithographic

(G-8783)
CAM CO INC (PA)
6270 Wolf Run Rd Se (44621-8914)
PHONE.................................740 922-4533
Randy Leishman, *President*
Daniel Leishman, *Corp Secy*
David Leishman, *Vice Pres*
EMP: 1
SALES (est): 1.4MM **Privately Held**
SIC: 1221 Auger mining, bituminous

(G-8784)
KENNETH MC BETH
Also Called: Blackstone Mining
514 Stillwater Ave (44621-1350)
PHONE.................................740 922-9494
Kenneth Mc Beth, *Owner*
EMP: 5
SALES (est): 369.5K **Privately Held**
SIC: 1221 Bituminous coal surface mining

GEOGRAPHIC SECTION

Dover - Tuscarawas County (G-8808)

(G-8785)
M3 MIDSTREAM LLC
Also Called: Leesville Plant
8349 Azalea Rd Sw (44621-9100)
PHONE..................................740 431-4168
EMP: 28
SALES (corp-wide): 54.9MM **Privately Held**
SIC: 1311 Natural gas production
PA: M3 Midstream Llc
    600 Travis St Ste 5600
    Houston TX 77002
    713 783-3000

(G-8786)
SERVICES ACQUISITION CO LLC
Also Called: Tank Services
4412 Pleasant Vly Rd Se (44621-9038)
P.O. Box 71 (44621-0071)
PHONE..................................330 479-9267
James Milano, *CEO*
EMP: 5 EST: 2014
SALES (est): 882.8K **Privately Held**
SIC: 3731 Tankers, building & repairing

Deshler
Henry County

(G-8787)
CAST METALS INCORPORATED
104 W North St (43516-1164)
P.O. Box 87 (43516-0087)
PHONE..................................419 278-2010
Scott Ferguson, *President*
Tom Downer, *President*
EMP: 15
SQ FT: 22,500
SALES (est): 5.5MM **Privately Held**
WEB: www.castmetals.com
SIC: 3321 Gray iron castings; ductile iron castings

(G-8788)
DESHLER METAL WORKING CO INC
140 S East Ave (43516-1302)
PHONE..................................419 278-0472
Judee Suber, *President*
EMP: 4
SQ FT: 11,000
SALES (est): 395.2K **Privately Held**
SIC: 3469 Spinning metal for the trade

(G-8789)
GRAMINEX LLC
2 300 County Rd C (43516)
PHONE..................................419 278-1023
Justin Ritter, *Manager*
EMP: 15
SALES (corp-wide): 3.8MM **Privately Held**
WEB: www.gmtfinechemicalssa.com
SIC: 2834 2833 Extracts of botanicals: powdered, pilular, solid or fluid; medicinals & botanicals
PA: Graminex, L.L.C.
    95 Midland St
    Saginaw MI 48638
    989 797-5502

(G-8790)
YARNELL BROS INC
103 E North St (43516-1283)
P.O. Box 81 (43516-0081)
PHONE..................................419 278-2831
Ron Yarnell, *President*
Richard L Yarnell, *Corp Secy*
Dave Yarnell, *Vice Pres*
EMP: 4 EST: 1948
SQ FT: 5,000
SALES (est): 454K **Privately Held**
SIC: 2048 Alfalfa or alfalfa meal, prepared as animal feed

Dexter City
Noble County

(G-8791)
AMES COMPANIES INC
21460 Ames Ln (45727-9702)
PHONE..................................740 783-2535
Jim Basham, *Branch Mgr*
EMP: 20
SALES (corp-wide): 1.5B **Publicly Held**
WEB: www.ames.com
SIC: 3423 Garden & farm tools, including shovels
HQ: The Ames Companies Inc
    465 Railroad Ave
    Camp Hill PA 17011
    717 737-1500

(G-8792)
B&N COAL INC
38455 Marietta Rte (45727)
P.O. Box 100 (45727-0100)
PHONE..................................740 783-3575
Carl Baker, *President*
Bob Cunningham, *Corp Secy*
Roger Osborne, *Vice Pres*
EMP: 64 EST: 1962
SQ FT: 21,000
SALES: 18MM **Privately Held**
SIC: 1221 8711 Strip mining, bituminous; engineering services

(G-8793)
BELDEX LAND COMPANY LLC (PA)
Also Called: Belpre Sand and Gravel Company
38455 State Rte 821 S (45727)
P.O. Box 100 (45727-0100)
PHONE..................................740 783-3575
Carl Baker, *Mng Member*
David Skinner, *Mng Member*
EMP: 6
SALES (est): 889.6K **Privately Held**
SIC: 1442 Construction sand & gravel

(G-8794)
DEXTER HARDWOODS INC
145 Jefferson St (45727)
PHONE..................................740 783-4141
Kenton Byrd, *President*
Carl Baker Jr, *Principal*
Robert P Cunningham, *Corp Secy*
Kevin Cimore, *Manager*
EMP: 4
SQ FT: 10,000
SALES: 1.5MM **Privately Held**
SIC: 2421 Lumber: rough, sawed or planed

(G-8795)
SHARON STONE CO
County Road 10 (45727)
P.O. Box 100 (45727-0100)
PHONE..................................740 374-3236
Carl Baker, *Owner*
EMP: 4
SALES (est): 251.8K **Privately Held**
SIC: 3295 5032 Slag, crushed or ground; stone, crushed or broken

(G-8796)
WARREN DRILLING CO INC
Also Called: Warren Trucking
305 Smithson St (45727-9749)
P.O. Box 103 (45727-0103)
PHONE..................................740 783-2775
Dan R Warren, *President*
Lewis D Warren, *Principal*
Paul H Warren, *Principal*
W T Warren, *Principal*
Randy C Warren, *Vice Pres*
EMP: 110 EST: 1939
SALES (est): 27.5MM **Privately Held**
WEB: www.warrendrilling.biz
SIC: 1381 Directional drilling oil & gas wells

Diamond
Portage County

(G-8797)
DEANGELO INSTRUMENT INC
3200 Mcclintocksburg Rd (44412-9732)
PHONE..................................330 654-9264
Thomas A Clark, *Principal*
EMP: 3 EST: 2001
SALES (est): 312.2K **Privately Held**
SIC: 3599 Machine shop, jobbing & repair

(G-8798)
INTERNATIONAL DIES CO INC
3400 Newton Falls Rd (44412-9630)
PHONE..................................330 744-7951
Ted Lyda, *President*
EMP: 6
SQ FT: 13,400
SALES (est): 625.7K **Privately Held**
SIC: 3544 Extrusion dies

(G-8799)
RINKER MATERIALS
4200 Universal Dr (44412-9700)
PHONE..................................330 654-2511
Chris Rowland, *Principal*
EMP: 7 EST: 1963
SALES (est): 594.5K **Privately Held**
SIC: 3273 Ready-mixed concrete

Donnelsville
Clark County

(G-8800)
BEACH MANUFACTURING CO
118 N Hampton Rd (45319-5011)
P.O. Box 129 (45319-0129)
PHONE..................................937 882-6372
Ted Beach, *President*
Louis Beach, *Principal*
Carrie M Ridenaur, *Principal*
Julia Bartlett, *Controller*
Todd Beach, *Supervisor*
EMP: 120
SQ FT: 20,000
SALES (est): 30.3MM **Privately Held**
WEB: www.beachmfgco.com
SIC: 3714 3231 Motor vehicle parts & accessories; mirrors, truck & automobile: made from purchased glass

(G-8801)
ECON-O-MACHINE PRODUCTS INC
160 E Main St (45319-5042)
P.O. Box 153 (45319-0153)
PHONE..................................937 882-6307
Annabelle Blumenschein, *President*
Roger A Blumenschein, *President*
Doug Blumenschein, *Vice Pres*
EMP: 3 EST: 1973
SQ FT: 8,440
SALES (est): 474.6K **Privately Held**
SIC: 3599 3549 7694 3621 Machine shop, jobbing & repair; metalworking machinery; armature rewinding shops; motors & generators

Dover
Tuscarawas County

(G-8802)
A W TIPKA OIL & GAS INC
2421 Johnstown Rd Ne (44622-7579)
PHONE..................................330 364-4333
Alan W Tipka, *President*
James Schumacher, *CFO*
EMP: 7
SALES (est): 460K **Privately Held**
SIC: 1389 Servicing oil & gas wells

(G-8803)
ALLIED MACHINE & ENGRG CORP (PA)
120 Deeds Dr (44622-9652)
P.O. Box 36 (44622-0036)
PHONE..................................330 343-4283
Bill Stokey, *CEO*
Terry Koester, *Regional Mgr*
Michael A Stokey, *Exec VP*
Steve Stokey, *Exec VP*
Gary Kropf, *Vice Pres*
▲ EMP: 235 EST: 1933
SALES (est): 65.6MM **Privately Held**
WEB: www.alliedmachine.com
SIC: 3545 Machine tool attachments & accessories

(G-8804)
ARIZONA CHEMICAL COMPANY LLC
875 Harger St (44622-9441)
PHONE..................................330 343-7701
Brian Hershberger, *Engineer*
Tom Wiegand, *Engineer*
John Trouts, *Branch Mgr*
Tina Manning, *Admin Asst*
EMP: 115
SQ FT: 3,000 **Publicly Held**
WEB: www.arizonachemical.com
SIC: 2861 2911 2821 2819 Wood distillation products; fractionation products of crude petroleum, hydrocarbons; plastics materials & resins; industrial inorganic chemicals
HQ: Kraton Chemical, Llc
    4600 Touchton Rd E # 1200
    Jacksonville FL 32246
    904 928-8700

(G-8805)
BAERLOCHER USA LLC (DH)
3676 Davis Rd Nw (44622-9771)
PHONE..................................330 364-6000
Ray Buehler, *CEO*
David Keubel, *CFO*
Mike Manzer, *Sales Staff*
Roberto Nunez, *Director*
▲ EMP: 10
SQ FT: 10,000
SALES (est): 32.8MM
SALES (corp-wide): 474.4MM **Privately Held**
SIC: 2819 Nonmetallic compounds
HQ: Baerlocher Gmbh
    Freisinger Str. 1
    UnterschleiBheim 85716
    891 437-30

(G-8806)
BAIR BODIES & TRAILERS INC
4562 Bair Rd Nw (44622-7070)
PHONE..................................330 343-4853
Lynn Corpman, *President*
D Corpman, *Vice Pres*
EMP: 3
SALES (est): 259.9K **Privately Held**
WEB: www.bairbodies.com
SIC: 3715 Truck trailers

(G-8807)
BARKETT FRUIT CO INC (PA)
Also Called: Farmer Smiths Market
1213 E 3rd St (44622-1227)
PHONE..................................330 364-6645
William Barkett, *CEO*
James Barkett, *President*
Thomas Barkett, *Vice Pres*
Ronald Barkett, *Treasurer*
EMP: 36
SQ FT: 20,000
SALES (est): 12.3MM **Privately Held**
WEB: www.barkettfruit.com
SIC: 5148 5143 5144 2099 Vegetables; fruits; dairy products, except dried or canned; eggs; salads, fresh or refrigerated

(G-8808)
BELDEN & BLAKE CORPORATION
1748 Saltwell Rd Nw (44622-7471)
PHONE..................................330 602-5551
Tim McConah, *Branch Mgr*
EMP: 30
SQ FT: 4,500 **Privately Held**

Dover - Tuscarawas County (G-8809) — GEOGRAPHIC SECTION

WEB: www.beldenblake.com
SIC: **1311** 1389 4922 5082 Crude petroleum production; natural gas production; oil field services; natural gas transmission; oil field equipment; oil & gas exploration services
HQ: Belden & Blake Corporation
1001 Fannin St Ste 800
Houston TX 77002
713 659-3500

(G-8809)
BLICK TOOL & DIE INC
117 E Front St (44622-2951)
PHONE.................................330 343-1277
James E Blickensderfer, *President*
Beth Blickensderfer, *Vice Pres*
EMP: 5
SQ FT: 6,000
SALES: 200K **Privately Held**
SIC: **3544** Special dies & tools

(G-8810)
BREITENBACH WINE CELLAR INC
Also Called: Breitenbach Bed & Breakfast
5934 Old Route 39 Nw (44622-7787)
PHONE.................................330 343-3603
Cynthia Bixler, *President*
EMP: 8
SALES (est): 1MM **Privately Held**
WEB: www.breitenbachwine.com
SIC: **2084** 5812 7011 Wines; eating places; bed & breakfast inn

(G-8811)
COMMERCIAL HONING LLC (PA)
Also Called: Commercial Fluid Power
2997 Progress St (44622-9639)
PHONE.................................330 343-8896
Jeff Headley, *Mng Member*
Rich Finnicum,
Kevin Reilly,
Mike Sims,
▲ EMP: 60 EST: 1946
SQ FT: 15,000
SALES (est): 25.5MM **Privately Held**
SIC: **3599** 3471 3317 Machine shop, jobbing & repair; plating & polishing; steel pipe & tubes

(G-8812)
COMMERCIAL HONING OHIO INC (PA)
2997 Progress St (44622-9639)
PHONE.................................330 343-8896
Jeff Headlee Mgr Member, *Principal*
Jeff Headlee, *Mng Member*
EMP: 60 EST: 1950
SALES (est): 9.6MM **Privately Held**
WEB: www.commercial-honing.com
SIC: **3492** Fluid power valves & hose fittings

(G-8813)
COMMERCIAL HONING OHIO INC
Commercial Fluid Power
2997 Progress St (44622-9639)
PHONE.................................330 343-8896
Melvin White, *Branch Mgr*
EMP: 25
SALES (corp-wide): 9.6MM **Privately Held**
WEB: www.commercial-honing.com
SIC: **3593** Fluid power cylinders, hydraulic or pneumatic
PA: Commercial Honing Of Ohio, Inc.
2997 Progress St
Dover OH 44622
330 343-8896

(G-8814)
CYCLONE SUPPLY COMPANY INC (PA)
524 River St (44622-1935)
P.O. Box 706 (44622-0706)
PHONE.................................330 204-0313
Tim Levengood, *President*
Dewain Horne, *Vice Pres*
EMP: 3
SQ FT: 60,000
SALES (est): 878.4K **Privately Held**
SIC: **3533** Oil & gas field machinery

(G-8815)
DEFLECTO LLC
303 Oxford St Ste A (44622-1977)
PHONE.................................330 602-0840
EMP: 39
SALES (corp-wide): 581.8MM **Privately Held**
SIC: **3089** Plastic hardware & building products
HQ: Deflecto, Llc
7035 E 86th St
Indianapolis IN 46250
317 849-9555

(G-8816)
DIRECT ACTION CO INC
Also Called: Dac
6668 Old Route 39 Nw (44622-7794)
PHONE.................................330 364-3219
Randy Jacobs, *President*
James Rhodes, *Vice Pres*
EMP: 15
SALES: 760K **Privately Held**
WEB: www.directaction.com
SIC: **5122** 2048 Vitamins & minerals; feed supplements

(G-8817)
DORIS KIMBLE
Also Called: Red Hill Development Company
3596 State Route 39 Nw (44622-7232)
PHONE.................................330 343-1226
Doris Kimble, *Owner*
EMP: 20
SALES: 3MM **Privately Held**
SIC: **1381** Drilling oil & gas wells

(G-8818)
DOVER CABINET INC
1568 State Route 39 Nw (44622-7346)
PHONE.................................330 343-9074
John A Perkowski, *President*
EMP: 18
SQ FT: 16,000
SALES (est): 2.1MM **Privately Held**
SIC: **2434** Wood kitchen cabinets

(G-8819)
DOVER CHEMICAL CORPORATION (HQ)
3676 Davis Rd Nw (44622-9771)
PHONE.................................330 343-7711
Jack Teat, *President*
Tom Freeman, *Exec VP*
Chuck Fletcher, *Vice Pres*
Don Stevenson, *Vice Pres*
Jiim Moore, *Safety Dir*
◆ EMP: 170 EST: 1949
SQ FT: 260,000
SALES: 107.8MM
SALES (corp-wide): 1.2B **Privately Held**
WEB: www.doverchem.com
SIC: **2819** 2869 2899 Industrial inorganic chemicals; industrial organic chemicals; chemical preparations
PA: Icc Industries Inc.
460 Park Ave Fl 7
New York NY 10022
212 521-1700

(G-8820)
DOVER FABRICATION AND BURN INC (HQ)
2996 Progress St (44622-9639)
PHONE.................................330 339-1057
Robert Sensel, *President*
EMP: 8 EST: 2012
SALES (est): 601.3K
SALES (corp-wide): 15.8MM **Privately Held**
SIC: **1799** 7692 7353 Welding on site; welding repair; oil well drilling equipment, rental or leasing
PA: Dover Hydraulics, Inc.
2996 Progress St
Dover OH 44622
330 364-1617

(G-8821)
DOVER HIGH PRFMCE PLAS INC
Also Called: Dhpp
140 Williams Dr Nw (44622-7662)
PHONE.................................330 343-3477
Mary L Schwab, *President*
Mike Poland, *Mfg Staff*
George Maksim, *Treasurer*
Kevin Kirkland, *Persnl Dir*
Paul Palmer, *Mktg Dir*
EMP: 36
SQ FT: 60,000
SALES (est): 8.3MM **Privately Held**
WEB: www.dhpp.net
SIC: **3089** Injection molding of plastics

(G-8822)
DOVER MACHINE CO
2208 State Route 516 Nw (44622-7081)
PHONE.................................330 343-4123
Wayne Amistadi, *President*
EMP: 14
SQ FT: 10,000
SALES: 740K **Privately Held**
SIC: **3599** 7692 3544 Machine shop, jobbing & repair; welding repair; special dies, tools, jigs & fixtures

(G-8823)
DOVER TANK AND PLATE COMPANY
5725 Crown Rd Nw (44622-9649)
P.O. Box 70 (44622-0070)
PHONE.................................330 343-4443
David Lawless, *President*
Earl Lawless, *Vice Pres*
Joseph Lawless, *Vice Pres*
Ray Schembechler, *Project Mgr*
Luke Lawless, *Treasurer*
EMP: 45
SQ FT: 40,000
SALES (est): 17.7MM **Privately Held**
WEB: www.dovertank.com
SIC: **3441** 3446 3444 3443 Fabricated structural metal; architectural metalwork; sheet metalwork; fabricated plate work (boiler shop)

(G-8824)
DUCK WATER BOATS INC
Also Called: Ice Water Airboats
3817 Blacksnake Hl Rd Ne (44622-7914)
PHONE.................................330 602-9008
Steve Hoover, *President*
EMP: 4 EST: 1999
SALES: 1.2MM **Privately Held**
WEB: www.duckwaterboats.com
SIC: **3732** 7699 5088 5551 Iceboats, building & repairing; boat repair; boats, non-recreational; boat dealers

(G-8825)
EXTREME TRAILERS LLC
317 E Broadway St (44622-1914)
PHONE.................................330 440-0026
Les Smith, *President*
EMP: 6
SQ FT: 100,000
SALES (est): 2.4MM **Privately Held**
SIC: **3715** Truck trailers

(G-8826)
FARSIGHT MANAGEMENT INC
6790 Middle Run Rd Nw (44622 7648)
PHONE.................................330 602-8338
Robert A Bennett, *President*
EMP: 4
SALES: 205K **Privately Held**
SIC: **1446** Molding sand mining

(G-8827)
G A SPRING ADVERTISING
Also Called: Pro-Print Business Center
2101 N Wooster Ave (44622-2403)
P.O. Box 673 (44622-0673)
PHONE.................................330 343-9030
Gerald A Spring, *Owner*
EMP: 4
SQ FT: 12,000
SALES: 180K **Privately Held**
SIC: **5112** 2752 Business forms; business form & card printing, lithographic

(G-8828)
GRAPHIC PUBLICATIONS INC
123 W 3rd St (44622-2968)
PHONE.................................330 343-4377
Michael Mast, *President*
Hunter Bargin, *Principal*
EMP: 60
SALES (est): 1.4MM **Privately Held**
SIC: **2711** Newspapers, publishing & printing

(G-8829)
HANNON COMPANY
Charles Rewinding Division
801 Commercial Pkwy (44622-3152)
P.O. Box 398 (44622-0398)
PHONE.................................330 343-7758
Timothy Welch, *Branch Mgr*
Tim J Welch, *Manager*
EMP: 14
SQ FT: 12,200
SALES (corp-wide): 25.8MM **Privately Held**
WEB: www.hanco.com
SIC: **7629** 5063 7699 7694 Electrical repair shops; motors, electric; motor controls, starters & relays: electric; welding equipment repair; electric motor repair; machine shop, jobbing & repair
PA: The Hannon Company
1605 Waynesburg Dr Se
Canton OH 44707
330 456-4728

(G-8830)
HVAC INC
Also Called: Dover Phila Heating & Cooling
133 W 3rd St (44622-2933)
PHONE.................................330 343-5511
David Kinsey, *President*
Dana Moser, *General Mgr*
James Moser, *Corp Secy*
EMP: 12
SQ FT: 10,000
SALES (est): 1.2MM **Privately Held**
WEB: www.hvac-inc.com
SIC: **1711** 3444 Warm air heating & air conditioning contractor; sheet metalwork

(G-8831)
INCA PRESSWOOD-PALLETS LTD (PA)
3005 Progress St (44622-9640)
P.O. Box 248 (44622-0248)
PHONE.................................330 343-3361
Wolfgang Ketzer, *Partner*
Hans Inselkammer, *Partner*
John Horning, *Exec VP*
Matt Doughty, *Plant Mgr*
Rae Powell, *Administration*
▲ EMP: 35 EST: 1979
SQ FT: 45,000
SALES (est): 5.6MM **Privately Held**
SIC: **2448** Pallets, wood

(G-8832)
INDUSTRIAL FINISHERS INC
3690 State Route 800 Ne (44622-7999)
P.O. Box 482 (44622-0482)
PHONE.................................330 343-7797
Paul Neiger, *President*
Tommie Wahl, *Corp Secy*
EMP: 4
SQ FT: 12,000
SALES (est): 125K **Privately Held**
WEB: www.industrial-finishers.com
SIC: **3479** Painting, coating & hot dipping

(G-8833)
J & J TOOL & DIE INC
203 W 4th St (44622-2905)
PHONE.................................330 343-4721
Scott Sherer, *President*
Carol Belt, *Corp Secy*
EMP: 7 EST: 1966
SQ FT: 5,000
SALES (est): 604.1K **Privately Held**
SIC: **3544** Mfg Dies & Tools

(G-8834)
KIM PHILLIPS SIGN CO LLC
Also Called: Signs To Go
812 Boulevard St (44622-2008)
PHONE.................................330 364-4280
Kim Phillips, *Principal*
EMP: 4
SALES (est): 442.4K **Privately Held**
SIC: **1522** 3993 Residential construction; signs & advertising specialties

(G-8835)
KRUZ INC
Also Called: Ravens Sales & Service
6332 Columbia Rd Nw (44622-7676)
PHONE.................................330 878-5595
Rufus Hall, *Manager*
EMP: 30

▲ = Import ▼= Export
◆ = Import/Export

GEOGRAPHIC SECTION

Dover - Tuscarawas County (G-8861)

SALES (est): 6.3MM
SALES (corp-wide): 10.9MM **Privately Held**
WEB: www.kruz.com
SIC: 3713 Dump truck bodies
PA: Kruz Inc.
1201 W Culver Rd
Knox IN 46534
574 772-6673

(G-8836)
LAVANDER BRIDAL SALON
218 W 3rd St (44622-2965)
PHONE.................330 602-0333
Karen Stokey, *Owner*
EMP: 10
SALES (est): 898K **Privately Held**
SIC: 2335 Bridal & formal gowns

(G-8837)
MARLITE INC
609 S Tuscarawas Ave (44622-2345)
PHONE.................330 343-6621
Darryl Rosser, *Branch Mgr*
EMP: 150 **Privately Held**
SIC: 2542 Partitions & fixtures, except wood
HQ: Marlite, Inc.
1 Marlite Dr
Dover OH 44622
330 343-6621

(G-8838)
MARLITE INC (DH)
1 Marlite Dr (44622-2361)
PHONE.................330 343-6621
Daryl Rosser, *President*
Mark Jutte, *Vice Pres*
Greg Leary, *Vice Pres*
Greg Triplett, *Vice Pres*
Kimberly McBride, *CFO*
◆ EMP: 150
SQ FT: 450,000
SALES (est): 70.9MM **Privately Held**
WEB: www.marlite.com
SIC: 2542 Partitions & fixtures, except wood
HQ: Nudo Products, Inc.
1500 Taylor Ave
Springfield IL 62703
217 528-5636

(G-8839)
MARMON HIGHWAY TECH LLC
6332 Columbia Rd Nw (44622-7676)
P.O. Box 525 (44622-0525)
PHONE.................330 878-5595
EMP: 40
SQ FT: 2,725
SALES (corp-wide): 210.8B **Publicly Held**
SIC: 7539 3714 Automotive Repair Mfg Motor Vehicle Parts/Accessories
HQ: Marmon Highway Technologies Llc
5915 Chalkville Rd 300
Birmingham AL 35235
205 508-2000

(G-8840)
METEOR SEALING SYSTEMS LLC
Also Called: Meteor Automotive
400 S Tuscarawas Ave (44622-2342)
PHONE.................330 343-9595
Joerg Busse, *Vice Pres*
Todd Smitt, *Purch Mgr*
Georgetta Byers, *Sales Executive*
John Scott, *Technology*
Juergen Wickert,
▲ EMP: 155
SALES (est): 45.7MM
SALES (corp-wide): 626.8K **Privately Held**
WEB: www.meteor-sealingsystems.com
SIC: 3069 Tubing, rubber
HQ: Meteor Gummiwerke K.H. Badje Gmbh & Co. Kg
Ernst-Deger-Str. 9
Bockenem 31167
506 725-0

(G-8841)
MIDDAUGH PRINTERS
226 W 2nd St (44622-2907)
P.O. Box 400, Sugarcreek (44681-0400)
PHONE.................330 852-2471
Jeri Middaugh, *Principal*
Mandy Middaugh, *Executive*
EMP: 4
SALES (est): 271.3K **Privately Held**
SIC: 2752 Commercial printing, offset

(G-8842)
MILLER WELDING INC
2718 Broad Run Dar Rd Nw (44622-7705)
PHONE.................330 364-6173
C Delon Miller, *President*
Robin Miller, *Vice Pres*
E Pauline Miller, *Treasurer*
EMP: 7
SQ FT: 1,320
SALES (est): 840.3K **Privately Held**
SIC: 7692 Welding repair

(G-8843)
MINTEQ INTERNATIONAL INC
5864 Crown Street Ext Nw (44622)
PHONE.................330 343-8821
Ron Nanni, *Branch Mgr*
EMP: 32
SQ FT: 150,000 **Publicly Held**
WEB: www.minteq.com
SIC: 3297 3255 3251 Brick refractories; clay refractories; brick & structural clay tile
HQ: Minteq International Inc.
35 Highland Ave
Bethlehem PA 18017

(G-8844)
NATURAL GAS CONSTRUCTION INC
Also Called: Ngc Red Hill
1737 Red Hill Rd Nw (44622-7113)
PHONE.................330 364-9240
Miles Pillar, *President*
Kathy Pillar, *Treasurer*
EMP: 3
SALES: 1MM **Privately Held**
SIC: 1389 Gas field services

(G-8845)
NEXT SALES LLC
3258 Dogwood Ln Nw (44622-6822)
PHONE.................330 704-4126
Michael R Ludwig, *Principal*
Mike Ludwig, *COO*
EMP: 8 EST: 2012
SALES (est): 916.5K **Privately Held**
SIC: 3275 Acoustical plaster, gypsum

(G-8846)
OERLIKON BLZERS CATING USA INC
120 Deeds Dr (44622-9652)
PHONE.................330 343-9892
EMP: 7
SALES (corp-wide): 2.6B **Privately Held**
SIC: 3479 Coating of metals & formed products
HQ: Oerlikon Balzers Coating Usa Inc.
1700 E Golf Rd Ste 200
Schaumburg IL 60173
847 619-5541

(G-8847)
R & J PRINTING ENTERPRISES INC
Also Called: Newhouse Printing Company
111 N Walnut St (44622-2939)
P.O. Box 280 (44622-0280)
PHONE.................330 343-1242
John S Carpenter, *President*
Tiffani Gerber, *Opers Mgr*
Stephanie Carpenter, *Mktg Coord*
EMP: 15 EST: 1917
SQ FT: 7,500
SALES (est): 1.6MM **Privately Held**
SIC: 2752 Commercial printing, offset

(G-8848)
RANGE RSURCES - APPALACHIA LLC
1748 Saltwell Rd Nw (44622-7471)
PHONE.................330 866-3301
Woody McDaniels, *Manager*
EMP: 41
SALES (corp-wide): 3.2B **Publicly Held**
WEB: www.gl-energy.com
SIC: 1382 Oil & gas exploration services
HQ: Range Resources - Appalachia, Llc.
3000 Town Center Blvd
Canonsburg PA 15317
724 743-6700

(G-8849)
REAM AND HAAGER LABORATORY
179 W Broadway St (44622-1916)
P.O. Box 706 (44622-0706)
PHONE.................330 343-3711
Tim Levengood, *President*
EMP: 13 EST: 1960
SQ FT: 4,300
SALES (est): 580K **Privately Held**
SIC: 8748 8734 0711 1389 Business consulting; water testing laboratory; soil testing services; pipe testing, oil field service

(G-8850)
SCHINDLERS BROAD RUN CHESE HSE
6011 Old Route 39 Nw (44622-7788)
PHONE.................330 343-4108
Chad Schindler, *President*
Nancy Schindler, *Treasurer*
Cindy Festi, *Office Mgr*
EMP: 10 EST: 1933
SQ FT: 16,600
SALES (est): 1.2MM **Privately Held**
WEB: www.broadruncheese.com
SIC: 2022 5451 5947 Natural cheese; cheese; gift shop

(G-8851)
SCHOOL HOUSE WINERY LLC
455 Schneiders Crssng Rd (44622-6922)
PHONE.................330 602-9463
Jennifer Jagunic, *Principal*
EMP: 5 EST: 2009
SALES (est): 186K **Privately Held**
SIC: 8299 2084 Schools & educational service; wines, brandy & brandy spirits

(G-8852)
SCHWAB INDUSTRIES INC (HQ)
2301 Progress St (44622-9641)
PHONE.................330 364-4411
Jerry A Schwab, *President*
David A Schwab, *Vice Pres*
Mary Lynn Hites, *Treasurer*
Donna Schwab, *Admin Sec*
EMP: 15 EST: 1950
SQ FT: 2,500
SALES: 39.8MM
SALES (corp-wide): 29.7B **Privately Held**
WEB: www.schwabindustries.com
SIC: 3273 5031 5032 Ready-mixed concrete; lumber, plywood & millwork; concrete & cinder block
PA: Crh Public Limited Company
Stonemasons Way
Dublin
140 410-00

(G-8853)
SHELLY MATERIALS INC
2301 Progress St (44622-9641)
P.O. Box 400 (44622-0400)
PHONE.................330 364-4411
Dave Moreland, *Branch Mgr*
EMP: 4
SALES (corp-wide): 29.7B **Privately Held**
SIC: 1422 Crushed & broken limestone
HQ: Shelly Materials, Inc.
80 Park Dr
Thornville OH 43076
740 246-6315

(G-8854)
SMITH CONCRETE CO (PA)
Also Called: Division of Selling Materials
2301 Progress St (44622-9641)
P.O. Box 356, Marietta (45750-0356)
PHONE.................740 373-7441
Mike Murphy, *General Mgr*
Dick Wilson, *Manager*
EMP: 50 EST: 1922
SQ FT: 2,000
SALES (est): 5.6MM **Privately Held**
WEB: www.smithconcreteco.com
SIC: 3272 3273 1442 Dry mixture concrete; ready-mixed concrete; construction sand & gravel

(G-8855)
SNYDER MANUFACTURING INC
3001 Progress St (44622-9640)
P.O. Box 188 (44622-0188)
PHONE.................330 343-4456
Dennis Snyder, *President*
Goerge Mokodean, *Admin Sec*
▲ EMP: 60
SQ FT: 50,000
SALES (est): 14.4MM **Privately Held**
SIC: 3083 Laminated plastics plate & sheet

(G-8856)
SNYDER MANUFACTURING CO LTD
3001 Progress St (44622-9640)
P.O. Box 188 (44622-0188)
PHONE.................330 343-4456
Dennis Snyder, *Partner*
EMP: 3 EST: 1960
SQ FT: 50,000
SALES (est): 439.2K **Privately Held**
WEB: www.snyderman.com
SIC: 7359 6512 3083 3081 Equipment rental & leasing; commercial & industrial building operation; laminated plastics plate & sheet; unsupported plastics film & sheet; broadwoven fabric mills, manmade

(G-8857)
SPEEDWAY LLC
Also Called: Speedway Superamerica 6243
225 S Wooster Ave (44622-1942)
PHONE.................330 343-9469
Bobbi Ward, *Branch Mgr*
EMP: 10 **Publicly Held**
WEB: www.speedwaynet.com
SIC: 1311 Crude petroleum production
HQ: Speedway Llc
500 Speedway Dr
Enon OH 45323
937 864-3000

(G-8858)
SUGARCREEK LIME SERVICE
Also Called: M B Trucking
2068 Gordon Rd Nw (44622-7741)
PHONE.................330 364-4460
Matthew Beachy, *Owner*
EMP: 8 EST: 1979
SALES (est): 721.5K **Privately Held**
SIC: 3274 Lime

(G-8859)
T V SPECIALTIES INC
Also Called: Dover Tower Company, The
320 W 3rd St (44622-3199)
PHONE.................330 364-6678
EMP: 10
SQ FT: 67,000
SALES (est): 1.8MM **Privately Held**
SIC: 5064 3663 5731 5065 Whol & Ret Radios Television Sets Tape Recorders & Parts

(G-8860)
TCB AUTOMATION LLC
601 W 15th St (44622-9763)
PHONE.................330 556-6444
Joseph Dalessandro, *Mng Member*
John Dalessandro,
EMP: 24
SALES: 3.5MM **Privately Held**
SIC: 1731 3613 General electrical contractor; control panels, electric

(G-8861)
TWIN CITIES CONCRETE CO (DH)
141 S Tuscarawas Ave (44622-1951)
PHONE.................330 343-4491
Jerry Schwab, *President*
Jerry Gwinn, *General Mgr*
David Schwab, *Vice Pres*
Mary Lynn Schwab, *Treasurer*
Donna Schwab, *Admin Sec*
EMP: 17 EST: 1949
SQ FT: 1,500
SALES (est): 20.7MM
SALES (corp-wide): 29.7B **Privately Held**
SIC: 3273 5072 Ready-mixed concrete; builders' hardware

Dover - Tuscarawas County (G-8862)

HQ: Schwab Industries, Inc.
2301 Progress St
Dover OH 44622
330 364-4411

(G-8862)
UNION CAMP CORP
875 Harger St (44622-9441)
PHONE.................................330 343-7701
Gary Craig, Director
▲ EMP: 3
SALES (est): 457.9K Privately Held
SIC: 2819 Industrial inorganic chemicals

(G-8863)
ZIMMER SURGICAL INC
Also Called: Zimmer Orthopaedic Surgical
200 W Ohio Ave (44622-9642)
PHONE.................................800 321-5533
Kenneth R Coonce, Vice Pres
James T Crines, Vice Pres
▲ EMP: 300
SALES (est): 80.2MM
SALES (corp-wide): 7.9B Publicly Held
SIC: 3842 Orthopedic appliances
PA: Zimmer Biomet Holdings, Inc.
345 E Main St
Warsaw IN 46580
574 267-6131

Doylestown
Wayne County

(G-8864)
COUNTER CONCEPTS INC
15535 Portage St (44230-1130)
PHONE.................................330 848-4848
Shawn Green, President
Dave Bartlett, Sales Mgr
EMP: 10
SALES (est): 1.9MM Privately Held
WEB: www.counterconcepts.com
SIC: 2541 3083 5211 Counters or counter display cases, wood; plastic finished products, laminated; lumber & other building materials

(G-8865)
MID-WEST POLY PAK INC
89 E Marion St (44230-1454)
P.O. Box 35 (44230-0035)
PHONE.................................330 658-2921
Dan Large, President
Julie Meeks, Principal
Sandra S Hubiak, Vice Pres
▲ EMP: 25
SQ FT: 26,000
SALES (est): 7.2MM Privately Held
WEB: www.midwestpolypak.com
SIC: 2673 Plastic bags: made from purchased materials

(G-8866)
STORAGE BUILDINGS UNLIMITED
12321 Hollow Ridge Rd (44230-9765)
PHONE.................................216 731-0010
Steve Rosser, Branch Mgr
EMP: 5
SALES (corp-wide): 1.2MM Privately Held
SIC: 3448 Prefabricated metal buildings
PA: Storage Buildings Unlimited Inc
278 Main St
Wadsworth OH
330 334-5803

(G-8867)
T J TARGET
235 Bailey Ct (44230-1596)
P.O. Box 171 (44230-0171)
PHONE.................................330 658-3057
Janet Siebeneck, Owner
EMP: 4
SALES (est): 325.7K Privately Held
SIC: 2621 5941 5091 Specialty papers; sporting goods & bicycle shops; sporting & recreation goods

Dresden
Muskingum County

(G-8868)
DRESDEN SPECIALTIES INC (PA)
Also Called: Social Supper
305 Main St (43821)
P.O. Box 110 (43821-0110)
PHONE.................................740 754-2451
M Dean Cole, CEO
Donna R Cole, President
EMP: 4 EST: 1956
SALES (est): 558.2K Privately Held
WEB: www.socialsupper.com
SIC: 3231 5947 5699 2752 Decorated glassware: chipped, engraved, etched, etc.; gift shop; formal wear; commercial printing, offset; letterpress printing; automotive & apparel trimmings

(G-8869)
MINING RECLAMATION INC
15953 State Route 60 S (43821-9657)
P.O. Box 555 (43821-0555)
PHONE.................................740 327-5555
John Shupert, President
EMP: 15 EST: 1997
SALES (est): 1MM Privately Held
SIC: 1081 Metal mining services

Dublin
Franklin County

(G-8870)
5874 SAWMILL LLC
5874 Sawmill Rd (43017-1589)
PHONE.................................614 795-1818
EMP: 3
SALES (est): 212.6K Privately Held
SIC: 2421 Sawmills & planing mills, general

(G-8871)
A GRADE NOTES INC (PA)
6385 Shier Rings Rd Ste 1 (43016-1261)
P.O. Box 4175 (43016-0617)
PHONE.................................614 766-9999
Gary Vander Stoep, CEO
Kathy Gatton Eshelman, President
Rita Wood, Corp Secy
David Kiess, Vice Pres
EMP: 8
SQ FT: 1,000
SALES (est): 1MM Privately Held
WEB: www.gradeanotes.com
SIC: 2752 7334 Lithographic Commercial Printing Photocopying Services

(G-8872)
ABHUSHAN LLC
2815 Festival Ln (43017-2363)
PHONE.................................614 789-0632
Tina Joshi, Principal
▲ EMP: 4
SALES (est): 357.4K Privately Held
SIC: 3423 Jewelers' hand tools

(G-8873)
ADNA INC
6866 Mcdougal Ct (43017-8898)
PHONE.................................614 397-4974
Rama P Ramenujam, President
EMP: 1
SALES: 1MM Privately Held
SIC: 2819 Chemicals, reagent grade: refined from technical grade

(G-8874)
ADVANCED PRGRM RESOURCES INC (PA)
Also Called: Touchmark
2715 Tuller Pkwy (43017-2310)
PHONE.................................614 761-9994
Danial Chacho, CEO
Larry Dado, President
Douglas Heagren, Treasurer
Jennifer Heagren, Director
EMP: 47
SQ FT: 5,100
SALES (est): 4.3MM Privately Held
SIC: 7379 7373 8742 7372 Computer related consulting services; systems integration services; management consulting services; application computer software; custom computer programming services

(G-8875)
AFI BRANDS LLC
Also Called: Ripple Swimwear
5575 Hayden Run Blvd (43016-7725)
PHONE.................................614 999-6426
Joanne Hopkins, Mng Member
EMP: 3
SALES (est): 314.3K Privately Held
SIC: 2329 2331 Men's & boys' sportswear & athletic clothing; women's & misses' blouses & shirts

(G-8876)
ALKON CORPORATION
6750 Crosby Ct (43016-7644)
PHONE.................................614 799-6650
Mark Marino, Branch Mgr
EMP: 35
SALES (corp-wide): 24.2MM Privately Held
WEB: www.alkoncorp.com
SIC: 3491 3082 5084 5085 Industrial valves; unsupported plastics profile shapes; industrial machinery & equipment; industrial supplies
PA: Alkon Corporation
728 Graham Dr
Fremont OH 43420
419 355-9111

(G-8877)
AMERICAN MITSUBA CORPORATION
4140 Tuller Rd Ste 106 (43017-5013)
PHONE.................................989 779-4962
Kenichi Hirano, Branch Mgr
EMP: 5
SALES (corp-wide): 3.6B Privately Held
SIC: 3621 Motors, electric
HQ: American Mitsuba Corporation
2945 Three Leaves Dr
Mount Pleasant MI 48858
989 779-4962

(G-8878)
AMERICAN MITSUBA CORPORATION
4140 Tuller Rd Ste 106 (43017-5013)
PHONE.................................989 779-4962
EMP: 5
SALES (corp-wide): 2.5B Privately Held
SIC: 3621 Mfg Motors/Generators
HQ: American Mitsuba Corporation
2945 Three Leaves Dr
Mount Pleasant MI 48858
989 773-0377

(G-8879)
AMERICAN RODPUMP LTD
5201 Indian Hill Rd (43017-9708)
PHONE.................................440 987-9457
John Van Krevel, President
EMP: 3
SALES (est): 271.7K Privately Held
SIC: 1311 Crude petroleum & natural gas

(G-8880)
APPALACHIAN FUELS LLC (PA)
6375 Riverside Dr Ste 200 (43017-5045)
PHONE.................................606 928-0460
Steven Addington, President
EMP: 8
SALES (est): 16.3MM Privately Held
SIC: 1241 Coal mining services

(G-8881)
APPORTIS LLC
90 S High St Ste C (43017-1171)
PHONE.................................614 832-8362
Philip Payne, President
EMP: 4
SALES (est): 81.1K Privately Held
SIC: 7372 Business oriented computer software

(G-8882)
AQ PRODUCTIONS INC
5945 Wilcox Pl Ste B (43016-8713)
PHONE.................................614 486-7700
Ronald Stiebler, President
Susan Trego, Treasurer
EMP: 3
SQ FT: 1,500
SALES (est): 29.1K Privately Held
WEB: www.aqproductions.com
SIC: 3993 Signs & advertising specialties

(G-8883)
ASHLAND LLC
Also Called: Ashland Distribution
5200 Blazer Pkwy (43017-3309)
P.O. Box 2219, Columbus (43216-2219)
PHONE.................................614 790-3333
Sherri Nelson, President
Ted Harris, Vice Pres
Fred Good, Vice Pres
Frank Pettus, Manager
Antonio Tong, Manager
EMP: 150
SALES (corp-wide): 3.7B Publicly Held
WEB: www.ashland.com
SIC: 2899 5169 Chemical preparations; chemicals & allied products
HQ: Ashland Llc
50 E Rivercenter Blvd # 1600
Covington KY 41011
859 815-3333

(G-8884)
ASHLAND SPECIALTY INGREDIENTS (PA)
Also Called: Ashland Spcalty Ingredients GP
5200 Laser Pkwy (43017)
PHONE.................................302 594-5000
James J O'Brien, CEO
▲ EMP: 47 EST: 2015
SALES (est): 20.4MM Privately Held
SIC: 2844 Shampoos, rinses, conditioners: hair

(G-8885)
ASK CHEMICALS LLC
Also Called: Ask Chemicals LP
495 Metro Pl S Ste 250 (43017-5319)
PHONE.................................800 848-7485
Frank Coenen, CEO
Stefan Sommer, Chairman
Scott Hoertz, COO
Michael Andrae, Vice Pres
Randy Helmick, Vice Pres
◆ EMP: 150
SQ FT: 3,200
SALES (est): 114MM Privately Held
SIC: 2899 Chemical preparations
HQ: Ask Chemicals Gmbh
Reisholzstr. 16-18
Hilden 40721
211 711-030

(G-8886)
AUTOMATION AND CTRL TECH INC
Also Called: Act
6141 Avery Rd (43016-8761)
P.O. Box 3667 (43016-0338)
PHONE.................................614 495-1120
Charles Totel, President
Dave Pond, COO
Michael Iaquinta, Vice Pres
EMP: 26
SQ FT: 21,000
SALES (est): 6.9MM Privately Held
WEB: www.autocontroltech.com
SIC: 3829 3823 Measuring & controlling devices; industrial instrmnts msrmnt display/control process variable

(G-8887)
BAMBECK INC
Also Called: Signs By Tomorrow
4362 Tuller Rd (43017-5029)
PHONE.................................614 766-1000
Mike Bambeck, President
EMP: 3
SALES (est): 262.6K Privately Held
SIC: 3993 Signs & advertising specialties

GEOGRAPHIC SECTION

Dublin - Franklin County (G-8914)

(G-8888)
BIOMETRIC INFORMATION MGT LLC
6059 Frantz Rd Ste 102 (43017-3322)
PHONE.....................614 456-1296
Bill Webb, *CEO*
Benjamin Powers, *President*
David W Babner,
EMP: 5
SALES (est): 751.2K **Privately Held**
SIC: 3674 Semiconductors & related devices

(G-8889)
BITES BAKING COMPANY LLC
8090 Summerhouse Dr W (43016-7066)
PHONE.....................614 457-6092
Diane Steiger, *Principal*
EMP: 4
SALES (est): 222.1K **Privately Held**
SIC: 2051 Bread, cake & related products

(G-8890)
BLACK BOX CORPORATION
5400 Frantz Rd Ste 240 (43016-6102)
PHONE.....................800 837-7777
Chris Tjotjos, *Branch Mgr*
EMP: 8
SALES (corp-wide): 1.8MM **Privately Held**
SIC: 3577 Computer peripheral equipment
HQ: Black Box Corporation
   1000 Park Dr
   Lawrence PA 15055
   724 746-5500

(G-8891)
BRASS TACKS CORPORATION LTD (PA)
Also Called: Tacpack
4177 Wyandotte Woods Blvd (43016-9611)
PHONE.....................614 599-7954
Dan Green, *Mng Member*
EMP: 4
SALES: 3MM **Privately Held**
SIC: 3949 Shooting equipment & supplies, general

(G-8892)
CAKE LLC
6724 Perimeter Loop Rd # 254 (43017-3202)
PHONE.....................614 592-7681
Lesley Blake, *Agent*
EMP: 7
SALES (est): 375.5K **Privately Held**
SIC: 7372 Home entertainment computer software

(G-8893)
CARDINAL HEALTH INC
7200 Cardinal Pl W (43017-1094)
PHONE.....................614 553-3830
EMP: 8
SALES (corp-wide): 136.8B **Publicly Held**
SIC: 5122 5047 8741 3842 Pharmaceuticals; druggists' sundries; blood plasma; surgical equipment & supplies; hospital equipment & supplies; management services; surgical appliances & supplies
PA: Cardinal Health, Inc.
   7000 Cardinal Pl
   Dublin OH 43017
   614 757-5000

(G-8894)
CARDINAL HEALTH INC (PA)
7000 Cardinal Pl (43017-1091)
PHONE.....................614 757-5000
Michael C Kaufmann, *CEO*
Gregory B Kenny, *Ch of Bd*
Michele A M Holcomb, *Exec VP*
Patricia B Morrison, *Exec VP*
Martin Alires, *Vice Pres*
◆ EMP: 2800 EST: 1979
SALES: 136.8B **Publicly Held**
WEB: www.cardinal.com
SIC: 5122 5047 8741 3842 Pharmaceuticals; blood plasma; druggists' sundries; surgical equipment & supplies; hospital equipment & supplies; management services; surgical appliances & supplies

(G-8895)
CARDINAL HEALTH 414 LLC (HQ)
7000 Cardinal Pl (43017-1091)
PHONE.....................614 757-5000
George S Barrett, *CEO*
Lisa Ashby, *President*
Shelley Bird, *Exec VP*
Mark Blake, *Exec VP*
Nick Augustinos, *Senior VP*
▲ EMP: 155 EST: 1974
SQ FT: 60,967
SALES (est): 332.9MM
SALES (corp-wide): 136.8B **Publicly Held**
WEB: www.syncor.com
SIC: 2834 2835 Pharmaceutical preparations; radioactive diagnostic substances
PA: Cardinal Health, Inc.
   7000 Cardinal Pl
   Dublin OH 43017
   614 757-5000

(G-8896)
CARDINAL HEALTH TECH LLC (HQ)
7000 Cardinal Pl (43017-1091)
PHONE.....................614 757-5000
Lisa Ashby, *President*
EMP: 9
SALES (est): 3.1MM
SALES (corp-wide): 136.8B **Publicly Held**
SIC: 3571 Electronic computers
PA: Cardinal Health, Inc.
   7000 Cardinal Pl
   Dublin OH 43017
   614 757-5000

(G-8897)
CATALENT PHARMA SOLUTIONS LLC
7000 Cardinal Pl (43017-1091)
PHONE.....................614 757-4757
EMP: 4 **Publicly Held**
WEB: www.fotiades.com
SIC: 2834 Pharmaceutical preparations
HQ: Catalent Pharma Solutions, Llc
   14 Schoolhouse Rd
   Somerset NJ 08873

(G-8898)
CENTRAL OHIO ORTHTIC PRSTHETIC
248 Bradenton Ave (43017-7504)
PHONE.....................614 659-1580
Brenda K Fowler, *Principal*
EMP: 3
SALES (est): 205.7K **Privately Held**
SIC: 3842 Orthopedic appliances

(G-8899)
CENTURY BIOTECH PARTNERS INC
7765 Dublin Rd (43017-9192)
PHONE.....................614 746-6998
Jinji Yue, *CFO*
EMP: 3
SALES: 250K **Privately Held**
SIC: 3845 Ultrasonic scanning devices, medical

(G-8900)
CHAMPA VENTURES LLC
6314 Belvedere Green Blvd (43016-8582)
P.O. Box 425 (43017-0425)
PHONE.....................614 726-1801
Champa Femando, *Principal*
EMP: 3 EST: 2013
SALES (est): 135.4K **Privately Held**
SIC: 2051 Bakery products, partially cooked (except frozen)

(G-8901)
COMMAND ALKON INCORPORATED
6750 Crosby Ct (43016-7644)
PHONE.....................614 799-0600
Randy Willaman, *Branch Mgr*
EMP: 60
SALES (corp-wide): 107.7MM **Privately Held**
WEB: www.commandalkon.com
SIC: 3823 7371 3625 Industrial process measurement equipment; custom computer programming services; relays & industrial controls
PA: Command Alkon Incorporated
   1800 Intl Pk Dr Ste 400
   Birmingham AL 35243
   205 879-3282

(G-8902)
COMPUTER WORKSHOP INC (PA)
5131 Post Rd Ste 102 (43017-1161)
PHONE.....................614 798-9505
Thelma Tippie, *President*
Terri Davy, *COO*
Terri Williams, *COO*
Kim McFarland, *Financial Exec*
Christa Partin, *Executive*
EMP: 20
SALES (est): 2.4MM **Privately Held**
WEB: www.tcworkshop.com
SIC: 8243 7371 2741 Operator training, computer; custom computer programming services; miscellaneous publishing

(G-8903)
CORDIS CORPORATION (HQ)
7000 Cardinal Pl (43017-1091)
PHONE.....................614 757-5000
Jon Gicomin, *CEO*
John M Adams Jr, *Vice Pres*
William Crates, *Vice Pres*
Warren Hastings, *Vice Pres*
Michele Holcomb, *Vice Pres*
◆ EMP: 1440 EST: 1959
SQ FT: 480,000
SALES (est): 414MM
SALES (corp-wide): 136.8B **Publicly Held**
WEB: www.cordis.com
SIC: 3841 3842 Surgical & medical instruments; catheters; surgical appliances & supplies; implants, surgical
PA: Cardinal Health, Inc.
   7000 Cardinal Pl
   Dublin OH 43017
   614 757-5000

(G-8904)
CRIMSON GATE CONSULTING CO (PA)
3274 Heatherstone Ct (43017-1806)
PHONE.....................614 805-0897
Brent Dyke, *CEO*
Brian Rogers, *Project Mgr*
Glenn Foote, *Director*
EMP: 4
SQ FT: 300
SALES (est): 901.9K **Privately Held**
SIC: 8742 7372 Business consultant; business oriented computer software; educational computer software; operating systems computer software

(G-8905)
DAISHIN INDUSTRIAL CO
6490 Shier Rings Rd Ste E (43016-6907)
PHONE.....................614 766-9535
Takeshi Okamaura, *President*
Aaron Schroeder, *Engineer*
▲ EMP: 3
SALES (est): 408.9K **Privately Held**
SIC: 3842 Braces, elastic

(G-8906)
DENSO AUTOMOTIVE OHIO
260 Cramer Creek Ct (43017-2584)
PHONE.....................614 336-1261
Akira Fukuda, *Principal*
▲ EMP: 3
SALES (est): 500.5K **Privately Held**
SIC: 3714 Motor vehicle parts & accessories

(G-8907)
DIOCESAN PUBLICATIONS INC OHIO (PA)
6161 Wilcox Rd (43016-1264)
PHONE.....................614 718-9500
Robert Zielke, *President*
Donald Zielke, *Treasurer*
EMP: 35
SALES (est): 4.7MM **Privately Held**
SIC: 2759 2741 Letterpress printing; miscellaneous publishing

(G-8908)
DUBLIN MILLWORK CO INC
7575 Fishel Dr S (43016-8821)
PHONE.....................614 889-7776
Wilbur C Strait, *Ch of Bd*
Scott Evisol, *General Mgr*
Scott Ebersole, *Manager*
Andy Castle, *Executive*
EMP: 30 EST: 1981
SQ FT: 100,000
SALES (est): 4.5MM
SALES (corp-wide): 39.1MM **Privately Held**
WEB: www.dublinmillwork.com
SIC: 5031 2431 Trim, sheet metal; doors & windows; millwork
PA: The Strait & Lamp Lumber Company Incorporated
   269 National Rd Se
   Hebron OH 43025
   740 928-4501

(G-8909)
DUNCAN DENTAL LAB LLC
6175 Shamrock Ct Ste A (43016-1200)
PHONE.....................614 793-0330
Gary Duncan, *Owner*
Brunhilde J Duncan, *Principal*
EMP: 4
SALES (est): 620K **Privately Held**
SIC: 3843 8072 Dental equipment & supplies; dental laboratories

(G-8910)
EBISYN MEDICAL INC
6474 Weston Cir W (43016-7724)
PHONE.....................609 759-1101
Dipanjan Nag, *President*
Jessica Morton, *Vice Pres*
EMP: 6 EST: 2014
SALES (est): 316.5K **Privately Held**
SIC: 3841 Diagnostic apparatus, medical

(G-8911)
ECI MACOLA/MAX LLC (DH)
5455 Rings Rd Ste 100 (43017-7519)
PHONE.....................978 539-6186
Lisa Wise, *General Mgr*
Mitchell Alcon,
Alex Braverman,
James A Workman,
EMP: 170
SQ FT: 30,000
SALES (est): 68MM
SALES (corp-wide): 216.4MM **Privately Held**
WEB: www.exactamerica.com
SIC: 7371 7372 5045 2759 Computer software development; prepackaged software; computer software; letterpress printing
HQ: Exact Holding B.V.
   Molengraaffsingel 33
   Delft 2629
   157 115-000

(G-8912)
ECO CHEM ALTERNATIVE FUELS LLC
565 Metro Pl S Ste 300 (43017-5382)
PHONE.....................614 764-3835
EMP: 6
SALES (est): 348.3K **Privately Held**
SIC: 2869 Mfg Industrial Organic Chemicals

(G-8913)
ELEMENT ONE HOME STAGING
2502 Starford Dr (43016-9247)
PHONE.....................740 972-4714
Lori Murphy, *Principal*
EMP: 4
SALES (est): 292.4K **Privately Held**
SIC: 2819 Mfg Industrial Inorganic Chemicals

(G-8914)
EVERRIS NA INC (DH)
4950 Blazer Pkwy (43017-3305)
PHONE.....................614 726-7100
Ariana Cohen, *President*

Dublin - Franklin County (G-8915)   GEOGRAPHIC SECTION

◆ EMP: 37 EST: 1966
SQ FT: 73,000
SALES (est): 22.4MM **Privately Held**
WEB: www.everris.com
SIC: 1479 Fertilizer mineral mining; fertilizer mineral mining

(G-8915)
FRANKLIN ELECTRIC CO INC
555 Metro Pl N (43017-5362)
PHONE.................614 794-2266
EMP: 563
SALES (corp-wide): 1.3B **Publicly Held**
SIC: 3621 Motors, electric
PA: Franklin Electric Co., Inc.
 9255 Coverdale Rd
 Fort Wayne IN 46809
 260 824-2900

(G-8916)
GOLD MINE INC
4951 Gillingham Way (43017-8644)
P.O. Box 385 (43017-0385)
PHONE.................614 378-8308
Ajay Pahouja, *President*
EMP: 4
SALES (est): 566.5K **Privately Held**
SIC: 3911 Jewelry, precious metal

(G-8917)
GORILLA DUMPSTERS
7686 Fishel Dr N B (43016-8746)
PHONE.................614 344-4677
Jeffrey E Fromson, *Principal*
EMP: 7
SALES (est): 1MM **Privately Held**
SIC: 3443 Dumpsters, garbage

(G-8918)
GREAT MIGRATIONS LLC
7453 Katesbridge Ct (43017-8281)
PHONE.................614 638-4632
Mark Juras, *Mng Member*
Fred Goodman,
George Juras,
EMP: 3
SALES: 600K **Privately Held**
WEB: www.greatmigrations.com
SIC: 7372 Prepackaged software

(G-8919)
GUILD ASSOCIATES INC (PA)
Also Called: Guild Biosciences
5750 Shier Rings Rd (43016-1234)
PHONE.................614 798-8215
Dominic Dinovo, *President*
Dolores Dinovo, *Treasurer*
◆ EMP: 80
SQ FT: 53,000
SALES: 33MM **Privately Held**
SIC: 8731 3559 Chemical machinery & equipment; chemical laboratory, except testing; biotechnical research, commercial

(G-8920)
GUILD ASSOCIATES INC
Also Called: Guild Biosciences
4412 Tuller Rd (43017-5033)
PHONE.................843 573-0095
Dominic Dinovo, *President*
Nick Dinovo, *Manager*
EMP: 7
SALES (est): 267.7K
SALES (corp-wide): 33MM **Privately Held**
SIC: 8731 3559 Chemical laboratory, except testing; chemical machinery & equipment
PA: Guild Associates, Inc.
 5750 Shier Rings Rd
 Dublin OH 43016
 614 798-8215

(G-8921)
HARTCO PRINTING COMPANY (PA)
Also Called: Hartco Products, The
4106 Delancy Park Dr (43016-7246)
PHONE.................614 761-1292
Carlton W Hartley, *President*
Louann Hartley, *Vice Pres*
EMP: 8 EST: 1955
SQ FT: 9,900
SALES (est): 1MM **Privately Held**
WEB: www.hartcoprinting.com
SIC: 2752 Commercial printing, offset

(G-8922)
HBD/THERMOID INC (HQ)
5200 Upper Metro Pl (43017-5377)
PHONE.................614 526-7000
Randy Lady, *General Mgr*
Wendy Jordan, *General Mgr*
Scott Kuhlman, *Plant Engr Mgr*
Dan Atwood, *Financial Exec*
Marie Vanhoy, *HR Admin*
▼ EMP: 113
SALES (est): 30.6MM
SALES (corp-wide): 261.6MM **Privately Held**
WEB: www.hbdelgin.com
SIC: 3429 3052 Manufactured hardware (general); rubber & plastics hose & beltings
PA: Hbd Industries Inc
 5200 Upper Metro
 Dublin OH 43017
 614 526-7000

(G-8923)
HIDAKA USA INC
5761 Shier Rings Rd (43016-1233)
PHONE.................614 889-8611
Yoshihiro Hidaka, *President*
Akihiro Hidaka, *Opers Staff*
Wayne Lloyd, *Purch Agent*
Diane Rosso, *Office Mgr*
Mikihiro Hidaka, *Admin Sec*
▲ EMP: 40
SQ FT: 90,000
SALES (est): 14.9MM
SALES (corp-wide): 72.6K **Privately Held**
WEB: www.hidakausainc.com
SIC: 3444 3469 Sheet metalwork; machine parts, stamped or pressed metal
HQ: Hidaka Seiki Co., Ltd.
 3-28-5, Nishirokugo
 Ota-Ku TKY 144-0
 337 326-421

(G-8924)
HOMESTAT FARM LTD (PA)
6065 Frantz Rd Ste 206 (43017-3372)
P.O. Box 1530 (43017-6530)
PHONE.................614 718-3060
Bill Stadtlander, *Maintenance Dir*
Jeanne Kelly, *Office Mgr*
Lance Archibald, *Mng Member*
EMP: 20
SQ FT: 1,152
SALES (est): 6.6MM **Privately Held**
WEB: www.homestatfarm.com
SIC: 5141 2099 Food brokers; food preparations

(G-8925)
HUNTSMAN
5407 Lanark Ct (43016-8540)
PHONE.................614 659-0155
EMP: 3
SALES (est): 267.3K **Privately Held**
SIC: 2821 Plastics materials & resins

(G-8926)
HUSKY ENERGY
Also Called: Husky Marketing and Supply Co
5550 Blazer Pkwy Ste 200 (43017-3478)
PHONE.................614 766-5633
Jerry Miller, *Manager*
EMP: 12
SALES (corp-wide): 14.8B **Privately Held**
SIC: 2911 Petroleum refining
PA: Husky Energy Inc
 707 8 Ave Sw
 Calgary AB T2P 1
 403 298-6111

(G-8927)
HUSKY MARKETING AND SUPPLY CO
Also Called: Husky Energy
5550 Blazer Pkwy Ste 200 (43017-3478)
PHONE.................614 210-2300
Scott Howard, *General Mgr*
Rod Cundiff, *Business Mgr*
Jon Frueh, *Engineer*
Julie Quatman, *Engineer*
Harrison Thompson, *Marketing Staff*
EMP: 40
SALES (est): 191.6K
SALES (corp-wide): 14.8B **Privately Held**
SIC: 1321 1382 Natural gasoline production; oil & gas exploration services
PA: Husky Energy Inc
 707 8 Ave Sw
 Calgary AB T2P 1
 403 298-6111

(G-8928)
IMPRESSIONS TO GO LLC
6121 Pirthshire St (43016-6705)
PHONE.................614 760-0600
Michael Kenny, *Mng Member*
Debra Kenny, *Manager*
EMP: 3
SQ FT: 1,800
SALES: 200K **Privately Held**
WEB: www.impressionstogo.com
SIC: 3993 Signs & advertising specialties

(G-8929)
INDEV GAUGING SYSTEMS INC
6141 Avery Rd (43016-8761)
PHONE.................815 282-4463
Jim Wickert, *Manager*
▲ EMP: 29 EST: 1999
SALES (est): 6.2MM
SALES (corp-wide): 20.7MM **Privately Held**
SIC: 3823 Draft gauges, industrial process type
PA: Jasch Industries Limited
 43/5 Bahalgarh Road,
 Sonepat HR 13102
 130 645-1517

(G-8930)
INTERSTATE GAS SUPPLY INC (PA)
6100 Emerald Pkwy (43016-3248)
P.O. Box 9060 (43017-0960)
PHONE.................614 659-5000
Scott White, *President*
Jim Baich, *COO*
Doug Austin, *Exec VP*
Barb C Dodge, *Opers Staff*
Kerry Dlugosz, *Accountant*
EMP: 87
SQ FT: 100,000
SALES: 1.4B **Privately Held**
WEB: www.igsenergy.com
SIC: 1311 Natural gas production

(G-8931)
INVENTUS POWER (OHIO) INC (DH)
Also Called: Nexergy, Inc.
5115 Prkcnter Ave Ste 275 (43017)
PHONE.................614 351-2191
Patrick Trippel, *President*
Carlos Gonzalez, *Opers Staff*
▲ EMP: 10
SQ FT: 46,000
SALES (est): 26MM
SALES (corp-wide): 404.3MM **Privately Held**
WEB: www.nexergy.com
SIC: 3679 Harness assemblies for electronic use; wire or cable

(G-8932)
JASSTEK INC
555 Metro Pl N Ste 100 (43017-1389)
PHONE.................614 808-3600
Sulakshana Singh, *President*
Ravi Paruchuri, *COO*
Praveen Tummala, *CFO*
EMP: 11
SQ FT: 1,200
SALES (est): 797.8K **Privately Held**
SIC: 7371 7372 7379 8748 Custom computer programming services; computer software development & applications; business oriented computer software; ; systems engineering consultant, ex. computer or professional

(G-8933)
JOHN STIEG & ASSOCIATES
8621 Kirkhill Ct (43017-9610)
PHONE.................614 889-7954
EMP: 4
SALES (est): 395.3K **Privately Held**
SIC: 3429 Mfg Hardware

(G-8934)
JUNIPER NETWORKS INC
545 Metro Pl S Ste 164 (43017-5316)
PHONE.................614 932-1432
Mike Isler, *Manager*
EMP: 72 **Publicly Held**
WEB: www.juniper.net
SIC: 7373 7372 Local area network (LAN) systems integrator; prepackaged software
PA: Juniper Networks, Inc.
 1133 Innovation Way
 Sunnyvale CA 94089

(G-8935)
KAD HOLDINGS INC
Also Called: Minuteman Press
5887 Karric Square Dr (43016-4243)
PHONE.................614 792-3399
Kenneth A Davis, *President*
Ken Davis, *Principal*
EMP: 3
SALES (est): 579.6K **Privately Held**
SIC: 2752 2791 2789 Commercial printing, offset; typesetting; bookbinding & related work

(G-8936)
KASAI NORTH AMERICA INC
655 Metro Pl S Ste 560 (43017-3382)
PHONE.................614 356-1494
Yoichi Yamaguchi, *Branch Mgr*
EMP: 14
SALES (corp-wide): 2.1B **Privately Held**
SIC: 3089 3714 3429 Injection molded finished plastic products; motor vehicle parts & accessories; manufactured hardware (general)
HQ: Kasai North America, Inc.
 1225 Garrison Dr
 Murfreesboro TN 37129
 615 546-6040

(G-8937)
KEHLER ENTERPRISES INC
323 W Bridge St (43017-2124)
PHONE.................614 889-8488
Eric N Kehler, *President*
Diane Kehler, *Admin Sec*
EMP: 3
SALES: 340K **Privately Held**
SIC: 3955 5734 Print cartridges for laser & other computer printers; printers & plotters: computers

(G-8938)
KENTROX INC (HQ)
5800 Innovation Dr (43016-3271)
PHONE.................614 798-2000
Richard S Cremona, *CEO*
Charlie Vogt, *Ch of Bd*
Jeffrey S Estuesta, *President*
Eric Langille, *President*
Michael P Keegan, *CFO*
▲ EMP: 100
SALES (est): 38.6MM **Publicly Held**
SIC: 3661 Telephone central office equipment, dial or manual

(G-8939)
KREMA PRODUCTS INC (PA)
Also Called: Krema Peanut Butter
45 N High St (43017-1130)
P.O. Box 715 (43017-0815)
PHONE.................614 889-4824
Craig Sonksen, *CEO*
Brent Morgan, *COO*
EMP: 3
SQ FT: 600
SALES (est): 6.5MM **Privately Held**
WEB: www.kremaproducts.com
SIC: 2099 5159 5441 5961 Peanut butter; nuts & nut by-products; nuts; gift items, mail order

(G-8940)
L C SYSTEMS INC
6135 Memorial Dr Ste 106f (43017-9005)
P.O. Box 437249, Louisville KY (40253-7249)
PHONE.................614 235-9430
Steve Brown, *President*
Deborah Brown, *Corp Secy*
EMP: 4
SALES (est): 680.1K **Privately Held**
WEB: www.lc-systems.com
SIC: 3444 Ventilators, sheet metal

▲ = Import ▼ = Export
◆ = Import/Export

GEOGRAPHIC SECTION

Dublin - Franklin County (G-8968)

(G-8941)
LEPPERT COMPANIES INC
8779 Tartan Fields Dr (43017-8771)
PHONE..................614 889-2818
Matthew Leppert, *Principal*
EMP: 3
SALES (est): 170K **Privately Held**
SIC: 2421 Furniture dimension stock, softwood

(G-8942)
LIMELGHT GRAPHIC SOLUTIONS INC
Also Called: Fastsigns
2829 Festival Ln (43017-2363)
PHONE..................614 793-1996
Geoffrey Smith, *Owner*
EMP: 5
SALES (est): 457.6K **Privately Held**
SIC: 3993 Signs & advertising specialties

(G-8943)
LLC KURTZ BROS CENTRAL OHIO
6279 Houchard Rd (43016-8817)
PHONE..................614 733-3074
Rick Serio, *Principal*
EMP: 3
SALES (est): 259.8K **Privately Held**
SIC: 2875 Fertilizers, mixing only

(G-8944)
LSP TECHNOLOGIES INC
6145 Scherers Pl (43016-1284)
PHONE..................614 718-3000
Jeff L Dulaney, *President*
David Lahrman, *Vice Pres*
Mark O'Loughlin, *Vice Pres*
Beth Mitchell, *Admin Sec*
EMP: 22
SQ FT: 18,000
SALES (est): 5.6MM **Privately Held**
WEB: www.lspt.com
SIC: 3724 Aircraft engines & engine parts

(G-8945)
MANCHIK ENGINEERING & CO
7070 Avery Rd (43017-2808)
PHONE..................740 927-4454
Joseph D Manchik, *Owner*
EMP: 5
SALES (est): 200K **Privately Held**
SIC: 7389 3663 Design services; radio broadcasting & communications equipment

(G-8946)
MIRUS ADAPTED TECH LLC
288 Cramer Creek Ct (43017-2584)
PHONE..................614 402-4585
Mason Takacs, *Opers Mgr*
Stephan Mertik, *Mng Member*
EMP: 20
SALES (est): 1.4MM **Privately Held**
SIC: 1731 7372 Electrical work; home entertainment computer software

(G-8947)
MODULAR ASSEMBLY INNOVATIONS (PA)
600 Stonehenge Pkwy # 100 (43017-6027)
PHONE..................614 389-4860
Billy R Vickers, *President*
EMP: 17
SALES (est): 55.8MM **Privately Held**
SIC: 3559 Automotive related machinery

(G-8948)
MONITORED THERAPEUTICS INC
6543 Commerce Pkwy Ste A (43017-5299)
P.O. Box 322 (43017-0322)
PHONE..................614 761-3555
William Ross, *Ch of Bd*
Michael Taylor, *Vice Pres*
Steve Han, *CTO*
EMP: 6
SALES (est): 766.4K **Privately Held**
SIC: 3845 7372 7389 Electromedical equipment; business oriented computer software;

(G-8949)
MUIRFIELD WINE COMPANY LLC
Also Called: Tutto Vino
7154 Muirfield Dr (43017-3801)
PHONE..................614 799-9222
EMP: 8
SALES (est): 690K **Privately Held**
SIC: 2084 Mfg Wines/Brandy/Spirits

(G-8950)
N8 MEDICAL INC
6000 Memorial Dr (43017-9767)
PHONE..................614 537-7246
David Richards, *CEO*
Kenneth B Leachman, *Principal*
Ronald Bracken, *Vice Pres*
Kenneth Leachman, *CFO*
EMP: 4
SALES (est): 1MM **Privately Held**
SIC: 2834 Pharmaceutical preparations

(G-8951)
NATIONAL GLASS SVC GROUP LLC
5500 Frantz Rd Ste 100 (43017-3545)
PHONE..................614 652-3699
Patric Fransko,
EMP: 10
SALES (est): 750K **Privately Held**
SIC: 2671 Packaging paper & plastics film, coated & laminated

(G-8952)
NAVIDEA BIOPHARMACEUTICALS INC
4995 Bradenton Ave # 240 (43017-3552)
PHONE..................614 793-7500
Jed A Latkin, *COO*
Michael Rosol, *Chief Mktg Ofcr*
EMP: 24
SQ FT: 5,000
SALES (est): 1.1MM **Privately Held**
WEB: www.neoprobe.com
SIC: 2834 Pharmaceutical preparations; in vitro & in vivo diagnostic substances

(G-8953)
NEIL BARTON
Also Called: Vendfriend
8215 Dublin Rd (43017-9712)
PHONE..................614 889-9933
Neil Barton, *Owner*
Susan Barton, *Partner*
EMP: 8 EST: 1984
SALES (est): 729.4K **Privately Held**
SIC: 3589 Water treatment equipment, industrial

(G-8954)
NELSON CONSTANTINELLI LTD
545 Metro Pl S Ste 100 (43017-5353)
PHONE..................800 680-1029
Constantinelli Nelson, *CEO*
EMP: 5
SALES (est): 59.1K **Privately Held**
SIC: 3172 Personal leather goods

(G-8955)
NEW BAKERY OF ZANESVILLE LLC
1 Dave Thomas Blvd (43017-5452)
P.O. Box 256 (43017-0256)
PHONE..................614 764-3100
EMP: 345 EST: 2015
SALES (est): 9.7MM **Privately Held**
SIC: 2051 Bread, cake & related products
HQ: Bimbo Qsr Ohio, Llc
3005 E Pointe Dr
Zanesville OH 43701
740 454-6876

(G-8956)
NEXEO SOLUTIONS LLC
5200 Blazer Pkwy (43017-3309)
PHONE..................800 531-7106
Pat Martinezwong, *Facilities Mgr*
Troy Sartors, *Warehouse Mgr*
Juan Rodriguez, *Production*
Janet Gibson, *Senior Buyer*
Ashley Isaacs, *Buyer*
EMP: 17
SALES (corp-wide): 8.6B **Publicly Held**
SIC: 5169 5162 2821 Industrial chemicals; plastics materials & basic shapes; plastics materials & resins
HQ: Nexeo Solutions, Llc
3 Waterway Square Pl # 1000
The Woodlands TX 77380

(G-8957)
ORACLE AMERICA INC
4378 Tuller Rd (43017-5030)
PHONE..................650 506-7000
EMP: 3
SALES (corp-wide): 39.8B **Publicly Held**
SIC: 7372 Prepackaged software
HQ: Oracle America, Inc.
500 Oracle Pkwy
Redwood City CA 94065
650 506-7000

(G-8958)
PARALLEL TECHNOLOGIES INC
4868 Blazer Pkwy (43017-3302)
PHONE..................614 798-9700
Joseph Redman, *President*
Martin B Jacobs, *Senior VP*
Jamie Baird, *Sales Executive*
Sarah Redman, *Executive*
EMP: 80
SQ FT: 8,500
SALES (est): 15.9MM **Privately Held**
WEB: www.paralleltech.com
SIC: 1623 7372 Telephone & communication line construction; business oriented computer software
PA: R C I Communications Inc
4868 Blazer Pkwy
Dublin OH

(G-8959)
PAYCARD USA INC
5854 Whitebark Pine Trl (43016-7456)
PHONE..................702 216-6801
Jim Hammer, *President*
EMP: 12
SALES (est): 1.2MM **Privately Held**
SIC: 2675 Cards: die-cut & unprinted: made from purchased materials

(G-8960)
PEARL TECH CORPORATION (PA)
545 Metro Pl S Ste 100 (43017-5353)
PHONE..................614 284-8357
Sirisha Nagireddi, *President*
Ben Nagireddi, *Vice Pres*
EMP: 4 EST: 2011
SQ FT: 2,000
SALES (est): 743.6K **Privately Held**
SIC: 7371 7372 Computer software development & applications; business oriented computer software

(G-8961)
PEEBLES CREATIVE GROUP INC
4260 Tuller Rd Ste 200 (43017-5026)
PHONE..................614 487-2011
Doug Peebles, *Principal*
EMP: 9
SQ FT: 3,500
SALES (est): 815.3K **Privately Held**
WEB: www.peeblescreativegroup.com
SIC: 2741 2759 Miscellaneous publishing; commercial printing

(G-8962)
PEERLESS-WINSMITH INC
Peerless Winsmith
5200 Upper Metro Pl # 110 (43017-5378)
PHONE..................330 399-3651
Paul Petrich, *Manager*
EMP: 328
SALES (corp-wide): 261.6MM **Privately Held**
WEB: www.peerlesswinsmith.com
SIC: 3621 Motors & generators
HQ: Peerless-Winsmith, Inc.
5200 Upper Metro Pl # 110
Dublin OH 43017
614 526-7000

(G-8963)
PEERLESS-WINSMITH INC (HQ)
Also Called: Ohio Electric Motors
5200 Upper Metro Pl # 110 (43017-5378)
PHONE..................614 526-7000
Thomas Pozdia, *Ch of Bd*
Eric Visnesky, *Mfg Staff*
John Crawford, *Design Engr*
Eric Houser, *CFO*
Robert A Sirak, *Treasurer*
◆ **EMP:** 3
SALES (est): 148.2MM
SALES (corp-wide): 261.6MM **Privately Held**
WEB: www.peerlesswinsmith.com
SIC: 3566 3621 3812 3559 Speed changers (power transmission equipment), except auto; motors & generators; magnetic field detection apparatus; separation equipment, magnetic
PA: Hbd Industries Inc
5200 Upper Metro
Dublin OH 43017
614 526-7000

(G-8964)
PENTAGON PROTECTION USA LLC
5500 Frantz Rd Ste 100 (43017-3545)
PHONE..................614 734-7240
Sam Elzein, *President*
EMP: 10
SQ FT: 2,000
SALES (est): 2MM **Privately Held**
SIC: 1793 3699 Glass & glazing work; security control equipment & systems

(G-8965)
PFIZER INC
8192 Bibury Ln (43016-7440)
PHONE..................614 496-0990
Todd Keiner, *Principal*
Jeff Barnes, *Manager*
EMP: 225
SALES (corp-wide): 53.6B **Publicly Held**
SIC: 2834 Pharmaceutical preparations
PA: Pfizer Inc.
235 E 42nd St
New York NY 10017
212 733-2323

(G-8966)
POWER ACQUISITION LLC (HQ)
5025 Bradenton Ave # 130 (43017-3506)
PHONE..................614 228-5000
John B Simmons, *CEO*
J Michael Kirksey, *CFO*
Cynthia Piper, *Credit Mgr*
EMP: 6
SALES (est): 219.2MM
SALES (corp-wide): 4.8B **Privately Held**
SIC: 3694 7538 7537 Distributors, motor vehicle engine; diesel engine repair: automotive; automotive transmission repair shops
PA: Oep Capital Advisors, L.P.
510 Madison Ave Fl 19
New York NY 10022
212 277-1552

(G-8967)
PRO ONCALL TECHNOLOGIES LLC
Also Called: Digital & Analog Design
4374 Tuller Rd Ste B (43017-5030)
PHONE..................614 761-1400
David Myers, *Sales/Mktg Mgr*
EMP: 15
SALES (est): 955.4K
SALES (corp-wide): 34.8MM **Privately Held**
SIC: 5065 3661 Telephone equipment; communication equipment; telephone & telegraph apparatus
PA: Pro Oncall Technologies, Llc
6902 E Kemper Rd
Cincinnati OH 45249
513 489-7660

(G-8968)
PROFESSIONAL PLASTICS CORP
4863 Rays Cir (43016-6069)
PHONE..................614 336-2498
Mark Casey, *VP Sales*

Dublin - Franklin County (G-8969)

EMP: 5
SALES (est): 279.7K Privately Held
SIC: 3089 Plastic processing

(G-8969)
PROFORMA PRINT & IMAGING
655 Metro Pl S Ste 600 (43017-3394)
PHONE..................................216 520-8400
Jim Pfaff, Owner
EMP: 3
SALES (est): 274.5K Privately Held
SIC: 2752 Commercial printing, offset

(G-8970)
QUEST SOFTWARE INC
Aeilita Div
6500 Emerald Pkwy Ste 400 (43017-6234)
PHONE..................................614 336-9223
Adam Hall, Regl Sales Mgr
Renee Chambers, Sales Associate
Ratmir Timashev, Manager
Erwin Bovens, Manager
Kelly Hardy, Manager
EMP: 70
SALES (corp-wide): 1.8B Privately Held
WEB: www.quest.com
SIC: 7372 Prepackaged software
HQ: Quest Software, Inc.
 4 Polaris Way
 Aliso Viejo CA 92656
 949 754-8000

(G-8971)
QUESTLINE INC
5500 Frantz Rd Ste 150 (43017-3548)
PHONE..................................614 255-3166
David Reim, CEO
Robert L Hines, COO
Julia Halterman, Accounts Mgr
Mary Nye, Business Dir
Joshua Platt, Account Dir
EMP: 36
SQ FT: 8,000
SALES: 4.7MM Privately Held
SIC: 2741 Business service newsletters; publishing & printing

(G-8972)
REICHARD SOFTWARE CORP
Also Called: Reichard Controls
655 Metro Pl S Ste 600 (43017-3394)
PHONE..................................614 537-8598
Steven Reichard, President
EMP: 3
SQ FT: 1,200
SALES (est): 310K Privately Held
WEB: www.reichard.com
SIC: 7372 7371 Prepackaged software; custom computer programming services

(G-8973)
RESIDENTS OF SAWMILL PARK
2765 Sawmill Park Dr (43017-1872)
PHONE..................................614 659-6678
Jennifer Offner, Principal
EMP: 9
SALES (est): 054.6K Privately Held
SIC: 2421 Sawmills & planing mills, general

(G-8974)
RIKENKAKI AMERICA CORPORATION
5985 Wilcox Pl Ste D (43016-6798)
PHONE..................................614 336-2744
Tetsuo Watanabe, President
▲ EMP: 3
SALES (est): 405.5K Privately Held
SIC: 3711 5012 Motor vehicles & car bodies; automobile auction

(G-8975)
ROBERT W JOHNSON INC (PA)
Also Called: Diamond Cellar, The
6280 Sawmill Rd (43017-1470)
PHONE..................................614 336-4545
R Andrew Johnson, CEO
Ron Croft, Vice Pres
Barb Tomcik, Vice Pres
Alex Johnson, Buyer
Doug Von Doersten, CFO
EMP: 70 EST: 1946
SQ FT: 23,000
SALES (est): 11.9MM Privately Held
SIC: 5944 3911 Jewelry, precious stones & precious metals; jewelry, precious metal

(G-8976)
RUSCILLI REAL ESTATE SERVICES
5100 Prkcnter Ave Ste 100 (43017)
PHONE..................................614 923-6400
Timothy Kelton, President
Timothy D Kelton, President
David C Wade, Treasurer
EMP: 10 EST: 1978
SQ FT: 1,000
SALES (est): 1MM Privately Held
WEB: www.ruscillire.com
SIC: 6531 1389 Real estate agent, residential; real estate agent, commercial; roustabout service

(G-8977)
SAGINOMIYA AMERICA INC
655 Metro Pl S Ste 700 (43017-3661)
PHONE..................................614 766-7390
Naoki Kando, President
▲ EMP: 1
SALES (est): 2.1MM Privately Held
SIC: 3829 Testing equipment: abrasion, shearing strength, etc.

(G-8978)
SAINT-GOBAIN PRFMCE PLAS CORP
Also Called: Medex
6250 Shier Rings Rd (43016-1270)
PHONE..................................614 889-2220
Ralph Dickman, Branch Mgr
EMP: 300
SALES (corp-wide): 215.9MM Privately Held
SIC: 3061 Mechanical rubber goods
HQ: Saint-Gobain Performance Plastics Corporation
 31500 Solon Rd
 Solon OH 44139
 440 836-6900

(G-8979)
SALIENT SYSTEMS INC
4393 Tuller Rd Ste K (43017-5106)
PHONE..................................614 792-5800
Robert Bower, President
EMP: 24
SQ FT: 16,000
SALES (est): 3.7MM
SALES (corp-wide): 626.9MM Publicly Held
WEB: www.salientsystems.com
SIC: 3674 8742 Microprocessors; business consultant
HQ: L. B. Foster Rail Technologies, Inc.
 415 Holiday Dr Ste 1
 Pittsburgh PA 15220
 412 928-3400

(G-8980)
SAWMILL STATION
3062 Sawdust Ln (43017-1695)
PHONE..................................614 434-6147
EMP: 3
SALES (est): 164.7K Privately Held
SIC: 2421 Sawmills & planing mills, general

(G-8981)
SCORPION CASE MFG LLC
329 Clover Ln (43017-1301)
PHONE..................................614 274-7246
Eric Epstine, Manager
Michael Pierce,
EMP: 10
SQ FT: 5,000
SALES: 500K Privately Held
WEB: www.scorpioncase.com
SIC: 2441 Shipping cases, wood: nailed or lock corner

(G-8982)
SELECTIVE MICRO TECH LLC
6200 Avery Rd Ste A (43016-3211)
PHONE..................................614 551-5974
Tanja Miller, Director
John Warner,
EMP: 5
SALES: 900K Privately Held
WEB: www.selectivemicro.com
SIC: 2819 Industrial inorganic chemicals

(G-8983)
SENSETRONICS LLC
8407 Gleneagles Ct (43017-9728)
PHONE..................................614 292-2833
EMP: 3
SALES (est): 152.5K Privately Held
SIC: 3845 8731 Mfg Electromedical Equipment Commercial Physical Research

(G-8984)
SERTEK LLC
6399 Shier Rings Rd (43016-3213)
PHONE..................................614 504-5828
Dave Crites, Manager
Tim Schiff,
EMP: 100
SALES (est): 32.1MM
SALES (corp-wide): 2.9B Privately Held
SIC: 3312 Blast furnaces & steel mills
HQ: Franke Foodservice Solutions, Inc.
 800 Aviation Pkwy
 Smyrna TN 37167
 615 287-8200

(G-8985)
SIGNPOST GAMES LLC
7108 Starkeys Ct (43017-1014)
PHONE..................................614 467-9025
Christopher Werner, Principal
EMP: 3
SALES (est): 137K Privately Held
SIC: 3993 Signs & advertising specialties

(G-8986)
SMITH & NEPHEW INC
4360 Tuller Rd (43017-5029)
PHONE..................................614 793-0581
Matt Smith, Branch Mgr
EMP: 3
SALES (corp-wide): 4.7B Privately Held
WEB: www.smith-nephew.com/us
SIC: 3842 Surgical appliances & supplies
HQ: Smith & Nephew, Inc.
 1450 E Brooks Rd
 Memphis TN 38116
 901 396-2121

(G-8987)
SMITHS MEDICAL ASD INC
5200 Upper Metro Pl # 200 (43017-5379)
P.O. Box 8106 (43016-2106)
PHONE..................................800 796-8701
Eller Erock, Manager
EMP: 23
SALES (corp-wide): 4.1B Privately Held
WEB: www.smith-medical.com
SIC: 3841 Surgical & medical instruments
HQ: Smiths Medical Asd, Inc.
 6000 Nathan Ln N Ste 100
 Plymouth MN 55442
 763 383-3000

(G-8988)
SMITHS MEDICAL ASD INC
6250 Shier Rings Rd (43016-1270)
PHONE..................................614 880 2220
Jill Freund, Human Resources
Heather Wise, Manager
Tim Fenner, Manager
EMP: 242
SALES (corp-wide): 4.1B Privately Held
SIC: 3841 IV transfusion apparatus
HQ: Smiths Medical Asd, Inc.
 6000 Nathan Ln N Ste 100
 Plymouth MN 55442
 763 383-3000

(G-8989)
SMITHS MEDICAL ASD INC
5200 Upper Metro Pl # 200 (43017-5379)
PHONE..................................614 210-6431
Lee Ann McKinney, Manager
EMP: 16
SALES (corp-wide): 4.2B Privately Held
SIC: 3841 Surgical & medical instruments
HQ: Smiths Medical Asd, Inc.
 6000 Nathan Ln N Ste 100
 Plymouth MN 55442
 763 383-3000

(G-8990)
SMITHS MEDICAL NORTH AMERICA
5200 Upper Metro Pl (43017-5377)
PHONE..................................614 210-7300
EMP: 8 EST: 2010
SALES (est): 1MM Privately Held
SIC: 3841 5047 Mfg Surgical/Medical Instruments Whol Medical/Hospital Equipment

(G-8991)
SMITHS MEDICAL PM INC (PA)
Also Called: BCI International
5200 Upper Metro Pl # 200 (43017-5379)
PHONE..................................614 210-7300
Jeff McCaulley, President
Don Alexander, Vice Pres
Jeff Baker, Vice Pres
Mark Sanderson, Vice Pres
Walter Orme, Treasurer
◆ EMP: 10 EST: 1976
SQ FT: 55,600
SALES (est): 42.7MM Privately Held
SIC: 3841 5047 Diagnostic apparatus, medical; electro-medical equipment

(G-8992)
SOCCER FIRST INC (PA)
6490 Dublin Park Dr (43016-8490)
PHONE..................................614 889-1115
Allen S Shepherd III, President
EMP: 7
SALES (est): 741.3K Privately Held
WEB: www.soccerfirst.net
SIC: 3949 Soccer equipment & supplies

(G-8993)
SOLEO HEALTH INC
6185 Shamrock Ct Ste A (43016-1275)
PHONE..................................844 467-8200
EMP: 10
SALES (corp-wide): 42.3MM Privately Held
SIC: 2834 5912 Druggists' preparations (pharmaceuticals); drug stores & proprietary stores
HQ: Soleo Health Inc.
 950 Calcon Hook Rd Ste 19
 Sharon Hill PA 19079
 888 244-2340

(G-8994)
STANLEY STEEMER INTL INC (PA)
Also Called: Stanley Steemer Carpet Cleaner
5800 Innovation Dr (43016-3271)
P.O. Box 8004 (43016-2004)
PHONE..................................614 764-2007
Wesley C Bates, CEO
Jack A Bates, President
Justin Bates, President
Ron Cochran, General Mgr
Anthony Eonta, General Mgr
▲ EMP: 250
SQ FT: 55,000
SALES: 240MM Privately Held
WEB: www.stanley-steemer.com
SIC: 7217 3635 6794 5713 Carpet & furniture cleaning on location; upholstery cleaning on customer premises; household vacuum cleaners; franchises, selling or licensing; carpets

(G-8995)
STERLING JEWELERS INC
5043 Tutle Crosng Blvd Ste 165 (43016)
PHONE..................................614 799-8000
EMP: 4 Privately Held
SIC: 3423 Jewelers' hand tools
HQ: Sterling Jewelers Inc.
 375 Ghent Rd
 Fairlawn OH 44333
 330 668-5000

(G-8996)
STRYKER ORTHOPEDIC
4420 Tuller Rd (43017-5033)
PHONE..................................614 766-2990
John Tripp, Principal
EMP: 8
SALES (est): 839.2K Privately Held
SIC: 3841 Surgical & medical instruments

GEOGRAPHIC SECTION

(G-8997)
STUDIUM LLC
4158 Bright Rd (43016-8229)
PHONE.................................614 402-0359
Christopher Asman, *Mng Member*
EMP: 3
SALES (est): 71.1K **Privately Held**
SIC: 7372 Educational computer software

(G-8998)
SUBARU OF A
565 Metro Pl S Ste 150 (43017-7312)
PHONE.................................614 793-2358
EMP: 5 EST: 2017
SALES (est): 197.7K **Privately Held**
SIC: 5511 5012 3711 Automobiles, new & used; automobile auction; motor vehicles & car bodies

(G-8999)
SUTPHEN CORPORATION (PA)
6450 Eiterman Rd (43016-8711)
P.O. Box 158, Amlin (43002-0158)
PHONE.................................800 726-7030
Drew Sutphen, *President*
Thomas C Sutphen, *Chairman*
Julie S Phelps, *Vice Pres*
Greg Mallon, *CFO*
Robert M Sutphen, *Shareholder*
◆ EMP: 180
SQ FT: 90,000
SALES: 117.1MM **Privately Held**
WEB: www.sutpheneast.com
SIC: 3711 5087 Fire department vehicles (motor vehicles), assembly of; firefighting equipment

(G-9000)
SYMANTEC CORPORATION
545 Metro Pl S Ste 100 (43017-5353)
PHONE.................................614 793-3060
Eric Hentshel, *Branch Mgr*
EMP: 5
SALES (corp-wide): 4.8B **Publicly Held**
WEB: www.symantec.com
SIC: 7372 Business oriented computer software
PA: Symantec Corporation
    350 Ellis St
    Mountain View CA 94043
    650 527-8000

(G-9001)
SYNSEI MEDICAL
6474 Weston Cir W (43016-7724)
PHONE.................................609 759-1101
Dipanjan Nag, *Partner*
EMP: 3
SALES (est): 143.3K **Privately Held**
SIC: 3845 Electrocardiographs

(G-9002)
TAUPE HOLDINGS CO
7758 Deercrest Ct (43016-9280)
PHONE.................................614 330-4600
Emmanuel Bate, *CEO*
Ajuseh Fortaboh, *President*
EMP: 3
SQ FT: 1,600
SALES (est): 94K **Privately Held**
SIC: 7349 7382 3991 4731 Building & office cleaning services; protective devices, security; street sweeping brooms, hand or machine; freight transportation arrangement

(G-9003)
TECHNICAL SALES & SOLUTION
4361 Wyandotte Woods Blvd (43016-8661)
PHONE.................................614 793-9612
Bob Kollins, *Principal*
EMP: 4
SALES (est): 310K **Privately Held**
SIC: 3699 Electrical welding equipment

(G-9004)
TITANIUM SALES GROUP LLC
7905 Melrue Ct (43016-7427)
PHONE.................................614 204-6098
Tim Mitchell, *Principal*
EMP: 4
SALES (est): 119.2K **Privately Held**
SIC: 3356 Titanium

(G-9005)
TMH INDUSTRIES LLC
5795 Baronscourt Way (43016-6046)
PHONE.................................954 232-7938
Todd M Hinze, *Principal*
EMP: 5
SALES (est): 306.1K **Privately Held**
SIC: 3999 Manufacturing industries

(G-9006)
TRU COMFORT MATTRESS
8994 Mediterra Pl (43016-6098)
PHONE.................................614 595-8600
Samuel Wang, *Administration*
EMP: 5
SALES (est): 533.3K **Privately Held**
SIC: 2515 Mattresses & foundations

(G-9007)
TURNER LIGHTNING PROTECTION CO
5193 Dry Creek Dr (43016-9727)
PHONE.................................614 738-6225
Bob Turner, *President*
Mike Adams, *Vice Pres*
EMP: 5
SALES (est): 600K **Privately Held**
WEB: www.lightningpro.com
SIC: 3643 Current-carrying wiring devices

(G-9008)
VIDA VE CORP
8210 Timber Mist Ct (43017-8673)
PHONE.................................614 203-2607
Kellie Smith-Hoover, *President*
Jeff Hoover, *Principal*
Barb Macdonald, *Principal*
EMP: 3
SALES (est): 166.3K **Privately Held**
SIC: 3612 Power transformers, electric

(G-9009)
VIOTEC LLC
5970 Pirthshire St (43016-6706)
P.O. Box 12743, Green Bay WI (54307-2743)
PHONE.................................614 596-2054
Michael Baenen,
EMP: 3
SALES (est): 125.2K **Privately Held**
SIC: 3699 Security devices

(G-9010)
VISIONTECH AUTOMATION LLC
6682 Weston Cir W (43016-7901)
PHONE.................................614 554-2013
Rakesh Mohan, *Partner*
EMP: 4
SQ FT: 2,000
SALES: 500K **Privately Held**
SIC: 3621 8711 Generating apparatus & parts, electrical; consulting engineer

(G-9011)
WEASTEC INCORPORATED
6195 Enterprise Ct (43016-3293)
PHONE.................................614 734-9645
Craig Miley, *Branch Mgr*
EMP: 42
SALES (corp-wide): 283.9MM **Privately Held**
SIC: 3711 8711 Automotive parts; engineering services
HQ: Weastec, Incorporated
    1600 N High St
    Hillsboro OH 45133
    937 393-6800

(G-9012)
WONDER-SHIRTS INC
7695 Crawley Dr (43017-8820)
PHONE.................................917 679-2336
Matthew Mohr, *President*
EMP: 6 EST: 2002
SALES: 1MM **Privately Held**
SIC: 2253 2211 T-shirts & tops, knit; apparel & outerwear fabrics, cotton

(G-9013)
Z TRACK MAGAZINE
6142 Northcliff Blvd (43016-6713)
PHONE.................................614 764-1703
Robert Clue, *President*
EMP: 3
SALES (est): 214.7K **Privately Held**
SIC: 2721 5945 Magazines: publishing only, not printed on site; hobby, toy & game shops

Dunbridge
Wood County

(G-9014)
BLAKO INDUSTRIES INC
10850 Middleton Pike (43414)
PHONE.................................419 246-6172
Ed Long, *President*
Paul J Leahy, *Principal*
Charles Hansen, *Vice Pres*
EMP: 28
SQ FT: 21,000
SALES (est): 6.6MM **Privately Held**
WEB: www.blako.com
SIC: 3081 Polyethylene film

(G-9015)
GELOK INTERNATIONAL CORP
20189 Pine Lake Rd (43414)
P.O. Box 69 (43414-0069)
PHONE.................................419 352-1482
Charles Stocking, *President*
Micheal Kirby, *CFO*
Carol Stocking, *Admin Sec*
▲ EMP: 15
SQ FT: 20,000
SALES (est): 4.7MM **Privately Held**
WEB: www.gelok.com
SIC: 3842 Surgical appliances & supplies

Dundee
Tuscarawas County

(G-9016)
A & M KILN DRY LTD
1711 County Road 200 (44624-9694)
PHONE.................................330 852-0505
Abe Raber, *President*
Daniel A Raber, *Vice Pres*
EMP: 3
SALES (est): 337.3K **Privately Held**
SIC: 3559 Kilns

(G-9017)
A & M KILN DRY LTD
10836 Lower Trail Rd Nw (44624-8922)
PHONE.................................330 852-0505
EMP: 10
SALES (est): 950K **Privately Held**
SIC: 3559 2435 Mfg Misc Industry Machinery Mfg Hardwood Veneer/Plywood

(G-9018)
DUTCH LEGACY LLC
2425 Us Route 62 (44624-9233)
PHONE.................................330 359-0270
Aaron Garber,
EMP: 8
SQ FT: 20,000
SALES: 12MM **Privately Held**
SIC: 2511 Wood household furniture

(G-9019)
HOLMES PRCUT/TROYER IMPRINTING
7540 Peabody Kent Rd (44624-9248)
PHONE.................................330 359-0000
EMP: 3
SALES (est): 305.7K **Privately Held**
SIC: 2759 Imprinting

(G-9020)
L AND J WOODWORKING
9035 Senff Rd (44624-9414)
PHONE.................................330 359-3216
Ray Yoder Jr, *Owner*
EMP: 14
SALES: 2MM **Privately Held**
SIC: 2431 Millwork

(G-9021)
LITTLE COTTAGE COMPANY
6673 State Route 515 (44624-9254)
P.O. Box 455, Berlin (44610-0455)
PHONE.................................330 893-4212
Daniel Schlabach, *President*
Lisa Schlabach, *Vice Pres*
EMP: 4
SALES (est): 664.1K **Privately Held**
WEB: www.littlecottagecompany.com
SIC: 3944 5945 Games, toys & children's vehicles; hobby, toy & game shops

(G-9022)
MILLWOOD INC
Also Called: Millwood Pallet Co
18279 Dover Rd (44624-9425)
PHONE.................................330 359-5220
Jim Caughey, *Manager*
EMP: 30 **Privately Held**
WEB: www.millwoodinc.com
SIC: 2448 Pallets, wood; cargo containers, wood
PA: Millwood, Inc.
    3708 International Blvd
    Vienna OH 44473

(G-9023)
MILLWOOD WHOLESALE INC
7969 Township Road 662 (44624-9602)
PHONE.................................330 359-6109
David Miller, *President*
EMP: 10
SALES: 1MM **Privately Held**
SIC: 1751 2431 2511 5021 Carpentry work; millwork; kitchen & dining room furniture; chairs

(G-9024)
NORTH VIEW WOODWORKING
8422 State Route 93 Nw (44624-8722)
PHONE.................................330 359-6286
Robert Miller, *Principal*
EMP: 4
SALES (est): 436K **Privately Held**
SIC: 2431 Millwork

(G-9025)
PRO FAB INDUSTRIES INC
9368 Massillon Rd (44624-9412)
P.O. Box 322, Mount Eaton (44659-0322)
PHONE.................................317 297-0461
Scott R Lowrie, *Principal*
EMP: 4
SALES (est): 265.5K **Privately Held**
SIC: 5271 3441 Mobile homes; fabricated structural metal

(G-9026)
RUBYS COUNTRY STORE
2467 Us Route 62 (44624-9233)
PHONE.................................330 359-0406
Ruby Mast, *Owner*
EMP: 3
SALES: 400K **Privately Held**
SIC: 5399 3089 5947 5945 Country general stores; plastic kitchenware, tableware & houseware; gifts & novelties; toys & games

(G-9027)
TRAIL CABINET
2270 Township Road 415 (44624-9654)
PHONE.................................330 893-3791
Robert Miller, *Principal*
EMP: 3
SALES (est): 289.2K **Privately Held**
SIC: 2434 Wood kitchen cabinets

(G-9028)
TRAILWAY WOOD
3173 Township Road 414 (44624-9274)
PHONE.................................330 893-9966
Jonas Miller, *Owner*
EMP: 14
SALES (est): 3MM **Privately Held**
SIC: 2511 Tables, household: wood

(G-9029)
TROYERS TRAIL BOLOGNA INC
6552 State Route 515 (44624-9226)
PHONE.................................330 893-2414
Dale Troyer, *President*
Darrin Troyer, *Vice Pres*
Greg Troyer, *Vice Pres*
Kevin Troyer, *Vice Pres*
Kenneth Troyer, *Treasurer*
EMP: 21 EST: 1925
SQ FT: 1,050

Dundee - Tuscarawas County (G-9030)

SALES (est): 4.5MM **Privately Held**
SIC: **2011** 5411 Cured meats from meat slaughtered on site; grocery stores, independent

(G-9030)
TWIN OAKS BARN
3337 Us Route 62 (44624-9270)
PHONE.................................330 893-3126
Melvin Miller, *Owner*
EMP: 10
SALES: 1.5MM **Privately Held**
SIC: **2452** 3999 Prefabricated buildings, wood; lawn ornaments

(G-9031)
WALNUT CREEK LUMBER CO LTD
10433 Pleasant Hill Rd Nw (44624-8775)
PHONE.................................330 852-4559
Dennis A Raber, *President*
EMP: 22
SQ FT: 864
SALES (est): 4.8MM **Privately Held**
SIC: **5031** 2421 Lumber: rough, dressed & finished; custom sawmill

(G-9032)
WENGERD WOOD INC
1760 County Road 200 (44624-9694)
PHONE.................................330 359-4300
Weyne Wengerd, *President*
Dean Wengerd, *Corp Secy*
EMP: 9 EST: 1998
SALES: 1.2MM **Privately Held**
SIC: **2499** Decorative wood & woodwork

(G-9033)
WINESBURG HARDWOOD LUMBER CO
2871 Us Route 62 (44624-9236)
PHONE.................................330 893-2705
Robert Coblentz, *Partner*
Levi Coblentz, *Partner*
Owen Coblentz, *Partner*
EMP: 25
SQ FT: 4,000
SALES (est): 4.3MM **Privately Held**
SIC: **2448** Pallets, wood

Dunkirk
Hardin County

(G-9034)
DIAMOND PLASTICS INC
211 W Geneva St (45836-1090)
P.O. Box 99 (45836-0099)
PHONE.................................419 759-3838
Fax: 419 759-3843
EMP: 82
SQ FT: 70,000
SALES (est): 8.9MM **Privately Held**
SIC: **3089** Mfg Plastic Products

(G-9035)
NORTH COAST CUSTOM MOLDING INC
211 W Geneva St (45836-1008)
PHONE.................................419 905-6447
Jim Braeunig, *President*
Chad Erick Miller, *Vice Pres*
Jane Miller, *Vice Pres*
EMP: 15
SQ FT: 9,700
SALES (est): 2.2MM **Privately Held**
SIC: **3089** Molding primary plastic

(G-9036)
OLDAKER MANUFACTURING CORP
Also Called: Oldaker M F G
301 N Main St (45836-1009)
P.O. Box 93 (45836-0093)
PHONE.................................419 759-3551
Linda Ream, *President*
Patrick M Ream, *President*
Patrick Ream, *Research*
John M Tudor, *Agent*
EMP: 8
SQ FT: 9,000

SALES (est): 1.1MM **Privately Held**
WEB: www.testleads.net
SIC: **3699** Lead-in wires, electric lamp

Dupont
Putnam County

(G-9037)
VILLAGE OF DUPONT
105 Liberty St (45837)
PHONE.................................419 596-3061
Robert L Heidenscher, *Mayor*
EMP: 9
SALES (est): 511.8K **Privately Held**
SIC: **2879** Agricultural chemicals

East Canton
Stark County

(G-9038)
BARBCO INC
315 Pekin Dr Se (44730-9462)
P.O. Box 30189, Canton (44730-0189)
PHONE.................................330 488-9400
Anthony R Barbera, *Principal*
John F Boggins, *Principal*
Richard C Kettler, *Principal*
David Barbera, *Vice Pres*
Tony Barbera, *Vice Pres*
▲ EMP: 46
SQ FT: 15,000
SALES (est): 19.1MM **Privately Held**
WEB: www.barbco.com
SIC: **3531** 3541 Tunnelling machinery; drilling & boring machines

(G-9039)
DLHBOWLES INC
336 Wood St S (44730-1348)
P.O. Box 6030, Canton (44706)
PHONE.................................330 488-0716
Debbie Seaburn, *Branch Mgr*
EMP: 75
SALES (corp-wide): 271.5MM **Privately Held**
WEB: www.dlh-inc.com
SIC: **3089** 3082 Injection molding of plastics; tubes, unsupported plastic
PA: Dlhbowles, Inc.
2422 Leo Ave Sw
Canton OH 44706
330 478-2503

(G-9040)
FTS INTERNATIONAL INC
1520 Wood Ave Se (44730-9591)
PHONE.................................330 754-2375
Richard Jelley, *Branch Mgr*
EMP: 628 **Publicly Held**
SIC: **1389** Measurement of well flow rates, oil & gas
PA: Fts International, Inc.
777 Main St Ste 2900
Fort Worth TX 76102

(G-9041)
KOCH KNIGHT LLC (DH)
5385 Orchardview Dr Se (44730-9568)
P.O. Box 30070 (44730-0070)
PHONE.................................330 488-1651
Mike Graeff, *President*
Mathew Phayer, *Vice Pres*
Teresa Falter, *Buyer*
Kevin Brooks,
◆ EMP: 80
SALES (est): 29.3MM
SALES (corp-wide): 42.4B **Privately Held**
WEB: www.kochknight.com
SIC: **2911** 5172 5169 4922 Petroleum refining; petroleum products; chemicals & allied products; natural gas transmission; crude petroleum production; natural gas production; refinery, chemical processing & similar machinery
HQ: Koch-Glitsch, Lp
4111 E 37th St N
Wichita KS 67220
316 828-5000

(G-9042)
OSNABURG QUILT FIBR ART GUILD
6855 Orchardview Dr Se (44730-9428)
PHONE.................................330 488-2591
Susan Jean Burgess, *Principal*
EMP: 4 EST: 2010
SALES (est): 285.9K **Privately Held**
SIC: **2211** Osnaburgs

(G-9043)
RECON SYSTEMS LLC (PA)
330 Wood St S (44730-1348)
P.O. Box 30100 (44730-0100)
PHONE.................................330 488-0368
Brandon Ballos, *Mng Member*
Rod Tussant,
EMP: 6
SALES (est): 1.4MM **Privately Held**
WEB: www.reconsystems.com
SIC: **3565** Packaging machinery

(G-9044)
RESCO PRODUCTS INC
6878 Osnaburg St Se (44730-9529)
P.O. Box 30169 (44730-0169)
PHONE.................................330 488-1226
Kurt Bletzacker, *Manager*
EMP: 65
SQ FT: 1,500
SALES (corp-wide): 210.1MM **Privately Held**
SIC: **3255** Clay refractories
PA: Resco Products, Inc.
6600 Steubenville Pike # 1
Pittsburgh PA 15205
888 283-5505

East Fultonham
Muskingum County

(G-9045)
CHESTERHILL STONE CO
Also Called: Shelly Materials
6305 Saltillo Rd (43735)
P.O. Box 28 (43735-0028)
PHONE.................................740 849-2338
Fax: 740 849-2599
EMP: 29
SALES (corp-wide): 9MM **Privately Held**
SIC: **1422** Limestone Quarry
PA: Chesterhill Stone Co
773 E State Route 60 Ne
Mcconnelsville OH

East Liberty
Logan County

(G-9046)
C & F FABRICATIONS INC
3100 State St (43319-9453)
P.O. Box 258 (43319-0258)
PHONE.................................937 666-3234
William D Mercer, *CEO*
Betty J Mercer, *President*
W Douglas Mercer, *Treasurer*
Karen Lyon, *Controller*
EMP: 20
SQ FT: 26,000
SALES (est): 1.1MM **Privately Held**
SIC: **3496** Miscellaneous fabricated wire products

(G-9047)
GREAT LAKES ASSEMBLIES LLC
11590 Tr 298 (43319)
PHONE.................................937 645-3900
Billy R Vickers, *President*
EMP: 70
SQ FT: 90,000
SALES (est): 55.1MM
SALES (corp-wide): 55.8MM **Privately Held**
WEB: www.gla-llc.com
SIC: **3711** Automobile assembly, including specialty automobiles

PA: Modular Assembly Innovations
600 Stonehenge Pkwy # 100
Dublin OH 43017
614 389-4860

(G-9048)
HARDING MACHINE ACQUISITION CO
Also Called: Global Precision Parts
13060 State Route 287 (43319-9439)
P.O. Box 752, Van Wert (45891-0752)
PHONE.................................937 666-3031
Dave Kriegel, *Ch of Bd*
Todd Kriegel, *President*
Susan Mosier, *CFO*
Yolanda Von Lehmden, *Controller*
EMP: 75
SALES (est): 11.1MM **Privately Held**
SIC: **3451** Screw machine products

(G-9049)
NISSIN BRAKE OHIO INC
25790 State Route 287 (43319-9500)
PHONE.................................937 642-7556
Aaron Riesen, *Branch Mgr*
EMP: 27
SALES (corp-wide): 1.7B **Privately Held**
SIC: **3714** Motor vehicle brake systems & parts
HQ: Nissin Brake Ohio, Inc.
1901 Industrial Dr
Findlay OH 45840
419 420-3800

East Liverpool
Columbiana County

(G-9050)
ASHCO
1250 Saint George St # 3 (43920-3400)
PHONE.................................330 385-2400
Robert L Ash, *Owner*
EMP: 2
SALES: 1MM **Privately Held**
SIC: **3556** Food products machinery

(G-9051)
C A JOSEPH CO (PA)
13712 Old Frdericktown Rd (43920-9531)
PHONE.................................330 385-6869
Charles Chuck Joseph, *President*
Chris Joseph, *Vice Pres*
Mike Joseph, *Vice Pres*
▲ EMP: 8
SQ FT: 200,000
SALES (est): 4.1MM **Privately Held**
WEB: www.cajoseph.com
SIC: **3089** 3599 Plastic processing; machine shop, jobbing & repair

(G-9052)
CAMPBELL SIGNS & APPAREL LLC
47366 Y And O Rd (43920-8747)
PHONE.................................330 386-4768
Jodi H Campbell, *CFO*
Jeff Campbell,
EMP: 15
SQ FT: 9,600
SALES: 12MM **Privately Held**
SIC: **3993** 2759 2395 Signs, not made in custom sign painting shops; screen printing; embroidery & art needlework

(G-9053)
COMMERCIAL DECAL OF OHIO INC
46686 Y And O Rd (43920-9710)
P.O. Box 2747 (43920-0747)
PHONE.................................330 385-7178
David Dunn, *President*
EMP: 25
SQ FT: 11,000
SALES (est): 2MM **Privately Held**
SIC: **2759** Decals: printing

(G-9054)
CUSTOM CRANKSHAFT INC
1730 Annesley Rd (43920-9410)
PHONE.................................330 382-1200
Scott Watson, *President*
EMP: 35

GEOGRAPHIC SECTION — East Palestine - Columbiana County (G-9081)

SALES (est): 4.4MM **Privately Held**
SIC: 3599 Crankshafts & camshafts, machining

(G-9055)
DECARIA BROTHERS INC
104 E 5th St (43920-3031)
PHONE..................................330 385-0825
Erin McCart, *Principal*
EMP: 5
SALES (corp-wide): 952K **Privately Held**
SIC: 2836 Vaccines & other immunizing products
PA: Decaria Brothers, Inc.
4201 Sunset Blvd
Steubenville OH 43952
740 264-5711

(G-9056)
DELTA MANUFACTURING INC
Also Called: Twister Displays
49207 Clctta Smthferry Rd (43920-9570)
P.O. Box 2704 (43920-0704)
PHONE..................................330 386-1270
Harry Smith, *President*
Jeff Smith, *Vice Pres*
EMP: 15 EST: 1972
SQ FT: 800,000
SALES (est): 3MM **Privately Held**
WEB: www.twisterdisplay.com
SIC: 3599 Amusement park equipment

(G-9057)
GROWMARK FS LLC
100 River Rd (43920)
PHONE..................................330 386-7626
Jan Punningham, *Manager*
EMP: 12
SALES (corp-wide): 7.2B **Privately Held**
WEB: www.growmarkfs.com
SIC: 2875 4225 4221 Fertilizers, mixing only; general warehousing & storage; farm product warehousing & storage
HQ: Growmark Fs, Llc
308 Ne Front St
Milford DE 19963
302 422-3002

(G-9058)
HALLS WELDING & SUPPLIES INC
49037 Clctta Smthferry Rd (43920-9206)
PHONE..................................330 385-9353
James Hall, *President*
Alicia Hall, *Vice Pres*
EMP: 4
SQ FT: 4,410
SALES (est): 689.7K **Privately Held**
WEB: www.hallswelding.com
SIC: 5084 1799 3699 3548 Welding machinery & equipment; welding on site; electrical equipment & supplies; welding apparatus

(G-9059)
INNOVATIVE CERAMIC CORP
Also Called: Quality Stamp Co
432 Walnut St (43920-3130)
PHONE..................................330 385-6515
Orville Steininger, *President*
EMP: 3
SQ FT: 5,000
SALES (est): 459.1K **Privately Held**
WEB: www.innovativeceramic.com
SIC: 3953 Pads, inking & stamping

(G-9060)
JOE BARRETT
Also Called: Barrett & Sons Pallet & Lbr Co
13583 Old Frdericktown Rd (43920-8941)
PHONE..................................216 385-2384
Roberta J Barrett, *Principal*
EMP: 4 EST: 2012
SALES (est): 315.3K **Privately Held**
SIC: 2448 Pallets, wood & wood with metal

(G-9061)
JOSEPH G PAPPAS
Also Called: J Pappas
3197 Forest Hills Dr (43920-1167)
PHONE..................................330 383-2917
Joseph G Pappas, *Principal*
EMP: 5 EST: 2011
SALES (est): 590K **Privately Held**
SIC: 1389 7389 Oil & gas field services;

(G-9062)
KENTAK PRODUCTS COMPANY
1230 Railroad St Ste 1 (43920-3406)
PHONE..................................330 386-3700
Doug Gomoll, *President*
Cheryl Smith, *Production*
EMP: 60
SALES (est): 6.7MM
SALES (corp-wide): 9MM **Privately Held**
SIC: 3082 3052 Tubes, unsupported plastic; plastic hose
PA: Kentak Products Company
1230 Railroad St Ste 1
East Liverpool OH 43920
330 382-2000

(G-9063)
KENTAK PRODUCTS COMPANY (PA)
1230 Railroad St Ste 1 (43920-3406)
PHONE..................................330 382-2000
Otto H Gomoll Jr, *Ch of Bd*
Douglas A Gomoll, *President*
William Mays, *Exec VP*
John Crago, *Plant Mgr*
Rex Johler, *Info Tech Dir*
▲ EMP: 45
SQ FT: 50,000
SALES: 9MM **Privately Held**
SIC: 3082 3052 Tubes, unsupported plastic; plastic hose

(G-9064)
KENTAK PRODUCTS COMPANY
1230 Railroad St Ste 1 (43920-3406)
PHONE..................................330 532-6211
Virginia Pickens, *Manager*
EMP: 5
SALES (est): 532.5K
SALES (corp-wide): 9MM **Privately Held**
SIC: 3082 3052 Tubes, unsupported plastic; plastic hose
PA: Kentak Products Company
1230 Railroad St Ste 1
East Liverpool OH 43920
330 382-2000

(G-9065)
KEYSTONE PRINTING CO
648 Saint Clair Ave (43920-3077)
P.O. Box 993 (43920-5993)
PHONE..................................330 385-9519
Craig Kidd, *President*
Dale Kidd, *Vice Pres*
EMP: 3
SQ FT: 2,250
SALES: 150K **Privately Held**
SIC: 2752 Commercial printing, offset

(G-9066)
KING WOLF ENTERPRISES LLC
1865 Park Way (43920-2065)
P.O. Box 5187 (43920-7187)
PHONE..................................330 853-0450
Ronald Wolf, *Mng Member*
Patrick King, *Mng Member*
EMP: 4
SQ FT: 11,000
SALES (est): 104.8K **Privately Held**
SIC: 3441 Fabricated structural metal

(G-9067)
OHIO VALLEY HERBAL PRODUCTS
1250 Saint George St # 5 (43920-3400)
PHONE..................................330 382-1229
Marina Schaum, *President*
EMP: 3
SALES (est): 419.1K **Privately Held**
WEB: www.wilderb.com
SIC: 2833 Drugs & herbs: grading, grinding & milling

(G-9068)
SH BELL COMPANY
2217 Michigan Ave (43920-3637)
PHONE..................................412 963-9910
Vince Monte, *Sales Staff*
Rusty Davis, *Manager*
Doris Thayer, *Director*
Chris McKenzie, *Assistant*
EMP: 37

SALES (corp-wide): 21.6MM **Privately Held**
SIC: 3479 4226 4225 Aluminum coating of metal products; special warehousing & storage; general warehousing & storage
PA: S.H. Bell Company
644 Alpha Dr
Pittsburgh PA 15238
412 963-9910

East Palestine
Columbiana County

(G-9069)
CARDINAL WELDING INC
895 E Taggart St (44413-2465)
P.O. Box 405 (44413-0405)
PHONE..................................330 426-2404
Daniel Shofstahl, *President*
Susanna Whaley, *Admin Sec*
EMP: 6
SQ FT: 25,000
SALES (est): 1.1MM **Privately Held**
SIC: 7692 3411 Welding repair; metal cans

(G-9070)
CARLSON AIRCRAFT INC
Also Called: Sky-Tek
51028 State Route 14 (44413-9747)
P.O. Box 88 (44413-0088)
PHONE..................................330 426-3934
Mary Carlson, *President*
EMP: 4
SALES (est): 290K **Privately Held**
SIC: 3721 7699 Aircraft; aircraft & heavy equipment repair services

(G-9071)
COLD DUCK SCREEN PRTG & EMB CO
540 Sugar Camp Dr (44413-1680)
PHONE..................................330 426-1900
John A Campagna, *Owner*
John Campagna, *Owner*
Connie Campagna, *Co-Owner*
EMP: 3
SQ FT: 2,400
SALES (est): 260.6K **Privately Held**
WEB: www.coldduckscreenprinting.com
SIC: 2759 2752 7389 2791 Screen printing; commercial printing, offset; sewing contractor; typesetting

(G-9072)
CUSTOMIZED VINYL SALES
50814 Hadley Rd (44413-9738)
PHONE..................................330 518-3238
Lauren McCambridgegruber, *Principal*
EMP: 6
SALES (est): 607.6K **Privately Held**
SIC: 3089 Fences, gates & accessories: plastic

(G-9073)
DILWORTH MACHINE
51552 Chain School Rd (44413-9742)
PHONE..................................330 427-1706
Fax: 330 427-1735
◆ EMP: 18
SQ FT: 10,000
SALES (est): 1.3MM **Privately Held**
SIC: 3599 Mfg Industrial Machinery

(G-9074)
DUNCAN BROTHERS DRILLING INC (PA)
1264 Howell Ave (44413-9784)
P.O. Box 8 (44413-0008)
PHONE..................................330 426-9507
Mark Duncan, *President*
EMP: 10
SQ FT: 2,500
SALES (est): 2.5MM **Privately Held**
SIC: 1241 Mining services: bituminous

(G-9075)
DUNCAN BROTHERS DRILLING INC
1264 Howell Ave (44413-9784)
P.O. Box 8 (44413-0008)
PHONE..................................330 426-9507
Mark Duncan, *President*
EMP: 10
SALES (corp-wide): 2.5MM **Privately Held**
SIC: 1241 Mining services: bituminous
PA: Duncan Brother's Drilling Inc
1264 Howell Ave
East Palestine OH 44413
330 426-9507

(G-9076)
E J BOGNAR INC
51887 E Taggart St (44413-2471)
P.O. Box 6 (44413-0006)
PHONE..................................330 426-9292
Mike Livingston, *Manager*
EMP: 12
SQ FT: 5,000
SALES (corp-wide): 8MM **Privately Held**
WEB: www.ejbognar.com
SIC: 1459 Fire clay mining
PA: E.J. Bognar Incorporated
733 Washington Rd Fl 5
Pittsburgh PA 15228
412 344-9900

(G-9077)
E R ADVANCED CERAMICS INC
Also Called: US Group
600 E Clark St (44413-2430)
P.O. Box 270 (44413-0270)
PHONE..................................330 426-9433
John Hayday, *President*
David A Early, *Exec VP*
Michael Dematteo, *CFO*
Jim Krebs, *Manager*
◆ EMP: 34
SQ FT: 68,274
SALES: 4.2MM **Privately Held**
WEB: www.usstoneware.com
SIC: 3531 3269 3547 3821 Construction machinery; grinding media, pottery; rolling mill machinery; particle size reduction apparatus, laboratory; filters; industrial pumps & parts

(G-9078)
EAST PALESTINE DECORATING LLC
870 W Main St (44413-1328)
PHONE..................................330 426-9600
Walter O'Malley,
Patrick Gaughan,
▲ EMP: 10
SALES (est): 297K **Privately Held**
SIC: 3231 Decorated glassware: chipped, engraved, etched, etc.

(G-9079)
EXOCHEM CORPORATION
90 Kemple Dr (44413-1501)
PHONE..................................330 426-9898
Randy Meraldi, *President*
EMP: 19
SALES (corp-wide): 12.3MM **Privately Held**
SIC: 2399 Cheese bandages, made from purchased materials
PA: Exochem Corporation
2421 E 28th St
Lorain OH 44055
800 807-7464

(G-9080)
LIQUID LUGGERS LLC
183 Edgeworth Ave (44413-1554)
PHONE..................................330 426-2538
Lynn Neely, *Principal*
EMP: 50
SALES (est): 8.9MM **Privately Held**
SIC: 3443 Tanks for tank trucks, metal plate

(G-9081)
MX SPRING INC
Also Called: Fcr Suspension
39 Wilderson Ave (44413-1163)
PHONE..................................330 426-4600
EMP: 5
SALES (est): 310K **Privately Held**
SIC: 3799 Transportation Equipment, Nec, Nsk

East Palestine - Columbiana County (G-9082)

(G-9082)
RBS MANUFACTURING INC
145 E Martin St (44413-2337)
P.O. Box 430 (44413-0430)
PHONE..................................330 426-9486
Dennis Garrett, *Principal*
George P Garrett, *Principal*
Rosemarie Garrett, *Principal*
John Wade, *Purch Mgr*
Leslie Allcorn, *Office Mgr*
EMP: 26
SALES (est): 3.2MM **Privately Held**
SIC: **3999** Barber & beauty shop equipment

(G-9083)
ROBERT MAYO INDUSTRIES
Also Called: Mayo, R A Industries
157 E Martin St (44413-2315)
PHONE..................................330 426-2587
Robert A Mayo, *Owner*
EMP: 6
SQ FT: 1,500
SALES (est): 767.4K **Privately Held**
SIC: **2512 7641** Upholstered household furniture; reupholstery & furniture repair

(G-9084)
STITCHES & STUFF
39 N Market St (44413-2053)
PHONE..................................330 426-9500
Kent Chapman, *Owner*
EMP: 4
SALES (est): 222K **Privately Held**
SIC: **2395** Embroidery & art needlework

(G-9085)
STROHECKER INCORPORATED
213 N Pleasant Dr (44413-2497)
PHONE..................................330 426-9496
Richard Strohecker, *President*
Tony J Moran, *Vice Pres*
John Felger, *Engineer*
Sharen Williams, *Office Mgr*
▲ EMP: 40 EST: 1947
SQ FT: 4,000
SALES (est): 11MM **Privately Held**
WEB: www.strohecker.com
SIC: **3567 3443** Industrial furnaces & ovens; metal parts

(G-9086)
TEST MARK INDUSTRIES INC
995 N Market St (44413-1109)
PHONE..................................330 426-2200
William F Tyger, *President*
Martin R Napolitano, *Corp Secy*
William Quinlan, *Director*
▼ EMP: 12
SQ FT: 8,500
SALES (est): 3.4MM **Privately Held**
WEB: www.testmark.net
SIC: **5049 3829** Laboratory equipment, except medical or dental; physical property testing equipment

(G-9087)
TUBETECH INC (PA)
Also Called: Tubetech North America
900 E Taggart St (44413-2424)
P.O. Box 470 (44413-0470)
PHONE..................................330 426-9476
Steve Oliphant, *CEO*
Stephen D Oliphant, *CEO*
Jon Roscow, *President*
Richard Downey, *Corp Secy*
EMP: 26
SQ FT: 80,000
SALES (est): 3.3MM **Privately Held**
WEB: www.tubetechnorthamerica.com
SIC: **3317 3471** Tubes, wrought: welded or lock joint; plating of metals or formed products

(G-9088)
UNITY TUBE INC
1862 State Route 165 (44413-9737)
P.O. Box 425 (44413-0425)
PHONE..................................330 426-4282
Dennis Kuhns, *President*
Lisa Travis, *Info Tech Mgr*
EMP: 18
SALES (est): 4.1MM **Privately Held**
WEB: www.unitytube.com
SIC: **3498** Tube fabricating (contract bending & shaping)

(G-9089)
WAYNES PRECISION MACHINE INC
Also Called: Wayne's Precision Mach Shop
354 N Liberty St (44413-2334)
PHONE..................................330 426-4626
Dave Myers, *President*
EMP: 3
SQ FT: 5,000
SALES (est): 250K **Privately Held**
SIC: **3599** Machine shop, jobbing & repair

East Rochester
Columbiana County

(G-9090)
HOOPES FERTILIZER WORKS INC (PA)
24104 Us Route 30 (44625-9701)
P.O. Box 74 (44625-0074)
PHONE..................................330 894-2121
Terry Hoopes, *President*
EMP: 5 EST: 1956
SQ FT: 30,000
SALES (est): 1.8MM **Privately Held**
WEB: www.hooverfence.com
SIC: **2875 5191** Fertilizers, mixing only; fertilizers & agricultural chemicals

(G-9091)
SUMMIT WELL SERVICES INC
28050 Speidel Rd (44625-9764)
P.O. Box 129, Hanoverton (44423-0129)
PHONE..................................330 223-1074
Alfred S Levine, *President*
Russell Miller, *Vice Pres*
Sandy Samoro, *Admin Sec*
EMP: 6
SALES (est): 551.5K **Privately Held**
SIC: **1382** Oil & gas exploration services

(G-9092)
VANGUARD OIL & GAS
28050 Speidel Rd (44625-9764)
P.O. Box 1300, East Lansing MI (48826-1300)
PHONE..................................330 223-1074
Alfred Levine, *Owner*
EMP: 5
SALES (est): 311.5K **Privately Held**
SIC: **1389** Oil & gas field services

East Sparta
Stark County

(G-9093)
ADAMS FABRICATING INC
10125 Sandyville Av (44626)
P.O. Box 325 (44626-0325)
PHONE..................................330 866-2986
Bill Adams, *President*
Elizabeth Adams, *Corp Secy*
Stephen Adams, *Vice Pres*
EMP: 4 EST: 1979
SQ FT: 5,600
SALES (est): 300K **Privately Held**
SIC: **3312** Plate, steel; structural shapes & pilings, steel

(G-9094)
CLARK SON ACTN LIQUIDATION INC
10233 Sandyville Ave Se (44626-9333)
PHONE..................................330 866-9330
Jona Rosks, *Principal*
▼ EMP: 8
SALES (est): 983.5K **Privately Held**
SIC: **2434** Wood kitchen cabinets

(G-9095)
SLATS AND NAILS INC
10465 Sandyville Ave Se (44626)
PHONE..................................330 866-1008
Richard Fioretto, *President*
Nicholas Incarnato, *Vice Pres*
Miklos Fioretto, *Treasurer*
EMP: 3
SQ FT: 80,000
SALES (est): 5.1MM **Privately Held**
SIC: **2448** Pallets, wood

Eastlake
Lake County

(G-9096)
2-M MANUFACTURING COMPANY
34560 Lakeland Blvd (44095-5221)
PHONE..................................440 269-1270
Mirko Cukelj, *President*
Katherine Cukelj, *Corp Secy*
EMP: 25
SALES (est): 4.5MM **Privately Held**
SIC: **3599** Machine shop, jobbing & repair

(G-9097)
ADVANCED CONTROLS INC
34300 Lakeland Blvd Frnt (44095-5237)
PHONE..................................440 354-5413
Paul O'Connor, *President*
EMP: 20 EST: 1974
SQ FT: 15,000
SALES (est): 3.9MM **Privately Held**
WEB: www.advancedcontrols.com
SIC: **3613** Control panels, electric

(G-9098)
AGILE SIGN & LTG MAINT INC
35280 Lakeland Blvd (44095-5302)
PHONE..................................440 918-1311
Tim Ruff, *President*
Iliana Kazandjieff, *Office Mgr*
EMP: 20
SQ FT: 10,000
SALES (est): 2.5MM **Privately Held**
WEB: www.agilesign.com
SIC: **3993** Signs & advertising specialties

(G-9099)
C & D TOOL INC
35595 Curtis Blvd Unit F (44095-4100)
PHONE..................................440 942-8463
Duane Seelinger, *President*
EMP: 5
SQ FT: 2,000
SALES (est): 475K **Privately Held**
SIC: **3544** Industrial molds

(G-9100)
C STONEMAN CORPORATION
Also Called: Stoneman Welding
100 E Shore Blvd (44095-1906)
PHONE..................................440 942-3325
Chuck Stoneman, *President*
EMP: 3
SQ FT: 11,831
SALES (est): 219.1K **Privately Held**
SIC: **7692 1799** Welding repair; welding on site

(G-9101)
CHAGRIN METAL FABRICATING INC
34201 Melinz Pkwy Unit B (44095-4018)
PHONE..................................440 946-6342
Bob Munaretto, *President*
Anthony Munaretto, *Principal*
EMP: 4
SALES (est): 320K **Privately Held**
SIC: **3444** Sheet metal specialties, not stamped

(G-9102)
CONSOLDTED PRECISION PDTS CORP
Also Called: Cpp Cleveland
34000 Lakeland Blvd (44095-5215)
PHONE..................................440 953-0053
Kevin Newcomb, *Facilities Mgr*
James Pultorak, *Facilities Mgr*
Amy Grald, *Buyer*
Mark Gaspari, *Engineer*
Sam Henninger, *Engineer*
EMP: 53
SALES (corp-wide): 8.4B **Privately Held**
SIC: **3369** Castings, except die-castings, precision
HQ: Consolidated Precision Products Corp.
    1621 Euclid Ave Ste 1850
    Cleveland OH 44115
    216 453-4800

(G-9103)
DEPENDABLE GEAR CORP
1422 E 363rd St (44095-4136)
PHONE..................................440 942-4969
John Luckay Jr, *President*
EMP: 4
SQ FT: 400
SALES: 150K **Privately Held**
WEB: www.dependablegear.com
SIC: **3566 3568 3462** Speed changers, drives & gears; pulleys, power transmission; construction or mining equipment forgings, ferrous

(G-9104)
DIE CO INC
1889 E 337th St (44095-5231)
PHONE..................................440 942-8856
Donald G Hawk, *President*
Michael T Hawk, *Vice Pres*
Diane Tyneski, *Marketing Staff*
Donna Corrigan, *Admin Sec*
▲ EMP: 48
SQ FT: 35,000
SALES (est): 10MM **Privately Held**
WEB: www.diecoinc.com
SIC: **3469 3496 3471 3429** Stamping metal for the trade; miscellaneous fabricated wire products; plating & polishing; manufactured hardware (general); metal heat treating

(G-9105)
DIVERSIFIED MCH COMPONENTS LLC
34099 Melinz Pkwy Unit D (44095-4001)
PHONE..................................440 942-5701
Gregory J O'Brien, *Mng Member*
EMP: 25
SALES (est): 5.6MM **Privately Held**
SIC: **3599** Machine shop, jobbing & repair

(G-9106)
EAGLEHEAD MANUFACTURING CO
35280 Lakeland Blvd (44095-5359)
PHONE..................................440 951-0400
Ray Westfall, *Principal*
EMP: 8 EST: 2009
SALES (est): 994.9K **Privately Held**
SIC: **3999** Manufacturing industries

(G-9107)
ENGINETICS CORPORATION
Also Called: Enginetics Aerospace
34000 Melinz Pkwy (44095-4054)
PHONE..................................440 946-8833
Don Maccanon, *Engineer*
Dale Pelfrey, *Manager*
EMP: 12
SALES (corp-wide): 868.3MM **Publicly Held**
SIC: **3446** Ornamental metalwork
HQ: Enginetics Corporation
    7700 New Carlisle Pike
    Huber Heights OH 45424
    937 878 3800

(G-9108)
ENPAC LLC
34355 Melinz Pkwy (44095-4033)
PHONE..................................440 975-0070
Dawn Lariccia, *Purch Mgr*
Larry Stanek, *Engineer*
Karen Moffett, *Accountant*
Brian Walters, *VP Sales*
Christopher Reed, *Accounts Mgr*
◆ EMP: 50
SQ FT: 66,500
SALES (est): 12.3MM **Privately Held**
SIC: **3089** Plastic containers, except foam

(G-9109)
ENPRESS LLC
34899 Curtis Blvd (44095-4015)
PHONE..................................440 510-0108
Douglas Honer, *Owner*
Timothy Reid,
▼ EMP: 40
SALES (est): 9.9MM **Privately Held**
WEB: www.enpress.com
SIC: **3089** Injection molding of plastics

GEOGRAPHIC SECTION

Eastlake - Lake County (G-9138)

(G-9110)
ESCO TURBINE TECH CLEVELAND
34000 Lakeland Blvd (44095-5215)
PHONE...................................440 953-0053
EMP: 11
SALES (est): 1.8MM Privately Held
SIC: 3535 Conveyors & conveying equipment

(G-9111)
EUCLID PRECISION GRINDING CO
35400 Lakeland Blvd (44095-5304)
PHONE...................................440 946-8888
Eric Barbe, *President*
Mary Lu Grycan, *Admin Sec*
EMP: 6 EST: 1945
SQ FT: 9,600
SALES (est): 1.1MM Privately Held
WEB: www.euclidprecision.com
SIC: 3599 Machine shop, jobbing & repair

(G-9112)
GRIP FORCE LLC
990 Quentin Rd (44095-2836)
P.O. Box 222, Willoughby (44096-0222)
PHONE...................................440 497-7014
Frank Royce, *Principal*
EMP: 4 EST: 2010
SALES (est): 349.3K Privately Held
SIC: 3494 Well adapters

(G-9113)
HIGH QUALITY TOOLS INC (PA)
34940 Lakeland Blvd (44095-5226)
PHONE...................................440 975-9684
Mirko Cukelj, *President*
▲ EMP: 12
SQ FT: 3,000
SALES: 5.5MM Privately Held
WEB: www.hqtinc.com
SIC: 5085 3545 Industrial tools; tools & accessories for machine tools

(G-9114)
INDUSTRIAL SHAFT AND MFG INC
34201 Melinz Pkwy Unit A (44095-4018)
PHONE...................................440 942-9104
Cleo Engbert, *President*
John Engbert, *Treasurer*
EMP: 4
SQ FT: 3,000
SALES: 180K Privately Held
SIC: 3599 Machine shop, jobbing & repair

(G-9115)
INTELLITRONIX CORPORATION
34099 Melinz Pkwy Unit E (44095-4001)
PHONE...................................440 359-7200
Paul Spivak, *President*
EMP: 20
SQ FT: 15,000
SALES (est): 3.7MM Privately Held
SIC: 3647 Automotive lighting fixtures
PA: Us Lighting Group, Inc.
    34099 Melinz Pkwy Unit E
    Eastlake OH 44095
    216 896-7000

(G-9116)
JONES PRINTING SERVICES INC
1519 E 367th St Ste 1 (44095-5351)
PHONE...................................440 946-7300
James E Jones, *President*
Bob Jones, *President*
Ralph Jones, *Treasurer*
EMP: 5
SALES: 700K Privately Held
WEB: www.printwithjones.com
SIC: 2752 Commercial printing, offset

(G-9117)
KILROY COMPANY (PA)
Also Called: Trust Technologies
34929 Curtis Blvd Ste 104 (44095-4053)
PHONE...................................440 951-8700
William S Kilroy II, *Ch of Bd*
Brett Jaffe, *President*
Mike Campbell, *President*
Paul Cardinale, *President*
Ron Dancer, *Facilities Mgr*
EMP: 75
SQ FT: 20,000
SALES (est): 21.4MM Privately Held
WEB: www.trust-tech.com
SIC: 3544 3549 3545 3541 Jigs & fixtures; metalworking machinery; machine tool accessories; machine tools, metal cutting type; sheet metalwork; nonferrous rolling & drawing

(G-9118)
KRENGEL EQUIPMENT LLC
Also Called: Krengel Manufacturing
34580 Lakeland Blvd (44095-5221)
PHONE...................................440 946-3570
Katherine Krengel,
EMP: 140
SALES: 20MM Privately Held
SIC: 3363 3544 Aluminum die-castings; dies & die holders for metal cutting, forming, die casting

(G-9119)
KYNTROL HOLDINGS INC (PA)
34700 Lakeland Blvd (44095-5223)
PHONE...................................440 220-5990
Wayne Foley, *President*
EMP: 1
SALES (est): 1.9MM Privately Held
SIC: 3593 Fluid power actuators, hydraulic or pneumatic

(G-9120)
LANGE EQUIPMENT
Also Called: Unit Dle
1585 E 361st St Unit D (44095-5329)
PHONE...................................440 953-1621
Dick Lang, *Owner*
EMP: 5
SALES (est): 337.6K Privately Held
SIC: 3559 Metal finishing equipment for plating, etc.

(G-9121)
MIDWEST PRECISION HOLDINGS INC (HQ)
34700 Lakeland Blvd (44095-5223)
PHONE...................................440 497-4086
Wayne Foley, *President*
EMP: 52
SALES: 1.5MM
SALES (corp-wide): 45.7MM Privately Held
SIC: 3812 Acceleration indicators & systems components, aerospace
PA: Tribus Aerospace Llc
    10 S Wacker Dr Ste 3300
    Chicago IL 60606
    312 876-7267

(G-9122)
MIDWEST PRECISION LLC
34700 Lakeland Blvd (44095-5223)
PHONE...................................440 951-2333
Carl Richter, *President*
Steve Zuzek, *Plant Mgr*
Eddie Schwartz, *Purch Mgr*
Adam Jones, *Engineer*
Dale King, *Engineer*
EMP: 52 EST: 2010
SQ FT: 38,000
SALES: 12.7MM
SALES (corp-wide): 45.7MM Privately Held
WEB: www.midwestllc.com
SIC: 3451 Screw machine products
HQ: Midwest Precision Holdings Inc.
    34700 Lakeland Blvd
    Eastlake OH 44095
    440 497-4086

(G-9123)
MOLD MASTERS INTL INC
34000 Melinz Pkwy (44095-4054)
PHONE...................................440 953-0220
Jim Allen, *CEO*
George Goodrich, *President*
Ron Kern, *Principal*
Vic Sirotek, *Principal*
Robert Soltis, *Vice Pres*
EMP: 170
SQ FT: 54,000
SALES (est): 38.2MM Privately Held
WEB: www.moldmastersintl.com
SIC: 3324 2842 Steel investment foundries; specialty cleaning, polishes & sanitation goods

(G-9124)
MRD SOLUTIONS LLC
34201 Melinz Pkwy Unit A (44095-4018)
PHONE...................................440 942-6969
Nicholas Merlini,
Eugene Rapp,
EMP: 8
SALES (est): 1.6MM Privately Held
SIC: 3541 Machine tools, metal cutting type

(G-9125)
NATIONAL BULLET CO
34971 Glen Dr (44095-2622)
PHONE...................................800 317-9506
Nick Sasso, *CEO*
Ken M Bayko, *President*
EMP: 9
SQ FT: 2,000
SALES: 850K Privately Held
WEB: www.nationalbullet.com
SIC: 3482 5941 Small arms ammunition; sporting goods & bicycle shops

(G-9126)
NORTHEAST BROACH & TOOL
990 Erie Rd Unit H (44095-1813)
PHONE...................................440 918-0048
Herb Eierman, *President*
Hannah Norder, *Corp Secy*
Tom Norder, *Exec VP*
EMP: 3 EST: 2000
SALES (est): 200K Privately Held
SIC: 3545 Broaches (machine tool accessories)

(G-9127)
NOVA METAL PRODUCTS INC
1455 E 328th St (44095-3457)
PHONE...................................440 269-1741
Dan Novak, *CEO*
Nick Novak, *Engineer*
EMP: 20
SALES: 400K Privately Held
SIC: 3449 Miscellaneous metalwork

(G-9128)
POLYMER & STEEL TECH INC
34899 Curtis Blvd (44095-4015)
PHONE...................................440 510-0108
Douglas Horner, *President*
Larry Stanek, *Engineer*
Brian Walters, *Chief Mktg Ofcr*
Paul M Hurd, *CTO*
▼ EMP: 50
SQ FT: 66,000
SALES (est): 8.4MM Privately Held
WEB: www.enpac.com
SIC: 3089 Plastic containers, except foam

(G-9129)
SAWYER RESEARCH PRODUCT
35400 Lakeland Blvd (44095-5304)
PHONE...................................440 951-8770
Gary R Johnson, *Principal*
EMP: 3
SALES (est): 355.8K Privately Held
SIC: 3679 Electronic circuits

(G-9130)
STAINLESS SPECIALTIES INC
33240 Lakeland Blvd (44095-5205)
PHONE...................................440 942-4242
Dennis O'Brien, *President*
Joan Podmore, *Vice Pres*
EMP: 25
SQ FT: 26,000
SALES (est): 4.9MM Privately Held
WEB: www.stainless-specialties.com
SIC: 3441 3312 Fabricated structural metal; blast furnaces & steel mills

(G-9131)
STEVENS AUTO GLAZE AND SEC LL
36250 Lkeland Blvd Unit 3 (44095)
PHONE...................................440 953-2900
Jeff Stevens, *President*
Joyce Stevens, *Corp Secy*
Dennis Klienherz, *CFO*
EMP: 2
SALES: 1MM Privately Held
SIC: 5531 5013 5169 3559 Automotive accessories; automotive supplies & parts; chemicals & allied products; automotive maintenance equipment

(G-9132)
STONEBROOK MACHINE
1572 E 365th St (44095-5325)
PHONE...................................440 951-5013
Donna Bowersock, *Owner*
EMP: 4
SQ FT: 3,000
SALES: 500K Privately Held
SIC: 3399 Metal fasteners

(G-9133)
SUBURBAN MANUFACTURING CO
1924 E 337th St (44095-5229)
PHONE...................................440 953-2024
Richard E Grice, *President*
EMP: 60 EST: 1979
SQ FT: 31,000
SALES (est): 11.4MM Privately Held
WEB: www.submfg.com
SIC: 3599 3546 3463 3561 Machine shop, jobbing & repair; power-driven handtools; metal stampings; pumps & pumping equipment; fluid power pumps; fluid power cylinders & actuators

(G-9134)
SUMMERS ACQUISITION CORP
1857 E 337th St Unit B (44095-5231)
PHONE...................................440 946-5611
Richard Brown, *Branch Mgr*
EMP: 3
SALES (corp-wide): 3.1B Privately Held
WEB: www.summersrubber.com
SIC: 5085 3429 Rubber goods, mechanical; manufactured hardware (general)
HQ: Summers Acquisition Corporation
    12555 Berea Rd
    Cleveland OH 44111
    216 941-7700

(G-9135)
T & D FABRICATING INC
1489 E 363rd St (44095-4137)
PHONE...................................440 951-5646
Dallas Adkins, *President*
Helen Adkins, *Corp Secy*
Todd Adkins, *Vice Pres*
Dona Stevens, *Office Mgr*
EMP: 20
SALES (est): 5.7MM Privately Held
WEB: www.tdfabricating.com
SIC: 3469 3498 3354 3351 Metal stampings; fabricated pipe & fittings; aluminum extruded products; copper rolling & drawing; steel pipe & tubes; welding machinery & equipment

(G-9136)
TRI-TECH RESEARCH LLC
Also Called: Watts Acquisition Company II
34099 Melinz Pkwy Unit K (44095-4001)
PHONE...................................440 946-6122
Ridley Watts, *Mng Member*
EMP: 16
SQ FT: 12,000
SALES: 1.3MM Privately Held
SIC: 3625 8711 Electric controls & control accessories, industrial; engineering services

(G-9137)
TYMOCA PARTNERS LLC
Also Called: Federal Gear
33220 Lakeland Blvd (44095-5205)
PHONE...................................440 946-4327
David Hegenbarth,
EMP: 10
SALES (est): 2.5MM Privately Held
SIC: 3566 Speed changers, drives & gears

(G-9138)
UNITED MACHINE AND TOOL INC
1956 E 337th St (44095-5229)
PHONE...................................440 946-7677
Martha Klatt, *CEO*
Harry Klatt, *President*
EMP: 8 EST: 1965
SQ FT: 10,000

Eastlake - Lake County (G-9139)

SALES (est): 490K *Privately Held*
WEB: www.unitedmachineandtool.com
SIC: 3599 Machine shop, jobbing & repair

(G-9139)
UNIVERSAL PROTOTYPE PRODUCT CO
36781 Lake Shore Blvd (44095-1146)
PHONE..................440 953-3550
Fax: 440 953-8099
EMP: 3
SQ FT: 2,500
SALES: 270K *Privately Held*
SIC: 3599 Machine Shop

(G-9140)
WEBER TECHNOLOGIES INC
34000 Melinz Pkwy (44095-4054)
PHONE..................440 946-8833
Wim Huijs, *CEO*
EMP: 25 **EST:** 1901
SQ FT: 54,000
SALES (est): 3.2MM
SALES (corp-wide): 868.3MM *Publicly Held*
WEB: www.weber-tech.com
SIC: 3469 3471 3444 Stamping metal for the trade; perforated metal, stamped; spinning metal for the trade; finishing, metals or formed products; sheet metalwork
HQ: Enginetics Corporation
7700 New Carlisle Pike
Huber Heights OH 45424
937 878-3800

Eaton
Preble County

(G-9141)
ABBY INDUSTRIES LLC
346 Frizzell Ave (45320-9375)
PHONE..................513 502-9865
Abigail Dahlinghaus, *Principal*
EMP: 3 **EST:** 2012
SALES (est): 240.1K *Privately Held*
SIC: 3999 Manufacturing industries

(G-9142)
AUKERMAN J F STEEL RULE DIE
5582 Ozias Rd (45320-9716)
P.O. Box 374 (45320-0374)
PHONE..................937 456-4498
John F Aukerman Jr, *President*
EMP: 7
SALES (est): 162.9K *Privately Held*
SIC: 3544 Dies, steel rule; special dies & tools

(G-9143)
BRUBAKER METALCRAFTS INC
209 N Franklin St (45320-1819)
PHONE..................937 456-5834
Paul Brubaker, *President*
Wilma Brubaker, *Admin Sec*
EMP: 7 **EST:** 1973
SQ FT: 3,000
SALES: 300K *Privately Held*
WEB: www.brubakertinware.com
SIC: 3229 Lantern globes

(G-9144)
BULLEN ULTRASONICS INC
1301 Miller Williams Rd (45320-8507)
PHONE..................937 456-7133
Mary A Bullen, *President*
Tom Fraga, *Sales Engr*
Gregory Fitch, *Director*
Mary A Moreland, *Admin Sec*
▲ **EMP:** 65 **EST:** 1969
SQ FT: 4,748
SALES (est): 12.1MM *Privately Held*
SIC: 3599 Machine shop, jobbing & repair

(G-9145)
CAMDEN CONCRETE PRODUCTS
Also Called: Shawnee Molds
4952 State Route 732 W (45320-9574)
PHONE..................937 456-1229
Everett J Gilbert,
Patricia Gilbert,
▼ **EMP:** 6
SALES: 450K *Privately Held*
SIC: 3544 Industrial molds

(G-9146)
CORNERSTONE MANUFACTURING INC
861 Us Route 35 (45320-8638)
P.O. Box 682 (45320-0682)
PHONE..................937 456-5930
Ronnie J Kutter, *President*
Trisha Kutter, *Vice Pres*
EMP: 9
SQ FT: 4,000
SALES: 1MM *Privately Held*
SIC: 3544 Special dies & tools

(G-9147)
DAILY AGENCY INC
309 N Barron St (45320-1705)
PHONE..................937 456-9808
William Daily, *President*
Rick Daily, *Corp Secy*
EMP: 15
SQ FT: 3,000
SALES (est): 793K *Privately Held*
WEB: www.dailyagency.com
SIC: 6531 2711 Real estate agents & managers; newspapers, publishing & printing

(G-9148)
ELECTRO-CAP INTERNATIONAL INC
1011 W Lexington Rd (45320-9290)
P.O. Box 87 (45320-0087)
PHONE..................937 456-6099
W Nelson Hardin, *President*
Janet L Hardin, *Admin Sec*
EMP: 18
SQ FT: 10,000
SALES (est): 2.6MM *Privately Held*
WEB: www.electro-cap.com
SIC: 3089 5047 Caps, plastic; hospital equipment & furniture

(G-9149)
FIRST IMPRESSION WEAR
120 E Main St (45320-1744)
PHONE..................937 456-3900
Pat Taylor, *Principal*
EMP: 3
SALES (est): 267.3K *Privately Held*
SIC: 2759 Screen printing

(G-9150)
GRILL
100 Morton Rd (45320-1633)
PHONE..................937 673-6768
EMP: 3
SALES (est): 119.9K *Privately Held*
SIC: 3625 Motor controls & accessories

(G-9151)
HEART WARMING CANDLES
6806 Cumbersville St (45320)
PHONE..................937 456-2720
Carol Gardner, *Owner*
EMP: 3
SALES (est): 197.4K *Privately Held*
SIC: 3999 Candles

(G-9152)
HENNY PENNY CORPORATION (PA)
1219 Us Route 35 (45320-8621)
P.O. Box 60 (45320-0060)
PHONE..................937 456-8400
Steve Cobb, *CEO*
Rob Connelly, *President*
◆ **EMP:** 508
SQ FT: 400,000
SALES (est): 174.4MM *Privately Held*
SIC: 3589 Cooking equipment, commercial

(G-9153)
I DREAM OF CAKES
995 Camden Rd (45320-9511)
PHONE..................937 533-6024
Julie Rosfeld, *Principal*
EMP: 6
SALES (est): 132.2K *Privately Held*
SIC: 5461 2041 Cakes; flour & other grain mill products

(G-9154)
INTERNATIONAL PAPER COMPANY
900 State Route 35 W (45320-8647)
PHONE..................937 456-4131
Dale Whitman, *Engineer*
John Winters, *Branch Mgr*
EMP: 120
SALES (corp-wide): 23.3B *Publicly Held*
SIC: 2621 Paper mills
PA: International Paper Company
6400 Poplar Ave
Memphis TN 38197
901 419-9000

(G-9155)
K-COLUMN LLC
438 7 Mile Rd (45320-9498)
PHONE..................937 269-3696
Lisa Novelli,
EMP: 4
SALES (est): 141.2K *Privately Held*
SIC: 3999 Manufacturing industries

(G-9156)
KEE PRINTING INC
118 W Monfort St (45320-1422)
PHONE..................937 456-6851
Richard McKee, *Owner*
Carol Fewell, *Manager*
EMP: 4 **EST:** 1978
SQ FT: 3,000
SALES: 275K *Privately Held*
SIC: 2752 2759 5999 Commercial printing, offset; letterpress printing; rubber stamps

(G-9157)
KRAMER POWER EQUIPMENT CO
2388 State Route 726 N (45320-9217)
PHONE..................937 456-2232
Joseph Kramer, *President*
C Jason Kramer, *Vice Pres*
Sharon Kramer, *Office Mgr*
EMP: 18
SQ FT: 20,000
SALES: 1.1MM *Privately Held*
WEB: www.kramerusa.com
SIC: 3599 3444 3441 7692 Machine shop, jobbing & repair; sheet metalwork; fabricated structural metal; welding repair

(G-9158)
LAM RESEARCH CORPORATION
960 S Franklin St (45320)
PHONE..................937 472-3311
Mike Snell, *General Mgr*
Patrick Bach, *Business Mgr*
Steve Joslin, *Opers Staff*
Haresh Siriwardane, *Research*
Kent Clay, *Engineer*
EMP: 220
SALES (corp-wide): 11B *Publicly Held*
WEB: www.lamrc.com
SIC: 3559 Semiconductor manufacturing machinery
PA: Lam Research Corporation
4650 Cushing Pkwy
Fremont CA 94538
510 572-0200

(G-9159)
LAS MOTOR SPORTS
1694 Eaton Lewisburg Rd (45320-9756)
PHONE..................937 456-2441
EMP: 3 **EST:** 2003
SALES (est): 150K *Privately Held*
SIC: 3599 Mfg Industrial Machinery

(G-9160)
LEE PLASTIC COMPANY LLC
1100 Us Route 35 (45320-8620)
P.O. Box 271 (45320-0271)
PHONE..................937 456-5720
Patricia Kutter, *CEO*
EMP: 8
SQ FT: 8,000
SALES: 750K *Privately Held*
SIC: 3089 Injection molding of plastics

(G-9161)
MARK DAILY
807 N Maple St (45320-1532)
PHONE..................937 369-5358
Mark Daily, *Administration*
EMP: 4
SALES (est): 139.2K *Privately Held*
SIC: 2711 Newspapers, publishing & printing

(G-9162)
NEATON AUTO PRODUCTS MFG INC (HQ)
975 S Franklin St (45320-9400)
PHONE..................937 456-7103
Naoki Horikawa, *President*
David Gulling, *Exec VP*
Craig Cole, *Vice Pres*
Kazuhiro Watanabe, *Vice Pres*
Dave Dunfee, *Prdtn Mgr*
▲ **EMP:** 277
SQ FT: 500,000
SALES (est): 99.7MM
SALES (corp-wide): 1B *Privately Held*
WEB: www.neaton.com
SIC: 3714 Motor vehicle engines & parts; steering mechanisms, motor vehicle
PA: Nihon Plast Co.,Ltd.
3507-15, Yamamiya
Fujinomiya SZO 418-0
544 586-830

(G-9163)
PARKER-HANNIFIN CORPORATION
Tube Fittings Division
725 N Beech St (45320-1499)
PHONE..................937 456-5571
Jay Studer, *Mfg Mgr*
Dan Quinn, *Engineer*
Patricia Combs, *Cust Mgr*
William Bowman, *Branch Mgr*
Gary Clyburn, *Manager*
EMP: 400
SALES (corp-wide): 14.3B *Publicly Held*
WEB: www.parker.com
SIC: 3494 5074 3498 3492 Pipe fittings; couplings, except pressure & soil pipe; plumbing & heating valves; plumbing fittings & supplies; tube fabricating (contract bending & shaping); fluid power valves & hose fittings
PA: Parker-Hannifin Corporation
6035 Parkland Blvd
Cleveland OH 44124
216 896-3000

(G-9164)
REGISTER HERALD OFFICE
200 Eaton Lewisburg Rd # 105 (45320-1191)
PHONE..................937 456-5553
Darron Newman, *Principal*
EMP: 15 **EST:** 2002
SALES (est): 712.7K *Privately Held*
SIC: 2711 Commercial printing & newspaper publishing combined; newspapers, publishing & printing

(G-9165)
SEVEN MILE CREEK CORPORATION
315 S Beech St (45320-2311)
P.O. Box 155 (45320-0155)
PHONE..................937 456-3320
William Cressell, *President*
Marqueeta Cressell, *Admin Sec*
EMP: 14 **EST:** 1935
SQ FT: 3,850
SALES (est): 350K *Privately Held*
WEB: www.sevenmilecreek.com
SIC: 2399 2392 2393 2326 Aprons, breast (harness); shower curtains: made from purchased materials; textile bags; men's & boys' work clothing

(G-9166)
SILFEX INC
950 S Franklin St (45320-9421)
PHONE..................937 472-3311
Rhoel Ramos, *Project Mgr*
Colleen Friedsberg, *Mfg Mgr*
Randall Hardin, *Opers Staff*
Randi Hollen, *Production*
Susie Parrish, *Senior Buyer*
▲ **EMP:** 142
SALES (est): 48.5MM
SALES (corp-wide): 11B *Publicly Held*
SIC: 3674 Semiconductors & related devices

PA: Lam Research Corporation
4650 Cushing Pkwy
Fremont CA 94538
510 572-0200

Edgerton
Williams County

(G-9167)
AIR-WAY MANUFACTURING COMPANY
303 W River St (43517-9670)
PHONE..............................419 298-2366
Ronald Hamm, *CEO*
Kim De Young, *General Mgr*
Pam Nester, *Office Mgr*
EMP: 150
SALES (corp-wide): 64MM **Privately Held**
WEB: www.air-way.com
SIC: 3492 Hose & tube fittings & assemblies, hydraulic/pneumatic
PA: Air-Way Manufacturing Company Inc
586 N Main St
Olivet MI 49076
269 749-2161

(G-9168)
ANDREW M FARNHAM
2112 County Road C60 (43517-9795)
PHONE..............................419 298-4300
Andrew M Farnham, *Principal*
EMP: 3
SALES (est): 176.5K **Privately Held**
SIC: 2834 Pharmaceutical preparations

(G-9169)
BUILDING CONCEPTS INC (PA)
Also Called: Cardinal Truss & Components
444 N Michigan Ave (43517-9811)
P.O. Box 579 (43517-0579)
PHONE..............................419 298-2371
William H Lutterbein, *President*
Dennis Imbrock, *Vice Pres*
Donald C Landel, *Vice Pres*
Shellie Thiel, *Sales Associate*
EMP: 16 **EST:** 1924
SQ FT: 14,000
SALES (est): 3.1MM **Privately Held**
WEB: www.lutterbein.com
SIC: 5211 1521 2439 Lumber & other building materials; single-family housing construction; trusses, wooden roof

(G-9170)
CENTER CONCRETE INC (PA)
8790 Us Rt 6 (43517)
P.O. Box 340 (43517-0340)
PHONE..............................800 453-4224
Don Pahl, *President*
Gary Weber, *Admin Sec*
EMP: 17
SQ FT: 800
SALES (est): 2.8MM **Privately Held**
SIC: 3273 Ready-mixed concrete

(G-9171)
EDGERTON FORGE INC (HQ)
257 E Morrison St (43517-9302)
PHONE..............................419 298-2333
Richard Horton, *CEO*
Skip Dietrick, *President*
Pam Fitzcharles, *General Mgr*
Mark A Cluadio, *Vice Pres*
Gordon Miller, *Vice Pres*
EMP: 46
SQ FT: 70,000
SALES (est): 14.6MM
SALES (corp-wide): 312.9MM **Privately Held**
WEB: www.edgertonforge.com
SIC: 3462 3714 3423 Iron & steel forgings; motor vehicle parts & accessories; hand & edge tools
PA: Avis Industrial Corporation
1909 S Main St
Upland IN 46989
765 998-2100

(G-9172)
ELLIOTT OREN PRODUCTS INC
113 Industrial Dr (43517-9666)
PHONE..............................419 298-0015
Matthew Elliott, *Branch Mgr*
EMP: 16
SALES (corp-wide): 6MM **Privately Held**
WEB: www.orenelliottproducts.com
SIC: 3451 Screw machine products
PA: Oren Elliott Products, Inc.
128 W Vine St
Edgerton OH 43517
419 298-2306

(G-9173)
ELLIOTT OREN PRODUCTS INC (PA)
128 W Vine St (43517-8606)
P.O. Box 638 (43517-0638)
PHONE..............................419 298-2306
June Elliott, *President*
Oren Elliott, *Vice Pres*
Matthew Elliott, *Prdtn Mgr*
EMP: 39
SQ FT: 24,000
SALES (est): 6MM **Privately Held**
WEB: www.orenelliottproducts.com
SIC: 3675 3451 3469 Electronic capacitors; screw machine products; metal stampings

(G-9174)
FERGUSON TOOLS INC
103 Industrial Dr (43517-9666)
PHONE..............................419 298-2327
William Ferguson, *President*
Darrin Ferguson, *Vice Pres*
Markc Ferguson, *Vice Pres*
Kathy Ferguson, *Admin Sec*
EMP: 30
SQ FT: 10,000
SALES (est): 4.8MM **Privately Held**
WEB: www.fergusontools.com
SIC: 3545 Cutting tools for machine tools

(G-9175)
FLEGAL BROTHERS INC
104 Industrial Dr (43517-9666)
PHONE..............................419 298-3539
Douglas Flegal, *President*
EMP: 15
SALES: 500K **Privately Held**
SIC: 2611 4213 Pulp mills, mechanical & recycling processing; trucking, except local

(G-9176)
MATSU OHIO INC
228 E Morrison St (43517-9389)
PHONE..............................419 298-2394
Dave Rutila, *President*
Art Artuso, *President*
Galliano Tiberini, *Vice Pres*
Becky Algeo, *Admin Sec*
▲ **EMP:** 122
SQ FT: 220,000
SALES (est): 27.7MM
SALES (corp-wide): 97.2MM **Privately Held**
SIC: 3465 Body parts, automobile: stamped metal
PA: Matsu Manufacturing Inc
7657 Bramalea Rd
Brampton ON L6T 5
905 291-5000

(G-9177)
MIDWEST STAMPING & MFG CO
228 E Morrison St (43517-9389)
PHONE..............................419 298-2394
John Carney, *Principal*
EMP: 9
SALES (est): 692.4K **Privately Held**
SIC: 3999 Manufacturing industries

(G-9178)
ROBERTSON EDM LLC
9294 State Route 249 (43517-9556)
PHONE..............................419 658-2219
Ronald Walker, *Mng Member*
Jeffrey Robertson,
EMP: 5
SALES: 675K **Privately Held**
SIC: 3599 Machine shop, jobbing & repair

(G-9179)
RURAL PRODUCTS INC
6266 Us Highway 6 (43517-9710)
PHONE..............................419 298-2677
John Curry, *President*
EMP: 4 **EST:** 1963
SALES (est): 400K **Privately Held**
SIC: 3451 3544 Screw machine products; special dies & tools

(G-9180)
STAFFORD GRAVEL INC
4225 Co Rd 79 (43517)
P.O. Box 340 (43517-0340)
PHONE..............................419 298-2440
Gerry Weber, *Principal*
EMP: 6
SALES (est): 587.1K **Privately Held**
SIC: 1442 Construction sand & gravel

(G-9181)
STARK TRUSS COMPANY INC
400 Component Dr (43517)
P.O. Box 535 (43517-0535)
PHONE..............................419 298-3777
Duane Miller, *Branch Mgr*
EMP: 75
SQ FT: 45,000
SALES (corp-wide): 186.7MM **Privately Held**
WEB: www.starktruss.com
SIC: 2439 2511 2411 Trusses, wooden roof; wood household furniture; logging
PA: Stark Truss Company, Inc.
109 Miles Ave Sw
Canton OH 44710
330 478-2100

(G-9182)
WEBER SAND & GRAVEL INC
2702 County Road 3b (43517-9692)
PHONE..............................419 298-2388
Thomas B Weber, *President*
Judy Weber, *Vice Pres*
EMP: 11
SQ FT: 2,000
SALES (est): 818.5K **Privately Held**
SIC: 1442 Common sand mining; gravel mining

Edon
Williams County

(G-9183)
AGRIDRY LLC
3460 Us Highway 20 (43518-9733)
P.O. Box 336 (43518-0336)
PHONE..............................419 459-4399
Eli P Troyer, *Mng Member*
EMP: 45
SALES (est): 10.7MM **Privately Held**
SIC: 3567 1541 Driers & redriers, industrial process; grain elevator construction

(G-9184)
DIMENSION HARDWOOD VENEERS INC
509 Woodville St (43518)
PHONE..............................419 272-2245
Paul Horstman, *President*
▲ **EMP:** 50 **EST:** 1977
SQ FT: 56,000
SALES (est): 8.4MM **Privately Held**
SIC: 2435 Hardwood veneer & plywood

(G-9185)
L & L MACHINE INC
2919 County Road 2l (43518-9771)
PHONE..............................419 272-5000
Laurie Lehman, *CEO*
Michael Lehman, *President*
EMP: 11
SQ FT: 40,000
SALES: 1.5MM **Privately Held**
SIC: 3599 Machine shop, jobbing & repair

(G-9186)
NORTHWEST MOLDED PLASTICS
14372 County Road 4 (43518-9765)
PHONE..............................419 459-4414
Richard L Lemmon, *Owner*
EMP: 9 **EST:** 1976
SQ FT: 25,000
SALES (est): 550K **Privately Held**
WEB: www.comtech2000.com
SIC: 3089 Molding primary plastic

(G-9187)
PLAS-TEC CORP
601 W Indiana St (43518-9645)
PHONE..............................419 272-2731
Kenneth Sharlow, *General Mgr*
Terry Carter, *Purchasing*
Dennis Cox, *Treasurer*
Troy Brock, *Maintence Staff*
EMP: 60
SQ FT: 85,000
SALES (est): 15.4MM **Privately Held**
WEB: www.plasteccorp.com
SIC: 3089 Injection molded finished plastic products; injection molding of plastics

(G-9188)
PTC ENTERPRISES INC
3047 County Road K (43518-9551)
PHONE..............................419 272-2524
Bill Patton, *President*
David C Newcomer, *Principal*
▲ **EMP:** 50
SALES (est): 8.9MM **Privately Held**
SIC: 3089 Injection molding of plastics

Eldorado
Preble County

(G-9189)
MIAMI VALLEY PLASTICS INC
310 S Main St (45321-9731)
PHONE..............................937 273-3200
George W Halderman, *CEO*
Alan Halderman, *Vice Pres*
▲ **EMP:** 35
SQ FT: 2,569
SALES (est): 6.3MM **Privately Held**
SIC: 3089 Injection molding of plastics

(G-9190)
OLDE SCHLHUSE VNYRD WINERY LLC
8538 State Route 726 (45321-9734)
P.O. Box 230 (45321-0230)
PHONE..............................937 273-6023
Angela S Zdobinski, *Owner*
EMP: 4
SALES (est): 289.7K **Privately Held**
SIC: 2084 Wines

(G-9191)
SUDS
160 Main Cross (45321)
PHONE..............................937 273-6007
Martin Ridge, *Principal*
EMP: 4
SALES (est): 362K **Privately Held**
SIC: 2599 Bar, restaurant & cafeteria furniture

Elida
Allen County

(G-9192)
A & D WOOD PRODUCTS INC (PA)
4220 Sherrick Rd (45807-9783)
PHONE..............................419 331-8859
Joseph Peters, *President*
EMP: 18
SALES (est): 2.5MM **Privately Held**
SIC: 2448 Pallets, wood

(G-9193)
AIRCRAFT DYNAMICS CORPORATION
418 E Kiracofe Ave (45807-1030)
P.O. Box 3038, Lima (45807-0038)
PHONE..............................419 331-0371
Jack D Jones, *President*
Alice White, *Corp Secy*
Steve Jones, *Exec VP*
Doug Thackery, *Vice Pres*
▲ **EMP:** 18 **EST:** 1935
SQ FT: 12,000
SALES (est): 2.4MM **Privately Held**
WEB: www.aircraftdynamics.com
SIC: 7359 3546 Equipment rental & leasing; power-driven handtools

Elida - Allen County (G-9194)

(G-9194)
BOWMAN CABINET SHOP
4880 N Cable Rd (45807-9518)
PHONE.............................419 331-8209
Kevin Bowman, *Owner*
EMP: 3 **EST:** 1959
SQ FT: 4,000
SALES (est): 396.9K **Privately Held**
SIC: 2434 Wood kitchen cabinets

(G-9195)
LIMA MILLWORK INC
4251 East Rd (45807-1534)
PHONE.............................419 331-3303
Mark Niemeyer, *President*
Thelma Neimeyer, *Vice Pres*
Hope Dawson, *Office Admin*
EMP: 26
SQ FT: 16,000
SALES: 3.5MM **Privately Held**
SIC: 2431 2511 2434 3281 Millwork; wood household furniture; wood kitchen cabinets; cut stone & stone products; wood partitions & fixtures; wood office furniture

(G-9196)
LIMA PIPE ORGAN CO INC
408 E Kiracofe Ave (45807-1030)
P.O. Box 3023 (45807-0023)
PHONE.............................419 331-5461
Larry Holycross, *President*
Tom Holycross, *Vice Pres*
EMP: 4
SQ FT: 3,500
SALES: 250K **Privately Held**
WEB: www.limapipeorgan.com
SIC: 3931 7699 Pipes, organ; organ tuning & repair

(G-9197)
ORICK STAMPING
614 E Kiracofe Ave (45807-1034)
PHONE.............................419 331-0600
Paul Orick, *CEO*
Greg Orick, *President*
Monica Orick, *Exec VP*
Bob Sheffield, *QC Mgr*
Rick Conmay, *Controller*
EMP: 80 **EST:** 1969
SQ FT: 100,000
SALES (est): 31.5MM **Privately Held**
WEB: www.oricktool.com
SIC: 3469 3544 Stamping metal for the trade; special dies, tools, jigs & fixtures

(G-9198)
PATTON INDUSTRIES INC
Also Called: Dimensional Equipment Div
1950 Beery Rd (45807-9514)
PHONE.............................419 331-5658
James E Patton, *President*
Sherry Patton, *Corp Secy*
Sandra L Patton, *Vice Pres*
EMP: 5
SQ FT: 40,000
SALES (est): 400K **Privately Held**
SIC: 5084 3599 Metalworking machinery; machine shop, jobbing & repair

(G-9199)
RANGE KLEEN MFG INC
4240 East Rd (45807-1533)
P.O. Box 696, Lima (45802-0696)
PHONE.............................419 331-8000
Patrick O'Connor, *President*
Patrick Oconnor, *Vice Pres*
Becky Hesseling, *Prdtn Mgr*
Sheri Strawn, *Finance*
Dana Swearengin, *Marketing Staff*
▲ **EMP:** 403 **EST:** 1971
SQ FT: 50,000
SALES (est): 73.1MM **Privately Held**
WEB: www.rangekleen.com
SIC: 3365 3469 Cooking/kitchen utensils, cast aluminum; metal stampings

(G-9200)
SHELDON ON SITE INC
4848 Gomer Rd (45807-9507)
PHONE.............................419 339-1381
Sheldon Bowman, *President*
Rebecca Bowman, *Admin Sec*
EMP: 5
SALES: 200K **Privately Held**
SIC: 7694 7699 Electric motor repair; engine repair & replacement, non-automotive

(G-9201)
SIEFKER SAWMILL
8705 W State Rd (45807-8730)
PHONE.............................419 339-1956
Gary Siefker, *Partner*
Dan Siefker, *Partner*
Ken Siefker, *Partner*
Ron Siefker, *Partner*
EMP: 8
SALES (est): 780K **Privately Held**
SIC: 2421 2426 Sawmills & planing mills, general; lumber, hardwood dimension

(G-9202)
ULRICH RUBBER STAMP COMPANY
Also Called: Tebben Rubber Stamp Company
2130 Larkspur Dr (45807-1489)
PHONE.............................419 339-9939
Jack Ulrich, *President*
Sally Ulrich, *Vice Pres*
EMP: 3 **EST:** 1953
SALES: 75K **Privately Held**
SIC: 2791 3953 7389 Typesetting; embossing seals & hand stamps;

Elmore
Ottawa County

(G-9203)
ALVIN L ROEPKE
Also Called: Vision Quest
329 Rice St (43416-9404)
P.O. Box 197 (43416-0197)
PHONE.............................419 862-3891
Alvin L Roepke, *Owner*
EMP: 16
SQ FT: 5,400
SALES: 850K **Privately Held**
SIC: 7336 2759 3993 2284 Silk screen design; screen printing; signs & advertising specialties; embroidery thread

(G-9204)
CALVIN J MAGSIG
Also Called: Elmore Mfg Co
343 Clinton St (43416-7703)
P.O. Box 32 (43416-0032)
PHONE.............................419 862-3311
Calvin J Magsig, *Owner*
EMP: 7
SQ FT: 15,000
SALES: 600K **Privately Held**
SIC: 3599 3494 Machine shop, jobbing & repair; valves & pipe fittings

(G-9205)
CHIPMATIC TOOL & MACHINE INC
212 Ottawa St (43416-7710)
P.O. Box 87 (43416-0087)
PHONE.............................419 862-2737
Mike Detzel, *President*
Duane Glase, *Purch Agent*
Kim M Detzel, *Admin Sec*
Kim Detzel, *Admin Sec*
EMP: 67
SQ FT: 30,000
SALES (est): 10.4MM **Privately Held**
WEB: www.chipmatic.com
SIC: 3599 8711 7692 3544 Machine shop, jobbing & repair; mechanical engineering; welding repair; special dies, tools, jigs & fixtures

(G-9206)
MACHINING TECHNOLOGIES INC (PA)
Also Called: M T
468 Maple St (43416-9423)
P.O. Box 287 (43416-0287)
PHONE.............................419 862-3110
William M Van Dorn, *CEO*
Thomas C Van Dorn, *CFO*
▲ **EMP:** 41
SQ FT: 32,000
SALES (est): 8.4MM **Privately Held**
SIC: 3082 3545 Unsupported plastics profile shapes; precision tools, machinists'

(G-9207)
MARTIN INDUSTRIES INC
473 Maple St (43416-9402)
P.O. Box 569 (43416-0569)
PHONE.............................419 862-2694
Tim Gerkensmeyer, *President*
EMP: 30
SQ FT: 10,000
SALES (est): 4.8MM **Privately Held**
SIC: 3069 3061 Hard rubber & molded rubber products; mechanical rubber goods

(G-9208)
MATERION BRUSH INC
14710 W Prtage River S Rd (43416-9500)
PHONE.............................419 862-2745
Thomas Piazza, *Vice Pres*
Lawrence Ryczek, *Vice Pres*
Dan Draper, *Maint Spvr*
Jeff Behm, *Production*
Eddie Deleon, *Production*
EMP: 700
SQ FT: 100,000
SALES (corp-wide): 1.2B **Publicly Held**
WEB: www.brushwellman.com
SIC: 3339 3369 3341 Beryllium metal; nonferrous foundries; secondary nonferrous metals
HQ: Materion Brush Inc.
   6070 Parkland Blvd Ste 1
   Mayfield Heights OH 44124
   216 486-4200

Elyria
Lorain County

(G-9209)
AEROWAVE INC
361 Windward Dr (44035-1633)
PHONE.............................440 731-8464
Bob Avon, *CEO*
EMP: 7
SALES: 700K **Privately Held**
SIC: 3548 Welding apparatus

(G-9210)
ALCO MANUFACTURING CORP LLC (PA)
10584 Middle Ave (44035-7812)
PHONE.............................440 458-5165
Kevin Koepp, *President*
EMP: 52
SALES (est): 18.8MM **Privately Held**
SIC: 3451 Screw machine products

(G-9211)
ALEXIS CONCRETE ENTERPRISE INC
672 Sugar Ln (44035-6310)
PHONE.............................440 366-0031
Edward Machovia, *President*
EMP: 11 **EST:** 2000
SALES (est): 1.6MM **Privately Held**
SIC: 3273 Ready-mixed concrete

(G-9212)
ALL STAR GROUP INC
Also Called: Signs N Ship
810 Taylor St (44035-6232)
PHONE.............................440 323-6060
Pam Melea, *President*
EMP: 4
SQ FT: 3,200
SALES (est): 310K **Privately Held**
WEB: www.signsnship.com
SIC: 3993 Signs, not made in custom sign painting shops

(G-9213)
ALLEN KENARD PRINTING INC
501 Clark St (44035-6109)
PHONE.............................440 323-7405
Fred A Rice, *President*
Judy L Rice, *Corp Secy*
EMP: 10
SQ FT: 10,000
SALES (est): 930K **Privately Held**
SIC: 2752 Commercial printing, offset

(G-9214)
AMERICAN COMMODORE TUXEDOS
Also Called: Ameritux
3574 Midway Mall (44035-2463)
PHONE.............................440 324-2889
Frank Simone Jr, *CEO*
Jose Rodriguez, *Manager*
EMP: 3
SALES (est): 101.3K **Privately Held**
SIC: 7299 2311 Tuxedo rental; tuxedos: made from purchased materials

(G-9215)
AMERICAN FLUID POWER INC
144 Reaser Ct (44035-6285)
PHONE.............................877 223-8742
Robert Weltman, *COO*
EMP: 7
SALES (est): 610K **Privately Held**
SIC: 3542 Bending machines

(G-9216)
AMIDAC WIND CORPORATION
151 Innovation Dr (44035-1675)
PHONE.............................213 973-4000
Ameer Alghusain, *CEO*
EMP: 5 **EST:** 2015
SALES (est): 363.7K **Privately Held**
SIC: 3643 Lightning protection equipment

(G-9217)
ANDRAS CORP
840 Infirmary Rd (44035-4819)
PHONE.............................440 323-2528
Ken Andras, *President*
EMP: 5 **EST:** 1964
SQ FT: 10,000
SALES: 500K **Privately Held**
SIC: 3272 Burial vaults, concrete or precast terrazzo

(G-9218)
APPLIED ENGNEERED SURFACES INC
535 Ternes Ln (44035-6286)
PHONE.............................440 366-0440
Lauren Yoakam, *President*
EMP: 18
SALES (est): 3.5MM **Privately Held**
SIC: 3441 Building components, structural steel

(G-9219)
ARNCO CORPORATION
860 Garden St (44035-4877)
PHONE.............................800 847-7661
Arlene P Tengel, *Principal*
William E Smith, *Corp Secy*
Dave Pampush, *VP Sales*
▲ **EMP:** 250
SALES (est): 42.4MM
SALES (corp-wide): 1.9B **Privately Held**
WEB: www.arncocorp.com
SIC: 3661 3829 3644 3429 Telephones & telephone apparatus; measuring & controlling devices; noncurrent-carrying wiring services; manufactured hardware (general); nonferrous wiredrawing & insulating
PA: Audax Group, L.P.
   101 Huntington Ave # 2450
   Boston MA 02199
   617 859-1500

(G-9220)
ATTRACTIVE KITCHENS & FLRG LLC
536 Cleveland St (44035-4055)
PHONE.............................440 406-9299
Byron Slater,
EMP: 5
SQ FT: 5,000
SALES: 2MM **Privately Held**
SIC: 2499 5211 1752 Woodenware, kitchen & household; counter tops; wood floor installation & refinishing

(G-9221)
B&B DISTRIBUTORS LLC
Also Called: Builders Straight Edge
150 Keep Ct Ste A (44035-2215)
PHONE.............................440 324-1293
George Hovanitz, *Mng Member*
EMP: 10

GEOGRAPHIC SECTION

Elyria - Lorain County (G-9250)

SALES (est): 1.4MM **Privately Held**
SIC: 3353 Aluminum sheet, plate & foil

(G-9222)
BASF CATALYSTS LLC
120 Pine St (44035-5228)
P.O. Box 4017 (44036-2017)
PHONE.....................440 322-3741
Randolph C Turk, *Branch Mgr*
EMP: 263
SALES (corp-wide): 71.7B **Privately Held**
SIC: 2819 Catalysts, chemical
HQ: Basf Catalysts Llc
33 Wood Ave S
Iselin NJ 08830
732 205-5000

(G-9223)
BASF CORPORATION
120 Pine St (44035-5228)
PHONE.....................440 329-2525
EMP: 7
SALES (est): 706K **Privately Held**
SIC: 2816 Inorganic pigments

(G-9224)
BENDIX SPCER FNDTION BRAKE LLC (DH)
901 Cleveland St (44035-4153)
PHONE.....................440 329-9709
Eddie Wilkinson, *President*
Aaron Schwass, *Vice Pres*
Mehmet Kocaarslan, *Buyer*
Greg Mazzella, *Buyer*
Jill Uhler, *Finance*
▲ EMP: 67
SALES (est): 61.4MM
SALES (corp-wide): 711.6K **Privately Held**
SIC: 3714 Air brakes, motor vehicle; brake drums, motor vehicle; motor vehicle brake systems & parts

(G-9225)
BIRGE HEAVY INDUSTRIES LTD
322 Furnace St (44035-5065)
PHONE.....................440 821-3249
Anthony Birge,
EMP: 20
SQ FT: 3,250
SALES (est): 837.5K **Privately Held**
SIC: 3999 Manufacturing industries

(G-9226)
BUCKEYE MOLDED PRODUCTS LTD
443 Oberlin Elyria Rd (44035-7761)
PHONE.....................440 323-2244
Carl R Kennedy, *Mng Member*
Fred Hugunin,
EMP: 10
SQ FT: 20,000
SALES (est): 1.6MM **Privately Held**
WEB: www.buckeyemoldedproducts.com
SIC: 3624 Brush blocks, carbon or molded graphite

(G-9227)
BUCKEYE STATE WELDING & FABG
175 Woodford Ave (44035-5436)
P.O. Box 837 (44036-0837)
PHONE.....................440 322-0344
Chris Reddinger, *Owner*
EMP: 22
SALES (corp-wide): 3.2MM **Privately Held**
SIC: 7692 Welding repair
PA: Buckeye State Welding & Fabricating, Inc.
131 Buckeye St
Elyria OH 44035
440 322-0319

(G-9228)
BUCKEYE STATE WLDG & FABG INC (PA)
131 Buckeye St (44035-5216)
P.O. Box 837 (44036-0837)
PHONE.....................440 322-0319
Kenneth E Reddinger, *President*
Christopher R Reddinger, *Corp Secy*
Patrick J Reddinger, *Vice Pres*
Elaine Benson, *Manager*
EMP: 13

SQ FT: 12,000
SALES (est): 3.2MM **Privately Held**
SIC: 3599 Machine shop, jobbing & repair

(G-9229)
CA PICARD SURFACE ENGRG INC
1206 E Broad St (44035-6308)
PHONE.....................440 366-5400
Mark Sink, *President*
▲ EMP: 12
SQ FT: 7,000
SALES (est): 2.2MM
SALES (corp-wide): 47.7MM **Privately Held**
SIC: 3469 5051 Machine parts, stamped or pressed metal; foundry products
HQ: Carl Aug. Picard Gmbh
Haster Aue 9
Remscheid 42857
219 189-30

(G-9230)
CABLETEK WIRING PRODUCTS INC
1150 Taylor St (44035-6281)
PHONE.....................800 562-9378
Stan Leonowigh, *President*
EMP: 25
SALES (est): 3.5MM **Privately Held**
SIC: 3444 Metal housings, enclosures, casings & other containers

(G-9231)
CASCADE PATTERN COMPANY INC
519 Ternes Ln (44035-6286)
PHONE.....................440 323-4300
Charles A Petek, *CEO*
Rick Petek, *President*
Nick Petek, *Vice Pres*
Corey Brooks, *Supervisor*
EMP: 32
SALES (est): 6.2MM **Privately Held**
WEB: www.cascadepattern.com
SIC: 3543 Industrial patterns

(G-9232)
CASCADE PLATING INC
Also Called: Lake Plating
210 Abbe Rd S (44035-6240)
PHONE.....................440 366-4931
Greg Lake, *President*
EMP: 3
SQ FT: 10,800
SALES (est): 333.7K **Privately Held**
SIC: 3471 Plating of metals or formed products

(G-9233)
CASTCO INC
527 Ternes Ln (44035-6286)
P.O. Box 1368, Delaware (43015-8368)
PHONE.....................440 365-2333
Dan Petek, *CEO*
EMP: 45
SALES (est): 6.8MM **Privately Held**
WEB: www.castco.com
SIC: 3321 Gray & ductile iron foundries

(G-9234)
CASTEK ALUMINUM INC
527 Ternes Ln (44035-6286)
PHONE.....................440 365-2333
Daniel C Petek, *President*
Harry Piero, *Sales Mgr*
EMP: 40
SALES (est): 9.6MM **Privately Held**
SIC: 3365 Aluminum foundries

(G-9235)
CENTRAL COCA-COLA BTLG CO INC
1410 Lake Ave (44035-3124)
PHONE.....................440 324-3335
Scott Dickerhoff, *Manager*
EMP: 52
SALES (corp-wide): 35.4B **Publicly Held**
WEB: www.colasic.net
SIC: 2086 Bottled & canned soft drinks
HQ: Central Coca-Cola Bottling Company, Inc.
555 Taxter Rd Ste 550
Elmsford NY 10523
914 789-1100

(G-9236)
CHALFANT MANUFACTURING COMPANY
7005 W River Rd S (44035-7058)
PHONE.....................440 323-9870
John Slaga, *Branch Mgr*
EMP: 17
SALES (corp-wide): 267.9K **Privately Held**
SIC: 3643 Current-carrying wiring devices
HQ: Chalfant Manufacturing Company
50 Pearl Rd Ste 212
Brunswick OH 44212
330 273-3510

(G-9237)
CITY ELYRIA COMMUNICATION
851 Garden St (44035-4874)
PHONE.....................440 322-3329
Larry Showalter, *Superintendent*
EMP: 6
SALES (est): 378.6K **Privately Held**
SIC: 3669 Traffic signals, electric

(G-9238)
CONSUN FOOD INDUSTRIES INC
Also Called: Sunshine Farms Dairy
123 Gateway Blvd N (44035-4923)
PHONE.....................440 322-6301
Dennis Walter, *President*
EMP: 60
SALES (corp-wide): 13.8MM **Privately Held**
SIC: 2026 Fluid milk
PA: Consun Food Industries, Inc.
123 Gateway Blvd N
Elyria OH 44035
440 322-6301

(G-9239)
CREATIVE POWDER COATINGS
6412 Gateway Blvd S (44035-5442)
PHONE.....................440 322-8197
Mark Brown, *CEO*
Gail Brown, *Treasurer*
EMP: 3
SQ FT: 6,000
SALES (est): 325.9K **Privately Held**
SIC: 3479 Painting of metal products; coating of metals & formed products

(G-9240)
CRYSTAL KOCH FINISHING INC
Also Called: Koch Crystal Finishing
630 Sugar Ln (44035-6310)
PHONE.....................440 366-7526
Martin Koch, *CEO*
Elizabeth Koch, *President*
Marty Koch, *General Mgr*
EMP: 5
SQ FT: 6,000
SALES (est): 456.7K **Privately Held**
SIC: 7699 3471 Scientific equipment repair service; plating & polishing

(G-9241)
DIAMOND PRODUCTS LIMITED
1111 Taylor St (44035-6245)
PHONE.....................440 323-4616
Don Williams, *Purch Agent*
EMP: 8
SALES (corp-wide): 3.7B **Privately Held**
WEB: www.diamondproducts.com
SIC: 3545 Machine tool accessories
HQ: Diamond Products, Limited
333 Prospect St
Elyria OH 44035
440 323-4616

(G-9242)
DIAMONDS PRODUCTS LLC
1250 E Broad St (44035-6311)
PHONE.....................440 323-4616
Tom Pfaff, *CIO*
Karl Moller,
▲ EMP: 7
SALES (est): 905K **Privately Held**
SIC: 3545 Diamond cutting tools for turning, boring, burnishing, etc.

(G-9243)
DICKS COUNTER D M
275 Warden Ave (44035-2649)
PHONE.....................440 322-3312

Horace Dicks, *Principal*
EMP: 3
SALES (est): 181.8K **Privately Held**
SIC: 3131 Counters

(G-9244)
DIY HOLSTER LLC
7836 Oberlin Rd (44035-1910)
PHONE.....................419 921-2168
C Patrick, *Mng Member*
EMP: 8
SALES (est): 973.1K **Privately Held**
SIC: 3199 5072 5961 Holsters, leather; hardware; tools & hardware, mail order

(G-9245)
DURA-LINE CORPORATION
860 Garden St (44035-4826)
PHONE.....................440 322-1000
Steven Sminth, *Branch Mgr*
EMP: 49 **Privately Held**
SIC: 3084 Plastics pipe
HQ: Dura-Line Corporation
11400 Parkside Dr Ste 300
Knoxville TN 37934
865 218-3460

(G-9246)
DYNATECH SYSTEMS INC
161 Reaser Ct (44035-6285)
P.O. Box 1589 (44036-1589)
PHONE.....................440 365-1774
Sue A Everett, *President*
EMP: 25
SQ FT: 5,000
SALES (est): 3.3MM **Privately Held**
WEB: www.diamonddrillbit.com
SIC: 3425 5085 Saw blades & handsaws; industrial supplies

(G-9247)
E C S CORP
Also Called: Elyria Concrete Step Company
8015 Murray Ridge Rd (44035-2071)
PHONE.....................440 323-1707
Betty Goad, *President*
Everett G Goad, *President*
Thomas Goad, *Vice Pres*
Thomas R Goad, *Vice Pres*
Gary Goad, *Treasurer*
EMP: 13 EST: 1957
SQ FT: 9,300
SALES: 745.9K **Privately Held**
SIC: 3446 3272 3271 Grillwork, ornamental metal; steps, prefabricated concrete; paving blocks, concrete

(G-9248)
E D M ELECTROFYING INC
34 Artemas Ct (44035-6167)
PHONE.....................440 322-8900
Timothy Koba, *President*
Jennifer Koba, *Vice Pres*
EMP: 5
SQ FT: 2,800
SALES: 380K **Privately Held**
WEB: www.electrofyingedm.com
SIC: 3541 3544 Electrical discharge erosion machines; special dies, tools, jigs & fixtures; industrial molds

(G-9249)
ELCOR INC
640 Sugar Ln (44035-6310)
P.O. Box 376, Amherst (44001-0376)
PHONE.....................440 365-5941
Jerry Mucha, *President*
Eddie Williams, *General Mgr*
Robert Zahratka, *Corp Secy*
Glen Hersteck, *Vice Pres*
Glen Hersteck, *Vice Pres*
EMP: 23
SQ FT: 7,500
SALES (est): 2MM **Privately Held**
WEB: www.elcor.net
SIC: 3694 3699 Harness wiring sets, internal combustion engines; electrical equipment & supplies

(G-9250)
ELITE PROPERTY GROUP LLC
Also Called: 1st Choice Contractor
1036 N Pasadena Ave (44035-2966)
PHONE.....................216 356-7469
Sean Webb,
EMP: 12

Elyria - Lorain County (G-9251)

SALES (est): 436.8K **Privately Held**
SIC: 8742 6531 6719 1389 Construction project management consultant; real estate managers; investment holding companies, except banks; construction, repair & dismantling services; construction management

(G-9251)
ELYRIA COPY CENTER INC
325 Lake Ave (44035-4903)
PHONE...................................440 323-4145
Summit Dukeman, *President*
EMP: 5
SQ FT: 2,000
SALES: 300K **Privately Held**
SIC: 2752 7334 Commercial printing, offset; photocopying & duplicating services

(G-9252)
ELYRIA MANUFACTURING CORP (PA)
Also Called: EMC Precision Machining
145 Northrup St (44035-6163)
P.O. Box 479 (44036-0479)
PHONE...................................440 365-4171
Larry Harrison, *President*
Bradley R Ohlemacher, *President*
Bob Graney, *CFO*
Jeff Badar, *Controller*
Mirinet Velez, *Sales Staff*
▲ EMP: 54 EST: 1925
SQ FT: 86,000
SALES (est): 11.3MM **Privately Held**
WEB: www.elyriamfg.com
SIC: 3451 Screw machine products

(G-9253)
ELYRIA METAL SPINNING FABG CO
Also Called: Metal Manufacturing
7511 W River Rd S (44035-6972)
P.O. Box 992 (44036-0992)
PHONE...................................440 323-8068
Donald Didomenico, *President*
EMP: 8 EST: 1962
SQ FT: 18,000
SALES (est): 1.5MM **Privately Held**
SIC: 3469 3599 Spinning metal for the trade; machine shop, jobbing & repair

(G-9254)
ELYRIA PATTERN CO INC
6785 W River Rd S (44035-7052)
PHONE...................................440 323-1526
James A Schroeder, *President*
James W Schroeder, *Vice Pres*
EMP: 7
SALES: 500K **Privately Held**
SIC: 3543 Industrial patterns

(G-9255)
ELYRIA PLATING CORPORATION
118 Olive St (44035-4000)
PHONE...................................440 365-8300
Kevin J Flanigan, *CEO*
E F Gookins, *President*
Eric Manuel, *Site Mgr*
Dick EPC, *Production*
EMP: 40 EST: 1937
SQ FT: 35,000
SALES (est): 5MM **Privately Held**
SIC: 3471 Electroplating of metals or formed products

(G-9256)
ELYRIA SPRING & SPECIALTY INC
123 Elbe St (44035-4879)
PHONE...................................440 323-5502
John Turk, *President*
Brian Reed, *Prdtn Mgr*
Brian King, *Purch Mgr*
Sue Shepard, *Sales Staff*
Mark Cicerchi, *Manager*
EMP: 45
SQ FT: 8,858
SALES (est): 8.6MM **Privately Held**
WEB: www.elyriaspring.com
SIC: 3495 3496 3493 3469 Wire springs; miscellaneous fabricated wire products; steel springs, except wire; metal stampings; automotive stampings

(G-9257)
EMC PRECISION MACHINING II LLC (PA)
145 Northrup St (44035-6147)
P.O. Box 479 (44036-0479)
PHONE...................................440 365-4171
Jack Zeman,
EMP: 18 EST: 2010
SALES (est): 13.6MM **Privately Held**
SIC: 3599 Machine shop, jobbing & repair

(G-9258)
ENGELHARD CORP
120 Pine St (44035-5228)
PHONE...................................440 322-3741
Al Brightwell, *Principal*
▲ EMP: 6
SALES (est): 640.2K **Privately Held**
SIC: 2819 Industrial inorganic chemicals

(G-9259)
ENVELOPE MART OF OHIO INC
1540 Lowell St (44035-4869)
P.O. Box 808 (44036-0808)
PHONE...................................440 365-8177
Robert T Thompson, *President*
EMP: 50
SALES (est): 9MM **Privately Held**
SIC: 5112 2677 Envelopes; envelopes

(G-9260)
ES THERMAL INC
Also Called: Brown Fired Heater Div
300 Ceran (44035)
P.O. Box 4030 (44036-4030)
PHONE...................................440 323-3291
David Hoecke, *President*
John Somodi, *Vice Pres*
Keith Phillips, *Chief Engr*
Jonathan Phillips, *Project Engr*
Keith J Phillips, *Admin Sec*
EMP: 25 EST: 1974
SQ FT: 48,000
SALES (est): 6MM **Privately Held**
SIC: 3433 Oil burners, domestic or industrial

(G-9261)
FLORIDA INVACARE HOLDINGS LLC
1 Invacare Way (44035-4190)
P.O. Box 4028 (44036-2028)
PHONE...................................800 333-6900
Matthew E Monaghan, *CEO*
EMP: 3
SALES (est): 104.8K
SALES (corp-wide): 972.3MM **Publicly Held**
SIC: 3842 Surgical appliances & supplies
PA: Invacare Corporation
   1 Invacare Way
   Elyria OH 44035
   440 329-6000

(G-9262)
GASFLUX COMPANY
32 Hawthorne St (44035-4008)
P.O. Box 1170 (44036-1170)
PHONE...................................440 365-1941
William K Farquhar, *Ch of Bd*
Robert C Farquhar, *President*
Richard Hoffman, *Vice Pres*
Mary Ann Farquhar, *Treasurer*
◆ EMP: 8 EST: 1938
SQ FT: 20,000
SALES (est): 1.7MM **Privately Held**
WEB: www.gasflux.com
SIC: 2899 Fluxes: brazing, soldering, galvanizing & welding

(G-9263)
GATEWAY INDUSTRIAL PDTS INC
160 Freedom Ct (44035-2245)
P.O. Box 95 (44036-0095)
PHONE...................................440 324-4112
Peter Delaporte, *President*
Gayle Delaporte, *General Mgr*
Rachel Sharp, *Sales Staff*
▼ EMP: 15
SQ FT: 25,000
SALES (est): 3.3MM **Privately Held**
WEB: www.gatewayindustrial.com
SIC: 3089 2431 Window screening, plastic; doors & door parts & trim, wood

(G-9264)
GREBER MACHINE TOOL INC
Also Called: Custom Powdr Coating By Greber
313 Clark St (44035-6105)
PHONE...................................440 322-3685
Ken Greber, *President*
Tammy Greber, *Treasurer*
EMP: 7
SQ FT: 600
SALES (est): 640K **Privately Held**
WEB: www.greberracing.com
SIC: 3479 7692 Coating of metals & formed products; welding repair

(G-9265)
HEALTHTECH PRODUCTS
Also Called: Invacare Rentals
1 Invacare Way (44035-4190)
PHONE...................................419 271-1761
Michael Will, *Principal*
EMP: 5
SALES (est): 494.7K **Privately Held**
SIC: 3842 Surgical appliances & supplies

(G-9266)
HUDAK MACHINE & TOOL INC
144 Eady Ct (44035-4124)
PHONE...................................440 366-8955
Frank P Hudak Jr, *President*
Barbara Schmittgen, *Corp Secy*
EMP: 3
SALES: 130K **Privately Held**
WEB: www.absolutemachine.com
SIC: 3544 3599 Jigs & fixtures; machine shop, jobbing & repair

(G-9267)
HYDRO-AIRE INC
Also Called: Lear Romec
241 Abbe Rd S (44035-6239)
PHONE...................................440 323-3211
Jay Higgs, *President*
David Hunger, *Engineer*
Tazewell Rowe, *Treasurer*
Ron Bosley, *Information Mgr*
EMP: 236
SALES (corp-wide): 3.3B **Publicly Held**
WEB: www.craneco.com
SIC: 3728 Aircraft parts & equipment
HQ: Hydro-Aire, Inc.
   3000 Winona Ave
   Burbank CA 91504

(G-9268)
INTERNATIONAL MULTIFOODS CORP
6325 Gateway Blvd S (44035-5447)
PHONE...................................440 323-5100
Mike Phippen, *Branch Mgr*
EMP: 4
SALES (corp-wide): 7.3B **Publicly Held**
SIC: 2051 Bakery: wholesale or wholesale/retail combined
HQ: International Multifoods Corporation
   1 Strawberry Ln
   Orrville OH 44667
   330 682-3000

(G-9269)
INTERTEK MACHINING & WLDG INC
6805 W River Rd S (44035-7054)
PHONE...................................440 323-3325
Mort Guerine, *President*
Dave W Dennis, *Vice Pres*
Andrea Monschein, *CFO*
EMP: 13
SQ FT: 24,000
SALES (est): 2.3MM **Privately Held**
WEB: www.intertekmachandweld.com
SIC: 3599 Machine shop, jobbing & repair

(G-9270)
INVACARE CANADIAN HOLDINGS INC
1 Invacare Way (44035-4190)
PHONE...................................440 329-6000
Matthew E Monaghan, *CEO*
EMP: 3
SALES (est): 155.7K
SALES (corp-wide): 972.3MM **Publicly Held**
SIC: 3842 Surgical appliances & supplies

PA: Invacare Corporation
   1 Invacare Way
   Elyria OH 44035
   440 329-6000

(G-9271)
INVACARE CANADIAN HOLDINGS LLC
1 Invacare Way (44035-4190)
PHONE...................................440 329-6000
EMP: 3 EST: 2015
SALES (est): 120.1K
SALES (corp-wide): 972.3MM **Publicly Held**
SIC: 3842 Surgical appliances & supplies
PA: Invacare Corporation
   1 Invacare Way
   Elyria OH 44035
   440 329-6000

(G-9272)
INVACARE CORPORATION (PA)
1 Invacare Way (44035-4190)
P.O. Box 4028 (44036-2028)
PHONE...................................440 329-6000
Matthew E Monaghan, *Ch of Bd*
Robert Hanley, *Business Mgr*
Anthony C Laplaca, *Senior VP*
Ralf Ledda, *Senior VP*
Laura Mahoney, *Vice Pres*
◆ EMP: 662
SALES: 972.3MM **Publicly Held**
WEB: www.invacare.com
SIC: 2514 2813 3842 Beds, including folding & cabinet, household: metal; industrial gases; oxygen, compressed or liquefied; wheelchairs

(G-9273)
INVACARE CORPORATION
Also Called: Invacare It & Financial Svcs
1320 Taylor St (44035-6250)
PHONE...................................800 333-6900
EMP: 97
SALES (corp-wide): 972.3MM **Publicly Held**
SIC: 2514 2813 3842 Beds, including folding & cabinet, household: metal; industrial gases; oxygen, compressed or liquefied; wheelchairs
PA: Invacare Corporation
   1 Invacare Way
   Elyria OH 44035
   440 329-6000

(G-9274)
INVACARE CORPORATION
1200 Taylor St (44035-6248)
PHONE...................................440 329-6000
John Dmytriw, *Branch Mgr*
EMP: 14
SQ FT: 13,000
SALES (corp-wide): 972.3MM **Publicly Held**
WEB: www.invacare.com
SIC: 3842 Wheelchairs; walkers
PA: Invacare Corporation
   1 Invacare Way
   Elyria OH 44035
   440 329-6000

(G-9275)
INVACARE HOLDINGS LLC
1 Invacare Way (44035-4190)
PHONE...................................440 329-6000
EMP: 4 EST: 2015
SALES (est): 258.3K
SALES (corp-wide): 972.3MM **Publicly Held**
SIC: 3842 Surgical appliances & supplies
PA: Invacare Corporation
   1 Invacare Way
   Elyria OH 44035
   440 329-6000

(G-9276)
INVACARE HOLDINGS CORPORATION
1 Invacare Way (44035-4190)
PHONE...................................440 329-6000
Gerald Blouch, *CEO*
A Malachi Mixon III, *Ch of Bd*
Joseph B Richey II, *President*
Anthony C Laplaca, *Senior VP*
▲ EMP: 3

GEOGRAPHIC SECTION

Elyria - Lorain County (G-9304)

SALES (est): 381.5K
SALES (corp-wide): 972.3MM **Publicly Held**
SIC: 2514 3841 3842 Beds, including folding & cabinet, household: metal; inhalation therapy equipment; wheelchairs
HQ: Invacare International Corporation
1 Invacare Way
Elyria OH 44035

(G-9277)
INVACARE INTERNATIONAL CORP (HQ)
1 Invacare Way (44035-4190)
PHONE..................440 329-6000
Sharon Corbett, *Principal*
EMP: 3
SALES (est): 23.3MM
SALES (corp-wide): 972.3MM **Publicly Held**
SIC: 2514 3841 3842 Beds, including folding & cabinet, household: metal; inhalation therapy equipment; wheelchairs
PA: Invacare Corporation
1 Invacare Way
Elyria OH 44035
440 329-6000

(G-9278)
INVACARE RESPIRATORY CORP
899 Cleveland St (44035-4100)
PHONE..................440 329-6000
Jeff Steiss, *Marketing Staff*
Dale A La Porte, *Admin Sec*
◆ EMP: 35 EST: 1979
SALES: 1.5MM
SALES (corp-wide): 972.3MM **Publicly Held**
WEB: www.invacare.com
SIC: 3842 Surgical appliances & supplies
PA: Invacare Corporation
1 Invacare Way
Elyria OH 44035
440 329-6000

(G-9279)
J & M PRECISION DIE CAST INC
1329 Taylor St (44035-6249)
PHONE..................440 365-7388
Michael Prokop, *President*
EMP: 12
SQ FT: 8,000
SALES: 1.2MM
SALES (corp-wide): 14.2MM **Privately Held**
SIC: 3599 Machine shop, jobbing & repair
PA: Rhenium Alloys, Inc.
38683 Taylor Pkwy
North Ridgeville OH 44035
440 365-7388

(G-9280)
J M SMUCKER COMPANY
6325 Gateway Blvd S (44035-5447)
PHONE..................440 323-5100
Mike Phippen, *Branch Mgr*
EMP: 36
SALES (corp-wide): 7.3B **Publicly Held**
WEB: www.smuckers.com
SIC: 2045 2099 2051 Cake mixes, prepared: from purchased flour; food preparations; bread, cake & related products
PA: The J M Smucker Company
1 Strawberry Ln
Orrville OH 44667
330 682-3000

(G-9281)
KASTLER & REICHLIN INC
Also Called: Phoenix Mold & Die
710 Taylor St (44035-6230)
PHONE..................440 322-0970
EMP: 50
SALES (est): 3.8MM **Privately Held**
SIC: 3544 3599 Mfg Plastic Injection Molds Fixtures Prototypes Cnc Machining & Stamping Dies

(G-9282)
KELCH MANUFACTURING CORP
626 Sugar Ln (44035-6396)
PHONE..................440 366-5060
Franklyn S Kelch, *President*
Joan Kelch, *Vice Pres*
EMP: 7
SQ FT: 9,000

SALES (est): 465.8K **Privately Held**
SIC: 3469 3544 Metal stampings; dies, plastics forming; diamond dies, metalworking

(G-9283)
L C SMITH CO
196 Morgan Ave (44035-2638)
PHONE..................440 327-1251
Francis Fife, *President*
Sheila Smith, *Vice Pres*
Jack Smith, *Manager*
EMP: 3
SQ FT: 4,200
SALES: 500K **Privately Held**
WEB: www.lcsmith.net
SIC: 3545 3715 Measuring tools & machines, machinists' metalworking type; trailer bodies

(G-9284)
LANXESS SOLUTIONS US INC
Also Called: Ingredient Technology Division
110 Liberty Ct (44035-2237)
PHONE..................440 324-6060
Ronald Nicolson, *Opers-Prdtn-Mfg*
EMP: 50
SQ FT: 10,000
SALES (corp-wide): 8.2B **Privately Held**
WEB: www.cromptoncorp.com
SIC: 2099 Emulsifiers, food
HQ: Lanxess Solutions Us Inc.
2 Armstrong Rd Ste 101
Shelton CT 06484
203 573-2000

(G-9285)
LAUREN YOAKAM
Also Called: Applied Engineered Surface
591 Ternes Ln (44035-6271)
PHONE..................440 365-3952
Lauren Yoakam, *Owner*
EMP: 8
SALES (est): 868.6K **Privately Held**
SIC: 3441 Fabricated structural metal

(G-9286)
LEAR MFG CO INC
147 Freedom Ct (44035-2245)
PHONE..................440 324-1111
Bonnie Lear, *President*
EMP: 15
SALES (est): 600K **Privately Held**
SIC: 3452 Nuts, metal

(G-9287)
LERNER ENTERPRISES INC
811 Taylor St (44035-6231)
PHONE..................440 323-5529
Arthur L Lerner, *Principal*
Paul Klug, *Admin Sec*
▲ EMP: 30
SQ FT: 30,000
SALES: 3.6MM **Privately Held**
WEB: www.masterbolt.com
SIC: 3452 Bolts, nuts, rivets & washers

(G-9288)
LORAIN MODERN PATTERN INC
159 Woodbury St (44035-4011)
PHONE..................440 365-6780
Todd R Roth, *President*
Sheila I Kelly-Roth, *Vice Pres*
EMP: 10
SQ FT: 5,500
SALES: 550K **Privately Held**
WEB: www.lorainmodern.com
SIC: 3543 Industrial patterns

(G-9289)
LOWER LIMB CENTERS LLC
1100 Abbe Rd N Ste D (44035-1667)
PHONE..................440 365-2502
Mark I Winters, *Principal*
EMP: 3 EST: 2008
SALES (est): 254K **Privately Held**
SIC: 3842 Limbs, artificial

(G-9290)
LTI POWER SYSTEMS
10800 Middle Ave Hngr B (44035-7893)
PHONE..................440 327-5050
Robert J Morog, *CEO*
Ken Potyrala, *QC Mgr*
Chuck Wallace, *Engineer*
Cris Desimone, *Accounting Mgr*

Mary Morog, *Admin Sec*
◆ EMP: 20
SQ FT: 35,000
SALES (est): 2MM **Privately Held**
WEB: www.ltipowersystems.com
SIC: 3612 Specialty transformers

(G-9291)
MARATHON INDUSTRIAL CNTRS INC
100 Freedom Ct (44035-2245)
PHONE..................440 324-2748
Richard L Sipley, *President*
▼ EMP: 12
SQ FT: 30,000
SALES (est): 1.4MM **Privately Held**
SIC: 3443 Industrial vessels, tanks & containers

(G-9292)
MCCONNELL READY MIX
37500 Butternut Ridge Rd (44039-8466)
PHONE..................440 458-4325
EMP: 6
SALES (est): 669K **Privately Held**
SIC: 3273 Ready-mixed concrete

(G-9293)
MENTOR RADIO LLC
151 Innovation Dr Ste 320 (44035-1677)
PHONE..................216 265-2315
Eric M Sadowski, *President*
EMP: 3
SALES (est): 280K **Privately Held**
WEB: www.mentorradio.com
SIC: 3663 Radio & TV communications equipment

(G-9294)
METAL BUILDING INTR PDTS CO
750 Adams St (44035)
PHONE..................440 322-6500
EMP: 12
SALES (corp-wide): 4.7MM **Privately Held**
SIC: 3296 Fiberglass insulation
PA: Metal Building Interior Products Co Inc
801 Bond St
Elyria OH
440 322-6500

(G-9295)
METRO DESIGN INC
10740 Middle Ave (44035-7816)
P.O. Box 248 (44036-0248)
PHONE..................440 458-4200
Jeffery Kraps, *President*
EMP: 14
SQ FT: 10,000
SALES (est): 2.2MM **Privately Held**
SIC: 3599 7699 3844 Custom machinery; machine shop, jobbing & repair; X-ray equipment repair; X-ray apparatus & tubes

(G-9296)
MINUTEMAN PRESS OF ELYRIA
631 Abbe Rd S (44035-7243)
PHONE..................440 365-9377
Donna Stein, *Owner*
Brenda Woodring, *Partner*
EMP: 4
SQ FT: 1,100
SALES (est): 340.9K **Privately Held**
SIC: 2752 Commercial printing, offset

(G-9297)
ML ERECTORS LLC
827 Walnut St (44035-3352)
PHONE..................440 328-3227
Paul Cook, *Opers Mgr*
Matthew J Loftin, *Mng Member*
EMP: 7 EST: 2003
SQ FT: 26,000
SALES: 1.2MM **Privately Held**
SIC: 2759 Publication printing

(G-9298)
MULTILINK INC
Also Called: Multifab
580 Ternes Ln (44035-6252)
PHONE..................440 366-6966
Steven Kaplan, *President*
Mike French, *Vice Pres*
Kathy Kaplan, *Vice Pres*
Steve Brown, *Engineer*

Sirisha Joish, *Accounts Exec*
▲ EMP: 140
SQ FT: 110,000
SALES (est): 147.4MM **Privately Held**
WEB: www.multilinkbroadband.com
SIC: 5063 3829 Wire & cable; cable testing machines

(G-9299)
NATIONAL MOLDED PRODUCTS INC
147 Kenwood St (44035-4009)
PHONE..................440 365-3400
Robert E Brown, *President*
Charlene Brown, *Corp Secy*
Brian Brown, *Vice Pres*
EMP: 30
SQ FT: 33,000
SALES: 1.5MM **Privately Held**
SIC: 3089 Injection molded finished plastic products

(G-9300)
NELSON STUD WELDING INC (DH)
7900 W Ridge Rd (44035-1952)
P.O. Box 4019 (44036-2019)
PHONE..................440 329-0400
Ken Caratelli, *President*
Doug Shantz, *General Mgr*
David Bubar, *Vice Pres*
Debbie Hunnel, *Vice Pres*
John Garmon, *Opers Mgr*
◆ EMP: 277 EST: 2000
SALES (est): 224.9MM
SALES (corp-wide): 3.4B **Privately Held**
SIC: 3452 3548 Bolts, nuts, rivets & washers; welding apparatus
HQ: Doncasters 456 Limited
Millennium Court
Burton-On-Trent STAFFS
133 286-4900

(G-9301)
NORTH COAST RIVET INC
700 Sugar Ln (44035-6312)
P.O. Box 1441 (44036-1441)
PHONE..................440 366-6829
Wesley L Shirley, *CEO*
Kathy Shirley, *Admin Sec*
EMP: 19
SQ FT: 6,000
SALES (est): 1MM **Privately Held**
SIC: 3452 Rivets, metal

(G-9302)
OAK TREE INTL HOLDINGS INC
1209 Lowell St (44035-4803)
PHONE..................702 462-7295
EMP: 5
SALES (est): 452.4K
SALES (corp-wide): 1.7MM **Privately Held**
SIC: 2834 Pharmaceutical preparations
PA: Oak Tree International Holdings, Inc.
9550 S Eastrn Ave Ste 253
Las Vegas NV 89123
702 462-7295

(G-9303)
OHIO DISPLAYS INC
Also Called: Odi
825 Leona St (44035-2300)
PHONE..................216 961-5600
Thomas R Mc Kay, *Ch of Bd*
Judy Miller, *Vice Pres*
Colleen Murray-Jones, *Office Mgr*
EMP: 15
SQ FT: 70,000
SALES (est): 2.3MM **Privately Held**
WEB: www.ohiodisplays.com
SIC: 3993 2542 Displays, paint process; partitions & fixtures, except wood

(G-9304)
OHIO METALLURGICAL SERVICE INC
Also Called: Ohiomet
1033 Clark St (44035-6257)
P.O. Box 1228 (44036-1228)
PHONE..................440 365-4104
Donald S Gaydosh, *President*
John Gaydosh, *President*
R E Baird, *Principal*
William D Latiano, *Principal*

Elyria - Lorain County (G-9305)

Glenn E Shoemaker, *Principal*
EMP: 69
SQ FT: 50,000
SALES: 10MM **Privately Held**
WEB: www.ohiomet.com
SIC: 3398 Metal heat treating

(G-9305)
OHIO SCREW PRODUCTS INC
818 Lowell St (44035-4876)
P.O. Box 4027 (44036-2027)
PHONE................................440 322-6341
Edward N Imbrogno, *Ch of Bd*
Daniel Imbrogno, *President*
Jim Fetcko, *President*
Dan Imbrogno, *President*
Elmer Brown, *Vice Pres*
EMP: 75 **EST:** 1945
SQ FT: 65,000
SALES (est): 23.7MM **Privately Held**
WEB: www.ohioscrew.com
SIC: 3541 3451 Screw machines, automatic; screw machine products

(G-9306)
P P E INC
Also Called: Elyria Plastic Products
710 Taylor St (44035-6230)
PHONE................................440 322-8577
Jim Kastler, *President*
R Stephen Laux, *Principal*
James M Reichlin, *Principal*
▲ **EMP:** 75
SQ FT: 6,000
SALES (est): 18.8MM **Privately Held**
WEB: www.elyriapp.com
SIC: 3089 Injection molded finished plastic products; injection molding of plastics

(G-9307)
P-AMERICAS LLC
Also Called: Pepsico
925 Lorain Blvd (44035-2819)
PHONE................................440 323-5524
Mike Schonberg, *Branch Mgr*
EMP: 123
SALES (corp-wide): 64.6B **Publicly Held**
SIC: 2086 Soft drinks: packaged in cans, bottles, etc.
HQ: P-Americas Llc
1 Pepsi Way
Somers NY 10589
336 896-5740

(G-9308)
PARKER-HANNIFIN CORPORATION
Gresen Hydraulics
520 Ternes Ln (44035-6266)
P.O. Box 4026 (44036-2026)
PHONE................................440 366-5100
Ted Bojanowski, *Vice Pres*
Chris Bulger, *Facilities Mgr*
Kurt Boey, *Engineer*
John Darmstadt, *Engineer*
Andy Ross, *Branch Mgr*
EMP: 300
SALES (corp-wide): 14.3B **Publicly Held**
WEB: www.parker.com
SIC: 3594 Fluid power pumps & motors
PA: Parker-Hannifin Corporation
6035 Parkland Blvd
Cleveland OH 44124
216 896-3000

(G-9309)
PARKER-HANNIFIN CORPORATION
Fluid Systems Division
711 Taylor St (44035-6229)
PHONE................................440 284-6277
Bryan Schue, *Safety Dir*
Paul Novak, *Facilities Mgr*
Mike Freeman, *QC Mgr*
Bill Heilman, *Engineer*
John Zielinski, *Design Engr*
EMP: 200
SALES (corp-wide): 14.3B **Publicly Held**
WEB: www.parker.com
SIC: 3728 3724 Aircraft assemblies, sub-assemblies & parts; aircraft engines & engine parts
PA: Parker-Hannifin Corporation
6035 Parkland Blvd
Cleveland OH 44124
216 896-3000

(G-9310)
PERFECTIONS FABRICATORS INC
680 Sugar Ln (44035-6310)
PHONE................................440 365-5850
James Ennes, *President*
David Ennes, *Vice Pres*
Dave Ennes, *Export Mgr*
Linda Stauffer, *Office Mgr*
EMP: 10 **EST:** 1973
SQ FT: 27,000
SALES (est): 998.2K **Privately Held**
SIC: 3441 Fabricated structural metal

(G-9311)
PERSONAL PLUMBER SERVICE CORP
Also Called: Value-Rooter
42343 N Ridge Rd (44035-1130)
PHONE................................440 324-4321
Russell Halstead, *President*
Russell Halstead, *President*
Russell A Halstead, *Owner*
Mellisa Holstead, *Treasurer*
EMP: 19
SALES (est): 1.6MM **Privately Held**
SIC: 1711 2842 1794 Plumbing contractors; drain pipe solvents or cleaners; excavation work

(G-9312)
PLASTIC ENTERPRISES INC (PA)
41520 Schadden Rd (44035-2227)
PHONE................................440 324-3240
John Leonowich, *President*
William Kaatz, *Vice Pres*
▲ **EMP:** 22 **EST:** 1959
SQ FT: 35,000
SALES (est): 4.7MM **Privately Held**
WEB: www.plastic-enterprises.com
SIC: 3089 3544 Injection molding of plastics; special dies, tools, jigs & fixtures

(G-9313)
PLASTIC ENTERPRISES INC
Also Called: Bee Valve
1150 Taylor St (44035-6281)
PHONE................................440 366-0220
Bill Kaatz, *Manager*
EMP: 9
SALES (corp-wide): 4.7MM **Privately Held**
WEB: www.plastic-enterprises.com
SIC: 3089 Injection molding of plastics
PA: Plastic Enterprises, Inc.
41520 Schadden Rd
Elyria OH 44035
440 324-3240

(G-9314)
PLASTO-TECH CORPORATION
708 Lowell St (44035-4843)
P.O. Box 226, Wooster (44691-0226)
PHONE................................440 323-6300
Bala Venkataraman, *President*
Laks Venkataraman, *Vice Pres*
Thomas Woodruff, *Treasurer*
EMP: 11
SQ FT: 50,000
SALES (est): 1.7MM
SALES (corp-wide): 43MM **Privately Held**
WEB: www.plasto-tech.com
SIC: 3082 Unsupported plastics profile shapes
PA: Magni- Power Company
5511 E Lincoln Way
Wooster OH 44691
330 264-3637

(G-9315)
QUALITY BLOW MOLDING INC
635 Oberlin Elyria Rd (44035-7727)
PHONE................................440 458-6550
Ronald E Matcham, *President*
Mary Anne Matcham, *Admin Sec*
EMP: 90
SQ FT: 30,000
SALES (est): 7.7MM **Privately Held**
SIC: 3089 Blow molded finished plastic products

(G-9316)
R V SPA LLC
42345 Oberlin Elyria Rd (44035-7415)
PHONE................................440 284-4800
Bill Gates, *Principal*
EMP: 4
SALES (est): 327.6K **Privately Held**
SIC: 3799 Recreational vehicles

(G-9317)
REAL ALLOY SPECIALTY PDTS LLC
440 Huron St (44035)
PHONE................................440 322-0072
EMP: 3
SALES (est): 99.9K **Privately Held**
SIC: 3355 Aluminum rolling & drawing

(G-9318)
REAL ALLOY SPECIALTY PRODUCTS
320 Huron St (44035-4829)
PHONE................................440 322-0072
Randy Collins, *Manager*
EMP: 28
SALES (corp-wide): 1.3B **Publicly Held**
SIC: 3341 Aluminum smelting & refining (secondary)
HQ: Real Alloy Specialty Products, Inc
3700 Park East Dr Ste 300
Beachwood OH 44122

(G-9319)
RECOGNITION ROBOTICS INC (PA)
151 Innovation Dr (44035-1675)
PHONE................................440 590-0499
Simon Melikian, *CEO*
Joe Cyrek, *Vice Pres*
EMP: 17
SALES (est): 11.8MM **Privately Held**
SIC: 3569 8742 Robots, assembly line: industrial & commercial; automation & robotics consultant

(G-9320)
RIDGE TOOL COMPANY (DH)
Also Called: Ridgid
400 Clark St (44035-6100)
P.O. Box 4023 (44036-2023)
PHONE................................440 323-5581
B J Jones, *Principal*
Dave Zink, *District Mgr*
David Botos, *Vice Pres*
Donna Calhoun, *Vice Pres*
Jim Carter, *Vice Pres*
◆ **EMP:** 800 **EST:** 1922
SQ FT: 600,000
SALES (est): 428.5MM
SALES (corp-wide): 17.4B **Publicly Held**
WEB: www.ridgid.com
SIC: 3423 3547 3546 3541 Hand & edge tools; rolling mill machinery; power-driven handtools; pipe cutting & threading machines

(G-9321)
RIDGE TOOL COMPANY
321 Sumner St (44035-6125)
PHONE................................440 329-4737
Ron Farkas, *Manager*
Bill Schramm, *Manager*
EMP: 20
SALES (corp-wide): 17.4B **Publicly Held**
WEB: www.ridgid.com
SIC: 3541 Machine tools, metal cutting type
HQ: Ridge Tool Company
400 Clark St
Elyria OH 44035
440 323-5581

(G-9322)
RIDGE TOOL MANUFACTURING CO
400 Clark St (44035-6100)
P.O. Box 4023 (44036-2023)
PHONE................................440 323-5581
Fred Pond, *President*
Scott Garfield, *Vice Pres*
Ralph Shaw, *CFO*
EMP: 1400
SQ FT: 400,000
SALES (est): 73.9MM
SALES (corp-wide): 17.4B **Publicly Held**
WEB: www.ridgid.com
SIC: 3541 3423 3547 3546 Machine tools, metal cutting type; hand & edge tools; rolling mill machinery; power-driven handtools; machine tool accessories; metal stampings
HQ: Ridge Tool Company
400 Clark St
Elyria OH 44035
440 323-5581

(G-9323)
RPM INDUSTRIES
1444 Lowell St (44035-4867)
PHONE................................440 268-8077
Erik Vanover, *Principal*
EMP: 3
SALES (est): 199.3K **Privately Held**
SIC: 3999 Manufacturing industries

(G-9324)
S A E MANUFACTURING
7880 W River Rd S (44035-6938)
PHONE................................440 322-9026
Mark Klier, *President*
Kevin Fenik, *Vice Pres*
EMP: 4
SQ FT: 6,000
SALES (est): 563.7K **Privately Held**
SIC: 3599 Machine shop, jobbing & repair

(G-9325)
SELZER TOOL & DIE INC
163 Kenwood St (44035-4096)
P.O. Box 1017 (44036-1017)
PHONE................................440 365-4124
David Selzer, *President*
Donna Selzer, *President*
Dale Selzer, *Vice Pres*
EMP: 3
SQ FT: 8,000
SALES (est): 300K **Privately Held**
SIC: 3599 7692 3544 Machine shop, jobbing & repair; welding repair; special dies, tools, jigs & fixtures

(G-9326)
SHALMET CORPORATION
164 Freedom Ct (44035-2245)
PHONE................................440 236-8840
Hugh O Donnell, *Branch Mgr*
EMP: 9
SALES (corp-wide): 2.1B **Publicly Held**
SIC: 3471 Polishing, metals or formed products
HQ: Shalmet Corporation
116 Pinedale Indus Rd
Orwigsburg PA 17961
570 366-1414

(G-9327)
SMART COMMERCIALIZATION CENTER
141 Innovation Dr (44035-1673)
PHONE................................440 300-4040
EMP: 3
SALES (est): 171.6K **Privately Held**
SIC: 3674 Semiconductors & related devices

(G-9328)
SMART MICROSYSTEMS LTD
141 Innovation Dr (44035-1673)
PHONE................................440 366-4257
Matt Apanius, *President*
EMP: 10
SALES (est): 570.4K **Privately Held**
SIC: 3674 Microcircuits, integrated (semiconductor)

(G-9329)
SMOKIN GUNS LLC
41458 Griswold Rd (44035-2351)
PHONE................................440 324-4003
Cory Eden, *President*
Melvin Eden, *Assistant VP*
Mary Melvin, *Vice Pres*
Mary Eden, *Exec Dir*
EMP: 3 **EST:** 2014
SALES: 70K **Privately Held**
SIC: 3484 7997 5941 Guns (firearms) or gun parts, 30 mm. & below; gun club, membership; firearms

▲ = Import ▼ = Export
◆ = Import/Export

GEOGRAPHIC SECTION

(G-9330)
SORTA 4 U LLC
267 Bon Air Ave (44035-4115)
PHONE...................................440 365-0091
EMP: 3
SALES (est): 190K **Privately Held**
SIC: 3448 Mfg Prefabricated Metal Buildings

(G-9331)
STAYS LIGHTING INC
Also Called: Best Fab Co.
936 Taylor St (44035-6234)
PHONE...................................440 328-3254
Joe Jingle, *President*
EMP: 8
SQ FT: 9,200
SALES (est): 1.3MM **Privately Held**
SIC: 3441 Fabricated structural metal

(G-9332)
SUZIN L CHOCOLATIERS
230 Broad St (44035-5502)
PHONE...................................440 323-3372
Suzin Stefanelli, *Owner*
EMP: 12
SQ FT: 26,000
SALES (est): 1.3MM **Privately Held**
WEB: www.suzinl.com
SIC: 2064 5441 5947 Chocolate candy, except solid chocolate; candy; gift shop

(G-9333)
SWARTZ MANUFACTURING INC
820 Walnut St (44035-3353)
PHONE...................................440 284-0297
Ira Swartz, *President*
Alissa Swartz, *Vice Pres*
EMP: 5
SQ FT: 10,000
SALES: 500K **Privately Held**
WEB: www.swartzmfg.com
SIC: 3599 Machine shop, jobbing & repair

(G-9334)
SYMRISE INC
110 Liberty Ct (44035-2237)
PHONE...................................440 324-6060
John Cassidy, *Branch Mgr*
Suzanne Blanchette, *Director*
EMP: 150
SALES (corp-wide): 3.6B **Privately Held**
WEB: www.symriseinc.com
SIC: 2869 Perfume materials, synthetic
HQ: Symrise Inc.
300 North St
Teterboro NJ 07608
201 288-3200

(G-9335)
TBH INTERNATIONAL
150 Ridge Circle Ln Apt A (44035-8711)
PHONE...................................440 323-4651
Thomas Heffner, *President*
Amy Heffner, *Vice Pres*
EMP: 3 EST: 2009
SALES (est): 230K **Privately Held**
SIC: 3861 Photographic equipment & supplies

(G-9336)
TE SIGNS AND SHIP LLC
810 Taylor St (44035-6232)
PHONE...................................440 281-9340
Pamela Melia,
EMP: 5
SALES (est): 267.1K **Privately Held**
SIC: 3993 7389 Letters for signs, metal;

(G-9337)
TEZ TOOL & FABRICATION INC
115 Buckeye St (44035-5216)
PHONE...................................440 323-2300
Matt Tezmer, *President*
EMP: 5
SQ FT: 4,900
SALES (est): 553.6K **Privately Held**
SIC: 3089 Injection molded finished plastic products

(G-9338)
THE RELIABLE SPRING WIRE FRMS
300 Abbe Rd S (44035-6276)
P.O. Box 58 (44036-0058)
PHONE...................................440 365-7400
Richard McBride, *President*
Sybil McBride, *Admin Sec*
EMP: 41 EST: 1937
SQ FT: 34,000
SALES (est): 9.3MM **Privately Held**
WEB: www.reliablespring.com
SIC: 3469 3495 Metal stampings; mechanical springs, precision

(G-9339)
TTR MANUFACTURING
740 Sugar Ln (44035-6312)
PHONE...................................440 366-5005
EMP: 3 EST: 2010
SALES (est): 297.1K **Privately Held**
SIC: 3999 Manufacturing industries

(G-9340)
ULTRA MACHINE INC
Also Called: Silver Machine Co
530 Lowell St (44035-4862)
PHONE...................................440 323-7632
Thomas C Guignette, *President*
EMP: 7
SQ FT: 2,500
SALES (est): 662.2K **Privately Held**
WEB: www.ultramachine.com
SIC: 3599 Machine shop, jobbing & repair

(G-9341)
UNITED INITIATORS INC (HQ)
555 Garden St (44035-4870)
PHONE...................................440 326-2416
Ed Hoozemans, *CEO*
William Clements, *Vice Pres*
Joe Ault, *Plant Mgr*
Paul Caldwell, *Plant Mgr*
Mark Mroz, *Plant Mgr*
◆ **EMP:** 63
SQ FT: 40,000
SALES (est): 70.1MM
SALES (corp-wide): 225.1MM **Privately Held**
SIC: 2819 2869 Catalysts, chemical; industrial organic chemicals
PA: United Initiators Gmbh
Dr.-Gustav-Adolph-Str. 3
Pullach I. Isartal 82049
897 442-20

(G-9342)
US MACHINE PRCSION GRNDING LLC
880 Taylor St (44035-6232)
PHONE...................................440 284-0711
Arrie Pritchard,
Leonard Miller,
EMP: 4
SALES: 850K **Privately Held**
SIC: 3599 Machine shop, jobbing & repair

(G-9343)
VECTRON INC
201 Perry Ct (44035-6149)
PHONE...................................440 323-3369
Robert Pustay, *President*
EMP: 100 EST: 1972
SQ FT: 48,000
SALES (est): 11.3MM **Privately Held**
SIC: 3599 3471 Machine shop, jobbing & repair; plating & polishing

(G-9344)
VTD SYSTEMS INC
7600 W River Rd S (44035-6934)
PHONE...................................440 323-4122
Robert Vilagi Jr, *President*
EMP: 20
SQ FT: 5,100
SALES (est): 3.5MM **Privately Held**
WEB: www.vtdsystems.com
SIC: 3599 Machine shop, jobbing & repair

(G-9345)
WAYNE PAK LTD
Also Called: Creative Packaging Concepts
214 Brace Ave (44035-2662)
PHONE...................................440 323-8744
Ron Young,
Diane Butler,
EMP: 15
SQ FT: 22,000
SALES (est): 2.5MM **Privately Held**
SIC: 3089 Plastic containers, except foam

(G-9346)
WESTVIEW CONCRETE CORP
Also Called: Avon Concrete
40105 Butternut Ridge Rd (44035-7903)
PHONE...................................440 458-5800
John Walls, *Vice Pres*
EMP: 20
SQ FT: 1,202
SALES (corp-wide): 8.9MM **Privately Held**
SIC: 3273 5211 Ready-mixed concrete; masonry materials & supplies
PA: Westview Concrete Corp.
26000 Sprague Rd
Olmsted Falls OH 44138
440 235-1800

(G-9347)
WOOSTER BRUSH COMPANY
870 Infirmary Rd (44035-4899)
PHONE...................................440 322-8081
Rick Dice, *Branch Mgr*
EMP: 6
SALES (corp-wide): 154.5MM **Privately Held**
SIC: 3991 Paint & varnish brushes
PA: The Wooster Brush Company
604 Madison Ave
Wooster OH 44691
330 264-4440

(G-9348)
ZAYTRAN CORPORATION
41535 Schadden Rd (44035-2226)
P.O. Box 1660 (44036-1660)
PHONE...................................440 324-2814
Theodore Zajac Jr, *President*
J C Wm Tattersall, *Principal*
Theodore Zajac Sr, *Chairman*
Chris Muehlheim, *Vice Pres*
Jerry Williams, *Plant Mgr*
EMP: 42
SQ FT: 80,000
SALES (est): 9.7MM **Privately Held**
WEB: www.zaytran.com
SIC: 3593 3492 Fluid power actuators, hydraulic or pneumatic; fluid power cylinders, hydraulic or pneumatic; fluid power valves & hose fittings

---

Englewood
Montgomery County

(G-9349)
AIMS-CMI TECHNOLOGY LLC
65 Haas Dr (45322-2842)
PHONE...................................937 832-2000
David A Delph, *President*
EMP: 17
SALES (est): 582.6K **Privately Held**
SIC: 3599 3544 Machine shop, jobbing & repair; special dies, tools, jigs & fixtures

(G-9350)
C&W SWISS INC
100 Lau Pkwy (45315-8787)
P.O. Box 65 (45315-0065)
PHONE...................................937 832-2889
Gregory Crabtree, *President*
Tammy Crabtree, *Vice Pres*
EMP: 18
SALES (est): 261.5K **Privately Held**
WEB: www.cwswiss.com
SIC: 3841 Surgical & medical instruments

(G-9351)
CECO MACHINE & TOOL
111 Quinter Farm Rd (45322-9705)
PHONE...................................937 264-3047
Steve Beck, *Owner*
Denis Beck, *Co-Owner*
EMP: 5
SQ FT: 5,000
SALES (est): 1MM **Privately Held**
SIC: 3599 Machine shop, jobbing & repair

(G-9352)
CREATIVE COUNTERTOPS OHIO LLC
477 E Wenger Rd (45322-2831)
PHONE...................................937 540-9450
Joe Kunk,
EMP: 10
SQ FT: 10,000
SALES: 1MM **Privately Held**
SIC: 3281 Granite, cut & shaped

(G-9353)
CREATIVE MICROSYSTEMS INC
Also Called: Civica CMI
52 Hillside Ct (45322-2745)
PHONE...................................937 836-4499
Lin Mallott, *CEO*
Missy Matherne, *Purchasing*
Arvind Kohli, *Finance*
David Swigart, *Finance*
Becky Chestnut, *Human Resources*
EMP: 80 EST: 1979
SQ FT: 14,400
SALES (est): 13.2MM **Privately Held**
WEB: www.creativemicrosystems.com
SIC: 7373 7372 Systems integration services; prepackaged software

(G-9354)
DAYTON ARTIFICIAL LIMB CLINIC
700 Harco Dr (45315-8793)
PHONE...................................937 836-1464
Tracy Slemker, *Owner*
EMP: 4
SALES: 950K **Privately Held**
WEB: www.dalconline.com
SIC: 3842 Surgical appliances & supplies

(G-9355)
DISPLAY DYNAMICS INC
1 Display Point Dr (45315-8857)
P.O. Box 27, Clayton (45315-0027)
PHONE...................................937 832-2830
Veit Von Parker, *President*
Jacqueline Parker, *General Mgr*
David Wells, *Prdtn Mgr*
EMP: 15
SQ FT: 40,000
SALES (est): 2MM **Privately Held**
WEB: www.disdyn.com
SIC: 7389 2541 7319 1751 Exhibit construction by industrial contractors; store fixtures, wood; display advertising service; cabinet & finish carpentry; partitions & fixtures, except wood; millwork

(G-9356)
DRIVEN INNOVATIONS LLC
140 Harrisburg Dr (45322-2836)
PHONE...................................330 818-7681
William Royer,
Martin Vance,
EMP: 6
SQ FT: 11,000
SALES (est): 308.8K **Privately Held**
SIC: 3634 Electric housewares & fans

(G-9357)
EATON COMPRSR FABRICATION INC
Also Called: Polar Air
1000 Cass Dr (45315-8844)
PHONE...................................877 283-7614
Matt Cain, *President*
◆ **EMP:** 25
SQ FT: 50,000
SALES (est): 10MM **Privately Held**
SIC: 3563 Air & gas compressors

(G-9358)
ETI TECH LLC
75 Holiday Dr (45322-2706)
PHONE...................................937 832-4200
Bill McLendon, *President*
Leonard Williams, *Project Engr*
Jeff Hartman, *CFO*
EMP: 13
SQ FT: 23,000

Englewood - Montgomery County (G-9359)

SALES (est): 3.5MM
SALES (corp-wide): 911.5K Privately Held
WEB: www.engineticstech.com
SIC: 3812 3679 8711 3629 Search & navigation equipment; electronic circuits; engineering services; electronic generation equipment; machine shop, jobbing & repair; aircraft parts & equipment
PA: Eti Mission Controls, Llc
 75 Holiday Dr
 Englewood OH 45322
 937 832-4200

(G-9359)
FRYES SOCCER SHOPPE
709 Taywood Rd (45322-1822)
PHONE..................................937 832-2230
Don Frye, *Owner*
EMP: 5
SQ FT: 2,400
SALES (est): 440.3K Privately Held
WEB: www.fryesoccer.com
SIC: 5941 2261 Soccer supplies; screen printing of cotton broadwoven fabrics

(G-9360)
GALACTIC PRECISION MFG LLC
345 Huls Dr (45315-8983)
PHONE..................................937 540-1800
Roger Mears,
Sivaram Gogineni,
Urmila Nath,
EMP: 3
SALES (est): 321.6K Privately Held
SIC: 3599 Crankshafts & camshafts, machining

(G-9361)
HART & COOLEY INC
1 Lau Pkwy (45315-8754)
PHONE..................................937 832-7800
Bob McDonald, *Branch Mgr*
EMP: 250 Privately Held
SIC: 3446 Registers (air), metal
HQ: Hart & Cooley, Inc.
 5030 Corp Exch Blvd Se
 Grand Rapids MI 49512
 616 656-8200

(G-9362)
HEMATITE INC
300 Lau Pkwy (45315-8826)
P.O. Box 249, Clayton (45315-0249)
PHONE..................................937 540-9889
John Charles Pavanel, *President*
EMP: 4
SALES (est): 307.6K
SALES (corp-wide): 72.7MM Privately Held
SIC: 3089 Automotive parts, plastic
PA: Pavaco Plastics Inc
 659 Speedvale Ave W
 Guelph ON N1K 1
 519 823-1383

(G-9363)
INNOVATIVE BUS CMPT SOLUTIONS
Also Called: I B C S
303 Shady Tree Ct (45315-9652)
PHONE..................................937 832-3969
Kent L Crabtree, *President*
EMP: 4
SQ FT: 2,400
SALES (est): 320K Privately Held
WEB: www.spasalon.com
SIC: 7372 Prepackaged software

(G-9364)
JACK A BYTE MLTMDIA GAMING LLC
Also Called: Jackabyte
893 S Main St 375 (45322-2814)
PHONE..................................937 321-1716
Sheri Yarbrough,
EMP: 5
SALES (est): 340.3K Privately Held
SIC: 7372 Home entertainment computer software

(G-9365)
KENT SWIGART
Also Called: Swigart Electric
301 W Wenger Rd (45322-1829)
PHONE..................................937 836-5292
Kent Swigart, *Owner*
Nevin E Swigart Sr, *Owner*
EMP: 3
SALES (est): 458.2K Privately Held
SIC: 7694 1799 3599 Electric motor repair; welding on site; machine shop, jobbing & repair

(G-9366)
KING KOLD INC
331 N Main St (45322-1333)
PHONE..................................937 836-2731
Douglas Smith, *President*
Robert L Smith, *Corp Secy*
EMP: 25
SQ FT: 5,210
SALES (est): 2.4MM Privately Held
SIC: 2038 2013 2011 5142 Frozen specialties; cooked meats from purchased meat; meat packing plants; fish, frozen: packaged

(G-9367)
LITEFLEX LLC (PA)
100 Holiday Dr (45322-2707)
P.O. Box 69 (45322-0069)
PHONE..................................937 836-7025
John Prikkel III, *President*
James Dean, *General Mgr*
Daniel Chien, *Vice Pres*
Ray Blatz, *CFO*
Jean Davis, *Chief Acct*
▲ EMP: 30
SQ FT: 70,000
SALES (est): 16.9MM Privately Held
SIC: 3493 Leaf springs: automobile, locomotive, etc.

(G-9368)
METRO TOOL & DIE CO INC
11974 Putnam Rd (45322-9721)
PHONE..................................937 836-8242
Michael Black, *CEO*
Karen Hergenrather, *Office Mgr*
EMP: 5 EST: 1959
SQ FT: 10,000
SALES: 500K Privately Held
SIC: 3544 Special dies & tools

(G-9369)
MIDWEST METROLOGY LLC
341 Smith Dr (45315-8705)
PHONE..................................937 832-0965
Bill Sierschula, *Mng Member*
EMP: 5 EST: 1999
SQ FT: 2,400
SALES (est): 462.7K Privately Held
WEB: www.midwest-metrology.com
SIC: 7699 3825 Industrial equipment services; test equipment for electronic & electric measurement

(G-9370)
NANOLAP TECHNOLOGIES LLC
85 Harrisburg Dr (45322-2835)
PHONE..................................877 658-4949
George Chang, *Mng Member*
EMP: 22
SQ FT: 19,000
SALES (est): 6MM Privately Held
SIC: 3291 Coated abrasive products

(G-9371)
NEWSPAPER SOLUTIONS LLC
116 Old Carriage Dr (45322-1168)
P.O. Box 398, Vandalia (45377-0398)
PHONE..................................937 694-9370
Douglas Gibson, *Mng Member*
EMP: 5
SALES: 25K Privately Held
SIC: 2711 Newspapers

(G-9372)
NISSIN PRECISION N AMER INC
375 Union Rd (45315-8802)
P.O. Box 399 (45322-0399)
PHONE..................................937 836-1910
Todd Shimizu, *President*
Kevin McCarthy, *General Mgr*
Mike Greer, *Vice Pres*
Cathy Sayer, *Vice Pres*
Akio Yamamoto, *Vice Pres*
▲ EMP: 80
SALES (est): 21.3MM
SALES (corp-wide): 88.4MM Privately Held
WEB: www.epinei.com
SIC: 3663 3444 Television broadcasting & communications equipment; sheet metalwork
PA: Nissin Kogyo Co.,Ltd.
 1-1-1, Tsukinowa
 Otsu SGA 520-2
 775 453-011

(G-9373)
PROSTHETIC DESIGN INC
Also Called: Pdi
700 Harco Dr (45315-8793)
PHONE..................................937 836-1464
Tracy Slemker, *President*
Don Mason, *Business Mgr*
▲ EMP: 4
SALES: 1.8MM Privately Held
WEB: www.prostheticdesign.com
SIC: 3842 5999 Limbs, artificial; orthopedic & prosthesis applications

(G-9374)
RATLIFF METAL SPINNING CO INC
40 Harrisburg Dr (45322-2834)
PHONE..................................937 836-3900
Michael K Ratliff, *President*
James D Ratliff, *Vice Pres*
Robin K Ratliff, *Treasurer*
EMP: 30
SQ FT: 40,000
SALES: 5.8MM Privately Held
WEB: www.ratliffmetal.com
SIC: 3469 Metal stampings

(G-9375)
SK TECH INC
200 Metro Dr (45315-8700)
PHONE..................................937 836-3535
Nobuyoshi Saigusa, *President*
Hideki Kawase, *President*
Hidki Kawase, *Principal*
Masatoshi Watanabe, *Vice Pres*
▲ EMP: 160
SQ FT: 48,000
SALES (est): 46.1MM Privately Held
SIC: 3694 Engine electrical equipment

(G-9376)
T K L LETTERING
300 W National Rd Ste C (45322-1442)
PHONE..................................937 832-2091
R Thomas Penny, *Owner*
EMP: 3
SALES (est): 139.1K Privately Held
SIC: 5941 5699 2759 Sporting goods & bicycle shops; sports apparel; screen printing

(G-9377)
TE-CO MANUFACTURING LLC
100 Quinter Farm Rd (45322-9705)
PHONE..................................937 836-0961
Tim Lindemuth, *Vice Pres*
Dan Parks, *Production*
Tyler Garland, *Purch Mgr*
Sam Lane, *Engineer*
Scott Johnston, *Regl Sales Mgr*
▲ EMP: 76 EST: 1926
SQ FT: 40,000
SALES (est): 14.6MM Privately Held
WEB: www.te-co.com
SIC: 3545 3829 3544 3429 Machine tool attachments & accessories; vises, machine (machine tool accessories); measuring & controlling devices; special dies, tools, jigs & fixtures; manufactured hardware (general); machine shop, jobbing & repair

(G-9378)
TOM SMITH INDUSTRIES INC
Also Called: T S I
500 Smith Dr (45315-8788)
PHONE..................................937 832-1555
Annette H Smith, *CEO*
Steven D Good, *President*
Steven Good, *President*
Tarra E Enochs, *Exec VP*
John A Shay, *Vice Pres*
▲ EMP: 130
SQ FT: 108,000
SALES (est): 40.1MM Privately Held
WEB: www.tomsmithindustries.com
SIC: 3544 3089 3714 Industrial molds; injection molded finished plastic products; motor vehicle parts & accessories

(G-9379)
TRIBUS INNOVATIONS LLC
Also Called: Tribus Enterprises
155 Haas Dr Englewood Oh (45322)
PHONE..................................509 992-4743
Kendell Bertagnole, *Mng Member*
Jay Byola, *Mng Member*
Tommy Mills, *Mng Member*
EMP: 4
SALES (est): 564.7K Privately Held
SIC: 3423 5084 Mechanics' hand tools; machine tools & metalworking machinery

(G-9380)
UNIFIED SCREENING & CRUSHING
Also Called: Ohio Wire Cloth
200 Cass Dr (45315-8834)
P.O. Box 280 (45322-0280)
PHONE..................................937 836-3201
Tom Lentsch, *President*
Devan Donalson, *Principal*
Michele Kleason, *Treasurer*
Dave Bozicevich, *Sales Staff*
James Georgantones, *Manager*
EMP: 6
SQ FT: 10,000
SALES (est): 900K
SALES (corp-wide): 15.6MM Privately Held
SIC: 3496 5082 7699 Wire cloth & woven wire products; mining machinery & equipment, except petroleum; welding equipment repair
PA: Unified Screening & Crushing - Mn, Inc.
 3350 Highway 149
 Eagan MN 55121
 651 454-8835

(G-9381)
VALUE ADDED PACKAGING INC
44 Lau Pkwy (45315-8777)
PHONE..................................937 832-9595
Jarod D Wenrick, *President*
▲ EMP: 15
SQ FT: 20,000
SALES (est): 4.5MM Privately Held
WEB: www.4vapack.com
SIC: 2653 Boxes, corrugated: made from purchased materials

(G-9382)
VANTAGE SPECIALTY INGREDIENTS
707 Harco Dr (45315-8854)
PHONE..................................937 264-1222
Louis Frischling, *President*
Patrick Bruegeman, *President*
Stephen Greenberg PHD, *Vice Pres*
Scott Hawkins, *Director*
▲ EMP: 24
SALES: 4.5MM Privately Held
WEB: www.lipotechnologies.com
SIC: 2869 Industrial organic chemicals

(G-9383)
WAGONER STORES INC (PA)
Also Called: Wagoners Red Wing Shs Fabrics
324 Union Blvd (45322-2115)
PHONE..................................937 836-3636
Carl Wagoner, *President*
Hazel Wagoner, *Vice Pres*
▲ EMP: 4
SQ FT: 4,000
SALES (est): 1.3MM Privately Held
SIC: 5331 5311 5661 2326 Variety Store Specializing In Men's And Boys Clothing Shoes Work Clothing Sewing Needlework And Manufacturer Of Hats

---

Enon
Clark County

(G-9384)
HARDWOOD STORE INC
340 Enon Rd (45323-1004)
PHONE..................................937 864-2899

John B Clark, *President*
Lisa L Clark, *Vice Pres*
Eric Shoopman, *Opers Mgr*
Cheryl Lewis, *Director*
EMP: 6
SQ FT: 16,000
SALES (est): 719.6K **Privately Held**
WEB: www.thelumberstore.com
SIC: 2499 5211 Decorative wood & woodwork; lumber products

(G-9385)
PROMAC INC
350 Conley Dr (45323-1002)
P.O. Box 158 (45323-0158)
PHONE..............................937 864-1961
Russell Foster, *President*
EMP: 25 EST: 1971
SQ FT: 22,000
SALES (est): 3.5MM **Privately Held**
SIC: 3599 3544 Machine shop, jobbing & repair; special dies, tools, jigs & fixtures

(G-9386)
SEEPEX INC
511 Speedway Dr (45323-1057)
P.O. Box 951454, Cleveland (44193-0016)
PHONE..............................937 864-7150
Mike Dillon, *President*
Euro Colombo, *President*
Daniel Lakovic, *President*
Ulrich Seeberger, *Managing Dir*
Tim Houseman, *Plant Supt*
◆ **EMP:** 115
SQ FT: 35,000
SALES (est): 37.6MM
SALES (corp-wide): 141.8MM **Privately Held**
WEB: www.seepex.com
SIC: 3586 3561 Measuring & dispensing pumps; pumps & pumping equipment
PA: Seepex Gmbh
   Scharnholzstr. 344
   Bottrop 46240
   204 199-60

(G-9387)
SPEEDWAY LLC (HQ)
500 Speedway Dr (45323-1056)
P.O. Box 1500, Springfield (45501-1500)
PHONE..............................937 864-3000
Anthony R Kenney, *President*
John Abbott, *General Mgr*
Jessy Box, *General Mgr*
Kyle Everett, *General Mgr*
Sasha Martin, *General Mgr*
EMP: 742
SALES (est): 3B **Publicly Held**
WEB: www.speedwaynet.net
SIC: 5411 5541 2869 Convenience stores, chain; filling stations, gasoline; fuels

Etna
Franklin County

(G-9388)
ALICE BEOUGHER
Also Called: Wagram
13255 National Rd Sw (43068-3396)
PHONE..............................740 927-2470
Alice Beougher, *Owner*
EMP: 3
SALES (est): 222.4K **Privately Held**
WEB: www.wagram.com
SIC: 3942 Miniature dolls, collectors'

(G-9389)
TERRY A JOHNSON
15094 Palmer Rd Sw (43068-3326)
PHONE..............................614 561-0706
Terry A Johnson, *Principal*
EMP: 5 EST: 2010
SALES (est): 270K **Privately Held**
SIC: 2048 Prepared feeds

(G-9390)
WAIBEL ELECTRIC CO INC
133 Humphries Dr (43068-6801)
PHONE..............................740 964-2956
Carl H Waibel Jr, *President*
Sherry Waibel, *Corp Secy*
EMP: 16
SQ FT: 5,200
SALES: 1MM **Privately Held**
WEB: www.waibelelectric.com
SIC: 1731 3621 General electrical contractor; motors & generators

Etna
Licking County

(G-9391)
AN BAICEIR BAKERY
116 Reader Ct (43062-9800)
PHONE..............................740 739-0501
Katrina Sheily, *Owner*
EMP: 9
SALES (est): 24K **Privately Held**
SIC: 2051 Bread, cake & related products

(G-9392)
BEST LIGHTING PRODUCTS INC (HQ)
1213 Etna Pkwy (43062-8041)
PHONE..............................740 964-0063
Jeffrey S Katz, *CEO*
George Jue, *President*
▲ **EMP:** 55 EST: 1997
SQ FT: 60,000
SALES (est): 12.5MM
SALES (corp-wide): 284.4MM **Privately Held**
WEB: www.bestlighting.net
SIC: 3646 5063 Commercial indusl & institutional electric lighting fixtures; electrical apparatus & equipment
PA: Corinthian Capital Group, Llc
   601 Lexington Ave Rm 5901
   New York NY 10022
   212 920-2300

(G-9393)
GUADALUPE PUBLISHING INC
60 Dellenbaugh Loop (43062-9642)
PHONE..............................614 450-2474
William Taylor, *Principal*
EMP: 3
SALES (est): 197.3K **Privately Held**
SIC: 2741 Miscellaneous publishing

(G-9394)
JELD-WEN INC
Also Called: Jeld-Wen Millwork Masters
91 Heritage Dr (43062-9805)
PHONE..............................740 964-1431
Scott Farrington, *Branch Mgr*
EMP: 136 **Publicly Held**
SIC: 2431 Doors, wood
HQ: Jeld-Wen, Inc.
   2645 Silver Crescent Dr
   Charlotte NC 28273
   800 535-3936

(G-9395)
JOULES ANGSTROM UV PRINTING (PA)
104 Heritage Dr (43062-8042)
PHONE..............................740 964-9113
Patrick T Carlisle, *President*
Jerry Duclos, *Marketing Staff*
Rick Klonowski, *Technical Staff*
Norris Duncan, *Shareholder*
Richard Klonowski, *Shareholder*
EMP: 24
SQ FT: 30,000
SALES (est): 7.7MM **Privately Held**
SIC: 2899 Chemical preparations

(G-9396)
LESS COST LIGHTING INC
1213 Etna Pkwy (43062-8041)
P.O. Box 394 (43018-0394)
PHONE..............................866 633-6883
Michael Katz, *President*
Dale McCain, *President*
Steve Smithson, *Sales Mgr*
EMP: 15
SALES (est): 1.6MM **Privately Held**
SIC: 3646 Commercial indusl & institutional electric lighting fixtures

(G-9397)
REX BURNETT
26 1st Ave Sw (43062-9441)
PHONE..............................740 927-4669
Rex Burnett, *Owner*
EMP: 3
SALES (est): 241.5K **Privately Held**
SIC: 3444 Awnings & canopies

(G-9398)
RIDGE CORPORATION
1201 Etna Pkwy (43062-8041)
PHONE..............................614 421-7434
Gary A Grandominico,
▲ **EMP:** 100
SALES (est): 23.8MM **Privately Held**
SIC: 3443 Liners/lining

(G-9399)
SCARRED HANDS WOOD CREATIONS
8484 Hazelton Etna Rd Sw (43062-9491)
PHONE..............................740 975-2835
Erik Rennie, *Administration*
EMP: 4
SALES (est): 217.5K **Privately Held**
SIC: 2431 Millwork

Euclid
Cuyahoga County

(G-9400)
ADVANCED EQUIPMENT SYSTEMS LLC
22800 Lakeland Blvd (44132-2606)
PHONE..............................216 289-6505
Frederic W Starr, *President*
EMP: 8
SQ FT: 65,000
SALES (est): 1.5MM **Privately Held**
SIC: 3535 Conveyors & conveying equipment

(G-9401)
AMD PLASTICS LLC (PA)
27600 Lakeland Blvd (44132-2152)
PHONE..............................216 289-4862
Brian Coll, *President*
▲ **EMP:** 19
SQ FT: 50,000
SALES (est): 4MM **Privately Held**
WEB: www.amdnet.com
SIC: 3089 Thermoformed finished plastic products

(G-9402)
AMERICAN METAL STAMPING CO LLC
20900 Saint Clair Ave (44117-1040)
PHONE..............................216 531-3100
Diane Rodgers, *CFO*
EMP: 17
SALES (est): 5.1MM **Privately Held**
SIC: 3441 Fabricated structural metal

(G-9403)
AMERICAN PUNCH CO INC
1655 Century Corners Pkwy (44132-3321)
PHONE..............................216 731-4501
Robert Olson, *President*
Larry Kern, *Opers Mgr*
Charles William Olson, *Controller*
Jovan Vucenovic, *VP Sales*
Paul Cassidy, *Sales Engr*
EMP: 21
SQ FT: 12,000
SALES (est): 4.1MM **Privately Held**
WEB: www.americanpunchco.com
SIC: 3599 3544 3421 Machine shop, jobbing & repair; special dies, tools, jigs & fixtures; cutlery

(G-9404)
BEAR CABINETRY LLC
23560 Lakeland Blvd (44132-2613)
PHONE..............................216 481-9282
Marsha Siha,
EMP: 6
SALES (est): 843.1K **Privately Held**
SIC: 2434 Wood kitchen cabinets

(G-9405)
BIC MANUFACTURING INC
Also Called: A-D Machine
26420 Cntury Corners Pkwy (44132-3310)
PHONE..............................216 531-9393
David D Carr, *President*

Gene Schein, *General Mgr*
Tom Levicky, *CFO*
EMP: 45
SQ FT: 42,000
SALES (est): 7.4MM **Privately Held**
SIC: 3599 Machine shop, jobbing & repair

(G-9406)
CALIFORNIA CERAMIC SUPPLY CO
Also Called: R Molds
19451 Roseland Ave Ste A (44117-1324)
PHONE..............................216 531-9185
Fax: 216 531-0070
EMP: 6 EST: 1950
SQ FT: 12,000
SALES (est): 380K **Privately Held**
SIC: 5945 3544 3275 Ret Hobbies/Toys/Games Mfg Dies/Tools/Jigs/Fixtures Mfg Gypsum Products

(G-9407)
CARE CABINETRY INC
1410 Chardon Rd Frnt (44117-1543)
PHONE..............................216 481-7445
Zolton Michal, *Vice Pres*
Michal Zolton, *Treasurer*
EMP: 5
SQ FT: 7,000
SALES (est): 480K **Privately Held**
SIC: 2434 Wood kitchen cabinets

(G-9408)
CENTER LINE MACHINING LLC
25700 Lakeland Blvd (44132-2635)
PHONE..............................216 289-6828
Marin Grman, *Mng Member*
Tusan Grman, *Mng Member*
EMP: 4
SALES: 700K **Privately Held**
SIC: 3541 Machine tool replacement & repair parts, metal cutting types

(G-9409)
CLEVELAND PLASTIC FABRICAT
25861 Tungsten Rd (44132-2817)
PHONE..............................216 797-7300
Mitchell Opalich, *President*
Lorraine Simer, *Vice Pres*
John Harrel, *Sales Staff*
EMP: 18
SQ FT: 21,500
SALES (est): 1.6MM **Privately Held**
WEB: www.clevelandplastic.com
SIC: 3599 3498 3561 3089 Machine shop, jobbing & repair; tube fabricating (contract bending & shaping); pumps & pumping equipment; fittings for pipe, plastic; industrial supplies; industrial fittings; pipes & fittings, plastic

(G-9410)
DETROIT FLAME HARDENING CO
Also Called: Cleveland Flame Hardening
24951 Tungsten Rd (44117-1237)
PHONE..............................216 531-4273
Greg Bybee, *General Mgr*
EMP: 5
SQ FT: 7,000
SALES (corp-wide): 2.9MM **Privately Held**
WEB: www.detroitflame.com
SIC: 3398 Metal heat treating
PA: Detroit Flame Hardening Company Inc
   17644 Mount Elliott St
   Detroit MI
   313 891-2936

(G-9411)
E D M SERVICES INC
21724 Saint Clair Ave (44117-1026)
PHONE..............................216 486-2068
Clifford Griffin, *President*
Nancy Griffin, *Corp Secy*
▲ **EMP:** 3
SQ FT: 4,400
SALES (est): 300.7K **Privately Held**
SIC: 3599 3544 Electrical discharge machining (EDM); special dies, tools, jigs & fixtures

Euclid - Cuyahoga County (G-9412)

(G-9412)
EAGLEHEAD MANUFACTURING CO
Also Called: Dejak Machine Tool Company
23555 Euclid Ave (44117-1703)
PHONE.................................216 692-1240
Harris Phillips, *CEO*
Ray Westfall, *President*
C Roger Cotman, *Shareholder*
EMP: 28
SQ FT: 25,000
SALES (est): 3.3MM **Privately Held**
SIC: 3965 Fasteners

(G-9413)
EUCLID HEAT TREATING CO
Also Called: E H T Company
1408 E 222nd St (44117-1108)
PHONE.................................216 481-8444
John H Vanas, *President*
Dan Lipnicki, *Vice Pres*
EMP: 55 **EST:** 1946
SQ FT: 45,000
SALES (est): 14MM **Privately Held**
WEB: www.euclidheattreating.com
SIC: 3398 1711 Metal heat treating; plumbing, heating, air-conditioning contractors

(G-9414)
GLOBAL GLASS BLOCK INC
23570 Lakeland Blvd (44132-2613)
PHONE.................................216 731-2333
Anthony Lacorte, *President*
▲ **EMP:** 8
SALES (est): 798K **Privately Held**
SIC: 3229 5039 Blocks & bricks, glass; glass construction materials

(G-9415)
GUARDIAN TECHNOLOGIES LLC
Also Called: GERM GUARDIAN
26251 Bluestone Blvd # 7 (44132-2826)
PHONE.................................216 706-2250
David Brickner, *Mng Member*
Richard Farone,
◆ **EMP:** 41
SQ FT: 72,000
SALES: 60.6MM **Privately Held**
WEB: www.guardiantechnologies.com
SIC: 3564 3585 Air purification equipment; humidifiers & dehumidifiers

(G-9416)
H & W TOOL CO
1363 Chardon Rd Ste 3 (44117-1558)
PHONE.................................216 795-5520
EMP: 3
SALES (est): 339.8K **Privately Held**
SIC: 3599 Machine shop, jobbing & repair

(G-9417)
H C STARCK INC
1250 E 222nd St (44117-1114)
PHONE.................................216 692-6990
Richard M Corry, *CEO*
EMP: 12
SALES (corp-wide): 354.1K **Privately Held**
SIC: 3339 Primary nonferrous metals
HQ: H. C. Starck Inc.
   45 Industrial Pl
   Newton MA 02461
   617 630-5800

(G-9418)
H C STARCK INC
21801 Tungsten Rd (44117-1117)
PHONE.................................216 692-3990
Greg Fuller, *Director*
EMP: 300
SALES (corp-wide): 354.1K **Privately Held**
WEB: www.hcstarck.com
SIC: 3356 3313 3339 Tungsten, basic shapes; molybdenum silicon, not made in blast furnaces; rhenium refining (primary)
HQ: H. C. Starck Inc.
   45 Industrial Pl
   Newton MA 02461
   617 630-5800

(G-9419)
HACIENDA PUBLICATIONS LLC
20970 Wilmore Ave (44123-2818)
PHONE.................................216 202-5440
Robin Boyd,
EMP: 3
SALES (est): 102.6K **Privately Held**
SIC: 2721 Periodicals: publishing & printing

(G-9420)
HOLISTIC MEASURES
26241 Lake Shore Blvd (44132-1177)
PHONE.................................216 261-0329
Patricia Carlisle, *Principal*
EMP: 4
SALES (est): 280.8K **Privately Held**
SIC: 2741 Miscellaneous publishing

(G-9421)
J W HARRIS CO INC
Also Called: Harris Products Group, The
22801 Saint Clair Ave (44117-2524)
PHONE.................................216 481-8100
David Nangle, *President*
Tom Tsiominas, *Engineer*
Betty Peltier, *Sales Mgr*
Robert Tefft, *Manager*
Randy Weise, *Technical Staff*
▲ **EMP:** 12
SALES (est): 4.8MM
SALES (corp-wide): 3B **Publicly Held**
SIC: 5051 3398 Copper; brazing (hardening) of metal
HQ: J. W. Harris Co., Inc.
   4501 Quality Pl
   Mason OH 45040
   513 754-2000

(G-9422)
JBJ TECHNOLOGIES INC
185 E 280th St (44132-1306)
PHONE.................................216 469-7297
Michael Johnston, *Senior VP*
EMP: 11
SALES (est): 1.5MM **Privately Held**
SIC: 3599 Machine shop, jobbing & repair

(G-9423)
JSM EXPRESS INC
27301 Markbarry Ave (44132-2109)
PHONE.................................216 331-2008
Jasmin Sakalic, *CEO*
EMP: 3 **EST:** 2005
SALES (est): 320.8K **Privately Held**
SIC: 3715 Truck trailers

(G-9424)
LINCOLN ELECTRIC INTL HOLDG CO (HQ)
22801 Saint Clair Ave (44117-2524)
PHONE.................................216 481-8100
John Stropki, *Chairman*
William Macdonald, *Vice Chairman*
Bob Blackstock, *Business Mgr*
Chris Brodnick, *Production*
Diane Lang, *Purch Mgr*
▲ **EMP:** 22
SALES (est): 391.2MM
SALES (corp-wide): 3B **Publicly Held**
SIC: 3548 Welding apparatus
PA: Lincoln Electric Holdings, Inc.
   22801 Saint Clair Ave
   Cleveland OH 44117
   216 481-8100

(G-9425)
MART PLUS FUEL
21820 Lake Shore Blvd (44123-1707)
PHONE.................................216 261-0420
Anil Uppal, *Principal*
EMP: 3
SALES (est): 191.5K **Privately Held**
SIC: 2869 Fuels

(G-9426)
MECHANICAL DYNAMICS ANALIS LTD
Also Called: Renewal Parts Maintenance
1250 E 222nd St (44117-1114)
PHONE.................................440 946-0082
John L Vanderhoef, *CEO*
EMP: 21
SALES (corp-wide): 38.5B **Privately Held**
SIC: 7699 3568 3053 Industrial machinery & equipment repair; power transmission equipment; gaskets, packing & sealing devices
HQ: Mechanical Dynamics & Analysis Llc
   19 British American Blvd
   Latham NY 12110
   518 399-3616

(G-9427)
MESOCOAT INC
Also Called: Mesocoat Advanced Coating Tech
24112 Rockwell Dr (44117-1252)
PHONE.................................216 453-0866
Stephen Goss, *CEO*
▲ **EMP:** 18
SALES (est): 748.8K
SALES (corp-wide): 1MM **Privately Held**
SIC: 3479 1799 5169 7699 Coating of metals & formed products; coating, rust preventive; aluminum coating of metal products; corrosion control installation; anti-corrosion products; industrial equipment services; industrial equipment cleaning
PA: Abakan Inc
   2665 S Byshr Dr Ste 450
   Miami FL 33133
   786 206-5368

(G-9428)
MULLIN PRINT SOLUTIONS
84 E 197th St (44119-1002)
PHONE.................................216 383-2901
Kevin Mullin, *Principal*
EMP: 3
SALES (est): 314K **Privately Held**
SIC: 2752 Commercial printing, lithographic

(G-9429)
NORMAN NOBLE INC
931 E 228th St (44123-3201)
PHONE.................................216 851-4007
Lawrence Noble, *President*
EMP: 50
SALES (corp-wide): 125.3MM **Privately Held**
SIC: 3841 Instruments, microsurgical: except electromedical
PA: Norman Noble, Inc.
   5507 Avion Park Dr
   Highland Heights OH 44143
   216 761-5387

(G-9430)
NORTH AMERICAN PLAS CHEM INC (PA)
Also Called: Noramco
1400 E 222nd St (44117-1108)
PHONE.................................216 531-3400
James Popela, *President*
EMP: 100
SQ FT: 25,000
SALES (est): 37.5MM **Privately Held**
WEB: www.nap-bag.com
SIC: 2673 2671 Plastic & pliofilm bags; packaging paper & plastics film, coated & laminated

(G-9431)
ORTHOTIC AND PROSTETIC SPC
20650 Lakeland Blvd (44119-3241)
PHONE.................................216 531-2773
Richard Gaudio, *President*
Tom Heckman, *Vice Pres*
Jeff Gerl, *Admin Sec*
EMP: 15 **EST:** 1972
SQ FT: 7,200
SALES (est): 1.3MM **Privately Held**
SIC: 3842 Orthopedic appliances; braces, elastic; splints, pneumatic & wood

(G-9432)
PARK-HIO FRGED MCHNED PDTS LLC
23000 Euclid Ave (44117-1729)
PHONE.................................216 692-7200
EMP: 11
SALES (est): 165.4K
SALES (corp-wide): 1.6B **Publicly Held**
SIC: 3291 Abrasive products
PA: Park-Ohio Holdings Corp.
   6065 Parkland Blvd Ste 1
   Cleveland OH 44124
   440 947-2000

(G-9433)
PIKE MACHINE PRODUCTS CO
23460 Lakeland Blvd (44132-2699)
PHONE.................................216 731-1880
Louis D Pike, *President*
Barbara Pike, *Vice Pres*
EMP: 30 **EST:** 1943
SQ FT: 10,000
SALES: 1MM **Privately Held**
SIC: 3599 3645 3451 3398 Machine shop, jobbing & repair; residential lighting fixtures; screw machine products; metal heat treating

(G-9434)
POWDERMET INC (PA)
24112 Rockwell Dr (44117-1252)
PHONE.................................216 404-0053
Andrew Sherman, *President*
Gabriel Santillan, *Engineer*
Ronald Nicholson, *Accounting Mgr*
Tammy Damico, *Human Res Mgr*
Haixiong Tang, *Marketing Staff*
EMP: 47
SQ FT: 7,800
SALES: 1.5MM **Privately Held**
WEB: www.powdermetinc.com
SIC: 3399 Powder, metal

(G-9435)
POWDERMET POWDER PRODUCTION
24112 Rockwell Dr Ste D (44117-1252)
PHONE.................................216 404-0053
Andrew Sherman, *CEO*
EMP: 10
SALES (est): 834.4K **Privately Held**
SIC: 3821 Crushing & grinding apparatus, laboratory

(G-9436)
PPG INDUSTRIES OHIO INC
Also Called: Pretreatment & Specialty Pdts
23000 Saint Clair Ave (44117-2503)
PHONE.................................216 486-5300
Jim Driddy, *Principal*
EMP: 66
SALES (corp-wide): 15.3B **Publicly Held**
WEB: www.ppgglass.com
SIC: 2851 Paints & allied products
HQ: Ppg Industries Ohio, Inc.
   3800 W 143rd St
   Cleveland OH 44111
   216 671-0050

(G-9437)
PRECISION HYDRAULIC CONNECTORS
Also Called: PHC Divison Bic Manufacturing
26420 Cntury Corners Pkwy (44132-3310)
PHONE.................................440 953-3778
Patrick De Capua, *President*
EMP: 15
SQ FT: 12,000
SALES (est): 1MM **Privately Held**
SIC: 3599 Machine & other job shop work

(G-9438)
R & A SPORTS INC
Also Called: Adler Team Sports
23780 Lakeland Blvd (44132-2615)
PHONE.................................216 289-2254
John Domo, *President*
Richard Domo, *Vice Pres*
Ruth Ann Domo, *Admin Sec*
EMP: 25
SQ FT: 16,000
SALES: 3.9MM **Privately Held**
SIC: 5091 5136 5137 2396 Sporting & recreation goods; sportswear, men's & boys'; sportswear, women's & children's; screen printing on fabric articles

(G-9439)
RALPHIE GIANNI MFG & CO
250 E 271st St (44132-1606)
PHONE.................................216 507-3873
Deshawn Massey Jr,
EMP: 10
SALES (est): 331.8K **Privately Held**
SIC: 2389 Apparel & accessories

GEOGRAPHIC SECTION

Fairborn - Greene County (G-9466)

(G-9440)
RISHER & CO
27011 Tungsten Rd (44132-2990)
PHONE..................................216 732-8351
William J Risher, *President*
Josh Mann, *Regional Mgr*
Brandon Plumlee, *Sales Mgr*
Jo Ann McNaughgon, *Manager*
EMP: 18 **EST:** 1942
SQ FT: 27,000
SALES (est): 2.8MM **Privately Held**
SIC: 3599 Machine shop, jobbing & repair

(G-9441)
S C INDUSTRIES INC
24460 Lakeland Blvd (44132-2622)
P.O. Box 32307 (44132-0307)
PHONE..................................216 732-9000
Earl Lauridsen, *President*
Gayle Wakefield, *Office Mgr*
▲ **EMP:** 20
SQ FT: 10,000
SALES (est): 5MM **Privately Held**
SIC: 3366 7389 Bushings & bearings; grinding, precision: commercial or industrial

(G-9442)
SCHWEBEL BAKING COMPANY
Also Called: Mill Brook
345 E 200th St (44119-1157)
PHONE..................................216 481-1880
Ray Paworwlski, *Manager*
EMP: 20
SALES (corp-wide): 170MM **Privately Held**
WEB: www.schwebels.com
SIC: 2051 Bread, cake & related products
PA: Schwebel Baking Company
965 E Midlothian Blvd
Youngstown OH 44502
330 783-2860

(G-9443)
SEME & SON AUTOMOTIVE INC
1320 E 260th St (44132-2816)
PHONE..................................216 261-0066
Frank Seme, *President*
Julie Seme, *Manager*
EMP: 4
SQ FT: 15,940
SALES (est): 594.6K **Privately Held**
WEB: www.seme-now.com
SIC: 3599 7538 Machine shop, jobbing & repair; engine rebuilding: automotive

(G-9444)
SUNSET INDUSTRIES INC
1272 E 286th St (44132-2191)
PHONE..................................216 731-8131
Ivan Hauptman, *President*
Peter Hauptman, *Vice Pres*
Clem Hren, *Vice Pres*
Rudy Hren, *Treasurer*
Frank Hren, *Shareholder*
EMP: 28
SQ FT: 14,500
SALES (est): 5.2MM **Privately Held**
WEB: www.sunsetindustries.com
SIC: 3599 3812 3594 Machine shop, jobbing & repair; search & navigation equipment; fluid power pumps & motors

(G-9445)
TECH-MED INC
Also Called: Shaker Numeric Mfg
1080 E 222nd St (44117-1101)
PHONE..................................216 486-0900
Gary White, *President*
Carty White, *Admin Sec*
EMP: 15 **EST:** 1953
SQ FT: 10,000
SALES (est): 2.6MM **Privately Held**
WEB: www.shakernumeric.com
SIC: 3469 Machine parts, stamped or pressed metal

(G-9446)
TECHALLOY INC
22801 Saint Clair Ave (44117-2524)
PHONE..................................216 481-8100
George Blankenship, *President*
Henry Lopes, *Vice Pres*
Richard Perlick, *Vice Pres*
Carl Reed, *Vice Pres*
Kurt Slacik, *Vice Pres*
▲ **EMP:** 50
SALES (est): 5.6MM
SALES (corp-wide): 3B **Publicly Held**
SIC: 3548 Welding wire, bare & coated
PA: Lincoln Electric Holdings, Inc.
22801 Saint Clair Ave
Cleveland OH 44117
216 481-8100

(G-9447)
TERMINAL OPTICAL LAB
26215 Tungsten Rd (44132-2998)
PHONE..................................216 289-7722
Rick Milam, *Principal*
EMP: 3
SALES (est): 305.5K **Privately Held**
SIC: 3851 Ophthalmic goods

(G-9448)
TRI COUNTY DOOR SERVICE INC
21701 Tungsten Rd (44117-1116)
PHONE..................................216 531-2245
Peter Look, *President*
Frank A Cigoy, *Vice Pres*
EMP: 11
SQ FT: 10,000
SALES (est): 1.9MM **Privately Held**
WEB: www.tricountydoor.com
SIC: 3442 1751 Garage doors, overhead: metal; carpentry work

(G-9449)
TRUST MANUFACTURING LLC
20080 Saint Clair Ave (44117-1015)
PHONE..................................216 531-8787
Paul S Novosel, *President*
Tim Corgan,
EMP: 15
SALES (est): 3.6MM **Privately Held**
SIC: 3429 Manufactured hardware (general)

Fairborn
Greene County

(G-9450)
ALI INDUSTRIES INC
Also Called: Abrasive Leaders & Innovators
747 E Xenia Dr (45324-8761)
PHONE..................................937 878-3946
Terry Ali, *President*
Christopher Ali, *Vice Pres*
Lee Kockentiet, *VP Finance*
Phillip Ali, *VP Sales*
◆ **EMP:** 200 **EST:** 1961
SQ FT: 260,360
SALES (est): 84.2MM **Privately Held**
WEB: www.gatorgrit.com
SIC: 3291 Abrasive products

(G-9451)
ALL SRVICE PLASTIC MOLDING INC
611 Yellw Spng Fairfld Rd (45324-9437)
PHONE..................................937 415-3674
Keller Phillip, *Branch Mgr*
EMP: 43
SALES (est): 2MM
SALES (corp-wide): 59.1MM **Privately Held**
SIC: 3089 Injection molding of plastics
PA: All Service Plastic Molding, Inc.
900 Fall Creek Dr
Vandalia OH 45377
937 890-0322

(G-9452)
BENS WELDING SERVICE INC
605 Middle St (45324-4828)
PHONE..................................937 878-4052
James Pile, *President*
Lisa Pile, *Admin Sec*
EMP: 4
SQ FT: 2,000
SALES (est): 350K **Privately Held**
SIC: 7692 7699 Welding repair; lawn mower repair shop

(G-9453)
BOEING COMPANY
2600 Paramount Pl Ste 400 (45324-6818)
PHONE..................................937 427-1767
Steve Teske, *Manager*
Gregory Hayes, *Post Master*
EMP: 15
SQ FT: 1,000
SALES (corp-wide): 101.1B **Publicly Held**
SIC: 3721 Aircraft
PA: The Boeing Company
100 N Riverside Plz
Chicago IL 60606
312 544-2000

(G-9454)
CEDAR CHEST
405 W Main St (45324-4816)
PHONE..................................937 878-9097
Bobby Jasoniski, *Owner*
EMP: 3
SALES (est): 189.5K **Privately Held**
SIC: 2499 Decorative wood & woodwork

(G-9455)
CEMEX USA INC
2600 Paramount Pl (45324-6819)
PHONE..................................937 879-8350
Don Clem, *Principal*
Gary Warner, *Supervisor*
EMP: 14 **EST:** 2010
SALES (est): 2.5MM **Privately Held**
SIC: 3273 Ready-mixed concrete

(G-9456)
CURTISS-WRIGHT CONTROLS
2600 Paramount Pl Ste 200 (45324-6816)
PHONE..................................937 252-5601
Cheryl Ullmer, *Buyer*
Boris Mikhaylenko, *Engineer*
Ron Taulton, *Branch Mgr*
Gorky Chin, *Manager*
Eric Freeman, *Info Tech Dir*
EMP: 50
SALES (corp-wide): 2.4B **Publicly Held**
SIC: 8711 8731 3769 3625 Consulting engineer; commercial physical research; guided missile & space vehicle parts & auxiliary equipment; relays & industrial controls
HQ: Curtiss-Wright Controls Electronic Systems, Inc.
28965 Avenue Penn
Santa Clarita CA 91355
661 702-1494

(G-9457)
DOMICONE PRINTING INC
854 Kauffman Ave (45324-3842)
P.O. Box 1 (45324-0001)
PHONE..................................937 878-3080
Fred Domicone, *President*
EMP: 5
SQ FT: 2,000
SALES: 600K **Privately Held**
WEB: www.domiconeprinting.com
SIC: 2752 7334 2759 Commercial printing, offset; photocopying & duplicating services; invitations: printing; announcements: engraved

(G-9458)
ERNST ENTERPRISES INC
Also Called: Valley Concrete Division
5325 Medway Rd (45324-9765)
PHONE..................................937 878-9378
John Macfee, *General Mgr*
EMP: 16
SALES (corp-wide): 227.2MM **Privately Held**
WEB: www.ernstconcrete.com
SIC: 3273 Ready-mixed concrete
PA: Ernst Enterprises, Inc.
3361 Successful Way
Dayton OH 45414
937 233-5555

(G-9459)
FOX LITE INC
8300 Dayton Rd (45324-5944)
PHONE..................................937 864-1966
Douglas Hoy, *President*
Mark Hopkins, *Vice Pres*
Walter Hoy, *Vice Pres*
Frank A Fox, *Comptroller*
▼ **EMP:** 30
SQ FT: 74,000
SALES (est): 6MM **Privately Held**
WEB: www.foxlite.com
SIC: 3089 Plastic hardware & building products; windows, plastic

(G-9460)
GLAWE MANUFACTURING CO INC
Also Called: Glawe Awnings
851 Zapata Dr (45324-5165)
PHONE..................................937 754-0064
L Vernon Schaefer, *President*
Thomas R Fridley, *Vice Pres*
Katherine Schaefer, *Vice Pres*
V Schaefer, *Vice Pres*
EMP: 20 **EST:** 1877
SQ FT: 20,500
SALES (est): 2.3MM **Privately Held**
WEB: www.glaweawnings.com
SIC: 2394 7359 Awnings, fabric: made from purchased materials; equipment rental & leasing

(G-9461)
HONEYWELL INTERNATIONAL INC
1232 Dytn Yllow Sprng Rd (45324-6360)
PHONE..................................937 754-4134
EMP: 60
SALES (corp-wide): 39B **Publicly Held**
SIC: 3822 3669 Mfg Environmntl Controls Mfg Communications Equip
PA: Honeywell International Inc.
101 Columbia Rd
Morristown NJ 07950
973 455-2000

(G-9462)
K & M HOME DEFENSE LLC
325 Wallace Dr (45324-5308)
PHONE..................................313 258-6142
Gregory Keith Alexander, *Owner*
EMP: 3
SALES (est): 161.4K **Privately Held**
SIC: 3812 Defense systems & equipment

(G-9463)
LASERLINC INC
777 Zapata Dr (45324-5160)
PHONE..................................937 318-2440
Dan Dixon, *President*
Kim Upton, *General Mgr*
Jeff Kohler, *Vice Pres*
Jack Weiss, *Vice Pres*
Paul Miller, *Finance*
▲ **EMP:** 20
SQ FT: 19,000
SALES (est): 5.3MM **Privately Held**
WEB: www.laserlinc.com
SIC: 3826 Analytical instruments

(G-9464)
NUVASIVE MANUFACTURING LLC
1 Herald Sq (45324-5153)
PHONE..................................937 343-0400
Antonio Marques, *Managing Dir*
Todd Tuckett, *Branch Mgr*
EMP: 26
SQ FT: 40,000
SALES (corp-wide): 1B **Publicly Held**
SIC: 3845 Ultrasonic scanning devices, medical
HQ: Nuvasive Manufacturing, Llc
7475 Lusk Blvd
San Diego CA 92121
858 909-1800

(G-9465)
P & B ELECTRIC
1835 Successful Dr (45324-9236)
PHONE..................................937 754-4695
Leonard Porter, *Principal*
EMP: 7
SALES (est): 1.1MM **Privately Held**
SIC: 3699 Electrical work

(G-9466)
RAPISCAN SYSTEMS HIGH ENERGY I
Also Called: Aracor
514 E Dytn Yllow Sprng Rd (45324-6432)
PHONE..................................937 879-4200
Robert Armistead, *President*
EMP: 4

Fairborn - Greene County (G-9467)   GEOGRAPHIC SECTION

SALES (corp-wide): 1B **Publicly Held**
WEB: www.aracor.com
SIC: 3845 Electromedical equipment
HQ: Rapiscan Systems High Energy Inspection Corporation
520 Almanor Ave
Sunnyvale CA 94085
408 733-7780

(G-9467)
REZAS ROAST LLC
Also Called: Roastery, The
611 Yellow Spgs (45324-9437)
P.O. Box 638, Yellow Springs (45387-0638)
PHONE.................................937 823-1193
Audria Ali-Maki, *Owner*
Audria Maki, *Mng Member*
EMP: 5
SQ FT: 2,000
SALES (est): 52.6K **Privately Held**
SIC: 2095 Roasted coffee

(G-9468)
STADCO INC
Also Called: Stadco Automatics
632 Yllow Sprng Frfeld Rd (45324)
PHONE.................................937 878-0911
Dennis C Trammell, *President*
Kenneth Wilson, *Vice Pres*
Jeffrey Lyon, *Director*
EMP: 45 EST: 1948
SQ FT: 42,000
SALES: 5.6MM **Privately Held**
WEB: www.stadcoautomatics.com
SIC: 3451 3541 Screw machine products; machine tools, metal cutting type

(G-9469)
STILLWRIGHTS DISTILLERY
5380 Intrastate Dr (45324-6159)
PHONE.................................937 879-4447
EMP: 4 EST: 2016
SALES (est): 240.2K **Privately Held**
SIC: 2085 Distilled & blended liquors

(G-9470)
SURFACE RECOVERY TECH LLC
833 Zapata Dr (45324-5165)
PHONE.................................937 879-5864
Thomas Brooks, *Mng Member*
EMP: 15
SQ FT: 20,000
SALES (est): 1.5MM **Privately Held**
SIC: 3441 Fabricated structural metal

(G-9471)
TANGIBLE SOLUTIONS INC
678 Yllow Sprng Frfeld Rd (45324)
PHONE.................................937 912-4603
Adam Clark, *CEO*
Roger Edwards, *Ch of Bd*
Christopher Collins, *COO*
Linda Terrill, *CFO*
EMP: 3
SALES (est): 188.2K **Privately Held**
SIC: 8748 8711 3544 8299 Systems engineering consultant, ex. computer or professional; engineering services; special dies, tools, jigs & fixtures; industrial molds; educational services; educational service, nondegree granting: continuing educ.

(G-9472)
TEE CREATIONS
Also Called: Tca Graphics
701 N Broad St Ste C (45324-5262)
PHONE.................................937 878-2822
Mike Brown, *Owner*
EMP: 9 EST: 1962
SQ FT: 5,000
SALES (est): 500K **Privately Held**
WEB: www.tcagraphics.com
SIC: 2396 5699 Screen printing on fabric articles; sports apparel

(G-9473)
VMETRO INC (DH)
Also Called: V Metro
2600 Paramount Pl Ste 200 (45324-6816)
PHONE.................................281 584-0728
James H Gerberman, *President*
▲ EMP: 6
SQ FT: 18,371

SALES (est): 2.2MM
SALES (est): 2.4B **Publicly Held**
WEB: www.vmetro.com
SIC: 3825 3672 3577 5065 Test equipment for electronic & electric measurement; printed circuit boards; computer peripheral equipment; electronic parts & equipment
HQ: Curtiss-Wright Controls, Inc.
15801 Brixham Hill Ave # 200
Charlotte NC 28277
704 869-4600

(G-9474)
VOLTAGE REGULATOR SALES & SVCS
Also Called: Electronic Services
590 E Dayton Dr (45324-5120)
PHONE.................................937 878-0673
Sarah Ruth Barnette, *Vice Pres*
▼ EMP: 4
SQ FT: 5,000
SALES (est): 684.4K **Privately Held**
WEB: www.gen-powercontrols.com
SIC: 7629 3612 Electrical repair shops; voltage regulating transformers, electric power

(G-9475)
WCR INC (PA)
Also Called: W C R
2377 Commerce Center Blvd B (45324-6378)
PHONE.................................937 223-0703
Kim Andreasen, *CEO*
Brad Stevens, *Owner*
Greg Pinasco, *Vice Pres*
Brandy McCarty, *Accountant*
Ben Hughes, *Sales Staff*
▲ EMP: 32 EST: 2007
SQ FT: 54,000
SALES (est): 39.9MM **Privately Held**
WEB: www.wcr-regasketing.com
SIC: 3443 Heat exchangers, condensers & components

(G-9476)
ZWF GOLF LLC
Also Called: Gem City Golf Club
920 N Broad St (45324)
PHONE.................................937 767-5621
Zachary Fink, *General Mgr*
Troy Martin, *Superintendent*
EMP: 20
SQ FT: 185
SALES: 600K **Privately Held**
SIC: 3949 Shafts, golf club

Fairfield
Butler County

(G-9477)
AAA LAMINATING AND BINDERY INC
Also Called: AAA Laminating & Bindery
7209 Dixie Hwy (45014-5544)
PHONE.................................513 860-2680
Gerald Randall, *Principal*
EMP: 3
SALES (est): 353K **Privately Held**
SIC: 2789 Bookbinding & related work

(G-9478)
AGFA CORPORATION
6104 Monastery Dr (45014-4460)
PHONE.................................513 829-6292
James Dixon, *Branch Mgr*
EMP: 220
SALES (corp-wide): 526.3MM **Privately Held**
SIC: 3861 Photographic equipment & supplies
HQ: Agfa Corporation
611 River Dr Ste 305
Elmwood Park NJ 07407
800 540-2432

(G-9479)
AKRO TOOL CO INC
240 Donald Dr (45014-3007)
PHONE.................................513 858-1555
Ken Johnson, *President*
Donna Johnson, *Treasurer*
EMP: 8
SQ FT: 10,000
SALES (est): 1MM **Privately Held**
SIC: 3599 Machine shop, jobbing & repair

(G-9480)
ALBA MANUFACTURING INC
8950 Seward Rd (45011-9109)
PHONE.................................513 874-0551
Tom Moon, *President*
Thomas N Inderhees, *President*
Mike Kroger, *Vice Pres*
Mike Kees, *Purchasing*
EMP: 52
SQ FT: 67,000
SALES (est): 30.3MM **Privately Held**
WEB: www.albamfg.com
SIC: 3535 5084 3312 Conveyors & conveying equipment; conveyor systems; blast furnaces & steel mills

(G-9481)
AMERICAN INKS AND COATINGS CO
575 Quality Blvd (45014-2294)
PHONE.................................513 552-7200
George Sickinger, *President*
EMP: 15
SALES (corp-wide): 3.2B **Privately Held**
SIC: 2893 Printing ink
HQ: American Inks And Coatings Company
3400 N Hutchinson St
Pine Bluff AR 71602
870 247-2080

(G-9482)
AMERICAN MANUFACTURING & EQP
Also Called: Cincinnati Retread Systems
4990 Factory Dr (45014-1945)
PHONE.................................513 829-2248
Albert Penter, *President*
Albert Penter Jr, *Vice Pres*
Carol Penter, *Treasurer*
EMP: 9
SQ FT: 12,000
SALES (est): 1.4MM **Privately Held**
WEB: www.cincinnatiretreadsystems.com
SIC: 3559 3714 3564 Tire retreading machinery & equipment; motor vehicle parts & accessories; blowers & fans

(G-9483)
AREA WIDE PROTECTIVE INC
9500 Le Saint Dr (45014-2253)
PHONE.................................513 321-9889
Fax: 513 321-9891
EMP: 48
SALES (corp-wide): 111.4MM **Privately Held**
SIC: 3669 7381 7382 Mfg Communications Equip Detective/Armor Car Svcs Security System Svcs
HQ: Area Wide Protective, Inc.
826 Overholt Rd
Kent OH 44240
330 644-0655

(G-9484)
BETH OTTO INDEPENDENT CASE EXA
544 Walter Ave (45014-1656)
PHONE.................................513 868-0484
Beth Otto, *Principal*
EMP: 3
SALES (est): 255.7K **Privately Held**
SIC: 3523 Mfg Farm Machinery/Equipment

(G-9485)
BK TOOL COMPANY INC
300 Security Dr (45014-4243)
PHONE.................................513 870-9622
Robert Reed Jr, *Treasurer*
EMP: 17
SQ FT: 10,200
SALES (est): 2.5MM **Privately Held**
SIC: 3544 Special dies & tools

(G-9486)
BYRON PRODUCTS INC
3781 Port Union Rd (45014-2207)
PHONE.................................513 870-9111
Mark Byron, *CEO*
Rick Henry, *President*
Don Vierling, *QC Mgr*

Mike Pavelka, *Department Mgr*
▲ EMP: 70
SQ FT: 44,000
SALES: 10.4MM **Privately Held**
WEB: www.byronproducts.com
SIC: 7692 Welding repair

(G-9487)
CALVARY INDUSTRIES INC (PA)
9233 Seward Rd (45014-5407)
PHONE.................................513 874-1113
John P Morelock Jr, *CEO*
Ivan Byers, *President*
Austin Morelock, *Business Mgr*
Thomas Rielage, *Vice Pres*
Les Paul, *Plant Mgr*
▲ EMP: 60
SQ FT: 100,000
SALES (est): 34.6MM **Privately Held**
WEB: www.calvaryindustries.com
SIC: 2819 5169 Industrial inorganic chemicals; chemicals & allied products

(G-9488)
CARR TOOL COMPANY
575 Security Dr (45014-4269)
PHONE.................................513 825-2900
Patricia Blum, *CEO*
Alex Blum, *President*
EMP: 30 EST: 1955
SQ FT: 13,000
SALES (est): 6.3MM **Privately Held**
WEB: www.carrtool.com
SIC: 3532 Mining machinery

(G-9489)
CENTRAL DESIGN SERVICES
5417 Dixie Hwy (45014-4107)
PHONE.................................513 829-7027
Donald C Blust, *Owner*
EMP: 4
SQ FT: 2,000
SALES (est): 260.3K **Privately Held**
SIC: 7641 2512 Reupholstery; upholstered household furniture

(G-9490)
CINCINNATI BABBITT INC
9217 Seward Rd (45014-5407)
PHONE.................................513 942-5088
Louis M Patterson, *President*
Dale A Frye, *Corp Secy*
▲ EMP: 15
SQ FT: 20,000
SALES (est): 2.5MM **Privately Held**
WEB: www.cinbab.com
SIC: 3599 Machine shop, jobbing & repair

(G-9491)
CKS SOLUTION INCORPORATED (PA)
4293 Muhlhauser Rd (45014-5450)
PHONE.................................513 947-1277
Peter Sung, *President*
James Braun, *CFO*
Jennifer Harris, *Cust Mgr*
▲ EMP: 35 EST: 2007
SQ FT: 72,000
SALES (est): 6.3MM **Privately Held**
SIC: 3679 Liquid crystal displays (LCD)

(G-9492)
CPC LOGISTICS INC
Also Called: Pds
8695 Seward Rd (45011-9716)
PHONE.................................513 874-5787
Fax: 513 682-7555
EMP: 51 EST: 1972
SALES (est): 1.9MM **Privately Held**
SIC: 8742 7363 3674 Management Consulting Services Help Supply Services Mfg Semiconductors/Related Devices

(G-9493)
DESIGN & SOFTWARE INTL (PA)
526 Nilles Rd Ste 2 (45014-2624)
PHONE.................................513 939-1800
James Caliguri, *President*
Donna Caliguri, *Vice Pres*
Jon Caliguri, *Sales Associate*
Casey Caliguri, *Office Mgr*
EMP: 10
SALES (est): 1.2MM **Privately Held**
WEB: www.designandsoftware.com
SIC: 7372 Prepackaged software

▲ = Import ▼ = Export
◆ = Import/Export

GEOGRAPHIC SECTION

Fairfield - Butler County (G-9519)

(G-9494)
DETROIT FLAME HARDENING CO
Also Called: Cincinnati Flame Hardening Co
375 Security Dr (45014-4250)
PHONE................513 942-1400
Allen Leach, *Manager*
EMP: 10
SALES (corp-wide): 2.9MM **Privately Held**
WEB: www.detroitflame.com
SIC: 3398 Metal heat treating
PA: Detroit Flame Hardening Company Inc
  17644 Mount Elliott St
  Detroit MI
  313 891-2936

(G-9495)
DPA INVESTMENTS INC
Also Called: Usalco
3700 Dixie Hwy (45014-1106)
PHONE................513 737-7100
Joseph Hickey, *Manager*
EMP: 10
SALES (corp-wide): 150MM **Privately Held**
WEB: www.usalco.com
SIC: 2819 Industrial inorganic chemicals
PA: Dpa Investments, Inc.
  2601 Cannery Ave
  Baltimore MD 21226
  410 918-2230

(G-9496)
DRESSER-RAND COMPANY
8655 Seward Rd (45011-9716)
PHONE................513 874-8388
Mel Harris, *Director*
EMP: 20
SALES (corp-wide): 95B **Privately Held**
WEB: www.dresser-rand.com
SIC: 3563 Air & gas compressors
HQ: Dresser-Rand Company
  500 Paul Clark Dr
  Olean NY 14760
  716 375-3000

(G-9497)
FLASHER LIGHT BARRICADE
4896 Factory Dr (45014-1915)
PHONE................513 554-1111
EMP: 3
SALES (est): 167.1K **Privately Held**
SIC: 3647 Vehicular lighting equipment

(G-9498)
FORCE CONTROL INDUSTRIES INC
3660 Dixie Hwy (45014-1105)
PHONE................513 868-0900
James C Besl, *President*
Steve Wissel, *General Mgr*
Robert Briede, *Principal*
Rick Fuhrman, *Principal*
Joseph E Besl, *Exec VP*
▲ **EMP:** 60
SQ FT: 60,000
SALES (est): 16.1MM **Privately Held**
WEB: www.forcecontrol.com
SIC: 3714 3594 3566 3568 Motor vehicle parts & accessories; fluid power pumps & motors; speed changers, drives & gears; clutches, except vehicular

(G-9499)
G & W PRODUCTS LLC
8675 Seward Rd (45011-9716)
PHONE................513 860-4050
Gary Johns, *CEO*
Wayde Hunker, *President*
Doug Henderson, *Vice Pres*
Douglas Henderson, *Vice Pres*
Randy Sagraves, *Vice Pres*
▲ **EMP:** 125
SQ FT: 120,000
SALES (est): 39.6MM **Privately Held**
WEB: www.gandwinc.com
SIC: 2541 3441 3469 Cabinets, lockers & shelving; fabricated structural metal; metal stampings

(G-9500)
GOTCHA COVERED
4854 Factory Dr (45014-1915)
PHONE................513 829-7555
Gregg Faestel, *Owner*
EMP: 5
SQ FT: 7,200
SALES (est): 290K **Privately Held**
SIC: 5719 2396 Window shades; screen printing on fabric articles

(G-9501)
GWP HOLDINGS INC
8675 Seward Rd (45011-9716)
PHONE................513 860-4050
Wayde Hunker, *CEO*
Douglas Henderson, *Vice Pres*
Elizabeth Sargent, *Purch Dir*
▲ **EMP:** 80 **EST:** 1968
SQ FT: 120,000
SALES (est): 12.4MM **Privately Held**
WEB: www.g-w-a.com
SIC: 3441 3479 3446 3469 Floor posts, adjustable: metal; building components, structural steel; railroad car racks, for transporting vehicles: steel; painting, coating & hot dipping; architectural metalwork; metal stampings; sheet metalwork; partitions & fixtures, except wood

(G-9502)
H S MORGAN LIMITED PARTNERSHIP (PA)
3158 Production Dr (45014-4228)
PHONE................513 870-4400
Thadius Jaroszewicz, *Mng Member*
James Vanderzwaag,
EMP: 2
SALES (est): 65.8MM **Privately Held**
SIC: 2521 2522 Panel systems & partitions (free-standing), office: wood; panel systems & partitions, office: except wood

(G-9503)
HAMILTON AIR PRODUCTS INC
3143 Production Dr (45014-4227)
PHONE................513 874-4030
EMP: 7
SQ FT: 20,000
SALES: 2MM
SALES (corp-wide): 11.1MM **Privately Held**
SIC: 3535 Mfg Pneumatic Bank Teller Systems
PA: Hamilton Products Group, Inc.
  7775 Cooper Rd
  Cincinnati OH 45242
  513 753-7773

(G-9504)
HIPSY LLC
4951 Dixie Hwy (45014-2994)
PHONE................513 403-5333
Lerin Buggs, *Branch Mgr*
EMP: 9
SALES (corp-wide): 654K **Privately Held**
SIC: 2339 Scarves, hoods, headbands, etc.: women's
PA: Hipsy Llc
  5321 Cleves Warsaw Pike
  Cincinnati OH 45238
  513 403-5333

(G-9505)
HONEYMOON PAPER PRODUCTS INC (PA)
7100 Dixie Hwy (45014-5543)
PHONE................513 755-7200
Betty Lou Cundall, *Principal*
John Kennedy, *Sales Staff*
EMP: 70
SQ FT: 68,000
SALES (est): 14.6MM **Privately Held**
WEB: www.honeymoonpaper.com
SIC: 2675 2653 Die-cut paper & board; corrugated & solid fiber boxes

(G-9506)
HOWDEN AMERICAN FAN COMPANY (HQ)
2933 Symmes Rd (45014-2001)
PHONE................513 874-2400
Greg Card, *President*
Dave Nadler, *Vice Pres*
Kathy Parry, *Vice Pres*
Jeff Robinson, *Vice Pres*
Rob Spade, *Controller*
▲ **EMP:** 123
SALES (est): 36.9MM
SALES (corp-wide): 3.6B **Publicly Held**
SIC: 3564 Exhaust fans: industrial or commercial; turbo-blowers, industrial; blowing fans: industrial or commercial; ventilating fans: industrial or commercial
PA: Colfax Corporation
  420 Natl Bus Pkwy Ste 500
  Annapolis Junction MD 20701
  301 323-9000

(G-9507)
HOWDEN AMERICAN FAN COMPANY
Woods Fan Division
3235 Homeward Way (45014-4237)
PHONE................513 874-2400
Kirk Shaper, *Manager*
EMP: 31
SALES (corp-wide): 3.6B **Publicly Held**
WEB: www.amfan-woods.com
SIC: 3564 Blowers & fans
HQ: Howden American Fan Company
  2933 Symmes Rd
  Fairfield OH 45014
  513 874-2400

(G-9508)
HOWDEN NORTH AMERICA INC
2933 Symmes Rd (45014-2001)
PHONE................513 874-2400
Karl Kimmerling, *President*
Kirk Schaeper, *Safety Mgr*
Guiseppe Blanchard, *Purch Mgr*
Jerry Brusman, *Engineer*
Blandina Jabbari, *Human Res Dir*
▲ **EMP:** 170
SALES (est): 25.2MM
SALES (corp-wide): 3.6B **Publicly Held**
WEB: www.howdenbuffalo.com
SIC: 3564 Blowers & fans
HQ: Howden North America Inc.
  2475 George Urban Blvd # 120
  Depew NY 14043
  803 741-2700

(G-9509)
ID IMAGES LLC
Also Called: HI Tech Printing
3741 Port Union Rd (45014-2207)
PHONE................513 874-5325
Brian Gale, *CEO*
EMP: 10
SALES (corp-wide): 1.1MM **Privately Held**
SIC: 2759 Commercial printing
PA: I.D. Images Llc
  2991 Interstate Pkwy
  Brunswick OH 44212

(G-9510)
INNMARK COMMUNICATIONS LLC
375 Northpointe Dr (45014-5474)
PHONE................513 285-1040
EMP: 107
SALES (corp-wide): 82.8MM **Privately Held**
SIC: 2759 Commercial printing
PA: Innomark Communications Llc
  420 Distribution Cir
  Fairfield OH 45014
  888 466-6627

(G-9511)
IPEX USA LLC
4507 Lesaint Ct (45014)
PHONE................513 942-9910
EMP: 3
SALES (corp-wide): 3.3MM **Privately Held**
SIC: 3084 Plastics pipe
HQ: Ipex Usa Llc
  10100 Rodney St
  Pineville NC 28134
  704 889-2431

(G-9512)
IWATA BOLT USA INC
102 Iwata Dr (45014-2298)
PHONE................513 942-5050
Nick Hiraga, *Branch Mgr*
EMP: 14
SALES (corp-wide): 22.5MM **Privately Held**
WEB: www.iwatabolt.com
SIC: 3452 Bolts, metal
PA: Iwata Bolt Usa Inc.
  7131 Orangewood Ave
  Garden Grove CA 92841
  714 897-0800

(G-9513)
J D B PARTNERS INC
Also Called: Minuteman Press
6601 Dixie Hwy Ste C (45014-5495)
PHONE................513 874-3056
Douglas Betz, *President*
Ken Ulm, *CFO*
Judy Betz, *Treasurer*
Angie Hamey, *Assistant*
EMP: 5
SALES (est): 695.6K **Privately Held**
SIC: 2752 2759 Commercial printing, offset; commercial printing

(G-9514)
JOHNSON-NASH METAL PDTS INC
9265 Seward Rd (45014-5407)
PHONE................513 874-7022
Craig Johnson, *CEO*
Charles Johnson, *President*
Colleen Johnson, *Chairman*
Carol Johnson Dreyer, *Corp Secy*
Ryan Faber, *Engineer*
EMP: 15
SQ FT: 21,000
SALES (est): 3.1MM **Privately Held**
WEB: www.johnsonnash.com
SIC: 3441 Fabricated structural metal

(G-9515)
JOURNAL NEWS
5120 Dixie Hwy (45014-3027)
PHONE................513 829-7900
EMP: 3
SALES (est): 95.7K **Privately Held**
SIC: 2711 Newspapers

(G-9516)
KAAA/HAMILTON ENTERPRISES INC
Also Called: K/H Enterprises
3143 Production Dr (45014-4227)
PHONE................513 874-5874
EMP: 30
SQ FT: 20,000
SALES (est): 3MM **Privately Held**
SIC: 3211 Mfg Flat Glass

(G-9517)
KNE LLC
12 Suffolk Ct (45014-3818)
PHONE................859 356-1690
Tom Elias, *Principal*
EMP: 4
SALES (est): 360.3K **Privately Held**
SIC: 3421 Table & food cutlery, including butchers'

(G-9518)
KOCH FOODS OF CINCINNATI LLC
4100 Port Union Rd (45014-2293)
PHONE................513 874-3500
Gary Tallent, *Superintendent*
Ted Davis, *Vice Pres*
Bill Kantola, *Vice Pres*
Howard Tallen, *Plant Mgr*
Michael Roach, *Safety Mgr*
▲ **EMP:** 1
SALES (est): 16.5MM
SALES (corp-wide): 2.1B **Privately Held**
SIC: 2099 Food preparations
PA: Koch Foods Incorporated
  1300 Higgins Rd Ste 100
  Park Ridge IL 60068
  601 732-8911

(G-9519)
KOCH MEAT CO INC
Also Called: Cooked Foods
4100 Port Union Rd (45014-2293)
PHONE................513 874-3500
Brian Reisen, *Manager*
EMP: 400
SALES (corp-wide): 2.1B **Privately Held**
SIC: 5142 5144 2015 Packaged frozen goods; poultry & poultry products; poultry slaughtering & processing

Fairfield - Butler County (G-9520)

HQ: Koch Meat Co., Inc.
1300 Higgins Rd Ste 100
Park Ridge IL 60068
847 384-8018

(G-9520)
KOLE SPECIALTIES INC
4695 Industry Dr Ste A (45014-1965)
PHONE.....................513 829-1111
John W Kole, *President*
Joyce Kole, *Treasurer*
EMP: 3
SQ FT: 11,000
SALES: 100K **Privately Held**
SIC: 3599 Machine shop, jobbing & repair

(G-9521)
L&M SHEET METAL LTD
5010 Factory Dr (45014-1919)
PHONE.....................513 858-6173
Keith Mobley, *Partner*
Terry Lawson, *Partner*
EMP: 5
SQ FT: 4,125
SALES: 361.2K **Privately Held**
SIC: 3444 Sheet metalwork

(G-9522)
MACHINTEK CO
3721 Port Union Rd (45014-2200)
PHONE.....................513 551-1000
Roger Hasler, *President*
Vaughn Burckard, *Principal*
Louis Solimine, *Admin Sec*
▲ **EMP:** 65
SQ FT: 37,000
SALES (est): 15MM **Privately Held**
WEB: www.machintek.com
SIC: 3599 Machine shop, jobbing & repair

(G-9523)
MASS-MARKETING INC
7209 Dixie Hwy (45014-5544)
PHONE.....................513 860-6200
Donald J Mueller, *President*
Betsy Engoe, *Manager*
Francine Fleming, *Executive*
◆ **EMP:** 140
SQ FT: 25,000
SALES (est): 15.5MM **Privately Held**
WEB: www.donmueller.com
SIC: 2752 Commercial printing, offset

(G-9524)
MASTER-HALCO INC
620 Commerce Center Dr (45011-8664)
PHONE.....................513 869-7600
Paul Smith, *Manager*
EMP: 35
SALES (corp-wide): 51.7B **Privately Held**
WEB: www.fenceonline.com
SIC: 5051 3315 Steel; fence gates posts & fittings: steel
HQ: Master-Halco, Inc.
3010 Lbj Fwy Ste 800
Dallas TX 75234
972 714-7300

(G-9525)
MASTERS PHARMACEUTICAL INC
8695 Seward Rd (45011-9716)
PHONE.....................513 290-2969
Ben Lazel, *President*
EMP: 6 **EST:** 2015
SALES (est): 689.1K **Privately Held**
SIC: 2834 Pharmaceutical preparations

(G-9526)
MATLY DIGITAL SOLUTIONS LLC
6625 Dixie Hwy Ste E (45014-5490)
PHONE.....................513 860-3435
George Matly, *Branch Mgr*
EMP: 5
SALES (corp-wide): 2.7MM **Privately Held**
SIC: 2741 7389 Business service newsletters: publishing & printing; personal service agents, brokers & bureaus
PA: Matly Digital Solutions, Llc
3432 Preston Hwy
Louisville KY 40213
502 375-2525

(G-9527)
MB MANUFACTURING CORP
2904 Symmes Rd (45014-2035)
PHONE.....................513 682-1461
Greg Kelley, *Principal*
EMP: 9 **EST:** 2003
SALES (est): 1.2MM **Privately Held**
SIC: 2421 Lumber: rough, sawed or planed

(G-9528)
MCNEILUS TRUCK AND MFG INC
8997 Lesaint Dr (45014)
PHONE.....................513 874-2022
Ken Shurboff, *Branch Mgr*
EMP: 23
SALES (corp-wide): 7.7B **Publicly Held**
WEB: www.mcneiluscompanies.com
SIC: 3713 3531 Cement mixer bodies; concrete plants
HQ: Mcneilus Truck And Manufacturing, Inc.
524 E Highway St
Dodge Center MN 55927
507 374-6321

(G-9529)
MIDWEST CONTAINER CORPORATION
375 Northpointe Dr (45014-5474)
PHONE.....................513 870-3000
Mike Brunst, *Owner*
Terry Pater, *Vice Pres*
Terry Evans, *Plant Mgr*
Kathy Henry, *Cust Svc Mgr*
EMP: 20
SQ FT: 52,200
SALES (est): 4.6MM **Privately Held**
SIC: 2653 Boxes, corrugated: made from purchased materials

(G-9530)
MOOSEHEAD CIGAR COMPANY LLC
5180 Potomac Dr (45014-2424)
PHONE.....................513 266-7207
Toney Vicars,
Richard Thomason,
EMP: 3
SALES (est): 334.3K **Privately Held**
SIC: 5194 5993 2121 Cigars; cigar store; cigars

(G-9531)
MOSS VALE INC
160 Donald Dr B (45014-3018)
P.O. Box 18759 (45018-0759)
PHONE.....................513 939-1970
Timothy J Morris, *President*
Janet Morris, *Corp Secy*
EMP: 18
SALES (est): 1MM **Privately Held**
SIC: 3498 Tube fabricating (contract bending & shaping)

(G-9532)
MT PLEASANT BLACKTOPPING INC
3199 Production Dr (45014-4227)
PHONE.....................513 874-3777
William House, *CEO*
Benjamin House, *President*
Anna House, *Vice Pres*
EMP: 8 **EST:** 1952
SQ FT: 3,200
SALES (est): 2.2MM **Privately Held**
SIC: 1623 1771 2951 Sewer line construction; water main construction; blacktop (asphalt) work; concrete repair; asphalt & asphaltic paving mixtures (not from refineries)

(G-9533)
MULHERN BELTING INC
310 Osborne Dr (45014-2247)
PHONE.....................201 337-5700
George Ober, *Manager*
EMP: 25
SQ FT: 10,000
SALES (corp-wide): 20MM **Privately Held**
SIC: 3021 3535 Rubber & plastics footwear; conveyors & conveying equipment
PA: Mulhern Belting, Inc.
148 Bauer Dr
Oakland NJ 07436
201 337-5700

(G-9534)
N C W NICOLOFF CAB WORKS LLC
3200 Profit Dr (45014-4238)
PHONE.....................513 821-1400
Shawn Nicoloff, *Mng Member*
Amy Nicoloff, *Mng Member*
EMP: 6
SALES (est): 284.6K **Privately Held**
SIC: 2434 1751 Wood kitchen cabinets; carpentry work

(G-9535)
NEXTGEN MATERIALS LLC
160a Donald Dr (45014-3023)
PHONE.....................513 858-2365
Danqing Zhu, *Manager*
Max Sorenson,
EMP: 3
SQ FT: 10,000 **Privately Held**
SIC: 2851 Paints & allied products

(G-9536)
NORTHEND GEAR & MACHINE INC
475 Security Dr (45014-4251)
PHONE.....................513 860-4334
Dan Rockenfelder, *President*
Duane Ratcliff, *Corp Secy*
David Shope, *Vice Pres*
Susan Mc Daniel, *Controller*
EMP: 18
SQ FT: 18,000
SALES: 2.2MM **Privately Held**
WEB: www.northendgear.com
SIC: 3599 Machine shop, jobbing & repair

(G-9537)
NORTHERN PRECISION INC
3245 Production Dr (45014-4232)
PHONE.....................513 860-4701
Harold W Jarvis, *President*
Dane A Kerby, *Senior VP*
EMP: 15
SQ FT: 5,000
SALES (est): 2.7MM **Privately Held**
SIC: 3599 Machine shop, jobbing & repair

(G-9538)
OBERSONS NURS & LANDSCAPES INC
Also Called: Obersons Snow and Ice MGT
3951 River Rd (45014-1008)
PHONE.....................513 894-0669
Chad Oberson, *President*
EMP: 11
SQ FT: 7,000
SALES (est): 1.9MM **Privately Held**
SIC: 0782 7349 2899 Landscape contractors; building maintenance services; salt

(G-9539)
OCS INTELLITRAK INC
8660 Seward Rd (45011-9716)
PHONE.....................513 742-5600
Thomas D Robertson, *President*
Charles P Tabler, *President*
Michelle Tabler, *Purch Mgr*
Kevin Collins, *Sr Project Mgr*
▲ **EMP:** 12
SQ FT: 14,500
SALES (est): 5.3MM
SALES (corp-wide): 46.9MM **Privately Held**
WEB: www.intellitrak.com
SIC: 3535 Conveyors & conveying equipment
PA: Lico, Inc.
9230 E 47th St
Kansas City MO 64133
816 356-0660

(G-9540)
P & G PRECISION LLC
3955 Kraus Ln (45014-5841)
PHONE.....................513 738-3500
Mark Puckett,
EMP: 5
SQ FT: 7,500

SALES: 500K **Privately Held**
WEB: www.pgprecision.com
SIC: 3599 Machine shop, jobbing & repair

(G-9541)
PACIFIC INDUSTRIES USA INC
8955 Seward Rd (45011-9109)
PHONE.....................513 860-3900
Toru Nishimura, *President*
James Johnson, *Manager*
Brad Bush, *Systs Prg Mgr*
Steve Schwartz, *Maintence Staff*
◆ **EMP:** 25
SQ FT: 53,000
SALES (est): 6MM
SALES (corp-wide): 1.1B **Privately Held**
SIC: 3714 Motor vehicle wheels & parts
PA: Pacific Industrial Co., Ltd.
100, Kyutokucho
Ogaki GIF 503-0
584 911-111

(G-9542)
PACIFIC MANUFACTURING OHIO INC
8955 Seward Rd (45011-9109)
PHONE.....................513 860-3900
Toshiteru Ando, *President*
Hiroshi Sakurada, *General Mgr*
Lance Bruce, *Traffic Mgr*
Eugene Bonsu, *Mfg Spvr*
Lea A Legg, *Production*
▲ **EMP:** 450
SALES (est): 194.5MM
SALES (corp-wide): 1.1B **Privately Held**
SIC: 3714 3469 Motor vehicle parts & accessories; metal stampings
PA: Pacific Industrial Co., Ltd.
100, Kyutokucho
Ogaki GIF 503-0
584 911-111

(G-9543)
PACKAGING CORPORATION AMERICA
Also Called: PCA
3840 Port Union Rd (45014-2202)
PHONE.....................513 860-1145
Susan Gardner, *Project Mgr*
Theresa Keene, *Sales Staff*
EMP: 4
SALES (corp-wide): 7B **Publicly Held**
SIC: 2653 Boxes, corrugated: made from purchased materials
PA: Packaging Corporation Of America
1 N Field Ct
Lake Forest IL 60045
847 482-3000

(G-9544)
PANELMATIC INC (PA)
258 Donald Dr (45014-3072)
P.O. Box 181446 (45018-1446)
PHONE.....................513 829-3666
Richard P Leach, *President*
Daphne Smith, *Business Mgr*
Cory Jones, *Vice Pres*
Dave Adamson, *CFO*
John Considine, *Manager*
EMP: 2 **EST:** 1957
SQ FT: 21,180
SALES (est): 38MM **Privately Held**
WEB: www.panelmatic.com
SIC: 3613 Control panels, electric; cubicles (electric switchboard equipment)

(G-9545)
PANELMATIC CINCINNATI INC
258 Donald Dr (45014-3072)
PHONE.....................513 829-1960
Richard E Dooley, *President*
Kevin Koch, *General Mgr*
Jeff Spencer, *General Mgr*
J P Stiffler Jr, *Vice Pres*
David D Adamson, *CFO*
EMP: 24 **EST:** 1962
SQ FT: 21,300
SALES (est): 4.1MM
SALES (corp-wide): 38MM **Privately Held**
WEB: www.panelmatic.com
SIC: 3613 8711 Control panels, electric; designing: ship, boat, machine & product

GEOGRAPHIC SECTION
Fairfield - Butler County (G-9571)

PA: Panelmatic, Inc.
258 Donald Dr
Fairfield OH 45014
513 829-3666

(G-9546)
PEASE INDUSTIES INC
7100 Dixie Hwy (45014-5543)
PHONE.................................513 870-3600
David H Pease Jr, *Ch of Bd*
Leonard W Cavens, *President*
David A Aluise, *Vice Pres*
Neil W Jackman, *Vice Pres*
EMP: 352
SQ FT: 220,000
SALES (est): 35.3MM
SALES (corp-wide): 1.8B **Privately Held**
WEB: www.peasedoors.com
SIC: 3442 3089 2431 Metal doors; doors, folding; plastic or plastic coated fabric; doors, wood; door frames, wood
PA: Pella Corporation
102 Main St
Pella IA 50219
641 621-1000

(G-9547)
PERFECTION PRINTING
9560 Le Saint Dr (45014-2253)
PHONE.................................513 874-2173
Steve Myers, *President*
Scott Myers, *Vice Pres*
Joe Myers, *Treasurer*
Dianna Haverland,
EMP: 14
SQ FT: 10,000
SALES: 1.4MM **Privately Held**
WEB: www.perfectionprinting.com
SIC: 2759 Screen printing

(G-9548)
PERKINS & MARIE CALLENDERS LLC
Also Called: Foxtail Foods
6880 Fairfield Bus Ctr Dr (45014)
PHONE.................................513 881-7900
Thomas Allender, *Engineer*
Steve Biederbeck, *Manager*
EMP: 130
SALES (corp-wide): 14.2MM **Privately Held**
WEB: www.perkinsrestaurants.com
SIC: 2051 Bread, cake & related products
HQ: Perkins & Marie Callender's, Llc
6075 Poplar Ave Ste 800
Memphis TN 38119
901 766-6400

(G-9549)
PPG INDUSTRIES INC
Also Called: PPG 4338
726 Nilles Rd (45014-3604)
PHONE.................................513 829-6006
Rick Smith, *Branch Mgr*
EMP: 24
SALES (corp-wide): 15.3B **Publicly Held**
WEB: www.ppg.com
SIC: 2851 Paints & allied products
PA: Ppg Industries, Inc.
1 Ppg Pl
Pittsburgh PA 15272
412 434-3131

(G-9550)
PREMIER CONSTRUCTION COMPANY
9361 Seward Rd (45014-5409)
PHONE.................................513 874-2611
Jan Gilkey, *President*
EMP: 35
SQ FT: 10,000
SALES (est): 8.2MM **Privately Held**
SIC: 5031 1751 2452 Lumber: rough, dressed & finished; plywood; carpentry work; panels & sections, prefabricated, wood

(G-9551)
PRESTIGE DISPLAY AND PACKG LLC
420 Distribution Cir (45014-5473)
PHONE.................................513 285-1040
Jeff Laking, *General Mgr*
Jerome Moore, *Maint Spvr*
Bill Witters, *Controller*
Victor Nelsen, *Human Res Dir*
Dave McGinnis, *Info Tech Mgr*
▲ **EMP:** 16
SQ FT: 200,000
SALES (est): 1.4MM
SALES (corp-wide): 82.8MM **Privately Held**
WEB: www.prestigedisplay.com
SIC: 2653 Mfg Corrugated/Solid Fiber Boxes
PA: Innomark Communications Llc
420 Distribution Cir
Fairfield OH 45014
888 466-6627

(G-9552)
PROMO SPARKS
1120 Hicks Blvd Ste 1 (45014-9401)
P.O. Box 181147 (45018-1147)
PHONE.................................513 844-2211
Mark Johnston, *President*
EMP: 8
SALES (est): 1MM **Privately Held**
SIC: 2759 Screen printing

(G-9553)
PROMOSPARK INC
1120 Hicks Blvd Ste 201 (45014-2876)
PHONE.................................513 844-2211
EMP: 9
SALES (est): 1.3MM **Privately Held**
SIC: 2759 Screen printing

(G-9554)
QUALITY GOLD INC (PA)
500 Quality Blvd (45014-2292)
P.O. Box 18490 (45018-0490)
PHONE.................................513 942-7659
Michael Langhammer, *CEO*
Jason Langhammer, *COO*
Kimberly Abrams, *Project Mgr*
Bonnie Cassett, *Purch Mgr*
Dennis Horn, *Controller*
▲ **EMP:** 278
SQ FT: 110,000
SALES (est): 77.3MM **Privately Held**
WEB: www.qgold.com
SIC: 3339 5944 Gold refining (primary); silver refining (primary); clock & watch stores

(G-9555)
QUEEN CITY TOOL WORKS INC
125 Constitution Dr Ste 2 (45014-2256)
PHONE.................................513 874-0111
Martin Oehler, *President*
Tim Mayes, *Vice Pres*
EMP: 6 **EST:** 1998
SQ FT: 5,200
SALES: 1.4MM **Privately Held**
WEB: www.queencitywebhosting.com
SIC: 3544 3599 Special dies & tools; machine & other job shop work

(G-9556)
R K METALS LTD
3235 Homeward Way (45014-4237)
PHONE.................................513 874-6055
Thomas McKee IV,
K C McKee,
EMP: 30 **EST:** 1997
SQ FT: 45,000
SALES (est): 6.6MM **Privately Held**
WEB: www.rkmetals.net
SIC: 3469 Stamping metal for the trade

(G-9557)
R K S TOOL & DIE INC
200 Security Dr (45014-4244)
PHONE.................................513 870-0225
Richard Strecker, *President*
David J Strecker Jr, *Corp Secy*
EMP: 3
SQ FT: 7,000
SALES (est): 366.5K **Privately Held**
WEB: www.rks-toolanddie.com
SIC: 3544 Special dies & tools

(G-9558)
RIVER CITY PHARMA
8695 Seward Rd (45011-9716)
PHONE.................................513 870-1680
Danny Smith, *President*
Jason Smith, *Vice Pres*
EMP: 75
SALES (est): 5.7MM **Privately Held**
SIC: 2834 5122 Pharmaceutical preparations; pharmaceuticals

(G-9559)
RODERER ENTERPRISES INC
Also Called: Fastsigns
6560 Dixie Hwy Ste E (45014-2238)
PHONE.................................513 942-3000
Richard A Roderer Jr, *President*
Steven Roderer, *Info Tech Dir*
EMP: 5
SQ FT: 1,400
SALES (est): 320K **Privately Held**
SIC: 3993 Signs & advertising specialties

(G-9560)
ROYAL WELDING INC
5000 Factory Dr (45014-1919)
PHONE.................................513 829-9353
Brett Barthel, *President*
Tom Klette, *Vice Pres*
Federico Robles, *Project Engr*
EMP: 4
SALES (est): 1.3MM **Privately Held**
SIC: 3441 Fabricated structural metal

(G-9561)
SCHOBER USA INC
4690 Industry Dr (45014-1923)
PHONE.................................513 489-7393
Karl Schober, *President*
Carl Schober, *President*
▲ **EMP:** 4
SQ FT: 2,000
SALES: 1.1MM
SALES (corp-wide): 1.6MM **Privately Held**
WEB: www.schoberusa.com
SIC: 3545 Precision tools, machinists'
PA: Schober Bau Gmbh
Dorfstr. 3
Konigstein/Sachs. Schw. 01824
350 216-8053

(G-9562)
SEA BIRD PUBLICATIONS INC
311 Nilles Rd Ste B (45014-2621)
PHONE.................................513 869-2200
Ginger Byrd, *Owner*
EMP: 4
SALES (est): 239.2K **Privately Held**
SIC: 2741 Miscellaneous publishing

(G-9563)
SIEB & MEYER AMERICA INC
Also Called: Sieb & Meyer America USA
3975 Port Union Rd (45014-2203)
PHONE.................................513 563-0860
John Endras, *General Mgr*
Jeff Endres, *Buyer*
Joe Beitzinger, *Engineer*
EMP: 14
SQ FT: 10,000
SALES (est): 2.7MM
SALES (corp-wide): 13.7MM **Privately Held**
WEB: www.pmcelectronics.com
SIC: 3625 5063 Relays & industrial controls; electrical apparatus & equipment; motors, electric; motor controls, starters & relays: electric
PA: First Tool Corp.
612 Linden Ave
Dayton OH 45403
937 254-6197

(G-9564)
SIGNIFICANT IMPRESSIONS INC
Also Called: Hightech Signs
4050 Thunderbird Ln (45014-2234)
PHONE.................................513 874-5223
Robert Steiner, *President*
Sarah Steiner, *Co-Owner*
Janet L Steiner, *Vice Pres*
EMP: 5
SQ FT: 8,000
SALES (est): 825K **Privately Held**
SIC: 3993 Signs, not made in custom sign painting shops

(G-9565)
SKYLINE CHILI INC (PA)
4180 Thunderbird Ln (45014-2235)
PHONE.................................513 874-1188
Kevin R Mc Donnell, *President*
Terry Donovan, *Exec VP*
Jim Konves, *Vice Pres*
Steve Gerwe, *Controller*
Sarah Lapham, *Marketing Mgr*
▲ **EMP:** 120 **EST:** 1949
SQ FT: 42,000
SALES (est): 60.8MM **Privately Held**
WEB: www.skylinechili.com
SIC: 5812 2038 6794 5149 Restaurant, family: chain; frozen specialties; franchises, selling or licensing; groceries & related products; dried or canned foods; canned goods: fruit, vegetables, seafood, meats, etc.; canned products

(G-9566)
SOFTWARE TO SYSTEMS INC
640 Glenna Dr (45014-2719)
PHONE.................................513 893-4367
Vicki Humphreys, *President*
Randy Adkins, *Engineer*
EMP: 8
SALES (est): 653.1K **Privately Held**
WEB: www.software2sys.com
SIC: 7372 Prepackaged software

(G-9567)
TEDIA COMPANY INC
1000 Tedia Way (45014-2003)
PHONE.................................513 874-5340
Hoon Choi, *President*
Elinora Park, *Chairman*
Chris Dendy, *Vice Pres*
John F Terbot II, *Vice Pres*
Will Mackie, *Opers Mgr*
◆ **EMP:** 88
SQ FT: 48,500
SALES (est): 36MM **Privately Held**
WEB: www.tedia.com
SIC: 2869 Solvents, organic

(G-9568)
TERON LIGHTING INC
33 Donald Dr Uppr (45014-3022)
PHONE.................................513 858-6004
Micheal Bellos, *President*
David Bellos, *Principal*
▲ **EMP:** 45
SQ FT: 51,100
SALES (est): 9MM
SALES (corp-wide): 8.3B **Publicly Held**
WEB: www.teronlight.com
SIC: 3646 Fluorescent lighting fixtures, commercial
HQ: Clare Sky, Inc.
7711 E Pleasant Valley Rd
Cleveland OH 44131
866 558-5706

(G-9569)
THE-FISCHER-GROUP
20282052 Bohlke Blvd (45014)
PHONE.................................513 285-1281
Vannessa Fisher, *Manager*
EMP: 21
SALES (est): 3.7MM **Privately Held**
SIC: 3915 Lapidary work, contract or other

(G-9570)
TSR MACHINERY SERVICES INC
100 Security Dr (45014-4245)
PHONE.................................513 874-9697
Todd Routh, *President*
Michael Clifford, *Engineer*
Steve Royalty, *Engineer*
Lisa Routh, *Treasurer*
EMP: 26
SQ FT: 26,000
SALES (est): 5.2MM **Privately Held**
SIC: 3541 Machine tools, metal cutting type

(G-9571)
USALCO FAIRFIELD PLANT LLC
3700 Dixie Hwy (45014-1106)
PHONE.................................513 737-7100
Les Gibson, *General Mgr*
Peter Askew,
David Askew,
EMP: 20
SALES (est): 846.9K **Privately Held**
SIC: 2899 Water treating compounds

Fairfield - Butler County (G-9572)   GEOGRAPHIC SECTION

(G-9572)
VIBRA FINISH CO
8411 Seward Rd (45011-8651)
PHONE 513 870-6300
Haskel Hall, *President*
EMP: 20
SALES (corp-wide): 4MM **Privately Held**
WEB: www.vibrafinish.com
SIC: 3291 Abrasive products
PA: Vibra Finish Co.
  2220 Shasta Way
  Simi Valley CA 93065
  805 578-0033

(G-9573)
VISTECH MFG SOLUTIONS LLC
4274 Thunderbird Ln (45014-5482)
PHONE 513 860-1408
Terry McLaughlin, *Vice Pres*
EMP: 8
SALES (corp-wide): 58.3MM **Privately Held**
SIC: 3565 Packaging machinery
PA: Vistech Manufacturing Solutions, Llc
  1156 Scenic Dr Ste 120
  Modesto CA 95350
  209 544-9333

(G-9574)
WAKE NATION
201 Joe Nuxhall Way (45014-1036)
PHONE 513 887-9253
Peter Kennedy, *Owner*
▲ EMP: 10 EST: 2009
SALES (est): 938.9K **Privately Held**
SIC: 3949 Water sports equipment

(G-9575)
WATCH-US INC
4450 Dixie Hwy (45014-1114)
PHONE 513 829-8870
Dan Graf, *President*
▲ EMP: 20
SQ FT: 90,000
SALES (est): 7.9MM **Privately Held**
WEB: www.watch-us.com
SIC: 3944 Automobile & truck models, toy & hobby

(G-9576)
WHOLESALE BAIT CO INC (PA)
2619 Bobmeyer Rd (45014-1217)
PHONE 513 863-2380
Gregory Fessel, *CEO*
Anthony G Fessel, *President*
Ron Robinson, *Buyer*
Benjamin Fessel, *Director*
EMP: 18 EST: 1950
SQ FT: 18,000
SALES (est): 4.9MM **Privately Held**
WEB: www.waxworms.com
SIC: 5199 3949 Bait, fishing; sporting & athletic goods

(G-9577)
WORKSTREAM INC (HQ)
Also Called: Maverick Desk
3158 Production Dr (45014-4228)
PHONE 513 870-4400
Thadius Jaroszewicz, *CEO*
Earl Crawford, *Opers Staff*
Barb Hausfeld, *Human Res Dir*
Brad Quick, *Cust Mgr*
Demitre Zelepuhin, *Info Tech Dir*
▼ EMP: 60
SQ FT: 50,000
SALES (est): 25.6MM **Privately Held**
SIC: 2521 2522 Panel systems & partitions (free-standing), office: wood; panel systems & partitions, office: except wood

(G-9578)
WYSONG CONCRETE PRODUCTS LLC
2138 Resor Rd (45014-3861)
PHONE 513 874-3109
John A Wysong, *Principal*
EMP: 5 EST: 2001
SALES (est): 523.7K **Privately Held**
SIC: 3272 Concrete products

(G-9579)
ZEBEC OF NORTH AMERICA INC
210 Donald Dr (45014-3007)
P.O. Box 181570 (45018-1570)
PHONE 513 829-5533
Ed Synder, *President*
Chris Snyder, *Vice Pres*
Scott Snyder, *Vice Pres*
▲ EMP: 35
SQ FT: 7,000
SALES (est): 3.6MM **Privately Held**
WEB: www.zebec.com
SIC: 3949 5091 Sporting & athletic goods; sporting & recreation goods

Fairfield Township
Butler County

(G-9580)
BUTLER TECH CAREER DEV SCHOOLS
Also Called: Southwest Ohio Computer Assn
3611 Hmlton Middletown Rd (45011-2241)
PHONE 513 867-1028
Mike Crumley, *Superintendent*
Donna Norris, *Asst Supt*
Chuck Adelsperger, *Administration*
Brad Pursell, *Tech/Comp Coord*
Donna Leroy, *Nurse*
EMP: 16
SALES (corp-wide): 45.6MM **Privately Held**
SIC: 8211 7372 Public combined elementary & secondary school; educational computer software
PA: Butler Technology & Career Development Schools
  3603 Hmlton Middletown Rd
  Fairfield Township OH 45011
  513 868-1911

(G-9581)
GE AIRCRAFT ENGINES
5871 Greenlawn Rd (45011-2233)
PHONE 513 868-9906
Robert Bombach, *Manager*
EMP: 3
SALES (est): 118.7K **Privately Held**
SIC: 3511 Turbines & turbine generator sets

(G-9582)
INNOVATIVE CONTROL SYSTEMS
5870 Fairham Rd (45011-2035)
PHONE 513 894-3712
Steven Saunders, *President*
Dave Edester, *Vice Pres*
EMP: 6
SALES (est): 812.3K **Privately Held**
SIC: 3613 Control panels, electric

(G-9583)
JUMP N SALES LLC
6745 Gilmore Rd Ste E (45011-5388)
P.O. Box 1683, West Chester (45071-1683)
PHONE 513 509-7661
Dena K Barger, *CEO*
Dena K Long, *Owner*
EMP: 1
SQ FT: 3,000
SALES: 1MM **Privately Held**
SIC: 3545 Cutting tools for machine tools

(G-9584)
M C L WINDOW COVERINGS INC
6741 Gilmore Rd Ste H (45011-5386)
PHONE 513 868-6000
Joe Lagedrost, *Branch Mgr*
EMP: 3
SALES (corp-wide): 2.5MM **Privately Held**
SIC: 2591 5714 7359 2221 Window blinds; drapery & upholstery stores; equipment rental & leasing; upholstery, tapestry & wall covering fabrics; drapery track installation
PA: M C L Window Coverings Inc
  11815 Technology Ln
  Fishers IN 46038
  317 577-2670

(G-9585)
SENSUS LLC
2991 Hamilton Mason Rd (45011-5355)
PHONE 513 892-7100
Dan Wampler, *Mng Member*
▲ EMP: 12
SQ FT: 25,000
SALES (est): 1.9MM **Privately Held**
WEB: www.sensusflavors.com
SIC: 2087 Pastes, flavoring
HQ: Synergy Flavors, Inc.
  1500 Synergy Dr
  Wauconda IL 60084
  847 487-1011

(G-9586)
SPR MACHINE INC
2130 Tuley Rd (45015-1333)
PHONE 513 737-8040
Scott Roth, *President*
Scott Pater, *Treasurer*
Rasmus Saile, *Admin Sec*
EMP: 5
SALES (est): 566.4K **Privately Held**
SIC: 3469 Machine parts, stamped or pressed metal

(G-9587)
SYNERGY FLAVORS (OH) LLC
Also Called: Sensus
2991 Hamilton Mason Rd (45011-5355)
PHONE 513 892-7100
Greg Bach, *CEO*
Kevin Goodner, *Director*
EMP: 1 EST: 2011
SALES (est): 4.3MM **Privately Held**
SIC: 2087 Extracts, flavoring
HQ: Synergy Flavors, Inc.
  1500 Synergy Dr
  Wauconda IL 60084
  847 487-1011

(G-9588)
THREE LEAF INC
3189 Princeton Rd Ste 123 (45011-5338)
PHONE 888 308-1007
Joseph Brandabur, *CEO*
David A Ferris, *President*
▲ EMP: 2
SALES: 1.2MM **Privately Held**
SIC: 2819 Copper compounds or salts, inorganic

Fairlawn
Summit County

(G-9589)
A SCHULMAN INC (HQ)
3637 Ridgewood Rd (44333-2699)
PHONE 330 666-3751
Bhavesh V Patel, *President*
Andreas K Gunther, *Exec VP*
Andrean R Horton, *Exec VP*
Gary D Phillips, *Exec VP*
Derck R Brictow, *Senior VP*
◆ EMP: 77 EST: 1928
SQ FT: 34,000
SALES: 2.4B
SALES (corp-wide): 34.5B **Privately Held**
WEB: www.aschulman.com
SIC: 2821 Molding compounds, plastics

(G-9590)
A SCHULMAN INC
3637 Ridgewood Rd (44333-2699)
PHONE 909 356-8091
EMP: 5
SALES (corp-wide): 2.4B **Publicly Held**
SIC: 2821 Mfg Plastic Materials & Resins
PA: A. Schulman, Inc.
  3637 Ridgewood Rd
  Fairlawn OH 44333
  330 666-3751

(G-9591)
A SCHULMAN INTERNATIONAL INC (DH)
3637 Ridgewood Rd (44333-3123)
PHONE 330 666-3751
Joseph M Gingo, *CEO*
EMP: 6

SALES (est): 2.3MM
SALES (corp-wide): 34.5B **Privately Held**
SIC: 2821 Plastics materials & resins
HQ: A. Schulman, Inc.
  3637 Ridgewood Rd
  Fairlawn OH 44333
  330 666-3751

(G-9592)
AKRO POLYCHEM INC
150 N Miller Rd Ste 300b (44333-3780)
PHONE 330 864-0360
Dave Murphy, *President*
▲ EMP: 3 EST: 2004
SALES (est): 319.3K **Privately Held**
SIC: 2296 Tire cord & fabrics

(G-9593)
ASI INVESTMENT HOLDING CO
3550 W Market St (44333-2658)
PHONE 330 666-3751
Joseph Gingo, *President*
Ron Andref, *Vice Pres*
Gary Elek, *Vice Pres*
Barry Rhodes, *Vice Pres*
Robert Stefanko, *CFO*
EMP: 80
SALES (est): 7.6MM
SALES (corp-wide): 34.5B **Privately Held**
WEB: www.aschulman.com
SIC: 2821 Elastomers, nonvulcanizable (plastics)
HQ: A. Schulman, Inc.
  3637 Ridgewood Rd
  Fairlawn OH 44333
  330 666-3751

(G-9594)
AURIS NOBLE LLC (PA)
3045 Smith Rd Ste 700 (44333-4458)
PHONE 330 321-6649
Patrick Deeringer, *COO*
Lou Britton, *Plant Mgr*
EMP: 10
SQ FT: 2,000
SALES (est): 1.5MM **Privately Held**
SIC: 3341 Secondary precious metals; platinum group metals, smelting & refining (secondary); silver smelting & refining (secondary); iridium smelting & refining (secondary)

(G-9595)
BEKAERT CORPORATION
3200 W Market St Ste 303 (44333-3326)
P.O. Box 92688t, Cleveland (44190-0002)
PHONE 330 835-5124
David Best, *Branch Mgr*
EMP: 35
SALES (corp-wide): 483.3MM **Privately Held**
WEB: www.bekaert.com
SIC: 3315 Wire & fabricated wire products; fencing made in wiredrawing plants
HQ: Bekaert Corporation
  1395 S Marietta Pkwy Se 500-100
  Marietta GA 30067
  770 421-8520

(G-9596)
BEKAERT CORPORATION
3200 W Market St Ste 303 (44333-3326)
PHONE 330 867-3325
Terese Crapanzano, *Branch Mgr*
EMP: 6
SQ FT: 11,000
SALES (corp-wide): 483.3MM **Privately Held**
WEB: www.bekaert.com
SIC: 3315 Wire & fabricated wire products; fencing made in wiredrawing plants
HQ: Bekaert Corporation
  1395 S Marietta Pkwy Se 500-100
  Marietta GA 30067
  770 421-8520

(G-9597)
BEKAERT NORTH AMERICA MGT CORP (HQ)
3200 W Market St Ste 303 (44333-3326)
PHONE 330 867-3325
Rick McWhirt, *President*
Bert Degraeve, *Chairman*
David Best, *CFO*
Boni Schreiber, *Admin Sec*
◆ EMP: 26

GEOGRAPHIC SECTION

Fairport Harbor - Lake County (G-9623)

SALES (est): 618.5MM
SALES (corp-wide): 483.3MM **Privately Held**
SIC: 3315 Wire & fabricated wire products
PA: Nv Bekaert Sa
Bekaertstraat 2
Zwevegem 8550
567 661-11

(G-9598)
BKT USA INC
2660 W Market St Ste 100 (44333-4209)
PHONE..................330 836-1090
Minoo Mehta, *President*
▲ **EMP:** 15
SQ FT: 3,000
SALES (est): 2.8MM
SALES (corp-wide): 675.2MM **Privately Held**
SIC: 5531 3011 Automotive tires; tires & inner tubes
PA: Balkrishna Industries Limited
Bkt House, C/15
Mumbai MH 40001
226 666-3800

(G-9599)
BUCKEYE CORRUGATED INC (PA)
Also Called: B C I
822 Kumho Dr Ste 400 (44333-9298)
PHONE..................330 576-0590
Douglas A Bosnik, *President*
Robert Butterfield, *President*
Mark A Husted, *CFO*
EMP: 9 **EST:** 1958
SQ FT: 11,000
SALES (est): 188.4MM **Privately Held**
WEB: www.buckeyecorrugated.com
SIC: 2653 Boxes, corrugated: made from purchased materials

(G-9600)
CEP HOLDINGS LLC
3560 W Market St Ste 340 (44333-2687)
PHONE..................330 665-2900
Mark Hamlin Jr,
James Van Tiem,
EMP: 5
SALES (est): 606.8K **Privately Held**
SIC: 3069 3089 Hard rubber & molded rubber products; extruded finished plastic products

(G-9601)
COLLABORATIVE FOR ADAPTIVE LIF
Also Called: Calm
3250 W Market St Ste 205 (44333-3320)
PHONE..................216 513-0572
EMP: 3
SALES (est): 117.4K **Privately Held**
SIC: 3841 7389 Mfg Surgical/Medical Instruments Business Services At Non-Commercial Site

(G-9602)
CONTITECH NORTH AMERICA INC (DH)
703 S Clvlnd Massillon Rd (44333-3023)
PHONE..................330 664-7180
Francisco Hidalgo, *CEO*
▲ **EMP:** 17
SALES (est): 18.9MM
SALES (corp-wide): 50.8B **Privately Held**
WEB: www.contitech-usa.com
SIC: 3061 Mechanical rubber goods
HQ: Contitech Ag
Vahrenwalder Str. 9
Hannover 30165
511 938-02

(G-9603)
CONTITECH USA INC (DH)
Also Called: Continental Contitech
703 S Clvlnd Mssillon Rd (44333-3023)
PHONE..................330 664-7000
Jim Hill, *President*
Hilary Byrne, *Sales Staff*
Brent Lloyd, *Marketing Staff*
Cory Walter, *Marketing Staff*
Stacie Barton, *Manager*
◆ **EMP:** 16
SQ FT: 100,000

SALES (est): 7.3MM
SALES (corp-wide): 50.8B **Privately Held**
WEB: www.veyance.com
SIC: 3069 Molded rubber products

(G-9604)
ELIOKEM INC
Also Called: Eliokem Materials and Concepts
175 Ghent Rd (44333-3330)
PHONE..................330 734-1100
Jerry Perfinger, *Branch Mgr*
EMP: 50
SQ FT: 103,766
SALES (corp-wide): 769.8MM **Publicly Held**
WEB: www.eliokem.com
SIC: 2822 Synthetic rubber
HQ: Eliokem, Inc.
175 Ghent Rd
Fairlawn OH 44333
330 734-1100

(G-9605)
FRISBY PRINTING COMPANY
Also Called: Minuteman Press
3571 Brookwall Dr Unit C (44333-9295)
PHONE..................330 665-4565
Parris Frisby, *President*
EMP: 3
SQ FT: 1,600
SALES: 400K **Privately Held**
SIC: 2752 Commercial printing, lithographic

(G-9606)
GOT GRAPHIX LLC
3265 W Market St (44333-3337)
PHONE..................330 703-9047
Meeran Shafeer, *Mng Member*
EMP: 10
SQ FT: 5,500
SALES: 700K **Privately Held**
SIC: 2759 2395 Screen printing; engraving; embroidery & art needlework

(G-9607)
HGGC CITADEL PLAS HOLDINGS INC (DH)
3637 Ridgewood Rd (44333-3123)
PHONE..................330 666-3751
Mike Huff, *CEO*
Kevin Andrews, *President*
Dennis Loughran, *CFO*
EMP: 6
SALES (est): 11.4MM
SALES (corp-wide): 34.5B **Privately Held**
SIC: 2821 Plastics materials & resins
HQ: A. Schulman, Inc.
3637 Ridgewood Rd
Fairlawn OH 44333
330 666-3751

(G-9608)
HPC HOLDINGS LLC (DH)
Also Called: Composite Group, The
3637 Ridgewood Rd (44333-3123)
PHONE..................330 666-3751
Terry Morgan, *CEO*
Tom Meola, *CFO*
Don Murdock, *Accounts Mgr*
EMP: 13
SALES (est): 134.4MM
SALES (corp-wide): 34.5B **Privately Held**
SIC: 2821 2655 Molding compounds, plastics; cans, composite: foil-fiber & other: from purchased fiber
HQ: Bulk Molding Compounds, Inc.
1600 Powis Ct
West Chicago IL 60185
630 377-1065

(G-9609)
ICO HOLDINGS LLC
3550 W Market St (44333-2658)
PHONE..................330 666-3751
Joseph M Gingo, *Principal*
EMP: 5
SALES (est): 1.8MM **Privately Held**
SIC: 2821 Plastics materials & resins

(G-9610)
ICO TECHNOLOGY INC
3550 W Market St (44333-2658)
PHONE..................330 666-3751
Jennifer K Beeman, *Principal*
EMP: 3 **EST:** 2014

SALES (est): 168.1K **Privately Held**
SIC: 3089 Extruded finished plastic products

(G-9611)
KOROSEAL INTERIOR PRODUCTS LLC (PA)
3875 Embassy Pkwy Ste 110 (44333-8334)
PHONE..................330 668-7600
Rich Runkel, *CEO*
Thomas Roche, *General Mgr*
John Farrell, *COO*
Barb Leyba, *Vice Pres*
Tracy Sheppard, *Project Dir*
▲ **EMP:** 130
SALES (est): 121MM **Privately Held**
SIC: 3081 3089 3069 Floor or wall covering, unsupported plastic; battery cases, plastic or plastic combination; wallcoverings, rubber

(G-9612)
LEADER PUBLICATIONS INC
Also Called: West Side Leader
3075 Smith Rd Ste 204 (44333-4454)
PHONE..................330 665-9595
Clark Burns, *General Mgr*
Kathleen Collins, *Senior Editor*
Maria Lindsay, *Assistant*
EMP: 20
SALES (est): 1.1MM **Privately Held**
WEB: www.akron.com
SIC: 2711 Newspapers: publishing only, not printed on site

(G-9613)
NEXT GENERATION PLASTICS LLC
3075 Smith Rd Ste 101 (44333-4453)
PHONE..................330 668-1200
Renee Heiney,
EMP: 4
SALES (est): 99K **Privately Held**
SIC: 2821 Plastics materials & resins

(G-9614)
OMNOVA OVERSEAS INC (HQ)
175 Ghent Rd (44333-3330)
PHONE..................330 869-4200
Kevin M McMullen, *CEO*
J L Heckel, *President*
Debra Arbaugh, *Supervisor*
Dave Kostrzewski, *IT/INT Sup*
EMP: 120
SALES (est): 7.3MM
SALES (corp-wide): 769.8MM **Publicly Held**
SIC: 2295 Chemically coated & treated fabrics
PA: Omnova Solutions Inc.
25435 Harvard Rd
Beachwood OH 44122
216 682-7000

(G-9615)
PROFUSION INDUSTRIES LLC (PA)
822 Kumho Dr Ste 202 (44333-5105)
PHONE..................800 938-2858
Jon Golden, *President*
Jack Woodyard, *Vice Pres*
Patrick Callahan, *QC Mgr*
William Hatch, *CFO*
Mike Struble, *Manager*
EMP: 8
SALES (est): 27.2MM **Privately Held**
SIC: 3081 3089 Unsupported plastics film & sheet; extruded finished plastic products

(G-9616)
SANCTUARY SOFTWARE STUDIO INC
3560 W Market St Ste 100 (44333-2660)
PHONE..................330 666-9690
Michael J Terry, *President*
Stacy Simontom, *Director*
EMP: 28
SQ FT: 2,200
SALES: 2MM **Privately Held**
WEB: www.sancsoft.com
SIC: 7372 7371 Application computer software; computer software development

(G-9617)
SIGNET GROUP INC
375 Ghent Rd (44333-4601)
PHONE..................330 668-5901
Charles E Scharff, *Principal*
Anne Minnello, *Advt Staff*
Trisha White, *Manager*
Lacey Warnement, *Director*
EMP: 43
SALES (est): 6MM **Privately Held**
SIC: 3911 Jewelry, precious metal

(G-9618)
SPECILTY FBRICS CONVERTING INC (DH)
703 S Clvlnd Mssillon Rd (44333-3023)
PHONE..................706 637-3000
Mark Daniels, *President*
▲ **EMP:** 37
SQ FT: 330,000
SALES (est): 32.4MM
SALES (corp-wide): 50.8B **Privately Held**
SIC: 2399 2281 Hand woven apparel; yarn spinning mills
HQ: Contitech Ag
Vahrenwalder Str. 9
Hannover 30165
511 938-02

(G-9619)
SSP INDUSTRIAL GROUP INC
3560 W Market St Ste 300 (44333-2687)
PHONE..................330 665-2900
Richard M Hamlin, *President*
Mark Hamlin Jr, *President*
James D Van Tiem, *Corp Secy*
James Gaul, *Admin Sec*
▲ **EMP:** 9
SALES (est): 1.4MM **Privately Held**
SIC: 3465 3412 3411 8742 Automotive stampings; metal barrels, drums & pails; food & beverage containers; management consulting services

(G-9620)
STEMCO AIR SPRINGS
3524 Southwestern Blvd (44333-3191)
PHONE..................234 466-7200
Dameon Vaughn, *Principal*
EMP: 24
SALES (est): 1MM **Privately Held**
SIC: 3714 Shock absorbers, motor vehicle

(G-9621)
SUNPRENE COMPANY
Also Called: Asi Investments Holding Co
3550 W Market St (44333-2658)
PHONE..................330 666-3751
Terry Haines, *President*
Anthony Johnson, *Project Mgr*
Robert Helteman, *Opers Mgr*
Rene Rombouts, *Director*
EMP: 120
SALES (est): 11.4MM **Privately Held**
SIC: 2821 Elastomers, nonvulcanizable (plastics)

(G-9622)
TCP INC
Also Called: Sir Speedy
2747 Crawfis Blvd Ste 108 (44333-2886)
PHONE..................330 836-4239
Thomas Delehanty, *President*
Connie Delehanty, *Vice Pres*
EMP: 5
SQ FT: 4,000
SALES (est): 822.6K **Privately Held**
WEB: www.printplususa.com
SIC: 2752 2761 2677 2671 Commercial printing, offset; manifold business forms; envelopes; packaging paper & plastics film, coated & laminated

---

Fairport Harbor
Lake County

(G-9623)
GEORGE WHALLEY COMPANY
Also Called: Cft Systems
1180 High St Ste 1 (44077-6921)
PHONE..................216 453-0099
George M Whalley, *President*
Howard M Whalley, *Vice Pres*

Fairport Harbor - Lake County (G-9624)   GEOGRAPHIC SECTION

Howard Whalley, *Sales Executive*
EMP: 20
SQ FT: 25,000
SALES (est): 3.9MM **Privately Held**
WEB: www.coolantfedtooling.com
SIC: 3545 Tool holders

(G-9624)
JM PERFORMANCE PRODUCTS INC
Also Called: J & M Machine
1234 High St (44077-5559)
PHONE.................................440 357-1234
John Stoneback, *President*
Linda Stoneback, *Vice Pres*
EMP: 19
SQ FT: 19,500
SALES (est): 2.7MM **Privately Held**
WEB: www.jmmachineinc.com
SIC: 3545 Milling machine attachments (machine tool accessories)

(G-9625)
LYONDELL CHEMICAL COMPANY
Also Called: Equistar
110 3rd St (44077-5837)
PHONE.................................440 352-9393
Jim Hillier, *Facilities Mgr*
Michael Step, *Enginr/R&D Mgr*
EMP: 42
SALES (corp-wide): 34.5B **Privately Held**
WEB: www.lyondell.com
SIC: 2869 Industrial organic chemicals
HQ: Lyondell Chemical Company
    1221 Mckinney St Ste 300
    Houston TX 77010
    713 309-7200

(G-9626)
MJM INDUSTRIES INC
1200 East St (44077-5571)
PHONE.................................440 350-1230
Thomas Roulston, *Ch of Bd*
Lois Roulston, *Vice Ch Bd*
Eric Wachob, *President*
▲ **EMP:** 58
SQ FT: 35,500
SALES (est): 14MM **Privately Held**
WEB: www.mjmindustries.com
SIC: 3643 Current-carrying wiring devices

(G-9627)
OURPETS COMPANY (HQ)
1300 East St (44077-5573)
PHONE.................................440 354-6500
Steven Tsengas, *President*
Konstantine S Tsengas, *COO*
Scott R Mendes, *CFO*
▲ **EMP:** 30
SQ FT: 64,000
SALES: 28.2MM **Publicly Held**
WEB: www.our-pets.com
SIC: 3999 Pet supplies
PA: Hyper Pet Llc
    1315 W Macarthur Rd
    Wichita KS 67217
    316 941-1100

(G-9628)
QUARTZ SCIENTIFIC INC (PA)
Also Called: Qsi
819 East St (44077-5596)
P.O. Box 1129 (44077-8129)
PHONE.................................360 574-6254
James R Atwell Jr, *President*
David North, *Accounting Mgr*
EMP: 25
SQ FT: 44,000
SALES (est): 2.8MM **Privately Held**
WEB: www.qsiquartz.com
SIC: 3679 Quartz crystals, for electronic application

(G-9629)
RAMPE MANUFACTURING COMPANY
Also Called: Torque Transmission
1246 High St (44077-5536)
PHONE.................................440 352-8995
John N Rampe, *CEO*
John W Rampe, *President*
Willam Patrick, *Controller*
EMP: 17 **EST:** 1947
SQ FT: 40,000
SALES (est): 1.9MM **Privately Held**
WEB: www.torquetrans.com
SIC: 3568 Power transmission equipment

(G-9630)
RITCHIE FOODS LLC
212 High St (44077-5827)
PHONE.................................440 354-7474
Erik Ritchie, *Principal*
EMP: 3
SALES (est): 225.8K **Privately Held**
SIC: 2099 Food preparations

Farmersville
Montgomery County

(G-9631)
QUALITY DURABLE INDUS FLOORS
Also Called: Q&D Indrustrial Floors
5005 Farmersvl German Pik (45325-9268)
PHONE.................................937 696-2833
Scott Carmack, *President*
Douglas Emrick, *Vice Pres*
Douglas A Emrick, *Vice Pres*
EMP: 14
SALES: 1MM **Privately Held**
SIC: 2851 7389 Epoxy coatings;

Fayette
Fulton County

(G-9632)
C & K MACHINE CO INC
604 N Park St (43521-9718)
P.O. Box 478 (43521-0478)
PHONE.................................419 237-3203
Ken Cassaubon, *President*
EMP: 7
SALES (est): 597.6K **Privately Held**
SIC: 3599 Machine shop, jobbing & repair

(G-9633)
K P PRECISION TOOL AND MCH CO
606 N Park St (43521)
PHONE.................................419 237-2596
EMP: 5
SQ FT: 7,500
SALES (est): 644.8K **Privately Held**
SIC: 3544 3599 Mfg Tools & Dies

(G-9634)
LAROSE INDUSTRIES LLC
Also Called: CRA-Z-Art, Palmer Paint
40 E Industrial Pkwy (43521)
PHONE.................................419 237-1600
Lawrence Rosen, *Branch Mgr*
EMP: 21 **Privately Held**
SIC: 5092 3944 3269 Arts & crafts equipment & supplies; craft & hobby kits & sets; stationery articles, pottery
PA: Larose Industries Llc
    1578 Sussex Tpke
    Randolph NJ 07869

(G-9635)
PHANTOM FIREWORKS INC
25840 Us Highway 20 (43521-9511)
PHONE.................................419 237-2185
Laurie Beaverson, *Manager*
EMP: 5
SALES (corp-wide): 37.5MM **Privately Held**
WEB: www.bjalan.com
SIC: 5999 2899 Fireworks; fireworks
PA: Phantom Ip, Llc
    2445 Belmont Ave
    Youngstown OH 44505
    330 746-1064

(G-9636)
RJR & ASSOCIATES INC
21550 County Road L (43521-9707)
PHONE.................................419 237-2220
Jon Rupp, *President*
Debra Rupp, *Corp Secy*
Jack Rupp, *Vice Pres*
EMP: 9
SQ FT: 6,600
SALES (est): 910K **Privately Held**
WEB: www.rjrassociates.net
SIC: 5999 5083 7692 Feed & farm supply; livestock equipment; welding repair

(G-9637)
TRW AUTOMOTIVE INC
Also Called: TRW Automotive Fayette Plant
705 N Fayette St (43521-9586)
PHONE.................................419 237-2511
Gary Predki, *General Mgr*
Joseph Blanchard, *Mfg Dir*
Rachel Konrad, *Safety Mgr*
Kendra Alcock, *Buyer*
Lynn Barnhart, *Engineer*
EMP: 212
SALES (corp-wide): 144.2K **Privately Held**
SIC: 3714 Motor vehicle parts & accessories
HQ: Trw Automotive Inc.
    12001 Tech Center Dr
    Livonia MI 48150
    734 855-2600

Fayetteville
Brown County

(G-9638)
DEUCE MACHINING LLC
3088 Us Highway 50 (45118-9012)
P.O. Box 57 (45118-0057)
PHONE.................................513 875-2291
Tim Boggs, *Principal*
EMP: 7
SALES (est): 779.6K **Privately Held**
SIC: 3599 Machine shop, jobbing & repair

(G-9639)
G B WELDING & METAL FABG CO
3288 Mcmullen Rd (45118-9748)
PHONE.................................937 444-2091
Greg Boler, *President*
Karen Boler, *Admin Sec*
EMP: 4
SALES (est): 320.2K **Privately Held**
SIC: 7692 Welding repair

(G-9640)
KILEY MACHINE COMPANY INC
4196 Anderson State Rd (45118-9777)
PHONE.................................513 875-3223
Dennis E Kiley, *President*
EMP: 8 **EST:** 1998
SALES (est): 150K **Privately Held**
SIC: 3599 Custom machinery

(G-9641)
KILEY MOLD COMPANY LLC
4200 Anderson State Rd (45118-9098)
PHONE.................................513 875-3223
Dennis Kiley,
Jerome Kiley,
EMP: 7
SALES (est): 983.7K **Privately Held**
SIC: 2821 Molding compounds, plastics

(G-9642)
WIEDERHOLD WLDG & FABRICATION
Also Called: W W F
1843 Us Highway 50 (45118-9661)
PHONE.................................513 875-3755
Dan Wiederhold, *Owner*
EMP: 4
SALES (est): 125K **Privately Held**
SIC: 7692 Welding repair

Felicity
Clermont County

(G-9643)
FELICITY PLASTICS MACHINERY
892 Neville Penn Schoolho (45120-9542)
PHONE.................................513 876-7003
Craig Rigdon, *President*
EMP: 25

SALES (est): 29.4K **Privately Held**
SIC: 3089 Injection molding of plastics

(G-9644)
L C LIMING & SONS INC
Also Called: L & L Plastics
3200 State Route 756 (45120-9766)
PHONE.................................513 876-2555
James C Liming, *President*
Margaret Laubach, *Treasurer*
Lance Liming, *Sales Staff*
EMP: 8
SQ FT: 9,250
SALES (est): 1.6MM **Privately Held**
WEB: www.landlplastics.com
SIC: 3089 6515 Injection molding of plastics; mobile home site operators

Findlay
Hancock County

(G-9645)
ADS
401 Olive St (45840-5358)
PHONE.................................419 422-6521
EMP: 8
SALES (est): 867.8K **Privately Held**
SIC: 3084 Plastics pipe

(G-9646)
ADS MTO ◆
12280 County Road 172 (45840-8904)
PHONE.................................419 424-5231
EMP: 5 **EST:** 2018
SALES (est): 365.1K **Privately Held**
SIC: 3471 Plating & polishing

(G-9647)
ADVANCE NOVELTY INCORPORATED
101 Stanford Pkwy (45840-1731)
P.O. Box 846 (45839-0846)
PHONE.................................419 424-0363
Tom Heimann, *Principal*
EMP: 7 **EST:** 2007
SALES (est): 648.6K **Privately Held**
SIC: 5092 3944 Toys & games; games, toys & children's vehicles

(G-9648)
ADVANCED DRAINAGE SYSTEMS INC
401 Olive St (45840-5358)
PHONE.................................419 424-8324
Bruce Rush, *Branch Mgr*
EMP: 36
SALES (corp-wide): 1.3B **Publicly Held**
WEB: www.ads-pipe.com
SIC: 3084 3083 Plastics pipe; laminated plastics plate & sheet
PA: Advanced Drainage Systems, Inc.
    4640 Trueman Blvd
    Hilliard OH 43026
    614 658-0050

(G-9649)
ALLEGRA PRINT & IMAGING
701 W Sandusky St (45840-2325)
P.O. Box 609 (45839-0609)
PHONE.................................419 427-8095
Karl Heminger, *Owner*
EMP: 12
SALES (est): 1MM **Privately Held**
SIC: 2752 Commercial printing, offset

(G-9650)
AMERICAN PLASTICS LLC
Also Called: Centrex Plastics
814 W Lima St (45840-2312)
PHONE.................................419 423-1213
EMP: 240
SALES (corp-wide): 35.2MM **Privately Held**
SIC: 3589 2673 Commercial cleaning equipment; food storage & trash bags (plastic)
HQ: American Plastics, Llc
    11840 Westline Indstrl Dr
    Saint Louis MO 63146
    800 325-1051

▲ = Import ▼ = Export
◆ = Import/Export

GEOGRAPHIC SECTION

Findlay - Hancock County (G-9677)

(G-9651)
ARCHIES TOO
2145 S Lake Ct (45840-1245)
PHONE....................419 427-2663
Mike Miller, *Owner*
EMP: 70
SALES (est): 4.1MM **Privately Held**
WEB: www.archiefans.com
SIC: 2024 Ice cream & frozen desserts

(G-9652)
AUSTIN POWDER COMPANY
3518 Township Road 142 (45840-9611)
PHONE....................419 299-3347
Rita Whelchel, *Manager*
EMP: 9
SALES (corp-wide): 567.4MM **Privately Held**
SIC: 2892 Explosives
HQ: Austin Powder Company
25800 Science Park Dr # 300
Cleveland OH 44122
216 464-2400

(G-9653)
BALL CORPORATION
1800 Production Dr (45840-5445)
PHONE....................419 423-3071
Rick Garcia, *Manager*
Hank Schroeder, *Manager*
Tom Martin, *Executive*
EMP: 151
SALES (corp-wide): 11.6B **Publicly Held**
SIC: 3411 Food & beverage containers
PA: Ball Corporation
10 Longs Peak Dr
Broomfield CO 80021
303 469-3131

(G-9654)
BALL METAL BEVERAGE CONT CORP
Also Called: Ball Metal Beverage Cont Div
12340 Township Rd 99 E (45840)
PHONE....................419 423-3071
Stephen White, *QC Mgr*
Sarzin Satari, *Engineer*
Tom Martin, *Branch Mgr*
Ron Jones, *Manager*
EMP: 204
SALES (corp-wide): 11.6B **Publicly Held**
SIC: 3411 Beer cans, metal
HQ: Ball Metal Beverage Container Corp.
9300 W 108th Cir
Westminster CO 80021

(G-9655)
BALLINGER INDUSTRIES INC (PA)
2500 Fostoria Ave (45840-8732)
PHONE....................419 422-4533
Jon Ballinger, *President*
Jeff Bisbee, *Plant Mgr*
John Harrigan, *QC Mgr*
Timothy Jones, *CFO*
Tom Fruth, *Manager*
▲ **EMP:** 16
SALES (est): 49.7MM **Privately Held**
WEB: www.fabco-inc.com
SIC: 3531 Construction machinery

(G-9656)
BIRD CORPORATION
Also Called: Envirnmntal Archtctral Signage
100 Stanford Pkwy (45840-1732)
PHONE....................419 424-3095
Jay Morehart, *President*
John Schafer, *Vice Pres*
EMP: 3
SALES (est): 257.2K **Privately Held**
SIC: 1799 3993 Sign installation & maintenance; signs & advertising specialties

(G-9657)
BLANCHARD REFINING COMPANY LLC
539 S Main St (45840-3229)
PHONE....................419 422-2121
Gary R Heminger, *CEO*
Timothy Griffith, *Treasurer*
EMP: 1 EST: 2012
SALES (est): 32.6MM **Publicly Held**
SIC: 2911 Petroleum refining
PA: Marathon Petroleum Corporation
539 S Main St
Findlay OH 45840

(G-9658)
BLANCHARD TERMINAL COMPANY LLC
539 S Main St (45840-3229)
PHONE....................419 422-2121
Gary R Heminger, *President*
EMP: 1
SALES (est): 1.6MM **Publicly Held**
SIC: 2911 Petroleum refining
PA: Marathon Petroleum Corporation
539 S Main St
Findlay OH 45840

(G-9659)
BOEHR PRINT
2703 N Main St Ste 1 (45840-4039)
PHONE....................419 358-1350
Grandy Ramond, *Owner*
Jeff Boehr, *Owner*
EMP: 3
SQ FT: 3,600
SALES: 130K **Privately Held**
SIC: 2752 Commercial printing, lithographic

(G-9660)
BOSSERMAN AUTOMOTIVE ENGRG LLC
Also Called: Aircraft-Refuelers.com
18919 Olympic Dr (45840-9453)
PHONE....................419 722-2879
Terry Bosserman, *President*
▼ **EMP:** 6 EST: 2012
SALES (est): 666.3K **Privately Held**
SIC: 3713 Tank truck bodies

(G-9661)
BREAD KNEADS INC
510 S Blanchard St (45840-5951)
PHONE....................419 422-3863
Kelley Smith, *President*
EMP: 9
SALES (est): 725.3K **Privately Held**
SIC: 5411 5149 2099 2051 Delicatessens; groceries & related products; food preparations; bread, cake & related products

(G-9662)
BRINKMAN TURKEY FARMS INC (PA)
Also Called: Brinkman's Country Corner
16314 State Route 68 (45840-9245)
PHONE....................419 365-5127
Larry Brinkman, *President*
Joe Ray Brinkman, *Vice Pres*
EMP: 18
SQ FT: 6,000
SALES (est): 8.6MM **Privately Held**
WEB: www.brinkmanfarms.com
SIC: 5411 2015 2013 0115 Grocery stores, independent; turkey, processed: canned; chicken, processed: canned; prepared beef products from purchased beef; prepared pork products from purchased pork; corn

(G-9663)
BROWN COMPANY OF FINDLAY LTD
225 Stanford Pkwy (45840-1733)
P.O. Box 1625 (45839-1625)
PHONE....................419 425-3002
Melvin J Brown, *President*
Matt Brown, *Manager*
Cheryl Grace, *Manager*
EMP: 20
SALES (est): 4.2MM **Privately Held**
SIC: 3089 7389 Injection molding of plastics; inspection & testing services

(G-9664)
CASCADE CUT STONE
41 Township Highway 87 (45839)
P.O. Box 120 (45839-0120)
PHONE....................419 422-4341
EMP: 3 EST: 2009
SALES (est): 150K **Privately Held**
SIC: 3281 Mfg Cut Stone/Products

(G-9665)
CENTENNIAL SCREEN PRINTING
1785 S Romick Pkwy (45840-5461)
PHONE....................419 422-5548
Ron Pehrson, *Partner*
Kathryn Pehrson,
EMP: 4
SQ FT: 32,000
SALES: 260K **Privately Held**
SIC: 2759 7389 Screen printing; embroidering of advertising on shirts, etc.

(G-9666)
CENTREX PLASTICS LLC
814 W Lima St (45840-2312)
P.O. Box 707 (45839-0707)
PHONE....................419 423-1213
Terrence L Reinhart, *President*
Ed Umin, *Plant Mgr*
Nick Reinhart, *Opers Mgr*
Mike Zimmerman, *Opers Mgr*
Pamela Fennell, *Human Res Mgr*
EMP: 240
SALES (est): 83.6MM
SALES (corp-wide): 35.2MM **Privately Held**
SIC: 3089 Injection molded finished plastic products
HQ: American Plastics, Llc
11840 Westline Indstrl Dr
Saint Louis MO 63146
800 325-1051

(G-9667)
CHATELAIN PLASTICS INC
413 N Main St (45840-3541)
P.O. Box 1464 (45839-1464)
PHONE....................419 422-4323
Jim Chatelain, *President*
Karen Detert, *Treasurer*
EMP: 5 EST: 1947
SQ FT: 2,400
SALES (est): 470K **Privately Held**
SIC: 3089 5162 3993 Boxes, plastic; plastics materials; signs, not made in custom sign painting shops

(G-9668)
CHEMWISE
1752 W Romick Pkwy (45840-5465)
PHONE....................419 425-3604
EMP: 3 EST: 2011
SALES (est): 340.6K **Privately Held**
SIC: 3312 Chemicals & other products derived from coking

(G-9669)
CLARK RM INC
400 Crystal Ave (45840-4770)
PHONE....................419 425-9889
Marshall Clark, *Manager*
EMP: 40 **Privately Held**
SIC: 2491 2449 2448 2441 Structural lumber & timber, treated wood; wood containers; wood pallets & skids; nailed wood boxes & shook
PA: Clark Rm Inc
1110 Summerlin Dr
Douglas GA

(G-9670)
CLASSIC SIGN COMPANY INC
112 Lagrange St (45840-1600)
PHONE....................419 420-0058
Patrick Gaswint, *President*
Lisa Gaswint, *Admin Sec*
EMP: 7
SQ FT: 10,000
SALES (est): 1.5MM **Privately Held**
SIC: 3993 Signs, not made in custom sign painting shops

(G-9671)
CONTROL INDUSTRIES INC
1700 Fostoria Ave Ste 300 (45840-6281)
P.O. Box 889, Urbana (43078-0889)
PHONE....................937 653-7694
James Long, *President*
James B Long, *Vice Pres*
EMP: 6 EST: 1962
SQ FT: 3,200
SALES (est): 530K **Privately Held**
SIC: 3663 Receiver-transmitter units (transceiver)

(G-9672)
COOPER TIRE & RUBBER COMPANY (PA)
701 Lima Ave (45840-2388)
PHONE....................419 423-1321
Thomas P Capo, *Ch of Bd*
Bradley E Hughes, *President*
Stephen Zamansky, *Senior VP*
Allen Tsaur, *Vice Pres*
Howard Colvin, *Research*
◆ **EMP:** 1000
SALES: 2.8B **Publicly Held**
WEB: www.coopertire.com
SIC: 3011 Automobile tires, pneumatic; truck or bus tires, pneumatic; motorcycle tires, pneumatic; retreading materials, tire

(G-9673)
COOPER TIRE & RUBBER COMPANY
900 Lima Ave (45840-2320)
PHONE....................419 424-4202
P Rooney, *Branch Mgr*
EMP: 21
SALES (corp-wide): 2.8B **Publicly Held**
SIC: 3011 Automobile tires, pneumatic
PA: Cooper Tire & Rubber Company Inc
701 Lima Ave
Findlay OH 45840
419 423-1321

(G-9674)
COOPER TIRE & RUBBER COMPANY
1625 Lake Casscade Pkwy (45840)
P.O. Box 550 (45839-0550)
PHONE....................419 424-4384
Stella Purewall, *Payroll Mgr*
John Ebert, *Manager*
EMP: 60
SALES (corp-wide): 2.8B **Publicly Held**
WEB: www.coopertire.com
SIC: 3011 Tires & inner tubes
PA: Cooper Tire & Rubber Company Inc
701 Lima Ave
Findlay OH 45840
419 423-1321

(G-9675)
COOPER TIRE VHCL TEST CTR INC (HQ)
701 Lima Ave (45840-2315)
PHONE....................419 423-1321
Brad Hughes, *President*
Stephen O Schrooder, *Treasurer*
James E Kline, *Admin Sec*
▲ **EMP:** 21
SQ FT: 2,500
SALES (est): 2.9MM
SALES (corp-wide): 2.8B **Publicly Held**
SIC: 3011 4225 Automobile tires, pneumatic; truck or bus tires, pneumatic; general warehousing & storage
PA: Cooper Tire & Rubber Company Inc
701 Lima Ave
Findlay OH 45840
419 423-1321

(G-9676)
CWC PARTNERS LLC
228 Stadium Dr (45840-2246)
PHONE....................567 208-1573
Cary Cox,
EMP: 4
SALES: 200K **Privately Held**
SIC: 0762 2084 5182 5921 Vineyard management & maintenance services; wines; wine; wine; dried fruit

(G-9677)
DIETSCH BROTHERS INCORPORATED (PA)
400 W Main Cross St (45840-3317)
PHONE....................419 422-4474
Jeffery Dietsch, *President*
Jeff Dietsch, *Vice Pres*
Thomas Dietsch, *Vice Pres*
Richard Dietsch, *Treasurer*
EMP: 53
SQ FT: 12,000
SALES: 4.6MM **Privately Held**
WEB: www.dietschs.com
SIC: 2066 2024 5441 Chocolate & cocoa products; ice cream & frozen desserts; confectionery

Findlay - Hancock County (G-9678)

(G-9678)
DISTINCTIVE BUILDING ELEM
15476 E State Route 12 (45840-8864)
PHONE..................................419 420-5528
EMP: 4
SALES (est): 300.8K Privately Held
SIC: 2819 Mfg Industrial Inorganic Chemicals

(G-9679)
DJM PLASTICS LTD
Also Called: DLM Plastics
1530 Harvard Ave (45840-1737)
PHONE..................................419 424-5250
Matt Badertscher,
◆ EMP: 10
SALES (est): 2MM Privately Held
SIC: 3089 3081 Injection molded finished plastic products; unsupported plastics film & sheet

(G-9680)
DOW CHEMICAL COMPANY
3441 N Main St (45840-4299)
PHONE..................................419 423-6500
John Harrison, Branch Mgr
EMP: 150
SQ FT: 250,000
SALES (corp-wide): 85.9B Publicly Held
WEB: www.dow.com
SIC: 2821 Plastics materials & resins
HQ: The Dow Chemical Company
   2211 H H Dow Way
   Midland MI 48642
   989 636-1000

(G-9681)
DS TECHSTAR INC
1219 W Main Cross St (45840-0707)
PHONE..................................419 424-0888
D Steve Brown, President
Warren Brown, Treasurer
D D Brown, Admin Sec
▲ EMP: 7
SQ FT: 1,000
SALES (est): 4MM Privately Held
WEB: www.techstar-inc.com
SIC: 3441 Bridge sections, prefabricated highway

(G-9682)
FABCO INC (HQ)
616 N Blanchard St (45840-5706)
P.O. Box 673 (45839-0673)
PHONE..................................419 421-4740
Lynn Roeder, Principal
Timothy A Jones, CFO
Kristina Vanbuskirk, Human Res Mgr
▲ EMP: 50
SQ FT: 35,000
SALES (est): 23.3MM
SALES (corp-wide): 49.7MM Privately Held
WEB: www.fabco-inc.com
SIC: 3535 3444 3443 3441 Conveyors & conveying equipment; sheet metalwork; fabricated plate work (boiler shop); fabricated structural metal; bucket or scarifier teeth
PA: Ballinger Industries, Inc.
   2500 Fostoria Ave
   Findlay OH 45840
   419 422-4533

(G-9683)
FINDLAY AMERICAN PROSTHETIC &
12474 County Road 99 (45840-9736)
PHONE..................................419 424-1622
Jeremy Berman, President
EMP: 6
SALES (est): 771.8K Privately Held
WEB: www.fapoc.com
SIC: 3842 3841 Braces, orthopedic; medical instruments & equipment, blood & bone work

(G-9684)
FINDLAY MACHINE & TOOL INC
Also Called: Fmt
2000 Industrial Dr (45840-5443)
P.O. Box 1562 (45839-1562)
PHONE..................................419 434-3100
Joseph Kirk, President
Kolleen Kirk, President
George Hay, Vice Pres
Andrew Rill, Vice Pres
Jay Armstrong, Project Engr
▲ EMP: 45
SQ FT: 200,000
SALES (est): 12.3MM Privately Held
WEB: www.fmtinc.com
SIC: 3559 Degreasing machines, automotive & industrial

(G-9685)
FINDLAY PALLET INC
300 Bell Ave (45840)
PHONE..................................419 423-0511
Robert Reed, President
EMP: 9
SALES (est): 660K Privately Held
SIC: 2448 Cargo containers, wood & wood with metal; skids, wood & wood with metal

(G-9686)
FINDLAY PALLETT INC
102 Crystal Ave (45840-4734)
PHONE..................................419 423-0511
David A Hackenberg, Principal
EMP: 3
SALES (est): 224.1K Privately Held
SIC: 2448 Wood pallets & skids

(G-9687)
FINDLAY PRODUCTS CORPORATION
2045 Industrial Dr (45840-5444)
P.O. Box 1006 (45839-1006)
PHONE..................................419 423-3324
James E Hoyt, President
Lloyd A Miller, Vice Pres
▲ EMP: 130
SQ FT: 224,000
SALES (est): 37.5MM Privately Held
SIC: 3465 3469 Automotive stampings; metal stampings
PA: Midway Products Group, Inc.
   1 Lyman E Hoyt Dr
   Monroe MI 48161

(G-9688)
FLEETMASTER EXPRESS INC
5250 Distribution Dr (45840-9814)
PHONE..................................419 425-0666
Rob Mahlman, Principal
EMP: 171
SALES (corp-wide): 90.8MM Privately Held
SIC: 2741 Miscellaneous publishing
PA: Fleetmaster Express, Incorporated
   1814 Hollins Rd Ne
   Roanoke VA 24012
   540 344-8834

(G-9689)
FREUDENBERG-NOK GENERAL PARTNR
555 Marathon Blvd (45840-1790)
P.O. Box 269 (45839-0269)
PHONE..................................419 427-5221
Roy Schrooder, General Mgr
EMP: 170
SALES (corp-wide): 11B Privately Held
WEB: www.freudenberg-nok.com
SIC: 3053 3492 Gaskets, all materials; fluid power valves & hose fittings
HQ: Freudenberg-Nok General Partnership
   47774 W Anchor Ct
   Plymouth MI 48170
   734 451-0020

(G-9690)
FRIENDS SERVICE CO INC (PA)
Also Called: Friends Business Source
2300 Bright Rd (45840-5432)
PHONE..................................419 427-1704
Kenneth J Schroeder, President
Dale Alt, President
Betsy Hughes, Vice Pres
Peg Schroeder, Human Res Dir
Jennifer Dysinger, Accounts Mgr
EMP: 80
SQ FT: 65,000
SALES (est): 30MM Privately Held
WEB: www.friendsoffice.com
SIC: 5112 5021 5044 5087 Stationery & office supplies; furniture; office equipment; janitors' supplies; photolithographic printing

(G-9691)
G S WIRING SYSTEMS INC (HQ)
1801 Production Dr (45840-5446)
P.O. Box 1045 (45839-1045)
PHONE..................................419 423-7111
George Suzuki, President
Shinichi Inagaki, President
Yukinobu Ukai, Treasurer
Masami Kunimi, Sales Mgr
Joji Suzuki, Admin Sec
▲ EMP: 412
SQ FT: 72,000
SALES (est): 46MM
SALES (corp-wide): 250.2MM Privately Held
WEB: www.gswiring.com
SIC: 3714 5013 Automotive wiring harness sets; motor vehicle supplies & new parts
PA: G.S.Electech,Inc.
   58-1, Hirako, Yoshiwaracho
   Toyota AIC 473-0
   565 782-800

(G-9692)
GARSITE/PROGRESS LLC
1005 Lima Ave (45840-2321)
PHONE..................................419 424-1100
EMP: 14
SALES (corp-wide): 1.8B Publicly Held
SIC: 3728 Mfg Aircraft Parts/Equipment
HQ: Garsite/Progress Llc
   539 S 10th St
   Kansas City KS 66105
   913 342-5600

(G-9693)
GILLIG CUSTOM WINERY INC
1720 Northridge Rd (45840-1905)
PHONE..................................419 202-6057
EMP: 3
SALES (est): 157.9K Privately Held
SIC: 2084 Wines

(G-9694)
GOULD FIRE PROTECTION INC
633 Bristol Dr (45840-6909)
PHONE..................................419 957-2416
Arthur Gould, President
James Amos, Vice Pres
EMP: 6
SALES (est): 550K Privately Held
SIC: 3569 Sprinkler systems, fire: automatic

(G-9695)
GRAHAM PACKG PLASTIC PDTS INC
170 Stanford Pkwy 7 (45840-1732)
PHONE..................................419 421-8037
John Linde, Principal
Allen Reinhart, Engineer
EMP: 180
SALES (corp-wide): 11.6B Publicly Held
SIC: 3085 Plastics bottles
HQ: Graham Packaging Plastic Products Inc.
   1 Seagate Ste 10
   Toledo OH 43604
   717 849-8500

(G-9696)
GSW MANUFACTURING INC
1801 Production Dr (45840-5446)
P.O. Box 1045 (45839-1045)
PHONE..................................419 423-7111
Yukinobu Ukai, President
Terry Veller, Maint Spvr
Teresa Patterson, Production
Michael Werst, Production
Jeremy Gerdemann, Engineer
▲ EMP: 412
SQ FT: 72,000
SALES (est): 142.5MM
SALES (corp-wide): 250.2MM Privately Held
WEB: www.gswiring.com
SIC: 3714 3694 Automotive wiring harness sets; engine electrical equipment
HQ: G S Wiring Systems, Inc
   1801 Production Dr
   Findlay OH 45840
   419 423-7111

(G-9697)
GVS FILTRATION INC (DH)
2150 Industrial Dr (45840-5402)
PHONE..................................419 423-9040
Hasnain R Merchant, CEO
Nick Galambos, Ch of Bd
Scott Salsburey, Principal
George Starring, Principal
Julie Graber, Business Mgr
▲ EMP: 400
SQ FT: 100,000
SALES (est): 168.3MM
SALES (corp-wide): 4.2MM Privately Held
SIC: 3569 Filters, general line: industrial
HQ: Gvs Spa
   Via Roma 50
   Zola Predosa BO 40069
   051 617-6311

(G-9698)
HAMLET PROTEIN INC
5289 Hamlet Dr (45840)
PHONE..................................567 525-5627
Scott Moore, President
Ryne Rich, Finance
▼ EMP: 40
SALES (est): 5MM Privately Held
SIC: 2048 Prepared feeds
HQ: Hamlet Protein A/S
   Saturnvej 51
   Horsens 8700
   756 310-20

(G-9699)
HANCOCK STRUCTURAL STEEL LLC
813 E Bigelow Ave (45840-4256)
P.O. Box 1546 (45839-1546)
PHONE..................................419 424-1217
Chalk Wenner, Owner
EMP: 10
SQ FT: 15,000
SALES (est): 2.5MM Privately Held
SIC: 3441 Fabricated structural metal

(G-9700)
HANCOR HOLDING CORPORATION (HQ)
401 Olive St (45840-5358)
PHONE..................................419 422-6521
Steven Anderson, President
◆ EMP: 330
SQ FT: 27,000
SALES (est): 190.1MM
SALES (corp-wide): 1.3B Publicly Held
SIC: 3084 Plastics pipe
PA: Advanced Drainage Systems, Inc.
   4640 Trueman Blvd
   Hilliard OH 43026
   614 658-0050

(G-9701)
HANCOR INC
Also Called: Hantech
433 Olive St (45840-5358)
P.O. Box 1047 (45839-1047)
PHONE..................................419 424-8225
Clark Inniger, Manager
EMP: 70
SALES (corp-wide): 1.3B Publicly Held
SIC: 3089 3084 2821 Septic tanks, plastic; plastics pipe; plastics materials & resins
HQ: Hancor, Inc.
   4640 Trueman Blvd
   Hilliard OH 43026
   614 658-0050

(G-9702)
HANCOR INC
12370 Jackson Township Rd (45839)
P.O. Box 1047 (45839-1047)
PHONE..................................419 424-8222
Steve Ferell, Manager
EMP: 100
SALES (corp-wide): 1.3B Publicly Held
SIC: 3084 Plastics pipe
HQ: Hancor, Inc.
   4640 Trueman Blvd
   Hilliard OH 43026
   614 658-0050

▲ = Import ▼ = Export
◆ = Import/Export

GEOGRAPHIC SECTION

Findlay - Hancock County (G-9728)

(G-9703)
HIGH QUALITY PLASTICS
2000 Fostoria Ave (45840-9775)
P.O. Box 269 (45839-0269)
PHONE..............................419 422-8290
Frits Vanderklooster, *Principal*
EMP: 7
SALES (est): 614.5K **Privately Held**
SIC: 3053 Gaskets, packing & sealing devices

(G-9704)
HOLTGRVEN SCALE ELCTRONIC CORP
Also Called: Loadmaster Scale Mfgr
420 E Lincoln St (45840-4945)
PHONE..............................419 422-4779
Leonard Holtgreven, *President*
Mark Holtgreven, *Vice Pres*
Janice Fullington, *Technology*
▲ **EMP:** 17 **EST:** 1958
SQ FT: 20,000
SALES (est): 3.7MM **Privately Held**
WEB: www.loadmasterscale.com
SIC: 3596 Industrial scales; truck (motor vehicle) scales

(G-9705)
HOMESTEAD COLLECTIONS
11300 Township Rd 99 (45840)
PHONE..............................419 422-8286
Bonnie Schey, *Partner*
Kreg Schey, *Partner*
EMP: 3
SALES (est): 391.3K **Privately Held**
SIC: 2499 Decorative wood & woodwork

(G-9706)
HOUSE OF AWARDS AND SPORTS
419 N Main St (45840-3378)
PHONE..............................419 422-7877
Jeff Crawford, *President*
Karen Crawford, *Vice Pres*
EMP: 7
SQ FT: 3,500
SALES (est): 991.9K **Privately Held**
SIC: 3949 5091 Sporting & athletic goods; sporting & recreation goods

(G-9707)
HOUSE OF HINDENACH
408 N Main St (45840-3542)
PHONE..............................419 422-0392
Donald W Hindenach, *Owner*
EMP: 4
SQ FT: 4,500
SALES (est): 400K **Privately Held**
SIC: 5731 3651 7622 1731 Consumer electronic equipment; audio electronic systems; speaker systems; communication equipment repair; radio repair & installation; home entertainment repair services; sound equipment specialization

(G-9708)
JAQUAS MONOGRAMMING & DESIGN
Also Called: Jacqua's Monogramming & Design
1016 Tiffin Ave Ste E (45840-6269)
PHONE..............................419 422-2244
Patrick Jaqua,
EMP: 4
SALES (est): 209.4K **Privately Held**
SIC: 2395 Embroidery products, except schiffli machine

(G-9709)
JIM H NIEMEYER
1004 W Sandusky St (45840-2332)
PHONE..............................419 422-2465
Jim Neimeyer, *Owner*
EMP: 15
SALES (est): 912.1K **Privately Held**
SIC: 2024 Ice cream & frozen desserts

(G-9710)
JK-CO LLC
16960 E State Route 12 (45840-9744)
PHONE..............................419 422-5240
Joseph L Kurtz, *President*
C Leon Thornton, *Vice Pres*
Tony Butz, *Project Mgr*
Chuck Brothers, *Buyer*

Chad Vogel, *Project Engr*
▼ **EMP:** 45
SQ FT: 40,000
SALES (est): 11.7MM **Privately Held**
SIC: 3743 4789 Railroad car rebuilding; railroad car repair

(G-9711)
KROGER CO
Also Called: Kroger 00510
101 6th St (45840-5143)
PHONE..............................419 423-2065
Richard Redick, *Branch Mgr*
EMP: 75
SALES (corp-wide): 121.1B **Publicly Held**
WEB: www.kroger.com
SIC: 5411 5912 2051 Supermarkets, chain; proprietary (non-prescription medicine) stores; bread, cake & related products
PA: The Kroger Co
1014 Vine St Ste 1000
Cincinnati OH 45202
513 762-4000

(G-9712)
LAWFT (PA)
1016 N Blanchard St (45840-4719)
PHONE..............................419 422-5293
Verl Warnimont, *Owner*
EMP: 4 **EST:** 2012
SALES (est): 518.4K **Privately Held**
SIC: 2326 Work uniforms

(G-9713)
LEGACY FARMERS COOPERATIVE (PA)
6566 County Road 236 (45840-9769)
PHONE..............................419 423-2611
Mark Sunderman, *President*
Dave Koch, *Opers Mgr*
Gary Herringshaw, *Treasurer*
Deborah Boger, *Controller*
Matt McGuire, *Accounts Mgr*
EMP: 15
SQ FT: 10,000
SALES (est): 278.4MM **Privately Held**
SIC: 5153 5191 5984 2875 Grains; farm supplies; seeds: field, garden & flower; fertilizer & fertilizer materials; liquefied petroleum gas dealers; fertilizers, mixing only; prepared feeds; flour & other grain mill products

(G-9714)
LEVEL PACKAGING LLC
12517 County Road 99 (45840-9736)
PHONE..............................614 392-2412
Chad Bartling, *Mng Member*
EMP: 5
SQ FT: 20,000
SALES (est): 120.7K **Privately Held**
SIC: 2671 Plastic film, coated or laminated for packaging

(G-9715)
LFG SPECIALTIES LLC
16406 E Us Route 224 (45840-9761)
PHONE..............................419 424-4999
De Arment,
Steve Martin,
EMP: 50 **EST:** 1988
SQ FT: 3,000
SALES (est): 7.8MM
SALES (corp-wide): 6.7B **Publicly Held**
WEB: www.lfgspecialties.com
SIC: 3585 2899 Evaporative condensers, heat transfer equipment; flares
HQ: The Shaw Group Inc
4171 Essen Ln
Baton Rouge LA 70809
225 932-2500

(G-9716)
MAGNESIUM ELEKTRON NORTH AMER
115 Stanford Pkwy (45840-1731)
P.O. Box 258, Madison IL (62060-0258)
PHONE..............................419 424-8878
Connie Kempf, *Manager*
EMP: 24

SALES (corp-wide): 441.3MM **Privately Held**
WEB: www.magnesium-elektron.com
SIC: 3364 Magnesium & magnesium-base alloy die-castings
HQ: Magnesium Elektron North America, Inc.
1001 College St
Madison IL 62060
618 452-5190

(G-9717)
MANUFCTRING BUS DEV SLTONS LLC
1950 Industrial Dr (45840-5441)
P.O. Box 1811 (45839-1811)
PHONE..............................419 294-1313
Brian Robertson, *President*
EMP: 60
SQ FT: 50,000
SALES (est): 2.4MM **Privately Held**
WEB: www.mbdsna.com
SIC: 3559 Automotive related machinery

(G-9718)
MARATHON OIL COMPANY
539 S Main St (45840-3229)
P.O. Box 151 (45839-0151)
PHONE..............................419 422-2121
Timothy Griffith, *Senior VP*
Amy Odonnell, *Engineer*
Melisa Zachrich, *Technology*
Daryl L Rotman, *Administration*
EMP: 27
SALES (corp-wide): 6.5B **Publicly Held**
WEB: www.marathonoilcompany.com
SIC: 2911 Petroleum refining
HQ: Marathon Oil Company
5555 San Felipe St B114
Houston TX 77056
713 629-6600

(G-9719)
MARATHON PETROLEUM COMPANY LP (HQ)
539 S Main St (45840-3229)
P.O. Box 1 (45839-7836)
PHONE..............................419 422-2121
Gary Heminger, *CEO*
Ronald G Becker, *President*
Brad Allsop, *Partner*
Mary Ellen Peters, *Partner*
J Michael Wilder, *Partner*
◆ **EMP:** 10
SQ FT: 621,000
SALES (est): 15.8B **Publicly Held**
WEB: www.mapllc.com
SIC: 2951 2865 Gasoline; asphalt paving mixtures & blocks; cyclic crudes & intermediates

(G-9720)
MARATHON PETROLEUM COPORATION
539 S Main St (45840-3229)
P.O. Box 7601, Springfield (45501-7601)
PHONE..............................419 422-2121
EMP: 3 **EST:** 2010
SALES (est): 99.8K **Privately Held**
SIC: 2911 Petroleum refining

(G-9721)
MARATHON PETROLEUM CORPORATION (PA)
539 S Main St (45840-3229)
PHONE..............................419 422-2121
Gary R Heminger, *Ch of Bd*
Donald C Templin, *President*
Glenn M Plumby, *COO*
C Michael Palmer, *Senior VP*
Suzanne Gagle, *Vice Pres*
EMP: 277
SALES: 75.3B **Publicly Held**
SIC: 2911 5172 Petroleum refining; gasoline

(G-9722)
MARBEE INC
Also Called: Marbee Printing & Graphic Art
2703 N Main St Ste 1 (45840-4039)
PHONE..............................419 422-9441
Randy Raymond, *President*
Teresa Raymond, *Corp Secy*
EMP: 6
SQ FT: 3,600

SALES (est): 978.4K **Privately Held**
WEB: www.marbeeprinting.com
SIC: 2752 2759 Commercial printing, offset; commercial printing

(G-9723)
MC BROWN INDUSTRIES INC
10534 Township Road 128 (45840-9315)
PHONE..............................419 963-2800
Lester Brown III, *President*
Dan Brown, *Vice Pres*
EMP: 10
SQ FT: 15,000
SALES (est): 690K **Privately Held**
SIC: 3441 3599 Fabricated structural metal; machine shop, jobbing & repair

(G-9724)
MICHIGAN SUGAR COMPANY
Also Called: Findlay Terminal
1343 Greenwood St (45840-1660)
PHONE..............................419 423-1666
Westley Thomas, *Branch Mgr*
EMP: 5
SALES (corp-wide): 600MM **Privately Held**
SIC: 4225 2063 General warehousing & storage; beet sugar
PA: Michigan Sugar Company
122 Uptown Dr Unit 300
Bay City MI 48708
989 686-0161

(G-9725)
MIDWAY PRODUCTS GROUP INC
2045 Industrial Dr (45840-5444)
PHONE..............................419 422-7070
Jane Myers, *Vice Pres*
Daryl Osburn, *Branch Mgr*
EMP: 3 **Privately Held**
SIC: 3469 Metal stampings
PA: Midway Products Group, Inc.
1 Lyman E Hoyt Dr
Monroe MI 48161

(G-9726)
MIDWEST LASER SYSTEMS INC
Also Called: MLS Systems
1101 Commerce Pkwy (45840-1997)
PHONE..............................419 424-0062
Chad Bouillon, *President*
William J Hunter, *President*
EMP: 40
SQ FT: 50,000
SALES (est): 7.4MM **Privately Held**
WEB: www.mlssystems.com
SIC: 3599 3549 Custom machinery; metalworking machinery

(G-9727)
MITEC POWERTRAIN INC
4000 Fostoria Ave (45840-8733)
PHONE..............................567 525-5606
Tim Hall, *President*
Bryan Little, *QC Mgr*
▲ **EMP:** 30
SQ FT: 100,000
SALES (est): 9.2MM
SALES (corp-wide): 230.9MM **Privately Held**
SIC: 3714 Motor vehicle parts & accessories
PA: Mitec Automotive Ag
Rennbahn 25
Eisenach 99817
369 168-40

(G-9728)
MOLTEN NORTH AMERICA CORP (HQ)
1835 Industrial Dr (45840-5440)
P.O. Box 1451 (45839-1451)
PHONE..............................419 425-2700
Hiddaki Miyamoto, *President*
Toshikazu Yamate, *Vice Pres*
Guy Crawford, *QC Mgr*
Ashley Fennell, *Human Resources*
Toshi Yamate, *Manager*
▲ **EMP:** 189
SQ FT: 100,814
SALES: 21.9MM
SALES (corp-wide): 375.1MM **Privately Held**
SIC: 3089 Automotive parts, plastic

Findlay - Hancock County (G-9729)

PA: Molten Corporation
1-8, Yokogawashimmachi, Nishi-Ku
Hiroshima HIR 733-0
822 921-381

(G-9729)
NATIONAL LIME AND STONE CO
9860 County Road 313 (45840-9003)
P.O. Box 120 (45839-0120)
PHONE...............................419 423-3400
Tim Federici, *Sales Staff*
Denny Swick, *Branch Mgr*
EMP: 31
SALES (corp-wide): 3.2B **Privately Held**
WEB: www.natlime.com
SIC: 3273 1422 Ready-mixed concrete; crushed & broken limestone
PA: The National Lime And Stone Company
551 Lake Cascade Pkwy
Findlay OH 45840
419 422-4341

(G-9730)
NICHIDAI AMERICA CORPORATION
Also Called: N A C
15630 E State Route 12 # 4 (45840-7771)
PHONE...............................419 423-7511
Yuzuru Mishimura, *President*
Kiyoshi Naaadawa, *Vice Pres*
EMP: 26
SALES (est): 3MM **Privately Held**
SIC: 3312 Tool & die steel

(G-9731)
NISSIN BRAKE OHIO INC (HQ)
1901 Industrial Dr (45840-5442)
P.O. Box 886 (45839-0886)
PHONE...............................419 420-3800
Itsuo Miyake, *President*
Wilson J Schroeder, *Vice Pres*
Hiro Sato, *Treasurer*
Norio Hirotani, *Admin Sec*
▲ EMP: 670
SQ FT: 228,000
SALES (est): 151.3MM
SALES (corp-wide): 1.7B **Privately Held**
WEB: www.nissinbrake.com
SIC: 3714 Motor vehicle brake systems & parts
PA: Nissin Kogyo Co., Ltd.
801, Kazawa
Tomi NAG 389-0
268 631-230

(G-9732)
NORTHWEST INSTALLATIONS INC
1903 Blanchard Ave (45840-6472)
P.O. Box 1563 (45839-1563)
PHONE...............................419 423-5738
Tracy Lopez, *President*
EMP: 23
SQ FT: 7,000
SALES (est): 4MM **Privately Held**
WFB: www.northwestinstallationsltd.com
SIC: 1796 3444 3443 3441 Machinery Installation; sheet metalwork; fabricated plate work (boiler shop); fabricated structural metal

(G-9733)
OHIO CONVEYOR AND SUPPLY INC
845 Hurd Ave (45840-3019)
PHONE...............................419 422-3825
John R Snyder, *President*
Annette Bowden, *Corp Secy*
Joseph P Snyder, *Vice Pres*
EMP: 5 EST: 1944
SALES: 1MM **Privately Held**
SIC: 3463 Mechanical power transmission forgings, nonferrous

(G-9734)
OLD MILL CUSTOM CABINETRY CO
Also Called: Diversified Woodworking
310 E Crawford St (45840-4807)
PHONE...............................419 423-8897
Robert Chiow, *President*
Diana Chiow, *Treasurer*
EMP: 4
SQ FT: 7,500
SALES (est): 387.4K **Privately Held**
SIC: 1799 2434 Kitchen cabinet installation; vanities, bathroom: wood

(G-9735)
OLDE MAN GRANOLA LLC
7227 W State Route 12 (45840-8802)
PHONE...............................419 819-9576
Fay Plaza, *Opers Staff*
Rebecca Green, *Manager*
Mark Plaza, *Manager*
Kelly Green, *Exec Dir*
Trevor Plaza, *Exec Dir*
EMP: 10 EST: 2013
SALES (est): 581.2K **Privately Held**
SIC: 2043 7389 Granola & muesli, except bars & clusters;

(G-9736)
OPERATIONAL SUPPORT SVCS LLC
1850 Industrial Dr (45840-5439)
P.O. Box 178 (45839-0178)
PHONE...............................419 425-0889
Donald J Holtgraven,
Gary Franks,
Paul Yates,
EMP: 15
SQ FT: 5,000
SALES (est): 4.9MM **Privately Held**
SIC: 2655 Fiber shipping & mailing containers

(G-9737)
OTTAWA OIL CO INC
Also Called: Findlay Party Mart
1100 Trenton Ave (45840-1920)
PHONE...............................419 425-3301
Karen Roberts, *Manager*
EMP: 11
SALES (corp-wide): 78.1MM **Privately Held**
WEB: www.putnamnet.com
SIC: 1389 Pumping of oil & gas wells
PA: Ottawa Oil Co., Inc.
10305 State Route 224
Ottawa OH
419 523-6441

(G-9738)
P & A INDUSTRIES INC
600 Crystal Ave (45840-4600)
P.O. Box 1446 (45839-1446)
PHONE...............................419 422-7070
Dean Trier, *Branch Mgr*
EMP: 200 **Privately Held**
SIC: 3465 3469 Automotive stampings; metal stampings
HQ: P & A Industries, Inc.
600 Crystal Ave
Findlay OH 45840
419 422-7070

(G-9739)
PARKINS ASPHALT SEALING
1710 Olney Ave (45840-1451)
PHONE...............................419 422-2399
Jim Heldman, *Owner*
Pat Heldman, *Principal*
EMP: 5
SALES (est): 424.1K **Privately Held**
SIC: 2851 1771 Paints, asphalt or bituminous; driveway contractor

(G-9740)
PARTITIONS PLUS LLC
12517 County Road 99 (45840-9736)
PHONE...............................419 422-2600
Chris Pollock, *Plant Mgr*
Ruan Yeager, *Marketing Staff*
Brian Robinson, *Office Mgr*
EMP: 13
SQ FT: 40,000
SALES (est): 4MM **Privately Held**
SIC: 5046 2541 5021 Partitions; wood partitions & fixtures; racks

(G-9741)
PIECO INC (PA)
Also Called: Superior Trim
2151 Industrial Dr (45840-5429)
P.O. Box 118 (45839-0118)
PHONE...............................419 422-5335
Michael Gardner, *President*
EMP: 50 EST: 1997
SQ FT: 50,000
SALES (est): 37.7MM **Privately Held**
WEB: www.suptrim.com
SIC: 2396 Automotive trimmings, fabric; furniture trimmings, fabric; trimming, fabric

(G-9742)
PMC ACQUISITIONS INC
2040 Industrial Dr (45840-5443)
PHONE...............................419 429-0042
Duane Jebbett, *President*
EMP: 65 EST: 2014
SALES (est): 4.1MM **Privately Held**
SIC: 3081 6719 Plastic film & sheet; investment holding companies, except banks

(G-9743)
PUKKA INC (PA)
Also Called: Pukka Headwear
337 S Main St Fl 4 (45840-3373)
P.O. Box 773 (45839-0773)
PHONE...............................419 429-7808
Shawn Rogers, *CEO*
Tate Miller, *President*
Andrea Rogers, *Vice Pres*
David Pruss, *CFO*
Justin Prior, *Sales Staff*
◆ EMP: 64
SALES (est): 7.3MM **Privately Held**
SIC: 2353 Caps: cloth, straw & felt

(G-9744)
RADAR LOVE CO
Also Called: Superior Trim Formed Products
5500 Fostoria Ave (45840-8739)
P.O. Box 578 (45840-0578)
PHONE...............................419 951-4750
Phillip D Gardner, *President*
Charles Henry, *Principal*
EMP: 19
SQ FT: 12,000
SALES (est): 3.9MM **Privately Held**
SIC: 3089 3714 3713 Injection molding of plastics; motor vehicle parts & accessories; truck & bus bodies

(G-9745)
RANDY R WILSON
5225 W State Route 12 (45840-9342)
PHONE...............................740 454-4440
Randy R Wilson, *Principal*
EMP: 3
SALES (est): 200.5K **Privately Held**
SIC: 3131 Quarters

(G-9746)
REITER DAIRY OF AKRON INC
10456 State Route 224 W (45840-1907)
PHONE...............................419 424-5060
Ed Bazile, *Manager*
EMP: 20 **Publicly Held**
SIC: 2026 2024 Mfg Fluid Milk Mfg Ice Cream/Frozen Desert
HQ: Reiter Dairy Of Akron, Inc.
1961 Commerce Cir
Springfield OH 45504
937 323 5777

(G-9747)
ROKI AMERICA CO LTD
2001 Production Dr (45840-5450)
P.O. Box 1044 (45839-1044)
PHONE...............................419 424-9713
Takaya Shimada, *CEO*
Toshifumi Sasamori, *President*
Hiromitsu Shimada Jr, *Chairman*
Bob Funkhouser, *Vice Pres*
Linda Samsal, *Purchasing*
▲ EMP: 350
SQ FT: 177,000
SALES (est): 186.8MM
SALES (corp-wide): 16MM **Privately Held**
WEB: www.filtechusa.com
SIC: 3714 Filters: oil, fuel & air, motor vehicle; power transmission equipment, motor vehicle
PA: Roki Holdings Co.,Ltd.
2396, Futamata, Futamatacho, Tenryu-Ku
Hamamatsu SZO 431-3

(G-9748)
ROWMARK LLC (PA)
5409 Hamlet Dr (45840-6618)
P.O. Box 1605 (45839-1605)
PHONE...............................419 425-8974
Duane E Jebbett, *CEO*
Beth Linhart, *Vice Pres*
Rich Zydonik, *Vice Pres*
Tom Makowski, *Purchasing*
Jamie Twining, *Engineer*
◆ EMP: 100
SQ FT: 65,000
SALES (est): 35MM **Privately Held**
WEB: www.rowmark.com
SIC: 3089 3083 Extruded finished plastic products; laminated plastics plate & sheet

(G-9749)
ROWMARK LLC
Also Called: Premier Material Concepts
2040 Industrial Dr (45840-5443)
PHONE...............................419 429-0042
EMP: 75
SALES (corp-wide): 79.6MM **Privately Held**
SIC: 3089 Mfg Plastic Products
PA: Rowmark Llc
5409 Hamlet Dr
Findlay OH 45840
419 425-8974

(G-9750)
ROYAL MFG
2447 Tiffin Ave (45840-8672)
PHONE...............................419 902-8222
James Herrington, *Principal*
EMP: 4
SALES (est): 750K **Privately Held**
SIC: 3999 Manufacturing industries

(G-9751)
SANOH AMERICA INC (HQ)
1849 Industrial Dr (45840-5440)
P.O. Box 1626 (45839-1626)
PHONE...............................419 425-2600
Masahiko Mizukami, *President*
Eric Carroll, *Vice Pres*
Jeff Hook, *Vice Pres*
Ronald Frisch, *CFO*
Ronald J Curry, *VP Mktg*
▲ EMP: 70
SQ FT: 303,000
SALES (est): 296.8MM
SALES (corp-wide): 1.3B **Privately Held**
WEB: www.sanoh-america.com
SIC: 3498 Tube fabricating (contract bending & shaping)
PA: Sanoh Industrial Co.,Ltd.
1-23-23, Ebisu
Shibuya-Ku TKY 150-0
357 938-411

(G-9752)
SAUSSER STEEL COMPANY INC
230 Crystal Ave (45840-4796)
PHONE...............................419 422-9632
Joo W Sausser, *President*
Dorothy M Garlow, *Corp Secy*
Larry Cherry, *Vice Pres*
Donald Hutton, *Vice Pres*
▲ EMP: 19 EST: 1941
SQ FT: 500,000
SALES (est): 3.7MM **Privately Held**
WEB: www.saussersteel.com
SIC: 3441 5084 5051 3446 Fabricated structural metal; welding machinery & equipment; steel; architectural metalwork; sheet metalwork; fabricated plate work (boiler shop)

(G-9753)
SHELLY COMPANY
Also Called: Findlay Division
1700 Fostoria Ave Ste 200 (45840-6218)
PHONE...............................419 422-8854
Don Webber, *Branch Mgr*
EMP: 70
SALES (corp-wide): 29.7B **Privately Held**
SIC: 2951 Asphalt paving mixtures & blocks
HQ: Shelly Company
80 Park Dr
Thornville OH 43076
740 246-6315

▲ = Import ▼ = Export
◆ = Import/Export

GEOGRAPHIC SECTION

Fleming - Washington County (G-9779)

(G-9754)
SIGNED BY JOSETTE LLC
303 E Sandusky St (45840-4941)
PHONE..........................419 796-9632
Josette Brinkman,
EMP: 3 **EST:** 2007
SALES (est): 229.9K **Privately Held**
SIC: 3993 Signs & advertising specialties

(G-9755)
SIMONA PMC LLC
2040 Industrial Dr (45840-5443)
P.O. Box 1123 (45839-1123)
PHONE..........................419 429-0042
Duane Jebbett, *CEO*
Tom Miller, *Senior VP*
Mike Freaney, *Opers Staff*
Greg Horton, *Regl Sales Mgr*
Roger Jean, *Sales Staff*
EMP: 65 **EST:** 2003
SALES: 25MM
SALES (corp-wide): 464.7MM **Privately Held**
SIC: 3081 Plastic film & sheet
PA: Simona Ag
Teichweg 16
Kirn 55606
675 214-0

(G-9756)
SMITH QUARTER HORSES
1116 Glen Meadow Dr (45840-6256)
PHONE..........................419 420-0112
Robert Smith, *Principal*
EMP: 3
SALES (est): 91.1K **Privately Held**
SIC: 3053 Gaskets, packing & sealing devices

(G-9757)
SMOKE RINGS INC
Also Called: Butt Hut
1928 Tiffin Ave (45840-6753)
PHONE..........................419 420-9966
Jean Dove, *President*
EMP: 7
SALES (est): 981.1K **Privately Held**
WEB: www.smokerings.com
SIC: 2131 5993 Chewing & smoking tobacco; tobacco stores & stands

(G-9758)
SONOCO PRTECTIVE SOLUTIONS INC
1900 Industrial Dr (45840-5441)
P.O. Box 714 (45839-0714)
PHONE..........................419 420-0029
EMP: 5
SALES (corp-wide): 4.9B **Publicly Held**
SIC: 2671 Manufactures Packaging Paper And Film
HQ: Sonoco Protective Solutions, Inc.
1 N 2nd St
Hartsville SC 29550
843 383-7000

(G-9759)
SONOCO PRTECTIVE SOLUTIONS INC
1900 Industrial Dr (45840-5441)
P.O. Box 714 (45839-0714)
PHONE..........................419 420-0029
Rod Williams, *Branch Mgr*
EMP: 100
SQ FT: 100,000
SALES (corp-wide): 5.3B **Publicly Held**
WEB: www.createcorp.com
SIC: 3089 3086 2821 Blister or bubble formed packaging, plastic; plastics foam products; plastics materials & resins
HQ: Sonoco Protective Solutions, Inc.
1 N 2nd St
Hartsville SC 29550
843 383-7000

(G-9760)
SOUTHSIDE WOLFIES
546 6th St (45840-5148)
PHONE..........................419 422-5450
Shawn Lalji, *Owner*
EMP: 3
SALES (est): 216.3K **Privately Held**
SIC: 2068 Salted & roasted nuts & seeds

(G-9761)
SQUARE ONE SOLUTIONS LLC
Also Called: Brown Box Company
105 Jefferson St (45840)
PHONE..........................419 425-5445
Stephen Chan, *President*
Kary Chan,
Kathryn Lewis,
Giannina Riblet,
EMP: 13
SQ FT: 7,000
SALES (est): 2.4MM **Privately Held**
SIC: 2653 Boxes, corrugated: made from purchased materials

(G-9762)
STONECO INC (DH)
1700 Fostoria Ave Ste 200 (45840-6218)
P.O. Box 865 (45839-0865)
PHONE..........................419 422-8854
John T Bearss, *President*
Don Weber, *Vice Pres*
Jack Zouhary, *Admin Sec*
EMP: 87
SQ FT: 34,000
SALES (est): 61.4MM
SALES (corp-wide): 29.7B **Privately Held**
WEB: www.stoneco.net
SIC: 2951 1411 Asphalt & asphaltic paving mixtures (not from refineries); limestone, dimension-quarrying
HQ: Shelly Company
80 Park Dr
Thornville OH 43076
740 246-6315

(G-9763)
STREAMSIDE MATERIALS LLC
7440 Township Road 95 (45840-9659)
PHONE..........................419 423-1290
Randall Tucker, *CEO*
Brian Halm, *Director*
EMP: 6
SALES (est): 310.5K **Privately Held**
SIC: 8742 1442 Materials mgmt. (purchasing, handling, inventory) consultant; construction sand & gravel

(G-9764)
STREICHERS ENTERPRISES INC
Also Called: Streicher's Quickprint
109 S Main St (45840-3423)
PHONE..........................419 423-8606
Thomas Day, *President*
Tammy Day, *Admin Sec*
Michael Streicher, *Admin Sec*
EMP: 5
SQ FT: 4,000
SALES: 500K **Privately Held**
SIC: 2752 Commercial printing, offset

(G-9765)
SUMMERS ACQUISITION CORP
16406 E Us Route 224 (45840-9761)
PHONE..........................419 423-5800
Gary Porcello, *Branch Mgr*
EMP: 5
SALES (corp-wide): 3.1B **Privately Held**
WEB: www.summersrubber.com
SIC: 5085 3498 3441 3429 Rubber goods, mechanical; fabricated pipe & fittings; fabricated structural metal; manufactured hardware (general); rubber & plastics hose & beltings
HQ: Summers Acquisition Corporation
12555 Berea Rd
Cleveland OH 44111
216 941-7700

(G-9766)
T & S ENTERPRISES
1616 Bliss Ave (45840-1512)
P.O. Box 305 (45839-0305)
PHONE..........................419 424-1122
Sharon A Nagy, *Owner*
EMP: 20
SQ FT: 60,000
SALES (est): 1.3MM **Privately Held**
SIC: 3596 3643 Scales & balances, except laboratory; connectors & terminals for electrical devices

(G-9767)
TEXSTONE INDUSTRIES
433 Oak Ave (45840-4750)
P.O. Box 1126 (45839-1126)
PHONE..........................419 722-4664
EMP: 3
SALES (est): 204K **Privately Held**
SIC: 3999 Manufacturing industries

(G-9768)
TH PLASTICS INC
1640 Westfield Dr (45840)
PHONE..........................419 425-5825
EMP: 15
SALES (corp-wide): 100.6MM **Privately Held**
SIC: 3089 Mfg Plastic Products
PA: Th Plastics, Inc.
106 E Main St
Mendon MI 49072
419 425-5825

(G-9769)
TH PLASTICS INC
101 Bentley Ct (45840-1799)
PHONE..........................419 425-5825
Stacy McCoy, *Buyer*
Maurisa Meyers, *Purchasing*
Elizabeth Mitchell, *Branch Mgr*
Shirley McGlothlen, *Administration*
EMP: 115
SALES (est): 14MM
SALES (corp-wide): 142MM **Privately Held**
SIC: 3089 Aquarium accessories, plastic; injection molding of plastics
PA: Th Plastics, Inc.
106 E Main St
Mendon MI 49072
269 496-8495

(G-9770)
THUNDER DREAMER PUBLISHING
2500 Crystal Ave (45840-4462)
PHONE..........................419 424-2004
Daniel Gerschutz, *President*
Deborah Gerschutz, *Vice Pres*
EMP: 3
SALES (est): 171K **Privately Held**
SIC: 2741 Music, sheet: publishing & printing

(G-9771)
TRIXIES PICKLES INC
Also Called: Firehouse Sub
1978 Tiffin Ave (45840-6753)
PHONE..........................817 658-6648
Brett Fredrick, *Principal*
EMP: 26
SALES (est): 127K **Privately Held**
SIC: 2035 5812 Pickled fruits & vegetables; eating places

(G-9772)
VALFILM LLC
3441 N Main St (45840-4206)
PHONE..........................419 423-6500
Alberto Geronomi, *CEO*
EMP: 100
SALES (est): 19.7MM **Privately Held**
SIC: 3081 Plastic film & sheet

(G-9773)
VEONEER NISSIN BRAKE
2001 Industrial Dr (45840-5444)
P.O. Box 886 (45840-0886)
PHONE..........................419 425-6725
Wilson Schroeder, *CEO*
EMP: 325
SALES: 150MM
SALES (corp-wide): 2.2B **Publicly Held**
SIC: 3714 Motor vehicle brake systems & parts
HQ: Veoneer Us, Inc.
26360 American Dr
Southfield MI 48034
248 223-8074

(G-9774)
WABASH NATIONAL CORPORATION
2000 Fostoria Ave (45840-9775)
PHONE..........................419 434-9409
EMP: 86
SALES (corp-wide): 2.2B **Publicly Held**
SIC: 3715 Truck trailers
PA: Wabash National Corporation
1000 Sagamore Pkwy S
Lafayette IN 47905
765 771-5300

(G-9775)
WERK-BRAU COMPANY
2800 Fostoria Ave (45840-8757)
P.O. Box 545 (45839-0545)
PHONE..........................419 422-2912
Paul Ballinger, *CEO*
Jon Ballinger, *President*
Jim Greulich, *Vice Pres*
Tim Jones, *Controller*
Kristina Buskirk, *Human Resources*
▲ **EMP:** 66
SQ FT: 104,000
SALES (est): 26.3MM
SALES (corp-wide): 49.7MM **Privately Held**
WEB: www.werkbrau.com
SIC: 3531 3412 Buckets, excavating: clamshell, concrete, dragline, etc.; backhoe mounted, hydraulically powered attachments; construction machinery attachments; metal barrels, drums & pails
PA: Ballinger Industries, Inc.
2500 Fostoria Ave
Findlay OH 45840
419 422-4533

(G-9776)
WHIRLPOOL CORPORATION
4901 N Main St (45840-9780)
PHONE..........................419 423-8123
Jeff Noelcorporate, *President*
Kelly Gierhart, *Materials Mgr*
Tom Buckleitner, *Opers Staff*
Brian Etzkorn, *Production*
John Fulcher, *Engineer*
EMP: 100
SALES (corp-wide): 21B **Publicly Held**
WEB: www.whirlpoolcorp.com
SIC: 3639 3632 Dishwashing machines, household; household refrigerators & freezers
PA: Whirlpool Corporation
2000 N M 63
Benton Harbor MI 49022
269 923-5000

Fleming
Washington County

(G-9777)
ANDERSON ENERGY INC
12959 State Route 550 (45729-5229)
P.O. Box 327, Vincent (45784-0327)
PHONE..........................740 678-8608
Den Anderson, *President*
EMP: 7
SALES (est): 348.5K **Privately Held**
SIC: 1381 Drilling oil & gas wells

(G-9778)
AZA ENTERPRISES LLC
1149 Fisher Ridge Rd (45729-5001)
PHONE..........................740 678-8482
EMP: 5
SALES: 350K **Privately Held**
SIC: 3325 Steel Foundry

(G-9779)
BT ENERGY CORPORATION (PA)
1635 Warren Chapel Rd (45729-5089)
P.O. Box 60, Marietta (45750-0060)
PHONE..........................740 373-6134
Jugal K Taneja, *CEO*
Eddie Beale, *President*
A Theodore Stautberg Jr, *President*
John Schneider, *Senior Engr*
R Stuyvesant Pierrepont, *VP Finance*
EMP: 1 **EST:** 1981
SQ FT: 4,000
SALES (est): 1MM **Privately Held**
SIC: 1311 Crude petroleum production; natural gas production

Fleming
Washington County

(G-9780)
PINE RIDGE PROCESSING
Also Called: Pine Ridge Meat Processing
4559 Anderson Rd (45729-5148)
PHONE...................740 749-3166
Douglas Sprague, *Owner*
EMP: 3
SQ FT: 1,800
SALES (est): 160K **Privately Held**
SIC: 2011 5421 Beef products from beef slaughtered on site; meat markets, including freezer provisioners

(G-9781)
STONEBRIDGE OPERATING CO LLC
1635 Warren Chapel Rd (45729-5089)
P.O. Box 60, Marietta (45750-0060)
PHONE...................740 373-6134
E Biehl,
EMP: 1
SALES (est): 1MM **Privately Held**
WEB: www.stonebridgeoperating.com
SIC: 1311 Crude petroleum production
PA: Bt Energy Corporation
1635 Warren Chapel Rd
Fleming OH 45729
740 373-6134

Fletcher
Miami County

(G-9782)
CREATIA INC
7990 Sodom Ballou Rd (45326-8772)
PHONE...................937 368-3100
Tim Deaton, *Branch Mgr*
EMP: 5 **Privately Held**
SIC: 7336 2262 Commercial art & graphic design; screen printing: manmade fiber & silk broadwoven fabrics
PA: Creatia, Inc.
8989 Lostcreek Shelby Rd
Fletcher OH 45326

Flushing
Belmont County

(G-9783)
GLENN MICHAEL BRICK
Also Called: Go For Broke Amusement
108 Wood St (43977-9727)
PHONE...................740 391-5735
Glenn M Brick, *Owner*
EMP: 11
SALES: 2.7MM **Privately Held**
SIC: 4212 7993 7699 3578 Mail carriers, contract; juke boxes; automated teller machine (ATM) repair; automatic teller machines (ATM)

(G-9784)
PATRIARCH TRUCKING LLC
68500 Mrrstown Flshing Rd (43977-9775)
PHONE...................877 875-5402
Paul Vandal,
EMP: 3
SQ FT: 8,000
SALES (est): 240K **Privately Held**
SIC: 1446 6513 Silica sand mining; apartment building operators

Forest
Hardin County

(G-9785)
BUCKEYE MCH FABRICATORS INC
610 E Lima St (45843-1182)
PHONE...................419 273-2521
D Ray Marshall, *President*
Nancy Marshall, *Admin Sec*
EMP: 50 **EST**: 1974
SQ FT: 65,000
SALES (est): 10.3MM **Privately Held**
SIC: 3599 Machine shop, jobbing & repair; custom machinery

(G-9786)
DPI INC
110 N Davis St (45843-1010)
PHONE...................419 273-1400
Fax: 419 273-2234
EMP: 6
SQ FT: 7,000
SALES (est): 520K **Privately Held**
SIC: 3199 5699 5713 Mfg Of Leather Steering Wheel Covers A Ret Of Embroidered Apparel & A Ret & Whol Of Carpets

(G-9787)
DUFF QUARRY INC
3798 State Route 53 (45843-9379)
PHONE...................419 273-2518
James E Duff, *President*
EMP: 10
SALES (corp-wide): 3.2MM **Privately Held**
SIC: 1422 Crushed & broken limestone
PA: Duff Quarry Inc
9042 State Route 117
Huntsville OH 43324
937 686-2811

(G-9788)
SHELLY MATERIALS INC
3798 State Route 53 (45843-9379)
PHONE...................419 273-2510
Norman Cochran, *Branch Mgr*
EMP: 6
SALES (corp-wide): 29.7B **Privately Held**
SIC: 2951 Asphalt paving mixtures & blocks
HQ: Shelly Materials, Inc.
80 Park Dr
Thornville OH 43076
740 246-6315

(G-9789)
TRIUMPH THERMAL SYSTEMS LLC (HQ)
200 Railroad St (45843-9193)
PHONE...................419 273-2511
Michael Perhay, *President*
Dawn Bailey, *Purch Mgr*
Kenneth Jackson, *Human Res Dir*
Lisa Butler, *Technology*
Mark Sievert, *Director*
EMP: 96
SQ FT: 125,000
SALES (est): 27.8MM **Publicly Held**
WEB: www.triumph-thermal.com
SIC: 3728 3443 Aircraft parts & equipment; heat exchangers, condensers & components

(G-9790)
VTS CO LTD
607 E Lima St (45843-1180)
PHONE...................419 273-4010
Lloyd Swavel, *President*
EMP: 7
SALES (est): 903.1K **Privately Held**
SIC: 3089 Extruded finished plastic products

Fort Jennings
Putnam County

(G-9791)
BCFAB INC (PA)
Also Called: Buckeye Custom Fab
15751 Road 19 (45844-9739)
PHONE...................419 532-2899
Mike Siebeneck, *Managing Prtnr*
Dan Wehri, *Partner*
Mark Wehri, *Principal*
EMP: 7
SALES (est): 770K **Privately Held**
SIC: 3441 Fabricated structural metal

(G-9792)
G & S CUSTOM TOOLING LLC
18406 Road 20 (45844-9106)
PHONE...................419 286-2888
German Darrin, *Administration*
EMP: 3
SALES (est): 313.2K **Privately Held**
SIC: 3544 Special dies & tools

Fort Loramie
Shelby County

(G-9793)
CROWN EQUIPMENT CORPORATION
Also Called: Crown Lift Trucks
300 S Tower St (45845)
P.O. Box 379 (45845-0379)
PHONE...................937 295-4062
Sheryl Gray, *Branch Mgr*
EMP: 70
SALES (corp-wide): 3.1B **Privately Held**
SIC: 3537 Lift trucks, industrial: fork, platform, straddle, etc.
PA: Crown Equipment Corporation
44 S Washington St
New Bremen OH 45869
419 629-2311

(G-9794)
CUSTOM FOAM PRODUCTS INC (PA)
900 Tower Dr (45845-8712)
PHONE...................937 295-2700
Nick Fullenkamp, *Owner*
Steve Sherman, *Vice Pres*
EMP: 20
SQ FT: 48,000
SALES (est): 5.6MM **Privately Held**
SIC: 3086 Packaging & shipping materials, foamed plastic

(G-9795)
EDWARDS MACHINE SERVICE INC
8800 State Route 66 (45845-9806)
P.O. Box 33 (45845-0033)
PHONE...................937 295-2929
Thomas Edwards, *President*
Ronald Edwards, *Treasurer*
EMP: 10
SQ FT: 7,500
SALES (est): 1.1MM **Privately Held**
WEB: www.edwardsmachine.net
SIC: 3542 Rebuilt machine tools, metal forming types

(G-9796)
EILEEN MUSSER SHIELA
80 S Main St (45845-9770)
PHONE...................937 295-4212
Eileen Musser, *Principal*
EMP: 4
SALES (est): 385.1K **Privately Held**
SIC: 2844 Toilet preparations

(G-9797)
FIVE STAR MACHINE & TOOL
403 S Main St (45845-8716)
PHONE...................937 420-2170
Jeff Albers, *President*
Michelle Albers, *Admin Sec*
EMP: 4
SALES (est): 200K **Privately Held**
SIC: 3599 Machine shop, jobbing & repair

(G-9798)
FORT LORAMIE CAST STONE PDTS
120 S Main St (45845-9781)
P.O. Box 322 (45845-0322)
PHONE...................937 420-2257
Charles Wendeln, *President*
Theodore Wendeln, *Corp Secy*
John Wendeln, *Vice Pres*
EMP: 3 **EST**: 1928
SQ FT: 20,000
SALES: 450K **Privately Held**
WEB: www.caststoneproducts.com
SIC: 3272 5231 5211 Concrete products; paint; lumber & other building materials

(G-9799)
INDUSTRIAL MACHINING SERVICES
700 Tower Dr (45845-8769)
P.O. Box 228 (45845-0228)
PHONE...................937 295-2022
John B Puthoff, *President*
Craig Rosengarten, *General Mgr*
EMP: 40
SQ FT: 13,500
SALES: 9.1MM **Privately Held**
WEB: www.ims-spi.com
SIC: 3599 Machine shop, jobbing & repair

(G-9800)
JEFFREY BRANDEWIE
30 E Park St (45845-9301)
PHONE...................937 726-7765
Jeffrey Brandewie, *Principal*
EMP: 3
SALES (est): 150K **Privately Held**
SIC: 3089 Plastics products

(G-9801)
PARTNERS IN RECOGNITION INC
405 S Main St (45845-8716)
PHONE...................937 420-2150
Gregory Short, *President*
Angela Speelman, *Vice Pres*
◆ **EMP**: 28
SQ FT: 10,000
SALES (est): 2.9MM **Privately Held**
WEB: www.partnersinrecognition.com
SIC: 3999 Identification plates

(G-9802)
R C FAMILY WOOD PRODUCTS
5590 State Route 47 (45845)
PHONE...................937 295-2393
Rick Schulze, *President*
Cindy Schulze, *Vice Pres*
EMP: 5
SQ FT: 1,664
SALES (est): 781.6K **Privately Held**
SIC: 2448 Pallets, wood; skids, wood

(G-9803)
ROL - TECH INC
Also Called: Marwil
4814 Calvert Dr (45845)
P.O. Box 547, Winter Park FL (32790-0547)
PHONE...................214 905-8050
Roberto Diaz Del Castillo, *President*
Mark Lang, *Principal*
Zachary Gillett, *Vice Pres*
Stephanie Eilerman, *Human Res Mgr*
▲ **EMP**: 170
SALES (est): 34.4MM **Privately Held**
SIC: 3545 Machine tool accessories

(G-9804)
SCHMITMEYER INC
Also Called: G W Tool & Die Co
195 Ben St (45845)
P.O. Box 227 (45845-0227)
PHONE...................937 295-2091
Jarett Schmitmeyer, *President*
Nicole Schmitmeyer, *Vice Pres*
Eric Grimm, *Prgrmr*
EMP: 9 **EST**: 1946
SQ FT: 7,200
SALES (est): 790K **Privately Held**
WEB: www.g-wtool.com
SIC: 3599 3544 Machine shop, jobbing & repair; special dies & tools

(G-9805)
SELECT-ARC INC (PA)
600 Enterprise Dr (45845)
P.O. Box 259 (45845-0259)
PHONE...................937 295-5215
Dale Stager, *President*
Scott Stager, *Vice Pres*
Ralph Clifton, *Purch Mgr*
Ottmar Marko, *CFO*
Stacy Tangeman, *Credit Staff*
◆ **EMP**: 150
SQ FT: 67,000
SALES: 20.5MM **Privately Held**
WEB: www.select-arc.com
SIC: 3548 Welding apparatus

(G-9806)
SHARP ENTERPRISES INC
Also Called: A & B Printing
400 Enterprise Dr (45845)
P.O. Box 2 (45845-0002)
PHONE...................937 295-2965
James R Sharp, *President*
EMP: 19
SQ FT: 8,000

GEOGRAPHIC SECTION

Fort Recovery - Mercer County (G-9831)

SALES (est): 3.7MM **Privately Held**
SIC: 2752 Commercial printing, offset

(G-9807)
SOUTH SIDE DRIVE THRU
9204 Hilgefort Rd (45845-9717)
PHONE..................937 295-2927
Ken Barhorst, *Owner*
Mary Barhorst, *Co-Owner*
EMP: 6
SALES (est): 305.1K **Privately Held**
SIC: 2082 Beer (alcoholic beverage)

(G-9808)
STUDIO ELEVEN INC (PA)
301 S Main St (45845-8755)
P.O. Box 315 (45845-0315)
PHONE..................937 295-2225
Tom Barhorst, *President*
Frances A Barhorst, *Corp Secy*
Paige Turner, *Mktg Coord*
Joyce Vehorn, *Executive*
Maria Quinter, *Shareholder*
▲ EMP: 20
SALES (est): 2.9MM **Privately Held**
WEB: www.studioeleven.net
SIC: 2759 Screen printing

(G-9809)
TOOLING TECH HOLDINGS LLC (HQ)
100 Enterprise Dr (45845-9407)
PHONE..................937 295-3672
Tony Seger, *CEO*
EMP: 5 EST: 2011
SALES (est): 32.8MM **Privately Held**
SIC: 3089 Thermoformed finished plastic products

(G-9810)
TOOLING TECHNOLOGY LLC (PA)
Also Called: Tooling Tech Group
100 Enterprise Dr (45845-9407)
P.O. Box 319 (45845-0319)
PHONE..................937 295-3672
Anthony Seger, *CEO*
Gary Peppelman, *President*
EMP: 80
SQ FT: 42,000
SALES (est): 36.5MM **Privately Held**
SIC: 3544 3363 3365 3322 Industrial molds; aluminum die-castings; aluminum foundries; malleable iron foundries

(G-9811)
WAYNE TRAIL TECHNOLOGIES INC
407 S Main St (45845-8716)
PHONE..................937 295-2120
David M Knapke, *President*
Don Goldschmidt, *Buyer*
Dave Ruhenkamp, *Purchasing*
Ron Luthman, *Engineer*
Phil Deschner, *Project Engr*
EMP: 100 EST: 1962
SQ FT: 82,000
SALES (est): 30.8MM
SALES (corp-wide): 3B **Publicly Held**
WEB: www.waynetrail.com
SIC: 3728 3599 7692 3544 Aircraft parts & equipment; tubing, flexible metallic; machine shop, jobbing & repair; welding repair; special dies, tools, jigs & fixtures
PA: Lincoln Electric Holdings, Inc.
22801 Saint Clair Ave
Cleveland OH 44117
216 481-8200

Fort Recovery
Mercer County

(G-9812)
BUCKEYE DESIGN & ENGR SVC LLC
2600 Wabash Rd (45846-9500)
P.O. Box 168 (45846-0168)
PHONE..................419 375-4241
James Westgerdes, *Partner*
EMP: 6
SALES (est): 998.8K **Privately Held**
WEB: www.buckeyedesign.com
SIC: 3089 Injection molding of plastics

(G-9813)
COOPER FARMS INC (PA)
2321 State Route 49 (45846-9501)
P.O. Box 339 (45846-0339)
PHONE..................419 375-4116
James R Cooper, *President*
Brian Donley, *General Ptnr*
Jim Meeks, *General Ptnr*
Gary A Cooper, *Vice Pres*
Nick Decker, *Safety Mgr*
EMP: 100 EST: 1940
SQ FT: 38,000
SALES (est): 26.4MM **Privately Held**
WEB: www.cooperfarms.com
SIC: 2048 5191 Poultry feeds; feed

(G-9814)
COOPER FARMS INC
Also Called: Cooper Farms East Mill
2351 Wabash Rd (45846-9586)
PHONE..................419 375-4119
Bill Alig, *Manager*
EMP: 64
SALES (corp-wide): 26.4MM **Privately Held**
SIC: 2048 Poultry feeds
PA: Cooper Farms, Inc.
2321 State Route 49
Fort Recovery OH 45846
419 375-4116

(G-9815)
COOPER FARMS INC
3310 State Route 49 (45846-9507)
P.O. Box 339 (45846-0339)
PHONE..................419 375-4619
Dianne Cooper, *Sales Staff*
Tom Staugler, *Branch Mgr*
EMP: 17
SALES (corp-wide): 26.4MM **Privately Held**
WEB: www.cooperfarms.com
SIC: 2048 5191 5153 Poultry feeds; feed; grains
PA: Cooper Farms, Inc.
2321 State Route 49
Fort Recovery OH 45846
419 375-4116

(G-9816)
FORT RECOVERY EQUIPMENT INC
1201 Industrial Dr (45846-8046)
P.O. Box 646 (45846-0646)
PHONE..................419 375-1006
Cyril G Le Fevre, *President*
Helen Le Fevre, *Vice Pres*
Greg Le Fevre, *Vice Pres*
◆ EMP: 50 EST: 1970
SQ FT: 30,000
SALES (est): 12.4MM **Privately Held**
WEB: www.fortrecoveryequipment.com
SIC: 5083 3523 Livestock equipment; barn, silo, poultry, dairy & livestock machinery

(G-9817)
FORT RECOVERY EQUITY INC (PA)
2351 Wabash Rd (45846-9586)
PHONE..................419 375-4119
William Glass, *CEO*
Arnie Sumner, *President*
EMP: 165
SQ FT: 15,000
SALES (est): 18.6MM **Privately Held**
SIC: 2015 5153 Egg processing; grain elevators

(G-9818)
FORT RECOVERY INDUSTRIES INC (PA)
2440 State Route 49 (45846)
P.O. Box 638 (45846-0638)
PHONE..................419 375-4121
Wesley M Jetter, *Ch of Bd*
Dean Jetter, *COO*
Barry Hounshell, *VP Mfg*
Jack Baughman, *Plant Mgr*
Tony Thees, *Site Mgr*
◆ EMP: 315 EST: 1945
SQ FT: 120,000
SALES (est): 78.1MM **Privately Held**
WEB: www.fortrecoveryindustries.com
SIC: 3432 3363 3429 Plumbing fixture fittings & trim; aluminum die-castings; manufactured hardware (general)

(G-9819)
FORT RECOVERY INDUSTRIES INC
1200 Industrial Park Dr (45846)
PHONE..................419 375-3005
Randy Petit, *Manager*
EMP: 30
SALES (corp-wide): 47.7MM **Privately Held**
WEB: www.fortrecoveryindustries.com
SIC: 3432 Plumbing fixture fittings & trim
PA: Fort Recovery Industries, Inc.
2440 State Route 49
Fort Recovery OH 45846
419 375-4121

(G-9820)
GS WOOD & METAL COATING LLC
2096 Saint Joe Rd (45846-9711)
P.O. Box 593 (45846-0593)
PHONE..................419 375-7708
Gary Steinbrunner, *Principal*
EMP: 4
SALES (est): 335.9K **Privately Held**
SIC: 3479 Painting, coating & hot dipping

(G-9821)
HOME IDEA CENTER INC
1100 Commerce St (45846-8003)
P.O. Box 649 (45846-0649)
PHONE..................419 375-4951
Dan Schoen, *President*
Travis Laux, *Vice Pres*
EMP: 18
SQ FT: 12,000
SALES: 2MM **Privately Held**
SIC: 2599 Cabinets, factory

(G-9822)
J & M MANUFACTURING CO INC
284 Railroad St (45846)
P.O. Box 547 (45846-0547)
PHONE..................419 375-2376
Michael Grieshop, *President*
Jeff Grieshop, *Vice Pres*
Eric Fullenkamp, *Engineer*
Chuck Wolf, *Human Res Mgr*
Shannon Grieshop, *Sales Mgr*
◆ EMP: 200 EST: 1950
SQ FT: 400,000
SALES (est): 61.4MM **Privately Held**
WEB: www.jm-inc.com
SIC: 3523 Farm machinery & equipment

(G-9823)
JR MANUFACTURING INC (PA)
900 Industrial Dr W (45846-8043)
P.O. Box 478 (45846-0478)
PHONE..................419 375-8021
Jeff Roessner, *President*
Tomo Yamamoto, *President*
Greg Lefevre, *Vice Pres*
Chad Guggenbiller, *CFO*
▲ EMP: 150
SQ FT: 48,000
SALES (est): 60.8MM **Privately Held**
WEB: www.jrmanufacturing.net
SIC: 3315 3441 Steel wire & related products; fabricated structural metal

(G-9824)
JW MANUFACTURING
317 Watkins Rd (45846-9125)
PHONE..................419 375-5536
Josh Wuebker, *Principal*
EMP: 3 EST: 2014
SALES (est): 327K **Privately Held**
SIC: 3999 Manufacturing industries

(G-9825)
MEL HEITKAMP BUILDERS LTD
635 Secret Judy Rd (45846)
P.O. Box 229 (45846-0229)
PHONE..................419 375-0405
Doug Heitkamp, *Partner*
Jack Heitkamp, *Partner*
Tony Heitkamp, *Partner*
Joe Heitkamp, *General Ptnr*

EMP: 9
SALES (est): 669.1K **Privately Held**
SIC: 8741 2521 5712 Construction management; cabinets, office: wood; customized furniture & cabinets

(G-9826)
ROESSNER HOLDINGS INC
482 State Route 119 (45846-9563)
P.O. Box 369, Saint Henry (45883-0369)
PHONE..................419 356-2123
Jeffrey D Roessner, *President*
EMP: 6
SQ FT: 5,000
SALES: 450K **Privately Held**
SIC: 3555 Printing trades machinery

(G-9827)
STEVE VORE WELDING AND STEEL
Also Called: Vores Steve Welding & Steel
3234 State Route 49 (45846)
P.O. Box 37 (45846-0037)
PHONE..................419 375-4087
Stephen Vore, *President*
EMP: 10
SQ FT: 5,400
SALES: 836.9K **Privately Held**
SIC: 3312 7692 1799 3444 Structural shapes & pilings, steel; welding repair; welding on site; sheet metalwork; fabricated plate work (boiler shop); fabricated structural metal

(G-9828)
SUSPENSION FEEDER CORPORATION
482 State Route 119 (45846-9563)
P.O. Box 369, Saint Henry (45883-0369)
PHONE..................419 763-1377
Gregory G Baron, *President*
Roberta Baron, *Treasurer*
EMP: 10
SQ FT: 12,000
SALES: 1MM **Privately Held**
SIC: 3555 Printing trades machinery

(G-9829)
V H COOPER & CO INC (HQ)
Also Called: Cooper Foods
2321 State Route 49 (45846-9501)
P.O. Box 339 (45846-0339)
PHONE..................419 375-4116
James R Cooper, *President*
Gary A Cooper, *COO*
Neil Diller, *CFO*
Anada E Cooper, *Treasurer*
Dianne L Cooper, *Admin Sec*
EMP: 150
SQ FT: 4,400
SALES (est): 124MM
SALES (corp-wide): 256.7MM **Privately Held**
WEB: www.cooperfoods.com
SIC: 0253 2015 2011 Turkeys & turkey eggs; chicken slaughtering & processing; pork products from pork slaughtered on site; hams & picnics from meat slaughtered on site
PA: Cooper Hatchery, Inc.
22348 Road 140
Oakwood OH 45873
419 594-3325

(G-9830)
WABASH RIVER CONSERVANCY
Also Called: Wabash River Conservancy Dst
14574 State Route 49 (45846-9104)
PHONE..................419 375-2577
Walter Broeing, *President*
Don Rose, *Vice Pres*
John Portcamp, *Treasurer*
EMP: 4 EST: 1999
SALES: 27.8K **Privately Held**
SIC: 3823 Water quality monitoring & control systems

(G-9831)
WESTGERDES CABINETS
2664 Sawmill Rd (45846-9707)
PHONE..................419 375-2113
Robert Westgerdes, *Owner*
EMP: 3
SQ FT: 8,200

Fostoria - Seneca County (G-9832)   **GEOGRAPHIC SECTION**

SALES (est): 150K Privately Held
SIC: 2434 Wood kitchen cabinets

Fostoria
Seneca County

(G-9832)
ALPHA COATINGS INC
622 S Corporate Dr W (44830-9447)
PHONE 419 435-5111
Terence White, *President*
EMP: 115
SQ FT: 48,000
SALES (est): 20MM
SALES (corp-wide): 15.3B **Publicly Held**
WEB: www.alpha-coatings.com
SIC: 3479 2891 Coating of metals & formed products; adhesives & sealants
HQ: Whitford Worldwide Company, Llc
  47 Park Ave
  Elverson PA 19520
  610 286-3500

(G-9833)
ARCHER-DANIELS-MIDLAND COMPANY
Also Called: ADM
608 Findlay St (44830-1850)
PHONE 419 435-6633
Dale Anderburry, *Manager*
EMP: 45
SALES (corp-wide): 64.3B **Publicly Held**
WEB: www.admworld.com
SIC: 2041 2077 2075 Flour & other grain mill products; animal & marine fats & oils; soybean oil mills
PA: Archer-Daniels-Midland Company
  77 W Wacker Dr Ste 4600
  Chicago IL 60601
  312 634-8100

(G-9834)
B & B PALLET CO
885 S State Route 587 (44830-9501)
PHONE 419 435-4530
Steve Bugner, *Owner*
EMP: 4
SALES (est): 247.4K **Privately Held**
SIC: 2448 Pallets, wood

(G-9835)
B&D TRUCK PARTS SLS & SVCS LLC
1498 Perrysburg Rd (44830-1351)
PHONE 419 701-7041
Bill J Bowling,
EMP: 6
SALES (est): 330K **Privately Held**
SIC: 8999 3751 Artists & artists' studios; motorcycle accessories

(G-9836)
DAILY FOSTORIA REVIEW CO
Also Called: Review Times, The
113 E Center St (44830-2905)
P.O. Box 947 (44830-0947)
PHONE 419 435-6641
Fax: 419 435-9073
EMP: 200
SALES (est): 5.3MM **Privately Held**
SIC: 2711 Newspaper Publisher

(G-9837)
FABRICATION SHOP INC
1395 Buckley St (44830-9459)
PHONE 419 435-7934
Bill Cronauer, *President*
Deborah Cronauer, *Vice Pres*
EMP: 18
SQ FT: 15,000
SALES (est): 2.2MM **Privately Held**
SIC: 7692 3443 3544 Welding repair; fabricated plate work (boiler shop); special dies & tools

(G-9838)
FILMTEC INC
1120 Sandusky St (44830-2761)
PHONE 419 435-1819
John P Hollingsworth, *President*
Jo Hollingsworth, *Vice Pres*
EMP: 20
SQ FT: 44,000
SALES (est): 3.6MM **Privately Held**
WEB: www.filmtecinc.com
SIC: 3549 Wiredrawing & fabricating machinery & equipment, ex. die

(G-9839)
FOSTORIA BSHNGS INSLATORS CORP
602 S Corporate Dr W D (44830-9456)
P.O. Box 1064 (44830-1064)
PHONE 419 435-7514
Philip C John, *President*
▲ EMP: 6
SALES (est): 750K **Privately Held**
SIC: 3612 Transformers, except electric

(G-9840)
FOSTORIA BUSHINGS INC
Also Called: FB Ins
602 S Corporate Dr W (44830-9456)
P.O. Box 1064 (44830-1064)
PHONE 419 435-7514
Philip C John, *President*
▲ EMP: 9
SALES (est): 1.3MM **Privately Held**
SIC: 3612 Transformers, except electric

(G-9841)
FOSTORIA ETHANOL LLC
Also Called: Poet Brfining- Fostoria 23200
2111 Sandusky St (44830-2790)
PHONE 419 436-0954
Art Thomas, *General Mgr*
Jeff Broin, *Principal*
EMP: 40
SALES (est): 15.5MM **Privately Held**
SIC: 2869 Ethyl alcohol, ethanol
PA: Poet, Llc
  4615 N Lewis Ave
  Sioux Falls SD 57104

(G-9842)
FOSTORIA FOCUS INC
112 N Main St (44830-2223)
P.O. Box 1158 (44830-1158)
PHONE 419 435-6397
Donald P Miller, *President*
EMP: 11
SALES (est): 424.9K **Privately Held**
WEB: www.fostoriafocus.com
SIC: 2711 Newspapers: publishing only, not printed on site

(G-9843)
FOSTORIA MACHINE PRODUCTS
425 S Union St (44830-2342)
P.O. Box 883 (44830-0883)
PHONE 419 435-4262
Bill Derck, *Owner*
EMP: 7 EST: 1954
SQ FT: 3,000
SALES (est): 673.1K **Privately Held**
SIC: 3544 3451 Special dies & tools; screw machine products

(G-9844)
FOSTORIA MONUMENT CO (PA)
Also Called: Tri County Marble & Granite
701 Van Buren St (44830-1538)
PHONE 419 435-0373
Gregory A Smith, *President*
Saundra Smith, *Admin Sec*
EMP: 3
SQ FT: 2,000
SALES (est): 941K **Privately Held**
SIC: 3281 5099 Monument or burial stone, cut & shaped; signs, except electric

(G-9845)
FRAM GROUP OPERATIONS LLC
Honeywell
1600 N Union St (44830-1958)
P.O. Box 880 (44830-0880)
PHONE 419 436-5827
Paul Humphrys, *Director*
EMP: 900 **Privately Held**
WEB: www.honeywell.com
SIC: 3714 3264 Motor vehicle parts & accessories; porcelain electrical supplies
HQ: Fram Group Operations Llc
  1900 W Field Ct 4w-516
  Lake Forest IL 60045

(G-9846)
MACHINE TOOL & FAB CORP
1401 Sandusky St (44830-2774)
PHONE 419 435-7676
Dick Kiser, *President*
EMP: 19
SQ FT: 20,400
SALES (est): 3.4MM **Privately Held**
WEB: www.machinetoolandfab.com
SIC: 3599 3441 3442 Custom machinery; fabricated structural metal; hangar doors, metal

(G-9847)
MACHINE TOOL DESIGN & FAB LLC
1401 Sandusky St (44830-2774)
PHONE 419 435-7676
Christopher Eastman, *Mng Member*
EMP: 19
SALES (est): 880.4K
SALES (corp-wide): 1.2MM **Privately Held**
SIC: 3544 7699 Special dies, tools, jigs & fixtures; metal reshaping & replating services
PA: Eastman Holding Llc
  1185 W Parkway Blvd
  Aurora OH 44202
  419 435-7676

(G-9848)
MENNEL MILLING COMPANY
320 Findlay St (44830-1854)
P.O. Box 806 (44830-0806)
PHONE 419 436-5130
Donald L Mennel, *Branch Mgr*
EMP: 60
SALES (corp-wide): 119.2MM **Privately Held**
WEB: www.troyelevator.com
SIC: 2041 Flour & other grain mill products
PA: The Mennel Milling Company
  319 S Vine St
  Fostoria OH 44830
  419 435-8151

(G-9849)
MORGAN ADVANCED MATERIALS
200 N Town St (44830-2835)
PHONE 419 435-8182
Randy Bishop, *Plant Mgr*
Brad Miehls, *Engineer*
John Roets, *Engineer*
Greg Smith, *CFO*
▼ EMP: 160
SALES (est): 18.5MM **Privately Held**
SIC: 3624 Carbon & graphite products

(G-9850)
NATIONAL ELEC CARBN PDTS INC
200 N Town St (44830-2835)
PHONE 419 435-8182
Greg Smith, *Finance Mgr*
John Stang, *Branch Mgr*
EMP: 100
SALES (corp-wide): 1.3B **Privately Held**
WEB: www.nationalspecialties.com
SIC: 3624 Carbon & graphite products
HQ: National Electrical Carbon Products, Inc.
  251 Forrester Dr
  Greenville SC 29607
  864 458-7777

(G-9851)
NEON PAINTBRUSH
461 W Lytle St Lot 153 (44830-3412)
PHONE 419 436-1202
Joseph McCartney, *Administration*
EMP: 3
SALES (est): 140K **Privately Held**
SIC: 2813 Neon

(G-9852)
NIPPON STL SMKIN CRNKSHAFT LLC
Also Called: Nsi Crankshaft
1815 Sandusky St (44830-2754)
PHONE 419 435-0411
Makoto Tsuruhara, *President*
Tim Hasegawa, *Exec VP*
Mitch Koboshi, *Exec VP*
James Siebenaller, *Maint Spvr*
Al Leonard, *Production*
EMP: 13
SQ FT: 225,000
SALES (est): 3.7MM
SALES (corp-wide): 53.2B **Privately Held**
SIC: 3599 3714 Crankshafts & camshafts, machining; crankshaft assemblies, motor vehicle
HQ: Nippon Steel & Sumitomo Metal U.S.A., Inc.
  1251 Ave Of The Ave Fl 23 Flr 23
  New York NY 10020
  212 486-7150

(G-9853)
NORTON MANUFACTURING CO INC
455 W 4th St (44830-1864)
P.O. Box 1127 (44830-1127)
PHONE 419 435-0411
EMP: 11
SALES (est): 1.2MM **Privately Held**
SIC: 3714 Motor vehicle parts & accessories

(G-9854)
OK INDUSTRIES INC
2307 W Corporate Dr W (44830-9449)
PHONE 419 435-2361
James Kenyon, *President*
Jim Kenyon, *President*
EMP: 45
SQ FT: 100,000
SALES (est): 8.8MM **Privately Held**
WEB: www.okindustries.com
SIC: 2821 Plastics materials & resins

(G-9855)
ROPPE CORPORATION
1602 N Union St (44830-1958)
PHONE 419 435-8546
Donald P Miller, *President*
Judy R Miller, *Vice Pres*
Judy Miller, *Vice Pres*
Bart Rogers, *Vice Pres*
Mark J Baker, *Treasurer*
◆ EMP: 300
SALES: 115MM
SALES (corp-wide): 189.7MM **Privately Held**
SIC: 3069 Flooring, rubber: tile or sheet
PA: Roppe Holding Company
  1602 N Union St
  Fostoria OH 44830
  419 435-8546

(G-9856)
ROPPE HOLDING COMPANY
J Miller and Co
106 N Main St (44830-2223)
PHONE 419 435-6601
Jessica Sheridan, *Manager*
EMP: 8
SALES (corp-wide): 189.7MM **Privately Held**
WEB: www.roppe.com
SIC: 3089 3069 Extruded finished plastic products; rubber floor coverings, mats & wallcoverings; wallcoverings, rubber; tile, rubber; stair treads, rubber
PA: Roppe Holding Company
  1602 N Union St
  Fostoria OH 44830
  419 435-8546

(G-9857)
SANDY CREEK MINING CO INC
522 S Poplar St (44830-3054)
P.O. Box 88 (44830-0088)
PHONE 419 435-5891
Patrick Woodruff, *President*
Jason Woodruff, *General Mgr*
▲ EMP: 4 EST: 1996
SALES (est): 572.8K **Privately Held**
WEB: www.sandycreekmining.com
SIC: 1481 Mine exploration, nonmetallic minerals

(G-9858)
SCHREINER CSTM STAIRS & MLLWK
1415 Sandusky St (44830-2774)
P.O. Box 750 (44830-0750)
PHONE 419 435-8935
Melvin Schreiner, *President*

▲ = Import ▼ = Export
◆ = Import/Export

Shirley Schreiner, *Corp Secy*
Greg Schreiner, *Vice Pres*
EMP: 5
SQ FT: 5,000
SALES (est): 638.7K **Privately Held**
SIC: 2431 Staircases & stairs, wood

(G-9859)
SENECA MILLWORK INC
300 Court Pl (44830-2453)
P.O. Box 429 (44830-0429)
PHONE.....................................419 435-6671
Donald Miller, *President*
Mark J Baker, *Principal*
Judy R Miller, *Principal*
Angela K Gillett, *Vice Pres*
▲ **EMP:** 50 **EST:** 1873
SQ FT: 120,000
SALES (est): 7.1MM **Privately Held**
WEB: www.senecamillwork.com
SIC: 2431 Moldings, wood: unfinished & prefinished; floor baseboards, wood

(G-9860)
TIME IS MONEY
1280 North Dr (44830-9780)
PHONE.....................................419 701-6098
EMP: 3 **EST:** 1999
SALES (est): 230K **Privately Held**
SIC: 3559 7389 Mfg Misc Industry Machinery

Frankfort
Ross County

(G-9861)
CONVEYOR METAL WORKS INC
2717 Bush Mill Rd (45628-9791)
PHONE.....................................740 477-8700
Scott P Kadish, *President*
Christy Wolfe, *Vice Pres*
EMP: 20 **EST:** 2000
SQ FT: 30,000
SALES (est): 5.4MM **Privately Held**
WEB: www.conveyormetalworks.com
SIC: 3535 Conveyors & conveying equipment

(G-9862)
JAY TACKETT
Also Called: T R C
387 Musselman Station Rd (45628-9761)
PHONE.....................................740 779-1715
Jay Takett, *Owner*
EMP: 5
SQ FT: 4,000
SALES: 200K **Privately Held**
SIC: 3955 5112 3861 2899 Print cartridges for laser & other computer printers; inked ribbons; photographic equipment & supplies; chemical preparations

(G-9863)
LIGHTLE ENTERPRISES OHIO LLC (PA)
22 E Springfield St (45628-8013)
P.O. Box 329 (45628-0329)
PHONE.....................................740 998-5363
David Lightle,
Dixie Lightle,
EMP: 4
SALES (est): 1MM **Privately Held**
SIC: 3669 7359 5099 Pedestrian traffic control equipment; work zone traffic equipment (flags, cones, barrels, etc.); reflective road markers

(G-9864)
ROCAL INC (PA)
3186 County Road 550 (45628-9503)
PHONE.....................................740 998-2122
Robert Lightle, *President*
Andrew Blazar, *Plant Mgr*
Maryl Greening, *Controller*
Rick Turner, *Accounts Mgr*
▲ **EMP:** 90
SQ FT: 200,000
SALES (est): 23MM **Privately Held**
SIC: 3993 Signs, not made in custom sign painting shops

Franklin
Warren County

(G-9865)
119C LANDIS DISPLAY CO
Also Called: C L D
346 Beam Dr (45005-2008)
PHONE.....................................937 307-9499
Charles H Landis Jr, *Owner*
Charlie Landis, *Owner*
EMP: 5 **EST:** 1980
SALES: 178.6K **Privately Held**
SIC: 2541 Store & office display cases & fixtures

(G-9866)
3-D TECHNICAL SERVICES COMPANY
Also Called: 3-Dmed
255 Industrial Dr (45005-4429)
PHONE.....................................937 746-2901
Robert Aumann, *President*
Jennifer Theriault, *Finance Mgr*
Becky Larson, *Sales Staff*
EMP: 25
SQ FT: 15,000
SALES (est): 3.1MM **Privately Held**
WEB: www.3-dtechnicalservices.com
SIC: 7389 2542 3999 Building scale models; design, commercial & industrial; partitions & fixtures, except wood; models, general, except toy

(G-9867)
ADVANCED WELDING CO
901 N Main St (45005-1650)
PHONE.....................................937 746-6800
Tony Ling, *Owner*
EMP: 20
SQ FT: 8,000
SALES (est): 500K **Privately Held**
SIC: 3443 3599 7692 3444 Fabricated plate work (boiler shop); machine & other job shop work; welding repair; sheet metalwork

(G-9868)
AM GENERAL LLC
2000 Watkins Glen Dr (45005-2392)
PHONE.....................................937 704-0160
Alasdair Young, *Chief Engr*
Charles M Hall, *Branch Mgr*
EMP: 4 **Privately Held**
SIC: 3711 3714 Military motor vehicle assembly; motor vehicle parts & accessories
HQ: Am General Llc
105 N Niles Ave
South Bend IN 46617
574 237-6222

(G-9869)
AMPLE INDUSTRIES INC
4000 Commerce Center Dr (45005-1897)
PHONE.....................................937 746-9700
Gregory K Pratt, *President*
William Akers Sr, *Vice Pres*
Vic Crainish, *Controller*
EMP: 210
SQ FT: 108,000
SALES (est): 25.4MM
SALES (corp-wide): 35.2B **Privately Held**
WEB: www.ampleindustries.com
SIC: 2657 Paperboard backs for blister or skin packages
PA: Huhtamaki Oyj
Revontulenkuja 1
Espoo 02100
106 867-000

(G-9870)
ATLAS ROOFING CORPORATION
Gypsum & Roofing Div
675 Oxford Rd (45005-3678)
PHONE.....................................937 746-9941
Kathy Cahall, *QC Mgr*
Rick Bielecki, *Plant Engr*
Robert Cipriano, *VP Human Res*
Cassandra Henry, *Accounts Exec*
Scott Karas, *Sales Staff*
EMP: 170 **Privately Held**
WEB: www.atlasroofing.com
SIC: 3086 2951 2952 Insulation or cushioning material, foamed plastic; asphalt paving mixtures & blocks; asphalt felts & coatings
HQ: Atlas Roofing Corporation
802 Highway 19 N Ste 190
Meridian MS 39307
601 484-8900

(G-9871)
BENNETT MECHANICAL SYSTEMS LLC
5157 Union Rd (45005-5140)
PHONE.....................................513 292-3506
Paul Bennett,
Justin Bennett,
EMP: 3
SALES (est): 291.1K **Privately Held**
SIC: 3585 Refrigeration & heating equipment

(G-9872)
BOND MACHINE COMPANY INC
921 N Main St (45005-1650)
PHONE.....................................937 746-4941
David Bond, *President*
Steve Bond, *Corp Secy*
John Bond Jr, *Vice Pres*
Tom Bond, *Admin Sec*
EMP: 14 **EST:** 1968
SQ FT: 12,000
SALES: 2.1MM **Privately Held**
WEB: www.bondmachineco.com
SIC: 3599 Machine shop, jobbing & repair

(G-9873)
CAST PLUS INC
415 Oxford Rd (45005-3639)
PHONE.....................................937 743-7278
Maurice R Meeker, *President*
Richard Devaney, *Vice Pres*
Scott Meeker, *Sales Executive*
EMP: 35
SQ FT: 40,000
SALES (est): 5.5MM **Privately Held**
WEB: www.castplus.com
SIC: 3479 Coating of metals & formed products

(G-9874)
CHENEY PULP AND PAPER COMPANY
1000 Anderson St (45005-2571)
P.O. Box 215 (45005-0215)
PHONE.....................................937 746-9991
Mark Snyder, *President*
Donald A Davies, *Principal*
▲ **EMP:** 30 **EST:** 1924
SQ FT: 30,000
SALES (est): 8.5MM **Privately Held**
WEB: www.cheneypulp.com
SIC: 2621 Paper mills

(G-9875)
CONTAINER GRAPHICS CORP
1 Miller St (45005-4455)
PHONE.....................................937 746-5666
Steve Woods, *Branch Mgr*
EMP: 25
SALES (corp-wide): 3MM **Privately Held**
WEB: www.containergraphics.com
SIC: 3544 Dies, steel rule
PA: Container Graphics Corp.
114 Ednbrgh S Dr Ste 104
Cary NC 27511
919 481-4200

(G-9876)
COUNTER- ADVICE INC
7002 State Route 123 (45005-2358)
PHONE.....................................937 291-1600
Brian Donley, *President*
Morgan Krapfel, *Receptionist*
EMP: 13
SQ FT: 13,000
SALES (est): 2.1MM **Privately Held**
WEB: www.counteradvice.com
SIC: 2541 Counter & sink tops

(G-9877)
COUNTRY TIN
228 S Main St (45005-2226)
PHONE.....................................937 746-7229
EMP: 3 **EST:** 2004
SALES (est): 160K **Privately Held**
SIC: 3645 Mfg Residential Lighting Fixtures

(G-9878)
DAYTON DAILEY NEWS
5000 Commerce Center Dr (45005-7200)
PHONE.....................................937 743-2387
Joe Mc Kinnon, *Principal*
Barbara Parker, *Purchasing*
Julie Campbell, *Admin Mgr*
Stan Richmond, *Executive*
EMP: 13
SALES (est): 1.5MM **Privately Held**
SIC: 2711 Commercial printing & newspaper publishing combined

(G-9879)
DCS TECHNOLOGIES CORPORATION
6501 State Route 123 (45005-4519)
PHONE.....................................937 743-4060
Phil Denlinger, *President*
Ned M Denlinger, *Vice Pres*
EMP: 35 **EST:** 1979
SQ FT: 15,000
SALES (est): 6MM **Privately Held**
WEB: www.dcs-tech.com
SIC: 2759 Laser printing

(G-9880)
F & G TOOL AND DIE CO
130 Industrial Dr (45005-4428)
PHONE.....................................937 746-3658
Dick Smith, *Branch Mgr*
EMP: 22
SALES (corp-wide): 14MM **Privately Held**
SIC: 3542 3469 Machine tools, metal forming type; metal stampings
PA: F & G Tool And Die Co.
3024 Dryden Rd
Moraine OH 45439
937 294-1405

(G-9881)
F P C PRINTING INC
Also Called: Franklin's Printing
119 Art Ave (45005-1601)
PHONE.....................................937 743-8136
Michael Patrick, *President*
Kathleen Patrick, *Corp Secy*
Chad Patrick, *Vice Pres*
EMP: 6
SQ FT: 10,000
SALES (est): 813.4K **Privately Held**
SIC: 2752 Commercial printing, lithographic

(G-9882)
FAURECIA EXHAUST SYSTEMS INC
Also Called: Franklin Mfg Div
2301 Commerce Center Dr (45005-1896)
PHONE.....................................937 743-0551
Parker Sykes, *Branch Mgr*
EMP: 400
SALES (corp-wide): 342.9MM **Privately Held**
WEB: www.franklin.faurecia.com
SIC: 3714 3053 Exhaust systems & parts, motor vehicle; manifolds, motor vehicle; gaskets, packing & sealing devices
HQ: Faurecia Emissions Control Systems Na, Llc
543 Matzinger Rd
Toledo OH 43612
812 341-2000

(G-9883)
FERCO TECH LLC
291 Conover Dr (45005-1944)
P.O. Box 607 (45005-0607)
PHONE.....................................937 746-6696
Bryan Perkins, *President*
Earl Larkin, *Co-CEO*
Vincent Bebko, *Plant Mgr*
Randy Harris, *Engineer*
Jim Clemons, *CFO*
EMP: 120
SQ FT: 30,000
SALES (est): 37.1MM
SALES (corp-wide): 168.5MM **Privately Held**
SIC: 3728 Aircraft parts & equipment

Franklin - Warren County (G-9884)

PA: Novaria Group, L.L.C.
6300 Ridglea Pl Ste 800
Fort Worth TX 76116
817 381-3810

(G-9884)
FRANKLIN CABINET COMPANY INC
2500 Commerce Center Dr (45005-1816)
PHONE...................937 743-9606
Mark Duncan, *President*
EMP: 29
SQ FT: 50,000
SALES (est): 4.3MM **Privately Held**
SIC: 3083 2541 2599 2531 Plastic finished products, laminated; cabinets, lockers & shelving; bar, restaurant & cafeteria furniture; public building & related furniture; upholstered household furniture; wood kitchen cabinets

(G-9885)
GAD-JETS INC
Also Called: Associated Technical Sales
323 Industrial Dr (45005-4431)
P.O. Box 13419, Dayton (45413-0419)
PHONE...................937 274-2111
Adryana Southerland, *President*
EMP: 8
SQ FT: 9,280
SALES: 350K **Privately Held**
WEB: www.gadjets.com
SIC: 3542 3089 Presses: hydraulic & pneumatic, mechanical & manual; fittings for pipe, plastic

(G-9886)
GENERAL ENGINE PRODUCTS LLC
2000 Watkins Glen Dr (45005-2392)
P.O. Box 488 (45005-0488)
PHONE...................937 704-0160
Charles M Hall, *President*
Daniel J Dell'orto, *Vice Pres*
Jeffery Adams, *Director*
James Armour,
▲ **EMP:** 80
SALES (est): 15.8MM **Privately Held**
WEB: www.amgmil.com
SIC: 3519 Diesel engine rebuilding
HQ: Am General Llc
105 N Niles Ave
South Bend IN 46617
574 237-6222

(G-9887)
GREEN POINT METALS INC (PA)
Also Called: GPM
301 Shotwell Dr (45005-4659)
PHONE...................937 743-4075
Brian D Williamson, *CEO*
Doug Everhart, *President*
Travis Hearn, *Vice Pres*
Gary Mockabee, *CFO*
Jeffrey Paugh, *Sales Staff*
FMP: 35
SQ FT: 150,000
SALES (est): 8.5MM **Privately Held**
WEB: www.greenpointmetals.com
SIC: 3441 Fabricated structural metal

(G-9888)
H & W SCREW PRODUCTS INC
335 Industrial Dr (45005-4431)
PHONE...................937 866-2577
Robert E Wray, *President*
Wendy Wray, *Treasurer*
Richard Carlisle, *Admin Sec*
EMP: 13
SQ FT: 10,000
SALES (est): 1.1MM **Privately Held**
SIC: 3451 Screw machine products

(G-9889)
HOMECARE MATTRESS INC
Also Called: Next Day Access-Central Ohio
303 Conover Dr (45005-1957)
PHONE...................937 746-2556
Debbie Lipps, *President*
P Scott Lipps, *Vice Pres*
Ryan Conde, *Accounts Mgr*
EMP: 15
SQ FT: 6,000
SALES (est): 3.4MM **Privately Held**
SIC: 3448 2515 5047 5712 Ramps: prefabricated metal; mattresses & foundations; medical & hospital equipment; mattresses

(G-9890)
HUHTAMAKI INC
4000 Commerce Center Dr (45005-1897)
PHONE...................937 746-9700
Phil Walker, *Manager*
Doug Pike, *Technology*
Sandra Kelly, *Planning*
Vanessa Thompson, *Personnel Assit*
EMP: 320
SALES (corp-wide): 35.2B **Privately Held**
SIC: 3565 2656 Labeling machines, industrial; ice cream containers: made from purchased material
HQ: Huhtamaki, Inc.
9201 Packaging Dr
De Soto KS 66018
913 583-3025

(G-9891)
IKO PRODUCTION INC
1200 S Main St (45005-2781)
PHONE...................937 746-4561
Randy Dalton, *Plant Supt*
David Foulkes, *Branch Mgr*
EMP: 47
SQ FT: 100,000 **Privately Held**
SIC: 2952 3083 Roofing felts, cements or coatings; laminated plastics plate & sheet
HQ: Iko Production, Inc.
120 Hay Rd
Wilmington DE 19809

(G-9892)
KEMPER AUTOMOTIVE
1380 E 2nd St (45005-1850)
P.O. Box 188 (45005-0188)
PHONE...................800 783-8004
EMP: 6
SQ FT: 11,000
SALES (est): 683.3K **Privately Held**
SIC: 2396 5531 Mfg Auto/Apparel Trimming & Ret Auto Accessories

(G-9893)
KLOCKNER PENTAPLAST AMER INC
400 Shotwell Dr (45005-4661)
PHONE...................937 743-8040
Klockner Pentaplast, *Principal*
John Coppock, *Opers Mgr*
Annie Globig, *Engineer*
EMP: 4
SALES (corp-wide): 672.8K **Privately Held**
SIC: 3554 3052 Fourdrinier machines, paper manufacturing; plastic hose
HQ: Klockner Pentaplast Of America, Inc.
3585 Kloeckner Rd
Gordonsville VA 22942
540 832-1400

(G-9894)
L&E ENGINEERING LLC
291 Conover Dr (45005-1944)
PHONE...................937 746-6696
EMP: 29
SALES (corp-wide): 4.7MM **Privately Held**
SIC: 3728 Aircraft parts & equipment
PA: L&E Engineering Llc
254 N Graham Rd
Greenwood IN 46143
937 746-6696

(G-9895)
LEGACY FINISHING INC
415 Oxford Rd (45005-3639)
P.O. Box 249 (45005-0249)
PHONE...................937 743-7278
Tom Custer, *Principal*
Kevin Dickerson, *Production*
Dick Meeker, *Benefits Mgr*
Christine Fischer, *Office Mgr*
Scott Meeker, *Manager*
EMP: 9
SALES (est): 1.5MM **Privately Held**
SIC: 3399 Powder, metal

(G-9896)
LYNX CHEMICAL
370 Industrial Dr (45005-4432)
PHONE...................513 856-9161
William Schmidt,
EMP: 4
SALES (corp-wide): 3MM **Privately Held**
SIC: 2899 Chemical supplies for foundries
PA: Lynx Chemical
2550 Bobmeyer Rd
Hamilton OH

(G-9897)
MARBLE ARCH PRODUCTS INC
263 Industrial Dr (45005-4429)
PHONE...................937 746-8388
Keenan Beauchamp, *President*
EMP: 14
SQ FT: 15,000
SALES (est): 2.6MM **Privately Held**
WEB: www.marblearchproducts.com
SIC: 3088 5211 Bathroom fixtures, plastic; bathroom fixtures, equipment & supplies

(G-9898)
MCS MIDWEST LLC (PA)
3876 Hendrickson Rd (45005-9726)
PHONE...................513 217-0805
Stanley J Streeter,
EMP: 17
SALES (est): 4.3MM **Privately Held**
SIC: 3089 7699 Garbage containers, plastic; agricultural equipment repair services

(G-9899)
MERIDIAN BRICK LLC
250 Industrial Dr (45005-4430)
PHONE...................937 294-1548
Troy Vaughn, *Manager*
EMP: 7
SALES (corp-wide): 441MM **Privately Held**
WEB: www.boralbricks.com
SIC: 3251 Structural brick & blocks
PA: Meridian Brick Llc
6455 Shiloh Rd D
Alpharetta GA 30005
770 645-4500

(G-9900)
MIAMI VALLEY PAPER LLC
Also Called: Miami Wabash
413 Oxford Rd (45005-3639)
P.O. Box 5651, Hartford CT (06102-5651)
PHONE...................937 746-6451
Bill Naser, *Manager*
EMP: 18
SALES (est): 100.3MM **Privately Held**
SIC: 2631 Paperboard mills
HQ: Miami Valley Paper Llc
108 Main St Ste 3
Norwalk CT 06851

(G-9901)
MIRACLE WELDING INC
Also Called: Miracle Air
141 Industrial Dr Ste 200 (45005-4427)
PHONE...................513 746-9977
David Miracle, *President*
Faun Miracle, *Vice Pres*
EMP: 6 **EST:** 1978
SQ FT: 12,000
SALES (est): 1MM **Privately Held**
WEB: www.miraclewelding.com
SIC: 3599 3441 Machine shop, jobbing & repair; fabricated structural metal

(G-9902)
NATION COATING SYSTEMS INC
501 Shotwell Dr (45005-4663)
PHONE...................937 746-7632
Larry F Grimenstein, *President*
Lois Grimenstein, *Corp Secy*
Jim Drumm, *Vice Pres*
EMP: 8
SALES (est): 1.3MM **Privately Held**
WEB: www.nationcoatingsystems.com
SIC: 3479 Coating of metals & formed products; painting, coating & hot dipping

(G-9903)
NC WORKS INC
3500 Commerce Center Dr (45005-7202)
PHONE...................937 514-7781

Simon Chen, *President*
Mikio Nishizu, *Principal*
Jim Reinert, *Maint Spvr*
▲ **EMP:** 27 **EST:** 2010
SALES (est): 4.6MM
SALES (corp-wide): 8.6MM **Privately Held**
SIC: 2299 Automotive felts; carpet cushions, felt
PA: Fehrer Enterprise Corporation.
1, Miao-Pu Lane, Shau Shin Lee,
Tainan City 74170
658 362-16

(G-9904)
NIKTEC LLC
127 Industrial Dr (45005-4427)
PHONE...................513 282-3747
Nicholas Campbell,
▼ **EMP:** 7
SALES (est): 550.8K **Privately Held**
SIC: 7629 3679 Electrical repair shops; electronic circuits

(G-9905)
NOVOLEX HOLDINGS INC
Also Called: Burrrows Paper Corroc Div
2000 Commerce Center Dr (45005-1477)
PHONE...................937 746-1933
Jef Hall, *Manager*
EMP: 337
SQ FT: 106,000
SALES (corp-wide): 3B **Privately Held**
WEB: www.burrowspaper.com
SIC: 2621 2656 2653 Tissue paper; sanitary food containers; boxes, corrugated: made from purchased materials
HQ: Novolex Holdings, Llc
101 E Carolina Ave
Hartsville SC 29550
843 857-4800

(G-9906)
OLIVAMED LLC
401 Shotwell Dr (45005-4660)
PHONE...................937 401-0821
Bernard Speeckaert, *President*
Larry Couchot, *General Mgr*
Franco Grasso, *Principal*
Mario Pop, *Opers Staff*
Kara Mastern, *Accountant*
▲ **EMP:** 16
SQ FT: 2,000
SALES (est): 1.7MM **Privately Held**
SIC: 2079 Olive oil

(G-9907)
P R U INDUSTRIES INC
8401 Claude Thomas Rd (45005-1497)
PHONE...................937 746-8702
James Riling, *President*
Marcie Marks, *Vice Pres*
Mark See, *Vice Pres*
EMP: 10
SALES: 4MM
SALES (corp-wide): 2.5MM **Privately Held**
SIC: 2448 Wood pallets & skids
PA: Industrial Holdings Group, Inc
7755 Paragon Rd Ste 104
Dayton OH 45459
937 434-8100

(G-9908)
PFIZER INC
160 Industrial Dr (45005-4428)
PHONE...................937 746-3603
Chris Gebhart, *Engineer*
Fred Haller, *Manager*
Ron Groh, *Director*
EMP: 146
SALES (corp-wide): 53.6B **Publicly Held**
WEB: www.pfizer.com
SIC: 2833 2844 2099 2834 Antibiotics; hair preparations, including shampoos; toilet preparations; oral preparations; cake fillings, except fruit; drugs acting on the cardiovascular system, except diagnostic
PA: Pfizer Inc.
235 E 42nd St
New York NY 10017
212 733-2323

Franklin Furnace - Scioto County (G-9935)

(G-9909)
PHARMACIA HEPAR LLC
160 Industrial Dr (45005-4428)
PHONE.....................................937 746-3603
Fred J Haller, *President*
EMP: 72
SQ FT: 35,000
SALES (est): 9.6MM
SALES (corp-wide): 53.6B **Publicly Held**
WEB: www.pfizer.com
SIC: **2833** 2834 Medicinal chemicals; pharmaceutical preparations
PA: Pfizer Inc.
235 E 42nd St
New York NY 10017
212 733-2323

(G-9910)
PHE MANUFACTURING
331 Industrial Dr (45005-4431)
PHONE.....................................937 790-1582
Xavier Avendano, *General Mgr*
Javier Avendano, *Principal*
EMP: 6
SALES (est): 154.4K **Privately Held**
SIC: **3999** Manufacturing industries

(G-9911)
PIETRA NATURALE INC
140 Industrial Dr (45005-4428)
PHONE.....................................937 438-8882
Michael Carnevale Jr, *President*
Robert Carnevale, *Vice Pres*
Michael Ricky Carnevale, *Treasurer*
EMP: 12
SQ FT: 15,000
SALES (est): 1.6MM **Privately Held**
WEB: www.pietranaturale.com
SIC: **1799** 3281 Counter top installation; marble, building: cut & shaped

(G-9912)
QUALITY ARCHITECTURAL AND FABR
8 Shotwell Dr (45005-4600)
PHONE.....................................937 743-2923
Demida Davis, *President*
Theodosa L Davis, *Vice Pres*
EMP: 18
SQ FT: 15,000
SALES (est): 3.9MM **Privately Held**
SIC: **3446** Architectural metalwork

(G-9913)
QUEST TECHNOLOGIES INC
Also Called: Quest Lasercut
600 Commerce Center Dr (45005-7205)
PHONE.....................................937 743-1200
John Wenning, *President*
Mike Wolters, *Vice Pres*
Rodney Inman, *Plant Mgr*
EMP: 10
SQ FT: 12,000
SALES (est): 2MM **Privately Held**
SIC: **3599** 3499 7389 Machine shop, jobbing & repair; fire- or burglary-resistive products; metal cutting services

(G-9914)
R L DRAKE COMPANY
230 Industrial Dr (45005-4496)
PHONE.....................................937 746-4556
Ronald E Wysong, *Ch of Bd*
Michael Brubaker, *Vice Pres*
Steve Koogler, *Vice Pres*
Steve Morgan, *Vice Pres*
EMP: 79
SQ FT: 90,000
SALES (est): 8.6MM **Privately Held**
WEB: www.rldrake.com
SIC: **3663** 3651 Radio broadcasting & communications equipment; television broadcasting & communications equipment; space satellite communications equipment; household audio & video equipment

(G-9915)
RIVERVIEW PACKAGING INC
101 Shotwell Dr (45005-4653)
P.O. Box 155 (45005-0155)
PHONE.....................................937 743-9530
Joan K Ferrell, *President*
Marshall D Ruchman, *Principal*
Robert S Ferrell, *Corp Secy*
Randal T Ferrell, *Vice Pres*
EMP: 40
SQ FT: 75,000
SALES (est): 9.1MM **Privately Held**
SIC: **2653** Boxes, corrugated: made from purchased materials

(G-9916)
RNM HOLDINGS INC (PA)
550 Conover Dr (45005-1953)
PHONE.....................................937 704-9900
Matt Milton, *President*
Stephen F Marsee, *President*
▲ EMP: 41
SQ FT: 13,500
SALES (est): 46.4MM **Privately Held**
WEB: www.crane1services.com
SIC: **3531** Crane carriers

(G-9917)
ROTATION DYNAMICS CORPORATION
Also Called: Rotadyne
315 Industrial Dr (45005-4431)
PHONE.....................................937 746-4069
Pat Lakes, *Office Mgr*
Pat Saunders, *Administration*
EMP: 10
SALES (corp-wide): 164.4MM **Privately Held**
SIC: **3555** Printing trades machinery
PA: Rotation Dynamics Corporation
1101 Windham Pkwy
Romeoville IL 60446
630 769-9255

(G-9918)
SERVING VETERANS MOBILITY INC
303 Conover Dr (45005-1957)
PHONE.....................................937 746-4788
Debra Lipps, *Vice Pres*
EMP: 8
SALES (est): 235K **Privately Held**
SIC: **3999** Wheelchair lifts

(G-9919)
SHUR FIT DISTRIBUTORS INC
Also Called: Shur-Form Laminates Division
221 N Main St (45005-1629)
PHONE.....................................937 746-0567
Paul Gross, *President*
Hershal Nichol, *Vice Pres*
Kent Gross, *Treasurer*
EMP: 30
SQ FT: 58,000
SALES (est): 3.7MM **Privately Held**
SIC: **2541** Table or counter tops, plastic laminated

(G-9920)
SHUTTER EXPRESSIONS
8460 Heather Ct (45005-3940)
PHONE.....................................937 626-0462
Theresa Cook, *Principal*
EMP: 3
SALES (est): 184.4K **Privately Held**
SIC: **3442** Shutters, door or window: metal

(G-9921)
SRS MANUFACTURING CORP
395 Industrial Dr (45005-4431)
PHONE.....................................937 746-3086
Carlos Robinson, *President*
Kevin Robinson, *Manager*
EMP: 18
SQ FT: 12,000
SALES (est): 2.2MM **Privately Held**
SIC: **3599** Machine shop, jobbing & repair

(G-9922)
SUN CHEMICAL CORPORATION
General Printing Ink Division
125 Jaygee Dr (45005-4446)
PHONE.....................................937 743-8055
Mike Grotha, *Branch Mgr*
EMP: 20
SQ FT: 22,500
SALES (corp-wide): 7.1B **Privately Held**
WEB: www.sunchemical.com
SIC: **2893** Printing ink
HQ: Sun Chemical Corporation
35 Waterview Blvd Ste 100
Parsippany NJ 07054
973 404-6000

(G-9923)
SUNSTAR ENGRG AMERICAS INC
Also Called: Sunstar Sprockets
700 Watkins Glen Dr (45005-2394)
PHONE.....................................937 743-9049
Naoki Achiwa, *Principal*
EMP: 13 **Privately Held**
SIC: **3751** Motorcycles, bicycles & parts
HQ: Sunstar Engineering Americas Inc.
85 S Pioneer Blvd
Springboro OH 45066

(G-9924)
TAPCO HOLDINGS INC
200 Shotwell Dr (45005-4656)
PHONE.....................................800 771-4486
Joseph Kelley, *Branch Mgr*
EMP: 15 **Privately Held**
WEB: www.atlanticshuttersystems.com
SIC: **3089** Shutters, plastic
HQ: Tapco Holdings, Inc.
29797 Beck Rd
Wixom MI 48393
248 668-6400

(G-9925)
TECH-WAY INDUSTRIES INC
301 Industrial Dr (45005-4431)
P.O. Box 517 (45005-0517)
PHONE.....................................937 746-1004
Kenneth Parker, *CEO*
Robin Parker, *Principal*
Brian Kress, *Vice Pres*
EMP: 55 EST: 1964
SQ FT: 90,000
SALES (est): 15.1MM **Privately Held**
SIC: **3089** Injection molding of plastics

(G-9926)
TOTAL QUALITY MACHINING INC
10 Shotwell Dr (45005-4600)
PHONE.....................................937 746-7765
Theodosa Davis, *President*
Demida Davis, *Treasurer*
EMP: 14
SQ FT: 25,000
SALES (est): 1.6MM **Privately Held**
WEB: www.totalqualitymachining.com
SIC: **3599** Machine shop, jobbing & repair

(G-9927)
TRI STATE PALLET INC (PA)
8401 Claude Thomas Rd # 57 (45005-1475)
PHONE.....................................937 746-8702
John Sickinger, *President*
EMP: 28
SALES (est): 3.5MM **Privately Held**
SIC: **2448** Pallets, wood & wood with metal

(G-9928)
VALUED RELATIONSHIPS INC (PA)
Also Called: V R I
1400 Commerce Center Dr B (45005-7203)
PHONE.....................................800 860-4230
Chris Hendriksen, *CEO*
Andy Schoonover, *President*
Salli Duncan, *Vice Pres*
Rich Filler, *CFO*
Dan Vogel, *CFO*
EMP: 106
SQ FT: 10,000
SALES (est): 62.6MM **Privately Held**
WEB: www.monitoringcare.com
SIC: **3845** Patient monitoring apparatus

(G-9929)
WAFFLE HOUSE INC
6840 Franklin Lebanon Rd (45005-4558)
PHONE.....................................937 746-6830
Steve Foreman, *Branch Mgr*
EMP: 20
SALES (corp-wide): 787.1MM **Privately Held**
SIC: **2096** 5145 Potato chips & similar snacks; snack foods
PA: Waffle House, Inc.
5986 Financial Dr
Norcross GA 30071
770 729-5700

(G-9930)
WALTER F STEPHENS JR INC
415 South Ave (45005-3647)
PHONE.....................................937 746-0521
Ruth Ann Stephens, *Ch of Bd*
Carla Baker, *President*
Walter F Stephens Jr, *President*
Diane Stephens Maloney, *Corp Secy*
Patty Gleason, *Vice Pres*
EMP: 50
SQ FT: 45,000
SALES (est): 6.8MM **Privately Held**
SIC: **5999** 2389 5122 5023 Police supply stores; uniforms & vestments; toiletries; toothbrushes, except electric; kitchenware; uniforms, men's & boys'; mattresses & foundations

(G-9931)
WALTHER ENGRG & MFG CO INC
Also Called: Walther EMC
3501 Shotwell Dr (45005-4667)
PHONE.....................................937 743-8125
Chris Walther, *President*
Phil Fensel, *Vice Pres*
Anthony Ridenour, *Engineer*
Cathy Brannan, *Cust Mgr*
EMP: 49
SQ FT: 35,000
SALES (est): 10.8MM **Privately Held**
WEB: www.waltheremc.com
SIC: **3714** Motor vehicle parts & accessories

(G-9932)
WAYTEK CORPORATION
400 Shotwell Dr (45005-4661)
PHONE.....................................937 743-6142
Stephen P Foley, *President*
William Le May, *Chairman*
William Crawford, *Vice Pres*
Sylvia Kessler, *Admin Sec*
▲ EMP: 42
SQ FT: 32,000
SALES (est): 12.4MM **Privately Held**
WEB: www.waytekcorp.com
SIC: **2672** 2891 Coated & laminated paper; adhesives & sealants

---

Franklin Furnace
Scioto County

(G-9933)
CECIL CAUDILL TRAILER SLS INC
6679 Gallia Pike (45629-8986)
PHONE.....................................740 574-0704
Richard Caudill, *President*
EMP: 10
SALES (est): 1.3MM **Privately Held**
SIC: **3792** 5561 Travel trailers & campers; camper & travel trailer dealers

(G-9934)
G & J PEPSI-COLA BOTTLERS INC
Also Called: Pepsico
4587 Gallia Pike (45629-8777)
P.O. Box 299 (45629-0299)
PHONE.....................................740 354-9191
Robert Ross, *Branch Mgr*
EMP: 350
SALES (corp-wide): 418.3MM **Privately Held**
WEB: www.gjpepsi.com
SIC: **2086** 5149 Carbonated soft drinks, bottled & canned; groceries & related products
PA: G & J Pepsi-Cola Bottlers Inc
9435 Waterstone Blvd # 390
Cincinnati OH 45249
513 785-6060

(G-9935)
HERES YOUR SIGN
304 Lafayette Ln (45629-9037)
PHONE.....................................740 574-1248
Buffy Goodwin, *Principal*
EMP: 3
SALES (est): 230.7K **Privately Held**
SIC: **3993** Signs, not made in custom sign painting shops

Franklin Furnace - Scioto County (G-9936)

(G-9936)
WOODWORKS UNLIMITED
330 Lambro Ln (45629-8994)
PHONE..................................740 574-4523
Gregory Chaffin, *Owner*
EMP: 4
SALES (est): 322.4K **Privately Held**
SIC: 2431 Millwork

Frazeysburg
Muskingum County

(G-9937)
CALVARY CHRISTIAN CH OF OHIO
Also Called: Frazeysburg Restaurant & Bky
338 W 3rd St (43822-9785)
PHONE..................................740 828-9000
Rev Scott Egbert, *President*
Robert McGraw, *Vice Pres*
Mari Anne Holbrook, *Treasurer*
EMP: 40
SQ FT: 2,500
SALES: 55.4K **Privately Held**
SIC: 2051 8661 5541 0241 Bakery: wholesale or wholesale/retail combined; Christian & Reformed Church; filling stations, gasoline; milk production

(G-9938)
DK MANFCTURING FRAZEYSBURG INC (HQ)
119 W 2nd St (43822-9675)
P.O. Box 409 (43822-0409)
PHONE..................................740 828-3291
Allen L Handlan, *Principal*
Brad Williams, *Vice Pres*
Nancy Campbell, *Purchasing*
Sharron Adair, *Manager*
EMP: 115
SALES (est): 17.5MM
SALES (corp-wide): 17.6MM **Privately Held**
SIC: 3089 Injection molded finished plastic products; injection molding of plastics
PA: Dak Enterprises, Inc.
18062 Timber Trails Rd
Marysville OH 43040
740 828-3291

(G-9939)
H & D DRILLING CO INC
11183 Pleasant Valley Rd (43822-9507)
PHONE..................................740 745-2236
Harold Donaker, *CEO*
Wanda Donaker, *Corp Secy*
EMP: 5
SALES (est): 475.1K **Privately Held**
SIC: 1381 Drilling oil & gas wells

(G-9940)
H & S DRILLING CO INC
101 E 3rd St (43822-9652)
P.O. Box 40 (43822-0040)
PHONE..................................740 828-2411
Robert Hullhorst, *President*
Thomas Hullhorst, *Treasurer*
EMP: 3
SQ FT: 2,500
SALES (est): 165K **Privately Held**
SIC: 1311 1382 1794 Crude petroleum production; oil & gas exploration services; excavation work

(G-9941)
R & J DRILLING COMPANY INC
18586 Pinewood Trl (43822-9502)
P.O. Box 86 (43822-0086)
PHONE..................................740 763-3991
Ronald F Moran, *President*
Brenda Moran, *Manager*
EMP: 5 EST: 1958
SQ FT: 6,000
SALES: 240K **Privately Held**
SIC: 1389 1381 Oil field services; directional drilling oil & gas wells

(G-9942)
WALNUT HILL SHOP
17388a Frampton Rd (43822-9510)
PHONE..................................740 828-3346
Mary Kanuckel, *Owner*
EMP: 3 EST: 2000
SALES (est): 100K **Privately Held**
SIC: 2395 Embroidery & art needlework

Fredericksburg
Wayne County

(G-9943)
BILL HALL WELL SERVICE
10180 James Rd (44627-9538)
PHONE..................................330 695-4671
Bill Hall, *Owner*
EMP: 3
SALES (est): 177.9K **Privately Held**
SIC: 1389 Swabbing wells; gas field services; oil field services

(G-9944)
CABINET SPECIALTIES INC
10738 Criswell Rd (44627-9719)
PHONE..................................330 695-3463
Ivan Weaver, *President*
Robert Weaver, *Vice Pres*
EMP: 20
SQ FT: 15,000
SALES (est): 2.1MM **Privately Held**
SIC: 2434 Wood kitchen cabinets

(G-9945)
CHORE ANDEN
Also Called: Hickory Lane Welding
11461 Salt Creek Rd (44627-9755)
PHONE..................................330 695-2300
Aden Chore, *Owner*
EMP: 8
SALES (est): 665.3K **Privately Held**
SIC: 7692 Welding repair

(G-9946)
COUNTRY COMFORT WOODWORKING
2 Mi Sw Of Mt Eaton (44627)
PHONE..................................330 695-4408
Crist Miller, *Principal*
EMP: 3
SALES (est): 404.4K **Privately Held**
SIC: 2431 Millwork

(G-9947)
CRISWELL FURNITURE LLC
8139 Criswell Rd (44627-9709)
PHONE..................................330 695-2082
Jonas Mast, *Mng Member*
David Mast, *Mng Member*
Eli Mast, *Mng Member*
EMP: 15
SALES (est): 3.5MM **Privately Held**
SIC: 2511 Wood household furniture

(G-9948)
DUTCH DESIGN PRODUCTS LLC
8216 State Route 241 (44627-9638)
PHONE..................................330 674-1167
Barbara Hershberger, *Owner*
EMP: 22
SALES (est): 950K **Privately Held**
SIC: 2521 Wood office furniture

(G-9949)
DUTCH VALLEY WOODCRAFT LTD
5833 Township Road 610 (44627-9640)
PHONE..................................330 695-2364
Levi A Weaver, *Principal*
EMP: 3
SALES (est): 221.5K **Privately Held**
SIC: 2511 Wood household furniture

(G-9950)
EVEN HEAT MFG LTD
8241 Tr 601 (44627)
PHONE..................................330 695-9351
John R Slater, *CEO*
▲ **EMP:** 10
SQ FT: 6,700
SALES (est): 1.2MM **Privately Held**
SIC: 3469 Metal stampings

(G-9951)
FARMSTEAD ACRES WOODWORKING
9106 County Road 201 (44627-9402)
PHONE..................................330 695-6492
Lester J Wengerd, *Principal*
EMP: 4 EST: 2010
SALES (est): 374.5K **Privately Held**
SIC: 2431 Millwork

(G-9952)
HOLMES PRINTING SOLUTIONS LLC
8757 County Road 77 (44627-9446)
PHONE..................................330 234-9699
Phillip Holmes, *President*
EMP: 4
SALES (est): 310K **Privately Held**
SIC: 2752 Commercial printing, lithographic

(G-9953)
MILLER CRIST
Also Called: Crosco Wood Products
10258 S Kansas Rd (44627-9754)
PHONE..................................330 359-7877
Crist Miller, *Owner*
Cris Miller, *Principal*
EMP: 16
SQ FT: 8,000
SALES (est): 1MM **Privately Held**
SIC: 2435 Hardwood plywood, prefinished

(G-9954)
MRS MLLERS HMMADE NOODLES LTD
9140 County Road 192 (44627-9436)
P.O. Box 289 (44627-0289)
PHONE..................................330 694-5814
Leon Miller, *Partner*
Esther Miller, *Partner*
Maria Miller, *Principal*
▲ **EMP:** 10
SQ FT: 11,000
SALES (est): 1.5MM **Privately Held**
WEB: www.mrsmillersnoodles.com
SIC: 2098 Noodles (e.g. egg, plain & water), dry

(G-9955)
PREMIUM PANEL & TREAD
4910 Harrison Rd (44627-9500)
PHONE..................................330 695-9979
Daniel Shetler, *Owner*
EMP: 5
SALES (est): 564.7K **Privately Held**
SIC: 2431 Stair railings, wood

(G-9956)
QUALITY FABRICATIONS LLC
7108 Township Road 569 (44627-9410)
PHONE..................................330 695-2478
Ivan Hochstetler, *Principal*
Sam Yoder, *Manager*
EMP: 5
SALES (est): 1.1MM **Privately Held**
SIC: 2512 Living room furniture: upholstered on wood frames

(G-9957)
RN CABINETS & MORE LTD
3916 County Road 200 (44627-9674)
PHONE..................................330 275-0203
Raymond J Miller, *Principal*
EMP: 4 EST: 2016
SALES (est): 184.6K **Privately Held**
SIC: 2434 Wood kitchen cabinets

(G-9958)
ROBIN INDUSTRIES INC
Also Called: Fredericksburg Facility
300 W Clay St (44627)
P.O. Box 242 (44627-0242)
PHONE..................................330 695-9300
Dave Wingett, *Principal*
Jeff Shedron, *Engineer*
Polly Yoder, *Personnel*
Cathy Graser, *Info Tech Mgr*
Brian Jokovich, *Info Tech Mgr*
EMP: 170
SALES (corp-wide): 81.6MM **Privately Held**
WEB: www.robin-industries.com
SIC: 3069 3061 Molded rubber products; mechanical rubber goods
PA: Robin Industries, Inc.
6500 Rockside Rd Ste 230
Independence OH 44131
216 631-7000

(G-9959)
SALT CREEK LUMBER COMPANY INC
11657 Salt Creek Rd (44627-9755)
PHONE..................................330 695-3500
Norman Boerman, *President*
Shirley Boerman, *Vice Pres*
EMP: 6
SQ FT: 8,000
SALES (est): 690K **Privately Held**
SIC: 5031 2421 Lumber: rough, dressed & finished; sawmills & planing mills, general

(G-9960)
SCENIC VALLEY SURPLUS LLC
10258 S Kansas Rd (44627-9754)
PHONE..................................330 359-0555
Rosanna Miller, *Principal*
EMP: 4
SALES (est): 203.6K **Privately Held**
SIC: 2711 Newspapers

(G-9961)
YODER WINDOW & SIDING LTD
Also Called: Glass Specialties
7165 Fredericksburg Rd (44627-9808)
PHONE..................................330 857-4530
Derryl Troyer, *Manager*
EMP: 5 **Privately Held**
SIC: 3211 Flat glass
PA: Yoder Window & Siding, Ltd.
7846 Harrison Rd
Fredericksburg OH 44627

(G-9962)
YODER WINDOW & SIDING LTD (PA)
Also Called: Yoder Window and Siding
7846 Harrison Rd (44627-9798)
PHONE..................................330 695-6960
Jonas Yoder, *Partner*
Derryl R Troyer, *Partner*
Jonas M Yoder, *Partner*
EMP: 13
SQ FT: 6,500
SALES (est): 1.9MM **Privately Held**
SIC: 2431 1751 1761 Windows, wood; window & door (prefabricated) installation; gutter & downspout contractor; siding contractor

Fredericktown
Knox County

(G-9963)
BENCHMARK CABINETS
97 Mount Vernon Ave (43019-7700)
PHONE..................................740 694-1144
Wesley Crum, *Owner*
EMP: 32
SQ FT: 29,000
SALES: 3MM **Privately Held**
WEB: www.benchmark-cabinets.com
SIC: 2434 2541 Wood kitchen cabinets; counter & sink tops

(G-9964)
COUNTRY MANUFACTURING INC
333 Salem Ave Ext (43019-9186)
P.O. Box 104 (43019-0104)
PHONE..................................740 694-9926
Joe Chattin, *President*
Karen Gay Chattin, *Corp Secy*
EMP: 15 EST: 1978
SQ FT: 15,000
SALES (est): 2.9MM **Privately Held**
WEB: www.countrymfg.com
SIC: 3523 Farm machinery & equipment

(G-9965)
DEE-JAYS CUSTOM BUTCHERING
17460 Ankneytown Rd (43019-8015)
PHONE..................................740 694-7492
Jenny Jessee, *Co-Owner*
Mike Jessee, *Mng Member*
EMP: 10
SALES (est): 330K **Privately Held**
SIC: 2011 5142 5421 Meat packing plants; meat, frozen: packaged; meat markets, including freezer provisioners

(G-9966)
DIVELBISS CORPORATION
9778 Mount Gilead Rd (43019-9161)
PHONE..................................800 245-2327
Terry L Divelbiss, *President*
Alan Divelbiss, *Vice Pres*
Don Divelbiss, *Engineer*
Christopher Bigler, *Technology*
EMP: 39 **EST:** 1974
SQ FT: 17,000
SALES (est): 8.3MM **Privately Held**
WEB: www.divelbiss.com
SIC: 3625 Relays & industrial controls

(G-9967)
EDWARDS SHEET METAL WORKS INC
Also Called: Edwards Culvert Co
10439 Sparta Rd (43019-9025)
P.O. Box 239 (43019-0239)
PHONE..................................740 694-0010
Richard Well, *President*
Catherine Chris Well, *Corp Secy*
EMP: 12 **EST:** 1907
SQ FT: 8,000
SALES: 1MM **Privately Held**
SIC: 3444 Culverts, sheet metal; pipe, sheet metal

(G-9968)
EPIK LTD
7196 Mount Gilead Rd (43019-9556)
PHONE..................................419 768-2498
Daniel Jagla, *Principal*
Lisa Shinaberry, *Admin Dir*
EMP: 3
SALES (est): 331.2K **Privately Held**
SIC: 3999 Manufacturing industries

(G-9969)
FOOTE FOUNDRY LLC
283 N Main St (43019-1111)
PHONE..................................740 694-1595
Joseph E Locanti, *Mng Member*
Todd Colman,
EMP: 65
SQ FT: 70,000
SALES (est): 10.5MM **Privately Held**
WEB: www.footefoundry.com
SIC: 3321 Gray iron castings

(G-9970)
FT PRECISION INC
Also Called: Ftp
9731 Mount Gilead Rd (43019-9167)
PHONE..................................740 694-1500
Tamami Nishimura, *President*
Ben Beeber, *President*
▲ **EMP:** 512
SQ FT: 150,000
SALES (est): 221.9MM
SALES (corp-wide): 360.4MM **Privately Held**
WEB: www.ftprecision.com
SIC: 3714 Motor vehicle engines & parts
PA: Tanaka Seimitsu Kogyo Co.,Ltd.
2-7-10, Shinjohommachi
Toyama TYM 930-0
764 517-651

(G-9971)
INDUSTRIAL AND MAR ENG SVC CO
Also Called: Imesco
13843 Armentrout Rd (43019-9717)
PHONE..................................740 694-0791
Theresa C Chandler, *CEO*
EMP: 10
SQ FT: 7,200
SALES (est): 950K **Privately Held**
WEB: www.imescomfg.com
SIC: 3613 3625 3479 3993 Control panels, electric; switchgear & switchgear accessories; generator control & metering panels; control circuit relays, industrial; name plates: engraved, etched, etc.; signs & advertising specialties; motors & generators

(G-9972)
LAGC LTD
11729 Leedy Rd (43019-9289)
PHONE..................................419 886-2141
Donnie Cataldo, *Principal*
EMP: 4

SALES (est): 312.6K **Privately Held**
SIC: 1311 Crude petroleum & natural gas

(G-9973)
M H LOGGING & LUMBER
14582 Montgomery Rd (43019-9772)
PHONE..................................740 694-1988
Mark Hulse, *Owner*
EMP: 5 **EST:** 2014
SALES (est): 409.2K **Privately Held**
SIC: 2411 Logging

(G-9974)
OHIO COMMUNITY MEDIA
59 W College St (43019-1042)
PHONE..................................740 848-4064
Leslie Bronstein, *Principal*
EMP: 3
SALES (est): 105.5K **Privately Held**
SIC: 2711 Newspapers, publishing & printing

(G-9975)
OPTIONS PLUS INCORPORATED
143 Tuttle Ave (43019-1029)
PHONE..................................740 694-9811
▼ **EMP:** 10 **EST:** 1976
SQ FT: 25,000
SALES (est): 1.4MM **Privately Held**
SIC: 3444 3496 Mfg Sheet Metalwork Mfg Misc Fabricated Wire Products

(G-9976)
SAUNDERS TRUCKING LCC
13 Boyd St (43019-9021)
PHONE..................................419 210-0551
Ted Saunders, *Mng Member*
Diane Saunders, *Mng Member*
EMP: 5
SALES (est): 763.8K **Privately Held**
SIC: 3537 Truck trailers, used in plants, docks, terminals, etc.

(G-9977)
SCHAFER DRIVELINE LLC (HQ)
123 Phoenix Pl (43019-9162)
PHONE..................................740 694-2055
Paul Meikle, *Accountant*
Bipin Doshi,
Stanley Blenke,
Linda Doshi,
Matt McClain,
◆ **EMP:** 57
SQ FT: 110,000
SALES (est): 13.3MM
SALES (corp-wide): 38.3MM **Privately Held**
SIC: 3714 Axles, motor vehicle
PA: Schafer Industries, Inc.
4701 Nimtz Pkwy
South Bend IN 46628
574 234-4116

(G-9978)
TD LANDSCAPE INC
16780 Pinkley Rd (43019-9302)
PHONE..................................740 694-0244
Scott Huvler, *President*
EMP: 15
SALES (est): 780.5K **Privately Held**
SIC: 3523 Grounds mowing equipment

(G-9979)
TENDA HORSE PRODUCTS LLC
18400 N Liberty Rd (43019-9742)
P.O. Box 614, Mount Vernon (43050-0614)
PHONE..................................740 694-8836
Todd Mizer, *Mng Member*
EMP: 3
SALES (est): 339.5K **Privately Held**
WEB: www.tendahorse.com
SIC: 2048 Mineral feed supplements

(G-9980)
TEXMASTER TOOLS INC
143 Tuttle Ave (43019-1029)
P.O. Box 132 (43019-0132)
PHONE..................................740 965-8778
John Capoccia, *President*
▲ **EMP:** 18
SQ FT: 25,000
SALES (est): 4.2MM **Privately Held**
SIC: 5072 3429 Hardware; manufactured hardware (general)

(G-9981)
U M D AUTOMATED SYSTEMS INC
9855 Salem Rd (43019-9301)
P.O. Box 317 (43019-0317)
PHONE..................................740 694-8614
Don Rogers, *President*
Laura Rogers, *Vice Pres*
Michael Rogers, *Engineer*
Troy Herbert, *Accounts Mgr*
EMP: 72
SQ FT: 55,000
SALES: 20MM **Privately Held**
SIC: 3441 Fabricated structural metal

(G-9982)
UMD CONTRACTORS INC
9855 Salem Rd (43019-9301)
P.O. Box 228 (43019-0228)
PHONE..................................740 694-8614
Don Rogers, *President*
Bill Vick, *Accounts Mgr*
EMP: 13
SALES (est): 2.1MM **Privately Held**
SIC: 3011 Tires & inner tubes

(G-9983)
WARD/KRAFT FORMS OF OHIO INC
700 Salem Ave Ext (43019-9188)
P.O. Box 211 (43019-0211)
PHONE..................................740 694-0015
Harold E Kraft, *President*
Robert A Horton, *Vice Pres*
David Young, *Treasurer*
Daryl Roller, *VP Mktg*
Fred Mitchelson, *Admin Sec*
EMP: 80
SQ FT: 41,400
SALES: 5.3MM
SALES (corp-wide): 97.8MM **Privately Held**
WEB: www.wardkraft.com
SIC: 2759 Commercial printing
HQ: Ward-Kraft, Inc.
2401 Cooper St
Fort Scott KS 66701
800 821-4021

Freeport
Harrison County

(G-9984)
BOND QUARTERS HORSES
23574 Cadiz Rd (43973-8602)
PHONE..................................614 354-4028
EMP: 3
SALES (est): 170.8K **Privately Held**
SIC: 3131 Mfg Footwear Cut Stock

(G-9985)
ROSEBUD MINING COMPANY
28490 Birmingham Rd (43973-9754)
PHONE..................................740 658-4217
EMP: 35
SALES (corp-wide): 605.3MM **Privately Held**
SIC: 1222 Bituminous coal-underground mining
PA: Rosebud Mining Company
301 Market St
Kittanning PA 16201
724 545-6222

(G-9986)
SCHROCK WOODWORKING
71444 Grapevine Rd (43973-8909)
PHONE..................................740 489-5229
Eli Schrock, *Owner*
EMP: 4
SALES: 400K **Privately Held**
SIC: 2434 Wood kitchen cabinets

Fremont
Sandusky County

(G-9987)
A BUN IN OVEN
1011 Hayes Ave (43420-2816)
PHONE..................................419 559-3056
Brooke Huber, *Principal*
EMP: 4 **EST:** 2011
SALES (est): 182.1K **Privately Held**
SIC: 2051 Bakery: wholesale or wholesale/retail combined

(G-9988)
ABC INOAC EXTERIOR SYSTEMS LLC
1410 Motor Ave (43420-1437)
PHONE..................................419 334-8951
Sandra Muehling, *QC Mgr*
Angelo Cesta, *Branch Mgr*
Todd Sherman, *Info Tech Mgr*
EMP: 250
SALES (est): 55.8MM
SALES (corp-wide): 95.2MM **Privately Held**
SIC: 2396 5531 Automotive & apparel trimmings; automotive parts
PA: Abc Inoac Exterior Systems Llc
24175 Northwestern Hwy
Southfield MI 48075
248 619-6057

(G-9989)
ACTION PRINTING & PHOTOGRAPHY
626 Grant St (43420-2259)
PHONE..................................419 332-9615
Dan Laity, *Owner*
EMP: 4
SALES: 180K **Privately Held**
SIC: 2752 Commercial printing, offset

(G-9990)
ALKON CORPORATION (PA)
728 Graham Dr (43420-4073)
PHONE..................................419 355-9111
Mark Winter, *President*
Wayne Morroney, *President*
Mike Caron, *Vice Pres*
▲ **EMP:** 60
SQ FT: 40,000
SALES (est): 24.2MM **Privately Held**
WEB: www.alkoncorp.com
SIC: 3491 3082 5084 5085 Valves, nuclear; tubes, unsupported plastic; industrial machinery & equipment; pistons & valves; valves & fittings; fluid power valves & hose fittings

(G-9991)
ARDAGH METAL PACKAGING USA INC
2145 Cedar St (43420-1007)
PHONE..................................419 334-4461
Jerry Allen, *Plant Mgr*
John Young, *Production*
Paulie Johnson, *Manager*
Todd Shilling, *Maintence Staff*
EMP: 4
SALES (corp-wide): 242.1K **Privately Held**
SIC: 3565 Packaging machinery
HQ: Ardagh Metal Packaging Usa Inc.
600 N Bell Ave
Carnegie PA 15106

(G-9992)
ART FREMONT IRON CO
307 E State St (43420-4151)
P.O. Box 652 (43420-0652)
PHONE..................................419 332-5554
Robert C Leaser, *Owner*
EMP: 4 **EST:** 1946
SQ FT: 5,000
SALES: 240K **Privately Held**
SIC: 3444 3446 Casings, sheet metal; architectural metalwork

(G-9993)
ATLAS INDUSTRIES INC (PA)
1750 E State St (43420-4056)
PHONE..................................419 355-1000
Jerald F Clark, *President*
Roman G Burnor Jr, *Principal*
J S Heyman, *Principal*
Merwyn G Leatherman, *Principal*
Stephen Clark, *COO*
◆ **EMP:** 134 **EST:** 1938
SQ FT: 150,000

Fremont - Sandusky County (G-9994)

GEOGRAPHIC SECTION

SALES (est): 133.9MM **Privately Held**
WEB: www.atlasindustries.com
SIC: 3599 Crankshafts & camshafts, machining; custom machinery

(G-9994)
AURIA FREMONT LLC
Also Called: Auria Solutions
400 S Stone St (43420-2658)
PHONE 419 332-1587
Brian Pour, *CEO*
EMP: 261 EST: 2007
SALES (est): 42.9MM
SALES (corp-wide): 571K **Privately Held**
WEB: www.iaaawards.com
SIC: 3714 Motor vehicle parts & accessories
HQ: Auria Solutions Usa Inc.
26999 Central Park Blvd
Southfield MI 48076
734 456-2800

(G-9995)
BAP MANUFACTURING INC
601 N Stone St Ste 1 (43420-1566)
PHONE 419 332-5041
W Scott Brown, *President*
EMP: 30
SQ FT: 10,000
SALES (est): 1.2MM **Privately Held**
WEB: www.bapman.com
SIC: 3545 Cutting tools for machine tools

(G-9996)
BEMIS COMPANY INC
730 Industrial Dr (43420-8678)
PHONE 419 334-9465
Russell John, *Engineer*
Ryan Richter, *Plant Engr*
William Kraut, *Manager*
EMP: 20
SALES (corp-wide): 4B **Publicly Held**
SIC: 2671 2672 Packaging paper & plastics film, coated & laminated; coated & laminated paper
PA: Bemis Company, Inc.
2301 Industrial Dr
Neenah WI 54956
920 527-5000

(G-9997)
BENCHMARK PRINTS
2252 W State St (43420-1439)
PHONE 419 332-7640
Kenn Bower, *Owner*
EMP: 11
SQ FT: 5,700
SALES (est): 590K **Privately Held**
WEB: www.benchmarkprints.com
SIC: 2759 5611 5199 Screen printing; men's & boys' clothing stores; advertising specialties

(G-9998)
BERLEKAMP PLASTICS INC
2587 County Road 99 (43420-9316)
PHONE 419 334-4401
Kenneth Berlekamp Jr, *President*
Sandra Berlekamp, *Corp Secy*
Kathy Macallister, *Office Mgr*
Vickie Willey,
EMP: 15 EST: 1929
SQ FT: 12,000
SALES (est): 2.5MM **Privately Held**
WEB: www.berlekamp.com
SIC: 3089 Injection molding of plastics

(G-9999)
BLACK SWAMP DISTILLERY
118 N Arch St (43420-2451)
PHONE 419 344-4347
Darrin Critchet, *Principal*
EMP: 3 EST: 2013
SALES (est): 150.4K **Privately Held**
SIC: 2085 Distilled & blended liquors

(G-10000)
BLONDE SWAN
307 W State St (43420-2527)
PHONE 419 307-8591
Elizabeth Martin, *Owner*
Alex Poznanski, *Owner*
EMP: 11
SALES (est): 756K **Privately Held**
SIC: 2371 2353 Hats, fur; hats, caps & millinery

(G-10001)
BOMB MFG LLC
530 S Taft Ave (43420-3234)
PHONE 419 559-9689
Kenneth F Flower, *CEO*
EMP: 4
SALES: 500K **Privately Held**
SIC: 3999 Manufacturing industries

(G-10002)
BURKETT INDUSTRIES INC
507 Vine St (43420-3493)
PHONE 419 332-4391
Richard B Burkett, *President*
EMP: 5 EST: 1870
SQ FT: 5,600
SALES (est): 796.9K **Privately Held**
WEB: www.burkettindustrieselectric.com
SIC: 1731 3643 General electrical contractor; lightning protection equipment

(G-10003)
C A KUSTOMS
524 N Stone St (43420-1531)
PHONE 419 332-4395
Clay Keim, *Owner*
EMP: 3
SALES: 200K **Privately Held**
WEB: www.cakustoms.com
SIC: 3993 Signs & advertising specialties

(G-10004)
CARBO FORGE INC
150 State Route 523 (43420-9364)
PHONE 419 334-9788
Jeffrey Woitha, *President*
Jeffrey Witham, *President*
Troy Lewis, *Engineer*
Rich Egbert, *Controller*
Gary Hatton, *Sales Staff*
EMP: 44 EST: 1920
SQ FT: 90,000
SALES (est): 9MM **Privately Held**
WEB: www.carboforge.com
SIC: 3462 Iron & steel forgings

(G-10005)
CENTURY DIE COMPANY LLC
215 N Stone St (43420-1505)
PHONE 419 332-2693
Timothy Myers,
EMP: 58
SALES (est): 13.9MM **Privately Held**
SIC: 3544 Industrial molds

(G-10006)
CERTIFIED POWER INC
Also Called: Toledo Driveline
1110 Napoleon St (43420-2328)
PHONE 419 355-1200
EMP: 79
SALES (corp-wide): 295.8MM **Privately Held**
SIC: 3714 7539 5013 Motor vehicle parts & accessories; automotive repair shops; automotive supplies & parts
PA: Certified Power, Inc.
970 Campus Dr
Mundelein IL 60060
847 573-3800

(G-10007)
CHRISTY MACHINE COMPANY
118 Birchard Ave (43420-3008)
P.O. Box 39 (43420-0039)
PHONE 419 332-6451
Randy Fielding, *President*
EMP: 11
SQ FT: 7,000
SALES (est): 2MM **Privately Held**
WEB: www.christydispensers.com
SIC: 3556 Food products machinery

(G-10008)
CLARK ASSOCIATES INC
702 W State St Ste A (43420-2592)
PHONE 419 334-3838
Gerald E Clark, *President*
Garry E Clark, *Vice Pres*
EMP: 4
SQ FT: 3,500
SALES: 300K **Privately Held**
SIC: 2752 5045 Commercial printing, offset; computers & accessories, personal & home entertainment

(G-10009)
CROWN BATTERY MANUFACTURING CO (PA)
1445 Majestic Dr (43420-9190)
P.O. Box 990 (43420-0990)
PHONE 419 334-7181
Hal Hawk, *CEO*
Tim Hack, *CFO*
◆ EMP: 450 EST: 1926
SQ FT: 220,000
SALES (est): 179.9MM **Privately Held**
WEB: www.crownbattery.com
SIC: 3691 Storage batteries

(G-10010)
CUSTOM FRESHENERS
423 Knapp St (43420-2512)
PHONE 888 241-9109
Ken Flowers, *Owner*
EMP: 4
SALES: 450K **Privately Held**
WEB: www.customfresheners.com
SIC: 2869 Perfume materials, synthetic

(G-10011)
DECKER CUSTOM WOOD LLC
Also Called: Decker Custom Wood Working
505 W Mcgormley Rd (43420-8672)
PHONE 419 332-3464
Adam Decker,
Jim Britner,
EMP: 6
SQ FT: 3,500
SALES: 200K **Privately Held**
WEB: www.deckerwoodworking.com
SIC: 2431 Millwork

(G-10012)
ENERGY MANUFACTURING LTD
1830 Old Oak Harbour Rd (43420)
P.O. Box 1127, Fostoria (44830-1127)
PHONE 419 355-9304
Richard Norton, *President*
EMP: 6
SQ FT: 40,000
SALES (est): 1MM **Privately Held**
SIC: 3586 Oil pumps, measuring or dispensing; gasoline pumps, measuring or dispensing

(G-10013)
ENGLER PRINTING CO
808 W State St (43420-2538)
PHONE 419 332-2181
Jay Engler, *Owner*
Marilyn Engler, *Co-Owner*
EMP: 9 EST: 1952
SQ FT: 4,000
SALES (est): 530K **Privately Held**
SIC: 2752 Commercial printing, offset

(G-10014)
FIRST CHOICE PACKAGING INC (PA)
Also Called: First Choice Packg Solutions
1501 W State St (43420-1629)
PHONE 419 333-4100
Paul W Tomick, *President*
Frank Wolfinger, *Vice Pres*
▲ EMP: 150
SALES (est): 32.6MM **Privately Held**
WEB: www.firstchoicepackaging.com
SIC: 3089 7389 Thermoformed finished plastic products; packaging & labeling services

(G-10015)
FREMONT COMPANY (PA)
802 N Front St (43420-1917)
PHONE 419 334-8995
Richard L Smith, *President*
Jeff Diehr, *Vice Pres*
Christopher Smith, *Vice Pres*
Dave Dariano, *QC Mgr*
James Kroner, *CFO*
▼ EMP: 180
SQ FT: 250,000
SALES (est): 59.9MM **Privately Held**
WEB: www.fremontcompany.com
SIC: 2033 Vegetables: packaged in cans, jars, etc.

(G-10016)
FREMONT COMPANY
802 N Front St (43420-1917)
PHONE 419 334-8995
Jerry Schuett, *Manager*
EMP: 40
SALES (corp-wide): 59.9MM **Privately Held**
WEB: www.fremontcompany.com
SIC: 2033 Vegetables: packaged in cans, jars, etc.
PA: The Fremont Company
802 N Front St
Fremont OH 43420
419 334-8995

(G-10017)
FREMONT CUTTING DIES INC
3179 Us 20 E (43420-9014)
PHONE 419 334-5153
Gregory Abdoo, *President*
EMP: 9 EST: 2000
SQ FT: 1,000
SALES (est): 1.4MM **Privately Held**
SIC: 3544 Die springs

(G-10018)
FREMONT DISCOVER LTD
315 Garrison St (43420-3031)
P.O. Box 172 (43420-0172)
PHONE 419 332-8696
Thomas McCrystal, *Principal*
EMP: 3
SALES (est): 137.4K **Privately Held**
SIC: 2711 Newspapers, publishing & printing

(G-10019)
FREMONT FLASK CO
1000 Wolfe Ave (43420-1670)
P.O. Box 594 (43420-0594)
PHONE 419 332-2231
Carl W Yeager Jr, *President*
John Yeager, *Treasurer*
James Yeager, *Admin Sec*
EMP: 16
SQ FT: 20,000
SALES (est): 2.2MM **Privately Held**
WEB: www.wwsusa.net
SIC: 3559 Foundry machinery & equipment

(G-10020)
GANNETT CO INC
News Herald
1700 Cedar St (43420-1114)
P.O. Box 550, Port Clinton (43452-0550)
PHONE 419 332-5511
C George-Dealer, *Principal*
EMP: 18
SALES (corp-wide): 2.9B **Publicly Held**
WEB: www.gannett.com
SIC: 2711 Newspapers: publishing only, not printed on site
PA: Gannett Co., Inc.
7950 Jones Branch Dr
Mc Lean VA 22102
703 854-6000

(G-10021)
GANNETT STLLITE INFO NTWRK LLC
News Messenger, The
1800 E State St Ste B (43420-4083)
P.O. Box 1230 (43420-8230)
PHONE 419 334-1012
Cindy Bealer, *Administration*
EMP: 60
SQ FT: 2,792
SALES (corp-wide): 2.9B **Publicly Held**
WEB: www.usatoday.com
SIC: 2711 2752 Newspapers; commercial printing, lithographic
HQ: Gannett Satellite Information Network, Llc
7950 Jones Branch Dr
Mc Lean VA 22102
703 854-6000

(G-10022)
GARVIN TOOL & DIE INC
3000 State Route 412 (43420-9599)
PHONE 419 334-2392
William Garvin, *President*
Ted Gardin, *Vice Pres*
Joe Garvin, *Shareholder*

▲ = Import ▼ =Export
◆ =Import/Export

GEOGRAPHIC SECTION
Fremont - Sandusky County (G-10050)

EMP: 5
SQ FT: 2,048
SALES (est): 550K Privately Held
WEB: www.garvintools.com
SIC: 3544 Special dies & tools

(G-10023)
GENERAL CUTLERY INC (PA)
1918 N County Road 232 (43420-9595)
PHONE.................................419 332-2316
David Reitz, *President*
Carleton R Reitz, *Vice Pres*
Donna Shoemaker, *Admin Sec*
EMP: 20 **EST:** 1945
SQ FT: 25,000
SALES (est): 2.7MM Privately Held
SIC: 3421 Cutlery

(G-10024)
GRAHAM PACKAGING COMPANY LP
725 Industrial Dr (43420-8679)
PHONE.................................419 334-4197
Rick Van, *Manager*
EMP: 43
SALES (corp-wide): 1MM Privately Held
WEB: www.grahampackaging.com
SIC: 3085 3089 Plastics bottles; plastic containers, except foam
HQ: Graham Packaging Company, L.P.
  700 Indian Springs Dr # 100
  Lancaster PA 17601
  717 849-8500

(G-10025)
GRAHAM PACKAGING PET TECH INC
725 Industrial Dr (43420-8679)
PHONE.................................419 334-4197
Lance Novotny, *Manager*
EMP: 113
SALES (corp-wide): 11.6B Publicly Held
SIC: 3085 Plastics bottles
HQ: Graham Packaging Pet Technologies Inc.
  1 Seagate Ste 10
  Toledo OH
  717 849-8500

(G-10026)
GREAT LAKES MCHY & AUTOMTN LLC
1839 Port Clinton Rd (43420-1313)
PHONE.................................419 208-2004
Matt McCabe,
Mike Paeth,
EMP: 2
SALES: 1MM Privately Held
SIC: 3089 Injection molded finished plastic products

(G-10027)
GREEN BAY PACKAGING INC
Fremont Division
2323 Commerce Dr (43420-1052)
PHONE.................................419 332-5593
Paul Hasemeyer, *Manager*
EMP: 129
SALES (corp-wide): 1.3B Privately Held
WEB: www.gbp.com
SIC: 2653 3412 Boxes, corrugated: made from purchased materials; metal barrels, drums & pails
PA: Green Bay Packaging Inc.
  1700 N Webster Ave
  Green Bay WI 54302
  920 433-5111

(G-10028)
INDUSTRIAL HANGER CONVEYOR CO
886 N County Road 232 (43420-9145)
P.O. Box 30, Clyde (43410-0030)
PHONE.................................419 332-2661
Paul W Fishbaugh, *President*
Donna Fishbaugh, *Admin Sec*
EMP: 4 **EST:** 1969
SALES (est): 1.1MM Privately Held
WEB: www.industrialhanger.com
SIC: 3599 3441 3444 Machine shop, jobbing & repair; fabricated structural metal; sheet metalwork

(G-10029)
JMJ PAPER INC
Also Called: Wolfe Paper Co
1900 Napoleon St (43420)
PHONE.................................419 332-6675
Duane Beckley, *Manager*
EMP: 10 Privately Held
SIC: 2621 Paper mills

(G-10030)
JOSEPH B STINSON CO
2300 Napoleon Rd (43420-2644)
P.O. Box 71 (43420-0071)
PHONE.................................419 334-4151
Adair Van Nette, *President*
EMP: 4
SALES (est): 400K Privately Held
SIC: 7389 3569 Design, commercial & industrial; assembly machines, non-metalworking

(G-10031)
JS FABRICATIONS INC
1400 E State St (43420-4061)
PHONE.................................419 333-0323
Jack Swint, *President*
EMP: 8
SALES (est): 1.3MM Privately Held
SIC: 3441 1795 1721 Fabricated structural metal; demolition, buildings & other structures; industrial painting

(G-10032)
KRAFT HEINZ FOODS COMPANY
Also Called: Quality Assurance
1200n N 5th St (43420-3935)
PHONE.................................419 332-7357
Bob Jurski, *Branch Mgr*
EMP: 40
SALES (corp-wide): 26.2B Publicly Held
SIC: 2033 Canned fruits & specialties
HQ: Kraft Heinz Foods Company
  1 Ppg Pl Ste 3200
  Pittsburgh PA 15222
  412 456-5700

(G-10033)
LESHER PRINTERS INC
810 N Wilson Ave (43420-2271)
P.O. Box 565 (43420-0565)
PHONE.................................419 332-8253
Emiel J Cool, *CEO*
Gary Cool, *President*
EMP: 28 **EST:** 1949
SQ FT: 24,000
SALES: 3MM Privately Held
WEB: www.lesherprinters.com
SIC: 2759 Letterpress printing

(G-10034)
LIGHT CRAFT MANUFACTURING INC
Also Called: Light Craft Direct
220 Sullivan Rd (43420-9671)
PHONE.................................419 332-0536
Jeffery R Matt, *President*
Susan L Wright, *Corp Secy*
Kenneth A Matt, *Vice Pres*
▲ **EMP:** 10
SQ FT: 14,370
SALES (est): 2.1MM Privately Held
WEB: www.lightcraftmfg.com
SIC: 3646 Commercial indusl & institutional electric lighting fixtures

(G-10035)
LINE TOOL & DIE INC
933 Napoleon St (43420-2323)
PHONE.................................419 332-2931
Albert Mader, *President*
EMP: 3 **EST:** 1920
SQ FT: 2,500
SALES (est): 518.5K Privately Held
SIC: 3544 3599 Special dies & tools; machine shop, jobbing & repair

(G-10036)
LOCKER KONNECTION SERVICES LLC
405 Jackson St (43420-2315)
P.O. Box 457 (43420-0457)
PHONE.................................419 334-3956
EMP: 6
SALES (est): 652K Privately Held
SIC: 3444 Mfg Sheet Metalwork

(G-10037)
LOUIS G FREEMAN CO
911 Graham Dr (43420-4086)
PHONE.................................419 334-9709
EMP: 50
SALES (corp-wide): 8.3MM Privately Held
SIC: 3312 3544 Blast Furnace-Steel Works Mfg Dies/Tools/Jigs/Fixtures
PA: Louis G Freeman Co Inc
  911 Graham Dr
  Fremont OH 43420
  419 334-9709

(G-10038)
LUDLOW COMPOSITES CORPORATION
Also Called: Crown Mats & Mating
2100 Commerce Dr (43420-1048)
PHONE.................................419 332-5531
Vincent J Dephillips, *President*
B Randall Dobbs, *President*
Joanne Boston, *Business Mgr*
Joann Northcott, *Vice Pres*
Barry Payne, *Vice Pres*
◆ **EMP:** 180
SQ FT: 190,000
SALES (est): 43.3MM Privately Held
SIC: 3069 3081 Mats or matting, rubber; latex, foamed; vinyl film & sheet

(G-10039)
MARK CARPENTER INDUSTRIES INC
Also Called: Mc Industries
2300 Napoleon Rd (43420-2644)
PHONE.................................419 294-4568
Fax: 419 355-8083
EMP: 8
SQ FT: 10,000
SALES: 600K Privately Held
SIC: 3559 Mfg Custom Foundry Equipment

(G-10040)
MICHIGAN SUGAR COMPANY
1101 N Front St (43420-1922)
PHONE.................................419 332-9931
Linda Orndorff, *Warehouse Mgr*
Mark Flegenheimer, *Manager*
EMP: 10
SALES (corp-wide): 600MM Privately Held
SIC: 2063 Beet sugar
PA: Michigan Sugar Company
  122 Uptown Dr Unit 300
  Bay City MI 48708
  989 686-0161

(G-10041)
O E MEYER CO
1005 Everett Rd (43420-1432)
PHONE.................................419 332-6931
Eric Wharton, *Branch Mgr*
EMP: 8
SALES (corp-wide): 92.8MM Privately Held
WEB: www.oemeyer.com
SIC: 3548 Welding & cutting apparatus & accessories
PA: O. E. Meyer Co.
  3303 Tiffin Ave
  Sandusky OH 44870
  419 625-1256

(G-10042)
ORBIS RPM LLC
2100 Cedar St (43420-1008)
PHONE.................................419 355-8310
Jay Neundorfer, *Branch Mgr*
EMP: 10
SALES (corp-wide): 1.7B Privately Held
WEB: www.cartonplast.com
SIC: 3081 Unsupported plastics film & sheet
HQ: Orbis Rpm, Llc
  1055 Corporate Center Dr
  Oconomowoc WI 53066
  262 560-5000

(G-10043)
P H GLATFELTER COMPANY
2275 Commerce Dr (43420-1045)
PHONE.................................419 333-6700
Lloyd Tuskan, *Opers-Prdtn-Mfg*
Cheryl Missler, *Human Res Dir*

EMP: 75
SALES (corp-wide): 866.2MM Publicly Held
WEB: www.glatfelter.com
SIC: 2761 2672 Manifold business forms; coated & laminated paper
PA: P. H. Glatfelter Company
  96 S George St Ste 520
  York PA 17401
  717 225-4711

(G-10044)
PALMER BROS TRANSIT MIX CON
210 N Stone St (43420)
PHONE.................................419 332-6363
Chuck Rapp, *Manager*
EMP: 10
SALES (corp-wide): 7MM Privately Held
SIC: 3273 Ready-mixed concrete
PA: Palmer Bros Transit Mix Concrete Inc
  12205 E Gypsy Lane Rd
  Bowling Green OH 43402
  419 352-4681

(G-10045)
PRECISION MACHINE & TOOL CO
1016 N 5th St (43420-3932)
PHONE.................................419 334-8405
Ken Ambrozy, *President*
Carolyn Ambrozy, *Corp Secy*
Eric Kiser, *Engineer*
Daniel Garza, *Project Engr*
Dan Long, *Finance Mgr*
EMP: 17 **EST:** 1979
SQ FT: 11,500
SALES (est): 2.9MM Privately Held
WEB: www.pmtcompany.com
SIC: 3599 Custom machinery; machine shop, jobbing & repair

(G-10046)
PROFESSIONAL SUPPLY INC
Also Called: Worthington Energy Innovations
504 Liberty St (43420-1929)
PHONE.................................419 332-7373
Thomas E Kiser, *President*
Dave Engeman, *Treasurer*
Steven Frederick, *Technical Staff*
EMP: 18 **EST:** 1979
SQ FT: 9,600
SALES (est): 6.2MM Privately Held
WEB: www.professionalsupplyinc.com
SIC: 3585 1711 Refrigeration & heating equipment; plumbing, heating, air-conditioning contractors

(G-10047)
RJM TOOL
1718 Sycamore St (43420-2258)
PHONE.................................419 355-0900
Robert Mason, *Owner*
EMP: 3
SALES (est): 100K Privately Held
SIC: 3599 Machine shop, jobbing & repair

(G-10048)
ROOTS POULTRY INC
3721 W State St (43420-9771)
PHONE.................................419 332-0041
Mark Damschroder, *CEO*
Annette Damschroder, *General Mgr*
EMP: 19
SQ FT: 8,000
SALES (est): 2.2MM Privately Held
WEB: www.rootspoultry.com
SIC: 2015 5144 5499 Chicken, processed: cooked; poultry & poultry products; eggs & poultry

(G-10049)
ROWEND INDUSTRIES INC
1035 Napoleon St Ste 101 (43420-2390)
PHONE.................................419 333-8300
Robert Jablonski, *President*
EMP: 8
SALES (est): 824K Privately Held
SIC: 3999 Barber & beauty shop equipment

(G-10050)
SEAWIN INC
728 Graham Dr (43420-4073)
PHONE.................................419 355-9111
Prakash Jog, *President*

Fremont - Sandusky County (G-10051)

EMP: 60
SALES (est): 5.4MM
SALES (corp-wide): 24.2MM **Privately Held**
WEB: www.seawin.com
SIC: 3491 Industrial valves
PA: Alkon Corporation
728 Graham Dr
Fremont OH 43420
419 355-9111

(G-10051)
STANDARD TECHNOLOGIES LLC
2641 Hayes Ave (43420-9715)
PHONE 419 332-6434
Max Valentine, *President*
Ian Feyedelem, *Engineer*
Clifford Pohlman, *Engineer*
Andy Price, *Sales Dir*
EMP: 75 **EST:** 1916
SQ FT: 35,000
SALES (est): 15.9MM **Privately Held**
SIC: 3444 Sheet metalwork

(G-10052)
STYLE CREST INC (HQ)
2450 Enterprise St (43420-8553)
P.O. Box A (43420-0555)
PHONE 419 332-7369
Thomas Kern, *CEO*
Henry Valle, *President*
Phillip Burton, *Corp Secy*
William Goad, *Exec VP*
Bryan T Kern, *Exec VP*
◆ **EMP:** 277
SALES (est): 165.5MM
SALES (corp-wide): 173.7MM **Privately Held**
SIC: 3089 5075 5031 8361 Siding, plastic; warm air heating & air conditioning; building materials, exterior; building materials, interior; residential care
PA: Style Crest Enterprises, Inc.
2450 Enterprise St
Fremont OH 43420
419 355-8586

(G-10053)
STYLE CREST ENTERPRISES INC (PA)
2450 Enterprise St (43420-8553)
P.O. Box A (43420-0555)
PHONE 419 355-8586
Thomas L Kern, *CEO*
Henry Valle, *President*
Greg Risk, *General Mgr*
Phillip Burton, *Corp Secy*
Bryan T Kern, *Exec VP*
EMP: 70
SQ FT: 40,000
SALES (est): 173.7MM **Privately Held**
SIC: 3089 5075 Plastic hardware & building products; awnings, fiberglass & plastic combination; siding, plastic; warm air heating & air conditioning

(G-10054)
TECHNIFORM INDUSTRIES INC
2107 Hayes Ave (43420-2695)
PHONE 419 332-8484
Clifford A Robinette, *President*
Michael Robinette, *Sales Mgr*
Jon Mistor, *Office Mgr*
EMP: 30
SQ FT: 16,000
SALES (est): 7.8MM **Privately Held**
WEB: www.techniform-plastics.com
SIC: 3083 3599 Thermoplastic laminates: rods, tubes, plates & sheet; custom machinery

(G-10055)
THE FREMONT KRAUT COMPANY
724 N Front St (43420-1915)
PHONE 419 332-6481
Russell G Sorg, *President*
Jan Sorg, *Corp Secy*
Orland H Hasselbach, *Vice Pres*
Richard L Smith, *VP Sales*
EMP: 70 **EST:** 1906
SALES (est): 3MM
SALES (corp-wide): 59.9MM **Privately Held**
WEB: www.fremontcompany.com
SIC: 2033 Canned fruits & specialties
PA: The Fremont Company
802 N Front St
Fremont OH 43420
419 334-8995

(G-10056)
TRUE KOTE INC
2132 E Cole Rd (43420-8754)
PHONE 419 334-8813
Donald C Bayless, *President*
Marie Bayless, *Corp Secy*
EMP: 8
SQ FT: 2,500
SALES: 500K **Privately Held**
SIC: 1752 3544 Floor laying & floor work; dies, steel rule

(G-10057)
TW TANK LLC
721 Graham Dr (43420-4074)
PHONE 419 334-2664
EMP: 5 **Privately Held**
SIC: 3443 Mfg Fabricated Plate Work

(G-10058)
TW TANK LLC
721 Graham Dr (43420-4074)
PHONE 419 334-2664
EMP: 5 **Privately Held**
SIC: 7692 Welding Repair

(G-10059)
UNICAN OHIO LLC
4600 Oak Harbor Rd (43420-9373)
PHONE 419 636-5461
Stig Rasmussen, *Mng Member*
▲ **EMP:** 5
SQ FT: 100,000
SALES (est): 1.2MM **Privately Held**
SIC: 3412 Metal barrels, drums & pails

(G-10060)
UNIQUE FABRICATIONS INC
2520 Hayes Ave (43420-2639)
PHONE 419 355-1700
Karl Honsperger, *President*
Anthony Doble, *Vice Pres*
Ellen Honsperger, *Treasurer*
Madeline Doble, *Admin Sec*
EMP: 17
SQ FT: 12,000
SALES: 4.9MM **Privately Held**
WEB: www.uniquefabrications.com
SIC: 3441 Building components, structural steel

(G-10061)
VALLEY ELECTRIC COMPANY
432 N Wood St (43420-2561)
PHONE 419 332-6405
Cynthia Auxter, *President*
Margaret Huffman, *Vice Pres*
EMP: 6 **EST:** 1957
SALES (est): 994.7K **Privately Held**
SIC: 1731 3679 General electrical contractor; electronic circuits; commutators, electronic; electronic loads & power supplies

(G-10062)
VANTAGE ATHLETIC
325 Cottage St (43420-4043)
PHONE 419 680-5274
Devon Mezinger, *Principal*
EMP: 4
SALES (est): 361K **Privately Held**
SIC: 3949 Sporting & athletic goods

(G-10063)
WAHL REFRACTORY SOLUTIONS LLC
767 S State Route 19 (43420-9260)
PHONE 419 334-2658
Timothy M Albertson, *President*
Cornerstone Industrial Group, *Managing Prtnr*
Andy Aelker, *Senior Buyer*
Tabatha Timmons, *QC Mgr*
Sarah Herman, *Controller*
▲ **EMP:** 65
SALES (est): 13.5MM **Privately Held**
SIC: 3297 3255 Nonclay refractories; mortars, clay refractory

(G-10064)
WOODBRIDGE GROUP
827 Graham Dr (43420-4075)
PHONE 419 334-3666
Don McFarland, *Senior Engr*
Mike Kohout, *Manager*
EMP: 150
SALES (corp-wide): 10.6B **Publicly Held**
SIC: 3069 3714 Hard rubber & molded rubber products; motor vehicle parts & accessories
HQ: Woodbridge Company Limited, The
65 Queen St W Suite 2400
Toronto ON M5H 2
416 364-8700

(G-10065)
WRIGHT LEATHER WORKS
2789 Hayes Ave (43420-9714)
PHONE 567 314-0019
EMP: 3 **EST:** 2016
SALES (est): 266.3K **Privately Held**
SIC: 3199 Leather goods

Fresno
Coshocton County

(G-10066)
ANDY RABER
Also Called: Deer Valley Woodworking
32441 County Rd Ste 12 (43824)
PHONE 740 622-1386
Andy Raber, *Owner*
EMP: 3 **EST:** 2001
SALES (est): 252.1K **Privately Held**
SIC: 2511 2541 Wood household furniture; wood partitions & fixtures

(G-10067)
CHILI LOGGING LTD
30240 County Road 10 (43824-9021)
PHONE 740 545-9502
Leroy Troyer, *Principal*
EMP: 3
SALES (est): 185.8K **Privately Held**
SIC: 2411 Logging

(G-10068)
PEARL VALLEY CHEESE INC
54760 Township Road 90 (43824-9796)
P.O. Box 68 (43824-0068)
PHONE 740 545-6002
John E Stalder, *President*
Charles Ellis, *General Mgr*
Sally Ellis, *Corp Secy*
EMP: 20
SQ FT: 8,000
SALES (est): 6.2MM **Privately Held**
WEB: www.pearlvalleycheese.com
SIC: 2022 Natural cheese

(G-10069)
PENWOOD MFG
30505 Tr 212 (43824)
PHONE 330 359-5600
Paul Nisley, *Owner*
EMP: 6
SALES (est): 290K **Privately Held**
SIC: 2511 Wood household furniture

(G-10070)
PRECISION INC
33725 County Road 10 (43824-9018)
PHONE 330 897-8860
Dan Miller, *President*
Martha Miller, *Admin Sec*
EMP: 4
SQ FT: 400
SALES: 100K **Privately Held**
SIC: 7389 3599 Design, commercial & industrial; electrical discharge machining (EDM)

(G-10071)
SUPERFINE MANUFACTURING INC
33715 County Road 10 (43824-9018)
PHONE 330 897-9024
Dan Miller, *Owner*
EMP: 10
SALES (est): 1.3MM **Privately Held**
WEB: www.superfineinc.com
SIC: 3469 Metal stampings

(G-10072)
TROYERS PALLET SHOP
31052 Township Road 227 (43824-8801)
PHONE 330 897-1038
Atlee Troyer, *Owner*
EMP: 3 **EST:** 2001
SALES (est): 262.1K **Privately Held**
SIC: 2448 Pallets, wood & wood with metal

Gahanna
Franklin County

(G-10073)
ADVANCED PLASTIC SYSTEMS INC
990 Gahanna Pkwy (43230-6613)
PHONE 614 759-6550
Wolfgang Doerschlag, *President*
EMP: 17
SQ FT: 25,000
SALES (est): 3.4MM **Privately Held**
SIC: 3089 Injection molding of plastics

(G-10074)
AJA INDUSTRIES LLC
3857 Wintergreen Blvd (43230-1058)
PHONE 614 216-9566
John D Chubb,
Tina L Chubb,
▲ **EMP:** 3
SALES (est): 169.9K **Privately Held**
SIC: 3599 7389 Custom machinery;

(G-10075)
AQUASURTECH OEM CORP
845 Claycraft Rd (43230-6665)
PHONE 614 577-1203
EMP: 3
SALES (est): 262.1K **Privately Held**
SIC: 3999 Manufacturing industries

(G-10076)
ARCHITCTRAL IDENTIFICATION INC (PA)
1170 Claycraft Rd (43230-6640)
PHONE 614 868-8400
William J Cooke, *President*
Barbara B Cooke, *Corp Secy*
James W Cooke, *COO*
Robert C Barnhart Jr, *Vice Pres*
Keri Schroeder, *Project Mgr*
EMP: 20
SQ FT: 5,000
SALES (est): 2.7MM **Privately Held**
WEB: www.archid.net
SIC: 8748 3993 Systems analysis or design; electric signs

(G-10077)
BUSINESS FNCTNALITY FORMS SVCS
4367 Grays Market Dr (43230-5425)
PHONE 614 557-9420
Kenyetta Bagby, *Principal*
EMP: 3
SALES: 3K **Privately Held**
SIC: 2754 Business form & card printing, gravure

(G-10078)
CDDS INC
Also Called: Embroidme
950 Taylor Station Rd U (43230-6670)
PHONE 614 626-8747
David Foresta, *President*
Scott Foresta, *Vice Pres*
EMP: 3
SALES: 1.3MM **Privately Held**
SIC: 3993 Advertising novelties

(G-10079)
DEEMSYS INC (PA)
800 Cross Pointe Rd Afg (43230-6687)
PHONE 614 322-9928
Vijiayarani Benjamin, *Ch of Bd*
Jacob Benjamin, *President*
Dexter Benjamin, *Vice Pres*

▲ = Import ▼ = Export
◆ = Import/Export

EMP: 52
SQ FT: 5,100
SALES: 7.8MM **Privately Held**
WEB: www.deemsysinc.com
SIC: 8748 2741 7373 8299 Business consulting; ; systems software development services; educational service, non-degree granting: continuing educ.; computer software development & applications

(G-10080)
DIVERSITY-VUTEQ LLC
1015 Taylor Rd (43230-6202)
PHONE..................614 490-5034
EMP: 5
SALES (est): 173.9K **Privately Held**
SIC: 3089 Plastics products

(G-10081)
EXIDE TECHNOLOGIES
861 Taylor Rd Unit G (43230-6275)
PHONE..................614 863-3866
Mark Patterson, *Manager*
EMP: 7
SALES (corp-wide): 2.4B **Privately Held**
WEB: www.exideworld.com
SIC: 5013 3629 Automotive batteries; battery chargers, rectifying or nonrotating
PA: Exide Technologies
13000 Deerfield Pkwy # 200
Milton GA 30004
678 566-9000

(G-10082)
HEAT TREATING INC
675 Cross Pointe Rd (43230-6689)
PHONE..................614 759-9963
Rod Ingram, *Vice Pres*
EMP: 8 **EST:** 2009
SALES (est): 694.7K **Privately Held**
SIC: 3398 Metal heat treating

(G-10083)
HOLLYWOOD IMPRINTS LLC
1000 Morrison Rd Ste D (43230-6669)
PHONE..................614 501-6040
Elvis Doss,
Davidee Doss,
Kim Mitchem,
EMP: 14
SALES (est): 1.5MM **Privately Held**
SIC: 7336 2396 7319 Silk screen design; fabric printing & stamping; screen printing on fabric articles; poster advertising service, except outdoor

(G-10084)
INK WELL
969 Claycraft Rd (43230-6635)
PHONE..................614 861-7113
Barbara Seay, *Owner*
EMP: 5
SQ FT: 3,000
SALES (est): 330K **Privately Held**
SIC: 2752 Commercial printing, lithographic

(G-10085)
INTO GREAT BRANDS INC
Also Called: Motorkote & Dura Lube
1010 Taylor Station Rd A (43230-6676)
PHONE..................888 771-5656
Bill Beichner, *CEO*
James Dolin Jr, *CFO*
▼ **EMP:** 10
SQ FT: 15,000
SALES (est): 1.9MM **Privately Held**
WEB: www.motorkote.com
SIC: 2992 Oils & greases, blending & compounding

(G-10086)
K PETROLEUM INC (PA)
81 Mill St Ste 205 (43230-1718)
PHONE..................614 532-5420
Jam Khorrami, *President*
EMP: 2
SQ FT: 3,000
SALES: 7.6MM **Privately Held**
WEB: www.kpetroleum.com
SIC: 1382 Oil & gas exploration services

(G-10087)
KAHIKI FOODS INC
1100 Morrison Rd (43230-6645)
PHONE..................614 322-3180
Alan L Hoover, *President*
Tim Tsao, *Vice Pres*
Frederick A Niebauer, *CFO*
Bob Helland, *VP Sales*
Debbie Kapes, *Office Mgr*
▲ **EMP:** 160
SQ FT: 119,000
SALES (est): 49.4MM
SALES (corp-wide): 361.4MM **Privately Held**
WEB: www.kahiki.com
SIC: 2038 Frozen specialties
PA: Abarta, Inc.
200 Alpha Dr
Pittsburgh PA 15238
412 963-6226

(G-10088)
LA BOIT SPECIALTY VEHICLES (PA)
700 Cross Pointe Rd (43230-6685)
PHONE..................614 231-7640
Gil Blais, *President*
Ryan Depriest, *General Mgr*
Wayne Henderson, *Plant Mgr*
Samson Cheng, *CFO*
Anne Blais, *Treasurer*
EMP: 35
SQ FT: 18,000
SALES (est): 9.1MM **Privately Held**
WEB: www.laboit.com
SIC: 3711 3713 Ambulances (motor vehicles), assembly of; ambulance bodies

(G-10089)
MCNEILUS TRUCK AND MFG INC
1130 Morrison Rd (43230-6646)
P.O. Box 30777 (43230-0777)
PHONE..................614 868-0760
Paul Ellingen, *Manager*
EMP: 6
SALES (corp-wide): 7.7B **Publicly Held**
WEB: www.mcneiluscompanies.com
SIC: 3713 5082 Cement mixer bodies; concrete processing equipment
HQ: Mcneilus Truck And Manufacturing, Inc.
524 E Highway St
Dodge Center MN 55927
507 374-6321

(G-10090)
MIDDLETON PRINTING CO INC
81 Mill St Ste 300 (43230-1718)
PHONE..................614 294-7277
David H Stewart, *President*
Reno Camerucci, *Vice Pres*
EMP: 9 **EST:** 1950
SQ FT: 14,000
SALES (est): 1.4MM **Privately Held**
WEB: www.middletonprinting.com
SIC: 2752 2791 2759 Commercial printing, offset; typesetting; commercial printing

(G-10091)
MILNOT COMPANY
735 Taylor Rd Ste 200 (43230-6274)
PHONE..................888 656-3245
Craig A Steinke, *CEO*
William J Bond, *Vice Pres*
▼ **EMP:** 4 **EST:** 1934
SALES (est): 403K
SALES (corp-wide): 7.3B **Publicly Held**
WEB: www.milnot.com
SIC: 2032 2023 Canned specialties; condensed milk
PA: The J M Smucker Company
1 Strawberry Ln
Orrville OH 44667
330 682-3000

(G-10092)
MRC GLOBAL (US) INC
700 Taylor Rd (43230-3318)
PHONE..................614 475-4733
Steven Park, *Branch Mgr*
EMP: 11 **Publicly Held**
SIC: 1311 Crude petroleum & natural gas
HQ: Mrc Global (Us) Inc.
1301 Mckinney St Ste 2300
Houston TX 77010
877 294-7574

(G-10093)
NATURYM LLC
1255 N Hamilton Rd (43230-6785)
PHONE..................614 284-3068
Ian Downes, *Mng Member*
EMP: 4
SALES (est): 477.5K **Privately Held**
SIC: 2873 5261 5191 Nitrogen solutions (fertilizer); fertilizer; fertilizers & agricultural chemicals

(G-10094)
NETPARK LLC
1182 Claycraft Rd (43230-6640)
PHONE..................614 866-2495
Jon Schmidt, *President*
Daniel Gump, *Director*
EMP: 10
SALES (est): 937.4K **Privately Held**
SIC: 7372 Business oriented computer software

(G-10095)
NETWORK COMMUNICATIONS INC
Also Called: Apartment Finder Magazine
467 Waterbury Ct Ste B (43230-5313)
PHONE..................614 934-1919
EMP: 150
SALES (corp-wide): 1.3B **Privately Held**
SIC: 2741 Misc Publishing
HQ: Network Communications, Inc.
2 Sun Ct Ste 300
Norcross GA 30092
678 346-9300

(G-10096)
NIAGARA BOTTLING LLC
1700 Eastgate Pkwy (43230-8602)
PHONE..................614 751-7420
Randell Presnell, *Principal*
Adrian Becker, *Production*
▲ **EMP:** 13
SALES (est): 2.4MM **Privately Held**
SIC: 2086 Bottled & canned soft drinks

(G-10097)
PAHUJA INC
Also Called: Alloy Polymers
1125 Gahanna Pkwy (43230-6612)
PHONE..................614 864-3989
Peter Ploumidis, *Manager*
EMP: 60
SALES (corp-wide): 57.3MM **Privately Held**
WEB: www.alloypolymers.com
SIC: 2821 3089 Polypropylene resins; extruded finished plastic products
PA: Pahuja, Inc.
3310 Deepwater Trml Rd
Richmond VA 23234
804 200-6624

(G-10098)
PERFECTION PACKAGING INC
885 Claycraft Rd (43230-6850)
PHONE..................614 866-8558
James W Cox, *President*
Evelyn Cox, *Vice Pres*
EMP: 3
SALES (est): 50K **Privately Held**
WEB: www.perfectionpkg.com
SIC: 2671 3577 Bar code (magnetic ink) printers; paper coated or laminated for packaging

(G-10099)
R&S CARBON TRADING LLC
146 N Hamilton Rd Ste 127 (43230-2600)
PHONE..................614 264-3083
Roger D Kinney, *Mng Member*
Sean Kinney,
▼ **EMP:** 4
SQ FT: 525
SALES: 1MM **Privately Held**
WEB: www.rscarbon.com
SIC: 3624 Carbon & graphite products

(G-10100)
RIBBON TECHNOLOGY CORPORATION
Also Called: Ribtec
825 Taylor Station Rd (43230-6654)
P.O. Box 30758 (43230-0758)
PHONE..................614 864-5444
Kevin Jackson, *President*
Scott Palmer, *Corp Secy*
◆ **EMP:** 11
SQ FT: 40,000
SALES (est): 2MM **Privately Held**
WEB: www.ribtec.com
SIC: 3357 Building wire & cable, nonferrous

(G-10101)
ROMANOFF ELC RESIDENTIAL LLC
1288 Research Rd (43230-6625)
PHONE..................614 755-4500
Matthew Romanoff, *CEO*
EMP: 63
SALES (est): 208.5K
SALES (corp-wide): 10MM **Privately Held**
SIC: 3699 Household electrical equipment
PA: The Romanoff Group Llc
1288 Research Rd
Gahanna OH 43230
614 755-4500

(G-10102)
SCOTTS COMPANY LLC
710 Cross Pointe Rd (43230-6685)
P.O. Box 307574 (43230-7574)
PHONE..................614 863-3920
Mike McClung, *Branch Mgr*
EMP: 20
SALES (corp-wide): 2.6B **Publicly Held**
WEB: www.scottscompany.com
SIC: 2873 Fertilizers: natural (organic), except compost
HQ: The Scotts Company Llc
14111 Scottslawn Rd
Marysville OH 43040
937 644-0011

(G-10103)
SIGN A RAMA
Also Called: Sign-A-Rama
64 Granville St (43230-3064)
PHONE..................614 337-6000
Bill Martin, *Owner*
EMP: 4 **EST:** 1999
SALES (est): 340.7K **Privately Held**
SIC: 3993 Signs & advertising specialties

(G-10104)
SJPM INC
Also Called: Metcalf Design & Printing Ctr
264 Agler Rd (43230-2546)
PHONE..................614 475-4571
Beverly Metcalf, *President*
David Metcalf, *Vice Pres*
Jeff Metcalf, *Manager*
EMP: 5
SQ FT: 1,200
SALES (est): 681.8K **Privately Held**
SIC: 2752 7336 2791 Commercial printing, offset; graphic arts & related design; typesetting

(G-10105)
SNOW AVIATION INTL INC
949 Creek Dr (43230)
PHONE..................614 588-2452
Harry T Snow, *President*
Bill Fergusson, *Exec VP*
Richard Heybes, *Vice Pres*
Donald Smith, *Vice Pres*
EMP: 129
SQ FT: 28,000
SALES: 10MM **Privately Held**
WEB: www.snowaviation.com
SIC: 3721 3728 3724 Aircraft; aircraft assemblies, subassemblies & parts; aircraft engines & engine parts

(G-10106)
SPECTRAMED INC
275 W Johnstown Rd (43230-2732)
PHONE..................740 263-3059
Richard Fisher, *President*
▲ **EMP:** 10

Gahanna - Franklin County (G-10107)

SQ FT: 3,000
SALES: 2.3MM **Privately Held**
WEB: www.spectramedonline.com
SIC: 3624 Electrodes, thermal & electrolytic uses: carbon, graphite

(G-10107)
SPHON ASSOCIATES INC
962 Bryn Mawr Dr (43230-3843)
PHONE 614 741-4002
Alicia Holloway, *Principal*
EMP: 3 **EST:** 2007
SALES (est): 223.5K **Privately Held**
SIC: 2421 Building & structural materials, wood

(G-10108)
SURPLUS FREIGHT INC (PA)
501 Morrison Rd Ste 100 (43230-3541)
PHONE 614 235-7660
David Belford, *CEO*
Alf Karzia, *President*
Douglas A Hanby, *Principal*
Mike Mess, *Treasurer*
EMP: 17
SALES (est): 3MM **Privately Held**
SIC: 3537 Trucks: freight, baggage, etc.: industrial, except mining

(G-10109)
THOMPSON PARTNERS INC
Also Called: Tpi Medical
82 Mill St Ste A (43230-3058)
P.O. Box 307687 (43230-7687)
PHONE 866 475-2500
Garret Thompson, *President*
EMP: 4
SALES (est): 339.3K **Privately Held**
SIC: 3841 Surgical & medical instruments

(G-10110)
VICTORY DIRECT LLC
750 Cross Pointe Rd Ste M (43230-6692)
PHONE 614 626-0000
Joy Clark, *Accounting Mgr*
Joe King, *Mng Member*
EMP: 7
SALES: 1MM **Privately Held**
SIC: 7331 2752 Mailing service; business form & card printing, lithographic

Galena
Delaware County

(G-10111)
ERIC MONDENE
4278 Harlem Rd (43021-9667)
PHONE 740 965-2842
Eric Mondene, *Principal*
EMP: 4
SALES (est): 265K **Privately Held**
SIC: 3423 Carpenters' hand tools, except saws: levels, chisels, etc.

(G-10112)
GALENA VAULT LTD
4909 Harlem Rd (43021-9302)
PHONE 740 965-2200
Marcia Jo M Eisenbrown, *Owner*
EMP: 3
SALES (est): 367K **Privately Held**
SIC: 3272 Burial vaults, concrete or precast terrazzo

(G-10113)
HALLS SHEET METAL FABRICATION
Also Called: Hall's Sheet Metal Fabricating
10001 Center Village Rd (43021-5002)
PHONE 740 965-9264
James Hall, *President*
Mary Hall, *Admin Sec*
EMP: 4
SQ FT: 6,000
SALES (est): 657.6K **Privately Held**
WEB: www.hallsheetmetal.com
SIC: 3444 Sheet metal specialties, not stamped

(G-10114)
JCP SIGNS & GRAPHIX INC
12920 Gorsuch Rd (43021-8620)
PHONE 740 965-3058
EMP: 3
SALES (est): 207.7K **Privately Held**
SIC: 3993 Mfg Signs/Advertising Specialties

(G-10115)
MASON PRODUCING INC
10010 Center Village Rd (43021-8605)
PHONE 740 913-0686
EMP: 3
SALES (est): 154.9K **Privately Held**
SIC: 1311 Crude petroleum & natural gas

(G-10116)
MIDWEST INDUSTRIAL SPECIALTIES
5521 Summer Blvd (43021-9549)
PHONE 740 815-0541
Steven B Davis, *Mng Member*
EMP: 3
SALES: 250K **Privately Held**
SIC: 3544 Dies & die holders for metal cutting, forming, die casting

(G-10117)
WARFIGHTER FCSED LOGISTICS INC (PA)
3894 Worthington Rd (43021-9705)
PHONE 740 513-4692
Darrell Kem, *CEO*
Morgan Ellington, *COO*
Valerie Hammond, *CFO*
EMP: 7
SALES (est): 2.2MM **Privately Held**
SIC: 3711 3724 3714 7389 Military motor vehicle assembly; universal carriers, military, assembly of; lubricating systems, aircraft; transmissions, motor vehicle; motor vehicle body components & frame;

(G-10118)
WS TRADING LLC
Also Called: Buy Truck Wheels
2623 S State Route 605 (43021-9457)
P.O. Box 327, New Albany (43054-0327)
PHONE 800 830-4547
EMP: 3
SQ FT: 5,000
SALES: 2.1MM **Privately Held**
SIC: 3011 Tires & inner tubes

Galion
Crawford County

(G-10119)
A & G MANUFACTURING CO INC (PA)
Also Called: A G Mercury
280 Gelsanliter Rd (44833-2234)
P.O. Box 935 (44833-0935)
PHONE 419 468-7433
Arvin Shifley, *President*
Glen Shifley Sr, *Principal*
Doug Shifley, *CFO*
Carol Carder, *Regl Sales Mgr*
Glen E Shifley Jr, *Admin Sec*
▲ **EMP:** 40
SQ FT: 100,000
SALES (est): 10.4MM **Privately Held**
WEB: www.agmercury.com
SIC: 3599 7692 3446 3444 Machine shop, jobbing & repair; welding repair; architectural metalwork; sheet metalwork; fabricated plate work (boiler shop); fabricated structural metal

(G-10120)
A & G MANUFACTURING CO INC
165 Gelsanliter Rd (44833)
PHONE 419 468-7433
Arvin Shifley, *Branch Mgr*
EMP: 70
SALES (est): 9.2MM
SALES (corp-wide): 10.4MM **Privately Held**
WEB: www.agmercury.com
SIC: 3599 Machine shop, jobbing & repair
PA: A. & G. Manufacturing Co., Inc.
  280 Gelsanliter Rd
  Galion OH 44833
  419 468-7433

(G-10121)
A-1 PRINTING INC
139 Harding Way W (44833-1727)
PHONE 419 468-5422
Becky Lloyd, *Branch Mgr*
EMP: 7
SALES (corp-wide): 1.3MM **Privately Held**
SIC: 2752 Commercial printing, offset
PA: A-1 Printing, Inc.
  825 S Sandusky Ave
  Bucyrus OH 44820
  419 562-3111

(G-10122)
ALEXANDER WILBERT VAULT CO (PA)
1263 State Hwy 598 (44833)
P.O. Box 177 (44833-0177)
PHONE 419 468-3477
C Phillip Longstreth, *President*
Sean Longstreth, *Vice Pres*
EMP: 10
SALES: 700K **Privately Held**
SIC: 3272 Burial vaults, concrete or precast terrazzo

(G-10123)
BAILLIE LUMBER CO LP
3953 County Road 51 (44833)
PHONE 419 462-2000
Russel Jones, *Branch Mgr*
EMP: 40
SALES (corp-wide): 344.3MM **Privately Held**
SIC: 5031 2426 2421 Lumber: rough, dressed & finished; hardwood dimension & flooring mills; sawmills & planing mills, general
PA: Baillie Lumber Co., L.P.
  4002 Legion Dr
  Hamburg NY 14075
  800 950-2850

(G-10124)
BROTHERS BODY AND EQP LLC
352 South St Bldg 24 (44833-2742)
P.O. Box 926 (44833-0926)
PHONE 419 462-1975
Michael Horn, *President*
Matt Horn, *Opers Mgr*
Tim Horn, *Bd of Directors*
▲ **EMP:** 15
SQ FT: 30,000
SALES (est): 4.2MM **Privately Held**
WEB: www.brothersbande.com
SIC: 3713 Truck bodies & parts

(G-10125)
CARTER MACHINE COMPANY INC (PA)
Also Called: Hydranamics
820 Edward St (44833-2223)
PHONE 419 468-3530
Juanita Carter, *Ch of Bd*
Andrea Carter, *President*
E V Keeler, *Principal*
EMP: 5 **EST:** 1941
SALES (est): 11.6MM **Privately Held**
SIC: 3593 3498 3471 Fluid power cylinders, hydraulic or pneumatic; fabricated pipe & fittings; plating & polishing

(G-10126)
CASS FRAMES INC
6052 State Route 19 (44833-9771)
P.O. Box 625 (44833-0625)
PHONE 419 468-2863
James Cass, *President*
Bart Cass, *Vice Pres*
Delores Cass, *Admin Sec*
EMP: 9
SQ FT: 4,200
SALES (est): 1.4MM **Privately Held**
SIC: 2499 Picture & mirror frames, wood; picture frame molding, finished

(G-10127)
CENTRAL STATE ENTERPRISES INC
1331 Freese Works Pl (44833-9368)
PHONE 419 468-8191
Donald E Kuenzli Jr, *President*
Sandra Kuenzli, *Corp Secy*
Gary Yetzer, *Engineer*
Teresa Osowski, *Office Mgr*
EMP: 37
SQ FT: 28,000
SALES (est): 7.7MM **Privately Held**
SIC: 3599 Machine shop, jobbing & repair

(G-10128)
CMI HOLDING COMPANY CRAWFORD
1310 Freese Works Pl (44833-9368)
PHONE 419 468-9122
Kevin Hessey, *President*
Brad Hessey, *Vice Pres*
Keith Hummel, *Vice Pres*
Tonya Hoepf, *Manager*
Joy Hessey, *Admin Sec*
◆ **EMP:** 70
SALES (est): 12.2MM
SALES (corp-wide): 110MM **Privately Held**
WEB: www.crawfordmachineinc.com
SIC: 3432 Plumbers' brass goods: drain cocks, faucets, spigots, etc.
HQ: Sloan L Tramec L C
  534 E 48th St
  Holland MI 49423
  616 395-5600

(G-10129)
COTTONWOOD PALLET INC
Also Called: Cotton Wood Pallet Co
9541 Mrral Krkptrick Rd E (44833-9789)
PHONE 419 468-9703
Eugene Stewart, *President*
Christopher Stewart, *Vice Pres*
EMP: 4
SALES (est): 382.5K **Privately Held**
SIC: 2448 Pallets, wood

(G-10130)
COVERT MANUFACTURING INC (PA)
328 S East St (44833-2729)
P.O. Box 608 (44833-0608)
PHONE 419 468-1761
Donald L Covert Sr, *CEO*
Kym Fox, *President*
Teri Williams, *President*
Donna Morrow, *Admin Sec*
▲ **EMP:** 370
SQ FT: 300,000
SALES (est): 65.9MM **Privately Held**
WEB: www.covertmfg.com
SIC: 3545 Machine tool accessories

(G-10131)
CRASE COMMUNICATIONS INC
120 Harding Way E Ste 104 (44833-1927)
PHONE 419 468-1173
Edward Crase, *President*
Linda Crase, *Corp Secy*
EMP: 13
SALES (est): 1.4MM **Privately Held**
WEB: www.crasecommunications.com
SIC: 1731 3661 Telephone & telephone equipment installation; toll switching equipment, telephone

(G-10132)
DINKMAR INC
9357 Township Road 48 (44833-9801)
PHONE 419 468-8516
Fax: 419 468-8417
EMP: 5
SQ FT: 5,200
SALES (est): 400K **Privately Held**
SIC: 3589 5084 Mfg Service Industry Machinery Whol Industrial Equipment

(G-10133)
DYENAMO DISTRIBUTING
6124 State Route 19 (44833-8931)
P.O. Box 759 (44833-0759)
PHONE 419 462-9474
Ken Dye, *Owner*
EMP: 12
SALES (est): 1.1MM **Privately Held**
SIC: 2759 Promotional printing

(G-10134)
E & E NAMEPLATES INC
760 E Walnut St (44833-2133)
PHONE 419 468-3617
Mike Enders, *Co-Owner*
EMP: 12 **EST:** 1976
SQ FT: 4,500

▲ = Import ▼ = Export
◆ = Import/Export

GEOGRAPHIC SECTION

Gallipolis - Gallia County (G-10160)

SALES (est): 1.1MM **Privately Held**
SIC: 2759 Screen printing

(G-10135)
EAGLE CRUSHER CO INC (PA)
525 S Market St (44833-2612)
P.O. Box 537 (44833-0537)
PHONE..............................419 468-2288
Susanne Cobey, *President*
Shawn Jury, *Vice Pres*
Scott Carpenter, *Purch Mgr*
Lisa Cain, *Engineer*
Ray Kilgore, *Engineer*
◆ **EMP:** 180 **EST:** 1915
SQ FT: 40,000
SALES (est): 59.8MM **Privately Held**
WEB: www.eaglecrusher.com
SIC: 3535 3532 3589 3531 Conveyors & conveying equipment; crushing, pulverizing & screening equipment; sewage & water treatment equipment; construction machinery

(G-10136)
ECLIPSE
126 N Union St (44833-1736)
PHONE..............................419 564-7482
Teresa Harris, *Principal*
EMP: 5
SALES (est): 331.2K **Privately Held**
SIC: 7372 Prepackaged software

(G-10137)
ELLIOTT MACHINE WORKS INC
1351 Freese Works Pl (44833-9368)
P.O. Box 955 (44833-0955)
PHONE..............................419 468-4709
Richard Ekin, *President*
Brad Ekin, *Vice Pres*
Brent Ekin, *VP Opers*
EMP: 48 **EST:** 1968
SQ FT: 54,000
SALES: 8MM **Privately Held**
WEB: www.elliottmachine.com
SIC: 3713 3443 3537 Truck bodies (motor vehicles); tanks for tank trucks, metal plate; trucks: freight, baggage, etc.: industrial, except mining; truck trailers, used in plants, docks, terminals, etc.

(G-10138)
GALION LLC
515 N East St (44833-2142)
P.O. Box 447 (44833-0447)
PHONE..............................419 468-5214
Richard Voorde, *CEO*
Stephen Koch, *Mng Member*
Cindy Shepherd,
Stan Will,
EMP: 105
SQ FT: 60,000
SALES (est): 51MM **Privately Held**
WEB: www.galion.net
SIC: 3482 3444 Small arms ammunition; sheet metalwork

(G-10139)
GALION CANVAS PRODUCTS (PA)
385 S Market St (44833-2608)
PHONE..............................419 468-5333
Steve Siclair, *Owner*
Scott Goldsmith, *Principal*
EMP: 12
SQ FT: 5,000
SALES: 300K **Privately Held**
WEB: www.galioncanvasproducts.com
SIC: 7359 2394 Tent & tarpaulin rental; canvas & related products; tarpaulins, fabric: made from purchased materials; awnings, fabric: made from purchased materials; tents: made from purchased materials

(G-10140)
GALION PACKAGING CO INC
340 S East St (44833-2731)
PHONE..............................419 468-2548
David La Chance, *President*
Richard Lachance, *Vice Pres*
EMP: 5
SQ FT: 15,000
SALES (est): 896.9K **Privately Held**
SIC: 2631 Container, packaging & boxboard; packaging board

(G-10141)
GEYERS MARKETS INC
Geyer's Market 5
230 Portland Way N (44833-1631)
PHONE..............................419 468-9477
Fax: 419 468-1826
EMP: 80
SALES (corp-wide): 60MM **Privately Held**
SIC: 5411 2051 Ret Groceries Mfg Bread/Related Products
PA: Geyers' Markets, Inc.
  131 Iberia St
  Mount Gilead OH 43338
  419 683-2925

(G-10142)
GINNYS CUSTOM FRAMING GALLERY
Also Called: Gathering Place
1135 Cherington Dr (44833-1004)
PHONE..............................419 468-7240
Ginny Barr, *Owner*
Donald Barr, *Co-Owner*
EMP: 3
SQ FT: 1,600
SALES (est): 150K **Privately Held**
SIC: 2499 Picture frame molding, finished

(G-10143)
GLEDHILL ROAD MACHINERY CO
765 Portland Way S (44833-2326)
P.O. Box 567 (44833-0567)
PHONE..............................419 468-4400
Garland Gledhill, *Ch of Bd*
Michael D Rarick, *President*
Sherrie Dill, *Treasurer*
EMP: 50 **EST:** 1930
SQ FT: 57,000
SALES (est): 17.8MM **Privately Held**
WEB: www.gledhillonline.com
SIC: 3531 Road construction & maintenance machinery; snow plow attachments

(G-10144)
HYDRANAMICS INC
Also Called: Hydranamics Div Carter Mch Co
820 Edward St (44833-2223)
PHONE..............................419 468-3530
Juanita Carter, *Ch of Bd*
Andrea Carter, *President*
EMP: 86
SALES (est): 7.1MM
SALES (corp-wide): 11.6MM **Privately Held**
WEB: www.hydranamics.com
SIC: 3593 3547 Fluid power cylinders, hydraulic or pneumatic; rolling mill machinery
PA: Carter Machine Company, Inc.
  820 Edward St
  Galion OH 44833
  419 468-3530

(G-10145)
IBERIA FIREARMS INC
3929 State Route 309 (44833-9408)
P.O. Box 236, Iberia (43325-0236)
PHONE..............................419 468-3746
James Cole, *President*
Jane Cole, *Corp Secy*
EMP: 4
SALES (est): 505.6K **Privately Held**
SIC: 3484 Guns (firearms) or gun parts, 30 mm. & below

(G-10146)
JUST PLASTICS INC
869 Smith St (44833-2761)
P.O. Box 645 (44833-0645)
PHONE..............................419 468-5506
Steve Eckstein, *President*
Judy Eckstein, *President*
EMP: 40
SQ FT: 11,000
SALES (est): 6.1MM **Privately Held**
SIC: 3089 Injection molded finished plastic products

(G-10147)
KNOX COUNTY PRINTING CO
Also Called: Knox County Citizen
129 Harding Way E (44833-1902)
PHONE..............................740 848-4032
Donald E Clark, *President*
Richard Brenneman, *Owner*
EMP: 5
SQ FT: 1,000
SALES (est): 109.1K **Privately Held**
SIC: 2711 2752 Commercial printing & newspaper publishing combined; commercial printing, lithographic

(G-10148)
LINDEN MONUMENTS
104 Linden Dr (44833-1526)
PHONE..............................419 468-4130
Charles E Jackson, *Owner*
EMP: 3
SALES (est): 249.7K **Privately Held**
SIC: 3281 5999 Monument or burial stone, cut & shaped; monuments & tombstones

(G-10149)
PARTNERS MANUFACTURING GROUP
9357 Township Road 48 (44833-9801)
PHONE..............................419 468-8516
Jeff Dinkel, *President*
Dave Dinkel, *Corp Secy*
Norm Dinkel, *Vice Pres*
EMP: 4
SQ FT: 7,500
SALES (est): 280K **Privately Held**
SIC: 3315 Steel wire & related products

(G-10150)
PIPELINE AUTOMATION SYSTE INC
215 Harding Way W (44833-1728)
PHONE..............................419 462-8833
EMP: 1
SALES: 1MM **Privately Held**
SIC: 3547 Mfg Misc Products

(G-10151)
PRINTS & PAINTS FLR CVG CO INC
Also Called: My Floors By Prints and Paints
888 Bucyrus Rd (44833-1549)
PHONE..............................419 462-5663
Gary Frankhouse Sr, *President*
Sandra Frankhouse, *Exec VP*
Gary Frankhouse Jr, *Treasurer*
Steve Frankhouse, *Admin Sec*
EMP: 23
SQ FT: 14,000
SALES (est): 3.7MM **Privately Held**
WEB: www.printsandpaints.com
SIC: 3996 5231 2295 1743 Asphalted-felt-base floor coverings: linoleum, carpet; paint; laminating of fabrics; tile installation, ceramic

(G-10152)
SAUTTER BROTHERS
Also Called: Sautter Bros Machine & Fabg
6443 Brandt Rd (44833-9395)
PHONE..............................419 468-7443
John M Sautter, *Partner*
Thomas E Sautter, *Partner*
EMP: 4
SQ FT: 100,000
SALES (est): 487.9K **Privately Held**
SIC: 3441 0116 0115 Fabricated structural metal; soybeans; corn

(G-10153)
SCENIC SCREEN
4463 State Route 309 (44833-9616)
PHONE..............................419 468-3110
Judy Sanders, *Owner*
EMP: 3
SQ FT: 1,000
SALES (est): 135.2K **Privately Held**
SIC: 2262 Screen printing: manmade fiber & silk broadwoven fabrics

(G-10154)
SCHILLING GRAPHICS INC (PA)
275 Gelsanliter Rd (44833-2235)
P.O. Box 978 (44833-0978)
PHONE..............................419 468-1037
Douglas Schilling, *President*
EMP: 33
SQ FT: 20,000
SALES (est): 8.8MM **Privately Held**
SIC: 2752 3552 3555 2759 Decals, lithographed; silk screens for textile industry; printing trades machinery; commercial printing; packaging paper & plastics film, coated & laminated; automotive & apparel trimmings

(G-10155)
SHOWPLACE INC
Also Called: Showplace Rental
201 S Market St (44833-2629)
PHONE..............................419 468-7368
Jacob Webb, *Manager*
EMP: 5
SALES (corp-wide): 13.2MM **Privately Held**
WEB: www.showplaceinc.biz
SIC: 3679 7359 Electronic circuits; stores & yards equipment rental
PA: Showplace, Inc.
  611 Bellefontaine Ave
  Marion OH 43302
  740 382-8891

(G-10156)
SPEEDWAY LLC
Also Called: Speedway Superamerica 3187
746 Harding Way W (44833-1616)
PHONE..............................419 468-9773
Carl Schieber, *Branch Mgr*
EMP: 10 **Publicly Held**
WEB: www.speedwaynet.com
SIC: 1311 Crude petroleum production
HQ: Speedway Llc
  500 Speedway Dr
  Enon OH 45323
  937 864-3000

(G-10157)
STARKEY MACHINERY INC
254 S Washington St (44833-2616)
P.O. Box 207 (44833-0207)
PHONE..............................419 468-2560
James D Starkey, *President*
Don Starkey, *Vice Pres*
EMP: 20 **EST:** 1881
SQ FT: 30,000
SALES (est): 4.1MM **Privately Held**
WEB: www.starkeymachinery.com
SIC: 3559 5084 3594 3544 Clay working & tempering machines; industrial machinery & equipment; fluid power pumps & motors; special dies, tools, jigs & fixtures; machine tools, metal forming type

(G-10158)
TRAMEC SLOAN LLC
1310 Freese Works Pl (44833-9368)
PHONE..............................419 468-9122
Kevin Hessey, *President*
EMP: 15
SALES (corp-wide): 110MM **Privately Held**
SIC: 3714 3625 3561 Motor vehicle parts & accessories; relays & industrial controls; pumps & pumping equipment
HQ: Sloan L Tramec L C
  534 E 48th St
  Holland MI 49423
  616 395-5600

(G-10159)
VULCAN PRODUCTS CO INC
208 S Washington St (44833-2616)
P.O. Box 216 (44833-0216)
PHONE..............................419 468-1039
Ralph Chamberlin, *President*
EMP: 13 **EST:** 1951
SALES (est): 1.7MM **Privately Held**
SIC: 3451 Screw machine products

Gallipolis
Gallia County

(G-10160)
BCMR PUBLICATIONS LLC
430 2nd Ave (45631-1130)
PHONE..............................740 441-7778
Christopher Rathburn, *Administration*
EMP: 4 **EST:** 2009
SQ FT: 2,080
SALES (est): 293.4K **Privately Held**
SIC: 2741 Miscellaneous publishing

Gallipolis - Gallia County (G-10161)

(G-10161)
BIG RIVER ELECTRIC INC
299 Upper River Rd (45631-1838)
P.O. Box 244 (45631-0244)
PHONE.................................740 446-4360
Kelly Counts, *President*
Debra Barcus, *Corp Secy*
Geraldine Counts, *Vice Pres*
EMP: 6
SQ FT: 8,500
SALES (est): 1MM **Privately Held**
SIC: 5999 7694 5063 Motors, electric; electric motor repair; motors, electric

(G-10162)
CREMEANS CONCRETE AND SUP CO
161 Georges Creek Rd (45631-8535)
P.O. Box 475 (45631-0475)
PHONE.................................740 446-1142
John Cremeans, *President*
Carol Cremeans, *Treasurer*
EMP: 6
SALES (est): 719.9K **Privately Held**
SIC: 3273 Ready-mixed concrete

(G-10163)
ELECTROCRAFT ARKANSAS INC
250 Mccormick Rd (45631-8745)
PHONE.................................501 268-4203
James Elsner, *CEO*
Logan D Delany Jr, *Ch of Bd*
Terry McKinniss, *General Mgr*
Mike Lawson, *Safety Mgr*
Rob Kerber, *Marketing Mgr*
▲ EMP: 65 EST: 2001
SQ FT: 50,000
SALES (est): 11.6MM
SALES (corp-wide): 126.2MM **Privately Held**
WEB: www.agimotors.com
SIC: 3621 Electric motor & generator parts
HQ: Electrocraft, Inc.
1 Progress Dr
Dover NH 03820
603 742-3330

(G-10164)
ELECTROCRAFT OHIO INC
250 Mccormick Rd (45631-8745)
PHONE.................................740 441-6200
James Elsner, *President*
Mike Karsonovich, *President*
Logan D Delany Jr, *Principal*
John Arico, *Vice Pres*
Marshall French, *Manager*
▲ EMP: 225
SQ FT: 160,000
SALES (est): 48.8MM
SALES (corp-wide): 126.2MM **Privately Held**
SIC: 3625 Relays & industrial controls
HQ: Electrocraft, Inc.
1 Progress Dr
Dover NH 03820
603 742-3330

(G-10165)
GKN PLC
Also Called: GKN Sinter Metals
2160 Eastern Ave (45631-1823)
PHONE.................................740 446-9211
David Knotts, *Engineer*
Daniel Swannigan, *Branch Mgr*
EMP: 9
SALES (corp-wide): 2.7B **Privately Held**
SIC: 3462 Iron & steel forgings
HQ: Gkn Limited
Po Box 55
Redditch WORCS B98 0
152 751-7715

(G-10166)
GKN SINTER METALS LLC
Also Called: Precision Forged Products
2160 Eastern Ave (45631-1823)
PHONE.................................740 441-3203
Jim McKinney, *Engineer*
Greg Landis, *Branch Mgr*
EMP: 130
SALES (corp-wide): 2.7B **Privately Held**
SIC: 3312 3568 3462 Sinter, iron; power transmission equipment; iron & steel forgings

HQ: Gkn Sinter Metals, Llc
2200 N Opdyke Rd
Auburn Hills MI 48326
248 296-7832

(G-10167)
HEARTLAND PUBLICATIONS LLC
Gallipolis Daily Tribune
825 3rd Ave (45631-1624)
PHONE.................................740 446-2342
Sammy Lopez, *Branch Mgr*
EMP: 11
SALES (corp-wide): 763.9MM **Privately Held**
WEB: www.heartlandpublications.com
SIC: 2759 2711 Publication printing; newspapers, publishing & printing
HQ: Heartland Publications, Llc
4500 Lyons Rd
Miamisburg OH 45342
860 664-1075

(G-10168)
JM LOGGING INC
1624 Graham School Rd (45631-8002)
PHONE.................................740 441-0941
J M Clagg, *Owner*
EMP: 3 EST: 2010
SALES (est): 235.2K **Privately Held**
SIC: 2411 Logging

(G-10169)
KING KUTTER II INC
Also Called: Sfs Truck Sales & Parts
2150 Eastern Ave (45631-1823)
P.O. Box 786 (45631-0786)
PHONE.................................740 446-0351
James Phillip Fraley, *President*
Jeff Fraley, *Vice Pres*
Deborah Swain, *Admin Sec*
▲ EMP: 50
SQ FT: 160
SALES (est): 17.2MM **Privately Held**
SIC: 5521 3713 Trucks, tractors & trailers: used; truck & bus bodies

(G-10170)
KSN CLEARING LLC
736 2nd Ave (45631-1514)
P.O. Box 796, Marietta (45750-0796)
PHONE.................................304 269-3306
Kristine Frame,
EMP: 15
SALES (est): 407.9K **Privately Held**
SIC: 1389 7389 Grading oil & gas well foundations;

(G-10171)
MARION CALDWELL
1262 Lincoln Pike Rear (45631)
PHONE.................................740 446-1042
Caldwell Marion, *Owner*
EMP: 3
SALES (est): 160K **Privately Held**
SIC: 3523 Driers (farm): grain, hay & seed

(G-10172)
O-KAN MARINE REPAIR INC
267 Upper River Rd (45631-1838)
PHONE.................................740 446-4686
Chris Preston, *President*
Randy Canaday, *General Mgr*
Tessa Haggerty, *General Mgr*
Jay Hall Jr, *Vice Pres*
Sandra Neal, *Treasurer*
EMP: 34
SALES (est): 4.8MM **Privately Held**
WEB: www.okanmarinerepair.com
SIC: 3732 3731 Boat building & repairing; barges, building & repairing

(G-10173)
PIP AND HUDS LLC
334 2nd Ave (45631-1414)
PHONE.................................740 208-5519
EMP: 4
SALES (est): 392.8K **Privately Held**
SIC: 2752 Commercial printing, offset

(G-10174)
RIVERVIEW PRODUCTIONS INC
Also Called: UNIQUE EXPRESSIONS
652 Jackson Pike (45631-1389)
P.O. Box 624, Wellston (45692-0624)
PHONE.................................740 441-1150

Thomas Meadows, *Chairman*
EMP: 9
SALES: 566.9K **Privately Held**
SIC: 5261 2611 Nurseries; pulp mills, mechanical & recycling processing

(G-10175)
SHELLY MATERIALS INC
1248 State Route 7 N (45631-9475)
PHONE.................................740 446-7789
Trevor Small, *Manager*
EMP: 4
SALES (corp-wide): 29.7B **Privately Held**
SIC: 2951 Asphalt & asphaltic paving mixtures (not from refineries)
HQ: Shelly Materials, Inc.
80 Park Dr
Thornville OH 43076
740 246-6315

(G-10176)
THOMAS DO-IT CENTER INC (PA)
Also Called: Thomas Rental
176 Mccormick Rd (45631-8745)
PHONE.................................740 446-2002
Jim Thomas, *President*
Lee Cyrus, *President*
Jay Hall, *Principal*
Marlene Hall, *Vice Pres*
▲ EMP: 85
SQ FT: 85,000
SALES (est): 12.4MM **Privately Held**
SIC: 5251 7359 2439 5211 Hardware; builders' hardware; equipment rental & leasing; lawn & garden equipment rental; trusses, wooden roof; lumber products

Galloway
Franklin County

(G-10177)
EL NUEVO NARANJO
6142 Glenworth Ct (43119-8559)
PHONE.................................614 863-4212
James Diaz De Leon, *Principal*
EMP: 3
SALES (est): 319.1K **Privately Held**
SIC: 3421 Table & food cutlery, including butchers'

(G-10178)
EM INNOVATIONS INC
6106 Bausch Rd (43119-9382)
P.O. Box 262 (43119-0262)
PHONE.................................614 853-1504
Connie Lewis, *President*
Jane Parr, *Corp Secy*
Joel Culp, *Vice Pres*
Spencer Fullerton, *Sales Staff*
Tom Parr, *Shareholder*
▲ EMP: 4
SALES (est): 401.6K **Privately Held**
WEB: www.eminnovations.com
SIC: 3841 Surgical & medical instruments

(G-10179)
GNI ERECTORS
8907 Stillwater Dr (43119-9082)
PHONE.................................614 465-7260
EMP: 5 EST: 1994
SALES (est): 200K **Privately Held**
SIC: 3444 Mfg Sheet Metalwork

(G-10180)
SNYDERS TOOL & DIE INC
6481 W Broad St (43119-9390)
PHONE.................................614 878-2205
William R Frey, *President*
EMP: 3
SQ FT: 3,000
SALES (est): 290K **Privately Held**
SIC: 3544 Special dies & tools

(G-10181)
ST JOHN LTD INC (PA)
Also Called: St John Chemical Dist Co
6299 George Fox Dr (43119-9075)
PHONE.................................614 851-8153
Wayne St John, *President*
Anita St John, *Corp Secy*
EMP: 4

SALES (est): 392.9K **Privately Held**
SIC: 3589 8721 5169 Water treatment equipment, industrial; accounting services, except auditing; chemicals & allied products

Gambier
Knox County

(G-10182)
KENYON REVIEW
104 College Dr Fl 2 (43022-5003)
PHONE.................................740 427-5208
David Lynn, *CEO*
Meg Galipault, *COO*
Diane Anci, *Vice Pres*
Terry Dunnavant, *Director*
Lee Schott, *Asst Director*
EMP: 6
SALES (est): 778.2K **Privately Held**
WEB: www.kenyonreview.com
SIC: 2721 Magazines: publishing & printing

(G-10183)
SMALL SAND & GRAVEL INC
10229 Killduff Rd (43022-9657)
P.O. Box 617 (43022-0617)
PHONE.................................740 427-3130
Michael W Small, *President*
William T Small, *Treasurer*
Carol Small, *Admin Sec*
EMP: 35
SALES (est): 8.6MM **Privately Held**
SIC: 1442 Sand mining; gravel mining

(G-10184)
SMALLS ASPHALT PAVING INC
10229 Killduff Rd (43022-9657)
P.O. Box 552 (43022-0552)
PHONE.................................740 427-4096
Robert E Small, *President*
Michael Small, *Vice Pres*
William T Small, *Treasurer*
Carol Small, *Admin Sec*
EMP: 25
SALES (est): 2.5MM **Privately Held**
SIC: 1771 2951 1611 Blacktop (asphalt) work; asphalt paving mixtures & blocks; highway & street construction

(G-10185)
SMALLS INC
Also Called: Small's Ready-Mixed Concrete
10229 Killduff Rd (43022-9657)
P.O. Box 503 (43022-0503)
PHONE.................................740 427-3633
Robert Small, *President*
Sharon Mills, *Admin Sec*
EMP: 10
SALES (est): 1.2MM **Privately Held**
WEB: www.smalls.com
SIC: 3273 Ready-mixed concrete

(G-10186)
YODERS CIDER BARN
Also Called: Yoder's Cider Barn
3361 Martinsburg Rd (43022-9737)
PHONE.................................740 668-4961
Sheldon Yoder, *Owner*
▲ EMP: 10
SALES (est): 1.3MM **Privately Held**
SIC: 2023 2033 Condensed, concentrated & evaporated milk products; jams, including imitation: packaged in cans, jars, etc.

Garrettsville
Portage County

(G-10187)
DISKIN ENTERPRISES LLC
Also Called: Four Seasons Manufacturing
10421 Industrial Dr (44231-9764)
PHONE.................................330 527-4308
Michael E Diskin, *President*
Micheal A Diskin, *Vice Pres*
Jean Nocera, *Controller*
Andy Baumanns, *Accountant*
EMP: 30
SALES (est): 1MM **Privately Held**
SIC: 3089 Injection molding of plastics

GEOGRAPHIC SECTION

Geneva - Ashtabula County (G-10217)

(G-10188)
EDGEWELL PER CARE BRANDS LLC
10545 Freedom St (44231-9237)
PHONE..................330 527-2191
Ronald R Taylor, *Branch Mgr*
EMP: 70
SQ FT: 50,000
SALES (corp-wide): 2.2B **Publicly Held**
WEB: www.eveready.com
SIC: 3691 Storage batteries
HQ: Edgewell Personal Care Brands, Llc
6 Research Dr
Shelton CT 06484
203 944-5500

(G-10189)
ENERGIZER BATTERY MFG INC
10545 Freedom St (44231-9237)
PHONE..................330 527-2191
Matt Smith, *Principal*
EMP: 3
SALES (est): 333.2K **Privately Held**
SIC: 3999 Manufacturing industries

(G-10190)
GRNTWRX LLC
8205 Clover Ln (44231-1060)
PHONE..................440 478-6160
Nicholas Hadzinsky,
EMP: 3
SALES (est): 136.3K **Privately Held**
SIC: 3452 Bolts, nuts, rivets & washers

(G-10191)
HARRISON MCH & PLASTIC CORP (PA)
11614 State Route 88 (44231-9105)
P.O. Box 1826, Hiram (44234-1826)
PHONE..................330 527-5641
Bryson Swanda, *President*
Bob Maynard, *Controller*
Robert Maynard, *CTO*
EMP: 25
SQ FT: 30,000
SALES (est): 5MM **Privately Held**
SIC: 3089 3444 3084 Plastic processing; sheet metalwork; plastics pipe

(G-10192)
HERMANN PICKLE COMPANY (PA)
11964 State Route 88 (44231-9115)
P.O. Box 347 (44231-0347)
PHONE..................330 527-2696
Larry Hermann, *President*
Ruth Hermann, *Treasurer*
EMP: 28
SALES (est): 9.5MM **Privately Held**
SIC: 2035 Pickles, sauces & salad dressings

(G-10193)
JC ELECTRIC
9717 State Route 88 (44231-9746)
P.O. Box 304 (44231-0304)
PHONE..................330 760-2915
Jason Carmichael, *Owner*
EMP: 22
SALES (est): 2.9MM **Privately Held**
SIC: 1731 3699 1521 Electrical work; door opening and closing devices, electrical; single-family home remodeling, additions & repairs

(G-10194)
KECAMM LLC
10404 Industrial Dr (44231-9764)
PHONE..................330 527-2918
Cheryl A Macek, *CEO*
George Macek, *President*
EMP: 7
SQ FT: 10,000
SALES (est): 744K **Privately Held**
SIC: 3479 5084 Bonderizing of metal or metal products; paint spray equipment, industrial

(G-10195)
KECOAT LLC
10610 Freedom St (44231-9763)
PHONE..................330 527-0215
Darrin Macek, *Mng Member*
EMP: 17
SQ FT: 10,000
SALES (est): 3.1MM **Privately Held**
SIC: 3441 Fabricated structural metal

(G-10196)
L & P MACHINE COMPANY
8488 State Route 305 (44231-9755)
PHONE..................330 527-2753
Terry Allen, *Owner*
EMP: 4 **EST:** 1967
SQ FT: 10,000
SALES (est): 350.6K **Privately Held**
WEB: www.lpmachine.net
SIC: 3599 Machine shop, jobbing & repair; custom machinery

(G-10197)
MACHINE TEK SYSTEMS INC
10400 Industrial Dr (44231-9764)
P.O. Box 187 (44231-0187)
PHONE..................330 527-4450
Tim Paul, *President*
EMP: 33
SQ FT: 22,000
SALES (est): 4.8MM **Privately Held**
SIC: 3544 3599 3451 Special dies & tools; machine shop, jobbing & repair; screw machine products

(G-10198)
MEGA PLASTICS CO
10610 Freedom St (44231-9763)
PHONE..................330 527-2211
Ronald Porter, *President*
Wendi Porter, *Vice Pres*
EMP: 20 **EST:** 1998
SQ FT: 25,000
SALES (est): 1.8MM **Privately Held**
SIC: 3089 Plastic processing

(G-10199)
MODERN RETAIL SOLUTIONS LLC
10421 Industrial Dr (44231-9764)
PHONE..................330 527-4308
Michael E Diskin,
▼ **EMP:** 24
SQ FT: 100,000
SALES (est): 2MM **Privately Held**
WEB: www.modernstorefixtures.com
SIC: 2542 Partitions & fixtures, except wood

(G-10200)
PHOENIX WELDING SOLUTIONS LLC
7606 Norton Rd (44231-9606)
PHONE..................330 569-7223
Scott P Sukey Jr, *Principal*
EMP: 8
SALES (est): 88.7K **Privately Held**
SIC: 7692 Welding repair

(G-10201)
PREMIER PROD SVC INDS INC
10384 Industrial Dr C (44231-9263)
PHONE..................330 527-0333
Heidi Piecuch, *President*
Brian Piecuch, *Vice Pres*
EMP: 4
SQ FT: 5,000
SALES (est): 661.4K **Privately Held**
SIC: 3599 Custom machinery; machine shop, jobbing & repair

(G-10202)
SUPERIOR QUALITY MACHINE CO
10500 Industrial Dr (44231-9250)
P.O. Box 303 (44231-0303)
PHONE..................330 527-7146
Joe Kenesky, *Owner*
▲ **EMP:** 20
SQ FT: 11,000
SALES (est): 2MM **Privately Held**
SIC: 3599 Machine shop, jobbing & repair

(G-10203)
THERM-O-LINK INC (PA)
10513 Freedom St (44231-9244)
PHONE..................330 527-2124
Ronald M Krisher, *Ch of Bd*
David Campbell, *President*
Thomas C B Letson, *Principal*
John Archer, *Info Tech Mgr*
▲ **EMP:** 100
SQ FT: 125,000
SALES (est): 41.2MM **Privately Held**
WEB: www.tolwire.com
SIC: 3357 3496 Nonferrous wiredrawing & insulating; miscellaneous fabricated wire products

(G-10204)
WEEKLY VILLAGER INC
Also Called: Weekly Villager, The
8088 Main St (44231-1214)
P.O. Box 331 (44231-0331)
PHONE..................330 527-5761
Jody Schroath, *President*
Roy Tancost, *Co-Owner*
EMP: 3
SALES (est): 273.8K **Privately Held**
SIC: 2711 2752 Newspapers: publishing only, not printed on site; commercial printing, lithographic

(G-10205)
WOOD KRAFT
8928 Ely Rd (44231-9613)
PHONE..................440 487-4634
Kenneth Bender, *Principal*
EMP: 4
SALES (est): 227.9K **Privately Held**
SIC: 2022 Mfg Cheese

(G-10206)
Z AND M SCREW MACHINE PRODUCTS
10232 Hopkins Rd (44231-9011)
PHONE..................330 467-5822
EMP: 5
SQ FT: 3,500
SALES (est): 320K **Privately Held**
SIC: 3451 Mfg Screw Machine Products

Gates Mills
Cuyahoga County

(G-10207)
ASHTECH CORPORATION
7155 Settlers Ridge Rd (44040-9631)
P.O. Box 24129, Cleveland (44124-0129)
PHONE..................440 646-9911
Gerald L Deroy, *President*
EMP: 5
SQ FT: 2,000
SALES: 5MM **Privately Held**
WEB: www.ashtechcorp.com
SIC: 3535 5084 Conveyors & conveying equipment; industrial machinery & equipment

(G-10208)
PROCHASKA INDUSTRIES LLC
7959 Gates Mills Est Dr (44040-9303)
PHONE..................440 423-0464
John Prochaska, *Owner*
EMP: 3
SALES (est): 133.2K **Privately Held**
SIC: 3999 Manufacturing industries

(G-10209)
TRANSDERMAL INC
Also Called: Lasercap
938 Chestnut Run (44040-9761)
PHONE..................440 241-1846
Robert Haber, *President*
▲ **EMP:** 10
SALES (est): 550K **Privately Held**
SIC: 3841 3699 Diagnostic apparatus, medical; laser systems & equipment

Geneva
Ashtabula County

(G-10210)
A SCHULMAN INC
Also Called: A Schulman Compression
110 N Eagle St (44041-1107)
PHONE..................440 224-7544
EMP: 3
SALES (corp-wide): 34.5B **Privately Held**
SIC: 2821 Plastics materials & resins
HQ: A. Schulman, Inc.
3637 Ridgewood Rd
Fairlawn OH 44333
330 666-3751

(G-10211)
ADRIA SCIENTIFIC GL WORKS CO
2683 State Route 534 S (44041)
P.O. Box 673 (44041-0673)
PHONE..................440 474-6691
Milan Krmpotic, *President*
Brigitte Krmpotic, *Corp Secy*
EMP: 6
SQ FT: 18,000
SALES: 500K **Privately Held**
SIC: 3231 Products of purchased glass

(G-10212)
ADVANCED TIME SYSTEMS
4591 Cork Cold Springs Rd (44041-9674)
PHONE..................440 466-2689
Charles McFarland, *Owner*
Christa McFarland, *Principal*
EMP: 3 **EST:** 1990
SALES: 300K **Privately Held**
WEB: www.advtime.com
SIC: 3579 Time clocks & time recording devices

(G-10213)
AITKEN PRODUCTS INC
566 N Eagle St (44041-1099)
P.O. Box 151 (44041-0151)
PHONE..................440 466-5711
Suzanne Aitken Shannon, *President*
Louis J Doria, *Principal*
Thomas A Grabien, *Principal*
Sue Aitken, *Executive*
EMP: 8 **EST:** 1957
SQ FT: 50,000
SALES (est): 1.5MM **Privately Held**
SIC: 3634 3433 Heating units, electric (radiant heat): baseboard or wall; gas infrared heating units

(G-10214)
ARC RUBBER INC
100 Water St (44041-1192)
PHONE..................440 466-4555
Robert Johnson, *President*
Robert Johnson III, *Vice Pres*
Josephine Johnson, *Admin Sec*
EMP: 10 **EST:** 1965
SQ FT: 20,000
SALES (est): 1.7MM **Privately Held**
WEB: www.arcrubber.com
SIC: 3069 3061 Molded rubber products; mechanical rubber goods

(G-10215)
C H R INDUSTRIES INC
185 Water St Ste 6 (44041-1199)
P.O. Box 269 (44041-0269)
PHONE..................440 361-0744
Carol Hein, *President*
Chammy Hein,
EMP: 4
SQ FT: 12,500
SALES (est): 364.8K **Privately Held**
SIC: 2399 Belting & belt products

(G-10216)
CLASSIC EXHAUST
805 Pro Gram Pkwy (44041-1172)
PHONE..................440 466-5460
Scott Thompson, *Partner*
Dwayne Hudson, *Partner*
EMP: 4
SQ FT: 6,200
SALES (est): 508.7K **Privately Held**
SIC: 3714 Exhaust systems & parts, motor vehicle

(G-10217)
DWAYNE BENNETT INDUSTRIES
Also Called: Bennett Displays
6708 N Ridge Rd W (44041-7663)
PHONE..................440 466-5724
Dwayne Bennett, *Owner*
EMP: 6
SALES (est): 555.7K **Privately Held**
SIC: 2542 3441 Racks, merchandise display or storage: except wood; fabricated structural metal

Geneva - Ashtabula County (G-10218)

(G-10218)
ELSTER PERFECTION CORPORATION (DH)
436 N Eagle St (44041-1157)
PHONE.....................440 428-1171
Barry O'Connell, *President*
Timothy Stevens, *Finance Dir*
◆ EMP: 100
SQ FT: 75,000
SALES (est): 50.6MM
SALES (corp-wide): 41.8B **Publicly Held**
WEB: www.perfectioncorp.com
SIC: **3498** 3089 3429 3312 Fabricated pipe & fittings; fittings for pipe, plastic; manufactured hardware (general); blast furnaces & steel mills; plastics pipe; laminated plastics plate & sheet
HQ: Elster American Meter Company, Llc
208 S Rogers Ln
Raleigh NC 27610
800 338-4800

(G-10219)
FERRANTE WINE FARM INC
558 Rte 307 (44041)
PHONE.....................440 466-8466
Nicholas Ferrante, *President*
Nicholas Farrante, *President*
Pete Ferrante, *Managing Dir*
Mary Jo Ferrante, *Principal*
Peter Ferrante, *Principal*
EMP: 40
SQ FT: 3,023
SALES (est): 2.4MM **Privately Held**
WEB: www.ferrantewinery.com
SIC: **0172** 2084 5812 Grapes; wines; eating places

(G-10220)
H & H ENGINEERED MOLDED PDTS
436 N Eagle St (44041-1157)
PHONE.....................440 415-1814
Barry O Connell, *President*
Roy Sutterfield, *President*
Tim Stevens, *Treasurer*
EMP: 55
SQ FT: 26,000
SALES (est): 5.6MM
SALES (corp-wide): 41.8B **Publicly Held**
WEB: www.perfectioncorp.com
SIC: **3089** Injection molding of plastics
HQ: Elster Perfection Corporation
436 N Eagle St
Geneva OH 44041
440 428-1171

(G-10221)
HADLOCK PLASTICS LLC
110 N Eagle St (44041-1196)
PHONE.....................440 466-4876
Terry Morgan, *President*
Mark Sjostrom, *Opers Dir*
Tim Clark, *QA Dir*
Donna J Hadlock, *Human Res Mgr*
Mary Jewell, *Sales Staff*
▲ EMP: 107
SQ FT: 110,000
SALES (est): 28.8MM
SALES (corp-wide): 34.5B **Privately Held**
WEB: www.hadlockplastics.com
SIC: **3089** Injection molded finished plastic products
HQ: Hpc Holdings, Llc
3637 Ridgewood Rd
Fairlawn OH 44333

(G-10222)
HDT EXPEDITIONARY SYSTEMS INC
5455 Route 307 W (44041)
PHONE.....................440 466-6640
James Maurer, *President*
EMP: 21 **Privately Held**
SIC: **3585** 3564 3433 Air conditioning units, complete: domestic or industrial; filters, air: furnaces, air conditioning equipment, etc.; heating equipment, except electric
HQ: Hdt Expeditionary Systems, Inc.
30500 Aurora Rd Ste 100
Solon OH 44139
216 438-6111

(G-10223)
HUNDLEY CELLARS LLC
6451 N River Rd W (44041-9312)
PHONE.....................843 368-5016
Larry Hundley,
EMP: 5
SALES (est): 315K **Privately Held**
SIC: **2084** 7389 Wines;

(G-10224)
LOUIS ARTHUR STEEL COMPANY (PA)
185 Water St (44041-1199)
P.O. Box 229 (44041-0229)
PHONE.....................440 997-5545
J Trombley Kanicki, *President*
J Matthew Kanicki, *Vice Pres*
Sandra Kanicki, *Vice Pres*
J Barton Kanicki, *Shareholder*
James H Kanicki, *Shareholder*
EMP: 8 EST: 1949
SQ FT: 80,000
SALES (est): 13MM **Privately Held**
SIC: **3441** 5051 3444 3443 Building components, structural steel; steel; sheet metalwork; fabricated plate work (boiler shop)

(G-10225)
LOUIS ARTHUR STEEL COMPANY
Also Called: Arthur Louis Steel Co
200 North Ave E (44041-1166)
PHONE.....................440 997-5545
Andy Housel, *General Mgr*
EMP: 50
SALES (corp-wide): 13MM **Privately Held**
SIC: **3441** Fabricated structural metal
PA: The Louis Arthur Steel Company
185 Water St
Geneva OH 44041
440 997-5545

(G-10226)
NORTH COAST VOICE MAG
143 S Cedar St (44041-1657)
P.O. Box 118 (44041-0118)
PHONE.....................440 415-0999
L Carol Stouder, *Principal*
EMP: 3
SALES (est): 142.4K **Privately Held**
SIC: **2711** Newspapers

(G-10227)
OLD MILL WINERY INC
403 S Broadway (44041-1844)
PHONE.....................440 466-5560
Al Snyder, *Partner*
Joanne Snyder, *Partner*
EMP: 12
SALES (est): 1.3MM **Privately Held**
SIC: **2084** Wines

(G-10228)
PHILLIPS & SONS WELDING & FABG
6720 N Ridge Rd W (44041)
PHONE.....................440 428-1625
Steven Phillips, *Owner*
EMP: 3
SQ FT: 20,000
SALES: 350K **Privately Held**
SIC: **7692** 3441 Welding repair; fabricated structural metal

(G-10229)
TEGAM INC (PA)
10 Tegam Way (44041-1144)
PHONE.....................440 466-6100
Andrew Brush, *CEO*
Adam Fleder, *President*
EMP: 43
SQ FT: 28,600
SALES (est): 9.1MM **Privately Held**
WEB: www.tegam.com
SIC: **3829** 7629 Measuring & controlling devices; electrical measuring instrument repair & calibration

(G-10230)
VIRANT FAMILY WINERY INC
541 Atkins Rd (44041-8352)
PHONE.....................440 466-6279
Charles Virant, *CEO*
Frank Virant, *President*
Martha Virant, *Treasurer*
Holly Virant, *Admin Sec*
EMP: 4 EST: 1998
SQ FT: 1,338
SALES (est): 146.4K **Privately Held**
WEB: www.starbeacon.com
SIC: **2084** Wines

(G-10231)
WINERY AT SPRING HILL INC
6062 S Ridge Rd W (44041-8375)
P.O. Box 47 (44041-0047)
PHONE.....................440 466-0626
Richard Trice, *Principal*
Jeffrey Piotrowski, *CFO*
EMP: 15
SALES (est): 1.6MM **Privately Held**
SIC: **2084** Wines

Genoa
Ottawa County

(G-10232)
GRAYMONT DOLIME (OH) INC
21880 W State Route 163 (43430-1679)
P.O. Box 158 (43430-0158)
PHONE.....................419 855-8682
Stephane Godin, *Principal*
J Graham Weir, *Chairman*
Mathieu Bouchard, *Vice Pres*
Mike Brown, *Vice Pres*
Kenneth J Lahti, *Vice Pres*
▼ EMP: 54
SALES (est): 10.8MM
SALES (corp-wide): 171.4MM **Privately Held**
SIC: **3274** Lime
PA: Graymont Inc
301 S 700 E 3950
Salt Lake City UT 84102
801 262-3942

(G-10233)
JBI CORPORATION
22325 State Route 51 W (43430-1123)
PHONE.....................419 855-3389
John Badger, *Ch of Bd*
Joseph Badger, *President*
Florence Badger, *Corp Secy*
Kathryn Miller, *Admin Sec*
EMP: 10
SQ FT: 7,500
SALES (est): 1.7MM **Privately Held**
WEB: www.jbicorp.com
SIC: **8711** 3544 8734 Civil engineering; consulting engineer; jigs & fixtures; testing laboratories

(G-10234)
M E P MANUFACTURING INC (PA)
214 E 4th St (43430-1651)
PHONE.....................419 855-7723
Michael J Pascaru, *President*
Diane Pascaru, *Vice Pres*
Patrick Brown, *Shareholder*
EMP: 7
SQ FT: 12,000
SALES (est): 1.1MM **Privately Held**
SIC: **3498** 3499 5051 Piping systems for pulp paper & chemical industries; nozzles, spray: aerosol, paint or insecticide; pipe & tubing, steel

(G-10235)
RCR PARTNERSHIP
Also Called: Paul Blausey Farms
424 N Martin Williston Rd (43430-9786)
PHONE.....................419 340-1202
Chad Gargas,
EMP: 6 EST: 2013
SALES (est): 834.5K **Privately Held**
SIC: **3443** Farm storage tanks, metal plate

(G-10236)
RIVERSIDE MCH & AUTOMTN INC (PA)
1240 N Genoa Clay Ctr Rd (43430-1206)
PHONE.....................419 855-8308
Gerald Giesler, *CEO*
Jerry Giesler, *President*
Lester Meyer, *Partner*
John Bennion, *Plant Mgr*
Glenn Burger, *Plant Mgr*
EMP: 60
SQ FT: 30,000
SALES (est): 9.7MM **Privately Held**
WEB: www.riverside-machine.com
SIC: **3599** 3549 Machine shop, jobbing & repair; machine & other job shop work; metalworking machinery

Georgetown
Brown County

(G-10237)
BROWN CNTY BD MNTAL RTARDATION
325 W State St Ste A2 (45121-1262)
PHONE.....................937 378-4891
Theresa Armstrong, *Principal*
Lena Bradford, *Principal*
EMP: 35
SQ FT: 100,000
SALES: 131.9K **Privately Held**
SIC: **8331** 3993 2396 Sheltered workshop; signs & advertising specialties; automotive & apparel trimmings

(G-10238)
THOMAS ENTPS OF GEORGETOWN
Also Called: Thomas Welding & Repair
933 S Main St (45121-8409)
PHONE.....................937 378-6300
Keith D Thomas, *President*
EMP: 3 EST: 1990
SQ FT: 1,820
SALES: 450K **Privately Held**
SIC: **7692** 3599 Welding repair; machine shop, jobbing & repair

(G-10239)
WATSON MEEKS AND COMPANY
10402 W Fork Rd (45121-8260)
P.O. Box 21700 (45121-0700)
PHONE.....................937 378-2355
William C Meeks, *Partner*
Richard M Watson, *Partner*
EMP: 4
SQ FT: 2,800
SALES (est): 558.4K **Privately Held**
SIC: **3931** 8711 Keyboard instruments & parts; carillon bells; consulting engineer

Germantown
Montgomery County

(G-10240)
ABSOLUTE CNC MACHINING LLC
2643 Dyton Grmantown Pike (45327-9625)
P.O. Box 47 (45327-0047)
PHONE.....................937 855-0406
Thomas Hodge,
EMP: 3
SQ FT: 1,500
SALES (est): 376.3K **Privately Held**
SIC: **3599** Machine shop, jobbing & repair

(G-10241)
ELI LILLY AND COMPANY
Also Called: Elanco Animal Health
7440 Weaver Rd (45327-9390)
PHONE.....................937 855-3300
Tom Epperson, *President*
EMP: 3
SALES (corp-wide): 24.5B **Publicly Held**
WEB: www.lilly.com
SIC: **2834** Pharmaceutical preparations
PA: Eli Lilly And Company
Lilly Corporate Ctr
Indianapolis IN 46285
317 276-2000

(G-10242)
HOSLER MAPS INC
115 N Plum St (45327-1359)
PHONE.....................937 855-4173
Gene Hosler, *President*
Susie Hosler, *President*
EMP: 3

▲ = Import ▼ = Export
◆ = Import/Export

GEOGRAPHIC SECTION

Girard - Trumbull County (G-10268)

SQ FT: 9,000
SALES: 385K **Privately Held**
SIC: 3613 Panel & distribution boards & other related apparatus

(G-10243)
L & H PRINTING
Also Called: L & H Printing Co
34 W Market St (45327-1354)
PHONE 937 855-4512
Nancy Havens, *Mng Member*
EMP: 4
SALES (est): 164.1K **Privately Held**
SIC: 8351 2752 Child day care services; commercial printing, lithographic

(G-10244)
OHIO ENGINEERING AND MFG SLS
Also Called: O E M Sales
11610 State Route 725 (45327-9760)
PHONE 937 855-6971
Harold Melampy, *President*
Harold E Melampy, *President*
Pamela S Melampy, *Treasurer*
EMP: 5
SQ FT: 4,400
SALES: 200K **Privately Held**
SIC: 5051 3599 Stampings, metal; grinding castings for the trade

(G-10245)
POINT SOURCE INC
7996 Butter St (45327)
PHONE 937 855-6020
Fax: 937 855-6020
EMP: 12
SQ FT: 3,000
SALES: 1.2MM **Privately Held**
SIC: 8731 3827 Commercial Physical Research Mfg Optical Instruments/Lenses

(G-10246)
THOMAS D EPPERSON
Also Called: Epco
7440 Weaver Rd (45327-9390)
P.O. Box 19 (45327-0019)
PHONE 937 855-3300
Thomas D Epperson, *Owner*
EMP: 7
SQ FT: 2,104
SALES (est): 649.4K **Privately Held**
SIC: 3751 Motorcycle accessories; motorcycles & related parts

Gettysburg
Darke County

(G-10247)
NORCOLD INC
1 Century Dr (45328-6002)
PHONE 937 447-2241
Jim Shaw, *Manager*
EMP: 200
SALES (corp-wide): 471.1MM **Privately Held**
SIC: 3822 3632 Refrigeration controls (pressure); household refrigerators & freezers
HQ: Norcold Inc.
600 S Kuther Rd
Sidney OH 45365

Gibsonburg
Sandusky County

(G-10248)
HENDERSON BUILDERS INC
1610 County Road 90 (43431-9717)
PHONE 419 665-2684
David R Henderson Jr, *President*
Kim Henderson, *Admin Sec*
EMP: 5
SALES (est): 583.6K **Privately Held**
SIC: 1521 2791 General remodeling, single-family houses; typesetting, computer controlled

(G-10249)
K DAVIS INC
526 N Webster St (43431-1044)
P.O. Box 162 (43431-0162)
PHONE 419 637-2859
Londa Davis, *President*
Kevin Davis, *Treasurer*
EMP: 6
SALES (est): 68.4K **Privately Held**
SIC: 3822 3596 Appliance controls except air-conditioning & refrigeration; scales & balances, except laboratory

Gilboa
Putnam County

(G-10250)
HILLSIDE WINERY
221 Main St (45875-9757)
PHONE 419 456-3108
Lou Schaublin, *Principal*
EMP: 7
SALES (est): 690.7K **Privately Held**
SIC: 2084 Wines

Girard
Trumbull County

(G-10251)
A J CONSTRUCTION CO
870 Shannon Rd (44420-2046)
PHONE 330 539-9544
Anthony Guerrieri, *President*
EMP: 6
SALES (est): 661.2K **Privately Held**
SIC: 2541 Cabinets, except refrigerated: show, display, etc.: wood; cabinets, lockers & shelving; counter & sink tops; counters or counter display cases, wood

(G-10252)
ALTRONIC LLC (DH)
712 Trumbull Ave (44420-3443)
PHONE 330 545-9768
Bruce R Beeghly, *President*
Joseph Lepley, *Vice Pres*
Kevin Gibson, *Representative*
▲ **EMP:** 150 **EST:** 1955
SQ FT: 80,000
SALES (est): 46.2MM **Privately Held**
WEB: www.altroniccontrols.com
SIC: 3694 3823 3613 3625 Ignition systems, high frequency; temperature instruments: industrial process type; control panels, electric; relays & industrial controls
HQ: Hoerbiger Holding Ag
Baarerstrasse 18
Zug ZG 6302
415 601-000

(G-10253)
AMEX DIES INC
932 N State St (44420-1796)
PHONE 330 545-9766
Ted Dudzik, *President*
Sam Bates, *General Mgr*
EMP: 17 **EST:** 1961
SQ FT: 6,000
SALES: 1.6MM **Privately Held**
SIC: 3544 Extrusion dies

(G-10254)
BRAINARD RIVET COMPANY
Also Called: BUCKEYE FASTENERS COMPANY
222 Harry St (44420-1759)
P.O. Box 30 (44420-0030)
PHONE 330 545-4931
Patrick Finnegan, *President*
Linda Kerekes, *Corp Secy*
William Chick, *QC Mgr*
Jan Hughes, *Finance*
Paul Kovach, *Sales Mgr*
EMP: 34
SQ FT: 61,000
SALES: 6.3MM
SALES (corp-wide): 42.3MM **Privately Held**
WEB: www.brainardrivet.com
SIC: 3452 Bolts, nuts, rivets & washers

PA: Fastener Industries, Inc.
1 Berea Cmns Ste 209
Berea OH 44017
440 243-0034

(G-10255)
CHECKERED EXPRESS INC
2501 W Liberty St (44420-3112)
PHONE 330 530-8169
Csaba Bujdoso, *President*
EMP: 15
SALES (est): 1.6MM **Privately Held**
SIC: 2741 Miscellaneous publishing

(G-10256)
DAFFINS CANDIES (PA)
Also Called: Daffin Candies
700 N State St (44420-1700)
PHONE 330 545-0325
Joseph Costello, *President*
Dorothy Costello, *Vice Pres*
EMP: 9
SQ FT: 4,000
SALES (est): 789.2K **Privately Held**
SIC: 2064 5947 Chocolate candy, except solid chocolate; gift shop

(G-10257)
FIRE FAB CORPORATION
999 Trumbull Ave (44420-3448)
PHONE 330 759-9834
Ernie Nicholas, *President*
Mary Nicholas, *Corp Secy*
Jamie Wilcox, *Accountant*
EMP: 6
SQ FT: 18,000
SALES: 1.1MM **Privately Held**
SIC: 3569 Sprinkler systems, fire: automatic

(G-10258)
FIRE FOE CORP
999 Trumbull Ave (44420-3400)
PHONE 330 759-9834
Earnest A Nicholas, *President*
Thomas Spain, *Safety Dir*
Mary Nicholas, *Admin Sec*
EMP: 35
SQ FT: 18,000
SALES: 4.5MM **Privately Held**
WEB: www.firefoe.com
SIC: 3569 7699 Sprinkler systems, fire: automatic; fire control (military) equipment repair

(G-10259)
FIVE STAR GRAPHICS INC
201 W Liberty St (44420-2846)
PHONE 330 545-5077
John Penza, *CEO*
Samuel Penza, *Vice Pres*
Robert Penza, *Treasurer*
James Penza, *Admin Sec*
EMP: 5
SQ FT: 14,400
SALES (est): 487.5K **Privately Held**
WEB: www.fivestargraphics.net
SIC: 2759 Screen printing

(G-10260)
GAS ANALYTICAL SERVICES INC
1688 Shannon Rd (44420-1121)
PHONE 330 539-4267
Bernie Vogel, *Manager*
EMP: 4
SALES (corp-wide): 22.8MM **Privately Held**
SIC: 1389 Gas field services
HQ: Gas Analytical Services, Inc.
8444 Water St
Stonewood WV 26301
304 623-0020

(G-10261)
GIRARD MACHINE COMPANY INC
700 Dot St (44420-1701)
P.O. Box 298 (44420-0298)
PHONE 330 545-9731
Carl Malito, *President*
Donald Malito, *Vice Pres*
Robert Malito, *Admin Sec*
EMP: 50 **EST:** 1948
SQ FT: 60,000

SALES: 13.7MM **Privately Held**
SIC: 3559 3599 Foundry, smelting, refining & similar machinery; machine shop, jobbing & repair

(G-10262)
MARSH TECHNOLOGIES INC
30 W Main St Ste A (44420-2520)
PHONE 330 545-0085
Sandra G Marsh, *President*
EMP: 12
SQ FT: 10,000
SALES (est): 1.2MM **Privately Held**
WEB: www.marshtechnologies.com
SIC: 3544 Special dies, tools, jigs & fixtures

(G-10263)
NEW DAWN DESIGNS
1282 Trumbull Ave Ste E (44420-3475)
PHONE 330 759-3500
Linda Barton, *President*
Scott Barton, *Vice Pres*
EMP: 2
SQ FT: 8,000
SALES: 1MM **Privately Held**
SIC: 2759 Letterpress & screen printing

(G-10264)
PETTIT W T & SONS CO INC
1670 Keefer Rd (44420-1434)
PHONE 330 539-6100
Francis Poe, *President*
Daniel De Genova, *Vice Pres*
EMP: 8
SQ FT: 57,000
SALES (est): 1.4MM **Privately Held**
WEB: www.wtpettit.com
SIC: 3469 7389 Metal stampings; metal slitting & shearing

(G-10265)
ROCKYS HINGE CO
1660 Harding Ave (44420-1514)
PHONE 330 539-6296
Rocky Shamlin, *Owner*
EMP: 6
SQ FT: 3,072
SALES (est): 481.7K **Privately Held**
WEB: www.rockyhin.ipower.com
SIC: 5251 3944 Hardware; child restraint seats, automotive

(G-10266)
SOFT TOUCH WOOD LLC
Also Called: Soft Tuch Furn Repr Rfinishing
1560 S State St (44420-3315)
PHONE 330 545-4204
Terry Chudakoff, *President*
Megan Vickers, *Vice Pres*
Tony Peluso, *Engineer*
Bob Leer, *Manager*
EMP: 40
SQ FT: 5,000
SALES (est): 2MM **Privately Held**
WEB: www.softtouchwood.com
SIC: 7641 2531 Furniture refinishing; public building & related furniture

(G-10267)
STANCORP INC
712 Trumbull Ave (44420-3443)
PHONE 330 545-6615
Fax: 330 545-6726
EMP: 4
SQ FT: 1,200
SALES (est): 576.9K **Privately Held**
SIC: 6411 3823 Insurance Agent/Broker Mfg Process Control Instruments

(G-10268)
VALLOUREC STAR LP
706 S State St (44420-3204)
PHONE 330 742-6227
EMP: 16
SALES (corp-wide): 2.6MM **Privately Held**
SIC: 3317 Steel pipe & tubes
HQ: Vallourec Star, Lp
2669 M L K J Blvd
Youngstown OH 44510
330 742-6300

Glandorf
Putnam County

(G-10269)
FIELD GYMMY INC
138-143 S Main St (45848)
P.O. Box 121, Ottawa (45875-0121)
PHONE.................................419 538-6511
Dennis Nienberg, *President*
Thomas Russell, *Corp Secy*
Melvin Nienberg, *Vice Pres*
EMP: 8
SQ FT: 15,300
SALES (est): 1.1MM **Privately Held**
WEB: www.fieldgymmy.com
SIC: 3523 3713 3563 3531 Farm machinery & equipment; truck & bus bodies; air & gas compressors; construction machinery

Glenford
Perry County

(G-10270)
JAMES RYAN SOLOMAN
Also Called: Buildcret Concrete
5471 High Point Rd (43739-9727)
PHONE.................................740 659-2304
Ryan Solomon, *Owner*
EMP: 3
SALES (est): 156.7K **Privately Held**
SIC: 1442 Construction sand & gravel

(G-10271)
PIONEER SANDS LLC
Also Called: Glassrock Plant
2446 State Route 204 (43739)
PHONE.................................740 659-2241
Wayn Dailey, *Manager*
EMP: 40
SALES (corp-wide): 9.4B **Publicly Held**
SIC: 3295 1446 Minerals, ground or treated; industrial sand
HQ: Pioneer Sands Llc
5205 N O Connor Blvd # 200
Irving TX 75039
972 444-9001

(G-10272)
PLASTIC REGRINDERS INC
3161 Cooperriders Rd Nw (43739-9648)
PHONE.................................740 659-2346
George West, *President*
Sharon West, *Corp Secy*
EMP: 4
SALES: 330K **Privately Held**
SIC: 2821 Plastics materials & resins

(G-10273)
VAN BURENS WELDING & MACHINE
11496 Cherry Hill Rd (43739-9620)
P.O. Box 85 (43739-0085)
PHONE.................................740 787-2636
Daniel V Buren, *Owner*
Daniel Van Buren, *Owner*
Jonathan Van Buren, *Co-Owner*
EMP: 4
SALES (est): 185.6K **Privately Held**
SIC: 7692 3542 Welding repair; machine tools, metal forming type

Glenmont
Holmes County

(G-10274)
BRIAR HILL STONE COMPANY
12470 State Route 520 (44628-9702)
P.O. Box 457 (44628-0457)
PHONE.................................330 377-5100
Frank Waller, *President*
Lowell M Shope, *General Mgr*
Connie D Scott, *Vice Pres*
EMP: 30
SQ FT: 4,000
SALES (est): 4.2MM **Privately Held**
WEB: www.briarhillstone.com
SIC: 3281 Stone, quarrying & processing of own stone products

Glouster
Athens County

(G-10275)
C & B LOGGING INC
9821 State Route 13 Se (45732-9623)
PHONE.................................740 347-4844
George J Post, *President*
Cameron Post, *Vice Pres*
EMP: 5
SALES (est): 507.1K **Privately Held**
SIC: 2411 0139 Logging camps & contractors; hay farm

(G-10276)
FROG RANCH FOODS LTD
5 S High St (45732-1051)
PHONE.................................740 767-3705
Craig Cornett, *President*
Kristi Hewitt, *CFO*
EMP: 10
SQ FT: 10,000
SALES: 1MM **Privately Held**
WEB: www.frogranch.com
SIC: 2099 Food preparations

Gnadenhutten
Tuscarawas County

(G-10277)
DAVID COX
Also Called: Dave's Welding & Excavation
9664 Gilmore Rd Se (44629-9637)
PHONE.................................740 254-4858
David Cox, *Owner*
Patricia Cox, *Co-Owner*
EMP: 3 **EST:** 1968
SALES: 200K **Privately Held**
SIC: 1794 7692 3444 Excavation work; welding repair; sheet metalwork

(G-10278)
ECHO DRILLING INC
Also Called: Crude Oil Buyer
367 Echo Rd Se (44629-9654)
PHONE.................................740 254-4127
Kenneth Ebersbach, *Branch Mgr*
EMP: 5
SALES (est): 395.6K
SALES (corp-wide): 1.3MM **Privately Held**
SIC: 1381 Drilling oil & gas wells
PA: Echo Drilling Inc
11 Crestview Mnr
Newcomerstown OH 43832
740 498-8560

(G-10279)
FIVECOAT LUMBER INC
2400 Larson Rd Se (44629-9500)
P.O. Box 871 (44629-0871)
PHONE.................................740 254-4681
John Fivecoat, *President*
Carl Fivecoat, *Vice Pres*
Karen Fivecoart, *Admin Sec*
EMP: 15
SALES (est): 781K **Privately Held**
SIC: 2421 5211 Lumber: rough, sawed or planed; planing mill products & lumber

(G-10280)
MILLWOOD LUMBER INC
Also Called: Millwood Logging
2400 Larson Rd Se (44629-9500)
P.O. Box 871 (44629-0871)
PHONE.................................740 254-4681
Jeffery Miller, *President*
Ervin Weaver, *Sales Staff*
EMP: 22
SALES (est): 3MM **Privately Held**
WEB: www.millwoodlumber.com
SIC: 2421 Sawmills & planing mills, general

(G-10281)
PEMJAY INC
318 E Tuscarawas Ave (44629)
P.O. Box 669 (44629-0669)
PHONE.................................740 254-4591
Yolanda Jagunic, *Ch of Bd*
David Jagunic, *President*
Mark Dummermuth, *Vice Pres*
EMP: 23
SQ FT: 8,000
SALES (est): 4.7MM **Privately Held**
WEB: www.pemjay.com
SIC: 3441 Fabricated structural metal

(G-10282)
PLYMOUTH FOAM LLC
1 Souther Gateway St (44629)
P.O. Box 177 (44629-0177)
PHONE.................................740 254-1188
Chris Coleman, *Manager*
EMP: 45
SALES (corp-wide): 31.8MM **Privately Held**
SIC: 3086 Insulation or cushioning material, foamed plastic
PA: Plymouth Foam Llc
1800 Sunset Dr
Plymouth WI 53073
800 669-1176

(G-10283)
STOCKER CONCRETE COMPANY
7574 Us Hwy 36 Se (44629)
P.O. Box 176 (44629-0176)
PHONE.................................740 254-4626
Thomas Stocker, *President*
Jeffrey Stocker, *Corp Secy*
Bryan Stocker, *Vice Pres*
William Stocker, *Shareholder*
EMP: 12
SQ FT: 15,000
SALES (est): 880K
SALES (corp-wide): 2.2MM **Privately Held**
SIC: 3273 5032 5211 3271 Ready-mixed concrete; concrete building products; masonry materials & supplies; concrete & cinder block; concrete block & brick; construction sand & gravel
PA: Stocker Sand & Gravel Co
Rr 36
Gnadenhutten OH 44629
740 254-4635

(G-10284)
STOCKER SAND & GRAVEL CO (PA)
Rr 36 (44629)
PHONE.................................740 254-4635
Bill Stocker, *President*
Jeffrey Stocker, *President*
Thomas Stocker, *Corp Secy*
Bryan Stocker, *Vice Pres*
Shane Casimir, *Manager*
EMP: 30 **EST:** 1933
SQ FT: 3,000
SALES (est): 2.2MM **Privately Held**
SIC: 1442 3271 Common sand mining; gravel mining; blocks, concrete or cinder: standard

Goshen
Clermont County

(G-10285)
BAPTIST HERITAGE REVIVAL SOC
10632 Eltzroth Rd (45122-9641)
P.O. Box 311 (45122-0311)
PHONE.................................915 526-2832
Theodore Alexander, *Director*
EMP: 4
SALES: 30K **Privately Held**
SIC: 8412 7372 Historical society; application computer software

(G-10286)
DANDY PRODUCTS INC
3314 State Route 131 (45122-8511)
PHONE.................................513 625-3000
Daniel R Reed, *President*
Colleen Reed, *Vice Pres*
EMP: 10
SQ FT: 15,000
SALES (est): 1.8MM **Privately Held**
SIC: 3069 Floor coverings, rubber; mats or matting, rubber; wallcoverings, rubber

(G-10287)
G S LINK & ASSOCIATES
1881 Main St (45122-9763)
PHONE.................................513 722-2457
S T Link, *Partner*
Goethe S Link, *Principal*
EMP: 5
SQ FT: 5,000
SALES (est): 290K **Privately Held**
SIC: 2752 Commercial printing, lithographic

(G-10288)
HONEY SWEETIE ACRES LLC
2710 Spring Hill Rd (45122-9497)
PHONE.................................513 456-6090
Regina Bauscher, *Mng Member*
Steven Bauscher, *Mng Member*
EMP: 3
SALES: 150K **Privately Held**
SIC: 0214 2844 Goat farm; toilet preparations

(G-10289)
LAB QUALITY MACHINING INC
6311 Roudebush Rd (45122-9571)
PHONE.................................513 625-0219
James Brath, *President*
Linda A Brath, *Principal*
EMP: 6
SQ FT: 5,200
SALES: 400K **Privately Held**
WEB: www.labqualitymachining.com
SIC: 3544 Special dies & tools

(G-10290)
TRIUMPHANT ENTERPRISES INC
7096 Hill Station Rd (45122-9728)
PHONE.................................513 617-1668
Richard G Hughes Sr, *President*
Jewell A Hughes, *Vice Pres*
EMP: 25
SALES (est): 4.9MM **Privately Held**
SIC: 3537 Trucks: freight, baggage, etc.: industrial, except mining

Grafton
Lorain County

(G-10291)
ADVANCE WEIGHT SYSTEM INC
409 Main St (44044-1205)
P.O. Box 6 (44044-0006)
PHONE.................................440 926-3691
Clarence G Lahl Jr, *President*
Roland Seaburn, *Vice Pres*
Martha Lahl, *Treasurer*
Martha Noel, *Manager*
EMP: 10
SQ FT: 3,000
SALES: 400K **Privately Held**
WEB: www.advancew8.com
SIC: 3596 Weighing machines & apparatus

(G-10292)
ARTISAN MOLD CO INC
1021 Commerce Dr 219 (44044-1279)
P.O. Box 219 (44044-0219)
PHONE.................................440 926-4511
Jerry Winson, *President*
John T Winson, *Vice Pres*
Gail Philion, *Admin Sec*
EMP: 4
SALES (est): 620K **Privately Held**
SIC: 3089 Injection molding of plastics

(G-10293)
BANKS MANUFACTURING COMPANY
40259 Banks Rd (44044-9750)
PHONE.................................440 458-8661
Tim Boyd, *President*
Sheila Boyd, *Vice Pres*
EMP: 10 **EST:** 1948
SQ FT: 10,000

Grand Rapids - Wood County (G-10321)

SALES: 954.2K **Privately Held**
WEB: www.banksmfg.com
SIC: 1799 1721 3441 Sandblasting of building exteriors; industrial painting; fabricated structural metal

(G-10294)
COMMTECH SOLUTIONS INC
38900 Arbor Ct (44044-1056)
PHONE 440 458-4870
Alan Gauvreau, *President*
EMP: 1
SALES: 1.8MM **Privately Held**
SIC: 3661 Communication headgear, telephone

(G-10295)
CREATIVE WOODWORKS
16940 Indian Hollow Rd (44044-9232)
PHONE 440 355-8155
Larry Babb, *Owner*
EMP: 4
SQ FT: 1,500
SALES: 67.3K **Privately Held**
SIC: 2521 Wood office furniture

(G-10296)
CUSTOMCHROME PLATING INC
Also Called: Custom Chrome Plating
963 Mechanic St (44044-1416)
PHONE 440 926-3116
Jon E Wright, *President*
EMP: 15
SQ FT: 12,500
SALES: 1MM **Privately Held**
SIC: 3471 Chromium plating of metals or formed products; plating of metals or formed products

(G-10297)
DAY INDUSTRIES INC
690 Island Rd (44044)
PHONE 216 577-6674
Philip Kauffman, *CEO*
Camilla Kaufmann, *Corp Secy*
Robert Kaufmann, *Vice Pres*
EMP: 3
SALES (est): 5MM **Privately Held**
SIC: 5131 5033 3599 Labels; fiberglass building materials; machine shop, jobbing & repair

(G-10298)
DOVE MANUFACTURING LLC
12900 Reed Rd (44044-9577)
PHONE 440 506-7935
David Dove, *Mng Member*
EMP: 3
SALES (est): 125.5K **Privately Held**
SIC: 3714 Screw machine products

(G-10299)
EATON CORPORATION
Also Called: Eaton Township
12043 Avon Belden Rd (44044-9417)
PHONE 440 748-2236
Linda Spitzer, *Principal*
EMP: 3 **Privately Held**
WEB: www.eaton.com
SIC: 3625 Motor controls & accessories
HQ: Eaton Corporation
1000 Eaton Blvd
Cleveland OH 44122
440 523-5000

(G-10300)
EATON FABRICATING COMPANY INC
1009 Mcalpin Ct (44044-1322)
PHONE 440 926-3121
Ray D Roach Jr, *President*
Lloyd H Roach Sr, *Principal*
Jack Schulman, *Principal*
Lloyd Roach, *Prdtn Mgr*
Todd Leissa, *Engineer*
▲ **EMP:** 50
SQ FT: 40,600
SALES (est): 10.7MM **Privately Held**
WEB: www.eatonfabricating.com
SIC: 3599 3444 3443 Machine shop, jobbing & repair; sheet metalwork; fabricated plate work (boiler shop)

(G-10301)
GENERAL PLUG AND MFG CO (PA)
455 Main St (44044-1257)
P.O. Box 26 (44044-0026)
PHONE 440 926-2411
Kevin J Flanigan, *President*
Jim Tyree, *General Mgr*
Ron Richmond, *Vice Pres*
Ryan Flanigan, *Purch Mgr*
John Bis, *Engineer*
▲ **EMP:** 125 **EST:** 1955
SQ FT: 70,000
SALES (est): 33.6MM **Privately Held**
WEB: www.generalplug.com
SIC: 3494 3599 3643 Pipe fittings; machine shop, jobbing & repair; current-carrying wiring devices

(G-10302)
GRAFTON READY MIX CONCRETE INC
1155 Elm St (44044-1303)
P.O. Box 37 (44044-0037)
PHONE 440 926-2911
Jeffrey Riddell, *President*
EMP: 22
SQ FT: 15,000
SALES: 1.4MM
SALES (corp-wide): 14.4MM **Privately Held**
WEB: www.graftonreadymix.com
SIC: 3273 5032 5211 Ready-mixed concrete; brick, stone & related material; concrete mixtures; masonry materials & supplies
PA: Consumeracq, Inc.
2509 N Ridge Rd E
Lorain OH 44055
440 277-9305

(G-10303)
GREAT WORKS PUBLISHING INC
Also Called: Donze Enterprises
1080 Cleveland St (44044-1319)
PHONE 440 926-1100
Christoher Donze, *President*
EMP: 15
SALES (est): 689.2K **Privately Held**
SIC: 2741 Music, sheet: publishing & printing

(G-10304)
JESCO PRODUCTS INC
11811 Robson Rd (44044-9157)
PHONE 440 233-5828
Eva Squires, *President*
Mary Jane Taylor, *Corp Secy*
EMP: 3
SQ FT: 800
SALES (est): 428.1K **Privately Held**
WEB: www.jescoproducts.com
SIC: 3599 Machine shop, jobbing & repair

(G-10305)
JOE GONDA COMPANY INC
Also Called: Gonda Wood Products
50000 Gondawood Dr (44044-9194)
P.O. Box 282 (44044-0282)
PHONE 440 458-6000
Michael Gonda, *President*
Patricia Marie Gonda, *Corp Secy*
EMP: 11
SQ FT: 7,500
SALES (est): 1.6MM **Privately Held**
SIC: 2448 2449 Pallets, wood; skids, wood; wood containers

(G-10306)
KEY MARKETING GROUP
11185 Arrowhead Dr (44044-9774)
PHONE 440 748-3479
David Pataky, *Owner*
Judy Pataky, *Co-Owner*
EMP: 4
SALES (est): 269.5K **Privately Held**
SIC: 7336 2759 Graphic arts & related design; commercial printing

(G-10307)
LUDWIG MUSIC PUBLISHING CO
1080 Cleveland St (44044-1319)
PHONE 440 926-1100
Christopher Donze, *President*
EMP: 12
SQ FT: 7,000
SALES (est): 830.5K **Privately Held**
WEB: www.ludwigmusic.com
SIC: 2741 Music, sheet: publishing only, not printed on site

(G-10308)
PALLET PROS
12500 Island Rd (44044-9550)
PHONE 440 537-9087
EMP: 3
SALES (est): 130K **Privately Held**
SIC: 2448 Mfg Wood Pallets/Skids

(G-10309)
POWER GROUNDING SOLUTIONS LLC
1001 Commerce Dr (44044-1278)
P.O. Box 66 (44044-0066)
PHONE 440 926-3219
Margaret McMillen, *President*
▲ **EMP:** 4
SQ FT: 10,000
SALES (est): 624.2K **Privately Held**
SIC: 3643 Current-carrying wiring devices

(G-10310)
SOUNDPROOF
15400 Highland Dr (44044-9028)
PHONE 440 864-8864
John Schneider, *Owner*
EMP: 5
SALES: 30K **Privately Held**
SIC: 3651 Household audio & video equipment

(G-10311)
SULO ENTERPRISES INC
Also Called: Magna Products
1017 Commerce Dr (44044-1279)
P.O. Box 97 (44044-0097)
PHONE 440 926-3322
Lowell L Snider, *President*
Suzanne Snider, *Vice Pres*
▲ **EMP:** 16
SQ FT: 6,000
SALES: 13.5MM **Privately Held**
WEB: www.shop-mag.com
SIC: 3499 Magnets, permanent: metallic

(G-10312)
UNITED CIRCUITS INC
1000 Commerce Dr (44044-1271)
PHONE 440 926-1000
Frank Schubert, *President*
Barbara Schubert, *Corp Secy*
Gary W Jump, *Vice Pres*
EMP: 10 **EST:** 1982
SQ FT: 17,000
SALES (est): 1.4MM **Privately Held**
SIC: 3672 Printed circuit boards

(G-10313)
WILLIS CNC
1008 Commerce Dr (44044-1275)
PHONE 440 926-0434
EMP: 7
SALES (est): 837.2K **Privately Held**
SIC: 3599 Machine shop, jobbing & repair

Grand Rapids
Wood County

(G-10314)
A+ ENGINEERING FABRICATION INC
17562 Beech St (43522-9728)
P.O. Box 470 (43522-0470)
PHONE 419 832-0748
David Arno, *President*
Linda Arno, *Vice Pres*
Ryan Arno, *Engineer*
EMP: 15
SQ FT: 23,500
SALES (est): 4.7MM **Privately Held**
WEB: www.aplusengineering.com
SIC: 3441 3599 8711 Fabricated structural metal; machine shop, jobbing & repair; engineering services

(G-10315)
INDUSTRIAL APPLICATION SVS
13453 Woodbrier Ln (43522-9681)
PHONE 419 875-5093
Marty Anderson, *President*
EMP: 4
SALES (est): 405.9K **Privately Held**
WEB: www.industrialapp.com
SIC: 3629 7389 Electrical industrial apparatus; business services

(G-10316)
LAKE WOOD PRODUCT INC (PA)
13020 Box Rd (43522-9233)
PHONE 419 832-0150
Jay Thomas, *President*
Donald W Pullen, *President*
Heidi Thomas, *Vice Pres*
Patty Miller, *Admin Sec*
EMP: 5
SQ FT: 11,648
SALES: 400K **Privately Held**
SIC: 2448 Pallets, wood; skids, wood

(G-10317)
PARAMOUNT PRODUCTS
10550 Prov Neap Swan Rd (43522-9668)
P.O. Box 429, Neapolis (43547-0429)
PHONE 419 832-0235
Roger A Kosch, *President*
Carolyn Kosch, *Corp Secy*
EMP: 5
SQ FT: 10,000
SALES (est): 796.8K **Privately Held**
WEB: www.paramountproducts.com
SIC: 2992 Lubricating oils & greases

(G-10318)
PIONEER HI-BRED INTL INC
15180 Henry Wood Rd (43522-9772)
PHONE 419 748-8051
Scott Millikan, *Manager*
EMP: 35
SQ FT: 6,000
SALES (corp-wide): 85.9B **Publicly Held**
WEB: www.pioneer.com
SIC: 5191 5153 2075 2041 Seeds: field, garden & flower; corn; soybeans; soybean oil mills; flour & other grain mill products
HQ: Pioneer Hi-Bred International, Inc.
7100 Nw 62nd Ave
Johnston IA 50131
515 535-3200

(G-10319)
Q S I FABRICATION
10333 S River Rd (43522-9350)
PHONE 419 832-1680
Tom Zitzelberger, *President*
Pete Wiederhold, *Sales Mgr*
EMP: 7
SQ FT: 400
SALES (est): 514.5K **Privately Held**
SIC: 3441 Fabricated structural metal

(G-10320)
SAYLOR PRODUCTS CORPORATION
17484 Saylor Ln (43522-9792)
PHONE 419 832-2125
Gregory Westhoven, *President*
EMP: 10 **EST:** 1902
SQ FT: 550
SALES: 1.4MM
SALES (corp-wide): 6.9MM **Privately Held**
SIC: 3644 Electric conduits & fittings
PA: Saylor Technical Products, Llc
17484 Saylor Ln
Grand Rapids OH 43522
713 884-0564

(G-10321)
SEEBURGER GREENHOUSE
Also Called: Usc Metal Fabricators
11480 S River Rd (43522-9341)
PHONE 419 832-1834
Larry Seeburger, *Owner*
EMP: 5
SALES (est): 377.9K **Privately Held**
SIC: 0181 3441 Bedding plants, growing of; flowers: grown under cover (e.g. greenhouse production); fabricated structural metal

---

(PA)=Parent Co (HQ)=Headquarters (DH)=Div Headquarters
✪ = New Business established in last 2 years

Grand River
Lake County

(G-10322)
GRAND RIVER ASPHALT
6 Coast Guard Rd (44045)
P.O. Box 249 (44045-0249)
PHONE..............................440 352-2254
Jerome T Osborne, *President*
EMP: 4
SALES (est): 530K **Privately Held**
SIC: 2951 Asphalt & asphaltic paving mixtures (not from refineries)

(G-10323)
JED INDUSTRIES INC
320 River St (44045-8214)
P.O. Box 369 (44045-0369)
PHONE..............................440 639-9973
Donald Nye, *President*
EMP: 25
SQ FT: 27,000
SALES (est): 3.7MM **Privately Held**
WEB: www.jedindustries.com
SIC: 3599 5084 Machine & other job shop work; industrial machinery & equipment

(G-10324)
KONGSBERG ACTUATION SYSTEMS
Also Called: Kongsberg Automotive
301 Olive St (44045-8221)
P.O. Box 98 (44045-0098)
PHONE..............................440 639-8778
EMP: 19
SALES (est): 377K
SALES (corp-wide): 1.2B **Privately Held**
WEB: www.teleflexfluidsystems.com
SIC: 3714 Motor vehicle parts & accessories
PA: Kongsberg Automotive Asa
Dyrmyrgata 48
Kongsberg 3611
327 705-00

(G-10325)
OSBORNE MATERIALS COMPANY (PA)
1 Williams St (44045-8253)
P.O. Box 248 (44045-0248)
PHONE..............................440 357-7026
Harold T Larned, *President*
Gary D Bradler, *President*
▼ **EMP:** 41
SQ FT: 2,500
SALES (est): 7.1MM **Privately Held**
SIC: 1442 Sand mining; gravel mining

(G-10326)
SUMITOMO ELC CARBIDE MFG INC (DH)
Also Called: Master Tool Div
210 River St (44045-8249)
P.O. Box 188 (44045-0188)
PHONE..............................440 354-0600
Yasuhisa Hashimoto, *President*
Takahiro Kimura, *Admin Sec*
EMP: 10
SQ FT: 25,000
SALES (est): 16MM
SALES (corp-wide): 28.9B **Privately Held**
SIC: 3541 3546 3545 3544 Machine tools, metal cutting type; power-driven handtools; machine tool accessories; special dies, tools, jigs & fixtures; hand & edge tools
HQ: Sumitomo Electric Carbide Inc
1001 E Business Center Dr
Mount Prospect IL 60056
847 635-0044

Granville
Licking County

(G-10327)
CARTER EVANS ENTERPRISES INC
Also Called: Pacer's Embroidery Barn
3354 Battee Rd (43023-9796)
PHONE..............................614 920-2276
Fax: 614 920-2277
EMP: 3
SQ FT: 2,500
SALES: 180K **Privately Held**
SIC: 2395 5949 Embroidery Or Art Needlework & Ret Embroidery Supplies

(G-10328)
CPIC AUTOMOTIVE INC
1226 Weaver Dr (43023-1257)
PHONE..............................740 587-3262
Cameron Cofer, *Vice Pres*
EMP: 3
SQ FT: 15,000
SALES (est): 126.4K **Privately Held**
SIC: 3296 Fiberglass insulation

(G-10329)
DOWNEY ENTERPRISES INC
Also Called: John Downey Company
2087 Jones Rd (43023-9542)
P.O. Box 565 (43023-0565)
PHONE..............................740 587-4258
John Downey, *President*
EMP: 5
SQ FT: 1,500
SALES: 140K **Privately Held**
SIC: 7217 2721 Carpet & furniture cleaning on location; magazines: publishing & printing

(G-10330)
ERATH VENEER CORP VIRGINIA
2825 Hallie Ln B (43023-9256)
PHONE..............................540 483-5223
Michael G Erath, *Chairman*
Rbobert C Moore, *Corp Secy*
◆ **EMP:** 14 **EST:** 1952
SALES (est): 2MM **Privately Held**
WEB: www.erathveneer.com
SIC: 2435 Veneer stock, hardwood

(G-10331)
HOLOPHANE CORPORATION (HQ)
3825 Columbus Rd Bldg A (43023-8604)
PHONE..............................866 759-1577
Vernon J Nagel, *CEO*
Jack BAC, *Sales Staff*
Sean Clare, *Sales Staff*
Kelly Fough, *Sales Staff*
◆ **EMP:** 107
SALES (est): 244.2MM
SALES (corp-wide): 3.6B **Publicly Held**
SIC: 3646 3648 Commercial indusl & institutional electric lighting fixtures; outdoor lighting equipment
PA: Acuity Brands, Inc.
1170 Peachtree St Ne
Atlanta GA 30309
404 853-1400

(G-10332)
MCDONALD & WOODWARD PUBG CO
431b E College St (43023-1319)
PHONE..............................740 321-1140
Jerry Mc Donald, *President*
Gavin Faulkner, *Vice Pres*
Trish Newcomb, *Admin Sec*
EMP: 3
SALES: 210K **Privately Held**
WEB: www.mwpubco.com
SIC: 2731 Books: publishing only

(G-10333)
MERITOR INC
Also Called: Arvinmrtor Commerical Vhcl Sys
4009 Columbus Rd Ste 111 (43023-8623)
PHONE..............................740 348-3498
Jim Corll, *Engineer*
Mike Deep, *Manager*
EMP: 157 **Publicly Held**
WEB: www.arvinmeritor.com
SIC: 3714 3713 Axles, motor vehicle; truck & bus bodies
PA: Meritor, Inc.
2135 W Maple Rd
Troy MI 48084

(G-10334)
MILESTONE VENTURES LLC (PA)
Also Called: Milestone Veneer
2924 Hallie Ln (43023-9516)
PHONE..............................317 908-2093
Dittmar Schaefer, *Mng Member*
John J McHugh III, *Mng Member*
Bernd Merkel, *Mng Member*
▼ **EMP:** 4
SALES (est): 1.7MM **Privately Held**
SIC: 2411 Veneer logs

(G-10335)
OOGEEP
1718 Columbus Rd (43023-1234)
P.O. Box 187 (43023-0187)
PHONE..............................740 587-0410
Rhonda Reda, *Principal*
Mark Bruce, *Comms Dir*
EMP: 3
SALES (est): 288.4K **Privately Held**
SIC: 1381 Drilling oil & gas wells

(G-10336)
OWENS CORNING SALES LLC
Owens Corning Science and Tech
2790 Columbus Rd (43023-1200)
PHONE..............................740 587-3562
Frank O'Brien Bernin, *Vice Pres*
EMP: 400 **Publicly Held**
WEB: www.owenscorning.com
SIC: 8731 2221 Commercial physical research; broadwoven fabric mills, manmade
HQ: Owens Corning Sales, Llc
1 Owens Corning Pkwy
Toledo OH 43659
419 248-8000

(G-10337)
RED VETTE PRINTING COMPANY
75 Fern Hill Dr (43023-9102)
P.O. Box 725, Newark (43058-0725)
PHONE..............................740 364-1766
Denna Brown, *President*
EMP: 5
SALES: 250K **Privately Held**
WEB: www.redvetteprinting.com
SIC: 2752 Commercial printing, lithographic

(G-10338)
TEKDOG INC
4813 Granview Rd (43023-9443)
P.O. Box 363 (43023-0363)
PHONE..............................614 737-3743
Jason Keller, *President*
Kerry Kicos, *Opers Staff*
Michelle Murphy, *Accounts Mgr*
EMP: 5
SALES (est): 455.3K **Privately Held**
SIC: 8331 7372 8243 Job training services; prepackaged software; business oriented computer software; software training, computer

(G-10339)
THERMAL VISIONS INC (PA)
Also Called: Threshhold
83 Stone Henge Dr (43023-9532)
PHONE..............................740 587-4025
Dwight Musgrave, *President*
Dean Musgrave, *Admin Sec*
▲ **EMP:** 5
SQ FT: 11,000
SALES: 17MM **Privately Held**
WEB: www.thermalvisions.com
SIC: 3086 Packaging & shipping materials, foamed plastic

Gratis
Preble County

(G-10340)
TOLSON PALLET MFG INC
10240 State Rte 122 (45330)
P.O. Box 151 (45330-0151)
PHONE..............................937 787-3511
Keith Tolson, *President*
Brent Tolson, *Vice Pres*
EMP: 10 **EST:** 1969
SQ FT: 30,000
SALES: 2.5MM **Privately Held**
SIC: 2448 Pallets, wood; skids, wood

Graysville
Washington County

(G-10341)
HARMON JOHN
Also Called: Harmon, John K
36300 Greenbrier Rd (45734-9725)
PHONE..............................740 934-2032
John Harmon, *Owner*
EMP: 4
SALES (est): 259.4K **Privately Held**
SIC: 1389 Servicing oil & gas wells

(G-10342)
WHITACRE ENTERPRISES INC
35651 State Route 537 (45734-7002)
PHONE..............................740 934-2331
Koy Whitacre, *President*
EMP: 16
SQ FT: 7,000
SALES (est): 2MM **Privately Held**
SIC: 5411 1382 Convenience stores, independent; oil & gas exploration services

Green
Summit County

(G-10343)
NEXT DESIGN & BUILD LLC
Also Called: Trident Polymer Solutions
4735 Massillon Rd # 520 (44232-0834)
PHONE..............................330 907-3042
Oscar Mascarenhas, *Mng Member*
EMP: 3
SALES (est): 500K **Privately Held**
SIC: 2671 Plastic film, coated or laminated for packaging

Green Springs
Seneca County

(G-10344)
JAMES W CUNNINGHAM
Also Called: Electrical Machinery & Repair
125 Baker St (44836-9306)
PHONE..............................419 639-2111
Fax: 419 639-2113
EMP: 15 **EST:** 1954
SQ FT: 15,000
SALES (est): 670K **Privately Held**
SIC: 7694 Electric Motor Repair

Greenfield
Highland County

(G-10345)
ADIENT US LLC
1147 N Washington St (45123-9782)
PHONE..............................937 383-5200
Joe Jones, *Prdtn Mgr*
EMP: 250
SQ FT: 65,000 **Privately Held**
SIC: 3714 Motor vehicle parts & accessories
HQ: Adient Us Llc
49200 Halyard Dr
Plymouth MI 48170
734 254-5000

(G-10346)
AMERICAN MADE CORRUGATED PACKG
Also Called: A M C P
1100 N 5th St (45123)
P.O. Box 186 (45123-0186)
PHONE..............................937 981-2111
Arden Fife, *President*
Pat Mc Allister, *Treasurer*
EMP: 15
SQ FT: 21,000

GEOGRAPHIC SECTION

Greenville - Darke County (G-10373)

SALES (est): 2.6MM **Privately Held**
SIC: 2653 5113 Boxes, corrugated: made from purchased materials; corrugated & solid fiber boxes

(G-10347)
CORVAC COMPOSITES LLC
1025 N Washington St (45123-9780)
PHONE..................248 807-0969
James Fitzell, *CEO*
EMP: 12
SALES (corp-wide): 177.4MM **Privately Held**
SIC: 3089 Thermoformed finished plastic products
HQ: Corvac Composites, Llc
   4450 36th St Se
   Kentwood MI 49512

(G-10348)
GMI COMPANIES INC
Woodware Furniture
512 S Washington St (45123-1645)
PHONE..................937 981-0244
George L Leasure, *President*
EMP: 3
SALES (corp-wide): 38.7MM **Privately Held**
SIC: 2531 2493 2599 2541 Blackboards, wood; bulletin boards, cork; bulletin boards, wood; boards: planning, display, notice, showcases, except refrigerated: wood; panel systems & partitions (free-standing), office: wood; panel systems & partitions, office: except wood
PA: Gmi Companies, Inc.
   2999 Henkle Dr
   Lebanon OH 45036
   513 932-3445

(G-10349)
GMI COMPANIES INC
Also Called: Waddell A Div GMI Companies
512 S Washington St (45123-1645)
P.O. Box 18 (45123-0018)
PHONE..................937 981-7724
Tom Septer, *Manager*
EMP: 25
SALES (corp-wide): 38.7MM **Privately Held**
WEB: www.ghent.com
SIC: 2541 Showcases, except refrigerated: wood; store fixtures, wood
PA: Gmi Companies, Inc.
   2999 Henkle Dr
   Lebanon OH 45036
   513 932-3445

(G-10350)
GREENFIELD RESEARCH INC (PA)
347 Edgewood Ave (45123-1149)
P.O. Box 239 (45123-0239)
PHONE..................937 981-7763
Michael Penn, *President*
Robert Snider, *Corp Secy*
Bob Snider, *Treasurer*
Chris Lewis, *Controller*
▼ EMP: 150 EST: 1966
SQ FT: 60,000
SALES (est): 43.1MM **Privately Held**
WEB: www.greenfieldresearch.com
SIC: 2396 Screen printing on fabric articles; automotive trimmings, fabric

(G-10351)
GREENFIELD RESEARCH INC
324 S Washington St (45123-1437)
PHONE..................937 876-9224
Michael Penn, *President*
EMP: 5
SALES (corp-wide): 43.1MM **Privately Held**
SIC: 2396 Automotive trimmings, fabric
PA: Greenfield Research, Inc.
   347 Edgewood Ave
   Greenfield OH 45123
   937 981-7763

(G-10352)
HISEY BELLS
Also Called: Inter Valley Communication
581 Capps Rd (45123-8356)
PHONE..................740 333-7669
Dave Hisey, *Owner*
EMP: 3

SALES: 80K **Privately Held**
WEB: www.hiseybells.com
SIC: 3931 Bells (musical instruments)

(G-10353)
JETTS EMBROIDERIES
Also Called: Jett's Professional Embroidery
1060 Jefferson St (45123-8319)
PHONE..................937 981-3716
Carla Jett, *Owner*
Ted Jett, *Manager*
EMP: 3
SALES: 180K **Privately Held**
SIC: 2395 2396 Embroidery & art needlework; screen printing on fabric articles

(G-10354)
LETTER SHOP
247 Jefferson St (45123-1345)
PHONE..................937 981-3117
Steve Pearce, *Owner*
EMP: 3
SQ FT: 6,300
SALES: 280K **Privately Held**
SIC: 2752 Commercial printing, offset

Greenford
Mahoning County

(G-10355)
SPOTTED HORSE STUDIO INC
6385 State Rte 165 (44422)
P.O. Box 5 (44422-0005)
PHONE..................330 533-2391
William Baird, *President*
EMP: 3
SALES (est): 208.2K **Privately Held**
SIC: 3993 Signs & advertising specialties

Greentown
Stark County

(G-10356)
ACTION SIGN INC
3140 Stage St (44630)
P.O. Box 341 (44630-0341)
PHONE..................330 966-0390
George Manos, *President*
EMP: 3
SALES (est): 341.2K **Privately Held**
SIC: 3993 Signs, not made in custom sign painting shops

(G-10357)
CANRON MANUFACTURING INC
3979 State St Nw (44630)
P.O. Box 356 (44630-0356)
PHONE..................330 497-1131
John Kettering, *President*
Heidi Michel, *Vice Pres*
EMP: 10 EST: 1981
SQ FT: 15,000
SALES (est): 2.7MM **Privately Held**
SIC: 3496 Miscellaneous fabricated wire products

(G-10358)
EXCALIBUR EXPLORATION INC
9720 Cleveland Ave Nw (44630)
P.O. Box 362 (44630-0362)
PHONE..................330 966-7003
David E Harker, *President*
Kurt Tyuluman, *Vice Pres*
Jennifer N Harker, *Treasurer*
EMP: 3
SALES (est): 549.9K **Privately Held**
WEB: www.excaliburexploration.com
SIC: 1311 Crude petroleum production; natural gas production

Greenville
Darke County

(G-10359)
ACTION PROSTHETICS LLC
1498 N Broadway St Ste 3 (45331-2454)
PHONE..................937 548-9100
Karl Burk, *Owner*

EMP: 3
SALES (est): 265.4K **Privately Held**
SIC: 3842 Prosthetic appliances

(G-10360)
BASF CORPORATION
1175 Martin St (45331-1886)
PHONE..................937 547-6700
Jim Bero, *Branch Mgr*
EMP: 150
SALES (corp-wide): 71.7B **Privately Held**
WEB: www.basf.com
SIC: 2869 Industrial organic chemicals
HQ: Basf Corporation
   100 Park Ave
   Florham Park NJ 07932
   973 245-6000

(G-10361)
BROTHERS PUBLISHING CO LLC
Also Called: Early Bird, The
100 Washington Ave (45331-1515)
PHONE..................937 548-3330
Ryan Berry, *Editor*
Louanna Gwinn, *Sales Staff*
Keith Foutz, *Mng Member*
Clinton Randall, *Webmaster*
EMP: 45
SALES (est): 2.7MM **Privately Held**
SIC: 2711 2791 7331 Newspapers: publishing only, not printed on site; typesetting; mailing list compilers

(G-10362)
CALMEGO SPECIALIZED PDTS LLC
1569 Martindale Rd (45331-9696)
PHONE..................937 669-5620
Clarence Neels,
EMP: 10
SALES (est): 1.2MM **Privately Held**
SIC: 3366 Copper foundries

(G-10363)
CARR SUPPLY CO
900 Sater St (45331-1637)
PHONE..................937 316-6300
Stive Werling, *Manager*
EMP: 5
SALES (corp-wide): 4.9B **Privately Held**
SIC: 5722 5074 3432 1521 Air conditioning room units, self-contained; plumbing fittings & supplies; plumbing fixture fittings & trim; single-family home remodeling, additions & repairs
HQ: Carr Supply Co.
   1415 Old Leonard Ave
   Columbus OH 43219
   614 252-7883

(G-10364)
CLASSIC REPRODUCTIONS
5315 Meeker Rd (45331-9751)
P.O. Box 916 (45331-0916)
PHONE..................937 548-9839
Thomas Jeffers, *Owner*
EMP: 8
SQ FT: 48,000
SALES (est): 854K **Privately Held**
WEB: www.classicreproductions.com
SIC: 3714 Motor vehicle body components & frame

(G-10365)
COMMERCIAL PRTG OF GREENVILL
314 S Broadway St (45331-1905)
PHONE..................937 548-3835
Jeff Campbell, *Owner*
Joan Brante, *Principal*
Marian Campbell, *Admin Sec*
EMP: 8
SQ FT: 2,200
SALES (est): 834.5K **Privately Held**
SIC: 2752 Commercial printing, lithographic

(G-10366)
CROMWELL ALEENE
Also Called: Mock Shoppe
101 W Main St (45331-1401)
PHONE..................937 547-2281
Aleene Cromwell, *Owner*
EMP: 3

SQ FT: 500
SALES: 75K **Privately Held**
SIC: 3199 Novelties, leather

(G-10367)
D A FITZGERALD CO INC
1045 Sater St (45331-1638)
P.O. Box 206 (45331-0206)
PHONE..................937 548-0511
Don S Fitzgerald, *President*
Janice Fitzgerald, *Corp Secy*
Scott Fitzgerald, *Admin Sec*
EMP: 9 EST: 1967
SQ FT: 10,000
SALES: 770K **Privately Held**
SIC: 3544 Special dies & tools; jigs & fixtures

(G-10368)
FOUREMANS SAND & GRAVEL INC
2791 Wildcat Rd (45331-9453)
PHONE..................937 547-1005
Gary B Foureman, *President*
John Foureman, *Vice Pres*
Susan Foureman, *Treasurer*
EMP: 6 EST: 1953
SQ FT: 14,000
SALES: 380K **Privately Held**
SIC: 1442 1794 Gravel mining; excavation & grading, building construction

(G-10369)
FRAM GROUP OPERATIONS LLC
Honeywell
851 Jackson St (45331-1277)
PHONE..................937 316-3000
Bernie Salles, *Manager*
EMP: 4 **Privately Held**
WEB: www.honeywell.com
SIC: 3714 3264 Filters: oil, fuel & air, motor vehicle; spark plugs, porcelain
HQ: Fram Group Operations Llc
   1900 W Field Ct 4w-516
   Lake Forest IL 60045

(G-10370)
FRIENDS OF BEARS MILL INC
6450 Arcanum Bearsmill Rd (45331-9617)
PHONE..................937 548-5112
Terry Clark, *President*
EMP: 4
SQ FT: 8,000
SALES: 126.4K **Privately Held**
WEB: www.bearsmill.com
SIC: 2041 5947 Flour mills, cereal (except rice); gift shop

(G-10371)
G S K INC
915 Front St (45331-1606)
P.O. Box 358 (45331-0358)
PHONE..................937 547-1611
Jack Besecker, *CEO*
Chris Besecker, *President*
Patricia Besecker, *Corp Secy*
EMP: 9
SQ FT: 6,600
SALES (est): 1.7MM **Privately Held**
SIC: 3089 2631 7389 Molding primary plastic; paperboard mills; packaging & labeling services

(G-10372)
GE INTELLIGENT PLATFORMS INC
5438 S State Route 49 (45331-3317)
PHONE..................937 459-5404
David Benton, *Branch Mgr*
EMP: 3
SALES (corp-wide): 17.4B **Publicly Held**
SIC: 3625 Numerical controls
HQ: Intelligent Platforms, Llc
   2500 Austin Dr
   Charlottesville VA 22911

(G-10373)
GOSPEL TRUMPET PUBLISHING
5065 S State Route 49 (45331-9750)
P.O. Box 1139 (45331-9139)
PHONE..................937 548-9876
Susan Mutch, *Owner*
EMP: 3
SALES: 70K **Privately Held**
SIC: 2741 Miscellaneous publishing

Greenville - Darke County (G-10374)

GEOGRAPHIC SECTION

(G-10374)
GREENVILLE TECHNOLOGY INC (HQ)
5755 State Route 571 (45331-9692)
P.O. Box 974 (45331-0974)
PHONE...................................937 548-3217
YAF Nakao, *President*
William Laframboise, *COO*
James Heiser, *Exec VP*
Akihiko Hirano, *Treasurer*
Bill Laframboise, *Executive*
▲ **EMP:** 672
SQ FT: 300,000
SALES: 20MM
SALES (corp-wide): 1.7B **Privately Held**
WEB: www.gtioh.com
SIC: 3089 Injection molded finished plastic products
PA: Moriroku Holdings Company, Ltd.
 1-1-1, Minamiaoyama
 Minato-Ku TKY 107-0
 334 036-102

(G-10375)
JAFE DECORATING CO INC
1250 Martin St (45331-1870)
PHONE...................................937 547-1888
Randy O'Dell, *President*
EMP: 28
SQ FT: 36,000
SALES (est): 4.2MM **Privately Held**
SIC: 3231 Decorated glassware: chipped, engraved, etched, etc.

(G-10376)
JOSH L DERKSEN
200 N Broadway St (45331-2223)
PHONE...................................937 548-0080
Josh Derksen, *Principal*
EMP: 4
SALES (est): 496.4K **Privately Held**
SIC: 3714 Mufflers (exhaust), motor vehicle

(G-10377)
JRB INDUSTRIES LLC
3425 State Route 571 (45331-3247)
PHONE...................................567 825-7022
James Bates,
EMP: 25
SALES (est): 1.1MM **Privately Held**
SIC: 3999 Atomizers, toiletry

(G-10378)
KLOCKNER PENTAPLAST AMER INC
Witt Plastics
1671 Martindale Rd (45331-9681)
PHONE...................................937 548-7272
Ryan Beatty, *Materials Mgr*
Todd Geyer, *Site Mgr*
Daryl Means, *Site Mgr*
Karen Tobias, *Manager*
EMP: 80
SALES (corp-wide): 672.8K **Privately Held**
WEB: www.kpafilms.com
SIC: 3089 Plastic containers, except foam
HQ: Klockner Pentaplast Of America, Inc.
 3585 Kloeckner Rd
 Gordonsville VA 22942
 540 832-1400

(G-10379)
KNITTING MACHINERY CORP
607 Riffle Ave (45331-1612)
P.O. Box 902 (45331-0902)
PHONE...................................937 548-2338
Chester Rice, *Manager*
EMP: 10
SALES (corp-wide): 7.2MM **Privately Held**
SIC: 3552 Knitting machines
PA: Knitting Machinery Corp.
 15625 Saranac Rd
 Cleveland OH 44110
 216 851-9900

(G-10380)
MARKWITH TOOL COMPANY INC
Also Called: Millmcrawley
5261 S State Route 49 (45331-1035)
PHONE...................................937 548-6808
Merlin Miller, *President*
Maxine Miller, *Vice Pres*
EMP: 13
SQ FT: 32,500
SALES (est): 1.8MM **Privately Held**
WEB: www.markwithtool.com
SIC: 3599 Custom machinery; machine shop, jobbing & repair

(G-10381)
MIAMI VALLEY PRESS INC
6132 Kruckeburg Rd (45331-9210)
PHONE...................................937 547-0771
Gerald Flora, *President*
Jane Flora, *Vice Pres*
EMP: 5 **EST:** 2001
SALES (est): 470K **Privately Held**
SIC: 2754 2759 2752 Invitations: gravure printing; envelopes: printing; business form & card printing, lithographic

(G-10382)
MILTON WEST FABRICATORS INC
4773 Hllnsburg Tampico Rd (45331-9515)
PHONE...................................937 547-3069
William Hoisington, *President*
Doug Subler, *Vice Pres*
John Mutschler, *Treasurer*
EMP: 6
SALES (est): 1MM **Privately Held**
SIC: 3444 Sheet metalwork

(G-10383)
MJS PLASTICS INC
1355 Sater St (45331-1640)
P.O. Box 26 (45331-0026)
PHONE...................................937 548-1000
Matthew J Steyer, *President*
EMP: 4
SQ FT: 30,000
SALES (est): 474.5K **Privately Held**
WEB: www.mjsplastics.com
SIC: 2821 Plastics materials & resins

(G-10384)
MONSANTO COMPANY
1051 Landsdowne Ave (45331-8381)
PHONE...................................937 548-7858
Jim Larkin, *Manager*
EMP: 10
SALES (corp-wide): 45.3B **Privately Held**
WEB: www.monsanto.com
SIC: 2879 Agricultural chemicals
HQ: Monsanto Company
 800 N Lindbergh Blvd
 Saint Louis MO 63167
 314 694-1000

(G-10385)
NEW CAN COMPANY INC
1367 Sater St (45331-1640)
PHONE...................................937 547-9050
Jamie Jamieson, *Branch Mgr*
EMP: 6
SALES (corp-wide): 8.4MM **Privately Held**
SIC: 3469 Metal stampings
HQ: The New Can Company Inc
 1 Mear Rd
 Holbrook MA 02343
 781 767-1650

(G-10386)
PFI USA
5963 Jysville St Johns Rd (45331-9398)
PHONE...................................937 547-0413
Albert Wiebe, *Principal*
EMP: 15
SALES (est): 4.8MM **Privately Held**
SIC: 3499 Automobile seat frames, metal

(G-10387)
POLYONE CORPORATION
1050 Landsdowne Ave (45331-8382)
PHONE...................................800 727-4338
John Dimino, *Plant Mgr*
EMP: 121 **Publicly Held**
WEB: www.spartech.com
SIC: 2821 Plastics materials & resins
PA: Polyone Corporation
 33587 Walker Rd
 Avon Lake OH 44012

(G-10388)
POLYONE CORPORATION
Also Called: Spartech Plastics
1050 Landsdowne Ave (45331-8382)
PHONE...................................937 548-2133
Julie A McAlindon, *Manager*
EMP: 50 **Publicly Held**
SIC: 2821 Plastics materials & resins
PA: Polyone Corporation
 33587 Walker Rd
 Avon Lake OH 44012

(G-10389)
RAMCO ELECTRIC MOTORS INC
5763 Jysville St Johns Rd (45331-9678)
PHONE...................................937 548-2525
Dave Dunaway, *President*
Jase Barhorst, *Human Res Mgr*
EMP: 85
SQ FT: 30,000
SALES: 20.9MM **Privately Held**
WEB: www.ramcorotors.com
SIC: 3621 3625 3363 Motors, electric; rotors, for motors; relays & industrial controls; aluminum die-castings

(G-10390)
REBSCO INC
4362 Us Route 36 (45331-9754)
P.O. Box 370 (45331-0370)
PHONE...................................937 548-2246
Tyeis L Baker-Baumann, *President*
EMP: 15 **EST:** 1965
SQ FT: 23,000
SALES: 2.1MM **Privately Held**
WEB: www.rebsco.com
SIC: 1542 2431 3448 3443 Nonresidential Cnstn Mfg Millwork Mfg Prefab Metal Bldgs Mfg Fabricated Plate Wrk

(G-10391)
REESERS MACHINE INC
2624 Fox Rd (45331-9467)
PHONE...................................937 548-5847
Daniel Reeser, *President*
Dan Reeser, *President*
Linda Reeser, *Corp Secy*
EMP: 4
SQ FT: 5,000
SALES: 500K **Privately Held**
SIC: 3599 Machine shop, jobbing & repair

(G-10392)
RIEGLE COLORS
3566 N Creek Dr (45331-3006)
PHONE...................................937 548-8444
James Riegle, *Owner*
EMP: 5
SALES (est): 220K **Privately Held**
WEB: www.rieglecolors.com
SIC: 2329 Riding clothes:, men's, youths' & boys'

(G-10393)
ROBERT WINNER SONS INC
Also Called: Winners Meat Farm
2259 State Route 502 (45331-9442)
PHONE...................................937 548-7513
Mike Winner, *Branch Mgr*
EMP: 4
SALES (corp-wide): 33.9MM **Privately Held**
SIC: 0213 2011 Hogs; pork products from pork slaughtered on site
PA: Robert Winner Sons, Inc.
 8544 State Route 705
 Yorkshire OH 45388
 419 582-4321

(G-10394)
RUSSELL L GARBER (PA)
Also Called: Garber Farms
4891 Clark Station Rd (45331-9562)
PHONE...................................937 548-6224
Russell L Garber, *Owner*
Etta Garber, *Co-Owner*
EMP: 12
SALES (est): 1.5MM **Privately Held**
WEB: www.garberfarms.com
SIC: 2448 0161 Pallets, wood; melon farms

(G-10395)
SPARTECH LLC
1050 Landsdowne Ave (45331-8382)
PHONE...................................937 548-1395
Julie A McAlindon, *Manager*
EMP: 100
SALES (corp-wide): 1.6B **Privately Held**
WEB: www.spartech.com
SIC: 3081 3089 Unsupported plastics film & sheet; plastic containers, except foam; plastic kitchenware, tableware & houseware
HQ: Spartech Llc
 11650 Lkeside Crossing Ct
 Saint Louis MO 63146
 314 569-7400

(G-10396)
ST HENRY TILE CO INC
Also Called: Wayne Builders Supply
5410 S State Route 49 (45331-1032)
PHONE...................................937 548-1101
Mike Homan, *Manager*
EMP: 12
SALES (corp-wide): 30MM **Privately Held**
SIC: 3271 5211 3272 Blocks, concrete or cinder: standard; masonry materials & supplies; concrete products, precast
PA: The St Henry Tile Co Inc
 281 W Washington St
 Saint Henry OH 45883
 419 678-4841

(G-10397)
STATELINE POWER CORP
Also Called: Southeast Diesl Acquisition Sub
650 Pine St (45331-1625)
PHONE...................................937 547-1006
Tom Tracy III, *President*
EMP: 15
SQ FT: 45,000
SALES (est): 7.1MM **Privately Held**
WEB: www.statelinepower.com
SIC: 3569 3621 Gas producers, generators & other gas related equipment; gas generators; motors & generators; power generators
HQ: Tradewinds Power Corp.
 5820 Nw 84th Ave
 Doral FL 33166

(G-10398)
TREATY CITY INDUSTRIES INC
Also Called: T C I
945 Sater St (45331-1636)
P.O. Box 39 (45331-0039)
PHONE...................................937 548-9000
Mike Jones, *President*
Sherri Jones, *Treasurer*
EMP: 19
SQ FT: 40,000
SALES (est): 3MM **Privately Held**
SIC: 3053 3469 Gaskets, packing & sealing devices; metal stampings

(G-10399)
WALLS BROS ASPHALT CO INC (PA)
Also Called: Walls Asphalt Manufacturing
3690 Hllnsburg Sampson Rd (45331-9721)
PHONE...................................937 548-7158
Perry Walls, *President*
James Jergensen, *Chairman*
EMP: 4 **EST:** 1961
SQ FT: 1,900
SALES (est): 765.1K **Privately Held**
SIC: 2951 1611 Asphalt & asphaltic paving mixtures (not from refineries); general contractor, highway & street construction

(G-10400)
WHIRLPOOL CORPORATION
1701 Kitchen Aid Way (45331-8331)
PHONE...................................937 548-4126
David Augsburger, *Project Mgr*
Jeff Postel, *Opers Staff*
Jerry Bell, *Purch Dir*
John Heck, *QC Dir*
Clarence Kammer, *Engineer*
EMP: 375
SALES (corp-wide): 21B **Publicly Held**
WEB: www.whirlpoolcorp.com
SIC: 3634 Electric household cooking appliances

▲ = Import ▼ = Export
◆ = Import/Export

PA: Whirlpool Corporation
2000 N M 63
Benton Harbor MI 49022
269 923-5000

(G-10401)
WHIRLPOOL CORPORATION
1301 Sater St (45331-1640)
PHONE.................................937 547-0773
EMP: 175
SALES (corp-wide): 21B Publicly Held
SIC: 3633 Household laundry machines, including coin-operated
PA: Whirlpool Corporation
2000 N M 63
Benton Harbor MI 49022
269 923-5000

(G-10402)
WOLF G T AWNING & TENT CO
3352 State Route 571 (45331-3229)
P.O. Box 248 (45331-0248)
PHONE.................................937 548-4161
Susan Miles, *President*
Maurie Miles, *Vice Pres*
EMP: 10 EST: 1896
SALES (est): 910.5K Privately Held
SIC: 7359 2394 Tent & tarpaulin rental; canvas & related products

Greenwich
Huron County

(G-10403)
F SQUARED INC
9 Sunset Dr (44837-1020)
PHONE.................................419 752-7273
William Shipman, *President*
Patricia Shipman, *Corp Secy*
EMP: 6
SALES: 450K Privately Held
SIC: 3825 Electrical power measuring equipment

(G-10404)
JOHNSON BROS RUBBER CO INC
Also Called: Johnson Bros Greenwich
41 Center St (44837-1049)
PHONE.................................419 752-4814
Ken Bostic, *Manager*
EMP: 30
SALES (corp-wide): 54.4MM Privately Held
SIC: 5199 3743 3634 3545 Foams & rubber; railroad equipment; electric housewares & fans; machine tool accessories; gaskets, packing & sealing devices
PA: Johnson Bros. Rubber Co., Inc.
42 W Buckeye St
West Salem OH 44287
419 853-4122

(G-10405)
K & L DIE & MANUFACTURING
7541 Olvsburg Ftchvlle Rd (44837)
PHONE.................................419 895-1301
Karl Kinstle, *President*
Lu Kinstle, *Corp Secy*
EMP: 5
SQ FT: 5,000
SALES (est): 721.4K Privately Held
SIC: 3469 3544 3441 Stamping metal for the trade; special dies & tools; tower sections, radio & television transmission

(G-10406)
LAKEPARK INDUSTRIES INC
Also Called: Midway Products Group
40 Seminary St (44837-1040)
PHONE.................................419 752-4471
James Hoyt, *President*
Lloyd A Miller, *Vice Pres*
Steve Anderson, *Manager*
EMP: 150
SQ FT: 60,000
SALES (est): 27.3MM Privately Held
SIC: 3469 3465 Stamping metal for the trade; automotive stampings
PA: Midway Products Group, Inc.
1 Lyman E Hoyt Dr
Monroe MI 48161

(G-10407)
RICHLAND LAMINATED COLUMNS LLC
8252 State Route 13 (44837-9638)
PHONE.................................419 895-0036
Elmer Sensenig,
EMP: 10
SQ FT: 40,000
SALES (est): 2MM Privately Held
SIC: 2439 Arches, laminated lumber

(G-10408)
S C MACHINE
116 Us Highway 224 W (44837-9400)
PHONE.................................419 752-6961
Steve Chuburko, *Owner*
EMP: 4
SALES (est): 340.4K Privately Held
WEB: www.scmachine.com
SIC: 3599 Machine shop, jobbing & repair

(G-10409)
TIMBERLANE WOODWORKING
8425 Olvsburg Ftchvlle Rd (44837)
PHONE.................................419 895-9945
Wilmer Martin, *Principal*
EMP: 4 EST: 2008
SALES (est): 400.1K Privately Held
SIC: 2434 Wood kitchen cabinets

Grove City
Franklin County

(G-10410)
ADVANCE APEX INC (PA)
Also Called: Advance Cnc Machining
2375 Harrisburg Pike (43123-1057)
PHONE.................................614 539-3000
Jeremy J Hamilton, *President*
Chet Colopy, *Vice Pres*
Kyle Dunaway, *Vice Pres*
Travis Hamilton, *Sales Mgr*
Tricia Hulse, *Sales Staff*
▲ EMP: 31
SQ FT: 40,000
SALES (est): 6.7MM Privately Held
WEB: www.advancemachining.com
SIC: 3599 Machine shop, jobbing & repair

(G-10411)
ADVANCE INDUSTRIAL MFG INC
1996 Longwood Ave (43123-1218)
P.O. Box 1296 (43123-6296)
PHONE.................................614 871-3333
James Wintzer, *President*
Katherine L Larimore, *Corp Secy*
Dr Christopher Wintzer, *Director*
Cynthia T Wintzer, *Director*
Douglas Wintzer, *Director*
EMP: 49
SQ FT: 35,000
SALES: 6MM Privately Held
SIC: 3441 3443 3449 Fabricated structural metal; fabricated plate work (boiler shop); miscellaneous metalwork

(G-10412)
AIM ATTACHMENTS
1720 Feddern Ave (43123-1206)
PHONE.................................614 539-3030
Dennis Hamilton, *Owner*
▼ EMP: 20 EST: 2008
SALES (est): 2.9MM Privately Held
WEB: www.aimattachments.com
SIC: 3531 Construction machinery attachments

(G-10413)
ALL PACK SERVICES LLC
3442 Grant Ave (43123-2513)
PHONE.................................614 935-0964
Billie Jo Grubb, *Accountant*
Brian Householder,
Tom Pack,
EMP: 13 EST: 2013
SALES: 60K Privately Held
SIC: 7349 3613 Building maintenance services; time switches, electrical switchgear apparatus

(G-10414)
AMERICAN AWARDS INC
Also Called: Reynoldsburg Trophy
2380 Harrisburg Pike (43123-1058)
PHONE.................................614 875-1850
Steve Gibson, *President*
Gary Gibson, *Corp Secy*
EMP: 13
SQ FT: 6,500
SALES: 1MM Privately Held
WEB: www.awardsohio.com
SIC: 5999 3993 Trophies & plaques; signs & advertising specialties

(G-10415)
AMIR INTERNATIONAL FOODS INC
3504 Broadway (43123-1941)
PHONE.................................614 332-1742
Basel Said, *Principal*
EMP: 6
SALES (est): 220K Privately Held
SIC: 2099 Food preparations

(G-10416)
BARBS EMBROIDERY
2700 Brunswick Dr (43123-2122)
PHONE.................................614 875-9933
Barbara Cantrell, *Principal*
EMP: 3
SALES (est): 95.7K Privately Held
SIC: 2395 Embroidery & art needlework

(G-10417)
BOEHM INC (PA)
2050 Hardy Parkway St (43123-1214)
PHONE.................................614 875-9010
Stuart Reeve, *President*
Michael Hutchison, *Vice Pres*
Jonda Lacy, *CFO*
EMP: 30
SQ FT: 12,000
SALES: 8.3MM Privately Held
WEB: www.boehminc.com
SIC: 2672 2759 Labels (unprinted), gummed; made from purchased materials; decals: printing

(G-10418)
BRICOLAGE INC
2989 Lewis Centre Way (43123-1782)
PHONE.................................614 853-6789
Phillip G Lilly, *President*
Jeff Spellacy, *Admin Sec*
EMP: 10
SALES (est): 1.6MM Privately Held
SIC: 2434 3399 2821 2752 Wood kitchen cabinets; metal fasteners; plastics materials & resins; commercial printing, lithographic

(G-10419)
BUCK EQUIPMENT INC
1720 Feddern Ave (43123-1206)
PHONE.................................614 539-3039
Dennis Hamilton, *CEO*
Jamie Odell, *Sales Executive*
▲ EMP: 35
SQ FT: 60,000
SALES (est): 9.4MM Privately Held
WEB: www.buckequipment.com
SIC: 3531 3743 3441 5088 Logging equipment; railroad equipment; fabricated structural metal; railroad equipment & supplies

(G-10420)
CLIENTRAX TECHNOLOGY SOLUTIONS
Also Called: Clientrax Software
3347 Mcdowell Rd (43123-2907)
PHONE.................................614 875-2245
Michael Mantkowski, *President*
EMP: 10 EST: 1987
SALES (est): 805.2K Privately Held
WEB: www.clientrax.com
SIC: 7372 Business oriented computer software

(G-10421)
CONCORD FABRICATORS INC
6511 Seeds Rd (43123-8431)
PHONE.................................614 875-2500
Gary Hammel, *President*
Lyn Blevins, *Project Mgr*
Andy Hoy, *Prdtn Mgr*
Bill Hitchcock, *Manager*
Chuck Purdom, *Officer*
EMP: 23
SQ FT: 21,500
SALES (est): 10MM Privately Held
SIC: 1791 3441 Structural steel erection; fabricated structural metal

(G-10422)
CONSUMERS NEWS SERVICES INC
Also Called: Grove City Record
4048 Broadway (43123-3026)
PHONE.................................614 875-2307
Jeff Donnayou, *Manager*
EMP: 6
SALES (corp-wide): 651.9MM Privately Held
SIC: 2711 Newspapers, publishing & printing
HQ: Consumers News Services Inc
5300 Crosswind Dr
Columbus OH 43228
740 888-6000

(G-10423)
CROWN EQUIPMENT CORPORATION
Also Called: Crown Lift Trucks
2100 Southwest Blvd (43123-1898)
PHONE.................................614 274-7700
Rusty Edwards, *Manager*
EMP: 65
SALES (corp-wide): 3.1B Privately Held
WEB: www.okisys.com
SIC: 3537 Lift trucks, industrial: fork, platform, straddle, etc.
PA: Crown Equipment Corporation
44 S Washington St
New Bremen OH 45869
419 629-2311

(G-10424)
CUMMINS INC
2297 Southwest Blvd Ste K (43123-1822)
P.O. Box 291989, Nashville TN (37229-1989)
PHONE.................................614 604-6004
Tammy Fawley, *Branch Mgr*
EMP: 4
SALES (corp-wide): 23.7B Publicly Held
SIC: 3519 3714 3694 3621 Internal combustion engines; motor vehicle parts & accessories; engine electrical equipment; generator sets: gasoline, diesel or dual-fuel
PA: Cummins Inc.
500 Jackson St
Columbus IN 47201
812 377-5000

(G-10425)
DEERFIELD VENTURES INC
Also Called: Ink Well
2224 Stringtown Rd (43123-3926)
P.O. Box 305 (43123-0305)
PHONE.................................614 875-0688
David Keil, *President*
Anna Keil, *Corp Secy*
EMP: 8 EST: 1982
SQ FT: 3,000
SALES (est): 1.1MM Privately Held
SIC: 2752 Commercial printing, offset

(G-10426)
DIMENSIONS THREE INC
6157 Enterprise Pkwy (43123-9539)
PHONE.................................614 539-5180
Tony Hart, *President*
Michael Charnier, *Vice Pres*
John Casey, *Treasurer*
EMP: 5 EST: 1997
SQ FT: 4,500
SALES (est): 322K Privately Held
SIC: 2395 Pleating & stitching

(G-10427)
DYNAMP LLC
3735 Gantz Rd Ste D (43123-4849)
PHONE.................................614 871-6900
Brad Seavoy, *General Mgr*
David Shepard, *Vice Pres*
Robert Mills, *Project Engr*
David Shepherd, *Marketing Mgr*
Gary Cooper, *Manager*

Grove City - Franklin County (G-10428)

GEOGRAPHIC SECTION

▲ EMP: 27
SQ FT: 16,000
SALES (est): 5.4MM **Privately Held**
SIC: 3825 Current measuring equipment

(G-10428)
EJ USA INC
1855 Feddern Ave (43123-1207)
PHONE..................614 871-2436
Brian Hall, *Sales/Mktg Mgr*
EMP: 6 **Privately Held**
WEB: www.ejiw.com
SIC: 3321 Manhole covers, metal
HQ: Ej Usa, Inc.
 301 Spring St
 East Jordan MI 49727
 800 874-4100

(G-10429)
ELECTR-GNRAL PLAS CORP CLUMBUS
6200 Enterprise Pkwy (43123-9286)
PHONE..................614 871-2915
Patrick A Castro Sr, *President*
Patrick A Castro Jr, *Vice Pres*
EMP: 8
SQ FT: 36,400
SALES (est): 2.3MM **Privately Held**
SIC: 3089 Injection molding of plastics; plastic processing

(G-10430)
FABCON COMPANIES LLC
3400 Jackson Pike (43123-8993)
PHONE..................614 875-8601
Michael Lejeune, *CEO*
Jeff Prewitt, *Vice Pres*
EMP: 100
SQ FT: 40,000 **Privately Held**
SIC: 3272 Prestressed concrete products
PA: Fabcon Companies, Llc
 6111 Highway 13 W
 Savage MN 55378

(G-10431)
GRAMAG LLC
2999 Lewis Centre Way (43123-1782)
PHONE..................614 875-8435
EMP: 50 **Privately Held**
SIC: 2531 Mfg Auto Seats
PA: Gramag Llc
 41700 Gardenbrook Rd # 150
 Novi MI

(G-10432)
GREEN CORP MAGNETIC INC
4342 Mcdowell Rd (43123-4000)
PHONE..................614 801-4000
Stephen Green, *President*
▲ EMP: 20
SALES (est): 2.8MM **Privately Held**
WEB: www.greencorp.com
SIC: 3542 Magnetic forming machines

(G-10433)
HALCORF GROUP INC (HQ)
Also Called: Horton Emergency Vehicles
3800 Mcdowell Rd (43123-4022)
PHONE..................614 539-8181
John Slawson, *President*
▼ EMP: 180 EST: 1997
SQ FT: 110,000
SALES (est): 66.5MM **Publicly Held**
WEB: www.hortonambulance.com
SIC: 3711 Motor vehicles & car bodies

(G-10434)
HORTON ENTERPRISES INC
3800 Mcdowell Rd (43123-4022)
PHONE..................614 539-8181
EMP: 3
SALES (est): 280K **Privately Held**
SIC: 3711 Mfg Motor Vehicle/Car Bodies

(G-10435)
INSTANTWHIP-COLUMBUS INC (HQ)
3855 Marlane Dr (43123-9224)
P.O. Box 249 (43123-0249)
PHONE..................614 871-9447
Douglas A Smith, *President*
Tom G Michaelides, *Senior VP*
Vinson Lewis, *Vice Pres*
G Fredrick Smith, *Admin Sec*
EMP: 32

SQ FT: 10,300
SALES (est): 5.9MM
SALES (corp-wide): 47.5MM **Privately Held**
SIC: 2026 5143 2023 8741 Whipped topping, except frozen or dry mix; dairy products, except dried or canned; dietary supplements, dairy & non-dairy based; management services
PA: Instantwhip Foods, Inc.
 2200 Cardigan Ave
 Columbus OH 43215
 614 488-2536

(G-10436)
INTEGRATED SYSTEMS PROFESSIONA
Also Called: Isp
4110 Demorest Rd (43123-9549)
PHONE..................614 875-0104
Tony Brackman, *Principal*
Mark Sell,
EMP: 3 EST: 2015
SALES (est): 342.2K **Privately Held**
SIC: 3357 Fiber optic cable (insulated)

(G-10437)
JOE SESTITO
Also Called: Varsity Sporting Goods
5553 Spring Hill Rd (43123-8907)
PHONE..................614 871-7778
EMP: 7
SALES (est): 293.3K **Privately Held**
SIC: 5941 5699 2759 Ret Sporting Goods/Bicycles Ret Misc Apparel/Accessories Commercial Printing

(G-10438)
KAMAN CORPORATION
3735 Gantz Rd Ste C (43123-4849)
PHONE..................614 871-1893
EMP: 42
SALES (corp-wide): 1.8B **Publicly Held**
SIC: 3812 Aircraft/aerospace flight instruments & guidance systems
PA: Kaman Corporation
 1332 Blue Hills Ave
 Bloomfield CT 06002
 860 243-7100

(G-10439)
KERN INC (DH)
3940 Gantz Rd Ste A (43123-4845)
PHONE..................614 317-2600
Thomas Brock, *President*
▲ EMP: 25
SQ FT: 30,000
SALES (est): 7MM
SALES (corp-wide): 134.3MM **Privately Held**
SIC: 3579 3577 Envelope stuffing, sealing & addressing machines; computer peripheral equipment
HQ: Kern Ag
 Hunigenstrasse 16
 Konolfingen BE 3510
 317 903-535

(G-10440)
KIRK WILLIAMS COMPANY INC
2734 Home Rd (43123-1701)
P.O. Box 189 (43123-0189)
PHONE..................614 875-9023
James K Williams Jr, *President*
James K Williams III, *Corp Secy*
EMP: 80
SQ FT: 40,000
SALES (est): 31.3MM **Privately Held**
WEB: www.kirkwilliamsco.com
SIC: 1711 3564 3444 Mechanical contractor; warm air heating & air conditioning contractor; ventilation & duct work contractor; sheet metalwork; blowers & fans

(G-10441)
LOGITECH INC
6423 Seeds Rd (43123-9524)
PHONE..................614 871-2822
Kirk Wallace, *President*
David W Ritchie III, *Treasurer*
▲ EMP: 20
SQ FT: 32,400
SALES (est): 6MM **Privately Held**
SIC: 3535 5084 Conveyors & conveying equipment; conveyor systems

(G-10442)
LOLLIPOP STOP
4595 Hunting Creek Dr (43123-3636)
PHONE..................614 991-5192
EMP: 3
SALES (est): 159.8K **Privately Held**
SIC: 2064 Lollipops & other hard candy

(G-10443)
MAGIC DRAGON MACHINE INC
3451 Grant Ave (43123-2512)
PHONE..................614 539-8004
Richard Burket, *President*
EMP: 6
SQ FT: 4,000
SALES (est): 360K **Privately Held**
SIC: 3711 Automobile assembly, including specialty automobiles

(G-10444)
MERRILL CORPORATION
3400 Southpark Pl Ste H (43123-4857)
PHONE..................614 801-4700
Robert Cook, *Branch Mgr*
EMP: 150
SALES (corp-wide): 566.6MM **Privately Held**
SIC: 2711 Job printing & newspaper publishing combined
PA: Merrill Corporation
 1 Merrill Cir
 Saint Paul MN 55108
 651 646-4501

(G-10445)
MESSER LLC
1699 Feddern Ave (43123-1205)
PHONE..................614 539-2259
Judy Rogers, *Manager*
EMP: 7
SALES (corp-wide): 1.4B **Privately Held**
SIC: 2813 Industrial gases
HQ: Messer Llc
 200 Somerset Corporate
 Bridgewater NJ 08807
 908 464-8100

(G-10446)
MID OHIO SCREEN PRINT INC
4163 Kelnor Dr (43123-2960)
PHONE..................614 875-1774
Mike Haughn, *President*
Steven Haughn, *Treasurer*
EMP: 6
SQ FT: 18,000
SALES: 800K **Privately Held**
SIC: 2759 Screen printing

(G-10447)
MOHAWK INDUSTRIES INC
3565 Urbancrest Indus Dr (43123-1766)
PHONE..................800 837-3812
Gary Miller, *Branch Mgr*
EMP: 156
SALES (corp-wide): 9.9B **Publicly Held**
WEB: www.mohawkind.com
SIC: 2273 3253 Finishers of tufted carpets & rugs; smyrna carpets & rugs, machine woven; ceramic wall & floor tile
PA: Mohawk Industries, Inc.
 160 S Industrial Blvd
 Calhoun GA 30701
 706 629-7721

(G-10448)
MURRAY DISPLAY FIXTURES LTD
2300 Southwest Blvd (43123-4829)
PHONE..................614 875-1594
Todd Murray, *CEO*
Glenn Murray, *Vice Pres*
Jonathan Murray, *Vice Pres*
Kim Ellen Murray, *Treasurer*
EMP: 12 EST: 2006
SQ FT: 11,000
SALES: 1.7MM **Privately Held**
SIC: 2541 1751 Display fixtures, wood; cabinet building & installation

(G-10449)
NATIONAL WELDING & TANKER REPR
2036 Hendrix Dr (43123-1215)
PHONE..................614 875-3399
Bryan Baker, *President*

EMP: 9
SALES (est): 345.3K **Privately Held**
SIC: 7692 7699 7389 9621 Welding repair; tank repair & cleaning services; inspection & testing services; licensing, inspection: transportation facilities, services

(G-10450)
NATIONAL WELDING & TANKER REPR
2036 Hendrix Dr (43123-1215)
PHONE..................614 875-3399
John Watterson, *President*
Nicole Watterson, *Vice Pres*
EMP: 6
SALES (est): 310K **Privately Held**
SIC: 7692 Welding repair

(G-10451)
NEW WAVE PROSTHETICS INC
3454 Grant Ave (43123-2515)
PHONE..................614 782-2361
Victoria Lawson, *Treasurer*
EMP: 5 EST: 2014
SQ FT: 3,000
SALES (est): 536.1K **Privately Held**
SIC: 3842 Surgical appliances & supplies

(G-10452)
NEXUS VISION GROUP LLC
2156 Southwest Blvd (43123-1893)
PHONE..................866 492-6499
Jerry Shaw,
▲ EMP: 30
SALES (est): 4.9MM **Privately Held**
SIC: 3851 Eyeglasses, lenses & frames

(G-10453)
OH-LI COMMERCIAL CLEANING LLC
1905 Lake Crest Dr (43123-4895)
PHONE..................614 390-3628
Ray West, *Mng Member*
EMP: 5
SALES (est): 239.4K **Privately Held**
SIC: 3589 Commercial cleaning equipment

(G-10454)
OLDE HOME MARKET LLC
2517 Old Home Rd (43123-1773)
PHONE..................614 738-3975
Steven Garner, *CEO*
EMP: 4
SQ FT: 3,000
SALES (est): 138.7K **Privately Held**
SIC: 2051 Bakery: wholesale or wholesale/retail combined

(G-10455)
OWENS CORNING SALES LLC
3750 Brookham Dr Ste K (43123-4850)
PHONE..................614 539-0830
Anne Depaeew, *Manager*
EMP: 50 **Publicly Held**
WEB: www.owenscorning.com
SIC: 3296 Fiberglass insulation
HQ: Owens Corning Sales, Llc
 1 Owens Corning Pkwy
 Toledo OH 43659
 419 248-8000

(G-10456)
PARABELLUM ARMAMENT CO LLC
3142 Broadway Ste 200 (43123-1780)
PHONE..................614 557-5987
Andrew Edge, *Mng Member*
Dave Waldmann,
EMP: 5
SALES: 530K **Privately Held**
SIC: 3484 Machine guns or machine gun parts, 30 mm. & below

(G-10457)
POSSIBLE PLASTICS INC
1620 Feddern Ave Bldg B (43123-1200)
PHONE..................614 277-2100
Shawn Lind, *CEO*
Cheryl Lind, *President*
EMP: 4
SQ FT: 5,000

▲ = Import ▼ = Export
♦ = Import/Export

GEOGRAPHIC SECTION

Groveport - Franklin County (G-10483)

SALES (est): 542K Privately Held
WEB: www.possibleplastics.com
SIC: 3089 5046 Injection molding of plastics; store fixtures & display equipment

(G-10458)
PPG INDUSTRIES INC
Also Called: PPG 5539
2362 Stringtown Rd (43123-3927)
PHONE..................614 277-0620
Jeff Baker, *Manager*
EMP: 3
SALES (corp-wide): 15.3B Publicly Held
WEB: www.ppg.com
SIC: 2851 Paints & allied products
PA: Ppg Industries, Inc.
1 Ppg Pl
Pittsburgh PA 15272
412 434-3131

(G-10459)
PRESTRESS SERVICES INDS LLC
3350 Jackson Pike (43123-8875)
PHONE..................614 871-2900
Kevin Chesshir, *General Mgr*
EMP: 23
SQ FT: 1,000
SALES (est): 3MM
SALES (corp-wide): 91.7MM Privately Held
SIC: 3272 Prestressed concrete products
PA: Prestress Services Industries Llc
2250 N Hartford Ave
Columbus OH 43222
859 299-0461

(G-10460)
PROCTER & GAMBLE COMPANY
2200 Southwest Blvd (43123-2854)
PHONE..................410 527-5735
EMP: 205
SALES (corp-wide): 66.8B Publicly Held
WEB: www.pg.com
SIC: 2844 Deodorants, personal
PA: The Procter & Gamble Company
1 Procter And Gamble Plz
Cincinnati OH 45202
513 983-1100

(G-10461)
PVM INCORPORATED
3515 Grove City Rd (43123-3054)
PHONE..................614 871-0302
Gary Curry, *President*
EMP: 8
SQ FT: 10,000
SALES (est): 780K Privately Held
SIC: 3599 Machine shop, jobbing & repair

(G-10462)
RICHARDSON SUPPLY LTD
2080 Hardy Parkway St (43123-1214)
PHONE..................614 539-3033
Sharon Fisher, *CEO*
Jeffrey W Richardson, *President*
EMP: 6 EST: 1968
SALES (est): 1.5MM Privately Held
WEB: www.richardsonsupply.com
SIC: 2759 Screen printing

(G-10463)
RUBEX INC
Also Called: Edge Adhesives-Oh
3709 Grove City Rd (43123-3020)
PHONE..................614 875-6343
Dave Burger, *CEO*
▼ EMP: 13
SALES (est): 2.9MM Privately Held
SIC: 2891 Adhesives & sealants
PA: Edge Adhesives Holdings, Inc.
5117 Northeast Pkwy
Fort Worth TX 76106
817 232-2026

(G-10464)
S&T AUTOMOTIVE AMERICA LLC
3900 Gantz Rd (43123-4834)
PHONE..................614 782-9041
JW Park,
▲ EMP: 4
SQ FT: 175,000
SALES: 2MM Privately Held
SIC: 3089 Automotive parts, plastic

(G-10465)
SC SOLUTIONS INC
4119 Ashgrove Dr (43123-3377)
PHONE..................614 317-7119
Amanda J Moore, *CEO*
Sara A Dugan, *COO*
Carolina E Petri, *Risk Mgmt Dir*
EMP: 3
SALES (est): 1.5K Privately Held
WEB: www.scsbooks.com
SIC: 2731 2721 2741 Book publishing; periodicals: publishing & printing; technical papers: publishing & printing

(G-10466)
SHELLY MATERIALS INC
3300 Jackson Pike (43123-8875)
PHONE..................614 871-6704
Craig Ferguson, *Branch Mgr*
EMP: 6
SALES (corp-wide): 29.7B Privately Held
SIC: 3273 Ready-mixed concrete
HQ: Shelly Materials, Inc.
80 Park Dr
Thornville OH 43076
740 246-6315

(G-10467)
SHERWIN-WILLIAMS COMPANY
3875 Brookham Dr (43123-4827)
PHONE..................614 539-8456
Timothy Sandor, *Manager*
EMP: 20
SALES (corp-wide): 17.5B Publicly Held
WEB: www.sherwin.com
SIC: 5231 2851 Paint; wallcoverings; paints & allied products; varnishes; lacquer: bases, dopes, thinner
PA: The Sherwin-Williams Company
101 W Prospect Ave # 1020
Cleveland OH 44115
216 566-2000

(G-10468)
SIMMONS COMPANY
3960 Brookham Dr (43123-9741)
PHONE..................614 871-8088
Williamson Barry, *Principal*
EMP: 4 EST: 2010
SALES (est): 335.1K Privately Held
SIC: 2511 Wood bedroom furniture

(G-10469)
SNYDERS-LANCE INC
4000 Gantz Rd Ste E (43123-4844)
PHONE..................614 856-4616
Erroll Elliott, *Manager*
EMP: 4
SALES (corp-wide): 8.6B Publicly Held
WEB: www.lancesnacks.com
SIC: 2052 2064 Cookies; crackers, dry; soda crackers; candy bars, including chocolate covered bars; granola & muesli, bars & clusters
HQ: Snyder's-Lance, Inc.
13515 Balntyn Corp Pl
Charlotte NC 28277
704 554-1421

(G-10470)
SOUND COMMUNICATIONS INC
3474 Park St (43123-2530)
P.O. Box 1148 (43123-6148)
PHONE..................614 875-8500
Garry Stephenson, *President*
James Jacobs, *General Mgr*
Toni Vanhorn, *Vice Pres*
Travis Bell, *Project Mgr*
Kay Bish, *Accounts Mgr*
EMP: 17
SQ FT: 6,000
SALES (est): 4.3MM Privately Held
WEB: www.soundcommunications.com
SIC: 3669 7382 7338 Intercommunication systems, electric; security systems services; secretarial & court reporting

(G-10471)
TAYLOR COMMUNICATIONS INC
3125 Lewis Centre Way (43123-1784)
PHONE..................614 277-7500
Jeff Wise, *Branch Mgr*
Lori Fraley, *Manager*
Susan Keller, *Supervisor*
EMP: 134

SALES (corp-wide): 3.2B Privately Held
SIC: 2759 Commercial printing
HQ: Taylor Communications, Inc.
1725 Roe Crest Dr
North Mankato MN 56003
507 625-2828

(G-10472)
TAYLOR COMMUNICATIONS INC
3545 Urbancrest Indus (43123-1766)
PHONE..................937 221-3347
Wesley Thompson, *Manager*
EMP: 60
SALES (corp-wide): 3.2B Privately Held
WEB: www.stdreg.com
SIC: 2761 Manifold business forms
HQ: Taylor Communications, Inc.
1725 Roe Crest Dr
North Mankato MN 56003
507 625-2828

(G-10473)
TIGERPOLY MANUFACTURING INC
6231 Enterprise Pkwy (43123-9271)
PHONE..................614 871-0045
Seiji Shiga, *President*
Michael S Crane, *Principal*
Yasuhiko Tomita, *Principal*
Takeo Kitamura, *Business Mgr*
Tammi Cross, *Vice Pres*
▲ EMP: 350
SQ FT: 196,000
SALES (est): 81.5MM
SALES (corp-wide): 401.4MM Privately Held
SIC: 3089 3714 3621 3061 Blow molded finished plastic products; motor vehicle parts & accessories; motors & generators; mechanical rubber goods
PA: Tigers Polymer Corporation
1-4-1, Higashimachi, Shinsenri
Toyonaka OSK 560-0
668 341-551

(G-10474)
TMARZETTI COMPANY
Also Called: Marzetti Distribution Center
5800 N Meadows Dr (43123-8600)
PHONE..................614 277-3577
Patrick Hopkins, *Warehouse Mgr*
Joyce Decker, *Purch Mgr*
Jake Dean, *Research*
Shelba Jackson, *Human Res Mgr*
Mark Norman, *Branch Mgr*
EMP: 122
SALES (corp-wide): 1.2B Publicly Held
SIC: 4225 2035 General warehousing & storage; pickles, sauces & salad dressings
HQ: T.Marzetti Company
380 Polaris Pkwy Ste 400
Westerville OH 43082
614 846-2232

(G-10475)
TOOLTEX INC
6160 Seeds Rd (43123-8603)
PHONE..................614 539-3222
Paul Spurgeon, *President*
EMP: 15
SQ FT: 140,000
SALES (est): 4.3MM Privately Held
WEB: www.tooltex.com
SIC: 3559 Plastics working machinery

(G-10476)
TOSOH AMERICA INC (HQ)
3600 Gantz Rd (43123-1895)
PHONE..................614 539-8622
Jan Top, *President*
Dan Minard, *Supervisor*
▲ EMP: 350
SQ FT: 250,000
SALES (est): 215.4MM
SALES (corp-wide): 7.7B Privately Held
SIC: 5169 3564 5047 5052 Industrial chemicals; blowers & fans; diagnostic equipment; medical; coal & other minerals & ores
PA: Tosoh Corporation
3-8-2, Shiba
Minato-Ku TKY 105-0
354 275-103

(G-10477)
TOSOH SMD INC
2050 Southpark Pl (43123-4819)
PHONE..................614 875-7912
Jason Akers, *Manager*
EMP: 5
SALES (corp-wide): 7.7B Privately Held
SIC: 3499 Aerosol valves, metal
HQ: Tosoh Smd Inc.
3600 Gantz Rd
Grove City OH 43123
614 875-7912

(G-10478)
TOSOH SMD INC (DH)
3600 Gantz Rd (43123-1895)
PHONE..................614 875-7912
Marten Blazic, *President*
▲ EMP: 166
SQ FT: 250,000
SALES (est): 78.2MM
SALES (corp-wide): 7.7B Privately Held
WEB: www.tsmd.com
SIC: 3674 Semiconductors & related devices
HQ: Tosoh America, Inc.
3600 Gantz Rd
Grove City OH 43123
614 539-8622

(G-10479)
TURNER PRESSURE
3997 Thistlewood Dr (43123-9048)
PHONE..................614 871-7775
Dale Turner, *Owner*
EMP: 5 EST: 2006
SQ FT: 1,200
SALES (est): 319.1K Privately Held
SIC: 3822 Steam pressure controls, residential or commercial type

(G-10480)
Z M O COMPANY INC (PA)
Also Called: Z M O Oil
4188 Alkire Rd (43123-1004)
PHONE..................614 875-0230
Ronald Johnson, *President*
Don Schaffner, *Vice Pres*
Doris Johnson, *Treasurer*
Marie Schaffner, *Admin Sec*
EMP: 6
SALES: 768.6K Privately Held
SIC: 2834 Liniments

Groveport
Franklin County

(G-10481)
AMSTED INDUSTRIES INCORPORATED
Also Called: Griffin Wheel
3900 Bixby Rd (43125-9510)
PHONE..................614 836-2323
Joe Cuske, *Plant Mgr*
EMP: 181
SALES (corp-wide): 2.4B Privately Held
SIC: 3321 5088 3743 3714 Railroad car wheels & brake shoes, cast iron; railroad equipment & supplies; railroad equipment; motor vehicle parts & accessories
PA: Amsted Industries Incorporated
180 N Stetson Ave # 1800
Chicago IL 60601
312 645-1700

(G-10482)
AMSTED RAIL COMPANY INC
3900 Bixby Rd (43125-9510)
PHONE..................614 836-2323
EMP: 14
SALES (corp-wide): 2.4B Privately Held
SIC: 3743 Railroad equipment
HQ: Amsted Rail Company, Inc.
311 S Wacker Dr Ste 5300
Chicago IL 60606

(G-10483)
AS AMERICA INC
Also Called: American Standard Brands
6600 Port Rd Ste 200 (43125-9129)
PHONE..................614 497-9384
Joe Coleman, *Manager*
Kendra Mahon, *Supervisor*

Groveport - Franklin County (G-10484)   GEOGRAPHIC SECTION

EMP: 125
SQ FT: 1,000,000
SALES (corp-wide): 15.6B **Privately Held**
SIC: 3432 Plumbing fixture fittings & trim
HQ: As America, Inc.
1 Centennial Ave Ste 101
Piscataway NJ 08854

(G-10484)
BECTON DICKINSON AND COMPANY
Also Called: Carefusion
2727 London Groveport Rd (43125-9304)
PHONE 858 617-4272
EMP: 3
SALES (est): 564.5K **Privately Held**
SIC: 3841 Surgical & medical instruments

(G-10485)
BELL OHIO INC
6300 Commerce Center Dr (43125-1183)
PHONE 605 332-6721
Benjamin Graham, *President*
EMP: 10 **EST:** 2015
SALES: 12MM
SALES (corp-wide): 70.3MM **Privately Held**
SIC: 2657 Folding paperboard boxes
PA: Bell Incorporated
617 W Algonquin St
Sioux Falls SD 57104
605 332-6721

(G-10486)
C & R INC (PA)
5600 Clyde Moore Dr (43125-1081)
PHONE 614 497-1130
Ronald E Murphy, *President*
Phillip Lee Mc Kitrick, *Vice Pres*
Christina M Murphy, *Treasurer*
EMP: 47
SALES (est): 9.7MM **Privately Held**
WEB: www.crproducts.com
SIC: 3444 7692 3443 3312 Sheet metal specialties, not stamped; welding repair; fabricated plate work (boiler shop); blast furnaces & steel mills

(G-10487)
CAKE DECOR
607 Main St (43125-1420)
PHONE 614 836-5533
Danielle Saunders,
EMP: 6
SALES: 140K **Privately Held**
SIC: 2064 7999 5999 Candy & other confectionery products; cake or pastry decorating instruction; cake decorating supplies

(G-10488)
CREATIVE TOOL & DIE
244 Main St (43125-1124)
PHONE 614 836-0080
James Newman Jr, *Partner*
Anita Raisley, *Partner*
EMP: 6
SQ FT: 2,600
SALES (est): 764K **Privately Held**
WEB: www.creativetooldie.com
SIC: 3599 Machine shop, jobbing & repair

(G-10489)
FLOOD HELIARC INC
4181 Venture Pl (43125-9207)
P.O. Box 237 (43125-0237)
PHONE 614 835-3929
Robert Flood, *President*
Suzanne Flood, *Corp Secy*
EMP: 10
SQ FT: 7,000
SALES: 1.2MM **Privately Held**
WEB: www.floodheliarc.com
SIC: 3444 3613 3469 Sheet metal specialties, not stamped; switchgear & switchboard apparatus; metal stampings

(G-10490)
FLUVITEX USA INC
6510 Pontius Rd (43125-7505)
PHONE 614 610-1199
Mark Roth, *CEO*
EMP: 3
SQ FT: 123,588

SALES (est): 23.5MM
SALES (corp-wide): 1.6MM **Privately Held**
SIC: 2392 Blankets, comforters & beddings
HQ: Masias Maquinaria SI
Calle Major De Santa Magdalena 1
Sant Joan Les Fonts 17857
972 293-150

(G-10491)
FRANK BRUNCKHORST COMPANY LLC
2225 Spiegel Dr (43125-9036)
PHONE 614 662-5300
Alexander Morris, *Principal*
EMP: 8
SALES (est): 4.7MM **Privately Held**
SIC: 5142 2013 Meat, frozen: packaged; frozen meats from purchased meat

(G-10492)
FRANKLIN EQUIPMENT LLC (PA)
4141 Hamilton Square Blvd (43125-9084)
PHONE 614 228-2014
Tony Repeta, *COO*
Joseph Moore, *Foreman/Supr*
Lori Johnson, *Controller*
Josh Kemmerer, *Sales Staff*
David Powell, *Sales Staff*
EMP: 24
SQ FT: 20,000
SALES (est): 50.2MM **Privately Held**
SIC: 5083 3524 Tractors, agricultural; lawn & garden equipment; cultivators (garden tractor equipment)

(G-10493)
HOME CITY ICE COMPANY
4505 S Hamilton Rd (43125-9416)
PHONE 614 836-2877
Tony Bakes, *Branch Mgr*
EMP: 50
SQ FT: 12,000
SALES (corp-wide): 232.5MM **Privately Held**
WEB: www.homecityice.com
SIC: 5199 5999 2097 Ice, manufactured or natural; ice; manufactured ice
PA: The Home City Ice Company
6045 Bridgetown Rd Ste 1
Cincinnati OH 45248
513 574-1800

(G-10494)
INNOVTIVE CRTIVE SOLUTIONS LLC
Also Called: I C S
5835 Green Pointe Dr S B (43125-2000)
PHONE 614 491-9638
Bob Pushay, *Mng Member*
EMP: 38
SALES (est): 1.2MM **Privately Held**
SIC: 2759 7336 Screen printing; commercial art & graphic design

(G-10495)
IOSIL ENERGY CORPORATION
5700 Green Pointe Dr N (43125-1082)
PHONE 614 295-8680
Dr Sudheer Pimputkar, *CEO*
Dr Karthik Balakrishnan, *Senior VP*
Geoffrey Flagg, *CFO*
EMP: 10 **EST:** 2010
SALES (est): 1.3MM **Privately Held**
SIC: 3433 Mfg Heating Equipment-Non-electric

(G-10496)
IRONMAN METALWORKS LLC
250 Lowery Ct Ste A (43125-9346)
PHONE 614 907-6629
Andrew Gussler, *Mng Member*
EMP: 4
SQ FT: 5,000
SALES (est): 288.4K **Privately Held**
SIC: 3443 Tanks for tank trucks, metal plate

(G-10497)
KOMAR INDUSTRIES INC (PA)
4425 Marketing Pl (43125-9556)
PHONE 614 836-2366
Larry E Koenig, *President*
Debra Koenig, *Vice Pres*

Mark Koenig, *Vice Pres*
◆ **EMP:** 50
SQ FT: 58,000
SALES (est): 8.8MM **Privately Held**
WEB: www.komarindustries.com
SIC: 3423 3523 3531 3567 Hand & edge tools; farm machinery & equipment; construction machinery; industrial furnaces & ovens; sewage & water treatment equipment

(G-10498)
KRAFT ELECTRICAL CONTG INC
4407 Professional Pkwy (43125-9228)
PHONE 614 836-9300
EMP: 36
SALES (corp-wide): 13.4MM **Privately Held**
SIC: 4813 3699 Telephone communication, except radio; electrical equipment & supplies
PA: Kraft Electrical Contracting, Inc.
5710 Hillside Ave
Cincinnati OH 45233
513 467-0500

(G-10499)
KUBOTA TRACTOR CORPORATION
6300 At One Kubota Way (43125-1186)
PHONE 614 835-3800
Ted Pederson, *General Mgr*
EMP: 13
SALES (corp-wide): 16.4B **Privately Held**
SIC: 3531 Construction machinery
HQ: Kubota Tractor Corporation
1000 Kubota Dr
Grapevine TX 76051
817 756-1171

(G-10500)
KURTZ BROS INC
Also Called: Branch 300
2850 Rohr Rd (43125-9311)
P.O. Box 207, Westerville (43086-0207)
PHONE 614 491-0868
Bonnie Straight, *Manager*
EMP: 20
SALES (corp-wide): 46.2MM **Privately Held**
WEB: www.kurtz-bros.com
SIC: 1241 5261 Coal mining services; top soil
PA: Kurtz Bros., Inc.
6415 Granger Rd
Independence OH 44131
216 986-7000

(G-10501)
LOMAR ENTERPRISES INC
Also Called: Ecc Company
5905 Green Pointe Dr S G (43125-2007)
PHONE 614 409-9104
Lou Onders, *President*
Mark Molnar, *Treasurer*
EMP: 15
SQ FT: 10,000
SALES: 1.8MM **Privately Held**
WEB: www.ecccco.com
SIC: 3825 3544 Test equipment for electronic & electrical circuits; special dies, tools, jigs & fixtures

(G-10502)
MANNINGS USA
351 Lowery Ct Ste 3 (43125-9344)
PHONE 614 836-0021
Scott Weese, *Principal*
EMP: 4
SALES (est): 109.9K **Privately Held**
SIC: 3398 Metal heat treating

(G-10503)
MCGILL AIRFLOW LLC (DH)
1 Mission Park (43125-1149)
PHONE 614 829-1200
James D McGill, *President*
John Montell, *Vice Pres*
▼ **EMP:** 2
SQ FT: 13,000
SALES (est): 32.9MM
SALES (corp-wide): 67.7MM **Privately Held**
WEB: www.mcgillairflow.com
SIC: 3444 Ducts, sheet metal

HQ: United Mcgill Corporation
1 Mission Park
Groveport OH 43125
614 829-1200

(G-10504)
MCGILL CORPORATION (PA)
1 Mission Park (43125-1149)
PHONE 614 829-1200
James D McGill, *Ch of Bd*
Jayne F McGill, *Admin Sec*
◆ **EMP:** 10
SQ FT: 13,000
SALES (est): 67.7MM **Privately Held**
WEB: www.themcgillcorp.com
SIC: 3564 3444 5169 Precipitators, electrostatic; air purification equipment; ducts, sheet metal; sealants

(G-10505)
MENASHA PACKAGING COMPANY LLC
2842 Spiegel Dr (43125-9012)
PHONE 740 773-8204
Robert Krajci, *Manager*
EMP: 18
SALES (corp-wide): 1.7B **Privately Held**
SIC: 2653 Boxes, corrugated: made from purchased materials
HQ: Menasha Packaging Company, Llc
1645 Bergstrom Rd
Neenah WI 54956
920 751-1000

(G-10506)
METAL MAN INC
4681 Homer Ohio Ln Ste A (43125-9231)
PHONE 614 830-0968
Robert Posey, *President*
Ken Gilkerson, *Vice Pres*
EMP: 6
SALES (est): 854.6K **Privately Held**
SIC: 3441 Fabricated structural metal

(G-10507)
NIFCO AMERICA CORPORATION
4485 S Hamilton Rd (43125-9334)
PHONE 614 836-8691
Allen Hofmann, *Principal*
EMP: 250
SALES (corp-wide): 2.5B **Privately Held**
SIC: 3089 Automotive parts, plastic
HQ: Nifco America Corporation
8015 Dove Pkwy
Canal Winchester OH 43110
614 920-6800

(G-10508)
PEERLESS LASER PROCESSORS INC
4353 Directors Blvd (43125-9504)
PHONE 614 836-5790
Tim Gase, *President*
Paul Duclos, *Sales Staff*
EMP: 45
SQ FT: 35,000
SALES (est): 4.2MM
SALES (corp-wide): 22.7MM **Privately Held**
SIC: 3699 Laser welding, drilling & cutting equipment
PA: The Peerless Saw Company
4353 Directors Blvd
Groveport OH 43125
614 836-5790

(G-10509)
PEERLESS SAW COMPANY (PA)
4353 Directors Blvd (43125-9350)
PHONE 614 836-5790
Tim Gase, *Owner*
Ken Lloyd, *Vice Pres*
Eric Beal, *Manager*
▲ **EMP:** 110 **EST:** 1931
SQ FT: 30,000
SALES (est): 22.7MM **Privately Held**
SIC: 3425 3541 Saw blades for hand or power saws; machine tools, metal cutting type

(G-10510)
PLAN B TOYS LTD
4036 London Lancaster Rd (43125-9202)
PHONE 614 751-6605
EMP: 3

GEOGRAPHIC SECTION

Hamilton - Butler County (G-10539)

SALES (est): 210K **Privately Held**
SIC: 3069 Mfg Toys And Statues

(G-10511)
SHOCKAKHAN EXPRESS LLC
4953 Bixby Ridge Dr W (43125-1167)
PHONE..................................614 432-3133
Tony Channakhon, *Principal*
EMP: 4
SALES (est): 547.8K **Privately Held**
SIC: 2655 Fiber shipping & mailing containers

(G-10512)
SKULD LLC
4324 Bennington Creek Ln (43125-9088)
PHONE..................................330 423-7339
Sarah Jordan, *Mng Member*
Mark Debruin,
Kalisata Jordan-Debruin,
EMP: 3 EST: 2015
SALES (est): 188.2K **Privately Held**
SIC: 3324 3321 3365 Steel investment foundries; gray & ductile iron foundries; aluminum foundries

(G-10513)
STABER INDUSTRIES INC
4800 Homer Ohio Ln (43125-9390)
PHONE..................................614 836-5995
William Staber, *President*
▲ EMP: 35
SQ FT: 55,000
SALES (est): 8MM **Privately Held**
WEB: www.staber.com
SIC: 3633 3444 Household laundry equipment; sheet metalwork

(G-10514)
TIMKEN COMPANY
3782 Potomac St (43125-9472)
PHONE..................................614 836-3337
James Ferguson, *Branch Mgr*
EMP: 15
SALES (corp-wide): 3.5B **Publicly Held**
SIC: 3562 Ball & roller bearings
PA: The Timken Company
4500 Mount Pleasant St Nw
North Canton OH 44720
234 262-3000

(G-10515)
TRANE US INC
6600 Port Rd Ste 200 (43125-9129)
PHONE..................................614 497-6300
Sean Strane, *Branch Mgr*
EMP: 150 **Privately Held**
SIC: 3585 Refrigeration & heating equipment
HQ: Trane U.S. Inc.
3600 Pammel Creek Rd
La Crosse WI 54601
608 787-2000

(G-10516)
UNITED MCGILL CORPORATION (HQ)
1 Mission Park (43125-1100)
PHONE..................................614 829-1200
James D McGill, *President*
Patrick Brooks, *QC Dir*
Jayne F McGill, *Admin Sec*
▲ EMP: 30 EST: 1951
SQ FT: 13,000
SALES (est): 67.7MM **Privately Held**
WEB: www.unitedmcgill.com
SIC: 3444 3564 5169 3567 Ducts, sheet metal; precipitators, electrostatic; air purification equipment; sealants; industrial furnaces & ovens; adhesives & sealants
PA: The Mcgill Corporation
1 Mission Park
Groveport OH 43125
614 829-1200

(G-10517)
XEROX CORPORATION C/O GENCO
6290 Opus Dr (43125-9633)
PHONE..................................503 582-6059
▲ EMP: 5
SALES (est): 854.9K **Privately Held**
SIC: 3861 Photographic equipment & supplies

Grover Hill
Paulding County

(G-10518)
FABSTAR TANKS INC
20302 Road 48 (45849-9324)
PHONE..................................419 587-3639
Mark Sinn, *President*
EMP: 18
SALES (est): 1.5MM **Privately Held**
SIC: 3443 7389 Fuel tanks (oil, gas, etc.); metal plate;

(G-10519)
R & L TRUSS INC
17985 Road 60 (45849-9400)
P.O. Box 130 (45849-0130)
PHONE..................................419 587-3440
Ron Treece, *CEO*
Larry Pressler, *President*
EMP: 10
SQ FT: 3,360
SALES (est): 1.6MM **Privately Held**
WEB: www.rltruss.com
SIC: 2439 Trusses, wooden roof

Guysville
Athens County

(G-10520)
ROBERT ASHCRAFT
4350 Bethany Ridge Rd (45735-9564)
PHONE..................................740 667-3690
Robert Ashcraft, *Principal*
EMP: 3
SALES (est): 232.6K **Privately Held**
SIC: 2411 Logging

Gypsum
Ottawa County

(G-10521)
UNITED STATES GYPSUM COMPANY
121 S Lake St (43433)
PHONE..................................419 734-3161
P V Savu, *Plant Mgr*
Bill Steleger, *Systems Staff*
EMP: 350
SALES (corp-wide): 3.3B **Publicly Held**
WEB: www.usg.com
SIC: 3275 Gypsum products
HQ: United States Gypsum Company
550 W Adams St Ste 1300
Chicago IL 60661
312 606-4000

Hamden
Vinton County

(G-10522)
CORBETT R CAUDILL CHIPPING INC
35887 State Route 324 (45634-8824)
PHONE..................................740 596-5984
Corbett R Caudill, *President*
Myrta Caudill, *Admin Sec*
EMP: 15 EST: 1971
SALES (est): 2.8MM **Privately Held**
SIC: 3546 4212 Hammers, portable: electric or pneumatic, chipping, etc.; local trucking, without storage

(G-10523)
INDUSTRIAL TIMBER & LAND CO
35748 State Route 93 (45634-8872)
PHONE..................................740 596-5294
Greg McKinniss, *Executive*
EMP: 9 EST: 2007
SALES (est): 1.3MM **Privately Held**
SIC: 2421 Sawmills & planing mills, general

(G-10524)
SANDS HILL COAL HAULING CO INC (PA)
38701 State Route 160 (45634)
PHONE..................................740 384-4211
Alan Arthur, *President*
EMP: 142
SQ FT: 3,500
SALES (est): 7.2MM **Privately Held**
SIC: 1221 Strip mining, bituminous

(G-10525)
SANDS HILL MINING LLC
38701 State Route 160 (45634)
PHONE..................................740 384-4211
Steve Garson,
EMP: 11
SALES (est): 889.2K **Privately Held**
SIC: 1429 Grits mining (crushed stone)

Hamilton
Butler County

(G-10526)
7 ROWE COURT PROPERTIES LLC
Also Called: Bren-Ko Patterns
7 Rowe Ct (45015-2211)
PHONE..................................513 874-7236
Debbie Johnson, *Corp Secy*
Randy Johnson, *Mng Member*
EMP: 5
SQ FT: 85,000
SALES (est): 1.2MM **Privately Held**
SIC: 3543 3089 Industrial patterns; air mattresses, plastic

(G-10527)
A & L MACHINE TOOL
3080 Darrtown Rd (45013-9331)
PHONE..................................513 863-2662
Steve Miller, *Owner*
EMP: 4
SQ FT: 1,500
SALES: 65K **Privately Held**
SIC: 3599 Machine shop, jobbing & repair

(G-10528)
ACCESS ENVELOPE INC
2348 Pleasant Ave (45015-1502)
PHONE..................................513 889-0888
Karen Testerman, *President*
EMP: 12
SALES (est): 500K **Privately Held**
SIC: 2677 Envelopes

(G-10529)
ADVANCED DRAINAGE SYSTEMS INC
ADS Hancor
2650 Hamilton Eaton Rd (45011-9502)
P.O. Box 718 (45012-0718)
PHONE..................................513 863-1384
Nathan Williams, *Branch Mgr*
EMP: 100
SALES (corp-wide): 1.3B **Publicly Held**
WEB: www.ads-pipe.com
SIC: 3084 Plastics pipe
PA: Advanced Drainage Systems, Inc.
4640 Trueman Blvd
Hilliard OH 43026
614 658-0050

(G-10530)
AIR ONE JET CENTER
2808 Bobmeyer Rd (45015-1308)
PHONE..................................513 867-9500
EMP: 3 EST: 2010
SALES (est): 130K **Privately Held**
SIC: 3721 Mfg Aircraft

(G-10531)
ALECO MACHINE LLC
233 N Martin L King Blvd (45011)
PHONE..................................513 894-6400
Bernard A Lemieux,
EMP: 3
SALES (est): 269.3K **Privately Held**
SIC: 3599 Machine shop, jobbing & repair

(G-10532)
AMERICAN QUALITY MOLDS LLC
2275 Millville Ave Ste E (45013-4256)
PHONE..................................513 276-7345
Jimmy A Hitchcock, *Mng Member*
EMP: 5
SALES (est): 719.1K **Privately Held**
SIC: 3465 Moldings or trim, automobile: stamped metal

(G-10533)
AMERICAN RUGGED ENCLOSURES (PA)
4 Standen Dr (45015-2208)
PHONE..................................513 942-3004
Raymond J Casey, *President*
Shawn Beckman, *Corp Secy*
EMP: 12
SQ FT: 13,500
SALES (est): 2MM **Privately Held**
WEB: www.areinc.com
SIC: 3469 Electronic enclosures, stamped or pressed metal

(G-10534)
AMERICAN TOOL WORKS INC
160 Hancock Ave (45011-4351)
PHONE..................................513 844-6363
Scott Lorance, *Manager*
EMP: 16
SALES (est): 1.1MM **Privately Held**
SIC: 3599 Machine shop, jobbing & repair
PA: American Tool Works, Inc.
160 Hancock Ave
Hamilton OH 45011

(G-10535)
AMERICAN TOOL WORKS INC (PA)
Also Called: ATW
160 Hancock Ave (45011-4351)
PHONE..................................513 844-6363
Michael Lorance, *President*
EMP: 19
SALES (est): 2.5MM **Privately Held**
SIC: 3599 Machine shop, jobbing & repair

(G-10536)
ART METALS GROUP INC
3795 Symmes Rd (45015-1373)
PHONE..................................513 942-8800
Marlon Bailey, *CEO*
Robert McCoy, *CFO*
▲ EMP: 60 EST: 1946
SQ FT: 40,000
SALES (est): 19.9MM **Privately Held**
SIC: 3469 Metal stampings

(G-10537)
BARNCRAFT STORAGE BUILDINGS
2527 Millville Shandon Rd (45013-8209)
PHONE..................................513 738-5654
Dennis Donovan, *Owner*
EMP: 3
SQ FT: 1,440
SALES (est): 378.1K **Privately Held**
SIC: 3448 1542 Farm & utility buildings; agricultural building contractors

(G-10538)
BAXTER HOLDINGS INC
3370 Port Union Rd (45014-4223)
PHONE..................................513 860-3593
Robert Kelly, *CEO*
EMP: 20
SQ FT: 32,000
SALES (est): 3.8MM **Privately Held**
WEB: www.baxterprecast.com
SIC: 3272 3443 Steps, prefabricated concrete; slabs, crossing: concrete; concrete products, precast; burial vaults, concrete or precast terrazzo; fabricated plate work (boiler shop)

(G-10539)
BELL BURIAL VAULT CO
804 Belle Ave (45015-1151)
PHONE..................................513 896-9044
Brian Bell, *Owner*
EMP: 5
SQ FT: 5,000

Hamilton - Butler County (G-10540) GEOGRAPHIC SECTION

SALES: 450K **Privately Held**
SIC: 3281 3272 5087 Burial vaults, stone; burial vaults, concrete or precast terrazzo; concrete burial vaults & boxes

(G-10540)
BETHART ENTERPRISES INC (PA)
Also Called: Bethart Printing Services
531 Main St (45013-3221)
PHONE.................513 863-6161
Richard Bethart, *President*
EMP: 14 EST: 1974
SQ FT: 4,400
SALES (est): 1.5MM **Privately Held**
SIC: 2752 7334 Commercial printing, offset; photocopying & duplicating services

(G-10541)
BISON USA CORP
5325 Muhlhauser Rd (45011-9349)
PHONE.................513 713-0513
EMP: 7
SALES (est): 89.1K
SALES (corp-wide): 19MM **Privately Held**
SIC: 8711 3999 3549 Engineering services; atomizers, toiletry; metalworking machinery
PA: Bison Chucks S A
  Ul. Mysliwska 13
  Bialystok 15-56

(G-10542)
BMC OF BARFIELD INC
3501 Symmes Rd (45015-1369)
PHONE.................513 860-4455
Mike Dill, *Principal*
EMP: 8
SALES (est): 1MM **Privately Held**
SIC: 3999 Manufacturing industries

(G-10543)
BROWN DAVE PRODUCTS INC
4560 Layhigh Rd (45013-9200)
PHONE.................513 738-1576
David Brown, *President*
EMP: 12 EST: 1979
SQ FT: 4,000
SALES (est): 1.4MM **Privately Held**
SIC: 3944 7371 Airplane models, toy & hobby; custom computer programming services

(G-10544)
CENTER MASS DEFENSE
4421 Hamilton Cleves Rd (45013-8688)
PHONE.................513 314-8401
Faron Addis, *President*
EMP: 3
SALES (est): 278K **Privately Held**
SIC: 3812 Defense systems & equipment

(G-10545)
CIMA INC
1010h Eaton Ave (45013-4640)
PHONE.................513 382-8976
Thomas Uhl, *Principal*
EMP: 20 EST: 1994
SALES (est): 578.4K **Privately Held**
SIC: 2449 2448 Wood containers; pallets, wood

(G-10546)
CIMA INC
1010 Eaton Ave (45013-4640)
PHONE.................513 382-8976
Tom Uhl, *President*
▲ **EMP:** 30
SALES (est): 4.8MM **Privately Held**
WEB: www.cima-kdt.com
SIC: 3561 7363 2449 Industrial pumps & parts; temporary help service; rectangular boxes & crates, wood

(G-10547)
CONNAUGHTON WLDG & FENCE LLC
440 Hensel Pl (45011-1702)
PHONE.................513 867-0230
Robert Singhoffer,
David Singhoffer,
EMP: 6
SQ FT: 5,000

SALES (est): 529.6K **Privately Held**
SIC: 1799 7692 3469 Fence construction; welding repair; ornamental metal stampings

(G-10548)
CONNECTOR MANUFACTURING CO (DH)
Also Called: C M C
3501 Symmes Rd (45015-1369)
PHONE.................513 860-4455
William J Boehm, *Ch of Bd*
Joe Klenk, *President*
Bob Batchelor, *Division Mgr*
Frank Privett, *Senior VP*
Alan Beck, *Vice Pres*
▲ **EMP:** 172
SQ FT: 103,000
SALES (est): 52.3MM
SALES (corp-wide): 4.4B **Publicly Held**
WEB: www.cmclugs.com
SIC: 3643 Electric connectors

(G-10549)
CUSC INTERNATIONAL LTD
3 Standen Dr (45015-2209)
PHONE.................513 881-2000
Caroline McIntosh, *CEO*
Agnes Parks, *Manager*
▲ **EMP:** 9
SALES (est): 757.1K **Privately Held**
SIC: 2299 4225 7389 Tops & top processing, manmade or other fiber; warehousing, self-storage; packaging & labeling services
PA: Bajoria Holdings Private Limited
  Mcleod House, 3, Netaji Subhas Road
  Kolkata WB 70000

(G-10550)
D B S STINLESS STL FABRICATORS
21 Standen Dr (45015-2209)
PHONE.................513 856-9600
Nick Bauer, *General Mgr*
Russell Bowermaster, *Shareholder*
▲ **EMP:** 9
SQ FT: 12,000
SALES (est): 1.5MM **Privately Held**
SIC: 3444 Restaurant sheet metalwork

(G-10551)
DURO DYNE MIDWEST CORP
3825 Symmes Rd (45015-1376)
PHONE.................513 870-6000
Randall Hinden, *President*
William Watman, *Corp Secy*
▲ **EMP:** 290
SQ FT: 51,000
SALES (est): 47.2MM
SALES (corp-wide): 125.5MM **Privately Held**
SIC: 3585 3564 3498 3469 Air conditioning equipment, complete; ventilating fans; industrial or commercial; fabricated pipe & fittings; metal stampings; sheet metalwork; heating equipment, except electric
PA: Dyne Duro National Corp
  81 Spence St
  Bay Shore NY 11706

(G-10552)
DYNAMIC CONTROL NORTH AMER INC (PA)
3042 Symmes Rd (45015-1331)
PHONE.................513 860-5094
Scott Whitaker, *President*
Beth Maranda, *Manager*
▲ **EMP:** 16
SQ FT: 15,000
SALES (est): 3.6MM **Privately Held**
WEB: www.dynamat.com
SIC: 3443 Baffles

(G-10553)
ELLISON TECHNOLOGIES INC
5333 Muhlhauser Rd (45011-9349)
PHONE.................513 874-2736
EMP: 9
SALES (corp-wide): 45.9B **Privately Held**
SIC: 3545 Machine tool attachments & accessories

HQ: Ellison Technologies, Inc.
  9912 Pioneer Blvd
  Santa Fe Springs CA 90670
  562 949-8311

(G-10554)
ELRA INDUSTRIES INC
550 S Erie Hwy (45011-4346)
PHONE.................513 868-6228
Eldon Smith, *President*
EMP: 8
SQ FT: 13,000
SALES: 750K **Privately Held**
WEB: www.elra.com
SIC: 3089 Injection molding of plastics

(G-10555)
EVAN RAGOUZIS CO
4 Standen Dr (45015-2208)
PHONE.................513 242-5900
Evan Ragouzis, *Owner*
EMP: 2
SQ FT: 8,464
SALES (est): 1MM **Privately Held**
SIC: 3272 Building materials, except block or brick: concrete

(G-10556)
FAB SHOP INC
1520 Bender Ave (45011-4075)
PHONE.................513 860-1332
Pamela Walden, *President*
Joseph Pate Jr, *President*
Annette H Pate, *Corp Secy*
Pamela Pate, *Vice Pres*
EMP: 3 EST: 1959
SQ FT: 12,000
SALES (est): 360K **Privately Held**
SIC: 3441 Fabricated structural metal

(G-10557)
FAIRFIELD LICENSE CENTER INC
530 Wessel Dr Ste L (45014-3651)
PHONE.................513 829-6224
Pamela Bock, *Principal*
EMP: 5
SALES (est): 482.8K **Privately Held**
SIC: 3469 Automobile license tags, stamped metal

(G-10558)
FIN PAN INC (PA)
3255 Symmes Rd (45015-1361)
P.O. Box 411 (45012-0411)
PHONE.................513 870-9200
Elisa Schafer, *President*
Louis A Beimford, *Principal*
Theodore Clear, *Treasurer*
Jason Clear, *Sales Staff*
▲ **EMP:** 18
SQ FT: 40,000
SALES (est): 8.5MM **Privately Held**
WEB: www.finpan.com
SIC: 3272 Concrete products, precast

(G-10559)
FUTURE FINISHES INC
40 Standen Dr (45015-2210)
PHONE.................513 860-0020
Daniel L Brown, *President*
Alison Fossette, *Production*
Barbara Brennan, *Financial Exec*
Teresa Brennan, *Office Mgr*
Renee Pellman, *Office Mgr*
EMP: 30
SQ FT: 25,000
SALES (est): 4.1MM **Privately Held**
WEB: www.futurefinishes.com
SIC: 3471 Plating of metals or formed products

(G-10560)
G & J PEPSI-COLA BOTTLERS INC
2580 Bobmeyer Rd (45015-1394)
PHONE.................513 896-3700
Don Chalfant, *Branch Mgr*
EMP: 145
SQ FT: 50,000
SALES (corp-wide): 418.3MM **Privately Held**
WEB: www.gjpepsi.com
SIC: 2086 Carbonated soft drinks, bottled & canned

PA: G & J Pepsi-Cola Bottlers Inc
  9435 Waterstone Blvd # 390
  Cincinnati OH 45249
  513 785-6060

(G-10561)
G & M METAL PRODUCTS INC
1001 Fairview Ave (45015-1629)
PHONE.................513 863-3353
Charles Garrod, *President*
Dawn Garrod, *Corp Secy*
William D Moore, *Vice Pres*
EMP: 5 EST: 1965
SQ FT: 6,800
SALES (est): 770.2K **Privately Held**
SIC: 3469 3499 Stamping metal for the trade; machine bases, metal

(G-10562)
G L INDUSTRIES INC
Also Called: Climax Packaging Machinery
25 Standen Dr (45015-2209)
P.O. Box 18097, Fairfield (45018-0097)
PHONE.................513 874-1233
William P George, *President*
EMP: 20
SQ FT: 18,000
SALES (est): 5.7MM **Privately Held**
WEB: www.climaxpackaging.com
SIC: 3565 7389 Packaging machinery; packaging & labeling services

(G-10563)
G R K MANUFACTURING CO INC
1200 Dayton St (45011-4220)
PHONE.................513 863-3131
Gary Kilday, *President*
Eileen K Kilday, *Corp Secy*
David S Kilday, *Vice Pres*
Lori E Kilday, *Vice Pres*
▲ **EMP:** 30 EST: 1917
SQ FT: 100,000
SALES (est): 3.9MM **Privately Held**
WEB: www.grkmfg.com
SIC: 2511 2499 2512 Wood household furniture; decorative wood & woodwork; upholstered household furniture

(G-10564)
GLOBAL HEALTH SERVICES INC
901 Boyle Rd (45013-1815)
PHONE.................513 777-8111
Beth Townsend, *CEO*
Dave Townsend, *Vice Pres*
EMP: 4
SALES (est): 557.8K **Privately Held**
WEB: www.ghs-inc.com
SIC: 2836 Vaccines

(G-10565)
GVS INDUSTRIES INC
Also Called: Cadillac Papers
1030 Beissinger Rd (45013-9322)
PHONE.................513 851-3606
Sharon Sheppard, *Office Mgr*
Donald Gillespie II, *Shareholder*
Ronald Green, *Shareholder*
EMP: 6
SALES (est): 831.5K **Privately Held**
SIC: 2621 3861 5113 5112 Specialty or chemically treated papers; toners, prepared photographic (not made in chemical plants); industrial & personal service paper; stationery & office supplies; printing & writing paper

(G-10566)
HACKER WOOD PRODUCTS INC
2144 Jackson Rd (45011-9534)
PHONE.................513 737-4462
Chris Hacker, *President*
EMP: 6 EST: 1998
SQ FT: 2,200
SALES (est): 233.5K **Privately Held**
SIC: 2448 Wood pallets & skids

(G-10567)
HAMILTON BRASS & ALUM CASTINGS
706 S 8th St (45011-3753)
P.O. Box 657 (45012-0657)
PHONE.................513 867-0400
Tom Koehler, *President*
EMP: 20 EST: 1918
SQ FT: 25,000

▲ = Import ▼ = Export
◆ = Import/Export

SALES (est): 4.1MM **Privately Held**
WEB: www.hamilton-litestat.com
SIC: 3364 3321 Brass & bronze die-castings; gray & ductile iron foundries

(G-10568)
HAMILTON CUSTOM MOLDING INC
1365 Shuler Ave (45011-4567)
PHONE..........................513 844-6643
Ed White, *President*
Dorothy White, *Corp Secy*
EMP: 7
SQ FT: 20,000
SALES: 700K **Privately Held**
WEB: www.hamiltoncm.com
SIC: 3089 3544 Plastic containers, except foam; special dies, tools, jigs & fixtures

(G-10569)
HANOVER WINERY INC
2121 Morman Rd (45013-9375)
PHONE..........................513 304-9702
Elizabeth McDonald, *Principal*
EMP: 3
SALES (est): 272.8K **Privately Held**
SIC: 2084 Wines

(G-10570)
HARTFORD STEEL SALES
6 S 2nd St Ste 214 (45011-2862)
P.O. Box 1236 (45012-1236)
PHONE..........................513 275-1744
Scott Hartford, *Mng Member*
EMP: 1
SQ FT: 100
SALES: 2MM **Privately Held**
SIC: 3449 Bars, concrete reinforcing: fabricated steel

(G-10571)
IMI-IRVING MATERIALS INC
600 Augspurger Rd (45011-6913)
PHONE..........................513 844-8444
Randy Jones, *Principal*
EMP: 3
SALES (est): 187.9K **Privately Held**
SIC: 3273 Ready-mixed concrete

(G-10572)
INTEGRATED POWER SERVICES LLC
2175a Schlichter Dr (45015-1482)
PHONE..........................513 863-8816
Jason Reynolds, *Branch Mgr*
EMP: 28
SQ FT: 20,500
SALES (corp-wide): 924.8MM **Privately Held**
WEB: www.integratedps.com
SIC: 7694 Electric motor repair
HQ: Integrated Power Services Llc
3 Independence Pt Ste 100
Greenville SC 29615

(G-10573)
IRVING MATERIALS INC
600 Augspurger Rd (45011-6913)
PHONE..........................513 844-8444
Randy Jones, *Branch Mgr*
EMP: 10
SALES (corp-wide): 814.4MM **Privately Held**
SIC: 3273 Ready-mixed concrete
PA: Irving Materials, Inc.
8032 N State Road 9
Greenfield IN 46140
317 326-3101

(G-10574)
J N LINROSE MFG LLC
999 East Ave (45011-3831)
P.O. Box 1187 (45012-1187)
PHONE..........................513 867-5500
Frank C Pfirman,
EMP: 5
SALES (est): 1MM **Privately Held**
WEB: www.jnlinrose.com
SIC: 3444 3446 1751 Studs & joists, sheet metal; lintels light gauge steel; lightweight steel framing (metal stud) installation

(G-10575)
J R CUSTOM UNLIMITED
2620 Bobmeyer Rd (45015-1306)
PHONE..........................513 894-9800
James Riesenberg, *President*
EMP: 10
SALES (est): 1.2MM **Privately Held**
SIC: 2499 Decorative wood & woodwork

(G-10576)
JASON INCORPORATED
Also Called: Jacksonlea
3440 Symmes Rd (45015-1359)
PHONE..........................513 860-3400
Ron Locher, *General Mgr*
EMP: 17
SALES (corp-wide): 612.9MM **Publicly Held**
WEB: www.jasoninc.com
SIC: 3446 3471 3291 2842 Ornamental metalwork; plating & polishing; abrasive products; specialty cleaning, polishes & sanitation goods
HQ: Jason Incorporated
833 E Michigan St Ste 900
Milwaukee WI 53202
414 277-9300

(G-10577)
KAIVAC INC (PA)
2680 Van Hook Ave (45015-1583)
PHONE..........................513 887-4600
Bob Robinson Jr, *President*
Dan Parker, *Vice Pres*
Josh Harrell, *Research*
Tom Chambers, *CFO*
Robert Toews, *CFO*
◆ **EMP:** 40
SALES (est): 4.6MM **Privately Held**
WEB: www.kaivac.com
SIC: 3589 Commercial cleaning equipment

(G-10578)
KAO USA INC
8778 Lesaint Dr (45011)
PHONE..........................513 421-1400
EMP: 5
SALES (corp-wide): 13.4B **Privately Held**
SIC: 2844 Toilet preparations
HQ: Kao Usa Inc.
2535 Spring Grove Ave
Cincinnati OH 45214
513 421-1400

(G-10579)
KATHOM MANUFACTURING CO INC
661 Williams Ave (45015-1158)
PHONE..........................513 868-8890
Thomas R Wells, *President*
EMP: 22
SALES (est): 4MM **Privately Held**
WEB: www.kathom.com
SIC: 3089 3643 2821 Injection molding of plastics; current-carrying wiring devices; plastics materials & resins

(G-10580)
KING RETAIL SOLUTIONS INC
3865 Symmes Rd (45015-1376)
PHONE..........................513 729-5858
EMP: 10
SALES (corp-wide): 39.8MM **Privately Held**
SIC: 7336 3993 Commercial Art/Graphic Design Mfg Signs/Advertising Specialties
HQ: King Retail Solutions, Inc.
3850 W 1st Ave
Eugene OR 97402
541 686-2848

(G-10581)
KUHLMANNS FABRICATION
1753 Millville Oxford Rd (45013-8931)
PHONE..........................513 967-4617
Mark Kuhlmann, *Principal*
EMP: 3 EST: 2008
SALES (est): 268.7K **Privately Held**
SIC: 3842 Welders' hoods

(G-10582)
LOUS MACHINE COMPANY INC
102 Hastings Ave (45011-4708)
PHONE..........................513 856-9199
G Danny Jackson, *President*
EMP: 10
SQ FT: 10,000
SALES (est): 1.5MM **Privately Held**
SIC: 3599 Machine shop, jobbing & repair

(G-10583)
M L C TECHNOLOGIES INC
4 Standen Dr (45015-2208)
PHONE..........................513 874-7792
Michael L Crompton, *President*
James Jackson,
Marty Todd,
EMP: 4
SQ FT: 6,000
SALES (est): 548.9K **Privately Held**
SIC: 3599 3089 Custom machinery; injection molding of plastics

(G-10584)
MA FLYNN ASSOCIATES LLC
Also Called: Flynn Metering
4115 Tonya Trl (45011-8535)
PHONE..........................513 893-7873
Marvin Flynn, *Mng Member*
Diana Flynn,
EMP: 5
SQ FT: 12,000
SALES (est): 2.4MM **Privately Held**
WEB: www.flynnmeteringsystems.com
SIC: 5084 3625 Meters, consumption registering; motor starters & controllers, electric

(G-10585)
MATANDY STEEL & METAL PDTS LLC
Also Called: Matandy Steel Sales
1200 Central Ave (45011-3825)
P.O. Box 1186 (45012-1186)
PHONE..........................513 844-2277
Andrew Schuster, *President*
Joanne Pfirman,
EMP: 100
SQ FT: 125,000
SALES (est): 32.1MM **Privately Held**
WEB: www.matandy.com
SIC: 4225 3312 3444 3399 General warehousing & storage; sheet or strip, steel, cold-rolled: own hot-rolled; studs & joists, sheet metal; nails: aluminum, brass or other nonferrous metal or wire

(G-10586)
MEMBRANE SPECIALISTS LLC (PA)
2 Rowe Ct (45015-2211)
PHONE..........................513 860-9490
Ryan Cage, *Engineer*
Pat Pelton, *Engineer*
Lyle Henson, *Manager*
David Pearson,
Peter Allan,
▲ **EMP:** 7 EST: 2009
SQ FT: 12,000
SALES (est): 1.4MM **Privately Held**
SIC: 3569 Filters, general line: industrial

(G-10587)
MINNICKS DRIVE-THRU
828 East Ave (45011-3808)
PHONE..........................513 868-6126
Ralph Minnick, *Principal*
EMP: 3 EST: 2010
SALES (est): 169.8K **Privately Held**
SIC: 2082 Beer (alcoholic beverage)

(G-10588)
MUNICIPAL BREW WORKS LLC
306 Ashley Brook Dr (45013-6349)
PHONE..........................513 889-8369
James Goodman, *Principal*
EMP: 5
SALES (est): 395.1K **Privately Held**
SIC: 2082 Malt beverages

(G-10589)
NETUREN AMERICA CORPORATION
2995 Moser Ct (45011-5430)
PHONE..........................513 863-1900
Etsla Yamamura, *CEO*
Makoto Nakahara, *Principal*
▲ **EMP:** 18
SALES (est): 3.6MM **Privately Held**
SIC: 3398 Metal heat treating

(G-10590)
NK MACHINE INC
1550 Pleasant Ave (45015-1035)
PHONE..........................513 737-8035
Nick Emenaker, *President*
Betty Emenaker, *Owner*
Edward Emenaker, *Owner*
EMP: 7
SQ FT: 6,000
SALES (est): 1MM **Privately Held**
SIC: 3599 Machine shop, jobbing & repair

(G-10591)
OHIO HEAT TRANSFER
3400 Port Union Rd (45014-4224)
PHONE..........................513 870-5323
Mark A Epure, *President*
EMP: 3
SALES (est): 282.6K **Privately Held**
SIC: 3443 Fabricated plate work (boiler shop)

(G-10592)
OLD WEST INDUSTRIES INC (PA)
Also Called: Moser Leather Company
1421 Boyle Rd Bldg B (45013-1825)
PHONE..........................513 889-0500
James Cox, *Principal*
▲ **EMP:** 5
SALES (est): 581.9K **Privately Held**
WEB: www.ket-moy.com
SIC: 5941 3111 Saddlery & equestrian equipment; leather tanning & finishing

(G-10593)
OLIVER PRODUCTS COMPANY
Also Called: Oliver-Tolas Healthcare Packg
3840 Symmes Rd (45015-1378)
PHONE..........................513 860-6880
Julian Benavides, *Regional Mgr*
Alyssa Hezmalhalch, *Regional Mgr*
Jeff Kinell, *Mfg Staff*
Tom Backs, *Engineer*
Jose Rivera, *Engineer*
EMP: 19
SALES (corp-wide): 2.9B **Privately Held**
SIC: 2672 Chemically treated papers: made from purchased materials; adhesive papers, labels or tapes: from purchased material
HQ: Oliver Products Company
445 6th St Nw
Grand Rapids MI 49504
616 456-7711

(G-10594)
OMNIBOOM LLC
20 High St (45011-2709)
PHONE..........................833 675-3987
Richie Brees,
EMP: 3 EST: 2017
SALES (est): 71.1K **Privately Held**
SIC: 7372 7371 Prepackaged software; computer software development

(G-10595)
ORBIS CORPORATION
1621 Hanover Ct (45013-4198)
PHONE..........................513 737-9489
EMP: 6
SALES (corp-wide): 1.7B **Privately Held**
SIC: 3089 Mfg Plastic Products
HQ: Orbis Corporation
1055 Corporate Center Dr
Oconomowoc WI 53066
262 560-5000

(G-10596)
PLAS-TANKS INDUSTRIES INC (PA)
39 Standen Dr (45015-2209)
PHONE..........................513 942-3800
J Kent Covey, *President*
Connie Royse, *Vice Pres*
EMP: 39
SQ FT: 33,000
SALES (est): 9.1MM **Privately Held**
WEB: www.plastanks.com
SIC: 3089 3564 3444 3084 Tubs, plastic (containers); blowers & fans; sheet metalwork; plastics pipe

Hamilton - Butler County (G-10597)

(G-10597)
PPG INDUSTRIES INC
91 N Brookwood Ave (45013-1209)
PHONE................513 737-1893
Rob Reniff, *Branch Mgr*
EMP: 4
SALES (corp-wide): 15.3B **Publicly Held**
SIC: 2851 Paints & allied products
PA: Ppg Industries, Inc.
1 Ppg Pl
Pittsburgh PA 15272
412 434-3131

(G-10598)
PROCTER GAMBLE CO
3550 Symmes Rd (45015-1497)
PHONE................513 698-7675
EMP: 3
SALES (est): 183.1K **Privately Held**
SIC: 2676 Sanitary paper products

(G-10599)
QLOG CORP
33 Standen Dr (45015-2209)
PHONE................513 874-1211
J Robert Warden, *President*
Thomas Rebel, *Vice Pres*
EMP: 9
SQ FT: 7,500
SALES: 2MM **Privately Held**
WEB: www.qlog.com
SIC: 8748 3679 Systems analysis or design; electronic circuits

(G-10600)
QUALITY PUBLISHING CO
Also Called: Quality Printing & Publishing
3200 Symmes Rd (45015-1357)
PHONE................513 863-8210
Jane Johnson, *President*
David Johnson, *Vice Pres*
Steve Clark, *Graphic Designe*
Jennifer Sapp, *Graphic Designe*
EMP: 10 **EST:** 1953
SQ FT: 10,000
SALES: 1.2MM **Privately Held**
WEB: www.qualitypublishing.com
SIC: 2752 Commercial printing, offset

(G-10601)
RUBBERDUCK 4X4
1622 Smith Rd (45013-8629)
PHONE................513 889-1735
Travis Depew, *Owner*
EMP: 6
SALES (est): 500K **Privately Held**
SIC: 3714 Motor vehicle parts & accessories

(G-10602)
SCC INSTRUMENTS
4436 Hamilton Scipio Rd (45013-9129)
PHONE................513 856-8444
William Sefton, *President*
EMP: 5
SALES (est): 580K **Privately Held**
SIC: 3625 Flow actuated electrical switches

(G-10603)
SCHAEFER BOX & PALLET CO
11875 Paddys Run Rd (45013-9365)
PHONE................513 738-2500
Stanley Schaefer, *CEO*
Tod Hollifield, *President*
EMP: 32 **EST:** 1968
SQ FT: 45,000
SALES (est): 5.3MM **Privately Held**
WEB: www.schaeferboxandpallet.com
SIC: 2449 2448 2441 Rectangular boxes & crates, wood; pallets, wood; nailed wood boxes & shook

(G-10604)
SHAPE SUPPLY INC
700 S Erie Hwy (45011-3904)
PHONE................513 863-6695
Eugene Lukjan, *President*
EMP: 4
SQ FT: 16,000
SALES: 500K **Privately Held**
SIC: 3444 5075 Pipe, sheet metal; warm air heating equipment & supplies

(G-10605)
SIGNERY2 LLC
2571 Millville Shandon Rd (45013-8218)
PHONE................513 738-3048
Lois Schmidt,
EMP: 3
SQ FT: 3,600
SALES (est): 210K **Privately Held**
WEB: www.schmidtsignery.com
SIC: 3993 Signs & advertising specialties

(G-10606)
SMART PAPERS HOLDINGS LLC
601 N B St (45013-2909)
PHONE................513 869-5583
Dan Maheu, *President*
EMP: 240
SALES (est): 59.3MM **Privately Held**
SIC: 2621 Fine paper

(G-10607)
SPECIALTY PLAS FABRICATIONS
Also Called: Custom Cases For Collectibles
1600 Irma Ave (45011-4419)
PHONE................513 856-9475
Betty Brickner, *President*
▲ **EMP:** 7
SQ FT: 12,000
SALES: 600K **Privately Held**
WEB: www.casesforcollectibles.com
SIC: 3089 Plastic containers, except foam

(G-10608)
STAT INDUSTRIES INC
3269 Profit Dr (45014-4239)
PHONE................513 860-4482
Robyn Kellough, *Manager*
EMP: 6
SALES (corp-wide): 930K **Privately Held**
WEB: www.statindex.com
SIC: 2675 Index cards, die-cut: made from purchased materials
PA: Stat Industries, Inc.
137 Stone Rd
Chillicothe OH 45601
740 779-6561

(G-10609)
TERRY ASPHALT MATERIALS INC (DH)
8600 Bilstein Blvd (45015-2204)
PHONE................513 874-6192
Dan Koeninger, *CEO*
Jim Monroe, *Terminal Mgr*
W Pierre Peltier, *Manager*
Ryan Terry, *Technical Staff*
Christopher Winter, *Administration*
EMP: 25
SALES (est): 38.3MM
SALES (corp-wide): 83.5MM **Privately Held**
SIC: 5082 2952 Road construction & maintenance machinery; asphalt felts & coatings
HQ: Barrett Industries Corporation
73 Headquarters Plz
Morristown NJ 07960
973 533-1001

(G-10610)
THYSSENKRUPP BILSTEIN AMER INC (HQ)
8685 Bilstein Blvd (45015-2205)
PHONE................513 881-7600
Fabian Schmahl, *President*
Brian Driscoll, *Warehouse Mgr*
Vincent Elisan, *Engineer*
Sebastian Kaemper, *Engineer*
Jade O'Mara, *Engineer*
◆ **EMP:** 212
SQ FT: 115,000
SALES (est): 106.1MM
SALES (corp-wide): 39.8B **Privately Held**
SIC: 3714 5013 Shock absorbers, motor vehicle; springs, shock absorbers & struts
PA: Thyssenkrupp Ag
Thyssenkrupp Allee 1
Essen 45143
201 844-0

(G-10611)
TIPCO PUNCH INC
6 Rowe Ct (45015-2211)
PHONE................513 874-9140
Jack Pickins, *CEO*
Scott Ellsworth, *Vice Pres*
Douglas Lee, *Opers Staff*
Dave Rudicil, *Research*
Tom Halpin, *Marketing Staff*
EMP: 30
SQ FT: 12,000
SALES (est): 5.1MM **Privately Held**
SIC: 3544 Punches, forming & stamping
HQ: Tipco Inc
1 Coventry Rd
Brampton ON L6T 4
905 791-9811

(G-10612)
TK MACHINING SPECIALTIES LLC
2677 Morgan Ln (45013-8650)
PHONE................513 368-3963
Troy Kordenbrock,
EMP: 5
SQ FT: 5,000
SALES: 1MM **Privately Held**
SIC: 3679 Electronic circuits

(G-10613)
TRI-MAC MFG & SVCS CO
Also Called: Tri-Mac Mfg & Serv
860 Belle Ave (45015-1151)
PHONE................513 896-4445
William Bates, *President*
Bill Galster, *Vice Pres*
EMP: 17
SQ FT: 40,000
SALES (est): 3.4MM **Privately Held**
SIC: 3714 3554 5084 3549 Motor vehicle parts & accessories; paper industries machinery; trucks, industrial; trailers, industrial; metalworking machinery; sheet metalwork

(G-10614)
TRI-STATE JET MFG LLC
1480 Beissinger Rd (45013-1110)
PHONE................513 896-4538
Jeff Pierson, *Principal*
EMP: 4 **EST:** 2012
SALES (est): 280.3K **Privately Held**
SIC: 3812 Aircraft/aerospace flight instruments & guidance systems

(G-10615)
TRIANGLE SIGN CO
221 N B St (45013-3195)
PHONE................513 863-2578
Donald K Whittlesey, *Partner*
Everett Hoskins Jr, *Partner*
Tim Hoskins, *Partner*
EMP: 9 **EST:** 1920
SQ FT: 6,695
SALES (est): 700K **Privately Held**
SIC: 3993 7389 Neon signs; sign painting & lettering shop

(G-10616)
UFP HAMILTON LLC
Also Called: Universal Forest Products
115 Distribution Dr (45014-4257)
PHONE................513 285-7190
Ken Rewa, *Principal*
EMP: 19
SALES (est): 2.8MM
SALES (corp-wide): 4.4B **Publicly Held**
SIC: 2491 2436 2431 Structural lumber & timber, treated wood; softwood veneer & plywood; stair railings, wood; woodwork, interior & ornamental
PA: Universal Forest Products, Inc.
2801 E Beltline Ave Ne
Grand Rapids MI 49525
616 364-6161

(G-10617)
VENICE CORNERSTONE NEWSPAPER
2640 Cncnnati Brkville Rd (45014-5973)
PHONE................513 738-7151
Lanny Leach, *Owner*
Treasa Leach, *Business Mgr*
EMP: 3
SALES (est): 166.5K **Privately Held**
SIC: 2711 Newspapers, publishing & printing

(G-10618)
VINYLMAX CORPORATION
2921 Mcbride Ct (45011-5420)
PHONE................800 847-3736
James Doerger, *CEO*
EMP: 90
SQ FT: 100,000
SALES (est): 15.7MM **Privately Held**
WEB: www.vinylmax.com
SIC: 3089 2431 Window frames & sash, plastic; doors & door parts & trim, wood

(G-10619)
W & W CUSTOM FABRICATION INC (PA)
143 E Fairway Dr (45013-3528)
PHONE................513 353-4617
Steven Webb, *President*
Mike Hutcheson, *Vice Pres*
EMP: 2
SQ FT: 600
SALES: 1MM **Privately Held**
SIC: 3444 Sheet metalwork

(G-10620)
WALLOVER OIL HAMILTON INC
Also Called: National Oil Products
1000 Forest Ave (45015-1632)
PHONE................513 896-6692
George Marquis, *Chairman*
EMP: 13 **EST:** 1963
SQ FT: 15,000
SALES (est): 2.5MM **Privately Held**
SIC: 2992 Re-refining lubricating oils & greases
HQ: Wallover Enterprises Inc.
21845 Drake Rd
Strongsville OH 44149
440 238-9250

(G-10621)
WATSON GRAVEL INC (PA)
2728 Hamilton Cleves Rd (45013-9452)
PHONE................513 863-0070
Ronald E Watson, *President*
Michael T Watson, *Vice Pres*
Janet L Meyers, *Treasurer*
Labreeska Stanifer, *Human Res Mgr*
Brian Bottoms, *Manager*
EMP: 55
SQ FT: 2,000
SALES (est): 10.6MM **Privately Held**
WEB: www.watsongravel.com
SIC: 1442 Gravel mining

(G-10622)
WILLIAM HARDING
5359 Jenkins Rd (45013-9122)
PHONE................513 738-3344
Darrin Harding, *Administration*
EMP: 3 **EST:** 2017
SALES (est): 123.2K **Privately Held**
SIC: 2813 Hydrogen

Hammondsville
Jefferson County

(G-10623)
SAM ABDALLAH
Also Called: Aquanaut Lounge
777 Hammondsville Rd (43930)
P.O. Box 114, Stratton (43961-0114)
PHONE................330 532-3900
Sam Abdallah, *Owner*
EMP: 30
SQ FT: 10,000
SALES (est): 2.5MM **Privately Held**
WEB: www.samabdallah.com
SIC: 2899 Fireworks; citronella oil

Hanging Rock
Lawrence County

(G-10624)
WORLEYS MACHINE & FAB INC
1003 State Rr 650 (45638)
P.O. Box 604, Ironton (45638-0604)
PHONE................740 532-3337
James Worley, *President*
Diana Worley, *Corp Secy*

GEOGRAPHIC SECTION

Harrison - Hamilton County (G-10650)

EMP: 8
SALES (est): 500K Privately Held
SIC: 3599 7692 Machine shop, jobbing & repair; welding repair

Hannibal
Monroe County

(G-10625)
TRIPLE J OILFIELD SERVICES LLC
42722 State Route 7 (43931)
PHONE..................................740 483-9030
EMP: 6
SALES (est): 784.1K Privately Held
SIC: 1389 Oil/Gas Field Services

Harpster
Wyandot County

(G-10626)
COONS HOMEMADE CANDIES
16451 County Highway 113 (43323-9331)
PHONE..................................740 496-4141
Charles W Coons, *President*
EMP: 4
SALES (est): 209.9K Privately Held
SIC: 2064 5961 5441 Candy & other confectionery products; food, mail order; candy

Harrison
Hamilton County

(G-10627)
ABRA AUTO BODY & GLASS LP
Also Called: ABRA Autobody & Glass
10106 Harrison Ave (45030-1925)
PHONE..................................513 367-9200
EMP: 7
SALES (corp-wide): 1.8B Privately Held
SIC: 5013 2851 Body repair or paint shop supplies, automotive; paint removers
HQ: Abra Auto Body & Glass Lp
   7225 Northland Dr N # 110
   Brooklyn Park MN 55428
   888 872-2272

(G-10628)
AERO PROPULSION SUPPORT INC
Also Called: Aero Propulsion Support Group
108 May Dr Ste A (45030-2005)
PHONE..................................513 367-9452
Allan Slattery, *President*
Rose Slattery, *Vice Pres*
Tara Slone, *Program Mgr*
Michelle Philpot, *Office Admin*
EMP: 49
SQ FT: 25,000
SALES (est): 11.3MM Privately Held
WEB: www.aeropropulsion.com
SIC: 3511 Turbines & turbine generator sets & parts

(G-10629)
AIR LOGIC POWER SYSTEMS LLC
10100 Progress Way (45030-1295)
PHONE..................................513 202-5130
David Huberfield, *CEO*
EMP: 5
SALES (est): 563K
SALES (corp-wide): 7.8MM Privately Held
SIC: 3823 Industrial flow & liquid measuring instruments
PA: Air Logic Power Systems, Llc
   2440 W Corp Prsrv Dr # 600
   Oak Creek WI 53154
   414 671-3332

(G-10630)
ALL-RITE RDYMX MIAMI VLY LLC
7466 New Haven Rd (45030-9280)
PHONE..................................513 738-1933
W Thomas Fisher,
EMP: 6
SALES (est): 677.4K Privately Held
SIC: 3273 Ready-mixed concrete

(G-10631)
ALLIANCE KNIFE INC
124 May Dr (45030-2024)
P.O. Box 729 (45030-0729)
PHONE..................................513 367-9000
William L Keith, *President*
Sharon Keith, *Corp Secy*
Steve Camden, *Plant Mgr*
Jackie Elmore, *Sales Staff*
Sue Lucas, *Office Mgr*
◆ EMP: 20
SALES: 5.9MM Privately Held
WEB: www.allianceknife.com
SIC: 5085 3545 Knives, industrial; machine knives, metalworking

(G-10632)
BELL INDUSTRIES
9843 New Haven Rd (45030-1836)
PHONE..................................513 353-2355
Edward Vierling, *Owner*
EMP: 10
SQ FT: 8,600
SALES (est): 889.6K Privately Held
WEB: www.bellindustries.net
SIC: 3931 Bells (musical instruments); carillon bells; chimes & parts (musical instruments)

(G-10633)
CHICAGO DENTAL SUPPLY INC
10051 Simonson Rd Unit 9 (45030-2001)
PHONE..................................800 571-5211
Paul E Myers III, *President*
▲ EMP: 9 EST: 2002
SALES (est): 745.4K Privately Held
SIC: 3843 Dental equipment & supplies

(G-10634)
CINCINNATI CRANE & HOIST LLC
10860 Paddys Run Rd (45030-9252)
P.O. Box 1072, Hamilton (45012-1072)
PHONE..................................513 202-1408
Richard Strobl, *CEO*
Russell York, *Engineer*
Joyce Cross, *Accountant*
Sarah Ashpaw, *Office Mgr*
Tiffany Parish, *Clerk*
EMP: 13
SQ FT: 36,000
SALES (est): 6MM Privately Held
SIC: 3536 1796 Hoists, cranes & monorails; installing building equipment

(G-10635)
CINCINNATI TEST SYSTEMS INC (PA)
10100 Progress Way (45030-1295)
PHONE..................................513 202-5100
Kevin Hansell, *General Mgr*
Barbara A Jackson, *Principal*
Joanna Moncivaiz, *Controller*
Lacey Davis, *Assistant*
EMP: 145
SQ FT: 25,000
SALES (est): 49.7MM Privately Held
WEB: www.cincinnati-test.com
SIC: 3823 Pressure measurement instruments, industrial

(G-10636)
CIRCUIT SERVICES LLC
351 Deerfield Dr (45030-2080)
PHONE..................................513 604-7405
Jeffery S Stewart,
EMP: 3
SALES (est): 250.5K Privately Held
SIC: 3672 Printed circuit boards

(G-10637)
COATING SYSTEMS INC
Also Called: C S I
150 Sales Ave (45030-1484)
PHONE..................................513 367-5600
Thomas W Ritter, *President*
John Ritter, *Vice Pres*
EMP: 17
SQ FT: 20,000
SALES (est): 2.7MM Privately Held
WEB: www.coatingsystems.com
SIC: 3479 Coating of metals & formed products

(G-10638)
CROWN PLASTICS CO
116 May Dr (45030-2095)
PHONE..................................513 367-0238
Robert H Ellerhorst, *Ch of Bd*
Gary Ellerhorst, *President*
Gregg Ellerhorst, *Vice Pres*
Ken Myers, *Shareholder*
▲ EMP: 52
SQ FT: 56,000
SALES (est): 17MM Privately Held
WEB: www.crownplastics.com
SIC: 2821 3081 Plastics materials & resins; polypropylene film & sheet

(G-10639)
EDELMANN PROVISION COMPANY
Also Called: Fresh Sausage Specialists
10000 Martins Way (45030-2090)
PHONE..................................513 881-5800
James Frondorf, *President*
James Burke, *Vice Pres*
Gary Willhite, *Vice Pres*
EMP: 80 EST: 1930
SQ FT: 10,000
SALES (est): 16.3MM Privately Held
SIC: 2013 Sausages from purchased meat; luncheon meat from purchased meat; frankfurters from purchased meat; prepared pork products from purchased pork

(G-10640)
FASTPATCH LTD
10774 Carolina Trace Rd (45030-2729)
P.O. Box 5 (45030-0005)
PHONE..................................513 367-1838
Mike Jacobs, *President*
EMP: 10
SALES (est): 519.2K Privately Held
SIC: 2395 Embroidery products, except schiffli machine; embroidery & art needlework

(G-10641)
FEILHAUERS MACHINE SHOP INC (PA)
421 Industrial Dr (45030-2104)
PHONE..................................513 202-0545
Don Feilhauer, *President*
EMP: 5 EST: 1979
SQ FT: 8,000
SALES (est): 864.8K Privately Held
WEB: www.feilhauers.com
SIC: 3599 Machine shop, jobbing & repair

(G-10642)
FRONTIER SIGNS & DISPLAYS INC
525 New Biddinger Rd (45030-1252)
P.O. Box 328 (45030-0328)
PHONE..................................513 367-0813
Jack S Wuesterfeld, *President*
Ruth Wuesterfeld, *Treasurer*
EMP: 7
SQ FT: 17,000
SALES (est): 965.8K Privately Held
SIC: 2521 2522 3993 Wood office furniture; office furniture, except wood; signs & advertising specialties

(G-10643)
GEOGRAPH INDUSTRIES INC
475 Industrial Dr (45030-2104)
PHONE..................................513 202-9200
George Freudiger, *President*
Mark Freudiger, *Vice Pres*
George Michael Freudiger, *Treasurer*
EMP: 26
SQ FT: 25,000
SALES: 4MM Privately Held
WEB: www.geograph-ind.com
SIC: 2541 3993 2521 2522 Wood partitions & fixtures; signs & advertising specialties; cabinets, office: wood; chairs, office: padded or plain, except wood

(G-10644)
GREER & WHITEHEAD CNSTR INC
510 S State St Ste D (45030-1494)
PHONE..................................513 202-1757
Steven Whitehead, *President*
Russell Whitehead, *General Mgr*
EMP: 35
SALES (est): 5.7MM Privately Held
SIC: 1711 1389 Mechanical contractor; building oil & gas well foundations on site

(G-10645)
HEARTLAND ENGINEERED PDTS LLC
355 Industrial Dr (45030-1483)
PHONE..................................513 367-0080
Tom Andres, *Prdtn Mgr*
Robert Parsons, *Regl Sales Mgr*
Julie Baker, *Marketing Staff*
Larry Race, *Manager*
EMP: 17
SALES (est): 2.4MM Privately Held
SIC: 3999 3537 Dock equipment & supplies, industrial; platforms, stands, tables, pallets & similar equipment

(G-10646)
HOLIDAY HOMES INC
Also Called: Holiday Hmes Rvrview Crossings
10620 Sand Run Rd (45030-9452)
PHONE..................................513 353-9777
Adam Perkins, *General Mgr*
EMP: 12
SQ FT: 1,781
SALES (corp-wide): 11.6MM Privately Held
SIC: 2451 6531 Mobile homes; real estate agents & managers
PA: Holiday Homes, Inc.
   1252 Goshen Pike
   Milford OH 45150
   513 575-7697

(G-10647)
HOME CITY ICE COMPANY
5709 State Rte 128 (45030)
PHONE..................................513 353-9346
Cliff Riegler, *Manager*
EMP: 10
SALES (corp-wide): 232.5MM Privately Held
WEB: www.homecityice.com
SIC: 2097 Manufactured ice
PA: The Home City Ice Company
   6045 Bridgetown Rd Ste 1
   Cincinnati OH 45248
   513 574-1800

(G-10648)
HUBERT ENTERPRISES INC
9555 Dry Fork Rd (45030-1994)
PHONE..................................513 367-8600
Bart Kohler, *President*
Ted Wimmel, *Manager*
EMP: 5
SQ FT: 372,500
SALES (est): 1.2MM Privately Held
SIC: 5046 2761 Store equipment; store fixtures; manifold business forms

(G-10649)
HULSMAN SIGNS
10001 State Route 128 (45030-9229)
PHONE..................................513 738-3389
Charlie Jones, *Owner*
EMP: 3
SALES (est): 156.4K Privately Held
SIC: 3993 Signs, not made in custom sign painting shops

(G-10650)
HUSAC PAVING
114 S Walnut St (45030-1373)
P.O. Box 409 (45030-0409)
PHONE..................................513 200-2818
Joe Wasinger, *Owner*
EMP: 5
SALES (est): 210.3K Privately Held
SIC: 2951 Paving blocks

Harrison - Hamilton County (G-10651)

(G-10651)
ILSCO CORPORATION
Glenmoor Company Division
119 May Dr (45030-2023)
PHONE....................513 367-9100
Russ Hensley, *Opers-Prdtn-Mfg*
John Telscher, *Controller*
EMP: 30
SQ FT: 37,068
SALES (corp-wide): 116.7MM **Privately Held**
WEB: www.ilsco.com
SIC: 3451 Screw machine products
HQ: Ilsco Corporation
 4730 Madison Rd
 Cincinnati OH 45227
 513 533-6200

(G-10652)
JAMTEK ENTERPRISES INC
10845 State Route 128 (45030-9236)
PHONE....................513 738-4700
Thomas Kroeger, *President*
Jerome Kroeger, *Vice Pres*
Paul Kroeger, *CFO*
▲ **EMP:** 4
SQ FT: 12,900
SALES (est): 1.2MM **Privately Held**
WEB: www.jamtek.net
SIC: 5085 5169 3566 Industrial supplies; industrial chemicals; drives, high speed industrial, except hydrostatic

(G-10653)
JTM PROVISIONS COMPANY INC
Also Called: Jtm Food Group
200 Sales Ave (45030-1485)
PHONE....................513 367-4900
Anthony A Maas, *President*
Jerome Maas, *Vice Pres*
John Maas Jr, *Vice Pres*
Joseph Maas, *Vice Pres*
EMP: 350 EST: 1963
SQ FT: 96,000
SALES: 154.8MM **Privately Held**
WEB: www.jtmfoodgroup.com
SIC: 2013 2051 Frozen meats from purchased meat; buns, bread type: fresh or frozen

(G-10654)
KAPLAN INDUSTRIES INC
6255 Kilby Rd (45030-9417)
PHONE....................513 386-7762
Dottie McLeer, *Branch Mgr*
EMP: 15
SALES (est): 3.2MM
SALES (corp-wide): 11.4MM **Privately Held**
SIC: 3491 Compressed gas cylinder valves
PA: Kaplan Industries, Inc.
 6255 Kilby Rd
 Harrison OH 45030
 856 779-8181

(G-10655)
KAPLAN INDUSTRIES INC (PA)
6255 Kilby Rd (45030-9417)
PHONE....................856 779-8181
Dean Kaplan, *President*
Rita Kaplan, *Vice Pres*
Devon Goodman, *Sales Staff*
Jim Johnston, *Director*
◆ **EMP:** 50
SQ FT: 6,000
SALES (est): 11.4MM **Privately Held**
WEB: www.kaplanindustries.com
SIC: 3491 Compressed gas cylinder valves

(G-10656)
MAB FABRICATION INC
320 N State St (45030-1146)
PHONE....................855 622-3221
James Rice, *Principal*
EMP: 4
SALES (est): 446.6K **Privately Held**
SIC: 3499 3999 Aerosol valves, metal; barber & beauty shop equipment

(G-10657)
MARTIN MARIETTA MATERIALS INC
Also Called: Martin Marietta Aggregates
170 Pilot Rd (45030)
PHONE....................513 200-2303
Dewey Powell, *Manager*
EMP: 3
SQ FT: 1,705 **Publicly Held**
WEB: www.martinmarietta.com
SIC: 1422 Crushed & broken limestone
PA: Martin Marietta Materials Inc
 2710 Wycliff Rd
 Raleigh NC 27607

(G-10658)
MCFEELYS INC
320 N State St (45030-1146)
PHONE....................800 443-7937
Peter Putterman, *President*
EMP: 15
SALES: 7.1MM **Privately Held**
SIC: 5085 3553 Fasteners & fastening equipment; woodworking machinery

(G-10659)
MIAMI VALLEY READY MIX INC
9540 Hamilton Cleves Hwy (45030-9706)
PHONE....................513 738-2616
Tom Norris, *Manager*
EMP: 30
SALES (corp-wide): 2.6MM **Privately Held**
SIC: 3273 Ready-mixed concrete
PA: Miami Valley Ready Mix, Inc.
 7466 New Haven Rd
 Harrison OH
 513 738-2616

(G-10660)
NAVPAR INC
11029 State Route 128 (45030-9710)
PHONE....................513 738-2230
Earl Keim, *President*
Jerome J Charls, *Principal*
Wendell Shallenberger, *Corp Secy*
Mike Ledars, *Vice Pres*
EMP: 3
SQ FT: 3,500
SALES (est): 481K **Privately Held**
SIC: 3441 Ship sections, prefabricated metal

(G-10661)
NEASE CO LLC
Also Called: Nease Performance Chemicals
10740 Paddys Run Rd (45030-9251)
PHONE....................513 738-1255
Ed Hamilton, *Engineer*
Frank Canepa, *Branch Mgr*
EMP: 60
SALES (corp-wide): 14.9MM **Privately Held**
SIC: 2869 Glycol ethers
HQ: Nease Co. Llc
 9774 Windisch Rd
 West Chester OH 45069
 513 587-2800

(G-10662)
PCS PHOSPHATE COMPANY INC
10818 Paddys Run Rd (45030-9252)
PHONE....................513 738-1261
Jack Sullivan, *Manager*
EMP: 24
SALES (corp-wide): 8.8B **Privately Held**
WEB: www.potashcorp.com
SIC: 2819 Phosphates, except fertilizers: defluorinated & ammoniated
HQ: Pcs Phosphate Company, Inc.
 1101 Skokie Blvd Ste 400
 Northbrook IL 60062
 847 849-4200

(G-10663)
POWEREX-IWATA AIR TECH INC
150 Production Dr (45030-1477)
PHONE....................888 769-7979
Gary Heman, *President*
Charles Heman, *President*
Pruce Jacobs, *President*
Mark David Wiwi, *Accountant*
▲ **EMP:** 70
SQ FT: 75,000
SALES: 35MM
SALES (corp-wide): 225.3B **Publicly Held**
WEB: www.powerexinc.com
SIC: 3563 Air & gas compressors
HQ: The Scott Fetzer Company
 28800 Clemens Rd
 Westlake OH 44145
 440 892-3000

(G-10664)
PREMIER INK SYSTEMS INC (PA)
10420 N State St (45030-9501)
P.O. Box 670 (45030-0670)
PHONE....................513 367-2300
Thomas Farmer, *President*
Judy Fritz, *Office Mgr*
EMP: 15
SALES (est): 16.5MM **Privately Held**
WEB: www.premierink.com
SIC: 2851 2893 2899 Lacquers, varnishes, enamels & other coatings; printing ink; chemical preparations

(G-10665)
PUTTMANN INDUSTRIES INC
Also Called: Atlas Dowel & Wood Products Co
320 N State St (45030-1146)
P.O. Box 327 (45030-0327)
PHONE....................513 202-9444
Peter Puttmann, *President*
▲ **EMP:** 15 EST: 1951
SQ FT: 65,000
SALES (est): 3MM **Privately Held**
WEB: www.atlasdowel.com
SIC: 2499 Dowels, wood

(G-10666)
QUIKRETE COMPANIES INC
Also Called: Quikrete Cincinnati
5425 Kilby Rd (45030-8910)
PHONE....................513 367-6135
Russ Smiley, *General Mgr*
Glen Lainhart, *Manager*
EMP: 40
SQ FT: 21,340 **Privately Held**
WEB: www.quikrete.com
SIC: 3272 3273 Dry mixture concrete; ready-mixed concrete
HQ: The Quikrete Companies Llc
 5 Concourse Pkwy Ste 1900
 Atlanta GA 30328
 404 634-9100

(G-10667)
R L TORBECK INDUSTRIES INC
355 Industrial Dr (45030-1483)
PHONE....................513 367-0080
Richard L Torbeck Jr, *President*
R Stephen Millbourn, *Vice Pres*
EMP: 90 EST: 1975
SQ FT: 67,000
SALES (est): 26.9MM **Privately Held**
WEB: www.torbeckind.com
SIC: 3441 3499 3444 3444 Fabricated structural metal; metal household articles; prefabricated metal buildings; sheet metalwork

(G-10668)
ROBERT E MOORE
Also Called: Valley Welding Service
10430 New Biddinger Rd (45030-8720)
PHONE....................513 367-0006
Robert E Moore, *Owner*
Robert Moore, *Owner*
Linda Moore, *Co-Owner*
EMP: 4 EST: 1945
SQ FT: 3,760
SALES (est): 420.1K **Privately Held**
SIC: 7692 Welding repair

(G-10669)
SCOTT FETZER COMPANY
Also Called: Halex
101 Production Dr (45030-1477)
PHONE....................440 439-1616
Cecil Medford, *Manager*
EMP: 120
SALES (corp-wide): 225.3B **Publicly Held**
SIC: 3635 Household vacuum cleaners
HQ: The Scott Fetzer Company
 28800 Clemens Rd
 Westlake OH 44145
 440 892-3000

(G-10670)
SIMPSON & SONS INC
10220 Harrison Ave (45030-1938)
PHONE....................513 367-0152
Joseph A Simpson, *President*
James Simpson, *Vice Pres*
EMP: 14
SQ FT: 10,500
SALES (est): 1.5MM **Privately Held**
SIC: 4789 7692 Railroad maintenance & repair services; welding repair

(G-10671)
SNYDER ELECTRONICS
5501 Lawrenceburg Rd # 100 (45030-8501)
P.O. Box 111 (45030-0111)
PHONE....................513 738-7200
William Snyder, *Owner*
◆ **EMP:** 5
SQ FT: 9,000
SALES (est): 395.3K **Privately Held**
SIC: 3651 Audio electronic systems

(G-10672)
STELTER AND BRINCK INC
201 Sales Ave (45030-1472)
PHONE....................513 367-9300
Joseph A Brinck II, *President*
Larry Brinck, *Principal*
Henry Stelter, *Principal*
Mary B Turpen, *Principal*
Tony Brinck, *Vice Pres*
EMP: 35 EST: 1940
SQ FT: 17,000
SALES (est): 9.1MM **Privately Held**
WEB: www.stelterbrinck.com
SIC: 3564 3567 3494 3433 Blowers & fans; industrial furnaces & ovens; valves & pipe fittings; heating equipment, except electric

(G-10673)
STOP STICK LTD
365 Industrial Dr (45030-1483)
PHONE....................513 202-5500
Andrew Morrison, *President*
Scott Trentel, *Accounts Mgr*
Louis M Groen, *Mng Member*
Andy Morrison, *Manager*
Ken French, *Technical Staff*
▲ **EMP:** 27
SQ FT: 10,000
SALES (est): 5.4MM **Privately Held**
WEB: www.stopstick.com
SIC: 3315 Nails, spikes, brads & similar items

(G-10674)
SUPERIOR STRUCTURES INC
320 N State St (45030-1146)
P.O. Box 26 (45030-0026)
PHONE....................513 942-5954
Chris Harrison, *General Mgr*
Tim Bischel, *Principal*
Brandon Vanderyt, *Office Mgr*
Charles Hatfield, *Admin Sec*
EMP: 10
SQ FT: 7,500
SALES (est): 2.2MM **Privately Held**
SIC: 3448 1531 Greenhouses: prefabricated metal; operative builders

(G-10675)
SUR-SEAL CORPORATION
10053 Simonson Rd (45030-2193)
PHONE....................513 574-8500
Mike Kasselmann, *Manager*
EMP: 5
SALES (corp-wide): 40MM **Privately Held**
SIC: 3053 Gaskets, all materials; packing, rubber
HQ: Sur-Seal, Llc
 6156 Wesselman Rd
 Cincinnati OH 45248
 513 574-8500

GEOGRAPHIC SECTION

Hartville - Stark County (G-10704)

(G-10676)
TASI HOLDINGS INC (PA)
Also Called: Tasi Group
10100 Progress Way (45030-1295)
PHONE.................513 202-5182
Jack Goffena, *CFO*
EMP: 27
SALES (est): 89.7MM **Privately Held**
SIC: 3823 3629 Industrial flow & liquid measuring instruments; electronic generation equipment

(G-10677)
TENKOTTE TOPS INC
11029 State Route 128 (45030-9710)
P.O. Box 592, Miamitown (45041-0592)
PHONE.................513 738-7300
Richard G Tenkotte, *President*
Diane Tenkotte, *Corp Secy*
EMP: 5
SQ FT: 4,300
SALES (est): 693.9K **Privately Held**
SIC: 2541 2434 Table or counter tops, plastic laminated; vanities, bathroom: wood

(G-10678)
VERITRACK INC
9487 Dry Fork Rd (45030-2900)
PHONE.................513 202-0790
EMP: 17
SALES: 2MM
SALES (corp-wide): 61MM **Privately Held**
SIC: 2754 Gravure Commercial Printing
PA: Diversified Labeling Solutions, Inc.
1285 Hamilton Pkwy
Itasca IL 60143
630 625-1225

(G-10679)
WAYNE/SCOTT FETZER COMPANY
Also Called: Wayne Water Systems
101 Production Dr (45030-1477)
PHONE.................800 237-0987
Duane Johnson, *President*
▲ **EMP:** 200
SQ FT: 160,000
SALES (est): 86MM
SALES (corp-wide): 225.3B **Publicly Held**
SIC: 3561 5074 Pumps, domestic: water or sump; water purification equipment
HQ: The Scott Fetzer Company
28800 Clemens Rd
Westlake OH 44145
440 892-3000

(G-10680)
WHITEWATER PROCESSING CO
10964 Campbell Rd (45030-8902)
PHONE.................513 367-4133
Kelly Kopp, *President*
Steve Kopp, *President*
Kevin Kopp, *Vice Pres*
EMP: 100
SQ FT: 7,500
SALES (est): 13.3MM **Privately Held**
SIC: 2015 Turkey, slaughtered & dressed

Hartford
Trumbull County

(G-10681)
JONES PROCESSING
State Rte 7 (44424)
P.O. Box 178 (44424-0178)
PHONE.................330 772-2193
Terry Jones, *President*
Sandra Jones, *Vice Pres*
EMP: 4 **EST:** 1964
SALES (est): 441.5K **Privately Held**
SIC: 2011 Meat packing plants

Hartville
Stark County

(G-10682)
A S NF PRODUCING INC
10539 Schlabach Ave Ne (44632-9134)
PHONE.................330 933-0622
Donna M Moyer, *Principal*
EMP: 3 **EST:** 2012
SALES (est): 162.7K **Privately Held**
SIC: 1311 Crude petroleum & natural gas

(G-10683)
AMERICAN COUNTERTOPS INC
7291 Swamp St Ne (44632-9324)
P.O. Box 535 (44632-0535)
PHONE.................330 877-0343
EMP: 9
SQ FT: 500
SALES: 1.6MM **Privately Held**
SIC: 2541 Mfg Wood Partitions/Fixtures

(G-10684)
AMERICRAFT STOR BUILDINGS LTD
1147 W Maple St (44632-8529)
PHONE.................330 877-6900
Scott Raymon, *President*
EMP: 5
SQ FT: 448
SALES (est): 286.9K **Privately Held**
SIC: 1521 2452 Patio & deck construction & repair; prefabricated wood buildings

(G-10685)
C AND J MACHINE INC
403 State Route 44 (44632-9202)
PHONE.................330 935-2170
Tim Wittensoldner, *President*
EMP: 5
SQ FT: 6,500
SALES: 1MM **Privately Held**
SIC: 3599 Machine shop, jobbing & repair

(G-10686)
C E KEGG INC (PA)
Also Called: Kegg Pipe Organ Builders
1184 Woodland St Sw (44632-8304)
PHONE.................330 877-8800
Charles E Kegg, *President*
Ellen Kegg, *Admin Sec*
Joyce Harper,
EMP: 6
SQ FT: 5,000
SALES (est): 777.8K **Privately Held**
WEB: www.kegggorgan.com
SIC: 3931 Pipes, organ

(G-10687)
CNB MACHINING AND MFG LLC
1052 Manning Rd Nw (44632-9505)
PHONE.................330 877-7920
Richard Reaven, *Principal*
EMP: 5
SALES (est): 387.9K **Privately Held**
SIC: 3999 Manufacturing industries

(G-10688)
DATA CONTROL SYSTEMS INC
13611 Kaufman Ave Nw (44632-9632)
PHONE.................330 877-4497
James R Shreve, *President*
EMP: 4
SALES (est): 678.1K **Privately Held**
WEB: www.dcsamerica.com
SIC: 3823 Industrial instrmnts msrmnt display/control process variable

(G-10689)
DMC WELDING INCORPORATED
9975 Market Ave N (44632-8720)
PHONE.................330 877-1935
Daniel Mihalik, *President*
EMP: 3
SALES (est): 250K **Privately Held**
SIC: 3441 1799 Fabricated structural metal; welding on site

(G-10690)
ENERVEST LTD
125 State Route 43 (44632-9500)
PHONE.................330 877-6747
EMP: 75 **Privately Held**
SIC: 1382 Oil & gas exploration services
PA: Enervest, Ltd.
1001 Fannin St Ste 800
Houston TX 77002

(G-10691)
GROW WITH ME- CREATIONS
Also Called: Grow With ME Bibs
14236 Wade Ave Ne (44632-9336)
PHONE.................800 850-1889
Diane Pullen, *Owner*
EMP: 5
SALES: 30K **Privately Held**
WEB: www.growwithme.com
SIC: 2385 2211 Bibs, waterproof: made from purchased materials; blankets & blanketings, cotton

(G-10692)
HARTVILLE CHOCOLATES INC
Also Called: Hartville Chocolate Factory
114 S Prospect Ave (44632-8906)
P.O. Box 1360 (44632-1360)
PHONE.................330 877-1999
Mary L Barton, *President*
EMP: 18
SQ FT: 3,200
SALES (est): 3.1MM **Privately Held**
WEB: www.hartvillechocolatefactory.com
SIC: 2066 5441 5999 Chocolate; candy; cake decorating supplies

(G-10693)
HARTVILLE LOCKER SERVICE INC
119 Sunnyside St Sw (44632-8933)
P.O. Box 7 (44632-0007)
PHONE.................330 877-9547
James Young, *President*
Jill E Young, *Corp Secy*
EMP: 8
SQ FT: 5,500
SALES (est): 815.7K **Privately Held**
SIC: 2011 Meat packing plants

(G-10694)
HARTVILLE PLASTICS INC
322 Lake Ave Ne (44632-9683)
PHONE.................330 877-9090
Robert Andrews, *President*
EMP: 8
SALES (est): 1MM **Privately Held**
SIC: 3089 Plastic processing

(G-10695)
HERITAGE TRUCK EQUIPMENT INC
661 Powell Ave (44632-7800)
PHONE.................330 699-4491
Eric Bontrager, *President*
Brian Bontrager, *Vice Pres*
EMP: 85
SALES (est): 34.7MM **Privately Held**
WEB: www.heritagetruck.com
SIC: 3537 Trucks, tractors, loaders, carriers & similar equipment

(G-10696)
HOME QUARTERS NORTH CANTO
1428 Edison St Nw (44632-9633)
PHONE.................330 806-5336
Rebecca Canto, *Principal*
EMP: 3
SALES (est): 147.9K **Privately Held**
SIC: 3131 Mfg Footwear Cut Stock

(G-10697)
JERRY MOORE INC (PA)
1010 Sunnyside St Sw (44632-9094)
P.O. Box 1180 (44632-1180)
PHONE.................330 877-1155
Gerald H Moore, *President*
Robert D Moore, *Vice Pres*
John N Teeple, *Admin Sec*
EMP: 4
SQ FT: 3,000
SALES (est): 1.7MM **Privately Held**
SIC: 1311 Crude petroleum production; natural gas production

(G-10698)
KINGSWAY ART & SIGN
1555 Andrews St Ne (44632-9018)
PHONE.................330 877-6241
Lloyd King, *President*
Mary J King, *Treasurer*
EMP: 3
SALES (est): 300.6K **Privately Held**
SIC: 3993 Signs & advertising specialties

(G-10699)
KNOWLES PRESS INC
Also Called: Hartville News
316 E Maple St (44632-8880)
P.O. Box 428 (44632-0428)
PHONE.................330 877-9345
Rosalee Haines, *President*
Jacquelin Vaughn, *Admin Sec*
EMP: 5
SQ FT: 2,400
SALES: 235K **Privately Held**
SIC: 2711 2752 Commercial printing & newspaper publishing combined; lithographing on metal

(G-10700)
L C F INC
Also Called: Love Chocolate Factory
114 S Prospect Ave (44632-8906)
P.O. Box 1360 (44632-1360)
PHONE.................330 877-3322
Robert M Barton, *President*
▼ **EMP:** 18
SQ FT: 12,000
SALES (est): 2.3MM **Privately Held**
SIC: 2066 Chocolate candy, solid

(G-10701)
LOUISVILLE MOLDED PRODUCTS
Also Called: Lmp
13122 Duquette Ave Ne (44632-8829)
PHONE.................330 877-9740
Robert Osolinski, *President*
Charles Lynn, *Vice Pres*
EMP: 6
SQ FT: 40,000
SALES (est): 660K **Privately Held**
WEB: www.lmp.com
SIC: 2821 Polyurethane resins

(G-10702)
MITCHELL PIPING LLC
1101 Sunnyside St Sw C (44632-9066)
PHONE.................330 245-0258
Scott Mitchell, *President*
EMP: 30
SALES (est): 1.2MM **Privately Held**
SIC: 3498 Fabricated pipe & fittings

(G-10703)
RANDOLPH TOOL COMPANY INC
750 Wales Dr (44632-8852)
PHONE.................330 877-4923
Patrick Franze, *President*
Lisa M Franze, *Treasurer*
EMP: 12
SQ FT: 5,800
SALES (est): 2.2MM **Privately Held**
WEB: www.randolphtool.com
SIC: 3599 3423 Machine shop, jobbing & repair; knives, agricultural or industrial

(G-10704)
SCANACON INCORPORATED
950 Wales Dr (44632-8856)
PHONE.................330 877-7600
Sven Hedman, *Ch of Bd*
Kevin Wolf, *President*
William Gower, *Vice Pres*
Shannon Gledhill, *Project Mgr*
Ken Setzler, *Engineer*
▲ **EMP:** 6
SALES (est): 1.9MM
SALES (corp-wide): 765.5K **Privately Held**
WEB: www.scanacon.com
SIC: 3565 Canning machinery, food
HQ: Scanacon Ab
Bergkallavagen 36c
Sollentuna 192 7
856 482-300

Hartville - Stark County (G-10705) GEOGRAPHIC SECTION

(G-10705)
SCOTT PROCESS SYSTEMS INC
Also Called: Spsi
1160 Sunnyside St Sw (44632-9098)
PHONE..................................330 877-2350
Frank Diener, *Vice Pres*
Jason Kinsley, *Plant Mgr*
◆ EMP: 240
SQ FT: 100,000
SALES (est): 65.7MM Privately Held
WEB: www.scottprocess.com
SIC: 3498 Pipe sections fabricated from purchased pipe
HQ: Industrial Piping, Inc.
212 S Tryon St Ste 1050
Charlotte NC 28281
704 588-1100

Harveysburg
Warren County

(G-10706)
TRANSEL CORPORATION
Also Called: Transel Technologies
123 E South St (45032)
PHONE..................................513 897-3442
Darrell McKinney, *President*
Kimberly McKinney, *Vice Pres*
EMP: 5
SQ FT: 3,792
SALES: 500K Privately Held
WEB: www.transeltech.com
SIC: 5999 3663 8742 Communication equipment; radio & TV communications equipment; management consulting services

Haverhill
Scioto County

(G-10707)
ALTIVIA PETROCHEMICALS LLC
1019 Haverhill Ohio (45636)
PHONE..................................740 532-3420
Mark Tipton, *Manager*
EMP: 50
SALES (corp-wide): 72.9MM Privately Held
SIC: 2865 Phenol, alkylated & cumene
PA: Altivia Petrochemicals, Llc
1100 La St Ste 4800
Houston TX 77002
713 658-9000

Haviland
Paulding County

(G-10708)
CUSTOM ASSEMBLY INC
2952 Road 107 (45851-9638)
PHONE..................................419 622-3040
George Keysor, *President*
Steven R Plummer, *Principal*
Gus A Schlatter, *Principal*
Sharon Keysor, *Vice Pres*
Jennifer Rigdon, *Human Res Mgr*
EMP: 50
SQ FT: 60,000
SALES (est): 9.7MM Privately Held
SIC: 3751 Motorcycles, bicycles & parts

(G-10709)
DRAINAGE PRODUCTS INC
100 W Main St (45851)
P.O. Box 61 (45851-0061)
PHONE..................................419 622-6951
Craig A Stoller, *President*
Thomas Coy, *Corp Secy*
EMP: 25 EST: 1978
SALES (est): 3.7MM Privately Held
SIC: 3084 Plastics pipe

(G-10710)
HAVILAND CULVERT COMPANY
100 W Main (45851)
P.O. Box 97 (45851-0097)
PHONE..................................419 622-6951
Russell W Stoller, *President*
Thomas A Gordon, *Corp Secy*
EMP: 7
SALES (est): 1.1MM Privately Held
SIC: 3272 Pipe, concrete or lined with concrete

(G-10711)
HAVILAND DRAINAGE PRODUCTS CO (PA)
100 W Main St (45851)
PHONE..................................419 622-4611
Russell Stoller, *President*
Todd Stoller, *Corp Secy*
EMP: 17 EST: 1924
SQ FT: 1,000
SALES (est): 50.8MM Privately Held
SIC: 3259 Drain tile, clay

(G-10712)
HAVILAND PLASTIC PRODUCTS CO
119 W Main St (45851)
P.O. Box 38 (45851-0038)
PHONE..................................419 622-3110
Craig Stoller, *President*
Todd Stoller, *Corp Secy*
▼ EMP: 26
SALES (est): 8MM Privately Held
WEB: www.havilandplastics.com
SIC: 3089 Fittings for pipe, plastic

(G-10713)
MODERN PLASTICS RECOVERY INC
100 Main St (45851)
P.O. Box 38 (45851-0038)
PHONE..................................419 622-4611
Craig Stoller, *President*
EMP: 16
SALES (est): 3.5MM Privately Held
SIC: 2821 Plastics materials & resins

Hayesville
Ashland County

(G-10714)
COBURN INC (PA)
636 Ashland Cnty Rd 30 A (44838)
P.O. Box 447, Ashland (44805-0447)
PHONE..................................419 368-4051
Charles Zimmerman, *CEO*
Todd Zimmerman, *President*
EMP: 65
SQ FT: 82,000
SALES (est): 15.3MM Privately Held
SIC: 2631 Container, packaging & boxboard; folding boxboard

(G-10715)
JBM TECHNOLOGIES INC
1926 State Rte 179 (44838)
P.O. Box 108 (44838-0108)
PHONE..................................419 368-4362
Leslie W Jordan, *President*
EMP: 5
SQ FT: 10,000
SALES (est): 596.1K Privately Held
SIC: 3053 Gaskets & sealing devices; gaskets, all materials

Heath
Licking County

(G-10716)
AMERICAN VNEER EDGEBANDING INC
Also Called: A.V.E.C.
1700 James Pkwy (43056-4027)
PHONE..................................740 928-2700
Germany Heigtz, *Principal*
Andrew Lenkei, *Sales Mgr*
▲ EMP: 6
SQ FT: 30,000
SALES (est): 987.8K
SALES (corp-wide): 1.9B Privately Held
WEB: www.avec-usa.com
SIC: 2435 2436 Veneer stock, hardwood; veneer stock, softwood
HQ: Heitz International Beteiligungs Gmbh
Maschweg 27
Melle 49324
542 296-80

(G-10717)
ATLANTIC INERTIAL SYSTEMS INC
781 Irving Wick Dr W (43056-9492)
PHONE..................................740 788-3800
Al Bonacci, *Branch Mgr*
EMP: 30
SALES (corp-wide): 66.5B Publicly Held
WEB: www.condorpacific.com
SIC: 3812 Gyroscopes
HQ: Atlantic Inertial Systems Inc.
250 Knotter Dr
Cheshire CT 06410
203 250-3500

(G-10718)
BIONETICS CORPORATION
Also Called: Bionetics-Desg-
781 Irving Wick Dr W # 1 (43056-9492)
PHONE..................................740 788-3800
Carolyn Matthews, *General Mgr*
EMP: 24
SQ FT: 160,000
SALES (corp-wide): 47.1MM Privately Held
WEB: www.bionetics.com
SIC: 3679 3829 Electronic circuits; measuring & controlling devices
PA: The Bionetics Corporation
101 Production Dr Ste 100
Yorktown VA 23693
757 873-0900

(G-10719)
HARTMAN DISTRIBUTING LLC
1262 Bluejack Ln (43056-8228)
PHONE..................................740 616-7764
Troy Hartman, *CEO*
EMP: 84
SALES (est): 4.9MM Privately Held
SIC: 2759 Screen printing

(G-10720)
HOMESTEAD BEER COMPANY
811 Irving Wick Dr W (43056-1199)
PHONE..................................740 522-8018
EMP: 7
SALES (est): 516.2K Privately Held
SIC: 2082 Malt beverages

(G-10721)
INTEC LLC
351 S 30th St Ste E (43056-1265)
P.O. Box 204, Crestwood KY (40014-0204)
PHONE..................................614 633-7430
John Kupka, *Mng Member*
EMP: 4
SQ FT: 2,500
SALES: 160K Privately Held
SIC: 3577 Printers & plotters

(G-10722)
ISO TECHNOLOGIES INC
1870 James Pkwy (43056-4003)
PHONE..................................740 928-0084
Alan Benton, *President*
EMP: 3 EST: 2013
SALES (est): 362.5K Privately Held
SIC: 3086 Plastics foam products

(G-10723)
KAISER ALUMINUM FAB PDTS LLC
Also Called: Kaiser Aluminum Newark Works
600 Kaiser Dr (43056-1088)
PHONE..................................740 522-1151
Dan Lilly, *Prdtn Mgr*
Larry Spring, *Purch Agent*
Cary Holmes, *Engineer*
Sean Hussey, *Human Res Mgr*
Renee McCann, *HR Admin*
EMP: 250
SALES (corp-wide): 1.4B Publicly Held
WEB: www.kaisertwd.com
SIC: 3355 3334 Rods, rolled, aluminum; primary aluminum
HQ: Kaiser Aluminum Fabricated Products, Llc
27422 Portola Pkwy # 200
Foothill Ranch CA 92610

(G-10724)
KOROSHI SCHOOL OF DEFENSE
12955 Fairview Rd (43056-9044)
PHONE..................................740 323-3582
EMP: 3
SALES (est): 170.8K Privately Held
SIC: 3812 Defense systems & equipment

(G-10725)
KPS NAPA
441 Hopewell Dr (43056-1547)
PHONE..................................740 522-9445
Howard Warner, *Owner*
EMP: 15
SALES (est): 640K Privately Held
SIC: 3711 Automobile bodies, passenger car, not including engine, etc.

(G-10726)
MATTERWORKS
2135 James Pkwy (43056-4002)
PHONE..................................740 200-0071
Thomas Miller, *President*
EMP: 3
SALES (est): 229.6K Privately Held
SIC: 2822 Ethylene-propylene rubbers, EPDM polymers

(G-10727)
POLYMER TECH & SVCS INC (PA)
Also Called: Pts
1835 James Pkwy (43056-1092)
PHONE..................................740 929-5500
Sharad Thakkar, *President*
EMP: 35
SQ FT: 50,000
SALES (est): 5.4MM Privately Held
WEB: www.polymertechnologiesinc.com
SIC: 3089 2611 Casting of plastic; pulp mills

(G-10728)
R D HOLDER OIL CO INC
1000 Keller Dr (43056-8055)
PHONE..................................740 522-3136
EMP: 5
SALES (corp-wide): 28.4MM Privately Held
SIC: 1311 Crude petroleum & natural gas
PA: R. D. Holder Oil Co., Inc.
600 N Dayton Lakeview Rd
New Carlisle OH 45344
800 243-0432

(G-10729)
RAMP CREEK III LTD
1100 Thornwood Dr Lot 1 (43056-9501)
P.O. Box 240, Reynoldsburg (43068-0240)
PHONE..................................740 522 0660
Roberto Ditommaso, *Principal*
EMP: 7
SALES (est): 513.4K Privately Held
SIC: 3272 Housing components, prefabricated concrete

(G-10730)
RESINOID ENGINEERING CORP
2040 James Pkwy (43056-1031)
PHONE..................................740 928-2220
R Young, *Controller*
John Maurer, *Branch Mgr*
EMP: 20
SALES (corp-wide): 21.7MM Privately Held
WEB: www.resinoid.com
SIC: 3089 3714 3625 Plastic hardware & building products; motor vehicle parts & accessories; relays & industrial controls
PA: Resinoid Engineering Corp
251 Oneill Dr
Hebron OH 43025
740 928-6115

(G-10731)
SAMUEL STRAPPING SYSTEMS INC
1455 James Pkwy (43056-4007)
PHONE..................................740 522-2500

Brad McConnell, *Production*
Matthew Taylor, *Controller*
Jay Jones, *Manager*
EMP: 100
SALES (corp-wide): 1.8B **Privately Held**
WEB: www.samuelstrapping.com
SIC: 3565 3089 5085 5084 Wrapping machines; plastic processing; industrial supplies; industrial machinery & equipment; packaging materials
HQ: Samuel, Son & Co. (Usa) Inc.
1401 Davey Rd Ste 300
Woodridge IL 60517
630 783-8900

(G-10732)
SAND HOLLOW WINERY
12558 Sand Hollow Rd (43056-9789)
PHONE...................740 323-3959
Jim Young, *Principal*
EMP: 3
SALES (est): 158.3K **Privately Held**
SIC: 2084 Wines

(G-10733)
SITE TECH (PA)
75 Central Pkwy (43056-1253)
PHONE...................740 522-0019
Phil Jones, *Principal*
EMP: 4
SALES (est): 723.9K **Privately Held**
SIC: 3571 Electronic computers

(G-10734)
W/S PACKAGING GROUP INC
1720 James Pkwy (43056-4027)
PHONE...................740 929-2210
Albert Ghiloni, *General Mgr*
Bob Braun, *Vice Pres*
Judy Ghiloni, *Cust Mgr*
Tim Newberry, *Manager*
EMP: 14
SALES (corp-wide): 734.8MM **Privately Held**
SIC: 2679 2752 Labels, paper: made from purchased material; commercial printing, lithographic
PA: W/S Packaging Group, Inc.
2571 S Hemlock Rd
Green Bay WI 54229
920 866-6300

(G-10735)
XPERION E&E USA LLC
1475 James Pkwy (43056-4007)
PHONE...................740 788-9560
Sean Ellen, *Mng Member*
EMP: 25
SQ FT: 50,000
SALES (est): 8.3MM
SALES (corp-wide): 173.4MM **Privately Held**
SIC: 3624 Fibers, carbon & graphite
HQ: Hexagon Purus Gmbh
Otto-Hahn-Str. 5
Kassel 34123
561 585-490

Hebron
Licking County

(G-10736)
4W SERVICES
7901 Minecaster Rd (43025)
PHONE...................614 554-5427
Donald White, *Owner*
EMP: 15
SALES: 300K **Privately Held**
SIC: 3715 8999 Semitrailers for truck tractors; artists & artists' studios

(G-10737)
ALLIED TUBE & CONDUIT CORP
250 Capital Dr (43025-9489)
PHONE...................740 928-1018
Scott Shipley, *Branch Mgr*
EMP: 12 **Publicly Held**
WEB: www.alliedtube.com
SIC: 3644 Electric conduits & fittings
HQ: Allied Tube & Conduit Corporation
16100 Lathrop Ave
Harvey IL 60426
708 339-1610

(G-10738)
ARMORSOURCE LLC
3600 Hebron Rd (43025-9664)
PHONE...................740 928-0070
Yoav Kapah, *CEO*
Donald Blake, *Exec VP*
Keith Gaskins, *Vice Pres*
Bob Pettinger, *Vice Pres*
Brian Leis, *Materials Mgr*
▼ **EMP:** 20
SQ FT: 120,000
SALES (est): 7.9MM **Privately Held**
SIC: 3469 Helmets, steel

(G-10739)
CLEARWATER WOOD GROUP LLC
4401 Hunts Landing Rd (43025-9493)
PHONE...................567 644-9951
Aaron Mayes, *Mng Member*
Girard Besanceney, *Mng Member*
▲ **EMP:** 4 **EST:** 2010
SALES (est): 2MM **Privately Held**
SIC: 2511 Wood household furniture

(G-10740)
COVESTRO LLC
Newark Industrial Park (43025)
PHONE...................740 929-2015
Lora Rand, *Manager*
EMP: 150
SALES (corp-wide): 16.7B **Privately Held**
SIC: 2822 2821 Synthetic rubber; plastics materials & resins
HQ: Covestro Llc
1 Covestro Cir
Pittsburgh PA 15205
412 413-2000

(G-10741)
DAVID OGILBEE
1881 Beaver Run Rd Se (43025-9651)
PHONE...................740 929-2638
David Ogilbee, *CEO*
EMP: 3
SALES (est): 196.2K **Privately Held**
SIC: 3715 Truck trailers

(G-10742)
DOW CHEMICAL COMPANY
3700 Hebron Rd (43025-9665)
PHONE...................740 929-5100
David Cook, *Branch Mgr*
EMP: 7
SALES (corp-wide): 85.9B **Publicly Held**
SIC: 2821 Thermoplastic materials
HQ: The Dow Chemical Company
2211 H H Dow Way
Midland MI 48642
989 636-1000

(G-10743)
FORCEONE LLC
3600 Hebron Rd (43025-9664)
PHONE...................513 939-1018
Dannie Dubley,
Don Blake,
Larry Dixon,
EMP: 30
SQ FT: 17,000
SALES (est): 4.1MM **Privately Held**
WEB: www.hardarmor.com
SIC: 3842 Bulletproof vests

(G-10744)
GE INFRASTRUCTURE SENSING INC
611 O Neill Dr (43025-9680)
PHONE...................740 928-7010
Elizabeth May, *Branch Mgr*
EMP: 301
SALES (corp-wide): 121.6B **Publicly Held**
SIC: 3823 Moisture meters, industrial process type
HQ: Ge Infrastructure Sensing, Llc
1100 Technology Park Dr # 100
Billerica MA 01821
978 437-1000

(G-10745)
GENERAL ELECTRIC COMPANY
611 O Neill Dr (43025-9659)
PHONE...................740 928-7010
EMP: 8

SALES (corp-wide): 121.6B **Publicly Held**
SIC: 3297 Crucibles: graphite, magnesite, chrome, silica, etc.
PA: General Electric Company
41 Farnsworth St
Boston MA 02210
617 443-3000

(G-10746)
GLUTEN-FREE EXPRESSIONS
520 E Main St (43025-9702)
PHONE...................740 928-0338
Cyndi Baughman, *Principal*
EMP: 4
SALES (est): 183.3K **Privately Held**
SIC: 2051 Cakes, bakery: except frozen

(G-10747)
HENDRICKSON INTERNATIONAL CORP
Also Called: Hendrickson Auxiliary Axles
277 N High St (43025-8008)
PHONE...................740 929-5600
Mike Keeler, *General Mgr*
Lisa Kirkingburg, *Accounting Dir*
EMP: 78
SALES (corp-wide): 916.4MM **Privately Held**
SIC: 3714 3493 3089 5084 Motor vehicle parts & accessories; steel springs, except wire; plastic containers, except foam; industrial machinery & equipment; truck & bus bodies
HQ: Hendrickson International Corporation
500 Park Blvd Ste 450
Itasca IL 60143
630 874-9700

(G-10748)
HOLLYS CUSTOM PRINT INC
1001 O Neill Dr (43025-9409)
P.O. Box 4454, Newark (43058-4454)
PHONE...................740 928-2697
Steve Hollingshead, *President*
EMP: 35
SQ FT: 22,500
SALES (est): 3.6MM **Privately Held**
SIC: 2752 2759 Commercial printing, lithographic; commercial printing

(G-10749)
ISO TECHNOLOGIES INC
200 Milliken Dr (43025-9657)
PHONE...................740 344-9554
Alan Benton, *President*
EMP: 30
SALES: 10MM **Privately Held**
SIC: 3069 Foam rubber

(G-10750)
LEAR CORPORATION
Also Called: Renosol Seating
180 N High St (43025-9011)
P.O. Box 640 (43025-0640)
PHONE...................740 928-4358
Jeff O'Sickey, *Plant Mgr*
Derek Bujak, *Materials Mgr*
Mark Dobransky, *Materials Mgr*
EMP: 50
SALES (corp-wide): 21.1B **Publicly Held**
SIC: 3714 Motor vehicle parts & accessories
PA: Lear Corporation
21557 Telegraph Rd
Southfield MI 48033
248 447-1500

(G-10751)
MCKINLEYS MEADERY LLC
4412 Keller Rd (43025-9630)
PHONE...................740 928-0229
Jarrod McKinley, *Principal*
EMP: 3 **EST:** 2016
SALES (est): 91.3K **Privately Held**
SIC: 2082 Malt beverages

(G-10752)
MOLDING TECHNOLOGIES LTD
85 N High St (43025)
PHONE...................740 929-2065
Angela Baumgartner,
EMP: 10 **EST:** 2017
SQ FT: 60,000
SALES (est): 1.1MM **Privately Held**
SIC: 3089 Plastics products

(G-10753)
MOMENTIVE PERFORMANCE MTLS INC
611 O Neill Dr (43025-9680)
PHONE...................740 928-7010
Dan Edson, *Engineer*
Mordhorst Steve, *Marketing Mgr*
Cherly Glaton, *Manager*
Angela Fenn-Garrett, *Info Tech Dir*
EMP: 195
SALES (corp-wide): 2.7B **Publicly Held**
SIC: 2869 3479 Silicones; coating of metals with silicon
HQ: Momentive Performance Materials Inc.
260 Hudson River Rd
Waterford NY 12188

(G-10754)
MPW INDUSTRIAL SVCS GROUP INC (PA)
9711 Lancaster Rd (43025-9764)
PHONE...................740 927-8790
Monte R Black, *CEO*
Jared Black, *President*
Jimmy Peck, *General Mgr*
Sean M Hutcheson, *Counsel*
Tyler Keathley, *Opers Mgr*
EMP: 86
SQ FT: 24,000
SALES (est): 208.7MM **Privately Held**
WEB: www.mpwgroup.com
SIC: 7349 8744 3589 Cleaning service, industrial or commercial; facilities support services; commercial cleaning equipment

(G-10755)
MTI ACQUISITION LLC
Also Called: Molding Technologies
85 N High St (43025)
P.O. Box 730 (43025-0730)
PHONE...................740 929-2065
Angela Baumgartner, *CFO*
Jesse Downhour, *Mng Member*
EMP: 25
SQ FT: 55,000
SALES (est): 4.4MM **Privately Held**
WEB: www.moldingtech.com
SIC: 3089 Plastic hardware & building products

(G-10756)
OHIO METAL TECHNOLOGIES INC
470 John Alford Pkwy (43025-9437)
PHONE...................740 928-8288
Toshi Hara, *President*
Masao Segawa, *Vice Pres*
Toshiyuki Hara, *Treasurer*
▲ **EMP:** 80
SQ FT: 20,600
SALES (est): 24.6MM **Privately Held**
WEB: www.ohiometal.net
SIC: 3462 Automotive & internal combustion engine forgings

(G-10757)
PLASTIPAK PACKAGING INC
Also Called: Constar International
610 O Neill Dr Bldg 22 (43025-9680)
PHONE...................740 928-4435
Paul Medley, *Plant Mgr*
Brian Dunlap, *Opers Mgr*
Michelle McClellen, *Human Res Mgr*
EMP: 125
SALES (corp-wide): 1.3B **Privately Held**
WEB: www.constarllc.com
SIC: 3089 3085 Plastic containers, except foam; plastics bottles
HQ: Plastipak Packaging, Inc.
41605 Ann Arbor Rd E
Plymouth MI 48170
734 455-3600

(G-10758)
POLYMERA INC
511 Milliken Dr (43025-9657)
PHONE...................740 527-2069
Maan Said, *President*
Herbert Hutchison, *Senior VP*
Jeffrey Brandt, *Vice Pres*
Matthew Kollar, *Vice Pres*
Michael Skoff, *CFO*
EMP: 9

Hebron - Licking County (G-10759)

SALES (est): 2.2MM **Privately Held**
SIC: 3087 Custom compound purchased resins

(G-10759)
RESINOID ENGINEERING CORP (PA)
251 Oneill Dr (43025)
PHONE...................................740 928-6115
Robert C Herbst, *President*
Tom Pitcock, *General Mgr*
Clarence A Herbst Jr, *Chairman*
Sam Mohn, *Manager*
Jeff Showers, *Senior Mgr*
▲ **EMP:** 100 **EST:** 1939
SQ FT: 70,000
SALES (est): 21.7MM **Privately Held**
WEB: www.resinoid.com
SIC: 2821 3083 3089 Molding compounds, plastics; laminated plastics plate & sheet; injection molding of plastics

(G-10760)
RR DONNELLEY & SONS COMPANY
Also Called: R R Donnelley
190 Milliken Dr (43025-9657)
PHONE...................................740 928-6110
Jeff Gebhart, *Branch Mgr*
EMP: 280
SALES (corp-wide): 6.8B **Publicly Held**
SIC: 2759 Business forms: printing
PA: R. R. Donnelley & Sons Company
35 W Wacker Dr Ste 3650
Chicago IL 60601
312 326-8000

(G-10761)
S R DOOR INC (PA)
Also Called: Seal-Rite Door
1120 O Neill Dr (43025-9409)
P.O. Box 2109, Columbus (43216-2109)
PHONE...................................740 927-3558
Scott A Miller, *President*
Glen Miller, *Vice Pres*
EMP: 106 **EST:** 1980
SQ FT: 75,000
SALES (est): 15.9MM **Privately Held**
WEB: www.seal-ritedoor.com
SIC: 2431 3442 3211 5031 Doors, wood; windows & window parts & trim, wood; metal doors; construction glass; lumber, plywood & millwork

(G-10762)
SCHWEBEL BAKING COMPANY
121 O Neill Dr (43025-9680)
PHONE...................................330 783-2860
John Phillips, *Manager*
Chuck Monroe, *Manager*
EMP: 74
SALES (corp-wide): 170MM **Privately Held**
WEB: www.schwebels.com
SIC: 5461 2051 Bread; bread, cake & related products
PA: Schwebel Baking Company
965 E Midlothian Blvd
Youngstown OH 44502
330 783-2860

(G-10763)
SMARTBILL LTD
1050 O Neill Dr (43025-9409)
PHONE...................................740 928-6909
Sherry Obrien, *Executive*
Robin Hess,
Randy W Hess,
EMP: 17
SQ FT: 10,000
SALES (est): 3.6MM **Privately Held**
WEB: www.smartbillcorp.com
SIC: 2759 Business forms: printing

(G-10764)
SUNFIELD INC
116 Enterprise Dr (43025-9200)
PHONE...................................740 928-0404
Norio Hirotani, *President*
Chuck Curran, *Plant Mgr*
Masashi Harana, *Plant Mgr*
Donna Estep, *Production*
Mike Bush, *Admin Sec*
▲ **EMP:** 70
SQ FT: 33,000

SALES (est): 29.6MM
SALES (corp-wide): 701.9K **Privately Held**
SIC: 3469 Stamping metal for the trade
HQ: Ikeda Manufacturing Co., Ltd.
135-3, Nishishinmachi
Ota GNM 373-0
276 313-131

(G-10765)
TENCATE ADVANCED ARMOR USA INC
1051 Oneill Dr (43025)
PHONE...................................740 928-0326
EMP: 83
SALES (corp-wide): 1.4B **Privately Held**
SIC: 3229 3795 Yarn, fiberglass; tanks & tank components
HQ: Tencate Advanced Armor Usa, Inc.
165 Castilian Dr
Goleta CA 93117

(G-10766)
THK MANUFACTURING AMERICA INC
471 N High St (43025-9012)
P.O. Box 759 (43025-0759)
PHONE...................................740 928-1415
Nobuyuki Maki, *President*
Andrew Lower, *Project Engr*
David Jacques, *Manager*
Clay Hooper, *Maintence Staff*
Chie Schuller, *Relations*
▲ **EMP:** 160
SQ FT: 400,000
SALES (est): 48.8MM
SALES (corp-wide): 3.1B **Privately Held**
WEB: www.thk.com
SIC: 3823 3469 Industrial instrmnts msrmnt display/control process variable; machine parts, stamped or pressed metal
HQ: T H K Holdings Of America Llc
200 Commerce Dr
Schaumburg IL 60173
847 310-1111

(G-10767)
TI GROUP AUTO SYSTEMS LLC
Bundy Tubing Div
3600 Hebron Rd (43025-9664)
PHONE...................................740 929-2049
Mark Lanancusa, *Manager*
EMP: 250
SALES (corp-wide): 4B **Privately Held**
WEB: www.tiautomotive.com
SIC: 3317 3714 3498 Steel pipe & tubes; motor vehicle parts & accessories; fabricated pipe & fittings
HQ: Ti Group Automotive Systems, Llc
2020 Taylor Rd
Auburn Hills MI 48326
248 296-8000

(G-10768)
TRANSCENDIA INC
Also Called: Dow Chemical
3700 Hebron Rd (43025-9665)
PHONE...................................740 929-5100
Andy Maynard, *Branch Mgr*
EMP: 105
SALES (corp-wide): 348.8MM **Privately Held**
WEB: www.dow.com
SIC: 3081 Unsupported plastics film & sheet
PA: Transcendia, Inc.
9201 Belmont Ave
Franklin Park IL 60131
847 678-1800

(G-10769)
UNIPAC INC
2109 National Rd Sw (43025-9639)
PHONE...................................740 929-2000
David L De Ment, *President*
Chris De Ment, *Treasurer*
EMP: 22 **EST:** 1973
SQ FT: 50,000
SALES (est): 8.6MM **Privately Held**
WEB: www.unipacinc.com
SIC: 2657 2653 Folding paperboard boxes; boxes, corrugated: made from purchased materials

(G-10770)
VIRGAIL INDUSTRIES INC
Also Called: Accufilm
145 S High St (43025-9690)
P.O. Box 277 (43025-0277)
PHONE...................................740 928-6001
Bradley Jay Smith, *President*
▲ **EMP:** 7
SQ FT: 11,200
SALES: 457.7K **Privately Held**
SIC: 2671 Packaging paper & plastics film, coated & laminated

Helena
Sandusky County

(G-10771)
FREMONT QUICK PRINT
2870 W Us Highway 6 (43435-9709)
PHONE...................................419 334-8808
Scott McConnell, *Owner*
EMP: 3
SALES: 120K **Privately Held**
SIC: 7334 2752 Photocopying & duplicating services; commercial printing, offset

(G-10772)
GLASS MIRROR AWARDS INC
703 County Road 26 (43435-9776)
PHONE...................................419 638-2221
Mark Leyerle, *President*
Laurie Leyerle, *Vice Pres*
EMP: 5
SALES (est): 600K **Privately Held**
SIC: 3999 5231 Plaques, picture, laminated; glass

Hicksville
Defiance County

(G-10773)
A & P TOOL INC
Also Called: APT Manufacturing Solutions
801 Industrial Dr (43526-1174)
P.O. Box 88 (43526-0088)
PHONE...................................419 542-6681
Anthony R Nighswander, *President*
Ben Nighswander, *Vice Pres*
Brent Staugler, *Purch Agent*
Mandy Ridgway, *Purchasing*
Travis Hughes, *Engineer*
EMP: 30
SALES (est): 8.6MM **Privately Held**
WEB: www.aptoolinc.com
SIC: 3541 3822 Machine tools, metal cutting type; building services monitoring controls, automatic

(G-10774)
ADROIT THINKING INC
Also Called: 5-Acre Mill
10860 State Route 2 (43526-9366)
PHONE...................................419 542-9363
Tim Becker, *President*
Mary Becker, *Vice Pres*
EMP: 17
SQ FT: 28,000
SALES (est): 2.3MM **Privately Held**
SIC: 2499 Decorative wood & woodwork

(G-10775)
ARC SOLUTIONS INC
605 Industrial Dr (43526-1177)
P.O. Box 264 (43526-0264)
PHONE...................................419 542-9272
Dennis Vetter, *President*
EMP: 10
SALES (est): 2.4MM **Privately Held**
WEB: www.arcsolutions.com
SIC: 7692 Welding repair; welding machinery & equipment

(G-10776)
AVALIGN TECHNOLOGIES INC (HQ)
801 Industrial Dr (43526-1174)
PHONE...................................419 542-7743
Forrest Whittaker, *CEO*
Kevin L Countryman, *President*
Kalli Countryman, *Vice Pres*

John Binz, *Plant Mgr*
John Rapes, *CFO*
EMP: 10
SQ FT: 50,000
SALES (est): 14.1MM
SALES (corp-wide): 270.1MM **Privately Held**
WEB: www.nemcomed.net
SIC: 3842 3841 Splints, pneumatic & wood; surgical & medical instruments
PA: Roundtable Healthcare Partners, Lp
272 E Deerpath Ste 350
Lake Forest IL 60045
847 739-3200

(G-10777)
BATTERSHELL CABINETS
312 Defiance Ave (43526-1210)
PHONE...................................419 542-6448
John Battershell, *Owner*
EMP: 4
SALES (est): 205.2K **Privately Held**
SIC: 1751 2511 Cabinet building & installation; wood household furniture

(G-10778)
FWT LLC
761 W High St (43526-1052)
P.O. Box 8597, Fort Worth TX (76124-0597)
PHONE...................................419 542-1420
Robert Krause, *Branch Mgr*
EMP: 9
SALES (corp-wide): 6.3B **Privately Held**
SIC: 3441 Building components, structural steel
HQ: Fwt, L.L.C.
5750 E Interstate 20
Fort Worth TX 76119
817 255-2965

(G-10779)
MST INC
Also Called: Modern Safety Techniques
11370 Breininger Rd (43526-9339)
P.O. Box 87 (43526-0087)
PHONE...................................419 542-6645
Charles Martin, *President*
James M Prickett, *Principal*
EMP: 7
SQ FT: 10,000
SALES (est): 740K **Privately Held**
WEB: www.modsafe.com
SIC: 3842 Respiratory protection equipment, personal

(G-10780)
NEMCO FOOD EQUIPMENT LTD (PA)
301 Meuse Argonne St (43526-1143)
P.O. Box 305 (43526-0305)
PHONE...................................419 542-7751
Kenny Moffatt, *Ch of Bd*
Stanley Guilliam, *President*
Don McGlaughlin, *Production*
Bruce Werling, *QC Mgr*
Larry Stowart, *CFO*
◆ **EMP:** 75 **EST:** 1976
SQ FT: 50,000
SALES (est): 17.2MM **Privately Held**
WEB: www.nemconet.com
SIC: 3556 Food products machinery

(G-10781)
PARKER-HANNIFIN CORPORATION
Hydraulic Valve Div
373 Meuse Argonne St (43526-1182)
PHONE...................................419 542-6611
Andy Ross, *Branch Mgr*
EMP: 161
SALES (corp-wide): 14.3B **Publicly Held**
WEB: www.parker.com
SIC: 3492 3491 Valves, hydraulic, aircraft; industrial valves
PA: Parker-Hannifin Corporation
6035 Parkland Blvd
Cleveland OH 44124
216 896-3000

(G-10782)
STEELES 5 ACRE MILL INC
10860 State Route 2 (43526-9366)
PHONE...................................419 542-9363
Cathy Steele, *President*
EMP: 17

SALES (est): 1.6MM **Privately Held**
SIC: 2499 Decorative wood & woodwork

(G-10783)
STOETT INDUSTRIES INC
Also Called: Libart North America
600 Defiance Ave (43526-9352)
PHONE.....................419 542-0247
Jack Stover, *President*
Jeff Manger, *Project Mgr*
Brooke Gordon, *Mktg Dir*
◆ EMP: 24
SQ FT: 68,000
SALES: 1.4MM **Privately Held**
WEB: www.stoett.com
SIC: 3442 Screen & storm doors & windows

(G-10784)
TRI STATE DAIRY LLC
210 Wendell Ave (43526-1405)
P.O. Box 284 (43526-0284)
PHONE.....................419 542-8788
Nelson Hershberger, *Principal*
EMP: 8
SALES (est): 1.1MM **Privately Held**
SIC: 2022 Cheese, natural & processed

(G-10785)
TRIBUNE PRINTING INC
Also Called: News Tribune
147 E High St (43526-1159)
P.O. Box 303 (43526-0303)
PHONE.....................419 542-7764
Mary Ann Barth, *President*
EMP: 9
SQ FT: 2,000
SALES (est): 605.4K **Privately Held**
WEB: www.hicksvillenewstribune.com
SIC: 2711 2752 Newspapers: publishing only, not printed on site; commercial printing, lithographic

Highland Heights
Cuyahoga County

(G-10786)
C & S ASSOCIATES INC
Also Called: National Lien Digest
729 Miner Rd (44143-2117)
P.O. Box 24101, Cleveland (44124-0101)
PHONE.....................440 461-9661
Mary B Cowan, *President*
Delores A Cowan, *President*
Cathleen M Cowan, *Principal*
Bernard J Cowan, *Exec VP*
Greg Powelson, *Vice Pres*
EMP: 50 EST: 1974
SQ FT: 9,000
SALES (est): 6.8MM **Privately Held**
SIC: 7322 2721 Collection agency, except real estate; periodicals: publishing only

(G-10787)
COTSWORKS LLC (PA)
749 Miner Rd (44143-2145)
PHONE.....................440 446-8800
Marc Simms, *Vice Pres*
Ken Applebaum, *Mng Member*
Eugen Artemie, *Manager*
Paul Hospodar, *Manager*
Charles IAMS, *Info Tech Mgr*
EMP: 36
SQ FT: 6,000
SALES (est): 7MM **Privately Held**
WEB: www.cotsworks.com
SIC: 3661 Fiber optics communications equipment

(G-10788)
EM4 INC
676 Alpha Dr (44143-2123)
PHONE.....................216 486-6100
EMP: 5
SALES (est): 809.4K **Privately Held**
SIC: 3674 Semiconductors & related devices

(G-10789)
FD ROLLS CORP
Also Called: Fd Machinery
5405 Avion Park Dr (44143-1918)
PHONE.....................216 536-1433
EMP: 4
SALES (est): 109.9K
SALES (corp-wide): 5.2MM **Privately Held**
SIC: 3317 Steel pipe & tubes
PA: Dalian Field Manufacturing Co., Ltd.
No.39-8, Yongjing Street, Shahekou District
Dalian 11602
411 831-9274

(G-10790)
FORKLIFTS OF AMERICAS LLC
28 Alpha Park (44143-2208)
PHONE.....................440 821-5143
Samuel Benavides, *CFO*
Steve Maniaci, *Sales Staff*
Ken Jecmen,
Henry Alvarado,
Maria Moyano,
EMP: 8
SALES (est): 1.3MM **Privately Held**
SIC: 3537 7359 5063 Forklift trucks; pallet rental services; batteries

(G-10791)
GLOBAL WOOD PRODUCTS LLC
734 Alpha Dr Ste J (44143-2135)
PHONE.....................440 442-5859
EMP: 3 EST: 2010
SALES (est): 180K **Privately Held**
SIC: 2499 Mfg Wood Products

(G-10792)
GOOCH & HOUSEGO (OHIO) LLC
Also Called: Clevelandcrystals
676 Alpha Dr (44143-2123)
PHONE.....................216 486-6100
Gareth Jones, *CEO*
Terry Scribbins, *COO*
Jon Fowler, *Exec VP*
Andrew Boteler, *CFO*
Jeff Luken, *Mng Member*
EMP: 65
SQ FT: 51,000
SALES (est): 15.2MM
SALES (corp-wide): 159.2MM **Privately Held**
WEB: www.clevelandcrystals.com
SIC: 3823 3827 Industrial instrmnts msrmnt display/control process variable; optical instruments & lenses
PA: Gooch & Housego Plc
Dowlish Ford
Ilminster TA19
146 025-6440

(G-10793)
HEICO AEROSPACE PARTS CORP (DH)
Also Called: Flight Specialties Components
375 Alpha Park (44143-2237)
PHONE.....................954 987-6101
Luis J Morell, *President*
David Flosdorf, *Engineer*
Carlos L Macau, *Treasurer*
Elizabeth R Letendre, *Admin Sec*
EMP: 294
SQ FT: 1,500
SALES (est): 43.5MM **Publicly Held**
WEB: www.inertial.com
SIC: 3728 Aircraft parts & equipment
HQ: Heico Aerospace Corporation
3000 Taft St
Hollywood FL 33021
954 987-6101

(G-10794)
NORMAN NOBLE INC (PA)
5507 Avion Park Dr (44143-1921)
PHONE.....................216 761-5387
Lawrence Noble, *President*
Bill Morad, *General Mgr*
Chris Noble, *Vice Pres*
Dan Stefano, *Vice Pres*
Don Beckett, *Engineer*
▲ EMP: 450 EST: 1962
SQ FT: 20,000
SALES (est): 125.3MM **Privately Held**
WEB: www.nnoble.com
SIC: 3841 Instruments, microsurgical: except electromedical

(G-10795)
NORMAN NOBLE INC
5340 Avion Park Dr (44143-1917)
PHONE.....................216 761-5387
Bryan Payne, *QC Mgr*
Dan Stefano, *Manager*
EMP: 287
SALES (corp-wide): 125.3MM **Privately Held**
WEB: www.nnoble.com
SIC: 3599 Machine shop, jobbing & repair
PA: Norman Noble, Inc.
5507 Avion Park Dr
Highland Heights OH 44143
216 761-5387

(G-10796)
OHIO SAFETY PRODUCTS LLC
Also Called: Ohio Safety Supply
675 Alpha Dr (44143-2139)
PHONE.....................216 255-3067
Seva Dorn, *COO*
EMP: 3
SALES (est): 121.7K **Privately Held**
SIC: 3842 Personal safety equipment

(G-10797)
PHILIPS HEALTHCARE CLEVELAND
595 Miner Rd (44143-2131)
PHONE.....................440 483-3235
George M Albertson, *Principal*
◆ EMP: 20
SALES (est): 2.6MM **Privately Held**
SIC: 3845 Electromedical equipment

(G-10798)
PHILIPS MEDICAL SYSTEMS MR
603 Alpha Dr (44143-2114)
PHONE.....................440 483-2499
EMP: 223
SALES (corp-wide): 20.9B **Privately Held**
SIC: 3674 3679 3845 Integrated circuits, semiconductor networks, etc.; cryogenic cooling devices for infrared detectors, masers; cores, magnetic; magnetic resonance imaging device, nuclear
HQ: Philips Medical Systems Mr, Inc
450 Old Niskayuna Rd
Latham NY 12110
518 782-1122

(G-10799)
PURE FOODS LLC
675 Alpha Dr Ste E (44143-2139)
PHONE.....................303 358-8375
Anthony Stedillie, *Mng Member*
EMP: 9
SALES (est): 259.5K **Privately Held**
SIC: 2099 Food preparations

(G-10800)
WG MOBILE WELDING LLC
6151 Wilson Mills Rd # 210 (44143-2153)
PHONE.....................440 720-1940
Wayne Greg, *Owner*
EMP: 5
SALES (est): 91.6K **Privately Held**
SIC: 7692 Welding repair

Hilliard
Franklin County

(G-10801)
ADS VENTURES INC (HQ)
4640 Trueman Blvd (43026-2438)
PHONE.....................614 658-0050
Joseph A Chlapaty, *Ch of Bd*
EMP: 7
SALES (est): 1.8MM
SALES (corp-wide): 1.3B **Publicly Held**
SIC: 3084 3086 Plastics pipe; plastics foam products
PA: Advanced Drainage Systems, Inc.
4640 Trueman Blvd
Hilliard OH 43026
614 658-0050

(G-10802)
ADVANCED DRAINAGE OF OHIO INC
4640 Trueman Blvd (43026-2438)
PHONE.....................614 658-0050
Franklin E Eck, *CEO*
Joseph A Chlapaty, *President*
EMP: 80
SALES (est): 5.2MM
SALES (corp-wide): 1.3B **Publicly Held**
WEB: www.ads-pipe.com
SIC: 3084 Plastics pipe
PA: Advanced Drainage Systems, Inc.
4640 Trueman Blvd
Hilliard OH 43026
614 658-0050

(G-10803)
ADVANCED DRAINAGE SYSTEMS INC (PA)
Also Called: ADS
4640 Trueman Blvd (43026-2438)
PHONE.....................614 658-0050
C Robert Kidder, *Ch of Bd*
D Scott Barbour, *President*
Robert M Klein, *Exec VP*
Ronald R Vitarelli, *Exec VP*
Ewout Leeuwenburg, *Senior VP*
▼ EMP: 100
SQ FT: 45,500
SALES: 1.3B **Publicly Held**
WEB: www.ads-pipe.com
SIC: 3084 3086 Plastics pipe; plastics foam products

(G-10804)
AMERICAN REGENT INC
4150 Lyman Dr (43026)
PHONE.....................614 436-2222
Joseph Kenneth Keller, *CEO*
Robert Vultaggio, *Controller*
Linda Romaine, *Manager*
EMP: 100 **Privately Held**
WEB: www.pharmaforceinc.com
SIC: 2834 5122 Pharmaceutical preparations; pharmaceuticals
HQ: American Regent, Inc.
5 Ramsey Rd
Shirley NY 11967
631 924-4000

(G-10805)
ARES SPORTSWEAR LTD
3704 Lacon Rd (43026-1207)
PHONE.....................614 767-1950
Steve Ritter, *Business Mgr*
Brandon Caylor, *QC Mgr*
Lauren Cook, *Accounts Mgr*
Christopher Mills, *Accounts Mgr*
Greg Barnard, *Mktg Dir*
▲ EMP: 55
SQ FT: 50,000
SALES (est): 19.4MM **Privately Held**
WEB: www.areswear.com
SIC: 2759 Screen printing

(G-10806)
ARMSTRONG WORLD INDUSTRIES INC
4241 Leap Rd Bldg A (43026-1125)
P.O. Box 580 (43026-0580)
PHONE.....................614 771-9307
David G Haggerty, *Opers-Prdtn-Mfg*
Martin Hammack, *Maintence Staff*
Greg Moore, *Maintence Staff*
EMP: 80
SQ FT: 225,000
SALES (corp-wide): 975.3MM **Publicly Held**
WEB: www.armstrong.com
SIC: 5713 3996 3251 Floor covering stores; hard surface floor coverings; brick & structural clay tile
PA: Armstrong World Industries, Inc.
2500 Columbia Ave
Lancaster PA 17603
717 397-0611

(G-10807)
ATLAS MACHINE AND SUPPLY INC
5040 Nike Dr (43026-7420)
PHONE.....................614 351-1603
Greg Dyky, *Branch Mgr*
EMP: 4

Hilliard - Franklin County (G-10808)

SALES (corp-wide): 43.5MM **Privately Held**
WEB: www.atlasmachine.com
SIC: 3599 5084 3563 Machine shop, jobbing & repair; industrial machinery & equipment; air & gas compressors
PA: Atlas Machine And Supply, Inc.
7000 Global Dr
Louisville KY 40258
502 584-7262

(G-10808)
AXALT POWDE COATI SYSTE USA I
4130 Lyman Dr (43026-1230)
PHONE 614 600-4104
EMP: 14
SALES (corp-wide): 4.7B **Publicly Held**
SIC: 2851 Paints & paint additives
HQ: Axalta Powder Coating Systems Usa, Inc.
9800 Genard Rd
Houston TX 77041

(G-10809)
AXALTA COATING SYSTEMS USA LLC
4130 Lyman Dr (43026-1230)
PHONE 614 777-7230
Brian Phillippi, *Prdtn Mgr*
Karyn E Rodriguez,
EMP: 58
SALES (est): 1.2MM **Privately Held**
SIC: 3999 Manufacturing industries

(G-10810)
BARNEY CORPORATION INC (PA)
Also Called: Filters.com
4089 Leap Rd (43026-1117)
P.O. Box 1270 (43026-6270)
PHONE 614 274-9069
Marshall Barney, *President*
Virginia L Barney, *Vice Pres*
◆ EMP: 7
SQ FT: 8,400
SALES (est): 1.3MM **Privately Held**
WEB: www.barneycorp.com
SIC: 3569 Filters

(G-10811)
BESTWAY CABINETS LLC
3525 Ridgewood Dr (43026-2455)
PHONE 614 306-3518
Mike E Dooper, *Principal*
EMP: 4 EST: 2015
SALES (est): 317.5K **Privately Held**
SIC: 2434 Wood kitchen cabinets

(G-10812)
BIAGINIS DRAPERIES
3082 Alton Darby Creek Rd (43026-8337)
PHONE 614 876-1706
Debra Biagini, *Owner*
Butch Biagini, *Co-Owner*
EMP: 3
SALES: 80K **Privately Held**
SIC: 2391 Curtains & draperies

(G-10813)
BIG BILLS TRUCKING LLC
6023 Homestead Ct (43026-7369)
PHONE 614 850-0626
William Davis, *Mng Member*
EMP: 4
SALES: 180K **Privately Held**
SIC: 1442 7389 Construction sand & gravel;

(G-10814)
BLIND FACTORY SHOWROOM
Also Called: The Blind Factory
3670 Parkway Ln Ste M (43026-1237)
PHONE 614 771-6549
Don Grove, *President*
Andrew Grove, *Vice Pres*
Ann Grove, *Treasurer*
EMP: 20
SQ FT: 16,000
SALES (est): 2.2MM **Privately Held**
WEB: www.theblindfactory.com
SIC: 2591 5719 5023 Blinds vertical; vertical blinds; vertical blinds

(G-10815)
BREIBACH ASSOCIATION
Also Called: Breibach & Associates
5117 Grandon Dr (43026-1715)
PHONE 614 876-6480
June Breibach, *Owner*
EMP: 7 EST: 1988
SALES (est): 328.2K **Privately Held**
SIC: 5099 3993 Signs, except electric; advertising novelties

(G-10816)
CITYSCAPES INTERNATIONAL INC
4200 Lyman Ct (43026-1213)
PHONE 614 850-2540
James Cullinan, *President*
EMP: 200
SQ FT: 30,000
SALES: 4.6MM **Privately Held**
WEB: www.cityscapesinc.com
SIC: 3531 Construction machinery

(G-10817)
CLOVERLEAF OFFICE SLUTIONS LLC
5394 Old Creek Ln (43026-8870)
PHONE 614 219-9050
Debbie Derenzo,
Derenzo Brian,
EMP: 3
SALES (est): 289.2K **Privately Held**
SIC: 2759 Commercial printing

(G-10818)
CNG BUSINESS GROUP
Also Called: Friday's Creations
4974 Scoto Darby Rd Ste A (43026)
PHONE 614 771-0877
Anthony Currie, *Owner*
EMP: 3
SQ FT: 2,200
SALES: 250K **Privately Held**
SIC: 2395 Embroidery products, except schiffli machine; embroidery & art needlework

(G-10819)
COLORAMICS LLC
Also Called: Mayco Colors
4077 Weaver Ct S (43026-1197)
PHONE 614 876-1171
Colleen Carey,
◆ EMP: 43
SQ FT: 75,000
SALES (est): 12.7MM **Privately Held**
WEB: www.maycocolors.com
SIC: 2851 Paints & paint additives

(G-10820)
CONNECT TELEVISION
4811 Northwest Pkwy (43026-1128)
PHONE 614 876-4402
Tamy Valkosky, *Principal*
EMP: 3
SALES (est): 176.8K **Privately Held**
SIC: 2298 Cable, fiber

(G-10821)
CRUISE QUARTERS
4013 Main St (43026-1422)
PHONE 614 777-6022
Steven Kirk Boganwright, *Principal*
EMP: 3
SALES (est): 315K **Privately Held**
SIC: 3131 Mfg Footwear Cut Stock

(G-10822)
CUMMINS BRIDGEWAY COLUMBUS LLC
4000 Lyman Dr (43026-1212)
PHONE 614 771-1000
Bill Bergner,
EMP: 60
SALES: 7.4MM
SALES (corp-wide): 23.7B **Publicly Held**
WEB: www.bridgewaypower.com
SIC: 5084 3519 Engines & parts, diesel; internal combustion engines
PA: Cummins Inc.
500 Jackson St
Columbus IN 47201
812 377-5000

(G-10823)
CUMMINS INC
4000 Lyman Dr (43026-1212)
PHONE 614 771-1000
Greg Bowl, *Branch Mgr*
William Bergner, *Branch Mgr*
EMP: 25
SALES (corp-wide): 23.7B **Publicly Held**
WEB: www.bridgewaypower.com
SIC: 5084 7538 3519 Engines & parts, diesel; diesel engine repair: automotive; internal combustion engines
PA: Cummins Inc.
500 Jackson St
Columbus IN 47201
812 377-5000

(G-10824)
DECENT HILL PUBLISHERS LLC
Also Called: Decent Hill Press
2825 Wynneleaf St (43026-8144)
PHONE 216 548-1255
Jude Odu,
EMP: 6
SALES (est): 310K **Privately Held**
SIC: 2731 Book music: publishing only, not printed on site

(G-10825)
GOULD GROUP LLC
4653 Trueman Blvd Ste 120 (43026-2597)
PHONE 740 807-4294
Brian Gould, *CEO*
Julie Gould, *COO*
EMP: 4
SALES (est): 219.8K **Privately Held**
SIC: 1711 1731 3585 4911 Plumbing, heating, air-conditioning contractors; electrical work; refrigeration & heating equipment; transmission, electric power; roofing, siding & insulation

(G-10826)
GREAT DANE LLC
Also Called: Great Dane Trailers
4080 Lyman Dr (43026-1287)
PHONE 614 876-0666
Gary Blackburn, *Manager*
EMP: 38
SQ FT: 21,088
SALES (corp-wide): 1.5B **Privately Held**
WEB: www.greatdanetrailers.com
SIC: 3715 Truck trailers
HQ: Great Dane Llc
222 N Lasalle St Ste 920
Chicago IL 60601

(G-10827)
HANCOR INC (DH)
4640 Trueman Blvd (43026-2438)
PHONE 614 658-0050
Steven A Anderson, *President*
William E Altermatt, *Vice Pres*
Pat Ferren, *Vice Pres*
Derek Kamp, *Vice Pres*
John Maag, *CFO*
◆ EMP: 330
SQ FT: 20,000
SALES (est): 190.1MM
SALES (corp-wide): 1.3B **Publicly Held**
SIC: 3084 3088 3089 3083 Plastics pipe; plastics plumbing fixtures; septic tanks, plastic; laminated plastics plate & sheet
HQ: Hancor Holding Corporation
401 Olive St
Findlay OH 45840
419 422-6521

(G-10828)
HIGHLIGHTS FOR CHILDREN INC
4555 Lyman Dr (43026-1282)
PHONE 614 486-0631
Kim Clements, *Manager*
EMP: 140
SALES (corp-wide): 216.2MM **Privately Held**
WEB: www.highlights.com
SIC: 2721 Magazines: publishing & printing; magazines: publishing only, not printed on site
PA: Highlights For Children, Inc.
1800 Watermark Dr
Columbus OH 43215
614 486-0631

(G-10829)
HILLIARD CAT SHACK LLC
5484 Pearson Ct (43026-7518)
PHONE 614 527-9711
Kimberly Mash,
EMP: 4
SALES (est): 320.3K **Privately Held**
SIC: 2329 Men's & boys' sportswear & athletic clothing

(G-10830)
INS ROBOTICS INC
3600 Parkway Ln (43026-1281)
PHONE 888 293-5325
Beth Harkins, *Principal*
EMP: 8
SALES (est): 804.8K **Privately Held**
SIC: 3535 Robotic conveyors

(G-10831)
INTERNATIONAL PRODUCTS (HQ)
Also Called: Ipsg / Micro Center
4119 Leap Rd (43026-1117)
PHONE 614 850-3000
Richard Mershad, *President*
▲ EMP: 21
SQ FT: 125,000
SALES: 30.2MM
SALES (corp-wide): 3.6B **Privately Held**
WEB: www.microcenter.com
SIC: 3571 Computers, digital, analog or hybrid
PA: Micro Electronics, Inc.
4119 Leap Rd
Hilliard OH 43026
614 850-3000

(G-10832)
J M S CUSTOM FINISHING
4468 Circle Dr (43026-1013)
PHONE 614 264-9916
EMP: 3 EST: 2017
SALES (est): 134.2K **Privately Held**
SIC: 3471 Plating & polishing

(G-10833)
JD POWER SYSTEMS LLC
Also Called: John Deere Authorized Dealer
3979 Parkway Ln (43026-1250)
PHONE 614 317-9394
Jeffrey D Mitchell, *Owner*
Glenn McIntosh, *General Mgr*
Adam Taylor, *Manager*
Amber Mitchell, *Clerk*
EMP: 12
SALES (est): 3MM **Privately Held**
SIC: 3621 5082 Motors & generators; construction & mining machinery

(G-10834)
JIT COMPANY INC
2180 Venus Dr (43026-8124)
PHONE 614 529-8010
Marcy Wu, *President*
Jom Pin Chen, *Vice Pres*
EMP: 13
SALES (est): 2.2MM **Privately Held**
SIC: 3599 Machine shop, jobbing & repair

(G-10835)
JOHNSON ENGINE & MACHINE
2899 Walcutt Rd (43026-8880)
PHONE 614 876-0724
Donald H Johnson, *Owner*
EMP: 7 EST: 1962
SQ FT: 10,000
SALES (est): 613.7K **Privately Held**
SIC: 3599 7538 Machine shop, jobbing & repair; general automotive repair shops; engine rebuilding: automotive; truck engine repair, except industrial

(G-10836)
KATIES SNACK FOODS LLC
3929 Hill Park Rd (43026-8080)
PHONE 614 440-0780
Katie Levesque, *Principal*
EMP: 4
SALES (est): 242.4K **Privately Held**
SIC: 5145 2013 Snack foods; sausages & other prepared meats

(G-10837)
LASERFLEX CORPORATION (HQ)
3649 Parkway Ln (43026-1214)
PHONE..................614 850-9600
Ken Kinkopf, *President*
Mary Beth Hagerty, *Finance Mgr*
EMP: 62
SQ FT: 75,000
SALES (est): 25.4MM **Publicly Held**
WEB: www.customlasercuttingservices.com
SIC: **7389** 7699 7692 3599 Metal cutting services; finishing services; industrial machinery & equipment repair; welding repair; machine shop, jobbing & repair; fabricated structural metal; metallizing of fabrics

(G-10838)
MARBLE CLIFF LIMESTONE INC
2650 Old Dublin Rd (43026)
PHONE..................614 488-3030
Paul D Rice, *President*
EMP: 3
SQ FT: 1,884
SALES (est): 207.6K **Privately Held**
SIC: **1411** Limestone & marble dimension stone

(G-10839)
MERRY X-RAY CHEMICAL CORP
Also Called: Baldwin
4770 Northwest Pkwy (43026-1131)
PHONE..................614 219-2011
Eric Cole, *Manager*
EMP: 6
SALES (corp-wide): 108MM **Privately Held**
SIC: **6411** 2899 Medical insurance claim processing, contract or fee basis; chemical supplies for foundries
PA: Merry X-Ray Chemical Corporation
    4909 Murphy Canyon Rd # 120
    San Diego CA 92123
    858 565-4472

(G-10840)
MID-OHIO PRODUCTS INC
4329 Reynolds Dr (43026-1261)
PHONE..................614 771-2795
Richard Coleman II, *President*
▲ EMP: 56 EST: 1980
SQ FT: 16,000
SALES (est): 10.4MM **Privately Held**
WEB: www.mid-ohioproducts.com
SIC: **3544** 3444 Dies & die holders for metal cutting, forming, die casting; punches, forming & stamping; sheet metalwork

(G-10841)
MIDWEST INDUSTRIAL RUBBER INC
Also Called: Mir
4847 Northwest Pkwy (43026-1128)
PHONE..................614 876-3110
George Binek, *Branch Mgr*
EMP: 14
SALES (corp-wide): 53.6MM **Privately Held**
SIC: **5085** 3535 3061 3053 Hose, belting & packing; power transmission equipment & apparatus; rubber goods, mechanical; conveyors & conveying equipment; mechanical rubber goods; gaskets, packing & sealing devices
PA: Midwest Industrial Rubber Inc
    10431 Midwest Indus Dr
    Saint Louis MO 63132
    314 890-0070

(G-10842)
MORLAN & ASSOCIATES INC (PA)
Also Called: Flex-Core Division
4970 Scioto Darby Rd D (43026-1548)
P.O. Box 6047 (43026-6047)
PHONE..................614 889-6152
Donald Morlan, *Ch of Bd*
Teri Shaw, *President*
Eric Whelan, *Vice Pres*
Amy McNabb, *Admin Sec*
▼ EMP: 29
SQ FT: 15,000
SALES: 10MM **Privately Held**
WEB: www.flex-core.com
SIC: **3612** Transformers, except electric

(G-10843)
NANOFIBER SOLUTIONS INC
4389 Weaver Ct N (43026-1132)
PHONE..................614 453-5877
Ross Kayuha, *CEO*
Jed Johnson, *CTO*
John Lannutti, *Security Dir*
EMP: 9
SQ FT: 20,000
SALES: 550K **Privately Held**
SIC: **2834** 2835 Liniments; in vitro & in vivo diagnostic substances

(G-10844)
OCS TELECOM LLC
4138 Weaver Ct E (43026-1299)
P.O. Box 291, Centerburg (43011-0291)
PHONE..................740 503-5939
Jeremy Funk, *Partner*
EMP: 12 EST: 2012
SALES (est): 912.3K **Privately Held**
SIC: **3661** Telephone station equipment & parts, wire

(G-10845)
OGR PUBLISHING INC
Also Called: O Gauge Railroading
5825 Redsand Rd (43026-8057)
P.O. Box 218 (43026-0218)
PHONE..................330 757-3020
Richard P Melvin, *President*
EMP: 7
SQ FT: 4,000
SALES (est): 659.8K **Privately Held**
WEB: www.webhostsvc.com
SIC: **2741** Miscellaneous publishing

(G-10846)
OHIO LAMINATING & BINDING INC
4364 Reynolds Dr (43026-1260)
PHONE..................614 771-4868
Jim Ondecko, *President*
Jimmy R Ondecko, *Vice Pres*
▲ EMP: 40
SQ FT: 5,000
SALES (est): 3.3MM **Privately Held**
WEB: www.ohiolaminatingandbinding.com
SIC: **7389** 2789 2672 Laminating service; bookbinding & related work; coated & laminated paper

(G-10847)
OHIO SEMITRONICS INC (PA)
Also Called: OSI
4242 Reynolds Dr (43026-1264)
PHONE..................614 777-1005
Warren E Bulman, *Ch of Bd*
Robert A Shaw, *President*
Bob Borghese, *Purch Agent*
Nick Adams, *Engineer*
David Baldock, *Engineer*
▲ EMP: 88
SQ FT: 49,000
SALES: 8.5MM **Privately Held**
WEB: www.ohiosemi.com
SIC: **3674** 3679 3663 3625 Semiconductors & related devices; transducers, electrical; radio & TV communications equipment; relays & industrial controls; motors & generators; transformers, except electric

(G-10848)
OHIO SYNCHRO SWIM CLUB
4405 Landmark Ln (43026-7821)
PHONE..................614 319-4667
Sadie Braun, *Principal*
EMP: 3 EST: 2017
SALES: 101.4K **Privately Held**
SIC: **3621** Synchros

(G-10849)
OPEN TEXT INC
3671 Ridge Mill Dr (43026-7752)
PHONE..................614 658-3588
Anik Ganguly, *Manager*
Mike Nappi, *Manager*
EMP: 50
SALES (corp-wide): 2.8B **Privately Held**
SIC: **7372** Prepackaged software
HQ: Open Text Inc.
    2950 S Delaware St
    San Mateo CA 94403
    650 645-3000

(G-10850)
PERDATUM INC
4098 Main St (43026-1437)
PHONE..................614 761-1578
Mark Tochtenhagen, *President*
Leo Renner, *CFO*
EMP: 8
SQ FT: 2,500
SALES: 306K **Privately Held**
SIC: **7372** Prepackaged software

(G-10851)
PHANTOM TECHNOLOGY LLC
Also Called: Pool Office Manager
3116 Scioto Darby Exec Ct (43026-8989)
P.O. Box 3211, Columbus (43210-0211)
PHONE..................614 710-0074
Mike Leone,
EMP: 6
SALES (est): 135.3K **Privately Held**
SIC: **7372** Business oriented computer software

(G-10852)
PHOENIX HYDRAULIC PRESSES INC
4329 Reynolds Dr (43026-1261)
P.O. Box 1048, Powell (43065-1048)
PHONE..................614 850-8940
Charles Sherman, *President*
EMP: 10
SQ FT: 6,000
SALES (est): 1.8MM **Privately Held**
WEB: www.phoenixhydraulic.com
SIC: **3542** Presses: hydraulic & pneumatic, mechanical & manual

(G-10853)
POWELL PRINTS LLC
3991 Main St (43026-1449)
PHONE..................614 771-4830
Larry Powell, *Mng Member*
EMP: 4
SALES (est): 538.3K **Privately Held**
SIC: **2759** Screen printing

(G-10854)
PPG INDUSTRIES INC
Also Called: PPG 9282
5054 Cemetery Rd (43026-1671)
PHONE..................614 921-9228
Randy Ridgeway, *Manager*
EMP: 3
SALES (corp-wide): 15.3B **Publicly Held**
WEB: www.ppg.com
SIC: **2851** 3011 Paints & allied products; tire sundries or tire repair materials, rubber
PA: Ppg Industries, Inc.
    1 Ppg Pl
    Pittsburgh PA 15272
    412 434-3131

(G-10855)
PRO LIGHTING LLC
5864 Hunting Haven Dr (43026-7992)
P.O. Box 1201 (43026-6201)
PHONE..................614 561-0089
Jeffrey J Treadway, *Principal*
EMP: 4
SALES (est): 426.7K **Privately Held**
SIC: **3648** Lighting equipment

(G-10856)
PROTO PRCSION MFG SLUTIONS LLC
Also Called: Proto Precision Fabricators
4101 Leap Rd (43026-1117)
PHONE..................614 771-0080
Sugu Suguness, *Principal*
EMP: 13
SALES (est): 463.4K **Privately Held**
SIC: **3999** Manufacturing industries

(G-10857)
RAGE CORPORATION (PA)
Also Called: Rage Plastics
3949 Lyman Dr (43026-1274)
P.O. Box 159 (43026-0159)
PHONE..................614 771-4771
George Saliaris, *President*
Dan Saliaris, *Vice Pres*
▲ EMP: 85
SQ FT: 65,000
SALES (est): 27.3MM **Privately Held**
SIC: **3089** 3544 Injection molding of plastics; special dies, tools, jigs & fixtures

(G-10858)
RICH PRODUCTS CORPORATION
4600 Northwest Pkwy (43026-1130)
P.O. Box 490 (43026-0490)
PHONE..................614 771-1117
John Maier, *Opers Mgr*
Jason Brooks, *Research*
Michael Callaway, *Manager*
Will Richards, *Manager*
Peg Robinette, *Asst Mgr*
EMP: 150
SALES (corp-wide): 3.9B **Privately Held**
WEB: www.richs.com
SIC: **2023** 2099 2051 2045 Dry, condensed, evaporated dairy products; food preparations; bread, cake & related products; prepared flour mixes & doughs
PA: Rich Products Corporation
    1 Robert Rich Way
    Buffalo NY 14213
    716 878-8000

(G-10859)
S & G MANUFACTURING GROUP LLC (PA)
Also Called: S&G Distribution
4830 Northwest Pkwy (43026-1131)
PHONE..................614 529-0100
Bret Klisares, *President*
Thomas Anderson, *Business Mgr*
Josh Ball, *VP Opers*
Ted Murphy, *Project Mgr*
Charles Klick, *Purch Agent*
EMP: 142
SQ FT: 105,500
SALES (est): 24.6MM **Privately Held**
WEB: www.sgmgroup.com
SIC: **3441** 3444 2435 2436 Fabricated structural metal; sheet metalwork; hardwood veneer & plywood; softwood veneer & plywood; vanities, bathroom: wood

(G-10860)
SENSOTEC LLC
Also Called: Sensorwerks
3450 Cemetery Rd (43026-8348)
PHONE..................614 481-8616
Jack Feil, *Sales Staff*
John L Priest,
EMP: 6
SALES: 500K **Privately Held**
WEB: www.sensorwerks.com
SIC: **3829** Pressure transducers

(G-10861)
SHUTTERBUS OHIO LLC ✪
3590 Smiley Rd (43026-8356)
PHONE..................937 726-9634
Benjamin Randolph, *Principal*
EMP: 3 EST: 2018
SALES (est): 180.1K **Privately Held**
SIC: **3442** Shutters, door or window: metal

(G-10862)
SMALL DOG PRINTING
3972 Brown Park Dr Ste E (43026-1167)
P.O. Box 750 (43026-0750)
PHONE..................614 777-7620
Amy Bias, *CEO*
Rebecca Dornsife, *Co-Owner*
EMP: 4
SALES (est): 468.8K **Privately Held**
WEB: www.smalldogprinting.com
SIC: **2759** Commercial printing

(G-10863)
STACEYS KITCHEN LIMITED
4350 Kerr Dr Ste B (43026-1055)
PHONE..................614 921-1290
EMP: 4 EST: 2005
SALES (est): 140K **Privately Held**
SIC: **2099** Mfg Food Preparations

Hilliard - Franklin County (G-10864)

(G-10864)
STAR DYNAMICS CORPORATION (PA)
Also Called: Aeroflex Powell
4455 Reynolds Dr (43026-1261)
PHONE.................................614 334-4510
Jerry Jost, *President*
Andy Bell, *General Mgr*
Glen Herchik, *VP Bus Dvlpt*
Julie West, *Controller*
Samantha Wolfert, *Human Res Mgr*
▲ **EMP:** 74
SQ FT: 20,000
SALES (est): 21.5MM Privately Held
WEB: www.isarinc.com
SIC: 3812 Search & navigation equipment

(G-10865)
STATE METAL HOSE INC
4171 Lyman Dr (43026-1228)
PHONE.................................614 527-4700
Ward Argust, *President*
EMP: 7 **EST:** 2007
SALES (est): 1.1MM Privately Held
SIC: 3492 Hose & tube fittings & assemblies, hydraulic/pneumatic

(G-10866)
STENCILSMITH LLC
3001 Stouenburgh Dr (43026-8862)
P.O. Box 401 (43026-0401)
PHONE.................................614 876-4350
April Dabaie,
EMP: 4
SALES (est): 340.6K Privately Held
SIC: 3953 Stencils, painting & marking

(G-10867)
SUNDAY SCHOOL SOFTWARE
4369 Brickwood Dr (43026-3420)
PHONE.................................614 527-8776
Neil Mac Queen, *President*
EMP: 3
SALES (est): 205.7K Privately Held
WEB: www.sundaysoftware.com
SIC: 7372 8661 Prepackaged software; religious organizations

(G-10868)
TEACHERS PUBLISHING GROUP
Also Called: Essential Learning Products
4200 Parkway Ct (43026-1200)
PHONE.................................614 486-0631
Gary Meyers, *President*
Thomas Mason, *Treasurer*
EMP: 10
SQ FT: 36,000
SALES (est): 946K
SALES (corp-wide): 216.2MM Privately Held
WEB: www.elpdealer.com
SIC: 7371 2731 Custom computer programming services; books: publishing only
PA: Highlights For Children, Inc.
  1800 Watermark Dr
  Columbus OH 43215
  614 486-0631

(G-10869)
TEXTILES INC
Also Called: Sales Office Rob Jordan Vp Sls
5892 Heritage Lakes Dr (43026-7617)
PHONE.................................614 529-8642
Rob Jordan, *Branch Mgr*
EMP: 8
SALES (est): 514.3K
SALES (corp-wide): 19.1MM Privately Held
SIC: 2511 2599 Wood household furniture; hotel furniture
PA: Textiles, Inc.
  23 Old Springfield Rd
  London OH 43140
  740 852-0782

(G-10870)
THERMOPLASTIC ACCESSORIES CORP
Also Called: T A C
3949 Lyman Dr (43026-1209)
P.O. Box 159 (43026-0159)
PHONE.................................614 771-4777
George Saliaris, *President*

Mary Lou Saliaris, *Admin Sec*
EMP: 45
SQ FT: 48,000
SALES (est): 3.8MM
SALES (corp-wide): 27.3MM Privately Held
SIC: 3089 Blow molded finished plastic products
PA: Rage Corporation
  3949 Lyman Dr
  Hilliard OH 43026
  614 771-4771

(G-10871)
TOUCH LIFE CENTERS LLC
3455 Mill Run Dr Ste 310 (43026-9082)
PHONE.................................614 388-8075
Stuart Mead,
Mark Ford,
EMP: 5
SALES (est): 371.5K Privately Held
SIC: 3842 Prosthetic appliances

(G-10872)
TUBULAR TECHNIQUES INC
3025 Scioto Darby Exec Ct (43026-8990)
PHONE.................................614 529-4130
Steve Harman, *President*
Amy Pope-Harman, *Admin Sec*
EMP: 6 **EST:** 1972
SQ FT: 7,500
SALES (est): 2.6MM Privately Held
WEB: www.tubulartechniques.com
SIC: 5051 3599 Tubing, metal; tubing, flexible metallic

(G-10873)
VANNER HOLDINGS INC
4282 Reynolds Dr (43026-1260)
PHONE.................................614 771-2718
Steven Funk, *President*
Merry H Pieper, *Principal*
Chris Collet, *Vice Pres*
Steve Speck, *Engineer*
Mary Wade, *Manager*
◆ **EMP:** 55
SQ FT: 20,000
SALES (est): 12.9MM Privately Held
WEB: www.vanner.com
SIC: 3629 3823 3699 3648 Inverters, nonrotating: electrical; power conversion units, a.c. to d.c.: static-electric; battery chargers, rectifying or nonrotating; industrial instrmnts msrmnt display/control process variable; electrical equipment & supplies; lighting equipment; motors & generators

(G-10874)
VICART PRCSION FABRICATORS INC
Also Called: Proto Precision Fabricators
4101 Leap Rd (43026-1117)
PHONE.................................614 771-0080
Arthur Handshy, *President*
Joe Luebbe, *Vice Pres*
Bryan Graham, *Engineer*
Debbie L Hedrick, *Financial Exec*
EMP: 35
SQ FT: 18,000
SALES (est): 6.9MM Privately Held
WEB: www.protoprecision.com
SIC: 3444 Sheet metal specialties, not stamped

(G-10875)
ZURN INDUSTRIES LLC
4501 Sutphen Ct (43026-1224)
PHONE.................................814 455-0921
Bob Armbrewster, *Manager*
EMP: 10 Publicly Held
WEB: www.zurn.com
SIC: 5074 3431 Plumbing & hydronic heating supplies; sinks: enameled iron, cast iron or pressed metal
HQ: Zurn Industries, Llc
  1801 Pittsburgh Ave
  Erie PA 16502
  814 455-0921

Hillsboro
Highland County

(G-10876)
ABBOTT SIGNS (PA)
251 John St (45133-1021)
PHONE.................................937 393-6600
Randy Abbott, *Owner*
EMP: 5
SALES: 300K Privately Held
SIC: 3993 Signs, not made in custom sign painting shops

(G-10877)
CAMECO COMMUNICATIONS
Also Called: Highland County Press
128 S High St (45133-1443)
P.O. Box 849 (45133-0849)
PHONE.................................937 840-9490
Rory Ryan, *President*
Angie Matticks, *Vice Pres*
Rosemary Ryan, *Manager*
EMP: 7
SQ FT: 1,000
SALES (est): 356.9K Privately Held
SIC: 2711 Commercial printing & newspaper publishing combined; newspapers, publishing & printing

(G-10878)
G FORDYCE CO
210 Hobart Dr (45133-9487)
P.O. Box 309 (45133-0309)
PHONE.................................937 393-3241
Bob Wilson, *Owner*
Stan Storts, *General Mgr*
EMP: 6
SQ FT: 12,000
SALES (est): 292.8K Privately Held
SIC: 3554 Folding machines, paper

(G-10879)
HIGHLAND COMPUTER FORMS INC (PA)
1025 W Main St (45133-8219)
P.O. Box 831 (45133-0831)
PHONE.................................937 393-4215
Robert D Wilson, *President*
Chris Brown, *General Mgr*
Philip D Wilson, *Chairman*
Robert Wilson, *COO*
Rob Jones, *Plant Mgr*
EMP: 130 **EST:** 1979
SQ FT: 70,000
SALES (est): 37.6MM Privately Held
WEB: www.hcf.com
SIC: 2761 Computer forms, manifold or continuous

(G-10880)
HIGHLAND PRECISION PLATING
6940 State Route 124 (45133-9435)
P.O. Box 784 (45133-0784)
PHONE.................................937 393-9501
Allen Brotherton, *President*
EMP: 3
SQ FT: 400
SALES (est): 585K Privately Held
SIC: 3471 Electroplating of metals or formed products

(G-10881)
INGERSOLL-RAND CO
8799 Peach Orchard Rd (45133-9657)
PHONE.................................704 655-4000
EMP: 3
SALES (est): 156.9K Privately Held
SIC: 3131 Rands

(G-10882)
ITW FOOD EQUIPMENT GROUP LLC
Also Called: Hobart
1495 N High St (45133-8203)
PHONE.................................937 393-4271
Bill Zinno, *Manager*
EMP: 241
SALES (corp-wide): 14.7B Publicly Held
SIC: 3556 Food products machinery
HQ: Itw Food Equipment Group Llc
  701 S Ridge Ave
  Troy OH 45374

(G-10883)
JERRYS WELDING SUPPLY INC
Also Called: Jerry's Welding Supply ICN
5367 Us Highway 50 (45133-7532)
PHONE.................................937 364-1500
Gerald Bonnet, *Owner*
EMP: 5
SALES (est): 519.2K Privately Held
SIC: 5084 7692 5169 Welding machinery & equipment; welding repair; oxygen

(G-10884)
MAC PRINTING COMPANY
406 N West St (45133-1088)
P.O. Box 1782 (45133-1782)
PHONE.................................937 393-1101
John R Mc Laughlin, *President*
Lois Mc Laughlin, *Corp Secy*
Linda Mc Laughlin, *Manager*
EMP: 5
SQ FT: 3,500
SALES (est): 646.4K Privately Held
WEB: www.macprintingcompany.com
SIC: 2759 2752 Commercial printing; commercial printing, lithographic

(G-10885)
MAINES BROTHERS TIN SHOP
Also Called: Maines, Clyde Sons Tin Shop
121 S West St (45133-1355)
PHONE.................................937 393-1633
Harley Maines, *Partner*
Clyde Maines, *Partner*
Roger Maines, *Partner*
EMP: 3
SALES (est): 66.5K Privately Held
WEB: www.windsorfair.com
SIC: 1761 3444 Roofing contractor; sheet metalwork

(G-10886)
OHIO ASPHALTIC LIMESTONE CORP
8591 Mad River Rd (45133-9451)
PHONE.................................937 364-2191
Toll Free:.............................888 -
Diana Jones, *President*
William C Mason, *President*
Dianna Jones, *Vice Pres*
Amy Huebner, *Office Mgr*
Tom Mason, *Technology*
EMP: 10
SQ FT: 1,200
SALES: 3.1MM
SALES (corp-wide): 7.3MM Privately Held
WEB: www.ohio-asphaltic-limestone.com
SIC: 1422 Limestones, ground
PA: Miller-Mason Paving Co (Inc)
  8591 Mad River Rd
  Hillsboro OH
  937 364-2369

(G-10887)
OHIO VALLEY TRUSS CO (PA)
6000 Us Highway 50 (45133-7546)
P.O. Box 365 (45133-0365)
PHONE.................................937 393-3995
Willard G Bohrer, *President*
Joann Bohrer, *Corp Secy*
EMP: 45
SQ FT: 12,000
SALES (est): 6.1MM Privately Held
SIC: 2439 Trusses, wooden roof; trusses, except roof: laminated lumber

(G-10888)
OHIO VALLEY TRUSS CO
887 1/2 W Main St (45133-7452)
P.O. Box 365 (45133-0365)
PHONE.................................937 393-3995
Willard Bohrer, *President*
EMP: 5
SQ FT: 3,000
SALES (corp-wide): 4.7MM Privately Held
SIC: 2439 Trusses, wooden roof
PA: Ohio Valley Truss Co
  6000 Us Highway 50
  Hillsboro OH 45133
  937 393-3995

(G-10889)
PAS TECHNOLOGIES INC
214 Hobart Dr (45133-9487)
PHONE.................................937 840-1000

GEOGRAPHIC SECTION

Joshua Ayers, *Engineer*
James Heiser, *Engineer*
Nathanael Young, *Engineer*
Mark Greene, *Manager*
Wayne Lowery, *Manager*
EMP: 100 **Privately Held**
WEB: www.pas-technologies.com
SIC: 3724 7699 Aircraft engines & engine parts; aircraft & heavy equipment repair services
HQ: Pas Technologies Inc.
  1234 Atlantic Ave
  North Kansas City MO 64116

(G-10890)
ROTARY FORMS PRESS INC (PA)
835 S High St (45133-9692)
PHONE.....................................937 393-3426
Jon Cassner, *President*
Brian Cassner, *Treasurer*
EMP: 50 **EST:** 1952
SQ FT: 24,500
SALES: 320K **Privately Held**
WEB: www.rotaryformspress.com
SIC: 2761 2752 Computer forms, manifold or continuous; commercial printing, lithographic

(G-10891)
SEAL TITE LLC
120 Moore Rd (45133-8523)
PHONE.....................................937 393-4268
Michael J Kelley, *CEO*
Eric Newswanger, *Opers Mgr*
Jeff Leasure, *Opers Staff*
Sherry Leasure, *Engineer*
Josh Ihme, *Sales Staff*
EMP: 100
SQ FT: 120,000
SALES (est): 23.9MM **Privately Held**
SIC: 3498 Fabricated pipe & fittings

(G-10892)
UNIT SETS INC
835 S High St (45133-9602)
PHONE.....................................937 840-6123
Jon Cassner, *President*
Jon H Cassner, *President*
Brian Cassner, *Treasurer*
Kathy Cassner, *Admin Sec*
EMP: 24
SQ FT: 25,000
SALES (est): 185.1K
SALES (corp-wide): 320K **Privately Held**
WEB: www.rotaryformspress.com
SIC: 2761 Unit sets (manifold business forms)
PA: Rotary Forms Press, Inc.
  835 S High St
  Hillsboro OH 45133
  937 393-3426

(G-10893)
WEASTEC INCORPORATED
1600 N High St (45133-9400)
PHONE.....................................937 393-6800
EMP: 158
SALES (corp-wide): 283.9MM **Privately Held**
WEB: www.weastec.com
SIC: 3714 3643 Motor vehicle electrical equipment; current-carrying wiring devices
HQ: Weastec, Incorporated
  1600 N High St
  Hillsboro OH 45133
  937 393-6800

(G-10894)
WEASTEC INCORPORATED (HQ)
1600 N High St (45133-9400)
PHONE.....................................937 393-6800
Yasusuke Sugino, *President*
Bill Smith, *Senior VP*
Loretta Leedom, *Mfg Spvr*
Joy Puckett, *Production*
Robert Moots, *Purch Agent*
▲ **EMP:** 222
SQ FT: 190,000
SALES (est): 62.1MM
SALES (corp-wide): 283.9MM **Privately Held**
WEB: www.weastec.com
SIC: 3714 Motor vehicle electrical equipment
PA: Toyo Denso Co., Ltd.
  2-10-4, Shimbashi
  Minato-Ku TKY 105-0
  335 020-151

(G-10895)
WILLIAMSON SAFE INC
5631 State Route 73 (45133-9005)
PHONE.....................................937 393-9919
J Edgar Williamson, *President*
Bing C Williamson, *Vice Pres*
EMP: 34 **EST:** 1979
SQ FT: 40,000
SALES (est): 4MM **Privately Held**
WEB: www.wsco.net
SIC: 3499 Safe deposit boxes or chests, metal; safes & vaults, metal

Hinckley
Medina County

(G-10896)
A-KOBAK CONTAINER COMPANY
1701 W 130th St (44233-9586)
P.O. Box 490 (44233-0490)
PHONE.....................................330 225-7791
Gerald H Dolph, *President*
Edward Clark, *Vice Pres*
Patrick Sullivan, *Sales Staff*
EMP: 15 **EST:** 1963
SQ FT: 40,000
SALES (est): 3.8MM **Privately Held**
SIC: 2653 Boxes, corrugated: made from purchased materials

(G-10897)
ALPINE CABINETS INC
1515 W 130th St Ste E (44233-9169)
PHONE.....................................330 273-2131
Jim Artel, *President*
EMP: 4
SQ FT: 6,000
SALES (est): 506K **Privately Held**
SIC: 2434 Wood kitchen cabinets

(G-10898)
AMERICAN CUBE MOLD INC
Also Called: Acm
1515 W 130th St Ste C (44233-9169)
PHONE.....................................330 558-0044
Frank J Kichurchak, *President*
Michael Kichurchak, *Opers Staff*
EMP: 6
SQ FT: 3,800
SALES (est): 1.5MM **Privately Held**
SIC: 3544 3829 Industrial molds; testing equipment: abrasion, shearing strength, etc.

(G-10899)
CONTROLLED ACCESS INC
Also Called: Sentronic
1515 W 130th St Ste A (44233-9169)
PHONE.....................................330 273-6185
Michelle Sherba, *President*
Sylvia Hayes, *Treasurer*
Paul Hendlin, *Sales Mgr*
Debbie Mercier, *Sales Staff*
Mike Sherba, *Shareholder*
▲ **EMP:** 16
SQ FT: 10,000
SALES (est): 2.6MM **Privately Held**
WEB: www.controlledaccess.com
SIC: 3829 Turnstiles, equipped with counting mechanisms

(G-10900)
GREAT LAKES STAIR & MLLWK CO
1545 W 130th St Ste A1 (44233-9168)
PHONE.....................................330 225-2005
Tim Noonan, *President*
Barb Noonan, *Corp Secy*
Marcy Noonan, *Admin Asst*
EMP: 7
SQ FT: 7,500
SALES (est): 1.1MM **Privately Held**
WEB: www.stair.com
SIC: 2431 5031 Staircases & stairs, wood; doors & windows; door frames, all materials; windows

(G-10901)
HIGHSCHOOLBALL INC
82 Wakefield Run Blvd (44233-9221)
PHONE.....................................330 321-8536
Matthew Zelinski, *President*
EMP: 3
SQ FT: 1,200
SALES (est): 117.5K **Privately Held**
SIC: 2711 Newspapers, publishing & printing

(G-10902)
HINCKLEY WOOD PRODUCTS
1545 W 130th St (44233-9121)
PHONE.....................................330 220-9999
Tim Noonan, *President*
EMP: 15
SALES (est): 1.6MM **Privately Held**
SIC: 2431 Staircases & stairs, wood

(G-10903)
JAMAR PRECISION GRINDING CO
2661 Center Rd (44233-9562)
PHONE.....................................330 220-0099
John Hatala, *President*
Jeff Miezin, *Plant Mgr*
EMP: 48
SALES (est): 7.9MM **Privately Held**
SIC: 3599 Grinding castings for the trade

(G-10904)
LIBERTY MOLD & MACHINE COMPANY
1369 Ridge Rd Ste B (44233-9297)
P.O. Box 193 (44233-0193)
PHONE.....................................330 278-7825
John Babich, *President*
Joel Babich, *President*
Jim Babich, *General Mgr*
EMP: 3
SQ FT: 2,200
SALES: 600K **Privately Held**
SIC: 3544 Dies, plastics forming; forms (molds), for foundry & plastics working machinery

(G-10905)
PERFORMANCE POINT GRINDING
1669 W 130th St Ste 302 (44233-9104)
PHONE.....................................330 220-0871
Aaron Vanke, *Owner*
EMP: 3
SALES: 300K **Privately Held**
SIC: 3599 Grinding castings for the trade

(G-10906)
TARANTULA PERFORMANCE RACG LLC
Also Called: Tpr
1669 W 130th St Ste 301 (44233-9104)
PHONE.....................................330 273-3456
Bryan Fredmonsky,
Jim Clopp,
Steve Fredmonsky,
◆ **EMP:** 3
SQ FT: 15,000
SALES (est): 119.7K **Privately Held**
SIC: 3751 Motorcycles, bicycles & parts

(G-10907)
TURNWOOD INDUSTRIES INC
365 State Rd (44233-9634)
PHONE.....................................330 278-2421
Peter Svilar, *President*
Steve Svilar, *Vice Pres*
▲ **EMP:** 26
SQ FT: 26,000
SALES: 1.7MM **Privately Held**
WEB: www.turnwoodinc.com
SIC: 2434 2431 Wood kitchen cabinets; interior & ornamental woodwork & trim

(G-10908)
ZS CREAM & BEAN
2706 Boston Rd (44233-9498)
PHONE.....................................440 652-6369
Lawrence Zirker, *Principal*
EMP: 5
SALES (est): 419.8K **Privately Held**
SIC: 2024 Ice cream, bulk

Hiram
Portage County

(G-10909)
DURAMAX GLOBAL CORP
Also Called: Duramax Marine
17990 Great Lakes Pkwy (44234-9681)
PHONE.....................................440 834-5400
Richard Spangler, *Director*
Tammy Simsa, *Director*
EMP: 90
SQ FT: 65,000
SALES (est): 4MM **Privately Held**
SIC: 3061 Mechanical rubber goods

(G-10910)
GREAT LAKES CHEESE CO INC (PA)
17825 Great Lakes Pkwy (44234-9677)
P.O. Box 1806 (44234-1806)
PHONE.....................................440 834-2500
Gary Vanic, *President*
Marcel Dasen, *Principal*
Hans Epprecht, *Principal*
Albert Z Meyers, *Principal*
John Epprecht, *Corp Secy*
◆ **EMP:** 500
SQ FT: 218,000
SALES (est): 1.6B **Privately Held**
WEB: www.greatlakescheese.com
SIC: 5143 2022 Cheese; natural cheese

(G-10911)
SAINT-GOBAIN CERAMICS PLAS INC
Saint-Gobain Crystals
17900 Great Lakes Pkwy (44234-9681)
PHONE.....................................440 834-5600
Tom Penninsky, *Manager*
EMP: 210
SALES (corp-wide): 215.9MM **Privately Held**
WEB: www.sgceramics.com
SIC: 2819 Industrial inorganic chemicals
HQ: Saint-Gobain Ceramics & Plastics, Inc.
  750 E Swedesford Rd
  Valley Forge PA 19482

Holgate
Henry County

(G-10912)
PEREZ FOODS LLC
515 Richholt St (43527-7731)
P.O. Box 65 (43527-0065)
PHONE.....................................419 264-0303
James McDaniel, *Mng Member*
EMP: 8
SQ FT: 5,000
SALES: 275K **Privately Held**
SIC: 2099 Tortillas, fresh or refrigerated

(G-10913)
ROZEVINK ENGINES LLC
14316 State Route 281 (43527-9775)
PHONE.....................................419 789-1159
Jonathan Rozevink, *Principal*
▼ **EMP:** 3
SALES (est): 289.5K **Privately Held**
SIC: 3519 Gas engine rebuilding

Holland
Lucas County

(G-10914)
ADDITIVE METAL ALLOYS LTD
1421 Holloway Rd Ste B (43528-8647)
PHONE.....................................800 687-6110
Richard Meklus, *Principal*
EMP: 8 **EST:** 2014
SQ FT: 1,100
SALES (est): 570.4K **Privately Held**
SIC: 3399 Powder, metal

Holland - Lucas County (G-10915)

(G-10915)
ALL COUNTY PHONE DIRECTORIES
Also Called: All County Phone Directory
7056 Wexford Hill Ln (43528-9101)
P.O. Box 130 (43528-0130)
PHONE.....................419 865-2464
EMP: 4
SQ FT: 800
SALES: 500K *Privately Held*
SIC: 2741 Misc Publishing

(G-10916)
BOLLINGER TOOL & DIE INC
959 Hamilton Dr (43528-8211)
PHONE.....................419 866-5180
Danny N Bollinger, *President*
Anne Bollinger, *Vice Pres*
EMP: 7
SQ FT: 6,700
SALES: 950K *Privately Held*
SIC: 3544 Special dies, tools, jigs & fixtures

(G-10917)
BUNTING BEARINGS LLC (PA)
1001 Holland Park Blvd (43528-9287)
P.O. Box 729 (43528-0729)
PHONE.....................419 866-7000
Thomas Kwiatkowski, *CEO*
George Mugford, *President*
Jody Engelhardt, *General Mgr*
George Rohloff, *General Mgr*
Keith Brown, *Chairman*
▲ EMP: 100
SQ FT: 94,000
SALES: 55MM *Privately Held*
SIC: 3366 3566 Brass foundry; speed changers, drives & gears

(G-10918)
CAMEO COUNTERTOPS INC (PA)
1610 Kieswetter Rd (43528-8678)
PHONE.....................419 865-6371
Brian Hudock, *President*
Tim Sorokin, *Vice Pres*
EMP: 9
SQ FT: 22,000
SALES (est): 3.7MM *Privately Held*
WEB: www.cameocountertops.com
SIC: 2541 5031 2821 Counter & sink tops; lumber, plywood & millwork; plastics materials & resins

(G-10919)
CGS SIGNS LLC
Also Called: Cgs Imaging
6950 Hall St (43528-9485)
PHONE.....................419 897-3000
Chuck Stranc,
Carol Stranc,
▲ EMP: 14
SQ FT: 14,000
SALES (est): 2.6MM *Privately Held*
WEB: www.cgssigns.net
SIC: 3993 7319 Signs & advertising specialties; display advertising service

(G-10920)
CREATIVE PRODUCTS INC
Also Called: CPI
1430 Kieswetter Rd (43528-9785)
PHONE.....................419 866-5501
Marvin Smith, *President*
EMP: 33
SQ FT: 26,000
SALES (est): 2.2MM *Privately Held*
SIC: 5023 5211 2541 Kitchen tools & utensils; cabinets, kitchen; counter tops; wood partitions & fixtures

(G-10921)
CUSTOM COLOR MATCH AND SPC
Also Called: Watkins Auto Body Shop
8930 Airport Hwy (43528-9604)
PHONE.....................419 868-5882
Menuel Fajardo, *Owner*
EMP: 3
SALES (est): 130K *Privately Held*
SIC: 3479 Painting, coating & hot dipping

(G-10922)
CUSTOM DESIGN & TOOL
8900 Geiser Rd (43528-9022)
PHONE.....................419 865-9773
Chuck Bolanger, *President*
EMP: 4
SQ FT: 6,719
SALES (est): 472.3K *Privately Held*
SIC: 3544 Special dies, tools, jigs & fixtures

(G-10923)
D & J DISTRIBUTING & MFG
Also Called: Exotica Fresheners Co
1302 Holloway Rd (43528-9538)
PHONE.....................419 865-2552
Oussama Elassir, *President*
Adnan Elassir, *Vice Pres*
◆ EMP: 20
SQ FT: 45,000
SALES (est): 4.2MM *Privately Held*
SIC: 2842 Sanitation preparations, disinfectants & deodorants

(G-10924)
DAILY DOG
8325 Hill Ave (43528-9192)
PHONE.....................419 708-4923
Jennifer Bettinger, *Principal*
EMP: 3
SALES (est): 143.2K *Privately Held*
SIC: 2711 Newspapers, publishing & printing

(G-10925)
DESIGNETICS INC (PA)
1624 Eber Rd (43528-9776)
PHONE.....................419 866-0700
Craig Williams, *President*
Jay Sanchez, *QC Mgr*
Donald Welch, *Controller*
Sheena Coleman, *Sales Staff*
Jeff Schnapp, *Manager*
EMP: 58
SQ FT: 20,000
SALES (est): 9MM *Privately Held*
WEB: www.designetics.com
SIC: 3559 3991 Automotive related machinery; brooms & brushes

(G-10926)
DOYLE MANUFACTURING INC
Also Called: Shamrock Molded Products
1440 Holloway Rd (43528-8608)
PHONE.....................419 865-2548
Michael A Doyle, *President*
Linda Doyle, *Corp Secy*
Chad Doyle, *Engineer*
Keith Parker, *Department Mgr*
Bryan Doyle, *Manager*
EMP: 70
SQ FT: 100,000
SALES: 10.3MM *Privately Held*
WEB: www.doyleshamrock.com
SIC: 3089 3544 Injection molding of plastics; special dies, tools, jigs & fixtures

(G-10927)
DREAMSCAPE MEDIA LLC (PA)
1417 Timber Wolf Dr (43528-8302)
PHONE.....................877 983-7326
Bradley Rose, *General Mgr*
Brad Rose, *Vice Pres*
John Holkeboer, *Prdtn Mgr*
Michael Olah, *Opers Staff*
EMP: 8
SALES (est): 845.2K *Privately Held*
SIC: 2731 Books: publishing only

(G-10928)
DRS INDUSTRIES INC
1067 Hamilton Dr (43528-8165)
PHONE.....................419 861-0334
J Peter Hottois, *President*
Tom Hillabrand, *Controller*
EMP: 65
SQ FT: 28,120
SALES (est): 28MM *Privately Held*
WEB: www.drsinc.com
SIC: 2819 3089 Aluminum compounds; injection molding of plastics

(G-10929)
DURA TEMP CORPORATION
949 S Mccord Rd (43528-8695)
PHONE.....................419 866-4348
Dave Rollins, *President*
EMP: 13
SQ FT: 6,000
SALES (est): 3MM *Privately Held*
WEB: www.duratemp.com
SIC: 3559 3221 Glass making machinery: blowing, molding, forming, etc.; glass containers

(G-10930)
ELECTRONIC CONCEPTS ENGRG INC
Also Called: E C E
1465 Timber Wolf Dr (43528-8302)
PHONE.....................419 861-9000
Karl W Swonger Jr, *President*
Rick Mills, *Technician*
EMP: 14
SQ FT: 17,900
SALES (est): 2.2MM *Privately Held*
WEB: www.eceinc.com
SIC: 7371 8731 3728 7373 Computer software development; electronic research; aircraft assemblies, subassemblies & parts; computer integrated systems design

(G-10931)
FINISHING MACHINE INC
707 Lost Lakes Dr (43528-8483)
PHONE.....................419 491-0197
Robert Motz, *President*
Christine Motz, *Treasurer*
John Ryan, *Manager*
EMP: 23
SQ FT: 12,000
SALES (est): 2.2MM *Privately Held*
WEB: www.finishingmachine.com
SIC: 3599 Machine shop, jobbing & repair

(G-10932)
GENERIC SYSTEMS INC
10560 Geiser Rd (43528-8506)
PHONE.....................419 841-8460
James Fletcher, *President*
Michael Dullum, *Engineer*
Daniel Ford, *Engineer*
Gina Konczal, *Marketing Mgr*
Melinda Fletcher, *Admin Sec*
EMP: 15
SQ FT: 18,000
SALES (est): 3MM *Privately Held*
WEB: www.genericsys.com
SIC: 3549 7373 7371 Assembly machines, including robotic; systems integration services; computer software development & applications

(G-10933)
HAMILTON MANUFACTURING CORP
1026 Hamilton Dr (43528-8210)
PHONE.....................419 867-4858
Robin Ritz, *CEO*
Steve Alt, *President*
Bonnie Osborne, *Exec VP*
Laura Harris, *Treasurer*
▲ EMP: 45 EST: 1921
SQ FT: 32,000
SALES (est): 10.2MM *Privately Held*
WEB: www.hamiltonmfg.com
SIC: 3172 8711 Coin purses; designing: ship, boat, machine & product

(G-10934)
ICO MOLD LLC
6415 Angola Rd (43528-8555)
PHONE.....................419 867-3900
Micheal Zhao,
EMP: 7
SALES (est): 335.3K *Privately Held*
SIC: 3089 Injection molding of plastics

(G-10935)
IMAGE GROUP OF TOLEDO INC
1255 Corporate Dr (43528-9590)
P.O. Box 1147 (43528-1147)
PHONE.....................419 866-3300
Jon M Levine, *CEO*
Tom Herman, *Principal*
Linda Gomez, *Prdtn Mgr*
Lisa Hoverson, *CFO*
Justin Herman, *Accounts Exec*
◆ EMP: 44 EST: 1989
SQ FT: 29,400
SALES (est): 8.5MM *Privately Held*
WEB: www.theimagegroup.net
SIC: 2261 Screen printing of cotton broadwoven fabrics

(G-10936)
JEFFREY A CLARK
Also Called: Bad Brush Design
148 N King Rd (43528-8768)
PHONE.....................419 866-8775
Jeffrey A Clark, *Owner*
EMP: 5
SQ FT: 2,800
SALES: 180K *Privately Held*
WEB: www.badbrush.com
SIC: 7336 3993 Graphic arts & related design; signs & advertising specialties

(G-10937)
JML HOLDINGS INC
Also Called: Bassett Nut Company
6210 Merger Dr (43528-9593)
PHONE.....................419 866-7500
Jon M Levine, *President*
Jeff Williams, *COO*
Larry J Robbins, *Vice Pres*
▲ EMP: 15
SQ FT: 12,000
SALES: 1.8MM *Privately Held*
WEB: www.bassettnut.com
SIC: 5441 5145 2064 Nuts; popcorn, including caramel corn; candy; nuts, salted or roasted; popcorn & supplies; candy; popcorn balls or other treated popcorn products

(G-10938)
JOHNSON CONTRLS BTRY GROUP INC
10300 Industrial St (43528-9791)
PHONE.....................419 865-0542
Aaron Byrne, *Opers-Prdtn-Mfg*
EMP: 600 *Privately Held*
SIC: 3691 Batteries, rechargeable
HQ: Johnson Controls Battery Group, Llc
5757 N Green Bay Ave
Milwaukee WI 53209

(G-10939)
JOHNSON POWER LTD
1236 Clark St (43528-7403)
PHONE.....................419 866-6692
Paul D Lumbrezer, *Branch Mgr*
EMP: 5
SALES (corp-wide): 17.8MM *Privately Held*
WEB: www.johnsonpower.com
SIC: 3714 Motor vehicle parts & accessories
PA: Johnson Power, Ltd.
2530 Braga Dr
Broadview IL 60155
708 345-4300

(G-10940)
KERN-LIEBERS TEXAS INC
1510 Albon Rd (43528-8684)
PHONE.....................419 865-2437
Hannes Stein, *CEO*
EMP: 30 EST: 1988
SALES: 67.8MM *Privately Held*
SIC: 3495 Wire springs

(G-10941)
KERN-LIEBERS USA INC (HQ)
1510 Albon Rd (43528-9159)
P.O. Box 396 (43528-0396)
PHONE.....................419 865-2437
Hans Jocheim Steim, *Ch of Bd*
Lothar Bauerle, *President*
Gert Wagner, *Treasurer*
Mack Holcomb, *VP Sales*
▲ EMP: 60 EST: 1977
SQ FT: 40,000
SALES (est): 18.1MM
SALES (corp-wide): 810.9MM *Privately Held*
SIC: 3495 3493 Mechanical springs, precision; steel springs, except wire
PA: Hugo Kern Und Liebers Gmbh & Co.
Kg Platinen- Und Federnfabrik
Dr.-Kurt-Steim-Str. 35
Schramberg 78713
742 251-10

GEOGRAPHIC SECTION

Holland - Lucas County (G-10968)

(G-10942)
KLUMM BROS
9241 W Bancroft St (43528-9731)
PHONE.................................419 829-3166
Karen Klumm, *Partner*
Crystal Howard, *Office Mgr*
EMP: 40
SALES (est): 99.5K **Privately Held**
SIC: 3531 Construction machinery

(G-10943)
MATHESON TRI-GAS INC
1720 Trade Rd (43528-8202)
PHONE.................................419 865-8881
Craig Morton, *Manager*
EMP: 13
SQ FT: 18,120 **Privately Held**
WEB: www.airliquide.com
SIC: 5084 2813 Welding machinery & equipment; safety equipment; nitrogen
HQ: Matheson Tri-Gas, Inc.
150 Allen Rd Ste 302
Basking Ridge NJ 07920
908 991-9200

(G-10944)
MESTEK INC
American Warming & Vent Div
7301 International Dr (43528-9412)
PHONE.................................419 288-2703
Paul Quinlan, *Manager*
EMP: 61
SQ FT: 18,000
SALES (corp-wide): 669.8MM **Privately Held**
SIC: 3822 3444 3442 Air flow controllers, air conditioning & refrigeration; sheet metalwork; metal doors, sash & trim
PA: Mestek, Inc.
260 N Elm St
Westfield MA 01085
413 568-9571

(G-10945)
NATIONAL ILLMINATION SIGN CORP
6525 Angola Rd (43528-9651)
P.O. Box 563 (43528-0563)
PHONE.................................419 866-1666
George L Jeakle, *President*
Neil Jeakle, *Vice Pres*
Cindy Studebaker, *Admin Mgr*
EMP: 9
SQ FT: 18,200
SALES: 1MM **Privately Held**
SIC: 3993 Electric signs

(G-10946)
NEON GOLDFISH MKTG SOLUTIONS
6912 Spring Valley Dr # 208 (43528-9677)
PHONE.................................419 842-4462
Justin Johnson, *Info Tech Mgr*
EMP: 3 **EST:** 2017
SALES (est): 178.2K **Privately Held**
SIC: 2813 Neon

(G-10947)
OTTAWA RUBBER COMPANY (PA)
1600 Commerce Rd (43528-8689)
P.O. Box 553 (43528-0553)
PHONE.................................419 865-1378
Mike Bugert, *President*
David Bishop, *Plant Mgr*
James H Bugert, *Plant Mgr*
Chuck Bodi, *Treasurer*
Jeff Bretz, *Sales Staff*
EMP: 17 **EST:** 1945
SQ FT: 12,000
SALES (est): 10.5MM **Privately Held**
WEB: www.ottawarubber.com
SIC: 3061 Mechanical rubber goods

(G-10948)
PATRIOT PRODUCTS INC
Also Called: Patriot Mobility
1133 Corporate Dr Ste B (43528-7405)
P.O. Box 88, Presque Isle MI (49777-0088)
PHONE.................................419 865-9712
Steven Grudzien, *President*
EMP: 15
SALES (est): 1.9MM **Privately Held**
SIC: 3841 Surgical & medical instruments

(G-10949)
PATTERSON COLBURNE (PA)
1100 S Hlland Sylvania Rd (43528)
PHONE.................................419 866-5544
Tony Colbourne, *Owner*
EMP: 6
SALES (est): 1.2MM **Privately Held**
WEB: www.rapatterson.com
SIC: 8721 7372 Accounting services, except auditing; prepackaged software

(G-10950)
PRECISION CUTOFF LLC
7400 Airport Hwy (43528-9545)
P.O. Box 1040 (43528-1040)
PHONE.................................419 866-8000
Jim Cannaley, *Mng Member*
EMP: 120
SQ FT: 150,000
SALES: 10MM **Privately Held**
WEB: www.woodsage.com
SIC: 3317 Steel pipe & tubes

(G-10951)
PRINCIPLED DYNAMICS INC
6920 Hall St (43528-9485)
PHONE.................................419 351-6303
Gene Gunderson, *Principal*
Michael W Holmes, *Principal*
Robert E Holmes, *Principal*
James Swartz, *Principal*
Patricia Earl, *Vice Pres*
EMP: 8 **EST:** 2012
SALES (est): 1.1MM **Privately Held**
SIC: 2834 Pharmaceutical preparations

(G-10952)
QUALITY CARE PRODUCTS LLC
Also Called: Qcp
6920 Hall St (43528-9485)
PHONE.................................734 847-2704
Michael Holmes,
Robert Holmes Sr,
James Swartz,
EMP: 40
SALES (est): 13.5K **Privately Held**
SIC: 2834 Pharmaceutical preparations

(G-10953)
RENNCO AUTOMATION SYSTEMS INC
971 Hamilton Dr (43528-8211)
PHONE.................................419 861-2340
Mike E Owens, *President*
Dave Miklos, *Vice Pres*
David Breese, *Engineer*
Josh Kreager, *Program Mgr*
EMP: 30
SQ FT: 15,000
SALES (est): 8MM **Privately Held**
SIC: 3569 Robots, assembly line: industrial & commercial

(G-10954)
RNM HOLDINGS INC
1810 Eber Rd Ste C (43528-7898)
PHONE.................................419 867-8712
Matthew Milton, *President*
EMP: 20
SQ FT: 15,000 **Privately Held**
SIC: 5084 3536 Cranes, industrial; hoists; hoists, cranes & monorails; cranes, industrial plant; cranes, overhead traveling; cranes & monorail systems
PA: Rnm Holdings, Inc.
550 Conover Dr
Franklin OH 45005

(G-10955)
SCHENA COMPANY LTD
Also Called: Midwest Granite & Stone
7710 Hill Ave Ste B (43528-7607)
PHONE.................................419 868-5207
Don Schena, *President*
David Schena, *Vice Pres*
EMP: 5
SQ FT: 8,000
SALES: 450K **Privately Held**
WEB: www.midwestgraniteandstone.com
SIC: 3281 Granite, cut & shaped

(G-10956)
SCHINDLER ELEVATOR CORPORATION
1530 Timber Wolf Dr (43528-9161)
P.O. Box 960 (43528-0960)
PHONE.................................419 861-5900
Mark Kershner, *Manager*
Holly Byington, *Associate*
EMP: 26
SALES (corp-wide): 10.9B **Privately Held**
WEB: www.us.schindler.com
SIC: 3534 7699 Elevators & equipment; escalators, passenger & freight; elevators: inspection, service & repair
HQ: Schindler Elevator Corporation
20 Whippany Rd
Morristown NJ 07960
973 397-6500

(G-10957)
SELCO INDUSTRIES INC
1590 Albon Rd Ste 1 (43528-9410)
PHONE.................................419 861-0336
Ruby Hill, *CEO*
Seldon Hill, *President*
EMP: 190
SQ FT: 17,000
SALES (est): 27.2MM **Privately Held**
SIC: 2678 Papeteries & writing paper sets

(G-10958)
SOLAR CON INC
7134 Railroad St (43528-9539)
P.O. Box 176 (43528-0176)
PHONE.................................419 865-5877
Donald Wells, *Ch of Bd*
Suzanna Wells, *Treasurer*
J Patrick Dooley Jr, *Marketing Staff*
EMP: 45
SQ FT: 26,725
SALES (est): 5.9MM **Privately Held**
WEB: www.solarcon.com
SIC: 3679 3663 Antennas, receiving; radio & TV communications equipment

(G-10959)
SPONSELLER GROUP INC (PA)
1600 Timber Wolf Dr (43528-8303)
PHONE.................................419 861-3000
Keith Sponseller, *President*
Harold P Sponseller, *Chairman*
Kevin R Nevius, *Vice Pres*
David Nowak, *Vice Pres*
Mike Jacobs, *Project Mgr*
EMP: 44
SQ FT: 8,900
SALES (est): 8.7MM **Privately Held**
SIC: 8711 3599 Consulting engineer; machine shop, jobbing & repair

(G-10960)
TEKNI-PLEX INC
Also Called: Global Technology Center
1445 Timber Wolf Dr (43528-8302)
PHONE.................................419 491-2399
Paul J Young, *CEO*
Phil Bourgeois, *Vice Pres*
Richard Rohrs, *Plant Mgr*
Edward McKinley, *Director*
Kimberly Neumeyer, *Executive Asst*
EMP: 28 **EST:** 1967
SALES (est): 6.1MM
SALES (corp-wide): 1.1B **Privately Held**
SIC: 2679 7389 2672 Egg cartons, molded pulp: made from purchased material; packaging & labeling services; cloth lined paper: made from purchased paper
PA: Tekni-Plex, Inc.
460 E Swedesford Rd # 3000
Wayne PA 19087
484 690-1520

(G-10961)
TMB ENTERPRISES LLC
Also Called: Haas Jordan Company
6509 Angola Rd (43528-9651)
PHONE.................................419 243-2189
David F Waltz, *President*
Thomas A Waltz, *Vice Pres*
Jeffrey Cohen, *Treasurer*
Todd Blackmar, *Mng Member*
EMP: 10 **EST:** 1899
SQ FT: 25,000
SALES (est): 1.8MM **Privately Held**
WEB: www.haas-jordan.com
SIC: 3999 Umbrellas, canes & parts

(G-10962)
TOLEDO TRANSDUCERS INC
Also Called: Toledo Integrated Systems
6834 Spring Valley Dr # 3 (43528-7864)
PHONE.................................419 724-4170
Mark Storer, *President*
Randall W Seed, *Treasurer*
Daniel N Falcone, *Admin Sec*
EMP: 40 **EST:** 1976
SQ FT: 16,000
SALES (est): 10MM **Privately Held**
WEB: www.toledointegratedsystems.com
SIC: 3823 3829 3625 3613 Industrial instrmnts msrmnt display/control process variable; measuring & controlling devices; relays & industrial controls; switchgear & switchboard apparatus

(G-10963)
TRANE COMPANY
Also Called: Ingersoll Rand
1001 Hamilton Dr (43528-8210)
PHONE.................................419 491-2278
Dennis Goldsmith, *Branch Mgr*
EMP: 12 **Privately Held**
SIC: 3585 Heating equipment, complete
HQ: The Trane Company
3600 Pammel Creek Rd
La Crosse WI 54601
608 787-2000

(G-10964)
TURBINE STANDARD LTD (PA)
10550 Industrial St (43528-7732)
PHONE.................................419 865-0355
David R Corwin, *Partner*
Patty Kops, *Partner*
Brandon Carman, *QC Mgr*
Dan Corwin, *Engineer*
▲ **EMP:** 17
SALES (est): 4.1MM **Privately Held**
WEB: www.turbinestandard.com
SIC: 3724 Aircraft engines & engine parts

(G-10965)
VINYL DESIGN CORPORATION
7856 Hill Ave (43528-9181)
PHONE.................................419 283-4009
Patrick J Trompeter, *President*
EMP: 29
SQ FT: 36,000
SALES (est): 5.4MM **Privately Held**
WEB: www.vinyldesigncorp.com
SIC: 3089 5033 2452 Windows, plastic; siding, except wood; prefabricated wood buildings

(G-10966)
WETTLE CORPORATION
952 Holland Park Blvd (43528-9279)
PHONE.................................419 865-6923
Heather Wettle, *Principal*
EMP: 3
SALES (est): 424K **Privately Held**
SIC: 3993 Signs & advertising specialties

(G-10967)
WOODSAGE CORPORATION
7400 Airport Hwy (43528-9545)
PHONE.................................419 476-3553
Curtis Bowers, *Branch Mgr*
EMP: 70
SALES (corp-wide): 3.5MM **Privately Held**
SIC: 3498 Tube fabricating (contract bending & shaping)
PA: Woodsage Corporation
7400 Airport Hwy
Holland OH 43528
419 866-8000

(G-10968)
WOODSAGE INDUSTRIES LLC
7400 Airport Hwy (43528-9545)
P.O. Box 1040 (43528-1040)
PHONE.................................419 866-8000
Daniel Brown, *Mng Member*
Mary Ellen Pisanelli,
EMP: 7
SALES (est): 1.4MM **Privately Held**
SIC: 3999 Atomizers, toiletry

Holland - Lucas County (G-10969)   GEOGRAPHIC SECTION

(G-10969)
WOODSAGE LLC
7400 Airport Hwy (43528-9545)
P.O. Box 1040 (43528-1040)
PHONE..................................419 866-8000
Daniel Brown, *CEO*
Curtis Bowers, *Vice Pres*
Mick Bryan, *Vice Pres*
EMP: 110
SQ FT: 150,000
SALES: 150K Privately Held
SIC: 3317 Steel pipe & tubes

(G-10970)
WREATHS & MASN JARS BY KRISSI
332 Saint James Cir (43528-9320)
PHONE..................................419 250-6606
Kris Rayman, *Principal*
EMP: 3
SALES (est): 113.2K Privately Held
SIC: 3999 Wreaths, artificial

Holmesville
Holmes County

(G-10971)
A&M COUNTRY WOODWORKING LLC
7920 Township Road 574 (44633-9802)
PHONE..................................330 674-1011
Andrew Miller, *Principal*
EMP: 3
SALES (est): 267.5K Privately Held
SIC: 2431 Millwork

(G-10972)
ACTION COUPLING & EQP INC
8248 County Road 245 (44633-9724)
P.O. Box 99 (44633-0099)
PHONE..................................330 279-4242
Scott Eliot, *President*
▲ **EMP:** 80
SQ FT: 75,000
SALES (est): 19.4MM Privately Held
WEB: www.actiongolfcarts.com
SIC: 3569 5087 3429 Firefighting apparatus & related equipment; firefighting equipment; manufactured hardware (general)

(G-10973)
AURIA HOLMESVILLE LLC
8281 County Road 245 (44633)
PHONE..................................330 279-4505
Brian Pour, *President*
Michael Norton, *Maint Spvr*
EMP: 271
SALES (est): 4MM
SALES (corp-wide): 571K Privately Held
WEB: www.iaaawards.com
SIC: 3714 Motor vehicle parts & accessories
HQ: Auria Solutions Usa Inc.
26999 Central Park Blvd
Southfield MI 48076
734 456-2800

(G-10974)
CLASSIC METALS LTD
7051 State Route 83 (44633-9603)
PHONE..................................330 763-1162
John E Yoder, *Principal*
EMP: 5 **EST:** 2008
SALES (est): 547.2K Privately Held
SIC: 2952 Roofing materials

(G-10975)
H I SMITH OIL & GAS INC
8255 County Road 192 (44633)
PHONE..................................330 279-2361
Kenny Jacobs, *President*
Tammy Haubenschield, *Corp Secy*
EMP: 3
SALES: 210K Privately Held
SIC: 1311 Crude petroleum production; natural gas production

(G-10976)
HEARTLAND STAIRWAYS INC
7964 Township Road 565 (44633-9702)
PHONE..................................330 279-2554
Roy Hostewtler, *President*
EMP: 4
SALES (corp-wide): 1.7MM Privately Held
SIC: 2431 Millwork
PA: Heartland Stairways, Inc.
8230 County Road 245
Holmesville OH 44633
330 279-2554

(G-10977)
HEARTLAND STAIRWAYS INC (PA)
8230 County Road 245 (44633-9724)
PHONE..................................330 279-2554
Roy Hostewtler, *President*
Delon Shetler, *Vice Pres*
EMP: 11
SQ FT: 17,000
SALES: 1.7MM Privately Held
SIC: 3534 Elevators & moving stairways

(G-10978)
HEARTLAND STAIRWAYS INC
Township Road 245 (44633)
PHONE..................................330 279-2554
Fax: 330 695-9905
EMP: 8
SALES: 1MM Privately Held
SIC: 3534 Mfg Elevators/Escalators

(G-10979)
HOLMES STAIR PARTS LTD
8614 Township Road 561 (44633-9706)
PHONE..................................330 279-2797
Ben R Hershberger, *Owner*
Arlyn Hershberger,
EMP: 20
SALES (est): 4.3MM Privately Held
SIC: 3534 Elevators & moving stairways

(G-10980)
HOLMES SUPPLY CORP
7571 State Route 83 (44633-9633)
PHONE..................................330 279-2634
Steve Schlabach, *President*
EMP: 9
SALES (est): 1.2MM Privately Held
SIC: 3299 2951 1442 Sand lime products; asphalt paving mixtures & blocks; construction sand & gravel

(G-10981)
HOLMES WHEEL SHOP INC
Also Called: American Stirrup
7969 County Road 189 (44633-9756)
P.O. Box 56 (44633-0056)
PHONE..................................330 279-2891
Ronald Clark, *President*
Paul Stutzman, *Vice Pres*
▲ **EMP:** 20
SQ FT: 32,000
SALES (est): 2.6MM Privately Held
SIC: 2499 3199 Spools, reels & pulleys: wood; stirrups, wood or metal

(G-10982)
INTERNATIONAL AUTOMOTIVE
8281 County Road 245 (44633-9724)
P.O. Box 115 (44633-0115)
PHONE..................................330 279-6557
Kim Landall, *Principal*
EMP: 10
SALES (est): 1.3MM Privately Held
SIC: 3069 Hard rubber products

(G-10983)
MILLER LOGGING INC
8373 State Route 83 (44633)
PHONE..................................330 279-4721
Roy A Miller Jr, *President*
Levi Miller, *Corp Secy*
Barbara Miller, *Vice Pres*
EMP: 28
SALES: 1.7MM Privately Held
SIC: 2421 1629 2411 Wood chips, produced at mill; land clearing contractor; logging

(G-10984)
ROTO SOLUTIONS INC
8300 County Rd 189 (44633)
PHONE..................................330 279-2424
Richard Cook, *President*
Ralph Kirkpatrick, *Vice Pres*
Mark Scheibe, *Vice Pres*
EMP: 100
SALES (est): 9.4MM Privately Held
WEB: www.rotosolutions.com
SIC: 3089 Blow molded finished plastic products; injection molded finished plastic products; extruded finished plastic products

Homer
Licking County

(G-10985)
OHIO STATE PALLET CORP
2175 Broehm Rd (43027)
PHONE..................................614 332-3961
Teresa Salyers, *Principal*
EMP: 4
SALES (est): 402.2K Privately Held
SIC: 2448 Pallets, wood

Homerville
Medina County

(G-10986)
PRINT MARKETING INC
11820 Black River Schl Rd (44235-9716)
PHONE..................................330 625-1500
Robert Rodman, *President*
▲ **EMP:** 20
SQ FT: 1,854
SALES (est): 5.5MM Privately Held
SIC: 2752 Commercial printing, offset

Homeworth
Columbiana County

(G-10987)
BUCKMAN MACHINE WORKS INC
24841 Georgetown Rd (44634-9522)
PHONE..................................330 525-7665
Dale L Buckman, *President*
Marylou Buckman, *Vice Pres*
EMP: 5
SALES (est): 100K Privately Held
WEB: www.ohiodrill.com
SIC: 3011 Tires & inner tubes

(G-10988)
HOMEWORTH FABRICATIONS & MCHS
23094 Georgetown Rd (44634)
P.O. Box 127 (44634-0127)
PHONE..................................330 525-5459
Ronald D Matz, *President*
Rocco Vizzuso, *Vice Pres*
EMP: 11
SQ FT: 3,000
SALES (est): 1.2MM Privately Held
SIC: 3823 3544 Industrial instrmnts msrmnt display/control process variable; jigs & fixtures

(G-10989)
OHIO DRILL & TOOL CO (PA)
Also Called: Homeworth Sales Service Div
23255 Georgetown Rd (44634)
P.O. Box 154 (44634-0154)
PHONE..................................330 525-7717
George Sanor, *Ch of Bd*
Connie Hallman, *President*
Dale Buckman, *General Mgr*
Daniel Matz, *Vice Pres*
Joseph Schopfer, *Sales Mgr*
EMP: 20
SQ FT: 5,000
SALES (est): 12MM Privately Held
SIC: 5085 5261 3546 3545 Industrial tools; lawn & garden equipment; power-driven handtools; machine tool accessories

(G-10990)
OHIO DRILL & TOOL CO
Also Called: Homeworth Sales & Services
23303 South St (44634)
P.O. Box 154 (44634-0154)
PHONE..................................330 525-7161
Dan Motz, *Manager*
EMP: 5
SALES (corp-wide): 12MM Privately Held
SIC: 3545 Machine tool accessories
PA: Ohio Drill & Tool Co
23255 Georgetown Rd
Homeworth OH 44634
330 525-7717

Hopedale
Harrison County

(G-10991)
HOPEDALE MINING LLC
86900 Sinfield Rd (43976)
P.O. Box 415 (43976-0415)
PHONE..................................740 937-2225
David G Zatezalo,
EMP: 40
SALES (est): 5.9MM Privately Held
SIC: 1081 Metal mining services

Hopewell
Muskingum County

(G-10992)
FLINT RIDGE VINEYARD LLC
3970 Pert Hill Rd (43746-9762)
PHONE..................................740 787-2116
Diane Jahnes, *Mng Member*
EMP: 3
SALES (est): 156.9K Privately Held
SIC: 2084 Wines

(G-10993)
J & M CONSTRUCTION LLP
8780 Hopewell National Rd (43746-9791)
PHONE..................................740 454-8986
Jonathan Mast, *Managing Prtnr*
Ervin Zook, *Partner*
EMP: 5
SALES (est): 673.1K Privately Held
SIC: 3089 Prefabricated plastic buildings

Houston
Shelby County

(G-10994)
GLAZIER PATTERN & COACH
3720 Loramie Wash Rd (45333-9714)
PHONE..................................937 492-7355
Steve R Glazier, *Owner*
EMP: 3
SALES: 130K Privately Held
WEB: www.gpcw.com
SIC: 3543 Industrial patterns

Howard
Knox County

(G-10995)
BAM FUEL INC
21191 Floralwood Dr (43028-9649)
PHONE..................................740 397-6674
Beth A Mickley, *Principal*
EMP: 3
SALES (est): 285.4K Privately Held
SIC: 2869 Fuels

(G-10996)
KACY STAIRS
Also Called: Kacy Architectural Millwork
19762 Nunda Rd (43028-9657)
PHONE..................................740 599-5201
Kevin Noble, *President*
Dave Noble, *Treasurer*
EMP: 11
SQ FT: 10,000
SALES (est): 1.3MM Privately Held
SIC: 2431 Staircases & stairs, wood

GEOGRAPHIC SECTION

Huber Heights - Montgomery County (G-11022)

(G-10997)
PIONEER SANDS LLC
Also Called: Millwood Plant
26900 Coshocton Rd (43028-9216)
PHONE.................................740 599-7773
Steven Bell, *Manager*
EMP: 30
SALES (corp-wide): 9.4B **Publicly Held**
SIC: 3295 1446 1442 Minerals, ground or treated; industrial sand; construction sand & gravel
HQ: Pioneer Sands Llc
5205 N O Connor Blvd # 200
Irving TX 75039
972 444-9001

(G-10998)
YODER MANUFACTURING
7679 Flack Rd (43028-9740)
PHONE.................................740 504-5028
Noah E Yoder, *Principal*
EMP: 3 **EST:** 2001
SALES (est): 247.9K **Privately Held**
SIC: 3999 Manufacturing industries

Hubbard
Trumbull County

(G-10999)
B W ELECTRICAL & MAINT SVC
6204 Yungstown Hubbard Rd (44425-1317)
P.O. Box 297 (44425-0297)
PHONE.................................330 534-7870
Bruce Wylie, *President*
EMP: 4
SQ FT: 625
SALES (est): 478.6K **Privately Held**
SIC: 7694 Electric motor repair

(G-11000)
BAKER HUGHES A GE COMPANY LLC
8008 Truck World Blvd (44425-3210)
PHONE.................................304 884-6442
EMP: 8
SALES (corp-wide): 121.6B **Publicly Held**
SIC: 3533 Oil & gas field machinery
HQ: Baker Hughes, A Ge Company, Llc
17021 Aldine Westfield Rd
Houston TX 77073
713 439-8600

(G-11001)
ELLWOOD ENGINEERED CASTINGS CO
7158 Hubbard Masury Rd (44425-9756)
PHONE.................................330 568-3000
Kevin Handerhan, *President*
Susan A Apel, *Vice Pres*
Lyda Force, *Vice Pres*
Robert Price, *Purch Mgr*
Chris Gatto, *Sales Staff*
◆ **EMP:** 135
SALES (est): 38.2MM
SALES (corp-wide): 775.5MM **Privately Held**
WEB: www.ellwoodgroup.com
SIC: 3321 3369 3322 Gray iron ingot molds, cast; nonferrous foundries; malleable iron foundries
PA: Ellwood Group, Inc.
600 Commercial Ave
Ellwood City PA 16117
724 752-3680

(G-11002)
INDEPENDENCE 2 LLC
Also Called: I2
623 W Liberty St (44425-1750)
P.O. Box 40 (44425-0040)
PHONE.................................800 414-0545
Ronald P Baldine, *Managing Prtnr*
Bonnie L Buchanan, *Partner*
Nick Ingoedue, *Partner*
▲ **EMP:** 10
SQ FT: 10,000
SALES (est): 2MM **Privately Held**
SIC: 3429 Door locks, bolts & checks

(G-11003)
JAMES J FAIRBANKS COMPANY INC
7342 Hubbard Bedford Rd (44425-9736)
PHONE.................................330 534-1374
James J Fairbanks, *President*
EMP: 3
SALES (est): 172.3K **Privately Held**
SIC: 8611 3999 Manufacturers' institute; barber & beauty shop equipment

(G-11004)
KILAR MANUFACTURING INC
2616 N Main St (44425-3246)
PHONE.................................330 534-8961
Marilyn Kilar, *President*
EMP: 30
SQ FT: 12,000
SALES (est): 5.6MM **Privately Held**
SIC: 3713 3714 Car carrier bodies; motor vehicle parts & accessories

(G-11005)
MAGEROS CANDIES
132 N Main St (44425-1654)
PHONE.................................330 534-1146
Manuel Mageros, *Owner*
Pasciala Boukis, *Owner*
Helen Magereros, *Owner*
EMP: 5
SQ FT: 1,800
SALES (est): 280.9K **Privately Held**
WEB: www.clevelandwedding.com
SIC: 2064 Candy & other confectionery products

(G-11006)
NANOLOGIX INC
843 N Main St (44425-1128)
PHONE.................................330 534-0800
Bret Barnhizer, *President*
Debby Miller, *Purchasing*
Carol Surrena, *Manager*
EMP: 9
SQ FT: 5,000
SALES: 24K **Privately Held**
WEB: www.nanologixinc.com
SIC: 3829 Testing equipment: abrasion, shearing strength, etc.

(G-11007)
OHIO STEEL SHEET & PLATE INC
7845 Chestnut Ridge Rd (44425-9702)
P.O. Box 1146, Warren (44482-1146)
PHONE.................................800 827-2401
John Rebhan, *President*
Mike Link, *Vice Pres*
Eric Rebhan, *Vice Pres*
EMP: 45
SQ FT: 320,000
SALES (est): 12.9MM **Privately Held**
WEB: www.ohiosteelplate.com
SIC: 3312 5051 3444 Sheet or strip, steel, hot-rolled; plate, steel; metals service centers & offices; sheet metalwork

(G-11008)
OMEGA LOGGING INC (PA)
2550 State Line Rd (44425-9749)
P.O. Box 524, West Middlesex PA (16159-0524)
PHONE.................................330 534-0378
Richard G Conti, *President*
Paul Chovan, *President*
Priscilla Iliss, *Corp Secy*
EMP: 15
SALES: 5MM **Privately Held**
WEB: www.omega-inc.biz
SIC: 2411 2421 Logging; sawmills & planing mills, general

(G-11009)
PSK STEEL CORP
2960 Gale Dr (44425-1099)
P.O. Box 308 (44425-0308)
PHONE.................................330 759-1251
Henry Kinast, *Ch of Bd*
Jerry Kinast, *President*
Steven R Anderson, *Vice Pres*
Steven Anderson, *Vice Pres*
▲ **EMP:** 40
SQ FT: 120,000
SALES (est): 10.7MM **Privately Held**
WEB: www.psksteel.com
SIC: 3544 Special dies & tools; industrial molds

(G-11010)
TAYLOR - WINFIELD CORPORATION (PA)
Also Called: Denton & Anderson Mktg Div
3200 Innovation Pl (44425)
PHONE.................................330 259-8500
John A Anderson II, *Ch of Bd*
Roger Bacon, *President*
Steve Zimmer, *QC Mgr*
Tim Vesey, *Engineer*
Justin Fain, *Design Engr*
▼ **EMP:** 90 **EST:** 1882
SQ FT: 45,000
SALES (est): 20.3MM **Privately Held**
WEB: www.coil-joining.com
SIC: 3548 3542 3567 Welding apparatus; machine tools, metal forming type; robots for metal forming: pressing, extruding, etc.; induction heating equipment

(G-11011)
WARREN FABRICATING CORPORATION (PA)
7845 Chestnut Ridge Rd (44425-9702)
PHONE.................................330 534-5017
Eric Rebhan, *CEO*
John C Rebhan, *President*
Todd Commons, *CFO*
◆ **EMP:** 90 **EST:** 1967
SQ FT: 380,000
SALES (est): 84.7MM **Privately Held**
WEB: www.warfab.com
SIC: 3441 3599 3547 3532 Fabricated structural metal; machine shop, jobbing & repair; rolling mill machinery; mining machinery; sheet metalwork; fabricated plate work (boiler shop)

(G-11012)
WILLIAMS MACHINE CO INC
461 N Main St (44425-1422)
P.O. Box 310 (44425-0310)
PHONE.................................330 534-3058
Fax: 330 534-4839
EMP: 6
SQ FT: 6,500
SALES (est): 300K **Privately Held**
SIC: 3599 Machine Shop

(G-11013)
WISE ENTERPRISES INC
1911 Wick Campbell Rd (44425-2868)
PHONE.................................330 568-7095
Ted Wise, *President*
Kathy Lesnak, *Treasurer*
Kathy Miller, *Admin Sec*
EMP: 4
SQ FT: 3,200
SALES: 275K **Privately Held**
SIC: 3599 Machine shop, jobbing & repair

(G-11014)
YOUNGSTOWN-KENWORTH INC (PA)
Also Called: All-Line Truck Sales
7255 Hubbard Masury Rd (44425-9757)
PHONE.................................330 534-9761
Tomiel Mikes, *President*
Geraldine Mikes, *Principal*
Randall R Fiest, *Vice Pres*
Randall Fiest, *Vice Pres*
Dave Claypool, *Sales Staff*
EMP: 35
SQ FT: 14,900
SALES (est): 8.4MM **Privately Held**
WEB: www.youngstownkenworth.com
SIC: 5013 5012 7538 3713 Truck parts & accessories; trucks, commercial; general automotive repair shops; truck & bus bodies; industrial trucks & tractors

---

Huber Heights
Montgomery County

(G-11015)
CONTINENTAL FAN MFG
6274 Executive Blvd (45424-1424)
PHONE.................................937 233-5524
Ken Grimes, *Principal*
Kenneth Grimes, *Office Mgr*
EMP: 3
SALES (est): 198.1K **Privately Held**
SIC: 3999 Manufacturing industries

(G-11016)
EIGHTY SIX INC
8823 Salon Cir (45424-1581)
PHONE.................................800 760-0722
Jonathan Annarino, *CEO*
Nitin Gautam, *COO*
Nick Hartwig, *Vice Pres*
EMP: 3
SALES (est): 155.5K **Privately Held**
SIC: 7371 7372 Computer software systems analysis & design, custom; computer software development & applications; application computer software

(G-11017)
ENGINETICS CORPORATION (DH)
Also Called: Enginetics Aero Space
7700 New Carlisle Pike (45424-1570)
PHONE.................................937 878-3800
Dale Pelfrey, *CEO*
Stan Matthews, *Vice Pres*
Sam Frazier, *VP Opers*
Samuel Battaglia, *Plant Mgr*
Cindy Howard, *Purch Mgr*
EMP: 108 **EST:** 1976
SQ FT: 57,000
SALES (est): 23.4MM
SALES (corp-wide): 868.3MM **Publicly Held**
WEB: www.enginetics.com
SIC: 3724 3728 3812 3519 Aircraft engines & engine parts; aircraft parts & equipment; search & navigation equipment; jet propulsion engines

(G-11018)
FISHER TESTERS LLC
5079 Kerridge Rd (45424)
PHONE.................................937 416-6554
James A Fisher,
EMP: 4 **Privately Held**
SIC: 3825 Instruments to measure electricity
PA: Fisher Testers, Llc
324 E Schantz Ave
Oakwood OH 45409

(G-11019)
HEIGHTS DUMPSTER SERVICES LLC
5742 Mallard Dr (45424-4148)
PHONE.................................937 321-0096
Steven Mitchum, *Principal*
EMP: 3 **EST:** 2015
SALES (est): 179.2K **Privately Held**
SIC: 3443 Dumpsters, garbage

(G-11020)
HESS ADVANCED TECHNOLOGY INC
7415 Chambersburg Rd (45424-3921)
P.O. Box 17669, Dayton (45417-0669)
PHONE.................................937 268-4377
Fred Edmonds, *CEO*
Delilah Stevens, *President*
EMP: 1
SQ FT: 38,000
SALES: 2MM **Privately Held**
SIC: 2851 Shellac (protective coating)

(G-11021)
INTEGRITY INDUSTRIAL EQP INC
7401 Bridgewater Rd (45424-2406)
PHONE.................................937 238-9275
Jeffrey Smith, *President*
EMP: 3
SQ FT: 8,000
SALES (est): 223.7K **Privately Held**
SIC: 3537 Forklift trucks

(G-11022)
MPE AEROENGINES INC (HQ)
Also Called: Enginetics
7700 New Carlisle Pike (45424-1512)
PHONE.................................937 878-3800
Dale Pelfrey, *CEO*

EMP: 4
SALES (est): 23.4MM
SALES (corp-wide): 868.3MM **Publicly Held**
SIC: 3365 Aerospace castings, aluminum
PA: Standex International Corporation
11 Keewaydin Dr Ste 300
Salem NH 03079
603 893-9701

(G-11023)
PVS PLASTICS TECHNOLOGY CORP
6290 Executive Blvd (45424-1424)
PHONE 937 233-4376
Juerden Frank, *President*
Chad Terrill, *Prdtn Mgr*
▲ **EMP:** 20
SQ FT: 25,000
SALES (est): 5.3MM **Privately Held**
WEB: www.pvs-plastics.net
SIC: 3089 Injection molding of plastics
PA: Pvs Kunststofftechnik Beteiligungsges. Mbh
Salzstr. 20
Niedernhall
794 091-260

(G-11024)
UPDIKE SUPPLY COMPANY (PA)
Also Called: Machine Tools Supply
8241 Expansion Way (45424-6381)
PHONE 937 482-4000
Steve Short, *President*
Shane Hannan, *Principal*
Jeff Butts, *Exec VP*
Rob Johnson, *Vice Pres*
Mike Flanagan, *Purchasing*
EMP: 36
SALES (est): 6MM **Privately Held**
SIC: 3541 Machine tools, metal cutting type

Hudson
Summit County

(G-11025)
ABOUT CATS & DOGS LLC
7600 Olde Eight Rd (44236-1057)
PHONE 440 263-8989
Derek Ruff, *Mng Member*
EMP: 4
SALES: 250K **Privately Held**
SIC: 2047 Dog & cat food

(G-11026)
ADVANCED MATERIALS PRODUCTS
Also Called: Adma Products
1890 Georgetown Rd (44236-4058)
PHONE 330 650-4000
Vladimir Moxson, *President*
Sophia Moxson, *Vice Pres*
▲ **EMP:** 6
SQ FT: 20,000
SALES (est): 1.2MM **Privately Held**
WEB: www.admaproducts.com
SIC: 3339 Titanium metal, sponge & granules

(G-11027)
ALPHA TECHNOLOGIES SVCS LLC (DH)
6279 Hudson Crossing Pkwy (44236-4348)
PHONE 330 745-1641
Jeff Ward, *Buyer*
Ken Brown, *Mng Member*
Peter Boogaard, *Technology*
Darin Myers, *Technical Staff*
Barbara Davidson,
◆ **EMP:** 60
SALES (est): 25.2MM
SALES (corp-wide): 5.1B **Publicly Held**
SIC: 3823 8748 Industrial instrmnts msrmnt display/control process variable; testing services
HQ: Dynisco Instruments Llc
38 Forge Pkwy
Franklin MA 02038
508 541-9400

(G-11028)
ALTEO NA LLC
46 Ravenna St Ste B3 (44236-3059)
P.O. Box 730 (44236-0730)
PHONE 440 460-4600
Scott Barnhouse,
▲ **EMP:** 5
SQ FT: 2,500
SALES: 30MM
SALES (corp-wide): 6.2MM **Privately Held**
SIC: 3295 Minerals, ground or treated
HQ: Alteo Holding
Route De Biver
Gardanne 13120

(G-11029)
ALTERA CORPORATION
591 Boston Mills Rd # 600 (44236-1195)
PHONE 330 650-5200
Donald Kautzman, *Branch Mgr*
EMP: 4
SALES (corp-wide): 70.8B **Publicly Held**
SIC: 3674 Semiconductors & related devices
HQ: Altera Corporation
101 Innovation Dr
San Jose CA 95134
408 544-7000

(G-11030)
AMERICAN ULTRA SPECIALTIES INC
6855 Industrial Pkwy (44236-1158)
PHONE 330 656-5000
Christi Yacinski, *President*
Michaela M Stofey, *Corp Secy*
Martin Yacinski, *Vice Pres*
John Ningard Sr, *Shareholder*
Albert Sivillo, *Shareholder*
EMP: 18
SQ FT: 37,500
SALES (est): 5MM **Privately Held**
SIC: 2992 5172 Re-refining lubricating oils & greases; lubricating oils & greases

(G-11031)
AMF BRUNS AMERICA LP
Also Called: AMF Bruns of America
1797 Georgetown Rd (44236-4192)
PHONE 877 506-3770
Peter Haarhuis, *CEO*
EMP: 5
SQ FT: 54,450
SALES (est): 380.4K **Privately Held**
SIC: 3443 Pressurizers or auxiliary equipment, nuclear: metal plate

(G-11032)
AVESTA SYSTEMS INC (PA)
5601 Hudson Dr Ste 200 (44236-3745)
PHONE 330 650-1800
Greg Lawton, *President*
Ron Myers, *Exec VP*
Beth Jokhio, *Director*
EMP: 9
SALES (est): 2MM **Privately Held**
SIC: 7372 8742 Business oriented computer software; human resource consulting services

(G-11033)
BECKER SIGNS INC
6381 Chittenden Rd Ste E9 (44236-2052)
PHONE 330 659-4504
Brian Becker, *President*
Karen Becker, *Principal*
EMP: 8
SALES (est): 762.3K **Privately Held**
SIC: 3993 5999 Signs & advertising specialties; alarm & safety equipment stores

(G-11034)
BEDFORD ANODIZING CO (PA)
82 Aurora St (44236-2945)
PHONE 330 650-6052
Thomas E De Weese, *President*
Thomas Deweese, *President*
EMP: 47 EST: 1978
SQ FT: 125,000
SALES (est): 18.4MM **Privately Held**
SIC: 3471 Anodizing (plating) of metals or formed products

(G-11035)
CAMBRIDGE MFG JEWELERS
Also Called: Cambridge Jewelers
76 Maple Dr Ste 1 (44236-3029)
PHONE 330 528-0207
O William Koke, *President*
EMP: 5
SQ FT: 1,800
SALES (est): 576.7K **Privately Held**
SIC: 3911 5094 5944 Jewelry apparel; jewelry; jewelry, precious stones & precious metals

(G-11036)
CLAFLIN COMPANY INC
5270 Hudson Dr (44236-3738)
PHONE 330 650-0582
James C Claflin, *President*
Howard Claflin, *President*
EMP: 8
SQ FT: 10,000
SALES (est): 1MM **Privately Held**
SIC: 3089 Injection molding of plastics

(G-11037)
CLEARSONIC MANUFACTURING INC
1223 Norton Rd (44236-4403)
PHONE 828 772-9809
Brian Smith, *President*
Larry Schedler, *VP Sales*
Caron Smith, *Office Mgr*
▲ **EMP:** 8
SQ FT: 10,000
SALES (est): 1.4MM **Privately Held**
SIC: 3089 Panels, building: plastic

(G-11038)
COMET TECHNOLOGIES USA INC
Also Called: Yxlon International
5675 Hudson Indus Pkwy (44236-5012)
PHONE 234 284-7849
Chris Warren, *COO*
Robert Jardim, *Vice Pres*
Roger Wende, *Sales Mgr*
Jason Robbins, *Officer*
EMP: 15
SALES (corp-wide): 443.3MM **Privately Held**
SIC: 3844 X-ray apparatus & tubes
HQ: Comet Technologies Usa Inc.
100 Trap Falls Road Ext
Shelton CT 06484
203 447-3200

(G-11039)
COSO MEDIA LLC
5603 Darrow Rd Ste 500 (44236-5039)
PHONE 330 904-5889
Matthew Dewees, *President*
Bernard Dewees, *Principal*
EMP: 4 EST: 2011
SQ FT: 1,146
SALES (est): 330K **Privately Held**
SIC: 7371 2759 Computer software development; commercial printing

(G-11040)
CURTIS CHEMICAL INC
6020 Ogilvy Dr (44236-3946)
P.O. Box 460 (44236-0460)
PHONE 330 656-2514
Ron G Frew, *President*
EMP: 8
SQ FT: 35,000
SALES (est): 1MM **Privately Held**
SIC: 2819 Industrial inorganic chemicals

(G-11041)
DELUXE CORPORATION
10030 Phillipp Pkwy (44236)
PHONE 330 342-1500
Robin Lebine, *Principal*
EMP: 200
SALES (corp-wide): 2B **Publicly Held**
WEB: www.dlx.com
SIC: 2782 Blankbooks & looseleaf binders
PA: Deluxe Corporation
3680 Victoria St N
Shoreview MN 55126
651 483-7111

(G-11042)
DESIGN MAGNETICS LTD
7941 Valley View Rd (44236-1250)
PHONE 234 380-5500
Margaret Obrien, *President*
EMP: 3
SALES (est): 168.5K **Privately Held**
SIC: 3429 Hangers, wall hardware

(G-11043)
ENVIRONMENTAL WALL SYSTEMS
77 Milford Dr Ste 283 (44236-2782)
P.O. Box 1388 (44236-0888)
PHONE 440 542-6600
EMP: 4
SQ FT: 46,000
SALES (est): 530K **Privately Held**
SIC: 2542 Mfg Movable Walls (Non Wood)

(G-11044)
FORTEC LITHO CENTRAL LLC
6245 Hudson Crossing Pkwy (44236-4348)
PHONE 330 463-1265
Maria Farro, *General Mgr*
Drew C Forhan, *Principal*
EMP: 4
SALES (est): 414.3K **Privately Held**
SIC: 2752 Commercial printing, lithographic

(G-11045)
GEO SPECIALTY CHEMICAL
2685 Blue Heron Dr (44236-1868)
PHONE 330 650-0237
Martin Gregor, *Manager*
EMP: 3
SALES (est): 188.8K **Privately Held**
SIC: 2869 Industrial organic chemicals

(G-11046)
GLC BIOTECHNOLOGY INC
7925 Megan Meadow Dr (44236-4536)
PHONE 440 349-2193
Baochuan Guo, *President*
EMP: 4
SALES (est): 503.2K **Privately Held**
SIC: 3829 Medical diagnostic systems, nuclear

(G-11047)
GLOBAL DESIGN FACTORY LLC
1227 Norton Rd 3b (44236-4403)
PHONE 330 322-8775
Valerie Miller, *President*
EMP: 3
SQ FT: 900
SALES (est): 449.5K **Privately Held**
SIC: 2521 Wood office furniture

(G-11048)
GRACE METALS LTD
685 Ashbrooke Way (44236-1280)
P.O. Box 712 (44236-0712)
PHONE 234 380-1433
Kristin Douglas, *President*
EMP: 5 EST: 2013
SALES: 10MM **Privately Held**
SIC: 3312 Stainless steel

(G-11049)
GRAPHIX JUNCTION
5170 Hudson Dr Ste B (44236-3797)
PHONE 234 284-8392
Cathy Andrade, *Owner*
EMP: 5 EST: 2010
SALES: 250K **Privately Held**
SIC: 7389 2759 2395 Apparel pressing service; screen printing; art goods for embroidering, stamped: purchased materials

(G-11050)
HALIFAX INDUSTRIES INC
2060 Garden Ln (44236-1320)
PHONE 216 990-8951
William J Dodson, *President*
EMP: 5
SQ FT: 8,000
SALES: 350K **Privately Held**
SIC: 3559 Frame straighteners, automobile (garage equipment)

GEOGRAPHIC SECTION — Hudson - Summit County (G-11079)

(G-11051)
HANDCRAFTED JEWELRY INC
Also Called: Jewelry Art
116 N Main St (44236-2827)
PHONE 330 650-9011
Georgianna Bojtos, *President*
Barbara Johnson, *Vice Pres*
EMP: 7 **EST:** 1977
SQ FT: 1,000
SALES: 500K **Privately Held**
WEB: www.handcraftedjewelry.com
SIC: 5944 5947 7699 2759 Jewelry, precious stones & precious metals; silverware; gift shop; customizing services; engraving

(G-11052)
HUDSON ACCESS GROUP II
2460 Bramfield Way (44236-4939)
PHONE 330 283-6214
Thomas Mendoza, *Owner*
EMP: 1
SQ FT: 1,100
SALES: 1.4MM **Privately Held**
SIC: 3651 5731 Household audio & video equipment; radio, television & electronic stores

(G-11053)
HUDSON EXTRUSIONS INC
1255 Norton Rd (44236-4403)
P.O. Box 255 (44236-0255)
PHONE 330 653-6015
Marylin Hansen, *President*
Dewey Hansen, *Shareholder*
EMP: 35 **EST:** 1956
SQ FT: 33,000
SALES (est): 8MM **Privately Held**
WEB: www.hudsonextrusions.com
SIC: 3089 Extruded finished plastic products

(G-11054)
IMPRINTS
77 Maple Dr (44236-3037)
PHONE 330 650-0467
William Stemple, *Owner*
EMP: 10
SQ FT: 1,100
SALES (est): 510K **Privately Held**
SIC: 2791 Typesetting

(G-11055)
INNAGO LLC
77 Milford Dr (44236-2781)
PHONE 330 554-3101
Yasir Drabu,
David Spooner,
EMP: 4
SALES (est): 98.3K **Privately Held**
SIC: 7372 Prepackaged software

(G-11056)
INTERNATIONAL PRECISION
1570 Terex Rd (44236-4069)
PHONE 330 342-0407
Uri Joseph, *Managing Dir*
Craig Mackey, *Vice Pres*
Charlotte Joseph, *Director*
▲ **EMP:** 7
SQ FT: 50,000
SALES: 10MM **Privately Held**
SIC: 3324 Aerospace investment castings, ferrous; commercial investment castings, ferrous

(G-11057)
ISOTOPX INC
12 Pinewood Ln (44236-3468)
PHONE 508 337-8467
Zenon Palancz, *Principal*
Stephen Shuttleworth, *Vice Pres*
Mark Yardley, *Treasurer*
EMP: 3
SALES: 950K **Privately Held**
SIC: 3826 Analytical instruments

(G-11058)
J R MACHINING INC
5170 Hudson Dr Ste G (44236-3797)
PHONE 330 528-3406
Mark Pasuit, *CEO*
Daniel Pasuit, *President*
Dolores Pasuit, *Admin Sec*
▼ **EMP:** 3
SQ FT: 3,000
SALES (est): 429.7K **Privately Held**
SIC: 3469 Machine parts, stamped or pressed metal

(G-11059)
JAMES O EMERT JR
7920 Princewood Dr (44236-1576)
PHONE 330 650-6990
James O Emert, *Principal*
EMP: 3
SALES (est): 375.6K **Privately Held**
SIC: 3317 Steel pipe & tubes

(G-11060)
KOBELCO STEWART BOLLING INC
1600 Terex Rd (44236-4086)
PHONE 330 655-3111
Atsushi Shigeno, *President*
John Schneider, *Vice Pres*
Scott Morgan, *Opers Mgr*
Lisa Weiss, *Safety Mgr*
Tom Fennell, *Purch Agent*
▲ **EMP:** 94
SQ FT: 270,000
SALES (est): 40.2MM
SALES (corp-wide): 17.6B **Privately Held**
WEB: www.ksbiusa.com
SIC: 3559 Rubber working machinery, including tires
HQ: Kobe Steel Usa Holdings Inc.
535 Madison Ave Fl 5
New York NY 10022
212 751-9400

(G-11061)
LOCAL INSIGHT YELLOW PAGES INC
100 Executive Pkwy (44236-1630)
P.O. Box 2502 (44236-0002)
PHONE 330 650-7100
EMP: 175 **EST:** 1984
SALES (est): 21.4MM **Privately Held**
SIC: 2741 Misc Publishing
PA: Berry
100 Executive Pkwy
Hudson OH
330 650-7100

(G-11062)
MAGNUM ASSET ACQUISITION LLC
Also Called: Magnum Innovations
5675 Hudson Industrial (44236-5012)
PHONE 330 915-2382
Ron Cozean, *Principal*
Maria Hughes, *Principal*
EMP: 28
SALES (est): 1.8MM **Privately Held**
SIC: 3646 Fluorescent lighting fixtures, commercial

(G-11063)
NCRX OPTICAL SOLUTIONS INC (PA)
105 Executive Pkwy # 401 (44236-1692)
P.O. Box 38004, Pittsburgh PA (15238-8004)
PHONE 330 239-5353
John Traina, *CEO*
Patrick Cook, *President*
Ed McCall, *COO*
Larry Siders, *CTO*
EMP: 12
SALES (est): 1.5MM **Privately Held**
SIC: 3827 Optical test & inspection equipment

(G-11064)
OILS BY NATURE INCORPORATED
5712 Abbyshire Dr 1a (44236-2678)
PHONE 330 468-8897
Marilyn Salvucci, *President*
Scott C Anderson, *Vice Pres*
◆ **EMP:** 5
SQ FT: 6,000
SALES (est): 917.7K **Privately Held**
WEB: www.oilsbynature.com
SIC: 2844 Cosmetic preparations

(G-11065)
OPTI VISION INC (PA)
5697 Darrow Rd (44236-4013)
P.O. Box 995 (44236-5995)
PHONE 330 650-0919
Pamela Mumick, *President*
EMP: 5
SQ FT: 2,790
SALES (est): 915.2K **Privately Held**
SIC: 5995 3851 Eyeglasses, prescription; ophthalmic goods; eyeglasses, lenses & frames

(G-11066)
OUCHLESS LURES INC
305 Kilbourne Dr (44236-3423)
PHONE 330 653-3867
Lee V Iken, *Principal*
EMP: 4
SALES (est): 277.6K **Privately Held**
SIC: 3949 Lures, fishing: artificial

(G-11067)
PLASTIC PALLET & CONTAINER INC
2239 Edgeview Dr (44236-1802)
PHONE 330 650-6700
Martin R Ackerman, *President*
David Ackerman, *VP Sales*
EMP: 2
SQ FT: 1,100
SALES (est): 1.2MM **Privately Held**
WEB: www.pp-c.com
SIC: 2448 Pallets, wood

(G-11068)
PRINTERS DEVIL INC
77 Maple Dr (44236-3037)
PHONE 330 650-1218
William Stemple, *President*
Maryann Fisher, *Graphic Designe*
EMP: 14
SQ FT: 800
SALES: 1MM **Privately Held**
WEB: www.printersdevil.com
SIC: 2752 7334 Commercial printing, offset; photocopying & duplicating services

(G-11069)
RAMCO SPECIALTIES INC (PA)
5445 Hudson Indus Pkwy (44236-3777)
PHONE 330 653-5135
Richard A Malson II, *President*
Mark Gamble, *CFO*
▲ **EMP:** 150
SQ FT: 165
SALES (est): 24.6MM **Privately Held**
WEB: www.ramconut.com
SIC: 3965 3452 3714 Fasteners; nuts, metal; motor vehicle parts & accessories

(G-11070)
REZKEM CHEMICALS LLC
56 Milford Dr Ste 100 (44236-2760)
PHONE 330 653-9104
Eric Gorze, *President*
▲ **EMP:** 10 **EST:** 2011
SALES (est): 1.6MM **Privately Held**
SIC: 2869 Laboratory chemicals, organic

(G-11071)
ROPER LOCKBOX LLC
7600 Olde Eight Rd (44236-1057)
PHONE 330 656-5148
John Evans, *President*
Joann Riddles, *Vice Pres*
EMP: 4 **EST:** 1997
SQ FT: 1,700
SALES (est): 642.8K **Privately Held**
WEB: www.roperlock.com
SIC: 3469 5099 Boxes, stamped metal; locks & lock sets

(G-11072)
SHERWIN-WILLIAMS COMPANY
5860 Darrow Rd (44236-3864)
PHONE 330 528-0124
Mindy Malone, *Manager*
EMP: 6
SALES (corp-wide): 17.5B **Publicly Held**
WEB: www.sherwin.com
SIC: 5231 2851 Paint; wallcoverings; paints & allied products; varnishes; lacquer: bases, dopes, thinner
PA: The Sherwin-Williams Company
101 W Prospect Ave # 1020
Cleveland OH 44115
216 566-2000

(G-11073)
SINTERED METAL INDUSTRIES INC
Also Called: Simet
1890 Georgetown Rd (44236-4058)
PHONE 330 650-4000
Vladimir Moxson, *President*
Sophia Moxson, *Vice Pres*
Cathy Tonkin, *Admin Mgr*
EMP: 10
SALES (est): 1.3MM **Privately Held**
SIC: 3441 3568 Fabricated structural metal; bearings, bushings & blocks

(G-11074)
SNS NANO FIBER TECHNOLOGY LLC
5633 Hudson Indus Pkwy (44236-5012)
PHONE 330 655-0030
Kim Stanley, *Plant Mgr*
Laura M Frazier, *Mng Member*
Sandra Flower, *Manager*
Darrell Reneker, *Technical Staff*
EMP: 9 **EST:** 2005
SALES (est): 879.2K **Privately Held**
SIC: 7379 3325 ; alloy steel castings, except investment

(G-11075)
SPEARFYSH INC
60 W Streetsboro St Ste 5 (44236-2868)
PHONE 330 487-0300
Marc Miller, *CEO*
Kim Lewis, *COO*
Rand Lennox, *Chief Engr*
EMP: 11
SQ FT: 1,900
SALES (est): 755.3K **Privately Held**
SIC: 7372 Business oriented computer software

(G-11076)
SPECIALTY METALS PROCESSING
837 Seasons Rd (44224-1027)
PHONE 330 656-2767
Michael Miniea, *President*
▲ **EMP:** 46
SQ FT: 170,000
SALES (est): 11.6MM **Privately Held**
SIC: 3541 Machine tools, metal cutting type

(G-11077)
STANDING ROCK DESIGNERY
Also Called: Standing Rock Gallery
5194 Darrow Rd (44236-4004)
PHONE 330 650-9089
Kaye McFarland, *Partner*
John Herring, *Partner*
Earl McFarland, *Partner*
EMP: 5
SALES (est): 280K **Privately Held**
SIC: 3231 5211 Stained glass: made from purchased glass; glass, leaded or stained

(G-11078)
SUMMIT RESOURCES GROUP INC
7476 Whitemarsh Way (44236-1289)
PHONE 330 653-3992
E Dennis Matecun Jr, *Vice Pres*
Dennis Matecun, *Vice Pres*
Tammy Matecun, *Vice Pres*
EMP: 3
SALES (est): 583.7K **Privately Held**
SIC: 3324 5051 Steel investment foundries; metals service centers & offices

(G-11079)
THOMPSON ASSOC HUDSON OHIO
Also Called: Handkerchief House, The
5771 Sunset Dr (44236-3836)
P.O. Box 268 (44236-0268)
PHONE 330 655-2142
Helen D Thompson, *President*
Pat Smith, *Principal*
Judith Maupin, *Vice Pres*

Hudson - Summit County (G-11080)

EMP: 5 EST: 1962
SALES (est): 390.5K **Privately Held**
SIC: 2395 Embroidery & art needlework

(G-11080)
TRU-HAR PRODUCTS
7946 Darrow Rd Unit 334 (44236-1314)
P.O. Box 1394 (44236-0894)
PHONE..................330 338-6826
John T Faulkner, *Office Mgr*
EMP: 5
SALES (est): 377.1K **Privately Held**
SIC: 3399 Metal fasteners

(G-11081)
UNIVERSAL DRECT FLFLLMENT CORP
5581 Hudson Indus Pkwy (44236-5019)
PHONE..................330 650-5000
Jared Florian, *President*
Regina Harper, *Purch Agent*
▲ EMP: 140
SQ FT: 78,000
SALES (est): 49.2MM
SALES (corp-wide): 51.5MM **Privately Held**
WEB: www.artandartifact.com
SIC: 5961 2741 2396 Catalog & mail-order houses; miscellaneous publishing; automotive & apparel trimmings
PA: Universal Screen Arts, Inc.
5581 Hudson Indus Pkwy
Hudson OH 44236
330 650-5000

(G-11082)
WBC GROUP LLC (PA)
Also Called: Meyerpt
6333 Hudson Crossing Pkwy (44236-4346)
PHONE..................866 528-2144
Ron Harrington, *CEO*
▲ EMP: 95
SQ FT: 50,000
SALES (est): 129.2MM **Privately Held**
WEB: www.indemed.com
SIC: 5122 5047 3843 Vitamins & minerals; pharmaceuticals; medical & hospital equipment; dental equipment & supplies

(G-11083)
WOLTERS KLUWER CLINICAL DRUG
1100 Terex Rd (44236-3771)
PHONE..................330 650-6506
Denise Basow, *President*
David A Del Toro, *Vice Pres*
Mike Hofherr, *Vice Pres*
EMP: 65
SQ FT: 24,000
SALES (est): 11.2MM
SALES (corp-wide): 5.2B **Privately Held**
SIC: 2731 2791 7379 Books: publishing only; typesetting, computer controlled; computer related maintenance services
HQ: Wolters Kluwer Health, Inc.
2001 Market St Ste 5
Philadelphia PA 19103
215 521-8300

(G-11084)
YXLON
5675 Hudson Indus Pkwy (44236-5012)
PHONE..................234 284-7862
Chris Warren, *Principal*
EMP: 3
SALES (est): 303.9K **Privately Held**
SIC: 3844 X-ray apparatus & tubes

Huntsville
Logan County

(G-11085)
DUFF QUARRY INC (PA)
9042 State Route 117 (43324-9617)
P.O. Box 305 (43324-0305)
PHONE..................937 686-2811
James E Duff, *President*
Scott Duff, *Vice Pres*
Sandy Duff, *Admin Sec*
EMP: 20 EST: 1953
SQ FT: 26,000
SALES (est): 3.2MM **Privately Held**
SIC: 1422 Crushed & broken limestone

(G-11086)
FIRE SAFETY SERVICES INC
6228 Township Road 95 (43324-9673)
PHONE..................937 686-2000
Steven Spath, *President*
Kay Spath, *Corp Secy*
Marcus Taylor, *Vice Pres*
EMP: 18
SQ FT: 6,400
SALES: 5.9MM **Privately Held**
WEB: www.fssohio.com
SIC: 5099 5012 5087 3999 Fire extinguishers; fireproof clothing; fire trucks; firefighting equipment; fire extinguishers, portable; fire extinguisher servicing

(G-11087)
GADGETS MANUFACTURING CO
9366 State Route 117 (43324-9617)
PHONE..................937 686-5371
Bill Page, *Owner*
EMP: 4
SALES (est): 220K **Privately Held**
SIC: 5731 3651 Antennas, satellite dish; household audio & video equipment

(G-11088)
RETENTION KNOB SUPPLY & MFG CO
4905 State Route 274 W (43324-9643)
P.O. Box 61, Bellefontaine (43311-0061)
PHONE..................937 686-6405
Thomas E Christen, *President*
Carrie Christen, *Admin Sec*
EMP: 10
SQ FT: 100,000
SALES (est): 1.5MM **Privately Held**
SIC: 3545 Machine tool attachments & accessories

Huron
Erie County

(G-11089)
ARTHUR CORPORATION
1305 Huron Avery Rd (44839-2429)
PHONE..................419 433-7202
Charles Hensel, *President*
Mark Svancara, *Vice Pres*
EMP: 65 EST: 1981
SQ FT: 65,000
SALES (est): 24.2MM **Privately Held**
SIC: 3089 3083 Thermoformed finished plastic products; laminated plastics plate & sheet

(G-11090)
ASSEMBLY WORKS INC
Also Called: Assembly Works Matrix Automtn
1705 Sawmill Pkwy (44839-2232)
PHONE..................419 433-5010
William E Kaman, *President*
Julie Smart, *Admin Sec*
EMP: 8 EST: 1998
SQ FT: 10,200
SALES (est): 996.5K **Privately Held**
SIC: 3613 Panelboards & distribution boards, electric

(G-11091)
CANTELLI BLOCK AND BRICK INC (PA)
1001 Sawmill Pkwy (44839-2297)
PHONE..................419 433-0102
Raymond J Cantelli, *President*
Anita Cantelli, *Co-President*
Ray A Cantelli, *Vice Pres*
Adriana Cantelli, *Treasurer*
John Mell, *Sales Mgr*
EMP: 23 EST: 1923
SQ FT: 43,580
SALES: 2.8MM **Privately Held**
SIC: 3271 Blocks, concrete or cinder: standard

(G-11092)
CENTRAL OHIO PAPER & PACKG INC (PA)
Also Called: Breckenridge Paper & Packaging
2350 University Dr E (44839-9173)
PHONE..................419 621-9239
Edward Pettegrew Jr, *President*

Linda Forrider, *Purchasing*
Tony Lowe, *Sales Mgr*
Jeff Griffith, *Sales Staff*
Bob Matthews, *Sales Staff*
EMP: 15
SQ FT: 12,000
SALES: (est): 4.6MM **Privately Held**
WEB: www.breckpack.com
SIC: 2671 Paper coated or laminated for packaging

(G-11093)
DENTON ATD INC (PA)
900 Denton Dr (44839-8922)
PHONE..................567 265-5200
David C Stein, *President*
Robert A Denton, *Chairman*
Micheal Beebe, *Vice Pres*
Craig Morgan, *Shareholder*
EMP: 46
SQ FT: 16,000
SALES (est): 6MM **Privately Held**
WEB: www.dentonatd.com
SIC: 3999 3821 3829 Mannequins; calibration tapes for physical testing machines; measuring & controlling devices

(G-11094)
GEOCORP INC
9010 River Rd (44839-9523)
PHONE..................419 433-1101
George Conrad, *President*
John Ochenas, *Vice Pres*
Niel Fleetwood, *Human Res Mgr*
Jeremy Milner, *Sales Staff*
EMP: 46
SQ FT: 6,000
SALES (est): 12.6MM **Privately Held**
WEB: www.geocorpinc.com
SIC: 3823 Thermocouples, industrial process type

(G-11095)
HEALTHCARE BENEFITS INC
1212 Cleveland Rd W (44839-1410)
P.O. Box 326 (44839-0326)
PHONE..................419 433-4499
Joan Norton, *CEO*
Ed Norton, *President*
EMP: 5
SQ FT: 20,000
SALES (est): 100K **Privately Held**
SIC: 1542 3732 Hospital construction; lifeboats, building & repairing

(G-11096)
HURON CEMENT PRODUCTS COMPANY (PA)
Also Called: H & C Building Supplies
617 Main St (44839-2593)
PHONE..................419 433-4161
John Caporini, *President*
EMP: 38 EST: 1914
SQ FT: 37,800
SALES (est): 9.4MM **Privately Held**
SIC: 5211 5032 3273 3546 Cement; sand & gravel; cement; gravel; ready-mixed concrete; power-driven handtools; concrete products; cement, hydraulic

(G-11097)
HURON HOMETOWN NEWS
304 Williams St (44839-1648)
PHONE..................419 433-1401
John Schaffner, *Principal*
EMP: 3
SALES (est): 117.8K **Privately Held**
SIC: 2711 Newspapers, publishing & printing

(G-11098)
HYBRID TRAILER CO LLC
912 University Dr S (44839-9172)
PHONE..................419 433-3022
Glenn Peterman,
EMP: 5 EST: 2010
SALES (est): 375.4K **Privately Held**
SIC: 3792 Travel trailers & campers

(G-11099)
INTERNATIONAL AUTOMOTIVE COMPO
Also Called: Automotive Industries Division
1608 Sawmill Pkwy (44839-2200)
PHONE..................419 433-5653
EMP: 700 **Privately Held**

WEB: www.iaaawards.com
SIC: 3089 3714 3429 3229 Injection molded finished plastic products; motor vehicle parts & accessories; manufactured hardware (general); pressed & blown glass
HQ: International Automotive Components Group North America, Inc.
28333 Telegraph Rd
Southfield MI 48034

(G-11100)
JCK INDUSTRIES
730 River Rd (44839-2623)
P.O. Box 486 (44839-0486)
PHONE..................419 433-6277
Jack Kenning, *President*
EMP: 30
SALES (est): 3MM **Privately Held**
SIC: 3312 Blast furnaces & steel mills

(G-11101)
KEVIN G RYBA INC
3727 Perkins Ave (44839-1058)
PHONE..................419 627-2010
Kevin G Ryba, *President*
EMP: 3 EST: 1995
SALES (est): 209.9K **Privately Held**
SIC: 2064 Candy & other confectionery products

(G-11102)
LABEL AID INC
608 Rye Beach Rd (44839-2064)
PHONE..................419 433-2888
Darlene Crooks, *President*
Carl S Hanson, *Vice Pres*
Lucille Hanson, *Treasurer*
Heather Feeney, *Admin Sec*
Patrick Gioffre, *Graphic Designe*
▲ EMP: 15
SQ FT: 40,000
SALES: 3.5MM **Privately Held**
WEB: www.labelaidinc.com
SIC: 2679 Labels, paper: made from purchased material

(G-11103)
LAKEWAY MFG INC (PA)
730 River Rd (44839-2623)
P.O. Box 486 (44839-0486)
PHONE..................419 433-3030
Jack Kenning, *President*
Barbara K Straka, *Corp Secy*
Veronica Lee, *Accounting Mgr*
Hugh Beggs, *Sales Staff*
Kathy Weaver, *Marketing Staff*
EMP: 30
SALES (est): 6.2MM **Privately Held**
SIC: 3567 3255 3446 3433 Industrial furnaces & ovens; clay refractories; architectural metalwork; heating equipment, except electric; steel foundries; cold finishing of steel shapes

(G-11104)
LATANICK EQUIPMENT INC
720 River Rd (44839-2623)
PHONE..................419 433-2200
Richard D Poorman, *President*
Richard Decker, *Vice Pres*
Gina Holt, *Purchasing*
Pam Neill, *Draft/Design*
Judy Poorman, *Manager*
EMP: 20
SQ FT: 32,000
SALES (est): 4.3MM **Privately Held**
WEB: www.latanickequipment.com
SIC: 8711 3599 Designing: ship, boat, machine & product; custom machinery

(G-11105)
MUDBROOK GOLF CENTER
1609 Mudbrook Rd (44839-8905)
PHONE..................419 433-2945
Fax: 419 433 0132
EMP: 6
SALES (est): 260K **Privately Held**
SIC: 3949 Mfg Sporting/Athletic Goods

(G-11106)
N2Y LLC
Also Called: Djc Holdings
909 University Dr S (44839-9172)
P.O. Box 550 (44839-0550)
PHONE..................419 433-9800

Jacquelyn Clark, *President*
David Clark, *Principal*
Michael Clark, *Principal*
Don Wostmann, *Principal*
Christin Wostmann, *Senior VP*
EMP: 20
SQ FT: 16,800
SALES: 3MM **Privately Held**
WEB: www.news-2-you.com
SIC: 3999 Education aids, devices & supplies

(G-11107)
ODYSSEY PRESS INC
913 Superior Dr (44839-1454)
PHONE..................614 410-0356
David L Trotter, *President*
Mark Bober, *Vice Pres*
EMP: 15
SQ FT: 10,000
SALES (est): 1.8MM **Privately Held**
WEB: www.odysseypress.com
SIC: 2752 2759 Commercial printing, offset; letterpress printing

(G-11108)
PLASTIC WORKS INC (PA)
10502 Mudbrook Rd (44839-9372)
P.O. Box 369 (44839-0369)
PHONE..................419 433-6576
Martin Kvame, *President*
EMP: 14
SALES (est): 1.7MM **Privately Held**
SIC: 3081 3089 Packing materials, plastic sheet; plastic processing

(G-11109)
PPG ARCHITECTURAL COATINGS LLC
350 Sprowl Rd (44839-2636)
PHONE..................419 433-5664
Michael H McGarry, *CEO*
EMP: 12
SALES (est): 1.8MM
SALES (corp-wide): 15.3B **Publicly Held**
SIC: 2851 Paints & allied products
PA: Ppg Industries, Inc.
   1 Ppg Pl
   Pittsburgh PA 15272
   412 434-3131

(G-11110)
PRECISION MACHINING CORP
9307 Wikel Rd (44839-9140)
PHONE..................419 433-3520
James Ebert, *President*
EMP: 4
SQ FT: 4,400
SALES (est): 423.4K **Privately Held**
SIC: 3599 Machine shop, jobbing & repair; custom machinery

(G-11111)
ROSWELL INC
9808 Barrows Rd (44839-9796)
PHONE..................419 433-4709
John Delamater, *President*
EMP: 5
SQ FT: 6,500
SALES (est): 855.7K **Privately Held**
WEB: www.roswellinc.com
SIC: 3089 Plastic containers, except foam

Iberia
Morrow County

(G-11112)
COREWORTH HOLDINGS LLC
8402 County Rd (43325)
PHONE..................419 468-7100
Rodney Whited, *Partner*
Randy Harper, *Partner*
Rich Kozlowski,
▲ **EMP:** 3
SALES (est): 358.9K **Privately Held**
SIC: 3469 Machine parts, stamped or pressed metal

(G-11113)
GLEN-GERY CORPORATION
County Rd 9 (43325)
P.O. Box 207 (43325-0207)
PHONE..................419 468-5002
George Robinson, *Manager*
EMP: 50
SALES (corp-wide): 1.2MM **Privately Held**
WEB: www.glengerybrick.com
SIC: 3251 3255 Structural brick & blocks; clay refractories
HQ: Glen-Gery Corporation
   1166 Spring St
   Reading PA 19610
   610 374-4011

(G-11114)
IBERIA MACHINE SHOP INC
8402 County Rd 30 (43325)
P.O. Box 205 (43325-0205)
PHONE..................419 468-7100
Rodney L Whited, *President*
EMP: 4
SQ FT: 6,000
SALES (est): 579.1K **Privately Held**
SIC: 3599 Machine shop, jobbing & repair

(G-11115)
YIZUMI-HPM CORPORATION
Also Called: HPM North America Corp
3424 State Rt 309 (43325)
P.O. Box 210 (43325-0210)
PHONE..................740 382-5600
Bill Duff, *General Mgr*
John Beary, *Sales Mgr*
Lori Baker, *Office Mgr*
Randy Clements, *Manager*
▲ **EMP:** 26
SALES (est): 6.1MM
SALES (corp-wide): 303.1MM **Privately Held**
SIC: 3542 Die casting machines; pressing machines
PA: Guangdong Yizumi Precision Machinery Co., Ltd.
   No.22, Keyuan 3 Rd., (Ronggui),
   Shunde High-Tech Zone
   Foshan 52830
   757 292-6200

Independence
Cuyahoga County

(G-11116)
7SIGNAL SOLUTIONS INC (PA)
6155 Rockside Rd Ste 110 (44131-2217)
PHONE..................216 777-2900
Thomas Barrett, *CEO*
Don Cook, *Chief Mktg Ofcr*
EMP: 24
SQ FT: 3,900
SALES (est): 5.5MM **Privately Held**
SIC: 3661 Telephone & telegraph apparatus

(G-11117)
ACCEL PERFORMANCE GROUP LLC (DH)
6100 Oak Tree Blvd # 200 (44131-6914)
PHONE..................216 658-6413
Robert Tobey, *CEO*
Robert Romanelli, *President*
Andrew Mazzarella, *CFO*
▲ **EMP:** 180
SQ FT: 200,000
SALES (est): 50.8MM
SALES (corp-wide): 109.9MM **Privately Held**
WEB: www.mrgasket.com
SIC: 3714 5013 3053 Motor vehicle parts & accessories; automotive supplies & parts; gaskets, packing & sealing devices
HQ: Msdp Group Llc
   1350 Pullman Dr Dr14
   El Paso TX 79936
   915 857-5200

(G-11118)
AGILE GLOBAL SOLUTIONS INC
5755 Granger Rd Ste 610 (44131-1458)
PHONE..................916 655-7745
EMP: 29
SALES (corp-wide): 5.2MM **Privately Held**
SIC: 7372 Business oriented computer software
PA: Agile Global Solutions, Inc.
   13405 Folsom Blvd Ste 515
   Folsom CA 95630
   916 353-1780

(G-11119)
AMARR COMPANY
Also Called: Amarr Garage Doors
800 Resource Dr Ste 3 (44131-1875)
PHONE..................216 573-7100
Luke Andress, *Branch Mgr*
EMP: 3
SALES (corp-wide): 9B **Privately Held**
WEB: www.amarr.com
SIC: 2431 3442 5211 Garage doors, overhead: wood; garage doors, overhead: metal; garage doors, sale & installation
HQ: Amarr Company
   165 Carriage Ct
   Winston Salem NC 27105
   336 744-5100

(G-11120)
AVTRON INC
7900 E Pleasant Valley Rd (44131-5529)
PHONE..................216 642-1230
John Brock, *President*
Ann Williams, *CFO*
Tom Lose, *Controller*
EMP: 32
SALES (est): 7.1MM **Privately Held**
SIC: 3629 Electrical industrial apparatus

(G-11121)
CARDIOINSIGHT TECHNOLOGIES INC
3 Summit Park Dr Ste 400 (44131-2582)
PHONE..................216 274-2221
Patrick J Wethington, *President*
Charu Ramanathan, *Founder*
EMP: 9
SALES (est): 1.7MM **Privately Held**
SIC: 3845 Electrocardiographs
PA: Medtronic Public Limited Company
   20 Lower Hatch Street
   Dublin

(G-11122)
CHALLENGER HARDWARE COMPANY
800 Resource Dr Ste 8 (44131-1875)
PHONE..................216 591-1141
Joe Ross, *President*
▲ **EMP:** 12 **EST:** 2005
SALES (est): 1.7MM **Privately Held**
SIC: 3312 Stainless steel

(G-11123)
COVIA HOLDINGS CORPORATION (HQ)
3 Summit Park Dr Ste 700 (44131-6901)
PHONE..................440 214-3284
Richard A Navarre, *Ch of Bd*
Jenniffer D Deckard, *President*
Campbell J Jones, *COO*
Andrew D Eich, *CFO*
Gerald L Clancey, *Ch Credit Ofcr*
◆ **EMP:** 90
SALES: 1.8B
SALES (corp-wide): 136.2MM **Publicly Held**
WEB: www.unimin.com
SIC: 1446 1499 1422 1459 Silica mining; quartz crystal (pure) mining; dolomite, crushed & broken-quarrying; nepheline syenite quarrying; steam railroads; construction sand & gravel
PA: Scr - Sibelco
   Plantin En Moretuslei 1a
   Antwerpen 2018
   322 366-11

(G-11124)
DUNHAM MACHINE INC
1311 E Schaaf Rd Bldg A (44131-1347)
PHONE..................216 398-4500
Ted Pawelec, *President*
Peter Pistell, *Vice Pres*
EMP: 9
SQ FT: 7,500
SALES (est): 1.4MM **Privately Held**
WEB: www.dunhammachine.com
SIC: 3599 Machine shop, jobbing & repair

(G-11125)
EMC CORPORATION
6480 Rckside Wds Blvd S # 330 (44131-2222)
PHONE..................216 606-2000
Tom Weldon, *Manager*
Tony Emanuel, *Senior Mgr*
EMP: 39
SALES (corp-wide): 90.6B **Publicly Held**
WEB: www.emc.com
SIC: 3572 7372 Computer storage devices; prepackaged software
HQ: Emc Corporation
   176 South St
   Hopkinton MA 01748
   508 435-1000

(G-11126)
FAIRMOUNT MINERALS LLC
Also Called: Fairmount Santrol
3 Summit Park Dr Ste 700 (44131-6901)
PHONE..................269 926-9450
Jenniffer Deckard, *CEO*
EMP: 200
SALES (est): 988MM
SALES (corp-wide): 136.2MM **Publicly Held**
SIC: 1446 Industrial sand
HQ: Fairmount Santrol Inc.
   3 Summit Park Dr Ste 700
   Independence OH 44131
   440 214-3200

(G-11127)
FAIRMOUNT SANTROL INC (DH)
Also Called: Fairmount Minerals
3 Summit Park Dr Ste 700 (44131-6901)
P.O. Box 87, Chardon (44024-0087)
PHONE..................440 214-3200
Charles D Fowler, *CEO*
Jenniffer D Deckard, *President*
William E Conway, *Chairman*
Joseph Fodo, *Vice Pres*
Tim Mc Millin, *Sls & Mktg Exec*
▼ **EMP:** 9
SALES (est): 1.1B
SALES (corp-wide): 136.2MM **Publicly Held**
WEB: www.fairmountminerals.com
SIC: 2891 Adhesives
HQ: Covia Holdings Corporation
   3 Summit Park Dr Ste 700
   Independence OH 44131
   440 214-3284

(G-11128)
FIRST PRODUCT TECHNOLOGIES LLC
6100 Oak Tree Blvd (44131-2544)
PHONE..................440 364-0664
Louis Novak,
Paul R Koontz,
Frank R Novak,
EMP: 3 **EST:** 2016
SALES (est): 138.3K **Privately Held**
SIC: 3571 Electronic computers

(G-11129)
FML RESIN LLC
3 Summit Park Dr Ste 700 (44131-6901)
PHONE..................440 214-3200
Jenniffer D Deckard, *President*
EMP: 27
SALES (est): 847.3K **Privately Held**
SIC: 1442 Construction sand & gravel

(G-11130)
FML SAND LLC
3 Summit Park Dr Ste 700 (44131-6901)
PHONE..................440 214-3200
Chris Navel, *Mng Member*
EMP: 4
SALES (est): 780.5K
SALES (corp-wide): 136.2MM **Publicly Held**
SIC: 1442 Common sand mining
HQ: Fairmount Santrol Inc.
   3 Summit Park Dr Ste 700
   Independence OH 44131
   440 214-3200

Independence - Cuyahoga County (G-11131)

(G-11131)
FML TERMINAL LOGISTICS LLC (DH)
3 Summit Park Dr Ste 700 (44131-6901)
PHONE..................................440 214-3200
Jennifer Deckard, *President*
EMP: 5
SALES (est): 5.5MM
SALES (corp-wide): 136.2MM **Publicly Held**
SIC: 1442 Construction sand & gravel
HQ: Fairmount Santrol Inc.
    3 Summit Park Dr Ste 700
    Independence OH 44131
    440 214-3200

(G-11132)
GLOBAL GRAPHITE GROUP LLC
4807 Rockside Rd (44131-2192)
PHONE..................................216 538-0362
Craig S Shular, *Mng Member*
Henry Yu,
EMP: 2 EST: 2017
SQ FT: 400
SALES: 70MM **Privately Held**
SIC: 3297 Graphite refractories: carbon bond or ceramic bond

(G-11133)
GOODRICH CORPORATION
Also Called: Goodrich Landing Gear Division
6225 Oak Tree Blvd (44131-2509)
PHONE..................................216 429-4018
Tarah Reiter, *General Mgr*
Michael Reese, *Production*
Tony Loncaric, *Engineer*
Brian Gora, *Manager*
EMP: 500
SQ FT: 27,772
SALES (corp-wide): 66.5B **Publicly Held**
WEB: www.bfgoodrich.com
SIC: 3728 Alighting (landing gear) assemblies, aircraft
HQ: Goodrich Corporation
    2730 W Tyvola Rd
    Charlotte NC 28217
    704 423-7000

(G-11134)
GRAFTECH HOLDINGS INC
6100 Oak Tree Blvd # 300 (44131-6970)
PHONE..................................216 676-2000
Joel L Hawthorne, *CEO*
Bill McFadden, *General Mgr*
Erick R Asmussen, *Vice Pres*
John D Moran, *Vice Pres*
Vicki Vesel, *Safety Mgr*
EMP: 310
SALES (est): 757.5K
SALES (corp-wide): 8.5B **Publicly Held**
SIC: 1499 3624 Graphite mining; carbon & graphite products
HQ: Graftech International Ltd.
    982 Keynote Cir Ste 6
    Brooklyn Heights OH 44131

(G-11135)
HONEYWELL INTERNATIONAL INC
950 Keynote Cir Ste 90 (44131-1885)
PHONE..................................216 459-6048
Jim Rosen, *General Mgr*
Dan Stankey, *CFO*
Sam Davis, *Consultant*
Jon Mansco, *Senior Mgr*
EMP: 657
SALES (corp-wide): 41.8B **Publicly Held**
WEB: www.honeywell.com
SIC: 3724 Turbines, aircraft type
PA: Honeywell International Inc.
    115 Tabor Rd
    Morris Plains NJ 07950
    973 455-2000

(G-11136)
INDY EQP INDEPENDENCE RECYCL
6220 E Schaaf Rd (44131-1332)
PHONE..................................216 524-0999
Victor Digeronimo, *President*
▲ EMP: 250
SQ FT: 15,000
SALES (est): 250MM **Privately Held**
SIC: 3531 Construction machinery

(G-11137)
JENCO MANUFACTURING INC
7682 Valley Vista Rd (44131-6643)
PHONE..................................216 898-9682
EMP: 24
SALES (est): 3MM **Privately Held**
SIC: 3452 Mfg Rivets

(G-11138)
KOHUT ENTERPRISES INC
Also Called: Mel-Ba Manufacturing
5281 Butternut Ridge Dr (44131-4688)
PHONE..................................440 366-6666
Kenneth M Kohut, *President*
EMP: 6
SQ FT: 23,000
SALES: 800K **Privately Held**
WEB: www.mel-ba.com
SIC: 3451 Screw machine products

(G-11139)
KOMATSU MINING CORP
981 Keynote Cir Ste 8 (44131-1842)
PHONE..................................216 503-5029
Edward L Doheny, *Branch Mgr*
EMP: 10
SALES (corp-wide): 23.4B **Privately Held**
SIC: 3532 Mining machinery
HQ: Komatsu Mining Corp.
    100 E Wisconsin Ave # 2780
    Milwaukee WI 53202
    414 319-8500

(G-11140)
KRONOS INCORPORATED
6100 Oak Tree Blvd # 410 (44131-6948)
PHONE..................................216 867-5609
Dianne Maupin, *Branch Mgr*
EMP: 4
SALES (corp-wide): 1.1B **Privately Held**
WEB: www.kronos.com
SIC: 7372 Business oriented computer software
HQ: Kronos Incorporated
    900 Chelmsford St # 312
    Lowell MA 01851
    978 250-9800

(G-11141)
LIQUID DEVELOPMENT COMPANY (PA)
Also Called: L D C
5708 E Schaaf Rd (44131-1308)
PHONE..................................216 641-9366
Doug Hutchinson, *President*
Beldon Hutchinson, *Vice Pres*
Lynn Hutchinson, *Treasurer*
Dawn Hutchinson, *Admin Sec*
▲ EMP: 9 EST: 1978
SQ FT: 18,000
SALES (est): 1.1MM **Privately Held**
WEB: www.ldcu.com
SIC: 2899 3559 Chemical preparations; electroplating machinery & equipment

(G-11142)
MAXON CORPORATION
950 Keynote Cir Ste 113 (44131-1880)
PHONE..................................216 459-6056
Joseph Pomykala, *Manager*
EMP: 3
SALES (corp-wide): 41.8B **Publicly Held**
WEB: www.maxoncorp.com
SIC: 3823 Combustion control instruments
HQ: Maxon Corporation
    201 E 18th St
    Muncie IN 47302
    765 284-3304

(G-11143)
NATURALLY SMART LABS LLC
7820 E Pleasant Valley Rd (44131-5531)
PHONE..................................216 503-9398
Keith A Vanderburg,
EMP: 3
SALES (est): 304.9K **Privately Held**
SIC: 2844 Cosmetic preparations

(G-11144)
NIDEC MOTOR CORPORATION
Also Called: Nidec Industrial Solutions
7555 E Pleasant Vly (44131-5562)
PHONE..................................216 642-1230
Anna Marie Kennedy, *Manager*
EMP: 150
SALES (corp-wide): 13.9B **Privately Held**
SIC: 3823 3829 Industrial instrmnts msrmnt display/control process variable; aircraft & motor vehicle measurement equipment
HQ: Nidec Motor Corporation
    8050 West Florissant Ave
    Saint Louis MO 63136

(G-11145)
OPTA MINERALS (USA) INC (DH)
Also Called: Rossborough
4807 Rockside Rd Ste 400 (44131-2159)
PHONE..................................330 659-3003
David J Kruse, *President*
Paul Uguccioni, *Vice Pres*
James Wilson, *Admin Sec*
▲ EMP: 7
SQ FT: 6,000
SALES (est): 4.4MM
SALES (corp-wide): 1.2B **Privately Held**
WEB: www.mgtechcorp.com
SIC: 2899 Metal treating compounds
HQ: Opta Minerals Inc
    407 Parkside Dr
    Waterdown ON L0R 2
    905 689-7361

(G-11146)
POLYMER ADDITIVES INC (DH)
Also Called: Valtris Specialty Chemicals
7500 E Pleasant Valley Rd (44131-5536)
PHONE..................................216 875-7200
Paul Angus, *CEO*
Kaval Patel, *President*
Humberto Goldoni, *Managing Dir*
Steve Hughes, *Vice Pres*
Jim Mason, *Vice Pres*
◆ EMP: 75
SQ FT: 30,000
SALES (est): 112MM
SALES (corp-wide): 727.7MM **Privately Held**
SIC: 2899 Fire retardant chemicals
HQ: Polymer Additives Holdings, Inc.
    7500 E Pleasant Valley Rd
    Independence OH 44131
    216 875-7200

(G-11147)
POLYMER ADDITIVES HOLDINGS INC (DH)
Also Called: Valtris
7500 E Pleasant Valley Rd (44131-5536)
PHONE..................................216 875-7200
Paul Angus, *President*
Anthony A Tamer, *President*
Steve Hughes, *Vice Pres*
Jay Xu, *Vice Pres*
Jim Mason, *VP Opers*
EMP: 200
SALES: 105MM **Privately Held**
SIC: 5169 2899 Chemicals & allied products; chemical preparations; fire retardant chemicals
HQ: H.I.G. Capital, Inc.
    1450 Brickell Ave Fl 31
    Miami FL 33131
    305 379-2322

(G-11148)
PRECISION METALFORMING ASSN (PA)
6363 Oak Tree Blvd (44131-2556)
PHONE..................................216 241-1482
William E Gaskin, *CEO*
Jody Fledderman, *Vice Ch Bd*
Roy Hardy, *President*
David C Klotz, *President*
Daniel E Ellashek, *Vice Pres*
▲ EMP: 41
SQ FT: 20,000
SALES: 6.3MM **Privately Held**
SIC: 8611 2731 Trade associations; book publishing

(G-11149)
QUEZ MEDIA MARKETING INC
6100 Oak Tree Blvd # 200 (44131-6914)
PHONE..................................216 910-0202
Jose A Vasquez, *CEO*
EMP: 11
SALES (est): 1.3MM **Privately Held**
SIC: 7374 2752 7336 7371 Computer graphics service; commercial printing, offset; commercial art & graphic design; computer software systems analysis & design, custom; direct mail advertising services; marketing consulting services

(G-11150)
SKILLSOFT CORPORATION
6645 Acres Dr (44131-4962)
PHONE..................................216 524-5200
Joe Garrison, *Branch Mgr*
EMP: 66
SALES (corp-wide): 352.2K **Privately Held**
SIC: 7372 Educational computer software
HQ: Skillsoft Corporation
    300 Innovative Way # 201
    Nashua NH 03062
    603 324-3000

(G-11151)
SYMANTEC CORPORATION
6100 Oak Tree Blvd (44131-2544)
PHONE..................................216 643-6700
EMP: 70
SALES (corp-wide): 4.8B **Publicly Held**
SIC: 7372 Prepackaged software
PA: Symantec Corporation
    350 Ellis St
    Mountain View CA 94043
    650 527-8000

(G-11152)
THYSSENKRUPP MATERIALS NA INC
6050 Oak Tree Blvd # 110 (44131-6927)
PHONE..................................216 883-8100
Randy Pacelli, *Branch Mgr*
EMP: 87
SQ FT: 65,000
SALES (corp-wide): 39.8B **Privately Held**
SIC: 5051 3341 Steel; secondary nonferrous metals
HQ: Thyssenkrupp Materials Na, Inc.
    22355 W 11 Mile Rd
    Southfield MI 48033
    248 233-5600

(G-11153)
UNITED COMPUTER GROUP INC (PA)
Also Called: Ucg Technologies
7100 E Pleasant Valley Rd # 250 (44131-5556)
PHONE..................................216 520-1333
James A Kandrac, *President*
Pamela Kandrac, *Vice Pres*
Michael D Powall, *Vice Pres*
EMP: 8
SQ FT: 3,200
SALES (est): 5.9MM **Privately Held**
SIC: 5045 7372 Computers, peripherals & software; prepackaged software

(G-11154)
USER FRIENDLY PHONE BOOK LLC
2 Summit Park Dr Ste 105 (44131-2558)
PHONE..................................216 674-6500
Jack Nelson, *Branch Mgr*
EMP: 45
SALES (corp-wide): 92MM **Privately Held**
WEB: www.ufpb.net
SIC: 2741 Directories, telephone: publishing & printing
PA: User Friendly Phone Book, Llc
    10200 Grogans Mill Rd # 440
    The Woodlands TX 77380
    281 465-5400

(G-11155)
VIASAT INC
5990 W Creek Rd Ste 1 (44131-2181)
PHONE..................................216 706-7800
Fax: 216 706-7801
EMP: 62
SQ FT: 11,000
SALES (est): 8.5MM
SALES (corp-wide): 1.5B **Publicly Held**
SIC: 3661 Mfg Digit Communications Equipment

GEOGRAPHIC SECTION

PA: Viasat, Inc.
6155 El Camino Real
Carlsbad CA 92009
760 476-2200

(G-11156)
WEED INSTRUMENT COMPANY INC
Also Called: Furnace Parts
6133 Rockside Rd Ste 300 (44131-2243)
PHONE.................................800 321-0796
Debbie Nieman, *General Mgr*
EMP: 30
SALES (corp-wide): 1B **Privately Held**
SIC: 3823 Industrial instrmnts msrmnt display/control process variable
HQ: Weed Instrument Company, Inc.
707 Jeffrey Way
Round Rock TX 78665
512 434-2900

(G-11157)
WESTMOUNT TECHNOLOGY INC
Also Called: Wmt
6100 Oak Tree Blvd (44131-2544)
PHONE.................................216 328-2011
Sowmia Mahesh, *CEO*
Timothy Luberger, *Director*
EMP: 5
SQ FT: 600
SALES (est): 209.4K **Privately Held**
SIC: 7371 7373 7372 7379 Computer software development & applications; office computer automation systems integration; business oriented computer software;

Irondale
Jefferson County

(G-11158)
C A JOSEPH CO
C A Joseph Machine Shop
170 Broadway St (43932)
PHONE.................................330 532-4646
Joe Smithbower, *Manager*
EMP: 14
SALES (corp-wide): 4.1MM **Privately Held**
WEB: www.cajoseph.com
SIC: 3599 3444 3443 3441 Machine shop, jobbing & repair; sheet metalwork; fabricated plate work (boiler shop); fabricated structural metal
PA: C. A. Joseph Co.
13712 Old Frdericktown Rd
East Liverpool OH 43920
330 385-6869

Ironton
Lawrence County

(G-11159)
ALLEN ENTERPRISES INC
Also Called: Tri-State Wilbert Vault Co
2900 S 9th St (45638)
P.O. Box 231 (45638-0231)
PHONE.................................740 532-5913
Douglas M Allen, *President*
Ronald Keener, *Treasurer*
Robin Robison, *Controller*
Gretchen A Allen, *Director*
EMP: 20
SQ FT: 22,000
SALES: 1.2MM **Privately Held**
SIC: 5039 3272 5087 Septic tanks; septic tanks, concrete; caskets

(G-11160)
ARROW COAL GROVE INC
300 Marion Pike (45638-2957)
PHONE.................................740 532-6143
EMP: 10
SALES (est): 775.4K **Privately Held**
SIC: 1542 3273 1794 Commercial Contractor Mfg Ready Mix Concrete And Excavation

(G-11161)
ARTHURS REFRIGERATION
2156 State Route 93 (45638-8176)
P.O. Box 272 (45638-0272)
PHONE.................................740 532-0206
Chris Arthur, *Owner*
EMP: 3
SALES (est): 384.3K **Privately Held**
SIC: 3585 5064 Refrigeration & heating equipment; refrigerators & freezers

(G-11162)
BRUCE BOX CO INC
161 Big Doney Rd Unit A (45638-8506)
PHONE.................................740 533-0670
Keith Bruce, *President*
Joyce Bruce, *President*
Sharon Bruce, *Vice Pres*
Debbie Crabtree, *Admin Sec*
EMP: 3 **EST:** 1970
SQ FT: 3,500
SALES: 330K **Privately Held**
SIC: 2653 Boxes, corrugated: made from purchased materials

(G-11163)
CRABRO PRINTING INC
314 Chestnut St (45638-1902)
P.O. Box 670 (45638-0670)
PHONE.................................740 533-3404
Steven G Cragar, *President*
Carl Brose, *Vice Pres*
EMP: 4
SALES (est): 398.2K **Privately Held**
SIC: 2759 Screen printing

(G-11164)
EMERSON NETWORK POWER
3040 S 9th St (45638-2895)
PHONE.................................614 841-8054
Steve Hassell, *President*
EMP: 3 **EST:** 2016
SALES (est): 106.9K **Privately Held**
SIC: 3613 3585 7629 Switchgear & switchboard apparatus; refrigeration & heating equipment; electrical repair shops

(G-11165)
G BIG INC
Also Called: Pickett Concrete
300 Marion Pike (45638-2957)
PHONE.................................740 532-9123
Ronald Jenkins, *Branch Mgr*
EMP: 6
SALES (est): 483.6K
SALES (corp-wide): 3.8MM **Privately Held**
WEB: www.gbig.com
SIC: 3273 Ready-mixed concrete
PA: G Big Inc
441 Rockwood Ave
Chesapeake OH 45619
740 867-5758

(G-11166)
IRONTON PUBLICATIONS INC
Also Called: Ironton Tribune The
2903 S 5th St (45638-2866)
P.O. Box 647 (45638-0647)
PHONE.................................740 532-1441
James B Boone Jr, *Director*
EMP: 508
SQ FT: 12,000
SALES (est): 18.8MM
SALES (corp-wide): 105.4MM **Privately Held**
WEB: www.irontontribune.com
SIC: 2711 Newspapers, publishing & printing
PA: Boone Newspapers, Inc.
1060 Fairfax Park Ste B
Tuscaloosa AL 35406
205 330-4100

(G-11167)
J & M MAYNARD ENTERPRISES INC (PA)
Also Called: J & M Steel
501 N 2nd St (45638-1349)
P.O. Box 478 (45638-0478)
PHONE.................................740 532-3032
Mark Maynard, *President*
Mary Jane Maynard, *Corp Secy*
John Maynard, *Vice Pres*
Joann Maynard, *Shareholder*
EMP: 19

SQ FT: 10,000
SALES (est): 2MM **Privately Held**
SIC: 3599 Machine shop, jobbing & repair

(G-11168)
JANELL INC
1014 S 2nd St (45638-1984)
PHONE.................................740 532-9111
Fax: 740 532-8300
EMP: 4
SALES (est): 326.1K **Privately Held**
SIC: 3272 Mfg Concrete Products

(G-11169)
MODULAR SECURITY SYSTEMS INC
Also Called: Mssi
1804 N 2nd St (45638-1048)
P.O. Box 402, Worthington KY (41183-0402)
PHONE.................................740 532-7822
Robert Rhett Slagel, *CEO*
David Slagel, *President*
Heath Brownstead, *Business Mgr*
Kevin Harrison, *Vice Pres*
Benjamin Pack Pe, *CFO*
▼ **EMP:** 5
SQ FT: 1,000
SALES (est): 1.6MM **Privately Held**
WEB: www.modularsecuritysystems.com
SIC: 3699 5065 Security control equipment & systems; security control equipment & systems

(G-11170)
PREMERE PRECAST PRODUCTS
317 Hecla St (45638-1370)
PHONE.................................740 533-3333
Evyian Terry, *Principal*
EMP: 12 **EST:** 2008
SALES (est): 1.5MM **Privately Held**
SIC: 3272 Precast terrazo or concrete products

(G-11171)
PRINTING EXPRESS INC
1229 S 3rd St (45638-2028)
P.O. Box 831 (45638-0831)
PHONE.................................740 532-7003
Mary Beth Nenni, *President*
Jennifer L Mays, *Vice Pres*
EMP: 7
SQ FT: 1,100
SALES: 700K **Privately Held**
SIC: 2752 Commercial printing, offset

(G-11172)
ROACH WOOD PRODUCTS & PLAS INC
25 Township Road 328 (45638-8171)
PHONE.................................740 532-4855
Bruce Roach Sr, *CEO*
Bruce Roach Jr, *President*
EMP: 8
SQ FT: 10,700
SALES (est): 1.2MM **Privately Held**
SIC: 3082 Unsupported plastics profile shapes

(G-11173)
SWIFT MANUFACTURING CO INC
700 Lorain St (45638-1088)
PHONE.................................740 237-4405
Michael Moore, *President*
Zachary Moore, *Vice Pres*
EMP: 6
SALES (est): 840.5K **Privately Held**
WEB: www.swiftmfg.net
SIC: 3339 Primary nonferrous metals

(G-11174)
UNDISCOVERED RADIO NETWORK
621 S 6th St (45638-1828)
PHONE.................................740 533-1032
Colleen Griffiths, *President*
EMP: 3
SALES (est): 292.7K **Privately Held**
SIC: 3651 Audio electronic systems

(G-11175)
VERTIV CORPORATION
3040 S 9th St (45638-2895)
PHONE.................................740 547-5100
Bob Walters, *General Mgr*
EMP: 300
SALES (corp-wide): 322.9MM **Privately Held**
WEB: www.liebert.com
SIC: 3823 Industrial instrmnts msrmnt display/control process variable
HQ: Vertiv Corporation
1050 Dearborn Dr
Columbus OH 43085
614 888-0246

(G-11176)
WELLS GROUP LLC
487 Gallia Pike (45638-8080)
PHONE.................................740 532-9240
Kimberly Cole, *Branch Mgr*
EMP: 10
SALES (corp-wide): 50.8MM **Privately Held**
SIC: 3273 Ready-mixed concrete
PA: The Wells Group Llc
611 W Main St
West Liberty KY 41472
606 743-3485

(G-11177)
WHEELER EMBROIDERY
Also Called: Cjt's
1007 N 2nd St (45638-1235)
PHONE.................................740 550-9751
Joshua Wheeler, *Principal*
EMP: 4
SALES (est): 398.6K **Privately Held**
SIC: 3999 Manufacturing industries

Jackson
Jackson County

(G-11178)
A E RUSTON ELECTRIC LLC
121 N David Ave (45640-1112)
PHONE.................................740 286-3022
Alfred T Ruston, *Mng Member*
EMP: 5 **EST:** 1922
SQ FT: 15,000
SALES (est): 1MM **Privately Held**
SIC: 7694 3599 Electric motor repair; machine shop, jobbing & repair

(G-11179)
A K READY MIX LLC
441 Dixon Run Rd (45640-8038)
PHONE.................................740 286-8900
Robert E Stewart,
EMP: 12
SALES (est): 1.4MM **Privately Held**
SIC: 3273 Ready-mixed concrete

(G-11180)
ALUCHEM OF JACKSON INC
14782 Beaver Pike (45640-9661)
PHONE.................................740 286-2455
Ronald P Zapletal, *President*
Edward L Butera, *Vice Pres*
Ronald L Bell, *Treasurer*
EMP: 50
SALES (est): 9.6MM **Privately Held**
SIC: 2819 Industrial inorganic chemicals

(G-11181)
BELLISIO
100 E Broadway St (45640-1347)
P.O. Box 550 (45640-0550)
PHONE.................................740 286-5505
Charlie Milliken, *Principal*
◆ **EMP:** 8
SALES (est): 540.7K **Privately Held**
SIC: 2038 Frozen specialties

(G-11182)
BELLISIO FOODS INC
100 E Broadway St (45640-1347)
P.O. Box 550 (45640-0550)
PHONE.................................740 286-5505
Jeff Wilson, *Branch Mgr*
EMP: 110

Jackson - Jackson County (G-11183)

SALES (corp-wide): 15.2B **Privately Held**
SIC: 2038 2033 Dinners, frozen & packaged; spaghetti & other pasta sauce: packaged in cans, jars, etc.
HQ: Bellisio Foods, Inc
  1201 Harmon Pl Ste 302
  Minneapolis MN 55403
  218 723-5555

(G-11183)
BRENMAR CONSTRUCTION INC
900 Morton St (45640-1089)
PHONE.................................740 286-2151
Todd Ghearing, *President*
Andy Graham, *Corp Secy*
Tim Ousley, *Vice Pres*
EMP: 60
SQ FT: 5,000
SALES: 8MM **Privately Held**
WEB: www.brenmarconstruction.com
SIC: 1542 3312 Commercial & office building contractors; structural shapes & pilings, steel

(G-11184)
BROWN PUBLISHING CO INC (PA)
1 Acy Ave Ste D (45640-9563)
P.O. Box 270 (45640-0270)
PHONE.................................740 286-2187
Roy Brown, *President*
EMP: 7 **EST:** 1925
SQ FT: 5,250
SALES (est): 1.4MM **Privately Held**
SIC: 2711 Newspapers: publishing only, not printed on site

(G-11185)
FOR EVERY HOME
Also Called: James Logan Logging
10381 Chillicothe Pike (45640-8743)
PHONE.................................740 710-1253
Kelly Logan, *Principal*
EMP: 3
SALES (est): 225.7K **Privately Held**
SIC: 2411 Logging

(G-11186)
HIGGINS BUILDING MTLS NO 2 LLC
2000 Acy Ave (45640-2506)
PHONE.................................740 395-5410
David Higgins, *Mng Member*
EMP: 3
SALES (est): 223.3K **Privately Held**
SIC: 3444 Siding, sheet metal

(G-11187)
JACKSON MONUMENT INC
14 Fairmount St (45640-1409)
PHONE.................................740 286-1590
Stan Louis, *President*
Darryl Radliff, *Principal*
EMP: 8
SALES (est): 760.3K **Privately Held**
SIC: 3272 5999 Monuments, concrete; monuments, finished to custom order

(G-11188)
JALCO INDUSTRIES INC
330 Athens St (45640-9433)
P.O. Box 947 (45640-0947)
PHONE.................................740 286-3808
Randal L Ridge, *President*
Susan R Ridge, *Treasurer*
EMP: 10
SQ FT: 10,000
SALES (est): 1MM **Privately Held**
SIC: 3281 5032 Building stone products; concrete building products

(G-11189)
LANTZ LUMBER & SAW SHOP
637 Industry Dr (45640-8737)
PHONE.................................740 286-5658
EMP: 3
SALES (est): 209.8K **Privately Held**
SIC: 2421 Sawmill/Planing Mill

(G-11190)
MARTIN BLOCK COMPANY
290 Twin Oaks Dr (45640-8608)
PHONE.................................740 286-7507
Richard L Coriell, *President*
EMP: 5 **EST:** 1946

SQ FT: 12,800
SALES (est): 610K **Privately Held**
SIC: 3271 5211 Blocks, concrete or cinder: standard; lumber & other building materials

(G-11191)
MONTGOMERY MCH & FABRICATION
206 Watts Blevins Rd (45640-9768)
P.O. Box 247 (45640-0247)
PHONE.................................740 286-2863
Carry E Montgomery, *President*
Bobbi D Montgomery, *Vice Pres*
Jason Montgomery, *Vice Pres*
Mary Montgomery, *Vice Pres*
EMP: 35
SQ FT: 20,000
SALES (est): 5.9MM **Privately Held**
WEB: www.montgomerymachineshop.com
SIC: 3599 Machine shop, jobbing & repair

(G-11192)
MOUNTAINEER MINING CORP
885 Sternberger Rd (45640-9601)
PHONE.................................740 418-1817
Jason E Adkins, *President*
Jason Adkins, *President*
EMP: 4
SALES (est): 258.5K **Privately Held**
SIC: 3535 Conveyors & conveying equipment

(G-11193)
OSCO INDUSTRIES INC
165 Athens St (45640-1306)
P.O. Box 327 (45640-0327)
PHONE.................................740 286-5004
Keith Denny, *Branch Mgr*
Chris Maness, *Risk Mgmt Dir*
Tom Stewart, *Maintence Staff*
EMP: 125
SALES (corp-wide): 90.2MM **Privately Held**
WEB: www.oscoind.com
SIC: 3321 3322 Gray iron castings; malleable iron foundries
PA: Osco Industries, Inc.
  734 11th St
  Portsmouth OH 45662
  740 354-3183

(G-11194)
PACIFIC MANUFACTURING TENN INC
555 Smith Ln (45640)
PHONE.................................513 900-7862
Hisaichi Seko, *President*
EMP: 20 **EST:** 2014
SQ FT: 189,000
SALES (est): 1.4MM **Privately Held**
SIC: 3469 Ornamental metal stampings

(G-11195)
STEVENS AUTO PARTS & TOWNG
2848 Big Rock Rd (45640-8798)
PHONE.................................740 988-2260
David Stevens, *President*
EMP: 3
SALES (est): 207K **Privately Held**
SIC: 5531 5015 7549 3546 Automotive parts; automotive parts & supplies, used; towing service, automotive; saws & sawing equipment; plumbing & heating supplies; sewer cleaning & rodding

(G-11196)
SUPERIOR HARDWOODS OF OHIO
78 Jackson Hill Rd (45640-9301)
P.O. Box 166 (45640-0166)
PHONE.................................740 384-6862
Ammet Tonway, *Owner*
EMP: 70
SALES (est): 4MM **Privately Held**
SIC: 2411 2421 Timber, cut at logging camp; sawmills & planing mills, general

(G-11197)
TELEGRAM
920 Veterans Dr Unit C (45640-2175)
P.O. Box 667 (45640-0667)
PHONE.................................740 286-3604
Jerry Mossbarger, *General Mgr*

EMP: 17
SALES (est): 481.6K **Privately Held**
WEB: www.thetelegram.com
SIC: 2711 Newspapers: publishing only, not printed on site

(G-11198)
TIM CRABTREE
Also Called: Tim's Woodshop
117 Athens St (45640-1306)
PHONE.................................740 286-4535
Tim Crabtree, *Owner*
EMP: 5
SALES (est): 566K **Privately Held**
WEB: www.timswoodshop.com
SIC: 2541 Display fixtures, wood

(G-11199)
TOW PATH READY MIX
1668 Kessinger School Rd (45640-9127)
PHONE.................................740 286-2131
Lonnie Lemaster, *Branch Mgr*
EMP: 10
SALES (est): 1MM **Privately Held**
SIC: 3273 Ready-mixed concrete
PA: Tow Path Ready Mix
  12360 State Route 104
  Lucasville OH 45648

(G-11200)
VALUE ADDED BUSINESS SVCS CO (PA)
120 Twin Oaks Dr (45640-9506)
PHONE.................................614 854-9755
Craig Lund, *President*
Diane Hill, *General Mgr*
Mark Burtrand, *Opers Mgr*
EMP: 6 **EST:** 1997
SALES (est): 4.1MM **Privately Held**
WEB: www.valueaddedbiz.com
SIC: 2759 8742 5112 Commercial printing; management consulting services; stationery & office supplies

(G-11201)
WILLIAMS JOHN F OIL FIELD SVCS
20669 Coshocton Co Rd 6 (45640)
P.O. Box 443, Coshocton (43812-0443)
PHONE.................................740 622-7692
John F Williams, *President*
EMP: 4
SALES (est): 503.1K **Privately Held**
SIC: 1389 Oil field services; gas field services

(G-11202)
WINTERS PRODUCTS INC
Also Called: Winters Concrete
109 Athens St (45640-1306)
PHONE.................................740 286-4149
David R Michael, *President*
EMP: 10 **EST:** 1955
SQ FT: 800
SALES (est): 680K **Privately Held**
SIC: 3273 Ready-mixed concrete

(G-11203)
ZIP LASER SYSTEMS INC
Also Called: Zip Systems of Jackson
345 E Main St Ste H (45640-1789)
P.O. Box 527 (45640-0527)
PHONE.................................740 286-6613
Nick Summers, *President*
EMP: 4
SQ FT: 3,000
SALES (est): 586.3K **Privately Held**
SIC: 2752 7334 Commercial printing, offset; photocopying & duplicating services

Jackson Center
Shelby County

(G-11204)
A G PARTS INC
Also Called: Quality Parts
500 N Linden St (45334)
P.O. Box 757 (45334-0757)
PHONE.................................937 596-6448
Charles Cole, *President*
Tony Nimeyer, *Vice Pres*
EMP: 16

SALES (est): 2.1MM **Privately Held**
WEB: www.agparts.com
SIC: 3714 Motor vehicle parts & accessories

(G-11205)
AIRSTREAM INC (HQ)
419 W Pike St (45334-9728)
P.O. Box 629 (45334-0629)
PHONE.................................937 596-6111
Lawrence J Huttle, *Ch of Bd*
Peter B Orthwein, *Ch of Bd*
Robert Wheeler, *President*
Rick March, *General Mgr*
Wade F B Thompson, *Principal*
◆ **EMP:** 350
SQ FT: 286,000
SALES: 101.8MM
SALES (corp-wide): 8.3B **Publicly Held**
WEB: www.airstream.com
SIC: 3716 3792 3714 3713 Motor homes; travel trailers & campers; motor vehicle parts & accessories; truck & bus bodies; motor vehicles & car bodies
PA: Thor Industries, Inc.
  601 E Beardsley Ave
  Elkhart IN 46514
  574 970-7460

(G-11206)
CREATIVE PLASTICS INTL
18163 Snider Rd (45334-9734)
PHONE.................................937 596-6769
Gerald B Wurm, *President*
Keith Korn, *Vice Pres*
Randolph Korn, *Vice Pres*
Randolph W Korn, *Vice Pres*
Richard Wurm, *Vice Pres*
EMP: 17 **EST:** 1968
SQ FT: 40,000
SALES (est): 3.3MM **Privately Held**
SIC: 3089 Thermoformed finished plastic products; plastic processing

(G-11207)
DESIGN ORIGINAL INC
402 Jackson St (45334-5057)
P.O. Box 727 (45334-0727)
PHONE.................................937 596-5121
Frank E Pusey, *President*
Glenn A Pusey, *Vice Pres*
EMP: 16
SQ FT: 25,000
SALES (est): 3.5MM **Privately Held**
WEB: www.design-original.com
SIC: 5136 5137 2396 2395 Sportswear, men's & boys'; men's & boys' outerwear; shirts, men's & boys'; sweaters, men's & boys'; sportswear, women's & children's; coats: women's, children's & infants'; hats: women's, children's & infants'; sweaters, women's & children's; automotive & apparel trimmings; pleating & stitching

(G-11208)
ELDORADO NATIONAL KANSAS INC
419 W Pike St (45334-9728)
PHONE.................................937 596-6849
Andrew Imanse, *CEO*
EMP: 3 **Publicly Held**
SIC: 3711 Buses, all types, assembly of
HQ: Eldorado National (Kansas), Inc.
  1655 Wall St
  Salina KS 67401

(G-11209)
EMI CORP (PA)
Also Called: E M I Plastic Equipment
801 W Pike St (45334-6037)
P.O. Box 590 (45334-0590)
PHONE.................................937 596-5511
James E Andraitis, *President*
Brad Wren, *Vice Pres*
Deb Herold, *Purch Agent*
Linda Andraitis-Varljen, *Treasurer*
Kay Friders, *Controller*
▲ **EMP:** 85 **EST:** 1980
SQ FT: 80,000
SALES (est): 16.3MM **Privately Held**
WEB: www.emiplastics.com
SIC: 3544 5084 Special dies, tools, jigs & fixtures; industrial machinery & equipment

▲ = Import ▼ = Export
◆ = Import/Export

GEOGRAPHIC SECTION

Jefferson - Ashtabula County (G-11236)

(G-11210)
LACAL EQUIPMENT INC
901 W Pike St (45334-6024)
P.O. Box 757 (45334-0757)
PHONE..................800 543-6161
Roger Dietrich, *President*
Tom Homan, *President*
Tony Niemeyer, *Principal*
Charles M Cole, *Vice Pres*
Roger Detrick, *Vice Pres*
▲ **EMP:** 30
SQ FT: 14,000
SALES (est): 8.2MM
SALES (corp-wide): 105.6MM **Privately Held**
WEB: www.lacal.com
SIC: 3714 Motor vehicle parts & accessories
PA: Jmac Inc.
200 W Nationwide Blvd # 1
Columbus OH 43215
614 436-2418

(G-11211)
MASTER SWAGING INC
210 Washington St (45334)
P.O. Box 550 (45334-0550)
PHONE..................937 596-6171
Daniel Gilroy, *President*
Cindy Gilroy, *Principal*
EMP: 6
SQ FT: 26,000
SALES (est): 976.9K **Privately Held**
WEB: www.mastersswaging.com
SIC: 3728 3599 Aircraft assemblies, sub-assemblies & parts; machine shop, jobbing & repair

(G-11212)
PLASTIPAK PACKAGING INC
18015 State Route 65 (45334-9434)
P.O. Box 789 (45334-0789)
PHONE..................937 596-6142
Bruce Rinehart, *Project Mgr*
Jeff Webster, *Opers Mgr*
Joe Kreitzer, *Purchasing*
Clint Schroeder, *Engineer*
Joyce Faler, *Persnl Mgr*
EMP: 500
SALES (corp-wide): 1.3B **Privately Held**
WEB: www.plastipak.com
SIC: 3085 2671 Plastics bottles; packaging paper & plastics film, coated & laminated
HQ: Plastipak Packaging, Inc.
41605 Ann Arbor Rd E
Plymouth MI 48170
734 455-3600

(G-11213)
PLASTIPAK PACKAGING INC
300 Washington St (45334)
PHONE..................937 596-5166
Lisa Zimpfer, *QC Mgr*
William P Young, *Branch Mgr*
EMP: 123
SALES (corp-wide): 1.3B **Privately Held**
WEB: www.plastipak.com
SIC: 3085 Plastics bottles
HQ: Plastipak Packaging, Inc.
41605 Ann Arbor Rd E
Plymouth MI 48170
734 455-3600

(G-11214)
PRECISION DETAILS INC
104 Washington St (45334-1101)
P.O. Box 696 (45334-0696)
PHONE..................937 596-0068
Jeff Winemiller, *President*
Katie Winemiller, *Vice Pres*
EMP: 15
SQ FT: 4,500
SALES (est): 1.4MM **Privately Held**
SIC: 3544 Special dies, tools, jigs & fixtures

(G-11215)
PRODEVA INC
100 Jerry Dr (45334-5075)
P.O. Box 729 (45334-0729)
PHONE..................937 596-6713
Steve Bunke, *President*
Shirley Bunke, *Treasurer*
Frederick Bunke, *Admin Sec*
EMP: 12
SQ FT: 21,000
SALES (est): 1.3MM **Privately Held**
WEB: www.prodeva.com
SIC: 3599 3559 Machine shop, jobbing & repair; recycling machinery

(G-11216)
STEVEN YANT
Also Called: Yant Beef Jerky
103 Jerry Dr (45334-5075)
P.O. Box 67 (45334-0067)
PHONE..................937 596-0497
Steven Yant, *Owner*
EMP: 3
SALES: 130K **Privately Held**
SIC: 2013 Sausages & other prepared meats

(G-11217)
THOR INDUSTRIES INC
419 W Pike St (45334-9728)
PHONE..................937 596-6111
Bekki Knox, *Accountant*
Emily Boothe, *Mktg Dir*
Steven Hileman, *Manager*
Penny Meyers, *General Counsel*
Brandy Ramsey, *Legal Staff*
EMP: 25
SALES (corp-wide): 8.3B **Publicly Held**
SIC: 3799 3711 Recreational vehicles; buses, all types, assembly of
PA: Thor Industries, Inc.
601 E Beardsley Ave
Elkhart IN 46514
574 970-7460

Jamestown
Greene County

(G-11218)
BROWN PRECISION MACHINE
13 S Buckles Ave (45335-1581)
PHONE..................937 675-6585
EMP: 5
SQ FT: 5,500
SALES: 300K **Privately Held**
SIC: 3599 Job Machine Shop

(G-11219)
CAESARCREEK PALLETS LTD
4392 Shawnee Trl (45335-1227)
PHONE..................937 416-4447
Larry Payton, *Principal*
Clarence Payton, *Principal*
Steve Payton, *Principal*
EMP: 14
SQ FT: 6,000
SALES: 1.5MM **Privately Held**
SIC: 2448 Pallets, wood

(G-11220)
MIKES WELDING
5589 Us Highway 35 E (45335-9588)
P.O. Box 221 (45335-0221)
PHONE..................937 675-6587
Michael Brown, *Owner*
EMP: 4
SALES (est): 304.9K **Privately Held**
SIC: 7692 3441 Welding repair; fabricated structural metal

(G-11221)
TWIST INC (PA)
47 S Limestone St (45335-9501)
P.O. Box 177 (45335-0177)
PHONE..................937 675-9581
Joe W Wright, *President*
Dan Coots, *Plant Mgr*
Vincent Liming, *Project Mgr*
Richard Tracy, *Purchasing*
Jim Church, *Engineer*
▲ **EMP:** 110
SQ FT: 50,000
SALES (est): 34.2MM **Privately Held**
SIC: 3495 3542 3469 3471 Mechanical springs, precision; machine tools, metal forming type; metal stampings; electroplating & plating

(G-11222)
TWIST INC
5100 Waynesville (45335)
PHONE..................937 675-9581
J Smith, *Branch Mgr*
EMP: 30
SALES (corp-wide): 34.2MM **Privately Held**
SIC: 3495 3542 3469 Mechanical springs, precision; machine tools, metal forming type; metal stampings
PA: Twist Inc.
47 S Limestone St
Jamestown OH 45335
937 675-9581

Jefferson
Ashtabula County

(G-11223)
ADA SOLUTIONS INC
901 Ftville Richmond Rd E (44047)
PHONE..................440 576-0423
David Chase, *President*
▼ **EMP:** 20
SALES (est): 2.2MM **Privately Held**
SIC: 2821 Molding compounds, plastics

(G-11224)
ALTERA POLYMERS LLC
222 S Sycamore St (44047-1434)
PHONE..................864 973-7000
Barry Rhodes, *Mng Member*
EMP: 9 **EST:** 2011
SALES (est): 1.2MM **Privately Held**
SIC: 2821 Elastomers, nonvulcanizable (plastics)

(G-11225)
BRAKERS PUBLISHING & PRTG SVC
166 W Cedar St (44047-1331)
P.O. Box 489 (44047-0489)
PHONE..................440 576-0136
Katherine Kermetz, *Owner*
EMP: 5
SALES (est): 261.1K **Privately Held**
SIC: 7379 2759 Computer related services; commercial printing

(G-11226)
CENTERRA CO-OP
161 E Jefferson St (44047-1113)
PHONE..................800 362-9598
Jim Reader, *Manager*
EMP: 28
SALES (corp-wide): 174.6MM **Privately Held**
SIC: 5172 5261 2048 5191 Gases, liquefied petroleum (propane); fertilizer; bird food, prepared; farm supplies
PA: Centerra Co-Op
813 Clark Ave
Ashland OH 44805
419 281-2153

(G-11227)
CHUCK MEADORS PLASTICS CO
150 S Cucumber St (44047-1439)
PHONE..................440 813-4466
Chuck Meadors, *President*
EMP: 10
SALES (est): 866.5K **Privately Held**
SIC: 3089 Hardware, plastic

(G-11228)
CLARENCE TUSSEL JR
141 E Jefferson St (44047-1186)
P.O. Box 126 (44047-0126)
PHONE..................440 576-3415
Clarence Tussel Jr, *Owner*
EMP: 1
SQ FT: 2,500
SALES (est): 1.3MM **Privately Held**
SIC: 1382 1381 Geological exploration, oil & gas field; drilling oil & gas wells

(G-11229)
EMERINE ESTATES INC
5689 Loveland Rd (44047-9531)
P.O. Box 273 (44047-0273)
PHONE..................440 293-8199
Jason Emerine, *Principal*
EMP: 3
SALES (est): 277K **Privately Held**
SIC: 2084 Wines

(G-11230)
K CUPCAKES
222 Elliott Ave (44047-1230)
PHONE..................440 576-3464
EMP: 4 **EST:** 2013
SALES (est): 198K **Privately Held**
SIC: 2051 Mfg Bread/Related Products

(G-11231)
KARLCO OILFIELD SERVICES INC
141 E Jefferson St (44047-1113)
P.O. Box 126 (44047-0126)
PHONE..................440 576-3415
Clarence Tussel Jr, *President*
EMP: 11
SQ FT: 3,000
SALES (est): 1.1MM **Privately Held**
SIC: 1389 Servicing oil & gas wells

(G-11232)
KEN FORGING INC
1049 Griggs Rd (44047-8772)
P.O. Box 277 (44047-0277)
PHONE..................440 993-8091
Richard Kovach, *President*
Ken Kovach, *Vice Pres*
Jo Stover, *Vice Pres*
Ken Powell, *Maint Spvr*
Bill Kahl, *Purch Mgr*
EMP: 115 **EST:** 1970
SQ FT: 150,000
SALES (est): 38.4MM **Privately Held**
WEB: www.kenforging.com
SIC: 3462 3544 Iron & steel forgings; special dies & tools

(G-11233)
KING LUMINAIRE COMPANY INC (HQ)
Also Called: Stresscrete
1153 State Route 46 N (44047-8748)
P.O. Box 266 (44047-0266)
PHONE..................440 576-9073
Greg Button, *President*
Yvonne Neubauer, *QC Mgr*
▲ **EMP:** 45
SQ FT: 18,000
SALES (est): 23.7MM
SALES (corp-wide): 27.4MM **Privately Held**
WEB: www.kingluminaire.com
SIC: 3646 Ornamental lighting fixtures, commercial
PA: Stress-Crete Holdings Inc
840 Walker's Line Suite 7
Burlington ON
905 632-9301

(G-11234)
METAL SALES MANUFACTURING CORP
352 E Erie St (44047-1406)
PHONE..................440 319-3779
Bill Mako, *Manager*
EMP: 35
SQ FT: 33,000
SALES (corp-wide): 390.6MM **Privately Held**
SIC: 3444 3449 3441 2952 Siding, sheet metal; miscellaneous metalwork; fabricated structural metal; asphalt felts & coatings
HQ: Metal Sales Manufacturing Corporation
545 S 3rd St Ste 200
Louisville KY 40202
502 855-4300

(G-11235)
NEXT DIMENSION COMPONENTS INC
223 S Spruce St (44047-8321)
PHONE..................440 576-0194
Rhine Blake, *CEO*
Virginia Padale, *Admin Asst*
EMP: 22 **EST:** 2007
SALES (est): 3.4MM **Privately Held**
SIC: 3272 Concrete window & door components, sills & frames

(G-11236)
PRESRITE CORPORATION
322 S Cucumber St (44047-1423)
P.O. Box 550 (44047-0550)
PHONE..................440 576-0015

Jefferson - Ashtabula County (G-11237)

Roy Stainfield, *General Mgr*
EMP: 115
SALES (est): 17.3MM
SALES (corp-wide): 187.6MM **Privately Held**
WEB: www.presrite.com
SIC: 3462 Iron & steel forgings
PA: Presrite Corporation
3665 E 78th St
Cleveland OH 44105
216 441-5990

(G-11237)
SHOOTING RANGE SUPPLY LLC
735 Fairway St (44047-8568)
P.O. Box 269, Andover (44003-0269)
PHONE 440 576-7711
Julie Cole, *Mng Member*
Martin Cole,
EMP: 4
SQ FT: 800
SALES (est): 429.2K **Privately Held**
WEB: www.perfectrubbermulch.com
SIC: 3949 Sporting & athletic goods

(G-11238)
SMOKIN TS SMOKEHOUSE
1550 Stnhpe Kllgsvlle (44047-8473)
PHONE 440 577-1117
Todd Neczeporenko, *Owner*
EMP: 3 **EST:** 1993
SALES: 750K **Privately Held**
SIC: 2011 Meat packing plants

(G-11239)
STRESS-CRETE COMPANY
Also Called: King Luminaire
1153 State Route 46 N (44047-8748)
P.O. Box 266 (44047-0266)
PHONE 440 576-9073
Jim Fultz, *Branch Mgr*
EMP: 17
SALES (corp-wide): 27.4MM **Privately Held**
WEB: www.stresscrete.com
SIC: 3646 Commercial indusl & institutional electric lighting fixtures
HQ: Stress-Crete Limited
840 Walker's Line Suite 7
Burlington ON L7N 2
905 827-6901

(G-11240)
THE GAZETTE PRINTING CO INC (PA)
Also Called: Tribune , The
46 W Jefferson St (44047-1028)
P.O. Box 166 (44047-0166)
PHONE 440 576-9125
Jeffrey Lampson, *President*
John E Lampson, *Publisher*
Marilyn Lampson, *Admin Sec*
EMP: 62 **EST:** 1876
SQ FT: 8,600
SALES (est): 10.7MM **Privately Held**
WFR: www.gazetteprinting.com
SIC: 2711 Newspapers, publishing & printing

(G-11241)
TMD WEK NORTH LLC
Also Called: Wek Industries
1085 Jffrsn Eagleville Rd (44047-1267)
PHONE 440 576-6940
William Hylan, *CFO*
Kimberly Schaefer, *Exec Sec*
EMP: 116 **EST:** 2014
SQ FT: 112,500
SALES (est): 18.5MM
SALES (corp-wide): 309.9MM **Privately Held**
SIC: 3089 Blow molded finished plastic products
HQ: Toledo Molding & Die, Inc.
1429 Coining Dr
Toledo OH 43612
419 470-3950

(G-11242)
TOD THIN BRUSHES INC
1152 State Route 46 N (44047-8748)
PHONE 440 576-6859
Michael R Oliver, *President*
Mildred Oliver, *President*
EMP: 10
SQ FT: 2,500
SALES (est): 1.7MM **Privately Held**
WEB: www.todthinbrushes.com
SIC: 3991 Brushes, household or industrial

(G-11243)
WORTHINGTON CYLINDER CORP
863 State Route 307 E (44047-9668)
PHONE 440 576-5847
Robert Pierce, *Purch Agent*
Shelly Degennaro, *Human Resources*
Dan Brubaker, *Branch Mgr*
Jim Williams, *Maintence Staff*
EMP: 187
SALES (corp-wide): 3.5B **Publicly Held**
SIC: 3443 Cylinders, pressure: metal plate
HQ: Worthington Cylinder Corporation
200 W Old Wlson Bridge Rd
Worthington OH 43085
614 840-3210

(G-11244)
ZEHRCO-GIANCOLA COMPOSITES INC
382 E Erie St (44047-1406)
PHONE 440 576-9941
James H Nevins, *Branch Mgr*
EMP: 5
SALES (corp-wide): 26MM **Privately Held**
SIC: 3089 Injection molding of plastics
PA: Zehrco-Giancola Composites, Inc.
1501 W 47th St
Ashtabula OH 44004
440 994-6317

Jeffersonville
Fayette County

(G-11245)
BUNGE NORTH AMERICA FOUNDATION
12574 State Route 41 (43128-9542)
PHONE 740 426-6332
Drew Walker, *Manager*
EMP: 7 **Privately Held**
WEB: www.bungemarion.com
SIC: 2075 Soybean protein concentrates & isolates
HQ: Bunge North America Foundation
1391 Timberlk Mnr Pkwy # 31
Chesterfield MO 63017
314 872-3030

(G-11246)
E R B ENTERPRISES INC
Also Called: Rocky Mountain Chocolate
8205 Factory Shops Blvd (43128-9602)
PHONE 740 948-9174
Nalynn Hall, *Manager*
EMP: 5
SALES (corp-wide): 1.5MM **Privately Held**
SIC: 5441 2066 2064 Candy; chocolate & cocoa products; candy & other confectionery products
PA: E. R. B. Enterprises, Inc.
1500 Polaris Pkwy # 2022
Columbus OH 43240
239 567-0585

(G-11247)
KEYNES BROTHERS INC
12574 State Route 41 (43128-9542)
PHONE 740 426-6332
Bill Keynes, *President*
Jim Schneider, *Manager*
EMP: 4
SALES (est): 243.5K **Privately Held**
SIC: 3523 Elevators, farm

(G-11248)
TFO TECH CO LTD
Also Called: T F O
221 State St (43128-1090)
PHONE 740 426-6381
Yoshio Saisharo, *President*
Curtis A Loveland, *Principal*
Katsumasa Toya, *Chairman*
Kanji Endo, *Exec VP*
▲ **EMP:** 140
SQ FT: 70,000
SALES (est): 23.7MM
SALES (corp-wide): 40.3MM **Privately Held**
WEB: www.tfotech.com
SIC: 3462 3465 3714 Automotive forgings, ferrous: crankshaft, engine, axle, etc.; automotive stampings; motor vehicle parts & accessories
PA: Tfo Corporation
2-16-4, Akabane
Kita-Ku TKY 115-0
364 544-651

Jeromesville
Ashland County

(G-11249)
BARTTER & SONS
1761 Township Road 85 (44840-9651)
PHONE 419 651-0374
Dave Bartter, *Principal*
Jody Bartter, *Office Mgr*
EMP: 3
SALES (est): 170K **Privately Held**
SIC: 3423 Plumbers' hand tools

(G-11250)
HEFFELFINGERS MEATS INC
469 County Road 30a (44840-9733)
PHONE 419 368-7131
Rick Heffelfinger, *President*
Gloria Heffelfinger, *Corp Secy*
Steve Heffelfinger, *Vice Pres*
EMP: 20 **EST:** 1963
SALES (est): 2.4MM **Privately Held**
SIC: 2011 Beef products from beef slaughtered on site

Jerusalem
Monroe County

(G-11251)
PROFIT ENERGY COMPANY INC
36829 Township Road 2067 (43747-9713)
PHONE 740 472-1018
Carl F Rousenberg III, *President*
L L Rousenberg, *Treasurer*
EMP: 4
SALES (est): 448.8K **Privately Held**
SIC: 1311 Crude petroleum production; natural gas production

Jewett
Harrison County

(G-11252)
MARKWEST UTICA EMG LLC
46700 Giacobbi Rd (43986-9553)
PHONE 740 942-4810
Frank M Semple, *Branch Mgr*
EMP: 7
SALES (corp-wide): 6.4B **Publicly Held**
SIC: 1321 Natural gas liquids
HQ: Markwest Utica Emg, L.L.C.
1515 Arapahoe St
Denver CO 80202
303 925-9200

Johnstown
Licking County

(G-11253)
ALL PRO ALUM CYLINDER HEADS
5370 Jhnstown Alxndria Rd (43031-9575)
P.O. Box 424 (43031-0424)
PHONE 740 967-7761
Robert P Williams, *President*
Susie Williams, *Corp Secy*
EMP: 4
SALES (est): 528.6K **Privately Held**
SIC: 3714 Cylinder heads, motor vehicle

(G-11254)
ALLIANCE CARPET CUSHION CO
143 Commerce Blvd (43031-9610)
PHONE 740 966-5001
Keith Anders, *Manager*
EMP: 60
SALES (corp-wide): 9.9B **Publicly Held**
SIC: 2282 2273 Carpet yarn: twisting, winding or spooling; carpets & rugs
HQ: Alliance Carpet Cushion Co
180 Church St
Torrington CT 06790
860 489-4273

(G-11255)
ANOMATIC CORPORATION (DH)
8880 Innvation Campus Way (43031)
PHONE 740 522-2203
William B Rusch, *President*
Pete McCallin, *President*
Kal Kalyanasundaram, *Business Mgr*
Don Perry, *Exec VP*
Scott Rusch, *Exec VP*
▲ **EMP:** 277 **EST:** 1974
SQ FT: 65,000
SALES (est): 113.9MM
SALES (corp-wide): 632.4MM **Privately Held**
WEB: www.anomatic.com
SIC: 3471 3469 2396 Anodizing (plating) of metals or formed products; metal stampings; automotive & apparel trimmings
HQ: Thyssen"sche Handelsgesellschaft Mit Beschrankter Haftung
Dohne 54
Mulheim An Der Ruhr 45468
208 992-180

(G-11256)
APEKS LLC
Also Called: Apeks Supercritical
150 Commerce Blvd (43031-9011)
PHONE 740 809-1160
Andy Joseph, *President*
Nick Yerico, *Manager*
Scott Sondles, *Technical Staff*
EMP: 20 **EST:** 2001
SQ FT: 10,000
SALES (est): 1.9MM **Privately Held**
SIC: 3542 Mechanical (pneumatic or hydraulic) metal forming machines

(G-11257)
ARMSTRONG WORLD INDUSTRIES INC
451 E Coshocton St (43031-9010)
PHONE 740 967-1063
Kent Vipond, *Principal*
EMP: 24
SALES (corp-wide): 975.3MM **Publicly Held**
SIC: 3272 Wall & ceiling squares, concrete
PA: Armstrong World Industries, Inc.
2500 Columbia Ave
Lancaster PA 17603
717 397-0611

(G-11258)
AUTUMN RUSH VINEYARD LLC
5686 Dutch Ln (43031-9450)
PHONE 614 312-5748
Jonathan Nappier, *Principal*
EMP: 3
SALES (est): 68.6K **Privately Held**
SIC: 2084 Wines

(G-11259)
BIGMAR INC
9711 Sportsman Club Rd (43031-9141)
PHONE 740 966-5800
John Tramontana, *CEO*
John Tramontata, *CEO*
Cynthia R May, *President*
Bernard Kramer, *COO*
Massimo Pedrani, *Exec VP*
EMP: 50
SQ FT: 8,600
SALES (est): 3.7MM **Privately Held**
SIC: 2834 8111 Pharmaceutical preparations; legal services

GEOGRAPHIC SECTION

Kensington - Columbiana County (G-11286)

(G-11260)
BUCKEYE READY-MIX LLC
7720 Jhnstown Alxndria Rd (43031-9340)
PHONE...............................740 967-4801
Larry Randles, *Vice Pres*
EMP: 8
SALES (corp-wide): 45.1MM **Privately Held**
SIC: 3273 Ready-mixed concrete
PA: Buckeye Ready-Mix, Llc
7657 Taylor Rd Sw
Reynoldsburg OH 43068
614 575-2132

(G-11261)
BUD CORP
158 Commerce Blvd (43031-9011)
PHONE...............................740 967-9992
Kelton Brown, *Principal*
EMP: 8
SALES (est): 1MM **Privately Held**
SIC: 1542 3444 5084 Nonresidential construction; sheet metalwork; materials handling machinery

(G-11262)
CHAM COR INDUSTRIES INC
117 W Coshocton St (43031-1108)
PHONE...............................740 967-9015
Michael Chambers, *CEO*
Gary H Chambers Jr, *President*
Michael Bailey, *Vice Pres*
EMP: 8
SQ FT: 6,000
SALES (est): 630K **Privately Held**
WEB: www.techtirerepairs.com
SIC: 2754 Job printing, gravure

(G-11263)
CONCEPT MANUFACTURING LLC
101 Butternut Cove Pl (43031-2506)
PHONE...............................812 677-2043
Henry Boggs Jr,
EMP: 7
SQ FT: 11,000
SALES (est): 269K **Privately Held**
SIC: 3086 Packaging & shipping materials, foamed plastic

(G-11264)
CRC METAL PRODUCTS
29 Greenscapes Ct (43031-8007)
PHONE...............................740 966-0475
Gary Pittman, *President*
EMP: 5
SALES: 210K **Privately Held**
WEB: www.crcmetalproducts.com
SIC: 3444 Sheet metal specialties, not stamped

(G-11265)
FLEETWOOD CUSTOM COUNTERTOPS (PA)
Also Called: Fleetwood Craftsman
15710 Center Village Rd (43031-9264)
PHONE...............................740 965-9833
James L Jacobus, *President*
EMP: 15
SQ FT: 16,000
SALES (est): 1.7MM **Privately Held**
SIC: 2511 2541 2434 Wood household furniture; wood partitions & fixtures; wood kitchen cabinets

(G-11266)
FORTRESS INDUSTRIES LLC
15710 Center Village Rd (43031-9264)
PHONE...............................614 402-3045
EMP: 4 **EST:** 2015
SALES (est): 199.6K **Privately Held**
SIC: 3999 Manufacturing industries

(G-11267)
GM LOGGING
204 Cole Dr (43031-1085)
PHONE...............................740 501-0819
Randy McFadden, *Principal*
EMP: 3 **EST:** 2010
SALES (est): 202.9K **Privately Held**
SIC: 2411 Logging

(G-11268)
HBK STONEWORKS
9292 Jhnstown Alxndria Rd (43031-9327)
PHONE...............................740 817-2244
Ben Keller, *Manager*
EMP: 3
SALES (est): 222.1K **Privately Held**
SIC: 3281 Granite, cut & shaped

(G-11269)
KDC US HOLDINGS INC
Also Called: Kdc Lynchburg
8825 Smiths Mill Rd N (43031)
PHONE...............................740 927-2817
Ian Kalinosky, *Branch Mgr*
EMP: 3
SALES (corp-wide): 603MM **Privately Held**
SIC: 2834 Pharmaceutical preparations
HQ: Kdc Us Holdings, Inc.
1000 Robins Rd
Lynchburg VA 24504

(G-11270)
MUNSON MACHINE COMPANY INC
80 E College Ave (43031-1204)
P.O. Box 304 (43031-0304)
PHONE...............................740 967-6867
Todd Thacker, *President*
Leroy Thacker, *Admin Sec*
EMP: 7
SQ FT: 4,500
SALES (est): 250K **Privately Held**
SIC: 3599 Machine shop, jobbing & repair

(G-11271)
SONOCO PRODUCTS COMPANY
8865 Smiths Mill Rd N (43031)
PHONE...............................740 927-2525
Theresa Biel, *General Mgr*
EMP: 92
SALES (corp-wide): 5.3B **Publicly Held**
SIC: 2631 Paperboard mills
PA: Sonoco Products Company
1 N 2nd St
Hartsville SC 29550
843 383-7000

(G-11272)
TECHNICAL RUBBER COMPANY INC (PA)
Also Called: Tech International
200 E Coshocton St (43031-1083)
P.O. Box 486 (43031-0486)
PHONE...............................740 967-9015
Micheal Chambers, *CEO*
Dan Layne, *President*
Diane Kirkpatrick, *General Mgr*
Robert Overs, *COO*
Gary Armstrong, *Senior VP*
◆ **EMP:** 270
SQ FT: 10,000
SALES (est): 113.6MM **Privately Held**
WEB: www.techtirerepairs.com
SIC: 3011 5014 2891 Tire sundries or tire repair materials, rubber; tire & tube repair materials; sealing compounds, synthetic rubber or plastic

(G-11273)
TRUFLEX RUBBER PRODUCTS CO
Also Called: Pang Rubber Company
200 E Coshocton St (43031-1096)
PHONE...............................740 967-9015
Pauline Chambers Yost, *President*
Mike Chambers, *COO*
Cheryl Poulton, *Vice Pres*
Robert Overs, *Treasurer*
EMP: 225
SQ FT: 75,000
SALES (est): 12.2MM **Privately Held**
SIC: 3011 3069 Tire & inner tube materials & related products; air-supported rubber structures

(G-11274)
WILLMAC ENTERPRISES INC
12200 Johnstown Utica Rd (43031-9562)
P.O. Box 541 (43031-0541)
PHONE...............................740 967-1979
Linda Williamson, *President*
Larry E Williamson, *Admin Sec*
EMP: 4

SQ FT: 2,500
SALES (est): 275K **Privately Held**
SIC: 3599 Machine shop, jobbing & repair

Junction City
Perry County

(G-11275)
R C POLING COMPANY INC
2105 Clay Rd (43748-9770)
PHONE...............................740 939-0023
Richard C Poling, *President*
Catherine Poling, *Vice Pres*
EMP: 3
SQ FT: 800
SALES (est): 1.8MM **Privately Held**
SIC: 1311 Crude petroleum production; natural gas production

Kalida
Putnam County

(G-11276)
B-K TOOL & DESIGN INC
480 W Main St (45853)
P.O. Box 416 (45853-0416)
PHONE...............................419 532-3890
Bob Kahle, *President*
Donna Horstman, *General Mgr*
Kevin M Kahle, *Vice Pres*
Jerry Schmenk, *Project Mgr*
Gale Bellmann, *Buyer*
EMP: 80
SQ FT: 12,000
SALES (est): 28.9MM **Privately Held**
SIC: 3544 Special dies, tools, jigs & fixtures

(G-11277)
K & L READY MIX INC
105 S 6th St (45853)
P.O. Box 300 (45853-0300)
PHONE...............................419 532-3585
Ron Kahle Jr, *Vice Pres*
EMP: 19
SALES (corp-wide): 7.6MM **Privately Held**
WEB: www.kandlreadymix.com
SIC: 3273 3271 Ready-mixed concrete; concrete block & brick
PA: K & L Ready Mix Inc
10391 State Route 15
Ottawa OH 45875
419 523-4376

(G-11278)
KALIDA MANUFACTURING INC
801 Ottawa St (45853)
P.O. Box 390 (45853-0390)
PHONE...............................419 532-2026
Bruce R Henke, *President*
Tim Inoue, *President*
Sho Akimoto, *Vice Pres*
▲ **EMP:** 250
SQ FT: 300,000
SALES (est): 77.3MM
SALES (corp-wide): 209.4MM **Privately Held**
WEB: www.kth.net
SIC: 3714 Motor vehicle parts & accessories
PA: Kth Parts Industries, Inc.
1111 State Route 235 N
Saint Paris OH 43072
937 663-5941

(G-11279)
NICANA CONSULTING INC
801 Oak Pkwy (45853)
PHONE...............................419 615-9703
Christopher Fortman, *Principal*
Jeffrey Krouse, *Principal*
William Romes, *Principal*
EMP: 4
SALES (est): 144.5K **Privately Held**
SIC: 3484 Small arms

(G-11280)
REMLINGER MANUFACTURING CO INC
16394 Us 224 (45853)
P.O. Box 299 (45853-0299)
PHONE...............................419 532-3647
Mildred C Remlinger, *Ch of Bd*
John Remlinger, *President*
Roger Westbeld, *Manager*
Mark Warnecke, *Executive*
▲ **EMP:** 32
SQ FT: 52,000
SALES: 9.9MM **Privately Held**
SIC: 3523 Harrows: disc, spring, tine, etc.

(G-11281)
SARKA BROS MACHINING INC
607 Ottawa St (45853)
P.O. Box 316 (45853-0316)
PHONE...............................419 532-2393
Bob Allen, *President*
Terry Burnett, *Vice Pres*
EMP: 8
SQ FT: 24,000
SALES (est): 1.4MM **Privately Held**
SIC: 3556 Food products machinery

(G-11282)
UNVERFERTH MFG CO INC (PA)
601 S Broad St (45853)
P.O. Box 357 (45853-0357)
PHONE...............................419 532-3121
R Steven Unverferth, *President*
Richard A Unverferth, *Chairman*
Daniel Fanger, *Vice Pres*
Gladys Unverferth, *Vice Pres*
Dennis Kapcar, *CFO*
◆ **EMP:** 249 **EST:** 1948
SQ FT: 828,501
SALES (est): 155.3MM **Privately Held**
WEB: www.unverferth.com
SIC: 3523 Farm machinery & equipment

Kelleys Island
Erie County

(G-11283)
KELLEYS ISLAND WINE CO
418 Woodford Rd (43438)
PHONE...............................419 746-2678
Kirt Zettler, *President*
Roberta Zettler, *Corp Secy*
EMP: 8
SQ FT: 7,000
SALES (est): 903.4K **Privately Held**
WEB: www.kelleysislandwine.com
SIC: 2084 5921 Wines; wine

Kensington
Columbiana County

(G-11284)
BRIAR HILL FURNITURE
7061 Bane Rd Ne (44427-9662)
PHONE...............................330 223-2109
Kenneth Yoder, *Partner*
Arthur Horst, *Partner*
EMP: 3
SALES (est): 240.6K **Privately Held**
SIC: 2511 Wood household furniture

(G-11285)
M3 MIDSTREAM LLC
Also Called: Kensington Plant
11543 Sr 644 (44427)
PHONE...............................330 223-2220
EMP: 28
SALES (corp-wide): 54.9MM **Privately Held**
SIC: 1311 Natural gas production
PA: M3 Midstream Llc
600 Travis St Ste 5600
Houston TX 77002
713 783-3000

(G-11286)
UTICA EAST OHIO MIDSTREAM
8194 Trout Rd Ne (44427-9666)
PHONE...............................330 223-1766
EMP: 3 **EST:** 2013

Kensington - Columbiana County (G-11287)

SALES (est): 201.2K **Privately Held**
SIC: 1382 Oil & gas exploration services

(G-11287)
WILLIAM S MILLER INC
11250 Montgomery Rd (44427-9702)
P.O. Box 145, Hanoverton (44423-0145)
PHONE 330 223-1794
William Miller, *CEO*
George Miller, *President*
Jane Todd, *Corp Secy*
David W Miller, *Vice Pres*
EMP: 9
SALES (est): 1.9MM **Privately Held**
SIC: 1311 Crude petroleum production

Kent
Portage County

(G-11288)
ACCURATE PLASTICS LLC
4430 Crystal Pkwy (44240-8006)
PHONE 330 346-0048
John Satina, *Principal*
EMP: 12
SALES (est): 1.8MM **Privately Held**
SIC: 3089 Injection molding of plastics

(G-11289)
ACTION SUPER ABRASIVE PDTS INC
945 Greenbriar Pkwy (44240-6478)
PHONE 330 673-7333
Joseph Haag, *President*
Dan Noonan, *Vice Pres*
EMP: 20
SQ FT: 27,000
SALES (est): 2.7MM **Privately Held**
WEB: www.actionsuper.com
SIC: 3291 Wheels, grinding: artificial

(G-11290)
AILES MILLWORK INC
1520 Enterprise Way (44240-7547)
PHONE 330 678-4300
Patrick Ailes, *President*
Margaret Ailes, *Corp Secy*
Ryan Ailes, *Vice Pres*
EMP: 18 EST: 1975
SQ FT: 13,000
SALES (est): 2.1MM **Privately Held**
WEB: www.ailesmillwork.com
SIC: 2431 2434 Millwork; wood kitchen cabinets

(G-11291)
AKRON CRATE AND PALLET LLC
1545 Mogadore Rd (44240-7540)
PHONE 330 524-8955
Matthew Breiding, *President*
EMP: 4
SALES (est): 370.4K **Privately Held**
SIC: 2448 Pallets, wood

(G-11292)
ALSICO USA INC (PA)
Also Called: Euclid Vidaro Mfg. Co.
333 Martinel Dr (44240-4370)
P.O. Box 550 (44240-0010)
PHONE 330 673-7413
Charles Rosenblatt, *President*
Edward Davis, *Vice Pres*
Howard Fleischmann, *Vice Pres*
▲ EMP: 100 EST: 1870
SQ FT: 29,000
SALES (est): 13.9MM **Privately Held**
WEB: www.euclidgarment.com
SIC: 2326 Men's & boys' work clothing

(G-11293)
AMETEK FLORCARE SPECIALTY MTRS
100 E Erie St Ste 200 (44240-2660)
PHONE 330 677-3786
Richard J Lamb, *President*
Earl Clausson, *Engineer*
Kris Diehl, *Engineer*
Harold Hughes, *Engineer*
David Pusker, *Project Engr*
EMP: 13
SALES (est): 2.1MM **Privately Held**
SIC: 3621 Mfg Motors/Generators

(G-11294)
AMETEK TCHNICAL INDUS PDTS INC (HQ)
Also Called: Ametek Electromechanical Group
100 E Erie St Ste 130 (44240-3587)
PHONE 330 677-3754
Todd Schlegel, *General Mgr*
Matt French, *Vice Pres*
Peter Smith, *CFO*
William D Burke, *Treasurer*
Kathryn E Sena, *Admin Sec*
EMP: 65 EST: 2009
SALES (est): 69MM
SALES (corp-wide): 4.8B **Publicly Held**
SIC: 3621 5063 3566 Motors, electric; motors, electric; speed changers, drives & gears
PA: Ametek, Inc.
1100 Cassatt Rd
Berwyn PA 19312
610 647-2121

(G-11295)
AMREX INC
431 W Elm St (44240-3717)
P.O. Box 456 (44240-0008)
PHONE 330 678-7050
Harold Carlson, *CEO*
David Carlson, *President*
EMP: 3
SALES (est): 165.4K **Privately Held**
SIC: 3089 Synthetic resin finished products

(G-11296)
AREA WIDE PROTECTIVE INC (HQ)
Also Called: Awp
826 Overholt Rd (44240-7530)
PHONE 330 644-0655
John P Sypek, *President*
Ron Brotherton, *Vice Pres*
Rusty Parrish, *Vice Pres*
Don Weidig, *CFO*
Suzette Cole, *Accounts Mgr*
EMP: 45 EST: 1991
SALES (est): 156.2MM
SALES (corp-wide): 172.7MM **Privately Held**
SIC: 3669 Pedestrian traffic control equipment; traffic signals, electric
PA: Awp, Inc.
4244 Mount Pleasant St Nw # 100
North Canton OH 44720
330 677-7401

(G-11297)
AYSCO SECURITY CONSULTANTS INC
4075 Karg Industrial Pkwy B (44240-6485)
PHONE 330 733-8183
Eric Frasier, *CEO*
Rod Bragg, *Principal*
EMP: 32
SALES (est): 129.4K **Privately Held**
SIC: 3699 5065 Security devices; security control equipment & systems

(G-11298)
BANG PRINTING OF OHIO INC
3765 Sunnybrook Rd (44240-7443)
PHONE 800 678-1222
Tom Campion, *Principal*
EMP: 11
SALES (est): 2.4MM **Privately Held**
SIC: 2752 Commercial printing, lithographic

(G-11299)
BECKWITH ORCHARDS INC
1617 Lake Rockwell Rd (44240-3019)
PHONE 330 673-6433
Charles Beckwith, *President*
Sally Beckwith, *General Mgr*
Marilyn Beckwith, *Vice Pres*
EMP: 12
SQ FT: 1,824
SALES (est): 1.4MM **Privately Held**
WEB: www.beckwithorchards.com
SIC: 2099 5431 5947 Cider, nonalcoholic; fruit stands or markets; gift shop

(G-11300)
BEEMER MACHINE COMPANY INC
1530 Enterprise Way (44240-7547)
PHONE 330 678-3822
Edward Burch, *President*
EMP: 8
SALES (est): 1.3MM **Privately Held**
SIC: 3599 Machine shop, jobbing & repair

(G-11301)
BOYCE MACHINE INC
3609 Mogadore Rd (44240-7431)
PHONE 330 678-3210
Shelby C Boyce, *President*
Patricia Boyce, *Corp Secy*
EMP: 9
SQ FT: 5,400
SALES (est): 1MM **Privately Held**
SIC: 3599 Machine shop, jobbing & repair

(G-11302)
C G C SYSTEMS INC
4763 Sherman Rd (44240-7054)
PHONE 330 678-3261
David Rose, *President*
John F Szwejk, *Vice Pres*
Betty Duncan, *Treasurer*
Joseph Bystricky Jr, *Asst Treas*
Daniel Holliday, *Admin Sec*
EMP: 4
SALES: 400K **Privately Held**
WEB: www.ccgsystems.com
SIC: 3444 Sheet metalwork

(G-11303)
CAMX OUTDOORS INC
1500 Enterprise Way (44240-7547)
PHONE 330 474-3969
David Choma, *Principal*
EMP: 3 EST: 2012
SALES (est): 169.4K **Privately Held**
SIC: 3949 Sporting & athletic goods

(G-11304)
CITY OF KENT
Also Called: Kent Parks Recreation
497 Middlebury Rd (44240-3409)
PHONE 330 673-8897
John Idone, *Director*
EMP: 10
SQ FT: 1,440 **Privately Held**
SIC: 2531 7349 Picnic tables or benches, park; building maintenance services
PA: City Of Kent
325 S Depeyster St
Kent OH 44240
330 676-4189

(G-11305)
COLONIAL MACHINE COMPANY INC
1041 Mogadore Rd (44240-7534)
P.O. Box 650 (44240-0012)
PHONE 330 673-5859
Roy Metcalf, *CEO*
James Rankin, *President*
Matt Metcalf, *VP Finance*
EMP: 71 EST: 1945
SQ FT: 35,000
SALES (est): 11.8MM **Privately Held**
WEB: www.colonial-machine.com
SIC: 3544 Special dies & tools; industrial molds

(G-11306)
COLONIAL PATTERNS INC
920 Overholt Rd (44240-7550)
PHONE 330 673-6475
Martin A Meluch, *President*
Valent Meluch, *Corp Secy*
▲ EMP: 30 EST: 1952
SQ FT: 4,800
SALES (est): 4.5MM **Privately Held**
WEB: www.colonialpatt.com
SIC: 3543 3544 Industrial patterns; special dies, tools, jigs & fixtures

(G-11307)
COPEN MACHINE INC
501 Dodge St (44240-3709)
PHONE 330 678-4598
Terry D Copen, *President*
John Pozzini, *Supervisor*
EMP: 13 EST: 1978

SQ FT: 13,000
SALES (est): 1.3MM **Privately Held**
SIC: 3599 Machine shop, jobbing & repair

(G-11308)
CUSTOMER SERVICE SYSTEMS INC
Also Called: Cssi & Quality Printing
1250 W Main St Ste A (44240-1979)
PHONE 330 677-2877
Carla Casky, *President*
EMP: 5
SALES (est): 447K **Privately Held**
WEB: www.matriximpact.com
SIC: 2759 2796 2791 2752 Commercial printing; platemaking services; typesetting; commercial printing, lithographic

(G-11309)
D & J PRINTING INC
Also Called: Hess Print Solutions
3765 Sunnybrook Rd (44240-7443)
PHONE 330 678-5868
Douglas Mann, *Branch Mgr*
EMP: 90
SALES (corp-wide): 514.8MM **Privately Held**
SIC: 2759 Commercial printing
HQ: D. & J. Printing, Inc.
3323 Oak St
Brainerd MN 56401
218 829-2877

(G-11310)
DAVEY KENT INC
Also Called: Davey Drill
200 W Williams St (44240-3797)
P.O. Box 400 (44240-0007)
PHONE 330 673-5400
J Thomas Myers II, *CEO*
Tom Myers, *President*
Chris Cooler, *Principal*
David Myers, *Vice Pres*
Jamie Hay, *Office Mgr*
▲ EMP: 20
SQ FT: 50,000
SALES (est): 6.7MM **Privately Held**
WEB: www.daveykent.com
SIC: 3532 Drills & drilling equipment, mining (except oil & gas)

(G-11311)
DE-LUX MOLD & MACHINE INC
6523 Pleasant Ave (44240)
P.O. Box 11163, Brady Lake (44211-1163)
PHONE 330 678-1030
EMP: 9
SQ FT: 4,200
SALES (est): 997.5K **Privately Held**
SIC: 3544 Mfg Plastic Molds

(G-11312)
DENNIS CORSO CO INC
266 Martinel Dr Bldg A (44240-4473)
PHONE 330 673-2411
Dennis Corso, *President*
EMP: 5
SQ FT: 5,000
SALES: 500K **Privately Held**
SIC: 3548 1799 Welding apparatus; welding on site

(G-11313)
DERMAMED COATIN
271 Progress Blvd (44240-8055)
PHONE 330 474-3786
▲ EMP: 5
SALES (est): 553.2K **Privately Held**
SIC: 2672 Coated & laminated paper

(G-11314)
DIPTECH SYSTEMS INC (PA)
4485 Crystal Pkwy Ste 100 (44240-8016)
P.O. Box 39 (44240-0001)
PHONE 330 673-4400
Tom Doland, *President*
Bill Mars, *President*
Mark Baskin, *Vice Pres*
Jeff Charlton, *Vice Pres*
Jeffrey Charlton, *Vice Pres*
EMP: 3
SALES (est): 3.5MM **Privately Held**
WEB: www.diptechsystems.com
SIC: 3559 Fiber optics strand coating machinery

GEOGRAPHIC SECTION

Kent - Portage County (G-11342)

(G-11315)
DON WARTKO CONSTRUCTION CO (PA)
Also Called: Design Concrete Surfaces
975 Tallmadge Rd (44240-6474)
PHONE 330 673-5252
Thomas Wartko, *President*
David Wartko, *Vice Pres*
Mike Wartko, *Vice Pres*
Ron Wartko, *Vice Pres*
Doris Wartko, *Admin Sec*
EMP: 60
SQ FT: 15,000
SALES (est): 18.4MM **Privately Held**
SIC: 1623 1794 3732 Oil & gas line & compressor station construction; sewer line construction; water main construction; excavation work; boat building & repairing

(G-11316)
DPM ORTHODONTICS INC
1519 Enterprise Way Ste H (44240-7524)
PHONE 330 673-0334
David J Marko, *President*
EMP: 6
SALES (est): 929.9K **Privately Held**
SIC: 3842 Orthopedic appliances

(G-11317)
EAST END WELDING COMPANY
357 Tallmadge Rd (44240-7201)
PHONE 330 677-6000
John E Susong, *President*
▲ **EMP:** 120 **EST:** 1967
SQ FT: 146,500
SALES (est): 36.4MM **Privately Held**
SIC: 3599 7692 Custom machinery; welding repair

(G-11318)
ELBEX CORPORATION
300 Martinel Dr (44240-4369)
PHONE 330 673-3233
Edward L Bittle, *President*
Lora Lie Jones, *Purch Mgr*
EMP: 90
SALES (est): 28.7MM **Privately Held**
WEB: www.elbex-us.com
SIC: 3061 Mechanical rubber goods

(G-11319)
EMERGENCY PRODUCTS & RES INC
Also Called: Epr
890 W Main St (44240-2284)
PHONE 330 673-5003
Jerold Ramsey, *President*
Jim Doherty, *Vice Pres*
▲ **EMP:** 6
SQ FT: 350,000
SALES (est): 1MM **Privately Held**
WEB: www.epandr.com
SIC: 2448 Wood pallets & skids

(G-11320)
ENTERPRISE PLASTICS INC
1500 Enterprise Way (44240-7547)
PHONE 330 346-0496
Martin Mulch, *President*
Valente Muluch, *Admin Sec*
▲ **EMP:** 20
SQ FT: 10,000
SALES (est): 4.5MM **Privately Held**
SIC: 3089 Injection molding of plastics

(G-11321)
FAITHFUL MOLD POLISHING EX
4485 Crystal Pkwy (44240-8013)
PHONE 330 678-8006
Houa Voe, *Owner*
EMP: 3
SALES: 40K **Privately Held**
SIC: 3471 Polishing, metals or formed products

(G-11322)
FRIENDS SERVICE CO INC
948 Cherry St (44240-7522)
PHONE 800 427-1704
Kenneth J Schroeder, *Branch Mgr*
EMP: 7 **Privately Held**
SIC: 5112 5021 5044 5087 Stationery & office supplies; furniture; office equipment; service establishment equipment; commercial printing, lithographic

PA: Friends Service Co., Inc.
2300 Bright Rd
Findlay OH 45840

(G-11323)
FROGS IN BLOOM
1112 Delores Ave (44240-2178)
PHONE 330 678-9508
Paulette Thurman, *Owner*
EMP: 3
SALES (est): 151.5K **Privately Held**
SIC: 2771 Greeting cards

(G-11324)
FURUKAWA ROCK DRILL USA INC (HQ)
Also Called: Gougler Industries Inc
705 Lake St (44240-2738)
PHONE 330 673-5826
Jeff Crane, *CEO*
Joe Burger, *Research*
Shoji Iguchi, *Director*
◆ **EMP:** 15
SQ FT: 240,000
SALES (est): 11.7MM
SALES (corp-wide): 1.5B **Privately Held**
WEB: www.gougler.com
SIC: 3533 3599 3546 Drilling tools for gas, oil or water wells; machine shop, jobbing & repair; power-driven handtools
PA: Furukawa Co., Ltd.
2-2-3, Marunouchi
Chiyoda-Ku TKY 100-0
332 126-570

(G-11325)
FURUKAWA ROCK DRILL USA CO LTD (PA)
Also Called: Frd
711 Lake St (44240-2738)
PHONE 330 673-5826
Jeff Krame, *Principal*
Shelly Branch, *Buyer*
▼ **EMP:** 20
SQ FT: 27,181
SALES (est): 4.7MM **Privately Held**
WEB: www.kenttool.com
SIC: 3545 3594 3546 3423 Tools & accessories for machine tools; fluid power pumps & motors; power-driven handtools; hand & edge tools

(G-11326)
GRAPHIC DETAIL INC
936 Greenbriar Pkwy (44240-6448)
PHONE 330 678-1724
Craig Lemasters, *President*
Randy Snyder, *Senior VP*
Lisa Lemasters, *Vice Pres*
Chad Migge, *Admin Sec*
EMP: 5
SALES (est): 757.1K **Privately Held**
SIC: 3993 Signs & advertising specialties

(G-11327)
GUYS BREWING GEAR
1325 Chelton Dr (44240-3264)
PHONE 330 554-9362
EMP: 3
SALES (est): 108.9K **Privately Held**
SIC: 2082 Malt beverages

(G-11328)
GWEN ROSENBERG ENTERPRISES LLC
175 E Erie St Ste 201 (44240-3595)
PHONE 330 678-1893
Gwen Rosenberg, *Mng Member*
EMP: 5
SALES (est): 180K **Privately Held**
SIC: 2064 5441 Candy bars, including chocolate covered bars; popcorn, including caramel corn

(G-11329)
H & S STEEL TREATING INC
Also Called: Peterson Heat Treating
4142 Mogadore Rd (44240-7263)
P.O. Box 2167, Stow (44224-0167)
PHONE 330 678-5245
William Sullivan, *President*
EMP: 10 **EST:** 1984
SQ FT: 14,000
SALES (est): 1.2MM **Privately Held**
SIC: 3398 Metal heat treating

(G-11330)
H W FAIRWAY INTERNATIONAL INC
716 N Mantua St (44240-2320)
P.O. Box 782 (44240-0016)
PHONE 330 678-2540
Lee J Strange, *President*
Alice Kandes, *Treasurer*
Charles Zuehmker, *Admin Sec*
EMP: 27 **EST:** 1940
SQ FT: 22,000
SALES (est): 4.1MM **Privately Held**
WEB: www.hwfairway.com
SIC: 3699 3823 3621 Laser systems & equipment; industrial instrmnts msrmnt display/control process variable; starters, for motors

(G-11331)
HAPCO INC
Also Called: Tarpco
390 Portage Blvd (44240-7283)
PHONE 330 678-9353
Charles George, *CEO*
Chuck George, *CEO*
Bernard Carpenter, *President*
John A Daily, *Principal*
Michael Szugye, *Sales Mgr*
◆ **EMP:** 11
SQ FT: 23,000
SALES (est): 2.5MM **Privately Held**
WEB: www.hapcoinc.com
SIC: 3545 5049 Diamond cutting tools for turning, boring, burnishing, etc.; precision tools

(G-11332)
HARDLINE WELDING LLC
2161 Mogadore Rd (44240-7261)
P.O. Box 241 (44240-0005)
PHONE 330 858-6289
Robert Nutter,
EMP: 5
SALES (est): 195.7K **Privately Held**
SIC: 7692 Welding repair

(G-11333)
HUGO SAND COMPANY
7055 State Route 43 (44240-6198)
PHONE 216 570-1212
Dorothy Strohm, *President*
Scott R Terhune, *Vice Pres*
Sythnia Terhune, *Vice Pres*
EMP: 7
SQ FT: 400
SALES (est): 680K **Privately Held**
SIC: 1442 Construction sand mining; gravel mining

(G-11334)
INDUSTRIAL MOLDED PLASTICS
425 1/2 W Grant St (44240-2311)
P.O. Box 726 (44240-0014)
PHONE 330 673-1464
Kelly Luli, *President*
Mary Ann Lewis, *Vice Pres*
EMP: 20
SQ FT: 11,000
SALES (est): 379.2K **Privately Held**
SIC: 3083 Thermosetting laminates: rods, tubes, plates & sheet

(G-11335)
J B MANUFACTURING INC
4465 Crystal Pkwy (44240-8005)
PHONE 330 676-9744
John L Anderson, *President*
EMP: 32
SQ FT: 36,000
SALES (est): 5.2MM **Privately Held**
WEB: www.taclatch.com
SIC: 3599 Machine shop, jobbing & repair

(G-11336)
J S MANUFACTURING LLC
4631 Mogadore Rd (44240-7249)
PHONE 330 815-2136
Debbie J Mills, *Principal*
EMP: 3
SALES (est): 191.1K **Privately Held**
SIC: 3999 Manufacturing industries

(G-11337)
JOS-TECH INC
852 W Main St (44240-2216)
P.O. Box 952 (44240-0019)
PHONE 330 678-3260
Bradford Joslyn, *President*
David Fox, *Vice Pres*
Caroline Mueller, *Admin Sec*
EMP: 25
SALES (est): 5.8MM **Privately Held**
WEB: www.jos-tech.com
SIC: 3089 Injection molding of plastics; plastic processing

(G-11338)
KENT ADHESIVE PRODUCTS CO
Also Called: K A P C O
1000 Cherry St (44240-7501)
P.O. Box 626 (44240-0011)
PHONE 330 678-1626
Edward Small, *President*
Jenifer Codrea, *Vice Pres*
Philip M Zavracky, *Vice Pres*
Nate Foltz, *Purch Mgr*
Steve Smigel, *Controller*
▼ **EMP:** 80 **EST:** 1974
SQ FT: 100,000
SALES (est): 38.4MM **Privately Held**
WEB: www.kapco.com
SIC: 2679 2672 2675 7389 Paper products, converted; adhesive papers, labels or tapes: from purchased material; tape, pressure sensitive: made from purchased materials; die-cut paper & board; laminating service; tape slitting

(G-11339)
KENT AUTOMATION INC
449 Dodge St (44240-3707)
PHONE 330 678-6343
Dennis Lyell, *President*
Gary Lyell, *Vice Pres*
EMP: 15
SQ FT: 12,000
SALES (est): 4.7MM **Privately Held**
SIC: 3599 Machine shop, jobbing & repair

(G-11340)
KENT DISPLAYS INC (PA)
Also Called: Improv Electronics
343 Portage Blvd (44240-9200)
PHONE 330 673-8784
Joel Domino, *President*
Brett Carey, *Sales Staff*
Chris Cooperider, *Manager*
Asad Khan, *CTO*
Sue Hensley, *Admin Asst*
▲ **EMP:** 105
SQ FT: 42,000
SALES (est): 32.3MM **Privately Held**
WEB: www.kentdisplays.com
SIC: 3679 Liquid crystal displays (LCD)

(G-11341)
KENT ELASTOMER PRODUCTS INC (HQ)
1500 Saint Clair Ave (44240-4364)
P.O. Box 668 (44240-0012)
PHONE 330 673-1011
Bob Oborn, *President*
Brad Walker, *Buyer*
April Butcher, *Supervisor*
Lee Ann Corp, *Administration*
▲ **EMP:** 150
SQ FT: 42,000
SALES (est): 31.7MM
SALES (corp-wide): 379.3MM **Privately Held**
WEB: www.kentelastomer.com
SIC: 3052 Rubber & plastics hose & beltings
PA: Meridian Industries, Inc.
735 N Water St Ste 630
Milwaukee WI 53202
414 224-0610

(G-11342)
KENT INFORMATION SERVICES INC
6185 2nd Ave (44240-2991)
PHONE 330 672-2110
John H Graves, *President*
John Graves, *President*
EMP: 6

Kent - Portage County (G-11343)

SALES (est): 377.3K **Privately Held**
SIC: **2721** 8721 Periodicals; accounting, auditing & bookkeeping

(G-11343)
KENT MOLD AND MANUFACTURING CO
1190 W Main St (44240-1942)
PHONE..................330 673-3469
Paul Ferder, *President*
Henry Trivelli, *Corp Secy*
EMP: 40 EST: 1944
SQ FT: 35,000
SALES (est): 7.3MM **Privately Held**
WEB: www.kentmold.com
SIC: **3544** Industrial molds

(G-11344)
KENT STATE UNIVERSITY
Kent State University Press
307 Lwry Hall Terrance Dr (44242-0001)
P.O. Box 5190
PHONE..................330 672-7913
Will Underwood, *Director*
EMP: 10
SALES (corp-wide): 474.6MM **Privately Held**
WEB: www.kenteliv.kent.edu
SIC: **2731** 8221 Book publishing; university
PA: Kent State University
    1500 Horning Rd
    Kent OH 44242
    330 672-3000

(G-11345)
KENT STATE UNIVERSITY
Also Called: Daily Kent Stater
205 Frlanklin Hall (44242-0001)
P.O. Box 5190
PHONE..................330 672-2586
Laurie Cantor, *General Mgr*
EMP: 3
SALES (corp-wide): 474.6MM **Privately Held**
WEB: www.kenteliv.kent.edu
SIC: **2711** 8221 Newspapers, publishing & printing; university
PA: Kent State University
    1500 Horning Rd
    Kent OH 44242
    330 672-3000

(G-11346)
LAND OLAKES INC
2001 Mogadore Rd (44240-7296)
PHONE..................330 678-1578
Steve Sehafer, *Opers-Prdtn-Mfg*
EMP: 177
SALES (corp-wide): 10.4B **Privately Held**
WEB: www.landolakes.com
SIC: **2022** Cheese, natural & processed
PA: Land O'lakes, Inc.
    4001 Lexington Ave N
    Arden Hills MN 55126
    651 375-2222

(G-11347)
MAAG AUTOMATIK INC
Also Called: Maag Reduction Engineering
235 Progress Blvd (44240-8055)
PHONE..................330 677-2225
EMP: 35
SALES (corp-wide): 6.9B **Publicly Held**
SIC: **3532** 5084 Crushing, pulverizing & screening equipment; pellet mills (mining machinery); pulverizing machinery & equipment
HQ: Maag Automatik, Inc.
    9401 Southern Pine Blvd Q
    Charlotte NC 28273

(G-11348)
MAC LTT INC
Also Called: Mac Liquid Tank Trailer
1400 Fairchild Ave (44240-1818)
PHONE..................330 474-3795
Jim Maiorana, *President*
Anthony Miller, *Purch Mgr*
Ryan Neff, *Engineer*
Lori Picicco, *Sales Staff*
Dennis Gauthier, *Manager*
EMP: 162
SALES (est): 91.3MM **Privately Held**
SIC: **3569** Assembly machines, non-metalworking

PA: Mac Trailer Manufacturing, Inc.
    14599 Commerce St Ne
    Alliance OH 44601

(G-11349)
MARK GRZIANIS ST TREATS EX INC (PA)
Also Called: Yaya's
1294 Windward Ln (44240-1895)
PHONE..................330 414-6266
Mark Graziani, *President*
Wendy Graziani, *Vice Pres*
EMP: 12
SALES: 50K **Privately Held**
SIC: **5812** 2035 7389 Cafeteria; dressings, salad: raw & cooked (except dry mixes);

(G-11350)
MASTERS PRCISION MACHINING INC
4465 Crystal Pkwy (44240-8005)
PHONE..................330 419-1933
Kenneth Rice, *President*
Charlotte Rice, *CFO*
EMP: 10 EST: 2014
SALES (est): 676.2K **Privately Held**
SIC: **3541** Numerically controlled metal cutting machine tools

(G-11351)
MERIDIAN INDUSTRIES INC
Also Called: Kent Elastomer Products
1500 Saint Clair Ave (44240-4364)
P.O. Box 668 (44240-0012)
PHONE..................330 673-1011
Vann Epp Murray, *President*
Murray V Epp, *Project Mgr*
EMP: 60
SALES (corp-wide): 379.3MM **Privately Held**
WEB: www.meridiancompanies.com
SIC: **3069** 3842 3083 3082 Tubing, rubber; surgical appliances & supplies; laminated plastics plate & sheet; unsupported plastics profile shapes; mechanical rubber goods
PA: Meridian Industries, Inc.
    735 N Water St Ste 630
    Milwaukee WI 53202
    414 224-0610

(G-11352)
METAL-MAX INC
1540 Enterprise Way (44240-7547)
PHONE..................330 673-9926
Richard La Mancusa, *President*
EMP: 8
SQ FT: 5,000
SALES: 900K **Privately Held**
SIC: **3444** Sheet metal specialties, not stamped

(G-11353)
MICHAEL KAUFMAN COMPANIES INC (PA)
Also Called: Educational Equipment
845 Overholt Rd (44240-7529)
P.O. Box 154 (44240-0003)
PHONE..................330 673-4881
Michael Kaufman, *President*
John T Waller, *Principal*
◆ EMP: 12
SQ FT: 60,000
SALES (est): 2.1MM **Privately Held**
SIC: **3281** 2599 2493 2541 Blackboards, slate; boards: planning, display, notice; bulletin boards, cork; store & office display cases & fixtures; display fixtures, wood

(G-11354)
MICHAEL KAUFMAN COMPANIES INC
Also Called: Educational Equipment
845 Overholt Rd (44240-7529)
P.O. Box 154 (44240-0003)
PHONE..................330 673-4881
Michael Kaufman, *President*
EMP: 10

SALES (corp-wide): 2.1MM **Privately Held**
SIC: **3281** 2599 2493 2541 Blackboards, slate; boards: planning, display, notice; bulletin boards, cork; store & office display cases & fixtures; display fixtures, wood
PA: Michael Kaufman Companies, Inc.
    845 Overholt Rd
    Kent OH 44240
    330 673-4881

(G-11355)
MIKE B CRAWFORD
Also Called: Advanced Display Systems
606 Mogadore Rd (44240-7533)
PHONE..................330 673-7944
Mike Crawford, *Owner*
EMP: 3
SQ FT: 3,200
SALES: 200K **Privately Held**
SIC: **3993** 5999 7532 2759 Signs, not made in custom sign painting shops; decals; truck painting & lettering; screen printing; commercial printing, lithographic

(G-11356)
MILLER BEARING COMPANY INC
420 Portage Blvd (44240-7285)
PHONE..................330 678-8844
Donald A Miller, *President*
Julie Miller, *Corp Secy*
EMP: 28 EST: 1978
SQ FT: 75,000
SALES (est): 3.3MM **Privately Held**
WEB: www.millerbearing.com
SIC: **3562** Ball bearings & parts

(G-11357)
MOLD SURFACE TEXTURES
Also Called: MST
4485 Crystal Pkwy Ste 300 (44240-8016)
PHONE..................330 678-8590
Joe Gendron, *President*
Kevin Gasaway, *Treasurer*
Sue Gasaway, *Office Mgr*
Aaron Pendergast, *Admin Sec*
EMP: 6
SALES (est): 1.1MM **Privately Held**
SIC: **3544** Industrial molds

(G-11358)
NEWELL BRANDS INC
Also Called: Rubbermaid
212 Progress Blvd (44240-8015)
PHONE..................330 733-1184
Amy Smith, *Branch Mgr*
EMP: 13
SALES (corp-wide): 8.6B **Publicly Held**
SIC: **3069** Medical & laboratory rubber sundries & related products
PA: Newell Brands Inc.
    221 River St Ste 13
    Hoboken NJ 07030
    201 610-6600

(G-11359)
P S P INC
Also Called: Petry Power Systems
7337 Westview Rd (44240-5911)
PHONE..................330 283-5635
Robert V Petry, *President*
EMP: 50
SALES: 3MM **Privately Held**
SIC: **2869** Fuels

(G-11360)
PARKER-HANNIFIN CORPORATION
Also Called: Fluid System Connectors Div
838 Overholt Rd (44240-7500)
PHONE..................330 673-2700
Russ Kalis, *Branch Mgr*
EMP: 90
SALES (corp-wide): 14.3B **Publicly Held**
WEB: www.parker.com
SIC: **3089** Fittings for pipe, plastic
PA: Parker-Hannifin Corporation
    6035 Parkland Blvd
    Cleveland OH 44124
    216 896-3000

(G-11361)
PEGASUS PRODUCTS COMPANY INC
315 Gougler Ave (44240-2405)
PHONE..................330 677-1123
Fax: 330 677-4130
EMP: 4
SQ FT: 24,000
SALES (est): 280K **Privately Held**
SIC: **2599** Mfg Furniture/Fixtures

(G-11362)
PODNAR PLASTICS INC
343 Portage Blvd Unit 3 (44240-9200)
PHONE..................330 673-2255
Scott Podnar, *President*
EMP: 50
SALES (corp-wide): 4.8MM **Privately Held**
WEB: www.rez-tech.com
SIC: **3089** Molding primary plastic
PA: Podnar Plastics, Inc.
    1510 Mogadore Rd
    Kent OH 44240
    330 673-2255

(G-11363)
PODNAR PLASTICS INC (PA)
1510 Mogadore Rd (44240-7599)
PHONE..................330 673-2255
Jack Podnar, *President*
Craig Podnar, *Vice Pres*
Scott Podnar, *Vice Pres*
EMP: 27 EST: 1977
SQ FT: 38,000
SALES: 4.8MM **Privately Held**
WEB: www.rez-tech.com
SIC: **3089** Injection molding of plastics; blow molded finished plastic products

(G-11364)
POLYMERICS INC
1540 Saint Clair Ave (44240-4364)
PHONE..................330 677-1131
Kim Marquis, *Opers Mgr*
Tony Bisesi, *Controller*
EMP: 21
SQ FT: 26,458
SALES (est): 5.7MM
SALES (corp-wide): 15.3MM **Privately Held**
WEB: www.polymericsinc.com
SIC: **2899** 2821 Chemical preparations; plastics materials & resins
PA: Polymerics, Inc.
    2828 2nd St
    Cuyahoga Falls OH 44221
    330 434-6665

(G-11365)
POPPED
175 E Erie St Ste 201 (44240-3595)
PHONE..................330 678-1893
Gwen Rosenberg, *Owner*
EMP: 10 EST: 2011
SALES (est): 755.3K **Privately Held**
SIC: **2064** 7389 Candy & other confectionery products;

(G-11366)
POST PRODUCTS INC
1600 Franklin Ave (44240-4308)
P.O. Box 777 (44240-0015)
PHONE..................330 678-0048
Jay McElravy, *President*
Nancy McElravy, *Corp Secy*
EMP: 7
SQ FT: 6,000
SALES (est): 968.1K **Privately Held**
WEB: www.postproducts.com
SIC: **3599** Machine shop, jobbing & repair

(G-11367)
PRESS OF OHIO INC
Also Called: Hess Print Solutions
3765 Sunnybrook Rd (44240-7443)
PHONE..................330 678-5868
Doug Mann, *President*
EMP: 28
SALES (est): 4.4MM **Privately Held**
SIC: **2759** Commercial printing

GEOGRAPHIC SECTION

Kent - Portage County (G-11393)

(G-11368)
PRIMAL SCREEN INC
Also Called: Alpha Strike
1021 Mason Ave (44240-2718)
PHONE..................330 677-1766
Terry Tasker, *President*
Tom Diroll, *Corp Secy*
Donald Emerson, *Director*
Fumi Yozawa, *Director*
EMP: 20
SQ FT: 10,000
SALES: 1.5MM **Privately Held**
WEB: www.primalscreen.net
SIC: 2759 Screen printing

(G-11369)
PROTO MACHINE & MFG INC
2190 State Route 59 (44240-7142)
PHONE..................330 677-1700
Edward L Dias, *President*
Marvin Maffett, *General Mgr*
Shelly Morgan, *Administration*
EMP: 15
SQ FT: 10,000
SALES (est): 2MM **Privately Held**
WEB: www.protomachine.com
SIC: 3599 Machine shop, jobbing & repair

(G-11370)
PYRAMID MOLD INC
Also Called: Pyramid Mold & Machine Company
222 Martinel Dr (44240-4321)
P.O. Box 634 (44240-0011)
PHONE..................330 673-5200
Joan Siciliano, *President*
Adolph Siciliano, *President*
Martin Cannistra, *Sr Project Mgr*
EMP: 15
SQ FT: 10,000
SALES (est): 2.6MM **Privately Held**
WEB: www.pyramidmold-machine.com
SIC: 3544 Special dies & tools

(G-11371)
QUANTUM JEWELRY DIST
4631 Mogadore Rd (44240-7249)
P.O. Box 55, Mogadore (44260-0055)
PHONE..................330 678-2222
Tammy Palmer, *President*
James Palmer, *Vice Pres*
EMP: 20
SQ FT: 8,000
SALES: 2MM **Privately Held**
SIC: 3914 Pewter ware

(G-11372)
QUICK SERVICE WELDING & MCH CO
117 E Summit St (44240-3556)
PHONE..................330 673-3818
Frank S Bowen, *President*
Wilma Bowen, *Corp Secy*
James M Bowen, *Vice Pres*
EMP: 11 **EST:** 1919
SQ FT: 11,200
SALES (est): 1.1MM **Privately Held**
SIC: 7692 3599 Welding repair; machine shop, jobbing & repair

(G-11373)
RASCHKE ENGRAVING INC
Also Called: Buckeye Engraving
4485 Crystal Pkwy Ste 200 (44240-8016)
PHONE..................330 677-5544
Steve Broadbent, *President*
George Botzman, *Vice Pres*
EMP: 7
SQ FT: 4,000
SALES (est): 688.3K **Privately Held**
SIC: 7389 3953 Engraving service; marking devices

(G-11374)
REZ-TECH CORPORATION
1510 Mogadore Rd (44240-7531)
PHONE..................330 673-4009
Jack Podnar, *CEO*
Jeanette M Podnar, *Corp Secy*
Craig Podnar, *Exec VP*
Scott Podnar, *Vice Pres*
▲ **EMP:** 47 **EST:** 1981
SQ FT: 38,000
SALES: 5.2MM **Privately Held**
SIC: 3089 Injection molding of plastics

(G-11375)
RHOADS PRINTING CENTER INC (PA)
Also Called: Copy Print
302 N Water St (44240-2423)
PHONE..................330 678-2042
Richard M Rhoads, *President*
Jill Rhoads, *Admin Sec*
EMP: 8 **EST:** 1971
SQ FT: 8,000
SALES (est): 1.3MM **Privately Held**
SIC: 2752 7334 Commercial printing, offset; photocopying & duplicating services

(G-11376)
ROBERT LONG MANUFACTURING INC
4192 Karg Industrial Pkwy (44240-6400)
PHONE..................330 678-0911
Robert Long, *President*
Doug Atkins, *Vice Pres*
EMP: 8
SQ FT: 7,200
SALES: 1.5MM **Privately Held**
SIC: 3599 Machine shop, jobbing & repair

(G-11377)
RON-AL MOLD & MACHINE INC
1057 Mason Ave (44240-2718)
PHONE..................330 673-7919
Ronald Siciliano, *President*
Alan Siciliano, *Treasurer*
Rosalee Hodge, *Office Mgr*
EMP: 12
SQ FT: 2,500
SALES (est): 1.6MM **Privately Held**
WEB: www.ronalmold.com
SIC: 3544 Industrial molds

(G-11378)
ROTOLINE USA LLC
4429 Crystal Pkwy Ste B (44240-8014)
PHONE..................330 677-3223
Alain Stpierre, *General Mgr*
Raphaeli Deluccas, *General Mgr*
EMP: 6
SALES (est): 906.6K **Privately Held**
SIC: 3524 Rototillers (garden machinery)

(G-11379)
RUB-R-ROAD INC
431 W Elm St (44240-3717)
P.O. Box 456 (44240-0008)
PHONE..................330 678-7050
David Carlson, *President*
Kenneth Banks, *Corp Secy*
EMP: 3
SQ FT: 8,000
SALES (est): 587.4K **Privately Held**
WEB: www.rub-r-road.com
SIC: 2951 Asphalt paving mixtures & blocks

(G-11380)
SCHNELLER LLC (HQ)
Also Called: Veritas
6019 Powdermill Rd (44240-7109)
PHONE..................330 676-7183
Heather Rinderle, *Opers Staff*
Mark Tennant, *Project Engr*
Brittany Sands, *Accountant*
Daryl Wong, *Accounts Mgr*
Gregory Hamilton, *Manager*
▲ **EMP:** 112
SQ FT: 125,000
SALES (est): 90.9MM
SALES (corp-wide): 3.8B **Publicly Held**
WEB: www.schneller.com
SIC: 2295 Resin or plastic coated fabrics; laminating of fabrics
PA: Transdigm Group Incorporated
1301 E 9th St Ste 3000
Cleveland OH 44114
216 706-2960

(G-11381)
SCHNELLER LLC
Polyplastex International
6019 Powdermill Rd (44240-7109)
PHONE..................330 673-1299
Tom Spseisser, *Manager*
EMP: 75
SALES (corp-wide): 3.8B **Publicly Held**
WEB: www.schneller.com
SIC: 3083 8731 3728 Laminated plastic sheets; commercial physical research; aircraft parts & equipment
HQ: Schneller Llc
6019 Powdermill Rd
Kent OH 44240
330 676-7183

(G-11382)
SCOTT MOLDERS INCORPORATED
7180 State Route 43 (44240-5940)
P.O. Box 645 (44240-0012)
PHONE..................330 673-5777
Scott Yahner, *President*
Glenn Russell, *Vice Pres*
Sherri Kershner, *Office Mgr*
EMP: 70
SQ FT: 23,000
SALES (est): 8.6MM **Privately Held**
SIC: 3089 2821 Thermoformed finished plastic products; plastics materials & resins

(G-11383)
SEAL MASTER CORPORATION
Also Called: Sealmaster
340 Martinel Dr (44240)
PHONE..................330 673-8410
Edward Bittle, *Branch Mgr*
EMP: 45
SALES (corp-wide): 11.9MM **Privately Held**
WEB: www.sealmasterseals.com
SIC: 2951 Asphalt paving mixtures & blocks
PA: Seal Master Corporation
368 Martinel Dr
Kent OH 44240
330 673-8410

(G-11384)
SELECT MACHINE CO INC
4125 Karg Industrial Pkwy (44240-6425)
PHONE..................330 678-7676
Bill Sagaser, *President*
William Sagaser, *Corp Secy*
Douglas Beavers, *Vice Pres*
EMP: 10
SQ FT: 7,000
SALES (est): 1.3MM **Privately Held**
SIC: 3544 3599 Special dies, tools, jigs & fixtures; machine shop, jobbing & repair

(G-11385)
SHELLY MATERIALS INC
1181 Cherry St (44240)
PHONE..................330 673-3646
Dennis Krohn, *Manager*
EMP: 4
SALES (corp-wide): 29.7B **Privately Held**
SIC: 1422 1442 2951 4492 Crushed & broken limestone; construction sand & gravel; concrete, asphaltic (not from refineries); tugboat service
HQ: Shelly Materials, Inc.
80 Park Dr
Thornville OH 43076
740 246-6315

(G-11386)
SMITHERS-OASIS COMPANY (PA)
295 S Water St Ste 201 (44240-3591)
PHONE..................330 945-5100
Charles F Walton, *CEO*
Robin M Kilbride, *President*
James Stull, *Treasurer*
▼ **EMP:** 15
SQ FT: 7,500
SALES (est): 52.7MM **Privately Held**
WEB: www.smithersoasis.com
SIC: 3086 Packaging & shipping materials, foamed plastic

(G-11387)
SMITHERS-OASIS COMPANY
Smithers-Oasis North America
919 Marvin St (44240-2436)
P.O. Box 118 (44240-0002)
PHONE..................330 673-5831
Charles Walton, *President*
Robert Williams, *Branch Mgr*
EMP: 11
SALES (corp-wide): 52.7MM **Privately Held**
WEB: www.smithersoasis.com
SIC: 3086 Plastics foam products
PA: Smithers-Oasis Company
295 S Water St Ste 201
Kent OH 44240
330 945-5100

(G-11388)
SORBOTHANE INC (PA)
2144 State Route 59 (44240-7142)
PHONE..................330 678-9444
David Church, *President*
Robert Whitlinger, *Principal*
Greg Seith, *Plant Supt*
EMP: 20
SQ FT: 60,000
SALES (est): 2.7MM **Privately Held**
WEB: www.sorbothane.com
SIC: 3069 3545 3296 2821 Molded rubber products; machine tool accessories; mineral wool; plastics materials & resins

(G-11389)
SPORTSGUARD LABORATORIES INC
821 W Main St (44240-2215)
PHONE..................330 673-3932
Dan Brett, *President*
EMP: 3
SQ FT: 1,500
SALES (est): 290K **Privately Held**
WEB: www.sportsguard.com
SIC: 3843 Dental equipment & supplies

(G-11390)
STEINERT INDUSTRIES INC
1507 Franklin Ave (44240-3770)
PHONE..................330 678-0028
John J Steinert, *President*
Laura Cheges, *Treasurer*
EMP: 15 **EST:** 1976
SQ FT: 11,000
SALES: 1MM **Privately Held**
WEB: www.steinertindustries.com
SIC: 3559 3599 Glass making machinery: blowing, molding, forming, etc.; machine shop, jobbing & repair

(G-11391)
SUNNY BROOK PRESSED CON CO
3586 Sunnybrook Rd (44240-7448)
PHONE..................330 673-7667
Joseph F Repasky Jr, *President*
EMP: 9
SALES (est): 2MM **Privately Held**
WEB: www.sunnybrookpressedconcrete.com
SIC: 3271 Architectural concrete: block, split, fluted, screen, etc.

(G-11392)
TARPCO INC
390 Portage Blvd (44240-7283)
PHONE..................330 677-8277
Chuck George, *President*
Harold A Neidlinger, *President*
Michael R Harrison, *Vice Pres*
Nathan Splitstone, *Sales Staff*
EMP: 18 **EST:** 1938
SQ FT: 6,500
SALES (est): 1.3MM **Privately Held**
WEB: www.tarpco.com
SIC: 2394 7359 3537 Tarpaulins, fabric: made from purchased materials; tent & tarpaulin rental; industrial trucks & tractors

(G-11393)
TECHNIDRILL SYSTEMS INC
429 Portage Blvd (44240-7286)
PHONE..................330 678-9980
Jim Kent, *President*
H Calhoun, *Corp Secy*
EMP: 36
SQ FT: 23,000
SALES (est): 6.5MM **Privately Held**
WEB: www.technidrillsystems.com
SIC: 3541 3546 3545 Drilling & boring machines; power-driven handtools; machine tool accessories

Kent - Portage County (G-11394)

(G-11394)
TMAC MACHINE INC
924 Overholt Rd (44240-7551)
PHONE..................................330 673-0621
Ray Thompson, *President*
EMP: 7
SQ FT: 10,400
SALES: 350K **Privately Held**
SIC: 3599 3069 Machine shop, jobbing & repair; platens, except printers': solid or covered rubber

(G-11395)
TORSION PLASTICS
1133 Windward Ln (44240-1897)
PHONE..................................812 453-9645
Joseph Sitzman, *Principal*
EMP: 3 **EST:** 2014
SALES (est): 161.6K **Privately Held**
SIC: 3089 Injection molding of plastics

(G-11396)
TREE CITY MOLD & MACHINE CO
6752 State Route 43 (44240-6197)
PHONE..................................330 673-9807
Robert M Zalewski, *President*
Terry Zalewski, *Corp Secy*
EMP: 6 **EST:** 1955
SQ FT: 12,000
SALES: 1MM **Privately Held**
SIC: 3544 Industrial molds

(G-11397)
U S DEVELOPMENT CORP
900 W Main St (44240-2285)
PHONE..................................570 966-5990
Brad Wertman, *Manager*
EMP: 30
SALES (est): 1.5MM
SALES (corp-wide): 10.2MM **Privately Held**
WEB: www.rotomold.net
SIC: 3089 3949 Injection molding of plastics; sporting & athletic goods
PA: U S Development Corp
900 W Main St
Kent OH 44240
330 673-6900

(G-11398)
U S DEVELOPMENT CORP (PA)
Also Called: Akro-Plastics
900 W Main St (44240-2285)
PHONE..................................330 673-6900
Jerold Ramsey, *President*
Fred Maurer, *Director*
EMP: 50
SQ FT: 185,000
SALES (est): 10.2MM **Privately Held**
WEB: www.rotomold.net
SIC: 3089 6512 Molding primary plastic; commercial & industrial building operation

(G-11399)
WEISS MOTORS
4554 State Route 43 (44240-6924)
PHONE..................................330 678-5585
Robert Knapp, *Owner*
EMP: 3
SALES: 260K **Privately Held**
SIC: 3711 7532 Automobile assembly, including specialty automobiles; top & body repair & paint shops

Kenton
Hardin County

(G-11400)
A & P WOOD PRODUCTS INC
15790 State Route 31 (43326-9016)
PHONE..................................419 673-1196
Walter Allsup, *President*
Debbie Allsup, *Corp Secy*
EMP: 3
SALES: 1MM **Privately Held**
SIC: 2411 Logging camps & contractors

(G-11401)
ALLMAX SOFTWARE INC
911 S Main St (43326-2207)
P.O. Box 40 (43326-0040)
PHONE..................................419 673-8863
Russell Maxwell, *President*
Patricia Maxwell, *Vice Pres*
Doug Klima, *Accounts Mgr*
EMP: 15
SQ FT: 5,000
SALES: 1.3MM **Privately Held**
WEB: www.allmaxsoftware.com
SIC: 7372 Prepackaged software

(G-11402)
ATMOSPHERE ANNEALING LLC
1501 Raff Rd Sw (43326)
PHONE..................................330 478-0314
Saminathan Ramaswamy, *Manager*
EMP: 65
SALES (corp-wide): 81.9MM **Privately Held**
SIC: 3398 Annealing of metal
HQ: Atmosphere Annealing, Llc
209 W Mount Hope Ave # 2
Lansing MI 48910
517 485-5090

(G-11403)
BAKELITE N SUMITOMO AMER INC
13717 Us Highway 68 (43326-9302)
PHONE..................................419 675-1282
Kurt Sandy, *Branch Mgr*
EMP: 3
SALES (corp-wide): 1.9B **Privately Held**
SIC: 3089 Plastic containers, except foam
HQ: Sumitomo Bakelite North America, Inc.
46820 Magellan Dr Ste C
Novi MI 48377

(G-11404)
DUREZ CORPORATION
13717 State Route 68 (43326-9302)
PHONE..................................567 295-6400
Bill Bazell, *Manager*
EMP: 150
SQ FT: 25,000
SALES (corp-wide): 1.9B **Privately Held**
WEB: www.durez.com
SIC: 2891 2295 2821 Adhesives; plastic; resin or plastic coated fabrics; plastics materials & resins
HQ: Durez Corporation
46820 Magellan Dr Ste C
Novi MI 48377
248 313-7000

(G-11405)
GOLDEN GIANT INC
Also Called: Golden Giants Building System
13300 S Vision Dr (43326-9599)
P.O. Box 389 (43326-0389)
PHONE..................................419 674-4038
Gene A Good, *CEO*
Wright McCullough, *Principal*
Paul N McKinley, *Principal*
Sharon J Good, *Corp Secy*
Chris Richards, *Vice Pres*
EMP: 35 **EST:** 1971
SQ FT: 80,000
SALES (est): 11.1MM **Privately Held**
WEB: www.goldengiant.com
SIC: 3448 Buildings, portable: prefabricated metal; prefabricated metal components

(G-11406)
GOLDEN GRAPHICS LTD
314 W Franklin St (43326-1702)
P.O. Box 208 (43326-0208)
PHONE..................................419 673-6260
Thomas G Carrig, *Principal*
Michael Carrig,
EMP: 10
SQ FT: 8,000
SALES (est): 1.4MM **Privately Held**
WEB: www.golden-graphics.com
SIC: 2752 7335 7336 2789 Commercial printing, offset; commercial photography; graphic arts & related design; bookbinding & related work; commercial printing

(G-11407)
GRAPHIC PACKAGING INTL LLC
Also Called: International Paper
1300 S Main St (43326-2298)
PHONE..................................419 673-0711
Vicky Winters, *Safety Mgr*
Heather Fleece, *Purchasing*
Don Gerling, *Engineer*
Ted Riggs, *Branch Mgr*
Matthew Alloway, *Manager*
EMP: 375 **Publicly Held**
WEB: www.internationalpaper.com
SIC: 2656 2621 Cups, paper: made from purchased material; paper mills
HQ: Graphic Packaging International, Llc
1500 Riveredge Pkwy # 100
Atlanta GA 30328

(G-11408)
HARDIN COUNTY PUBLISHING CO (HQ)
Also Called: Kenton Times, The
201 E Columbus St (43326-1583)
P.O. Box 230 (43326-0230)
PHONE..................................419 674-4066
Jeff Barnes, *President*
EMP: 36 **EST:** 1953
SQ FT: 9,600
SALES (est): 3.7MM
SALES (corp-wide): 8.7MM **Privately Held**
SIC: 2711 Job printing & newspaper publishing combined; newspapers: publishing only, not printed on site
PA: Ray Barnes Newspaper Inc
201 E Columbus St 207
Kenton OH 43326
419 674-4066

(G-11409)
HENSEL READY MIX INC (PA)
9925 County Road 265 (43326-9773)
PHONE..................................419 675-1808
Rodney Hensel, *President*
Linda Hensel, *Vice Pres*
EMP: 10 **EST:** 1963
SQ FT: 5,000
SALES (est): 1.5MM **Privately Held**
WEB: www.t3hw00t.com
SIC: 3273 Ready-mixed concrete

(G-11410)
INTERNATIONAL PAPER COMPANY
808 Fontaine St (43326-2160)
PHONE..................................800 422-4657
Brett Bahr, *Controller*
Al Kayler, *Branch Mgr*
EMP: 143
SALES (corp-wide): 23.3B **Publicly Held**
WEB: www.internationalpaper.com
SIC: 2656 Paper cups, plates, dishes & utensils
PA: International Paper Company
6400 Poplar Ave
Memphis TN 38197
901 419-9000

(G-11411)
KENTON IRON PRODUCTS INC (PA)
347 Vine St (43326-1253)
PHONE..................................419 674-4178
Jerry Harmeyer, *President*
Michael Heyne, *Corp Secy*
Mark Brown, *Supervisor*
EMP: 75
SQ FT: 70,000
SALES (est): 14.7MM **Privately Held**
WEB: www.kentoniron.com
SIC: 3321 3322 Gray iron ingot molds, cast; malleable iron foundries

(G-11412)
MCCULLOUGH INDUSTRIES INC
13047 County Road 175 (43326-9022)
P.O. Box 222 (43326-0222)
PHONE..................................419 673-0767
Stephen McCullough, *CEO*
Donna Morrison, *Sales Executive*
Bob Osbun, *Manager*
Cathy Rogers, *Manager*
Royce Van Scoit, *Supervisor*
EMP: 25 **EST:** 1969
SQ FT: 75,000
SALES (est): 8.2MM **Privately Held**
SIC: 3537 Mfg Industrial Trucks/Tractors

(G-11413)
MID OHIO WOOD RECYCLING INC
16289 State Route 31 (43326-8819)
PHONE..................................419 673-8470
Leo Smithberger, *Owner*
Carla Smithberger, *Vice Pres*
EMP: 8
SQ FT: 30,000
SALES: 650K **Privately Held**
SIC: 2448 Pallets, wood

(G-11414)
MOLDMAKERS INC
13608 Us Highway 68 (43326-9302)
P.O. Box 372 (43326-0372)
PHONE..................................419 673-0902
Gene R Longbrake, *President*
Shari K Longbrake, *Treasurer*
Kim Kaufman, *Admin Sec*
EMP: 10
SQ FT: 12,000
SALES (est): 1.3MM **Privately Held**
WEB: www.moldmakersinc.com
SIC: 3544 3089 Special dies & tools; injection molding of plastics

(G-11415)
MORTON BUILDINGS INC
Also Called: Morton Buildings Plant
14483 State Route 31 (43326-9055)
P.O. Box 223 (43326-0223)
PHONE..................................419 675-2311
Paul Hudson, *General Mgr*
Karen Baker, *Plant Mgr*
Marc Hale, *Engineer*
Garry Shirk, *Manager*
EMP: 70
SALES (corp-wide): 463.7MM **Privately Held**
SIC: 3448 5039 2452 Farm & utility buildings; prefabricated structures; prefabricated wood buildings
PA: Morton Buildings, Inc.
252 W Adams St
Morton IL 61550
800 447-7436

(G-11416)
NALCON READY MIX INC
12484 State Route 701 (43326-9225)
P.O. Box 120, Findlay (45839-0120)
PHONE..................................419 422-4341
Matthew R Pfirsch, *President*
EMP: 5
SALES (est): 293.5K
SALES (corp-wide): 3.2B **Privately Held**
WEB: www.natlime.com
SIC: 3273 Ready-mixed concrete
PA: The National Lime And Stone Company
551 Lake Cascade Pkwy
Findlay OH 45840
419 422-4341

(G-11417)
OCCIDENTAL CHEMICAL DUREZ
13717 Us Highway 68 (43326-9590)
PHONE..................................419 675-5300
Bill Bazell, *Principal*
▲ **EMP:** 8
SALES (est): 1MM **Privately Held**
SIC: 2819 Industrial inorganic chemicals

(G-11418)
PRECISION STRIP INC
190 Bales Rd (43326)
PHONE..................................419 674-4186
Don Bornhorst, *Branch Mgr*
EMP: 180
SALES (corp-wide): 11.5B **Publicly Held**
WEB: www.precision-strip.com
SIC: 4225 3341 General warehousing & storage; secondary nonferrous metals
HQ: Precision Strip Inc.
86 S Ohio St
Minster OH 45865
419 628-2343

(G-11419)
RADIO HOSPITAL
30 N Main St (43326-1552)
PHONE..................................419 679-1103
David Pearson, *Branch Mgr*
EMP: 5
SALES (corp-wide): 1.3MM **Privately Held**
SIC: 3663 Cellular radio telephone
PA: Radio Hospital
2308 Harding Hwy
Lima OH 45804
419 225-9202

GEOGRAPHIC SECTION

Kettlersville - Shelby County (G-11445)

(G-11420)
RAY BARNES NEWSPAPER INC (PA)
Also Called: Kenton Times
201 E Columbus St 207 (43326-1583)
P.O. Box 230 (43326-0230)
PHONE..................................419 674-4066
Charles Barnes, *President*
Kendrick Jesionowski, *Editor*
Jeff Barnes, *Vice Pres*
Judith K Barnes, *Treasurer*
EMP: 4
SQ FT: 5,600
SALES (est): 8.7MM **Privately Held**
WEB: www.kentontimes.com
SIC: 2711 Job printing & newspaper publishing combined; newspapers, publishing & printing

(G-11421)
ROBINSON FIN MACHINES INC
13670 Us Highway 68 (43326-9302)
PHONE..................................419 674-4152
Ruth A Haushalter, *President*
David Haushalter, *Vice Pres*
Sheryl Haushalter, *Vice Pres*
▲ **EMP:** 46
SQ FT: 27,000
SALES (est): 11.6MM **Privately Held**
WEB: www.robfin.com
SIC: 3444 Sheet metalwork

(G-11422)
SCIOTO SIGN CO INC
6047 Us Highway 68 (43326-9218)
PHONE..................................419 673-1261
Sandra A Pruden, *Ch of Bd*
Shawn Moore, *President*
Ronald Klesmit, *Manager*
EMP: 30
SQ FT: 52,500
SALES (est): 4.8MM **Privately Held**
WEB: www.sciotosigns.com
SIC: 3993 Signs, not made in custom sign painting shops; advertising novelties

(G-11423)
SPECIALTY PALLET ENTPS LLC
18031 State Route 309 (43326-9541)
PHONE..................................419 673-0247
Russ Cahill, *Principal*
EMP: 4
SALES (est): 496.2K **Privately Held**
SIC: 2448 Wood pallets & skids

(G-11424)
SPECIALTY STEEL SOLUTIONS
14574 State Route 292 (43326-9063)
PHONE..................................567 674-0011
Jonathan Diem, *Principal*
EMP: 4
SALES (est): 561.8K **Privately Held**
SIC: 3441 Fabricated structural metal

(G-11425)
SUPERIOR MACHINE TOOL INC
13606 Us Highway 68 (43326-9302)
PHONE..................................419 675-2363
Bill Clum, *President*
Richard L Rapp, *President*
Brad Clum, *Prgrmr*
EMP: 10
SQ FT: 7,200
SALES (est): 650K **Privately Held**
SIC: 3599 Machine shop, jobbing & repair

Kettering
Montgomery County

(G-11426)
ACCO BRANDS USA LLC
Mead Products
4751 Hempstead Station Dr (45429-5165)
PHONE..................................937 495-6323
Eric Brecht, *Technology*
Maria Pasquel, *Art Dir*
Kevin McNulty, *Creative Dir*
Katie Guggenbiller, *Graphic Designe*
EMP: 1264
SALES (corp-wide): 1.9B **Publicly Held**
SIC: 3089 Injection molding of plastics

HQ: Acco Brands Usa Llc
4 Corporate Dr
Lake Zurich IL 60047
800 222-6462

(G-11427)
BWI CHASSIS DYNAMICS NA INC
3100 Research Blvd (45420-4022)
PHONE..................................937 455-5100
Jeff Zhao, *Branch Mgr*
EMP: 13
SALES (corp-wide): 7.3MM **Privately Held**
SIC: 3714 Motor vehicle parts & accessories
HQ: Bwi Chassis Dynamics (Na), Inc.
12501 Grand River Rd
Brighton MI 48116
937 455-5308

(G-11428)
BWI NORTH AMERICA INC
Ahg - Global Ride Dynamics
3100 Res Blvd Ste 210 (45420)
PHONE..................................937 455-5190
Thomas P Gold, *Branch Mgr*
EMP: 130
SALES (corp-wide): 7.3MM **Privately Held**
SIC: 3714 Motor vehicle parts & accessories
HQ: Bwi North America Inc.
3100 Res Blvd Ste 240
Kettering OH 45420

(G-11429)
BWI NORTH AMERICA INC (DH)
Also Called: Bwi Group
3100 Res Blvd Ste 240 (45420)
PHONE..................................937 253-1130
Zhong Wang, *President*
Izabela Fiszer, *Purch Mgr*
Michael Hurtt, *Chief Engr*
David Barta, *Engineer*
Darin Dellinger, *Engineer*
▲ **EMP:** 20
SQ FT: 60,000
SALES (est): 50.6MM
SALES (corp-wide): 7.3MM **Privately Held**
SIC: 3714 5511 Motor vehicle parts & accessories; new & used car dealers
HQ: Beijing West Industries Co., Ltd.
No.85 Puan Road, Doudian Town,
Fangshan District
Beijing 10242
105 753-7300

(G-11430)
COMPOSITE TECHNICAL SVCS LLC
Also Called: CTS
2000 Composite Dr (45420-1493)
PHONE..................................937 660-3783
Deborah Goenner, *Accounting Mgr*
Charlene Kneer, *Office Mgr*
Enrico Ferri,
EMP: 5
SQ FT: 1,580
SALES (est): 804.6K **Privately Held**
SIC: 2821 Polyethylene resins; epoxy resins

(G-11431)
EASTMAN KODAK COMPANY
3100 Research Blvd # 250 (45420-4019)
PHONE..................................937 259-3000
Bonnie Saravullo, *Branch Mgr*
EMP: 20
SALES (corp-wide): 1.3B **Publicly Held**
SIC: 3861 Photographic equipment & supplies
PA: Eastman Kodak Company
343 State St
Rochester NY 14650
585 724-4000

(G-11432)
GREENE FUEL PLAZA INC
3151 E Dorothy Ln (45420-3819)
PHONE..................................937 532-4826
Jagtar Singh, *Principal*
EMP: 3
SALES (est): 208.7K **Privately Held**
SIC: 2869 Fuels

(G-11433)
INFINITY TRICHOLOGY CENTER
5250 Far Hills Ave (45429-2382)
PHONE..................................937 281-0555
Nancy Bellard, *Vice Pres*
EMP: 5
SALES (est): 327.3K **Privately Held**
SIC: 3845 Laser systems & equipment, medical

(G-11434)
MIDMARK CORPORATION (PA)
1700 S Patterson Blvd # 400 (45409-2141)
PHONE..................................937 526-3662
Anne Eiting Klamar, *CEO*
Greg Blackmore, *COO*
Mike Walker, *COO*
Bill Zulauf, *Mfg Dir*
Max Geittmann, *Project Mgr*
◆ **EMP:** 600 **EST:** 1915
SQ FT: 400,000
SALES (est): 327.4MM **Privately Held**
WEB: www.midmark.com
SIC: 3648 3842 3843 2542 Lighting equipment; stretchers; dental equipment & supplies; partitions & fixtures, except wood; operating tables

(G-11435)
NANOSPERSE LLC
2000 Composite Dr (45420-1493)
PHONE..................................937 296-5030
James Hartings, *Opers Mgr*
Arthur Fritts,
▼ **EMP:** 9
SQ FT: 10,000
SALES (est): 1.4MM **Privately Held**
WEB: www.nanosperse.com
SIC: 3087 2891 2851 2821 Custom compound purchased resins; epoxy adhesives; epoxy coatings; epoxy resins

(G-11436)
NANOTECHLABS INC (PA)
Also Called: Buckeye Composites
2000 Composite Dr (45420-1493)
PHONE..................................937 297-9518
Jessica Ravine, *CEO*
Richard Czerw, *Principal*
EMP: 13
SALES (est): 1.5MM **Privately Held**
SIC: 3955 Carbon paper & inked ribbons

(G-11437)
NCR INTERNATIONAL INC (HQ)
1700 S Patterson Blvd (45409-2140)
PHONE..................................937 445-5000
Gerald Schul, *Engineer*
John Boudreau, *Treasurer*
Bob Milanesi, *Sales Staff*
Joseph Stuber, *Consultant*
Linda M Sherman, *Director*
EMP: 6 **EST:** 1980
SALES (est): 2.3MM
SALES (corp-wide): 6.4B **Publicly Held**
SIC: 3575 3578 7371 7374 Computer terminals; calculating & accounting equipment; custom computer programming services; data processing & preparation
PA: Ncr Corporation
864 Spring St Nw
Atlanta GA 30308
937 445-5000

(G-11438)
NORTH AMERICAN RESEARCH CORP
1700 S Patterson Blvd (45409-2140)
PHONE..................................937 445-5000
Jonathan Hoak, *Principal*
EMP: 3
SALES (est): 19.6K
SALES (corp-wide): 6.4B **Publicly Held**
WEB: www.ncr.com
SIC: 3571 3578 Electronic computers; calculating & accounting equipment
PA: Ncr Corporation
864 Spring St Nw
Atlanta GA 30308
937 445-5000

(G-11439)
OHIO LAB PHARMA LLC
4738 Gateway Cir J184 (45440-1724)
PHONE..................................484 522-2601
Ghassan Alshami, *Manager*

EMP: 5
SALES (est): 443.6K **Privately Held**
SIC: 2834 Pharmaceutical preparations

(G-11440)
RESONETICS LLC
Also Called: Mound Laser Photonics Center
2941 College Dr (45420-1172)
PHONE..................................937 865-4070
Tom Burns, *CEO*
Jodi Wolfe, *QC Mgr*
Kevin Hartke, *CTO*
EMP: 63 **Privately Held**
SIC: 3699 3841 Laser systems & equipment; medical instruments & equipment, blood & bone work
PA: Resonetics, Llc
44 Simon St
Nashua NH 03060

(G-11441)
ROTAIRTECH INC
4668 Gateway Cir (45440-1714)
PHONE..................................937 435-8178
Mark D Swinford, *President*
EMP: 4
SALES (est): 293.7K **Privately Held**
SIC: 3545 Tools & accessories for machine tools

(G-11442)
TENNECO AUTOMOTIVE OPER CO INC
2555 Woodman Dr (45420-1487)
PHONE..................................937 781-4940
Mike Andreatta, *Branch Mgr*
EMP: 60
SQ FT: 18,000
SALES (corp-wide): 11.7B **Publicly Held**
WEB: www.tenneco-automotive.com
SIC: 3714 Motor vehicle engines & parts; shock absorbers, motor vehicle
HQ: Tenneco Automotive Operating Company, Inc.
500 N Field Dr
Lake Forest IL 60045
847 482-5000

(G-11443)
WESTROCK MWV LLC
Also Called: Meadwestvaco
4751 Hempstead Station Dr (45429-5165)
PHONE..................................937 495-6323
Neil McLachlan, *Branch Mgr*
EMP: 240
SALES (corp-wide): 16.2B **Publicly Held**
WEB: www.meadwestvaco.com
SIC: 2631 Paperboard mills
HQ: Westrock Mwv, Llc
501 S 5th St
Richmond VA 23219
804 444-1000

(G-11444)
XERION ADVANCED BATTERY CORP
3100 Res Blvd Ste 320 (45420)
PHONE..................................720 229-0697
John Busbee, *President*
Paul Braun, *Principal*
Christopher Kolb, *Exec VP*
EMP: 10 **EST:** 2012
SALES (est): 1.1MM **Privately Held**
SIC: 3691 Batteries, rechargeable

Kettlersville
Shelby County

(G-11445)
ROETTGER HARDWOOD INC
17066 Kettlersville Rd (45336)
PHONE..................................937 693-6811
Viola Roettger, *President*
EMP: 12 **EST:** 1947
SQ FT: 74,000
SALES: 1MM **Privately Held**
SIC: 2431 2434 Millwork; wood kitchen cabinets

Kidron
Wayne County

(G-11446)
GERBER FARM DIVISION INC
5889 Kidron Rd (44636)
PHONE..................................800 362-7381
John R Metzger, *President*
Kelly Mora, *Human Res Mgr*
Sue Gerber, *Administration*
EMP: 7
SALES (est): 720.1K **Privately Held**
SIC: 2015 Chicken, processed: fresh

(G-11447)
GERBER WOOD PRODUCTS INC
6075 Kidron Rd (44636)
P.O. Box 250 (44636-0250)
PHONE..................................330 857-3901
Steve Gerber, *President*
Jerry Staples, *Plant Mgr*
Eldon Gerber, *Admin Sec*
EMP: 9
SALES (est): 1MM **Privately Held**
WEB: www.gerberwood.com
SIC: 3993 3999 Advertising novelties; plaques, picture, laminated

Killbuck
Holmes County

(G-11448)
BAKERWELL INC (PA)
10420 County Road 620 (44637-9728)
P.O. Box 425 (44637-0425)
PHONE..................................330 276-2161
W Rex Baker, *President*
Robert K Baker, *CFO*
EMP: 21
SQ FT: 126,000
SALES (est): 5.8MM **Privately Held**
SIC: 1311 1389 Crude petroleum production; servicing oil & gas wells

(G-11449)
BAKERWELL SERVICE RIGS INC (HQ)
10420 County Road 620 (44637-9728)
P.O. Box 425 (44637-0425)
PHONE..................................330 276-2161
W Rex Baker, *President*
Jeffrey Baker, *Corp Secy*
Andrew Baker, *Vice Pres*
EMP: 18
SALES (est): 1.4MM
SALES (corp-wide): 5.8MM **Privately Held**
SIC: 1381 Service well drilling
PA: Bakerwell, Inc.
10420 County Road 620
Killbuck OH 44637
330 276-2161

(G-11450)
CROW WORKS LLC
179 Straits Ln (44637-9549)
PHONE..................................888 811-2769
Dennis Blankemeyer, *President*
Denise Blankemeyer, *Vice Pres*
Belinda Hughes, *CFO*
EMP: 50
SQ FT: 4,800
SALES (est): 14MM **Privately Held**
SIC: 2521 2599 Wood office furniture; bar, restaurant & cafeteria furniture; hotel furniture

(G-11451)
DANIELS AMISH COLLECTION LLC
100 Straits Ln (44637-9549)
PHONE..................................330 276-0110
Christopher Karman, *Branch Mgr*
EMP: 120
SALES (est): 3.1MM
SALES (corp-wide): 20MM **Privately Held**
SIC: 2519 Fiberglass furniture, household: padded or plain

PA: Daniel's Amish Collection, Llc
9190 Massillon Rd
Dundee OH 44624
330 359-0400

(G-11452)
JH WOODWORKING LLC
11259 Township Road 71 (44637-9444)
PHONE..................................330 276-7600
Joni Hostetler, *Principal*
EMP: 4 **EST:** 2011
SALES (est): 440.9K **Privately Held**
SIC: 2431 Millwork

(G-11453)
KILLBUCK OILFIELD SERVICES
9277 Township Road 92 (44637-9707)
PHONE..................................330 276-6706
Paul R Baker, *Partner*
Robert P Baker, *Partner*
Roger Baker, *Partner*
EMP: 4
SALES: 96.5K **Privately Held**
SIC: 1389 Oil field services; gas field services

(G-11454)
SHREINER SOLE CO INC
1 Taylor Dr (44637)
P.O. Box 347 (44637-0347)
PHONE..................................330 276-6135
David Shreiner, *President*
Donna Shreiner, *Admin Sec*
▲ **EMP:** 10
SQ FT: 56,750
SALES: 500K **Privately Held**
WEB: www.shreinerco.com
SIC: 3069 3061 Soles, boot or shoe: rubber, composition or fiber; mechanical rubber goods

(G-11455)
WILSON CABINET CO
Straits Industrial Park (44637)
P.O. Box 305 (44637-0305)
PHONE..................................330 276-8711
Carl De Maria, *President*
Rebecca Stover, *Corp Secy*
EMP: 35 **EST:** 1950
SQ FT: 75,000
SALES: 3.5MM **Privately Held**
WEB: www.wilsoncabinet.com
SIC: 2434 Vanities, bathroom: wood

(G-11456)
WILSONS COUNTRY CREATIONS
13248 County Road 6 (44637-9434)
PHONE..................................330 377-4190
Tom Wilson, *Owner*
EMP: 13
SQ FT: 3,500
SALES (est): 1.5MM **Privately Held**
WEB: www.wilsoncc.com
SIC: 5199 5261 3272 Statuary; lawn ornaments; concrete products

Kimbolton
Guernsey County

(G-11457)
SIMONDS INTERNATIONAL LLC
76000 Old Twenty One Rd (43749-9610)
PHONE..................................978 424-0100
John Fogle, *Branch Mgr*
EMP: 47
SALES (corp-wide): 88MM **Privately Held**
WEB: www.simondsinternational.com
SIC: 3423 5251 Hand & edge tools; tools
HQ: Simonds International L.L.C.
135 Intervale Rd
Fitchburg MA 01420
978 343-3731

Kingston
Ross County

(G-11458)
GT MACHINE & FAB
16655 Charleston Pike (45644-9584)
PHONE..................................740 701-9607
Melissa Congrove, *Principal*
EMP: 3
SALES (est): 122.5K **Privately Held**
SIC: 3541 Machine tools, metal cutting type

Kingsville
Ashtabula County

(G-11459)
HYDRANT HAT LLC
5759 S Wright St (44048-5804)
PHONE..................................440 224-1007
David Laugen, *EMP:* 3
SALES (est): 215.1K **Privately Held**
WEB: www.hydrant-hat.com
SIC: 3089 Plastic containers, except foam

(G-11460)
LYONS
5231 State Route 193 (44048-7713)
P.O. Box 554 (44048-0554)
PHONE..................................440 224-0676
Elijah Lyons, *Owner*
EMP: 6
SALES (est): 422.4K **Privately Held**
SIC: 3715 Truck trailers

(G-11461)
NELSON SAND & GRAVEL INC
5720 State Route 193 (44048-9715)
P.O. Box 466 (44048-0466)
PHONE..................................440 224-0198
Thomas Nelson, *President*
Donna J Nelson, *Corp Secy*
EMP: 10
SQ FT: 6,000
SALES (est): 1.1MM **Privately Held**
SIC: 1442 Common sand mining; gravel mining

(G-11462)
R W SIDLEY INC
3062 E Center St (44068)
PHONE..................................440 224-2664
Robert Buescher, *President*
EMP: 15
SALES (est): 1MM **Privately Held**
SIC: 3273 Ready-mixed concrete

Kinsman
Trumbull County

(G-11463)
BAYLOFF STMPED PDTS KNSMAN INC
8091 State Route 5 (44428-9628)
PHONE..................................330 876-4511
Richard Bayer, *President*
Rufus S Day Jr, *Principal*
Dixon Morgan, *Principal*
M E Newcomer, *Principal*
Dan Moore, *Vice Pres*
EMP: 80
SQ FT: 115,000
SALES (est): 14.6MM **Privately Held**
SIC: 3469 7692 3444 3315 Stamping metal for the trade; welding repair; sheet metalwork; steel wire & related products

(G-11464)
HANDLE LIGHT INC
5533 State Route 7 (44428-9751)
PHONE..................................330 772-8901
Daniel Bozzo, *President*
EMP: 9
SALES (est): 962.3K **Privately Held**
WEB: www.handlelight.com
SIC: 3559 Automotive maintenance equipment

(G-11465)
MCGILL SEPTIC TANK CO
8913 State St (44428-9706)
PHONE..................................330 876-2171
Charles McGill, *President*
James McElhinny, *Vice Pres*
EMP: 30
SQ FT: 10,000
SALES (est): 3.9MM **Privately Held**
SIC: 3272 2531 Concrete products, precast; public building & related furniture

(G-11466)
STRATTON CREEK WOOD WORKS LLC
5915 Burnett East Rd (44428-9757)
PHONE..................................330 876-0005
Bill Sandrock,
Kathy Marie,
EMP: 11
SALES (est): 1.5MM **Privately Held**
WEB: www.strattoncreek.com
SIC: 2431 Millwork

Kirtland
Lake County

(G-11467)
ENDURA PLASTICS INC
7955 Euclid Chardon Rd (44094-9014)
PHONE..................................440 951-4466
Mark Di Lillo, *President*
Susan Thomas, *Buyer*
Mary Kenny, *QC Mgr*
Don Kitchen, *Engineer*
Grant Edwards, *Sales Mgr*
EMP: 85 **EST:** 1961
SQ FT: 26,000
SALES (est): 14.5MM **Privately Held**
WEB: www.endura.com
SIC: 3089 3544 Injection molded finished plastic products; special dies, tools, jigs & fixtures

(G-11468)
EZSHRED LLC (PA)
7621 Euclid Chardon Rd (44094-8740)
P.O. Box 8, Chesterland (44026-0008)
PHONE..................................440 256-7640
Ronald Ray,
EMP: 5
SALES (est): 603.7K **Privately Held**
SIC: 5734 7371 7372 Computer software & accessories; computer software development & applications; publishers' computer software

(G-11469)
MIDWEST TELEMETRY INC
7935 Chardon Rd B7 (44094-9008)
PHONE..................................440 725-5718
Roger Rankin, *President*
EMP: 3 **EST:** 2012
SALES (est): 162.7K **Privately Held**
SIC: 8711 3825 Electrical or electronic engineering; instruments to measure electricity

(G-11470)
SPEC MASK OHIO LLC
7899 Euclid Chardon Rd (44094-9536)
PHONE..................................440 522-3055
Thomas Dicillo, *Principal*
Teresa Dicillo, *Principal*
EMP: 3 **EST:** 2010
SALES (est): 198.2K **Privately Held**
SIC: 2992 Lubricating oils & greases

(G-11471)
STEWART ACQUISITION LLC
Also Called: Endura Plastics
7955 Euclid Chardon Rd (44094-9014)
PHONE..................................800 376-4466
James Stewart, *President*
EMP: 30
SALES (corp-wide): 11.7MM **Privately Held**
SIC: 3089 Injection molding of plastics
PA: Stewart Acquisition Llc
2146 Enterprise Pkwy
Twinsburg OH 44087
330 963-0322

GEOGRAPHIC SECTION

(G-11472)
VILLAGE OUTDOORS
7875 Euclid Chardon Rd (44094)
PHONE.................................440 256-1172
Anne Difranco, *Owner*
Steve Blackburn, *Sales Staff*
EMP: 5
SALES (est): 703.3K **Privately Held**
SIC: 3524 Lawn & garden equipment

(G-11473)
WHOLESALE CHANNEL LETTERS
8603 Euclid Chardon Rd (44094-9586)
PHONE.................................440 256-3200
Dale Heigley, *Owner*
EMP: 8
SALES (est): 732K **Privately Held**
WEB: www.wholesalesignsuperstore.com
SIC: 3993 Neon signs

Kitts Hill
Lawrence County

(G-11474)
DAVID ADKINS LOGGING
1260 Township Road 256 (45645-8885)
PHONE.................................740 533-0297
David A Adkins, *Admin Sec*
EMP: 6
SALES (est): 476K **Privately Held**
SIC: 2411 Logging camps & contractors

(G-11475)
MILLWRGHT WLDG FBRICATION SVCS
1590 County Road 105 (45645-8632)
PHONE.................................740 533-1510
Mike Moore, *President*
Stephen H Thompson, *Vice Pres*
EMP: 11
SALES (est): 443.1K **Privately Held**
SIC: 7692 Welding repair

La Rue
Marion County

(G-11476)
POWERMOUNT SYSTEMS INC
1602 Larue Marseilles Rd (43332-8928)
PHONE.................................740 499-4330
Ronald Abbott, *Principal*
EMP: 9
SALES (est): 983.9K **Privately Held**
SIC: 3355 Extrusion ingot, aluminum: made in rolling mills

(G-11477)
VICTORY STORE FIXTURES INC
3153 Winnemac Pike S (43332-8818)
PHONE.................................740 499-3494
EMP: 16
SQ FT: 1,200
SALES (est): 1.3MM **Privately Held**
SIC: 3083 Assembly & Fabrication Of Laminated Store Fixtures

Lagrange
Lorain County

(G-11478)
COLONIAL CABINETS INC
337 S Center St (44050-9014)
P.O. Box 62 (44050-0062)
PHONE.................................440 355-9663
Jerry Duelley, *President*
Barry Ickes, *Vice Pres*
Kenneth Sooy, *Treasurer*
EMP: 13
SQ FT: 10,000
SALES: 900K **Privately Held**
SIC: 2434 Wood kitchen cabinets

(G-11479)
DYNAMIC MACHINE CONCEPTS INC
Also Called: D M C
233 Commerce Dr Unit A (44050-9227)
PHONE.................................216 470-0270
Andrew Miller, *President*
Holly Miller, *Vice Pres*
EMP: 4
SQ FT: 7,500
SALES: 600K **Privately Held**
WEB: www.webservertools.com
SIC: 3599 Custom machinery

(G-11480)
FREAK-N-FRIES INC
204 Taylor Blvd (44050-9304)
PHONE.................................440 453-1877
Rob Dirne, *President*
EMP: 3
SALES (est): 217.4K **Privately Held**
SIC: 2015 Sausage, poultry

(G-11481)
GREY HAWK GOLF LLC
665 U S Grant St (44050-8508)
PHONE.................................440 355-4844
David D Benadetto, *Mng Member*
EMP: 3
SALES (est): 210.9K **Privately Held**
SIC: 3949 Sporting & athletic goods

(G-11482)
GREY HAWK GOLF CLUB
665 U S Grant St (44050-8508)
PHONE.................................440 355-4844
David De Benadetto, *Owner*
EMP: 50
SALES (est): 2.8MM **Privately Held**
WEB: www.greyhawkgolf.com
SIC: 3949 Shafts, golf club

(G-11483)
INSERVCO INC (DH)
Also Called: Staci Lagrange
110 Commerce Dr (44050-9491)
P.O. Box 106 (44050-0106)
PHONE.................................847 855-9600
Jere Simonson, *Corp Secy*
Greg Hebson, *Vice Pres*
Mike Nargi, *Vice Pres*
▲ **EMP:** 71
SQ FT: 26,300
SALES (est): 17.4MM **Privately Held**
WEB: www.inservco.com
SIC: 3679 Electronic circuits
HQ: Staci Corp.
110 Commerce Dr
Lagrange OH 44050
440 355-5102

(G-11484)
JEHM TECHNOLOGIES INC
612 N Center St Ste 201 (44050-9000)
P.O. Box 202, Amherst (44001-0202)
PHONE.................................440 355-5558
Jeff Pufnock, *Principal*
EMP: 5
SALES (est): 385.1K **Privately Held**
SIC: 7372 Prepackaged software

(G-11485)
KECK ENGINEERING INC
39610 Whitney Rd (44050-9753)
PHONE.................................440 355-9855
Reinhard Keck, *President*
EMP: 7 **EST:** 1966
SALES (est): 506.7K **Privately Held**
WEB: www.keckengineering.com
SIC: 3599 Machine shop, jobbing & repair

(G-11486)
LA GRANGE ELEC ASSEMBLIES CO
349 S Center St (44050-9014)
P.O. Box 555 (44050-0555)
PHONE.................................440 355-5388
W Robin Mc Clain, *President*
Richard M Mc Clain, *Vice Pres*
Don Tolbert, *Plant Mgr*
EMP: 22
SQ FT: 40,000
SALES (est): 2.5MM **Privately Held**
WEB: www.lagrangeelectrical.com
SIC: 3679 Harness assemblies for electronic use: wire or cable; power supplies, all types: static

(G-11487)
M C INDUSTRIES INC
111 Commerce Dr (44050-9491)
P.O. Box 116 (44050-0116)
PHONE.................................440 355-4040
Dave Mick, *President*
Karen Mick, *Vice Pres*
EMP: 15
SQ FT: 10,000
SALES (est): 1.7MM **Privately Held**
SIC: 3452 Bolts, nuts, rivets & washers

(G-11488)
MADER MACHINE CO INC
Also Called: Mader Dampers
422 Commerce Dr E (44050-9316)
PHONE.................................440 355-4505
Lon Zeager, *President*
Nancy Zeager, *Corp Secy*
Lon James Zeager, *Vice Pres*
EMP: 32 **EST:** 1963
SQ FT: 45,000
SALES (est): 10.4MM **Privately Held**
SIC: 3822 Damper operators: pneumatic, thermostatic, electric; controls, combination limit & fan

(G-11489)
MICRON MANUFACTURING INC
186 Commerce Dr (44050-8926)
PHONE.................................440 355-4200
Mark A Zupan, *President*
Anne Zupan, *Vice Pres*
Scott Slosier, *Opers Mgr*
Sue Gessner, *Purch Dir*
Bill Stewart, *Engineer*
EMP: 60
SQ FT: 50,000
SALES (est): 15.8MM **Privately Held**
WEB: www.micmfg.com
SIC: 3541 Machine tools, metal cutting type

(G-11490)
NEW AGE DESIGN & TOOL INC
162 Commerce Dr (44050-8926)
PHONE.................................440 355-5400
Glen Allen, *President*
Donald Youngblood, *Corp Secy*
EMP: 15
SQ FT: 10,000
SALES: 1.9MM **Privately Held**
SIC: 3312 Tool & die steel

(G-11491)
PANEL MASTER LLC
191 Commerce Dr (44050-8926)
PHONE.................................440 355-4442
Cheryl Watts, *Finance Mgr*
Ridley Watts, *Mng Member*
EMP: 30
SQ FT: 24,000
SALES (est): 6.9MM **Privately Held**
WEB: www.panelmaster.com
SIC: 3613 3625 Control panels, electric; relays & industrial controls

(G-11492)
QUALITY METAL PRODUCTS INC
210 Commerce Dr (44050-9492)
PHONE.................................440 355-6165
Mark Duplata, *President*
Robert Yunker, *President*
Mark Duplaga, *Vice Pres*
Kathleen Norton Fox, *Services*
EMP: 5
SQ FT: 5,000
SALES (est): 624.5K **Privately Held**
SIC: 3599 3469 Machine shop, jobbing & repair; metal stampings

(G-11493)
SLADE GARDNER
233 Commerce Dr Unit B (44050-9227)
P.O. Box 595 (44050-0595)
PHONE.................................440 355-8015
Mark Pinto, *Owner*
EMP: 3
SALES (est): 429.6K **Privately Held**
SIC: 3542 7692 Machine tools, metal forming type; welding repair

(G-11494)
TRIMLINE DIE CORPORATION
421 Commerce Dr E (44050-9316)
P.O. Box 66 (44050-0066)
PHONE.................................440 355-6900
Dave Gido, *President*
EMP: 20
SQ FT: 10,000
SALES (est): 4.3MM **Privately Held**
WEB: www.trimlinedie.com
SIC: 3544 Special dies & tools

(G-11495)
TRUE TURN INDUSTRIES
233 Commerce Dr Unit D (44050-9227)
PHONE.................................440 355-6256
Joe Maloney, *Owner*
EMP: 3
SALES: 500K **Privately Held**
SIC: 3469 Machine parts, stamped or pressed metal

(G-11496)
VEXOS ELECTRONIC MFG SVCS
110 Commerce Dr (44050-9491)
PHONE.................................855 711-3227
Paul Jona, *President*
Greg Collins, *Senior VP*
EMP: 7
SALES (est): 335K **Privately Held**
SIC: 3672 Printed circuit boards

(G-11497)
VIRGILS KITCHENS INC
18800 Whitehead Rd (44050-9434)
PHONE.................................440 355-5058
James Rader, *President*
Barb Rader, *Corp Secy*
Virgil Rader, *Vice Pres*
EMP: 9 **EST:** 1961
SQ FT: 5,000
SALES (est): 346.2K **Privately Held**
SIC: 2434 5712 Wood kitchen cabinets; cabinet work, custom; cabinets, except custom made: kitchen

Lake Milton
Mahoning County

(G-11498)
DISCIPLE TOOL & MACHINE
189 Se River Rd (44429-9613)
PHONE.................................330 503-7879
John E Lorent, *Owner*
EMP: 5
SALES (est): 333.2K **Privately Held**
SIC: 3544 Special dies, tools, jigs & fixtures

Lakemore
Summit County

(G-11499)
FOUR GENERATIONS INC
Also Called: Ideal Baking Co
1320 Main St (44250-9805)
PHONE.................................330 784-2243
Greg Godar, *President*
EMP: 7 **EST:** 1920
SQ FT: 10,000
SALES (est): 665K **Privately Held**
WEB: www.idealbakeryequipment.com
SIC: 2051 Bread, cake & related products

(G-11500)
ROBAN INC
1319 Main St (44250-9803)
P.O. Box 526 (44250-0526)
PHONE.................................330 794-1059
Karen Medzi, *President*
EMP: 9
SQ FT: 7,000
SALES: 1MM **Privately Held**
WEB: www.robansignage.com
SIC: 2796 7336 3479 Engraving platemaking services; silk screen design; etching on metals; etching, photochemical

Lakeside
Ottawa County

(G-11501)
CUSTOM CANVAS & BOAT REPAIR
Also Called: Custom Canvas & Upholstery
29 S Bridge Rd (43440-9483)
PHONE..................419 732-3314
Shawn Harrison, *President*
Von Ellis, *Vice Pres*
David Walter, *Treasurer*
Carol Ellis, *Admin Sec*
EMP: 11
SQ FT: 4,800
SALES: 500K **Privately Held**
SIC: 2394 Liners & covers, fabric: made from purchased materials

Lakeside Marblehead
Ottawa County

(G-11502)
FINE PRINT LLC
508 Oak Ave (43440-1744)
PHONE..................419 702-7087
Beverly Bartczak, *Owner*
EMP: 4
SALES (est): 408.5K **Privately Held**
SIC: 2752 Commercial printing, lithographic

(G-11503)
HEADSET WHOLESALERS LTD
2411 S Commodore Ct (43440-9825)
PHONE..................419 798-5200
Marilyn Minto,
EMP: 2
SALES (est): 1MM **Privately Held**
SIC: 3661 Headsets, telephone

Lakeview
Logan County

(G-11504)
DRAIN PRODUCTS LLC (PA)
13051 County Road 301 (43331-9502)
PHONE..................419 230-4549
Jonathan Myers, *Owner*
EMP: 4
SQ FT: 20,000
SALES: 600K **Privately Held**
SIC: 5162 3084 Plastics materials & basic shapes; plastics pipe

(G-11505)
UNITED TOOL AND MACHINE INC
490 N Main St (43331-9398)
P.O. Box 307 (43331-0307)
PHONE..................937 843-5603
Claude Heintz, *President*
Sylvia Heintz, *Treasurer*
Chris Shrader, *Admin Sec*
EMP: 13 **EST:** 1973
SQ FT: 41,000
SALES (est): 2.7MM **Privately Held**
WEB: www.united-tm.com
SIC: 3599 Machine shop, jobbing & repair

Lakeville
Holmes County

(G-11506)
INTERDEN INDUSTRIES INC
2377 County Road 175 (44638-9610)
PHONE..................419 368-9011
Terra Studer, *President*
Boett Grogen, *Vice Pres*
EMP: 5
SALES: 280K **Privately Held**
SIC: 1381 1389 Drilling oil & gas wells; oil & gas wells: building, repairing & dismantling

Lakewood
Cuyahoga County

(G-11507)
717 INC
Also Called: 717 Ink
13000 Athens Ave Ste 110 (44107-6256)
PHONE..................440 925-0402
Joseph Haddad, *President*
Jonn Horning, *Administration*
EMP: 7
SALES: 150K **Privately Held**
SIC: 2262 Screen printing: manmade fiber & silk broadwoven fabrics

(G-11508)
ABC LETTERING & EMBROIDERY
13727 Madison Ave (44107-4744)
PHONE..................216 321-8338
Michael J Martin, *Owner*
EMP: 5
SALES: 150K **Privately Held**
SIC: 2396 Screen printing on fabric articles

(G-11509)
ALLENBAUGH FOODS LLC
14305 Bayes Ave (44107-6011)
PHONE..................216 952-3984
Craig Allenbaugh, *Principal*
EMP: 3
SALES (est): 252.9K **Privately Held**
SIC: 2099 Food preparations

(G-11510)
AMERICAN ICON DEFENSE LTD
1510 W Clifton Blvd (44107-3311)
PHONE..................216 233-5184
Ian Conant, *Principal*
EMP: 4
SALES (est): 387K **Privately Held**
SIC: 3812 Defense systems & equipment

(G-11511)
AMPLIFIED SOLAR INC
1453 Wayne Ave (44107-3422)
PHONE..................216 236-4225
Justin Walker, *President*
EMP: 4
SALES (est): 265.3K **Privately Held**
SIC: 3629 Electrical industrial apparatus

(G-11512)
BENSAN JEWELERS INC
Also Called: Broestl & Wallis Fine Jewelers
14410 Madison Ave (44107-4513)
PHONE..................216 221-1434
Daniel D Wallis, *President*
Jeffery Broestl, *Admin Sec*
EMP: 7
SQ FT: 2,106
SALES (est): 999.5K **Privately Held**
WEB: www.broestlwallis.com
SIC: 5944 3911 7631 Jewelry, precious stones & precious metals; jewelry apparel; jewelry repair services

(G-11513)
BLUE COTTAGE BAKERY LLC
15612 Lake Ave (44107-1222)
PHONE..................216 221-9733
Carole Rojas, *Principal*
EMP: 4
SALES (est): 166.2K **Privately Held**
SIC: 2051 Bread, cake & related products

(G-11514)
CAHILL SERVICES INC
13000 Athens Ave Ste 104e (44107-6256)
P.O. Box 811132, Cleveland (44181-1132)
PHONE..................216 410-5595
Christine M Cahill, *Principal*
EMP: 4
SALES (est): 440.7K **Privately Held**
SIC: 2851 Removers & cleaners

(G-11515)
COMPUTER ENTERPRISE INC
Also Called: Enterprise Electric
1530 Saint Charles Ave (44107-4341)
PHONE..................216 228-7156
Vera Prete, *President*
Peter Prete, *Vice Pres*
EMP: 15
SALES (est): 1.3MM **Privately Held**
WEB: www.computerenterprise.com
SIC: 1731 7372 Computerized controls installation; computer installation; business oriented computer software

(G-11516)
EUCLID STEEL & WIRE INC
Also Called: ES&w
13000 Athens Ave Ste 101 (44107-6233)
PHONE..................216 731-6744
Donald J Anzells, *President*
Daniel R Corcoran, *Principal*
Charles D Mc Bride, *Principal*
T P Mc Mahon, *Principal*
EMP: 12
SQ FT: 10,400
SALES (est): 1.5MM **Privately Held**
SIC: 3315 Wire, steel: insulated or armored

(G-11517)
FERRY CAP & SET SCREW COMPANY (HQ)
13300 Bramley Ave (44107-6248)
PHONE..................216 649-7400
Joseph Mc Auliffe, *President*
Gerald O Mullin, *Corp Secy*
Donald E Johnson, *VP Sales*
▲ **EMP:** 175
SQ FT: 130,000
SALES (est): 100.7MM
SALES (corp-wide): 13.9B **Publicly Held**
WEB: www.ferrycap.com
SIC: 3452 Bolts, metal
PA: Stanley Black & Decker, Inc.
1000 Stanley Dr
New Britain CT 06053
860 225-5111

(G-11518)
GLASS FABRICATORS INC
2160 Halstead Ave (44107-6244)
P.O. Box 347251, Cleveland (44134-7251)
PHONE..................216 529-1919
Fax: 216 529-1922
EMP: 5
SQ FT: 28,000
SALES: 1MM **Privately Held**
SIC: 3211 Fabricates Glass

(G-11519)
HAWTHORNE WIRE LTD
13000 Athens Ave Ste 101 (44107-6233)
PHONE..................216 712-4747
Christopher Whiting, *President*
EMP: 13 **EST:** 2005
SALES (est): 2MM **Privately Held**
SIC: 3315 Wire & fabricated wire products

(G-11520)
HAWTHORNE WIRE SERVICES LTD
13000 Athens Ave Ste 101 (44107-6233)
PHONE..................216 712-4747
Christopher Whiting, *Principal*
EMP: 5
SALES (est): 909.6K **Privately Held**
SIC: 3315 Steel wire & related products

(G-11521)
INITIALLY YOURS
15028 Madison Ave (44107-4014)
PHONE..................216 228-4478
Gary Galauner, *Owner*
Richard Ebert, *Co-Owner*
Andy Hess, *Co-Owner*
EMP: 3
SALES: 60K **Privately Held**
WEB: www.initiallyyoursengravers.com
SIC: 5999 2395 Trophies & plaques; decorative & novelty stitching, for the trade

(G-11522)
INSTARIDE CLE LLC
15026 Madison Ave (44107-4014)
PHONE..................216 801-4542
Cliston Jackson, *CEO*
Nandee Jackson, *CFO*
EMP: 3
SALES: 50K **Privately Held**
SIC: 7372 Application computer software

(G-11523)
JOE THE PRINTER GUY LLC
1590 Parkwood Rd (44107-4739)
PHONE..................216 651-3880
Joseph E McHugh, *Principal*
EMP: 6 **EST:** 2008
SALES (est): 654.6K **Privately Held**
SIC: 2752 Commercial printing, lithographic

(G-11524)
LA DUA INC
17123 Hilliard Rd (44107-5428)
PHONE..................440 243-9600
Albert Kishman, *President*
Audry Kishman, *Chairman*
Kimber L Neuendorf, *Vice Pres*
EMP: 6
SQ FT: 2,400
SALES (est): 447.8K **Privately Held**
WEB: www.laduainc.com
SIC: 7336 2791 Commercial art & graphic design; typesetting

(G-11525)
LAKE ERIE INDUSTRIES LLC
13000 Athens Ave Ste 101 (44107-6233)
P.O. Box 771392 (44107-0057)
PHONE..................216 255-1867
Hugh J Campbell,
▲ **EMP:** 4
SALES: 750K **Privately Held**
SIC: 3451 Screw machine products

(G-11526)
LAKEWOOD OBSERVER INC
14900 Detroit Ave Ste 205 (44107-3922)
PHONE..................216 712-7070
Jim O'Bryan, *Principal*
EMP: 7
SALES (est): 363.1K **Privately Held**
SIC: 2711 Newspapers, publishing & printing

(G-11527)
MADISON PRESS INC
1381 Summit Ave (44107-2495)
PHONE..................216 521-3789
Alton Willcox, *President*
Frank Underwood, *Admin Sec*
EMP: 4
SQ FT: 1,500
SALES (est): 386.2K **Privately Held**
WEB: www.madisonpress.net
SIC: 2759 Letterpress printing

(G-11528)
MALLEYS CANDIES (PA)
Also Called: Malley's Chocolates
1685 Victoria Ave (44107-4054)
PHONE..................216 362-8700
William Malley, *President*
Mike Malley, *Principal*
Dan Malloy, *COO*
Daniel Malley, *Vice Pres*
Jason Smith, *Plant Supt*
▲ **EMP:** 101
SQ FT: 60,000
SALES (est): 53.5MM **Privately Held**
WEB: www.malleys.com
SIC: 5441 5451 2064 2068 Candy; nuts; ice cream (packaged); candy bars, including chocolate covered bars; chocolate candy, except solid chocolate; nuts: dried, dehydrated, salted or roasted; ice cream & ice milk; chocolate & cocoa products

(G-11529)
MCGAW TECHNOLOGY INC
17439 Lake Ave (44107-1147)
P.O. Box 26268, Cleveland (44126-0268)
PHONE..................216 521-3490
Mike McGraw, *President*
EMP: 3
SALES: 500K **Privately Held**
WEB: www.mcgawtech.com
SIC: 7372 Prepackaged software

(G-11530)
NEOGRAF SOLUTIONS LLC
11709 Madison Ave (44107-5230)
PHONE..................216 529-3777
Robert Reynolds, *President*
Brian Bartos, *Vice Pres*
EMP: 180

GEOGRAPHIC SECTION   Lancaster - Fairfield County (G-11557)

SALES (est): 1.6MM **Privately Held**
SIC: 3624 Electrodes, thermal & electrolytic uses: carbon, graphite
PA: Aterian Investment Partners, Lp
11 E 44th St Rm 1803
New York NY 10017

(G-11531)
NEXT STEP SOCKS LLC
2042 Richland Ave (44107-6002)
PHONE 216 534-8077
Mickey Haba, *Principal*
EMP: 3 EST: 2016
SALES (est): 86.2K **Privately Held**
SIC: 2252 Socks

(G-11532)
NORTON INDUSTRIES INC
1366 W 117th St (44107-3011)
PHONE 888 357-2345
Trisha Rhea, *President*
Alan Rhea, *Vice Pres*
Carlonna Gerber, *Accounting Mgr*
Jessica Archer, *Manager*
Eric Johnston, *Manager*
EMP: 25
SQ FT: 30,000
SALES: 8MM **Privately Held**
WEB: www.nortonceilings.com
SIC: 3646 2541 Ceiling systems, luminous; store fixtures, wood; display fixtures, wood

(G-11533)
PROCOMSOL LTD
13001 Athens Ave Ste 220 (44107-6246)
PHONE 216 221-1550
Jeffrey A Dobos, *Principal*
Irena Wasylyk, *Sales Staff*
EMP: 5
SALES (est): 910.6K **Privately Held**
SIC: 3661 3695 Modems; computer software tape & disks: blank, rigid & floppy

(G-11534)
RAD-CON INC (PA)
Also Called: Entec International Systems
13001 Athens Ave Ste 300 (44107-6246)
PHONE 440 871-5720
David R Blackman, *President*
Christopher Messina, *President*
Michael McDonald, *Vice Pres*
Sean McGreer, *Vice Pres*
EMP: 26
SQ FT: 6,000
SALES (est): 10MM **Privately Held**
WEB: www.rad-con.com
SIC: 8711 3567 Engineering services; industrial furnaces & ovens

(G-11535)
SENTRY PROTECTION LLC
Also Called: Sentry Protection Products
16927 Detroit Ave Ste 3 (44107-3642)
PHONE 216 228-3200
James Ryan, *Mng Member*
▼ **EMP:** 5 EST: 1998
SQ FT: 1,500
SALES (est): 877.7K **Privately Held**
WEB: www.sentrypro.com
SIC: 3089 Molding primary plastic

(G-11536)
VOLL HOCKEY INC
11820 Edgewater Dr # 418 (44107-1798)
PHONE 216 521-4625
Gregory Voloshen, *President*
Ann Miholovic, *Manager*
EMP: 3 EST: 1998
SQ FT: 250
SALES: 10K **Privately Held**
SIC: 3949 Sporting & athletic goods

(G-11537)
WESTERN RESERVE DISTILLERS LLC
14221 Madison Ave (44107-4509)
PHONE 330 780-9599
Kevin Thomas, *Mng Member*
Ann Thomas, *Mng Member*
EMP: 7 EST: 2014
SALES (est): 280.1K **Privately Held**
SIC: 2085 Distilled & blended liquors

Lancaster
Fairfield County

(G-11538)
ACCURATE MECHANICAL INC
566 Mill Park Dr (43130-7744)
PHONE 740 681-1332
EMP: 49
SALES (corp-wide): 26.3MM **Privately Held**
SIC: 5074 5063 3499 1711 Heating equipment (hydronic); electrical supplies; aerosol valves, metal; septic system construction
PA: Accurate Mechanical, Inc.
3001 River Rd
Chillicothe OH
740 775-5005

(G-11539)
AMERICAN PENNEKAMP MFG INC
1495 Longwood Dr Ne (43130-1373)
PHONE 740 687-0096
Robert Muckensturm, *Manager*
EMP: 3
SALES (corp-wide): 1.8MM **Privately Held**
SIC: 3496 Conveyor belts
PA: American Pennekamp Mfg, Inc
2502 Shelburn Rd
Millville NJ
856 327-5290

(G-11540)
ANCHI INC
Also Called: Anchor Hocking
1115 W 5th Ave (43130-2938)
PHONE 740 653-2527
Mark R Eichhorn, *CEO*
◆ **EMP:** 1500
SALES (est): 171.5MM
SALES (corp-wide): 682.6MM **Privately Held**
SIC: 3231 Products of purchased glass
HQ: Anchor Hocking, Llc
519 N Pierce Ave
Lancaster OH 43130

(G-11541)
ANCHOR HOCKING LLC (HQ)
Also Called: Anchor Hocking Company, The
519 N Pierce Ave (43130-2969)
PHONE 740 681-6478
Mark Eichhorn, *President*
Bert Filice, *Senior VP*
Joe Sundberg, *Senior VP*
Mark Hedstrom, *CFO*
◆ **EMP:** 1200
SALES (est): 446MM
SALES (corp-wide): 682.6MM **Privately Held**
WEB: www.anchor.com
SIC: 3229 3089 3411 3221 Tableware, glass or glass ceramic; cooking utensils, glass or glass ceramic; cups, plastic, except foam; plates, plastic; bottle caps, molded plastic; metal cans; glass containers
PA: The Oneida Group Inc
519 N Pierce Ave
Lancaster OH 43130
740 687-2500

(G-11542)
ANCHOR HOCKING LLC
Also Called: Anchor Hocking Company
1115 W 5th Ave (43130-2900)
PHONE 740 687-2500
EMP: 5
SALES (corp-wide): 682.6MM **Privately Held**
SIC: 3229 3089 3411 3221 Tableware, glass or glass ceramic; cups, plastic, except foam; metal cans; glass containers
HQ: Anchor Hocking, Llc
519 N Pierce Ave
Lancaster OH 43130

(G-11543)
ANCHOR HOCKING CONSMR GL CORP
1115 W 5th Ave (43130-2900)
PHONE 740 653-2527
Mark Eichorn, *President*
▼ **EMP:** 7
SALES (est): 1.5MM **Privately Held**
SIC: 3229 Glassware, art or decorative

(G-11544)
ANCHOR HOCKING GLASS COMPANY
Plant 1 1115 W Fifth Ave Nt St Pla (43130)
PHONE 740 681-6025
Mark Eichhorn, *President*
EMP: 3
SALES (est): 536.2K **Privately Held**
SIC: 5023 3263 2821 Glassware; commercial tableware or kitchen articles, fine earthenware; plastics materials & resins

(G-11545)
B & T WELDING AND MACHINE CO
423 S Mount Pleasant Ave (43130-3913)
P.O. Box 987 (43130-0987)
PHONE 740 687-1908
Alvin R Brown, *President*
Patricia Brown, *Vice Pres*
Darlene Baker, *Treasurer*
EMP: 6
SQ FT: 8,500
SALES (est): 733.2K **Privately Held**
SIC: 3599 Machine shop, jobbing & repair

(G-11546)
BABCOCK & WILCOX COMPANY
2600 E Main St (43130-8490)
P.O. Box 415 (43130-0415)
PHONE 740 687-6500
Chris McKeown, *Superintendent*
Mark Molnar, *Project Mgr*
Mark Meadows, *Materials Mgr*
Breck Hardy, *Purch Agent*
Adam Wharton, *Buyer*
EMP: 33
SALES (est): 9.9MM **Privately Held**
SIC: 3511 Turbines & turbine generator sets

(G-11547)
BAINTER MACHINING COMPANY (PA)
1230 Rainbow Dr Ne (43130-1137)
PHONE 740 653-2422
Daniel A Bainter, *President*
Reda L Bainter, *Corp Secy*
EMP: 21
SQ FT: 2,000
SALES: 600K **Privately Held**
SIC: 3444 3599 Sheet metalwork; machine shop, jobbing & repair

(G-11548)
BROOKE PRINTERS INC
Also Called: First Impressions Printing
358 Lincoln Ave Ste C (43130-3747)
P.O. Box 764 (43130-0764)
PHONE 614 235-6800
Gary N Brooke, *President*
EMP: 3
SQ FT: 1,800
SALES: 250K **Privately Held**
SIC: 2752 7334 Commercial printing, offset; photocopying & duplicating services

(G-11549)
BUCKEYE READY-MIX LLC
Fairfield Concrete
1750 Logan Langster Rd (43130-9001)
PHONE 740 654-4423
Jerry Culp, *Manager*
EMP: 15
SALES (corp-wide): 45.1MM **Privately Held**
WEB: www.buckeyereadymix.com
SIC: 3273 Ready-mixed concrete
PA: Buckeye Ready-Mix, Llc
7657 Taylor Rd Sw
Reynoldsburg OH 43068
614 575-2132

(G-11550)
BWX TECHNOLOGIES INC
2600 E Main St (43130-8490)
PHONE 740 687-4180
Dave Keller, *Branch Mgr*
EMP: 9 **Publicly Held**
SIC: 3621 Power generators
PA: Bwx Technologies, Inc.
800 Main St Ste 4
Lynchburg VA 24504

(G-11551)
C J KRAFT ENTERPRISES INC
Also Called: Bay Packing
301 S Maple St (43130-4406)
PHONE 740 653-9606
Kathleen Kraft, *President*
David Kraft, *Vice Pres*
Karen Kraft, *Admin Sec*
EMP: 21
SQ FT: 2,000
SALES (est): 2.3MM **Privately Held**
SIC: 5411 2011 5148 Grocery stores, independent; meat packing plants; fruits, fresh; vegetables, fresh

(G-11552)
CAMERON INTERNATIONAL CORP
471 Quarry Rd Se (43130-8272)
PHONE 740 654-4260
EMP: 8 **Publicly Held**
SIC: 3533 Oil & gas field machinery
HQ: Cameron International Corporation
4646 W Sam Houston Pkwy N
Houston TX 77041

(G-11553)
CARELESS HEART ENTERPRISES (PA)
600 N Columbus St (43130-2535)
PHONE 740 654-9999
Mason Reta, *Principal*
EMP: 4
SALES (est): 238.5K **Privately Held**
SIC: 3949 Skateboards

(G-11554)
CITY OF LANCASTER
Also Called: Lancaster Municipal Gas
1424 Campground Rd (43130-9503)
PHONE 740 687-6670
Michael R Pettit, *Superintendent*
Bill Burrows, *Superintendent*
Michael Pettit, *Manager*
Carrie Woody, *Admin Asst*
EMP: 25 **Privately Held**
WEB: www.ci.lancaster.oh.us
SIC: 1311 4924 Crude petroleum & natural gas; natural gas distribution
PA: City Of Lancaster
104 E Main St
Lancaster OH 43130
740 687-6617

(G-11555)
COMPLETE FILTER MEDIA LLC
1000 Mcgrery Rd Se (43130-7854)
PHONE 740 438-0929
Mike Beier,
EMP: 45
SALES (est): 2.4MM **Privately Held**
SIC: 3564 Filters, air: furnaces, air conditioning equipment, etc.

(G-11556)
CONSOLIDATED GRAPHICS INC
Also Called: Cyril-Scott Company, The
3950 Lancaster New Lxngtn (43130-7899)
PHONE 740 654-2112
Chad Stephenson, *President*
Amy Carbaugh, *Financial Analy*
EMP: 155
SALES (corp-wide): 6.8B **Publicly Held**
SIC: 2759 Commercial printing
HQ: Consolidated Graphics, Inc.
5858 Westheimer Rd # 200
Houston TX 77057
713 787-0977

(G-11557)
CREATIVE CABINETS LTD
1807 Snoke Rd Sw (43130-8902)
PHONE 740 689-0603
Kenny Mitchell, *Partner*

Lancaster - Fairfield County (G-11558)

Jerry Meldrum, *General Ptnr*
EMP: 10
SQ FT: 15,000
SALES (est): 1.4MM **Privately Held**
WEB: www.creativecabinetsltd.com
SIC: 2434 Wood kitchen cabinets

(G-11558)
CRISTS MACHINING INC
Also Called: CMI
1910 Hamburg Rd Sw (43130-8904)
PHONE..................740 653-0041
Arthur Crist, *President*
Pamala Crist, *Treasurer*
Art C Crist, *Manager*
EMP: 3
SQ FT: 2,000
SALES: 120K **Privately Held**
SIC: 3599 Machine shop, jobbing & repair

(G-11559)
CROWN CLOSURES MACHINERY
1765 W Fair Ave (43130-2325)
PHONE..................740 681-6593
John Conway, *CEO*
Dominic Capretta, *Design Engr*
▲ **EMP**: 40
SALES (est): 8.6MM
SALES (corp-wide): 11.1B **Publicly Held**
WEB: www.crownholdings.net
SIC: 3565 Packaging machinery
PA: Crown Holdings Inc.
770 Township Line Rd # 100
Yardley PA 19067
215 698-5100

(G-11560)
CROWN CORK & SEAL USA INC
940 Mill Park Dr (43130-9576)
PHONE..................740 681-3000
Ed Schott, *Manager*
EMP: 90
SALES (corp-wide): 11.1B **Publicly Held**
WEB: www.crowncork.com
SIC: 3089 3466 3411 Closures, plastic; closures, stamped metal; jar tops & crowns, stamped metal; metal cans
HQ: Crown Cork & Seal Usa, Inc.
770 Township Line Rd # 100
Yardley PA 19067
215 698-5100

(G-11561)
CROWN CORK & SEAL USA INC
1765 W Fair Ave (43130-2325)
PHONE..................740 681-6593
Shelia Heath, *Branch Mgr*
EMP: 35
SALES (corp-wide): 11.1B **Publicly Held**
WEB: www.crowncork.com
SIC: 3411 Metal cans
HQ: Crown Cork & Seal Usa, Inc.
770 Township Line Rd # 100
Yardley PA 19067
215 698-5100

(G-11562)
D K MANUFACTURING
2118 Commerce St (43130-9363)
PHONE..................740 654-5566
Daniel Keifer, *President*
Kelly Rees, *Business Mgr*
Brad Williams, *Vice Pres*
Ginny King, *Human Res Dir*
EMP: 90
SALES (est): 16.4MM **Privately Held**
SIC: 3089 Injection molded finished plastic products; injection molding of plastics

(G-11563)
DEVAULT MACHINE & MOULD CO LLC
Also Called: General Machine and Mould Co
2294 Commerce St (43130-9363)
P.O. Box 785 (43130-0785)
PHONE..................740 654-5925
Terris E Devault, *Mng Member*
EMP: 7 **EST**: 1966
SQ FT: 5,000
SALES (est): 1.2MM **Privately Held**
WEB: www.genmach.com
SIC: 3599 Machine & other job shop work

(G-11564)
DIAMOND ELECTRONICS INC
Also Called: Honeywell
1858 Cedar Hill Rd (43130-4178)
PHONE..................740 652-9222
George K Broady, *Ch of Bd*
EMP: 118
SQ FT: 72,000
SALES (est): 1.4MM **Privately Held**
SIC: 3663 Television closed circuit equipment

(G-11565)
DIAMOND POWER INTL INC
Also Called: Diamond Electronics
2530 E Main St (43130-8490)
PHONE..................740 687-4001
Ron Burris, *Manager*
EMP: 13
SALES (corp-wide): 1B **Publicly Held**
WEB: www.diamondpower.com
SIC: 3823 Industrial instrmnts msrmnt display/control process variable
HQ: Diamond Power International, Inc.
2600 E Main St
Lancaster OH 43130
740 687-6500

(G-11566)
DIAMOND POWER INTL INC (DH)
Also Called: Diamond Power Specialty
2600 E Main St (43130-9366)
P.O. Box 415 (43130-0415)
PHONE..................740 687-6500
Eileen M Competti, *President*
◆ **EMP**: 277
SALES (est): 138MM
SALES (corp-wide): 1B **Publicly Held**
WEB: www.diamondpower.com
SIC: 3564 Blowers & fans
HQ: The Babcock & Wilcox Company
20 S Van Buren Ave
Barberton OH 44203
330 753-4511

(G-11567)
DITTMAR SALES AND SERVICE
132 W 6th Ave (43130-2505)
PHONE..................740 653-7933
Fax: 740 653-7602
EMP: 5
SQ FT: 7,600
SALES: 900K **Privately Held**
SIC: 3261 5251 5261 3432 Mfg Vetreous Plmbng Fxtr Ret Hardware Ret Nursery/Garden Supp Mfg Plumbing Fxtr Fittng

(G-11568)
DK MANUFACTURING LANCASTER INC
2118 Commerce St (43130-9363)
PHONE..................740 654-5566
Daniel Keifer, *President*
EMP: 85
SALES (est): 11.5MM
SALES (corp-wide): 17.6MM **Privately Held**
SIC: 3089 Injection molded finished plastic products
PA: Dak Enterprises, Inc.
18062 Timber Trails Rd
Marysville OH 43040
740 828-3291

(G-11569)
FABRICATED PACKAGING MTLS INC
296 Quarry Rd Se (43130)
PHONE..................740 681-1750
Dale Statter, *Manager*
EMP: 5
SALES (corp-wide): 5.6MM **Privately Held**
SIC: 3086 Packaging & shipping materials, foamed plastic
PA: Fabricated Packaging Materials, Inc.
2109 Commerce St
Lancaster OH 43130
740 654-3492

(G-11570)
FABRICATED PACKAGING MTLS INC (PA)
Also Called: F P M
2109 Commerce St (43130-9363)
PHONE..................740 654-3492
Jeff Gross, *President*
Dale Stalter, *Treasurer*
▲ **EMP**: 13
SALES: 5.6MM **Privately Held**
SIC: 3086 Packaging & shipping materials, foamed plastic

(G-11571)
FAIRFIELD WOODWORKS LTD
1612 E Main St (43130-3472)
PHONE..................740 689-1953
Ron Smith, *President*
Ben Smith, *Vice Pres*
Jed Smith, *Vice Pres*
EMP: 7 **EST**: 1998
SQ FT: 5,000
SALES (est): 500K **Privately Held**
SIC: 2434 2431 Wood kitchen cabinets; moldings & baseboards, ornamental & trim

(G-11572)
FEDEX CORPORATION
1612 N Memorial Dr (43130-1631)
PHONE..................740 687-0334
Fax: 740 687-0297
EMP: 4
SALES (corp-wide): 47.4B **Publicly Held**
SIC: 2752 Lithographic Commercial Printing
PA: Fedex Corporation
942 Shady Grove Rd S
Memphis TN 38120
901 818-7500

(G-11573)
FUNCTIONAL IMAGING LTD
2368 Pine Crest Dr (43130-7731)
PHONE..................740 689-2466
Theresa Spiers, *Partner*
Carla Conkey, *Partner*
EMP: 3
SALES (est): 237.4K **Privately Held**
SIC: 2759 3299 Thermography; images, small; gypsum, clay or papier mache

(G-11574)
GANNETT CO INC
Also Called: Lancaster Eagle Gazette
123 S Broad St Ste 233 (43130-4304)
P.O. Box 848 (43130-0848)
PHONE..................740 654-1321
Rick Zabrak, *Branch Mgr*
EMP: 50
SALES (corp-wide): 2.9B **Publicly Held**
WEB: www.gannett.com
SIC: 2711 Newspapers: publishing only, not printed on site
PA: Gannett Co., Inc.
7950 Jones Branch Dr
Mc Lean VA 22102
703 854-6000

(G-11575)
GHP II LLC (DH)
Also Called: Anchor Hocking Indus GL Div
1115 W 5th Ave (43130-2938)
PHONE..................740 687-2500
Mark Eichorn, *CEO*
Mark Hedstrom, *CFO*
George Hamilton,
▼ **EMP**: 200 **EST**: 1905
SQ FT: 41,900
SALES (est): 149.7MM
SALES (corp-wide): 682.6MM **Privately Held**
WEB: www.anchorhocking.com
SIC: 3229 3089 3411 3221 Tableware, glass or glass ceramic; cooking utensils, glass or glass ceramic; cups, plastic, except foam; plates, plastic; bottle caps, molded plastic; bowl covers, plastic; metal cans; glass containers

(G-11576)
GHP II LLC
2893 W Fair Ave (43130-8993)
P.O. Box 600 (43130-0600)
PHONE..................740 681-6825
Tom Gilligan, *Manager*

EMP: 280
SQ FT: 1,300,000
SALES (corp-wide): 682.6MM **Privately Held**
WEB: www.anchorhocking.com
SIC: 5023 3231 China; glassware; products of purchased glass
HQ: Ghp Ii, Llc
1115 W 5th Ave
Lancaster OH 43130
740 687-2500

(G-11577)
GLASFLOSS INDUSTRIES INC (PA)
2168 Commerce St (43130-9363)
P.O. Box 789, Desoto TX (75123-0789)
PHONE..................740 687-1100
Scott Lange, *President*
Cheryl Thompson, *Principal*
Donald Kingston, *Vice Pres*
Janet Peterson, *Purch Mgr*
Bill McKnight, *Purchasing*
▼ **EMP**: 250 **EST**: 1956
SALES (est): 45MM **Privately Held**
WEB: www.glasflossindustries.com
SIC: 3564 Filters, air: furnaces, air conditioning equipment, etc.

(G-11578)
HANGER PRSTHETCS & ORTHO INC
111 N Ewing St (43130-3364)
PHONE..................740 654-1884
Curt Hoellrich, *Manager*
Kurt Hoellrich, *Manager*
EMP: 4
SALES (corp-wide): 1B **Publicly Held**
SIC: 5999 3842 Orthopedic & prosthesis applications; prosthetic appliances
HQ: Hanger Prosthetics & Orthotics, Inc.
10910 Domain Dr Ste 300
Austin TX 78758
512 777-3800

(G-11579)
HEDGES PRINTING CO
6490 Revenge Rd Sw (43130-8270)
PHONE..................740 422-8500
Jessica R Hedges, *Administration*
EMP: 4
SALES (est): 148.6K **Privately Held**
SIC: 2752 Commercial printing, offset

(G-11580)
INCESSANT SOFTWARE INC
8577 Ohio Wesleyan Ct Nw (43130-9329)
PHONE..................614 206-2211
Al Pruden, *President*
EMP: 9
SALES (est): 670K **Privately Held**
WEB: www.incessant.com
SIC: 7372 Prepackaged software

(G-11581)
JOHNSON TOOL DISTRIBUTORS
1059 Rockmill Rd Nw (43130-9517)
PHONE..................740 653-6959
Gary Johnson, *Owner*
EMP: 5
SQ FT: 7,000
SALES: 142K **Privately Held**
SIC: 3524 5083 Lawn & garden equipment; lawn & garden machinery & equipment

(G-11582)
LANCASTER WEST SIDE COAL CO (PA)
700 Van Buren Ave (43130-2339)
PHONE..................740 862-4713
Jerry H Fahrer, *President*
Mary K Cann, *Vice Pres*
Bruce Fahrer, *Treasurer*
William Cann, *Admin Sec*
EMP: 12 **EST**: 1925
SQ FT: 1,600
SALES (est): 1.2MM **Privately Held**
SIC: 3273 5211 5032 Ready-mixed concrete; lumber & other building materials; brick, stone & related material

▲ = Import ▼ = Export
◆ = Import/Export

GEOGRAPHIC SECTION
Lancaster - Fairfield County (G-11613)

(G-11583)
LANCE INDUSTRIES INC
1361 Sugar Grove Rd Se (43130-4861)
PHONE.................................740 243-6657
Lance Alspaugh, *Principal*
EMP: 3
SALES (est): 185.2K **Privately Held**
SIC: 3999 Manufacturing industries

(G-11584)
LITHCHEM INTL TOXCO INC
265 Quarry Rd Se (43130-8271)
PHONE.................................740 653-6290
Ed Green, *Principal*
EMP: 3 **EST:** 1998
SALES (est): 266.4K **Privately Held**
SIC: 3691 Storage batteries

(G-11585)
MARGO TOOL TECHNOLOGY INC
2616 Setter Ct Nw (43130-9151)
PHONE.................................740 653-8115
John Porter, *President*
Jeff Ellis, *Corp Secy*
EMP: 10
SQ FT: 7,500
SALES (est): 1.8MM **Privately Held**
SIC: 3599 Custom machinery

(G-11586)
MEMAC INDUSTRIES INC
324 Quarry Rd Se (43130-8055)
P.O. Box 231 (43130-0231)
PHONE.................................740 653-4815
Carol L Figgins-Clarke, *President*
Danny Clarke, *Vice Pres*
EMP: 8
SQ FT: 5,900
SALES (est): 1.2MM **Privately Held**
WEB: www.memacindustries.com
SIC: 3599 Machine shop, jobbing & repair

(G-11587)
MID-WEST FABRICATING CO
885 Mill Park Dr (43130-8061)
PHONE.................................740 277-7021
Ann Custer, *Vice Pres*
EMP: 20
SALES (corp-wide): 25.5MM **Privately Held**
SIC: 3452 Bolts, metal
PA: Mid-West Fabricating Co.
   313 N Johns St
   Amanda OH 43102
   740 969-4411

(G-11588)
MID-WEST FABRICATING CO
Also Called: Rock Mill Division
3115 W Fair Ave (43130-9568)
PHONE.................................740 681-4411
Chad Shuttleworth, *Branch Mgr*
Lonnie White, *Manager*
EMP: 9
SALES (corp-wide): 25.5MM **Privately Held**
WEB: www.midwestfab.com
SIC: 3714 3452 Tie rods, motor vehicle; bolts, metal
PA: Mid-West Fabricating Co.
   313 N Johns St
   Amanda OH 43102
   740 969-4411

(G-11589)
MINUTMAN PRESS FRFELD CNTY LLC
135 N Columbus St (43130-3704)
PHONE.................................740 689-1992
Pam O'Connor, *Human Resources*
Dan O'Connor,
EMP: 3
SQ FT: 1,400
SALES (est): 362.7K **Privately Held**
SIC: 2752 Commercial printing, lithographic

(G-11590)
NEIL R SCHOLL INC
54 Snoke Hill Rd Ne (43130-9315)
PHONE.................................740 653-6593
Neil R Scholl, *President*
Betty Scholl, *Vice Pres*
EMP: 10

SQ FT: 2,000
SALES (est): 1MM **Privately Held**
SIC: 3599 5084 Custom machinery; industrial machinery & equipment

(G-11591)
NORTH END PRESS INCORPORATED
235 S Columbus St (43130-4315)
PHONE.................................740 653-6514
Richard Benadum, *President*
Brad A Benadum, *Vice Pres*
Greg Benadum, *Vice Pres*
EMP: 20 **EST:** 1933
SQ FT: 55,000
SALES (est): 1.4MM **Privately Held**
SIC: 2789 Bookbinding & related work

(G-11592)
NORWESCO INC
3111 Wilson Rd (43130-8144)
PHONE.................................740 654-6402
Darrin Dittman, *Manager*
EMP: 20
SQ FT: 15,000
SALES (corp-wide): 44.1MM **Privately Held**
WEB: www.ncmmolding.com
SIC: 3089 Plastic & fiberglass tanks
PA: Norwesco, Inc.
   4365 Steiner St
   Saint Bonifacius MN 55375
   952 446-1945

(G-11593)
OHIO MATTRESS
1408 Ety Rd Nw (43130-7745)
PHONE.................................740 739-8219
Lee Winters, *Principal*
EMP: 5 **EST:** 2012
SALES (est): 803.9K **Privately Held**
SIC: 2515 Mattresses & foundations

(G-11594)
ONE-WRITE COMPANY
3750 Lancaster New Lexing (43130-9314)
PHONE.................................740 654-2128
Norman Boyd, *President*
▼ **EMP:** 28
SALES (est): 4MM **Privately Held**
WEB: www.onewriteco.com
SIC: 2752 Commercial printing, offset

(G-11595)
ONEIDA GROUP INC (PA)
519 N Pierce Ave (43130-2927)
PHONE.................................740 687-2500
Patrick Lockwood-Taylor, *CEO*
Daniel J Collin, *Ch of Bd*
Thomas J Baldwin, *Vice Ch Bd*
Erika Schoenberger, *Principal*
Anthony Reisig, *Senior VP*
EMP: 129
SALES (est): 682.6MM **Privately Held**
SIC: 3089 3469 Plastic kitchenware, tableware & houseware; kitchen fixtures & equipment, porcelain enameled

(G-11596)
PHILLIPS AWNING CO
2052 W Fair Ave (43130-9672)
PHONE.................................740 653-2433
Patricia Probasco, *Owner*
EMP: 3
SQ FT: 1,800
SALES (est): 240K **Privately Held**
SIC: 5211 2394 3444 Jalousies; awnings, fabric: made from purchased materials; sheet metalwork

(G-11597)
PHOENIX/ELECTROTEK LLC
890 Mill Park Dr (43130-2572)
PHONE.................................740 681-1412
Duane Astrauskas, *Mng Member*
EMP: 25
SALES: 1.7MM
SALES (corp-wide): 8.9MM **Privately Held**
SIC: 2298 Ropes & fiber cables
PA: Phoenix/Edt Inc
   1080 Meyerside Dr
   Mississauga ON L5T 1
   905 678-9400

(G-11598)
PRECISION CNC LLC
1858 Cedar Hill Rd (43130-4178)
PHONE.................................740 689-9009
Paul Davis, *Mng Member*
Nathan Hawkins,
EMP: 28
SQ FT: 10,000
SALES (est): 3MM **Privately Held**
WEB: www.metalforce.net
SIC: 3599 Machine shop, jobbing & repair

(G-11599)
PRO-KLEEN INDUSTRIAL SVCS INC
Also Called: Porta-Kleen
1030 Mill Park Dr (43130-9576)
PHONE.................................740 689-1886
Monte Black, *Ch of Bd*
EMP: 45
SALES (est): 7.5MM **Privately Held**
WEB: www.portakleen.com
SIC: 7359 7699 5963 3088 Portable toilet rental; septic tank cleaning service; bottled water delivery; tubs (bath, shower & laundry), plastic

(G-11600)
PROFESSIONAL SCREEN PRINTING
731 N Pierce Ave (43130-2416)
PHONE.................................740 687-0760
Jeff Uhl, *President*
John Uhl,
EMP: 8
SQ FT: 3,000
SALES (est): 800K **Privately Held**
WEB: www.promotionalproducts-promotionalitems.co
SIC: 7336 2752 Silk screen design; commercial printing, lithographic

(G-11601)
RESIDENTIAL ELECTRONIC SVCS
3155 Lancstr Kirkrsvll Nw (43130-8599)
PHONE.................................740 681-9150
Daniel Miller, *President*
EMP: 3 **EST:** 1998
SALES: 25K **Privately Held**
SIC: 3699 Security devices

(G-11602)
RETRIEV TECHNOLOGIES INC
265 Quarry Rd Se (43130-8271)
PHONE.................................740 653-6290
Ed Green, *Branch Mgr*
EMP: 100
SALES (corp-wide): 37.2MM **Privately Held**
SIC: 3691 Batteries, rechargeable
PA: Retriev Technologies Incorporated
   125 E Commercial St Ste A
   Anaheim CA 92801
   714 738-8516

(G-11603)
ROBERT ALTEN INC
449 S Ewing St (43130-9400)
P.O. Box 731 (43130-0731)
PHONE.................................740 653-2640
Jan C Alten, *President*
Mary Ann Alten, *Vice Pres*
EMP: 5 **EST:** 1933
SQ FT: 3,000
SALES: 450K **Privately Held**
SIC: 3599 7692 Machine shop, jobbing & repair; welding repair

(G-11604)
ROCKBRIDGE OUTFITTERS
Also Called: Ohio Valley Trading and Exch
2805 Clmbus Lncster Rd Nw (43130-8663)
PHONE.................................740 654-1956
EMP: 7
SALES (est): 439.2K **Privately Held**
SIC: 3949 Mfg Sporting/Athletic Goods

(G-11605)
ROCKSIDE WINERY & VINEYARDS LL
2363 Lncster Newark Rd Ne (43130-8200)
PHONE.................................740 687-4414
Lynn Rutter, *Principal*
EMP: 4

SALES (est): 278K **Privately Held**
SIC: 2084 Wines

(G-11606)
SHELLY COMPANY
Also Called: Shelly Materials
3232 Lgan Lancaster Rd Se (43130-9007)
PHONE.................................740 687-4420
Tony Marks, *Manager*
EMP: 14
SALES (corp-wide): 29.7B **Privately Held**
SIC: 1442 Construction sand mining; gravel mining
HQ: Shelly Company
   80 Park Dr
   Thornville OH 43076
   740 246-6315

(G-11607)
SHERIDAN ONE STOP CARRYOUT
1510 Sheridan Dr (43130-1303)
PHONE.................................740 687-1300
Eric Molzan, *Owner*
EMP: 7 **EST:** 1981
SALES (est): 394.3K **Privately Held**
SIC: 1311 Crude petroleum & natural gas

(G-11608)
SILVER EXPRESSIONS
1635 River Valley Cir S # 5078 (43130-5712)
PHONE.................................740 687-0144
Diane Rosenberger, *Principal*
EMP: 4
SALES (est): 315.2K **Privately Held**
SIC: 3423 Jewelers' hand tools

(G-11609)
SMITH RN SHEET METAL SHOP INC
1312 Campground Rd (43130-9503)
PHONE.................................740 653-5011
Patrick Smith, *President*
Sue Smith, *Treasurer*
Mary Jo Smith, *Admin Sec*
EMP: 25
SQ FT: 1,800
SALES: 3MM **Privately Held**
SIC: 3444 Sheet metalwork

(G-11610)
SOUTHSTERN MACHINING FIELD SVC (PA)
500 Lincoln Ave (43130-4243)
PHONE.................................740 689-1147
John Treitmaier, *President*
Bob Hines, *Foreman/Supr*
EMP: 37
SQ FT: 6,500
SALES (est): 5.3MM **Privately Held**
WEB: www.semohio.com
SIC: 3599 Custom machinery

(G-11611)
SRI OHIO INC
1061 Mill Park Dr (43130-9577)
PHONE.................................740 653-5800
Bonnita Heston, *Principal*
Bob Muckensturm, *VP Opers*
▲ **EMP:** 51
SALES (est): 12.6MM **Privately Held**
SIC: 2759 Screen printing

(G-11612)
STELLAR INDUSTRIAL TECH CO
Also Called: Stellar I T Co
1918 York Town Ct (43130-1242)
PHONE.................................740 654-7052
Michael Vawter, *President*
Carolyn Vawter, *Vice Pres*
EMP: 4
SQ FT: 1,500
SALES: 300K **Privately Held**
SIC: 8742 4953 3694 Industrial consultant; liquid waste, collection & disposal; distributors, motor vehicle engine

(G-11613)
THORWALD HOLDINGS INC
Also Called: Martins Partitions
866 Mill Park Dr (43130-2572)
P.O. Box 102, Carroll (43112-0102)
PHONE.................................740 756-9271
Tamara Miller, *President*

Lancaster - Fairfield County (G-11614)

Bruce Miller, *Treasurer*
Sean Miller, *Manager*
EMP: 25
SALES (est): 3.9MM **Privately Held**
SIC: 2631 Packaging board

(G-11614)
TOXCO INC
265 Quarry Rd Se (43130-8271)
PHONE..................740 653-6290
Ed Green, *Branch Mgr*
EMP: 71
SALES (corp-wide): 18.2MM **Privately Held**
WEB: www.toxco.com
SIC: 3691 Batteries, rechargeable
PA: Toxco, Inc.
   125 E Commercial St Ste A
   Anaheim CA 92801
   714 738-8516

(G-11615)
TREEHOUSE PRIVATE BRANDS INC
Also Called: Ralston Food
3775 Lanc New Lex Rd Se (43130-9314)
PHONE..................740 654-8880
Andy Rohrbach, *Branch Mgr*
EMP: 350
SALES (corp-wide): 5.8B **Publicly Held**
SIC: 2043 Cereal breakfast foods
HQ: Treehouse Private Brands, Inc.
   800 Market St Ste 2600
   Saint Louis MO 63101

(G-11616)
TREEHOUSE PRIVATE BRANDS INC
276 Bremen Rd (43130-7873)
PHONE..................740 654-8880
Gary Rodkin, *CEO*
EMP: 5
SALES (corp-wide): 5.8B **Publicly Held**
SIC: 2043 Cereal breakfast foods
HQ: Treehouse Private Brands, Inc.
   800 Market St Ste 2600
   Saint Louis MO 63101

(G-11617)
VIC MAR MANUFACTURING INC
Also Called: S&S Manufactruing
730 Lawrence St (43130-9401)
PHONE..................740 687-5434
Stephen R Shumaker, *President*
Lawrence H Smith, *Vice Pres*
EMP: 5
SQ FT: 4,600
SALES: 300K **Privately Held**
SIC: 3599 Machine shop, jobbing & repair

(G-11618)
WESTROCK USC INC
1290 Campground Rd (43130-9503)
PHONE..................740 681-1600
Rick Morgan, *General Mgr*
EMP: 107
SQ FT: 314,000
SALES (corp-wide): 16.2B **Publicly Held**
SIC: 2653 Boxes, corrugated: made from purchased materials
HQ: Westrock Usc, Inc.
   1000 Abernathy Rd
   Atlanta GA 30328
   770 448-2193

(G-11619)
WIZARD PUBLICATIONS INC
Also Called: Hawaii Revealed
1979 Wilshire Ln Nw (43130-7957)
P.O. Box 991, Lihue HI (96766-0991)
PHONE..................808 821-1214
Andrew Doughty, *President*
EMP: 10
SALES (est): 12.1K **Privately Held**
SIC: 2741 Miscellaneous publishing

(G-11620)
ZEBCO INDUSTRIES INC
211 N Columbus St (43130-3006)
PHONE..................740 654-4510
Kevin Stalter, *President*
Jill Stalter, *Vice Pres*
Madonna Christy, *Admin Sec*
EMP: 19
SQ FT: 128,000
SALES (est): 3.6MM **Privately Held**
WEB: www.zebcoindustries.com
SIC: 3086 5113 2671 Packaging & shipping materials, foamed plastic; industrial & personal service paper; packaging paper & plastics film, coated & laminated

Langsville
Meigs County

(G-11621)
DUFF FARM
30762 Old Dexter Rd (45741-9554)
PHONE..................740 742-2182
Robin Duff, *Owner*
EMP: 3
SALES (est): 147.1K **Privately Held**
SIC: 3949 Hooks, fishing

Latham
Pike County

(G-11622)
LATHAM LIMESTONE LLC
6424 State Route 124 (45646-9703)
PHONE..................740 493-2677
Dennis Garrison,
EMP: 8
SQ FT: 500
SALES (est): 555.5K **Privately Held**
SIC: 1422 Limestones, ground

(G-11623)
LATHAM LUMBER & PALLET CO INC
9445 Street Rte 124 (45646)
P.O. Box 147 (45646-0147)
PHONE..................740 493-2707
Karen Chandler, *President*
EMP: 15
SQ FT: 12,000
SALES: 4MM **Privately Held**
SIC: 2499 Mulch, wood & bark

Latty
Paulding County

(G-11624)
AL-CO PRODUCTS INC
485 2nd St (45855)
P.O. Box 74 (45855-0074)
PHONE..................419 399-3867
Russell W Stoller, *President*
Trent Stoller, *Corp Secy*
John F Kohler, *Vice Pres*
EMP: 13
SQ FT: 11,000
SALES (est): 1.9MM
SALES (corp-wide): 50.8MM **Privately Held**
WEB: www.al-coproducts.com
SIC: 3281 3949 2821 2434 Marble, building: cut & shaped; sporting & athletic goods; plastics materials & resins; wood kitchen cabinets
PA: Haviland Drainage Products Co.
   100 W Main St
   Haviland OH 45851
   419 622-4611

Laura
Miami County

(G-11625)
PRESTONS REPAIR & WELDING
11611 State Route 571 (45337-9836)
P.O. Box M (45337-0808)
PHONE..................937 947-1883
Kevin Mote, *President*
EMP: 3
SQ FT: 4,800
SALES (est): 318.6K **Privately Held**
SIC: 7538 7692 General automotive repair shops; automotive welding

Laurelville
Hocking County

(G-11626)
C & L ERECTORS & RIGGERS INC
16412 Thompson Ridge Rd (43135-9238)
P.O. Box 98 (43135-0098)
PHONE..................740 332-7185
Chris Riddle, *President*
Craig Riddle, *Vice Pres*
Dale W Riddle, *Shareholder*
EMP: 20
SQ FT: 1,500
SALES (est): 1.8MM **Privately Held**
SIC: 1629 2411 Land clearing contractor; logging; wood chips, produced in the field

(G-11627)
T & D THOMPSON INC
Also Called: Hocking Hills Hardwoods
15952 State Route 56 E (43135-9741)
P.O. Box 88 (43135-0088)
PHONE..................740 332-8515
Terry L Thompson, *President*
David R Thompson, *Vice Pres*
Chuck Karr, *Human Res Mgr*
EMP: 50
SQ FT: 50,000
SALES (est): 6.9MM **Privately Held**
WEB: www.hockinghillshardwoods.com
SIC: 2448 2449 2431 2426 Pallets, wood; wood containers; millwork; hardwood dimension & flooring mills; sawmills & planing mills, general

Lebanon
Warren County

(G-11628)
A A A PROFESSIONAL HTG & COOLG
535 N Broadway St (45036-1736)
PHONE..................513 933-0564
Mitch Underwood, *President*
Chris Smith, *Vice Pres*
EMP: 5
SALES (est): 519.2K **Privately Held**
SIC: 1711 3444 Heating & air conditioning contractors; ducts, sheet metal

(G-11629)
ADDISONMCKEE INC (PA)
1637 Kingsview Dr (45036-8395)
PHONE..................513 228-7000
Jim Sabine, *CEO*
Lonnie McGrew, *Vice Pres*
Mike Burnett, *VP Mfg*
Claud Lessard, *CFO*
Nancy A McKee,
▲ **EMP:** 142
SQ FT: 78,000
SALES: 8MM **Privately Held**
WEB: www.addisonmckee.com
SIC: 3542 3599 5084 3549 Bending machines; machine shop, jobbing & repair; industrial machinery & equipment; metalworking machinery; rolling mill machinery; special dies, tools, jigs & fixtures

(G-11630)
ADDITION MFG TECH LLC (PA)
1637 Kingsview Dr (45036-8395)
PHONE..................513 228-7000
EMP: 9
SALES (est): 6.2MM **Privately Held**
SIC: 3498 Mfg Fabricated Pipe/Fittings

(G-11631)
ADVICS MANUFACTURING OHIO INC
1650 Kingsview Dr (45036-8390)
PHONE..................513 932-7878
Atsuo Matsumoto, *President*
Ron Lipps, *Vice Pres*
Rob Seiler, *Opers Mgr*
Johnny Troxell, *Opers Mgr*
Billy Collins, *Facilities Mgr*
▲ **EMP:** 625
SQ FT: 323,000
SALES (est): 188.9MM
SALES (corp-wide): 36.6B **Privately Held**
WEB: www.advics-ohio.com
SIC: 3714 Motor vehicle brake systems & parts
HQ: Advics North America, Inc.
   1650 Kingsview Dr
   Lebanon OH 45036
   513 696-5450

(G-11632)
ALLEN FIELDS ASSOC INC
3525 Grant Ave Ste D (45036-6431)
PHONE..................513 228-1010
Raymond Watson, *Owner*
EMP: 6
SALES (est): 728.4K **Privately Held**
SIC: 3699 5063 Electrical equipment & supplies; electrical apparatus & equipment

(G-11633)
AMA FUEL SERVICES LLC
3053 Hart Rd (45036-9123)
PHONE..................513 836-3800
Danielle Bingman,
EMP: 5
SQ FT: 9,000
SALES (est): 605.4K **Privately Held**
SIC: 2869 Fuels

(G-11634)
ARI PHOENIX INC (PA)
4119 Binion Way (45036-9336)
PHONE..................513 229-3750
Gareth Hudson, *CEO*
James Mock, *CFO*
EMP: 27
SALES (est): 14.3MM **Privately Held**
SIC: 3536 3564 Hoists; exhaust fans: industrial or commercial

(G-11635)
AWS INDUSTRIES INC
Also Called: Tomak Precision
2600 Henkle Dr (45036-8026)
PHONE..................513 932-7941
Alvin W Schaeper, *President*
Paul Balash, *Admin Sec*
EMP: 45 EST: 1953
SQ FT: 20,000
SALES (est): 10.3MM **Privately Held**
WEB: www.tomak.com
SIC: 3728 3841 Aircraft parts & equipment; surgical & medical instruments

(G-11636)
BENNERS CUSTOM WOODWORKING (PA)
1004 W Main St (45036-9512)
PHONE..................513 932-9159
Michael Benner, *President*
Chris Benner, *Manager*
EMP: 9
SQ FT: 3,700
SALES (est): 1.3MM **Privately Held**
SIC: 2511 Wood household furniture

(G-11637)
BIG CHIEF MANUFACTURING LTD
250 Harmon Ave (45036-8800)
PHONE..................513 934-3888
James Howe Jr, *Partner*
▲ **EMP:** 25
SQ FT: 20,000
SALES (est): 1.8MM
SALES (corp-wide): 8.2MM **Privately Held**
SIC: 3545 Machine tool accessories
PA: Big Chief, Inc.
   5150 Big Chief Dr
   Cincinnati OH 45227
   513 271-7411

(G-11638)
C T CHEMICALS INC
4110 Columbia Rd (45036-9588)
PHONE..................513 459-9744
Gregory Lalonde, *President*
Robert Bokon, *Vice Pres*
EMP: 6
SQ FT: 97,000

GEOGRAPHIC SECTION

Lebanon - Warren County (G-11663)

SALES (est): 1.1MM
SALES (corp-wide): 60.6MM **Privately Held**
SIC: 2819 Industrial inorganic chemicals
PA: Avidity Science, Llc
  819 Bakke Ave
  Waterford WI 53185
  262 534-5181

(G-11639)
CADILLAC PRODUCTS INC
265 S West St (45036-2152)
PHONE.....................................248 813-8255
Jeff Yezzi, *Branch Mgr*
EMP: 20
SALES (corp-wide): 168.4MM **Privately Held**
SIC: 3714 Motor vehicle parts & accessories
PA: Cadillac Products, Inc.
  5800 Crooks Rd Ste 100
  Troy MI 48098
  248 813-8200

(G-11640)
CARL E OEDER SONS SAND & GRAV
1000 Mason Morrow Rd (45036-9271)
PHONE.....................................513 494-1555
Carl Edward Oeder, *President*
David Oeder, *Vice Pres*
Diane Browning, *Treasurer*
Verna Rae Oeder, *Admin Sec*
EMP: 30 EST: 1955
SQ FT: 23,600
SALES (est): 2.1MM **Privately Held**
WEB: www.oeder.com
SIC: 1442 4212 7538 Sand mining; gravel mining; dump truck haulage; truck engine repair, except industrial

(G-11641)
CCTM INC
838 Carson Dr (45036-1316)
PHONE.....................................513 934-3533
Dan Collins, *President*
Gregory Collins, *Vice Pres*
Connie Collins, *Admin Sec*
EMP: 5
SQ FT: 7,500
SALES (est): 507.4K **Privately Held**
WEB: www.cctmath.org
SIC: 3544 7389 3499 3599 Special dies, tools, jigs & fixtures; metal slitting & shearing; automobile seat frames, metal; machine shop, jobbing & repair

(G-11642)
COLONIAL WOODCRAFT INC
Also Called: River Bend Chair Co
1004 W Main St (45036-9512)
PHONE.....................................513 779-8088
Kenneth Shannon, *President*
Ruth Shannon, *Vice Pres*
EMP: 11
SQ FT: 9,000
SALES: 500K **Privately Held**
SIC: 2511 Chairs, household, except upholstered: wood

(G-11643)
CONNOR ELECTRIC INC
605 N Liberty Keuter Rd (45036-9755)
PHONE.....................................513 932-5798
Warren Conner, *President*
Donna Conner, *Admin Sec*
EMP: 3
SALES (est): 240K **Privately Held**
SIC: 3531 1731 Construction machinery; electrical work

(G-11644)
CONTEMPRARY IMAGE LABELING INC
2034 Mckinley Blvd (45036-6425)
PHONE.....................................513 583-5699
Doug Weideman, *Principal*
Kurt Wiedeman, *Vice Pres*
EMP: 6
SQ FT: 18,000
SALES (est): 965.6K **Privately Held**
SIC: 2759 Labels & seals: printing

(G-11645)
CVC LIMITED 1 LLC
568 S Liberty Keuter Rd (45036-9337)
PHONE.....................................740 605-3853
Carl Cardi,
EMP: 5
SALES (est): 321.1K **Privately Held**
SIC: 3629 Electronic generation equipment

(G-11646)
D & E MACHINE CO
962 S Us Route 42 (45036-7918)
PHONE.....................................513 932-2184
Kent P Coomer, *President*
Tim Wilkerson, *Opers Mgr*
Kimberly A Coomer, *Treasurer*
EMP: 9
SQ FT: 12,000
SALES: 1.6MM **Privately Held**
WEB: www.demachine.com
SIC: 3599 Machine shop, jobbing & repair

(G-11647)
DAVIDSON JEWELERS INC
726 E Main St (45036-1900)
PHONE.....................................513 932-3936
John Davidson, *Owner*
Mary Davidson, *Co-Owner*
EMP: 3
SQ FT: 800
SALES (est): 180K **Privately Held**
SIC: 5944 3911 7631 Jewelry, precious stones & precious metals; jewelry, precious metal; jewelry repair services

(G-11648)
E-BEAM SERVICES INC
2775 Henkle Dr Unit B (45036-8256)
PHONE.....................................513 933-0031
Peter Tuozzolo, *General Mgr*
Dave Keenan, *Branch Mgr*
Jennifer Griggs, *Technical Staff*
EMP: 20
SQ FT: 129,116
SALES (corp-wide): 5MM **Privately Held**
WEB: www.e-beamservices.com
SIC: 3699 Electronic training devices
PA: E-Beam Services, Inc.
  270 Duffy Ave Ste H
  Hicksville NY 11801
  516 622-1422

(G-11649)
ECOLAB INC
726 E Main St Ste F (45036-1900)
PHONE.....................................513 932-0830
Dan Elam, *District Mgr*
EMP: 8
SALES (corp-wide): 14.6B **Publicly Held**
WEB: www.ecolab.com
SIC: 2842 Sanitation preparations, disinfectants & deodorants
PA: Ecolab Inc.
  1 Ecolab Pl
  Saint Paul MN 55102
  800 232-6522

(G-11650)
ENGINRED PLSTIC COMPONENTS INC
315 S West St (45036-2182)
PHONE.....................................513 228-0298
Wanda Boyle, *Branch Mgr*
EMP: 128 **Privately Held**
SIC: 3089 Injection molding of plastics
PA: Engineered Plastic Components, Inc.
  4500 Westown Pkwy Ste 277
  West Des Moines IA 50266

(G-11651)
ERNST ENTERPRISES INC
4250 Columbia Rd (45036-9589)
PHONE.....................................513 874-8300
Robert Himes, *Manager*
EMP: 50
SQ FT: 2,822
SALES (corp-wide): 227.2MM **Privately Held**
WEB: www.ernstconcrete.com
SIC: 3273 Ready-mixed concrete
PA: Ernst Enterprises, Inc.
  3361 Successful Way
  Dayton OH 45414
  937 233-5555

(G-11652)
FLINT GROUP US LLC
Also Called: Flint Group Global Packaging
2675 Henkle Dr (45036-8027)
PHONE.....................................513 934-6500
Steve Proper, *Maint Spvr*
Philip Ernest, *Chief Mktg Ofcr*
Michael Hackett, *Branch Mgr*
David Roark, *Technical Staff*
Jeff Deatherage, *Maintence Staff*
EMP: 5
SALES (corp-wide): 3.2B **Privately Held**
WEB: www.flintink.com
SIC: 2893 Printing ink
PA: Flint Group Us Llc
  14909 N Beck Rd
  Plymouth MI 48170
  734 781-4600

(G-11653)
GEORGE & UNDERWOOD LLP
530 N Broadway St (45036-1735)
PHONE.....................................513 409-5631
George Andy, *Principal*
EMP: 3 EST: 2016
SALES (est): 50.2K **Privately Held**
SIC: 2499 Wood products

(G-11654)
GEORGE MANUFACTURING INC
160 Harmon Ave (45036-9511)
PHONE.....................................513 932-1067
Erin George, *President*
Dan George, *Shareholder*
EMP: 28
SQ FT: 60,000
SALES (est): 4.1MM **Privately Held**
WEB: www.georgemfg.com
SIC: 3312 3479 3444 Pipes & tubes; painting, coating & hot dipping; sheet metalwork

(G-11655)
GEORGE STEEL FABRICATING INC
1207 S Us Route 42 (45036-8198)
PHONE.....................................513 932-2887
John George, *President*
Brad Frost, *Corp Secy*
Kevin Nickell, *Vice Pres*
Tom Bausmith, *Project Mgr*
Blake Berryman, *Project Mgr*
EMP: 35
SQ FT: 32,100
SALES (est): 7.1MM **Privately Held**
WEB: www.georgesteel.com
SIC: 7692 3441 3599 Welding repair; fabricated structural metal; machine shop, jobbing & repair

(G-11656)
GEYGAN ENTERPRISES INC
Also Called: Minuteman Press
101 Dave Ave Ste E (45036-2293)
PHONE.....................................513 932-4222
Michael Geygan, *President*
EMP: 12
SALES: 1.2MM **Privately Held**
WEB: www.mmpressleb.com
SIC: 2752 7334 2759 5999 Commercial printing, lithographic; photocopying & duplicating services; labels & seals: printing; invitations: printing; rubber stamps; typesetting; manifold business forms

(G-11657)
GMI COMPANIES INC (PA)
Also Called: Ghent Manufacturing
2999 Henkle Dr (45036-9260)
PHONE.....................................513 932-3445
George L Leasure, *Chairman*
Mary Alice Leasure, *Admin Sec*
▲ EMP: 160
SQ FT: 101,000
SALES (est): 38.7MM **Privately Held**
WEB: www.ghent.com
SIC: 2531 2493 2599 2541 Blackboards, wood; bulletin boards, wood; bulletin boards, cork; boards: planning, display, notice; showcases, except refrigerated: wood; panel systems & partitions (free-standing), office: wood; panel systems & partitions, office: except wood

(G-11658)
GOLDEN TURTLE CHOCOLATE FCTRY
120 S Broadway St Ste 1 (45036-1729)
P.O. Box 647 (45036-0647)
PHONE.....................................513 932-1990
Joy Kossouji, *Owner*
Ted Kossouji, *Partner*
EMP: 6
SQ FT: 3,000
SALES: 200K **Privately Held**
WEB: www.goldenturtlechocolatefactory.com
SIC: 2066 5441 5947 Chocolate; candy, nut & confectionery stores; gifts & novelties

(G-11659)
GRAFISK MSKNFABRIK-AMERICA LLC
603 Norgal Dr Ste F (45036-9382)
PHONE.....................................630 432-4370
Mark Rogers, *President*
▲ EMP: 8
SALES (est): 1MM
SALES (corp-wide): 50MM **Privately Held**
SIC: 2759 Commercial printing
PA: Grafisk Maskinfabrik A/S
  Bregnerodvej 92
  BirkerOd 3460
  458 123-00

(G-11660)
GREEN BAY PACKAGING INC
Cincinnati Division
760 Kingsview Dr (45036-9554)
PHONE.....................................513 228-5560
Craig Erickson, *Prdtn Mgr*
Dwayne Owens, *Production*
Wayne Petersen, *Manager*
EMP: 71
SQ FT: 103,000
SALES (corp-wide): 1.3B **Privately Held**
WEB: www.gbp.com
SIC: 2653 3412 Boxes, corrugated: made from purchased materials; metal barrels, drums & pails
PA: Green Bay Packaging Inc.
  1700 N Webster Ave
  Green Bay WI 54302
  920 433-5111

(G-11661)
HEAT AND SENSOR TECH LLC
Also Called: Heat & Sensor
627 Norgal Dr (45036-9275)
PHONE.....................................513 228-0481
Gary Shackeford, *Mng Member*
Michelle Shackeford,
▲ EMP: 53
SQ FT: 12,000
SALES: 3.7MM **Privately Held**
WEB: www.heatandsensortech.com
SIC: 3567 Heating units & devices, industrial: electric

(G-11662)
HESS TECHNOLOGIES INC
Also Called: Rotex Silver Recovery Co
200 Harmon Ave (45036-8800)
PHONE.....................................513 228-0909
Paul Hess, *President*
Bernadine Hess, *Corp Secy*
EMP: 4
SQ FT: 29,000
SALES: 165K **Privately Held**
WEB: www.rotexsilver.com
SIC: 3559 Silver recovery equipment

(G-11663)
INX INTERNATIONAL INK CO
350 Homan Rd (45036-1181)
PHONE.....................................707 693-2990
EMP: 10
SALES (corp-wide): 1.4B **Privately Held**
SIC: 2893 Printing ink
HQ: Inx International Ink Co.
  150 N Martingale Rd # 700
  Schaumburg IL 60173
  630 382-1800

Lebanon - Warren County (G-11664) — GEOGRAPHIC SECTION

(G-11664)
INX INTERNATIONAL INK CO
350 Homan Rd (45036-1181)
PHONE................................513 282-2920
Randy Robinson, *Manager*
EMP: 12
SALES (corp-wide): 1.4B **Privately Held**
SIC: 2893 Printing ink
HQ: Inx International Ink Co.
150 N Martingale Rd # 700
Schaumburg IL 60173
630 382-1800

(G-11665)
JIT PACKAGING INC
1550 Kingsview Dr (45036-8389)
PHONE................................513 934-0905
Jeff Jones, *Manager*
EMP: 3
SALES (est): 483.1K
SALES (corp-wide): 11.7MM **Privately Held**
SIC: 2653 Boxes, corrugated: made from purchased materials
PA: J.I.T. Packaging, Inc.
250 Page Rd
Aurora OH 44202
330 562-8080

(G-11666)
KADANT BLACK CLAWSON INC
1425 Kingsview Dr (45036-7591)
PHONE................................251 653-8558
Les Pouliot, *Manager*
EMP: 60
SALES (corp-wide): 633.7MM **Publicly Held**
WEB: www.kadantbc.com
SIC: 3554 3523 Sandpaper manufacturing machines; cleaning machines for fruits, grains & vegetables
HQ: Kadant Black Clawson Inc.
1425 Kingsview Dr
Lebanon OH 45036
513 229-8100

(G-11667)
KADANT BLACK CLAWSON INC (HQ)
1425 Kingsview Dr (45036-7591)
PHONE................................513 229-8100
Jonathan W Painter, *President*
Thomas M Obrie, *President*
Wayne South, *Business Mgr*
Eklund John, *Vice Pres*
Tom Golden, *Opers Staff*
▲ **EMP:** 75
SQ FT: 26,000
SALES (est): 39.5MM
SALES (corp-wide): 633.7MM **Publicly Held**
WEB: www.kadantbc.com
SIC: 3554 Paper industries machinery
PA: Kadant Inc.
1 Technology Park Dr # 210
Westford MA 01886
978 776-2000

(G-11668)
KANDO OF CINCINNATI INC
Also Called: Franklin Brazing Met Treating
2025 Mckinley Blvd (45036-8075)
PHONE................................513 459-7782
Timothy Mathile, *CEO*
Blake Michaels, *President*
EMP: 50
SQ FT: 53,000
SALES (est): 9.9MM **Privately Held**
WEB: www.franklinbrazing.com
SIC: 3398 Brazing (hardening) of metal

(G-11669)
KIRBYS AUTO & TRUCK REPAIR
Also Called: Warren Welding and Fabrication
875 Columbus Ave (45036-1692)
PHONE................................513 934-3999
Glen Kirby, *President*
Jennifer Kirby, *Treasurer*
EMP: 8 **EST:** 1996
SQ FT: 12,510
SALES: 650K **Privately Held**
SIC: 7538 7692 General automotive repair shops; welding repair

(G-11670)
LEBANON ELECTRIC MOTOR SVC LLC
602 E Main St (45036-1916)
P.O. Box 156 (45036-0156)
PHONE................................513 932-2889
Tom Carter, *Owner*
EMP: 3
SQ FT: 3,000
SALES (est): 280K **Privately Held**
SIC: 5063 7694 5999 Motors, electric; electric motor repair; motors, electric

(G-11671)
MANE INC (DH)
Also Called: Mane Calafornia
2501 Henkle Dr (45036-7794)
PHONE................................513 248-9876
Jean Mane, *Ch of Bd*
Ken Hunter, *President*
Estelle Klein, *Business Mgr*
Brad Kelley, *COO*
Jill Fleury, *Vice Pres*
◆ **EMP:** 70
SQ FT: 70,000
SALES (est): 115.9MM **Privately Held**
SIC: 2087 2099 Extracts, flavoring; food preparations
HQ: Mane Usa Inc.
60 Demarest Dr
Wayne NJ 07470
973 633-5533

(G-11672)
MANE INC
1093 Mane Way (45036-8049)
PHONE................................513 248-9876
EMP: 70 **Privately Held**
SIC: 2087 Mfg Flavor Extracts/Syrup
HQ: Mane, Inc.
2501 Henkle Dr
Lebanon OH 45036
513 248-9876

(G-11673)
MIX-MASTERS INC
Also Called: Jbs Industries
2550 Henkle Dr (45036-7793)
PHONE................................513 228-2800
Scott Baeten, *President*
John T Hufford, *Vice Pres*
Laurie Baeten, *CFO*
EMP: 17 **EST:** 2000
SQ FT: 18,000
SALES (est): 4.4MM **Privately Held**
SIC: 2841 2842 Soap & other detergents; polishing preparations & related products

(G-11674)
NEWMAN INTERNATIONAL INC
Also Called: Newman Sanitary Gasket
964 W Main St (45036-9173)
P.O. Box 222 (45036-0222)
PHONE................................513 932-7379
Thomas C Moore, *President*
David Wj Newman, *Vice Pres*
▲ **EMP:** 52
SALES (est): 5.4MM **Privately Held**
SIC: 3053 Gaskets, all materials

(G-11675)
NEWMAN SANITARY GASKET COMPANY
964 W Main St (45036-9173)
P.O. Box 222 (45036-0222)
PHONE................................513 932-7379
David William Newman, *President*
Thomas Moore, *Vice Pres*
Justin Todd, *Plant Mgr*
EMP: 41
SQ FT: 38,000
SALES (est): 6MM **Privately Held**
WEB: www.newmangasket.com
SIC: 3053 Gaskets, all materials

(G-11676)
NIBCO INC
2800 Henkle Dr (45036-8894)
PHONE................................513 228-1426
Chris Mason, *Branch Mgr*
EMP: 47
SALES (corp-wide): 713.7MM **Privately Held**
SIC: 3088 Plastics plumbing fixtures

PA: Nibco Inc.
1516 Middlebury St
Elkhart IN 46516
574 295-3000

(G-11677)
OEDER CARL E SONS SAND & GRAV
1000 Mason Mrrow Mlgrv Rd (45036-9271)
PHONE................................513 494-1238
Carl E Oeder, *President*
EMP: 35
SALES (est): 3.5MM **Privately Held**
SIC: 4213 1442 Trucking, except local; construction sand & gravel

(G-11678)
OHIO FLAME HARDENING COMPANY (PA)
4110 Columbia Rd (45036-9588)
PHONE................................513 336-6160
Robert Bokon, *President*
EMP: 7
SQ FT: 65,000
SALES (est): 1.4MM **Privately Held**
SIC: 3398 Brazing (hardening) of metal

(G-11679)
ON-POWER INC
3525 Grant Ave Ste A (45036-6431)
PHONE................................513 228-2100
Larry D Davis, *President*
Joe Back, *Purchasing*
Tim Quackenbush, *Electrical Engi*
Thomas Mergy, *CFO*
Tom Mergy, *CFO*
EMP: 32
SQ FT: 41,350
SALES: 8MM **Privately Held**
WEB: www.onpowerinc.com
SIC: 3511 8711 Gas turbines, mechanical drive; consulting engineer

(G-11680)
OPW ENGINEERED SYSTEMS INC (DH)
2726 Henkle Dr (45036-8209)
PHONE................................888 771-9438
Robert B Nicholson III, *CEO*
Tim Warning, *President*
Mike Krauser, *Vice Pres*
▲ **EMP:** 1
SALES (est): 15MM
SALES (corp-wide): 6.9B **Publicly Held**
WEB: www.opw-es.com
SIC: 3494 3825 3625 3568 Valves & pipe fittings; instruments to measure electricity; relays & industrial controls; power transmission equipment; conveyors & conveying equipment
HQ: Opw Fluid Transfer Group
4304 Nw Mattox Rd
Kansas City MO 64150
816 741-6600

(G-11681)
OVERLY HAUTZ MOTOR BASE CO
Also Called: Overly Hautz Company
285 S West St (45036-2152)
P.O. Box 837 (45036-0837)
PHONE................................513 932-0025
Thomas Copanas, *President*
Trevor Ahlert, *Vice Pres*
Edward Bees, *Vice Pres*
Pete Gough, *Plant Mgr*
Clara Mendez, *Finance*
▲ **EMP:** 50
SQ FT: 27,000
SALES (est): 9.9MM **Privately Held**
WEB: www.overlyhautz.com
SIC: 3699 Electrical equipment & supplies

(G-11682)
PAX CORRUGATED PRODUCTS INC
Also Called: P A X
1899 Kingsview Dr (45036-8397)
PHONE................................513 932-9855
Stan Bernard, *CEO*
James E Cory II, *President*
Pete Magrino, *Maintence Staff*
EMP: 100
SQ FT: 119,457

SALES: 25.8MM
SALES (corp-wide): 42.4B **Privately Held**
WEB: www.paxbox.com
SIC: 2653 Boxes, corrugated: made from purchased materials
HQ: Georgia-Pacific Llc
133 Peachtree St Nw
Atlanta GA 30303
404 652-4000

(G-11683)
PEREGRINE OUTDOOR PRODUCTS LLC (PA)
Also Called: Peregrine Field Gear
4317 N State Route 48 # 3 (45036-1052)
PHONE................................800 595-3850
Steve Kawamoto, *CEO*
Steven Kawamoto, *Mng Member*
Steve Hurt,
Larry Kramer,
James Lua,
EMP: 7
SQ FT: 2,500
SALES (est): 385K **Privately Held**
SIC: 5091 5699 2387 3949 Sharpeners, sporting goods; sports apparel; apparel belts; shooting equipment & supplies, general; target shooting equipment

(G-11684)
PIONEER PRECISION TOOL INC
5100 Bunnell Hill Rd (45036-9052)
PHONE................................513 932-8805
Glenn Johnson, *President*
Cyndi Johnson, *Vice Pres*
EMP: 3
SALES (est): 199.9K **Privately Held**
SIC: 3544 Special dies & tools

(G-11685)
PKG TECHNOLOGIES INC
212 N Broadway St Ste 7 (45036-2736)
P.O. Box 267, Ashburn VA (20146-0267)
PHONE................................513 967-2783
David Wallace, *CEO*
Mihkael Denola, *Ch of Bd*
Mary Schaefer, *CFO*
Paul Denola, *Treasurer*
EMP: 4
SALES (est): 596.1K **Privately Held**
SIC: 7372 Prepackaged software

(G-11686)
PRESS FOR LESS PRINTING FIRM I
1836 Stubbs Mill Rd (45036-9654)
PHONE................................931 912-4606
EMP: 4 **EST:** 2008
SALES (est): 320K **Privately Held**
SIC: 2752 Lithographic Commercial Printing

(G-11687)
QUAD/GRAPHICS INC
760 Fujitec Dr (45036)
PHONE................................513 932-1064
Mike Lehky, *Branch Mgr*
EMP: 509
SALES (corp-wide): 4.1B **Publicly Held**
SIC: 2752 2754 3823 2721 Commercial printing, offset; commercial printing, gravure; controllers for process variables, all types; magazines: publishing & printing
PA: Quad/Graphics Inc.
N61w23044 Harrys Way
Sussex WI 53089
414 566-6000

(G-11688)
RACEWAY BEVERAGE LLC
11 S Broadway St (45036-1769)
PHONE................................513 932-2214
James P Smith Jr, *Principal*
EMP: 3 **EST:** 2008
SALES (est): 142.1K **Privately Held**
SIC: 3644 Raceways

(G-11689)
RED LION NURSERY INC
3505 N State Route 741 (45036-9783)
P.O. Box 67, Franklin (45005-0067)
PHONE................................937 704-9840
Dennis Myers, *President*
EMP: 5
SALES (est): 41.1K **Privately Held**
SIC: 2499 Saddle trees, wood

▲ = Import ▼ = Export
◆ = Import/Export

GEOGRAPHIC SECTION

Leetonia - Columbiana County (G-11716)

(G-11690)
RF LINX INC
2142 Greentree Rd (45036-8129)
PHONE..................513 777-2774
Joe Janning, *President*
▲ EMP: 6
SQ FT: 5,000
SALES (est): 966.3K **Privately Held**
SIC: 3663 Amplifiers, RF power & IF

(G-11691)
ROYCE CO
2340 Lebanon Rd (45036-9681)
PHONE..................513 933-0344
Royce Burton, *Owner*
EMP: 3
SQ FT: 4,000
SALES: 140K **Privately Held**
SIC: 3599 Machine shop, jobbing & repair

(G-11692)
RPMI PACKAGING INC
3899 S Us Route 42 (45036-9530)
P.O. Box 105, Mason (45040-0105)
PHONE..................513 398-4040
Robert Hillerich, *President*
Jane Ribarsky, *Accountant*
Terry Christman, *Sales Executive*
Gary Young, *Marketing Staff*
Sandra Dahling, *IT/INT Sup*
EMP: 10
SALES (est): 1.4MM **Privately Held**
WEB: www.rpmipackaging.com
SIC: 3565 Packaging machinery

(G-11693)
SCHMIDT PROGRESSIVE LLC
Also Called: Food Furniture
360 Harmon Ave (45036-8801)
P.O. Box 380 (45036-0380)
PHONE..................513 934-2600
Don Blades, *Vice Pres*
Stephen Moore, *Sales Executive*
Julia Rodenbeck, *Mng Member*
Joeseph Pardy,
EMP: 20
SQ FT: 55,000
SALES (est): 2.2MM **Privately Held**
WEB: www.schmidtprogressive.com
SIC: 3089 Fiberglass doors

(G-11694)
SCHNEDER ELC BLDNGS AMRCAS INC
1770 Masn Mrrw Millgrv Rd (45036-9688)
PHONE..................513 398-9800
Bill Korn, *Branch Mgr*
Jeffrey Owens, *Manager*
EMP: 80
SALES (corp-wide): 355.8K **Privately Held**
SIC: 1731 3822 Electrical work; auto controls regulating residntl & coml environmt & applncs
HQ: Schneider Electric Buildings Americas, Inc.
1650 W Crosby Rd
Carrollton TX 75006
972 323-1111

(G-11695)
SIEMENS INDUSTRY INC
4170 Columbia Rd (45036-9588)
PHONE..................513 336-2267
Fax: 513 494-5120
EMP: 87
SALES (corp-wide): 96B **Privately Held**
SIC: 3822 Mfg Environmntl Controls
HQ: Siemens Industry, Inc.
1000 Deerfield Pkwy
Buffalo Grove IL 60089
847 215-1000

(G-11696)
SIGNERY
1002 W Main St Apt D (45036-8267)
PHONE..................513 932-1938
Richard Freed, *Owner*
EMP: 3
SQ FT: 1,444
SALES (est): 175.5K **Privately Held**
SIC: 7389 3993 Sign painting & lettering shop; signs & advertising specialties

(G-11697)
SOFFSEAL INC
2175 Deerfield Rd (45036-6422)
PHONE..................513 934-0815
Gary Anderson, *President*
Donna Anderson, *Admin Sec*
▲ EMP: 40
SQ FT: 24,000
SALES (est): 6.6MM **Privately Held**
WEB: www.soffseal.com
SIC: 3069 3061 3053 Rubber automotive products; mechanical rubber goods; gaskets, packing & sealing devices

(G-11698)
SOFTWARE SOLUTIONS INC (PA)
420 E Main St (45036-2234)
PHONE..................513 932-6667
John Rettig, *President*
Rick Fortman, *Vice Pres*
Kevin Nye, *Regl Sales Mgr*
Larry Hollingshead, *Manager*
Monica Scott, *Manager*
EMP: 32 EST: 1978
SQ FT: 12,200
SALES (est): 4.5MM **Privately Held**
WEB: www.elocalgovernment.com
SIC: 5045 7372 7373 Computer software; disk drives; application computer software; computer integrated systems design

(G-11699)
STC INTERNATIONAL CO LTD (PA)
1499 Shaker Run Blvd (45036-4041)
PHONE..................561 308-6002
Frank Ferguson, *President*
EMP: 8
SALES (est): 1.9MM **Privately Held**
SIC: 3541 3545 2821 Machine tools, metal cutting type; machine tool accessories; plastics materials & resins

(G-11700)
TELEMPU N HAYASHI AMER CORP
1500 Kingsview Dr (45036-8389)
PHONE..................513 932-9319
Harry Okamoto, *Director*
EMP: 6
SALES (corp-wide): 1.7B **Privately Held**
SIC: 2396 Automotive trimmings, fabric
HQ: Hayashi Telempu North America Corporation
14328 Genoa Ct
Plymouth MI 48170
734 456-5221

(G-11701)
TOTAL MAINTENANCE MANAGEMENT
320 Harmon Ave (45036-8801)
PHONE..................513 228-2345
Thomas Koerner, *President*
EMP: 6
SQ FT: 14,700
SALES (est): 1.4MM **Privately Held**
SIC: 7694 Electric motor repair

(G-11702)
TRIM PARTS INC
2175 Deerfield Rd (45036-6422)
PHONE..................513 934-0815
Carl Chadwell, *President*
Daniel Jenkins, *Controller*
▲ EMP: 35
SQ FT: 55,000
SALES (est): 6.9MM
SALES (corp-wide): 6.5MM **Privately Held**
WEB: www.trimparts.com
SIC: 3714 3544 3429 Motor vehicle parts & accessories; special dies, tools, jigs & fixtures; manufactured hardware (general)
PA: Restoration Parts Unlimited, Inc.
2175 Deerfield Rd
Lebanon OH 45036
513 934-0815

(G-11703)
TURTLECREEK TOWNSHIP
670 N Rte 123 (45036-7016)
PHONE..................513 932-4080
Steven Flint, *Chief*
EMP: 16 **Privately Held**
SIC: 9199 3621 General government administration; ; generating apparatus & parts, electrical
PA: Turtlecreek Township
670 N State Route 123
Lebanon OH 45036
513 932-4902

(G-11704)
UGN INC
201 Exploration Dr (45036)
PHONE..................513 360-3500
Peter Anthony, *President*
EMP: 160
SALES (corp-wide): 2.2B **Privately Held**
SIC: 3714 Motor vehicle parts & accessories
HQ: U.G.N., Inc.
18410 Crossing Dr Ste C
Tinley Park IL 60487
773 437-2400

(G-11705)
UNITHERM INC
601 Norgal Dr (45036-9308)
P.O. Box 1189 (45036-5189)
PHONE..................937 278-1900
Ronald D Messer, *President*
Brian Messer, *Software Dev*
EMP: 5
SQ FT: 12,000
SALES: 899.4K **Privately Held**
SIC: 2672 Labels (unprinted), gummed: made from purchased materials; adhesive papers, labels or tapes: from purchased material

(G-11706)
VISTECH MFG SOLUTIONS LLC
265 S West St (45036-2152)
PHONE..................513 933-9300
Dylan Roundtree, *Plant Mgr*
Steve Campbell, *Plant Mgr*
Jeff Yezzi, *Sales Mgr*
EMP: 10
SALES (corp-wide): 58.3MM **Privately Held**
SIC: 3565 Packaging machinery
PA: Vistech Manufacturing Solutions, Llc
1156 Scenic Dr Ste 120
Modesto CA 95350
209 544-9333

(G-11707)
WRAY PRECISION PRODUCTS INC
3650 Turtlecreek Rd (45036-9685)
PHONE..................513 228-5000
Steven Dorgan, *President*
Steve Dorgan, *Plant Mgr*
EMP: 7
SQ FT: 12,000
SALES (est): 286K **Privately Held**
SIC: 3599 Machine shop, jobbing & repair

Leesburg
Highland County

(G-11708)
CANDLE-LITE COMPANY LLC
250 Eastern Ave (45135-9783)
P.O. Box 385 (45135-0385)
PHONE..................937 780-2711
EMP: 50
SQ FT: 900,000
SALES (corp-wide): 259.4MM **Privately Held**
WEB: www.lancastercolony.com
SIC: 3999 Candles
HQ: Candle-Lite Company, Llc
10521 Millington Ct Ste B
Blue Ash OH 45242
513 563-1113

(G-11709)
CREATIVE FAB & WELDING LLC
Also Called: Valley Trailers
9691 Stafford Rd (45135-9464)
PHONE..................937 780-5000
Keith Becker, *Production*
Cameron Dyck, *Mng Member*
Jeremy Dyck, *Manager*
EMP: 22
SQ FT: 800
SALES (est): 2.2MM **Privately Held**
SIC: 3441 7692 Fabricated structural metal; welding repair

(G-11710)
JAYRON FABRICATION LLC
13140 New Martinsburg Rd (45135-9623)
PHONE..................740 335-3184
James Gingerich, *Mng Member*
EMP: 5
SALES (est): 590K **Privately Held**
SIC: 3441 7699 Fabricated structural metal; agricultural equipment repair services

(G-11711)
JR KENNEL MFG
12196 Wilmington Ave (45135-9453)
PHONE..................937 780-6104
John Russell, *Owner*
EMP: 5
SALES: 300K **Privately Held**
SIC: 2679 Adding machine rolls, paper: made from purchased material

(G-11712)
LEESBURG MODERN SALES INC
12607 Monroe Rd (45135)
PHONE..................937 780-2613
Janet Dove, *President*
EMP: 3 EST: 1957
SQ FT: 7,200
SALES (est): 409.4K **Privately Held**
WEB: www.fivestarproducts.com
SIC: 2891 2842 Sealing compounds, synthetic rubber or plastic; adhesives; degreasing solvent

(G-11713)
MASON COMPANY LLC
260 Depot Ln (45135-8438)
P.O. Box 365 (45135-0365)
PHONE..................937 780-2321
Greg Taylor, *CEO*
Ked Sturgill, *Safety Dir*
Jeff Ballman, *Plant Mgr*
Gary Silvis, *Engineer*
Elaine Schmidt, *Manager*
EMP: 44
SQ FT: 35,000
SALES (est): 13.4MM **Privately Held**
SIC: 3496 Cages, wire

(G-11714)
MM OUTSOURCING LLC
355 S South St (45135-9473)
P.O. Box 29 (45135-0029)
PHONE..................937 661-4300
Toni May,
EMP: 10
SALES (est): 381.9K **Privately Held**
SIC: 3052 3061 4212 Automobile hose, rubber; automotive rubber goods (mechanical); local trucking, without storage

(G-11715)
PRIEST MILLWRIGHT SERVICE
101 Miller St (45135-0377)
P.O. Box 169 (45135-0169)
PHONE..................937 780-3405
Forrest Priest, *Owner*
EMP: 8
SQ FT: 3,000
SALES (est): 728.7K **Privately Held**
SIC: 3444 Sheet metalwork

Leetonia
Columbiana County

(G-11716)
BUCKEYE FBRICATORS OF LEETONIA
38009 Butcher Rd (44431-9746)
PHONE..................330 427-0330
Frank Grimes, *President*
EMP: 4
SQ FT: 4,950

Leetonia - Columbiana County (G-11717)

SALES (est): 410K **Privately Held**
WEB: www.buckeyemachine.com
SIC: 3441 Fabricated structural metal

(G-11717)
DEIBEL MANUFACTURING LLC
41659 Esterly Dr (44431-9676)
PHONE.....................330 482-3351
Andrew C Deibel, *Mng Member*
Jane M Deibel,
EMP: 6
SALES: 500K **Privately Held**
SIC: 3443 Fabricated plate work (boiler shop)

(G-11718)
LEETONIA TOOL COMPANY
142 Main St (44431-1181)
PHONE.....................330 427-6944
Robert L Holt, *President*
Dennis J Holt, *Vice Pres*
J W Holt, *Treasurer*
EMP: 12 EST: 1907
SQ FT: 25,000
SALES: 450K **Privately Held**
SIC: 3429 Builders' hardware; marine hardware

(G-11719)
PENNEX ALUMINUM
1 Commerce Ave (44431-8720)
PHONE.....................330 427-6704
Thomas Hutchinson, *Principal*
EMP: 100
SALES (est): 4.2MM **Privately Held**
SIC: 2819 Aluminum compounds

(G-11720)
QUAKER CITY SEPTIC TANKS LLC
290 E High St (44431-9653)
PHONE.....................330 427-2239
Jeff Foust, *Mng Member*
EMP: 8
SQ FT: 4,000
SALES (est): 1.7MM **Privately Held**
SIC: 3272 Septic tanks, concrete

(G-11721)
STAINLESS MACHINE ENGINEERING
5275 Woodville Rd (44431-9622)
PHONE.....................330 501-1992
Ken Baun, *President*
EMP: 4
SALES (est): 220K **Privately Held**
WEB: www.stainlessmachine-engineering.com
SIC: 3599 5719 Machine shop, jobbing & repair; metalware

(G-11722)
SUPER SHEET METAL
40811 Bonesville Schl Rd (44431-8623)
PHONE.....................330 482-9045
Wilma J Bolton, *Owner*
Tom Bolton, *Co-Owner*
EMP: 3
SQ FT: 3,000
SALES: 200K **Privately Held**
SIC: 3444 Sheet metalwork

Leipsic
Putnam County

(G-11723)
CRABAR/GBF INC (HQ)
Also Called: Ennis-Leispic
68 Vine St (45856-1488)
PHONE.....................419 943-2141
Keith Walters, *CEO*
EMP: 51
SALES (est): 125.1MM
SALES (corp-wide): 370.1MM **Publicly Held**
SIC: 2752 Business form & card printing, lithographic
PA: Ennis, Inc.
2441 Presidential Pkwy
Midlothian TX 76065
972 775-9801

(G-11724)
CRABAR/GBF INC
Also Called: Crabar Business Systems
68 Vine St (45856-1488)
P.O. Box 66 (45856-0066)
PHONE.....................419 943-2141
Roger Hermiller, *Manager*
EMP: 15
SALES (corp-wide): 370.1MM **Publicly Held**
SIC: 2759 2791 2761 2752 Business forms: printing; typesetting; manifold business forms; commercial printing, lithographic; packaging paper & plastics film, coated & laminated; automotive & apparel trimmings
HQ: Crabar/Gbf, Inc.
68 Vine St
Leipsic OH 45856
419 943-2141

(G-11725)
DILLER METALS INC
507 S Eastom St (45856-1300)
PHONE.....................419 943-3364
Pete Diller, *President*
EMP: 6
SALES (est): 1.5MM **Privately Held**
SIC: 3443 Metal parts

(G-11726)
IAMS COMPANY
3700 State Route 65 (45856-9231)
P.O. Box 87 (45856-0087)
PHONE.....................419 943-4267
Greg Wolking, *Manager*
EMP: 140
SALES (corp-wide): 34.2B **Privately Held**
WEB: www.iams.com
SIC: 2047 Dog food
HQ: The Iams Company
8700 S Masn Montgomery Rd
Mason OH 45040
800 675-3849

(G-11727)
K & L READY MIX INC
300 Putnam Dr (45856-9222)
PHONE.....................419 943-2200
Tyler Kahle, *Manager*
EMP: 6
SALES (est): 419.5K
SALES (corp-wide): 7.6MM **Privately Held**
SIC: 3273 Ready-mixed concrete
PA: K & L Ready Mix Inc
10391 State Route 15
Ottawa OH 45875
419 523-4376

(G-11728)
LAUREATE MACHINE & AUTOMTN LLC
100 Laureate Dr (45856-8710)
P.O. Box 55 (45856-0055)
PHONE.....................419 615-4601
John Mullett, *Mng Member*
▲ EMP: 5
SQ FT: 11,000
SALES (est): 715K **Privately Held**
SIC: 3569 Liquid automation machinery & equipment

(G-11729)
MICKENS INC
Also Called: Leipsic Messenger Newspaper
117 E Main St (45856-1428)
P.O. Box 65 (45856-0065)
PHONE.....................419 943-2590
Keith Mickens, *Branch Mgr*
EMP: 5
SALES (est): 334.4K
SALES (corp-wide): 470.1K **Privately Held**
WEB: www.mickens.com
SIC: 2711 Newspapers, publishing & printing
PA: Mickens Inc
107 East St Ste 1
Liberty Center OH 43532
419 533-2401

(G-11730)
PATRICK PRODUCTS INC
150 S Werner St (45856-1363)
PHONE.....................419 943-4137
Robert S Patrick, *President*
Thomas M Patrick, *Vice Pres*
Dewayne Utrup, *Plant Engr*
Nathan Christman, *Electrical Engi*
Roger Selhorst, *CFO*
▲ EMP: 145 EST: 1999
SQ FT: 300,000
SALES (est): 52.9MM **Privately Held**
WEB: www.patrickproducts.com
SIC: 3089 Plastic containers, except foam

(G-11731)
PRECISION LASER & FORMING
6500 Road 5 (45856-9763)
PHONE.....................419 943-4350
Thomas Koenig, *CEO*
Howard Hermiller, *Treasurer*
EMP: 13
SQ FT: 17,000
SALES (est): 2MM **Privately Held**
SIC: 3312 Blast furnaces & steel mills

(G-11732)
PRETIUM PACKAGING LLC
Also Called: Patrick's
150 S Werner St (45856-1363)
PHONE.....................419 943-3733
EMP: 145
SALES (corp-wide): 141MM **Privately Held**
SIC: 3089 Plastic containers, except foam
HQ: Pretium Packaging, L.L.C.
15450 S Outer Forty Dr St
Chesterfield MO 63017
314 727-8200

(G-11733)
PRO-TEC COATING COMPANY LLC
5000 Pro-Tec Pkwy (45856-8212)
PHONE.....................419 943-1100
Richard Veitch, *President*
EMP: 80
SALES (corp-wide): 108MM **Privately Held**
SIC: 3398 Annealing of metal
PA: Pro-Tec Coating Company, Llc
5500 Pro-Tec Pkwy
Leipsic OH 45856
419 943-1211

(G-11734)
PRO-TEC COATING COMPANY LLC
4500 Protec Pkwy (45856)
PHONE.....................419 943-1100
Richard Veitch, *President*
EMP: 80
SALES (corp-wide): 108MM **Privately Held**
SIC: 3479 Galvanizing of iron, steel or end-formed products
PA: Pro-Tec Coating Company, Llc
5500 Pro-Tec Pkwy
Leipsic OH 45856
419 943-1211

(G-11735)
PRO-TEC COATING COMPANY LLC (PA)
5500 Pro-Tec Pkwy (45856-8215)
PHONE.....................419 943-1211
Richard E Veitch, *President*
Robert M Stanton, *Principal*
Brent Rosebrook, *Vice Pres*
▲ EMP: 230
SQ FT: 725,000
SALES (est): 108MM **Privately Held**
WEB: www.proteccoating.com
SIC: 3479 Galvanizing of iron, steel or end-formed products

(G-11736)
RUHE SALES INC (PA)
5450 State Route 109 (45856-9438)
PHONE.....................419 943-3357
Marilyn Ruhe, *President*
Robert G Ruhe, *Vice Pres*
EMP: 15
SQ FT: 10,000
SALES (est): 828.5K **Privately Held**
SIC: 0721 3721 4581 4512 Crop dusting services; aircraft; airports, flying fields & services; air transportation, scheduled

(G-11737)
SUMMIT ETHANOL LLC
Also Called: Poet Biorefining-Leipsic
3875 State Rd 65 (45856)
PHONE.....................419 943-7447
Jeff Lautt, *CEO*
Mark Borer, *General Mgr*
Daniel Loveland, *CFO*
EMP: 40
SALES (est): 14.5MM **Privately Held**
SIC: 2869 Ethyl alcohol, ethanol; ethanolamines
PA: Poet, Llc
4615 N Lewis Ave
Sioux Falls SD 57104

(G-11738)
WAGNER FARMS & SAWMILL LLC
13201 Road X (45856-9295)
PHONE.....................419 653-4126
James Wagner, *Partner*
Jeffrey Wagner, *Partner*
Martin Wagner, *Partner*
Michael Wagner, *Partner*
Steven Wagner, *Partner*
EMP: 13 EST: 1940
SALES (est): 1.7MM **Privately Held**
WEB: www.wagnerfarms.com
SIC: 2421 0191 2426 Sawmills & planing mills, general; general farms, primarily crop; hardwood dimension & flooring mills

(G-11739)
WARD CONSTRUCTION CO (PA)
385 Oak St (45856-1358)
PHONE.....................419 943-2450
Arnold W Rosebrock, *President*
Patricia A Newell, *Corp Secy*
Barry A Rosebrock, *Vice Pres*
Daniel A Rosebrock, *Vice Pres*
EMP: 19
SALES: 9.4MM **Privately Held**
SIC: 1611 4212 1442 1771 General contractor, highway & street construction; local trucking, without storage; sand mining; gravel mining; concrete work

Lewis Center
Delaware County

(G-11740)
ABRASIVE TECHNOLOGY INC (PA)
8400 Green Meadows Dr N (43035-9453)
P.O. Box 545 (43035-0545)
PHONE.....................740 548-4100
Loyal M Peterman Jr, *President*
Daryl L Peterman, *Principal*
Stephan Koknat, *Research*
James Weldon, *CFO*
Ricardo Fonseca, *Sales Staff*
▲ EMP: 200 EST: 1971
SQ FT: 100,000
SALES (est): 99.5MM **Privately Held**
WEB: www.abrasive-tech.com
SIC: 3291 Abrasive stones, except grinding stones: ground or whole; abrasive wheels & grindstones, not artificial

(G-11741)
ABRASIVE TECHNOLOGY LAPIDARY
Also Called: Crystalite
8400 Green Meadows Dr N (43035-9453)
P.O. Box 545 (43035-0545)
PHONE.....................740 548-4855
Loyal M Peterman, *President*
EMP: 200
SQ FT: 50,000
SALES (est): 13.3MM **Privately Held**
WEB: www.crystalite.com
SIC: 3541 Machine tools, metal cutting type

(G-11742)
ABSOLUTE IMPRESSIONS INC (PA)
281 Enterprise Dr (43035-9418)
PHONE.....................614 840-0599
Keith Hamilton, *President*
Jeff Vigar, *Vice Pres*

GEOGRAPHIC SECTION
Lewis Center - Delaware County (G-11767)

EMP: 14
SQ FT: 15,000
SALES (est): 1.5MM **Privately Held**
WEB: www.absoluteimpressions.com
SIC: 2759 Screen printing

(G-11743)
AIR WAVES LLC
7750 Green Meadows Dr A (43035-8381)
PHONE..................................740 548-1200
Kyle Kantner, *President*
Kim Betz, *Opers Staff*
Daniel Kaiser, *CFO*
◆ EMP: 250 **EST:** 2016
SQ FT: 50,000
SALES (est): 63.6MM **Privately Held**
WEB: www.airwavesinc.com
SIC: 2261 Screen printing of cotton broad-woven fabrics

(G-11744)
AMERIHUA INTL ENTPS INC
707 Radio Dr (43035-7134)
PHONE..................................740 549-0300
Stephen S Chen, *Ch of Bd*
David W Chen, *Vice Pres*
Leighton L Chen, *Vice Pres*
◆ EMP: 7 **EST:** 1984
SQ FT: 3,000
SALES: 5MM **Privately Held**
WEB: www.amerihua.com
SIC: 5149 8742 3231 Specialty food items; management consulting services; Christmas tree ornaments: made from purchased glass

(G-11745)
ATS ATMTION GLOBL SVCS USA INC
425 Enterprise Dr (43035-9424)
PHONE..................................519 653-4483
EMP: 3
SALES (est): 114.7K
SALES (corp-wide): 769.5MM **Privately Held**
SIC: 3823 Industrial instrmnts msrmnt display/control process variable
PA: Ats Automation Tooling Systems Inc
730 Fountain St Suite 2b
Cambridge ON N3H 4
519 653-6500

(G-11746)
ATS OHIO INC
Also Called: Automation Tooling Systems
425 Enterprise Dr (43035-9424)
PHONE..................................614 888-2344
Anthony Caputo, *CEO*
Carl Galloway, *Vice Pres*
▼ EMP: 125 **EST:** 1974
SQ FT: 99,000
SALES: 22.5MM
SALES (corp-wide): 769.5MM **Privately Held**
WEB: www.ats-ohio.com
SIC: 3563 Robots for industrial spraying, painting, etc.
PA: Ats Automation Tooling Systems Inc
730 Fountain St Suite 2b
Cambridge ON N3H 4
519 653-6500

(G-11747)
ATS SYSTEMS OREGON INC
425 Enterprise Dr (43035-9424)
PHONE..................................541 738-0932
Anthony Caputo, *CEO*
Maria Perrella, *President*
Stewart McCvaig, *Admin Sec*
▲ EMP: 300
SQ FT: 85,000
SALES (est): 81.1MM
SALES (corp-wide): 769.5MM **Privately Held**
SIC: 3569 5084 Robots, assembly line: industrial & commercial; industrial machinery & equipment
PA: Ats Automation Tooling Systems Inc
730 Fountain St Suite 2b
Cambridge ON N3H 4
519 653-6500

(G-11748)
AUNTIES ATTIC
1550 Lewis Center Rd G (43035-8232)
PHONE..................................740 548-5059
EMP: 35
SQ FT: 3,500
SALES (est): 1.5MM **Privately Held**
SIC: 2392 5199 Mfg Household Furnishings Whol Nondurable Goods

(G-11749)
AUTOMATION TOOLING SYSTEMS (HQ)
Also Called: Ats Ohio
425 Enterprise Dr (43035-9424)
PHONE..................................614 781-8063
Jeff Brennan, *General Mgr*
Joe Moreno, *Principal*
Jeff Amrine, *Engineer*
Kevin Fairchild, *Engineer*
Dawn Martinski, *Administration*
◆ EMP: 140
SQ FT: 150,000
SALES (est): 594MM
SALES (corp-wide): 769.5MM **Privately Held**
SIC: 3569 Assembly machines, non-metalworking; robots, assembly line: industrial & commercial
PA: Ats Automation Tooling Systems Inc
730 Fountain St Suite 2b
Cambridge ON N3H 4
519 653-6500

(G-11750)
AVURE TECHNOLOGIES INC
8270 Green Meadows Dr N (43035-9450)
PHONE..................................614 891-2732
Melanie Harter, *Branch Mgr*
EMP: 16 **Publicly Held**
SIC: 3823 Industrial process control instruments
HQ: Avure Technologies Incorporated
1830 Airport Exchange Blv
Erlanger KY 41018

(G-11751)
BLACK BOX CORPORATION
Also Called: Black Box Network Services
255 Enterprise Dr (43035-9418)
P.O. Box 327 (43035-0327)
PHONE..................................614 825-7400
Jessica Kwaczala, *Purchasing*
Brendon Gilbert, *Engineer*
Dave Oddo, *Branch Mgr*
John Kuczkowski, *Technology*
EMP: 17
SALES (corp-wide): 1.8MM **Privately Held**
SIC: 3577 3679 3661 Computer peripheral equipment; electronic switches; modems
HQ: Black Box Corporation
1000 Park Dr
Lawrence PA 15055
724 746-5500

(G-11752)
BREAKING BREAD PIZZA COMPANY
9042 Cotter St (43035-7101)
PHONE..................................614 754-4777
Thomas Dumit, *President*
Micheal Scott, *Vice Pres*
William York, *Vice Pres*
EMP: 35
SALES (est): 3.7MM **Privately Held**
SIC: 2051 Bread, cake & related products

(G-11753)
BTC INC
8842 Whitney Dr (43035-8297)
PHONE..................................740 549-2722
Sheldon Lambert, *President*
Jerold S Cook, *Principal*
Robin Mills, *Admin Mgr*
Keith Channels, *Technician*
EMP: 23
SALES (est): 4.8MM **Privately Held**
SIC: 3812 Search & navigation equipment

(G-11754)
BTC TECHNOLOGY SERVICES INC
617 Carle Ave (43035-8294)
PHONE..................................740 549-2722
Sheldon Lambert, *CEO*
EMP: 3
SALES (est): 186.7K **Privately Held**
SIC: 3812 Search & navigation equipment

(G-11755)
DICKMAN DIRECTORIES INC
6145 Columbus Pike (43035-9008)
PHONE..................................740 548-6130
Toll Free:.............................877
William L Michel, *President*
Gerry Michel, *Corp Secy*
EMP: 6
SQ FT: 5,000
SALES (est): 594.8K **Privately Held**
SIC: 2741 Directories: publishing & printing

(G-11756)
DINOL US INC
8520 Cotter St (43035-7138)
PHONE..................................740 548-1656
Joe Renzi, *Business Mgr*
EMP: 6
SALES (est): 108.9K
SALES (corp-wide): 15B **Privately Held**
SIC: 2899 Corrosion preventive lubricant
HQ: Wurth Group Of North America Inc.
93 Grant St
Ramsey NJ 07446
201 818-8877

(G-11757)
DISPATCH PRINTING COMPANY
Also Called: Columbus Dispatch
7801 N Central Dr (43035-9407)
PHONE..................................740 548-5331
Don Patton, *Branch Mgr*
EMP: 238
SALES (corp-wide): 651.9MM **Privately Held**
SIC: 2711 4833 Commercial printing & newspaper publishing combined; television broadcasting stations
PA: The Dispatch Printing Company
62 E Broad St
Columbus OH 43215
614 461-5000

(G-11758)
DURACORP LLC
Also Called: Solut
7787 Graphics Way (43035-8000)
PHONE..................................740 549-3336
Bill Shepard, *CEO*
Scott Rechel, *President*
Jason Kauffman, *Vice Pres*
Erik O Neil, *Vice Pres*
Jo Rodgers, *Cust Mgr*
▼ EMP: 75
SALES (est): 16.7MM **Privately Held**
SIC: 2621 2656 Packaging paper; sanitary food containers

(G-11759)
ELECTRONIC IMAGING SVCS INC
Also Called: Vestcom Retail Solutions
8273 Green Meadows Dr N # 400 (43035-7373)
PHONE..................................740 549-2487
EMP: 6
SALES (corp-wide): 22.7MM **Privately Held**
SIC: 8742 2759 Marketing consulting services; commercial printing; labels & seals: printing; promotional printing
HQ: Electronic Imaging Services, Inc.
2800 Cantrell Rd Ste 400
Little Rock AR 72202
501 663-0100

(G-11760)
EOI INC
Also Called: Medical Resources
8377 Green Meadows Dr N C (43035-9506)
PHONE..................................740 201-3300
Suzi Reichenbach, *CEO*
Randy Reichenbach, *Vice Pres*
Dianne Risch, *CFO*
Tyler Reichenbach, *Sales Staff*
▼ EMP: 16
SQ FT: 18,000
SALES (est): 6MM **Privately Held**
SIC: 5712 5021 5047 3841 Furniture stores; office & public building furniture; medical equipment & supplies; hospital equipment & furniture; instruments, surgical & medical; diagnostic apparatus, medical; electromedical equipment

(G-11761)
GRANDVIEW MATERIALS INC
8598 Cotter St (43035-7137)
PHONE..................................614 488-6998
Jonathan Qian, *President*
▲ EMP: 4
SALES (est): 3MM **Privately Held**
WEB: www.grandviewmaterials.com
SIC: 3341 Secondary nonferrous metals

(G-11762)
INDUSTRIAL SOLUTIONS INC
Also Called: I S I
8333 Green Meadows Dr N A (43035-8497)
PHONE..................................614 431-8118
James D Cooke, *President*
Susan Cooke, *Vice Pres*
Steve Lance, *Purch Mgr*
EMP: 21
SALES (est): 5.3MM **Privately Held**
SIC: 3613 Panelboards & distribution boards, electric

(G-11763)
INPOWER LLC
8311 Green Meadows Dr N (43035-9451)
P.O. Box 2520, Westerville (43086-2520)
PHONE..................................740 548-0965
John Melvin, *Engineer*
Robert Ladow, *Natl Sales Mgr*
Chuck Bennett, *VP Mktg*
Karen Sullivan, *Marketing Mgr*
Jim Sullivan, *Mng Member*
EMP: 15
SQ FT: 14,000
SALES: 59MM **Privately Held**
WEB: www.inpowerdirect.com
SIC: 3559 Electronic component making machinery

(G-11764)
INTERNATIONAL NOODLE COMPANY
341 Enterprise Dr (43035-9418)
PHONE..................................614 888-0665
Ridge Cheung, *President*
Jerry Cheung, *Vice Pres*
Ning Ho Cheung, *Admin Sec*
▲ EMP: 15
SQ FT: 12,000
SALES (est): 2.3MM **Privately Held**
SIC: 2098 Noodles (e.g. egg, plain & water), dry

(G-11765)
LAPEL PINS UNLIMITED LLC
5649 Ketch St (43035-8233)
PHONE..................................614 562-3218
Dean M Kuhn, *Principal*
EMP: 3
SALES (est): 250.2K **Privately Held**
SIC: 3452 Pins

(G-11766)
LUMENOMICS INC
Also Called: Inside Outfitters
8333 Green Meadows Dr N (43035-8496)
PHONE..................................614 798-3500
Carlee Swihart, *Vice Pres*
EMP: 46 **Privately Held**
SIC: 5023 2591 2221 2211 Draperies; venetian blinds; vertical blinds; window covering parts & accessories; drapery hardware & blinds & shades; window shades; draperies & drapery fabrics, man-made fiber & silk; draperies & drapery fabrics, cotton; shades, canvas: made from purchased materials
PA: Lumenomics, Inc.
500 Mercer St C2
Seattle WA 98109

(G-11767)
MICROCOM CORPORATION
8220 Green Meadows Dr N (43035-9450)
PHONE..................................740 548-6262
Steven Wolfe, *CEO*

Lewis Center - Delaware County (G-11768)

James R Larson, *CEO*
David Dezse, *Vice Pres*
John Collins, *Warehouse Mgr*
Greg Melick, *Design Engr*
▲ **EMP:** 24
SQ FT: 29,000
SALES (est): 7.2MM **Privately Held**
WEB: www.microcomcorp.com
SIC: 3577 5111 5112 3953 Printers, computer; bar code (magnetic ink) printers; printing & writing paper; inked ribbons; marking devices

(G-11768)
MIDWEST ENERGY EMISSIONS CORP
670 Enterprise Dr Ste D (43035-9441)
PHONE..................................614 505-6115
Christopher Greenberg, *Ch of Bd*
Richard Macpherson, *President*
John Pavlish, *Senior VP*
James Trettel, *Vice Pres*
Richard H Gross, *CFO*
EMP: 17
SALES: 12.3MM **Privately Held**
SIC: 3822 Auto controls regulating residntl & coml environmt & applncs

(G-11769)
NEURORESCUE LLC
2004 Alum Village Dr (43035-8139)
PHONE..................................614 354-6453
Robert Michael Maher,
Christian Bonasso,
Phillip Immesoete,
William Zerick,
EMP: 4
SALES (est): 149.2K **Privately Held**
SIC: 3841 7389 Medical instruments & equipment, blood & bone work;

(G-11770)
PELTON ENVIRONMENTAL PRODUCTS
8638 Cotter St (43035-7136)
PHONE..................................440 838-1221
Edward Pelton, *Vice Pres*
John Pelton, *Sales Engr*
Janis Gaither, *Manager*
EMP: 8
SALES (est): 920K **Privately Held**
WEB: www.peltonenv.com
SIC: 5074 3589 Water purification equipment; sewage & water treatment equipment

(G-11771)
PHARMA TEGIX LLC
3177 Mccammon Chase Dr (43035-8175)
PHONE..................................740 879-4015
EMP: 3
SALES (est): 188.6K **Privately Held**
SIC: 2834 Pharmaceutical preparations

(G-11772)
PINK CORNER OFFICE INC
8595 Columbus Pike # 106 (43035-9614)
PHONE..................................614 547-9350
Mary Young, *CEO*
EMP: 3 **EST:** 2012
SQ FT: 3,000
SALES (est): 216.9K **Privately Held**
SIC: 2721 Magazines: publishing only, not printed on site

(G-11773)
POWERWASH OF OHIO
8029 Cranes Crossing Dr (43035-8633)
PHONE..................................614 260-2756
Leo Santillo, *Owner*
EMP: 3
SALES: 83K **Privately Held**
SIC: 3589 Car washing machinery

(G-11774)
QUINTUS TECHNOLOGIES LLC
8270 Green Meadows Dr N (43035-9450)
PHONE..................................614 891-2732
Dennis Schwegel, *Manager*
Ed Williams,
EMP: 28
SALES (est): 3.7MM **Privately Held**
SIC: 7699 7389 3443 Industrial equipment services; industrial & commercial equipment inspection service; industrial vessels, tanks & containers

(G-11775)
READY MADE RC LLC
7719 Graphics Way Ste F (43035-9667)
PHONE..................................740 936-4500
Timothy J Stanfield, *President*
▲ **EMP:** 4
SQ FT: 2,400
SALES (est): 220K **Privately Held**
SIC: 5945 3944 Children's toys & games, except dolls; airplane models, toy & hobby; automobile & truck models, toy & hobby

(G-11776)
RETAIL MANAGEMENT PRODUCTS
Also Called: Rxscan
8851 Whitney Dr (43035-7107)
PHONE..................................740 548-1725
Max J Peoples, *Partner*
Bill Peoples, *Partner*
Santanu Lahin, *CIO*
Rachel Reed, *Director*
EMP: 15
SALES (est): 1.8MM **Privately Held**
WEB: www.rxscan.com
SIC: 7372 Business oriented computer software

(G-11777)
ROYAL SPA COLUMBUS
9022 Cotter St (43035-7101)
PHONE..................................614 529-8569
Dan Wilson, *Principal*
EMP: 4
SALES (est): 208K **Privately Held**
SIC: 3949 5091 5999 Water sports equipment; hot tubs; hot tub & spa chemicals, equipment & supplies

(G-11778)
RUBBERTEC INDUSTRIAL PDTS CO
Elledge Gasket
7580 Commerce Ct (43035-9702)
PHONE..................................740 657-3345
Mark Knore, *Manager*
Jeff Severe, *Manager*
EMP: 8 **Privately Held**
SIC: 3053 Gaskets, packing & sealing devices
PA: Rubbertec Industrial Products Company
7580 Commerce Ct
Lewis Center OH 43035

(G-11779)
SHALLOW LAKE CORP
Also Called: Minuteman Press
8958 Cotter St (43035-7103)
PHONE..................................614 883-6350
Mark Werner, *President*
EMP: 3
SQ FT: 1,200
SALES (est): 400.9K **Privately Held**
SIC: 2752 Commercial printing, lithographic

(G-11780)
SIGNMASTER INC
758 Radio Dr (43035-7112)
PHONE..................................614 777-0670
Sandy Beatner, *President*
EMP: 5 **EST:** 1997
SALES (est): 504.1K **Privately Held**
SIC: 3993 Signs & advertising specialties

(G-11781)
SOLID LIGHT COMPANY INC
Also Called: Airwaves
7750 Green Meadows Dr A (43035-8380)
PHONE..................................740 548-1219
EMP: 28
SQ FT: 12,000
SALES (est): 3.9MM **Privately Held**
SIC: 3552 Decorates Apparel And Silk Screeing

(G-11782)
SUN COMMUNITIES INC
5277 Columbus Pike (43035-9710)
PHONE..................................740 548-1942
EMP: 3
SQ FT: 7,942
SALES (corp-wide): 471.6MM **Publicly Held**
SIC: 6798 2451 Real Estate Investment Trust & Mobile Homes
PA: Sun Communities, Inc.
27777 Franklin Rd Ste 200
Southfield MI 48034
248 208-2500

(G-11783)
TEC LINE INC
8020 Strawberry Hill Rd (43035-7030)
PHONE..................................740 881-5948
Richard Edgar, *President*
EMP: 4
SALES: 792K **Privately Held**
SIC: 2819 Industrial inorganic chemicals

(G-11784)
TESA INC
544 Enterprise Dr Ste A (43035-9704)
PHONE..................................614 847-8200
John Truitt, *President*
Becky Rowland, *Sales Staff*
EMP: 7 **EST:** 1973
SALES (est): 1MM **Privately Held**
SIC: 3612 5063 Distribution transformers, electric; electrical apparatus & equipment

(G-11785)
THINK SIGNS LLC
689 Radio Dr (43035-7132)
PHONE..................................614 384-0333
Cynthia Johnson,
Carl Johnson,
EMP: 6
SALES (est): 232.9K **Privately Held**
SIC: 3993 Signs & advertising specialties

(G-11786)
TITANIUM LACROSSE LLC
2671 Coltsbridge Dr (43035-8754)
PHONE..................................614 562-8082
Andrew J Auld, *CEO*
EMP: 12
SALES (est): 1.5MM **Privately Held**
SIC: 3356 Titanium

(G-11787)
TRACEWELL SYSTEMS INC (PA)
567 Enterprise Dr (43035-9431)
PHONE..................................614 846-6175
Larry Tracewell, *President*
Matt Tracewell, *Exec VP*
Betty Tracewell, *Vice Pres*
EMP: 61
SQ FT: 10,000
SALES (est): 26.3MM **Privately Held**
WEB: www.tracewellsystems.com
SIC: 3572 3571 3728 Computer storage devices; electronic computers; aircraft parts & equipment

(G-11788)
WORLDWIDE MACHINE TOOL LLC
9000 Cotter St (43035-7101)
PHONE..................................614 496-9414
Bill Garbe, *President*
◆ **EMP:** 3
SALES (est): 625.8K **Privately Held**
SIC: 3545 Machine tool accessories

Lewisburg
Preble County

(G-11789)
ANDERSON PALLET & PACKG INC
Also Called: Anderson Pallet Service
210 Western Ave (45338-9584)
P.O. Box 669 (45338-0669)
PHONE..................................937 962-2614
Ross Anderson, *President*
Marc Anderson, *Vice Pres*
Grace Anderson, *Treasurer*
EMP: 25
SQ FT: 10,000
SALES (est): 3.2MM **Privately Held**
SIC: 2448 Pallets, wood

(G-11790)
D M TOOL & PLASTICS INC (PA)
4140 Us Route 40 E (45338-9506)
P.O. Box 309, Brookville (45309-0309)
PHONE..................................937 962-4140
Dennis Meyer, *President*
Bill Meyer, *Vice Pres*
Pat Meyer, *Treasurer*
Dan Hickey, *Sales Mgr*
EMP: 18
SQ FT: 35,000
SALES (est): 4.2MM **Privately Held**
WEB: www.bulldogtools.com
SIC: 3089 3599 Injection molding of plastics; machine shop, jobbing & repair

(G-11791)
FETZER MACHINING CO INC
5192 Pyrmont Rd (45338-8759)
PHONE..................................937 962-4019
Don Fetzer, *President*
Linda Joy Fetzer, *Vice Pres*
EMP: 4
SQ FT: 1,728
SALES (est): 399.1K **Privately Held**
SIC: 3599 Machine shop, jobbing & repair

(G-11792)
HEALTHY LIVING
4248 New Market Banta Rd (45338-7739)
PHONE..................................937 962-4705
Thomas Apple, *Owner*
Pam Apple, *Co-Owner*
EMP: 3
SALES (est): 205.4K **Privately Held**
SIC: 2023 Dietary supplements, dairy & non-dairy based

(G-11793)
IAMS COMPANY
6571 State Route 503 N (45338-6713)
P.O. Box 862 (45338)
PHONE..................................937 962-7782
Kurt Petry, *Manager*
EMP: 90
SQ FT: 35,000
SALES (corp-wide): 34.2B **Privately Held**
WEB: www.iams.com
SIC: 2047 5199 Dog food; pet supplies
HQ: The Iams Company
8700 S Masn Montgomery Rd
Mason OH 45040
800 675-3849

(G-11794)
LEWISBURG CONTAINER COMPANY (DH)
275 W Clay St (45338-8107)
P.O. Box 39 (45338-0039)
PHONE..................................937 962-2681
Anthony Pratt, *President*
Davis Kyles, *Corp Secy*
David Wiser, *CFO*
Nedra Beare, *Human Res Mgr*
▲ **EMP:** 235
SQ FT: 384,000
SALES (est): 42.1MM
SALES (corp-wide): 2.5B **Privately Held**
WEB: www.lpgdesign.com
SIC: 2653 Boxes, corrugated: made from purchased materials; display items, corrugated: made from purchased materials
HQ: Pratt Properties, Inc.
1800 Sarasot Bus Pkwy Ne
Conyers GA 30013
770 918-5678

(G-11795)
MANCO INC
6531 State Route 503 N (45338-6713)
PHONE..................................937 962-2661
Dwight Armstrong, *President*
EMP: 4
SALES (est): 320.5K **Privately Held**
WEB: www.akey.com
SIC: 2048 5499 Bone meal, prepared as animal feed; health & dietetic food stores

(G-11796)
PARKER-HANNIFIN CORPORATION
Also Called: Tube Fitting
700 W Cumberland St (45338-8903)
PHONE..................................937 962-5301
William Bowman, *Branch Mgr*

▲ = Import ▼ = Export
◆ = Import/Export

Ron Roohian, *Analyst*
EMP: 150
SALES (corp-wide): 14.3B **Publicly Held**
WEB: www.parker.com
SIC: 3594 Fluid power pumps & motors
PA: Parker-Hannifin Corporation
6035 Parkland Blvd
Cleveland OH 44124
216 896-3000

(G-11797)
PARKER-HANNIFIN CORPORATION
Also Called: Tube Fittings Division
704 W Cumberland St (45338-8903)
PHONE.................................937 962-5566
William Bowman, *Branch Mgr*
Freddy Sykes, *Manager*
EMP: 200
SALES (corp-wide): 14.3B **Publicly Held**
WEB: www.parker.com
SIC: 3492 Hose & tube fittings & assemblies, hydraulic/pneumatic
PA: Parker-Hannifin Corporation
6035 Parkland Blvd
Cleveland OH 44124
216 896-3000

(G-11798)
PROVIMI NORTH AMERICA INC
6531 State Route 503 N (45338-6713)
PHONE.................................937 770-2400
Dwight Armstrong, *President*
Dave Norby, *Exec VP*
Dan Brouse, *Plant Mgr*
Charles Shininger, *Site Mgr*
Lonnie Beisner, *Buyer*
EMP: 55
SALES (corp-wide): 114.7B **Privately Held**
SIC: 2048 Prepared feeds
HQ: Provimi North America, Inc.
10 Collective Way
Brookville OH 45309
937 770-2400

(G-11799)
WYSONG STONE CO
5897 State Route 503 N (45338-6733)
P.O. Box 159 (45338-0159)
PHONE.................................937 962-2559
John D Wysong, *Corp Secy*
Carroll Wysong, *Vice Pres*
EMP: 13 EST: 1965
SQ FT: 1,500
SALES (est): 1MM **Privately Held**
SIC: 1422 Limestones, ground

Lewistown
Logan County

(G-11800)
BLOOM CENTER BIODIESEL LLC
4974 Township Road 79 (43333-9739)
PHONE.................................937 585-6412
Timothy Knief,
EMP: 4
SQ FT: 18,000
SALES: 150K **Privately Held**
SIC: 2911 Diesel fuels

(G-11801)
KNIEF FARMS A PARTNERSHIP
10532 County Road 13 (43333-9740)
PHONE.................................937 585-4810
Jerry Knief, *Partner*
Kevin Knief, *Partner*
Kyle Knief, *Partner*
EMP: 3
SALES (est): 336.9K **Privately Held**
SIC: 3523 Driers (farm): grain, hay & seed

Lewisville
Monroe County

(G-11802)
BOLON TIMBER LLC
45436 Smithberger Rd (43754-9605)
PHONE.................................740 567-4102
Bill Bolon, *Mng Member*
Becky Bolon,
EMP: 5
SALES: 400K **Privately Held**
SIC: 2411 Logging camps & contractors

(G-11803)
GERALD CHRISTMAN
Also Called: Christman Quarry
47278 Swazey Rd (43754-9410)
PHONE.................................740 838-2475
Gerald Christman, *Owner*
EMP: 5 EST: 1949
SQ FT: 1,000
SALES: 597K **Privately Held**
SIC: 1411 1422 Limestone, dimension-quarrying; crushed & broken limestone

Lexington
Richland County

(G-11804)
CONTACT INDUSTRIES INC
25 Industrial Dr (44904-1372)
P.O. Box 3086, Mansfield (44904-0086)
PHONE.................................419 884-9788
James Arnholt, *President*
E R Mc Intyre, *Vice Pres*
EMP: 36
SQ FT: 12,000
SALES (est): 5.4MM **Privately Held**
WEB: www.contactind.com
SIC: 3625 3825 3612 Switches, electronic applications; instruments to measure electricity; transformers, except electric

(G-11805)
NEXT GENERATION FILMS INC (PA)
230 Industrial Dr (44904-1346)
PHONE.................................419 884-8150
David A Frecka, *CEO*
Dan Niss, *President*
Brian Ellis, *Plant Mgr*
Jason Frecka, *Plant Mgr*
Brandon Hall, *Opers Staff*
▲ **EMP:** 166
SALES (est): 61.3MM **Privately Held**
SIC: 2673 2671 3089 Plastic & pliofilm bags; plastic film, coated or laminated for packaging; floor coverings, plastic

(G-11806)
SMH MANUFACTURING INC
Also Called: Deca Manufacturing
300 S Mill St (44904-8519)
PHONE.................................419 884-0071
Mark Huffman, *President*
Scott Huffman, *Vice Pres*
EMP: 11
SALES (est): 1.1MM **Privately Held**
SIC: 3643 3714 3679 Current-carrying wiring devices; booster (jump-start) cables, automotive; harness assemblies for electronic use: wire or cable

(G-11807)
STONERIDGE INC
Also Called: Hi-Stat A Stoneridge Co
345 S Mill St (44904-9573)
PHONE.................................419 884-1219
Tom Morell, *Plant Mgr*
EMP: 700
SALES (corp-wide): 866.2MM **Publicly Held**
WEB: www.stoneridge.com
SIC: 3714 Motor vehicle electrical equipment
PA: Stoneridge, Inc.
39675 Mackenzie Dr # 400
Novi MI 48377
248 489-9300

(G-11808)
SUPPORT SVC LLC
Also Called: Support Service
25 Walnut St Rear (44904-1260)
PHONE.................................419 617-0660
William Purcell, *Owner*
EMP: 7 EST: 2010
SQ FT: 450,000
SALES (est): 1MM **Privately Held**
SIC: 5531 7539 7536 8711 Automotive & home supply stores; alternators & generators, rebuilding & repair; machine shop, automotive; tune-up service, automotive; automotive springs, rebuilding & repair; automotive glass replacement shops; engineering services; nonferrous die-castings except aluminum

Liberty Center
Henry County

(G-11809)
MICKENS INC (PA)
Also Called: Deshler Flag
107 East St Ste 1 (43532-9423)
P.O. Box 6 (43532-0006)
PHONE.................................419 533-2401
Donald Mickens, *President*
Susan Mickens, *Vice Pres*
EMP: 8 EST: 1984
SQ FT: 2,000
SALES (est): 470.1K **Privately Held**
WEB: www.mickens.com
SIC: 2711 Newspapers: publishing only, not printed on site

(G-11810)
TRIPLE DIAMOND PLASTICS LLC
405 N Pleasantview Dr (43532-9376)
P.O. Box 1967, Nokomis FL (34274-1967)
PHONE.................................419 533-0085
N Berry Taylor, *CEO*
Michael Wheeler, *Vice Pres*
Kristine Taylor, *CFO*
EMP: 75
SQ FT: 40,000
SALES (est): 11MM **Privately Held**
SIC: 3089 Boxes, plastic; pallets, plastic

Liberty Township
Butler County

(G-11811)
BOATFUN SPORTS INC
Also Called: Funsports Brands
6548 Westminster Ct (45044-8793)
PHONE.................................513 379-0506
Albert F Buchweitz III, *President*
Stephanie Buchweitz, *Treasurer*
EMP: 3
SQ FT: 400
SALES: 121.4K **Privately Held**
SIC: 3949 Basketball equipment & supplies, general

(G-11812)
COX NEWSPAPERS LLC
Also Called: Western Star Newspaper
200 Harmon Ave (45044)
PHONE.................................513 696-4500
Thomas Barr, *Principal*
EMP: 25
SALES (corp-wide): 32.5B **Privately Held**
WEB: www.coxnewspapers.com
SIC: 2711 Newspapers, publishing & printing
HQ: Cox Newspapers, Inc.
6205 Peachtree Dunwoody
Atlanta GA 30328

(G-11813)
COX NEWSPAPERS LLC
Also Called: Hamilton Journalnews
7320 Yankee Rd (45044-9168)
PHONE.................................513 863-8200
EMP: 60
SALES (corp-wide): 32.5B **Privately Held**
SIC: 2711 Newspapers, publishing & printing
HQ: Cox Newspapers, Inc.
6205 Peachtree Dunwoody
Atlanta GA 30328

(G-11814)
FLEXTRONICS INTERNATIONAL USA
6224 Windham Ct (45044-8659)
PHONE.................................513 755-2500
EMP: 535
SALES (corp-wide): 23.8B **Privately Held**
SIC: 3672 Printed circuit boards
HQ: Flextronics International Usa, Inc.
6201 America Center Dr
San Jose CA 95002

(G-11815)
HAMILTON JOURNAL NEWS INC
7320 Yankee Rd (45044-9168)
PHONE.................................513 863-8200
Anne Hoffman, *President*
EMP: 75
SALES (est): 2.5MM **Privately Held**
SIC: 2711 Commercial printing & newspaper publishing combined; newspapers, publishing & printing

(G-11816)
HAMPTON PUBLISHING COMPANY
7739 Derbyshire Ct (45044-9028)
PHONE.................................513 777-9543
Mike McNeil, *President*
Barbara McNeil, *Director*
EMP: 5
SALES (est): 533.8K **Privately Held**
SIC: 2741 Maps: publishing & printing

(G-11817)
PULSE JOURNAL
7320 Yankee Rd (45044-9168)
PHONE.................................513 829-7900
Ann Hoffman, *Principal*
EMP: 25
SALES (est): 960.6K **Privately Held**
SIC: 2711 Newspapers, publishing & printing

(G-11818)
QUEST SOLUTIONS GROUP LLC
8046 Green Lake Dr (45044-9474)
PHONE.................................513 703-4520
Larry Thomas, *Mng Member*
P Diana Thomas, *Mng Member*
EMP: 6
SALES: 500K **Privately Held**
SIC: 2891 2621 Adhesives & sealants; waterproof paper

(G-11819)
SCHNEIDER ELECTRIC USA INC
5425 Longhunter Chase Dr (45044-9817)
PHONE.................................513 755-5503
Alan Turner, *Branch Mgr*
EMP: 152
SALES (corp-wide): 355.8K **Privately Held**
SIC: 3613 Switchgear & switchboard apparatus
HQ: Schneider Electric Usa, Inc.
201 Wshington St Ste 2700
Boston MA 02108
978 975-9600

(G-11820)
SHUR CLEAN USA LLC
7568 Wyandot Ln Unit 3 (45044-9609)
P.O. Box 8406, West Chester (45069-8406)
PHONE.................................513 341-5486
David Kling,
EMP: 4 EST: 2011
SQ FT: 5,000
SALES (est): 307.2K **Privately Held**
SIC: 1799 2842 3471 Exterior cleaning, including sandblasting; steam cleaning of building exteriors; specialty cleaning preparations; cleaning, polishing & finishing; cleaning & descaling metal products; decontaminating & cleaning of missile or satellite parts

Liberty Twp
Butler County

(G-11821)
APOSTROPHE APPS LLC
4452 Millikin Rd (45011-2309)
PHONE.................513 608-4399
Mark Seremet,
EMP: 3
SALES (est): 149.1K **Privately Held**
SIC: 7372 7389 Application computer software;

(G-11822)
COFFING CORPORATION (PA)
5336 Lesourdsville Rd (45011-9740)
PHONE.................513 919-2813
Chris Coffing, *President*
EMP: 15
SQ FT: 5,000
SALES (est): 2.8MM **Privately Held**
SIC: 7372 7389 Prepackaged software;

(G-11823)
D M L STEEL TECH
6974 Zenith Ct (45011-7207)
PHONE.................513 737-9911
Suguna Bommaraju, *Partner*
Rama Bommaraju, *Partner*
EMP: 13
SALES (est): 1.5MM **Privately Held**
SIC: 3315 8748 Steel wire & related products; business consulting

(G-11824)
DALACO MATERIALS LLC
4805 Hamilton Middltwn (45011-2686)
PHONE.................513 893-5483
Dallas Myers,
EMP: 15
SQ FT: 120,000
SALES (est): 3.1MM **Privately Held**
SIC: 3272 Concrete products

(G-11825)
FEATHER LITE INNOVATIONS INC
Also Called: Tuf-N-Lite
4805 Hmlton Middletown Rd (45011-2686)
PHONE.................513 893-5483
Randy Ledford, *General Mgr*
EMP: 11 **Privately Held**
SIC: 3444 Concrete forms, sheet metal
PA: Feather Lite Innovations, Inc.
650 Pleasant Valley Dr
Springboro OH 45066

(G-11826)
KENNETH SHANNON
5438 Kyles Station Rd (45011-9741)
PHONE.................513 777-8888
Kenneth Shannon, *Principal*
EMP: 3
SALES (est): 165.2K **Privately Held**
SIC: 2512 Upholstered household furniture

(G-11827)
KUWATCH PRINTING LLC
Also Called: Corporate Printing
7163 Ashview Ln (45011-8723)
PHONE.................513 759-5850
Kurt Kuwatch,
EMP: 4
SQ FT: 6,500
SALES: 500K **Privately Held**
WEB: www.corp-print.com
SIC: 2752 Commercial printing, lithographic

Lima
Allen County

(G-11828)
3 BROTHERS TORCHING INC
4915 Dutch Hollow Rd (45807-9703)
PHONE.................419 339-9985
Donnie Gipson, *Mng Member*
EMP: 3
SALES (est): 336K **Privately Held**
SIC: 3541 Machine tools, metal cutting type

(G-11829)
ACCUBUILT INC (PA)
2550 Cent Point Pkwy (45804)
PHONE.................419 224-3910
Gregory J Corona, *President*
Ronald Reagan, *Principal*
Kevin Grady, *CFO*
▼ **EMP:** 216
SQ FT: 168,000
SALES: 81.3MM **Privately Held**
SIC: 3711 Hearses (motor vehicles), assembly of

(G-11830)
ACCUBUILT INC
Also Called: Eureeka
2550 Central Point Pkwy (45804-3890)
PHONE.................419 224-3910
Rob Hubbard, *CEO*
Ed McDonald, *VP Sls/Mktg*
EMP: 119
SQ FT: 168,000
SALES: 16MM
SALES (corp-wide): 81.3MM **Privately Held**
SIC: 3711 Hearses (motor vehicles), assembly of
PA: Accubuilt, Inc.
2550 Cent Point Pkwy
Lima OH 45804
419 224-3910

(G-11831)
AIRGAS USA LLC
1590 Mcclain Rd (45804-1974)
PHONE.................419 228-2828
Jason Morsow, *Manager*
EMP: 16
SALES (corp-wide): 125.9MM **Privately Held**
WEB: www.us.linde-gas.com
SIC: 2813 5084 Argon; welding machinery & equipment
HQ: Airgas Usa, Llc
259 N Radnor Chester Rd # 100
Radnor PA 19087
610 687-5253

(G-11832)
AIRWAVE COMMUNICATIONS CONS
Also Called: Cell 4less
1209 Allentown Rd (45805-2432)
P.O. Box 5216 (45802-5216)
PHONE.................419 331-1526
Dominic Sementelli, *President*
Jeff Lunguy, *Exec VP*
EMP: 8
SQ FT: 2,700
SALES (est): 510.6K **Privately Held**
SIC: 4813 4812 3577 7371 Local & long distance telephone communications; radio pager (beeper) communication services; computer peripheral equipment; computer software systems analysis & design, custom

(G-11833)
AKZO NOBEL CHEMICALS LLC
1747 Fort Amanda Rd (45804-1864)
PHONE.................419 229-0088
Kathy Scott, *Manager*
EMP: 4
SALES (corp-wide): 11.3B **Privately Held**
WEB: www.akzo-nobel.com
SIC: 2869 2899 Industrial organic chemicals; chemical preparations
HQ: Akzo Nobel Chemicals Llc
525 W Van Buren St # 1600
Chicago IL 60607
312 544-7000

(G-11834)
ALLEN COUNTY FABRICATION INC
Also Called: A C F
999 Industry Ave (45804-4171)
PHONE.................419 227-7447
Kevin E Hall, *President*
Ronald M Kennedy, *President*
Patricia Kennedy, *Treasurer*
Billie Neal, *Manager*
EMP: 20
SQ FT: 16,800
SALES (est): 4.1MM **Privately Held**
WEB: www.allencountyfab.com
SIC: 3444 Sheet metal specialties, not stamped

(G-11835)
ALPHA BUS FORMS & PRTG LLC
4330 East Rd (45807-1535)
PHONE.................419 999-5138
Kris Griss, *Manager*
Karen E Burgoon,
Pam Baker,
Phillip Kleman,
Karen McElroy,
EMP: 3
SQ FT: 6,000
SALES (est): 285.3K **Privately Held**
WEB: www.alphaprintingforms.com
SIC: 2759 Commercial Printing

(G-11836)
AMERICAN BOTTLING COMPANY
Also Called: 7 Up Bottling Co
2350 Central Point Pkwy (45804-3806)
PHONE.................419 229-7777
Mike Hoenie, *Manager*
EMP: 26 **Publicly Held**
WEB: www.cs-americas.com
SIC: 2086 Bottled & canned soft drinks
HQ: The American Bottling Company
5301 Legacy Dr
Plano TX 75024

(G-11837)
AMERICAN TRIM LLC
Also Called: Superior Metal Products
999 W Grand Ave (45801-3427)
PHONE.................419 996-4703
Randy Fosnaugh, *Branch Mgr*
EMP: 3
SALES (corp-wide): 445.1MM **Privately Held**
SIC: 3469 Porcelain enameled products & utensils
HQ: American Trim, L.L.C.
1005 W Grand Ave
Lima OH 45801

(G-11838)
AMERICAN TRIM LLC
651 N Baxter St (45801-3953)
PHONE.................419 996-4729
Gary Fosnaugh, *Branch Mgr*
EMP: 100
SALES (corp-wide): 445.1MM **Privately Held**
SIC: 3469 Porcelain enameled products & utensils
HQ: American Trim, L.L.C.
1005 W Grand Ave
Lima OH 45801

(G-11839)
AMERICAN TRIM LLC
625 Victory Ave (45801-3952)
PHONE.................419 996-4703
Randy Fosnaugh, *Manager*
EMP: 73
SALES (corp-wide): 445.1MM **Privately Held**
SIC: 3469 Porcelain enameled products & utensils
HQ: American Trim, L.L.C.
1005 W Grand Ave
Lima OH 45801

(G-11840)
AMERICAN TRIM LLC (HQ)
1005 W Grand Ave (45801-3429)
PHONE.................419 228-1145
Jeffrey A Hawk, *CEO*
Mick Berning, *President*
Marcelo Gonzalez, *General Mgr*
Leo J Hawk, *Chairman*
Paul Whitfield, *COO*
▲ **EMP:** 50
SQ FT: 15,000
SALES: 275.5MM
SALES (corp-wide): 445.1MM **Privately Held**
SIC: 3469 Porcelain enameled products & utensils
PA: Superior Metal Products, Inc.
1005 W Grand Ave
Lima OH 45801
419 228-1145

(G-11841)
AMERIX NUTRA-PHARMA
904 N Cable Rd (45805-1704)
PHONE.................567 204-7756
EMP: 3
SALES (est): 216.9K **Privately Held**
SIC: 2834 Pharmaceutical preparations

(G-11842)
AREA WIDE PROTECTIVE INC
413 Flanders Ave (45801-4117)
PHONE.................419 221-2997
EMP: 5
SALES (corp-wide): 172.7MM **Privately Held**
SIC: 3669 Pedestrian traffic control equipment
HQ: Area Wide Protective, Inc.
826 Overholt Rd
Kent OH 44240
330 644-0655

(G-11843)
ARTS ROLLOFFS & REFUSE INC
108 Cheshire Cir (45804-3316)
P.O. Box 2039, Cridersville (45806-0039)
PHONE.................419 991-3730
Arthor Recker, *President*
EMP: 3
SALES (est): 455.8K **Privately Held**
SIC: 3713 Garbage, refuse truck bodies

(G-11844)
ASHLAND LLC
1220 S Metcalf St (45804-1171)
PHONE.................419 998-8728
Charley Gaspereppi, *Manager*
EMP: 40
SALES (corp-wide): 3.7B **Publicly Held**
WEB: www.ispcorp.com
SIC: 2899 Chemical preparations
HQ: Ashland Llc
50 E Rivercenter Blvd # 1600
Covington KY 41011
859 815-3333

(G-11845)
BRANDON SCREEN PRINTING
326 S West St (45801-4844)
PHONE.................419 229-9837
Robert L Liddle, *Owner*
EMP: 10
SQ FT: 12,000
SALES: 1MM **Privately Held**
SIC: 2396 3993 2752 Screen printing on fabric articles; signs & advertising specialties; commercial printing, lithographic

(G-11846)
BRINKMAN LLC
Also Called: American Paint Recyclers
1524 Adak Ave (45805-3905)
PHONE.................419 204-5934
Jeremy Brinkman, *Mng Member*
Joshua Brinkman,
EMP: 10 **EST:** 2007
SALES (est): 354.3K **Privately Held**
SIC: 2851 5812 7359 Paints & paint additives; pizzeria, independent; equipment rental & leasing

(G-11847)
BRP MANUFACTURING COMPANY
Also Called: Buckeye Rubber Products
637 N Jackson St (45801-4125)
PHONE.................800 858-0482
Kendall House, *President*
Steve Pendergast, *Vice Pres*
Matthew Henderson, *Controller*
Jim Ward, *Sales Mgr*
Donovan Lonsway, *Manager*
◆ **EMP:** 44 **EST:** 1997
SQ FT: 190,000
SALES (est): 10.8MM **Privately Held**
WEB: www.brpmfg.com
SIC: 3069 3061 2822 Sheeting, rubber or rubberized fabric; friction tape, rubber; mechanical rubber goods; synthetic rubber

GEOGRAPHIC SECTION
Lima - Allen County (G-11873)

(G-11848)
CAMERON PACKAGING INC
250 E Hanthorn Rd (45804-2344)
PHONE.............................419 222-9404
Michael Cameron, *CEO*
Grant Morgenstern, *President*
Bridget Cribben, *Treasurer*
Diane Cameron, *Admin Sec*
▲ EMP: 9
SQ FT: 56,000
SALES (est): 2MM **Privately Held**
WEB: www.cameronpackaging.com
SIC: 2653 Boxes, corrugated: made from purchased materials

(G-11849)
COCA-COLA BOTTLING CO CNSLD
201 N Shore Dr (45801-4822)
P.O. Box 268, Findlay (45839-0268)
PHONE.............................419 422-3743
John Iafolla, *Branch Mgr*
EMP: 9
SALES (corp-wide): 4.6B **Publicly Held**
WEB: www.colasic.net
SIC: 2086 Soft drinks: packaged in cans, bottles, etc.
PA: Coca-Cola Consolidated, Inc.
    4100 Coca Cola Plz # 100
    Charlotte NC 28211
    704 557-4400

(G-11850)
CSS PUBLISHING CO INC
5450 N Dixie Hwy (45807-9559)
PHONE.............................419 227-1818
Wesley T Runk, *President*
Patti Furr, *Vice Pres*
Elen Shockey, *Treasurer*
David Runk, *VP Sales*
EMP: 30
SQ FT: 50,000
SALES (est): 2.6MM **Privately Held**
WEB: www.csspub.com
SIC: 2731 5192 Books: publishing only; books

(G-11851)
CUSTOM BLAST & COAT INC
1511 S Dixie Hwy (45804-1844)
PHONE.............................419 225-6024
G J Gossard, *President*
Bruce Dukeman, *Admin Sec*
EMP: 8
SALES (est): 937.7K **Privately Held**
SIC: 3312 Blast furnace & related products

(G-11852)
DANA DRIVE SHAFT PDTS GROUP
Also Called: Corp, Dana
777 Bible Rd (45801-2025)
PHONE.............................419 227-2001
Mark Neidert, *Engineer*
Tim Johns, *Manager*
Ron Mertz, *Maintence Staff*
EMP: 3
SALES (est): 813.9K **Privately Held**
SIC: 3714 Motor vehicle parts & accessories

(G-11853)
DANA DRIVESHAFT MFG LLC
Also Called: Dana Driveshaft Products
777 Bible Rd (45801-2025)
PHONE.............................419 222-9708
Nick Fasone, *Branch Mgr*
EMP: 118 **Publicly Held**
SIC: 3714 Motor vehicle parts & accessories
HQ: Dana Driveshaft Manufacturing, Llc
    3939 Technology Dr
    Maumee OH 43537

(G-11854)
DESTER CORPORATION
1200 E Kibby St Bldg 32 (45804-3163)
PHONE.............................419 362-8020
Stef Vandeperre, *President*
Deborah Lesly, *Manager*
◆ EMP: 12 EST: 2006
SQ FT: 157,000
SALES (est): 1.9MM **Privately Held**
SIC: 3089 Plastic containers, except foam

HQ: Gategroup Holding Ag
    Sagereistrasse 20
    Glattbrugg ZH 8152
    445 337-000

(G-11855)
DESTER CORPORATION
1200 E Kibby St Bldg 6 (45804-3163)
PHONE.............................419 362-8020
Patricia Hopkins, *President*
Vernon Hines, *Production*
EMP: 12
SALES (est): 776.5K **Privately Held**
SIC: 3089 Air mattresses, plastic

(G-11856)
DR PEPPER SNAPPLE GROUP
2480 Saint Johns Rd (45804-4003)
PHONE.............................419 223-0072
Larry Young, *President*
EMP: 4
SALES (est): 218K **Privately Held**
SIC: 2086 Bottled & canned soft drinks

(G-11857)
DR PEPPER/SEVEN UP INC
2350 Central Point Pkwy (45804-3806)
PHONE.............................419 229-7777
Marvin Lehman, *Principal*
EMP: 68 **Publicly Held**
SIC: 2086 Soft drinks: packaged in cans, bottles, etc.
HQ: Dr Pepper/Seven Up, Inc.
    5301 Legacy Dr Fl 1
    Plano TX 75024
    972 673-7000

(G-11858)
DYNACO USA INC
1075 Prosperity Rd (45801-3127)
PHONE.............................419 227-3000
Deb Kruger, *Branch Mgr*
EMP: 3
SALES (corp-wide): 9B **Privately Held**
SIC: 3442 Rolling doors for industrial buildings or warehouses, metal
HQ: Dynaco Usa, Inc.
    935 Campus Dr
    Mundelein IL 60060
    847 562-4910

(G-11859)
E S INDUSTRIES INC (PA)
110 Brookview Ct (45801-2070)
PHONE.............................419 643-2625
Charles Dale, *President*
Charles L Dale, *President*
EMP: 5
SALES (est): 7.2MM **Privately Held**
SIC: 3535 3556 4221 Conveyors & conveying equipment; food products machinery; grain elevator, storage only

(G-11860)
ERIE CERAMIC ARTS COMPANY LLC
1005 W Grand Ave (45801-3429)
PHONE.............................419 228-1145
Rick Pfeifer,
Jeffrey Hawk,
Leo J Hawk,
Dana Morgan,
EMP: 5 EST: 1946
SQ FT: 200,000
SALES (est): 742.5K
SALES (corp-wide): 445.1MM **Privately Held**
SIC: 3479 Enameling, including porcelain, of metal products
PA: Superior Metal Products, Inc.
    1005 W Grand Ave
    Lima OH 45801
    419 228-1145

(G-11861)
ERNST ENTERPRISES INC
Also Called: Ernst Ready Mix Division
377 S Central Ave (45804-1301)
PHONE.............................419 222-2015
Edward Bryam, *Manager*
EMP: 17
SALES (corp-wide): 227.2MM **Privately Held**
WEB: www.ernstconcrete.com
SIC: 5211 3275 Concrete & cinder block; gypsum products

PA: Ernst Enterprises, Inc.
    3361 Successful Way
    Dayton OH 45414
    937 233-5555

(G-11862)
F3 DEFENSE SYSTEMS LLC
1601 S Dixie Hwy (45804-1842)
P.O. Box 344, Ellenton FL (34222-0344)
PHONE.............................419 982-2020
Shefali Vibhakar, *Partner*
EMP: 9
SQ FT: 24,600
SALES (est): 557.3K **Privately Held**
SIC: 3599 Machine & other job shop work; machine shop, jobbing & repair

(G-11863)
FMH ELECTRIC INC
Also Called: Mac Electric
1240 Fairgreen Ave (45805-4432)
PHONE.............................419 782-0671
EMP: 12
SQ FT: 6,400
SALES (est): 1.2MM **Privately Held**
SIC: 7694 7699 5063 Electric Motor Repair

(G-11864)
FORD MOTOR COMPANY
1155 Bible Rd (45801-3193)
PHONE.............................419 226-7000
Parker Kronour, *Safety Mgr*
Colleen Stein, *Purch Mgr*
Jim Hare, *Engineer*
Paul A Edwards, *Branch Mgr*
Mike Rafferty, *Manager*
EMP: 1949
SQ FT: 2,424,360
SALES (corp-wide): 160.3B **Publicly Held**
WEB: www.ford.com
SIC: 3714 3519 Motor vehicle engines & parts; internal combustion engines
PA: Ford Motor Company
    1 American Rd
    Dearborn MI 48126
    313 322-3000

(G-11865)
FORT AMANDA SPECIALTIES LLC
1747 Fort Amanda Rd (45804-1864)
PHONE.............................419 229-0088
Bouke Ankone, *Opers Mgr*
Angie Neeld, *Production*
Lisa Goodin, *Engineer*
Owen Griffiths, *Manager*
BASF Corp,
▲ EMP: 85
SALES (est): 36.6MM
SALES (corp-wide): 11.3B **Privately Held**
WEB: www.fortamanda.com
SIC: 2899 Chemical preparations
PA: Akzo Nobel N.V.
    Christian Neefestraat 2
    Amsterdam

(G-11866)
FULTZ SIGN CO INC
3350 Slabtown Rd (45804-2212)
PHONE.............................419 225-6000
Chris Fultz, *President*
Evelyn Fultz, *Vice Pres*
EMP: 4
SQ FT: 1,492
SALES (est): 413.3K **Privately Held**
SIC: 3993 Electric signs

(G-11867)
GASDORF TOOL AND MCH CO INC
445 N Mcdonel St (45801-4266)
P.O. Box 1194 (45802-1194)
PHONE.............................419 227-0103
Richard R Rapp, *President*
Lynn Krohn, *Corp Secy*
EMP: 30 EST: 1953
SQ FT: 20,000
SALES (est): 5.1MM **Privately Held**
SIC: 3599 3544 Custom machinery; special dies & tools; jigs & fixtures; industrial molds

(G-11868)
GASLAMP POPCORN COMPANY
6575 Bellefontaine Rd (45804-4415)
PHONE.............................951 684-6767
Leslie Accuar, *CEO*
George Wiley, *Ch of Bd*
EMP: 5
SALES (est): 455.7K
SALES (corp-wide): 138.3MM **Privately Held**
SIC: 2099 Food preparations
PA: Rudolph Foods Company, Inc.
    6575 Bellefontaine Rd
    Lima OH 45804
    909 383-7463

(G-11869)
GENERAL DYNAMICS LAND
Also Called: General Dyn Lima Army T P
1161 Buckeye Rd (45804-1825)
PHONE.............................419 221-7000
Tom Beining, *Engineer*
David Biller, *Engineer*
Dan Cassidy, *Engineer*
Brian Westerfield, *Engineer*
Gregory Bonifas, *Senior Engr*
EMP: 400
SALES (corp-wide): 36.1B **Publicly Held**
WEB: www.gdls.com
SIC: 3795 Tanks, military, including factory rebuilding
HQ: General Dynamics Land Systems Inc.
    38500 Mound Rd
    Sterling Heights MI 48310
    586 825-4000

(G-11870)
GREATER OHIO ETHANOL LLC (PA)
7227 Harding Hwy (45801-8719)
PHONE.............................567 940-9500
Gregory A Kruger, *Mng Member*
James Blair,
EMP: 8
SQ FT: 3,000
SALES (est): 559K **Privately Held**
WEB: www.go-ethanol.com
SIC: 2869 Ethyl alcohol, ethanol

(G-11871)
GROSS & SONS CUSTOM MILLWORK
1219 Grant St (45803-3735)
PHONE.............................419 227-0214
James H Gross, *President*
Debra Gross, *Treasurer*
EMP: 6
SQ FT: 8,000
SALES (est): 791.4K **Privately Held**
SIC: 2431 2541 2434 Millwork; counter & sink tops; wood kitchen cabinets

(G-11872)
GUARDIAN LIMA LLC
2485 Houx Pkwy (45804-3901)
PHONE.............................567 940-9500
Don Dales, *CEO*
Jack Wolfcale, *Prdtn Mgr*
Adam Spees, *Supervisor*
Chris Kaufman, *Maintence Staff*
EMP: 34
SALES (est): 13.1MM
SALES (corp-wide): 27.9MM **Privately Held**
SIC: 2869 Ethyl alcohol, ethanol
PA: Guardian Energy, Llc
    4745 380th Ave
    Janesville MN 56048
    507 234-5000

(G-11873)
HEAT TREATING TECHNOLOGIES
1799 E 4th St (45804-2713)
PHONE.............................419 224-8324
Chester L Walthall, *CEO*
Richard W Deibel, *President*
Judith Walthall, *Admin Sec*
EMP: 23
SQ FT: 33,000
SALES (est): 4.9MM **Privately Held**
WEB: www.httlima.com
SIC: 3398 Metal heat treating

Lima - Allen County (G-11874)

(G-11874)
HIGH TECH METAL PRODUCTS LLC
2300 Central Point Pkwy (45804-3806)
PHONE...........................419 227-9414
Jerry Neuman, *Owner*
EMP: 8
SQ FT: 25,000
SALES (est): 660K **Privately Held**
SIC: 3599 Machine shop, jobbing & repair

(G-11875)
HUSKY LIMA REFINERY
1150 S Metcalf St (45804-1145)
PHONE...........................419 226-2300
Don Deley, *District Mgr*
Thomas Langer, *District Mgr*
Patrick Conrath, *Opers Mgr*
Jay Patel, *Warehouse Mgr*
Anthony Underwood, *Opers Staff*
EMP: 55 EST: 2016
SALES (est): 9.7MM **Privately Held**
SIC: 2911 Oils, fuel

(G-11876)
IHEARTCOMMUNICATIONS INC
Also Called: Clear Channel
667 W Market St (45804-4603)
PHONE...........................419 223-2060
Kim Field, *General Mgr*
EMP: 65 **Publicly Held**
SIC: 4832 2711 Radio broadcasting stations; newspapers
HQ: Iheartcommunications, Inc.
20880 Stone Oak Pkwy
San Antonio TX 78258
210 822-2828

(G-11877)
INEOS LLC (PA)
1900 Fort Amanda Rd (45804-1827)
P.O. Box 628 (45802-0628)
PHONE...........................419 226-1200
Dennis Seith, *President*
Tracey Maag, *COO*
Mike Hazel, *Mfg Mgr*
Don Ramsey, *Facilities Mgr*
Mark Rush, *Buyer*
▲ EMP: 73
SALES (est): 34.1MM **Privately Held**
SIC: 2899 Chemical preparations

(G-11878)
INEOS NITRILES USA LLC
1900 Fort Amanda Rd (45804-1827)
P.O. Box 628 (45802-0628)
PHONE...........................419 226-1200
Phil Popovec, *Principal*
EMP: 157
SALES (est): 4.7MM **Privately Held**
SIC: 2824 2869 Acrylonitrile fibers; industrial organic chemicals

(G-11879)
INTERNATIONAL BRAKE INDS INC (DH)
Also Called: Carlson Quality Brake
1840 Mccullough St (45801-3098)
PHONE...........................419 227-4421
Greg Andes, *President*
Steve Mart, *Vice Pres*
Anthony Armaly, *Opers Staff*
Bryan Stroth, *Opers Staff*
Greg Miller, *Purch Mgr*
▲ EMP: 153
SQ FT: 91,000
SALES (est): 92.1MM **Privately Held**
WEB: www.ibilima.com
SIC: 3713 3714 Truck & bus bodies; motor vehicle brake systems & parts
HQ: Qualitor, Inc.
1840 Mccullough St
Lima OH 45801
248 204-8600

(G-11880)
ISP LIMA LLC
12220 S Metcalf St (45804)
PHONE...........................419 998-8700
Sunil Kumar,
▲ EMP: 36
SALES (est): 8MM **Privately Held**
SIC: 2911 Petroleum refining
HQ: Isp Chemicals Llc
455 N Main St
Calvert City KY 42029
270 395-4165

(G-11881)
J M HAMILTON GROUP INC
Also Called: Metal Coating Company
1700 Elida Rd (45805-1511)
PHONE...........................419 229-4010
Howell D Glover Jr, *President*
Marie L Glover, *Principal*
James I Hunt, *Principal*
John H Romey, *Principal*
Richard W Hussey, *Vice Pres*
EMP: 18
SQ FT: 25,000
SALES (est): 2.6MM **Privately Held**
WEB: www.metalcoatingcompany.com
SIC: 3479 3559 3471 Painting, coating & hot dipping; glass making machinery: blowing, molding, forming, etc.; plating & polishing

(G-11882)
JOINT SYSTEMS MFG CTR
1155 Buckeye Rd Bldg 147 (45804-1815)
PHONE...........................419 221-9580
▲ EMP: 4
SALES (est): 216.4K **Privately Held**
SIC: 3795 Tanks & tank components

(G-11883)
KENNEDY GRAPHICS INC (PA)
1640 N Main St (45801-2825)
PHONE...........................419 223-9825
Mary Sprague-Mccourt, *President*
EMP: 5
SALES (est): 607.3K **Privately Held**
SIC: 2752 Offset Printing

(G-11884)
KW SERVICES LLC
1864 Mccullough St (45801-3059)
PHONE...........................419 228-1325
Kermit Caudill Jr, *General Mgr*
EMP: 6
SALES (corp-wide): 40MM **Privately Held**
WEB: www.koontz-wagner.com
SIC: 7694 Electric motor repair
PA: Kw Services, Llc
3801 Voorde Dr Ste B
South Bend IN 46628
574 232-2051

(G-11885)
LEADAR ROLL INC (PA)
893 Shawnee Rd (45805-3437)
PHONE...........................419 227-2200
Gary Stanklus, *President*
Darlene Stanklus, *Corp Secy*
Steve Hull, *Vice Pres*
Rob Monnin, *Controller*
▲ EMP: 25
SQ FT: 12,000
SALES (est): 6.1MM **Privately Held**
SIC: 3599 Machine shop, jobbing & repair

(G-11886)
LEE A WILLIAMS JR
205 W Elm St (45801-4811)
P.O. Box 267 (45802-0267)
PHONE...........................419 225-6751
Lee A Wiliams Jr, *Owner*
EMP: 3
SALES (est): 206.1K **Privately Held**
SIC: 1311 Crude petroleum & natural gas production

(G-11887)
LIMA ARMATURE WORKS INC
Also Called: Double Eagle
142 E Pearl St (45801-4149)
PHONE...........................419 222-4010
James W Smith, *Ch of Bd*
Rick Smith, *President*
Margaret E Smith, *Corp Secy*
EMP: 7 EST: 1927
SQ FT: 41,000
SALES (est): 1.5MM **Privately Held**
WEB: www.limaarmature.com
SIC: 7694 5063 Electric motor repair; motors, electric; motor controls, starters & relays: electric; transformers & transmission equipment; electrical supplies

(G-11888)
LIMA EQUIPMENT CO
895 Shawnee Rd (45805-3437)
P.O. Box 943 (45802-0943)
PHONE...........................419 222-4181
James Gideon, *President*
Angie Mox, *Office Mgr*
▲ EMP: 5
SQ FT: 20,000
SALES (est): 400K **Privately Held**
SIC: 3548 5063 5085 Welding & cutting apparatus & accessories; generators; industrial supplies

(G-11889)
LIMA PALLET COMPANY INC
1470 Neubrecht Rd (45801-3122)
PHONE...........................419 229-5736
Tracie Sanchez, *President*
Kelly Sarno, *Vice Pres*
Jeff Sanchez, *Opers Mgr*
Brian Cunningham, *Sales Staff*
EMP: 21
SQ FT: 25,000
SALES (est): 3.5MM **Privately Held**
WEB: www.limapallet.com
SIC: 2448 2441 Pallets, wood; nailed wood boxes & shook

(G-11890)
LIMA REFINING COMPANY (HQ)
1150 S Metcalf St (45804-1145)
P.O. Box 4505 (45802-4505)
PHONE...........................419 226-2300
William Kalsse, *CEO*
Gregory King, *President*
Sean Curtis, *Chief*
Todd Neu, *Senior VP*
Jorge Coelho, *Plant Mgr*
▲ EMP: 277
SALES (est): 173.4MM
SALES (corp-wide): 14.8B **Privately Held**
WEB: www.premcor.com
SIC: 2911 Petroleum refining
PA: Husky Energy Inc
707 8 Ave Sw
Calgary AB T2P 1
403 298-6111

(G-11891)
LIMA REFINING COMPANY
1150 S Metcalf St (45804-1145)
P.O. Box 4505 (45802-4505)
PHONE...........................419 226-2300
Patty Chapman, *Branch Mgr*
EMP: 60
SALES (corp-wide): 14.8B **Privately Held**
WEB: www.premcor.com
SIC: 2911 Petroleum refining
HQ: Lima Refining Company
1150 S Metcalf St
Lima OH 45804
419 226-2300

(G-11892)
LIMA SANDBLASTING & PNTG CO
4310 East Rd (45807-1535)
P.O. Box 3037 (45807-0037)
PHONE...........................419 331-2939
Larry Smith, *President*
Laura Smith, *Vice Pres*
EMP: 5
SQ FT: 17,000
SALES (est): 646.9K **Privately Held**
SIC: 3471 3479 Sand blasting of metal parts; painting of metal products

(G-11893)
LIMA SHEET METAL MACHINE & MFG
1001 Bowman Rd (45804-3409)
PHONE...........................419 229-1161
Michael R Emerick, *President*
Ann Emerick, *Corp Secy*
Thomas Emerick, *Exec VP*
EMP: 31 EST: 1974
SQ FT: 26,250
SALES (est): 6.6MM **Privately Held**
WEB: www.limasheetmetal.com
SIC: 3589 3599 7349 7692 Commercial cooking & foodwarming equipment; machine shop, jobbing & repair; building maintenance, except repairs; welding repair; food products machinery; sheet metalwork

(G-11894)
LIMA SPORTING GOODS INC
1404 Allentown Rd (45805-2204)
PHONE...........................419 222-1036
David Kirian, *President*
EMP: 20
SQ FT: 12,900
SALES: 2.9MM **Privately Held**
SIC: 2759 5941 Screen printing; team sports equipment

(G-11895)
LONGS CUSTOM DOORS
229 S Greenlawn Ave (45807-1339)
PHONE...........................419 339-2331
Darrell Long, *Owner*
EMP: 4
SALES (est): 475K **Privately Held**
SIC: 2431 Doors & door parts & trim, wood

(G-11896)
MAC ELECTRIC INC
1240 Fairgreen Ave (45805-4432)
PHONE...........................419 782-0671
EMP: 9
SQ FT: 6,500
SALES: 748.7K **Privately Held**
SIC: 7694 Electric Motor Repair

(G-11897)
MARTIN PRINTING CO
1804 Wendell Ave (45805-3161)
PHONE...........................419 224-9176
Margaret Whitlatch, *Owner*
EMP: 3 EST: 1923
SQ FT: 2,000
SALES (est): 245.1K **Privately Held**
SIC: 2759 2752 Letterpress printing; commercial printing, offset

(G-11898)
ME SIGNS INC
Also Called: Fastsigns
2155 Elida Rd (45805-1518)
PHONE...........................419 222-7446
Mark E Engle, *President*
EMP: 5 EST: 2010
SALES: 650K **Privately Held**
SIC: 3993 Signs & advertising specialties

(G-11899)
MENARD INC
2614 N Eastown Rd (45807-1601)
PHONE...........................419 998-4348
Timothy Bart, *Manager*
EMP: 50
SALES (corp-wide): 12.5B **Privately Held**
WEB: www.menards.com
SIC: 2431 Millwork
PA: Menard, Inc.
5101 Menard Dr
Eau Claire WI 54703
715 876-5911

(G-11900)
MESSER LLC
961 Industry Ave (45804-4171)
PHONE...........................419 227-9585
Carl Frommer, *Branch Mgr*
EMP: 23
SALES (corp-wide): 1.4B **Privately Held**
SIC: 2813 Industrial gases
HQ: Messer Inc
200 Somerset Corporate
Bridgewater NJ 08807
908 464-8100

(G-11901)
MESSER LLC
1680 Buckeye Rd (45804-1826)
PHONE...........................419 221-5043
Stuart Emmons, *Branch Mgr*
EMP: 22
SALES (corp-wide): 1.4B **Privately Held**
SIC: 2813 Nitrogen

GEOGRAPHIC SECTION
Lima - Allen County (G-11927)

HQ: Messer Llc
200 Somerset Corporate
Bridgewater NJ 08807
908 464-8100

(G-11902)
METOKOTE CORPORATION
1340 Neubrecht Rd (45801-3120)
PHONE 270 889-9907
Kermit Rowe, *Manager*
EMP: 25
SALES (corp-wide): 15.3B **Publicly Held**
WEB: www.metokote.com
SIC: 3479 Coating of metals & formed products
HQ: Metokote Corporation
1340 Neubrecht Rd
Lima OH 45801
419 996-7800

(G-11903)
METOKOTE CORPORATION (HQ)
Also Called: Ppg-Metokote
1340 Neubrecht Rd (45801-3120)
PHONE 419 996-7800
Jeffrey J Oravitz, *President*
▲ **EMP:** 445
SQ FT: 30,000
SALES (est): 500.3MM
SALES (corp-wide): 15.3B **Publicly Held**
WEB: www.metokote.com
SIC: 3479 Coating of metals & formed products
PA: Ppg Industries, Inc.
1 Ppg Pl
Pittsburgh PA 15272
412 434-3131

(G-11904)
METOKOTE CORPORATION
Also Called: Plant 25
1340 Neubrecht Rd (45801-3120)
PHONE 419 227-1100
Jim Bender, *Principal*
EMP: 59
SALES (corp-wide): 15.3B **Publicly Held**
WEB: www.metokote.com
SIC: 3479 Coating of metals & formed products
HQ: Metokote Corporation
1340 Neubrecht Rd
Lima OH 45801
419 996-7800

(G-11905)
METOKOTE CORPORATION
1340 Neubrecht Rd (45801-3120)
PHONE 419 221-2754
Jay Binder, *Manager*
EMP: 120
SQ FT: 118,500
SALES (corp-wide): 15.3B **Publicly Held**
WEB: www.metokote.com
SIC: 3479 3471 Coating of metals with plastic or resins; plating & polishing
HQ: Metokote Corporation
1340 Neubrecht Rd
Lima OH 45801
419 996-7800

(G-11906)
METOKOTE CORPORATION
1340 Neubrecht Rd (45801-3120)
PHONE 319 232-6994
Chad Dirks, *Manager*
EMP: 60
SALES (corp-wide): 15.3B **Publicly Held**
WEB: www.metokote.com
SIC: 3479 Coating of metals with plastic or resins
HQ: Metokote Corporation
1340 Neubrecht Rd
Lima OH 45801
419 996-7800

(G-11907)
METOKOTE CORPORATION
1340 Neubrecht Rd (45801-3120)
PHONE 419 996-7800
Lewis Phillipson, *Manager*
EMP: 7
SALES (corp-wide): 15.3B **Publicly Held**
WEB: www.metokote.com
SIC: 1081 Metal mining services

HQ: Metokote Corporation
1340 Neubrecht Rd
Lima OH 45801
419 996-7800

(G-11908)
MODERN INK TECHNOLOGY LLC
Also Called: Organic Coating Products
1005 W Grand Ave (45801-3429)
PHONE 419 738-9664
Dana Morgan,
EMP: 11
SQ FT: 12,000
SALES (est): 853.4K
SALES (corp-wide): 445.1MM **Privately Held**
SIC: 3952 Ink, drawing: black & colored
PA: American Trim, L.L.C.
1005 W Grand Ave
Lima OH 45801

(G-11909)
MURPHY TRACTOR & EQP CO INC
Also Called: John Deere Authorized Dealer
3550 Saint Johns Rd (45804-4017)
PHONE 419 221-3666
Chris Cron, *Branch Mgr*
EMP: 8 **Privately Held**
SIC: 3531 5082 Construction machinery; construction & mining machinery
HQ: Murphy Tractor & Equipment Co., Inc.
5375 N Deere Rd
Park City KS 67219
855 246-9124

(G-11910)
NATIONAL LIME AND STONE CO
1314 Findlay Rd (45801-3106)
PHONE 419 228-3434
Debbie Montooth, *Human Res Dir*
Nick Morris, *Manager*
EMP: 22
SQ FT: 1,200
SALES (corp-wide): 3.2B **Privately Held**
WEB: www.natlime.com
SIC: 1422 Crushed & broken limestone
PA: The National Lime And Stone Company
551 Lake Cascade Pkwy
Findlay OH 45840
419 422-4341

(G-11911)
NEWS GAZETTE PRINTING COMPANY
Also Called: Ngp Printing Professional
324 W Market St (45801-4714)
P.O. Box 1017 (45802-1017)
PHONE 419 227-2527
Dan Mills, *President*
James Honegger, *Vice Pres*
Jim Honegger, *Vice Pres*
Peter Paulik, *Vice Pres*
Pete Paulik, *VP Prdtn*
EMP: 11
SQ FT: 2,800
SALES (est): 1.4MM **Privately Held**
WEB: www.ngpco.com
SIC: 2752 Commercial printing, offset

(G-11912)
NWC HUD CORP II
1404 N West St (45801-2828)
PHONE 419 228-8400
EMP: 5
SALES (est): 25.6K **Privately Held**
SIC: 3021 Rubber & plastics footwear

(G-11913)
P-AMERICAS LLC
1750 Greely Chapel Rd (45804-4122)
PHONE 419 227-3541
Rob Rosser, *Manager*
EMP: 25
SALES (corp-wide): 64.6B **Publicly Held**
SIC: 5149 2086 Soft drinks; bottled & canned soft drinks
HQ: P-Americas Llc
1 Pepsi Way
Somers NY 10589
336 896-5740

(G-11914)
PCS NITROGEN INC
Also Called: Arcadian Ohio
1900 Fort Amanda Rd (45804-1827)
P.O. Box 628 (45802-0628)
PHONE 419 226-1200
Chuck Treloar, *Manager*
EMP: 370
SALES (corp-wide): 8.8B **Privately Held**
SIC: 2873 Nitrogen solutions (fertilizer)
HQ: Pcs Nitrogen, Inc.
1101 Skokie Blvd Ste 400
Northbrook IL 60062
847 849-4200

(G-11915)
PCS NITROGEN OHIO LP
2200 Fort Amanda Rd (45804-1801)
P.O. Box 628 (45802-0628)
PHONE 419 879-8989
Jochen Tilk, *President*
Wayne Brownlee, *CFO*
EMP: 3
SALES (est): 1.6MM
SALES (corp-wide): 8.8B **Privately Held**
SIC: 2873 Nitrogenous fertilizers
HQ: Potash Corporation Of Saskatchewan Inc
122 1st Ave S Suite 500
Saskatoon SK S7K 7
306 933-8500

(G-11916)
PERFECTION BAKERIES INC
1278 W Robb Ave (45801-2406)
PHONE 419 221-2359
Carol Moyer, *Principal*
EMP: 58
SALES (corp-wide): 515.3MM **Privately Held**
SIC: 2051 Bakery: wholesale or wholesale/retail combined
PA: Perfection Bakeries, Inc.
350 Pearl St
Fort Wayne IN 46802
260 424-8245

(G-11917)
PRAXAIR INC
961 Industry Ave (45804-4171)
PHONE 419 422-1353
Terry Peyton, *Opers-Prdtn-Mfg*
EMP: 4 **Privately Held**
SIC: 2813 Industrial gases
HQ: Praxair, Inc.
10 Riverview Dr
Danbury CT 06810
203 837-2000

(G-11918)
PRAXAIR DISTRIBUTION INC
961 Industry Ave (45804-4171)
PHONE 419 422-1353
Barrow Turner, *Manager*
EMP: 4 **Privately Held**
SIC: 2813 5084 5999 Carbon dioxide; dry ice, carbon dioxide (solid); oxygen, compressed or liquefied; welding machinery & equipment; welding supplies
HQ: Praxair Distribution, Inc.
10 Riverview Dr
Danbury CT 06810
203 837-2000

(G-11919)
PRECISION WOOD & METAL CO
3960 E Bluelick Rd (45801-1555)
PHONE 419 221-1512
Leo Robert Schneider, *Owner*
EMP: 4
SALES: 89K **Privately Held**
SIC: 3312 Tool & die steel

(G-11920)
PROCTER & GAMBLE COMPANY
840 N Thayer Rd (45801)
PHONE 419 998-5891
Chris Horn, *Network Mgr*
EMP: 404
SALES (corp-wide): 66.8B **Publicly Held**
SIC: 2844 2676 3421 2842 Deodorants, personal; towels, napkins & tissue paper products; razor blades & razors; specialty cleaning preparations; soap: granulated, liquid, cake, flaked or chip
PA: The Procter & Gamble Company
1 Procter And Gamble Plz
Cincinnati OH 45202
513 983-1100

(G-11921)
PROCTER & GAMBLE MFG CO
3875 Reservoir Rd (45801-3310)
P.O. Box 1900 (45802-1900)
PHONE 419 226-5500
Scott Hamilton, *Project Mgr*
Bruce Hoffman, *Project Mgr*
Shane Hites, *Mfg Spvr*
Jamey Truex, *Buyer*
James Wireman, *Buyer*
EMP: 250
SALES (corp-wide): 66.8B **Publicly Held**
SIC: 2844 Toilet preparations
HQ: The Procter & Gamble Manufacturing Company
1 Procter And Gamble Plz
Cincinnati OH 45202
513 983-1100

(G-11922)
PROFORMA SYSTEMS ADVANTAGE
1207 Findlay Rd (45801-3103)
PHONE 419 224-8747
Robert McPheron, *President*
Michelle McPheron, *Vice Pres*
Cathy Richard, *Admin Sec*
EMP: 6
SALES (est): 807.6K **Privately Held**
SIC: 2759 Calendars: printing

(G-11923)
PURINA ANIMAL NUTRITION LLC
1111 N Cole St (45805-2003)
PHONE 419 224-2015
Robert Geir, *Branch Mgr*
EMP: 35
SALES (corp-wide): 10.4B **Privately Held**
SIC: 2048 Prepared feeds
HQ: Purina Animal Nutrition Llc
100 Danforth Dr
Gray Summit MO 63039

(G-11924)
QUALITOR INC (HQ)
1840 Mccullough St (45801-3059)
PHONE 248 204-8600
Gary Cohen, *CEO*
Scott Gibaratz, *CFO*
▲ **EMP:** 6 **EST:** 1999
SQ FT: 2,500
SALES (est): 173.9MM **Privately Held**
WEB: www.qualitorinc.com
SIC: 3714 5013 Motor vehicle engines & parts; motor vehicle brake systems & parts; air brakes, motor vehicle; wipers, windshield, motor vehicle; motor vehicle supplies & new parts

(G-11925)
QUALITY WLDG & FABRICATION LLC
4330 East Rd (45807-1535)
PHONE 419 225-6208
Ashley M Miller, *Principal*
EMP: 55
SALES (est): 76.2K **Privately Held**
SIC: 7692 Welding repair

(G-11926)
QUICK AS A WINK PRINTING CO
321 W High St (45801-4701)
PHONE 419 224-9786
David S Beck, *President*
Deb Gerding, *Purchasing*
Andrew Beck, *Manager*
Julie Kirk, *Manager*
EMP: 18
SQ FT: 5,000
SALES (est): 2.4MM **Privately Held**
SIC: 2752 2791 7389 5099 Commercial printing, offset; typesetting; sign painting & lettering shop; rubber stamps; marking devices; commercial printing

(G-11927)
RANDALL BEARINGS INC (PA)
1046 S Greenlawn Ave (45804-1100)
P.O. Box 1258 (45802-1258)
PHONE 419 223-1075
Kent Morgan, *President*

Jeff Hager, *Vice Pres*
Pat Ridenour, *Mfg Staff*
Jennifer Rode, *Purch Dir*
Doug Hamilton, *Engineer*
▲ **EMP:** 90
SQ FT: 117,400
SALES (est): 29.3MM **Privately Held**
WEB: www.randallbearings.com
SIC: 3568 3624 3366 Bearings, bushings & blocks; carbon & graphite products; copper foundries

(G-11928)
REGAL BELOIT AMERICA INC
200 E Chapman Rd (45801-2012)
PHONE.................................608 364-8800
William Conway, *Plant Mgr*
EMP: 230
SALES (corp-wide): 3.6B **Publicly Held**
WEB: www.marathonelect.com
SIC: 3621 3625 Motors & generators; relays & industrial controls
HQ: Regal Beloit America, Inc.
200 State St
Beloit WI 53511
608 364-8800

(G-11929)
RESOURCE RECYCLING INC
1596 Neubrecht Rd (45801-3124)
PHONE.................................419 222-2702
Micah Hollinger, *President*
EMP: 15
SALES: 4.2MM **Privately Held**
SIC: 4953 3999 4214 Recycling, waste materials; custom pulverizing & grinding of plastic materials; local trucking with storage

(G-11930)
REVENUE MANAGEMENT GROUP LLC
2348 Baton Rouge (45805-1167)
P.O. Box 747 (45802-0747)
PHONE.................................419 993-2200
Ned Kaning, *Mng Member*
Scott G Koenig
EMP: 3 **EST:** 2000
SALES (est): 200.9K **Privately Held**
WEB: www.easypmts.com
SIC: 2754 Invitations: gravure printing

(G-11931)
REX MANUFACTURING CO
Also Called: Rex Auto Seat Covers
805 S Cable Rd (45805-3467)
P.O. Box 1294 (45802-1294)
PHONE.................................419 224-5751
James M Rex, *Owner*
EMP: 5 **EST:** 1930
SQ FT: 4,500
SALES (est): 383.3K **Privately Held**
SIC: 5013 5531 2399 2394 Automotive supplies & parts; automotive accessories; seat covers, automobile; convertible tops, canvas or boat: from purchased materials

(G-11932)
RIGHTWAY FOOD SERVICE
3255 Saint Johns Rd (45804-4022)
PHONE.................................419 223-4075
Jason Dorsten, *General Mgr*
EMP: 3
SALES (est): 270K **Privately Held**
SIC: 5046 2599 2499 Restaurant equipment & supplies; restaurant furniture, wood or metal; food handling & processing products, wood

(G-11933)
RMT HOLDINGS INC
1025 Findlay Rd (45801-3171)
P.O. Box 5183 (45802-5183)
PHONE.................................419 221-1168
Richard Toth, *President*
Cathi Toth, *Vice Pres*
Steven A Romey
Dale M Vandemark
Judy L Yoh
EMP: 15
SQ FT: 15,000
SALES (est): 2.5MM **Privately Held**
SIC: 2789 Paper cutting

(G-11934)
RUDA PRINT & GRAPHICS
4129 Elida Rd (45807-1549)
PHONE.................................419 331-7832
Fax: 419 331-2329
EMP: 4
SALES: 400K **Privately Held**
SIC: 2752 Lithographic Commercial Printing

(G-11935)
RUDOLPH FOODS COMPANY INC (PA)
6575 Bellefontaine Rd (45804-4415)
PHONE.................................909 383-7463
P.O. Box 509 (45802-0509)
James Rudolph, *CEO*
Richard Rudolph, *President*
Philip Rudolph, *Corp Secy*
Barbara Snyder, *Vice Pres*
◆ **EMP:** 160
SQ FT: 110,000
SALES (est): 138.3MM **Privately Held**
SIC: 2096 2099 Pork rinds; food preparations

(G-11936)
SCHWANS HOME SERVICE INC
2545 Saint Johns Rd (45804-4004)
PHONE.................................419 222-9977
Mark Cornwell, *Branch Mgr*
EMP: 25
SALES (corp-wide): 5.3B **Privately Held**
SIC: 5963 2024 2037 Food services, direct sales; ice cream, packaged: molded, on sticks, etc.; fruit juice concentrates, frozen
HQ: Schwan's Home Service, Inc.
115 W College Dr
Marshall MN 56258
507 532-3274

(G-11937)
SEWER RODDING EQUIPMENT CO
Also Called: Sreco Flexible
3434 S Dixie Hwy (45804-3756)
PHONE.................................419 991-2065
Larry Drain, *Manager*
EMP: 30
SALES (corp-wide): 17.6MM **Privately Held**
SIC: 5032 3546 3423 Sewer pipe, clay; power-driven handtools; hand & edge tools
PA: Sewer Rodding Equipment Co Inc
3217 Carter Ave
Marina Del Rey CA 90292
310 301-9009

(G-11938)
SHELLY MATERIALS INC
600 N Sugar St (45804-4184)
PHONE.................................419 229-2741
Lyle Snyder, *Manager*
EMP: 5
SALES (corp-wide): 29.7B **Privately Held**
SIC: 1422 Crushed & broken limestone
HQ: Shelly Materials, Inc.
80 Park Dr
Thornville OH 43076
740 246-6315

(G-11939)
SIGN PRO OF LIMA
404 Brower Rd (45801-2502)
PHONE.................................419 222-7767
Michelle Sterling, *Manager*
EMP: 5
SQ FT: 1,700
SALES (est): 340K **Privately Held**
WEB: www.signproimaging.com
SIC: 3993 Signs, not made in custom sign painting shops

(G-11940)
SIGN SOURCE USA INC
1700 S Dixie Hwy (45804-1834)
P.O. Box 776 (45802-0776)
PHONE.................................419 224-1130
Jeff Pisel, *President*
Sompahkoun Southibounnorath, *Vice Pres*
Grant Pisel, *Production*
Joe Pisel, *Purch Mgr*
Karen Hoblein, *Admin Secy*
EMP: 55
SALES (est): 25MM **Privately Held**
WEB: www.signsourceusa.com
SIC: 5085 3993 Signmaker equipment & supplies; signs & advertising specialties

(G-11941)
SNOW PRINTING CO INC
1000 W Grand Ave Frnt (45801-3498)
PHONE.................................419 229-7669
Donald L Kohl, *President*
Joyce Kohl, *Corp Secy*
Daniel Kohl, *Vice Pres*
EMP: 10
SQ FT: 4,200
SALES (est): 980K **Privately Held**
SIC: 2752 2759 Commercial printing, offset; letterpress printing

(G-11942)
SPALLINGER MILLWRIGHT SVC CO
Also Called: Spall Autoc Syste / US Millwr
1155 E Hanthorn Rd (45804-3929)
PHONE.................................419 225-5830
Scott Spallinger, *President*
▲ **EMP:** 85
SQ FT: 80,000
SALES (est): 31.7MM **Privately Held**
WEB: www.spallinger.com
SIC: 3446 1796 Stairs, staircases, stair treads: prefabricated metal; railings, prefabricated metal; machinery installation

(G-11943)
SPECIALIZED PHARMACEUTICALS
799 S Main St (45804-1519)
PHONE.................................419 371-2081
EMP: 4 **EST:** 2012
SALES (est): 325.7K **Privately Held**
SIC: 5912 2834 Drug stores & proprietary stores; pharmaceutical preparations

(G-11944)
STAR SPANGLED SPECTACULAR INC
4230 Elida Rd (45807-1550)
PHONE.................................419 879-3502
Kurt Neeper, *Principal*
EMP: 4 **EST:** 2011
SALES: 97.6K **Privately Held**
SIC: 2836 Culture media

(G-11945)
SUEVER STONE COMPANY (PA)
706 E Main St (45807-1071)
PHONE.................................419 331-1945
Neil Lause, *President*
Glen Lause, *Vice Pres*
Eileen Lause, *Treasurer*
EMP: 15
SQ FT: 10,000
SALES: 3MM **Privately Held**
SIC: 1422 1611 Crushed & broken limestone; surfacing & paving

(G-11946)
SUPERIOR FORGE & STEEL CORP (PA)
1820 Mcclain Rd (45804-1978)
PHONE.................................419 222-4412
James C Markovitz, *CEO*
Anthony Bartley, *Treasurer*
◆ **EMP:** 100
SQ FT: 350,000
SALES (est): 26MM **Privately Held**
WEB: www.qrolls.com
SIC: 3312 3316 Sheet or strip, steel, cold-rolled: own hot-rolled; cold finishing of steel shapes

(G-11947)
SUPERIOR METAL PRODUCTS INC (PA)
Also Called: American Trim
1005 W Grand Ave (45801-3400)
PHONE.................................419 228-1145
Leo Hawk, *CEO*
Richard Pfeifer, *President*
Dana Morgan, *Treasurer*
◆ **EMP:** 50 **EST:** 1958
SQ FT: 15,000
SALES (est): 445.1MM **Privately Held**
SIC: 3429 3469 Manufactured hardware (general); porcelain enameled products & utensils

(G-11948)
T J ELLIS ENTERPRISES INC
1505 Neubrecht Rd (45801-3123)
PHONE.................................419 224-1969
Johnnie Small, *Manager*
EMP: 5
SALES (corp-wide): 3.6MM **Privately Held**
SIC: 2411 Logging
PA: T J Ellis Enterprises Inc
1505 Neubrecht Rd
Lima OH 45801
419 999-5026

(G-11949)
TELEDOOR LLC
1075 Prosperity Rd (45801-3127)
PHONE.................................419 227-3000
Deb Kruger, *Business Mgr*
John Recker, *Mng Member*
Mike Schulte
EMP: 7
SQ FT: 22,000
SALES (est): 430K **Privately Held**
WEB: www.teledoor.net
SIC: 2431 Doors, wood

(G-11950)
TERRY & JACK NEON SIGN CO
225 S Collins Ave (45804-3001)
PHONE.................................419 229-0674
Jack L Pisel Jr, *President*
Patricia Woods, *Corp Secy*
Mike Strange, *Vice Pres*
EMP: 26 **EST:** 1947
SQ FT: 40,000
SALES (est): 2.1MM **Privately Held**
SIC: 3993 Electric signs

(G-11951)
THREE AS INC
Also Called: Allen County Pallet
1605 E 4th St (45804-2711)
P.O. Box 277 (45802-0277)
PHONE.................................419 227-4240
O Roger Wright, *President*
EMP: 5
SQ FT: 15,000
SALES (est): 677.8K **Privately Held**
SIC: 6512 3089 2448 Commercial & industrial building operation; extruded finished plastic products; wood pallets & skids

(G-11952)
TILTON CORPORATION
330 S Pine St (45804)
P.O. Box 839 (45802-0839)
PHONE.................................419 227-6421
Kevin Wiechart, *President*
Harry Coy, *Treasurer*
Gretchen Morin, *Manager*
Judy Tilton, *Admin Sec*
EMP: 125
SQ FT: 7,000
SALES: 13.1MM **Privately Held**
WEB: www.tiltonindustries.com
SIC: 1711 1761 3498 3444 Mechanical contractor; sheet metalwork; fabricated pipe & fittings; sheet metalwork; fabricated structural metal
PA: Tilton Industries, Inc.
330 S Pine St
Lima OH
419 227-6421

(G-11953)
TRINITY HIGHWAY PRODUCTS LLC
425 E O Connor Ave (45801)
PHONE.................................419 227-1296
Keith Hamburg, *Branch Mgr*
John Hickman, *Manager*
EMP: 19
SALES (corp-wide): 2.5B **Publicly Held**
SIC: 3743 Railroad equipment
HQ: Trinity Highway Products, Llc.
2525 N Stemmons Fwy
Dallas TX 75207

▲ = Import ▼ = Export
◆ = Import/Export

GEOGRAPHIC SECTION

Lisbon - Columbiana County (G-11980)

(G-11954)
TYSEKA
1021 Brower Rd (45801-2301)
PHONE...............................419 860-9585
Jason Dancs, *Owner*
EMP: 5
SALES (est): 232.1K **Privately Held**
SIC: 3231 Cut & engraved glassware: made from purchased glass

(G-11955)
UNITED STATES DEPT OF ARMY
Also Called: Lima Army Tank Plant
1155 Buckeye Rd (45804-1815)
PHONE...............................419 221-9500
Ted Epple, *Branch Mgr*
EMP: 75 **Publicly Held**
SIC: 9711 3795 Army; ; tanks, military, including factory rebuilding
HQ: United States Department Of The Army
101 Army Pentagon
Washington DC 20310

(G-11956)
VINNIES DRIVE THRU
864 W North St (45801-3925)
PHONE...............................419 225-5272
James Faircloth, *Principal*
EMP: 4
SALES (est): 336.8K **Privately Held**
SIC: 2086 Mfg Bottled/Canned Soft Drinks

(G-11957)
W T INC
Also Called: Midwest Plastics
606 N Jackson St (45801-4126)
P.O. Box 1687 (45802-1687)
PHONE...............................419 224-6942
William M Taflinger, *President*
Rebecca Taflinger, *Vice Pres*
William S Taflinger, *Treasurer*
Stephen C Talfinger, *Admin Sec*
▼ **EMP:** 11
SQ FT: 7,500
SALES (est): 2MM **Privately Held**
SIC: 3089 Injection molding of plastics

(G-11958)
WAHLIES CSTM CFT DRAPERY UPHL
605 W Kibby St (45804-1018)
PHONE...............................419 229-1731
Tim Marshall, *President*
Carol Marshall, *Manager*
EMP: 5
SQ FT: 1,000
SALES: 350K **Privately Held**
SIC: 7641 2391 5712 Reupholstery; draperies, plastic & textile: from purchased materials; furniture stores

(G-11959)
WHEMCO-OHIO FOUNDRY INC
1600 Mcclain Rd (45804-1979)
PHONE...............................419 222-2111
Charles R Novelli, *President*
John Hirbar, *Managing Dir*
Michael P Nakon, *Principal*
Anthony J Poli, *Principal*
Anthony Poli, *Principal*
EMP: 140
SALES (est): 31.1MM
SALES (corp-wide): 574.3MM **Privately Held**
WEB: www.whemco.com
SIC: 3321 3325 3322 Gray iron castings; steel foundries; malleable iron foundries
HQ: Whemco Inc.
5 Hot Metal St Ste 300
Pittsburgh PA 15203
412 390-2700

Lima
Auglaize County

(G-11960)
ALPLA INC
3320 Fort Shwnee Indus Dr (45806-1843)
PHONE...............................419 991-9484
Keith Wagner, *Principal*
▲ **EMP:** 18
SALES (est): 4.8MM **Privately Held**
SIC: 3085 Plastics bottles

HQ: Alpla - Werke Lehner Gmbh & Co Kg
Daimlerstr. 4-6
Markdorf 88677
754 450-80

(G-11961)
BASIC PACKAGING LTD
2986 Indian Hill Dr (45806-1362)
PHONE...............................330 634-9665
Hal Johnson, *President*
Bob Moodie, *Shareholder*
EMP: 10
SQ FT: 30,000
SALES: 650K **Privately Held**
WEB: www.basicpackaging.com
SIC: 2653 Boxes, corrugated: made from purchased materials

(G-11962)
PRECISION THRMPLSTC COMPONTS
Also Called: P T C
3765 Saint Johns Rd (45806-2629)
P.O. Box 1296 (45802-1296)
PHONE...............................419 227-4500
Randy E Carter, *President*
◆ **EMP:** 100
SQ FT: 62,000
SALES: 13MM **Privately Held**
WEB: www.ptclima.com
SIC: 3089 Injection molding of plastics; injection molded finished plastic products; extruded finished plastic products

Lisbon
Columbiana County

(G-11963)
AMERICAN BUILT CUSTOM PALLETS
42120 Glasgow Rd (44432-9665)
PHONE...............................330 532-4780
EMP: 4
SALES (est): 180K **Privately Held**
SIC: 2448 Mfg Wood Pallets/Skids

(G-11964)
AMERICAN CLIMBER & MCH CORP
38294 Industrial Park Rd (44432-8325)
P.O. Box 471 (44432-0471)
PHONE...............................330 420-0019
Louis Horvath Sr, *President*
Peter Horvath, *Admin Sec*
EMP: 5
SQ FT: 5,000
SALES (est): 560.1K **Privately Held**
SIC: 3536 Hoists

(G-11965)
COLUMBUS MCKINNON CORPORATION
Chester Hoist
7573 State Route 45 (44432-8382)
PHONE...............................330 424-7248
Bob Burkey, *General Mgr*
Chris Mull, *Plant Mgr*
Joe Runyon, *Sales Staff*
Deb Tipton, *Manager*
Bruce Pastore, *CIO*
EMP: 57
SALES (corp-wide): 839.4MM **Publicly Held**
WEB: www.cmworks.com
SIC: 3536 3713 3568 3496 Hoists, cranes & monorails; truck & bus bodies; power transmission equipment; miscellaneous fabricated wire products
PA: Columbus Mckinnon Corporation
205 Crosspoint Pkwy
Getzville NY 14068
716 689-5400

(G-11966)
D W DICKEY AND SON INC (PA)
Also Called: D W Dickey
7896 Dickey Dr (44432-9391)
P.O. Box 189 (44432-0189)
PHONE...............................330 424-1441
Gary Neville, *President*
Timothy Dickey, *President*
David Dickey, *Vice Pres*

Janet Blosser, *Admin Sec*
EMP: 52
SALES (est): 62.6MM **Privately Held**
SIC: 5169 3273 5172 Explosives; ready-mixed concrete; fuel oil

(G-11967)
GRANT STREET PALLET INC
39196 Grant St (44432-9781)
P.O. Box 268 (44432-0268)
PHONE...............................330 424-0355
Kenneth Miller, *President*
EMP: 8
SALES: 1MM **Privately Held**
SIC: 2448 Wood pallets & skids

(G-11968)
HEIM SHEET METAL INC
525 E Chestnut St (44432-1319)
PHONE...............................330 424-7820
David Belaney, *President*
Melinda Belaney, *Corp Secy*
EMP: 6 **EST:** 1928
SQ FT: 11,100
SALES: 516K **Privately Held**
SIC: 3444 Sheet metalwork

(G-11969)
HOUSING & EMRGNCY LGSTCS PLNNR
36905 State Route 30 (44432-9413)
PHONE...............................209 201-7511
Janice Regalo,
EMP: 20
SALES (est): 685.2K **Privately Held**
SIC: 3999 Manufacturing industries

(G-11970)
J & A MACHINE
8362 Thomas Rd (44432-9475)
PHONE...............................330 424-5235
Fax: 330 424-9028
EMP: 4
SQ FT: 12,000
SALES (est): 370K **Privately Held**
SIC: 4212 7692 5082 7389 Local Trucking Operator Welding Repair Whol Construction/Mining Equipment Business Services

(G-11971)
J I T PALLETS INC
39196 Grant St (44432-9781)
P.O. Box 268 (44432-0268)
PHONE...............................330 424-0355
Kenneth Miller, *President*
EMP: 4
SALES (est): 221.9K **Privately Held**
SIC: 2448 Wood pallets & skids

(G-11972)
J P INDUSTRIAL PRODUCTS INC (PA)
Also Called: JP Industrial
11988 State Route 45 (44432-8625)
PHONE...............................330 424-1110
James E Pastore, *President*
Kurt Kessler, *Opers Staff*
Rebecca Brown, *Manager*
▲ **EMP:** 8
SQ FT: 5,000
SALES (est): 12MM **Privately Held**
WEB: www.jpindustrial.com
SIC: 2821 Plastics materials & resins

(G-11973)
J P INDUSTRIAL PRODUCTS INC
State Rte 518 (44432)
PHONE...............................330 424-3388
Beccy Brown, *Manager*
EMP: 22
SALES: 3.1MM
SALES (corp-wide): 12MM **Privately Held**
WEB: www.jpindustrial.com
SIC: 3086 Padding, foamed plastic
PA: J. P. Industrial Products, Inc.
11988 State Route 45
Lisbon OH 44432
330 424-1110

(G-11974)
LISBON HOIST INC
321 S Beaver St (44432)
P.O. Box 462 (44432-0462)
PHONE...............................330 424-7283
Michael Burlingame, *President*
Connie Burlingame, *Finance Mgr*
EMP: 18
SQ FT: 35,000
SALES: 2.2MM **Privately Held**
WEB: www.lisbonhoist.com
SIC: 3536 Hoists

(G-11975)
LISBON PATTERN LIMITED
7629 State Route 45 (44432-9394)
P.O. Box 506 (44432-0506)
PHONE...............................330 424-7676
David Tolson, *Owner*
Kenneth Lovett, *Owner*
EMP: 5
SALES (est): 484.4K **Privately Held**
SIC: 3543 Industrial patterns

(G-11976)
OGDEN NEWSPAPERS OHIO INC (DH)
Also Called: Morning Journal
308 Maple St (44432-1205)
PHONE...............................330 424-9541
Beth Todd, *Controller*
Beth Bentley, *Human Resources*
Janet Marker, *Supervisor*
Heidi Grimm, *Director*
EMP: 23 **EST:** 1852
SQ FT: 13,000
SALES (est): 2.4MM **Privately Held**
WEB: www.morningjournalnews.com
SIC: 2711 Job printing & newspaper publishing combined
HQ: The Ogden Newspapers Inc
1500 Main St
Wheeling WV 26003
304 233-0100

(G-11977)
OHIO PET FOODS INC (HQ)
38251 Indl Pk Rd (44432)
PHONE...............................330 424-1431
Jim Golladay, *President*
Matthew Golladay, *Vice Pres*
Don Grimm, *Foreman/Supr*
Travis Golladay, *Treasurer*
James Golladay, *Human Res Dir*
◆ **EMP:** 37 **EST:** 1978
SQ FT: 50,000
SALES (est): 6.8MM **Privately Held**
WEB: www.ohiopetfoods.com
SIC: 2048 2047 Feeds, specialty: mice, guinea pig, etc.; dog food

(G-11978)
PAPER SERVICE INC
12022 Leslie Rd (44432-9531)
PHONE...............................330 227-3546
Randy Barnard, *President*
Dean Barnard, *Vice Pres*
EMP: 17 **EST:** 1968
SQ FT: 20,000
SALES (est): 3.4MM **Privately Held**
SIC: 2679 Paperboard products, converted

(G-11979)
PAUL E CEKOVICH
Also Called: Pallet Man The
9403 Black Rd (44432-9685)
PHONE...............................330 424-3213
Paul E Cekovich, *Principal*
EMP: 3 **EST:** 2012
SALES (est): 212K **Privately Held**
SIC: 2448 Pallets, wood & wood with metal

(G-11980)
R L CRAIG INC
6496 State Route 45 (44432-8357)
PHONE...............................330 424-1525
Richard L Craig, *President*
Charles-Aliso Bell, *Vice Pres*
Katheryn A Craig, *Vice Pres*
EMP: 13
SQ FT: 7,600
SALES (est): 3.2MM **Privately Held**
WEB: www.rlcraig.com
SIC: 3599 Machine shop, jobbing & repair

Lisbon - Columbiana County (G-11981)

(G-11981)
VANCE ADAMS
Also Called: Frontiers Unlimited
123 E Lincoln Way (44432-1405)
PHONE..................................330 424-9670
Vance A Adams, *Owner*
EMP: 3
SQ FT: 950
SALES (est): 185.2K Privately Held
SIC: 5941 3827 Camping equipment; binoculars

(G-11982)
WELDING IMPROVEMENT COMPANY
10070 Stookesberry Rd (44432-8639)
PHONE..................................330 424-9666
Tina Strong, *President*
Scott Strong, *Vice Pres*
John Anderson, *CFO*
EMP: 8
SALES (est): 2MM Privately Held
SIC: 3441 Fabricated structural metal

(G-11983)
WRIGHT BUFFING WHEEL COMPANY
300 S Market St (44432-1236)
PHONE..................................330 424-7887
Kent Brennemen, *President*
Frederick L Brenneman, *President*
Linda Brenneman, *Admin Sec*
EMP: 4
SQ FT: 6,000
SALES (est): 270K Privately Held
WEB: www.wrightbuffingwheel.com
SIC: 7389 3291 3545 Grinding, precision: commercial or industrial; buffing or polishing wheels, abrasive or nonabrasive; machine tool accessories

Litchfield
Medina County

(G-11984)
ARTISTIC COMPOSITE & MOLD CO
9225 Stone Rd (44253-8700)
PHONE..................................330 352-6632
Bryan Whittenberger, *President*
Nicole Whittenberger, *Vice Pres*
EMP: 4
SQ FT: 4,000
SALES (est): 276.5K Privately Held
SIC: 3356 2655 Welding rods; cans, composite: foil-fiber & other: from purchased fiber

(G-11985)
MEDINA FOODS INC
Also Called: Gold Rush Jerky
9706 Crow Rd (44253-9549)
PHONE..................................330 725-1390
Abdalla Nimer, *President*
Cathy Fobes, *Vice Pres*
EMP: 45
SQ FT: 50,000
SALES (est): 7.2MM Privately Held
WEB: www.medinafoods.com
SIC: 2013 Sausages & other prepared meats

(G-11986)
PARKN MANUFACTURING LLC
8035 Norwalk Rd Ste 107 (44253-9135)
PHONE..................................330 723-8172
Willard Robert Scandlon, *CEO*
Bob Scandlon,
EMP: 12
SQ FT: 10,000
SALES: 4.5MM Privately Held
SIC: 3541 Machine tool replacement & repair parts, metal cutting types

(G-11987)
SHARPER TOOLING
9473 Smith Rd (44253-9737)
PHONE..................................330 667-2960
Brad O'Donnell, *Owner*
EMP: 4
SQ FT: 7,500
SALES: 132K Privately Held
SIC: 3545 Machine tool accessories

Little Hocking
Washington County

(G-11988)
7 UP OF MARIETTA INC
871 State Route 618 (45742-5377)
PHONE..................................740 423-9230
Bruce Freeman, *Manager*
Robert Deeds, *Manager*
Lisa Pettit, *Admin Sec*
EMP: 30
SALES (est): 2MM Privately Held
SIC: 2086 Bottled & canned soft drinks

(G-11989)
AGE GRAPHICS LLC
678 Collins Rd (45742-5397)
PHONE..................................740 989-0006
Jim Bushong,
EMP: 10 EST: 1997
SALES (est): 2MM Privately Held
WEB: www.agegraphics.com
SIC: 3577 Graphic displays, except graphic terminals

(G-11990)
AMERICAN BOTTLING COMPANY
871 State Route 618 (45742-5377)
PHONE..................................740 423-9230
Robert Deeds, *Principal*
EMP: 70 Publicly Held
WEB: www.cs-americas.com
SIC: 2086 Bottled & canned soft drinks
HQ: The American Bottling Company
    5301 Legacy Dr
    Plano TX 75024

(G-11991)
CREATIVE STITCHES MONOGRAMMING
87 Cornes Rd (45742-5197)
PHONE..................................740 667-3592
Linda Chevalier, *Owner*
EMP: 4
SALES (est): 100K Privately Held
WEB: www.creative-stitches.com
SIC: 2395 Embroidery & art needlework

Lockbourne
Franklin County

(G-11992)
AMERISOURCEBERGEN CORPORATION
6301 Lasalle Dr (43137-9280)
PHONE..................................614 497-3665
Frank Dicenso, *Director*
EMP: 100
SALES (corp-wide): 167.9B Publicly Held
SIC: 2834 5122 Pharmaceutical preparations; pharmaceuticals; druggists' sundries
PA: Amerisourcebergen Corporation
    1300 Morris Dr Ste 100
    Chesterbrook PA 19087
    610 727-7000

(G-11993)
CITY OF COLUMBUS
Also Called: Compost Facility
7000 State Route 104 (43137-9712)
PHONE..................................614 645-3152
John Hoff, *Branch Mgr*
EMP: 23 Privately Held
WEB: www.cityofcolumbus.org
SIC: 2875 9511 Compost; air, water & solid waste management;
PA: City Of Columbus
    90 W Broad St Rm B33
    Columbus OH 43215
    614 645-7671

(G-11994)
HIKMA PHARMACEUTICALS USA INC
2130 Rohr Rd (43137-9243)
PHONE..................................732 542-1191
Michael Raya, *Manager*
EMP: 5
SALES (corp-wide): 1.9B Privately Held
SIC: 2834 Pharmaceutical preparations
HQ: Hikma Pharmaceuticals Usa Inc.
    246 Industrial Way W
    Eatontown NJ 07724
    732 542-1191

(G-11995)
J P SAND & GRAVEL COMPANY
Also Called: Marble Cliff Block & Bldrs Sup
5911 Lockbourne Rd (43137-9256)
P.O. Box 2 (43137-0002)
PHONE..................................614 497-0083
Herbert Hartshorn, *Ch of Bd*
Richard A Roberts, *President*
Mike Craiglow, *Vice Pres*
Joann Roberts, *Treasurer*
EMP: 28 EST: 1925
SQ FT: 6,200
SALES (est): 3MM Privately Held
SIC: 3271 1442 Blocks, concrete or cinder: standard; construction sand mining; gravel mining

(G-11996)
LOCKBOURNE AG CENTER INC
10 Commerce St (43137-9279)
P.O. Box 11 (43137-0011)
PHONE..................................614 491-0635
Kenneth R Gregory, *President*
Vicky Gregory, *Treasurer*
EMP: 4
SQ FT: 20,000
SALES (est): 563.9K Privately Held
SIC: 3199 Feed bags for horses

(G-11997)
LUXOTTICA OF AMERICA INC
Also Called: Luxottica Optical Mfg
2150 Bixby Rd (43137-9273)
PHONE..................................614 409-9381
Chip Sexton, *Branch Mgr*
EMP: 102
SALES (corp-wide): 283.5MM Privately Held
SIC: 3851 Ophthalmic goods
HQ: Luxottica Of America Inc.
    4000 Luxottica Pl
    Mason OH 45040

(G-11998)
NATIONAL LIME AND STONE CO
5911 Lockbourne Rd (43137-9256)
PHONE..................................614 497-0083
Martin Cudoc, *Plant Mgr*
Richard Roberts, *Branch Mgr*
EMP: 25
SQ FT: 4,032
SALES (corp-wide): 3.2B Privately Held
WEB: www.natlime.com
SIC: 3271 1442 Blocks, concrete or cinder: standard; construction sand mining; gravel mining
PA: The National Lime And Stone Company
    551 Lake Cascade Pkwy
    Findlay OH 45840
    419 422-4341

(G-11999)
VSP LAB COLUMBUS
2605 Rohr Rd (43137-9281)
PHONE..................................614 409-8900
Ed Morris, *Principal*
EMP: 23
SALES (est): 4.5MM Privately Held
SIC: 3827 Optical instruments & lenses

(G-12000)
WHIRLPOOL CORPORATION
6241 Shook Rd (43137-9306)
PHONE..................................614 409-4340
EMP: 175
SALES (corp-wide): 21B Publicly Held
SIC: 3585 3632 3633 Air conditioning units, complete: domestic or industrial; refrigerators, mechanical & absorption: household; freezers, home & farm; household laundry machines, including coin-operated
PA: Whirlpool Corporation
    2000 N M 63
    Benton Harbor MI 49022
    269 923-5000

Lockland
Hamilton County

(G-12001)
POST
312 Elm St (45215-5540)
PHONE..................................513 768-8000
Margaret Buchanan, *Principal*
EMP: 3
SALES (est): 158.1K Privately Held
SIC: 2711 Newspapers

Lodi
Medina County

(G-12002)
ABC PLASTICS INC
140 West Dr (44254-1062)
PHONE..................................330 948-3322
Barbara Lohmier, *President*
EMP: 40
SQ FT: 66,000
SALES (est): 6.6MM Privately Held
SIC: 3089 Injection molded finished plastic products

(G-12003)
ADVANCE BRONZE INC (PA)
139 Ohio St (44254-1047)
P.O. Box 280 (44254-0280)
PHONE..................................330 948-1231
David Del Propost, *President*
Dave Delpropost, *General Mgr*
Brett Fehrenbach, *Engineer*
Vincent J Del Propost, *Treasurer*
Herbert Herschbach, *Controller*
▲ EMP: 60
SQ FT: 150,000
SALES (est): 11.1MM Privately Held
WEB: www.advancebronze.com
SIC: 3568 3366 Power transmission equipment; bushings & bearings

(G-12004)
ADVANCE BRONZEHUBCO DIV (HQ)
139 Ohio St (44254-1047)
PHONE..................................304 232-4414
Thomas Seringer,
David Delpropost,
EMP: 20
SALES (est): 2.3MM
SALES (corp-wide): 11.1MM Privately Held
WEB: www.hubcobronze.com
SIC: 3366 Bronze foundry
PA: Advance Bronze, Inc.
    139 Ohio St
    Lodi OH 44254
    330 948-1231

(G-12005)
ALLOY FABRICATORS INC
700 Wooster St (44254-1340)
PHONE..................................330 948-3535
Lance Yurich, *President*
Dan Dietrick, *General Mgr*
EMP: 21
SQ FT: 15,000
SALES (est): 3.6MM Privately Held
WEB: www.alloyfab.net
SIC: 3441 Fabricated structural metal

(G-12006)
ARTISTIC FOODS INCORPORATED
355 Elyria St (44254-1077)
PHONE..................................330 401-1313
Nicole Whittenberger, *Principal*
EMP: 3
SALES (est): 156.1K Privately Held
SIC: 2099 Food preparations

GEOGRAPHIC SECTION

Logan - Hocking County (G-12034)

(G-12007)
BACK RD CANDLES & HM DECOR LLC
9970 Sanford Rd (44254-9761)
PHONE 330 461-6075
Jennifer Wooley, *Principal*
EMP: 3
SALES (est): 63.5K **Privately Held**
SIC: 3999 Candles

(G-12008)
BUCKEYE POLYMERS INC (PA)
104 Lee St (44254-1056)
PHONE 330 948-3007
Jeffery Fisher, *President*
▲ **EMP:** 37
SQ FT: 35,000
SALES (est): 9.9MM **Privately Held**
WEB: www.buckeyepolymers.com
SIC: 2821 2824 Molding compounds, plastics; polyethylene resins; acrylonitrile fibers

(G-12009)
CROPKING INCORPORATED
134 West Dr (44254-1062)
PHONE 330 302-4203
Paul Brentlinger, *President*
Marilyn Brentlinger, *Corp Secy*
◆ **EMP:** 16
SQ FT: 40,000
SALES (est): 4MM **Privately Held**
WEB: www.cropking.com
SIC: 3448 3999 Greenhouses; prefabricated metal; hydroponic equipment

(G-12010)
FASTFEED CORP
124 S Academy St (44254-1345)
PHONE 330 948-7333
Dan Reed, *President*
EMP: 6
SALES (est): 1.1MM **Privately Held**
SIC: 3441 Fabricated structural metal

(G-12011)
FEINKOST INGREDIENT CO U S A
Also Called: Feinkost Ingredients
103 Billman St (44254-1029)
PHONE 330 948-3006
Mark Sandridge, *President*
EMP: 5
SALES: 150K **Privately Held**
SIC: 2099 Emulsifiers, food

(G-12012)
HERALD LOOMS
118 Lee St (44254-1056)
PHONE 330 948-1080
Alan Anderson, *Principal*
EMP: 3
SALES (est): 108.6K **Privately Held**
SIC: 2711 Newspapers, publishing & printing

(G-12013)
L C I INC
101 West Dr (44254-1061)
P.O. Box 205 (44254-0205)
PHONE 330 948-1922
Elias A Sutton Jr, *President*
Diana L Sutton, *Corp Secy*
EMP: 3
SQ FT: 16,000
SALES (est): 439.9K **Privately Held**
SIC: 3469 3599 Stamping metal for the trade; machine shop, jobbing & repair

(G-12014)
LODI FOUNDRY CO INC
106 Billman St (44254-1030)
P.O. Box 185 (44254-0185)
PHONE 330 948-1516
Fax: 330 948-2112
EMP: 24
SQ FT: 14,000
SALES: 1.2MM **Privately Held**
SIC: 3365 Aluminum Foundry

(G-12015)
LOWELL MARCUM
Also Called: Marcum Machine Shop
328 Bank St (44254-1006)
P.O. Box 337 (44254-0337)
PHONE 330 948-2353
Lowell Marcum, *Owner*
EMP: 5
SALES (est): 410.6K **Privately Held**
SIC: 3599 Job Machine Shop

(G-12016)
MAGNACO INDUSTRIES INC (PA)
140 West Dr (44254-1062)
PHONE 216 961-3636
Ken Geith, *President*
Magdalaine Geith, *Treasurer*
EMP: 20
SQ FT: 43,000
SALES: 1,000K **Privately Held**
SIC: 3714 7389 Motor vehicle parts & accessories; packaging & labeling services

(G-12017)
OAK FRONT INC
Also Called: Bent Nail Millwork
830 Bank St (44254-1028)
P.O. Box 217 (44254-0217)
PHONE 330 948-4500
David Fetherolf, *Vice Pres*
EMP: 5
SQ FT: 8,000
SALES (est): 655.1K **Privately Held**
SIC: 2431 Doors, wood

(G-12018)
PIONEER MACHINE INC
104 S Prospect St (44254-1313)
PHONE 330 948-6500
Don Gray, *President*
Sherry Gray, *Vice Pres*
EMP: 8
SQ FT: 8,400
SALES (est): 766.4K **Privately Held**
SIC: 3441 3599 Fabricated structural metal; machine shop, jobbing & repair

(G-12019)
SHILLING TRANSPORT
9718 Avon Lake Rd (44254-9639)
PHONE 330 948-1105
Gary Frank, *President*
EMP: 7
SALES (est): 420K **Privately Held**
SIC: 3715 Truck trailers

(G-12020)
STEPHEN ANDREWS INC
Also Called: Camelot Printing
7634 Lafayette Rd (44254-9607)
PHONE 330 725-2672
Stephen Andrews, *President*
EMP: 7
SQ FT: 1,700
SALES (est): 894K **Privately Held**
SIC: 2759 2752 Commercial printing; commercial printing, lithographic; commercial printing, offset

Logan
Hocking County

(G-12021)
AMANDA BENT BOLT COMPANY
Also Called: Amanda Manufacturing
1120 C I C Dr (43138-9153)
P.O. Box 1027 (43138-4027)
PHONE 740 385-6893
Robert Gruschow, *President*
Sandra Zwayer, *Controller*
▲ **EMP:** 212
SQ FT: 139,000
SALES: 86MM
SALES (corp-wide): 99.2MM **Privately Held**
WEB: www.amandabentbolt.com
SIC: 3496 3452 Miscellaneous fabricated wire products; bolts, nuts, rivets & washers

PA: Deshler Group, Inc.
34450 Industrial Rd
Livonia MI 48150
734 525-9100

(G-12022)
CLAY LOGAN PRODUCTS COMPANY
Also Called: LOGAN FOUNDRY & MACHINE
201 S Walnut St (43138-1376)
PHONE 740 385-2184
Richard H Brandt, *Ch of Bd*
William R Brandt, *President*
William Heft, *Vice Pres*
Bill Heft, *Manager*
Donald Hoobler, *Director*
EMP: 80
SQ FT: 266,000
SALES: 19.3MM **Privately Held**
WEB: www.claypipe.com
SIC: 3259 Clay sewer & drainage pipe & tile

(G-12023)
COLUMBUS WASHBOARD COMPANY LTD
14 Gallagher Ave (43138-1666)
PHONE 740 380-3828
Jacqueline M Barnett, *Owner*
Bevan Barnett,
Joyce Gerstner,
Larry Gerstner,
James Martin,
▲ **EMP:** 8
SQ FT: 15,000
SALES: 500K **Privately Held**
SIC: 2499 Washboards, wood & part wood

(G-12024)
GABRIEL LOGAN LLC (PA)
1689 E Front St (43138-9290)
PHONE 740 380-6809
Troy L Gabriel, *CEO*
Tom Richardson, *Exec VP*
Sam Stump, *Plant Mgr*
Nancy Cox, *Purchasing*
Sharon McKinley, *Manager*
▲ **EMP:** 61
SQ FT: 300,000
SALES (est): 8.9MM **Privately Held**
WEB: www.gabriellogan.com
SIC: 2541 Display fixtures, wood; pedestals & statuary, wood; store & office display cases & fixtures

(G-12025)
GENERAL ELECTRIC COMPANY
Hc 93 Box N (43138)
PHONE 740 385-2114
John Davis, *Manager*
Michael Wilhite, *Manager*
EMP: 100
SALES (corp-wide): 121.6B **Publicly Held**
SIC: 3231 3229 Products of purchased glass; pressed & blown glass
PA: General Electric Company
41 Farnsworth St
Boston MA 02210
617 443-3000

(G-12026)
HOCKING HILLS ENERGY & WELL SE
32919 Logan Horns Mill Rd (43138-8497)
PHONE 740 385-6690
David Poling, *Mng Member*
EMP: 7
SALES: 3.5MM **Privately Held**
SIC: 1382 1381 Geophysical exploration, oil & gas field; drilling oil & gas wells

(G-12027)
HOCKING VALLEY CONCRETE INC (PA)
35255 Hocking Dr (43138-9482)
PHONE 740 385-2165
William Vaughn, *President*
David Vaughn, *Vice Pres*
Mark Vaughn, *Vice Pres*
Doug Dicken, *Sales Staff*
Jeff Cupp, *Manager*
EMP: 20 **EST:** 1956
SQ FT: 2,000

SALES (est): 3.8MM **Privately Held**
SIC: 3273 1442 Ready-mixed concrete; construction sand mining; gravel mining

(G-12028)
HOCKING VALLEY CONCRETE INC
35255 Hocking Dr (43138-9482)
PHONE 740 385-2165
William Laughn, *Manager*
EMP: 8
SALES (corp-wide): 4MM **Privately Held**
SIC: 3273 Ready-mixed concrete
PA: Hocking Valley Concrete, Inc.
35255 Hocking Dr
Logan OH 43138
740 385-2165

(G-12029)
JUDITH C ZELL
21313 State Route 93 S (43138-7508)
PHONE 740 385-0386
Edward Zell, *President*
Judith Zell, *Owner*
EMP: 3
SALES: 300K **Privately Held**
SIC: 3993 2499 Signs & advertising specialties; decorative wood & woodwork

(G-12030)
KILBARGER CONSTRUCTION INC
Also Called: C & L Supply
450 Gallagher Ave (43138-1893)
P.O. Box 946 (43138-0946)
PHONE 740 385-6019
Edward Kilbarger, *CEO*
Anthony Kilbarger, *Vice Pres*
James E Kilbarger, *Vice Pres*
Tony Kilbarger, *Vice Pres*
Daniel Stohs, *Opers Mgr*
EMP: 120
SQ FT: 2,500
SALES (est): 23.2MM **Privately Held**
WEB: www.kilbarger.com
SIC: 1381 Drilling oil & gas wells

(G-12031)
KILBARGER INVESTMENTS INC
Also Called: Kilbarger Investment Co
450 Gallagher Ave (43138-1893)
P.O. Box 946 (43138-0946)
PHONE 740 385-6019
Edward F Kilbarger, *President*
Anthony Kilbarger, *Vice Pres*
James E Kilbarger, *Vice Pres*
Ann Kilbarger, *Admin Sec*
EMP: 4
SQ FT: 2,500
SALES (est): 645.2K **Privately Held**
SIC: 1311 Crude petroleum production; natural gas production

(G-12032)
LOGAN COATINGS LLC
2255 E Front St (43138-8637)
P.O. Box 202 (43138-0202)
PHONE 740 380-0047
James M Johnson, *Principal*
EMP: 10
SALES (est): 1.1MM **Privately Held**
SIC: 3479 Coating of metals & formed products

(G-12033)
LOGAN SCREEN PRINTING
Also Called: Logan Screen Printing & EMB
119 W Main St (43138-1605)
PHONE 740 385-3303
Bob Schrader, *Owner*
EMP: 5
SQ FT: 3,200
SALES (est): 438K **Privately Held**
WEB: www.loganscreenprinting.com
SIC: 2759 2396 2395 Screen printing; automotive & apparel trimmings; pleating & stitching

(G-12034)
LOGAN WELDING INC
37062 Hocking Dr (43138-9465)
PHONE 740 385-9651
Mark E Brandon, *President*
Dan Brandon, *Vice Pres*
Juanita Brandon, *Admin Sec*
EMP: 6

Logan - Hocking County (G-12035)   GEOGRAPHIC SECTION

SQ FT: 5,100
SALES (est): 727.5K **Privately Held**
SIC: 7692 Welding repair

(G-12035)
MENNEL MILLING COMPANY
Also Called: Mennel Milling Logan
1 W Front St (43138-1825)
PHONE..................................740 385-6824
Larry Hawkins, *Branch Mgr*
EMP: 37
SALES (corp-wide): 119.2MM **Privately Held**
SIC: 5191 2041 Feed; flour mills, cereal (except rice)
PA: The Mennel Milling Company
   319 S Vine St
   Fostoria OH 44830
   419 435-8151

(G-12036)
MENNEL MILLING COMPANY
Also Called: Mennel Milling Logan
1 W Front St (43138-1825)
PHONE..................................740 385-6824
EMP: 65
SALES (corp-wide): 119.2MM **Privately Held**
SIC: 2041 5191 Flour mills, cereal (except rice); feed
PA: The Mennel Milling Company
   319 S Vine St
   Fostoria OH 44830
   419 435-8151

(G-12037)
OAK DALE DRILLING INC
149 Ruth Ave (43138-1851)
PHONE..................................740 385-5888
Dale Tucker, *President*
Teddy Tucker, *Treasurer*
EMP: 5
SALES (est): 347.2K **Privately Held**
SIC: 1381 Directional drilling oil & gas wells

(G-12038)
OSBURN ASSOCIATES INC (PA)
9383 Vanatta Rd (43138-8719)
P.O. Box 912 (43138-0912)
PHONE..................................740 385-5732
Harry Osburn, *Director*
Charles A Gerken, *Director*
Donna Osburn, *Director*
▲ EMP: 40
SQ FT: 39,360
SALES (est): 15.7MM **Privately Held**
WEB: www.osburnassociates.com
SIC: 3089 5063 Fittings for pipe, plastic; boxes & fittings, electrical

(G-12039)
PATTONS TRUCK & HEAVY EQP SVC
Also Called: K & K Auto & Truck Parts
35640 Hocking Dr (43138-9467)
P.O. Box 963 (43138-0963)
PHONE..................................740 385-4067
Paul Patton, *President*
EMP: 16
SQ FT: 3,400
SALES (est): 2.8MM **Privately Held**
SIC: 3599 7538 5531 Machine shop, jobbing & repair; general automotive repair shops; automotive & home supply stores

(G-12040)
PAUL A GRIM INC
15104 State Route 328 (43138-9445)
PHONE..................................740 385-9637
Paul A Grim, *President*
Joyce Grim, *Admin Sec*
EMP: 5
SQ FT: 7,200
SALES: 500K **Privately Held**
SIC: 1381 Drilling oil & gas wells

(G-12041)
QUALITY CONCEPTS TELECOM
19485 Harble Rd (43138-9772)
PHONE..................................740 385-2003
Chris Warren, *Office Mgr*
Richard J Warren,
EMP: 20
SQ FT: 1,400
SALES (est): 2.4MM **Privately Held**
SIC: 3452 Bolts, nuts, rivets & washers

(G-12042)
RALPH ROBINSON INC
Also Called: Oil Enterprises
700 Ohio Ave (43138-8469)
P.O. Box 84 (43138-0084)
PHONE..................................740 385-2747
Michael Robinson, *President*
EMP: 6 EST: 1962
SQ FT: 4,700
SALES (est): 756.7K **Privately Held**
SIC: 1389 5084 Oil & gas wells: building, repairing & dismantling; oil refining machinery, equipment & supplies

(G-12043)
SIGNS UNLIMITED THE GRAPHIC (PA)
Also Called: Advent Designs
21313 State Route 93 S (43138-7508)
PHONE..................................614 836-7446
Judy Zell, *CEO*
Ed Zell, *President*
EMP: 8
SQ FT: 20,000
SALES: 300K **Privately Held**
WEB: www.adventdesigns.com
SIC: 3993 7389 Signs & advertising specialties; design services

(G-12044)
SMEAD MANUFACTURING COMPANY
851 Smead Rd (43138-9500)
PHONE..................................740 385-5601
EMP: 175
SALES (corp-wide): 233.3MM **Privately Held**
SIC: 2675 Folders, filing, die-cut: made from purchased materials
PA: Smead Manufacturing Company Inc
   600 Smead Blvd
   Hastings MN 55033
   651 437-4111

(G-12045)
TYJEN INC (PA)
Also Called: Slater's Builders Supplies
35255 Hocking Dr (43138-9482)
PHONE..................................740 380-3215
Mark Vaughn, *President*
David Vaughn, *Vice Pres*
EMP: 3 EST: 1931
SQ FT: 2,000
SALES (est): 3.1MM **Privately Held**
SIC: 3271 5211 Blocks, concrete or cinder: standard; lumber & other building materials

(G-12046)
WRIGHTS WELL SERVICE
37940 Scout Rd (43138-8832)
PHONE..................................740 380-9602
Ken Wright, *Owner*
EMP: 6
SALES (est): 210.2K **Privately Held**
SIC: 1389 Servicing oil & gas wells

London
Madison County

(G-12047)
ADVANCED DRAINAGE SYSTEMS INC
288 Lafayette St (43140-9069)
PHONE..................................740 852-9554
Barry Trimble, *Manager*
EMP: 30
SALES (corp-wide): 1.3B **Publicly Held**
WEB: www.ads-pipe.com
SIC: 3084 Plastics pipe
PA: Advanced Drainage Systems, Inc.
   4640 Trueman Blvd
   Hilliard OH 43026
   614 658-0050

(G-12048)
ADVANCED DRAINAGE SYSTEMS INC
400 E High St (43140-9501)
PHONE..................................740 852-2980
Robert Sensabaugh, *Branch Mgr*
EMP: 52
SALES (corp-wide): 1.3B **Publicly Held**
WEB: www.ads-pipe.com
SIC: 3084 Plastics pipe
PA: Advanced Drainage Systems, Inc.
   4640 Trueman Blvd
   Hilliard OH 43026
   614 658-0050

(G-12049)
ARMALY LLC
Also Called: Armaly Brands
110 W 1st St (43140-1484)
PHONE..................................740 852-3621
Annmarie Armaly, *Treasurer*
▼ EMP: 40
SALES (est): 7.7MM
SALES (corp-wide): 8.2MM **Privately Held**
SIC: 3089 5199 3086 Floor coverings, plastic; sponges (animal); plastics foam products
PA: Armaly Sponge Company
   1900 Easy St
   Commerce Township MI 48390
   248 669-2100

(G-12050)
BODYCOTE IMT INC
443 E High St (43140-9501)
PHONE..................................740 852-5000
Chris Gattie, *Manager*
EMP: 27
SALES (corp-wide): 911.9MM **Privately Held**
SIC: 3398 3269 Metal heat treating; pottery household articles, except kitchen articles
HQ: Bodycote Imt, Inc.
   155 River St
   Andover MA 01810
   978 470-0876

(G-12051)
BODYCOTE THERMAL PROC INC
Also Called: Bodycote Kolsterising
443 E High St (43140-9501)
PHONE..................................740 852-4955
Doug Ridgeway, *General Mgr*
Daniel Kane, *Plant Engr*
EMP: 7
SALES (corp-wide): 911.9MM **Privately Held**
SIC: 3398 Metal heat treating
HQ: Bodycote Thermal Processing, Inc.
   12700 Park Central Dr # 700
   Dallas TX 75251
   214 904-2420

(G-12052)
CENTRAL OHIO PRINTING CORP
Also Called: Madison Press
55 W High St (43140-1074)
PHONE..................................740 852-1616
Donald Hartley, *President*
EMP: 55 EST: 1961
SQ FT: 20,000
SALES (est): 2.7MM
SALES (corp-wide): 2MM **Privately Held**
WEB: www.madison-press.com
SIC: 2711 2752 Newspapers, publishing & printing; commercial printing, lithographic
PA: Walls Newspapers Inc
   525 Office Park Dr
   Mountain Brk AL 35223
   205 870-1684

(G-12053)
CHURCH & DWIGHT CO INC
Also Called: Arm & Hammer
110 W 1st St (43140-1484)
PHONE..................................740 852-3621
Neil Parrish, *Opers Mgr*
Richard Newberry, *Purch Mgr*
Sandra Wood, *Supervisor*
EMP: 70
SALES (corp-wide): 4.1B **Publicly Held**
WEB: www.churchdwight.com
SIC: 2812 Sodium bicarbonate
PA: Church & Dwight Co., Inc.
   500 Charles Ewing Blvd
   Ewing NJ 08628
   609 806-1200

(G-12054)
COLD STORAGE SERVICES LLC
54 S Main St (43140-1212)
PHONE..................................740 837-0858
Jeffrey M Johnson, *Mng Member*
EMP: 5 EST: 2016
SALES: 360K **Privately Held**
SIC: 3632 Household refrigerators & freezers

(G-12055)
COLUMBUS MESSENGER COMPANY
Also Called: Madison Messenger
78 S Main St (43140-1212)
PHONE..................................740 852-0809
Jim Durban, *Manager*
EMP: 4
SALES (corp-wide): 2MM **Privately Held**
SIC: 2711 Newspapers, publishing & printing; newspapers: publishing only, not printed on site
PA: The Columbus Messenger Company
   3500 Sullivant Ave
   Columbus OH 43204
   614 272-5422

(G-12056)
CREAMER METAL PRODUCTS (PA)
77 S Madison Rd (43140-1444)
PHONE..................................740 852-1752
Kennison Sims, *Partner*
Scott Sims, *Partner*
Thomas Hurley, *Prdtn Mgr*
Gary Beatty, *Purch Agent*
Mark Wilson, *Sales Mgr*
EMP: 20 EST: 1945
SQ FT: 31,000
SALES (est): 1B **Privately Held**
WEB: www.creamermetal.com
SIC: 3523 Farm machinery & equipment

(G-12057)
DEER CREEK HONEY FARMS LTD
551 E High St (43140-9304)
PHONE..................................740 852-0899
Christopher L Dunham, *Partner*
Lee T Dunham, *Partner*
Mark L Dunham, *Partner*
EMP: 8 EST: 1938
SQ FT: 22,000
SALES (est): 1MM **Privately Held**
SIC: 2099 0279 Honey, strained & bottled; apiary (bee & honey farm)

(G-12058)
DIGIONYX LLC
8420 Opossum Run Rd (43140-9437)
PHONE..................................614 594-9897
Timothy Fleming,
Harold Goings,
EMP: 5
SALES (est): 188.8K **Privately Held**
SIC: 7372 7389 Prepackaged software;

(G-12059)
ELITE FTSCOM INC
Also Called: Elitefts
1402 State Route 665 (43140-8796)
PHONE..................................740 845-0987
Dave Tate, *CEO*
Steven Diel, *CEO*
Josh Goedker, *Editor*
Tracey Tate, *Vice Pres*
Lori Nutter, *Warehouse Mgr*
▲ EMP: 5
SQ FT: 3,000
SALES (est): 1.1MM **Privately Held**
WEB: www.elitefts.com
SIC: 5961 3949 Fitness & sporting goods, mail order; exercise equipment; dumbbells & other weightlifting equipment

GEOGRAPHIC SECTION

Lorain - Lorain County (G-12087)

(G-12060)
GARY I TEACH JR
4855 Rsdale Mlford Ctr Rd (43140)
PHONE..................................614 582-7483
Gary L Teach, *Principal*
EMP: 4
SALES (est): 437K **Privately Held**
SIC: 2672 Coated & laminated paper

(G-12061)
GRA-MAG TRUCK INTR SYSTEMS LLC (DH)
470 E High St (43140-9303)
PHONE..................................740 490-1000
Colleen Uhrig, *Accountant*
Rick Chefer, *Mng Member*
▲ **EMP:** 30
SQ FT: 60,000
SALES (est): 9.8MM
SALES (corp-wide): 38.9B **Privately Held**
WEB: www.gramag.com
SIC: 2531 Seats, automobile

(G-12062)
INTELLIGRATED PRODUCTS LLC
475 E High St (43140-9303)
P.O. Box 899 (43140-0899)
PHONE..................................740 490-0300
Chris Cole, *CEO*
Jim McCarthy,
▲ **EMP:** 33
SQ FT: 210,000
SALES (est): 11.2MM
SALES (corp-wide): 41.8B **Publicly Held**
SIC: 3535 Conveyors & conveying equipment
HQ: Intelligrated Systems, Inc.
7901 Innovation Way
Mason OH 45040
866 936-7300

(G-12063)
JOHN C STARR
Also Called: Starr Trophy & Awards
15 S Main St (43140-1243)
P.O. Box 615 (43140-0615)
PHONE..................................740 852-5592
John C Starr, *Owner*
EMP: 3
SQ FT: 2,400
SALES (est): 260.4K **Privately Held**
SIC: 5999 5947 7389 2759 Trophies & plaques; gift shop; engraving service; imprinting

(G-12064)
KMAK GROUP LLC
480 E High St (43140-9303)
P.O. Box 496 (43140-0496)
PHONE..................................937 308-1023
Kevin Henry, *President*
EMP: 11 **EST:** 2009
SQ FT: 15,000
SALES (est): 1.7MM **Privately Held**
SIC: 2448 Cargo containers, wood & wood with metal

(G-12065)
NISSEN CHEMITEC AMERICA INC
350 E High St (43140-9773)
PHONE..................................740 852-3200
Shawn Hendrix, *President*
Shinya Kawakami, *President*
Richard Hendrix, *Exec VP*
Kunihiko Nagura, *Vice Pres*
Damion Manns, *Plant Mgr*
▲ **EMP:** 230
SQ FT: 155,000
SALES (est): 48.5MM
SALES (corp-wide): 281.5MM **Privately Held**
WEB: www.londonind.com
SIC: 3089 Injection molding of plastics
PA: Nissen Chemitec Corporation
2-4-34, Nishiharacho
Niihama EHM 792-0
897 334-171

(G-12066)
O CONNOR OFFICE PDTS & PRTG
60 W High St (43140-1075)
PHONE..................................740 852-2209
Gary Feliks, *Owner*
EMP: 8
SQ FT: 3,200
SALES (est): 560K **Privately Held**
SIC: 5943 2752 Office forms & supplies; commercial printing, offset

(G-12067)
OAKVALE FARM CHEESE INC
1283 State Route 29 Ne (43140-9545)
PHONE..................................740 857-1230
Dale King, *President*
Randall Finke, *Vice Pres*
Elizabeth Finke, *Treasurer*
Jean King, *Admin Sec*
EMP: 5
SALES (est): 384.5K **Privately Held**
SIC: 2022 Cheese, natural & processed

(G-12068)
OLIVE BRANCH
2337 Finley Guy Rd (43140-9529)
PHONE..................................614 563-3139
Olive Branch, *Principal*
EMP: 3
SALES (est): 139.1K **Privately Held**
SIC: 2079 Olive oil

(G-12069)
STANLEY ELECTRIC US CO INC (HQ)
420 E High St (43140-9799)
PHONE..................................740 852-5200
Shinomiya Masahiro, *President*
Brian Boldman, *Plant Mgr*
Shad Russell, *Production*
Doug McCaw, *QC Mgr*
Nicholas Finnegan, *Engineer*
▲ **EMP:** 277
SQ FT: 733,000
SALES: 40MM
SALES (corp-wide): 4.1B **Privately Held**
WEB: www.stanleyus.com
SIC: 3647 3694 3089 Automotive lighting fixtures; automotive electrical equipment; injection molding of plastics
PA: Stanley Electric Co.,Ltd.
2-9-13, Nakameguro
Meguro-Ku TKY 153-0
368 662-222

(G-12070)
TEXTILES INC (PA)
Also Called: Jordan Young International
23 Old Springfield Rd (43140-2033)
PHONE..................................740 852-0782
Phillip Jordan, *President*
Catherine Jordan, *Vice Pres*
Rob Jordan, *Vice Pres*
▲ **EMP:** 200
SQ FT: 4,000
SALES (est): 19.1MM **Privately Held**
SIC: 2511 Wood household furniture

(G-12071)
UNDER HILL WATER WELL
1789 Itawamba Trl (43140-8737)
PHONE..................................740 852-0858
Timothy Underhill, *Principal*
EMP: 3
SALES (est): 368.7K **Privately Held**
SIC: 3533 Drilling tools for gas, oil or water wells

(G-12072)
WILSON PRTG GRAPHICS OF LONDON (PA)
158 S Main St (43140-1439)
PHONE..................................740 852-5934
Tim Wilson, *President*
EMP: 5
SQ FT: 4,800
SALES (est): 692.2K **Privately Held**
SIC: 2752 Commercial printing, offset

Londonderry
Ross County

(G-12073)
ALBRIGHT SAW COMPANY INC
Also Called: Albright Supply Company
33535 Us Highway 50 (45647-9715)
PHONE..................................740 887-2107
EMP: 3
SALES (est): 226.2K **Privately Held**
SIC: 3524 5261 Mfg Lawn/Garden Equipment Ret Nursery/Garden Supplies

(G-12074)
CLARK MACHINE SERVICE
33926 Us Highway 50 (45647-9704)
P.O. Box 203 (45647-0203)
PHONE..................................740 887-2396
Barry L Clark, *Owner*
Patty Clark, *Bookkeeper*
EMP: 3
SQ FT: 3,696
SALES (est): 267.1K **Privately Held**
SIC: 3599 Machine shop, jobbing & repair

(G-12075)
DON PUCKETT LUMBER INC
31263 Beech Grove Rd (45647-8942)
PHONE..................................740 887-4191
Tim Puckett, *President*
Jeff Puckett, *Vice Pres*
EMP: 17
SALES (est): 1.4MM **Privately Held**
SIC: 2421 Sawmills & planing mills, general

Lorain
Lorain County

(G-12076)
A CLASS COATINGS INC
4481 Oakhill Blvd (44053-1959)
PHONE..................................440 960-6869
Lee Bolber, *President*
EMP: 12
SQ FT: 20,000
SALES (est): 810K **Privately Held**
SIC: 3479 Coating of metals & formed products; aluminum coating of metal products

(G-12077)
A-1 WELDING & FABRICATION
1005 E 32nd St (44055-1598)
PHONE..................................440 233-8474
Kenneth J Balko, *President*
Wayne Balko, *Vice Pres*
Holly Herbert, *Admin Sec*
EMP: 10
SQ FT: 60,000
SALES (est): 2MM **Privately Held**
SIC: 3443 3312 Weldments; structural shapes & pilings, steel

(G-12078)
AMERICAN METAL CHEMICAL CORP
Also Called: Amcor Marine
200 E 9th St (44052-1903)
PHONE..................................440 244-1800
Debbie Smith, *Branch Mgr*
EMP: 5
SALES (corp-wide): 14.9MM **Privately Held**
SIC: 2899 Fluxes: brazing, soldering, galvanizing & welding
PA: American Metal Chemical Corporation
3546 S Morgan St
Chicago IL 60609
773 254-1818

(G-12079)
ATLANTIC INVESTMENT
6117 Antler Xing (44053-1879)
PHONE..................................440 567-5054
Jose Moquete, *Principal*
EMP: 4
SQ FT: 2,450
SALES: 144K **Privately Held**
SIC: 2099 Food preparations

(G-12080)
BODNAR PRINTING CO INC
3480 Colorado Ave (44052-2818)
PHONE..................................440 277-8295
Ralph Woodward, *President*
Bonnie Woodward, *Corp Secy*
EMP: 12 **EST:** 1948
SQ FT: 5,000
SALES (est): 2.1MM **Privately Held**
WEB: www.bodnarprinting.com
SIC: 2752 Commercial printing, offset

(G-12081)
BUSES INTERNATIONAL
702 N Ridge Rd E (44055-3018)
PHONE..................................440 233-4091
Todd Rainey, *COO*
Tom Szychowicz, *Director*
Norman Beetler, *Director*
EMP: 12
SALES: 723.2K **Privately Held**
WEB: www.busesinternational.org
SIC: 8661 3711 8011 Christian & Reformed Church; bus & other large specialty vehicle assembly; medical centers

(G-12082)
CAMACO LLC
Also Called: Camaco Lorain
3400 River Indus Pk Rd (44052-2900)
PHONE..................................440 288-4444
Ruby Srivastava, *Buyer*
Kevin Behm, *Engineer*
Chris Galligan, *Engineer*
Colleen Walsh, *Engineer*
Thomas Rockwell, *CFO*
EMP: 560
SALES (corp-wide): 535.7MM **Privately Held**
WEB: www.camaco.com
SIC: 3499 Automobile seat frames, metal
HQ: Camaco, Llc
37000 W 12 Mile Rd # 105
Farmington Hills MI 48331
248 442-6800

(G-12083)
CASE PLATING INC
736 Idaho Ave (44052-3354)
PHONE..................................440 288-8304
Bonnie Pickett, *President*
EMP: 4
SQ FT: 12,000
SALES: 300K **Privately Held**
SIC: 3471 Plating of metals or formed products

(G-12084)
CONSUMERACQ INC (PA)
2509 N Ridge Rd E (44055-3772)
P.O. Box 823 (44052-0823)
PHONE..................................440 277-9305
Jeffrey Riddell, *President*
Steve Holovacs, *Sales Staff*
Jacqueline Riddell, *Admin Sec*
EMP: 150
SQ FT: 4,000
SALES (est): 14.4MM **Privately Held**
SIC: 3273 5211 Ready-mixed concrete; lumber & other building materials

(G-12085)
CONSUMERS BUILDERS SUPPLY CO (PA)
2509 N Ridge Rd E (44055-3772)
P.O. Box 824 (44052-0824)
PHONE..................................440 277-9306
Jeffrey Riddell, *President*
Charlie Houdeshell, *Traffic Dir*
Jacqueline Riddell, *Admin Sec*
Scott Herrington, *Assistant*
EMP: 20
SALES (est): 5.3MM **Privately Held**
WEB: www.consumersbuilderssupply.com
SIC: 3273 5211 Ready-mixed concrete; lumber & other building materials

(G-12086)
CRAWFORD RESOURCES INC
1326 Coper Foster Pk Rd W (44053-3614)
PHONE..................................419 624-8400
Dale Crawford, *President*
Elizabeth Jane Crawford, *Vice Pres*
EMP: 3
SALES (est): 385.1K **Privately Held**
SIC: 3677 Filtration devices, electronic

(G-12087)
CUSTOM SINK TOP MFG
Also Called: C S T Geometric Forms
302 W 12th St (44052-3406)
PHONE..................................440 245-6220
Greg Luca, *Principal*
EMP: 11

Lorain - Lorain County (G-12088) — GEOGRAPHIC SECTION

SALES (est): 1.2MM **Privately Held**
SIC: **5031** 2599 Structural assemblies, prefabricated: wood; factory furniture & fixtures; cabinets, factory

(G-12088)
DAYTON HEIDELBERG DISTRG CO
5901 Baumhart Rd (44053-2012)
PHONE..................................440 989-1027
EMP: 90
SALES (corp-wide): 369.4MM **Privately Held**
SIC: **2082** Beer (alcoholic beverage)
PA: Dayton Heidelberg Distributing Co.
3601 Dryden Rd
Moraine OH 45439
937 222-8692

(G-12089)
EMERSON ELECTRIC CO
1509 Iowa Ave (44052-3379)
PHONE..................................440 288-1122
EMP: 21
SALES (corp-wide): 17.4B **Publicly Held**
SIC: **3823** Industrial instrmnts msrmnt display/control process variable
PA: Emerson Electric Co.
8000 West Florissant Ave
Saint Louis MO 63136
314 553-2000

(G-12090)
ERDIE INDUSTRIES INC
1205 Colorado Ave (44052-3313)
PHONE..................................440 288-0166
Jason Erdie, *President*
Jeffrey Erdie, *Vice Pres*
EMP: 40
SQ FT: 50,000
SALES (est): 9.3MM **Privately Held**
WEB: www.erdiepaper.com
SIC: **2655** Tubes, fiber or paper: made from purchased material

(G-12091)
EXOCHEM CORPORATION (PA)
2421 E 28th St (44055-2198)
PHONE..................................800 807-7464
Randall Miraldi, *President*
Lois Miraldi, *Corp Secy*
Kathleen Roark, *Vice Pres*
▲ EMP: 54 EST: 1968
SQ FT: 21,000
SALES (est): 12.3MM **Privately Held**
SIC: **3299** Insulsleeves (foundry materials)

(G-12092)
FELLER TOOL CO INC
7405 Industrial Pkwy Dr (44052-2064)
PHONE..................................440 324-6277
Doug Feller, *President*
Deborah Feller, *Vice Pres*
EMP: 10 EST: 1959
SQ FT: 2,400
SALES (est): 770K **Privately Held**
SIC: **3544** 3599 Special dies & tools; machine shop, jobbing & repair

(G-12093)
GLOBAL PLASTIC TECH INC
1657 Broadway (44052-3439)
PHONE..................................440 879-6045
Makki Odeh, *President*
Adey Shanap, *General Mgr*
EMP: 4
SALES (est): 253.3K **Privately Held**
SIC: **2673** Food storage & frozen food bags, plastic

(G-12094)
H P NIELSEN INC
Also Called: Nielsen Jewelers
753 Broadway (44052-1805)
PHONE..................................440 244-4255
Carl G Nielsen, *President*
Krystina Nielsen, *Vice Pres*
EMP: 6 EST: 1877
SQ FT: 2,600
SALES (est): 762.4K **Privately Held**
SIC: **5944** 3911 7631 Jewelry, precious stones & precious metals; jewelry, precious metal; jewelry repair services

(G-12095)
HPC MANUFACTURING INC
7405 Industrial Pkwy Dr (44053-2064)
PHONE..................................440 322-8334
Robert Drake, *CEO*
EMP: 3
SQ FT: 20,000
SALES (est): 504.7K **Privately Held**
SIC: **3561** Industrial pumps & parts

(G-12096)
JOURNAL REGISTER COMPANY
Also Called: Morning Journal
2500 W Erie Ave (44053-1056)
PHONE..................................440 245-6901
Jeff Schell, *Publisher*
Jeff Sudbrook, *Manager*
EMP: 115
SALES (corp-wide): 661.2MM **Privately Held**
SIC: **2711** 5994 Newspapers, publishing & printing; newsstand
PA: Journal Register Company
5 Hanover Sq Fl 25
New York NY 10004
212 257-7212

(G-12097)
KTS-MET BAR PRODUCTS INC
967 G St (44052-3329)
PHONE..................................440 288-9308
Delvis Kerns, *President*
EMP: 9
SQ FT: 8,500
SALES (est): 1.4MM **Privately Held**
SIC: **3451** Screw machine products

(G-12098)
KUHN FABRICATING INC
1637 E 28th St (44055-1701)
PHONE..................................440 277-4182
Lewis Kuhn, *President*
Rosemary Kuhn, *Vice Pres*
EMP: 6 EST: 1958
SQ FT: 18,000
SALES (est): 1MM **Privately Held**
SIC: **3444** Sheet metal specialties, not stamped

(G-12099)
LAKE SCREEN PRINTING INC
1924 Broadway (44052-3682)
PHONE..................................440 244-5707
Ben Zientarski Jr, *President*
Annette Zientarski, *Corp Secy*
Teresa Zientarski, *Vice Pres*
EMP: 8
SQ FT: 10,000
SALES (est): 1.1MM **Privately Held**
WEB: www.lakescreen.com
SIC: **2759** Screen printing

(G-12100)
LEVIT JEWELERS INC
4274 Oberlin Ave (44053-2925)
PHONE..................................440 985-1685
Rob M Levit, *President*
Katrina Levit, *Vice Pres*
EMP: 4
SALES (est): 459K **Privately Held**
WEB: www.levitjewelers.com
SIC: **3911** Jewelry, precious metal

(G-12101)
LORAIN COUNTY AUTO SYSTEMS INC
3400 River Indus Pk Rd (44052-2900)
PHONE..................................248 442-6800
Thomas Rockwell, *CFO*
EMP: 60
SALES (corp-wide): 535.7MM **Privately Held**
SIC: **3714** Motor vehicle engines & parts
HQ: Lorain County Automotive Systems, Inc.
7470 Industrial Pkwy Dr
Lorain OH 44053
440 960-7470

(G-12102)
LORAIN COUNTY AUTO SYSTEMS INC (HQ)
Also Called: Lcas
7470 Industrial Pkwy Dr (44053-2070)
PHONE..................................440 960-7470
Arvind Pradhan, *CEO*
Keith Brenning, *Opers Mgr*
Tom Rockwell, *CFO*
▲ EMP: 50
SQ FT: 36,000
SALES (est): 213.6MM
SALES (corp-wide): 535.7MM **Privately Held**
WEB: www.lcas.com
SIC: **3714** Motor vehicle engines & parts
PA: P & C Group I, Inc.
37000 W 12 Mile Rd
Farmington Hills MI 48331
248 442-6800

(G-12103)
LORAIN PRINTING COMPANY
1310 Colorado Ave (44052-3322)
PHONE..................................440 288-6000
Brian Koethe, *CEO*
Edwin Koethe II, *Ch of Bd*
Jon Koethe, *President*
Lisa Koethe-Harrison, *Admin Sec*
EMP: 40 EST: 1905
SQ FT: 31,000
SALES (est): 3.7MM **Privately Held**
SIC: **2752** Commercial printing, offset

(G-12104)
MARIOTTI PRINTING CO LLC
513 E 28th St (44055-1396)
PHONE..................................440 245-4120
Martin Mariotti, *Mng Member*
Eileen Mariotti,
EMP: 6
SQ FT: 15,000
SALES (est): 578.2K **Privately Held**
WEB: www.mariottiprinting.com
SIC: **2752** 2759 Commercial printing, offset; letterpress printing

(G-12105)
MATERION BRUSH INC
7375 Industrial Pkwy (44053-4800)
PHONE..................................440 960-5660
Bill Bishop, *Manager*
EMP: 21
SALES (corp-wide): 1.2B **Publicly Held**
WEB: www.brushwellman.com
SIC: **2821** 5051 Plastics materials & resins; metals service centers & offices
HQ: Materion Brush Inc.
6070 Parkland Blvd Ste 1
Mayfield Heights OH 44124
216 486-4200

(G-12106)
NATIONAL BRONZE MTLS OHIO INC
Also Called: Aviva Metals
5311 W River Rd (44055-3735)
PHONE..................................440 277-1226
Michael Greathead, *President*
Norman M Lazarus, *Exec VP*
Jill Conyer, *Admin Sec*
▲ EMP: 27
SALES (est): 7.8MM **Privately Held**
SIC: **3366** 3341 5051 Copper foundries; secondary nonferrous metals; copper
PA: Metchem Anstalt
Feger Treuunternehmen Reg.
Vaduz
237 454-5

(G-12107)
NORLAB INC
Also Called: Norlab Dyes
7465 Industrial Pkwy Dr (44053-2079)
P.O. Box 380, Amherst (44001-0380)
PHONE..................................440 282-5265
John Azok, *President*
EMP: 5
SQ FT: 10,000
SALES (est): 1MM
SALES (corp-wide): 18.9B **Privately Held**
WEB: www.norlabdyes.com
SIC: **2865** Dyes & pigments
HQ: Bio-Medical Applications Of Missouri, Inc.
920 Winter St
Waltham MA 02451

(G-12108)
NORTH CAST ORTHTICS PRSTHETICS (PA)
6100 S Broadway Ste 104 (44053-3875)
PHONE..................................440 233-4314
Jeffrey J Yakovich, *President*
Kathleen Yakovich, *Vice Pres*
Craig Williams,
EMP: 15
SQ FT: 5,000
SALES (est): 2MM **Privately Held**
SIC: **3842** Braces, orthopedic; limbs, artificial

(G-12109)
NOVEX PRODUCTS INCORPORATED
2707 Toledo Ave Ste A (44055-1465)
PHONE..................................440 244-3330
Peyman Pakdel, *President*
▲ EMP: 30
SQ FT: 30,000
SALES (est): 6.5MM **Privately Held**
SIC: **2676** Towels, napkins & tissue paper products

(G-12110)
OKEEFE CASTING CO
2401 E 28th St (44055-2197)
PHONE..................................440 277-5427
Patrick O'Keefe, *Owner*
Lawrence O'Keefe, *Owner*
EMP: 5
SQ FT: 1,200
SALES (est): 572.7K **Privately Held**
WEB: www.okeefecasting.com
SIC: **3365** 3366 Aluminum & aluminum-based alloy castings; castings (except die); bronze; castings (except die)

(G-12111)
PC CAMPANA INC (PA)
6155 Park Square Dr Ste 1 (44053-4145)
PHONE..................................440 246-6500
David Campana, *President*
Michael Marsico, *COO*
Robert M Campana, *CFO*
▲ EMP: 130
SQ FT: 250,000
SALES (est): 32.8MM **Privately Held**
WEB: www.pccampana.com
SIC: **3441** Fabricated structural metal

(G-12112)
PERKINS MOTOR SERVICE LTD (PA)
Also Called: Standard Welding & Lift Truck
1864 E 28th St (44055-1804)
PHONE..................................440 277-1256
Thomas L Shumaker,
EMP: 38
SQ FT: 10,200
SALES (est): 5.4MM **Privately Held**
SIC: **5013** 5531 7692 7539 Truck parts & accessories; automotive supplies & parts; truck equipment & parts; automotive parts; automotive welding; radiator repair shop, automotive; brake repair, automotive; automotive springs, rebuilding & repair; hydraulic equipment repair

(G-12113)
PRIME INDUSTRIES INC
1817 Iowa Ave (44052-3359)
PHONE..................................440 288-3626
Richard Persico, *President*
Joseph Persico Jr, *Vice Pres*
EMP: 35
SQ FT: 53,000
SALES (est): 5.3MM **Privately Held**
WEB: www.primeindustries.net
SIC: **3086** 3544 2821 2671 Plastics foam products; special dies, tools, jigs & fixtures; plastics materials & resins; packaging paper & plastics film, coated & laminated

(G-12114)
QUALITY SECURITY DOOR & MFG CO (PA)
1925 Broadway (44052-3626)
PHONE..................................440 246-0770
Barbara Jacobs, *President*
Robert Jacobs, *Corp Secy*
Bob Jacobs, *Treasurer*

EMP: 6
SQ FT: 25,000
SALES (est): 604.7K **Privately Held**
WEB: www.qualitysecuritydoor.com
SIC: 3442 3446 Metal doors; storm doors or windows, metal; gates, ornamental metal; railings, prefabricated metal

(G-12115)
RACEWAY PETROLEUM INC
3040 Oberlin Ave (44052-4563)
PHONE..................440 989-2660
Imran Nazir, *Principal*
EMP: 7
SALES (est): 879.5K **Privately Held**
SIC: 3644 Raceways

(G-12116)
REPUBLIC ENGINEERED PRODUCTS
Also Called: Republic Steel
1807 E 28th St (44055-1803)
PHONE..................440 277-2000
Jim Kuntz, *President*
EMP: 31
SALES (est): 6.2MM **Privately Held**
SIC: 3312 Bars, iron: made in steel mills

(G-12117)
REPUBLIC STEEL INC
1807 E 28th St (44055-1803)
PHONE..................440 277-2000
Joseph Lapinsky, *Branch Mgr*
Richard Wildman, *Manager*
Gregg Kruth, *Technology*
Jon Sosnowski, *IT/INT Sup*
EMP: 40 **Privately Held**
SIC: 3312 Blast furnaces & steel mills
HQ: Republic Steel
2633 8th St Ne
Canton OH 44704
330 438-5435

(G-12118)
ROCKWELL METALS COMPANY LLC
3709 W Erie Ave (44053-1237)
PHONE..................440 242-2420
Chris Harrington, *Mng Member*
▲ **EMP:** 15
SQ FT: 54,000
SALES: 40MM **Privately Held**
SIC: 5051 3444 Sheets, metal; sheet metalwork

(G-12119)
SENTINEL MANAGEMENT INC
Also Called: Semco Carbon
3000 Leavitt Rd (44052-4167)
PHONE..................440 821-7372
Vincent L Thompson, *President*
Nancy Thompson, *Corp Secy*
Matt Thompson, *Vice Pres*
Kirk Filker, *Prdtn Mgr*
Filip Cujba, *Manager*
EMP: 28
SALES: 7MM **Privately Held**
SIC: 3624 Carbon & graphite products

(G-12120)
SHERWIN-WILLIAMS COMPANY
2280 Coper Foster Pk Rd W (44053-3610)
PHONE..................440 282-2310
Jameson Maag, *Manager*
EMP: 4
SALES (corp-wide): 17.5B **Publicly Held**
SIC: 2851 5231 Paints & allied products; paint & painting supplies
PA: The Sherwin-Williams Company
101 W Prospect Ave # 1020
Cleveland OH 44115
216 566-2000

(G-12121)
SKY RIDERS INC
3736 Dallas Ave (44055-2354)
PHONE..................440 310-6819
Charles Brown, *CEO*
EMP: 4
SALES (est): 196.3K **Privately Held**
SIC: 3721 Aircraft

(G-12122)
SKYLIFT INC
3000 Leavitt Rd Ste 6 (44052-4166)
PHONE..................440 960-2100
George Wojnowski, *President*
Nicholas Jarmoszuk, *Vice Pres*
EMP: 8
SQ FT: 6,000
SALES (est): 2.2MM **Privately Held**
WEB: www.skyliftus.com
SIC: 3537 Cranes, industrial truck

(G-12123)
SLUTZKERS QUICKPRINT CENTER
Also Called: Quick Print
721 Broadway (44052-1805)
PHONE..................440 244-0330
Roger Slutzker, *President*
Jane Slutzker, *Vice Pres*
EMP: 4
SQ FT: 2,000
SALES: 150K **Privately Held**
SIC: 2752 2789 2759 Commercial printing, offset; bookbinding & related work; commercial printing

(G-12124)
STAINWOOD PRODUCTS
2803 Toledo Ave (44055-1445)
PHONE..................440 244-1352
William Hoag, *Ch of Bd*
Michael Hoag, *Vice Pres*
Richard Hoag, *Vice Pres*
Thomas Hoag, *Vice Pres*
EMP: 13
SQ FT: 14,000
SALES (est): 1MM
SALES (corp-wide): 800MM **Privately Held**
WEB: www.stainwood.com
SIC: 2431 Millwork
HQ: Nilco, Llc
1221 W Maple St Ste 100
Hartville OH 44632
888 248-5151

(G-12125)
SUPERPRINTER INC
1925 N Ridge Rd E (44055-3344)
PHONE..................440 277-0787
Michael Potts, *President*
EMP: 3
SALES (est): 399.3K **Privately Held**
SIC: 2752 Commercial printing, offset

(G-12126)
SUPERPRINTER LTD
1901 N Ridge Rd E (44055-3344)
PHONE..................440 277-0787
Michael Potts, *Partner*
Karen Potts, *Partner*
EMP: 3
SQ FT: 2,000
SALES: 200K **Privately Held**
SIC: 2752 Commercial printing, offset

(G-12127)
SWOCAT DESIGN INC
Also Called: Shoreway Sports
4325 Oberlin Ave Uppr (44052-2958)
PHONE..................440 282-4700
Jim Swope, *President*
Gay Swope, *Corp Secy*
EMP: 5
SQ FT: 910
SALES (est): 1.2MM **Privately Held**
WEB: www.shorewaysports.com
SIC: 5136 5137 2396 5699 Shirts, men's & boys'; women's & children's outerwear; screen printing on fabric articles; sports apparel

(G-12128)
SYSCO GUEST SUPPLY LLC
7395 Lorain Indus Pkwy (44052)
PHONE..................440 960-2515
Jeff Dubois, *Manager*
EMP: 18
SALES (corp-wide): 58.7B **Publicly Held**
SIC: 5122 2844 5131 5139 Drugs, proprietaries & sundries; toilet preparations; piece goods & notions; footwear
HQ: Sysco Guest Supply, Llc
300 Davidson Ave
Somerset NJ 08873
732 537-2297

(G-12129)
TERMINAL READY-MIX INC
524 Colorado Ave (44052-2198)
PHONE..................440 288-0181
Theresa Pelton, *President*
John Falbo, *Vice Pres*
Russ Rosso, *Plant Mgr*
Pete Falbo, *Treasurer*
Nora Lewis, *Bookkeeper*
▲ **EMP:** 45 **EST:** 1954
SQ FT: 1,000
SALES (est): 9.6MM **Privately Held**
WEB: www.falboconstruction.com
SIC: 3273 1611 Ready-mixed concrete; highway & street paving contractor

(G-12130)
TUBOSCOPE PIPELINE SVCS INC
Also Called: Nov Tuboscope
2199 E 28th St (44055-1932)
PHONE..................530 695-3569
EMP: 4
SALES (corp-wide): 8.4B **Publicly Held**
SIC: 1389 Testing, measuring, surveying & analysis services
HQ: Tuboscope Pipeline Services Inc.
2835 Holmes Rd
Houston TX 77051

(G-12131)
UNITED STATES STEEL CORP
Lorain Pipe Mill
2199 E 28th St (44055-1932)
PHONE..................440 240-2500
Sarah Casalla, *Manager*
Jeff Bailey, *Administration*
Sam Lutz, *Administration*
Jessica Potts, *Maintence Staff*
EMP: 550
SALES (corp-wide): 14.1B **Publicly Held**
SIC: 3312 Blast furnaces & steel mills
PA: United States Steel Corp
600 Grant St Ste 468
Pittsburgh PA 15219
412 433-1121

(G-12132)
V & A PROCESS INC
2345 E 28th St (44055-2003)
PHONE..................440 288-8137
Albert Di Luciano, *President*
Gilbert Rothman, *Vice Pres*
EMP: 11
SALES (est): 1.8MM **Privately Held**
WEB: www.vandaprocess.com
SIC: 2821 Plastics materials & resins

(G-12133)
VARCO LP
1807 E 28th St (44055-1803)
PHONE..................440 277-8696
Randy Hamilton, *Branch Mgr*
EMP: 35
SALES (corp-wide): 8.4B **Publicly Held**
WEB: www.tuboscope.com
SIC: 1389 Running, cutting & pulling casings, tubes & rods
HQ: Varco, L.P.
2835 Holmes Rd
Houston TX 77051
713 799-5272

(G-12134)
VERTIV ENERGY SYSTEMS INC
1510 Kansas Ave (44052-3364)
PHONE..................440 288-1122
Dennis Del Campo, *Vice Pres*
Dave Smith, *Opers Mgr*
Michael Neeley, *CFO*
Adam White, *Technical Staff*
◆ **EMP:** 800
SALES (est): 1.2MM
SALES (corp-wide): 2.1B **Privately Held**
SIC: 3661 3644 7629 Telephone & telegraph apparatus; noncurrent-carrying wiring services; telecommunication equipment repair (except telephones)
HQ: Vertiv Group Corporation
1050 Dearborn Dr
Columbus OH 43085
614 888-0246

(G-12135)
VERTIV GROUP CORPORATION
1510 Kansas Ave (44052-3364)
PHONE..................440 288-1122
Dave Smith, *Opers Mgr*
EMP: 9
SALES (corp-wide): 322.9MM **Privately Held**
SIC: 3661 3644 7629 Telephone & telegraph apparatus; noncurrent-carrying wiring services; telecommunication equipment repair (except telephones)
HQ: Vertiv Group Corporation
1050 Dearborn Dr
Columbus OH 43085
614 888-0246

(G-12136)
VISUAL EXPRESSIONS SIGN CO
901 Broadway (44052-1949)
PHONE..................440 245-6660
Thomas Ott, *President*
Brian Bartlebaugh, *Vice Pres*
EMP: 5
SQ FT: 600
SALES (est): 523.9K **Privately Held**
SIC: 3993 Signs & advertising specialties

(G-12137)
WEST ERIE FUEL
4935 W Erie Ave (44053-1333)
PHONE..................440 282-3493
EMP: 5 **EST:** 2013
SALES (est): 246.3K **Privately Held**
SIC: 2869 Fuels

(G-12138)
WS THERMAL PROCESS TECH INC
8301 W Erie Ave (44053-2090)
PHONE..................440 385-6829
Joachin G Wunning, *President*
Lee Rabe, *Vice Pres*
Helen Tuttle, *VP Finance*
Steven Mickey, *Sales Engr*
EMP: 9
SALES (est): 1.3MM **Privately Held**
SIC: 3433 Gas burners, industrial

Lore City
Guernsey County

(G-12139)
QES PRESSURE CONTROL LLC
64201 Wintergreen Rd (43755-9704)
PHONE..................740 489-5721
Charles Jones, *Branch Mgr*
EMP: 25
SALES (corp-wide): 991.3MM **Privately Held**
SIC: 1381 Drilling oil & gas wells
HQ: Qes Pressure Control Llc
4500 Se 59th St
Oklahoma City OK 73135

(G-12140)
SABRE ENERGY CORPORATION
175 Main St Nw (43755-9798)
P.O. Box 113 (43755-0113)
PHONE..................740 685-8266
Mike Rawlings, *Vice Pres*
EMP: 3
SQ FT: 1,200
SALES (est): 369.2K **Privately Held**
SIC: 8742 1381 Public utilities consultant; drilling oil & gas wells

Loudonville
Ashland County

(G-12141)
EASTERN GRAPHIC ARTS
214 N Jefferson St (44842-1316)
P.O. Box 477 (44842-0477)
PHONE..................419 994-5815

Loudonville - Ashland County (G-12142)

Carla Goudy, *Owner*
EMP: 3
SALES (est): 233.1K **Privately Held**
SIC: 2759 Commercial printing

(G-12142)
GOLF BALL MANUFACTURERS LLC
Also Called: Gbm Golf
326 N Water St (44842-1263)
PHONE 419 994-5563
Tim Deighan, *Managing Prtnr*
EMP: 5
SQ FT: 35,000
SALES: 350K **Privately Held**
SIC: 3949 Golf equipment

(G-12143)
HOCHSTETLER MILLING LLC
552 State Route 95 (44842-9611)
PHONE 419 368-0004
Levi Hochstetler,
EMP: 22
SQ FT: 13,000
SALES (est): 1.8MM **Privately Held**
SIC: 7389 2452 Log & lumber broker; log cabins, prefabricated, wood

(G-12144)
MOHICAN LOG HOMES INC
Also Called: H&H Custom Homes
2441 State Route 60 (44842-9673)
PHONE 419 994-4088
Levi Hostetler, *President*
EMP: 3
SALES (est): 230.7K **Privately Held**
SIC: 1521 1522 2452 New construction, single-family houses; residential construction; log cabins, prefabricated, wood; modular homes, prefabricated, wood

(G-12145)
OAKBRIDGE TIMBER FRAMING
9001 Township Road 461 (44842-9701)
P.O. Box 89 (44842-0089)
PHONE 419 994-1052
Johnny Miller, *Owner*
EMP: 6 **Privately Held**
SIC: 2411 Timber, cut at logging camp
PA: Oakbridge Timber Framing
20857 Earnest Rd
Howard OH 43028

(G-12146)
OHIO BIOSYSTEMS COOP INC
135 N Market St (44842-1216)
P.O. Box 381, Nashville (44661-0381)
PHONE 419 980-7663
EMP: 7
SALES: 500K **Privately Held**
SIC: 2869 Mfg Industrial Organic Chemicals

(G-12147)
R D THOMPSON PAPER PDTS CO INC
1 Madison St (44842-9786)
P.O. Box 88 (44842-0088)
PHONE 419 994-3614
Thomas Thompson, *President*
EMP: 35 **EST:** 1953
SQ FT: 25,000
SALES (est): 6.8MM **Privately Held**
WEB: www.rdthompsonpaper.com
SIC: 2675 Manila folders

(G-12148)
ROWTAC INC
16125 Township Road 458 (44842-9732)
PHONE 419 994-4777
Frank Nestich, *President*
Aaron Nestich, *Vice Pres*
Annete Nestich, *Admin Sec*
EMP: 5
SALES: 350K **Privately Held**
SIC: 3599 Machine shop, jobbing & repair

(G-12149)
TRUAX PRINTING INC
425 E Haskell St (44842-1312)
PHONE 419 994-4166
Bruce Truax, *Ch of Bd*
Tom Truax, *President*
Zack Truax, *Vice Pres*
Dan Truax, *Vice Pres*
Jay Hollinger, *Safety Dir*
EMP: 45
SQ FT: 56,000
SALES (est): 5.7MM **Privately Held**
WEB: www.truaxprinting.com
SIC: 2711 Commercial printing & newspaper publishing combined

(G-12150)
YOUNG SAND & GRAVEL CO INC
689 State Route 39 (44842)
P.O. Box 117 (44842-0117)
PHONE 419 994-3040
Myron Oswalt, *President*
EMP: 14 **EST:** 1946
SQ FT: 2,400
SALES (est): 780K **Privately Held**
SIC: 1442 Construction sand & gravel

Louisville
Stark County

(G-12151)
ALLEGHENY LUDLUM LLC
Also Called: ATI Allegheny Ludlum
1500 W Main St (44641-2325)
PHONE 330 875-2244
Gerry Campbell, *Human Resources*
Tony Denoi, *Manager*
EMP: 26 **Publicly Held**
WEB: www.alleghenyludlum.com
SIC: 3312 3471 3398 3316 Stainless steel; plating & polishing; metal heat treating; cold finishing of steel shapes
HQ: Allegheny Ludlum, Llc
1000 Six Ppg Pl
Pittsburgh PA 15222
412 394-2800

(G-12152)
BIERY CHEESE CO (PA)
6544 Paris Ave (44641-9544)
PHONE 330 875-3381
Dennis Biery, *President*
Benjamin Biery, *Vice Pres*
Roger Foulk, *Transptn Dir*
Peter Sluman, *Plant Mgr*
Edwin Felger, *Facilities Mgr*
▲ **EMP:** 216
SQ FT: 110,000
SALES (est): 86.4MM **Privately Held**
WEB: www.bierycheese.com
SIC: 2022 Natural cheese

(G-12153)
BRADLEY ENTERPRISES INC (PA)
Also Called: Family Fun
3750 Beck Ave (44641-9455)
PHONE 330 875-1444
Scott Cook, *President*
Pamela Halgreen, *Corp Secy*
Terry McKimm, *Vice Pres*
EMP: 5 **EST:** 1958
SQ FT: 1,500
SALES (est): 4.3MM **Privately Held**
SIC: 3949 5091 Swimming pools, except plastic; swimming pools, equipment & supplies

(G-12154)
H & H QUICK MACHINE INC
7816 Edison St (44641-8325)
PHONE 330 935-0944
Martin Hustead, *President*
Anthony Hustead, *Vice Pres*
EMP: 10 **EST:** 1997
SALES (est): 300K **Privately Held**
SIC: 3599 Machine shop, jobbing & repair

(G-12155)
H-P PRODUCTS INC
2000 W Main St (44641-2344)
PHONE 330 875-7193
Paul Bishop, *Branch Mgr*
EMP: 50
SQ FT: 24,000
SALES (corp-wide): 96.5MM **Privately Held**
WEB: www.metflo.com
SIC: 3498 3635 Tube fabricating (contract bending & shaping); household vacuum cleaners
PA: H-P Products, Inc.
512 W Gorgas St
Louisville OH 44641
330 875-5556

(G-12156)
HOPPEL FABRICATION SPECIALTIES
9481 Columbus Rd Ste 1 (44641-8546)
PHONE 330 823-5700
Steffon Hoppel, *President*
Sheryl Hoppel, *Vice Pres*
Renee Heilman, *Treasurer*
EMP: 10 **EST:** 1987
SALES (est): 1MM **Privately Held**
SIC: 3441 Fabricated structural metal

(G-12157)
INK INC
200 S Bauman Ct (44641-1602)
P.O. Box 223 (44641-0223)
PHONE 330 875-4789
Bruce Leone, *President*
Jennifer Leone, *Vice Pres*
Dave Norris, *Prdtn Mgr*
EMP: 6
SALES (est): 1MM **Privately Held**
WEB: www.planetink.com
SIC: 2752 Commercial printing, offset

(G-12158)
J & L SPECIALTY STEEL INC
1500 W Main St (44641-2325)
P.O. Box 3920 (44641-3920)
PHONE 330 875-6200
Victor Fusco, *Principal*
Ken Fay, *Controller*
EMP: 5
SALES (est): 651.8K **Privately Held**
SIC: 3441 Fabricated structural metal

(G-12159)
JOHANNINGS INC
3244 S Nickelplate St (44641-9654)
PHONE 330 875-1706
Curtis Bates, *President*
Christy Bates, *Office Mgr*
EMP: 9 **EST:** 1964
SALES: 1MM **Privately Held**
WEB: www.johanningsinc.com
SIC: 2434 Wood kitchen cabinets

(G-12160)
LOUISVILLE HERALD INC
308 S Mill St (44641-1643)
P.O. Box 170 (44641-0170)
PHONE 330 875-5610
Frank Clapper, *President*
Shirley Clapper, *Advt Staff*
Paula Fether, *MIS Dir*
EMP: 5 **EST:** 1887
SQ FT: 2,800
SALES (est): 441.6K **Privately Held**
WEB: www.louisvilleherald.com
SIC: 2711 Newspapers: publishing only, not printed on site

(G-12161)
MIDLAKE PRODUCTS & MFG CO
819 N Nickelplate St (44641-2455)
PHONE 330 875-4202
Jeffrey Rich, *President*
Greg Duplin, *Vice Pres*
Jane Pukys, *CFO*
EMP: 60
SQ FT: 28,000
SALES (est): 13.4MM **Privately Held**
WEB: www.midlake.com
SIC: 3429 Manufactured hardware (general)

(G-12162)
OHIO ROLL GRINDING INC
5165 Louisville St (44641-8630)
P.O. Box 7099, Canton (44705-0099)
PHONE 330 453-1884
James P Robinson, *President*
Catherine Robinson, *Treasurer*
EMP: 26
SQ FT: 14,000
SALES (est): 4.9MM **Privately Held**
SIC: 3599 3471 Machine shop, jobbing & repair; plating & polishing

(G-12163)
OTC SERVICES INC
1776 Constitution Ave (44641-1362)
P.O. Box 188 (44641-0188)
PHONE 330 871-2444
Robert Ganser Jr, *President*
William Bruner, *General Mgr*
Brad McDonald, *Project Mgr*
Joe Faherty, *Sales Mgr*
Gary George, *Regl Sales Mgr*
▲ **EMP:** 80 **EST:** 2012
SQ FT: 98,000
SALES: 22MM **Privately Held**
SIC: 3612 Transformers, except electric

(G-12164)
PERFORMANCE TECHNOLOGIES LLC
3690 Tulane Ave (44641-7960)
PHONE 330 875-1216
Andy Connolly, *Branch Mgr*
EMP: 8
SALES (corp-wide): 3.3B **Publicly Held**
SIC: 1389 Pumping of oil & gas wells
HQ: Performance Technologies Llc
3715 S Radio Rd
El Reno OK 73036

(G-12165)
SALCO MACHINE INC
3822 Victory Ave (44641-8601)
PHONE 330 456-8281
Annette Rosenverg, *President*
John Saliol, *Vice Pres*
Susanna Saliola, *Treasurer*
EMP: 11
SQ FT: 8,900
SALES (est): 1.8MM **Privately Held**
WEB: www.salcomachine.com
SIC: 3599 Machine shop, jobbing & repair

(G-12166)
SHERWOOD RTM CORP
4043 Beck Ave (44641-9458)
P.O. Box 211 (44641-0211)
PHONE 330 875-7151
Ronald Brookes, *President*
EMP: 6
SQ FT: 15,000
SALES (est): 1.3MM **Privately Held**
WEB: www.sherwoodcorp.com
SIC: 2821 3543 Plastics materials & resins; industrial patterns

(G-12167)
SMITH P K WOODCARVING LLC
2021 A Riverside Drv Stea (44641)
PHONE 513 271-7077
Philip K Smith, *Mng Member*
EMP: 3
SQ FT: 3,000
SALES (est): 269.7K **Privately Held**
WEB: www.pksmithwoodcarving.com
SIC: 2499 Carved & turned wood

(G-12168)
SOUTHWEST ELECTRIC CO
609 Enterprise Cir (44641-7947)
P.O. Box 82639, Oklahoma City OK (73148-0639)
PHONE 330 875-7000
John Saylor, *Manager*
EMP: 13
SALES (corp-wide): 75.6MM **Privately Held**
SIC: 7694 Electric motor repair
PA: Southwest Electric Co.
6503 Se 74th St
Oklahoma City OK 73135
800 364-4445

(G-12169)
UNIWALL MANUFACTURING CO (HQ)
3750 Beck Ave (44641-9455)
PHONE 330 875-1444
Scott Cook, *President*
Pamela Hellgren, *Corp Secy*
Terry McKimm, *Vice Pres*
EMP: 10
SQ FT: 4,500

GEOGRAPHIC SECTION

Loveland - Clermont County (G-12197)

SALES (est): 1.7MM
SALES (corp-wide): 4.3MM **Privately Held**
SIC: 3949 Swimming pools, except plastic
PA: Bradley Enterprises Inc
   3750 Beck Ave
   Louisville OH 44641
   330 875-1444

(G-12170)
VACUFLO FACTORY
512 W Gorgas St (44641-1332)
PHONE..................................330 875-2450
Paul Bishop, *Principal*
EMP: 3
SALES (est): 226.5K **Privately Held**
SIC: 2241 Braids, textile

(G-12171)
WASHITA VALLEY ENTERPRISES INC
3707 Tulane Ave Bldg 9 (44641-7949)
P.O. Box 409 (44641-0409)
PHONE..................................330 510-1568
Tiffany Midgett, *President*
EMP: 14
SALES (corp-wide): 47.2MM **Privately Held**
SIC: 1389 Oil consultants
PA: Washita Valley Enterprises, Inc.
   1705 Se 59th St
   Oklahoma City OK 73129
   405 670-5338

(G-12172)
XPRESS PRINT INC
Also Called: Xpress Print & Bus Systems
6424 Easton St (44641-9054)
PHONE..................................330 494-7246
William Mullen, *President*
M Dianne Mullen, *Vice Pres*
EMP: 14
SALES (est): 1.3MM **Privately Held**
SIC: 2752 5044 Commercial printing, offset; duplicating machines

Loveland
Clermont County

(G-12173)
A&M WOODWORKING
1924 W Loveland Ave (45140-2629)
PHONE..................................513 722-5415
Melba Schultz, *Principal*
EMP: 8
SALES (est): 77.4K **Privately Held**
SIC: 8041 2431 Offices & clinics of chiropractors; millwork

(G-12174)
ABM DRIVES INC
394 Wards Corner Rd # 110 (45140-8300)
PHONE..................................513 576-1300
Gabriel Venzin, *President*
Bettina Place, *Admin Sec*
▲ EMP: 3
SQ FT: 2,300
SALES (est): 606.9K
SALES (corp-wide): 494.2MM **Privately Held**
WEB: www.abm-drives.com
SIC: 3621 Motors, electric
HQ: Abm Greiffenberger Antriebstechnik Gmbh
   Friedenfelser Str. 24
   Marktredwitz 95615
   923 167-0

(G-12175)
ALCON INC (PA)
6522 Snider Rd (45140-9587)
PHONE..................................513 722-1037
C G Sorflaten, *President*
David Nieto, *CFO*
EMP: 20
SQ FT: 15,000
SALES (est): 4MM **Privately Held**
SIC: 3643 Connectors & terminals for electrical devices

(G-12176)
AMANO CINCINNATI INCORPORATED
130 Commerce Dr (45140-7726)
PHONE..................................513 697-9000
Kash Gokli, *Vice Pres*
Rick Wright, *Materials Mgr*
John Gutapfel, *Manager*
EMP: 70
SQ FT: 52,200
SALES (corp-wide): 1.1B **Privately Held**
SIC: 3559 3873 3829 3625 Parking facility equipment & supplies; watches, clocks, watchcases & parts; measuring & controlling devices; relays & industrial controls
HQ: Amano Cincinnati Incorporated
   140 Harrison Ave
   Roseland NJ 07068
   973 403-1900

(G-12177)
AMP ELECTRIC VEHICLES INC
100 Commerce Dr (45140-7726)
PHONE..................................513 360-4704
Stephen S Burns, *CEO*
Martin J Rucidlo, *President*
Chuck Strasser, *Buyer*
Alan Arkus, *Engineer*
Don Wires, *Engineer*
EMP: 18 EST: 2007
SALES (est): 116.4K **Publicly Held**
SIC: 3711 3714 Motor vehicles & car bodies; motor vehicle parts & accessories
PA: Workhorse Group Inc.
   100 Commerce Dr
   Loveland OH 45140

(G-12178)
AXATRONICS LLC ✪
422 Wards Corner Rd E (45140-6964)
PHONE..................................513 239-5898
Claudia Cagle, *Principal*
EMP: 4 EST: 2018
SALES (est): 673.6K **Privately Held**
SIC: 3549 Assembly machines, including robotic

(G-12179)
BASEBALL CARD CORNER
1812 Arrowhead Trl (45140-8517)
PHONE..................................513 677-0464
EMP: 3
SALES (est): 140K **Privately Held**
SIC: 5947 3949 Ret Gifts/Novelties Mfg Sporting/Athletic Goods

(G-12180)
BAY ISLAND COMPANY INC
Also Called: Point Five Golf Co
585 Ibold Rd (45140-6901)
PHONE..................................513 248-0356
Duane Peterson, *President*
Dale Peterson, *Vice Pres*
Willis Peterson, *Vice Pres*
EMP: 3
SALES (est): 75K **Privately Held**
SIC: 3949 1629 Golf equipment; golf course construction

(G-12181)
BRENTMOOR HAMS LLC
10367 Brentmoor Dr (45140-4804)
PHONE..................................513 677-0813
Richard Neuenschwander, *Principal*
EMP: 6 EST: 2010
SALES (est): 599.6K **Privately Held**
SIC: 2013 Prepared pork products from purchased pork

(G-12182)
BROGAN MACHINE SHOP
501 Lovelnd Madera Rd # 2 (45140-2740)
PHONE..................................513 683-9054
Richard J Brogan, *President*
Joan Brogan, *Corp Secy*
EMP: 4
SQ FT: 2,500
SALES (est): 260K **Privately Held**
SIC: 3599 2431 Machine shop, jobbing & repair; millwork

(G-12183)
COLD JET LLC (PA)
455 Wards Corner Rd # 100 (45140-9033)
PHONE..................................513 831-3211
Eugene L Cooke III, *CEO*
Scott Gatje, *COO*
Cristy Morris, *VP Accounting*
◆ EMP: 130
SQ FT: 40,000
SALES (est): 65MM **Privately Held**
WEB: www.coldjet.com
SIC: 3559 Chemical machinery & equipment

(G-12184)
CREATIVE COMMERCIAL FINISHING
1298 State Route 28 Ste B (45140-8817)
PHONE..................................513 722-9393
Robert Hattersley, *Owner*
EMP: 5
SQ FT: 12,000
SALES (est): 700K **Privately Held**
SIC: 2269 2899 2851 Chemical coating or treating of narrow fabrics; chemical preparations; paints & allied products

(G-12185)
DEXPORT TOOL MANUFACTURING CO
855 Carpenter Rd (45140-8102)
PHONE..................................513 625-1600
Elizabeth Hite, *President*
Richard Hite, *Vice Pres*
John Lanoue, *Shareholder*
EMP: 4
SALES (est): 473K **Privately Held**
WEB: www.dexport-tool.com
SIC: 3541 5085 Machine tools, metal cutting type; industrial supplies

(G-12186)
ESTEE LAUDER COMPANIES INC
6279 Tri Ridge Blvd # 250 (45140-8396)
PHONE..................................310 994-9651
Patrick Thompson, *Branch Mgr*
EMP: 6 **Publicly Held**
SIC: 2844 Toilet preparations
PA: The Estee Lauder Companies Inc
   767 5th Ave Fl 1
   New York NY 10153

(G-12187)
FISCHER GLOBAL ENTERPRISES LLC
Also Called: Periflo/Px Pumps USA
155 Commerce Dr (45140-7727)
PHONE..................................513 583-4900
Phil Douglas,
Ken Fischer,
▲ EMP: 25
SALES (est): 3MM **Privately Held**
WEB: www.fpv.com
SIC: 3561 Industrial pumps & parts

(G-12188)
FLOWSERVE CORPORATION
422 Wards Corner Rd F (45140-6964)
PHONE..................................513 874-6990
Brad Harrellson, *General Mgr*
EMP: 6
SALES (corp-wide): 3.8B **Publicly Held**
SIC: 3561 Industrial pumps & parts
PA: Flowserve Corporation
   5215 N Oconnor Blvd Connor
   Irving TX 75039
   972 443-6500

(G-12189)
FRESH PRESS LLC
6567 Estate Ln (45140-5911)
PHONE..................................513 378-1402
Katie Patterson, *Principal*
EMP: 3 EST: 2016
SALES (est): 100.8K **Privately Held**
SIC: 2711 Newspapers

(G-12190)
GARYS CLASSIC GUITARS
6692 Sandy Shores Dr (45140-5851)
PHONE..................................513 891-0555
Gary S Dick, *Owner*
EMP: 4

SALES (est): 200K **Privately Held**
WEB: www.garysguitars.com
SIC: 3931 7389 Guitars & parts, electric & nonelectric;

(G-12191)
GEOTECH PATTERN & MOLD INC
272 E Kemper Rd (45140-8601)
P.O. Box 276 (45140-0276)
PHONE..................................513 683-2600
Jonathan D Ledford, *President*
Frank Schilling, *Opers-Prdtn-Mfg*
Frank Diedrichs, *Admin Sec*
EMP: 9 EST: 1946
SQ FT: 9,000
SALES (est): 1.8MM **Privately Held**
WEB: www.geotech-pattern.com
SIC: 3543 Industrial patterns

(G-12192)
GL NAUSE CO INC
1971 Phoenix Dr (45140-9241)
PHONE..................................513 722-9500
Gregory L Nause, *President*
Jodie K Nause, *Admin Sec*
Jodie Nause, *Admin Sec*
EMP: 25
SQ FT: 30,000
SALES (est): 5.2MM **Privately Held**
WEB: www.glnause.com
SIC: 3441 3443 1791 7699 Building components, structural steel; fabricated plate work (boiler shop); structural steel erection; industrial equipment services; industrial machinery & equipment repair; architectural metalwork; sheet metalwork

(G-12193)
GREENLIGHT OPTICS LLC
8940 Glendale Milford Rd (45140-8908)
PHONE..................................513 247-9777
Todd Rutherford,
Michael Okeefe,
Bill Phillips,
EMP: 20
SQ FT: 8,000
SALES (est): 6.1MM **Privately Held**
SIC: 3827 3089 Optical instruments & apparatus; lenses, except optical: plastic

(G-12194)
GREGORY AUTO SERVICE
Also Called: Dragon Racing Service
224 Beech Rd (45140-8827)
PHONE..................................513 248-0423
Nicholas Gregory, *Partner*
David Gregory, *Partner*
EMP: 4
SALES (est): 300K **Privately Held**
SIC: 7538 3714 General automotive repair shops; motor vehicle engines & parts

(G-12195)
HAECO INC (PA)
6504 Snider Rd (45140-9228)
PHONE..................................513 722-1030
Jerry Henline, *President*
Clement Au, *Manager*
▲ EMP: 12
SQ FT: 7,200
SALES (est): 1.7MM **Privately Held**
WEB: www.haeco.us
SIC: 3559 Pack-up assemblies, wheel overhaul

(G-12196)
HEALTHPRO BRANDS INC
12044 Millstone Ct (45140-6295)
P.O. Box 867, Mason (45040-0867)
PHONE..................................513 492-7512
Todd Wichmann, *CEO*
Mark Winterhalter, *CFO*
Durk Jager, *Shareholder*
▼ EMP: 5
SQ FT: 2,000
SALES (est): 1MM **Privately Held**
WEB: www.healthprobrands.com
SIC: 3523 Cleaning machines for fruits, grains & vegetables

(G-12197)
HERITAGE TOOL
6225 N Shadow Hill Way (45140-9187)
PHONE..................................513 753-7300
Mark J Myers, *Owner*

Loveland - Clermont County (G-12198) GEOGRAPHIC SECTION

EMP: 12
SALES (est): 515.7K Privately Held
SIC: 3599 3751 Machine shop, jobbing & repair; motorcycles & related parts

(G-12198)
HEULE TOOL CORPORATION
131 Commerce Dr (45140-7727)
PHONE................513 860-9900
Heinrich Heule, President
Gary Brown, Vice Pres
Joe Stokes, Opers-Prdtn-Mfg
Ulf Heule, Treasurer
Andrew Cook, Manager
EMP: 6
SQ FT: 3,500
SALES (est): 930.3K Privately Held
WEB: www.heuletool.com
SIC: 3599 Machine shop, jobbing & repair
PA: Heule Werkzeug Ag
    Wegenstrasse 11
    Balgach SG
    717 263-838

(G-12199)
INNERWOOD & COMPANY
688 Elizabeth Ln (45140-9172)
PHONE................513 677-2229
Janine V Melink-Hueber, CEO
J V Melink-Hueber, Principal
EMP: 17
SALES (est): 2MM Privately Held
WEB: www.innerwood.com
SIC: 2517 2521 Wood television & radio cabinets; wood office filing cabinets & bookcases

(G-12200)
INTELLIGENT SIGNAL TECH
Also Called: Ist International
6318 Dustywind Ln (45140-7730)
PHONE................614 530-4784
Sheldyn K Armstrong, President
Matthew Bolton, CFO
EMP: 8
SQ FT: 2,500
SALES (est): 1MM Privately Held
WEB: www.intelligentsignals.com
SIC: 3669 Traffic signals, electric

(G-12201)
INTERNATIONAL PAPER COMPANY
6283 Tri Ridge Blvd (45140-8318)
PHONE................513 248-6000
EMP: 4
SALES (corp-wide): 23.3B Publicly Held
SIC: 2621 Paper mills
PA: International Paper Company
    6400 Poplar Ave
    Memphis TN 38197
    901 419-9000

(G-12202)
JACO INC
Also Called: Cincinnati Stair
1451 State Route 28 Ste D (45140-8442)
PHONE................513 722-3947
Marc Tirey, President
EMP: 3
SQ FT: 5,000
SALES (est): 133.1K Privately Held
WEB: www.cincinnatistair.com
SIC: 2431 Staircases & stairs, wood

(G-12203)
KBC SERVICES
9993 Union Cemetery Rd (45140-7187)
PHONE................513 693-3743
Kevin Brown, Principal
EMP: 10
SALES (est): 352.5K Privately Held
SIC: 1389 8742 Construction, repair & dismantling services; construction project management consultant

(G-12204)
KESSLER STUDIOS INC
273 E Broadway St (45140-3121)
PHONE................513 683-7500
Bob Kessler, President
Cindy Kessler, Vice Pres
EMP: 3 EST: 1981

SALES (est): 170K Privately Held
WEB: www.kesslerstudios.com
SIC: 3231 Stained glass; made from purchased glass

(G-12205)
KLEENLINE LLC
6279 Tri Ridge Blvd # 410 (45140-8396)
PHONE................800 259-5973
William M Shult, Principal
EMP: 3
SALES (est): 171.2K Privately Held
SIC: 3535 Conveyors & conveying equipment

(G-12206)
KMGRAFX INC
Also Called: Asi Sign Systems
394 Wards Corner Rd # 100 (45140-8339)
PHONE................513 248-4100
Kimberly Moscarino, President
Heather Knox, Project Mgr
Kenneth Knarr, Treasurer
Suzi Roth, Sr Project Mgr
Lisa Hartman, Manager
EMP: 8
SQ FT: 2,700
SALES (est): 1.1MM Privately Held
WEB: www.kmgrafx.com
SIC: 3993 Signs & advertising specialties

(G-12207)
KYS WELDING & FABRICATION
154 Shoemaker Dr (45140-7786)
PHONE................513 702-9081
KY Nguyen, Owner
EMP: 3
SALES (est): 63.5K Privately Held
SIC: 7692 Welding repair

(G-12208)
L & I NATURAL RESOURCES INC
10369 Cones Rd (45140-7211)
PHONE................513 683-2045
Alvin Walker, President
Marjorie Walker, Corp Secy
Jerry Walker, Vice Pres
EMP: 5
SQ FT: 1,000
SALES (est): 341.7K Privately Held
SIC: 1442 Sand mining; gravel mining

(G-12209)
LANDEN DESKTOP PUBG CTR INC
Also Called: Landen Digital Publishing
8976 Columbia Rd (45140-1114)
P.O. Box 468 (45140-0468)
PHONE................513 683-5181
Martha Hines, President
Linda G Dorn, Principal
Frances E Hober, Principal
EMP: 6
SQ FT: 5,000
SALES (est): 715.2K Privately Held
WEB: www.landendigital.com
SIC: 2759 2752 2791 7338 Commercial printing; commercial printing, lithographic; typesetting; secretarial & court reporting

(G-12210)
LIFO ENTERPRISES INC
Also Called: Fontova Mexican Foods
810 Carrington Pl Apt 206 (45140-8693)
P.O. Box 236 (45140-0236)
PHONE................513 225-8801
Pevro Fontova, President
EMP: 3 EST: 1981
SALES (est): 480K Privately Held
SIC: 2032 7389 Mexican foods: packaged in cans, jars, etc.;

(G-12211)
MACPRO INC
Also Called: Machine Products
1456 Fay Rd Unit B (45140-9771)
PHONE................513 575-3000
D Wayne Hughes, President
David Hughes, Vice Pres
EMP: 10 EST: 1967
SQ FT: 20,000
SALES (est): 1MM Privately Held
WEB: www.macpro.com
SIC: 3599 Machine shop, jobbing & repair

(G-12212)
MAINSTREAM WATERJET LLC
108 Northeast Dr (45140-7144)
PHONE................513 683-5426
Thomas Harbin, Vice Pres
Jayson Daus,
Ray Schilderink,
EMP: 10
SQ FT: 25,000
SALES (est): 2MM Privately Held
SIC: 3599 Machine shop, jobbing & repair

(G-12213)
MAULL TOOL & DIE SUPPLY LLC
112 Pheasantlake Dr (45140-7136)
PHONE................513 646-4229
Charlie Maull, Mng Member
EMP: 2
SALES (est): 5MM Privately Held
SIC: 3312 Tool & die steel

(G-12214)
MENARD INC
Also Called: Menards
3787 W State Route 22 3 (45140-3515)
PHONE................513 583-1444
Bert Marsh, Manager
EMP: 150
SALES (corp-wide): 12.5B Privately Held
SIC: 2431 5211 Millwork; lumber & other building materials
PA: Menard, Inc.
    5101 Menard Dr
    Eau Claire WI 54703
    715 876-5911

(G-12215)
MICHAELS PRE-CAST CON PDTS
1917 Adams Rd (45140-7236)
PHONE................513 683-1292
Vernon Michael, President
Mary Jane Micheal, Corp Secy
Donald Michael, Vice Pres
Vernon Jim Michael, Vice Pres
EMP: 10
SQ FT: 5,000
SALES (est): 1.3MM Privately Held
SIC: 5032 5999 3446 3272 Concrete building products; concrete products, pre-cast; architectural metalwork; concrete products; public building & related furniture; wood household furniture

(G-12216)
NEPTUNE AQUATIC SYSTEMS INC
6641 Smith Rd (45140-6508)
PHONE................513 575-2989
Jeffrey Quint, President
EMP: 4
SALES (est): 343.2K Privately Held
SIC: 3841 Surgical & medical instruments

(G-12217)
NESTLE USA INC
6279 Tri Ridge Blvd # 100 (45140-8396)
PHONE................513 576-4930
Teresa Donley, Branch Mgr
EMP: 25
SALES (corp-wide): 90.8B Privately Held
WEB: www.nestleusa.com
SIC: 2064 5141 Candy & other confectionery products; groceries, general line
HQ: Nestle Usa, Inc.
    1812 N Moore St
    Rosslyn VA 22209
    818 549-6000

(G-12218)
NEWWAVE TECHNOLOGIES INC
968 Paxton Guinea Rd (45140-8575)
PHONE................513 683-1211
William Stevens, President
Linda Stevens, Vice Pres
EMP: 5
SQ FT: 2,000
SALES (est): 900K Privately Held
WEB: www.newwavetechnologies.net
SIC: 3955 7378 Print cartridges for laser & other computer printers; computer maintenance & repair

(G-12219)
OCEAN SPRAY CRANBERRIES INC
6281 Tri Ridge Blvd # 300 (45140-8345)
PHONE................513 455-5770
Greg Fairbanks, Principal
EMP: 3
SALES (est): 229.4K Privately Held
SIC: 2033 Canned fruits & specialties

(G-12220)
PAUL MIRACLE
Also Called: Air Shop, The
6749 Oakland Rd (45140-9455)
PHONE................513 575-3113
Paul Miracle, Owner
EMP: 5
SQ FT: 1,440
SALES: 370K Privately Held
SIC: 3442 Metal doors, sash & trim

(G-12221)
PHOENIX INDUSTRIES & APPARATUS
6466 Snider Rd Apt C (45140-9542)
PHONE................513 722-1085
Sheri L Nause, President
Carl D Nause, Vice Pres
EMP: 15
SQ FT: 8,550
SALES (est): 1.4MM Privately Held
WEB: www.phoenixdottank.com
SIC: 7692 Welding repair

(G-12222)
POLYGROUP INC
9341 Hickory Hill Ct (45140-1089)
PHONE................877 476-5972
Paul Jackson, President
▲ EMP: 50
SALES (est): 7.4MM Privately Held
SIC: 2821 Plastics materials & resins

(G-12223)
POWDER ALLOY CORPORATION
101 Northeast Dr (45140-7145)
PHONE................513 984-4016
E Stephen Payne, President
Darlene Payne, Vice Pres
Kimberly R Gatto, CFO
▲ EMP: 40
SQ FT: 20,000
SALES (est): 12.9MM Privately Held
WEB: www.powderalloy.com
SIC: 3399 Powder, metal

(G-12224)
R & W PRINTING COMPANY
1394 Stella Dr (45140-8714)
PHONE................513 575-0131
Steve Poole, President
EMP: 3 EST: 1969
SALES (est): 325.2K Privately Held
SIC: 2752 2791 Commercial printing, offset; typesetting

(G-12225)
R G C INC
Also Called: Donisi Mirror Company
507 Loveland Madeira Rd (45140-2713)
PHONE................513 683-3110
Thomas G Crawford, President
Bill Ward, Office Mgr
EMP: 10
SQ FT: 30,000
SALES: 1.6MM Privately Held
WEB: www.donisimirror.com
SIC: 3229 3231 Pressed & blown glass; mirrored glass

(G-12226)
RAY MEYER SIGN COMPANY INC
8942 Glendale Milford Rd (45140-8908)
PHONE................513 984-5446
Ray A Meyer, President
Barbara A Meyer, Corp Secy
John A Meyer, Vice Pres
Barbara Meyer, Treasurer
Michael A Meyer, VP Sales
EMP: 25
SQ FT: 12,000
SALES: 1.8MM Privately Held
WEB: www.raymeyersigns.com
SIC: 3993 Signs & advertising specialties

GEOGRAPHIC SECTION

Lowellville - Mahoning County (G-12253)

(G-12227)
ROBERDS CONVERTING CO INC
113 Northeast Dr (45140-7145)
PHONE..................513 683-6667
James J Achberger, *President*
Mike Scherder, *General Mgr*
John M Achberger, *Vice Pres*
Will Achberger, *Vice Pres*
Phil Weinrich, *Vice Pres*
EMP: 38 EST: 1905
SQ FT: 72,000
SALES (est): 12.1MM **Privately Held**
WEB: www.roberdsconverting.com
SIC: 2679 Paperboard products, converted; paper products, converted

(G-12228)
ROZZI COMPANY INC (PA)
118 Karl Brown Way (45140-2902)
P.O. Box 5 (45140-0005)
PHONE..................513 683-0620
Joseph Rozzi, *President*
Michael Lutz, *Vice Pres*
Arthur Rozzi, *Treasurer*
William Zeilman, *Manager*
Nancy Rozzi, *Admin Sec*
▲ EMP: 30 EST: 1931
SQ FT: 5,000
SALES (est): 5MM **Privately Held**
SIC: 2899 Fireworks

(G-12229)
SAFE-GRAIN INC (PA)
417 Wards Corner Rd Ste B (45140-9083)
PHONE..................513 398-2500
Scott Chant, *President*
EMP: 7
SALES: 3.4MM **Privately Held**
SIC: 3829 1731 Temperature sensors, except industrial process & aircraft; electronic controls installation

(G-12230)
SCRIP-SAFE SECURITY PRODUCTS
Also Called: Scrip-Safe International
136 Commerce Dr (45140-7726)
PHONE..................513 697-7789
Joseph E Orndorff, *President*
Bill Varney, *Production*
Joanne Orndorff, *CFO*
Kevin Hickey, *Sales Dir*
Carolyn Deangelis, *Art Dir*
▼ EMP: 20
SQ FT: 15,000
SALES: 5MM **Privately Held**
WEB: www.scrip-safe.com
SIC: 2752 7389 Commercial printing, offset; printing broker

(G-12231)
SHAWCOR INC
Also Called: Dsg-Canusa
173 Commerce Dr (45140-7727)
P.O. Box 498830, Cincinnati (45249-8830)
PHONE..................513 683-7800
Jim Raussen, *Sales Staff*
EMP: 40
SALES (corp-wide): 1.6B **Privately Held**
SIC: 3317 Steel pipe & tubes
HQ: Shawcor Inc.
5875 N Sam Houston Pkwy W
Houston TX 77086
281 886-2350

(G-12232)
SIGNODE INDUSTRIAL GROUP LLC
Also Called: Angleboard
396 Wards Corner Rd # 100 (45140-9060)
PHONE..................513 248-2990
Shane Harrisson, *Manager*
EMP: 20
SALES (corp-wide): 11.1B **Publicly Held**
SIC: 2679 2671 Paper products, converted; packaging paper & plastics film, coated & laminated
HQ: Signode Industrial Group Llc
3650 W Lake Ave
Glenview IL 60026
847 724-6100

(G-12233)
SIRRUS INC
422 Wards Corner Rd (45140-6964)
PHONE..................513 448-0308
Jeff Uhrig, *CEO*
▲ EMP: 34
SALES (est): 8.5MM **Privately Held**
SIC: 2891 Adhesives & sealants

(G-12234)
SST CONVEYOR COMPONENTS INC
185 Commerce Dr (45140-7727)
PHONE..................513 583-5500
Winfield Scott, *President*
Thomas C Hamm, *Principal*
Joe Schuetz, *CFO*
▲ EMP: 20
SALES (est): 5.9MM **Privately Held**
SIC: 3535 Conveyors & conveying equipment

(G-12235)
SST PRECISION MANUFACTURING
154 Commerce Dr (45140-7726)
PHONE..................513 583-5500
Winfield Scott, *President*
Joe Schuetz, *CFO*
Glen Stidham, *Sales Mgr*
Faye Bess, *Manager*
Pam Catron, *Info Tech Mgr*
EMP: 10
SALES (est): 1.4MM **Privately Held**
SIC: 3599 7699 Crankshafts & camshafts, machining; industrial tool grinding

(G-12236)
STEEL IT LLC
11793 Enyart Rd (45140-8274)
PHONE..................513 253-3111
Craig Freeman, *Mng Member*
EMP: 10
SQ FT: 8,500
SALES (est): 1.1MM **Privately Held**
SIC: 3441 Fabricated structural metal

(G-12237)
SUN & SOIL LLC
1357 State Route 28 (45140-8426)
PHONE..................513 575-5900
Karl Scheidler,
EMP: 3
SALES: 230K **Privately Held**
SIC: 2899 Chemical preparations

(G-12238)
SUPPLY DYNAMICS INC
6279 Tr Rdge Blvd Ste 310 (45140)
PHONE..................513 965-2000
Trevor Stansbury, *President*
EMP: 24
SALES (est): 934.7K **Privately Held**
WEB: www.supplydynamics.com
SIC: 5051 3544 3541 2836 Iron & steel (ferrous) products; copper sheets, plates, bars, rods, pipes, etc.; aluminum bars, rods, ingots, sheets, pipes, plates, etc.; foundry products; computer software development; biological products, except diagnostic; sawmills & planing mills, general

(G-12239)
T&T WELDING
1469 State Route 28 (45140-8778)
P.O. Box 115 (45140-0115)
PHONE..................513 615-1156
Tom Politt, *Owner*
EMP: 3 EST: 2001
SALES (est): 324K **Privately Held**
SIC: 7692 Welding repair

(G-12240)
TRANSDUCERS DIRECT LLC
112 Lakeview Ct (45140-7745)
PHONE..................513 583-7597
Connie Clark, *Principal*
EMP: 3
SALES (est): 311.5K **Privately Held**
SIC: 3674 Ultra-violet sensors, solid state

(G-12241)
VACCA INC (PA)
9501 Union Cemetery Rd # 100 (45140-9686)
PHONE..................513 697-0270
Giampaolo Vacca, *CEO*
Lawrence Weber, *President*
EMP: 4
SALES (est): 384.7K **Privately Held**
WEB: www.vaccainc.com
SIC: 3999 Heating pads, nonelectric

(G-12242)
VALVE RELATED CONTROLS INC
Also Called: Vrc
143 Commerce Dr (45140-7727)
PHONE..................513 677-8724
Fred Tasch, *CEO*
Ed Lester, *President*
Jason Lester, *Design Engr*
▲ EMP: 12
SQ FT: 12,000
SALES (est): 2.9MM **Privately Held**
WEB: www.vrc-usa.com
SIC: 5084 3625 Industrial machinery & equipment; positioning controls, electric

(G-12243)
VENUS TRADING LLC
10965 Rednor Ct (45140-7763)
PHONE..................513 374-0066
Vinit Trivedi, *Partner*
▼ EMP: 5
SALES (est): 227.4K **Privately Held**
SIC: 3479 Coating of metals & formed products

(G-12244)
WASHING SYSTEMS LLC (HQ)
167 Commerce Dr (45140-7727)
PHONE..................800 272-1974
John Walroth, *CEO*
Jonathan C Dill, *CFO*
▼ EMP: 110
SALES (est): 90MM
SALES (corp-wide): 13.4B **Privately Held**
WEB: www.washingsystems.com
SIC: 5169 2841 Detergents; industrial chemicals; soap & other detergents
PA: Kao Corporation
1-14-10, Nihombashikayabacho
Chuo-Ku TKY 103-0
336 607-111

(G-12245)
WORKHORSE GROUP INC (PA)
100 Commerce Dr (45140-7726)
PHONE..................513 297-3640
Stephen S Burns, *CEO*
Raymond J Chess, *Ch of Bd*
Duane Hughes, *President*
Robert Willison, *COO*
Phillip Crawford, *Engineer*
EMP: 94
SQ FT: 7,500
SALES: 763.1K **Publicly Held**
SIC: 3714 Motor vehicle parts & accessories

Lowell
Washington County

(G-12246)
J & J LOGGING
7100 Highland Ridge Rd (45744-7605)
PHONE..................740 896-2827
John Seevers, *Principal*
EMP: 3
SALES (est): 256.8K **Privately Held**
SIC: 2411 Logging camps & contractors

(G-12247)
OAKWOOD FURNITURE INC
10105 State Route 60 (45744-7272)
P.O. Box 241 (45744-0241)
PHONE..................740 896-3162
Robert Huck, *President*
Rhonda Huck, *Vice Pres*
EMP: 4
SQ FT: 3,500
SALES: 235K **Privately Held**
SIC: 2434 5712 5211 1751 Wood kitchen cabinets; furniture stores; cabinets, kitchen; cabinet & finish carpentry

Lowellville
Mahoning County

(G-12248)
ALUMINUM COLOR INDUSTRIES INC (PA)
369 W Wood St (44436-1039)
PHONE..................330 536-6295
Trude Stoeckel-Spinosa, *President*
Tina Spinosa, *Treasurer*
Lorna Willard, *Admin Sec*
EMP: 65
SQ FT: 30,000
SALES (est): 7.5MM **Privately Held**
SIC: 3442 3471 3444 Moldings & trim, except automobile: metal; finishing, metals or formed products; sheet metalwork

(G-12249)
ARS RECYCLING SYSTEMS LLC
Also Called: Advanced Recycling Systems,
4000 Mccartney Rd (44436-9413)
PHONE..................330 536-8210
Gus G Lyras, *President*
Elio Mussullo, *Vice Pres*
Victor Pallotta, *Vice Pres*
Patsy Pilorusso, *Shareholder*
EMP: 14
SQ FT: 25,000
SALES (est): 3.5MM **Privately Held**
WEB: www.arsrecycling.com
SIC: 7699 3559 Welding equipment repair; recycling machinery

(G-12250)
FALCON FOUNDRY COMPANY
96 6th St (44436-1264)
P.O. Box 301 (44436-0301)
PHONE..................330 536-6221
Gary S Slaven, *President*
John Lopatta, *Principal*
William R Lopatta, *Exec VP*
Lisa Mendozzi, *Treasurer*
◆ EMP: 90
SQ FT: 175,000
SALES (est): 27MM **Privately Held**
WEB: www.falconfoundry.com
SIC: 3366 Castings (except die): copper & copper-base alloy; castings (except die): bronze

(G-12251)
GARLAND WELDING CO INC
804 E Liberty St (44436-1266)
PHONE..................330 536-6506
Rose Del Signore, *President*
Vincent Del Signore, *Principal*
Ralph Signore, *Vice Pres*
Joanne Del Signore, *Admin Sec*
Nick Del Signore, *Admin Sec*
EMP: 12
SQ FT: 6,880
SALES (est): 2.4MM **Privately Held**
WEB: www.garlandwelding.com
SIC: 3441 7692 Fabricated structural metal; welding repair

(G-12252)
GENNARO PAVERS
6065 Arrel Smith Rd (44436-9545)
PHONE..................330 536-6825
David Gennaro, *President*
Ray Gennaro, *Vice Pres*
EMP: 6
SALES (est): 640K **Privately Held**
SIC: 1771 3271 Concrete work; paving blocks, concrete

(G-12253)
LYCO CORPORATION
Also Called: Pilorusso Construction Div
1089 N Hubbard Rd (44436-9737)
PHONE..................412 973-9176
Patsy Pilorusso, *President*
Elio Massullo, *Owner*
W C Pilorusso, *Vice Pres*
Mike Pallotto, *Treasurer*
EMP: 20 EST: 1947

Lowellville - Mahoning County (G-12254)

SQ FT: 25,000
SALES (est): 3.7MM **Privately Held**
WEB: www.lyco-mfg.com
SIC: 7699 3441 Welding equipment repair; fabricated structural metal

(G-12254)
RAVANA INDUSTRIES INC
6170 Center Rd (44436-9521)
P.O. Box 152 (44436-0152)
PHONE..................................330 536-4015
Danette J St Vincent, *CEO*
William St Vincent, *President*
EMP: 8
SALES (est): 860K **Privately Held**
WEB: www.ridingtheelephant.blogs.fortune.cnn.co
SIC: 3541 3363 Machine tool replacement & repair parts, metal cutting types; aluminum die-castings

(G-12255)
RC OUTSOURCING LLC
102 E Water St (44436-1117)
PHONE..................................330 536-8500
Raymond Carlson,
EMP: 3 EST: 2015
SQ FT: 4,500
SALES (est): 198.5K **Privately Held**
SIC: 2834 Pharmaceutical preparations

(G-12256)
SAFEWAY CONTACT LENS INC
1212 Bedford Rd (44436-8705)
PHONE..................................330 536-6469
John A Kizar, *President*
Mariruth Stewart, *Treasurer*
EMP: 6 EST: 1960
SQ FT: 1,832
SALES (est): 793.2K **Privately Held**
SIC: 3851 Contact lenses

(G-12257)
WELDING EQUIPMENT REPAIR CO
142 E Water St (44436-1117)
P.O. Box 143 (44436-0143)
PHONE..................................330 536-2125
Merle Holloway, *President*
EMP: 5
SQ FT: 2,000
SALES (est): 423.6K **Privately Held**
SIC: 7692 Welding repair

Lower Salem
Washington County

(G-12258)
BLAIR LOGGING
30530 Lebanon Rd (45745-9733)
PHONE..................................740 934-2730
Ronald Blair, *Owner*
EMP: 6
SALES: 150K **Privately Held**
SIC: 2411 Logging camps & contractors

(G-12259)
WARNER VESS INC
12 Warner Second St (45745-8844)
PHONE..................................740 585-2481
Ronald Vess, *President*
EMP: 4
SALES (est): 240K **Privately Held**
SIC: 3541 Machine tool replacement & repair parts, metal cutting types

Lucasville
Scioto County

(G-12260)
C & D COUNTERS
359b Back St (45648)
P.O. Box 1131 (45648-1131)
PHONE..................................740 259-5529
Darrell Spriggs, *President*
EMP: 3
SALES (est): 304.8K **Privately Held**
SIC: 2541 Counter & sink tops

(G-12261)
COX INC
Also Called: Cox Precast
11201 State Route 104 (45648-7512)
PHONE..................................740 858-4400
Forest Arbaugh, *President*
Keith Gallimore, *Office Mgr*
EMP: 12
SALES (est): 619.4K **Privately Held**
SIC: 3272 Concrete products, precast

(G-12262)
E A COX INC
11201 State Route 104 (45648-7512)
P.O. Box 819 (45648-0819)
PHONE..................................740 858-4400
Forrest Arbaugh, *President*
EMP: 8 EST: 1970
SALES (est): 1.2MM **Privately Held**
SIC: 3272 Septic tanks, concrete; manhole covers or frames, concrete; tanks, concrete

(G-12263)
FALCON FAB AND FINISHES LLC
Also Called: Falcon Fabrication
3368 Piketon Rd (45648-8767)
P.O. Box 285, Minford (45653-0285)
PHONE..................................740 820-4458
Deron M Brisker, *President*
EMP: 3
SALES (est): 80K **Privately Held**
SIC: 3312 3449 3315 3496 Wire products, steel or iron; hot-rolled iron & steel products; bars, concrete reinforcing; fabricated steel; wire & fabricated wire products; miscellaneous fabricated wire products

(G-12264)
HERFF JONES LLC
37 Lucasville Mdfrd Rd (45648)
PHONE..................................740 357-2160
Jeffrey Webb, *CEO*
EMP: 4
SALES (corp-wide): 1.1B **Privately Held**
SIC: 2752 Commercial printing, lithographic
HQ: Herff Jones, Llc
4501 W 62nd St
Indianapolis IN 46268
800 419-5462

(G-12265)
LAWRENCE PALLETS & SOLUTIONS
620 Owensville Rd (45648-8476)
PHONE..................................740 259-4283
EMP: 4 EST: 2006
SALES (est): 250K **Privately Held**
SIC: 2448 Mfg Wood Pallets/Skids

(G-12266)
MITCHELL WELDING LLC
11761 State Route 104 (45648-8583)
PHONE..................................740 259-2211
James Richard Mitchell, *Partner*
Timothy T Mitchell, *Partner*
EMP: 3
SALES (est): 223.5K **Privately Held**
SIC: 7692 Welding repair

(G-12267)
RAY L LUTE LL
494 Coldicott Hill Rd (45648-9595)
PHONE..................................740 372-7703
EMP: 3
SALES (est): 228.2K **Privately Held**
SIC: 2411 0811 Logging Timber Tract Operation

(G-12268)
TOW PATH READY MIX (PA)
Also Called: Tow Path Materials
12360 State Route 104 (45648-8201)
PHONE..................................740 259-3222
Mark Salisbury, *Owner*
EMP: 4
SALES (est): 1.4MM **Privately Held**
SIC: 3273 Ready-mixed concrete

Ludlow Falls
Miami County

(G-12269)
MARMAX MACHINE CO
Also Called: Meiring Precision
2425 S State Route 48 (45339-9792)
P.O. Box 99 (45339-0099)
PHONE..................................937 698-9900
David M Shepherd, *Owner*
EMP: 7
SQ FT: 7,200
SALES (est): 291.3K **Privately Held**
SIC: 3599 Machine shop, jobbing & repair

(G-12270)
WALL POLISHING LLC
1953 S State Route 48 (45339-8760)
PHONE..................................937 698-1330
Kenneth Wall, *Principal*
EMP: 3 EST: 2011
SALES (est): 212K **Privately Held**
SIC: 3471 Polishing, metals or formed products

Lynchburg
Highland County

(G-12271)
GT MOTORSPORTS
7323 Oh 135 (45142)
PHONE..................................937 763-7272
Greg Tholen, *Owner*
EMP: 3 **Privately Held**
SIC: 3714 Motor vehicle parts & accessories

Lyons
Fulton County

(G-12272)
AEROTECH STYLING INC
14181 County Road 10 2 (43543-9709)
PHONE..................................419 923-6970
Bently Shaw, *President*
Todd Shaw, *Vice Pres*
EMP: 5
SQ FT: 11,700
SALES: 330K **Privately Held**
WEB: www.aerotechstyling.com
SIC: 3714 7532 Motor vehicle parts & accessories; customizing services, non-factory basis

(G-12273)
B W GRINDING CO
Also Called: Bw Supply Co.
15048 County Road 10 3 (43533-9713)
P.O. Box 307 (43533-0307)
PHONE..................................419 923-1376
Martin Welch, *President*
EMP: 35
SQ FT: 30,000
SALES (est): 13.2MM **Privately Held**
WEB: www.bwsupplyco.com
SIC: 5085 3324 Industrial tools; commercial investment castings, ferrous

(G-12274)
MCS MFG LLC
15210 County Road 10 3 (43533-9713)
PHONE..................................419 923-0169
Aaron R Call, *Principal*
EMP: 5 EST: 2008
SALES (est): 359.4K **Privately Held**
SIC: 3999 Manufacturing industries

Macedonia
Summit County

(G-12275)
AGS CUSTOM GRAPHICS INC
Also Called: A G S Ohio
8107 Bavaria Rd (44056)
PHONE..................................330 963-7770
John Green, *President*
Laura Williams, *Project Mgr*
Stephan Kolakowski, *Production*
Todd Henkel, *Accounts Mgr*
Bozena French, *Cust Mgr*
EMP: 74
SQ FT: 70,000
SALES (est): 20.6MM
SALES (corp-wide): 6.8B **Publicly Held**
WEB: www.automatedgraphic.com
SIC: 2752 2721 7375 2791 Commercial printing, offset; periodicals; information retrieval services; typesetting; bookbinding & related work; commercial printing
PA: R. R. Donnelley & Sons Company
35 W Wacker Dr Ste 3650
Chicago IL 60601
312 326-8000

(G-12276)
ALPHABET SOUP INC
981 Cessna Dr (44056-1105)
PHONE..................................330 467-4418
Wanda Glowacki, *President*
Robert Glowacki, *Vice Pres*
Robert Scott, *Vice Pres*
EMP: 3
SALES: 100K **Privately Held**
SIC: 2395 Embroidery & art needlework

(G-12277)
AMERICAN LIGHT METALS LLC
Also Called: Empire Die Casting Company
635 Highland Rd E (44056-2109)
PHONE..................................330 908-3065
Yogen Rahangdale, *Mng Member*
Paul Christensen, *Prgrmr*
EMP: 200 EST: 2013
SQ FT: 200,000
SALES: 28MM
SALES (corp-wide): 34MM **Privately Held**
SIC: 3363 3364 Aluminum die-castings; zinc & zinc-base alloy die-castings
HQ: Srs Die Casting Holdings, Llc
635 Highland Rd E
Macedonia OH 44056
330 467-0750

(G-12278)
BANCEQUITY PETROLEUM CORP
8821 Freeway Dr (44056-1506)
P.O. Box 560200 (44056-0200)
PHONE..................................330 468-5935
Thomas J Fischietto, *President*
Brenda S Eilbeck, *Director*
EMP: 4
SALES (est): 482.6K **Privately Held**
SIC: 1381 Drilling oil & gas wells

(G-12279)
BILZ VIBRATION TECHNOLOGY INC
895 Highland Rd E Ste F (44056-2128)
P.O. Box 241305, Cleveland (44124-8305)
PHONE..................................330 468-2459
Marc A Brower, *President*
Bill Granchi, *Vice Pres*
William Granchi, *Sales Staff*
▲ EMP: 15
SQ FT: 8,000
SALES: 1.3MM **Privately Held**
SIC: 5084 3829 Machinists' precision measuring tools; vibration meters, analyzers & calibrators

(G-12280)
BLUE CUBE OPERATIONS LLC
9456 Freeway Dr (44056-1000)
PHONE..................................440 248-1223
EMP: 3
SALES (corp-wide): 6.9B **Publicly Held**
SIC: 2819 Industrial inorganic chemicals
HQ: Blue Cube Operations Llc
190 Carondelet Plz # 1530
Saint Louis MO 63105
314 480-1400

(G-12281)
BUDGET MOLDERS SUPPLY INC
8303 Corporate Park Dr (44056-2300)
PHONE..................................216 367-7050
Ed Kuchar Sr, *President*
Ed Kuchar Jr, *Vice Pres*
Raymond A Kuchar, *Vice Pres*

GEOGRAPHIC SECTION

Macedonia - Summit County (G-12308)

Francis E Kuchar, *Treasurer*
Jeff Hauff, *Manager*
EMP: 25
SALES (est): 1.9MM **Privately Held**
WEB: www.budgetmolders.com
SIC: 3559 Plastics working machinery

(G-12282)
CENTRAL COCA-COLA BTLG CO INC
8295 Bavaria Dr E (44056-2259)
PHONE.................................330 487-0212
EMP: 3
SALES (corp-wide): 41.8B **Publicly Held**
SIC: 5149 2086 8741 Whol Groceries Mfg Bottled/Canned Soft Drinks Management Services
HQ: Central Coca-Cola Bottling Company, Inc.
555 Taxter Rd Ste 550
Elmsford NY 10523
914 789-1100

(G-12283)
CHAMPION WIN CO CLEVELAND LLC
9011 Freeway Dr Ste 1 (44056-1524)
PHONE.................................440 899-2562
Chris Maple, *President*
◆ **EMP:** 45
SALES (est): 5.5MM **Privately Held**
SIC: 3081 3442 Vinyl film & sheet; storm doors or windows, metal

(G-12284)
COBRA PLASTICS INC
1244 Highland Rd E (44056-2308)
PHONE.................................330 425-3669
Kent Houser, *President*
George Sehringer, *Corp Secy*
Vic Gullatta, *Prdtn Mgr*
Chris Ippolito, *Accounts Mgr*
Colleen Thrasher, *Accounts Mgr*
◆ **EMP:** 100
SQ FT: 95,000
SALES (est): 28.5MM **Privately Held**
WEB: www.cobraplastics.com
SIC: 3089 Molding primary plastic; plastic processing

(G-12285)
CONNELLY INDUSTRIES LLC
9651 N Bedford Rd (44056-1007)
PHONE.................................330 468-0675
M K Connelly, *Principal*
EMP: 3
SALES (est): 149.3K **Privately Held**
SIC: 3999 Manufacturing industries

(G-12286)
CSC SERVICEWORKS HOLDINGS
8515 Freeway Dr Ste D (44056-1589)
PHONE.................................800 362-3182
EMP: 3
SALES (corp-wide): 378.9MM **Privately Held**
SIC: 3633 Household laundry equipment
PA: Csc Serviceworks Holdings, Inc.
303 Sunnyside Blvd # 70
Plainview NY 11803
516 349-8555

(G-12287)
CUSTOM GRAPHICS INC
Also Called: AGS Custom Graphics
8107 Bavaria Dr E (44056-2252)
PHONE.................................330 963-7770
Stan Ritter, *President*
Chuck Straka, *VP Opers*
Elaine Ramos, *Production*
Ellen Backs, *Human Res Dir*
Roger Lozinski, *Accounts Exec*
EMP: 120
SQ FT: 85,000
SALES (est): 10.8MM
SALES (corp-wide): 6.8B **Publicly Held**
WEB: www.agscustomgraphics.com
SIC: 2752 Commercial printing, lithographic
HQ: Consolidated Graphics, Inc.
5858 Westheimer Rd # 200
Houston TX 77057
713 787-0977

(G-12288)
DESIGN MOLDED PLASTICS INC
8220 Bavaria Rd (44056)
PHONE.................................330 963-4400
Jay Honsaker, *President*
Bob Beesley, *General Mgr*
Diane Hanson, *Corp Secy*
Robert Beesley, *Opers Staff*
Sue Kahley, *Purch Agent*
▲ **EMP:** 132 **EST:** 1985
SALES (est): 34.6MM **Privately Held**
SIC: 3089 Injection molded finished plastic products; injection molding of plastics

(G-12289)
DIEMASTER TOOL & MOLD INC
895 Highland Rd E 5 (44056-2128)
PHONE.................................330 467-4281
Paul Badovick, *President*
Dorothy Badovick, *Corp Secy*
EMP: 12 **EST:** 1966
SQ FT: 7,200
SALES (est): 1.4MM **Privately Held**
SIC: 3544 Forms (molds), for foundry & plastics working machinery

(G-12290)
DON BASCH JEWELERS INC
8210 Mcidonia Comm Blvd36 (44056-1861)
PHONE.................................330 467-2116
Don Basch, *President*
Denise Basch, *Admin Sec*
EMP: 13
SALES (est): 2.3MM **Privately Held**
WEB: www.donbaschjewelers.com
SIC: 3911 7631 Jewelry, precious metal; watch, clock & jewelry repair

(G-12291)
ELITE MFG SOLUTIONS LLC
7792 Capital Blvd Ste 6 (44056-2132)
PHONE.................................330 612-7434
Dean O'Malley, *Partner*
EMP: 5 **EST:** 2009
SALES (est): 751.5K **Privately Held**
SIC: 3549 Metalworking machinery

(G-12292)
ETS SCHAEFER LLC
8050 Highland Pointe Pkwy (44056-2147)
PHONE.................................330 468-6600
EMP: 4
SALES (corp-wide): 78MM **Privately Held**
SIC: 3297 3433 Nonclay refractories; heating equipment, except electric
HQ: Ets Schaefer, Llc
3700 Park East Dr Ste 300
Beachwood OH 44122
330 468-6600

(G-12293)
EXPERT GASKET & SEAL LLC
9011 Freeway Dr Ste 5 (44056-1524)
PHONE.................................330 468-0066
Gail Aleck,
David Smith,
Seth Yellen,
EMP: 3
SQ FT: 8,500
SALES (est): 401.6K **Privately Held**
WEB: www.expertgasket.com
SIC: 3053 Gaskets, packing & sealing devices

(G-12294)
FINAL FINISH CORP
596 Highland Rd E (44056-2108)
PHONE.................................440 439-3303
William R Griffith, *President*
Gisele Griffith, *Vice Pres*
Deena Weber, *Marketing Mgr*
EMP: 5
SQ FT: 11,700
SALES (est): 266.2K **Privately Held**
SIC: 3479 Painting of metal products; coating of metals & formed products

(G-12295)
FORTERRA PIPE & PRECAST LLC
7925 Empire Pkwy (44056-2144)
PHONE.................................330 467-7890
Sue Waters, *Branch Mgr*
EMP: 9
SALES (corp-wide): 1.5B **Publicly Held**
SIC: 3272 Culvert pipe, concrete
HQ: Forterra Pipe & Precast, Llc
511 E John Carpenter Fwy
Irving TX 75062
469 458-7973

(G-12296)
FUNCTIONAL PRODUCTS INC
8282 Bavaria Dr E (44056-2248)
PHONE.................................330 963-3060
David Devore, *President*
Diane Costas, *Vice Pres*
Jeff Plumley, *Plant Mgr*
▲ **EMP:** 20
SQ FT: 24,000
SALES (est): 5.9MM **Privately Held**
WEB: www.functionalproducts.com
SIC: 2992 Lubricating oils

(G-12297)
G & G HEADER DIE INC
1200 Saybrook Dr (44056-2408)
PHONE.................................330 468-3458
George Giles, *President*
Candice Giles, *Vice Pres*
EMP: 6
SQ FT: 3,000
SALES: 320K **Privately Held**
SIC: 3544 Special dies & tools

(G-12298)
G W STEFFEN BOOKBINDERS INC
8212 Bavaria Dr E (44056-2248)
PHONE.................................330 963-0300
William Turoczy, *President*
Elizabeth L Turoczy, *Corp Secy*
EMP: 50 **EST:** 1904
SQ FT: 45,000
SALES (est): 6.1MM **Privately Held**
WEB: www.steffenbookbinders.com
SIC: 2789 Binding only: books, pamphlets, magazines, etc.

(G-12299)
GASPAR SERVICES LLC
Also Called: Akland Printing
7791 Capital Blvd Ste 2 (44056-2186)
PHONE.................................330 467-8292
Jane Altman, *Office Mgr*
Gregory Apanasewicz,
EMP: 6
SQ FT: 4,200
SALES (est): 1.1MM **Privately Held**
SIC: 2752 Commercial printing, offset

(G-12300)
GREAT DAY IMPROVEMENTS LLC (HQ)
Also Called: Patio Enclosures
700 Highland Rd E (44056-2160)
PHONE.................................330 468-0700
Steve White, *CEO*
Craig Cox, *President*
Kent Nusser, *Plant Mgr*
Kristie Nekl, *Production*
Kevin Dow, *CFO*
EMP: 9
SALES (est): 46.4MM **Privately Held**
SIC: 3231 3448 3444 5712 Products of purchased glass; prefabricated metal buildings; sunrooms, prefabricated metal; sheet metalwork; outdoor & garden furniture; window furnishings

(G-12301)
HANSON AGGREGATES EAST LLC
7925 Empire Pkwy (44056-2144)
PHONE.................................330 467-7890
Geoff Richardson, *Manager*
EMP: 25
SALES (corp-wide): 20.6B **Privately Held**
SIC: 3272 Concrete products used to facilitate drainage
HQ: Hanson Aggregates East Llc
3131 Rdu Center Dr
Morrisville NC 27560
919 380-2500

(G-12302)
IER FUJIKURA INC (PA)
Also Called: I E R Industries
8271 Bavaria Dr E (44056-2259)
PHONE.................................330 425-7121
John Elsley, *President*
Athur E Lange, *President*
Carol Braunschweig, *Principal*
Sara Hammond, *Purch Agent*
Pat Breen, *Technical Staff*
▲ **EMP:** 128
SQ FT: 60,000
SALES (est): 34.9MM **Privately Held**
WEB: www.ierindustries.com
SIC: 3069 3061 3053 2821 Molded rubber products; mechanical rubber goods; gaskets, packing & sealing devices; plastics materials & resins

(G-12303)
INOVENT ENGINEERING INC
8877 Freeway Dr (44056-1506)
P.O. Box 560314 (44056-0314)
PHONE.................................330 468-0005
P Clark Hungerford Jr, *President*
Ron Fenn, *Vice Pres*
Jim Eucker, *Shareholder*
EMP: 8
SQ FT: 7,000
SALES: 537K **Privately Held**
WEB: www.inoventengineering.com
SIC: 8711 3599 Professional engineer; custom machinery

(G-12304)
INSIGHTFUEL LLC
Also Called: Afv
1333 Highland Rd E Ste P (44056-2445)
PHONE.................................330 998-7380
Kevin Dickey, *General Mgr*
Jeffrey King,
EMP: 15
SQ FT: 16,500
SALES: 5.5MM **Privately Held**
SIC: 2869 Industrial organic chemicals

(G-12305)
J & D BERDINE SIGNS INC
746 E Aurora Rd Ste 3 (44056-2733)
PHONE.................................330 468-0556
Joseph V Berdine II, *President*
EMP: 4
SALES (est): 359.2K **Privately Held**
SIC: 3993 Signs & advertising specialties

(G-12306)
JAMES THOMAS SHIVELEY
Also Called: Innovative Industries
585 Highland Rd E (44056-2107)
P.O. Box 41205, Cleveland (44141-0205)
PHONE.................................330 468-2601
James Thomas Shiveley, *President*
EMP: 4
SQ FT: 30,000
SALES: 125K **Privately Held**
WEB: www.innovativeindustries.com
SIC: 3567 Heating units & devices, industrial: electric

(G-12307)
JAY DEE SERVICE CORPORATION
Also Called: Bearing & Transm Sup Co Div
1320 Highland Rd E (44056-2310)
P.O. Box 560185 (44056-0185)
PHONE.................................330 425-1546
John Zimmerman Sr, *CEO*
Constance A Zimmerman, *President*
Julia Hall, *Principal*
Alfred Palay, *Principal*
Julia Zimmerman, *Principal*
▲ **EMP:** 8 **EST:** 1979
SQ FT: 13,000
SALES: 28MM **Privately Held**
WEB: www.bearingtrans.com
SIC: 5084 3562 Hydraulic systems equipment & supplies; ball bearings & parts

(G-12308)
JOHNSTON-MOREHOUSE-DICKEY CO
1290 Highland Rd E (44056-2308)
PHONE.................................330 405-6050
Tony Blaknik, *Branch Mgr*
EMP: 5

Macedonia - Summit County (G-12309)

SALES (corp-wide): 33.8MM **Privately Held**
SIC: **2299** 3089 5039 Narrow woven fabrics: linen, jute, hemp & ramie; plastic hardware & building products; netting, plastic; soil erosion control fabrics
PA: Johnston-Morehouse-Dickey Co Inc
5401 Progress Blvd
Bethel Park PA 15102
412 833-7100

(G-12309)
JOSLYN MANUFACTURING COMPANY
9400 Valley View Rd (44056-2060)
PHONE...................330 467-8111
Bret Joslyn, *President*
Charles B Joslyn, *Principal*
Brain Joslyn, *Vice Pres*
Brian Joslyn, *Vice Pres*
Scott Price, *Opers Staff*
▲ EMP: 25 EST: 1946
SQ FT: 105,000
SALES (est): 6.8MM **Privately Held**
WEB: www.joslyn-mfg.com
SIC: **3089** Injection molding of plastics; plastic processing

(G-12310)
KIMPTON PRINTING & SPC CO
Also Called: Kimpton Prtg & Specialities
400 Highland Rd E (44056-2133)
PHONE...................330 467-1640
Dale Kimpton, *President*
Don Kimpton, *Vice Pres*
Helen Kimpton, *Vice Pres*
EMP: 10
SQ FT: 2,400
SALES (est): 1.8MM **Privately Held**
WEB: www.kimptonprinting.com
SIC: **2752** 7336 Commercial printing, offset; silk screen design

(G-12311)
M & M CERTIFIED WELDING INC
556 Highland Rd E Ste 3 (44056-2162)
PHONE...................330 467-1729
Matthew B McCann, *President*
Stephany Meek, *Manager*
EMP: 10
SQ FT: 16,000
SALES (est): 2.2MM **Privately Held**
WEB: www.mmcertifiedwelding.com
SIC: **3443** 1799 Weldments; welding on site

(G-12312)
OLD ES LLC
8050 Highland Pointe Pkwy (44056-2147)
PHONE...................330 468-6600
Terrance H Hogan, *CEO*
Dennis Guilmette, *General Mgr*
Hugh Storms, *Engineer*
Michael Hobey, *CFO*
Michael J Hobey,
EMP: 40
SQ FT: 73,000
SALES (est): 11.5MM
SALES (corp-wide): 273.3MM **Privately Held**
WEB: www.etsschaefer.com
SIC: **3297** 3433 2221 Nonclay refractories; heating equipment, except electric; broadwoven fabric mills, manmade
PA: Old Rar, Inc.
3700 Park East Dr Ste 300
Beachwood OH 44122
216 910-3400

(G-12313)
PARKER-HANNIFIN CORPORATION
1390 Highland Rd E (44056-2310)
PHONE...................330 963-0601
EMP: 120
SALES (corp-wide): 14.3B **Publicly Held**
SIC: **3594** Fluid power pumps & motors
PA: Parker-Hannifin Corporation
6035 Parkland Blvd
Cleveland OH 44124
216 896-3000

(G-12314)
PARKER-HANNIFIN CORPORATION
1390 Highland Rd E (44056-2310)
PHONE...................216 896-3000
Achilleas Dorotheou, *Manager*
EMP: 12
SALES (corp-wide): 14.3B **Publicly Held**
SIC: **3594** Fluid power pumps
PA: Parker-Hannifin Corporation
6035 Parkland Blvd
Cleveland OH 44124
216 896-3000

(G-12315)
PLASTIC MATERIALS INC (PA)
775 Highland Rd E (44056-2111)
PHONE...................330 468-5706
William Speaks, *Principal*
EMP: 26
SALES (est): 12.3MM **Privately Held**
SIC: **3089** Air mattresses, plastic

(G-12316)
PLASTIC MATERIALS INC
Also Called: PMI
775 Highland Rd E (44056-2111)
PHONE...................330 468-0184
EMP: 31
SALES (corp-wide): 12.3MM **Privately Held**
SIC: **3089** Air mattresses, plastic
PA: Plastic Materials Inc
775 Highland Rd E
Macedonia OH 44056
330 468-5706

(G-12317)
PLASTIC PROCESS EQUIPMENT INC (PA)
Also Called: Ppe
8303 Corporate Park Dr (44056-2300)
PHONE...................216 367-7000
Edward Kuchar, *President*
Henry G Roethel, *Engineer*
Brian Jones, *Administration*
▲ EMP: 20
SALES (est): 7.8MM **Privately Held**
SIC: **3559** 5085 5084 Plastics working machinery; industrial supplies; industrial machinery & equipment

(G-12318)
POLY-CARB INC
9456 Freeway Dr (44056-1000)
P.O. Box 39278, Solon (44139-0278)
PHONE...................440 248-1223
Puneet Singh, *President*
▲ EMP: 40
SQ FT: 55,000
SALES (est): 7.9MM
SALES (corp-wide): 85.9B **Publicly Held**
WEB: www.poly-carb.com
SIC: **2821** Silicone resins
HQ: The Dow Chemical Company
2211 H H Dow Way
Midland MI 48642
989 636-1000

(G-12319)
PRECISION REPLACEMENT LLC
9009 Freeway Dr Unit 7 (44056-1523)
PHONE...................330 908-0410
Joseph D Lukes, *Principal*
EMP: 6
SQ FT: 5,500
SALES (est): 2MM **Privately Held**
SIC: **3565** 5999 Vacuum packaging machinery; electronic parts & equipment

(G-12320)
PRO QUIP INC
850 Highland Rd E (44056-2190)
PHONE...................330 468-1850
Harry J Abraham, *CEO*
George Braun, *Principal*
Brian Abraham, *Vice Pres*
Rosalyn Abraham, *Treasurer*
Al Gilenko, *Controller*
▲ EMP: 55 EST: 1969
SQ FT: 26,000
SALES (est): 20.5MM **Privately Held**
WEB: www.proquipinc.com
SIC: **3559** Refinery, chemical processing & similar machinery

(G-12321)
PROGRESSIVE MACHINE DIE INC
8406 Bavaria Dr E (44056-2275)
PHONE...................330 405-6600
Julius Feitl, *President*
EMP: 40 EST: 1963
SQ FT: 70,000
SALES (est): 7.1MM **Privately Held**
WEB: www.pmd-inc.com
SIC: **3429** 3544 3469 Manufactured hardware (general); special dies, tools, jigs & fixtures; metal stampings

(G-12322)
RALPH FELICE INC
Also Called: Far Associates
1532 Newport Dr (44056-1970)
PHONE...................330 468-0482
Ralph A Felice, *President*
EMP: 4
SALES (est): 693.9K **Privately Held**
WEB: www.pyrometry.com
SIC: **3823** Pyrometers, industrial process type

(G-12323)
REINECKERS BAKERY LTD
Also Called: Reinecker Party Center & Catrg
8575 Freeway Dr (44056-1534)
PHONE...................330 467-2221
Caroline Davis, *Partner*
Heidi Reinecker, *Partner*
Richard Reinecker, *Partner*
EMP: 3 EST: 1959
SALES: 200K **Privately Held**
SIC: **2051** 5812 Bakery: wholesale or wholesale/retail combined; caterers

(G-12324)
SC FIRE PROTECTION LTD
Also Called: S C Fastening Systems
8531 Freeway Dr (44056-1534)
PHONE...................330 468-3300
Chuck Domonkos, *CEO*
Scott Filips, *President*
▲ EMP: 7
SALES: 680K **Privately Held**
SIC: **2899** Fire extinguisher charges

(G-12325)
SILVERCOTE LLC
9600b Valley View Rd (44056-2059)
PHONE...................330 748-8500
Jodi Shankweiler, *Branch Mgr*
EMP: 9
SALES (corp-wide): 8.2B **Privately Held**
SIC: **3296** Insulation: rock wool, slag & silica minerals
HQ: Silvercote, Llc
25 Logue Ct
Greenville SC 29615
844 232-3701

(G-12326)
SOURCE3MEDIA INC
9085 Freeway Dr (44056-1508)
PHONE...................330 467-9003
Gary Began, *President*
Ronald S Marshek, *Director*
◆ EMP: 35 EST: 1967
SQ FT: 17,000
SALES (est): 8MM **Privately Held**
WEB: www.hudsonpr.com
SIC: **2752** Commercial printing, offset

(G-12327)
SPECIALTY MAGNETICS LLC
440 Highland Rd E (44056-2106)
PHONE...................330 468-8834
Shawn Grill, *Mng Member*
Jeff Glen, *Mng Member*
▲ EMP: 3
SQ FT: 800
SALES (est): 535K **Privately Held**
SIC: **3612** Transformers, except electric

(G-12328)
SPEEDWAY LLC
Also Called: Speedway Superamerica 1848
757 E Aurora Rd (44056)
PHONE...................330 468-3320
Jerry Kurinsky, *Branch Mgr*
EMP: 14 **Publicly Held**
WEB: www.speedwaynet.com
SIC: **1311** Crude petroleum production
HQ: Speedway Llc
500 Speedway Dr
Enon OH 45323
937 864-3000

(G-12329)
SR PRODUCTS
1380 Highland Rd E (44056-2310)
PHONE...................330 998-6500
Steve Harnish, *President*
Stephen Duke, *CFO*
EMP: 7
SALES (est): 823.9K **Privately Held**
SIC: **2952** Asphalt felts & coatings

(G-12330)
SRS DIE CASTING HOLDINGS LLC (HQ)
Also Called: Empire Diecasting
635 Highland Rd E (44056-2109)
PHONE...................330 467-0750
Yogen Rahangdale,
EMP: 6
SALES (est): 28MM
SALES (corp-wide): 34MM **Privately Held**
SIC: **3363** 3364 Aluminum die-castings; zinc & zinc-base alloy die-castings
PA: Srs Light Metals Inc.
635 Highland Rd E
Macedonia OH 44056
330 467-0750

(G-12331)
SRS LIGHT METALS INC (PA)
635 Highland Rd E (44056-2109)
PHONE...................330 467-0750
Yogen Rahangdale,
EMP: 3 EST: 2013
SALES (est): 34MM **Privately Held**
SIC: **3363** 3364 Aluminum die-castings; zinc & zinc-base alloy die-castings

(G-12332)
STANDARD SIGNS INCORPORATED (PA)
Also Called: Lumacurve Airfield Signs
9115 Freeway Dr (44056-1543)
PHONE...................330 467-2030
John A Messner, *President*
Dave Benson, *Accounts Mgr*
Melanie Rostankowski, *Accounts Mgr*
Liz Humpage, *Marketing Staff*
EMP: 19 EST: 1936
SQ FT: 27,000
SALES (est): 3.4MM **Privately Held**
WEB: www.standardsigns.com
SIC: **3993** Signs, not made in custom sign painting shops

(G-12333)
STANEK E F AND ASSOC INC
Also Called: Stanek Windows
700 Highland Rd E (44056-2160)
PHONE...................216 341-7700
Mark Davis, *President*
Jerry Donatelli, *Exec VP*
Ron Stanek, *Vice Pres*
Robert Van Schoonhaven, *CFO*
Victor Perri, *Sales Staff*
EMP: 120
SQ FT: 35,000
SALES (est): 18.3MM **Privately Held**
WEB: www.stanekwindows.com
SIC: **3089** Windows, plastic; window frames & sash, plastic

(G-12334)
SUNLESS INC (PA)
8909 Freeway Dr Ste A (44056-1574)
PHONE...................440 836-0199
Peter Van Niekerk, *CEO*
▼ EMP: 120
SQ FT: 68,000

SALES (est): 29.4MM **Privately Held**
WEB: www.sunlessinc.com
SIC: 3648 Sun tanning equipment, incl. tanning beds

(G-12335)
SUPERFINISHERS INC
380 Highland Rd E (44056-2139)
PHONE..................................330 467-2125
Frank Bucar, *President*
EMP: 7
SQ FT: 5,000
SALES: 700K **Privately Held**
SIC: 3471 3599 Finishing, metals or formed products; machine shop, jobbing & repair

(G-12336)
SYSTEMS PACK INC
649 Highland Rd E (44056-2109)
PHONE..................................330 467-5729
Ray Attwell, *President*
Laurene Neval, *CFO*
Sean Freeman, *Consultant*
Jeff Vranic, *Consultant*
EMP: 30 EST: 1977
SQ FT: 62,131
SALES: 8MM **Privately Held**
WEB: www.systemspackinc.com
SIC: 5199 7389 5113 2653 Packaging materials; packaging & labeling services; shipping supplies; corrugated & solid fiber boxes

(G-12337)
TIN WIZARD HEATING AND COOLING
8853 Robinwood Ter (44056-2719)
PHONE..................................330 468-7884
James Plush, *Principal*
EMP: 3 EST: 2010
SALES (est): 28.5K **Privately Held**
SIC: 3356 Tin

(G-12338)
WILLARD MACHINE & WELDING INC
556 Highland Rd E Ste 3 (44056-2162)
PHONE..................................330 467-0642
Margaret Willard, *President*
George C Willard, *Vice Pres*
EMP: 10
SQ FT: 9,600
SALES (est): 759.1K **Privately Held**
SIC: 3713 7532 Specialty motor vehicle bodies; top & body repair & paint shops

Madison
Lake County

(G-12339)
ALLPASS CORPORATION
222 N Lake St (44057-3118)
P.O. Box 10 (44057-0010)
PHONE..................................440 998-6300
Joseph Passerell, *CEO*
David Passerell, *CEO*
Joe Passerell, *President*
Steve Passerell, *COO*
Mike Passerell, *Vice Pres*
▲ EMP: 12
SALES (est): 3.8MM **Privately Held**
SIC: 3443 Metal parts

(G-12340)
BUCKEYE ALUMINUM FOUNDRY INC (PA)
457 N Lake St (44057-3139)
PHONE..................................440 428-7180
Peter Otterman Jr, *President*
EMP: 3 EST: 1973
SALES (est): 2MM **Privately Held**
WEB: www.buckeyealuminum.com
SIC: 3366 Copper foundries

(G-12341)
CASE PATTERN CO INC
2380 Forest Glen Rd (44057-2366)
PHONE..................................216 531-0744
Timothy B Gorka, *President*
Lawrence E Gorka, *Corp Secy*
EMP: 5 EST: 1963

SALES (est): 703.9K **Privately Held**
SIC: 3543 3544 Foundry patternmaking; forms (molds), for foundry & plastics working machinery

(G-12342)
CENTER MASS AMMO LLC
6642 Middle Ridge Rd (44057-2904)
PHONE..................................440 796-6207
Christopher Sanford, *CEO*
Jason Bosworth, *Co-Owner*
Scott Graham, *Co-Owner*
EMP: 3
SALES (est): 222.6K **Privately Held**
SIC: 3483 3482 Ammunition loading & assembling plant; small arms ammunition; cartridge cases for ammunition, 30 mm. & below

(G-12343)
CHALET DEBONNE VINEYARDS INC
7840 Doty Rd (44057-9511)
PHONE..................................440 466-3485
Anthony Paul Debevc, *President*
Tony J Debevc, *Vice Pres*
Beth Debevc, *Admin Sec*
EMP: 12
SQ FT: 14,000
SALES (est): 1.9MM **Privately Held**
SIC: 2084 Wines

(G-12344)
CHEMMASTERS INC
300 Edwards St (44057-3112)
PHONE..................................440 428-2105
Daniel Schodowski, *President*
John Fauth, *General Mgr*
Greg Myers, *Vice Pres*
Roblyn Jericho, *Opers Mgr*
Brenda Carr, *Safety Mgr*
◆ EMP: 20
SQ FT: 25,000
SALES (est): 7.6MM **Privately Held**
WEB: www.chemmasters.net
SIC: 2899 2891 5169 2851 Concrete curing & hardening compounds; sealants; chemicals & allied products; paints & allied products; paints, waterproof; coating, air curing

(G-12345)
COUNTY OF LAKE
Also Called: Waste Water Treatment Plant
7815 Cashen Rd (44057-1651)
PHONE..................................440 428-1794
Terry Rascke, *Manager*
EMP: 10
SQ FT: 650 **Privately Held**
WEB: www.lakecountyohio.gov
SIC: 3589 Water treatment equipment, industrial
PA: County Of Lake
8 N State St Ste 215
Painesville OH 44077
440 350-2500

(G-12346)
D & L MANUFACTURING INC
2715 Bennett Rd (44057-2657)
PHONE..................................440 428-1627
Richard W Kuehnle, *President*
EMP: 5 EST: 1973
SQ FT: 1,200
SALES (est): 545.4K **Privately Held**
SIC: 3469 Stamping metal for the trade

(G-12347)
DEE LEE MACHINE INC
3921 Townline Rd (44057-3326)
PHONE..................................440 259-2245
Dale Broadwater, *President*
Sally Broadwater, *Vice Pres*
EMP: 3
SQ FT: 1,876
SALES (est): 500K **Privately Held**
SIC: 3599 Machine shop, jobbing & repair

(G-12348)
EAE LOGISTICS COMPANY LLC
5907 S Ridge Rd (44057-9741)
PHONE..................................440 417-4788
Daniel T Larned,
EMP: 3

SALES (est): 500K **Privately Held**
SIC: 3542 4491 4731 7389 Presses; forming, stamping, punching, sizing (machine tools); marine cargo handling; freight transportation arrangement;

(G-12349)
EMPIRE POWER SYSTEMS CO
6211 Shore Dr (44057-1945)
P.O. Box 1893, Mentor (44061-1893)
PHONE..................................440 796-4401
Ronald Lapham, *Principal*
EMP: 4
SALES (est): 450K **Privately Held**
SIC: 3643 3613 3694 3679 Power line cable; switchgear & switchboard apparatus; battery cable wiring sets for internal combustion engines; harness assemblies for electronic use: wire or cable

(G-12350)
FORZZA CORPORATION (PA)
222 N Lake St (44057-3118)
PHONE..................................440 998-6300
Joseph C Passerell, *President*
EMP: 5 EST: 2010
SALES (est): 1.7MM **Privately Held**
SIC: 3585 Parts for heating, cooling & refrigerating equipment

(G-12351)
INTERNATIONAL PAPER COMPANY
3200 County Line Rd (44057-9731)
PHONE..................................440 428-5116
EMP: 3
SALES (corp-wide): 23.3B **Publicly Held**
SIC: 2621 Paper mills
PA: International Paper Company
6400 Poplar Ave
Memphis TN 38197
901 419-9000

(G-12352)
KG TOOL COMPANY
5640 Middle Ridge Rd (44057-2814)
PHONE..................................440 428-8633
Greg Giecerich, *Principal*
EMP: 4
SALES (est): 457.5K **Privately Held**
SIC: 3544 Special dies, tools, jigs & fixtures

(G-12353)
LAURENTIA WINERY
6869 River Rd (44057-9008)
PHONE..................................440 296-9170
EMP: 3
SALES (est): 214.1K **Privately Held**
SIC: 2084 Wines

(G-12354)
NYP CORP (FRMR NY-PTERS CORP)
2711 Bennett Rd (44057-2657)
PHONE..................................440 428-0129
Mike Rider, *General Mgr*
EMP: 5
SALES (est): 296.6K
SALES (corp-wide): 16.8MM **Privately Held**
SIC: 2393 Textile bags
PA: Nyp Corp. (Formerly New Yorker-Peters Corporation)
805 E Grand St
Elizabeth NJ 07201
908 351-6550

(G-12355)
PUMPHREY MACHINE CORP
7240 N Ridge Rd (44057-2629)
P.O. Box 477 (44057-0477)
PHONE..................................440 417-0481
Herbert Pumphrey, *President*
EMP: 9
SQ FT: 9,000
SALES (est): 1.4MM **Privately Held**
SIC: 3599 Machine shop, jobbing & repair

(G-12356)
SCC WINE COMPANY LLC
Also Called: Silver Crest
4511 Bates Rd (44057-8210)
PHONE..................................216 374-3740
Eric Cotton, *Mng Member*

EMP: 3
SALES (est): 84.8K **Privately Held**
SIC: 2084 Wines

(G-12357)
TOPKOTE INC
404 N Lake St (44057-3151)
PHONE..................................440 428-0525
Shane Slattman, *Principal*
EMP: 9
SALES (est): 720K **Privately Held**
SIC: 3399 Silver powder

(G-12358)
UNIVERSAL SCIENTIFIC INC
6210 Campbell Dr (44057-2003)
PHONE..................................440 428-1777
Thomas W Heckman, *President*
Phoebe Heckman, *Corp Secy*
EMP: 8
SQ FT: 2,500
SALES (est): 1.5MM **Privately Held**
WEB: www.universalscientific.com
SIC: 3821 Laboratory equipment: fume hoods, distillation racks, etc.

Magnolia
Stark County

(G-12359)
CREEKSIDE COTTAGE WINERY LLC
8818 Cleveland Ave Se (44643-9706)
PHONE..................................330 694-1013
Stephen Miller, *Principal*
EMP: 3
SALES (est): 125.1K **Privately Held**
SIC: 2084 Wines, brandy & brandy spirits

(G-12360)
MAGNOLIA MACHINE & REPAIR INC
3315 Magnolia Rd Nw (44643-9528)
PHONE..................................330 866-4200
Daniel Fedeli, *President*
EMP: 5
SQ FT: 3,000
SALES (est): 430K **Privately Held**
SIC: 3599 Machine shop, jobbing & repair

(G-12361)
OLDE WOOD LTD
7557 Willowdale Ave Se (44643-9718)
PHONE..................................330 866-1441
Thomas Sancic, *CEO*
EMP: 35
SQ FT: 70,000
SALES (est): 7MM **Privately Held**
SIC: 3272 Building materials, except block or brick: concrete

(G-12362)
PHOENIX ASPHALT COMPANY INC
18025 Imperial Rd (44643)
PHONE..................................330 339-4935
James R Demuth, *President*
EMP: 6
SALES (est): 223.5K **Privately Held**
SIC: 1442 5032 Construction sand & gravel; sand, construction

(G-12363)
SMITH SMITH & DEYARMAN
9260 Bachelor Rd Nw (44643-9564)
P.O. Box 406 (44643-0406)
PHONE..................................330 866-5521
D Michael Smith, *Partner*
Charles Deyarman, *Partner*
EMP: 3
SALES (est): 205.8K **Privately Held**
SIC: 1381 Drilling oil & gas wells

Maineville
Warren County

(G-12364)
ABCO BAR & TUBE CUTTING SVC
7685 S State Route 48 # 1 (45039-8802)
PHONE..................513 697-9487
Kris Martin, *President*
Jason Martin, *Vice Pres*
Nathan Huff, *VP Opers*
Amanda Martin, *Office Mgr*
EMP: 30
SQ FT: 40,000
SALES (est): 7.7MM **Privately Held**
WEB: www.abcomachining.com
SIC: 3451 3452 3599 Screw machine products; bolts, nuts, rivets & washers; machine & other job shop work; machine shop, jobbing & repair

(G-12365)
CJR DESSERTS
7272 Northgate Dr (45039-8110)
PHONE..................513 549-6403
Christopher Rogers, *Founder*
EMP: 4
SALES (est): 197.4K **Privately Held**
SIC: 2051 Bread, cake & related products

(G-12366)
CONTINGNCY PRCREMENT GROUP LLC
Also Called: Cpg Armor Company
2800 Millbank Row (45039-9711)
PHONE..................513 204-9590
William Cornett, *CEO*
Irina Khusainova-Cornett, *Principal*
EMP: 4
SALES (est): 362K **Privately Held**
SIC: 2311 7382 7381 Military uniforms, men's & youths': purchased materials; policemen's uniforms: made from purchased materials; protective devices, security; detective & armored car services

(G-12367)
ELIZABETHS CLOSET
8847 Dover Dr (45039-9738)
PHONE..................513 646-5025
Liz Cook, *Owner*
EMP: 2
SALES: 92K **Privately Held**
SIC: 5632 5812 2032 Costume jewelry; American restaurant; Mexican foods: packaged in cans, jars, etc.

(G-12368)
ELKEN CO
2905 Afton Valley Ct (45039-8847)
PHONE..................513 459-7207
Kenneth Lippert, *President*
EMP: 5
SALES (est): 626.3K **Privately Held**
WEB: www.clearviewbinders.com
SIC: 2782 2396 Blankbooks & looseleaf binders; bindings, cap & hat: made from purchased materials

(G-12369)
FABACRAFT INC
Also Called: Fabacraft Co
201 Grandin Rd (45039-9762)
PHONE..................513 677-0500
Edward F Bavis, *Ch of Bd*
William Sieber, *President*
Dolly Mattingly, *Corp Secy*
Michael Brown, *Vice Pres*
David McCartt, *Purch Mgr*
EMP: 35 **EST:** 1958
SQ FT: 44,000
SALES (est): 7.4MM **Privately Held**
WEB: www.bavis.com
SIC: 3535 Conveyors & conveying equipment

(G-12370)
HENKEL ADHESIVE CORPORATION
1356 Tecumseh Dr (45039-7993)
PHONE..................513 677-5800
EMP: 3
SALES (est): 123.2K **Privately Held**
SIC: 2891 Adhesives

(G-12371)
JMR ENTERPRISES LLC
Also Called: Robinson Ordnance
7808 Hyatts Ln (45039-7285)
PHONE..................937 618-1736
Joseph Robinson, *Agent*
EMP: 3
SALES (est): 150.2K **Privately Held**
SIC: 5961 3484 3482 Catalog sales; guns (firearms) or gun parts, 30 mm. & below; small arms ammunition

(G-12372)
KROGER CO
2900 W Us Hwy 22 3 Unit 1 (45039)
PHONE..................513 683-4001
Bob Oaters, *Manager*
EMP: 80
SALES (corp-wide): 121.1B **Publicly Held**
WEB: www.kroger.com
SIC: 5411 5992 5912 2052 Supermarkets, chain; florists; drug stores & proprietary stores; cookies & crackers; bread, cake & related products
PA: The Kroger Co
1014 Vine St Ste 1000
Cincinnati OH 45202
513 762-4000

(G-12373)
LAUGHING STAR MONTESSORY
8725 Davis Rd (45039-8329)
PHONE..................513 683-5682
Susan Barker, *President*
EMP: 3
SALES (est): 260.4K **Privately Held**
WEB: www.laughingstarmontessori.com
SIC: 2759 Commercial printing

(G-12374)
MARKET READY
1129 Avalon Dr (45039-9131)
PHONE..................513 289-9231
Dan H Letzler, *Owner*
EMP: 6
SALES (est): 571.9K **Privately Held**
SIC: 3273 Ready-mixed concrete

(G-12375)
NAIL SECRET
3187 Wstn Row Rd Ste 105 (45039)
PHONE..................513 459-3373
Stacey Chau, *Owner*
EMP: 3
SALES (est): 126.9K **Privately Held**
SIC: 3999 Fingernails, artificial

(G-12376)
OHIO FIRST DEFENSE
3530 Arbor Hill Ln (45039-9028)
PHONE..................513 571-9461
Kenneth Bertz, *Principal*
EMP: 3 **EST:** 2015
SALES (est): 157.1K **Privately Held**
SIC: 3812 Defense systems & equipment

(G-12377)
SVM AMERICA LTD
1004 River Forest Dr (45039-7717)
PHONE..................937 218-7591
Timothy Homan,
EMP: 50
SALES (est): 3.1MM **Privately Held**
SIC: 3711 Cars, armored, assembly of

(G-12378)
UTV HITCHWORKS LLC
1295 W Us Highway 22 & 3 (45039-8218)
PHONE..................513 615-8568
Dale McOsker, *Vice Pres*
Mark Altemeier,
EMP: 4
SALES (est): 562.6K **Privately Held**
SIC: 3714 Motor vehicle electrical equipment

Malinta
Henry County

(G-12379)
GILSON SCREEN INCORPORATED
8-810 K 2 Rd (43535)
P.O. Box 99 (43535-0199)
PHONE..................419 256-7711
David A Cody, *President*
Steven J Roby, *Vice Pres*
Trent Smith, *Vice Pres*
Richard Franz, *Site Mgr*
James A Cody, *Treasurer*
EMP: 42 **EST:** 1961
SQ FT: 30,000
SALES (est): 9.9MM **Privately Held**
WEB: www.globalgilson.com
SIC: 3829 3444 Testing equipment: abrasion, shearing strength, etc.; sheet metalwork

(G-12380)
JAD MACHINE COMPANY INC
10620 County Road J (43535-9713)
PHONE..................419 256-6332
Jim Hastedt, *President*
Diane Hastedt, *Corp Secy*
EMP: 12
SQ FT: 12,000
SALES (est): 1MM **Privately Held**
WEB: www.jadmachine.com
SIC: 3451 Screw machine products

Malta
Morgan County

(G-12381)
E Z GROUT CORPORATION
Also Called: Ezg Manufacturing
1833 N Riverview Rd (43758-9303)
PHONE..................740 749-3512
Damian Lang, *President*
Daniel Kern, *Plant Mgr*
Kevin Brooker, *Production*
Douglas Taylor, *CFO*
▲ **EMP:** 25
SALES: 9.7MM **Privately Held**
WEB: www.ezgrout.com
SIC: 3423 3531 Masons' hand tools; construction machinery

(G-12382)
EZ GROUT CORPORATION INC
Also Called: Ezg Manufacturing
1833 N Riverview Rd (43758-9303)
PHONE..................740 962-2024
Damian Lang, *Owner*
Steve Wheeler, *Marketing Staff*
EMP: 40 **EST:** 2007
SALES (est): 13MM **Privately Held**
SIC: 5082 3499 3549 Masonry equipment & supplies; chests, fire or burglary resistive: metal; wiredrawing & fabricating machinery & equipment, ex. die

(G-12383)
J VALTIER GAS AND OIL CO INC
10416 State Route 37 (43758-9417)
PHONE..................740 342-2839
Joseph N Altier Jr, *President*
EMP: 5
SALES (est): 501.5K **Privately Held**
SIC: 1381 1389 Directional drilling oil & gas wells; servicing oil & gas wells

(G-12384)
WOLFE CREEK FARMS
Also Called: Wilson Well Service
433 Wilson Dr (43758-9286)
PHONE..................740 962-4563
Jerry R Wilson, *Owner*
Alan Wilson, *Partner*
Azcal Wilson, *Partner*
Mark Wilson, *Partner*
EMP: 4
SALES (est): 282K **Privately Held**
SIC: 1389 0115 0116 0212 Oil field services; gas field services; corn; soybeans; beef cattle except feedlots; hogs

Malvern
Carroll County

(G-12385)
CAMBRIDGE MILL PRODUCTS INC
6005 Alliance Rd Nw (44644-9439)
P.O. Box 490 (44644-0490)
PHONE..................330 863-1121
Charles Lebeau III, *President*
Jerry W Morris II, *Vice Pres*
EMP: 7
SQ FT: 2,400
SALES (est): 1.9MM **Privately Held**
WEB: www.cambridgemillproducts.com
SIC: 2992 Oils & greases, blending & compounding; re-refining lubricating oils & greases

(G-12386)
CEDAR OUTDOOR FURNITURE INC
8229 Old Canal Ln Nw (44644-9706)
PHONE..................330 863-2580
Gary Pearce, *President*
Elizabeth Pearce, *Admin Sec*
EMP: 5
SQ FT: 9,400
SALES (est): 250K **Privately Held**
WEB: www.cedaroutdoor.com
SIC: 2511 Wood lawn & garden furniture; porch furniture & swings: wood

(G-12387)
COLFOR MANUFACTURING INC
3255 Alliance Rd Nw (44644-9756)
PHONE..................330 863-7500
David C Dauch, *Chairman*
Michael K Simonte, *Exec VP*
Alberto Satine, *Senior VP*
▲ **EMP:** 691
SALES (est): 228.8MM
SALES (corp-wide): 7.2B **Publicly Held**
SIC: 3462 3599 3463 Iron & steel forgings; machine shop, jobbing & repair; nonferrous forgings
HQ: American Axle & Manufacturing, Inc.
1 Dauch Dr
Detroit MI 48211

(G-12388)
DUNN S TANK SERVICE INC
6036 Alliance Rd Nw (44644-9445)
PHONE..................330 863-2200
EMP: 3 **EST:** 2012
SALES (est): 130K **Privately Held**
SIC: 1382 Oil/Gas Exploration Services

(G-12389)
ELASTON COMPANY
448 E Mohawk Dr (44644-9510)
PHONE..................330 863-2865
Theodore J Dettling, *President*
Ted Dettling Jr, *Vice Pres*
Marlyn Dettling, *Treasurer*
EMP: 10 **EST:** 1980
SALES (est): 850K **Privately Held**
SIC: 2891 Adhesives

(G-12390)
FOR CALL INC
3255 Alliance Rd Nw (44644-9756)
PHONE..................330 863-0404
Inacio Moriguchi, *President*
EMP: 500 **EST:** 1967
SALES (est): 32.8MM **Privately Held**
SIC: 3462 Iron & steel forgings

(G-12391)
GBS CORP
Also Called: GBS Filing Solutions
224 Morges Rd (44644-9736)
P.O. Box 308 (44644-0308)
PHONE..................330 863-1828
Pat Lieser, *VP Mktg*
Michele Benson, *Branch Mgr*
Alan Bartlett, *Executive*
EMP: 116

SALES (corp-wide): 72.8MM **Privately Held**
SIC: **2675** 2752 2672 2761 Folders, filing, die-cut: made from purchased materials; business forms, lithographed; adhesive papers, labels or tapes: from purchased material; manifold business forms
PA: Gbs Corp.
7233 Freedom Ave Nw
North Canton OH 44720
330 494-5330

(G-12392)
GORDONS GRAPHICS INC
123 S Reed Ave (44644-9496)
P.O. Box 586 (44644-0586)
PHONE..................................330 863-2322
Brad Lewis, *President*
Jerry Hinton, *Corp Secy*
EMP: 7
SQ FT: 1,500
SALES (est): 325K **Privately Held**
SIC: **2752** 2759 5734 5943 Commercial printing, offset; engraving; computer & software stores; office forms & supplies

(G-12393)
MECHANICAL ELASTOMERICS INC
Also Called: MEI
3266 Coral Rd Nw (44644-9467)
P.O. Box 588 (44644-0588)
PHONE..................................330 863-1014
Jonathan Walters, *President*
Dale Olbon, *General Mgr*
Meg Walters, *Treasurer*
EMP: 5
SQ FT: 1,932
SALES (est): 649.8K **Privately Held**
SIC: **3052** Rubber & plastics hose & beltings

Manchester
Adams County

(G-12394)
HEADWATERS INCORPORATED
745 Us Route 52 (45144-8450)
PHONE..................................989 671-1500
Sam Jackson, *Manager*
EMP: 18 **Privately Held**
SIC: **3272** Siding, precast stone
HQ: Headwaters Incorporated
10701 S River Front Pkwy # 300
South Jordan UT 84095

(G-12395)
MOYER VINEYARDS INC
Also Called: Moyer Winery & Restaurant
3859 Us Highway 52 (45144-8338)
P.O. Box 235 (45144-0235)
PHONE..................................937 549-2957
Carol White, *President*
EMP: 22 EST: 1973
SQ FT: 5,000
SALES (est): 2.8MM **Privately Held**
SIC: **2084** 5812 Wines; restaurant, family: independent

(G-12396)
PETERSON RADIO INC
9711 Us Highway 52 (45144-9577)
PHONE..................................937 549-3731
Neil Peterson, *President*
EMP: 3
SQ FT: 8,000
SALES (est): 703.3K **Privately Held**
SIC: **5064** 7622 3663 Radios; radio repair & installation; radio broadcasting & communications equipment

(G-12397)
VANCES DEPARTMENT STORE (PA)
Also Called: Vance's Wonder Store
37 E 2nd St (45144-1301)
P.O. Box 326 (45144-0326)
PHONE..................................937 549-2188
David A Scott, *Owner*
EMP: 6
SQ FT: 5,000

SALES (est): 1.6MM **Privately Held**
SIC: **5651** 5661 5211 2541 Family clothing stores; shoe stores; lumber & other building materials; cabinets, except refrigerated: show, display, etc.: wood

(G-12398)
VANCES DEPARTMENT STORE
Also Called: Adams County Lumber
600 Washington St (45144-1362)
PHONE..................................937 549-3033
Gregory B Scott, *Principal*
EMP: 11
SALES (corp-wide): 1.6MM **Privately Held**
SIC: **5651** 5661 5211 2541 Family clothing stores; shoe stores; lumber & other building materials; cabinets, except refrigerated: show, display, etc.: wood
PA: Vance's Department Store
37 E 2nd St
Manchester OH 45144
937 549-2188

Mansfield
Richland County

(G-12399)
A L CALLAHAN DOOR SALES
35 Industrial Dr (44904-1372)
PHONE..................................419 884-3667
Don Callahan, *Owner*
EMP: 7
SQ FT: 3,000
SALES (est): 1.1MM **Privately Held**
SIC: **5211** 7699 3699 Garage doors, sale & installation; garage door repair; door opening & closing devices, electrical

(G-12400)
AARONYX PUBLISHING
Also Called: Aaronyx Design
1924 Springmill Rd (44903-8908)
PHONE..................................419 747-2400
Michael Holloway, *Owner*
EMP: 4
SALES: 90K **Privately Held**
WEB: www.aaronyx.com
SIC: **2741** Miscellaneous publishing

(G-12401)
AK MANSFIELD
913 Bowman St (44903-4109)
PHONE..................................419 755-3011
Randy Hartman, *Principal*
EMP: 350
SALES (est): 9.4MM **Privately Held**
SIC: **3999** Bleaching & dyeing of sponges

(G-12402)
AK STEEL CORPORATION
Also Called: Mansfield Operations
913 Bowman St (44903-4109)
P.O. Box 247 (44901-0247)
PHONE..................................419 755-3011
Lee Price, *Maint Mgr*
Richard Dray, *Engineer*
Sarah Gilley, *Engineer*
Bradley Tilton, *Engineer*
Randy Hartman, *CPA*
EMP: 500 **Publicly Held**
WEB: www.ketnar.org
SIC: **3312** Stainless steel
HQ: Ak Steel Corporation
9227 Centre Pointe Dr
West Chester OH 45069
513 425-4200

(G-12403)
AMAROQ INC
Also Called: Guetle Die & Stamping
648 N Trimble Rd (44906-2002)
PHONE..................................419 747-2110
Rt Mong, *President*
EMP: 7
SQ FT: 8,000
SALES (est): 1MM **Privately Held**
SIC: **3469** 3544 Stamping metal for the trade; special dies, tools, jigs & fixtures

(G-12404)
AMERASCREW INC
653 Lida St (44903-1242)
P.O. Box 1407 (44901-1407)
PHONE..................................419 522-2232
John R Keith, *President*
EMP: 21
SQ FT: 37,000
SALES (est): 4.4MM **Privately Held**
WEB: www.amerascrew.com
SIC: **3451** Screw machine products

(G-12405)
AMERICAN TOOL & MFG CO
Also Called: American Tool & Manufacturing
211 Newman St (44902-1461)
P.O. Box 1242 (44901-1242)
PHONE..................................419 522-2452
Myron Brenner, *President*
EMP: 14 EST: 1966
SQ FT: 40,000
SALES (est): 2.1MM **Privately Held**
WEB: www.americantoolmfg.com
SIC: **3469** Stamping metal for the trade

(G-12406)
AMERICAS BEST SIDING CO
1395 W Longview Ave (44906-1802)
PHONE..................................419 589-5900
Darlow C Bartram, *Owner*
Beth Horfey, *Manager*
EMP: 5
SQ FT: 5,000
SALES (est): 610.5K **Privately Held**
SIC: **3444** Metal flooring & siding

(G-12407)
APPLIED GRAPHICS LTD
1717 Mccarrick Pkwy (44903-6533)
PHONE..................................419 756-6882
Natalie Beckert, *President*
EMP: 7
SALES (est): 544.2K **Privately Held**
SIC: **3993** 7311 2791 Signs & advertising specialties; advertising agencies; typesetting

(G-12408)
AS AMERICA INC
Also Called: American Standard Brands
41 Cairns Rd (44903-8992)
PHONE..................................419 522-4211
Kevin Oak, *Manager*
EMP: 20
SALES (corp-wide): 15.6B **Privately Held**
WEB: www.sanymetal.com
SIC: **3261** 3431 3281 2541 Plumbing fixtures, vitreous china; metal sanitary ware; cut stone & stone products; wood partitions & fixtures; wood kitchen cabinets
HQ: As America, Inc.
1 Centennial Ave Ste 101
Piscataway NJ 08854

(G-12409)
AUTOMATIC PARTS
433 Springmill St (44903-7008)
P.O. Box 1505 (44901-1505)
PHONE..................................419 524-5841
Robert H Wittmer, *President*
David A Wittmer, *Vice Pres*
Bill Briggs, *Prdtn Mgr*
Justin Constable, *Manager*
EMP: 20
SQ FT: 17,000
SALES (est): 3.2MM **Privately Held**
WEB: www.automaticparts.com
SIC: **3599** Machine shop, jobbing & repair

(G-12410)
BAY WORLD INTERNATIONAL INC
395 Reed St (44903-1084)
PHONE..................................419 525-2222
Jon P Ralph, *CEO*
Jay Ralph, *Vice Pres*
EMP: 40
SQ FT: 30,000
SALES (est): 6.1MM **Privately Held**
WEB: www.bayworldmfg.com
SIC: **2431** Window frames, wood

(G-12411)
BLACK RIVER GROUP INC (PA)
Also Called: Black River Display Group
140 Park Ave E (44902-1830)
P.O. Box 876 (44901-0876)
PHONE..................................419 524-6699
Terry Neff, *President*
Kurt Myers, *Prdtn Mgr*
Steve Winters, *Safety Mgr*
Chris Baldasare, *Accounting Mgr*
Chaz Schroeder, *Accounts Exec*
EMP: 65
SQ FT: 74,000
SALES: 120MM **Privately Held**
WEB: www.ds-creative.com
SIC: **7311** 2752 2791 2789 Advertising agencies; commercial printing, lithographic; typesetting; bookbinding & related work

(G-12412)
BLEVINS METAL FABRICATION INC
Also Called: Blevins Fabrication
288 Illinois Ave S (44905-2827)
PHONE..................................419 522-6082
Lloyd T Blevins, *President*
Sharon Thomas, *Buyer*
EMP: 25 EST: 1997
SQ FT: 13,000
SALES (est): 4.7MM **Privately Held**
SIC: **7692** 3446 3444 3443 Welding repair; architectural metalwork; sheet metalwork; fabricated plate work (boiler shop); fabricated structural metal

(G-12413)
BRANDTS CUSTOM MACHINING LLC
1183 Stewart Rd N (44905-1551)
PHONE..................................419 566-3192
Benjamin Brandt, *Principal*
EMP: 7
SALES (est): 540.4K **Privately Held**
SIC: **3599** Custom machinery

(G-12414)
BREITINGER COMPANY
595 Oakenwaldt St (44905-1900)
PHONE..................................419 526-4255
Milo Breitinger, *President*
Breitinger Kim, *CFO*
Kim Breitinger, *Manager*
Nikki Williams, *Admin Asst*
EMP: 120 EST: 1954
SQ FT: 106,000
SALES (est): 35.9MM **Privately Held**
WEB: www.breitingercompany.com
SIC: **3441** 3469 7692 3444 Fabricated structural metal; metal stampings; welding repair; sheet metalwork; fabricated plate work (boiler shop)

(G-12415)
BROST FOUNDRY COMPANY
198 Wayne St (44902-1433)
PHONE..................................419 522-1133
Chuck Horvath, *Manager*
EMP: 15
SALES (est): 1.9MM
SALES (corp-wide): 5.3MM **Privately Held**
WEB: www.brostfoundry.com
SIC: **3366** Brass foundry
PA: Brost Foundry Company (Inc)
2934 E 55th St
Cleveland OH 44127
216 641-1131

(G-12416)
BUCKEYE VAULT SERVICE INC
Also Called: Buckeye Delivery
2253 Stiving Rd (44903-8900)
P.O. Box 1261 (44901-1261)
PHONE..................................419 747-1976
Don Neighbors, *President*
Jill Neighbors, *Corp Secy*
Douglas Neighbors, *Vice Pres*
EMP: 7
SALES (est): 1.2MM **Privately Held**
SIC: **3272** Burial vaults, concrete or precast terrazzo

Mansfield - Richland County (G-12417)

(G-12417)
BUNTING BEARINGS LLC
153 E 5th St (44902-1407)
P.O. Box 1053 (44901-1053)
PHONE...........................419 522-3323
Kim J Keogh, *Branch Mgr*
EMP: 47
SQ FT: 68,000
SALES (corp-wide): 55MM **Privately Held**
SIC: 3366 3568 3369 3356 Bushings & bearings, bronze (nonmachined); power transmission equipment; nonferrous foundries; nonferrous rolling & drawing
PA: Bunting Bearings, Llc
    1001 Holland Park Blvd
    Holland OH 43528
    419 866-7000

(G-12418)
C & G ASSOCIATES INC
3130 Hastings Newville Rd (44903-7740)
P.O. Box 3954 (44907-3954)
PHONE...........................419 756-6583
Paul M Cocanour, *President*
EMP: 4
SQ FT: 3,200
SALES (est): 300K **Privately Held**
WEB: www.cg-associates.org
SIC: 2381 Fabric dress & work gloves

(G-12419)
CAPITAL PROSTHETIC &
625 Cline Ave (44907-1038)
PHONE...........................567 560-2051
David Kozersky, *Branch Mgr*
EMP: 25
SALES (est): 308K
SALES (corp-wide): 2.9MM **Privately Held**
SIC: 3842 Limbs, artificial; braces, orthopedic
PA: Capital Prosthetic And Orthotic Center, Inc.
    4678 Larwell Dr
    Columbus OH 43220
    614 451-0446

(G-12420)
CAROUSEL MAGIC LLC
44 W 4th St (44902-1206)
PHONE...........................419 522-6456
Sherell Anderson,
Pauline Anderson,
Andrea Clark,
Ross Clark,
EMP: 4
SQ FT: 16,000
SALES: 300K **Privately Held**
WEB: www.carouselmagic.com
SIC: 3599 7699 Carousels (merry-go-rounds); antique repair & restoration, except furniture, automobiles

(G-12421)
CAROUSEL WORKS INC
1285 Pollock Pkwy (44905-1374)
PHONE...........................419 522-7558
Art Ritchie, *President*
Daniel Jones, *Vice Pres*
Kate Blakely, *Treasurer*
Ryan D Jones, *Admin Sec*
EMP: 23
SQ FT: 25,000
SALES: 2.1MM **Privately Held**
WEB: www.carouselworks.com
SIC: 3599 Carousels (merry-go-rounds)

(G-12422)
CASE-MAUL MANUFACTURING CO
30 Harker St (44903-1395)
PHONE...........................419 524-1061
Craig Case, *President*
Sandra Collins, *Corp Secy*
Helen Witschi, *Office Mgr*
Debbie Johnson, *Manager*
Joann Case,
▲ EMP: 10 EST: 1953
SQ FT: 18,000
SALES (est): 1.5MM **Privately Held**
WEB: www.case-maulmfg.com
SIC: 3599 7692 Machine shop, jobbing & repair; welding repair

(G-12423)
CEMENT PRODUCTS INC
389 Park Ave E (44905-2896)
PHONE...........................419 524-4342
Toll Free:.........................877 -
David Schmitz, *President*
Douglas Schmitz, *Vice Pres*
Daniel Schmitz, *Treasurer*
Dwight Schmitz, *Admin Sec*
EMP: 26 EST: 1916
SQ FT: 82,778
SALES (est): 4.2MM **Privately Held**
WEB: www.cementproducts.com
SIC: 3271 3273 3272 Blocks, concrete or cinder: standard; ready-mixed concrete; concrete products

(G-12424)
CENTRAL COCA-COLA BTLG CO INC
100 Industrial Pkwy (44903-8999)
PHONE...........................419 522-2653
Mike Dewalt, *Manager*
EMP: 45
SALES (corp-wide): 35.4B **Publicly Held**
WEB: www.colasic.net
SIC: 2086 Bottled & canned soft drinks
HQ: Central Coca-Cola Bottling Company, Inc.
    555 Taxter Rd Ste 550
    Elmsford NY 10523
    914 789-1100

(G-12425)
CITY OF MANSFIELD
2010 S Lexngtn Sprngml Rd (44904)
PHONE...........................419 884-3310
Llydia Ride, *Branch Mgr*
EMP: 12 **Privately Held**
WEB: www.metrich.com
SIC: 3569 Filters & strainers, pipeline
PA: City Of Mansfield
    30 N Diamond St
    Mansfield OH 44902
    419 755-9626

(G-12426)
CLEANING LADY INC
190 Stewart Rd N (44905-2639)
PHONE...........................419 589-5566
Suzanne Stewart, *Principal*
EMP: 15
SQ FT: 7,360
SALES (est): 470.8K **Privately Held**
SIC: 7349 5169 2841 Janitorial service, contract basis; detergents; detergents, synthetic organic or inorganic alkaline

(G-12427)
COMMERCIAL CUTNG GRAPHICS LLC
208 Central Ave (44905-2410)
PHONE...........................419 526-4800
Barbara Lindsay, *President*
Matt Seifert, *Production*
Chuck Johnson, *Design Engr*
Matt Patrick, *Manager*
Jeffrey A Burkhart,
EMP: 62
SQ FT: 45,000
SALES (est): 16.7MM **Privately Held**
WEB: www.commercialcutting.com
SIC: 2675 Die-cut paper & board

(G-12428)
CORNS QUALITY WOODWORKING LLC
1525 Chew Rd (44903-9231)
PHONE...........................419 589-4899
Jeff Corns, *Principal*
EMP: 4
SALES (est): 240K **Privately Held**
SIC: 2431 Millwork

(G-12429)
CORPAD COMPANY INC
555 Park Ave E (44905-2871)
P.O. Box 1492 (44901-1492)
PHONE...........................419 522-7818
Dane Arlen Bonecutter, *Principal*
EMP: 55
SQ FT: 97,500
SALES (est): 16.4MM **Privately Held**
SIC: 2631 Paperboard mills

(G-12430)
CSM HORVATH LEDGEBROOK
Also Called: Rost Boundry
198 Wayne St (44902-1433)
PHONE...........................419 522-1133
Chuck Horvath, *President*
EMP: 4
SALES (est): 343.9K **Privately Held**
SIC: 3363 Aluminum die-castings

(G-12431)
DALLAS DESIGN & TECHNOLOGY INC
184 Industrial Dr (44904-1339)
P.O. Box 3043 (44904-0043)
PHONE...........................419 884-9750
Mark Stevens, *President*
EMP: 9
SQ FT: 8,500
SALES: 2MM **Privately Held**
WEB: www.dallasdesigntech.com
SIC: 3599 Machine shop, jobbing & repair

(G-12432)
DAVIES SINCE 1900
Also Called: Davies Interiors
913 S Main St (44907-2037)
PHONE...........................419 756-4212
David J Davies, *Owner*
EMP: 3
SQ FT: 8,000
SALES: 500K **Privately Held**
SIC: 5713 1721 2273 1743 Floor covering stores; interior commercial painting contractor; carpets & rugs; marble installation, interior

(G-12433)
DND EMULSIONS INC
270 Park Ave E (44902-1849)
PHONE...........................419 525-4988
Delbert Dawson, *President*
EMP: 5
SQ FT: 2,940
SALES (est): 464.7K **Privately Held**
SIC: 2869 2952 2992 Industrial organic chemicals; coating compounds, tar; cutting oils, blending: made from purchased materials

(G-12434)
DTE INC
110 Baird Pkwy (44903-7909)
PHONE...........................419 522-3428
Rob Nelson, *CEO*
Dean Russell, *President*
Burke Melching, *Vice Pres*
EMP: 30
SQ FT: 45,000
SALES (est): 3.8MM **Privately Held**
WEB: www.dteinc.com
SIC: 7629 3661 Telephone set repair; telephone & telegraph apparatus

(G-12435)
EDGE PLASTICS INC (PA)
449 Newman St (44902-1123)
PHONE...........................419 522-6696
Shelley Fisher, *President*
▲ EMP: 150
SQ FT: 146,000
SALES (est): 32.8MM **Privately Held**
SIC: 3089 Injection molded finished plastic products; injection molding of plastics

(G-12436)
ELTOOL CORPORATION
1400 Park Ave E (44905-2989)
PHONE...........................513 723-1772
Edward Crotty, *President*
Vicky Young, *Office Mgr*
EMP: 7
SALES (est): 551.5K **Privately Held**
WEB: www.eltool.com
SIC: 8742 3599 5084 Marketing consulting services; machine shop, jobbing & repair; industrial machinery & equipment

(G-12437)
ENERGY TECHNOLOGIES INC
Also Called: E T I
219 Park Ave E (44902-1845)
PHONE...........................419 522-4444
Paul C Madden, *President*
Sam Kehl, *Research*
Rhonda Reeder, *Info Tech Mgr*
John S Madden, *Admin Sec*
EMP: 80
SQ FT: 30,000
SALES (est): 16.8MM **Privately Held**
WEB: www.ruggedsystems.com
SIC: 3629 3625 3621 Electronic generation equipment; relays & industrial controls; motors & generators

(G-12438)
FAMILY VALUES MAGAZINE
3027 Fox Rd (44904-9707)
P.O. Box 9012 (44904-9012)
PHONE...........................419 566-1102
Shane Hostetler, *Principal*
EMP: 4 EST: 2009
SALES (est): 321.4K **Privately Held**
SIC: 2721 Periodicals

(G-12439)
FIVE HANDICAP INC (PA)
Also Called: Mansfield Graphics
127 N Walnut St (44901-1221)
P.O. Box 7 (44901-0007)
PHONE...........................419 525-2511
Chuck B McCartney, *President*
EMP: 15 EST: 1929
SQ FT: 20,000
SALES (est): 3.2MM **Privately Held**
WEB: www.mansfieldgraphics.com
SIC: 3469 Metal stampings

(G-12440)
FORBES REHAB SERVICES INC (PA)
49 Illinois Ave S (44905-2824)
PHONE...........................419 589-7688
Paul Forbes, *President*
EMP: 5
SQ FT: 2,400
SALES (est): 764.7K **Privately Held**
WEB: www.frs-solutions.com
SIC: 3842 Technical aids for the handicapped

(G-12441)
FORREST MACHINE PDTS CO LTD
Also Called: Forrest Scrw Machine
139 Illinois Ave S (44905-2825)
P.O. Box 3648 (44907-0648)
PHONE...........................419 589-3774
Cyd McCready, *Principal*
Donald Holmes, *Engineer*
Steve Fellows, *Manager*
Mark Whitaker, *Manager*
Joseph Scali, *Prgrmr*
EMP: 22
SALES: 950K **Privately Held**
SIC: 3549 3451 Metalworking machinery; screw machine products

(G-12442)
FRIEND ENGRG & MCH CO INC
67 Illinois Ave S (44905-2824)
PHONE...........................419 589-5066
David Friend, *President*
Beth Friend, *Corp Secy*
EMP: 3
SQ FT: 10,000
SALES (est): 450K **Privately Held**
SIC: 3599 Custom machinery

(G-12443)
GANNETT CO INC
News Journal
70 W 4th St (44903-1676)
P.O. Box 25 (44901-0025)
PHONE...........................419 522-3311
Tom Brennen, *Principal*
EMP: 165
SALES (corp-wide): 2.9B **Publicly Held**
WEB: www.gannett.com
SIC: 2711 Newspapers, publishing & printing
PA: Gannett Co., Inc.
    7950 Jones Branch Dr
    Mc Lean VA 22102
    703 854-6000

Mansfield - Richland County (G-12470)

(G-12444)
GANNETT PUBLISHING SVCS LLC
70 W 4th St (44903-1676)
PHONE..................419 522-3311
EMP: 8
SALES (corp-wide): 2.9B Publicly Held
SIC: 2711 Commercial printing & newspaper publishing combined; newspapers, publishing & printing
HQ: Gannett Publishing Services, Llc
7950 Jones Branch Dr
Mc Lean VA 22102
703 854-6000

(G-12445)
GENERAL TECHNOLOGIES INC
855 W Longview Ave (44906-2131)
P.O. Box 1726 (44901-1726)
PHONE..................419 747-1800
Susan L Moran, Principal
Margaret Marlow, Vice Pres
▲ EMP: 20 EST: 1957
SQ FT: 40,000
SALES: 5MM Privately Held
WEB: www.general-technologies.com
SIC: 3469 7692 3444 3443 Metal stampings; welding repair; sheet metalwork; fabricated plate work (boiler shop)

(G-12446)
GLOBAL OILFIELD SERVICES LLC
Also Called: Gofs
3401 State Route 13 (44904-9394)
PHONE..................419 756-8027
Jim Jackson, President
Annette Jones, Admin Sec
EMP: 3
SALES (est): 288K Privately Held
SIC: 1389 5082 1623 Oil field services; oil field equipment; oil & gas line & compressor station construction

(G-12447)
GORMAN-RUPP COMPANY (PA)
600 S Airport Rd (44903-7831)
P.O. Box 1217 (44901-1217)
PHONE..................419 755-1011
James C Gorman, Ch of Bd
Jeffrey S Gorman, President
Tim Cline, Engineer
Travis Eighinger, Electrical Engi
James C Kerr, CFO
EMP: 277 EST: 1933
SALES: 414.3MM Publicly Held
WEB: www.gormanrupp.com
SIC: 3594 3561 Fluid power pumps & motors; industrial pumps & parts

(G-12448)
GORMAN-RUPP COMPANY
Ipt Pumps Division
305 Bowman St (44903-1689)
P.O. Box 1217 (44901-1217)
PHONE..................419 755-1011
James Robinette, Engineer
Angie Morehead, Controller
Tina Spearman, Marketing Staff
Cindy Hoffner, Manager
James A Lomax, Director
EMP: 500
SALES (corp-wide): 414.3MM Publicly Held
WEB: www.gormanrupp.com
SIC: 3561 Industrial pumps & parts
PA: Gorman-Rupp Company
600 S Airport Rd
Mansfield OH 44903
419 755-1011

(G-12449)
GORMAN-RUPP COMPANY
Also Called: Warehouse
100 Rump Rd (44903)
P.O. Box 1217 (44901-1217)
PHONE..................419 755-1245
Jeffrey Gorman, President
EMP: 8
SALES (corp-wide): 414.3MM Publicly Held
WEB: www.gormanrupp.com
SIC: 5084 3561 Pumps & pumping equipment; pumps & pumping equipment
PA: Gorman-Rupp Company
600 S Airport Rd
Mansfield OH 44903
419 755-1011

(G-12450)
GORMAN-RUPP COMPANY
100 Rupp Rd (44903-6512)
PHONE..................419 755-1011
Judith Sorine, Principal
EMP: 3
SALES (corp-wide): 414.3MM Publicly Held
SIC: 3594 Fluid power pumps & motors
PA: Gorman-Rupp Company
600 S Airport Rd
Mansfield OH 44903
419 755-1011

(G-12451)
GOYAL INDUSTRIES INC
382 Park Ave E (44905-2843)
PHONE..................419 522-7099
Prakash R Goyal, President
▲ EMP: 21
SQ FT: 18,000
SALES (est): 3.7MM Privately Held
SIC: 3599 3441 Machine shop, jobbing & repair; fabricated structural metal

(G-12452)
GRASAN EQUIPMENT COMPANY INC
440 S Illinois Ave (44907-1809)
PHONE..................419 526-4440
Marian L Eilenfeld, President
Ed Eilenfeld, Vice Pres
Edward Eilenfeld Jr, Vice Pres
Chuck Ferguson, Engineer
Aaron Niswander, Engineer
▼ EMP: 65 EST: 1970
SQ FT: 62,000
SALES (est): 20.2MM Privately Held
WEB: www.grasan.com
SIC: 4953 3532 3559 3535 Recycling, waste materials; crushers, stationary; rock crushing machinery, stationary; screeners, stationary; recycling machinery; conveyors & conveying equipment; construction machinery

(G-12453)
GRAYWACKE INC
300 S Mill St (44904-8519)
PHONE..................419 884-7014
Scott Huffman, President
Mark Huffman, Vice Pres
EMP: 15
SQ FT: 14,000
SALES (est): 3.3MM Privately Held
WEB: www.graywacke.net
SIC: 3691 Batteries, rechargeable

(G-12454)
GROWCO INC
844 Kochheiser Rd (44904-8637)
PHONE..................419 886-4628
Jeff Mason, Principal
EMP: 3
SALES (est): 239.1K Privately Held
SIC: 3272 Concrete products

(G-12455)
HAYFORD TECHNOLOGIES
Also Called: Milark Industries
500 S Airport Rd (44903-8067)
PHONE..................419 524-7627
Matt Breitinger, President
Brooke Breitinger,
Mary Breitinger,
Trisha Breitinger,
EMP: 99
SALES (est): 2.8MM Privately Held
SIC: 3465 3469 Automotive stampings; metal stampings; perforated metal, stamped

(G-12456)
HEARTLAND DESIGN CONCEPTS
29 Illinois Ave S (44905-2824)
PHONE..................419 774-0199
Kristen Dalownia, Principal
EMP: 3

SALES (est): 54.5K Privately Held
SIC: 7389 2499 7336 Design services; signboards, wood; commercial art & graphic design; art design services

(G-12457)
HERGATT MACHINE INC
2530 Pavonia Rd (44903-7807)
PHONE..................419 589-2931
Neil N Hergatt, President
Becky Hergatt, Corp Secy
EMP: 8
SQ FT: 4,000
SALES (est): 600K Privately Held
SIC: 3599 Machine shop, jobbing & repair

(G-12458)
HESS INDUSTRIES LTD
108 Sawyer Pkwy (44903-6514)
PHONE..................419 525-4000
Mark A Hess, President
Pamela Hess, Vice Pres
EMP: 10
SQ FT: 12,000
SALES: 1MM Privately Held
WEB: www.hessindltd.com
SIC: 3544 Special dies & tools

(G-12459)
HIGHPOINT FIREARMS
Also Called: Hi-Point Firearms
1015 Springmill St (44906-1571)
PHONE..................419 747-9444
Tom Deeb, President
Shirley Deeb, Admin Sec
EMP: 28
SQ FT: 24,000
SALES (est): 4.5MM Privately Held
SIC: 3484 5941 Guns (firearms) or gun parts, 30 mm. & below; sporting goods & bicycle shops

(G-12460)
IDEAL ELECTRIC POWER CO
330 E 1st St (44902-7756)
PHONE..................419 522-3611
Jim Petersen, President
Bill Evans, President
Michael Gordon, Accountant
◆ EMP: 11
SQ FT: 280,000
SALES (est): 51MM Privately Held
WEB: www.hhi.co.kr
SIC: 3621 3613 3625 Generators & sets, electric; motors, electric; switchgear & switchgear accessories; relays & industrial controls

(G-12461)
JAY INDUSTRIES INC
Also Called: Broshco Fabricated Products
1595 W Longview Ave (44906-1806)
PHONE..................419 747-4161
Rick R Taylor, President
R G Taylor, Principal
Dave Benick, Exec VP
Paul Shatlock, Vice Pres
Josh Taylor, Vice Pres
▲ EMP: 930
SQ FT: 125,000
SALES (est): 1.8MM Privately Held
WEB: www.jayindinc.com
SIC: 2531 3089 Seats, automobile; injection molding of plastics

(G-12462)
JAY MID-SOUTH LLC
150 Longview Ave E (44903-4206)
PHONE..................256 439-6600
Rick Taylor, Mng Member
▲ EMP: 150
SQ FT: 65,000
SALES (est): 22.2MM Privately Held
SIC: 3499 Automobile seat frames, metal

(G-12463)
JOHN L GARBER MATERIALS CORP
2745 Gass Rd (44904-8715)
PHONE..................419 884-1567
John L Garber, President
Matthew Garber, Vice Pres
Donna West, Admin Sec
EMP: 13
SQ FT: 500

SALES (est): 979.3K Privately Held
SIC: 1442 Gravel mining

(G-12464)
JONES POTATO CHIP CO (PA)
823 Bowman St (44903-4107)
PHONE..................419 529-9424
Robert Jones, President
Charles K Hellinger, Principal
Frederick W Jones, Principal
Darryl Jones, Vice Pres
Bob Martin, Sales Mgr
EMP: 46 EST: 1940
SQ FT: 50,000
SALES (est): 8.8MM Privately Held
WEB: www.joneschips.com
SIC: 2096 5145 Potato chips & other potato-based snacks; potato chips

(G-12465)
JOTCO INC
1400 Park Ave E (44905-2989)
PHONE..................513 721-4943
John Young, President
Vicki Young, Admin Sec
EMP: 6
SQ FT: 100,000
SALES (est): 691.1K Privately Held
WEB: www.jotco-inc.com
SIC: 3471 8711 3599 Finishing, metals or formed products; engineering services; machine & other job shop work

(G-12466)
KARMA METAL PRODUCTS INC
556 Caldwell Ave (44905-1401)
PHONE..................419 524-4371
Thomas Taska, President
Ron Kocher, Vice Pres
Judy Taska, Treasurer
EMP: 10
SQ FT: 6,800
SALES (est): 1.4MM Privately Held
WEB: www.karmametalproducts.com
SIC: 3451 3545 Screw machine products; measuring tools & machines, machinists' metalworking type

(G-12467)
KOKOSING MATERIALS INC
215 Oak St (44907-1439)
PHONE..................419 522-2715
Bill Burgett, Branch Mgr
EMP: 6
SALES (corp-wide): 19.9MM Privately Held
SIC: 2951 Asphalt & asphaltic paving mixtures (not from refineries)
PA: Kokosing Materials, Inc.
17531 Waterford Rd
Fredericktown OH 43019
740 694-9585

(G-12468)
LENNOX MACHINE INC
Also Called: Lennox Machine Shop
1471 Sprang Pkwy (44903-6531)
P.O. Box 1643 (44901-1643)
PHONE..................419 525-1020
Terry L Eighinger, President
David Eighinger, Vice Pres
EMP: 11
SALES (est): 1.7MM Privately Held
SIC: 3599 Machine shop, jobbing & repair

(G-12469)
LESCH BTRY & PWR SOLUTION LLC
2744 Lexington Ave (44904-1429)
PHONE..................419 884-0219
Tom Lesch, Manager
Brian Lesch,
Sandra Lesch,
EMP: 4
SALES (est): 511.1K Privately Held
SIC: 3621 7389 Storage battery chargers, motor & engine generator type; business services

(G-12470)
LONG VIEW STEEL CORP
1555 W Longview Ave (44906-1806)
P.O. Box 2839 (44906-0839)
PHONE..................419 747-1108
David Jacko, President
EMP: 12

Mansfield - Richland County (G-12471)   GEOGRAPHIC SECTION

SALES (est): 3.4MM **Privately Held**
WEB: www.longviewsteel.com
SIC: 3312 Blast furnaces & steel mills

(G-12471)
M GRAFIX LLC
384 Gatewood Dr Apt 2 (44907-2349)
PHONE 419 528-8665
Maurice Byrd,
EMP: 14
SALES: 34K **Privately Held**
WEB: www.mgrafix.net
SIC: 7374 2741 Computer graphics service; shopping news; publishing & printing

(G-12472)
MAJOR METALS COMPANY
844 Kochheiser Rd (44904-8637)
PHONE 419 886-4600
Jeffrey C Mason, *President*
Wayne Riffe, *Vice Pres*
Jason Dials, *Sales Mgr*
EMP: 30
SQ FT: 60,000
SALES (est): 13.7MM **Privately Held**
WEB: www.majormetalscompany.com
SIC: 3312 5051 3317 Plate, sheet & strip, except coated products; iron or steel flat products; steel pipe & tubes

(G-12473)
MALABAR PROPERTIES LLC
Also Called: Deca Manufacturing
300 S Mill St (44904-8519)
PHONE 419 884-0071
Hansford R Williams, *President*
Carolyn Williams, *Corp Secy*
Karen M Cashell, *Vice Pres*
EMP: 15
SQ FT: 33,000
SALES (est): 16.7MM **Privately Held**
WEB: www.decamfgcables.com
SIC: 3679 3544 3672 Harness assemblies for electronic use; wire or cable; industrial molds; printed circuit boards

(G-12474)
MANAIRCO INC
28 Industrial Pkwy (44903-8999)
P.O. Box 111 (44901-0111)
PHONE 419 524-2121
James C Gorman, *Ch of Bd*
Gayle Gorman Freeman, *President*
Marjorie Gorman, *Corp Secy*
Joel Beinbrech, *Vice Pres*
Leroy Blizzard, *Design Engr*
EMP: 9 **EST:** 1953
SQ FT: 14,000
SALES (est): 1.6MM **Privately Held**
WEB: www.manairco.com
SIC: 3648 3645 Airport lighting fixtures; runway approach, taxi or ramp; residential lighting fixtures

(G-12475)
MANSFIELD BRICK & SUPPLY CO (PA)
320 N Diamond St (44902-1008)
P.O. Box 1273 (44901-1273)
PHONE 419 526-1191
Toll Free: .... 888 -
Mike Anderson, *President*
Jane Anderson, *Corp Secy*
EMP: 8
SQ FT: 3,500
SALES (est): 1.4MM **Privately Held**
SIC: 5211 5032 3272 Brick; brick, except refractory; concrete products, precast

(G-12476)
MANSFIELD IMAGING CENTER LLC
536 S Trimble Rd Ste A (44906-3418)
PHONE 419 756-8899
Michael R Viau,
EMP: 12
SALES (est): 1.3MM **Privately Held**
SIC: 3826 Magnetic resonance imaging apparatus

(G-12477)
MANSFIELD INDUSTRIES INC
1776 Harrington Mem Rd (44903-8996)
PHONE 419 524-1300
Otis M Cummins, *Chairman*
Greg Beal, *Mfg Mgr*
EMP: 29
SALES (est): 5.7MM **Privately Held**
WEB: www.mansfieldindustries.com
SIC: 3469 Stamping metal for the trade

(G-12478)
MCDANIEL PRODUCTS INC
Also Called: Automatic Parts
433 Springmill St (44903-7008)
P.O. Box 1505 (44901-1505)
PHONE 419 524-5841
Justin Constable, *Branch Mgr*
EMP: 31 **Privately Held**
SIC: 3451 Screw machine products
PA: Mcdaniel Products, Inc.
1775 Liberty Ave
Vermilion OH 44089

(G-12479)
MERRICO INC
541 Grant St (44903-1215)
P.O. Box 156 (44901-0156)
PHONE 419 525-2711
Sandy Powers, *President*
EMP: 4
SQ FT: 15,000
SALES (est): 520K **Privately Held**
WEB: www.merrico.com
SIC: 3644 3069 Insulators & insulation materials, electrical; hard rubber & molded rubber products

(G-12480)
MID OHIO TROPHY & AWARDS
131 W Cook Rd (44907-2403)
PHONE 419 756-2266
Charlotte Brown, *Owner*
EMP: 3
SALES (est): 232.1K **Privately Held**
SIC: 3499 5999 Trophies, metal, except silver; trophies & plaques

(G-12481)
MIDWEST AIRCRAFT PRODUCTS CO
Also Called: Mapco
125 S Mill St (44904-9571)
PHONE 419 884-2164
Jerry Miller, *CEO*
▼ **EMP:** 17
SQ FT: 25,000
SALES (est): 1.5MM **Privately Held**
WEB: www.midwestaircraft.com
SIC: 3728 Aircraft parts & equipment

(G-12482)
MINNICH MANUFACTURING CO INC
1444 State Route 42 (44903-9509)
P.O. Box 367 (44901-0367)
PHONE 419 903-0010
James R Minnich, *President*
Allen Bragg, *Engineer*
Todd Jurjevic, *Manager*
▲ **EMP:** 25
SQ FT: 43,000
SALES (est): 9.2MM **Privately Held**
WEB: www.minnich-mfg.com
SIC: 3531 Vibrators for concrete construction

(G-12483)
MIP INTERENT ENTERPRISES LLC
Also Called: Boxdrop Mansfield Mattress
720c 5th Ave (44905-1421)
PHONE 614 917-8705
Baron Johnson,
EMP: 35
SQ FT: 900
SALES (est): 2.9MM **Privately Held**
SIC: 2759 7336 Commercial printing; commercial art & graphic design

(G-12484)
MK METAL PRODUCTS INC (PA)
Also Called: Mavericks Stainless
90 Sawyer Pkwy (44903-6514)
P.O. Box 878 (44901-0878)
PHONE 419 756-3644
Richard L Kemp, *CEO*
J Douglas Drusbal, *Principal*
David Cole, *Vice Pres*
EMP: 35 **EST:** 1956
SQ FT: 39,000
SALES (est): 6.3MM **Privately Held**
WEB: www.mkmetalproducts.com
SIC: 3441 Fabricated structural metal

(G-12485)
MODERN BUILDERS SUPPLY INC
85 Smith Ave (44905-2854)
PHONE 419 526-0002
Rich Graham, *Manager*
EMP: 12
SALES (corp-wide): 347.7MM **Privately Held**
WEB: www.polaristechnologies.com
SIC: 5032 3089 5033 5031 Brick, stone & related material; doors, folding; plastic or plastic coated fabric; windows, plastic; roofing, asphalt & sheet metal; kitchen cabinets
PA: Modern Builders Supply, Inc.
3500 Phillips Ave
Toledo OH 43608
419 241-3961

(G-12486)
MORITZ CONCRETE INC
362 N Trimble Rd (44906-2541)
P.O. Box 1342 (44901-1342)
PHONE 419 529-3232
Martin F Moritz Jr, *President*
Peter Moritz, *Assistant VP*
James Moritz, *Vice Pres*
Robert Moritz, *Treasurer*
Joe Moritz, *Admin Sec*
EMP: 47
SQ FT: 260,000
SALES (est): 7.5MM **Privately Held**
WEB: www.moritzconcrete.com
SIC: 3273 Ready-mixed concrete

(G-12487)
MORITZ INTERNATIONAL INC
665 N Main St (44902-4201)
PHONE 419 526-5222
Frank Moritz, *President*
Carol Moritz, *Vice Pres*
Thomas R Moritz, *Vice Pres*
Dan Teutschmann, *Manager*
EMP: 37
SQ FT: 50,000
SALES (est): 11.5MM **Privately Held**
WEB: www.moritzinternational.com
SIC: 3715 Truck trailers

(G-12488)
MR ELECTRIC
24 Bell St (44906)
P.O. Box 572, Bellville (44813-0572)
PHONE 419 289-7474
Tom Lamp, *Owner*
EMP: 5
SALES (est): 379.2K **Privately Held**
SIC: 5063 3699 1731 Generators; electrical equipment & supplies; electrical work

(G-12489)
NATIONAL PATENT ANALYTICAL SYS
2090 Harrington Mem Rd (44903-8051)
P.O. Box 1435 (44901-1435)
PHONE 419 526-6727
John Fusco, *President*
EMP: 31
SQ FT: 2,000
SALES (est): 6.2MM **Privately Held**
WEB: www.npas.com
SIC: 3829 Breathalyzers

(G-12490)
NEWMAN TECHNOLOGY INC (HQ)
100 Cairns Rd (44903-8990)
PHONE 419 525-1856
Takuji Shimizu, *President*
Yukihisa Murata, *Exec VP*
Stephen Rourke, *Senior VP*
Mike Blevins, *QC Mgr*
Tom Bader, *Finance Mgr*
▲ **EMP:** 217
SQ FT: 450,000
SALES (est): 404.8MM
SALES (corp-wide): 12.3MM **Privately Held**
WEB: www.newmantech.com
SIC: 3714 3751 Mufflers (exhaust), motor vehicle; motorcycle accessories
PA: Sankei Giken Co.,Ltd.
1024-10, Niihori
Kawaguchi STM 334-0
482 959-460

(G-12491)
NEWSPAPER NETWORK CENTRAL OH
70 W 4th St (44903-1676)
PHONE 419 524-3545
Tom Brennan, *Principal*
EMP: 8
SALES (est): 555.4K **Privately Held**
WEB: www.nncogannett.com
SIC: 2711 Newspapers, publishing & printing

(G-12492)
NEXT GENERATION BAG INC
230 Industrial Dr (44904-1346)
PHONE 419 884-1327
John D Frecka, *CEO*
EMP: 350
SALES (est): 28.8MM **Privately Held**
SIC: 2673 Plastic bags; made from purchased materials

(G-12493)
NEXT GENERATION FILMS INC
215 Industrial Dr (44904-1347)
PHONE 419 884-8150
David Frecka, *Manager*
Dody Matthews, *Manager*
Jodi Mooney, *Receptionist*
EMP: 284 **Privately Held**
WEB: www.nextgenfilms.com
SIC: 2671 Plastic film, coated or laminated for packaging
PA: Next Generation Films, Inc.
230 Industrial Dr
Lexington OH 44904

(G-12494)
NORMANT CANDY CO
Also Called: Normant's Salt Water Taffy
1821 Mock Rd (44904-9302)
PHONE 419 886-4214
Richard Normant, *Owner*
EMP: 18
SALES (est): 1.5MM **Privately Held**
SIC: 2064 5441 Candy & other confectionery products; candy

(G-12495)
OGS TOOL & MANUFACTURING
3520 N Main St (44903-9735)
PHONE 419 524-6200
Scott Miller, *Owner*
EMP: 5
SQ FT: 4,000
SALES (est): 388.2K **Privately Held**
SIC: 3544 Special dies, tools, jigs & fixtures

(G-12496)
OHIO ELECTRIC MOTOR SVC LLC
311 E 3rd St (44902-1511)
PHONE 419 525-2225
EMP: 4
SALES (corp-wide): 1.7MM **Privately Held**
SIC: 7699 7694 5063 3699 Repair Services Armature Rewinding Whol Electrical Equip Mfg Elec Mach/Equip/Supp
PA: Ohio Electric Motor Service, Llc
1909 E Livingston Ave
Columbus OH 43209
614 444-1451

(G-12497)
OHIO VALLEY MANUFACTURING INC
1501 Harrington Mem Rd (44903-8995)
PHONE 419 522-5818
Michael C Fanello, *President*
John Fanello, *President*
Jeff Fanello, *Vice Pres*
Steven Fanello, *Vice Pres*

Thom Weber, *CFO*
EMP: 80
SQ FT: 75,000
SALES (est): 30.8MM **Privately Held**
WEB: www.ohiovalleymfg.com
SIC: 3469 3399 Stamping metal for the trade; flakes, metal

(G-12498)
OHIO VLY STMPNG-ASSEMBLIES INC
500 Newman St (44902-1122)
PHONE.................419 522-0983
Todd J Flagel, *Principal*
Bob Ganfield, *Engineer*
EMP: 30
SALES (est): 4.6MM **Privately Held**
SIC: 3297 Nonclay refractories

(G-12499)
OMEGA TEK INC
649 Old Mill Run Rd (44906-3474)
P.O. Box 185, Shelby (44875-0185)
PHONE.................419 756-9580
James C Hudson, *President*
Marguerite Hudson, *Vice Pres*
EMP: 6
SALES: 500K **Privately Held**
SIC: 3625 Control circuit relays, industrial

(G-12500)
OUR DETERGENT INC
Also Called: D.B.G. Cleaners
101 Knight Pkwy (44903-6548)
PHONE.................419 589-5571
Suzanne Stewart, *President*
James C Stewart, *Principal*
John C Stewart, *Vice Pres*
EMP: 3
SQ FT: 6,000
SALES (est): 350K **Privately Held**
SIC: 2841 Detergents, synthetic organic or inorganic alkaline

(G-12501)
P C R RESTORATIONS INC
Also Called: Lehr Awning Co
933 W Longview Ave (44906-2133)
PHONE.................419 747-7957
Phillip E Russell, *President*
Debbie Russell, *Vice Pres*
EMP: 16
SQ FT: 11,000
SALES (est): 1.9MM **Privately Held**
WEB: www.pcr-lehrawning.com
SIC: 2394 3089 2221 5999 Canvas awnings & canopies; awnings, fiberglass & plastic combination; upholstery, tapestry & wall covering fabrics; awnings

(G-12502)
PRECISION SWITCHING INC
2090 Harrington Mem Rd (44903-8051)
P.O. Box 1435 (44901-1435)
PHONE.................800 800-8143
John Fusco, *President*
Daniel Fusco, *Vice Pres*
EMP: 7
SQ FT: 10,000
SALES (est): 896.1K **Privately Held**
SIC: 3613 3677 3672 3625 Switchgear & switchboard apparatus; electronic coils, transformers & other inductors; printed circuit boards; relays & industrial controls; transformers, except electric

(G-12503)
R M DAVIS INC
Also Called: Mall Compan, The
517 Walfield Dr (44904-1649)
PHONE.................419 756-6719
Richard Byus, *President*
Dora Byus, *Admin Sec*
Amanda Neuts, *Admin Asst*
EMP: 3
SQ FT: 4,900
SALES: 275K **Privately Held**
SIC: 3993 1799 Electric signs; sign installation & maintenance

(G-12504)
R M INDUSTRIES INC
95 Ohio Brass Rd (44902-1029)
PHONE.................419 529-8970
Robert Mc Coy, *President*
Linda S Mc Coy, *Corp Secy*

EMP: 5
SQ FT: 11,000
SALES (est): 505.5K **Privately Held**
SIC: 3999 Education aids, devices & supplies

(G-12505)
RICHLAND BLUE PRINTCOM INC
1069 Park Ave W (44906-2811)
P.O. Box 903 (44901-0903)
PHONE.................419 524-2781
Toll Free:...............888 -
Mary Beth Motta, *President*
Kristen Lackey, *Corp Secy*
Kristen McGuire, *Manager*
EMP: 3
SQ FT: 3,000
SALES (est): 750.1K **Privately Held**
WEB: www.richlandblueprint.com
SIC: 7334 7389 5999 2759 Blueprinting service; printers' services: folding, collating; architectural supplies; commercial printing; engineers' equipment & supplies

(G-12506)
RICHLAND NEWHOPE INDUSTRIES (PA)
150 E 4th St (44902-1520)
P.O. Box 916 (44901-0916)
PHONE.................419 774-4400
Peggy Hamblin, *Vice Pres*
Greg Young, *Prdtn Mgr*
Elizabeth Prather, *Exec Dir*
EMP: 250
SQ FT: 63,000
SALES: 6.4MM **Privately Held**
SIC: 0782 2448 7349 8331 Lawn & garden services; wood pallets & skids; building maintenance services; job training & vocational rehabilitation services; packaging & labeling services

(G-12507)
RICHLAND SCREW MACHINE PDTS
531 Grant St (44903-1213)
P.O. Box 696 (44901-0696)
PHONE.................419 524-1272
Randall L Schoenman, *President*
EMP: 22 **EST:** 1946
SQ FT: 15,000
SALES (est): 3.6MM **Privately Held**
WEB: www.richlandscrewmachine.com
SIC: 3451 Screw machine products

(G-12508)
RURAL FARM DISTRIBUTORS CO
2690 Bowman Street Rd (44903-7429)
PHONE.................419 747-6807
EMP: 3
SALES (corp-wide): 3.3MM **Privately Held**
SIC: 2875 5191 Mfg Fertilizers-Mix Only Whol Farm Supplies
PA: Rural Farm Distributors, Co.
2680 Olivesburg Rd
Mansfield OH

(G-12509)
RUSSELL T BUNDY ASSOCIATES INC
Also Called: Pan-Glo
1711 N Main St (44903-8111)
PHONE.................419 526-4454
William Matzke, *Manager*
EMP: 30
SALES (corp-wide): 62MM **Privately Held**
SIC: 3479 Pan glazing
PA: Russell T. Bundy Associates, Inc.
417 E Water St Ste 1
Urbana OH 43078
937 652-2151

(G-12510)
S & S MACHINING LTD
76 Atenway St (44902-1025)
PHONE.................419 524-9525
Cliff Shindeldecker, *Partner*
Rhonda Shindeldecker, *Partner*
EMP: 10
SQ FT: 7,000

SALES: 600K **Privately Held**
SIC: 3451 Screw machine products

(G-12511)
SASH FOAM WORKS INC
555 Park Ave E (44905-2871)
P.O. Box 1494 (44901-1494)
PHONE.................419 522-4074
Gary Haverfield, *President*
EMP: 3
SALES (est): 414.5K **Privately Held**
SIC: 3086 Packaging & shipping materials, foamed plastic

(G-12512)
SHELLY FISHER
Also Called: P P C Greatstuff Co
449 Newman St (44902-1123)
PHONE.................419 522-6696
Shelley Fisher, *Principal*
EMP: 100
SALES (est): 7.4MM **Privately Held**
SIC: 3089 Injection molding of plastics

(G-12513)
SIR STEAK MACHINERY INC
40 Baird Pkwy (44903-7908)
PHONE.................419 526-9181
James Munroe, *President*
Michael J Biro, *Vice Pres*
Richard C Biro, *Vice Pres*
Dean Schlichting, *Treasurer*
Barbara Burkhardt, *Office Mgr*
EMP: 20
SQ FT: 37,500
SALES (est): 4MM
SALES (corp-wide): 22MM **Privately Held**
WEB: www.birosaw.com
SIC: 3549 Metalworking machinery
PA: The Biro Manufacturing Company
1114 W Main St
Marblehead OH 43440
419 798-4451

(G-12514)
SKYBOX INVESTMENTS INC
Also Called: Brasspack Packing Supply
1275 Pollock Pkwy (44905-1374)
P.O. Box 1567 (44901-1567)
PHONE.................419 525-6013
James Miller, *CEO*
Marc Miller, *Corp Secy*
Marty Ross, *Vice Pres*
Rodney Robertson, *Vice Pres*
Joseph R Murach, *CFO*
EMP: 45
SQ FT: 60,000
SALES (est): 15MM **Privately Held**
SIC: 2653 Boxes, corrugated: made from purchased materials

(G-12515)
SKYBOX PACKAGING LLC
Also Called: Mr Box
1275 Pollock Pkwy (44905-1374)
P.O. Box 1567 (44901-1567)
PHONE.................419 525-7209
Marc Miller, *President*
Jan Piko, *Regl Sales Mgr*
EMP: 73
SALES (est): 15.7MM
SALES (corp-wide): 882.3MM **Privately Held**
SIC: 3086 5199 Packaging & shipping materials, foamed plastic; packaging materials
PA: Atlantic Packaging Products Ltd
111 Progress Ave
Scarborough ON M1P 2
416 298-8101

(G-12516)
SLATER SILK SCREEN
323 Lenox Ave (44906-2521)
P.O. Box 9440, Fresno CA (93792-9440)
PHONE.................419 755-8337
Michael Slater, *Principal*
EMP: 3 **EST:** 2014
SALES (est): 215.7K **Privately Held**
SIC: 2759 Screen printing

(G-12517)
SNYDER MACHINE CO INC
256 N Diamond St (44902-1006)
PHONE.................419 526-1527

Joseph E Greene, *CEO*
Joseph A Greene, *President*
Joy Greene, *Corp Secy*
EMP: 5 **EST:** 1960
SQ FT: 9,000
SALES: 500K **Privately Held**
SIC: 3599 Machine shop, jobbing & repair

(G-12518)
SOLSYS INC
96 Vanderbilt Rd (44904-8603)
PHONE.................419 886-4683
Jeffrey C Mason, *President*
EMP: 7
SALES (est): 754.8K **Privately Held**
SIC: 3572 Computer storage devices

(G-12519)
STEIN INC
1490 Old Bowman St (44903-8805)
PHONE.................419 747-2611
EMP: 17 **EST:** 2010
SALES (est): 1.4MM **Privately Held**
SIC: 2431 Millwork

(G-12520)
STERLING COLLECTABLES INC
862 Pugh Rd (44903-8755)
PHONE.................419 892-5708
Kelly Spencer, *President*
EMP: 6 **EST:** 2011
SALES (est): 318.8K **Privately Held**
SIC: 3999 5199 Christmas tree ornaments, except electrical & glass; Christmas novelties; Christmas trees, including artificial

(G-12521)
STRASSELLS MACHINE INC
1015 Springmill St (44906-1571)
PHONE.................419 747-1088
Michael Strassell, *President*
Kimberly Strassell, *Vice Pres*
EMP: 10
SQ FT: 1,600
SALES (est): 1.8MM **Privately Held**
SIC: 3599 Machine shop, jobbing & repair

(G-12522)
SUGAR SHACK
4703 Flowers Rd (44903-7780)
PHONE.................419 961-4016
Jessica Slusher, *Administration*
EMP: 4 **EST:** 2015
SALES (est): 152.2K **Privately Held**
SIC: 2051 Cakes, pies & pastries

(G-12523)
SUMMERS ACQUISITION CORP
10 W Piper Rd (44903-8116)
PHONE.................419 526-5800
Bill Atkins, *Branch Mgr*
EMP: 5
SALES (corp-wide): 3.1B **Privately Held**
WEB: www.summersrubber.com
SIC: 5085 3429 3052 Rubber goods, mechanical; manufactured hardware (general); rubber & plastics hose & beltings
HQ: Summers Acquisition Corporation
12555 Berea Rd
Cleveland OH 44111
216 941-7700

(G-12524)
SYSTEMS JAY LLC NANOGATE
Rohr Manufacturing Div
1555 W Longview Ave (44906-1806)
PHONE.................419 747-1096
David Jacot, *Branch Mgr*
EMP: 50
SALES (corp-wide): 219.6MM **Privately Held**
WEB: www.jayindinc.com
SIC: 3312 Tubes, steel & iron
HQ: Jay Nanogate Systems Llc
150 Longview Ave E
Mansfield OH 44903
419 524-3778

(G-12525)
SYSTEMS JAY LLC NANOGATE
Crestline Paint
515 Newman St (44902-1160)
PHONE.................419 522-7745
Steve Kunz, *Branch Mgr*
EMP: 130

Mansfield - Richland County (G-12526) GEOGRAPHIC SECTION

SALES (corp-wide): 219.6MM Privately Held
WEB: www.jayindinc.com
SIC: 3714 Motor vehicle parts & accessories
HQ: Jay Nanogate Systems Llc
 150 Longview Ave E
 Mansfield OH 44903
 419 524-3778

(G-12526)
TAYLOR METAL PRODUCTS CO
700 Springmill St (44903-1199)
PHONE.................419 522-3471
Richard G Taylor, President
Helen F Taylor, Vice Pres
Rich Storms, Maint Spvr
Greg Roach, Purch Agent
Scott Taylor, Sales Dir
▲ EMP: 155 EST: 1923
SQ FT: 160,000
SALES (est): 35.5MM Privately Held
WEB: www.tmpind.com
SIC: 3469 3465 Stamping metal for the trade; automotive stampings

(G-12527)
TE CONNECTIVITY CORPORATION
Cii Technologies Hartman Pdts
175 N Diamond St (44902-1004)
PHONE.................419 521-9500
Kathy Castor, Branch Mgr
EMP: 235
SALES (corp-wide): 13.1B Privately Held
WEB: www.raychem.com
SIC: 3613 3625 3812 3769 Power switching equipment; control panels, electric; relays, for electronic use; search & navigation equipment; guided missile & space vehicle parts & auxiliary equipment
HQ: Te Connectivity Corporation
 1050 Westlakes Dr
 Berwyn PA 19312
 610 893-9800

(G-12528)
THE MANSFIELD STRL & ERCT CO (PA)
Also Called: Mansfield Fabricated Products
429 Park Ave E (44905-2844)
P.O. Box 427 (44901-0427)
PHONE.................419 522-5911
Richard Gash, President
Barbara Gash, Corp Secy
EMP: 25 EST: 1924
SQ FT: 60,000
SALES (est): 6.3MM Privately Held
SIC: 3441 5051 Fabricated structural metal; metals service centers & offices

(G-12529)
THE MANSFIELD STRL & ERCT CO
Also Called: Mansfield Fabricated Products
817 Belmont Ave (44906-2022)
PHONE.................419 747-6571
Bill Kent, Office Mgr
EMP: 5
SALES (corp-wide): 6.3MM Privately Held
SIC: 3441 Fabricated structural metal
PA: Mansfield Structural And Erecting Company, The (Inc)
 429 Park Ave E
 Mansfield OH 44905
 419 522-5911

(G-12530)
THERM-O-DISC INCORPORATED (DH)
1320 S Main St (44907-5500)
PHONE.................419 525-8500
Charles C G, CEO
Scott Klonowski, Vice Pres
Martin Leslie, Vice Pres
Steve Richardson, Marketing Staff
▲ EMP: 900 EST: 1945
SQ FT: 333,400

SALES (est): 589.6MM
SALES (corp-wide): 17.4B Publicly Held
WEB: www.thermodisc.com
SIC: 3822 3823 Built-in thermostats, filled system & bimetal types; industrial instrmts msrmnt display/control process variable

(G-12531)
THORNTON POWDER COATINGS INC
2300 N Main St (44903-6703)
P.O. Box 1119 (44901-1119)
PHONE.................419 522-7183
James Thornton, President
Dawn Thornton, Vice Pres
EMP: 15
SQ FT: 20,000
SALES (est): 2MM Privately Held
SIC: 3479 Coating of metals & formed products

(G-12532)
TMS INTERNATIONAL LLC
1344 Bowman St (44903-4009)
P.O. Box 2000, Glassport PA (15045-0600)
PHONE.................419 747-5500
EMP: 5 Privately Held
SIC: 3312 Blast Furnace-Steel Works
HQ: Tms International, Llc
 12 Monongahela Ave
 Glassport PA 15045
 412 678-6141

(G-12533)
TRI R TOOLING INC
220 Piper Rd (44905-1370)
PHONE.................419 522-8665
Robert John, President
Rudy John, Vice Pres
Renee John, Treasurer
EMP: 12
SQ FT: 6,500
SALES (est): 1.8MM Privately Held
WEB: www.trirtooling.com
SIC: 3599 Machine shop, jobbing & repair

(G-12534)
TRIDICO SILK SCREEN & SIGN CO
162 N Diamond St (44902-1326)
PHONE.................419 526-1695
Michael T Tridico, Owner
EMP: 3 EST: 1976
SQ FT: 25,000
SALES (est): 275.6K Privately Held
SIC: 3993 7336 5198 Signs & advertising specialties; silk screen design; stain

(G-12535)
VIDONISH STUDIOS
Also Called: Vidonish Stained Glass Studio
20 E Main St (44904-1223)
PHONE.................419 884-1119
Cherri Vidonish, Managing Prtnr
Bill Vidonish, Partner
EMP: 4
SQ FT: 1,700
SALES: 220K Privately Held
SIC: 3231 Stained glass: made from purchased glass

(G-12536)
WALTER GRAPHICS INC
850 Oak St (44907-1452)
P.O. Box 3781 (44907-0781)
PHONE.................419 522-5261
Herbert F Walter, President
Susan Walter, Corp Secy
Phillip Walter, Vice Pres
EMP: 3
SQ FT: 5,000
SALES (est): 381K Privately Held
SIC: 2752 Commercial printing, offset

(G-12537)
WARREN RUPP INC
800 N Main St (44902-4209)
P.O. Box 1568 (44901-1568)
PHONE.................419 524-8388
Scott Aiello, President
John Carter, President
Dan Johnston, Vice Pres
David Marsh, Maint Spvr
Robyn Montgomery, Buyer
▲ EMP: 224

SQ FT: 80,000
SALES (est): 67.1MM
SALES (corp-wide): 2.4B Publicly Held
WEB: www.warrenrupp.com
SIC: 3561 Pumps & pumping equipment
PA: Idex Corporation
 1925 W Field Ct Ste 200
 Lake Forest IL 60045
 847 498-7070

(G-12538)
WATERSOURCE LLC
1225 W Longview Ave (44906-1907)
PHONE.................419 747-9552
Craig Bodell, Branch Mgr
EMP: 5
SALES (est): 545.8K
SALES (corp-wide): 2.1MM Privately Held
SIC: 3261 Plumbing fixtures, vitreous china
PA: Watersource, L.L.C.
 330 Milan Ave
 Norwalk OH 44857
 419 747-9552

(G-12539)
WEISS INDUSTRIES INC
Also Called: Weiss Metallurgical Services
2480 N Main St (44903-8555)
P.O. Box 157 (44901-0157)
PHONE.................419 526-2480
Rudolph Weiss, President
Robert Nikolaus, Principal
Maria Weiss, Principal
Paul Jamieson, Opers Mgr
John Schutte, Engineer
EMP: 30 EST: 1954
SQ FT: 40,000
SALES: 5MM Privately Held
WEB: www.weissind.com
SIC: 3469 3398 3544 Metal stampings; metal heat treating; special dies & tools

(G-12540)
WESTINGHOUSE A BRAKE TECH CORP
472 Rembrandt St (44902-7015)
PHONE.................419 526-5323
EMP: 96
SALES (corp-wide): 4.3B Publicly Held
SIC: 3743 Brakes, air & vacuum: railway
PA: Westinghouse Air Brake Technologies Corporation
 1001 Airbrake Ave
 Wilmerding PA 15148
 412 825-1000

Mantua
Portage County

(G-12541)
AETNA PLASTICS CORP
Also Called: Vanguard Fabrication Division
4466 Orchard St (44255-9049)
PHONE.................330 274-2855
James Bailey, Manager
EMP: 5
SALES (corp-wide): 16.2MM Privately Held
WEB: www.aetnaplastics.com
SIC: 3272 3089 3443 7389 Panels & sections, prefabricated concrete; ducting, plastic; tanks, standard or custom fabricated: metal plate; metal cutting services; plastics pipe; laminated plastics plate & sheet
PA: Aetna Plastics Corp.
 9075 Bank St
 Cleveland OH 44125
 330 762-1901

(G-12542)
ASSOCIATED ASSOCIATES INC
Also Called: Associated Ready Mix Concrete
9551 Elliman Rd (44255-9440)
P.O. Box 670538, Northfield (44067-0538)
PHONE.................330 626-3300
Harold Joslin, President
Sandra Riha, Admin Sec
EMP: 20
SQ FT: 2,700

SALES (est): 3.1MM Privately Held
SIC: 3273 5211 Ready-mixed concrete; masonry materials & supplies

(G-12543)
BEARDED SHUTTER ◆
10821 John Edward Dr (44255-9411)
PHONE.................440 567-8568
Stewart Thompson, Owner
EMP: 3 EST: 2018
SALES (est): 183K Privately Held
SIC: 3442 Shutters, door or window: metal

(G-12544)
CREATIVE PROCESSING INC
17540 Rapids Rd (44255)
P.O. Box 708, Burton (44021-0708)
PHONE.................440 834-4070
Daniel Piscura Jr, President
Freida Piscura, Admin Sec
EMP: 12
SQ FT: 10,000
SALES (est): 1.9MM Privately Held
SIC: 3599 Machine shop, jobbing & repair

(G-12545)
DESIGN FABRICATORS OF MANTUA
10612 Main St (44255-9636)
PHONE.................330 274-5353
Paul Janson, President
Cindy Janson, Corp Secy
EMP: 4
SQ FT: 6,800
SALES (est): 880.1K Privately Held
SIC: 3559 Chemical machinery & equipment

(G-12546)
GALLAGHER LUMBER CO
10272 Vaughn Rd (44255-9745)
P.O. Box 698 (44255-0698)
PHONE.................330 274-2333
Lel Gallagher, Owner
Terry Gallagher, Owner
EMP: 3
SALES (est): 252.4K Privately Held
SIC: 2448 Pallets, wood

(G-12547)
GOODELL FARMS
5212 Goodell Rd (44255-9746)
PHONE.................330 274-2161
Jay Goodell, Partner
EMP: 5
SALES (est): 343.6K Privately Held
SIC: 0241 0134 2099 Dairy farms; Irish potatoes; maple syrup

(G-12548)
HYDRA AIR EQUIPMENT INC
9222 State Route 44 (44255-9709)
P.O. Box 1324, Kent (44240-0025)
PHONE.................330 274-2222
Dennis Marn, President
Ann Marn, Vice Pres
Shirley Stanley, Treasurer
EMP: 4
SQ FT: 6,000
SALES: 190K Privately Held
SIC: 3545 5084 Machine tool attachments & accessories; hydraulic systems equipment & supplies

(G-12549)
INDUSTRIAL CONNECTIONS INC
11730 Timber Point Trl (44255-9694)
PHONE.................330 274-2155
Wendy Carlton, President
▼ EMP: 6
SQ FT: 7,000
SALES: 4MM Privately Held
SIC: 5085 3492 Industrial fittings; lapidary equipment; hose & tube fittings & assemblies, hydraulic/pneumatic

(G-12550)
LAKESIDE SAND & GRAVEL INC
3498 Frost Rd (44255-9136)
PHONE.................330 274-2569
Larry Kotkowski, President
Ronald Kotkowski, Corp Secy
EMP: 25
SQ FT: 4,200

GEOGRAPHIC SECTION

Maple Heights - Cuyahoga County (G-12576)

SALES: 1.6MM **Privately Held**
SIC: 1442 Construction sand mining; gravel mining

(G-12551)
MANTALINE CORPORATION
Also Called: Transportation Group
4754 E High St (44255-9201)
PHONE..................................330 274-2264
Bryan Fink, *Manager*
Bryan N Fink, *Manager*
EMP: 75
SALES (corp-wide): 35.2MM **Privately Held**
WEB: www.mantaline.com
SIC: 5169 3061 Synthetic rubber; mechanical rubber goods
PA: Mantaline Corporation
  4754 E High St
  Mantua OH 44255
  330 274-2264

(G-12552)
MAR-ZANE INC
9551 Elliman Rd (44255-9440)
PHONE..................................330 626-2079
Jeff Parks, *Superintendent*
EMP: 3
SALES (corp-wide): 276.3MM **Privately Held**
SIC: 2951 1611 Asphalt paving mixtures & blocks; surfacing & paving
HQ: Mar-Zane, Inc.
  3570 S River Rd
  Zanesville OH 43701
  740 453-0721

(G-12553)
MEDICAL IMAGING DIST LLC
Also Called: Mid
11823 State Route 44 (44255-9647)
PHONE..................................800 898-3392
Donald Mori, *CEO*
Stephen Hayes, *President*
Brett Schaeffer, *COO*
Craig McCowin, *Vice Pres*
Matt Wurm, *CFO*
EMP: 5
SALES (est): 327.6K **Privately Held**
SIC: 3826 Magnetic resonance imaging apparatus

(G-12554)
MERIDIENNE INTERNATIONAL INC
Also Called: Atlantic Water Gardens
4494 Orchard St (44255-9049)
PHONE..................................330 274-8317
William Lynne, *President*
Kyle Weemhoff, *Sales Staff*
Brandon Dwyer, *Manager*
◆ EMP: 7
SQ FT: 15,000
SALES: 2.5MM **Privately Held**
SIC: 3083 1799 3271 0781 Laminated plastics plate & sheet; fountain installation; blocks, concrete; landscape or retaining wall; landscape services
PA: Oase Living Water Gmbh
  Tecklenburger Str. 161
  Horstel
  545 480-0

(G-12555)
O K BRUGMANN JR & SONS INC
4083 Mennonite Rd (44255-9413)
PHONE..................................330 274-2106
Oscar Brugmann Jr, *President*
Mark Brugmann, *Principal*
Gail Brugmann, *Vice Pres*
EMP: 12
SALES (est): 2.2MM **Privately Held**
SIC: 5032 5211 3273 3272 Concrete & cinder building products; concrete & cinder block; ready-mixed concrete; concrete products

(G-12556)
OSCAR BRUGMANN SAND & GRAVEL
3828 Dudley Rd (44255-9426)
PHONE..................................330 274-8224
Roy Brugmann, *President*
Olga Van Auken, *Admin Sec*
Joan Martin, *Asst Sec*
EMP: 14

SQ FT: 1,000
SALES (est): 3.4MM **Privately Held**
SIC: 1442 Construction sand mining; gravel mining

(G-12557)
P & S WELDING CO
11611 Mantua Center Rd (44255-9447)
P.O. Box 842 (44255-0842)
PHONE..................................330 274-2850
Victor Grimm, *President*
EMP: 3
SQ FT: 3,200
SALES (est): 331K **Privately Held**
SIC: 3089 1799 Plastic processing; welding on site

(G-12558)
SHELLY MATERIALS INC
3943 Beck Rd (44255-9471)
PHONE..................................330 274-0802
Bruce Ahrens, *Branch Mgr*
EMP: 4
SALES (corp-wide): 29.7B **Privately Held**
SIC: 1422 Crushed & broken limestone
HQ: Shelly Materials, Inc.
  80 Park Dr
  Thornville OH 43076
  740 246-6315

(G-12559)
SINGLETON REELS INC
11783 Timber Point Trl (44255-9694)
PHONE..................................330 274-2961
Scott Hamilton, *President*
Kelly Brode, *Office Mgr*
Rob Garro, *Director*
Dave Miller, *Executive*
EMP: 20 EST: 1972
SQ FT: 28,000
SALES (est): 5.6MM **Privately Held**
WEB: www.singletonreels.com
SIC: 2499 Reels, plywood

(G-12560)
STAMM CONTRACTING CO INC
4566 Orchard St (44255-9701)
P.O. Box 450 (44255-0450)
PHONE..................................330 274-8230
Hal Stamm, *President*
Elva Novotny, *Corp Secy*
Quinn Novotny, *Exec VP*
Jason Hielman, *Purch Agent*
Matt Tucek, *Sales Executive*
EMP: 40 EST: 1913
SQ FT: 1,500
SALES (est): 5.9MM **Privately Held**
WEB: www.stammcontracting.com
SIC: 3273 1541 1542 5211 Ready-mixed concrete; industrial buildings & warehouses; commercial & office building contractors; lumber & other building materials; brick, stone & related material; concrete work

(G-12561)
VICTORY ATHLETICS INC
10702 Second St (44255-8300)
PHONE..................................330 274-2854
Butch Schultz, *President*
EMP: 3
SALES (est): 243.3K **Privately Held**
WEB: www.victoryathleticsinc.com
SIC: 3949 Sporting & athletic goods

(G-12562)
VISUAL ART GRAPHIC SERVICES
5244 Goodell Rd (44255-9746)
PHONE..................................330 274-2775
George South, *President*
EMP: 30
SQ FT: 35,000
SALES (est): 3MM **Privately Held**
WEB: www.evisualarts.com
SIC: 2752 7336 Commercial printing, lithographic; commercial art & graphic design

---

Maple Heights
Cuyahoga County

(G-12563)
A-1 MANUFACTURING CORP
5446 Dunham Rd (44137-3653)
PHONE..................................216 475-6084
Robert Hill, *President*
Marlene Hill, *Treasurer*
EMP: 9
SQ FT: 20,000
SALES (est): 1.7MM **Privately Held**
SIC: 3469 Stamping metal for the trade

(G-12564)
ALTERNATE DEFENSE LLC
19101 Watercrest Ave (44137-3152)
PHONE..................................216 225-5889
Ronald Mitchell, *Administration*
EMP: 3
SALES (est): 160K **Privately Held**
SIC: 3812 Defense systems & equipment

(G-12565)
BARNES SERVICES LLC
20677 Centuryway Rd (44137-3116)
PHONE..................................440 319-2088
Leon Barnes, *Principal*
EMP: 6
SALES (est): 149.9K **Privately Held**
SIC: 1389 Construction, repair & dismantling services

(G-12566)
BOGGS GRAPHIC EQUIPMENT LLC
14901 Broadway Ave (44137-1107)
P.O. Box 544, Newbury (44065-0544)
PHONE..................................888 837-8101
Christopher Boggs, *Vice Pres*
Jack L Boggs,
▼ EMP: 9
SALES (est): 2MM **Privately Held**
WEB: www.boggsgraphics.com
SIC: 3565 3555 5084 Packaging machinery; printing presses; printing trades machinery, equipment & supplies

(G-12567)
BROWN-CAMPBELL COMPANY
Also Called: Brown-Campbell Steel
14400 Industrial Ave S (44137-3253)
PHONE..................................216 332-0101
Raymond Gualtier, *Manager*
EMP: 10
SQ FT: 12,000
SALES (est): 1.3MM
SALES (corp-wide): 100.1MM **Privately Held**
WEB: www.brown-campbell.com
SIC: 3446 Gratings, open steel flooring
PA: Brown-Campbell Company
  11800 Investment Dr
  Shelby Township MI 48315
  586 884-2180

(G-12568)
CHARLES SVEC INC (PA)
Also Called: Rock Lite
5470 Dunham Rd (44137-3690)
PHONE..................................216 662-5200
Michael Svec, *President*
Dean Svec, *Corp Secy*
Thann Peacock, *Plant Supt*
John Sanuk, *Sales Mgr*
Keith Chipchase, *Office Mgr*
EMP: 20
SQ FT: 25,000
SALES (est): 2.3MM **Privately Held**
SIC: 3271 3272 Concrete block & brick; concrete products

(G-12569)
CLIFTON STEEL COMPANY (PA)
16500 Rockside Rd (44137-4324)
PHONE..................................216 662-6111
Herbert C Neides, *President*
Howard Feldenkris, *Vice Pres*
Bruce Goodman, *Vice Pres*
Pamela Neides, *Human Res Mgr*
▲ EMP: 95
SQ FT: 160,000

SALES (est): 62.8MM **Privately Held**
WEB: www.cliftonsteel.com
SIC: 5051 3441 3443 3398 Steel; structural shapes, iron or steel; fabricated structural metal; metal parts; metal heat treating

(G-12570)
DEWITT INC
Also Called: Non-Ferrous Heat Treating
14450 Industrial Ave N (44137-3249)
PHONE..................................216 662-0800
John Whittaker, *President*
Joe Frankhauser, *Treasurer*
EMP: 8 EST: 1957
SQ FT: 10,000
SALES: 580K **Privately Held**
SIC: 3398 Metal heat treating

(G-12571)
DR Z AMPS INC
Also Called: Dr Z Amplification
17011 Broadway Ave (44137-3407)
PHONE..................................216 475-1444
Michael D Zaite, *President*
EMP: 10
SQ FT: 3,500
SALES: 2MM **Privately Held**
WEB: www.drzamps.com
SIC: 3651 Amplifiers: radio, public address or musical instrument

(G-12572)
EUCLID WELDING CO INC
16500 Rockside Rd (44137-4324)
PHONE..................................216 289-0714
John Varljen, *Principal*
EMP: 5
SALES (est): 704.1K **Privately Held**
SIC: 7692 Welding repair

(G-12573)
HANGER PRSTHETCS & ORTHO INC
16480 Broadway Ave (44137-2659)
PHONE..................................216 475-4211
Matt Manolio, *Manager*
EMP: 8
SALES (corp-wide): 1B **Publicly Held**
SIC: 3842 Orthopedic appliances
HQ: Hanger Prosthetics & Orthotics, Inc.
  10910 Domain Dr Ste 300
  Austin TX 78758
  512 777-3800

(G-12574)
JR LARRY KNIGHT
Also Called: High Kinky Plastic
5260 Cato St (44137-1416)
PHONE..................................216 762-3141
Larry Knight Jr, *Owner*
EMP: 4
SALES: 410K **Privately Held**
SIC: 3089 Kitchenware, plastic

(G-12575)
OHIO MAGNETICS INC
5400 Dunham Rd (44137-3653)
PHONE..................................216 662-8484
Thomas J Pozda, *CEO*
Randy L Greely, *Ch of Bd*
▲ EMP: 36
SQ FT: 140,000
SALES (est): 9.2MM
SALES (corp-wide): 261.6MM **Privately Held**
WEB: www.ohiomagnetics.com
SIC: 3499 3559 3669 3625 Magnets, permanent: metallic; separation equipment, magnetic; metal detectors; relays & industrial controls; motors & generators; conveyors & conveying equipment
HQ: Peerless-Winsmith, Inc.
  5200 Upper Metro Pl # 110
  Dublin OH 43017
  614 526-7000

(G-12576)
OR-TEC INC
14500 Industrial Ave S (44137-3255)
PHONE..................................216 475-5225
Ciaran O-Mezia, *President*
David Marriott, *General Mgr*
▲ EMP: 9

Maple Heights - Cuyahoga County (G-12577)

SALES (est): 1.7MM **Privately Held**
SIC: 3589 Water treatment equipment, industrial

(G-12577)
R AND D INCORPORATED
16645 Granite Rd (44137-4301)
PHONE 216 581-6328
Mary Lou Jester, *Ch of Bd*
Kerry Keyes, *President*
EMP: 27 **EST:** 1962
SQ FT: 20,000
SALES: 6.1MM **Privately Held**
SIC: 2653 2652 Boxes, corrugated: made from purchased materials; setup paperboard boxes

(G-12578)
RACELITE SOUTH COAST INC
16518 Broadway Ave (44137-2602)
P.O. Box 370076 (44137-9076)
PHONE 216 581-4600
James Sima, *President*
Mary Sima, *Vice Pres*
Maryann Sima, *Admin Sec*
EMP: 10 **EST:** 1967
SQ FT: 5,000
SALES (est): 720K **Privately Held**
SIC: 3429 3732 3469 3312 Marine hardware; boat building & repairing; metal stampings; blast furnaces & steel mills

(G-12579)
SALON STYLING CONCEPTS LTD
Also Called: One Styling
20900 Libby Rd (44137-2929)
PHONE 216 539-0437
Eun Joo Park, *President*
▲ **EMP:** 20 **EST:** 2011
SALES (est): 1.7MM **Privately Held**
SIC: 3999 Hair curlers, designed for beauty parlors

(G-12580)
ST LAWRENCE HOLDINGS LLC
16500 Rockside Rd (44137-4324)
PHONE 330 562-9000
Herbert Neides, *President*
Jonh Zanin, *Controller*
Eileen Radcliffe, *Accounts Mgr*
EMP: 34
SALES: 8MM **Privately Held**
SIC: 5051 3443 3441 Steel; iron & steel (ferrous) products; fabricated plate work (boiler shop); fabricated structural metal

(G-12581)
SUNTWIST CORP
5461 Dunham Rd (44137-3644)
PHONE 800 935-3534
▲ **EMP:** 46
SQ FT: 38,000
SALES (est): 4.9MM **Privately Held**
SIC: 2759 Commercial Printing, Nec

(G-12582)
UNITED METAL FABRICATORS INC
14301 Industrial Ave S (44137-3252)
PHONE 216 662-2000
James A Martis, *Ch of Bd*
Stephen B Martis, *President*
Debra Perdue, *Office Mgr*
Roald Amundson, *Info Tech Mgr*
EMP: 30 **EST:** 1945
SQ FT: 16,500
SALES (est): 7.1MM **Privately Held**
WEB: www.unitedmetalfabricators.com
SIC: 3441 Fabricated structural metal

(G-12583)
US CORRUGATED OF MASSILLON
16645 Granite Rd (44137-4301)
PHONE 216 663-3344
Charles Messina, *CEO*
EMP: 15
SALES (est): 3.4MM **Privately Held**
SIC: 2653 Boxes, corrugated: made from purchased materials

Marblehead
Ottawa County

(G-12584)
BIRO MANUFACTURING COMPANY (PA)
1114 W Main St (43440-2099)
PHONE 419 798-4451
Richard C Biro, *President*
Carl G Biro, *Principal*
Michael J Biro, *Vice Pres*
Robert S Biro, *Vice Pres*
Bill Lacure, *Plant Mgr*
◆ **EMP:** 80
SQ FT: 76,000
SALES (est): 22MM **Privately Held**
SIC: 3556 Choppers, commercial, food

(G-12585)
FERGUSONS CUT GLASS WORKS
5890 East Harbor Rd (43440-9612)
PHONE 419 734-0808
Cary Ferguson, *President*
Jackie Ferguson, *Vice Pres*
EMP: 5
SQ FT: 10,000
SALES (est): 516.2K **Privately Held**
SIC: 3231 Leaded glass; furniture tops, glass: cut, beveled or polished; mirrored glass; decorated glassware: chipped, engraved, etched, etc.

(G-12586)
LAFARGE NORTH AMERICA INC
831 S Quarry Rd (43440-2576)
PHONE 419 798-4486
Jeff Grashel, *Manager*
EMP: 64
SALES (corp-wide): 26.4B **Privately Held**
WEB: www.lafargenorthamerica.com
SIC: 3273 Ready-mixed concrete
HQ: Lafarge North America Inc.
8700 W Bryn Mawr Ave
Chicago IL 60631
773 372-1000

(G-12587)
REEF RUNNER TACKLE CO INC
102 Cherry St (43440-2209)
P.O. Box 450 (43440-0450)
PHONE 419 798-9125
Scott Stecher, *President*
Elizabeth Stecher, *Corp Secy*
EMP: 6
SALES (est): 300K **Privately Held**
WEB: www.reefrunner.com
SIC: 3949 Lures, fishing: artificial

Marengo
Morrow County

(G-12588)
CHAMPION MANUFACTURING INC
4025 Bennington Way (43334-9536)
P.O. Box 2003, Westerville (43086-2003)
PHONE 419 253-7930
Mike Mills, *President*
Michael Mills, *General Mgr*
Dave Rose, *Director*
EMP: 4
SALES (est): 593.5K **Privately Held**
WEB: www.champion-mfg.com
SIC: 3069 Floor coverings, rubber

(G-12589)
CLEAR RUN LUMBER CO
2830 State Route 229 (43334-9456)
PHONE 740 747-2665
Millard Fisher, *Owner*
EMP: 3
SALES (est): 190.8K **Privately Held**
SIC: 2421 Sawmills & planing mills, general

(G-12590)
D & L MACHINING LLC
4621 Township Road 21 (43334-9706)
PHONE 419 253-1351
Don M Blair, *Principal*
EMP: 3 **EST:** 2001
SALES (est): 369.9K **Privately Held**
SIC: 3599 Machine shop, jobbing & repair

(G-12591)
FISHBURN TANK TRUCK SERVICE
5012 State Route 229 (43334-9634)
P.O. Box 278 (43334-0278)
PHONE 419 253-6031
Jack Fishburn, *Owner*
EMP: 60
SALES (est): 2.1MM **Privately Held**
SIC: 1389 Haulage, oil field

(G-12592)
HENSEL READY MIX
4050 Bennington Way (43334-9535)
PHONE 419 253-9200
EMP: 4
SALES (est): 29.5K **Privately Held**
SIC: 3273 5211 Ready-mixed concrete; concrete & cinder block

(G-12593)
MARENGO FABRICATED STEEL LTD (PA)
1089 County Road 26 (43334-9643)
P.O. Box 179 (43334-0179)
PHONE 800 919-2652
Rick Howell, *Partner*
Robert C Howell, *Partner*
Bob Howell, *General Ptnr*
Charlotte Howell, *Controller*
Michelle Mounts, *Office Mgr*
EMP: 17
SQ FT: 60,000
SALES (est): 3.4MM **Privately Held**
SIC: 3713 Tank truck bodies; dump truck bodies

(G-12594)
SELECT LOGGING
5739 Township Road 21 (43334-9710)
PHONE 419 564-0361
Jason Pauley, *Principal*
EMP: 3 **EST:** 2010
SALES (est): 219.2K **Privately Held**
SIC: 2411 Logging

(G-12595)
SIGN SMITH LLC
2760 County Road 26 (43334-9666)
PHONE 614 519-9144
Michael Shawn Smith, *Principal*
EMP: 5
SALES (est): 727.3K **Privately Held**
SIC: 3993 Signs & advertising specialties

(G-12596)
TWG NOODLE COMPANY LLC
1151 State Route 61 (43334-9498)
PHONE 419 560-2033
James Halpin,
EMP: 3
SALES (est): 91.3K **Privately Held**
SIC: 2098 Macaroni & spaghetti

Maria Stein
Mercer County

(G-12597)
3WAY MACHINE AND TOOL COMPANY
2411 Cssella Montezuma Rd (45860-9797)
PHONE 419 925-7222
David L Moorman, *President*
Lily Heart, *Vice Pres*
Dave Pottkotter, *Admin Sec*
EMP: 6
SQ FT: 3,500
SALES: 450K **Privately Held**
SIC: 3599 Machine shop, jobbing & repair

(G-12598)
BERGMAN TOOL & MACHINE CO
8066 Industrial Dr (45860-9546)
PHONE 419 925-4963
Ted Bergman, *President*
John Bergman, *Vice Pres*
EMP: 8
SQ FT: 8,000
SALES: 830K **Privately Held**
SIC: 3599 Mfg Industrial Machinery

(G-12599)
MANCO MANUFACTURING CO
2411 Rolfes Rd (45860-9708)
PHONE 419 925-4152
Nancy Nieberding, *President*
Patrick R Nieberding, *Vice Pres*
Eric Nieberding, *Treasurer*
EMP: 8
SQ FT: 14,000
SALES (est): 1.3MM **Privately Held**
SIC: 3441 Fabricated structural metal

(G-12600)
MOELLER BREW BARN LLC
8595 Irwin St (45860-9550)
PHONE 419 925-3005
Monica M Wright, *Principal*
EMP: 4
SALES (est): 96.1K **Privately Held**
SIC: 2082 Malt beverages

(G-12601)
UNIQUE COVERS
8758 State Route 119 (45860-9521)
PHONE 419 925-9600
Patricia Unrast, *Owner*
EMP: 4
SALES (est): 282.9K **Privately Held**
SIC: 2679 Book covers, paper

Marietta
Washington County

(G-12602)
ALPHA OMEGA IMPORT EXPORT LLC
1135 Browns Rd (45750-9074)
PHONE 740 885-9155
Gerry Dallimore, *Principal*
EMP: 4
SALES (est): 401K **Privately Held**
SIC: 3089 Lamp bases & shades, plastic

(G-12603)
ANTERO RESOURCES CORPORATION
2335 State Route 821 (45750-5362)
PHONE 740 760-1000
EMP: 60 **Publicly Held**
SIC: 1382 Oil & gas exploration services
PA: Antero Resources Corporation
1615 Wynkoop St
Denver CO 80202

(G-12604)
ARNOLDS REPAIR SHOP
101 Simpson St (45750-6759)
PHONE 740 373-5313
Gary J Arnold, *Partner*
Ivan F Arnold, *Partner*
Richard P Arnold, *Partner*
EMP: 3
SQ FT: 2,400
SALES (est): 270K **Privately Held**
SIC: 3599 7692 Machine shop, jobbing & repair; welding repair

(G-12605)
ARTEX OIL COMPANY
2337 State Route 821 (45750-5475)
PHONE 740 373-3313
Arthur Rupe, *CEO*
Jerry James, *President*
Gene Huck, *Vice Pres*
EMP: 20
SALES (est): 3.9MM **Privately Held**
WEB: www.artexoil.com
SIC: 1381 Drilling oil & gas wells

(G-12606)
ASPHALT MATERIALS INC
505 River Ln (45750-8481)
PHONE 740 373-3040
Josh Gregory, *Plant Mgr*
EMP: 4

GEOGRAPHIC SECTION

Marietta - Washington County (G-12632)

SALES (corp-wide): 248.2MM **Privately Held**
SIC: **2951** Asphalt & asphaltic paving mixtures (not from refineries)
PA: Asphalt Materials, Inc.
5400 W 86th St
Indianapolis IN 46268
317 872-6010

(G-12607)
ASPHALT MATERIALS INC
13925 State Route 7 (45750-8244)
PHONE.................................740 374-5100
Josh Gregory, *Plant Mgr*
EMP: 10
SALES (corp-wide): 248.2MM **Privately Held**
SIC: **2951** Asphalt & asphaltic paving mixtures (not from refineries)
PA: Asphalt Materials, Inc.
5400 W 86th St
Indianapolis IN 46268
317 872-6010

(G-12608)
BALDWIN B AA DESIGN
256 Front St (45750-2908)
P.O. Box 542 (45750-0542)
PHONE.................................740 374-5844
Anthony A Baldwin, *Owner*
Rebecca Baldwin, *Co-Owner*
EMP: 4
SALES: 225K **Privately Held**
SIC: **3911** Jewelry, precious metal

(G-12609)
BOB LANES WELDING INC
545 Rummer Rd (45750-6710)
PHONE.................................740 373-3567
Robert Lane, *President*
Sandra Lane, *Corp Secy*
EMP: 12
SQ FT: 6,700
SALES: 750K **Privately Held**
SIC: **1799** 1623 7692 3444 Welding on site; pipe laying construction; welding repair; sheet metalwork; metal heat treating

(G-12610)
BROUGHTON FOODS COMPANY (HQ)
1701 Greene St (45750)
PHONE.................................740 373-4121
Michael McCullum, *Principal*
David Broughton, *Manager*
EMP: 160 EST: 1910
SQ FT: 8,000
SALES (est): 54.6MM **Publicly Held**
SIC: **2026** 2024 5451 Cottage cheese; half & half; milk processing (pasteurizing, homogenizing, bottling); yogurt; ice cream, packaged: molded, on sticks, etc.; dairy products stores

(G-12611)
C L W INC
1201 Gilman Ave (45750-9499)
PHONE.................................740 374-8443
David Armstrong, *President*
Frederick L Burge, *Corp Secy*
Fred Burge, *Manager*
EMP: 9
SQ FT: 7,500
SALES (est): 1.2MM **Privately Held**
SIC: **3444** Concrete forms, sheet metal

(G-12612)
CARON PRODUCTS AND SVCS INC
27640 State Route 7 (45750-5146)
P.O. Box 715 (45750-0715)
PHONE.................................740 373-6809
Jon F Bergen, *Principal*
Bob Beckelman, *Principal*
Sue Eckberg, *Principal*
Spencer Krigsman, *Principal*
Paul Sereni, *Principal*
▲ EMP: 22
SQ FT: 12,000
SALES (est): 5.8MM **Privately Held**
WEB: www.caronproducts.com
SIC: **3823** 3821 Temperature instruments: industrial process type; laboratory apparatus, except heating & measuring

(G-12613)
CARPER WELL SERVICE INC
30745 State Route 7 (45773-5177)
P.O. Box 273, Reno (45773-0273)
PHONE.................................740 374-2567
Millard E Carper, *President*
Ryan Carper, *Treasurer*
EMP: 10
SQ FT: 3,500
SALES (est): 1MM **Privately Held**
SIC: **1389** Construction, repair & dismantling services

(G-12614)
CC INVESTORS MANAGEMENT CO LLC
30765 State Route 7 (45750-5177)
PHONE.................................740 374-8129
David Scott Farrar, *Mng Member*
EMP: 2
SQ FT: 1,000
SALES: 8MM **Privately Held**
SIC: **3497** Foil containers for bakery goods & frozen foods

(G-12615)
CITY OF MARIETTA
Also Called: Water Treatment Plant
2000 4th St (45750)
PHONE.................................740 374-6864
David Sands, *Director*
EMP: 40 **Privately Held**
SIC: **3589** 9111 Water treatment equipment, industrial; mayors' offices
PA: City Of Marietta
301 Putnam St Frnt Frnt
Marietta OH 45750
740 373-0473

(G-12616)
COIL SPECIALTY CHEMICALS LLC
2375 Glendale Rd (45750-8038)
PHONE.................................740 236-2407
Robert Coil, *Mng Member*
EMP: 8
SQ FT: 5,000
SALES (est): 1.3MM **Privately Held**
SIC: **2869** Glycerin

(G-12617)
COMMUNITY ACTION PROGRAM CORP
Also Called: Community Action Wic Hlth Svc
696 Wayne St (45750-3265)
PHONE.................................740 374-8501
Kathleen Boersma, *Director*
EMP: 10
SALES (corp-wide): 9.9MM **Privately Held**
WEB: www.wmcap.org
SIC: **8399** 8093 8011 2241 Community action agency; family planning & birth control clinics; offices & clinics of medical doctors; wicking
PA: Community Action Program Corp
218 Putnam St
Marietta OH 45750
740 373-3745

(G-12618)
DAVIDS STONE COMPANY LLC
514 4th St (45750-1901)
PHONE.................................740 373-1996
David B Paige,
EMP: 3
SALES (est): 112.3K **Privately Held**
SIC: **3281** Building stone products

(G-12619)
DIMEX LLC
28305 State Route 7 (45750-5151)
PHONE.................................740 374-3100
David Wesel, *CEO*
Melissa Jarvis, *Safety Dir*
Maurice Lecompte, *QA Dir*
Jeff Cain, *Engineer*
William Dopp, *CFO*
◆ EMP: 120
SQ FT: 224,000
SALES (est): 50.7MM
SALES (corp-wide): 460.4MM **Privately Held**
WEB: www.dimexcorp.com
SIC: **3089** Extruded finished plastic products
PA: Grey Mountain Partners, Llc
1470 Walnut St Ste 400
Boulder CO 80302
303 449-5692

(G-12620)
DIRECTIONAL ONE SVCS INC USA
2163a-1 Gwb Complex (45750)
PHONE.................................740 371-5031
Kevin Onishenko, *CEO*
EMP: 6
SALES (est): 565.4K **Privately Held**
SIC: **1381** Directional drilling oil & gas wells

(G-12621)
DOAK LASER
2801 Waterford Rd (45750-6910)
PHONE.................................740 374-0090
Bill Doak, *Principal*
EMP: 4
SALES (est): 313.2K **Privately Held**
SIC: **3479** Etching & engraving

(G-12622)
EAGLE FIREWORKS CO (PA)
26400 State Route 7 (45750-5111)
PHONE.................................740 373-3357
Fred Wells, *Owner*
▲ EMP: 5
SALES (est): 656.3K **Privately Held**
WEB: www.wvfireworks.net
SIC: **5999** 2899 Fireworks; fireworks

(G-12623)
ELPRO SERVICES INC
210 Mill Creek Rd (45750-1394)
PHONE.................................740 568-9900
Sylvain Riendeau, *President*
Madleina Collenberg, *Sales Staff*
Leah Harris, *Training Spec*
EMP: 4
SQ FT: 1,200
SALES (est): 862.8K **Privately Held**
WEB: www.elpro.us
SIC: **3823** Industrial instrmnts msrmnt display/control process variable
PA: Elpro-Buchs Ag
Langaulistrasse 45
Buchs SG
815 520-808

(G-12624)
FLEXMAG INDUSTRIES INC (DH)
Also Called: Arnold Magnetic Technologies
107 Industry Rd (45750-9355)
PHONE.................................740 373-3492
Tim Wilson, *President*
James McNerney, *Plant Mgr*
▲ EMP: 100
SQ FT: 84,619
SALES (est): 18.6MM **Publicly Held**
WEB: www.arnoldmagnetics.com
SIC: **3499** Magnets, permanent: metallic
HQ: Arnold Magnetic Technologies Corporation
770 Linden Ave
Rochester NY 14625
585 385-9010

(G-12625)
FULL CIRCLE OIL FIELD SVCS INC
2327 State Route 821 B (45750-5362)
PHONE.................................740 371-5422
Mitch Fouss, *Principal*
Danny Warren, *Principal*
Renee Warren, *Principal*
EMP: 6
SALES (est): 734.1K **Privately Held**
SIC: **1389** Oil field services

(G-12626)
GHOSTBLIND INDUSTRIES INC
2347a State Route 821 (45750-5362)
P.O. Box 644 (45750-0644)
PHONE.................................740 374-6766
Kevin Pottmeyer, *CEO*
Greg Thieman, *Natl Sales Mgr*
▲ EMP: 6
SQ FT: 7,500
SALES (est): 1.7MM **Privately Held**
SIC: **5091** 3949 Hunting equipment & supplies; hunting equipment

(G-12627)
GILLARD CONSTRUCTION INC
Also Called: Cypress Valley Log Homes
1308 Greene St (45750-9809)
PHONE.................................740 376-9744
John Gillard, *President*
Debra Gillard, *Vice Pres*
Jill Wright, *Treasurer*
Kelly Gillard, *Admin Sec*
EMP: 16
SALES (est): 2.4MM **Privately Held**
WEB: www.cypressvalleyloghomes.com
SIC: **1521** 2434 5211 2452 General remodeling, single-family houses; wood kitchen cabinets; cabinets, kitchen; log cabins, prefabricated, wood

(G-12628)
GREENE STREET WHOLESALE LLC
1310 Greene St (45750-9809)
PHONE.................................740 374-5206
Jill Wright, *Mng Member*
Chance Wright, *Mng Member*
EMP: 3
SALES: 250K **Privately Held**
SIC: **5031** 5211 3446 Kitchen cabinets; counter tops; stairs, fire escapes, balconies, railings & ladders

(G-12629)
GRIMM SCIENTIFIC INDUSTRIES
1403 Pike St (45750-5106)
P.O. Box 2143 (45750-7143)
PHONE.................................740 374-3412
Joseph E Grimm, *President*
Edmund Dutton, *Vice Pres*
Jon Grimm, *Vice Pres*
Walt Brothers, *Treasurer*
Launa Morus, *Sales Mgr*
EMP: 10
SQ FT: 5,000
SALES: 750K **Privately Held**
WEB: www.grimmscientific.com
SIC: **3841** Physiotherapy equipment, electrical

(G-12630)
HAESSLY LUMBER SALES CO (PA)
25 Sheets Run Rd (45750-5186)
PHONE.................................740 373-6681
Norman E Haessly Jr, *President*
Mark Haessly, *Vice Pres*
Steve Haessly, *Vice Pres*
Julie Haessly, *Treasurer*
Jim Tidd, *Manager*
EMP: 55 EST: 1941
SQ FT: 160
SALES (est): 8MM **Privately Held**
SIC: **2421** 2449 2448 2435 Lumber: rough, sawed or planed; wood containers; wood pallets & skids; hardwood veneer & plywood; hardwood dimension & flooring mills; logging

(G-12631)
HARDMAGIC
125 Frederick St (45750-3407)
PHONE.................................415 390-6232
Matt Hackney, *Owner*
EMP: 12
SQ FT: 4,000
SALES: 726.5K **Privately Held**
SIC: **7336** 7372 Commercial art & graphic design; publishers' computer software

(G-12632)
HI-VAC CORPORATION
27895 State Route 7 (45750)
PHONE.................................740 374-2306
Philip Coerper, *Branch Mgr*
EMP: 4
SALES (corp-wide): 20.2MM **Privately Held**
SIC: **3589** Vacuum cleaners & sweepers, electric: industrial

Marietta - Washington County (G-12633)

PA: Hi-Vac Corporation
117 Industry Rd
Marietta OH 45750
740 374-2306

(G-12633)
HUNTER EUREKA PIPELINE LLC
125 Putnam St (45750-2936)
PHONE.................740 374-2940
EMP: 8
SALES (est): 1.1MM
SALES (corp-wide): 515.1MM **Publicly Held**
SIC: 1311 Crude petroleum & natural gas production
HQ: Blue Ridge Mountain Resources, Inc.
122 W John Carpenter Fwy # 300
Irving TX 75039
469 444-1647

(G-12634)
HYDE BROTHERS PRTG & MKTG LLC (PA)
2343 State Route 821 E (45750-5465)
PHONE.................740 373-2054
Richard Kulick, *President*
Steve Flaughers, *Vice Pres*
EMP: 4
SALES (est): 592.2K **Privately Held**
SIC: 2759 Promotional printing

(G-12635)
INLAND HARDWOOD CORPORATION
Also Called: Inland Wood Products
25 Sheets Run Rd (45750-5186)
PHONE.................740 373-7187
Norman E Haessly Jr, *President*
Mark Haessly, *Vice Pres*
Steve Haessly, *Treasurer*
Julie Haessly, *Admin Sec*
EMP: 72
SALES (est): 7.8MM
SALES (corp-wide): 8MM **Privately Held**
SIC: 2448 Pallets, wood
PA: Haessly Lumber Sales Co.
25 Sheets Run Rd
Marietta OH 45750
740 373-6681

(G-12636)
JAMES ENGINEERING INC
Also Called: Artex Oil Company
2163 State Route 821 (45750-5462)
PHONE.................740 373-9521
Jerry James, *President*
Rhonda James, *Corp Secy*
EMP: 5
SQ FT: 2,000
SALES (est): 380K **Privately Held**
SIC: 8711 1389 Consulting engineer; oil field services

(G-12637)
KETELI TEAMWEAR LLC
313 Greene St (45750-3134)
PHONE.................740 373-7969
Brian Ketelsen, *Owner*
EMP: 3
SALES (est): 251.1K **Privately Held**
SIC: 2759 Screen printing

(G-12638)
KROGER CO
40 Acme St (45750-3306)
PHONE.................740 374-2523
Stan Ness, *Manager*
EMP: 100
SALES (corp-wide): 121.1B **Publicly Held**
WEB: www.kroger.com
SIC: 5411 5992 5912 5812 Supermarkets, chain; florists; drug stores & proprietary stores; eating places; cookies & crackers; bread, cake & related products
PA: The Kroger Co
1014 Vine St Ste 1000
Cincinnati OH 45202
513 762-4000

(G-12639)
LOKEN OIL FIELD SERVICES LLC
2190 Olinn Rd (45750-6525)
PHONE.................740 749-3495
Curtis L Loken, *Principal*
EMP: 3
SALES (est): 133.1K **Privately Held**
SIC: 1389 Oil field services

(G-12640)
LONGYEAR COMPANY
1010 Greene St (45750-2409)
PHONE.................740 373-2190
EMP: 35 **Privately Held**
SIC: 1481 Test boring for nonmetallic minerals
HQ: Longyear Company
2455 S 3600 W
West Valley City UT 84119

(G-12641)
MAGNUM MAGNETICS CORPORATION (PA)
Also Called: Magnum Inks & Coatings
801 Masonic Park Rd (45750-9357)
PHONE.................740 373-7770
Allen Love, *President*
Bruce Dean, *General Mgr*
Tom Love, *COO*
Bob Perkins, *Transportation*
Ryan Watters, *Opers Staff*
◆ **EMP:** 160
SQ FT: 30,000
SALES (est): 30.3MM **Privately Held**
WEB: www.magnummagnetics.com
SIC: 3499 Magnets, permanent: metallic

(G-12642)
MARIETTA ERAMET INC
16705 State Route 7 (45750-8519)
P.O. Box 299 (45750-0299)
PHONE.................740 374-1000
Michel Masci, *CFO*
Marc Blanquart, *CFO*
▲ **EMP:** 205
SALES (est): 113.3MM
SALES (corp-wide): 819MM **Privately Held**
WEB: www.emspecialproducts.com
SIC: 3313 Ferroalloys
HQ: Eramet Holding Manganese
10 Boulevard De Grenelle
Paris 75015

(G-12643)
MARIETTA RESOURCES CORPORATION
704 Pike St (45750-3501)
PHONE.................740 373-6305
Lynn Foster, *President*
Cathy Binegar, *Sales Associate*
EMP: 10
SALES (est): 970K **Privately Held**
SIC: 1311 Crude petroleum production; natural gas production

(G-12644)
MARTYS PRINT SHOP
307 3rd St (45750-2902)
PHONE.................740 373-3454
Marty Margolis, *Owner*
EMP: 3
SQ FT: 1,700
SALES (est): 327K **Privately Held**
SIC: 2752 Commercial printing, offset

(G-12645)
MASTER MAGNETICS INC
Also Called: Magnetic Source
108 Industry Rd (45750-9355)
PHONE.................740 373-0909
Dewayne Collins, *Branch Mgr*
EMP: 12
SALES (corp-wide): 21.6MM **Privately Held**
WEB: www.magnetsource.com
SIC: 3357 Magnet wire, nonferrous
PA: Master Magnetics, Inc.
1211 Atchison Ct
Castle Rock CO 80109
303 688-3966

(G-12646)
MC ALARNEY POOL SPAS AND BILLD
Also Called: McAlarney Pols Spas Billd More
908 Pike St (45750-3505)
PHONE.................740 373-6698
Cheryl McAlarney, *President*
Wayne Mc Alarney, *Exec VP*
EMP: 25 **EST:** 1975
SQ FT: 6,500
SALES: 1.2MM **Privately Held**
WEB: www.mcalarney.com
SIC: 5091 3949 Swimming pools, equipment & supplies; spa equipment & supplies; billiard equipment & supplies; sporting & athletic goods

(G-12647)
MIDWAY MACHINING INC
1060 Gravel Bank Rd (45750-8370)
PHONE.................740 373-8976
Robert L Casto, *President*
Katherine E Murphy, *Corp Secy*
Gary Hendershot, *Vice Pres*
Katherine Casto, *Manager*
Brooke Proffitt, *Admin Sec*
EMP: 11
SQ FT: 3,000
SALES (est): 1.9MM **Privately Held**
WEB: www.midwaymachininginc.net
SIC: 3599 Machine shop, jobbing & repair

(G-12648)
NEW MULCH IN A BOTTLE LIMITED
140 Gross St Ste 116 (45750-2031)
PHONE.................724 290-2341
Russell Coffin,
EMP: 4
SALES (est): 282.5K **Privately Held**
SIC: 2869 Carbon disulfide

(G-12649)
OHIO VALLEY ALLOY SERVICES INC
100 Westview Ave (45750-9403)
PHONE.................740 373-1900
Randall Henthorn, *President*
Richard J Henthorn Jr, *Treasurer*
▲ **EMP:** 20
SQ FT: 2,500
SALES (est): 4.7MM **Privately Held**
SIC: 3312 3341 Blast furnaces & steel mills; general warehousing; secondary nonferrous metals

(G-12650)
OHIO VALLEY SPECIALTY COMPANY
115 Industry Rd (45750-9355)
PHONE.................740 373-2276
Larry G Hawkins, *President*
Frank D Mendicino, *Vice Pres*
John Schafer, *Prdtn Mgr*
Jay Brown, *Purch Mgr*
Arthur Mendicino, *Info Tech Mgr*
EMP: 12
SQ FT: 7,000
SALES (est): 2.4MM **Privately Held**
WEB: www.ovsc.com
SIC: 3339 Silicon, pure

(G-12651)
PARDSON INC
Also Called: Bird Watcher's Digest
149 Acme St (45750-3402)
P.O. Box 110 (45750-0110)
PHONE.................740 373-5285
William Thompson III, *President*
Andy Thompson, *President*
Mollee Brown, *General Mgr*
Jim Cirigliano, *Editor*
Elsa Thompson, *Treasurer*
EMP: 13 **EST:** 1978
SQ FT: 3,400
SALES: 1.3MM **Privately Held**
SIC: 2721 2731 5961 Magazines: publishing only, not printed on site; book publishing; mail order house

(G-12652)
PAWNEE MAINTENANCE INC
101 Rathbone Rd (45750-1437)
P.O. Box 269 (45750-0269)
PHONE.................740 373-6861
Ted R Szabo, *President*
EMP: 60
SQ FT: 3,000
SALES (est): 4.5MM **Privately Held**
WEB: www.pawnee.com
SIC: 1541 3272 Industrial buildings & warehouses; concrete products

(G-12653)
PIONEER PIPE INC
Also Called: Pioneer Group
2021 Hanna Rd (45750-8255)
PHONE.................740 376-2400
David M Archer, *President*
Matthew Hilverding, *Corp Secy*
Arlene M Archer, *Vice Pres*
Karl Robinson, *Vice Pres*
Larry Silvus, *Transptn Dir*
▲ **EMP:** 600
SQ FT: 24,800
SALES (est): 163.7MM **Privately Held**
WEB: www.pioneerpipeinc.com
SIC: 3498 1711 3443 3441 Pipe sections fabricated from purchased pipe; pipe fittings, fabricated from purchased pipe; plumbing contractors; warm air heating & air conditioning contractor; mechanical contractor; fabricated plate work (boiler shop); fabricated structural metal; blast furnaces & steel mills

(G-12654)
PIP ENTERPRISES LLC
220 Indian Run Rd (45750-6690)
PHONE.................740 373-5276
Judith Lang, *Principal*
EMP: 4
SALES (est): 101.5K **Privately Held**
SIC: 2752 Commercial printing, lithographic

(G-12655)
PITNEY BOWES INC
111 Marshall Rd (45750-1160)
PHONE.................740 374-5535
Marcia Pawloski, *Branch Mgr*
EMP: 60
SALES (corp-wide): 3.5B **Publicly Held**
SIC: 3579 7359 Postage meters; business machine & electronic equipment rental services
PA: Pitney Bowes Inc.
3001 Summer St Ste 3
Stamford CT 06905
203 356-5000

(G-12656)
PRAXAIR INC
10 Morris Loop Rd (45750)
PHONE.................740 373-6449
Dallas Shelton, *Branch Mgr*
EMP: 4 **Privately Held**
SIC: 2813 Industrial gases
HQ: Praxair, Inc.
10 Riverview Dr
Danbury CT 06810
203 837-2000

(G-12657)
PRAXAIR INC
2034 Blue Knob Rd (45750-8287)
PHONE.................740 374-5525
Chip Green, *Manager*
EMP: 12 **Privately Held**
SIC: 2813 Industrial gases
HQ: Praxair, Inc.
10 Riverview Dr
Danbury CT 06810
203 837-2000

(G-12658)
PREMIER PRINTING SOLUTIONS
115 Pineview Cir (45750-9433)
PHONE.................740 374-2836
Max Huck, *Owner*
EMP: 4
SALES (est): 319.5K **Privately Held**
SIC: 2752 Commercial printing, lithographic

(G-12659)
PRESSMARK INC
641 State Route 821 Ste A (45750-8042)
P.O. Box 931, Cornelius NC (28031-0931)
PHONE.................740 373-6005
Richard F Cataldo, *President*
Barbara Cataldo, *Admin Sec*
EMP: 5
SQ FT: 3,500
SALES (est): 650.3K **Privately Held**
WEB: www.pressmarkprinting.com
SIC: 2752 Commercial printing, offset

▲ = Import ▼ = Export
◆ = Import/Export

GEOGRAPHIC SECTION
Marietta - Washington County (G-12685)

(G-12660)
PROFUSION INDUSTRIES LLC
700 Bf Goodrich Rd (45750-7849)
P.O. Box 657 (45750-0657)
PHONE..................................740 374-6400
Nick Garst, *Research*
Jon Golden, *Branch Mgr*
Keith Bell, *Business Dir*
EMP: 20
SALES (est): 4.7MM
SALES (corp-wide): 27.2MM **Privately Held**
SIC: 3081 Unsupported plastics film & sheet
PA: Profusion Industries, Llc
822 Kumho Dr Ste 202
Fairlawn OH 44333
800 938-2858

(G-12661)
R R DONNELLEY & SONS COMPANY
88 Products Ln (45750-9212)
PHONE..................................740 376-9276
EMP: 3
SALES (corp-wide): 6.8B **Publicly Held**
SIC: 2754 Commercial printing, gravure
PA: R. R. Donnelley & Sons Company
35 W Wacker Dr Ste 3650
Chicago IL 60601
312 326-8000

(G-12662)
RAMPP COMPANY (PA)
20445 State Route 550 Ofc (45750-6900)
P.O. Box 608 (45750-0608)
PHONE..................................740 373-7886
Mark E Fulton, *President*
Charles D Fogle, *Principal*
David Fox, *Principal*
Charles Hall, *Principal*
Martin J Ramp, *Principal*
EMP: 45 **EST:** 1950
SQ FT: 50,000
SALES (est): 9.9MM **Privately Held**
WEB: www.ramppco.com
SIC: 3533 3443 3325 Drilling tools for gas, oil or water wells; crane hooks, laminated plate; alloy steel castings, except investment

(G-12663)
RICHARDSON PRINTING CORP (PA)
Also Called: Zip Center, The-Division
201 Acme St (45750-3404)
P.O. Box 663 (45750-0663)
PHONE..................................740 373-5362
Dennis E Valentine, *President*
Robert Richardson Jr, *Shareholder*
Charles E Schwab, *Admin Sec*
▲ **EMP:** 65
SQ FT: 100,000
SALES (est): 4.4MM **Privately Held**
WEB: www.rpcprint.com
SIC: 7389 2752 Business Services Lithographic Commercial Printing

(G-12664)
ROCKBOTTOM OIL & GAS
Also Called: Gibson, Jo K
1 Court House Ln Ste 3 (45750-2900)
PHONE..................................740 374-2478
Charles Kiser, *Partner*
EMP: 3
SALES (est): 216.6K **Privately Held**
SIC: 1381 Drilling oil & gas wells

(G-12665)
ROSSI PASTA FACTORY INC
106 Front St (45750-3163)
P.O. Box 930 (45750-0930)
PHONE..................................740 376-2065
Frank Christy, *Ch of Bd*
John Hammat, *President*
Sophia Lesher, *Manager*
EMP: 15
SQ FT: 8,000
SALES (est): 1.8MM **Privately Held**
WEB: www.rossipasta.com
SIC: 2099 5499 Pasta, uncooked: packaged with other ingredients; gourmet food stores

(G-12666)
SEWAH STUDIOS INC
190 Mill Creek Rd (45750-1381)
P.O. Box 298 (45750-0298)
PHONE..................................740 373-2087
Bradford Smith, *President*
David Smith, *Vice Pres*
EMP: 15 **EST:** 1927
SQ FT: 6,000
SALES (est): 1.3MM **Privately Held**
WEB: www.sewahstudios.com
SIC: 3446 Architectural metalwork

(G-12667)
SHELLY AND SANDS INC
Hc 7 Box S (45750)
P.O. Box 1 (45750-0001)
PHONE..................................740 373-6495
Roger Thomas, *Manager*
EMP: 10
SALES (corp-wide): 276.3MM **Privately Held**
WEB: www.shellyandsands.com
SIC: 2951 Asphalt & asphaltic paving mixtures (not from refineries)
PA: Shelly And Sands, Inc.
3570 S River Rd
Zanesville OH 43701
740 453-0721

(G-12668)
SHIRT FAMILY
23 Garden City Rd (45750-5405)
PHONE..................................740 706-1284
Molly Korn, *Administration*
EMP: 3 **EST:** 2015
SALES (est): 335.7K **Privately Held**
SIC: 2759 Screen printing

(G-12669)
SILVESCO INC
2985 State Route 26 (45750-7586)
P.O. Box 161 (45750-0161)
PHONE..................................740 373-6661
Rodney Paxton, *President*
Michele Paxton, *Vice Pres*
EMP: 10 **EST:** 1964
SQ FT: 11,800
SALES (est): 1.3MM **Privately Held**
SIC: 2448 2449 Pallets, wood; rectangular boxes & crates, wood

(G-12670)
SKUTTLE MFG CO
Also Called: Skuttle Indoor Air Qulty Pdts
101 Margaret St (45750-9052)
PHONE..................................740 373-9169
Davis Powers, *President*
Debby Romick, *Corp Secy*
Jenny Powers, *Technology*
▲ **EMP:** 14 **EST:** 1917
SQ FT: 96,500
SALES (est): 3.5MM **Privately Held**
WEB: www.skuttle.com
SIC: 3634 3564 3822 Humidifiers, electric: household; filters, air: furnaces, air conditioning equipment, etc.; auto controls regulating residntl & coml environmt & applncs

(G-12671)
SMITH BROTHERS ERECTION INC
101 Industry Rd (45750-9355)
PHONE..................................740 373-3575
Robert A Gribben Jr, *President*
Robert A Gribben III, *Director*
EMP: 45 **EST:** 2011
SALES (est): 1.2MM **Privately Held**
SIC: 1791 3449 Structural steel erection; bars, concrete reinforcing; fabricated steel

(G-12672)
SOLVAY ADVANCED POLYMERS LLC
17005 State Route 7 (45750-8248)
P.O. Box 446 (45750-0446)
PHONE..................................740 373-9242
Joseph D Greulich, *President*
EMP: 19
SALES (est): 3.6MM **Privately Held**
SIC: 2819 Radium, luminous compounds

(G-12673)
SOLVAY SPCLTY POLYMERS USA LLC
17005 State Route 7 (45750-8248)
P.O. Box 446 (45750-0446)
PHONE..................................740 373-9242
Craig Wade, *Buyer*
Wally Kandell, *Branch Mgr*
Vincent Nedeff, *Technician*
EMP: 20
SALES (corp-wide): 10MM **Privately Held**
WEB: www.solvayadvancedpolymers.com
SIC: 2821 Plastics materials & resins
HQ: Solvay Specialty Polymers Usa, L.L.C.
4500 Mcginnis Ferry Rd
Alpharetta GA 30005
770 772-8200

(G-12674)
SOMERVILLE MANUFACTURING INC
15 Townhall Rd (45750-5374)
PHONE..................................740 336-7847
Steve Somerville, *President*
Peggy Somerville, *Vice Pres*
EMP: 20
SALES (est): 3.9MM **Privately Held**
SIC: 3441 3444 7692 Fabricated structural metal; sheet metalwork; welding repair

(G-12675)
STEVENS OIL & GAS LLC
110 Lynch Church Rd (45750-7545)
PHONE..................................740 374-4542
Matthew Stevens, *Principal*
EMP: 8
SALES (est): 636.5K **Privately Held**
SIC: 1389 Oil & gas field services

(G-12676)
STEVES VANS & ACCESSORIES LLC
Also Called: Marietta Mobility
221 Pike St (45750-3320)
PHONE..................................740 374-3154
Stephen K Hesson,
EMP: 9
SQ FT: 3,700
SALES (est): 3.4MM **Privately Held**
SIC: 5511 7532 5531 5999 Vans, new & used; van conversion; automotive accessories; technical aids for the handicapped; recreational vehicle parts & accessories; wheelchair lifts

(G-12677)
STRATAGRAPH NE INC
116 Ellsworth Ave (45750-8607)
P.O. Box 59, Reno (45773-0059)
PHONE..................................740 373-3091
Walt Teer, *President*
EMP: 32
SQ FT: 2,400
SALES (est): 700K **Privately Held**
SIC: 1389 1381 Oil field services; drilling oil & gas wells

(G-12678)
SUMMERS ACQUISITION CORP
Also Called: Summers Rubber Co Branch 06
100 Tennis Center Dr (45750-8802)
PHONE..................................740 373-0303
Betty Malcolm, *Sales Staff*
Mel Shipley, *Branch Mgr*
EMP: 4
SALES (corp-wide): 3.1B **Privately Held**
WEB: www.summersrubber.com
SIC: 3052 3492 Rubber hose; hose & tube fittings & assemblies, hydraulic/pneumatic
HQ: Summers Acquisition Corporation
12555 Berea Rd
Cleveland OH 44111
216 941-7700

(G-12679)
TERRA SONIC INTERNATIONAL LLC
27825 State Route 7 (45750-9060)
PHONE..................................740 374-6608
John Walsh, *Mng Member*
James Savinkoff, *Supervisor*
◆ **EMP:** 22 **EST:** 1998
SQ FT: 600,000
SALES (est): 4.3MM **Privately Held**
SIC: 1623 7353 3533 Oil & gas pipeline construction; oil field equipment, rental or leasing; oil & gas drilling rigs & equipment

(G-12680)
THERMO FISHER SCIENTIFIC
401 Mill Creek Rd (45750-4304)
P.O. Box 649 (45750-0649)
PHONE..................................740 373-4763
David Leister, *Production*
Carrie Conley, *Purch Agent*
Mark Spence, *Engineer*
Tricia Tortoreti, *Sales Staff*
Jamie Keefer, *Branch Mgr*
EMP: 592
SQ FT: 287
SALES (corp-wide): 24.3B **Publicly Held**
WEB: www.thermo.com
SIC: 3826 Analytical instruments
HQ: Thermo Fisher Scientific (Ashville) Llc
28 Schenck Pkwy Ste 400
Asheville NC 28803
828 658-2711

(G-12681)
TKN OILFIELD SERVICES LLC
108 Woodcrest Dr (45750-1352)
PHONE..................................740 516-2583
Nick S Flowers,
Cheryl B Cobb,
Tisha D Voland,
EMP: 12
SQ FT: 1,500
SALES (est): 5MM **Privately Held**
SIC: 1389 Oil field services

(G-12682)
TOP DRILLING CORPORATION (PA)
107 Lancaster St 301 (45750-2734)
PHONE..................................304 477-3333
Doug Haught, *President*
Robin J Cook, *Director*
EMP: 15
SQ FT: 1,000
SALES (est): 2.4MM **Privately Held**
WEB: www.topdrilling.com
SIC: 1381 Directional drilling oil & gas wells

(G-12683)
TRIAD ENERGY CORPORATION
125 Putnam St (45750-2936)
PHONE..................................740 374-2940
Kean Weaver, *President*
James R Bryden, *Vice Pres*
Brent Powell, *Safety Mgr*
Kim Arnold, *Human Res Mgr*
EMP: 26
SALES (est): 3.3MM **Privately Held**
SIC: 2992 1382 Lubricating oils & greases; oil & gas exploration services

(G-12684)
TRIAD HUNTER LLC (DH)
125 Putnam St (45750-2936)
PHONE..................................740 374-2940
Richard S Farrell, *Senior VP*
James W Denny III, *Vice Pres*
Sam Miracle, *Project Mgr*
Tracy Miskofsky, *Manager*
EMP: 16
SALES (est): 29.5MM
SALES (corp-wide): 515.1MM **Publicly Held**
SIC: 1311 Crude petroleum production
HQ: Blue Ridge Mountain Resources, Inc.
122 W John Carpenter Fwy # 300
Irving TX 75039
469 444-1647

(G-12685)
TRIAD HUNTER LLC
125 Putnam St (45750-2936)
PHONE..................................740 374-2940
Rodney Boron, *Production*
Kimberly R Arnold, *Branch Mgr*
EMP: 8
SALES (corp-wide): 515.1MM **Publicly Held**
SIC: 1311 Crude petroleum & natural gas
HQ: Triad Hunter, Llc
125 Putnam St
Marietta OH 45750

Marietta - Washington County (G-12686)

(G-12686)
UNITED CHART PROCESSORS INC
1461 Masonic Park Rd (45750-5393)
PHONE..................................740 373-5801
David Graham, *President*
Barbara Graham, *Vice Pres*
EMP: 8
SALES (est): 969.7K **Privately Held**
SIC: 1389 Gas field services

(G-12687)
VIKING FABRICATORS INC
2021 Hanna Rd (45750-8255)
PHONE..................................740 374-5246
David M Archer, *President*
James S Huggins, *Principal*
Matthew Hilverding, *Corp Secy*
Arlene M Archer, *Vice Pres*
EMP: 25
SQ FT: 20,000
SALES (est): 5.1MM **Privately Held**
SIC: 3441 7692 3446 3443 Fabricated structural metal; welding repair; architectural metalwork; fabricated plate work (boiler shop)

(G-12688)
VIKING INTL RESOURCES CO INC
Also Called: Virco
125 Putnam St (45750-2936)
PHONE..................................304 628-3878
Thomas G Palmer, *President*
EMP: 5
SQ FT: 1,200
SALES (est): 975.3K
SALES (corp-wide): 515.1MM **Publicly Held**
WEB: www.vircoinc.net
SIC: 1311 Crude petroleum & natural gas production
HQ: Triad Hunter, Llc
  125 Putnam St
  Marietta OH 45750

(G-12689)
WINSTON OIL CO INC
1 Court House Ln Ste 3 (45750-2900)
P.O. Box 754 (45750-0754)
PHONE..................................740 373-9664
Deborah Cunningham, *Principal*
EMP: 7
SALES (est): 647K **Privately Held**
SIC: 3569 Gas producers, generators & other gas related equipment

(G-12690)
ZIDE SPORT SHOP OF OHIO INC
Also Called: Zide Screen Printing
118 Industry Rd (45750-9255)
PHONE..................................740 373-8199
Randy Schneeberger, *Manager*
EMP: 14
SALES (corp-wide): 7.4MM **Privately Held**
SIC: 2396 Screen printing on fabric articles
PA: Zide Sport Shop Of Ohio, Inc.
  253 2nd St
  Marietta OH 45750
  740 373-6446

Marion
Marion County

(G-12691)
ALIN MACHINING COMPANY INC
875 E Mark St (43302-2748)
PHONE..................................740 223-0200
Ryan Dballinger, *Branch Mgr*
EMP: 75
SALES (corp-wide): 50MM **Privately Held**
SIC: 3511 Turbines & turbine generator sets
PA: Alin Machining Company, Inc.
  3131 W Soffel Ave
  Melrose Park IL 60160
  708 681-1043

(G-12692)
AMBASSADOR STEEL CORPORATION
850 Barks Rd W (43302-7270)
PHONE..................................740 382-9969
Gene Baker, *Manager*
EMP: 12
SALES (corp-wide): 25B **Publicly Held**
WEB: www.ambassadorsteel.com
SIC: 3441 5051 Fabricated structural metal; bars, metal
HQ: Ambassador Steel Corporation
  1340 S Grandstaff Dr
  Auburn IN 46706
  260 925-5440

(G-12693)
ARCELORMITTAL TUBULAR
686 W Fairground St (43302-1706)
PHONE..................................740 382-3979
Jerome Granboulan, *CEO*
Mark Bryer, *CFO*
▲ EMP: 100
SQ FT: 410,000
SALES (est): 19.2MM **Privately Held**
WEB: www.dofascomarion.com
SIC: 3317 Steel pipe & tubes
PA: Arcelormittal Tubular Products Luxembourg Sa
  Boulevard D'avranches 24-26
  Luxembourg

(G-12694)
ARCELORMITTAL USA LLC
686 W Fairground St (43302-1706)
PHONE..................................740 375-2299
Bernard Buchanan, *General Mgr*
Carl Spitzer, *Safety Mgr*
George J Cavender, *Buyer*
George Cavender, *Buyer*
David Snively, *Buyer*
EMP: 14
SALES (corp-wide): 9.1B **Privately Held**
SIC: 3312 Blast furnaces & steel mills
HQ: Arcelormittal Usa Llc
  1 S Dearborn St Ste 1800
  Chicago IL 60603
  312 346-0300

(G-12695)
BERT RADEBAUGH
Also Called: American Quality Door
1544 Marion Marysville Rd (43302-7332)
PHONE..................................740 382-8134
Bert Radebaugh, *Owner*
EMP: 3
SALES: 350K **Privately Held**
SIC: 5031 1751 7699 5211 Doors & windows; window & door installation & erection; door & window repair; door & window products; door opening & closing devices, electrical

(G-12696)
BUCKEYE READY-MIX LLC
627 Likens Rd (43302-8653)
PHONE..................................740 387-8846
Kevin McCoy, *Manager*
EMP: 10
SALES (corp-wide): 45.1MM **Privately Held**
WEB: www.buckeyereadymix.com
SIC: 3273 Ready-mixed concrete
PA: Buckeye Ready-Mix, Llc
  7657 Taylor Rd Sw
  Reynoldsburg OH 43068
  614 575-2132

(G-12697)
BUNGE NORTH AMERICA FOUNDATION
751 E Farming St (43302-3113)
P.O. Box 1805 (43301-1805)
PHONE..................................740 383-1181
EMP: 63 **Privately Held**
SIC: 2075 Soybean Oil Mill
HQ: Bunge North America Foundation
  11720 Borman Dr
  Saint Louis MO 63017
  314 872-3030

(G-12698)
BUZZ N SHUTTLE SERVICE
333 Executive Dr Apt 1 (43302-6351)
PHONE..................................740 223-0567
EMP: 3 EST: 2000
SALES (est): 170K **Privately Held**
SIC: 3532 Mfg Mining Machinery

(G-12699)
CENTRAL MACHINERY COMPANY LLC
Also Called: Denmac Metalworks
1339 E Fairground Rd (43302-8873)
PHONE..................................740 387-1289
Rod Galbreath, *President*
EMP: 17 EST: 2000
SQ FT: 25,000
SALES (est): 4.3MM **Privately Held**
SIC: 3544 Subpresses, metalworking

(G-12700)
COUNTRY CATERERS INC (PA)
Also Called: Riverside Homemade Ice Cream
409 Mrion Cardington Rd W (43302-7313)
PHONE..................................740 389-1013
Rob Lill, *President*
Vickie Lill, *Vice Pres*
EMP: 4
SQ FT: 2,000
SALES (est): 283.8K **Privately Held**
WEB: www.countrycaterers.net
SIC: 5812 2024 Caterers; ice cream, bulk

(G-12701)
CREATIVE DOCUMENTS SOLUTIONS
1629 Marion Waldo Rd (43302-7425)
PHONE..................................740 389-4252
Lorraine Corbin, *Principal*
Teri Austin, *Sales Staff*
EMP: 6
SALES (est): 1MM **Privately Held**
SIC: 2759 Commercial printing

(G-12702)
FOLKS CREATIVE PRINTERS INC
101 E George St (43302-2304)
PHONE..................................740 383-6326
Trudi E Maish, *Ch of Bd*
James L Saiter, *President*
Dixon Ericson, *Manager*
Linda M Maish, *Admin Sec*
EMP: 27 EST: 1922
SALES (est): 3.6MM **Privately Held**
WEB: www.folksprinting.com
SIC: 2752 3993 2789 2759 Commercial printing, offset; signs & advertising specialties; bookbinding & related work; commercial printing

(G-12703)
GANNETT CO INC
Also Called: Marion Star
163 E Center St (43302-3813)
PHONE..................................419 521-7341
Tom Brennan, *Editor*
EMP: 41
SALES (corp-wide): 2.9B **Publicly Held**
WEB: www.gannett.com
SIC: 2711 Newspapers: publishing only, not printed on site
PA: Gannett Co., Inc.
  7950 Jones Branch Dr
  Mc Lean VA 22102
  703 854-6000

(G-12704)
GENERAL MACHINE & SAW COMPANY (PA)
740 W Center St (43302-3550)
P.O. Box 587 (43301-0587)
PHONE..................................740 382-1104
Joseph Murphy, *President*
Jack Dean, *Vice Pres*
Matt Murphy, *Vice Pres*
Kathy Smith, *Office Mgr*
Beth Murphy, *Admin Sec*
EMP: 96
SQ FT: 100,000
SALES (est): 19.5MM **Privately Held**
SIC: 3312 Blast furnaces & steel mills

(G-12705)
GENERAL MACHINE & SAW COMPANY
305 Davis St (43302)
P.O. Box 587 (43301-0587)
PHONE..................................740 375-5730
Matt Murphy, *Branch Mgr*
EMP: 21
SALES (est): 3.2MM
SALES (corp-wide): 19.5MM **Privately Held**
SIC: 3599 Machine shop, jobbing & repair
PA: General Machine & Saw Company
  740 W Center St
  Marion OH 43302
  740 382-1104

(G-12706)
GEYER TRANSPORT & MFG
1443 N Main St (43302-1551)
PHONE..................................740 382-9008
EMP: 18
SALES (est): 1.3MM **Privately Held**
SIC: 3799 1799 Mfg Transportation Equipment Trade Contractor

(G-12707)
GRAPHIC PACKAGING INTL LLC
1171 W Center St (43302-3465)
PHONE..................................740 387-6543
Bill Campagna, *Manager*
Sonya Gibson, *Manager*
EMP: 150
SQ FT: 100,000 **Publicly Held**
SIC: 2657 Folding paperboard boxes
HQ: Graphic Packaging International, Llc
  1500 Riveredge Pkwy # 100
  Atlanta GA 30328

(G-12708)
HANGER PRSTHETCS & ORTHO INC
1136 Independence Ave (43302-6318)
PHONE..................................419 522-0055
Bill Neu, *Manager*
EMP: 3
SALES (corp-wide): 1B **Publicly Held**
SIC: 8071 3842 5999 Medical laboratories; limbs, artificial; orthopedic & prosthesis applications
HQ: Hanger Prosthetics & Orthotics, Inc.
  10910 Domain Dr Ste 300
  Austin TX 78758
  512 777-3800

(G-12709)
HANGER PRSTHETCS & ORTHO INC
1136 Independence Ave (43302-6318)
PHONE..................................740 383-2163
Tim Riedlinger, *Manager*
EMP: 3
SALES (corp-wide): 1B **Publicly Held**
SIC: 3842 5999 Limbs, artificial; orthopedic & prosthesis applications
HQ: Hanger Prosthetics & Orthotics, Inc.
  10910 Domain Dr Ste 300
  Austin TX 78758
  512 777-3800

(G-12710)
HARSCO CORPORATION
Also Called: Patent Construction Systems
3477 Harding Hwy E (43302-8534)
PHONE..................................740 387-1150
Don Broadwater, *Branch Mgr*
EMP: 24
SALES (corp-wide): 1.6B **Publicly Held**
SIC: 3537 3536 3535 3531 Industrial trucks & tractors; hoists, cranes & monorails; conveyors & conveying equipment; construction machinery; architectural metalwork
PA: Harsco Corporation
  350 Poplar Church Rd
  Camp Hill PA 17011
  717 763-7064

(G-12711)
HIGHWAY SAFETY CORP
473 W Fairground St (43302-1701)
PHONE..................................740 387-6991
Larry Ross, *Sales Staff*
Jim Chick, *Manager*
EMP: 15
SALES (corp-wide): 50.4MM **Privately Held**
SIC: 3444 3479 Guard rails, highway; sheet metal; galvanizing of iron, steel or end-formed products

PA: Highway Safety Corp.
239 Commerce St Ste C
Glastonbury CT 06033
860 659-4330

(G-12712)
HILDRETH MFG LLC
1657 Cascade Dr (43302-8509)
P.O. Box 905 (43301-0905)
PHONE..................................740 375-5832
Gerald Hildreth, *Vice Pres*
Eric Perini, *Maint Spvr*
Teresa Tebbe, *Bookkeeper*
Gerald Selan, *VP Sales*
Terry Hildreth,
EMP: 25
SALES (est): 9.7MM **Privately Held**
WEB: www.hildrethmfg.com
SIC: 3331 Blocks, copper

(G-12713)
INTERNATIONAL PAPER COMPANY
1600 Cascade Dr (43302-8509)
PHONE..................................740 383-4061
Ron Iden, *Principal*
EMP: 163
SALES (corp-wide): 23.3B **Publicly Held**
SIC: 2631 Paperboard mills
PA: International Paper Company
6400 Poplar Ave
Memphis TN 38197
901 419-9000

(G-12714)
KA WANNER INC
Also Called: Robotworx
370 W Fairground St (43302-1728)
PHONE..................................740 251-4636
Keith Wanner, *President*
Ricky Glass, *Purch Agent*
EMP: 30
SQ FT: 75,000
SALES (est): 11.7MM **Privately Held**
WEB: www.robotsforwelding.com
SIC: 3535 Robotic conveyors

(G-12715)
LAIPPLYS PRTG MKTG SLTIONS INC
270 E Center St (43302-4124)
P.O. Box 777 (43301-0777)
PHONE..................................740 387-9282
Ronald E Laipply, *President*
Effie Laipply, *Corp Secy*
Jacque Laipply, *Vice Pres*
EMP: 9
SQ FT: 5,000
SALES (est): 1.5MM **Privately Held**
WEB: www.laipplyprint.com
SIC: 2789 7336 7331 Bookbinding & related work; graphic arts & related design; direct mail advertising services

(G-12716)
LOBO AWRDS SCREEN PRTG GRAPHIX
627 Bellefontaine Ave (43302-6101)
PHONE..................................740 972-9087
Jeff Roberts, *Owner*
EMP: 3
SALES: 50K **Privately Held**
SIC: 2752 Commercial printing, lithographic

(G-12717)
MARION ETHANOL LLC
Also Called: Poet Biorefining
1660 Hillman Ford Rd (43302-9475)
PHONE..................................740 383-4400
Joe Bouza, *Marketing Staff*
Rick Fox, *Manager*
EMP: 45
SALES: 144MM **Privately Held**
SIC: 2869 2046 Ethyl alcohol, ethanol; corn oil products
PA: Poet, Llc
4615 N Lewis Ave
Sioux Falls SD 57104

(G-12718)
MARION INDUSTRIES INC
999 Kellogg Pkwy (43302-1791)
PHONE..................................740 223-0075
Rick Charville, *CEO*

James R Conway, *Ch of Bd*
Jerome Curtis, *President*
Gerald Lehrke, *Vice Pres*
Tim Stapleton, *Administration*
EMP: 753
SQ FT: 144,000
SALES (est): 228.8MM
SALES (corp-wide): 582.7MM **Privately Held**
WEB: www.egreeninc.com
SIC: 3714 Motor vehicle wheels & parts
PA: Ernie Green Industries, Inc.
2030 Dividend Dr
Columbus OH 43228
614 219-1423

(G-12719)
MID OHIO PACKAGING LLC
Also Called: Mopac
2135 Innovation Dr (43302-8261)
PHONE..................................740 383-9200
Tim Tootle, *General Mgr*
Jack Schwarz,
EMP: 30
SQ FT: 78,000
SALES (est): 6.2MM
SALES (corp-wide): 702.7MM **Privately Held**
WEB: www.mopac-ssp.com
SIC: 2653 Boxes, corrugated: made from purchased materials; sheets, solid fiber: made from purchased materials
HQ: Schwarz Partners Packaging, Llc
3600 Woodview Trce # 300
Indianapolis IN 46268
317 290-1140

(G-12720)
MILLS COMPANY
3007 Harding Hwy E 4n (43302-8370)
PHONE..................................740 375-0770
Donald H Mullett, *Ch of Bd*
John Kleczka, *Admin Sec*
▲ **EMP:** 25 **EST:** 1921
SALES (est): 12.6MM
SALES (corp-wide): 173.7MM **Privately Held**
WEB: www.mills-co.com
SIC: 2542 Partitions for floor attachment, prefabricated: except wood
PA: Bradley Corporation
W142n9101 Fountain Blvd
Menomonee Falls WI 53051
262 251-6000

(G-12721)
MISSION INDUSTRIAL GROUP LLC
Also Called: Drum Runner
3602 Harding Hwy E (43302-8534)
PHONE..................................740 387-2287
Mark Snow, *Mng Member*
▼ **EMP:** 10
SQ FT: 17,000
SALES: 500K **Privately Held**
WEB: www.drumrunner.com
SIC: 3599 Machine & other job shop work

(G-12722)
MURPHY INDUSTRIES INC
1650 Cascade Dr (43302-8509)
PHONE..................................740 387-7890
Theodore J Murphy Sr, *CEO*
Theodore J Murphy Jr, *President*
Michael J Murphy, *Vice Pres*
Paul Murphy, *Vice Pres*
▲ **EMP:** 35
SQ FT: 25,000
SALES (est): 6.3MM **Privately Held**
WEB: www.murphyind.com
SIC: 3315 3357 Cable, steel: insulated or armored; nonferrous wiredrawing & insulating

(G-12723)
NACHURS ALPINE SOLUTIONS CORP (HQ)
421 Leader St (43302-2225)
PHONE..................................740 382-5701
Jeffrey Barnes, *CEO*
Robert Hopp, *Vice Pres*
Scott Moon, *Vice Pres*
Reiny Packull, *Vice Pres*
David Rose, *Vice Pres*
◆ **EMP:** 25

SALES (est): 48.7MM
SALES (corp-wide): 105.4MM **Privately Held**
WEB: www.nachurs.com
SIC: 2875 2869 2819 Fertilizers, mixing only; industrial organic chemicals; industrial inorganic chemicals
PA: Trans-Resources, Llc
17780 Collins Ave
Sunny Isles Beach FL 33160
305 933-8301

(G-12724)
NATIONAL LIME AND STONE CO
700 Likens Rd (43302-8601)
P.O. Box 144 (43301-0144)
PHONE..................................740 387-3485
Richard Seifert, *Plant Mgr*
Scott Silver, *Manager*
EMP: 20
SALES (corp-wide): 3.2B **Privately Held**
WEB: www.natlime.com
SIC: 1422 5999 Limestones, ground; rock & stone specimens
PA: The National Lime And Stone Company
551 Lake Cascade Pkwy
Findlay OH 45840
419 422-4341

(G-12725)
NEWSAFE TRANSPORT SERVICE INC
979 Pole Lane Rd (43302-8524)
P.O. Box 749 (43301-0749)
PHONE..................................740 387-1679
Rachpal Sangh, *Owner*
EMP: 11
SQ FT: 400
SALES: 2.7MM **Privately Held**
SIC: 3537 Trucks: freight, baggage, etc.: industrial, except mining

(G-12726)
OHIO GALVANIZING CORP
467 W Fairground St (43302-1701)
PHONE..................................740 387-6474
W Patric Gregory, *CEO*
Robert J West, *CFO*
EMP: 50
SQ FT: 57,000
SALES: 10.6MM **Privately Held**
WEB: www.ohgalv.com
SIC: 3479 Galvanizing of iron, steel or end-formed products

(G-12727)
OVERHEAD DOOR CORPORATION
Todco
1332 E Fairground Rd (43302-8505)
PHONE..................................740 383-6376
Daniel C Rengert, *President*
Heather Munsell, *Plant Mgr*
Michael Hahn, *Manager*
EMP: 100
SALES (corp-wide): 3.6B **Privately Held**
WEB: www.overheaddoor.com
SIC: 3442 2431 3441 Garage doors, overhead: metal; doors, wood; fabricated structural metal
HQ: Overhead Door Corporation
2501 S State Hwy 121 Ste
Lewisville TX 75067
469 549-7100

(G-12728)
PROMO COSTUMES INC
381 W Center St (43302-3651)
P.O. Box 37 (43301-0037)
PHONE..................................740 383-5176
Lyn Giles, *Vice Pres*
Daniel Giles, *Vice Pres*
Adam Giles, *Office Admin*
EMP: 19
SALES: 750K **Privately Held**
WEB: www.promocostumes.com
SIC: 2389 7299 Costumes; costume rental

(G-12729)
R ANTHONY ENTERPRISES LLC
2626 Whetstone River Rd S (43302-8937)
PHONE..................................419 341-0961
Rocco Piacentino, *Mng Member*
EMP: 10
SQ FT: 10,000

SALES: 1MM **Privately Held**
SIC: 1389 Construction, repair & dismantling services

(G-12730)
RI ALTO MFG INC
1632 Cascade Dr (43302-8509)
PHONE..................................740 914-4230
Rick Mattix, *President*
Maryann Mattix, *Corp Secy*
Sam Hawkins, *Vice Pres*
EMP: 19 **EST:** 1981
SQ FT: 9,000
SALES (est): 3.6MM **Privately Held**
WEB: www.rialtomfg.com
SIC: 3599 7692 Machine shop, jobbing & repair; welding repair

(G-12731)
ROY I KAUFMAN INC
1672 Marion Uppr Sndsk Rd (43302-1531)
PHONE..................................740 382-0643
Beth Kaufman, *Treasurer*
Martin T Kaufman II, *Director*
EMP: 8 **EST:** 1956
SQ FT: 12,000
SALES (est): 1.6MM **Privately Held**
SIC: 3496 Woven wire products

(G-12732)
SAKAMURA USA INC
970 Kellogg Pkwy (43302-1783)
PHONE..................................740 223-7777
Takayuki Nakano, *President*
Jun Kobayashi, *Vice Pres*
Naomi Taniguchi, *Treasurer*
▲ **EMP:** 14
SQ FT: 10,000
SALES (est): 3.4MM
SALES (corp-wide): 65.1MM **Privately Held**
WEB: www.sakamura.net
SIC: 3462 Iron & steel forgings
PA: Sakamura Machine Co.,Ltd.
46, Tominoshiro, Shimotsuya, Kumiyamacho
Kuse-Gun KYO 613-0
774 437-000

(G-12733)
SCOTT SYSTEMS INTL INC
Also Called: Robotworx
370 W Fairground St (43302-1728)
PHONE..................................740 383-8383
Stacey McGill, *Principal*
Greg Chiles, *CFO*
EMP: 12
SALES (est): 430.5K
SALES (corp-wide): 30.1MM **Privately Held**
SIC: 3549 8742 Assembly machines, including robotic; automation & robotics consultant
HQ: Scott Technology Limited
630 Kaikorai Valley Road
Dunedin 9011

(G-12734)
SEMCO
1025 Pole Ln Rd (43302-8524)
P.O. Box 561 (43301-0561)
PHONE..................................800 848-5764
Bob Diersing, *Principal*
J Douglass Schrim, *Principal*
Leonard Furman, *Chairman*
Randy Furman, *Vice Pres*
Shelby Furman, *Vice Pres*
▲ **EMP:** 60
SQ FT: 40,000
SALES (est): 14.1MM **Privately Held**
WEB: www.semcotips.com
SIC: 3599 3366 Machine shop, jobbing & repair; copper foundries

(G-12735)
SIKA CORPORATION
1682 Mrn Williamsprt Rd E (43302-8694)
PHONE..................................740 387-9224
Todd Petrie, *VP Opers*
Ray Gear, *Purch Mgr*
Doug White, *Branch Mgr*
EMP: 62

Marion - Marion County (G-12736)

SALES (corp-wide): 6.3B Privately Held
WEB: www.sikacorp.com
SIC: 2899 5169 3566 Concrete curing & hardening compounds; concrete additives; speed changers, drives & gears
HQ: Sika Corporation
    201 Polito Ave
    Lyndhurst NJ 07071
    201 933-8800

(G-12736)
SIMCOTE INC
Also Called: Simcote of Ohio Division
250 N Greenwood St (43302-3177)
PHONE.................................740 382-5000
Art Tofte, Branch Mgr
EMP: 26
SALES (corp-wide): 14.5MM Privately Held
WEB: www.simcote.com
SIC: 3479 3449 Painting, coating & hot dipping; miscellaneous metalwork
PA: Simcote, Inc.
    1645 Red Rock Rd
    Saint Paul MN 55119
    651 735-9660

(G-12737)
STEAM TURB ALTE RESO
Also Called: Star
116 Latourette St (43302-3429)
P.O. Box 862 (43301-0862)
PHONE.................................740 387-5535
Sue B Flaherty, Ch of Bd
Tammy Flaherty, President
Ken Kubinski, Vice Pres
Donna Macgregor Rambin, Vice Pres
EMP: 45
SQ FT: 12,000
SALES (est): 10.3MM Privately Held
WEB: www.starturbine.com
SIC: 3511 Steam turbines; industrial supplies

(G-12738)
STORAD LABEL CO
126 Blaine Ave (43302-3612)
P.O. Box 493 (43301-0493)
PHONE.................................740 382-6440
Bob Hord, President
Andrew Hord, General Mgr
Ann Hord, Vice Pres
Ryan Hord, VP Sls/Mktg
EMP: 13 EST: 1966
SQ FT: 7,000
SALES (est): 2.2MM Privately Held
WEB: www.storadlabel.com
SIC: 2672 Labels (unprinted), gummed: made from purchased materials; tape, pressure sensitive: made from purchased materials

(G-12739)
TA DIE FOR GOURMET CUPCAKES
2094 Harding Hwy E (43302-8527)
PHONE.................................740 751-4586
Missy Meddins,
EMP: 4
SALES (est): 296.9K Privately Held
SIC: 2051 Bakery: wholesale or wholesale/retail combined

(G-12740)
TEMPLE-INLAND INC
1600 Cascade Dr (43302-8509)
PHONE.................................614 221-1522
EMP: 4
SALES (est): 109.8K Privately Held
SIC: 2653 Mfg Corrugated/Solid Fiber Boxes

(G-12741)
TMS INTERNATIONAL CORPORATION
Also Called: International Mill Service
912 Cheney Ave (43302-6208)
PHONE.................................740 223-0091
George Post, General Mgr
EMP: 12 Privately Held
WEB: www.envirosources.com
SIC: 3312 Blast furnaces & steel mills
HQ: Tms International Corporation
    12 Monongahela Ave
    Glassport PA 15045
    412 675-8251

(G-12742)
TODCO
1295 E Fairground Rd (43302-8503)
PHONE.................................740 223-2542
Dennis Stone, CEO
Margaret Roush, CTO
EMP: 12 EST: 2017
SALES (est): 1.6MM Privately Held
SIC: 2431 Millwork

(G-12743)
TODD W GOINGS
Also Called: Carousel Carvings
360 Summit St (43302-5228)
PHONE.................................740 389-5842
Todd W Goings, Owner
EMP: 3
SALES (est): 200K Privately Held
WEB: www.carouselsandcarvings.com
SIC: 7641 7299 5812 2499 Antique furniture repair & restoration; banquet hall facilities; caterers; carved & turned wood

(G-12744)
TREE FREE RESOURCES LLC
Also Called: Tfr Printing
175 Park Blvd (43302-3534)
PHONE.................................740 751-4844
Dale G Haddad,
EMP: 12
SALES (est): 1.6MM Privately Held
SIC: 2759 Commercial printing

(G-12745)
TRI COUNTY QUALITY WTR SYSTEMS
659 N Main St (43302-2332)
PHONE.................................740 751-4764
Jessica Bosh, General Mgr
EMP: 5
SALES (est): 319.5K Privately Held
SIC: 3589 Water filters & softeners, household type

(G-12746)
US YACHIYO INC
1177 Kellogg Pkwy (43302-1779)
PHONE.................................740 375-4687
Hiroshi Sasamoto, President
Kazuyoshi Itai, Vice Pres
Everett Lawrence, Production
Mike Hogan, Sales Staff
Kazuhiro Asabuki, Director
◆ EMP: 232
SQ FT: 125,000
SALES (est): 94MM
SALES (corp-wide): 144.1B Privately Held
SIC: 3795 Tanks & tank components
HQ: Yachiyo Of America Inc.
    2285 Walcutt Rd
    Columbus OH 43228

(G-12747)
WARREN ZACHMAN CONTRACTING
5005 Marion Edison Rd (43302-8979)
PHONE.................................740 389-4503
H Warren Zachman, President
David Schrote, Vice Pres
M Joyce Zachman, Treasurer
EMP: 3
SALES: 93K Privately Held
SIC: 3523 Farm machinery & equipment

(G-12748)
WHIRLPOOL CORPORATION
1300 Marion Agosta Rd (43302-9577)
PHONE.................................740 383-7122
Brian Gahr, President
Stan Kenneth, Vice Pres
David Strzalka, Mfg Dir
Barbara Klee, Safety Dir
Burl Davis, Safety Mgr
EMP: 250
SALES (corp-wide): 21B Publicly Held
WEB: www.whirlpoolcorp.com
SIC: 3633 5064 3632 Laundry dryers, household or coin-operated; washing machines; household refrigerators & freezers
PA: Whirlpool Corporation
    2000 N M 63
    Benton Harbor MI 49022
    269 923-5000

(G-12749)
WILLIAMS LEATHER PRODUCTS INC
Also Called: McKinley Leather
1476 Likens Rd Ste 104 (43302-8788)
PHONE.................................740 223-1604
Derek Williams, President
EMP: 6
SQ FT: 8,000
SALES (est): 1.4MM Privately Held
WEB: www.mckinleyleather.com
SIC: 3172 Personal leather goods

(G-12750)
WILSON BOHANNAN COMPANY
Also Called: W B
621 Buckeye St (43302-6121)
P.O. Box 504 (43301-0504)
PHONE.................................740 382-3639
Howard Smith, President
Josiah Bindley, Principal
G B Knapp, Principal
E J Schoenlaub, Principal
Pamela Smith, Corp Secy
EMP: 65 EST: 1860
SQ FT: 40,000
SALES (est): 21.2MM Privately Held
WEB: www.padlocks.com
SIC: 3429 Padlocks

(G-12751)
WYANDOT INC
135 Wyandot Ave (43302-1538)
PHONE.................................740 383-4031
Nick R Chilton, CEO
Wayne Cook, Area Mgr
Sam Prince, Area Mgr
Bryan Hensel, Vice Pres
Dan McGrady, Vice Pres
▲ EMP: 350 EST: 1936
SQ FT: 250,000
SALES (est): 116.7MM Privately Held
WEB: www.wyandotsnacks.com
SIC: 2096 Corn chips & other corn-based snacks

Marshallville
Wayne County

(G-12752)
D & R SUPPLY INC
18228 Fulton Rd (44645-9716)
PHONE.................................330 855-3781
Lindsey Schmitt, President
Jane Lavis, Manager
EMP: 3 EST: 1955
SALES (est): 407.6K Privately Held
WEB: www.drsupply.com
SIC: 2951 Asphalt & asphaltic paving mixtures (not from refineries)

(G-12753)
MARSHALLVILLE PACKING CO INC
50 E Market St (44645-9468)
P.O. Box 276 (44645-0276)
PHONE.................................330 855-2871
Frank T Tucker, President
Jeannette Tucker, Corp Secy
EMP: 29 EST: 1960
SQ FT: 35,000
SALES (est): 1.9MM Privately Held
SIC: 5421 5147 2013 2011 Meat markets, including freezer provisioners; meats, fresh; sausages & other prepared meats; meat packing plants

(G-12754)
NANCYS DRAPERIES
57 S Main St (44645-9773)
P.O. Box 305 (44645-0305)
PHONE.................................330 855-7751
Nancy Yoder, Owner
EMP: 12
SALES (est): 1MM Privately Held
SIC: 2211 5714 1799 Draperies & drapery fabrics, cotton; draperies; drapery track installation

(G-12755)
RUPP CONSTRUCTION INC
18228 Fulton Rd (44645-9716)
PHONE.................................330 855-2781
Gary Radabaugh, President
Dorothea Radabaugh, Corp Secy
EMP: 10
SQ FT: 20,000
SALES (est): 1.4MM Privately Held
WEB: www.ruppconstruction.com
SIC: 1442 Construction sand & gravel

Martins Ferry
Belmont County

(G-12756)
ARROWSTRIP INC
1st & Locust St S (43935)
P.O. Box 37 (43935-0037)
PHONE.................................740 633-2609
W Quay Mull II, Ch of Bd
Pete Mysliwic, President
Gary A Butler, Exec VP
Lisa M Leach, Vice Pres
▼ EMP: 21
SQ FT: 25,000
SALES (est): 5.2MM Privately Held
WEB: www.arrowstrip.com
SIC: 3312 Iron & steel: galvanized, pipes, plates, sheets, etc.

(G-12757)
AYERS LIMESTONE QUARRY INC
2002 Colerain Pike (43935)
PHONE.................................740 633-2958
Thomas E Ayers Jr, President
Patricia Ayers, Corp Secy
John Ayers, Vice Pres
EMP: 10
SQ FT: 8,000
SALES (est): 759.3K Privately Held
SIC: 1422 3274 Whiting mining, crushed & broken-quarrying; lime

(G-12758)
BLENDZALL INC
310 S 1st St (43935-1774)
PHONE.................................740 633-1333
Larry Eagle, President
Linda Parsons, Vice Pres
James Parsons, Treasurer
EMP: 5
SQ FT: 3,500
SALES (est): 750.5K Privately Held
WEB: www.blendzall.com
SIC: 2992 Oils & greases, blending & compounding

(G-12759)
CRUMMITT & SON VAULT CORP (PA)
329 N 2nd St (43935-2514)
P.O. Box 277 (43935-0277)
PHONE.................................304 281-2420
Michael Crummitt Jr, President
EMP: 9 EST: 1947
SQ FT: 10,000
SALES (est): 1.2MM Privately Held
SIC: 3272 Burial vaults, concrete or precast terrazzo

(G-12760)
EASTERN OHIO NEWSPAPERS INC
200 S 4th St (43935-1312)
PHONE.................................740 633-1131
G O Nutting, President
EMP: 5
SALES (est): 361.8K Privately Held
SIC: 2711 Newspapers, publishing & printing

(G-12761)
LESCO INC
100 Picoma Rd (43935-9700)
PHONE.................................740 633-6366
Frank Damato, Manager
EMP: 10
SALES (corp-wide): 37.3B Publicly Held
WEB: www.lesco.com
SIC: 5191 2875 Limestone, agricultural; seeds: field, garden & flower; fertilizers, mixing only

GEOGRAPHIC SECTION

Marysville - Union County (G-12788)

HQ: Lesco, Inc.
　　1385 E 36th St
　　Cleveland OH 44114
　　216 706-9250

(G-12762)
ULTIMATE SIGNS AND GRAPHICS
904 Indiana St (43935-2039)
PHONE....................740 633-8928
Jeff Rehberg, *Owner*
EMP: 3
SALES (est): 131K **Privately Held**
SIC: 3993 Signs & advertising specialties

(G-12763)
UNITED DAIRY INC (PA)
Also Called: United Quality Chekd Dairy
300 N 5th St (43935-1647)
P.O. Box 280 (43935-0280)
PHONE....................740 633-1451
Joseph L Carson, *President*
Joseph M Carson Jr, *Chairman*
George Wood, *Corp Secy*
Gary Cowell, *Vice Pres*
Philip Morris, *Opers Mgr*
EMP: 200 **EST**: 1903
SQ FT: 20,000
SALES (est): 202.7MM **Privately Held**
WEB: www.uniteddairy.com
SIC: 2026 2024 Milk processing (pasteurizing, homogenizing, bottling); ice cream, bulk

(G-12764)
WILSON BLACKTOP CORPORATION
915 Carlisle St Rear (43935-1511)
PHONE....................740 635-3566
Dale M Wilson, *President*
Janice L Wilson, *Corp Secy*
Mark E Wilson, *Vice Pres*
EMP: 20
SQ FT: 1,000
SALES (est): 4.2MM **Privately Held**
SIC: 2951 1611 1771 Asphalt & asphaltic paving mixtures (not from refineries); highway & street paving contractor; blacktop (asphalt) work; driveway contractor

Martinsburg
Knox County

(G-12765)
COVER UP BUILDING SYSTEMS
101 N Market St (43037)
P.O. Box 133 (43037-0133)
PHONE....................740 668-8985
Stephen Kidwell, *Owner*
EMP: 3
SALES (est): 247.3K **Privately Held**
SIC: 3448 Prefabricated metal buildings

Martinsville
Clinton County

(G-12766)
JOHN MCCULLOCH DISTILLERY
414 Cemetery Rd (45146-9654)
P.O. Box 112 (45146-0112)
PHONE....................937 725-5588
John McCulloch, *Principal*
EMP: 3 **EST**: 2011
SALES (est): 143.4K **Privately Held**
SIC: 2085 Distilled & blended liquors

(G-12767)
ROZZI COMPANY INC
6047 State Route 350 (45146-9539)
PHONE....................513 683-0620
Matthew Sheeley, *Principal*
EMP: 10
SALES (corp-wide): 5MM **Privately Held**
SIC: 2899 Chemical preparations
PA: The Rozzi Company Inc
　　118 Karl Brown Way
　　Loveland OH 45140
　　513 683-0620

(G-12768)
WILLIAM OEDER READY MIX INC
8807 State Route 134 (45146-9533)
PHONE....................513 899-3901
William Oeder, *President*
Robert Oeder, *Vice Pres*
Ronald Oeder, *Vice Pres*
Alma Oeder, *Treasurer*
Jo Ann Parker, *Admin Sec*
EMP: 20 **EST**: 1939
SQ FT: 3,000
SALES (est): 1.7MM **Privately Held**
SIC: 3273 Ready-mixed concrete

Marysville
Union County

(G-12769)
ALPHA CONTAINER CO INC
16789 Square Dr (43040-9496)
PHONE....................937 644-5511
Fred L McClellan Sr, *President*
Fred L Mc Clellan Sr, *President*
Chris McClellan, *Vice Pres*
▲ **EMP**: 12
SQ FT: 40,000
SALES (est): 4.1MM **Privately Held**
WEB: www.alphacontainer.net
SIC: 2653 Boxes, corrugated: made from purchased materials

(G-12770)
AMERICAN AGRITECH LLC
Also Called: Botanicare
14111 Scottslawn Rd (43040-7800)
PHONE....................480 777-2000
Treg Bradley,
◆ **EMP**: 30
SQ FT: 21,000
SALES (est): 8.3MM
SALES (corp-wide): 2.6B **Publicly Held**
WEB: www.americanagritech.com
SIC: 3423 Garden & farm tools, including shovels
PA: The Scotts Miracle-Gro Company
　　14111 Scottslawn Rd
　　Marysville OH 43040
　　937 644-0011

(G-12771)
BAR1 MOTORSPORTS
1757 Creekview Dr (43040-8556)
PHONE....................614 284-3732
Brian J Alder, *Owner*
EMP: 10
SALES (est): 723.3K **Privately Held**
SIC: 7694 Motor repair services

(G-12772)
BUCKEYE DIAMOND LOGISTICS INC
21963 Northwest Pkwy (43040-9147)
PHONE....................937 644-2194
Kenneth La Chey, *Branch Mgr*
EMP: 6
SALES (corp-wide): 32MM **Privately Held**
WEB: www.buckeyegroup.com
SIC: 3081 Packing materials, plastic sheet
PA: Buckeye Diamond Logistics, Inc.
　　15 Sprague Rd
　　South Charleston OH 45368
　　937 462-8361

(G-12773)
BUCKEYE READY-MIX LLC
838 N Main St (43040-9701)
P.O. Box 31, Reynoldsburg (43068-0031)
PHONE....................937 642-2951
Larry Randels, *Vice Pres*
EMP: 30
SQ FT: 3,000
SALES (corp-wide): 45.1MM **Privately Held**
WEB: www.buckeyereadymix.com
SIC: 3273 Ready-mixed concrete
PA: Buckeye Ready-Mix, Llc
　　7657 Taylor Rd Sw
　　Reynoldsburg OH 43068
　　614 575-2132

(G-12774)
CLOUTH SPRENGER LLC
14681 Industrial Pkwy (43040-9596)
PHONE....................937 642-8390
Tim Combs,
▲ **EMP**: 3 **EST**: 2010
SALES (est): 210.4K **Privately Held**
SIC: 3316 Strip steel, razor blade, cold-rolled: purchased hot-rolled

(G-12775)
CONNOLLY CONSTRUCTION CO INC
179 Emmaus Rd (43040-5524)
P.O. Box 271 (43040-0271)
PHONE....................937 644-8831
Phillip F Connolly, *President*
John Eufinger, *Treasurer*
Bonnie Spurling, *Receptionist*
EMP: 5
SQ FT: 2,244
SALES (est): 774.3K **Privately Held**
WEB: www.connollyconstruction.com
SIC: 1623 1521 1411 Sewer line construction; new construction, single-family houses; dimension stone

(G-12776)
CONTITECH USA INC
Also Called: Continental Contitech
13601 Industrial Pkwy (43040-8890)
PHONE....................937 644-8900
Ken Kontely, *Enginr/R&D Mgr*
Cheryl McCreary, *Empl Rel Mgr*
Lou Dizenzo, *Manager*
Bryan Mandzak, *Executive*
EMP: 39
SALES (corp-wide): 50.8B **Privately Held**
WEB: www.veyance.com
SIC: 3496 Conveyor belts
HQ: Contitech Usa, Inc.
　　703 S Clvland Mssillon Rd
　　Fairlawn OH 44333

(G-12777)
CONTRACT BUILDING COMPONENTS
Also Called: C B C
14540 Industrial Pkwy (43040-9595)
PHONE....................937 644-0739
Steven Yoder, *Vice Pres*
Jeff Coulter, *Manager*
EMP: 20
SALES (est): 2.9MM **Privately Held**
SIC: 2439 Trusses, wooden roof

(G-12778)
COPY SOURCE INC
108 N Main St (43040-1106)
PHONE....................937 642-7140
Joan Izzard, *CEO*
EMP: 3
SQ FT: 8,680
SALES (est): 367.7K **Privately Held**
SIC: 2759 2741 Commercial printing; miscellaneous publishing

(G-12779)
D C RAMEY PIANO CO
17768 Woodview Dr (43040-9711)
PHONE....................708 602-3961
David Ramey Jr, *Owner*
EMP: 3
SALES: 300K **Privately Held**
WEB: www.dcramey.com
SIC: 3931 Keyboards, piano or organ

(G-12780)
DAK ENTERPRISES INC (PA)
18062 Timber Trails Rd (43040-8158)
P.O. Box 409, Frazeysburg (43822-0409)
PHONE....................740 828-3291
Daniel Keifer, *President*
EMP: 200
SALES (est): 17.6MM **Privately Held**
SIC: 3089 Injection molded finished plastic products

(G-12781)
ENGINEERED MFG & EQP CO
Also Called: E M E C
11611 Industrial Pkwy (43040-9522)
PHONE....................937 642-7776
Raymond A Grigorenko, *President*
Thomas Walter, *General Mgr*
Leslie Grigorenko, *Vice Pres*
EMP: 8
SQ FT: 9,000
SALES (est): 1.2MM **Privately Held**
SIC: 3544 3699 Special dies, tools, jigs & fixtures; electrical equipment & supplies

(G-12782)
FILE 13 INC
232 N Main St Ste K (43040-1160)
P.O. Box 626 (43040-0626)
PHONE....................937 642-4855
Mark Ropp, *Principal*
EMP: 12
SALES (est): 1.8MM **Privately Held**
SIC: 3559 Tire shredding machinery

(G-12783)
FRANKES WOOD PRODUCTS LLC
825 Collins Ave (43040-1330)
PHONE....................937 642-0706
William Franke, *President*
Christopher S Franke, *Shareholder*
Kevin Franke, *Shareholder*
Michelle R Franke, *Shareholder*
EMP: 33
SQ FT: 93,800
SALES (est): 6.5MM **Privately Held**
SIC: 2448 2449 2493 3061 Cargo containers, wood; shipping cases & drums, wood: wirebound & plywood; fiberboard, other vegetable pulp; mechanical rubber goods; rubber scrap; marketing consulting services

(G-12784)
GRAPHIC STITCH INC
169 Grove St Rm A (43040-1342)
PHONE....................937 642-6707
Todd M Hoge, *President*
EMP: 9
SQ FT: 2,800
SALES (est): 883.5K **Privately Held**
WEB: www.graphicstitch.com
SIC: 2395 2759 Embroidery products, except schiffli machine; commercial printing

(G-12785)
GREENVILLE TECHNOLOGY INC
15000 Industrial Pkwy (43040-9547)
PHONE....................937 642-6744
EMP: 6 **EST**: 2015
SALES (est): 396K **Privately Held**
SIC: 3089 Automotive parts, plastic

(G-12786)
GUARDIAN STRATEGIC DEFENSE LLC
1540 Horizon Dr (43040-2551)
PHONE....................937 707-8985
Paul Sprague, *Principal*
EMP: 3
SALES (est): 159.6K **Privately Held**
SIC: 3812 Defense systems & equipment

(G-12787)
HAWTHORNE HYDROPONICS LLC
Also Called: Hawthorne Hydroponics/Botanic
14111 Scottslawn Rd (43040-7800)
PHONE....................480 777-2000
Chris Hagedorn,
Ross Haley,
▲ **EMP**: 100 **EST**: 1987
SALES: 1.3MM
SALES (corp-wide): 2.6B **Publicly Held**
SIC: 5083 2879 Hydroponic equipment & supplies; lawn & garden machinery & equipment; agricultural chemicals
HQ: The Hawthorne Garden Company
　　800 Port Washington Blvd
　　Port Washington NY 11050
　　516 883-6550

(G-12788)
HAWTHORNE HYDROPONICS LLC (DH)
14111 Scottslawn Rd (43040-7800)
PHONE....................800 221-1760
Chris Hagedorn, *Mng Member*
Amanda Green, *Manager*
EMP: 9

Marysville - Union County (G-12789)

SQ FT: 50,000
SALES (est): 71.6MM
SALES (corp-wide): 2.6B **Publicly Held**
SIC: 2873 Mfg Nitrogenous Fertilizers
HQ: The Hawthorne Garden Company
   800 Port Washington Blvd
   Port Washington NY 11050
   516 883-6550

(G-12789)
HONDA ENGINEERING N AMER INC
24000 Honda Pkwy (43040-9251)
PHONE..................................937 642-5000
Akira Takeshita, *President*
Ramesh Doddi, *Project Mgr*
Kevin Brletic, *Engineer*
Glenn Gonzales, *Regl Sales Mgr*
Bruce Drye, *Manager*
▲ EMP: 350
SALES (est): 182.6MM
SALES (corp-wide): 144.1B **Privately Held**
SIC: 3544 Special dies & tools; industrial molds
HQ: Honda Engineering Co.,Ltd.
   6-1, Hagadai, Hagamachi
   Haga-Gun TCG 321-3
   286 775-511

(G-12790)
HONDA ENGINEERING NA INC
24000 Honda Pkwy (43040-9251)
PHONE..................................937 707-5357
EMP: 10
SALES (est): 291.3K
SALES (corp-wide): 144.1B **Privately Held**
SIC: 3544 Special dies & tools
HQ: Honda Engineering Co.,Ltd.
   6-1, Hagadai, Hagamachi
   Haga-Gun TCG 321-3
   286 775-511

(G-12791)
HONDA OF AMERICA MFG INC (HQ)
Also Called: Marysville Auto Plant
24000 Honda Pkwy (43040-9251)
PHONE..................................937 642-5000
Tomomi Kosaka, *CEO*
Akio Hamada, *President*
John Adams, *Principal*
Deborah Gardner, *Purch Mgr*
Chris Walker, *Buyer*
◆ EMP: 750
SQ FT: 2,235,000
SALES (est): 3.6B
SALES (corp-wide): 144.1B **Privately Held**
WEB: www.hondamfg.com
SIC: 3711 Automobile assembly, including specialty automobiles
PA: Honda Motor Co., Ltd.
   2-1-1, Minamiaoyama
   Minato-Ku TKY 107-0
   334 231-111

(G-12792)
HONDA OF AMERICA MFG INC
Also Called: Honda Support Office
19900 State Route 739 (43040-9256)
PHONE..................................937 644-0724
EMP: 200
SALES (corp-wide): 144.1B **Privately Held**
SIC: 3714 3711 3465 8742 Motor vehicle parts & accessories; motor vehicles & car bodies; automotive stampings; training & development consultant
HQ: Honda Of America Mfg., Inc.
   24000 Honda Pkwy
   Marysville OH 43040
   937 642-5000

(G-12793)
HONDA OF AMERICA MFG INC
25000 Honda Pkwy (43040-9190)
PHONE..................................937 642-5000
EMP: 500
SALES (corp-wide): 144.1B **Privately Held**
SIC: 3711 Automobile assembly, including specialty automobiles

HQ: Honda Of America Mfg., Inc.
   24000 Honda Pkwy
   Marysville OH 43040
   937 642-5000

(G-12794)
HYPONEX CORPORATION (DH)
Also Called: Scotts- Hyponex
14111 Scottslawn Rd (43040-7800)
PHONE..................................937 644-0011
James Hagedorn, *President*
David M Brockman, *Exec VP*
Christopher Nagel, *Exec VP*
David C Evans, *CFO*
Donna Jones, *Administration*
EMP: 100 EST: 1980
SQ FT: 73,000
SALES (est): 595.8MM
SALES (corp-wide): 2.6B **Publicly Held**
SIC: 2873 2875 Fertilizers: natural (organic), except compost; plant foods, mixed: from plants making nitrog. fertilizers; fertilizers, mixing only; potting soil, mixed
HQ: The Scotts Company Llc
   14111 Scottslawn Rd
   Marysville OH 43040
   937 644-0011

(G-12795)
INFRARED IMAGING SYSTEMS INC
22718 Holycross Epps Rd (43040-9144)
PHONE..................................614 989-1148
James W Sharpe, *CEO*
Dale Siegel, *President*
Greg Miller, *Vice Pres*
Robert L Crane PHD, *Officer*
EMP: 4
SQ FT: 1,200
SALES (est): 330K **Privately Held**
SIC: 3823 Infrared instruments, industrial process type

(G-12796)
INTERNATIONAL PAPER COMPANY
13307 Industrial Pkwy (43040-9589)
PHONE..................................937 578-7718
EMP: 3
SALES (corp-wide): 23.3B **Publicly Held**
SIC: 2621 Paper mills
PA: International Paper Company
   6400 Poplar Ave
   Memphis TN 38197
   901 419-9000

(G-12797)
MAGNETIC SCREW MACHINE PDTS
23241 State Route 37 (43040-9749)
PHONE..................................937 348-2807
Bryan Bayes, *President*
EMP: 7 EST: 1971
SQ FT: 16,000
SALES (est): 1.1MM **Privately Held**
SIC: 3451 Screw machine products

(G-12798)
MARYSVILLE MONUMENT COMPANY
703 E 5th St (43040-1219)
PHONE..................................937 642-7039
EMP: 3
SALES (est): 95.7K **Privately Held**
SIC: 2711 Newspapers, publishing & printing

(G-12799)
MARYSVILLE NEWSPAPER INC (PA)
Also Called: Richwood Gazette
207 N Main St (43040-1161)
P.O. Box 226 (43040-0226)
PHONE..................................937 644-9111
Daniel Behrens, *President*
Kevin Behrens, *Principal*
EMP: 30
SQ FT: 10,000
SALES (est): 2.4MM **Privately Held**
WEB: www.marysvillejt.com
SIC: 2711 2731 Newspapers, publishing & printing; books: publishing & printing

(G-12800)
MARYSVILLE PRINTING COMPANY
127 S Main St (43040-1551)
PHONE..................................937 644-4959
William S Lithgo, *Owner*
EMP: 3
SQ FT: 3,600
SALES (est): 371.4K **Privately Held**
SIC: 2752 2759 Commercial printing, offset; commercial printing

(G-12801)
MARYSVILLE STEEL INC
323 E 8th St (43040)
P.O. Box 383 (43040-0383)
PHONE..................................937 642-5971
Steven J Clayman, *CEO*
EMP: 31
SQ FT: 50,000
SALES (est): 10.6MM **Privately Held**
SIC: 3441 1791 5039 Fabricated structural metal; structural steel erection; joists

(G-12802)
MCDANNALD WELDING & MACHINING
11879 State Route 736 (43040-9516)
PHONE..................................937 644-0300
Keith E McDannald, *President*
Susan McDannald, *Vice Pres*
EMP: 4
SALES (est): 275K **Privately Held**
SIC: 7692 3599 1799 1542 Welding repair; machine shop, jobbing & repair; welding on site; design & erection, combined: non-residential

(G-12803)
NEW REPUBLIC INDUSTRIES LLC
Also Called: My Second Home Early Lrng Schl
497 Bridle Dr (43040-1658)
PHONE..................................614 580-9927
Scott Weigand,
EMP: 11
SALES (est): 571.1K **Privately Held**
SIC: 3999 Manufacturing industries

(G-12804)
NKC OF AMERICA INC
24000 Honda Pkwy Gate E (43040)
PHONE..................................937 642-4033
Frederick Sheward, *Manager*
EMP: 5
SALES (est): 390.3MM **Privately Held**
WEB: www.nkcusa.com
SIC: 3535 Belt conveyor systems, general industrial use
HQ: Nkc Of America, Inc.
   1584 E Brooks Rd
   Memphis TN 38116
   901 396-6334

(G-12805)
PARKER-HANNIFIN CORPORATION
Hydraulic Pump Division
14249 Industrial Pkwy (43040-9504)
PHONE..................................937 644-3915
Ken Theiss, *Branch Mgr*
EMP: 230
SALES (corp-wide): 14.3B **Publicly Held**
WEB: www.parker.com
SIC: 3594 3491 3679 Pumps, hydraulic power transfer; industrial valves; electronic circuits
PA: Parker-Hannifin Corporation
   6035 Parkland Blvd
   Cleveland OH 44124
   216 896-3000

(G-12806)
PRECISION COATINGS SYSTEMS
948 Columbus Ave (43040-9501)
PHONE..................................937 642-4727
Fred Myers Jr, *President*
Mark Myers, *Vice Pres*
Sherry Myers, *Vice Pres*
Wendy Myers, *Vice Pres*
EMP: 30

SQ FT: 26,000
SALES: 2.4MM **Privately Held**
WEB: www.precisioncoatingsystems.com
SIC: 3479 7532 7549 7514 Painting of metal products; paint shop, automotive; collision shops, automotive; towing services; rent-a-car service

(G-12807)
RAY LEWIS & SON INCORPORATED
916 Delaware Ave (43040-1726)
P.O. Box 399 (43040-0399)
PHONE..................................937 644-4015
Robert Lewis, *President*
Nancy Lewis, *Corp Secy*
Bruce Valentino, *CFO*
Charles Lewis, *Shareholder*
EMP: 40 EST: 1944
SQ FT: 75,000
SALES (est): 7.1MM **Privately Held**
WEB: www.raylewisandson.com
SIC: 3364 3369 Zinc & zinc-base alloy die-castings; nonferrous foundries

(G-12808)
SAY DUMPSTERS
22665 Drby Pottersburg Rd (43040-8546)
PHONE..................................937 578-3744
Stanley Yanczura, *President*
EMP: 4
SALES (est): 439.9K **Privately Held**
SIC: 3443 Dumpsters, garbage

(G-12809)
SCOTTS COMPANY LLC (HQ)
Also Called: Scotts Miracle-Gro Products
14111 Scottslawn Rd (43040-7801)
P.O. Box 418 (43040-0418)
PHONE..................................937 644-0011
James Hagedorn, *CEO*
Ann Aquillo, *Vice Pres*
James Iovino, *Vice Pres*
Craig Izzo, *Vice Pres*
Jim King, *Vice Pres*
◆ EMP: 427
SALES (est): 1.6B
SALES (corp-wide): 2.6B **Publicly Held**
WEB: www.scottscompany.com
SIC: 2873 2874 2879 0782 Fertilizers: natural (organic), except compost; phosphates; fungicides, herbicides, insecticides, agricultural or household; lawn services; mulch, wood & bark; lawn & garden equipment; lawnmowers, residential: hand or power
PA: The Scotts Miracle-Gro Company
   14111 Scottslawn Rd
   Marysville OH 43040
   937 644-0011

(G-12810)
SCOTTS MIRACLE-GRO COMPANY (PA)
14111 Scottslawn Rd (43040-7801)
PHONE..................................937 644-0011
James Hagedorn, *Ch of Bd*
Michael C Lukemire, *President*
Melanie Spare, *Business Mgr*
Tim Veasman, *Business Mgr*
Denise S Stump, *Exec VP*
▲ EMP: 277
SALES: 2.6B **Publicly Held**
WEB: www.scotts.com
SIC: 3542 0782 7342 2879 Machine tools, metal forming type; lawn & garden services; pest control services; insecticides & pesticides

(G-12811)
SCOTTS MIRACLE-GRO COMPANY
Also Called: East Chemical Plant
14101 Industrial Pkwy (43040-9591)
PHONE..................................937 578-5065
Mike Henkel, *Branch Mgr*
Richard Briggs, *Manager*
EMP: 29
SALES (corp-wide): 2.6B **Publicly Held**
SIC: 2873 2879 Fertilizers: natural (organic), except compost; fungicides, herbicides
PA: The Scotts Miracle-Gro Company
   14111 Scottslawn Rd
   Marysville OH 43040
   937 644-0011

GEOGRAPHIC SECTION

Mason - Warren County (G-12836)

(G-12812)
SCOTTS MIRACLE-GRO PRODUCTS
14111 Scottslawn Rd (43040-7801)
PHONE....................937 644-0011
John Kenlon, *President*
Paul Duval, *Senior VP*
Patrick Norton, *CFO*
Lee Eadie, *Marketing Staff*
Brian Finney, *Manager*
EMP: 45
SQ FT: 10,000
SALES (est): 5.4MM
SALES (corp-wide): 2.6B **Publicly Held**
SIC: 2873 3432 Nitrogenous fertilizers; plumbing fixture fittings & trim
PA: The Scotts Miracle-Gro Company
  14111 Scottslawn Rd
  Marysville OH 43040
  937 644-0011

(G-12813)
SMG GROWING MEDIA INC (HQ)
14111 Scottslawn Rd (43040-7800)
PHONE....................937 644-0011
EMP: 7
SALES (est): 32.3MM
SALES (corp-wide): 2.6B **Publicly Held**
SIC: 3524 5083 Lawn & garden equipment; farm & garden machinery
PA: The Scotts Miracle-Gro Company
  14111 Scottslawn Rd
  Marysville OH 43040
  937 644-0011

(G-12814)
ST MARYS CEMENT INC (US)
14531 Industrial Pkwy (43040-9596)
PHONE....................937 642-4573
John Coolidge, *Manager*
EMP: 7
SALES (corp-wide): 1.1MM **Privately Held**
SIC: 3241 Cement, hydraulic
HQ: St. Marys Cement U.S. Llc
  9333 Dearborn St
  Detroit MI 48209
  313 842-4600

(G-12815)
STRAIGHT 72 INC
Also Called: MAI Manufacturing
20078 State Route 4 (43040-9723)
PHONE....................740 943-5730
Chris Vogelsang, *President*
Linda Wolf, *Vice Pres*
Mike Thomas, *QC Mgr*
Thomas J Muselin, *Hum Res Coord*
EMP: 60
SALES (est): 7.6MM **Privately Held**
SIC: 8711 3544 Acoustical engineering; special dies, tools, jigs & fixtures

(G-12816)
SUMITOMO ELC WIRG SYSTEMS INC
14800 Industrial Pkwy (43040-7507)
PHONE....................937 642-7579
Federico Menendez, *QC Mgr*
EMP: 33
SALES (corp-wide): 28.9B **Privately Held**
SIC: 3714 5063 3694 Automotive wiring harness sets; wire & cable; engine electrical equipment
HQ: Sumitomo Electric Wiring Systems, Inc.
  1018 Ashley St
  Bowling Green KY 42103
  270 782-7397

(G-12817)
TOOL TECHNOLOGIES VAN DYKE
639 Clymer Rd (43040-9502)
P.O. Box 256, Milford Center (43045-0256)
PHONE....................937 349-4900
Steven Vand Yke, *Owner*
Amy Rock, *Executive Asst*
EMP: 10
SQ FT: 5,000
SALES (est): 930K **Privately Held**
WEB: www.tooltechohio.com
SIC: 3829 3544 Measuring & controlling devices; special dies, tools, jigs & fixtures

(G-12818)
TRIPLE ARROW INDUSTRIES INC
Also Called: Arch Polymers
13311 Industrial Pkwy (43040-9589)
PHONE....................614 437-5588
Howard WEI, *President*
Ben Xu, *Principal*
George Wu, *Vice Pres*
◆ **EMP:** 7
SALES (est): 1.6MM **Privately Held**
SIC: 2821 5093 Plastics materials & resins; metal scrap & waste materials; nonferrous metals scrap

(G-12819)
Z LINE KITCHEN AND BATH LLC (PA)
Also Called: Range Hood Store, The
916 Delaware Ave (43040-1726)
PHONE....................614 777-5004
Andy Zuro,
EMP: 12
SQ FT: 13,000
SALES (est): 6.5MM **Privately Held**
SIC: 3444 5722 Hoods, range: sheet metal; gas ranges; electric ranges

Mason
Warren County

(G-12820)
AERO FULFILLMENT SERVICES CORP (PA)
3900 Aero Dr (45040-8840)
PHONE....................800 225-7145
Jon T Gimpel, *Ch of Bd*
Brenda Conaway, *VP Finance*
EMP: 100
SQ FT: 125,000
SALES: 23MM **Privately Held**
WEB: www.aerofulfillment.com
SIC: 4225 7374 7331 2759 General warehousing; data processing service; mailing service; commercial printing

(G-12821)
AEROSERV INC
201 Industrial Row Dr (45040-2600)
PHONE....................513 932-9227
Steve Michael, *President*
EMP: 10
SQ FT: 14,000
SALES (est): 1.9MM **Privately Held**
WEB: www.aeroserv.com
SIC: 3599 Machine shop, jobbing & repair

(G-12822)
AKOS PROMOTIONS INC
668 Reading Rd Ste C (45040-1583)
P.O. Box 78 (45040-0078)
PHONE....................513 398-6324
Christine Smith, *President*
EMP: 3
SQ FT: 2,500
SALES (est): 460K **Privately Held**
WEB: www.akospromo.com
SIC: 5199 2759 Advertising specialties; commercial printing

(G-12823)
AMPACET CORP
4705 Duke Dr Ste 400 (45040-9502)
PHONE....................513 247-5403
Morgan Gibbs, *Manager*
EMP: 4
SALES (est): 90K **Privately Held**
SIC: 2821 Plastics materials & resins

(G-12824)
ANDRE CORPORATION
4600 N Masn Montgomery Rd (45040-9176)
PHONE....................574 293-0207
David Andre, *President*
EMP: 50
SQ FT: 50,000
SALES (est): 15.6MM **Privately Held**
WEB: www.andrecorp.com
SIC: 3452 3469 5085 Washers, metal; stamping metal for the trade; fasteners, industrial: nuts, bolts, screws, etc.

(G-12825)
ARC BLINDS INC
3850 Bethany Rd (45040-9172)
PHONE....................513 889-4864
Dan Tichenor, *Principal*
EMP: 4 **EST:** 2012
SALES (est): 461.8K **Privately Held**
SIC: 2591 Window blinds

(G-12826)
ARMOR CONSOLIDATED INC (PA)
4600 N Mson Montgomery Rd (45040-9176)
PHONE....................513 923-5260
David K Schmitt, *CEO*
EMP: 2
SALES (est): 60.8MM **Privately Held**
SIC: 3441 3446 3443 6719 Fabricated structural metal; architectural metalwork; fabricated plate work (boiler shop); investment holding companies, except banks

(G-12827)
ARMOR GROUP INC (HQ)
4600 N Masn Montgomery Rd (45040-9176)
PHONE....................513 923-5260
David K Schmitt, *CEO*
Katherine D Schmitt, *Chairman*
Jane Martin, *Purch Mgr*
Joe Kennedy, *Buyer*
▲ **EMP:** 102
SALES: 60MM
SALES (corp-wide): 60.8MM **Privately Held**
WEB: www.cinind.com
SIC: 3441 3446 3444 3443 Fabricated structural metal; architectural metalwork; sheet metalwork; fabricated plate work (boiler shop)
PA: Armor Consolidated, Inc.
  4600 N Mson Montgomery Rd
  Mason OH 45040
  513 923-5260

(G-12828)
ARMOR METAL GROUP MASON INC (DH)
Also Called: Armormetal
4600 N Masn Montgomery Rd (45040-9176)
PHONE....................513 769-0700
David K Schmitt, *CEO*
Frank Ahaus, *President*
Jeffrey G Stagnaro, *Principal*
Dave Moses, *Sales Staff*
▲ **EMP:** 200
SALES (est): 58.8MM
SALES (corp-wide): 60.8MM **Privately Held**
SIC: 3441 3446 3444 3443 Fabricated structural metal; architectural metalwork; sheet metalwork; fabricated plate work (boiler shop)

(G-12829)
ASHLEY F WARD INC (PA)
Also Called: Precision Tek Manufacturing
7490 Easy St (45040-9423)
PHONE....................513 398-1414
Bill Ward, *Ch of Bd*
William H Ward, *Ch of Bd*
Terry Bien, *President*
Brian Scalf, *Vice Pres*
Bruce Snyder, *Plant Mgr*
▲ **EMP:** 116
SQ FT: 150,000
SALES (est): 46.5MM **Privately Held**
WEB: www.ashleyward.com
SIC: 3451 Screw machine products

(G-12830)
ATRICURE INC (PA)
7555 Innovation Way (45040-9695)
PHONE....................513 755-4100
Scott W Drake, *Ch of Bd*
Michael H Carrel, *President*
Douglas J Seith, *COO*
Justin J Noznesky, *Senior VP*
M Andrew Wade, *CFO*
EMP: 235 **EST:** 2000
SQ FT: 92,000
SALES: 201.6MM **Publicly Held**
WEB: www.atricure.com
SIC: 3841 Surgical instruments & apparatus; clamps, surgical

(G-12831)
BASCO MANUFACTURING COMPANY (PA)
Also Called: Basco Shower Enclosures
7201 Snider Rd (45040-9601)
PHONE....................513 573-1900
George W Rohde Jr, *President*
G William Rohde Sr, *Chairman*
Steve Lotz, *Vice Pres*
Kiersten Jung, *Purch Agent*
Jennifer Gress, *Purchasing*
◆ **EMP:** 177 **EST:** 1946
SQ FT: 80,000
SALES (est): 36.1MM **Privately Held**
WEB: www.bascoshowerdoor.com
SIC: 3231 Doors, glass: made from purchased glass; mirrored glass

(G-12832)
BEARCAT CONSTRUCTION INC
4457 Bethany Rd (45040-8128)
PHONE....................513 314-0867
Mike Gates, *Owner*
Irwin Vanwinkle, *General Mgr*
EMP: 4
SALES (est): 150K **Privately Held**
SIC: 1389 1522 Building oil & gas well foundations on site; residential construction

(G-12833)
BEAUMONT MACHINE LLC
7697 Innovation Way (45040-9605)
PHONE....................513 701-0421
Ramish Malhotra,
EMP: 15
SQ FT: 21,000
SALES (est): 3.7MM **Privately Held**
WEB: www.beaumontmachine.com
SIC: 3823 7699 Industrial process measurement equipment; precision instrument repair

(G-12834)
BEELINE PURCHASING LLC
4454 N Mallard Cv (45040-9041)
PHONE....................513 703-3733
Cathleen Holden, *President*
Kevin Holden, *Principal*
EMP: 3 **EST:** 2010
SALES (est): 235.5K **Privately Held**
SIC: 5999 5047 3842 Alarm & safety equipment stores; auction rooms (general merchandise); industrial safety devices: first aid kits & masks; personal safety equipment

(G-12835)
BERRY FILM PRODUCTS CO INC (DH)
Also Called: Clopay Plastic Products Co Inc
8585 Duke Blvd (45040-3100)
PHONE....................800 225-6729
Alan H Koblin, *President*
Ken Callow, *Vice Pres*
Danny Kelly, *Maint Spvr*
Jim Johnson, *Design Engr*
Tom Givens, *Treasurer*
◆ **EMP:** 100
SQ FT: 35,000
SALES (est): 90.6MM **Publicly Held**
SIC: 3081 Plastic film & sheet
HQ: Berry Global, Inc.
  101 Oakley St
  Evansville IN 47710
  812 424-2904

(G-12836)
BOSTON SCNTFIC NRMDLATION CORP
4267 S Haven Dr (45040-8629)
PHONE....................513 377-6160
EMP: 3
SALES (corp-wide): 9.8B **Publicly Held**
SIC: 3841 Surgical & medical instruments
HQ: Boston Scientific Neuromodulation Corporation
  25155 Rye Canyon Loop
  Valencia CA 91355

Mason - Warren County (G-12837)

(G-12837)
CARDEN DOOR COMPANY LLC
1224 Castle Dr (45040-9433)
PHONE 513 459-2233
Deb Stamper, *Accounts Mgr*
Adam Sylvester, *Manager*
John Jackson, *Council Mbr*
Cody Carden, *CIO*
Bruce Carden,
EMP: 7
SQ FT: 10,000
SALES (est): 760K **Privately Held**
SIC: 2431 Doors & door parts & trim, wood; doors, combination screen-storm, wood

(G-12838)
CARTER MANUFACTURING CO INC
4220 State Route 42 (45040-1931)
PHONE 513 398-7303
Chris Carter, *President*
EMP: 26
SALES (est): 885.7K **Privately Held**
WEB: www.cartermanufacturing.com
SIC: 3544 7692 3541 Dies & die holders for metal cutting, forming, die casting; jigs & fixtures; welding repair; machine tools, metal cutting type

(G-12839)
CARTER SCOTT-BROWNE
4220 State Route 42 (45040-1931)
PHONE 513 398-3970
Christopher Carter, *President*
Don Bullock, *Vice Pres*
EMP: 25
SALES (est): 1.7MM **Privately Held**
SIC: 3312 Tool & die steel

(G-12840)
CENGAGE LEARNING INC
770 Broadway (45040)
PHONE 513 234-5967
EMP: 143
SALES (corp-wide): 141.3MM **Privately Held**
SIC: 2731 Text Book Publishing
PA: Cengage Learning Inc
  20 Channel Ctr St
  Boston MA 02210
  203 965-8600

(G-12841)
CINCINNATI FTN SQ NEWS INC
Also Called: Fountain News
8739 S Shore Pl (45040-5044)
PHONE 513 421-4049
Diane Witte, *President*
Wanda Mauge, *Corp Secy*
James Witte, *Vice Pres*
Vido Patel, *Manager*
EMP: 10
SQ FT: 2,200
SALES (est): 517.3K **Privately Held**
SIC: 2711 Newspapers, publishing & printing

(G-12842)
CINCINNATI HEAT EXCHANGERS INC
6404 Thornberry Ct # 440 (45040-3502)
PHONE 513 874-7232
Timothy J Stillson, *President*
Elizabeth Stillson, *Admin Sec*
William Taylor,
▲ **EMP:** 6
SQ FT: 2,121
SALES (est): 1MM **Privately Held**
WEB: www.cinheats.com
SIC: 3443 Fabricated plate work (boiler shop)

(G-12843)
CINCINNATI INDUSTRIAL MCHY INC
4600 N Masn Montgomery Rd (45040-9176)
PHONE 513 923-5600
Joshua Donay, *President*
▲ **EMP:** 200
SQ FT: 200,000
SALES (est): 21.2MM
SALES (corp-wide): 60.8MM **Privately Held**
SIC: 3441 Fabricated structural metal
HQ: Armor Metal Group Mason, Inc.
  4600 N Masn Montgomery Rd
  Mason OH 45040

(G-12844)
CINCINNATI WINDOW SHADE INC
Also Called: Blinds Plus and More
5633 Tylersville Rd Ste 1 (45040-2533)
PHONE 513 398-8510
Cheri Burns, *Sales Staff*
EMP: 3
SALES (corp-wide): 5.4MM **Privately Held**
SIC: 5023 5719 2591 Window covering parts & accessories; window shades; venetian blinds; vertical blinds; window shades; venetian blinds; vertical blinds; window shades; venetian blinds; blinds vertical
PA: Cincinnati Window Shade, Inc.
  3004 Harris Ave
  Cincinnati OH 45212
  513 631-7200

(G-12845)
CINCOM SYSTEMS INC
4605 Duke Dr (45040-9410)
PHONE 513 459-1470
Thomas M Nies, *Branch Mgr*
EMP: 200
SALES (corp-wide): 109.6MM **Privately Held**
SIC: 7372 Business oriented computer software
PA: Cincom Systems, Inc.
  55 Merchant St Ste 100
  Cincinnati OH 45246
  513 612-2300

(G-12846)
CLOPAY BUILDING PDTS CO INC (DH)
Also Called: Ideal Door
8585 Duke Blvd (45040-3100)
PHONE 513 770-4800
Gene Colleran, *President*
Dan Beckley, *Vice Pres*
Alan R Leist, *Vice Pres*
Mr Pat Lohse, *Vice Pres*
Edward Shin, *Vice Pres*
◆ **EMP:** 36
SQ FT: 35,000
SALES (est): 234.3MM
SALES (corp-wide): 1.5B **Publicly Held**
SIC: 2431 3442 2436 Garage doors, overhead: wood; garage doors, overhead: metal; plywood, softwood
HQ: Clopay Corporation
  8585 Duke Blvd
  Mason OH 45040
  800 282-2260

(G-12847)
CLOPAY CORPORATION (HQ)
8585 Duke Blvd (45040-3100)
PHONE 800 282-2260
Gary Abyad, *President*
Eugene Colleran, *Senior VP*
Ellen Shoemaker, *Senior VP*
John Green, *Vice Pres*
Kevin Preston, *Opers Mgr*
▲ **EMP:** 231
SQ FT: 130,587
SALES (est): 981.8MM
SALES (corp-wide): 1.5B **Publicly Held**
WEB: www.clopay.com
SIC: 3081 3442 2431 1796 Plastic film & sheet; garage doors, overhead: metal; garage doors, overhead: wood; doors, wood; power generating equipment installation
PA: Griffon Corporation
  712 5th Ave Fl 18
  New York NY 10019
  212 957-5000

(G-12848)
CLOROX COMPANY
4680 Parkway Dr 130 (45040-8296)
PHONE 513 445-1840
Gina Kelly, *Manager*
EMP: 19
SALES (corp-wide): 6.1B **Publicly Held**
WEB: www.clorox.com
SIC: 2842 2812 Laundry cleaning preparations; chlorine, compressed or liquefied
PA: The Clorox Company
  1221 Broadway Ste 1300
  Oakland CA 94612
  510 271-7000

(G-12849)
CM PAULA COMPANY (PA)
Also Called: Geocentral
6049 Hi Tek Ct (45040-2603)
PHONE 513 759-7473
Charles W Mc Cullough, *Ch of Bd*
Greg Ionna, *President*
William Creager II, *Exec VP*
Monika Brandrup-Thomas, *Vice Pres*
Bill Ash, *CFO*
◆ **EMP:** 25 **EST:** 1958
SQ FT: 56,000
SALES (est): 12.9MM **Privately Held**
WEB: www.upwithpaper.com
SIC: 3089 2678 2499 3999 Novelties, plastic; stationery: made from purchased materials; decorative wood & woodwork; bric-a-brac

(G-12850)
CMC ELECTRONICS CINCINN
7500 Innovation Way (45040-9695)
PHONE 513 573-6316
Alan Scalf, *Engineer*
EMP: 3
SALES (est): 274.4K **Privately Held**
SIC: 3679 Electronic circuits

(G-12851)
CNC INDEXING FEEDING TECH LLC (PA)
7944 Innovation Way Ste B (45040-9396)
PHONE 513 770-4200
Steven Smith, *President*
Jamie Schwarz, *Natl Sales Mgr*
EMP: 7
SALES (est): 839.9K **Privately Held**
SIC: 3545 Machine tool accessories

(G-12852)
COMPOSITE CONCEPTS INC
615 Bunker Ln (45040-2044)
PHONE 440 247-3844
Dan Tomalin, *President*
Gary Meader, *Vice Pres*
EMP: 3
SALES (est): 286.7K **Privately Held**
SIC: 3357 Nonferrous wiredrawing & insulating

(G-12853)
CONAGRA BRANDS INC
7300 Central Parke Blvd (45040-6802)
PHONE 513 229-0305
Roland Rubio, *Branch Mgr*
EMP: 120
SALES (corp-wide): 7.9B **Publicly Held**
SIC: 2099 Food preparations
PA: Conagra Brands, Inc.
  222 Merchandise Mart Plz
  Chicago IL 60654
  312 549-5000

(G-12854)
DANONE US LLC
7577 Central Parke Blvd (45040-6810)
PHONE 513 229-0092
George Denmen, *Manager*
EMP: 390
SALES (corp-wide): 762.4MM **Privately Held**
WEB: www.dannon.com
SIC: 2024 Yogurt desserts, frozen
HQ: Danone Us, Llc
  1 Maple Ave
  White Plains NY 10605
  914 872-8400

(G-12855)
DEERFIELD MANUFACTURING INC
Also Called: Ice Industries Deerfield
320 N Mason Montgomery Rd (45040-7528)
PHONE 513 398-2010
Howard Ice, *President*
Paul Bishop, *COO*
Jeff Boger, *Exec VP*
EMP: 24 **EST:** 1946
SQ FT: 80,000
SALES (est): 13.6MM
SALES (corp-wide): 100MM **Privately Held**
WEB: www.iceindustries.com
SIC: 3469 Stamping metal for the trade
PA: Ice Industries, Inc.
  3810 Herr Rd
  Sylvania OH 43560
  419 842-3612

(G-12856)
DEERFIELD MEDICAL IMAGING LLC
9311 S Masn Montgomery Rd (45040)
PHONE 513 271-5717
Diane Bebout, *CFO*
Linda Stamper,
M Patricia Braeuning, *Radiology*
Robert V Bulas, *Radiology*
EMP: 3
SQ FT: 1,332
SALES (est): 375.2K **Privately Held**
SIC: 3845 CAT scanner (Computerized Axial Tomography) apparatus

(G-12857)
DOVER CORPORATION
Also Called: Opw Fluid Transfer Group
4680 Parkway Dr Ste 203 (45040-8296)
PHONE 513 696-1790
David Crouse, *Branch Mgr*
EMP: 10
SALES (corp-wide): 6.9B **Publicly Held**
SIC: 3531 3542 3565 Construction machinery; machine tools, metal forming type; packaging machinery
PA: Dover Corporation
  3005 Highland Pkwy # 200
  Downers Grove IL 60515
  630 541-1540

(G-12858)
DOWN-LITE INTERNATIONAL INC (PA)
Also Called: Downlite
8153 Duke Blvd (45040-8104)
PHONE 513 229-3696
James P Lape, *CEO*
Chad Altbaier, *Vice Pres*
Robert Altbaier, *Vice Pres*
Janna Ragan, *CFO*
Lisa Pruett, *Officer*
▲ **EMP:** 230 **EST:** 1983
SQ FT: 20,000
SALES (est): 78.8MM **Privately Held**
WEB: www.downbuyingguide.com
SIC: 2392 5719 Pillows, bed: made from purchased materials; comforters & quilts: made from purchased materials; bedding (sheets, blankets, spreads & pillows)

(G-12859)
EBSCO INDUSTRIES INC
1111 Western Row Rd (45040-1365)
PHONE 513 398-2149
Randy Sam, *Manager*
EMP: 15
SQ FT: 27,140
SALES (corp-wide): 2.8B **Privately Held**
WEB: www.ebscoind.com
SIC: 3949 Fishing tackle, general
PA: Ebsco Industries, Inc.
  5724 Highway 280 E
  Birmingham AL 35242
  205 991-6600

(G-12860)
EBSCO INDUSTRIES INC
Also Called: Imagen Brands
4680 Parkway Dr Ste 200 (45040-8173)
PHONE 513 398-3695
Lori Kates, *General Mgr*
Douglas Mayhugh, *Vice Pres*
Beth Banfill, *Controller*
Priscilla Wagner, *Human Res Dir*
Mike Qualters, *Sales Dir*
EMP: 15
SALES (corp-wide): 2.8B **Privately Held**
WEB: www.ebscoind.com
SIC: 2741 Miscellaneous publishing

PA: Ebsco Industries, Inc.
5724 Highway 280 E
Birmingham AL 35242
205 991-6600

(G-12861)
ELLISON GROUP INC (PA)
8118 Corp Way Ste 201 (45040)
PHONE..................513 770-4900
C Michael Ellison, *President*
Denny Myers, *Engineer*
Kevin Michael, *CFO*
EMP: 15
SALES (est): 54.2MM **Privately Held**
SIC: 3479 Painting, coating & hot dipping

(G-12862)
ELLISON SRFC TECH - MEXICO LLC
8093 Columbia Rd Ste 201 (45040-9560)
PHONE..................513 770-4900
Michael Ellison, *President*
Kevin Michael, *CFO*
EMP: 25
SQ FT: 13,000
SALES: 47MM **Privately Held**
SIC: 3479 Coating of metals & formed products

(G-12863)
ELLISON SURFACE TECH - W LLC (HQ)
8093 Columbia Rd Ste 201 (45040-9560)
PHONE..................513 770-4900
C Michael Ellison, *Mng Member*
EMP: 5
SALES (est): 2.5MM **Privately Held**
SIC: 3479 Painting, coating & hot dipping

(G-12864)
ELLISON SURFACE TECH INC (HQ)
8118 Corp Way Ste 201 (45040)
PHONE..................513 770-4922
C Michael Ellison, *President*
Ron Hall, *Opers Mgr*
Andy McCort, *Engineer*
Kevin Michael, *CFO*
Ben Watson, *Accounting Mgr*
EMP: 15
SQ FT: 27,000
SALES: 50MM **Privately Held**
WEB: www.ellisonsurfacetech.com
SIC: 3479 Coating of metals & formed products; painting, coating & hot dipping

(G-12865)
EMPIRE PACKING COMPANY LP
4780 Alliance Dr (45040-7832)
PHONE..................901 948-4788
Din Kirk, *Branch Mgr*
EMP: 800
SALES (corp-wide): 117.1MM **Privately Held**
SIC: 2011 Meat packing plants
PA: Empire Packing Company, L.P.
1837 Harbor Ave
Memphis TN 38113
901 948-4788

(G-12866)
ENGSTROM MANUFACTURING INC
4503b State Route 42 (45040-1936)
PHONE..................513 573-0010
Steve Engstrom, *President*
Joe Tako, *Corp Secy*
Jack Horstman, *Vice Pres*
Dave Tenny, *Vice Pres*
EMP: 14
SALES: 780K **Privately Held**
WEB: www.engstromprecision.com
SIC: 3452 3451 Screws, metal; screw machine products

(G-12867)
EPIC TECHNOLOGIES LLC
4240 Irwin Simpson Rd (45040-9859)
PHONE..................513 683-5455
Cameron Mc Gillivary, *VP Sls/Mktg*
John Smith, *Manager*
EMP: 100
SALES (corp-wide): 1.2B **Privately Held**
SIC: 3577 3679 Computer peripheral equipment; electronic circuits

HQ: Epic Technologies, Llc
9340 Owensmouth Ave
Chatsworth CA 91311
701 426-2192

(G-12868)
EVOKES LLC
8118 Corp Way Ste 212 (45040)
PHONE..................513 947-8433
Daniel Lincoln, *President*
Tony Leslie, *Office Mgr*
EMP: 50 **EST:** 2015
SQ FT: 900
SALES (est): 2.4MM **Privately Held**
SIC: 3822 8011 Building services monitoring controls, automatic; surgeon

(G-12869)
FAG BEARINGS CORPORATION
4035 N Ascot Pl (45040-1850)
PHONE..................513 398-1139
EMP: 200
SALES (corp-wide): 68.1B **Privately Held**
SIC: 3562 Ball & roller bearings
HQ: Fag Bearings Llc
200 Park Ave
Danbury CT 06810

(G-12870)
FANUC AMERICA CORPORATION
7700 Innovation Way (45040-9696)
PHONE..................513 754-2400
Eric Cahall, *Engineer*
John Roemisch, *Branch Mgr*
EMP: 35
SQ FT: 40,000
SALES (corp-wide): 6.8B **Privately Held**
WEB: www.fanucrobotics.com
SIC: 3559 3548 3559 Metal finishing equipment for plating, etc.; electric welding equipment; robots, assembly line: industrial & commercial
HQ: Fanuc America Corporation
3900 W Hamlin Rd
Rochester Hills MI 48309
248 377-7000

(G-12871)
FORTE INDUS EQP SYSTEMS INC
Also Called: Forte Industries
6037 Commerce Ct (45040-8819)
PHONE..................513 398-2800
Eugene A Forte, *President*
Doug Stamper, *Controller*
Eric Clark, *CIO*
Phyllis Forte, *Admin Sec*
EMP: 32
SQ FT: 16,000
SALES (est): 24.1MM
SALES (corp-wide): 36.3B **Privately Held**
WEB: www.forte-industries.com
SIC: 5084 8711 3537 Materials handling machinery; consulting engineer; industrial trucks & tractors
HQ: Swisslog Holding Ag
Webereiweg 3
Buchs AG 5033
628 379-537

(G-12872)
FRITO-LAY NORTH AMERICA INC
5181 Natorp Blvd Ste 400 (45040-2184)
PHONE..................513 229-3000
John Boes, *VP Human Res*
Chuck Shields, *Branch Mgr*
EMP: 160
SALES (corp-wide): 64.6B **Publicly Held**
SIC: 2096 Potato chips & similar snacks
HQ: Frito-Lay North America, Inc.
7701 Legacy Dr
Plano TX 75024

(G-12873)
FUJITEC AMERICA INC (HQ)
7258 Innovation Way (45040-8015)
PHONE..................513 755-6100
Takakazu Uchiyama, *CEO*
Katsuji Okuda, *President*
Masashi Tsuchihata, *Vice Pres*
Ray Gibson, *CFO*
Melissa Kawahara, *Admin Sec*
▲ **EMP:** 200

SQ FT: 300,000
SALES (est): 219.2MM
SALES (corp-wide): 1.5B **Privately Held**
WEB: www.fujiteceurope.com
SIC: 3534 Elevators & equipment; escalators, passenger & freight; walkways, moving
PA: Fujitec Co., Ltd.
591-1, Miyatacho
Hikone SGA 522-0
749 307-111

(G-12874)
FUN-IN-GAMES INC
Also Called: Fig- Games
9378 Mason Montgomery Rd (45040-8827)
PHONE..................866 587-1004
Mark Cohen,
▲ **EMP:** 5
SALES: 560.3K **Privately Held**
SIC: 2321 2752 7389 Sport shirts, men's & boys': from purchased materials; playing cards, lithographed;
PA: Global Consolidated Holdings Inc.
3965 Marble Ridge Ln
Mason OH 45040

(G-12875)
GATESAIR INC (HQ)
5300 Kings Island Dr (45040-2353)
PHONE..................513 459-3400
Bruce Swail, *CEO*
John Howell, *Principal*
Bryant Burke, *Vice Pres*
Joe Mack, *Vice Pres*
Joseph Mack, *Vice Pres*
▲ **EMP:** 52
SQ FT: 30,000
SALES (est): 16.5MM
SALES (corp-wide): 4B **Privately Held**
SIC: 1731 3663 7371 Communications specialization; radio & TV communications equipment; computer software development & applications
PA: The Gores Group Llc
9800 Wilshire Blvd
Beverly Hills CA 90212
310 209-3010

(G-12876)
GENERAL MILLS INC
5181 Natorp Blvd Ste 540 (45040-2183)
PHONE..................513 770-0558
Peter Baruk, *Branch Mgr*
EMP: 55
SALES (corp-wide): 15.7B **Publicly Held**
WEB: www.generalmills.com
SIC: 5141 2041 Food brokers; flour mixes
PA: General Mills, Inc.
1 General Mills Blvd
Minneapolis MN 55426
763 764-7600

(G-12877)
GEORGIA-PACIFIC LLC
5181 Natorp Blvd Ste 520 (45040-5907)
PHONE..................513 336-4200
James Hannan, *Manager*
EMP: 12
SALES (corp-wide): 42.4B **Privately Held**
SIC: 2621 Paper mills
HQ: Georgia-Pacific Llc
133 Peachtree St Nw
Atlanta GA 30303
404 652-4000

(G-12878)
GLASSLIGHT CANDLES LLC
8706 Charleston Ridge Dr (45040-8032)
PHONE..................443 509-5505
Carri Brown, *Principal*
EMP: 3
SALES (est): 196.1K **Privately Held**
SIC: 3999 Candles

(G-12879)
GLOBAL INNOVATIVE PRODUCTS LLC
7697 Innovation Way # 200 (45040-9605)
PHONE..................513 701-0441
Ramesh Malhotra, *Mng Member*
▲ **EMP:** 7
SQ FT: 25,000
SALES (est): 360.8K **Privately Held**
SIC: 3621 Electric motor & generator parts

(G-12880)
GLOBAL LASER TEK
7697 Innovation Way # 700 (45040-9605)
PHONE..................513 701-0452
Dan Polto, *Director*
EMP: 28 **EST:** 2014
SALES (est): 1.9MM
SALES (corp-wide): 5MM **Privately Held**
SIC: 3699 Laser systems & equipment
PA: Global Specialty Machines Llc
7697 Innovation Way # 700
Mason OH 45040
513 701-0452

(G-12881)
GLOBAL SPECIALTY MACHINES LLC (PA)
7697 Innovation Way # 700 (45040-9605)
PHONE..................513 701-0452
Ramesh Malhotra, *Mng Member*
Dan Polto, *Mng Member*
▲ **EMP:** 12
SQ FT: 3,000
SALES (est): 5MM **Privately Held**
SIC: 3541 Electron-discharge metal cutting machine tools

(G-12882)
GRAHAM PACKAGING CO EUROPE LLC
1225 Castle Dr (45040-9672)
PHONE..................513 398-5000
Jerry Hammons, *Engineer*
Jay Tharp, *Plant Engr*
Lee Banks, *Branch Mgr*
EMP: 125
SALES (corp-wide): 1MM **Privately Held**
WEB: www.liquidcontainer.com
SIC: 3089 Buckets, plastic; plastic containers, except foam
HQ: Graham Packaging Company Europe Llc
2401 Pleasant Valley Rd # 2
York PA 17402

(G-12883)
HAAG-STREIT HOLDING US INC (DH)
3535 Kings Mills Rd (45040-2303)
PHONE..................513 336-7255
Dennis Imwalle, *President*
David R Edenfield, *Vice Pres*
EMP: 20
SALES (est): 52.7MM
SALES (corp-wide): 1.2B **Privately Held**
SIC: 5047 3841 Surgical equipment & supplies; surgical & medical instruments; ophthalmic instruments & apparatus
HQ: Haag-Streit Holding Ag
Gartenstadtstrasse 10
KOniz BE 3098
319 780-100

(G-12884)
HANDS ON INTERNATIONAL LLC
8541 Charleston Ridge Dr (45040-7995)
PHONE..................513 502-9000
Micheal Proctor, *Accounting Mgr*
Fessel Khan,
Julie Khan,
▲ **EMP:** 7
SALES (est): 402.6K **Privately Held**
SIC: 5136 2326 7389 Work clothing, men's & boys'; work apparel, except uniforms;

(G-12885)
HARRIS HAWK
306 W Main St (45040-1622)
PHONE..................800 459-4295
Frank Batscie, *President*
Frank Geers, *Principal*
EMP: 5
SALES: 1MM **Privately Held**
WEB: www.harrishawk.com
SIC: 5199 2752 8999 Advertising specialties; commercial printing, offset; communication services

(G-12886)
HI-TEK MANUFACTURING INC
Also Called: System EDM of Ohio
6050 Hi Tek Ct (45040-2602)
PHONE..................513 459-1094

Cletis Jackson, *President*
Scott Stang, *Plant Mgr*
George Carrington, *QC Mgr*
Michael Beech, *Engineer*
Craig Enderle, *Engineer*
▲ **EMP:** 180
SQ FT: 71,000
SALES (est): 69MM **Privately Held**
WEB: www.hitekmfg.com
SIC: 3599 7692 3724 3714 Machine shop, jobbing & repair; welding repair; aircraft engines & engine parts; motor vehicle parts & accessories; special dies, tools, jigs & fixtures

(G-12887)
IAMS COMPANY (HQ)
8700 S Masn Montgomery Rd (45040-9760)
PHONE 800 675-3849
AG Losley, *CEO*
Brian Robson, *CFO*
Jan Dinges, *Admin Sec*
▲ **EMP:** 300
SQ FT: 50,000
SALES (est): 311MM
SALES (corp-wide): 34.2B **Privately Held**
WEB: www.iams.com
SIC: 2047 2048 Dog food; cat food; prepared feeds
PA: Mars, Incorporated
   6885 Elm St Ste 1
   Mc Lean VA 22101
   703 821-4900

(G-12888)
IBIZA HOLDINGS INC
7901 Innovation Way (45040-9498)
PHONE 513 701-7300
Chris Cole, *CEO*
EMP: 50
SALES (est): 3.7MM **Privately Held**
SIC: 3535 Conveyors & conveying equipment

(G-12889)
ICE INDUSTRIES INC
320 N Mason Montgomery Rd (45040-7528)
PHONE 513 398-2010
Ken Kneip, *Controller*
Jene Swick, *Branch Mgr*
EMP: 5
SALES (corp-wide): 100MM **Privately Held**
SIC: 3469 Metal stampings
PA: Ice Industries, Inc.
   3810 Herr Rd
   Sylvania OH 43560
   419 842-3612

(G-12890)
IMAGINE COMMUNICATIONS CORP
Also Called: Harris Broadcast
5300 Kings Island Dr # 101 (45040-2353)
PHONE 513 459-3400
P Harris Morris, *CEO*
Rich Lohmueller, *Principal*
EMP: 75
SQ FT: 17,000
SALES (corp-wide): 4B **Privately Held**
SIC: 3663 Radio broadcasting & communications equipment; television broadcasting & communications equipment
HQ: Imagine Communications Corp.
   7950 Legacy Dr Ste 400
   Plano TX 75024
   469 803-4900

(G-12891)
INTELLIGRATED INC (HQ)
7901 Innovation Way (45040-9498)
PHONE 866 936-7300
Chris Cole, *CEO*
Jim McCarthy, *President*
Edward Puisis, *CFO*
▲ **EMP:** 29 **EST:** 2001
SALES (est): 27MM
SALES (corp-wide): 41.8B **Publicly Held**
SIC: 3535 Conveyors & conveying equipment
PA: Honeywell International Inc.
   115 Tabor Rd
   Morris Plains NJ 07950
   973 455-2000

(G-12892)
INTELLIGRATED HEADQUARTERS LLC
7901 Innovation Way (45040-9498)
PHONE 866 936-7300
EMP: 9 **EST:** 2014
SALES (est): 553.9K
SALES (corp-wide): 41.8B **Publicly Held**
SIC: 3535 Conveyors & conveying equipment
HQ: Intelligrated Systems, Inc.
   7901 Innovation Way
   Mason OH 45040
   866 936-7300

(G-12893)
INTELLIGRATED SUB HOLDINGS INC (PA)
7901 Innovation Way (45040-9498)
PHONE 513 701-7300
Chris Cole, *CEO*
Derek Nemeth, *Credit Mgr*
EMP: 21
SQ FT: 250,000
SALES (est): 8.5MM **Privately Held**
SIC: 3535 Conveyors & conveying equipment

(G-12894)
INTELLIGRATED SYSTEMS INC (HQ)
7901 Innovation Way (45040-9498)
PHONE 866 936-7300
Chris Cole, *CEO*
Jim McCarthy, *President*
Ed Puisis, *CFO*
▲ **EMP:** 800 **EST:** 1996
SQ FT: 390,000
SALES: 800MM
SALES (corp-wide): 41.8B **Publicly Held**
SIC: 3535 5084 7371 Conveyors & conveying equipment; industrial machinery & equipment; computer software development
PA: Honeywell International Inc.
   115 Tabor Rd
   Morris Plains NJ 07950
   973 455-2000

(G-12895)
INTELLIGRATED SYSTEMS LLC
7901 Innovation Way (45040-9498)
PHONE 513 701-7300
Chris Cole, *CEO*
Jim McCarthy, *President*
Jim McKnight, *Senior VP*
Bryan Jones, *Vice Pres*
Ed Puisis, *CFO*
EMP: 2300
SQ FT: 260,000
SALES (est): 228.8MM
SALES (corp-wide): 41.8B **Publicly Held**
SIC: 3535 5084 7371 Conveyors & conveying equipment; materials handling machinery; computer software development
HQ: Intelligrated Systems, Inc.
   7901 Innovation Way
   Mason OH 45040
   866 936-7300

(G-12896)
INTELLIGRATED SYSTEMS OHIO LLC (DH)
7901 Innovation Way (45040-9498)
PHONE 513 701-7300
Jim McCarthy, *President*
Stephen Ackerman, *Exec VP*
Stephen Causey, *Vice Pres*
◆ **EMP:** 600 **EST:** 2010
SQ FT: 332,000
SALES (est): 287.7MM
SALES (corp-wide): 41.8B **Publicly Held**
WEB: www.fkilogistex.com
SIC: 3535 5084 3537 Conveyors & conveying equipment; industrial machinery & equipment; palletizers & depalletizers
HQ: Intelligrated Systems, Inc.
   7901 Innovation Way
   Mason OH 45040
   866 936-7300

(G-12897)
INTERSTATE CONTRACTORS LLC
Also Called: Ic Roofing
762 Reading Rd G (45040-1362)
PHONE 513 372-5393
Young Chon Jung,
Jiah Jung,
EMP: 40
SALES (est): 2.8MM **Privately Held**
SIC: 8611 3444 Business associations; metal roofing & roof drainage equipment

(G-12898)
K & K PRECISION INC
5001 N Masn Montgomery Rd (45040-9148)
PHONE 513 336-0032
David J Kappes, *President*
Larry G Hixson, *Vice Pres*
Melinda Kappes, *Admin Sec*
EMP: 21 **EST:** 1991
SALES (est): 4.7MM **Privately Held**
WEB: www.kkprecision.com
SIC: 3599 Machine shop, jobbing & repair

(G-12899)
KLOSTERMAN BAKING CO
1130 Reading Rd (45040-9156)
PHONE 513 398-2707
Chip Klosterman, *President*
EMP: 19
SQ FT: 60,000
SALES (corp-wide): 207.2MM **Privately Held**
SIC: 2051 4225 Bakery: wholesale or wholesale/retail combined; general warehousing
PA: Klosterman Baking Co.
   4760 Paddock Rd
   Cincinnati OH 45229
   513 242-5667

(G-12900)
KNEADING DOUGH LLC
7912 S Masn Montgomery Rd (45040-8249)
PHONE 719 310-5774
Corbin G Koepke,
EMP: 4 **EST:** 2015
SALES (est): 201.2K **Privately Held**
SIC: 2051 Bakery: wholesale or wholesale/retail combined

(G-12901)
L-3 CMMNCATIONS NOVA ENGRG INC
4393 Digital Way (45040-7604)
P.O. Box 16850, Salt Lake City UT (84116-0850)
PHONE 877 282-1168
Mark Fischer, *President*
EMP: 150
SQ FT: 80,000
SALES (est): 8.7MM
SALES (corp-wide): 10.2B **Publicly Held**
WEB: www.l-3com.com
SIC: 8711 3663 Electrical or electronic engineering; carrier equipment, radio communications
PA: L3 Technologies, Inc.
   600 3rd Ave Fl 34
   New York NY 10016
   212 697-1111

(G-12902)
L3 CINCINNATI ELECTRONICS CORP (HQ)
Also Called: L-3 Communications Cincinnati
7500 Innovation Way (45040-9695)
PHONE 513 573-6100
Russ Walker, *CEO*
Patrick J Sweeney, *Chairman*
Doug Becker, *Vice Pres*
Mark Dapore, *Vice Pres*
Ed English, *Vice Pres*
EMP: 600
SQ FT: 230,000
SALES (est): 136MM
SALES (corp-wide): 10.2B **Publicly Held**
WEB: www.cinele.com
SIC: 3812 3769 3823 Detection apparatus: electronic/magnetic field, light/heat; missile guidance systems & equipment; guided missile & space vehicle parts & auxiliary equipment; infrared instruments, industrial process type
PA: L3 Technologies, Inc.
   600 3rd Ave Fl 34
   New York NY 10016
   212 697-1111

(G-12903)
LANTEK SYSTEMS INC
5155 Financial Way Ste 2 (45040-0055)
PHONE 513 988-8708
Juan Louis Larranaga, *President*
Alberto Martinez, *Vice Pres*
Adria Iles, *Director*
EMP: 6
SQ FT: 2,750
SALES (est): 644.8K
SALES (corp-wide): 101.8K **Privately Held**
SIC: 7373 7372 5734 7371 Computer system selling services; turnkey vendors, computer systems; business oriented computer software; computer software & accessories; computer software development & applications
HQ: Lantek Sheet Metal Solutions SI
   Calle Ferdinand Zeppelin 2
   Vitoria-Gasteiz 01510
   945 298-705

(G-12904)
M C SYSTEMS INC
4455 Bethany Rd Unit C (45040-9688)
PHONE 513 336-6007
Mark Chrostowski, *President*
Drew Chrostowski, *Vice Pres*
EMP: 4
SALES (est): 403.5K **Privately Held**
SIC: 3577 7699 Bar code (magnetic ink) printers; repair services

(G-12905)
MAKINO INC (HQ)
7680 Innovation Way (45040-9695)
P.O. Box 8003 (45040-8003)
PHONE 513 573-7200
Donald Lane, *President*
Bob Henry, *Vice Pres*
F Matsubara, *Admin Sec*
◆ **EMP:** 356 **EST:** 1887
SQ FT: 320,000
SALES (est): 169MM
SALES (corp-wide): 1.7B **Privately Held**
WEB: www.moldmakermag.com
SIC: 3541 Machine tools, metal cutting type
PA: Makino Milling Machine Co., Ltd.
   2-3-19, Nakane
   Meguro-Ku TKY 152-0
   337 171-151

(G-12906)
MAMMAS MANDEL
7952 Hedgewood Cir (45040-6008)
PHONE 513 827-2457
Howard Pinsky, *Principal*
EMP: 3 **EST:** 2011
SALES (est): 169.5K **Privately Held**
SIC: 2053 Cakes, bakery: frozen

(G-12907)
MARTIN MARIETTA MATERIALS INC
4900 Parkway Dr (45040-8430)
PHONE 513 701-1120
Michael Hunt, *Principal*
EMP: 10 **Publicly Held**
SIC: 1423 Crushed & broken granite
PA: Martin Marietta Materials Inc
   2710 Wycliff Rd
   Raleigh NC 27607

(G-12908)
MAUSER USA LLC
1229 Castle Dr (45040-9672)
P.O. Box 350 (45040-0350)
PHONE 513 398-1300
Carolyn Russell, *Transptn Dir*
Steve Haunert, *Plant Mgr*

Tom Knapp, *Manager*
EMP: 90
SALES (corp-wide): 1.1B **Privately Held**
SIC: 3412 Drums, shipping: metal
HQ: Mauser Usa, Llc
 35 Cotters Ln Ste C
 East Brunswick NJ 08816
 732 353-7100

(G-12909)
MICROSOFT CORPORATION
4605 Duke Dr Ste 800 (45040-7627)
PHONE..................513 339-2800
Tom Taylor, *Partner*
Jack Lapan, *Branch Mgr*
EMP: 54
SALES (corp-wide): 110.3B **Publicly Held**
WEB: www.microsoft.com
SIC: 7372 Application computer software
PA: Microsoft Corporation
 1 Microsoft Way
 Redmond WA 98052
 425 882-8080

(G-12910)
MILLER AND SLAY WDWKG LLC
8284 Winters Ln (45040-9100)
PHONE..................513 265-3816
Jon Miller, *Principal*
EMP: 4
SALES (est): 246.5K **Privately Held**
SIC: 2431 Millwork

(G-12911)
MITSUBISHI ELC AUTO AMER INC (DH)
4773 Bethany Rd (45040-8344)
PHONE..................513 573-6614
Takeo Sasaki, *President*
Kelle Sanders, *Opers Staff*
Tina Appelman, *Production*
Athar Siddiqui, *Production*
Tom Wylie, *Purch Mgr*
◆ EMP: 422
SQ FT: 220,000
SALES (est): 249.2MM
SALES (corp-wide): 41.5B **Privately Held**
SIC: 3694 3651 3714 Motors, starting: automotive & aircraft; alternators, automotive; household audio & video equipment; motor vehicle parts & accessories
HQ: Mitsubishi Electric Us Holdings, Inc.
 5900 Katella Ave Ste A
 Cypress CA 90630
 714 220-2500

(G-12912)
MORSE ENTERPRISES INC
Also Called: AlphaGraphics Cincinnati
6678 Tri Way Dr (45040-2605)
PHONE..................513 229-3600
Cinda Morse, *Principal*
Steven Morse, *Principal*
Sherry Taylor, *Director*
EMP: 7 EST: 2013
SQ FT: 3,200
SALES (est): 480K **Privately Held**
SIC: 2759 7334 2752 7336 Commercial printing; photocopying & duplicating services; commercial printing, offset; business form & card printing, lithographic; commercial art & graphic design; pamphlets: printing & binding, not published on site

(G-12913)
MULTI-COLOR CORPORATION
5510 Courseview Dr (45040-2366)
PHONE..................513 459-3283
Bob Feldman, *Branch Mgr*
EMP: 9
SALES (corp-wide): 1.3B **Publicly Held**
SIC: 2759 2679 2672 Labels & seals: printing; labels, paper: made from purchased material; labels (unprinted), gummed: made from purchased materials
PA: Multi-Color Corporation
 4053 Clough Woods Dr
 Batavia OH 45103
 513 381-1480

(G-12914)
NEO TECHNOLOGY SOLUTIONS
4240 Irwin Simpson Rd (45040-9859)
PHONE..................513 234-5725
EMP: 6

SALES (est): 778.3K **Privately Held**
SIC: 3672 Circuit boards, television & radio printed

(G-12915)
NORITAKE CO INC
4990 Alliance Dr (45040-4516)
PHONE..................513 234-0770
Nori Kambayashi, *Branch Mgr*
EMP: 30
SALES (corp-wide): 1.1B **Privately Held**
WEB: www.noritake.com
SIC: 3291 Synthetic abrasives
HQ: Noritake Co., Inc.
 15-22 Fair Lawn Ave
 Fair Lawn NJ 07410
 201 796-2222

(G-12916)
NORWICH OVERSEAS INC (HQ)
8700 S Masn Montgomery Rd (45040-9760)
PHONE..................513 983-1100
▲ EMP: 10
SALES (est): 5MM
SALES (corp-wide): 259.8MM **Privately Held**
SIC: 2834 Mfg Pharmaceutical Preparations
PA: Warner Chilcott Pharmaceuticals Inc.
 1 Procter And Gamble Plz
 Cincinnati OH 45202
 513 983-1100

(G-12917)
O C TANNER COMPANY
Also Called: O.c Tanner Recognition
8569 S Mason Montgomery R (45040-9806)
PHONE..................513 583-1100
Debbie Phipps, *Manager*
EMP: 5
SALES (corp-wide): 341.9MM **Privately Held**
WEB: www.octanner.com
SIC: 3911 Pins (jewelry), precious metal
PA: O. C. Tanner Company
 1930 S State St
 Salt Lake City UT 84115
 801 486-2430

(G-12918)
OAKLEY DIE & MOLD CO
Also Called: O D M
7595 Innovation Way (45040-9052)
PHONE..................513 754-8500
Ernest Petrinowitsch, *CEO*
Harry Petrinowitsch, *President*
Peggy Braun, *Admin Sec*
▲ EMP: 35 EST: 1948
SQ FT: 80,950
SALES (est): 6.6MM **Privately Held**
WEB: www.odm.com
SIC: 3599 3544 3545 Machine shop, jobbing & repair; industrial molds; tools & accessories for machine tools

(G-12919)
OSG USA INC
3611 Socialvl Fstr Rd # 102 (45040-7361)
PHONE..................513 755-3360
Rick Jones, *Branch Mgr*
EMP: 10
SALES (corp-wide): 1.1B **Privately Held**
WEB: www.osgtool.com
SIC: 3544 Special dies, tools, jigs & fixtures
HQ: Osg Usa, Inc.
 676 E Fullerton Ave
 Glendale Heights IL 60139
 630 790-1400

(G-12920)
PHANTOM SOUND
104 Reading Rd (45040-1634)
PHONE..................513 759-4477
Howard Mc Gurdy, *Owner*
◆ EMP: 12
SALES: 810K **Privately Held**
WEB: www.phantomsound.com
SIC: 3651 5731 Speaker systems; radio, television & electronic stores

(G-12921)
PILOT PRODUCTION SOLUTIONS LLC
Also Called: Pps
6253 Crooked Creek Dr (45040-2443)
PHONE..................513 602-1467
Michael Ullom,
EMP: 3
SALES (est): 206.2K **Privately Held**
SIC: 2672 7389 Coated & laminated paper;

(G-12922)
PORTION PAC INC (DH)
7325 Snider Rd (45040-9193)
PHONE..................513 398-0400
Jeffrey Berger, *President*
Pete Jack, *President*
Timothy E Hoberg, *Principal*
Leslie Boettcher, *Vice Pres*
▼ EMP: 400
SQ FT: 100,000
SALES (est): 138.5MM
SALES (corp-wide): 26.2B **Publicly Held**
WEB: www.portionpac.com
SIC: 2033 2035 Catsup: packaged in cans, jars, etc.; jams, including imitation: packaged in cans, jars, etc.; jellies, edible, including imitation: in cans, jars, etc.; marmalade: packaged in cans, jars, etc.; seasonings & sauces, except tomato & dry; mustard, prepared (wet); horseradish, prepared; dressings, salad: raw & cooked (except dry mixes)
HQ: Kraft Heinz Foods Company
 1 Ppg Pl Fl 34
 Pittsburgh PA 15222
 412 456-5700

(G-12923)
PRASCO LLC (PA)
Also Called: Prasco Laboratories
6125 Commerce Ct (45040-6723)
PHONE..................513 204-1100
Christopher H Arington, *CEO*
Jonathan Lapps, *President*
David Vucurevich, *President*
Patrick Christensen, *Vice Pres*
Otis Ranson, *Vice Pres*
▲ EMP: 118
SALES (est): 19MM **Privately Held**
WEB: www.prasco.com
SIC: 2834 Pharmaceutical preparations

(G-12924)
PRATT INDUSTRIES INC
Also Called: Pratt Displays
4700 Duke Dr Ste 140 (45040-9507)
PHONE..................513 770-0851
Dave Connors, *Manager*
Debbie Richey, *Manager*
EMP: 66
SALES (corp-wide): 2.5B **Privately Held**
SIC: 2653 Display items, corrugated: made from purchased materials
PA: Pratt Industries, Inc.
 1800 Sarasota Busin Ste C
 Conyers GA 30013
 770 918-5678

(G-12925)
PRESTIGE FIREWORKS LLC
222 Van Buren Dr (45040-2138)
PHONE..................513 492-7726
Kevin Shew, *President*
Martin Schaefer, *Vice Pres*
EMP: 19
SALES: 250K **Privately Held**
WEB: www.prestigefireworks.com
SIC: 2899 Fireworks

(G-12926)
PROCTER & GAMBLE COMPANY
8700 Mason Montgomery Rd (45040-9760)
P.O. Box 8006 (45040-8006)
PHONE..................513 622-1000
Bonnie Bowman, *General Mgr*
Kim Harvey, *General Mgr*
Shirley Pfeifer, *Vice Pres*
Mary Haver, *Project Mgr*
Murthy Jayanthi, *Project Mgr*
EMP: 113

SALES (corp-wide): 66.8B **Publicly Held**
WEB: www.pg.com
SIC: 2844 2676 3421 2842 Deodorants, personal; towels, napkins & tissue paper products; razor blades & razors; specialty cleaning preparations; soap: granulated, liquid, cake, flaked or chip
PA: The Procter & Gamble Company
 1 Procter And Gamble Plz
 Cincinnati OH 45202
 513 983-1100

(G-12927)
PROPHARMA SALES LLC
5770 Gateway Ste 203 (45040-1897)
PHONE..................513 486-3353
EMP: 7 EST: 2016
SALES (est): 934.3K **Privately Held**
SIC: 2834 Pharmaceutical preparations

(G-12928)
PULSE WORLDWIDE LTD
7554 Central Parke Blvd (45040-6816)
PHONE..................513 234-7829
Julie Gutterman, *Principal*
EMP: 9
SALES: 380K **Privately Held**
SIC: 3841 Surgical & medical instruments

(G-12929)
R-K ELECTRONICS INC
7405 Industrial Row Dr (45040-1301)
PHONE..................513 204-6060
John L Keller, *President*
Claudia McElroy, *Partner*
Carolyn R Keller, *Exec VP*
▲ EMP: 14 EST: 1949
SQ FT: 11,200
SALES (est): 2.9MM **Privately Held**
WEB: www.rke.com
SIC: 3625 3672 Control equipment, electric; control circuit relays, industrial; timing devices, electronic; wiring boards

(G-12930)
RELIANCE MEDICAL PRODUCTS INC (DH)
3535 Kings Mills Rd (45040-2303)
PHONE..................513 398-3937
Ernest Cavin, *President*
Russ Stearns, *President*
Mark Pabst, *Safety Mgr*
Frank Wolfe, *QA Dir*
Tony Lanza, *Engineer*
◆ EMP: 85
SQ FT: 100,000
SALES (est): 18.4MM
SALES (corp-wide): 1.2B **Privately Held**
SIC: 3841 Surgical & medical instruments

(G-12931)
REMTEC CORP
6049 Hi Tek Ct (45040-2603)
PHONE..................513 860-4299
Teri Campbell, *Principal*
EMP: 4
SALES (est): 945.9K **Privately Held**
SIC: 3569 Assembly machines, non-metalworking

(G-12932)
REMTEC ENGINEERING
Also Called: Mbs Acquisition
6049 Hi Tek Ct (45040-2603)
PHONE..................513 860-4299
Keith Rosnell, *CEO*
EMP: 45
SQ FT: 25,000
SALES (est): 8.2MM **Privately Held**
WEB: www.remtecautomation.com
SIC: 3569 5084 Assembly machines, non-metalworking; robots, assembly line: industrial & commercial; robots, industrial

(G-12933)
RHINESTAHL CORPORATION (PA)
Also Called: Rhinestahl AMG
1111 Western Row Rd (45040-1365)
PHONE..................513 229-5300
Dieter Moeller, *President*
Alan Oak, *COO*
Scott Crislip, *Vice Pres*
Chris Hanna, *Vice Pres*
Dave Rettenmaier, *Vice Pres*
▲ EMP: 72

Mason - Warren County (G-12934)

SQ FT: 120,000
SALES (est): 42.7MM **Privately Held**
SIC: 3523 Turf & grounds equipment

(G-12934)
RHINESTAHL CORPORATION
7687 Innovation Way (45040-9695)
PHONE 513 229-5300
Tom Hohnston, *Branch Mgr*
EMP: 25
SALES (corp-wide): 42.7MM **Privately Held**
SIC: 3544 Special dies, tools, jigs & fixtures
PA: Rhinestahl Corporation
 1111 Western Row Rd
 Mason OH 45040
 513 229-5300

(G-12935)
SARA LEE FOODS
4680 Parkway Dr Ste 305 (45040-8198)
PHONE 513 204-4941
EMP: 3
SALES (est): 142.2K **Privately Held**
SIC: 2013 Sausages & other prepared meats

(G-12936)
SARA WOOD PHARMACEUTICALS LLC
4518 Margaret Ct (45040-2922)
PHONE 513 833-5502
Keith Kociba, *CEO*
Mina Pathel, *Principal*
Thomas Docherty, *COO*
Eileen Rogers, *Officer*
David Schultenover, *Officer*
EMP: 8
SALES (est): 411.4K **Privately Held**
SIC: 2834 Solutions, pharmaceutical

(G-12937)
SCICOMPRO - LLC
4861 Hampton Pond Ln (45040-5698)
PHONE 513 680-8686
Kurt W Weingand,
EMP: 3
SALES (est): 195.8K **Privately Held**
SIC: 2834 Veterinary pharmaceutical preparations

(G-12938)
SEAPINE SOFTWARE INC (HQ)
6960 Cintas Blvd (45040-8922)
PHONE 513 754-1655
Richard Riccetti, *President*
Richard Clyde, *President*
Kelly Riccetti, *Exec VP*
Judy Test, *CFO*
Matthew Disher, *CIO*
EMP: 50
SQ FT: 36,000
SALES (est): 12.5MM **Privately Held**
WEB: www.seapine.net
SIC: 7371 7372 Custom computer programming services; operating systems computer software

(G-12939)
SINGLE SOURCE TECHNOLOGIES LLC
Also Called: Makino
7680 Innovation Way (45040-9695)
PHONE 513 573-7200
Dun Lane, *President*
▲ **EMP:** 500
SALES (est): 53.2MM **Privately Held**
SIC: 3541 Machine tools, metal cutting: exotic (explosive, etc.)

(G-12940)
SOUND CONCEPTS LLC
1233 Castle Dr Ste A5 (45040-6984)
PHONE 513 703-0147
James B Murphy, *Mng Member*
EMP: 5
SQ FT: 600
SALES: 150K **Privately Held**
SIC: 5999 5099 3651 Audio-visual equipment & supplies; video & audio equipment; audio electronic systems

(G-12941)
SPEAR USA INC (HQ)
Also Called: Multi-Color
5510 Courseview Dr (45040-2366)
PHONE 513 459-1100
Richard Spear, *CEO*
Randall Spear, *President*
Michael Henry, *CFO*
▲ **EMP:** 125
SQ FT: 80,000
SALES (est): 82MM
SALES (corp-wide): 1.3B **Publicly Held**
SIC: 2759 Screen printing
PA: Multi-Color Corporation
 4053 Clough Woods Dr
 Batavia OH 45103
 513 381-1480

(G-12942)
STAR COMBUSTION SYSTEMS LLC
6506 Castle Dr (45040-9413)
P.O. Box 636 (45040-0636)
PHONE 513 282-0810
Tom Ballman, *Project Mgr*
Tim Daugherty, *Prdtn Mgr*
Andrew J Kemppainen, *Mng Member*
Brandon Moore, *Technician*
EMP: 3
SQ FT: 3,000
SALES (est): 590.1K **Privately Held**
SIC: 3823 Combustion control instruments

(G-12943)
SUGAR FOODS CORPORATION
4398 Wilderness Way (45040-7242)
PHONE 513 336-9748
Jeff Denzel, *Principal*
EMP: 3
SALES (corp-wide): 294.2MM **Privately Held**
SIC: 2869 Sweeteners, synthetic
PA: Sugar Foods Corporation
 950 3rd Ave Fl 21
 New York NY 10022
 212 753-6900

(G-12944)
SUPERIOR LABEL SYSTEMS INC (HQ)
Also Called: Superior Machine Systems
7500 Industrial Row Dr (45040-1307)
PHONE 513 336-0825
Kenneth Kidd, *Ch of Bd*
Thomas Braig, *Vice Pres*
Randy Barlow, *Director*
EMP: 275
SQ FT: 30,000
SALES (est): 29.6MM
SALES (corp-wide): 734.8MM **Privately Held**
SIC: 3565 2759 3993 3577 Labeling machines, industrial; flexographic printing; signs & advertising specialties; computer peripheral equipment; coated & laminated paper; packaging paper & plastics film, coated & laminated
PA: W/S Packaging Group, Inc.
 2571 S Hemlock Rd
 Green Bay WI 54229
 920 866-6300

(G-12945)
SYNERGY HEALTH NORTH AMER INC
7086 Industrial Row Dr (45040-1363)
PHONE 513 398-6406
Mike Vell, *Manager*
EMP: 75
SALES (corp-wide): 2.6B **Privately Held**
SIC: 3841 7213 Surgical & medical instruments; linen supply
HQ: Synergy Health North America, Inc.
 3903 Northdale Blvd 100e
 Tampa FL 33624
 813 891-9550

(G-12946)
TELEDYNE INSTRUMENTS INC
Also Called: Teledyne Tekmar
4736 Scialville Foster Rd (45040-8265)
PHONE 513 229-7000
Martin Motz, *Engineer*
Cindy Leichty, *Human Res Dir*
Tammy Rellar, *Manager*
EMP: 25
SALES (corp-wide): 2.9B **Publicly Held**
SIC: 5049 3826 3829 3821 Laboratory equipment, except medical or dental; analytical instruments; environmental testing equipment; measuring & controlling devices; laboratory apparatus & furniture
HQ: Teledyne Instruments, Inc.
 1049 Camino Dos Rios
 Thousand Oaks CA 91360
 805 373-4545

(G-12947)
TELEDYNE INSTRUMENTS INC
Also Called: Teledyne Instruments
4736 Scialville Foster Rd (45040-8265)
PHONE 603 886-8400
Peter Brown, *Manager*
EMP: 65
SALES (corp-wide): 2.9B **Publicly Held**
SIC: 3826 Spectrometers
HQ: Teledyne Instruments, Inc.
 1049 Camino Dos Rios
 Thousand Oaks CA 91360
 805 373-4545

(G-12948)
TELEDYNE TEKMAR COMPANY (HQ)
Also Called: Tekmar-Dohrmann
4736 Scialville Foster Rd (45040-8265)
PHONE 513 229-7000
Robert Mehrabian, *Ch of Bd*
Ron Uchtman, *Opers Mgr*
Cindy Cancel, *Purchasing*
Stephen Proffitt, *Research*
Heather Beale, *Engineer*
EMP: 25
SQ FT: 40,000
SALES (est): 34.2MM
SALES (corp-wide): 2.9B **Publicly Held**
WEB: www.teledynetekmar.com
SIC: 5049 3826 3829 3821 Laboratory equipment, except medical or dental; analytical instruments; environmental testing equipment; measuring & controlling devices; laboratory apparatus & furniture
PA: Teledyne Technologies Inc
 1049 Camino Dos Rios
 Thousand Oaks CA 91360
 805 373-4545

(G-12949)
TENNESSEE COATINGS INC (HQ)
Also Called: Ellison Surfc Technologies-Tn
8093 Columbia Rd Ste 201 (45040-9560)
PHONE 513 770-4900
Andrew Ellison, *CEO*
Tim Perkins, *President*
Kevin Michael, *CFO*
EMP: 14
SALES (est): 1.7MM **Privately Held**
SIC: 3479 Coating of metals & formed products

(G-12950)
TERRENE LABS LLC
5939 Deerfield Blvd (45040-2671)
PHONE 513 445-3539
Piyush Sing, *CEO*
James Carpenter, *COO*
EMP: 5
SALES (est): 156K **Privately Held**
SIC: 7372 Prepackaged software

(G-12951)
TRUECHOICEPACK CORP
5155 Financial Way Ste 6 (45040-0055)
PHONE 937 630-3832
Heena Rathore, *President*
Christopher Che, *Chairman*
Rakesh Rathore, *COO*
EMP: 44
SALES (est): 2.4MM
SALES (corp-wide): 9.6MM **Privately Held**
SIC: 3089 3086 8748 7389 Blister or bubble formed packaging, plastic; packaging & shipping materials, foamed plastic; business consulting; field warehousing
PA: Che International Group, Llc
 9435 Waterstone Blvd # 140
 Cincinnati OH 45249
 513 444-2072

(G-12952)
VELOCITY CONCEPT DEV GROUP LLC (PA)
4393 Digital Way (45040-7604)
PHONE 513 204-2100
John D Speridakos,
EMP: 9
SALES (est): 4.4MM **Privately Held**
SIC: 3999 Atomizers, toiletry

(G-12953)
W/S PACKAGING GROUP INC
7500 Industrial Row Dr (45040-1307)
PHONE 513 459-2400
Mark Lutz, *Vice Pres*
John Arshem, *Vice Pres*
Deb Kaplan, *Production*
Scott Oestreicher, *Production*
Jason Helton, *Engineer*
EMP: 150
SALES (corp-wide): 734.8MM **Privately Held**
WEB: www.wspackaging.com
SIC: 2679 3565 Labels, paper: made from purchased material; packaging machinery
PA: W/S Packaging Group, Inc.
 2571 S Hemlock Rd
 Green Bay WI 54229
 920 866-6300

(G-12954)
WEST POINT OPTICAL GROUP LLC
4680 Parkway Dr Ste 455 (45040-8199)
PHONE 614 395-9775
Bill Noble, *Mng Member*
EMP: 3 **EST:** 2015
SALES (est): 114.7K **Privately Held**
SIC: 3827 Optical instruments & lenses

(G-12955)
WITT INDUSTRIES INC (DH)
Also Called: Witt Products
4600 N Masn Montgomery Rd (45040-9176)
PHONE 513 871-5700
Tim Harris, *President*
Gary Brown, *Sales Mgr*
Anna Horton, *Sales Staff*
▼ **EMP:** 50
SQ FT: 71,500
SALES (est): 21.1MM
SALES (corp-wide): 60.8MM **Privately Held**
WEB: www.witt.com
SIC: 3479 3469 3441 3412 Galvanizing of iron, steel or end-formed products; garbage cans, stamped & pressed metal; fabricated structural metal; metal barrels, drums & pails; metal cans; blast furnaces & steel mills

Massillon
Stark County

(G-12956)
3-D SERVICE LTD (PA)
Also Called: Magnetech
800 Nave Rd Se (44646-9476)
PHONE 330 830-3500
Bernie Dewees, *President*
Tracy Tucker, *Human Res Mgr*
▲ **EMP:** 120
SQ FT: 85,000
SALES (est): 6.4MM **Privately Held**
WEB: www.3-dservice.com
SIC: 7694 7699 Electric motor repair; industrial equipment services

(G-12957)
A & R MACHINE CO INC
13212 Vega St Sw (44647-9200)
PHONE 330 832-4631
Rollin Shriner, *President*
Patsy Shriner, *Vice Pres*
EMP: 6
SQ FT: 10,000
SALES: 350K **Privately Held**
SIC: 3599 Custom machinery

GEOGRAPHIC SECTION
Massillon - Stark County (G-12985)

(G-12958)
ABP INDUCTION LLC
607 1st St Sw (44646-6729)
PHONE.................................330 830-6252
Todd Alley, *Branch Mgr*
EMP: 12
SALES (corp-wide): 8.1MM **Privately Held**
SIC: 3567 Industrial furnaces & ovens
PA: Abp Induction, Llc
　　1440 13th Ave
　　Union Grove WI 53182
　　262 317-5300

(G-12959)
ANOINTED DESIGN & TECHNOLOGIES
1766 Huron Rd Se (44646-8362)
PHONE.................................330 826-1493
Greg Streator, *Principal*
EMP: 4
SALES: 10K **Privately Held**
SIC: 3325 Steel foundries

(G-12960)
APPLIED INNOVATIONS
1245 Cleveland St Sw (44647-7955)
PHONE.................................330 837-5694
Scott Brown, *Owner*
EMP: 6
SALES (est): 330K **Privately Held**
SIC: 3312 Tool & die steel

(G-12961)
AUTO PRO & DESIGN
356 27th St Se (44646-5036)
PHONE.................................330 833-9237
Dean Masters, *Owner*
EMP: 3
SALES: 170K **Privately Held**
WEB: www.autoprodesign.com
SIC: 3993 Signs & advertising specialties

(G-12962)
BATES PRINTING INC
150 23rd St Se (44646-7046)
PHONE.................................330 833-5830
Dan Bates, *President*
John Bates, *President*
Daniel Bates, *Vice Pres*
EMP: 10
SQ FT: 3,000
SALES: 800K **Privately Held**
WEB: www.batesprinting.com
SIC: 2752 2759 Commercial printing, offset; commercial printing

(G-12963)
BRINKLEY TECHNOLOGY GROUP LLC
Also Called: Hercules Engine Components
2770 Erie St S (44646-7943)
PHONE.................................330 830-2498
Douglas Brinkley, *President*
EMP: 17 EST: 2015
SQ FT: 34,000
SALES (est): 1.5MM **Privately Held**
SIC: 3599 3519 3621 3694 Oil filters, internal combustion engine, except automotive; governors, diesel engine; diesel engine rebuilding; storage battery chargers, motor & engine generator type; distributors, motor vehicle engine

(G-12964)
C MASSOUH PRINTING CO INC
Also Called: C Massouh Printing Services
9589 Portage St Nw (44646-9074)
PHONE.................................330 832-6334
Carl Massouh, *President*
Cheryl Massouh, *Admin Sec*
EMP: 3
SALES: 700K **Privately Held**
SIC: 7389 2752 Printing broker; commercial printing, lithographic

(G-12965)
C-N-D INDUSTRIES INC
Also Called: Cnd Machine
359 State Ave Nw (44647-4269)
PHONE.................................330 478-8811
Clyde Shetler, *President*
Don Rossbach, *CFO*
EMP: 42
SQ FT: 28,000
SALES (est): 8.6MM **Privately Held**
WEB: www.cndinc.com
SIC: 3441 3599 7692 3444 Fabricated structural metal; machine shop, jobbing & repair; welding repair; sheet metalwork

(G-12966)
CANTON FABRICATORS INC (PA)
Also Called: Breining Mechanical Sytems
1115 Industrial Ave Sw (44647-7611)
PHONE.................................330 830-2900
Patricia Mc Elroy, *CEO*
Charlotte Sickle, *Ch of Bd*
Lauren Ehmer, *President*
EMP: 8 EST: 1947
SQ FT: 7,500
SALES (est): 886.5K **Privately Held**
SIC: 3444 Sheet metalwork

(G-12967)
CARBONLESS ON DEMANDCOM
332 Erie St S (44646-6740)
PHONE.................................330 837-8611
David Mathis, *Owner*
EMP: 19
SALES: 3MM **Privately Held**
SIC: 2752 Business form & card printing, lithographic

(G-12968)
COLD HEADED FAS ASSEMBLIES INC
1875 Harsh Ave Se Ste 3 (44646-7182)
P.O. Box 547 (44648-0547)
PHONE.................................330 833-0800
Oscar Lee, *President*
Gwen Hemperly, *Admin Sec*
▲ **EMP:** 12
SQ FT: 30,000
SALES (est): 1.8MM **Privately Held**
WEB: www.coldheaded.us
SIC: 3452 3599 Bolts, metal; machine shop, jobbing & repair

(G-12969)
COPLEY OHIO NEWSPAPERS INC
Also Called: Independent The
729 Lincoln Way E (44646-6829)
PHONE.................................330 833-2631
Kevin Coffey, *Principal*
EMP: 70
SQ FT: 9,221
SALES (corp-wide): 1.5B **Publicly Held**
WEB: www.timesreporter.com
SIC: 2711 2752 Commercial printing & newspaper publishing combined; commercial printing, lithographic
HQ: Copley Ohio Newspapers Inc
　　500 Market Ave S
　　Canton OH 44702
　　585 598-0030

(G-12970)
CORRCHOICE INC (HQ)
777 3rd St Nw (44647-4203)
P.O. Box 934 (44648-0934)
PHONE.................................330 833-5705
Geoffrey Jollay, *Ch of Bd*
Geoffrey A Jollay, *President*
Daniel J Gunseft, *Principal*
Chris Krumm, *VP Mfg*
▲ **EMP:** 80
SALES (est): 66.7MM
SALES (corp-wide): 3.8B **Publicly Held**
SIC: 2679 Paperboard products, converted
PA: Greif, Inc.
　　425 Winter Rd
　　Delaware OH 43015
　　740 549-6000

(G-12971)
CROWN CORK & SEAL USA INC
700 16th St Se (44646-7152)
PHONE.................................330 833-1011
James Skinner, *Engineer*
Bernard Baumann, *Manager*
Mike Danby, *Administration*
EMP: 300
SALES (corp-wide): 11.1B **Publicly Held**
WEB: www.crowncork.com
SIC: 3411 Aluminum cans
HQ: Crown Cork & Seal Usa, Inc.
　　770 Township Line Rd # 100
　　Yardley PA 19067
　　215 698-5100

(G-12972)
CUSTER PRODUCTS LIMITED
1320 Sanders Ave Sw (44647-7631)
PHONE.................................330 490-3158
Bradley Custer, *President*
▲ **EMP:** 15
SQ FT: 12,500
SALES (est): 3.7MM **Privately Held**
WEB: www.custerproducts.com
SIC: 3714 5013 5072 Motor vehicle parts & accessories; motor vehicle supplies & new parts; hardware

(G-12973)
DAVID A AND MARY A MATHIS
Also Called: D & M Printing
332 Erie St S (44646-6740)
PHONE.................................330 837-8611
David A Mathis, *Owner*
Mary A Mathis, *Co-Owner*
EMP: 6
SALES (est): 490K **Privately Held**
SIC: 2752 Commercial printing, lithographic

(G-12974)
DOTCENTRAL LLC
1650 Deerford Ave Sw (44647)
PHONE.................................330 809-0112
Daniel Swartz, *Mng Member*
Paul Atwell, *Officer*
EMP: 10
SALES (est): 261K **Privately Held**
SIC: 2741

(G-12975)
DOVER ATWOOD CORP
1875 Harsh Ave Se Ste 1 (44646-7182)
PHONE.................................330 809-0630
John Levengood, *President*
EMP: 4
SALES (est): 580K **Privately Held**
SIC: 1389 Oil field services; gas field services

(G-12976)
DRAIME ENTERPRISES INC
1300 Erie St S Unit C (44646-7997)
PHONE.................................330 837-2254
John E Draime, *President*
David Draime, *Treasurer*
EMP: 5 EST: 1970
SALES (est): 420K **Privately Held**
SIC: 3519 Internal combustion engines

(G-12977)
DW HERCULES LLC
Also Called: Hercules Engine Components
2770 Erie St S (44646-7943)
P.O. Box 451 (44648-0451)
PHONE.................................330 830-2498
Doug Brinkley, *President*
Jack Dienes,
Bruce Weick,
▲ **EMP:** 40
SQ FT: 22,000
SALES (est): 7.5MM **Privately Held**
WEB: www.herculesengine.com
SIC: 3519 5999 Parts & accessories, internal combustion engines; engine & motor equipment & supplies

(G-12978)
EARTHWALK ORTHOTIC
500 Vista Ave Se (44646-7949)
P.O. Box 1196 (44648-1196)
PHONE.................................330 837-6569
Brigham Wilson, *President*
EMP: 16
SQ FT: 9,000
SALES: 1,000K **Privately Held**
SIC: 3842 Orthopedic appliances

(G-12979)
ELECTRA - CORD INC
1320 Sanders Ave Sw (44647-7631)
P.O. Box 875 (44648-0875)
PHONE.................................330 832-8124
Randall A Hutsell, *President*
▲ **EMP:** 75
SQ FT: 33,000
SALES (est): 13MM
SALES (corp-wide): 1.9B **Privately Held**
SIC: 3699 3357 Extension cords; nonferrous wiredrawing & insulating
HQ: Tpc Wire & Cable Corp.
　　9600 Valley View Rd
　　Macedonia OH 44056

(G-12980)
ENGRAVERS GALLERY & SIGN CO
10 Lincoln Way E (44646-6632)
PHONE.................................330 830-1271
Bonnie Fall, *Owner*
EMP: 6
SQ FT: 1,600
SALES: 250K **Privately Held**
SIC: 3993 7389 Letters for signs, metal; engraving service

(G-12981)
FIBERCORR MILLS LLC
670 17th St Nw (44647-5343)
P.O. Box 453 (44648-0453)
PHONE.................................330 837-5151
Scott Shew, *Vice Pres*
Scott Sanders, *Purch Agent*
Ralph Reisinger, *CFO*
Allan Lynch, *Cust Mgr*
Frank Shew, *Mng Member*
▲ **EMP:** 77
SQ FT: 87,500
SALES (est): 30.1MM **Privately Held**
WEB: www.fibercorr.com
SIC: 2679 2631 Paper products, converted; paperboard mills

(G-12982)
FRANKS CASING
607 1st St Sw (44646-6729)
PHONE.................................330 236-4264
Brandon Veberica, *General Mgr*
EMP: 5
SALES (est): 293.9K **Privately Held**
SIC: 1389 Oil field services

(G-12983)
FRESH MARK INC (PA)
Also Called: Superior's Brand Meats
1888 Southway St Se (44646)
P.O. Box 571 (44648-0571)
PHONE.................................330 834-3669
Neil Genshaft, *CEO*
David Cochenour, *President*
Tim Cranor, *President*
Richard Foster, *General Mgr*
Bob Goode, *Superintendent*
◆ **EMP:** 500 EST: 1932
SQ FT: 80,000
SALES: 1.3B **Privately Held**
WEB: www.freshmark.com
SIC: 2013 5147 2011 Prepared beef products from purchased beef; prepared pork products from purchased pork; sausages & related products, from purchased meat; meats & meat products; meat packing plants

(G-12984)
FRESH MARK INC
Also Called: Fresh Mark Sugardale
1888 Southway St Sw (44646-9429)
P.O. Box 571 (44648-0571)
PHONE.................................330 832-7491
Tim Craner, *President*
Ryan Cucerzan, *Production*
Sherry Chidester, *Senior Engr*
Diane Doyle, *Accountant*
Mark Slaughter, *Director*
EMP: 350
SALES (corp-wide): 1.3B **Privately Held**
WEB: www.freshmark.com
SIC: 5147 2013 Meats & meat products; sausages & other prepared meats
PA: Fresh Mark, Inc.
　　1888 Southway St Se
　　Massillon OH 44646
　　330 834-3669

(G-12985)
GAMEDAY VISION
1147 Oberlin Ave Sw (44647-7665)
PHONE.................................330 830-4550
Krista Simcic, *President*
EMP: 10

Massillon - Stark County (G-12986)

SALES (est): 665.5K **Privately Held**
SIC: 3577 Printers & plotters

(G-12986)
GARY LAWRENCE ENTERPRISES INC
Also Called: Lawrence Machine
21 Charles Ave Sw (44646-6621)
P.O. Box 727 (44648-0727)
PHONE..................................330 833-7181
Gary Lawrence, *President*
Christopher Lawrence, *Vice Pres*
Eric Lawrence, *Treasurer*
EMP: 8
SQ FT: 15,000
SALES (est): 1.2MM **Privately Held**
WEB: www.lawrencemachineinc.com
SIC: 3993 5199 Signs & advertising specialties; advertising specialties

(G-12987)
GERSTENSLAGER CONSTRUCTION
Also Called: Gerstenslager Hardwood Pdts
343 16th St Se (44646-7177)
PHONE..................................330 832-3604
Mike Gerstenslager, *Owner*
Myron F Gerstenslager Jr, *Owner*
EMP: 6
SQ FT: 12,000
SALES (est): 330K **Privately Held**
SIC: 2431 Millwork

(G-12988)
GOLD N KRISP CHIPS & PRETZELS
1900 Erie Ave Nw (44646-4050)
PHONE..................................330 832-8395
Odell Gainey, *President*
Doug Roudebush, *Manager*
EMP: 5
SQ FT: 2,400
SALES (est): 667.4K **Privately Held**
SIC: 2096 Potato chips & other potato-based snacks

(G-12989)
GQI INC
2650 Richville Dr Sw # 105 (44646-8397)
PHONE..................................330 830-9805
Axel Dannoritzer, *President*
Richard Hassel, *Vice Pres*
EMP: 4
SALES (est): 449.3K **Privately Held**
SIC: 3841 Surgical instruments & apparatus

(G-12990)
GREGS EAGLE TIRE CO INC
3425 Lincoln Way E (44646-3762)
PHONE..................................330 837-1983
Greg Lawley, *Principal*
EMP: 4
SQ FT: 792
SALES (est): 617.8K **Privately Held**
SIC: 5531 3011 Automotive tires; tires & inner tubes

(G-12991)
GREIF INC
787 Warmington Rd Se (44646-8830)
P.O. Box 675 (44648-0675)
PHONE..................................330 879-2936
Jack Eschliman, *Plant Engr*
Susan Straughn, *Office Mgr*
Matt Sullivan, *Manager*
Eddie Moore, *Maintence Staff*
EMP: 110
SALES (corp-wide): 3.8B **Publicly Held**
WEB: www.greif.com
SIC: 2655 Fiber cans, drums & similar products
PA: Greif, Inc.
425 Winter Rd
Delaware OH 43015
740 549-6000

(G-12992)
GREIF PACKAGING LLC
787 Warmington Rd Sw (44646)
PHONE..................................330 879-2101
Chip Shew, *Manager*
EMP: 110
SALES (corp-wide): 3.8B **Publicly Held**
SIC: 2611 Pulp manufactured from waste or recycled paper
HQ: Greif Packaging Llc
366 Greif Pkwy
Delaware OH 43015
740 549-6000

(G-12993)
H P E INC
2025 Harsh Ave Se (44646-7127)
PHONE..................................330 833-3161
Robert Boley, *President*
Robert N Boley, *President*
Sandra Boley, *Treasurer*
EMP: 12
SQ FT: 12,000
SALES (est): 790K **Privately Held**
SIC: 3533 3569 3547 3494 Oil & gas field machinery; gas separators (machinery); gas producers, generators & other gas related equipment; rolling mill machinery; valves & pipe fittings; fabricated plate work (boiler shop)

(G-12994)
HEINZ FOREIGN INVESTMENT CO (HQ)
1301 Oberlin Ave Sw (44647-7669)
P.O. Box 15222, Pittsburgh PA (15237-0222)
PHONE..................................330 837-8331
Bernardo Hees, *CEO*
▲ EMP: 10
SALES (est): 34.2MM
SALES (corp-wide): 26.2B **Publicly Held**
SIC: 2037 Frozen fruits & vegetables
PA: The Kraft Heinz Company
1 Ppg Pl Fl 34
Pittsburgh PA 15222
412 456-5700

(G-12995)
HENDRICKS VACUUM FORMING INC (PA)
3500 17th St Sw (44647-9700)
PHONE..................................330 837-2040
Donald G Hendricks, *President*
Rob Hendricks, *Vice Pres*
Quinton Wratchford, *Plant Supt*
Bonnie Hendricks, *CPA*
George Hendricks, *Sales Associate*
EMP: 20 EST: 1978
SQ FT: 40,000
SALES (est): 2.1MM **Privately Held**
WEB: www.hvfi.com
SIC: 3993 Electric signs

(G-12996)
HENDRICKS VACUUM FORMING INC
Also Called: Massillon Machine & Die
3536 17th St Sw (44647-9211)
PHONE..................................330 833-8913
Gary Burkholder, *Branch Mgr*
EMP: 7
SALES (corp-wide): 2.1MM **Privately Held**
WEB: www.hvfi.com
SIC: 3542 Die casting machines
PA: Hendricks Vacuum Forming, Inc.
3500 17th St Sw
Massillon OH 44647
330 837-2040

(G-12997)
HJ HEINZ COMPANY LP (DH)
Also Called: Heinz Frozen Foods
1301 Oberlin Ave Sw (44647-7669)
PHONE..................................330 837-8331
Allan Briggs, *Managing Prtnr*
Mike Parks, *Manager*
Rick Uriguem, *Manager*
▲ EMP: 600
SALES (est): 62.4MM
SALES (corp-wide): 26.2B **Publicly Held**
SIC: 2037 Frozen fruits & vegetables
HQ: Kraft Heinz Foods Company
1 Ppg Pl Fl 34
Pittsburgh PA 15222
412 456-5700

(G-12998)
HK ENGINE COMPONENTS LLC (HQ)
800 Nave Rd Se (44646-9476)
PHONE..................................330 830-3500
J Cullen Burdette, *President*
James I Depew, *Admin Sec*
▲ EMP: 2
SALES (est): 8.3MM
SALES (corp-wide): 322.2MM **Privately Held**
SIC: 3519 Governors, diesel engine
PA: National Railway Equipment Co.
1100 Shawnee St
Mount Vernon IL 62864
618 242-6590

(G-12999)
HUTH READY MIX & SUPPLY CO
Also Called: Huth Ready-Mix & Supply Co
501 5th St Nw (44647-5473)
P.O. Box 524 (44648-0524)
PHONE..................................330 833-4191
Roger L Huth, *President*
Alice H Huth, *Admin Sec*
EMP: 15
SQ FT: 3,000
SALES (est): 2.9MM **Privately Held**
SIC: 3273 5211 Ready-mixed concrete; brick; concrete & cinder block

(G-13000)
HYDRO-DYNE INC
225 Wetmore Ave Se (44646-6788)
P.O. Box 318 (44648-0318)
PHONE..................................330 832-5076
Rose Ann Dare, *President*
Lynn Neel, *Vice Pres*
Jean Holiday, *Manager*
Sherri McMillen, *Manager*
Ken Yeaman, *Manager*
▲ EMP: 30
SQ FT: 130,000
SALES (est): 8.2MM **Privately Held**
WEB: www.hydrodyneinc.com
SIC: 3585 8711 Evaporative condensers, heat transfer equipment; engineering services

(G-13001)
HYDRO-THRIFT CORPORATION
Also Called: Hydrothrift
1301 Sanders Ave Sw (44647-7632)
P.O. Box 1037 (44648-1037)
PHONE..................................330 837-5141
T K Heston, *President*
Robby Strock, *Design Engr*
Paul Heston, *Treasurer*
▼ EMP: 23 EST: 1973
SQ FT: 27,000
SALES: 5.3MM **Privately Held**
WEB: www.hydrothrift.com
SIC: 3443 3585 Heat exchangers, condensers & components; air conditioning equipment, complete

(G-13002)
IDENTITEK SYSTEMS INC
Also Called: Adams Signs
1100 Industrial Ave Sw (44647-7608)
P.O. Box 347 (44648-0347)
PHONE..................................330 832-9844
Joseph Pugliese, *President*
Paul Boyer, *VP Sales*
EMP: 53
SQ FT: 70,000
SALES (est): 8MM **Privately Held**
WEB: www.adamssigns.com
SIC: 1799 3993 Sign installation & maintenance; signs & advertising specialties; electric signs

(G-13003)
INDEPENDENT PROTECTION SYSTEMS
2510 Upland Ave Sw (44647-7270)
P.O. Box 214 (44648-0214)
PHONE..................................330 832-7992
Randall P Ross, *Owner*
EMP: 5 EST: 1975
SALES (est): 298.2K **Privately Held**
SIC: 1731 2381 Fire detection & burglar alarm systems specialization; glove linings, except fur

(G-13004)
J L R PRODUCTS INC
1212 Oberlin Ave Sw (44647-7668)
PHONE..................................330 832-9557
Matthew Radocaj, *President*
EMP: 15
SALES: 1.6MM **Privately Held**
SIC: 3429 3568 Pulleys metal; pulleys, power transmission

(G-13005)
JACODAR INC
1212 Oberlin Ave Sw (44647-7668)
PHONE..................................330 832-9557
Matthew Radocaj, *President*
EMP: 10
SQ FT: 24,000
SALES (est): 770.8K
SALES (corp-wide): 358.5MM **Privately Held**
SIC: 3452 Bolts, metal
PA: Ojim, Inc.
1212 Oberlin Ave Sw
Massillon OH 44647
330 832-9557

(G-13006)
JOSEPH KNAPP
Also Called: Knapp Enterprises
151 Lennox Ave Sw (44646-3807)
PHONE..................................330 832-3515
Joseph Knapp, *Owner*
EMP: 11
SQ FT: 15,000
SALES (est): 938.9K **Privately Held**
SIC: 2599 7213 5046 Restaurant furniture, wood or metal; table cover supply; restaurant equipment & supplies

(G-13007)
JP SELF DEFENSE LLC
2870 Lincoln Way E (44646)
PHONE..................................330 356-1541
Jonathan Porter,
EMP: 3
SALES (est): 121.7K **Privately Held**
SIC: 3812 Defense systems & equipment

(G-13008)
KENDEL WELDING & FABRICATION
1700 Navarre Rd Se (44646)
PHONE..................................330 834-2429
Bettina M Kendel, *President*
Donald R Kendel, *Vice Pres*
EMP: 8 EST: 1999
SALES (est): 856.6K **Privately Held**
SIC: 7692 Welding repair

(G-13009)
KENMORE CONSTRUCTION CO INC
Also Called: American Sand & Gravel Div
9500 Forty Corners Rd Nw (44647-9309)
PHONE..................................330 832-8888
Chris Scala, *Manager*
EMP: 48
SALES (corp-wide): 93MM **Privately Held**
WEB: www.kenmorecompanies.com
SIC: 1611 1442 General contractor, highway & street construction; construction sand & gravel
PA: Kenmore Construction Co., Inc.
700 Home Ave
Akron OH 44310
330 762-8936

(G-13010)
KENNEWEGS WOOD PRODUCTS
973 Vindell Ave Nw (44647-5273)
PHONE..................................330 832-1540
John Kenneweg, *Owner*
Brenda Kenneweg, *Co-Owner*
EMP: 3
SALES (est): 210K **Privately Held**
SIC: 5712 2499 Custom made furniture, except cabinets; wood products

(G-13011)
KING MACHINE AND TOOL CO
1237 Sanders Ave Sw (44647-7684)
PHONE..................................330 833-7217
William Kapper, *President*

GEOGRAPHIC SECTION

Massillon - Stark County (G-13037)

Tracy Kapper, *Vice Pres*
Kelly Kapper, *Treasurer*
Judith A Kapper, *Admin Sec*
▲ **EMP:** 18 **EST:** 1949
SQ FT: 22,000
SALES (est): 4.3MM **Privately Held**
WEB: www.kmtco.com
SIC: 3544 Dies & die holders for metal cutting, forming, die casting

(G-13012)
KRAFT HEINZ COMPANY
Also Called: Kraft Heinz Company
1301 Oberlin Ave Sw (44647-7669)
PHONE.................................330 837-8331
Ken Stiffler, *Manager*
EMP: 700
SQ FT: 1,196
SALES (corp-wide): 26.2B **Publicly Held**
SIC: 2033 2099 Tomato sauce: packaged in cans, jars, etc.; food preparations
PA: The Kraft Heinz Company
1 Ppg Pl Fl 34
Pittsburgh PA 15222
412 456-5700

(G-13013)
LAND OLAKES INC
8485 Navarre Rd Sw (44646-8814)
PHONE.................................330 879-2158
Gary Hauenstin, *Manager*
EMP: 41
SALES (corp-wide): 10.4B **Privately Held**
WEB: www.landolakes.com
SIC: 2048 5191 2047 Livestock feeds; animal feeds; dog & cat food
PA: Land O'lakes, Inc.
4001 Lexington Ave N
Arden Hills MN 55126
651 375-2222

(G-13014)
LLC RING MASTERS
240 6th St Nw (44647-5413)
PHONE.................................330 832-1511
Jeffrey Headlee,
Randy Hunt,
Tony Lee,
John Nelson,
EMP: 34
SQ FT: 51,000
SALES (est): 3.5MM **Privately Held**
WEB: www.ring-masters.net
SIC: 3316 Cold finishing of steel shapes

(G-13015)
LTG POLYMERS LIMITED
7612 Onyx Ave Nw (44646-9206)
PHONE.................................330 854-5609
Howard Galberach, *Principal*
EMP: 3 **EST:** 2010
SALES (est): 233K **Privately Held**
SIC: 2821 Plastics materials & resins

(G-13016)
MAGNETECH INDUSTRIAL SVCS INC
800 Nave Rd Se (44646-9476)
PHONE.................................330 830-3500
Mike Rice, *Branch Mgr*
EMP: 120 **Publicly Held**
SIC: 7694 7699 Electric motor repair; industrial equipment services
HQ: Magnetech Industrial Services, Inc.
800 Nave Rd Se
Massillon OH 44646
330 830-3500

(G-13017)
MAINTENANCE AND REPAIR FABG CO
427 Harding Ave Nw (44646-3295)
PHONE.................................330 478-1149
James A Paulus, *President*
Jackie Paulus, *Admin Sec*
EMP: 5 **EST:** 1979
SQ FT: 8,580
SALES (est): 157.8K **Privately Held**
SIC: 7692 Welding repair

(G-13018)
MARTIN PALLET INC
Also Called: M P I Logistics
1414 Industrial Ave Sw (44647-7663)
PHONE.................................330 832-5309
Richard D Miller, *President*

Judith A Miller, *Vice Pres*
EMP: 21
SQ FT: 16,500
SALES (est): 4.2MM **Privately Held**
WEB: www.martinpallet.com
SIC: 2448 7699 Pallets, wood; pallet repair

(G-13019)
MASSILLON ASPHALT CO
1833 Riverside Dr Nw (44647-9300)
PHONE.................................330 833-6330
Dave Aventino, *Manager*
EMP: 3
SALES (corp-wide): 620.4K **Privately Held**
SIC: 1771 2951 Blacktop (asphalt) work; asphalt paving mixtures & blocks
PA: Massillon Asphalt Co
5947 Whipple Ave Nw
Canton OH 44720
330 494-5472

(G-13020)
MASSILLON MACHINE & DIE INC
3536 17th St Sw (44647-9211)
PHONE.................................330 833-8913
Gary Burkholder, *President*
EMP: 9
SQ FT: 7,000
SALES: 750K **Privately Held**
SIC: 3599 1799 Custom machinery; welding on site

(G-13021)
MASSILLON METAPHYSICS
912 Amherst Rd Ne (44646-4568)
P.O. Box 1305 (44648-1305)
PHONE.................................330 837-1653
Lena Fain, *Principal*
EMP: 3 **EST:** 2011
SALES (est): 153.3K **Privately Held**
SIC: 1499 Gemstone & industrial diamond mining

(G-13022)
MATCH MOLD & MACHINE INC
1100 Nova Dr Se (44646-8867)
PHONE.................................330 830-5503
Timothy V Lidderdale, *President*
Thomas Knipfer, *Vice Pres*
Ruth Lidderdale, *Treasurer*
EMP: 40 **EST:** 1981
SALES (est): 3.7MM **Privately Held**
SIC: 3544 Forms (molds), for foundry & plastics working machinery

(G-13023)
MATRIX SYS AUTO FINISHES LLC
600 Nova Dr Se (44646-8884)
PHONE.................................248 668-8135
W Kent Gardner, *President*
Sean Hook, *Director*
EMP: 100
SQ FT: 26,000
SALES (est): 37MM
SALES (corp-wide): 116.6MM **Privately Held**
WEB: www.matrixsystem.com
SIC: 5198 2851 Paints; paints & allied products
PA: Quest Specialty Chemicals, Inc.
225 Sven Farms Dr Ste 204
Charleston SC 29492
800 966-7580

(G-13024)
MEL WACKER SIGN INC
13076 Barrs Rd Sw (44647-9746)
PHONE.................................330 832-1726
Bonnie Maier, *President*
Melville Maier, *Vice Pres*
EMP: 6
SALES (est): 887.5K **Privately Held**
WEB: www.wackersigns.com
SIC: 3993 1799 5999 Signs, not made in custom sign painting shops; sign installation & maintenance; flags

(G-13025)
MELANDA INC
Also Called: Express Lube
2646 Lincoln Way Nw (44647-5119)
PHONE.................................330 833-0517

Louis Brio, *President*
Larry Grim, *Manager*
EMP: 9
SQ FT: 4,000
SALES: 300K **Privately Held**
SIC: 2992 Lubricating oils

(G-13026)
MIDWESTERN INDUSTRIES INC (PA)
915 Oberlin Ave Sw (44647-7661)
P.O. Box 810 (44648-0810)
PHONE.................................330 837-4203
W A Blackwell, *Principal*
Laverne J Riesbeck, *Principal*
Mary E Riesbeck, *Principal*
David Weaver, *Vice Pres*
William J Crone, *Vice Pres*
▼ **EMP:** 104
SQ FT: 148,000
SALES: 19MM **Privately Held**
WEB: www.midwesternind.com
SIC: 3559 3496 3564 3443 Screening equipment, electric; mesh, made from purchased wire; screening, woven wire: made from purchased wire; blowers & fans; fabricated plate work (boiler shop); steel wire & related products

(G-13027)
MOMENTS TO REMEMBER USA LLC
1250 Sanders Ave Sw (44647-7683)
PHONE.................................330 830-0839
Nancy Schmidt, *Partner*
Karl Schmidt, *Partner*
Jen Wetvel, *Administration*
EMP: 7
SALES (est): 1MM **Privately Held**
WEB: www.momentsusa.com
SIC: 3993 7313 7331 3555 Signs & advertising specialties; electronic media advertising representatives; printed media advertising representatives; direct mail advertising services; mats, advertising & newspaper

(G-13028)
MONOVISION MACHINE
125 Walnut Rd Se (44647-7934)
PHONE.................................330 833-2146
Glen Marthy, *Principal*
EMP: 7
SALES (est): 962.2K **Privately Held**
SIC: 3599 Machine shop, jobbing & repair

(G-13029)
NFM/WELDING ENGINEERS INC (PA)
Also Called: N F M
577 Oberlin Ave Sw (44647-7820)
PHONE.................................330 837-3868
Philip A Roberson, *President*
Ronald Pribich, *Senior VP*
John Roberson, *Vice Pres*
Paul Roberson, *Vice Pres*
Scott Swallen, *Vice Pres*
▲ **EMP:** 140
SQ FT: 150,000
SALES (est): 43.2MM **Privately Held**
WEB: www.nfmwe.com
SIC: 3599 Machine shop, jobbing & repair

(G-13030)
OHIO METALIZING LLC
2519 Erie St S (44646-7918)
P.O. Box 1182 (44648-1182)
PHONE.................................330 830-1092
George Pribich,
EMP: 5
SQ FT: 17,000
SALES (est): 573.2K
SALES (corp-wide): 43.2MM **Privately Held**
SIC: 2295 3599 3471 Metallizing of fabrics; machine & other job shop work; plating & polishing
PA: Nfm/Welding Engineers, Inc.
577 Oberlin Ave Sw
Massillon OH 44647
330 837-3868

(G-13031)
OHIO PACKAGING (DH)
777 3rd St Nw (44647-4203)
PHONE.................................330 833-2884
Dale Kiaski, *Vice Pres*
Ray Shelton, *Maintence Staff*
Rick Hazen,
▲ **EMP:** 20 **EST:** 1964
SQ FT: 1,800
SALES (est): 17.7MM
SALES (corp-wide): 3.8B **Publicly Held**
SIC: 2679 5199 Paperboard products, converted; packaging materials
HQ: Corrchoice, Inc.
777 3rd St Nw
Massillon OH 44647
330 833-5705

(G-13032)
OJIM INC (PA)
1212 Oberlin Ave Sw (44647-7668)
PHONE.................................330 832-9557
Mijo Radocaj, *Ch of Bd*
Matt Radocaj, *President*
EMP: 15
SQ FT: 39,500
SALES: 358.5MM **Privately Held**
SIC: 3599 Machine shop, jobbing & repair

(G-13033)
OMNI DIE CASTING INC
1100 Nova Dr Se (44646-8867)
PHONE.................................330 830-5500
Timothy Lidderdale, *President*
Derek Lidderdale, *Vice Pres*
Darin Jacobs, *Project Mgr*
Dan Swab, *Purch Agent*
Barbara Houck, *Office Mgr*
▼ **EMP:** 30 **EST:** 1958
SQ FT: 10,000
SALES (est): 7.6MM **Privately Held**
SIC: 3363 Aluminum die-castings

(G-13034)
OMNI USA INC
1100 Nova Dr Se (44646-8867)
PHONE.................................330 830-5500
Timothy V Lidderdale, *President*
Theodore Buss, *Treasurer*
EMP: 100
SALES (est): 16.1MM **Privately Held**
SIC: 3364 Zinc & zinc-base alloy die-castings

(G-13035)
OSTER SAND AND GRAVEL INC
Also Called: Oster Enterprises
1955 Riverside Dr Nw (44647-9300)
PHONE.................................330 833-2649
Bruce Bickel, *Manager*
EMP: 8
SALES (corp-wide): 4.1MM **Privately Held**
SIC: 1442 1422 Construction sand & gravel; crushed & broken limestone
PA: Oster Sand And Gravel, Inc.
5947 Whipple Ave Nw
Canton OH 44720
330 494-5472

(G-13036)
P-AMERICAS LLC
Also Called: Pepsico
815 Oberlin Ave Sw (44647-7876)
PHONE.................................330 837-4224
Bob Joyce, *Warehouse Mgr*
Jenny Plummet, *Manager*
EMP: 123
SALES (corp-wide): 64.6B **Publicly Held**
SIC: 2086 Carbonated soft drinks, bottled & canned
HQ: P-Americas Llc
1 Pepsi Way
Somers NY 10589
336 896-5740

(G-13037)
PACE MOLD & MACHINE LLC
8225 Navarre Rd Sw (44646-8813)
P.O. Box 6, Navarre (44662-0006)
PHONE.................................330 879-1777
Patrick Nolan,
Marilyn Hurst, *Admin Sec*
Leonard Buckner,
EMP: 6 **EST:** 1977
SQ FT: 14,000

Massillon - Stark County (G-13038)

SALES (est): 868.1K **Privately Held**
SIC: **3544** 2821 3089 Forms (molds), for foundry & plastics working machinery; molding compounds, plastics; injection molding of plastics; molding primary plastic

(G-13038)
PER-TECH INC
113 Erie St S (44646-6649)
PHONE..................330 833-8824
Robert Phillips, *Vice Pres*
Randall Hutsell, *Admin Sec*
Rex Kick, *Technician*
EMP: 28
SQ FT: 90,000
SALES: 2MM **Privately Held**
SIC: **3679** 3694 Harness assemblies for electronic use; wire or cable; engine electrical equipment

(G-13039)
PLASTIC FORMING COMPANY INC
201 Vista Ave Se (44646-7938)
PHONE..................330 830-5167
David Norcia, *Prdtn Mgr*
Mike Warth, *Manager*
EMP: 25
SALES (corp-wide): 7.4MM **Privately Held**
WEB: www.plasticformingcompany.com
SIC: **3089** 3086 3161 Blow molded finished plastic products; plastics foam products; luggage
PA: The Plastic Forming Company Inc
20 S Bradley Rd
Woodbridge CT 06525
203 397-1338

(G-13040)
POLYMER PACKAGING INC (PA)
Also Called: Polymer Protective Packaging
8333 Navarre Rd Se (44646-9652)
PHONE..................330 832-2000
Larry L Lanham, *CEO*
Ronald Reagan, *President*
William D Lanham, *Exec VP*
Chris Thomazin, *Vice Pres*
Jeffrey S Davis, *CFO*
▲ **EMP:** 65
SQ FT: 36,000
SALES (est): 58.1MM **Privately Held**
WEB: www.polymerpkg.com
SIC: **5113** 5162 2621 2821 Paper & products, wrapping or coarse; plastics products; wrapping & packaging papers; plastics materials & resins

(G-13041)
POLYONE CORPORATION
1675 Navarre Rd Se (44646-9607)
PHONE..................330 834-3812
Steve Strover, *Manager*
EMP: 75 **Publicly Held**
WEB: www.polyone.com
SIC: **2821** Plastics materials & resins
PA: Polyone Corporation
33587 Walker Rd
Avon Lake OH 44012

(G-13042)
PREMIER BUILDING SOLUTIONS INC (PA)
480 Nova Dr Se (44646-9597)
PHONE..................330 244-2907
Derek J Miller, *President*
Rebecca J Miller, *Vice Pres*
◆ **EMP:** 75
SALES (est): 20.4MM **Privately Held**
SIC: **2891** Adhesives

(G-13043)
PURINA ANIMAL NUTRITION LLC
8485 Navarre Rd Sw (44646-8814)
PHONE..................330 879-2158
Gary Hauenstein, *Manager*
EMP: 35
SALES (corp-wide): 10.4B **Privately Held**
SIC: **2048** Prepared feeds
HQ: Purina Animal Nutrition Llc
100 Danforth Dr
Gray Summit MO 63039

(G-13044)
R W SCREW PRODUCTS INC
999 Oberlin Ave Sw (44647-7698)
P.O. Box 310 (44648-0310)
PHONE..................330 837-9211
James Woolley, *CEO*
Larry Longworth, *President*
Tim Longworth, *Human Res Dir*
Debby Sickafoose, *Human Res Mgr*
John Fetzer, *Manager*
EMP: 240 **EST:** 1948
SQ FT: 180,000
SALES (est): 56.8MM **Privately Held**
SIC: **3451** Screw machine products

(G-13045)
REPUBLIC STEEL
401 Rose Ave Se (44646-6870)
PHONE..................330 837-7024
Pamela Kovick, *Sales Mgr*
K W Hazard, *Branch Mgr*
EMP: 16 **Privately Held**
SIC: **3312** Blast furnaces & steel mills
HQ: Republic Steel
2633 8th St Ne
Canton OH 44704
330 438-5435

(G-13046)
SCASSA ASPHALT INC
4167 Beaumont Ave Nw (44647-9556)
PHONE..................330 830-2039
Nicholas Scassa, *President*
EMP: 10
SALES (est): 1.3MM **Privately Held**
SIC: **1389** Construction, repair & dismantling services

(G-13047)
SHEARERS FOODS LLC (PA)
Also Called: Shearer's Snacks
100 Lincoln Way E (44646-6634)
PHONE..................330 834-4030
C J Fraleigh, *CEO*
Christopher Fraleigh, *CEO*
Montgomery Pooley, *Exec VP*
Dennis Herod, *Prdtn Mgr*
Derrick Johnson, *Prdtn Mgr*
◆ **EMP:** 700 **EST:** 1980
SQ FT: 200,000
SALES (est): 590.9MM **Privately Held**
SIC: **2096** 5145 Potato chips & similar snacks; snack foods

(G-13048)
SHERWIN-WILLIAMS COMPANY
600 Nova Dr Se (44646-8884)
P.O. Box 709 (44648-0709)
PHONE..................330 830-6000
Thomas M Perry, *President*
EMP: 192
SQ FT: 139,645
SALES (corp-wide): 17.5B **Publicly Held**
WEB: www.alcoind.com
SIC: **2851** 3087 2842 2891 Paints & paint additives; epoxy coatings; custom compound purchased resins; stain removers; adhesives & sealants
PA: The Sherwin-Williams Company
101 W Prospect Ave # 1020
Cleveland OH 44115
216 566-2000

(G-13049)
SNACK ALLIANCE INC (HQ)
100 Lincoln Way E (44646-6634)
P.O. Box 70, Hermiston OR (97838-0070)
PHONE..................330 767-3426
Robert Shearer, *CEO*
Scott Smith, *President*
Thomas Shearer, *Exec VP*
Fredric Kohmann, *CFO*
◆ **EMP:** 20
SALES (est): 124.2MM
SALES (corp-wide): 590.9MM **Privately Held**
SIC: **2096** Potato chips & similar snacks
PA: Shearer's Foods, Llc
100 Lincoln Way E
Massillon OH 44646
330 834-4030

(G-13050)
STANDARDS TESTING LABS INC (PA)
1845 Harsh Ave Se (44646-7123)
P.O. Box 758 (44648-0758)
PHONE..................330 833-8548
Anthony E Efremoff, *President*
Darryl Fuller, *President*
Tim Dietz, *General Mgr*
Jason Sumney, *General Mgr*
Tim Flood, *Chief Engr*
▲ **EMP:** 60 **EST:** 1972
SQ FT: 84,000
SALES (est): 14.9MM **Privately Held**
WEB: www.stllabs.com
SIC: **3829** 8734 8071 Testing equipment: abrasion, shearing strength, etc.; product testing laboratory, safety or performance; automobile proving & testing ground; medical laboratories

(G-13051)
STERILITE CORPORATION
4495 Sterilite St Se (44646-7400)
PHONE..................330 830-2204
Dennis Forgues, *Plant Mgr*
Dennis Forges, *Manager*
EMP: 355
SALES (corp-wide): 380.5MM **Privately Held**
WEB: www.sterilite.com
SIC: **3089** Plastic kitchenware, tableware & houseware; plastic containers, except foam
PA: Sterilite Corporation
30 Scales Ln
Townsend MA 01469
978 597-1000

(G-13052)
TIGER SAND & GRAVEL LLC
411 Oberlin Ave Sw (44647-7826)
PHONE..................330 833-6325
Lee Cush, *Office Mgr*
David M Dipietro, *Mng Member*
Leenn Cush, *Manager*
Steven P Dipeitro,
EMP: 10
SALES (est): 1.8MM **Privately Held**
SIC: **1442** Construction sand & gravel

(G-13053)
TORTILLERIA EL MAIZAL LLP
1895 Greentree Pl Se (44646-8181)
PHONE..................330 209-9344
Dawn Mora, *Principal*
EMP: 5
SALES (est): 143.5K **Privately Held**
SIC: **2099** Tortillas, fresh or refrigerated

(G-13054)
TOWER INDUSTRIES LTD
2101 9th St Sw (44647-7651)
PHONE..................330 837-2216
Todd Werstler,
Robert Werstler,
EMP: 43
SQ FT: 15,000
SALES (est): 11MM **Privately Held**
SIC: **3088** Plastics plumbing fixtures

(G-13055)
U S CHEMICAL & PLASTICS
600 Nova Dr Se (44646-8884)
PHONE..................740 254-4311
John Nelson, *Plant Mgr*
◆ **EMP:** 6
SALES (est): 628.7K **Privately Held**
SIC: **2899** Chemical preparations

(G-13056)
VEHICLE SYSTEMS INC
Also Called: V S I
7130 Lutz Ave Nw (44646-9343)
PHONE..................330 854-0535
Ervin Van Denberg, *President*
Vivian Vandenberg, *Corp Secy*
Scott Vandenberg, *Vice Pres*
EMP: 7
SALES (est): 1.5MM **Privately Held**
WEB: www.vehiclesys.com
SIC: **3714** 8742 8731 Motor vehicle brake systems & parts; management consulting services; commercial physical research

(G-13057)
WASHINGTON PRODUCTS INC
1875 Harsh Ave Se Ste 1 (44646-7182)
P.O. Box 644 (44646-0644)
PHONE..................330 837-5101
John A Boring, *President*
EMP: 11
SQ FT: 30,000
SALES (est): 2.1MM **Privately Held**
SIC: **3443** 3647 3429 2656 Fabricated plate work (boiler shop); automotive lighting fixtures; manufactured hardware (general); sanitary food containers; kitchen fixtures & equipment: metal, except cast aluminum

(G-13058)
YANKE BIONICS INC
2400 Wales Ave Nw (44646-0804)
PHONE..................330 833-0955
Steven Simko, *Branch Mgr*
EMP: 5
SALES (corp-wide): 10.1MM **Privately Held**
SIC: **3842** Prosthetic appliances
PA: Yanke Bionics, Inc.
303 W Exchange St
Akron OH 44302
330 762-6411

Masury
Trumbull County

(G-13059)
BULL MOOSE TUBE COMPANY
1433 Standard Ave (44438-1558)
P.O. Box 67 (44438-0067)
PHONE..................330 448-4878
Dave Thompson, *Manager*
EMP: 8 **Privately Held**
WEB: www.bullmoosetube.com
SIC: **3317** Steel pipe & tubes
HQ: Bull Moose Tube Company
1819 Clarkson Rd Ste 100
Chesterfield MO 63017
636 537-1249

(G-13060)
CUSTOM CNTRWGHT PLATE PROC INC
7799 Locust St (44438-1567)
P.O. Box 594, Cortland (44410-0594)
PHONE..................330 448-2347
Timothy Gearhart, *President*
EMP: 5
SQ FT: 22,000
SALES (est): 450K **Privately Held**
SIC: **2796** Platemaking services

(G-13061)
PIPELINES INC
7800 Addison Rd (44438-1207)
PHONE..................330 448-0000
William Bilske, *Manager*
EMP: 6
SALES (corp-wide): 25.3MM **Privately Held**
WEB: www.corp.enbridge.com
SIC: **3494** 1794 Line strainers, for use in piping systems; excavation work
PA: Pipelines, Inc.
16363 Saint Clair Ave
East Liverpool OH 43920
330 386-3646

(G-13062)
ROEMER INDUSTRIES INC
1555 Masury Rd (44438-1702)
PHONE..................330 448-2000
Joseph L O'Toole, *President*
Faith Otoole, *Admin Sec*
EMP: 71
SQ FT: 52,000
SALES (est): 9.1MM **Privately Held**
WEB: www.roemerind.com
SIC: **3479** 3469 3993 3613 Name plates: engraved, etched, etc.; metal stampings; signs & advertising specialties; switchgear & switchboard apparatus; coated & laminated paper

GEOGRAPHIC SECTION

Maumee - Lucas County (G-13088)

(G-13063)
T N T TECHNOLOGIES INC
7848 Locust St (44438-1533)
PHONE.................330 448-4744
Thomas Caldwell, *President*
EMP: 3
SQ FT: 7,500
SALES (est): 406.9K **Privately Held**
SIC: 3599 Machine shop, jobbing & repair; custom machinery

(G-13064)
WESTERN RESERVE METALS INC
7775 Addison Rd (44438-1208)
P.O. Box 126 (44438-0126)
PHONE.................330 448-4092
Tod Theodore, *President*
EMP: 22 EST: 1972
SQ FT: 24,000
SALES (est): 6.8MM **Privately Held**
SIC: 5051 3312 3316 Metals Service Center Blast Furnace-Steel Works Mfg Cold-Rolled Steel Shapes

Maumee
Lucas County

(G-13065)
ABBOTT MECHANICAL SERVICES LLC
804 W Wayne St (43537-1925)
PHONE.................419 460-4315
Gerry Abbott, *Owner*
Gary Abbott,
EMP: 4
SALES: 100K **Privately Held**
SIC: 1711 5074 3433 Heating & air conditioning contractors; refrigeration contractor; boilers, hot water heating; boilers, low-pressure heating: steam or hot water

(G-13066)
ADVANCED DSTRBTED GNRATION LLC
1331 Conant St Ste 107 (43537-4214)
PHONE.................419 530-3792
John Witte, *President*
EMP: 3
SALES (est): 108.3K **Privately Held**
SIC: 3674 Semiconductors & related devices

(G-13067)
AFFYMETRIX INC
434 W Dussel Dr (43537-1685)
PHONE.................419 887-1233
Kristin Yakimow, *Branch Mgr*
EMP: 12
SALES (corp-wide): 24.3B **Publicly Held**
SIC: 3826 Analytical instruments
HQ: Affymetrix, Inc.
3380 Central Expy
Santa Clara CA 95051

(G-13068)
ALTON PRODUCTS INC
425 W Sophia St (43537-1845)
P.O. Box 1115 (43537-8115)
PHONE.................419 893-0201
Marcia Janicki, *President*
Joseph M Albright, *Vice Pres*
Karen S Prala, *Treasurer*
Cindy Albright, *Admin Sec*
EMP: 13 EST: 1949
SQ FT: 21,000
SALES (est): 1.2MM **Privately Held**
SIC: 3599 Machine shop, jobbing & repair

(G-13069)
AMERICAN FRAME CORPORATION (PA)
400 Tomahawk Dr (43537-1695)
PHONE.................419 893-5595
Ronald J Mickel, *President*
Michael Cromly, *Vice Pres*
Larry Haddad, *Vice Pres*
Ronald Mickel, *Research*
Dana Dunbar, *Treasurer*
▲ EMP: 44
SQ FT: 33,000
SALES (est): 5.6MM **Privately Held**
WEB: www.americanframe.com
SIC: 7699 5961 5023 3444 Picture framing, custom; mail order house; home furnishings; sheet metalwork

(G-13070)
AMERICAN HEART ASSOCIATION INC
4331 Keystone Dr Ste D (43537-8797)
PHONE.................419 740-6180
Christine Colvin, *Branch Mgr*
EMP: 12
SALES (corp-wide): 780.2MM **Privately Held**
SIC: 8399 2721 Health systems agency; periodicals
PA: American Heart Association, Inc.
7272 Greenville Ave
Dallas TX 75231
214 373-6300

(G-13071)
ANATRACE PRODUCTS LLC (HQ)
434 W Dussel Dr (43537-1624)
PHONE.................419 740-6600
Ben Travis, *President*
Connie Cupilary, *General Mgr*
Ken Kreh, *VP Opers*
Mike Drury, *CFO*
Judy McCormick, *Manager*
EMP: 34
SALES (est): 7.3MM **Privately Held**
SIC: 5169 3585 Detergents & soaps, except specialty cleaning; refrigeration & heating equipment

(G-13072)
ANDERSONS INC (PA)
1947 Briarfield Blvd (43537-1690)
P.O. Box 119 (43537-0119)
PHONE.................419 893-5050
Daniel T Anderson, *President*
Patrick E Bowe, *President*
Michael S Irmen, *President*
Corbett Jorgenson, *President*
Rasesh H Shah, *President*
EMP: 150
SQ FT: 245,000
SALES: 3B **Publicly Held**
WEB: www.andersonsinc.com
SIC: 0723 5191 2874 4789 Crop preparation services for market; cash grain crops market preparation services; farm supplies; fertilizers & agricultural chemicals; seeds & bulbs; phosphatic fertilizers; plant foods, mixed: from plants making phosphatic fertilizer; railroad car repair; rental of railroad cars; grains

(G-13073)
ANDERSONS INC
Also Called: Fabrication Division
415 Illinois Ave (43537-1705)
P.O. Box 119 (43537-0119)
PHONE.................419 891-2930
Andrea Gay, *Sales Staff*
Michael Andersons, *Branch Mgr*
EMP: 36
SALES (corp-wide): 3B **Publicly Held**
WEB: www.andersonsinc.com
SIC: 3599 Machine shop, jobbing & repair
PA: The Andersons Inc
1947 Briarfield Blvd
Maumee OH 43537
419 893-5050

(G-13074)
ANDERSONS CLYMERS ETHANOL LLC (HQ)
1947 Briarfield Blvd (43537-1690)
PHONE.................574 722-2627
Phil Huffman, *Mng Member*
EMP: 25
SALES (est): 5MM
SALES (corp-wide): 3B **Publicly Held**
SIC: 2869 Ethyl alcohol, ethanol
PA: The Andersons Inc
1947 Briarfield Blvd
Maumee OH 43537
419 893-5050

(G-13075)
APPLIED ENERGY TECH INC
Also Called: A E T
1720 Indian Wood Cir E (43537-4041)
PHONE.................419 537-9052
Terence Seikel, *Ch of Bd*
Craig Winn, *President*
Aaron Faust, *Vice Pres*
John Harberts, *Vice Pres*
Lori Pierson, *CFO*
EMP: 26
SQ FT: 16,100
SALES (est): 9.5MM **Privately Held**
SIC: 3441 Fabricated structural metal

(G-13076)
B & B PRINTING GRAPHICS INC
1689 Lance Pointe Rd (43537-1603)
PHONE.................419 893-7068
Beth Stewart, *President*
Barney Stewart, *Vice Pres*
EMP: 10
SQ FT: 6,000
SALES (est): 1.7MM **Privately Held**
WEB: www.printinggraphics.com
SIC: 2752 Commercial printing, offset

(G-13077)
BARNES GROUP INC
Associated Spring Raymond
370 W Dussel Dr Ste A (43537-1604)
PHONE.................419 891-9292
Peter Korczynski, *Opers Mgr*
Tracy Allison, *Controller*
EMP: 33
SALES (corp-wide): 1.5B **Publicly Held**
WEB: www.barnesgroupinc.com
SIC: 5072 3495 Hardware; wire springs
PA: Barnes Group Inc.
123 Main St
Bristol CT 06010
860 583-7070

(G-13078)
BARTON-CAREY MEDICAL PRODUCTS (PA)
1331 Conant St Ste 102 (43537-1665)
P.O. Box 421, Perrysburg (43552-0421)
PHONE.................419 887-1285
John H Mays, *President*
EMP: 28
SALES (est): 2.4MM **Privately Held**
WEB: www.bartoncarey.com
SIC: 3842 2339 2326 Clothing, fire resistant & protective; women's & misses' outerwear; men's & boys' work clothing

(G-13079)
BAY CONTROLS LLC
6528 Weatherfield Ct (43537-9468)
PHONE.................419 891-4390
Brian Bee, *Opers Mgr*
Gary Ruff, *Senior Engr*
Mike Bavis, *CFO*
Wendy Beitzel, *Accounting Mgr*
Jason Modlin, *Sales Engr*
▼ EMP: 30
SQ FT: 12,000
SALES (est): 5.9MM
SALES (corp-wide): 89.4K **Privately Held**
WEB: www.baycontrols.com
SIC: 3625 Industrial controls: push button, selector switches, pilot
PA: Entelco Corporation
6528 Weatherfield Ct
Maumee OH 43537
419 872-4620

(G-13080)
BERRY GLOBAL INC
1695 Indian Wood Cir (43537-4003)
PHONE.................419 887-1602
Estelle Berry, *Branch Mgr*
EMP: 10 **Publicly Held**
SIC: 3089 3081 Bottle caps, molded plastic; unsupported plastics film & sheet
HQ: Berry Global, Inc.
101 Oakley St
Evansville IN 47710
812 424-2904

(G-13081)
CDC CORPORATION
1445 Holland Rd (43537-1617)
PHONE.................715 532-5548
James M Roenitz, *President*
David R Sachse, *Vice Pres*
▲ EMP: 100
SQ FT: 80,000
SALES (est): 11.3MM **Publicly Held**
WEB: www.conweddesignscape.com
SIC: 2542 Partitions & fixtures, except wood
HQ: Owens Corning Sales, Llc
1 Owens Corning Pkwy
Toledo OH 43659
419 248-8000

(G-13082)
CDC FAB CO
1445 Holland Rd (43537-1617)
PHONE.................419 866-7705
Peter A Dewhirst, *Principal*
EMP: 16 EST: 2016
SALES (est): 3.6MM **Privately Held**
SIC: 3448 Prefabricated metal buildings

(G-13083)
CONWED DESIGNSCAPE
1445 Holland Rd (43537-1617)
PHONE.................715 532-5548
James Roenitz,
▲ EMP: 14
SALES (est): 2.4MM **Privately Held**
SIC: 2542 Mfg Partitions/Fixtures-Non-wood

(G-13084)
CUMMINS BRIDGEWAY TOLEDO LLC
801 Illinois Ave (43537-1713)
PHONE.................419 893-8711
Holly Roesch,
EMP: 9
SALES (est): 2.7MM
SALES (corp-wide): 23.7B **Publicly Held**
WEB: www.bridgewaypower.com
SIC: 5084 3519 Engines & parts, diesel; internal combustion engines
PA: Cummins Inc.
500 Jackson St
Columbus IN 47201
812 377-5000

(G-13085)
DAN K WILLIAMS INC
1350 Ford St (43537-1733)
P.O. Box 147 (43537-0147)
PHONE.................419 893-3251
Dan K Williams, *President*
EMP: 22
SALES (est): 3.8MM **Privately Held**
SIC: 3273 Ready-mixed concrete

(G-13086)
DANA AUTO SYSTEMS GROUP LLC (DH)
3939 Technology Dr (43537-9194)
PHONE.................419 887-3000
Rick Harman,
◆ EMP: 88
SALES (est): 581.5MM **Publicly Held**
SIC: 3714 Motor vehicle parts & accessories

(G-13087)
DANA AUTOMOTIVE AFTERMARKET (DH)
3939 Technology Dr (43537-9194)
PHONE.................419 887-3000
James K Kamsickas, *CEO*
Susan Herring, *General Mgr*
James Laisure, *Div Sub Head*
Terry McCormack, *Div Sub Head*
D Butcher, *Vice Pres*
EMP: 5
SALES (est): 23.2MM **Publicly Held**
SIC: 3714 Motor vehicle parts & accessories

(G-13088)
DANA BRAZIL HOLDINGS I LLC (DH)
3939 Technology Dr (43537-9194)
PHONE.................419 887-3000
Roger Wood, *CEO*
Beatriz Jimenez, *Vice Pres*
Ken Koncilja, *Vice Pres*
Seth Metzger, *Vice Pres*
Craig Price, *Vice Pres*
EMP: 5

Maumee - Lucas County (G-13089)

SALES (est): 762.7K **Publicly Held**
SIC: **3714** Motor vehicle parts & accessories
HQ: Dana World Trade Corporation
3939 Technology Dr
Maumee OH 43537
419 887-3000

(G-13089)
DANA COMMERCIAL VHCL MFG LLC (DH)
Also Called: Dana Commercial Vehicle Pdts
3939 Technology Dr (43537-9194)
PHONE.............................419 887-3000
Nick Stanage,
Tom Wilgus,
◆ EMP: 2
SALES (est): 55.6MM **Publicly Held**
SIC: **3714** Motor vehicle parts & accessories

(G-13090)
DANA COMMERCIAL VHCL PDTS LLC (DH)
3939 Technology Dr (43537-9194)
PHONE.............................419 887-3000
Ben Passino, *Engineer*
Haley Bollman, *Manager*
Lewis Nickell, *Manager*
Marvin Franklin,
◆ EMP: 95
SALES (est): 106.9MM **Publicly Held**
SIC: **3714** Motor vehicle parts & accessories

(G-13091)
DANA DRIVESHAFT MFG LLC (DH)
Also Called: Dana Driveshaft Products
3939 Technology Dr (43537-9194)
PHONE.............................419 887-3000
Margot Hoffman,
▲ EMP: 61
SALES (est): 48.5MM **Publicly Held**
SIC: **3714** Motor vehicle parts & accessories

(G-13092)
DANA DRIVESHAFT PRODUCTS LLC (DH)
3939 Technology Dr (43537-9194)
PHONE.............................419 887-3000
Rod Filcek,
▲ EMP: 57
SALES (est): 66.2MM **Publicly Held**
SIC: **3714** Motor vehicle parts & accessories

(G-13093)
DANA GLOBAL PRODUCTS INC (DH)
3939 Technology Dr (43537-9194)
P.O. Box 1000 (43537-7000)
PHONE.............................419 887-3000
Rodney R Filcek, *President*
Jeffrey S Bowen, *Vice Pres*
Lillian Etzkorn, *Treasurer*
Marc S Levin, *Admin Sec*
◆ EMP: 7
SALES (est): 3.2MM **Publicly Held**
SIC: **3714** Motor vehicle parts & accessories

(G-13094)
DANA HEAVY VEHICLE SYSTEMS (DH)
Also Called: Dana Heavy Vhcl Systems Group
3939 Technology Dr (43537-9194)
PHONE.............................419 887-3000
Nick Cole, *President*
◆ EMP: 2
SALES (est): 252.3MM **Publicly Held**
SIC: **3714** Motor vehicle parts & accessories

(G-13095)
DANA INCORPORATED (PA)
3939 Technology Dr (43537-9194)
P.O. Box 1000 (43537-7000)
PHONE.............................419 887-3000
Keith E Wandell, *Ch of Bd*
James K Kamsickas, *President*
Dwayne E Matthews, *President*
Robert D Pyle, *President*
Mark E Wallace, *Exec VP*
EMP: 300
SALES: 8.1B **Publicly Held**
SIC: **3714** Motor vehicle parts & accessories; motor vehicle transmissions, drive assemblies & parts

(G-13096)
DANA LIGHT AXLE MFG LLC (DH)
Also Called: Dana Light Axle Products
3939 Technology Dr (43537-9194)
PHONE.............................419 887-3000
Thomas Stone, *Mng Member*
▲ EMP: 19
SALES: 130MM **Publicly Held**
SIC: **3714** Motor vehicle parts & accessories

(G-13097)
DANA LIMITED
6515 Maumee Western Rd (43537-9367)
PHONE.............................419 887-3000
EMP: 3
SALES (est): 183.3K **Privately Held**
SIC: **3714** Motor vehicle parts & accessories

(G-13098)
DANA LIMITED
Also Called: Dana Information Technology
580 Longbow Dr (43537-1759)
PHONE.............................419 482-2000
Al Henderson, *Manager*
Luciano Satine, *Manager*
EMP: 100 **Publicly Held**
WEB: www.intelligentcooling.com
SIC: **3714** Motor vehicle parts & accessories
HQ: Dana Limited
3939 Technology Dr
Maumee OH 43537

(G-13099)
DANA LIMITED (HQ)
3939 Technology Dr (43537-9194)
P.O. Box 1000 (43537-7000)
PHONE.............................419 887-3000
James Sweetnam, *President*
Siddharth Petkar, *General Mgr*
John Devine, *Chairman*
Marc S Levin, *Senior VP*
Kyle Albertson, *Engineer*
▲ EMP: 500
SALES (est): 5.7B **Publicly Held**
WEB: www.intelligentcooling.com
SIC: **3714** 3053 3593 3492 Motor vehicle parts & accessories; gaskets & sealing devices; fluid power cylinders, hydraulic or pneumatic; control valves, fluid power: hydraulic & pneumatic

(G-13100)
DANA OFF HIGHWAY PRODUCTS LLC (DH)
3939 Technology Dr (43537-9194)
P.O. Box 1000 (43537-7000)
PHONE.............................419 887-3000
Nick Stanage, *President*
◆ EMP: 45
SALES (est): 47.5MM **Publicly Held**
SIC: **3714** Motor vehicle parts & accessories

(G-13101)
DANA SEALING MANUFACTURING LLC (DH)
Also Called: Dana Sealing Products
3939 Technology Dr (43537-9194)
PHONE.............................419 887-3000
Rod Filcek,
Ralf Goettel,
▲ EMP: 87
SALES (est): 93.2MM **Publicly Held**
SIC: **3714** Motor vehicle parts & accessories

(G-13102)
DANA SEALING PRODUCTS LLC (DH)
3939 Technology Dr (43537-9194)
P.O. Box 1000 (43537-7000)
PHONE.............................419 887-3000
Karla Zoeller, *Controller*
Jim Zabojnik, *Accounts Mgr*
Ralf Goettel,
▲ EMP: 26
SALES (est): 119.8MM **Publicly Held**
SIC: **3714** Motor vehicle parts & accessories

(G-13103)
DANA STRUCTURAL PRODUCTS LLC (DH)
3939 Technology Dr (43537-9194)
PHONE.............................419 887-3000
Gilberto Ceretti,
EMP: 4
SALES (est): 678.5K **Publicly Held**
SIC: **3714** Motor vehicle parts & accessories

(G-13104)
DANA THERMAL PRODUCTS LLC (DH)
3939 Technology Dr (43537-9194)
PHONE.............................419 887-3000
Ralf Goettel,
▲ EMP: 20
SALES (est): 10.8MM **Publicly Held**
SIC: **3714** Motor vehicle parts & accessories

(G-13105)
DANA WORLD TRADE CORPORATION (DH)
3939 Technology Dr (43537-9194)
PHONE.............................419 887-3000
Kenneth A Hiltz, *CFO*
EMP: 5
SALES (est): 10.3MM **Publicly Held**
SIC: **3714** Motor vehicle parts & accessories

(G-13106)
DEFENSE SURPLUS LLC
706 Waite Ave (43537-3464)
PHONE.............................419 460-9906
Vincent Porter, *Principal*
EMP: 3 EST: 2012
SALES (est): 329.7K **Privately Held**
SIC: **3812** Defense systems & equipment

(G-13107)
DENTSPLY SIRONA INC
520 Illinois Ave (43537-1708)
PHONE.............................419 893-5672
Garyn Livecchi, *General Mgr*
EMP: 50
SQ FT: 4,000
SALES (corp-wide): 3.9B **Publicly Held**
WEB: www.dentsply.com
SIC: **3843** Teeth, artificial (not made in dental laboratories)
PA: Dentsply Sirona Inc.
221 W Philadelphia St
York PA 17401
717 845-7511

(G-13108)
DENTSPLY SIRONA INC
Ransom & Randolph
3535 Briarfield Blvd (43537-9383)
PHONE.............................419 865-9497
Dan Nixon, *Branch Mgr*
Casey Wolfe, *Manager*
EMP: 72
SALES (corp-wide): 3.9B **Publicly Held**
SIC: **3844** 2821 3915 3843 X-ray apparatus & tubes; beta-ray irradiation equipment; radiographic X-ray apparatus & tubes; molding compounds, plastics; jewelers' castings; impression material, dental
PA: Dentsply Sirona Inc.
221 W Philadelphia St
York PA 17401
717 845-7511

(G-13109)
EATON-AEROQUIP LLC
1660 Indian Wood Cir (43537-4004)
PHONE.............................419 891-7775
Howard Selland, *President*
EMP: 90 **Privately Held**
SIC: **8711** 3594 3593 3561 Professional engineer; fluid power pumps & motors; fluid power cylinders & actuators; pumps & pumping equipment; fluid power valves & hose fittings; rubber & plastics hose & beltings
HQ: Eaton Aeroquip Llc
1000 Eaton Blvd
Cleveland OH 44122
216 523-5000

(G-13110)
FOUR FIRES MEADERY LLC
1683 Lance Pointe Rd # 106 (43537-1681)
PHONE.............................419 704-9573
Andrew Lynch,
Christopher Clarke,
Joshua Kirk,
Athreya Rajan,
EMP: 4
SALES (est): 177.9K **Privately Held**
SIC: **2084** Neutral spirits, fruit

(G-13111)
FRIPRO ENERGY LLC
7008 Garden Rd (43537-1010)
PHONE.............................419 865-0002
Thomas E Fairbairin, *CEO*
Terrence J Sherman, *President*
EMP: 3
SQ FT: 43,560
SALES (est): 173K **Privately Held**
SIC: **8731** 3671 Energy research; electron beam (beta ray) generator tubes

(G-13112)
FYPON LTD
1750 Indian Wood Cir (43537-4049)
P.O. Box 301, Archbold (43502-0301)
PHONE.............................800 446-3040
Merle G Beck, *President*
Marcia Ostrowski, *Sales Mgr*
Jim Moore, *Director*
▲ EMP: 200
SQ FT: 150,000
SALES (est): 27.7MM
SALES (corp-wide): 76.5MM **Privately Held**
SIC: **3089** Plastic hardware & building products
HQ: Simonton Holdings, Inc.
520 Lake Cook Rd
Deerfield IL 60015
304 428-8261

(G-13113)
GREAT LAKES ENGRAVING CORP
Also Called: Great Lakes Reprographic
1736 Henthorne Dr (43537-1350)
PHONE.............................419 867-1607
Jack P Kerin, *President*
Jill Weiser, *Vice Pres*
EMP: 4
SQ FT: 7,500
SALES (est): 520.6K **Privately Held**
WEB: www.greatlakesengraving.net
SIC: **7334** 2752 Photocopying & duplicating services; commercial printing, lithographic

(G-13114)
HALL-TOLEDO INC
525 W Sophia St (43537-1881)
P.O. Box 1501 (43537-8501)
PHONE.............................419 893-4334
Andrew F Boesel, *President*
EMP: 10
SQ FT: 5,000
SALES (est): 1.2MM **Privately Held**
SIC: **3546** 3714 Power-driven handtools; motor vehicle parts & accessories
PA: Michabo Inc
525 W Sophia St
Maumee OH 43537

(G-13115)
HAMMILL MANUFACTURING CO (PA)
Also Called: Impact Cutoff Div
360 Tomahawk Dr (43537-1612)
P.O. Box 1450 (43537-8450)
PHONE.............................419 476-0789
John Hammill, *Ch of Bd*
John E Hamill Jr, *President*
Robert Doubler, *Exec VP*

Carl Barnard, *Vice Pres*
Jeff McFarland, *Plant Supt*
EMP: 100 **EST:** 1955
SQ FT: 80,000
SALES (est): 27.8MM **Privately Held**
WEB: www.hammillmfg.com
SIC: 3842 3545 Implants, surgical; chucks: drill, lathe or magnetic (machine tool accessories)

(G-13116)
HELM INSTRUMENT COMPANY INC
361 W Dussel Dr (43537-1649)
PHONE.............................419 893-4356
Richard T Wilhelm, *President*
Mary L Tice, *Vice Pres*
Mary Tice, *Vice Pres*
Michael Wilhelm, *Vice Pres*
Mike Wilhelm, *Vice Pres*
EMP: 34 **EST:** 1962
SQ FT: 12,500
SALES (est): 7.4MM **Privately Held**
WEB: www.helminstrument.com
SIC: 3829 3825 3823 3822 Measuring & controlling devices; instruments to measure electricity; industrial instrmnts msrmnt display/control process variable; auto controls regulating residntl & coml environmt & applncs; relays & industrial controls

(G-13117)
HENRY-GRIFFITTS LIMITED (HQ)
Also Called: About Golf
352 Tomahawk Dr (43537-1612)
PHONE.............................419 482-9095
Bill Bales, *CEO*
▲ **EMP:** 9
SALES (est): 3.4MM
SALES (corp-wide): 4.3MM **Privately Held**
SIC: 3999 Atomizers, toiletry
PA: Aboutgolf, Limited
352 Tomahawk Dr
Maumee OH 43537
419 482-9095

(G-13118)
IMAGE BY J & K LLC
1575 Henthorne Dr (43537-1372)
PHONE.............................888 667-6929
James Land IV, *Mng Member*
EMP: 400
SQ FT: 10,000
SALES (est): 51.6MM **Privately Held**
SIC: 3589 7217 7349 7342 Floor washing & polishing machines, commercial; carpet & upholstery cleaning; building & office cleaning services; service station cleaning & degreasing; air duct cleaning; rest room cleaning service

(G-13119)
ISHOS BROS FUEL VENTURES INC
1289 Conant St (43537-1607)
PHONE.............................586 634-0187
Michael Isho, *Owner*
EMP: 5 **EST:** 2011
SALES (est): 364.4K **Privately Held**
SIC: 2869 Fuels

(G-13120)
J-M DESIGNS LLC
128 W Wayne St (43537-2151)
PHONE.............................419 794-2114
Mary Ellen Gedert,
Francis R Gedert,
EMP: 5
SQ FT: 4,500
SALES (est): 393.6K **Privately Held**
SIC: 5949 5099 2759 Sewing & needlework; signs, except electric; screen printing

(G-13121)
JAZZ TEXTILE IMPRESSIONS
1425 Holland Rd (43537-1617)
P.O. Box 6778, Toledo (43612-0778)
PHONE.............................419 242-5940
Daniel Burke, *President*
EMP: 5

SALES (est): 420K **Privately Held**
WEB: www.jazztextiles.com
SIC: 2759 Screen printing

(G-13122)
JOHNS MANVILLE CORPORATION
1020 Ford St (43537-1820)
PHONE.............................419 467-8189
EMP: 224
SALES (corp-wide): 225.3B **Publicly Held**
WEB: www.jm.com
SIC: 3296 Fiberglass insulation
HQ: Johns Manville Corporation
717 17th St Ste 800
Denver CO 80202
303 978-2000

(G-13123)
JOHNSON CONTROLS
3661 Brrfeld Blvd Ste 101 (43537)
PHONE.............................419 861-0662
Jim Ravaf, *Manager*
EMP: 50 **Privately Held**
WEB: www.simplexgrinnell.com
SIC: 3669 Emergency alarms
HQ: Johnson Controls Fire Protection Lp
6600 Congress Ave
Boca Raton FL 33487
561 988-7200

(G-13124)
KUHLMAN CORPORATION (PA)
Also Called: Kuhlman Construction Products
1845 Indian Wood Cir (43537-4072)
P.O. Box 714, Toledo (43697-0714)
PHONE.............................419 897-6000
Timothy L Goligoski, *President*
Kenneth Kuhlman, *Vice Pres*
Terry Schaefer, *CFO*
Tim Casey, *Sales Mgr*
▲ **EMP:** 150 **EST:** 1901
SQ FT: 18,000
SALES (est): 50.1MM **Privately Held**
WEB: www.kuhlman-corp.com
SIC: 4226 5032 3273 Special warehousing & storage; brick, stone & related material; brick, except refractory; building blocks; sewer pipe, clay; ready-mixed concrete

(G-13125)
LAFARGE NORTH AMERICA INC
1645 Indian Wood Cir (43537-4400)
PHONE.............................419 897-7656
Larry Papenfuss, *Manager*
EMP: 14
SQ FT: 2,088
SALES (corp-wide): 26.4B **Privately Held**
WEB: www.lafargenorthamerica.com
SIC: 3241 Cement, hydraulic
HQ: Lafarge North America Inc.
8700 W Bryn Mawr Ave
Chicago IL 60631
773 372-1000

(G-13126)
LARRYS WATER CONDITIONING
Also Called: Lwc
720 Illinois Ave Ste I (43537-1750)
PHONE.............................419 887-0290
Larry Kohlenberg,
Sandra Kohlenberg,
EMP: 3
SQ FT: 2,400
SALES (est): 360K **Privately Held**
SIC: 3589 Water treatment equipment, industrial

(G-13127)
LINE DRIVE SPORTZ-LCRC LLC
2901 Key St Ste 1 (43537-2421)
PHONE.............................419 794-7150
Elizabeth Beck,
James Hanna,
EMP: 6
SALES (est): 752.7K **Privately Held**
SIC: 3949 Sporting & athletic goods

(G-13128)
MAGNESIUM PRODUCTS GROUP INC
Also Called: M P G
3928 Azalea Cir (43537-9191)
PHONE.............................310 971-5799

Bradley A Hirou, *President*
Steve Hubble, *COO*
Ronald W Banks, *Exec VP*
EMP: 6
SALES (est): 301.2K **Privately Held**
WEB: www.mpg-mfg.com
SIC: 3441 Fabricated structural metal

(G-13129)
MAUMEE ASSEMBLY & STAMPING LLC
920 Illinois Ave (43537-1716)
PHONE.............................419 304-2887
Stanley Chlebowski, *CEO*
Travis Barta, *Vice Pres*
Joseph W Weiss, *Controller*
Mike Lowery, *Manager*
EMP: 100
SALES (est): 25.8MM **Privately Held**
SIC: 3469 Stamping metal for the trade

(G-13130)
MAUMEE HOSE & FITTING INC
Also Called: Maumee Hose & Belting Co
720 Illinois Ave Ste H (43537-1750)
PHONE.............................419 893-7252
James C Walsh, *President*
Karen Walsh, *Vice Pres*
EMP: 7
SQ FT: 10,000
SALES (est): 1MM **Privately Held**
WEB: www.maumeehose.com
SIC: 3429 5085 Clamps, couplings, nozzles & other metal hose fittings; hose, belting & packing

(G-13131)
MAUMEE QUICK PRINT INC
406 Illinois Ave (43537-2180)
PHONE.............................419 893-4321
Peggy Masters, *President*
Jennifer Starr, *Vice Pres*
EMP: 5 **EST:** 1976
SQ FT: 1,400
SALES: 150K **Privately Held**
SIC: 2752 Commercial printing, offset

(G-13132)
METAL FORMING & COINING CORP (PA)
Also Called: MFC
1007 Illinois Ave (43537-1752)
PHONE.............................419 897-9530
Thomas Wienrich, *President*
Tim Cripsey, *General Mgr*
Paul Kessler, *Exec VP*
Jerry Lagger, *Vice Pres*
Katherine Church, *Engineer*
EMP: 100 **EST:** 1953
SQ FT: 103,000
SALES (est): 26.9MM **Privately Held**
WEB: www.mfccorp.com
SIC: 3462 Iron & steel forgings

(G-13133)
MICHABO INC (PA)
525 W Sophia St (43537-1847)
PHONE.............................419 893-4334
Milton C Boesel Jr, *President*
Andrew Boesel, *Vice Pres*
EMP: 1
SQ FT: 5,000
SALES (est): 1.3MM **Privately Held**
SIC: 3546 Power-driven handtools

(G-13134)
MIRROR
Also Called: Community Mirror, The
113 W Wayne St (43537-2150)
PHONE.............................419 893-8135
Michael Mc Carthy, *Owner*
Carol McCarthy, *Persnl Dir*
Mike McCarthy, *Pub Rel Staff*
Dan Lawrence, *Technology*
EMP: 20
SQ FT: 5,000
SALES (est): 1MM **Privately Held**
SIC: 2711 Commercial printing & newspaper publishing combined; newspapers: publishing only, not printed on site

(G-13135)
MIRROR PUBLISHING CO INC
Also Called: Mirror, The
113 W Wayne St (43537-2150)
PHONE.............................419 893-8135

Michael McCarthy, *President*
EMP: 20
SQ FT: 3,000
SALES (est): 1.2MM **Privately Held**
SIC: 2711 Newspapers, publishing & printing

(G-13136)
MITCHS WELDING & HITCHES
802 Kingsbury St (43537-1826)
PHONE.............................419 893-3117
James Mitchell, *President*
EMP: 8
SQ FT: 5,000
SALES (est): 852.5K **Privately Held**
SIC: 3537 5561 Industrial trucks & tractors; recreational vehicle parts & accessories

(G-13137)
MOLECULAR DIMENSIONS INC
434 W Dussel Dr (43537-1685)
PHONE.............................419 740-6600
Ben Travis, *President*
James Schmalz, *Vice Pres*
Mike Drury, *CFO*
▲ **EMP:** 4
SALES (est): 200K **Privately Held**
WEB: www.moleculardimensions.com
SIC: 3944 3585 Science kits: microscopes, chemistry sets, etc.; refrigeration & heating equipment
HQ: Anatrace Products, Llc
434 W Dussel Dr
Maumee OH 43537
419 740-6600

(G-13138)
PLASTEX INDUSTRIES INC
7106 Country Creek Rd (43537-9727)
PHONE.............................419 531-0189
Susan Smotherman, *President*
▲ **EMP:** 30
SQ FT: 12,000
SALES (est): 5.3MM **Privately Held**
WEB: www.plastex-industries.com
SIC: 3089 Injection molding of plastics

(G-13139)
PRO-PAK INDUSTRIES INC (PA)
1125 Ford St (43537-1703)
P.O. Box 1176 (43537-8176)
PHONE.............................419 729-0751
Leo Deiger, *President*
Charles M Deiger, *Corp Secy*
Anthony Deiger, *Vice Pres*
Randy Deiger, *Vice Pres*
Josh Baum, *Plant Mgr*
EMP: 110 **EST:** 1948
SALES (est): 35.6MM **Privately Held**
SIC: 2653 Boxes, corrugated: made from purchased materials

(G-13140)
PROTEL SYSTEMS AND SVCS LLC (PA)
1298 Conant St Ste 504 (43537-1608)
PHONE.............................419 913-0825
Denny McBroom,
EMP: 3
SALES (est): 455.8K **Privately Held**
SIC: 7372 Business oriented computer software

(G-13141)
RANSOM & RANDOLPH
520 Illinois Ave (43537-1708)
PHONE.............................419 794-1210
EMP: 4
SALES (est): 316.8K
SALES (corp-wide): 706.7K **Privately Held**
SIC: 2241 Bindings, textile
PA: Ransom & Randolph
3535 Briarfield Blvd
Maumee OH 43537
419 794-1212

(G-13142)
S E JOHNSON COMPANIES INC (DH)
1360 Ford St (43537-1733)
PHONE.............................419 893-8731
John T Bearss, *CEO*
Donald Weber, *Vice Pres*
Mark W Karchner, *CFO*

Maumee - Lucas County (G-13143) GEOGRAPHIC SECTION

Terry J Moore, *Treasurer*
Jack Zouhary, *Admin Sec*
EMP: 15 **EST:** 1924
SQ FT: 34,000
SALES (est): 45.6MM
SALES (corp-wide): 29.7B **Privately Held**
WEB: www.sejohnson.com
SIC: 1611 1622 2951 1411 General contractor, highway & street construction; bridge construction; asphalt & asphaltic paving mixtures (not from refineries); limestone, dimension-quarrying
HQ: Shelly Company
80 Park Dr
Thornville OH 43076
740 246-6315

(G-13143)
SENATOR INTERNATIONAL INC (PA)
Also Called: Allermuir
4111 N Jerome Rd (43537-7100)
PHONE 419 887-5806
Mark Brettschneider, *President*
Philip Callahan, *General Mgr*
Colin Mustoe, *Managing Dir*
Jeff Rogers, *Controller*
Paul Hoelzle, *Accountant*
▲ **EMP:** 38
SALES (est): 15MM **Privately Held**
SIC: 5712 2522 2521 Office furniture; office furniture, except wood; wood office furniture

(G-13144)
SERVICE SPRING CORP (PA)
1703 Toll Gate Dr (43537-1673)
PHONE 419 838-6081
Michael McAlear, *CEO*
Clarence J Veigel, *Principal*
Evelyn F Veigel, *Principal*
Scott Simpson, *Facilities Mgr*
Jeff Reau, *Engineer*
▼ **EMP:** 87 **EST:** 1962
SQ FT: 98,000
SALES (est): 21.8MM **Privately Held**
WEB: www.sscorp.com
SIC: 3493 Steel springs, except wire

(G-13145)
SKR ENTERPRISES LLC
Also Called: Always Promoting Co.
127 W Wayne St (43537-2150)
PHONE 419 891-1112
Scott Sterns, *Mng Member*
Kevin Sterns,
EMP: 8
SALES: 700K **Privately Held**
WEB: www.alwayspromoting.com
SIC: 3999 Advertising display products

(G-13146)
SOCCER CENTRE OWNERS LTD
1620 Market Place Dr (43537-4318)
PHONE 419 893-5425
Brant Smith, *President*
EMP: 30 **EST:** 2012
SQ FT: 300,000
SALES (est): 970.8K **Privately Held**
SIC: 3949 7999 Pads: football, basketball, soccer, lacrosse, etc.; indoor court clubs

(G-13147)
SPARTAN CHEMICAL COMPANY INC (PA)
1110 Spartan Dr (43537-1725)
PHONE 419 897-5551
Stephen H Swigart, *CEO*
John Swigart, *President*
Jack Ellison, *Division Mgr*
Jay Anderson, *Regional Mgr*
Derek Awalt, *Regional Mgr*
◆ **EMP:** 48 **EST:** 1956
SQ FT: 450,000
SALES (est): 71.7MM **Privately Held**
WEB: www.spartanchemical.com
SIC: 2842 Floor waxes

(G-13148)
SPOSIE LLC
4064 Technology Dr (43537-9310)
PHONE 888 977-2229
Ryan Wright, *Mng Member*
EMP: 12

SQ FT: 35,000
SALES: 3MM **Privately Held**
SIC: 2676 Infant & baby paper products

(G-13149)
STONECO INC
Also Called: Shelley Company
1360 Ford St (43537-1733)
PHONE 419 893-7645
Lee Wehner, *Manager*
EMP: 15
SALES (corp-wide): 29.7B **Privately Held**
WEB: www.stoneco.net
SIC: 1422 5032 Crushed & broken limestone; stone, crushed or broken
HQ: Stoneco, Inc.
1700 Fostoria Ave Ste 200
Findlay OH 45840
419 422-8854

(G-13150)
SUN CHEMICAL CORPORATION
Ink & Plates
1380 Ford St (43537-1733)
PHONE 419 891-3514
Tara Dimauro, *Purch Mgr*
Tom Owarzak, *Buyer*
Wes Lucas, *Manager*
EMP: 80
SQ FT: 68,000
SALES (corp-wide): 7.1B **Privately Held**
WEB: www.sunchemical.com
SIC: 2893 Printing ink
HQ: Sun Chemical Corporation
35 Waterview Blvd Ste 100
Parsippany NJ 07054
973 404-6000

(G-13151)
SURFACE COMBUSTION INC (PA)
1700 Indian Wood Cir (43537-4067)
P.O. Box 428 (43537-0428)
PHONE 419 891-7150
William J Bernard Jr, *President*
Lori Lingle, *President*
Randy Behnfeldt, *Regional Mgr*
Bill Bernard, *Vice Pres*
Max Hoetzl, *Vice Pres*
▲ **EMP:** 110
SQ FT: 36,000
SALES (est): 23.8MM **Privately Held**
WEB: www.surfacecombustion.com
SIC: 3567 Industrial furnaces & ovens

(G-13152)
THERMA-TRU CORP
6214 Monclova Rd (43537-9761)
PHONE 419 740-5193
EMP: 80
SALES (corp-wide): 5.4B **Publicly Held**
SIC: 3089 Window frames & sash, plastic
HQ: Therma-Tru Corp.
1750 Indian Wood Cir # 100
Maumee OH 43537
419 891-7400

(G-13153)
TIAMA AMERICAS INC
6500 Weatherfield Ct (43537-9468)
PHONE 269 274-3107
EMP: 5
SALES (est): 164.1K **Privately Held**
SIC: 3221 Glass containers
HQ: Tiama
Zone Artisanale Des Plattes
Vourles 69390
437 201-500

(G-13154)
TILT-OR-LIFT INC (PA)
124 E Dudley St (43537-3366)
P.O. Box 8728 (43537-8728)
PHONE 419 893-6944
Dennis Rober, *President*
Christine Hammer, *Office Mgr*
EMP: 6
SQ FT: 1,400
SALES: 1MM **Privately Held**
SIC: 3537 5084 Lift trucks, industrial: fork, platform, straddle, etc.; industrial machinery & equipment

(G-13155)
TOP NOTCH FLEET SERVICES LLC
801 Wall St (43537-3567)
PHONE 419 260-4057
Tom J Laurie, *Mng Member*
EMP: 5
SALES: 297.2K **Privately Held**
SIC: 7692 7549 7538 Automotive welding; road service, automotive; general truck repair

(G-13156)
TUPPAS SOFTWARE CORPORATION
1690 Woodlands Dr (43537-4045)
PHONE 419 897-7902
Paul Tupciauskas, *CEO*
Bob Brewster, *Sales Staff*
EMP: 200
SALES (est): 12.6MM **Privately Held**
WEB: www.tuppas.com
SIC: 3829 Medical diagnostic systems, nuclear

(G-13157)
TWENTY SECOND CNTURY FOODS LLC
Also Called: Petit Gourmet
6546 Weatherfield Ct C (43537-9252)
PHONE 419 866-6343
Jason E Dzierwa, *Principal*
EMP: 3
SALES (est): 110K **Privately Held**
SIC: 2099 Food preparations

(G-13158)
US COEXCELL INC
400 W Dussel Dr Ste C (43537-1636)
PHONE 419 897-9110
Christopher Nelson, *President*
Dennis Puening, *Vice Pres*
▲ **EMP:** 41
SQ FT: 40,000
SALES (est): 10.8MM
SALES (corp-wide): 131.9MM **Privately Held**
WEB: www.uscoxl.com
SIC: 3089 Plastic containers, except foam
PA: Cleveland Steel Container Corporation
30310 Emerald Valley Pkwy
Solon OH 44139
440 349-8000

(G-13159)
VICKERS INTERNATIONAL INC (DH)
3000 Strayer Rd (43537-9529)
PHONE 419 867-2200
Darryl F Allen, *President*
James Oathout, *Vice Pres*
Gary J Findling, *Treasurer*
EMP: 10
SQ FT: 21,000
SALES (est): 2.1MM **Privately Held**
SIC: 3561 3594 3491 Pumps & pumping equipment; motors, pneumatic; motors: hydraulic, fluid power or air; industrial valves
HQ: Eaton Corporation
1000 Eaton Blvd
Cleveland OH 44122
440 523-5000

(G-13160)
WILLIAMS CONCRETE INC
1350 Ford St (43537-1733)
PHONE 419 893-3251
Mark Williams, *President*
Terry Schaefer, *VP Finance*
EMP: 14
SALES: 2.8MM
SALES (corp-wide): 50.1MM **Privately Held**
WEB: www.kuhlman-corp.com
SIC: 3273 Ready-mixed concrete
PA: Kuhlman Corporation
1845 Indian Wood Cir
Maumee OH 43537
419 897-6000

(G-13161)
Y Z ENTERPRISES INC
Also Called: Almondina Brand Biscuits
1930 Indian Wood Cir # 100 (43537-4001)
PHONE 419 893-8777
Yuval N Zaliouk, *CEO*
Jack Hunter, *Vice Pres*
Christopher Moody, *Vice Pres*
Susan M Zaliouk, *Treasurer*
EMP: 20
SQ FT: 12,500
SALES (est): 4.2MM **Privately Held**
WEB: www.zaliouk.com
SIC: 2052 Cookies

Mayfield Heights
Cuyahoga County

(G-13162)
DATATRAK INTERNATIONAL INC
5900 Landerbrook Dr # 170 (44124-4085)
PHONE 440 443-0082
Alex Tabatabai, *Ch of Bd*
James R Ward, *President*
Varnesh Sritharan, *Vice Pres*
Shyla Jones, *Project Mgr*
Osman Muhammad, *Project Mgr*
EMP: 47
SQ FT: 4,300
SALES: 7.4MM **Privately Held**
WEB: www.datatrak.net
SIC: 7374 7372 Data processing & preparation; prepackaged software

(G-13163)
FERRO CORPORATION (PA)
6060 Parkland Blvd # 250 (44124-4225)
PHONE 216 875-5600
Peter T Thomas, *Ch of Bd*
Mark H Duesenberg, *Vice Pres*
Benjamin J Schlater, *CFO*
▲ **EMP:** 90
SALES: 1.6B **Publicly Held**
WEB: www.ferro.com
SIC: 3479 2816 2851 3399 Coating of metals & formed products; color pigments; enamels; plastics base paints & varnishes; paste, metal; plastics materials & resins; carbohydrate plastics; proprietary drug products

(G-13164)
FERRO INTERNATIONAL SVCS INC
6060 Parkland Blvd # 250 (44124-4225)
PHONE 216 875-5600
EMP: 4
SALES (est): 285.8K
SALES (corp-wide): 1.6B **Publicly Held**
WEB: www.ferro.com
SIC: 2816 Color pigments
PA: Ferro Corporation
6060 Parkland Blvd # 250
Mayfield Heights OH 44124
216 875-5600

(G-13165)
HANGER PRSTHETCS & ORTHO INC
6001 Landerhaven Dr Ste A (44124-4190)
PHONE 440 605-0232
EMP: 7
SALES (corp-wide): 1B **Publicly Held**
SIC: 3842 Surgical appliances & supplies
HQ: Hanger Prosthetics & Orthotics, Inc.
10910 Domain Dr Ste 300
Austin TX 78758
512 777-3800

(G-13166)
KERRY INC
5800 Landerbrook Dr # 300 (44124-6509)
PHONE 440 229-5200
EMP: 21 **Privately Held**
SIC: 2834 Pharmaceutical preparations
HQ: Kerry Inc.
3330 Millington Rd
Beloit WI 53511
608 363-1200

GEOGRAPHIC SECTION

(G-13167)
MATERION BRUSH INC (HQ)
6070 Parkland Blvd Ste 1 (44124-4191)
PHONE..................216 486-4200
B R Harman, *Principal*
E A Levine, *Principal*
Michael C Hasychak, *Corp Secy*
Steve Perlaky, *Engineer*
John D Grampa, *CFO*
▲ **EMP:** 100 **EST:** 1931
SALES (est): 379.4MM
SALES (corp-wide): 1.2B **Publicly Held**
WEB: www.brushwellman.com
SIC: 3351 3356 3264 3339 Copper & copper alloy sheet, strip, plate & products; strip, copper & copper alloy; plates, copper & copper alloy; tubing, copper & copper alloy; nickel & nickel alloy pipe, plates, sheets, etc.; porcelain parts for electrical devices, molded; beryllium metal; secondary precious metals; semiconductors & related devices
PA: Materion Corporation
6070 Parkland Blvd Ste 1
Mayfield Heights OH 44124
216 486-4200

(G-13168)
MATERION CORPORATION (PA)
6070 Parkland Blvd Ste 1 (44124-4191)
PHONE..................216 486-4200
Richard J Hipple, *Ch of Bd*
Clive A Grannum, *President*
Michael P Newell, *President*
Jugal Vijayvargiya, *President*
Nic Baloi, *Vice Pres*
◆ **EMP:** 150
SQ FT: 79,130
SALES: 1.2B **Publicly Held**
SIC: 3339 3351 3356 3341 Beryllium metal; copper & copper alloy sheet, strip, plate & products; nickel & nickel alloy pipe, plates, sheets, etc.; secondary precious metals; semiconductors & related devices

(G-13169)
NATURAL BEAUTY HC EXPRESS
6809 Mayfield Rd Apt 550 (44124-2262)
PHONE..................440 459-1776
Stacey Carlton, *Manager*
EMP: 7 **EST:** 2010
SALES (est): 254.4K **Privately Held**
SIC: 3999 Furniture, barber & beauty shop

(G-13170)
PRIEST SERVICES INC (PA)
1127 Linda St 5885 (44124)
P.O. Box 16307, Rocky River (44116-0307)
PHONE..................440 333-1123
Howard E Priest, *Ch of Bd*
Homer S Taft, *President*
Donald W Farley, *Principal*
Carol Kuehnle, *Principal*
Judy Oneacre, *Principal*
EMP: 25 **EST:** 1950
SQ FT: 40,000
SALES (est): 4.1MM **Privately Held**
WEB: www.floorprep.com
SIC: 3275 2891 2851 Gypsum products; adhesives & sealants; paints & allied products

(G-13171)
TMW SYSTEMS INC (HQ)
6085 Parkland Blvd (44124-4184)
PHONE..................216 831-6606
David Wangler, *President*
Rod Strata, *COO*
David Mook, *Exec VP*
Jeffrey Ritter, *Exec VP*
Scott Vanselous, *Exec VP*
EMP: 125
SQ FT: 32,500
SALES (est): 79.8MM
SALES (corp-wide): 3.1B **Publicly Held**
WEB: www.bulktrucker.com
SIC: 7372 Business oriented computer software
PA: Trimble Inc.
935 Stewart Dr
Sunnyvale CA 94085
408 481-8000

(G-13172)
TRUE NORTH ENERGY LLC
Also Called: Truenorth Energy
6411 Mayfield Rd (44124-3214)
PHONE..................440 442-0060
EMP: 29
SALES (corp-wide): 265.4MM **Privately Held**
SIC: 5541 1382 Filling stations, gasoline; oil & gas exploration services
PA: True North Energy, Llc
10346 Brecksville Rd
Brecksville OH 44141
877 245-9336

Mayfield Hts
Cuyahoga County

(G-13173)
GSC NEON
6301 Aldenham Dr (44143-3331)
PHONE..................216 310-6243
Sander Wolfe, *Principal*
EMP: 3
SALES (est): 123.2K **Privately Held**
SIC: 2813 Neon

Mayfield Village
Cuyahoga County

(G-13174)
PREFORMED LINE PRODUCTS CO (PA)
660 Beta Dr (44143-2398)
P.O. Box 91129, Cleveland (44101-3129)
PHONE..................440 461-5200
Robert G Ruhlman, *Ch of Bd*
Dennis F McKenna, *Exec VP*
Michael A Weisbarth, *Treasurer*
J Cecil Curlee Jr, *VP Human Res*
J Ryan Ruhlman, *VP Mktg*
EMP: 277
SALES: 420.8MM **Publicly Held**
WEB: www.preformed.com
SIC: 3644 3661 Pole line hardware; fiber optics communications equipment

(G-13175)
PROFORMA ADVANTAGE
640 Som Center Rd (44143-2311)
PHONE..................440 781-5255
David Littlefield, *President*
EMP: 5 **EST:** 2011
SALES (est): 370K **Privately Held**
SIC: 2759 Commercial printing

(G-13176)
QUALITY ELECTRODYNAMICS LLC
6655 Beta Dr Ste 100 (44143-2380)
PHONE..................440 638-5106
Hiroyuki Fujita, *CEO*
Michael P Esposito Jr, *Chairman*
Albert B Ratner, *Chairman*
Nholas Castrilla, *Plant Mgr*
Megan Crouch, *Buyer*
EMP: 115
SALES (est): 23MM **Privately Held**
SIC: 3841 Surgical & medical instruments

(G-13177)
SURGICAL THEATER LLC (PA)
781 Beta Dr Ste A (44143-2360)
PHONE..................216 452-2177
Mordechai Avifar, *CEO*
Guy Geri, *Vice Pres*
Todd Goldberg, *VP Sales*
Alon Geri, *CTO*
Michael Conditt, *Director*
EMP: 9
SQ FT: 5,000
SALES (est): 3.7MM **Privately Held**
SIC: 3841 Surgical & medical instruments

Mc Arthur
Vinton County

(G-13178)
APPALACHIA WOOD INC (PA)
Also Called: McArthur Lumber and Post
31310 State Route 93 (45651-8924)
PHONE..................740 596-2551
Fax: 740 596-2555
EMP: 30 **EST:** 1951
SQ FT: 150,000
SALES: 3.6MM **Privately Held**
SIC: 2491 2421 5031 2411 Wood Preserving Sawmill/Planing Mill Whol Lumber/Plywd/Millwk Logging

(G-13179)
AUSTIN POWDER COMPANY
Also Called: Red Diamond Plant
430 Powder Plant Rd (45651)
P.O. Box 317 (45651-0317)
PHONE..................740 596-5286
Keith Mills, *Manager*
Larry Mc Corkle, *Manager*
EMP: 225
SALES (corp-wide): 567.4MM **Privately Held**
SIC: 2892 Explosives
HQ: Austin Powder Company
25800 Science Park Dr # 300
Cleveland OH 44122
216 464-2400

(G-13180)
CROWNOVER LUMBER CO INC (PA)
501 Fairview Ave (45651)
P.O. Box 301 (45651-0301)
PHONE..................740 596-5229
Lundy Crownover, *President*
Cheryl Crownover, *Personnel*
EMP: 60
SQ FT: 2,000
SALES: 9MM **Privately Held**
WEB: www.crownoverlumber.com
SIC: 2421 2426 Lumber: rough, sawed or planed; hardwood dimension & flooring mills

(G-13181)
ERICKSON-HUFF TOOL AND DIE
61698 Locker Plant Rd (45651)
PHONE..................740 596-4036
Frank Erickson, *President*
David Huff, *Vice Pres*
EMP: 5
SQ FT: 3,200
SALES (est): 200K **Privately Held**
WEB: www.ehtool.com
SIC: 3544 Industrial molds; special dies & tools

(G-13182)
NIMCO INC
Also Called: LP Propane Gas
33711 State Route 93 (45651-1280)
PHONE..................740 596-4477
Alfred Robertson, *President*
EMP: 4 **EST:** 1987
SALES (est): 284K **Privately Held**
WEB: www.nimco.com
SIC: 1321 Propane (natural) production

(G-13183)
NORMAN KNEPP ✪
Also Called: Knepp's Power Equipment
62969 Us Highway 50 (45651-8410)
PHONE..................740 978-6339
Norman Knepp, *Owner*
EMP: 3 **EST:** 2018
SALES (est): 118.7K **Privately Held**
SIC: 3524 Lawn & garden mowers & accessories

(G-13184)
SUPERIOR HARDWOODS OF OHIO
62581 Us Highway 50 (45651-8414)
P.O. Box 320 (45651-0320)
PHONE..................740 596-2561
Emmett Conway Jr, *President*
Adam Conway, *Vice Pres*
EMP: 32 **EST:** 1979
SQ FT: 11,000
SALES (est): 3.5MM **Privately Held**
WEB: www.superior-hardwoods.com
SIC: 2421 2426 Sawmills & planing mills, general; hardwood dimension & flooring mills

Mc Clure
Henry County

(G-13185)
C DCAP MODEM LINE
232 S East St (43534-9900)
PHONE..................419 748-7409
Barry Connly, *Principal*
EMP: 3 **EST:** 2010
SALES (est): 154.9K **Privately Held**
SIC: 3661 Modems

(G-13186)
M & R REDI MIX INC
L207 County Road 1c (43534-9769)
P.O. Box 53038, Pettisville (43553-0038)
PHONE..................419 748-8442
Scott Bergman, *Director*
EMP: 5
SQ FT: 2,400
SALES (est): 427.4K
SALES (corp-wide): 3MM **Privately Held**
SIC: 3273 Ready-mixed concrete
PA: M & R Redi Mix Inc
521 Commercial St
Pettisville OH 43553
419 445-7771

Mc Comb
Hancock County

(G-13187)
CONSOLIDATED BISCUIT COMPANY
312 Rader Rd (45858-9751)
PHONE..................419 293-2911
Derrick Presley, *Manager*
EMP: 14
SQ FT: 136,806
SALES (est): 1.8MM **Privately Held**
WEB: www.consolidatedcreditservices.com
SIC: 2052 Biscuits, dry

(G-13188)
CRUSHPROOF TUBING CO
100 North St (45858)
P.O. Box 668 (45858-0668)
PHONE..................419 293-2111
Vance M Kramer Jr, *President*
Richard Hollington, *Admin Sec*
EMP: 35 **EST:** 1950
SQ FT: 28,000
SALES: 5.7MM **Privately Held**
WEB: www.crushproof.com
SIC: 3052 Rubber & plastics hose & beltings

(G-13189)
HEARTHSIDE FOOD SOLUTIONS LLC
Also Called: Consolidated Biscuit Company
312 Rader Rd (45858-9751)
PHONE..................419 293-2911
Robert Cummings,
EMP: 2500 **Privately Held**
SIC: 2052 Cookies; crackers, dry
PA: Hearthside Food Solutions, Llc
3500 Lacey Rd Ste 300
Downers Grove IL 60515

(G-13190)
K & L READY MIX INC
5511 State Route 613 (45858-9345)
PHONE..................419 293-2937
Gary Langhals, *Director*
EMP: 10
SALES (corp-wide): 7.6MM **Privately Held**
WEB: www.kandlreadymix.com
SIC: 3273 Ready-mixed concrete

Mc Cutchenville
Wyandot County

(G-13191)
BUCKYS MACHINE AND FAB LTD
8376 S County Road 47 (44844-9620)
PHONE..................................419 981-5050
Daniel L Buckingham,
EMP: 7
SQ FT: 5,500
SALES: 200K **Privately Held**
SIC: 3599 Machine shop, jobbing & repair

Mc Dermott
Scioto County

(G-13192)
DALE LUTE LOGGING
2696 Henley Deemer Rd (45652-9061)
PHONE..................................740 352-1779
Dale F Lute, *Owner*
EMP: 5
SALES (est): 150K **Privately Held**
SIC: 4789 3537 Cargo loading & unloading services; platforms, stands, tables, pallets & similar equipment

(G-13193)
J M MEAT PROCESSING
360 S Zuefle Dr (45652-8938)
PHONE..................................740 259-3030
Jerry Montavon, *Administration*
EMP: 3
SALES (est): 211.3K **Privately Held**
SIC: 2011 Meat packing plants

(G-13194)
TAYLOR LUMBER WORLDWIDE INC
18253 State Route 73 (45652-8925)
P.O. Box 279 (45652-0279)
PHONE..................................740 259-6222
Edward Robbins, *President*
Greg Lute, *Vice Pres*
Art Robbins, *VP Opers*
Shery Spriggs, *CFO*
Tom Imm, *Sales Associate*
◆ **EMP:** 132 **EST:** 1882
SQ FT: 290
SALES (est): 26.1MM **Privately Held**
WEB: www.taylorlumberinc.com
SIC: 2421 Sawmills & planing mills, general

(G-13195)
WALLER BROTHERS STONE COMPANY
744 Mcdermott Rushtown Rd (45652)
PHONE..................................740 858-1948
Frank L Waller, *President*
Lowell M Shope, *Vice Pres*
EMP: 45
SQ FT: 5,175
SALES (est): 6.5MM **Privately Held**
SIC: 3281 3821 2511 Stone, quarrying & processing of own stone products; building stone products; laboratory apparatus & furniture; wood household furniture

Mc Donald
Trumbull County

(G-13196)
AMROD BRIDGE & IRON LLC
105 Ohio Ave (44437-1900)
P.O. Box 749, Youngstown (44501-0749)
PHONE..................................330 530-8230
Jonathan M Dorma, *Mng Member*
Alex Benyo,
Brian Benyo,
EMP: 24
SALES (est): 5.2MM **Privately Held**
SIC: 3441 Structural Metal Fabrication

(G-13197)
GENERAL ELECTRIC COMPANY
3159 Wildwood Dr (44437-1354)
P.O. Box 688, Conneaut (44030-0688)
PHONE..................................440 593-1156
Jeff Adams, *Manager*
EMP: 140
SALES (corp-wide): 121.6B **Publicly Held**
SIC: 3641 5719 Electric lamps; lighting, lamps & accessories
PA: General Electric Company
41 Farnsworth St
Boston MA 02210
617 443-3000

(G-13198)
GENERAL ELECTRIC COMPANY
3159 Wildwood Dr (44437-1354)
PHONE..................................330 297-0861
Kent Snyder, *Manager*
Willie Cooper, *Manager*
Robert Koblenzer, *Project Leader*
EMP: 600
SALES (corp-wide): 121.6B **Publicly Held**
SIC: 3641 Electric lamps
PA: General Electric Company
41 Farnsworth St
Boston MA 02210
617 443-3000

(G-13199)
GENERAL ELECTRIC COMPANY
3159 Wildwood Dr (44437-1354)
PHONE..................................330 373-1400
David Martin, *Branch Mgr*
EMP: 600
SALES (corp-wide): 121.6B **Publicly Held**
SIC: 3641 3648 3229 Lamps, sealed beam; lighting equipment; pressed & blown glass
PA: General Electric Company
41 Farnsworth St
Boston MA 02210
617 443-3000

(G-13200)
GLOBAL OIL & GAS SERVICES LLC
2337 Watson Marshall Rd (44437-1212)
P.O. Box 209, Girard (44420-0209)
PHONE..................................330 807-1490
Cory Jursik, *Vice Pres*
EMP: 3
SALES (est): 145.1K **Privately Held**
SIC: 1382 Aerial geophysical exploration oil & gas

(G-13201)
MCDONALD STEEL CORPORATION
100 Ohio Ave (44437-1954)
P.O. Box 416 (44437-0416)
PHONE..................................330 530-9118
Tim Egnot, *President*
Daniel B Roth, *Chairman*
William K Clark, *VP Opers*
Joe Jenyk, *Engineer*
Michael J Havalo, *CFO*
▲ **EMP:** 105
SQ FT: 680,000
SALES (est): 21.1MM **Privately Held**
WEB: www.mcdonaldsteel.com
SIC: 3312 Bars & bar shapes, steel, hot-rolled

(G-13202)
STEEL & ALLOY UTILITY PDTS INC
110 Ohio Ave (44437-1900)
PHONE..................................330 530-2220
Nathan Gallo, *President*
Nick Gallo, *Vice Pres*
▼ **EMP:** 50
SQ FT: 60,000
SALES (est): 16.5MM **Privately Held**
SIC: 3569 3443 3444 3441 Assembly machines, non-metalworking; fabricated plate work (boiler shop); sheet metalwork; fabricated structural metal

McConnelsville
Morgan County

(G-13203)
EAGLES CLUB
407 W Riverside Dr (43756)
PHONE..................................740 962-6490
John Rex, *President*
Jeck Ciurtis, *President*
Gary Woodard, *Admin Sec*
EMP: 8
SALES (est): 394.7K **Privately Held**
SIC: 2082 8641 Beer (alcoholic beverage); civic social & fraternal associations

(G-13204)
FOLLOW RIVER DESIGNS LLC
4330 E Hppole Ridge Rd Ne (43756-9505)
PHONE..................................614 325-9954
Karla Voyten, *Owner*
Jennifer Ponchak, *Owner*
EMP: 4 **EST:** 2006
SALES (est): 686.3K **Privately Held**
SIC: 3822 Auto controls regulating residntl & coml environmt & applncs

(G-13205)
HANN BOX WORKS
Also Called: Hann Construction
4678 N State Route 60 Nw (43756-9317)
P.O. Box 400, Malta (43758-0400)
PHONE..................................740 962-3752
Darl Hann, *Owner*
Mitchell Downing, *Manager*
EMP: 25
SALES (est): 1.2MM **Privately Held**
WEB: www.hannmfg.com
SIC: 2449 2448 Wood containers; wood pallets & skids

(G-13206)
HANN MANUFACTURING INC
4678 N State Route 60 Nw (43756-9317)
P.O. Box 400, Malta (43758-0400)
PHONE..................................740 962-3752
Darl Hann, *President*
Toni Eckert, *Financial Exec*
Cory Hann, *Sales Executive*
EMP: 26
SQ FT: 30,000
SALES (est): 4.6MM **Privately Held**
SIC: 2531 2448 2441 Public building & related furniture; wood pallets & skids; nailed wood boxes & shook

(G-13207)
MAHLE INDUSTRIES INCORPORATED
5130 N State Route 60 Nw (43756-9021)
PHONE..................................740 962-2040
John Feather, *Branch Mgr*
EMP: 115
SALES (corp-wide): 336.4K **Privately Held**
WEB: www.glacier-vandervell.com
SIC: 3714 Camshafts, motor vehicle
HQ: Mahle Industries, Incorporated
23030 Mahle Dr
Farmington Hills MI 48335
248 305-8200

(G-13208)
MIBA SINTER USA LLC
5045 N State Route 60 Nw (43756-9640)
PHONE..................................740 962-4242
Jason Rayner, *Engineer*
Rick Walker, *Engineer*
Dan Jones, *Controller*
Rebecca Stofan, *Accountant*
Steve Krise, *Mng Member*
▲ **EMP:** 10
SALES: 27.2MM
SALES (corp-wide): 1B **Privately Held**
SIC: 3312 Sinter, iron
PA: Mitterbauer Beteiligungs - Aktiengesellschap
Dr. Mitterbauer-StraBe 3
Laakirchen 4663
761 325-41

(G-13209)
MORGAN COUNTY PUBLISHING CO
Also Called: Morgan County Herald
89 W Main St (43756-1264)
P.O. Box 268 (43756-0268)
PHONE..................................740 962-3377
Jack Barnes, *President*
Don Keller, *Editor*
EMP: 9
SQ FT: 5,000
SALES (est): 694.9K **Privately Held**
WEB: www.mchnews.com
SIC: 2711 Newspapers: publishing only, not printed on site

Mechanicsburg
Champaign County

(G-13210)
ADVANCED TECHNOLOGY PRODUCTS
282 E Sandusky St (43044-1051)
PHONE..................................937 349-5221
EMP: 4
SALES (est): 119.8K **Privately Held**
SIC: 3674 Semiconductors & related devices

(G-13211)
MECHANICSBURG SAND & GRAVEL
5734 State Route 4 (43044-9748)
PHONE..................................937 834-2606
James Cushman, *President*
Charles Wibright Jr, *Corp Secy*
EMP: 12 **EST:** 1957
SQ FT: 3,400
SALES (est): 1.3MM **Privately Held**
SIC: 1442 Construction sand mining; gravel mining

Mechanicstown
Carroll County

(G-13212)
KINGS WELDING AND FABG INC
5259 Bane Rd Ne (44651-9020)
PHONE..................................330 738-3592
Glen Richard King Sr, *President*
Diane Garrett, *Corp Secy*
Pat Sica, *Exec Dir*
EMP: 45
SQ FT: 9,500
SALES (est): 6.1MM **Privately Held**
SIC: 3599 7692 3498 3441 Machine shop, jobbing & repair; welding repair; fabricated pipe & fittings; fabricated structural metal

(G-13213)
MILLER & SON LOGGING
8521 Clover Rd Ne (44651-9041)
PHONE..................................330 738-2031
Ruth Miller, *Principal*
EMP: 3
SALES (est): 238.3K **Privately Held**
SIC: 2411 Logging camps & contractors

Medina
Medina County

(G-13214)
3M COMPANY
1030 Lake Rd (44256-2450)
PHONE..................................330 725-1444
Jason Borza, *Engineer*
Maurice Jefferson, *Engineer*
Joe Petrie, *Sls & Mktg Exec*
Tom Gregory, *Branch Mgr*
EMP: 100
SALES (corp-wide): 32.7B **Publicly Held**
WEB: www.mmm.com
SIC: 2672 Tape, pressure sensitive: made from purchased materials

PA: K & L Ready Mix Inc
10391 State Route 15
Ottawa OH 45875
419 523-4376

GEOGRAPHIC SECTION
Medina - Medina County (G-13240)

PA: 3m Company
3m Center
Saint Paul MN 55144
651 733-1110

(G-13215)
7D MARKETING INC
345 N State Rd (44256-1405)
PHONE..................................330 721-8822
Patrick Spoerndle, *President*
EMP: 12
SQ FT: 60,000
SALES (est): 1.9MM **Privately Held**
SIC: 2541 2431 Display fixtures, wood; millwork

(G-13216)
ABBEY MACHINE PRODUCTS CO
1011 Lake Rd (44256-2450)
PHONE..................................216 481-0080
David L Bennett, *President*
Gregory Bennett, *Vice Pres*
Cynthia Bennett, *Controller*
EMP: 5
SALES: 650K **Privately Held**
SIC: 3599 Machine shop, jobbing & repair

(G-13217)
ADVANCED CHEMICAL SOLUTIONS (PA)
1114 N Court St 196 (44256-1579)
PHONE..................................330 283-5157
Gerry Groudle, *President*
David Fidel, *Vice Pres*
EMP: 9 EST: 2001
SQ FT: 12,000
SALES (est): 3.5MM **Privately Held**
WEB: www.advancedchemicalsolutions.com
SIC: 2899 Metal treating compounds

(G-13218)
AGRATI - MEDINA LLC (DH)
941-955 Lake Rd (44256)
PHONE..................................330 725-8853
Philip Johnson, *CEO*
Matt Kerschner, *Principal*
David Kaminski, *COO*
Amro Hassan, *Prdtn Mgr*
Mark Davis, *Production*
◆ **EMP:** 146
SALES (est): 46.2MM **Privately Held**
WEB: www.jacobsonmfg.com
SIC: 3452 Screws, metal
HQ: Agrati - Park Forest, Llc
24000 S Western Ave
Park Forest IL 60466
708 228-5193

(G-13219)
AI ROOT COMPANY (PA)
Also Called: West Liberty Commons
623 W Liberty St (44256-2225)
P.O. Box 706 (44258-0706)
PHONE..................................330 723-4359
John A Root, *Ch of Bd*
Rob Graham, *Business Mgr*
Brad I Root, *Senior VP*
Andy Cutlip, *Plant Mgr*
Chuck Schloss, *Warehouse Mgr*
▲ **EMP:** 190
SQ FT: 182,000
SALES (est): 39.4MM **Privately Held**
WEB: www.beeculture.com
SIC: 3999 3085 Candles; plastics bottles

(G-13220)
AI ROOT COMPANY
Also Called: Root Candles
234 S State Rd (44256-2697)
PHONE..................................330 725-6677
Brad Root, *President*
EMP: 150
SALES (corp-wide): 39.4MM **Privately Held**
WEB: www.beeculture.com
SIC: 3999 3085 Candles; plastics bottles
PA: The A I Root Company
623 W Liberty St
Medina OH 44256
330 723-4359

(G-13221)
ALCHEM CORPORATION
525 W Liberty St (44256-2223)
PHONE..................................330 725-2436
B George Buskin, *President*
▲ **EMP:** 8
SQ FT: 28,000
SALES (est): 1.6MM **Privately Held**
WEB: www.alcheminc.com
SIC: 2819 Industrial inorganic chemicals

(G-13222)
ALLFASTENERS USA LLC (HQ)
959 Lake Rd (44256-2453)
PHONE..................................440 232-6060
Michael Strange, *President*
Christina Wade, *Controller*
▲ **EMP:** 26
SALES: 25MM **Privately Held**
SIC: 3429 Builders' hardware

(G-13223)
AMERI-CAL CORPORATION
1001 Lake Rd (44256-2760)
PHONE..................................330 725-7735
Jay D Vigneault, *President*
Jacqueline Avigneault, *Manager*
▲ **EMP:** 13
SQ FT: 15,000
SALES (est): 3.7MM **Privately Held**
WEB: www.americalcorp.com
SIC: 2672 Adhesive papers, labels or tapes: from purchased material; tape, pressure sensitive: made from purchased materials

(G-13224)
ANCHOR LAMINA AMERICA INC
445 W Liberty St (44256-2273)
PHONE..................................330 952-1595
EMP: 31
SALES (corp-wide): 2.9B **Privately Held**
SIC: 3545 Machine tool accessories
HQ: Anchor Lamina America, Inc.
39830 Grand River Ave B-2
Novi MI 48375
248 489-9122

(G-13225)
ARCHITECTURAL DAYLIGHTING LLC
Also Called: Archday
879 S Progress Dr Ste C (44256-3926)
PHONE..................................330 460-5000
Victoria Tifft, *Mng Member*
EMP: 5
SQ FT: 8,000
SALES (est): 697.7K **Privately Held**
SIC: 3444 Skylights, sheet metal

(G-13226)
AXON MEDICAL LLC
1484 Medina Rd Ste 117 (44256-5378)
PHONE..................................216 276-0262
Christopher Hardin, *Principal*
Joel Hawley, *Principal*
EMP: 20
SALES (est): 1.4MM **Privately Held**
SIC: 3841 3842 5047 Surgical & medical instruments; surgical appliances & supplies; abdominal supporters, braces & trusses; braces, orthopedic; instruments, surgical & medical

(G-13227)
B & B BINDERY INC
4381 Pine Lake Dr (44256-7641)
PHONE..................................330 722-5430
EMP: 6
SQ FT: 8,000
SALES (est): 500K **Privately Held**
SIC: 2789 Bookbinding

(G-13228)
B C COMPOSITES CORPORATION
777 W Smith Rd (44256-3501)
PHONE..................................330 262-3070
Mark McConnell, *President*
EMP: 11
SQ FT: 50,000
SALES: 1.3MM
SALES (corp-wide): 10.1MM **Privately Held**
WEB: www.bccomposites.com
SIC: 3499 Metal ladders
PA: Bc Investment Corporation
1505 E Bowman St
Wooster OH 44691
330 262-3070

(G-13229)
BIL-JAC FOODS INC (PA)
3337 Medina Rd (44256-9631)
PHONE..................................330 722-7888
Robert Kelly, *President*
Bonnie Phillip, *General Mgr*
William Kelly, *Chairman*
Lynn Bingham, *Vice Pres*
James Kelly, *Vice Pres*
EMP: 25
SQ FT: 6,000
SALES (est): 23.5MM **Privately Held**
WEB: www.biljac.com
SIC: 2047 Dog food; cat food

(G-13230)
BOND CHEMICALS INC
1154 W Smith Rd (44256-2443)
PHONE..................................330 725-5935
Thomas Goslee Jr, *President*
Carol Goslee, *Vice Pres*
EMP: 16 EST: 1960
SQ FT: 24,000
SALES (est): 2.8MM **Privately Held**
WEB: www.bondchemicals.com
SIC: 2899 2819 Water treating compounds; corrosion preventive lubricant; rust resisting compounds; industrial inorganic chemicals

(G-13231)
BPR-RICO ELC TRCK SPCALIST INC
691 W Liberty St (44256-2225)
PHONE..................................330 723-4050
Dave Mueller, *President*
EMP: 75
SALES (est): 7.5MM
SALES (corp-wide): 37.5MM **Privately Held**
WEB: www.bpr-rico.com
SIC: 3537 Lift trucks, industrial: fork, platform, straddle, etc.
PA: Bpr-Rico Equipment, Inc.
691 W Liberty St
Medina OH 44256
330 723-4050

(G-13232)
BPR-RICO MANUFACTURING INC
Also Called: Bpr/Rico
691 W Liberty St (44256-2225)
PHONE..................................330 723-4050
Dave Mueller, *CEO*
Steve Shuck, *President*
Sandy Mueller, *Corp Secy*
Kent Stelmasczuk, *CFO*
▲ **EMP:** 100
SQ FT: 175,000
SALES: 30MM
SALES (corp-wide): 37.5MM **Privately Held**
SIC: 3537 Lift trucks, industrial: fork, platform, straddle, etc.
PA: Bpr-Rico Equipment, Inc.
691 W Liberty St
Medina OH 44256
330 723-4050

(G-13233)
BREW KETTLE STRONGSVILLE LLC
3520 Longwood Dr (44256-8400)
P.O. Box 360893, Strongsville (44136-0015)
PHONE..................................440 915-7074
EMP: 6
SALES (est): 566.2K **Privately Held**
SIC: 2082 Malt beverages

(G-13234)
CARLISLE BRAKE & FRICTION INC
920 Lake Rd (44256-2453)
PHONE..................................330 725-4941
EMP: 32
SALES (corp-wide): 4.4B **Publicly Held**
SIC: 3751 Brakes, friction clutch & other: bicycle
HQ: Carlisle Brake & Friction, Inc.
6180 Cochran Rd
Solon OH 44139
440 528-4000

(G-13235)
CHICK MASTER INCUBATOR COMPANY (PA)
945 Lafayette Rd (44256-3510)
P.O. Box 704 (44258-0704)
PHONE..................................330 722-5591
Robert Holzer, *CEO*
Larry Stevens, *General Mgr*
Chad Daniels, *Vice Pres*
Alan Shandler, *Vice Pres*
Lou Sharp, *Vice Pres*
◆ **EMP:** 118
SQ FT: 100,000
SALES (est): 26.5MM **Privately Held**
WEB: www.chickmaster.com
SIC: 3523 1711 Incubators & brooders, farm; plumbing, heating, air-conditioning contractors

(G-13236)
CHRONICLE TELEGRAM
885 W Liberty St (44256-1312)
PHONE..................................330 725-4166
George Hudnutt, *Owner*
EMP: 3
SALES (est): 116.4K **Privately Held**
SIC: 2711 Newspapers

(G-13237)
CLETRONICS INC
2262 Port Centre Dr (44256-5994)
PHONE..................................330 239-2002
David Sands, *President*
Steve Garfield, *Vice Pres*
Ed Wurgler, *Plant Mgr*
▼ **EMP:** 19
SQ FT: 12,500
SALES: 2.4MM **Privately Held**
WEB: www.cletronics.com
SIC: 3677 Transformers power supply, electronic type

(G-13238)
COMMERCIAL GRINDING SERVICES
Also Called: Cgs
1155 Industrial Pkwy # 1 (44256-2492)
P.O. Box 1121 (44258-1121)
PHONE..................................330 273-5040
Kevin T Butas, *President*
Steve Bruns, *General Mgr*
EMP: 20
SQ FT: 3,600
SALES (est): 1.4MM **Privately Held**
WEB: www.cgstool.com
SIC: 7699 3541 3545 Knife, saw & tool sharpening & repair; machine tools, metal cutting type; end mills

(G-13239)
CONCORD DESIGN INC
3382 S Weymouth Rd (44256-9227)
PHONE..................................330 722-5133
Gerald Smith, *President*
Dina Smith, *Treasurer*
EMP: 3
SQ FT: 800
SALES: 33.2K **Privately Held**
SIC: 3544 Special dies & tools; jigs & fixtures

(G-13240)
CONTROLS INC
5204 Portside Dr (44256-5966)
P.O. Box 368, Sharon Center (44274-0368)
PHONE..................................330 239-4345
Robert Cowen, *President*
Scott Izzo, *Vice Pres*
David Steinberg, *Engineer*
EMP: 25

Medina - Medina County (G-13241) GEOGRAPHIC SECTION

SALES: 1.8MM **Privately Held**
WEB: www.controlsinc.com
SIC: 3625 7389 1731 Control equipment, electric; industrial controls: push button, selector switches, pilot; design services; electronic controls installation

(G-13241)
CONVIBER INC
Also Called: Heintz Conveying Belt Service
1066 Industrial Pkwy (44256-2449)
PHONE.................................330 723-6006
Rich Serrena, *Manager*
EMP: 10
SALES (corp-wide): 13.3MM **Privately Held**
WEB: www.conviber.com
SIC: 7699 3559 Rubber product repair; rubber working machinery, including tires
PA: Conviber, Inc.
644 Garfield St
Springdale PA 15144
724 274-6300

(G-13242)
CORRPRO COMPANIES INC (DH)
1055 W Smith Rd (44256-2444)
PHONE.................................330 723-5082
David H Kroon, *President*
Jennifer Chrosniak, *General Mgr*
Jesse Corona, *Superintendent*
Sam Jeffery, *Area Mgr*
Dorwin Hawn, *Exec VP*
▼ EMP: 50
SQ FT: 8,000
SALES: 198.7MM
SALES (corp-wide): 1.3B **Publicly Held**
WEB: www.corrpro.com
SIC: 3699 8711 Electrical equipment & supplies; engineering services
HQ: Insituform Technologies, Llc
17988 Edison Ave
Chesterfield MO 63005
636 530-8000

(G-13243)
CORRPRO COMPANIES INC
Also Called: Corrpro Waterworks
1055 W Smith Rd (44256-2444)
PHONE.................................330 725-6681
George Giannakos, *Branch Mgr*
EMP: 15
SALES (corp-wide): 1.3B **Publicly Held**
WEB: www.corrpro.com
SIC: 3699 8711 Electrical equipment & supplies; engineering services
HQ: Corrpro Companies, Inc.
1055 W Smith Rd
Medina OH 44256
330 723-5082

(G-13244)
CORRPRO COMPANIES INTL INC
1055 W Smith Rd (44256-2444)
PHONE.................................330 723-5082
EMP: 4 EST: 2013
SALES (est): 279.5K
SALES (corp-wide): 1.3B **Publicly Held**
SIC: 3699 Electrical equipment & supplies
HQ: Insituform Technologies, Llc
17988 Edison Ave
Chesterfield MO 63005
636 530-8000

(G-13245)
COUNTY OF MEDINA
Also Called: Medina County Recorders
144 N Broadway St Ste 117 (44256-1928)
PHONE.................................330 723-3641
Colleen Swedyk, *Principal*
EMP: 13 **Privately Held**
WEB: www.mcbmrdd.org
SIC: 3825 Recorders, oscillographic
PA: County Of Medina
144 N Brdwy St Rm 201
Medina OH 44256
330 722-9208

(G-13246)
CREATIVE CONCEPTS
620 E Smith Rd Ste W1 (44256-3648)
PHONE.................................216 513-6463
Ryan Fairbanks, *Owner*
EMP: 3

SALES (est): 277.9K **Privately Held**
SIC: 3444 2426 Concrete forms, sheet metal; dimension, hardwood

(G-13247)
CUSTOM CHEMICAL PACKAGING LLC
4086 Watercourse Dr (44256-7897)
PHONE.................................330 331-7416
Scott Sandusky,
EMP: 21
SALES (est): 3.4MM **Privately Held**
SIC: 2842 Automobile polish

(G-13248)
D O TECHNOLOGIES INC
667 Lafayette Rd (44256-3700)
PHONE.................................330 725-4561
Douglas R Piskac, *President*
Douglas Piskac, *President*
EMP: 10
SQ FT: 14,700
SALES (est): 1.6MM **Privately Held**
SIC: 3599 Machine shop, jobbing & repair

(G-13249)
DAIRY FARMERS AMERICA INC
1035 Medina Rd Ste 300 (44256-5398)
PHONE.................................330 670-7800
Glenn Wallace, *Chief*
EMP: 30
SALES (corp-wide): 14.6B **Privately Held**
WEB: www.dfamilk.com
SIC: 2022 2026 2021 0211 Cheese, natural & processed; fluid milk; creamery butter; beef cattle feedlots
PA: Dairy Farmers Of America, Inc.
1405 N 98th St
Kansas City KS 66111
816 801-6455

(G-13250)
DDG INCORPORATED
Also Called: Davis Design Group
3593 Medina Rd (44256-8182)
PHONE.................................440 343-5060
Wayne Davis, *CEO*
EMP: 4
SALES: 600K **Privately Held**
SIC: 2759 7336 Commercial printing; art design services

(G-13251)
DEBANDALE PRINTING INC
Also Called: Minuteman Press
2785 Sharon Copley Rd (44256-9718)
PHONE.................................330 725-5122
Dale Heufner, *President*
EMP: 4
SQ FT: 1,100
SALES (est): 354.9K **Privately Held**
SIC: 2752 2759 2791 2789 Commercial printing, offset; screen printing; engraving; typesetting; bookbinding & related work

(G-13252)
DIE GUYS INC
5238 Portside Dr (44256-5966)
PHONE.................................330 239-3437
Jeri Potts, *CEO*
Cathy Greenwald, *President*
Luke Darling, *Admin Sec*
EMP: 24 EST: 2000
SQ FT: 14,000
SALES: 2.7MM **Privately Held**
WEB: www.dieguys.com
SIC: 3544 Dies, steel rule

(G-13253)
DIVERSIFIED TECHNOLOGY INC
650 W Smith Rd Ste 10 (44256-3717)
PHONE.................................330 722-4995
William F Musal, *President*
EMP: 3
SQ FT: 5,500
SALES: 400K **Privately Held**
SIC: 2992 Lubricating oils

(G-13254)
ELKINS EARTHWORKS LLC
865 W Liberty St Ste 220 (44256-3950)
PHONE.................................330 725-7766
Charles D Elkins, *Principal*
Daniel Duncan, *Sales Mgr*
EMP: 5 EST: 2010

SALES (est): 1.6MM **Privately Held**
SIC: 3826 Gas analyzing equipment

(G-13255)
ENGINEERED POLYMER SYSTEMS LLC
2600 Medina Rd (44256-8145)
P.O. Box 370, Sharon Center (44274-0370)
PHONE.................................216 255-2116
EMP: 3 EST: 2009
SALES (est): 227.5K **Privately Held**
SIC: 2821 Plastics materials & resins

(G-13256)
ENI USA R & M CO INC
Also Called: ENI USA R & M CO. INC.
740 S Progress Dr (44256-1368)
PHONE.................................330 723-6457
Joe Krisky, *Vice Pres*
EMP: 10
SQ FT: 6,000
SALES (corp-wide): 34.1B **Privately Held**
WEB: www.americanagip.com
SIC: 2992 5172 Lubricating oils & greases; petroleum products
HQ: Eni Usa R&M Co. Inc.
485 Madison Ave Fl 6
New York NY 10022
646 264-2100

(G-13257)
ERIE COPPER WORKS INC
230 N State Rd (44256-1404)
P.O. Box 309 (44258-0309)
PHONE.................................330 725-5590
David A Surgeon, *President*
David Berg, *Vice Pres*
Jesse Barrowcliff, *Opers Staff*
EMP: 4 EST: 1967
SQ FT: 2,200
SALES (est): 736.1K **Privately Held**
SIC: 3643 Current-carrying wiring devices

(G-13258)
ERODETECH INC
4986 Gateway Dr (44256-8637)
P.O. Box 1643 (44258-1643)
PHONE.................................330 725-9181
EMP: 6
SALES (est): 298.4K **Privately Held**
SIC: 1389 Oil/Gas Field Services

(G-13259)
FACULTATIEVE TECH AMERICAS INC
Also Called: Incinerator Specialists
940 Lake Rd (44256-2453)
PHONE.................................330 723-6339
Henri Keizer, *CEO*
▲ EMP: 27
SALES (est): 6.5MM **Privately Held**
SIC: 3567 Fuel-fired furnaces & ovens; incinerators, metal: domestic or commercial

(G-13260)
FALCON INDUSTRIES INC (PA)
180 Commerce Dr (44256-3949)
PHONE.................................330 723-0099
J Don Fitzgerald, *CEO*
EMP: 27
SQ FT: 24,000
SALES (est): 11.5MM **Privately Held**
WEB: www.falconindustries.com
SIC: 3541 3535 3444 3423 Machine tools, metal cutting type; conveyors & conveying equipment; sheet metalwork; hand & edge tools

(G-13261)
FASTSIGNS
2736 Medina Rd (44256-9660)
PHONE.................................330 952-2626
Tob Coss, *Owner*
EMP: 3
SALES (est): 305.8K **Privately Held**
SIC: 3993 Signs & advertising specialties

(G-13262)
FIRE-DEX LLC
780 S Progress Dr (44256-1368)
PHONE.................................330 723-0000
Brett Jaffe, *CEO*
Larry Haught, *Production*
Amanda Macklin, *Engineer*
Dee Ocallaghan, *Accounting Mgr*

Adam Hogan, *Regl Sales Mgr*
◆ EMP: 100
SQ FT: 28,000
SALES (est): 25.3MM **Privately Held**
WEB: www.firedex.com
SIC: 2389 Uniforms & vestments

(G-13263)
FORGING EQP SOLUTIONS INC
1486 Medina Rd Ste 209 (44256-5384)
PHONE.................................330 239-2222
Jeff Jones, *President*
EMP: 4
SQ FT: 1,000
SALES (est): 652K **Privately Held**
SIC: 3462 Iron & steel forgings

(G-13264)
FOUNDATIONS WORLDWIDE INC (PA)
5216 Portside Dr (44256-5966)
PHONE.................................330 722-5033
Joseph A Lawlor, *President*
Stan Argabrite, *Vice Pres*
Alan Lytle, *Engineer*
Lisa Vanadia, *CFO*
Margo Miller, *Marketing Staff*
◆ EMP: 34
SQ FT: 60,000
SALES (est): 18MM **Privately Held**
WEB: www.shamrock-industries.com
SIC: 5999 2511 3944 Children's furniture; children's wood furniture; strollers, baby (vehicle); walkers, baby (vehicle); structural toy sets; scooters, children's

(G-13265)
FRICTION PRODUCTS CO
Also Called: Hawk Performance
920 Lake Rd (44256-2453)
PHONE.................................330 725-4941
Chris Disantis, *CEO*
Ronald E Weinberg, *Chairman*
Thomas A Gilbride, *Vice Pres*
◆ EMP: 266
SQ FT: 176,000
SALES (est): 86.4MM
SALES (corp-wide): 4.4B **Publicly Held**
WEB: www.hawkperformance.com
SIC: 3728 3714 Aircraft landing assemblies & brakes; motor vehicle brake systems & parts
HQ: Carlisle Brake & Friction, Inc.
6180 Cochran Rd
Solon OH 44139
440 528-4000

(G-13266)
GASKO FABRICATED PRODUCTS LLC (HQ)
4049 Ridge Rd (44256-8618)
P.O. Box 1050, Middlefield (44062-1050)
PHONE.................................330 239-1781
Randy Guernsey, *President*
Gregory Nemecek, *President*
Ed Bosken, *Vice Pres*
EMP: 32
SQ FT: 12,000
SALES: 6.5MM
SALES (corp-wide): 8.5MM **Privately Held**
WEB: www.gasko.com
SIC: 3053 Gaskets, all materials
PA: Cornerstone Industrial Holdings Inc
100 Park Pl
Chagrin Falls OH 44022
440 893-9144

(G-13267)
GLAXOSMITHKLINE LLC
6250 Highland Meadows Dr (44256-6528)
PHONE.................................330 241-4447
EMP: 26
SALES (corp-wide): 39.8B **Privately Held**
SIC: 2834 Pharmaceutical preparations
HQ: Glaxosmithkline Llc
5 Crescent Dr
Philadelphia PA 19112
215 751-4000

(G-13268)
GLORIOUS CUPCAKES
3132 Sterling Lake Dr (44256-6241)
PHONE.................................216 544-2325
Lori L Stagliano, *Administration*
EMP: 4 EST: 2014

GEOGRAPHIC SECTION

Medina - Medina County (G-13298)

SALES (est): 157.9K **Privately Held**
SIC: 2051 Bread, cake & related products

(G-13269)
GLOUCESTER ENGINEERING CO INC
220 Lafayette Rd (44256-2334)
PHONE.................................330 722-5168
EMP: 7 **Privately Held**
SIC: 3559 Plastics working machinery
HQ: Gloucester Engineering Co., Inc.
11 Dory Rd
Gloucester MA 01930
978 281-1800

(G-13270)
HAWTHORNE BOLT WORKS CORP
Also Called: Manufacturer
1020 Industrial Pkwy (44256-2449)
PHONE.................................330 723-0555
Nick Gentile, *President*
EMP: 4
SALES (est): 505.4K **Privately Held**
SIC: 3429 Manufactured hardware (general)

(G-13271)
HEINTZ MANUFACTURERS INC
Also Called: Conviber
1066 Industrial Pkwy (44256-2449)
P.O. Box 301, Springdale PA (15144-0301)
PHONE.................................724 274-6300
Frank Pucciarelli, *President*
Kenneth Gangl, *President*
Kirk Gangl, *Vice Pres*
▲ EMP: 3 **EST:** 1918
SALES (est): 395.5K **Privately Held**
SIC: 7699 3559 Rubber product repair; rubber working machinery, including tires

(G-13272)
HERAEUS ELECTRO-NITE CO LLC
6469 Fenn Rd (44256-9463)
PHONE.................................330 725-1419
EMP: 6
SALES (corp-wide): 96.1K **Privately Held**
WEB: www.electro-nite.com
SIC: 3829 3674 Thermocouples; semiconductors & related devices
HQ: Heraeus Electro-Nite Co., Llc
541 S Industrial Dr
Hartland WI 53029
215 944-9000

(G-13273)
HIGH LOW WINERY
588 Medina Rd (44256-8127)
PHONE.................................844 466-4456
EMP: 4
SALES (est): 307.1K **Privately Held**
SIC: 2084 Wines

(G-13274)
HOWDEN NORTH AMERICA INC
411 Independence Dr (44256-2406)
PHONE.................................330 867-8540
Ben Goss, *Engineer*
Anthony Hall, *Engineer*
Jenaro Arjemi, *Manager*
Bruce Ott, *Technical Staff*
EMP: 92
SALES (corp-wide): 3.6B **Publicly Held**
SIC: 3564 3822 Blowers & fans; purification & dust collection equipment; damper operators: pneumatic, thermostatic, electric
HQ: Howden North America Inc.
2475 George Urban Blvd # 120
Depew NY 14043
803 741-2700

(G-13275)
HOWDEN NORTH AMERICA INC
935 Heritage Dr (44256-2404)
PHONE.................................330 721-7374
Edward Biesiada, *Branch Mgr*
EMP: 22
SALES (corp-wide): 3.6B **Publicly Held**
SIC: 3564 Blowers & fans
HQ: Howden North America Inc.
2475 George Urban Blvd # 120
Depew NY 14043
803 741-2700

(G-13276)
HUDSON PRINTING OF MEDINA LLC
2425 Medina Rd Ste 206 (44256-5381)
PHONE.................................330 591-4800
Steve Vojvodich, *Principal*
Byron Nemeth, *Master*
EMP: 4
SALES (est): 250K **Privately Held**
SIC: 2752 Commercial printing, lithographic

(G-13277)
ICANDI GRAPHICS LLC
650 W Smith Rd Ste 3 (44256-2397)
PHONE.................................330 723-8337
Benjamin D Schmid, *Owner*
EMP: 4
SALES (est): 478.8K **Privately Held**
SIC: 2752 Commercial printing, lithographic

(G-13278)
INDUSTRIAL WIRE CO INC
6867 Wooster Pike (44256-8859)
PHONE.................................330 723-7471
George Zimmerman, *Manager*
EMP: 3
SALES (corp-wide): 570.3K **Privately Held**
WEB: www.ind-wire.com
SIC: 3496 Miscellaneous fabricated wire products
PA: Industrial Wire Co Inc
2805 Superior Ave E
Cleveland OH 44114
216 781-2230

(G-13279)
INNOVATION SALES LLC
803 E Washington St # 210 (44256-3326)
PHONE.................................330 239-0400
Pamela Blackburn, *Manager*
EMP: 7
SALES (est): 330K **Privately Held**
SIC: 3291 Abrasive metal & steel products

(G-13280)
INTERACTIVE ENGINEERING CORP
884 Medina Rd (44256-9615)
PHONE.................................330 239-6888
Ming Zhang, *President*
Andy Dan, *Purchasing*
EMP: 25
SQ FT: 200,000
SALES (est): 3.3MM **Privately Held**
SIC: 8748 3672 Systems analysis & engineering consulting services; printed circuit boards

(G-13281)
INTERNATIONAL METAL SUPPLY LLC
3995 Medina Rd Ste 200 (44256-5958)
PHONE.................................330 764-1004
Kevin Eales,
EMP: 11
SALES (est): 1.8MM **Privately Held**
SIC: 3313 Ferroalloys

(G-13282)
J R GOSLEE CO
1154 W Smith Rd (44256-2443)
PHONE.................................330 723-4904
Carol Goslee, *President*
Tom Goslee Jr, *Vice Pres*
EMP: 10 **EST:** 1928
SQ FT: 1,164
SALES (est): 674.1K **Privately Held**
SIC: 3295 Clay, ground or otherwise treated

(G-13283)
JROLL LLC
Also Called: Sushi On The Roll
985 Boardman Aly (44256-1599)
PHONE.................................330 661-0600
Kenneth Oppenheimer,
Jon Roller,
EMP: 12
SQ FT: 3,000
SALES: 990K **Privately Held**
SIC: 2048 5146 Fish food; fish & seafoods

(G-13284)
KATHYS KRAFTS AND KOLLECTIBLES
3303 Hamilton Rd (44256-7633)
PHONE.................................423 787-3709
Kathy Hayes, *Principal*
EMP: 3 **EST:** 2013
SALES (est): 213.6K **Privately Held**
SIC: 2022 Mfg Cheese

(G-13285)
KELLY FOODS CORPORATION (PA)
3337 Medina Rd (44256-9631)
PHONE.................................330 722-8855
Robert Kelly, *President*
Jim Kelly, *Corp Secy*
▼ EMP: 22
SALES (est): 14.9MM **Privately Held**
WEB: www.kellyfoodscorp.com
SIC: 2048 2047 Dry pet food (except dog & cat); dog & cat food

(G-13286)
KURTS AUTO PARTS LLC
4093 Watercourse Dr (44256-7895)
PHONE.................................330 723-0166
Kurt Morse, *President*
EMP: 3
SALES (est): 240K **Privately Held**
SIC: 3714 Motor vehicle parts & accessories

(G-13287)
LSQ MANUFACTURING INC
1140 Industrial Pkwy (44256-2486)
PHONE.................................330 725-4905
Richard L Rauckhorst III, *President*
Richard L Rauckhorst III, *President*
Judith L Coffman, *Vice Pres*
EMP: 10 **EST:** 1946
SQ FT: 8,000
SALES: 1MM **Privately Held**
WEB: www.arthurproducts.com
SIC: 3494 3563 3432 Valves & pipe fittings; air & gas compressors; plumbing fixture fittings & trim

(G-13288)
LUXX ULTRA-TECH INC
7334 Lonesome Pine Trl (44256-7133)
PHONE.................................330 483-6051
Mary Matejka, *President*
Rudolph Matejka, *Principal*
Cathy Johnson, *Vice Pres*
EMP: 5
SQ FT: 5,500
SALES: 1.5MM **Privately Held**
SIC: 3069 Molded rubber products

(G-13289)
MANSFIELD PAINT CO INC
525 W Liberty St (44256-2223)
PHONE.................................330 725-2436
George Bufkin, *CEO*
EMP: 8
SQ FT: 24,000
SALES (est): 2.1MM **Privately Held**
SIC: 2851 Paints: oil or alkyd vehicle or water thinned; lacquer: bases, dopes, thinner; enamels

(G-13290)
MATRIX PLASTICS CO INC
171 Granger Rd Unit 156 (44256-7308)
PHONE.................................330 666-7730
Bill Mann, *Partner*
William D Mann, *General Ptnr*
Joan Mann, *Vice Pres*
EMP: 3
SALES: 300K **Privately Held**
SIC: 3089 Injection molding of plastics

(G-13291)
MATRIX PLASTICS CO INC
171 Granger Rd Unit 156 (44256-7308)
PHONE.................................330 666-2395
William D Mann, *President*
Susan M Mann, *Corp Secy*
Joan C Mann, *Vice Pres*
Susan Mann, *Treasurer*
EMP: 3
SQ FT: 1,500
SALES: 500K **Privately Held**
WEB: www.matrixplastics.com
SIC: 3089 Injection molding of plastics

(G-13292)
MCJAK CANDY COMPANY LLC
1087 Branch Rd (44256-8900)
PHONE.................................330 722-3531
Denise Kyle, *Sales Staff*
Larry Johns,
Francine Johns,
▲ EMP: 44
SQ FT: 27,000
SALES: 3MM **Privately Held**
WEB: www.mcjakcandy.com
SIC: 2064 Candy & other confectionery products

(G-13293)
MEDINA COUNTY PUBLICATIONS INC
Also Called: Gazzette, The
885 W Liberty St (44256-1396)
P.O. Box 407 (44258-0407)
PHONE.................................330 721-4040
George Hudnutt, *Publisher*
EMP: 5
SALES (corp-wide): 27.9MM **Privately Held**
SIC: 2711 Newspapers, publishing & printing
HQ: Medina County Publications, Inc.
225 East Ave
Elyria OH
440 329-7000

(G-13294)
MEDINA PLATING CORP
940 Lafayette Rd (44256-3504)
PHONE.................................330 725-4155
Shawn Ritchie, *President*
Susan Kohanski, *Corp Secy*
Stephanie Miller, *Controller*
EMP: 28 **EST:** 1962
SQ FT: 10,000
SALES: 7MM **Privately Held**
WEB: www.medinaplating.com
SIC: 3471 Electroplating of metals or formed products

(G-13295)
MEDINA POWDER COATING CORP
930 Lafayette Rd Unit C (44256-3509)
PHONE.................................330 952-1977
EMP: 8 **EST:** 2013
SALES (est): 904K **Privately Held**
SIC: 3479 Coating of metals & formed products

(G-13296)
MEDINA POWDER GROUP
910 Lake Rd Ste B (44256-2765)
PHONE.................................330 952-2711
EMP: 7
SALES (est): 880.2K **Privately Held**
SIC: 3479 Coating of metals & formed products

(G-13297)
MEDINA SIGNS POST INC
411 W Smith Rd (44256-2354)
PHONE.................................330 723-2484
David A Sterrett, *President*
Carol Sterrett, *Vice Pres*
EMP: 5
SQ FT: 6,000
SALES: 414.5K **Privately Held**
SIC: 3993 7389 Neon signs; sign painting & lettering shop

(G-13298)
MEDINA SUPPLY COMPANY (DH)
230 E Smith Rd (44256-3616)
PHONE.................................330 723-3681
Jerry A Schwab, *President*
David Schwab, *Vice Pres*
Mary Lynn Schwab, *Treasurer*
Donna L Schwab, *Admin Sec*
EMP: 20 **EST:** 1974
SQ FT: 2,000

Medina - Medina County (G-13299) — GEOGRAPHIC SECTION

SALES (est): 52.2MM
SALES (corp-wide): 29.7B Privately Held
SIC: 1442 3273 3281 5211 Construction sand & gravel; ready-mixed concrete; cut stone & stone products; brick; concrete & cinder block
HQ: Shelly Materials, Inc.
80 Park Dr
Thornville OH 43076
740 246-6315

(G-13299)
MEDINVENT LLC
1133 Medina Rd Ste 500 (44256-5914)
PHONE.................................330 247-0921
William John Flickinger,
Steven F Isenberg MD,
▲ EMP: 4
SQ FT: 200
SALES (est): 581.6K Privately Held
SIC: 3841 3845 Surgical & medical instruments; respiratory analysis equipment, electromedical

(G-13300)
METAL MERCHANTS USA INC
445 W Liberty St (44256-2273)
P.O. Box 302 (44258-0302)
PHONE.................................330 723-3228
Jerry Moody, Principal
EMP: 7
SALES (est): 759.8K Privately Held
SIC: 3356 Nonferrous rolling & drawing

(G-13301)
MIGRAINE PROOF LLC
6890 Meadowood Dr (44256-9447)
PHONE.................................330 635-7874
Lynn Urbanic, Principal
EMP: 4
SALES (est): 317.1K Privately Held
SIC: 2834 Pharmaceutical preparations

(G-13302)
MINUTEMAN PRESS
455 W Liberty St (44256-2267)
PHONE.................................330 725-4121
Dale Huefner, Principal
EMP: 4
SALES (est): 200K Privately Held
SIC: 2752 Commercial printing, offset

(G-13303)
MOLDING MACHINE SERVICES INC
301 Lake Rd (44256-2458)
P.O. Box 8, Chippewa Lake (44215-0008)
PHONE.................................330 461-2270
William Waite, President
EMP: 5 EST: 2007
SALES (est): 650.6K Privately Held
SIC: 1796 3541 Machinery installation; machine tool replacement & repair parts, metal cutting types

(G-13304)
MONTVIEW CORPORATION
Also Called: Repro Depot
404 W Liberty St (44256-2222)
PHONE.................................330 723-3409
Diane Korfhage, President
EMP: 2
SQ FT: 3,200
SALES: 1.1MM Privately Held
SIC: 2752 7334 2791 2789 Commercial printing, offset; photocopying & duplicating services; typesetting; bookbinding & related work

(G-13305)
MSLS GROUP LLC
Also Called: Main Street Lighting Standards
1080 Industrial Pkwy (44256-2449)
PHONE.................................330 723-4431
Bernard McRae, Mng Member
EMP: 39
SALES (est): 13.4MM Privately Held
SIC: 3312 Fence posts, iron & steel

(G-13306)
NASONEB INC
1133 Medina Rd Ste 500 (44256-5914)
PHONE.................................330 247-0921
William Flickinger, President
EMP: 3
SALES (est): 497.2K Privately Held
SIC: 3845 Electromedical apparatus

(G-13307)
NORTHSTAR PUBLISHING
437 Lafayette Rd Ste 310 (44256-2398)
P.O. Box 1166 (44258-1166)
PHONE.................................330 721-9126
Rodney Auth, President
EMP: 7
SQ FT: 500
SALES: 1MM Privately Held
WEB: www.camp-business.com
SIC: 2731 Books: publishing only

(G-13308)
O P SERVICES INC
799 N Court St (44256-1765)
PHONE.................................330 723-6679
Justin D Proctor, Principal
EMP: 3
SALES (est): 282.2K Privately Held
SIC: 3842 Orthopedic appliances

(G-13309)
OCCIDENTAL CHEMICAL CORP
3984 Dogleg Trl (44256-7208)
PHONE.................................330 764-3441
Roger Hirl, President
EMP: 35
SALES (corp-wide): 18.9B Publicly Held
WEB: www.oxychem.com
SIC: 2812 Alkalies & chlorine
HQ: Occidental Chemical Corporation
14555 Dallas Pkwy Ste 400
Dallas TX 75254
972 404-3800

(G-13310)
OFFICE MAGIC INC (PA)
Also Called: Electrocoat
2290 Wilbur Rd (44256-8496)
PHONE.................................510 782-6100
Craig Codding, President
EMP: 14
SALES (est): 1.6MM Privately Held
SIC: 3479 2522 7641 2519 Painting, coating & hot dipping; office desks & tables: except wood; reupholstery; fiberglass & plastic furniture

(G-13311)
OLIVE TAP (PA)
30 Public Sq (44256-2203)
PHONE.................................330 721-6500
John Petrocelloy, Owner
EMP: 1
SALES (est): 21.9MM Privately Held
SIC: 2079 Olive oil

(G-13312)
OPTEM INC
1030 W Smith Rd (44256-2445)
PHONE.................................330 723-5686
A Banerjie, Principal
Abby Kamleh, Office Mgr
EMP: 5
SALES (est): 670.5K Privately Held
SIC: 2821 Plastics materials & resins

(G-13313)
ORTHOTIC AND PROSTHETIC I
799 N Court St Ste 1 (44256-1766)
PHONE.................................330 723-6679
Justin D Proctor, Principal
EMP: 3
SALES (est): 265.3K Privately Held
SIC: 3842 Orthopedic appliances

(G-13314)
OVATION POLYMER TECHNOLOGY AND
Also Called: Optem
1030 W Smith Rd (44256-2445)
PHONE.................................330 723-5686
Asis Banerjie, President
Delbert Henderson, COO
▲ EMP: 23
SQ FT: 55,000
SALES (est): 2MM Privately Held
WEB: www.opteminc.com
SIC: 2821 Plastics materials & resins

(G-13315)
OWENS CORNING SALES LLC
890 W Smith Rd (44256-2484)
PHONE.................................330 764-7800
Jerry Moore, Manager
EMP: 125 Publicly Held
WEB: www.owenscorning.com
SIC: 3296 Mineral wool
HQ: Owens Corning Sales, Llc
1 Owens Corning Pkwy
Toledo OH 43659
419 248-8000

(G-13316)
PACKAGING SPECIALTIES INC
300 Lake Rd (44256-2459)
PHONE.................................330 723-6000
Robert Syme, Ch of Bd
James Munson, President
Joe Lorenz, General Mgr
Tony Canterbury, Warehouse Mgr
John Syme, Planning
▲ EMP: 50 EST: 1959
SQ FT: 59,000
SALES (est): 10.6MM Privately Held
WEB: www.packspec.com
SIC: 3412 3411 Metal barrels, drums & pails; metal cans
PA: Syme Inc
300 Lake Rd
Medina OH 44256
330 723-6000

(G-13317)
PHASE LINE DEFENSE LLC
2610 Lester Rd (44256-9477)
P.O. Box 214, Valley City (44280-0214)
PHONE.................................440 219-0046
James Banks, Administration
EMP: 4
SALES (est): 216.7K Privately Held
SIC: 3812 Defense systems & equipment

(G-13318)
PLASTI-KEMM INC
Also Called: Plastic-Kemm
2805 Stony Hill Rd (44256-8693)
PHONE.................................330 239-1555
Joseph Kemmerling, President
EMP: 5
SALES (est): 340K Privately Held
SIC: 2821 Plastics materials & resins

(G-13319)
PLASTICS CONVERTING SOLUTIONS
5341 River Styx Rd (44256-8725)
P.O. Box 88 (44258-0088)
PHONE.................................330 722-2537
Victor R Balest, Principal
Victor Balest, Principal
EMP: 3
SALES (est): 311.6K Privately Held
SIC: 3089 Injection molding of plastics

(G-13320)
PLATE ENGRAVING CORPORATION
2324 Sharon Copley Rd (44256-9773)
PHONE.................................330 239-2155
James Michael Brobeck, President
Malissa Nutter, General Mgr
Von Brobeck, Vice Pres
EMP: 12
SQ FT: 4,018
SALES (est): 1.4MM Privately Held
WEB: www.plate-engraving.com
SIC: 2796 3089 Engraving on copper, steel, wood or rubber: printing plates; engraving of plastic

(G-13321)
POST NEWSPAPERS
5164 Normandy Park Dr # 100 (44256-5901)
PHONE.................................330 721-7678
Bruce Trogdon, Principal
Jerry Obney, Marketing Staff
Diane Chaffee, Advt Staff
Vicki Sulzener, Office Mgr
Ronnie Zack, Manager
EMP: 3 EST: 2009
SALES (est): 216.6K Privately Held
SIC: 2711 Newspapers, publishing & printing

(G-13322)
PROFORMA STEINBACHER & ASSOC
3745 Medina Rd Ste A (44256-9510)
PHONE.................................330 241-5370
Larry Steinbacher, Principal
EMP: 3 EST: 2007
SALES (est): 301.6K Privately Held
SIC: 2759 Commercial printing

(G-13323)
PROGRESSIVE MOLDING TECH
5234 Portside Dr (44256-5966)
PHONE.................................330 220-7030
Laird Daubenspeck, CEO
EMP: 8
SQ FT: 8,900
SALES (est): 1.5MM Privately Held
SIC: 3089 Injection molding of plastics

(G-13324)
PROSTHETIC & ORTHOTIC SERVICES
799 N Court St Ste 1 (44256-1766)
PHONE.................................330 723-6679
Justin Proctor, President
EMP: 5
SALES (est): 686.9K Privately Held
SIC: 3842 Orthopedic appliances

(G-13325)
QPMR INC
Also Called: Quality Plastic Machine Repair
7599 Hidden Acres Dr (44256-8813)
PHONE.................................330 723-1739
Jennifer Shurratt, President
EMP: 13
SALES (est): 560K Privately Held
SIC: 7699 3599 Industrial machinery & equipment repair; machine shop, jobbing & repair

(G-13326)
QUALITY TOOLING SYSTEMS INC
650 W Smith Rd Ste 4 (44256-2397)
PHONE.................................330 722-5025
Mrs Robert Kacic, Owner
Joe Schuld, Engrg Mgr
EMP: 11
SQ FT: 12,000
SALES (est): 1.9MM Privately Held
SIC: 3544 Special dies & tools

(G-13327)
REPUBLIC POWDERED METALS INC (HQ)
2628 Pearl Rd (44256-9099)
P.O. Box 777 (44258-0777)
PHONE.................................330 225-3192
Thomas Sullivan, Ch of Bd
Frank C Sullivan, President
Ken Armstrong, Vice Pres
Lonny Dirusso, Vice Pres
John Kramer, Vice Pres
◆ EMP: 61
SQ FT: 20,000
SALES (est): 1.5B
SALES (corp-wide): 5.3B Publicly Held
SIC: 2851 2891 3069 2899 Paints & allied products; adhesives & sealants; roofing, membrane rubber; waterproofing compounds; dyes & pigments; specialty cleaning preparations
PA: Rpm International Inc.
2628 Pearl Rd
Medina OH 44256
330 273-5090

(G-13328)
ROBERT GOREY
Also Called: Gorey Construction
6811 Stone Rd (44256-8991)
PHONE.................................330 725-7272
Robert Gorey, Owner
EMP: 3
SALES (est): 269.6K Privately Held
SIC: 2951 1623 Concrete, asphaltic (not from refineries); sewer line construction; water main construction

▲ = Import ▼=Export
◆ =Import/Export

(G-13329)
ROBLOC INC
Also Called: UPS Stores, The
3593 Medina Rd (44256-8182)
PHONE.................................330 723-5853
Brett Robertson, *Branch Mgr*
EMP: 3 **Privately Held**
SIC: 7389 2759 Mailbox rental & related service; commercial printing
PA: Robloc Inc
    1114 N Court St
    Medina OH 44256

(G-13330)
RPM CONSUMER HOLDING COMPANY (HQ)
2628 Pearl Rd (44256-7623)
P.O. Box 777 (44258-0777)
PHONE.................................330 273-5090
Frank C Sullivan, *President*
Ron Rice, *President*
Ronald A Rice, *Vice Pres*
Keith R Smiley, *Treasurer*
Edward W Moore, *Admin Sec*
EMP: 9
SALES (est): 12.1MM
SALES (corp-wide): 5.3B **Publicly Held**
SIC: 2891 3089 3952 3944 Adhesives; cement, except linoleum & tile; kits, plastic; brushes, air, artists'; games, toys & children's vehicles; enamels
PA: Rpm International Inc.
    2628 Pearl Rd
    Medina OH 44256
    330 273-5090

(G-13331)
RPM INTERNATIONAL INC (PA)
2628 Pearl Rd (44256-7623)
P.O. Box 777 (44258-0777)
PHONE.................................330 273-5090
Frank C Sullivan, *Ch of Bd*
Lonny Dirusso, *Vice Pres*
Matthew Franklin, *Vice Pres*
Randell McShepard, *Vice Pres*
Gordon Hyde, *VP Opers*
◆ **EMP:** 61 **EST:** 1947
SALES: 5.3B **Publicly Held**
WEB: www.rpminc.com
SIC: 2891 3069 2899 2865 Adhesives & sealants; sealants; adhesives; roofing, membrane rubber; waterproofing compounds; concrete curing & hardening compounds; corrosion preventive lubricant; dyes & pigments; specialty cleaning preparations; lacquers, varnishes, enamels & other coatings

(G-13332)
S F S STADLER INC
5201 Portside Dr (44256-5966)
PHONE.................................330 239-7100
EMP: 6
SALES (est): 576K **Privately Held**
SIC: 3452 Pins

(G-13333)
S&V INDUSTRIES INC (PA)
5054 Paramount Dr (44256-5363)
PHONE.................................330 666-1986
Senthil Sundarapandian, *CEO*
Senthil Kumar Sundarapandian, *CEO*
Mahesh Douglas, *President*
Joan Owens, *Vice Pres*
▲ **EMP:** 40
SQ FT: 1,618
SALES (est): 50MM **Privately Held**
WEB: www.svindustries.com
SIC: 5049 3089 3312 Engineers' equipment & supplies; casting of plastic; forgings, iron & steel

(G-13334)
SANDRIDGE FOOD CORPORATION (PA)
Also Called: Sandridge Gourmet Salads
133 Commerce Dr (44256-1333)
PHONE.................................330 725-2348
Mark D Sandridge, *CEO*
William G Frantz, *President*
Brad Chapman, *General Mgr*
Jordan Sandridge, *General Mgr*
Roger Coy, *Area Mgr*
▲ **EMP:** 5
SQ FT: 130,000
SALES (est): 114.5MM **Privately Held**
WEB: www.sandridge.com
SIC: 2099 Salads, fresh or refrigerated

(G-13335)
SANDRIDGE FOOD CORPORATION
Also Called: Sandridge Gourmet Salads
133 Commerce Dr (44256-1333)
PHONE.................................330 725-8883
Barry Pioski, *Manager*
EMP: 225
SALES (corp-wide): 114.5MM **Privately Held**
WEB: www.sandridge.com
SIC: 2099 5141 Salads, fresh or refrigerated; groceries, general line
PA: Sandridge Food Corporation
    133 Commerce Dr
    Medina OH 44256
    330 725-2348

(G-13336)
SCIS AEROSPACE LLC
1179 Alexandria Ln (44256-3262)
PHONE.................................216 533-8533
Robert Boyd, *President*
Brian Jaskiewicz, *Vice Pres*
James Ralph, *Treasurer*
Jeffrey Jaskiewicz, *Admin Sec*
EMP: 4
SALES (est): 149.8K **Privately Held**
SIC: 3724 3728 Research & development on aircraft engines & parts; military aircraft equipment & armament; research & dev by manuf., aircraft parts & auxiliary equip

(G-13337)
SEALY MATTRESS COMPANY
1070 Lake Rd (44256-2450)
PHONE.................................330 725-4146
Larry Schedler, *Branch Mgr*
EMP: 180
SQ FT: 143,000
SALES (corp-wide): 2.7B **Publicly Held**
SIC: 2515 Mattresses, containing felt, foam rubber, urethane, etc.; box springs, assembled
HQ: Sealy Mattress Company
    1 Office Parkway Rd
    Trinity NC 27370
    336 861-3500

(G-13338)
SEALY MATTRESS MFG CO INC
1070 Lake Rd (44256-2450)
PHONE.................................800 697-3259
Vicky Avans, *Manager*
EMP: 100
SALES (corp-wide): 2.7B **Publicly Held**
SIC: 2515 Mattresses, innerspring or box spring
HQ: Sealy Mattress Manufacturing Company, Llc
    1 Office Parkway Rd
    Trinity NC 27370
    336 861-3500

(G-13339)
SFS GROUP USA INC
Also Called: Sfs Intec
5201 Portside Dr (44256-5966)
PHONE.................................330 239-7100
URS Langenauer, *Vice Pres*
Shawn Varney, *Maint Spvr*
Tim Myers, *IT/INT Sup*
Debbie Moore, *Executive*
EMP: 186
SALES (corp-wide): 1.6B **Privately Held**
SIC: 3714 Motor vehicle parts & accessories
HQ: Sfs Group Usa, Inc.
    1045 Spring St
    Wyomissing PA 19610
    610 376-5751

(G-13340)
SHARK SOLAR LLC
4386 Belmont Ct (44256-7486)
PHONE.................................216 630-7395
EMP: 5
SALES (est): 185.7K **Privately Held**
SIC: 1711 3433 Plumbing/Heating/Air Cond Contractor Mfg Heating Equipment-Nonelectric

(G-13341)
SHELLY MATERIALS INC
300 N State Rd (44256-1406)
PHONE.................................330 722-2190
EMP: 4
SALES (est): 23.7B **Privately Held**
SIC: 1422 Crushed/Broken Limestone
HQ: Shelly Materials, Inc.
    80 Park Dr
    Thornville OH 43076
    740 246-6315

(G-13342)
SHERWN-WLLAMS INTL HLDINGS INC (HQ)
4603 Ledgewood Dr (44256-9034)
PHONE.................................216 566-2000
Henry Sherwin, *Principal*
EMP: 5
SALES (est): 1.6MM
SALES (corp-wide): 17.5B **Publicly Held**
SIC: 5231 2851 Paint & painting supplies; wallcoverings; paints & allied products
PA: The Sherwin-Williams Company
    101 W Prospect Ave # 1020
    Cleveland OH 44115
    216 566-2000

(G-13343)
SINFUL SWEETS LLC
3862 Turnberry Dr (44256-6885)
PHONE.................................330 721-0916
Judi Campobenedetto, *Principal*
EMP: 4 **EST:** 2010
SALES (est): 184.7K **Privately Held**
SIC: 2051 Cakes, bakery: except frozen

(G-13344)
SKINNER SALES GROUP INC
Also Called: Skinner Metal Products
3860 Deer Lake Dr (44256-7697)
PHONE.................................440 572-8455
EMP: 20
SQ FT: 24,000
SALES (est): 1.2MM **Privately Held**
SIC: 3441 3443 3449 Steel Aluminum Stainless Steel Custom Metal Fabricated Prdts

(G-13345)
SOLUTIONS IN POLYCARBONATE LLC
6353 Norwalk Rd (44256-9455)
PHONE.................................330 572-2860
Bruce Gold, *President*
EMP: 6
SQ FT: 24,000
SALES (est): 329.1K **Privately Held**
SIC: 3089 Windows, plastic

(G-13346)
STANDARD WELDING & STEEL PDTS
260 S State Rd (44256-2474)
P.O. Box 297 (44258-0297)
PHONE.................................330 273-2777
Charles Coleman, *CEO*
Christopher Coleman, *President*
Charles F Coleman, *President*
Jack Colman, *Vice Pres*
Jayne Coleman, *Treasurer*
EMP: 18 **EST:** 1939
SQ FT: 30,000
SALES (est): 4.2MM **Privately Held**
WEB: www.stdwelding.com
SIC: 3441 Fabricated structural metal

(G-13347)
STANDOUT STICKERS INC
4930 Chippewa Rd Unit A (44256-8824)
PHONE.................................877 449-7703
Jeffrey Nemecek, *CEO*
Josh Hippley, *Marketing Staff*
EMP: 6
SALES: 650.6K **Privately Held**
SIC: 2759 Screen printing

(G-13348)
STRAIGHT RAZOR DESIGNES
4307 Belmont Ct (44256-7484)
PHONE.................................330 598-1414
Don Addlean, *Owner*
EMP: 3
SALES (est): 244.3K **Privately Held**
SIC: 3199 Razor strops

(G-13349)
SUPRO SPRING & WIRE FORMS INC
6440 Norwalk Rd Ste N (44256-7154)
PHONE.................................330 722-5628
Kevin Provagna, *President*
James Gensert, *Vice Pres*
▲ **EMP:** 35
SQ FT: 12,000
SALES: 5MM **Privately Held**
WEB: www.suprospring.com
SIC: 3495 Wire springs

(G-13350)
SYME INC (PA)
300 Lake Rd (44256-2459)
PHONE.................................330 723-6000
Robert P Syme, *CEO*
Jim L Munson, *President*
EMP: 21
SQ FT: 58,000
SALES (est): 10.6MM **Privately Held**
WEB: www.syme.com
SIC: 3412 Metal barrels, drums & pails

(G-13351)
THERMO VENT MANUFACTURING INC
Also Called: Therm-O-Vent
1213 Medina Rd (44256-8135)
PHONE.................................330 239-0239
Stephen Boesch, *President*
Charles R Boesch, *Vice Pres*
Jeffery W Boesch, *Vice Pres*
▲ **EMP:** 11
SQ FT: 6,800
SALES (est): 1.1MM **Privately Held**
SIC: 3444 3564 Ventilators, sheet metal; blowers & fans

(G-13352)
THOMAS ROSS ASSOCIATES INC
303 N Broadway St (44256-1930)
PHONE.................................330 723-1110
Thomas Ross, *President*
Melody A Ross, *Project Mgr*
Melody Ross, *Office Mgr*
Jenny Scheidler, *Analyst*
EMP: 3
SALES (est): 150K **Privately Held**
SIC: 3571 1731 7378 5045 Electronic computers; computer installation; computer & data processing equipment repair/maintenance; computers; computer software; accounting machines using machine readable programs

(G-13353)
TIGER GENERAL LLC
6867 Wooster Pike (44256-8859)
PHONE.................................330 239-4949
Mark Overholt, *President*
Mickey Manack, *Vice Pres*
Sherry Overholt, *Vice Pres*
EMP: 70
SQ FT: 18,000
SALES (est): 14.2MM **Privately Held**
SIC: 3533 5511 Oil & gas drilling rigs & equipment; oil field machinery & equipment; trucks, tractors & trailers: new & used

(G-13354)
TRAILER ONE INC
6378 Norwalk Rd (44256-9455)
PHONE.................................330 723-7474
Kenneth Smith, *President*
Bradley Thomas, *Vice Pres*
▼ **EMP:** 10
SQ FT: 250
SALES: 7.8MM **Privately Held**
WEB: www.trailerone.com
SIC: 5511 3715 7359 Trucks, tractors & trailers: new & used; truck trailers; equipment rental & leasing

(G-13355)
TROGDON PUBLISHING INC
Also Called: Ohio Standard Bread
5164 Normandy Park Dr # 100 (44256-5901)
PHONE.................................330 721-7678
Bruce Trogdon, *President*
Mike Trogdon, *Publisher*

Medina - Medina County (G-13356)

(G-13356)
UNISAND INCORPORATED
1097 Industrial Pkwy (44256-2448)
PHONE..................................330 722-0222
David W Bullock, *President*
Douglas Bullock, *Vice Pres*
Todd Seefeldt, *Plant Mgr*
▲ **EMP:** 26
SQ FT: 3,000
SALES (est): 4.1MM **Privately Held**
WEB: www.unisand.com
SIC: 3291 Abrasive wheels & grindstones, not artificial

(G-13357)
UNITED SPORT APPAREL
229 Harding St Ste B (44256-1288)
PHONE..................................330 722-0818
David A Bricker, *Owner*
EMP: 10
SQ FT: 6,000
SALES (est): 1MM **Privately Held**
WEB: www.unitedsportapparel.com
SIC: 2759 2395 Screen printing; embroidery products, except schiffli machine

(G-13358)
UNITED TUBE CORPORATION
960 Lake Rd (44256-2453)
PHONE..................................330 725-4196
Frank J Sadowski, *President*
Harvey O Yoder, *Principal*
Angelina Chaplain, *Vice Pres*
Mark Segedi, *Sales Staff*
Patti McCormick, *Executive Asst*
EMP: 54 **EST:** 1945
SALES (est): 12.7MM **Privately Held**
SIC: 3317 Tubes, wrought: welded or lock joint; welded pipe & tubes

(G-13359)
VALUE STREAM SYSTEMS INC
2575 Medina Rd Ste B (44256-6606)
PHONE..................................330 907-0064
Kevin Archer, *President*
Nathan Jones, *Principal*
EMP: 4 **EST:** 2016
SQ FT: 1,500
SALES (est): 45K **Privately Held**
SIC: 7372 7379 7371 Business oriented computer software; computer related consulting services; computer software development & applications

(G-13360)
VALVOLE AMERICA LLC
2550 Medina Rd (44256-8144)
PHONE..................................330 464-8872
Steven A Huzyak, *Mng Member*
▲ **EMP:** 5 **EST:** 2015
SQ FT: 7,600
SALES (est): 1.4MM **Privately Held**
SIC: 3492 3491 Valves, hydraulic, aircraft; valves, automatic control

(G-13361)
VINTAGE MACHINE SUPPLY INC
650 W Smith Rd Ste 9 (44256-2397)
PHONE..................................330 723-0800
Tom Hastings, *President*
EMP: 3
SQ FT: 3,000
SALES (est): 464.2K **Privately Held**
WEB: www.vintagemachinesupplies.com
SIC: 3599 Machine shop, jobbing & repair

(G-13362)
W G MACHINE TOOL SERVICE CO
7735 Spieth Rd (44256-8914)
PHONE..................................330 723-3428
EMP: 9
SQ FT: 10,000
SALES (est): 978.8K **Privately Held**
SIC: 3542 Rebuilds Machine Tools

(G-13363)
WOODBINE PRODUCTS COMPANY
Also Called: Powrkleen
915 W Smith Rd (44256-2446)
PHONE..................................330 725-0165
Phillip Navratil, *President*
Stephen A Kuzyk Jr, *Corp Secy*
▲ **EMP:** 14 **EST:** 1961
SQ FT: 20,000
SALES (est): 4.2MM **Privately Held**
WEB: www.powrkleen.com
SIC: 2842 2844 Cleaning or polishing preparations; toilet preparations

(G-13364)
X-TREME FINISHES INC
Also Called: Line-X of Akron/Medina
387 Medina Rd Ste 1000 (44256-9681)
PHONE..................................330 474-0614
Tawny R Zajc, *Principal*
EMP: 10 **EST:** 2013
SALES (est): 174.8K **Privately Held**
SIC: 3479 2851 1752 7549 Etching & engraving; epoxy coatings; polyurethane coatings; access flooring system installation; undercoating/rustproofing cars; exterior cleaning, including sandblasting

Medway
Clark County

(G-13365)
AERO COMPOSITES INC
3400 Spangler Rd (45341-9752)
P.O. Box 404 (45341-0404)
PHONE..................................937 849-0244
David Patko, *President*
Patricia Ann Scully, *President*
Dave Scully, *Vice Pres*
EMP: 4
SQ FT: 6,000
SALES (est): 512.4K **Privately Held**
WEB: www.aerocomposites.com
SIC: 3721 8711 Aircraft; consulting engineer

(G-13366)
PROTOFAB MANUFACTURING INC
8 University Rd (45341-1260)
PHONE..................................937 849-4983
EMP: 5
SALES (est): 27.1K **Privately Held**
SIC: 3552 Mfg Industrial Machinery

(G-13367)
WAYNE CONCRETE COMPANY
223 Western Dr (45341-9521)
PHONE..................................937 545-9919
Wayne Gibson, *Owner*
EMP: 10 **EST:** 1987
SALES (est): 258K **Privately Held**
SIC: 1442 Construction sand & gravel

Mentor
Lake County

(G-13368)
1 888 U PITCH IT
7176 Fillmore Ct (44060-4816)
PHONE..................................440 796-9028
Frank A Jurkoshek, *Principal*
EMP: 4
SALES (est): 449.1K **Privately Held**
SIC: 3089 Garbage containers, plastic

(G-13369)
ABSOLUTE GRINDING CO INC
7007 Spinach Dr (44060-4959)
PHONE..................................440 974-4030
Rob Murnyack, *President*
EMP: 11
SQ FT: 8,100
SALES: 671.5K **Privately Held**
WEB: www.absolutegrinding.com
SIC: 3599 Machine shop, jobbing & repair

(G-13370)
ACCU-TECH MFG & SUPPORT
8875 East Ave (44060-4305)
PHONE..................................440 205-8882
Jeff Moore, *President*
Ron Curtiss, *Vice Pres*
EMP: 10
SQ FT: 6,500
SALES (est): 732K **Privately Held**
SIC: 3599 Machine shop, jobbing & repair

(G-13371)
ACCURATE METAL SAWING SVC CO (PA)
8989 Tyler Blvd (44060-2184)
PHONE..................................440 205-3205
Thomas C Blue, *Incorporator*
EMP: 21 **EST:** 2001
SALES (est): 2MM **Privately Held**
WEB: www.accuratemetalsawing.com
SIC: 3541 Plasma process metal cutting machines

(G-13372)
ACCURATE TECH INC
7230 Industrial Park Blvd (44060-5316)
PHONE..................................440 951-9153
Micheal Karcic Jr, *President*
Glen Yamamoto, *Business Mgr*
EMP: 6
SQ FT: 3,000
SALES (est): 550K **Privately Held**
SIC: 3599 Machine shop, jobbing & repair

(G-13373)
ACO POLYMER PRODUCTS INC (DH)
Also Called: Quartz
9470 Pinecone Dr (44060-1863)
PHONE..................................440 285-7000
Derek Humphries, *President*
Jason Jonke, *Engineer*
Kevin Taylor, *CFO*
Cheryl Barta, *Human Res Mgr*
Mary Moe, *Sales Staff*
◆ **EMP:** 50 **EST:** 1978
SQ FT: 30,000
SALES (est): 25.4MM
SALES (corp-wide): 850.8MM **Privately Held**
WEB: www.acousa.com
SIC: 3272 3089 3312 Concrete products, precast; plastic & fiberglass tanks; stainless steel
HQ: Severin Ahlmann Holding Gmbh
Am Ahlmannkai
Budelsdorf 24782
433 135-40

(G-13374)
ACTIVITIES PRESS INC
Also Called: AP Direct
7181 Industrial Park Blvd (44060-5327)
PHONE..................................440 953-1200
Graydon Bullard, *President*
Leroy Bridges, *Vice Pres*
Linda Bridges, *Treasurer*
Kathy Byers, *Sales Staff*
Bill Hilston, *Sales Staff*
▲ **EMP:** 28 **EST:** 1947
SQ FT: 24,000
SALES (est): 4.8MM **Privately Held**
WEB: www.activitiespress.com
SIC: 2752 2791 2789 Commercial printing, offset; typesetting; bookbinding & related work

(G-13375)
ADVANCED PNEUMATICS INC
Also Called: Advanced F.M.e Products
9413 Hamilton Dr (44060-8709)
PHONE..................................440 953-0700
Thomas Nalfi, *President*
Ed Diebold, *Sales Staff*
EMP: 5
SQ FT: 1,200
SALES (est): 1MM **Privately Held**
WEB: www.advancedpneumatics.com
SIC: 3568 Power transmission equipment

(G-13376)
ADVANCED SLEEVE CORP
8767 East Ave (44060-4303)
PHONE..................................440 205-1055
Robert Anderson, *Owner*
Jeff Zaugg, *Executive*
EMP: 9
SALES (est): 1MM **Privately Held**
SIC: 3599 Machine shop, jobbing & repair

(G-13377)
AIR POWER DYNAMICS LLC
7350 Corporate Blvd (44060-4856)
PHONE..................................440 701-2100
Edward F Crawford, *CEO*
Boya Belasic,
EMP: 200
SQ FT: 73,000
SALES (est): 36.1MM **Privately Held**
WEB: www.beechtechnology.com
SIC: 3543 Industrial patterns

(G-13378)
AIR TECHNICAL INDUSTRIES INC
7501 Clover Ave (44060-5297)
P.O. Box 149 (44061-0149)
PHONE..................................440 951-5191
Pero Novak, *CEO*
Cyndi McCloud, *General Mgr*
Vida Novak, *Vice Pres*
Nick Oriti, *Foreman/Supr*
Bob Hughes, *Sales Mgr*
◆ **EMP:** 40 **EST:** 1964
SQ FT: 80,000
SALES (est): 12.5MM **Privately Held**
WEB: www.airtechnical.com
SIC: 3537 3569 3536 3421 Stacking machines, automatic; robots, assembly line; industrial & commercial; hoists, cranes & monorails; cutlery; bulk handling conveyor systems

(G-13379)
AIR TOOL SERVICE COMPANY (PA)
7722 Metric Dr (44060-4862)
PHONE..................................440 701-1021
Rick J Sabath, *President*
Henry Brueggeman, *Principal*
Betty J Gerhard, *Principal*
James Becker, *Vice Pres*
EMP: 14 **EST:** 1956
SQ FT: 30,000
SALES (est): 1.7MM **Privately Held**
WEB: www.atsco.com
SIC: 3494 3546 Valves & pipe fittings; power-driven handtools

(G-13380)
AJ FLUID POWER SALES & SUP INC
Also Called: Safe Air Valve Co.
8766 Tyler Blvd (44060-4329)
PHONE..................................440 255-7960
Adam Jenkins, *President*
EMP: 5
SQ FT: 4,000
SALES (est): 868.9K **Privately Held**
WEB: www.safeairvalve.com
SIC: 7699 3492 Valve repair, industrial; control valves, fluid power: hydraulic & pneumatic

(G-13381)
ALAMARRA INC
8788 Tyler Blvd (44060-4328)
PHONE..................................800 336-3007
Lawrence Boros, *President*
Markay Boros, *CFO*
EMP: 3
SALES (est): 380.2K **Privately Held**
WEB: www.alamarra.com
SIC: 2099 Food preparations

(G-13382)
ALL - FLO PUMP COMPANY
8989 Tyler Blvd (44060-2184)
PHONE..................................440 354-1700
Robert Brizes, *President*
Bob Eklund, *Manager*
Ronald Robinson, *Shareholder*
▲ **EMP:** 22
SALES (est): 4.2MM **Privately Held**
WEB: www.allflo.com
SIC: 3594 3561 Fluid power pumps; pumps & pumping equipment

GEOGRAPHIC SECTION
Mentor - Lake County (G-13410)

(G-13383)
ALL AMERICAN INDUS SVCS LLC
8171 Tyler Blvd (44060-4826)
PHONE..................440 255-7525
Renee Roland,
Patrick Studnicka,
EMP: 4
SQ FT: 20,000
SALES (est): 112K **Privately Held**
SIC: 7692 Welding repair

(G-13384)
ALL STATE GL BLOCK FCTRY INC
8781 East Ave (44060-4303)
PHONE..................440 205-8410
Vince Tassone, *President*
Vince Tasone, *President*
EMP: 8
SQ FT: 3,000
SALES: 720K **Privately Held**
SIC: 1793 5231 3229 Glass & glazing work; glass; blocks & bricks, glass

(G-13385)
AMERICAN METAL COATINGS INC (PA)
7700 Tyler Blvd (44060-4964)
PHONE..................216 451-3131
Konstantinos Dotsikas, *President*
John Obratil, *Office Mgr*
EMP: 40
SQ FT: 180,000
SALES (est): 7.6MM **Privately Held**
SIC: 3471 Electroplating of metals or formed products

(G-13386)
AMERICAN POLYMER STANDARDS
8680 Tyler Blvd (44060-4348)
P.O. Box 901 (44061-0901)
PHONE..................440 255-2211
John E Armonas, *President*
EMP: 5
SQ FT: 5,600
SALES (est): 644.3K **Privately Held**
WEB: www.ampolymer.com
SIC: 8734 2821 Water testing laboratory; plastics materials & resins

(G-13387)
ANGSTROM AUTOMOTIVE GROUP LLC
8229 Tyler Blvd (44060-4218)
PHONE..................440 255-6700
EMP: 5 **Privately Held**
SIC: 3714 Axle housings & shafts, motor vehicle
PA: Angstrom Automotive Group, Llc
 26980 Trolley Indus Dr
 Taylor MI 48180

(G-13388)
ANGSTROM PRECISION METALS LLC
8229 Tyler Blvd (44060-4218)
PHONE..................440 255-6700
Nagesh K Palakurthi, *CEO*
Mario Manocchio, *President*
David Berg, *General Mgr*
Sandy Bradford, *COO*
▲ EMP: 60
SALES (est): 12MM **Privately Held**
SIC: 3545 Precision tools, machinists'
PA: Angstrom Automotive Group, Llc
 26980 Trolley Indus Dr
 Taylor MI 48180

(G-13389)
ANODIZING SPECIALISTS INC
7547 Tyler Blvd (44060-4869)
PHONE..................440 951-0257
David J Pecjak, *President*
Michael T Pecjak, *Vice Pres*
EMP: 18
SQ FT: 11,000
SALES: 1.5MM **Privately Held**
WEB: www.anodizingspecialists.com
SIC: 3471 Finishing, metals or formed products; anodizing (plating) of metals or formed products

(G-13390)
APOLLO MANUFACTURING CO LLC
7911 Enterprise Dr (44060-5311)
PHONE..................440 951-9972
Draga Marusic, *Vice Pres*
Allen Sandy, *Mng Member*
Ronald Jack,
EMP: 30
SQ FT: 25,000
SALES (est): 6.8MM **Privately Held**
WEB: www.apollo-mfg.com
SIC: 3545 Precision tools, machinists'

(G-13391)
APOLLO PLASTICS INC
7555 Tyler Blvd Ste 11 (44060-4866)
PHONE..................440 951-7774
Stanley Skrbis, *President*
Maria Skrbis, *Corp Secy*
EMP: 10 EST: 1973
SQ FT: 8,000
SALES (est): 708.6K **Privately Held**
WEB: www.apolloplastics.net
SIC: 3544 3089 Industrial molds; plastic processing

(G-13392)
ARCH PARENT INC
9215 Mentor Ave (44060-6477)
PHONE..................440 701-7420
EMP: 1904
SALES (corp-wide): 3B **Privately Held**
SIC: 2752 Commercial printing, lithographic
PA: Arch Parent Inc.
 9 W 57th St Fl 31
 New York NY 10019
 212 796-8500

(G-13393)
AREM CO
Also Called: Jaytee Division
7234 Justin Way (44060-4881)
PHONE..................440 974-6740
Bob Myotte, *President*
Becky Uyesugi, *Vice Pres*
Jack Kurant, *Admin Sec*
EMP: 14
SALES (est): 3MM **Privately Held**
WEB: www.arema.net
SIC: 3498 3949 3354 3471 Fabricated pipe & fittings; sporting & athletic goods; aluminum extruded products; plating & polishing; tubing, copper & copper alloy

(G-13394)
ATS MACHINE & TOOL CO INC
7750 Division Dr (44060-4860)
PHONE..................440 255-1120
Robert E Dutko, *President*
Denise Dutko, *Vice Pres*
Paul Motiejunas, *Plant Mgr*
EMP: 12
SQ FT: 15,000
SALES: 2MM **Privately Held**
WEB: www.atsmachine.com
SIC: 3599 Machine shop, jobbing & repair

(G-13395)
AUTOMATION METROLOGY INTL LLC (PA)
8808 Tyler Blvd (44060-4361)
PHONE..................440 354-6436
David Denman,
▼ EMP: 5
SQ FT: 5,000
SALES (est): 2MM **Privately Held**
WEB: www.auto-met.com
SIC: 5084 3823 3699 Measuring & testing equipment, electrical; industrial process measurement equipment; digital displays of process variables; laser systems & equipment

(G-13396)
AVERY DENNISON CORPORATION
8100 Tyler Blvd (44060-4865)
PHONE..................440 534-6527
EMP: 6
SALES (corp-wide): 7.1B **Publicly Held**
SIC: 2672 Coated & laminated paper
PA: Avery Dennison Corporation
 207 N Goode Ave Ste 500
 Glendale CA 91203
 626 304-2000

(G-13397)
AVERY DENNISON CORPORATION
7100 Lindsay Dr (44060-4923)
PHONE..................440 358-2828
John Siegel, *Accountant*
Frederick Buse, *Branch Mgr*
EMP: 115
SALES (corp-wide): 7.1B **Publicly Held**
SIC: 2672 Adhesive backed films, foams & foils
PA: Avery Dennison Corporation
 207 N Goode Ave Ste 500
 Glendale CA 91203
 626 304-2000

(G-13398)
AVERY DENNISON CORPORATION
7236 Justin Way (44060-4881)
PHONE..................440 266-2500
Rob Dibble, *Branch Mgr*
EMP: 115
SALES (corp-wide): 7.1B **Publicly Held**
SIC: 2672 Adhesive backed films, foams & foils
PA: Avery Dennison Corporation
 207 N Goode Ave Ste 500
 Glendale CA 91203
 626 304-2000

(G-13399)
AVERY DENNISON CORPORATION
7070 Spinach Dr Bldg 19 (44060-4958)
PHONE..................440 358-2930
EMP: 115
SALES (corp-wide): 7.1B **Publicly Held**
SIC: 2672 Adhesive backed films, foams & foils
PA: Avery Dennison Corporation
 207 N Goode Ave Ste 500
 Glendale CA 91203
 626 304-2000

(G-13400)
B & G MACHINE COMPANY INC
7205 Commerce Dr (44060-5307)
PHONE..................440 946-8787
Donald Kuchenbecker, *President*
EMP: 4 EST: 1954
SQ FT: 25,000
SALES (est): 280K **Privately Held**
SIC: 3599 Machine shop, jobbing & repair

(G-13401)
B N MACHINE INC
8853 East Ave (44060-4305)
PHONE..................440 255-5200
Bill Nicholl, *President*
EMP: 4
SQ FT: 4,000
SALES (est): 403.7K **Privately Held**
WEB: www.bnmachine.com
SIC: 3599 Machine shop, jobbing & repair

(G-13402)
BESTLIGHT LED CORPORATION
8909 East Ave (44060-4305)
PHONE..................440 205-1552
James Moll, *President*
EMP: 4
SALES (est): 469.9K **Privately Held**
SIC: 3674 Light emitting diodes

(G-13403)
BILL WYATT INC
Also Called: Wyatt Printing
8857 Lake Shore Blvd (44060-1521)
PHONE..................330 535-1113
Bill Wyatt, *President*
EMP: 7
SQ FT: 10,000
SALES (est): 570K **Privately Held**
WEB: www.oneguyandadog.com
SIC: 2752 2791 2789 Commercial printing, offset; typesetting; bookbinding & related work

(G-13404)
BLEIL CHAN
Also Called: Bleil Manufacturing Company
9451 Jackson St (44060-4513)
PHONE..................440 352-6012
Chan Bleil, *President*
Mary Ann Bleil, *Treasurer*
EMP: 5
SQ FT: 2,000
SALES: 300K **Privately Held**
SIC: 3599 Machine shop, jobbing & repair

(G-13405)
BOBS GRINDING INC
7564 Tyler Blvd Ste D (44060-4870)
PHONE..................440 946-6179
Dennis Murnyack, *President*
EMP: 4
SALES: 160K **Privately Held**
SIC: 3599 Machine shop, jobbing & repair; grinding castings for the trade

(G-13406)
BRUMALL MFG CORPORATION
7850 Division Dr (44060-4874)
PHONE..................440 974-2622
Rod Brumberg, *President*
Wanda Brumberg, *Corp Secy*
Yvonne Brumberg, *Vice Pres*
▲ EMP: 40
SQ FT: 25,000
SALES (est): 7.2MM **Privately Held**
WEB: www.brumall.com
SIC: 3643 Connectors & terminals for electrical devices

(G-13407)
BURTON INDUSTRIES INC
7875 Division Dr (44060-4877)
PHONE..................440 974-1700
Chris Burton, *Branch Mgr*
EMP: 25
SALES (corp-wide): 27.6MM **Privately Held**
WEB: www.burtonind.com
SIC: 3599 Machine shop, jobbing & repair
PA: Burton Industries, Inc.
 9821 Cedar Falls Rd
 Hazelhurst WI 54531
 906 932-5970

(G-13408)
BUYERS PRODUCTS COMPANY (PA)
9049 Tyler Blvd (44060-4800)
PHONE..................440 974-8888
Mark Saltzman, *President*
Dave Durst, *General Mgr*
Brian Smith, *COO*
Jeff Mueller, *Vice Pres*
Brian Lanican, *Mfg Dir*
▲ EMP: 160 EST: 1947
SQ FT: 172,000
SALES (est): 149MM **Privately Held**
WEB: www.buyersproducts.com
SIC: 5013 3714 Truck parts & accessories; motor vehicle parts & accessories

(G-13409)
BUYERS PRODUCTS COMPANY
8120 Tyler Blvd (44060-4852)
PHONE..................440 974-8888
James Kleinman, *Branch Mgr*
EMP: 5
SALES (corp-wide): 149MM **Privately Held**
SIC: 3465 Body parts, automobile: stamped metal
PA: Buyers Products Company
 9049 Tyler Blvd
 Mentor OH 44060
 440 974-8888

(G-13410)
BUYERS PRODUCTS COMPANY
7700 Tyler Blvd (44060-4964)
PHONE..................440 974-8888
James Kleinman, *Branch Mgr*
EMP: 5
SALES (est): 434K
SALES (corp-wide): 149MM **Privately Held**
SIC: 5013 3714 Truck parts & accessories; motor vehicle parts & accessories

Mentor - Lake County (G-13411)

PA: Buyers Products Company
9049 Tyler Blvd
Mentor OH 44060
440 974-8888

(G-13411)
CEMEX CONSTRUCTION CORPORATION
10176 Page Dr (44060-6816)
PHONE................................440 449-0872
Gianmichele Bruno, *President*
EMP: 6
SALES (est): 220K **Privately Held**
SIC: 3273 Ready-mixed concrete

(G-13412)
CHEMSULTANTS INTERNATIONAL INC (PA)
9079 Tyler Blvd (44060-1868)
P.O. Box 1118 (44061-1118)
PHONE................................440 974-3080
Judith Muny, *Corp Secy*
Keith Muny, *Vice Pres*
Mark Van Ness, *Prdtn Mgr*
Jennifer Muny, *Director*
Bonnie Cole-King, *Director*
EMP: 25
SQ FT: 10,000
SALES (est): 5.4MM **Privately Held**
SIC: 3821 8734 8742 Laboratory apparatus & furniture; product testing laboratory; safety or performance; industry specialist consultants

(G-13413)
CLARK RBR PLASTIC INTL SLS INC (PA)
8888 East Ave (44060-4306)
P.O. Box 299 (44061-0299)
PHONE................................440 255-9793
Gregory Clark, *Treasurer*
James T Clark II, *Vice Pres*
Jeff Lippus, *Sales Mgr*
Julie Clark, *Director*
EMP: 75 **EST:** 1970
SQ FT: 16,000
SALES (est): 21.3MM **Privately Held**
WEB: www.clarkrandp.com
SIC: 3061 3069 3089 Mechanical rubber goods; molded rubber products; extruded finished plastic products

(G-13414)
CLEVELAND CARBIDE TOOL CO
7755 Division Dr (44060-4861)
PHONE................................440 974-1155
John Halick, *President*
Barbara Halick, *Vice Pres*
EMP: 4 **EST:** 1941
SQ FT: 5,000
SALES (est): 400K **Privately Held**
SIC: 3545 Cutting tools for machine tools; milling cutters

(G-13415)
CLEVELAND SPECIALTY INSPTN SVC
8562 East Ave (44060-4302)
PHONE................................440 578-1046
James Popovic, *President*
EMP: 13
SQ FT: 3,200
SALES (est): 920K **Privately Held**
WEB: www.clevelandspecialty.com
SIC: 7389 3545 Inspection & testing services; threading tools (machine tool accessories); gauges (machine tool accessories)

(G-13416)
CLIMAX METAL PRODUCTS COMPANY
8141 Tyler Blvd (44060-4855)
PHONE................................440 943-8898
Jerry Wheaton, *CEO*
Gerald R Wheaton, *President*
L G Knecht, *Principal*
John T White, *Principal*
Steve Wolfe, *Plant Mgr*
▲ **EMP:** 65 **EST:** 1946
SQ FT: 25,000

SALES (est): 16.1MM
SALES (corp-wide): 674.9MM **Publicly Held**
WEB: www.climaxmetal.com
SIC: 3366 3568 Bushings & bearings; couplings, shaft: rigid, flexible, universal joint, etc.; collars, shaft (power transmission equipment)
PA: Rbc Bearings Incorporated
102 Willenbrock Rd
Oxford CT 06478
203 267-7001

(G-13417)
COASTAL DIAMOND INCORPORATED
7255 Industrial Park Blvd A (44060-5331)
PHONE................................440 946-7171
Art Bastulli, *President*
Kathleen Potts, *Corp Secy*
Jody Kamenshy, *Vice Pres*
Jeff Bastulli, *Sales Mgr*
EMP: 9
SQ FT: 7,500
SALES (est): 1MM **Privately Held**
WEB: www.coastaldiamond.com
SIC: 3291 5085 Abrasive products; industrial supplies

(G-13418)
COBB INDUSTRIES INC
7605 Saint Clair Ave (44060-5235)
PHONE................................440 946-4695
Lawrence Rokosky, *President*
Marcia Rokosky, *Vice Pres*
EMP: 4
SQ FT: 4,000
SALES: 500K **Privately Held**
SIC: 3544 Special dies, tools, jigs & fixtures

(G-13419)
COMMERCIAL DOCK & DOOR INC
7653 Saint Clair Ave (44060-5235)
PHONE................................440 951-1210
Allen A Kovar, *President*
Raymond M Strumbly, *Vice Pres*
Tom Liebhardt, *CFO*
EMP: 22
SALES (est): 3.8MM **Privately Held**
SIC: 3448 Docks: prefabricated metal

(G-13420)
COMMERCIAL MFG SVCS INC
Also Called: Cmsi
7123 Industrial Park Blvd (44060-5313)
PHONE................................440 953-2701
▼ **EMP:** 8
SQ FT: 20,000
SALES (est): 1.8MM **Privately Held**
SIC: 3679 3672 Mfg Electronic Components Mfg Printed Circuit Boards

(G-13421)
COMPETETIVE CARBIDE INC
Also Called: Competitive Carbide
9332 Pinecone Dr (44060-1861)
PHONE................................440 350-9393
Tom Cirino, *President*
Charlie Novak, *General Mgr*
Erik Hennie, *Engineer*
Craig Krivoy, *Sales Mgr*
Ralph Lehman, *Sales Engr*
▲ **EMP:** 40
SQ FT: 10,000
SALES (est): 6.6MM **Privately Held**
WEB: www.competitivecarbide.com
SIC: 3541 Machine tools, metal cutting type

(G-13422)
CORE MANUFACTURING LLC
8878 East Ave (44060-4306)
PHONE................................440 946-8002
Ted Wolf, *President*
Richard Stark, *Director*
David Sukenik, *Director*
Theodore Wolf, *Director*
EMP: 9
SALES (est): 1.5MM **Privately Held**
SIC: 3452 Bolts, nuts, rivets & washers

(G-13423)
CORE-TECH INC
7850 Enterprise Dr (44060-5310)
PHONE................................440 946-8324
Jim Corbett, *President*
Paul Lynch, *Manager*
Bob Salo, *Manager*
EMP: 5
SQ FT: 14,000
SALES (est): 1MM **Privately Held**
WEB: www.core-tech-inc.com
SIC: 3599 Machine shop, jobbing & repair

(G-13424)
CORY ELECTRONICS
7665 Mentor Ave 335 (44060-5409)
PHONE................................440 951-9424
Jason Fiore, *Engineer*
EMP: 3
SALES (est): 112.8K **Privately Held**
SIC: 3357 Aircraft wire & cable, nonferrous

(G-13425)
CR SUPPLY LLC
7661 Ohio St (44060-4848)
PHONE................................440 759-5408
Robert Hemly, *Mng Member*
EMP: 1
SQ FT: 2,500
SALES: 1MM **Privately Held**
SIC: 3545 Cutting tools for machine tools

(G-13426)
CRESCENT METAL PRODUCTS INC (PA)
Also Called: Cres Cor
5925 Heisley Rd (44060-1833)
PHONE................................440 350-1100
Clifford D Baggott, *Principal*
Rio Degennaro, *Vice Pres*
Gregory D Baggott, *Treasurer*
Heather B Stewart, *Admin Sec*
▲ **EMP:** 176 **EST:** 1936
SALES (est): 70.4MM **Privately Held**
WEB: www.crescor.com
SIC: 3556 3567 3537 2542 Food products machinery; industrial furnaces & ovens; industrial trucks & tractors; partitions & fixtures, except wood

(G-13427)
CREST PRODUCTS INC
Also Called: Crest Aluminum Products
8287 Tyler Blvd (44060-4218)
PHONE................................440 942-5770
John M Allin, *President*
Timothy Antos, *Vice Pres*
Peter Antos, *Treasurer*
Nancy Worden, *Admin Sec*
EMP: 18 **EST:** 1966
SQ FT: 41,500
SALES (est): 4.3MM **Privately Held**
WEB: www.crestproducts.com
SIC: 3444 7389 Awnings, sheet metal; metal slitting & shearing

(G-13428)
DANAHER CORPORATION
7171 Industrial Park Blvd (44060-5351)
PHONE................................440 995-3025
Mary Niederer, *Principal*
EMP: 173
SALES (corp-wide): 19.8B **Publicly Held**
SIC: 3823 Water quality monitoring & control systems
PA: Danaher Corporation
2200 Penn Ave Nw Ste 800w
Washington DC 20037
202 828-0850

(G-13429)
DAVENPORT SERVICE GROUP INC
7561 Tyler Blvd Ste 9 (44060-4867)
PHONE................................440 487-9353
Bart Davenport, *President*
Jennifer Davenport, *Treasurer*
EMP: 2
SALES: 1MM **Privately Held**
SIC: 7692 Welding repair

(G-13430)
DOC HOWARDS DISTILLERY
7737 Lucretia Ct (44060-5964)
PHONE................................440 488-9463

Sherri Howard, *Principal*
EMP: 3
SALES (est): 117.7K **Privately Held**
SIC: 2085 Distilled & blended liquors

(G-13431)
DOVER CORPORATION
7201 Industrial Park Blvd (44060-5315)
PHONE................................440 951-6600
Theodore Caldwell, *Branch Mgr*
EMP: 5
SALES (corp-wide): 6.9B **Publicly Held**
SIC: 3592 Pistons & piston rings
PA: Dover Corporation
3005 Highland Pkwy # 200
Downers Grove IL 60515
630 541-1540

(G-13432)
DRUMMOND DOLOMITE INC
Also Called: Drummond Dolomite Quarry
7954 Reynolds Rd (44060-5334)
P.O. Box 658 (44061-0658)
PHONE................................440 942-7000
Jerome T Osborne, *President*
Harold T Larned, *Vice Pres*
Ilda Hayden, *Admin Sec*
EMP: 10
SALES (est): 740K **Privately Held**
SIC: 1422 Dolomite, crushed & broken-quarrying

(G-13433)
DRYCAL INC
7355 Production Dr (44060-4858)
PHONE................................440 974-1999
Margus Sweigard, *President*
Lembit Sweigard, *Vice Pres*
EMP: 8
SQ FT: 14,500
SALES: 900K **Privately Held**
WEB: www.drycal.com
SIC: 2759 Screen printing

(G-13434)
DYNA-FLEX INC
7300 Industrial Park Blvd (44060-5318)
PHONE................................440 946-9424
James D'Amico, *President*
Bob Ritchie, *General Mgr*
Barbara D'Amico, *Vice Pres*
Jim Ritchie, *Engineer*
Laura Curtis, *Treasurer*
▲ **EMP:** 10
SALES (est): 1MM **Privately Held**
WEB: www.flexinc.com
SIC: 3492 Hose & tube couplings, hydraulic/pneumatic

(G-13435)
DYNAMIC SPECIALTIES INC
7471 Tyler Blvd Ste E (44060-5413)
PHONE................................440 946-2838
Charles Heinrich, *CEO*
Dorothy Heinrich, *Admin Sec*
EMP: 3 **EST:** 1970
SQ FT: 3,500
SALES: 100K **Privately Held**
SIC: 7692 Welding repair

(G-13436)
EASTERN SLIPCOVER COMPANY INC
6399 Cumberland Dr (44060-2465)
PHONE................................440 951-2310
John E Bolden, *President*
Pat Bolden, *Vice Pres*
EMP: 5
SQ FT: 1,300
SALES (est): 447.3K **Privately Held**
SIC: 2392 Slipcovers: made of fabric, plastic etc.

(G-13437)
EASY BOARD INC
8621 Station St (44060-4336)
PHONE................................440 205-8836
Sean Meaney, *President*
EMP: 5
SQ FT: 4,000
SALES: 400K **Privately Held**
WEB: www.easyboardinc.com
SIC: 2542 Office & store showcases & display fixtures

▲ = Import ▼ = Export
◆ = Import/Export

GEOGRAPHIC SECTION
Mentor - Lake County (G-13464)

(G-13438)
ELLEN L ELLSWORTH
9930 Johnnycake Ridge Rd 4b (44060-6752)
PHONE 440 352-8031
Ellen L Ellsworth, *Owner*
EMP: 5
SALES (est): 500.8K **Privately Held**
SIC: 3841 Optometers

(G-13439)
EMBROIDERED ID INC
Also Called: Embroidered Identity
7845 Hidden Hollow Dr (44060-7316)
PHONE 440 974-8113
Jacklyn Fatica, *President*
Diana Palmer, *Vice Pres*
EMP: 3
SQ FT: 1,200
SALES: 500K **Privately Held**
SIC: 5131 5949 2395 Sewing accessories; sewing, needlework & piece goods; embroidery products, except schiffli machine

(G-13440)
ENTERPRISE C N C INC
9280 Pineneedle Dr (44060-1824)
PHONE 440 354-3868
Ivan Katic, *President*
Michael Katic, *Vice Pres*
Slavko Katic, *Treasurer*
Gail Goll, *Finance Mgr*
Chris Weinkamer, *Admin Sec*
EMP: 4
SQ FT: 5,000
SALES: 150K **Privately Held**
SIC: 3599 Machine shop, jobbing & repair

(G-13441)
ENTERPRISE WELDING & FABG INC
6257 Heisley Rd (44060-1887)
PHONE 440 354-4128
Ivan Katic, *President*
Chris Weinkamer, *General Mgr*
Albert R Amigoni, *Principal*
Slavko Katic, *Treasurer*
Joe Katic, *CTO*
EMP: 170 **EST:** 1975
SQ FT: 100,000
SALES (est): 45.7MM **Privately Held**
WEB: www.enterprisewelding.com
SIC: 3444 Sheet metalwork

(G-13442)
EYE LIGHTING INTL N AMER INC
9150 Hendricks Rd (44060-2146)
PHONE 440 350-7000
Tsuneo Kobayashi, *CEO*
Tatsuyuki Kawajiri, *CEO*
Tom Salpietra, *President*
Greg Barry, *Vice Pres*
Greg R Barry, *Vice Pres*
▲ **EMP:** 170
SQ FT: 100,000
SALES: 29.4MM
SALES (corp-wide): 538MM **Privately Held**
WEB: www.eyelighting.com
SIC: 3229 3641 Pressed & blown glass; electric lamps & parts for generalized applications
PA: Iwasaki Electric Co.,Ltd.
1-4-16, Nihombashibakurocho
Chuo-Ku TKY 103-0
358 478-611

(G-13443)
FISCHER SPECIAL TOOLING CORP
7219 Commerce Dr (44060-5307)
PHONE 440 951-8411
Kevin Johnson, *President*
Molly Johnson, *Corp Secy*
Kathi McNichol, *Software Dev*
EMP: 14 **EST:** 1959
SQ FT: 5,000
SALES: 3MM **Privately Held**
WEB: www.fischerspecialtooling.com
SIC: 3541 3545 3544 Machine tools, metal cutting: exotic (explosive, etc.); drilling machine tools (metal cutting); reaming machines; machine tool accessories; special dies, tools, jigs & fixtures

(G-13444)
FMT REPAIR SERVICE CO
6374 Dawson Blvd (44060-3648)
PHONE 330 347-7374
Steve Shearer, *President*
Tom Warnick, *Vice Pres*
EMP: 3
SALES (est): 329.6K **Privately Held**
SIC: 3549 7699 1796 Wiredrawing & fabricating machinery & equipment, ex. die; mechanical instrument repair; installing building equipment

(G-13445)
FORMASTERS CORPORATION
5959 Pinecone Dr (44060-1866)
PHONE 440 639-9206
John J Ferguson, *President*
EMP: 12
SQ FT: 10,500
SALES (est): 2.6MM **Privately Held**
SIC: 3469 3449 Metal stampings; custom roll formed products

(G-13446)
FOUNDRY SUPPORT OPERATION
7849 Enterprise Dr (44060-5309)
PHONE 440 951-4142
Joshua Corvett, *Principal*
EMP: 15
SALES (est): 1MM **Privately Held**
SIC: 3471 Finishing, metals or formed products

(G-13447)
FRANTZ MEDICAL DEVELOPMENT LTD (PA)
7740 Metric Dr (44060-4862)
PHONE 440 255-1155
Mark G Frantz, *President*
J Paul Hanson, *Vice Pres*
Jeffrey Dunlop, *CFO*
EMP: 160
SQ FT: 3,750
SALES (est): 16MM **Privately Held**
WEB: www.frantz.com
SIC: 3841 3089 Surgical & medical instruments; injection molding of plastics

(G-13448)
FRANTZ MEDICAL DEVELOPMENT LTD
7740 Metric Dr (44060-4862)
PHONE 440 205-9026
Joe Lasher, *Opers-Prdtn-Mfg*
EMP: 75
SQ FT: 3,000
SALES: 5.8MM
SALES (corp-wide): 16MM **Privately Held**
WEB: www.frantz.com
SIC: 3841 3561 Surgical & medical instruments; pumps & pumping equipment
PA: Frantz Medical Development Ltd.
7740 Metric Dr
Mentor OH 44060
440 255-1155

(G-13449)
FRANTZ MEDICAL GROUP
7740 Metric Dr (44060-4862)
PHONE 440 974-8522
Mark Frantz, *Principal*
EMP: 32
SALES (est): 2.9MM **Privately Held**
SIC: 3841 Surgical & medical instruments

(G-13450)
FREDON CORPORATION
8990 Tyler Blvd (44060-5368)
P.O. Box 600 (44061-0600)
PHONE 440 951-5200
Roger J Sustar, *CEO*
Alyson Scott, *President*
Richard Ditto, *Vice Pres*
Chris Sustar, *Vice Pres*
▼ **EMP:** 80
SQ FT: 70,000
SALES (est): 16.2MM **Privately Held**
WEB: www.fredon.com
SIC: 3599 3541 Custom machinery; grinding machines, metalworking

(G-13451)
FREPEG INDUSTRIES INC
8624 East Ave (44060-4365)
PHONE 440 255-8595
Fred Stout, *President*
Peggy Stout, *Vice Pres*
EMP: 15
SQ FT: 8,000
SALES (est): 1.5MM **Privately Held**
SIC: 3469 Metal stampings

(G-13452)
FULTON SIGN & DECAL INC
7144 Industrial Park Blvd (44060-5314)
PHONE 440 951-1515
Charles Fulton, *President*
Gary Fulton, *General Mgr*
Gertrude Fulton, *Vice Pres*
Robert B Fulton, *Treasurer*
EMP: 6 **EST:** 1969
SQ FT: 5,000
SALES: 500K **Privately Held**
SIC: 3993 Signs & advertising specialties

(G-13453)
G & T MANUFACTURING CO
6085 Pinecone Dr (44060-1866)
PHONE 440 639-7777
Gerald Cutts, *President*
Thomas B Cutts, *President*
Pat Caticchio, *Principal*
Beverly Cutts, *Treasurer*
EMP: 19
SQ FT: 6,200
SALES (est): 3.1MM **Privately Held**
WEB: www.gtmanufacturingco.com
SIC: 3531 3537 Aerial work platforms: hydraulic/elec. truck/carrier mounted; industrial trucks & tractors

(G-13454)
G T M ASSOCIATES INC
7112 Industrial Park Blvd (44060-5314)
PHONE 440 951-0006
Antone Mutter, *President*
EMP: 4
SALES (est): 340K **Privately Held**
WEB: www.gtmassociates.com
SIC: 3599 Machine shop, jobbing & repair

(G-13455)
GDJ INC
Also Called: Technology Explortation Pdts
7585 Tyler Blvd (44060-4869)
PHONE 440 975-0258
Jack Gilbert, *President*
Deborah Gilbert, *Vice Pres*
EMP: 6
SQ FT: 6,500
SALES (est): 660K **Privately Held**
SIC: 3821 Laboratory equipment: fume hoods, distillation racks, etc.

(G-13456)
GENERAL GLASS & SCREEN INC
6095 Pinecone Dr (44060-1866)
PHONE 440 350-9033
Stephen Rostar, *President*
Heidi Rostar, *Vice Pres*
EMP: 4
SQ FT: 3,900
SALES (est): 625.6K **Privately Held**
SIC: 5231 3231 Glass; products of purchased glass

(G-13457)
GENESIS QUALITY PRINTING INC
7250 Commerce Dr Ste G (44060-5332)
P.O. Box 5157, Eastlake (44095-0157)
PHONE 440 975-5700
Edward Dulzer, *President*
EMP: 3
SQ FT: 1,700
SALES (est): 261.7K **Privately Held**
SIC: 2759 2791 2752 Commercial printing; typesetting; commercial printing, lithographic

(G-13458)
GENII INC
5976 Heisley Rd (44060-1873)
PHONE 651 501-4810
Marcia Morris, *CEO*
EMP: 5
SQ FT: 1,500
SALES (est): 873.6K
SALES (corp-wide): 2.6B **Privately Held**
WEB: www.genii-gi.com
SIC: 3845 Ultrasonic scanning devices, medical
HQ: United States Endoscopy Group, Inc.
5976 Heisley Rd
Mentor OH 44060
440 639-4494

(G-13459)
GLO-QUARTZ ELECTRIC HEATER CO
7084 Maple St (44060-4932)
P.O. Box 358 (44061-0358)
PHONE 440 255-9701
George T Strokes, *President*
Nancy L Strokes, *Corp Secy*
Thomas M Strokes, *Exec VP*
EMP: 25 **EST:** 1952
SQ FT: 22,000
SALES (est): 5.8MM **Privately Held**
SIC: 3567 3823 3634 3433 Heating units & devices, industrial: electric; industrial instrmnts msrmnt display/control process variable; electric housewares & fans; heating equipment, except electric

(G-13460)
GLOBAL MANUFACTURING TECH LLC
8671 Tyler Blvd Unit F (44060-4347)
PHONE 440 205-1001
Jeffrey T Rose,
Kenny Anderson,
EMP: 5
SQ FT: 6,000
SALES: 234K **Privately Held**
SIC: 3469 Machine parts, stamped or pressed metal

(G-13461)
GOAL MEDICAL LLC
7555 Tyler Blvd (44060-4866)
PHONE 541 654-5951
Scott Cottrell, *President*
EMP: 25 **EST:** 2013
SQ FT: 5,000
SALES (est): 1.3MM **Privately Held**
SIC: 3841 Surgical & medical instruments

(G-13462)
GREAT LAKES POWER PRODUCTS INC (PA)
Also Called: John Deere Authorized Dealer
7455 Tyler Blvd (44060-8389)
PHONE 440 951-5111
Harry Allen Jr, *CEO*
Harry L Allen Jr, *Ch of Bd*
Richard J Pennza, *President*
David Bell, *Vice Pres*
Sam Profio, *Vice Pres*
▲ **EMP:** 60
SQ FT: 55,000
SALES (est): 31.9MM **Privately Held**
WEB: www.glpowerlift.com
SIC: 5085 5084 3566 Power transmission equipment & apparatus; materials handling machinery; speed changers (power transmission equipment), except auto

(G-13463)
HABCO TOOL AND DEV CO INC
7725 Metric Dr (44060-4863)
PHONE 440 946-5546
Steven Sanders, *President*
Ron Giannetti, *Exec VP*
James Patchin, *Plant Mgr*
Kathy Fulmer, *Purchasing*
EMP: 46 **EST:** 1955
SQ FT: 24,000
SALES: 3MM **Privately Held**
WEB: www.habcotool.com
SIC: 3599 7692 Machine shop, jobbing & repair; welding repair

(G-13464)
HENKEL US OPERATIONS CORP
7405 Production Dr (44060-4876)
PHONE 440 255-8900
Tim Viskocil, *Plant Mgr*
Brian Elston, *Engineer*
Robert Kern, *Branch Mgr*

Mentor - Lake County (G-13465)

Stephen Sicree, *Manager*
EMP: 35
SALES (corp-wide): 22.7B **Privately Held**
SIC: 2891 Adhesives
HQ: Henkel Us Operations Corporation
1 Henkel Way
Rocky Hill CT 06067
860 571-5100

(G-13465)
HI TEK MOLD
7777 Saint Clair Ave (44060-5237)
PHONE..................440 942-4090
EMP: 7
SQ FT: 7,500
SALES (est): 370K **Privately Held**
SIC: 3089 Mfg Plastic Injection Molds

(G-13466)
HIGHLAND PRODUCTS CORP
9331 Mercantile Dr (44060-4523)
PHONE..................440 352-4777
Mark Erickson, *President*
Jeanne Wojciechowicz, *Corp Secy*
Matt Nolan, *Plant Mgr*
EMP: 10
SQ FT: 11,000
SALES (est): 1.7MM **Privately Held**
SIC: 3599 Machine shop, jobbing & repair

(G-13467)
HOLLOW BORING INC
7832 Enterprise Dr (44060-5310)
P.O. Box 58 (44061-0058)
PHONE..................440 951-2929
Joseph Cerne, *President*
EMP: 4
SQ FT: 3,000
SALES (est): 468.3K **Privately Held**
SIC: 3599 Machine shop, jobbing & repair

(G-13468)
HYPROLAP FINISHING CO
9300 Pinecone Dr (44060-1861)
PHONE..................440 352-0270
Elmer Guiher, *President*
EMP: 5
SQ FT: 7,000
SALES: 600K **Privately Held**
SIC: 3599 Machine shop, jobbing & repair

(G-13469)
INDUSTRIAL QUARTZ CORP
7552 Saint Clair Ave D (44060-5201)
PHONE..................440 942-0909
Richard Intihar, *President*
Robert Intihar, *General Mgr*
Bob Intihar, *Sales Executive*
Sue Kozlowski, *Office Mgr*
▲ **EMP:** 19
SQ FT: 10,000
SALES: 3.6MM **Privately Held**
SIC: 3295 3769 3677 3498 Minerals, ground or treated; guided missile & space vehicle parts & auxiliary equipment; electronic coils, transformers & other inductors; fabricated pipe & fittings

(G-13470)
INDUSTRIAL SYSTEMS & SOLUTIONS
Also Called: ISS
8812 Tyler Blvd (44060-4361)
PHONE..................440 205-1658
David Kelley, *President*
Dawn Hoban, *CFO*
EMP: 3
SQ FT: 2,200
SALES: 100K **Privately Held**
WEB: www.industrialss.com
SIC: 3694 Distributors, motor vehicle engine

(G-13471)
INDUSTRIAL THERMOSET PLAS INC
Also Called: I.T. Plastics
7675 Jenther Dr (44060-4872)
PHONE..................440 975-0411
Jack Schriner, *President*
EMP: 10
SQ FT: 8,000
SALES (est): 1.3MM **Privately Held**
WEB: www.itplastics.com
SIC: 2821 Plastics materials & resins

(G-13472)
INTEGRA ENCLOSURES LIMITED
8989 Tyler Blvd (44060-2184)
PHONE..................440 269-4966
EMP: 100
SALES (est): 3.2MM **Privately Held**
SIC: 2821 Thermoplastic materials

(G-13473)
INTEGRATED MED SOLUTIONS INC
7124 Industrial Park Blvd (44060-5314)
PHONE..................440 269-6984
Mike Watts, *President*
Lee Dwyer, *Principal*
Gus Deangelo, *CFO*
EMP: 60
SALES (est): 10.7MM **Privately Held**
WEB: www.astromodel.com
SIC: 3841 3842 Diagnostic apparatus, medical; surgical appliances & supplies

(G-13474)
INTERNATIONAL HYDRAULICS INC
Also Called: Ihi Connectors R
7700 Saint Clair Ave (44060-5238)
PHONE..................440 951-7186
Charles Ridley, *President*
Paul Ridley, *Business Mgr*
Lori Silvis, *QC Mgr*
Karen Rist, *Manager*
▲ **EMP:** 50
SQ FT: 62,000
SALES (est): 11.7MM **Privately Held**
WEB: www.ihiconnectors.com
SIC: 3643 Electric connectors

(G-13475)
INTERPAK INC
Also Called: Roto Mold
7278 Justin Way (44060-4881)
PHONE..................440 974-8999
Mark Shaw, *President*
Tad Heyman, *Vice Pres*
Mark Eubank, *Sales Mgr*
▼ **EMP:** 43
SQ FT: 65,000
SALES (est): 6.8MM **Privately Held**
WEB: www.rotomold.com
SIC: 3089 Injection molding of plastics

(G-13476)
ISOMEDIX INC
5960 Heisley Rd (44060-1834)
PHONE..................440 354-2600
Mike Tokich, *Senior VP*
Clint Olsen, *Plant Mgr*
Michelle Zirngible, *Plant Mgr*
▲ **EMP:** 9
SALES (est): 1.9MM
SALES (corp-wide): 2.6B **Privately Held**
WEB: www.steris.com
SIC: 3842 Surgical appliances & supplies
HQ: Steris Corporation
5960 Heisley Rd
Mentor OH 44060
440 354-2600

(G-13477)
ITECGRAPHIX INC
7417 Mentor Ave (44060-5405)
PHONE..................440 951-5020
Virginia Forbes, *Principal*
David Forbes, *Principal*
EMP: 4
SALES (est): 100K **Privately Held**
SIC: 3993 Signs & advertising specialties

(G-13478)
J & C GROUP INC OF OHIO
6781 Hopkins Rd (44060-4311)
PHONE..................440 205-9658
James J Smolik, *President*
Christine Smolik, *Shareholder*
▲ **EMP:** 22
SQ FT: 13,000
SALES (est): 4.1MM **Privately Held**
SIC: 3679 Electronic circuits

(G-13479)
J & L MANAGEMENT CORPORATION
Also Called: Kramer Printing
8634 Station St (44060-4316)
PHONE..................440 205-1199
Leonard Kramer, *Partner*
Gerald Kramer, *Partner*
EMP: 6
SQ FT: 7,000
SALES (est): 932.2K **Privately Held**
SIC: 2752 2732 Commercial printing, offset; book printing

(G-13480)
J & M CUTTING TOOLS INC
9401 Hamilton Dr (44060-8709)
PHONE..................440 622-3900
Fax: 440 354-2325
EMP: 8
SQ FT: 3,200
SALES (est): 790K **Privately Held**
SIC: 3451 Mfg Screw Machine Products

(G-13481)
J & M INDUSTRIES INC
7775 Division Dr (44060-4861)
PHONE..................440 951-1985
David Martin, *President*
EMP: 8 **EST:** 2000
SQ FT: 8,000
SALES: 500K **Privately Held**
WEB: www.jandmmold.com
SIC: 3544 Dies & die holders for metal cutting, forming, die casting

(G-13482)
J & P PRODUCTS INC
Also Called: Specialties Unlimited
8865 East Ave (44060-4305)
PHONE..................440 974-2830
Paul Jonke, *President*
Dennis Jonke, *Admin Sec*
EMP: 34
SQ FT: 18,000
SALES (est): 5.3MM **Privately Held**
WEB: www.specialtiesunlimited.net
SIC: 3599 Machine shop, jobbing & repair

(G-13483)
JACK WALKER PRINTING CO
9517 Jackson St (44060-4515)
PHONE..................440 352-4222
Jack G Walker, *President*
Mike Walker, *Vice Pres*
Jim Whitlow, *Opers Staff*
▲ **EMP:** 18
SQ FT: 3,500
SALES (est): 2.1MM **Privately Held**
SIC: 2752 2791 2789 2759 Commercial printing, offset; typesetting; bookbinding & related work; commercial printing

(G-13484)
JADE PRODUCTS INC
9309 Mercantile Dr (44060-4523)
PHONE..................440 352-1700
John Erickson, *President*
Joseph Erickson, *Engineer*
Elyse Pietravoia, *Clerk*
EMP: 17
SQ FT: 5,500
SALES (est): 3.2MM **Privately Held**
SIC: 3599 Machine shop, jobbing & repair

(G-13485)
JJ SLEEVES INC
6850 Patterson Dr (44060-4331)
PHONE..................440 205-1055
Allen Beach, *Sales Mgr*
EMP: 8
SALES: 800K **Privately Held**
WEB: www.advancedsleeve.com
SIC: 3599 Machine shop, jobbing & repair

(G-13486)
JOHN D OIL AND GAS COMPANY
7001 Center St (44060-4933)
P.O. Box 5069 (44061-5069)
PHONE..................440 255-6325
Richard M Osborne, *Ch of Bd*
Timothy P Reilly, *President*
Carolyn Coatoam, *CFO*
EMP: 7

SALES (est): 1.8MM **Privately Held**
SIC: 1382 1311 4225 Oil & gas exploration services; crude petroleum & natural gas production; warehousing, self-storage

(G-13487)
JOHNSTON MANUFACTURING INC
Also Called: J M C Rollmasters
7611 Saint Clair Ave (44060-5235)
PHONE..................440 269-1420
Dennis Johnston, *President*
Marsha Johnston, *Corp Secy*
EMP: 8 **EST:** 1968
SQ FT: 8,500
SALES (est): 1.5MM **Privately Held**
SIC: 3544 Special dies & tools

(G-13488)
KAEPER MACHINE INC
8680 Twinbrook Rd (44060-4341)
PHONE..................440 974-1010
Kye Hwang, *President*
Mike Kidner, *Principal*
EMP: 20
SALES (est): 3.5MM **Privately Held**
SIC: 3545 3484 Precision tools, machinists'; small arms; machine guns or machine gun parts, 30 mm. & below; pistols or pistol parts, 30 mm. & below; shotguns or shotgun parts, 30 mm. & below

(G-13489)
KICHER AND COMPANY (PA)
6942 Spinach Dr (44060-4958)
PHONE..................440 266-1663
Thomas P Kicher, *President*
Thomas Kicher, *VP Engrg*
EMP: 9
SALES (est): 950.8K **Privately Held**
SIC: 3829 Measuring & controlling devices

(G-13490)
KITCHEN & BATH FACTORY INC
7170 Hawthorne Dr (44060-4631)
PHONE..................440 510-8111
Louis Hundza, *President*
EMP: 3
SALES (est): 278.3K **Privately Held**
SIC: 2541 Counter & sink tops

(G-13491)
KSI DISTRIBUTION INC (PA)
8724 Tyler Blvd (44060-4350)
PHONE..................440 256-2500
Lynn Keegan, *Principal*
James P Keegan, *Principal*
EMP: 3
SALES (est): 407.6K **Privately Held**
SIC: 3465 Body parts, automobile: stamped metal

(G-13492)
L B WEISS CONSTRUCTION INC
Also Called: Weiss Construction & Sewer
8677 Twinbrook Rd (44060-4340)
PHONE..................440 205-1774
L Weiss, *President*
Lavele Weiss, *President*
Shirley Weiss, *Admin Sec*
EMP: 4
SQ FT: 3,600
SALES (est): 600.5K **Privately Held**
SIC: 3272 Sewer pipe, concrete

(G-13493)
L J MANUFACTURING INC
9436 Mercantile Dr (44060-1889)
PHONE..................440 352-1979
Michael Ball, *President*
Darlene Ball, *Admin Sec*
EMP: 8
SQ FT: 10,000
SALES (est): 1.1MM **Privately Held**
WEB: www.ljmfg.com
SIC: 3599 Machine shop, jobbing & repair

(G-13494)
LAKE COUNTY PLATING CORP
7790 Division Dr (44060-4860)
PHONE..................440 255-8835
Charles H Dowling, *President*
Janet Dowling, *Vice Pres*
EMP: 10 **EST:** 1958
SQ FT: 20,000

▲ = Import ▼ = Export
◆ = Import/Export

GEOGRAPHIC SECTION

Mentor - Lake County (G-13522)

SALES (est): 660K **Privately Held**
WEB: www.lakecountyplating.com
SIC: **3471** Plating of metals or formed products

(G-13495)
LAKE PUBLISHING INC
Also Called: Callender Group, The
9853 Johnnycake Ridge Rd # 107 (44060-6700)
PHONE..............................440 299-8500
James S Callender Jr, *Principal*
Heidi Callender, *Officer*
EMP: 7 EST: 2009
SQ FT: 1,100
SALES (est): 387.6K **Privately Held**
SIC: **2741 8748** Miscellaneous publishing; business consulting

(G-13496)
LANKO INDUSTRIES INC
7301 Industrial Park Blvd (44060-5317)
PHONE..............................440 269-1641
John Lanphier, *President*
Susan Lanphier, *Admin Sec*
EMP: 8
SQ FT: 9,000
SALES (est): 1.2MM **Privately Held**
SIC: **3544** Wire drawing & straightening dies; special dies & tools

(G-13497)
LASERDEALER INC
9323 Hamilton Dr (44060-4559)
PHONE..............................440 357-8419
R Burns, *Principal*
EMP: 3
SALES (est): 120.3K **Privately Held**
WEB: www.laserdealer.com
SIC: **3479** Name plates: engraved, etched, etc.

(G-13498)
LIBRA INDUSTRIES INC (PA)
7770 Division Dr (44060-4860)
PHONE..............................440 974-7770
Rod Howell, *CEO*
Albert Catani, *COO*
EMP: 120 EST: 1980
SQ FT: 52,000
SALES (est): 41.1MM **Privately Held**
WEB: www.libraind.com
SIC: **3699** Electrical equipment & supplies

(G-13499)
LIBRA INDUSTRIES INC
7715 Metric Dr (44060-4863)
PHONE..............................440 974-7770
Ron Rehberger, *Mfg Mgr*
EMP: 40
SALES (corp-wide): 41.1MM **Privately Held**
WEB: www.libraind.com
SIC: **3672** Printed circuit boards
PA: Libra Industries, Inc.
7770 Division Dr
Mentor OH 44060
440 974-7770

(G-13500)
LINCOLN ELECTRIC HOLDINGS INC
Mentor Mfg Fcility Div
6500 Heisley Rd (44060-1805)
PHONE..............................440 255-7696
Jeff Iannini, *Plant Mgr*
Bill Cooper, *Engineer*
Michael Sorine, *Maintence Staff*
EMP: 540
SALES (corp-wide): 3B **Publicly Held**
WEB: www.lincolnelectric.com
SIC: **3548** Welding wire, bare & coated
PA: Lincoln Electric Holdings, Inc.
22801 Saint Clair Ave
Cleveland OH 44117
216 481-8100

(G-13501)
LINTERN CORPORATION (PA)
8685 Station St (44060-4336)
P.O. Box 90 (44061-0090)
PHONE..............................440 255-9333
Richard K Lintern, *President*
Tyler Smith, *COO*
Ray Ohler, *Vice Pres*
Beixiong Zhang, *Vice Pres*
Louann Zook, *Purch Agent*
◆ EMP: 38 EST: 1903
SQ FT: 22,500
SALES: 6MM **Privately Held**
WEB: www.lintern.com
SIC: **3585 3714 3648** Air conditioning units, complete: domestic or industrial; heaters, motor vehicle; filters: oil, fuel & air, motor vehicle; lanterns: electric, gas, carbide, kerosene or gasoline

(G-13502)
LOECY PRECISION MANUFACTURING
9180 Hilo Farm Dr (44060-7935)
PHONE..............................440 358-0551
EMP: 14
SQ FT: 15,000
SALES (est): 2MM **Privately Held**
SIC: **3599** Mfg Industrial Machinery

(G-13503)
LUMINAUD INC
8688 Tyler Blvd (44060-4348)
PHONE..............................440 255-9082
Thomas Lennox, *President*
Dorothy Lennox, *Vice Pres*
EMP: 7
SQ FT: 5,000
SALES (est): 1.1MM **Privately Held**
SIC: **3842** Limbs, artificial

(G-13504)
M P MACHINE INC
8743 East Ave (44060-4303)
PHONE..............................440 255-8355
Bennie Barbera, *President*
Cettina Barbera, *Admin Sec*
EMP: 3
SQ FT: 4,000
SALES (est): 411.1K **Privately Held**
SIC: **3599** Machine shop, jobbing & repair

(G-13505)
MAC DHUI PROBE OF AMERICA INC
7867 Enterprise Dr 9 (44060-5309)
PHONE..............................440 942-5597
Raymond Janasek, *President*
EMP: 3 EST: 1980
SQ FT: 1,200
SALES (est): 366.8K **Privately Held**
SIC: **3841** Probes, surgical

(G-13506)
MACEK INDUSTRIES
8830 Tyler Blvd (44060-4361)
PHONE..............................440 205-8711
James Macek, *Owner*
EMP: 4
SQ FT: 2,000
SALES: 450K **Privately Held**
SIC: **3544** Special dies, tools, jigs & fixtures

(G-13507)
MAG MACHINE INC
7243 Industrial Park Blvd (44060-5315)
PHONE..............................440 946-3381
Michael R Spehar, *President*
EMP: 4
SQ FT: 1,640
SALES (est): 514.6K **Privately Held**
SIC: **3599** Machine shop, jobbing & repair

(G-13508)
MAG-NIF INC
8820 East Ave (44060-4390)
P.O. Box 720 (44061-0720)
PHONE..............................440 255-9366
William W Knox Jr, *Ch of Bd*
Dennis Delaat, *Vice Pres*
Jim Weiss, *Treasurer*
▲ EMP: 100
SQ FT: 180,000
SALES (est): 18.7MM **Privately Held**
WEB: www.magnif.com
SIC: **3944 3089** Banks, toy; puzzles; injection molding of plastics

(G-13509)
MALISH CORPORATION (PA)
7333 Corporate Blvd (44060-4857)
PHONE..............................440 951-5356
Jeffery J Malish, *President*
Ken Shary, *President*
Fred Lombardi, *Vice Pres*
Mark Ray, *Treasurer*
◆ EMP: 115 EST: 1948
SQ FT: 82,000
SALES (est): 23.5MM **Privately Held**
WEB: www.malish.com
SIC: **3991 3089** Brushes, household or industrial; extruded finished plastic products

(G-13510)
MALONE SPECIALTY INC
8900 East Ave (44060-4306)
PHONE..............................440 255-4200
Steven Malone, *President*
▲ EMP: 12
SQ FT: 10,000
SALES (est): 3.6MM **Privately Held**
WEB: www.malonespecialtyinc.com
SIC: **5013 3492** Truck parts & accessories; hose & tube fittings & assemblies, hydraulic/pneumatic

(G-13511)
MARTIN & MARIANNE TOOLS INC
9335 Kathleen Dr (44060-4479)
PHONE..............................440 255-5107
Martin Sherman, *President*
EMP: 6
SALES (est): 656.2K **Privately Held**
SIC: **3541** Drilling machine tools (metal cutting)

(G-13512)
MATRIX TOOL & MACHINE INC
7870 Division Dr (44060-4874)
PHONE..............................440 255-0300
Richard Wilson, *President*
George Maust, *Vice Pres*
Rich Wilson, *Opers Mgr*
John Bourne, *Materials Mgr*
Patty Wilson, *Office Mgr*
EMP: 24
SQ FT: 20,000
SALES (est): 3.8MM **Privately Held**
SIC: **3599 3545** Custom machinery; machine tool accessories

(G-13513)
MEAK SOLUTIONS LLC
7315 Industrial Park Blvd (44060-5317)
PHONE..............................440 796-8209
Eric Kettani, *Mng Member*
Amir Kettani, *Mng Member*
EMP: 2
SALES: 1.2MM **Privately Held**
SIC: **3728 6799 3569 3724** Blades, aircraft propeller: metal or wood; refueling equipment for use in flight, airplane; commodity contract trading companies; baling machines, for scrap metal, paper or similar material; turbo-superchargers, aircraft

(G-13514)
MEDALLION LIGHTING CORPORATION
Also Called: Complements Lighting
8710 East Ave (44060-4304)
P.O. Box 51 (44061-0051)
PHONE..............................440 255-8383
William A Knuff, *President*
Kenneth Maclean, *COO*
Greg Swan, *Manager*
◆ EMP: 40 EST: 1982
SQ FT: 50,000
SALES (est): 7.4MM **Privately Held**
WEB: www.medallionlighting.com
SIC: **3645 3641 2514** Table lamps; floor lamps; wall lamps; electric lamps; metal household furniture

(G-13515)
MENTOR GLASS SUPPLIES AND REPR
8985 Osborne Dr (44060-4326)
PHONE..............................440 255-9444
David Reed, *President*
Robert Reed, *Vice Pres*
EMP: 3
SQ FT: 2,000
SALES (est): 279.5K **Privately Held**
SIC: **3211 7536 1793** Insulating glass, sealed units; automotive glass replacement shops; glass & glazing work

(G-13516)
MENTOR SIGNS & GRAPHICS INC
Also Called: Soulsby, John
7522a Tyler Blvd Ste A (44060-5450)
PHONE..............................440 951-7446
John Soulsby, *President*
Chas Irish, *Graphic Designe*
EMP: 4
SQ FT: 2,600
SALES: 180K **Privately Held**
SIC: **3993** Signs, not made in custom sign painting shops

(G-13517)
METAL SEAL PRECISION LTD (PA)
8687 Tyler Blvd (44060-4346)
PHONE..............................440 255-8888
John L Habe IV, *President*
Allan B Pirnat, *Vice Pres*
James Snyder, *Controller*
▼ EMP: 75
SQ FT: 158,000
SALES (est): 34.3MM **Privately Held**
SIC: **3444** Sheet metalwork

(G-13518)
MICRO LABORATORIES INC
7158 Industrial Park Blvd (44060-5314)
PHONE..............................440 918-0001
Keith Kokal, *President*
Kirk Kokal, *Vice Pres*
EMP: 6
SQ FT: 1,500
SALES (est): 670K **Privately Held**
SIC: **3829 8734** Measuring & controlling devices; testing laboratories

(G-13519)
MILL ROSE LABORATORIES INC
7310 Corp Blvd (44060)
PHONE..............................440 974-6730
Paul M Miller, *President*
Stephen W Kovalcheck Jr, *CFO*
Lawrence W Miller, *Admin Sec*
▲ EMP: 40 EST: 1977
SQ FT: 59,000
SALES (est): 6.3MM
SALES (corp-wide): 32.4MM **Privately Held**
WEB: www.millrose.com
SIC: **3991 5047** Brooms & brushes; medical equipment & supplies
PA: The Mill-Rose Company
7995 Tyler Blvd
Mentor OH 44060
440 255-9171

(G-13520)
MILL-ROSE COMPANY (PA)
7995 Tyler Blvd (44060-4896)
PHONE..............................440 255-9171
Paul M Miller, *President*
Lawrence W Miller, *Vice Pres*
Diane Miller, *Admin Sec*
▲ EMP: 160
SQ FT: 61,000
SALES (est): 32.4MM **Privately Held**
WEB: www.millrose.com
SIC: **3841 5085 3991 3624** Surgical instruments & apparatus; industrial supplies; brushes, industrial; brushes, household or industrial; carbon & graphite products; abrasive products

(G-13521)
MINUTEMAN PRESS
7450 Mentor Ave (44060-5406)
PHONE..............................440 946-3311
Steven Shaeffer, *Owner*
EMP: 4
SQ FT: 1,400
SALES (est): 409.2K **Privately Held**
SIC: **2752** Commercial printing, lithographic

(G-13522)
MONODE MARKING PRODUCTS INC (PA)
Also Called: Waldorf Marking Devices Div
9200 Tyler Blvd (44060-1882)
PHONE..............................440 975-8802
Tom Mackey, *President*

EMP: 65
SQ FT: 15,000
SALES (est): 12.3MM **Privately Held**
SIC: 3542 5084 Marking machines; printing trades machinery, equipment & supplies

(G-13523)
MONODE STEEL STAMP INC
7620 Tyler Blvd (44060-4853)
PHONE.................................440 975-8802
Chris Lillstrung, *Manager*
EMP: 15
SALES (corp-wide): 1.8MM **Privately Held**
WEB: www.monode.com
SIC: 3542 3469 Marking machines; metal stampings
PA: Monode Steel Stamp, Inc
  149 High St
  New London OH 44851
  419 929-3501

(G-13524)
MSD PRODUCTS INC
7842 Enterprise Dr (44060-5310)
PHONE.................................440 946-0040
Mark Davis, *President*
EMP: 4
SQ FT: 3,000
SALES: 300K **Privately Held**
SIC: 3599 Machine shop, jobbing & repair

(G-13525)
MUM INDUSTRIES INC
8989 Tyler Blvd (44060-2184)
P.O. Box 1870 (44061-1870)
PHONE.................................440 269-4966
Jim Cooney, *President*
Chris Brizes, *Vice Pres*
Tricia Stokes, *Project Mgr*
William Tidwell, *Engineer*
Maggie Donnelly, *Controller*
▲ **EMP:** 32
SALES (est): 8.1MM **Privately Held**
WEB: www.mumindustries.com
SIC: 2821 Plasticizer/additive based plastic materials

(G-13526)
NEW TRANSCON LLC
Also Called: Transcon Conveyor
8824 Twinbrook Rd (44060-4335)
PHONE.................................440 255-7600
Robert W Bruml, *Mng Member*
Roger Breedlove,
◆ **EMP:** 26 **EST:** 1959
SQ FT: 45,000
SALES (est): 6.4MM **Privately Held**
WEB: www.transconinc.com
SIC: 3535 Belt conveyor systems, general industrial use

(G-13527)
NHVS INTERNATIONAL INC
7600 Tyler Blvd (44060-4853)
PHONE.................................440 527-8610
Sherry Richcreek, *CEO*
Asija Buljan, *Plant Mgr*
Heather Richcreek, *Plant Mgr*
Kelly Cameron, *Controller*
Chris Bonney, *Asst Controller*
EMP: 325
SQ FT: 100,000
SALES (est): 28.6MM **Privately Held**
SIC: 3812 Acceleration indicators & systems components, aerospace

(G-13528)
NIFTECH INC
Also Called: Niftech Precision Race Pdts
5565 Wilson Dr (44060-1555)
PHONE.................................440 257-6018
Julie Knaus, *President*
Raymond Knaus, *Vice Pres*
EMP: 10
SALES: 200K **Privately Held**
SIC: 3699 Electrical equipment & supplies

(G-13529)
NORTH COAST MEDI-TEK INC
8603 East Ave (44060-4366)
PHONE.................................440 974-0750
Teri Sokolowski, *President*
Robert Sokolowski, *Vice Pres*
EMP: 11
SQ FT: 6,600
SALES (est): 1.8MM **Privately Held**
SIC: 3841 Surgical & medical instruments

(G-13530)
NORTHCOAST VALVE AND GATE INC
9437 Mercantile Dr (44060-4524)
PHONE.................................440 392-9910
Anthony Fistek, *President*
EMP: 8
SALES (est): 1.4MM **Privately Held**
SIC: 3494 Valves & pipe fittings

(G-13531)
O H TECHNOLOGIES INC
9300 Progress Pkwy (44060-1859)
P.O. Box 5039 (44061-5039)
PHONE.................................440 354-8780
Dwight Bowden, *President*
EMP: 3 **EST:** 1975
SQ FT: 5,000
SALES (est): 511.8K **Privately Held**
WEB: www.ohtech.com
SIC: 3825 Test equipment for electronic & electric measurement

(G-13532)
OE EXCHANGE LLC (PA)
8200 Tyler Blvd (44060-4252)
PHONE.................................440 266-1639
Peter L Mooney,
EMP: 8
SALES (est): 1.2MM **Privately Held**
SIC: 3714 Wheels, motor vehicle

(G-13533)
OLD SALT TEES
9777 Little Mountain Rd (44060-8227)
PHONE.................................440 463-0628
Dawn Bokar, *Principal*
EMP: 3
SALES (est): 121.7K **Privately Held**
SIC: 2759 Screen printing

(G-13534)
OMEGA MACHINE & TOOL INC
7590 Jenther Dr (44060-4872)
PHONE.................................440 946-6846
Dolf Litschel, *President*
Ema Litschel, *Vice Pres*
EMP: 10
SQ FT: 9,000
SALES: 1MM **Privately Held**
SIC: 3599 Machine shop, jobbing & repair

(G-13535)
ORBIS CORPORATION
7212 Justin Way (44060-4881)
PHONE.................................440 974-3857
Kim Holland, *Marketing Staff*
Kim Cantwell, *Manager*
Dwayne Hughes, *Manager*
EMP: 120
SALES (corp-wide): 1.7B **Privately Held**
WEB: www.orbiscorporation.com
SIC: 3089 Synthetic resin finished products
HQ: Orbis Corporation
  1055 Corporate Center Dr
  Oconomowoc WI 53066
  262 560-5000

(G-13536)
ORDNANCE CLEANING SYSTEMS LLC
7895 Division Dr (44060-4877)
PHONE.................................440 205-0677
Jeffrey Allenby,
EMP: 5
SQ FT: 14,000
SALES (est): 205.8K **Privately Held**
SIC: 3489 Ordnance & accessories

(G-13537)
OSAIR INC (PA)
7001 Center St (44060-4933)
P.O. Box 1020 (44061-1020)
PHONE.................................440 974-6500
Richard Osborne, *President*
Jon Magnusson, *Vice Pres*
EMP: 9
SQ FT: 4,000
SALES (est): 15.5MM **Privately Held**
SIC: 1381 2813 Drilling oil & gas wells; nitrogen

(G-13538)
OSAIR INC
8649 East Ave (44060-4366)
PHONE.................................440 255-8238
John Magnusson, *Manager*
EMP: 3
SALES (corp-wide): 15.5MM **Privately Held**
SIC: 3569 Separators for steam, gas, vapor or air (machinery)
PA: Osair, Inc.
  7001 Center St
  Mentor OH 44060
  440 974-6500

(G-13539)
OSBORNE INC (PA)
7954 Reynolds Rd (44060-5334)
P.O. Box 658 (44061-0658)
PHONE.................................440 942-7000
Jerome T Osborne, *Principal*
William Mackey, *Treasurer*
▲ **EMP:** 25
SQ FT: 4,500
SALES (est): 15MM **Privately Held**
SIC: 5211 3273 3271 Lumber & other building materials; ready-mixed concrete; blocks, concrete or cinder: standard

(G-13540)
PAKO INC
7615 Jenther Dr (44060-4872)
PHONE.................................440 946-8030
Paul Kosir, *President*
Drazen Blazevic, *Production*
Stan Krulc, *Production*
Adam Perusek, *Purch Mgr*
Dave Dudor, *Buyer*
▲ **EMP:** 246
SQ FT: 142,000
SALES (est): 80.6MM **Privately Held**
WEB: www.pako.com
SIC: 3728 3714 Aircraft parts & equipment; motor vehicle parts & accessories

(G-13541)
PANELBLOC INC
8665 Tyler Blvd (44060-4346)
PHONE.................................440 974-8877
Betty Gotliebowski, *President*
Raymond Gotliebowski Jr, *Exec VP*
EMP: 10
SQ FT: 7,800
SALES: 400K **Privately Held**
WEB: www.panelbloc.com
SIC: 3433 Gas infrared heating units

(G-13542)
PARKER-HANNIFIN CORPORATION
Also Called: Gas Turbine Fuel Systems
8940 Tyler Blvd (44060-2185)
PHONE.................................440 266-2300
Chuck Bovard, *Engineer*
Andrew McClelland, *Engineer*
Jeff Melzak, *Engineer*
Phil Tate, *Engineer*
Glen Weis, *Engineer*
EMP: 50
SALES (corp-wide): 14.3B **Publicly Held**
WEB: www.parker.com
SIC: 3594 Fluid power pumps
PA: Parker-Hannifin Corporation
  6035 Parkland Blvd
  Cleveland OH 44124
  216 896-3000

(G-13543)
PARKER-HANNIFIN CORPORATION
Gas Turbine Fuel Systems Div
8940 Tyler Blvd (44060-2185)
PHONE.................................440 205-8230
Less Conner, *Manager*
EMP: 168
SALES (corp-wide): 12B **Publicly Held**
WEB: www.parker.com
SIC: 3594 Fluid power pumps & motors
PA: Parker-Hannifin Corporation
  6035 Parkland Blvd
  Cleveland OH 44124
  216 896-3000

(G-13544)
PAXAR CORPORATION (HQ)
Also Called: Avery Dennison
8080 Norton Pkwy 22 (44060-5990)
PHONE.................................845 398-3229
Susan C Miller, *Ch of Bd*
Robert Van Der Merwe, *President*
Richard A Maue, *Vice Pres*
Robert S Stone, *Vice Pres*
Anthony Colatrella, *CFO*
◆ **EMP:** 50
SQ FT: 30,000
SALES (est): 18.2MM
SALES (corp-wide): 7.1B **Publicly Held**
WEB: www.paxar.com
SIC: 2269 2752 3555 3577 Labels, cotton: printed; tags, lithographed; printing trades machinery; bar code (magnetic ink) printers
PA: Avery Dennison Corporation
  207 N Goode Ave Ste 500
  Glendale CA 91203
  626 304-2000

(G-13545)
PCC AIRFOILS LLC
8607 Tyler Blvd (44060-4222)
PHONE.................................440 255-9770
Armand Lauzon, *General Mgr*
EMP: 108
SQ FT: 55,000
SALES (corp-wide): 225.3B **Publicly Held**
WEB: www.pccairfoils.com
SIC: 3369 3324 3724 Castings, except die-castings, precision; steel investment foundries; airfoils, aircraft engine
HQ: Pcc Airfoils Llc
  3401 Entp Pkwy Ste 200
  Cleveland OH 44122
  216 831-3590

(G-13546)
PELOTON MANUFACTURING CORP
Also Called: SSC Controls Company
8909 East Ave (44060-4305)
PHONE.................................440 205-1600
James E Moll, *President*
Brent Moll, *Officer*
▲ **EMP:** 15
SQ FT: 8,500
SALES: 5MM **Privately Held**
WEB: www.ssccontrols.com
SIC: 3625 8742 Relays & industrial controls

(G-13547)
PERFORMANCE SUPERABRASIVES LLC
Also Called: Coastal Diamond
7255 Industrial Park Blvd A (44060-5331)
PHONE.................................440 946-7171
Scott Kaplan, *Mng Member*
Tim Rash,
EMP: 9
SQ FT: 5,200
SALES (est): 680.2K **Privately Held**
SIC: 3291 3545 Wheels, grinding: artificial; wheel turning equipment, diamond point or other

(G-13548)
PLATING PROCESS SYSTEMS INC
7561 Tyler Blvd Ste 5 (44060-4867)
P.O. Box 808 (44061-0808)
PHONE.................................440 951-9667
John Salyards, *President*
Rosalie Salyards, *Corp Secy*
Louis Gianelos, *Vice Pres*
▼ **EMP:** 9
SQ FT: 9,880
SALES: 2.5MM **Privately Held**
WEB: www.platingprocess.com
SIC: 2899 Plating compounds

(G-13549)
POLYCHEM CORPORATION (HQ)
6277 Heisley Rd (44060-1899)
PHONE.................................440 357-1500
Brian Jeckering, *CEO*
Barry Clifford, *CFO*
Joe Bazelides, *Controller*
◆ **EMP:** 180

GEOGRAPHIC SECTION
Mentor - Lake County (G-13577)

SQ FT: 165,000
SALES: 130MM **Privately Held**
SIC: 2671 Plastic film, coated or laminated for packaging

(G-13550)
POLYCHEM CORPORATION
7214 Justin Way (44060-4881)
PHONE.................................440 357-1500
EMP: 5 **Privately Held**
SIC: 2671 Plastic film, coated or laminated for packaging
HQ: Polychem Corporation
6277 Heisley Rd
Mentor OH 44060
440 357-1500

(G-13551)
POLYMER CONCEPTS INC
7555 Tyler Blvd Ste 1 (44060-4866)
PHONE.................................440 953-9605
Chris Callsen, *President*
▼ EMP: 7 EST: 1999
SQ FT: 6,000
SALES (est): 1.4MM **Privately Held**
WEB: www.polymerconcept.com
SIC: 2821 Polyurethane resins

(G-13552)
PRECISION DIE MASTERS
8724 East Ave (44060-4304)
P.O. Box 263 (44061-0263)
PHONE.................................440 255-1204
Frank E Carmichael, *President*
EMP: 16
SQ FT: 16,000
SALES (est): 1.2MM **Privately Held**
SIC: 3544 Special dies & tools

(G-13553)
PRECISION WOODWORK LTD
6385 Mentor Park Blvd (44060-3721)
PHONE.................................440 257-3002
Patrick D Foss, *Partner*
Linda J Foss, *Partner*
EMP: 3
SQ FT: 1,500
SALES: 450K **Privately Held**
WEB: www.precisionwoodwork.com
SIC: 2431 Millwork

(G-13554)
PRO MOLD DESIGN INC
9853 Johnnycake Ridge Rd # 308 (44060-6792)
PHONE.................................440 352-1212
Ronald Kowalski, *President*
Russ Kowalski, *Vice Pres*
EMP: 3
SALES: 125K **Privately Held**
SIC: 2821 Molding compounds, plastics

(G-13555)
PROFAC INC
Also Called: Merritt Woodwork
7198 Industrial Park Blvd (44060-5328)
PHONE.................................440 942-0205
G Michael Merritt, *CEO*
Tony Aoun, *President*
Janet E Bowden, *Principal*
Harold M Chattman, *Principal*
Keith E Merritt, *Vice Pres*
▲ EMP: 135
SQ FT: 90,000
SALES (est): 33.4MM **Privately Held**
WEB: www.merrittwoodwork.com
SIC: 2431 Millwork

(G-13556)
PROFICIENT MACHINING CO
7522 Tyler Blvd Unit B-G (44060-5450)
PHONE.................................440 942-4942
Kenneth Putman, *President*
Carol Putman, *Corp Secy*
Kenneth Putman Jr, *Exec VP*
EMP: 22
SQ FT: 15,000
SALES (est): 4.5MM **Privately Held**
WEB: www.proficientmachining.com
SIC: 3599 Machine shop, jobbing & repair

(G-13557)
PROFICIENT PLASTICS INC
7777 Saint Clair Ave (44060-5237)
P.O. Box 5053 (44061-5053)
PHONE.................................440 205-9700
Robert W Wisen, *President*
Greg Wisen, *Vice Pres*
Joe Wesley, *Plant Mgr*
EMP: 10
SQ FT: 1,500
SALES (est): 1.8MM **Privately Held**
SIC: 3089 Injection molding of plastics

(G-13558)
PROGAGE INC
7555 Tyler Blvd Ste 6 (44060-4866)
PHONE.................................440 951-4477
Edward Vadakin, *President*
Paul Paliobeis, *Engineer*
Allison Urbanek, *Engineer*
EMP: 19
SQ FT: 14,000
SALES (est): 2.5MM **Privately Held**
WEB: www.progage.com
SIC: 3544 Jigs & fixtures

(G-13559)
PROGRESSIVE POWDER COATING INC
7742 Tyler Blvd (44060-4802)
PHONE.................................440 974-3478
Mark Saltzman, *President*
Thomas Gries, *Vice Pres*
EMP: 25
SQ FT: 24,024
SALES (est): 3.8MM **Privately Held**
SIC: 3479 Coating of metals & formed products

(G-13560)
PROLINE SCREENWEAR
8586 East Ave (44060-4302)
PHONE.................................440 205-3700
David Juka, *Principal*
EMP: 3
SALES (est): 307.3K **Privately Held**
SIC: 2759 Screen printing

(G-13561)
PYROMATICS CORP (PA)
9321 Pineneedle Dr (44060-1825)
PHONE.................................440 352-3500
Andre Ezis, *CEO*
Cyndi St Julian, *CFO*
EMP: 11
SQ FT: 27,000
SALES (est): 1.6MM **Privately Held**
WEB: www.pyromatics.com
SIC: 3221 3231 3297 Glass containers; products of purchased glass; nonclay refractories

(G-13562)
QUADREL INC
Also Called: Quadrel Labeling Systems
7670 Jenther Dr (44060-4872)
PHONE.................................440 602-4700
Lon Deckard, *President*
Charles Wepler, *Vice Pres*
Joseph P Rouse, *Admin Sec*
◆ EMP: 43
SQ FT: 3,842
SALES (est): 13.8MM **Privately Held**
WEB: www.quadrel.com
SIC: 3565 Labeling machines, industrial

(G-13563)
QUALITY COMPONENTS INC
8825 East Ave (44060-4305)
P.O. Box 956 (44061-0956)
PHONE.................................440 255-0606
William Dennison Sr, *President*
EMP: 15
SQ FT: 10,000
SALES (est): 2.5MM
SALES (corp-wide): 548.1MM **Publicly Held**
WEB: www.qccompany.com
SIC: 7699 3548 Welding equipment repair; welding & cutting apparatus & accessories
HQ: Stratos International, Inc.
299 Johnson Ave Sw
Waseca MN 56093
507 833-8822

(G-13564)
QUALITY DESIGN MACHINING INC
9349 Hamilton Dr (44060-4559)
PHONE.................................440 352-7290
Robert Fletcher, *President*
EMP: 8
SQ FT: 5,000
SALES: 574.5K **Privately Held**
SIC: 3599 Amusement park equipment

(G-13565)
QUALITY MACHINE SYSTEMS LLC
7875 Enterprise Dr (44060-5309)
PHONE.................................440 223-2217
Paul Kinczel, *Partner*
Steve Vucic, *Partner*
St Jepan Vucic,
EMP: 8
SQ FT: 10,000
SALES (est): 974.1K **Privately Held**
WEB: www.qualitymachineairtools.com
SIC: 3599 Machine shop, jobbing & repair

(G-13566)
QUALITY QUARTZ OF AMERICA INC
9362 Hamilton Dr (44060-4558)
PHONE.................................440 352-2851
Carmella Petruziello, *Owner*
EMP: 3
SQ FT: 11,130
SALES (est): 320K **Privately Held**
WEB: www.qualityquartz.com
SIC: 3679 Quartz crystals, for electronic application

(G-13567)
QUALTEK ELECTRONICS CORP
7610 Jenther Dr (44060-4872)
PHONE.................................440 951-3300
John Hallums, *President*
▲ EMP: 120
SQ FT: 20,000
SALES (est): 23.3MM **Privately Held**
WEB: www.qualtekusa.com
SIC: 3634 3643 3577 3612 Electric housewares & fans; current-carrying wiring devices; power outlets & sockets; computer peripheral equipment; transformers, except electric; blowers & fans; miscellaneous fabricated wire products

(G-13568)
R C PACKAGING SYSTEMS
6277 Heisley Rd (44060-1858)
PHONE.................................248 684-6363
▲ EMP: 15
SQ FT: 12,000
SALES (est): 2.9MM **Privately Held**
SIC: 2298 Mfg Cordage/Twine

(G-13569)
R J K ENTERPRISES INC
Also Called: Niftech
5565 Wilson Dr (44060-1555)
PHONE.................................440 257-6018
Raymond Knaus, *President*
Ellen Cook, *Vice Pres*
Julie Knaus, *Vice Pres*
EMP: 10
SQ FT: 1,500
SALES: 1MM **Privately Held**
WEB: www.niftech.com
SIC: 7389 3599 Design, commercial & industrial; custom machinery

(G-13570)
R S MANUFACTURING INC
8878 East Ave (44060-4306)
PHONE.................................440 946-8002
Richard Stark Sr, *President*
Richard Stark Jr, *Vice Pres*
David Stark, *Shareholder*
Dee Ann Stark, *Shareholder*
Robyn Stark, *Shareholder*
EMP: 15
SQ FT: 4,800
SALES: 400K **Privately Held**
SIC: 3452 Bolts, metal; nuts, metal; screws, metal; washers

(G-13571)
R T & T MACHINING CO INC
8195 Tyler Blvd (44060-4854)
PHONE.................................440 974-8479
F Paul Thompson, *President*
Ellen Thompson, *Vice Pres*
EMP: 14
SQ FT: 12,000
SALES (est): 1.1MM **Privately Held**
SIC: 3451 3599 3545 3544 Screw machine products; machine shop, jobbing & repair; machine tool accessories; special dies, tools, jigs & fixtures

(G-13572)
RACE WINNING BRANDS INC (HQ)
Also Called: Wiseco
7201 Industrial Park Blvd (44060-5315)
PHONE.................................440 951-6600
Brian Reese, *President*
Ted Caldwell, *Vice Pres*
Josh Vogel, *CFO*
EMP: 320
SQ FT: 150,000
SALES (est): 70.2MM
SALES (corp-wide): 275.1MM **Privately Held**
SIC: 3592 3714 Pistons & piston rings; motor vehicle parts & accessories
PA: Kinderhook Industries, Llc
505 5th Ave Fl 25
New York NY 10017
212 201-6780

(G-13573)
RKI INC (PA)
Also Called: Roll-Kraft
8901 Tyler Blvd (44060-2184)
PHONE.................................888 953-9400
George C Gehrisch Jr, *President*
Sanjay Singh, *President*
Dennis M Langer, *Exec VP*
Chaz Rau, *Vice Pres*
Chuck Summerhill, *Vice Pres*
EMP: 121 EST: 1964
SQ FT: 100,000
SALES (est): 22.7MM **Privately Held**
WEB: www.roll-kraft.com
SIC: 3547 Primary rolling mill equipment

(G-13574)
RLR INDUSTRIES INC
Also Called: Rainbow Plastics
8677 Tyler Blvd Unit B (44060-4346)
PHONE.................................440 951-9501
Richard Rodgers Jr, *President*
EMP: 38
SQ FT: 25,000
SALES: 2.2MM **Privately Held**
SIC: 3089 Thermoformed finished plastic products; plastic processing

(G-13575)
ROYAL PLASTICS INC
9410 Pineneedle Dr (44060-1880)
PHONE.................................440 352-1357
Gary Connell, *President*
Gary Mc Connell, *President*
Song Crawford, *Vice Pres*
Patricia Garner, *Vice Pres*
Bruce Usnik, *Vice Pres*
▲ EMP: 225 EST: 1966
SQ FT: 135,000
SALES (est): 60.9MM **Privately Held**
SIC: 3089 3643 Injection molding of plastics; current-carrying wiring devices

(G-13576)
S T TOOL & DESIGN INC
9452 Mercantile Dr (44060-1889)
PHONE.................................440 357-1250
John Fifa, *General Mgr*
Tony Sisa, *Manager*
EMP: 14
SQ FT: 6,000
SALES (est): 2.5MM **Privately Held**
SIC: 3599 Machine shop, jobbing & repair

(G-13577)
SEABISCUIT MOTORSPORTS INC (DH)
Also Called: Wiseco Piston Company, Inc.
7201 Industrial Park Blvd (44060-5315)
PHONE.................................440 951-6600
▲ EMP: 320 EST: 1980
SQ FT: 150,000
SALES (est): 70MM
SALES (corp-wide): 275.1MM **Privately Held**
WEB: www.wiseco.com
SIC: 3592 3714 Pistons & piston rings; motor vehicle parts & accessories

Mentor - Lake County (G-13578)

HQ: Race Winning Brands, Inc.
7201 Industrial Park Blvd
Mentor OH 44060
440 951-6600

(G-13578)
SEMPER QUALITY INDUSTRY INC
Also Called: Mc Cartney Industries
9411 Mercantile Dr (44060-4524)
PHONE 440 352-8111
Dale B McCartney, *President*
Duane McCartney, *Vice Pres*
EMP: 8
SQ FT: 12,000
SALES: 750K **Privately Held**
WEB: www.semperquality.com
SIC: 1721 3479 Industrial painting; coating of metals & formed products

(G-13579)
SENTINEL CONSUMER PRODUCTS INC (PA)
7750 Tyler Blvd (44060-4802)
PHONE 801 825-5671
Michael S Klein, *President*
EMP: 80
SQ FT: 53,000
SALES (est): 20.5MM **Privately Held**
WEB: www.sentinelconsumer.com
SIC: 3842 3131 2844 First aid, snake bite & burn kits; dressings, surgical; swabs, sanitary cotton; inner soles, leather; toilet preparations

(G-13580)
SGM CO INC
9000 Tyler Blvd (44060-1897)
PHONE 440 255-1190
Patrick L Gerboth, *CEO*
Laura L Gerboth, *President*
Brian Kerslake, *Engineer*
EMP: 40 **EST:** 1967
SQ FT: 45,000
SALES (est): 6.4MM **Privately Held**
SIC: 3433 Heating equipment, except electric

(G-13581)
SHEET METAL PRODUCTS CO INC
5950 Pinecone Dr (44060-1865)
PHONE 440 392-9000
Joseph J Mahovlic, *CEO*
James F Saxa, *President*
Steven H Sneiderman, *Principal*
Tom Elliott, *Prdtn Mgr*
Brian Panko, *Mfg Staff*
EMP: 25
SALES (est): 7.4MM **Privately Held**
WEB: www.sheetmetalproductsco.com
SIC: 3444 3429 Sheet metal specialties, not stamped; manufactured hardware (general)
PA: The Providence Group Inc
9290 Metcalf Rd
Willoughby OH

(G-13582)
SIGNS N STUFF INC
9354 Mentor Ave Ste 4 (44060-6467)
PHONE 440 974-3151
William Budziak, *President*
EMP: 5
SALES (est): 452.9K **Privately Held**
SIC: 3993 Signs & advertising specialties

(G-13583)
SKRIBS TOOL AND DIE INC
Also Called: Apollo Plastic
7555 Tyler Blvd Ste 11 (44060-4866)
PHONE 440 951-7774
Stanley Skrbis, *President*
Maria Skrbis, *Corp Secy*
Stanley Skrbis Jr, *Vice Pres*
EMP: 28 **EST:** 1973
SQ FT: 24,000
SALES (est): 3.5MM **Privately Held**
SIC: 3544 3089 Forms (molds), for foundry & plastics working machinery; injection molding of plastics

(G-13584)
SMP WELDING LLC
8171 Tyler Blvd (44060-4826)
PHONE 440 205-9353
Joe Demarco, *Opers Staff*
Renee Roland, *Marketing Mgr*
Patrick Studnicka,
EMP: 12
SQ FT: 10,000
SALES (est): 4.5MM **Privately Held**
SIC: 7692 Welding repair

(G-13585)
SPANG & COMPANY
Spang Power Electronic
9305 Progress Pkwy (44060-1855)
PHONE 440 350-6108
Timothy J Lindey, *Division Pres*
EMP: 31
SALES (corp-wide): 103.9MM **Privately Held**
SIC: 3699 3625 3674 3566 Electron linear accelerators; control equipment, electric; controls for adjustable speed drives; semiconductors & related devices; speed changers, drives & gears
PA: Spang & Company
110 Delta Dr
Pittsburgh PA 15238
412 963-9363

(G-13586)
SPORTSMASTER
9140 Lake Shore Blvd (44060-1637)
PHONE 440 257-3900
Ronald Micchia DDS, *Owner*
EMP: 13
SQ FT: 1,800
SALES (est): 821.5K **Privately Held**
SIC: 2891 Adhesives & sealants

(G-13587)
STAM INC
7350 Production Dr (44060-4859)
P.O. Box 951108, Cleveland (44193-0005)
PHONE 440 974-2500
Kent Marvin, *President*
H James Sheedy, *Principal*
David Baumgardner, *Engineer*
Brendan Anderson, *CFO*
▲ **EMP:** 45
SQ FT: 28,000
SALES (est): 9.9MM **Privately Held**
WEB: www.staminc.com
SIC: 3498 Tube fabricating (contract bending & shaping)

(G-13588)
STAR PRECISION TECH LLC
6989 Lindsay Dr (44060-4928)
PHONE 440 266-7700
Michael Canty, *President*
EMP: 60
SQ FT: 45,000
SALES (est): 9.2MM
SALES (corp-wide): 34.7MM **Privately Held**
WEB: www.starprecision.net
SIC: 3599 Machine shop, jobbing & repair
PA: Alloy Bellows & Precision Welding, Inc.
653 Miner Rd
Cleveland OH 44143
440 684-3000

(G-13589)
STERIS CORPORATION
Also Called: Research & Development II
5900 Heisley Rd (44060-1834)
PHONE 440 354-2600
EMP: 6
SALES (corp-wide): 2.6B **Privately Held**
SIC: 3842 Surgical appliances & supplies
HQ: Steris Corporation
5960 Heisley Rd
Mentor OH 44060
440 354-2600

(G-13590)
STERIS CORPORATION (HQ)
5960 Heisley Rd (44060-1834)
PHONE 440 354-2600
Walter M Rosebrough Jr, *President*
Robert E Moss, *President*
Loyal W Wilson, *Principal*
Michael B Wood, *Principal*
Bill Evennou, *District Mgr*
◆ **EMP:** 843
SALES (est): 2B
SALES (corp-wide): 2.6B **Privately Held**
WEB: www.steris.com
SIC: 3842 3845 3841 Sterilizers, hospital & surgical; endoscopic equipment, electromedical; diagnostic apparatus, medical
PA: Steris Limited
Rutherford House Stephensons Way
Derby DE21
133 238-7100

(G-13591)
STERIS CORPORATION
6100 Heisley Rd (44060-1838)
PHONE 440 354-2600
Rick Lee, *Business Mgr*
Mark Furlong, *Senior Buyer*
CPS, *Manager*
Chuck Biese, *Director*
EMP: 126
SALES (corp-wide): 2.6B **Privately Held**
WEB: www.steris.com
SIC: 3842 Surgical appliances & supplies
HQ: Steris Corporation
5960 Heisley Rd
Mentor OH 44060
440 354-2600

(G-13592)
STERIS CORPORATION
6515 Hopkins Rd (44060-4307)
PHONE 440 354-2600
Toby Duff, *Project Engr*
Jeff Kiessel, *Sales Staff*
Les Vinney, *Manager*
Toby Soots, *Manager*
EMP: 100
SALES (corp-wide): 2.6B **Privately Held**
WEB: www.steris.com
SIC: 3842 Sterilizers, hospital & surgical; surgical appliances & supplies
HQ: Steris Corporation
5960 Heisley Rd
Mentor OH 44060
440 354-2600

(G-13593)
STERIS CORPORATION
9325 Pinecone Dr (44060-1862)
P.O. Box 75044, Cleveland (44101-2199)
PHONE 440 354-2600
EMP: 10
SALES (corp-wide): 2.6B **Privately Held**
WEB: www.steris.com
SIC: 3842 Surgical appliances & supplies
HQ: Steris Corporation
5960 Heisley Rd
Mentor OH 44060
440 354-2600

(G-13594)
STRATEGIC TECHNOLOGY ENTP
5960 Heisley Rd (44060-1834)
PHONE 440 354-2600
Les Binney, *President*
Gerry Reis, *Vice Pres*
Ken Barnes, *Manager*
EMP: 20
SALES (est): 1.7MM **Privately Held**
SIC: 3821 Clinical laboratory instruments, except medical & dental

(G-13595)
STROUSE INDUSTRIES INC
8090 Danbury Ct (44060-2421)
PHONE 440 257-2520
Joseph Strouse, *President*
Judy Strouse, *Treasurer*
EMP: 4 **EST:** 1971
SALES (est): 481.1K **Privately Held**
SIC: 3541 Machine tools, metal cutting type

(G-13596)
SULECKI PRECISION PRODUCTS
8785 East Ave (44060-4303)
PHONE 440 255-5454
Daniel Sulecki, *President*
David Sulecki, *Corp Secy*
John Sulecki, *Vice Pres*
Ed Sulecki, *Purch Dir*
EMP: 10
SQ FT: 4,500
SALES (est): 1.4MM **Privately Held**
SIC: 3599 3544 3444 3441 Machine shop, jobbing & repair; special dies, tools, jigs & fixtures; sheet metalwork; fabricated structural metal

(G-13597)
SUNBRIGHT USA INC
8909 East Ave (44060-4305)
PHONE 440 205-0600
James E Moll, *President*
Deb Kaiger, *QC Mgr*
Jay Santamaria, *Marketing Staff*
Jan Myers, *Administration*
▲ **EMP:** 3
SALES (est): 377.1K **Privately Held**
SIC: 3999 Combs, except hard rubber

(G-13598)
SUTTERLIN MACHINE & TOOL CO
9445 Pineneedle Dr (44060-1827)
PHONE 440 357-0817
Claude Sutterlin, *President*
Dan Sutterlin, *Manager*
EMP: 17 **EST:** 1966
SQ FT: 6,000
SALES (est): 3.2MM **Privately Held**
WEB: www.sutterlinmachine.com
SIC: 3544 Special dies & tools

(G-13599)
T-N-T CONCRETE INC
6032 W Valleyview Ct (44060-2241)
PHONE 540 480-4040
Caleb Shifflett, *Manager*
EMP: 4
SALES (est): 311.8K **Privately Held**
SIC: 1771 1794 2951 1741 Concrete work; excavation work; excavation & grading, building construction; composition blocks for paving; concrete block masonry laying; blocks, concrete: landscape or retaining wall

(G-13600)
TAYLOR COMMUNICATIONS INC
7200 Justin Way (44060-4881)
PHONE 440 974-1611
James Larson, *Manager*
EMP: 7
SQ FT: 10,000
SALES (corp-wide): 3.2B **Privately Held**
WEB: www.stdreg.com
SIC: 2761 Manifold business forms
HQ: Taylor Communications, Inc.
1725 Roe Crest Dr
North Mankato MN 56003
507 625-2828

(G-13601)
TECMARK CORPORATION (PA)
7745 Metric Dr (44060-4863)
PHONE 440 205-7600
Walter Swick, *CEO*
Ron Sayles, *President*
Sean Swick, *President*
Chuck Stein, *Vice Pres*
Matthew Duncan, *Engineer*
▲ **EMP:** 60 **EST:** 1999
SQ FT: 23,000
SALES (est): 9.1MM **Privately Held**
WEB: www.tecmarkcorp.com
SIC: 3629 3823 3643 Electronic generation equipment; industrial instrmnts msrmnt display/control process variable; current-carrying wiring devices

(G-13602)
TECMARK CORPORATION
Also Called: North Shore Safety
7335 Production Dr (44060-4858)
PHONE 440 205-9188
Matt Moon, *Controller*
EMP: 25
SALES (corp-wide): 9.1MM **Privately Held**
SIC: 3823 Industrial instrmnts msrmnt display/control process variable
PA: Tecmark Corporation
7745 Metric Dr
Mentor OH 44060
440 205-7600

GEOGRAPHIC SECTION

Mentor - Lake County (G-13630)

(G-13603)
TEN MFG LLC
7675 Saint Clair Ave A (44060-5235)
PHONE..................................440 487-1100
Anthony Smith,
EMP: 10
SALES (est): 395.4K **Privately Held**
SIC: 3273 Ready-mixed concrete

(G-13604)
TERSUS PHARMACEUTICALS
5966 Heisley Rd (44060-1886)
PHONE..................................440 951-2451
Jeffrey A Green, *Principal*
Brian Seifert, *CFO*
EMP: 10
SALES (est): 480K **Privately Held**
SIC: 2834 Pharmaceutical preparations

(G-13605)
THERMOTION CORP
Also Called: Thermotion-Madison
6520 Hopkins Rd (44060-4308)
PHONE..................................440 639-8325
Gary Swanson, *President*
EMP: 15
SALES (est): 2.7MM **Privately Held**
WEB: www.thermotion.com
SIC: 3625 Actuators, industrial

(G-13606)
TIMOTHY ALLEN JEWELERS INC
8925 Mentor Ave Ste D (44060-6350)
PHONE..................................440 974-8885
Timothy Allen Sobonya, *President*
Michelle Sobonya, *Vice Pres*
EMP: 5
SQ FT: 2,072
SALES: 400K **Privately Held**
WEB: www.timothyallenjewelers.com
SIC: 3911 5944 Jewelry apparel; jewelry stores

(G-13607)
TOM RICHARDS INC (PA)
Also Called: Process Technology
7010 Lindsay Dr (44060-4921)
PHONE..................................440 974-1300
Jody Richards, *President*
Laurie Hinton, *Buyer*
Howard Base, *Engineer*
Dan Kosta, *Engineer*
Leslie N Thomas, *VP Finance*
▲ EMP: 150
SQ FT: 72,000
SALES (est): 24.7MM **Privately Held**
WEB: www.process-technology.com
SIC: 3559 Metal finishing equipment for plating, etc.; semiconductor manufacturing machinery

(G-13608)
TOP SHELF EMBROIDERY
9450 Mentor Ave (44060-4520)
PHONE..................................440 209-8566
Tim Ferrell, *Principal*
EMP: 3
SALES (est): 136.8K **Privately Held**
SIC: 2395 Embroidery products, except schiffli machine

(G-13609)
TOPS INC
Also Called: Tops Auto Interiors
7564 Tyler Blvd Ste A (44060-4870)
PHONE..................................440 954-9451
Frank Frazza, *President*
EMP: 5
SALES (est): 502K **Privately Held**
SIC: 2299 7641 7542 Tops, combing & converting; upholstery work; carwashes

(G-13610)
TOTAL MANUFACTURING CO INC
7777 Saint Clair Ave (44060-5237)
P.O. Box 5053 (44061-5053)
PHONE..................................440 205-9700
Robert W Wisen, *President*
Greg Wisen, *Opers Mgr*
EMP: 22
SALES (est): 4.5MM **Privately Held**
SIC: 3599 Machine shop, jobbing & repair

(G-13611)
TQ MANUFACTURING COMPANY INC
7345 Production Dr (44060-4858)
PHONE..................................440 255-9000
James Klopp, *President*
Thomas Cooper, *General Mgr*
EMP: 11
SQ FT: 10,000
SALES (est): 1.5MM **Privately Held**
WEB: www.tqmfg.com
SIC: 3599 Machine shop, jobbing & repair

(G-13612)
TRAILER COMPONENT MFG INC
8120 Tyler Blvd (44060-4852)
PHONE..................................440 255-2888
James Kleinman, *President*
Thomas Gries, *Vice Pres*
Mark Saltzman, *Treasurer*
Violeta Sikora, *Manager*
▲ EMP: 30
SQ FT: 42,000
SALES (est): 8.4MM **Privately Held**
SIC: 3714 3599 3537 Motor vehicle parts & accessories; machine & other job shop work; industrial trucks & tractors

(G-13613)
TRANSFER EXPRESS INC
7650 Tyler Blvd (44060-4853)
PHONE..................................440 918-1900
Ted Stahl, *President*
Jason Ziga, *General Mgr*
Devin Hart, *Production*
Paul Fultz, *Senior Buyer*
Matt Cook, *CFO*
◆ EMP: 65
SQ FT: 85,000
SALES (est): 16MM
SALES (corp-wide): 33.4MM **Privately Held**
WEB: www.txpress.com
SIC: 2759 2752 Screen printing; transfers, decalcomania or dry; lithographed
PA: Stahls' Inc.
6353 E 14 Mile Rd
Sterling Heights MI 48312
800 478-2457

(G-13614)
TROY SCREW PRODUCTS
7455 Clover Ave (44060-5211)
PHONE..................................440 946-3381
Mark Work, *Vice Pres*
EMP: 4
SALES (est): 442.7K **Privately Held**
SIC: 3452 Bolts, nuts, rivets & washers

(G-13615)
TYLER HAVER INC (DH)
Also Called: W S Tyler
8570 Tyler Blvd (44060-4232)
PHONE..................................440 974-1047
Randy A Bakeberg, *President*
Becky Martin, *Export Mgr*
Ben Gimal, *VP Sales*
Bill Lucas, *Regl Sales Mgr*
William Lucas, *Sales Staff*
▲ EMP: 50
SQ FT: 65,000
SALES (est): 10.2MM
SALES (corp-wide): 579.2MM **Privately Held**
SIC: 3496 Miscellaneous fabricated wire products
HQ: Tylinter, Inc.
8570 Tyler Blvd
Mentor OH 44060
800 321-6188

(G-13616)
TYLER HAVER INC
W S Tyler
8570 Tyler Blvd (44060-4232)
PHONE..................................800 255-1259
Kevin Deighan, *Manager*
EMP: 60
SALES (corp-wide): 579.2MM **Privately Held**
SIC: 3569 Sifting & screening machines
HQ: Tyler Haver Inc
8570 Tyler Blvd
Mentor OH 44060
440 974-1047

(G-13617)
ULTRA IMPRESSIONS INC
Also Called: PIP Printing
7533 Tyler Blvd Ste D (44060-5415)
PHONE..................................440 951-4777
Wayne G Reese, *President*
James E Reese, *Vice Pres*
EMP: 5
SQ FT: 2,600
SALES (est): 857.2K **Privately Held**
SIC: 2752 Commercial printing, offset

(G-13618)
UNIQUE PACKAGING & PRINTING
9086 Goldfinch Ct (44060-1810)
P.O. Box 417, Grand River (44045-0417)
PHONE..................................440 785-6730
Robert F Bradach, *President*
Madeline Bradach, *Vice Pres*
EMP: 10
SQ FT: 20,000
SALES (est): 100K **Privately Held**
SIC: 7389 3991 Packaging & labeling services; brooms & brushes

(G-13619)
UNITED STATES ENDOSCOPY
6091 Heisley Rd (44060-1835)
PHONE..................................440 639-4494
EMP: 3
SALES (corp-wide): 2.6B **Privately Held**
SIC: 3841 Surgical instruments & apparatus
HQ: United States Endoscopy Group, Inc.
5976 Heisley Rd
Mentor OH 44060
440 639-4494

(G-13620)
US POWDER COATING INC
8665 Tyler Blvd (44060-4346)
PHONE..................................440 255-3090
Ray Gotliewbowski, *Principal*
EMP: 4
SALES (est): 320K **Privately Held**
SIC: 3499 Friction material, made from powdered metal

(G-13621)
V K C INC
Also Called: Fab Form
7667 Jenther Dr (44060-4872)
PHONE..................................440 951-9634
Joseph Chmielewski, *President*
Raymond Gotliebowski, *Vice Pres*
Pete Deatsch, *Production*
Brandin Maxwell, *Purchasing*
Chad Gotliebowski, *Sales Staff*
EMP: 19
SQ FT: 10,000
SALES (est): 4.7MM **Privately Held**
SIC: 3469 Stamping metal for the trade

(G-13622)
VAST MOLD & TOOL CO INC
7154 Industrial Park Blvd (44060-5314)
PHONE..................................440 942-7585
Vincent Romano, *President*
EMP: 5
SQ FT: 8,000
SALES: 600K **Privately Held**
SIC: 3089 Molding primary plastic

(G-13623)
VECTOR INTERNATIONAL CORP
Also Called: Vector Screenprinting & EMB
7404 Tyler Blvd (44060-5402)
PHONE..................................440 942-2002
Doug Anderson, *President*
EMP: 8
SQ FT: 6,000
SALES (est): 825.3K **Privately Held**
WEB: www.vectorproimage.com
SIC: 2396 2395 Screen printing on fabric articles; embroidery & art needlework

(G-13624)
VICON FABRICATING COMPANY LTD
7200 Justin Way (44060-4881)
PHONE..................................440 205-6700
Robert S Seidemann, *CEO*
Jeffrey Conforte, *President*
Joseph M Geitz, *Sales Mgr*
Michael Conforte, *Executive*
Anita R Seidemann,
EMP: 35 EST: 1965
SQ FT: 40,000
SALES (est): 8.9MM **Privately Held**
WEB: www.viconfab.com
SIC: 3441 3398 Fabricated structural metal; metal heat treating

(G-13625)
VOLK OPTICAL INC
7893 Enterprise Dr (44060-5309)
PHONE..................................440 942-6161
Jyoti Gupta, *President*
Terry Cooper, *Regional Mgr*
Gary Webel, *Vice Pres*
Ezequiel Lukin, *Regl Sales Mgr*
Diane Drodouski, *Executive*
▲ EMP: 70 EST: 1974
SQ FT: 18,000
SALES (est): 12.5MM
SALES (corp-wide): 1.5B **Privately Held**
SIC: 8011 3851 3827 Offices & clinics of medical doctors; lenses, ophthalmic; optical instruments & lenses
HQ: Halma Holdings Inc.
11500 Northlake Dr # 306
Cincinnati OH 45249
513 772-5501

(G-13626)
WILSON OPTICAL LABORATORY INC
Also Called: North American Coating Labs
9450 Pineneedle Dr (44060-1828)
PHONE..................................440 357-7000
John H Wilson, *CEO*
Brian Wilson, *President*
EMP: 50
SQ FT: 30,000
SALES (est): 8.5MM **Privately Held**
WEB: www.nacl.com
SIC: 3851 3827 3229 Lens coating, ophthalmic; optical instruments & lenses; pressed & blown glass

(G-13627)
WINES FOR YOU
7344 Mentor Ave (44060-7543)
PHONE..................................440 946-1420
Debbie Iacofano, *Principal*
EMP: 4
SALES (est): 239K **Privately Held**
SIC: 2084 Wines

(G-13628)
WIRE SHOP INC
5959 Pinecone Dr (44060-1866)
PHONE..................................440 354-6842
John Ferguson, *President*
Howard Pindale, *Vice Pres*
EMP: 20
SQ FT: 20,000
SALES (est): 3.1MM **Privately Held**
WEB: www.thewireshop.com
SIC: 3544 3599 Special dies & tools; machine & other job shop work

(G-13629)
WOOD SPECIALISTS
9485 Pinecone Dr (44060-1864)
PHONE..................................440 639-9797
Ken Demarchi, *Owner*
EMP: 4 EST: 1977
SQ FT: 7,000
SALES (est): 572.3K **Privately Held**
SIC: 2653 2541 Corrugated boxes, partitions, display items, sheets & pad; cabinets, lockers & shelving

(G-13630)
WS TYLER SCREENING INC
8570 Tyler Blvd (44060-4232)
PHONE..................................440 974-1047
Florian Festge, *President*
Caroline Mann, *Director*
EMP: 23
SALES (est): 1.3MM
SALES (corp-wide): 579.2MM **Privately Held**
SIC: 3496 Miscellaneous fabricated wire products
PA: Haver & Boecker Ohg
Carl-Haver-Platz 3
Oelde 59302
252 230-0

Mentor On The Lake
Lake County

(G-13631)
AQUA PENNSYLVANIA INC
Also Called: Aqua Ohio
7748 Twilight Dr (44060-2629)
PHONE.....................440 257-6190
Bill Bowers, *Branch Mgr*
EMP: 6
SALES (corp-wide): 838MM **Publicly Held**
SIC: 5499 4941 3589 Water: distilled mineral or spring; water supply; water treatment equipment, industrial
HQ: Aqua Pennsylvania, Inc.
762 W Lancaster Ave
Bryn Mawr PA 19010
610 525-1400

(G-13632)
MENTOR INC
Also Called: Action Door
5983 Andrews Rd (44060-2819)
PHONE.....................440 255-1250
Shelly Mastanuono, *CEO*
Michael Whittwer, *President*
Dino Mastanuono, *Vice Pres*
▲ **EMP**: 9
SALES (est): 1.6MM **Privately Held**
WEB: www.mentor.net
SIC: 3732 Dories, building & repairing

Mesopotamia
Trumbull County

(G-13633)
INNOVATIVE INTEGRATIONS INC
Also Called: I3
7877 Girdle Rd (44439)
P.O. Box 222 (44439-0222)
PHONE.....................216 533-5353
Matthew Toddy, *President*
EMP: 3
SALES (est): 287.4K **Privately Held**
SIC: 3625 7373 7389 Relays, for electronic use; office computer automation systems integration; systems software development services;

Metamora
Fulton County

(G-13634)
PARKER-HANNIFIN CORPORATION
Hydraulic Filter Division
16810 Fulton County Rd 2 (43540)
PHONE.....................419 644-4311
Jack Atkinson, *Principal*
Tom Brooks, *Principal*
D Crooks, *Principal*
Al Zingaro, *Principal*
Debra Johnston, *Vice Pres*
EMP: 150
SALES (corp-wide): 14.3B **Publicly Held**
WEB: www.parker.com
SIC: 3542 Presses: hydraulic & pneumatic, mechanical & manual
PA: Parker-Hannifin Corporation
6035 Parkland Blvd
Cleveland OH 44124
216 896-3000

Miamisburg
Montgomery County

(G-13635)
A & T ORNAMENTAL IRON COMPANY
415 E Sycamore St (45342-2331)
PHONE.....................937 859-6006
Terry L Wagerman, *Owner*
EMP: 4
SALES (est): 405.3K **Privately Held**
SIC: 3446 Railings, prefabricated metal; gates, ornamental metal

(G-13636)
A-1 SPRINKLER COMPANY INC
2383 Northpointe Dr (45342-2989)
PHONE.....................937 859-6198
Bill Hausmann, *CEO*
EMP: 68
SQ FT: 15,000
SALES (est): 9.6MM **Privately Held**
WEB: www.spkr.com
SIC: 3569 5087 Firefighting apparatus & related equipment; firefighting equipment

(G-13637)
ADVANCED INDUSTRIAL MEASUREMNT
2580 Kohnle Dr (45342-3669)
P.O. Box 341118, Beavercreek (45434-1118)
PHONE.....................937 320-4930
David A Delph, *President*
Mark Gerading, *Vice Pres*
▲ **EMP**: 21
SALES (est): 4.3MM **Privately Held**
SIC: 3829 Measuring & controlling devices

(G-13638)
ALDRICH CHEMICAL
Also Called: Sigma-Aldrich
3858 Benner Rd (45342-4304)
PHONE.....................937 859-1808
Bob Becker, *Engineer*
John Shay, *Engineer*
Diane Szydell, *Manager*
Breet Eshbaugh, *Supervisor*
Michael Ferdelman, *Supervisor*
EMP: 70
SQ FT: 30,000
SALES (corp-wide): 16.9B **Privately Held**
SIC: 2819 5084 2899 2869 Isotopes, radioactive; chemical process equipment; chemical preparations; industrial organic chemicals
HQ: Aldrich Chemical
3050 Spruce St
Saint Louis MO 63103
314 771-5765

(G-13639)
ALEGRE INC
Also Called: Alegre Global Supply Solutions
3101 W Tech Blvd (45342-0819)
PHONE.....................937 885-6786
Lilly Phillips, *President*
Don Phillips, *Vice Pres*
Sue Buzard, *Materials Mgr*
Sue Peterson, *Materials Mgr*
EMP: 14
SQ FT: 24,000
SALES (est): 2.7MM **Privately Held**
SIC: 4225 5013 3714 General warehousing; automotive supplies & parts; motor vehicle engines & parts

(G-13640)
ANDERSON PUBLISHING CO (PA)
9443 Springboro Pike (45342-4425)
PHONE.....................513 474-9305
John L Mason, *Ch of Bd*
Dale Hartig, *President*
Diane Perry, *CFO*
Greg Arvanetes, *VP Sales*
EMP: 84 **EST**: 1887
SQ FT: 22,000
SALES (est): 5.6MM **Privately Held**
WEB: www.andersonpublishing.com
SIC: 2731 2741 Books: publishing only; pamphlets: publishing only, not printed on site; textbooks: publishing only, not printed on site; miscellaneous publishing; technical papers: publishing only, not printed on site

(G-13641)
APPLEHEART
2240 E Central Ave (45342-7601)
PHONE.....................937 384-0430
Tom Robbins, *President*
EMP: 6
SQ FT: 4,500
SALES (est): 380K **Privately Held**
WEB: www.tomrobbins.com
SIC: 5699 2759 2395 Uniforms & work clothing; commercial printing; embroidery products, except schiffli machine

(G-13642)
AVERY DENNISON
200 Monarch Ln (45342-3639)
PHONE.....................937 865-2439
Jan Watson, *Design Engr*
EMP: 13
SALES (est): 1.7MM **Privately Held**
SIC: 2672 Coated & laminated paper

(G-13643)
BELL VAULT & MONUMENT WORKS
1019 S Main St (45342-3148)
PHONE.....................937 866-2444
Timothy Bell, *President*
Greg Bell, *Corp Secy*
Jane Minges, *Sales Staff*
EMP: 24 **EST**: 1928
SQ FT: 17,000
SALES (est): 4.1MM **Privately Held**
SIC: 3272 5999 7261 3281 Burial vaults, concrete or precast terrazzo; monuments, finished to custom order; gravestones, finished; funeral service & crematories; cut stone & stone products; public building & related furniture

(G-13644)
BRAINERD INDUSTRIES INC (PA)
680 Precision Ct (45342-6138)
PHONE.....................937 228-0488
Gregory W Fritz, *President*
Rhonda Reynolds, *Vice Pres*
EMP: 50 **EST**: 1997
SQ FT: 72,000
SALES (est): 30MM **Privately Held**
WEB: www.brainerdindustries.com
SIC: 3469 3993 3442 Stamping metal for the trade; name plates: except engraved, etched, etc.: metal; metal doors, sash & trim

(G-13645)
BROWN CNC MACHINERY INC
433 E Maple Ave (45342-2343)
PHONE.....................937 865-9191
Mike Brown, *President*
Steve Brown, *Exec VP*
EMP: 28
SQ FT: 20,000
SALES (est): 1.7MM **Privately Held**
SIC: 3599 Machine shop, jobbing & repair

(G-13646)
C B & S SPOUTING INC
4609 Slders Hm Mmsburg Rd (45342-1127)
PHONE.....................937 866-1600
Penny Bullock, *President*
EMP: 3
SALES (est): 250K **Privately Held**
SIC: 3089 Spouting, plastic & glass fiber reinforced

(G-13647)
C B MFG & SLS CO INC (PA)
4455 Infirmary Rd (45342-1299)
PHONE.....................937 866-5986
Charles S Biehn Jr, *CEO*
Richard Porter, *President*
Donald M Cain, *Vice Pres*
Roger Adams, *Plant Mgr*
Amanda Morris, *Production*
▲ **EMP**: 67
SQ FT: 90,000
SALES (est): 35.8MM **Privately Held**
WEB: www.cbmfg.com
SIC: 5085 3423 Knives, industrial; knives, agricultural or industrial

(G-13648)
CERTIFIED TOOL & GRINDING INC
Also Called: Ctg
4455 Infirmary Rd (45342-1233)
PHONE.....................937 865-5934
Charles Biehn, *President*
Joseph Biehn, *Vice Pres*
▲ **EMP**: 7 **EST**: 1972
SALES (est): 1.1MM
SALES (corp-wide): 2.4MM **Privately Held**
WEB: www.certifiedindustrialservices.com
SIC: 3545 Cutting tools for machine tools; tools & accessories for machine tools
PA: Certified Heat Treating, Inc
4475 Infirmary Rd
Dayton OH 45449
937 866-0245

(G-13649)
CESO INC (PA)
3601 Rigby Rd Ste 310 (45342-5040)
PHONE.....................937 435-8584
David Oakes, *President*
James I Weprin, *Principal*
EMP: 51
SQ FT: 30,000
SALES (est): 16.2MM **Privately Held**
SIC: 8711 3674 8712 Civil engineering; light emitting diodes; architectural services

(G-13650)
CHRISTIAN BLUE PAGES (PA)
521 Byers Rd Ste 102 (45342-5379)
PHONE.....................937 847-2583
Darrel Geis, *President*
Brian Hegyi, *Sales Dir*
EMP: 10
SALES (est): 713.4K **Privately Held**
WEB: www.cbpgs.com
SIC: 2741 Directories, telephone: publishing only, not printed on site

(G-13651)
CONNECTIVE DESIGN INCORPORATED
Also Called: C D I
3010 S Tech Blvd (45342-4860)
PHONE.....................937 746-8252
Danya A Chandler, *President*
Mike Chandler, *Treasurer*
EMP: 11
SQ FT: 8,500
SALES (est): 2.5MM **Privately Held**
WEB: www.cdinc.us
SIC: 3678 3714 3679 Electronic connectors; automotive wiring harness sets; harness assemblies for electronic use: wire or cable

(G-13652)
COX NEWSPAPERS LLC
Also Called: Miamisburg News
230 S 2nd St (45342-2925)
P.O. Box 108 (45343-0108)
PHONE.....................937 866-3331
Donald J Miller, *President*
EMP: 10
SALES (corp-wide): 32.5B **Privately Held**
WEB: www.coxnewspapers.com
SIC: 2711 Newspapers, publishing & printing
HQ: Cox Newspapers, Inc.
6205 Peachtree Dunwoody
Atlanta GA 30328

(G-13653)
CUSTOMFORMED PRODUCTS INC
Also Called: Custom Formed Products
645 Precision Ct (45342-6138)
PHONE.....................937 388-0480
Michael Schindler, *President*
EMP: 15
SQ FT: 15,000
SALES (est): 2.1MM **Privately Held**
SIC: 2789 3469 3544 Paper cutting; metal stampings; dies, steel rule

(G-13654)
DAY-TEC TOOL & MFG INC
4900 Lyons Rd Unit A (45342-6417)
PHONE.....................937 847-0022
Gerald Whitehead, *President*
Dana Whitehead, *President*
Joseph Baylogh, *Vice Pres*
Jack Meyers, *Plant Mgr*
EMP: 12
SQ FT: 15,000
SALES: 2MM **Privately Held**
WEB: www.dtma.org
SIC: 3599 Machine shop, jobbing & repair

Miamisburg - Montgomery County (G-13679)

(G-13655)
DAYTON SUPERIOR CORPORATION (DH)
1125 Byers Rd (45342-5765)
PHONE..................................937 866-0711
James McRickard, *President*
Jay Requarth, *General Mgr*
Randy Brown, *Senior VP*
Peter Viens, *Senior VP*
Richard Lindstrom, *Vice Pres*
◆ EMP: 115 EST: 1924
SQ FT: 72,000
SALES (est): 353MM **Publicly Held**
WEB: www.daytonsuperior.com
SIC: 3315 3452 3462 3089 Steel wire & related products; dowel pins, metal; construction or mining equipment forgings, ferrous; plastic hardware & building products; chemical preparations

(G-13656)
DAYTON SUPERIOR CORPORATION
Also Called: Dayton Richmond
1125 Byers Rd (45342-5765)
PHONE..................................815 732-3136
Kevin Miller, *Sales/Mktg Mgr*
EMP: 20 **Publicly Held**
WEB: www.daytonsuperior.com
SIC: 2899 3496 Concrete curing & hardening compounds; miscellaneous fabricated wire products
HQ: Dayton Superior Corporation
1125 Byers Rd
Miamisburg OH 45342
937 866-0711

(G-13657)
DAYTON SYSTEMS GROUP INC
3003 S Tech Blvd (45342-4864)
PHONE..................................937 885-5665
Henry C Bachmann, *President*
Brad Bachmann, *COO*
Steve Cook, *Vice Pres*
EMP: 55
SQ FT: 23,000
SALES (est): 11.8MM **Privately Held**
WEB: www.dsgtech.com
SIC: 3565 Canning machinery, food

(G-13658)
DAYTRONIC CORPORATION (HQ)
2566 Kohnle Dr (45342-3669)
PHONE..................................937 866-3300
Robert Hart, *President*
EMP: 10 EST: 1954
SQ FT: 5,000
SALES (est): 1.1MM **Privately Held**
WEB: www.daytronic.com
SIC: 3829 Measuring & controlling devices

(G-13659)
DIGITAL CONTROLS CORPORATION (PA)
444 Alexandersville Rd (45342-3658)
PHONE..................................513 746-8118
EMP: 52 EST: 1969
SQ FT: 24,000
SALES (est): 9.1MM **Privately Held**
SIC: 7379 7372 5045 8742 Computer Related Svcs Prepackaged Software Svc Whol Computer/Peripheral Mgmt Consulting Svcs

(G-13660)
DOUBLE DIPPIN INC
949 Blanche Dr (45342-2027)
PHONE..................................937 847-2572
Don Smith, *Principal*
EMP: 4
SALES (est): 269.3K **Privately Held**
SIC: 2024 Ice cream & ice milk

(G-13661)
DSI PARTS LLC
2133 Lyons Rd (45342-4463)
PHONE..................................937 746-4678
Doug Smith, *President*
EMP: 3
SALES (est): 48K **Privately Held**
SIC: 3999 Manufacturing industries

(G-13662)
EAGLE MFG SOLUTIONS LLC
2585 Belvo Rd (45342-3911)
PHONE..................................937 865-0366
Dave Batner, *Mng Member*
Scott Lovelace, *Mng Member*
EMP: 12
SALES (est): 2.3MM **Privately Held**
SIC: 3599 Machine shop, jobbing & repair; custom machinery

(G-13663)
ELECTRIPACK INC
2064 Byers Rd (45342-1167)
PHONE..................................937 433-2602
Jeanne Wright, *CEO*
Paul Wise, *Facilities Mgr*
Roger Blankenship, *Warehouse Mgr*
Kari Nettleship, *Accountant*
◆ EMP: 40
SQ FT: 20,000
SALES (est): 7MM **Privately Held**
WEB: www.electripack.com
SIC: 3694 Harness wiring sets, internal combustion engines

(G-13664)
EPLUNO LLC
4501 Lyons Rd (45342-6444)
PHONE..................................800 249-5275
Paul Scapatici,
EMP: 17
SQ FT: 10,000
SALES (est): 1.5MM **Privately Held**
SIC: 2326 Men's & boys' work clothing

(G-13665)
ESKO-GRAPHICS INC (HQ)
Also Called: Eskoartwork
8535 Gander Creek Dr (45342-5436)
PHONE..................................937 454-1721
Kurt Demeuleneere, *CEO*
Jill Gehrhardt, *President*
Mark Quinlan, *President*
Tony Wiley, *President*
Ellen Schipper, *General Mgr*
▲ EMP: 70
SQ FT: 27,000
SALES (est): 133.7MM
SALES (corp-wide): 19.8B **Publicly Held**
SIC: 5084 7372 Printing trades machinery, equipment & supplies; prepackaged software
PA: Danaher Corporation
2200 Penn Ave Nw Ste 800w
Washington DC 20037
202 828-0850

(G-13666)
EVENFLO COMPANY INC (HQ)
225 Byers Rd (45342-3614)
PHONE..................................937 415-3300
Jon Chamberlain, *CEO*
Peter Banat, *Vice Pres*
Josh Korth, *CFO*
David McGillivary, *Treasurer*
Anthony Chip Gaetano, *Info Tech Dir*
◆ EMP: 150
SQ FT: 1,250,000
SALES (est): 257.5MM
SALES (corp-wide): 914.5MM **Privately Held**
WEB: www.evenflo.com
SIC: 2519 3944 Fiberglass & plastic furniture; child restraint seats, automotive
PA: Goodbaby International Holdings Limited
Rm 2001 20/F Two Chinachem Exchange Sq
North Point HK
280 603-38

(G-13667)
EXCELITAS TECHNOLOGIES CORP
1100 Vanguard Blvd (45342-0312)
PHONE..................................866 539-5916
Steven Cornett, *Electrical Engi*
Doug Benner, *Branch Mgr*
Steven Damian, *Manager*
EMP: 120 **Privately Held**
SIC: 3829 3489 Thermometers & temperature sensors; ordnance & accessories
HQ: Excelitas Technologies Corp.
200 West St
Waltham MA 02451

(G-13668)
FINASTRA USA CORPORATION
8555 Gander Creek Dr (45342-5436)
PHONE..................................937 435-2335
Connie Bruce, *Manager*
EMP: 49
SALES (corp-wide): 5.2B **Privately Held**
WEB: www.harlandfinancialsolutions.com
SIC: 7372 7389 Prepackaged software; personal service agents, brokers & bureaus
HQ: Finastra Usa Corporation
1320 Sw Broadway Ste 100
Portland OR 97201
407 804-6600

(G-13669)
FLORIDA TILE INC
Florida Tile 79
2105 Lyons Rd (45342-4463)
PHONE..................................937 293-5151
Michelle Clary, *Manager*
EMP: 6
SQ FT: 2,000
SALES (corp-wide): 147.6MM **Privately Held**
WEB: www.floridatile.com
SIC: 3253 Wall tile, ceramic
PA: Florida Tile, Inc.
998 Governors Ln Ste 300
Lexington KY 40513
859 219-5200

(G-13670)
FOXTRONIX INC
2240 E Central Ave Ste 4 (45342-3683)
PHONE..................................937 866-2112
Christopher Sweeney, *Owner*
EMP: 5
SQ FT: 2,200
SALES (est): 2.1MM **Privately Held**
WEB: www.foxtronix.com
SIC: 5065 3069 Electronic parts; hard rubber & molded rubber products

(G-13671)
FREEDOM ASPHALT SEALANT & LINE
1241 Stephens St (45342-1745)
PHONE..................................937 416-1053
Larry West, *Principal*
EMP: 3
SALES (est): 149.6K **Privately Held**
SIC: 2891 Sealants

(G-13672)
GAYSTON CORPORATION
Also Called: Mulch Masters of Ohio
721 Richard St (45342-1840)
P.O. Box 523 (45343-0523)
PHONE..................................937 743-6050
Adam Stone, *CEO*
Andrew Sheldrick, *COO*
Keith Bowers, *Engineer*
Paul Stone, *Engineer*
Ed Wach, *Engineer*
◆ EMP: 125 EST: 1951
SQ FT: 280,000
SALES (est): 44.5MM **Privately Held**
WEB: www.gayston.com
SIC: 1794 2819 3443 2499 Excavation & grading, building construction; aluminum compounds; cylinders, pressure: metal plate; mulch, wood & bark; military insignia

(G-13673)
HAMMELMANN CORPORATION (HQ)
436 Southpointe Dr (45342-6459)
PHONE..................................937 859-8777
Kathy Miller, *General Mgr*
Peter Englehardt, *Corp Secy*
Gisela Hammelmann, *Vice Pres*
Michael Goecke, *Vice Pres*
John Tsolis, *Vice Pres*
▲ EMP: 17
SQ FT: 10,000
SALES (est): 21.3MM
SALES (corp-wide): 118MM **Privately Held**
WEB: www.hammelmann.com
SIC: 5084 3443 Pumps & pumping equipment; fabricated plate work (boiler shop)
PA: Interpump Group Spa
Via Enrico Fermi 25
Sant'ilario D'enza RE 42049
052 290-4311

(G-13674)
HARTZELL MFG CO
2533 Technical Dr (45342-6108)
PHONE..................................937 859-5955
Gary Van Gundy, *CEO*
Eric Giese, *Plant Mgr*
Joe Gauthier, *QC Mgr*
Fred Issenmann, *QC Mgr*
Steve Smith, *Controller*
EMP: 36
SQ FT: 35,000
SALES (est): 6.5MM **Privately Held**
WEB: www.hartzellmfg.com
SIC: 3444 3479 3471 Sheet metal specialties, not stamped; coating of metals & formed products; plating & polishing
HQ: Drt Precision Mfg., Llc
1985 Campbell Rd
Sidney OH 45365
937 507-4308

(G-13675)
HEARTLAND PUBLICATIONS LLC (HQ)
Also Called: Civitas Media
4500 Lyons Rd (45342-6447)
PHONE..................................860 664-1075
Michael Bush, *President*
Bob Bertz, *CFO*
EMP: 11
SALES (est): 9MM
SALES (corp-wide): 763.9MM **Privately Held**
WEB: www.heartlandpublications.com
SIC: 2759 Publication printing
PA: Civitas Media, Llc
130 Harbour Place Dr # 300
Davidson NC 28036
704 897-6020

(G-13676)
HILLTOP BASIC RESOURCES INC
Also Called: Riverbend Sand Rock and Gravel
4710 Soldiers Home W (45342)
PHONE..................................937 859-3616
Mike Oliver, *Manager*
EMP: 15
SALES (corp-wide): 116.7MM **Privately Held**
WEB: www.hilltopbasicresources.com
SIC: 5032 1442 Gravel; sand, construction; construction sand & gravel
PA: Hilltop Basic Resources, Inc.
1 W 4th St Ste 1100
Cincinnati OH 45202
513 651-5000

(G-13677)
HOOVEN - DAYTON CORP (PA)
Also Called: H D C
511 Byers Rd (45342-5337)
P.O. Box 507, Mason (45040-0507)
PHONE..................................937 233-4473
Christopher Che, *President*
Al Abolofia, *Senior VP*
▲ EMP: 73
SQ FT: 40,000
SALES: 22MM **Privately Held**
WEB: www.hoovendayton.com
SIC: 2679 2672 2671 2759 Tags & labels, paper; tape, pressure sensitive: made from purchased materials; packaging paper & plastics film, coated & laminated; labels & seals: printing

(G-13678)
III OLIVE LLC SPICY
3650 Rigby Rd (45342-4974)
PHONE..................................937 247-5969
EMP: 3
SALES (est): 166.4K **Privately Held**
SIC: 2079 Olive oil

(G-13679)
INNOMARK COMMUNICATIONS LLC
3233 S Tech Blvd (45342-0843)
PHONE..................................937 454-5555

Miamisburg - Montgomery County (G-13680)

Rob Jones, *Manager*
EMP: 42
SALES (corp-wide): 82.8MM **Privately Held**
SIC: 2752 2789 Commercial printing, offset; bookbinding & related work
PA: Innomark Communications Llc
420 Distribution Cir
Fairfield OH 45014
888 466-6627

(G-13680)
INVOTEC ENGINEERING INC (PA)
10909 Industry Ln (45342-0818)
PHONE 937 886-3232
John C Hanna, *President*
Thomas Hahn, *Principal*
Mark Goode, *Safety Mgr*
Karen Brunke, *Engrg Dir*
Zachary Berger, *Engineer*
EMP: 60
SQ FT: 63,000
SALES (est): 21.4MM **Privately Held**
WEB: www.invotec.com
SIC: 8711 3599 Machine tool design; custom machinery

(G-13681)
JATRODIESEL INC
845 N Main St (45342-1871)
PHONE 937 847-8050
Rajesh Mosali, *President*
Rahul Bobbili, *Vice Pres*
▼ **EMP:** 17
SALES: 4.5MM **Privately Held**
WEB: www.jatrodiesel.com
SIC: 2869 3519 Mfg Industrial Organic Chemicals Mfg Internal Combustion Engines

(G-13682)
JOHNSON MACHINING SERVICES LLC
4505 Infirmary Rd (45342-1235)
PHONE 937 866-4744
Tom Johnson, *Mng Member*
Robert Mason,
EMP: 7
SQ FT: 2,500
SALES (est): 1MM **Privately Held**
SIC: 3599 3499 8711 Machine shop, jobbing & repair; machine bases, metal; mechanical engineering

(G-13683)
KINGSCOTE CHEMICALS INC
Also Called: Kingscote-Formulabs
3334 S Tech Blvd (45342-0823)
PHONE 937 886-9100
Robert Ciulla, *President*
Mark Hoover, *Manager*
EMP: 4
SALES: 900K **Privately Held**
WEB: www.kingscotechemicals.com
SIC: 2865 Cyclic crudes & intermediates

(G-13684)
LEXISNEXIS GROUP (DH)
9443 Springboro Pike (45342-5490)
PHONE 937 865-6800
Kurt Sanford, *CEO*
Doug Kaplan, *CEO*
▲ **EMP:** 148
SALES (est): 456.7MM
SALES (corp-wide): 9.7B **Privately Held**
SIC: 7375 2741 Data base information retrieval; miscellaneous publishing
HQ: Relx Inc.
230 Park Ave Ste 700
New York NY 10169
212 309-8100

(G-13685)
LIQUID LOGIC LLC
720 Mound Rd Ste 250 (45342)
PHONE 937 865-3068
Bill Merten, *CEO*
EMP: 3
SALES (est): 142.2K **Privately Held**
WEB: www.liquidlogicdispensers.com
SIC: 3841 Surgical & medical instruments

(G-13686)
MATTHEW BENDER & COMPANY INC
9443 Springboro Pike (45342-4425)
PHONE 518 487-3000
George Bearse, *Vice Pres*
EMP: 240
SALES (corp-wide): 9.7B **Privately Held**
SIC: 2721 2731 Periodicals; book publishing
HQ: Matthew Bender & Company, Inc.
744 Broad St Fl 8
Newark NJ 07102
518 487-3000

(G-13687)
MAX DAETWYLER CORP
2133 Lyons Rd (45342-4463)
PHONE 937 428-1781
Peter Daetwyler, *President*
EMP: 11
SALES (corp-wide): 75MM **Privately Held**
SIC: 3599 Electrical discharge machining (EDM)
HQ: Max Daetwyler Corp.
13420 Reese Blvd W
Huntersville NC 28078
704 875-1200

(G-13688)
MDI OF OHIO INC
Also Called: Formco
802 N 4th St (45342-1812)
PHONE 937 866-2345
John E Dempsey, *President*
EMP: 34
SALES (est): 6.9MM
SALES (corp-wide): 17.3MM **Privately Held**
SIC: 3089 Injection molded finished plastic products; injection molding of plastics
PA: Molded Devices, Inc.
6918 Ed Perkic St
Riverside CA 92504
480 785-9100

(G-13689)
METAL SHREDDERS INC
5101 Farmersville W (45342)
P.O. Box 244, Dayton (45449)
PHONE 937 866-0777
Ken Cohen, *President*
Wilbur Cohen, *Chairman*
EMP: 30
SQ FT: 8,000
SALES (est): 3.5MM **Privately Held**
WEB: www.metalshredders.com
SIC: 7389 3341 Metal slitting & shearing; secondary nonferrous metals

(G-13690)
MIAMI VALLEY COUNTERS & SPC
8515 Dyton Cncinnati Pike (45342-3168)
PHONE 937 865-0562
Ron James, *President*
Robert Dennis, *Vice Pres*
EMP: 6
SQ FT: 2,987
SALES (est): 805.1K **Privately Held**
SIC: 2541 Counter & sink tops

(G-13691)
MIAMI VALLEY PRECISION INC
456 Alexandersville Rd (45342-3658)
PHONE 937 866-1804
Michael Smith, *President*
Brian Smith, *Vice Pres*
Christine Smith, *Treasurer*
EMP: 22
SQ FT: 16,000
SALES (est): 3.5MM **Privately Held**
SIC: 3599 Machine shop, jobbing & repair

(G-13692)
MIAMI-CAST INC
901 N Main St (45342-1873)
PHONE 937 866-2951
George Deckebach, *President*
C Thomas Koehler, *Vice Pres*
Charles Koehler, *Treasurer*
EMP: 26
SQ FT: 20,000
SALES (est): 5.6MM **Privately Held**
WEB: www.miami-cast.com
SIC: 3321 Gray iron castings

(G-13693)
MIAMISBURG COATING
925 N Main St (45342-1873)
PHONE 937 866-1323
William Sizemore, *Partner*
Opal Sizemore, *Partner*
EMP: 10
SQ FT: 15,000
SALES (est): 1MM **Privately Held**
SIC: 3479 Coating of metals & formed products

(G-13694)
MIL-MAR CENTURY CORPORATION
8641 Washington Church Rd (45342-4470)
PHONE 937 275-4860
Trib Tewari, *President*
Beth Corwin, *Controller*
Bob Wehmeier, *Manager*
▲ **EMP:** 15
SALES (est): 2.6MM **Privately Held**
SIC: 3599 Machine shop, jobbing & repair

(G-13695)
MILLER PUBLISHING COMPANY
230 S 2nd St (45342-2925)
P.O. Box 1085 (45343-1085)
PHONE 937 866-3331
Donald J Miller, *Principal*
EMP: 3
SALES (est): 272.8K **Privately Held**
SIC: 2721 Magazines: publishing only, not printed on site

(G-13696)
MOUND PRINTING COMPANY INC
Also Called: Promotional Spring
2455 Belvo Rd (45342-3909)
PHONE 937 866-2872
Wade Riggs, *President*
Dennis Riggs, *General Mgr*
Frances Riggs, *Vice Pres*
Jason George, *Project Mgr*
Jeff Crowe, *Opers Mgr*
EMP: 25
SQ FT: 30,000
SALES (est): 5.2MM **Privately Held**
WEB: www.goldenbooks.com
SIC: 2759 Screen printing

(G-13697)
NAUTILUS HYOSUNG AMERICA INC
2076 Byers Rd (45342-1167)
PHONE 937 203-4900
Justin Kim, *Director*
EMP: 3
SALES (est): 289.9K **Privately Held**
SIC: 3612 Power transformers, electric

(G-13698)
NEWPAGE GROUP INC
8540 Gander Creek Dr (45342-5439)
PHONE 937 242-9500
George F Martin, *President*
Chan W Galbato, *Chairman*
James C Tyrone, *Exec VP*
Daniel A Clark, *Senior VP*
Douglas K Cooper, *Senior VP*
EMP: 6000
SALES (est): 228.8MM
SALES (corp-wide): 30.7B **Privately Held**
SIC: 2621 Paper mills
PA: Cerberus Capital Management, L.P.
875 3rd Ave
New York NY 10022
212 891-2100

(G-13699)
NEWPAGE HOLDING CORPORATION
8540 Gander Creek Dr (45342-5439)
PHONE 877 855-7243
George F Martin, *President*
James C Tyrone, *Exec VP*
Daniel A Clark, *Senior VP*
Laszlo M Lukacs, *Senior VP*
Douglas K Cooper, *Vice Pres*
◆ **EMP:** 1
SALES (est): 361.5MM **Publicly Held**
SIC: 2621 2672 2611 Fine paper; coated & laminated paper; pulp mills
PA: Verso Corporation
8540 Gander Creek Dr
Miamisburg OH 45342

(G-13700)
NONA COMPOSITES LLC
510 Earl Blvd (45342-6411)
PHONE 937 490-4814
Benjamin Dietsch, *Principal*
Patrick Hood, *Principal*
EMP: 5 **EST:** 2016
SALES (est): 336.4K **Privately Held**
SIC: 2821 3728 8711 Epoxy resins; aircraft parts & equipment; engineering services

(G-13701)
OCM LLC (HQ)
Also Called: Ohio Community Media
4500 Lyons Rd (45342-6447)
PHONE 937 247-2700
Roy Brown, *CEO*
EMP: 25
SALES (est): 89.7MM
SALES (corp-wide): 763.9MM **Privately Held**
SIC: 2711 Newspapers: publishing only, not printed on site
PA: Civitas Media, Llc
130 Harbour Place Dr # 300
Davidson NC 28036
704 897-6020

(G-13702)
OEM CORPORATION
3660 Benner Rd (45342-4368)
PHONE 937 859-7492
Randy Shupert, *President*
▼ **EMP:** 14
SQ FT: 38,000
SALES: 3MM **Privately Held**
WEB: www.oem-corp.com
SIC: 3564 Blowers & fans

(G-13703)
OHIO GRAVURE TECHNOLOGIES INC
1241 Byers Rd (45342-5770)
PHONE 937 439-1582
Eric Serenius, *President*
Chris Winter, *Mfg Staff*
Jeff Hemmelgarn, *Sr Ntwrk Engine*
Donna Aker, *Admin Asst*
Thomas Mader, *Associate*
▲ **EMP:** 30
SALES (est): 4.5MM **Privately Held**
SIC: 2754 Commercial printing, gravure
HQ: Heliograph Holding Gmbh
Konrad-Zuse-Bogen 18
Krailling 82152
897 859-6179

(G-13704)
ONEIL & ASSOCIATES INC (PA)
495 Byers Rd (45342-3798)
PHONE 937 865-0800
Bob Heilman, *President*
Ralph E Heyman, *Principal*
Gerald D Rapp, *Principal*
Howard N Thiele Jr, *Principal*
John Staten, *Chairman*
EMP: 300 **EST:** 1947
SQ FT: 75,000
SALES (est): 33.9MM **Privately Held**
WEB: www.oneil.com
SIC: 2741 8999 7336 Technical manuals: publishing only, not printed on site; technical manual preparation; commercial art & illustration

(G-13705)
PRINTING SERVICE COMPANY
3233 S Tech Blvd (45342-0843)
PHONE 937 425-6100
William Fair, *President*
Gary Boens, *Exec VP*
Paul Molyneaux, *Treasurer*
EMP: 70
SQ FT: 40,000
SALES: 16.6MM **Privately Held**
SIC: 2752 Commercial printing, offset

GEOGRAPHIC SECTION

Miamisburg - Montgomery County (G-13730)

(G-13706)
PROJECT ENGINEERING COMPANY
3010 S Tech Blvd (45342-4860)
PHONE..................937 743-9114
John L Michael, *President*
Trey Michael, *General Mgr*
EMP: 12
SQ FT: 8,000
SALES (est): 2MM **Privately Held**
WEB: www.projectengineeringcompany.com
SIC: 3469 Machine parts, stamped or pressed metal

(G-13707)
QUALITY CHANNEL LETTERS
1115 N 11th St (45342-1931)
PHONE..................859 866-6500
John M Wells, *Owner*
EMP: 3
SQ FT: 3,000
SALES (est): 254.7K **Privately Held**
SIC: 3993 Electric signs

(G-13708)
RELX INC
Also Called: Lexis Nexis
9443 Springboro Pike (45342-4425)
PHONE..................937 865-6800
Michael Weber, *Branch Mgr*
EMP: 49
SALES (corp-wide): 9.7B **Privately Held**
WEB: www.lexis-nexis.com
SIC: 2721 2731 7389 7999 Trade journals: publishing only, not printed on site; books: publishing only; trade show arrangement; exposition operation
HQ: Relx Inc.
 230 Park Ave Ste 700
 New York NY 10169
 212 309-8100

(G-13709)
RELX INC
4700 Lyons Rd (45342-6453)
PHONE..................937 865-6800
Bill Wheeler, *Manager*
EMP: 15
SALES (corp-wide): 9.7B **Privately Held**
WEB: www.lexis-nexis.com
SIC: 2721 Periodicals
HQ: Relx Inc.
 230 Park Ave Ste 700
 New York NY 10169
 212 309-8100

(G-13710)
RELX INC
Also Called: Lexisnexis
9333 Springboro Pike (45342-4424)
PHONE..................937 865-6800
Doug Kaplan, *Branch Mgr*
EMP: 128
SALES (corp-wide): 9.7B **Privately Held**
WEB: www.lexis-nexis.com
SIC: 2731 Books: publishing only
HQ: Relx Inc.
 230 Park Ave Ste 700
 New York NY 10169
 212 309-8100

(G-13711)
RENEGADE MATERIALS CORPORATION
3363 S Tech Blvd (45342-0826)
PHONE..................508 579-7888
Robert Gray, *President*
Susan Robitaille, *General Mgr*
Ron Garcia, *Opers Mgr*
Raymund Serranzana, *Engineer*
Eric Collins, *CFO*
▲ EMP: 22
SQ FT: 25,000
SALES (est): 5MM **Privately Held**
SIC: 3081 2891 2821 Plastic film & sheet; epoxy adhesives; epoxy resins; polyimides (skybond, kaplon); nylon resins

(G-13712)
RETALIX INC
2490 Technical Dr (45342-6136)
PHONE..................937 384-2277
Barry Shake, *CEO*
Barry Shaked, *President*
Karen Weaver, *Treasurer*
EMP: 155
SQ FT: 72,000
SALES (est): 9.8MM
SALES (corp-wide): 6.4B **Publicly Held**
SIC: 5734 7372 Software, business & non-game; prepackaged software
HQ: Ncr Global Ltd
 9 Dafna
 Raanana 43662
 747 756-677

(G-13713)
RUMFORD PAPER COMPANY
8540 Gander Creek Dr (45342-5439)
PHONE..................937 242-9230
George F Martin, *President*
EMP: 4 EST: 2010
SALES (est): 391.5K **Privately Held**
SIC: 2621 Paper mills

(G-13714)
SEELAUS INSTRUMENT CO
422 Alexandersville Rd (45342-3658)
PHONE..................513 733-8222
Hank Seelaus, *President*
Beth Seelaus, *Vice Pres*
EMP: 5
SQ FT: 1,500
SALES (est): 2.5MM **Privately Held**
SIC: 3823 Industrial process measurement equipment

(G-13715)
SGI MATRIX LLC (PA)
1041 Byers Rd (45342-5487)
PHONE..................937 438-9033
James Young, *President*
Jeffrey S Young, *Vice Pres*
John Schomburg, *CFO*
Jeff Stout, *VP Sales*
Bruce Rogoff,
EMP: 68 EST: 1977
SQ FT: 12,000
SALES (est): 30.5MM **Privately Held**
WEB: www.matrixsys.com
SIC: 8711 7373 3873 Engineering services; computer integrated systems design; watches, clocks, watchcases & parts

(G-13716)
SIGNATURE TECHNOLOGIES INC (DH)
Also Called: Com-Net Software Specialists
3728 Benner Rd (45342-4302)
PHONE..................937 859-6323
Elie Geva, *President*
David Michaels, *COO*
EMP: 40
SQ FT: 25,000
SALES (est): 20MM
SALES (corp-wide): 1.1B **Privately Held**
WEB: www.comnetsoftware.com
SIC: 3669 3674 3577 Transportation signaling devices; semiconductors & related devices; computer peripheral equipment
HQ: Sita Information Networking Computing Uk Limited
 C/O The Old Vinyl Factory
 Hayes MIDDX UB3 1
 800 026-0256

(G-13717)
SILVER TOOL INC
2440 Cross Pointe Dr (45342-3584)
PHONE..................937 865-0012
Marty Gebhardt, *Principal*
EMP: 40
SALES (corp-wide): 5.2MM **Privately Held**
WEB: www.silvertool.com
SIC: 3599 3545 3559 Machine shop, jobbing & repair; gauges (machine tool accessories); precision measuring tools; metal finishing equipment for plating, etc.
PA: Silver Tool, Inc.
 2440 Crosspointe Dr
 Miamisburg OH
 937 865-0067

(G-13718)
SOURCELINK OHIO LLC
3303 W Tech Blvd (45342-0817)
PHONE..................937 885-8000
Don Landrum, *CEO*
Jim Wisnionski, *President*
Mike Dolan, *COO*
Scott Wolford, *Production*
Gordon Anderson, *CFO*
EMP: 120
SQ FT: 140,000
SALES (est): 29.9MM
SALES (corp-wide): 86.9MM **Privately Held**
SIC: 7331 7374 2752 Direct mail advertising services; data processing service; commercial printing, lithographic
PA: Sourcelink Acquisition, Llc
 500 Park Blvd Ste 1425
 Itasca IL 60143
 866 947-6872

(G-13719)
STACO ENERGY PRODUCTS CO (HQ)
2425 Technical Dr (45342-6137)
PHONE..................937 253-1191
Cary M Maguire, *Ch of Bd*
Jim Clark, *President*
Jeff Hoffman, *Principal*
Richard K Hoesterey, *Principal*
Dan Hinkle, *Vice Pres*
◆ EMP: 6 EST: 1944
SALES: 15MM
SALES (corp-wide): 44.2MM **Privately Held**
WEB: www.stacoenergy.com
SIC: 3677 3612 3999 Electronic coils, transformers & other inductors; generator voltage regulators; military insignia
PA: Components Corporation Of America
 5950 Berkshire Ln # 1500
 Dallas TX 75225
 214 969-0166

(G-13720)
STAR CITY ART CO
421 S 9th St (45342-3340)
PHONE..................937 865-9792
EMP: 15
SALES (est): 770K **Privately Held**
SIC: 3577 Mfg Computer Peripheral Equipment

(G-13721)
STEINER EOPTICS INC (PA)
Also Called: Sensor Technology Systems
3475 Newmark Dr (45342-5426)
PHONE..................937 426-2341
Alan Page, *General Mgr*
Doris Byerly Anderson, *Office Mgr*
EMP: 80
SQ FT: 50,000
SALES (est): 13.9MM **Privately Held**
SIC: 8731 3851 Electronic research; ophthalmic goods

(G-13722)
SYNAGRO MIDWEST INC
4515 Infirmary Rd (45342-1235)
PHONE..................937 384-0669
Jim Rosendall, *Vice Pres*
EMP: 10
SALES (est): 2.3MM
SALES (corp-wide): 12.5MM **Privately Held**
SIC: 4953 2873 Recycling, waste materials; nitrogenous fertilizers
HQ: Synagro Technologies, Inc.
 435 Williams Ct Ste 100
 Baltimore MD 21220

(G-13723)
TECH PRODUCTS CORPORATION (DH)
2215 Lyons Rd (45342-4465)
PHONE..................937 438-1100
Dan Rork, *President*
Hugh E Wall Jr, *Principal*
Peirce Wood, *Principal*
A M Zimmerman, *Principal*
Bryan Strayer, *Prdtn Mgr*
EMP: 29
SQ FT: 25,000
SALES (est): 5.4MM
SALES (corp-wide): 2.6MM **Privately Held**
WEB: www.tpcdayton.com
SIC: 3625 5084 3829 3651 Noise control equipment; noise control equipment; measuring & controlling devices; household audio & video equipment
HQ: Fabreeka International Holdings, Inc.
 1023 Turnpike St
 Stoughton MA 02072
 781 341-3655

(G-13724)
TECHNICOTE INC (PA)
222 Mound Ave (45342-2996)
P.O. Box 188 (45343-0188)
PHONE..................800 358-4448
Doug O'Connell, *President*
Dorothy L Chapman, *Principal*
Peggy Curtiss, *Principal*
Michael A Ogline, *Principal*
Roger Poteet, *QC Mgr*
◆ EMP: 46
SQ FT: 35,000
SALES (est): 78.2MM **Privately Held**
WEB: www.technicote.com
SIC: 2672 Adhesive papers, labels or tapes: from purchased material; labels (unprinted), gummed: made from purchased materials

(G-13725)
TECHNICOTE WESTFIELD INC
222 Mound Ave (45342-2996)
PHONE..................937 859-4448
Dirk Desanzo, *President*
Douglas Garwood, *Corp Secy*
John L Mc Cormick, *Vice Pres*
John Petel, *Vice Pres*
EMP: 60
SQ FT: 35,000
SALES (est): 6.5MM **Privately Held**
SIC: 2672 Adhesive papers, labels or tapes: from purchased material

(G-13726)
TERADATA OPERATIONS INC
2461 Rosina Dr (45342-6431)
PHONE..................937 866-0032
EMP: 3 **Publicly Held**
SIC: 3571 Electronic computers
HQ: Teradata Operations, Inc.
 10000 Innovation Dr
 Miamisburg OH 45342

(G-13727)
TERADATA OPERATIONS INC (HQ)
10000 Innovation Dr (45342-4927)
PHONE..................937 242-4030
Victor Lund, *President*
John Emanuel, *President*
John Huffman, *Partner*
Paul Majchrzak, *Partner*
Oliver Ratzesberger, *COO*
EMP: 100
SALES (est): 396.9MM **Publicly Held**
SIC: 3571 7379 Electronic computers; computer related consulting services

(G-13728)
TRI DLTA METAL FABRICATION LLC
643 Dunraven Pass (45342-2204)
PHONE..................937 499-4315
Steven Dicken, *Principal*
EMP: 3
SALES (est): 48K **Privately Held**
SIC: 3999 Manufacturing industries

(G-13729)
UNCLE JESTERS FINE FOODS LLC
2564 Kohnle Dr (45342-3669)
P.O. Box 751953, Dayton (45475-1953)
PHONE..................937 550-1025
Jeffrey Stevenson, *President*
EMP: 4 EST: 2010
SQ FT: 5,000
SALES (est): 307.1K **Privately Held**
SIC: 2033 5141 2035 5149 Barbecue sauce: packaged in cans, jars, etc.; jams, jellies & preserves: packaged in cans, jars, etc.; groceries, general line; pickles, sauces & salad dressings; seasonings, sauces & extracts

(G-13730)
UNITED GRINDING NORTH AMER INC (DH)
2100 United Grinding Blvd (45342-6804)
PHONE..................937 859-1975

Miamisburg - Montgomery County (G-13731)

Mr Terry Derrico, *CEO*
Rodger Pinney, *President*
Simon Bramhall, *General Mgr*
Joseph Szenay, *General Mgr*
Michael Martin, *Regional Mgr*
▲ **EMP:** 66
SALES (est): 38.6MM
SALES (corp-wide): 2.8MM **Privately Held**
WEB: www.grinding.com
SIC: 3541 Machine tools, metal cutting type
HQ: United Grinding Gmbh
  Kurt-A.-Korber-Chaussee 63-71
  Hamburg 21033
  407 250-07

(G-13731)
VENTARI CORPORATION
8641 Washington Church Rd (45342-4470)
PHONE.................................937 278-4269
Trib Tawari, *President*
Bob Pelfrey, *General Mgr*
EMP: 25
SALES (est): 2.3MM **Privately Held**
SIC: 3449 Miscellaneous metalwork

(G-13732)
VERSO CORPORATION (PA)
8540 Gander Creek Dr (45342-5439)
PHONE.................................877 855-7243
Leslie T Lederer, *CEO*
Robert M Amen, *Ch of Bd*
Michael A Weinhold, *President*
Peter H Kesser, *Senior VP*
Kenneth D Sawyer, *Senior VP*
EMP: 277
SALES: 2.6B **Publicly Held**
SIC: 2621 Specialty papers

(G-13733)
VERSO CORPORATION
Also Called: Verso Paper
8540 Gander Creek Dr (45342-5439)
PHONE.................................901 369-4105
Tom Huber, *Manager*
EMP: 58 **Publicly Held**
SIC: 2653 2656 2631 2611 Boxes, corrugated: made from purchased materials; food containers (liquid tight), including milk cartons; cartons, milk: made from purchased material; container, packaging & boxboard; container board; packaging board; pulp mills; printing paper
PA: Verso Corporation
  8540 Gander Creek Dr
  Miamisburg OH 45342

(G-13734)
VERSO CORPORATION
8540 Gander Creek Dr (45342-5439)
PHONE.................................901 369-4100
Gary Romanski, *Opers Mgr*
Matthew Archambeau, *Mfg Staff*
Marilyn Foley, *Purchasing*
Matt Riggle, *Engineer*
Loretta Baker, *Accountant*
EMP: 400 **Publicly Held**
SIC: 2621 Paper mills
PA: Verso Corporation
  8540 Gander Creek Dr
  Miamisburg OH 45342

(G-13735)
VERSO PAPER HOLDING LLC (HQ)
8540 Gander Creek Dr (45342-5439)
PHONE.................................877 855-7243
Mike Jackson, *CEO*
Mark A Angelson, *Chairman*
James C Tyrone, *Exec VP*
J Mark Lukacs, *Senior VP*
David L Santez, *Senior VP*
◆ **EMP:** 380
SALES (est): 797.2MM **Publicly Held**
SIC: 2621 2611 Fine paper; uncoated paper; pulp manufactured from waste or recycled paper

(G-13736)
VERSO PAPER HOLDING LLC
8540 Gander Creek Dr (45342-5439)
PHONE.................................901 369-4100
Pat Gibney, *Branch Mgr*
David Michaud, *Manager*
EMP: 840 **Publicly Held**

SIC: 2671 Paper coated or laminated for packaging
HQ: Verso Paper Holding Llc
  8540 Gander Creek Dr
  Miamisburg OH 45342
  877 855-7243

(G-13737)
WALTER GRINDERS INC
510 Earl Blvd (45342-6411)
PHONE.................................937 859-1975
Joe Szenay, *Principal*
Michael Gebhardt, *Vice Pres*
EMP: 4
SALES (est): 355.4K **Privately Held**
SIC: 3541 Crankshaft regrinding machines

(G-13738)
WARREN FIRE EQUIPMENT INC
2240 E Central Ave (45342-7601)
PHONE.................................937 866-8918
Robert Keefer, *Branch Mgr*
EMP: 5
SALES (corp-wide): 4.7MM **Privately Held**
WEB: www.warrenfireequip.com
SIC: 5087 5012 7389 3569 Firefighting equipment; automobiles & other motor vehicles; fire extinguisher servicing; firefighting apparatus & related equipment
PA: Warren Fire Equipment, Inc.
  6880 Tod Ave Sw
  Warren OH 44481
  330 824-3523

(G-13739)
WAUSEON MACHINE & MFG INC
Also Called: Autmotion Rbtic Intgration Div
2495 Technical Dr (45342-6137)
PHONE.................................419 337-0940
Jack Fisher, *Principal*
EMP: 5
SALES (corp-wide): 18.4MM **Privately Held**
SIC: 3599 Machine shop, jobbing & repair
PA: Wauseon Machine & Manufacturing, Inc.
  995 Enterprise Ave
  Wauseon OH 43567
  419 337-0940

(G-13740)
WAXCO INTERNATIONAL INC
Also Called: Dacraft
727 Dayton Oxford Rd (45342)
P.O. Box 147 (45343-0147)
PHONE.................................937 746-4845
Roger Wax, *President*
Bill Wax, *Vice Pres*
EMP: 10
SALES (est): 1.8MM **Privately Held**
SIC: 3355 1521 5211 1761 Structural shapes, rolled, aluminum; general remodeling, single-family houses; door & window products; siding contractor

(G-13741)
WILLIAMS PRECISION TOOL INC
6855 Gillen Ln (45342-1507)
PHONE.................................937 384-0608
EMP: 12
SALES (est): 870K **Privately Held**
SIC: 3599 Mfg Industrial Machinery

(G-13742)
YASKAWA AMERICA INC
Motoman Robotics Division
100 Automation Way (45342-4962)
PHONE.................................937 847-6200
Steve Barhorst, *Division Pres*
EMP: 180
SQ FT: 304,815
SALES (corp-wide): 4B **Privately Held**
WEB: www.motoman.com
SIC: 3569 Robots, assembly line: industrial & commercial
HQ: Yaskawa America, Inc.
  2121 Norman Dr
  Waukegan IL 60085
  847 887-7000

Miamitown
Hamilton County

(G-13743)
BICKERS METAL PRODUCTS INC
5825 State Rte128 (45041)
P.O. Box 648 (45041-0648)
PHONE.................................513 353-4000
Robert C Graff, *President*
Roger Coffaro, *Vice Pres*
Charles Coffaro, *Shareholder*
EMP: 40 **EST:** 1964
SQ FT: 30,000
SALES (est): 10.8MM **Privately Held**
SIC: 3441 3444 Fabricated structural metal; sheet metalwork

(G-13744)
BROTHERS TOOL AND MFG LTD
8300 Harrison Ave (45041)
P.O. Box 89 (45041-0089)
PHONE.................................513 353-9700
Grant Schutte, *Partner*
John Schutte, *Partner*
EMP: 12
SQ FT: 6,000
SALES (est): 1.2MM **Privately Held**
WEB: www.brotherstool.net
SIC: 3544 Special dies, tools, jigs & fixtures

(G-13745)
CHARGER PRESS INC
6088 Rte128 (45041)
P.O. Box 117 (45041-0117)
PHONE.................................513 542-3113
Gerald J Laake, *President*
EMP: 18 **EST:** 1956
SALES (est): 1.8MM **Privately Held**
SIC: 2752 Commercial printing, offset

(G-13746)
GATEWAY CONCRETE FORMING SVCS
5938 Hamilton Cleves Rd (45041)
P.O. Box 130 (45041-0130)
PHONE.................................513 353-2000
Robert Bilz, *President*
Tim Hughey, *President*
Brandon Erfman, *Vice Pres*
Jean C Hughey, *Treasurer*
J Robert Hughey, *Shareholder*
EMP: 75
SQ FT: 3,000
SALES (est): 8MM **Privately Held**
WEB: www.gatewaybuildingproducts.com
SIC: 1771 3449 3496 3429 Foundation & footing contractor; bars, concrete reinforcing: fabricated steel; miscellaneous fabricated wire products; manufactured hardware (general)

(G-13747)
JACP INC (PA)
5928 Hamilton Cleves Rd (45041)
PHONE.................................513 353-3660
Michael Baltes, *President*
EMP: 4
SQ FT: 25,000
SALES (est): 890K **Privately Held**
WEB: www.jacp.com
SIC: 3541 3443 3564 Grinding machines, metalworking; tanks for tank trucks, metal plate; dust or fume collecting equipment, industrial

(G-13748)
MACLEOD INC
5928 Hamilton Cleves Rd (45041)
PHONE.................................513 771-9560
Robert J Wallace, *President*
EMP: 5
SQ FT: 22,000
SALES (est): 445K **Privately Held**
WEB: www.macleod.com
SIC: 3443 Tanks for tank trucks, metal plate
PA: Jacp Inc
  5928 Hamilton Cleves Rd
  Miamitown OH 45041

(G-13749)
MODERN SHEET METAL WORKS INC
6037 State Rte 128 (45041)
P.O. Box 445 (45041-0445)
PHONE.................................513 353-3666
Dorothy Johnson, *President*
Cynthia Freppon, *Vice Pres*
Pamela Rosenacher, *Treasurer*
William Freppon, *Sales Executive*
EMP: 25 **EST:** 1936
SQ FT: 16,000
SALES (est): 5.5MM **Privately Held**
WEB: www.modernsheetmetal.com
SIC: 3444 Sheet metalwork

(G-13750)
RHINO ROBOTICS LTD
5928 State Rte 128 (45041)
P.O. Box 230 (45041-0230)
PHONE.................................513 353-9772
EMP: 4
SQ FT: 25,000
SALES (est): 390K **Privately Held**
SIC: 3535 5084 Mfg Conveyors/Equipment Whol Industrial Equipment

(G-13751)
SEILKOP INDUSTRIES INC
A-G Tool & Die Company
5927 State Route 128 (45041)
P.O. Box 250 (45041-0250)
PHONE.................................513 353-3090
Ken Seilkop, *Owner*
John Mason, *Engineer*
George Meister, *Engineer*
EMP: 40
SQ FT: 19,000
SALES (corp-wide): 24.1MM **Privately Held**
WEB: www.epcorfoundry.com
SIC: 3312 3544 Tool & die steel; special dies, tools, jigs & fixtures
PA: Seilkop Industries, Inc.
  425 W North Bend Rd
  Cincinnati OH 45216
  513 761-1035

Miamiville
Clermont County

(G-13752)
IRVINE WOOD RECOVERY INC
110 Glendale Milford Rd (45147)
PHONE.................................513 831-0060
Les Irvine, *President*
Elizabeth Hovis, *Bookkeeper*
EMP: 40
SQ FT: 15,000
SALES (est): 6.4MM **Privately Held**
SIC: 2499 Mulch, wood & bark

(G-13753)
MESSER LLC
Boc Gases
State Road 126160 St State Ro (45147)
PHONE.................................513 831-4742
John L Seibert, *Manager*
EMP: 23
SALES (corp-wide): 1.4B **Privately Held**
SIC: 2813 Nitrogen
HQ: Messer Llc
  200 Somerset Corporate
  Bridgewater NJ 08807
  908 464-8100

Middle Point
Van Wert County

(G-13754)
ADDITIVE TECHNOLOGY INC
Also Called: Adtec
404 W Railroad St (45863-9779)
P.O. Box 221 (45863-0221)
PHONE.................................419 968-2777
John Sheeran, *President*
H Daniel Sheeran, *Vice Pres*
▲ **EMP:** 4
SQ FT: 15,000

▲ = Import ▼ = Export
◆ = Import/Export

SALES (est): 560.3K **Privately Held**
SIC: 2899 Chemical preparations

(G-13755)
AMERICAN PAINT RECYCLERS LLC
4664 Mddle Pint Wetzel Rd (45863-9536)
PHONE..........................888 978-6558
Jeremy Brinkman, *Principal*
EMP: 4
SALES (est): 189.6K **Privately Held**
SIC: 2851 Paints & paint additives

(G-13756)
B & B WELDING
6647 Middle Pt Wetzel Rd (45863-9635)
PHONE..........................419 968-2743
Larry Black, *Owner*
EMP: 3 EST: 1992
SALES (est): 90.9K **Privately Held**
SIC: 7692 Welding repair

(G-13757)
TRAVELING & RECYCLE WOOD PDTS
Also Called: T&R Wood Products
19590 Bellis Rd (45863-9721)
P.O. Box 143 (45863-0143)
PHONE..........................419 968-2649
Eddy Miller, *President*
Scott Miller, *Vice Pres*
EMP: 12
SQ FT: 13,680
SALES (est): 1.2MM **Privately Held**
SIC: 2441 2448 2449 Boxes, wood; cases, wood; pallets, wood; wood containers

Middlebranch
Stark County

(G-13758)
KARG FIBERGLASS INC
2831 Diamond St (44652)
P.O. Box 35 (44652-0035)
PHONE..........................330 494-2611
George L Karg, *President*
EMP: 4
SQ FT: 7,000
SALES: 380K **Privately Held**
WEB: www.kargfiberglass.com
SIC: 3714 Motor vehicle body components & frame

(G-13759)
LEHIGH CEMENT COMPANY LLC
8282 Middlebranch Ave Ne (44652)
PHONE..........................330 499-9100
EMP: 3
SALES (corp-wide): 20.6B **Privately Held**
SIC: 3273 Ready-mixed concrete
HQ: Lehigh Cement Company Llc
  300 E John Carpenter Fwy
  Irving TX 75062
  877 534-4442

(G-13760)
LEHIGH HANSON ECC INC
8282 Middlebranch Ave Ne (44652)
P.O. Box 234 (44652-0234)
PHONE..........................330 499-9100
Dale Lewis, *Branch Mgr*
EMP: 18
SALES (corp-wide): 20.6B **Privately Held**
WEB: www.essroc.com
SIC: 3273 Ready-mixed concrete
HQ: Lehigh Hanson Ecc, Inc.
  3251 Bath Pike
  Nazareth PA 18064
  610 837-6725

Middleburg Heights
Cuyahoga County

(G-13761)
ASSOCIATED SOFTWARE CONS INC
Also Called: A S C
7251 Engle Rd Ste 400 (44130-3400)
PHONE..........................440 826-1010
Tim Liston, *President*
John H Liston, *Corp Secy*
Danny Liggett, *Project Mgr*
Dave Stricklen, *Manager*
John Liston, *Software Dev*
EMP: 17
SQ FT: 7,500
SALES (est): 4.8MM **Privately Held**
WEB: www.asconline.com
SIC: 7371 7372 Computer software systems analysis & design, custom; prepackaged software

(G-13762)
CLEVELAND DIE & MFG CO (PA)
Also Called: Cleveland Die & Mfg
20303 1st Ave (44130-2433)
PHONE..........................440 243-3404
Juan Chahda, *President*
Liliana Chahda, *Vice Pres*
Vladimir Haoui, *Plant Mgr*
Stela Mimis, *Purch Mgr*
Viorica Tepes, *Controller*
▲ EMP: 25
SQ FT: 165,000
SALES: 16MM **Privately Held**
WEB: www.clevelanddie.com
SIC: 3469 3544 Stamping metal for the trade; special dies, tools, jigs & fixtures

(G-13763)
COATING SYSTEMS GROUP INC
6909 Engle Rd Bldg C (44130-3473)
PHONE..........................440 816-9306
Frank Popiel, *President*
Dawn Kaminski, *Principal*
EMP: 10
SALES (est): 212.6K **Privately Held**
SIC: 8711 3535 Engineering services; conveyors & conveying equipment

(G-13764)
DUBOSE ENERGY FASTENERS & MACH
18737 Sheldon Rd (44130-2472)
PHONE..........................216 362-1700
Carl Rogers, *CEO*
Martin Kossick, *President*
Richard Rogers, *Treasurer*
EMP: 18
SALES (est): 2.5MM
SALES (corp-wide): 11.5B **Publicly Held**
SIC: 3965 Fasteners
PA: Reliance Steel & Aluminum Co.
  350 S Grand Ave Ste 5100
  Los Angeles CA 90071
  213 687-7700

(G-13765)
IEC INFRARED SYSTEMS INC
7803 Freeway Cir (44130-6308)
PHONE..........................440 234-8000
Rick Pettergrew, *President*
Arthur Stachowicz, *Electrical Engi*
Ron Austin, *Business Dir*
EMP: 25
SQ FT: 2,300
SALES (est): 3.9MM **Privately Held**
WEB: www.iecinfrared.com
SIC: 3826 Infrared analytical instruments

(G-13766)
IEC INFRARED SYSTEMS LLC
7803 Freeway Cir (44130-6308)
PHONE..........................440 234-8000
Richard Pettegrew, *Mng Member*
EMP: 22
SALES (est): 2.6MM **Privately Held**
SIC: 7389 3826 Design services; infrared analytical instruments

(G-13767)
NOVA MACHINE PRODUCTS INC (HQ)
18001 Sheldon Rd (44130-2465)
PHONE..........................216 267-3200
David Linton, *CEO*
Martin R Benante, *Ch of Bd*
Greg Jackson, *Safety Mgr*
Jim Skufca, *Sales Mgr*
Terri Dienes, *Manager*
▲ EMP: 70
SALES (est): 17.5MM
SALES (corp-wide): 2.4B **Publicly Held**
SIC: 3452 3429 3369 3356 Bolts, metal; washers; nuts, metal; lock washers; manufactured hardware (general); nonferrous foundries; nonferrous rolling & drawing
PA: Curtiss-Wright Corporation
  130 Harbour Place Dr # 300
  Davidson NC 28036
  704 869-4600

(G-13768)
PRECISION REMOTES LLC
7803 Freeway Cir (44130-6308)
PHONE..........................510 215-6474
Bob Whiteaker, *Office Mgr*
EMP: 20
SQ FT: 5,000
SALES (est): 3.6MM **Privately Held**
SIC: 3861 Tripods, camera & projector

(G-13769)
RIVALS SPORTS GRILLE LLC
6710 Smith Rd (44130-2656)
PHONE..........................216 267-0005
John Simmons,
EMP: 48
SQ FT: 4,368
SALES: 1.9MM **Privately Held**
SIC: 5812 7372 Grills (eating places); application computer software

(G-13770)
SOLUTION INDUSTRIES LLC
17830 Englewood Dr Ste 11 (44130-3485)
PHONE..........................440 816-9500
John Radel, *President*
Jim Jordan, *Regl Sales Mgr*
EMP: 39
SALES (est): 5.5MM **Privately Held**
SIC: 3965 Fasteners, buttons, needles & pins

(G-13771)
VERANTIS CORPORATION (HQ)
7251 Engle Rd Ste 300 (44130-3400)
PHONE..........................440 243-0700
William Jackson, *Senior VP*
▼ EMP: 30
SALES (est): 17.8MM **Privately Held**
SIC: 3564 5075 Air purification equipment; blowers & fans; air pollution control equipment & supplies
PA: Tanglewood Investments Inc.
  5051 Westheimer Rd # 300
  Houston TX 77056
  713 629-5525

Middlefield
Geauga County

(G-13772)
A & M PALLET SHOP INC
14550 Madison Rd (44062-9499)
P.O. Box 765 (44062-0765)
PHONE..........................440 632-1941
Andy A Miller, *President*
EMP: 11
SQ FT: 4,200
SALES (est): 1.1MM **Privately Held**
SIC: 2448 Pallets, wood

(G-13773)
ADVANCING ECO-AGRICULTURE LLC
4551 Parks West Rd (44062-9345)
P.O. Box 683 (44062-0683)
PHONE..........................800 495-6603
Jason Hobson, *CEO*
P Van Den Bossche, *Chairman*
Philippe Van Den Bossche, *Chairman*
John Kempf,
EMP: 5 EST: 2008
SALES (est): 1.4MM **Privately Held**
SIC: 2873 8748 Fertilizers: natural (organic), except compost; agricultural consultant

(G-13774)
AIRWOLF AEROSPACE LLC
15369 Madison Rd (44062-8404)
PHONE..........................440 632-1687
John Kochy, *Mng Member*
EMP: 5
SALES (est): 571.1K **Privately Held**
SIC: 3728 Research & dev by manuf., aircraft parts & auxiliary equip

(G-13775)
ALL FOAM PRODUCTS CO
15005 Enterprise Way (44062-9369)
PHONE..........................330 849-3636
Darrell McNair, *Principal*
EMP: 3
SALES (est): 316.6K **Privately Held**
SIC: 3086 Plastics foam products

(G-13776)
ALL FOAM PRODUCTS CO (PA)
Also Called: All Foam Pdts Safety Foam Proc
15005 Enterprise Way (44062-9369)
PHONE..........................330 849-3636
Darrell McNair, *President*
Sue Kagebein, *General Mgr*
Shelly Silver, *Corp Secy*
Debbie Irlbacker, *Vice Pres*
Marvin Steinlauf, *Vice Pres*
EMP: 6
SQ FT: 3,200
SALES: 795K **Privately Held**
WEB: www.allfoam.com
SIC: 3086 Plastics foam products

(G-13777)
AMERICAN PLASTIC TECH INC
Also Called: A P T
15229 S State Ave (44062-9468)
P.O. Box 37 (44062-0037)
PHONE..........................440 632-5203
Joseph A Bergen, *President*
Duncan M Simpson Jr, *Senior VP*
Edd Hiksman, *CFO*
Tony Mosko, *Controller*
Pauline Anderson, *Manager*
▲ EMP: 182
SQ FT: 178,000
SALES (est): 59.7MM **Privately Held**
WEB: www.sajar.com
SIC: 3089 3559 Injection molding of plastics; plastics working machinery

(G-13778)
ARROWHEAD PALLETS LLC
7851 Parkman Mespo Rd (44062-9328)
PHONE..........................440 693-4241
Ervin C Byler,
EMP: 16
SALES (est): 172.7K **Privately Held**
SIC: 2448 Wood pallets & skids

(G-13779)
BASETEK LLC (PA)
14975 White Rd (44062-9216)
PHONE..........................877 712-2273
Scott Sapita, *Mng Member*
Timothy E Marklay,
EMP: 16
SALES: 5MM **Privately Held**
SIC: 3531 5032 Construction machinery; concrete & cinder block

(G-13780)
BENTRONIX CORP
14999 Madison Rd (44062-8403)
P.O. Box 1297 (44062-1297)
PHONE..........................440 632-0606
Ludmilla Benins, *President*
Peter Benins, *Vice Pres*
Brian Lanstrum, *Vice Pres*
EMP: 7
SQ FT: 2,500
SALES: 600K **Privately Held**
SIC: 3613 7629 Control panels, electric; electronic equipment repair

(G-13781)
BRADFORD NEAL MACHINERY INC
14503 Old State Rd (44062-9703)
P.O. Box 1237 (44062-1237)
PHONE..........................440 632-1393
James Skinner, *President*
Ruth Skinner, *Corp Secy*
EMP: 3
SQ FT: 6,000

Middlefield - Geauga County (G-13782)

SALES (est): 471.8K **Privately Held**
WEB: www.bradfordneal.com
SIC: 3559 7699 Plastics working machinery; robots, molding & forming plastics; industrial machinery & equipment repair

(G-13782)
CARTER-JONES LUMBER COMPANY
14601 Kinsman Rd (44062-9245)
PHONE.................................440 834-8164
Lenny Barciskoi, *Manager*
EMP: 15
SALES (corp-wide): 1.4B **Privately Held**
SIC: 2452 5074 5211 Prefabricated buildings, wood; plumbing & hydronic heating supplies; lumber products
HQ: The Carter-Jones Lumber Company
601 Tallmadge Rd
Kent OH 44240
330 673-6100

(G-13783)
CHEM TECHNOLOGIES LTD
14875 Bonner Dr (44062-8493)
PHONE.................................440 632-9311
S James Schill, *Principal*
Janet Cline, *Purch Mgr*
Patrick Roddy, *Director*
EMP: 30
SQ FT: 120,000
SALES (est): 13.8MM **Privately Held**
WEB: www.chemtechnologiesltd.com
SIC: 2819 2899 Industrial inorganic chemicals; chemical preparations

(G-13784)
CHEROKEE HARDWOODS INC (PA)
Also Called: Amish Heritg WD Floors & Furn
16741 Newcomb Rd (44062-8248)
PHONE.................................440 632-0322
Wallace D Byler, *President*
Bill W Byler, *Vice Pres*
EMP: 10 EST: 1997
SQ FT: 12,500
SALES (est): 813.9K **Privately Held**
SIC: 2421 2426 Sawmills & planing mills, general; hardwood dimension & flooring mills

(G-13785)
CHIPMUNK LOGGING & LUMBER LLC
15810 Chipmunk Ln (44062-7205)
PHONE.................................440 537-5124
Jacob Detweiler, *Mng Member*
EMP: 3
SALES (est): 260.2K **Privately Held**
SIC: 2411 Logging

(G-13786)
COMPANY FRONT AWARDS
12653 Madison Rd (44062-9749)
PHONE.................................440 636-5493
Alan Byrne, *Partner*
EMP: 3
SQ FT: 2,800
SALES: 150K **Privately Held**
SIC: 3499 2499 Trophies, metal, except silver; trophy bases, wood

(G-13787)
CREATION INDUSTRIES LLC
15236 Shedd Rd (44062-9222)
PHONE.................................440 554-6286
Alba Whiteside, *Principal*
EMP: 3 EST: 2009
SALES (est): 279.3K **Privately Held**
SIC: 3999 Manufacturing industries

(G-13788)
CROSSCREEK PALLET CO
14530 Madison Rd (44062-9499)
PHONE.................................440 632-1940
Michael Yoder, *Owner*
EMP: 3
SALES (est): 394.7K **Privately Held**
SIC: 2448 Pallets, wood & wood with metal

(G-13789)
CUSTOM PALET MANUFACTURING
9291 N Girdle Rd (44062-9531)
PHONE.................................440 693-4603
Lester Mullet, *Owner*
EMP: 7
SALES (est): 526.8K **Privately Held**
SIC: 2448 Pallets, wood

(G-13790)
D MARTONE INDUSTRIES INC
Also Called: Jaco Products
15060 Madison Rd (44062-9450)
PHONE.................................440 632-5800
Frank Defino, *President*
David B Cathcart, *Principal*
Samuel R Martillotta, *Principal*
EMP: 30
SQ FT: 38,000
SALES (est): 5.1MM **Privately Held**
WEB: www.jacoproducts.com
SIC: 3089 Injection molded finished plastic products; plastic processing
PA: A.J.D. Holding Co.
2181 Enterprise Pkwy
Twinsburg OH 44087

(G-13791)
D P PRODUCTS INC
14790 Brkshire Ind Pkwy (44062)
PHONE.................................440 834-9663
Ken Ashba, *Principal*
EMP: 3 EST: 2011
SALES (est): 207K **Privately Held**
SIC: 2448 Wood pallets & skids

(G-13792)
D T KOTHERA INC
Also Called: Liberty Fabricating & Steel
15422 Georgia Rd (44062-9011)
P.O. Box 1048 (44062-1048)
PHONE.................................440 632-1651
Dave Kothera, *President*
EMP: 4
SQ FT: 9,600
SALES (est): 750K **Privately Held**
SIC: 5051 3441 Metals service centers & offices; fabricated structural metal

(G-13793)
DAVID J FISHER (PA)
Also Called: D & E Cut Stock
9794 State Route 534 (44062-9516)
PHONE.................................440 636-2256
David J Fisher, *Owner*
EMP: 3
SALES: 275K **Privately Held**
SIC: 2448 Pallets, wood

(G-13794)
DRUMMOND CORP
14990 Brkshire Indus Pkwy (44062)
P.O. Box 389, Burton (44021-0389)
PHONE.................................440 834-9660
Paul Spangler Sr, *President*
Joan Spangler, *Vice Pres*
Paul Spangler Jr, *Vice Pres*
EMP: 15
SQ FT: 10,000
SALES (est): 2MM **Privately Held**
WEB: www.drummondcorp.com
SIC: 3089 Injection molding of plastics; plastic processing

(G-13795)
DYNAMIC TOOL DIE
14925 White Rd (44062-9216)
PHONE.................................440 834-0007
David Mance, *Owner*
EMP: 3
SALES: 100K **Privately Held**
SIC: 3544 Special dies & tools

(G-13796)
E & L SPRING SHOP
16035 Nauvoo Rd (44062-9766)
PHONE.................................440 632-1439
Ervin Byler, *President*
William Byler, *Partner*
Walter Miller, *Vice Pres*
EMP: 3
SALES (est): 365.1K **Privately Held**
SIC: 3493 Leaf springs: automobile, locomotive, etc.

(G-13797)
EEI ACQUISITION CORP
Also Called: Engineered Endeavors
15175 Kinsman Rd (44062-9471)
PHONE.................................440 564-5484
Patrick Deloney, *President*
Gerry Truax, *CFO*
EMP: 45 EST: 1988
SALES (est): 13.3MM **Privately Held**
SIC: 3663 Mobile communication equipment

(G-13798)
FISHER PALLET
8496 Bundysburg Rd (44062-9303)
PHONE.................................440 632-0863
Daniel Fisher Jr, *Owner*
EMP: 3
SQ FT: 3,148
SALES (est): 191.4K **Privately Held**
SIC: 2448 Pallets, wood & wood with metal

(G-13799)
FLAMBEAU INC
15981 Valplast St (44062-9399)
P.O. Box 97 (44062-0097)
PHONE.................................440 632-6131
Jason Sauey, *President*
Carolyn Corley, *Branch Mgr*
Melissa Blankenship, *Manager*
EMP: 97
SALES (corp-wide): 320MM **Privately Held**
SIC: 3089 Plastic containers, except foam
HQ: Flambeau, Inc.
801 Lynn Ave
Baraboo WI 53913
800 352-6266

(G-13800)
GOLD KEY PROCESSING INC
14910 Madison Rd (44062-8403)
PHONE.................................440 632-0901
Tracy Garrison, *President*
Randy Simpson, *COO*
Don Picard, *Vice Pres*
Jamey Petrik, *Purch Agent*
Doug Thomas, *Buyer*
▲ EMP: 170
SQ FT: 160,000
SALES (est): 76.4MM
SALES (corp-wide): 1.4B **Privately Held**
WEB: www.goldkeyltd.com
SIC: 3069 2891 Reclaimed rubber & specialty rubber compounds; adhesives & sealants
HQ: Hexpol Holding Inc.
14330 Kinsman Rd
Burton OH 44021
440 834-4644

(G-13801)
H & H TREE SERVICE LLC
15530 Old State Rd (44062-8208)
P.O. Box 179 (44062-0179)
PHONE.................................440 632-0551
Kimberly Heiss, *President*
EMP: 3
SQ FT: 6,000
SALES (est): 224K **Privately Held**
SIC: 2411 Timber, cut at logging camp

(G-13802)
HANS ROTHENBUHLER & SON INC
15815 Nauvoo Rd (44062-8501)
PHONE.................................440 632-6000
John Rothenbuhler, *President*
Joyce Filla, *General Mgr*
Gary Schoenwald, *Marketing Staff*
▲ EMP: 40
SALES (est): 12.3MM **Privately Held**
SIC: 2022 5451 5143 2023 Natural cheese; dairy products stores; dairy products, except dried or canned; dry, condensed, evaporated dairy products

(G-13803)
HARDWOOD FLRG & PANELING INC
Also Called: SHEOGA HARDWOOD FLOORING & PAN
15320 Burton Windsor Rd (44062-9785)
P.O. Box 248 (44062-0248)
PHONE.................................440 834-1710
Pete C Miller, *President*
Steve Trudick, *Chairman*
Larry Yoder, *Corp Secy*
Barbara Titus, *CFO*
▼ EMP: 72
SQ FT: 135,000
SALES: 15.8MM **Privately Held**
WEB: www.sheogaflooring.com
SIC: 2426 Flooring, hardwood

(G-13804)
HAUSER SERVICES LLC
Also Called: Hauser Landscaping
15668 Old State Rd (44062-8488)
P.O. Box 1161 (44062-1161)
PHONE.................................440 632-5126
Monique Hauser, *Mng Member*
Dave Hauser, *Manager*
EMP: 20
SQ FT: 10,000
SALES: 2.6MM **Privately Held**
SIC: 2499 0781 Mulch, wood & bark; landscape services

(G-13805)
HERBERT WOOD PRODUCTS INC
15089 White Rd (44062-9216)
PHONE.................................440 834-1410
Bryan Herbert, *President*
EMP: 3
SQ FT: 5,000
SALES (est): 295.1K **Privately Held**
SIC: 1541 2499 Renovation, remodeling & repairs: industrial buildings; decorative wood & woodwork

(G-13806)
HK LOGGING & LUMBER LTD
16465 Farley Rd (44062-8290)
PHONE.................................440 632-1997
Henry Kuhns, *President*
EMP: 7
SALES (est): 923.6K **Privately Held**
SIC: 2411 Logging

(G-13807)
J D L HARDWOODS
9024 N Girdle Rd (44062-9604)
PHONE.................................440 272-5630
Joe Miller, *Partner*
Dan Miller, *Partner*
Levi Yoder, *Partner*
EMP: 4
SQ FT: 4,120
SALES (est): 339.5K **Privately Held**
SIC: 2448 5211 Pallets, wood; lumber products

(G-13808)
J S COMPANY
16351 Nauvoo Rd (44062-9769)
PHONE.................................440 632-0052
Jones Sputzman, *Owner*
EMP: 3
SALES (est): 145.2K **Privately Held**
SIC: 3599 Machine shop, jobbing & repair

(G-13809)
J S STAIRS
16118 Old State Rd (44062-8205)
PHONE.................................440 632-5680
John Stutzman, *Owner*
EMP: 4
SALES: 300K **Privately Held**
SIC: 3446 Stairs, staircases, stair treads: prefabricated metal

(G-13810)
JOBAP ASSEMBLY INC
16090 Industrial Pkwy # 9 (44062-6302)
PHONE.................................440 632-5393
Rebecca Portman, *President*
Jeannine Reeves, *General Mgr*
Judith Mellenger, *Treasurer*
▲ EMP: 16
SQ FT: 6,000
SALES (est): 3.1MM **Privately Held**
SIC: 3699 1731 Electrical equipment & supplies; electrical work

(G-13811)
JOHNSONITE INC
Also Called: Johnsonite Rubber Flooring
16035 Industrial Pkwy (44062-9386)
P.O. Box 880 (44062-0880)
PHONE.................................440 632-3441
Jeff Buttitta, *President*
Tom Dowling, *CFO*
▲ EMP: 500

SALES (est): 70.3MM
SALES (corp-wide): 589.6K Privately Held
SIC: 3086 Carpet & rug cushions, foamed plastic
HQ: Tarkett
  Tour Initiale
  Puteaux

(G-13812)
KRAFTMAID TRUCKING INC (PA)
16052 Industrial Pkwy (44062-9382)
P.O. Box 1055 (44062-1055)
PHONE....................................440 632-2531
Tom Chieffe, *President*
EMP: 100
SQ FT: 12,000
SALES (est): 16.7MM Privately Held
SIC: 4813 2517 Telephone communication, except radio; wood television & radio cabinets

(G-13813)
LA ROSE PAVING CO INC
16590 Nauvoo Rd (44062-9408)
P.O. Box 146 (44062-0146)
PHONE....................................440 632-0330
Toll Free:................................888 -
Linda Rose, *President*
Jim Rose, *Vice Pres*
EMP: 8
SALES: 500K Privately Held
SIC: 2951 Paving blocks

(G-13814)
M A MILLER
16790 Pioneer Rd (44062-8716)
PHONE....................................440 636-5697
Mark Miller, *Owner*
Barbara Miller, *Co-Owner*
EMP: 4
SALES (est): 260K Privately Held
SIC: 2434 Wood kitchen cabinets

(G-13815)
MAINE RUBBER PREFORMS LLC
16090 Industrial Pkwy # 1 (44062-6300)
PHONE....................................216 210-2094
Wesley L Hellegers, *Partner*
EMP: 3
SALES (est): 366.2K Privately Held
SIC: 3069 Custom compounding of rubber materials

(G-13816)
MARSH VALLEY FOREST PDTS LTD
14141 Old State Rd (44062-9740)
PHONE....................................440 632-1889
Mervin P Miller, *President*
Pete Miller, *General Ptnr*
EMP: 7
SQ FT: 16,000
SALES (est): 1.3MM Privately Held
SIC: 2426 5211 Flooring, hardwood; lumber products

(G-13817)
MASCO CABINETRY LLC
15535 S State Ave (44062)
PHONE....................................440 632-2547
Mike Newton, *Manager*
EMP: 601
SALES (corp-wide): 8.3B Publicly Held
SIC: 2434 Wood kitchen cabinets
HQ: Masco Cabinetry Llc
  4600 Arrowhead Dr
  Ann Arbor MI 48105
  734 205-4600

(G-13818)
MASCO CBINETRY MIDDLEFIELD LLC (DH)
15535 S State Ave (44062)
P.O. Box 1055 (44062-1055)
PHONE....................................440 632-5333
Keith Scherzer, *President*
Andrew Rattray, *Vice Pres*
◆ EMP: 2533

SALES (est): 555.8MM
SALES (corp-wide): 8.3B Publicly Held
WEB: www.kraftmaid.com
SIC: 2434 Wood household furniture; wood kitchen cabinets; vanities, bathroom: wood
HQ: Masco Cabinetry Llc
  4600 Arrowhead Dr
  Ann Arbor MI 48105
  734 205-4600

(G-13819)
MASCO CBINETRY MIDDLEFIELD LLC
16052 Industrial Pkwy (44062-9382)
P.O. Box 1055 (44062-1055)
PHONE....................................440 632-5058
Keith Scherzer, *Branch Mgr*
EMP: 100
SALES (corp-wide): 8.3B Publicly Held
SIC: 2511 2434 Wood household furniture; wood kitchen cabinets; general warehousing & storage
HQ: Masco Cabinetry Middlefield Llc
  15535 S State Ave
  Middlefield OH 44062
  440 632-5333

(G-13820)
MERCURY PLASTICS LLC
15760 Madison Rd (44062-8408)
P.O. Box 989 (44062-0989)
PHONE....................................440 632-5281
William Rowley Jr,
EMP: 3
SALES (est): 708.5K
SALES (corp-wide): 8.3B Publicly Held
SIC: 3089 Extruded finished plastic products
PA: Masco Corporation
  17450 College Pkwy
  Livonia MI 48152
  313 274-7400

(G-13821)
MESPO WOODWORKING
4421 Donley Rd (44062-9549)
PHONE....................................440 693-4041
Jacob Miller, *Owner*
EMP: 3 EST: 1997
SALES (est): 200K Privately Held
SIC: 2541 Cabinets, except refrigerated: show, display, etc.: wood

(G-13822)
MIDDLEFIELD CHEESE HOUSE INC
15815 Nauvoo Rd (44062-8501)
PHONE....................................440 632-5228
Ann Rothenbuhler, *President*
Steve Ilg, *Engineer*
Joel Sloan, *Manager*
EMP: 20
SQ FT: 2,000
SALES (est): 3.5MM Privately Held
SIC: 2022 Natural cheese

(G-13823)
MIDDLEFIELD GLASS INCORPORATED
17447 Kinsman Rd (44062-9433)
P.O. Box 1266 (44062-1266)
PHONE....................................440 632-5699
Michael Lyons, *President*
Carol Lyons, *President*
EMP: 20
SQ FT: 9,000
SALES (est): 1.9MM Privately Held
WEB: www.middlefieldglass.com
SIC: 3231 5231 Stained glass: made from purchased glass; glass, leaded or stained

(G-13824)
MIDDLEFIELD MIX INC
15815 Nauvoo Rd (44062-8501)
PHONE....................................440 632-0157
John Rothenbuhler, *President*
EMP: 15
SQ FT: 1,364
SALES (est): 2.3MM Privately Held
SIC: 2022 Natural cheese

(G-13825)
MIDDLEFIELD PALLET INC
15940 Burton Windsor Rd (44062-9791)
PHONE....................................440 632-0553
Robert J Troyer, *President*
John A Yoder, *Exec VP*
EMP: 42
SQ FT: 30,000
SALES (est): 7.3MM Privately Held
WEB: www.middlefieldpallet.com
SIC: 2448 Pallets, wood

(G-13826)
MIDDLEFIELD PLASTICS INC
15235 Burton Windsor Rd (44062-9784)
P.O. Box 708 (44062-0708)
PHONE....................................440 834-4638
John D Fisher, *President*
Edward Minick, *Vice Pres*
Angie Fischbach, *Controller*
EMP: 45
SQ FT: 44,000
SALES (est): 11MM Privately Held
WEB: www.middlefieldplastics.com
SIC: 3089 3053 Extruded finished plastic products; gaskets; packing & sealing devices

(G-13827)
MIDDLEFIELD SIGN CO
14895 N State Ave Unit G (44062-9724)
P.O. Box 490 (44062-0490)
PHONE....................................440 632-0708
Larry Lasich, *Owner*
EMP: 3
SALES: 140K Privately Held
SIC: 3993 7336 7335 Signs, not made in custom sign painting shops; commercial art & graphic design; commercial photography

(G-13828)
MIDDLFELD ORIGINAL CHEESE COOP
Also Called: Das Deutsch Cheese
16942 Kinsman Rd (44062-9484)
P.O. Box 237 (44062-0237)
PHONE....................................440 632-5567
Eli D L Miller, *President*
Nevin R Byler, *Vice Pres*
EMP: 20
SQ FT: 12,000
SALES (est): 2.6MM Privately Held
SIC: 2022 Natural cheese; processed cheese

(G-13829)
MILLER LOGGING
5327 Parks West Rd (44062-9352)
PHONE....................................440 693-4001
Eli P Miller, *Principal*
EMP: 3 EST: 1998
SALES (est): 315.4K Privately Held
SIC: 2411 Logging camps & contractors

(G-13830)
MILLER TRUSS LLC
15345 Georgia Rd (44062-8231)
PHONE....................................440 321-0126
Noah W Miller, *Principal*
EMP: 4
SALES (est): 342.1K Privately Held
SIC: 2439 Trusses, wooden roof

(G-13831)
MILLERS LINIMENTS LLC
17150 Bundysburg Rd (44062-9247)
PHONE....................................440 548-5800
Albert Miller, *Principal*
EMP: 3
SALES (est): 216.1K Privately Held
SIC: 2834 Liniments

(G-13832)
MK ENTERPRISES INC
11162 Industrial Pkwy (44062)
PHONE....................................440 632-0121
Mark W Frieling, *President*
Rodney W Hurd, *Vice Pres*
Kimberly H Frieling, *Treasurer*
Nancy W Hurd, *Admin Sec*
EMP: 30
SQ FT: 6,000

SALES (est): 4.9MM Privately Held
WEB: www.mkenter.com
SIC: 3679 Harness assemblies for electronic use: wire or cable

(G-13833)
MOLTEN MTAL EQP INNVATIONS LLC
Also Called: Mmei
15510 Old State Rd (44062-8208)
PHONE....................................440 632-9119
Paul Cooper, *President*
Kevin Doherty, *Treasurer*
▲ EMP: 28
SALES (est): 7.6MM Privately Held
SIC: 3561 Industrial pumps & parts

(G-13834)
MULTI-WING AMERICA INC
15030 Brkshire Indus Pkwy (44062-9390)
P.O. Box 425, Burton (44021-0425)
PHONE....................................440 834-9400
Jim Crowley, *President*
Terese Crowley, *Corp Secy*
Bill Crowley, *Vice Pres*
John Crowley, *Vice Pres*
Jerry Harris, *Vice Pres*
▲ EMP: 45
SQ FT: 27,500
SALES (est): 13.6MM Privately Held
WEB: www.mw-america.com
SIC: 3564 Exhaust fans: industrial or commercial

(G-13835)
MVP PLASTICS INC (PA)
15005 Enterprise Way (44062-9369)
PHONE....................................440 834-1790
Darrell McNair, *President*
Frank Druschel, *Opers Staff*
Joe Bayus, *Buyer*
Ed Kalbfell, *QC Mgr*
Penny Amato, *Engineer*
EMP: 10
SQ FT: 5,000
SALES (est): 3MM Privately Held
SIC: 3089 Injection molding of plastics

(G-13836)
MYERS INDUSTRIES INC
Also Called: Dillen Products
15150 Madison Rd (44062-9495)
P.O. Box 738 (44062-0738)
PHONE....................................440 632-1006
Dexter Chumley, *General Mgr*
EMP: 40
SALES (corp-wide): 566.7MM Publicly Held
WEB: www.myersind.com
SIC: 3089 3423 Injection molded finished plastic products; hand & edge tools
PA: Myers Industries, Inc.
  1293 S Main St
  Akron OH 44301
  330 253-5592

(G-13837)
NAUVOD MACHINE CO
16254 Nauvoo Rd (44062-9731)
PHONE....................................440 632-1990
Lester Byler, *Principal*
EMP: 3 EST: 2008
SALES (est): 281.9K Privately Held
SIC: 3599 Machine & other job shop work

(G-13838)
NAUVOO CUSTOM WOODWORKING
17231 Nauvoo Rd (44062-8416)
PHONE....................................440 632-9502
EMP: 3
SALES (est): 519.1K Privately Held
SIC: 2431 Millwork

(G-13839)
NEFF-PERKINS COMPANY
16080 Industrial Pkwy (44062-9382)
PHONE....................................440 632-1658
Robert Elly, *Branch Mgr*
EMP: 170
SQ FT: 12,800

Middlefield - Geauga County (G-13840)

SALES (corp-wide): 40MM **Privately Held**
WEB: www.neffp.com
SIC: 3069 3061 3053 Molded rubber products; mechanical rubber goods; gaskets, packing & sealing devices
PA: Neff-Perkins Company
16080 Industrial Pkwy
Middlefield OH 44062
440 632-1658

(G-13840)
NORMANDY PRODUCTS COMPANY
16125 Industrial Pkwy (44062-9393)
P.O. Box 52 (44062-0052)
PHONE..............................440 632-5050
Carl Arysiak, *Principal*
EMP: 60
SQ FT: 64,000
SALES (est): 8.3MM
SALES (corp-wide): 12.5MM **Privately Held**
WEB: www.normandyproducts.com
SIC: 3082 3498 Tubes, unsupported plastic; fabricated pipe & fittings
HQ: Normandy Products Company
1150 Freeport Rd
Pittsburgh PA 15238
412 826-1825

(G-13841)
NORSTAR ALUMINUM MOLDS INC
Also Called: Starwood
15986 Valplast St (44062-9399)
PHONE..............................440 632-0853
Erik Adams, *Engineer*
Brian Gresch, *Branch Mgr*
EMP: 60
SALES (corp-wide): 8MM **Privately Held**
SIC: 7011 3444 Hotels & motels; sheet metalwork
PA: Norstar Aluminum Molds, Inc.
W66n622 Madison Ave
Cedarburg WI 53012
262 375-5600

(G-13842)
O A R VINYL WINDOWS & SIDING
Also Called: O A R Vinyl Window Co
12880 Clay St (44062-8733)
PHONE..............................440 636-5573
Andy Byler, *Owner*
Mary W Bylar, *Owner*
EMP: 4
SALES (est): 421.8K **Privately Held**
SIC: 3089 5211 5033 1761 Windows, plastic; siding; siding, except wood; siding contractor

(G-13843)
PARKS WEST PALLET LLC
4566 Parks West Rd (44062-9345)
PHONE..............................440 693-4651
Joe Bricker,
Rebecca Bricker,
EMP: 4
SQ FT: 2,348
SALES (est): 300K **Privately Held**
SIC: 2448 Pallets, wood

(G-13844)
PCKD ENTERPRISES INC
Also Called: Molten Metals
15510 Old State Rd (44062-8208)
PHONE..............................440 632-9119
Paul Cooper, *President*
Mark Andes, *Principal*
Sarah Mikash, *Principal*
John Winland, *Purchasing*
Vince Fontana, *Engineer*
▲ EMP: 22
SQ FT: 16,000
SALES (est): 4.5MM **Privately Held**
WEB: www.mmei-inc.com
SIC: 3561 Industrial pumps & parts

(G-13845)
PERFORMA LA MAR PRINTING INC
15912 W High St (44062)
PHONE..............................440 632-9800
David Chase, *President*
Kathy McClure, *President*
Lamar McClure, *Vice Pres*
EMP: 8
SALES (est): 700K **Privately Held**
SIC: 2752 2791 Commercial printing, offset; typesetting

(G-13846)
PLASTIC EXTRUSION TECH LTD
15229 S State Ave (44062-9468)
P.O. Box 92 (44062-0092)
PHONE..............................440 632-5611
William E Spencer, *President*
Diane Spencer, *Admin Sec*
▼ EMP: 25
SQ FT: 38,500
SALES: 10MM **Privately Held**
SIC: 3089 Extruded finished plastic products; plastic processing

(G-13847)
PLEASANT VALLEY WDWKG LLC
13424 Clay St (44062-8741)
PHONE..............................440 636-5860
Lester L Mullet Jr, *Mng Member*
Andy M Byler,
EMP: 5
SALES (est): 599K **Privately Held**
SIC: 2431 2434 Interior & ornamental woodwork & trim; wood kitchen cabinets

(G-13848)
POLYCHEM DISPERSIONS INC
16066 Industrial Pkwy (44062-9382)
PHONE..............................800 545-3530
William Nichols, *CEO*
Anthony Vanni, *President*
Jeff Nichols, *Director*
EMP: 45 EST: 1981
SQ FT: 30,000
SALES (est): 13.9MM **Privately Held**
WEB: www.dispersions.com
SIC: 2869 Industrial organic chemicals

(G-13849)
RESOURCE MTL HDLG & RECYCL INC (PA)
14970 Brkshire Indus Pkwy (44062-9390)
PHONE..............................440 834-0727
Josh Jones, *President*
Stacey Cremers, *COO*
▼ EMP: 20
SQ FT: 50,000
SALES (est): 7.6MM **Privately Held**
SIC: 5099 3089 Containers: glass, metal or plastic; plastic containers, except foam

(G-13850)
SCHNIDER PALLET LLC
9782 Bundysburg Rd (44062-9362)
PHONE..............................440 632-5346
Fred Schnider,
EMP: 9
SALES (est): 548.3K **Privately Held**
SIC: 2448 Pallets, wood & wood with metal

(G-13851)
SELINICK CO
15879 Madison Rd (44062-8409)
PHONE..............................440 632-1788
Merv Miller, *Owner*
EMP: 3
SQ FT: 3,600
SALES (est): 280.5K **Privately Held**
SIC: 7537 7692 Automotive transmission repair shops; welding repair

(G-13852)
SHAWNEE WOOD PRODUCTS INC
8918 Bundysburg Rd (44062-9525)
PHONE..............................440 632-1771
Raymond C Miller, *President*
Michael Byler, *Vice Pres*
Douglas King, *Admin Sec*
EMP: 5
SQ FT: 6,000
SALES (est): 532K **Privately Held**
SIC: 2434 2431 Wood kitchen cabinets; staircases & stairs, wood

(G-13853)
SIMON DE YOUNG CORPORATION
15010 Brkshire Indus Pkwy (44062-9390)
P.O. Box 217 (44062-0217)
PHONE..............................440 834-3000
Simon D Young, *President*
Margaret D Young, *Corp Secy*
EMP: 8
SALES: 500K **Privately Held**
WEB: www.braidingmachinery.com
SIC: 3552 3549 Braiding machines, textile; wiredrawing & fabricating machinery & equipment, ex. die

(G-13854)
STUTZMAN BROTHERS SAWMILL
15991 Nauvoo Rd (44062-9765)
PHONE..............................440 272-5179
EMP: 8 EST: 1995
SALES (est): 750K **Privately Held**
SIC: 2421 5031 Sawmill/Planing Mill Whol Lumber/Plywood/Millwork

(G-13855)
SUBURBAN COMMUNICATIONS INC
Also Called: Good News
14905 N State Ave (44062-9747)
P.O. Box 95 (44062-0095)
PHONE..............................440 632-0130
Thomas Henry, *President*
Don Cimorell, *Chairman*
Neil Belcher, *Vice Pres*
Gayle Moore, *Prdtn Mgr*
EMP: 30 EST: 1979
SALES (est): 2MM **Privately Held**
WEB: www.good-news.com
SIC: 2721 2741 Magazines: publishing only, not printed on site; miscellaneous publishing

(G-13856)
SUGARBUSH CREEK FARM
13034 Madison Rd (44062-9753)
PHONE..............................440 636-5371
Pam Cermak, *Owner*
EMP: 3
SALES: 130K **Privately Held**
SIC: 2099 Maple syrup

(G-13857)
THE HC COMPANIES INC (DH)
Also Called: Pro Cal
15150 Madison Rd (44062-9495)
P.O. Box 738 (44062-0738)
PHONE..............................440 632-3333
Chris Koscho, *President*
Bob Quinlan, *Engineer*
John Landefeld, *CFO*
Jessica Treece, *Accountant*
Jim Sandy, *Info Tech Mgr*
▲ EMP: 40
SQ FT: 11,000
SALES (est): 228.7MM
SALES (corp-wide): 384.2MM **Privately Held**
SIC: 3089 5261 Planters, plastic; flower pots, plastic; lawn & garden supplies

(G-13858)
TIMBER PRODUCTS INC
8652 Parkman Mespo Rd (44062-9334)
PHONE..............................440 693-4098
George A Chittle Jr, *President*
George Chittle III, *Corp Secy*
John Rowland, *Vice Pres*
EMP: 4
SQ FT: 7,500
SALES (est): 340K **Privately Held**
SIC: 2448 Pallets, wood; skids, wood

(G-13859)
TROY INNOVATIVE INSTRS INC
15111 White Rd (44062-9216)
P.O. Box 1328 (44062-1328)
PHONE..............................440 834-9567
Thomas Cseplo, *President*
August Deangelo, *Principal*
Randall Hampton, *Principal*
Carol Cseplo, *Admin Sec*
EMP: 40
SQ FT: 12,000
SALES (est): 7.3MM **Privately Held**
SIC: 3841 Medical instruments & equipment, blood & bone work

(G-13860)
TROYMILL MANUFACTURING INC (PA)
Also Called: Troymill Wood Products
17055 Kinsman Rd (44062-9485)
P.O. Box 306 (44062-0306)
PHONE..............................440 632-5580
Marvin Schaefer, *President*
Brian Schaefer, *Exec VP*
Steven Belman, *Vice Pres*
Michael Leuchtag, *Manager*
EMP: 12
SQ FT: 19,500
SALES (est): 14.5MM **Privately Held**
SIC: 5031 2448 Lumber, plywood & millwork; wood pallets & skids

(G-13861)
TRUMBULL COUNTY HARDWOODS
9446 Bundysburg Rd (44062-9300)
PHONE..............................440 632-0555
John Betweiler, *Partner*
Rudy Detweiler, *Partner*
▼ EMP: 23
SQ FT: 600
SALES: 5.2MM **Privately Held**
WEB: www.tchardwoods.com
SIC: 2421 2426 Lumber: rough, sawed or planed; hardwood dimension & flooring mills

(G-13862)
ULTIMATE PALLET & TRUCKING LLC
4774 Parks West Rd (44062-9347)
PHONE..............................440 693-4090
David Miller, *Principal*
EMP: 4
SALES (est): 280K **Privately Held**
SIC: 2448 Wood pallets & skids

(G-13863)
UNIVERSAL PLASTICS - SAJAR
Also Called: Sajar Plastics, Inc.
15285 S State Ave (44062-9468)
P.O. Box 37 (44062-0037)
PHONE..............................440 632-5203
Jay Kumar, *President*
EMP: 5
SALES (est): 194.4K
SALES (corp-wide): 21.3MM **Privately Held**
SIC: 3089 Injection molding of plastics
PA: Universal Plastics Corporation
75 Whiting Farms Rd
Holyoke MA 01040
413 592-4791

(G-13864)
UNIVERSAL POLYMER & RUBBER LTD (PA)
15730 Madison Rd (44062-8408)
P.O. Box 767 (44062-0767)
PHONE..............................440 632-1691
Joe Colebank, *President*
Andrew Cavanagh, *Vice Pres*
▲ EMP: 109
SQ FT: 56,000
SALES (est): 46.5MM **Privately Held**
WEB: www.universalpolymer.com
SIC: 3069 3089 Molded rubber products; extruded finished plastic products

(G-13865)
VITAMIN LAC
17642 Tavern Rd (44062-9191)
PHONE..............................440 548-5294
Melvin Yoder, *Owner*
EMP: 11
SALES (est): 576.5K **Privately Held**
SIC: 2399 Horse & pet accessories, textile

(G-13866)
VLCHEK PLASTICS
15981 Valplast St (44062-9399)
P.O. Box 5 (44062-0005)
PHONE..............................440 632-1631
Jason Sauey, *Principal*
EMP: 3

GEOGRAPHIC SECTION   Middletown - Butler County (G-13893)

SALES (est): 215.9K **Privately Held**
SIC: 3089 Injection molding of plastics

(G-13867)
WINSPEC INC
15470 Chipmunk Ln (44062-9218)
PHONE..................................440 834-9068
Gregory Klausner, *President*
Joan Klausner, *Vice Pres*
EMP: 4
SQ FT: 12,000
SALES (est): 486.9K **Privately Held**
WEB: www.winspec.com
SIC: 2211 Draperies & drapery fabrics, cotton

(G-13868)
WOODCRAFT INDUSTRIES INC
15351 S State Ave (44062-9469)
P.O. Box 250 (44062-0250)
PHONE..................................440 632-9655
Dan Miller, *Manager*
EMP: 160 **Publicly Held**
SIC: 2434 2431 2426 Wood kitchen cabinets; millwork; dimension, hardwood
HQ: Woodcraft Industries, Inc.
    525 Lincoln Ave Se
    Saint Cloud MN 56304
    320 656-2345

(G-13869)
WOODWORKS DESIGN
9005 N Girdle Rd (44062-9502)
PHONE..................................440 693-4414
Todd Armfelt, *Principal*
EMP: 7
SALES (est): 1.4MM **Privately Held**
SIC: 2431 Millwork

(G-13870)
XYZ PLASTICS INC
15760 Madison Rd (44062-8408)
P.O. Box 989 (44062-0989)
PHONE..................................440 632-5281
William Rowley Sr, *Ch of Bd*
William Rowley Jr, *President*
Bob Yunk, *General Mgr*
Mark Baker, *Corp Secy*
Don Covey, *Plant Mgr*
◆ EMP: 225 EST: 1964
SQ FT: 130,000
SALES (est): 53.5MM **Privately Held**
SIC: 3089 Extruded finished plastic products; plastic processing

(G-13871)
YODERS HARNESS SHOP
14698 Bundysburg Rd (44062-9775)
PHONE..................................440 632-1505
Levi J Yoder, *Owner*
Fannie J Yoder, *Co-Owner*
EMP: 3
SQ FT: 2,500
SALES: 180K **Privately Held**
SIC: 3199 5191 5948 Harness or harness parts; harness equipment; leather goods, except luggage & shoes

Middleport
Meigs County

(G-13872)
FACEMYER FOREST PRODUCTS INC
State Rte 7 (45760)
P.O. Box 89 (45760-0089)
PHONE..................................740 992-7425
William L Facemyer, *President*
Tammy Capehart, *Admin Sec*
EMP: 15
SALES (est): 1.9MM **Privately Held**
SIC: 2421 Lumber: rough, sawed or planed

(G-13873)
QUALITY PRINT SHOP INC
255 Mill St (45760-1163)
PHONE..................................740 992-3345
Dwane Weber, *President*
EMP: 3 EST: 1993
SQ FT: 4,200
SALES: 150K **Privately Held**
SIC: 2759 Commercial printing

Middletown
Butler County

(G-13874)
3D SALES & CONSULTING INC
Also Called: M R T
408 Vanderveer St (45044-4239)
PHONE..................................513 422-1198
Talbert Selby, *President*
David Poe, *Vice Pres*
EMP: 25
SQ FT: 25,000
SALES (est): 5.9MM **Privately Held**
SIC: 3599 Machine shop, jobbing & repair

(G-13875)
ADONAI TECHNOLOGIES LLC
1223 Hook Dr (45042-1734)
PHONE..................................513 560-9020
Jerran Adkins, *President*
EMP: 3
SQ FT: 9,000
SALES (est): 152.1K **Privately Held**
SIC: 3672 Printed circuit boards

(G-13876)
AIR PRODUCTS AND CHEMICALS INC
2500 Yankee Rd (45044-7652)
PHONE..................................513 420-3663
Wallace Brashear, *Branch Mgr*
EMP: 51
SALES (corp-wide): 8.9B **Publicly Held**
WEB: www.airproducts.com
SIC: 2813 Oxygen, compressed or liquefied
PA: Air Products And Chemicals, Inc.
    7201 Hamilton Blvd
    Allentown PA 18195
    610 481-4911

(G-13877)
AK STEEL CORPORATION
801 Crawford St (45044-4537)
PHONE..................................513 425-3694
Robert Jordan, *General Mgr*
Jim Funk, *Senior Buyer*
Daniel Scherrer, *Research*
Robert Hilbert, *Engineer*
Paul Janavicius, *Engineer*
EMP: 298 **Publicly Held**
SIC: 3312 Stainless steel
HQ: Ak Steel Corporation
    9227 Centre Pointe Dr
    West Chester OH 45069
    513 425-4200

(G-13878)
AK STEEL CORPORATION
622 Box (45042)
PHONE..................................513 425-3593
EMP: 10 **Publicly Held**
WEB: www.ketnar.org
SIC: 3312 Blast furnaces & steel mills
HQ: Ak Steel Corporation
    9227 Centre Pointe Dr
    West Chester OH 45069
    513 425-4200

(G-13879)
AKERS PACKAGING SERVICE INC (PA)
Also Called: Akers Packaging Service Group
2820 Lefferson Rd (45044-6999)
P.O. Box 610 (45042-0610)
PHONE..................................513 422-6312
James F Akers, *Ch of Bd*
William C Akers II, *President*
Marilyn R Akey, *Corp Secy*
Michael S Akey, *Vice Pres*
Mike Blatt, *Sales Mgr*
▲ EMP: 235
SQ FT: 220,000
SALES (est): 90.2MM **Privately Held**
WEB: www.akers-pkg.com
SIC: 2653 Boxes, corrugated: made from purchased materials

(G-13880)
AKERS PACKAGING SOLUTIONS INC (PA)
Also Called: Akers Packaging Service Group
2820 Lefferson Rd (45044-6999)
P.O. Box 610 (45042-0610)
PHONE..................................513 422-6312
James F Akers, *Ch of Bd*
William C Akers, *President*
Alfred J Pedicone, *Corp Secy*
Michael Shannon Akey, *Vice Pres*
EMP: 75 EST: 2014
SALES (est): 11.1MM **Privately Held**
SIC: 2653 Boxes, corrugated: made from purchased materials

(G-13881)
AKERS PACKAGING SOLUTIONS INC
2820 Lefferson Rd (45044-6999)
PHONE..................................304 525-0342
Randall Fields, *Manager*
Ben Cox, *Maintence Staff*
EMP: 29
SALES (corp-wide): 11.1MM **Privately Held**
SIC: 2653 Boxes, corrugated: made from purchased materials
PA: Akers Packaging Solutions, Inc.
    2820 Lefferson Rd
    Middletown OH 45044
    513 422-6312

(G-13882)
AL BRADSHAW JR
Also Called: Machine Doctors
5009 Oxford Middleton Rd (45042)
PHONE..................................513 422-8870
Al Bradshaw Jr, *Owner*
EMP: 3 EST: 1987
SALES (est): 272.9K **Privately Held**
SIC: 7694 Electric motor repair

(G-13883)
ALLIANCE PRINTING & PUBLISHING
2520 Atco Ave (45042-2517)
PHONE..................................513 422-7611
Greg Brauch, *President*
Mike Fakes, *Vice Pres*
Ed McConnell, *Vice Pres*
Barry Henry, *CFO*
Janis Nein, *Sales Staff*
EMP: 15
SQ FT: 20,000
SALES (est): 1.5MM **Privately Held**
WEB: www.allianceprinting.net
SIC: 2752 Commercial printing, offset

(G-13884)
AMTECO INC
5773 Elk Creek Rd (45042-9669)
P.O. Box 1458, West Chester (45071-1458)
PHONE..................................513 217-4430
Jeffrey L Myers, *President*
EMP: 3 EST: 1993
SALES (est): 404.8K **Privately Held**
WEB: www.amtecoincorporated.com
SIC: 3821 Laboratory apparatus & furniture

(G-13885)
AVURE TECHNOLOGIES INC
2601 S Verity Pkwy # 13 (45044-7482)
PHONE..................................513 433-2500
Keith Cripe, *Branch Mgr*
EMP: 54 **Publicly Held**
SIC: 3556 Food products machinery
HQ: Avure Technologies Incorporated
    1830 Airport Exchange Blv
    Erlanger KY 41018

(G-13886)
BACKYARD SCOREBOARDS LLC
Also Called: Nifty Promo Products
431 Kenridge Dr (45042-4930)
PHONE..................................513 702-6561
Keith Bailey, *Sales Mgr*
Douglas Poffenderger,
EMP: 9
SQ FT: 11,000
SALES: 275K **Privately Held**
SIC: 3949 Team sports equipment

(G-13887)
BOGDEN INDUSTRIAL COATINGS LLC
5020 Eck Rd (45042-1614)
PHONE..................................513 267-5101
Jennifer Bogden, *Principal*
EMP: 3
SALES (est): 168.9K **Privately Held**
SIC: 3479 Metal coating & allied service

(G-13888)
BROWN-SINGER CO
108 Dorset Dr (45044-4948)
PHONE..................................513 422-9619
James Brown, *President*
EMP: 15 EST: 1875
SQ FT: 16,800
SALES (est): 1.8MM **Privately Held**
SIC: 3443 Fabricated plate work (boiler shop)

(G-13889)
C RC AUTOMOTIVE
460 N Verity Pkwy (45042-2129)
PHONE..................................513 422-4775
Ron Cole, *Principal*
EMP: 3
SALES (est): 169K **Privately Held**
SIC: 7539 5013 3599 Electrical services; automotive servicing equipment; machine shop, jobbing & repair

(G-13890)
CARROLL DISTRG & CNSTR SUP INC
6688 Georgetown Ln (45042-1315)
PHONE..................................513 422-3327
Steve Carroll, *President*
EMP: 5
SALES (corp-wide): 116.5MM **Privately Held**
SIC: 5082 3444 Contractors' materials; concrete forms, sheet metal
PA: Carroll Distributing & Construction Supply, Inc.
    1502 E Main St
    Ottumwa IA 52501
    641 683-1888

(G-13891)
CENTURY MOLD COMPANY INC
55 Wright Dr (45044-3287)
PHONE..................................513 539-9283
Ron Ricotta, *Branch Mgr*
EMP: 89
SALES (corp-wide): 203.7MM **Privately Held**
WEB: www.centurymold.com
SIC: 3089 Injection molding of plastics
PA: Century Mold Company, Inc.
    25 Vantage Point Dr
    Rochester NY 14624
    585 352-8600

(G-13892)
CHAUTAUQUA FIBERGLASS & PLASTI
2601 S Verity Pkwy (45044-7482)
PHONE..................................513 423-8840
Adam Bennett, *Principal*
EMP: 5
SALES (est): 474.3K
SALES (corp-wide): 475K **Privately Held**
SIC: 2221 Fiberglass fabrics
PA: Reinforced Plastic Systems
    740 Main St S
    Mahone Bay NS B0J 2
    902 624-8383

(G-13893)
CHEMTRADE CHEMICALS US LLC
305 Richmond St (45044-4322)
PHONE..................................513 422-6319
Steve Combs, *Plant Supt*
Steve Combes, *Manager*
EMP: 4
SALES (corp-wide): 1.1B **Privately Held**
SIC: 2819 Aluminum sulfate
HQ: Chemtrade Chemicals Us Llc
    90 E Halsey Rd
    Parsippany NJ 07054

Middletown - Butler County (G-13894)   GEOGRAPHIC SECTION

(G-13894)
CITY OF MIDDLETOWN
Also Called: Water Treatment
805 Columbia Ave (45042-1907)
PHONE.................513 425-7781
Scott Belcher, *Manager*
EMP: 12 **Privately Held**
WEB: www.trentonlibrary.net
SIC: 3589 4941 Water treatment equipment, industrial; water supply
PA: City Of Middletown
1 Donham Plz
Middletown OH 45042
513 425-7766

(G-13895)
COHEN BROTHERS INC (PA)
1520 14th Ave (45044-5801)
P.O. Box 957 (45044-0957)
PHONE.................513 422-3696
Wilbur Cohen, *Ch of Bd*
Kenneth Cohen, *President*
Mose Cohen, *Principal*
Philip Cohen, *Principal*
Ken Cohen, *COO*
EMP: 9 **EST:** 1924
SQ FT: 90,000
SALES (est): 77.5MM **Privately Held**
WEB: www.cohenbrothersinc.com
SIC: 5093 3441 3341 3312 Ferrous metal scrap & waste; nonferrous metals scrap; fabricated structural metal; secondary nonferrous metals; blast furnaces & steel mills

(G-13896)
CONTECH ENGNERED SOLUTIONS LLC
1001 Grove St (45044-5890)
PHONE.................513 645-7000
EMP: 70 **Privately Held**
SIC: 3084 3317 3441 3443 Plastics pipe; steel pipe & tubes; fabricated structural metal; fabricated plate work (boiler shop); culverts, sheet metal
HQ: Contech Engineered Solutions Llc
9025 Centre Pointe Dr # 400
West Chester OH 45069
513 645-7000

(G-13897)
CONTECH ENGNERED SOLUTIONS LLC
1001 Grove St (45044-5890)
PHONE.................513 425-5337
Keith Wingfield, *Branch Mgr*
EMP: 10 **Privately Held**
SIC: 3443 Culverts, metal plate
HQ: Contech Engineered Solutions Llc
9025 Centre Pointe Dr # 400
West Chester OH 45069
513 645-7000

(G-13898)
CROWN ELECTRIC ENGRG & MFG LLC
175 Edison Dr (45044-3269)
PHONE.................513 539-7394
Chad Shell, *Mng Member*
Bruce Hack,
▲ **EMP:** 25
SQ FT: 48,000
SALES (est): 8.6MM **Privately Held**
WEB: www.crown-electric.com
SIC: 3643 3444 Bus bars (electrical conductors); sheet metal specialties, not stamped

(G-13899)
DAUBENMIRES PRINTING
1527 Central Ave (45044-4135)
PHONE.................513 425-7223
Gary Daubenmire, *Owner*
EMP: 8
SQ FT: 4,000
SALES (est): 869.2K **Privately Held**
WEB: www.daubenmiresprinting.com
SIC: 2752 2791 Commercial printing, offset; typesetting

(G-13900)
DIGITAL VISUALS INC
Also Called: Dvi Retail
15 N Clinton St (45042-2003)
PHONE.................513 420-9466
Debra S Edwards, *President*
James L Edwards, *Vice Pres*
Jim Edwards, *Vice Pres*
EMP: 3
SQ FT: 5,000
SALES (est): 353.4K **Privately Held**
WEB: www.dvisuals.com
SIC: 2759 Commercial printing

(G-13901)
DMK INDUSTRIES INC
1801 Made Dr (45044-8948)
PHONE.................513 727-4549
Dennis Kuna, *President*
Mary Beth Ferree, *Office Mgr*
EMP: 15
SALES (est): 2.2MM **Privately Held**
SIC: 3369 Nonferrous foundries

(G-13902)
DYNAMIC DIES INC
1310 Hook Dr (45042-1712)
PHONE.................513 705-9524
EMP: 33
SALES (corp-wide): 26.9MM **Privately Held**
SIC: 3544 Special dies, tools, jigs & fixtures
PA: Dynamic Dies, Inc.
1705 Commerce Rd
Holland OH 43528
419 865-0249

(G-13903)
DYNAMIC DIES INC
1310 Hook Dr (45042-1712)
PHONE.................513 705-9524
EMP: 33
SALES (corp-wide): 26.9MM **Privately Held**
SIC: 3544 Special dies, tools, jigs & fixtures
PA: Dynamic Dies, Inc.
1705 Commerce Rd
Holland OH 43528
419 865-0249

(G-13904)
ELECTRO-METALLICS CO
3004 Lefferson Rd (45044-6903)
PHONE.................513 423-8091
Hamilton Watkins, *President*
Jane M Watkins, *Corp Secy*
EMP: 8 **EST:** 1965
SQ FT: 2,500
SALES (est): 783.8K **Privately Held**
WEB: www.electrometallics.net
SIC: 3471 Electroplating of metals or formed products; plating of metals or formed products

(G-13905)
ERNST ENTERPRISES INC
2504 S Main St (45044-7446)
PHONE.................513 422-3651
EMP: 11
SALES (corp-wide): 227.2MM **Privately Held**
SIC: 3273 Ready-mixed concrete
PA: Ernst Enterprises, Inc.
3361 Successful Way
Dayton OH 45414
937 233-5555

(G-13906)
ESSITY PROF HYGIENE N AMER LLC
Also Called: ESSITY PROFESSIONAL HYGIENE NORTH AMERICA LLC
700 Columbia Ave (45042-1931)
PHONE.................513 217-3644
EMP: 4
SALES (corp-wide): 7.6B **Privately Held**
SIC: 2621 Paper mills
HQ: Essity Professional Hygiene North America Llc
984 Winchester Rd
Neenah WI 54956
920 727-3770

(G-13907)
EVERTZ TECHNOLOGY SERVICE USA
2601 S Verity Pkwy # 102 (45044-7481)
PHONE.................513 422-8400
Egon Evertz, *President*
▲ **EMP:** 31
SALES (est): 6MM **Privately Held**
WEB: www.etsusainc.net
SIC: 3325 Steel foundries

(G-13908)
FIXTURE DIMENSIONS INC
4355 Salzman Rd (45044-9741)
PHONE.................513 360-7512
Linda F Schaffeld, *President*
▼ **EMP:** 30
SQ FT: 10,000
SALES (est): 5MM **Privately Held**
SIC: 2541 2431 Store & office display cases & fixtures; display fixtures, wood; millwork

(G-13909)
GENOA HEALTHCARE LLC
1036 S Verity Pkwy (45044-5513)
PHONE.................513 727-0471
EMP: 7
SALES (corp-wide): 226.2B **Publicly Held**
SIC: 2834 Pharmaceutical preparations
HQ: Genoa Healthcare Llc
707 S Grady Way Ste 700
Renton WA 98057

(G-13910)
GRANGER PLASTIC COMPANY
1600 M A D E Indus Dr (45044)
PHONE.................513 424-1955
James Cravens, *President*
Jeffrey T Witschey, *Principal*
Jack Cobb, *Vice Pres*
EMP: 20
SALES (est): 4.2MM **Privately Held**
WEB: www.rotocasting.com
SIC: 3089 Injection molding of plastics

(G-13911)
GRAPHIC PACKAGING INTL INC
Also Called: Altivity Packaging
407 Charles St (45042-2107)
PHONE.................513 424-4200
Kevin Nobiling, *Mfg Mgr*
Carl Yeakel, *Production*
Earl Hill, *Plant Engr*
Neil Shockey, *Controller*
Scott Lebeau, *Manager*
EMP: 143 **Publicly Held**
SIC: 2631 2657 Folding boxboard; packaging board; folding paperboard boxes
HQ: Graphic Packaging International, Llc
1500 Riveredge Pkwy # 100
Atlanta GA 30328

(G-13912)
HY-BLAST INC
70 Enterprise Dr (45044-8925)
P.O. Box 602 (45042-0602)
PHONE.................513 424-0704
Robert Cunningham, *President*
Betty Jane Cunningham, *Corp Secy*
Donald Ray Cunningham, *Vice Pres*
Thomas Cunningham, *Vice Pres*
EMP: 16
SQ FT: 25,000
SALES (est): 1.3MM **Privately Held**
WEB: www.hyblastinc.com
SIC: 1799 3471 7699 Epoxy application; polishing, metals or formed products; industrial equipment cleaning

(G-13913)
HYTEK COATINGS INC
1700 S University Blvd (45044-5972)
PHONE.................513 424-0131
James Hammer, *President*
EMP: 5
SQ FT: 13,300
SALES: 400K **Privately Held**
SIC: 2851 Mfg Paints/Allied Products

(G-13914)
INJECTION ALLOYS INCORPORATED
1700 Made Industrial Dr (45044-8937)
PHONE.................513 422-8819
Chris Jackson, *CEO*
Manuel Franco, *CFO*
Michelle Shockley, *Controller*
Weijuan Du, *Supervisor*
▲ **EMP:** 10
SQ FT: 29,000
SALES: 6MM **Privately Held**
SIC: 3315 Wire & fabricated wire products
HQ: Injection Alloys Limited
The Way
Royston HERTS

(G-13915)
INLINE LABEL COMPANY
4720 Emerald Way (45044-8962)
PHONE.................513 217-5662
David S Heckler, *President*
EMP: 14 **EST:** 1997
SALES (est): 2.7MM **Privately Held**
SIC: 2679 Labels, paper: made from purchased material

(G-13916)
INTERNATIONAL PAPER COMPANY
912 Nelbar St (45042-2529)
PHONE.................800 473-0830
EMP: 160
SALES (corp-wide): 23.3B **Publicly Held**
SIC: 2621 Paper mills
PA: International Paper Company
6400 Poplar Ave
Memphis TN 38197
901 419-9000

(G-13917)
INTERSCOPE MANUFACTURING INC
2901 Carmody Blvd (45042-1761)
PHONE.................513 423-8866
John Michael Brill, *CEO*
◆ **EMP:** 50
SQ FT: 175,000
SALES (est): 6.6MM **Privately Held**
WEB: www.interscopemfg.com
SIC: 3599 7389 Custom machinery; repossession service

(G-13918)
JOHN H HOSKING INC
Also Called: Diamond Aluminum Co
4665 Emerald Way (45044-8966)
PHONE.................513 821-1080
James Hodde Jr, *President*
EMP: 6
SQ FT: 6,725
SALES: 900K **Privately Held**
WEB: www.diamond-aluminum.net
SIC: 3498 Fabricated pipe & fittings

(G-13919)
LAYNE HEAVY CIVIL INC
6451 Germantown Rd (45042-1352)
PHONE.................513 424-7287
Ron Alexander, *Branch Mgr*
EMP: 20
SALES (corp-wide): 2.9B **Publicly Held**
WEB: www.ranneymethod.com
SIC: 1781 3589 5251 Water well drilling; water treatment equipment, industrial; pumps & pumping equipment
HQ: Reynolds Construction, Llc.
4544 N State Road 37
Orleans IN 47452
812 865-3232

(G-13920)
LIM SERVICES LLC
Also Called: Locke Industrial Maint Svcs
3351 Cincinnati Dayton Rd (45044-8955)
PHONE.................513 217-0801
Beau Hoy, *Branch Mgr*
David Locke, *Admin Mgr*
EMP: 10
SQ FT: 2,200
SALES (est): 560K **Privately Held**
SIC: 1799 7699 3498 1721 Welding on site; boiler & heating repair services; fabricated pipe & fittings; residential painting

(G-13921)
LOXCREEN COMPANY INC
100 Westheimer Dr (45044-3242)
PHONE.................513 539-2255
Carrie Taylor, *Manager*
EMP: 10

GEOGRAPHIC SECTION

Middletown - Butler County (G-13946)

SALES (corp-wide): 270.2MM **Privately Held**
WEB: www.loxcreen.com
SIC: **5051** 5031 3354 3442 Aluminum bars, rods, ingots, sheets, pipes, plates, etc.; doors; aluminum extruded products; screens, window, metal
HQ: The Loxcreen Company Inc
    1630 Old Dunbar Rd
    West Columbia SC 29172
    803 822-1600

(G-13922)
M-D BUILDING PRODUCTS INC
100 Westheimer Dr (45044-3242)
PHONE.....................513 539-2255
Carrie Taylor-Lane, *Principal*
EMP: 288
SALES (corp-wide): 270.2MM **Privately Held**
SIC: **3442** Weather strip, metal
PA: M-D Building Products, Inc.
    4041 N Santa Fe Ave
    Oklahoma City OK 73118
    405 528-4411

(G-13923)
MAGELLAN AROSPC MIDDLETOWN INC (HQ)
2320 Wedekind Dr (45042-2390)
PHONE.....................513 422-2751
James S Butyniec, *CEO*
Arvel Delong, *Opers Staff*
Susan Glenn, *Buyer*
John Furbay, *Finance Dir*
John Foy, *Human Res Dir*
EMP: 100
SALES (est): 17.8MM
SALES (corp-wide): 759.1MM **Privately Held**
WEB: www.aeroncainc.com
SIC: **3724** 3728 Aircraft engines & engine parts; aircraft body assemblies & parts
PA: Magellan Aerospace Corporation
    3160 Derry Rd E
    Mississauga ON L4T 1
    905 677-1889

(G-13924)
MANUFACTURERS EQUIPMENT CO
Also Called: Meco
35 Enterprise Dr (45044-8928)
PHONE.....................513 424-3573
Adam W Miller, *President*
David Meyer, *General Mgr*
Frank B Carraher, *Vice Pres*
Bryan Sicking, *Project Mgr*
Joe Mahlmeister, *CFO*
▲ EMP: 14
SQ FT: 16,000
SALES: 2.6MM **Privately Held**
WEB: www.mecoservices.com
SIC: **3496** 3535 Wire chain; belt conveyor systems, general industrial use; bucket type conveyor systems

(G-13925)
MATHESON TRI-GAS INC
Also Called: AK Steel Door 360
1801 Crawford St (45044-4572)
PHONE.....................513 727-9638
John Green, *Branch Mgr*
Don Pierce, *Manager*
EMP: 11 **Privately Held**
SIC: **5084** 2813 Welding machinery & equipment; safety equipment; nitrogen
HQ: Matheson Tri-Gas, Inc.
    150 Allen Rd Ste 302
    Basking Ridge NJ 07920
    908 991-9200

(G-13926)
MECCO INC
2100 S Main St (45044-7345)
PHONE.....................513 422-3651
David T Morgan, *President*
Charles E Morgan, *Vice Pres*
Ron Price, *Vice Pres*
Stephen Rains, *Treasurer*
Brenda Burns, *Admin Sec*
EMP: 45 EST: 1956
SQ FT: 2,000
SALES (est): 4.3MM **Privately Held**
WEB: www.meccoconcrete.com
SIC: **3273** 1442 Ready-mixed concrete; construction sand mining; gravel mining

(G-13927)
METAL MATIC
1701 Made Dr (45044-8939)
PHONE.....................513 422-6007
Bruce Petschen, *Principal*
EMP: 3
SALES (est): 607.4K **Privately Held**
SIC: **3317** Steel pipe & tubes

(G-13928)
MIDDLETOWN LICENSE AGENCY INC
3232 Roosevelt Blvd (45044-6424)
PHONE.....................513 422-7225
Cristy Gamble, *President*
EMP: 12
SALES (est): 887.5K **Privately Held**
WEB: www.middletownlicenseagency.com
SIC: **3469** Automobile license tags, stamped metal

(G-13929)
MIDDLETOWN PHARMACY INC
4421 Roosevelt Blvd Ste H (45044-9024)
PHONE.....................513 705-6252
Raef Hamaed, *President*
EMP: 9
SALES (est): 1.5MM **Privately Held**
SIC: **2834** Pharmaceutical preparations

(G-13930)
MIDDLETOWN TUBE WORKS INC
2201 Trine St (45044-5766)
PHONE.....................513 727-0080
Angela Phillips, *President*
Kevin Hart, *Purch Mgr*
Kathy Young, *Purch Agent*
Scott King, *QC Mgr*
Paul Anderson, *CFO*
EMP: 80
SQ FT: 230,000
SALES (est): 23.1MM
SALES (corp-wide): 29.7MM **Privately Held**
WEB: www.middletowntube.com
SIC: **3312** Blast furnaces & steel mills
PA: Phillips Mfg. And Tower Co.
    5578 State Route 61 N
    Shelby OH 44875
    419 347-1720

(G-13931)
MOORCHILD LLC
Also Called: Murphy's Landing Casual Dining
6 S Broad St (45044-4000)
PHONE.....................513 649-8867
Linda Moorman, *Mng Member*
Nancy Fairchild, *Mng Member*
EMP: 10
SALES (est): 542.2K **Privately Held**
SIC: **2599** Bar, restaurant & cafeteria furniture

(G-13932)
MTR MARTCO LLC
3350 Yankee Rd (45044-8927)
PHONE.....................513 424-5307
Raymond McIntosh, *President*
Ottie Craycraft, *Foreman/Supr*
John Bowers, *Engineer*
Dan Miller, *Engineer*
Randy Yoder, *Controller*
▼ EMP: 55 EST: 1998
SQ FT: 60,000
SALES (est): 16.9MM **Privately Held**
WEB: www.mtrmartco.com
SIC: **3554** 3312 Paper industries machinery; stainless steel

(G-13933)
MUELLER GAS PRODUCTS
1800 Clayton Ave (45042-2200)
PHONE.....................513 424-5311
Doug Murdock, *Owner*
EMP: 100
SALES (est): 7.4MM **Privately Held**
SIC: **3714** Manifolds, motor vehicle

(G-13934)
N-STOCK BOX INC
1500 S University Blvd (45044-5968)
PHONE.....................513 423-0319
Jeff Pennington, *President*
Lori Combs, *Vice Pres*
Jon Combs, *Human Res Mgr*
Jed Brubaker, *VP Sales*
Lisa Langhorne, *Sales Staff*
EMP: 40
SQ FT: 70,000
SALES (est): 10.9MM **Privately Held**
WEB: www.n-stockbox.com
SIC: **2653** Boxes, corrugated: made from purchased materials

(G-13935)
NATURAL BEAUTY PRODUCTS INC
Also Called: Decaplus
50 S Main St (45044-4060)
P.O. Box 1566 (45042-7383)
PHONE.....................513 420-9400
Kenneth Alsop, *President*
David Haddix, *Vice Pres*
James Webb, *Treasurer*
Michelle Randall, *Office Mgr*
EMP: 10
SALES (est): 911.4K **Privately Held**
WEB: www.deccaplus.com
SIC: **5999** 2844 Hair care products; hair preparations, including shampoos

(G-13936)
NCI BUILDING SYSTEMS INC
2400 Yankee Rd (45044-8301)
PHONE.....................937 584-3300
John Wallace, *General Mgr*
Drew Dearman, *QC Mgr*
Michael Thornburg, *QC Mgr*
Duane Appel, *Manager*
Mike Rosenberry, *Manager*
EMP: 164
SALES (corp-wide): 2B **Publicly Held**
SIC: **3448** Prefabricated metal buildings
PA: Nci Building Systems, Inc.
    10943 N Sam Huston Pkwy W
    Houston TX 77064
    281 897-7788

(G-13937)
NEW CENTURY SALES LLC
2905 Lopane Ave (45044-6063)
PHONE.....................513 422-3631
Tony Dicristoforo, *Principal*
EMP: 4
SALES (est): 340.9K **Privately Held**
SIC: **2741** Miscellaneous publishing

(G-13938)
PAC WORLDWIDE CORPORATION
Also Called: Pac Manufacturing
3131 Cincinnati Dayton Rd (45044-8965)
PHONE.....................800 610-9367
EMP: 77 **Privately Held**
SIC: **5112** 2677 Whol Stationery/Office Supplies Mfg Envelopes
HQ: Pac Worldwide Corporation
    15435 Ne 92nd St
    Redmond WA 98052
    425 202-4000

(G-13939)
PACKAGING CORPORATION AMERICA
Also Called: Pca/Middletown 353
1824 Baltimore Rd (45044-5902)
P.O. Box 127 (45042-0127)
PHONE.....................513 424-3542
Minnie Griffin, *Vice Pres*
Glenn Hicks, *Plant Mgr*
Matthew Mancz, *Controller*
Bob Garland, *VP Sales*
Joe Burley, *Sales Staff*
EMP: 100
SQ FT: 200,000
SALES (corp-wide): 7B **Publicly Held**
WEB: www.packagingcorp.com
SIC: **2653** Boxes, corrugated: made from purchased materials
PA: Packaging Corporation Of America
    1 N Field Ct
    Lake Forest IL 60045
    847 482-3000

(G-13940)
PHONAK LLC
2951 Cincinnati Dayton Rd (45044-9313)
PHONE.....................513 420-4568
EMP: 4
SALES (corp-wide): 2.8B **Privately Held**
SIC: **3842** Hearing aids
HQ: Phonak, Llc
    4520 Weaver Pkwy Ste 1
    Warrenville IL 60555
    630 821-5000

(G-13941)
PILOT CHEMICAL CORP
3439 Yankee Rd (45044-8931)
PHONE.....................513 424-9700
Jeff Russell, *Branch Mgr*
EMP: 50
SQ FT: 25,000
SALES (corp-wide): 108.9MM **Privately Held**
WEB: www.pilotchemical.com
SIC: **2841** 2842 Detergents, synthetic organic or inorganic alkaline; specialty cleaning, polishes & sanitation goods
HQ: Pilot Chemical Corp.
    2744 E Kemper Rd
    Cincinnati OH 45241
    513 326-0600

(G-13942)
PIXSLAP INC
1634 Central Ave (45044-4191)
PHONE.....................937 559-2671
Adam Ali, *CEO*
EMP: 5
SQ FT: 2,500
SALES (est): 326.6K **Privately Held**
SIC: **7311** 7319 7371 2741 Advertising agencies; media buying service; custom computer programming services;

(G-13943)
PPG INDUSTRIES INC
Also Called: PPG 4335
4480 Marie Dr (45044-6248)
PHONE.....................513 424-1241
Brian Wright, *Branch Mgr*
EMP: 24
SALES (corp-wide): 15.3B **Publicly Held**
WEB: www.ppg.com
SIC: **2851** Paints & allied products
PA: Ppg Industries, Inc.
    1 Ppg Pl
    Pittsburgh PA 15272
    412 434-3131

(G-13944)
PROGRESSIVE RIBBON INC (PA)
1533 Central Ave (45044-4135)
PHONE.....................513 705-9319
Darryl Bowen, *President*
Dan Bush, *Vice Pres*
EMP: 20
SQ FT: 20,000
SALES (est): 4.8MM **Privately Held**
SIC: **3955** Ribbons, inked: typewriter, adding machine, register, etc.

(G-13945)
PROPIPE TECHNOLOGIES INC
1800 Clayton Ave (45042-2200)
PHONE.....................513 424-5311
John Blount, *President*
EMP: 43
SQ FT: 52,500
SALES (est): 6.8MM
SALES (corp-wide): 2.5B **Publicly Held**
WEB: www.muellerbrass.com
SIC: **3498** Manifolds, pipe: fabricated from purchased pipe
HQ: Mueller Brass Co.
    8285 Tournament Dr # 150
    Memphis TN 38125
    901 753-3200

(G-13946)
PURE SPORTS DESIGN
Also Called: Pro Sign Design
3125 Yankee Rd Ste 1 (45044-7793)
PHONE.....................937 935-5595
Jerry Van Horn, *Owner*
EMP: 5

Middletown - Butler County (G-13947)

SALES (est): 194.8K *Privately Held*
WEB: www.prosigndesign.com
SIC: 3993 Signs, not made in custom sign painting shops

(G-13947)
QUAKER CHEMICAL CORPORATION (HQ)
3431 Yankee Rd (45044-8931)
PHONE.................................513 422-9600
Michael F Barry, *President*
D Jeffry Benoliel, *Corp Secy*
Patrick J Piccioni, *Vice Pres*
Tracie Hunt, *Buyer*
Naryan RAO, *QC Mgr*
▲ EMP: 60
SALES (est): 15.1MM
SALES (corp-wide): 820MM *Publicly Held*
WEB: www.quakerchem.com
SIC: 2992 2899 Lubricating oils & greases; chemical preparations
PA: Quaker Chemical Corporation
 901 E Hector St
 Conshohocken PA 19428
 610 832-4000

(G-13948)
REBILTCO INC
8775 Thomas Rd (45042-1233)
PHONE.................................513 424-2024
Larry Eckhardt, *President*
EMP: 6
SQ FT: 25,000
SALES (est): 1.1MM *Privately Held*
SIC: 3554 Corrugating machines, paper

(G-13949)
ROSS HX LLC
2908 Cincinnati Dayton Rd (45044-9313)
PHONE.................................513 217-1565
Ted Osner, *Human Resources*
Richard Ross,
EMP: 7
SQ FT: 9,000
SALES: 100K *Privately Held*
SIC: 3443 Heat exchangers, plate type

(G-13950)
RUS POWER STORAGE LLC
3210 S Main St (45044-7423)
PHONE.................................937 999-8121
Allen Ely, *President*
EMP: 1
SQ FT: 1,000
SALES: 2.5MM *Privately Held*
SIC: 3691 3692 Storage batteries; dry cell batteries, single or multiple cell

(G-13951)
SHADETREE MACHINE
5994 Kalbfleisch Rd (45042-8937)
PHONE.................................513 727-8771
John Bridges, *Owner*
EMP: 4
SALES (est): 210K *Privately Held*
WEB: www.shadetreemachine.com
SIC: 3549 Wiredrawing & fabricating machinery & equipment, ex. die

(G-13952)
SHEPHERD CHEMICAL COMPANY
Also Called: Shepherd Middletown Co
3444 Yankee Rd (45044-8931)
PHONE.................................513 424-7276
Bayard Pelsor, *Branch Mgr*
EMP: 15
SQ FT: 945
SALES (corp-wide): 90MM *Privately Held*
SIC: 2819 Metal salts & compounds, except sodium, potassium, aluminum
HQ: The Shepherd Chemical Company
 4900 Beech St
 Norwood OH 45212
 513 731-1110

(G-13953)
SPURLINO MATERIALS LLC (PA)
4000 Oxford State Rd (45044-8973)
PHONE.................................513 705-0111
Jim Spurlino, *President*
EMP: 50
SQ FT: 10,000
SALES (est): 27MM *Privately Held*
WEB: www.spurlino.net
SIC: 3273 Ready-mixed concrete

(G-13954)
START PRINTING
3140 Cincinnati Dayton Rd (45044-8921)
PHONE.................................513 424-2121
Teresa Lytle, *Principal*
EMP: 4
SALES (est): 472.5K *Privately Held*
SIC: 2752 Commercial printing, lithographic

(G-13955)
SUNCOKE ENERGY NC
Also Called: Mto Suncoke
3353 Yankee Rd (45044-8927)
PHONE.................................513 727-5571
Frederick Fritz A Henderson, *CEO*
Brian Bokovoy, *Safety Mgr*
David O'Brien, *Manager*
EMP: 40
SALES (est): 5.4MM *Privately Held*
SIC: 1241 Coal mining services

(G-13956)
TEMPLE INLAND
912 Nelbar St (45042-2529)
PHONE.................................513 425-0830
Kent Kimmel, *Personnel Exec*
EMP: 8
SALES (est): 637.8K *Privately Held*
SIC: 2653 Corrugated & solid fiber boxes

(G-13957)
THOMPSON DISTRIBUTING CO INC
3227 Seneca St (45044-7755)
PHONE.................................513 422-9011
Clark L Thompson, *President*
EMP: 3
SALES (est): 169K *Privately Held*
SIC: 3582 Drycleaning equipment & machinery, commercial

(G-13958)
TMS INTERNATIONAL LLC
1801 Crawford St (45044-4572)
PHONE.................................513 425-6462
EMP: 4 *Privately Held*
SIC: 3312 Blast furnaces & steel mills
HQ: Tms International, Llc
 12 Monongahela Ave
 Glassport PA 15045
 412 678-6141

(G-13959)
TMS INTERNATIONAL LLC
3018 Oxford State Rd (45044-8900)
PHONE.................................513 422-4572
EMP: 5 *Privately Held*
SIC: 3312 Blast furnaces & steel mills
HQ: Tms International, Llc
 12 Monongahela Ave
 Glassport PA 15045
 412 678-6141

(G-13960)
TOMSON STEEL COMPANY
1400 Made Industrial Dr (45044-8936)
P.O. Box 940 (45044-0940)
PHONE.................................513 420-8600
Stephen Lutz, *President*
Larry L Knapp, *Principal*
Thomas Lutz, *Vice Pres*
Kelly Malone, *Sales Staff*
Jim Strok, *Sales Staff*
EMP: 25
SQ FT: 94,000
SALES (est): 22.6MM *Privately Held*
WEB: www.tomsonsteel.com
SIC: 5051 3291 Steel; abrasive metal & steel products

(G-13961)
UNBRIDLED BREWING COMPANY LLC
Also Called: Figleaf Brewing Company
3387 Cincinnati Dayton Rd (45044-8905)
PHONE.................................937 361-2573
Brian Yavorsky,
Andrew Allgeyer,
Tasha Brown,
Paul Jeff Fortney,
EMP: 12
SQ FT: 8,400
SALES (est): 482.7K *Privately Held*
SIC: 2082 Beer (alcoholic beverage)

(G-13962)
VAIL RUBBER WORKS INC
Also Called: Midwest Service
605 Clark St (45042-2117)
PHONE.................................513 705-2060
Donald Bown, *Branch Mgr*
EMP: 18
SALES (corp-wide): 30.3MM *Privately Held*
WEB: www.vailrubber.com
SIC: 3554 Paper industries machinery
PA: Vail Rubber Works, Inc.
 521 Langley Ave
 Saint Joseph MI 49085
 877 350-0441

(G-13963)
VANDERPOOL MOTOR SPORTS
6315 Howe Rd (45042-1657)
PHONE.................................513 424-2166
Daniel Vanderpool, *Owner*
EMP: 5
SALES (est): 304.8K *Privately Held*
SIC: 3714 Motor vehicle engines & parts

(G-13964)
WATSON GRAVEL INC
2100 S Main St (45044-7345)
PHONE.................................513 422-3781
Steve Rains, *Safety Mgr*
Ron Price, *Manager*
EMP: 20
SALES (corp-wide): 10.6MM *Privately Held*
SIC: 1442 Gravel mining
PA: Watson Gravel, Inc.
 2728 Hamilton Cleves Rd
 Hamilton OH 45013
 513 863-0070

(G-13965)
WAUSAU PAPER CORP
Also Called: Wausau Mosinee Paper
700 Columbia Ave (45042-1931)
PHONE.................................513 217-3623
Younette Sleet, *Marketing Mgr*
Douglas Zirbel, *Manager*
EMP: 200
SALES (corp-wide): 7.6B *Privately Held*
SIC: 2621 Paper mills
HQ: Wausau Paper Corp.
 2929 Arch St Ste 2600
 Philadelphia PA 19104
 866 722-8675

(G-13966)
WAUSAU PPR TOWEL & TISSUE LLC
700 Columbia Ave (45042-1931)
PHONE.................................513 424-2999
Pat Bradley, *Manager*
EMP: 220
SALES (corp-wide): 7.6B *Privately Held*
SIC: 2621 2676 Towels, tissues & napkins: paper & stock; sanitary paper products
HQ: Wausau Paper Towel & Tissue Llc
 1150 Industry Rd
 Harrodsburg KY 40330

(G-13967)
WHITT MACHINE INC
806 Central Ave (45044-1718)
PHONE.................................513 423-7624
Dean Whitt, *President*
Wendy Whitt, *Vice Pres*
Angie Snarski, *Treasurer*
EMP: 15
SQ FT: 35,000
SALES: 1.2MM *Privately Held*
SIC: 3599 7692 Machine shop, jobbing & repair; welding repair

(G-13968)
WIKOFF COLOR CORPORATION
1330 Hook Dr (45042-1712)
PHONE.................................513 423-0727
Bill Dishman, *Sales/Mktg Mgr*
Janice Kolker, *Info Tech Dir*
EMP: 9
SQ FT: 3,600
SALES (corp-wide): 150MM *Privately Held*
WEB: www.wikoff.com
SIC: 2893 Printing ink
PA: Wikoff Color Corporation
 1886 Merritt Rd
 Fort Mill SC 29715
 803 548-2210

(G-13969)
WORTHINGTON STEEL COMPANY
1501 Made Dr (45044-8938)
PHONE.................................513 702-0130
Tim Glaab, *Branch Mgr*
EMP: 8
SALES (corp-wide): 3.5B *Publicly Held*
SIC: 5051 3444 Steel; sheet metalwork
HQ: The Worthington Steel Company
 200 W Old Wilson Bridge Rd
 Worthington OH 43085
 614 438-3210

Middletown
Warren County

(G-13970)
BARRETT PAVING MATERIALS INC
3751 Commerce Dr (45005-5234)
PHONE.................................513 271-6200
Janice Misch, *Human Res Mgr*
Gerald Bushelman, *Manager*
EMP: 200
SALES (corp-wide): 83.5MM *Privately Held*
WEB: www.barrettpaving.com
SIC: 5032 2951 1771 1611 Asphalt mixture; asphalt paving mixtures & blocks; driveway, parking lot & blacktop contractors; surfacing & paving; construction sand & gravel
HQ: Barrett Paving Materials Inc.
 3 Becker Farm Rd Ste 307
 Roseland NJ 07068
 973 533-1001

(G-13971)
MIDDLETOWNUSACOM
6730 Roosevelt Ave (45005-5730)
PHONE.................................513 594-2831
EMP: 3
SALES (est): 100.1K *Privately Held*
SIC: 2711 Newspapers, publishing & printing

(G-13972)
NL MFG & DISTRIBUTION SYS IN
6107 Market Ave (45005-5238)
PHONE.................................513 422-5216
Tom Frederick, *Principal*
▲ EMP: 8
SALES (est): 1.1MM *Privately Held*
SIC: 3999 Manufacturing industries

Midvale
Tuscarawas County

(G-13973)
ALTERNTIVE SPPORT APPRATUS LLC
5609 Gundy Dr (44653)
P.O. Box 556 (44653-0556)
PHONE.................................740 922-2727
Erica Wright, *Info Tech Mgr*
Mark Natoli,
Cheryl Price,
Kurt Shelley,
EMP: 3
SQ FT: 10,000
SALES (est): 592.8K *Privately Held*
WEB: www.asap911.com
SIC: 3713 Ambulance bodies

GEOGRAPHIC SECTION

Milford - Clermont County (G-13998)

(G-13974)
AMERICAN BOTTLING COMPANY
Also Called: 7 Up Bottling Co
Old Rte 250 (44653)
P.O. Box 535 (44653-0535)
PHONE.................................740 922-5253
Nick Kazocoff, *Manager*
EMP: 35 **Publicly Held**
WEB: www.cs-americas.com
SIC: 2086 Bottled & canned soft drinks
HQ: The American Bottling Company
5301 Legacy Dr
Plano TX 75024

(G-13975)
AMKO SERVICE COMPANY (DH)
Also Called: Dover Cryogenics
3211 Brightwood Rd (44653)
P.O. Box 280 (44653-0280)
PHONE.................................330 364-8857
Darren Nippard, *President*
Duane R Yant, *Principal*
▲ **EMP:** 50
SALES (est): 6.2MM **Privately Held**
SIC: 7699 3443 7629 Tank repair & cleaning services; cryogenic tanks, for liquids & gases; electrical repair shops
HQ: Praxair, Inc.
10 Riverview Dr
Danbury CT 06810
203 837-2000

(G-13976)
DOVER CONVEYOR INC
3323 Brightwood Rd (44653)
P.O. Box 300 (44653-0300)
PHONE.................................740 922-9390
Joseph Coniglio, *President*
Tim Frank, *Project Engr*
EMP: 25
SQ FT: 40,000
SALES (est): 6.6MM **Privately Held**
WEB: www.doverconveyor.com
SIC: 3535 3441 3532 Conveyors & conveying equipment; fabricated structural metal; cages, mine shaft

(G-13977)
FIBA TECHNOLOGIES INC
Also Called: Amko Service Company
3211 Brightwood Rd (44653)
P.O. Box 280 (44653-0280)
PHONE.................................330 602-7300
David Ohl, *Branch Mgr*
EMP: 55
SALES (corp-wide): 53.5MM **Privately Held**
SIC: 3443 Cryogenic tanks, for liquids & gases
PA: Fiba Technologies, Inc.
53 Ayer Rd
Littleton MA 01460
508 887-7100

(G-13978)
HYDRAULIC SPECIALISTS INC
5655 Gundy Dr (44653)
PHONE.................................740 922-3343
Dale Burkholder, *President*
Laraine Burkholder, *Corp Secy*
EMP: 25
SQ FT: 15,000
SALES (est): 3.7MM **Privately Held**
SIC: 3443 7699 3593 Industrial vessels, tanks & containers; hydraulic equipment repair; fluid power cylinders & actuators

(G-13979)
IMAGE ARMOR LLC
3509 Brightwood Rd Se (44653)
PHONE.................................877 673-4377
Bryan Walker, *CEO*
◆ **EMP:** 5
SQ FT: 3,000
SALES: 850K **Privately Held**
SIC: 2869 Accelerators, rubber processing: cyclic or acyclic

(G-13980)
MAINTENANCE REPAIR SUPPLY INC
Also Called: Convertapax
5539 Gundy Dr (44653)
P.O. Box 540 (44653-0540)
PHONE.................................740 922-3006
Brad Mathias, *President*
▲ **EMP:** 20
SQ FT: 48,000
SALES (est): 6.7MM **Privately Held**
WEB: www.m-r-sinc.com
SIC: 5085 2821 5084 Industrial supplies; polyesters; plastic products machinery

Milan
Erie County

(G-13981)
CERTAINTEED CORPORATION
11519 Us Highway 250 N (44846-9708)
PHONE.................................419 499-2581
Mark Hyde, *Manager*
EMP: 247
SALES (corp-wide): 215.9MM **Privately Held**
WEB: www.certainteed.net
SIC: 2952 Roofing materials
HQ: Certainteed Corporation
20 Moores Rd
Malvern PA 19355
610 893-5000

(G-13982)
EDISON SOLAR INC
3809 State Route 113 E (44846-9430)
PHONE.................................419 499-0000
David Miller, *President*
EMP: 10
SALES (est): 1.6MM **Privately Held**
SIC: 3585 1711 Heating equipment, complete; solar energy contractor

(G-13983)
FREUDENBERG-NOK SEALING TECH
11617 State Route 13 (44846-9725)
PHONE.................................877 331-8427
EMP: 13 EST: 2015
SALES (est): 1.6MM **Privately Held**
SIC: 3315 Steel wire & related products

(G-13984)
HEMCO INC
Also Called: Bay Manufacturing
1413 State Route 113 E (44846-9527)
P.O. Box 1250 (44846-1250)
PHONE.................................419 499-4602
Michael J Mc Guire, *President*
Joyce Mc Guire, *Corp Secy*
▲ **EMP:** 4
SQ FT: 20,000
SALES (est): 619.8K **Privately Held**
WEB: www.baymfg.com
SIC: 3519 Outboard motors; parts & accessories, internal combustion engines

(G-13985)
JASON INCORPORATED
Janesville-Sackner Group
12406 Us Rte 250 (44846)
P.O. Box 349, Norwalk (44857-0349)
PHONE.................................419 668-4474
David Cataldi, *CEO*
James Schultz, *Principal*
Kevin Dow, *Manager*
EMP: 53
SQ FT: 2,000
SALES (corp-wide): 612.9MM **Publicly Held**
WEB: www.jasoninc.com
SIC: 3086 Mfg Plastic Foam Products
HQ: Jason Incorporated
833 E Michigan St Ste 900
Milwaukee WI 53202
414 277-9500

(G-13986)
JOHNS MANVILLE CORPORATION
49 Lockwood Rd (44846-9734)
PHONE.................................419 499-1400
Brian Keyser, *General Mgr*
EMP: 75
SALES (corp-wide): 225.3B **Publicly Held**
SIC: 2952 Roofing materials
HQ: Johns Manville Corporation
717 17th St Ste 800
Denver CO 80202
303 978-2000

(G-13987)
PULLMAN COMPANY
Also Called: Tenneco
33 Lockwood Rd (44846-9734)
PHONE.................................419 499-2541
Casey McElwain, *Branch Mgr*
EMP: 50
SALES (corp-wide): 11.7B **Publicly Held**
WEB: www.tenneco-automotive.com
SIC: 3714 Shock absorbers, motor vehicle
HQ: The Pullman Company
1 International Dr
Monroe MI 48161
734 243-8000

(G-13988)
SCHLESSMAN SEED CO (PA)
11513 Us Highway 250 N (44846-9708)
PHONE.................................419 499-2572
Daryl Deering, *Ch of Bd*
Vicki Zorn, *Plant Mgr*
Dave Herzer, *Treasurer*
Mark Skaggs, *Controller*
David Schlessman, *Finance Mgr*
EMP: 25
SQ FT: 100,000
SALES (est): 23.5MM **Privately Held**
WEB: www.schlessman-seed.com
SIC: 5191 2075 0723 0116 Seeds: field, garden & flower; soybean oil mills; crop preparation services for market; soybeans; corn; wheat

(G-13989)
SIEMENS INDUSTRY INC
21 N Main St (44846-9733)
PHONE.................................419 499-4616
Caleb Richmond, *Manager*
EMP: 20
SALES (corp-wide): 95B **Privately Held**
WEB: www.srt-ar.com
SIC: 3613 Switchgear & switchboard apparatus
HQ: Siemens Industry, Inc.
1000 Deerfield Pkwy
Buffalo Grove IL 60089
800 743-6367

(G-13990)
TRADITIONAL MARBLE & GRAN LTD
10105 Us Highway 250 N (44846-9570)
PHONE.................................419 625-3966
Albert T Gasparini, *President*
▲ **EMP:** 12
SQ FT: 12,000
SALES (est): 1.6MM **Privately Held**
WEB: www.traditionalmarblengranite.com
SIC: 3281 Granite, cut & shaped

Milford
Clermont County

(G-13991)
3M COMPANY
910 Lila Ave (45150-1631)
PHONE.................................513 248-1749
Beth Gramza, *Branch Mgr*
EMP: 324
SALES (corp-wide): 32.7B **Publicly Held**
SIC: 3841 Surgical instruments & apparatus
PA: 3m Company
3m Center
Saint Paul MN 55144
651 733-1110

(G-13992)
AB PLASTICS INC
1287 Us Route 50 (45150-9688)
PHONE.................................513 576-6333
Robert Basile, *President*
Kimberlee Basile, *Controller*
Kim Basille, *Admin Sec*
EMP: 9
SQ FT: 5,000
SALES (est): 1.9MM **Privately Held**
WEB: www.ab-plastics.com
SIC: 3089 Plastic & fiberglass tanks; ducting, plastic; plastic hardware & building products

(G-13993)
AMERICAN INSULATION TECH LLC
6071 Branch Hill Guinea P (45150-1567)
PHONE.................................513 733-4248
Jerome Napier, *Mng Member*
EMP: 12
SALES (est): 796.2K **Privately Held**
SIC: 3296 3081 Fiberglass insulation; film base, cellulose acetate or nitrocellulose plastic

(G-13994)
APPLIED SYSTEMS INC
Also Called: Ivans Insurance Solutions
5300 Dupont Cir Ste B (45150-2791)
PHONE.................................513 943-0000
EMP: 20
SALES (corp-wide): 362MM **Privately Held**
SIC: 7371 7372 Computer software development; prepackaged software
PA: Applied Systems, Inc.
200 Applied Pkwy
University Park IL 60484
708 534-5575

(G-13995)
B & D MACHINISTS INC
1350 Us Route 50 (45150-9205)
PHONE.................................513 831-8588
Tonson Boone Jr, *President*
Velma Boone, *Corp Secy*
Gary W Boone, *Vice Pres*
Steven Boone, *Vice Pres*
EMP: 11
SQ FT: 16,000
SALES: 1.3MM **Privately Held**
SIC: 3599 Machine shop, jobbing & repair

(G-13996)
BEARING PRECIOUS SEED (PA)
1369 Woodville Pike B (45150-2260)
PHONE.................................513 575-1706
William Duttry, *President*
Alan Braley, *Director*
▼ **EMP:** 6
SALES (est): 1.8MM **Privately Held**
SIC: 2731 Books: publishing & printing

(G-13997)
BECK STUDIOS INC
1001 Tech Dr (45150-9780)
PHONE.................................513 831-6650
Dan L Ilhardt, *President*
Matt Mullen, *General Mgr*
Merrel Ludlow, *Vice Pres*
Matthew Mullen, *Vice Pres*
Mark Wolfson, *Sales Staff*
EMP: 20
SQ FT: 9,000
SALES: 4.9MM **Privately Held**
WEB: www.beckstudios.com
SIC: 1799 3999 Rigging, theatrical; stage hardware & equipment, except lighting; theatrical scenery

(G-13998)
BKHN INC
Also Called: Buckhorn
55 W Techne Center Dr (45150-8901)
PHONE.................................513 831-4402
Bill Tonachio, *General Mgr*
Greg Stodnick, *Treasurer*
Milton I Wiskind, *Admin Sec*
EMP: 68
SQ FT: 29,000
SALES (est): 10.6MM
SALES (corp-wide): 566.7MM **Publicly Held**
WEB: www.buckhorninc.com
SIC: 3089 Plastic containers, except foam
HQ: Buckhorn Inc.
55 W Techne Center Dr A
Milford OH 45150
513 831-4402

Milford - Clermont County (G-13999)

(G-13999)
BREWER COMPANY (PA)
Also Called: Brewercote
1354 Us Route 50 (45150-9205)
PHONE..................................800 394-0017
Pinckney W Brewer, *President*
Michael T Dooley, *Vice Pres*
Bill Maclean, *Prdtn Mgr*
Carl Nickulis, *Engineer*
Gail Menzel, *Hum Res Coord*
▲ **EMP:** 8
SQ FT: 8,000
SALES: 50MM **Privately Held**
WEB: www.thebrewerco.com
SIC: 2952 0782 2951 Coating compounds, tar; roofing materials; seeding services, lawn; turf installation services, except artificial; asphalt paving mixtures & blocks

(G-14000)
BUCKHORN INC (HQ)
55 W Techne Center Dr A (45150-9779)
PHONE..................................513 831-4402
Joel Grant, *Senior VP*
Matt Gerstner, *Opers Staff*
Jason Jatsko, *Buyer*
Michelle Keener, *Human Res Mgr*
Lance Schickling, *Cust Mgr*
◆ **EMP:** 37
SQ FT: 19,000
SALES (est): 179.2MM
SALES (corp-wide): 566.7MM **Publicly Held**
WEB: www.buckhorninc.com
SIC: 3089 Plastic containers, except foam
PA: Myers Industries, Inc.
   1293 S Main St
   Akron OH 44301
   330 253-5592

(G-14001)
BUCKHORN MATERIAL HDLG GROUP
Also Called: Nestier
55 W Techne Center Dr A (45150-9779)
PHONE..................................513 831-4402
Bill Tonachio, *President*
Greg Stodnick, *Treasurer*
Milt Wiskind, *Admin Sec*
▼ **EMP:** 68
SQ FT: 29,000
SALES (est): 6.9MM
SALES (corp-wide): 566.7MM **Publicly Held**
SIC: 3089 Plastic containers, except foam
PA: Myers Industries, Inc.
   1293 S Main St
   Akron OH 44301
   330 253-5592

(G-14002)
CHRIS STEPP
Also Called: Stepp Sewing Service
927 State Route 28 Unit B (45150-1948)
PHONE..................................513 248-0822
Chris Stepp, *Owner*
EMP: 6
SQ FT: 1,200
SALES (est): 150K **Privately Held**
SIC: 2395 5651 Embroidery & art needlework; unisex clothing stores

(G-14003)
CINCY SAFE COMPANY
1607 State Route 131 (45150-2667)
PHONE..................................513 900-9152
Gary Krug, *President*
EMP: 20
SQ FT: 12,400
SALES (est): 3.2MM **Privately Held**
SIC: 3499 Safes & vaults, metal

(G-14004)
COMBINED INDUSTRIAL SOLUTIONS
944 Klondyke Rd (45150-9683)
PHONE..................................513 659-3091
Dwayne Dixie, *Owner*
EMP: 5
SALES: 300K **Privately Held**
SIC: 3599 Industrial machinery

(G-14005)
CONVEYOR TECHNOLOGIES LTD
501 Techne Center Dr B (45150-2796)
PHONE..................................513 248-0663
Charles Mitchell, *President*
Tim Mitchell, *Vice Pres*
Tony Mitchell, *Vice Pres*
Debbie Damaska, *Office Mgr*
EMP: 8
SQ FT: 7,000
SALES (est): 1.6MM **Privately Held**
WEB: www.conveyortechltd.com
SIC: 3535 Conveyors & conveying equipment

(G-14006)
CUSTOM BUILT CRATES INC
1700 Victory Park Dr (45150-1812)
PHONE..................................513 248-4422
Glen Brandenburg, *President*
Eric Douglas Bradenburg, *Vice Pres*
EMP: 20
SALES (est): 4.5MM **Privately Held**
SIC: 4213 2449 7389 Trucking, except local; rectangular boxes & crates, wood;

(G-14007)
DIGIMAX SIGNS
759 Us Route 50 (45150-9510)
PHONE..................................513 576-0747
Rick Seissiger, *President*
EMP: 3
SALES (est): 318.6K **Privately Held**
WEB: www.digimaxsigns.com
SIC: 3993 Signs & advertising specialties

(G-14008)
FLUID CONSERVATION SYSTEMS (DH)
Also Called: Fcs
502 Techne Center Dr B (45150-8780)
PHONE..................................513 831-9335
Andrew Richardson, *Ch of Bd*
Neal Summers, *President*
Kevin Calhoun, *Manager*
Teresa Fischer, *Manager*
Allison Grelle, *Manager*
EMP: 11 EST: 1981
SQ FT: 4,500
SALES (est): 1.3MM
SALES (corp-wide): 1.5B **Privately Held**
WEB: www.fluidconservation.com
SIC: 3599 7389 3812 Water leak detectors; inspection & testing services; search & navigation equipment
HQ: Halma Holdings Inc.
   11500 Northlake Dr # 306
   Cincinnati OH 45249
   513 772-5501

(G-14009)
FOUNTAIN SPECIALISTS INC
226 Main St (45150-1124)
PHONE..................................513 831-5717
Lois Sedacca, *President*
Mark Sedacca, *Vice Pres*
EMP: 8 EST: 1960
SQ FT: 5,000
SALES (est): 1MM **Privately Held**
SIC: 5261 3272 3499 3089 Fountains, outdoor; fountains, concrete; fountains (except drinking), metal; plastic processing; lighting, lamps & accessories; pumps & pumping equipment

(G-14010)
GB LIQUIDATING COMPANY INC
22 Whitney Dr (45150-9783)
PHONE..................................513 248-7600
Cory Sherman, *Editor*
Leon Lovette, *Regional Mgr*
Kathy Kluska, *Human Res Dir*
Joe Leahy, *Marketing Staff*
Robert Sherman Jr,
EMP: 50
SALES (est): 4.5MM **Privately Held**
WEB: www.gordonbernard.com
SIC: 7371 2759 2741 2752 Custom computer programming services; commercial printing; miscellaneous publishing; calendar & card printing, lithographic

(G-14011)
GOLDEN SIGNS AND LIGHTING LLC
120-150 Olympic Rd (45150)
PHONE..................................513 248-0895
Harold Golden, *Owner*
EMP: 3
SALES (est): 281.6K **Privately Held**
SIC: 3993 Signs & advertising specialties

(G-14012)
GOOD BEANS COFFEE ROASTERS LLC
1381 Cottonwood Dr (45150-2455)
PHONE..................................513 310-9516
Chris Bean, *Principal*
EMP: 3 EST: 2015
SALES (est): 123.1K **Privately Held**
SIC: 2095 Roasted coffee

(G-14013)
GORDON BERNARD COMPANY LLC
22 Whitney Dr (45150-9781)
PHONE..................................513 248-7600
Robert Sherman Jr, *President*
Cory Sherman, *Editor*
Leon Lovette, *Regional Mgr*
Kathy Kluska, *Human Res Dir*
Karyl Menchen, *Regl Sales Mgr*
EMP: 45
SQ FT: 25,000
SALES (est): 5.6MM **Privately Held**
SIC: 5199 2752 2741 Calendars; commercial printing, lithographic; miscellaneous publishing

(G-14014)
GREGG MACMILLAN
Also Called: Macmillan Graphics
2002 Ford Cir Ste A (45150-2748)
PHONE..................................513 248-2121
Gregg J Macmillan, *CEO*
Gregg Macmillan, *Owner*
EMP: 8
SQ FT: 4,000
SALES (est): 445.2K **Privately Held**
WEB: www.macgra.com
SIC: 2752 7336 Commercial printing, offset; graphic arts & related design

(G-14015)
H & H OF MILFORD OHIO LLC
1194 Wintercrest Cir (45150-2600)
PHONE..................................513 576-9004
Mark Hartwell, *President*
▲ **EMP:** 5
SQ FT: 10,000
SALES (est): 1.2MM **Privately Held**
SIC: 3949 5092 Sporting & athletic goods; playing cards

(G-14016)
HASON USA CORP
1262 Us Highway 50 (45150-9767)
PHONE..................................513 248-0287
Dennis Blain, *Principal*
EMP: 25 EST: 2014
SALES (est): 6MM **Privately Held**
SIC: 3443 Tanks, standard or custom fabricated: metal plate

(G-14017)
HYDRO SYSTEMS COMPANY
401 Milford Pkwy (45150-1298)
PHONE..................................513 271-8800
Joe Stamter, *Manager*
EMP: 5
SALES (corp-wide): 6.9B **Publicly Held**
SIC: 3586 Measuring & dispensing pumps
HQ: Hydro Systems Company
   3798 Round Bottom Rd
   Cincinnati OH 45244

(G-14018)
INTERNATIONAL PAPER COMPANY
5806 Jeb Stuart Dr (45150-2117)
P.O. Box 5383, Portland OR (97228-5383)
PHONE..................................877 447-2737
EMP: 277
SALES (corp-wide): 23.3B **Publicly Held**
WEB: www.internationalpaper.com
SIC: 2621 Paper mills
PA: International Paper Company
   6400 Poplar Ave
   Memphis TN 38197
   901 419-9000

(G-14019)
INTERPLEX MEDICAL LLC
25 Whitney Dr Ste 114 (45150-8400)
PHONE..................................513 248-5120
Karen G Granik, *Mng Member*
EMP: 24
SALES (est): 4.4MM **Privately Held**
WEB: www.interplexmedical.com
SIC: 3842 Grafts, artificial: for surgery

(G-14020)
JAMES G MOREHOUSE
Also Called: Morehouse Welding
4814a Woodlawn Dr (45150-9735)
PHONE..................................513 752-2236
James Morehouse, *Owner*
EMP: 5
SQ FT: 1,200
SALES (est): 312.8K **Privately Held**
SIC: 7692 Welding repair

(G-14021)
JEFF PENDERGRASS
Also Called: Titan Chemical
6037 Mill Row Ct (45150-2258)
PHONE..................................513 575-1226
Jeff Pendergrass, *Owner*
EMP: 3
SALES (est): 52.7K **Privately Held**
SIC: 2899 5087 5169 5999 Chemical preparations; carpet & rug cleaning equipment & supplies, commercial; detergents & soaps, except specialty cleaning; cleaning equipment & supplies;

(G-14022)
JOURNEY SYSTEMS LLC (PA)
25 Whitney Dr Ste 100 (45150-8400)
PHONE..................................513 831-6200
John L Whittley, *CEO*
Nancy Whittley, *Manager*
Richard Graham,
Nancy C Whittley,
EMP: 14
SQ FT: 9,875
SALES (est): 1.3MM **Privately Held**
SIC: 3571 5045 5734 Electronic computers; computers, peripherals & software; computer software; computer & software stores; computer software & accessories

(G-14023)
KANAWHA SCALES & SYSTEMS INC
26 Whitney Dr (45150-9783)
PHONE..................................513 576-0700
James Bradbury, *President*
EMP: 19
SALES (corp-wide): 51.1MM **Privately Held**
SIC: 5046 7699 3822 3596 Scales, except laboratory; scale parts service; auto controls regulating residntl & coml environmt & applncs; scales & balances, except laboratory
PA: Kanawha Scales & Systems, Inc.
   111 Jacobson Dr
   Poca WV 25159
   304 755-8321

(G-14024)
LORE INC
5526 Garrett Dr (45150-2824)
PHONE..................................513 969-8481
Igor Haheu, *Principal*
EMP: 3
SALES (est): 104.9K **Privately Held**
SIC: 2711 Newspapers

(G-14025)
MARTIN BAUDER WOODWORKING LLC
1498 Binning Rd (45150-9113)
PHONE..................................513 735-0659
Martin Bauder, *Principal*
EMP: 4
SALES (est): 221.9K **Privately Held**
SIC: 2431 Millwork

GEOGRAPHIC SECTION

Millbury - Wood County (G-14050)

(G-14026)
MELINK CORPORATION (PA)
5140 River Valley Rd (45150-9108)
PHONE.................................513 685-0958
Stephen K Melink, *President*
EMP: 12
SQ FT: 36,000
SALES (est): 19.6MM **Privately Held**
WEB: www.melinkcorp.com
SIC: 8711 8748 3822 Heating & ventilation engineering; energy conservation consultant; appliance controls except air-conditioning & refrigeration

(G-14027)
MILFORD PRINTERS (PA)
317 Main St (45150-1125)
P.O. Box 674 (45150-0674)
PHONE.................................513 831-6630
Robert M Heichel, *Owner*
EMP: 20
SQ FT: 8,000
SALES (est): 1.9MM **Privately Held**
WEB: www.milfordprinters.com
SIC: 2752 Commercial printing, offset; lithographing on metal

(G-14028)
MILFORD PRINTERS
18 Locust St (45150-1024)
PHONE.................................513 831-6630
Ron Woodruff, *Manager*
EMP: 3
SALES (corp-wide): 1.9MM **Privately Held**
WEB: www.milfordprinters.com
SIC: 2752 Commercial printing, offset
PA: Milford Printers
317 Main St
Milford OH 45150
513 831-6630

(G-14029)
MOTOR SYSTEMS INCORPORATED
Also Called: MSI
460 Milford Pkwy (45150-9104)
PHONE.................................513 576-1725
Fred Daniel Freshley, *President*
Kevin Salm, *President*
Bev Walsh, *Purchasing*
Randon Rose, *Engineer*
Daryl Zielinski, *Engineer*
EMP: 32
SQ FT: 16,000
SALES (est): 9.3MM **Privately Held**
WEB: www.motorsystems.com
SIC: 3569 Robots, assembly line: industrial & commercial

(G-14030)
OVERHOFF TECHNOLOGY CORP
1160 Us Route 50 (45150-9517)
P.O. Box 182 (45150-0182)
PHONE.................................513 248-2400
Robert Goldstein, *President*
Ivan Mitev, *Engineer*
EMP: 14
SQ FT: 8,000
SALES (est): 2.9MM
SALES (corp-wide): 1.4MM **Privately Held**
WEB: www.overhoff.com
SIC: 3829 3823 Nuclear instrument modules; controllers for process variables, all types
PA: U.S. Nuclear Corp.
7051 Eton Ave
Canoga Park CA 91303
818 296-0746

(G-14031)
PARKER-HANNIFIN CORPORATION
Also Called: Electromechanical North Amer
50 W Techne Center Dr H (45150-8403)
PHONE.................................513 831-2340
Kenneth Sweet, *Branch Mgr*
EMP: 75
SALES (corp-wide): 14.3B **Publicly Held**
WEB: www.parker.com
SIC: 3577 7371 3575 3571 Computer peripheral equipment; computer software development; computer terminals; electronic computers
PA: Parker-Hannifin Corporation
6035 Parkland Blvd
Cleveland OH 44124
216 896-3000

(G-14032)
PHANTASM VAPORS LLC (PA)
951 Lila Ave (45150-1617)
PHONE.................................513 248-2431
Tim Jacobs,
EMP: 5
SALES (est): 1MM **Privately Held**
SIC: 5731 3911 Consumer electronic equipment; cigar & cigarette accessories

(G-14033)
PPG INDUSTRIES INC
Also Called: P P G
500 Techne Center Dr (45150-2763)
PHONE.................................513 576-0360
Greg Wagner, *Manager*
EMP: 50
SALES (corp-wide): 15.3B **Publicly Held**
WEB: www.ppg.com
SIC: 2851 Shellac (protective coating)
PA: Ppg Industries, Inc.
1 Ppg Pl
Pittsburgh PA 15272
412 434-3131

(G-14034)
PPG INDUSTRIES INC
500 Techne Center Dr (45150-2763)
PHONE.................................513 576-3100
Eckhardt Pohl, *Branch Mgr*
EMP: 24
SALES (corp-wide): 15.3B **Publicly Held**
WEB: www.ppg.com
SIC: 2851 Paints & allied products
PA: Ppg Industries, Inc.
1 Ppg Pl
Pittsburgh PA 15272
412 434-3131

(G-14035)
PRIMEX
400 Techne Center Dr # 104 (45150-2792)
PHONE.................................513 831-9959
Douglas Strief, *President*
Catherine Strief, *Corp Secy*
EMP: 40
SQ FT: 20,000
SALES (est): 5.2MM **Privately Held**
WEB: www.controlworksinc.com
SIC: 3613 3823 3699 3625 Control panels, electric; industrial instrmnts msrmnt display/control process variable; electrical equipment & supplies; relays & industrial controls

(G-14036)
REDI ROCK STRUCTURES OKI LLC
1050 Round Bottom Rd (45150-9740)
PHONE.................................513 965-9221
Kenny Swanson, *Sales Staff*
Tim Turton, *Mng Member*
EMP: 6
SALES (est): 490K **Privately Held**
SIC: 3272 Floor slabs & tiles, precast concrete

(G-14037)
REMINGTON ENGRG MACHINING INC
5105 River Valley Rd (45150-9117)
PHONE.................................513 965-8999
Dan Mallaley, *President*
Valerie Mallaley, *Corp Secy*
EMP: 6 **EST:** 1996
SQ FT: 2,500
SALES (est): 879.4K
SALES (corp-wide): 65MM **Privately Held**
WEB: www.remingtonengineering.com
SIC: 3599 Machine & other job shop work
PA: Cold Jet, Llc
455 Wards Corner Rd # 100
Loveland OH 45140
513 831-3211

(G-14038)
S & S PALLETS
1536 Pointe Dr (45150-2695)
PHONE.................................513 967-7432
EMP: 4 **EST:** 2010
SALES (est): 386.2K **Privately Held**
SIC: 2448 Pallets, wood & wood with metal

(G-14039)
SARDINIA CONCRETE COMPANY (PA)
911 Us Route 50 (45150-9703)
PHONE.................................513 248-0090
James Fraley, *Managing Prtnr*
Al Grill, *Opers Mgr*
Chad Kelley, *QC Mgr*
Chad Kelly, *Engineer*
Jerry Ziegelmeyer, *Controller*
EMP: 40
SQ FT: 12,500
SALES (est): 10.7MM **Privately Held**
SIC: 3273 Ready-mixed concrete

(G-14040)
SIGN GRAPHICS & DESIGN
420 Main St Unit A (45150-1170)
PHONE.................................513 576-1639
K Scot Conover, *Owner*
EMP: 4
SALES (est): 359.7K **Privately Held**
WEB: www.signgraphics-design.com
SIC: 3993 Signs, not made in custom sign painting shops

(G-14041)
SILER EXCAVATION SERVICES
6025 Catherine Dr (45150-2203)
PHONE.................................513 400-8628
Mike Siler,
EMP: 40 **EST:** 2007
SALES (est): 1.1MM **Privately Held**
SIC: 1794 1389 Excavation work; construction, repair & dismantling services

(G-14042)
TACTICAL ENVMTL SYSTEMS INC
Also Called: T E S
1156 Us Route 50 (45150-9517)
PHONE.................................513 831-2663
Dillard Pegg Jr, *President*
Randel West, *Vice Pres*
EMP: 4
SALES (est): 1.2MM **Privately Held**
WEB: www.tacticalsys.com
SIC: 3585 5075 Air conditioning equipment, complete; air conditioning & ventilation equipment & supplies

(G-14043)
TATA AMERICA INTL CORP
Also Called: Tata Consultancy Services
1000 Summit Dr Unit 1 (45150-2724)
PHONE.................................513 677-6500
Sumanta Roy, *Regional Mgr*
Vikas Gupta, *Manager*
Brian Purvis, *Manager*
Alex Kellerman, *Software Dev*
EMP: 300
SALES (corp-wide): 81.3MM **Privately Held**
SIC: 7372 7373 7371 Prepackaged software; computer integrated systems design; custom computer programming services
HQ: Tata America International Corporation
101 Park Ave Rm 2603
New York NY 10178
212 557-8038

(G-14044)
TOOMEY INC
Also Called: Toomey Natural Foods
914 Lila Ave (45150-1631)
PHONE.................................513 831-4771
Mimi Toomey, *President*
J Patrick Toomey, *President*
EMP: 6
SQ FT: 2,400
SALES (est): 550K **Privately Held**
WEB: www.toomeynaturalfoods.com
SIC: 2023 Dietary supplements, dairy & non-dairy based

(G-14045)
TRI-TECH MACHINING LLC
1885 Seven Lands Dr (45150-2668)
PHONE.................................513 575-3959
Timothy Crawford,
EMP: 5
SQ FT: 4,000
SALES (est): 275K **Privately Held**
SIC: 3821 1731 Laboratory equipment: fume hoods, distillation racks, etc.; sound equipment specialization

(G-14046)
TRIUMPH SIGNS & CONSULTING INC
480 Milford Pkwy (45150-9104)
PHONE.................................513 576-8090
William Downey, *President*
Vinay Duncan, *Project Mgr*
Anne Keener, *Project Mgr*
Antonio Whittle, *Purch Agent*
Sheri S Iker, *Controller*
EMP: 39
SALES (est): 5.9MM **Privately Held**
SIC: 3993 Signs & advertising specialties

Milford Center
Union County

(G-14047)
NUTRIEN AG SOLUTIONS INC
9972 State Route 38 (43045-9760)
PHONE.................................614 873-4253
Jason Hess, *Principal*
EMP: 6
SALES (corp-wide): 8.8B **Privately Held**
SIC: 5261 5191 2875 Fertilizer; fertilizers & agricultural chemicals; fertilizers, mixing only
HQ: Nutrien Ag Solutions, Inc.
3005 Rocky Mountain Ave
Loveland CO 80538
970 685-3300

Millbury
Wood County

(G-14048)
CUSTOM GL SLTIONS MILLBURY LLC
Also Called: Guardian Millbury
24145 W Moline Martin Rd (43447-9568)
PHONE.................................419 855-7706
Michael Morrison, *President*
Paul Zeille, *Plant Mgr*
EMP: 225
SQ FT: 25,000
SALES (est): 27.8MM
SALES (corp-wide): 106.6MM **Privately Held**
SIC: 3211 3231 Plate glass, polished & rough; tempered glass; insulating glass, sealed units; products of purchased glass
PA: Custom Glass Solutions, Llc
600 Lkview Plz Blvd Ste A
Worthington OH 43085
248 340-1800

(G-14049)
FORMLABS OHIO INC
Also Called: Spectra Photopolymers Inc.
27800 Lemoyne Rd Ste J (43447-9683)
PHONE.................................419 837-9783
Alex Mejiritski, *President*
EMP: 28
SALES (est): 1.5MM **Privately Held**
SIC: 2899 5169 Chemical preparations; chemicals & allied products

(G-14050)
LAKE TOWNSHIP TRUSTEES
3800 Ayers Rd (43447-9745)
PHONE.................................419 836-1143
Dan McLargin, *Manager*
EMP: 9 **Privately Held**
WEB: www.laketwp.com
SIC: 9111 7997 3531 City & town managers' offices; baseball club, except professional & semi-professional; road construction & maintenance machinery

Millbury - Wood County (G-14051)

PA: Lake Township Trustees
27975 Cummings Rd
Millbury OH 43447

(G-14051)
LEVISON ENTERPRISES LLC
Also Called: Epi Global
4470 Moline Martin Rd (43447-9201)
PHONE...........................419 838-7365
David Levison, *President*
EMP: 20
SQ FT: 14,000
SALES (est): 4.3MM **Privately Held**
SIC: 3672 Printed circuit boards

(G-14052)
SPECTRA GROUP LIMITED INC
Also Called: Sgl
27800 Lemoyne Rd Ste J (43447-9683)
PHONE...........................419 837-9783
Douglas C Neckers, *Ch of Bd*
Oleg Greiwich, *President*
Alex Mejiritski, *President*
EMP: 7
SQ FT: 5,680
SALES (est): 1.8MM **Privately Held**
WEB: www.sglinc.com
SIC: 2891 Adhesives

Millersburg
Holmes County

(G-14053)
77 COACH SUPPLY LTD
7426 County Road 77 (44654-9279)
PHONE...........................330 674-1454
Atlee Kaufman,
EMP: 26
SALES (est): 3MM **Privately Held**
SIC: 5099 2499 Wood & wood by-products; decorative wood & woodwork

(G-14054)
A & M WOODWORKING
6440 State Route 515 (44654-8854)
PHONE...........................330 893-1331
Andrew Yoder, *Principal*
EMP: 3
SALES (est): 208K **Privately Held**
SIC: 2431 Millwork

(G-14055)
AFFORDABLE BARN CO LTD
Also Called: Southern Wholesale
4260 Township Road 617 (44654-7913)
PHONE...........................330 674-3001
Robert Yoder, *Manager*
Japheth Yoder,
Gabriel Schlabach,
EMP: 14 **EST:** 2012
SALES: 2.7MM **Privately Held**
SIC: 3448 Buildings, portable: prefabricated metal

(G-14056)
AL YODER CONSTRUCTION COMPANY
Also Called: Fairview Log Homes
3375 County Road 160 (44654-8366)
P.O. Box 275, Winesburg (44690-0275)
PHONE...........................330 359-5726
Alvin A Yoder, *President*
Ruth Yoder, *Corp Secy*
Sarah Troyer, *Admin Sec*
EMP: 6
SALES: 1.2MM **Privately Held**
SIC: 1521 2452 New construction, single-family houses; log cabins, prefabricated, wood

(G-14057)
ALONOVUS CORP
7368 County Road 623 (44654-9256)
P.O. Box 358 (44654-0358)
PHONE...........................330 674-2300
Michael Mast, *Principal*
David Mast, *Principal*
John Mast, *Principal*
Andy Vernon, *Manager*
Jim Marshall, *Author*
EMP: 56

SALES: 7.2MM **Privately Held**
SIC: 8742 2741 7371 Marketing consulting services; miscellaneous publishing; computer software development & applications

(G-14058)
AMERICAS BEST BOWSTRINGS LLC (PA)
3149 Ohio 39 (44654)
PHONE...........................330 893-7155
Jerry Mullet, *Principal*
EMP: 7
SALES (est): 680.6K **Privately Held**
SIC: 3949 Sporting & athletic goods

(G-14059)
AMISH COUNTRY ESSENTIALS LLC
4663 Us Rt 62 Millersburg (44654)
PHONE...........................330 674-3088
Tracy Cultice,
Shane Cultice,
▼ **EMP:** 3
SQ FT: 8,000
SALES (est): 129K **Privately Held**
SIC: 2844 2841 2834 Face creams or lotions; shampoos, rinses, conditioners: hair; soap: granulated, liquid, cake, flaked or chip; lip balms

(G-14060)
AMISH WEDDING FOODS INC
316 S Mad Anthony St (44654-1388)
PHONE...........................330 674-9199
John R Troyer, *CEO*
James Troyer, *President*
Aaron Yoder, *General Mgr*
EMP: 40
SALES (est): 6.8MM
SALES (corp-wide): 806.3MM **Privately Held**
SIC: 2022 2099 2013 Cheese, natural & processed; food preparations; noodles, uncooked: packaged with other ingredients; sausages & other prepared meats; beef, dried: from purchased meat
PA: Lipari Foods Operating Company Llc
26661 Bunert Rd
Warren MI 48089
586 447-3500

(G-14061)
B AND L SALES INC (PA)
3149 State Rte Ste 39 (44654)
P.O. Box 172, Walnut Creek (44687-0172)
PHONE...........................330 279-2007
Ben Mast, *President*
EMP: 4
SALES (est): 563.7K **Privately Held**
SIC: 2273 Floor coverings: paper, grass, reed, coir, sisal, jute, etc.

(G-14062)
BANDS COMPANY INC
164 E Jackson St (44654-1235)
P.O. Box 328 (44654-0328)
PHONE...........................330 674-0446
Michael Brown, *President*
Brent Smith, *Vice Pres*
Susan Hager, *Treasurer*
Ann Brown, *Admin Sec*
EMP: 8
SQ FT: 3,000
SALES (est): 932.2K **Privately Held**
SIC: 1382 Oil & gas exploration services

(G-14063)
BARKMAN PRODUCTS LLC
2550 Township Road 121 (44654-8909)
PHONE...........................330 893-2520
Albert Barkman, *Principal*
EMP: 4 **EST:** 2008
SALES (est): 298.6K **Privately Held**
SIC: 2499 Decorative wood & woodwork

(G-14064)
BEECHVALE LAMINATING
7241 Township Road 572 (44654-9160)
PHONE...........................330 674-2804
Jonas Hochstetler, *Owner*
EMP: 11
SALES (est): 840.9K **Privately Held**
SIC: 2431 Millwork

(G-14065)
BENT WOOD SOLUTIONS LLC
7426 County Road 77 (44654-9279)
PHONE...........................330 674-1454
Atlee N Kaufman, *Principal*
EMP: 4
SALES (est): 593K **Privately Held**
SIC: 1542 3553 Commercial & office building contractors; woodworking machinery

(G-14066)
BERLIN CUSTOM LEATHER LTD
5085 Township Road 353 (44654-8715)
PHONE...........................330 674-3768
EMP: 3
SALES (est): 404.9K **Privately Held**
SIC: 3199 Leather goods

(G-14067)
BERLIN TRUCK CAPS LTD
Also Called: Berlin Parts
4560 State Route 39 (44654-9600)
PHONE...........................330 893-2811
Wayne Beachy Jr, *Partner*
James Beachy, *Partner*
EMP: 10
SQ FT: 12,000
SALES (est): 800K **Privately Held**
SIC: 5199 3792 Tarpaulins; pickup covers, canopies or caps

(G-14068)
BERLIN WOODWORKING
4575 Township Road 366 (44654-9102)
PHONE...........................330 893-3234
Gary Troyer, *Principal*
EMP: 4
SALES (est): 422.8K **Privately Held**
SIC: 2431 Millwork

(G-14069)
BROTY ENTERPRISES INC (PA)
Also Called: Thoughts That Count
88 W Jackson St (44654-1302)
PHONE...........................330 674-6900
Victoria Curren, *President*
Kelly Curren, *Vice Pres*
EMP: 3
SQ FT: 5,000
SALES (est): 443.5K **Privately Held**
SIC: 5947 2411 Gift shop; logging

(G-14070)
BUCKEYE PALLETT
3463 County Road 160 (44654-8369)
PHONE...........................330 359-5919
Merlin Miller, *Principal*
EMP: 4 **EST:** 2008
SALES (est): 375.6K **Privately Held**
SIC: 2448 Wood pallets & skids

(G-14071)
BUCKEYE SEATING LLC
6960 County Road 672 (44654-8350)
P.O. Box 128, Berlin (44610-0128)
PHONE...........................330 473-2379
Emanuel Weaver, *Mng Member*
EMP: 10
SALES (est): 1MM **Privately Held**
SIC: 2399 Seat covers, automobile

(G-14072)
BUCKEYE WELDING
2507 Township Road 110 (44654-9085)
PHONE...........................330 674-0944
Alvin Wengerd, *Principal*
EMP: 5
SALES (est): 292.2K **Privately Held**
SIC: 7692 Welding repair

(G-14073)
BUNKER HILL CHEESE CO INC
Also Called: Heinis Cheese Chalet
6005 County Road 77 (44654-9045)
PHONE...........................330 893-2131
Peter Dauwalder, *President*
P H C Dauwalder, *Principal*
T D Gindlesberger, *Principal*
Mark Schlabach, *Purchasing*
EMP: 60
SQ FT: 80,000
SALES (est): 13.2MM **Privately Held**
SIC: 2022 5451 5812 Natural cheese; cheese; snack shop

(G-14074)
BURKHOLDER BUGGY SHOP
7400 County Road 77 (44654-9279)
PHONE...........................330 674-5891
EMP: 3
SALES (est): 200K **Privately Held**
SIC: 3799 Mfg Transportation Equipment

(G-14075)
BUSY BEE LUMBER
5965 Township Road 355 (44654-8880)
P.O. Box 16, Berlin (44610-0016)
PHONE...........................330 674-1305
Alvin Miller, *Owner*
EMP: 6
SALES (est): 382.9K **Privately Held**
SIC: 2411 Logging

(G-14076)
CANAL DOVER FURNITURE LLC
8211 Township Road 652 (44654-8341)
PHONE...........................330 359-5375
Karen Yoder, *General Mgr*
Dan Mast, *Mng Member*
▼ **EMP:** 60
SQ FT: 60,000
SALES: 7.6MM **Privately Held**
SIC: 2511 Dining room furniture: wood

(G-14077)
CARTER-JONES LUMBER COMPANY
6139 State Route 39 (44654-8845)
PHONE...........................330 674-9060
EMP: 104
SALES (corp-wide): 1.4B **Privately Held**
SIC: 5031 5211 2439 2434 Lumber, plywood & millwork; lumber & other building materials; structural wood members; wood kitchen cabinets; millwork; hardwood dimension & flooring mills
HQ: The Carter-Jones Lumber Company
601 Tallmadge Rd
Kent OH 44240
330 673-6100

(G-14078)
DOVETAIL DIMENSIONS
6534 Township Road 603 (44654-7010)
PHONE...........................330 674-9533
Timon Miller, *Partner*
David Miller, *Partner*
EMP: 4
SALES (est): 458.6K **Privately Held**
SIC: 2541 Cabinets, lockers & shelving

(G-14079)
DS WELDING LLC
3982 State Route 39 (44654-8382)
PHONE...........................330 893-4049
David Shetler, *Principal*
EMP: 8
SALES (est): 88.7K **Privately Held**
SIC: 7692 Welding repair

(G-14080)
EDUCATIONAL ELECTRONICS INC
Also Called: Artsinheaven.com
101 Lakeview Dr Apt 28 (44654-6800)
PHONE...........................234 301-9077
Ed Bedford, *CEO*
Kathleen Bedford, *Admin Sec*
EMP: 5
SALES: 240K **Privately Held**
WEB: artsinheaven.com
SIC: 3679 Electronic circuits

(G-14081)
EUROCASE ARCHITECTURAL CABINET
7488 State Route 241 (44654-8383)
PHONE...........................330 674-0681
Garrett M Roach, *Mng Member*
EMP: 15
SALES (est): 1MM **Privately Held**
SIC: 3469 Architectural panels or parts, porcelain enameled

GEOGRAPHIC SECTION — Millersburg - Holmes County (G-14112)

(G-14082) FEIKERT SAND & GRAVEL CO INC
Also Called: Feikert Concrete
6971 County Road 189 (44654-9186)
PHONE.................330 674-0038
Lynn Feikert, *President*
James Feikert, *Vice Pres*
John T Feikert, *Treasurer*
Sheila Feikert, *Executive*
EMP: 20 EST: 1932
SQ FT: 6,000
SALES (est): 4.4MM Privately Held
SIC: 1442 3273 1422 Common sand mining; ready-mixed concrete; crushed & broken limestone

(G-14083) G & H DRILLING INC
Also Called: Land & Shore Drilling
5550 County Road 314 (44654-9713)
P.O. Box 149 (44654-0149)
PHONE.................330 674-4868
Brian Galford, *President*
EMP: 20
SQ FT: 300
SALES (est): 2.7MM Privately Held
SIC: 1381 Service well drilling

(G-14084) GALION-GODWIN TRUCK BDY CO LLC
Also Called: Galion Dump Bodies
7415 Peabody Kent Rd (44654)
P.O. Box 208, Winesburg (44690-0208)
PHONE.................330 359-5495
James P Godwin,
▲ EMP: 64
SALES (est): 14.2MM Privately Held
WEB: www.galion-godwin.com
SIC: 3536 3713 5531 3711 Hoists, cranes & monorails; truck & bus bodies; truck equipment & parts; motor vehicles & car bodies; fabricated structural metal; sheet metalwork

(G-14085) GRAPHIC PUBLICATIONS INC
Also Called: Bargain Hunter
7368 County Road 623 (44654-9256)
P.O. Box 358 (44654-0358)
PHONE.................330 674-2300
Michael Mast, *President*
Frances Mast, *Corp Secy*
▲ EMP: 45
SQ FT: 12,000
SALES (est): 5.9MM Privately Held
WEB: www.gpubs.com
SIC: 2721 7336 Periodicals: publishing only; graphic arts & related design

(G-14086) GUGGISBERG CHEESE INC (PA)
Also Called: Chalet In The Valley
5060 State Route 557 (44654-9266)
PHONE.................330 893-2550
Richard Guggisberg, *President*
Cynthia Mellor, *Principal*
Paul A Miller, *Principal*
Rosanne Parrot, *Principal*
Diane Melloe, *Treasurer*
EMP: 50
SQ FT: 10,000
SALES (est): 11.2MM Privately Held
WEB: www.guggisberg.com
SIC: 2022 5812 5961 5451 Natural cheese; eating places; cheese, mail order; cheese

(G-14087) HEARTLAND STAIRWAY LTD
7080 Township Road 601 (44654-8892)
PHONE.................330 279-2554
Roy Hochstetler, *Partner*
Emanuel Hochstetler, *Partner*
Mark Wengerd, *Partner*
EMP: 4
SALES (est): 280K Privately Held
SIC: 2431 Staircases & stairs, wood

(G-14088) HERSHBERGER LAWN STRUCTURES
Also Called: Play Mor
8990 State Route 39 (44654-9791)
PHONE.................330 674-3900
Paul Hershberger, *Partner*
Amos Stoltzfus Jr, *Partner*
EMP: 17
SQ FT: 21,000
SALES (est): 2.2MM Privately Held
WEB: www.playmorswingsets.com
SIC: 3944 5941 5091 Structural toy sets; playground equipment; sporting & recreation goods

(G-14089) HERSHEY MACHINE
5502 State Route 557 (44654-9488)
PHONE.................330 674-2718
Atlee Hershberger, *Owner*
EMP: 4 EST: 1996
SALES (est): 547.2K Privately Held
SIC: 3443 Tanks, standard or custom fabricated: metal plate

(G-14090) HERSHY WAY LTD
5918 County Road 201 (44654-9294)
PHONE.................330 893-2809
Aden Hershberger, *Partner*
Jay Hershberger, *Partner*
Steven Hershberger, *Partner*
EMP: 7
SALES (est): 773.3K Privately Held
WEB: www.hershyway.com
SIC: 2519 3523 Lawn furniture, except wood, metal, stone or concrete; cattle feeding, handling & watering equipment

(G-14091) HILL FINISHING
32795 Township Road 219 (44654-9509)
PHONE.................740 623-0650
EMP: 4 EST: 2012
SALES (est): 267.3K Privately Held
SIC: 2511 Wood household furniture

(G-14092) HILLSIDE WOOD LTD
8413 Township Road 652 (44654-8343)
PHONE.................330 359-5991
Aden Troyer, *Manager*
EMP: 20
SALES: 3MM Privately Held
SIC: 2426 Chair seats, hardwood

(G-14093) HOCHSTETLER WOOD
Also Called: H W Chair Co
6791 County Road 77 (44654-7901)
PHONE.................330 893-2384
Eli Hochstetler, *Partner*
David Hochstetler, *Partner*
Ivan Hochstetler, *Partner*
Mark Hochstetler, *Partner*
Wayne Hochstetler, *Partner*
EMP: 16
SQ FT: 35,500
SALES (est): 2.1MM Privately Held
SIC: 2426 2511 Hardwood dimension & flooring mills; chairs, bentwood

(G-14094) HOCHSTETLER WOOD LTD
6791 County Road 77 (44654-7901)
PHONE.................330 893-1601
Eli Hochstetler, *President*
EMP: 17
SALES (est): 2MM Privately Held
SIC: 2511 Wood household furniture

(G-14095) HOLMES BY PRODUCTS CO
3175 Township Road 411 (44654-9176)
PHONE.................330 893-2322
Abe Miller, *President*
Brian Miller, *Vice Pres*
Mary Miller, *Treasurer*
▲ EMP: 50
SQ FT: 15,000
SALES (est): 7.6MM Privately Held
SIC: 2077 Animal & marine fats & oils

(G-14096) HOLMES CHEESE CO
9444 State Route 39 (44654-9764)
PHONE.................330 674-6451
Robert J Ramseyer, *President*
Walter P Ramseyer, *Vice Pres*
▲ EMP: 35 EST: 1941
SQ FT: 42,000
SALES (est): 12MM Privately Held
WEB: www.holmescheese.com
SIC: 2022 Natural cheese; whey, raw or liquid

(G-14097) HOLMES COUNTY HUB INC
Also Called: Daily Record, The
6 W Jackson St Ste C (44654-1396)
PHONE.................330 674-1811
V Dix, *Publisher*
Cindy Hinkle, *Manager*
EMP: 9
SALES (est): 382.3K Privately Held
WEB: www.the-daily-record.com
SIC: 2711 Newspapers, publishing & printing

(G-14098) HOLMES LUMBER & BLDG CTR INC
Also Called: Holmes Lumber & Supply
6139 Hc 39 (44654)
PHONE.................330 674-9060
Paul Miller, *President*
D Tim Yoder, *Credit Mgr*
EMP: 150 EST: 1952
SQ FT: 16,000
SALES (est): 971.4K Privately Held
WEB: www.holmeslumber.com
SIC: 5031 5211 2439 2434 Lumber, plywood & millwork; lumber & other building materials; structural wood members; wood kitchen cabinets; millwork; hardwood dimension & flooring mills

(G-14099) HOLMES REDIMIX INC
5420 County Road 349 (44654-9761)
PHONE.................330 674-0865
Daniel L Mathie, *President*
EMP: 10
SALES (est): 1.5MM Privately Held
SIC: 1442 Construction sand & gravel

(G-14100) HOPEWOOD INC
8087 Township Road 652 (44654-8898)
PHONE.................330 359-5656
Ronald Clark, *President*
EMP: 20
SALES (est): 1.5MM Privately Held
WEB: www.hopewoodinc.com
SIC: 2512 2511 Upholstered household furniture; wood household furniture

(G-14101) J & R WOODWORKING
4925 Private Road 386 (44654-9235)
PHONE.................330 893-0713
Joe Troyer, *Owner*
EMP: 7
SALES (est): 695.4K Privately Held
SIC: 2499 Decorative wood & woodwork

(G-14102) JLM LOGGING LLC
3334 County Road 160 (44654-8390)
PHONE.................330 340-4863
Junior Miller, *Principal*
EMP: 3
SALES (est): 211.5K Privately Held
SIC: 2411 Logging

(G-14103) KAUFMAN MULCH INC
Also Called: Kaufman Trucking
3988 County Road 135 (44654-9217)
PHONE.................330 893-3676
Larry Kaufman, *President*
Kim Kaufman, *Vice Pres*
EMP: 4
SALES (est): 519.3K Privately Held
SIC: 2499 2421 Mulch, wood & bark; sawmills & planing mills, general

(G-14104) LAB ELECTRONICS INC
5640 Township Road 353 (44654-8759)
PHONE.................330 674-9818
Lawrence Lamp, *Principal*
William Baker, *Principal*
EMP: 8
SQ FT: 200
SALES (est): 618.4K Privately Held
SIC: 3571 Electronic computers

(G-14105) LAMAR D STEINER
Also Called: D & K Designs
6815 State Route 39 (44654-9796)
PHONE.................330 466-1479
Lamar Steiner, *Owner*
EMP: 4
SQ FT: 1,000
SALES (est): 153.7K Privately Held
SIC: 2759 Screen printing

(G-14106) LBC CLAY CO LLC
4501 Township Road 307 (44654-9656)
PHONE.................330 674-0674
Larry L Clark, *Principal*
EMP: 8 EST: 2010
SALES (est): 765.8K Privately Held
SIC: 3251 Brick & structural clay tile

(G-14107) LLC BOWMAN LEATHER
6705 Private Road 387 (44654-8249)
PHONE.................330 893-1954
Dan Bowman,
EMP: 7
SALES (est): 552K Privately Held
SIC: 3199 5699 Leather goods; leather garments

(G-14108) M H WOODWORKING LLC
Also Called: Buckeye Rocker
2789 County Rd Ste 600 (44654)
PHONE.................330 893-3929
Mose V Hershberger,
EMP: 8
SALES (est): 1MM Privately Held
SIC: 2431 Millwork

(G-14109) MAC OIL FIELD SERVICE INC
7861 Township Road 306 (44654-9666)
P.O. Box 211 (44654-0211)
PHONE.................330 674-7371
Robert G Mc Vicker Jr, *President*
Patricia Mc Vicker, *Vice Pres*
EMP: 15
SQ FT: 1,376
SALES: 1.6MM Privately Held
SIC: 1389 4212 Oil field services; liquid haulage, local

(G-14110) MAPLE HILL WOODWORKING
2726 Trl 128 (44654)
PHONE.................330 674-2500
Mark Miller, *Principal*
EMP: 4 EST: 2008
SALES (est): 291.3K Privately Held
SIC: 2431 Millwork

(G-14111) MIDFLOW SERVICES LLC
812 S Washington St (44654-1398)
PHONE.................330 674-2399
EMP: 19
SALES (corp-wide): 3.5MM Privately Held
SIC: 3533 Oil & gas field machinery
PA: Midflow Services, Llc
  10774 Township Road 506
  Shreve OH 44676
  330 567-3108

(G-14112) MILLER LUMBER CO INC
7101 State Route 39 (44654-8828)
PHONE.................330 674-0273
Myron Miller, *President*
Scott Miller, *Treasurer*
EMP: 22 EST: 1949
SQ FT: 5,000

Millersburg - Holmes County (G-14113)

SALES: 5.5MM **Privately Held**
WEB: www.millerlumberco.com
SIC: **2421** Kiln drying of lumber; planing mills

(G-14113)
MILLERS STORAGE BARNS LLC
4230 State Route 39 (44654-9682)
PHONE 330 893-3293
Owen Miller, *Mng Member*
Linda Kuhns,
Marlin Kuhns,
EMP: 23
SQ FT: 15,928
SALES (est): 5MM **Privately Held**
WEB: www.millersstoragebuildings.com
SIC: **2452** Farm buildings, prefabricated or portable: wood

(G-14114)
MILLERSBURG ICE CO
25 S Grant St (44654-1322)
PHONE 330 674-3016
Lewis Ritchey, *President*
Phillip Ritchey, *Treasurer*
EMP: 20 EST: 1936
SQ FT: 18,000
SALES (est): 2.6MM **Privately Held**
SIC: **2097** 5921 Manufactured ice; beer (packaged); wine

(G-14115)
MOUNT HOPE PLANING
Also Called: Mhp Flooring
7598 Tr652 (44654)
PHONE 330 359-0538
John Miller Jr, *Owner*
EMP: 16
SQ FT: 36,000
SALES: 2.7MM **Privately Held**
SIC: **2431** 1771 Millwork; flooring contractor

(G-14116)
MT EATON PALLET LTD
4761 County Road 207 (44654-9055)
PHONE 330 893-2986
Dwain Schlabach, *Partner*
Roger Chenevey, *Sales Mgr*
EMP: 40
SQ FT: 12,000
SALES (est): 5.6MM **Privately Held**
SIC: **2448** Pallets, wood; pallets, wood & wood with metal

(G-14117)
MULTI PRODUCTS COMPANY
7188 State Route 39 (44654-9204)
P.O. Box 1597, Gainesville TX (76241-1597)
PHONE 330 674-5981
Jeff Berlin, *CEO*
William T Baker, *President*
Bud Doty, *Corp Secy*
Greg Guthrie, *Vice Pres*
▲ EMP: 42
SQ FT: 30,000
SALES (est): 12.5MM **Privately Held**
SIC: **3533** 5084 Oil field machinery & equipment; industrial machinery & equipment

(G-14118)
NJM FURNITURE OUTLET INC
6899 County Road 672 (44654-8349)
PHONE 330 893-3514
James Kandell, *Principal*
EMP: 10
SALES (est): 627.5K **Privately Held**
SIC: **2512** Upholstered household furniture

(G-14119)
PLAINS PRECUT LTD
4917 County Road 207 (44654-8221)
PHONE 330 893-3300
Abe Weaver, *Principal*
EMP: 4
SALES (est): 403.9K **Privately Held**
SIC: **2448** Pallets, wood & wood with metal

(G-14120)
PRECISION GEOPHYSICAL INC (PA)
2695 State Route 83 (44654-9455)
PHONE 330 674-2198
Steven Mc Crossin, *President*
EMP: 32
SALES (est): 4.8MM **Privately Held**
WEB: www.precisiongeophysical.com
SIC: **1382** Oil & gas exploration services

(G-14121)
R & B ENTERPRISES USA INC
1868 County Road 150 (44654-8922)
PHONE 330 674-2227
Roger Patterson, *President*
EMP: 3
SALES: 700K **Privately Held**
SIC: **1389** 1794 Roustabout service; excavation work

(G-14122)
REXAM PLC
Rexam Prescription Products
5091 County Road 120 (44654-9231)
PHONE 330 893-2451
Paul Arsenault, *Manager*
EMP: 9
SALES (corp-wide): 11.6B **Publicly Held**
SIC: **3085** Plastics bottles
HQ: Rexam Limited
4 Millbank
London SW1P
158 240-8999

(G-14123)
RIDGEVIEW SHEET METAL
4772 Township Road 352 (44654-9099)
PHONE 330 674-3768
EMP: 4 EST: 2013
SALES (est): 250.4K **Privately Held**
SIC: **3444** Sheet metalwork

(G-14124)
ROCKWOOD PRODUCTS LTD
Also Called: Rockwood Door & Millwork
5264 Township Road 401 (44654-8740)
PHONE 330 893-2392
Roger Schrock, *President*
Paul Schrock, *Partner*
Esther Schrock, *Co-Owner*
Twila Beachy, *Project Mgr*
Marcus Willey, *Sales Associate*
EMP: 18
SALES: 1.5MM **Privately Held**
WEB: www.rockwooddoor.com
SIC: **5211** 2431 5031 Door & window products; doors & door parts & trim, wood; doors & windows

(G-14125)
SALTCREEK INDUSTRIES
420 W Jones St (44654-1087)
PHONE 330 674-2816
EMP: 3
SALES (est): 158.7K **Privately Held**
SIC: **3999** Manufacturing industries

(G-14126)
SALTILLO CORPORATION (PA)
2143 Township Road 112 (44654-9410)
PHONE 330 674-6722
Leona Hershberger, *President*
Fanie Herb Miller, *Corp Secy*
David H Hershberger, *Vice Pres*
Melissa Malani, *Consultant*
Michelle Retzlaff, *Consultant*
▲ EMP: 8 EST: 1996
SALES: 2.2MM **Privately Held**
WEB: www.saltillo.com
SIC: **3669** Intercommunication systems, electric

(G-14127)
SCENIC RIDGE MANUFACTURING LLC
5749 County Rd Ste 349 (44654)
PHONE 330 674-0557
Delbert Miller, *Mng Member*
Mary Miller,
EMP: 3
SQ FT: 1,200
SALES (est): 124.4K **Privately Held**
SIC: **2399** Horse harnesses & riding crops, etc.: non-leather

(G-14128)
SCHLABACH WOODWORKS LTD
6678 State Route 241 (44654-8826)
PHONE 330 674-7488
David Schlabach, *Owner*
EMP: 20
SALES (est): 2.8MM **Privately Held**
SIC: **3996** Hard surface floor coverings

(G-14129)
SIMPLE PRODUCTS LLC
Also Called: Design Farm
10336 Township Road 262 (44654-8746)
P.O. Box 94 (44654-0094)
PHONE 330 674-2448
Michael Jaeb, *Principal*
EMP: 3
SALES (est): 180K **Privately Held**
SIC: **2099** Syrups

(G-14130)
STAR BRITE EXPRESS CAR WA
887 S Washington St (44654-1707)
PHONE 330 674-0062
Rodney J Starr, *Principal*
EMP: 9
SALES (est): 543.8K **Privately Held**
SIC: **2741** Miscellaneous publishing

(G-14131)
STUTZMAN MANUFACTURING LTD
7727 Township Road 604 (44654-8352)
PHONE 330 674-4359
Bert L Stutzman, *Mng Member*
EMP: 6
SALES (est): 1MM **Privately Held**
SIC: **3542** 7389 Nail heading machines;

(G-14132)
SWARTZ WOODWORKING
7136 Township Road 654 (44654-8367)
PHONE 330 359-6359
Paul Swartz, *Principal*
EMP: 4
SALES (est): 324.3K **Privately Held**
SIC: **2431** Millwork

(G-14133)
TECH TOOL INC
2901 County Road 150 (44654-8510)
PHONE 330 674-1176
David M Kauffman, *President*
Elizabeth Kauffman, *Corp Secy*
Beth Kauffman, *Treasurer*
▲ EMP: 10 EST: 1981
SQ FT: 4,800
SALES: 900K **Privately Held**
SIC: **3533** 3498 3494 Oil & gas field machinery; fabricated pipe & fittings; valves & pipe fittings

(G-14134)
TGS INTERNATIONAL INC
4464 State Route 39 (44654-9677)
P.O. Box 355, Berlin (44610-0355)
PHONE 330 893-4828
Paul Weaver, *Vice Pres*
Roman Mullet, *Treasurer*
David Troyer, *Exec Dir*
EMP: 50
SALES (est): 2.6MM
SALES (corp-wide): 130.1MM **Privately Held**
SIC: **4731** 2731 Freight forwarding; book publishing
PA: Christian Aid Ministries
4464 State Route 39
Millersburg OH 44654
330 893-2428

(G-14135)
TH MANUFACTURING INC
4674 County Road 120 (44654-9280)
PHONE 330 893-3572
Jeff Tomski, *President*
Don Troyer, *Plant Supt*
EMP: 9
SQ FT: 60,000
SALES (est): 1.7MM **Privately Held**
SIC: **3543** Industrial patterns

(G-14136)
TMARZETTI COMPANY
Inn Maid Products Div
7445 County Road 68 (44654-9668)
P.O. Box 27 (44654-0027)
PHONE 330 674-2993
Theodore Zuercher, *Manager*
EMP: 14
SQ FT: 35,000
SALES (corp-wide): 1.2B **Publicly Held**
SIC: **2098** Noodles (e.g. egg, plain & water), dry
HQ: T.Marzetti Company
380 Polaris Pkwy Ste 400
Westerville OH 43082
614 846-2232

(G-14137)
TOPE PRINTING INC
1056 S Washington St (44654-9438)
PHONE 330 674-4993
John C Tope, *President*
Vanessa Tope, *Corp Secy*
Andrew P Tope, *Vice Pres*
EMP: 7 EST: 1974
SQ FT: 6,000
SALES (est): 530.9K **Privately Held**
SIC: **2752** 2759 Commercial printing, off-set; letterpress printing

(G-14138)
TRICO ENTERPRISES LLC
6430 Township Road 348 (44654-9754)
PHONE 330 674-1157
Ed Miller, *Mng Member*
EMP: 22
SQ FT: 20,000
SALES (est): 4.1MM **Privately Held**
SIC: **3553** 5999 Sawmill machines; alarm & safety equipment stores

(G-14139)
TROYER CHEESE INC
6597 County Road 625 (44654-9071)
PHONE 330 893-2479
James A Troyer, *President*
Aaron Yoder, *Purch Mgr*
Steve Yoder, *Buyer*
Rob Ervin, *Controller*
Lori Durkin, *Financial Analy*
EMP: 45
SQ FT: 59,500
SALES (est): 20.5MM
SALES (corp-wide): 806.3MM **Privately Held**
WEB: www.troyercheese.com
SIC: **5147** 2032 5143 5149 Meats, cured or smoked; ethnic foods: canned, jarred, etc.; cheese; specialty food items
PA: Lipari Foods Operating Company Llc
26661 Bunert Rd
Warren MI 48089
586 447-3500

(G-14140)
UNIVERSAL WELL SERVICES INC
11 S Washington St (44654-1341)
PHONE 814 333-2656
Rick Sloan, *Manager*
EMP: 24
SALES (corp-wide): 3.3B **Publicly Held**
WEB: www.univwell.com
SIC: **1389** Hydraulic fracturing wells; cementing oil & gas well casings
HQ: Universal Well Services, Inc.
13549 S Mosiertown Rd
Meadville PA 16335
814 337-1983

(G-14141)
V & W WOODCRAFT
5071 Township Road 353 (44654-8715)
PHONE 330 674-0073
Vernon Weaver, *Principal*
EMP: 3
SALES: 110K **Privately Held**
SIC: **2431** Woodwork, interior & ornamental

(G-14142)
VALLEYVIEW WOOD TURNING CO
8260 Township Road 652 (44654-8341)
PHONE 330 763-0407

Ervin Hershberger, *Owner*
Leon Hershberger, *General Mgr*
EMP: 18
SQ FT: 15,000
SALES: 2.2MM **Privately Held**
SIC: 2426 Stock, chair, hardwood: turned, shaped or carved

(G-14143)
VINYL TECH STORAGE BARN
5930 State Route 39 (44654-8331)
PHONE.................................330 674-5670
Eugene Miller, *Owner*
EMP: 4
SALES (est): 1MM **Privately Held**
SIC: 3448 Farm & utility buildings

(G-14144)
W H PATTEN DRILLING CO INC
6336 County Road 207 (44654-9153)
P.O. Box 10 (44654-0010)
PHONE.................................330 674-3046
William H Patten III, *President*
William H Patten Jr, *Shareholder*
Kim Mathie, *Admin Sec*
EMP: 8 **EST:** 1940
SQ FT: 1,200
SALES: 600K **Privately Held**
SIC: 1311 Crude petroleum production

(G-14145)
WALNUT CREEK CART SHOP
3309 State Route 39 (44654-8848)
PHONE.................................330 893-1097
Clyde Yoder, *Owner*
EMP: 3
SALES: 7K **Privately Held**
SIC: 3799 Carriages, horse drawn

(G-14146)
WALNUT CREEK PLANING LTD
5778 State Route 515 (44654-8807)
PHONE.................................330 893-3244
Dwight Kratzer, *President*
Charles Kratzer, *General Mgr*
Marie Miller, *General Mgr*
Brad Smith, *General Mgr*
Ken Kratzer, *Vice Pres*
◆ **EMP:** 100
SQ FT: 90,000
SALES: 30MM **Privately Held**
WEB: www.walnutcreekplaning.com
SIC: 5211 2421 2499 2426 Millwork & lumber; planing mills; decorative wood & woodwork; hardwood dimension & flooring mills

(G-14147)
WASTE PARCHMENT INC
4510 Township Road 307 (44654-9656)
PHONE.................................330 674-6868
Robert Smith, *President*
Elaine Smith, *Admin Sec*
EMP: 30
SQ FT: 80,000
SALES (est): 1MM **Privately Held**
SIC: 4953 2611 Recycling, waste materials; pulp mills

(G-14148)
WASTEQUIP MANUFACTURING CO LLC
930 Massillon Rd (44654-8200)
PHONE.................................330 674-1119
Larry Mohler, *Manager*
EMP: 49
SALES (corp-wide): 574.7MM **Privately Held**
WEB: www.rayfo.com
SIC: 3443 Dumpsters, garbage
HQ: Wastequip Manufacturing Company Llc
1901 Roxborough Rd # 300
Charlotte NC 28211

(G-14149)
WEEKLY BROTHERS CNTY LINE FAR
1533 Township Road 110 (44654-9616)
PHONE.................................330 674-4195
Paul Weekley, *Principal*
EMP: 4
SALES (est): 222.2K **Privately Held**
SIC: 2711 Newspapers

(G-14150)
WENGERD CABINETS
6605 Township Road 362 (44654-8248)
PHONE.................................330 231-0879
Roy Wengerd, *Principal*
EMP: 4 **EST:** 2009
SALES (est): 352.6K **Privately Held**
SIC: 2434 Wood kitchen cabinets

(G-14151)
WILKSHIRE DRY CLEANERS LLC
5660 County Road 203 (44654-8275)
PHONE.................................330 674-7696
Ryan Torrence, *Mng Member*
EMP: 5
SALES (est): 317.2K **Privately Held**
SIC: 2842 Drycleaning preparations

(G-14152)
WOOD WORKS
9210 Township Road 304 (44654-8523)
PHONE.................................330 674-0333
Don Hubener, *Owner*
EMP: 3
SALES (est): 200.7K **Privately Held**
SIC: 2599 Bar furniture

(G-14153)
YODER LUMBER CO INC (PA)
4515 Township Road 367 (44654-8885)
PHONE.................................330 893-3121
Eli J Yoder, *President*
Robert Mapes, *President*
Ken Grate, *Corp Secy*
Melvin Yoder, *Vice Pres*
Roy Yoder, *Vice Pres*
▼ **EMP:** 55 **EST:** 1947
SQ FT: 15,000
SALES (est): 30.3MM **Privately Held**
WEB: www.yoderlumber.com
SIC: 2421 2448 2499 2431 Lumber: rough, sawed or planed; pallets, wood; mulch, wood & bark; millwork; hardwood dimension & flooring mills

(G-14154)
YODER LUMBER CO INC
7100 County Road 407 (44654-9628)
PHONE.................................330 674-1435
Mel Yoder, *Manager*
EMP: 50
SALES (corp-wide): 30.3MM **Privately Held**
WEB: www.yoderlumber.com
SIC: 2421 2448 Lumber: rough, sawed or planed; wood pallets & skids
PA: Yoder Lumber Co., Inc.
4515 Township Road 367
Millersburg OH 44654
330 893-3121

(G-14155)
YODERS NYLON HALTER SHOP
7682 Township Road 652 (44654-8337)
PHONE.................................330 893-3479
Daniel O Yoder, *Owner*
EMP: 3
SALES (est): 203.5K **Privately Held**
SIC: 2221 Nylon broadwoven fabrics

(G-14156)
YODERS WOODWORKING
2249 Township Road 112 (44654-8226)
PHONE.................................888 818-0568
Phillip L Yoder, *Owner*
EMP: 6
SQ FT: 6,000
SALES: 865.6K **Privately Held**
SIC: 2511 Bed frames, except water bed frames: wood

(G-14157)
YUTZY WOODWORKING LTD
6995 Township Road 654 (44654-8815)
PHONE.................................330 359-6166
Dennis Yutzy, *Owner*
▲ **EMP:** 230
SALES (est): 21.8MM **Privately Held**
SIC: 2431 Millwork

Millersport
Fairfield County

(G-14158)
AGRATI - MEDINA LLC
Also Called: Minuteman Distribution
2140 Refugee Rd Ne (43046)
PHONE.................................740 467-3199
EMP: 4
SALES (corp-wide): 927.2K **Privately Held**
SIC: 3452 Mfg Bolts/Screws/Rivets
HQ: Agrati - Medina, Llc
941-955 Lake Rd
Medina OH 44256
330 725-8853

(G-14159)
GRAVEL DOCTOR OF OHIO LLC
Also Called: Gravel Doctor of Ohio, The
2985 Canal Dr (43046-8044)
PHONE.................................844 472-8353
EMP: 3 **EST:** 2014
SALES (est): 240K **Privately Held**
SIC: 1442 Construction sand & gravel

(G-14160)
HEFTY HOIST INC
Also Called: Aqua Marine Supply
2397a Refugee St (43046-9748)
P.O. Box 44 (43046-0044)
PHONE.................................740 467-2515
Chet Hauck, *President*
Jason Moore, *Purch Mgr*
▲ **EMP:** 20
SQ FT: 14,000
SALES (est): 3.3MM **Privately Held**
SIC: 3566 Reduction gears & gear units for turbines, except automotive

(G-14161)
SEE YA THERE INC
Also Called: See Ya There Vacation and Trvl
12710 W Bank Dr Ne (43046-9738)
PHONE.................................614 856-9037
John J Allen, *President*
Michael Hatem, *Vice Pres*
George Lindsey, *Treasurer*
EMP: 7
SQ FT: 800
SALES (est): 400K **Privately Held**
WEB: www.seeyathere.com
SIC: 2741 Newsletter publishing

(G-14162)
WELDON ICE CREAM COMPANY
2887 Canal Dr (43046-9701)
PHONE.................................740 467-2400
David Pierce, *Principal*
EMP: 8
SQ FT: 10,800
SALES (est): 497.1K **Privately Held**
WEB: www.weldons.com
SIC: 2024 Ice cream, bulk

Millersville
Sandusky County

(G-14163)
CARMEUSE LIME INC
Also Called: Carmeuse Lime & Stone
3964 County Road 41 (43435-9619)
PHONE.................................419 638-2511
Tim Haubert, *Purchasing*
Mike Klenda, *Branch Mgr*
EMP: 37 **Privately Held**
SIC: 1422 Crushed & broken limestone
HQ: Carmeuse Lime, Inc.
11 Stanwix St Fl 21
Pittsburgh PA 15222
412 995-5500

Mineral City
Tuscarawas County

(G-14164)
HILLTOP ENERGY INC
6978 Lindentree Rd Ne (44656-8973)
P.O. Box 395 (44656-0395)
PHONE.................................330 859-2108
Brandy Caterley, *Director*
EMP: 22
SQ FT: 3,200
SALES (corp-wide): 62.6MM **Privately Held**
SIC: 2892 2819 Explosives; industrial inorganic chemicals
HQ: Hilltop Energy, Inc.
7896 Dickey Dr
Lisbon OH 44432
330 424-1441

Mineral Ridge
Trumbull County

(G-14165)
FBR INDUSTRIES INC
1336 Seaborn St Ste 7 (44440-9006)
PHONE.................................330 701-7425
Stephen Fbrown, *Principal*
EMP: 5
SALES (est): 382.2K **Privately Held**
SIC: 3999 Manufacturing industries

(G-14166)
J & K POWDER COATING
1336 Seaborn St (44440-9006)
PHONE.................................330 540-6145
Jeffrey A Christy, *Principal*
EMP: 4
SALES (est): 498.3K **Privately Held**
SIC: 3399 Powder, metal

(G-14167)
J & W CANVAS COMPANY
1386 Church St (44440-9532)
PHONE.................................330 652-7678
Timothy J McNeil, *Owner*
EMP: 4
SQ FT: 1,600
SALES: 250K **Privately Held**
SIC: 7699 2394 Tent repair shop; canvas & related products

(G-14168)
L B FOSTER COMPANY
Also Called: Relay Rail Div.
1193 Salt Springs Rd (44440-9318)
PHONE.................................330 652-1461
Scott Calahoun, *Manager*
EMP: 25
SQ FT: 3,000
SALES (corp-wide): 626.9MM **Publicly Held**
WEB: www.lbfoster.com
SIC: 1799 3743 Coating of metal structures at construction site; railroad equipment
PA: L. B. Foster Company
415 Holiday Dr Ste 1
Pittsburgh PA 15220
412 928-3400

(G-14169)
MASHEEN SPECIALTIES
3519 Union St (44440-9008)
PHONE.................................330 652-7535
EMP: 20
SALES (est): 1.6MM **Privately Held**
SIC: 3541 Die sinking machines

(G-14170)
P & S ENERGY INC
3729 Union St (44440-9004)
P.O. Box 523 (44440-0523)
PHONE.................................330 652-2525
Martin Solomon, *President*
Ben Z Post, *Corp Secy*
Howard Solomon, *Vice Pres*
EMP: 3
SQ FT: 4,500

Mineral Ridge - Trumbull County (G-14171)

SALES (est): 270K **Privately Held**
SIC: 1311 1381 Crude petroleum & natural gas; drilling oil & gas wells

(G-14171)
SPECIALTY PIPE & TUBE INC (HQ)
3600 Union St (44440-9000)
P.O. Box 516 (44440-0516)
PHONE.................................330 505-8262
Steven J Baroff, *President*
◆ EMP: 19
SQ FT: 18,600
SALES (est): 11.3MM
SALES (corp-wide): 280.8MM **Publicly Held**
WEB: www.specialtypipe.com
SIC: 3317 Welded pipe & tubes; tubes, wrought; welded or lock joint
PA: Synalloy Corporation
    4510 Cox Rd Ste 201
    Glen Allen VA 23060
    804 822-3260

(G-14172)
TOMCO INDUSTRIES
1660 E County Line Rd (44440-9404)
PHONE.................................330 652-7531
Lloyd Tompkins Jr, *President*
EMP: 5
SALES: 600K **Privately Held**
SIC: 3544 Extrusion dies; industrial molds

(G-14173)
VALLEY CONTAINERS INC
3515 Union St (44440-9007)
PHONE.................................330 544-2244
Steve Hershfeldt, *President*
EMP: 14
SQ FT: 15,000
SALES (est): 2.7MM **Privately Held**
SIC: 2653 Corrugated boxes, partitions, display items, sheets & pad

(G-14174)
WHOLE SOLUTIONS
1217 Salt Springs Rd (44440-9331)
PHONE.................................330 652-1725
Jeffrey Hattendorf, *Principal*
EMP: 3
SALES (est): 379.1K **Privately Held**
SIC: 3541 Drilling & boring machines

Minerva
Stark County

(G-14175)
ABRASIVE SUPPLY COMPANY INC
25240 State Route 172 (44657-9430)
PHONE.................................330 894-2818
Rob Miller, *President*
▲ EMP: 16
SQ FT: 16,000
SALES (est): 1.9MM **Privately Held**
WEB: www.polyblast.com
SIC: 3291 Abrasive products

(G-14176)
B & H MACHINE INC
15001 Lincoln St Se (44657-8900)
P.O. Box 96 (44657-0096)
PHONE.................................330 868-6425
J Timothy Bush, *President*
Ron Willhelm, *Engineer*
Christine Logan, *Accounting Mgr*
Brady Koble, *VP Sales*
EMP: 36 EST: 1951
SQ FT: 70,000
SALES (est): 7.7MM **Privately Held**
WEB: www.bhcylinders.com
SIC: 3593 3599 Fluid power cylinders, hydraulic or pneumatic; machine shop, jobbing & repair

(G-14177)
CARAUSTAR INDUSTRIAL AND CON
Also Called: Minerva Tube Plant
460 Knox Ct (44657-1528)
PHONE.................................330 868-4111
Steve Lacher, *Manager*
EMP: 35
SQ FT: 45,000
SALES (corp-wide): 3.8B **Publicly Held**
SIC: 2655 Tubes, fiber or paper: made from purchased material; cores, fiber: made from purchased material
HQ: Caraustar Industrial And Consumer Products Group Inc
    5000 Austell Powder Ste
    Austell GA 30106
    803 548-5100

(G-14178)
DUTCHCRAFT TRUSS COMPONENT INC
2212 Fox Ave Se (44657-9146)
PHONE.................................330 862-2220
Reginald Stoltzfus, *Principal*
Jennette Stolzfus, *Principal*
Dan Kienzle, *Manager*
EMP: 16
SALES (est): 2.4MM **Privately Held**
SIC: 2439 Trusses, wooden roof

(G-14179)
ERVIN LEE LOGGING
8555 Stump Rd (44657-9002)
PHONE.................................330 771-0039
Ervin Lee, *Administration*
EMP: 3
SALES (est): 162.6K **Privately Held**
SIC: 2411 Logging camps & contractors

(G-14180)
GENERAL COLOR INVESTMENTS INC
Also Called: Plastic Color Division
250 Bridge St (44657-1509)
P.O. Box 7 (44657-0007)
PHONE.................................330 868-4161
Holly Gartner, *President*
Keith W Gartner, *Vice Pres*
EMP: 100 EST: 1938
SQ FT: 142,800
SALES (est): 26.4MM **Privately Held**
WEB: www.generalcolor.com
SIC: 2816 3087 Color pigments; custom compound purchased resins

(G-14181)
HARBISONWALKER INTL INC
1316 Alliance Rd Nw (44657-9767)
P.O. Box 240 (44657-0240)
PHONE.................................330 868-4141
Jan Smith, *Branch Mgr*
EMP: 12
SALES (corp-wide): 703.8MM **Privately Held**
WEB: www.hwr.com
SIC: 3255 Clay refractories
HQ: Harbisonwalker International, Inc.
    1305 Cherrington Pkwy # 100
    Moon Township PA 15108

(G-14182)
HARN VAULT SERVICE INC (PA)
422 East St (44657-1429)
PHONE.................................330 832-1995
Karen Harn, *President*
EMP: 12 EST: 1945
SQ FT: 4,872
SALES (est): 1.3MM **Privately Held**
SIC: 3272 Burial vaults, concrete or pre-cast terrazzo

(G-14183)
HOFFEE JOHN
Also Called: Lion's Den Sport Shop
207 N Market St (44657-1615)
PHONE.................................330 868-3553
John Hoffee, *Owner*
Rita Hoffee, *Co-Owner*
EMP: 5
SQ FT: 2,500
SALES (est): 240K **Privately Held**
SIC: 5941 2759 Sporting goods & bicycle shops; screen printing

(G-14184)
IMPERIAL ALUM - MINERVA LLC
217 Roosevelt St (44657-1541)
PHONE.................................330 868-7765
Mike Chenoweth, *Vice Pres*
David Riddell, *Vice Pres*
Gary Grim, *Plant Supt*
Shaun McLaughlin, *Manager*
David Kozin,
EMP: 55
SALES (est): 12.7MM **Privately Held**
SIC: 3334 5093 Slabs (primary), aluminum; scrap & waste materials

(G-14185)
JERICO PLASTIC INDUSTRIES INC (PA)
Also Called: Jerico Industries
250 Bridge St Bldg 92 (44657-1509)
PHONE.................................330 868-4600
Steve Copeland, *Owner*
Brenda Copeland, *Vice Pres*
EMP: 20
SQ FT: 53,000
SALES (est): 8.5MM **Privately Held**
WEB: www.jericoplastic.com
SIC: 2821 Plastics materials & resins

(G-14186)
KEPCOR INC
Also Called: Ssi Tiles
215 Bridge St (44657-1508)
P.O. Box 119 (44657-0119)
PHONE.................................330 868-6434
Robert B Keplinger, *President*
Connie Keplinger, *Vice Pres*
EMP: 10
SQ FT: 121,500
SALES (est): 700K **Privately Held**
SIC: 3253 3251 Ceramic wall & floor tile; brick & structural clay tile

(G-14187)
KMI PROCESSING LLC (PA)
15383 Lisbon St Ne (44657-9191)
PHONE.................................330 862-2185
Randy Kuttler,
EMP: 7 EST: 2011
SALES (est): 2.7MM **Privately Held**
SIC: 3541 Sawing & cutoff machines (metalworking machinery)

(G-14188)
KMI PROCESSING LLC
15441 Lisbon St Ne (44657-9191)
PHONE.................................330 862-2185
EMP: 19
SALES (corp-wide): 2.7MM **Privately Held**
SIC: 3541 Sawing & cutoff machines (metalworking machinery)
PA: Kmi Processing, Llc
    15383 Lisbon St Ne
    Minerva OH 44657
    330 862-2185

(G-14189)
KOUNTRY PRIDE ENTERPRISES
10167 Malibu Rd Ne (44657-9750)
PHONE.................................330 868-3345
Corwin W Stahler, *Partner*
Marian Stahler, *Partner*
EMP: 3
SALES (est): 380.2K **Privately Held**
SIC: 2448 Wood pallets & skids

(G-14190)
MACHINE DYNAMICS & ENGRG INC
Also Called: Energy Transfer
9312 Arrow Rd Nw (44657-8742)
PHONE.................................330 868-5603
Kenneth Barkan II, *President*
Kevin Pasiuk, *Engineer*
Paul D Barkan, *Treasurer*
Patricia Barkan, *Info Tech Mgr*
◆ EMP: 75
SQ FT: 240,000
SALES (est): 19.7MM **Privately Held**
WEB: www.machinedynamics.com
SIC: 3498 Tube fabricating (contract bending & shaping); coils, pipe: fabricated from purchased pipe

(G-14191)
MCDANIEL ENVELOPE CO INC
1400 Union Ave Se (44657-9171)
P.O. Box 355, Damascus (44619-0355)
PHONE.................................330 868-5929
James H Pidgeon, *President*
Barry Pidgeon, *Vice Pres*
Michael J Pidgeon, *Admin Sec*
EMP: 17 EST: 1973
SALES (est): 2.2MM **Privately Held**
SIC: 2759 Envelopes: printing

(G-14192)
MCGUIRE MACHINE LLC
1400 Union Ave Se (44657-9171)
PHONE.................................330 868-3072
Patrick McGuire, *Partner*
Kimberly McGuire, *Partner*
EMP: 5
SALES (est): 762.2K **Privately Held**
SIC: 3599 7699 Machine shop, jobbing & repair; industrial machinery & equipment repair

(G-14193)
MINERVA DAIRY INC
Also Called: Minerva Maid
430 Radloff Ave (44657-1400)
P.O. Box 60 (44657-0060)
PHONE.................................330 868-4196
Phillip Muller, *President*
Venae Watts, *Corp Secy*
Adam Muller, *Vice Pres*
EMP: 65 EST: 1970
SQ FT: 53,000
SALES (est): 26.3MM **Privately Held**
WEB: www.minervacheese.com
SIC: 2023 2021 2022 Dry, condensed, evaporated dairy products; creamery butter; processed cheese

(G-14194)
MINERVA WELDING AND FABG INC
22133 Us Route 30 (44657-9401)
P.O. Box 369 (44657-0369)
PHONE.................................330 868-7731
James A Gram, *President*
Stephen J Gram, *Treasurer*
Mike Gasper, *Manager*
Daniel E Gram, *Admin Sec*
Margie Wilson, *Admin Asst*
EMP: 40 EST: 1949
SQ FT: 10,000
SALES (est): 18.7MM **Privately Held**
WEB: www.minweld.com
SIC: 5084 3599 Industrial machinery & equipment; machine shop, jobbing & repair

(G-14195)
MONARCH PRODUCTS CO
105 Short St (44657-1698)
P.O. Box 118 (44657-0118)
PHONE.................................330 868-7717
Gene Mercarelli, *Vice Pres*
EMP: 26
SQ FT: 16,000
SALES (est): 3.6MM **Privately Held**
SIC: 3544 Special dies & tools; jigs & fixtures

(G-14196)
PCC AIRFOILS LLC
3860 Union Ave Se (44657-8944)
PHONE.................................330 868-6441
Ken Buck, *Vice Pres*
EMP: 214
SQ FT: 300,000
SALES (corp-wide): 225.3B **Publicly Held**
WEB: www.pccairfoils.com
SIC: 3369 3324 Nonferrous foundries; steel investment foundries
HQ: Pcc Airfoils Llc
    3401 Entp Pkwy Ste 200
    Cleveland OH 44122
    216 831-3590

(G-14197)
PCC AIRFOILS LLC
3860 Union Ave Se (44657-8901)
PHONE.................................330 868-7376
John Jerse, *Manager*
EMP: 7
SALES (est): 1MM **Privately Held**
SIC: 7372 Application computer software

(G-14198)
REGAL METAL PRODUCTS CO (PA)
3615 Union Ave Se (44657-8972)
P.O. Box 207 (44657-0207)
PHONE.................................330 868-6343
J Ted Tomak Sr, *President*
Ted Tomak, *Vice Pres*
Charlie Walker, *Plant Mgr*

GEOGRAPHIC SECTION

Roy Berger, *Prdtn Mgr*
EMP: 44 **EST:** 1965
SQ FT: 125,000
SALES (est): 7.6MM **Privately Held**
SIC: 3469 3544 Stamping metal for the trade; special dies, tools, jigs & fixtures

(G-14199)
REGAL METAL PRODUCTS CO
162 Arbor Rd Ne (44657-9746)
P.O. Box 207 (44657-0207)
PHONE..................................330 868-6343
John Theodore, *Vice Pres*
EMP: 17
SALES (est): 1.4MM
SALES (corp-wide): 7.6MM **Privately Held**
SIC: 3469 3544 Stamping metal for the trade; special dies & tools
PA: Regal Metal Products Co.
3615 Union Ave Se
Minerva OH 44657
330 868-6343

(G-14200)
RESCAR COMPANIES INC
177 Curry St (44657-1817)
P.O. Box 310, Ashtabula (44005-0310)
PHONE..................................630 963-1114
Barb Thomas, *Branch Mgr*
EMP: 19
SALES (corp-wide): 21.8MM **Privately Held**
SIC: 3743 Railroad car rebuilding
PA: Rescar Companies, Inc.
1101 31st St Ste 250
Downers Grove IL 60515
630 963-1114

(G-14201)
SHANEWAY INC (PA)
1032 Brush Rd Ne (44657-9755)
P.O. Box 357, Tallmadge (44278-0357)
PHONE..................................330 868-2220
Paul A Weick, *CEO*
Judith A Miller, *President*
Sam Keller, *Vice Pres*
Jerry Shane, *Vice Pres*
Judy Bell, *Treasurer*
EMP: 5
SQ FT: 800
SALES (est): 570.3K **Privately Held**
SIC: 3341 4953 7361 Recovery & refining of nonferrous metals; recycling, waste materials; labor contractors (employment agency)

(G-14202)
SUMMITVILLE TILES INC
1310 Alliance Rd Nw (44657-9767)
P.O. Box 283 (44657-0283)
PHONE..................................330 868-6771
James A Miller, *Manager*
EMP: 130
SALES (corp-wide): 34.5MM **Privately Held**
WEB: www.summitville.com
SIC: 3253 Floor tile, ceramic; wall tile, ceramic
PA: Summitville Tiles, Inc
15364 State Rte 644
Summitville OH 43962
330 223-1511

(G-14203)
SUMMITVILLE TILES INC
Also Called: Summitville Lab
81 Arbor Rd Ne (44657-8755)
P.O. Box 90 (44657-0090)
PHONE..................................330 868-6463
Joseph Dutt, *Manager*
EMP: 23
SALES (corp-wide): 34.5MM **Privately Held**
WEB: www.summitville.com
SIC: 2891 3255 2899 Epoxy adhesives; clay refractories; chemical preparations
PA: Summitville Tiles, Inc
15364 State Rte 644
Summitville OH 43962
330 223-1511

(G-14204)
THREE SONS MINERVA HARDWARE
16400 Bayard Rd (44657-8675)
PHONE..................................330 868-7709
David Ables, *Owner*
Dave Ables, *Owner*
EMP: 14
SALES (est): 3.2MM **Privately Held**
SIC: 3429 Manufactured hardware (general)

(G-14205)
WESTMONT INC
3035 Union Ave Ne (44657-8667)
PHONE..................................330 862-3080
Michael Zawaski, *President*
EMP: 8
SQ FT: 5,000
SALES (est): 1.2MM **Privately Held**
WEB: www.westmontinc.com
SIC: 3824 Mechanical & electromechanical counters & devices

(G-14206)
WILKS INDUSTRIES
4010 Robertsville Ave Se (44657-8930)
PHONE..................................330 868-5105
EMP: 3
SALES (est): 137.5K **Privately Held**
SIC: 3999 Manufacturing industries

Minford
Scioto County

(G-14207)
SWARTZ AUDIE
Also Called: Swartz Race Cars
527 Flower Ison Rd (45653-7900)
PHONE..................................740 820-2341
Audie Swartz, *Owner*
Tammy Swartz, *Admin Sec*
EMP: 3
SALES (est): 286.8K **Privately Held**
SIC: 3799 Off-road automobiles, except recreational vehicles

Mingo Junction
Jefferson County

(G-14208)
EASTERN AUTOMATED PIPING
424 State St (43938-1053)
P.O. Box 249 (43938-0249)
PHONE..................................740 535-8184
Ron Kleineke, *Owner*
▼ **EMP:** 6
SALES (est): 1.1MM **Privately Held**
SIC: 3499 3312 1711 1623 Fabricated metal products; blast furnaces & steel mills; plumbing, heating, air-conditioning contractors; pipeline construction

Minster
Auglaize County

(G-14209)
ALBERT FREYTAG INC
306 Executive Dr (45865)
P.O. Box 5 (45865-0005)
PHONE..................................419 628-2018
William Freytag, *President*
Joseph Freytag, *Vice Pres*
EMP: 25
SQ FT: 1,200
SALES (est): 6.7MM **Privately Held**
SIC: 3441 1741 Fabricated structural metal; masonry & other stonework

(G-14210)
BENDCO MACHINE & TOOL INC
283 W 1st St (45865-1251)
P.O. Box 6 (45865-0006)
PHONE..................................419 628-3802
Norman Tidwell, *President*
Kenneth C Wolaver, *President*
Norman E Tidwell, *Corp Secy*
Jennifer Axe, *Manager*
EMP: 13
SQ FT: 19,500
SALES (est): 1.2MM **Privately Held**
WEB: www.bendcomachine.com
SIC: 3542 3547 Bending machines; rolling mill machinery

(G-14211)
DANONE US LLC
216 Southgate (45865-9552)
P.O. Box 122 (45865-0122)
PHONE..................................419 628-3861
Nick Keiser, *Materials Mgr*
Lois Dietz, *Engineer*
Jill Eilerman, *Engineer*
Dane Thrush, *Engineer*
Matt Wiley, *Engineer*
EMP: 390
SALES (corp-wide): 762.4MM **Privately Held**
WEB: www.dannon.com
SIC: 2024 Yogurt desserts, frozen
HQ: Danone Us, Llc
1 Maple Ave
White Plains NY 10605
914 872-8400

(G-14212)
DUCO TOOL & DIE INC
19 S Main St (45865-1349)
PHONE..................................419 628-2031
Dale J Dues, *President*
Margaret Dues, *Corp Secy*
EMP: 10
SQ FT: 10,000
SALES (est): 1.3MM **Privately Held**
WEB: www.ducotoolanddie.com
SIC: 3544 7692 Special dies & tools; welding repair

(G-14213)
EGYPT STRUCTURAL STEEL PROC
480 Osterloh Rd (45865-9750)
P.O. Box 124 (45865-0124)
PHONE..................................419 628-2375
Kenneth Osterloh, *President*
Doris Osterloh, *Vice Pres*
EMP: 40
SQ FT: 36,360
SALES (est): 3.9MM **Privately Held**
SIC: 3441 3312 Fabricated structural metal; blast furnaces & steel mills

(G-14214)
FOX SUPPLY LLC
40 Columbia Dr (45865-9415)
P.O. Box 194 (45865-0194)
PHONE..................................419 628-3051
Wesley Thieman, *President*
Mark Thieman, *Vice Pres*
Wes Thieman, *Vice Pres*
EMP: 5
SQ FT: 16,000
SALES: 2MM **Privately Held**
SIC: 5999 2676 5113 Cleaning equipment & supplies; sanitary paper products; industrial & personal service paper

(G-14215)
GB IMAGE MACHINE INCORPORATED (PA)
351 Industrial Dr (45865-1258)
P.O. Box 181 (45865-0181)
PHONE..................................419 628-4150
Lynn Bergman, *President*
Jerry Bergman, *Vice Pres*
EMP: 5
SQ FT: 12,000
SALES (est): 330K **Privately Held**
SIC: 3599 Machine shop, jobbing & repair

(G-14216)
GLOBUS PRINTING & PACKG CO INC (PA)
1 Executive Pkwy (45865-1274)
P.O. Box 114 (45865-0114)
PHONE..................................419 628-2381
Dennis Schmiesing, *President*
Tim Schmiesing, *Corp Secy*
Lyle Sanvido, *Production*
Lisa Albers, *Sales Staff*
Larry Luebke, *Sales Staff*
EMP: 70 **EST:** 1957
SQ FT: 100,000
SALES (est): 19.9MM **Privately Held**
WEB: www.globusprinting.com
SIC: 2752 Commercial printing, offset

(G-14217)
HORIZON PUBLICATIONS INC
Also Called: Community Post
326 N Main St Ste 200 (45865)
PHONE..................................419 628-2369
Deb Zwez, *Manager*
EMP: 4
SALES (corp-wide): 71.5MM **Privately Held**
WEB: www.malvern-online.com
SIC: 2711 Newspapers, publishing & printing
PA: Horizon Publications, Inc.
1120 N Carbon St Ste 100
Marion IL 62959
618 993-1711

(G-14218)
KARD WELDING INC
Also Called: Kard Bridge Products
480 Osterloh Rd (45865-9750)
P.O. Box 124 (45865-0124)
PHONE..................................419 628-2598
Doris Osterloh, *President*
Ken Osterloh, *Owner*
Kenneth H Osterloh, *Vice Pres*
EMP: 20
SQ FT: 36,360
SALES (est): 5.6MM **Privately Held**
SIC: 3499 3443 Machine bases, metal; fabricated plate work (boiler shop)

(G-14219)
MACHINE CONCEPTS INC
2167 State Route 66 (45865-9401)
P.O. Box 127 (45865-0127)
PHONE..................................419 628-3498
John Eiting, *President*
Randy May, *Draft/Design*
▲ **EMP:** 32
SQ FT: 30,000
SALES (est): 8.5MM **Privately Held**
WEB: www.machineconcepts.com
SIC: 3599 Machine shop, jobbing & repair

(G-14220)
MARK ONE MANUFACTURING LTD
351 Industrial Dr Ste 9 (45865-1258)
PHONE..................................419 628-4405
Doug Larger, *President*
EMP: 4
SALES (est): 331.7K **Privately Held**
SIC: 3443 Plate work for the metalworking trade

(G-14221)
NIDEC MINSTER CORPORATION
115 N Ohio St (45865-1072)
PHONE..................................419 628-1652
EMP: 3
SALES (est): 256.1K **Privately Held**
SIC: 3568 Power transmission equipment

(G-14222)
POST PRINTING CO (PA)
205 W 4th St (45865-1062)
P.O. Box 101 (45865-0101)
PHONE..................................859 254-7714
Tim Thompson, *President*
Glenn Thompson II, *Vice Pres*
Jeff Ahlers, *Manager*
Jane Thompson, *Director*
EMP: 54 **EST:** 1896
SQ FT: 14,400
SALES (est): 12.3MM **Privately Held**
WEB: www.postprinting.com
SIC: 2759 2752 Letterpress printing; commercial printing, offset

(G-14223)
PROGRESS TOOL & STAMPING INC
Also Called: Progress Tool Co
207 Southgate (45865-9552)
P.O. Box 53 (45865-0053)
PHONE..................................419 628-2384
Lee H Westerheide, *President*
Keith Westerheide, *Design Engr*
EMP: 20
SQ FT: 22,000

Minster - Auglaize County (G-14224)

SALES (est): 3.6MM **Privately Held**
SIC: **3544** 3469 Special dies & tools; jigs & fixtures; metal stampings

(G-14224)
SECURCOM INC
307 W 1st St (45865-1210)
P.O. Box 116 (45865-0116)
PHONE..............................419 628-1049
Bill Bergman, *President*
James R Shenk, *Principal*
Amy Winner, *Office Mgr*
Marlene Hoying, *Admin Sec*
EMP: 22 EST: 1997
SALES (est): 3.6MM **Privately Held**
WEB: www.securcom.com
SIC: **5999** 7382 3699 5065 Telephone & communication equipment; security systems services; security control equipment & systems; communication equipment

(G-14225)
SUNRISE COOPERATIVE INC
Also Called: Minster Farmers
292 W 4th St (45865-1024)
P.O. Box 100 (45865-0100)
PHONE..............................419 628-4705
Mike Bensman, *Branch Mgr*
EMP: 11
SALES (corp-wide): 56.3MM **Privately Held**
SIC: **5191** 5153 5172 2041 Feed; grain elevators; grains; field beans; engine fuels & oils; flour & other grain mill products
PA: Sunrise Cooperative, Inc.
   2025 W State St Ste A
   Fremont OH 43420
   419 332-6468

(G-14226)
THIEMAN MACHINE
5395 State Route 119 (45865-9404)
PHONE..............................419 628-2474
Ken Thieman, *President*
EMP: 3
SALES (est): 428.8K **Privately Held**
SIC: **3599** Machine shop, jobbing & repair

(G-14227)
TRADEMARK DESIGNS INC
17 Jackson St (45865-1144)
P.O. Box 217 (45865-0217)
PHONE..............................419 628-3897
Mark Nolan, *President*
Jerry Henkaline, *Corp Secy*
EMP: 20
SQ FT: 3,700
SALES: 2.8MM **Privately Held**
SIC: **3999** Identification plates

Mogadore
Portage County

(G-14228)
AKRON CULTURED MARBLE PDTS LLC
3992 Mogadore Rd (44260-1303)
PHONE..............................330 628-6757
Chris Stiffler,
EMP: 3
SALES: 200K **Privately Held**
SIC: **3281** Marble, building: cut & shaped

(G-14229)
AMERIMOLD INC
595a Waterloo Rd Ste A (44260-8710)
PHONE..............................330 628-2190
Bill Wensel, *President*
EMP: 6
SQ FT: 2,000
SALES: 550K **Privately Held**
WEB: www.amerimold.com
SIC: **3544** 3599 Industrial molds; machine shop, jobbing & repair

(G-14230)
ARCONIC INC
Also Called: Alcoa
3340 Gilchrist Rd (44260-1254)
PHONE..............................330 835-6000
Kevin Matske, *Manager*
EMP: 135
SALES (corp-wide): 14B **Publicly Held**
SIC: **3353** Aluminum sheet & strip
PA: Arconic Inc.
   390 Park Ave Fl 12
   New York NY 10022
   212 836-2758

(G-14231)
BICO AKRON INC
Also Called: Bico Steel Service Centers
3100 Gilchrist Rd (44260-1246)
PHONE..............................330 794-1716
Michael A Ensminger, *President*
▲ EMP: 65
SQ FT: 90,000
SALES (est): 28.5MM **Privately Held**
SIC: **5051** 3443 Steel; fabricated plate work (boiler shop)

(G-14232)
CORNWELL QUALITY TOOLS COMPANY
200 N Cleveland Ave (44260-1205)
PHONE..............................330 628-2627
Bill Nobley, *Branch Mgr*
Dianna Stump, *Executive*
EMP: 75
SQ FT: 3,000
SALES (corp-wide): 173.8MM **Privately Held**
WEB: www.cornwelltools.com
SIC: **3423** 5085 Hand & edge tools; industrial supplies
PA: The Cornwell Quality Tools Company
   667 Seville Rd
   Wadsworth OH 44281
   330 336-3506

(G-14233)
COUNTRYSIDE PUMPING INC
1496 Martin Rd (44260-1558)
PHONE..............................330 628-0058
Melissa Rufener, *President*
Mary J Roth, *Corp Secy*
EMP: 3
SALES: 50.4K **Privately Held**
SIC: **1389** Service And Maintenance Of Oil & Gas Wells

(G-14234)
DUMA DEER PROCESSING LLC
831 Waterloo Rd (44260-9503)
PHONE..............................330 805-3429
David Duma, *General Mgr*
EMP: 3
SALES (est): 177.2K **Privately Held**
SIC: **2011** Meat packing plants

(G-14235)
DUMAS MEATS INC
857 Randolph Rd (44260-9343)
P.O. Box 54 (44260-0054)
PHONE..............................330 628-3438
Dave Duma, *President*
Beverley Duma, *Treasurer*
EMP: 8
SQ FT: 3,000
SALES (est): 814.2K **Privately Held**
WEB: www.dumameatsfarmmarket.com
SIC: **5421** 2013 Freezer provisioners, meat; meat markets, including freezer provisioners; sausages & other prepared meats

(G-14236)
ENDURANCE MANUFACTURING INC
213 Randolph Rd (44260-1341)
PHONE..............................330 628-2600
Thomas J Turkalj, *Principal*
EMP: 6
SALES (est): 572.8K **Privately Held**
SIC: **2813** Industrial gases

(G-14237)
EXTRUDED SILICON PRODUCTS INC
3300 Gilchrist Rd (44260-1254)
PHONE..............................330 733-0101
Joseph E Foreman, *President*
EMP: 48
SALES (est): 7MM **Privately Held**
SIC: **3061** Mechanical rubber goods

(G-14238)
GEORGIA-PACIFIC LLC
3265 Gilchrist Rd (44260-1247)
PHONE..............................330 794-4444
Craig McNeil, *Manager*
EMP: 150
SALES (corp-wide): 42.4B **Privately Held**
WEB: www.gp.com
SIC: **2621** Paper mills
HQ: Georgia-Pacific Llc
   133 Peachtree St Nw
   Atlanta GA 30303
   404 652-4000

(G-14239)
HEXPOL COMPOUNDING LLC
Also Called: Hexpol Silicone
3939a Mogadore Indus Pkwy (44260-1224)
PHONE..............................440 682-4038
EMP: 4
SALES (corp-wide): 1.4B **Privately Held**
SIC: **2821** Thermoplastic materials
HQ: Hexpol Compounding Llc
   14330 Kinsman Rd
   Burton OH 44021
   440 834-4644

(G-14240)
HUNTERS MANUFACTURING CO INC (PA)
Also Called: Tenpoint Crossbow Technologies
1325 Waterloo Rd (44260-9608)
PHONE..............................330 628-9245
Richard L Bednar, *CEO*
Philip Bednar, *Exec VP*
Steve Bednar, *Exec VP*
Robert Seymour, *Warehouse Mgr*
Grant Fritz, *Buyer*
▲ EMP: 32
SALES (est): 5.9MM **Privately Held**
WEB: www.tenpointcrossbows.com
SIC: **3949** 3999 Crossbows; arrows, archery; cigarette lighters, except precious metal

(G-14241)
JANORPOT LLC
3175 Gilchrist Rd (44260-1245)
PHONE..............................330 564-0232
Norm Belliveau, *President*
Ron Vandiver, *Vice Pres*
Ann Saccone, *Office Mgr*
Charles Snyder,
▲ EMP: 35
SQ FT: 40,000
SALES (est): 9.2MM **Privately Held**
WEB: www.janorpot.com
SIC: **3089** Flower pots, plastic

(G-14242)
KENT ELASTOMER PRODUCTS INC
3890 Mogadore Indus Pkwy (44260-1223)
PHONE..............................800 331-4762
Murrey Vanepp, *Principal*
EMP: 7
SALES (corp-wide): 379.3MM **Privately Held**
SIC: **3052** Rubber & plastics hose & beltings
HQ: Kent Elastomer Products, Inc.
   1500 Saint Clair Ave
   Kent OH 44240
   330 673-1011

(G-14243)
LABEL PRINT TECHNOLOGIES LLC
3380 Gilchrist Rd (44260-1254)
PHONE..............................800 475-4030
Dennis Corrado,
▲ EMP: 15
SALES (est): 4.1MM **Privately Held**
SIC: **2754** Labels: gravure printing

(G-14244)
MOORE WELL SERVICES INC
246 N Cleveland Ave (44260-1205)
PHONE..............................330 650-4443
Jeff Moore, *President*
Jeita Moore, *Vice Pres*
EMP: 21
SQ FT: 8,000
SALES (est): 4.9MM **Privately Held**
SIC: **1381** Drilling oil & gas wells

(G-14245)
NEWELL BRANDS INC
Also Called: Newell Rubbermaid
3200 Gilchrist Rd (44260-1248)
PHONE..............................330 733-7771
Joe Soldano, *Branch Mgr*
Mark Yerian, *Supervisor*
Matthew Rees, *Technology*
Christine Zaleha,
EMP: 14
SALES (corp-wide): 8.6B **Publicly Held**
SIC: **3089** Plastic kitchenware, tableware & houseware
PA: Newell Brands Inc.
   221 River St Ste 13
   Hoboken NJ 07030
   201 610-6600

(G-14246)
OMNOVA SOLUTIONS INC
Gencorp Specialty Polmers
165 S Cleveland Ave (44260-1593)
PHONE..............................330 628-6550
Marvin Zima, *President*
Jim Wood, *Opers Spvr*
EMP: 150
SALES (corp-wide): 769.8MM **Publicly Held**
WEB: www.omnova.com
SIC: **2824** 3087 Organic fibers, noncellulosic; custom compound purchased resins
PA: Omnova Solutions Inc.
   25435 Harvard Rd
   Beachwood OH 44122
   216 682-7000

(G-14247)
RUBBERMAID INCORPORATED
3200 Gilchrist Rd (44260-1248)
PHONE..............................330 733-7771
Donna Neal, *Senior Buyer*
John Bias, *Manager*
EMP: 182
SALES (corp-wide): 8.6B **Publicly Held**
WEB: www.rubbermaid.com
SIC: **3089** Planters, plastic; plastic kitchenware, tableware & houseware
HQ: Rubbermaid Incorporated
   3 Glenlake Pkwy Ste D
   Atlanta GA 30328
   770 418-7000

(G-14248)
SAM AMERICAS INC
3555 Gilchrist Rd (44260-1240)
P.O. Box 8 (44260-0008)
PHONE..............................330 628-1118
Kaz Nakai, *CEO*
Kenji Saito, *President*
Jay Theiss, *Vice Pres*
Steve Ensch, *Purch Agent*
Rob Owsiany, *QC Mgr*
EMP: 33 EST: 2006
SQ FT: 60,000
SALES (est): 6.2MM
SALES (corp-wide): 964.4MM **Privately Held**
SIC: **3369** Castings, except die-castings, precision
PA: Shinagawa Refractories Co.,Ltd.
   2-2-1, Otemachi
   Chiyoda-Ku TKY 100-0
   362 651-600

(G-14249)
SHINAGAWA ADVANCED MATERIALS A
3555 Gilchrist Rd (44260-1240)
P.O. Box 8 (44260-0008)
PHONE..............................330 628-1118
K G Keiji Saito, *President*
◆ EMP: 28
SQ FT: 28,800
SALES (est): 5.5MM **Privately Held**
WEB: www.fmpinc.net
SIC: **3399** Metal powders, pastes & flakes

(G-14250)
SUMMIT MACHINE LTD
3991 Mogadore Rd (44260-1367)
PHONE..............................330 628-2663
Clement Knapp, *General Mgr*
Craig Yates, *Plant Mgr*

GEOGRAPHIC SECTION

Jim Burns,
▲ **EMP:** 20
SQ FT: 23,000
SALES (est): 3.5MM **Privately Held**
WEB: www.summitmachine.com
SIC: 3599 Machine shop, jobbing & repair

(G-14251)
SUMMIT PLASTIC COMPANY
3175 Gilchrist Rd (44260-1245)
P.O. Box 117, Tallmadge (44278-0117)
PHONE...................................330 633-3668
Norman Belliveau, *CEO*
Jim Pfeiffer, *General Mgr*
George Collins, *Vice Pres*
Chuck Snyder, *Vice Pres*
Lou Mokodean, *Materials Mgr*
▲ **EMP:** 70 **EST:** 1990
SQ FT: 55,000
SALES (est): 15.9MM **Privately Held**
SIC: 3081 Unsupported plastics film & sheet

(G-14252)
VERTEX INC
3956 Mogadore Indus Pkwy (44260-1201)
PHONE...................................330 628-6230
Dean Hansen, *President*
Ronald Mayfield, *President*
Salvatore Brugnano, *Chairman*
James Westhoff, *Corp Secy*
Richard Bowers, *Vice Pres*
▲ **EMP:** 30
SQ FT: 20,000
SALES (est): 8.2MM **Privately Held**
SIC: 3069 3061 3053 Valves, hard rubber; mechanical rubber goods; gaskets, packing & sealing devices

Monclova
Lucas County

(G-14253)
ADVANCED LITHO SYSTEMS
4429 Weckerly Rd (43542-9483)
PHONE...................................419 865-2652
Marty McClanahan, *Owner*
EMP: 4
SALES (est): 240K **Privately Held**
WEB: www.advancedlithosystems.com
SIC: 3861 Printing equipment, photographic

Monroe
Butler County

(G-14254)
AM RETAIL GROUP INC
628 Premium Outlets Dr (45050-1836)
PHONE...................................513 539-7837
EMP: 3
SALES (corp-wide): 3B **Publicly Held**
SIC: 3199 Leather garments
HQ: Am Retail Group, Inc.
7401 Boone Ave N
Brooklyn Park MN 55428

(G-14255)
BITS & CHIPS MACHINING COMPANY
730 Lebanon St (45050-1439)
PHONE...................................513 539-0800
Kimberly A Ludwig, *President*
EMP: 8
SQ FT: 6,000
SALES (est): 1.5MM **Privately Held**
SIC: 3599 Machine shop, jobbing & repair

(G-14256)
CELLERA LLC
1045 Reed Dr Ste C (45050-1717)
PHONE...................................513 539-1500
Dick Moon, *CFO*
Ken Heyl, *Officer*
▲ **EMP:** 5
SALES (est): 245.2K **Privately Held**
SIC: 2844 Face creams or lotions

(G-14257)
CHROME DEPOSIT CORPORATION
341 Lawton Ave (45050-1215)
PHONE...................................513 539-8486
Dan Zimmerman, *Manager*
Tonya Chapman, *Manager*
Dana Ewing, *Manager*
LI Lu, *Technology*
Benita Paulsen, *Technology*
EMP: 27
SALES (corp-wide): 23.7MM **Privately Held**
WEB: www.cdcportage.com
SIC: 3471 Chromium plating of metals or formed products
PA: Chrome Deposit Corporation
6640 Melton Rd
Portage IN 46368
219 763-1571

(G-14258)
CHROME DEPOSIT CORPORATION
341 Lawton Ave (45050-1215)
PHONE...................................513 539-8486
EMP: 40
SALES (corp-wide): 24.7MM **Privately Held**
SIC: 3471 Plating And Polishing
PA: Chrome Deposit Corporation
6640 Melton Rd
Portage IN 46368
219 763-1571

(G-14259)
DAYTON TECHNOLOGIES
351 N Garver Rd (45050-1292)
PHONE...................................513 539-5474
Darwin Brown, *Principal*
EMP: 11
SALES (est): 1.3MM **Privately Held**
SIC: 3082 Unsupported plastics profile shapes

(G-14260)
DECEUNINCK NORTH AMERICA LLC (PA)
351 N Garver Rd (45050-1233)
PHONE...................................513 539-4444
Filip Geeraert, *President*
Roy Frost, *Managing Dir*
Frank Perna, *Vice Pres*
Heather Slaton, *Safety Dir*
Jeremy Green, *Production*
▲ **EMP:** 269 **EST:** 1969
SALES (est): 125.3MM **Privately Held**
WEB: www.daytech.com
SIC: 3082 Unsupported plastics profile shapes

(G-14261)
DIXIE MACHINERY INC
Also Called: Dixitech Cnc
845 Todhunter Rd (45050-1032)
P.O. Box 1019, Mason (45040-6019)
PHONE...................................513 360-0091
Richard Patrick, *President*
EMP: 12
SQ FT: 23,000
SALES (est): 3.5MM **Privately Held**
WEB: www.dixiemachineryinc.com
SIC: 3541 Machine tools, metal cutting type

(G-14262)
FLEETCHEM LLC
651 N Garver Rd (45050-1207)
PHONE...................................513 539-1111
Angela Lovejoy, *Controller*
Tj Blakemor, *Branch Mgr*
EMP: 10 **Privately Held**
WEB: www.fleetchem.com
SIC: 2045 Blended flour: from purchased flour
PA: Fleetchem, Llc
1222 Brassie Ave Ste 19
Flossmoor IL 60422

(G-14263)
GARDNER METAL CRAFT INC
490 S Main St (45050-1415)
P.O. Box 176 (45050-0176)
PHONE...................................513 539-4538
Jack Blevins, *President*

Gail Blevins, *Vice Pres*
EMP: 5
SQ FT: 8,000
SALES (est): 879.7K **Privately Held**
WEB: www.gardnermetalcraft.net
SIC: 3441 Fabricated structural metal

(G-14264)
GLASS COATINGS & CONCEPTS LLC
300 Lawton Ave (45050-1216)
PHONE...................................513 539-5300
Jeff Nixon,
▲ **EMP:** 25
SALES (est): 5.8MM
SALES (corp-wide): 58.2MM **Privately Held**
WEB: www.gcconcepts.com
SIC: 2893 Printing ink
PA: The Shepherd Color Company
4539 Dues Dr
West Chester OH 45246
513 874-0714

(G-14265)
GREAN TECHNOLOGIES LLC
Also Called: Kemex Laboratories
902 N Garver Rd (45050-1241)
PHONE...................................513 510-7116
David L Moats,
EMP: 5
SALES (est): 48.9K **Privately Held**
SIC: 2899 Chemical preparations

(G-14266)
HI TECH TOOL CORPORATION
415 Breaden Dr Ste 1 (45050-2479)
PHONE...................................513 346-4061
James Gregory, *Ch of Bd*
Kelly Thompson, *Exec VP*
EMP: 5
SALES (est): 613.3K **Privately Held**
SIC: 3545 Cutting tools for machine tools

(G-14267)
HONEY CELL INC MID WEST
6480 Hamilton Lebanon Rd (45044-9285)
PHONE...................................513 360-0280
Rick Gillette, *General Mgr*
EMP: 27
SQ FT: 40,000
SALES (est): 5.4MM **Privately Held**
SIC: 2621 Paper mills
PA: Honey Cell, Inc.
850 Union Ave
Bridgeport CT 06607

(G-14268)
HONEYCOMB MIDWEST
6480 Hamilton Lebanon Rd (45044-9285)
PHONE...................................513 360-0280
Robert Neidermieir, *General Mgr*
EMP: 30
SALES (est): 2.3MM **Privately Held**
SIC: 2621 Art paper

(G-14269)
JOURNEY ELECTRONICS CORP
902 N Garver Rd (45050-1241)
P.O. Box 465 (45050-0465)
PHONE...................................513 539-9836
Michael Gorden, *President*
Kris Gorden, *Opers Mgr*
EMP: 7
SQ FT: 3,000
SALES: 400K
SALES (corp-wide): 544.6K **Privately Held**
WEB: www.gorden.org
SIC: 3672 3823 Printed circuit boards; industrial process control instruments
PA: Gorden Inc.
201 Inspiration Blvd # 400
Reading PA 19607
610 644-4476

(G-14270)
KERRY FLAVOR SYSTEMS US LLC
Also Called: Kerry Ingredients & Flavours
1055 Reed Dr (45050-1725)
PHONE...................................513 539-7373
David Moats, *Vice Pres*
EMP: 28 **Privately Held**
WEB: www.cargill.com

SIC: 2869 2819 Flavors or flavoring materials, synthetic; industrial inorganic chemicals
PA: Kerry Flavor Systems Us, Llc
10261 Chester Rd
Cincinnati OH 45215

(G-14271)
KLW PLASTICS INC
930 Deneen Ave (45050-1210)
PHONE...................................678 674-2990
EMP: 8
SALES (corp-wide): 789.2M **Privately Held**
SIC: 3089 Mfg Plastic Products
HQ: Klw Plastics, Inc.
980 Deneen Ave
Monroe OH 45050
513 539-2673

(G-14272)
KLW PLASTICS INC (DH)
980 Deneen Ave (45050-1210)
PHONE...................................513 539-2673
Kenneth M Roessler, *President*
Don Pearson, *CFO*
▲ **EMP:** 6
SQ FT: 37,000
SALES (est): 7MM
SALES (corp-wide): 1.1B **Privately Held**
WEB: www.klwplastics.com
SIC: 3089 5099 Blow molded finished plastic products; containers: glass, metal or plastic

(G-14273)
LEVI STRAUSS & CO
211 Premium Outlets Dr (45050-1829)
PHONE...................................513 539-7822
EMP: 19
SALES (corp-wide): 5.5B **Publicly Held**
SIC: 2325 Jeans: men's, youths' & boys'
PA: Levi Strauss & Co.
1155 Battery St
San Francisco CA 94111
415 501-6000

(G-14274)
ORORA PACKAGING SOLUTIONS
Also Called: Landsberg Cincinnati Div 1017
930 Deneen Ave (45050-1210)
PHONE...................................513 539-8274
Bob Firenze, *Manager*
EMP: 5 **Privately Held**
SIC: 5113 2653 Paper & products, wrapping or coarse; boxes, corrugated: made from purchased materials
HQ: Orora Packaging Solutions
6600 Valley View St
Buena Park CA 90620
714 562-6000

(G-14275)
RIVERTOWN BREWING COMPANY LLC
6550 Hamilton Lebanon Rd (45044-9285)
PHONE...................................513 827-9280
Tim Bales, *Director*
Jason D Roeper,
Randy Schiltz,
▲ **EMP:** 20
SALES (est): 2MM **Privately Held**
SIC: 2082 Brewers' grain

(G-14276)
SNYDER CONCRETE PRODUCTS INC
Also Called: Snyder Brick and Block
233 Senate Dr (45050-1716)
PHONE...................................513 539-7686
Dan Trettel, *Office Mgr*
Lee Snyder, *Manager*
EMP: 12
SQ FT: 37,984
SALES (corp-wide): 12.6MM **Privately Held**
WEB: www.snyderonline.com
SIC: 5999 5211 3272 Concrete products, pre-cast; brick; concrete products, precast
PA: Snyder Concrete Products, Inc.
2301 W Dorothy Ln
Moraine OH 45439
937 885-5176

Monroe - Butler County (G-14277)

(G-14277)
STEWARTS MACHINING INC
960 Holman Dr (45050-1077)
PHONE..................513 422-5000
Karen Stewart, *President*
Kenneth Stewart, *Vice Pres*
EMP: 5
SQ FT: 4,000
SALES (est): 390K **Privately Held**
SIC: 3599 Machine shop, jobbing & repair

(G-14278)
TEREX UTILITIES INC
Also Called: Cincinnati Division
920 Deneen Ave (45050-1210)
PHONE..................513 539-9770
Rick Girffis, *Branch Mgr*
EMP: 53
SALES (corp-wide): 5.1B **Publicly Held**
WEB: www.craneamerica.com
SIC: 3531 7629 3536 Cranes; electrical repair shops; hoists, cranes and monorails
HQ: Terex Utilities, Inc.
12805 Sw 77th Pl
Tigard OR 97223
503 620-0611

(G-14279)
VALVSYS LLC
421 Breaden Dr Ste 15 (45050-1575)
PHONE..................513 539-1234
Brad Frank, *President*
Lak Frank,
▲ EMP: 8 EST: 2000
SQ FT: 1,200
SALES (est): 1.1MM **Privately Held**
WEB: www.valvsys.com
SIC: 2812 Alkalies

(G-14280)
VINYL BUILDING PRODUCTS LLC
351 N Garver Rd (45050-1233)
PHONE..................513 539-4444
Ralph Weiss, *President*
EMP: 265 EST: 2003
SALES (est): 13.8MM **Privately Held**
WEB: www.tkvbp.com
SIC: 3081 Mfg Unsupported Plastic Film/Sheet

(G-14281)
WAFFLE HOUSE INC
1225 Hamilton Lebanon Rd (45050-1705)
PHONE..................513 539-8372
Rob Helton, *Branch Mgr*
EMP: 19
SALES (corp-wide): 787.1MM **Privately Held**
SIC: 2096 5145 Potato chips & similar snacks; snack foods
PA: Waffle House, Inc.
5986 Financial Dr
Norcross GA 30071
770 729-5700

(G-14282)
WORTHINGTON INDUSTRIES INC
Worthington Steel
350 Lawton Ave (45050-1216)
PHONE..................513 539-9291
Dave Kleimeyer, *General Mgr*
David Kleimeyer, *Sales/Mktg Mgr*
EMP: 165
SQ FT: 120,000
SALES (corp-wide): 3.5B **Publicly Held**
WEB: www.worthingtonindustries.com
SIC: 3325 5051 3471 3441 Steel foundries; metals service centers & offices; plating & polishing; fabricated structural metal; blast furnaces & steel mills
PA: Worthington Industries, Inc.
200 W Old Wlson Bridge Rd
Worthington OH 43085
614 438-3210

(G-14283)
XEROX CORPORATION
6500 Hamilton Lebanon Rd (45044-9702)
PHONE..................513 539-4858
Greg Bafaoyga, *Manager*
William Detcher, *Manager*
EMP: 84
SALES (corp-wide): 9.8B **Publicly Held**
SIC: 3577 Computer peripheral equipment
PA: Xerox Corporation
201 Merritt 7
Norwalk CT 06851
203 968-3000

(G-14284)
XEROX CORPORATION
6490 Hamilton Lebanon Rd (45044-9285)
PHONE..................513 539-4808
Jerry Cook, *Manager*
EMP: 5
SALES (corp-wide): 9.8B **Publicly Held**
SIC: 3577 Computer peripheral equipment
PA: Xerox Corporation
201 Merritt 7
Norwalk CT 06851
203 968-3000

Monroeville
Huron County

(G-14285)
2ND ROE LLC
12014 Thomas Rd (44847-9692)
PHONE..................419 499-3031
Cheryl Roe, *Principal*
EMP: 3
SALES (est): 178.7K **Privately Held**
SIC: 2048 Poultry feeds

(G-14286)
ALBRIGHT MACHINE
4296 Us Highway 20 W (44847-9758)
P.O. Box 514 (44847-0514)
PHONE..................419 483-1088
Terry Albright, *Owner*
EMP: 3
SQ FT: 6,000
SALES (est): 283.7K **Privately Held**
SIC: 3599 Custom machinery

(G-14287)
BORES MANUFACTURING CO INC
Also Called: Bores, J F Mfg
300 Sandusky St (44847)
P.O. Box 216 (44847-0216)
PHONE..................419 465-2606
Kevin Bores, *President*
Shirley Bores, *Vice Pres*
EMP: 12
SQ FT: 9,200
SALES (est): 1.9MM **Privately Held**
WEB: www.boresmfg.com
SIC: 3714 3713 Motor vehicle parts & accessories; truck & bus bodies

(G-14288)
HBE MACHINE INC
1100 State Route 61 N (44847-9202)
PHONE..................419 668-9426
Thomas R Hedrick, *President*
EMP: 6
SQ FT: 10,000
SALES (est): 931.3K **Privately Held**
SIC: 3599 Machine shop, jobbing & repair

(G-14289)
NARI INC
Also Called: Lorain Quickprint
5190 State Route 99 N (44847-9426)
PHONE..................440 960-2280
Richard Gfell, *President*
EMP: 4
SQ FT: 1,800
SALES (est): 230K **Privately Held**
WEB: www.lorainquickprint.com
SIC: 2752 2791 2789 Commercial printing, offset; typesetting; bookbinding & related work

(G-14290)
SCOTTRODS LLC
2512 Higbee Rd (44847-9617)
PHONE..................419 499-2705
Scott Leber,
EMP: 7
SALES (est): 280K **Privately Held**
SIC: 3229 7389 3711 Glass fiber products; ; automobile bodies, passenger car, not including engine, etc.

(G-14291)
SMS TECHNOLOGIES INC
3531 Everingin Rd (44847-9726)
PHONE..................419 465-4175
Stanley Schug, *President*
Nickie Schug, *Vice Pres*
EMP: 10
SALES (est): 1.5MM **Privately Held**
WEB: www.smstechnologies.com
SIC: 3646 Commercial indusl & institutional electric lighting fixtures

(G-14292)
VENTURE PACKAGING INC
311 Monroe St (44847-9406)
PHONE..................419 465-2534
Ira Boots, *President*
James Kratochuil, *Vice Pres*
John Rathbun, *Vice Pres*
EMP: 360 EST: 1976
SQ FT: 112,000
SALES (est): 48.7MM **Publicly Held**
WEB: www.6sens.com
SIC: 3089 Injection molded finished plastic products
HQ: Berry Global, Inc.
101 Oakley St
Evansville IN 47710
812 424-2904

(G-14293)
VENTURE PACKAGING MIDWEST INC
311 Monroe St (44847-9406)
PHONE..................419 465-2534
Kurt Klodnick, *Principal*
EMP: 7
SALES (est): 697.1K **Publicly Held**
SIC: 3089 Bottle caps, molded plastic
HQ: Berry Global, Inc.
101 Oakley St
Evansville IN 47710
812 424-2904

Montgomery
Hamilton County

(G-14294)
HAUTE CHOCOLATE INC
9424 Shelly Ln (45242-7610)
PHONE..................513 793-9999
Lisa Holmes, *President*
John Holmes, *Managing Dir*
Linda Obrian, *Manager*
EMP: 4
SQ FT: 2,000
SALES (est): 280K **Privately Held**
SIC: 2066 5441 Chocolate & cocoa products; candy

(G-14295)
KEMPF SURGICAL APPLIANCES INC
10567 Montgomery Rd (45242-4451)
PHONE..................513 984-5758
Steven Kempf, *President*
Susan Kempf, *Treasurer*
EMP: 22
SALES (est): 3.2MM **Privately Held**
SIC: 5999 5047 7352 3842 Hospital equipment & supplies; hospital equipment & supplies; medical equipment rental; surgical appliances & supplies

(G-14296)
O & P OPTIONS LLC
10547 Montgomery Rd # 600 (45242-4418)
PHONE..................513 791-7767
Douglas B Van Atta, *Mng Member*
EMP: 3
SALES (est): 260.2K **Privately Held**
SIC: 3842 Prosthetic appliances; braces, orthopedic

(G-14297)
OFFICE BSED ANSTHESIA SVCS LLC
10296 Gentlewind Dr (45242-5813)
PHONE..................513 582-5170
Brian Kasson, *President*
EMP: 3
SALES (est): 219.1K **Privately Held**
SIC: 3841 Surgical & medical instruments

(G-14298)
POLISHED PEARL LLP
11419 Brattle Ln (45249-3608)
PHONE..................513 659-8824
Teresa Eklund, *Partner*
Nicole Robyn, *Partner*
EMP: 4
SQ FT: 1,000
SALES (est): 144K **Privately Held**
SIC: 2335 Wedding gowns & dresses

(G-14299)
THERMO FISHER SCIENTIFIC INC
8761 Arcturus Dr (45249-3521)
PHONE..................513 489-2926
Steve Collins, *Branch Mgr*
EMP: 14
SALES (corp-wide): 24.3B **Publicly Held**
WEB: www.thermo.com
SIC: 3826 Analytical instruments
PA: Thermo Fisher Scientific Inc.
168 3rd Ave
Waltham MA 02451
781 622-1000

Montpelier
Williams County

(G-14300)
20/20 CUSTOM MOLDED PLAST (PA)
14620 Selwyn Dr (43543-9237)
PHONE..................419 485-2020
Ron Ernsberger, *President*
Kami Bentley, *QC Mgr*
Doug Lude, *Engineer*
David Rupp, *Treasurer*
Chad Adams, *Controller*
EMP: 81 EST: 2000
SQ FT: 40,000
SALES (est): 36.4MM **Privately Held**
WEB: www.2020cmp.com
SIC: 3089 Injection molding of plastics

(G-14301)
ADVANCE REPORTER (PA)
Also Called: Williams County Publishing
115 Broad St (43543-1325)
PHONE..................419 485-4851
Forrest R Church, *Owner*
Casey Church, *Co-Owner*
EMP: 3
SALES (est): 548.1K **Privately Held**
SIC: 2711 5994 Commercial printing & newspaper publishing combined; news dealers & newsstands

(G-14302)
BRYAN PUBLISHING COMPANY
Also Called: Northwest Realty
319 W Main St (43543-1017)
P.O. Box 149 (43543-0149)
PHONE..................419 485-3113
Paul Miller, *Manager*
EMP: 3
SQ FT: 1,740
SALES (est): 172.2K
SALES (corp-wide): 4MM **Privately Held**
WEB: www.bryantimes.com
SIC: 2711 Newspapers-Publishing/Printing
PA: The Bryan Publishing Company
127 S Walnut St
Bryan OH 43506
419 636-1111

(G-14303)
BULLSEYE MACHINES LLC
1224 Charlies Way (43543-1933)
PHONE..................419 485-5951
Harry Croft,
EMP: 3
SALES (est): 351.6K **Privately Held**
SIC: 3599 Machine shop, jobbing & repair

(G-14304)
CHASE BRASS AND COPPER CO LLC (DH)
14212 Selwyn Dr (43543-9595)
PHONE..................419 485-3193

GEOGRAPHIC SECTION

Devin Denner, *President*
Daniel Goehler, *President*
James Palmour, *President*
◆ **EMP:** 304
SQ FT: 129,000
SALES (est): 64.9MM **Publicly Held**
WEB: www.chasebrass.com
SIC: 3351 Copper rolling & drawing

(G-14305)
CK TECHNOLOGIES LLC (HQ)
1701 Magda Dr (43543-9368)
PHONE................................419 485-1110
Jeremie Thiel, *Plant Mgr*
Amanda Bell, *Materials Mgr*
Bob Houston, *Facilities Mgr*
Rick Smith, *Opers Staff*
Shane Lantz, *Production*
▲ **EMP:** 300
SQ FT: 164,000
SALES (est): 150MM
SALES (corp-wide): 577.9MM **Privately Held**
WEB: www.cktech.biz
SIC: 3089 Plastic containers, except foam; injection molding of plastics
PA: Cascade Engineering, Inc.
   3400 Innovation Ct Se
   Grand Rapids MI 49512
   616 975-4800

(G-14306)
DECO PLAS PROPERTIES LLC
700 Randolph St (43543-1464)
PHONE................................419 485-0632
Michael Kreps,
John Simon,
EMP: 50
SALES (est): 10MM **Privately Held**
SIC: 2851 Paints & allied products

(G-14307)
DYCO MANUFACTURING INC
12708 State Route 576 (43543-9242)
PHONE................................419 485-5525
Alan M Dye, *President*
Wes Dye, *Vice Pres*
Crystal Tyre, *Admin Sec*
EMP: 14
SALES (est): 2.4MM **Privately Held**
WEB: www.chwchospital.com
SIC: 3469 3544 Stamping metal for the trade; special dies & tools

(G-14308)
ENGELS MACHINING LLC
13299 State Route 107 (43543-9102)
P.O. Box 73 (43543-0073)
PHONE................................419 485-1500
James Engels, *Owner*
EMP: 4
SQ FT: 5,000
SALES (est): 487.6K **Privately Held**
WEB: www.engelsmachining.com
SIC: 3451 3931 Screw machine products; musical instruments

(G-14309)
ENGINEERING COATINGS LLC
1826 Magda Dr (43543-9374)
PHONE................................419 485-0077
EMP: 3
SALES (est): 139K **Privately Held**
SIC: 3471 Plating/Polishing Service

(G-14310)
INDIGO 48 LLC
1607 Magda Dr (43543-9348)
PHONE................................419 551-6931
Mark Hillman, *General Mgr*
John D Jackson, *Principal*
EMP: 3 **EST:** 2011
SALES (est): 266.7K **Privately Held**
SIC: 3471 Polishing, metals or formed products; cleaning & descaling metal products; cleaning, polishing & finishing

(G-14311)
KIMBLE MACHINES INC
124 S Jonesville St (43543-1337)
PHONE................................419 485-8449
Robert J Kimble, *President*
Margaret Kimble, *Corp Secy*
EMP: 14
SQ FT: 8,200
SALES (est): 2.1MM **Privately Held**
WEB: www.kimblemachines.com
SIC: 3599 Custom machinery

(G-14312)
MARTIN SPROCKET & GEAR INC
350 S Airport Rd (43543-9329)
PHONE................................419 485-5515
Deb Reese, *Purchasing*
Thomas H Kurtz, *Branch Mgr*
EMP: 75
SALES (corp-wide): 456MM **Privately Held**
SIC: 3566 3537 3535 3462 Gears, power transmission, except automotive; industrial trucks & tractors; conveyors & conveying equipment; iron & steel forgings; hand & edge tools; sprockets (power transmission equipment)
PA: Martin Sprocket & Gear, Inc.
   3100 Sprocket Dr
   Arlington TX 76015
   817 258-3000

(G-14313)
MOORE INDUSTRIES INC
1317 Hendricks Dr (43543-1951)
P.O. Box 316 (43543-0316)
PHONE................................419 485-5572
Michael Moore, *President*
Rebecca Moore, *Vice Pres*
▲ **EMP:** 65
SQ FT: 40,000
SALES (est): 15.4MM **Privately Held**
WEB: www.mooreindustries.com
SIC: 3089 Molding primary plastic; injection molding of plastics

(G-14314)
POWERS AND SONS LLC (DH)
1613 Magda Dr (43543-9359)
PHONE................................419 485-3151
Doug Link, *COO*
Sandy Howard, *Mfg Mgr*
Jeff Baden, *Engineer*
Cheree Lee, *Engineer*
Frank Martin, *Engineer*
▲ **EMP:** 220
SQ FT: 200,000
SALES (est): 58.9MM
SALES (corp-wide): 2.9B **Privately Held**
WEB: www.powersandsonsllc.com
SIC: 3714 Motor vehicle parts & accessories
HQ: Wanxiang (Usa) Holdings Corporation
   88 Airport Rd Ste 100
   Elgin IL 60123
   847 622-8838

(G-14315)
RANTEK PRODUCTS LLC
1826 Magda Dr Ste A (43543-9366)
PHONE................................419 485-2421
Randy Wyman,
EMP: 6 **EST:** 2001
SALES (est): 994.5K **Privately Held**
SIC: 3199 Harness or harness parts

(G-14316)
RASSINI CHASSIS SYSTEMS LLC
1812 Magda Dr (43543-9373)
PHONE................................419 485-1524
Robert Anderson, *Mng Member*
Pam Vandermoon,
EMP: 60
SQ FT: 100,000
SALES (est): 40.6MM **Privately Held**
SIC: 3493 Coiled flat springs
HQ: Sanluis Rassini, S.A. De C.V.
   Monte Pelvoux No. 220, Piso 8
   Ciudad De Mexico CDMX 11000

(G-14317)
RAYMONDS TOOL & GAUGE LLC
6726 County Road N30 (43543-9773)
P.O. Box 106 (43543-0106)
PHONE................................419 485-8340
Steve Raymond, *Mng Member*
Melissa Raymond,
EMP: 5
SQ FT: 3,600
SALES (est): 627K **Privately Held**
SIC: 3544 Special dies & tools

(G-14318)
RICHMOND MACHINE CO
1528 Travis Dr (43543-9524)
PHONE................................419 485-5740
Lee Richmond, *President*
Robert Richmond, *Vice Pres*
EMP: 32 **EST:** 1965
SQ FT: 60,000
SALES (est): 7.1MM **Privately Held**
SIC: 3599 3535 Custom machinery; conveyors & conveying equipment

(G-14319)
TOMAHAWK TOOL SUPPLY
1604 Magda Dr (43543-9206)
PHONE................................419 485-8737
Jeff Thomas, *President*
EMP: 9
SALES (est): 991.6K **Privately Held**
WEB: www.tomahawktoolservice.com
SIC: 3544 Special dies & tools

(G-14320)
VILLAGE REPORTER
115 Broad St (43543-1325)
PHONE................................419 485-4851
Forrest Church, *Principal*
EMP: 4
SALES (est): 205.8K **Privately Held**
SIC: 2711 Newspapers, publishing & printing

(G-14321)
W C HELLER & CO INC
Also Called: Heller Sports Center
201 W Wabash St (43543-1840)
PHONE................................419 485-3176
Robert L Heller, *President*
Andrew Heller, *Vice Pres*
Patricia Heller, *Treasurer*
EMP: 12 **EST:** 1891
SQ FT: 25,500
SALES (est): 1.3MM **Privately Held**
WEB: www.wcheller.com
SIC: 2531 School furniture; library furniture

(G-14322)
WINZELER STAMPING CO
129 W Wabash St (43543-1881)
PHONE................................419 485-3147
Mike Winzeler, *Branch Mgr*
EMP: 80
SALES (corp-wide): 32MM **Privately Held**
WEB: www.winzelerstamping.com
SIC: 3429 3492 3469 Clamps & couplings, hose; fluid power valves & hose fittings; metal stampings
PA: Winzeler Stamping Co.
   129 W Wabash St
   Montpelier OH 43543
   419 485-3147

Montville
Geauga County

(G-14323)
5S INC
9755 Plank Rd (44064-9712)
P.O. Box 188 (44064-0188)
PHONE................................440 968-0212
Tom Sparks, *President*
EMP: 7
SALES (est): 787.3K **Privately Held**
SIC: 3599 Machine shop, jobbing & repair

(G-14324)
NT MACHINE INC
Also Called: Nt Machine Inorp
10080 Clay St (44064-9738)
PHONE................................440 968-3506
Nicholas Saris Jr, *President*
Darlene Sparks, *Corp Secy*
Tom Sparks, *Vice Pres*
EMP: 3
SALES (est): 360.6K **Privately Held**
SIC: 3599 Machine shop, jobbing & repair

(G-14325)
RAY TOWNSEND
Also Called: Townsend Machinery
9168 Clay St (44064-9700)
PHONE................................440 968-3617
Ray Townsend, *Owner*
EMP: 5
SQ FT: 35,000
SALES (est): 435.9K **Privately Held**
WEB: www.townsendmachinery.com
SIC: 3599 7692 Machine shop, jobbing & repair; welding repair

(G-14326)
YAUGHER ENTERPRIZES INC
9755 Plank Rd Ste A (44064-9712)
PHONE................................440 968-0151
Karen Yaugher, *President*
EMP: 5
SQ FT: 12,000
SALES (est): 407K **Privately Held**
SIC: 3599 Machine shop, jobbing & repair

Moraine
Montgomery County

(G-14327)
3JD INC
Also Called: Stone Center of Dayton
2823 Northlawn Ave (45439-1645)
PHONE................................513 324-9655
Jerry Berkemeyer, *Principal*
▲ **EMP:** 15
SALES (est): 1.9MM **Privately Held**
SIC: 2541 Counter & sink tops

(G-14328)
ACCUPHASE METAL TREATING LLC
2490 Arbor Blvd (45439-1780)
PHONE................................937 610-5934
Randy Benson,
Christopher Panetta,
EMP: 4
SQ FT: 500
SALES (est): 495K **Privately Held**
SIC: 3398 Metal heat treating

(G-14329)
ACUTEMP THERMAL SYSTEMS
2900 Dryden Rd (45439-1618)
PHONE................................937 312-0114
Marshall Griffin, *CFO*
EMP: 10
SALES (est): 1.9MM **Privately Held**
SIC: 3822 Temperature controls, automatic

(G-14330)
ANGELS LANDING INC
Also Called: Compass
3430 S Dixie Dr Ste 301 (45439-2316)
PHONE................................513 687-3681
John Riedl, *Principal*
Dan Jackson, *CFO*
Mark Jovanovic, *Asst Broker*
Scott Hustis, *Associate*
▲ **EMP:** 6
SQ FT: 2,000
SALES (est): 631K **Privately Held**
SIC: 2514 Juvenile furniture, household: metal

(G-14331)
ANTHONY DECORATIVE FABRICS AND
Also Called: Anthony's Fabric
2701 Lance Dr (45409-1519)
PHONE................................937 299-4637
Marion Scrimenti, *President*
Charlene Scrimenti, *Corp Secy*
EMP: 3 **EST:** 1977
SQ FT: 6,000
SALES (est): 503.4K **Privately Held**
SIC: 5131 2391 Drapery material, woven; curtains, window: made from purchased materials

(G-14332)
BAYARD INC
2621 Dryden Rd Ste 300 (45439-1600)
PHONE................................937 293-1415
John P Koize, *Principal*

Moraine - Montgomery County (G-14333)

EMP: 11 Privately Held
SIC: 2759 Publication printing
HQ: Bayard, Inc.
1 Montauk Ave Ste 3
New London CT 06320
860 437-3012

(G-14333)
BDS PACKAGING INC
3155 Elbee Rd Ste 201 (45439-2046)
PHONE.....................937 643-0530
Wendell T Bryant, *President*
Jeff Sloneker, *Vice Pres*
EMP: 58
SQ FT: 78,264
SALES (est): 11.6MM Privately Held
WEB: www.bdspackaging.com
SIC: 2653 3993 7389 Boxes, corrugated: made from purchased materials; displays & cutouts, window & lobby; packaging & labeling services

(G-14334)
BERRY INVESTMENTS INC
3055 Kettering Blvd # 418 (45439-1900)
PHONE.....................937 293-0398
John W Berry Sr, *CEO*
William T Lincoln, *President*
EMP: 6
SQ FT: 2,500
SALES (est): 1.1MM Privately Held
WEB: www.berryinvestments.com
SIC: 5091 3679 Sporting & recreation goods; microwave components

(G-14335)
BOS ELECTRIC SUPPLY LLC
2388 Arbor Blvd (45439-1745)
PHONE.....................937 426-0578
Ross Owens, *Store Mgr*
Michael Sizemore, *Sales Staff*
Alex Barnes,
EMP: 5 EST: 2017
SALES: 1.3MM Privately Held
SIC: 3699 Electrical work

(G-14336)
BRONT MACHINING INC
2601 W Dorothy Ln (45439-1831)
PHONE.....................937 228-4551
Gary Warlaumont, *President*
Brian Warlaumont, *Vice Pres*
EMP: 20 EST: 1975
SQ FT: 25,000
SALES: 4MM Privately Held
SIC: 3451 3599 Screw machine products; machine shop, jobbing & repair

(G-14337)
CHAMPION WIN ENCLOSURE DAYTON
2012 Springboro W Bldg 4 (45439-1648)
PHONE.....................937 299-6800
Brian Copple, *Owner*
EMP: 20
SALES (est): 1.8MM Privately Held
SIC: 3442 Metal doors, sash & trim

(G-14338)
CLIPPER MAGAZINE LLC
2360 W Dorothy Ln Ste 101 (45439-1861)
PHONE.....................937 534-0470
Bob Levine, *Principal*
EMP: 4 Privately Held
SIC: 2754 2721 Coupons: gravure printing; periodicals
HQ: Clipper Magazine, Llc
3708 Hempland Rd
Mountville PA 17554
717 569-5100

(G-14339)
CROWN CORK & SEAL USA INC
5005 Springboro Pike (45439-2974)
PHONE.....................937 299-2027
EMP: 121
SQ FT: 50,000
SALES (corp-wide): 11.1B Publicly Held
WEB: www.crowncork.com
SIC: 3411 Metal cans
HQ: Crown Cork & Seal Usa, Inc.
770 Township Line Rd # 100
Yardley PA 19067
215 698-5100

(G-14340)
CSAFE LLC
2900 Dryden Rd (45439-1618)
PHONE.....................937 312-0114
Brian Kohr,
▲ EMP: 8
SALES (est): 1.8MM Privately Held
SIC: 3585 Refrigeration & heating equipment

(G-14341)
DADDY KATZ LLC
3250 Kettering Blvd (45439-1926)
PHONE.....................937 296-0347
William Winger Jr, *Principal*
EMP: 7 EST: 2008
SALES (est): 850.1K Privately Held
SIC: 3089 Automotive parts, plastic

(G-14342)
DAPSCO
3110 Kettering Blvd (45439-1972)
PHONE.....................937 294-5331
Richard Schwartz, *Vice Pres*
Bruce Anderson, *CPA*
Dave Benedict, *Technical Staff*
EMP: 13
SALES (est): 2.5MM Privately Held
SIC: 3571 Electronic computers

(G-14343)
DAYTON AIR CONTROL PDTS LLC
2785 Lance Dr (45409-1519)
PHONE.....................937 254-4441
Robin Haviland, *Mng Member*
EMP: 3
SQ FT: 6,000
SALES (est): 358.8K Privately Held
SIC: 3491 Industrial valves

(G-14344)
DAYTON BRICK COMPANY INC
Also Called: D & M Welding
2300 Arbor Blvd (45439-1724)
PHONE.....................937 293-4189
Jeffrey McCarroll, *President*
Jeffrey Mc Carroll, *President*
Brian Mc Carroll, *Corp Secy*
Justin McCarroll, *Opers Mgr*
Tona Potter, *Office Mgr*
EMP: 15
SQ FT: 15,000
SALES (est): 2.2MM Privately Held
SIC: 7692 Welding repair

(G-14345)
DEUER DEVELOPMENTS INC
Also Called: Tuf-Tug Products Div
3434 Encrete Ln (45439-1946)
PHONE.....................937 299-1213
Joseph F Deuer Jr, *President*
Louise Deuer, *Treasurer*
▲ EMP: 18
SQ FT: 27,000
SALES (est): 3.5MM Privately Held
WEB: www.tuf-tug.com
SIC: 3544 7539 Special dies, tools, jigs & fixtures; machine shop, automotive

(G-14346)
DMAX LTD (DH)
3100 Dryden Rd (45439-1622)
PHONE.....................937 425-9700
Lawrence R Sessoms, *Principal*
Susumu Hosoi, *Principal*
Tim Young, *Controller*
♦ EMP: 100
SQ FT: 700,000
SALES (est): 92.7MM Publicly Held
WEB: www.dmax-ltd.com
SIC: 3519 Engines, diesel & semi-diesel or dual-fuel

(G-14347)
DOUBLEDAY ACQUISITIONS LLC
Also Called: Acutemp
2900 Dryden Rd (45439-1618)
PHONE.....................937 242-6768
Brian Kohr, *CEO*
Nadine Siqueland, *Vice Pres*
Patrick Schafer, *CFO*
▲ EMP: 110
SQ FT: 30,000

SALES (est): 30.4MM Privately Held
WEB: www.acutemp.com
SIC: 3823 Temperature instruments: industrial process type

(G-14348)
EAGLE WRIGHT INNOVATIONS INC
2591 Lance Dr (45409-1513)
PHONE.....................937 640-8093
Mary F Catanzaro, *President*
Ronald Catanzaro, *President*
EMP: 5
SQ FT: 12,600
SALES (est): 766.5K Privately Held
WEB: www.eaglewright.com
SIC: 2621 5045 Printing paper; computer peripheral equipment; disk drives

(G-14349)
EICOM CORPORATION
3249 Dryden Rd (45439-1423)
PHONE.....................937 294-5692
Lisa S Pierce, *Principal*
EMP: 34
SALES (est): 11.5MM Privately Held
SIC: 3568 Couplings, shaft: rigid, flexible, universal joint, etc.

(G-14350)
ENTING WATER CONDITIONING INC (PA)
Also Called: Superior Water Conditioning Co
3211 Dryden Rd Frnt Frnt (45439-1400)
PHONE.....................937 294-5100
Mel Entingh, *CEO*
Dan Entingh, *President*
Amber Entingh, *Purchasing*
Karen Entingh, *Treasurer*
Doris Entingh, *Admin Sec*
▲ EMP: 31 EST: 1965
SQ FT: 43,440
SALES (est): 3.2MM Privately Held
WEB: www.enting.com
SIC: 3589 5999 5074 Water filters & softeners, household type; water purification equipment, household type; water treatment equipment, industrial; water purification equipment; water softeners

(G-14351)
ERNST METAL TECHNOLOGIES LLC (DH)
2920 Kreitzer Rd (45439-1644)
PHONE.....................937 434-3133
Neil Cordonnier, *President*
Dana Fultz, *Purchasing*
Jolene Calladine, *Treasurer*
▲ EMP: 44
SALES (est): 21.2MM
SALES (corp-wide): 664.2K Privately Held
SIC: 3469 3312 Stamping metal for the trade; tool & die steel & alloys
HQ: Ernst Umformtechnik Gmbh
Am Wiesenbach 1
Oberkirch 77704
780 540-60

(G-14352)
F & G TOOL AND DIE CO (PA)
3024 Dryden Rd (45439-1690)
PHONE.....................937 294-1405
Jeff Johnson, *President*
Gary M Fischer, *President*
John Grady, *VP Mfg*
Ed Scharer, *CFO*
Ed Scharrer, *Human Res Dir*
EMP: 50 EST: 1948
SQ FT: 60,000
SALES (est): 14MM Privately Held
SIC: 3544 3599 Special dies & tools; custom machinery

(G-14353)
FALCON TOOL & MACHINE INC
2795 Lance Dr (45409-1519)
PHONE.....................937 534-9999
Don Voehringer, *President*
John Noble, *Treasurer*
Mark Metter, *Admin Sec*
EMP: 7
SQ FT: 7,000

SALES (est): 500K Privately Held
SIC: 3541 3599 Machine tools, metal cutting type; machine shop, jobbing & repair

(G-14354)
FORGELINE INC
3522 Kettering Blvd Ste B (45439-2035)
PHONE.....................937 299-0298
David Schardt, *President*
Steven Schardt, *Sales Mgr*
EMP: 10
SQ FT: 5,600
SALES (est): 1.6MM Privately Held
WEB: www.forgeline.com
SIC: 3714 Wheels, motor vehicle

(G-14355)
GARDA CL TECHNICAL SVCS INC
2690 Lance Dr (45409-1527)
PHONE.....................937 294-4099
Steve Fosnot, *Branch Mgr*
EMP: 34 Privately Held
SIC: 7381 3578 4513 Armored car services; coin counters; air courier services
HQ: Garda Cl Technical Services, Inc.
700 S Federal Hwy Ste 300
Boca Raton FL 33432

(G-14356)
GLOBAL GAUGE CORPORATION
3200 Kettering Blvd (45439-1926)
PHONE.....................937 254-3500
Tim McCormick, *President*
Mark Cosculluela, *Production*
Brad Bernard, *Engineer*
Tom Fairchild, *Engineer*
Mike Welch, *Sales Staff*
EMP: 18
SQ FT: 45,000
SALES: 3.8MM Privately Held
WEB: www.globalgauge.com
SIC: 3829 Gauging instruments, thickness ultrasonic

(G-14357)
HAMILTON ANIMAL PRODUCTS LLC
2425 W Dorothy Ln (45439-1827)
PHONE.....................937 293-9994
Ashley Knowlton, *Accountant*
Dana Kilner, *HR Admin*
William Sherk,
▲ EMP: 20
SQ FT: 85,000
SALES (est): 2.7MM
SALES (corp-wide): 21MM Privately Held
WEB: www.hamiltonproducts.com
SIC: 3199 Harness or harness parts; dog furnishings: collars, leashes, muzzles, etc.: leather
PA: Miraclecorp Products
2425 W Dorothy Ln
Moraine OH 45439
937 293-9994

(G-14358)
HANGER PRSTHETCS & ORTHO INC
Also Called: Orpro Prosthetics & Orthotics
2000 Springboro W (45439-1648)
PHONE.....................937 643-1557
Ken Diskete, *Branch Mgr*
EMP: 15
SALES (corp-wide): 1B Publicly Held
SIC: 3842 Orthopedic & prosthesis applications
HQ: Hanger Prosthetics & Orthotics, Inc.
10910 Domain Dr Ste 300
Austin TX 78758
512 777-3800

(G-14359)
HARCO MANUFACTURING GROUP LLC (PA)
3535 Kettering Blvd (45439-2014)
PHONE.....................937 528-5000
Dennis Snider, *Controller*
Larry Harris,
Christina Harris,
▲ EMP: 300
SQ FT: 300,000

SALES (est): 57MM Privately Held
SIC: 3714 Motor vehicle brake systems & parts

(G-14360)
HARCO MANUFACTURING GROUP LLC
3535 Kettering Blvd 200 (45439-2014)
PHONE..................................937 528-5000
Tom Mc Nulty, *Branch Mgr*
EMP: 150 Privately Held
SIC: 3714 Motor vehicle brake systems & parts
PA: Harco Manufacturing Group, Llc
    3535 Kettering Blvd
    Moraine OH 45439

(G-14361)
JENA TOOL INC
5219 Springboro Pike (45439-2970)
PHONE..................................937 296-1122
George J Derr, *Chairman*
Dirk Unger, *Project Mgr*
Craig Johnson, *Engineer*
Shawn Miller, *CFO*
Susan Wolf, *Supervisor*
EMP: 74
SQ FT: 45,000
SALES (est): 12.8MM Privately Held
SIC: 3544 Special dies & tools

(G-14362)
JONES OLD RUSTIC SIGN
Also Called: Jones Signs
2758 Viking Ln (45439-1720)
PHONE..................................937 643-1695
Lorna Jones, *President*
Kenneth Jones, *Corp Secy*
Ken Jones, *Vice Pres*
Teresa Rutland, *Controller*
EMP: 40
SQ FT: 9,000
SALES: 1.2MM Privately Held
SIC: 3993 Signs, not made in custom sign painting shops

(G-14363)
KRAMER GRAPHICS INC
2408 W Dorothy Ln (45439-1828)
PHONE..................................937 296-9600
John Kramer Jr, *President*
David Vermette, *General Mgr*
Mary Lou Kramer, *Chairman*
Damon Davis, *Business Mgr*
Kelley Kramer, *Vice Pres*
▲ EMP: 50
SALES (est): 10.1MM Privately Held
WEB: www.kramergraphics.com
SIC: 2759 Commercial printing

(G-14364)
L M BERRY AND COMPANY (PA)
3170 Kettering Blvd (45439-1924)
PHONE..................................937 296-2121
Daniel J Graham, *President*
Greg Prince, *Opers Staff*
Joleen Neeley, *Manager*
Sonya Crocker, *Training Dir*
EMP: 650
SQ FT: 141,000
SALES (est): 69.2MM Privately Held
WEB: www.lmberry.com
SIC: 7311 2741 Advertising agencies; miscellaneous publishing

(G-14365)
L&H THREADED RODS CORP
3050 Dryden Rd (45439-1620)
PHONE..................................937 294-6666
John C Gray, *President*
Rob Herrmann, *QA Dir*
Jeff Schroder, *CFO*
Joe Young, *Sales Staff*
▲ EMP: 125
SQ FT: 45,000
SALES (est): 22.1MM
SALES (corp-wide): 45.1MM Privately Held
WEB: www.lhrods.com
SIC: 3312 Rods, iron & steel: made in steel mills
PA: Gray America Corp.
    3050 Dryden Rd
    Moraine OH 45439
    937 293-9213

(G-14366)
LANDIS DEFENSE SOLUTIONS
5335 Springboro Pike (45439-2913)
PHONE..................................937 938-0688
EMP: 3
SALES (est): 224.4K Privately Held
SIC: 3812 Defense systems & equipment

(G-14367)
MAR-CON TOOL COMPANY INC
2301 Arbor Blvd (45439-1788)
PHONE..................................937 299-2244
Gene A Hamrick, *President*
Gene Hamrick, *President*
Rodney Byrnes, *General Mgr*
Jeffrey Hecht, *COO*
Jeff Hamrick, *Vice Pres*
EMP: 25 EST: 1959
SQ FT: 15,500
SALES: 6MM Privately Held
WEB: www.marcontool.com
SIC: 3599 3728 3544 Machine shop, jobbing & repair; aircraft parts & equipment; special dies, tools, jigs & fixtures

(G-14368)
METALLURGICAL SERVICE INC
2221 Arbor Blvd (45439-1575)
PHONE..................................937 294-2681
William R Miller, *Ch of Bd*
Alice L Miller, *Corp Secy*
Robert Miller, *Vice Pres*
Thomas Miller, *Vice Pres*
EMP: 50
SQ FT: 45,000
SALES (est): 9.6MM
SALES (corp-wide): 19.3MM Privately Held
WEB: www.millerconsolidated.com
SIC: 3398 Metal heat treating
PA: Miller Consolidated Industries Inc
    2221 Arbor Blvd
    Moraine OH 45439
    937 294-2681

(G-14369)
METRO FLEX INC
3304 Encrete Ln (45439-1944)
PHONE..................................937 299-5360
Scot Terry, *CEO*
Charleston Cline, *Admin Sec*
EMP: 8
SALES (est): 1MM Privately Held
SIC: 2759 Screen printing

(G-14370)
MILLER CONSOLIDATED INDUSTRIES (PA)
2221 Arbor Blvd (45439-1521)
PHONE..................................937 294-2681
Larry Cartwright, *Vice Pres*
Tom Miller, *CFO*
Ben Eisbart, *Human Res Dir*
Kelly Henderson, *Director*
EMP: 106
SQ FT: 55,000
SALES (est): 19.3MM Privately Held
WEB: www.millerconsolidated.com
SIC: 5051 3398 Steel; metal heat treating

(G-14371)
MILLWORK FABRICATORS INC
3176 Kettering Blvd (45439-1924)
PHONE..................................937 299-5452
Dennis D Williams, *President*
EMP: 4 EST: 1979
SQ FT: 5,000
SALES (est): 505.3K
SALES (corp-wide): 14.4MM Privately Held
WEB: www.wilconcorp.com
SIC: 2431 Millwork
PA: Ddw Consulting, Inc.
    3176 Kettering Blvd
    Moraine OH 45439
    937 299-9920

(G-14372)
MIRACLECORP PRODUCTS (PA)
2425 W Dorothy Ln (45439-1827)
PHONE..................................937 293-9994
William M Sherk Jr, *President*
Patricia Weimer, *CFO*
Debbie Wietzel, *Sales Mgr*
Ron Castonguay, *Sales Staff*
Susie Lovy, *Mktg Dir*

◆ EMP: 55
SQ FT: 11,500
SALES: 21MM Privately Held
WEB: www.miraclecorp.com
SIC: 3999 0752 5999 Pet supplies; animal specialty services; pet supplies

(G-14373)
NEW DIMENSION METALS CORP
3050 Dryden Rd (45439-1620)
PHONE..................................937 299-2233
John Gray, *President*
Phil Huston, *Materials Mgr*
Kevin Lavery, *Opers Staff*
Jeff Schroder, *CFO*
Holly McReynolds, *Human Res Mgr*
▲ EMP: 40
SQ FT: 110,000
SALES (est): 19.2MM
SALES (corp-wide): 45.1MM Privately Held
WEB: www.grayamerica.com
SIC: 3316 Bars, steel, cold finished, from purchased hot-rolled
PA: Gray America Corp.
    3050 Dryden Rd
    Moraine OH 45439
    937 293-9313

(G-14374)
PARKER TRIAD STORE
2402 Springboro Pike (45439)
PHONE..................................937 293-4080
EMP: 99
SALES (est): 5.5MM Privately Held
SIC: 3511 Mfg Turbines/Generator Sets

(G-14375)
PERFORMNCE PLYMR SOLUTIONS INC
Also Called: Proof Research Acd
2711 Lance Dr (45409-1519)
PHONE..................................937 298-3713
Larry Murphy, *CEO*
David B Curliss, *President*
Jason Lincoln, *Vice Pres*
EMP: 14
SQ FT: 25,000
SALES: 1.5MM Privately Held
WEB: www.p2si.com
SIC: 8733 8731 8711 2821 Scientific research agency; commercial research laboratory; mechanical engineering; plastics materials & resins
PA: Proof Research, Inc.
    10 Western Village Ln
    Columbia Falls MT 59912

(G-14376)
PFLAUM PUBLISHING GROUP
3055 Kettering Blvd # 100 (45439-1900)
PHONE..................................937 293-1415
EMP: 5
SALES (est): 10.4K Privately Held
SIC: 2741 Miscellaneous publishing

(G-14377)
PJL ENTERPRISE INC (DH)
Also Called: Peter LI Education Group
3055 Kettering Blvd # 100 (45439-1989)
PHONE..................................937 293-1415
Peter J LI, *President*
Blair Downey, *Sales Staff*
EMP: 65 EST: 1971
SQ FT: 17,500
SALES (est): 8MM Privately Held
SIC: 2721 Magazines: publishing only, not printed on site
HQ: Bayard, Inc.
    1 Montauk Ave Ste 3
    New London CT 06320
    860 437-3012

(G-14378)
PJL ENTERPRISE INC
2019 Springboro W (45439-1665)
PHONE..................................937 293-1415
Peter LI, *President*
EMP: 25 Privately Held
SIC: 2721 Magazines: publishing only, not printed on site
HQ: Pjl Enterprise, Inc.
    3055 Kettering Blvd # 100
    Moraine OH 45439
    937 293-1415

(G-14379)
PLACECRETE INC
2475 Arbor Blvd (45439-1776)
PHONE..................................937 298-2121
Donald L Phlipot, *President*
EMP: 15
SQ FT: 17,000
SALES: 3MM Privately Held
SIC: 3273 Ready-mixed concrete

(G-14380)
POLAR INC
2297 N Moraine Dr (45439-1507)
P.O. Box 2995, Elkhart IN (46515-2995)
PHONE..................................937 297-0911
Robert J Crawford, *President*
Shaery Eilon, *Accounting Mgr*
▼ EMP: 10
SQ FT: 3,000
SALES (est): 2.6MM Privately Held
WEB: www.polarcompanies.com
SIC: 5169 5172 2841 Industrial chemicals; petroleum products; soap & other detergents

(G-14381)
PREMIER INV CAST GROUP LLC
3034 Dryden Rd (45439-1620)
PHONE..................................937 299-7333
Harry Greenhouse, *Partner*
Peter Tur, *Partner*
EMP: 35 EST: 2017
SALES: 6MM Privately Held
SIC: 3325 Steel foundries

(G-14382)
PREMIER INV CAST GROUP LLC
3034 Dryden Rd (45439-1620)
PHONE..................................413 727-2860
EMP: 35
SALES (est): 1.4MM Privately Held
SIC: 3324 Steel Investment Foundries

(G-14383)
PRINTING EXPRESS
3350 Kettering Blvd (45439-2011)
P.O. Box 456, Springboro (45066-0456)
PHONE..................................937 276-7794
James Armstrong, *Owner*
EMP: 6
SALES (est): 519.1K Privately Held
SIC: 2752 Commercial printing, lithographic

(G-14384)
PRO FAB WELDING SERVICE LLC (PA)
2765 Lance Dr (45409-1519)
PHONE..................................937 272-2142
Stephen Brandenburg, *Mng Member*
EMP: 5
SQ FT: 5,500
SALES (est): 419.4K Privately Held
SIC: 7692 Welding repair

(G-14385)
PRODUCTION CONTROL UNITS INC
2280 W Dorothy Ln (45439-1892)
PHONE..................................937 299-5594
Thomas Hoge, *President*
Jeff King, *Prdtn Mgr*
Jeff Elrod, *Mfg Mgr*
Nathan Baugh, *Purchasing*
William Sims, *Engineer*
▼ EMP: 100 EST: 1946
SQ FT: 58,000
SALES: 15MM Privately Held
WEB: www.sterlingpcu.com
SIC: 3829 3823 Measuring & controlling devices; industrial process control instruments

(G-14386)
PRODUCTION TURNING LLC
2490 Arbor Blvd Unit A (45439-1780)
PHONE..................................937 424-0034
Basil Morrison, *President*
Bob Kirk, *General Mgr*
Michael Turner, *Vice Pres*
EMP: 8
SALES (est): 1.1MM Privately Held
WEB: www.productionturning.com
SIC: 3714 Motor vehicle parts & accessories

Moraine - Montgomery County (G-14387)

(G-14387)
RACK PROCESSING COMPANY INC (PA)
2350 Arbor Blvd (45439-1760)
PHONE................................937 294-1911
Craig Coy, *President*
Kevyn Coy, *Vice Pres*
EMP: 50
SQ FT: 24,000
SALES: 21MM **Privately Held**
WEB: www.rackprocessing.com
SIC: 2542 3471 Partitions & fixtures, except wood; plating & polishing

(G-14388)
RACK PROCESSING COMPANY INC
Also Called: Pique Stripping Division
2350 Arbor Blvd (45439-1760)
PHONE................................937 294-1911
Dan Grammer, *Branch Mgr*
EMP: 45
SALES (corp-wide): 21MM **Privately Held**
WEB: www.rackprocessing.com
SIC: 3471 3479 2542 Plating & polishing; coating of metals with plastic or resins; racks, merchandise display or storage: except wood
PA: Rack Processing Company, Inc.
   2350 Arbor Blvd
   Moraine OH 45439
   937 294-1911

(G-14389)
RACO CUTTING INC (PA)
2230 E River Rd (45439-1519)
PHONE................................937 293-1228
Paul Etter, *President*
Mike Etter, *Treasurer*
Steve Etter, *Admin Sec*
EMP: 4
SQ FT: 5,000
SALES (est): 570.3K **Privately Held**
SIC: 3316 Cold finishing of steel shapes

(G-14390)
ROLLING ENTERPRISES INC
Also Called: Cat-Wood Metalworks
2701 Lance Dr (45409-1519)
PHONE................................937 866-4917
August Jay Rolling, *President*
EMP: 25
SALES (corp-wide): 2.5MM **Privately Held**
SIC: 3599 Machine shop, jobbing & repair
PA: Rolling Enterprises Inc
   2701 Lance Dr
   Moraine OH 45409
   719 659-6722

(G-14391)
S & J PRECISION INC
2015 Dryden Rd (45439-1741)
P.O. Box 562, Miamisburg (45343-0562)
PHONE................................937 296-0068
Forest Freeze, *President*
Judy Freeze, *Corp Secy*
EMP: 4
SALES (est): 300K **Privately Held**
SIC: 3312 Tool & die steel

(G-14392)
SANTOS INDUSTRIAL LTD (PA)
Also Called: Bimac
3034 Dryden Rd (45439-1620)
PHONE................................937 299-7333
Roberto Santos, *President*
EMP: 42 EST: 1958
SQ FT: 33,280
SALES (est): 5.2MM **Privately Held**
WEB: www.bimac.com
SIC: 3366 Copper foundries

(G-14393)
SANTOS INDUSTRIAL LTD
Also Called: Bimac Machine
2960 Springboro W (45439-1764)
PHONE................................937 299-7333
Bill Jordan, *Manager*
EMP: 3
SQ FT: 10,200
SALES (corp-wide): 5.2MM **Privately Held**
WEB: www.bimac.com
SIC: 3599 Machine shop, jobbing & repair
PA: Santos Industrial Ltd
   3034 Dryden Rd
   Moraine OH 45439
   937 299-7333

(G-14394)
SNYDER CONCRETE PRODUCTS INC (PA)
Also Called: Snyder Brick and Block
2301 W Dorothy Ln (45439-1825)
PHONE................................937 885-5176
Lee E Snyder, *CEO*
Mark Snyder, *Vice Pres*
Julie Flory, *Treasurer*
Todd Hopf, *Controller*
Joe Rohrer, *Sales Mgr*
▲ EMP: 25
SQ FT: 50,000
SALES (est): 12.6MM **Privately Held**
WEB: www.snyderonline.com
SIC: 5032 3271 3272 Brick, except refractory; concrete & cinder building products; blocks, concrete or cinder: standard; concrete products

(G-14395)
SOUTHPAW ENTERPRISES INC
2350 Dryden Rd (45439-1736)
P.O. Box 1047, Dayton (45401-1047)
PHONE................................937 252-7676
Frank Howard, *President*
Alex Moore, *VP Opers*
Mark Hamilton, *Engineer*
Paul Lauzau, *CFO*
▼ EMP: 34 EST: 1975
SQ FT: 37,500
SALES (est): 7.2MM **Privately Held**
WEB: www.southpawenterprises.com
SIC: 3842 Technical aids for the handicapped

(G-14396)
SUMMIT FINISHING TECHNOLOGIES
2490 Arbor Blvd Unit B (45439-1780)
PHONE................................937 424-5512
Robert Bauer, *CEO*
Christopher Panetta, *President*
EMP: 5
SALES (est): 266.2K **Privately Held**
SIC: 2796 Electrotype plates

(G-14397)
SUNSONG NORTH AMERICA INC
3535 Kettering Blvd (45439-2014)
PHONE................................919 365-3825
EMP: 4
SALES (est): 120K **Privately Held**
SIC: 3069 3999 Medical & laboratory rubber sundries & related products; atomizers, toiletry

(G-14398)
TAILORED SYSTEMS INC
Also Called: Vibrodyne Division
2853 Springboro W (45439-2045)
PHONE................................937 299-3900
Joseph Riess, *President*
Ron Logan, *Corp Secy*
John Riess, *Vice Pres*
Karen Berry, *Treasurer*
EMP: 7
SQ FT: 12,000
SALES (est): 800K **Privately Held**
WEB: www.vibrodyne.com
SIC: 3541 3599 Deburring machines; machine shop, jobbing & repair

(G-14399)
TKO MFG SERVICES INC
2360 W Dorothy Ln Ste 111 (45439-1861)
P.O. Box 2246, Dayton (45401-2246)
PHONE................................937 299-1637
Gary Keithley, *President*
Agripina Boettcher, *Vice Pres*
EMP: 22
SQ FT: 10,000
SALES (est): 2.5MM **Privately Held**
SIC: 3714 7389 Motor vehicle parts & accessories; packaging & labeling services

(G-14400)
WORLDWIDE MACHINING & MFG LLC
2300 Arbor Blvd (45439-1724)
PHONE................................937 902-5629
Justin McCarroll, *Principal*
Alica Irwin, *Principal*
EMP: 3 EST: 2017
SALES (est): 131.8K **Privately Held**
SIC: 3999 Manufacturing industries

Moreland Hills
Cuyahoga County

(G-14401)
BOWS BARRETTES & BAUBLES
4180 Chagrin River Rd (44022-1111)
PHONE................................440 247-2697
Cherrie Miller, *Owner*
EMP: 10
SALES (est): 300K **Privately Held**
SIC: 2353 Hats, trimmed: women's, misses' & children's

(G-14402)
PRECISION POLYMER CASTING LLC
140 Greentree Rd (44022-2424)
PHONE................................440 343-0461
Terry Capuano, *Principal*
EMP: 7
SALES (est): 907.9K **Privately Held**
SIC: 3325 Alloy steel castings, except investment

Morral
Marion County

(G-14403)
CONAGRA BRANDS INC
Golden Valley Microwave Foods
2970 County Highway 74 (43337-9206)
PHONE................................740 465-3912
William Harris, *Branch Mgr*
EMP: 13
SALES (corp-wide): 7.9B **Publicly Held**
WEB: www.conagra.com
SIC: 2099 Mfg Food Preparations
PA: Conagra Brands, Inc.
   222 Merchandise Mart Plz
   Chicago IL 60654
   312 549-5000

(G-14404)
J-LENCO INC
664 N High St (43337)
P.O. Box 346, La Rue (43332-0346)
PHONE................................740 499-2260
Edward P Murphy, *President*
Thomas A Frericks, *Principal*
Nancy Murphy, *Corp Secy*
Stephanie Forry, *Executive*
▲ EMP: 55
SALES (est): 11.6MM **Privately Held**
WEB: www.jlenco.com
SIC: 3543 Industrial patterns

(G-14405)
ROAD MAINTENANCE PRODUCTS
194 Center St (43337-7504)
P.O. Box 526 (43337-0526)
PHONE................................740 465-7181
James E Forry Jr, *President*
Barbara Forry, *Vice Pres*
EMP: 4 EST: 1994
SALES (est): 333.9K **Privately Held**
SIC: 1611 8742 2951 2911 Gravel or dirt road construction; industrial consultant; road materials, bituminous (not from refineries); road oils

Morristown
Belmont County

(G-14406)
BUCKEYE BRAKE MANUFACTURING
40168 National Rd W (43759)
PHONE................................740 782-1379
Greg Beckett, *President*
EMP: 10
SALES: 500K **Privately Held**
SIC: 3714 Motor vehicle brake systems & parts

Morrow
Warren County

(G-14407)
ACTION MACHINE & MANUFACTURING
6788 E Us Highway 22 & 3 (45152-9713)
PHONE................................513 899-3889
Delores Nadine Hartman, *President*
Nick Hartman, *Corp Secy*
Daryl Hartman, *Vice Pres*
EMP: 8 EST: 1963
SQ FT: 14,000
SALES (est): 568.1K **Privately Held**
SIC: 3599 Machine shop, jobbing & repair

(G-14408)
ARETE INNOVATIVE SOLUTIONS LLC
3050 Shawhan Rd (45152-8360)
PHONE................................513 503-2712
William Herman,
EMP: 5
SALES (est): 178.7K **Privately Held**
SIC: 3499 3544 3511 3563 Welding tips, heat resistant: metal; special dies, tools, jigs & fixtures; turbines & turbine generator sets; air & gas compressors; oil & gas drilling rigs & equipment

(G-14409)
CHRISTMAS RANCH LLC
3205 S Waynesville Rd (45152-8222)
PHONE................................513 505-3865
Debbie Fuchs, *Owner*
Michael Fuchs, *Owner*
EMP: 22
SALES (est): 2.8MM **Privately Held**
SIC: 3699 5999 Christmas tree lighting sets, electric; Christmas lights & decorations

(G-14410)
GRAVEL-TECH
4005 E Fster Mineville Rd (45152-8502)
PHONE................................513 703-3672
Michael Engel, *Principal*
EMP: 3
SALES (est): 195.6K **Privately Held**
SIC: 1442 Construction sand & gravel

(G-14411)
H E LONG COMPANY
3910 Anderson Rd (45152-7117)
P.O. Box 197 (45152-0197)
PHONE................................513 899-2610
Michael E Long, *President*
Richard Long, *Vice Pres*
Rick Long, *Software Dev*
EMP: 10
SALES (est): 1.2MM **Privately Held**
WEB: www.helongco.com
SIC: 3545 5084 Shaping tools (machine tool accessories); metalworking tools (such as drills, taps, dies, files)

(G-14412)
ISAACS JR FLOYD THOMAS
Also Called: 4 Him Sales
3480 E Us Highway 22 & 3 (45152-8237)
PHONE................................513 899-2342
Floyd Isaacs Jr, *Mng Member*
EMP: 9 EST: 2010
SALES: 500K **Privately Held**
SIC: 5561 3792 Camper & travel trailer dealers; tent-type camping trailers

▲ = Import ▼ = Export
◆ = Import/Export

GEOGRAPHIC SECTION

Mount Hope - Holmes County (G-14438)

(G-14413)
MORROW GRAVEL COMPANY INC
Also Called: Valley Asphalt
4850 Stubbs Mills Rd (45152-8340)
PHONE..................513 899-2000
Rick Dostal, *Superintendent*
EMP: 14
SALES (corp-wide): 26MM **Privately Held**
SIC: 1442 Gravel mining
PA: Morrow Gravel Company Inc
11641 Mosteller Rd
Cincinnati OH 45241
513 771-0820

(G-14414)
OZONE SYSTEMS SVCS GROUP INC
6687 State Route 132 (45152-8143)
PHONE..................513 899-4131
Ataur C Rehman, *President*
EMP: 3 EST: 1999
SALES (est): 1MM **Privately Held**
SIC: 8711 3441 7349 Consulting engineer; fabricated structural metal; chemical cleaning services

(G-14415)
STEPHEN R LILLEY
Also Called: Lilleys Fabrication and Design
2900 S Waynesville Rd (45152-9619)
PHONE..................513 899-4400
Stephen R Lilley, *Owner*
EMP: 4
SQ FT: 5,000
SALES: 300K **Privately Held**
SIC: 3299 2541 Moldings, architectural: plaster of paris; store & office display cases & fixtures

(G-14416)
VALLEY ASPHALT CORPORATION
Also Called: Morrow Gravel
4850 Stubbs Mills Rd (45152-8340)
PHONE..................513 381-0652
Bob Ftayton, *Manager*
EMP: 8
SALES (corp-wide): 84MM **Privately Held**
SIC: 2951 Asphalt paving mixtures & blocks
HQ: Valley Asphalt Corporation
11641 Mosteller Rd
Cincinnati OH 45241
513 771-0820

(G-14417)
VALLEY MACHINE TOOL CO INC
9773 Morrow Cozaddale Rd (45152-8589)
PHONE..................513 899-2737
Larry R Wilson, *President*
Douglas Wilson, *Corp Secy*
Ralph Wilson, *Vice Pres*
EMP: 40
SQ FT: 11,000
SALES (est): 6.5MM **Privately Held**
SIC: 3599 7692 Machine shop, jobbing & repair; welding repair

Mount Cory
Hancock County

(G-14418)
SNAPS INC
2557 Township Road 35 (45868-9701)
PHONE..................419 477-5100
Nancy Ruppright, *President*
Gary Ruppright, *Vice Pres*
EMP: 6
SALES: 100K **Privately Held**
SIC: 2389 Theatrical costumes

Mount Eaton
Wayne County

(G-14419)
DUTCH QUALITY STONE INC
18012 Dover Rd (44659)
P.O. Box 308 (44659-0308)
PHONE..................877 359-7866
Freeman H Mullet, *President*
▲ EMP: 30
SQ FT: 40,000
SALES (est): 4.6MM **Privately Held**
WEB: www.dutchqualitystone.com
SIC: 3281 Cut stone & stone products
HQ: Headwaters Incorporated
10701 S River Front Pkwy # 300
South Jordan UT 84095

(G-14420)
FLEX TECHNOLOGIES INC
Also Called: Mount Eaton Division
16183 E Main St (44659)
P.O. Box 223 (44659-0223)
PHONE..................330 359-5415
Jim Eichel, *Manager*
EMP: 80
SALES (corp-wide): 6MM **Privately Held**
WEB: www.flextechnologies.com
SIC: 3089 3714 3694 3564 Injection molding of plastics; motor vehicle parts & accessories; engine electrical equipment; blowers & fans
PA: Flex Technologies, Inc.
5479 Gundy Dr
Midvale OH 44653
740 922-5992

(G-14421)
QUALITY BLOCK & SUPPLY INC (DH)
Rr 250 (44659)
PHONE..................330 364-4411
Jerry A Schwab, *President*
David Schwab, *Vice Pres*
Donna Schwab, *Admin Sec*
EMP: 27
SQ FT: 4,000
SALES (est): 2.2MM
SALES (corp-wide): 29.7B **Privately Held**
SIC: 3271 3273 5032 Blocks, concrete or cinder: standard; ready-mixed concrete; concrete & cinder block
HQ: Schwab Industries, Inc.
2301 Progress St
Dover OH 44622
330 364-4411

Mount Gilead
Morrow County

(G-14422)
CONSOLIDATED GAS COOP INC
5255 State Route 95 (43338-9763)
PHONE..................419 946-6600
Nancy Salyer, *CFO*
EMP: 6
SALES (est): 721.9K **Privately Held**
SIC: 1321 Propane (natural) production

(G-14423)
EDCO PRODUCING
869 Meadow Dr (43338-1069)
P.O. Box 329 (43338-0329)
PHONE..................419 947-2515
Alan Jones, *President*
Eric Brown, *Vice Pres*
Wanda Jones, *Admin Sec*
EMP: 3
SQ FT: 3,000
SALES (est): 337.9K **Privately Held**
SIC: 1311 Natural gas production

(G-14424)
GERICH FIBERGLASS INC
7004 Us Highway 42 (43338-9638)
PHONE..................419 362-4591
Anton J Gerich, *President*
Lila S Gerich, *Vice Pres*
EMP: 30
SQ FT: 20,000
SALES (est): 1.5MM **Privately Held**
WEB: www.fibrecore.com
SIC: 3714 3713 3715 3792 Motor vehicle body components & frame; bus bodies (motor vehicles); trailer bodies; travel trailers & campers

(G-14425)
HARTMAN PRINTING CO
425 W Marion St (43338-1386)
PHONE..................419 946-2854
Steve Hartman, *Owner*
Karen Hartman, *Co-Owner*
EMP: 4
SQ FT: 5,000
SALES (est): 357K **Privately Held**
WEB: www.hartmanprinting.com
SIC: 2752 Commercial printing, offset

(G-14426)
HIRT PUBLISHING CO INC
Also Called: Marrow County Sentinel
245 Neal Ave Ste A (43338-9372)
P.O. Box 149 (43338-0149)
PHONE..................419 946-3010
Vicki Taylor, *Manager*
EMP: 25
SALES (corp-wide): 5.4MM **Privately Held**
SIC: 2711 5999 Newspapers, publishing & printing; rubber stamps
PA: Hirt Publishing Co, Inc
224 E Main St
Ottawa OH 45875
419 523-5709

(G-14427)
LILLY INDUSTRIES INC (PA)
Also Called: Lightning Bolt Fastners
6437 County Road 20 (43338-9624)
PHONE..................419 946-7908
Phil Lilly, *President*
Alvin Lilly, *Vice Pres*
EMP: 20
SQ FT: 8,000
SALES (est): 2.7MM **Privately Held**
SIC: 3441 Fabricated structural metal

(G-14428)
MARROW COUNTY SENTINEL
245 Neal Ave Ste A (43338-9372)
PHONE..................419 946-3010
EMP: 4
SALES (est): 182.5K **Privately Held**
SIC: 2711 Newspapers

(G-14429)
MEANS OF DEFENSE
7326 State Route 19 (43338-9354)
PHONE..................740 513-6210
Donna Schoonard, *Principal*
EMP: 3
SALES (est): 199.7K **Privately Held**
SIC: 3812 Defense systems & equipment

(G-14430)
POP A TOP CRUISE THRU
157 S Main St (43338-1409)
PHONE..................419 947-5855
Nikki Farson, *Owner*
EMP: 3
SALES (est): 181.2K **Privately Held**
SIC: 2082 Beer (alcoholic beverage)

(G-14431)
R M WOOD CO
5795 County Road 30 (43338-9701)
PHONE..................419 845-2661
Roy Murphey, *Administration*
EMP: 5
SALES (est): 279.8K **Privately Held**
SIC: 2421 2499 Sawmills & planing mills, general; wood products

(G-14432)
SHOPPERS COMPASS
114 Iberia St (43338-1263)
P.O. Box 109 (43338-0109)
PHONE..................419 947-9234
James Walsh, *Partner*
EMP: 3 EST: 1995
SALES (est): 229.6K **Privately Held**
SIC: 2741 Guides: publishing only, not printed on site; shopping news: publishing only, not printed on site

(G-14433)
SIGN CITY INC
5357 State Route 95 (43338-9764)
PHONE..................614 486-6700
EMP: 4
SALES (est): 460.1K **Privately Held**
SIC: 7336 3993 Commercial Art/Graphic Design Mfg Signs/Advertising Specialties

(G-14434)
SNYDER FABRICATION LLC
6145 County Road 30 (43338-9705)
PHONE..................419 946-6616
Terri Snyder,
Robert T Snyder,
EMP: 5
SQ FT: 1,800
SALES (est): 1MM **Privately Held**
WEB: www.snyderfab.com
SIC: 3599 Machine shop, jobbing & repair

(G-14435)
TS SALES LLC
Also Called: Top Shot Ammunition
255 Neal Ave (43338-9787)
PHONE..................727 804-8060
Mark Schneider, *Mng Member*
EMP: 15
SALES: 2MM **Privately Held**
SIC: 5941 3484 Firearms; guns (firearms) or gun parts, 30 mm. & below

Mount Hope
Holmes County

(G-14436)
ERVIN YODER
Also Called: Mount Hope Harness & Shoe
7700 County Rd 77 (44660)
P.O. Box 32 (44660-0032)
PHONE..................330 359-5862
Ervin S Yoder, *Owner*
EMP: 3 EST: 1986
SALES (est): 362.1K **Privately Held**
SIC: 5661 3199 Shoe stores; harness or harness parts

(G-14437)
GMI HOLDINGS INC (DH)
Also Called: Genie Company, The
1 Door Dr (44660)
P.O. Box 67 (44660-0067)
PHONE..................330 821-5360
Mike Kridel, *President*
Carl Adrien, *Principal*
Craig Smith, *Vice Pres*
David Osso, *Marketing Staff*
Brandie Stanley, *Planning*
▲ EMP: 350
SQ FT: 230,000
SALES (est): 142.1MM
SALES (corp-wide): 3.6B **Privately Held**
WEB: www.geniecompany.com
SIC: 3699 3635 Door opening & closing devices, electrical; household vacuum cleaners
HQ: Overhead Door Corporation
2501 S State Hwy 121 Ste
Lewisville TX 75067
469 549-7100

(G-14438)
HRH DOOR CORP (PA)
Also Called: Wayne Dalton
1 Door Dr (44660)
PHONE..................850 208-3400
Willis Mullet, *CEO*
Thomas B Bennett III, *President*
E E Muller, *Principal*
Alma Mullet, *Principal*
W C Pyers, *Principal*
◆ EMP: 650
SQ FT: 1,000,000
SALES (est): 621.6MM **Privately Held**
WEB: www.waynedalton.com
SIC: 3442 2431 Garage doors, overhead: metal; garage doors, overhead: wood

Mount Orab
Brown County

(G-14439)
CINCINNATI DOWEL & WD PDTS CO
135 Oak St (45154-9090)
PHONE.................................937 444-2502
William Streight, *President*
Eric Frey, *Sales Staff*
Melissa Hacker, *Admin Mgr*
Jerry Streight, *Technology*
◆ **EMP:** 25
SQ FT: 2,400
SALES (est): 3.5MM **Privately Held**
WEB: www.cincinnatidowel.com
SIC: 2499 Dowels, wood; carved & turned wood

(G-14440)
CINDOCO WOOD PRODUCTS CO
Also Called: Craftwood
410 Mount Clifton Dr (45154-9353)
PHONE.................................937 444-2504
Melissa Hacker, *President*
EMP: 6
SALES (est): 255.6K **Privately Held**
SIC: 5099 2431 Wood & wood by-products; millwork

(G-14441)
CLERMONT SUN PUBLISHING CO
Also Called: Brown County Press
219 S High St (45154-9039)
PHONE.................................937 444-3441
Steve Large, *Manager*
EMP: 4
SALES (corp-wide): 2.9MM **Privately Held**
WEB: www.clermontsun.com
SIC: 2711 Commercial printing & newspaper publishing combined
PA: Clermont Sun Publishing Company, Inc.
465 E Main St
Batavia OH
513 732-2511

(G-14442)
HAWKLINE NEVADA LLC
200 Front St (45154-8964)
PHONE.................................937 444-4295
John Burgess,
Larry Danna,
▲ **EMP:** 50
SQ FT: 150,000
SALES (est): 6.7MM **Privately Held**
WEB: www.gohawkline.com
SIC: 3523 3799 Cabs, tractors & agricultural machinery; trailers & trailer equipment

(G-14443)
HIGHLAND TECHNOLOGIES LLC
630 Harwood Rd (45154-8797)
PHONE.................................513 739-3510
Lester E McFarland, *Principal*
EMP: 4
SALES: 250K **Privately Held**
SIC: 3999 Manufacturing industries

(G-14444)
HIRONS MEMORIAL WORKS INC
14950 Us Highway 68 (45154-9701)
PHONE.................................937 444-2917
Ronald Hirons, *President*
Jane Hirons, *Corp Secy*
John Hirons, *Vice Pres*
EMP: 5
SQ FT: 10,000
SALES (est): 640.6K **Privately Held**
WEB: www.hironsmemorials.com
SIC: 5999 5084 3589 Monuments, finished to custom order; industrial machinery & equipment; sandblasting equipment

(G-14445)
HM DEFENSE
222 Homan Way (45154-8269)
P.O. Box 253 (45154-0253)
PHONE.................................513 260-6200
Clay Barker, *Principal*
EMP: 3 **EST:** 2017
SALES (est): 207.1K **Privately Held**
SIC: 3812 Defense systems & equipment

(G-14446)
LUXUS PRODUCTS LLC
Also Called: Luxus Arms
222 Homan Way (45154-8269)
P.O. Box 11 (45154-0011)
PHONE.................................937 444-6500
Clay Barker, *Principal*
EMP: 6
SALES (est): 400K **Privately Held**
SIC: 2491 Structural lumber & timber, treated wood

(G-14447)
MILACRON PLAS TECH GROUP LLC
418 W Main St (45154-9596)
PHONE.................................937 444-2532
James Kinzie, *General Mgr*
Dick Colwell, *Manager*
EMP: 183
SALES (corp-wide): 1.2B **Publicly Held**
SIC: 3544 Forms (molds), for foundry & plastics working machinery
HQ: Milacron Plastics Technologies Group Llc
4165 Half Acre Rd
Batavia OH 45103

(G-14448)
NORTH HIGH MARATHON
570 N High St (45154-7902)
PHONE.................................937 444-1894
Imad Shattya, *Owner*
EMP: 4
SALES (est): 252.4K **Privately Held**
SIC: 3443 Fuel tanks (oil, gas, etc.): metal plate

(G-14449)
PRECISION WELDING & MFG
101 Day Rd (45154-8924)
P.O. Box 369 (45154-0369)
PHONE.................................937 444-6925
Dan Fisher, *President*
EMP: 18
SQ FT: 20,000
SALES (est): 1.4MM **Privately Held**
WEB: www.danfisher.com
SIC: 3441 Fabricated structural metal

(G-14450)
PRO-TECH MANUFACTURING INC
14944 Hillcrest Rd (45154-8513)
PHONE.................................937 444-6484
Patrick Gregory, *President*
Jeff Roades, *Vice Pres*
EMP: 10
SQ FT: 9,000
SALES (est): 1.4MM **Privately Held**
SIC: 3599 Machine shop, jobbing & repair

(G-14451)
R K COMBUSTION & CONTROLS
212 Hughes Blvd (45154-8325)
PHONE.................................937 444-9700
Robert Krueger, *President*
Kathleen E Krueger, *Vice Pres*
EMP: 8
SALES (est): 82.1K **Privately Held**
WEB: www.rkcombustion.com
SIC: 3567 3823 Industrial furnaces & ovens; combustion control instruments

(G-14452)
WEDCO LLC
Also Called: Bardwell Winery
716 N High St (45154-8349)
P.O. Box 391 (45154-0391)
PHONE.................................513 309-0781
Roy R Weddle, *Mng Member*
EMP: 6
SALES: 130K **Privately Held**
SIC: 6531 2082 5182 Real estate brokers & agents; brewers' grain; wine

(G-14453)
X-MIL INC
220 Homan Way (45154-8269)
P.O. Box 452 (45154-0452)
PHONE.................................937 444-1323
Steven E Seibert, *President*
Erica Carpenter, *General Mgr*
Joel Scott Dalton, *Vice Pres*
Steve Dalton, *Info Tech Mgr*
Angie Kreidler, *Admin Sec*
EMP: 20
SALES (est): 1.2MM **Privately Held**
WEB: www.x-mil.com
SIC: 3599 Machine shop, jobbing & repair

Mount Perry
Perry County

(G-14454)
B & D COMMISSARY LLC
5705 State Route 204 Ne (43760)
PHONE.................................740 743-3890
William Dugas, *Partner*
David Dugas, *Partner*
EMP: 30
SALES (est): 3.2MM **Privately Held**
SIC: 2045 Pizza doughs, prepared: from purchased flour

(G-14455)
MAYSVILLE MATERIALS LLC
6535 Old Town Rd (43760-1100)
PHONE.................................740 849-0474
EMP: 6
SALES (est): 429.1K **Privately Held**
SIC: 1422 Crushed & broken limestone

(G-14456)
MT PERRY FOODS INC
5705 State Route 204 Ne (43760-9733)
P.O. Box 159, Glenford (43739-0159)
PHONE.................................740 743-3890
Reg Martin, *President*
John Largent, *Vice Pres*
Ron Pratt, *Maintence Staff*
EMP: 75 **EST:** 2000
SALES (est): 15.6MM **Privately Held**
WEB: www.perrycountyohiocofc.com
SIC: 2499 Food handling & processing products, wood

(G-14457)
PRECISION GEOPHYSICAL INC
4700 Rucker Rd (43760-9613)
PHONE.................................740 849-3044
EMP: 10
SALES (corp-wide): 4.8MM **Privately Held**
SIC: 1382 Gas And Oil Exploration
PA: Precision Geophysical Inc
2695 State Route 83
Millersburg OH 44654
330 674-2198

(G-14458)
S & S SPRING SHOP
1755 Mount Perry Rd (43760-9641)
PHONE.................................800 619-4652
Fred Bates, *Owner*
Gary Smith, *Owner*
James D Smith, *Partner*
EMP: 4
SQ FT: 2,400
SALES (est): 152.4K **Privately Held**
SIC: 7692 0721 Welding repair; planting services

(G-14459)
SMITH SPRINGS INC
1755 Mount Perry Rd (43760-9641)
PHONE.................................800 619-4652
Gary B Smith, *President*
Roxy R Smith, *Vice Pres*
EMP: 4
SALES (est): 345.1K **Privately Held**
SIC: 7692 7539 Welding repair; automotive repair shops

Mount Sterling
Madison County

(G-14460)
BLESCO SERVICES
8905 Mckendree Rd (43143-9120)
PHONE.................................614 871-4900
Brian Spangler, *President*
EMP: 4
SALES (est): 286.7K **Privately Held**
SIC: 3444 Sheet metalwork

(G-14461)
FURNISS CORPORATION LTD
15812 State Route 56 W (43143-9532)
P.O. Box 128 (43143-0128)
PHONE.................................614 871-1470
Andy Furniss, *Managing Prtnr*
Elizabeth Furniss, *Info Tech Mgr*
EMP: 19 **EST:** 1997
SQ FT: 27,000
SALES (est): 3.3MM **Privately Held**
WEB: www.furnisscorp.com
SIC: 3845 Electromedical apparatus

(G-14462)
KEIHIN THERMAL TECH AMER INC
10500 Oday Harrison Rd (43143-9474)
PHONE.................................740 869-3000
Tatsuhiko Arai, *President*
Scott Amortimer, *Vice Pres*
◆ **EMP:** 475
SALES (est): 133.1MM
SALES (corp-wide): 3.3B **Privately Held**
SIC: 5013 3714 Automotive engines & engine parts; motor vehicle engines & parts
PA: Keihin Corporation
1-26-2, Nishishinjuku
Shinjuku-Ku TKY 160-0
333 453-411

(G-14463)
LANDSCAPE GROUP LLC
15740 Scioto Darby Rd (43143-9036)
PHONE.................................614 302-4537
Greg Whaley,
EMP: 3
SALES (est): 241.4K **Privately Held**
SIC: 3523 Grounds mowing equipment

(G-14464)
OHIO WILLOW WOOD COMPANY
Also Called: Willowwood
15441 Scioto Darby Rd (43143-9036)
P.O. Box 130 (43143-0130)
PHONE.................................740 869-3377
Ryan Arbogast, *President*
John Choi, *General Mgr*
C Joseph Arbogast, *Exec VP*
Robert E Arbogast, *Vice Pres*
Mitchell Neff, *Facilities Dir*
▲ **EMP:** 205 **EST:** 1907
SQ FT: 90,000
SALES: 25MM **Privately Held**
WEB: www.owwco.com
SIC: 3842 Limbs, artificial; prosthetic appliances

(G-14465)
STEPHENS PIPE & STEEL LLC
10732 Schadel Ln (43143-9731)
P.O. Box 237 (43143-0237)
PHONE.................................740 869-2257
Rick Redman, *Principal*
Don Bowsher, *Manager*
Barb Stephens, *Executive Asst*
EMP: 150 **Privately Held**
WEB: www.stephenspipeandsteel.com
SIC: 3315 3523 3496 3494 Chain link fencing; farm machinery & equipment; miscellaneous fabricated wire products; valves & pipe fittings; architectural metalwork
HQ: Stephens Pipe & Steel, Llc
2224 E Highway 619
Russell Springs KY 42642
270 866-3331

Mount Vernon - Knox County (G-14495)

(G-14466)
WATERSHED MANGEMENT LLC
Also Called: Nancy Blanket
10460 State Route 56 Se (43143-9429)
PHONE.................................740 852-5607
Carl Hamman,
EMP: 10
SALES: 500K Privately Held
SIC: 5023 2399 Blankets; aprons, breast (harness)

Mount Vernon
Knox County

(G-14467)
AMG INDUSTRIES LLC
200 Commerce Dr (43050-4699)
PHONE.................................740 397-4044
David J McElroy, *President*
James McElroy, *COO*
Dennis McElroy, *Exec VP*
Mike Miller, *Vice Pres*
Jodean Pagani, *Purch Mgr*
EMP: 100
SQ FT: 120,000
SALES (est): 47.8MM Privately Held
WEB: www.amgindustries.com
SIC: 3469 Metal stampings
PA: Reserve Group Management Company
3560 W Market St Ste 300
Fairlawn OH 44333

(G-14468)
ARIEL CORPORATION
35 Blackjack Road Ext (43050-9482)
PHONE.................................740 397-0311
Karen Buchwald Wright, *President*
EMP: 8
SALES (corp-wide): 138.7MM Privately Held
SIC: 3563 Air & gas compressors
PA: Ariel Corporation
35 Blackjack Road Ext
Mount Vernon OH 43050
740 397-0311

(G-14469)
ARIEL CORPORATION
8405 Blackjack Rd (43050-2781)
PHONE.................................740 397-0311
EMP: 14
SALES (est): 2.1MM Privately Held
SIC: 3563 Air & gas compressors

(G-14470)
BENCHMARK CABINETS
17239 Sycamore Rd (43050-8527)
PHONE.................................740 397-4615
Wesley Crum, *Owner*
EMP: 22
SALES (est): 834.1K Privately Held
SIC: 2434 Wood kitchen cabinets

(G-14471)
C-H TOOL & DIE
Also Called: Ch Tool & Die
711 N Sandusky St (43050-1034)
P.O. Box 889 (43050-0889)
PHONE.................................740 397-7214
David Davison, *Owner*
EMP: 5
SQ FT: 10,000
SALES (est): 435.2K Privately Held
WEB: www.ch4d.com
SIC: 3423 3544 Tools or equipment for use with sporting arms; special dies & tools

(G-14472)
CAMERON INTERNATIONAL CORP
Also Called: Cooper Energy Services
8043 Columbus Rd (43050-9358)
PHONE.................................740 397-4888
Barry Thompson, *Principal*
EMP: 5 Publicly Held
SIC: 3519 Internal combustion engines
HQ: Cameron International Corporation
4646 W Sam Houston Pkwy N
Houston TX 77041

(G-14473)
CAPITAL CITY OIL INC
Also Called: American Energy Pdts Inc Ind
375 Columbus Rd (43050-4427)
PHONE.................................740 397-4483
Roy Bailey, *President*
EMP: 6
SALES (est): 750K Privately Held
SIC: 2911 4953 Oils, fuel; refuse systems

(G-14474)
CENTRAL OHIO FABRICATORS LLC
105 Progress Dr (43050-4772)
PHONE.................................740 393-3892
Barry Jacobs,
EMP: 50
SQ FT: 22,000
SALES (est): 9.4MM Privately Held
SIC: 3441 Fabricated structural metal

(G-14475)
CITY OF MOUNT VERNON
Also Called: Water & Waste Water Dept.
1550 Old Delaware Rd (43050-8631)
PHONE.................................740 393-9508
Judie Scott, *Administration*
EMP: 8 Privately Held
WEB: www.mountvernonohio.org
SIC: 2899 Water treating compounds
PA: City Of Mount Vernon
40 Public Sq Ste 206
Mount Vernon OH 43050
740 393-9520

(G-14476)
CLIFFS HIGH PERFORMANCE
20579 Berry Rd (43050-9226)
PHONE.................................740 397-2921
Cliff Ruggles, *Owner*
EMP: 3
SALES (est): 203.8K Privately Held
SIC: 3462 Automotive & internal combustion engine forgings

(G-14477)
DANDY PRODUCTS INC
1095 Harcourt Rd Ste C (43050-4476)
PHONE.................................800 591-2284
Dan Cleveland, *Branch Mgr*
EMP: 5 Privately Held
WEB: www.dandyproducts.com
SIC: 3531 Construction machinery
PA: Dandy Products Inc
Dublin OH 43016

(G-14478)
DIVERSIFIED PRODUCTS & SVCS
1250 Vernonview Dr (43050-1447)
PHONE.................................740 393-6202
Louis Ohara, *Director*
EMP: 118
SALES (est): 6.6MM Privately Held
SIC: 5199 2541 2511 Packaging materials; wood partitions & fixtures; wood household furniture

(G-14479)
DOWN HOME
Also Called: Down Home Leather
9 N Main St (43050-3203)
PHONE.................................740 393-1186
Laurel Lee Wagoner, *Owner*
EMP: 8
SQ FT: 5,000
SALES (est): 300K Privately Held
WEB: www.downhomeleather.com
SIC: 5947 3172 Gift shop; personal leather goods

(G-14480)
ENERGY MACHINE INC
100 Commerce Dr (43050-4641)
PHONE.................................740 397-1155
Brian Meier, *Manager*
Karen Buchwald Wright,
▲ EMP: 50
SQ FT: 60,000
SALES (est): 6.5MM Privately Held
WEB: www.energy-machine.com
SIC: 3599 Machine shop, jobbing & repair; crankshafts & camshafts, machining

(G-14481)
FAMOUS INDUSTRIES INC
Also Called: Heating & Cooling Products
325 Commerce Dr (43050-4643)
PHONE.................................740 397-8842
Don Smith, *General Mgr*
N M Greenberger, *Principal*
Harold J Rothwell, *Principal*
H A Sullivan, *Principal*
Donnie Hyatt, *Plant Mgr*
EMP: 160 Privately Held
WEB: www.jfgoodco.com
SIC: 3444 3585 3312 Sheet metalwork; refrigeration & heating equipment; blast furnaces & steel mills
HQ: Famous Industries, Inc.
2620 Ridgewood Rd Ste 200
Akron OH 44313
330 535-1811

(G-14482)
GOOD IMPRESSIONS LLC
205 S Mulberry St (43050-3329)
PHONE.................................740 392-4327
Ellen L Smith,
EMP: 3
SALES: 130K Privately Held
WEB: www.goodpress.biz
SIC: 2752 Commercial printing, offset

(G-14483)
INTERNATIONAL PAPER COMPANY
8800 Granville Rd (43050-9192)
PHONE.................................740 397-5215
Mark Smith, *Branch Mgr*
EMP: 180
SALES (corp-wide): 23.3B Publicly Held
WEB: www.internationalpaper.com
SIC: 2621 Paper mills
PA: International Paper Company
6400 Poplar Ave
Memphis TN 38197
901 419-9000

(G-14484)
J B KEPPLE SHEET METAL
1010 Vernonview Dr (43050-1451)
PHONE.................................740 393-2971
Michael Kepple, *Owner*
EMP: 3
SALES: 250K Privately Held
SIC: 3444 3496 3443 3429 Sheet metal specialties, not stamped; miscellaneous fabricated wire products; fabricated plate work (boiler shop); manufactured hardware (general)

(G-14485)
JELD-WEN INC
Also Called: Jeld-Wen Windows
1201 Newark Rd (43050-4728)
PHONE.................................740 397-1144
Brad Hunter, *Manager*
EMP: 345 Publicly Held
WEB: www.jeld-wen.com
SIC: 2431 Doors, wood
HQ: Jeld-Wen, Inc.
2645 Silver Crescent Dr
Charlotte NC 28273
800 535-3936

(G-14486)
JELD-WEN INC
335 Commerce Dr (43050-4643)
PHONE.................................740 397-3403
Ted Schnormeier, *Branch Mgr*
EMP: 20 Publicly Held
WEB: www.jeld-wen.com
SIC: 2431 Doors, wood
HQ: Jeld-Wen, Inc.
2645 Silver Crescent Dr
Charlotte NC 28273
800 535-3936

(G-14487)
KNOX MACHINE & TOOL
250 Columbus Rd (43050-4428)
PHONE.................................740 392-3133
Korby Bricker, *President*
Trent Hauke, *Corp Secy*
EMP: 9
SALES (est): 1MM Privately Held
SIC: 3599 Machine shop, jobbing & repair

(G-14488)
LANES WELDING & REPAIR
9180 Kinney Rd (43050-9333)
PHONE.................................740 397-2525
Frank H Lane, *Owner*
EMP: 3
SQ FT: 2,400
SALES (est): 121.6K Privately Held
SIC: 7692 Welding repair

(G-14489)
LONGRIDERS TRUCKING COMPANY
7 Delano St (43050-4503)
P.O. Box 4006, Newark (43058-4006)
PHONE.................................740 975-7863
Debra Smith, *Principal*
EMP: 5
SALES: 67K Privately Held
SIC: 3715 Truck trailers

(G-14490)
MARKT
1095 Harcourt Rd Ste A (43050-4476)
PHONE.................................740 397-5900
Mary Koscielniak, *Accounts Mgr*
Kaycee Chang, *Manager*
Taylor Todd, *Administration*
EMP: 7 EST: 2012
SALES: 860K Privately Held
SIC: 5699 2395 2759 Uniforms & work clothing; embroidery & art needlework; screen printing

(G-14491)
MAUSER USA LLC
219 Commerce Dr (43050-4645)
PHONE.................................614 856-5982
EMP: 45
SALES (corp-wide): 1.1B Privately Held
SIC: 3412 Mfg Metal Barrels/Pails
HQ: Mauser Usa, Llc
2 Tower Center Blvd 20-1
East Brunswick NJ 08816
732 353-7100

(G-14492)
MAUSER USA LLC
219 Commerce Dr (43050-4645)
PHONE.................................614 856-5982
Brad Strawser, *General Ptnr*
Bradley Strawser, *Manager*
EMP: 25 EST: 1985
SQ FT: 70,000
SALES (est): 6.3MM Privately Held
SIC: 3412 Metal barrels, drums & pails

(G-14493)
MOHAWK MANUFACTURING INC
306 E Gambier St (43050-3514)
PHONE.................................860 632-2345
Walter Nacey, *President*
EMP: 8
SALES (est): 649.9K Privately Held
SIC: 3469 Stamping metal for the trade

(G-14494)
MOUNT VERNON PACKAGING INC
135 Progress Dr (43050-4772)
P.O. Box 950 (43050-0950)
PHONE.................................740 397-3221
Donald Nuce, *President*
Margo Nuce, *Vice Pres*
EMP: 10
SALES (est): 2.2MM Privately Held
SIC: 2653 Boxes, corrugated: made from purchased materials

(G-14495)
MT VERNON CY WASTEWATER TRTMNT
3 Cougar Dr Unit 3 # 3 (43050-3866)
PHONE.................................740 393-9502
Mathias Orndorf, *Director*
Judi Scott, *Administration*
EMP: 12
SALES (est): 1.9MM Privately Held
SIC: 3589 Water treatment equipment, industrial

Mount Vernon - Knox County

(G-14496)
NOVOLEX HOLDINGS INC
Also Called: Packaging Div
101 Commerce Dr (43050-4646)
PHONE..................740 397-2555
Andy Frazee, *Production*
EMP: 78
SALES (corp-wide): 3B **Privately Held**
WEB: www.burrowspaper.com
SIC: 2621 2672 2671 Tissue paper; coated & laminated paper; waxed paper: made from purchased material
HQ: Novolex Holdings, Llc
101 E Carolina Ave
Hartsville SC 29550
843 857-4800

(G-14497)
OWENS CORNING SALES LLC
100 Blackjack Road Ext (43050-9194)
PHONE..................614 399-3915
Bob Demory, *Manager*
EMP: 54 **Publicly Held**
WEB: www.owenscorning.com
SIC: 2621 3296 Building paper, insulation; mineral wool
HQ: Owens Corning Sales, Llc
1 Owens Corning Pkwy
Toledo OH 43659
419 248-8000

(G-14498)
PACS SWITCHGEAR LLC
8405 Blackjack Rd (43050-2781)
PHONE..................740 397-5021
EMP: 22
SALES (corp-wide): 5MM **Privately Held**
SIC: 3613 Mfg Switchgear/Switchboards
PA: Pacs Switchgear, Llc
1211 Stewart Ave
Bethpage NY 11714
516 465-7100

(G-14499)
PAGE ONE GROUP
10 E Vine St Ste C (43050-3244)
PHONE..................740 397-4240
Jana Burson, *Partner*
Inez Maria, *Editor*
EMP: 7
SQ FT: 800
SALES: 516K **Privately Held**
SIC: 2752 8742 Commercial printing, off-set; marketing consulting services

(G-14500)
PERFORMACE DIESEL INC
16901 Mcvay Rd (43050)
PHONE..................740 392-3693
Stephen Harsany, *President*
Angel Harsany, *Treasurer*
EMP: 10
SQ FT: 7,000
SALES: 530K **Privately Held**
SIC: 3519 Diesel engine rebuilding

(G-14501)
POTEMKIN INDUSTRIES INC (PA)
8043 Columbus Rd (43050-9358)
PHONE..................740 397-4888
Horst Krajenski, *President*
Debbie Hamilton, *Vice Pres*
Jim Wells, *Engineer*
Mike Radermacher, *Project Engr*
Thomas Frye, *Accountant*
EMP: 30 EST: 1980
SQ FT: 14,000
SALES (est): 4.8MM **Privately Held**
WEB: www.potemkinindustries.com
SIC: 3563 Air & gas compressors including vacuum pumps

(G-14502)
PRINTING ARTS PRESS
8028 Newark Rd (43050-8155)
P.O. Box 431 (43050-0431)
PHONE..................740 397-6106
Robert Vogt, *Principal*
Theresa Kauser, *Accounts Mgr*
Charles Gherman, *Manager*
Rhonda Gherman, *Exec Dir*
EMP: 10 EST: 1945
SQ FT: 15,000
SALES (est): 1.6MM **Privately Held**
WEB: www.printingartspress.com
SIC: 2752 2791 Commercial printing, off-set; typesetting

(G-14503)
PROGRESSIVE COMMUNICATIONS
Also Called: Mount Vernon News
18 E Vine St (43050-3226)
P.O. Box 791 (43050-0791)
PHONE..................740 397-5333
Kay H Culbertson, *President*
Michelle L Hartman, *Vice Pres*
Elizabeth Lutwick, *Treasurer*
Corby Wise, *Adv Mgr*
Emily Butler, *Advt Staff*
EMP: 65
SQ FT: 30,000
SALES (est): 5.1MM **Privately Held**
SIC: 2711 2752 2791 Commercial printing & newspaper publishing combined; job printing & newspaper publishing combined; commercial printing, offset; typesetting

(G-14504)
REPLEX MIRROR COMPANY
Also Called: Replex Plastics
11 Mount Vernon Ave (43050-4163)
PHONE..................740 397-5535
Mark Schuetz, *President*
Blumensheid Tammy, *Accountant*
◆ EMP: 21
SQ FT: 100,000
SALES (est): 7MM **Privately Held**
WEB: www.replex.com
SIC: 3089 Thermoformed finished plastic products; injection molding of plastics

(G-14505)
SANOH AMERICA INC
7905 Industrial Park Dr (43050-2776)
PHONE..................740 392-9200
Eric Carroll, *Principal*
EMP: 220
SALES (corp-wide): 1.3B **Privately Held**
WEB: www.sanoh-america.com
SIC: 7539 3714 Automotive repair shops; motor vehicle parts & accessories
HQ: Sanoh America, Inc.
1849 Industrial Dr
Findlay OH 45840
419 425-2600

(G-14506)
SANT SAND & GRAVEL CO
14220 Parrott Ext (43050-4500)
P.O. Box 750 (43050-0750)
PHONE..................740 397-0000
Fax: 740 397-0862
EMP: 8 EST: 1959
SQ FT: 2,000
SALES: 366.8K
SALES (corp-wide): 28.7MM **Privately Held**
SIC: 1442 Sand & Gravel Mining
PA: United Precast Inc.
400 Howard St
Mount Vernon OH 43050
740 393-1121

(G-14507)
SELECTIVE MED COMPONENTS INC
504 Harcourt Rd Ste 3 (43050-3945)
PHONE..................740 397-7838
Richard Fisher III, *President*
EMP: 30
SQ FT: 6,000
SALES (est): 3.6MM **Privately Held**
WEB: www.selectivemed.com
SIC: 3823 Electrodes used in industrial process measurement

(G-14508)
SHAMROCK PLASTICS INC
633 Howard St (43050-3709)
PHONE..................740 392-5555
Tom Ruffner, *President*
Jay Ruffner, *General Mgr*
EMP: 10
SALES (est): 1.6MM **Privately Held**
WEB: www.shamrockplasticsinc.com
SIC: 2796 3083 Platemaking services; laminated plastic sheets

(G-14509)
SHELLENBARGER EXCAVATING & LOG
9260 Fairview Rd (43050-9307)
PHONE..................740 397-9949
Francis Shellenbarger, *Principal*
EMP: 3 EST: 2001
SALES (est): 231.4K **Privately Held**
SIC: 2411 Logging camps & contractors

(G-14510)
SIEMENS ENERGY INC
105 N Sandusky St (43050-2447)
PHONE..................740 393-8897
EMP: 252
SALES (corp-wide): 95B **Privately Held**
SIC: 1629 1731 3511 Power plant construction; energy management controls; turbines & turbine generator sets
HQ: Siemens Energy, Inc.
4400 N Alafaya Trl
Orlando FL 32826
407 736-2000

(G-14511)
SIEMENS ENERGY INC
607 W Chestnut St (43050-2335)
PHONE..................740 393-8464
EMP: 7
SALES (corp-wide): 89.6B **Privately Held**
SIC: 3661 Mfg Telephone/Telegraph Apparatus
HQ: Siemens Energy, Inc.
4400 N Alafaya Trl
Orlando FL 32826
407 736-2000

(G-14512)
SIEMENS ENERGY INC
Also Called: Siemens Power and Gas
105 N Sandusky St (43050-2447)
PHONE..................740 504-1947
Steven Charles Conner, *CEO*
EMP: 26
SALES (corp-wide): 95B **Privately Held**
SIC: 3511 Steam turbines
HQ: Siemens Energy, Inc.
4400 N Alafaya Trl
Orlando FL 32826
407 736-2000

(G-14513)
SIGNLINE GRAPHICS & LETTERING
114 Clinton Rd (43050-8601)
P.O. Box 254 (43050-0254)
PHONE..................740 397-5806
Charles Blubaugh, *President*
Candi L Blubaugh, *Vice Pres*
EMP: 4
SQ FT: 1,400
SALES: 200K **Privately Held**
WEB: www.signline1.com
SIC: 3993 Signs & advertising specialties

(G-14514)
SMARTCOPY INC (PA)
Also Called: Blue Fox Group, The
50 Parrott St Ste A (43050-4568)
PHONE..................740 392-6162
Michael Hajjar, *President*
EMP: 9
SQ FT: 20,000
SALES (est): 1.2MM **Privately Held**
SIC: 8999 3861 Art related services; processing equipment, photographic

(G-14515)
STEWARDSHIP TECHNOLOGY INC
201 W High St (43050-2427)
PHONE..................866 604-8880
Stuart Washington, *CEO*
Nina Vellayan, *President*
EMP: 4
SALES (est): 697.2K
SALES (corp-wide): 266.9MM **Privately Held**
SIC: 7372 Application computer software
HQ: Paya, Inc.
12120 Sunset Hills Rd # 500
Reston VA 20190
470 447-4066

(G-14516)
UNITED PRECAST INC
400 Howard St (43050-3547)
PHONE..................740 393-1121
John D Ellis, *President*
John P Ellis, *General Mgr*
Rick Sobers, *Manager*
George Ellis, *Shareholder*
Linda Ellis, *Shareholder*
EMP: 226
SQ FT: 4,000
SALES (est): 34.4MM **Privately Held**
WEB: www.unitedprecast.com
SIC: 3272 Concrete products, precast

(G-14517)
VER-MAC INDUSTRIES INC
100 Progress Dr (43050-4700)
PHONE..................740 397-6511
Dennis McElroy, *President*
William D Heichel, *Principal*
Mitch Durbin, *Vice Pres*
Stephanie Burson, *Project Mgr*
Jeff McElroy, *Project Mgr*
▲ EMP: 40
SQ FT: 26,000
SALES (est): 7.6MM **Privately Held**
WEB: www.ver-macindustries.com
SIC: 3599 3496 3449 Machine shop, jobbing & repair; air intake filters, internal combustion engine, except auto; miscellaneous fabricated wire products; miscellaneous metalwork

(G-14518)
WEYERHAEUSER CO CONTAINEERBOAR
8800 Granville Rd (43050-9192)
PHONE..................740 397-5215
Larry Tignor, *Principal*
EMP: 9 EST: 2009
SALES (est): 955K **Privately Held**
SIC: 2653 Boxes, corrugated: made from purchased materials

(G-14519)
WOLFF HOUSE ART PAPERS INC
133 S Main St (43050-3323)
PHONE..................740 501-3766
Jess Gabric, *President*
Thomas Wise, *Principal*
Dixie Gabric, *Vice Pres*
EMP: 3
SQ FT: 3,640
SALES: 120K **Privately Held**
SIC: 2679 Wallpaper

Mount Victory
Hardin County

(G-14520)
OHIO FRESH EGGS LLC
20449 County Road 245 (43340-9710)
P.O. Box 118 (43340-0118)
PHONE..................937 354-2233
Brian Kinter, *Manager*
EMP: 30
SALES (est): 1.5MM
SALES (corp-wide): 25.9MM **Privately Held**
SIC: 5144 2015 0252 Eggs; poultry slaughtering & processing; chicken eggs
PA: Ohio Fresh Eggs, Llc
11212 Croton Rd
Croton OH 43013
740 893-7200

(G-14521)
RAVENWORKS DEER SKIN
34477 Shertzer Rd (43340-9615)
P.O. Box 6 (43340-0006)
PHONE..................937 354-5151
Charles Harris, *Partner*
Nina Harris, *Partner*
EMP: 6
SALES (est): 628.6K **Privately Held**
SIC: 3171 3172 Women's handbags & purses; personal leather goods

GEOGRAPHIC SECTION

Napoleon - Henry County (G-14548)

(G-14522)
ROEHLERS MACHINE PRODUCTS
117 Taylor St E (43340-8811)
P.O. Box 366 (43340-0366)
PHONE.................................937 354-4401
Scott Roehler, *Owner*
EMP: 3
SQ FT: 5,500
SALES: 300K **Privately Held**
SIC: 3451 3545 3452 Screw machine products; machine tool accessories; bolts, nuts, rivets & washers

Munroe Falls
Summit County

(G-14523)
HARDCOATING TECHNOLOGIES LTD
103 S Main St (44262-1637)
PHONE.................................330 686-2136
James Haag, *President*
EMP: 20
SQ FT: 10,000
SALES (est): 2.4MM **Privately Held**
WEB: www.hardcoatingtech.com
SIC: 3479 Coating of metals & formed products

(G-14524)
KYOCERA SGS PRECISION TOOLS (PA)
55 S Main St (44262-1635)
P.O. Box 187 (44262-0187)
PHONE.................................330 688-6667
Thomas Haag, *President*
Chris Sparks, *Engineer*
Aaron Holb, *Treasurer*
Raymond Gibson, *Chief Mktg Ofcr*
▲ **EMP:** 50
SQ FT: 45,000
SALES: 78.5MM **Privately Held**
WEB: www.sgstool.com
SIC: 3545 5084 Cutting tools for machine tools; industrial machinery & equipment

(G-14525)
LEM INCORPORATED
71 S River Rd (44262-1654)
PHONE.................................330 535-6422
Anne Mc Gaughey, *President*
EMP: 4 EST: 1947
SQ FT: 3,200
SALES (est): 509.7K **Privately Held**
SIC: 3599 Machine shop, jobbing & repair

(G-14526)
M S B MACHINE INC
36 Castle Dr (44262-1602)
PHONE.................................330 686-7740
Jim Burkart, *President*
EMP: 6
SQ FT: 3,880
SALES (est): 639.2K **Privately Held**
SIC: 3599 Machine shop, jobbing & repair

(G-14527)
SONOCO PRODUCTS COMPANY
59 N Main St (44262-1064)
P.O. Box 217 (44262-0217)
PHONE.................................330 688-8247
John Parman, *Manager*
EMP: 110
SALES (corp-wide): 5.3B **Publicly Held**
WEB: www.sonoco.com
SIC: 2631 2655 Paperboard mills; fiber cans, drums & similar products
PA: Sonoco Products Company
1 N 2nd St
Hartsville SC 29550
843 383-7000

(G-14528)
SUPERIOR MOLD & DIE CO
449 N Main St (44262-1007)
PHONE.................................330 688-8251
Richard Yamokoski, *President*
Jeffery Yamokoski, *Owner*
Gale Young, *Vice Pres*
EMP: 40
SQ FT: 43,000
SALES (est): 6.1MM **Privately Held**
SIC: 3544 3599 Industrial molds; machine shop, jobbing & repair

(G-14529)
VADOSE SYN FUELS INC
323 S Main St (44262-1658)
PHONE.................................330 564-0545
Sheri A Peters, *Principal*
EMP: 7
SALES (est): 889.9K **Privately Held**
SIC: 2869 Fuels

Napoleon
Henry County

(G-14530)
ADVANCED DRAINAGE SYSTEMS INC
1075 Independence Dr (43545-9717)
PHONE.................................419 599-9565
Jason Hartland, *Manager*
EMP: 30
SQ FT: 14,000
SALES (corp-wide): 1.3B **Publicly Held**
WEB: www.ads-pipe.com
SIC: 3084 3083 Plastics pipe; laminated plastics plate & sheet
PA: Advanced Drainage Systems, Inc.
4640 Trueman Blvd
Hilliard OH 43026
614 658-0050

(G-14531)
AMCOR RIGID PLASTICS USA LLC
12993 State Route 110 (43545-5899)
PHONE.................................419 592-1998
Ray Behm, *Manager*
EMP: 33 **Privately Held**
WEB: www.slpcamericas.com
SIC: 3089 Plastic containers, except foam
HQ: Amcor Rigid Plastics Usa, Llc
935 Technology Dr Ste 100
Ann Arbor MI 48108

(G-14532)
AUTOMATIC FEED CO (PA)
Also Called: Automatic Feed Company
476 E Riverview Ave (43545-1899)
PHONE.................................419 592-0050
William L Beck, *Principal*
Peter Beck, *Vice Pres*
Erik Fretz, *Project Mgr*
Todd Jurski, *Project Mgr*
Ben Pescara, *Project Mgr*
▲ **EMP:** 94 EST: 1949
SQ FT: 160,000
SALES (est): 19.8MM **Privately Held**
WEB: www.automaticfeed.com
SIC: 3549 Cutting-up lines

(G-14533)
AVINA SPECIALTIES INC
116 W Washington St (43545-1740)
PHONE.................................419 592-5646
Nicholas Avina, *President*
Susan Avina, *Vice Pres*
EMP: 5
SALES (est): 500K **Privately Held**
SIC: 2395 Embroidery & art needlework

(G-14534)
CAMPBELL SOUP COMPANY
110 E Maumee Ave (43545)
PHONE.................................419 592-1010
Dale Morrison, *Principal*
EMP: 100
SALES (corp-wide): 8.6B **Publicly Held**
WEB: www.campbellsoups.com
SIC: 2032 2038 2033 2052 Spaghetti: packaged in cans, jars, etc.; frozen specialties; canned fruits & specialties; cookies & crackers; bread, cake & related products; potato chips & similar snacks
PA: Campbell Soup Company
1 Campbell Pl
Camden NJ 08103
856 342-4800

(G-14535)
CARSON INDUSTRIES LLC
1675 Industrial Dr (43545-9734)
PHONE.................................419 592-2309
Rich Gordinier, *Principal*
EMP: 6
SALES (est): 414.9K **Privately Held**
SIC: 3089 Injection molding of plastics

(G-14536)
CUSTAR STONE CO
9072 County Road 424 (43545-9732)
PHONE.................................419 669-4327
Brent Gerken, *President*
Jon Myers, *Corp Secy*
Mike Gerken, *Vice Pres*
Julian Gerken, *Shareholder*
EMP: 11
SQ FT: 3,000
SALES (est): 1.1MM **Privately Held**
SIC: 3281 Stone, quarrying & processing of own stone products

(G-14537)
DEFIANCE STAMPING CO
800 Independence Dr (43545-9192)
PHONE.................................419 782-5781
Tony Stuart, *President*
Brian Callan, *Principal*
Greg Yeager, *QC Mgr*
Vince Baker, *Engineer*
Michael Figy, *Engineer*
▲ **EMP:** 65 EST: 1927
SQ FT: 60,000
SALES (est): 16.9MM **Privately Held**
WEB: www.defiancestamping.com
SIC: 3469 Metal stampings

(G-14538)
FLAT ROCKS BREWING COMPANY
127 W Washington St (43545-1739)
PHONE.................................419 270-3582
EMP: 4 EST: 2015
SALES (est): 82.3K **Privately Held**
SIC: 5181 2082 Beer & ale; malt beverages

(G-14539)
GILSON MACHINE & TOOL CO INC
529 Freedom Dr (43545-5945)
PHONE.................................419 592-2911
William E Gilson Jr, *President*
Glen Gilson, *Corp Secy*
Karen Bunke, *Office Mgr*
EMP: 20 EST: 1946
SQ FT: 11,000
SALES (est): 3MM **Privately Held**
WEB: www.gilsonmachine.com
SIC: 3599 7692 3549 3544 Machine shop, jobbing & repair; welding repair; metalworking machinery; special dies, tools, jigs & fixtures; fabricated structural metal

(G-14540)
GRAEBENER GROUP TECH LTD
476 E Riverview Ave (43545-1855)
PHONE.................................419 591-7033
Richard Marando, *President*
▲ **EMP:** 2
SQ FT: 10,000
SALES: 1MM **Privately Held**
SIC: 3547 Pipe & tube mills

(G-14541)
HIGH PRODUCTION TECHNOLOGY LLC (HQ)
476 E Riverview Ave (43545-1855)
PHONE.................................419 591-7000
Marlowe Witt,
EMP: 15 EST: 1997
SQ FT: 6,000
SALES: 3MM
SALES (corp-wide): 19.8MM **Privately Held**
WEB: www.hiprotech.com
SIC: 3542 3441 Presses: hydraulic & pneumatic, mechanical & manual; fabricated structural metal
PA: Automatic Feed Co.
476 E Riverview Ave
Napoleon OH 43545
419 592-0050

(G-14542)
HIGH PRODUCTION TECHNOLOGY LLC
13068 County Road R (43545-5964)
PHONE.................................419 599-1511
Marlow Witt, *Branch Mgr*
EMP: 8
SALES (corp-wide): 19.8MM **Privately Held**
WEB: www.hiprotech.com
SIC: 3542 Machine tools, metal forming type
HQ: High Production Technology, Llc
476 E Riverview Ave
Napoleon OH 43545
419 591-7000

(G-14543)
HOLGATE METAL FAB INC
555 Independence Dr (43545-9656)
PHONE.................................419 599-2000
Jeff Spangler, *President*
Denise Spangler, *Vice Pres*
Randy Elling, *Sales Engr*
Jake Kraegel, *Supervisor*
EMP: 15
SQ FT: 16,000
SALES (est): 3.5MM **Privately Held**
WEB: www.holgatemetalfab.com
SIC: 1711 1761 3444 3441 Boiler maintenance contractor; sheet metalwork; sheet metalwork; fabricated structural metal; blast furnaces & steel mills

(G-14544)
HP2G LLC
2611 Scott St Napoleon (43545)
PHONE.................................419 906-1525
Sheila Kay, *Vice Pres*
Jen Rodgers, *Controller*
Douglas Pelmear,
EMP: 30
SALES: 950K **Privately Held**
SIC: 3714 Motor vehicle parts & accessories

(G-14545)
INNOVATIVE TOOL & DIE INC
1700 Industrial Dr (43545-9282)
PHONE.................................419 599-0492
Loren Sonnenberg, *President*
Larry Huber, *Corp Secy*
EMP: 8
SQ FT: 5,000
SALES (est): 1.1MM **Privately Held**
SIC: 3544 3599 Special dies & tools; machine & other job shop work

(G-14546)
ISOFOTON NORTH AMERICA INC
800 Independence Dr (43545-9192)
PHONE.................................419 591-4330
Michael A Peck, *President*
Joseph M Garton, *Vice Pres*
▲ **EMP:** 10
SQ FT: 185,000
SALES (est): 1.8MM **Privately Held**
SIC: 3674 Solar cells

(G-14547)
JACKSON DELUXE CLEANERS LTD (PA)
522 Hobson St (43545-1802)
PHONE.................................419 592-2826
Robert Jackson, *Owner*
EMP: 7
SQ FT: 2,500
SALES: 350K **Privately Held**
SIC: 7216 2842 Drycleaning Plant Mfg Polish/Sanitation Goods

(G-14548)
KOESTER CORPORATION (PA)
813 N Perry St (43545-1521)
PHONE.................................419 599-0291
Michael Koester, *President*
Jeanette Spiller, *Admin Sec*
EMP: 60
SQ FT: 40,000
SALES: 15.6MM **Privately Held**
WEB: www.koester-corp.com
SIC: 3569 3823 3613 Lubricating equipment; pressure measurement instruments, industrial; control panels, electric

Napoleon - Henry County (G-14549)

(G-14549)
LEADER ENGNRNG-
FABRICATION INC (PA)
695 Independence Dr (43545-9191)
P.O. Box 670 (43545-0670)
PHONE.................................419 592-0008
Charles Leader, *President*
Calvin Leader, *Shareholder*
Truus Leader, *Shareholder*
Dianna Schelmyer, *Admin Sec*
EMP: 46
SQ FT: 23,800
SALES: 8.2MM **Privately Held**
WEB:
www.leaderengineeringfabrication.com
SIC: 3599 Machine shop, jobbing & repair

(G-14550)
MARY JAMES INC
1025 Clairmont Ave (43545-1240)
PHONE.................................419 599-2941
James E Lammy Sr, *Principal*
EMP: 20
SALES (est): 1.3MM **Privately Held**
SIC: 2211 Apparel & outerwear fabrics, cotton

(G-14551)
MUSTANG PRINTING
Also Called: Turkeyfoot Printing
119 W Washington St (43545-1739)
P.O. Box 413, Wauseon (43567-0413)
PHONE.................................419 592-2746
Jerry Dehnbostel, *President*
EMP: 10
SQ FT: 4,800
SALES (est): 1.1MM **Privately Held**
SIC: 2752 Commercial printing, offset
HQ: Mustang Corporation
    229 N Fulton St
    Wauseon OH
    419 335-9070

(G-14552)
NAPOLEON INC
Also Called: Northwest Signal
595 E Riverview Ave (43545-1865)
PHONE.................................419 592-5055
Christopher Cullis, *President*
EMP: 40 EST: 1852
SQ FT: 7,200
SALES (est): 2.5MM **Privately Held**
WEB: www.northwestsignal.net
SIC: 2711 Newspapers: publishing only, not printed on site

(G-14553)
NAPOLEON MACHINE LLC
476 E Riverview Ave (43545-1855)
PHONE.................................419 591-7010
Dave Rakay, *Project Mgr*
Anita Febrey, *Controller*
Kyle Rickner, *Marketing Staff*
Kevin Febrey,
EMP: 35
SALES: 2MM **Privately Held**
SIC: 3599 1721 Crankshafts & camshafts, machining; electrical discharge machining (EDM); commercial painting; exterior commercial painting contractor; industrial painting

(G-14554)
OLDCASTLE PRECAST INC
1675 Industrial Dr (43545-9734)
PHONE.................................419 592-2309
Beverly Smith, *Purch Mgr*
EMP: 35
SALES (corp-wide): 29.7B **Privately Held**
WEB: www.oldcastle-precast.com
SIC: 3089 Boxes, plastic
HQ: Oldcastle Infrastructure, Inc.
    1002 15th St Sw Ste 110
    Auburn WA 98001
    253 833-2777

(G-14555)
PANDROL INC
Also Called: Railtech Boutet, Inc.
25 Interstate Dr (43545-8700)
P.O. Box 69 (43545-0069)
PHONE.................................419 592-5050
David C Barrett Jr, *Principal*
Oliver Dolder, *Exec VP*
◆ EMP: 43
SQ FT: 60,000
SALES (est): 10.8MM **Privately Held**
SIC: 3355 Rails, rolled & drawn, aluminum
HQ: Delachaux Sa
    Immeuble West Plaza
    Colombes 92700
    146 520-519

(G-14556)
PULLMAN COMPANY
Also Called: Tenneco
11800 County Road 424 (43545-5778)
PHONE.................................419 592-2055
Tom Weaver, *Branch Mgr*
EMP: 204
SQ FT: 220,000
SALES (corp-wide): 11.7B **Publicly Held**
WEB: www.tenneco-automotive.com
SIC: 3714 Motor vehicle engines & parts
HQ: The Pullman Company
    1 International Dr
    Monroe MI 48161
    734 243-8000

(G-14557)
R S V WLDG FBRCATION MACHINING
M063 County Road 12 (43545-9366)
P.O. Box 430 (43545-0430)
PHONE.................................419 592-0993
Ralph F Vocke, *President*
Randy Vocke, *Vice Pres*
Steve Vocke, *Admin Sec*
EMP: 10 EST: 1979
SQ FT: 10,400
SALES: 750K **Privately Held**
WEB: www.rsvwelding.com
SIC: 3441 7692 Fabricated structural metal; welding repair

(G-14558)
RAILTECH MATWELD INC
15 Interstate Dr (43545)
PHONE.................................419 592-5050
Oliver Dolder, *President*
EMP: 5 **Privately Held**
SIC: 2899 Chemical preparations
HQ: Railtech Matweld, Inc.
    25 Interstate Dr
    Napoleon OH 43545

(G-14559)
RAILTECH MATWELD INC (DH)
25 Interstate Dr (43545-8700)
P.O. Box 69 (43545-0069)
PHONE.................................419 591-3770
Oliver Dolder, *CEO*
Gregory B Minter, *President*
EMP: 21
SALES (est): 1.8MM **Privately Held**
SIC: 2899 Chemical preparations
HQ: Pandrol
    Zone Industrielle
    Raismes 59590
    327 228-480

(G-14560)
RETTIG FAMILY PALLETS INC
12484 State Route 110 (43545-9340)
PHONE.................................419 264-1540
Robert Rettig, *President*
EMP: 10
SQ FT: 30,000
SALES (est): 1.3MM **Privately Held**
SIC: 2448 Pallets, wood & wood with metal

(G-14561)
SCOTT PORT-A-FOLD INC
5963 State Route 110 (43545-9332)
PHONE.................................419 748-8880
James Lammy Jr, *President*
James E Lammy Jr, *President*
▲ EMP: 30
SQ FT: 45,000
SALES: 1MM **Privately Held**
SIC: 3086 3531 Plastics foam products; construction machinery

(G-14562)
TOY & SPORT TRENDS INC
Also Called: Scott Port-A-Fold
5963 State Route 110 (43545-9332)
PHONE.................................419 748-8880
James E Lammy Jr, *President*
Diane Smucker, *Admin Sec*
EMP: 20
SQ FT: 45,000
SALES: 1.5MM **Privately Held**
SIC: 5091 5092 3949 3086 Sporting & recreation goods; toys & hobby goods & supplies; sporting & athletic goods; plastics foam products

(G-14563)
UNITED AUTO WORKER AFL CIO
Also Called: Napoleon Products Co
410 Fillmore St (43545-1614)
PHONE.................................419 592-0434
EMP: 15
SALES (est): 1.1MM **Privately Held**
SIC: 3451 Mfg Screw Machine Products

Nashport
Muskingum County

(G-14564)
B D P SERVICES INC
Also Called: Sports Art
8255 Blackrun Rd (43830-9774)
PHONE.................................740 828-9685
Stephen Baum, *President*
Vince Paul, *Corp Secy*
EMP: 60
SQ FT: 28,000
SALES (est): 4.9MM **Privately Held**
WEB: www.sportsart-online.com
SIC: 2396 2395 Screen printing on fabric articles; embroidery products, except schiffli machine

(G-14565)
BROCKS CHIMNEY
4620 Gorsuch Rd (43830-9738)
PHONE.................................740 819-2489
Dean Brocklehurst, *Principal*
EMP: 3 EST: 2008
SALES (est): 239.1K **Privately Held**
SIC: 3281 Flagstones

(G-14566)
DARIN JORDAN
3460 Gorsuch Rd (43830-9492)
PHONE.................................740 819-3525
Darin Jordan, *Principal*
EMP: 7
SALES (est): 947.7K **Privately Held**
SIC: 1389 Oil field services

(G-14567)
HANBY FARMS INC
10790 Newark Rd (43830-9066)
P.O. Box 97 (43830-0097)
PHONE.................................740 763-3554
Ralph F Hanby, *President*
David R Hanby, *President*
Doug Hanby, *CFO*
Carol Hanby, *Admin Sec*
EMP: 34
SQ FT: 10,000
SALES (est): 7.8MM **Privately Held**
SIC: 2048 5153 5191 Livestock feeds; corn; soybeans; fertilizer & fertilizer materials

(G-14568)
MUSCLE FEAST LLC (PA)
1320 Boston Rd (43830-9603)
PHONE.................................740 877-8808
Jonathan Sean Gillespie,
▲ EMP: 11
SQ FT: 16,000
SALES: 2.3MM **Privately Held**
SIC: 5149 2023 Health foods; dietary supplements, dairy & non-dairy based

(G-14569)
PETE EMMERT CO
5580 Pleasant Valley Rd (43830-9570)
PHONE.................................740 455-3924
Peter Emmert, *Owner*
EMP: 5
SALES (est): 412.5K **Privately Held**
SIC: 2431 Interior & ornamental woodwork & trim

(G-14570)
RJ DRILLING COMPANY INC
5755 Licking Valley Rd Se (43830-2500)
PHONE.................................740 763-3991
Ronald F Moran, *President*
EMP: 3
SALES (est): 185K **Privately Held**
SIC: 1381 Drilling oil & gas wells

Navarre
Stark County

(G-14571)
ALFRED NICKLES BAKERY INC (PA)
26 Main St N (44662-1158)
PHONE.................................330 879-5635
David A Gardner, *President*
Mark Sponseller, *Senior VP*
Matthew Boxrucker, *Vice Pres*
Ernest Brideweser, *Vice Pres*
Christian Gardner, *Vice Pres*
▲ EMP: 500 EST: 1909
SQ FT: 110,000
SALES: 205MM **Privately Held**
WEB: www.nicklesbakery.com
SIC: 2051 Bread, cake & related products

(G-14572)
B & S TRANSPORT INC (PA)
11325 Lawndell Rd Sw (44662-8804)
P.O. Box 2678, North Canton (44720-0678)
PHONE.................................330 767-4319
Ronald Harris, *President*
Irvin Jackson, *Vice Pres*
EMP: 15 EST: 1977
SQ FT: 6,000
SALES (est): 2.3MM **Privately Held**
SIC: 3011 5014 5052 5045 Tires & inner tubes; tires & tubes; coal & other minerals & ores; computers, peripherals & software; books, periodicals & newspapers; book publishing

(G-14573)
CENTRAL ALLIED ENTERPRISES INC
Also Called: Massillon Washed Gravel Co
6331 Blough Ave Sw (44662-8506)
P.O. Box 80718, Canton (44708-0718)
PHONE.................................330 879-2132
Jerry Orn, *Div Sub Head*
Gary Miller, *Branch Mgr*
EMP: 8
SQ FT: 2,056
SALES (corp-wide): 60.2MM **Privately Held**
SIC: 1442 Construction sand mining; gravel mining
PA: Central Allied Enterprises, Inc.
    1243 Raff Rd Sw
    Canton OH 44710
    330 477-6751

(G-14574)
GREEN ACRES FURNITURE LTD
7412 Massillon Rd Sw (44662-9318)
PHONE.................................330 359-6251
Paul Swartzentruber, *Principal*
EMP: 12
SQ FT: 7,200
SALES (est): 1.5MM **Privately Held**
WEB: www.greenacresfurniture.com
SIC: 5712 2511 Beds & accessories; wood household furniture

(G-14575)
GREIF INC
9420 Warmington St Sw (44662-9670)
P.O. Box 675 (44662-0675)
PHONE.................................330 879-2101
Chip Shew, *Branch Mgr*
EMP: 100
SALES (corp-wide): 3.8B **Publicly Held**
WEB: www.greif.com
SIC: 2655 Fiber cans, drums & similar products
PA: Greif, Inc.
    425 Winter Rd
    Delaware OH 43015
    740 549-6000

(G-14576)
HARRYS PALLETS LLC
7029 Flenner St Sw (44662-9407)
PHONE.................................330 704-1056
Harry Dettweiler, *Principal*
EMP: 3 EST: 2014

GEOGRAPHIC SECTION

SALES (est): 171K **Privately Held**
SIC: 2448 Pallets, wood & wood with metal

(G-14577)
IMAGINE THIS RENOVATIONS
4220 Alabama Ave Sw (44662-9618)
PHONE.................................330 833-6739
Scott Miller, *Principal*
EMP: 8
SALES (est): 524K **Privately Held**
SIC: 2759 Commercial printing

(G-14578)
L N BRUT MANUFACTURING CO
4680 Alabama Ave Sw (44662-8708)
PHONE.................................330 833-9045
Lynn Neiss, *President*
Dolores J Schmidt, *Corp Secy*
EMP: 8
SQ FT: 11,000
SALES (est): 726K **Privately Held**
SIC: 3589 Sandblasting equipment

(G-14579)
L N S PALLETS
6144 Smith Rd Sw (44662-8107)
PHONE.................................330 936-7507
Scott Hargrove, *Administration*
EMP: 4
SALES (est): 301.5K **Privately Held**
SIC: 2448 Pallets, wood & wood with metal

(G-14580)
MILLER WELDMASTER CORPORATION (PA)
4220 Alabama Ave Sw (44662-9618)
PHONE.................................330 833-6739
Scott Miller, *President*
Jeff Dimos, *CFO*
◆ EMP: 91 EST: 1973
SQ FT: 20,000
SALES (est): 15MM **Privately Held**
WEB: www.weldmaster.com
SIC: 3548 Welding & cutting apparatus & accessories

(G-14581)
MYSTA EQUIPMENT CO
6434 Werstler Ave Sw (44662-9140)
PHONE.................................330 879-5353
Stanley Josefczyk, *Owner*
EMP: 6
SALES: 175K **Privately Held**
SIC: 3599 Machine & other job shop work

(G-14582)
NAVARRE INDUSTRIES INC
10384 Navarre Rd Sw (44662-9462)
PHONE.................................330 767-3003
Paul Miller, *President*
Gregory Miller, *Vice Pres*
EMP: 25
SQ FT: 45,000
SALES (est): 5.7MM **Privately Held**
WEB: www.navarreindustries.com
SIC: 3354 Aluminum extruded products

(G-14583)
NAVARRE TRAILER SALES INC
Also Called: Haul, Mark Sales/Service/Parts
4633 Erie Ave Sw (44662-8622)
PHONE.................................330 879-2406
Dina Jones, *President*
Amos Painter, *Vice Pres*
EMP: 3
SQ FT: 20,000
SALES (est): 1MM **Privately Held**
SIC: 5599 3715 Utility trailers; truck trailers

(G-14584)
OWENS CORNING
9318 Erie Ave Sw (44662-9448)
PHONE.................................419 248-8000
Jeannie Bender, *Vice Pres*
EMP: 6 **Publicly Held**
SIC: 3296 Fiberglass insulation
PA: Owens Corning
   1 Owens Corning Pkwy
   Toledo OH 43659

(G-14585)
PREMIER PALLET & RECYCLING
11361 Lawndell Rd Sw (44662)
P.O. Box 31, Brewster (44613-0031)
PHONE.................................330 767-2221
Pete Grove, *President*
EMP: 17 EST: 2004
SALES (est): 2.8MM **Privately Held**
SIC: 2448 Pallets, wood

(G-14586)
RC INDUSTRIES INC
Also Called: Mid's Spaghetti Sauce
620 Main St N (44662-8556)
P.O. Box 5 (44662-0005)
PHONE.................................330 879-5486
Steve Cress, *CEO*
Scott Ricketts, *President*
EMP: 25
SQ FT: 10,000
SALES (est): 5.6MM **Privately Held**
SIC: 2033 2035 Spaghetti & other pasta sauce: packaged in cans, jars, etc.; pickles, sauces & salad dressings

(G-14587)
RUEGG MFG LLC
13955 Elton St Sw (44662-9663)
PHONE.................................330 418-5617
Bill Ruegg, *Owner*
EMP: 5
SALES: 300K **Privately Held**
SIC: 3643 Power line cable

(G-14588)
TERYDON INC
7260 Erie Ave Sw (44662-8807)
PHONE.................................330 879-2448
Terry Gromes Sr, *President*
Jamie Gromes, *Office Mgr*
Gordon East, *Technology*
EMP: 12
SQ FT: 800
SALES: 1.5MM **Privately Held**
SIC: 3599 8711 Custom machinery; machine tool design

Negley
Columbiana County

(G-14589)
CUSTOM COILS
51305 Carmel Achor Rd (44441-9708)
PHONE.................................330 426-3797
Allen Mackall,
EMP: 4
SALES (est): 630.7K **Privately Held**
SIC: 3567 Induction heating equipment

(G-14590)
MAGNECO/METREL INC
51365 State Route 154 (44441-9728)
P.O. Box 176 (44441-0176)
PHONE.................................330 426-9468
Paul Painter, *Branch Mgr*
EMP: 38
SALES (corp-wide): 65.8MM **Privately Held**
WEB: www.magneco-metrel.com
SIC: 3255 3297 Clay refractories; nonclay refractories
PA: Magneco/Metrel, Inc.
   223 W Interstate Rd
   Addison IL 60101
   630 543-6660

(G-14591)
MELT INC
51621 Darlington Rd (44441-9701)
PHONE.................................330 426-3545
Ellen Beagle, *Principal*
EMP: 5
SALES (est): 470.6K **Privately Held**
SIC: 2448 Pallets, wood & wood with metal

(G-14592)
X L SAND AND GRAVEL CO
9289 Jackman Rd (44441)
P.O. Box 255 (44441-0255)
PHONE.................................330 426-9876
Raymond Lansberry, *President*
James Lansberry, *Treasurer*
EMP: 15

SQ FT: 1,000
SALES (est): 2.8MM **Privately Held**
SIC: 1442 Common sand mining; gravel mining

Nelsonville
Athens County

(G-14593)
GEORGIA-BOOT INC
Also Called: Durango Boot
39 E Canal St (45764-1247)
PHONE.................................740 753-1951
Gerald M Cohn, *CEO*
Thomas R Morrison, *President*
EMP: 100
SALES (est): 17.7MM **Privately Held**
WEB: www.durangoboot.com
SIC: 5139 3144 3143 3021 Shoes; women's footwear, except athletic; men's footwear, except athletic; rubber & plastics footwear

(G-14594)
QUICK LOADZ DELIVERY SYS LLC
185 W Canal St (45764-1144)
P.O. Box 272, The Plains (45780-0272)
PHONE.................................888 304-3946
Sean Jones,
Judy Vogelsang, *Administration*
▲ EMP: 20 EST: 2014
SALES (est): 632.3K **Privately Held**
SIC: 3715 Trailer bodies

(G-14595)
ROCKY BRANDS INC (PA)
39 E Canal St (45764-1247)
PHONE.................................740 753-1951
Mike Brooks, *Ch of Bd*
Jason Brooks, *President*
Richard Simms, *President*
Thomas Robertson, *Officer*
Curtis A Loveland, *Admin Sec*
EMP: 277
SQ FT: 25,000
SALES: 252.6MM **Publicly Held**
WEB: www.rockybrands.com
SIC: 3143 3144 2329 2331 Men's footwear, except athletic; women's footwear, except athletic; men's & boys' sportswear & athletic clothing; women's & misses' blouses & shirts; women's & misses' accessories; men's miscellaneous accessories

(G-14596)
ROCKY BRANDS INC
39 E Canal St (45764-1247)
PHONE.................................740 753-1951
Becky Steenrod, *Branch Mgr*
EMP: 60
SALES (corp-wide): 252.6MM **Publicly Held**
SIC: 3143 Men's footwear, except athletic
PA: Rocky Brands, Inc.
   39 E Canal St
   Nelsonville OH 45764
   740 753-1951

(G-14597)
SHOT-FORCE PRO LLC
13580 Kimberley Rd (45764-9511)
PHONE.................................740 753-3927
Stephen Davis,
EMP: 4
SALES (est): 172.9K **Privately Held**
SIC: 3462 7389 Armor plate, forged iron or steel;

(G-14598)
STARR MACHINE INC
226 Sylvania Ave (45764)
PHONE.................................740 753-0009
Brian Kasler, *President*
EMP: 24
SQ FT: 34,000
SALES (est): 4.1MM **Privately Held**
WEB: www.starrmachine.com
SIC: 3599 Machine shop, jobbing & repair

(G-14599)
T & M MACHINE PRODUCTS INC
14265 State Route 691 (45764-9428)
PHONE.................................740 753-2960
Darrow M Tolliver, *President*
Darrow G Tolliver Jr, *Vice Pres*
EMP: 5 EST: 1969
SQ FT: 11,000
SALES (est): 548.3K **Privately Held**
SIC: 3599 Machine shop, jobbing & repair

(G-14600)
TAT PUMPS INC
Also Called: Tat Engineering
398 Poplar St (45764-1425)
P.O. Box 268, Logan (43138-0268)
PHONE.................................740 385-0008
Kay Your, *President*
Robert Your, *Vice Pres*
EMP: 5 EST: 1998
SQ FT: 8,000
SALES (est): 150K **Privately Held**
WEB: www.tatpumps.com
SIC: 3561 Pumps, oil well & field

Nevada
Wyandot County

(G-14601)
STIGER PRE CAST INC
17793 State Highway 231 (44849-9710)
PHONE.................................740 482-2313
Jim Riedlinger, *President*
Cathy Scheffler, *Corp Secy*
Eva Mae Riedlinger, *Vice Pres*
EMP: 8 EST: 1943
SQ FT: 2,200
SALES (est): 1.2MM **Privately Held**
SIC: 3272 3271 Septic tanks, concrete; steps, prefabricated concrete; blocks, concrete or cinder: standard

New Albany
Franklin County

(G-14602)
614 CUPCAKES LLC
4045 Chelsea Grn W (43054-6027)
PHONE.................................614 245-8800
Dawn Freeman,
EMP: 6
SALES (est): 465.2K **Privately Held**
SIC: 2051 Bread, cake & related products

(G-14603)
ACE PRINTING LLC
7788 Central College Rd B (43054-7072)
PHONE.................................614 855-7227
Rebecca Lynn Alley, *Manager*
EMP: 3
SQ FT: 2,500
SALES: 190K **Privately Held**
SIC: 2752 Commercial printing, lithographic

(G-14604)
AMERICAN REGENT INC
6610 New Albany Rd E (43054-8730)
PHONE.................................614 436-2222
Joseph Kenneth Keller, *CEO*
Robert Vultaggio, *Controller*
Linda Romaine, *Manager*
EMP: 13 **Privately Held**
SIC: 2834 Adrenal pharmaceutical preparations
HQ: American Regent, Inc.
   5 Ramsey Rd
   Shirley NY 11967
   631 924-4000

(G-14605)
AROMAIR FINE FRAGRANCE COMPANY
8860 Smiths Mill Rd # 500 (43054-6653)
PHONE.................................614 984-2896
Richard Nihei, *CFO*
EMP: 500
SALES (est): 51.9MM **Privately Held**
SIC: 2842 Cleaning or polishing preparations

New Albany - Franklin County (G-14606)

(G-14606)
AUTOMATIC TIMING & CONTROLS (PA)
Also Called: Automatic Timing & Cntrls Div
7795 Walton Pkwy Ste 175 (43054-0002)
P.O. Box 305, Newell WV (26050-0305)
PHONE................................614 888-8855
Arnold B Siemer, *President*
Thomas Villano, *Vice Pres*
Roger D Bailey, *CFO*
Russell Gertmenian, *Admin Sec*
Barbara Johnson Siemer, *Asst Sec*
EMP: 8
SQ FT: 5,500
SALES (est): 15.9MM **Privately Held**
WEB: www.automatictiming.com
SIC: 3824 3823 3625 Fluid meters & counting devices; counters, revolution; tachometer, centrifugal; temperature instruments: industrial process type; timing devices, electronic

(G-14607)
AVERY DENNISON CORPORATION
7795 Walton Pkwy Ste 370 (43054-8246)
PHONE................................614 418-7740
EMP: 115
SALES (corp-wide): 6.3B **Publicly Held**
SIC: 2672 Mfg Coated/Laminated Paper
PA: Avery Dennison Corporation
    207 N Goode Ave Fl 6
    Glendale CA 91203
    626 304-2000

(G-14608)
BLACK RADISH CREAMERY LTD
7064 Cunningham Dr (43054-9063)
PHONE................................614 323-6016
John Reese, *Principal*
EMP: 6
SALES (est): 510.9K **Privately Held**
SIC: 2021 Creamery butter

(G-14609)
BOB EVANS FARMS INC (HQ)
8111 Smiths Mill Rd (43054-1183)
PHONE................................614 491-2225
Mike Townsley, *CEO*
Colin M Daly, *Exec VP*
Beth A Rauschenberger, *Senior VP*
Amy Gosiorowski, *Vice Pres*
Mark E Hood, *CFO*
EMP: 325
SALES: 394.8MM **Publicly Held**
WEB: www.bobevans.com
SIC: 5812 2011 2099 2035 Restaurant, family: chain; sausages from meat slaughtered on site; salads, fresh or refrigerated; pickles, sauces & salad dressings

(G-14610)
BOCCHI LABORATORIES OHIO LLC
9200 Smiths Mill Rd N (43054-6703)
PHONE................................614 741-7458
Joe Pender, *CEO*
Patrick Kelley, *CFO*
EMP: 300
SQ FT: 125,000
SALES (est): 14.3MM
SALES (corp-wide): 79.4MM **Privately Held**
SIC: 2844 Toilet preparations
PA: Shadow Holdings, Llc
    26455 Ruether Ave
    Santa Clarita CA 91350
    661 252-3807

(G-14611)
BSM COLUMBUS LLP
2677 Harrison Rd (43054-7440)
PHONE................................740 755-2380
Toby Baker, *Managing Prtnr*
Shannon Baker, *Managing Dir*
EMP: 3
SALES (est): 160.2K **Privately Held**
SIC: 3599 Custom machinery

(G-14612)
BUCKEYE PREP REPORT MAGAZINE
Also Called: Buckeye Prep Magazine
8599 Swisher Creek Xing (43054-8385)
PHONE................................614 855-6977
Richard Crockett, *Partner*
Robert Taylor, *Partner*
EMP: 3
SALES (est): 153K **Privately Held**
SIC: 2721 Periodicals

(G-14613)
CAPITAL CITY MILLWORK INC
150 E Dublin Granville Rd (43054-8593)
PHONE................................614 939-0670
Mark J Gundling, *President*
Jim Gundling, *Treasurer*
Aj Panzone, *Marketing Staff*
Alex Perez, *Manager*
EMP: 15
SQ FT: 12,000
SALES (est): 1.8MM **Privately Held**
WEB: www.capcitymillwork.com
SIC: 2431 Millwork

(G-14614)
COLUMBUS KDC
8825 Smiths Mill Rd (43054-6649)
PHONE................................614 656-1130
Mariann Brooks, *Principal*
EMP: 16 EST: 2015
SALES (est): 4.9MM **Privately Held**
SIC: 2844 Toilet preparations

(G-14615)
COMMERCIAL VEHICLE GROUP INC (PA)
7800 Walton Pkwy (43054-8233)
PHONE................................614 289-5360
Scott C Arves, *Ch of Bd*
Patrick E Miller, *President*
Dale M McKillop, *Senior VP*
Greg Boese, *Vice Pres*
Santosh Gadewar, *Opers Staff*
EMP: 1850
SALES: 897.7MM **Publicly Held**
WEB: www.commercialvehiclegroup.com
SIC: 3231 3714 Mirrors, truck & automobile: made from purchased glass; windshield wiper systems, motor vehicle

(G-14616)
COMPLETE EXPRESSIONS WD WORKS
6718 Albany Station Dr (43054-8093)
PHONE................................614 245-4152
Steve Fannin, *Principal*
EMP: 3
SALES (est): 222.6K **Privately Held**
SIC: 2431 Millwork

(G-14617)
CONTRACTOR TOOLS ONLINE LLC
Uknown (43054)
P.O. Box 942 (43054-0942)
PHONE................................614 264-9392
EMP: 3
SALES (est): 136.3K **Privately Held**
SIC: 7372 7374 Prepackaged Software Services Data Processing/Preparation

(G-14618)
CUSTOM AUTOMATION TECHNOLOGIES
1267 Bayboro Dr (43054-9411)
PHONE................................614 939-4228
Daniel D Hoehnen, *President*
Sally Hoehnen, *Vice Pres*
EMP: 3
SALES (est): 429.9K **Privately Held**
WEB: www.customautomationtech.com
SIC: 5999 3651 Audio-visual equipment & supplies; home entertainment equipment, electronic

(G-14619)
CUSTOM METAL PRODUCTS INC
Also Called: Do All Sheetmetal
5037 Babbitt Rd (43054-8301)
P.O. Box 119 (43054-0119)
PHONE................................614 855-2263
Dan Clark, *Plant Mgr*
Sherry Mechling, *QC Mgr*
EMP: 9 **Privately Held**
SIC: 3444 Housings for business machines, sheet metal
PA: Custom Metal Products Inc.
    5037 Babbitt Rd
    New Albany OH 43054

(G-14620)
CUSTOM METAL PRODUCTS INC (PA)
Also Called: Do All Sheet Metal
5037 Babbitt Rd (43054-8301)
P.O. Box 149 (43054-0149)
PHONE................................614 855-2263
Sheri Brock, *President*
Darrell Brock, *Corp Secy*
Carolyn Clark, *Controller*
Jana Cottrill, *Human Res Mgr*
EMP: 7
SQ FT: 24,000
SALES (est): 733K **Privately Held**
WEB: www.do-all-precision.com
SIC: 3444 Metal housings, enclosures, casings & other containers

(G-14621)
CVG NATIONAL SEATING CO LLC
7800 Walton Pkwy (43054-8233)
PHONE................................219 872-7295
Mervin Dunn, *President*
Jimmy Harris, *Vice Pres*
▲ EMP: 67
SALES (est): 72.4MM
SALES (corp-wide): 897.7MM **Publicly Held**
SIC: 2392 Chair covers & pads: made from purchased materials
PA: Commercial Vehicle Group, Inc.
    7800 Walton Pkwy
    New Albany OH 43054
    614 289-5360

(G-14622)
DESCO CORPORATION (PA)
7795 Walton Pkwy Ste 175 (43054-0002)
PHONE................................614 888-8855
Arnold B Siemer, *President*
Mc Connell A Coakwell, *Principal*
James M Smith, *Principal*
Thomas Villano, *Vice Pres*
Juan Hueso, *Opers Mgr*
EMP: 9
SQ FT: 5,500
SALES (est): 180.1MM **Privately Held**
WEB: www.descocapitalpartners.com
SIC: 3442 3825 3643 3531 Window & door frames; metal doors; instruments to measure electricity; current-carrying wiring devices; construction machinery; manufactured hardware (general)

(G-14623)
FAITH GUIDING CAFE LLC
Also Called: Renegade Candle Company
5195 Hampsted Vlg Ctr Way (43054-8331)
PHONE................................614 245-8451
William Lavanier, *President*
Kathy Lavan, *Mng Member*
▲ EMP: 10 EST: 2010
SALES: 400K **Privately Held**
SIC: 3999 8742 Candles; general management consultant

(G-14624)
FLEXCART LLC
5868 Kitzmiller Rd (43054-8576)
PHONE................................614 348-2517
Edward Guirlinger, *President*
James Marable, *Exec VP*
EMP: 5 EST: 2014
SQ FT: 4,200
SALES (est): 4MM **Privately Held**
SIC: 3589 Janitors' carts

(G-14625)
GIBBS E & ASSOCIATES LLC
7386 Hampsted Sq S (43054-8741)
PHONE................................614 939-1672
EMP: 7
SALES (est): 468.1K **Privately Held**
SIC: 7319 2253 Advertising Services Knit Outerwear Mill

(G-14626)
INNOVATIVE APPS LTD
8000 Walton Pkwy Ste 208 (43054-7073)
PHONE................................330 687-2888
Kevin Ly,
EMP: 3
SALES (est): 73.4K **Privately Held**
SIC: 7372 Prepackaged software

(G-14627)
ISOCHEM INCORPORATED
7721 Sutton Pl (43054-8757)
PHONE................................614 775-9328
Kevin E Klingerman, *President*
▲ EMP: 5
SALES (est): 601K **Privately Held**
SIC: 2821 Plastics materials & resins

(G-14628)
JANOVA LLC
7570 N Goodrich Sq (43054-8983)
PHONE................................614 638-6785
Jeffrey Lusenhop, *CEO*
Brian Lusenhop, *Vice Pres*
Kelly Di Cesare, *Human Resources*
Brian Steel, *VP Sales*
EMP: 19 EST: 2010
SALES (est): 1.2MM **Privately Held**
SIC: 7372 Application computer software; business oriented computer software

(G-14629)
JETFUEL SPORTS INC
8000 Walton Pkwy (43054-7073)
PHONE................................614 327-3300
EMP: 3 EST: 2016
SALES (est): 120.7K **Privately Held**
SIC: 2911 Jet fuels

(G-14630)
MAYFLOWER VEHICLE SYSTEMS LLC
Also Called: Stratos Seating,
7800 Walton Pkwy (43054-8233)
PHONE................................419 668-8132
EMP: 7
SALES (est): 1MM **Privately Held**
SIC: 2531 Mfg Public Building Furniture

(G-14631)
MUELLER ELECTRIC COMPANY INC
7795 Walton Pkwy Ste 175 (43054-0002)
PHONE................................614 888-8855
Rodger Bailey, *CEO*
EMP: 30 EST: 2011
SALES: 6.2MM **Privately Held**
SIC: 3679 3678 3825 Harness assemblies for electronic use: wire or cable; electronic connectors; test equipment for electronic & electric measurement

(G-14632)
NOW SOFTWARE INC
3720 Head Of Pond Rd (43054-8992)
PHONE................................614 783-4517
John Wallace Click, *Principal*
EMP: 5
SALES (est): 376.7K **Privately Held**
SIC: 7372 Prepackaged software

(G-14633)
PEN PAL LLC
5868 Kitzmiller Rd (43054-8576)
PHONE................................614 348-2517
Edward G Guirlinger, *Mng Member*
EMP: 3
SQ FT: 4,200
SALES: 1MM **Privately Held**
SIC: 3952 Pencil holders

(G-14634)
PINKY & THUMB LLC
Also Called: Project Aloha
5216 Sugar Run Dr (43054-9471)
PHONE................................614 939-5216
Michael Paz, *Principal*
EMP: 4
SALES (est): 100K **Privately Held**
SIC: 2396 Screen printing on fabric articles

▲ = Import ▼=Export
◆ =Import/Export

GEOGRAPHIC SECTION

(G-14635)
PWI INC
Also Called: Privacyware
5195 Hampsted Vlg Ctr Way (43054-8331)
PHONE 732 212-8110
Gregory Salvato, *CEO*
EMP: 15
SALES (est): 1.1MM **Privately Held**
WEB: www.pwicorp.com
SIC: 7372 7371 8742 Prepackaged software; software programming applications; corporation organizing

(G-14636)
SAMUEL CLARK (PA)
Also Called: Do All Sheet Metal
5037 Babbitt Rd (43054-8301)
P.O. Box 119 (43054-0119)
PHONE 614 855-2263
Fax: 614 855-7161
EMP: 18
SQ FT: 77,000
SALES: 1MM **Privately Held**
SIC: 3444 Mfg Sheet Metalwork

(G-14637)
TRI-TECH LABORATORIES INC
Also Called: Kdc Innovation
8825 Smiths Mill Rd (43054-6649)
PHONE 614 656-1130
Matt Unger, *Vice Pres*
EMP: 3
SALES (corp-wide): 603MM **Privately Held**
SIC: 2834 Pharmaceutical preparations
HQ: Kdc Us Holdings, Inc.
  1000 Robins Rd
  Lynchburg VA 24504

(G-14638)
TRIM SYSTEMS OPERATING CORP (HQ)
Also Called: Cvg Trim Systems
7800 Walton Pkwy (43054-8233)
PHONE 614 289-5360
Gerald L Armstrong, *President*
Linda Knockel, *Purch Mgr*
Josh Dippo, *Engineer*
Carl Kajder, *Engineer*
Cory Strait, *Engineer*
▲ **EMP:** 80
SALES (est): 137.1MM
SALES (corp-wide): 897.7MM **Publicly Held**
SIC: 3714 Motor vehicle parts & accessories
PA: Commercial Vehicle Group, Inc.
  7800 Walton Pkwy
  New Albany OH 43054
  614 289-5360

(G-14639)
TRIM SYSTEMS OPERATING CORP
7800 Walton Pkwy (43054-8233)
PHONE 614 289-5360
Russ Jansen, *Manager*
EMP: 240
SALES (corp-wide): 897.7MM **Publicly Held**
SIC: 2295 3713 3429 3083 Laminating of fabrics; truck & bus bodies; manufactured hardware (general); laminated plastics plate & sheet; public building & related furniture
HQ: Trim Systems Operating Corp.
  7800 Walton Pkwy
  New Albany OH 43054
  614 289-5360

(G-14640)
VENTURE THERAPEUTICS INC
10739 Johnstown Rd (43054-9752)
PHONE 614 430-3300
Peter Stoelzle, *CEO*
Hung Truong, *Research*
Michael Medors, *CFO*
EMP: 5
SALES (est): 621.4K **Privately Held**
SIC: 2834 Pharmaceutical preparations

(G-14641)
VERIANO FINE FOODS SPIRITS LTD
5175 Zarley St Ste A (43054)
P.O. Box 617 (43054-0617)
PHONE 614 745-7705
George Vergies,
Lynda Vergies,
EMP: 15
SQ FT: 10,000
SALES: 2.8MM **Privately Held**
SIC: 2085 5182 Distilled & blended liquors; liquor

(G-14642)
VETGRAFT LLC
7590 Brandon Rd (43054-9059)
PHONE 614 203-0603
Claire Wasielewski,
EMP: 3
SALES (est): 235.3K **Privately Held**
SIC: 2835 Veterinary diagnostic substances

New Bavaria
Henry County

(G-14643)
VERHOFF ALFALFA MILLS INC
1577 Henry Y (43548)
PHONE 419 653-4161
Larry A Mansfield, *Treasurer*
Darwin Verhoff, *Branch Mgr*
EMP: 3
SALES (corp-wide): 6.1MM **Privately Held**
SIC: 2048 Alfalfa or alfalfa meal, prepared as animal feed
PA: Verhoff Alfalfa Mills, Inc.
  1188 Sugar Mill Dr
  Ottawa OH 45875
  419 523-4767

New Bloomington
Marion County

(G-14644)
DIA ENTERPRISES INC
731 Decliff Rd N (43341-9533)
PHONE 740 802-7075
Doug Greenwood, *General Mgr*
Ike Greenwood,
EMP: 3
SALES: 100K **Privately Held**
SIC: 2421 Sawmills & planing mills, general

New Boston
Scioto County

(G-14645)
A & M REFRACTORIES INC
202 West Ave (45662-4946)
PHONE 740 456-8020
Michael Cartee, *President*
Richard Bobst, *Vice Pres*
EMP: 20
SQ FT: 60,000
SALES (est): 2.5MM **Privately Held**
SIC: 3297 Nonclay refractories

(G-14646)
BEAUTY SYSTEMS GROUP LLC
3606 Rhodes Ave (45662-4935)
PHONE 740 456-5434
Hollie Hale, *Branch Mgr*
EMP: 4 **Publicly Held**
SIC: 5087 3999 Beauty parlor equipment & supplies; barber & beauty shop equipment
HQ: Beauty Systems Group Llc
  3001 Colorado Blvd
  Denton TX 76210

New Bremen
Auglaize County

(G-14647)
AUGLAIZE ERIE MACHINE COMPANY
07148 Quellhorst Rd (45869-9632)
P.O. Box 72 (45869-0072)
PHONE 419 629-2068
Tom W Slife, *President*
Elaine Slife, *Treasurer*
Jeremy Homan, *Admin Sec*
Mark Slife, *Maintence Staff*
EMP: 25
SQ FT: 7,500
SALES (est): 5.2MM **Privately Held**
WEB: www.aemcnc.com
SIC: 3599 Machine shop, jobbing & repair

(G-14648)
CISCO SYSTEMS INC
130 S Washington St (45869-1249)
PHONE 419 977-2404
EMP: 656
SALES (corp-wide): 48B **Publicly Held**
SIC: 3577 Computer peripheral equipment
PA: Cisco Systems, Inc.
  170 W Tasman Dr
  San Jose CA 95134
  408 526-4000

(G-14649)
CROWN CREDIT COMPANY
44 S Washington St (45869-1288)
P.O. Box 640352, Cincinnati (45264-0352)
PHONE 419 629-2311
James Dicke III, *President*
EMP: 17
SQ FT: 2,492
SALES: 4.5MM
SALES (corp-wide): 3.1B **Privately Held**
SIC: 3537 Lift trucks, industrial: fork, platform, straddle, etc.
PA: Crown Equipment Corporation
  44 S Washington St
  New Bremen OH 45869
  419 629-2311

(G-14650)
CROWN EQUIPMENT CORPORATION
Also Called: Crown Lift Trucks
120 W Monroe St (45869-1149)
PHONE 419 629-9201
Dave Besser, *Branch Mgr*
EMP: 4
SALES (corp-wide): 3.1B **Privately Held**
SIC: 3537 Lift trucks, industrial: fork, platform, straddle, etc.
PA: Crown Equipment Corporation
  44 S Washington St
  New Bremen OH 45869
  419 629-2311

(G-14651)
CROWN EQUIPMENT CORPORATION
Also Called: Crown Lift Trucks
624 W Monroe St (45869-1351)
PHONE 419 629-2311
Rodrigo Flores, *QC Mgr*
Nick Siebert, *Design Engr*
Jennifer Henning, *Credit Staff*
Tj Shelters, *Sales Mgr*
Brian Botta, *Sales Staff*
EMP: 65
SALES (corp-wide): 3.1B **Privately Held**
SIC: 3537 Lift trucks, industrial: fork, platform, straddle, etc.
PA: Crown Equipment Corporation
  44 S Washington St
  New Bremen OH 45869
  419 629-2311

(G-14652)
CROWN EQUIPMENT CORPORATION
40 S Washington St (45869-1247)
PHONE 419 629-2311
EMP: 65
SALES (corp-wide): 1.3B **Privately Held**
SIC: 5084 3537 Whol Industrial Equipment Mfg Industrial Trucks/Tractors
PA: Crown Equipment Corporation
  44 S Washington St
  New Bremen OH 45869
  419 629-2311

(G-14653)
CROWN EQUIPMENT CORPORATION
Also Called: Crown Lift Trucks
510 W Monroe St (45869-1300)
PHONE 419 629-2311
EMP: 62
SALES (corp-wide): 3.1B **Privately Held**
SIC: 3537 Lift trucks, industrial: fork, platform, straddle, etc.
PA: Crown Equipment Corporation
  44 S Washington St
  New Bremen OH 45869
  419 629-2311

(G-14654)
FASTENAL COMPANY
575 W Monroe St (45869-1323)
PHONE 419 629-3024
Mark Suseland, *Branch Mgr*
EMP: 3
SALES (corp-wide): 4.9B **Publicly Held**
SIC: 5085 3429 Fasteners & fastening equipment; manufactured hardware (general)
PA: Fastenal Company
  2001 Theurer Blvd
  Winona MN 55987
  507 454-5374

(G-14655)
KINNINGER PROD WLDG CO INC
710 Kuenzel Dr (45869-9699)
P.O. Box 33 (45869-0033)
PHONE 419 629-3491
Kevin Thobe, *President*
Donna Thobe, *Treasurer*
Cheryl Thobe, *Admin Sec*
EMP: 53
SQ FT: 54,000
SALES (est): 10MM **Privately Held**
WEB: www.kinningerwelding.com
SIC: 3599 Machine shop, jobbing & repair

(G-14656)
MARKETING ESSENTIALS LLC
14 N Washington St (45869-1150)
PHONE 419 629-0080
Haley Dillon, *Marketing Staff*
Brooke Taylor, *Marketing Staff*
Patricia Cisco,
EMP: 13 **EST:** 2009
SALES (est): 388.8K **Privately Held**
SIC: 8743 2741 2721 2711 Public relations & publicity; ; magazines: publishing only, not printed on site; magazines: publishing & printing; newspapers: publishing only, not printed on site

(G-14657)
NEW BREMEN MACHINE & TOOL CO
705 Kuenzel Dr (45869-8600)
PHONE 419 629-3295
Joan Leffel, *CEO*
Jay Bergman, *Vice Pres*
Randy Bergman, *Vice Pres*
Robert Roth, *Vice Pres*
EMP: 25 **EST:** 1928
SQ FT: 45,000
SALES (est): 6.3MM **Privately Held**
WEB: www.newbremenmachine.com
SIC: 3469 3544 Metal stampings; special dies & tools

(G-14658)
NUPCO INC
06561 County Road 66a (45869-9615)
PHONE 419 629-2259
Luke Wilker, *President*
Virginia Dickie, *Vice Pres*
EMP: 6 **EST:** 1946
SQ FT: 3,750
SALES (est): 670.5K **Privately Held**
SIC: 3084 Plastics pipe

New Bremen - Auglaize County (G-14659)

(G-14659)
PRECISION REFLEX INC
710 Streine Dr (45869-8608)
P.O. Box 95 (45869-0095)
PHONE.............................419 629-2603
N David Dunlap, *President*
Mary Dunlap, *Corp Secy*
EMP: 12 **EST:** 1978
SQ FT: 2,100
SALES (est): 1MM **Privately Held**
WEB: www.pri-mounts.com
SIC: 3599 2796 7692 Machine shop, jobbing & repair; engraving on copper, steel, wood or rubber; printing plates; welding repair

(G-14660)
SAFEWAY PACKAGING INC (PA)
300 White Mountain Dr (45869-8621)
PHONE.............................419 629-3200
Kevin Manor, *President*
Ralph Stoner, *Vice Pres*
EMP: 82
SQ FT: 100,000
SALES (est): 19.9MM **Privately Held**
WEB: www.safewaypkg.com
SIC: 2653 2673 2671 2631 Boxes, corrugated: made from purchased materials; boxes, solid fiber: made from purchased materials; bags: plastic, laminated & coated; packaging paper & plastics film, coated & laminated; paperboard mills

(G-14661)
THIEMAN QUALITY METAL FAB INC
05140 Dicke Rd (45869-9750)
P.O. Box 45 (45869-0045)
PHONE.............................419 629-2612
Doug Broering, *Human Resources*
EMP: 80 **EST:** 1951
SQ FT: 90,000
SALES (est): 14MM **Privately Held**
WEB: www.thieman.com
SIC: 3441 Fabricated structural metal

(G-14662)
VISIONMARK NAMEPLATE CO LLC
100 White Mountain Dr (45869-8626)
P.O. Box 280, New Knoxville (45871-0280)
PHONE.............................419 977-3131
Jerry Merges, *President*
Mark Nolan, *Vice Pres*
EMP: 27
SQ FT: 20,000
SALES (est): 2.2MM **Privately Held**
SIC: 3479 Name plates: engraved, etched, etc.

New Carlisle
Clark County

(G-14663)
BEACH MFG PLASTIC MOLDING DIV
7816 W National Rd (45344)
PHONE.............................937 882-6400
Theodore Beach, *President*
EMP: 75
SALES (est): 7.1MM **Privately Held**
SIC: 3089 Molding primary plastic

(G-14664)
CARLISLE PLASTICS COMPANY INC
320 Ohio St (45344-1630)
P.O. Box 146 (45344-0146)
PHONE.............................937 845-9411
Cynthia A Thomas, *President*
Howard M Clay, *President*
Shannan Stewart, *General Mgr*
Cynthia Group, *VP Opers*
James Thomas, *Admin Sec*
EMP: 7
SQ FT: 12,000
SALES (est): 1.1MM **Privately Held**
WEB: www.carlisleplastics.com
SIC: 3089 Injection molding of plastics

(G-14665)
CUSTOM WAY WELDING INC
2217 N Dayton Lakeview Rd (45344-9578)
PHONE.............................937 845-9469
Brian Bonham, *President*
Amy Bonham, *Treasurer*
EMP: 11
SQ FT: 12,052
SALES: 3.3MM **Privately Held**
SIC: 1799 7692 5599 Ornamental metal work; welding repair; utility trailers

(G-14666)
G KEENER & CO
2936 Liberty Rd (45344-8511)
PHONE.............................937 846-1210
Gary Keener, *President*
Andrea Keener, *Vice Pres*
EMP: 4
SALES (est): 100K **Privately Held**
WEB: www.gkeenerco.com
SIC: 2519 Lawn & garden furniture, except wood & metal

(G-14667)
HTCI CO
12170 Milton Carlisle Rd (45344-9701)
P.O. Box 486 (45344-0486)
PHONE.............................937 845-1204
Kevin King, *President*
Deborah Jenkins, *Corp Secy*
Raymond Franks, *Exec VP*
Allen Partlow, *QC Mgr*
Ryan Storey, *Engineer*
EMP: 18
SALES: 2MM **Privately Held**
WEB: www.htc-inc.com
SIC: 3365 Aerospace castings, aluminum

(G-14668)
INDIAN CREEK DISTILLERY
7095 Staley Rd (45344-9416)
PHONE.............................937 846-1443
Julianne Staley, *Principal*
EMP: 5
SALES (est): 323.9K **Privately Held**
SIC: 2085 Distillers' dried grains & solubles & alcohol

(G-14669)
KAFFENBARGER TRUCK EQP CO (PA)
10100 Ballentine Pike (45344-9534)
PHONE.............................937 845-3804
Larry Kaffenbarger, *President*
Edward W Dunn, *Principal*
Everett L Kaffenbarger, *Principal*
◆ **EMP:** 110
SQ FT: 30,000
SALES (est): 38.4MM **Privately Held**
WEB: www.kaffenbarger.com
SIC: 3713 5013 Truck bodies (motor vehicles); truck parts & accessories

(G-14670)
KRAM PRECISION MACHINING INC
1751 Dalton Dr (45344-2309)
PHONE.............................937 849-1301
Greg Flory, *President*
Douglas Flory, *Treasurer*
▲ **EMP:** 6
SQ FT: 6,000
SALES: 500K **Privately Held**
SIC: 3599 Machine shop, jobbing & repair

(G-14671)
MAD RIVER STEEL LTD
Also Called: Mad River Steel Company
2141 N Dayton Lakeview Rd (45344-9578)
P.O. Box 411 (45344-0411)
PHONE.............................937 845-4046
John Bobo, *President*
EMP: 8
SQ FT: 10,200
SALES (est): 1.1MM **Privately Held**
SIC: 3441 Building components, structural steel

(G-14672)
MAJESTIC ENGINEERING & TL LLC
107 W Washington St (45344-1844)
PHONE.............................937 845-1079
Brad Hornback, *Managing Prtnr*

Mike Notestine, *Managing Prtnr*
EMP: 4 **EST:** 2012
SQ FT: 2,500
SALES: 275K **Privately Held**
SIC: 8711 3599 Engineering services; machine & other job shop work

(G-14673)
NCT TECHNOLOGIES GROUP INC (PA)
7867 W National Rd (45344-8268)
P.O. Box 37 (45344-0037)
PHONE.............................937 882-6800
Andrew Flora, *President*
Curtis Flora, *Vice Pres*
EMP: 25
SQ FT: 7,500
SALES (est): 5.4MM **Privately Held**
WEB: www.newcarlisletool.com
SIC: 3441 Fabricated structural metal

(G-14674)
NEO TECH
123 S Main St (45344-1952)
PHONE.............................937 845-0999
Ted Buskirk, *Owner*
EMP: 3
SALES (est): 211.3K **Privately Held**
SIC: 2813 Neon

(G-14675)
NUMERICS UNLIMITED INC
1700 Dalton Dr (45344-2307)
PHONE.............................937 849-0100
Wayne Atkins, *President*
Derick Simmons, *Opers Mgr*
Richard Rice, *Purchasing*
EMP: 22
SQ FT: 15,000
SALES (est): 4.1MM **Privately Held**
WEB: www.numericsunlimited.com
SIC: 3544 Industrial molds

(G-14676)
PATTON ALUMINUM PRODUCTS INC
65 Quick Rd (45344-9253)
PHONE.............................937 845-9404
Edward E Patton, *President*
Angie King, *Opers Mgr*
EMP: 15 **EST:** 1965
SQ FT: 14,000
SALES (est): 2.7MM **Privately Held**
WEB: www.pattonaluminum.com
SIC: 3354 3448 Shapes, extruded aluminum; screen enclosures; sunrooms, prefabricated metal

(G-14677)
PFI PRECISION INC
Also Called: Pfi Precision Machining
2011 N Dayton Lakeview Rd (45344-9550)
PHONE.............................937 845-3563
Colleen Janek, *President*
▲ **EMP:** 30
SQ FT: 16,000
SALES: 4.1MM **Privately Held**
WEB: www.pfiprecision.com
SIC: 3451 Screw machine products

(G-14678)
TAYLOR TOOL & DIE INC
306 N Main St (45344-1839)
PHONE.............................937 845-1491
Michael L Taylor, *President*
Jim Elrod, *Vice Pres*
Vern Young, *Admin Sec*
EMP: 7 **EST:** 1982
SQ FT: 3,900
SALES (est): 670K **Privately Held**
SIC: 3544 Special dies & tools

(G-14679)
TETRA MOLD & TOOL INC
51 Quick Rd (45344-9294)
PHONE.............................937 845-1651
Brent Hughes, *President*
Arleen Hughes, *Vice Pres*
Ronald L Hughes, *Vice Pres*
EMP: 25 **EST:** 1966
SQ FT: 10,000
SALES (est): 6.4MM **Privately Held**
WEB: www.tetramold.com
SIC: 3089 3544 3714 Injection molding of plastics; special dies, tools, jigs & fixtures; motor vehicle parts & accessories

(G-14680)
TIG WOOD & DIE INC
1760 Dalton Dr (45344-2307)
PHONE.............................937 849-6741
Richard Levally, *President*
Betty Levally, *Vice Pres*
EMP: 19
SQ FT: 12,000
SALES: 1.3MM **Privately Held**
SIC: 3544 5051 Paper cutting dies; dies, steel rule; stampings, metal

(G-14681)
VANSCOYK SHEET METAL CORP
475 Quick Rd (45344-9255)
PHONE.............................937 845-0581
David Van Scoyk, *President*
David Van Skoyk, *Corp Secy*
Wilma V Skoyk, *Vice Pres*
Wilma Van Skoyk, *Vice Pres*
Rachel Van Scoyk, *Marketing Mgr*
EMP: 7
SQ FT: 10,000
SALES: 500K **Privately Held**
SIC: 3441 Fabricated structural metal

New Concord
Muskingum County

(G-14682)
CAMPTON ELECTRIC SALES & SVC
11615 Norfield Rd (43762-9756)
PHONE.............................740 826-4429
Clara Campton, *Partner*
John Campton, *Partner*
Richard Campton, *General Ptnr*
EMP: 3
SALES (est): 310K **Privately Held**
SIC: 5063 7694 Motors, electric; electric motor repair

(G-14683)
CARBONLESS & CUT SHEET FORMS
1948 John Glenn Hwy (43762-9485)
PHONE.............................740 826-1700
Jason Killiany, *President*
David A Killainy, *President*
EMP: 18
SQ FT: 6,000
SALES: 500K **Privately Held**
SIC: 2759 5722 Business forms: printing; vacuum cleaners

(G-14684)
CASHMERE & TWIG LLC
181 Lowery Ln (43762-9795)
PHONE.............................740 404-8468
Jacqueline B Matheney, *Principal*
EMP: 12
SALES (est): 1.9MM **Privately Held**
SIC: 2844 Toilet preparations

(G-14685)
PENDAFORM COMPANY
200 S Friendship Dr (43762-9641)
PHONE.............................740 826-5000
EMP: 200
SALES (corp-wide): 477.9MM **Privately Held**
SIC: 3089 Mfg Plastic Products
PA: The Pendaform Company
200 S Friendship Dr
New Concord OH 53901
740 826-5000

(G-14686)
ROBERT BARR
Also Called: Big Sky Petroleum
1245 Friendship Dr (43762-1023)
PHONE.............................740 826-7325
Robert Barr, *Principal*
EMP: 12
SALES: 1.2MM **Privately Held**
WEB: www.robertbarr.com
SIC: 1311 5812 Crude petroleum production; natural gas production; restaurant, family: independent

(G-14687)
TK GAS SERVICES INC
2303 John Glenn Hwy (43762-9310)
PHONE..................................740 826-0303
Ted Korte, *President*
Jill Pattison, *Corp Secy*
EMP: 50
SQ FT: 4,000
SALES (est): 6.6MM Privately Held
SIC: 1389 Oil field services

New Franklin
Stark County

(G-14688)
VILLERS ENTERPRISES LIMITED
Also Called: Simxperience
980 Dunning Rd Bldg B (44614-9509)
PHONE..................................330 818-9838
Bernard L Villers Jr, *Mng Member*
Bernard Villers Sr,
EMP: 4
SQ FT: 2,500
SALES (est): 550.5K Privately Held
SIC: 3699 Automotive driving simulators (training aids), electronic

New Franklin
Summit County

(G-14689)
FISHERMANS CENTRAL LLC
5461 Manchester Rd (44319-4208)
PHONE..................................330 644-5346
EMP: 4
SALES (est): 343.2K Privately Held
SIC: 3949 Bait, artificial; fishing

(G-14690)
G & J EXTRUSIONS INC
1580 Turkeyfoot Lake Rd (44203-4852)
P.O. Box 275, Hessel MI (49745-0275)
PHONE..................................330 753-0162
Garry Dumbauld, *President*
Julie Dumbauld, *Vice Pres*
EMP: 6
SQ FT: 10,000
SALES (est): 654.7K Privately Held
WEB: www.gjextrude.com
SIC: 3089 Extruded finished plastic products

(G-14691)
J MCCAMAN ENTERPRISES INC
Also Called: J M Machinery
3032 Franks Rd (44216-9327)
P.O. Box 378, Wadsworth (44282-0378)
PHONE..................................330 825-2401
Michael L Dyer, *President*
Jason Breth, *Sales Mgr*
EMP: 15
SQ FT: 2,500
SALES (est): 2.4MM Privately Held
WEB: www.jmktm.com
SIC: 3559 5084 Plastics working machinery; rubber working machinery, including tires; industrial machinery & equipment

(G-14692)
JCI JONES CHEMICALS INC
2500 Vanderhoof Rd (44203-4650)
PHONE..................................330 825-2531
Dan Casmey, *Manager*
EMP: 15
SQ FT: 22,848
SALES (corp-wide): 179MM Privately Held
WEB: www.jcichem.com
SIC: 2812 8734 Chlorine, compressed or liquefied; testing laboratories
PA: Jci Jones Chemicals, Inc.
1765 Ringling Blvd
Sarasota FL 34236
941 330-1537

(G-14693)
MARTINS STEEL FABRICATION
2115 Center Rd (44216-8807)
PHONE..................................330 882-4311
Jason Darrah, *President*
Bryan Rossiter, *General Mgr*
Beverly Martin, *Vice Pres*
EMP: 20
SQ FT: 6,000
SALES: 4MM Privately Held
SIC: 3441 Fabricated structural metal

(G-14694)
OHIO PLASTICS & SAFETY PDTS
6140 Manchester Rd (44319-4615)
P.O. Box 593, Columbia Station (44028-0593)
PHONE..................................330 882-6764
Leanne Keith, *President*
EMP: 5
SQ FT: 3,850
SALES (est): 477.2K Privately Held
SIC: 3993 Signs & advertising specialties

(G-14695)
OHIO PLASTICS BELTING CO
6140 Manchester Rd (44319-4615)
P.O. Box 593, Columbia Station (44028-0593)
PHONE..................................330 882-6764
John David Satink, *Owner*
John G David, *Co-Owner*
Le-Anne Keith, *Co-Owner*
EMP: 6
SALES (est): 550K Privately Held
WEB: www.ohiothane.com
SIC: 2821 Plastics materials & resins

(G-14696)
PHILLIPS MCH & STAMPING CORP
5290 S Main St (44319-4997)
PHONE..................................330 882-6714
Wilda Phillips, *President*
Craig Phillips, *Vice Pres*
EMP: 8
SQ FT: 16,000
SALES (est): 1.4MM Privately Held
SIC: 3469 3544 Stamping metal for the trade; special dies & tools

(G-14697)
PRISTINE EXTERIORS
5925 Renninger Rd (44319-4833)
PHONE..................................330 957-5664
Jerry Largent, *Owner*
EMP: 3 EST: 2015
SALES (est): 73.7K Privately Held
SIC: 2381 Dyeing gloves, woven or knit: for the trade

(G-14698)
RUBBER ASSOCIATES INC
1522 Turkeyfoot Lake Rd (44203-4898)
PHONE..................................330 745-2186
Eugene Fiocca, *President*
Joe Machek, *Manager*
Shirley Graver, *MIS Mgr*
Kris Fiocca, *Executive*
Ronald Allan, *Asst Sec*
▲ EMP: 100
SQ FT: 76,000
SALES (est): 16.3MM Privately Held
WEB: www.rubberassociates.com
SIC: 3069 Molded rubber products

New Hampshire
Auglaize County

(G-14699)
BETHEL ENGINEERING AND EQP INC (PA)
13830 Mcbeth Rd (45870)
P.O. Box 67 (45870-0067)
PHONE..................................419 568-1100
David Whitaker, *President*
Kathy Whitaker, *Treasurer*
EMP: 34
SQ FT: 51,000
SALES: 5.6MM Privately Held
WEB: www.bethelengr.com
SIC: 3559 3441 Paint making machinery; fabricated structural metal

(G-14700)
BETHEL ENGINEERING AND EQP INC
13830 Mcbeth Rd (45870)
P.O. Box 67 (45870-0067)
PHONE..................................419 568-7976
David Whitaker, *Branch Mgr*
EMP: 20 Privately Held
WEB: www.bethelengr.com
SIC: 3559 Paint making machinery
PA: Bethel Engineering And Equipment, Inc.
13830 Mcbeth Rd
New Hampshire OH 45870

New Holland
Pickaway County

(G-14701)
DEER CREEK CUSTOM CANVAS LLC
23799 State Route 207 (43145-9705)
PHONE..................................740 495-9239
Zazchry Neff, *Mng Member*
EMP: 3
SALES (est): 159K Privately Held
SIC: 2394 7538 Canvas & related products; engine repair

(G-14702)
NEW HOLLAND ENGINEERING INC
43 E Front St (43145-9662)
P.O. Box 125 (43145-0125)
PHONE..................................740 495-5200
John Berker, *President*
Beverly Berker, *Vice Pres*
EMP: 7
SQ FT: 7,000
SALES (est): 900K Privately Held
WEB: www.gutterhangers.net
SIC: 3469 3541 Metal stampings; machine tools, metal cutting type

New Knoxville
Auglaize County

(G-14703)
HOGE LUMBER COMPANY (PA)
Also Called: Hoge Brush
701 S Main St State (45871)
PHONE..................................419 753-2263
John H Hoge, *President*
Jack R Hoge, *Exec VP*
Clark T Froning, *Vice Pres*
Bruce L Hoge, *Vice Pres*
Bruce Eschmeyer, *Sales Mgr*
▲ EMP: 35
SQ FT: 400,000
SALES (est): 6.4MM Privately Held
WEB: www.hoge.com
SIC: 3448 1521 2521 Prefabricated metal buildings; new construction, single-family houses; cabinets, office: wood

(G-14704)
HOGE LUMBER COMPANY
Hoge Brush Co
202 E South St (45871)
PHONE..................................419 753-2351
Dave Zwiep, *Manager*
EMP: 10
SQ FT: 80
SALES (corp-wide): 6.4MM Privately Held
WEB: www.hoge.com
SIC: 3991 Brooms & brushes
PA: Hoge Lumber Company
701 S Main St State
New Knoxville OH 45871
419 753-2263

(G-14705)
MODERN AG SUPPLY INC
302 S Main St (45871)
P.O. Box 249 (45871-0249)
PHONE..................................419 753-3484
Jack Leffel, *President*
EMP: 3
SALES (est): 320K Privately Held
SIC: 2879 Chemicals, agricultural

New Lebanon
Montgomery County

(G-14706)
A-BUCK MANUFACTURING INC
12251 Eagle Rd (45345-9122)
PHONE..................................937 687-3738
EMP: 3
SALES (est): 147.4K Privately Held
SIC: 3999 Mfg Misc Products

(G-14707)
B & B GEAR & MACHINE CO INC
440 W Main St (45345-1426)
PHONE..................................937 687-1771
Kevin Brinson, *President*
Jennifer Brinson, *Owner*
Jerry Brinson, *Director*
EMP: 12
SQ FT: 15,000
SALES (est): 3.7MM Privately Held
SIC: 3566 3599 Gears, power transmission, except automotive; machine shop, jobbing & repair

(G-14708)
DISTINCT CBNTRY INNVATIONS LLC
31 S Church St (45345-1213)
PHONE..................................937 661-1051
Brian Stoner,
EMP: 3
SALES: 250K Privately Held
SIC: 2434 1799 Wood kitchen cabinets; home/office interiors finishing, furnishing & remodeling

(G-14709)
DIXIE FLYER & PRINTING CO
424 Rosetta St (45345-1520)
PHONE..................................937 687-0088
Roger Salyer, *Principal*
EMP: 4
SALES (est): 240K Privately Held
SIC: 2752 Commercial printing, lithographic

(G-14710)
H DUANE LEIS ACQUISITIONS
Also Called: Micro Tool Service
443 S Diamond Mill Rd (45345)
PHONE..................................937 835-5621
H Duane Leis Jr, *President*
Duane Leis, *Vice Pres*
EMP: 20
SALES: 3MM Privately Held
SIC: 3545 Cutting tools for machine tools

(G-14711)
MARTIN WELDING LLC (PA)
1472 W Main St (45345-9772)
PHONE..................................937 687-3602
Mike Martin,
EMP: 10
SALES (est): 958.6K Privately Held
SIC: 7692 Welding repair

(G-14712)
MCINTOSH MACHINE
11 S Church St (45345-1213)
P.O. Box 164 (45345-0164)
PHONE..................................937 687-3936
Terry McIntosh, *Owner*
EMP: 5
SQ FT: 3,000
SALES (est): 210K Privately Held
SIC: 7692 5571 5013 3599 Welding repair; motorcycle parts & accessories; motorcycle parts; machine & other job shop work

New Lexington
Perry County

(G-14713)
C S A ENTERPRISES
Also Called: Tla Designs
932 S Main St (43764-1552)
PHONE.................................740 342-9367
Corlyn Speake Altier, *Owner*
EMP: 5
SALES: 100K **Privately Held**
SIC: 8721 2221 Billing & bookkeeping service; wall covering fabrics, manmade fiber & silk

(G-14714)
COOPER-STANDARD AUTOMOTIVE INC
2378 State Route 345 Ne (43764)
PHONE.................................740 342-3523
Mr B Dickens, *Branch Mgr*
Betty Lucas, *Technology*
EMP: 352
SQ FT: 80,000
SALES (corp-wide): 3.6B **Publicly Held**
WEB: www.cooperstandard.com
SIC: 3714 3443 Motor vehicle brake systems & parts; fuel systems & parts, motor vehicle; heat exchangers, condensers & components
HQ: Cooper-Standard Automotive Inc.
207 S West St
Auburn IN 46706
248 596-5900

(G-14715)
DNL OIL CORP
Also Called: Dusty's Salvage & Supply
7913 State Route 37 E (43764-9512)
PHONE.................................740 342-4970
N L Altier Jr, *President*
EMP: 7
SQ FT: 4,230
SALES (est): 800.6K **Privately Held**
SIC: 1381 5211 Drilling oil & gas wells; lumber & other building materials

(G-14716)
HOCKING VALLEY CONCRETE INC
1500 Commerce Dr (43764-9432)
PHONE.................................740 342-1948
William Laughn, *Principal*
Jim Thomas, *Manager*
EMP: 4
SALES (est): 324.6K
SALES (corp-wide): 3.8MM **Privately Held**
SIC: 3273 Ready-mixed concrete
PA: Hocking Valley Concrete, Inc.
35255 Hocking Dr
Logan OH 43138
740 385-2165

(G-14717)
LORI HOLDING CO (PA)
Also Called: Siemer Distributing
1400 Commerce Dr (43764-9500)
PHONE.................................740 342-3230
Joseph A Siemer III, *President*
EMP: 30
SALES (est): 10.8MM **Privately Held**
SIC: 5147 5143 5199 5142 Meats, fresh; cheese; ice, manufactured or natural; packaged frozen goods; manufactured ice

(G-14718)
LUDOWICI ROOF TILE INC
4757 Tile Plant Rd Se (43764-9630)
P.O. Box 69 (43764-0069)
PHONE.................................740 342-1995
Herve Gastinel, *President*
Guillaume Latil, *Vice Pres*
Kyle Riggle, *Project Mgr*
Shelby Stevenson, *Project Mgr*
David Kunkler, *Maint Spvr*
◆ **EMP:** 80
SQ FT: 100,000
SALES (est): 14.6MM
SALES (corp-wide): 3.7MM **Privately Held**
WEB: www.ludowici.com
SIC: 3259 Roofing tile, clay
HQ: Terreal
13 17
Suresnes 92150

(G-14719)
OXFORD MINING COMPANY INC
Also Called: Tunnell Hill Reclamation
2500 Township Rd 205 (43764)
PHONE.................................740 342-7666
Jeff Williams, *Superintendent*
EMP: 58
SALES (corp-wide): 1.3B **Privately Held**
SIC: 1221 Strip mining, bituminous
HQ: Oxford Mining Company, Inc.
544 Chestnut St
Coshocton OH 43812
740 622-6302

(G-14720)
PERRY COUNTY TRIBUNE
Also Called: Tribune Shopping News, The
399 Lincoln Park Dr Ste A (43764-1078)
P.O. Box 312 (43764-0312)
PHONE.................................740 342-4121
Deb Hutmire, *General Mgr*
Bill Rockwell, *Editor*
EMP: 10
SALES (est): 407.4K **Privately Held**
SIC: 2711 6512 Newspapers, publishing & printing; property operation, retail establishment

(G-14721)
R & D HILLTOP LUMBER INC
2126 State Route 93 Se (43764-9666)
PHONE.................................740 342-3051
Russell Howdyshell, *President*
Polly Howdyshell, *Vice Pres*
EMP: 23
SQ FT: 8,000
SALES (est): 2.9MM **Privately Held**
SIC: 2421 Lumber: rough, sawed or planed

(G-14722)
R CARNEY THOMAS
Also Called: T C Woodworking
1600 Commerce Dr (43764-9562)
PHONE.................................740 342-3388
Thomas Carney, *Owner*
EMP: 5
SQ FT: 13,000
SALES (est): 348.4K **Privately Held**
SIC: 1751 2521 2434 2431 Cabinet building & installation; cabinets, office: wood; wood kitchen cabinets; millwork

(G-14723)
SOUTHEASTERN SHAFTING MFG
402 W Broadway St (43764-1007)
P.O. Box 168 (43764-0168)
PHONE.................................740 342-4629
Scott Jones Sr, *President*
Theresa M Jones, *Admin Sec*
EMP: 18
SALES (est): 2.3MM **Privately Held**
WEB: www.seshafting.com
SIC: 3568 3599 Collars, shaft (power transmission equipment); machine shop, jobbing & repair

(G-14724)
STAR ENGINEERING INC
701 Madison St (43764-1086)
P.O. Box 71 (43764-0071)
PHONE.................................740 342-3514
Bill Mooney, *CEO*
Christopher Mooney, *President*
William J Mooney, *Vice Pres*
Daniel P Mooney, *Vice Pres*
John Mooney, *Vice Pres*
EMP: 35 **EST:** 1941
SQ FT: 36,000
SALES (est): 9.7MM **Privately Held**
WEB: www.starengineering.com
SIC: 3567 Ceramic kilns & furnaces

(G-14725)
SURVEYING CANNON LAND
7945 Township Road 114 Ne (43764-9608)
PHONE.................................740 342-2835
Kevin Cannon, *Owner*
EMP: 3
SALES (est): 158.5K **Privately Held**
SIC: 1389 Oil field services

(G-14726)
T & R NOODLES LLC
11400 State Route 37 E (43764-9655)
PHONE.................................614 537-4710
Joseph Metz, *COO*
Donald Metz, *CFO*
Donna Metz, *Chief Mktg Ofcr*
Andrew Metz, *Security Dir*
EMP: 4
SQ FT: 900
SALES (est): 240K **Privately Held**
SIC: 2098 Noodles (e.g. egg, plain & water), dry

(G-14727)
TERREAL NORTH AMERICA LLC
4757 Tile Plant Rd Se (43764-9630)
P.O. Box 309 (43764-0309)
PHONE.................................888 582-9052
Mike Ade, *Sales Staff*
Herve Gastinel, *Mng Member*
EMP: 175
SALES (est): 8.8MM **Privately Held**
SIC: 3259 Roofing tile, clay

New London
Huron County

(G-14728)
APPLIED AUTOMATION ENTERPRISE
24 Cedar St (44851-1218)
PHONE.................................419 929-2428
Timothy Hedrick, *President*
Vaughn Lucal, *Treasurer*
Susan Dooley, *Office Mgr*
Stephan Pabst, *Admin Sec*
EMP: 11
SQ FT: 15,000
SALES (est): 1.7MM **Privately Held**
WEB: www.automationent.com
SIC: 3541 Chucking machines, automatic

(G-14729)
FITCHVILLE EAST CORP
Also Called: Fitchville East Storage
1732 Us Highway 250 S (44851-9372)
PHONE.................................419 929-1510
Gene Rieske, *President*
Leonard Leach, *Vice Pres*
Lewis Rieske, *Manager*
EMP: 22
SALES (est): 1.3MM **Privately Held**
SIC: 3799 Trailers & trailer equipment

(G-14730)
KENT SPORTING GOODS CO INC (PA)
433 Park Ave (44851-1314)
PHONE.................................419 929-7021
Robert Archer, *CEO*
J Robert Tipton, *President*
Marlene Sipp, *Vice Pres*
Wayne Walters, *Vice Pres*
Hank Wiggins, *Vice Pres*
▲ **EMP:** 100
SQ FT: 25,000
SALES (est): 135.8MM **Privately Held**
SIC: 3949 Water sports equipment

(G-14731)
MONODE MARKING PRODUCTS INC
Also Called: Waldorf Marking Devices
149 High St (44851-1118)
PHONE.................................419 929-0346
Thomas Mackey, *President*
EMP: 10
SALES (corp-wide): 12.3MM **Privately Held**
SIC: 3542 3953 Marking machines; marking devices
PA: Monode Marking Products, Inc.
9200 Tyler Blvd
Mentor OH 44060
440 975-8802

(G-14732)
MONODE STEEL STAMP INC (PA)
149 High St (44851-1118)
PHONE.................................419 929-3501
Thomas Mackey, *President*
William Vickery, *Vice Pres*
EMP: 26
SQ FT: 3,000
SALES: 1.8MM **Privately Held**
WEB: www.monode.com
SIC: 3542 3469 3953 Marking machines; metal stampings; marking devices

(G-14733)
NEW LONDON FOUNDRY INC
80 Walnut St (44851-1240)
P.O. Box 227 (44851-0227)
PHONE.................................419 929-2073
Keith Gregory, *President*
Dorothy Gregory, *Corp Secy*
EMP: 15 **EST:** 1949
SQ FT: 21,000
SALES (est): 2.4MM **Privately Held**
SIC: 3365 3369 Aluminum & aluminum-based alloy castings; nonferrous foundries

(G-14734)
NEW LONDON REGALIA MFG CO
1 Harmony Pl (44851-1248)
PHONE.................................419 929-1516
Glen Hammersmith, *President*
S George Kurz, *Corp Secy*
EMP: 14
SQ FT: 7,500
SALES (est): 620K **Privately Held**
WEB: www.newlondonregalia.com
SIC: 2389 Regalia

(G-14735)
RANKIN MFG INC
201 N Main St (44851-1015)
PHONE.................................419 929-8338
Eric Rankine, *President*
Michael Rankine, *Corp Secy*
EMP: 22
SQ FT: 52,500
SALES (est): 4.4MM **Privately Held**
WEB: www.rankinmfg.com
SIC: 3441 3799 3599 Fabricated structural metal; trailers & trailer equipment; machine & other job shop work

(G-14736)
ROERIG MACHINE
27348 State Route 511 (44851-9667)
PHONE.................................440 647-4718
William Roerig, *Partner*
Ron Roerig, *Partner*
EMP: 6
SALES: 200K **Privately Held**
SIC: 3599 Machine shop, jobbing & repair

(G-14737)
SDG NEWS GROUP INC
Also Called: Firelands Farmer, The
43 E Main St (44851-1213)
P.O. Box 146 (44851-0146)
PHONE.................................419 929-3411
Scott Glove, *President*
Scott Gove, *President*
EMP: 10
SALES (est): 454.1K **Privately Held**
SIC: 2711 2752 Newspapers: publishing only, not printed on site; commercial printing, lithographic

(G-14738)
SEWLINE PRODUCTS INC
30 S Railroad St (44851-1243)
PHONE.................................419 929-1114
Duane E Mills, *President*
Alana Mills, *Admin Sec*
EMP: 12
SQ FT: 30,980
SALES: 350K **Privately Held**
SIC: 2392 2399 Blankets, comforters & beddings; infant carriers

GEOGRAPHIC SECTION

New Philadelphia - Tuscarawas County (G-14765)

(G-14739)
THOMAS CREATIVE APPAREL INC
1 Harmony Pl (44851-1248)
PHONE.....................419 929-1506
Vickie Hall, *President*
EMP: 35
SQ FT: 14,000
SALES (est): 3.7MM **Privately Held**
WEB: www.thomasrobes.com
SIC: 2384 2389 2353 Robes & dressing gowns; lodge costumes; hats, caps & millinery

(G-14740)
TIERRA-DERCO INTERNATIONAL LLC
40 S Main St (44851-1138)
PHONE.....................419 929-2240
Heath White, *Manager*
EMP: 7 **Privately Held**
SIC: 3524 Lawn & garden equipment
PA: Tierra-Derco International, Llc
  1000 S Saint Charles St
  Jasper IN 47546

New Madison
Darke County

(G-14741)
FLORIDA PRODUCTION ENGRG INC
Ernie Green Industries
1855 State Route 121 N (45346-9716)
PHONE.....................937 996-4361
Eric Opicka, *Enginr/R&D Mgr*
EMP: 90
SALES (corp-wide): 580.4MM **Privately Held**
SIC: 3465 3714 3429 Moldings or trim, automobile; stamped metal; motor vehicle parts & accessories; manufactured hardware (general)
HQ: Florida Production Engineering, Inc.
  2 E Tower Cir
  Ormond Beach FL 32174
  386 677-2566

(G-14742)
LUDY GREENHOUSE MFG CORP (PA)
122 Railroad St (45346-5016)
P.O. Box 141 (45346-0141)
PHONE.....................800 255-5839
Stephan A Scantland, *President*
Deborah Scantland, *Vice Pres*
EMP: 62 EST: 1957
SQ FT: 2,500
SALES (est): 18.3MM **Privately Held**
SIC: 1542 3448 Greenhouse construction; greenhouses: prefabricated metal

New Marshfield
Athens County

(G-14743)
DIESEL FLTRTION SPCIALISTS LLC
Also Called: Timothy A. Lyons
5475 Ste Rte 681 (45766)
P.O. Box 312, Albany (45710-0312)
PHONE.....................740 698-0255
Timothy A Lyons,
EMP: 3 EST: 2014
SALES (est): 200.5K **Privately Held**
SIC: 1389 Bailing, cleaning, swabbing & treating of wells

(G-14744)
SCHARENBERG SHEET METAL
2261 Scott Rd (45766-9502)
PHONE.....................740 664-2431
William Scharenberg, *Owner*
EMP: 4
SALES (est): 362.9K **Privately Held**
SIC: 3444 1711 Ducts, sheet metal; ventilation & duct work contractor; warm air heating & air conditioning contractor

New Matamoras
Washington County

(G-14745)
CREIGHTON SPORTS CENTER INC (PA)
205 Broadway Ave (45767-1193)
P.O. Box 400 (45767-0400)
PHONE.....................740 865-2521
Bill Creighton, *President*
Pam Creighton, *Corp Secy*
Chris Creighton, *Vice Pres*
EMP: 7
SQ FT: 2,400
SALES (est): 733K **Privately Held**
SIC: 3949 Sporting & athletic goods

(G-14746)
GRIMES SAND & GRAVEL
165 Holdren Ln (45767-6104)
PHONE.....................740 865-3990
Lewis Grimes, *Owner*
EMP: 6
SALES (est): 614.9K **Privately Held**
SIC: 1442 Construction sand & gravel

New Middletown
Mahoning County

(G-14747)
CC IRONWORKS LLC
10613 Main St (44442-8762)
PHONE.....................330 542-0500
Robert Pacella,
EMP: 3
SALES: 100K **Privately Held**
SIC: 3441 Fabricated structural metal

(G-14748)
COLUMBIA MIDSTREAM GROUP LLC
10846 Stateline Rd (44442-9727)
PHONE.....................330 542-1095
Stepanie Jones, *Office Mgr*
Scott Singer,
EMP: 18
SALES (est): 9.4MM
SALES (corp-wide): 10.5B **Privately Held**
SIC: 1311 Natural gas production
HQ: Columbia Pipeline Group, Inc.
  5151 San Felipe St
  Houston TX 77056
  713 386-3701

(G-14749)
CONTROL SYSTEM MANUFACTURING
10725 Struthers Rd (44442-9704)
PHONE.....................330 542-0000
Rex Cyrus, *Owner*
EMP: 50
SQ FT: 7,500
SALES (est): 7.4MM **Privately Held**
WEB: www.controlsystemmfg.com
SIC: 3699 Electrical equipment & supplies

(G-14750)
HITCH-HIKER MFG INC
10065 Rapp Rd (44442-9753)
PHONE.....................330 542-3052
Jeffrey Swartz, *President*
Holly Swartz, *Vice Pres*
EMP: 11 EST: 1973
SQ FT: 38,000
SALES (est): 2.1MM **Privately Held**
WEB: www.hitch-hikermfg.com
SIC: 3799 Boat trailers; trailers & trailer equipment

(G-14751)
PARAGON PLASTICS
5551 E Calla Rd (44442-9768)
P.O. Box 22 (44442-0022)
PHONE.....................330 542-9825
Michelle Rothrauff, *Principal*
EMP: 10
SALES (est): 1.1MM **Privately Held**
SIC: 3089 Injection molding of plastics

New Paris
Preble County

(G-14752)
BYEDAK CONSTRUCTION LTD
7406 New Pris Gttysbrg Rd (45347-8065)
PHONE.....................937 414-6153
Jon Milligan, *Principal*
EMP: 3
SALES (est): 320.8K **Privately Held**
SIC: 2621 1771 Building & roofing paper, felts & insulation siding; foundation & footing contractor

(G-14753)
DYNAMIC PLASTICS INC
Also Called: H & H Sailcraft
8207 H W Rd (45347-9241)
PHONE.....................937 437-7261
Paul Hemker, *President*
Heide Hemker, *Admin Sec*
EMP: 8
SQ FT: 20,000
SALES: 500K **Privately Held**
WEB: www.dynamicplastics.com
SIC: 3089 3732 3531 5551 Injection molding of plastics; sailboats, building & repairing; construction machinery; boat dealers

(G-14754)
H & S PRECISION SCREW PDTS INC
8205 H W Rd (45347)
PHONE.....................937 437-0316
Jerry J Winkle, *President*
EMP: 20
SQ FT: 10,000
SALES (est): 3.6MM **Privately Held**
SIC: 3451 Screw machine products

(G-14755)
RUTHIE ANN INC
Also Called: Admaster Supply
313 New Paris Ave (45347-1324)
PHONE.....................800 231-3567
▲ EMP: 18
SQ FT: 47,000
SALES (est): 1.9MM **Privately Held**
SIC: 3993 2759 Mfg Signs/Advertising Specialties Commercial Printing

New Philadelphia
Tuscarawas County

(G-14756)
ADVANCED INNOVATION & MFG INC
326 Pearl Ave Ne (44663-3918)
PHONE.....................330 308-6360
Frank J Michal, *President*
Bobie Stein, *Info Tech Mgr*
EMP: 4
SALES (est): 220K **Privately Held**
SIC: 3489 Ordnance & accessories

(G-14757)
ALLEN GREEN ENTERPRISES LLC
Also Called: UPS
513 Mill Ave Se (44663-3864)
PHONE.....................330 339-0200
Allen Green, *Mng Member*
EMP: 4
SALES: 300K **Privately Held**
SIC: 7389 3555 Mailing & messenger services; mailbox rental & related service; printing presses

(G-14758)
AQUABLUE INC
1776 Tech Park Dr Ne (44663-9410)
P.O. Box 446 (44663-0446)
PHONE.....................330 343-0220
Don Whittingham, *President*
EMP: 8
SALES (est): 1.9MM **Privately Held**
SIC: 2899 5169 Water treating compounds; chemicals & allied products

(G-14759)
ATLAS AMERICA INC
1026a Cookson Ave Se (44663-9500)
PHONE.....................330 339-3155
Rich Weber, *President*
EMP: 20
SALES (est): 1.6MM **Privately Held**
SIC: 1382 Oil & gas exploration services

(G-14760)
BRIDGES SHEET METAL
1184 Tuscarawas Ave Nw (44663-1024)
PHONE.....................330 339-3185
EMP: 3 EST: 2008
SALES (est): 227.8K **Privately Held**
SIC: 3444 Sheet metalwork

(G-14761)
BROWN WOOD PRODUCTS COMPANY
7783 Crooked Run Rd Sw (44663-6411)
PHONE.....................330 339-8000
Todd Dennison, *Manager*
EMP: 8
SALES (corp-wide): 3.2MM **Privately Held**
SIC: 2499 Decorative wood & woodwork
PA: Brown Wood Products Company
  7040 N Lawndale Ave
  Lincolnwood IL 60712
  847 673-4780

(G-14762)
BULK CARRIER TRNSP EQP CO
2743 Brightwood Rd Se (44663-6773)
PHONE.....................330 339-3333
Richard S Hartrick, *President*
Marcia Hartrick, *Vice Pres*
EMP: 26
SALES (est): 4.4MM **Privately Held**
WEB: www.bcte.com
SIC: 5012 2519 Trailers for trucks, new & used; household furniture, except wood or metal: upholstered

(G-14763)
CADO DOOR & DESIGN INC
Also Called: Cado Woodworking
5964 Main St Se (44663-8859)
PHONE.....................330 343-4288
Brian Cadele, *President*
EMP: 3
SALES: 400K **Privately Held**
WEB: www.cadomotus.com
SIC: 2499 Decorative wood & woodwork

(G-14764)
CASTINGS USA INC
2061 Brightwood Rd Se (44663-7724)
P.O. Box 202, Midvale (44653-0202)
PHONE.....................330 339-3611
Gregory M Dean, *President*
Terry Yahard, *Admin Sec*
EMP: 7 EST: 1974
SQ FT: 8,000
SALES (est): 1.1MM **Privately Held**
WEB: www.reymondproducts.com
SIC: 3321 3325 Gray iron castings; steel foundries

(G-14765)
COPLEY OHIO NEWSPAPERS INC
Also Called: Times Reporter/Midwest Offset
629 Wabash Ave Nw (44663-4145)
P.O. Box 667 (44663-0667)
PHONE.....................330 364-5577
Kevin Kampman, *Publisher*
EMP: 245
SALES (corp-wide): 1.5B **Publicly Held**
WEB: www.timesreporter.com
SIC: 2711 2752 7313 2791 Commercial printing & newspaper publishing combined; commercial printing, offset; newspaper advertising representative; typesetting; bookbinding & related work
HQ: Copley Ohio Newspapers Inc
  500 Market Ave S
  Canton OH 44702
  585 598-0030

New Philadelphia - Tuscarawas County (G-14766) — GEOGRAPHIC SECTION

(G-14766)
DENNEY PLASTICS MACHINING LLC
149 Stonecreek Rd Nw (44663-6902)
PHONE....................330 308-5300
Nicole Denney,
David Denney,
EMP: 12
SALES (est): 1.4MM **Privately Held**
SIC: 2821 Thermoplastic materials

(G-14767)
ELLIS LAUNDRY & LINEN SUPPLY
213 8th Street Ext Sw (44663-2088)
PHONE....................330 339-4941
Katherine Ellis, *President*
Jerry Ellis, *Admin Sec*
EMP: 6
SALES (est): 266.2K **Privately Held**
SIC: 3582 Ironers, commercial laundry & drycleaning

(G-14768)
FENTON BROS ELECTRIC CO
Also Called: Fenton's Festival of Lights
235 Ray Ave Ne (44663-2813)
P.O. Box 996 (44663-0996)
PHONE....................330 343-0093
Tom Fenton, *President*
Dennis Fenton, *Vice Pres*
Brian Fenton, *Treasurer*
Jim Hines, *Sales Staff*
Nancy Glenn, *Office Mgr*
EMP: 30 EST: 1947
SQ FT: 37,000
SALES (est): 23.4MM **Privately Held**
WEB: www.fentonbros.com
SIC: 5063 7694 Electrical supplies; electric motor repair

(G-14769)
FIRST STOP SIGNS AND DECALS
1347 4th St Nw (44663-1205)
PHONE....................330 343-1859
Todd Kinsey, *Owner*
Todd Kensey, *Owner*
EMP: 3
SQ FT: 8,250
SALES (est): 232K **Privately Held**
SIC: 3993 5999 2759 Signs & advertising specialties; decals; screen printing

(G-14770)
FREEPORT PRESS INC (PA)
2127 Reiser Ave Se (44663-3331)
P.O. Box 198, Freeport (43973-0198)
PHONE....................330 308-3300
David G Pilcher, *President*
Tom Dixon, *Purch Dir*
Todd Palkowitsh, *Purchasing*
Missy Hawkins, *Regl Sales Mgr*
Ed Parker, *Regl Sales Mgr*
EMP: 150
SQ FT: 36,000
SALES (est): 70.9MM **Privately Held**
WEB: www.freeportpress.com
SIC: 2752 Commercial printing, offset

(G-14771)
FREEPORT PRESS INC
2127 Reiser Ave Se (44663-3331)
PHONE....................740 658-4000
EMP: 13
SALES (est): 1.9MM
SALES (corp-wide): 70.9MM **Privately Held**
SIC: 2759 Commercial printing
PA: The Freeport Press Inc
2127 Reiser Ave Se
New Philadelphia OH 44663
330 308-3300

(G-14772)
GLENN O HAWBAKER INC
2565 Mthias Raceway Rd Sw (44663-6968)
PHONE....................330 308-0533
Daniel R Hawbaker, *President*
EMP: 3
SALES (est): 268.5K **Privately Held**
SIC: 2951 Asphalt & asphaltic paving mixtures (not from refineries)

(G-14773)
GRADALL INDUSTRIES INC (HQ)
406 Mill Ave Sw (44663-3835)
PHONE....................330 339-2211
Michael Haberman, *President*
Daniel Kaltenbaugh, *Vice Pres*
Joseph H Keller, *Vice Pres*
Damon Gould, *Facilities Mgr*
Eric Dietrich, *Regl Sales Mgr*
◆ EMP: 163 EST: 1992
SQ FT: 429,320
SALES (est): 93.3MM
SALES (corp-wide): 1B **Publicly Held**
WEB: www.gradall.com
SIC: 3537 3531 Industrial trucks & tractors; construction machinery
PA: Alamo Group Inc.
1627 E Walnut St
Seguin TX 78155
830 379-1480

(G-14774)
HYDRAULIC PARTS STORE INC
145 1st Dr Ne (44663-2857)
P.O. Box 808 (44663-0808)
PHONE....................330 364-6667
Robert M Henning Sr, *President*
EMP: 30
SQ FT: 25,000
SALES (est): 14.6MM **Privately Held**
SIC: 5084 3594 3593 3492 Hydraulic systems equipment & supplies; fluid power pumps & motors; fluid power cylinders & actuators; fluid power valves & hose fittings

(G-14775)
I-GROUP TECHNOLOGIES LLC
3509 Brightwood Rd Se (44663-7411)
P.O. Box 675, Midvale (44653-0675)
PHONE....................877 622-3377
Brian A Walker,
EMP: 5
SQ FT: 4,000
SALES: 500K **Privately Held**
SIC: 2211 Decorative trim & specialty fabrics, including twist weave

(G-14776)
J & D MINING INC
3497 University Dr Ne (44663-6711)
PHONE....................330 339-4935
John R Demuth, *President*
James R Demuth, *Vice Pres*
EMP: 38
SQ FT: 1,000
SALES (est): 4.3MM **Privately Held**
SIC: 1221 Bituminous coal surface mining

(G-14777)
KAY ZEE INC
1279 Crestview Ave Sw (44663-9642)
P.O. Box 95 (44663-0095)
PHONE....................330 339-1268
John Stratton, *President*
Kathryn Stratton, *Vice Pres*
EMP: 7
SALES (est): 853.6K **Privately Held**
WEB: www.kay-zee.com
SIC: 3861 Lens shades, camera

(G-14778)
KIMBLE CUSTOM CHASSIS COMPANY
Also Called: Kimble Manufacturing Company
1951 Reiser Ave Se (44663-3348)
PHONE....................877 546-2537
James C Cahill, *President*
Philip Keegan, *Vice Pres*
Jim Moberg, *Vice Pres*
Gregory Stohler, *Vice Pres*
Amie Guy, *CFO*
▲ EMP: 100
SQ FT: 100,000
SALES (est): 21.7MM
SALES (corp-wide): 196.6MM **Privately Held**
SIC: 3713 Truck bodies & parts
PA: Hines Corporation
1218 E Pontaluna Rd Ste B
Norton Shores MI 49456
231 799-6240

(G-14779)
KIMBLE MIXER COMPANY
Also Called: Hines Specialty Vehicle Group
1951 Reiser Ave Se (44663-3348)
PHONE....................330 308-6700
James C Cahill, *President*
Philip Keegan, *President*
Jim Moberg, *Vice Pres*
Jill Hamilton, *Purch Mgr*
Scott Johnson, *CFO*
▲ EMP: 75
SQ FT: 100,000
SALES (est): 37.6MM
SALES (corp-wide): 196.6MM **Privately Held**
WEB: www.kimblemixer.com
SIC: 3713 Cement mixer bodies
PA: Hines Corporation
1218 E Pontaluna Rd Ste B
Norton Shores MI 49456
231 799-6240

(G-14780)
LAUREN INTERNATIONAL LTD (HQ)
Also Called: Lauren Manufacturing
2228 Reiser Ave Se (44663-3334)
PHONE....................330 339-3373
Kevin E Gray, *President*
Jim Hummel, *COO*
Shelly Friedrichsen, *Project Mgr*
Wayne Burley, *Safety Mgr*
Greg Halterman, *Purchasing*
▲ EMP: 200 EST: 1965
SQ FT: 160,000
SALES (est): 93.8MM
SALES (corp-wide): 3.6B **Publicly Held**
WEB: www.laureninternational.com
SIC: 3069 Molded rubber products
PA: Cooper-Standard Holdings Inc.
39550 Orchard Hill Pl
Novi MI 48375
248 596-5900

(G-14781)
LAUREN MANUFACTURING LLC
2228 Reiser Ave Se (44663-3334)
PHONE....................330 339-3373
Kevin E Gray, *CEO*
Dale Foland, *Ch of Bd*
Lisa Huntsman, *President*
Chuck Laney, *President*
Jim Hummel, *Vice Pres*
▲ EMP: 288
SQ FT: 160,000
SALES (est): 46.5MM
SALES (corp-wide): 3.6B **Publicly Held**
WEB: www.lauren.com
SIC: 3069 3061 Molded rubber products; mechanical rubber goods
HQ: Lauren International, Ltd.
2228 Reiser Ave Se
New Philadelphia OH 44663
330 339-3373

(G-14782)
MANSFIELD JOURNAL CO
Also Called: Times Reporter
629 Wabash Ave Nw (44663-4145)
P.O. Box 667 (44663-0667)
PHONE....................330 364-8641
Brent Kettlewell, *Controller*
Nancy Molnar, *Relations*
EMP: 1 EST: 1930
SQ FT: 65,000
SALES (est): 3.5MM
SALES (corp-wide): 661.2MM **Privately Held**
SIC: 2711 2752 Newspapers, publishing & printing; commercial printing, offset
PA: Journal Register Company
5 Hanover Sq Fl 25
New York NY 10004
212 257-7212

(G-14783)
MARATHON MFG & SUP CO
5165 Main St Ne (44663-8802)
P.O. Box 701 (44663-0701)
PHONE....................330 343-2656
Emory Brumit, *President*
Peggy Brumit, *Treasurer*
EMP: 60 EST: 1969
SALES (est): 5.5MM **Privately Held**
SIC: 5199 3953 Advertising specialties; screens, textile printing

(G-14784)
MARSH INDUSTRIES INC
Marsh Chalk Board Co Div
1117 Bowers Ave Nw (44663-4129)
P.O. Box 1000 (44663-5100)
PHONE....................330 308-8667
Brian Marsh, *Manager*
EMP: 32
SALES (corp-wide): 20.5MM **Privately Held**
WEB: www.marsh-ind.com
SIC: 2431 5211 5943 3281 Millwork; planing mill products & lumber; school supplies; cut stone & stone products; office furniture, except wood; wood kitchen cabinets
PA: Marsh Industries, Inc,
2301 E High Ave
New Philadelphia OH 44663
330 308-5515

(G-14785)
MERIDIAN MACHINE INC
702 Steele Hill Rd Nw (44663-6512)
PHONE....................330 308-0296
EMP: 3
SALES (est): 266.8K **Privately Held**
SIC: 3599 5162 Mfg Industrial Machinery Whol Plastic Materials/Shapes

(G-14786)
MILLER PRODUCTS INC
Also Called: Beech Engineering & Mfg
642 Wabash Ave Nw (44663-4146)
P.O. Box 947 (44663-0947)
PHONE....................330 308-5934
Naomi Downend, *General Mgr*
EMP: 35
SALES (corp-wide): 36.3MM **Privately Held**
SIC: 3537 3535 Industrial trucks & tractors; conveyors & conveying equipment
PA: Miller Products, Inc.
450 Courtney Rd
Sebring OH 44672
330 938-2134

(G-14787)
MILLER STUDIO INC
734 Fair Ave Nw (44663-1589)
P.O. Box 997 (44663-0997)
PHONE....................330 339-1100
Jeff Miller, *President*
John A Basiletti, *Vice Pres*
▲ EMP: 60 EST: 1934
SALES (est): 8.8MM
SALES (corp-wide): 36.3MM **Privately Held**
WEB: www.miller-studio.com
SIC: 3299 2672 3452 3429 Plaques: clay, plaster or papier mache; adhesive papers, labels or tapes: from purchased material; bolts, nuts, rivets & washers; manufactured hardware (general)
PA: Miller Products, Inc.
450 Courtney Rd
Sebring OH 44672
330 938-2134

(G-14788)
MPS MANUFACTURING COMPANY LLC
326 Pearl Ave Ne (44663-3918)
PHONE....................330 343-1435
Mike Stein,
Jeff Powers,
EMP: 6
SALES (est): 1MM **Privately Held**
SIC: 3069 Molded rubber products

(G-14789)
MR TRAILER SALES INC
1565 Steele Hill Rd Nw (44663)
P.O. Box 562, Dover (44622-0562)
PHONE....................330 339-7701
Roger Rostad, *President*
Sharon Rostad, *President*
Don Rostad, *Director*
EMP: 8
SALES: 1MM **Privately Held**
SIC: 5012 5599 3441 3715 Trailers for passenger vehicles; utility trailers; fabricated structural metal; trailers or vans for transporting horses

▲ = Import ▼ = Export
◆ = Import/Export

GEOGRAPHIC SECTION

New Riegel - Seneca County (G-14817)

(G-14790)
NATIONAL LIME AND STONE CO
2942 Brightwood Rd Se (44663-7728)
PHONE..................................330 339-2144
David Weber, *Branch Mgr*
EMP: 3
SALES (corp-wide): 3.2B **Privately Held**
WEB: www.natlime.com
SIC: 1499 1442 3273 1423 Asphalt (native) mining; sand mining; gravel mining; ready-mixed concrete; crushed & broken granite
PA: The National Lime And Stone Company
551 Lake Cascade Pkwy
Findlay OH 45840
419 422-4341

(G-14791)
OAKTREE WIRELINE LLC
1825 E High Ave (44663-3280)
PHONE..................................330 352-7250
Tim Canter,
Sean Casey,
Dan Krawczyk,
Mark Miller,
Gary Reese,
EMP: 9
SQ FT: 3,000
SALES (est): 340.3K **Privately Held**
SIC: 1389 Well logging

(G-14792)
PARAMONT MACHINE COMPANY LLC
963 Commercial Ave Se (44663-2355)
PHONE..................................330 339-3489
Thomas Garrett, *CEO*
Michael Goldberg, *Vice Pres*
Scott Stephens, *Treasurer*
EMP: 35
SQ FT: 11,000
SALES (est): 4.8MM
SALES (corp-wide): 869.1MM **Privately Held**
WEB: www.paramontmachinecompany.com
SIC: 3599 3451 3053 Machine shop, jobbing & repair; screw machine products; gaskets, packing & sealing devices
HQ: Total Plastics Resources Llc
2810 N Burdick St Ste A
Kalamazoo MI 49004
269 344-0009

(G-14793)
PERFORMANCE ADDITIVES AMER LLC
906 Cookson Ave Se (44663-6859)
PHONE..................................330 365-9256
Dan Flynn, *General Mgr*
Daniel Flynn, *Mng Member*
♦ **EMP:** 5
SALES (est): 813.2K **Privately Held**
SIC: 3069 Rubber automotive products

(G-14794)
R & J CYLINDER & MACHINE INC
464 Robinson Dr Se (44663-3336)
PHONE..................................330 364-8263
Ronald Sandy, *President*
Jeffrey Shepherd, *Vice Pres*
Rick Pauline, *Manager*
Don Sandy, *Shareholder*
Kraig Warther, *Administration*
EMP: 53
SQ FT: 33,500
SALES (est): 11.9MM **Privately Held**
WEB: www.rjcylinder.com
SIC: 3593 3599 Fluid power cylinders, hydraulic or pneumatic; machine & other job shop work

(G-14795)
RED BONE SERVICES LLC
1213 Stonecreek Rd Sw (44663)
PHONE..................................330 364-0022
EMP: 4
SALES (corp-wide): 495.3MM **Publicly Held**
SIC: 1389 Oil field services
HQ: Red Bone Services, L.L.C.
1700 Enterprise Rd
Elk City OK 73644

(G-14796)
REYMOND PRODUCTS INTL INC
2066 Brightwood Rd Se (44663-7724)
P.O. Box 202, Midvale (44653-0202)
PHONE..................................330 339-3583
Greg Dean, *President*
Jonathon Baker, *Engineer*
Greg Camp, *Sales Staff*
Mark Milburn, *Sales Staff*
Bob Schatz, *Executive*
▲ **EMP:** 20
SQ FT: 15,000
SALES (est): 3.7MM **Privately Held**
SIC: 3599 3544 Machine shop, jobbing & repair; special dies, tools, jigs & fixtures

(G-14797)
RICH INDUSTRIES INC
2384 Brightwood Rd Se (44663-6772)
PHONE..................................330 339-4113
Rita Contini, *Corp Secy*
William Arnold, *Vice Pres*
Anthony Contini, *Vice Pres*
Scott Trammell, *Vice Pres*
Jeffrey Contini, *CFO*
▲ **EMP:** 50
SQ FT: 28,000
SALES (est): 10.2MM **Privately Held**
WEB: www.richindustriesinc.com
SIC: 2389 2393 2326 Disposable garments & accessories; textile bags; men's & boys' work clothing

(G-14798)
RICHMONDS WOODWORKS INC
1115 Oak Shadows Dr Ne (44663-7078)
PHONE..................................330 343-8184
EMP: 15
SALES (est): 880K **Privately Held**
SIC: 2511 Mfg Wood Household Furniture

(G-14799)
ROBERT H SHACKELFORD (PA)
Also Called: Quick Print Center
147 Ashwood Ln Ne (44663-2841)
PHONE..................................330 364-2221
Robert H Shackelford, *Owner*
EMP: 5 **EST:** 1977
SQ FT: 2,000
SALES (est): 500K **Privately Held**
WEB: www.quickprint-center.com
SIC: 2752 2796 2789 2759 Commercial printing, offset; platemaking services; bookbinding & related work; commercial printing

(G-14800)
SPEEDWAY LLC
Also Called: Speedway Superamerica 6246
1260 W High Ave (44663-6943)
PHONE..................................330 339-7770
Joy Cladwell, *Manager*
EMP: 8 **Publicly Held**
WEB: www.speedwaynet.com
SIC: 1311 Crude petroleum production
HQ: Speedway Llc
500 Speedway Dr
Enon OH 45323
937 864-3000

(G-14801)
STICK-IT GRAPHICS LLC
3161 Egypt Rd Ne (44663-7055)
PHONE..................................330 407-0142
Curtis Edward, *Owner*
Curtis Seward, *Principal*
EMP: 3
SALES (est): 193.2K **Privately Held**
SIC: 7336 2752 Commercial art & graphic design; commercial printing, lithographic; commercial printing, offset

(G-14802)
SUEZ WTS USA INC
Also Called: GE Water & Process Tech
2118 Reiser Ave Se (44663-3332)
PHONE..................................330 339-2292
Tom Johnston, *Branch Mgr*
EMP: 50
SALES (corp-wide): 94.7MM **Privately Held**
SIC: 2899 Water treating compounds
HQ: Suez Wts Usa, Inc.
4636 Somerton Rd
Trevose PA 19053
215 355-3300

(G-14803)
T-TOP SHOPPE
138 E High Ave (44663-2540)
PHONE..................................330 343-3481
Todd A Kensey, *Owner*
EMP: 5
SALES (est): 210K **Privately Held**
SIC: 5699 3993 Sports apparel; signs & advertising specialties

(G-14804)
TIMKEN COMPANY
1957 E High Ave (44663-3240)
PHONE..................................330 339-1151
Cindy Johnson, *General Mgr*
John Carr, *Opers-Prdtn-Mfg*
Craig Wilcoxon, *Electrical Engi*
EMP: 115
SALES (corp-wide): 3.5B **Publicly Held**
SIC: 3562 Ball & roller bearings
PA: The Timken Company
4500 Mount Pleasant St Nw
North Canton OH 44720
234 262-3000

(G-14805)
TOLLOTI PIPE LLC
102 Barnhill Rd Se (44663-8864)
P.O. Box 129, Uhrichsville (44683-0129)
PHONE..................................330 364-6627
Kyle Miller, *Principal*
Susan Morehead, *Office Mgr*
EMP: 12
SALES (est): 1.7MM **Privately Held**
SIC: 3084 Plastics pipe

(G-14806)
TOLLOTI PLASTIC PIPE INC (PA)
102 Barnhill Rd Se (44663-8864)
P.O. Box 40 (44663-0040)
PHONE..................................330 364-6627
Theodore Tolloti, *President*
John Tolloti, *President*
Doris Tolloti, *Corp Secy*
EMP: 38
SQ FT: 5,000
SALES (est): 3.8MM **Privately Held**
SIC: 3084 Plastics pipe

(G-14807)
UNDER PRESSURE SYSTEMS INC
322 North Ave Ne (44663-2714)
PHONE..................................330 602-4466
Cynthia J Valentine, *President*
EMP: 9
SQ FT: 10,000
SALES (est): 2.6MM **Privately Held**
SIC: 3589 Water treatment equipment, industrial

(G-14808)
WELL SERVICE GROUP INC
1490 Truss Rd Sw (44663-7530)
PHONE..................................330 308-0880
Bil Woessner, *General Mgr*
Jeff Atkinson, *Manager*
EMP: 13
SALES (est): 1.9MM **Privately Held**
SIC: 1381 Service well drilling

New Plymouth
Vinton County

(G-14809)
ON GUARD DEFENSE LLC
66211 Bethel Rd (45654-8934)
PHONE..................................740 596-1984
EMP: 4
SALES (est): 265.1K **Privately Held**
SIC: 3812 Defense systems & equipment

New Richmond
Clermont County

(G-14810)
B & S BLACKTOP CO
1704 Lndale Nchlsville Rd (45157)
PHONE..................................513 797-5759
Steve Brock, *Owner*
EMP: 4
SALES: 300K **Privately Held**
SIC: 2951 3271 Paving blocks; paving blocks, concrete

(G-14811)
LIVINGSTON & COMPANY LTD
1103 Ten Mile Rd (45157-9156)
PHONE..................................513 553-6430
EMP: 4
SALES: 4MM **Privately Held**
SIC: 3441 Structural Metal Fabrication

(G-14812)
MASTER DISPOSERS INC
Also Called: Market-Master
2128 Idlett Hill Rd (45157-8658)
PHONE..................................513 553-2289
EMP: 10
SQ FT: 8,000
SALES (est): 1MM **Privately Held**
SIC: 3589 Mfr Commercial Waste Disposers

(G-14813)
MIDWEST PLASTIC SYSTEMS INC
100 Front St (45157-1403)
PHONE..................................513 553-4380
Dale Werle, *Branch Mgr*
EMP: 4
SALES (corp-wide): 1.1MM **Privately Held**
SIC: 3089 Plastic containers, except foam
PA: Midwest Plastic Systems Inc
326 1/2 N Main St
Piqua OH 45356
513 553-2900

(G-14814)
RAPID SIGNS & MORE INC
Also Called: Rapid Signs & Sportswear
1044 Old Us Highway 52 (45157-9773)
PHONE..................................513 553-4040
William R Gilpin, *President*
Deborah Gilpin, *Admin Sec*
EMP: 4
SALES (est): 424.7K **Privately Held**
SIC: 3993 7336 2261 Signs & advertising specialties; art design services; printing of cotton broadwoven fabrics

New Riegel
Seneca County

(G-14815)
LUCIUS FENCE DECKING IRRIGAT
8146 Us Highway 224 (44853-9729)
PHONE..................................419 450-9907
Matthew Burgert,
EMP: 5
SALES (est): 149.1K **Privately Held**
SIC: 2499 Fencing, docks & other outdoor wood structural products

(G-14816)
NEW RIEGEL CAFE INC
Also Called: Boes, Wilbert J
14 N Perry St (44853-9776)
P.O. Box 237 (44853-0237)
PHONE..................................419 595-2255
Wilbert J Boes, *President*
Hildegarde Boes, *Principal*
Tom Boes, *Vice Pres*
Richard Boes, *Admin Sec*
EMP: 32
SQ FT: 4,500
SALES (est): 1.3MM **Privately Held**
SIC: 5812 2011 Barbecue restaurant; meat packing plants

(G-14817)
SCHREINER MANUFACTURING
1997 Township Road 66 (44853-9728)
PHONE..................................419 937-0300
Brandan Schreiner, *Principal*
EMP: 4 **EST:** 2012
SALES (est): 161.9K **Privately Held**
SIC: 3999 Barber & beauty shop equipment

New Springfield
Mahoning County

(G-14818)
B V MFG INC
13426 Woodworth Rd (44443-9789)
P.O. Box 176 (44443-0176)
PHONE.................................330 549-5331
Robert Maine, *President*
EMP: 18
SQ FT: 6,200
SALES (est): 2.6MM **Privately Held**
SIC: 3544 Extrusion dies; special dies & tools

(G-14819)
D & D MINING CO INC
3379 E Garfield Rd (44443-9743)
PHONE.................................330 549-3127
Donald Thompson, *President*
David Thompson, *Vice Pres*
EMP: 10
SQ FT: 1,000
SALES (est): 756.1K **Privately Held**
SIC: 1241 Coal mining services

(G-14820)
MANTAPART
1161 E Garfield Rd Unit 2 (44443-8709)
P.O. Box 2206 (44443-2206)
PHONE.................................330 549-2389
Tim Meehan, *Owner*
EMP: 3
SQ FT: 5,000
SALES (est): 239.3K **Privately Held**
WEB: www.mantapart.com
SIC: 5013 3519 5961 Automotive engines & engine parts; parts & accessories, internal combustion engines; cards, mail order

(G-14821)
THOMPSON BROTHERS MINING CO
3379 E Garfield Rd (44443-9743)
PHONE.................................330 549-3979
Don Thompson, *President*
Dave Thompson, *Vice Pres*
EMP: 10
SQ FT: 1,000
SALES (est): 770K **Privately Held**
SIC: 1221 Strip mining, bituminous

(G-14822)
TRINITY DOOR SYSTEMS
13886 Woodworth Rd (44443-8725)
PHONE.................................877 603-2018
Bill Warden, *President*
Bill Veon, *Manager*
EMP: 3
SALES (est): 240K **Privately Held**
SIC: 3699 1796 1793 Door opening & closing devices, electrical; installing building equipment; glass & glazing work

New Vienna
Clinton County

(G-14823)
ALLEN TOOL CO INC
300 S 2nd St (45159-9083)
P.O. Box 311 (45159-0311)
PHONE.................................937 987-2037
David Allen, *President*
Bill Allen, *Vice Pres*
Shirley Allen, *Treasurer*
EMP: 4 **EST:** 1979
SQ FT: 2,500
SALES (est): 539K **Privately Held**
SIC: 3544 Special dies & tools

(G-14824)
HUHTAMAKI INC
Also Called: Huhtamaki Plastics
5566 New Vienna Rd (45159-9533)
PHONE.................................937 987-3078
Julie Ivey, *Human Res Mgr*
Howard Liming, *Branch Mgr*
EMP: 350
SALES (corp-wide): 35.2B **Privately Held**
SIC: 3089 Plastic containers, except foam
HQ: Huhtamaki, Inc.
9201 Packaging Dr
De Soto KS 66018
913 583-3025

(G-14825)
OHIO VLY LIGHTNING PROTECTION
520 Leeka Rd (45159-9052)
PHONE.................................937 987-0245
Lucia Riley, *President*
EMP: 4
SQ FT: 1,500
SALES (est): 363K **Privately Held**
WEB: www.lightning-systems.com
SIC: 3643 Lightning protection equipment

(G-14826)
WELLS MANUFACTURING CO LLC
280 W Main St (45159)
P.O. Box 325 (45159-0325)
PHONE.................................937 987-2481
Grant Douglas, *President*
Glenn Douglas, *Vice Pres*
EMP: 10
SQ FT: 100,000
SALES (est): 3.5MM **Privately Held**
SIC: 3944 Games, toys & children's vehicles

New Washington
Crawford County

(G-14827)
C E WHITE CO (HQ)
417 N Kibler St (44854-9426)
P.O. Box 308 (44854-0308)
PHONE.................................419 492-2157
Tony Everett, *President*
Bob Knapp, *President*
Chad Novak, *Vice Pres*
Danny Maxwell, *Manager*
David Murphy, *Manager*
▲ **EMP:** 48 **EST:** 1937
SQ FT: 65,000
SALES (est): 15.5MM
SALES (corp-wide): 898MM **Privately Held**
WEB: www.cewhite.com
SIC: 2531 Seats, miscellaneous public conveyances
PA: Hickory Springs Manufacturing Company
235 2nd Ave Nw
Hickory NC 28601
828 328-2201

(G-14828)
CREST BENDING INC
108 John St (44854-9702)
P.O. Box 458 (44854-0458)
PHONE.................................419 492-2108
Robert E Studer, *President*
EMP: 45 **EST:** 1966
SQ FT: 50,000
SALES (est): 8.8MM **Privately Held**
WEB: www.crestbending.com
SIC: 3312 7692 3498 3317 Tubes, steel & iron; welding repair; fabricated pipe & fittings; steel pipe & tubes

(G-14829)
HERALD INC
625 S Kibler St (44854-9541)
P.O. Box 367 (44854-0367)
PHONE.................................419 492-2133
Suzanne Stump, *CEO*
Carol Aurand, *Human Res Mgr*
EMP: 35
SALES (est): 8.5MM **Privately Held**
SIC: 2752 Commercial printing, offset

(G-14830)
NEW MANSFIELD BRASS & ALUM CO
636 S Center St (44854-9711)
PHONE.................................419 492-2166
EMP: 30
SALES (est): 4.1MM **Privately Held**
SIC: 3365 Aluminum Foundry

(G-14831)
OHIO FOAM CORPORATION
529 S Kibler St (44854-9524)
P.O. Box 61, Bucyrus (44820-0061)
PHONE.................................419 492-2151
Rob Alderich, *Division Mgr*
Diane Swartzmiller, *Principal*
Terri Lady, *Administration*
EMP: 10
SQ FT: 15,000
SALES (corp-wide): 11.7MM **Privately Held**
WEB: www.ohiofoam.com
SIC: 3069 2821 Foam rubber; plastics materials & resins
PA: Ohio Foam Corporation
820 Plymouth St
Bucyrus OH 44820
419 563-0399

(G-14832)
SHEEP & FARM LIFE INC
Also Called: Shepherd, The
5696 Johnston Rd (44854-9736)
PHONE.................................419 492-2364
Ken Kark, *President*
Guy Flora, *Vice Pres*
Kathy Kark, *Treasurer*
Pat Flora, *Admin Sec*
EMP: 4
SALES (est): 280K **Privately Held**
SIC: 2721 Magazines: publishing only, not printed on site

(G-14833)
STUMPS CONVERTING INC
742 W Mansfield St (44854-9449)
PHONE.................................419 492-2542
Suzanne Stump, *President*
Dave Q Stump, *Vice Pres*
EMP: 10
SALES (est): 500K **Privately Held**
WEB: www.stumpsconverting.com
SIC: 2679 5149 Paper products, converted; syrups, except for fountain use

(G-14834)
WURMS WOODWORKING COMPANY
Also Called: Gr Golf
725 W Mansfield St (44854-9403)
P.O. Box 275 (44854-0275)
PHONE.................................419 492-2184
Gerald B Wurm, *President*
Richard Wurm, *Vice Pres*
Valerie Sanderson, *Treasurer*
Mary Wurm, *Admin Sec*
EMP: 36 **EST:** 1947
SQ FT: 60,000
SALES (est): 6MM **Privately Held**
WEB: www.wurmsproducts.com
SIC: 2499 2531 3082 3083 Furniture inlays (veneers); vehicle furniture; unsupported plastics profile shapes; laminated plastics plate & sheet; wood kitchen cabinets

New Waterford
Columbiana County

(G-14835)
AMERICAN PIONEER MANUFACTURING
3672 Silliman St (44445-9658)
PHONE.................................330 457-1400
EMP: 3
SALES (est): 160K **Privately Held**
SIC: 3999 Mfg Misc Products

(G-14836)
AMRON LLC
Also Called: Amron Testing
47287 State Route 558 (44445-9628)
PHONE.................................330 457-8570
Ronald Allen Hodge, *Owner*
Krista Cutter, *Manager*
EMP: 3
SALES (est): 88.6K **Privately Held**
SIC: 8734 3829 Product testing laboratory, safety or performance; ultrasonic testing equipment

(G-14837)
CENTURY CONTAINER LLC (HQ)
5331 State Route 7 (44445-9787)
PHONE.................................330 457-2367
Mark Brothers, *President*
EMP: 42
SALES (est): 17.6MM
SALES (corp-wide): 89.9MM **Privately Held**
SIC: 3089 Plastic containers, except foam
PA: Thorworks Industries, Inc.
2520 Campbell St
Sandusky OH 44870
419 626-4375

(G-14838)
CENTURY INDUSTRIES CORPORATION
5331 State Route 7 (44445-9787)
PHONE.................................330 457-2367
Don R Brothers, *CEO*
Jill Brothers, *President*
Budd Brothers, *Principal*
Roland Brothers, *Principal*
William G Houser, *Principal*
EMP: 25 **EST:** 1944
SQ FT: 100,000
SALES (est): 769.9K **Privately Held**
SIC: 2891 2952 Sealants; caulking compounds; sealing compounds for pipe threads or joints; asphalt felts & coatings

(G-14839)
DYNAMIC LEASING LTD
3790 State Route 7 (44445-9784)
PHONE.................................330 892-0164
Scott McCrea, *President*
EMP: 3 **EST:** 1998
SQ FT: 10,000
SALES (est): 476.8K
SALES (corp-wide): 7.2MM **Privately Held**
SIC: 3533 Oil & gas drilling rigs & equipment
PA: Dynamic Structures, Inc.
3790 State Route 7 Ste B
New Waterford OH 44445
330 892-0164

(G-14840)
GILLAM MACHINE COMPANY
1888 Macklin Rd (44445-9776)
PHONE.................................330 457-2557
Earon Gillam, *Owner*
EMP: 3
SALES (est): 178.4K **Privately Held**
SIC: 3599 Machine shop, jobbing & repair

(G-14841)
MAJESTIC MANUFACTURING INC
4536 State Route 7 (44445-9785)
P.O. Box 128 (44445-0128)
PHONE.................................330 457-2447
Paul Kudler, *President*
Jeff Kudler, *Vice Pres*
Rick Steed, *Purch Agent*
Vincent Kudler, *Treasurer*
▲ **EMP:** 45
SQ FT: 68,000
SALES (est): 8MM **Privately Held**
WEB: www.majesticrides.com
SIC: 3599 5087 Carnival machines & equipment, amusement park; carnival & amusement park equipment

(G-14842)
REISER MANUFACTURING
4571 Millrock Rd (44445-9627)
PHONE.................................330 846-8003
Lori Reiser, *Principal*
Lori L Reiser, *Officer*
Karen Renier,
EMP: 3
SALES (est): 282K **Privately Held**
SIC: 3999 Barber & beauty shop equipment

(G-14843)
STEELCON LLC
47287 State Route 558 (44445-9628)
PHONE.................................330 457-4003
Ronald Allen Hodge,
EMP: 6

GEOGRAPHIC SECTION

SALES (est): 598.5K **Privately Held**
SIC: 3441 Building components, structural steel

(G-14844)
WILLOUGHBY MANUFACTURING INC
47415 Heck Rd (44445-9729)
PHONE..................330 402-8217
Willoughby Renee, *Administration*
EMP: 3
SALES (est): 241K **Privately Held**
SIC: 3999 Candles

New Weston
Darke County

(G-14845)
FRED WINNER
Also Called: Winner Welding Fabricating
7860 Cohn Rd (45348-9715)
PHONE..................419 582-2421
Fred Winner, *Owner*
EMP: 8
SQ FT: 10,000
SALES: 750K **Privately Held**
SIC: 3443 3444 7692 Weldments; sheet metalwork; welding repair

Newark
Licking County

(G-14846)
3DNSEW LLC
11813 Wilkins Run Rd Ne (43055-9736)
P.O. Box 8638 (43058-8638)
PHONE..................740 618-8005
Jessica Ricket,
EMP: 4
SALES (est): 108.3K **Privately Held**
SIC: 2741

(G-14847)
ACTION ENTERPRISE
Also Called: Action Signs
416 W Main St (43055-4168)
PHONE..................740 522-1678
Robert B Rickard, *Owner*
EMP: 3
SALES (est): 184.8K **Privately Held**
SIC: 3993 Signs & advertising specialties

(G-14848)
ACUITY BRANDS LIGHTING INC
Also Called: ACUITY BRANDS LIGHTING, INC.
214 Oakwood Ave (43055-6716)
PHONE..................740 349-4343
Steve Hummel, *Plant Mgr*
EMP: 500
SALES (corp-wide): 3.6B **Publicly Held**
SIC: 3646 3648 3645 3612 Commercial indusl & institutional electric lighting fixtures; lighting equipment; residential lighting fixtures; transformers, except electric; aluminum foundries
HQ: Acuity Brands Lighting, Inc.
1 Acuity Way
Conyers GA 30012

(G-14849)
ACUITY BRANDS LIGHTING INC
Also Called: Hollphane
465 Mckinley Ave (43055-6735)
PHONE..................740 349-4409
EMP: 150
SALES (corp-wide): 2.7B **Publicly Held**
SIC: 3646 3645 3641 Mfg Commercial Lighting Fixtures Mfg Residential Lighting Fixtures Mfg Electric Lamps
HQ: Acuity Brands Lighting, Inc.
1 Acuity Way
Conyers GA 30012
800 922-9641

(G-14850)
AMPACET CORPORATION
1855 James Pkwy (43056-1092)
PHONE..................740 929-5521
Jim Edge, *Branch Mgr*
EMP: 150
SALES (corp-wide): 584.5MM **Privately Held**
WEB: www.ampacet.com
SIC: 2869 2816 Industrial organic chemicals; inorganic pigments
PA: Ampacet Corporation
660 White Plains Rd # 360
Tarrytown NY 10591
914 631-6600

(G-14851)
ANOMATIC CORPORATION
1650 Tamarack Rd (43055-1359)
PHONE..................740 522-2203
Chris Wilson, *Branch Mgr*
EMP: 500
SALES (corp-wide): 632.4MM **Privately Held**
SIC: 3471 Anodizing (plating) of metals or formed products
HQ: Anomatic Corporation
8880 Innvation Campus Way
Johnstown OH 43031
740 522-2203

(G-14852)
ARBORIS LLC
1780 Tamarack Rd (43055-1359)
PHONE..................740 522-9350
Tom Lindow, *Branch Mgr*
EMP: 34
SALES (corp-wide): 17.6MM **Privately Held**
WEB: www.arboris-us.com
SIC: 2819 Chemicals, high purity: refined from technical grade
PA: Arboris, Llc
1101 W Lathrop Ave
Savannah GA 31415
912 238-6355

(G-14853)
ASHCRAFT MACHINE & SUPPLY INC
185 Wilson St (43055-4099)
PHONE..................740 349-8110
Larry G Ashcraft, *President*
Jerry Ashcraft, *President*
Mike Ashcraft, *Vice Pres*
John Balster, *Manager*
EMP: 12 EST: 1949
SQ FT: 15,000
SALES (est): 1.2MM **Privately Held**
WEB: www.ashcraftmachine.com
SIC: 3599 Machine shop, jobbing & repair

(G-14854)
BOEING COMPANY
801 Irving Wick Dr W (43056-1199)
PHONE..................740 788-4000
Stephen Feller, *Partner*
Jeremy Addy, *Engineer*
Daryl Dickerson, *Engineer*
Tony Hensley, *Engineer*
Mike Michaelian, *Engineer*
EMP: 25
SALES (corp-wide): 101.1B **Publicly Held**
SIC: 7629 3812 Electrical repair shops; search & navigation equipment
PA: The Boeing Company
100 N Riverside Plz
Chicago IL 60606
312 544-2000

(G-14855)
BOEING COMPANY
801 Irving Wick Dr W (43056-1199)
PHONE..................740 788-5805
Charles Dutch, *Manager*
EMP: 600
SALES (corp-wide): 101.1B **Publicly Held**
SIC: 3721 Aircraft
PA: The Boeing Company
100 N Riverside Plz
Chicago IL 60606
312 544-2000

(G-14856)
BOWERSTON SHALE COMPANY
1329 Seven Hills Rd (43055-8964)
PHONE..................740 763-3921
Beth Hillyer, *Manager*
EMP: 35
SQ FT: 100,000
SALES (corp-wide): 36.8MM **Privately Held**
SIC: 3251 Brick clay: common face, glazed, vitrified or hollow; paving brick, clay
PA: Bowerston Shale Company (Inc)
515 Main St
Bowerston OH 44695
740 269-2921

(G-14857)
BURDENS MACHINE & WELDING
94 S 5th St (43055-5302)
P.O. Box 177 (43058-0177)
PHONE..................740 345-9246
Donald Burden Sr, *President*
Robert Burden, *Corp Secy*
Darrell Burden, *Vice Pres*
Donald Burden Jr, *Vice Pres*
EMP: 26
SQ FT: 4,400
SALES: 1.9MM **Privately Held**
SIC: 1799 3599 Welding on site; machine shop, jobbing & repair

(G-14858)
BURGIE BRAUEREI INC
860 Village Pkwy (43055-2851)
PHONE..................740 344-1620
Robert Burgie, *Principal*
EMP: 3
SALES (est): 187K **Privately Held**
SIC: 2082 Malt beverages

(G-14859)
CAPITAL PROSTHETIC &
Also Called: Capital Prsthetic Orthotic Ctr
55 S Terrace Ave (43055-1355)
PHONE..................740 522-3331
Lisa Craford, *Manager*
EMP: 6
SALES (corp-wide): 2.9MM **Privately Held**
SIC: 5999 3842 Orthopedic & prosthesis applications; limbs, artificial
PA: Capital Prosthetic And Orthotic Center, Inc.
4678 Larwell Dr
Columbus OH 43220
614 451-0446

(G-14860)
CARDINAL ELECTRIC LLC
1725 Mount Vernon Rd (43055-3499)
PHONE..................740 366-6850
Patricia C Bates, *President*
Cathy Kyle, *Mng Member*
Amanda Hart, *Manager*
Nancy Sutton,
EMP: 5
SQ FT: 26,000
SALES: 380K **Privately Held**
SIC: 5063 7694 Motors, electric; transformers, electric; motor controls, starters & relays: electric; electric motor repair

(G-14861)
CITY OF NEWARK
Also Called: Newark Water Plant
164 Waterworks Rd (43055-6057)
PHONE..................740 349-6765
Mike Buskirk, *Human Res Dir*
Steve Rhodes, *Manager*
EMP: 16 **Privately Held**
SIC: 3561 Pumps, domestic: water or sump
PA: City Of Newark
40 W Main St
Newark OH 43055
740 670-7512

(G-14862)
COLUMBUS ROOF TRUSSES INC
Also Called: Central Ohio Bldg Components
400 Marne Rd (43055-8817)
PHONE..................740 763-3000
Bill Walker, *Branch Mgr*
EMP: 10
SALES (corp-wide): 4.1MM **Privately Held**
SIC: 2439 Trusses, wooden roof; trusses, except roof: laminated lumber
PA: Columbus Roof Trusses, Inc.
2525 Fisher Rd
Columbus OH 43204
614 272-6464

(G-14863)
COMP-U-CHEM INC
195 Dayton Rd Ne (43055-8879)
PHONE..................740 345-3332
Warren G Knorr, *President*
EMP: 5
SALES: 750K **Privately Held**
WEB: www.comp-u-chem.com
SIC: 3589 1711 Sewage & water treatment equipment; plumbing, heating, air-conditioning contractors

(G-14864)
CONTOUR FORMING INC
215 Oakwood Ave (43055-6751)
P.O. Box 727 (43058-0727)
PHONE..................740 345-9777
Terrie Lee Hill, *President*
Garrie Hill, *VP Mfg*
Tracie Hill, *VP Sales*
EMP: 24 EST: 1955
SQ FT: 100,000
SALES (est): 5.2MM **Privately Held**
SIC: 3315 3356 3469 3444 Steel wire & related products; nonferrous rolling & drawing; metal stampings; sheet metalwork

(G-14865)
CP INDUSTRIES INC
Also Called: Pilot Chemical
11047 Lambs Ln (43055-9779)
PHONE..................740 763-2886
Kent Pitcher, *President*
Brian Pitcher, *Corp Secy*
Jeff Pitcher, *Vice Pres*
Martin Solomon, *Vice Pres*
▲ EMP: 12
SALES (est): 2MM **Privately Held**
SIC: 2891 Adhesives

(G-14866)
CRAIN-THARP PRINTING INC
Also Called: A Printed Impression
11 W Main St (43055-5503)
PHONE..................740 345-9823
Donna Corbett, *President*
Cheryl Tharp, *Corp Secy*
EMP: 3
SQ FT: 1,800
SALES: 185K **Privately Held**
SIC: 2752 Commercial printing, offset

(G-14867)
DENNIS LAVENDER
Also Called: Western Star Rail Services
200 Maholm St (43055-3832)
PHONE..................740 344-3336
Dennis Lavender, *Owner*
EMP: 5
SALES: 300K **Privately Held**
SIC: 3743 Railroad equipment

(G-14868)
DOUG SMITH
Also Called: Roger's Quick Print
55 W Church St (43055-5013)
PHONE..................740 345-1398
Doug Smith, *Owner*
EMP: 4
SQ FT: 3,300
SALES: 120K **Privately Held**
SIC: 2752 7334 2759 Commercial printing, offset; photocopying & duplicating services; invitations: printing

(G-14869)
EAGLE MACHINE AND WELDING INC
18 W Walnut St (43055-5408)
PHONE..................740 345-5210
Wade Ranck, *President*
Janet Ranck, *Treasurer*
Kristie E Ranck, *Admin Sec*
EMP: 3
SALES: 150K **Privately Held**
WEB: www.eaglemw.com
SIC: 3599 7692 Machine shop, jobbing & repair; welding repair

Newark - Licking County (G-14870)

(G-14870)
ELKHEAD GAS & OIL CO
12163 Marne Rd (43055-8810)
PHONE.................................740 763-3966
Maurice Dale Chapin, *President*
James Chapin, *Corp Secy*
Michael Chapin, *Vice Pres*
EMP: 6 **EST:** 1964
SQ FT: 1,000
SALES (est): 773.1K **Privately Held**
SIC: 1382 1311 Oil & gas exploration services; crude petroleum production; natural gas production

(G-14871)
ENZYME INDUSTRIES OF THE U S A
2090 James Pkwy (43056-1031)
P.O. Box 2242 (43056-0242)
PHONE.................................740 929-4975
Thomas G Gregg, *President*
Robert T Gregg, *Vice Pres*
Carol Gregg, *Treasurer*
EMP: 4
SQ FT: 3,750
SALES: 400K **Privately Held**
SIC: 2869 Enzymes

(G-14872)
EQUIPMENT GUYS INC
185 Westgate Dr (43055-9313)
PHONE.................................614 871-9220
Matthew A Purdy, *President*
Becky Twaddell, *Cust Mgr*
Shari L Purdy, *Incorporator*
EMP: 11
SALES (est): 1.1MM **Privately Held**
SIC: 3949 5084 Dumbbells & other weightlifting equipment; industrial machinery & equipment

(G-14873)
ES MANUFACTURING INC
55 Builders Dr (43055-1343)
PHONE.................................888 331-3443
Kenneth Walls, *President*
Rick Ault, *Plant Mgr*
EMP: 4
SQ FT: 13,000
SALES (est): 427.8K **Privately Held**
SIC: 2869 Methyl alcohol, synthetic methanol

(G-14874)
FAMILY MEDICAL CLINIC & LASER
44 S 29th St (43055-2564)
PHONE.................................740 345-2767
EMP: 5
SALES (est): 556.8K **Privately Held**
SIC: 2834 Mfg Pharmaceutical Preparations

(G-14875)
FRANKLIN FRAMES AND CYCLES
7179 Reform Rd (43055-9120)
PHONE.................................740 763-3838
John Trumbull, *Owner*
EMP: 3 **EST:** 1976
SALES (est): 232K **Privately Held**
SIC: 3751 3498 3444 Frames, motorcycle & bicycle; fabricated pipe & fittings; sheet metalwork

(G-14876)
GANNETT CO INC
Newark Advocate
22 N 1st St (43055-5608)
PHONE.................................740 345-4053
Bob Robins, *Branch Mgr*
EMP: 135
SALES (corp-wide): 2.9B **Publicly Held**
WEB: www.gannett.com
SIC: 2711 Newspapers, publishing & printing
PA: Gannett Co., Inc.
7950 Jones Branch Dr
Mc Lean VA 22102
703 854-6000

(G-14877)
GANNETT CO INC
Also Called: Newspaper Network Central Ohio
2 N 1st St (43055-5608)
PHONE.................................740 349-1100
Gale Betz, *Manager*
EMP: 19
SALES (corp-wide): 2.9B **Publicly Held**
WEB: www.gannett.com
SIC: 2711 Newspapers: publishing only, not printed on site
PA: Gannett Co., Inc.
7950 Jones Branch Dr
Mc Lean VA 22102
703 854-6000

(G-14878)
GARNER INDUSTRIES INC
767 Country Club Dr (43055-1605)
PHONE.................................740 349-0238
Daniel Garner, *President*
EMP: 4 **EST:** 1999
SALES (est): 529.1K **Privately Held**
SIC: 3089 Injection molding of plastics

(G-14879)
GEMCO MACHINE & TOOL INC
88 Decrow Ave (43055-3870)
PHONE.................................740 344-3111
Steve Hays, *President*
Faye Hays, *Admin Sec*
EMP: 10
SQ FT: 8,500
SALES (est): 1.6MM **Privately Held**
SIC: 3599 Machine shop, jobbing & repair

(G-14880)
GOLF GALAXY GOLFWORKS INC
Also Called: Golfworks, The
4820 Jacksontown Rd (43056-9377)
P.O. Box 3008 (43058-3008)
PHONE.................................740 328-4193
Mark McCormick, *CEO*
Richard C Nordvoid, *Principal*
Mark Wilson, *Vice Pres*
Jerry Datz, *CFO*
▲ **EMP:** 150 **EST:** 1974
SQ FT: 80,000
SALES (corp-wide): 8.4B **Publicly Held**
WEB: www.golfworks.com
SIC: 5091 2731 3949 5941 Golf equipment; books: publishing only; golf equipment; shafts, golf club; golf, tennis & ski shops
HQ: Golf Galaxy, Llc
345 Court St
Coraopolis PA 15108

(G-14881)
GRANVILLE MILLING CO
Also Called: Granville Milling Drive-Thru
145 N Cedar St (43055-6705)
PHONE.................................740 345-1305
Trent Smith, *Manager*
EMP: 6
SALES (corp-wide): 5.1MM **Privately Held**
WEB: www.granvillemilling.com
SIC: 2048 5191 Prepared feeds; animal feeds
PA: Granville Milling Co.
400 S Main St
Granville OH 43023
740 587-0221

(G-14882)
H & N INSTRUMENTS INC
219 N Westmoor Ave (43055-1837)
P.O. Box 4338 (43058-4338)
PHONE.................................740 344-4351
Gary M Nishioka, *President*
Charles K Holloway, *Vice Pres*
EMP: 5
SQ FT: 4,000
SALES (est): 450K **Privately Held**
SIC: 8731 3821 Commercial physical research; industrial laboratory, except testing; computer (hardware) development; chemical laboratory apparatus; physics laboratory apparatus; time interval measuring equipment, electric (lab type)

(G-14883)
HOLOPHANE CORPORATION
Also Called: Unique Solutions
515 Mckinley Ave (43055-6737)
PHONE.................................740 349-4194
Richard Peterson, *Manager*
EMP: 10
SALES (corp-wide): 3.6B **Publicly Held**
SIC: 3646 Commercial indusl & institutional electric lighting fixtures
HQ: Holophane Corporation
3825 Columbus Rd Bldg A
Granville OH 43023
866 759-1577

(G-14884)
HOPE TIMBER & MARKETING GROUP (PA)
Also Called: Wood Recovery
141 Union St (43055-3976)
P.O. Box 502, Granville (43023-0502)
PHONE.................................740 344-1788
Thomas J Harvey, *President*
Deborah L Harvey, *Chairman*
EMP: 18
SQ FT: 40,000
SALES (est): 2.1MM **Privately Held**
SIC: 2499 2448 Mulch or sawdust products, wood; pallets, wood

(G-14885)
HOPE TIMBER MULCH INC
141 Union St (43055-3976)
P.O. Box 502, Granville (43023-0502)
PHONE.................................740 344-1788
Thomas Harvey, *President*
Deborah L Harvey, *Exec VP*
EMP: 6
SQ FT: 20,000
SALES (est): 742.4K **Privately Held**
SIC: 2499 Mulch or sawdust products, wood

(G-14886)
HOPE TIMBER PALLET RECYCL INC
141 Union St (43055-3976)
P.O. Box 502, Granville (43023-0502)
PHONE.................................740 344-1788
Thomas J Harvey, *President*
▼ **EMP:** 24
SALES (est): 3.8MM **Privately Held**
SIC: 2448 4953 Pallets, wood; recycling, waste materials

(G-14887)
I G BRENNER INC
Also Called: Brenner International
32 E North St (43055-5823)
PHONE.................................740 345-8845
Robert M Fitzgerald, *President*
Robert Fitzgerald, *COO*
Jennifer Fitzgerald, *Admin Sec*
EMP: 10 **EST:** 1950
SQ FT: 12,000
SALES (est): 880K **Privately Held**
WEB: www.igbint.com
SIC: 3559 Plastics working machinery

(G-14888)
INTERNATIONAL PAPER COMPANY
1851 Tamarack Rd (43055-1350)
PHONE.................................740 522-3123
Bill Hartshorn, *General Mgr*
Jeff Lee, *Maintence Staff*
EMP: 70
SALES (corp-wide): 23.3B **Publicly Held**
WEB: www.internationalpaper.com
SIC: 2653 Boxes, corrugated: made from purchased materials
PA: International Paper Company
6400 Poplar Ave
Memphis TN 38197
901 419-9000

(G-14889)
JETT INDUSTRIES INC
180 Grant St (43055-3845)
PHONE.................................740 344-4140
Jodi E Priest, *President*
Timothy W Priest, *Vice Pres*
EMP: 4
SQ FT: 4,500
SALES (est): 380K **Privately Held**
SIC: 3599 5084 Machine shop, jobbing & repair; machine tools & accessories

(G-14890)
KATHY EDIE
Also Called: Kam Services
2737 Licking Valley Rd (43055-9105)
PHONE.................................740 763-4887
Kathy Edie, *Owner*
EMP: 3 **EST:** 2009
SALES: 115K **Privately Held**
SIC: 3271 Blocks, concrete: landscape or retaining wall

(G-14891)
KLARITY MEDICAL PRODUCTS LLC
1987 Coffman Rd (43055-1361)
PHONE.................................740 788-8107
Peter Larson, *President*
Susan Larson, *Vice Pres*
Logan Johnson, *QC Mgr*
EMP: 10
SALES (est): 1.8MM **Privately Held**
SIC: 3841 Surgical & medical instruments

(G-14892)
L & T COLLINS INC
Also Called: Minuteman of Heath
44 S 4th St (43055-5436)
PHONE.................................740 345-4494
Timothy M Collins, *President*
Laura Collins, *CFO*
EMP: 6
SQ FT: 12,500
SALES: 470K **Privately Held**
SIC: 2752 Commercial printing, offset

(G-14893)
LIBIDO EDGE LABS LLC
4331 Rock Haven Rd (43055-7999)
P.O. Box 253 (43058-0253)
PHONE.................................740 344-1401
Tammy Miller, *Managing Dir*
Tammy Creel, *Mng Member*
Ruth Moran, *Partner*
EMP: 5 **EST:** 2006
SQ FT: 4,000
SALES: 427.5K **Privately Held**
SIC: 2834 Vitamin preparations

(G-14894)
M & H SCREEN PRINTING
1486 Hebron Rd (43056-1035)
PHONE.................................740 522-1957
Douglas Moore, *Partner*
Stan Hall, *Partner*
Laurie Moore, *Partner*
EMP: 6
SQ FT: 4,000
SALES: 280K **Privately Held**
SIC: 2396 Screen printing on fabric articles

(G-14895)
M & R PHILLIPS ENTERPRISES
Also Called: Serappers Gallery
6242 Jacksontown Rd (43056-8303)
PHONE.................................740 323-0580
Mary Phillips, *President*
Rick Phillips, *Corp Secy*
EMP: 10
SALES (est): 680K **Privately Held**
SIC: 2782 Scrapbooks, albums & diaries

(G-14896)
MCDONALD & WOODWARD PUBLISHING
695 Tall Oaks Dr (43055-1679)
PHONE.................................740 641-2691
EMP: 3
SALES (est): 139.1K **Privately Held**
SIC: 2741 Miscellaneous publishing

(G-14897)
MID OHIO WOOD PRODUCTS INC
535 Franklin Ave (43056-1610)
PHONE.................................740 323-0427
Jay Parkinson, *President*
Nancy Parkinson, *Corp Secy*
EMP: 33
SQ FT: 16,000

▲ = Import ▼ = Export
◆ = Import/Export

GEOGRAPHIC SECTION

Newark - Licking County (G-14924)

SALES (est): 3.7MM **Privately Held**
SIC: 2448 2426 Pallets, wood; skids, wood; hardwood dimension & flooring mills

(G-14898)
MODERN WELDING CO OHIO INC
1 Modern Way (43055-3921)
P.O. Box 4430 (43058-4430)
PHONE..................740 344-9425
John W Jones, *President*
Doug Routher, *General Mgr*
Bob Weidner, *COO*
James M Ruth, *Exec VP*
Doug Rothert, *Vice Pres*
EMP: 30
SQ FT: 52,000
SALES (est): 7.4MM
SALES (corp-wide): 126.3MM **Privately Held**
WEB: www.modweldco.net
SIC: 3443 5051 Tanks, lined: metal plate; metals service centers & offices
PA: Modern Welding Company, Inc.
2880 New Hartford Rd
Owensboro KY 42303
270 685-4400

(G-14899)
NATIONAL GAS & OIL COMPANY (DH)
1500 Granville Rd (43055-1500)
P.O. Box 4970 (43058-4970)
PHONE..................740 344-2102
William H Sullivan Jr, *Ch of Bd*
Patrick J Mc Gonagle, *President*
Todd Ware, *Vice Pres*
EMP: 2
SQ FT: 20,000
SALES (est): 65.2MM **Privately Held**
SIC: 4922 4924 1311 Natural gas transmission; natural gas distribution; natural gas production

(G-14900)
NATIONAL GAS & OIL CORPORATION (DH)
Also Called: Permian Oil & Gas Division
1500 Granville Rd (43055-1500)
P.O. Box 4970 (43058-4970)
PHONE..................740 344-2102
William H Sullivan Jr, *Ch of Bd*
Patrick J Mc Gonagle, *President*
Gordon M King, *Vice Pres*
Todd P Ware, *Vice Pres*
EMP: 36
SQ FT: 10,000
SALES: 37.1MM
SALES (corp-wide): 65.2MM **Privately Held**
WEB: www.theenergycoop.com
SIC: 4922 4924 4932 4911 Natural gas transmission; natural gas distribution; gas & other services combined; electric services; industrial gases
HQ: National Gas & Oil Company Inc
1500 Granville Rd
Newark OH 43055
740 344-2102

(G-14901)
NEW WORLD ENERGY RESOURCES (PA)
1500 Granville Rd (43055-1536)
PHONE..................740 344-4087
John Manczak, *CEO*
EMP: 488
SALES (est): 18.8MM **Privately Held**
SIC: 1382 Geological exploration, oil & gas field

(G-14902)
NEWARK DOWNTOWN CENTER INC
8 Arcade Pl (43055-5546)
PHONE..................740 403-5454
Thomas W Cotton, *President*
EMP: 3
SALES (est): 136.6K **Privately Held**
SIC: 2711 Newspapers, publishing & printing

(G-14903)
NGO DEVELOPMENT CORPORATION (HQ)
Also Called: National Production
1500 Granville Rd (43055-1536)
P.O. Box 4970 (43058-4970)
PHONE..................740 344-3790
Dave Potter, *President*
Daniel S Mc Vey, *COO*
Todd P Ware, *CFO*
▲ EMP: 13 EST: 1975
SALES (est): 1.4MM
SALES (corp-wide): 18.8MM **Privately Held**
SIC: 4922 1381 Pipelines, natural gas; directional drilling oil & gas wells
PA: New World Energy Resources Inc
1500 Granville Rd
Newark OH 43055
740 344-4087

(G-14904)
NORTHEL USA LLC
5772 Bear Hollow Rd Se (43056-9464)
PHONE..................740 973-0309
EMP: 4 EST: 2015
SALES (est): 137K **Privately Held**
SIC: 4911 3511 Electric Services Mfg Turbines/Generator Sets

(G-14905)
OHIO PLASTICS COMPANY
3933 Price Rd Ne (43055-9507)
PHONE..................740 828-3291
Allen L Handlan, *President*
EMP: 4 EST: 1938
SQ FT: 10,000
SALES (est): 483.5K **Privately Held**
SIC: 3089 Injection molded finished plastic products

(G-14906)
OHIO RIVER VALLEY CABINET
4 Waterworks Rd (43055-6060)
PHONE..................740 975-8846
Bob Bachmann, *Owner*
EMP: 6
SALES (est): 240K **Privately Held**
SIC: 2434 Wood kitchen cabinets

(G-14907)
OWENS CORNING SALES LLC
400 Case Ave (43055-5805)
P.O. Box 3012 (43058-3012)
PHONE..................740 328-2300
Fred Ramquist, *Branch Mgr*
EMP: 148 **Publicly Held**
WEB: www.owenscorning.com
SIC: 3296 Fiberglass insulation
HQ: Owens Corning Sales, Llc
1 Owens Corning Pkwy
Toledo OH 43659
419 248-8000

(G-14908)
PACKAGING CORPORATION AMERICA
Also Called: PCA/Newark 365
205 S 21st St (43055-3879)
PHONE..................740 344-1126
Scott Robinson, *Sls & Mktg Exec*
Pom Watson, *Branch Mgr*
EMP: 115
SALES (corp-wide): 7B **Publicly Held**
WEB: www.packagingcorp.com
SIC: 2653 Boxes, corrugated: made from purchased materials
PA: Packaging Corporation Of America
1 N Field Ct
Lake Forest IL 60045
847 482-3000

(G-14909)
PENICK GAS & OIL
1504 Blue Jay Rd (43056-1767)
PHONE..................740 323-3040
EMP: 5 EST: 1939
SALES (est): 318.6K **Privately Held**
SIC: 1311 Crude petroleum production; natural gas production

(G-14910)
PHAGEVAX INC
855 Sharon Valley Rd # 101 (43055-2860)
PHONE..................740 502-9010
Clark Tibbs, *President*
EMP: 3
SALES (est): 89.5K **Privately Held**
WEB: www.phagevax.com
SIC: 2836 Vaccines & other immunizing products

(G-14911)
PLUS PUBLICATIONS INC
Also Called: Independent Restauratuer
57 S 3rd St (43055-5433)
P.O. Box 917 (43058-0917)
PHONE..................740 345-5542
James T Young, *Owner*
EMP: 5
SALES (est): 270K **Privately Held**
SIC: 2721 Magazines: publishing only, not printed on site

(G-14912)
POWER CORP SIGN PRODUCTS INC
632 Swansea Rd (43055-1526)
PHONE..................740 344-0468
Jeff Jones, *President*
EMP: 3
SQ FT: 10,000
SALES (est): 297.1K **Privately Held**
SIC: 3993 Electric signs

(G-14913)
PRESTON
42 Sandalwood Dr (43055-9233)
PHONE..................740 788-8208
Judith Preston, *Principal*
EMP: 12
SALES (est): 1.9MM **Privately Held**
SIC: 3545 Collars (machine tool accessories)

(G-14914)
PUGHS DESIGNER JEWELERS INC
44 S 2nd St (43055-5432)
PHONE..................740 344-9259
Kevin Pugh, *President*
Sandi Johnson, *Associate*
Marilyn Krebs, *Associate*
EMP: 8
SQ FT: 2,500
SALES: 900K **Privately Held**
WEB: www.diamondstodiefor.com
SIC: 5944 3961 7389 7631 Jewelry, precious stones & precious metals; costume jewelry; appraisers, except real estate; jewelry repair services

(G-14915)
QUANTUM
400 Case Ave (43055-5805)
PHONE..................740 328-2548
EMP: 3
SALES (est): 165.3K **Privately Held**
SIC: 3572 Computer storage devices

(G-14916)
RYANS NEWARK LEADER EX PRTG
Also Called: Leader Printing
56 Westgate Dr (43055-9313)
P.O. Box 4902 (43058-4902)
PHONE..................740 522-2149
Andrew T Ryan, *President*
Gary Ryan, *Treasurer*
EMP: 10 EST: 1895
SQ FT: 9,600
SALES (est): 1.1MM **Privately Held**
WEB: www.leaderprinting1895.com
SIC: 2752 2791 2789 2759 Commercial printing, offset; typesetting; bookbinding & related work; commercial printing

(G-14917)
SENTINEL USA INC
Also Called: Sentinel Utility Services
1285 Granville Rd (43055-2130)
PHONE..................740 345-6412
EMP: 12
SQ FT: 2,400
SALES (est): 693.8K
SALES (corp-wide): 8.6MM **Privately Held**
SIC: 2741 7371 Automated Or Digital Distribution Mapping Company & Field Inventory Services
PA: Irth Solutions, Inc.
5009 Horizons Pkwy Dr Ste 100
Columbus OH 43220
614 459-2328

(G-14918)
SHELLY MATERIALS INC
6824 Mount Vernon Rd (43055-9625)
PHONE..................740 745-5965
Wayne Spray, *Manager*
EMP: 5
SALES (corp-wide): 29.7B **Privately Held**
SIC: 1422 Crushed & broken limestone
HQ: Shelly Materials, Inc.
80 Park Dr
Thornville OH 43076
740 246-6315

(G-14919)
SPECTRUM ADHESIVES INC
11047 Lambs Ln (43055-9779)
PHONE..................740 763-2886
Kent Pitcher, *Branch Mgr*
EMP: 13
SALES (est): 1.6MM
SALES (corp-wide): 5.8MM **Privately Held**
SIC: 2891 Glue
PA: Spectrum Adhesives, Inc.
5611 Universal Dr
Memphis TN 38118
901 795-1943

(G-14920)
SPENCER-WALKER PRESS INC (PA)
1433 Amesbury Ln (43055-1894)
PHONE..................740 344-6110
David B Sinclair, *President*
EMP: 12
SQ FT: 16,000
SALES: 1.5MM **Privately Held**
SIC: 2752 2791 2789 2759 Commercial printing, offset; typesetting; bookbinding & related work; commercial printing; die-cut paper & board

(G-14921)
SPENCER-WALKER PRESS INC
Also Called: Print Shop, The
44 S 4th St (43055-5436)
PHONE..................740 345-4494
David Sinclair, *Owner*
EMP: 3
SALES (corp-wide): 1.5MM **Privately Held**
SIC: 2759 Commercial printing
PA: Spencer-Walker Press Inc
1433 Amesbury Ln
Newark OH 43055
740 344-6110

(G-14922)
STAR WIPERS INC (PA)
1125 E Main St (43055-8869)
PHONE..................724 695-2721
Todd Wilson, *President*
▲ EMP: 5
SALES (est): 1.6MM **Privately Held**
SIC: 2211 Scrub cloths

(G-14923)
STEPHEN R WHITE
Also Called: Carat Patch, The
800 Hebron Rd (43056-1443)
PHONE..................740 522-1512
Stephen R White, *Owner*
EMP: 3
SALES (est): 230.8K **Privately Held**
WEB: www.srwesq.com
SIC: 5944 3911 Jewelry, precious stones & precious metals; jewelry apparel

(G-14924)
STONEWORKD
1050 Harris Ave (43055-2429)
PHONE..................740 920-4099
Ericeh Horvath,
EMP: 10
SALES (est): 850K **Privately Held**
SIC: 3559 Stone working machinery

Newark - Licking County (G-14925)

(G-14925)
STRATEGIC MATERIALS INC
101 S Arch St (43055-6202)
P.O. Box 816 (43058-0816)
PHONE...................740 349-9523
Michael Back, *Manager*
EMP: 6
SALES (corp-wide): 430.6MM **Privately Held**
SIC: 3231 Products of purchased glass
HQ: Strategic Materials, Inc.
17220 Katy Fwy Ste 150
Houston TX 77094
281 647-2700

(G-14926)
SUGARTREE SQUARE MERCANTILE
5541 Grumms Ln Ne (43055-9755)
PHONE...................740 345-3882
Shirley Simms, *Partner*
EMP: 3
SALES (est): 236.1K **Privately Held**
SIC: 3795 Tanks & tank components

(G-14927)
SUMMIT CUSTOM CABINETS
10430 Hoover Rd Ne (43055-9751)
PHONE...................740 345-1734
Bill Guisinger, *Owner*
Scott Thomas, *Owner*
EMP: 3 EST: 1998
SALES (est): 180K **Privately Held**
SIC: 1751 2541 2434 Cabinet & finish carpentry; table or counter tops, plastic laminated; wood kitchen cabinets

(G-14928)
TECH WEAR EMBROIDERY COMPANY
738 W Main St (43055-2512)
PHONE...................740 344-1276
Chris McInturf, *President*
EMP: 5 EST: 1997
SALES (est): 184K **Privately Held**
WEB: www.embroideryshop.net
SIC: 2395 Embroidery products, except schiffli machine

(G-14929)
TECTUM INC
105 S 6th St (43055-4908)
P.O. Box 3002 (43058-3002)
PHONE...................740 345-9691
Michael Massaro, *President*
Wayne Chester, *Exec VP*
Stephen M Mihaly, *Shareholder*
John M Scott, *Shareholder*
▼ EMP: 120
SQ FT: 100,000
SALES: 12.9MM **Privately Held**
WEB: www.tectum.com
SIC: 2493 3444 3296 Fiberboard, other vegetable pulp; sheet metalwork; mineral wool

(G-14930)
TRAFFIC CNTRL SGNLS SIGNS & MA
Also Called: City of Newark
1195 E Main St (43055-8869)
PHONE...................740 670-7763
Gary Snavely, *Director*
EMP: 7 EST: 2007
SALES (est): 713.2K **Privately Held**
SIC: 3993 Signs & advertising specialties

(G-14931)
UNIVERSAL VENEER PRODUCTION
1776 Tamarack Rd (43055-1384)
PHONE...................740 522-1147
Klaus Krajewski, *President*
▼ EMP: 200
SQ FT: 98,000
SALES (est): 17.6MM **Privately Held**
SIC: 2436 Softwood veneer & plywood

(G-14932)
UNIVERSAL VENEER SALES CORP (PA)
1776 Tamarack Rd (43055-1384)
PHONE...................740 522-1147
Klaus Krajewski, *President*

Patty Showalter, *Sales Staff*
◆ EMP: 200
SQ FT: 75,000
SALES (est): 21.8MM **Privately Held**
SIC: 2435 Veneer stock, hardwood

(G-14933)
WYETH-SCOTT COMPANY
85 Dayton Rd Ne (43055-8814)
P.O. Box 888 (43058-0888)
PHONE...................740 345-4528
Amy L Kent, *President*
▲ EMP: 3 EST: 1909
SQ FT: 7,692
SALES: 595K **Privately Held**
WEB: www.wyeth-scott.com
SIC: 3546 3531 Power-driven handtools; winches

Newburgh Heights
Cuyahoga County

(G-14934)
ARCONIC INC
Also Called: Alcoa
1600 Harvard Ave (44105-3040)
PHONE...................216 641-3600
Alfredo Tinoco, *Buyer*
Susan Tooley, *Buyer*
John Ruhrkraut, *Engineer*
Danielle Vasas, *Human Res Mgr*
Kathleen Newell, *Empl Rel Mgr*
EMP: 1200
SALES (corp-wide): 14B **Publicly Held**
SIC: 3463 3321 Aluminum forgings; gray & ductile iron foundries
PA: Arconic Inc.
390 Park Ave Fl 12
New York NY 10022
212 836-2758

(G-14935)
ARCONIC INC
Also Called: Forged Wheels Division
1616 Harvard Ave (44105-3040)
PHONE...................216 641-3600
Merrick Murphy, *President*
EMP: 1200
SALES (corp-wide): 14B **Publicly Held**
SIC: 3463 Aluminum forgings
PA: Arconic Inc.
390 Park Ave Fl 12
New York NY 10022
212 836-2758

(G-14936)
H GOODMAN INC
Also Called: White Dove Mattress
3201 Harvard Ave (44105-3060)
PHONE...................216 341-0200
Bruce Goodman, *President*
Henry J Goodman, *Chairman*
Dennis Spohn, *Accounts Mgr*
Clark Pajak, *Marketing Staff*
▲ EMP: 90 EST: 1916
SQ FT: 270,000
SALES (est): 13MM **Privately Held**
WEB: www.whitedoveusa.com
SIC: 2515 2512 Mattresses & foundations; mattresses, innerspring or box spring; box springs, assembled; upholstered household furniture

(G-14937)
HOWMET ALUMINUM CASTING INC (HQ)
Also Called: Sigma Div
1600 Harvard Ave (44105-3040)
PHONE...................216 641-4340
Raymond B Mitchell, *President*
EMP: 50
SQ FT: 10,000
SALES (est): 44.7MM
SALES (corp-wide): 14B **Publicly Held**
SIC: 3365 Aerospace castings, aluminum
PA: Arconic Inc.
390 Park Ave Fl 12
New York NY 10022
212 836-2758

(G-14938)
HOWMET CASTINGS & SERVICES INC (DH)
1616 Harvard Ave (44105-3040)
PHONE...................216 641-4400
Eric M Brzostek, *President*
EMP: 274 EST: 2004
SALES (est): 642.7MM
SALES (corp-wide): 14B **Publicly Held**
SIC: 3324 Commercial investment castings, ferrous
HQ: Howmet Corporation
1616 Harvard Ave
Newburgh Heights OH 44105
757 825-7086

(G-14939)
HOWMET CORPORATION (DH)
Also Called: Alcoa Power & Propulsion
1616 Harvard Ave (44105-3040)
PHONE...................757 825-7086
David L Squier, *President*
Marklin Lasker, *Senior VP*
James R Stanley, *Senior VP*
Roland A Paul, *Vice Pres*
B Dennis Albrechtsen, *VP Mfg*
◆ EMP: 30
SQ FT: 10,000
SALES (est): 1.8B
SALES (corp-wide): 14B **Publicly Held**
WEB: www.alcoa.com
SIC: 3324 3542 5051 3479 Commercial investment castings, ferrous; machine tools, metal forming type; ferroalloys; ingots; coating of metals & formed products
HQ: Howmet Holdings Corporation
1 Misco Dr
Whitehall MI 49461
231 894-5686

(G-14940)
HUNT PRODUCTS INC
3982 E 42nd St (44105-3165)
PHONE...................440 667-2457
Jo Ann Hunt, *President*
Laura Hunt, *Vice Pres*
EMP: 35 EST: 1970
SQ FT: 30,000
SALES (est): 2.2MM **Privately Held**
SIC: 7389 3544 3053 2675 Packaging & labeling services; special dies, tools, jigs & fixtures; gaskets, packing & sealing devices; die-cut paper & board; packaging paper & plastics film, coated & laminated; automotive & apparel trimmings

(G-14941)
MCGEAN-ROHCO INC
2910 Harvard Ave (44105-3010)
PHONE...................216 441-4900
Kerry May, *Branch Mgr*
EMP: 60
SQ FT: 350,000
SALES (corp-wide): 62.8MM **Privately Held**
WEB: www.mcgean.com
SIC: 2899 2819 3471 2842 Chemical preparations; industrial inorganic chemicals; plating & polishing; specialty cleaning, polishes & sanitation goods
PA: Mcgean-Rohco, Inc.
2910 Harvard Ave
Newburgh Heights OH 44105
216 441-4900

(G-14942)
PARK-OHIO INDUSTRIES INC
Also Called: Ohio Crankshaft Div
3800 Harvard Ave (44105-3208)
PHONE...................216 341-2300
Felix Parorick, *Principal*
EMP: 150
SQ FT: 427,000
SALES (corp-wide): 1.6B **Publicly Held**
WEB: www.pkoh.com.cn
SIC: 3714 Camshafts, motor vehicle
HQ: Park-Ohio Industries, Inc.
6065 Parkland Blvd Ste 1
Cleveland OH 44124
440 947-2000

(G-14943)
PQ CORPORATION
5200 Harvard Ave (44105-4855)
PHONE...................216 341-2578
EMP: 3

SALES (est): 172.5K **Privately Held**
SIC: 2819 Industrial inorganic chemicals

(G-14944)
SAMCO TECHNOLOGIES INC
1600 Harvard Ave (44105-3040)
PHONE...................216 641-5288
Jim Batter, *Manager*
EMP: 6
SALES (corp-wide): 8.8MM **Privately Held**
WEB: www.samcotech.com
SIC: 3589 4941 Water treatment equipment, industrial; water supply
PA: Samco Technologies, Inc.
1 River Rock Dr
Buffalo NY 14207
716 743-9000

(G-14945)
WHITE DOVE MATTRESS LTD
3201 Harvard Ave (44105-3060)
PHONE...................216 341-0200
Karen Morchak, *Purch Mgr*
Arlene Turocy, *Controller*
Les McNair, *Sales Staff*
Bruce H Goodman,
▲ EMP: 43
SALES (est): 10MM **Privately Held**
SIC: 2515 Mattresses & foundations

Newbury
Geauga County

(G-14946)
BOGGS RECYCLING INC
12355 Kinsman Rd Unit J (44065-9620)
P.O. Box 576, Burton (44021-0576)
PHONE...................800 837-8101
Kimberly Boggs, *President*
Christopher A Boggs, *Principal*
EMP: 8
SQ FT: 10,000
SALES (est): 1.6MM **Privately Held**
SIC: 3334 Primary aluminum

(G-14947)
CHESTERLAND CABINET COMPANY
10389 Kinsman Rd (44065-9701)
P.O. Box 69 (44065-0069)
PHONE...................440 564-1157
Joe Mazzurco, *President*
Madeline Mazzurco, *Vice Pres*
EMP: 3
SQ FT: 1,500
SALES: 100K **Privately Held**
SIC: 2434 1751 Wood kitchen cabinets; cabinet & finish carpentry

(G-14948)
COUNTRY MOLDING
12375 Kinsman Rd (44065-9684)
PHONE...................440 564-5235
EMP: 3
SALES (est): 162.8K **Privately Held**
SIC: 3089 Molding primary plastic

(G-14949)
COUNTY WIDE WELDING LLC
14999 Cross Creek Pkwy (44065-9788)
PHONE...................440 564-1333
David Smith,
EMP: 3
SQ FT: 5,000
SALES: 300K **Privately Held**
SIC: 7692 Welding repair

(G-14950)
CREATIVE MOLD AND MACHINE INC
10385 Kinsman Rd (44065-9701)
P.O. Box 323 (44065-0323)
PHONE...................440 338-5146
Ray Lyons, *President*
Greg Davis, *Vice Pres*
Mishal Dedeck, *Vice Pres*
EMP: 25
SQ FT: 39,000
SALES (est): 4.3MM **Privately Held**
SIC: 7692 3599 Welding repair; machine shop, jobbing & repair

GEOGRAPHIC SECTION

Newcomerstown - Tuscarawas County (G-14979)

(G-14951)
DEM MANUFACTURING LLC
10357 Kinsman Rd (44065-9701)
P.O. Box 220 (44065-0220)
PHONE...............................440 564-7160
▲ **EMP:** 10
SALES (est): 1.3MM **Privately Held**
SIC: 3999 Manufacturing Industries, Nec, Nsk

(G-14952)
GEAUGA CONCRETE INC
10509 Kinsman Rd (44065-9803)
P.O. Box 249, Grand River (44045-0249)
PHONE...............................440 338-4915
Hal Larned, *President*
EMP: 10
SALES (est): 1.4MM
SALES (corp-wide): 3.5MM **Privately Held**
WEB: www.osdocks.com
SIC: 3273 Ready-mixed concrete
PA: Osborne Concrete & Stone Co.
1 Williams St
Grand River OH 44045
440 357-5562

(G-14953)
GEAUGA FEED AND GRAIN SUPPLY
11030 Kinsman Rd (44065-9744)
P.O. Box 654 (44065-0654)
PHONE...............................440 564-5000
Kevin Oreilly, *Owner*
EMP: 5 EST: 2002
SALES (est): 552.4K **Privately Held**
SIC: 5153 2048 Grains; livestock feeds

(G-14954)
GREEN VISION MATERIALS INC
11220 Kinsman Rd (44065-9676)
PHONE...............................440 564-5500
Beau Gibney, *Owner*
EMP: 15 EST: 2010
SALES (est): 2.5MM **Privately Held**
SIC: 4953 3271 Recycling, waste materials; blocks, concrete: landscape or retaining wall

(G-14955)
H2O MECHANICS LLC
15708 Park View Dr (44065-9574)
PHONE...............................440 554-9515
Chris Hansen, *Mng Member*
▼ **EMP:** 4
SQ FT: 4,000
SALES: 90K **Privately Held**
SIC: 3599 Custom machinery

(G-14956)
HAUETER CONSTRUCTION CO
Haueter Sand & Gravel Division
15349 Ravenna Rd (44065)
PHONE...............................440 834-8220
Tom Bevington, *Manager*
EMP: 8
SALES (corp-wide): 2.4MM **Privately Held**
SIC: 1442 Gravel mining
PA: Haueter Construction Co
Grant Street Ext
Chardon OH
440 286-9482

(G-14957)
HOSTAR INTERNATIONAL INC (PA)
15000 Cross Creek Pkwy (44065-9726)
PHONE...............................440 564-5362
Claudia Berg, *President*
Todd Bush, *President*
Ron Vitale, *Exec VP*
Dolores Lapalio, *Vice Pres*
Andy McCabe, *Vice Pres*
EMP: 11
SALES (est): 3.6MM **Privately Held**
WEB: www.hostar.com
SIC: 3535 Unit handling conveying systems

(G-14958)
JAC CONSTRUCTION OHIO LLC
14985 Cross Creek Pkwy (44065-9788)
PHONE...............................440 564-5005
Richard Fletcher,

EMP: 3
SALES: 500K **Privately Held**
SIC: 1381 1731 Directional drilling oil & gas wells; fiber optic cable installation

(G-14959)
L & N OLDE CAR CO
Also Called: Newbury Sandblasting & Pntg
9992 Kinsman Rd (44065)
P.O. Box 378 (44065-0378)
PHONE...............................440 564-7204
Nelson Peterson, *President*
Pamela Peterson, *Corp Secy*
EMP: 7
SQ FT: 25,000
SALES (est): 805K **Privately Held**
SIC: 3471 7532 Sand blasting of metal parts; paint shop, automotive

(G-14960)
NEWBURY WOODWORKS
10958 Kinsman Rd Unit 2 (44065-8602)
PHONE...............................440 564-5273
Aloysius Hoenigman Jr, *Owner*
EMP: 7
SQ FT: 8,000
SALES (est): 581.1K **Privately Held**
SIC: 5712 2499 Cabinet work, custom; decorative wood & woodwork

(G-14961)
OREILLY EQUIPMENT LLC
14555 Ravenna Rd (44065-9513)
PHONE...............................440 564-1234
Mikaela Klein, *Marketing Staff*
Jeffery M O'Reilly,
EMP: 6
SQ FT: 6,000
SALES (est): 2.5MM **Privately Held**
WEB: www.oreillyequipment.com
SIC: 5599 3714 Utility trailers; ice scrapers & window brushes, motor vehicle

(G-14962)
R W SIDLEY INCORPORATED
10688 Kinsman Rd (44065-9761)
PHONE...............................440 564-2221
Dan Craver, *Branch Mgr*
EMP: 21
SALES (corp-wide): 132.6MM **Privately Held**
WEB: www.rwsidleyinc.com
SIC: 3273 3272 3271 1442 Ready-mixed concrete; concrete products; concrete block & brick; construction sand & gravel
PA: R. W. Sidley Incorporated
436 Casement Ave
Painesville OH 44077
440 352-9343

(G-14963)
RALSTON INSTRUMENTS LLC
15035 Cross Creek Pkwy (44065-9726)
P.O. Box 340, Novelty (44072-0340)
PHONE...............................440 564-1430
Douglas Ralston, *CEO*
Corey Ralston,
EMP: 20
SALES (est): 3.7MM **Privately Held**
WEB: www.ralstoninst.com
SIC: 3829 Measuring & controlling devices

(G-14964)
S J K METALWORKING INC
Also Called: S K Industries
14940 Cross Creek Pkwy (44065-9788)
P.O. Box 267 (44065-0267)
PHONE...............................440 564-7877
Katherina Kekedy, *President*
Steven Kekedy, *Vice Pres*
EMP: 4
SQ FT: 8,000
SALES (est): 482.7K **Privately Held**
SIC: 3599 Machine shop, jobbing & repair

(G-14965)
SHARON JAMES CELLERS
11303 Kinsman Rd (44065-9693)
PHONE...............................440 739-4065
Sharon James, *Principal*
EMP: 3
SALES (est): 213.9K **Privately Held**
SIC: 2084 Wines

(G-14966)
SPEED CITY LLC
12361 Kinsman Rd Ste A (44065-8811)
P.O. Box 963, Willoughby (44096-0963)
PHONE...............................440 975-1969
John Bojec, *Principal*
Diana Harker, *Mng Member*
EMP: 4
SQ FT: 7,000
SALES (est): 707.8K **Privately Held**
SIC: 5531 3089 Automotive parts; automotive parts, plastic

(G-14967)
STEVEN DOUGLAS CORP
10420 Kinsman Rd (44065-9724)
PHONE...............................440 564-5200
Stephen Belliveau, *President*
Paul Belliveau, *Exec VP*
Deborah Belliveau, *Admin Sec*
EMP: 22 EST: 1998
SQ FT: 27,000
SALES (est): 7.7MM **Privately Held**
WEB: www.s-d-c.com
SIC: 3569 Assembly machines, non-metalworking

Newcomerstown
Tuscarawas County

(G-14968)
31 INC
Also Called: Extra Seal
100 Enterprise Dr (43832-9242)
P.O. Box 278 (43832-0278)
PHONE...............................740 498-8324
Charles Muhs, *President*
Robert Hendry, *Vice Pres*
Barbara Simms, *Opers Staff*
Tim Lint, *Technology*
◆ **EMP:** 100 EST: 1961
SQ FT: 130,000
SALES (est): 20MM **Privately Held**
WEB: www.31inc.com
SIC: 3011 3714 Tire sundries or tire repair materials, rubber; tire valve cores

(G-14969)
ACCURATE PRODUCTS COMPANY
98 Elizabeth St (43832-1432)
P.O. Box 106 (43832-0106)
PHONE...............................740 498-7202
Clark H Smith, *President*
R Clark Smith, *Vice Pres*
Annette Parks, *Manager*
EMP: 6 EST: 1946
SALES (est): 600K **Privately Held**
SIC: 3366 Castings (except die): brass; castings (except die): bronze

(G-14970)
BOLTARON INC
Also Called: A Simona Group Company
1 General St (43832-1230)
PHONE...............................740 498-5900
Lawrence J Schorr, *CEO*
Kevin Asti, *Vice Pres*
Jay Coventry, *Engineer*
Dean LI, *CFO*
Tyler Albertson, *Cust Mgr*
▲ **EMP:** 100
SQ FT: 175,000
SALES (est): 42MM **Privately Held**
WEB: www.empireplastics.com
SIC: 3081 2891 Film base, cellulose acetate or nitrocellulose plastic; adhesives & sealants

(G-14971)
BUCKEYE BOP LLC
Also Called: Buckeye Blow Out Preventer
401 Enterprise Dr (43832-9239)
PHONE...............................740 498-9898
EMP: 3
SALES (est): 250.6K **Privately Held**
SIC: 3564 3592 5719 Blowers & fans; valves; brushes

(G-14972)
CLAY LBC CO
59260 County Road 9 (43832-9702)
PHONE...............................740 492-5055

Chad Clark, *CEO*
EMP: 5
SALES (est): 198.8K **Privately Held**
SIC: 1442 Construction sand & gravel

(G-14973)
ECHO DRILLING INC (PA)
11 Crestview Mnr (43832-9654)
PHONE...............................740 498-8560
Kenneth E Ebersbach, *President*
Virgil Ebersbach, *Admin Sec*
EMP: 3
SQ FT: 100
SALES (est): 1.3MM **Privately Held**
SIC: 5172 1389 Crude oil; oil field services

(G-14974)
H3D TOOL CORPORATION (PA)
Also Called: High Definition Tooling
295 Enterprise Dr (43832-8954)
P.O. Box 314 (43832-0314)
PHONE...............................740 498-5181
Gary Dyer, *President*
Chris Dyer, *Vice Pres*
Jim Edsall, *Mfg Dir*
Bill Ludwig, *Engineer*
Bob Arick, *Sales Staff*
EMP: 9
SQ FT: 20,000
SALES (est): 1.4MM **Privately Held**
SIC: 3545 5085 Diamond cutting tools for turning, boring, burnishing, etc.; industrial supplies

(G-14975)
HERCO INC
295 Enterprise Dr (43832-8954)
P.O. Box 314 (43832-0314)
PHONE...............................740 498-5181
Gary Dyer, *President*
Chris Dyer, *Vice Pres*
James P Edsall, *Mfg Staff*
Jim Conlon, *Production*
Bob Arick, *Sales Mgr*
EMP: 40
SQ FT: 20,000
SALES (est): 5.5MM **Privately Held**
WEB: www.herco.net
SIC: 3545 Cutting tools for machine tools

(G-14976)
KURZ-KASCH INC
Kurz-Kasch Newcomerstown Div
199 E State St (43832-1468)
PHONE...............................740 498-8343
Jeff Smith, *Branch Mgr*
EMP: 175 **Privately Held**
WEB: www.kurz-kasch.com
SIC: 3089 Molding primary plastic
HQ: Kurz-Kasch, Inc.
199 E State St
Newcomerstown OH 43832
740 498-8343

(G-14977)
KURZ-KASCH INC (HQ)
199 E State St (43832-1468)
PHONE...............................740 498-8343
George E Kochanowski, *CEO*
Chad Merkel, *CEO*
▲ **EMP:** 84 EST: 1916
SQ FT: 6,000
SALES (est): 17.6MM **Privately Held**
WEB: www.kurz-kasch.com
SIC: 3089 3677 Thermoformed finished plastic products; injection molded finished plastic products; electronic coils, transformers & other inductors

(G-14978)
KURZKASCH INC WILM DIV
199 E State St (43832-1468)
PHONE...............................740 498-8345
Julie Nay, *Principal*
▲ **EMP:** 16 EST: 2011
SALES (est): 2.7MM **Privately Held**
SIC: 3089 Molding primary plastic

(G-14979)
OAK POINTE STAIR SYSTEMS INC
96 New Pace Rd (43832-1287)
PHONE...............................740 498-9820
Davis Weissman, *President*
Bernard Booth, *President*
EMP: 30

Newcomerstown - Tuscarawas County (G-14980)

GEOGRAPHIC SECTION

SALES (est): 3.6MM **Privately Held**
WEB: www.oakpointestair.com
SIC: 2431 Staircases, stairs & railings

(G-14980)
RAINBOW HILLS VINEYARDS INC
Also Called: Rainbow Hills Vineyards
26349 Township Road 251 (43832-9631)
PHONE.................................740 545-9305
Leland Wyse, *President*
Glenna Wyse, *Vice Pres*
EMP: 3
SALES (est): 226.1K **Privately Held**
SIC: 2084 Wines

(G-14981)
SHAW PALLETS & SPECIALTIES
12269 Lick Brown Rd (43832)
PHONE.................................740 498-7892
Kenneth Shaw, *President*
Rhea Shaw, *Vice Pres*
EMP: 4
SQ FT: 1,440
SALES (est): 481K **Privately Held**
WEB: www.shawpallet.com
SIC: 2448 Pallets, wood

(G-14982)
SHAW WILBERT VAULTS LLC
Also Called: Wilbert Shaw Valts
12269 Lick Run Rd (43832-9145)
PHONE.................................740 498-7438
Kenneth Shaw, *Mng Member*
EMP: 5
SALES (est): 519.5K **Privately Held**
SIC: 5087 3272 Concrete burial vaults & boxes; burial vaults, concrete or precast terrazzo

Newport
Washington County

(G-14983)
CARLTON OIL CORP
961 Greene St (45768-5057)
PHONE.................................740 473-2629
EMP: 8
SQ FT: 900
SALES: 1.5MM **Privately Held**
SIC: 1311 Producer & Driller

Newton Falls
Trumbull County

(G-14984)
AMERICAN MOLDED PLASTICS INC
3876 Newton Fls Bailey Rd (44444-9746)
P.O. Box 434 (44444-0434)
PHONE.................................330 872-3838
Ray Allen, *President*
Bertha Allen, *Vice Pres*
EMP: 10
SQ FT: 6,000
SALES (est): 1.5MM **Privately Held**
WEB: www.americanmoldedplastic.com
SIC: 3089 Injection molding of plastics

(G-14985)
BAR PROCESSING CORPORATION
1000 Windham Rd (44444-9586)
P.O. Box 280 (44444-0280)
PHONE.................................330 872-0914
Jack Starkey, *Sales Dir*
Jack Stacky, *Manager*
Rich Scheidly, *Maintence Staff*
EMP: 100
SALES (corp-wide): 39.9MM **Privately Held**
SIC: 3471 3316 Finishing, metals or formed products; polishing, metals or formed products; cold finishing of steel shapes
HQ: Bar Processing Corporation
26601 W Huron River Dr
Flat Rock MI 48134
734 782-4454

(G-14986)
CRISSMAN TOOL & MACHINE INC
3877 Hallock Sook Rd (44444-8716)
PHONE.................................330 872-1412
Lionel Crissman, *President*
Scott Crissman, *Admin Sec*
EMP: 3
SQ FT: 5,000
SALES (est): 220K **Privately Held**
SIC: 3599 Machine shop, jobbing & repair

(G-14987)
GUYS BARBEQUE INC
Also Called: Guy's Award Winning Barbeque
4498 W Oakland St Sw (44446-9535)
P.O. Box 431 (44444-0431)
PHONE.................................330 872-7256
Ira Hughes, *President*
Lyn Hughes, *Principal*
EMP: 9 EST: 2001
SALES (est): 500K **Privately Held**
WEB: www.guysbbq.com
SIC: 2033 Barbecue sauce: packaged in cans, jars, etc.

(G-14988)
KENS HIS & HERS SHOP INC
Also Called: Positive Images
5 S Milton Blvd Ste C (44444-1780)
PHONE.................................330 872-3190
Doug Cochran, *President*
Dawn Cochran, *Vice Pres*
EMP: 6
SQ FT: 5,200
SALES (est): 819.9K **Privately Held**
SIC: 2759 2395 Screen printing; embroidery & art needlework

(G-14989)
LUXAIRE CUSHION CO
2410 S Center St (44444-9408)
P.O. Box 156 (44444-0156)
PHONE.................................330 872-0995
Alan E Rathbun Jr, *President*
Steve Fackelman, *Vice Pres*
Julie Miller, *Shareholder*
EMP: 10 EST: 1946
SQ FT: 55,000
SALES (est): 1.2MM **Privately Held**
WEB: www.luxairecushion.com
SIC: 2393 Cushions, except spring & carpet: purchased materials

(G-14990)
NEWTON FALLS PRINTING
27 E Broad St (44444-1604)
PHONE.................................330 872-3532
Robert Staunton, *Owner*
EMP: 3
SQ FT: 4,275
SALES: 300K **Privately Held**
SIC: 2759 2752 Commercial printing; commercial printing, lithographic

(G-14991)
QUALITY SWITCH INC
715 Arlington Blvd (44444-8765)
P.O. Box 250 (44444-0250)
PHONE.................................330 872-5707
Russell Sewell, *President*
Rick Sewell, *Vice Pres*
Doug Senne, *Engineer*
Laura Whitmore, *Admin Sec*
EMP: 29
SQ FT: 31,200
SALES (est): 5.5MM **Privately Held**
WEB: www.qualityswitch.com
SIC: 3679 Electronic switches; electronic circuits

(G-14992)
R S IMPRINTS
5 S Milton Blvd (44444-1780)
PHONE.................................330 872-5905
Ross Sherlock, *Principal*
EMP: 10
SALES (est): 1.3MM **Privately Held**
SIC: 2752 Commercial printing, lithographic

(G-14993)
S & S WLDG FABG MACHINING INC
2587 Miller Graber Rd (44444-9724)
PHONE.................................330 392-7878
R Saxton, *CEO*
Jonathan Saxton, *President*
Steven Saxton, *Administration*
EMP: 25
SALES (est): 3.2MM **Privately Held**
WEB: www.sandsweb.com
SIC: 3315 Welded steel wire fabric

(G-14994)
TRANSCO RAILWAY PRODUCTS INC
2310 S Center St (44444-9406)
PHONE.................................330 872-0934
Stephanie Tresino, *Human Res Dir*
Robert Ewing, *Manager*
EMP: 60
SQ FT: 100,000
SALES (corp-wide): 96.7MM **Privately Held**
SIC: 3441 3743 Fabricated structural metal; railroad equipment
HQ: Transco Railway Products Inc.
200 N La Salle St # 1550
Chicago IL 60601
312 427-2818

(G-14995)
VENTURE PLASTICS INC (PA)
Also Called: V P
4000 Warren Rd (44444)
P.O. Box 249 (44444-0249)
PHONE.................................330 872-5774
Kenneth M Groff, *CEO*
J Stephen Trapp, *President*
David S Dennison, *Principal*
Deborah D Meyer, *Principal*
Charles E Wern Jr, *Principal*
▲ EMP: 115 EST: 1969
SQ FT: 60,000
SALES (est): 37.5MM **Privately Held**
WEB: www.ventureplastics.com
SIC: 3089 Injection molding of plastics

(G-14996)
VENTURE PLASTICS INC
4325 Warren Ravenna Rd (44444-8736)
PHONE.................................330 872-6262
EMP: 25
SALES (corp-wide): 37.5MM **Privately Held**
SIC: 3089 Injection molding of plastics
PA: Venture Plastics, Inc.
4000 Warren Rd
Newton Falls OH 44444
330 872-5774

Ney
Defiance County

(G-14997)
JANET SULLIVAN
Also Called: Real Products Manufacturing
3480 State Route 15 (43549-9713)
PHONE.................................419 658-2333
Janet Sullivan, *Owner*
EMP: 4
SQ FT: 9,000
SALES (est): 440K **Privately Held**
SIC: 2851 Removers & cleaners

Niles
Trumbull County

(G-14998)
ARCONIC INC
Also Called: Rti
1000 Warren Ave (44446-1168)
PHONE.................................330 544-7633
Kenneth Wilson, *General Mgr*
EMP: 3
SALES (corp-wide): 14B **Publicly Held**
SIC: 3355 3353 3463 Aluminum rolling & drawing; aluminum sheet & strip; coils, sheet aluminum; foil, aluminum; plates, aluminum; aluminum forgings
PA: Arconic Inc.
390 Park Ave Fl 12
New York NY 10022
212 836-2758

(G-14999)
ARCONIC TITANIUM
1000 Warren Ave (44446-1168)
PHONE.................................330 544-7633
EMP: 3
SALES (est): 99.9K **Privately Held**
SIC: 3356 Nonferrous Rolling/Drawing

(G-15000)
AUNTIE ANNES
5555 Youngstown Warren Rd # 637 (44446-4830)
PHONE.................................330 652-1939
Debra Barbara, *Manager*
EMP: 3 EST: 2001
SALES (est): 89.9K **Privately Held**
SIC: 5461 5999 2051 5812 Pretzels; miscellaneous retail stores; bread, cake & related products; eating places

(G-15001)
BRT EXTRUSIONS INC
Also Called: Building Rlationships Together
1818 N Main St Unit 1 (44446-1285)
P.O. Box 309 (44446-0309)
PHONE.................................330 544-0177
Roy Smith, *President*
William Fusco, *Vice Pres*
EMP: 220
SQ FT: 92,000
SALES (est): 53.3MM **Privately Held**
WEB: www.brtextrusions.com
SIC: 3354 Aluminum extruded products

(G-15002)
CHIEFFOS FROZEN FOODS INC
406 S Main St (44446-1454)
PHONE.................................330 652-1222
Richard Yannucci, *President*
EMP: 8
SQ FT: 7,200
SALES: 760K **Privately Held**
WEB: www.chieffopasta.com
SIC: 2038 Frozen specialties

(G-15003)
CLEVELAND STEEL CONTAINER CORP
412 Mason St (44446-2349)
PHONE.................................330 544-2271
Chistopher Page, *Owner*
Owen Muse, *QC Mgr*
EMP: 50
SALES (corp-wide): 131.9MM **Privately Held**
SIC: 3412 Barrels, shipping: metal; drums, shipping: metal; milk (fluid) shipping containers, metal; pails, shipping: metal
PA: Cleveland Steel Container Corporation
30310 Emerald Valley Pkwy
Solon OH 44139
440 349-8000

(G-15004)
CONDO INC
49 W Federal St (44446-5122)
PHONE.................................330 505-0485
John Condoleon, *Principal*
EMP: 3
SALES (est): 116.6K **Privately Held**
SIC: 3451 Screw machine products

(G-15005)
DINESOL PLASTICS INC
195 E Park Ave (44446-2352)
P.O. Box 470 (44446-0470)
PHONE.................................330 544-7171
Kenneth Fibus, *President*
Robert Hendricks Jr, *Vice Pres*
Kenneth Leonard, *Vice Pres*
Michael Janak, *CFO*
Bud Greathouse, *Maintence Staff*
▲ EMP: 125 EST: 1976
SQ FT: 120,000
SALES: 86MM **Privately Held**
WEB: www.dinesol.com
SIC: 3089 Injection molding of plastics

GEOGRAPHIC SECTION

Niles - Trumbull County (G-15031)

(G-15006)
DURSO BAKERY INC
212 S Cedar Ave (44446-2308)
P.O. Box 605 (44446-0605)
PHONE..................330 652-4741
Dominic D' Urso, *President*
Anthony D'Urso, *Shareholder*
Tony D'Urso, *Admin Sec*
EMP: 18
SQ FT: 7,000
SALES: 1.5MM **Privately Held**
SIC: 2051 Bakery: wholesale or wholesale/retail combined

(G-15007)
ENGINE MACHINE SERVICE INC
865 Summit Ave Unit 2 (44446-3661)
PHONE..................330 505-1804
Randall Gains, *President*
Paul Gains, *Treasurer*
EMP: 4
SQ FT: 400
SALES: 210K **Privately Held**
WEB: www.enginemachineservice.com
SIC: 3599 7539 Air intake filters, internal combustion engine, except auto; machine shop, automotive

(G-15008)
FAULL & SON LLC
515 Holford Ave (44446-1796)
P.O. Box 627 (44446-0627)
PHONE..................330 652-4341
James K Faull, *Principal*
Jim Faull, *Engineer*
Ted Faull,
EMP: 10 **EST:** 1949
SQ FT: 16,000
SALES (est): 439.2K **Privately Held**
WEB: www.faullandson.com
SIC: 3469 3544 3498 3429 Stamping metal for the trade; special dies & tools; fabricated pipe & fittings; manufactured hardware (general)

(G-15009)
FRAME DEPOT INC
1043 Youngstown Warren Rd (44446-4620)
PHONE..................330 652-7865
Robert Fowler, *President*
Jill Fowler, *Vice Pres*
Joe Fowler, *Vice Pres*
EMP: 5
SALES (est): 356.3K **Privately Held**
SIC: 7699 2499 7999 Picture framing, custom; picture & mirror frames, wood; arts & crafts instruction

(G-15010)
GLENWOOD ERECTORS INC
905 Summit Ave (44446-3612)
PHONE..................330 652-9616
Linda L Trunick, *President*
Michael E Trunick, *Vice Pres*
EMP: 7
SQ FT: 4,000
SALES (est): 1.1MM **Privately Held**
SIC: 3441 Fabricated structural metal

(G-15011)
HAMILTON RTI INC
1000 Warren Ave (44446-1168)
PHONE..................330 652-9951
Allyn E Mathews, *Principal*
EMP: 6
SALES (est): 517.8K
SALES (corp-wide): 14B **Publicly Held**
SIC: 3339 Titanium metal, sponge & granules
HQ: Rmi Titanium Company, Llc
1000 Warren Ave
Niles OH 44446
330 652-9952

(G-15012)
HOWLAND MACHINE CORP
947 Summit Ave (44446-3612)
PHONE..................330 544-4029
Bruce V Dewey, *President*
Carl Ford, *General Mgr*
Dennis Courtney, *Engineer*
Elliot Dewey, *Marketing Staff*
Dave Mooney, *Manager*
EMP: 20
SQ FT: 22,000
SALES (est): 3.9MM **Privately Held**
WEB: www.howland-machine.com
SIC: 3469 Machine parts, stamped or pressed metal

(G-15013)
INDUCTION SERVICES INC
1713 N Main St (44446-1249)
PHONE..................330 652-4494
Merle N Money, *President*
Brian Money, *Corp Secy*
Nora Money, *Marketing Staff*
EMP: 7
SQ FT: 11,000
SALES: 750K **Privately Held**
SIC: 3567 Induction heating equipment

(G-15014)
INTER-POWER CORPORATION
1713 N Main St (44446-1249)
PHONE..................330 652-4494
Merle Money, *President*
EMP: 8 **Privately Held**
WEB: www.interpwr.com
SIC: 3567 Induction heating equipment
PA: Inter-Power Corporation
3578 Van Dyke Rd
Almont MI 48003

(G-15015)
INTERNATIONAL TECHNICAL
Also Called: Itps
852 Ann Ave (44446-2924)
P.O. Box 111 (44446-0111)
PHONE..................330 505-1218
Samuel H Berkowitz, *CEO*
Richard L Goodman, *President*
▲ **EMP:** 23
SQ FT: 5,000
SALES (est): 5.5MM **Privately Held**
WEB: www.itps-inc.com
SIC: 2821 Plastics materials & resins

(G-15016)
IRONICS INC
750 S Main St (44446-1372)
P.O. Box 292 (44446-0292)
PHONE..................330 652-0583
Pete Tominey Jr, *President*
Mary Jane Tominey, *Shareholder*
EMP: 9
SQ FT: 10,000
SALES (est): 1.6MM **Privately Held**
WEB: www.ironics.com
SIC: 2816 3295 Iron oxide pigments (ochers, siennas, umbers); blast furnace slag

(G-15017)
J A MCMAHON INCORPORATED
6 E Park Ave (44446-5058)
PHONE..................330 652-2588
John A McMahon III, *President*
EMP: 26
SQ FT: 32,000
SALES: 12.9MM **Privately Held**
WEB: www.jamcmahon.com
SIC: 3441 Building components, structural steel

(G-15018)
JET STREAM INTERNATIONAL INC
931 Summit Ave Unit 3 (44446-3662)
PHONE..................330 505-9988
Edgar B Rumble Jr, *President*
John Isbill, *Vice Pres*
James E Constas, *Opers Mgr*
▲ **EMP:** 45 **EST:** 2000
SQ FT: 70,000
SALES (est): 9.3MM **Privately Held**
WEB: www.jetstr.com
SIC: 3469 3272 Metal stampings; concrete stuctural support & building material

(G-15019)
JOHN MANEELY COMPANY
Also Called: Wheatland Tube Company
1800 Hunter Ave (44446-1671)
PHONE..................724 342-6851
Mark Bahrey, *Branch Mgr*
EMP: 35 **Privately Held**
SIC: 3498 3317 3312 Pipe sections fabricated from purchased pipe; steel pipe & tubes; blast furnaces & steel mills
HQ: Wheatland Tube, Llc
700 S Dock St
Sharon PA 16146
800 257-8182

(G-15020)
KRONER PUBLICATIONS INC (PA)
1123 W Park Ave (44446-1188)
P.O. Box 150 (44446-0150)
PHONE..................330 544-5500
John Kroner Jr, *President*
Nick Poorbaugh, *General Mgr*
EMP: 30
SALES: 540K **Privately Held**
SIC: 2711 Commercial printing & newspaper publishing combined

(G-15021)
METAL PRODUCTS COMPANY (PA)
Also Called: Stamtex Metal Stampings
112 Erie St (44446-2320)
PHONE..................330 652-2558
Philip Frankle, *President*
EMP: 43 **EST:** 1921
SQ FT: 50,000
SALES (est): 8.6MM **Privately Held**
WEB: www.stamtexmp.com
SIC: 3469 Metal stampings

(G-15022)
METAL PRODUCTS COMPANY
Also Called: Stamtex
1818 N Main St Unit 4 (44446-1285)
PHONE..................330 652-6201
Philip Frankel, *President*
EMP: 20
SALES (est): 1.4MM
SALES (corp-wide): 8.6MM **Privately Held**
WEB: www.stamtexmp.com
SIC: 3469 Stamping metal for the trade
PA: The Metal Products Company
112 Erie St
Niles OH 44446
330 652-2558

(G-15023)
MICHAELS STORES INC
Also Called: Michaels 9837
5555 Youngstown Warren Rd # 914 (44446-4804)
PHONE..................330 505-1168
Paul Rockenfelder, *Branch Mgr*
EMP: 35
SALES (corp-wide): 5.2B **Publicly Held**
WEB: www.michaels.com
SIC: 3944 5945 Craft & hobby kits & sets; hobby, toy & game shops
HQ: Michaels Stores, Inc.
8000 Bent Branch Dr
Irving TX 75063
972 409-1300

(G-15024)
NILES MANUFACTURING & FINSHG
465 Walnut Ave (44446-2374)
PHONE..................330 544-0402
Robert Hendricks, *President*
Richard Hendricks, *Opers Mgr*
Beth Hall, *CFO*
EMP: 110
SQ FT: 150,000
SALES (est): 24.9MM **Privately Held**
WEB: www.nilesmfg.com
SIC: 3469 3479 3471 3444 Metal stampings; coating of metals & formed products; plating & polishing; sheet metalwork

(G-15025)
NILES ROLL SERVICE INC (PA)
704 Warren Ave (44446-1643)
PHONE..................330 544-0026
Timothy L Boggs, *President*
Beverly Boggs, *Corp Secy*
EMP: 11
SQ FT: 4,964
SALES (est): 1MM **Privately Held**
SIC: 3069 Roll coverings, rubber

(G-15026)
PHILLIPS MANUFACTURING CO
504 Walnut St (44446-2961)
PHONE..................330 652-4335
Steve Dalrymple, *Branch Mgr*
Susan Zimmerman, *Administration*
Ken Rupert, *Maintence Staff*
EMP: 90
SALES (corp-wide): 58.3MM **Privately Held**
WEB: www.phillipsmfg.com
SIC: 3442 3444 3541 Metal doors, sash & trim; sheet metalwork; machine tools, metal cutting type
PA: Phillips Manufacturing Co.
4949 S 30th St
Omaha NE 68107
402 339-3800

(G-15027)
PLUGGERS INC
1617 Warren Ave (44446-1170)
P.O. Box 474, Columbiana (44408-0474)
PHONE..................330 383-7692
Orville Nicholas, *Vice Pres*
EMP: 5
SALES (est): 336.3K **Privately Held**
WEB: www.pluggers.com
SIC: 1389 Well plugging & abandoning, oil & gas

(G-15028)
RMI TITANIUM COMPANY LLC (HQ)
Also Called: Rti Niles
1000 Warren Ave (44446-1168)
PHONE..................330 652-9952
Dawn S Hickton, *President*
John H Odle, *Exec VP*
Bob Babyak, *Purch Mgr*
Lawrence W Jacobs, *Treasurer*
Theodore Zalac, *Manager*
◆ **EMP:** 20
SQ FT: 677,605
SALES (est): 359.3MM
SALES (corp-wide): 14B **Publicly Held**
WEB: www.rti-intl.com
SIC: 3399 3356 1741 3533 Powder, metal; titanium; masonry & other stonework; oil & gas drilling rigs & equipment
PA: Arconic Inc.
390 Park Ave Fl 12
New York NY 10022
212 836-2758

(G-15029)
RMI TITANIUM COMPANY LLC
Also Called: Rti
2000 Warren Ave (44446-1148)
PHONE..................330 544-9470
EMP: 7
SALES (corp-wide): 14B **Publicly Held**
SIC: 3441 Fabricated structural metal
HQ: Rmi Titanium Company, Llc
1000 Warren Ave
Niles OH 44446
330 652-9952

(G-15030)
RMI TITANIUM COMPANY LLC
Also Called: Rti Niles
1000 Warren Ave (44446-1168)
P.O. Box 269 (44446-0269)
PHONE..................330 544-7633
Diane S Seman, *Principal*
Michael Jacques, *Research*
Eric Marsh, *Research*
Karl Haff, *Engineer*
Frank Spadafora, *Engineer*
EMP: 33
SALES (corp-wide): 14B **Publicly Held**
SIC: 3356 Titanium & titanium alloy: rolling, drawing or extruding
HQ: Rmi Titanium Company, Llc
1000 Warren Ave
Niles OH 44446
330 652-9952

(G-15031)
RMI TITANIUM COMPANY LLC
Rti Hermitage
1000 Warren Ave (44446-1168)
PHONE..................330 652-9955
Larry Jancay, *Engineer*
Paul Mandell, *Branch Mgr*

Niles - Trumbull County (G-15032)

MEI Guo, *Technical Staff*
Gordon Jack, *Analyst*
EMP: 9
SALES (corp-wide): 14B **Publicly Held**
SIC: 3356 Titanium
HQ: Rmi Titanium Company, Llc
 1000 Warren Ave
 Niles OH 44446
 330 652-9952

(G-15032)
RTI ALLOYS
1000 Warren Ave (44446-1168)
PHONE.................................330 652-9952
Robert G Helwig, *Administration*
▲ **EMP:** 8
SALES (est): 1.2MM **Privately Held**
SIC: 3312 Blast furnaces & steel mills

(G-15033)
RTI FINANCE CORP
Also Called: Rti Niles
1000 Warren Ave (44446-1168)
PHONE.................................330 652-9952
Dawne S Hickton, *CEO*
EMP: 4
SALES (est): 798.4K
SALES (corp-wide): 14B **Publicly Held**
SIC: 3339 Primary nonferrous metals
HQ: Rmi Titanium Company, Llc
 1000 Warren Ave
 Niles OH 44446
 330 652-9952

(G-15034)
RTI NILES
1000 Warren Ave (44446-1168)
PHONE.................................330 455-4010
EMP: 4
SALES (est): 288.5K **Privately Held**
SIC: 2816 Inorganic pigments

(G-15035)
RYMAN GRINDERS INC
704 Warren Ave (44446-1643)
PHONE.................................330 652-5080
Timothy L Boggs, *President*
Tim L Boggs, *President*
EMP: 19
SALES (est): 3.1MM **Privately Held**
SIC: 3531 Grinders, stone: portable

(G-15036)
S AND K PAINTING
1346 Clark St (44446-3446)
PHONE.................................330 505-1910
Stephen Hrosar, *President*
EMP: 4
SALES (est): 429.1K **Privately Held**
SIC: 2752 Commercial printing, lithographic

(G-15037)
TRAICHAL CONSTRUCTION COMPANY (PA)
Also Called: Warren Door
332 Plant St (44446-1895)
P.O. Box 70 (44446-0070)
PHONE.................................800 255-3667
Edward Traichal, *President*
EMP: 30
SQ FT: 15,000
SALES (est): 7.8MM **Privately Held**
WEB: www.plantia.com
SIC: 3442 1751 5199 5031 Metal doors; rolling doors for industrial buildings or warehouses, metal; window & door installation & erection; advertising specialties; doors & windows

(G-15038)
VALLEY GRAPHICS
1494 Salt Springs Rd (44446-1348)
PHONE.................................330 652-0484
James S Fentules, *Owner*
EMP: 4
SALES: 210K **Privately Held**
WEB: www.valley-services.com
SIC: 2752 Color lithography

(G-15039)
WARREN FABRICATING CORPORATION
907 S Main St (44446-1352)
P.O. Box 1032, Warren (44482-1032)
PHONE.................................330 544-4101
EMP: 25
SQ FT: 40,000
SALES (corp-wide): 84.7MM **Privately Held**
SIC: 3441 3544 Structural Metal Fabrication Mfg Dies/Tools/Jigs/Fixtures
PA: Warren Fabricating Corporation
 7845 Chestnut Ridge Rd
 Hubbard OH 44425
 330 534-5017

(G-15040)
WEST & BARKER INC
950 Summit Ave (44446-3693)
PHONE.................................330 652-9923
Samuel M Barker III, *President*
Suzanne Leone, *Treasurer*
June Barker, *Admin Sec*
EMP: 25 **EST:** 1971
SQ FT: 106,000
SALES (est): 5.2MM **Privately Held**
WEB: www.westandbarker.com
SIC: 3089 2396 3069 3714 Plastic hardware & building products; automotive & apparel trimmings; thread, rubber; motor vehicle parts & accessories

(G-15041)
YAR CORPORATION
406 S Main St (44446-1454)
PHONE.................................330 652-1222
Richard A Yannucci, *President*
EMP: 7
SALES: 800K **Privately Held**
SIC: 2098 Macaroni & spaghetti

North Baltimore
Wood County

(G-15042)
AUTOMATED BLDG COMPONENTS INC (PA)
2359 Grant Rd (45872-9662)
PHONE.................................419 257-2152
Harold L McCarty, *CEO*
Marshal McCarty, *President*
Jerry Reisgraf, *Info Tech Dir*
Jennifer Buckingham, *Shareholder*
EMP: 30
SQ FT: 10,000
SALES (est): 22.3MM **Privately Held**
WEB: www.abctruss.com
SIC: 2421 2439 2541 2435 Building & structural materials, wood; trusses, wooden roof; wood partitions & fixtures; hardwood veneer & plywood; millwork

(G-15043)
CONTINENTAL STRL PLAS INC
Also Called: CSP North Baltimore
100 S Poe Rd (45872-9551)
PHONE.................................419 257-2231
Gary Dickson, *Branch Mgr*
Daisy Lucas, *Manager*
EMP: 234
SALES (corp-wide): 7.8B **Privately Held**
WEB: www.cs-plastics.com
SIC: 3089 3714 Injection molding of plastics; motor vehicle parts & accessories
HQ: Continental Structural Plastics, Inc.
 255 Rex Blvd
 Auburn Hills MI 48326
 248 237-7800

(G-15044)
KEYSTONE FOODS LLC
Equity Group-Ohio Div
2208 Grant Rd (45872-9663)
P.O. Box 307 (45872-0307)
PHONE.................................419 257-2341
Steven Alberts, *Manager*
EMP: 250
SQ FT: 60,000 **Privately Held**
WEB: www.keystonefoods.com
SIC: 2013 Sausages & other prepared meats
HQ: Keystone Foods Llc
 905 Airport Rd Ste 400
 West Chester PA 19380
 610 667-6700

(G-15045)
MABAR PRINTING SERVICE
400 N Tarr St (45872-1157)
PHONE.................................419 257-3659
Eric Mays, *Owner*
EMP: 3 **EST:** 1960
SALES: 90K **Privately Held**
SIC: 2752 Commercial printing, offset

(G-15046)
MID-WOOD INC
Also Called: True Value
101 E State St (45872-1358)
PHONE.................................419 257-3331
Joe Smith, *Manager*
EMP: 10
SALES (corp-wide): 80MM **Privately Held**
SIC: 5153 5261 5251 5531 Grains; fertilizer; hardware; automotive tires; prepared feeds; lawn & garden services
PA: Mid-Wood, Inc.
 12965 Defiance Pike
 Cygnet OH
 419 352-5231

(G-15047)
POLYONE CORPORATION
733 E Water St (45872-1434)
P.O. Box 247 (45872-0247)
PHONE.................................440 930-1000
Pete Jacob, *Vice Pres*
EMP: 80 **Publicly Held**
WEB: www.polyone.com
SIC: 2821 5169 3087 Vinyl resins; synthetic resins, rubber & plastic materials; custom compound purchased resins
PA: Polyone Corporation
 33587 Walker Rd
 Avon Lake OH 44012

(G-15048)
TRUCK STOP EMBROIDERY (PA)
12906 Deshler Rd (45872-9650)
PHONE.................................419 257-2860
Phillip Johnson, *Principal*
EMP: 5
SALES (est): 1.5MM **Privately Held**
SIC: 3552 Embroidery machines

(G-15049)
TRUCK STOP EMBROIDERY
Also Called: Innovative Stiching
12906 Deshler Rd (45872-9650)
PHONE.................................419 257-2860
Jen Fackler, *Manager*
EMP: 5
SALES (corp-wide): 1.5MM **Privately Held**
SIC: 2395 Embroidery products, except schiffli machine
PA: Truck Stop Embroidery
 12906 Deshler Rd
 North Baltimore OH 45872
 419 257-2860

North Bend
Hamilton County

(G-15050)
BALECO INTERNATIONAL INC
3200 State Line Rd (45052-9731)
P.O. Box 11331, Cincinnati (45211-0331)
PHONE.................................513 353-3000
E Bernard Haviland, *President*
▲ **EMP:** 20 **EST:** 1958
SQ FT: 72,000
SALES (est): 10.1MM
SALES (corp-wide): 173.8MM **Privately Held**
SIC: 5091 3589 Swimming pools, equipment & supplies; swimming pool filter & water conditioning systems
PA: Haviland Enterprises, Inc.
 421 Ann St Nw
 Grand Rapids MI 49504
 616 361-6691

(G-15051)
IMPACT SPORTS WEAR INC
Also Called: Impact Promotions
99 St Annes Ave (45052-9655)
PHONE.................................513 922-7406
David J Becker, *President*
EMP: 3
SQ FT: 800
SALES (est): 358.9K **Privately Held**
SIC: 3552 5137 5136 Silk screens for textile industry; uniforms, women's & children's; uniforms, men's & boys'

(G-15052)
MARTIN MARIETTA MATERIALS INC
Martin Marietta Aggregates
10905 Us 50 (45052)
PHONE.................................513 353-1400
Bernie Jelen, *Branch Mgr*
EMP: 55 **Publicly Held**
WEB: www.martinmarietta.com
SIC: 1422 Crushed & broken limestone
PA: Martin Marietta Materials Inc
 2710 Wycliff Rd
 Raleigh NC 27607

(G-15053)
NUTRIEN AG SOLUTIONS INC
10743 Brower Rd (45052-9761)
PHONE.................................513 941-4100
Bill Chokran, *Manager*
EMP: 30
SALES (corp-wide): 8.8B **Privately Held**
WEB: www.cropproductionservices.com
SIC: 2873 2875 2819 Nitrogenous fertilizers; fertilizers, mixing only; industrial inorganic chemicals
HQ: Nutrien Ag Solutions, Inc.
 3005 Rocky Mountain Ave
 Loveland CO 80538
 970 685-3300

(G-15054)
RACK DRAFT SERVICE INC
11109 Guard Ln (45052-9413)
PHONE.................................513 353-5520
James M Rack, *President*
Jimmy Rack, *Vice Pres*
Melissa Seal, *Treasurer*
EMP: 11
SQ FT: 3,000
SALES (est): 1.8MM **Privately Held**
SIC: 3585 Beer dispensing equipment

(G-15055)
STEEL SERVICES INC
Also Called: Marky Welding
3150 State Line Rd (45052-9731)
PHONE.................................513 353-4173
Jeff Wernke, *President*
John Wernke, *Corp Secy*
EMP: 3
SALES (est): 310K **Privately Held**
WEB: www.wernkesteel.com
SIC: 3441 Expansion joints (structural shapes), iron or steel

(G-15056)
SUPER SIGNS INC
9890 Mount Nebo Rd (45052-9480)
PHONE.................................480 968-2200
Sammy Boner, *President*
EMP: 36
SQ FT: 1,500
SALES: 1MM **Privately Held**
WEB: www.supersigns.com
SIC: 3993 Signs & advertising specialties

(G-15057)
VEOLIA NA REGENERATION SRVCS
11215 Brower Rd (45052-9755)
PHONE.................................513 941-4121
Gerald Thomas, *Branch Mgr*
EMP: 19
SALES (corp-wide): 600.9MM **Privately Held**
WEB: www.dupont.com
SIC: 2819 Sulfuric acid, oleum
HQ: Veolia North America Regeneration Services, Llc
 53 State St
 Boston MA 02109
 312 552-2800

GEOGRAPHIC SECTION

(G-15058)
WERNKE WLDG & STL ERECTION CO
3150 State Line Rd (45052-9731)
PHONE.....................513 353-4173
Jeff Wernke, *President*
James Wernke, *Chairman*
John Wernke, *Corp Secy*
Jerry Wernke, *Vice Pres*
EMP: 14
SQ FT: 4,800
SALES (est): 2MM **Privately Held**
SIC: 1791 3441 Iron work, structural; fabricated structural metal

North Benton
Portage County

(G-15059)
ALLIANCE DRILLING INC
20388 N Benton West Rd (44449-9636)
PHONE.....................330 584-2781
EMP: 10
SALES (est): 940K **Privately Held**
SIC: 3541 Drilling

(G-15060)
BELOIT FUEL LLC
9379 First East St (44449)
PHONE.....................330 584-1915
Charles R Pierce, *Principal*
EMP: 7
SALES (est): 878K **Privately Held**
SIC: 2869 Fuels

(G-15061)
PAUL J TATULINSKI LTD
1595 W Main St (44449)
P.O. Box 382 (44449-0382)
PHONE.....................330 584-8251
Paul J Tatulinski, *President*
EMP: 10
SQ FT: 4,704
SALES: 700K **Privately Held**
SIC: 3053 Gaskets, all materials

(G-15062)
THEISS UAV SOLUTIONS LLC
10881 Johnson Rd (44449-9652)
P.O. Box 1086, Salem (44460-8086)
PHONE.....................330 584-2070
Chad Kapper, *President*
Richard Theiss, *Production*
EMP: 8 **EST:** 1992
SQ FT: 4,600
SALES (est): 1.2MM
SALES (corp-wide): 3.6B **Publicly Held**
WEB: www.theissaviation.com
SIC: 3721 7363 Aircraft; pilot service, aviation
HQ: Lauren International, Ltd.
2228 Reiser Ave Se
New Philadelphia OH 44663
330 339-3373

North Bloomfield
Trumbull County

(G-15063)
C DCAP MODEM LINE
8829 State Route 45 (44450-9800)
PHONE.....................440 685-4302
EMP: 3
SALES (est): 156.2K **Privately Held**
SIC: 3661 Mfg Telephone/Telegraph Apparatus

(G-15064)
DELUCA VINEYARDS
8954 State Route 45 (44450-9777)
PHONE.....................440 685-4242
Randy Deluca, *Partner*
Joe Deluca, *Partner*
EMP: 4
SQ FT: 1,765
SALES (est): 98.7K **Privately Held**
SIC: 0172 2084 Grapes; wines

(G-15065)
KUHNS MFG LLC
4210 Kinsman Rd Nw (44450-9710)
PHONE.....................440 693-4630
Ken Kuhns,
EMP: 6
SALES (est): 1.5MM **Privately Held**
SIC: 3523 Farm machinery & equipment

North Canton
Stark County

(G-15066)
A SCHULMAN INC
8562 Port Jackson Ave Nw (44720-5467)
PHONE.....................330 498-4840
A Maghes, *Branch Mgr*
EMP: 50
SALES (corp-wide): 34.5B **Privately Held**
SIC: 2821 Plastics materials & resins
HQ: A. Schulman, Inc.
3637 Ridgewood Rd
Fairlawn OH 44333
330 666-3751

(G-15067)
A STUCKI COMPANY
7376 Whipple Ave Nw (44720-7140)
PHONE.....................412 424-0560
Todd Woofter, *Regional*
EMP: 5
SALES (corp-wide): 26.7MM **Privately Held**
SIC: 3743 Railroad equipment
PA: A. Stucki Company
360 Wright Brothers Dr
Coraopolis PA 15108
412 424-0560

(G-15068)
AIRTEX INDUSTRIES LLC
Also Called: Pumps Group
2100 International Pkwy (44720-1373)
PHONE.....................330 899-0340
EMP: 5
SALES (est): 13.8MM
SALES (corp-wide): 753MM **Privately Held**
SIC: 3714 Motor vehicle parts & accessories; fuel pumps, motor vehicle; oil pump, motor vehicle; water pump, motor vehicle
HQ: Uci-Airtex Holdings, Inc.
2100 International Pkwy
North Canton OH 44720
330 899-0340

(G-15069)
ASC HOLDCO INC (PA)
Also Called: Pumps Group, The
2100 International Pkwy (44720-1373)
PHONE.....................330 899-0340
David Peace, *CEO*
Ted Swaldo, *President*
Tom Blackerby, *CFO*
▲ **EMP:** 6
SALES (est): 117.1MM **Privately Held**
WEB: www.ucinc.com
SIC: 3714 Water pump, motor vehicle

(G-15070)
ASC INDUSTRIES INC (HQ)
2100 International Pkwy (44720-1373)
PHONE.....................330 899-0340
David Peace, *CEO*
Don Wise, *Safety Mgr*
Yinghua LI, *VP Engrg*
Jason Busse, *Engineer*
Scott Strunk, *Engineer*
◆ **EMP:** 119
SQ FT: 200,000
SALES (est): 117.1MM **Privately Held**
WEB: www.asc-ind.com
SIC: 3714 Water pump, motor vehicle
PA: Asc Holdco, Inc.
2100 International Pkwy
North Canton OH 44720
330 899-0340

(G-15071)
B2 INCORPORATED (PA)
Also Called: B-Squared Prtg Mktg Solutions
8324c Cleveland Ave Nw (44720-4820)
PHONE.....................330 244-9510
Brent Belles, *CEO*
EMP: 9
SALES (est): 1.5MM **Privately Held**
SIC: 2752 Commercial printing, lithographic

(G-15072)
BALL CORPORATION
3075 Brookline Rd (44720-1526)
PHONE.....................330 244-2313
EMP: 12
SALES (corp-wide): 11.6B **Publicly Held**
SIC: 3411 Food & beverage containers
PA: Ball Corporation
10 Longs Peak Dr
Broomfield CO 80021
303 469-3131

(G-15073)
BIRO MANUFACTURING COMPANY
6658 Promway Ave Nw (44720-7316)
PHONE.....................419 798-4451
Sharon Edwards, *Manager*
EMP: 10
SALES (est): 1.8MM
SALES (corp-wide): 22MM **Privately Held**
SIC: 3556 Food products machinery
PA: The Biro Manufacturing Company
1114 W Main St
Marblehead OH 43440
419 798-4451

(G-15074)
C & S TURF CARE EQUIPMENT INC
6207 Dressler Rd Nw (44720-7607)
P.O. Box 36717, Canton (44735-6717)
PHONE.....................330 966-4511
Ted Shackelford, *President*
Karen Shackelford, *Admin Sec*
▼ **EMP:** 15
SQ FT: 6,000
SALES: 840K **Privately Held**
WEB: www.csturfequip.com
SIC: 3523 Farm machinery & equipment

(G-15075)
CALVERT WIRE & CABLE CORP
4276 Strausser St Nw (44720-7114)
PHONE.....................330 494-3248
Rich Geissinger, *Sales Staff*
Steve Hilson, *Manager*
EMP: 9 **Publicly Held**
SIC: 3357 Nonferrous wiredrawing & insulating
HQ: Calvert Wire & Cable Corporation
17909 Cleve Pkwy Ste 180
Cleveland OH 44142
216 433-7600

(G-15076)
CANTON ELEVATOR INC
2575 Greensburg Rd (44720-1419)
PHONE.....................330 833-3600
Robert A Kazar, *CEO*
Michael J Paschke, *President*
Greg Rinehart, *General Mgr*
Jared Heitger, *Foreman/Supr*
Don Barnes, *Project Engr*
◆ **EMP:** 75
SQ FT: 80,000
SALES (est): 20.6MM
SALES (corp-wide): 13.9B **Privately Held**
WEB: www.cantonelevator.com
SIC: 3534 3537 Elevators & equipment; industrial trucks & tractors
HQ: Nidec Motor Corporation
8050 West Florissant Ave
Saint Louis MO 63136

(G-15077)
DANSIZEN PRINTING CO INC
4525 Aultman Ave Nw (44720-8235)
PHONE.....................330 966-4962
James Dansizen, *President*
EMP: 4
SALES: 175K **Privately Held**
SIC: 2752 Commercial printing, offset

(G-15078)
DIEBOLD NIXDORF INCORPORATED (PA)
5995 Mayfair Rd (44720-1550)
P.O. Box 3077 (44720-8077)
PHONE.....................330 490-4000
Gary G Greenfield, *Ch of Bd*
Gerrard B Schmid, *President*
Olaf Heyden, *Senior VP*
Alan Kerr, *Senior VP*
Julian Sparkes, *Senior VP*
EMP: 900 **EST:** 1859
SALES: 4.5B **Publicly Held**
WEB: www.diebold.com
SIC: 3578 3699 3499 Automatic teller machines (ATM); banking machines; security control equipment & systems; safes & vaults, metal; safe deposit boxes or chests, metal

(G-15079)
DIEBOLD NIXDORF INCORPORATED
5995 Mayfair Rd (44720-1550)
PHONE.....................330 490-4000
Kelly Karnes, *Partner*
Daniel Hu, *Managing Dir*
Rick Baggot, *Vice Pres*
Natalie Gainer, *Vice Pres*
Jamie Lambo, *Vice Pres*
EMP: 59
SALES (corp-wide): 4.5B **Publicly Held**
WEB: www.diebold.com
SIC: 3578 Automatic teller machines (ATM)
PA: Diebold Nixdorf, Incorporated
5995 Mayfair Rd
North Canton OH 44720
330 490-4000

(G-15080)
ENVIRONMENTAL SAMPLING SUP INC (DH)
Also Called: E S S
4101 Shuffel St Nw (44720-6900)
PHONE.....................330 497-9396
Rachel Brydon Jannetta, *President*
Heather Collins Villemaire, *CFO*
Marsha Hemmerich, *Credit Staff*
Dave Behr, *Accounts Mgr*
Jenny L Stewart, *Admin Sec*
▲ **EMP:** 27
SALES (est): 5.3MM
SALES (corp-wide): 983.9MM **Privately Held**
SIC: 3089 3231 Plastic containers, except foam; products of purchased glass
HQ: Testamerica Holdings, Inc.
4101 Shuffel St Nw
North Canton OH 44720
330 497-9396

(G-15081)
FAIRWAY CARTS PARTS & MORE LLC
6944 Wales Ave Nw (44720-6333)
PHONE.....................234 209-9008
Timothy Doug Schuller,
EMP: 4
SALES (est): 607.1K **Privately Held**
SIC: 3537 4789 4212 Trucks, tractors, loaders, carriers & similar equipment; cargo loading & unloading services; local trucking, without storage

(G-15082)
FANNIE MAY CONFECTIONS INC
5353 Lauby Rd (44720-1572)
PHONE.....................330 494-0833
Terry Michell, *President*
Leanna Cole, *District Mgr*
Charles Irvine, *Vice Pres*
Jason Whalen, *Mktg Coord*
Bridget Marshall, *Manager*
EMP: 800
SALES (est): 65.6MM
SALES (corp-wide): 230.1MM **Privately Held**
SIC: 5441 2066 Candy; chocolate bars, solid
HQ: Fannie May Confections Brands, Inc.
9 W Washington St
Chicago IL 60602
330 494-0833

North Canton - Stark County (G-15083)   GEOGRAPHIC SECTION

(G-15083)
FIVES BRONX INC
Also Called: Bronx Taylor Wilson
8817 Pleasantwood Ave Nw (44720-4759)
PHONE..................................330 244-1960
Brian Lombardi, *CEO*
Dave Macneilll, *Vice Pres*
Curt Sabin, *CFO*
Doug Nidy, *Marketing Staff*
◆ **EMP:** 70 **EST:** 1988
SQ FT: 10,000
SALES (est): 21.5MM
SALES (corp-wide): 4.5MM **Privately Held**
WEB: www.btwcorp.com
SIC: 3547 Finishing equipment, rolling mill
HQ: Fives
3 Rue Drouot
Paris 75009
145 237-575

(G-15084)
FLUID AUTOMATION INC
8400 Port Jackson Ave Nw (44720-5464)
PHONE..................................248 912-1970
Lance H Daby, *President*
Beverly Daby, *Corp Secy*
Leon L Daby, *Vice Pres*
EMP: 25 **EST:** 1974
SQ FT: 16,000
SALES (est): 3.8MM **Privately Held**
WEB: www.fluidautomation.com
SIC: 3561 3569 Industrial pumps & parts; liquid automation machinery & equipment

(G-15085)
GBS CORP (PA)
Also Called: GBS Printech Solutions
7233 Freedom Ave Nw (44720-7123)
P.O. Box 2340, Canton (44720-0340)
PHONE..................................330 494-5330
Eugene Calabria, *President*
Ryan Hamsher, *General Mgr*
Laurence Merriman, *Chairman*
Bob Campolito, *Opers Staff*
Michele Benson, *CFO*
▲ **EMP:** 150 **EST:** 1971
SQ FT: 115,000
SALES (est): 72.8MM **Privately Held**
WEB: www.gbscorp.com
SIC: 5045 5112 2675 2672 Computers, peripherals & software; business forms; folders, filing, die-cut: made from purchased materials; labels (unprinted), gummed: made from purchased materials; tape, pressure sensitive: made from purchased materials; manifold business forms; commercial printing

(G-15086)
GLASCRAFT INC
8400 Port Jackson Ave Nw (44720-5464)
PHONE..................................330 966-3000
Morris Wheeler, *President*
Byron Bradley, *Vice Pres*
EMP: 65 **EST:** 1959
SQ FT: 51,200
SALES (est): 8.1MM
SALES (corp-wide): 1.6B **Publicly Held**
WEB: www.glascraft.com
SIC: 3563 Spraying outfits: metals, paints & chemicals (compressor)
PA: Graco Inc.
88 11th Ave Ne
Minneapolis MN 55413
612 623-6000

(G-15087)
GLENS BEDFORD GARDEN CENTER
9486 Cleveland Ave Nw (44720-4520)
PHONE..................................330 305-1971
Jason Hawley, *Manager*
EMP: 3 **EST:** 2017
SALES (est): 136.5K **Privately Held**
SIC: 1411 Dimension stone

(G-15088)
GRACO OHIO INC (HQ)
Also Called: Liquid Control
8400 Port Jackson Ave Nw (44720-5464)
PHONE..................................330 494-1313
William C Schiltz, *Ch of Bd*
Kenneth Jacobs, *President*
Ronald W Dougherty, *Principal*
Barbara Schiltz, *Treasurer*
▲ **EMP:** 100
SQ FT: 73,000
SALES (est): 24.6MM
SALES (corp-wide): 1.6B **Publicly Held**
WEB: www.dispensit.com
SIC: 3824 3586 5251 Predetermining counters; measuring & dispensing pumps; pumps & pumping equipment
PA: Graco Inc.
88 11th Ave Ne
Minneapolis MN 55413
612 623-6000

(G-15089)
GRADY MCCAULEY INC
Also Called: LSI Graphic Solutions Plus
9260 Pleasantwood Ave Nw (44720-9006)
PHONE..................................330 494-9444
David McCauley, *President*
Rick McFarren, *Mfg Staff*
Tyler Cobb, *Natl Sales Mgr*
Mark McKean, *Supervisor*
Dave Moeglin, *Director*
EMP: 100 **EST:** 1963
SQ FT: 212,000
SALES (est): 25.9MM
SALES (corp-wide): 342MM **Publicly Held**
WEB: www.gradymccauley.com
SIC: 3993 2759 Signs & advertising specialties; screen printing
PA: Lsi Industries Inc.
10000 Alliance Rd
Blue Ash OH 45242
513 793-3200

(G-15090)
HAINES & COMPANY INC (PA)
Also Called: Criss Cross Directories
8050 Freedom Ave Nw A (44720-6985)
P.O. Box 2117 (44720-0117)
PHONE..................................330 494-9111
William K Haines Jr, *Ch of Bd*
Leonard W Haines, *Principal*
Harriett E Jones, *Principal*
Delores Ball, *Treasurer*
Elizabeth Lowe, *Accounts Exec*
▲ **EMP:** 130 **EST:** 1932
SQ FT: 20,000
SALES (est): 35MM **Privately Held**
WEB: www.haines.com
SIC: 2741 7331 2752 2759 Directories: publishing & printing; mailing list compilers; commercial printing, lithographic; commercial printing

(G-15091)
HAINES CRISS CROSS (PA)
8050 Freedom Ave Nw (44720-6912)
PHONE..................................330 494-9111
John Segherd, *Principal*
EMP: 5
SALES (est): 559K **Privately Held**
SIC: 2741 Miscellaneous publishing

(G-15092)
HARRY LONDON CANDIES INC (DH)
Also Called: Harry London Chocolates
5353 Lauby Rd (44720-1572)
PHONE..................................330 494-0833
Terry Michell, *President*
Ed Seibolt, *Vice Pres*
Matthew J Anderson, *CFO*
▲ **EMP:** 94
SQ FT: 200,000
SALES (est): 67.2MM
SALES (corp-wide): 230.1MM **Privately Held**
WEB: www.londoncandies.com
SIC: 2066 5441 Chocolate & cocoa products; candy
HQ: Fannie May Confections Brands, Inc.
9 W Washington St
Chicago IL 60602
330 494-0833

(G-15093)
HSM WIRE INTERNATIONAL INC
820 S Valley Blvd Nw (44720-2770)
P.O. Box 2153 (44720-0153)
PHONE..................................330 244-8501
Hal Marker, *Principal*
EMP: 5
SALES (est): 258.5K **Privately Held**
SIC: 3315 Fencing made in wiredrawing plants

(G-15094)
JANE VALENTINE
Also Called: Colors
912 Woodside Ave Se (44720-3768)
PHONE..................................330 452-3154
Jane Valentine, *Owner*
EMP: 3
SALES (est): 120K **Privately Held**
SIC: 2395 Embroidery products, except schiffli machine

(G-15095)
JANI AUTO PARTS INC
Also Called: NAPA Auto Parts
6434 Wise Ave Nw (44720-7351)
PHONE..................................330 494-2975
John Pisani, *Principal*
EMP: 1
SALES (est): 3.8MM **Privately Held**
SIC: 3524 5999 1799 7699 Lawn & garden equipment; farm equipment & supplies; hydraulic equipment, installation & service; industrial equipment services

(G-15096)
KIRK KEY INTERLOCK COMPANY LLC
9048 Meridian Cir Nw (44720-8387)
PHONE..................................330 833-8223
Scott Life, *President*
Greg Wise, *Production*
Emily McDaniel, *Marketing Staff*
James G Owens, *Mng Member*
James R Fink,
▲ **EMP:** 47
SQ FT: 26,000
SALES (est): 12.4MM
SALES (corp-wide): 1.5B **Privately Held**
WEB: www.kirkkey.com
SIC: 3429 5063 Keys, locks & related hardware; electrical apparatus & equipment
PA: Halma Public Limited Company
Misbourne Court
Amersham BUCKS HP7 0
149 472-1111

(G-15097)
LETS GOLF DAILY INC
3199 Whitewood St Nw (44720-8362)
PHONE..................................330 966-3373
EMP: 3 **EST:** 2011
SALES (est): 110.7K **Privately Held**
SIC: 2711 Newspapers, publishing & printing

(G-15098)
LSI RETAIL GRAPHICS LLC
Also Called: Bob Ready
9260 Pleasantwood Ave Nw (44720-9006)
PHONE..................................401 766-7446
Jeff Stearns, *President*
Ronald S Stowell, *Corp Secy*
EMP: 65
SQ FT: 28,000
SALES (est): 9.2MM
SALES (corp-wide): 342MM **Publicly Held**
WEB: www.lsi-industries.com
SIC: 3993 Signs & advertising specialties
PA: Lsi Industries Inc.
10000 Alliance Rd
Blue Ash OH 45242
513 793-3200

(G-15099)
LT ENTERPRISES OF OHIO LLC
334 Orchard Ave Ne (44720-2556)
PHONE..................................330 526-6908
John D Larke, *Mng Member*
Nil Tyburk,
▲ **EMP:** 24
SQ FT: 10,000
SALES (est): 3.1MM **Privately Held**
SIC: 3444 Sheet metalwork

(G-15100)
LYNN TRUCK PARTS & SERVICE
2690 Missenden St Nw (44720-8218)
PHONE..................................330 966-1470
Lynn Hetrick, *President*
Melanie Hetrick, *Vice Pres*
EMP: 2
SQ FT: 10,000
SALES: 1MM **Privately Held**
WEB: www.lynntruckparts.com
SIC: 3714 Motor vehicle parts & accessories

(G-15101)
MICROPLEX INC
7568 Whipple Ave Nw (44720-6922)
PHONE..................................330 498-0600
Valerie Walters, *President*
John Walters, *Vice Pres*
Jo A Schwenning, *Purch Agent*
Susan Harst, *Treasurer*
Cheri Rowlands, *Accounts Mgr*
EMP: 30
SQ FT: 12,000
SALES (est): 6.2MM **Privately Held**
WEB: www.microplex.com
SIC: 3496 3679 5045 Cable, uninsulated wire: made from purchased wire; harness assemblies for electronic use: wire or cable; computer peripheral equipment

(G-15102)
MOHLER LUMBER COMPANY
4214 Portage St Nw (44720-7399)
PHONE..................................330 499-5461
Jennifer Hamilton, *Ch of Bd*
Richard Rohrer, *Ch of Bd*
Willidam Leed, *President*
Gary Leed, *Corp Secy*
Jed Rohrer, *Vice Pres*
EMP: 20 **EST:** 1911
SQ FT: 8,320
SALES (est): 2.2MM **Privately Held**
SIC: 2435 5211 2421 2426 Hardwood veneer & plywood; millwork & lumber; sawmills & planing mills, general; hardwood dimension & flooring mills

(G-15103)
MOTION MOBILITY & DESIGN INC
6490 Promler St Nw (44720-7625)
PHONE..................................330 244-9723
Paul V Pettini, *President*
Martin Giles, *General Mgr*
Steve Williams, *Vice Pres*
EMP: 11
SQ FT: 12,000
SALES (est): 2.5MM **Privately Held**
WEB: www.motionmobility.com
SIC: 3842 Braces, elastic

(G-15104)
MRO BUILT INC
6410 Promway Ave Nw (44720-7622)
PHONE..................................330 526-0555
Alfred Olivieri, *President*
Dean Olivieri, *Vice Pres*
Virginia Olivieri, *Treasurer*
Timothy Feller, *Admin Sec*
EMP: 75 **EST:** 1977
SQ FT: 55,000
SALES (est): 13.1MM
SALES (corp-wide): 87.5MM **Privately Held**
WEB: www.fredolivieri.com
SIC: 2599 2542 2434 Cabinets, factory; partitions & fixtures, except wood; wood kitchen cabinets
PA: Fred Olivieri Construction Company
6315 Promway Ave Nw
North Canton OH 44720
330 494-1007

(G-15105)
MYERS CONTROLLED POWER LLC (HQ)
219 E Maple St 100-200e (44720-2586)
PHONE..................................330 834-3200
James Owens, *President*
Gary Coury, *Managing Dir*
Gregory Kimbrough, *Engineer*
Martyn Sonnefeld, *Engineer*
Scott Hadley, *Info Tech Mgr*
▲ **EMP:** 105
SALES (est): 31MM
SALES (corp-wide): 196MM **Privately Held**
SIC: 3613 Control panels, electric

GEOGRAPHIC SECTION

North Canton - Stark County (G-15133)

PA: Myers Power Products, Inc.
2950 E Philadelphia St
Ontario CA 91761
909 923-1800

(G-15106)
NAVIGATOR CONSTRUCTION LLC
Also Called: Cabinet 2 Countertops
7530 Tim Ave Nw Ste B (44720-6960)
PHONE.................330 244-0221
Kurt Bonk, Mng Member
EMP: 3
SALES (est): 391.7K Privately Held
SIC: 2434 Wood kitchen cabinets

(G-15107)
NEW RIVER EQUIPMENT CORP
7793 Pittsburg Ave Nw (44720-6947)
PHONE.................330 669-0040
EMP: 3
SALES: 800K Privately Held
SIC: 3531 Mfg Construction Machinery Attachments

(G-15108)
P3LABS LLC
6545 Market Ave N Ste 100 (44720)
PHONE.................800 259-8059
Ewa Olsen,
EMP: 5
SALES (est): 216K Privately Held
SIC: 3699 5065 7371 Security devices; security control equipment & systems; computer software development

(G-15109)
PATENTHEALTH LLC
8000 Freedom Ave Nw (44720-6912)
PHONE.................330 208-1111
Michael Moorhead, Vice Pres
Dean Petersen, CFO
EMP: 5
SQ FT: 5,000
SALES (est): 1.6MM Privately Held
WEB: www.patenthealth.com
SIC: 2834 2833 Pharmaceutical preparations; medicinals & botanicals
PA: Arthur Middleton Capital Holdings, Inc.
8000 Freedom Ave Nw
North Canton OH 44720

(G-15110)
PAUL STIPKOVICH
Also Called: Franklin Graphics
515 Browning Ave Nw (44720-2341)
PHONE.................330 499-7391
Paul Stipkovich, Owner
EMP: 3 EST: 1973
SQ FT: 3,500
SALES (est): 243.8K Privately Held
SIC: 2752 Commercial printing, offset

(G-15111)
PORTAGE ELECTRIC PRODUCTS INC
Also Called: Pepi
7700 Freedom Ave Nw (44720-6906)
P.O. Box 2170, Canton (44720-0170)
PHONE.................330 499-2727
Brandon Wehl, Ch of Bd
Robert E Mylett, Principal
W Donald Reader, Principal
Edward J Zink, Principal
Omar R Givler, Senior VP
▲ EMP: 220 EST: 1963
SQ FT: 11,000
SALES (est): 39.5MM Privately Held
WEB: www.pepiusa.com
SIC: 3822 3829 Appliance controls except air-conditioning & refrigeration; measuring & controlling devices

(G-15112)
R R R DEVELOPMENT CO (PA)
8817 Pleasantwood Ave Nw (44720-4759)
PHONE.................330 966-8855
Ronald Dillard, President
Gene Emerick, President
Tom Dillard, COO
Thomas Dillard, Vice Pres
Robert Irwin, Vice Pres
▲ EMP: 85
SQ FT: 60,000
SALES (est): 16MM Privately Held
WEB: www.rrrdev.com
SIC: 3599 Machine shop, jobbing & repair

(G-15113)
RAIL BEARING SERVICE LLC
Also Called: Rail Bearing Service Inc
4500 Mount Pleasant St Nw (44720-5450)
P.O. Box 6929, Canton (44706-0929)
PHONE.................234 262-3000
Mervyn Cronje, Controller
EMP: 350
SQ FT: 6,000
SALES (est): 21K
SALES (corp-wide): 3.5B Publicly Held
SIC: 3568 Railroad car journal bearings
PA: The Timken Company
4500 Mount Pleasant St Nw
North Canton OH 44720
234 262-3000

(G-15114)
RESTLESS NOGGINS MFG LLC
334 Orchard Ave Ne (44720-2556)
P.O. Box 2995 (44720-0995)
PHONE.................330 526-6908
Dawn Tyburk, Principal
EMP: 3
SALES (est): 214.7K Privately Held
SIC: 3999 Manufacturing industries

(G-15115)
RHINO RUBBER LLC (PA)
7054 Meadowlands Ave Nw (44720-8813)
PHONE.................877 744-6603
Tim Ryan, President
▲ EMP: 15
SALES (est): 4.7MM Privately Held
SIC: 3089 3559 5014 Tires, plastic; rubber working machinery, including tires; tires & tubes

(G-15116)
SECO MACHINE INC
7376 Whipple Ave Nw (44720-7140)
PHONE.................330 499-2150
Mary Seccombe, President
Richard Seccombe, General Mgr
Delano F Rossio, Treasurer
Annette M Rossio, Admin Sec
EMP: 30
SALES (est): 6.2MM Privately Held
WEB: www.secomachine.com
SIC: 3599 Machine shop, jobbing & repair

(G-15117)
SHERWIN-WILLIAMS COMPANY
6483 Dressler Rd Nw (44720-7637)
PHONE.................330 253-6625
EMP: 4
SALES (corp-wide): 11.3B Publicly Held
SIC: 5231 2851 Ret Paint/Glass/Wallpaper Mfg Paints/Allied Products
PA: The Sherwin-Williams Company
101 W Prospect Ave # 1020
Cleveland OH 44115
216 566-2000

(G-15118)
SIGN A RAMA
Also Called: Sign-A-Rama
435 Applegrove St Nw (44720-1617)
PHONE.................330 499-4653
Jeff Cyfrod, Owner
EMP: 3
SALES (est): 196.5K Privately Held
WEB: www.lsti.net
SIC: 3993 Signs & advertising specialties

(G-15119)
SIMS-LOHMAN INC
Also Called: Canton Cut Stone
6570 Promway Ave Nw (44720-7314)
PHONE.................330 456-8408
EMP: 4
SALES (corp-wide): 127.4MM Privately Held
SIC: 3281 5032 Stone, quarrying & processing of own stone products; stone, crushed or broken
PA: Sims-Lohman, Inc.
6325 Este Ave
Cincinnati OH 45232
513 651-3510

(G-15120)
STANDARD ENGINEERING GROUP INC
3516 Highland Park Nw (44720-4532)
PHONE.................330 494-4300
Ronald Schlemmer, President
William Simmons, Vice Pres
▲ EMP: 5
SQ FT: 15,000
SALES (est): 2.3MM Privately Held
SIC: 3542 Machine tools, metal forming type

(G-15121)
STARK AIRWAYS
5430 Lauby Rd Bldg 27 (44720-1576)
PHONE.................330 526-6416
Ton Lambis, Manager
EMP: 3 EST: 2009
SALES (est): 300.3K Privately Held
SIC: 3721 Aircraft

(G-15122)
STARK INDUSTRIAL LLC
5103 Stoneham Rd (44720-1540)
P.O. Box 3030 (44720-8030)
PHONE.................330 493-9773
Ray Wilkof,
Samuel Wilkof,
▼ EMP: 40
SQ FT: 25,000
SALES (est): 24.2MM Privately Held
WEB: www.starkindustrial.com
SIC: 5085 3545 Industrial supplies; machine tool accessories

(G-15123)
SUN COLOR CORPORATION
1325 Irondale Cir Ne (44720-2157)
PHONE.................330 499-7010
David Smetana, President
EMP: 3
SALES (est): 327.2K Privately Held
SIC: 2851 2821 Paints & paint additives; plasticizer/additive based plastic materials

(G-15124)
THE NATIONAL LIME AND STONE CO
5377 Lauby Rd Ste 201 (44720-1529)
PHONE.................330 455-5722
Dave Weber, Principal
Ken Dinwiddie, Vice Pres
EMP: 5
SALES (corp-wide): 3.2B Privately Held
WEB: www.natlime.com
SIC: 1422 Crushed & broken limestone
PA: The National Lime And Stone Company
551 Lake Cascade Pkwy
Findlay OH 45840
419 422-4341

(G-15125)
THERMTROL CORPORATION (PA)
8914 Pleasantwood Ave Nw (44720-4762)
PHONE.................330 497-4148
Mark Jeffries Sr, President
Mark A Jeffries Jr, Exec VP
John Komer, Senior VP
Dan Curren, Vice Pres
Jim Kuch, Vice Pres
◆ EMP: 30
SQ FT: 24,000
SALES: 22MM Privately Held
WEB: www.thermtrol.com
SIC: 3679 3822 Harness assemblies for electronic use: wire or cable; thermostats & other environmental sensors

(G-15126)
TIMKEN COMPANY (PA)
4500 Mount Pleasant St Nw (44720-5450)
P.O. Box 6929, Canton (44706-0929)
PHONE.................234 262-3000
John M Timken Jr, Ch of Bd
Richard G Kyle, President
David Nolin, General Mgr
Steve Oswald, District Mgr
Christopher A Coughlin, Exec VP
◆ EMP: 4800 EST: 1899
SALES: 3.5B Publicly Held
SIC: 3562 Roller bearings & parts

(G-15127)
TIMKEN COMPANY
4500 Mount Pleasant St Nw (44720-5450)
PHONE.................234 262-3000
EMP: 6
SALES (corp-wide): 3B Publicly Held
SIC: 3562 Mfg Ball Bearings
PA: The Timken Company
4500 Mount Pleasant St Nw
North Canton OH 44720
234 262-3000

(G-15128)
TIMKEN RECEIVABLES CORPORATION
4500 Mount Pleasant St Nw (44720-5450)
PHONE.................234 262-3000
Glenn Eisenberg, President
EMP: 4
SALES (est): 410.8K
SALES (corp-wide): 3.5B Publicly Held
SIC: 3312 Blast furnaces & steel mills
PA: The Timken Company
4500 Mount Pleasant St Nw
North Canton OH 44720
234 262-3000

(G-15129)
TIMOTHY C GEORGES
4900 Massillon Rd Apt 6 (44720-1473)
PHONE.................330 933-9114
Timothy C Georges, Principal
EMP: 3
SALES (est): 112.6K Privately Held
SIC: 2711 Newspapers, publishing & printing

(G-15130)
TMSI LLC
9073 Pleasantwood Ave Nw (44720-4763)
P.O. Box 5414, Akron (44334-0414)
PHONE.................888 867-4872
Gerald R Potts, President
◆ EMP: 14
SQ FT: 24,000
SALES (est): 6.8MM
SALES (corp-wide): 412.6MM Privately Held
WEB: www.tmsi-usa.com
SIC: 5013 3825 Testing equipment, electrical: automotive; instruments to measure electricity
PA: Mesnac Co., Ltd.
No.43 Zhengzhou Road
Qingdao 26604
532 688-6262

(G-15131)
TRI - FLEX OF OHIO INC (PA)
2701 Applegrove St Nw (44720-6213)
PHONE.................330 705-7084
Paul Lili, President
EMP: 13 EST: 2011
SALES (est): 2.2MM Privately Held
SIC: 3365 Machinery castings, aluminum

(G-15132)
TRISTAN RUBBER MOLDING INC (PA)
7255 Whipple Ave Nw (44720-7137)
PHONE.................330 499-4055
Peter Fritz, President
Larry W Ball, Principal
Christina Fritz, Treasurer
EMP: 28
SQ FT: 20,000
SALES (est): 8.6MM Privately Held
SIC: 3069 Molded rubber products

(G-15133)
UNITED COMPONENTS LLC (DH)
Also Called: UCI
2100 International Pkwy (44720-1373)
PHONE.................812 867-4516
Bruce M Zorich, President
Ian I Fujiyama, Principal
Paul R Lederer, Principal
Gregory S Ledford, Principal
Raymond A Ranelli, Principal
◆ EMP: 50

North Canton - Stark County (G-15134)

SALES (est): 449.4MM
SALES (corp-wide): 753MM **Privately Held**
WEB: www.ucinc.com
SIC: 3714 Motor vehicle parts & accessories

(G-15134)
UPL INTERNATIONAL INC
Also Called: Universal Plastics
7661 Freedom Ave Nw (44720-6903)
PHONE.................................330 433-2860
Jeffrey Scarpitti, *President*
Wade Scarpitti, *President*
EMP: 20 **EST:** 1976
SQ FT: 18,000
SALES (est): 5MM **Privately Held**
WEB: www.universalplasticsmachine.com
SIC: 3089 5162 Plastic processing; plastics products

(G-15135)
VEGA TECHNOLOGY GROUP LLC
412 Sheraton Dr Nw (44720-2225)
PHONE.................................216 772-1434
Kevin D Busto, *Owner*
EMP: 3
SALES (est): 199.3K **Privately Held**
SIC: 3674 Semiconductors & related devices

(G-15136)
W3 ULTRASONICS LLC
5288 Huckleberry St Nw (44720-6876)
PHONE.................................330 284-3667
Scott Miller, *President*
EMP: 4
SQ FT: 5,000
SALES (est): 311.2K **Privately Held**
SIC: 3589 Commercial cleaning equipment

(G-15137)
WILLIAMS PARTNERS LP
7235 Whipple Ave Nw (44720-7137)
PHONE.................................330 966-3674
EMP: 245 **Publicly Held**
SIC: 1311 Natural gas production
PA: Williams Partners L.P.
1 Williams Ctr
Tulsa OK 74172

North Fairfield
Huron County

(G-15138)
FLY RACE FUELS LLC
1905 Maple Ridge Rd (44855-9653)
PHONE.................................419 744-9402
Brenda Ooten, *Principal*
EMP: 3
SALES (est): 180.4K **Privately Held**
SIC: 2869 Fuels

North Georgetown
Columbiana County

(G-15139)
ANTRAM FIRE EQUIPMENT
27970 Winona Rd (44665)
PHONE.................................330 525-7171
Paul Antram, *Owner*
EMP: 3 **EST:** 1972
SQ FT: 4,040
SALES (est): 240.9K **Privately Held**
SIC: 5087 7389 3711 Firefighting equipment; fire extinguisher servicing; fire department vehicles (motor vehicles), assembly of

North Jackson
Mahoning County

(G-15140)
AMERICAN PLASTECH LLC
11635 Mahoning Ave (44451-9688)
P.O. Box 399 (44451-0399)
PHONE.................................330 538-0576
Rick Amato, *Mng Member*
EMP: 6 **EST:** 2016
SALES (est): 692.7K **Privately Held**
SIC: 2431 Windows & window parts & trim, wood

(G-15141)
BCI AND V INVESTMENTS INC
11675 Mahoning Ave (44451-9688)
P.O. Box 698 (44451-0698)
PHONE.................................330 538-0660
Harold Bartels, *President*
Randy Vegso, *Vice Pres*
EMP: 55
SQ FT: 26,000
SALES (est): 9MM **Privately Held**
SIC: 2821 3356 Vinyl resins; nonferrous rolling & drawing

(G-15142)
BLUE RIBBON TRAILERS LTD
12800 Leonard Pkwy (44451-8611)
PHONE.................................330 538-4114
Clint Leonard, *President*
EMP: 19
SALES (est): 3.8MM **Privately Held**
WEB: www.blueribbontrailers.com
SIC: 3799 Trailers & trailer equipment

(G-15143)
CANFIELD MANUFACTURING CO INC
Also Called: Wilson Specialties
489 Rosemont Rd (44451-9717)
PHONE.................................330 533-3333
M J Stewart, *CEO*
Mary Mc Mahon, *Office Mgr*
Joe Campbell, *Branch Mgr*
Debbie Costa, *Admin Asst*
Jack Moore, *Representative*
EMP: 7 **EST:** 1800
SQ FT: 20,000
SALES (est): 420K **Privately Held**
SIC: 2426 2499 Lumber, hardwood dimension; handles, wood

(G-15144)
CLEVELAND CORETEC INC
Also Called: Ttm
12080 Debartolo Dr (44451-9642)
P.O. Box 216 (44451-0216)
PHONE.................................314 727-2087
Jonathan Schofield, *Principal*
EMP: 6
SALES (est): 669.7K **Privately Held**
SIC: 3672 Printed circuit boards

(G-15145)
DDI NORTH JACKSON CORP
12080 Debartolo Dr (44451-9642)
P.O. Box 216 (44451-0216)
PHONE.................................330 538-3900
Mark Curry, *CEO*
EMP: 7 **EST:** 2014
SALES (est): 873.8K **Privately Held**
SIC: 3672 Printed circuit boards

(G-15146)
EXTRUDEX ALUMINUM INC
12051 Mahoning Ave (44451-9617)
P.O. Box 697 (44451-0697)
PHONE.................................330 538-4444
Andrew Gucciardi, *President*
Brian Carder, *General Mgr*
Dick Gargasz, *Controller*
Bernadette Hoffman, *Cust Mgr*
Paul Love, *Manager*
▲ **EMP:** 120
SQ FT: 110,000
SALES (est): 36.4MM **Privately Held**
WEB: www.extrudexohio.com
SIC: 3354 Aluminum extruded products
PA: Placements Cir-Real Limitee
411 Chrislea Rd
Woodbridge ON L4L 8
416 745-4444

(G-15147)
INNOVAR SYSTEMS LIMITED
12155 Commissioner Dr (44451-9640)
P.O. Box 486 (44451-0486)
PHONE.................................330 538-3942
John Frano, *CEO*
Paul Graff, *President*
EMP: 11
SQ FT: 15,000
SALES (est): 2.8MM **Privately Held**
SIC: 3699 Laser welding, drilling & cutting equipment

(G-15148)
LEARNING EGG LLC
Also Called: Learning Egg, The
9332 Silica Rd (44451-9670)
PHONE.................................330 207-8663
Elijah Stambaugh,
EMP: 4
SQ FT: 1,000
SALES (est): 212.6K **Privately Held**
SIC: 7372 Educational computer software

(G-15149)
LIBERTY STEEL PRESSED PDTS LLC
11650 Mahoning Ave (44451-9688)
PHONE.................................330 538-2236
Jim Grasso, *President*
EMP: 3
SALES (est): 144.4K **Privately Held**
SIC: 3399 Primary metal products

(G-15150)
NORTH JCKSON SPECIALTY STL LLC
Also Called: Universal Stainless
2058 S Bailey Rd (44451-9639)
PHONE.................................330 538-9621
EMP: 12 **Publicly Held**
SIC: 3312 Stainless steel
HQ: North Jackson Specialty Steel, Llc
600 Mayer St
Bridgeville PA 15017
412 257-7600

(G-15151)
OHIO SPECIALTY DIES LLC
293 Rosemont Rd (44451-9632)
P.O. Box 428 (44451-0428)
PHONE.................................330 538-3396
Joseph P Baco, *Mng Member*
Jeff Baco,
EMP: 16 **EST:** 2011
SQ FT: 4,000
SALES: 1.3MM **Privately Held**
SIC: 3544 Special dies & tools

(G-15152)
PATRIOT SPECIAL METALS INC
2058 S Bailey Rd (44451-9639)
PHONE.................................330 538-9621
▲ **EMP:** 6
SALES (est): 1MM **Privately Held**
SIC: 3356 Nonferrous rolling & drawing

(G-15153)
PMC SYSTEMS LIMITED
12155 Commissioner Dr (44451-9640)
P.O. Box 486 (44451-0486)
PHONE.................................330 538-2268
John Frano, *President*
Randy G Yakubek, *President*
Paul Graff, *Vice Pres*
EMP: 30
SQ FT: 3,000
SALES (est): 5.7MM **Privately Held**
SIC: 3625 8711 Electric controls & control accessories, industrial; electrical or electronic engineering

(G-15154)
SOVEREIGN CIRCUITS INC
12080 Debartolo Dr (44451-9642)
P.O. Box 216 (44451-0216)
PHONE.................................330 538-3900
Robert Buss, *Principal*
EMP: 9
SALES (est): 1MM **Privately Held**
SIC: 3679 Electronic circuits

(G-15155)
STAMPED STEEL PRODUCTS INC
151 S Bailey Rd (44451-9636)
P.O. Box 5224, Poland (44514-0224)
PHONE.................................330 538-3951
William Robinson Jr, *President*
Micheal D Geiger, *Corp Secy*
EMP: 11 **EST:** 2001
SQ FT: 59,000
SALES (est): 4.3MM **Privately Held**
SIC: 3469 5051 Stamping metal for the trade; stampings, metal

(G-15156)
TTM TECHNOLOGIES INC
12080 Debartolo Dr (44451-9642)
P.O. Box 216 (44451-0216)
PHONE.................................330 538-3900
Tony Mrvelj, *Facilities Mgr*
Marty Cormier, *Purch Mgr*
Rick Gilder, *Engineer*
Mark Curry, *Controller*
Mike Hoffman, *Info Tech Mgr*
EMP: 118
SALES (corp-wide): 2.8B **Publicly Held**
WEB: www.sovereign-circuits.com
SIC: 3672 Printed circuit boards
PA: Ttm Technologies, Inc.
1665 Scenic Ave Ste 250
Costa Mesa CA 92626
714 327-3000

(G-15157)
VINYL PROFILES ACQUISITION LLC
11675 Mahoning Ave (44451-9688)
P.O. Box 698 (44451-0698)
PHONE.................................330 538-0660
Randy Vegso, *President*
EMP: 29
SALES (est): 7.5MM **Privately Held**
SIC: 2821 Plastics materials & resins

(G-15158)
VINYLTECH INC
11635 Mahoning Ave (44451-9688)
P.O. Box 127 (44451-0127)
PHONE.................................330 538-0369
Rick Amato, *President*
Mike Buchanan, *Vice Pres*
EMP: 30
SALES (est): 4.4MM **Privately Held**
SIC: 3544 Forms (molds), for foundry & plastics working machinery

North Kingsville
Ashtabula County

(G-15159)
BUHI IMPORTS
3210 E Center St (44068)
P.O. Box 420 (44068-0420)
PHONE.................................440 224-0013
Paul Buhite, *General Mgr*
Gemma Buhite, *Vice Pres*
▲ **EMP:** 4
SALES (est): 291.9K **Privately Held**
SIC: 5199 2499 5945 Baskets; reed, rattan, wicker & willow ware, except furniture; hobby, toy & game shops

(G-15160)
PREMIX INC (DH)
Also Called: Molded Parts Division
3365 E Center St (44068)
P.O. Box 281 (44068-0281)
PHONE.................................440 224-2181
Thomas J Meola, *President*
Edward Galda, *Purch Dir*
Martha Jones, *Buyer*
Mark Cartellone, *QC Mgr*
Ralph Varckette, *Plant Engr*
▼ **EMP:** 144
SQ FT: 300,000
SALES (est): 105.6MM
SALES (corp-wide): 34.5B **Privately Held**
WEB: www.premix.com
SIC: 3089 2821 Thermoformed finished plastic products; injection molding of plastics; plastic kitchenware, tableware & houseware; plastics materials & resins

(G-15161)
WHOLESALE IMPRINTS INC
Also Called: Ringer Screen Print
6259 Hewitt Ln (44068)
P.O. Box 507 (44068-0507)
PHONE.................................440 224-3527
John Ringer, *Principal*
EMP: 40 **EST:** 2013

SALES (est): 2.9MM **Privately Held**
SIC: **2395** 2396 Embroidery & art needlework; fabric printing & stamping

North Lawrence
Stark County

(G-15162)
KELBLYS RIFLE RANGE INC
7222 Dalton Fox Lake Rd (44666-9543)
PHONE..................................330 683-0070
George Kelbly Sr, *President*
Karen Kelbly, *Corp Secy*
George Kelbly Jr, *Vice Pres*
James Kelbly, *Vice Pres*
EMP: 8
SALES (est): 1.6MM **Privately Held**
WEB: www.kelbly.com
SIC: **3484** 7999 Rifles or rifle parts, 30 mm. & below; shooting range operation

(G-15163)
US TUBULAR PRODUCTS INC
Also Called: Benmit Division
14852 Lincoln Way W (44666)
PHONE..................................330 832-1734
Jeffrey J Cunningham, *President*
Connye Cunningham, *Corp Secy*
Brian Cunningham, *Vice Pres*
EMP: 60 EST: 1973
SQ FT: 100,000
SALES (est): 9.2MM **Privately Held**
SIC: **8734** 3498 Hydrostatic testing laboratory; tube fabricating (contract bending & shaping)

North Lewisburg
Champaign County

(G-15164)
PREHISTORIC ANTIQUITIES
7045 State Route 245 (43060-9720)
P.O. Box 100, Winchester (45697-0100)
PHONE..................................937 747-2225
Bill Ballinger, *President*
Linda Ballinger, *Vice Pres*
EMP: 3
SALES (est): 140K **Privately Held**
SIC: **2721** Magazines: publishing & printing

(G-15165)
WORTHNGTON STELPAC SYSTEMS LLC
5256 Burton Rd (43060-7000)
PHONE..................................937 747-2370
Paul Mc, *Branch Mgr*
EMP: 8
SALES (corp-wide): 3.5B **Publicly Held**
SIC: **3441** Fabricated structural metal
HQ: Worthington Steelpac Systems, Llc
1205 Dearborn Dr
Columbus OH 43085

North Lima
Mahoning County

(G-15166)
BIRD EQUIPMENT LLC
Also Called: Specialty Fab
11950 South Ave (44452-9744)
PHONE..................................330 549-1004
Joe Colletti, *President*
Brian Dwyer, *Vice Pres*
EMP: 28
SQ FT: 49,500
SALES: 2.6MM
SALES (corp-wide): 180.1MM **Privately Held**
SIC: **3441** Fabricated structural metal
PA: Desco Corporation
7795 Walton Pkwy Ste 175
New Albany OH 43054
614 888-2855

(G-15167)
COBRA MOTORCYCLES MFG
11511 Springfield Rd (44452-9755)
PHONE..................................330 207-3844
Bud Maimone, *President*
▲ EMP: 25
SALES (est): 3.2MM **Privately Held**
WEB: www.cobramotorcycle.com
SIC: **3751** Motorcycles & related parts

(G-15168)
COMMERCIAL MINERALS INC
10900 South Ave (44452-9792)
P.O. Box 217 (44452-0217)
PHONE..................................330 549-2165
Thomas Mackall, *President*
Melanie Dunn, *Treasurer*
EMP: 6 EST: 1981
SQ FT: 6,000
SALES (est): 512.6K **Privately Held**
SIC: **1221** Bituminous coal surface mining

(G-15169)
CULTURED MARBLE INC
11331 South Ave (44452-9772)
P.O. Box 284 (44452-0284)
PHONE..................................330 549-2282
Todd Worsencroft, *President*
David Worsencroft, *President*
Arthur D Worsencroft, *Corp Secy*
EMP: 8
SQ FT: 12,000
SALES: 400K **Privately Held**
SIC: **3299** 3088 Synthetic stones, for gem stones & industrial use; plastics plumbing fixtures

(G-15170)
DUO-CORP
280 Miley Rd (44452-8581)
P.O. Box 313 (44452-0313)
PHONE..................................330 549-2149
William G Kinkade, *CEO*
Bradley W Kinkade, *President*
Stephen De Capua, *CFO*
Stephen Decapua, *CFO*
Laureen Alderman, *Admin Sec*
EMP: 30
SQ FT: 70,000
SALES (est): 5.3MM **Privately Held**
WEB: www.duo-corp.com
SIC: **3089** 3442 Windows, plastic; screen & storm doors & windows

(G-15171)
HUNTER LIFT LTD
11233 South Ave (44452-9731)
PHONE..................................330 549-3347
Douglas R Verenski,
EMP: 21
SQ FT: 50,000
SALES (est): 641.1K **Privately Held**
WEB: www.hunterlift.com
SIC: **3537** Lift trucks, industrial: fork, platform, straddle, etc.

(G-15172)
J AND N INC
80 Eastgate Dr (44452-8563)
PHONE..................................234 759-3741
Joseph Tesiz, *President*
EMP: 15
SALES (est): 292.8K **Privately Held**
SIC: **2679** Plates, pressed & molded pulp: from purchased material

(G-15173)
KTSDI LLC
801 E Middletown Rd (44452-9761)
PHONE..................................330 783-2000
Ken Timmings, *Principal*
Bryon Gotham, *Accountant*
Duke Siddle, *Manager*
EMP: 7
SALES (est): 460K **Privately Held**
SIC: **8748** 3714 Business consulting; axle housings & shafts, motor vehicle

(G-15174)
L AND S EXPRESS FUEL CENTER
10125 Market St (44452-9556)
PHONE..................................330 549-9566
Lee Padula, *Principal*
EMP: 4
SALES (est): 431.7K **Privately Held**
SIC: **2869** Fuels

(G-15175)
LATELIER CUSTOM WOODWORKING
11905 Woodworth Rd (44452-9794)
PHONE..................................234 759-3359
Fax: 330 549-2029
EMP: 5
SALES (est): 675K **Privately Held**
SIC: **2521** 2512 2431 Mfg Custom Woodworkings

(G-15176)
PRINT FACTORY PLL
Also Called: Poland Print Shop
11471 South Ave (44452-9772)
P.O. Box 312 (44452-0312)
PHONE..................................330 549-9640
John Primm, *Partner*
Doris Primm, *Partner*
EMP: 7
SALES: 100K **Privately Held**
SIC: **2752** Commercial printing, offset

(G-15177)
R A M PLASTICS CO INC
11401 South Ave (44452)
P.O. Box 402 (44452-0402)
PHONE..................................330 549-3107
Richard Mallory, *President*
EMP: 35
SQ FT: 20,000
SALES (est): 5.2MM **Privately Held**
SIC: **3089** Injection molded finished plastic products; injection molding of plastics

(G-15178)
STERLING MINING CORPORATION (HQ)
10900 South Ave (44452-9792)
P.O. Box 217 (44452-0217)
PHONE..................................330 549-2165
W Thomas Mackall, *President*
Denise Mackall, *Treasurer*
EMP: 12
SQ FT: 6,000
SALES (est): 16.2MM
SALES (corp-wide): 113.6MM **Privately Held**
SIC: **1222** Bituminous coal-underground mining
PA: The East Fairfield Coal Co
10900 South Ave
North Lima OH
330 549-2165

(G-15179)
SUBTROPOLIS MINING CO
10900 South Ave (44452-9792)
P.O. Box 217 (44452-0217)
PHONE..................................330 549-2165
EMP: 5 EST: 2010
SALES (est): 412K **Privately Held**
SIC: **1221** Bituminous coal & lignite-surface mining

North Olmsted
Cuyahoga County

(G-15180)
ABSORBCORE LLC
30275 Lorain Rd (44070-3925)
PHONE..................................440 614-0457
Charles Flury,
EMP: 3
SALES (est): 302.9K **Privately Held**
SIC: **2273** Mats & matting

(G-15181)
ANAHEIM MANUFACTURING COMPANY
Also Called: Waste King
25300 Al Moen Dr (44070-5619)
P.O. Box 4146, Anaheim CA (92803-4146)
PHONE..................................800 767-6293
Steve Lattman, *President*
Robert A Schneider, *Vice Pres*
▲ EMP: 50
SALES (est): 7MM
SALES (corp-wide): 5.4B **Publicly Held**
WEB: www.anaheimmfg.com
SIC: **3639** Garbage disposal units, household

HQ: Moen Incorporated
25300 Al Moen Dr
North Olmsted OH 44070
440 962-2000

(G-15182)
BTA OF MOTORCARS INC
27500 Lorain Rd (44070-4038)
PHONE..................................440 716-1000
Gary Tamerlano, *Principal*
EMP: 8
SALES (est): 815.7K **Privately Held**
SIC: **3479** Painting of metal products

(G-15183)
CAPPCO TUBULAR PRODUCTS INC
26777 Lorain Rd Ste 216 (44070-3226)
PHONE..................................216 641-2218
EMP: 5
SALES (est): 262.9K **Privately Held**
SIC: **1741** 1629 3541 3446 Foundation building; dredging contractor; drilling & boring machines; fences, gates, posts & flagpoles

(G-15184)
DAMSEL IN DEFENSE
7484 Willow Woods Dr (44070-6326)
PHONE..................................561 307-4177
Yvonne Pelino, *Principal*
EMP: 3
SALES (est): 196.6K **Privately Held**
SIC: **3812** Defense systems & equipment

(G-15185)
DEL HOLDASH
29891 Westminster Dr (44070-5083)
PHONE..................................440 427-0611
Del Holdash, *Principal*
EMP: 3
SALES (est): 213.2K **Privately Held**
SIC: **2421** Sawmills & planing mills, general

(G-15186)
E T & K INC
Also Called: American Speedy Printing
23545 Lorain Rd (44070-2219)
PHONE..................................440 777-7375
Edward Scully, *President*
Theresa Scully, *Treasurer*
EMP: 3
SQ FT: 1,600
SALES: 310K **Privately Held**
SIC: **2752** Commercial printing, offset

(G-15187)
EMTA INC
Also Called: Joe D'S Printing
28875 Lorain Rd (44070-4043)
P.O. Box 503 (44070-0503)
PHONE..................................440 734-6464
Joe Delamielleure, *President*
Ron Dale, *Corp Secy*
Timothy Smith, *Vice Pres*
Ronald Deyo, *Treasurer*
EMP: 3
SQ FT: 1,200
SALES: 140K **Privately Held**
SIC: **2759** 2791 2752 Commercial printing; typesetting; commercial printing, lithographic

(G-15188)
EW PUBLISHING COMPANY
Also Called: Fastsigns
24181 Lorain Rd (44070-2163)
PHONE..................................440 979-0025
Paul Girgash, *Owner*
EMP: 3
SQ FT: 4,500
SALES (est): 382.8K **Privately Held**
SIC: **3993** Signs & advertising specialties

(G-15189)
FORM-A-TOP PRODUCTS INC
25044 Chase Dr (44070-1217)
PHONE..................................440 779-9452
Richard Drozdz, *President*
Harriet Drozdz, *Vice Pres*
EMP: 9 EST: 1952
SQ FT: 10,000
SALES (est): 753K **Privately Held**
SIC: **2541** Table or counter tops, plastic laminated

North Olmsted - Cuyahoga County (G-15190)

(G-15190)
FRAGAPANE BAKERIES INC (PA)
Also Called: Fragapane Bakery & Deli
28625 Lorain Rd (44070-4009)
PHONE.................................440 779-6050
John Fragapane, *President*
Nick Fragapane, *Vice Pres*
Victoria Fragapane, *Treasurer*
Rose Fragapane, *Admin Sec*
EMP: 8 **EST:** 1971
SQ FT: 4,000
SALES (est): 1.8MM **Privately Held**
SIC: 5411 5461 2051 Delicatessens; bakeries; bread, cake & related products

(G-15191)
GC CONTROLS INC
Also Called: Eurotherm
3926 Pine Cir (44070-1766)
P.O. Box 450799, Westlake (44145-0617)
PHONE.................................440 779-4777
Bob Roberts, *President*
Joanne Albers, *Treasurer*
Gary Albers, *Director*
EMP: 7
SALES (est): 864.4K **Privately Held**
SIC: 3625 Industrial controls: push button, selector switches, pilot

(G-15192)
HILO TECH INC
31532 Lorain Rd (44070-4733)
PHONE.................................440 979-1155
Gerald Potchatek, *President*
Debbie Heck, *Corp Secy*
EMP: 3
SALES (est): 414.9K **Privately Held**
SIC: 1796 3589 Machinery installation; car washing machinery

(G-15193)
HOMETOWN THREADS
Also Called: Abl Enterprises
4636 Great Northern Blvd (44070-3425)
PHONE.................................440 779-6053
Arnold Lantor, *President*
EMP: 4
SALES (est): 314.8K **Privately Held**
SIC: 2395 Embroidery & art needlework

(G-15194)
KELLY PRINTS LLC
Also Called: Minuteman Press
24112 Lorain Rd (44070-2116)
PHONE.................................440 356-6361
William Loyd Kelly,
EMP: 4
SALES (est): 591K **Privately Held**
SIC: 2752 Commercial printing, lithographic

(G-15195)
P C POWER INC
23792 Lorain Rd Ste 300 (44070-2225)
PHONE.................................440 779-4080
Arthur Bibbs, *President*
EMP: 4
SQ FT: 1,000
SALES: 500K **Privately Held**
SIC: 7378 3643 Computer & data processing equipment repair/maintenance; electric connectors

(G-15196)
Q MUSIC USA LLC
Also Called: Music Systems
5730 Great Northern Blvd E1 (44070-5626)
P.O. Box 60474, Fort Myers FL (33906-6474)
PHONE.................................239 995-5888
Allison Kox,
EMP: 4
SALES (est): 299.7K **Privately Held**
WEB: www.quebbie.com
SIC: 3651 Music distribution apparatus

(G-15197)
SCREEN IMAGES INC
6122 Croton Dr (44070-4430)
PHONE.................................440 779-7356
Karl Kullik, *President*
Carol Guncer, *Manager*
EMP: 3
SQ FT: 500
SALES (est): 170K **Privately Held**
SIC: 3993 Signs & advertising specialties

(G-15198)
SERVO SYSTEMS INC
31375 Lorain Rd (44070-4730)
P.O. Box 45552, Westlake (44145-0552)
PHONE.................................440 779-2780
Peter Ganczarski, *President*
EMP: 4
SQ FT: 2,000
SALES (est): 827.9K **Privately Held**
WEB: www.servo-systems.com
SIC: 5063 3678 Motor controls, starters & relays: electric; electronic connectors

(G-15199)
SMILE BRANDS INC
Also Called: Bright Now Dental
25102 Brookpark Rd (44070-6414)
PHONE.................................440 471-6133
Diane Ulichney, *Branch Mgr*
EMP: 6
SALES (corp-wide): 565MM **Privately Held**
HQ: Smile Brands Of Tennessee, Inc.
100 Spectrum Center Dr # 1500
Irvine CA 92618
714 668-1300
SIC: 3843 Dental equipment & supplies

(G-15200)
SPECIAL MTLS RES & TECH INC
Also Called: Specmat
27390 Lusandra Cir (44070-1747)
PHONE.................................440 777-4024
Maria Faur, *CEO*
EMP: 3
SQ FT: 3,000
SALES (est): 265.1K **Privately Held**
SIC: 8741 3674 8732 Management services; semiconductors & related devices; research services, except laboratory

(G-15201)
THERM-ALL INC (PA)
31387 Industrial Pkwy (44070-4764)
PHONE.................................440 779-9494
Robert Smigel, *President*
Ann Sliwa, *Principal*
Jared Welsh, *District Mgr*
Richard Sobiech, *CFO*
Dennis Kaczmarek, *Treasurer*
EMP: 20
SQ FT: 56,000
SALES (est): 18.3MM **Privately Held**
WEB: www.columnsentry.com
SIC: 3211 Building glass, flat; plate & sheet glass

(G-15202)
US VIDEO
23551 Westchester Dr (44070-1431)
PHONE.................................440 734-6463
Shailesh Shah,
EMP: 3
SALES: 80K **Privately Held**
SIC: 7841 3695 Video tape rental; video recording tape, blank

(G-15203)
WESTERN RESERVE FURNITURE CO
Also Called: William F Kelly
29701 Wellington Dr (44070-5063)
PHONE.................................440 235-6216
William Kelly, *Owner*
EMP: 3
SALES: 128K **Privately Held**
SIC: 1752 2511 Floor laying & floor work; wood household furniture

(G-15204)
YOST & SON INC
5502 Barton Rd (44070-3836)
PHONE.................................440 779-8025
Diana Yost, *President*
Marie Glasby, *Vice Pres*
EMP: 5
SALES: 1.1MM **Privately Held**
SIC: 3559 Chemical machinery & equipment

North Ridgeville
Lorain County

(G-15205)
8888 BUTLER INVESTMENTS INC
8888 Riverwood Dr (44039-6311)
PHONE.................................440 748-0810
Larry D Butler, *President*
Bradley A Butler, *Vice Pres*
EMP: 9 **EST:** 1960
SQ FT: 10,000
SALES (est): 1.2MM **Privately Held**
WEB: www.jlcapital.com
SIC: 3728 3599 Aircraft parts & equipment; machine shop, jobbing & repair

(G-15206)
ALANOD WESTLAKE METAL IND INC
36696 Sugar Ridge Rd (44039-3832)
PHONE.................................440 327-8184
John R Johnston Jr, *President*
Franke Lee, *President*
James Gula, *Vice Pres*
Greg Seeley, *Admin Sec*
◆ **EMP:** 21
SQ FT: 80,000
SALES (est): 50MM
SALES (corp-wide): 133.2MM **Privately Held**
WEB: www.westlakemetals.com
SIC: 5051 3354 Aluminum bars, rods, ingots, sheets, pipes, plates, etc.; aluminum extruded products
PA: Alanod Gmbh & Co. Kg
Egerstr. 12
Ennepetal 58256
233 398-6500

(G-15207)
ALL AROUND GARAGE DOOR INC
33434 Liberty Pkwy (44039-2670)
PHONE.................................440 759-5079
Steve Mazur, *President*
EMP: 4
SQ FT: 2,500
SALES (est): 308K **Privately Held**
SIC: 3442 3089 2431 Garage doors, overhead: metal; fences, gates & accessories: plastic; garage doors, overhead: wood

(G-15208)
APS ACCURATE PRODUCTS & SVCS
39050 Center Ridge Rd (44039-2742)
PHONE.................................440 353-9353
Tom Stemmer, *President*
EMP: 3
SALES (est): 276K **Privately Held**
SIC: 7389 7338 3824 Office facilities & secretarial service rental; secretarial & typing service; liquid meters

(G-15209)
BECKETT AIR INCORPORATED (PA)
Also Called: PM Motor Fan Blade Company
37850 Taylor Pkwy (44039-3600)
P.O. Box 1236, Elyria (44036-1236)
PHONE.................................440 327-9999
Scribner L Fauver, *Principal*
Ken Behner, *Engineer*
Greg Bloomfield, *Engineer*
John D Beckett, *Treasurer*
Yvonne Muck, *Human Res Dir*
▲ **EMP:** 90
SALES (est): 32.9MM **Privately Held**
WEB: www.beckettair.com
SIC: 3433 3585 3564 Heating equipment, except electric; refrigeration & heating equipment; blowers & fans

(G-15210)
BECKETT GAS INC (PA)
38000 Beckett Pkwy (44039-3645)
P.O. Box 4037, Elyria (44036-4037)
PHONE.................................440 327-3141
John D Beckett, *Ch of Bd*
Morrison J Carter, *President*
Kevin A Beckett, *Corp Secy*
Dennis Zemanek, *Mfg Spvr*
Mike O'Donnell, *Engineer*
◆ **EMP:** 226
SQ FT: 140,000
SALES (est): 47.5MM **Privately Held**
SIC: 3433 Burners, furnaces, boilers & stokers

(G-15211)
BINDERY TECH INC
35205 Center Ridge Rd (44039-3013)
PHONE.................................440 934-3247
Dave Sexton, *Principal*
Gordon B Loux, *Incorporator*
EMP: 14
SALES (est): 1.8MM **Privately Held**
SIC: 2789 Binding only: books, pamphlets, magazines, etc.

(G-15212)
BIOTHANE COATED WEBBING CORP
34655 Mills Rd (44039-1843)
PHONE.................................440 327-0485
Frank Boron, *President*
Robert Krebs, *Purchasing*
▲ **EMP:** 35 **EST:** 1976
SQ FT: 25,000
SALES (est): 8.8MM **Privately Held**
WEB: www.bioplastics.us
SIC: 2295 3083 2821 Resin or plastic coated fabrics; laminated plastics plate & sheet; plastics materials & resins

(G-15213)
BRACEMART LLC
36097 Westminister Ave (44039-4537)
PHONE.................................440 353-2830
Aaron Dibucci, *President*
William Hagy, *Principal*
EMP: 4 **EST:** 2015
SALES (est): 191.3K **Privately Held**
SIC: 3842 3949 Braces, orthopedic; supports: abdominal, ankle, arch, kneecap, etc.; sporting & athletic goods; exercise equipment

(G-15214)
BRG SPORTS INC
7501 Performance Ln (44039-2765)
PHONE.................................217 891-1429
EMP: 3
SALES (est): 162.7K **Privately Held**
SIC: 3949 Sporting & athletic goods

(G-15215)
BRUCK MANUFACTURING CO INC
33471 Liberty Pkwy (44039-3298)
PHONE.................................440 327-6619
George Bruck Jr, *CEO*
Kevin Bruck, *President*
George Bruck III, *Corp Secy*
EMP: 5 **EST:** 1957
SQ FT: 6,500
SALES: 300K **Privately Held**
SIC: 3599 3544 Machine shop, jobbing & repair; special dies, tools, jigs & fixtures

(G-15216)
CONTOUR TOOL INC
38830 Taylor Pkwy (44035-6254)
PHONE.................................440 365-7333
Paul Reichlin, *President*
R Stephen Laux, *Principal*
Yvonne D Reichlin, *Vice Pres*
Mark Schroeder, *VP Opers*
Sue Mims, *Admin Asst*
EMP: 35
SQ FT: 11,000
SALES (est): 6.4MM **Privately Held**
WEB: www.contourtool.com
SIC: 3545 3544 Machine tool accessories; special dies & tools

(G-15217)
CUPCAKE DIVAZ
5480 Autumn Ln (44039-1177)
PHONE.................................216 509-3850
Gina King, *Principal*
EMP: 4
SALES (est): 217.4K **Privately Held**
SIC: 2051 Bread, cake & related products

▲ = Import ▼ = Export
◆ = Import/Export

North Ridgeville - Lorain County (G-15247)

(G-15218)
CUPCAKE WISHES
34340 Bainbridge Rd (44039-4101)
PHONE.................................440 315-3856
Holly Kennedy, *Principal*
EMP: 4
SALES (est): 240.3K **Privately Held**
SIC: 2051 Bread, cake & related products

(G-15219)
CUYAHOGA VENDING CO INC
Also Called: Cuyahoga Group, The
39405 Taylor Pkwy (44035-6264)
PHONE.................................440 353-9595
EMP: 15
SALES (est): 2.5MM
SALES (corp-wide): 50.8MM **Privately Held**
SIC: 7359 2099 Vending machine rental; food preparations
PA: Cuyahoga Vending Co., Inc.
14250 Industrial Ave S # 104
Maple Heights OH 44137
216 663-2457

(G-15220)
DIRECT IMAGE SIGNS INC
7820 Maddock Rd (44039-3714)
PHONE.................................440 327-5575
Brett Smith, *President*
EMP: 3
SALES (est): 304.5K **Privately Held**
SIC: 3993 Electric signs

(G-15221)
DRECO INC
7887 Root Rd (44039-4013)
P.O. Box 39328 (44039-0328)
PHONE.................................440 327-6021
Christopher A Draudt, *President*
Russell Draudt, *President*
H T Ammerman, *Principal*
Harold F Ellsworth, *Principal*
Johanna S Rolfe, *Principal*
▲ EMP: 130 EST: 1932
SQ FT: 135,000
SALES (est): 18.5MM **Privately Held**
SIC: 3089 Injection molding of plastics

(G-15222)
ECHOGRAPHICS INC
9454 Grist Mill Dr (44039-9702)
P.O. Box 742, Berea (44017-0742)
PHONE.................................440 846-2330
James Fogleson, *President*
Linda Fogleson, *Corp Secy*
Carl Mieyal, *Vice Pres*
Jim Fogleson, *Human Res Mgr*
▲ EMP: 3
SQ FT: 2,000
SALES (est): 466.6K **Privately Held**
WEB: www.echographics.com
SIC: 2752 2759 5199 7336 Commercial printing, offset; business forms: printing; screen printing; advertising specialties; commercial art & graphic design

(G-15223)
FATE INDUSTRIES INC
36682 Sugar Ridge Rd (44039-3832)
PHONE.................................440 327-1770
Rick Fate, *President*
Julie Fate, *Admin Sec*
EMP: 8
SQ FT: 2,800
SALES (est): 1MM **Privately Held**
SIC: 3599 Machine shop, jobbing & repair

(G-15224)
FEDERAL BARCODE LABEL SYSTEMS
33438 Liberty Pkwy (44039-2670)
PHONE.................................440 748-8060
James K Jenkins, *President*
James Jenkins Jr, *Vice Pres*
EMP: 5
SQ FT: 5,200
SALES: 330K **Privately Held**
WEB: www.federalbarcode.com
SIC: 2679 2759 5045 Tags & labels, paper; labels & seals: printing; computer software

(G-15225)
FINE WOOD DESIGN INC
35535 Center Ridge Rd (44039-3019)
PHONE.................................440 327-0751
Uwe Neumann, *Principal*
EMP: 5
SALES (est): 653.7K **Privately Held**
SIC: 2434 5712 Wood kitchen cabinets; customized furniture & cabinets

(G-15226)
FROHOCK-STEWART INC
39400 Taylor Pkwy (44035-6263)
PHONE.................................440 329-6000
▲ EMP: 40 EST: 1954
SALES (est): 3.2MM
SALES (corp-wide): 1B **Publicly Held**
SIC: 3842 Manufactures Orthopedic Prosthetic Or Surgical Appliances Or Supplies
PA: Invacare Corporation
1 Invacare Way
Elyria OH 44035
440 329-6000

(G-15227)
GLAXOSMITHKLINE LLC
37381 Stone Creek Dr (44039-1243)
PHONE.................................440 552-2895
EMP: 26
SALES (corp-wide): 39.8B **Privately Held**
SIC: 2834 Pharmaceutical preparations
HQ: Glaxosmithkline Llc
5 Crescent Dr
Philadelphia PA 19112
215 751-4000

(G-15228)
HEIL ENGNEERED PROCESS EQP INC
37000 Center Ridge Rd (44039-2804)
PHONE.................................440 327-6051
Kyle Hankinson, *President*
James Hark, *Controller*
EMP: 13
SALES (est): 573.4K **Privately Held**
SIC: 3559 Chemical machinery & equipment

(G-15229)
HOISTECH LLC
5131 Mills Indus Pkwy (44039-1957)
PHONE.................................440 327-5379
Ray Mack,
EMP: 6 EST: 2010
SALES (est): 588.8K **Privately Held**
SIC: 3949 Sporting & athletic goods

(G-15230)
IMPACT INDUSTRIES INC
5120 Mills Indus Pkwy (44039-1958)
PHONE.................................440 327-2360
William Nestor, *President*
Leslie Nestor, *Vice Pres*
EMP: 41
SQ FT: 25,000
SALES (est): 6.5MM **Privately Held**
WEB: www.impactindustries.com
SIC: 3469 3544 Stamping metal for the trade; special dies & tools; jigs & fixtures

(G-15231)
INVACARE CORPORATION
Also Called: Invacare Hme
38683 Taylor Pkwy (44035-6200)
PHONE.................................440 329-6000
Brad Kushner, *Branch Mgr*
EMP: 14
SALES (corp-wide): 972.3MM **Publicly Held**
WEB: www.invacare.com
SIC: 3842 Surgical appliances & supplies
PA: Invacare Corporation
1 Invacare Way
Elyria OH 44035
440 329-6000

(G-15232)
INVACARE CORPORATION (TW)
39400 Taylor Pkwy (44035-6270)
PHONE.................................440 329-6000
A Malachi Mixon III, *President*
Mary Whitesel, *Manager*
◆ EMP: 45
SALES (est): 1.6B **Privately Held**
SIC: 3842 Surgical appliances & supplies

(G-15233)
IRONHOUSE PALLETS
5212 Mills Indus Pkwy (44039-1960)
P.O. Box 39161 (44039-0161)
PHONE.................................330 635-5218
EMP: 4
SALES (est): 325.8K **Privately Held**
SIC: 2448 Pallets, wood & wood with metal

(G-15234)
JBC TECHNOLOGIES INC
7887 Bliss Pkwy (44039-3475)
PHONE.................................440 327-4522
Joe Bliss, *CEO*
Brenda Doskocil, *VP Bus Dvlpt*
Jill Wallace, *Manager*
▲ EMP: 55
SALES (est): 14.1MM **Privately Held**
WEB: www.jbc-tech.com
SIC: 3423 Cutting dies, except metal cutting

(G-15235)
KALT MANUFACTURING COMPANY
36700 Sugar Ridge Rd (44039-3800)
PHONE.................................440 327-2102
Joseph W Kalt, *President*
William E Kalt, *Principal*
John Lowstetter, *Prdtn Mgr*
Matthew Skladan, *Purch Mgr*
Jeanne M Kalt, *Treasurer*
▲ EMP: 54
SQ FT: 60,000
SALES (est): 13.6MM **Privately Held**
WEB: www.kaltmfg.com
SIC: 3544 3545 3549 3599 Special dies & tools; machine tool accessories; metalworking machinery; machine shop, jobbing & repair

(G-15236)
KITCHEN WORKS INC
34425 Lorain Rd Ste 5 (44039-4492)
PHONE.................................440 353-0939
Dan Vaneck, *President*
Lisa Stoltz, *Vice Pres*
Jose Cendelero, *Treasurer*
EMP: 3
SQ FT: 7,500
SALES: 320K **Privately Held**
SIC: 2434 2522 1799 1521 Wood kitchen cabinets; cabinets, office: except wood; kitchen & bathroom remodeling; general remodeling, single-family houses; cabinet work, custom

(G-15237)
LAKE ERIE MACHINE
5165 Mills Indus Pkwy (44039-1957)
PHONE.................................440 353-9191
Jeff Reed, *Owner*
EMP: 4
SALES (est): 383.8K **Privately Held**
SIC: 3599 Machine shop, jobbing & repair

(G-15238)
LEAR MANUFACTURING INC
7855 Race Rd (44039-3615)
PHONE.................................440 327-4545
Bonnie Lear, *President*
John Lear, *Corp Secy*
EMP: 5
SQ FT: 2,688
SALES (est): 666.1K **Privately Held**
SIC: 3451 3545 Screw machine products; machine tool attachments & accessories

(G-15239)
LORAIN RULED DIE PRODUCTS INC
6287 Lear Nagle Rd Ste 4 (44039-3369)
PHONE.................................440 281-8607
Roger Galippo, *President*
EMP: 6
SQ FT: 2,800
SALES: 600K **Privately Held**
SIC: 3544 Dies, steel rule

(G-15240)
MAXIMUM GRAPHIX INC
33426 Liberty Pkwy (44039-2670)
PHONE.................................440 353-3301
Gregory Comwell, *President*
Kimberly Cromwell, *Vice Pres*
EMP: 5
SQ FT: 2,200
SALES: 300K **Privately Held**
SIC: 2752 7336 Commercial printing, offset; commercial art & graphic design

(G-15241)
NORLAKE MANUFACTURING COMPANY
39301 Taylor Pkwy (44035-6272)
P.O. Box 215, Elyria (44036-0215)
PHONE.................................440 353-3200
James Markus, *President*
Daryl Jackson, *Vice Pres*
▼ EMP: 90 EST: 1963
SQ FT: 50,000
SALES (est): 36.2MM **Privately Held**
WEB: www.norlakemfg.com
SIC: 3677 3714 3612 Transformers power supply, electronic type; motor vehicle parts & accessories; transformers, except electric

(G-15242)
NORTH EAST TECHNOLOGIES INC
5127 Mills Indus Pkwy (44039-1957)
PHONE.................................440 327-9278
Harry Salverson, *President*
EMP: 5 EST: 1995
SQ FT: 2,500
SALES (est): 703.4K **Privately Held**
SIC: 3541 Gear cutting & finishing machines

(G-15243)
P M MOTOR COMPANY
Also Called: P M Motor -Fan Blade Company
37850 Taylor Pkwy (44039-3643)
PHONE.................................440 327-9999
Michael Macken, *President*
Catherine E Macken, *Corp Secy*
Joan B Macken, *Vice Pres*
EMP: 14 EST: 1952
SQ FT: 10,000
SALES (est): 1.6MM **Privately Held**
WEB: www.pmfan.com
SIC: 3469 Machine parts, stamped or pressed metal

(G-15244)
PLEXTRUSIONS INC
38870 Taylor Pkwy (44035-6254)
PHONE.................................330 668-2587
Eve Gribble, *Principal*
EMP: 9
SALES (est): 1.3MM **Privately Held**
SIC: 3083 Thermoplastic laminates: rods, tubes, plates & sheet

(G-15245)
POPPEES POPCORN INC
38727 Taylor Pkwy (44035-6275)
PHONE.................................440 327-0775
Tim McGuir, *President*
Jennifer McGuire, *Vice Pres*
Tom McGuire, *Sales Staff*
EMP: 32 EST: 1948
SQ FT: 20,000
SALES (est): 6.3MM **Privately Held**
SIC: 2096 Potato chips & similar snacks

(G-15246)
PROTECTIVE INDUSTRIAL POLYMERS
7875 Bliss Pkwy (44039-3475)
PHONE.................................440 327-0015
Patrick Scudder, *President*
Jason Tobias, *Business Mgr*
Don Batke, *Opers Mgr*
Craig Scudder, *Finance Dir*
Sean Walsh, *Manager*
EMP: 10
SALES (est): 845.8K **Privately Held**
SIC: 1771 2515 2822 8741 Flooring contractor; mattresses, containing felt, foam rubber, urethane, etc.; ethylene-propylene rubbers, EPDM polymers; construction management

(G-15247)
PURITAS METAL PRODUCTS INC
7720 Race Rd (44039-3614)
PHONE.................................440 353-1917

North Ridgeville - Lorain County (G-15248)

Richard Cook, *CEO*
EMP: 15
SQ FT: 15,000
SALES (est): 2.4MM **Privately Held**
WEB: www.puritasmetal.com
SIC: 3599 Ties, form: metal

(G-15248)
QUALITY COMPOUND MFG
5212 Mills Indus Pkwy (44039-1960)
PHONE................................440 353-0150
Jeff Hopkins, *Mng Member*
EMP: 5
SALES (est): 538.6K **Privately Held**
SIC: 3999 Manufacturing industries

(G-15249)
RAVEN CONCEALMENT SYSTEMS LLC
7889 Root Rd (44039-4013)
PHONE................................440 508-9000
John Chapman, *CEO*
Kelly Laurence, *General Mgr*
Vicky Sawyer, *General Mgr*
John K Famlacher, *Principal*
Dotson Burton, *Principal*
EMP: 11
SALES (est): 388.3K **Privately Held**
SIC: 5399 3949 3089 Army-Navy goods; cases, gun & rod (sporting equipment); injection molding of plastics

(G-15250)
RETAYS WELDING COMPANY
7650 Race Rd (44039-3612)
PHONE................................440 327-4100
Allen Retay, *President*
Marilyn Hoskinson, *Admin Sec*
EMP: 25 EST: 1973
SQ FT: 28,000
SALES: 1.8MM **Privately Held**
SIC: 3443 3441 Fabricated plate work (boiler shop); fabricated structural metal

(G-15251)
RHENIUM ALLOYS INC (PA)
38683 Taylor Pkwy (44035-6200)
P.O. Box 245, Elyria (44036-0245)
PHONE................................440 365-7388
Mike Prokop, *President*
Todd Leonhardt, *Vice Pres*
William McVicker, *Controller*
Tim Carlson, *Sales Executive*
Martin Buck, *CTO*
▲ EMP: 60 EST: 1994
SQ FT: 35,500
SALES (est): 14.2MM **Privately Held**
WEB: www.rhenium.com
SIC: 3313 3356 3498 3339 Electrometallurgical products; tungsten, basic shapes; fabricated pipe & fittings; primary nonferrous metals; chemical preparations; ferroalloy ores, except vanadium

(G-15252)
RW BECKETT CORPORATION (PA)
38251 Center Ridge Rd (44039-2895)
P.O. Box 1289, Elyria (44036-1289)
PHONE................................440 327-1060
John D Beckett, *Ch of Bd*
John Beckett, *Ch of Bd*
Kevin D Beckett, *Ch of Bd*
Mark Kasinec, *Vice Pres*
Brendan Grace, *VP Opers*
◆ EMP: 193 EST: 1937
SQ FT: 40,000
SALES (est): 32.7MM **Privately Held**
WEB: www.lovingmonday.com
SIC: 3433 Oil burners, domestic or industrial

(G-15253)
SAVANNA TOOL AND MANUFACTURING
34395 Mills Rd (44039-2060)
PHONE................................440 327-8330
Stephen Santa, *President*
Phil Santa, *Vice Pres*
EMP: 5
SQ FT: 5,000
SALES (est): 500K **Privately Held**
SIC: 3599 Machine shop, jobbing & repair

(G-15254)
TANGO ECHO BRAVO MFG INC
4915 Mills Indus Pkwy (44039-1953)
PHONE................................440 937-3800
Timothy E Bennett, *President*
EMP: 6
SQ FT: 2,800
SALES (est): 575.6K **Privately Held**
SIC: 3999 Barber & beauty shop equipment

(G-15255)
THE METAL MARKER MFG CO
6225 Lear Nagle Rd (44039-3223)
PHONE................................440 327-2300
William Primrose, *President*
Mike Solarz, *Vice Pres*
Brian Rice, *Production*
Robin Dunbar, *Accountant*
Dave Odonnell, *Sales Mgr*
EMP: 13
SQ FT: 16,000
SALES (est): 1.2MM **Privately Held**
WEB: www.metalmarkermfg.com
SIC: 3953 Marking devices

(G-15256)
TOOL & DIE SYSTEMS INC
38900 Taylor Indus Pkwy (44039)
PHONE................................440 327-5800
Leonard Sikora, *President*
William T Flickinger, *Vice Pres*
Frank Greszler, *Manager*
Tom Sibert, *Network Analyst*
Jim Beal, *Associate*
EMP: 28
SQ FT: 60,000
SALES (est): 5.9MM **Privately Held**
WEB: www.tooldiesystems.com
SIC: 3444 3469 3599 3479 Sheet metalwork; metal stampings; machine shop, jobbing & repair; painting of metal products

(G-15257)
UNIVERSITY ACCESSORIES INC
Also Called: Avetec Products Group
5152 Mills Indus Pkwy (44039-1958)
PHONE................................440 327-4151
Douglas J Cook, *President*
Justin Simon, *Warehouse Mgr*
Moe Jemiola, *Purch Mgr*
Alice Linn, *Treasurer*
▲ EMP: 5
SQ FT: 5,500
SALES (est): 2.5MM **Privately Held**
WEB: www.usecure.com
SIC: 5065 5577 Electronic parts & equipment; computer peripheral equipment

(G-15258)
US REFRACTORY PRODUCTS LLC
7660 Race Rd (44039-3612)
PHONE................................440 386-4580
William Drake, *Vice Pres*
Gary M Demarco, *Mng Member*
▲ EMP: 25
SQ FT: 30,000
SALES (est): 5.5MM **Privately Held**
SIC: 3297 Nonclay refractories

North Royalton
Cuyahoga County

(G-15259)
AMCLO GROUP INC
9721 York Alpha Dr (44133-3505)
PHONE................................216 791-8400
William Harkins, *President*
Karl Morganthaler, *Admin Sec*
EMP: 101
SQ FT: 39,000
SALES (est): 15.3MM **Privately Held**
WEB: www.amclo.com
SIC: 3469 3089 Stamping metal for the trade; injection molding of plastics

(G-15260)
ANDREW TOOL CO INC
12146 York Rd Unit 2 (44133-3678)
PHONE................................440 237-4340
Kevin Yeo, *President*
Alice Yeo, *Treasurer*
EMP: 3
SQ FT: 3,400
SALES (est): 408.6K **Privately Held**
SIC: 3599 Machine shop, jobbing & repair

(G-15261)
AXEL AUSTIN LLC
10147 Royalton Rd Ste I (44133-4462)
PHONE................................440 237-1610
▼ EMP: 3 EST: 2012
SQ FT: 1,200
SALES (est): 330K **Privately Held**
SIC: 3625 Mfg Relays/Industrial Controls

(G-15262)
BARTAN DESIGN INC
10316 Edgerton Rd (44133-5543)
PHONE................................216 267-6474
Mircea S Bartan, *President*
Rabu Bartan, *Vice Pres*
Maria Bartan, *Admin Sec*
EMP: 3 EST: 1999
SALES (est): 220K **Privately Held**
WEB: www.bartandesign.com
SIC: 3281 Granite, cut & shaped

(G-15263)
BEST EQUIPMENT CO INC
12620 York Delta Dr (44133-3559)
PHONE................................440 237-3515
Mike Dahlman, *Mng Member*
EMP: 8
SALES (est): 1.1MM
SALES (corp-wide): 24MM **Privately Held**
SIC: 3589 Sewer cleaning equipment, power
PA: Best Equipment Co Inc
5550 Poindexter Dr
Indianapolis IN 46235
317 823-3050

(G-15264)
BSK INDUSTRIES INC (PA)
10143 Royalton Rd Ste C (44133-4463)
P.O. Box 33697 (44133-0697)
PHONE................................440 230-9299
Stephen Kisan, *President*
EMP: 10
SALES (est): 1.9MM **Privately Held**
WEB: www.bskindustries.com
SIC: 3823 8711 Industrial process control instruments; consulting engineer

(G-15265)
CARDINAL PRODUCTS INC
11929 Abbey Rd Ste D (44133-2664)
PHONE................................440 237-8280
Janet Stanley, *President*
EMP: 8
SQ FT: 10,000
SALES (est): 950K **Privately Held**
SIC: 3089 Molding primary plastic

(G-15266)
CHARLES V SNIDER & ASSOC INC
10139 Royalton Rd Ste K (44133-4473)
PHONE................................440 877-9151
Charles V Snider, *President*
EMP: 10
SQ FT: 3,200
SALES (est): 1.4MM **Privately Held**
WEB: www.cvsniderlaw.com
SIC: 3949 Playground equipment

(G-15267)
CPMG
12955 York Delta Dr Ste G (44133-3550)
PHONE................................440 263-2780
Michael W Johns, *Owner*
EMP: 5
SALES (est): 348.1K **Privately Held**
SIC: 3499 Fabricated metal products

(G-15268)
D J METRO MOLD & DIE INC
9841 York Alpha Dr Ste J (44133-3554)
PHONE................................440 237-1130
David Metro, *President*
EMP: 5
SALES (est): 524.1K **Privately Held**
SIC: 3544 3089 Special dies & tools; injection molding of plastics

(G-15269)
DENTAL SEALANTS
7029 Royalton Rd (44133-4874)
PHONE................................440 582-3466
EMP: 3
SALES (est): 123.2K **Privately Held**
SIC: 2891 Sealants

(G-15270)
EAGLE PRECISION PRODUCTS LLC
13800 Progress Pkwy Ste J (44133-4354)
PHONE................................440 582-9393
Joshua Reger, *Vice Pres*
Bruce Reger, *CFO*
EMP: 9
SQ FT: 18,000
SALES: 2MM **Privately Held**
WEB: www.eagleprecisionproducts.com
SIC: 3469 3544 Stamping metal for the trade; special dies & tools

(G-15271)
ENVIRNMNTAL CMPLIANCE TECH LLC
Also Called: Ect
13953 Progress Pkwy (44133-4305)
PHONE................................216 634-0400
Amin Mohammad,
EMP: 6
SALES (est): 608.6K **Privately Held**
WEB: www.enviro-ctech.com
SIC: 1799 4959 3826 Petroleum storage tanks, pumping & draining; environmental cleanup services; environmental testing equipment

(G-15272)
FGM MEDIA INC
13981 Stoney Creek Dr (44133-4114)
P.O. Box 33411 (44133-0411)
PHONE................................440 376-0487
Frank Malec, *President*
Paulette Holland, *Admin Sec*
EMP: 5
SALES (est): 400K **Privately Held**
WEB: www.fgmmedia.com
SIC: 2741 7371 7389 Technical manual & paper publishing; custom computer programming services;

(G-15273)
GARDELLA JEWELRY LLC
Also Called: Earth Dreams Jewelry
7432 Julia Dr (44133-3715)
PHONE................................440 877-9261
Jacqueline Magyar, *COO*
David Magyar, *CFO*
EMP: 6 EST: 2011
SALES (est): 576.2K **Privately Held**
SIC: 3961 7389 Jewelry apparel, non-precious metals; business services

(G-15274)
GRABER METAL WORKS INC
9664 Akins Rd Ste 1 (44133-4595)
PHONE................................440 237-8422
Steve M Graber Sr, *President*
Michael R Horvath, *Vice Pres*
Katherine Graber, *Treasurer*
EMP: 30 EST: 1965
SQ FT: 25,000
SALES (est): 3MM **Privately Held**
WEB: www.grabermetal.com
SIC: 3599 5051 3446 3444 Machine shop, jobbing & repair; tubing, flexible metallic; metals service centers & offices; architectural metalwork; sheet metalwork; fabricated plate work (boiler shop); fabricated structural metal

(G-15275)
H & D STEEL SERVICE INC
Also Called: H & D Steel Service Center
9960 York Alpha Dr (44133-3588)
PHONE................................440 237-3390
Raymond Gary Schreiber, *Ch of Bd*
Joseph Bubba, *President*
Joseph A Cachat, *Principal*
R M Jones, *Principal*
R G Schreiber, *Principal*
▲ EMP: 50
SQ FT: 125,000

▲ = Import ▼ = Export
◆ = Import/Export

GEOGRAPHIC SECTION — North Royalton - Cuyahoga County (G-15306)

SALES (est): 53.9MM **Privately Held**
WEB: www.hdsteel.com
SIC: 5051 3541 5085 Iron or steel flat products; sheets, metal; tubing, metal; bars, metal; home workshop machine tools, metalworking; industrial tools

(G-15276)
HAWK ENGINE & MACHINE
12166 York Rd Unit 1 (44133-3689)
PHONE..................................440 582-0900
Terry R Hawk, *President*
Denise Hawk, *Admin Sec*
EMP: 3 EST: 1975
SQ FT: 3,200
SALES: 200K **Privately Held**
SIC: 3599 2431 Machine & other job shop work; millwork

(G-15277)
INDUCTION TOOLING INC
12510 York Delta Dr (44133-3543)
PHONE..................................440 237-0711
William Stuehr, *President*
John Chesna, *Engineer*
John Gadus, *Engineer*
Sherry Stuehr, *Human Res Dir*
David Lynch, *Mktg Dir*
EMP: 20
SQ FT: 25,000
SALES (est): 4.8MM **Privately Held**
WEB: www.inductiontooling.com
SIC: 3567 Induction heating equipment

(G-15278)
INDUSTRIAL PARTS DEPOT LLC
Also Called: I P D
11266 Royalton Rd (44133-4474)
PHONE..................................440 237-9164
Jeff Guiliano, *Branch Mgr*
EMP: 6
SALES (corp-wide): 76MM **Privately Held**
SIC: 3519 5084 Parts & accessories, internal combustion engines; engines & parts, diesel
HQ: Industrial Parts Depot, Llc
    23231 Normandie Ave
    Torrance CA 90501
    310 530-1900

(G-15279)
JAGUAR MEDICAL SUPPLIES INC
12955 York Delta Dr Ste G (44133-3550)
PHONE..................................440 263-2780
Michael Johns, *President*
EMP: 3
SALES (est): 138.5K **Privately Held**
SIC: 3499 Machine bases, metal

(G-15280)
KENT CORPORATION
9601 York Alpha Dr (44133-3503)
PHONE..................................440 582-3400
Dean Costello, *CEO*
David Tsai, *President*
Mark Costello, *Admin Sec*
▲ EMP: 31
SQ FT: 22,000
SALES (est): 9.3MM **Privately Held**
WEB: www.kenttesgo.com
SIC: 3549 Coiling machinery

(G-15281)
KRIST KRENZ MACHINE INC
9801 York Alpha Dr (44133-3507)
PHONE..................................440 237-1800
Richard Krenz Jr, *President*
Alfred Krist, *Vice Pres*
Adam Krenz, *Treasurer*
Paul Krenz, *Admin Sec*
EMP: 65
SQ FT: 35,000
SALES (est): 9.4MM **Privately Held**
WEB: www.krenzkristmachine.com
SIC: 3451 Screw machine products

(G-15282)
L B FOLDING CO INC
12126 York Rd Unit F (44133-3688)
PHONE..................................216 961-0870
Richard Happensack, *President*
Geraldine Happensack, *Corp Secy*
EMP: 3
SQ FT: 25,260
SALES: 500K **Privately Held**
SIC: 2789 3554 Binding only: books, pamphlets, magazines, etc.; folding machines, paper

(G-15283)
LASZERAY TECHNOLOGY LLC
12315 York Delta Dr (44133-3544)
PHONE..................................440 582-8430
Greg Clark, *CEO*
Steve Patton, *Vice Pres*
▲ EMP: 81 EST: 1997
SQ FT: 60,000
SALES (est): 26.2MM **Privately Held**
WEB: www.laszeray.com
SIC: 3089 3544 Injection molding of plastics; special dies, tools, jigs & fixtures

(G-15284)
LOZINAK & SONS INC
8695 York Rd (44133-1506)
PHONE..................................440 877-1819
Jerry Liveneck, *President*
EMP: 3
SALES (est): 286.8K **Privately Held**
SIC: 3241 Masonry cement

(G-15285)
LUNAR TOOL & MOLD INC
9860 York Alpha Dr (44133-3586)
PHONE..................................440 237-2141
Friedrich Hoffman Jr, *President*
Kyle Shane, *Design Engr*
EMP: 19 EST: 1965
SQ FT: 20,000
SALES (est): 2.8MM **Privately Held**
WEB: www.lunarmold.com
SIC: 3544 7692 Special dies & tools; industrial molds; welding repair

(G-15286)
MAY CONVEYOR INC
9981 York Theta Dr (44133-3545)
PHONE..................................440 237-8012
Leonard May, *President*
Matias Dost, *Vice Pres*
▲ EMP: 15
SQ FT: 55,000
SALES (est): 2MM **Privately Held**
WEB: www.mayconveyor.com
SIC: 3496 Conveyor belts

(G-15287)
MDF TOOL CORPORATION
10166 Royalton Rd (44133-4427)
PHONE..................................440 237-2277
John Bunjevac, *CEO*
Larry Jackson, *President*
Jason Panaro, *Engineer*
Mark Geiger, *Design Engr*
EMP: 18 EST: 1980
SQ FT: 8,000
SALES (est): 3.2MM **Privately Held**
WEB: www.mdftool.com
SIC: 3544 3545 Special dies & tools; machine tool accessories

(G-15288)
NEXT GERENATION CRIMPING
Also Called: N G C
9880 York Alpha Dr (44133-3508)
PHONE..................................440 237-6300
Fred Krist, *Partner*
EMP: 8
SALES (est): 949K **Privately Held**
SIC: 3432 Plumbing fixture fittings & trim

(G-15289)
NU-TOOL INDUSTRIES INC
9920 York Alpha Dr (44133-3510)
PHONE..................................440 237-9240
Bruce Thompson, *President*
Richard Kuper, *Vice Pres*
Daniel Worthington, *Vice Pres*
EMP: 14
SQ FT: 8,000
SALES (est): 2.5MM **Privately Held**
WEB: www.nutoolind.com
SIC: 3599 Machine shop, jobbing & repair

(G-15290)
OAK INDUSTRIAL INC
12955 York Delta Dr Ste G (44133-3550)
PHONE..................................440 263-2780
Michael Johns, *CEO*
Russ Karla, *COO*
EMP: 7
SQ FT: 5,000
SALES: 500K **Privately Held**
SIC: 3599 Machine & other job shop work

(G-15291)
OIL SKIMMERS INC
12800 York Rd Ste G (44133-3682)
P.O. Box 33092 (44133-0092)
PHONE..................................440 237-4600
William R Townsend, *President*
Jim Petrucci, *Vice Pres*
Peter King, *Opers Mgr*
Craig Riley, *Purch Mgr*
Ken Gray, *Sales Mgr*
EMP: 22
SQ FT: 100,000
SALES: 6.2MM **Privately Held**
WEB: www.oilskim.com
SIC: 3569 3564 3533 3443 Filters; blowers & fans; oil & gas field machinery; fabricated plate work (boiler shop); filters, air & oil

(G-15292)
PALLET GUYS
12720 N Star Dr (44133-5945)
PHONE..................................440 897-3001
Josh Wentz, *Principal*
EMP: 4 EST: 2010
SALES (est): 295.8K **Privately Held**
SIC: 2448 Pallets, wood & wood with metal

(G-15293)
PARMA INTERNATIONAL INC
13927 Progress Pkwy (44133-4394)
PHONE..................................440 237-8650
Michael S Macdowell, *President*
Haydee Cooke, *Principal*
Giuseppe Franza, *Purchasing*
Mark Mathis, *Art Dir*
▲ EMP: 45
SQ FT: 17,000
SALES (est): 6MM **Privately Held**
WEB: www.parmapse.com
SIC: 3944 Automobile & truck models, toy & hobby

(G-15294)
PART RITE INC
12855 York Delta Dr (44133-3539)
PHONE..................................216 362-4100
Daniel W Mihovk, *President*
Sharon C Mihovk, *Corp Secy*
EMP: 3 EST: 1964
SQ FT: 5,000
SALES (est): 346.7K **Privately Held**
SIC: 3599 3544 Machine shop, jobbing & repair; special dies, tools, jigs & fixtures

(G-15295)
PAUL POPOV
Also Called: Product Machine Company
13800 Progress Pkwy Ste A (44133-4354)
PHONE..................................440 582-6677
Fax: 440 582-6680
EMP: 3
SALES (est): 250K **Privately Held**
SIC: 3599 Mfg Industrial Machinery

(G-15296)
PRECISE TUBE FORMING INC
9591 York Alpha Dr Ste 7 (44133-3555)
P.O. Box 425, East Palestine (44413-0425)
PHONE..................................440 237-3956
EMP: 7 EST: 1996
SQ FT: 6,000
SALES (est): 830K **Privately Held**
SIC: 3498 Mfg Fabricated Pipe/Fittings Specialzies In Assembling

(G-15297)
ROYAL WIRE PRODUCTS INC (PA)
13450 York Delta Dr (44133-3584)
PHONE..................................440 237-8787
William F Peshina, *President*
William Nelson, *Vice Pres*
Paige Peshina, *Vice Pres*
Victor Grima, *Plant Mgr*
▲ EMP: 100
SQ FT: 35,000
SALES: 19MM **Privately Held**
SIC: 3496 Cages, wire

(G-15298)
ROYALTON ARCHTCTRAL FBRICATION
13155 York Delta Dr (44133-3522)
PHONE..................................440 582-0400
Stefan Winkler, *President*
EMP: 13
SQ FT: 10,000
SALES (est): 1.6MM **Privately Held**
WEB: www.rafpanels.com
SIC: 3444 3446 Sheet metalwork; architectural metalwork

(G-15299)
ROYALTON FOOD SERVICE EQP CO
9981 York Theta Dr (44133-3545)
PHONE..................................440 237-0806
Leonard May, *President*
Hannelore May, *Corp Secy*
EMP: 20
SQ FT: 40,000
SALES (est): 3.7MM **Privately Held**
SIC: 3556 3631 Food products machinery; household cooking equipment

(G-15300)
ROYALTON RECORDER
13737 State Rd (44133-3907)
PHONE..................................440 237-2235
Maria Magmelli, *President*
EMP: 5
SALES (est): 292.7K **Privately Held**
SIC: 2711 Newspapers

(G-15301)
S & D ARCHITECTURAL METALS
12955 York Delta Dr (44133-3534)
PHONE..................................440 582-2560
Cynthia Blessing, *President*
Keith Blessing, *Vice Pres*
EMP: 7
SALES (est): 832.5K **Privately Held**
SIC: 3444 Sheet metalwork

(G-15302)
SPA POOL COVERS INC
7806 Royalton Rd (44133-4708)
PHONE..................................440 235-9981
Rudy J Martinez, *President*
Gail A Martinez, *Vice Pres*
Theresa L Jedlinsky, *Admin Sec*
EMP: 5
SQ FT: 1,000
SALES: 150K **Privately Held**
SIC: 3423 1799 Leaf skimmers or swimming pool rakes; swimming pool construction

(G-15303)
SYLVAN FORGE INC
7420 James Dr (44133-3703)
PHONE..................................440 237-3626
Mike Mason, *President*
Eric Blackmore, *Vice Pres*
EMP: 7
SALES (est): 623.5K **Privately Held**
SIC: 2431 Woodwork, interior & ornamental

(G-15304)
SYMBOL TOOL & DIE INC
11000 Industrial First Av (44133-2678)
PHONE..................................440 582-5989
Jon Ardelian, *President*
EMP: 6
SQ FT: 4,000
SALES (est): 794.6K **Privately Held**
SIC: 3544 Special dies & tools

(G-15305)
SYSTEMATIC MACHINE CORP
12955 York Delta Dr Ste F (44133-3550)
PHONE..................................440 877-9884
Richard Locker, *President*
EMP: 3
SQ FT: 5,200
SALES: 228K **Privately Held**
SIC: 3541 Machine tools, metal cutting type

(G-15306)
TRAVELERS VACATION GUIDE
10143 Royalton Rd (44133-4470)
PHONE..................................440 582-4949

North Royalton - Cuyahoga County (G-15307)

Pam Voigt, *President*
EMP: 7
SQ FT: 1,400
SALES (est): 531.7K **Privately Held**
SIC: 2711 Newspapers: publishing only, not printed on site

(G-15307)
TRENDCO INC (PA)
8043 Corporate Cir Ste 1 (44133-1279)
P.O. Box 33397 (44133-0397)
PHONE..................................216 661-6903
Michael Lombardo, *President*
EMP: 4
SQ FT: 400
SALES (est): 1.8MM **Privately Held**
SIC: 3949 1799 Sporting & athletic goods; artificial turf installation

(G-15308)
TRIAXIS MACHINE & TOOL LLC
11941 Abbey Rd Ste H (44133-2663)
PHONE..................................440 230-0303
Mark Timura, *General Mgr*
Ray Timura, *Mng Member*
EMP: 5
SALES: 800K **Privately Held**
SIC: 5251 3089 7389 3599 Tools; injection molding of plastics; grinding, precision: commercial or industrial; chemical milling job shop; electrical discharge machining (EDM); blades, aircraft propeller: metal or wood

(G-15309)
VALLEY TOOL & DIE INC
Also Called: Valco Division
10020 York Theta Dr (44133-3581)
PHONE..................................440 237-0160
Adolf Eisenloeffel, *President*
Helmut Eisenloeffel, *Principal*
Ernst Peters, *Principal*
Phillip S Eisenloeffel, *Vice Pres*
EMP: 65 **EST:** 1968
SQ FT: 54,000
SALES (est): 12.9MM **Privately Held**
WEB: www.valcocleve.com
SIC: 3465 3451 3452 3542 Automotive stampings; screw machine products; bolts, nuts, rivets & washers; machine tools, metal forming type; metal stampings; special dies & tools

(G-15310)
WESTGATE MACHINE CO INC
10665 Knights Way (44133-1998)
PHONE..................................216 889-9745
Terry Macho, *President*
Michael Macho, *Vice Pres*
Larry Oster, *Treasurer*
Cindy De Groot, *CPA*
Carolyn Macho, *Admin Sec*
EMP: 5
SQ FT: 1,600
SALES: 300K **Privately Held**
SIC: 3599 Machine shop, jobbing & repair

(G-15311)
WHITE MACHINE INC
9621 York Alpha Dr (44133-3594)
PHONE..................................440 237-3282
Larry White, *President*
Ronald White, *Exec VP*
Ruth White, *Vice Pres*
Marita Castle, *Finance Mgr*
Ron White, *Consultant*
EMP: 8 **EST:** 1971
SQ FT: 7,600
SALES (est): 700K **Privately Held**
SIC: 3599 3728 3544 Machine shop, jobbing & repair; aircraft parts & equipment; special dies, tools, jigs & fixtures

(G-15312)
ZIEGLER ENGINEERING INC
9840 York Alpha Dr Ste F (44133-3553)
PHONE..................................440 582-8515
Ed Ziegler, *President*
EMP: 5
SQ FT: 5,400
SALES: 600K **Privately Held**
SIC: 3441 Fabricated structural metal

Northfield
Summit County

(G-15313)
BENCHMARK SIGNS AND GIFTS
80 Hazel Dr (44067-2820)
PHONE..................................216 973-3718
Salvatore Lardomita Jr, *Administration*
EMP: 3
SALES (est): 89.8K **Privately Held**
SIC: 3993 Signs & advertising specialties

(G-15314)
BULK HANDLING EQUIPMENT CO
28 W Aurora Rd (44067-2073)
P.O. Box 670855 (44067-0855)
PHONE..................................330 468-5703
Joseph Stakes, *President*
Joanne Stakes, *Vice Pres*
Mary Anne Stakes, *Admin Sec*
EMP: 7
SALES (est): 745.6K **Privately Held**
WEB: www.bulkhand.com
SIC: 3535 Bulk handling conveyor systems

(G-15315)
COLUMBIA STEEL AND WIRE INC
30 W Aurora Rd (44067-2004)
PHONE..................................330 468-2709
Marty Koppleman, *President*
Betty Koppleman, *Vice Pres*
EMP: 4
SQ FT: 8,000
SALES: 3.8MM **Privately Held**
WEB: www.columbiasteelandwire.com
SIC: 3316 5051 Bars, steel, cold finished, from purchased hot-rolled; steel

(G-15316)
CONNELL LIMITED PARTNERSHIP
Danly Die Set
154 E Aurora Rd Pmb 186 (44067-2053)
PHONE..................................877 534-8986
Dave Lowum, *President*
Tony Wolverton, *Purchasing*
John Coppolino, *Manager*
EMP: 60
SALES (corp-wide): 500MM **Privately Held**
WEB: www.connell-lp.com
SIC: 3544 3542 3568 3366 Die sets for metal stamping (presses); die springs; punches, forming & stamping; forms (molds), for foundry & plastics working machinery; presses: hydraulic & pneumatic, mechanical & manual; bearings, bushings & blocks; bushings & bearings; bushings & bearings, bronze (nonmachined); spring washers, metal; cams (machine tool accessories)
PA: Connell Limited Partnership
 1 International Pl Fl 31
 Boston MA 02110
 617 737-2700

(G-15317)
E Z ROUT INC
102 E Aurora Rd (44067-2019)
PHONE..................................330 467-4814
Keith Johnson, *President*
EMP: 3 **EST:** 1991
SALES (est): 307.9K **Privately Held**
SIC: 3423 Edge tools for woodworking: augers, bits, gimlets, etc.

(G-15318)
GENERAL DIE CASTERS INC
6212 Akron Peninsula Rd (44067)
PHONE..................................330 467-6700
Tom Lenin, *Branch Mgr*
EMP: 55
SQ FT: 45,136
SALES (corp-wide): 31.3MM **Privately Held**
WEB: www.generaldie.com
SIC: 3363 3364 Aluminum die-castings; zinc & zinc-base alloy die-castings
PA: General Die Casters, Inc.
 2150 Highland Rd
 Twinsburg OH 44087
 330 678-2528

(G-15319)
IN GOOD HLTH & ANIMAL WELLNESS
9425 Olde 8 Rd Ste 4 (44067-1944)
PHONE..................................330 908-1234
Susan Glassner, *Owner*
EMP: 3
SALES (est): 141.8K **Privately Held**
SIC: 2047 3199 Dog & cat food; dog furnishings: collars, leashes, muzzles, etc.: leather

(G-15320)
MOSBRO MACHINE AND TOOL INC
8135 Crystal Creek Rd (44067-1802)
PHONE..................................330 467-0913
Neal J Moss, *President*
Kenneth S Moss, *Vice Pres*
EMP: 3 **EST:** 1978
SQ FT: 8,000
SALES: 150K **Privately Held**
SIC: 3544 3559 Special dies, tools, jigs & fixtures; foundry machinery & equipment

(G-15321)
PARKSIDE & EATON ESTATE
8689 Parkside Dr (44067-1889)
PHONE..................................330 467-2995
William J Weigand, *Principal*
EMP: 3
SALES (est): 230K **Privately Held**
SIC: 3625 Mfg Relays/Industrial Controls

(G-15322)
PROGRESSIVE FOLDING BINDING CO
Also Called: Progressive Book Binding Co
8082 Augusta Ln (44067-1171)
PHONE..................................216 621-1893
Fax: 216 621-4434
EMP: 5 **EST:** 1944
SQ FT: 10,692
SALES (est): 420K **Privately Held**
SIC: 2789 Bookbinding/Related Work

(G-15323)
REXEL INC
805 Millstream Run (44056-1564)
PHONE..................................330 468-1122
EMP: 4
SALES (corp-wide): 3MM **Privately Held**
SIC: 5063 3699 3645 Whol Electrical Equipment Mfg Electrical Equipment/Supplies Mfg Residential Lighting Fixtures
HQ: Rexel, Inc.
 14951 Dallas Pkwy # 1000
 Dallas TX 75254
 972 387-3600

(G-15324)
SENTRY GRAPHICS INC
114 Hiram College Dr (44067-2415)
PHONE..................................440 735-0850
Thomas Uridel, *President*
David Uridel, *Vice Pres*
EMP: 8
SQ FT: 7,200
SALES: 1MM **Privately Held**
SIC: 2752 5112 Commercial printing, offset; business forms; stationers, commercial; envelopes

(G-15325)
SMARTRONIX INC
416 Apple Hill Dr (44067-1107)
PHONE..................................216 378-3300
Gyorgy M Kovacs, *President*
EMP: 12
SQ FT: 4,500
SALES: 1MM **Privately Held**
WEB: www.cablawonline.com
SIC: 3571 5045 7373 7378 Electronic computers; computers, peripherals & software; systems integration services; computer peripheral equipment repair & maintenance

(G-15326)
STEVES SPORTS INC
10333 Northfield Rd # 136 (44067-1443)
PHONE..................................440 735-0044
Steve Baraona, *Owner*
EMP: 6 **EST:** 2010
SALES (est): 816K **Privately Held**
SIC: 2759 Screen printing

(G-15327)
SUMMIT AEROSPACE PRODUCTS
159 Ballantrae Dr (44067-2481)
PHONE..................................330 612-7341
Henry Prusinski, *Principal*
EMP: 3
SALES (est): 311K **Privately Held**
SIC: 3721 Aircraft

(G-15328)
TERMINAL EQUIPMENT INDUSTRIES
64 Privet Ln (44067-2883)
PHONE..................................330 468-0322
Ernest Pugh, *President*
Priscilla Pugh, *Treasurer*
EMP: 6
SQ FT: 1,100
SALES (est): 669.1K **Privately Held**
SIC: 3542 Machine tools, metal forming type

(G-15329)
UNIQUE LED PRODUCTS LLC
200 Chestnut Ave (44067-1523)
PHONE..................................440 520-4959
Darrell Frycz, *Mng Member*
Linda Frycz,
EMP: 3
SALES (est): 182K **Privately Held**
SIC: 3993 Signs & advertising specialties

Northwood
Wood County

(G-15330)
ADIENT US LLC
7560 Arbor Dr (43619-7500)
PHONE..................................419 662-4950
Jeffrey Ryan Arnold, *Branch Mgr*
EMP: 250 **Privately Held**
SIC: 3714 Motor vehicle parts & accessories
HQ: Adient Us Llc
 49200 Halyard Dr
 Plymouth MI 48170
 734 254-5000

(G-15331)
AMERICAN COLD FORGE LLC
5650 Woodville Rd (43619-2322)
PHONE..................................419 836-1062
Dave Huber, *President*
Jeffrey Leverenz, *Treasurer*
Jim Babel, *Consultant*
EMP: 29
SALES (est): 1.1MM **Privately Held**
SIC: 5531 3462 3463 Automotive parts; automobile & truck equipment & parts; speed shops, including race car supplies; automotive & internal combustion engine forgings; automotive forgings, ferrous: crankshaft, engine, axle, etc.; automotive forgings, nonferrous

(G-15332)
ANALYTIC STRESS RELIEVING INC
Also Called: Western Stress
6944 Mcnerney Dr (43619-1079)
PHONE..................................804 271-7198
Martin Kellie, *Branch Mgr*
EMP: 7
SALES (corp-wide): 250MM **Privately Held**
SIC: 3398 5084 Metal heat treating; metalworking machinery
PA: Analytic Stress Relieving, Inc.
 3118 W Pinhook Rd Ste 202
 Lafayette LA 70508
 337 237-8790

GEOGRAPHIC SECTION

(G-15333)
AUTO-TRONIC CONTROL CO
240 W Andrus Rd (43619-1206)
PHONE..................................419 666-5100
Harold M Kowalka, *President*
Kenneth Kowalka, *Vice Pres*
Sharon A Kowalka, *Treasurer*
Thomas Balyat, *Admin Sec*
EMP: 15
SQ FT: 28,000
SALES (est): 3.3MM **Privately Held**
WEB: www.auto-tronic.com
SIC: 3613 Control panels, electric

(G-15334)
BERGMAN SAFETY SPANNER CO INC
3002 Woodville Rd Ste B (43619-1469)
PHONE..................................419 691-1462
Virginia Schlicher, *President*
Edythe Pocse, *Corp Secy*
Wayne F Bergman, *Vice Pres*
Beth Woodruff, *Manager*
EMP: 5
SQ FT: 1,198
SALES (est): 930.5K **Privately Held**
SIC: 3423 Wrenches, hand tools

(G-15335)
CONDOS AND TREES LLC
2674 Woodville Rd (43619-1446)
PHONE..................................419 691-2287
Donna McClellan, *Principal*
EMP: 3 **EST:** 2011
SALES (est): 251.2K **Privately Held**
SIC: 3999 Pet supplies

(G-15336)
ENK TENOFOUR LLC
2533 Tracy Rd (43619-1083)
PHONE..................................419 661-1465
Ron Flazingski,
▲ **EMP:** 8 **EST:** 2012
SALES (est): 869.1K **Privately Held**
SIC: 3443 Cylinders, pressure: metal plate

(G-15337)
FAB STEEL CO INC
240 W Andrus Rd (43619-1206)
PHONE..................................419 666-5100
Harold M Kowalka, *President*
Sharon A Kowalka, *Vice Pres*
Jerry Oblenis, *Vice Pres*
Thomas Balyat, *Admin Sec*
EMP: 14
SQ FT: 13,000
SALES: 546.7K **Privately Held**
WEB: www.fab-steel.com
SIC: 3444 Metal housings, enclosures, casings & other containers

(G-15338)
HIRZEL CANNING COMPANY (PA)
Also Called: Dei Fratelli
411 Lemoyne Rd (43619-1699)
PHONE..................................419 693-0531
Karl A Hirzel Jr, *President*
Bill Hirzel, *Plant Mgr*
Rick Kopec, *Plant Mgr*
Emily Neuenschwander, *QA Dir*
Isaac Schroeder, *Plant Engr*
▲ **EMP:** 100 **EST:** 1923
SQ FT: 250,000
SALES (est): 29.6MM **Privately Held**
WEB: www.hirzel.com
SIC: 2033 8611 2034 Tomato products: packaged in cans, jars, etc.; tomato juice: packaged in cans, jars, etc.; tomato paste: packaged in cans, jars, etc.; tomato purees: packaged in cans, jars, etc.; business associations; dehydrated fruits, vegetables, soups

(G-15339)
HOT GRAPHIC SERVICES INC
2595 Tracy Rd (43619-1004)
P.O. Box 307, Toledo (43697-0307)
PHONE..................................419 242-7000
Gregory D Shapiro, *President*
Flora I Shapiro, *Chairman*
Norman Shapiro, *Corp Secy*
Myron Shapiro, *Vice Pres*
EMP: 30 **EST:** 1976
SQ FT: 11,000
SALES (est): 5.2MM **Privately Held**
WEB: www.h-o-tgraphics.com
SIC: 2791 2752 Photocomposition, for the printing trade; commercial printing, offset

(G-15340)
MAGNA EXTERIORS AMERICA INC
Also Called: Norplas Industries
7825 Caple Blvd (43619-1078)
PHONE..................................419 662-3256
WEI Chua, *QC Mgr*
Chris Orchard, *Controller*
EMP: 600
SALES (corp-wide): 38.9B **Privately Held**
SIC: 3544 Special dies, tools, jigs & fixtures
HQ: Magna Exteriors Of America, Inc.
750 Tower Dr
Troy MI 48098
248 631-1100

(G-15341)
NORPLAS INDUSTRIES INC (DH)
Also Called: Magna
7825 Caple Blvd (43619-1070)
PHONE..................................419 662-3317
Donald J Walker, *CEO*
Ray Beil, *General Mgr*
Graham Burrow, *Vice Pres*
Corey Honisko, *Foreman/Supr*
Greg Garrow, *Engineer*
▲ **EMP:** 277
SQ FT: 450,000
SALES (est): 370.4MM
SALES (corp-wide): 38.9B **Privately Held**
SIC: 3714 Motor vehicle parts & accessories
HQ: Magna Exteriors Of America, Inc.
750 Tower Dr
Troy MI 48098
248 631-1100

(G-15342)
OAKLEY INDUSTRIES SUB ASSEMBLY
6317 Fairfield Dr (43619-7508)
PHONE..................................419 661-8888
Dick Schmeltz, *President*
EMP: 50
SALES (corp-wide): 129.2MM **Privately Held**
SIC: 3714 Motor vehicle body components & frame
PA: Oakley Industries Sub Assembly Division, Inc.
4333 Matthew
Flint MI 48507
810 720-4444

(G-15343)
PAWS & REMEMBER NWO
2121 Tracy Rd (43619-1324)
PHONE..................................419 662-9000
Kenny Chan, *Administration*
EMP: 3
SALES (est): 167.9K **Privately Held**
SIC: 3272 Burial vaults, concrete or pre-cast terrazzo

(G-15344)
PILKINGTON NORTH AMERICA INC
2401 E Broadway St (43619-1318)
PHONE..................................800 547-9280
Rodney Baker, *Research*
John N Tomik, *Senior Engr*
David Wagner, *Senior Engr*
Stephen Weidner, *VP Sls/Mktg*
Dan Lubelski, *Branch Mgr*
EMP: 125
SALES (corp-wide): 5.6B **Privately Held**
WEB: www.low-eglass.com
SIC: 3211 Flat glass
HQ: Pilkington North America, Inc.
811 Madison Ave Fl 3
Toledo OH 43604
419 247-3731

(G-15345)
ROYAL TOOL AND MACHINE LLC
5740 Woodville Rd (43619-2398)
PHONE..................................419 836-7781
Marco Vallera, *Mng Member*
EMP: 5
SQ FT: 10,000
SALES: 250K **Privately Held**
SIC: 3599 Machine shop, jobbing & repair

(G-15346)
TL INDUSTRIES INC (PA)
2541 Tracy Rd (43619-1097)
PHONE..................................419 666-8144
Joseph Young, *Vice Pres*
Theodore Stetschulte, *Vice Pres*
Paul Rodgers, *Prdtn Mgr*
Keith Kogler, *Purch Agent*
EMP: 105
SQ FT: 36,000
SALES (est): 31.6MM **Privately Held**
SIC: 8711 3444 3629 3679 Electrical or electronic engineering; sheet metalwork; battery chargers, rectifying or nonrotating; loads, electronic

(G-15347)
TOLEDO METAL FINISHING INC
Also Called: Toledo Deburring Co
7880 Caple Blvd (43619-1099)
PHONE..................................419 661-1422
Robert E Van Schoick Jr, *President*
EMP: 8
SQ FT: 18,000
SALES (est): 1MM **Privately Held**
SIC: 3471 Finishing, metals or formed products

(G-15348)
TRI COUNTY WHEEL AND RIM LTD
6943 Wales Rd Ste A (43619-1073)
PHONE..................................419 666-1760
Doug Montion, *Principal*
EMP: 4 **EST:** 2012
SALES (est): 475.7K **Privately Held**
SIC: 3715 Truck trailers

(G-15349)
TURNER VAULT CO
2121 Tracy Rd (43619-1324)
PHONE..................................419 537-1133
Steven Turner, *President*
EMP: 30
SALES (est): 5.3MM **Privately Held**
SIC: 3272 Burial vaults, concrete or pre-cast terrazzo

(G-15350)
WC SALES INC
Also Called: Whitney Company
5732 Woodville Rd Ste C (43619-2300)
P.O. Box 218, Williston (43468-0218)
PHONE..................................419 836-2300
David Whitney, *CEO*
EMP: 5
SALES (est): 798.9K **Privately Held**
WEB: www.greasetrapsales.com
SIC: 3599 5074 Machine & other job shop work; plumbing & hydronic heating supplies

(G-15351)
WESCO DISTRIBUTION INC
6519 Fairfield Dr (43619-7507)
PHONE..................................419 666-1670
Chad Marrison, *Branch Mgr*
EMP: 28 **Publicly Held**
SIC: 5085 3699 Industrial supplies; electrical equipment & supplies
HQ: Wesco Distribution, Inc.
225 W Station Square Dr # 700
Pittsburgh PA 15219

(G-15352)
WHITAKER FINISHING LLC
2707 Tracy Rd (43619-1050)
PHONE..................................419 666-7746
Greg Heminger, *President*
Jeffrey E Cooley,
Scott Helmke,
Scott Hilty,
▲ **EMP:** 30
SALES (est): 3.9MM **Privately Held**
SIC: 3471 Electroplating of metals or formed products

(G-15353)
XENOTRONIX/TLI INC
2541 Tracy Rd (43619-1004)
PHONE..................................407 331-4793
Joseph Young, *President*
▲ **EMP:** 3
SALES (est): 307.1K
SALES (corp-wide): 31.6MM **Privately Held**
WEB: www.xenotronix.com
SIC: 3629 Battery chargers, rectifying or nonrotating
PA: T.L. Industries, Inc.
2541 Tracy Rd
Northwood OH 43619
419 666-8144

(G-15354)
YANFENG US AUTOMOTIVE
Also Called: Johnson Contrls Authorized Dlr
7560 Arbor Dr (43619-7500)
PHONE..................................419 662-4905
Keith Wandell, *President*
EMP: 96
SALES (corp-wide): 55MM **Privately Held**
SIC: 2531 5075 Public building & related furniture; warm air heating & air conditioning
HQ: Yanfeng Us Automotive Interior Systems I Llc
41935 W 12 Mile Rd
Novi MI 48377
248 319-7333

Norton
Summit County

(G-15355)
ACCENT MANUFACTURING INC (PA)
Also Called: Accent Showroom & Design Ctr
1026 Gardner Blvd (44203-6670)
PHONE..................................330 724-7704
Timothy Bush, *CEO*
Tim Bush, *President*
Betty Bush, *Corp Secy*
Anthony Piatko, *Sales Mgr*
Tom Baum, *Manager*
EMP: 18 **EST:** 1962
SQ FT: 12,500
SALES (est): 1.3MM **Privately Held**
WEB: www.accentmanufacturing.com
SIC: 1751 3433 3431 3261 Cabinet building & installation; heating equipment, except electric; metal sanitary ware; vitreous plumbing fixtures; wood partitions & fixtures; table tops, marble

(G-15356)
ACE READY MIX LLC
3826 Summit Rd (44203-5380)
PHONE..................................330 745-8125
Cliff Perren, *Vice Pres*
Albert C Perren Jr, *Mng Member*
Rhonda Regan, *Admin Sec*
EMP: 5
SQ FT: 5,100
SALES: 750K **Privately Held**
SIC: 3273 Ready-mixed concrete

(G-15357)
ACE READY MIX CONCRETE CO INC
3826 Summit Rd (44203-5380)
PHONE..................................330 745-8125
Clifford Perren, *Vice Pres*
EMP: 10
SALES (est): 802.3K **Privately Held**
SIC: 3273 Ready-mixed concrete

(G-15358)
ACTION SPORTS APPAREL INC
3070 Wadsworth Rd (44203-5265)
PHONE..................................330 848-9300
Thomas Gough, *President*
EMP: 3
SQ FT: 4,500
SALES: 460K **Privately Held**
WEB: www.seisports.com
SIC: 2396 5091 2395 Screen printing on fabric articles; bowling equipment; pleating & stitching

Norton - Summit County (G-15359)

(G-15359)
AKRON INDUS MTR SLS & SVC INC
3041 Barber Rd (44203-1009)
PHONE.................................330 753-7624
Kevin Mitchell, *President*
EMP: 4
SQ FT: 10,000
SALES: 750K **Privately Held**
SIC: 7694 5063 Electric motor repair; motors, electric

(G-15360)
ALBERTS SCREEN PRINT INC
Also Called: Albert Screenprint
3704 Summit Rd (44203-5378)
P.O. Box 1041 (44203-9441)
PHONE.................................330 753-7559
Margaret Falkenstein, *CEO*
Albert Falkenstein Sr, *Ch of Bd*
Albert S Falkenstein, *President*
Patrick Finn, *Mfg Dir*
Mike Rybarczyk, *Purch Mgr*
▲ EMP: 115 EST: 1962
SQ FT: 103,000
SALES (est): 19.9MM **Privately Held**
WEB: www.albertinc.com
SIC: 2759 3993 2752 Screen printing; signs & advertising specialties; commercial printing, lithographic

(G-15361)
ALLEN MORGAN TRUCKING & REPAIR
Also Called: Pro Street Chassis Shop
4162 Greenwich Rd (44203-5434)
PHONE.................................330 336-5192
Al Morgan, *President*
Deborah Morgan, *Corp Secy*
EMP: 3
SQ FT: 4,000
SALES: 200K **Privately Held**
SIC: 3711 3354 Chassis, motor vehicle; aluminum rod & bar

(G-15362)
BUCKEYE FIELD MACHINING INC
Also Called: Tech Group
2131 Wadsworth Rd Ste 500 (44203-5317)
PHONE.................................330 336-7036
Ben Riley, *President*
Pauline Riley, *Manager*
EMP: 3
SALES: 140K **Privately Held**
SIC: 3599 Machine shop, jobbing & repair

(G-15363)
COMPASS SYSTEMS & SALES LLC
5185 New Haven Cir (44203-4672)
PHONE.................................330 733-2111
Robert S Sherrod, *President*
Mark Rubin, *Vice Pres*
Brenda Pavlantos, *Treasurer*
Phil Hart, *Admin Sec*
▼ EMP: 56
SQ FT: 43,500
SALES (est): 14.6MM **Privately Held**
SIC: 3542 0724 Mechanical (pneumatic or hydraulic) metal forming machines; cotton ginning

(G-15364)
CUSTOM FAB
5281 S Hametown Rd (44203-6159)
PHONE.................................330 825-3586
Charles Gilbertson, *Owner*
EMP: 3
SQ FT: 1,472
SALES: 125K **Privately Held**
SIC: 3714 Motor vehicle engines & parts

(G-15365)
E L STONE COMPANY
Also Called: Stonecote
2998 Eastern Rd (44203-3902)
P.O. Box 1012 (44203-9412)
PHONE.................................330 825-4565
Mark Micire, *President*
Elma Micire, *Vice Pres*
EMP: 50 EST: 1955
SQ FT: 135,000
SALES: 3.5MM **Privately Held**
WEB: www.elstonecoinc.com
SIC: 3479 3471 Aluminum coating of metal products; plating & polishing

(G-15366)
EARTH ANATOMY FABRICATION LLC
4092 Greenwich Rd (44203-5432)
PHONE.................................740 244-5316
Chad Williams,
EMP: 1 EST: 2013
SALES: 1MM **Privately Held**
SIC: 5032 3281 7389 Marble building stone; granite building stone; building stone; stone, quarrying & processing of own stone products; dimension stone for buildings;

(G-15367)
ETKO MACHINE INC
2796 Barber Rd (44203-1002)
P.O. Box 710, Barberton (44203-0710)
PHONE.................................330 745-4033
Julius J Koroshazi, *President*
Etelka Koroshazi, *Corp Secy*
George J Koroshazi, *Vice Pres*
EMP: 9
SQ FT: 4,000
SALES (est): 1.4MM **Privately Held**
WEB: www.etko.com
SIC: 3599 Machine shop, jobbing & repair

(G-15368)
FISHER SAND & GRAVEL INC
Also Called: Flesher Sand & Gravel
3322 Clark Mill Rd (44203-1028)
PHONE.................................330 745-9239
James Fisher, *President*
EMP: 7 EST: 1968
SQ FT: 3,888
SALES: 500K **Privately Held**
SIC: 1442 Construction sand & gravel

(G-15369)
ICP ADHESIVES AND SEALANTS INC (HQ)
Also Called: Fomo Products, Inc.
2775 Barber Rd (44203-1001)
P.O. Box 1078 (44203-9478)
PHONE.................................330 753-4585
Stefan Miczka, *CEO*
Stefan Gantenbein, *President*
Kerry Armes, *Vice Pres*
Mojee Cline, *Vice Pres*
Tamie Seifert, *Opers Mgr*
▲ EMP: 18
SQ FT: 45,000
SALES (est): 6.3MM
SALES (corp-wide): 140.9MM **Privately Held**
WEB: www.fomo.com
SIC: 3086 2891 3296 2821 Plastics foam products; sealants; mineral wool; plastics materials & resins
PA: Innovative Chemical Products Group, Llc
150 Dascomb Rd
Andover MA 01810
978 623-9980

(G-15370)
INDEPENDENT DIGITAL CONSULTING
2081 Wadsworth Rd (44203-5305)
P.O. Box 697, Akron (44309-0697)
PHONE.................................330 753-0777
Thomas H Schurr, *President*
Emily J Schurr, *Corp Secy*
Nathan Schurr, *Shareholder*
EMP: 4
SQ FT: 4,200
SALES: 500K **Privately Held**
WEB: www.idconline.com
SIC: 8711 3625 Consulting engineer; designing: ship, boat, machine & product; relays & industrial controls

(G-15371)
J E DOYLE COMPANY
Also Called: Doyle Systems
5186 New Haven Cir (44203-4671)
PHONE.................................330 564-0743
Joseph M Lynch, *President*
▲ EMP: 23
SQ FT: 10,000
SALES (est): 4MM **Privately Held**
WEB: www.doylesystems.com
SIC: 3554 Paper industries machinery

(G-15372)
JJC PLASTICS LTD
4021 Deerspring Ct (44203-5481)
PHONE.................................330 334-3637
Michael Primovero, *President*
Barbara K Primovero, *Vice Pres*
EMP: 3
SALES (est): 457K **Privately Held**
SIC: 2821 Plastics materials & resins

(G-15373)
LASER HORIZONS
1879 Caroline Ave (44203-1401)
PHONE.................................330 208-0575
Joseph Maier, *Partner*
June Maier, *Partner*
Denise Sautters, *Partner*
Dennis Sautters, *Partner*
EMP: 3 EST: 1998
SALES (est): 214.4K **Privately Held**
WEB: www.laserhorizons.com
SIC: 2823 Cuprammonium fibers

(G-15374)
NVISION TECHNOLOGY INC
2769 Pinegate Dr (44203-3963)
PHONE.................................412 254-4668
Nicholas Vitalbo, *President*
EMP: 5
SALES (est): 318.2K **Privately Held**
SIC: 8748 3826 7371 Systems analysis & engineering consulting services; laser scientific & engineering instruments; computer software systems analysis & design, custom

(G-15375)
SPARTON ENTERPRISES INC
3717 Clark Mill Rd (44203-1035)
PHONE.................................330 745-6088
James E Little Jr, *President*
Andy Little, *Vice Pres*
▲ EMP: 25
SQ FT: 110,000
SALES (est): 5.7MM **Privately Held**
WEB: www.spartonenterprises.com
SIC: 3069 Reclaimed rubber (reworked by manufacturing processes)

(G-15376)
STARPOINT EXTRUSIONS LLC
3985 Eastern Rd C (44203-6215)
PHONE.................................330 825-2373
Greg Bilek, *Mng Member*
▲ EMP: 25
SALES: 5MM **Privately Held**
SIC: 3069 Hard rubber & molded rubber products

(G-15377)
WAGNER MACHINE INC
5151 Wooster Rd W (44203-6261)
PHONE.................................330 706-0700
Michael Wagner, *President*
Courtney Wagner, *Admin Sec*
▲ EMP: 35
SQ FT: 20,000
SALES (est): 7.4MM **Privately Held**
WEB: www.wagnermachine.com
SIC: 3599 Machine shop, jobbing & repair

Norwalk
Huron County

(G-15378)
ACCU-FEED ENGINEERING
50 Newton St (44857-1224)
P.O. Box 404 (44857-0404)
PHONE.................................419 668-7990
Jim Tracht, *Owner*
EMP: 9
SQ FT: 14,000
SALES (est): 1.3MM **Privately Held**
WEB: www.accu-feed.com
SIC: 3825 Meters: electric, pocket, portable, panelboard, etc.

(G-15379)
ALLIED PEDESTAL BOOM SYS LLC
75 Norwalk Commons Dr (44857-2637)
PHONE.................................419 663-0279
EMP: 3
SALES (est): 327.9K **Privately Held**
SIC: 3599 Machine shop, jobbing & repair

(G-15380)
AMERICRAFT CARTON INC
209 Republic St (44857-1157)
PHONE.................................419 668-1006
Dwight Henry, *Purch Mgr*
Darrin Carlson, *Manager*
EMP: 40
SALES (corp-wide): 194.1MM **Privately Held**
WEB: www.americraft.com
SIC: 2657 Food containers, folding: made from purchased material; paperboard backs for blister or skin packages
PA: Americraft Carton, Inc.
7400 State Line Rd # 206
Prairie Village KS 66208
913 387-3700

(G-15381)
ARMETON US CO
205 Republic St (44857-1157)
P.O. Box 234 (44857-0234)
PHONE.................................419 660-9296
Primoz Seljak, *Manager*
EMP: 11
SALES (est): 850K **Privately Held**
SIC: 3089 5084 Billfold inserts, plastic; machine tools & metalworking machinery

(G-15382)
BENNETT ELECTRIC INC
211 Republic St (44857-1157)
PHONE.................................800 874-5405
Daniel L Stewart, *President*
Jean Stewart, *Corp Secy*
Charles Avarello, *Vice Pres*
Laura Mack, *Office Mgr*
EMP: 14 EST: 1925
SQ FT: 15,000
SALES (est): 8.8MM **Privately Held**
WEB: www.bennett-electric.com
SIC: 5063 7694 Motors, electric; electric motor repair

(G-15383)
BROOKER BROS FORGING CO INC
102 Jefferson St (44857-1969)
P.O. Box 498 (44857-0498)
PHONE.................................419 668-2535
Rickard E Brooker, *President*
EMP: 20 EST: 1946
SQ FT: 16,000
SALES (est): 3.6MM **Privately Held**
WEB: www.brookerbros.com
SIC: 3462 Iron & steel forgings

(G-15384)
CASE-MAUL CLAMPS INC
69 N West St (44857-1213)
P.O. Box 605 (44857-0605)
PHONE.................................419 668-6563
James R Maul, *President*
Dr Peggy Maul, *Vice Pres*
▲ EMP: 17
SALES (est): 2.9MM **Privately Held**
WEB: www.case-maulclamps.com
SIC: 3429 Clamps, metal

(G-15385)
CUSTOM METAL WORKS INC (PA)
193 Akron Rd (44857)
PHONE.................................419 668-7831
Lawrence A Skinn, *President*
Bradley Skinn, *Vice Pres*
L Andrew Skinn, *Vice Pres*
Cynthia Skinn, *Treasurer*
EMP: 14 EST: 1981
SQ FT: 19,400
SALES (est): 1.9MM **Privately Held**
SIC: 7699 3599 3429 Industrial machinery & equipment repair; farm machinery repair; machine shop, jobbing & repair; manufactured hardware (general)

GEOGRAPHIC SECTION
Norwalk - Huron County (G-15410)

(G-15386)
DAN-MAR COMPANY INC
Also Called: Danmarco
200 Bluegrass Dr E (44857-1169)
PHONE..................................419 660-8830
James D Heckelman, *President*
Margaret Heckelman, *Vice Pres*
Don Nowicki, *Opers Mgr*
Cheryl Randleman, *Purch Mgr*
Nancy Heckelman, *Treasurer*
EMP: 26
SQ FT: 50,000
SALES: 2.4MM **Privately Held**
WEB: www.danmarco.com
SIC: 3674 3629 Solid state electronic devices; blasting machines, electrical

(G-15387)
DAVID PRICE METAL SERVICES INC
360 Eastpark Dr (44857-9500)
PHONE..................................419 668-3358
Christopher C Price, *President*
Faith A Price, *Corp Secy*
R David Smith, *CFO*
▲ **EMP:** 130
SQ FT: 100,000
SALES: 59.4MM **Privately Held**
WEB: www.dpms-inc.com
SIC: 3599 Machine shop, jobbing & repair

(G-15388)
DS EXPRESS CARRIERS INC (PA)
203 Republic St (44857-1157)
PHONE..................................419 433-6200
Daniela Stankic, *President*
EMP: 6
SALES (est): 2.3MM **Privately Held**
SIC: 4213 3669 8742 3715 Trucking, except local; transportation signaling devices; transportation consultant; semitrailers for missile transportation; rocket transportation casings; freight transportation arrangement

(G-15389)
DURABLE CORPORATION
75 N Pleasant St (44857-1218)
P.O. Box 290 (44857-0290)
PHONE..................................800 537-1603
Jon M Anderson, *CEO*
Tom Secor, *President*
Marcia Norris, *Principal*
Cathy McGinn, *Human Res Mgr*
Kaci White, *Mktg Dir*
◆ **EMP:** 60
SQ FT: 3,000
SALES (est): 12.6MM **Privately Held**
WEB: www.durablecorp.com
SIC: 3069 2273 5013 Mats or matting, rubber; molded rubber products; rubber automotive products; mats & matting; bumpers

(G-15390)
DURAMAX MARINE INDUSTRIES
53 Saint Marys St (44857-1841)
PHONE..................................419 668-3728
Tom Rice, *Principal*
EMP: 3
SALES (est): 302.9K **Privately Held**
SIC: 3999 Manufacturing industries

(G-15391)
EXTOL OF OHIO INC (PA)
208 Republic St (44857-1185)
PHONE..................................419 668-2072
Robin L Degraff, *President*
Mergie Simon, *Treasurer*
Maureen Ringle, *Payroll Mgr*
▼ **EMP:** 35
SQ FT: 45,000
SALES: 7.4MM **Privately Held**
WEB: www.norwalkohio.com
SIC: 3296 Insulation: rock wool, slag & silica minerals

(G-15392)
EXTOL OF OHIO INC
208 Republic St (44857-1185)
PHONE..................................419 668-2072
Robin L Degraff, *President*
Brian Eisenhower, *Vice Pres*
Margie Simon, *Treasurer*
Robert Baldwin, *Admin Sec*
EMP: 35
SQ FT: 45,000
SALES: 7.4MM **Privately Held**
WEB: www.extolohio.com
SIC: 3086 Plastics foam products
PA: Extol Of Ohio, Inc.
  208 Republic St
  Norwalk OH 44857

(G-15393)
FABRIWELD CORPORATION
360 Eastpark Dr (44857-9500)
PHONE..................................419 668-3358
Christopher C Price, *President*
David C Price, *Chairman*
Faith A Price, *Corp Secy*
David Smith, *Vice Pres*
Karen Krupp, *Executive Asst*
EMP: 9
SQ FT: 8,400
SALES (est): 1.9MM **Privately Held**
WEB: www.fabriweldcorp.com
SIC: 3625 3613 3549 3542 Relays & industrial controls; switchgear & switchboard apparatus; metalworking machinery; presses: hydraulic & pneumatic, mechanical & manual

(G-15394)
FAIR PUBLISHING HOUSE INC
15 Schauss Ave (44857-1851)
P.O. Box 350 (44857-0350)
PHONE..................................419 668-3746
Charles Doyle, *President*
Kevin F Doyle, *President*
EMP: 27
SQ FT: 25,000
SALES (est): 3.5MM
SALES (corp-wide): 3.9MM **Privately Held**
SIC: 2759 3993 2752 Imprinting; signs & advertising specialties; commercial printing, lithographic
PA: Rotary Printing Company
  15 Schauss Ave
  Norwalk OH 44857
  419 668-4821

(G-15395)
FIRELANDS FAS-PRINT LLC
59 Benedict Ave (44857-2127)
PHONE..................................419 668-3045
Sandra Reitezel,
Michael Reitezel,
EMP: 3
SQ FT: 2,600
SALES: 208K **Privately Held**
SIC: 2759 Letterpress printing

(G-15396)
GYRUS ACMI LP
93 N Pleasant St (44857-1218)
PHONE..................................419 668-8201
Tom Motta, *General Mgr*
EMP: 190
SQ FT: 55,000
SALES (corp-wide): 7.3B **Privately Held**
WEB: www.circoncorp.com
SIC: 3841 3845 Surgical & medical instruments; electromedical equipment
HQ: Gyrus Acmi, L.P.
  9600 Louisiana Ave N
  Minneapolis MN 55445
  763 416-3000

(G-15397)
HART ADVERTISING INC
6975 E Seminary St (44857)
P.O. Box 499 (44857-0499)
PHONE..................................419 668-1194
W Taylor Hart, *President*
Gay Hart-Sanders, *Corp Secy*
EMP: 12
SALES (est): 1.2MM **Privately Held**
SIC: 7312 3993 Billboard advertising; signs & advertising specialties

(G-15398)
HEN HOUSE INC
Also Called: Ditz Designs
100 Northwest St (44857-1273)
P.O. Box 586 (44857-0586)
PHONE..................................419 663-3377
Robert Ludwig, *President*
Jon Ditz, *Treasurer*
Joyce Ditz, *Bd of Directors*
Deborah Ludwig, *Admin Sec*
▲ **EMP:** 35
SQ FT: 37,000
SALES (est): 3.9MM **Privately Held**
WEB: www.ditzdesigns.com
SIC: 2511 Stools, household: wood

(G-15399)
HERALD REFLECTOR INC (PA)
Also Called: Norwalk Reflector
61 E Monroe St (44857-1532)
P.O. Box 71 (44857-0071)
PHONE..................................419 668-3771
David Rau, *President*
Alice Rau, *Treasurer*
EMP: 55 EST: 1829
SQ FT: 10,000
SALES (est): 3MM **Privately Held**
WEB: www.goreflector.com
SIC: 2711 Commercial printing & newspaper publishing combined; newspapers, publishing & printing

(G-15400)
HUG MANUFACTURING CORPORATION
2858 Arcade Rd (44857-9525)
P.O. Box 667 (44857-0667)
PHONE..................................419 668-5086
John Hug, *President*
EMP: 3
SQ FT: 3,375
SALES (est): 300K **Privately Held**
WEB: www.truckstriper.com
SIC: 3531 5084 Road construction & maintenance machinery; industrial machinery & equipment

(G-15401)
INTELLIWORKS HT
61 Saint Marys St (44857-1841)
P.O. Box 899 (44857-0899)
PHONE..................................419 660-9050
Dave Nunez, *Principal*
Tina Seiling, *Office Mgr*
▲ **EMP:** 6
SALES (est): 1.2MM **Privately Held**
SIC: 3559 Sewing machines & attachments, industrial

(G-15402)
KUHLMAN INSTRUMENT COMPANY
54 Summit St (44857-2134)
P.O. Box 468 (44857-0468)
PHONE..................................419 668-9533
Mark Lacy, *CEO*
Caryl Humphreys, *Administration*
EMP: 6
SQ FT: 5,000
SALES (est): 1MM **Privately Held**
WEB: www.kuhlmaninstrument.com
SIC: 3823 Industrial instrmnts msrmnt display/control process variable

(G-15403)
LASER IMAGES INC
28 W Main St (44857-1440)
P.O. Box 524 (44857-0524)
PHONE..................................419 668-8348
Ilene Tracht, *President*
EMP: 4
SQ FT: 3,200
SALES (est): 639.3K **Privately Held**
WEB: www.drc-mn.com
SIC: 2752 Commercial printing, offset

(G-15404)
LESCH BOAT COVER CANVAS CO LLC
43 1/2 Saint Marys St (44857-1809)
PHONE..................................419 668-6374
Daniel Lesch, *Owner*
EMP: 4
SQ FT: 3,000
SALES (est): 430.8K **Privately Held**
SIC: 2394 2396 Tarpaulins, fabric: made from purchased materials; convertible tops, canvas or boat: from purchased materials; automotive trimmings, fabric

(G-15405)
MAPLE CITY RUBBER COMPANY
Also Called: Tuf-Tex
55 Newton St (44857-1298)
P.O. Box 587 (44857-0587)
PHONE..................................419 668-8261
Michael Kilbane, *President*
Paul Bennett, *COO*
Jim Prater, *Plant Mgr*
Trisha Cross, *Purch Mgr*
Willam Chandler, *Controller*
▲ **EMP:** 44 EST: 1915
SQ FT: 104,000
SALES: 5.2MM **Privately Held**
WEB: www.maplecityrubber.com
SIC: 3069 Balloons, advertising & toy: rubber

(G-15406)
MOTO-ELECTRIC INC
262 Cleveland Rd (44857-9024)
PHONE..................................419 668-7894
Nicholas McCall, *President*
EMP: 8
SQ FT: 8,000
SALES: 1.4MM **Privately Held**
WEB: www.motoelectric.com
SIC: 7694 5063 Electric motor repair; motors, electric

(G-15407)
NEW HORIZONS BAKING COMPANY (PA)
211 Woodlawn Ave (44857-2276)
PHONE..................................419 668-8226
Ronald Jones, *President*
Trina Bediako, *Vice Pres*
Robert Creighton, *Vice Pres*
Mark Duke, *Vice Pres*
Mike Porter, *Vice Pres*
EMP: 350
SQ FT: 4,526
SALES: 94MM **Privately Held**
SIC: 2051 Buns, bread type: fresh or frozen; breads, rolls & buns

(G-15408)
NORWALK CONCRETE INDS INC (PA)
80 Commerce Dr (44857-9003)
P.O. Box 563 (44857-0563)
PHONE..................................419 668-8167
John A Lendrum, *President*
Terry Boose, *General Mgr*
Jeffrey S Malcolm, *Vice Pres*
Dennis Paakkonen, *Opers Mgr*
Gerry Schafer, *Purchasing*
▲ **EMP:** 40 EST: 1906
SALES (est): 13.7MM **Privately Held**
WEB: www.nciprecast.com
SIC: 3272 Concrete products, precast

(G-15409)
NORWALK CONCRETE INDS INC
80 Commerce Dr (44857-9003)
PHONE..................................419 668-8167
John Lendrum, *Branch Mgr*
EMP: 50
SALES (corp-wide): 13.7MM **Privately Held**
WEB: www.nciprecast.com
SIC: 3272 Concrete products, precast
PA: Norwalk Concrete Industries, Inc.
  80 Commerce Dr
  Norwalk OH 44857
  419 668-8167

(G-15410)
NORWALK PRECAST MOLDS INC
205 Industrial Pkwy (44857-3105)
P.O. Box 293 (44857-0293)
PHONE..................................419 668-1639
Jan Graves, *President*
Gregory D Graves, *President*
Loren Schild, *Accounts Mgr*
EMP: 20
SQ FT: 75,000
SALES (est): 3.5MM **Privately Held**
WEB: www.norwalkprecastmolds.com
SIC: 3544 Industrial molds

Norwalk - Huron County (G-15411)

(G-15411)
NORWALK WASTEWATER EQP CO
Also Called: Norweco
220 Republic St (44857-1156)
P.O. Box 410 (44857-0410)
PHONE..................................419 668-4471
Jan Graves, *Ch of Bd*
Gregory Graves, *President*
Michele Graves, *Corp Secy*
Jennifer Jenne, *Vice Pres*
James Meyer, *Vice Pres*
◆ **EMP:** 50 **EST:** 1906
SQ FT: 70,000
SALES (est): 23.8MM **Privately Held**
WEB: www.norweco.com
SIC: 3589 Water treatment equipment, industrial

(G-15412)
POLYONE CORPORATION
80 N West St (44857-1239)
PHONE..................................419 668-4844
Bob Mc Elsresh, *Plant Mgr*
Gary Weaver, *Purchasing*
EMP: 126 **Publicly Held**
WEB: www.polyone.com
SIC: 2865 3087 2851 2816 Dyes & pigments; custom compound purchased resins; paints & allied products; inorganic pigments
PA: Polyone Corporation
33587 Walker Rd
Avon Lake OH 44012

(G-15413)
R & D EQUIPMENT INC
206 Republic St (44857-1185)
PHONE..................................419 668-8439
George Gilbert, *President*
Chuck Plumb, *Vice Pres*
▲ **EMP:** 13 **EST:** 1977
SQ FT: 18,000
SALES (est): 2.9MM **Privately Held**
WEB: www.rdequipment.com
SIC: 3555 Printing trades machinery

(G-15414)
ROTARY PRINTING COMPANY (PA)
Also Called: Fair Publishing
15 Schauss Ave (44857-1851)
P.O. Box 350 (44857-0350)
PHONE..................................419 668-4821
Kevin F Doyle, *President*
EMP: 2
SQ FT: 25,000
SALES (est): 3.9MM **Privately Held**
SIC: 5112 2759 Business forms; letterpress printing; embossing on paper

(G-15415)
SOLID DIMENSIONS INC
Also Called: Solid Dimensions Line
720 Townline Road 151 (44857-9535)
PHONE..................................419 663-1134
Tim Parcher, *President*
Darla Parcher, *Vice Pres*
▲ **EMP:** 9
SALES: 900K **Privately Held**
WEB: www.soliddimensions.com
SIC: 2499 Engraved wood products; novelties, wood fiber; trophy bases, wood

(G-15416)
VERTEX REFINING OH LLC (HQ)
4376 State Route 601 (44857-9128)
PHONE..................................281 486-4182
Benjamin Cowart, *CEO*
EMP: 46
SALES (est): 800.8K **Publicly Held**
SIC: 2911 Petroleum refining

(G-15417)
WHEELER SHEET METAL INC
4640 Plank Rd (44857-9792)
PHONE..................................419 668-0481
Deloris Wheeler, *President*
Delores Wheeler, *President*
Wilma Collier, *Corp Secy*
EMP: 5
SQ FT: 14,000
SALES (est): 775.8K **Privately Held**
SIC: 1711 3444 Warm air heating & air conditioning contractor; ventilation & duct work contractor; sheet metalwork

(G-15418)
WILLIAM DAUCH CONCRETE COMPANY (PA)
84 Cleveland Rd (44857-9020)
P.O. Box 204 (44857-0204)
PHONE..................................419 668-4458
William Dauch, *President*
Mona E Dauch, *Corp Secy*
Monica McDonald, *Human Resources*
Duane Graffice, *Sales Staff*
Denver Ramsey, *Technical Staff*
EMP: 15 **EST:** 1966
SQ FT: 2,000
SALES (est): 23.2MM **Privately Held**
WEB: www.dauchconcrete.com
SIC: 5032 3273 3272 3271 Brick, stone & related material; ready-mixed concrete; concrete products; concrete block & brick

(G-15419)
WOODEN HORSE CORPORATION
819 Dublin Rd (44857-9746)
PHONE..................................419 663-1472
Sandy Lovato, *President*
Frank Lovato Jr, *Vice Pres*
EMP: 3
SALES: 350K **Privately Held**
SIC: 3949 Exercise equipment

Norwich
Muskingum County

(G-15420)
HECKMANN WTR RESOURCES CVR INC
9350 East Pike (43767-9726)
PHONE..................................740 844-0045
Scott Gibson, *Manager*
EMP: 3 **Publicly Held**
SIC: 1389 Removal of condensate gasoline from field (gathering) lines
HQ: Heckmann Water Resources (Cvr), Inc.
525 Park Rd
Frierson LA 71027
281 203-3434

(G-15421)
LUMI-LITE CANDLE COMPANY
Also Called: Lumi Craft
102 Sundale Rd (43767-9717)
P.O. Box 97 (43767-0097)
PHONE..................................740 872-3248
George Pappas, *President*
William W Wilson, *Chairman*
Tina Bales, *Vice Pres*
Pete Pappas, *Vice Pres*
▲ **EMP:** 100
SQ FT: 50,000
SALES (est): 12.3MM **Privately Held**
SIC: 3999 Candles

Norwood
Hamilton County

(G-15422)
ARCHITECTURAL DOOR SYSTEMS LLC
2810 Highland Ave (45212-2410)
PHONE..................................513 808-9900
Richard Beckman, *President*
Charles Beckman, *Vice Pres*
EMP: 5
SALES (est): 314.6K **Privately Held**
SIC: 2431 3429 Door frames, wood; manufactured hardware (general)

(G-15423)
AUTORENTALSYSTEMSCOM LLC
1776 Mentor Ave Ste 427 (45212-3586)
PHONE..................................513 334-1040
Laura Tierney, *Sales Mgr*
Chris Irwin,
Bryon Tierney,
EMP: 3
SQ FT: 482
SALES (est): 94.8K **Privately Held**
SIC: 7372 Business oriented computer software

(G-15424)
BLT INC
Also Called: Uptown Graphics
2834 Highland Ave (45212-2410)
PHONE..................................513 631-5050
Ronald Bush, *President*
Luigi Lavalle, *Vice Pres*
EMP: 13
SQ FT: 8,000
SALES (est): 1.6MM **Privately Held**
WEB: www.q-c-p.com
SIC: 2752 3083 2791 Commercial printing, offset; plastic finished products, laminated; typesetting

(G-15425)
COX INTERIOR INC
4080 Webster Ave (45212-2706)
PHONE..................................270 789-3129
Robert Mears, *Branch Mgr*
EMP: 10
SALES (corp-wide): 39.5MM **Privately Held**
WEB: www.coxinterior.com
SIC: 2431 Moldings, wood: unfinished & prefinished; trim, wood; staircases, stairs & railings; doors & door parts & trim, wood
PA: Cox Interior, Inc.
1751 Old Columbia Rd
Campbellsville KY 42718
270 789-3129

(G-15426)
EMD MILLIPORE CORPORATION
2909 Highland Ave (45212-2411)
PHONE..................................513 631-0445
Michael Mulligan, *Vice Pres*
Daryl Hayslip, *Info Tech Dir*
Sandra Heyob, *Associate*
EMP: 150
SQ FT: 100,000
SALES (corp-wide): 16.9B **Privately Held**
WEB: www.emdchemicals.com
SIC: 8731 3295 2899 2842 Biotechnical research, commercial; minerals, ground or treated; chemical preparations; specialty cleaning, polishes & sanitation goods; biological products, except diagnostic
HQ: Emd Millipore Corporation
400 Summit Dr
Burlington MA 01803
781 533-6000

(G-15427)
PALLET SPECS PLUS LLC
1701 Mills Ave (45212-2825)
P.O. Box 15236, Cincinnati (45215-0236)
PHONE..................................513 351-3200
Scott M Senter, *President*
Jake Catron, *COO*
Jason Catron, *COO*
EMP: 10
SQ FT: 20,000
SALES: 500K **Privately Held**
SIC: 2448 Pallets, wood

(G-15428)
SHEPHERD MATERIAL SCIENCE CO (PA)
4900 Beech St (45212-2316)
PHONE..................................513 731-1110
Thomas L Shepherd, *President*
Jeffrey M Stenger, *Controller*
EMP: 12
SALES (est): 90MM **Privately Held**
SIC: 2819 2869 Metal salts & compounds, except sodium, potassium, aluminum; industrial organic chemicals

(G-15429)
SINGLE PHASE PWR SOLUTIONS LLC (PA)
1917 Tilden Ave (45212-2519)
P.O. Box 12803, Cincinnati (45212-0803)
PHONE..................................513 722-5098
Drew Abbott, *Principal*
EMP: 4
SALES (est): 1.7MM **Privately Held**
SIC: 3621 Coils, for electric motors or generators

Nova
Ashland County

(G-15430)
AMP-TECH INC
910 County Road 40 (44859-9723)
PHONE..................................419 652-3444
Dana White, *Principal*
EMP: 3
SALES (est): 343.2K **Privately Held**
SIC: 7692 Welding repair

(G-15431)
AMPTECH MACHINING & WELDING
910 County Road 40 (44859-9723)
PHONE..................................419 652-3444
Dana White, *Owner*
EMP: 9
SALES (est): 285.5K **Privately Held**
WEB: www.amptechwelding.com
SIC: 7692 Welding repair

(G-15432)
DANA WHITE MACHINING WLDG INC
910 County Road 40 (44859-9723)
PHONE..................................419 652-3444
Dana White, *President*
Tammy White, *Admin Sec*
EMP: 6
SQ FT: 1,000
SALES (est): 510K **Privately Held**
SIC: 3599 Machine shop, jobbing & repair

(G-15433)
GRAPHITE SALES INC (PA)
220 Township Road 791 (44859-9703)
P.O. Box 23009, Chagrin Falls (44023-0009)
PHONE..................................419 652-3388
Kevin Burmeister, *CEO*
Michael Dwaileebe, *General Mgr*
Thomas Hoffman, *Plant Mgr*
Scott Taylor, *Opers Mgr*
Michael Slabe, *CFO*
◆ **EMP:** 15
SQ FT: 16,000
SALES (est): 14.3MM **Privately Held**
WEB: www.graphitesales.com
SIC: 3624 Electrodes, thermal & electrolytic uses: carbon, graphite

(G-15434)
GRAPHITE SALES INC
220 Township Road 791 (44859-9703)
PHONE..................................419 652-3388
Thomas Hoffman, *Branch Mgr*
EMP: 38
SALES (corp-wide): 14.3MM **Privately Held**
WEB: www.graphitesales.com
SIC: 2819 3624 Industrial inorganic chemicals; carbon & graphite products
PA: Graphite Sales, Inc.
220 Township Road 791
Nova OH 44859
419 652-3388

(G-15435)
PATTERSON & SONS INC
10 Township Road 1031 (44859-9721)
PHONE..................................419 281-0897
EMP: 10 **EST:** 1945
SQ FT: 30,000
SALES (est): 1.4MM **Privately Held**
SIC: 3444 Mfg Sheet Metalwork

(G-15436)
ULTRABUILT PLAY SYSTEMS INC
1114 Us Highway 224 (44859-9773)
PHONE..................................419 652-2294
Stephen Bennet, *President*
EMP: 10
SQ FT: 6,200
SALES (est): 1MM **Privately Held**
SIC: 3949 2541 Playground equipment; display fixtures, wood

▲ = Import ▼=Export
◆ =Import/Export

GEOGRAPHIC SECTION

Oakwood - Montgomery County (G-15464)

Novelty
Geauga County

(G-15437)
ARROW FABRICATING CO
7355 Calley Ln (44072-9585)
PHONE..................................216 641-0490
Ramesh Gavhane, *President*
Gaye Gavhane, *Corp Secy*
EMP: 30
SQ FT: 40,000
SALES (est): 5.5MM **Privately Held**
SIC: 3441 Fabricated structural metal

(G-15438)
ASM INTERNATIONAL
9639 Kinsman Rd (44073-0002)
PHONE..................................440 338-5151
Thomas Dudley, *CEO*
William Mahoney, *Managing Dir*
Amy Nolan, *Editor*
Joanne Miller, *Prdtn Mgr*
Veronica Becker, *Controller*
▲ EMP: 80
SQ FT: 55,000
SALES (est): 8.3MM **Privately Held**
WEB: www.aeromat.com
SIC: 2731 2721 7389 7999 Books: publishing only; periodicals: publishing only; advertising, promotional & trade show services; promoters of shows & exhibitions; trade show arrangement; exhibition operation

(G-15439)
NORAMAR COMPANY INC
8501 Kinsman Rd (44072-9640)
P.O. Box 771, Chagrin Falls (44022-0771)
PHONE..................................440 338-5740
Norm Tomiello, *President*
Marilyn Tomiello, *Corp Secy*
EMP: 7
SALES (est): 1MM **Privately Held**
WEB: www.noramar.com
SIC: 3823 Industrial instrmnts msrmnt display/control process variable

(G-15440)
WHITE CO DAVID
10161 Music St (44072-9622)
PHONE..................................440 247-2920
EMP: 3 EST: 2015
SALES (est): 162.8K **Privately Held**
SIC: 3089 Mfg Plastic Products

Oak Harbor
Ottawa County

(G-15441)
AYLING AND REICHERT CO CONSENT
411 S Railroad St (43449-1053)
P.O. Box 389 (43449-0389)
PHONE..................................419 898-2471
Robert G Wilson, *President*
Evelyn Wilson, *Vice Pres*
EMP: 35 EST: 1926
SQ FT: 23,000
SALES (est): 7.3MM **Privately Held**
SIC: 3469 3561 3443 Metal stampings; industrial pumps & parts; floating covers, metal plate

(G-15442)
C NELSON MANUFACTURING CO
265 N Lake Winds Pkwy (43449-9012)
PHONE..................................419 898-3305
Kelley Smith, *President*
Michele Huffman, *Purch Agent*
Paul Cox, *Senior Engr*
▼ EMP: 36
SQ FT: 1,200
SALES: 5MM **Privately Held**
WEB: www.cnelson.com
SIC: 3585 Refrigeration & heating equipment

(G-15443)
DAVIS FABRICATORS INC
15765 W State Route 2 (43449-9488)
PHONE..................................419 898-5297
Todd Davis, *CEO*
Walter Davis, *President*
Sandra Davis, *Vice Pres*
EMP: 20
SQ FT: 25,000
SALES (est): 4MM **Privately Held**
WEB: www.davisfabricators.com
SIC: 3441 Fabricated structural metal

(G-15444)
ESPERIA HOLDINGS LLC (PA)
Also Called: S T A
8035 W Lake Winds Dr (43449-8903)
PHONE..................................714 249-7888
Dennis M Liebman,
Anthony L Hunter,
EMP: 0 EST: 2015
SALES (est): 21.9MM **Privately Held**
SIC: 6719 2671 5084 Investment holding companies, except banks; packaging paper & plastics film, coated & laminated; processing & packaging equipment

(G-15445)
FORMETAL INC
220 Houghton St Ste 36 (43449-1123)
P.O. Box 416 (43449-0416)
PHONE..................................419 898-2211
William L Briggs, *CEO*
Patrick A Briggs, *President*
Stanley A Simon, *Admin Sec*
Eileen M Hasselbach, *Asst Sec*
EMP: 10
SQ FT: 52,000
SALES (est): 730K **Privately Held**
WEB: www.formetal.com
SIC: 3316 3469 Cold finishing of steel shapes; metal stampings

(G-15446)
NORTHERN MANUFACTURING CO INC
150 N Lake Winds Pkwy (43449-8921)
PHONE..................................419 898-2821
Quintin R Smith, *President*
Harry Bethel, *Principal*
Joe Bodner, *Principal*
Paul Schmitt, *Principal*
Matthew Adamcio, *Opers Staff*
▲ EMP: 145 EST: 1951
SQ FT: 120,000
SALES (est): 71.7MM **Privately Held**
WEB: www.versagage.com
SIC: 3441 Fabricated structural metal

(G-15447)
PRIESMAN PRINTERY
218 W Water St (43449-1334)
P.O. Box 233 (43449-0233)
PHONE..................................419 898-2526
James Priesman, *Owner*
EMP: 4
SQ FT: 3,640
SALES (est): 240K **Privately Held**
WEB: www.priesmanprintery.com
SIC: 2752 Commercial printing, offset

(G-15448)
WADSWORTH EXCAVATING INC
7869 W State Route 163 (43449-8705)
PHONE..................................419 898-0771
Calvin Wadsworth, *President*
Deloris Kay Wadsworth, *Treasurer*
EMP: 3
SQ FT: 2,400
SALES: 290K **Privately Held**
SIC: 1794 4493 3731 Excavation work; marinas; submarines, building & repairing

---

Oak Hill
Jackson County

(G-15449)
ART SAYLOR LOGGING
343 Slab Hill Rd (45656-9638)
PHONE..................................740 682-6188
Art Saylor, *Owner*
EMP: 10
SALES: 1MM **Privately Held**
SIC: 2411 Logging camps & contractors

(G-15450)
DENVER ADKINS
Also Called: Adkins & Sons
642 Phillip Kuhn Rd (45656-9645)
PHONE..................................740 682-3123
Denver Adkins, *Partner*
EMP: 12
SALES (est): 820K **Privately Held**
SIC: 2411 Logging camps & contractors; timber, cut at logging camp

(G-15451)
H & H INDUSTRIES INC
5400 State Route 93 (45656-9361)
PHONE..................................740 682-7721
Noah Hickman, *President*
Lisa Hickman, *Admin Sec*
EMP: 9
SALES (est): 1.9MM **Privately Held**
SIC: 3011 Retreading materials, tire

(G-15452)
JACKSON MACHINE & FABRICATION
6679 State Route 93 (45656-9301)
PHONE..................................740 682-3994
John H Shriver, *Owner*
EMP: 5
SALES (est): 351.7K **Privately Held**
SIC: 1799 3599 Welding on site; machine shop, jobbing & repair

(G-15453)
KCS CLEANING SERVICE
7550 State Route 93 (45656-9359)
PHONE..................................740 418-5479
Kathleen Strickland, *Principal*
EMP: 10
SALES: 85K **Privately Held**
SIC: 2842 Specialty cleaning, polishes & sanitation goods

(G-15454)
L&L EXCAVATING & LAND CLEARING
56 Jim Reese Rd (45656-9656)
PHONE..................................740 682-7823
Larry E Strickland, *Principal*
EMP: 4
SALES (est): 421.2K **Privately Held**
SIC: 1629 2411 5082 Land clearing contractor; logging; timber, cut at logging camp; logging & forestry machinery & equipment

(G-15455)
LEE SAYLOR LOGGING LLC
565 Cress Rd (45656-9423)
PHONE..................................740 682-0479
Garrett Saylor, *Principal*
EMP: 3
SALES (est): 108.7K **Privately Held**
SIC: 2411 Wooden logs; logging camps & contractors

(G-15456)
MICHAEL D STRICKLAND
Also Called: Mike Strickland Logging
2730 Hickory Grove Rd (45656-8986)
PHONE..................................740 682-6902
EMP: 3
SALES (est): 180K **Privately Held**
SIC: 2411 Logging

(G-15457)
NOCK AND SON COMPANY
4138 Monroe Hollow Rd (45656-8995)
PHONE..................................740 682-7741
Hayden Hammond, *Opers-Prdtn-Mfg*
EMP: 15
SALES (est): 2.2MM
SALES (corp-wide): 3.6MM **Privately Held**
WEB: www.nockandson.com
SIC: 3255 Clay refractories
PA: The Nock And Son Company
   27320 W Oviatt Rd
   Cleveland OH 44140
   440 871-5525

(G-15458)
PLIBRICO COMPANY LLC
454 County Road 33 (45656-8900)
PHONE..................................740 682-7755
Patrick Barry, *CEO*
EMP: 31
SALES (corp-wide): 35MM **Privately Held**
SIC: 3297 Brick refractories
PA: Plibrico Company, Llc
   1935 Techny Rd Ste 16
   Northbrook IL 60062
   312 337-9000

(G-15459)
RESCO PRODUCTS INC
Cedar Heights Clay Division
3542 State Route 93 (45656-8548)
P.O. Box 295 (45656-0295)
PHONE..................................740 682-7794
Ron Stowers, *Sales Mgr*
Linda Simpson, *Manager*
EMP: 35
SALES (corp-wide): 210.1MM **Privately Held**
SIC: 3255 3297 3251 Ladle brick, clay; nonclay refractories; brick & structural clay tile
PA: Resco Products, Inc.
   6600 Steubenville Pike # 1
   Pittsburgh PA 15205
   888 283-5505

(G-15460)
ROMAR METAL FABRICATING INC
201 Zane Oak Rd (45656-9742)
PHONE..................................740 682-7731
Wayne R Newsom, *President*
Robert H Newsom, *President*
EMP: 6
SQ FT: 3,700
SALES: 1MM **Privately Held**
SIC: 3441 7692 3444 Fabricated structural metal; welding repair; sheet metalwork

---

Oakwood
Montgomery County

(G-15461)
FACIAL SENSATION PRODUCTS
12 Beverly Pl (45419-3401)
P.O. Box 9191, Dayton (45409-9191)
PHONE..................................937 293-2280
Karl Stein, *Owner*
EMP: 4
SALES (est): 245.7K **Privately Held**
SIC: 2844 Toilet preparations

(G-15462)
JOHNSON ENERGY COMPANY
Also Called: Jec Forest & Paper Related Co
127 Lookout Dr (45409-2238)
PHONE..................................937 435-5401
Michael D Johnson, *President*
Frank V Surico, *Vice Pres*
EMP: 3 EST: 1978
SQ FT: 1,800
SALES: 42.5MM **Privately Held**
SIC: 5052 2671 Coal; plastic film, coated or laminated for packaging

(G-15463)
LEE OIL & GAS INC
326 Spirea Dr (45419-3541)
PHONE..................................937 223-8891
Richard Akers, *President*
James Adcock, *Vice Pres*
John H Thoma, *Vice Pres*
EMP: 3
SALES (est): 250K **Privately Held**
SIC: 1381 Drilling oil & gas wells

(G-15464)
MEDICAL SOFT INC
1800 Southwood Ln W (45419-1378)
PHONE..................................937 293-2575
M M Hall, *Owner*
Bruce Hall, *Owner*
EMP: 3 EST: 1990

Oakwood - Montgomery County (G-15465)

SALES (est): 292.7K **Privately Held**
SIC: **3695** Computer software tape & disks: blank, rigid & floppy

(G-15465)
OBSIDIAN BIODENT
260 Ridgewood Ave (45409-2218)
PHONE 937 938-9244
Sean Cahill, *Principal*
EMP: 4
SALES (est): 352.5K **Privately Held**
SIC: **3843** Dental equipment & supplies

(G-15466)
TRANSIMAGE INC
314 Spirea Dr (45419-3541)
PHONE 937 293-0261
Mark Roll, *President*
Carol Ackerman, *Corp Secy*
EMP: 4
SQ FT: 6,000
SALES: 500K **Privately Held**
WEB: www.transimageinc.com
SIC: **3861** **7384** Photographic paper & cloth, all types; photofinish laboratories

(G-15467)
TRIGON INDUSTRIES INC
1616 Delaine Ave (45419-3209)
PHONE 937 299-1350
Charles J Blank Jr, *President*
EMP: 5
SALES: 500K **Privately Held**
SIC: **2842** Industrial plant disinfectants or deodorants

Oakwood
Paulding County

(G-15468)
ACME MACHINE TECHNOLOGY LLC
115 Main St (45873)
P.O. Box 70 (45873-0070)
PHONE 419 594-3349
David Dangler, *Mng Member*
EMP: 3 EST: 2008
SQ FT: 120
SALES: 400K **Privately Held**
SIC: **3599** Machine shop, jobbing & repair

(G-15469)
COOPER HATCHERY INC (PA)
Also Called: Cooper Farms
22348 Road 140 (45873)
PHONE 419 594-3325
James R Cooper, *President*
Gary A Cooper, *COO*
Emily Smith, *COO*
Neil Diller, *Vice Pres*
Janice Fiely, *CFO*
EMP: 225 EST: 1934
SQ FT: 47,000
SALES (est): 256.7MM **Privately Held**
WEB: www.cooperfarm.com
SIC: **0254** **0253** **2015** **5153** Poultry hatcheries; turkey farm; turkey, processed; grains; prepared feeds

(G-15470)
END SEPARATION LLC
12742 Road 191 (45873-9136)
PHONE 419 438-0879
Christopher Pessefall, *Mng Member*
EMP: 4
SALES: 400K **Privately Held**
SIC: **3523** Loaders, farm type: manure, general utility

(G-15471)
MANSFIELD WELDING SERVICES LLC
20027 State Route 613 (45873-9437)
PHONE 419 594-2738
Randy Mansfield, *Mng Member*
Jan Mansfield,
EMP: 7
SALES (est): 870.6K **Privately Held**
SIC: **3499** **3548** Machine bases, metal; welding apparatus

(G-15472)
OLDCASTLE COMPANIES
13762 Road 179 (45873-9012)
PHONE 800 899-8455
EMP: 3
SALES (est): 181.3K **Privately Held**
SIC: **3272** Concrete products

(G-15473)
ROBERTS MANUFACTURING CO INC
24338 Road 148 (45873-9115)
PHONE 419 594-2712
Brian Bauer, *President*
Brian Miller, *Corp Secy*
Charles Louis Behrens, *Vice Pres*
Chuck Behrens, *Vice Pres*
Bob Ward, *Engineer*
▲ EMP: 50
SQ FT: 15,000
SALES: 4.5MM **Privately Held**
SIC: **3599** Machine shop, jobbing & repair

(G-15474)
STONECO INC
13762 Road 179 (45873-9012)
PHONE 419 393-2555
Rick Welch, *Superintendent*
EMP: 25
SALES (corp-wide): 29.7B **Privately Held**
WEB: www.stoneco.net
SIC: **1422** **2951** Crushed & broken limestone; asphalt paving mixtures & blocks
HQ: Stoneco, Inc.
1700 Fostoria Ave Ste 200
Findlay OH 45840
419 422-8854

(G-15475)
TOOLING CONNECTION INC
N Ste 12603 Hc 66 (45873)
P.O. Box 238 (45873-0238)
PHONE 419 594-3339
Klee Dangler, *President*
EMP: 9
SQ FT: 12,000
SALES (est): 610K **Privately Held**
SIC: **3541** **3544** Machine tools, metal cutting type; special dies & tools

Oakwood Village
Cuyahoga County

(G-15476)
AGMET METALS INC
7800 Medusa Rd (44146-5549)
PHONE 440 439-7400
Dana J Cassidy, *CEO*
Timothy A Andel, *CFO*
EMP: 20
SALES (est): 4.3MM **Privately Held**
SIC: **3559** Recycling machinery

(G-15477)
AIRGAS USA LLC
21610 Alexander Rd (44146-5509)
PHONE 440 232-6397
Todd Testa, *Branch Mgr*
Christopher Williams, *Director*
EMP: 6
SALES (corp-wide): 125.9MM **Privately Held**
SIC: **5169** **5084** **5085** **2813** Industrial gases; gases, compressed & liquefied; carbon dioxide; dry ice; welding machinery & equipment; safety equipment; welding supplies; industrial gases; carbon dioxide; nitrous oxide; dry ice, carbon dioxide (solid); industrial inorganic chemicals; calcium carbide
HQ: Airgas Usa, Llc
259 N Radnor Chester Rd # 100
Radnor PA 19087
610 687-5253

(G-15478)
BOSS PET PRODUCTS INC (HQ)
7730 First Pl Ste E (44146-6720)
PHONE 216 332-0832
Chris Miller, *President*
▲ EMP: 17
SQ FT: 20,000
SALES (est): 86MM **Publicly Held**
WEB: www.bossholdings.com
SIC: **3999** Pet supplies

(G-15479)
CROWN EQUIPMENT CORPORATION
Also Called: Crown Lift Trucks
26240 Broadway Ave Ste B (44146-6538)
PHONE 440 232-7772
Chuck Rammel, *Branch Mgr*
EMP: 23
SALES (corp-wide): 3.1B **Privately Held**
SIC: **3537** Lift trucks, industrial: fork, platform, straddle, etc.
PA: Crown Equipment Corporation
44 S Washington St
New Bremen OH 45869
419 629-2311

(G-15480)
GOOD NUTRITION LLC
Also Called: Good Greens
7710 First Pl (44146-6717)
P.O. Box 201727, Cleveland (44120-8112)
PHONE 216 534-6617
John Huff, *CEO*
Bill Ross, *Chairman*
Natalie Alesci, *Treasurer*
EMP: 10
SQ FT: 3,000
SALES: 5MM **Privately Held**
SIC: **2064** Granola & muesli, bars & clusters

(G-15481)
N-MOLECULAR INC
Also Called: Sofie
7650 Frst Pl Bldg B Ste A (44146)
PHONE 440 439-5356
Kenneth Smithmier, *CEO*
Timothy Stone, *President*
EMP: 15
SALES (corp-wide): 1.7MM **Privately Held**
SIC: **2834** Pharmaceutical preparations
PA: N-Molecular, Inc.
21000 Atl Blvd Ste 730
Dulles VA 20166
703 547-8161

(G-15482)
OAKWOOD LABORATORIES LLC (PA)
7670 First Pl Ste A (44146-6721)
PHONE 440 359-0000
Edward C Smith, *Ch of Bd*
Larry Johnson, *President*
Mark T Smith, *President*
Bc Thanoo, *Vice Pres*
Beverly Hill, *Human Res Mgr*
EMP: 38 EST: 1997
SQ FT: 15,000
SALES (est): 13.2MM **Privately Held**
SIC: **2834** Pharmaceutical preparations

(G-15483)
SHARPYS FOOD SYSTEMS LLC
26245 Broadway Ave (44146-6523)
PHONE 440 232-9601
Rajesh R Nair, *President*
Leela Nair, *Director*
EMP: 7
SQ FT: 13,600
SALES: 250K **Privately Held**
SIC: **2099** Food preparations

(G-15484)
SWIFT FILTERS INC (PA)
24040 Forbes Rd (44146-5650)
PHONE 440 735-0995
Edwin C Swift Jr, *President*
Charles C Swift, *Vice Pres*
Michelle Pacino, *Purchasing*
Cheryl Segulin, *Info Tech Mgr*
EMP: 38
SQ FT: 6,000
SALES (est): 6.9MM **Privately Held**
WEB: www.swiftfilters.com
SIC: **3569** **5075** Filters; air filters

(G-15485)
THERMO EBERLINE LLC
Also Called: Thermo Fisher Scientific
1 Thermo Fisher Way (44146-6536)
PHONE 440 703-1400

Gary Magyar, *Branch Mgr*
EMP: 122
SALES (corp-wide): 24.3B **Publicly Held**
SIC: **3829** Measuring & controlling devices
HQ: Thermo Eberline Llc
27 Forge Pkwy
Franklin MA 02038

(G-15486)
THERMO FISHER SCIENTIFIC INC
Also Called: Remel Products
1 Thermo Fisher Way (44146-6536)
PHONE 800 871-8909
Debra Dicillo, *Manager*
EMP: 150
SALES (corp-wide): 24.3B **Publicly Held**
SIC: **5047** **2835** **3841** Diagnostic equipment, medical; in vitro & in vivo diagnostic substances; surgical & medical instruments
PA: Thermo Fisher Scientific Inc.
168 3rd Ave
Waltham MA 02451
781 622-1000

(G-15487)
VIEWRAY TECHNOLOGIES INC
2 Thermo Fisher Way (44146-6536)
PHONE 440 703-3210
Scott Drake, *President*
Chris A Raanes, *President*
Shar Matin, *COO*
Peter Sullivan, *Exec VP*
Robert Bea, *Senior VP*
▲ EMP: 70
SALES: 80.9MM **Privately Held**
SIC: **3845** **5047** Electromedical equipment; therapy equipment

(G-15488)
WEBER TOOL & MFG INC
7761 First Pl (44146-6715)
PHONE 440 786-0221
Emery Teller, *President*
EMP: 4 EST: 1963
SQ FT: 6,000
SALES (est): 350K **Privately Held**
SIC: **3599** Machine shop, jobbing & repair

(G-15489)
WELDON PUMP ACQUITION LLC
640 Golden Oak Pkwy (44146-6504)
PHONE 440 232-2282
Jeffrey Kelly, *President*
Jim Craig, *Prdtn Mgr*
Jennifer Kelly, *Comptroller*
Lydia Bohm, *Marketing Mgr*
John Dematteis, *Products*
EMP: 28
SQ FT: 16,000
SALES (est): 2.5MM **Privately Held**
SIC: **3694** **3728** **3795** **9661** Distributors, motor vehicle engine; research & dev by manuf., aircraft parts & auxiliary equip; tanks & tank components; space research & technology

Oberlin
Lorain County

(G-15490)
ARGES
275 N Pleasant St (44074-1124)
PHONE 440 574-1305
Daniel Solorzano, *CEO*
Daniel Bulhosa Solorzano, *CEO*
Andrew Moran, *Chief Engr*
EMP: 3
SALES (est): 71.1K **Privately Held**
SIC: **7372** **4581** **8731** Prepackaged software; airport control tower operation, except government; commercial physical research

(G-15491)
BIG PRODUCTIONS INC
45300b Us Highway 20 (44074-9262)
PHONE 440 775-0015
Joanne Douglas, *President*
EMP: 6
SQ FT: 7,000

SALES: 573.9K **Privately Held**
WEB: www.bigproductionsinc.com
SIC: 2299 Jute & flax textile products

(G-15492)
CHAOS MATRIX LTD
44451 Kipton Nickle Plate (44074-9519)
PHONE..........................614 638-4748
David Clark,
Karrie Pontius,
EMP: 4
SALES (est): 225.6K **Privately Held**
WEB: www.chaosmatrix.com
SIC: 3571 Electronic computers

(G-15493)
EAST OBERLIN CABINETS
13184 Hale Rd (44074-9741)
PHONE..........................440 775-1166
Dennis Luttrell, *Owner*
EMP: 7 **EST:** 1976
SALES (est): 694.1K **Privately Held**
SIC: 2511 2434 Silverware chests: wood; desks, household: wood; vanities, bathroom: wood

(G-15494)
ENERGY DEVELOPMENTS INC
43550 Oberlin Elyria Rd (44074-9591)
PHONE..........................440 774-6816
EMP: 4
SALES (est): 410K **Privately Held**
SIC: 3612 Mfg Transformers

(G-15495)
GAZETTE PUBLISHING COMPANY (PA)
Also Called: Bellevue Gazette
42 S Main St (44074-1627)
PHONE..........................419 483-4190
Rick Miller, *President*
Thomas R Smith, *President*
Donald Reiderman, *Principal*
Greg Callaghan, *Admin Sec*
EMP: 117 **EST:** 1867
SQ FT: 6,000
SALES (est): 6.8MM **Privately Held**
WEB: www.theoberlinnews.com
SIC: 2711 2791 2752 Newspapers, publishing & printing; typesetting; commercial printing, lithographic

(G-15496)
GIBSON BROS INC
Also Called: Gibson Bakery
23 W College St (44074-1543)
PHONE..........................440 774-2401
Allyn Gibson, *President*
David Gibson, *Treasurer*
Melba Gibson, *Admin Sec*
EMP: 23 **EST:** 1885
SQ FT: 3,010
SALES (est): 2.2MM **Privately Held**
WEB: www.gibsonbros.com
SIC: 5411 2051 2064 2024 Grocery stores, independent; bakery: wholesale or wholesale/retail combined; candy & other confectionery products; ice cream & ice milk

(G-15497)
GOPOWERX INC
283 Eastern Ave (44074-1054)
P.O. Box 37 (44074-0037)
PHONE..........................440 707-6029
Neil Sater, *President*
EMP: 30
SALES (est): 3.4MM
SALES (corp-wide): 324.5K **Privately Held**
SIC: 5211 3674 Solar heating equipment; semiconductors & related devices
PA: Mh Gopower Company Limited
 6-2, Luke 3rd Rd.,
 Kaohsiung City
 769 559-00

(G-15498)
HAMCO MANUFACTURING INC
48882 State Route 511 (44074-9496)
PHONE..........................440 774-1637
Maurice H Hand, *President*
David Hand, *Vice Pres*
EMP: 4 **EST:** 1963
SQ FT: 4,000

SALES: 300K **Privately Held**
SIC: 3451 Screw machine products

(G-15499)
HYDRO TUBE ENTERPRISES INC (PA)
137 Artino St (44074-1265)
PHONE..........................440 774-1022
Mike Prokop, *President*
Richard Cooks, *Vice Pres*
Thomas E Hamel, *Vice Pres*
Tim Althaus, *VP Opers*
Barry Spreng, *Plant Supt*
▲ **EMP:** 70 **EST:** 1922
SQ FT: 67,000
SALES (est): 21.7MM **Privately Held**
WEB: www.hydrotube.com
SIC: 3498 Tube fabricating (contract bending & shaping)

(G-15500)
J RETTENMAIER USA LP
216 Oberlin Rd (44074-1202)
PHONE..........................440 385-6701
EMP: 6
SALES (corp-wide): 355.8K **Privately Held**
SIC: 2823 2299 Cellulosic manmade fibers; flock (recovered textile fibers)
HQ: J. Rettenmaier Usa Lp
 16369 Us Highway 131 S
 Schoolcraft MI 49087
 269 679-2340

(G-15501)
JB POLYMERS INC
55 S Main St Ste 204 (44074-1626)
PHONE..........................216 941-7041
John Busa, *President*
Jamie Fryberger, *Opers Mgr*
EMP: 9
SQ FT: 40,000
SALES (est): 1.5MM **Privately Held**
WEB: www.jbpolymers.com
SIC: 2821 Plastics materials & resins

(G-15502)
MOLD SOLUTIONS
55 S Main St Ste 131 (44074-1626)
PHONE..........................800 948-4947
Charles Bodey, *Principal*
EMP: 4
SALES (est): 360.4K **Privately Held**
SIC: 3544 Industrial molds

(G-15503)
NANOTECH INNOVATIONS LLC
132 Artino St (44074-1206)
PHONE..........................440 926-4888
Dennis Flood,
▼ **EMP:** 4
SQ FT: 2,000
SALES (est): 407.2K **Privately Held**
SIC: 3821 Laboratory equipment: fume hoods, distillation racks, etc.

(G-15504)
R R DONNELLEY & SONS COMPANY
Also Called: R & S Label
450 Sterns Rd (44074-1209)
PHONE..........................440 774-2101
Jake Martin, *Manager*
EMP: 50
SQ FT: 23,141
SALES (corp-wide): 6.8B **Publicly Held**
WEB: www.moore.com
SIC: 2752 2759 2672 2761 Commercial printing, lithographic; promotional printing, lithographic; tickets, lithographed; tags, lithographed; letterpress printing; promotional printing; schedule, ticket & tag printing & engraving; tags: printing; coated & laminated paper; continuous forms, office & business
PA: R. R. Donnelley & Sons Company
 35 W Wacker Dr Ste 3650
 Chicago IL 60601
 312 326-8000

(G-15505)
SWITZER PERFORMANCE ENGRG
Also Called: Switzer Performance Innovation
44800 Us Highway 20 (44074-9702)
P.O. Box 66 (44074-0066)
PHONE..........................440 774-4219
Tymme Switzer, *President*
Neil Switzer, *Consultant*
▲ **EMP:** 11
SALES (est): 1.7MM **Privately Held**
SIC: 3714 Motor vehicle engines & parts

Obetz
Franklin County

(G-15506)
CAPITOL CITY MFG CO INC
3881 Groveport Rd (43207-5126)
PHONE..........................614 491-1192
Matthew Peters, *President*
EMP: 4
SQ FT: 5,000
SALES: 500K **Privately Held**
SIC: 3452 Bolts, nuts, rivets & washers

(G-15507)
CAPITOL CITY TRAILERS INC
3960 Groveport Rd (43207-5127)
PHONE..........................614 491-2616
Buck Stewart, *President*
Scott Brown, *Vice Pres*
Tim Stewart, *Vice Pres*
Jeff Steen, *Sales Engr*
Rob Ryder, *Director*
EMP: 58
SQ FT: 20,000
SALES (est): 10.8MM **Privately Held**
WEB: www.capitolcitytrailers.net
SIC: 7539 3792 Trailer repair; travel trailers & campers

(G-15508)
CENTRAL ALUMINUM COMPANY LLC
2045 Broehm Rd (43207-5206)
PHONE..........................614 491-5700
Lee Grove, *General Mgr*
Kory Brockman, *CFO*
Jeannie Dawson, *Accounts Mgr*
EMP: 50 **EST:** 1963
SQ FT: 94,000
SALES (est): 16.7MM **Privately Held**
WEB: www.centralaluminum.com
SIC: 3354 3479 Aluminum extruded products; painting, coating & hot dipping
PA: Gdic Group, Llc
 1300 E 9th St Fl 20
 Cleveland OH 44114

(G-15509)
CHERYL & CO
4465 Industrial Center Dr (43207-4589)
PHONE..........................614 776-1500
Jodi Dixon, *Branch Mgr*
EMP: 80 **Publicly Held**
WEB: www.cherylandco.com
SIC: 2052 2066 Cookies & crackers; chocolate & cocoa products
HQ: Cheryl & Co.
 646 Mccorkle Blvd
 Westerville OH 43082
 614 776-1500

(G-15510)
MASONS SAND AND GRAVEL CO
2385 Rathmell Rd (43207-4835)
PHONE..........................614 491-3611
George C Smith, *President*
EMP: 9 **EST:** 1951
SQ FT: 3,000
SALES (est): 972.4K **Privately Held**
SIC: 1442 Construction sand mining; gravel mining

(G-15511)
MICHAEL R KELLY
Also Called: Kelly Printing
1657 Victor Ave (43207-4364)
PHONE..........................614 491-1745
Michael Kelly, *Principal*

EMP: 5
SQ FT: 2,000
SALES: 300K **Privately Held**
SIC: 2752 Lithographing on metal; commercial printing, offset

(G-15512)
NATIONAL BEVERAGE CORP
Also Called: Shasta Beverges
4685 Groveport Rd (43207-5216)
PHONE..........................614 491-5415
Thomas Watson, *Opers Mgr*
Monte Hale, *Manager*
EMP: 50
SALES (corp-wide): 975.7MM **Publicly Held**
WEB: www.natbev.com
SIC: 2086 Soft drinks: packaged in cans, bottles, etc.
PA: National Beverage Corp.
 8100 Sw 10th St Ste 4000
 Plantation FL 33324
 954 581-0922

(G-15513)
SHASTA BEVERAGES INC
Also Called: National Beverage
4685 Groveport Rd (43207-5295)
PHONE..........................614 491-5415
Monty Hale, *Manager*
EMP: 30
SALES (corp-wide): 975.7MM **Publicly Held**
SIC: 2086 Soft drinks: packaged in cans, bottles, etc.
HQ: Shasta Beverages, Inc.
 26901 Indl Blvd
 Hayward CA 94545
 954 581-0922

Ohio City
Van Wert County

(G-15514)
BAKER BUILT PRODUCTS INC
Also Called: Foot Wings
11877 Walnut Grove Ch Rd (45874-9244)
PHONE..........................419 965-2646
John A Baker Sr, *President*
Bruce L Baker, *President*
Barbara Baker, *Corp Secy*
John Baker, *Vice Pres*
EMP: 3 **EST:** 1974
SQ FT: 3,600
SALES (est): 500K **Privately Held**
WEB: www.bakerbuilt.com
SIC: 2851 7692 3523 Polyurethane coatings; welding repair; farm machinery & equipment

Okeana
Butler County

(G-15515)
AC SHINERS INC
5747 Jenkins Rd (45053-9688)
PHONE..........................513 738-1573
Arthur Schoultheis, *President*
William Schoultheis, *President*
Joseph Schoultheis, *Corp Secy*
EMP: 4
SQ FT: 3,500
SALES: 125K **Privately Held**
WEB: www.acshiners.com
SIC: 3949 Lures, fishing: artificial

(G-15516)
CHRISNIK INC
7461 Cncnnati Brkville Rd (45053-9780)
P.O. Box 516, Ross (45061-0516)
PHONE..........................513 738-2920
Robert Zaenkert, *President*
EMP: 6
SQ FT: 10,000
SALES: 300K **Privately Held**
SIC: 3423 5072 Masons' hand tools; hardware

Okeana - Butler County (G-15517)

(G-15517)
CUSTOM FABRICATION BY FISHER
100 Weaver Rd (45053-9711)
PHONE...................513 738-4600
Rodney Fisher, *Principal*
EMP: 7
SALES (est): 877.1K **Privately Held**
SIC: 3499 Novelties & giftware, including trophies

(G-15518)
D & E ELECTRIC INC
7055 Okana Drewersburg Rd (45053-9651)
PHONE...................513 738-1172
Douglas E Fritz, *President*
Edward H Fritz, *Vice Pres*
EMP: 15
SALES: 2MM **Privately Held**
SIC: 1731 3643 General electrical contractor; current-carrying wiring devices

(G-15519)
L B MACHINE & MFG CO INC
6624 Layhigh Rd (45053-9414)
PHONE...................513 471-6137
Gary Skora, *Owner*
Glenn Skora, *Vice Pres*
EMP: 8
SALES: 800K **Privately Held**
SIC: 3544 3542 Special dies, tools, jigs & fixtures; die casting machines

(G-15520)
WAGERS INC
2464 California Rd (45053-9618)
PHONE...................513 825-6300
Jim Wagers, *President*
EMP: 6
SALES (est): 540K **Privately Held**
WEB: www.wagers.com
SIC: 2899 Ink or writing fluids

(G-15521)
WHITMAN CORPORATION
2530 Joyce Ln (45053-9746)
PHONE...................513 541-3223
Toll Free:............................888 -
James Erhardt, *President*
Susan Erhardt, *Treasurer*
EMP: 6
SQ FT: 8,016
SALES: 500K **Privately Held**
WEB: www.taxidermist.net
SIC: 3161 3199 Cases, carrying; saddles or parts

(G-15522)
ZAENKERT SURVEYING ESSENTIALS
7461a Cncnnati Brkvlle Rd (45053-9780)
PHONE...................513 738-2917
Robert Zaenkert, *President*
Michelle Zaenkert, *Vice Pres*
EMP: 8
SQ FT: 2,100
SALES (est): 1.2MM **Privately Held**
SIC: 2499 5049 5211 Surveyors' stakes, wood; surveyors' instruments; lumber & other building materials

Okolona
Henry County

(G-15523)
REPUBLIC MILLS INC
Also Called: Hudson Feeds
888 School St (43545-9246)
PHONE...................419 758-3511
William H Koon II, *President*
Richard Lange, *General Mgr*
Becky Hardy, *Principal*
Sandy Wagner, *Principal*
Ronald Wingfield, *Corp Secy*
▼ **EMP:** 14
SQ FT: 30,000
SALES (est): 2.5MM **Privately Held**
WEB: www.republicmills.com
SIC: 2048 5191 Livestock feeds; feed

Old Fort
Seneca County

(G-15524)
CHURCH & DWIGHT CO INC
2501 E County Rd 34 (44861)
P.O. Box 122 (44861-0122)
PHONE...................419 992-4244
Bruce Neeley, *Branch Mgr*
EMP: 14
SALES (corp-wide): 4.1B **Publicly Held**
WEB: www.churchdwight.com
SIC: 2812 Sodium bicarbonate
PA: Church & Dwight Co., Inc.
500 Charles Ewing Blvd
Ewing NJ 08628
609 806-1200

(G-15525)
M & B ASPHALT COMPANY INC
Also Called: Maple Grove Stone
1525 W County Road 42 (44861)
P.O. Box 136 (44861-0136)
PHONE...................419 992-4236
EMP: 9
SALES (corp-wide): 69.4MM **Privately Held**
SIC: 2951 Asphalt paving mixtures & blocks
PA: M & B Asphalt Company, Inc.
1525 W Seneca Cnty Rd 42
Tiffin OH 44883
419 992-4235

Old Washington
Guernsey County

(G-15526)
HERSHBERGERS DUTCH MARKET LLP
Also Called: Dutch Barn Builders
228 Old National Rd (43768-9901)
PHONE...................740 489-5322
EMP: 22
SQ FT: 8,400
SALES (est): 1.1MM **Privately Held**
SIC: 5251 5411 5499 2452 Hardware & Grocery Store Ret Dried Fruit Spices & Herbs & Mfg Wood Storage Buildings

Olmsted Falls
Cuyahoga County

(G-15527)
ADAMS AUTOMATIC INC
26070 N Depot St (44138-1647)
P.O. Box 38156 (44138-0156)
PHONE...................440 235-4416
Edward Bond, *President*
Eric Dales, *President*
Adria Bond, *Vice Pres*
Kathy Bolek, *Executive Asst*
EMP: 10 **EST:** 1952
SQ FT: 7,200
SALES (est): 1.1MM **Privately Held**
WEB: www.adamsautomatic.com
SIC: 3451 Screw machine products

(G-15528)
AMERIPRINT
8119 Columbia Rd (44138-2023)
PHONE...................440 235-6094
Anthoney Giancaterino, *Principal*
EMP: 3
SALES (est): 180K **Privately Held**
SIC: 2759 Commercial printing

(G-15529)
BLUE RIDGE PAPER PRODUCTS INC
Also Called: Dairy Pak Div
7920 Mapleway Dr (44138-1626)
PHONE...................440 235-7200
Dave Lewallen, *Branch Mgr*
EMP: 200
SQ FT: 161,146
SALES (corp-wide): 1MM **Privately Held**
WEB: www.blueridgepaper.com
SIC: 2621 Fine paper; kraft paper
HQ: Blue Ridge Paper Products Inc.
41 Main St
Canton NC 28716
828 454-0676

(G-15530)
EVERGREEN PACKAGING INC
Also Called: Olmsted Falls Plant
7920 Mapleway Dr (44138-1626)
PHONE...................440 235-7200
William Shroka, *Safety Dir*
Marlene Smith, *Plant Mgr*
Greg Jones, *Branch Mgr*
EMP: 5
SALES (corp-wide): 1MM **Privately Held**
SIC: 2621 5199 Paper mills; packaging materials
HQ: Evergreen Packaging Llc
5350 Poplar Ave Ste 600
Memphis TN 38119

(G-15531)
THERMAFAB ALLOY INC
25367 Water St (44138-2015)
PHONE...................216 861-0540
George M Donnelly, *CEO*
Gilbert Sherman, *COO*
Daniel P Conway, *CFO*
EMP: 35
SQ FT: 58,000
SALES (est): 4.9MM **Privately Held**
WEB: www.tfaballoy.com
SIC: 3087 Custom compound purchased resins

Olmsted Twp
Cuyahoga County

(G-15532)
AMERICAN WIRE & CABLE COMPANY (PA)
7951 Bronson Rd (44138-1088)
PHONE...................440 235-1140
Richard M McClain, *President*
Kim R McClain, *Vice Pres*
▲ **EMP:** 30 **EST:** 1955
SQ FT: 80,000
SALES (est): 24.4MM **Privately Held**
WEB: www.americanwireandcable.com
SIC: 3357 3351 3315 Nonferrous wire-drawing & insulating; wire, copper & copper alloy; steel wire & related products

(G-15533)
LIBER LIMITED LLC
7162 Windwood Way (44138-1167)
PHONE...................440 427-0647
David C Liber, *President*
EMP: 5
SALES: 1.2MM **Privately Held**
SIC: 3465 5531 Body parts, automobile: stamped metal; automotive parts

(G-15534)
NEBULATRONICS INC
24542 Nobottom Rd (44138-1540)
PHONE...................440 243-2370
Kenneth Rados, *President*
Steve Harris, *Vice Pres*
Mike Panfil, *Vice Pres*
EMP: 26
SQ FT: 5,000
SALES (est): 3MM **Privately Held**
SIC: 3825 3829 Transducers for volts, amperes, watts, vars, frequency, etc.; measuring & controlling devices

(G-15535)
OLMSTED ICE INC
8134 Bronson Rd (44138-1033)
PHONE...................440 235-8411
Norman Dickson, *President*
Tom Dickson, *Vice Pres*
Ted Dickson, *Treasurer*
Tony Dickson, *Admin Sec*
EMP: 20
SQ FT: 3,000
SALES (est): 3MM **Privately Held**
WEB: www.olmstedice.com
SIC: 2097 Manufactured ice

(G-15536)
SSO INC
27064 Dogwood Ln (44138-3253)
PHONE...................440 235-3500
EMP: 15
SALES (est): 1.1MM **Privately Held**
SIC: 3554 Mfg Paper Industrial Machinery

Ontario
Richland County

(G-15537)
ADDED TOUCH DECORATING GALLERY
1162 Cobblefield Dr (44903-8257)
PHONE...................419 747-3146
Lorretta Compton, *Owner*
Lori Mc Clintock, *Manager*
EMP: 3
SQ FT: 3,150
SALES (est): 238.8K **Privately Held**
SIC: 3263 5719 7389 Semivitreous table & kitchenware; kitchenware; lighting, lamps & accessories; window furnishings; pictures & mirrors; interior designer

(G-15538)
CHILD EVNGELISM FELLOWSHIP INC
Also Called: Ashland R Crawford Knox
535 Beer Rd (44906-1214)
P.O. Box 67, Mansfield (44901-0067)
PHONE...................419 756-7799
Dale Baer, *Manager*
EMP: 41
SALES (corp-wide): 24.4MM **Privately Held**
SIC: 2752 Commercial printing, lithographic
PA: Child Evangelism Fellowship Incorporated
17482 Highway M
Warrenton MO 63383
636 456-4321

(G-15539)
CNB LLC
Also Called: Minuteman Press
84 Briggs Dr (44906-3829)
PHONE...................419 528-3109
Rachel Carter, *Accounts Exec*
Bonnie Brody, *Mng Member*
Mark Cooper, *Manager*
Mark A Cooper,
EMP: 3
SQ FT: 1,300
SALES: 25K **Privately Held**
SIC: 2752 Commercial printing, offset

(G-15540)
COLE TOOL & DIE COMPANY
Also Called: Oil Tooling and Stamping
466 State Route 314 N (44903-6555)
P.O. Box 150 (44862-0150)
PHONE...................419 522-1272
Alan D Cole, *CEO*
Dave Harmon, *President*
David Hammer, *Sales Staff*
Denice Crowner, *Administration*
EMP: 40 **EST:** 1953
SQ FT: 28,000
SALES (est): 11.1MM **Privately Held**
SIC: 3544 3469 3465 Special dies & tools; metal stampings; automotive stampings

(G-15541)
EMERSON PROCESS MANAGEMENT
Also Called: Shafer Valve Company
2500 Park Ave W (44906-1235)
PHONE...................419 529-4311
Dale Opperman, *Regl Sales Mgr*
Denise McQuade, *Info Tech Mgr*
EMP: 37
SALES (corp-wide): 17.4B **Publicly Held**
SIC: 3594 3593 Fluid power pumps & motors; fluid power actuators, hydraulic or pneumatic

HQ: Emerson Process Management Valve
Automation, Inc.
8100 West Florissant Ave
Saint Louis MO 63136
314 553-2000

(G-15542)
IRON VAULT DISTILLERY LLC
3880 Horizon Dr (44903-6540)
PHONE.....................................419 747-7560
John C Bassett, *Owner*
EMP: 3 **EST:** 2017
SALES (est): 112.6K **Privately Held**
SIC: 2085 Distilled & blended liquors

(G-15543)
MAR-ZANE INC
1300 W 4th St (44906-1828)
P.O. Box 1321, Mansfield (44901-1321)
PHONE.....................................419 529-2086
Herb Jarsar, *Manager*
EMP: 3
SALES (corp-wide): 276.3MM **Privately Held**
SIC: 1499 Asphalt (native) mining
HQ: Mar-Zane, Inc.
3570 S River Rd
Zanesville OH 43701
740 453-0721

(G-15544)
ONTARIO MECHANICAL LLC
2880 Park Ave W (44906-1026)
PHONE.....................................419 529-2578
Dave Baker, *Vice Pres*
Kenneth Earhart, *Mng Member*
EMP: 30 **EST:** 2012
SALES (est): 6.8MM **Privately Held**
SIC: 3449 1761 1791 Custom roll formed products; sheet metalwork; structural steel erection

(G-15545)
OXYRASE INC
3000 Park Ave W (44906-1050)
P.O. Box 1345, Mansfield (44901-1345)
PHONE.....................................419 589-8800
James Copeland, *Ch of Bd*
Casey Zace, *President*
EMP: 10
SQ FT: 7,000
SALES: 1MM **Privately Held**
WEB: www.oxyrase.com
SIC: 2869 Enzymes

(G-15546)
P R MACHINE WORKS INC
1825 Nussbaum Pkwy (44906-2360)
PHONE.....................................419 529-5748
Mark Romanchuk, *President*
Mark J Romanchuk, *President*
Jerry Schwall, *Vice Pres*
Mike Strench, *Purch Mgr*
Andrea Dill, *Human Res Mgr*
▲ **EMP:** 75
SQ FT: 14,100
SALES: 9.5MM **Privately Held**
WEB: www.prmachineworks.com
SIC: 3599 1531 Machine shop, jobbing & repair;

(G-15547)
POLY GREEN TECHNOLOGIES LLC
1237 W 4th St (44906-1825)
PHONE.....................................419 529-9909
Jeffrey Schultheis,
EMP: 5
SALES (est): 483.5K **Privately Held**
SIC: 2821 Plastics materials & resins

(G-15548)
STUMBO PUBLISHING CO
Also Called: Tribune Courier
347 Allen Dr (44906-1001)
P.O. Box 127 (44862-0127)
PHONE.....................................419 529-2847
Frank Stumbo, *President*
Jim Warne, *Editor*
Jenna Wolford, *Production*
Betty Stumbo, *Treasurer*
EMP: 3 **EST:** 1961
SQ FT: 800
SALES (est): 359.6K **Privately Held**
WEB: www.tribunecourier.com
SIC: 2791 2711 Typesetting; newspapers

(G-15549)
UNISPORT INC
Also Called: Johnny Johnson Sports
2254 Stumbo Rd (44906-3804)
PHONE.....................................419 529-4727
H Kim Baird, *President*
Todd Baird, *Vice Pres*
EMP: 10
SALES: 1.5MM **Privately Held**
SIC: 5136 5137 5699 2759 Sportswear, men's & boys'; sportswear, women's & children's; sports apparel; screen printing; embroidery products, except schiffli machine

(G-15550)
WHITE MULE COMPANY
2420 W 4th St (44906-1207)
PHONE.....................................740 382-9008
EMP: 21
SQ FT: 15,000
SALES (est): 4.2MM **Privately Held**
SIC: 3714 1791 Mfg Motor Vehicle Parts/Accessories Steel Erection

Oregon
Lucas County

(G-15551)
A & L INDUSTRIES
Also Called: A & L Inds Machining & Repr
2054 Grange St (43616-4442)
PHONE.....................................419 698-3733
Allen Hoar Jr, *Owner*
EMP: 30
SALES (est): 2.8MM **Privately Held**
SIC: 3599 Machine shop, jobbing & repair

(G-15552)
ABC APPLIANCE INC
3012 Navarre Ave (43616-3308)
PHONE.....................................419 693-4414
J R Pruss, *Manager*
EMP: 30
SALES (corp-wide): 300.7MM **Privately Held**
WEB: www.abcwarehouse.com
SIC: 3639 5722 5731 5065 Major kitchen appliances, except refrigerators & stoves; vacuum cleaners; high fidelity stereo equipment; telephone equipment; photocopy machines
PA: Abc Appliance, Inc.
1 W Silverdome Indus Park
Pontiac MI 48342
248 335-4222

(G-15553)
AECOM ENERGY & CNSTR INC
Also Called: Washington Group
4001 Cedar Point Rd (43616-1310)
P.O. Box 696, Toledo (43697-0696)
PHONE.....................................419 698-6277
EMP: 125
SALES (corp-wide): 20.1B **Publicly Held**
WEB: www.wgint.com
SIC: 1542 2911 Nonresidential construction; petroleum refining
HQ: Aecom Energy & Construction, Inc.
1999 Avenue Of The Stars
Los Angeles CA 90067
213 593-8100

(G-15554)
ASPHALT MATERIALS INC
940 N Wynn Rd (43616-1428)
PHONE.....................................419 693-0626
Chris Arman, *Manager*
EMP: 13
SQ FT: 5,600
SALES (corp-wide): 248.2MM **Privately Held**
SIC: 2951 Asphalt paving mixtures & blocks
PA: Asphalt Materials, Inc.
5400 W 86th St
Indianapolis IN 46268
317 872-6010

(G-15555)
AUTONEUM NORTH AMERICA INC
4131 Spartan Dr (43616-1300)
PHONE.....................................419 690-8924
EMP: 5
SALES (corp-wide): 2.2B **Privately Held**
SIC: 3714 Motor vehicle parts & accessories
HQ: Autoneum North America, Inc.
29293 Haggerty Rd
Novi MI 48377
248 848-0100

(G-15556)
AUTONEUM NORTH AMERICA INC
Also Called: Rieter Automotive-Oregon Plant
645 N Lallendorf Rd (43616-1334)
PHONE.....................................419 693-0511
Gordon Shaw, *Branch Mgr*
EMP: 350
SQ FT: 150,000
SALES (corp-wide): 2.2B **Privately Held**
WEB: www.rieter.com
SIC: 3625 3714 3444 3296 Relays & industrial controls; motor vehicle parts & accessories; sheet metalwork; mineral wool; nonwoven fabrics
HQ: Autoneum North America, Inc.
29293 Haggerty Rd
Novi MI 48377
248 848-0100

(G-15557)
BRANAM ORAL HEALTH TECH INC (PA)
3140 Dustin Rd (43616-4341)
PHONE.....................................248 670-0040
Michael J Janness, *President*
EMP: 4
SQ FT: 5,000
SALES (est): 599.6K **Privately Held**
SIC: 3843 Abrasive points, wheels & disks, dental

(G-15558)
CITGO PETROLEUM CORPORATION
1840 Otter Creek Rd (43616-1212)
PHONE.....................................419 698-8055
Pete Krivas, *Manager*
EMP: 5 **Privately Held**
WEB: www.citgo.com
SIC: 2911 Petroleum refining
HQ: Citgo Petroleum Corporation
1293 Eldridge Pkwy
Houston TX 77077
832 486-4000

(G-15559)
CTS SIGNS & SALES
1030 Cresceus Rd (43616-3123)
PHONE.....................................419 407-5534
Charles Baptista, *Owner*
EMP: 3
SALES (est): 143.9K **Privately Held**
SIC: 3993 Signs & advertising specialties

(G-15560)
FOUTY & COMPANY INC
5003 Bayshore Rd (43616-4478)
P.O. Box 167544 (43616-7544)
PHONE.....................................419 693-0017
Marion L Fouty, *President*
Ken Fouty, *President*
Ken Poupard, *Accounts Mgr*
▲ **EMP:** 20
SQ FT: 20,000
SALES (est): 4.2MM **Privately Held**
WEB: www.foutywaterjet.com
SIC: 5085 3053 Rubber goods, mechanical; gaskets, all materials

(G-15561)
MR EMBLEM INC
3209 Navarre Ave (43616-3311)
PHONE.....................................419 697-1888
Pat Slygh, *CEO*
Annette Clair, *Bookkeeper*
Connie Black, *Manager*
EMP: 7
SQ FT: 3,600
SALES: 950K **Privately Held**
WEB: www.mremblem.com
SIC: 2395 2396 5199 Embroidery & art needlework; screen printing on fabric articles; advertising specialties

(G-15562)
NISSEN LUMBER & COAL CO INC (PA)
5700 Navarre Ave (43616-3546)
PHONE.....................................419 836-8035
Jerry Nissen, *President*
Alan Nissen, *Vice Pres*
Eugene Nissen, *Treasurer*
Dennis Nissen, *Admin Sec*
EMP: 5
SQ FT: 1,200
SALES (est): 3.2MM **Privately Held**
SIC: 3273 5211 Ready-mixed concrete; sand & gravel; concrete & cinder block

(G-15563)
NORFOLK SOUTHERN CORPORATION
3830 Corduroy Rd (43616-1810)
PHONE.....................................419 697-5070
James Swider, *Manager*
EMP: 20
SALES (corp-wide): 11.4B **Publicly Held**
WEB: www.nscorp.com
SIC: 3743 4789 Railroad car rebuilding; railroad car repair
PA: Norfolk Southern Corporation
3 Commercial Pl Ste 1a
Norfolk VA 23510
757 629-2680

(G-15564)
PRAXAIR INC
3742 Cedar Point Rd (43616)
PHONE.....................................419 698-8005
Bill Engberg, *Manager*
EMP: 8 **Privately Held**
SIC: 2813 Industrial gases
HQ: Praxair, Inc.
10 Riverview Dr
Danbury CT 06810
203 837-2000

(G-15565)
R-MED INC
Also Called: Endoglobe
3465 Navarre Ave (43616-3427)
P.O. Box 167636 (43616-7636)
PHONE.....................................419 693-7481
Erol Riza, *President*
Burak Riza, *Manager*
▲ **EMP:** 7
SQ FT: 2,500
SALES (est): 972.1K **Privately Held**
SIC: 3841 Surgical & medical instruments

(G-15566)
RBM ENVIRONMENTAL AND CNSTR
4526 Bayshore Rd (43616-1035)
PHONE.....................................419 693-5840
Bob J Petty, *President*
Mike S Petty, *Vice Pres*
EMP: 40
SALES (est): 4.9MM **Privately Held**
SIC: 1794 7699 7692 3498 Excavation work; tank & boiler cleaning service; welding repair; fabricated pipe & fittings; fabricated structural metal

(G-15567)
SNOWS WOOD SHOP INC (PA)
7220 Brown Rd (43616-5805)
PHONE.....................................419 836-3805
Vernon Snow, *President*
Minda Snow, *Corp Secy*
Kurt Snow, *Vice Pres*
EMP: 22
SQ FT: 10,380
SALES (est): 2.3MM **Privately Held**
SIC: 2434 1751 Wood kitchen cabinets; cabinet & finish carpentry

(G-15568)
STANDARD OIL COMPANY
4001 Cedar Point Rd (43616-1310)
P.O. Box 696, Toledo (43697-0696)
PHONE.....................................419 698-6200
Terri Harlan, *Manager*

Oregon - Lucas County (G-15569)

EMP: 50
SALES (corp-wide): 240.2B **Privately Held**
WEB: www.crystal-enterprise.com
SIC: 2911 5541 Petroleum refining; gasoline service stations
HQ: The Standard Oil Company
  4101 Winfield Rd Ste 100
  Warrenville IL 60555
  630 836-5000

(G-15569)
STANDARD OIL COMPANY
Also Called: Pipeline Dept
4151 Cedar Point Rd (43616-1312)
PHONE 419 691-2460
Dennis Lahey, *Manager*
EMP: 5
SALES (corp-wide): 240.2B **Privately Held**
WEB: www.crystal-enterprise.com
SIC: 1382 1389 Oil & gas exploration services; gas field services
HQ: The Standard Oil Company
  4101 Winfield Rd Ste 100
  Warrenville IL 60555
  630 836-5000

(G-15570)
SWANSON ORTHOTIC & PROSTHETIC
Also Called: Novacare Prosthetics Orthotics
3048 Navarre Ave (43616-3308)
PHONE 419 690-0026
Vern Swanson, *Principal*
John Duggan, *Principal*
Robert Ortenzio, *Principal*
Scott Romberger, *Principal*
Michael Tarvin, *Principal*
EMP: 5
SALES (est): 355.6K **Privately Held**
SIC: 3842 Limbs, artificial

(G-15571)
TOLEDO ALFALFA MILLS INC
861 S Stadium Rd (43616-5898)
PHONE 419 836-3705
Kathryn Lumbrezes, *President*
Gary Lumbrezer, *Vice Pres*
Becky Lumbrezer-Box, *Admin Sec*
EMP: 8
SQ FT: 6,000
SALES (est): 758.2K **Privately Held**
SIC: 2048 Alfalfa or alfalfa meal, prepared as animal feed

(G-15572)
VORLAGE SPECIAL TOOL
205 Utah St (43605-2243)
PHONE 419 697-1201
Donald F Arnold, *Principal*
EMP: 3
SALES (est): 266.5K **Privately Held**
SIC: 3599 Machine shop, jobbing & repair

Oregonia
Warren County

(G-15573)
PROCTER & GAMBLE COMPANY
600 S Waynesville Rd (45054-9405)
PHONE 513 934-3406
C C Grabowski-Flaherty, *Manager*
EMP: 150
SALES (corp-wide): 66.8B **Publicly Held**
WEB: www.pg.com
SIC: 2844 2676 3421 2842 Deodorants, personal; towels, napkins & tissue paper products; razor blades & razors; specialty cleaning preparations; soap: granulated, liquid, cake, flaked or chip
PA: The Procter & Gamble Company
  1 Procter And Gamble Plz
  Cincinnati OH 45202
  513 983-1100

Orient
Pickaway County

(G-15574)
B & B INDUSTRIES INC
7001 Harrisburg Pike (43146-9468)
PHONE 614 871-3883
Bernard Harwood, *Owner*
Ken Webb, *General Mgr*
EMP: 4
SALES (est): 160K **Privately Held**
SIC: 3799 Golf carts, powered

(G-15575)
KMJ LEASING LTD
Also Called: B & B Industries
7001 Harrisburg Pike (43146-9468)
PHONE 614 871-3883
Kenneth A Harwood,
Mary A Harwood,
EMP: 38 **EST:** 1971
SQ FT: 5,000
SALES (est): 6.6MM **Privately Held**
WEB: www.bandbindustriesinc.com
SIC: 4213 3799 Contract haulers; golf carts, powered

(G-15576)
PETTITS PALLETS INC
11812 London Rd (43146)
PHONE 614 351-4920
Brenda Pettit, *President*
Tim Pettit, *Vice Pres*
EMP: 7
SALES (est): 679.3K **Privately Held**
SIC: 2448 Pallets, wood

(G-15577)
SCIOTO DARBY QUARTER HORSES
8701 Scioto Darby Rd (43146-9712)
PHONE 614 464-7290
EMP: 3
SALES (est): 159.6K **Privately Held**
SIC: 3131 Quarters

(G-15578)
SPECIALTEE SPORTSWEAR & DESIGN
9819 Us Highway 62 (43146-9175)
PHONE 614 877-0976
Randy Hill, *Mng Member*
EMP: 5
SALES (est): 559.5K **Privately Held**
SIC: 2759 5199 Screen printing; advertising specialties

(G-15579)
WONDER WELD INC
6127 Harrisburg Pike (43146-9409)
PHONE 614 875-1447
Doris Jean, *President*
Branden Timothy, *Manager*
EMP: 4
SQ FT: 17,000
SALES (est): 468.3K **Privately Held**
WEB: www.wonderweld.com
SIC: 7692 3677 3548 Welding repair; electronic coils, transformers & other inductors; welding apparatus

Orrville
Wayne County

(G-15580)
AAA PLASTICS AND PALLETS LTD
3505 York Rd (44667-9278)
PHONE 330 844-2556
Dan A Hargrove, *Principal*
EMP: 8 **EST:** 2008
SALES (est): 1MM **Privately Held**
SIC: 2448 Pallets, wood

(G-15581)
ACCURATE ELECTRONICS INC
169 S Main St (44667-1801)
P.O. Box 900 (44667-0900)
PHONE 330 682-7015
Jeffrey Evans, *CEO*
EMP: 250
SQ FT: 6,000
SALES (est): 17MM
SALES (corp-wide): 63.8MM **Privately Held**
WEB: www.willburt.com
SIC: 3679 3621 3812 3672 Electronic circuits; generators & sets, electric; search & navigation equipment; printed circuit boards; radio & TV communications equipment; current-carrying wiring devices
PA: The Will-Burt Company
  169 S Main St
  Orrville OH 44667
  330 682-7015

(G-15582)
ADVANCED CHEM SOLUTIONS INC
150 Allen Ave (44667-9021)
PHONE 216 692-3005
Gerry Groudle, *Branch Mgr*
EMP: 5
SALES (corp-wide): 3.5MM **Privately Held**
SIC: 2899 Chemical preparations
PA: Advanced Chemical Solutions Inc
  1114 N Court St 196
  Medina OH 44256
  330 283-5157

(G-15583)
BEKAERT CORPORATION
Also Called: Contours
322 E Pine St (44667-1853)
PHONE 330 683-5060
Otto Simmerman, *Principal*
EMP: 190
SQ FT: 260,000
SALES (corp-wide): 483.3MM **Privately Held**
WEB: www.bekaert.com
SIC: 3315 3316 3398 3479 Wire & fabricated wire products; fencing made in wiredrawing plants; cold-rolled strip or wire; wire, flat, cold-rolled strip: not made in hot-rolled mills; metal heat treating; coating of metals & formed products
HQ: Bekaert Corporation
  1395 S Marietta Pkwy Se 500-100
  Marietta GA 30067
  770 421-8520

(G-15584)
BEKAERT CORPORATION
510 Collins Blvd (44667-9796)
PHONE 330 683-5060
Otto Simmerman, *Principal*
EMP: 15
SALES (corp-wide): 483.3MM **Privately Held**
SIC: 3315 Wire & fabricated wire products; fencing made in wiredrawing plants
HQ: Bekaert Corporation
  1395 S Marietta Pkwy Se 500-100
  Marietta GA 30067
  770 421-8520

(G-15585)
BUCKEYE COUNTERS
10207 Ely Rd (44667-9510)
PHONE 330 682-0902
David A Miller, *Principal*
EMP: 3
SALES (est): 262.9K **Privately Held**
SIC: 3131 Counters

(G-15586)
CASKEYS INC
Also Called: Caskey's Recreation
14847 Fosnight Rd (44667-9716)
PHONE 330 683-0249
Jonathan Caskey, *President*
Donald Caskey, *Vice Pres*
Sandra Caskey, *Treasurer*
Beulah Caskey, *Admin Sec*
Bonnie Good, *Administration*
EMP: 4
SALES: 300K **Privately Held**
SIC: 3599 7033 Machine shop, jobbing & repair; campgrounds

(G-15587)
CHEMSPEC USA LLC
9287 Smucker Rd (44667-9795)
PHONE 330 669-8512
Ron Snow, *President*
Imelda Darin, *Credit Mgr*
Michael Hall, *Director*
▼ **EMP:** 60 **EST:** 2016
SALES (est): 93.1K
SALES (corp-wide): 4.7B **Publicly Held**
SIC: 2851 Paints & paint additives
HQ: Axalta Coating Systems, Llc
  2001 Market St Ste 3600
  Philadelphia PA 19103
  215 255-4347

(G-15588)
COUNTRY SALES & SERVICE LLC
255 Tracy Bridge Rd (44667-9383)
PHONE 330 683-2500
Scott Schlabach, *Mng Member*
EMP: 15
SALES (est): 2.8MM **Privately Held**
SIC: 3519 5999 5084 Engines, diesel & semi-diesel or dual-fuel; engine & motor equipment & supplies; industrial machinery & equipment

(G-15589)
DALTON WOOD PRODUCTS INC
101 N Swinehart Rd (44667-9532)
PHONE 330 682-0727
Robert Swartzentruber, *Manager*
EMP: 5
SALES: 475K **Privately Held**
SIC: 2499 Laundry products, wood

(G-15590)
FERRO CORPORATION
1560 N Main St (44667-9170)
P.O. Box 602 (44667-0602)
PHONE 330 682-8015
Kenneth Ackerman, *Branch Mgr*
EMP: 19
SALES (corp-wide): 1.6B **Publicly Held**
WEB: www.ferro.com
SIC: 2865 Cyclic crudes & intermediates
PA: Ferro Corporation
  6060 Parkland Blvd # 250
  Mayfield Heights OH 44124
  216 875-5600

(G-15591)
FOLGER COFFEE COMPANY (HQ)
Also Called: Folgers
1 Strawberry Ln (44667-1241)
PHONE 800 937-9745
Susan E Arnold, *President*
Alan G Lafley, *President*
J M Smucker, *Principal*
D R Walker, *Principal*
Joseph H Etter, *Senior VP*
▲ **EMP:** 15 **EST:** 1850
SQ FT: 1,600,000
SALES (est): 232MM
SALES (corp-wide): 7.3B **Publicly Held**
SIC: 2095 Coffee roasting (except by wholesale grocers); instant coffee; coffee, ground: mixed with grain or chicory; freeze-dried coffee
PA: The J M Smucker Company
  1 Strawberry Ln
  Orrville OH 44667
  330 682-3000

(G-15592)
GRAND UNIFICATION PRESS INC
2380 Wayne St (44667-9626)
PHONE 330 683-1187
Tim Brenneman, *President*
EMP: 4
SALES (est): 206.4K **Privately Held**
WEB: www.grandupress.com
SIC: 2731 Books: publishing only

(G-15593)
HEARTLAND EDUCATION COMMUNITY
200 N Main St (44667-1640)
P.O. Box 280 (44667-0280)
PHONE 330 684-3034
Carol Ubelhart, *Principal*

EMP: 14
SALES: 439.4K **Privately Held**
SIC: 2711 Newspapers, publishing & printing

(G-15594)
HEAT EXCHANGE APPLIED TECH
150b Allen Ave (44667-9021)
PHONE..................................330 682-4328
Bharat Patel, *President*
EMP: 10
SQ FT: 19,000
SALES (est): 2.2MM **Privately Held**
WEB: www.heat-voss.com
SIC: 3443 Fabricated plate work (boiler shop)

(G-15595)
INTERNATIONAL MULTIFOODS CORP (HQ)
Also Called: J M Smucker
1 Strawberry Ln (44667-1241)
P.O. Box 280 (44667-0280)
PHONE..................................330 682-3000
Gary Costley PHD, *CEO*
Dan C Swander, *President*
Frank W Bonvino, *Senior VP*
John E Byom, *CFO*
Jackie Borges, *Manager*
◆ EMP: 5 EST: 2000
SQ FT: 20,000
SALES (est): 219.1MM
SALES (corp-wide): 7.3B **Publicly Held**
WEB: www.multifoods.com
SIC: 5145 5149 5143 2048 Candy; snack foods; chewing gum; coffee, green or roasted; tea bagging; baking supplies; pizza supplies; cheese; livestock feeds; pizza dough, prepared; flour; flour mixes
PA: The J M Smucker Company
 1 Strawberry Ln
 Orrville OH 44667
 330 682-3000

(G-15596)
J M SMUCKER COMPANY (PA)
Also Called: SMUCKER'S
1 Strawberry Ln (44667-1298)
PHONE..................................330 682-3000
Richard K Smucker, *Ch of Bd*
Mark T Smucker, *President*
Barry C Dunaway, *President*
David J Lemmon, *President*
Tina R Floyd, *Senior VP*
▼ EMP: 1700
SALES: 7.3B **Publicly Held**
WEB: www.smuckers.com
SIC: 2033 2099 2023 2087 Jams, jellies & preserves: packaged in cans, jars, etc.; jellies, edible, including imitation: in cans, jars, etc.; vegetable juices: packaged in cans, jars, etc.; fruit juices: packaged in cans, jars, etc.; syrups; frosting, ready-to-use; sandwiches, assembled & packaged: for wholesale market; peanut butter; canned milk, whole; beverage bases, concentrates, syrups, powders & mixes; pickles, sauces & salad dressings

(G-15597)
J M SMUCKER COMPANY
333 Wadsworth Rd (44667-9214)
PHONE..................................330 684-1500
EMP: 19
SALES (corp-wide): 7.3B **Publicly Held**
SIC: 2033 Canned fruits & specialties
PA: The J M Smucker Company
 1 Strawberry Ln
 Orrville OH 44667
 330 682-3000

(G-15598)
JLG INDUSTRIES INC
2927 Paradise St (44667-9628)
PHONE..................................330 684-0132
EMP: 122
SALES (corp-wide): 7.7B **Publicly Held**
SIC: 3531 Construction machinery
HQ: Jlg Industries, Inc.
 1 J L G Dr
 Mc Connellsburg PA 17233
 717 485-5161

(G-15599)
JLG INDUSTRIES INC
600 E Chestnut St (44667-1951)
PHONE..................................330 684-0200
Wade Jones, *Branch Mgr*
EMP: 125
SALES (corp-wide): 6.8B **Publicly Held**
WEB: www.jlg.com
SIC: 3531 Construction machinery
HQ: Jlg Industries, Inc.
 1 J L G Dr
 Mc Connellsburg PA 17233
 717 485-5161

(G-15600)
JM SMUCKER CO
918 N Main St (44667-1222)
PHONE..................................330 684-8274
EMP: 6
SALES (est): 451.8K **Privately Held**
SIC: 2099 Food preparations

(G-15601)
LEHMAN & SONS
3328 S Kohler Rd (44667-9604)
PHONE..................................330 857-7404
Albert Lehman, *Owner*
EMP: 6 EST: 1969
SALES (est): 1.5MM **Privately Held**
SIC: 2431 Exterior & ornamental woodwork & trim

(G-15602)
LETTER GRAPHICS SIGN CO INC
400 W Market St (44667-1823)
P.O. Box 613 (44667-0613)
PHONE..................................330 683-3903
Jim R Webster, *CEO*
Frank Wessels, *President*
Chris Butdorf, *Finance*
EMP: 8
SQ FT: 1,500
SALES (est): 1MM **Privately Held**
SIC: 3993 Electric signs

(G-15603)
MOOG INC
1701 N Main St (44667-9172)
PHONE..................................330 682-0010
James King, *Principal*
EMP: 63
SALES (corp-wide): 2.7B **Publicly Held**
SIC: 3625 Actuators, industrial
PA: Moog Inc.
 400 Jamison Rd
 Elma NY 14059
 716 652-2000

(G-15604)
MYRON D BUDD
Also Called: Orrcast Aluminum Foundry
480 S Crown Hill Rd (44667-9553)
P.O. Box 277 (44667-0277)
PHONE..................................330 682-5866
Mary Budd, *Owner*
EMP: 3 EST: 1952
SQ FT: 3,000
SALES (est): 268.4K **Privately Held**
SIC: 3365 Aluminum foundries

(G-15605)
NATIONAL PATTERN MFG CO
1318 N Main St (44667-9761)
P.O. Box 58 (44667-0058)
PHONE..................................330 682-6871
Anthony J Yonto, *President*
Anthony A Nicholas, *President*
Robert C Nicholas, *Admin Sec*
EMP: 10
SQ FT: 3,000
SALES (est): 1.5MM
SALES (corp-wide): 94.8MM **Privately Held**
WEB: www.qcfoundry.com
SIC: 3544 3543 Dies, plastics forming; foundry patternmaking
PA: Quality Castings Company
 1200 N Main St
 Orrville OH 44667
 330 682-6871

(G-15606)
NU PET COMPANY (HQ) ✪
1 Strawberry Ln (44667-1241)
PHONE..................................330 682-3000
Barry C Dunaway, *President*
EMP: 201 EST: 2018
SALES (est): 4.6MM
SALES (corp-wide): 7.3B **Publicly Held**
SIC: 2099 2033 2023 2087 Syrups; frosting, ready-to-use; sandwiches, assembled & packaged: for wholesale market; peanut butter; jams, jellies & preserves: packaged in cans, jars, etc.; jellies, edible, including imitation: in cans, jars, etc.; vegetable juices: packaged in cans, jars, etc.; fruit juices: packaged in cans, jars, etc.; canned milk, whole; beverage bases, concentrates, syrups, powders & mixes; pickles, sauces & salad dressings
PA: The J M Smucker Company
 1 Strawberry Ln
 Orrville OH 44667
 330 682-3000

(G-15607)
NUCOR BRIGHT BAR ORVILLE LLC
555 Collins Blvd (44667-9796)
PHONE..................................330 682-5555
David A Sumoski, *President*
EMP: 19
SALES (est): 1.2MM
SALES (corp-wide): 25B **Publicly Held**
SIC: 3316 Bars, steel, cold finished, from purchased hot-rolled
PA: Nucor Corporation
 1915 Rexford Rd Ste 400
 Charlotte NC 28211
 704 366-7000

(G-15608)
ORRVILLE PRINTING CO INC
1645 N Main St (44667-9171)
PHONE..................................330 682-5066
Eric Badertscher, *President*
Ron Badertscher, *President*
Brittany Armentrout, *District Mgr*
EMP: 8
SALES: 500K **Privately Held**
SIC: 2752 2791 2789 Commercial printing, offset; typesetting; bookbinding & related work

(G-15609)
ORRVILLE TRUCKING & GRADING CO (PA)
475 Orr St (44667-9764)
P.O. Box 220 (44667-0220)
PHONE..................................330 682-4010
Auvil Richmond, *President*
John H Wilson, *Treasurer*
EMP: 50
SQ FT: 15,000
SALES (est): 7.4MM **Privately Held**
SIC: 3273 3272 5031 Ready-mixed concrete; concrete products; building materials, exterior; building materials, interior

(G-15610)
ORRVILON INC
1400 Dairy Ln (44667-2505)
PHONE..................................330 684-9400
K P Singh, *President*
Alan Soler, *Exec VP*
Frank Bongrazio, *CFO*
▲ EMP: 110 EST: 2009
SQ FT: 350,000
SALES (est): 41.3MM
SALES (corp-wide): 364.9MM **Privately Held**
SIC: 3354 3442 Aluminum extruded products; metal doors
PA: Holtec International
 1001 N Us Highway 1
 Jupiter FL 33477
 561 745-7772

(G-15611)
PURINA ANIMAL NUTRITION LLC
635 Collins Blvd (44667-9796)
PHONE..................................330 682-1951
Ken Schwarvrock, *Manager*
EMP: 35
SALES (corp-wide): 10.4B **Privately Held**
SIC: 2048 Prepared feeds
HQ: Purina Animal Nutrition Llc
 100 Danforth Dr
 Gray Summit MO 63039

(G-15612)
PURINA MILLS LLC
635 Collins Blvd (44667-9796)
PHONE..................................330 682-1951
Ken Fchwarzrock, *Manager*
EMP: 9
SALES (corp-wide): 10.4B **Privately Held**
WEB: www.purina-mills.com
SIC: 2048 Prepared feeds
HQ: Purina Mills, Llc
 555 Maryvle Univ Dr 200
 Saint Louis MO 63141

(G-15613)
QUALITY CASTINGS COMPANY (PA)
1200 N Main St (44667-1017)
P.O. Box 58 (44667-0058)
PHONE..................................330 682-6871
Di CK Nicholas, *CEO*
Richard Nicholas, *Ch of Bd*
David Yonto, *President*
Robert Nicholas, *General Mgr*
F L Strauss, *Principal*
EMP: 350 EST: 1927
SALES (est): 94.8MM **Privately Held**
WEB: www.qcfoundry.com
SIC: 3321 Gray iron castings; ductile iron castings

(G-15614)
REFRACTORY COATING TECH INC
Also Called: Refcotec
542 Collins Blvd (44667-9796)
PHONE..................................330 683-2200
William Dewood, *President*
Tim Sheehan, *Vice Pres*
Timothy P Sheehan, *Vice Pres*
Collin Dewood, *Sales Staff*
Matt Dewood, *Sales Staff*
EMP: 25
SQ FT: 23,400
SALES (est): 5.5MM **Privately Held**
WEB: www.refcotec.com
SIC: 3297 Heat resistant mixtures

(G-15615)
ROCK DECOR COMPANY
2877 Kidron Rd (44667-9603)
P.O. Box 148, Apple Creek (44606-0148)
PHONE..................................330 857-7625
Gary Miller, *Owner*
EMP: 5
SALES (est): 590.5K **Privately Held**
SIC: 3272 Stone, cast concrete

(G-15616)
ROGER HOOVER
571 Kidron Rd (44667-9203)
PHONE..................................330 857-1815
Roger Hoover, *Principal*
EMP: 3
SALES (est): 252.9K **Privately Held**
SIC: 2851 Removers & cleaners

(G-15617)
S & S PANEL
3314 S Kohler Rd (44667-9604)
PHONE..................................330 412-6735
Philip Schrock, *Owner*
EMP: 5
SALES (est): 274.7K **Privately Held**
SIC: 2431 Panel work, wood

(G-15618)
SCHANTZ ORGAN COMPANY (PA)
626 S Walnut St (44667-2238)
P.O. Box 156 (44667-0156)
PHONE..................................330 682-6065
Victor B Schantz, *President*
Jeff Dexter, *Vice Pres*
Eric Gastier, *Vice Pres*
EMP: 30 EST: 1873
SQ FT: 45,600
SALES (est): 7.2MM **Privately Held**
WEB: www.schantzorgan.com
SIC: 3931 Organs, all types: pipe, reed, hand, electronic, etc.

Orrville - Wayne County (G-15619) GEOGRAPHIC SECTION

(G-15619)
SCOTTS MIRACLE-GRO COMPANY
1220 Schrock Rd (44667-9582)
PHONE................................330 684-0421
Ark Dish, *Branch Mgr*
EMP: 70
SALES (corp-wide): 2.6B **Publicly Held**
SIC: 2873 Nitrogenous fertilizers
PA: The Scotts Miracle-Gro Company
   14111 Scottslawn Rd
   Marysville OH 43040
   937 644-0011

(G-15620)
SMITHFOODS INC (PA)
1381 Dairy Ln (44667-2503)
P.O. Box 87 (44667-0087)
PHONE................................330 683-8710
Nathan Schmid, *CEO*
Daniel Brimm, *Principal*
Vic Clesceri, *VP Sales*
Jim Breck, *Manager*
Mindy Mencl, *Manager*
EMP: 9
SALES (est): 202.1MM **Privately Held**
SIC: 2026 2024 Fluid milk; ice cream & frozen desserts

(G-15621)
SMUCKER INTERNATIONAL INC (HQ)
Also Called: Smucker's
1 Strawberry Ln (44667-1241)
PHONE................................330 682-3000
Richard Smucker, *CEO*
Tim Smucker, *Ch of Bd*
Jaclyn Welch, *Counsel*
Vince Byrd, *Vice Pres*
John Stangel, *Opers Mgr*
▼ **EMP:** 4
SALES (est): 595.5K
SALES (corp-wide): 7.3B **Publicly Held**
WEB: www.smuckers.com
SIC: 2033 2099 2086 Canned fruits & specialties; syrups; bottled & canned soft drinks
PA: The J M Smucker Company
   1 Strawberry Ln
   Orrville OH 44667
   330 682-3000

(G-15622)
SMUCKER MANUFACTURING INC
1 Strawberry Ln (44667-1241)
P.O. Box 280 (44667-0280)
PHONE................................888 550-9555
Peter Farah, *President*
EMP: 7 EST: 2012
SALES (est): 610.4K
SALES (corp-wide): 7.3B **Publicly Held**
SIC: 2033 Jams, jellies & preserves: packaged in cans, jars, etc.
PA: The J M Smucker Company
   1 Strawberry Ln
   Orrville OH 44667
   330 682-3000

(G-15623)
SMUCKER NATURAL FOODS INC
Strawberry Ln (44667)
PHONE................................330 682-3000
Robert Ferguson, *Vice Pres*
Don Ilg, *Opers Staff*
H Wagstaff, *Branch Mgr*
Jill Kauffman, *Manager*
Florence Videau, *Education*
EMP: 44
SALES (corp-wide): 7.3B **Publicly Held**
WEB: www.knudsenjuices.com
SIC: 2086 Bottled & canned soft drinks
HQ: Smucker Natural Foods, Inc.
   37 Speedway Ave
   Chico CA 95928
   530 899-5000

(G-15624)
SPECIALTY PALLET & DESIGN LTD
2600 Kidron Rd (44667-9645)
PHONE................................330 857-0257
Anthony Weaver, *Manager*
Shawn Loft,
Dan Andrews,
David Gruttle,
EMP: 30
SALES (est): 5.1MM **Privately Held**
SIC: 2448 Pallets, wood

(G-15625)
WILL-BURT ADVNCED CMPSITES INC
356 Collins Blvd (44667-9727)
PHONE................................330 684-5286
Vicki Oravec, *Principal*
EMP: 15
SALES (est): 1.5MM
SALES (corp-wide): 63.8MM **Privately Held**
SIC: 3448 Mfg Prefabricated Metal Buildings
PA: The Will-Burt Company
   169 S Main St
   Orrville OH 44667
   330 682-7015

(G-15626)
WILL-BURT COMPANY (PA)
169 S Main St (44667-1801)
P.O. Box 900 (44667-0900)
PHONE................................330 682-7015
Jeffrey Evans, *President*
Phil Tryon, *General Mgr*
John Glenn, *Regional Mgr*
Thomas Howard, *Business Mgr*
Travis Powell, *Business Mgr*
▲ **EMP:** 275 EST: 1918
SQ FT: 170,000
SALES (est): 63.8MM **Privately Held**
WEB: www.willburt.com
SIC: 3599 5039 3443 3449 Machine shop, jobbing & repair; prefabricated structures; fabricated plate work (boiler shop); miscellaneous metalwork; lighting equipment; sheet metalwork

(G-15627)
WILL-BURT COMPANY
150 Allen Ave (44667-9021)
PHONE................................330 683-9991
John Yurkschatt, *General Mgr*
EMP: 5
SALES (corp-wide): 63.8MM **Privately Held**
SIC: 3599 Machine shop, jobbing & repair
PA: The Will-Burt Company
   169 S Main St
   Orrville OH 44667
   330 682-7015

(G-15628)
WILL-BURT COMPANY
312 Collins Blvd (44667-9727)
P.O. Box 900 (44667-0900)
PHONE................................330 682-7015
Andrew Wasson, *Engineer*
Jeffrey O Evans, *Manager*
EMP: 37
SALES (corp-wide): 63.8MM **Privately Held**
WEB: www.willburt.com
SIC: 3443 3449 3599 5039 Fabricated plate work (boiler shop); miscellaneous metalwork; machine shop, jobbing & repair; prefabricated structures
PA: The Will-Burt Company
   169 S Main St
   Orrville OH 44667
   330 682-7015

(G-15629)
XL PATTERN SHOP INC
242 N Kansas Rd (44667-9638)
PHONE................................330 682-2981
Gary Snyder, *President*
EMP: 5
SALES (est): 300K **Privately Held**
WEB: www.xlpatternshop.com
SIC: 3543 Industrial patterns

Orwell
Ashtabula County

(G-15630)
FASCO MACHINE PRODUCTS INC
554 E Main St (44076)
P.O. Box 187 (44076-0187)
PHONE................................440 437-6242
Richard Fularz, *President*
EMP: 3
SQ FT: 2,400
SALES: 340.4K **Privately Held**
WEB: www.fascomachine.com
SIC: 3599 Machine shop, jobbing & repair

(G-15631)
HERITAGE SLEEP PRODUCTS LLC
243 Staley Rd (44076-8380)
P.O. Box 459 (44076-0459)
PHONE................................440 437-4425
Eli Schnucker, *Mng Member*
EMP: 26 EST: 2015
SALES (est): 2.5MM **Privately Held**
SIC: 2515 Mattresses & bedsprings

(G-15632)
HIT & MISS ENTERPRISES
Also Called: Hit & Miss Ent Antiq Engs Prts
4461 Montgomery Rd (44076-9744)
P.O. Box 157 (44076-0157)
PHONE................................440 272-5335
Ed Deis, *Owner*
Donna Deis, *Partner*
EMP: 4
SQ FT: 2,736
SALES (est): 368.9K **Privately Held**
SIC: 3714 Motor vehicle parts & accessories

(G-15633)
KENNAMETAL INC
180 Penniman Rd (44076-9500)
PHONE................................440 437-5131
David Orth, *Manager*
William Seger, *Maintence Staff*
EMP: 126
SALES (corp-wide): 2.3B **Publicly Held**
WEB: www.kennametal.com
SIC: 3545 Cutting tools for machine tools
PA: Kennametal Inc.
   600 Grant St Ste 5100
   Pittsburgh PA 15219
   412 248-8000

(G-15634)
MASCO CBINETRY MIDDLEFIELD LLC
Also Called: Kraftmaid Cabinetry
150 Grand Valley Ave (44076-9419)
P.O. Box 1055, Middlefield (44062-1055)
PHONE................................440 437-8537
Paul Schamrock, *Manager*
EMP: 500
SALES (corp-wide): 8.3B **Publicly Held**
SIC: 2431 2434 Doors, wood; wood kitchen cabinets
HQ: Masco Cabinetry Middlefield Llc
   15535 S State Ave
   Middlefield OH 44062
   440 632-5333

(G-15635)
TEP BEDDING GRP INC
Also Called: Therapedic Mattress
161 Grand Valley Ave (44076-9420)
PHONE................................440 437-7700
Scott Rogers, *Principal*
Michael J Teitelbaum, *Principal*
EMP: 20 EST: 2004
SALES (est): 2.4MM **Privately Held**
SIC: 2515 Mattresses & foundations

(G-15636)
WECALL INC
64 Penniman Rd (44076-9557)
P.O. Box 39 (44076-0039)
PHONE................................440 437-8202
Paul David Doherty, *President*
Bernard Doherty, *Vice Pres*
Vishal Dongare, *Project Engr*
EMP: 9
SQ FT: 7,400
SALES (est): 1.5MM **Privately Held**
WEB: www.wecallinc.com
SIC: 3429 3452 Metal fasteners; bolts, nuts, rivets & washers

(G-15637)
WELDED TUBES INC (PA)
135 Penniman Rd (44076-9535)
PHONE................................216 378-2092
Robert C Lewis Jr, *Ch of Bd*
Lewis L Guarnieri, *Principal*
George W Secrest, *Principal*
Charles A Young, *Principal*
Larry Lamphier, *Vice Pres*
▲ **EMP:** 2 EST: 1958
SQ FT: 400
SALES (est): 17.8MM **Privately Held**
WEB: www.weldedtubes.com
SIC: 3317 Tubes, wrought: welded or lock joint

(G-15638)
WELDED TUBES INC
135 Penniman Rd (44076-9535)
PHONE................................440 437-5144
Larry N Lamphier, *Vice Pres*
EMP: 10
SQ FT: 100,000
SALES (corp-wide): 17.8MM **Privately Held**
WEB: www.weldedtubes.com
SIC: 3317 3498 Steel pipe & tubes; fabricated pipe & fittings
PA: Welded Tubes, Inc.
   135 Penniman Rd
   Orwell OH 44076
   216 378-2092

(G-15639)
WELDED TUBES LLC
135 Penniman Rd (44076-9535)
PHONE................................210 278-3757
Joseph Frandanisa, *President*
Robert C Lewis Jr, *Owner*
EMP: 25
SALES: 100K **Privately Held**
SIC: 3317 Welded pipe & tubes

(G-15640)
WOODCRAFT INDUSTRIES INC
131 Grand Valley Ave (44076-9420)
P.O. Box 128 (44076-0128)
PHONE................................440 437-7811
Brain Richie, *Branch Mgr*
EMP: 100 **Publicly Held**
SIC: 2434 2426 2431 Wood kitchen cabinets; dimension, hardwood; millwork
HQ: Woodcraft Industries, Inc.
   525 Lincoln Ave Se
   Saint Cloud MN 56304
   320 656-2345

(G-15641)
Y&B LOGGING
3647 Montgomery Rd (44076-9742)
PHONE................................440 437-1053
Urie Yoder, *Principal*
EMP: 3
SALES (est): 132.3K **Privately Held**
SIC: 2411 Logging

Osgood
Darke County

(G-15642)
DYNAMIC WELD CORPORATION
242 N St (45351)
P.O. Box 127 (45351-0127)
PHONE................................419 582-2900
Harry Heitkamp, *President*
Sue Heitkamp, *Finance Mgr*
EMP: 44
SQ FT: 35,000
SALES (est): 11.8MM **Privately Held**
WEB: www.dynamicweld.com
SIC: 3444 7692 Sheet metalwork; welding repair

Ostrander
Delaware County

(G-15643)
ENVIRNMNTAL PRTCTIVE CTNGS LLC
5999 Houseman Rd (43061)
P.O. Box 8 (43061-0008)
PHONE.................................740 363-6180
Brian Parish, *General Mgr*
Robert W Stone, *Mng Member*
EMP: 4
SQ FT: 4,500
SALES (est): 351K **Privately Held**
SIC: 2851 2899 Paints & allied products; chemical preparations

(G-15644)
K L M MANUFACTURING COMPANY
56 Huston St (43061-9618)
PHONE.................................740 666-5171
K Leroy Moore, *President*
EMP: 6 EST: 1971
SQ FT: 5,000
SALES: 270K **Privately Held**
WEB: www.klmmfg.com
SIC: 3541 Machine tools, metal cutting type

(G-15645)
LIBERTY DIE CAST MOLDS INC
57 2nd St (43061-9441)
P.O. Box 2 (43061-0002)
PHONE.................................740 666-7492
Kenny L Nicol, *President*
Jack Fryman, *Corp Secy*
Duane C Glick, *Vice Pres*
Duane Glick, *Vice Pres*
EMP: 15
SQ FT: 6,544
SALES: 1.7MM **Privately Held**
WEB: www.libertydiecastmolds.com
SIC: 3544 Industrial molds

(G-15646)
SHELLY MATERIALS INC
8328 Watkins Rd (43061-9311)
PHONE.................................740 666-5841
Keith Siler, *Vice Pres*
EMP: 25
SALES (corp-wide): 29.7B **Privately Held**
SIC: 2951 1611 3274 1422 Asphalt & asphaltic paving mixtures (not from refineries); surfacing & paving; lime; crushed & broken limestone
HQ: Shelly Materials, Inc.
80 Park Dr
Thornville OH 43076
740 246-6315

Ottawa
Putnam County

(G-15647)
ACOH INC
210 Selhorst Dr Apt 213 (45875-1576)
PHONE.................................419 741-3195
Owen Hinkle Jr, *Principal*
EMP: 4 EST: 2017
SALES (est): 180K **Privately Held**
SIC: 3679 Electronic components

(G-15648)
BROOKHILL CENTER INDUSTRIES
7989 State Route 108 (45875-9678)
PHONE.................................419 876-3932
Bill Unterbink, *President*
EMP: 115
SQ FT: 16,000
SALES: 1.8MM **Privately Held**
SIC: 8331 2448 Sheltered workshop; wood pallets & skids

(G-15649)
CUSTOM WOODWORKING INC
214 S Main St (45875-9416)
PHONE.................................419 456-3330
Jerry Hovest, *President*
EMP: 9
SALES (est): 1MM **Privately Held**
SIC: 2434 Wood kitchen cabinets

(G-15650)
D 4 INDUSTRIES INC
685 Woodland Dr (45875-8627)
PHONE.................................419 523-9555
Jim Bibler, *President*
EMP: 9
SALES (est): 670K **Privately Held**
SIC: 3599 Machine shop, jobbing & repair

(G-15651)
DRAINAGE PIPE & FITTING
450 Tile Company St (45875-9217)
PHONE.................................419 538-6337
Floyd Tony Meyer, *Principal*
Crystal Solano, *Principal*
EMP: 8 EST: 2012
SALES: 300K **Privately Held**
SIC: 3494 Pipe fittings

(G-15652)
HIRT PUBLISHING CO INC (PA)
Also Called: Putnam County Sentinel
224 E Main St (45875-1944)
P.O. Box 149 (45875-0149)
PHONE.................................419 523-5709
Tim Garry, *President*
Gary L Hirt, *Chairman*
Karen L Hirt, *Corp Secy*
Brian Hirt, *Vice Pres*
EMP: 4
SQ FT: 1,800
SALES (est): 5.4MM **Privately Held**
SIC: 2711 Commercial printing & newspaper publishing combined

(G-15653)
HIRT PUBLISHING CO INC
Also Called: Putnam County Sentinel
224 E Main St (45875-1944)
P.O. Box 149 (45875-0149)
PHONE.................................419 523-5709
Don Hemple, *Manager*
EMP: 15
SALES (corp-wide): 5.4MM **Privately Held**
SIC: 2711 Newspapers, publishing & printing
PA: Hirt Publishing Co, Inc
224 E Main St
Ottawa OH 45875
419 523-5709

(G-15654)
HIRZEL CANNING COMPANY
Ottawa Foods, Div of
325 E Williamstown Rd (45875-1802)
PHONE.................................419 523-3225
Karl E Hirzel, *Plant Mgr*
EMP: 18
SALES (est): 3MM
SALES (corp-wide): 29.6MM **Privately Held**
WEB: www.hirzel.com
SIC: 2033 Tomato products: packaged in cans, jars, etc.; tomato juice: packaged in cans, jars, etc.; tomato paste: packaged in cans, jars, etc.; tomato purees: packaged in cans, jars, etc.
PA: Hirzel Canning Company
411 Lemoyne Rd
Northwood OH 43619
419 693-0531

(G-15655)
JB MACHINING CONCEPTS LLC
995 Sugar Mill Dr (45875-8526)
PHONE.................................419 523-0096
Alexander Blankemeyer, *Engineer*
John Blankemeyer, *President*
EMP: 8 EST: 2007
SQ FT: 18,000
SALES: 921.5K **Privately Held**
SIC: 3646 3645 Commercial indusl & institutional electric lighting fixtures; residential lighting fixtures

(G-15656)
K & L READY MIX INC (PA)
10391 State Route 15 (45875-8641)
P.O. Box 325 (45875-0325)
PHONE.................................419 523-4376
Ron Kahle Jr, *President*
EMP: 19
SQ FT: 12,000
SALES (est): 7.6MM **Privately Held**
WEB: www.kandlreadymix.com
SIC: 3273 Ready-mixed concrete

(G-15657)
KAHLE TECHNOLOGIES INC
1204 E 3rd St (45875-2022)
P.O. Box 127 (45875-0127)
PHONE.................................419 523-3951
Jameson Kahle, *President*
John Kahle II, *Vice Pres*
Robert Kahle, *Treasurer*
Randal Kahle, *Admin Sec*
EMP: 3
SQ FT: 2,400
SALES (est): 527.7K **Privately Held**
SIC: 3625 Relays & industrial controls

(G-15658)
MC ELWAIN INDUSTRIES INC
17941 Road L (45875-9455)
PHONE.................................419 532-3126
Amelia McElwain, *President*
EMP: 14
SALES (est): 1.4MM **Privately Held**
SIC: 7692 3441 Welding repair; building components, structural steel

(G-15659)
MIKES MILL SHOP INC
14768 Road J (45875-9441)
PHONE.................................419 538-6091
Michael Huffman, *President*
EMP: 3
SALES (est): 228.8K **Privately Held**
SIC: 1521 2499 General remodeling, single-family houses; decorative wood & woodwork

(G-15660)
NELSON MANUFACTURING COMPANY
6448 State Route 224 (45875-9789)
PHONE.................................419 523-5321
Anthony Niese, *President*
Chad Stall, *Vice Pres*
Patricia Taylor, *Treasurer*
Amy Niece, *Admin Sec*
▼ **EMP:** 80 EST: 1947
SQ FT: 46,000
SALES: 17.6MM **Privately Held**
WEB: www.nelsontrailer.com
SIC: 3715 7539 Semitrailers for truck tractors; trailer repair

(G-15661)
PALPAC INDUSTRIES INC
610 N Agner St (45875-1533)
P.O. Box 109 (45875-0109)
PHONE.................................419 523-3230
Danny E Meyer, *President*
Mike Meyer, *Treasurer*
Rene Langhals, *Admin Sec*
EMP: 18 EST: 1968
SQ FT: 62,000
SALES (est): 1.4MM **Privately Held**
SIC: 3089 3086 Molding primary plastic; plastics foam products

(G-15662)
PHANTASM DESIGNS
112 W Main St (45875-1722)
PHONE.................................419 538-6737
Don Huber, *Owner*
Holly Huber, *Co-Owner*
EMP: 9
SALES (est): 744.2K **Privately Held**
WEB: www.phantasmdesigns.com
SIC: 2262 2261 2395 7336 Screen printing: manmade fiber & silk broadwoven fabrics; screen printing of cotton broadwoven fabrics; embroidery & art needlework; emblems, embroidered; graphic arts & related design; silk screen design

(G-15663)
R K INDUSTRIES INC
725 N Locust St (45875-1466)
P.O. Box 306 (45875-0306)
PHONE.................................419 523-5001
Ann Woodyard, *President*
Joe Maag, *Vice Pres*
Barry Woodyard, *Manager*
Kimberly French, *Admin Sec*
▲ **EMP:** 85
SQ FT: 45,000
SALES (est): 8.8MM **Privately Held**
WEB: www.rkindustries.org
SIC: 7692 3465 Automotive welding; automotive stampings

(G-15664)
SILGAN PLASTICS LLC
690 Woodland Dr (45875-8627)
PHONE.................................419 523-3737
Russ Zervais, *President*
John Young, *Engineer*
Bob Martin, *Senior Engr*
Dawn Schnipke, *Human Res Mgr*
Mike Schneeg, *Manager*
EMP: 200
SALES (corp-wide): 4.4B **Publicly Held**
WEB: www.silganplastics.com
SIC: 3089 Plastic containers, except foam
HQ: Silgan Plastics Llc
14515 North Outer 40 Rd # 210
Chesterfield MO 63017
800 274-5426

(G-15665)
STEEL TECHNOLOGIES LLC
740 E Williamstown Rd (45875-1873)
PHONE.................................419 523-5199
Rick Furber, *Manager*
EMP: 50 **Privately Held**
WEB: www.steeltechnologies.com
SIC: 3312 Sheet or strip, steel, cold-rolled: own hot-rolled
HQ: Steel Technologies Llc
700 N Hurstbourne Pkwy # 400
Louisville KY 40222
502 245-2110

(G-15666)
STERLING INDUSTRIES INC
740 E Main St (45875-2029)
PHONE.................................419 523-3788
Marilyn Kulhman, *President*
Keith Kuhlman, *Vice Pres*
EMP: 10
SQ FT: 9,600
SALES (est): 1.1MM **Privately Held**
SIC: 2441 2448 Boxes, wood; pallets, wood

(G-15667)
STOEPFEL DRILLING CO
12245 State Route 115 (45875-9488)
PHONE.................................419 532-3307
John H Stoepfel Jr, *Partner*
Roger Winkle, *Partner*
EMP: 7 EST: 1954
SQ FT: 6,000
SALES (est): 515.6K **Privately Held**
SIC: 1481 1781 Mine & quarry services, nonmetallic minerals; water well drilling

(G-15668)
TACTICAL REVOLUTION LLC
10436 Country Acres Dr # 7 (45875-9400)
P.O. Box 651, Kalida (45853-0651)
PHONE.................................419 348-9526
William Romes,
EMP: 3
SALES (est): 158.2K **Privately Held**
SIC: 2389 Apparel & accessories

(G-15669)
TITAN BUS LLC
804 N Pratt St (45875-1556)
P.O. Box 468 (45875-0468)
PHONE.................................419 523-3593
Ed Verhoff,
Brian Barrington,
Joe Verhoff,
EMP: 5
SQ FT: 180,000
SALES: 5MM **Privately Held**
SIC: 3711 Buses, all types, assembly of

(G-15670)
VERHOFF ALFALFA MILLS INC (PA)
Also Called: Alfa Green Supreme
1188 Sugar Mill Dr (45875-8518)
PHONE.................................419 523-4767
Constance A Verhoff, *President*
Judith Fullenkamp, *Corp Secy*
Donald Verhoff, *Vice Pres*
▼ **EMP:** 7 EST: 1940

Ottawa - Putnam County (G-15671)

SQ FT: 500
SALES (est): 6.1MM **Privately Held**
SIC: 0723 2048 Crop preparation services for market; alfalfa or alfalfa meal, prepared as animal feed

(G-15671)
WARREN PRINTING & OFF PDTS INC
250 E Main St (45875-1944)
P.O. Box 229 (45875-0229)
PHONE.................................419 523-3635
Robert E Warren Jr, *President*
EMP: 10
SALES (est): 1.4MM **Privately Held**
SIC: 2752 2759 5943 2679 Commercial printing, offset; flexographic printing; office forms & supplies; tags & labels, paper

(G-15672)
WHIRLPOOL CORPORATION
677 Woodland Dr (45875-8627)
PHONE.................................419 523-5100
Glenn Kaufman, *Engineer*
Douglas Recker, *Engineer*
Al Inkrott, *Branch Mgr*
Keith Schimmoeller, *Technician*
EMP: 175
SALES (corp-wide): 21B **Publicly Held**
SIC: 3633 3632 3639 Household laundry machines, including coin-operated; washing machines, household: including coin-operated; laundry dryers, household or coin-operated; refrigerators, mechanical & absorption: household; freezers, home & farm; dishwashing machines, household; garbage disposal units, household; trash compactors, household
PA: Whirlpool Corporation
2000 N M 63
Benton Harbor MI 49022
269 923-5000

Ottawa Hills
Lucas County

(G-15673)
INTEGRATED SENSORS LLC
2403 Evergreen Rd (43606-2323)
PHONE.................................419 536-3212
Peter Friedman, *Mng Member*
EMP: 6
SALES (est): 750K **Privately Held**
WEB: www.isensors.net
SIC: 3674 Radiation sensors

(G-15674)
LIFT AI LLC
2348 Manchester Blvd (43606-2458)
PHONE.................................419 345-7831
Rob Wurth, *CEO*
EMP: 3
SALES (est): 52.3K **Privately Held**
SIC: 7699 7372 Elevators: inspection, service & repair; application computer software

(G-15675)
PHOENIX PARTNERS LLC
Also Called: Clevland Valve & Gauge Co
3464 Brookside Rd (43606-2609)
PHONE.................................734 654-2201
James Rorick, *CEO*
EMP: 40
SALES (est): 4.3MM **Privately Held**
SIC: 3491 Industrial valves

(G-15676)
PRECISION PALLET INC
3919 W Bancroft St (43606-2534)
PHONE.................................419 381-8191
Linwood Miller, *President*
EMP: 4
SQ FT: 5,000
SALES (est): 555K **Privately Held**
SIC: 2448 Pallets, wood

(G-15677)
SACKS BRUCE & ASSOCIATES
4959 Damascus Dr (43615-2151)
PHONE.................................419 537-0623
Bruce Sacks, *Owner*
EMP: 4

SALES (est): 506.9K **Privately Held**
SIC: 2329 Men's & boys' clothing

(G-15678)
TIDEWATER PRODUCTS INC
4520 Brookside Rd (43615-2206)
P.O. Box 23181, Toledo (43623-0181)
PHONE.................................419 534-9870
Steven Karakas, *President*
EMP: 3
SALES (est): 398.3K **Privately Held**
SIC: 2899 Water treating compounds

Ottoville
Putnam County

(G-15679)
ACME MACHINE AUTOMATICS INC
Also Called: Global Precision Parts
111 Progressive Dr (45876)
P.O. Box 579 (45876-0579)
PHONE.................................419 453-0010
Randy Mueller, *President*
EMP: 86
SQ FT: 62,500
SALES (est): 16.8MM **Privately Held**
WEB: www.acmemachine.net
SIC: 3451 3484 Screw machine products; small arms; guns (firearms) or gun parts, 30 mm. & below
PA: Kriegel Holding Company, Inc.
7600 Us Route 127
Van Wert OH 45891

(G-15680)
H & M MACHINE SHOP INC
290 State Route 189 (45876)
P.O. Box 207 (45876-0207)
PHONE.................................419 453-3414
Todd Horstman, *President*
Roger A Horstman, *Corp Secy*
Diane Horstman, *Vice Pres*
EMP: 16
SQ FT: 50,000
SALES: 2MM **Privately Held**
SIC: 3599 Machine shop, jobbing & repair

(G-15681)
J L WANNEMACHER SALES & SVC
26992 Us 224 W (45876)
PHONE.................................419 453-3445
James P Wannemacher, *President*
Ruth Wannemacher, *Corp Secy*
Lisa Wannemacher, *Vice Pres*
EMP: 14 EST: 1867
SQ FT: 10,000
SALES (est): 4MM **Privately Held**
SIC: 5083 7699 2452 Farm & garden machinery; farm machinery repair; modular homes, prefabricated, wood

(G-15682)
M & W TRAILERS INC
525 E Main St (45876)
P.O. Box 519 (45876-0519)
PHONE.................................419 453-3331
Kenneth Markward, *President*
Elmer A Markward, *Principal*
Elenor Wannemacher, *Principal*
Lavern S Wannemacher, *Principal*
Thomas Markward, *Vice Pres*
EMP: 10
SQ FT: 10,000
SALES: 2MM **Privately Held**
SIC: 7539 3715 5012 7538 Trailer repair; truck trailers; trailers for trucks, new & used; general truck repair

(G-15683)
PROGRESSIVE STAMPING INC
200 Progressive Dr (45876)
P.O. Box 549 (45876-0549)
PHONE.................................419 453-1111
Lloyd Miller, *President*
◆ EMP: 250
SALES (est): 64.4MM **Privately Held**
SIC: 3465 Automotive stampings
PA: Midway Products Group, Inc.
1 Lyman E Hoyt Dr
Monroe MI 48161

Otway
Scioto County

(G-15684)
BLANKENSHIP LOGGING LLC
433 Curtis Smith Rd (45657-8936)
PHONE.................................740 372-3833
Harold Blankenship, *Owner*
Harold L Blankenship Jr,
EMP: 6
SALES (est): 400K **Privately Held**
SIC: 2411 Logging camps & contractors

(G-15685)
BLANKENSHIP LUMBER INC
5356 State Route 348 (45657-8937)
PHONE.................................740 372-0191
Harold Blandkenship, *Principal*
EMP: 3
SALES (est): 279K **Privately Held**
SIC: 2421 Sawmills & planing mills, general

(G-15686)
BROWN FOREST PRODUCTS
652 State Route 348 (45657-8973)
PHONE.................................937 544-1515
Thomas Brown, *Owner*
EMP: 5
SALES: 500K **Privately Held**
SIC: 2411 Pulpwood contractors engaged in cutting

(G-15687)
COX WOOD PRODUCT INC
5715 State Route 348 (45657-8938)
PHONE.................................740 372-4735
Shelby Kratzer, *President*
Eric Kratzer, *Vice Pres*
EMP: 10 EST: 1950
SALES (est): 500K **Privately Held**
SIC: 2448 5211 Pallets, wood; planing mill products & lumber

(G-15688)
GARY BROWN FARM & SAWMILL
3575 State Route 348 (45657-8966)
PHONE.................................740 372-5022
Gary Brown, *Owner*
Cathy Brown, *Co-Owner*
EMP: 4
SALES (est): 220K **Privately Held**
SIC: 2421 Sawmills & planing mills, general

(G-15689)
POWELL LOGGING
7593 State Route 348 (45657-9078)
PHONE.................................740 372-6131
Russell Powell, *Principal*
EMP: 3
SALES (est): 177.7K **Privately Held**
SIC: 2411 Logging

Owensville
Clermont County

(G-15690)
R & M GRINDING INC
5080 State Rd 132 (45160)
PHONE.................................513 732-3330
Roger Gadzinski, *President*
Michael Gadzinski, *President*
Mike Gadzinski, *Vice Pres*
EMP: 4
SQ FT: 9,000
SALES (est): 675K **Privately Held**
SIC: 3599 7699 Machine shop, jobbing & repair; knife, saw & tool sharpening & repair

Oxford
Butler County

(G-15691)
CITY OF OXFORD
Also Called: Maintenance Building
945 Collins Run Rd (45056)
PHONE.................................513 523-8412
Eric Keebler, *Manager*
EMP: 16 **Privately Held**
WEB: www.cityofoxford.org
SIC: 3531 Road construction & maintenance machinery
PA: City Of Oxford
15 S College Ave
Oxford OH 45056
513 524-5200

(G-15692)
COX NEWSPAPERS LLC
Also Called: Oxford Press
30 W Park Pl Uppr Uppr (45056-2658)
PHONE.................................513 523-4139
Fax: 513 523-1935
EMP: 7 **Publicly Held**
SIC: 2711 Newspapers-Publishing/Printing
HQ: Cox Newspapers, Inc.
6205 Pchtree Dnwody Rd Ne
Atlanta GA 30328
678 645-0000

(G-15693)
GALLAGHER WOOD & CRAFTS
2715 Scott Rd (45056-9154)
PHONE.................................513 523-2748
Shawn Gallagher, *President*
EMP: 3
SALES (est): 233K **Privately Held**
SIC: 3732 Tenders (small motor craft), building & repairing

(G-15694)
HYQ TECHNOLOGIES LLC
Also Called: Hyq Teq
2897 Miamiview Ct Apt A (45056-8004)
PHONE.................................513 225-6911
EMP: 4
SALES (est): 206.5K **Privately Held**
SIC: 3711 3443 3441 3663 Mfg Motor Vehicle Bodies Mfg Fabricated Plate Wrk Structural Metal Fabrctn Mfg Communications Equip

(G-15695)
IRVING MATERIALS INC
6601 Ringwood Rd (45056-9047)
P.O. Box 15 (45056-0015)
PHONE.................................513 523-7127
Eddie G Moster, *Administration*
EMP: 11
SALES (corp-wide): 814.4MM **Privately Held**
SIC: 3273 Ready-mixed concrete
PA: Irving Materials, Inc.
8032 N State Road 9
Greenfield IN 46140
317 326-3101

(G-15696)
LETTERMAN PRINTING INC
316 S College Ave (45056-2225)
PHONE.................................513 523-1111
Jon C Rupel, *President*
Rhonda Rupel, *Admin Sec*
EMP: 8
SQ FT: 1,500
SALES (est): 925.9K **Privately Held**
SIC: 2752 2759 Commercial printing, offset; commercial printing

(G-15697)
MOONSHINE SCREEN PRINTING INC
23 N College Ave (45056-1108)
PHONE.................................513 523-7775
John Brosier, *President*
EMP: 13
SQ FT: 7,500
SALES (est): 600K **Privately Held**
WEB: www.moonshinescreenprinting.com
SIC: 2759 3993 Screen printing; neon signs

GEOGRAPHIC SECTION

(G-15698)
MORNING SUN TECHNOLOGIES INC
7191 Morning Sun Rd (45056-8846)
PHONE 513 461-1417
Harold Elliot, *Principal*
EMP: 3 **EST:** 2010
SALES (est): 155.6K **Privately Held**
SIC: 1221 Bituminous coal & lignite-surface mining

(G-15699)
RELEVIUM LABS INC (PA)
4663 Katie Ln Ste O (45056-9525)
PHONE 614 568-7000
Brent Reider, *President*
EMP: 4 **EST:** 2015
SALES (est): 2.4MM **Privately Held**
SIC: 5047 5999 3845 Electro-medical equipment; medical apparatus & supplies; electromedical apparatus

(G-15700)
SCHNEIDER ELECTRIC USA INC
5735 College Corner Pike (45056-9715)
PHONE 513 523-4171
Pat Mc Donald, *Div Sub Head*
Ed Westhaver, *Mfg Mgr*
John Wittwer, *Safety Mgr*
Connie Nielsen, *Buyer*
Darren Bailey, *Engineer*
EMP: 500
SALES (corp-wide): 355.8K **Privately Held**
WEB: www.squared.com
SIC: 3643 3699 3677 3612 Bus bars (electrical conductors); electrical equipment & supplies; electronic coils, transformers & other inductors; transformers, except electric; nonferrous wiredrawing & insulating
HQ: Schneider Electric Usa, Inc.
201 Wshington St Ste 2700
Boston MA 02108
978 975-9600

(G-15701)
TOM FUCITO INC
21 Lynn Ave (45056-1598)
PHONE 513 273-2092
Joe Engelhard, *Branch Mgr*
EMP: 25
SALES (corp-wide): 1.5MM **Privately Held**
SIC: 3421 Table & food cutlery, including butchers'
PA: Tom Fucito Inc
2111 Beechmont Ave
Cincinnati OH 45230
513 347-1111

(G-15702)
WATER SYSTEMS SERVICES
4164 Miami Western Dr (45056-9033)
P.O. Box 588 (45056-0588)
PHONE 513 523-6766
Dave Judy, *President*
EMP: 4
SALES (est): 250K **Privately Held**
SIC: 3589 1711 Water filters & softeners, household type; plumbing, heating, air-conditioning contractors

(G-15703)
WILD BERRY INCENSE INC
Also Called: Wild Berry Incense Factory
5475 College Corner Pike (45056-1010)
PHONE 513 523-8583
Mark Biales, *President*
Roger Atkin, *Vice Pres*
Jenny Gorenflo, *Marketing Mgr*
▲ **EMP:** 19
SQ FT: 20,000
SALES (est): 4.3MM **Privately Held**
WEB: www.wildberryincense.com
SIC: 2899 5947 Incense; novelties

Painesville
Lake County

(G-15704)
ACCURATE METAL MACHINING INC
882 Callendar Blvd (44077-1218)
PHONE 440 350-8225
John Racic, *President*
Gabriel Loiczly, *Vice Pres*
Thomas Loiczly, *Vice Pres*
Anita M Webb, *Purch Mgr*
Chris Miller, *Purch Agent*
EMP: 171 **EST:** 1976
SQ FT: 15,000
SALES (est): 33.4MM **Privately Held**
WEB: www.accuratemetalmachining.com
SIC: 3599 Machine shop, jobbing & repair

(G-15705)
ADVANCED DEFENSE PRODUCTS LLC
11162 Spear Rd (44077-9542)
PHONE 440 571-2277
Steven Frank, *Principal*
EMP: 3
SALES (est): 150.8K **Privately Held**
SIC: 3812 Defense systems & equipment

(G-15706)
AEROCONTROLEX GROUP INC (DH)
313 Gillett St (44077-2918)
PHONE 440 352-6182
Raymond Laubenthal, *President*
Mario Jurcevic, *Engineer*
Robert George, *Treasurer*
Michael Carney, *Sales Dir*
Bob Miller, *IT/INT Sup*
EMP: 99
SQ FT: 55,000
SALES (est): 18.7MM
SALES (corp-wide): 3.8B **Publicly Held**
WEB: www.aerocontrolex.com
SIC: 3492 5084 3594 Valves, hydraulic, aircraft; industrial machinery & equipment; fluid power pumps & motors

(G-15707)
AEROCONTROLEX GROUP INC
Also Called: Aero Fluid Products
313 Gillett St (44077-2918)
PHONE 440 352-6182
Rodger Jones, *Branch Mgr*
EMP: 98
SALES (corp-wide): 3.8B **Publicly Held**
SIC: 3728 Aircraft parts & equipment
HQ: Aerocontrolex Group, Inc.
313 Gillett St
Painesville OH 44077
440 352-6182

(G-15708)
ALPHA OMEGA DEV & MCH CO
Also Called: Accesories Tools
10395 Squires Ct (44077-2040)
PHONE 440 352-9915
Tibor Korosi, *Owner*
EMP: 3
SQ FT: 1,100
SALES (est): 100K **Privately Held**
SIC: 3599 Custom machinery

(G-15709)
ALTANA
830 E Erie St (44077-4453)
P.O. Box 747 (44077-0747)
PHONE 440 954-7600
Ameo Anthony, *President*
EMP: 3
SALES (est): 152.7K **Privately Held**
SIC: 3399 Primary metal products

(G-15710)
AMERICAN FOAM PRODUCTS INC
753 Liberty St (44077-3623)
PHONE 440 352-3434
Bruce Rosenbaum, *President*
EMP: 24 **EST:** 1977
SQ FT: 50,000
SALES (est): 6.1MM **Privately Held**
WEB: www.americanfoamproducts.com
SIC: 3086 Packaging & shipping materials, foamed plastic; insulation or cushioning material, foamed plastic

(G-15711)
ASBEKA CUSTOM PRODUCTS LLC
11288 Saint Andrews Way (44077-9332)
PHONE 440 352-0839
Harold Arrowsmith, *President*
Harold F Arrowsmith Jr, *Admin Sec*
EMP: 10
SQ FT: 20,000
SALES (est): 750K **Privately Held**
WEB: www.asbeka.com
SIC: 3821 Laboratory apparatus & furniture

(G-15712)
ASSOCIATED ENTERPRISES
1382 W Jackson St (44077-1306)
P.O. Box 110 (44077-0110)
PHONE 440 354-2106
John T Venaleck, *President*
EMP: 3 **EST:** 1977
SALES (est): 285.3K **Privately Held**
SIC: 3678 Electronic connectors

(G-15713)
AUTOSYTE
829 Callendar Blvd (44077-1218)
PHONE 440 858-3226
Richard Rose, *Owner*
EMP: 5
SALES (est): 549.6K **Privately Held**
SIC: 3679 Electronic components

(G-15714)
AVERY DENNISON CORPORATION
670 Hardy Rd (44077-4573)
PHONE 440 358-3466
Matthew Khanna, *Research*
Linda E Chandler, *Branch Mgr*
EMP: 20
SALES (corp-wide): 7.1B **Publicly Held**
SIC: 2672 Coated & laminated paper
PA: Avery Dennison Corporation
207 N Goode Ave Ste 500
Glendale CA 91203
626 304-2000

(G-15715)
AVERY DENNISON CORPORATION
7600 Auburn Rd Bldg 18 (44077-9608)
PHONE 440 358-4691
Ram Mukkamala, *Research*
Rich White, *Engineer*
Martina McIssac, *Manager*
EMP: 115
SALES (corp-wide): 7.1B **Publicly Held**
WEB: www.avery.com
SIC: 2672 2679 Adhesive papers, labels or tapes: from purchased material; building, insulating & packaging paper
PA: Avery Dennison Corporation
207 N Goode Ave Ste 500
Glendale CA 91203
626 304-2000

(G-15716)
AVERY DENNISON CORPORATION
Avery Dennison Graphic Div
250 Chester St (44077-4129)
PHONE 440 358-3700
Erica Getzendiner, *Human Resources*
Rick Olszewski, *Branch Mgr*
Harold Houston, *Technical Staff*
EMP: 300
SALES (corp-wide): 7.1B **Publicly Held**
WEB: www.avery.com
SIC: 2672 2891 Adhesive papers, labels or tapes: from purchased material; adhesives & sealants
PA: Avery Dennison Corporation
207 N Goode Ave Ste 500
Glendale CA 91203
626 304-2000

(G-15717)
AVERY DENNISON CORPORATION
250 Chester St Bldg 11 (44077-4129)
PHONE 440 358-3408
Tony Hume, *Manager*
EMP: 100
SALES (corp-wide): 7.1B **Publicly Held**
WEB: www.avery.com
SIC: 2672 3081 Adhesive papers, labels or tapes: from purchased material; unsupported plastics film & sheet
PA: Avery Dennison Corporation
207 N Goode Ave Ste 500
Glendale CA 91203
626 304-2000

(G-15718)
B B BRADLEY COMPANY INC (PA)
7755 Crile Rd (44077-9702)
PHONE 440 354-2005
Bruce Beaty, *President*
EMP: 50
SALES (est): 9.9MM **Privately Held**
WEB: www.bbbradley.com
SIC: 3086 Packaging & shipping materials, foamed plastic

(G-15719)
BEASLEY FIBERGLASS INC
799 Lakeshore Blvd (44077-1125)
PHONE 440 357-6644
Benjamin Beasley, *President*
Claudia Beasley, *Admin Sec*
EMP: 3
SQ FT: 4,500
SALES (est): 328K **Privately Held**
WEB: www.beasleycomposites.com
SIC: 3714 3751 Motor vehicle body components & frame; motorcycles & related parts

(G-15720)
BRUCE HIGH PERFORMANCE TRAN
1 High Tech Ave (44077-3701)
PHONE 440 357-8964
Laurie Dibiase, *Principal*
Keith Shima, *Facilities Mgr*
Gary Horst, *Manager*
EMP: 21 **EST:** 2013
SALES (est): 4.1MM **Privately Held**
SIC: 3715 Truck trailers

(G-15721)
CASCADE UNLIMITED LLC
2510 Hale Rd (44077-4926)
PHONE 440 352-7995
EMP: 6
SALES (est): 280.4K **Privately Held**
SIC: 3599 Machine shop, jobbing & repair

(G-15722)
COE MANUFACTURING COMPANY (HQ)
Also Called: Automated Systems Div
70 W Erie St Ste 150 (44077-3279)
P.O. Box 520 (44077-0520)
PHONE 440 352-9381
Shawn Casey, *CEO*
John Kucharik, *President*
Lucy P Coe Et Al, *Principal*
Harry P Coe, *Principal*
Jeffrey Darbut, *CFO*
EMP: 100
SQ FT: 300,000
SALES (est): 44MM
SALES (corp-wide): 317.6MM **Privately Held**
WEB: www.coemfg.com
SIC: 3553 3531 Construction machinery; presses for making particleboard, hardboard, plywood, etc.
PA: Usnr, Llc
1981 Schurman Way
Woodland WA 98674
360 225-8267

Painesville - Lake County (G-15723)

(G-15723)
CONCORD ROAD EQUIPMENT MFG INC
348 Chester St (44077-4154)
P.O. Box 772 (44077-0772)
PHONE..................440 357-5344
Glen Warfield, *President*
Jeffrey Warfield, *Vice Pres*
EMP: 30
SALES (est): 11.6MM Privately Held
WEB: www.concordroadequipment.com
SIC: 3531 Road construction & maintenance machinery

(G-15724)
CONNECTORS UNLIMITED INC (PA)
1359 W Jackson St (44077-1341)
PHONE..................440 357-1161
Martin Ignasiak, *President*
Ralph Victor, *Treasurer*
Don Barber, *Admin Sec*
▲ EMP: 23
SALES (est): 2.1MM Privately Held
WEB: www.connectorsunlimited.com
SIC: 3357 3678 Nonferrous wiredrawing & insulating; electronic connectors

(G-15725)
CONTROL MEASUREMENT INC
1400 Mentor Ave Ste 5 (44077-1840)
PHONE..................440 639-0020
Steve J Kovach, *President*
EMP: 3
SQ FT: 1,400
SALES (est): 409.1K Privately Held
WEB: www.controlmeasurement.com
SIC: 3829 Measuring & controlling devices

(G-15726)
CORA CUPCAKES
95 Park Rd (44077-5012)
PHONE..................440 227-7145
Wendy Savot, *Principal*
EMP: 4
SALES (est): 314.6K Privately Held
SIC: 2051 Bread, cake & related products

(G-15727)
COUNTERTOP XPRESS
381 Fountain Ave (44077-1209)
PHONE..................440 358-0500
Joe Trunkely, *Principal*
EMP: 5
SALES (est): 466.4K Privately Held
SIC: 2541 Counter & sink tops

(G-15728)
CUSTOM DESIGN CABINETS & TOPS
Also Called: Custom Design Kitchen & Bath
379 Fountain Ave (44077-1209)
PHONE..................440 639-9900
George Lehtonen, *President*
Kaarina Lehtonen, *Vice Pres*
EMP: 8
SQ FT: 11,000
SALES (est): 1.3MM Privately Held
SIC: 5031 2541 Kitchen cabinets; cabinets, except refrigerated: show, display, etc.: wood; sink tops, plastic laminated; table or counter tops, plastic laminated

(G-15729)
DE NORA HOLDINGS US INC
7590 Discovery Ln (44077-9190)
PHONE..................440 710-5300
Paolo Dellacha, *President*
Angelo Ferrari, *Treasurer*
Silvia Bertini, *Admin Sec*
EMP: 370
SALES (est): 14.6MM Privately Held
SIC: 3589 Water purification equipment, household type; water treatment equipment, industrial
HQ: De Nora Holding (Uk) Limited
    C/O Hackwood Secretaries Limited
    London

(G-15730)
DE NORA NORTH AMERICA INC
7590 Discovery Ln (44077-9190)
PHONE..................440 357-4000
Lucieno Iacopepti, *CEO*
▲ EMP: 10 EST: 1998
SQ FT: 70,000
SALES (est): 2.1MM Privately Held
SIC: 3479 Coating electrodes
HQ: Oronzio De Nora International B.V.
    Prins Bernhardplein 200
    Amsterdam 1097
    205 214-777

(G-15731)
DE NORA TECH LLC (DH)
7590 Discovery Ln (44077-9190)
PHONE..................440 710-5300
Paolo Dellacha, *CEO*
Charlotte Valencic, *General Mgr*
Frank J McGorty, *COO*
Tony Friedrich, *Plant Mgr*
Donna Shipman, *Buyer*
◆ EMP: 80 EST: 1982
SQ FT: 20,000
SALES (est): 40.9MM Privately Held
WEB: www.eltechsystems.com
SIC: 3624 3589 7359 Electrodes, thermal & electrolytic uses: carbon, graphite; sewage & water treatment equipment; equipment rental & leasing
HQ: Industrie De Nora Spa
    Via Leonardo Bistolfi 35
    Milano MI 20134
    022 129-1

(G-15732)
DUKES AEROSPACE INC
Also Called: Aero Fluid Products
313 Gillett St (44077-2918)
PHONE..................818 998-9811
Greg Rufus, *CEO*
James Riley, *CEO*
EMP: 79
SALES (est): 27.3MM
SALES (corp-wide): 3.8B Publicly Held
SIC: 3728 Aircraft parts & equipment
HQ: Transdigm, Inc.
    4223 Monticello Blvd
    Cleveland OH 44121

(G-15733)
EAGLE LABORATORY GLASS CO LLC
440 W Prospect St (44077-3268)
PHONE..................440 354-8350
Yvonne Drake, *Mng Member*
EMP: 3
SALES (est): 23.4K Privately Held
SIC: 3229 5023 5719 Pressed & blown glass; glassware; glassware

(G-15734)
ECKART AMERICA CORPORATION (DH)
Also Called: Eckart Aluminum
830 E Erie St (44077-4453)
P.O. Box 747 (44077-0747)
PHONE..................440 954-7600
Anthony J Ameo Jr, *President*
Thomas Meola, *CFO*
Andrew Toth, *Controller*
◆ EMP: 100
SALES (est): 48.7MM
SALES (corp-wide): 501.4K Privately Held
SIC: 3399 2893 2816 Powder, metal; printing ink; inorganic pigments

(G-15735)
ECM BIOFILMS INC
Victoria Pl Ste 225 (44077)
PHONE..................440 350-1400
Robert Sinclair, *President*
Timothy Gooding, *Admin Sec*
EMP: 4 EST: 1998
SQ FT: 1,200
SALES (est): 716.3K Privately Held
WEB: www.ecmbiofilms.com
SIC: 2824 Organic fibers, noncellulosic

(G-15736)
EXECUTIVE WINGS INC
13550 Carter Rd (44077-9171)
PHONE..................440 254-1812
Michael Toman, *Owner*
EMP: 8 EST: 2001
SALES (est): 508.8K Privately Held
SIC: 3721 Aircraft

(G-15737)
EXTRUDEX LIMITED PARTNERSHIP (PA)
310 Figgie Dr (44077-3028)
PHONE..................440 352-7101
Tod Oliva, *Partner*
George Humphrey, *General Ptnr*
Tom Jacobs, *Engineer*
Cindy Obrien, *CFO*
Wendy White, *Human Res Mgr*
EMP: 35
SQ FT: 27,120
SALES (est): 4.3MM Privately Held
WEB: www.extrudex.net
SIC: 3089 3524 3431 Extruded finished plastic products; lawn & garden equipment; metal sanitary ware

(G-15738)
FARETEC INC
1610 W Jackson St Unit 6 (44077-1388)
PHONE..................440 350-9510
Tod C R Sackett, *President*
Constance Sackett, *Treasurer*
George Sackett, *Admin Sec*
▲ EMP: 10
SQ FT: 7,000
SALES (est): 1.9MM Privately Held
WEB: www.faretec.com
SIC: 3842 5047 Braces, orthopedic; splints, pneumatic & wood; medical equipment & supplies

(G-15739)
FIRST FRANCIS COMPANY INC (HQ)
Also Called: Federal Hose Manufacturing
25 Florence Ave (44077-1103)
PHONE..................440 352-8927
Ron George, *President*
Dave Lally, *Vice Pres*
Debbie Middleton, *Vice Pres*
John Lally, *Controller*
EMP: 28 EST: 1997
SALES (est): 6.8MM
SALES (corp-wide): 66.3MM Publicly Held
WEB: www.federalhose.com
SIC: 5085 3599 3444 3429 Hose, belting & packing; hose, flexible metallic; sheet metalwork; manufactured hardware (general)
PA: Hickok Incorporated
    10514 Dupont Ave
    Cleveland OH 44108
    216 541-8060

(G-15740)
FIVES LANDIS CORP
Also Called: Citco Diamond & Cbn Products
7605 Discovery Ln (44077-9396)
PHONE..................440 709-0700
Michael Sweeney, *Vice Pres*
S A Sitler, *Engineer*
Thomas W Toaddy, *Persnl Mgr*
EMP: 75
SQ FT: 7,000
SALES (corp-wide): 4.5MM Privately Held
SIC: 3541 Grinding machines, metalworking
HQ: Fives Landis Corp.
    16778 Halfway Blvd
    Hagerstown MD 21740
    301 797-3400

(G-15741)
GENESIS LAMP CORP
375 N Saint Clair St (44077-4053)
PHONE..................440 354-0095
Edward C Zukowski, *President*
Mark Zukowski, *General Mgr*
Margaret Zukowski, *Corp Secy*
Donna Williams, *Admin Sec*
▲ EMP: 15 EST: 1979
SQ FT: 6,400
SALES (est): 3.5MM Privately Held
WEB: www.genesislamp.com
SIC: 3646 3648 Commercial indusl & institutional electric lighting fixtures; lighting equipment

(G-15742)
GRAND-ROCK COMPANY INC
395 Fountain Ave (44077-1209)
PHONE..................440 639-2000
William H Stoneman, *President*
Gerard Arth, *CFO*
Adam Sullivan, *Regl Sales Mgr*
John Polz, *Admin Mgr*
▲ EMP: 50
SQ FT: 52,000
SALES (est): 11.1MM Privately Held
SIC: 3714 3621 2531 Motor vehicle parts & accessories; motors & generators; public building & related furniture

(G-15743)
GREAT LAKES GLASSWERKS INC
360 W Prospect St (44077-3258)
PHONE..................440 358-0460
Richard Chaykowsky, *President*
Julie Patterson, *Vice Pres*
John Wolfe, *Treasurer*
▲ EMP: 7
SQ FT: 10,000
SALES (est): 1MM Privately Held
WEB: www.glglasswerks.com
SIC: 3679 Electronic circuits

(G-15744)
GUYER PRECISION INC
280 W Prospect St (44077-3256)
PHONE..................440 354-8024
Thomas Guyer, *President*
EMP: 11
SQ FT: 12,500
SALES (est): 2.5MM Privately Held
SIC: 3599 Machine shop, jobbing & repair

(G-15745)
HARDY INDUSTRIAL TECH LLC
Also Called: H I T
679 Hardy Rd (44077-4574)
PHONE..................440 350-6300
Eric Lofquist, *CEO*
Scott Forster, *Vice Pres*
▲ EMP: 67
SALES (est): 13.9MM
SALES (corp-wide): 60.7MM Privately Held
SIC: 2869 Fuels
PA: Magnus International Group, Inc.
    16533 Chillicothe Rd A
    Chagrin Falls OH 44023
    216 592-8355

(G-15746)
HIGH TECH PRFMCE TRLRS INC
1 High Tech Ave (44077-3701)
PHONE..................440 357-8964
Bruce C Hanusosky, *President*
Judy Hanusosky, *Exec VP*
Caity Hanusosky, *Director*
Steve Lewis, *Director*
Adam Olenchick, *Director*
EMP: 65
SQ FT: 84,000
SALES (est): 11.4MM Privately Held
SIC: 3715 Truck trailers

(G-15747)
IMAX INDUSTRIES INC
117 W Walnut Ave (44077-2925)
PHONE..................440 639-0242
Mike Miller, *President*
EMP: 10
SALES (est): 2.4MM Privately Held
WEB: www.imaxindustries.com
SIC: 8711 3548 Engineering services; welding apparatus

(G-15748)
INJECTION MOLDING SPECIALIST
251 W Prospect St (44077-3257)
PHONE..................440 639-7896
Lee Albers, *Owner*
EMP: 5
SQ FT: 4,500
SALES: 120K Privately Held
SIC: 3089 Injection molding of plastics

GEOGRAPHIC SECTION

Painesville - Lake County (G-15774)

(G-15749)
INTERNATIONAL CNTR ARTFCIAL OR
Also Called: Icaot
10 W Erie St Ste 200 (44077-3270)
PHONE..................................440 358-1102
Paul S Malcheski, *President*
EMP: 3
SALES: 149K **Privately Held**
SIC: 2752 8299 Publication printing, lithographic; educational services

(G-15750)
ISK AMERICAS INCORPORATED (HQ)
7474 Auburn Rd (44077-9703)
PHONE..................................440 357-4600
Fujio Tamara, *Ch of Bd*
Marvin Hosokawa, *Managing Dir*
F O Hicks, *Vice Pres*
R C Andrews, *Admin Sec*
Beth Fellenstein, *Administration*
EMP: 40
SQ FT: 4,400
SALES (est): 14.3MM
SALES (corp-wide): 1B **Privately Held**
WEB: www.woodguard.com
SIC: 2816 2491 Titanium dioxide, anatase or rutile (pigments); wood preserving
PA: Ishihara Sangyo Kaisha, Ltd.
1-3-15, Edobori, Nishi-Ku
Osaka OSK 550-0
664 441-451

(G-15751)
J & H CORPORATION
Also Called: US Mold Machine Tool Company
444 Newell St (44077-1254)
PHONE..................................440 357-5982
Jeff Hughes, *President*
Doug Hughes, *Corp Secy*
Dan Hobson, *Design Engr*
John Langelier, *Design Engr*
EMP: 8
SQ FT: 10,000
SALES (est): 1.2MM **Privately Held**
WEB: www.superiormfgcorp.com
SIC: 3544 Industrial molds

(G-15752)
KEENEY SAND & STONE INC
13320 Girdled Rd (44077-8715)
PHONE..................................330 254-4582
Dennis Keeney, *President*
Kim Keeney, *General Mgr*
Kevin Keeney, *Superintendent*
Kathy Keeney, *Admin Sec*
EMP: 4
SQ FT: 1,332
SALES (est): 630.5K **Privately Held**
SIC: 1442 Sand mining; gravel mining

(G-15753)
KELCO HARDWOOD FLOORS INC
10137 Johnnycake Ridge Rd (44077-2163)
P.O. Box 1421 (44077-7332)
PHONE..................................440 354-0974
David Kelly, *Owner*
Weeberly Kelly, *Vice Pres*
EMP: 4 **EST:** 1994
SALES (est): 302.2K **Privately Held**
SIC: 2426 Flooring, hardwood

(G-15754)
KLIVLEND CASK DISTILLING LLC
149 Hayer Dr (44077-1241)
PHONE..................................216 926-1682
Sylvester Williams, *Principal*
EMP: 3
SALES (est): 81.6K **Privately Held**
SIC: 2085 Distilled & blended liquors

(G-15755)
L B L LITHOGRAPHERS INC (PA)
Also Called: L B L Printing
365 W Prospect St (44077-3259)
PHONE..................................440 350-0106
Lawrence Gidley, *CEO*
Brian Gidley, *President*
Lois Gidley, *Treasurer*
EMP: 14
SQ FT: 4,500
SALES (est): 2.5MM **Privately Held**
WEB: www.lblprinting.com
SIC: 2752 Commercial printing, offset

(G-15756)
LAD TECHNOLOGY INC
7830 Hermitage Rd (44077-9114)
PHONE..................................440 461-8002
Donna Marie Domanovics, *President*
Louis Domanovics, *Vice Pres*
EMP: 25
SALES (est): 3.9MM **Privately Held**
WEB: www.ladtechnology.com
SIC: 3672 Printed circuit boards

(G-15757)
LAKE COUNTY AUTO RECYCLERS
427 Newell St (44077-1253)
PHONE..................................440 428-2886
Joseph Woitella Sr, *Owner*
EMP: 5 **EST:** 1974
SQ FT: 2,000
SALES (est): 430.6K **Privately Held**
SIC: 5093 3341 Ferrous metal scrap & waste; automotive wrecking for scrap; secondary nonferrous metals

(G-15758)
LUBRIZOL CORPORATION
Also Called: Lubrizol Production Plant
155 Freedom Rd (44077-1234)
PHONE..................................440 357-7064
Tanya Travis, *General Mgr*
Dave Giancola, *Plant Supt*
Lubrizol Cpvc, *Accountant*
Charlie Sinatra, *Manager*
Wayne Sample, *Maintence Staff*
EMP: 44
SQ FT: 1,524
SALES (corp-wide): 225.3B **Publicly Held**
WEB: www.lubrizol.com
SIC: 2899 2992 Chemical preparations; rust arresting compounds, animal or vegetable oil base
HQ: The Lubrizol Corporation
29400 Lakeland Blvd
Wickliffe OH 44092
440 943-4200

(G-15759)
MADISON TOOL & DIE INC
147 Elevator Ave (44077-3609)
PHONE..................................440 354-8642
C L Graniteo, *President*
Chris B Graniteo, *Vice Pres*
EMP: 4 **EST:** 1973
SQ FT: 5,500
SALES (est): 480K **Privately Held**
SIC: 3599 Machine shop, jobbing & repair

(G-15760)
MASTER CARBIDE TOOLS COMPANY
Also Called: Mastertech Diamond Products Co
55 Florence Ave (44077-1103)
PHONE..................................440 352-1112
Thomas Frakes, *President*
Cynthia Frakes, *Vice Pres*
EMP: 16 **EST:** 1946
SQ FT: 5,000
SALES (est): 3MM **Privately Held**
WEB: www.mastertechdiamond.com
SIC: 3545 Cutting tools for machine tools

(G-15761)
MATPLUS LTD
76 Burton St (44077-3011)
PHONE..................................440 352-7201
Jeffrey M Bednar, *President*
Eric Stutzman, *Opers Mgr*
Nicole Cooke, *Accounts Mgr*
MO Neading, *Accounts Mgr*
Holly Fulmer, *Info Tech Mgr*
▲ **EMP:** 8
SALES (est): 1.3MM **Privately Held**
SIC: 3842 Orthopedic appliances

(G-15762)
MCNEIL INDUSTRIES INC
835 Richmond Rd Ste 2 (44077-1123)
PHONE..................................440 951-7756
Randall J McNeil, *President*
Jordan Owens, *Exec VP*
Robert Madden, *Vice Pres*
Sandy Warner, *Receptionist*
▲ **EMP:** 30
SQ FT: 18,000
SALES (est): 8.4MM **Privately Held**
WEB: www.mcneilindustries.com
SIC: 3366 5085 Bushings & bearings; seals, industrial

(G-15763)
METAL CRAFT DOCKS INC
156 Burton St (44077-4137)
PHONE..................................440 286-7135
Dave Bender, *President*
EMP: 5 **EST:** 1935
SQ FT: 15,000
SALES (est): 843.4K **Privately Held**
WEB: www.metalcraftdocks.com
SIC: 3448 3446 Docks: prefabricated metal; architectural metalwork

(G-15764)
MORTON SALT INC
570 Headlands Rd (44077)
PHONE..................................440 354-9901
Paul Shank, *Branch Mgr*
EMP: 15
SALES (corp-wide): 4.6B **Privately Held**
SIC: 2899 Packers' salt
HQ: Morton Salt, Inc.
404 W Lake St Ste 3000
Chicago IL 60606

(G-15765)
NEL-ACK SHEET METAL INC
546 Hoyt St Ste 18 (44077-3674)
PHONE..................................440 357-7844
A William Nelson, *President*
EMP: 3
SALES (est): 260K **Privately Held**
SIC: 3444 Sheet metalwork

(G-15766)
NOVA CHEMICALS INC
786 Hardy Rd (44077-4524)
PHONE..................................440 352-3381
Ronda Senskey, *Finance Mgr*
Paul Pollo, *Branch Mgr*
EMP: 56 **Privately Held**
SIC: 2821 Polystyrene resins
HQ: Nova Chemicals Inc.
1555 Coraopolis Hts Rd
Moon Township PA 15108
412 490-4000

(G-15767)
OBRON ATLANTIC CORPORATION
Also Called: Eckart America
830 E Erie St (44077-4453)
P.O. Box 747 (44077-0747)
PHONE..................................440 954-7600
Anthony Ameo, *President*
Mark Wallace, *CFO*
EMP: 60 **EST:** 1912
SALES (est): 3.9MM
SALES (corp-wide): 501.4K **Privately Held**
WEB: www.eckart.net
SIC: 2816 3399 Metallic & mineral pigments; powder, metal
HQ: Eckart America Corporation
830 E Erie St
Painesville OH 44077
440 954-7600

(G-15768)
OHIO ASSOCIATED ENTPS LLC (PA)
97 Corwin Dr (44077-1802)
P.O. Box 110 (44077-0110)
PHONE..................................440 354-2106
John Hartman, *Vice Pres*
Barabra Recart, *Purch Mgr*
Ken Brand, *Engineer*
Mark Kappel, *Engineer*
Laura Graham, *Human Res Mgr*
▲ **EMP:** 20
SQ FT: 123,000
SALES (est): 37.3MM **Privately Held**
WEB: www.meritec.com
SIC: 3678 Electronic connectors

(G-15769)
OHIO ASSOCIATED ENTPS LLC
Also Called: Omnitec
1359 W Jackson St (44077-1341)
P.O. Box 110 (44077-0110)
PHONE..................................440 354-3148
James T Walch, *Branch Mgr*
EMP: 125
SQ FT: 25,000
SALES (corp-wide): 37.3MM **Privately Held**
WEB: www.meritec.com
SIC: 3643 Electric connectors; connectors & terminals for electrical devices
PA: Ohio Associated Enterprises Llc
97 Corwin Dr
Painesville OH 44077
440 354-2106

(G-15770)
OHIO ASSOCIATED ENTPS LLC
Also Called: Meritech
72 Corwin Dr (44077-1802)
PHONE..................................440 354-3148
John T Venaleck, *Branch Mgr*
EMP: 50
SALES (corp-wide): 37.3MM **Privately Held**
WEB: www.meritec.com
SIC: 3678 3544 3469 3357 Electronic connectors; special dies, tools, jigs & fixtures; metal stampings; communication wire
PA: Ohio Associated Enterprises Llc
97 Corwin Dr
Painesville OH 44077
440 354-2106

(G-15771)
PANAMA JEWELERS LLC
Also Called: Aero Refining
7250 Brakeman Rd (44077-9326)
PHONE..................................440 376-6987
Jabra Deir,
EMP: 5 **EST:** 2010
SALES (est): 225.5K **Privately Held**
SIC: 5944 3341 Jewelry stores; gold smelting & refining (secondary)

(G-15772)
PATH TECHNOLOGIES INC
437 W Prospect St (44077-3269)
PHONE..................................440 358-1500
David Princic, *President*
Dorothy Princic, *Shareholder*
Mike Princic, *Shareholder*
Barbara Sespico, *Shareholder*
EMP: 8
SQ FT: 7,000
SALES (est): 1.2MM **Privately Held**
WEB: www.path-tech.com
SIC: 3599 Machine shop, jobbing & repair; machine & other job shop work

(G-15773)
PCC AIRFOILS LLC
870 Renaissance Pkwy (44077-1287)
PHONE..................................440 350-6150
EMP: 10
SALES (corp-wide): 225.3B **Publicly Held**
SIC: 3369 Nonferrous foundries
HQ: Pcc Airfoils Llc
3401 Entp Pkwy Ste 200
Cleveland OH 44122
216 831-3590

(G-15774)
PENCA DESIGN GROUP LTD
1325 Yale Pl (44077-5492)
PHONE..................................440 210-4422
Patricia Penca, *Manager*
EMP: 3
SQ FT: 500
SALES (est): 186.8K **Privately Held**
SIC: 2759 7389 3993 7336 Advertising literature: printing; advertising, promotional & trade show services; advertising artwork; commercial art & graphic design; art design services; graphic arts & related design; graphic displays, except graphic terminals; advertising consultant

(PA)=Parent Co (HQ)=Headquarters (DH)=Div Headquarters
✪ = New Business established in last 2 years

2019 Harris Ohio Industrial Directory

Painesville - Lake County (G-15775)

(G-15775)
PET PROCESSORS LLC
1350 Bacon Rd (44077-4781)
PHONE..................440 354-4321
Ken Noble, *Purchasing*
Juliana Levi, *Engineer*
Renee Keener, *Human Resources*
Gary Laughlin, *Sales Dir*
Ken Berlin, *Accounts Mgr*
◆ **EMP:** 77
SQ FT: 350,000
SALES (est): 19.2MM **Privately Held**
WEB: www.petuk.com
SIC: 2821 Polyesters
PA: Diefenthal Holdings, Llc
1750 South Ln Ste 1
Mandeville LA 70471

(G-15776)
PRESSURE TECHNOLOGY OHIO INC
7996 Auburn Rd (44077-9701)
P.O. Box 92, Sewickley PA (15143-0092)
PHONE..................215 628-1975
David Bowles, *President*
EMP: 20
SALES (est): 3.5MM **Privately Held**
WEB: www.pressuretechnology.com
SIC: 3398 Metal heat treating

(G-15777)
R W SIDLEY INCORPORATED (PA)
436 Casement Ave (44077-3817)
P.O. Box 150 (44077-0150)
PHONE..................440 352-9343
Robert C Sidley, *Ch of Bd*
Robert J Buescher, *President*
Brad Busher, *General Mgr*
Iola Black, *Principal*
R H Bostick, *Principal*
▲ **EMP:** 30
SQ FT: 10,000
SALES (est): 132.6MM **Privately Held**
WEB: www.rwsidleyinc.com
SIC: 1771 3299 Concrete work; blocks & brick, sand lime

(G-15778)
R W SIDLEY INCORPORATED
Mining & Materials Division
436 Casement Ave (44077-3817)
P.O. Box 150 (44077-0150)
PHONE..................440 352-9343
Bob Buscher, *President*
EMP: 30
SALES (corp-wide): 132.6MM **Privately Held**
WEB: www.rwsidleyinc.com
SIC: 1422 Cement rock, crushed & broken-quarrying
PA: R. W. Sidley Incorporated
436 Casement Ave
Painesville OH 44077
440 352-9343

(G-15779)
RAILING CRAFTERS LTD
632 Argonne Dr (44077-4304)
PHONE..................440 506-9336
Ken Kotnik, *Owner*
EMP: 3
SALES: 50K **Privately Held**
SIC: 3441 Fabricated structural metal

(G-15780)
REGAL INDUSTRIES INC
857 Richmond Rd (44077-1143)
PHONE..................440 352-9600
Richard Lutzke, *President*
Kristin Lutzke V Pres-Cfo, *CFO*
EMP: 3
SQ FT: 3,000
SALES (est): 1.8MM **Privately Held**
WEB: www.regal-industries.com
SIC: 3568 3821 3559 Power transmission equipment; crushing & grinding apparatus, laboratory; chemical machinery & equipment

(G-15781)
ROPAMA INC
Also Called: Roco Industries
380 W Prospect St (44077-3258)
PHONE..................440 358-1304
Ron Mahoney, *President*
Pat Mahoney, *Vice Pres*
EMP: 15
SALES (est): 1MM **Privately Held**
SIC: 3398 Metal heat treating

(G-15782)
RUFF NEON & LIGHTING MAINT INC
295 W Prospect St (44077-3257)
PHONE..................440 350-6267
Thomas A Ruff, *President*
EMP: 10 **EST:** 1991
SALES (est): 1.4MM **Privately Held**
SIC: 3993 Neon signs

(G-15783)
SPECTRUM BRANDS INC
447 Lexington Ave (44077)
PHONE..................440 357-2600
EMP: 15
SALES (corp-wide): 5B **Publicly Held**
SIC: 3714 Mfg Motor Vehicle Parts/Accessories
HQ: Spectrum Brands, Inc.
3001 Deming Way
Middleton WI 53562
608 275-3340

(G-15784)
STAFAST PRODUCTS INC (PA)
Also Called: Stafast West
505 Lakeshore Blvd (44077-1197)
PHONE..................440 357-5546
Donald S Selle, *President*
Elmer T Elbrecht, *Principal*
John G Roberts, *Principal*
Joan Selle, *Corp Secy*
Kirk Hedger, *Opers Mgr*
▲ **EMP:** 40
SQ FT: 20,600
SALES (est): 27.3MM **Privately Held**
WEB: www.stafast.com
SIC: 5085 3452 Fasteners, industrial: nuts, bolts, screws, etc.; bolts, nuts, rivets & washers

(G-15785)
T & T MACHINE INC
892 Callendar Blvd (44077-1218)
PHONE..................440 354-0605
Tony Padovic, *President*
EMP: 14 **EST:** 1993
SQ FT: 13,000
SALES (est): 1.5MM **Privately Held**
WEB: www.terrymgt.com
SIC: 3599 Machine shop, jobbing & repair

(G-15786)
TECHNICAL GLASS PRODUCTS INC (PA)
881 Callendar Blvd (44077-1218)
PHONE..................440 639-6399
Jim Horvath, *President*
Halle Ricciardo, *Corp Secy*
Robert Singer, *Vice Pres*
▲ **EMP:** 17
SQ FT: 10,500
SALES: 6MM **Privately Held**
WEB: www.technicalglass.com
SIC: 3559 Glass making machinery: blowing, molding, forming, etc.

(G-15787)
TEKRAFT INDUSTRIES INC
244 Latimore St (44077-3903)
PHONE..................440 352-8321
Terrence Tekavec, *President*
Victor Tekavec, *Shareholder*
EMP: 8
SQ FT: 3,500
SALES (est): 332.7K **Privately Held**
SIC: 3599 Machine shop, jobbing & repair

(G-15788)
TESSA PRECISION PRODUCT INC
850 Callendar Blvd (44077-1218)
PHONE..................440 392-3470
Paul Battaglia, *President*
Mark Kawasaki, *Engineer*
Ron Hartman, *Manager*
Erika Battaglia, *Executive*
EMP: 36
SQ FT: 25,000
SALES (est): 7.6MM **Privately Held**
WEB: www.tessaprecision.com
SIC: 3599 Machine shop, jobbing & repair

(G-15789)
THE MAX
759 Lakeshore Blvd (44077-1176)
PHONE..................440 357-0036
Ray Minger, *Owner*
Connie Maxey, *Principal*
EMP: 4
SALES (est): 412.5K **Privately Held**
SIC: 2211 Print cloths, cotton

(G-15790)
THIRION BROTHERS EQP CO LLC
Also Called: Tbec
340 W Prospect St (44077-3258)
PHONE..................440 357-8004
David Thirion, *Principal*
EMP: 6
SQ FT: 1,015
SALES (est): 646.4K **Privately Held**
SIC: 3694 7699 5082 Distributors, motor vehicle engine; pumps & pumping equipment repair; general construction machinery & equipment

(G-15791)
TRANSDIGM INC
Aero Fluid Products
313 Gillett St (44077-2918)
PHONE..................440 352-6182
Paula Wheeler, *President*
Jennifer Griffin, *Manager*
EMP: 30
SALES (corp-wide): 3.8B **Publicly Held**
WEB: www.electromotion.com
SIC: 3561 Pumps & pumping equipment
HQ: Transdigm, Inc.
4223 Monticello Blvd
Cleveland OH 44121

(G-15792)
TURBO-MOLD INC
440 Blackbrook Rd (44077-1219)
PHONE..................440 352-2530
George Tirak, *President*
Greg Tirak, *Vice Pres*
EMP: 3 **EST:** 1967
SQ FT: 3,000
SALES: 135K **Privately Held**
SIC: 3544 Industrial molds

(G-15793)
TWIN RVERS TECH - PNSVILLE LLC
Also Called: Twin Rivers Technologies Mfg
679 Hardy Rd (44077-4574)
PHONE..................440 350-6300
Ken Morreale, *Project Mgr*
Hasni Ahmad, *Opers Staff*
Kimberly Sullivan, *Project Engr*
Michael Fechner, *Accounts Mgr*
Chris Schneider, *Sales Staff*
EMP: 70
SALES (est): 11.2MM **Privately Held**
WEB: www.twinriverstechnologies.com
SIC: 2869 Industrial organic chemicals

(G-15794)
VAL-CON INC
7201 Hermitage Rd (44077-9718)
PHONE..................440 357-1898
Richard Vertocnik, *President*
Jonell Vertocnik, *Vice Pres*
EMP: 7
SALES: 750K **Privately Held**
SIC: 3825 Energy measuring equipment, electrical

(G-15795)
VERSITEC MANUFACTURING INC
152 Elevator Ave (44077-3610)
PHONE..................440 354-4283
Royce Reinhart, *President*
Mark Neal, *Vice Pres*
Shawn Humphrey, *Accounts Mgr*
EMP: 16
SQ FT: 3,600
SALES (est): 2.7MM **Privately Held**
WEB: www.versitecinc.com
SIC: 3672 Printed circuit boards

(G-15796)
VISION PRESS INC
1634 W Jackson St (44077-1312)
P.O. Box 1308 (44077-8308)
PHONE..................440 357-6362
Douglas Advey, *President*
Ronald Advey, *Vice Pres*
EMP: 6
SALES: 750K **Privately Held**
SIC: 2759 Screen printing

(G-15797)
WATER STAR INC
7590 Discovery Ln (44077-9190)
PHONE..................440 996-0800
Dan Longhenry, *President*
Andrew Niksa, *Vice Pres*
▲ **EMP:** 14
SALES (est): 1.8MM
SALES (corp-wide): 1.1B **Publicly Held**
WEB: www.waterstarinc.com
SIC: 3356 3479 Titanium; coating of metals & formed products
PA: Tennant Company
701 Lilac Dr N
Minneapolis MN 55422
763 540-1200

(G-15798)
WESTERN RESERVE LUBRICANTS
13981 Leroy Center Rd (44077-9782)
PHONE..................440 951-5700
EMP: 3
SALES (est): 252.9K **Privately Held**
SIC: 2992 Lubricating oils

(G-15799)
WHOLESALE PRINTERS LTD
195 N Doan Ave (44077-1445)
PHONE..................440 354-5788
Elizabeth Kincaid, *Principal*
EMP: 4
SALES (est): 527.8K **Privately Held**
SIC: 2752 Commercial printing, lithographic

(G-15800)
WILLOW WATER TREATMENT INC
7855 Jennings Dr (44077-9383)
PHONE..................440 254-6313
Fax: 440 254-4845
EMP: 3
SALES (est): 240K **Privately Held**
SIC: 3589 Mfg Service Industry Machinery

(G-15801)
XPONET INC
Also Called: Mold Tech
20 Elberta Rd (44077-1231)
PHONE..................440 354-6617
Ralph Victor, *Ch of Bd*
Don Barber, *President*
Rick Clark, *Accounts Mgr*
Jane Mahoney, *Sales Mgr*
Sarah Marinc, *Admin Asst*
EMP: 50
SQ FT: 25,000
SALES (est): 8.5MM **Privately Held**
WEB: www.moldtech.com
SIC: 3357 3678 3643 3577 Communication wire; electronic connectors; current-carrying wiring devices; computer peripheral equipment

(G-15802)
YOKOHAMA INDS AMRICAS OHIO INC
474 Newell St (44077-1254)
P.O. Box 388 (44077-0388)
PHONE..................440 352-3321
Yoshahisa Makabayopshi, *President*
Pat Fleming, *Exec VP*
Don Patt, *Exec VP*
Walter Mason, *Production*
Larry Tremaglio, *Treasurer*
▲ **EMP:** 92
SQ FT: 132,000
SALES (est): 16.9MM
SALES (corp-wide): 5.7B **Privately Held**
WEB: www.sasrubber.com
SIC: 3069 Molded rubber products; rubber automotive products

GEOGRAPHIC SECTION

HQ: Yokohama Corporation Of North America
1500 Indiana St
Salem VA 24153
540 389-5426

(G-15803)
YOKOHAMA TIRE CORPORATION
Also Called: S A S Rubber
474 Newell St (44077-1254)
PHONE...................................440 352-3321
Donald A Patt, *Principal*
EMP: 132
SQ FT: 50,000
SALES (est): 7.7MM
SALES (corp-wide): 5.7B **Privately Held**
WEB: www.yrc.co.jp
SIC: 3061   Mechanical rubber goods
PA: Yokohama Rubber Company, Limited, The
5-36-11, Shimbashi
Minato-Ku TKY 105-0
354 004-520

(G-15804)
YOUR DAILY MOTIVATION YDM FITN
6631 Vrooman Rd (44077-8841)
PHONE...................................440 954-1038
Thomas Salvatore, *Principal*
EMP: 4
SALES (est): 213.3K **Privately Held**
SIC: 2711   Newspapers, publishing & printing

(G-15805)
ZSI MANUFACTURING INC
Also Called: American Belleville
8059 Crile Rd (44077-9180)
PHONE...................................440 266-0701
Steve Fowler, *CEO*
Christopher P Blossom, *CFO*
EMP: 9
SQ FT: 21,500
SALES (est): 59.9K **Privately Held**
SIC: 3493   Steel springs, except wire

Pandora
Putnam County

(G-15806)
ADVANCED DRAINAGE SYSTEMS INC
501 Basinger Rd (45877-8772)
PHONE...................................419 384-3140
Ryan Felt, *Branch Mgr*
EMP: 14
SALES (corp-wide): 1.3B **Publicly Held**
SIC: 3084   Plastics pipe
PA: Advanced Drainage Systems, Inc.
4640 Trueman Blvd
Hilliard OH 43026
614 658-0050

(G-15807)
UNARCO MATERIAL HANDLING INC
407 E Washington St (45877-8770)
P.O. Box 266 (45877-0266)
PHONE...................................419 384-3211
Joe Steinmetz, *Opers Mgr*
Bruce Ontrop, *Engineer*
Jerry Hight, *Engineer*
EMP: 4
SALES (corp-wide): 3.8B **Privately Held**
WEB: www.unarcorack.com
SIC: 2542 5084   Racks, merchandise display or storage; except wood; industrial machinery & equipment
HQ: Unarco Material Handling, Inc.
701 16th Ave E
Springfield TN 37172

Paris
Stark County

(G-15808)
CAR-NATION INC
1216 Fox Ave Se (44669-9794)
PHONE...................................330 862-9001
Doug Hosterman, *President*
EMP: 4
SQ FT: 1,000
SALES: 300K **Privately Held**
SIC: 3589   Car washing machinery

(G-15809)
STALLION OILFIELD CNSTR LLC
3361 Baird Ave Se (44669-9769)
PHONE...................................330 868-2083
Chrysta Dansby, *Branch Mgr*
EMP: 27 **Privately Held**
SIC: 1389   Oil field services
PA: Stallion Oilfield Construction, Llc
950 Corbindale Rd Ste 400
Houston TX 77024

Parkman
Geauga County

(G-15810)
C N C PRECISION MACHINE INC
18360 Industrial Cir (44080)
PHONE...................................440 548-3880
Alex Szkoe, *President*
EMP: 63
SALES (est): 12.7MM **Privately Held**
WEB: www.cncprecisionmachine.com
SIC: 3599   Machine shop, jobbing & repair

(G-15811)
DAN SHROCK CEMENT
9344 Pritchard Rd (44080)
PHONE...................................440 548-2498
Dan Shrock, *Principal*
EMP: 3
SALES (est): 157.5K **Privately Held**
SIC: 1771 3273 5211   Concrete work; ready-mixed concrete; cement

(G-15812)
MONTVILLE PLASTICS & RBR LLC
Also Called: Iron Horse Engineering
15567 Main Market Rd (44080)
P.O. Box 527 (44080-0527)
PHONE...................................440 548-3211
Jay Roberts, *Partner*
Tracy Roberts, *Vice Pres*
Larry Margolin, *Engineer*
Russ Nidy, *CFO*
EMP: 55
SQ FT: 50,000
SALES: 4.9MM **Privately Held**
SIC: 3089   Injection molding of plastics

(G-15813)
REVONOC INC
18125 Madison Rd (44080)
PHONE...................................440 548-3491
Ernest Conover III, *Principal*
EMP: 3
SQ FT: 3,500
SALES (est): 180.5K **Privately Held**
WEB: www.conoverworkshops.com
SIC: 8249 8999 2499   Vocational schools; technical manual preparation; decorative wood & woodwork

Parma
Cuyahoga County

(G-15814)
AMAC ENTERPRISES INC (PA)
5909 W 130th St (44130-1040)
PHONE...................................216 362-1880
George Chimples, *Ch of Bd*
Constantine Chimples, *President*
Thomas Chimples, *Vice Pres*
Carol Sojka, *Purch Agent*
Janet Chimples, *Treasurer*
▲ **EMP:** 112 **EST:** 1951
SQ FT: 190,000
SALES (est): 16.2MM **Privately Held**
WEB: www.amacent.com
SIC: 3398 3471   Metal heat treating; finishing, metals or formed products

(G-15815)
COWGILL PRINTING CO
4427 Brookpark Rd (44134-1163)
P.O. Box 30033, Cleveland (44130-0033)
PHONE...................................216 741-2076
Jeff Cowgill, *President*
EMP: 4 **EST:** 1926
SQ FT: 8,000
SALES: 575K **Privately Held**
WEB: www.cowgillprinting.com
SIC: 2752   Commercial printing, offset

(G-15816)
DYNAMIC TEMPERATURE SUPS LLC
Also Called: Dts
12448 Plaza Dr (44130-1057)
PHONE...................................216 767-5799
Gary Kloock,
▲ **EMP:** 3 **EST:** 2010
SALES: 1.5MM **Privately Held**
SIC: 3823   Industrial instrmnts msrmnt display/control process variable

(G-15817)
ELECTRA SOUND INC (PA)
Also Called: Electrasound TV & Appl Svc
5260 Commerce Pkwy W (44130-1271)
PHONE...................................216 433-9600
Robert C Masa Jr, *CEO*
Charles C Masa, *President*
Patricia Masa, *Vice Pres*
Rodger Miller, *Asst Controller*
Nancy Reschke, *VP Mktg*
EMP: 70
SQ FT: 28,000
SALES (est): 31MM **Privately Held**
WEB: www.electrasound.com
SIC: 3694 7622 5065 5731   Automotive electrical equipment; television repair shop; radio repair shop; video repair; sound equipment, electronic; sound equipment, automotive

(G-15818)
FDC MACHINE REPAIR INC
5585 Venture Dr (44130-9300)
PHONE...................................216 362-1082
Fred Di Censo, *President*
Ferdinando Di Censo, *President*
Maria Di Censo, *Vice Pres*
EMP: 30
SQ FT: 32,000
SALES (est): 5.7MM **Privately Held**
SIC: 3599   Machine shop, jobbing & repair

(G-15819)
FOURJAYS INC
Also Called: Minuteman Press
5341 Broadview Rd (44134-1628)
PHONE...................................216 741-8258
Gary Blevins, *President*
EMP: 4 **EST:** 2007
SQ FT: 1,800
SALES (est): 242K **Privately Held**
SIC: 2752   Commercial printing, lithographic

(G-15820)
GMR FURNITURE SERVICES LTD
Also Called: PDQ Installation Co
7403 Dorothy Ave (44129-3604)
PHONE...................................216 244-5072
Eric Liss,
EMP: 18
SALES (est): 1.6MM **Privately Held**
SIC: 2542   Cabinets: show, display or storage: except wood

(G-15821)
GRAFTECH INTL HOLDINGS INC
12300 Snow Rd (44130-1001)
PHONE...................................330 239-3023
EMP: 132
SALES (corp-wide): 8.5B **Publicly Held**
SIC: 3624   Electrodes, thermal & electrolytic uses: carbon, graphite

HQ: Graftech International Holdings Inc.
982 Keynote Cir
Brooklyn Heights OH 44131
216 676-2000

(G-15822)
HILLMAN GROUP INC
Needa Parts
12400 Plaza Dr (44130-1057)
PHONE...................................800 800-4900
EMP: 3
SALES (corp-wide): 484.2MM **Privately Held**
SIC: 3429 5162   Keys & key blanks; plastics materials
HQ: The Hillman Group Inc
10590 Hamilton Ave
Cincinnati OH 45231
513 851-4900

(G-15823)
HYFAST AEROSPACE LLC
12313 Plaza Dr (44130-1044)
PHONE...................................216 712-4158
Henry Ford, *Principal*
EMP: 3
SALES (est): 171.7K **Privately Held**
SIC: 3721   Aircraft

(G-15824)
NORTH AMRCN SSTNABLE ENRGY LTD
Also Called: Renewable Energy
1360 Grant Dr (44134-5327)
PHONE...................................440 539-7133
Michael Pasela,
EMP: 4
SALES (est): 260K **Privately Held**
SIC: 3433   Heating equipment, except electric

(G-15825)
OSG-STERLING DIE INC
12502 Plaza Dr (44130-1045)
PHONE...................................216 267-1300
Denise L Lucas, *Principal*
Stacey Cooper, *Supervisor*
▲ **EMP:** 70
SALES (est): 11.2MM
SALES (corp-wide): 1.1B **Privately Held**
WEB: www.sterlingdie.com
SIC: 3545   Cutting tools for machine tools
HQ: Osg Usa, Inc.
676 E Fullerton Ave
Glendale Heights IL 60139
630 790-1400

(G-15826)
PAULIN INDUSTRIES INC
12400 Plaza Dr U1 (44130-1057)
PHONE...................................216 433-7633
Richard Paulin, *President*
Bill Davis, *Principal*
Jessica Woon, *Sales Staff*
Barbara Marin, *Manager*
▲ **EMP:** 23
SQ FT: 800
SALES (est): 8.5MM
SALES (corp-wide): 838.3MM **Privately Held**
WEB: www.hpaulin.com
SIC: 5072 3452   Hardware; bolts, nuts, rivets & washers
HQ: The Hillman Group Inc
10590 Hamilton Ave
Cincinnati OH 45231
513 851-4900

Pataskala
Licking County

(G-15827)
ALBIN SALES INC
81 Brandon Dr (43062-8291)
PHONE...................................740 927-7210
Frederick D Albin, *President*
Sheley Albin, *Vice Pres*
EMP: 2 **EST:** 2001
SALES: 7MM **Privately Held**
SIC: 3585 8611   Heating & air conditioning combination units; manufacturers' institute

Pataskala - Licking County (G-15828)

GEOGRAPHIC SECTION

(G-15828)
AMERICAN POWER HOIST INC
63 E Mill St (43062-8203)
PHONE..................................740 964-2035
Thomas Jones, *President*
EMP: 5
SALES (est): 846.4K **Privately Held**
SIC: 3536 Boat lifts

(G-15829)
DLWOODWORKING
9330 Hollow Rd Sw (43062-9134)
PHONE..................................740 927-2693
EMP: 4 **EST:** 2013
SALES (est): 217K **Privately Held**
SIC: 2431 Millwork

(G-15830)
DRAGONFLIES AND ANGELS PRESS
103 Venetian Way Sw (43062-9147)
PHONE..................................740 964-9149
Saralee Etter, *Principal*
EMP: 3
SALES (est): 75.8K **Privately Held**
SIC: 2711 Newspapers

(G-15831)
EXCELSIOR PRINTING CO
1014 Putnam Rd Sw (43062-9754)
PHONE..................................740 927-2934
David Fannon, *President*
Melissa Fannon, *Vice Pres*
EMP: 9
SQ FT: 8,200
SALES (est): 1.2MM **Privately Held**
WEB: www.xlcr.com
SIC: 2752 Commercial printing, offset

(G-15832)
INNOVATIVE LAB SERVICES LLC
7123 National Rd Sw Rear (43062-8610)
PHONE..................................614 554-6446
Alan Miller,
EMP: 4
SQ FT: 4,000
SALES (est): 179K **Privately Held**
SIC: 3826 Spectroscopic & other optical properties measuring equipment; spectrometers; liquid chromatographic instruments

(G-15833)
J COM DATA INC
Also Called: Jcd
6706 Watkins Rd Sw (43062-9538)
PHONE..................................614 304-1455
April Standinger, *Principal*
Jason Standinger,
EMP: 3
SALES (est): 69.7K **Privately Held**
SIC: 7379 7389 3663 8748 Disk & diskette conversion service; ; carrier equipment, radio communications; telecommunications consultant; telephone/video communications; data entry service

(G-15834)
KARS OHIO LLC
6359 Summit Rd Sw (43062-8763)
P.O. Box 34, Summit Station (43073-0034)
PHONE..................................614 655-1099
Lisa Keyser Vega,
EMP: 8
SALES (est): 904K **Privately Held**
SIC: 2851 3479 1721 1629 Undercoatings, paint; painting of metal products; industrial painting; blasting contractor, except building demolition; tank repair & cleaning services

(G-15835)
KNOX ENERGY INC (PA)
11872 Worthington Rd Nw (43062-9770)
P.O. Box 705, New Albany (43054-0705)
PHONE..................................740 927-6731
Mark Jordan, *President*
Andy Merkle, *Vice Pres*
Terry Wade, *Prdtn Mgr*
EMP: 17
SALES (est): 1.6MM **Privately Held**
SIC: 2911 Oils, fuel

(G-15836)
OHIO STEEL INDUSTRIES INC
Also Called: Structural Steel Fabrication
13792 Broad St Sw (43062-9189)
P.O. Box 197, Summit Station (43073-0197)
PHONE..................................740 927-9500
Joe Leggett, *General Mgr*
Robet Eaton, *Branch Mgr*
EMP: 50
SQ FT: 200,000
SALES (corp-wide): 24.4MM **Privately Held**
WEB: www.ohiosteel.com
SIC: 3441 Fabricated structural metal
PA: Ohio Steel Industries, Inc.
2575 Ferris Rd
Columbus OH 43224
614 471-4800

(G-15837)
PATASKALA POST
Also Called: Heartland Communications Div
190 E Broad St Ste 2 (43062-7106)
P.O. Box 722 (43062-0722)
PHONE..................................740 964-6226
Randall Almendinger, *Owner*
EMP: 10
SALES (est): 381.3K **Privately Held**
SIC: 2711 Newspapers, publishing & printing

(G-15838)
PROGRAMMABLE CONTROL SERVICE
Also Called: P C S
6900 Blacks Rd Sw (43062-9512)
PHONE..................................740 927-0744
Phil Fraley, *President*
EMP: 12
SALES (est): 2.4MM **Privately Held**
WEB: www.programmablecontrol.com
SIC: 3569 5084 7378 Robots, assembly line: industrial & commercial; robots, industrial; computer maintenance & repair

(G-15839)
REDHAWK ENERGY SYSTEMS LLC
10340 Palmer Rd Sw (43062-9449)
P.O. Box 36, Etna (43018-0036)
PHONE..................................740 927-8244
William J Ulrich, *Sales Staff*
Thomas J Ulrich,
Arthur J Ulrich,
James J Ulrich,
John Ulrich,
EMP: 6
SQ FT: 5,000
SALES (est): 1.1MM **Privately Held**
SIC: 3674 Solar cells

(G-15840)
RIGHTER PLUMBING
1451 Galway Bnd N (43062-7099)
PHONE..................................614 604-7197
John Righter, *General Ptnr*
EMP: 5
SALES (est): 558K **Privately Held**
SIC: 3088 Plastics plumbing fixtures

(G-15841)
RONA ENTERPRISES INC
30 W Broad St (43062-8180)
P.O. Box 1498 (43062-1498)
PHONE..................................740 927-9971
Ronald A Thomas, *President*
EMP: 7
SQ FT: 1,500
SALES (est): 1.1MM **Privately Held**
WEB: www.ronahomes.com
SIC: 2452 6531 Prefabricated wood buildings; real estate agents & managers

(G-15842)
RYDER ENGRAVING INC
1029 Hazelton Etna Rd Sw (43062-8528)
PHONE..................................740 927-7193
Jill Gosnell, *President*
Chris Gosnell, *Admin Sec*
EMP: 6
SALES (est): 675.9K **Privately Held**
WEB: www.ryderengraving.com
SIC: 3479 7389 Name plates: engraved, etched, etc.; engraving service

(G-15843)
SCIOTO READY MIX LLC
6214 Taylor Rd Sw (43062-8885)
PHONE..................................740 924-9273
Steve W Edmund,
Steve Edmond,
EMP: 60 **EST:** 2005
SALES (est): 12MM **Privately Held**
SIC: 5211 3273 Cement; ready-mixed concrete

(G-15844)
SCREEN MACHINE INDUSTRIES LLC
10685 Columbus Pkwy (43062-7421)
PHONE..................................740 927-3464
Steve Cohen, *President*
EMP: 4
SALES (est): 469.8K **Privately Held**
SIC: 3531 5084 Construction machinery; industrial machinery & equipment

(G-15845)
SMI HOLDINGS INC
Also Called: Screen Machine
10685 Columbus Pkwy (43062-7421)
P.O. Box 423 (43062-0423)
PHONE..................................740 927-3464
Steven Cohen, *President*
Bernard Cohen, *Chairman*
La June Cohen, *Corp Secy*
Douglas Cohen, *Vice Pres*
◆ **EMP:** 100 **EST:** 1966
SALES (est): 34.7MM **Privately Held**
WEB: www.screenmach.com
SIC: 3532 Mining machinery

(G-15846)
TRANSPORTATION OHIO DEPARTMENT
Also Called: Pataskala License Bureau
318 S Township Rd (43062-7700)
PHONE..................................740 927-2285
Dottie Schirtzinger, *Manager*
EMP: 5 **Privately Held**
SIC: 3469 9621 Automobile license tags, stamped metal;
HQ: Ohio Department Of Transportation
1980 W Broad St
Columbus OH 43223

(G-15847)
TRI-CO INDUSTRIES
13804 Refugee Rd Sw (43062-9422)
PHONE..................................740 927-1928
Bob Byers, *Owner*
Robert Byers, *Owner*
EMP: 4
SQ FT: 1,000
SALES (est): 180K **Privately Held**
SIC: 2599 2541 Cabinets, factory; table or counter tops, plastic laminated

(G-15848)
VAMPIRE OPTICAL COATINGS INC
Also Called: Voci
63 E Mill St Unit B (43062-8203)
P.O. Box 240, Kirkersville (43033-0240)
PHONE..................................740 919-4596
Tom V Faris Jr, *President*
Thuy Nguyen, *Principal*
▲ **EMP:** 5
SQ FT: 16,000
SALES (est): 1.2MM **Privately Held**
WEB: www.v-coat.com
SIC: 3827 Optical test & inspection equipment

Patriot
Gallia County

(G-15849)
CHESTER F HALE
Also Called: Hale Logging
60 Dry Ridge Rd (45658-9250)
PHONE..................................740 379-2437
Chester F Hale, *Principal*
EMP: 3
SALES (est): 180.1K **Privately Held**
SIC: 2411 Logging camps & contractors

(G-15850)
CRISENBERY LOGGING LLC
7818 Lincoln Pike (45658-8914)
PHONE..................................740 256-1439
Joshua Crisenbery, *Principal*
EMP: 3
SALES (est): 137.9K **Privately Held**
SIC: 2411 Logging

(G-15851)
INGLES LOGGING
19094 State Route 141 (45658-9132)
PHONE..................................740 379-2909
Richard Ingles, *Owner*
EMP: 3
SALES (est): 120K **Privately Held**
SIC: 2411 5411 Logging; grocery stores

(G-15852)
INGLES LOGGING
17748 State Route 141 (45658-9206)
PHONE..................................740 379-2760
EMP: 4
SALES (est): 303.1K **Privately Held**
SIC: 2411 1794 Logging & Excavation Work

(G-15853)
PATRIOTIC BUILDINGS LLC
1753 Patriot Rd (45658-7504)
PHONE..................................740 853-3970
Denver McMillion,
Denver Mc Million,
EMP: 4
SALES (est): 100K **Privately Held**
SIC: 2449 Food containers, wood: wirebound

Paulding
Paulding County

(G-15854)
A PLUS PROPANE LLC
8622 Us Route 127 (45879-9406)
PHONE..................................419 399-4445
Jim Stoller, *Principal*
EMP: 4
SALES (est): 381.9K **Privately Held**
SIC: 1321 Propane (natural) production

(G-15855)
ALEX PRODUCTS INC
810 W Gasser Rd (45879-8770)
PHONE..................................419 399-4500
Dave Dondeylon, *Manager*
EMP: 110
SALES (corp-wide): 110.3MM **Privately Held**
WEB: www.alexproducts.com
SIC: 3499 5013 3714 Automobile seat frames, metal; automotive supplies & parts; motor vehicle parts & accessories
PA: Alex Products, Inc.
19911 County Rd T
Ridgeville Corners OH 43555
419 267-5240

(G-15856)
BAUGHMAN TILE COMPANY
8516 Road 137 (45879-9753)
PHONE..................................800 837-3160
Gene A Baughman, *President*
Mary A Baughman, *Corp Secy*
Brad Baughman, *Exec VP*
Eric Baughman, *Vice Pres*
Scott Kemler, *Marketing Staff*
EMP: 100 **EST:** 1883
SQ FT: 100,000
SALES (est): 30.6MM **Privately Held**
WEB: www.baughmantile.com
SIC: 3084 3259 Plastics pipe; clay sewer & drainage pipe & tile

(G-15857)
BLUE CREEK RENEWABLES LLC
7909 Broughton Pike (45879-9639)
PHONE..................................419 576-7855
Tom Sinn,
Howard Proctor,
EMP: 3
SALES (est): 139.5K **Privately Held**
SIC: 3999 Manufacturing industries

GEOGRAPHIC SECTION

(G-15858)
BRUNE PRINTING CO
310 W Perry St (45879-1454)
P.O. Box 232 (45879-0232)
PHONE.....................419 399-2756
Mark Brant, *CEO*
EMP: 5 **EST:** 1920
SQ FT: 3,000
SALES: 65K **Privately Held**
SIC: 2752 Commercial printing, offset

(G-15859)
DELPHOS HERALD INC
Paulding Progress
113 S Williams St (45879-1429)
P.O. Box 180 (45879-0180)
PHONE.....................419 399-4015
Doug Nutter, *Manager*
EMP: 7
SQ FT: 7,000
SALES (corp-wide): 1.1MM **Privately Held**
WEB: www.delphosherald.com
SIC: 2711 Newspapers, publishing & printing
PA: Herald Delphos Inc
   405 N Main St
   Delphos OH 45833
   419 695-0015

(G-15860)
HERBERT E ORR COMPANY
335 W Wall St (45879-1163)
P.O. Box 209 (45879-0209)
PHONE.....................419 399-4866
Greg Johnson, *President*
Bruce Whitman, *Supervisor*
Ken Metzger, *Admin Sec*
EMP: 125
SQ FT: 48,000
SALES (est): 46.1MM **Privately Held**
WEB: www.heorr.com
SIC: 5013 3479 Wheels, motor vehicle; painting of metal products

(G-15861)
INNOVATIVE ASSEMBLY SVCS LLC
400 W Wall St (45879)
P.O. Box 301 (45879-0301)
PHONE.....................419 399-3886
Phillip Hall, *Mng Member*
EMP: 17
SALES (est): 2.5MM **Privately Held**
SIC: 3569 Assembly machines, non-metalworking

(G-15862)
INSOURCE TECH INC
12124 Road 111 (45879-9000)
PHONE.....................419 399-3600
Roger Manz, *Principal*
Ken Manz, *Principal*
EMP: 15
SQ FT: 11,500
SALES: 7.6MM **Privately Held**
SIC: 3585 Heating & air conditioning combination units

(G-15863)
INSOURCE TECHNOLOGIES INC
12124 Road 111 (45879-9000)
PHONE.....................419 399-3600
Roger Manz, *Vice Pres*
Will Manz, *Prdtn Mgr*
Larry Manz, *Sales Mgr*
Michael Schneider, *IT/INT Sup*
Marvin Manz, *Director*
▲ **EMP:** 170
SQ FT: 11,500
SALES: 26.6MM **Privately Held**
WEB: www.insource-tech.com
SIC: 3699 Electrical equipment & supplies

(G-15864)
LAFARGE NORTH AMERICA INC
Also Called: Lafargeholcim
11435 County Rd 176 (45879-8834)
P.O. Box 160 (45879-0160)
PHONE.....................419 399-4861
Kim Musch, *Human Res Mgr*
Geoff Fehr, *Manager*
Terence Belland, *Maintence Staff*
EMP: 105

SALES (corp-wide): 26.4B **Privately Held**
WEB: www.lafargenorthamerica.com
SIC: 3241 Cement, hydraulic
HQ: Lafarge North America Inc.
   8700 W Bryn Mawr Ave
   Chicago IL 60631
   773 372-1000

(G-15865)
LAPHAM-HICKEY STEEL CORP
815 W Gasser Rd (45879-8765)
PHONE.....................419 399-4803
Douglas Fiske, *Branch Mgr*
EMP: 53
SQ FT: 400,000
SALES (corp-wide): 279.5MM **Privately Held**
WEB: www.thompsonsteelco.com
SIC: 3316 3398 Cold finishing of steel shapes; metal heat treating
PA: Lapham-Hickey Steel Corp.
   5500 W 73rd St
   Chicago IL 60638
   708 496-6111

(G-15866)
MORTON BUILDINGS INC
1099 N Williams St (45879-8847)
PHONE.....................419 399-4549
Jeff Dawson, *Manager*
EMP: 7
SALES (corp-wide): 463.7MM **Privately Held**
WEB: www.mortonbuildings.com
SIC: 3448 Prefabricated metal buildings
PA: Morton Buildings, Inc.
   252 W Adams St
   Morton IL 61550
   800 447-7436

(G-15867)
OHIO MIRROR TECHNOLOGIES INC (PA)
114 W Jackson St (45879-1264)
P.O. Box 223 (45879-0223)
PHONE.....................419 399-5903
Dennis R Krick, *President*
Tom Krick, *Treasurer*
EMP: 14
SQ FT: 2,700
SALES: 800K **Privately Held**
SIC: 3231 Products of purchased glass

(G-15868)
OHIO MIRROR TECHNOLOGIES INC
384 W Wall St (45879-1162)
PHONE.....................419 399-5903
Thomas Krick, *Manager*
EMP: 11
SALES (corp-wide): 800K **Privately Held**
SIC: 3231 Products of purchased glass
PA: Ohio Mirror Technologies Inc
   114 W Jackson St
   Paulding OH 45879
   419 399-5903

(G-15869)
P C WORKSHOP INC
900 W Caroline St (45879-1381)
P.O. Box 390 (45879-0390)
PHONE.....................419 399-4805
Megan Sierra, *CEO*
Brenda Miller, *Director*
EMP: 100
SALES: 1.2MM **Privately Held**
WEB: www.pcworkshop.com
SIC: 7389 3711 Document & office record destruction; automobile assembly, including specialty automobiles

(G-15870)
PRICE MANAGEMENT SERVICES LTD
10307 Road 107 (45879-9205)
PHONE.....................419 298-5423
EMP: 3
SALES (est): 119.9K **Privately Held**
SIC: 2448 Wood pallets & skids

(G-15871)
SPARTECH LLC
Also Called: Spartech Plastics
925 W Gasser Rd (45879-8765)
P.O. Box 420 (45879-0420)
PHONE.....................419 399-4050
Michelle Gawronski, *Human Res Dir*
Julie A McAlindon, *Manager*
EMP: 114
SALES (corp-wide): 1.6B **Privately Held**
WEB: www.spartech.com
SIC: 3081 3089 3083 Unsupported plastics film & sheet; extruded finished plastic products; laminated plastics plate & sheet
HQ: Spartech Llc
   11650 Lkeside Crossing Ct
   Saint Louis MO 63146
   314 569-7400

Payne
Paulding County

(G-15872)
GORDON TOOL INC
1301 State Route 49 (45880-9727)
PHONE.....................419 263-3151
William J Gordon, *President*
Lori Gordon, *Treasurer*
EMP: 15
SQ FT: 15,625
SALES (est): 2.3MM **Privately Held**
SIC: 5251 3544 Tools; special dies, tools, jigs & fixtures

(G-15873)
MARANATHA INDUSTRIES INC
102 S Main St (45880)
P.O. Box 209 (45880-0209)
PHONE.....................419 263-2013
Peggy Lee, *President*
Kevin Lee, *Vice Pres*
▲ **EMP:** 5
SQ FT: 6,700
SALES (est): 2.6MM **Privately Held**
SIC: 3663 Radio broadcasting & communications equipment

(G-15874)
TAYLOR PRODUCTS INC
230 S Laura St (45880)
PHONE.....................419 263-2313
Denise Reed, *Principal*
EMP: 22
SALES (est): 2.5MM
SALES (corp-wide): 5.4MM **Privately Held**
SIC: 3231 Products of purchased glass
PA: Taylor Products Inc
   66 Kingsboro Ave
   Gloversville NY 12078
   518 773-9312

(G-15875)
TAYLOR PRODUCTS INC
Also Called: Taylor Made Glass Systems
407 N Maple St (45880-9021)
PHONE.....................419 263-2313
Brian Castleman, *Plant Mgr*
Michelle Garrison, *Purch Mgr*
Jim Murlin, *Buyer*
Brian Lichty, *Engineer*
Sherry Good, *Sales Executive*
EMP: 42
SALES (corp-wide): 5.4MM **Privately Held**
SIC: 3231 3211 Products of purchased glass; flat glass
PA: Taylor Products Inc
   66 Kingsboro Ave
   Gloversville NY 12078
   518 773-9312

(G-15876)
WILDCAT CREEK FARMS INC
Also Called: Wildcat Creek Popcorn
4633 Road 94 (45880-9124)
PHONE.....................419 263-2549
Don Benschneider, *President*
Marge Yenser, *Corp Secy*
Dave Yenser, *Vice Pres*
EMP: 15
SQ FT: 4,320

SALES (est): 1.6MM **Privately Held**
WEB: www.wildcatcreekpopcorn.com
SIC: 2099 0111 0119 0115 Popcorn, packaged: except already popped; wheat; popcorn farm; corn; soybeans

Peebles
Adams County

(G-15877)
CEDAR PRODUCTS LLC
380 Duffey Rd (45660-9768)
PHONE.....................937 892-0070
Dennis Miller Jr, *Mng Member*
◆ **EMP:** 2
SALES: 1MM **Privately Held**
SIC: 2499 7389 Mulch, wood & bark;

(G-15878)
HANSON AGGREGATES EAST LLC
Plum Run Stone Division
848 Plum Run Rd (45660-9706)
PHONE.....................937 587-2671
Terry Lauderback, *Manager*
Terry Louderback, *Manager*
EMP: 50
SALES (corp-wide): 20.6B **Privately Held**
SIC: 1422 3274 3273 Crushed & broken limestone; lime; ready-mixed concrete
HQ: Hanson Aggregates East Llc
   3131 Rdu Center Dr
   Morrisville NC 27560
   919 380-2500

(G-15879)
J MCCOY LUMBER CO LTD (PA)
6 N Main St (45660-1243)
P.O. Box 306 (45660-0306)
PHONE.....................937 587-3423
Jack McCoy, *Owner*
EMP: 40
SQ FT: 2,400
SALES (est): 4.4MM **Privately Held**
SIC: 5031 2426 2431 Lumber: rough, dressed & finished; dimension, hardwood; moldings, wood: unfinished & prefinished

(G-15880)
PEEBLES MESSENGER NEWSPAPER
58 S Main St (45660-1189)
PHONE.....................937 587-1451
Pamela Syroney, *Owner*
EMP: 8
SALES (est): 357.5K **Privately Held**
SIC: 2711 Newspapers: publishing only, not printed on site

(G-15881)
RYAN DEVELOPMENT CORP
1 Ryan Rd (45660)
PHONE.....................937 587-2266
G William Ryan, *President*
W Mark Ryan, *Vice Pres*
EMP: 20
SQ FT: 20,000
SALES (est): 2.7MM **Privately Held**
SIC: 3089 Extruded finished plastic products

(G-15882)
SOUTHERN OHIO LUMBER LLC
11855 State Route 73 (45660-9556)
P.O. Box 145, Worthington (43085-0145)
PHONE.....................614 436-4472
Chuck Mainous, *President*
EMP: 30
SQ FT: 25,000
SALES (est): 3.7MM **Privately Held**
SIC: 2448 Pallets, wood

Pemberville
Wood County

(G-15883)
COUNTYLINE CO-OP INC (PA)
425 E Front St (43450-7039)
P.O. Box C (43450-0430)
PHONE.....................419 287-3241

Pemberville - Wood County (G-15884)

Donald Kline, *President*
Robert Rahrig, *General Mgr*
Robert Schroder, *Vice Pres*
Thomas Sieving, *Admin Sec*
EMP: 10
SQ FT: 10,000
SALES (est): 13.1MM **Privately Held**
SIC: 5153 5191 2875 2041 Grains; farm supplies; fertilizers, mixing only; flour & other grain mill products

(G-15884)
HERCULES ACQUISITION CORP
Also Called: Hercules Stamping Co
850 W Front St (43450-9703)
P.O. Box F (43450-0433)
PHONE.................................419 287-3223
James Akers, *Ch of Bd*
Wes Walters, *President*
James Gale, *President*
EMP: 30
SQ FT: 30,000
SALES (est): 4MM **Privately Held**
SIC: 3465 3469 Automotive stampings; metal stampings

(G-15885)
HIRZEL CANNING COMPANY
Pemberville Foods
115 Columbus St (43450-7029)
P.O. Box D (43450-0431)
PHONE.................................419 287-3288
Joe Hirzel, *General Mgr*
Jessica Jackson, *Purchasing*
Joseph Hirzel, *Manager*
Heidi Kopeck, *Officer*
EMP: 30
SALES (corp-wide): 29.6MM **Privately Held**
WEB: www.hirzel.com
SIC: 2033 Tomato products: packaged in cans, jars, etc.
PA: Hirzel Canning Company
411 Lemoyne Rd
Northwood OH 43619
419 693-0531

(G-15886)
JONES INDUSTRIAL SERVICE LLC
17221 Eisenhour Rd (43450-9667)
PHONE.................................419 287-4553
John Dibling,
EMP: 4
SQ FT: 576
SALES (est): 781K **Privately Held**
WEB: www.jonesindustrialservice.com
SIC: 3545 5084 Gauges (machine tool accessories); industrial machinery & equipment

(G-15887)
UNIVERSAL METAL PRODUCTS INC
850 W Front St (43450-9703)
P.O. Box F (43450-0433)
PHONE.................................419 287-3223
Gordon Daugherty, *President*
Stefan Gerlica, *Plant Mgr*
Ted Rossman, *Plant Mgr*
Enrique Dryere, *Manager*
John Vitale, *Manager*
EMP: 35
SALES (est): 5.5MM
SALES (corp-wide): 60MM **Privately Held**
WEB: www.ump-inc.com
SIC: 3469 Stamping metal for the trade
PA: Universal Metal Products, Inc.
29980 Lakeland Blvd
Wickliffe OH 44092
440 943-3040

Peninsula
Summit County

(G-15888)
A & C WELDING INC
80 Cuyhoga Fls Indus Pkwy (44264-9568)
PHONE.................................330 762-4777
Carl Lamancusa, *President*
Michael Lamancusa, *Vice Pres*
Timothy Gorbach, *Treasurer*
EMP: 25
SALES (est): 5.9MM **Privately Held**
SIC: 3444 7692 Sheet metalwork; welding repair

(G-15889)
ANSCO MACHINE COMPANY
60 Cuyhoga Fls Indus Pkwy (44264-9568)
PHONE.................................330 929-8181
Michael D Sterling, *President*
▲ **EMP:** 45
SQ FT: 48,000
SALES (est): 11.3MM **Privately Held**
WEB: www.ansco-machine.com
SIC: 3599 Machine shop, jobbing & repair

(G-15890)
CENTER FOR INQUIRY INC
6413 Riverview Rd (44264-9624)
PHONE.................................330 671-7192
Bill Stalker, *Principal*
EMP: 3
SALES (est): 188.6K **Privately Held**
SIC: 2721 Periodicals

(G-15891)
DIMENSIONAL WORKS OF ART
2355 Main St (44264-9666)
PHONE.................................330 657-2681
Carol Adams, *Owner*
EMP: 4
SALES (est): 25K **Privately Held**
SIC: 8999 3911 Artist; jewelry, precious metal

(G-15892)
DUFFY FAMILY PARTNER
356 Kendall Park Rd (44264-9523)
PHONE.................................330 650-6716
Arthur R Duffy, *Partner*
EMP: 3
SALES (est): 186.5K **Privately Held**
SIC: 2452 Log cabins, prefabricated, wood

(G-15893)
EAGLE ELASTOMER INC
70 Cuyhoga Fls Indus Pkwy (44264-9568)
P.O. Box 939, Cuyahoga Falls (44223-0939)
PHONE.................................330 923-7070
Neil X Mc Hale, *Ch of Bd*
Regan Mc Hale, *President*
Gene H McKenna, *Principal*
Vertina Ashling, *Vice Pres*
Charlie Christie, *QC Mgr*
EMP: 45
SQ FT: 26,000
SALES (est): 13.3MM **Privately Held**
WEB: www.eagleelastomer.com
SIC: 3069 2821 Tubing, rubber; rubber tape; rapping, rubber; plastics materials & resins

(G-15894)
INDUCTION HRDNING SPCLISTS INC
75 Cuyhoga Fls Indus Pkwy (44264-9567)
PHONE.................................234 678-6820
Mark Farley, *President*
EMP: 3
SQ FT: 3,000
SALES: 800K **Privately Held**
SIC: 3398 Metal heat treating

(G-15895)
LEDOW COMPANY INC
3011 Oak Hill Rd (44264-9670)
PHONE.................................330 657-2837
Leon Downing, *President*
Beverly Downing, *Admin Sec*
EMP: 3 **EST:** 1978
SQ FT: 10,000
SALES: 350K **Privately Held**
WEB: www.ledow.com
SIC: 3535 Conveyors & conveying equipment

(G-15896)
NATIONAL HWY MAINT SYSTEMS LLC
4361 State Rd (44264-9717)
P.O. Box 5315, Akron (44334-0315)
PHONE.................................330 922-3649
Michael Leahy,
Juliann Cronin,
EMP: 3
SALES (est): 289.6K **Privately Held**
SIC: 5099 2911 Safety equipment & supplies; asphalt or asphaltic materials, made in refineries; road materials, bituminous

(G-15897)
PILOT PLASTICS INC
200 Cyhoga Fls Indus Pkwy (44264-9572)
PHONE.................................330 920-1718
Ted Jendrisak, *President*
Nikolas P Andreef, *Principal*
EMP: 25
SALES (est): 5.6MM **Privately Held**
SIC: 3089 Injection molding of plastics

(G-15898)
STILLWELL EQUIPMENT CO INC
5398 Akron Cleveland Rd (44264-9767)
PHONE.................................330 650-1029
Donald L Stillwell, *President*
Toni Musgrave, *Treasurer*
EMP: 5
SQ FT: 1,100
SALES: 2MM **Privately Held**
WEB: www.stillwelleqpmt.com
SIC: 3531 Construction machinery; heavy construction equipment rental

(G-15899)
TERRY LUMBER AND SUPPLY CO
1710 Mill St W (44264-9701)
P.O. Box 216 (44264-0216)
PHONE.................................330 659-6800
Judy Lahoski, *Corp Secy*
James Montaquilla, *Vice Pres*
John Lahoski, *Manager*
EMP: 11
SQ FT: 20,000
SALES (est): 1.6MM **Privately Held**
SIC: 5251 5211 2448 2449 Hardware; lumber & other building materials; pallets, wood; rectangular boxes & crates, wood

(G-15900)
TRAIL MIX
1565 Boston Mills Rd W (44264-9617)
PHONE.................................330 657-2277
Pamela Good, *Manager*
EMP: 3
SALES (est): 191.3K **Privately Held**
SIC: 3273 Ready-mixed concrete

(G-15901)
WCCV FLOOR COVERINGS LLC (PA)
4535 State Rd (44264-9799)
PHONE.................................330 688-0114
John F Martin, *President*
EMP: 24
SALES (est): 12.1MM **Privately Held**
SIC: 5713 3253 Carpets; ceramic wall & floor tile

(G-15902)
WHOLECYCLE INC
Also Called: State 8 Motorcycle & Atv
100 Cyhoga Fls Indus Pkwy (44264-9569)
PHONE.................................330 929-8123
R Kirk Compton, *President*
Brett H Huff, *Business Mgr*
Gar Compton, *Corp Secy*
Paul Compton, *Vice Pres*
Chris Geiger, *Sales Mgr*
◆ **EMP:** 40
SQ FT: 25,000
SALES (est): 12.9MM **Privately Held**
SIC: 5012 5571 3799 Motorcycles; motorcycles; all terrain vehicles (ATV)

Perry
Lake County

(G-15903)
ALL WRIGHT ENTERPRISES LLC
Fidanza Performance
4285 Main St (44081-9635)
PHONE.................................440 259-5656
Jeffrey Jenkins, *President*
EMP: 9
SALES (corp-wide): 1.4MM **Privately Held**
SIC: 5013 3714 Clutches; wheels, motor vehicle; gears, motor vehicle
PA: All Wright Enterprises, Llc
5 Bisbee Ct Ste 109-313
Santa Fe NM 87508
440 259-5656

(G-15904)
DOGLOK INC
3512 River Rd (44081-8603)
PHONE.................................440 223-1836
Jerry Hagan, *President*
EMP: 4 **EST:** 2010
SALES (est): 225.4K **Privately Held**
SIC: 3089 Fences, gates & accessories: plastic

(G-15905)
GREAT LAKES POWER SERVICE CO
Also Called: John Deere Authorized Dealer
3691 Shepard Rd (44081-9694)
PHONE.................................440 259-0025
Harry Allen, *Owner*
EMP: 7
SALES (corp-wide): 15.1MM **Privately Held**
SIC: 3699 5082 Laser welding, drilling & cutting equipment; construction & mining machinery
PA: Great Lakes Power Service Co.
7455 Tyler Blvd
Mentor OH 44060
440 951-5111

(G-15906)
JOINING METALS INC
3314 Blackmore Rd (44081-9320)
PHONE.................................440 259-1790
Jeff Beckwith, *President*
EMP: 12
SALES (est): 2.3MM **Privately Held**
SIC: 3444 Sheet metalwork

(G-15907)
LEES MACHINERY INC
4089 N Ridge Rd (44081-9755)
PHONE.................................440 259-2222
Mike Zinn, *CEO*
Lee Zinn, *Owner*
EMP: 4
SQ FT: 10,000
SALES: 400K **Privately Held**
SIC: 5084 3599 3541 7699 Machine tools & accessories; machine shop, jobbing & repair; machine tools, metal cutting type; industrial machinery & equipment repair; tools, power

(G-15908)
M M I SERVICES INC
3235 Elizabeth Dr Unit 34 (44081-9102)
PHONE.................................440 259-2939
Michael D'Aquila, *President*
EMP: 19
SQ FT: 8,000
SALES (est): 4.2MM **Privately Held**
SIC: 3446 1799 Stairs, staircases, stair treads: prefabricated metal; railings, prefabricated metal; welding on site

(G-15909)
MACDIVITT RUBBER COMPANY LLC
3291 Center Rd (44081-9589)
P.O. Box 129 (44081-0129)
PHONE.................................440 259-5937
Bob McDivitt, *President*
Heather Collins, *Sales Associate*
EMP: 20
SQ FT: 20,000
SALES (est): 3.7MM **Privately Held**
WEB: www.macdivittrubber.com
SIC: 3061 3069 Mechanical rubber goods; molded rubber products

(G-15910)
OHIO ELASTOMERS
3470 Blackmore Rd (44081-9534)
PHONE.................................440 354-9750
William H Jaques, *Owner*
EMP: 4

▲ = Import ▼ = Export
◆ = Import/Export

SALES (est): 469.6K **Privately Held**
SIC: 3061 8731 Mechanical rubber goods; commercial physical research

(G-15911)
PRECISION CONVEYOR TECHNOLOGY
Also Called: Pct Industries
3785 Lane Rd Ext (44081-9549)
PHONE...................440 352-3601
Robert J Eder, *President*
Carol Eder, *Admin Sec*
EMP: 15
SQ FT: 15,000
SALES (est): 3.2MM **Privately Held**
WEB: www.precisionconveyor.com
SIC: 3535 3586 Conveyors & conveying equipment; measuring & dispensing pumps

(G-15912)
SIVON MANUFACTURING LLC
Also Called: Sivon Manufacturing Company
3131 Perry Park Rd (44081-9582)
PHONE...................440 259-5505
Charlotte Kieffer, *President*
Alta L Lahner, *Vice Pres*
Shawn Ritts, *Mng Member*
Bonnie Kieffer Judd, *Admin Sec*
EMP: 3 EST: 1931
SQ FT: 7,500
SALES (est): 599.3K **Privately Held**
WEB: www.sivonmfg.com
SIC: 3567 3599 3544 2891 Heating units & devices, industrial: electric; machine shop, jobbing & repair; special dies, tools, jigs & fixtures; epoxy adhesives

(G-15913)
SOUTH SHORE CONTROLS INC
4485 N Ridge Rd (44081-9760)
PHONE...................440 259-2500
Rick Stark, *President*
George Strekal, *Vice Pres*
EMP: 45
SQ FT: 22,000
SALES: 7MM **Privately Held**
WEB: www.southshorecontrols.com
SIC: 3549 5084 Metalworking machinery; instruments & control equipment

(G-15914)
TCE INTERNATIONAL LTD
Also Called: Cutting Edge, The
4843 N Ridge Rd (44081-9767)
PHONE...................800 962-2376
Joseph J Fellows, *President*
Angie Scheff, *COO*
Deborah J Fellows, *Vice Pres*
Elizabeth Krueger, *Opers Staff*
Debi Fellows, *Executive*
▼ EMP: 15
SQ FT: 20,000
SALES: 1.9MM **Privately Held**
WEB: www.cuttingedgeinc.com
SIC: 3479 3993 2752 2671 Etching & engraving; signs & advertising specialties; commercial printing, lithographic; packaging paper & plastics film, coated & laminated

Perrysburg
Wood County

(G-15915)
7 LITTLE CUPCAKES
1021 Sandusky St Ste C (43551-3120)
PHONE...................419 252-0858
Erin Liedigk, *Principal*
EMP: 4
SALES (est): 106.5K **Privately Held**
SIC: 2051 Bakery: wholesale or wholesale/retail combined

(G-15916)
A SCHULMAN INC
12600 Eckel Rd (43551-1204)
PHONE...................419 872-1408
EMP: 5
SALES (corp-wide): 34.5B **Privately Held**
SIC: 2821 Plastics materials & resins
HQ: A. Schulman, Inc.
   3637 Ridgewood Rd
   Fairlawn OH 44333
   330 666-3751

(G-15917)
ADR FUEL INC
353 Elm St (43551-2177)
PHONE...................419 872-2178
Glen Hefflinger, *Principal*
EMP: 3
SALES (est): 175.3K **Privately Held**
SIC: 2869 Fuels

(G-15918)
ALL OHIO READY MIX CONCRETE
622 Eckel Rd (43551-1202)
PHONE...................419 841-3838
Rick Stanley, *Principal*
EMP: 5
SALES (est): 709.4K **Privately Held**
SIC: 3273 Ready-mixed concrete

(G-15919)
AMERICAN STEEL TREATING INC (PA)
525 W 6th St (43551-1554)
PHONE...................419 874-2044
Roy Waits, *CEO*
Jeff Blanker, *President*
Susan Sears, *Accountant*
EMP: 40
SALES (est): 10MM **Privately Held**
WEB: www.americansteeltreating.com
SIC: 3398 Metal heat treating

(G-15920)
AMPP INCORPORATED
28271 Cedar Park Blvd # 5 (43551-4883)
PHONE...................419 666-4747
Daniel A Worline, *Principal*
▲ EMP: 200
SQ FT: 53,000
SALES (est): 22.5MM
SALES (corp-wide): 31.6MM **Privately Held**
WEB: www.ampp-inc.com
SIC: 3444 Sheet metalwork
PA: T.L. Industries, Inc.
   2541 Tracy Rd
   Northwood OH 43619
   419 666-8144

(G-15921)
ARTISTIC MEMORIALS LTD
12551 Jefferson St (43551-1906)
PHONE...................419 873-0433
Jeff Pettit, *President*
EMP: 5
SALES (est): 576.9K **Privately Held**
SIC: 3281 5999 Monument or burial stone, cut & shaped; monuments & tombstones

(G-15922)
B & B BOX COMPANY INC
26490 Southpoint Rd (43551-1370)
PHONE...................419 872-5600
Gregory B Hammer, *President*
EMP: 18
SQ FT: 32,500
SALES (est): 2.4MM **Privately Held**
WEB: www.b-n-bbox.com
SIC: 2653 Boxes, corrugated: made from purchased materials

(G-15923)
BOTTOMLINE INK CORPORATION
7829 Ponderosa Rd (43551-4854)
PHONE...................419 897-8000
Mike Davison, *President*
Nicholas J Cron, *Principal*
Darla Lay, *Accounts Mgr*
Emily Schwab, *Accounts Mgr*
Dave Tulk, *Info Tech Mgr*
▲ EMP: 29
SQ FT: 58,000
SALES (est): 6.8MM **Privately Held**
WEB: www.bottomlineink.com
SIC: 2759 5199 Advertising literature: printing; advertising specialties

(G-15924)
BPREX HALTHCARE BROOKVILLE INC (DH)
Also Called: Rexam Closure Systems
1899 N Wilkinson Way (43551-1685)
PHONE...................847 541-9700
Steve Wirrig, *CEO*
▲ EMP: 135
SALES (est): 195.2MM **Publicly Held**
SIC: 3089 Caps, plastic; closures, plastic
HQ: Berry Global, Inc.
   101 Oakley St
   Evansville IN 47710
   812 424-2904

(G-15925)
BUDERER DRUG COMPANY INC
26611 Dixie Hwy Ste 119 (43551-1749)
PHONE...................419 873-2800
Matthew Buderer, *Branch Mgr*
EMP: 13
SALES (corp-wide): 9.5MM **Privately Held**
SIC: 5122 2834 Drugs & drug proprietaries; animal medicines; proprietary (patent) medicines; proprietary drug products
PA: Buderer Drug Company, Inc.
   633 Hancock St
   Sandusky OH 44870
   419 627-2800

(G-15926)
BULK MOLDING COMPOUNDS INC
Also Called: BMC
12600 Eckel Rd (43551-1204)
PHONE...................419 874-7941
Larry Myers, *Manager*
EMP: 59
SALES (corp-wide): 34.5B **Privately Held**
WEB: www.bulkmolding.com
SIC: 3083 2834 3842 3841 Thermoplastic laminates: rods, tubes, plates & sheet; pharmaceutical preparations; surgical appliances & supplies; surgical & medical instruments; ophthalmic goods; chemical preparations
HQ: Bulk Molding Compounds, Inc.
   1600 Powis Ct
   West Chicago IL 60185
   630 377-1065

(G-15927)
CALPHALON CORPORATION (HQ)
310 3rd St (43551-4496)
PHONE...................770 418-7100
William A Burke, *CEO*
John K Stipancich, *Admin Sec*
▲ EMP: 93
SQ FT: 200,000
SALES (est): 104.7MM
SALES (corp-wide): 8.6B **Publicly Held**
WEB: www.calphalon.com
SIC: 3365 3469 Cooking/kitchen utensils, cast aluminum; metal stampings
PA: Newell Brands Inc.
   221 River St Ste 13
   Hoboken NJ 07030
   201 610-6600

(G-15928)
CALPHALON CORPORATION
310 3rd St (43551-4496)
PHONE...................419 666-8700
Jason Case, *Branch Mgr*
EMP: 23
SALES (corp-wide): 8.6B **Publicly Held**
SIC: 3365 Cooking/kitchen utensils, cast aluminum
HQ: Calphalon Corporation
   310 3rd St
   Perrysburg OH 43551
   770 418-7100

(G-15929)
CAMELA NITSCHKE RIBBONRY
119 Louisiana Ave (43551-1458)
PHONE...................419 872-0073
Camela Nitschke, *Owner*
EMP: 5
SQ FT: 3,960
SALES (est): 246K **Privately Held**
WEB: www.ribbonry.com
SIC: 5949 2396 Notions, including trim; ribbons & bows, cut & sewed

(G-15930)
CAMEO INC
995 3rd St (43551-4355)
PHONE...................419 661-9611
E Lee Ison, *President*
Brandon Ison, *Vice Pres*
▲ EMP: 40
SALES (est): 5.8MM **Privately Held**
WEB: www.cameopaxit.com
SIC: 2844 Toilet preparations; shampoos, rinses, conditioners: hair; mouthwashes; lipsticks

(G-15931)
CARDINAL AGGREGATE
8026 Fremont Pike (43551-9733)
PHONE...................419 872-4380
Mark Murray, *CEO*
Philip Bisel, *VP Opers*
EMP: 13
SALES (est): 1.5MM **Privately Held**
SIC: 3281 Stone, quarrying & processing of own stone products

(G-15932)
CENTOR INC (HQ)
1899 N Wilkinson Way (43551-1685)
PHONE...................567 336-8094
Ben Scheu, *President*
Michael Hope, *Manager*
EMP: 19
SALES (est): 10.7MM
SALES (corp-wide): 1.5B **Privately Held**
SIC: 2631 Container, packaging & boxboard
PA: Gerresheimer Ag
   Klaus-Bungert-Str. 4
   Dusseldorf 40468
   211 618-100

(G-15933)
CHAMPION WINDOW CO OF TOLEDO
7546 Ponderosa Rd Ste A (43551-5637)
PHONE...................419 841-0154
Toby Tokes, *President*
Ed Levine, *President*
EMP: 40
SQ FT: 8,500
SALES (est): 7.1MM **Privately Held**
SIC: 5211 3444 3442 3231 Doors, storm: wood or metal; windows, storm: wood or metal; sheet metalwork; metal doors, sash & trim; products of purchased glass

(G-15934)
CONTAINMENT SOLUTIONS INC
103 Secor Woods Ln (43551-2749)
PHONE...................419 874-8765
Jack Bushmeyer, *Branch Mgr*
EMP: 128 **Privately Held**
WEB: www.containmentsolutions.com
SIC: 3443 Fabricated plate work (boiler shop)
HQ: Containment Solutions, Inc.
   333 N Rivershire Dr # 190
   Conroe TX 77304

(G-15935)
COOL SEAL USA LLC
232 J St (43551-4416)
PHONE...................419 666-1111
Mike Jaeck, *CFO*
Tim Wisnewski, *CFO*
Tab Hinkle, *Mng Member*
EMP: 16
SALES (est): 5.3MM **Privately Held**
SIC: 3081 3083 Packing materials, plastic sheet; laminated plastics plate & sheet

(G-15936)
CUPCAKES FOR A CURE
26595 Woodmont Dr (43551-7222)
PHONE...................419 764-1719
Madison Cano, *Principal*
EMP: 7
SALES (est): 274.6K **Privately Held**
SIC: 2051 Bread, cake & related products

Perrysburg - Wood County (G-15937) GEOGRAPHIC SECTION

(G-15937)
CUTTING EDGE COUNTERTOPS INC
1300 Flagship Dr (43551-1375)
PHONE.....................419 873-9500
Brad Burns, *President*
Jon Cousino, *Principal*
Rob Loughridge, *Principal*
Jeff Erickson, *COO*
Brian Burns, *Vice Pres*
▼ **EMP:** 32
SQ FT: 24,000
SALES (est): 6.1MM **Privately Held**
WEB: www.cectops.com
SIC: 3281 1743 Granite, cut & shaped; marble installation, interior

(G-15938)
DCO LLC (HQ)
900 E Boundary St Ste 8a (43551-2406)
PHONE.....................419 931-9086
Michael L Debacker, *Mng Member*
Bricy Stringham,
◆ **EMP:** 277 **EST:** 1904
SALES (est): 3.1MM
SALES (corp-wide): 35.6MM **Privately Held**
WEB: www.dana.com
SIC: 3751 8741 Motor scooters & parts; financial management for business
PA: Enstar Holdings (Us) Llc
 150 2nd Ave N Fl 3
 Saint Petersburg FL 33701
 727 217-2900

(G-15939)
DELAFOIL PENNSYLVANIA INC
1775 Progress Dr (43551-2014)
PHONE.....................610 327-9565
James Cash, *President*
EMP: 70
SQ FT: 35,000
SALES (est): 5.1MM **Privately Held**
SIC: 3444 3469 Sheet metalwork; metal stampings

(G-15940)
DILLIN ENGINEERED SYSTEMS CORP
8030 Broadstone Rd (43551-4856)
PHONE.....................419 666-6789
David A Smith, *President*
Mike Brickner, *Project Mgr*
Kathy McCormick, *Finance*
Chris Mc Ilroy, *Manager*
Marty Shaffer, *Data Proc Dir*
EMP: 50
SQ FT: 40,000
SALES (est): 10.9MM **Privately Held**
SIC: 8711 3535 Mechanical engineering; conveyors & conveying equipment

(G-15941)
DRIFTER MARINE INC
28271 Cedar Park Blvd # 6 (43551-3846)
PHONE.....................419 666-8144
Jon B Liebenthal, *Principal*
▲ **EMP:** 8
SALES (est): 788.3K **Privately Held**
SIC: 2399 Fishing nets

(G-15942)
DYNALITE CORP
26040a Glenwood Rd Ste A (43551-4870)
PHONE.....................419 873-1706
Denny Emch, *President*
EMP: 8
SALES (est): 1.1MM **Privately Held**
SIC: 3691 Storage batteries

(G-15943)
ELECTRICAL CONTROL DESIGN INC
25571 Fort Meigs Rd Ste D (43551-2078)
PHONE.....................419 443-9290
Frank Smith, *President*
EMP: 4
SALES: 200K **Privately Held**
SIC: 3625 Electric controls & control accessories, industrial

(G-15944)
ELECTRONIC SOLUTIONS INC
28271 Cedar Park Blvd (43551-4883)
PHONE.....................419 666-4700
Joseph Young, *President*
Theodore Stechschulte, *President*
EMP: 11
SQ FT: 10,000
SALES (est): 5MM
SALES (corp-wide): 31.6MM **Privately Held**
SIC: 3679 Loads, electronic
PA: T.L. Industries, Inc.
 2541 Tracy Rd
 Northwood OH 43619
 419 666-8144

(G-15945)
EMHART GLASS MANUFACTURING INC
1899 N Wilkinson Way (43551-1685)
PHONE.....................567 336-7733
Jared Burke, *Manager*
EMP: 78
SALES (corp-wide): 3B **Privately Held**
SIC: 3559 Glass making machinery: blowing, molding, forming, etc.
HQ: Emhart Glass Manufacturing Inc.
 123 Great Pond Dr
 Windsor CT 06095
 860 298-7340

(G-15946)
EMHART GLASS MANUFACTURING INC
7401 Fremont Pike 6 (43551-9432)
PHONE.....................567 336-8784
Terry Wolfe, *Manager*
EMP: 5
SALES (corp-wide): 3B **Privately Held**
SIC: 3559 Glass making machinery: blowing, molding, forming, etc.
HQ: Emhart Glass Manufacturing Inc.
 123 Great Pond Dr
 Windsor CT 06095
 860 298-7340

(G-15947)
ENCOMPASS AUTOMATION &
622 Eckel Rd (43551-1202)
P.O. Box 2912, Toledo (43606-0912)
PHONE.....................419 873-0000
Carter Stewart, *Design Engr*
Mark Weihs,
John Cheney,
EMP: 10
SQ FT: 3,200
SALES (est): 1.9MM **Privately Held**
WEB: www.eaetech.com
SIC: 3823 Industrial instrmnts msrmnt display/control process variable

(G-15948)
EPRAD INC
28271 Cedar Park Blvd # 1 (43551-3846)
PHONE.....................419 666-3266
Ham-HI Lee, *President*
Theodore Steschulte, *Vice Pres*
Joseph L Young, *Vice Pres*
Jason Trzcinski, *Technology*
EMP: 8
SQ FT: 2,000
SALES (est): 660K **Privately Held**
WEB: www.eprad.com
SIC: 3861 3651 Motion picture apparatus & equipment; sound recording & reproducing equipment, motion picture; household audio & video equipment

(G-15949)
FCA US LLC
Toledo Machining Plant
8000 Chrysler Dr (43551-4813)
PHONE.....................419 661-3500
David Arndt, *Principal*
William Cayson, *Engineer*
Ted Lippert, *Maintence Staff*
EMP: 1600
SALES (corp-wide): 130.8B **Privately Held**
SIC: 3714 Motor vehicle transmissions, drive assemblies & parts
HQ: Fca Us Llc
 1000 Chrysler Dr
 Auburn Hills MI 48326

(G-15950)
FIBRETUFF MED BIOPOLYMERS LLC
238 W 7th St (43551-1555)
P.O. Box 353211, Toledo (43635-3211)
PHONE.....................419 346-8728
Robert Joyce, *Mng Member*
Tom Hughes,
Brian Jones,
Lisa Kelly,
Ted Walkowski,
EMP: 3 **EST:** 2014
SQ FT: 8,000
SALES: 30K **Privately Held**
SIC: 2821 Plastics materials & resins

(G-15951)
FIRST FILTER LLC
620 1st St Ampoint (43551)
PHONE.....................419 666-5260
Bob Righi, *Vice Pres*
Larry Walton, *Manager*
Chris Righi, *Admin Sec*
EMP: 3
SALES (est): 444.4K **Privately Held**
SIC: 3564 Filters, air: furnaces, air conditioning equipment, etc.

(G-15952)
FIRST SOLAR INC
Also Called: First Solar Electric
28101 Cedar Park Blvd (43551-4871)
P.O. Box 1032, Toledo (43697-1032)
PHONE.....................419 661-1478
Richard Romero, *Vice Pres*
Heather Murnen, *Buyer*
Eric Holt, *Engineer*
Brandon Russell, *Engineer*
Charlie Dahlke, *Controller*
EMP: 277
SALES (corp-wide): 2.2B **Publicly Held**
WEB: www.firstsolar.com
SIC: 3674 3433 Solar cells; heating equipment, except electric
PA: First Solar, Inc.
 350 W Washington St # 600
 Tempe AZ 85281
 602 414-9300

(G-15953)
FRAM GROUP OPERATIONS LLC
Also Called: Honeywell
28399 Cedar Park Blvd (43551-4864)
P.O. Box 981729, El Paso TX (79998-1729)
PHONE.....................419 661-6700
Jerry Bolser, *Principal*
Jim Lamb, *Vice Pres*
Daniel Groszkiewicz, *VP Opers*
Cyndi Holt, *Sales Staff*
Lee Bennett, *Branch Mgr*
EMP: 100 **Privately Held**
WEB: www.honeywell.com
SIC: 3714 3694 8734 8731 Motor vehicle engines & parts; filters: oil, fuel & air, motor vehicle; spark plugs for internal combustion engines; testing laboratories; commercial physical research
HQ: Fram Group Operations Llc
 1900 W Field Ct 4w-516
 Lake Forest IL 60045

(G-15954)
FRAZIER MACHINE AND PROD INC
26489 Southpoint Rd (43551-1371)
PHONE.....................419 661-1656
Boyd M Frazier Jr, *CEO*
Jeffrey B Frazier, *President*
EMP: 23
SQ FT: 18,000
SALES (est): 4.2MM **Privately Held**
SIC: 3599 3541 Mfg Industrial Machinery Mfg Machine Tools-Cutting

(G-15955)
FRESH PRODUCTS LLC
30600 Oregon Rd (43551-4544)
PHONE.....................419 531-9741
Douglas S Brown,
Doug Brown,
Robert B Brown,
◆ **EMP:** 55 **EST:** 1971
SQ FT: 48,000
SALES (est): 19.9MM **Privately Held**
WEB: www.freshproducts.com
SIC: 2842 Deodorants, nonpersonal

(G-15956)
FROZEN SPECIALTIES INC (DH)
Also Called: FSI
8600 S Wilkinson Way G (43551-2598)
P.O. Box 930 (43552-0930)
PHONE.....................419 445-9015
Daniel Bender, *CEO*
Gary Swartzbeck, *CFO*
▼ **EMP:** 25
SALES (est): 25.6MM
SALES (corp-wide): 15.2B **Privately Held**
WEB: www.frozenspecialties.com
SIC: 2038 Pizza, frozen
HQ: Bellisio Foods, Inc
 1201 Harmon Pl Ste 302
 Minneapolis MN 55403
 218 723-5555

(G-15957)
GIVENS LIFTING SYSTEMS INC
26437 Southpoint Rd (43551-1371)
PHONE.....................419 724-9001
Ray Givens, *President*
EMP: 50 **EST:** 2015
SALES (est): 770K
SALES (corp-wide): 11.5MM **Privately Held**
SIC: 3599 Custom machinery
PA: Givens Engineering Inc
 327 Sovereign Rd
 London ON N6M 1
 519 453-9008

(G-15958)
GLASSLINE CORPORATION (PA)
Also Called: Secure Pak
28905 Glenwood Rd (43551-3020)
P.O. Box 147 (43552-0147)
PHONE.....................419 666-9712
Tom S Ziems, *President*
Mark Opfer, *Vice Pres*
Lisa Lewandowski, *Purchasing*
Tammy Simkus, *Purchasing*
Jeff Gerity, *Engineer*
◆ **EMP:** 131
SQ FT: 90,125
SALES (est): 32.2MM **Privately Held**
WEB: www.secure-pak.com
SIC: 3545 3565 3535 3541 Diamond dressing & wheel crushing attachments; bottling machinery: filling, capping, labeling; bag opening, filling & closing machines; carton packing machines; conveyors & conveying equipment; machine tools, metal cutting type

(G-15959)
GLASSTECH INC (PA)
995 4th St (43551-4321)
PHONE.....................419 661-9500
Mark D Christman, *President*
Ken Wetmore, *Vice Pres*
Diane Tymiak, *CFO*
◆ **EMP:** 112 **EST:** 1971
SQ FT: 80,000
SALES (est): 25.9MM **Privately Held**
WEB: www.glasstech.com
SIC: 3211 3229 3231 Tempered glass; structural glass; glass tubes & tubing; tubing, glass; glass sheet, bent: made from purchased glass

(G-15960)
GRACE IMAGING LLC
28400 Cedar Park Blvd C (43551-4921)
PHONE.....................419 874-2127
Robert Petrie, *Principal*
Jeremiah Tipping, *Opers Mgr*
EMP: 3
SALES: 500K **Privately Held**
SIC: 2759 Commercial printing

(G-15961)
HIAB USA INC (HQ)
12233 Williams Rd (43551-6802)
PHONE.....................419 482-6000
Roland Sunden, *President*
Lennart Brelin, *President*
John Pielli, *Regional Mgr*
Joakim Andersson, *Vice Pres*
Conor Magee, *Vice Pres*
◆ **EMP:** 70 **EST:** 1962

SQ FT: 56,000
SALES (est): 89.5MM
SALES (corp-wide): 3.8B Privately Held
SIC: 5084 3536 Cranes, industrial; hoists; cranes, industrial plant; hoists
PA: Cargotec Oyj
Porkkalankatu 5
Helsinki 00180
207 774-000

(G-15962)
HINKLE MANUFACTURING LLC (PA)
348 5th St (43551-4922)
PHONE.................313 584-0400
Taber Hinkle,
EMP: 13 EST: 1971
SALES: 2MM Privately Held
WEB: www.carrollpackaging.com
SIC: 3089 Mfg Plastic Products

(G-15963)
HOLLAND SPRINGFIELD JOURNAL
117 E 2nd St (43551-2102)
PHONE.................419 874-2528
John B Welch, Principal
EMP: 3
SALES (est): 122.4K Privately Held
SIC: 2711 Job printing & newspaper publishing combined

(G-15964)
IMAGE INTEGRATIONS SYSTEMS (PA)
885 Commerce Dr Ste B (43551-5268)
PHONE.................419 872-0003
Bradley White, President
Ronald Kelley, VP Sales
Bob Kearney, VP Mktg
EMP: 11
SQ FT: 2,142
SALES (est): 3.9MM Privately Held
WEB: www.managedocs.com
SIC: 7374 7379 7372 7373 Data processing service; data processing consultant; prepackaged software; systems software development services

(G-15965)
IMCO CARBIDE TOOL INC
Also Called: Toledo Cutting Tools
28170 Cedar Park Blvd (43551-4872)
PHONE.................419 661-6313
Perry L Osburn, Ch of Bd
Matthew S Osburn, Vice Pres
Julie Whitlow, Admin Sec
EMP: 90
SQ FT: 25,000
SALES (est): 38.5MM Privately Held
WEB: www.imcousa.com
SIC: 5084 3545 Machine tools & accessories; tools & accessories for machine tools

(G-15966)
INDUSTRIAL HARDWOOD INC
Also Called: AAA
521 F St (43551-4313)
PHONE.................419 666-2503
Ashvin Shah, President
EMP: 7
SQ FT: 8,300
SALES (est): 1.2MM Privately Held
WEB: www.industrialhardwood.com
SIC: 2448 Pallets, wood; cargo containers, wood

(G-15967)
INNERAPPS LLC
Also Called: Identity Syncronizer
28350 Kensington Ln # 200 (43551-4174)
PHONE.................419 467-3110
Toby W Miller,
James Delverne,
Deborah Gordon,
Martin Rini,
Ben Trumbull,
EMP: 8 EST: 2009
SALES (est): 663.9K Privately Held
SIC: 7372 Business oriented computer software

(G-15968)
J C LOGAN BARIE LLC
Also Called: Erie Shores Mattress
194 E South Boundary St (43551-2527)
PHONE.................567 336-6523
John Mendofik,
EMP: 3
SALES (est): 249.6K Privately Held
SIC: 2515 Mattresses, containing felt, foam rubber, urethane, etc.

(G-15969)
JERL MACHINE INC
11140 Avenue Rd (43551-2825)
PHONE.................419 873-0270
Robert L Brossia, CEO
Carol Coe, President
Eileen Brossia, Vice Pres
David Kessler, Foreman/Supr
Rodney Burris, CFO
EMP: 61
SQ FT: 76,000
SALES (est): 10.6MM Privately Held
WEB: www.jerl.com
SIC: 7692 3599 Welding repair; machine shop, jobbing & repair

(G-15970)
JOSHUA ENTERPRISES INC
Also Called: Joshua Label Company
12900 Eckel Junction Rd (43551-1309)
PHONE.................419 872-9699
Keith Aschliman, President
Robert Aschliman, Treasurer
EMP: 3
SQ FT: 2,000
SALES (est): 380K Privately Held
SIC: 2679 Labels, paper: made from purchased material

(G-15971)
JOSTENS INC
1833 Eaglecrest Rd (43551-5478)
PHONE.................419 874-5835
Steven Dufrane, Manager
EMP: 39
SALES (corp-wide): 1.3B Privately Held
WEB: www.jostens.com
SIC: 3911 Rings, finger: precious metal
HQ: Jostens, Inc.
7760 France Ave S Ste 400
Minneapolis MN 55435
952 830-3300

(G-15972)
KIEMLE-HANKINS COMPANY (PA)
94 H St (43551-4497)
P.O. Box 507, Toledo (43697-0507)
PHONE.................419 661-2430
Tim Martindale, President
Kevin Napierala, Division Mgr
Stephen Martindale, Chairman
Robert Schuck, Purchasing
Jeffrey Lee, CFO
EMP: 50
SQ FT: 50,000
SALES: 20MM Privately Held
WEB: www.kiemlehankins.com
SIC: 7694 7629 3699 Electric motor repair; electrical equipment repair services; electrical equipment & supplies

(G-15973)
LAKO TOOL & MFG
7400 Ponderosa Rd (43551-4857)
P.O. Box 425 (43552-0425)
PHONE.................419 662-5256
Larry E Smith, President
Tony Capron, Production
Timothy Witzler, Project Engr
Joi Montano, Sales Staff
▲ EMP: 15 EST: 1974
SQ FT: 6,500
SALES (est): 3.2MM Privately Held
WEB: www.lakotool.com
SIC: 3599 Machine shop, jobbing & repair

(G-15974)
MACK INDUSTRIAL LLC
3258 Sterlingwood Ln (43551-3125)
PHONE.................800 918-9986
Scott E Charpie, Principal
EMP: 4
SQ FT: 30,000
SALES (est): 458.1K Privately Held
SIC: 3563 Air & gas compressors

(G-15975)
MARSHAS BUCKEYES LLC
25631 Fort Meigs Rd Ste E (43551-2098)
PHONE.................419 872-7666
Marsha E Smith, Mng Member
EMP: 22
SALES (est): 750K Privately Held
SIC: 2064 Candy & other confectionery products

(G-15976)
MASTER CHEMICAL CORPORATION (PA)
Also Called: Master Fluid Solutions
501 W Boundary St (43551-1200)
PHONE.................419 874-7902
Mike McHenry, CEO
Joe H Wright, Ch of Bd
Michael Deel, District Mgr
Z Ahmed Tahir, Vice Pres
Rich Jiannuzzi, Plant Mgr
◆ EMP: 338 EST: 1951
SQ FT: 100,000
SALES (est): 159.6MM Privately Held
WEB: www.masterchemical.com
SIC: 2992 Cutting oils, blending: made from purchased materials; oils & greases, blending & compounding

(G-15977)
MILO BENNETT CORP
12922 Eckel Junction Rd (43551-1309)
P.O. Box 217 (43552-0217)
PHONE.................419 874-1492
Gerome Rollins, President
EMP: 4
SQ FT: 3,000
SALES (est): 545.6K Privately Held
SIC: 2752 Commercial printing, offset

(G-15978)
MULCH WORLD
8232 Fremont Pike (43551-9705)
PHONE.................419 873-6852
Tim Welch, Principal
EMP: 4
SALES (est): 311.4K Privately Held
SIC: 2448 5031 5261 Pallets, wood & wood with metal; pallets, wood; nurseries & garden centers

(G-15979)
NATIONWIDE CHEMICAL PRODUCTS
24851 E Broadway Rd (43551-8947)
PHONE.................419 714-7075
Joe Bassett, Principal
EMP: 4 EST: 2012
SALES (est): 494.1K Privately Held
SIC: 2869 Laboratory chemicals, organic

(G-15980)
NEAL PUBLICATIONS INC
127 W Indiana Ave (43551-1578)
P.O. Box 451 (43552-0451)
PHONE.................419 874-4787
Dorothy J Neal, President
James Neal, Admin Sec
EMP: 5
SQ FT: 5,000
SALES (est): 615K Privately Held
SIC: 2731 Textbooks: publishing only, not printed on site; books: publishing only

(G-15981)
NEW WASTE CONCEPTS INC
26624 Glenwood Rd (43551-4846)
PHONE.................877 736-6924
Milton F Knight, CEO
Allan Wolf, Vice Pres
EMP: 10
SQ FT: 5,000
SALES: 5MM Privately Held
SIC: 2842 Sanitation preparations

(G-15982)
NORTHWEST PRINT INC
12900 Eckel Junction Rd C (43551-1309)
PHONE.................419 385-3375
Dean Warner, President
EMP: 5
SQ FT: 1,500
SALES (est): 300K Privately Held
WEB: www.northwestprint.com
SIC: 2752 Commercial printing, offset

(G-15983)
NORTHWOOD INDUSTRIES INC
7650 Ponderosa Rd (43551-4861)
PHONE.................419 666-2100
Kurt Miller, President
Laura Miller, Treasurer
Joe Bates, Supervisor
EMP: 18
SALES (est): 3.5MM Privately Held
SIC: 3469 3541 7699 8711 Machine parts, stamped or pressed metal; machine tools, metal cutting type; industrial equipment services; designing: ship, boat, machine & product

(G-15984)
ODYSSEY MACHINE COMPANY LTD
26675 Eckel Rd 5 (43551-1209)
PHONE.................419 455-6621
Ronald Leroux, President
EMP: 7
SALES (est): 1.1MM Privately Held
SIC: 3599 7699 Custom machinery; industrial machinery & equipment repair

(G-15985)
OHIO TABLE PAD COMPANY
Also Called: Southern Division
350 3 Meadows Dr (43551-3138)
P.O. Box 914 (43552-0914)
PHONE.................419 872-6400
Don Unger, Branch Mgr
EMP: 25
SALES (corp-wide): 9.5MM Privately Held
WEB: www.otpc.com
SIC: 2392 Pads & padding, table: except asbestos, felt or rattan
PA: The Ohio Table Pad Company
350 3 Meadows Dr
Perrysburg OH 43551
419 872-6400

(G-15986)
OHIO TABLE PAD COMPANY (PA)
Also Called: Ohio Table Pad Co Georgia Div
350 3 Meadows Dr (43551-3138)
P.O. Box 914 (43552-0914)
PHONE.................419 872-6400
Christopher P Krauser, President
Della B Bricker, Principal
N E Bricker, Principal
Jeffrey Lavoy, Treasurer
Stephen R Krauser, Shareholder
▲ EMP: 75
SQ FT: 15,000
SALES (est): 9.5MM Privately Held
WEB: www.otpc.com
SIC: 2299 5712 3949 2392 Felts & felt products; furniture stores; sporting & athletic goods; household furnishings

(G-15987)
OHIO TABLE PAD OF INDIANA
350 3 Meadows Dr (43551-3138)
P.O. Box 914 (43552-0914)
PHONE.................419 872-6400
Stephen Krauser, President
Christopher Krauser, Vice Pres
Jeffrey Lavoy, Treasurer
▲ EMP: 32
SQ FT: 15,000
SALES (est): 2.8MM
SALES (corp-wide): 9.5MM Privately Held
SIC: 2299 Wool felts, pressed or needle loom; tow to top mills
PA: The Ohio Table Pad Company
350 3 Meadows Dr
Perrysburg OH 43551
419 872-6400

(G-15988)
OLDCASTLE BUILDINGENVELOPE INC
291 M St (43551-4409)
PHONE.................419 661-5079
Scott Switzer, Manager
EMP: 51

Perrysburg - Wood County (G-15989)

SALES (corp-wide): 29.7B Privately Held
WEB: www.oldcastleglass.com
SIC: 3231 5231 Tempered glass: made from purchased glass; insulating glass: made from purchased glass; glass
HQ: Oldcastle Buildingenvelope, Inc.
5005 Lndn B Jnsn Fwy 10
Dallas TX 75244
214 273-3400

(G-15989)
ONESEAL INC (DH)
1300 3rd St (43551-4349)
PHONE..................973 599-1155
Michael Remark, *Owner*
Soren Lund, *General Mgr*
Lars Berenth, *Vice Pres*
▲ EMP: 3
SQ FT: 2,500
SALES: 2.5MM
SALES (corp-wide): 526.4K Privately Held
WEB: www.onesealusa.com
SIC: 3731 Shipbuilding & repairing
HQ: Oneseal Aps
Vibe Alle 2
Kokkedal 2980
491 488-00

(G-15990)
ONIX CORPORATION (PA)
27100 Oakmead Dr (43551-2670)
PHONE..................800 844-0076
Charles Verhoff, *CEO*
Richard Allen, *President*
John Halderman, *Vice Pres*
Todd Mroczkowski, *Controller*
▲ EMP: 37
SALES (est): 6.1MM Privately Held
SIC: 3433 Heating equipment, except electric

(G-15991)
ONIX CORPORATION
27100 Oakmead Dr (43551-2670)
PHONE..................800 844-0076
EMP: 30
SALES (corp-wide): 3.6MM Privately Held
SIC: 3714 Manufacturing Alternative Fuel Systems
PA: The Onix Corporation
27100 Oakmead Dr
Perrysburg OH 43551
800 844-0076

(G-15992)
OPTIMAIR LTD
Also Called: Air Compressor Exchange
29102 Glenwood Rd (43551-5644)
PHONE..................419 661-9568
Michael J Staczek,
EMP: 5
SALES (est): 529.5K Privately Held
WEB: www.optimair.com
SIC: 3563 Air & gas compressors

(G-15993)
OPTIME AIR MSP LTD
29102 Glenwood Rd (43551-5644)
PHONE..................419 661-9568
Mike Stacezek, *President*
EMP: 4
SALES (est): 390.3K Privately Held
SIC: 3563 Air & gas compressors

(G-15994)
ORBIS CORPORATION
Also Called: Hinkle Manufacturing
348 5th St (43551-4920)
PHONE..................262 560-5000
Jeff Wolens, *Branch Mgr*
EMP: 96
SALES (corp-wide): 1.7B Privately Held
SIC: 3086 2653 Packaging & shipping materials, foamed plastic; corrugated boxes, partitions, display items, sheets & pad
HQ: Orbis Corporation
1055 Corporate Center Dr
Oconomowoc WI 53066
262 560-5000

(G-15995)
OWENS-BROCKWAY GLASS CONT INC (DH)
Also Called: O-I
1 Michael Owens Way (43551-2999)
PHONE..................567 336-8449
Steve McCracken, *CEO*
Mathew Longthorne, *President*
Mr Albert P L Stroucken, *Chairman*
Jim Baehren, *Senior VP*
Steve Bramlage, *Senior VP*
◆ EMP: 250
SQ FT: 900,000
SALES (est): 5.5B
SALES (corp-wide): 6.8B Publicly Held
SIC: 3221 Glass containers

(G-15996)
OWENS-BROCKWAY PACKAGING INC (HQ)
1 Michael Owens Way (43551-2999)
PHONE..................567 336-5000
Al Stroucken, *CEO*
Gary Szymanski, *Sales Staff*
◆ EMP: 5
SQ FT: 100,000
SALES (est): 5.5B
SALES (corp-wide): 6.8B Publicly Held
WEB: www.owens-brockway.com
SIC: 3221 Glass containers
PA: Owens-Illinois, Inc.
1 Michael Owens Way
Perrysburg OH 43551
567 336-5000

(G-15997)
OWENS-ILLINOIS INC (PA)
1 Michael Owens Way (43551-2999)
PHONE..................567 336-5000
Andres A Lopez, *CEO*
Giancarlo Currarino, *Chairman*
Jeremy Frisco, *COO*
Marybeth Wilkinson, *Senior VP*
Juan Amezquita, *Vice Pres*
EMP: 277 EST: 1903
SALES: 6.8B Publicly Held
WEB: www.owens-brockway.com
SIC: 3221 Glass containers; food containers, glass; bottles for packing, bottling & canning: glass; medicine bottles, glass

(G-15998)
OWENS-ILLINOIS GENERAL INC (HQ)
Also Called: O-1
1 Michael Owens Way (43551-2999)
PHONE..................567 336-5000
Al Stroucken, *CEO*
Thomas L Young, *President*
Sharon Carino, *Business Mgr*
Carol Record, *Business Mgr*
Paul Jarrell, *Senior VP*
▲ EMP: 500
SQ FT: 900,000
SALES (est): 153.6K
SALES (corp-wide): 6.8B Publicly Held
SIC: 3221 Glass containers
PA: Owens-Illinois, Inc.
1 Michael Owens Way
Perrysburg OH 43551
567 336-5000

(G-15999)
OWENS-ILLINOIS GROUP INC (HQ)
1 Michael Owens Way (43551-2999)
PHONE..................567 336-5000
Albert P L Stroucken, *Ch of Bd*
Stephen P Bramlage Jr, *President*
James W Baehren, *Vice Pres*
Paul A Jarrell, *Vice Pres*
◆ EMP: 23
SALES: 6.8B Publicly Held
SIC: 3221 Glass containers
PA: Owens-Illinois, Inc.
1 Michael Owens Way
Perrysburg OH 43551
567 336-5000

(G-16000)
PALLET WORLD INC
8272 Fremont Pike (43551-9705)
PHONE..................419 874-9333
Timothy Welch, *President*
Ken Welch, *Corp Secy*
Michelle Boldman, *CFO*
EMP: 26
SQ FT: 3,000
SALES (est): 6MM Privately Held
WEB: www.palletworldinc.com
SIC: 2448 Pallets, wood

(G-16001)
PRECISION BUSINESS SOLUTIONS
447 J St (43551-4303)
PHONE..................419 661-8700
EMP: 3
SALES (est): 333.4K Privately Held
SIC: 2759 Commercial printing

(G-16002)
QUANEX SCREENS LLC
7597 Broadmoor Rd (43551-4875)
PHONE..................419 662-5001
EMP: 7 Publicly Held
SIC: 3442 Screen & storm doors & windows
HQ: Quanex Screens Llc
1800 West Loop S Ste 1500
Houston TX 77027
713 961-4600

(G-16003)
REACTIVE RESIN PRODUCTS CO
327 5th St (43551-4919)
PHONE..................419 666-6119
Jeff Freiburger, *President*
Robert L Hinkle, *Vice Pres*
Joe Leonard, *Admin Sec*
▲ EMP: 30
SQ FT: 150,000
SALES (est): 5.5MM Privately Held
WEB: www.rrp-mfg.com
SIC: 3565 3714 3089 Packaging machinery; motor vehicle parts & accessories; synthetic resin finished products

(G-16004)
SCHAEFER GROUP INC
Also Called: Frank W Schaefer
29102 Glenwood Rd Ste A (43551-5644)
PHONE..................419 897-2883
Kurt Cohan, *Branch Mgr*
EMP: 5
SALES (corp-wide): 40.4MM Privately Held
WEB: www.theschaefergroup.com
SIC: 3312 Blast furnaces & steel mills
PA: The Schaefer Group Inc
1300 Grange Hall Rd
Beavercreek OH 45430
937 253-3342

(G-16005)
SCHUTZ CONTAINER SYSTEMS INC
2105 S Wilkinson Way (43551-1599)
PHONE..................419 872-2477
Louis Tomchak, *Plant Mgr*
Keith Neubert, *Inv Control Mgr*
Otilia Alexa, *QC Mgr*
Pat Gillespe, *Branch Mgr*
Jeff Taylor, *Maintence Staff*
EMP: 80
SALES (corp-wide): 1.9B Privately Held
SIC: 2448 Cargo containers, wood & metal combination
HQ: Schutz Container Systems, Inc.
200 Aspen Hill Rd
Branchburg NJ 08876
908 429-1637

(G-16006)
SENSOPART USA INC
28400 Cedar Park Blvd (43551-4900)
PHONE..................419 931-7696
Daniel Simmons, *President*
Rochelle Gozdowski, *Office Mgr*
Rachelle Vrabvski, *Office Mgr*
EMP: 4
SALES (est): 437.5K Privately Held
SIC: 3861 Cameras & related equipment

(G-16007)
SPB GLOBAL LLC
26611 Nawash Dr (43551-5463)
PHONE..................419 931-6559
Susan Bernard, *CEO*
EMP: 4
SALES (est): 466.6K Privately Held
SIC: 3674 5064 5063 3613 Semiconductors & related devices; electrical appliances, television & radio; electrical apparatus & equipment; switchgear & switchboard apparatus

(G-16008)
SYSTEM PACKAGING OF GLASSLINE
28905 Glenwood Rd (43551-3020)
P.O. Box 109 (43552-0109)
PHONE..................419 666-9712
Tom Wims, *President*
EMP: 131
SALES (est): 9.6MM
SALES (corp-wide): 32.2MM Privately Held
WEB: www.secure-pak.com
SIC: 3565 Packaging machinery
PA: Glassline Corporation
28905 Glenwood Rd
Perrysburg OH 43551
419 666-9712

(G-16009)
TARPSTOP LLC (PA)
12000 Williams Rd (43551-6809)
P.O. Box 548 (43552-0548)
PHONE..................419 873-7867
Greg Nusbaum, *Controller*
Janet Harpest, *Human Res Mgr*
Doug Mikolajczak, *Branch Mgr*
Andrew M Knepper, *Mng Member*
Suzan Weschke, *Info Tech Mgr*
▲ EMP: 35
SALES (est): 8.5MM Privately Held
WEB: www.tarpstop.com
SIC: 3713 Truck & bus bodies

(G-16010)
TECH DYNAMICS INC
361 D St Ste B (43551-5645)
PHONE..................419 666-1666
John W Zimmerman, *President*
David G Fielding, *Vice Pres*
John Z Zimmerman, *Manager*
David Fielding, *Executive*
EMP: 16
SQ FT: 18,000
SALES (est): 4.1MM Privately Held
WEB: www.techdynamics.com
SIC: 3441 Fabricated structural metal

(G-16011)
TECHNEGLAS INC (HQ)
2100 N Wilkinson Way (43551-1598)
PHONE..................419 873-2000
Jeffrey T Lowry, *President*
John Bobinski, *Prdtn Mgr*
James Maiolo, *Supervisor*
▲ EMP: 5
SQ FT: 18,000
SALES (est): 3.2MM
SALES (corp-wide): 2.6B Privately Held
SIC: 3479 3674 Coating of metals with plastic or resins; silicon wafers, chemically doped
PA: Nippon Electric Glass Co., Ltd.
2-7-1, Seiran
Otsu SGA 520-0
775 371-700

(G-16012)
TECHNEGLAS INC
25875 Dixie Hwy Bldg 52 (43551-1918)
PHONE..................419 873-2000
Leyshon Townsend, *Branch Mgr*
EMP: 5
SALES (corp-wide): 2.6B Privately Held
SIC: 3229 Glass tubes & tubing
HQ: Techneglas, Inc.
2100 N Wilkinson Way
Perrysburg OH 43551
419 873-2000

(G-16013)
TECHNICAL GLASS PRODUCTS INC
7460 Ponderosa Rd (43551-4857)
PHONE..................425 396-8420
Joseph Murray, *President*
EMP: 3
SALES (est): 228.2K Privately Held
SIC: 3229 Scientific glassware

▲ = Import ▼ = Export
◆ = Import/Export

GEOGRAPHIC SECTION
Pickerington - Fairfield County (G-16039)

(G-16014)
THERMODYN CORPORATION
Sealing Resource
12265 Williams Rd Ste B (43551-6807)
PHONE.................................419 874-5100
Scott Sherwood, *Branch Mgr*
EMP: 6
SALES (corp-wide): 15MM **Privately Held**
SIC: 3053 Gaskets & sealing devices
PA: Thermodyn Corporation
   3550 Silica Rd
   Sylvania OH 43560
   419 841-7782

(G-16015)
THIRD PARTY SERVICE LTD
1205 Louisiana Ave (43552-9701)
PHONE.................................419 872-2312
Ronald L Brewer, *President*
Pamela Brewer, *Vice Pres*
EMP: 10
SALES (est): 920K **Privately Held**
SIC: 2631 4783 4212 Specialty board; packing & crating; local trucking, without storage

(G-16016)
TIDEWATER PRODUCTS INC
12305 Williams Rd (43551-1981)
P.O. Box 23181, Toledo (43623-0181)
PHONE.................................419 873-0223
Steven Karakas, *President*
EMP: 4
SALES (est): 787.2K **Privately Held**
SIC: 2899 Water treating compounds

(G-16017)
TINY LION MUSIC GROUPS
Also Called: Groovemaster Music
144 E 5th St (43551-2235)
PHONE.................................419 874-7353
Gaylord Richardson, *Owner*
Julie Richardson, *Co-Owner*
EMP: 8
SALES (est): 331.8K **Privately Held**
WEB: www.tinymixtapes.com
SIC: 2741 7389 Miscellaneous publishing; music recording producer

(G-16018)
TMT INC
Also Called: Tmt Logistics
655 D St (43551-4908)
P.O. Box 408 (43552-0408)
PHONE.................................419 592-1041
Tony Marks, *President*
EMP: 250
SALES (est): 9.6MM **Privately Held**
SIC: 4789 3999 Railroad maintenance & repair services; dock equipment & supplies, industrial

(G-16019)
TOLEDO ELECTROMOTIVE INC
28765 White Rd (43551-3657)
PHONE.................................419 874-7751
Tony Palumbo, *President*
EMP: 6
SALES (est): 466.8K **Privately Held**
SIC: 3625 Motor controls, electric

(G-16020)
UNIVERSAL HYDRAULIK USA CORP
25651 Fort Meigs Rd Ste A (43551-2076)
PHONE.................................419 873-6340
Michael Uhl, *CEO*
Ral Uhl, *CFO*
EMP: 3
SQ FT: 4,500
SALES: 100K
SALES (corp-wide): 23MM **Privately Held**
SIC: 3443 Heat exchangers: coolers (after, inter), condensers, etc.
PA: universal Hydraulik Gmbh
   Siemensstr. 33
   Neu-Anspach 61267
   608 194-180

(G-16021)
VIRTUAL BOSS INC
517 Prairie Rose Dr (43551-5715)
PHONE.................................419 872-7686
Patrick Forester, *President*
EMP: 4
SALES (est): 330K **Privately Held**
SIC: 7372 Prepackaged software

(G-16022)
VISUAL ADVANTAGE LLC
13010 Five Point Rd (43551-1338)
P.O. Box 1221 (43552-1221)
PHONE.................................714 671-0988
Eric Hennan,
EMP: 3
SALES (est): 461.5K **Privately Held**
WEB: www.avisualadvantage.com
SIC: 3993 Signs & advertising specialties

(G-16023)
WALDO & ASSOCIATES INC
28214 Glenwood Rd (43551-4855)
PHONE.................................419 666-3662
Richard Cottier, *President*
Kimberley Bunge, *Vice Pres*
Martin Cipriani, *Vice Pres*
Kenneth Lawandowski, *Vice Pres*
Richard Weis, *Sales Staff*
▲ **EMP:** 20
SQ FT: 30,000
SALES (est): 4.3MM **Privately Held**
WEB: www.waldoinc.com
SIC: 2879 Insecticides & pesticides

(G-16024)
WALKER TOOL & MACHINE CO
7700 Ponderosa Rd (43551-4851)
PHONE.................................419 661-8000
Tarry F Beard, *President*
Larry L Beard, *Corp Secy*
EMP: 13 **EST:** 1941
SQ FT: 18,500
SALES (est): 2.2MM **Privately Held**
WEB: www.walkertm.com
SIC: 3544 Special dies & tools

(G-16025)
WELCH PUBLISHING CO (PA)
Also Called: Perrysburg Messenger-Journal
117 E 2nd St (43551-2102)
P.O. Box 267 (43552-0267)
PHONE.................................419 874-2528
Matt H Welch, *President*
John B Welch, *Vice Pres*
EMP: 20
SQ FT: 6,000
SALES (est): 2.2MM **Privately Held**
WEB: www.rossford.com
SIC: 2711 2721 7375 2752 Job printing & newspaper publishing combined; periodicals; magazines: publishing & printing; information retrieval services; commercial printing, lithographic

(G-16026)
WHELCO INDUSTRIAL LTD (PA)
28210 Cedar Park Blvd (43551-4865)
PHONE.................................419 385-4627
Michael Farrar, *President*
Tom Fisher, *General Mgr*
Farrar G Richard,
EMP: 15
SQ FT: 12,000
SALES (est): 5.1MM **Privately Held**
WEB: www.whelco.com
SIC: 7694 Electric motor repair

(G-16027)
WHELCO INDUSTRIAL LTD
28210 Cedar Park Blvd (43551-4865)
PHONE.................................419 873-6134
Mike Farar, *Branch Mgr*
EMP: 36
SALES (corp-wide): 5.1MM **Privately Held**
WEB: www.whelco.com
SIC: 7694 Electric motor repair
PA: Whelco Industrial, Ltd
   28210 Cedar Park Blvd
   Perrysburg OH 43551
   419 385-4627

(G-16028)
WILLARD KELSEY SOLAR GROUP LLC
1775 Progress Dr (43551-2014)
PHONE.................................419 931-2001
Michael Cicak, *CEO*
Maurice Murphy, *CFO*
James Appold,
Gary T Faykosh,
James Heider,
▼ **EMP:** 45 **EST:** 2007
SALES (est): 7.9MM **Privately Held**
SIC: 3433 Solar heaters & collectors

(G-16029)
WORLD WIDE MEDICAL PHYSICS INC
26302 Thompson Rd (43551-9355)
PHONE.................................419 266-7530
Andrew Schneider, *President*
EMP: 4 **EST:** 2011
SALES (est): 238.2K **Privately Held**
SIC: 3841 Diagnostic apparatus, medical

Perrysville
Ashland County

(G-16030)
MANSFIELD PLUMBING PDTS LLC (HQ)
150 E 1st St (44864-9421)
P.O. Box 620 (44864-0620)
PHONE.................................419 938-5211
Jim Morando, *President*
◆ **EMP:** 600
SQ FT: 700,000
SALES (est): 177.7MM **Privately Held**
SIC: 3261 3463 3088 3431 Vitreous plumbing fixtures; plumbing fixture forgings, nonferrous; plastics plumbing fixtures; bathtubs: enameled iron, cast iron or pressed metal; shower stalls, metal; plumbing fixture fittings & trim; plumbing fittings & supplies

(G-16031)
S & S AGGREGATES INC
Also Called: Shelly & Sands Zanesville OH
4540 State Route 39 (44864-9600)
PHONE.................................419 938-5604
Kent Ewers, *Manager*
EMP: 12
SALES (corp-wide): 276.3MM **Privately Held**
SIC: 1442 Construction sand mining
HQ: S & S Aggregates, Inc
   3570 S River Rd
   Zanesville OH 43701
   740 453-0721

(G-16032)
STEP2 COMPANY LLC
2 Step 2 Dr 2nd (44864)
P.O. Box 300 (44864-0300)
PHONE.................................419 938-6343
Buster Cyrus, *Maint Spvr*
Kevin Long, *Manager*
EMP: 270
SALES (corp-wide): 219.9MM **Privately Held**
WEB: www.step2.com
SIC: 3089 3944 3423 Molding primary plastic; games, toys & children's vehicles; hand & edge tools
PA: The Step2 Company Llc
   10010 Aurora Hudson Rd
   Streetsboro OH 44241
   866 429-5200

Petersburg
Mahoning County

(G-16033)
EAST FAIRFIELD COAL CO
13699 Youngstown Pittsbur (44454-9713)
P.O. Box 217, North Lima (44452-0217)
PHONE.................................330 542-1010
Dave Conrad, *Manager*
EMP: 20
SQ FT: 1,248
SALES (corp-wide): 113.6MM **Privately Held**
WEB: www.eastfairfield.com
SIC: 1221 Bituminous coal surface mining
PA: The East Fairfield Coal Co
   10900 South Ave
   North Lima OH
   330 549-2165

Pettisville
Fulton County

(G-16034)
M & R REDI MIX INC (PA)
521 Commercial St (43553)
P.O. Box 53038 (43553-0038)
PHONE.................................419 445-7771
Kurt Nofziger, *President*
Connie Nofziger, *Vice Pres*
EMP: 20
SQ FT: 2,000
SALES (est): 3MM **Privately Held**
SIC: 3273 4212 Ready-mixed concrete; local trucking, without storage

(G-16035)
PETTISVILLE GRAIN CO (PA)
Also Called: Pgc Feeds
18251 County Road D E (43553)
PHONE.................................419 446-2547
Neil E Rupp, *President*
Corwin D Rufenacht, *Principal*
James L Rufenacht, *Principal*
EMP: 21
SALES (est): 11.8MM **Privately Held**
SIC: 5153 5999 2048 2041 Grain elevators; feed & farm supply; prepared feeds; flour & other grain mill products

(G-16036)
PETTISVILLE MEATS INC
3082 Main St (43553)
PHONE.................................419 445-0921
Steve Mc Intosh, *President*
EMP: 11 **EST:** 1967
SQ FT: 7,500
SALES: 250K **Privately Held**
SIC: 2013 4222 5421 Sausages & other prepared meats; storage, frozen or refrigerated goods; meat markets, including freezer provisioners

Phillipsburg
Montgomery County

(G-16037)
LAWHORN MACHINE & TOOL INC
25 E Walnut St (45354)
P.O. Box 36 (45354-0036)
PHONE.................................937 884-5674
Elizabeth Lawhorn, *President*
Steve Quist, *General Mgr*
EMP: 5
SQ FT: 5,600
SALES: 250K **Privately Held**
SIC: 3829 3825 Instrument board gauges, automotive: computerized; measuring instruments & meters, electric

Pickerington
Fairfield County

(G-16038)
ABOUT TIME SOFTWARE INC
12790 Pickerington Rd (43147-9457)
PHONE.................................614 759-6295
Mark Miller, *President*
EMP: 15
SALES: 1.2MM **Privately Held**
SIC: 7372 Prepackaged software

(G-16039)
ASHTON LLC
77 E Columbus St (43147-1382)
PHONE.................................614 833-4165
EMP: 11
SALES (est): 970.3K
SALES (corp-wide): 2.1MM **Privately Held**
SIC: 2759 Commercial printing
PA: Ashton Llc
   309 Bethel St
   Gibsonville NC 27249
   336 447-4951

Pickerington - Fairfield County (G-16040)

(G-16040)
BAGGALLINI INC
13405 Yarmouth Dr (43147-8493)
PHONE..........................800 628-0321
▼ EMP: 4 EST: 2011
SALES (est): 78K
SALES (corp-wide): 94.2MM **Privately Held**
SIC: 2393 5199 5948 Bags & containers, except sleeping bags: textile; canvas bags; bags, textile; luggage & leather goods stores
HQ: R. G. Barry Corporation
13405 Yarmouth Rd Nw
Pickerington OH 43147
614 864-6400

(G-16041)
BANDIT CHOPPERS LLC
237 Lillian Dr (43147-2057)
PHONE..........................614 556-4416
Dean Bandavanis, *Principal*
EMP: 3
SALES (est): 106.4K **Privately Held**
SIC: 3751 Motorcycles & related parts

(G-16042)
BOSCO PUP CO LLC
290 Parkwood Ave (43147-2016)
PHONE..........................614 833-0349
Ward R Phillips, *Principal*
EMP: 3
SALES (est): 119.7K **Privately Held**
SIC: 3269 Pottery products

(G-16043)
CLEMENS LICENSE AGENCY
12825 Wheaton Ave (43147-8591)
PHONE..........................614 288-8007
Jennifer Clemens, *Owner*
EMP: 7
SALES (est): 479.9K **Privately Held**
WEB: www.clemensrealty.com
SIC: 3469 Automobile license tags, stamped metal

(G-16044)
D AND D ASP SEALCOATING LLC
13199 E Crosset Hill Dr (43147-8943)
PHONE..........................614 288-3597
James Davis McGee Jr,
Russell Taylor,
EMP: 4
SALES (est): 260K **Privately Held**
SIC: 2951 Asphalt paving mixtures & blocks

(G-16045)
DELTA H TECHNOLOGIES LLC
8847 Easton Dr (43147-8871)
PHONE..........................614 561-8860
Richard Conway, *Owner*
EMP: 3
SALES: 200K **Privately Held**
SIC: 3567 Industrial furnaces & ovens

(G-16046)
ECHO MOBILE SOLUTIONS LLC
108 Leasure Dr (43147-8001)
PHONE..........................614 282-3756
Trent McMurray, *CEO*
EMP: 6
SALES: 1.5MM **Privately Held**
SIC: 7372 7389 Business oriented computer software;

(G-16047)
EVOQUA WATER TECHNOLOGIES LLC
Also Called: US Filter
1154 Hill Rd N (43147-8876)
PHONE..........................614 861-5440
Tim Swansonsn, *Manager*
EMP: 33
SALES (corp-wide): 1.3B **Publicly Held**
SIC: 3569 Filters
HQ: Evoqua Water Technologies Llc
210 6th Ave Ste 3300
Pittsburgh PA 15222
724 772-0044

(G-16048)
FOOT PETALS INC
13405 Yarmouth Rd Nw (43147)
PHONE..........................614 729-7205
Greg A Tunney, *President*
EMP: 9 EST: 2016
SALES (est): 832.4K **Privately Held**
SIC: 3144 Dress shoes, women's

(G-16049)
J & A AUTO SERVICE
101 E Columbus St (43147-3100)
PHONE..........................614 837-6820
Julie Kern, *Owner*
EMP: 3
SQ FT: 3,600
SALES (est): 260K **Privately Held**
SIC: 5541 3599 Gasoline service stations; machine shop, jobbing & repair

(G-16050)
JECH TECHNOLOGIES INC
13962 Olde Post Rd (43147-9438)
PHONE..........................740 927-3495
John Carter, *President*
Edward Cogan, *Vice Pres*
James Heidenreich, *Vice Pres*
EMP: 3
SALES: 150K **Privately Held**
WEB: www.jechtech.com
SIC: 3699 Electrical equipment & supplies

(G-16051)
JEFF KATZ (PA)
Also Called: Aquatic Lighting Systems
6265 Mamie Dr (43147-8564)
PHONE..........................614 834-0404
Jeff Katz, *Owner*
EMP: 3
SQ FT: 900
SALES (est): 626.5K **Privately Held**
SIC: 3648 Underwater lighting fixtures

(G-16052)
JUST NAME IT INC
268 Drexel Pl (43147-1437)
PHONE..........................614 626-8662
Joe Grubbs, *President*
EMP: 7
SALES (est): 468.3K **Privately Held**
SIC: 2395 Embroidery & art needlework

(G-16053)
MARBLELIFE OF CENTRAL OHIO
8440 Blacklick Eastern Rd (43147-7513)
P.O. Box 98, Reynoldsburg (43068-0098)
PHONE..........................614 837-6146
Deborah Allen, *Owner*
EMP: 5
SALES (est): 409.6K **Privately Held**
SIC: 3272 Art marble, concrete

(G-16054)
MIRION TECHNOLOGIES IST CORP
12954 Stonecreek Dr Ste C (43147-8840)
PHONE..........................614 367-2050
Daniel Messer, *Branch Mgr*
EMP: 7 **Privately Held**
SIC: 3559 Kilns
HQ: Mirion Technologies (Ist) Corporation
315 Daniel Zenker Dr # 204
Horseheads NY 14845
607 562-4300

(G-16055)
OUR FIFTH STREET LLC
Also Called: Target Business Services
12920 Stonecreek Dr Ste A (43147-8844)
PHONE..........................614 866-4065
Craig Maxey, *Mng Member*
EMP: 4
SALES (est): 803.4K **Privately Held**
WEB: www.targetbusinessservices.com
SIC: 2791 7331 7336 7389 Typesetting; direct mail advertising services; commercial art & graphic design; advertising, promotional & trade show services

(G-16056)
POLYSHIELD CORPORATION
8643 Chateau Dr (43147-9072)
PHONE..........................614 755-7674
Richard Allen, *CEO*
EMP: 10
SALES (est): 855.1K **Privately Held**
SIC: 3144 Ethylene-propylene rubbers, EPDM polymers

(G-16057)
PRO COMPANIES INC
1162 Hill Rd N (43147-8657)
PHONE..........................614 738-1222
Greg Rodoski,
EMP: 4
SQ FT: 4,000
SALES (est): 176.3K **Privately Held**
SIC: 3993 5131 2396 2752 Letters for signs, metal; flags & banners; fabric printing & stamping; screen printing on fabric articles; business form & card printing, lithographic

(G-16058)
QUAYLE CONSULTING INC
8572 N Spring Ct (43147-9096)
PHONE..........................614 868-1363
Stanley F Quayle, *President*
EMP: 2 EST: 1992
SALES: 1.9MM **Privately Held**
WEB: www.stanq.com
SIC: 8711 7389 7371 7372 Electrical or electronic engineering; ; custom computer programming services; prepackaged software; value-added resellers; computer systems; computer related consulting services

(G-16059)
RHINO TECH SOFTWARE LLC
13938 Nantucket Ave (43147-9313)
PHONE..........................614 456-9321
Scott M Whitt, *Principal*
EMP: 4
SALES (est): 415.4K **Privately Held**
SIC: 7372 Prepackaged software

(G-16060)
STANDARD PROTOTYPING IDEALS
70 Cross St 100 (43147-1261)
PHONE..........................614 837-9180
George Carney,
Robert Nieves,
Don Smallwood,
EMP: 3
SQ FT: 25,000
SALES (est): 328.6K **Privately Held**
SIC: 2396 Automotive & apparel trimmings

(G-16061)
SWEET PERSUASIONS LLC
9636 Circle Dr (43147-9650)
PHONE..........................614 216-9052
Melissa Lewis, *Principal*
EMP: 8
SALES (est): 859.3K **Privately Held**
SIC: 2051 Bakery: wholesale or wholesale/retail combined

(G-16062)
VACALON COMPANY INC
12960 Stonecreek Dr Ste D (43147-8799)
PHONE..........................614 577-1945
Bryan Frazier, *President*
Josh Andrachek, *Senior VP*
▲ EMP: 4
SQ FT: 8,000
SALES (est): 646.6K **Privately Held**
WEB: www.vacalon.com
SIC: 3843 Dental equipment & supplies

Pierpont
Ashtabula County

(G-16063)
A W TAYLOR LUMBER INCORPORATED
1114 State Route 7 S (44082-9643)
PHONE..........................440 577-1889
Allen Taylor, *President*
Maryjo Taylor, *Principal*
Angela Taylor, *Vice Pres*
EMP: 12
SALES (est): 1.7MM **Privately Held**
SIC: 2448 Wood pallets & skids

(G-16064)
COMPLETE ENERGY SERVICES INC
7338 Us Route 6 (44082-9725)
PHONE..........................440 577-1070
Gary Lauer, *Partner*
EMP: 9
SALES (est): 1.3MM **Privately Held**
SIC: 1389 Oil field services

(G-16065)
K S W C INC
Also Called: Kodiak Springs Water Co
697 State Line Rd (44082-9728)
PHONE..........................440 577-1114
James L Bushman, *President*
Lisa Bushman, *Vice Pres*
EMP: 4
SALES: 300K **Privately Held**
WEB: www.kswc.com
SIC: 3589 5999 Water treatment equipment, industrial; water purification equipment, household type; water purification equipment

(G-16066)
NATIONAL OILWELL VARCO INC
7338 N Richmond Rd (44082-9725)
PHONE..........................440 577-1225
Jerry Lower, *Owner*
EMP: 23
SALES (corp-wide): 8.4B **Publicly Held**
SIC: 3533 Oil & gas field machinery
PA: National Oilwell Varco, Inc.
7909 Parkwood Circle Dr
Houston TX 77036
713 346-7500

Piketon
Pike County

(G-16067)
BEEKMAN LOGGING
204 Wyckoff Rd (45661-9629)
PHONE..........................740 493-2763
Gary Beekman, *Partner*
Lisa Beekman, *Partner*
EMP: 3
SALES (est): 277.7K **Privately Held**
SIC: 2411 Logging camps & contractors

(G-16068)
CUSTOM HITCH AND TRAILER/OVER
Also Called: Custom Hitch & Trailer
4237 Us Highway 23 (45661-9703)
PHONE..........................740 289-3925
Della Nier, *Owner*
Jim Nier, *Co-Owner*
EMP: 7
SALES (est): 377.1K **Privately Held**
SIC: 3442 5531 5031 1751 Garage doors, overhead: metal; trailer hitches, automotive; lumber, plywood & millwork; carpentry work

(G-16069)
DOLGENCORP LLC
Also Called: Dollar General
7095 Us Highway 23 (45661-9004)
PHONE..........................740 289-4790
Linda Perdue, *Site Mgr*
Michelle Tribbey, *Branch Mgr*
EMP: 8
SALES (corp-wide): 25.6B **Publicly Held**
SIC: 5331 2851 Variety stores; removers & cleaners
HQ: Dolgencorp, Llc
100 Mission Rdg
Goodlettsville TN 37072
615 855-4000

(G-16070)
FAMILY WOODWORKS LLC
286 Taylor Hollow Rd (45661-9686)
PHONE..........................740 289-4071
George A Barlow, *Mng Member*
EMP: 3
SALES (est): 300K **Privately Held**
SIC: 2499 Decorative wood & woodwork

▲ = Import ▼=Export
◆ =Import/Export

GEOGRAPHIC SECTION

Pioneer - Williams County (G-16097)

(G-16071)
JIM NIER CONSTRUCTION INC
3877 Us Highway 23 (45661)
PHONE.................................740 289-2629
Della Nier, *Manager*
EMP: 11
SALES (est): 359K
SALES (corp-wide): 2.2MM **Privately Held**
SIC: 1446 1411 Industrial sand; dimension stone
PA: Jim Nier Construction, Inc.
340 Bailey Chapel Rd
Piketon OH 45661
740 289-3925

(G-16072)
JIM NIER CONSTRUCTION INC (PA)
Also Called: Jnc,
340 Bailey Chapel Rd (45661-9673)
PHONE.................................740 289-3925
Della Nier, *President*
Jim Nier, *Vice Pres*
EMP: 13
SQ FT: 7,000
SALES (est): 2.2MM **Privately Held**
SIC: 1761 3444 1542 1541 Sheet metalwork; sheet metalwork; nonresidential construction; industrial buildings & warehouses

(G-16073)
LANSING BROS SAWMILL
897 Chenoweth Fork Rd (45661-9565)
PHONE.................................937 588-4291
Lloyd Lansing, *Principal*
EMP: 3 EST: 2010
SALES (est): 229.5K **Privately Held**
SIC: 2421 Sawmills & planing mills, general

(G-16074)
MIDWEST TIMBER & LAND CO INC
88 Jasper Rd (45661-9732)
P.O. Box 338 (45661-0338)
PHONE.................................740 493-2400
David Smith, *President*
EMP: 21
SALES (est): 4.3MM **Privately Held**
SIC: 3553 Sawmill machines

(G-16075)
NO NAME LUMBER LLC
165 No Name Rd (45661-9736)
PHONE.................................740 289-3722
Marty Moore, *Principal*
EMP: 6
SALES (est): 765.2K **Privately Held**
SIC: 2421 Sawmills & planing mills, general

(G-16076)
OHIO VALLEY VENEER INC
Also Called: Ohio Valley Veneer Co
16523 State Route 124 (45661-9728)
PHONE.................................740 493-2901
Ed Robbins, *Owner*
▼ EMP: 49
SALES (est): 7.6MM **Privately Held**
SIC: 2426 2435 2421 Lumber, hardwood dimension; hardwood veneer & plywood; sawmills & planing mills, general

(G-16077)
P H GLATFELTER COMPANY
200 Schuster Rd (45661-9687)
PHONE.................................740 289-5100
Robert Browm, *Branch Mgr*
EMP: 7
SALES (corp-wide): 866.2MM **Publicly Held**
SIC: 3829 Electrogamma ray loggers
PA: P. H. Glatfelter Company
96 S George St Ste 520
York PA 17401
717 225-4711

(G-16078)
PARADIGM INTERNATIONAL INC
4239 Us Highway 23 (45661-9703)
PHONE.................................740 370-2428
Jeff Humble, *President*
EMP: 5
SALES (est): 87.6K **Privately Held**
SIC: 2385 Gowns, plastic: made from purchased materials

(G-16079)
S&R LUMBER LLC
207 Sugar Run Rd (45661-9740)
P.O. Box 275, Jasper (45642-0275)
PHONE.................................740 352-6135
Paul Henderson, *Mng Member*
EMP: 16
SQ FT: 1,524,600
SALES (est): 560.3K **Privately Held**
SIC: 2421 Lumber: rough, sawed or planed

(G-16080)
SIGNS 2 GRAPHICS
746 State Route 220 (45661-9722)
PHONE.................................740 493-2049
Tim Shockey, *Owner*
EMP: 5
SALES (est): 303.5K **Privately Held**
SIC: 3993 Signs, not made in custom sign painting shops

(G-16081)
WELLSGROUP
3293 Us Highway 23 (45661-8120)
PHONE.................................740 289-1000
EMP: 3 EST: 2017
SALES (est): 197.8K **Privately Held**
SIC: 3273 Ready-mixed concrete

(G-16082)
WOOLDRIDGE LUMBER CO
3264 Laurel Ridge Rd (45661-9620)
PHONE.................................740 289-4912
Mick Wooldridge, *Partner*
Mick Wooldridge, *Partner*
Alva Wooldridge, *Partner*
Dora Ransey, *Admin Sec*
EMP: 60
SQ FT: 6,000
SALES (est): 6MM **Privately Held**
SIC: 2421 Sawmills & planing mills, general

Pioneer
Williams County

(G-16083)
ACTION PRECISION PRODUCTS INC
100 E North Ave (43554-7808)
P.O. Box 188 (43554-0188)
PHONE.................................419 737-2348
Linda Heisler, *President*
Gary Beggs, *Vice Pres*
Vonnie Beggs, *Treasurer*
EMP: 20
SQ FT: 9,000
SALES (est): 3MM **Privately Held**
SIC: 3599 Machine shop, jobbing & repair

(G-16084)
ARCELORMITTAL TAILORED BLANKS
Also Called: Powerlasers
2 Kexon Dr (43554-9200)
P.O. Box 939 (43554-0939)
PHONE.................................419 737-3180
Joe Neri, *President*
Ed Pace, *President*
EMP: 65
SQ FT: 167,000
SALES (est): 22.6MM
SALES (corp-wide): 9.1B **Privately Held**
WEB: www.dofasco.ca
SIC: 3465 Automotive stampings
HQ: Arcelormittal Usa Llc
1 S Dearborn St Ste 1800
Chicago IL 60603
312 346-0300

(G-16085)
HUDSON LEATHER LTD
Also Called: Hudson Leather Co
14700 State Route 15 (43554-9765)
PHONE.................................419 485-8531
Dogan J Aldemdar,
EMP: 7
SQ FT: 10,000
SALES (est): 970.7K **Privately Held**
WEB: www.hudsonleather.com
SIC: 3131 5139 5661 Footwear cut stock; boots; men's boots; women's boots

(G-16086)
N N METAL STAMPINGS INC (PA)
Also Called: Pennant
510 S Maple St (43554-7956)
P.O. Box 248 (43554-0248)
PHONE.................................419 737-2311
Rob Harger, *President*
Nelson Melillo, *President*
Larry Martin, *CFO*
EMP: 30 EST: 1976
SQ FT: 60,000
SALES (est): 7.6MM **Privately Held**
WEB: www.pennantcompanies.com
SIC: 3469 3544 3465 Electronic enclosures, stamped or pressed metal; special dies, tools, jigs & fixtures; automotive stampings

(G-16087)
PIONEER CUSTOM COATING LLC
255 Industrial Ave Bldg D (43554-9510)
P.O. Box 337 (43554-0337)
PHONE.................................419 737-3152
Deniss Sentle, *Mng Member*
Dennis Sentle, *Mng Member*
Merry Sentle, *Mng Member*
EMP: 9
SQ FT: 2,400
SALES (est): 670K **Privately Held**
SIC: 3479 Coating of metals & formed products

(G-16088)
PIONEER CUSTOM MOLDING INC
3 Kexon Dr (43554-9200)
P.O. Box 463 (43554-0463)
PHONE.................................419 737-3252
Terry Hendricks, *CEO*
Bill Peterson, *President*
David Roth, *Vice Pres*
EMP: 23 EST: 1997
SQ FT: 22,500
SALES (est): 2.2MM **Privately Held**
SIC: 3089 Injection molding of plastics

(G-16089)
PIONEER HOMES INC
1018 Lakeshore Dr (43554-9641)
P.O. Box 275 (43554-0275)
PHONE.................................419 737-2371
Margaret G Thorp, *President*
Dorothy Ragland, *Corp Secy*
Norman Dean Thorp, *Vice Pres*
EMP: 4
SALES (est): 341.1K **Privately Held**
SIC: 2439 Trusses, wooden roof

(G-16090)
PIONEER TRANSFORMER COMPANY
Also Called: Dongan Electric Mfg Co
500 Cedar St (43554-7874)
P.O. Box 158 (43554-0158)
PHONE.................................419 737-2304
Steven E Hicks, *President*
Michael Lillard, *Plant Mgr*
Carey Christenson, *Safety Mgr*
Gary H Hicks, *Admin Sec*
▲ EMP: 6
SALES (est): 1.1MM
SALES (corp-wide): 9.9MM **Privately Held**
WEB: www.dongan.com
SIC: 3612 Machine tool transformers; control transformers; signaling transformers, electric
PA: Dongan Electric Manufacturing Co Inc
34760 Garfield Rd
Fraser MI 48026
313 567-8500

(G-16091)
POWERS AND SONS LLC
Also Called: Pioneer Forge Div
101 Industrial Ave (43554)
P.O. Box 598 (43554-0598)
PHONE.................................419 737-2373
Jeffrey Wilson, *Branch Mgr*
EMP: 100
SALES (corp-wide): 2.9B **Privately Held**
WEB: www.powersandsonsllc.com
SIC: 3462 3714 3463 Iron & steel forgings; motor vehicle parts & accessories; nonferrous forgings
HQ: Powers And Sons, Llc
1613 Magda Dr
Montpelier OH 43543
419 485-3151

(G-16092)
PREMIERE CON SOLUTIONS LLC
Also Called: Con-Cure
508 Cedar St (43554-7874)
P.O. Box 157 (43554-0157)
PHONE.................................419 737-9808
Douglas C Wittler, *Mng Member*
Theodore P Kill,
William W Maize Jr,
EMP: 13
SQ FT: 100,000
SALES (est): 2.5MM **Privately Held**
SIC: 3272 Concrete products

(G-16093)
PURE WATER GLOBAL INC
50 Industrial Ave (43554)
P.O. Box 567 (43554-0567)
PHONE.................................419 737-2352
EMP: 3 EST: 2008
SALES (est): 220K **Privately Held**
SIC: 3085 5085 Mfg Plastic Bottles Whol Industrial Supplies

(G-16094)
RAPID MACHINE INC
610 N State St (43554-9506)
P.O. Box 365 (43554-0365)
PHONE.................................419 737-2377
Jim F Spangler, *President*
Jennifer Wines, *Corp Secy*
EMP: 12 EST: 1978
SQ FT: 10,000
SALES (est): 1.4MM **Privately Held**
WEB: www.spanglersuperiortool.com
SIC: 3544 3541 3469 3444 Special dies, tools, jigs & fixtures; grinding, polishing, buffing, lapping & honing machines; pointing & burring machines; metal stampings; sheet metalwork

(G-16095)
REIFEL INDUSTRIES INC
201 Ohio St (43554-7934)
PHONE.................................419 737-2138
Thomas Reifel, *President*
M Kathleen Reifel, *Corp Secy*
Louis Reifel, *Vice Pres*
Kevin Wells, *Project Mgr*
Cullan Wilkerson, *Manager*
▲ EMP: 65
SQ FT: 60,000
SALES (est): 9.7MM **Privately Held**
WEB: www.reifel.com
SIC: 3479 3471 Coating of metals & formed products; plating & polishing

(G-16096)
RELIABLE METAL BUILDINGS LLC
16570 Us Highway 20ns (43554-9614)
PHONE.................................419 737-1300
Ivan Cruz Castillo,
EMP: 4
SALES (est): 486.6K **Privately Held**
SIC: 3448 Prefabricated metal buildings

(G-16097)
UNIVERSAL INDUSTRIAL PDTS INC
1 Coreway Dr (43554)
P.O. Box 628 (43554-0628)
PHONE.................................419 737-9584
Neil Marko, *President*
Scott Dye, *Mfg Mgr*
Randy Herriman, *CFO*
Mike Nowakowski, *Sales Mgr*
Deidre Whitman, *Info Tech Mgr*
▲ EMP: 18
SQ FT: 86,000

Piqua - Miami County (G-16098)

SALES: 7.2MM **Privately Held**
WEB: www.hinge.com
SIC: 3429 Manufactured hardware (general)

Piqua
Miami County

(G-16098)
AESTHETIC FINISHERS INC
1502 S Main St (45356-8319)
PHONE.................................937 778-8777
Sally Coomer, *CEO*
William Coomer III, *Vice Pres*
EMP: 35
SQ FT: 72,000
SALES (est): 4.3MM **Privately Held**
WEB: www.afipowder.com
SIC: 3479 Coating of metals & formed products

(G-16099)
APEX ALUMINUM DIE CAST CO INC
8877 Sherry Dr (45356-9111)
P.O. Box 617 (45356-0617)
PHONE.................................937 773-0432
Mark Zimmerman, *Incorporator*
EMP: 50
SALES (est): 12MM **Privately Held**
WEB: www.apexdiecasting.com
SIC: 3363 3369 Aluminum die-castings; nonferrous foundries

(G-16100)
ARKANSAS FACE VENEER CO INC (HQ)
1025 S Roosevelt Ave (45356-3713)
P.O. Box 919 (45356-0919)
PHONE.................................937 773-6295
Jeffery A Bannister, *CEO*
James Robert Hartzell, *Ch of Bd*
Jon Snyder, *President*
R Ward Harris III, *General Mgr*
Michael Bardo, *CFO*
▲ **EMP:** 20
SQ FT: 20,000
SALES (est): 3.6MM
SALES (corp-wide): 12.5MM **Privately Held**
SIC: 2435 Veneer stock, hardwood
PA: Hartzell Industries, Inc.
1025 S Roosevelt Ave
Piqua OH 45356
937 773-6295

(G-16101)
ATLANTIS SPORTSWEAR INC
Also Called: College Issue
344 Fox Dr (45356-8298)
PHONE.................................937 773-0680
David Reardon, *President*
David Scott Reardon, *President*
Gail Reardon, *Vice Pres*
Kyle Reardon, *VP Opers*
Susan Libbee, *Human Resources*
▲ **EMP:** 35
SQ FT: 65,000
SALES (est): 5.7MM **Privately Held**
SIC: 2261 2395 2396 Screen printing of cotton broadwoven fabrics; emblems, embroidered; automotive & apparel trimmings

(G-16102)
ATLAS PRECISION MACHINING INC
8899 Sherry Dr (45356-9111)
PHONE.................................937 615-9585
Patrick Zimmerman, *Principal*
Bryan Cooper, *Principal*
Lamar K Harris, *Principal*
EMP: 3
SALES (est): 328.5K **Privately Held**
SIC: 3599 Machine shop, jobbing & repair

(G-16103)
B & L LABELS AND PACKG CO INC
421 Fox Dr (45356-8237)
PHONE.................................937 773-9080
William Saddler, *President*
Lynn Saddler, *Vice Pres*
EMP: 7
SQ FT: 7,000
SALES (est): 1.3MM **Privately Held**
WEB: www.bllabels.com
SIC: 2672 2657 Labels (unprinted), gummed; made from purchased materials; folding paperboard boxes

(G-16104)
BORNHORST MOTOR SERVICE INC
Also Called: Electric Motor Service
8270 N Dixie Dr (45356-8636)
P.O. Box 110 (45356-0110)
PHONE.................................937 773-0426
Regina Owen, *President*
EMP: 8
SQ FT: 6,000
SALES (est): 1MM **Privately Held**
SIC: 7694 5063 Electric motor repair; motors, electric

(G-16105)
C A P INDUSTRIES INC
Also Called: Custom Aerosol Packaging
543 Staunton St (45356-3947)
P.O. Box 1411 (45356-1011)
PHONE.................................937 773-1824
Robert A Heckman, *President*
Eric Heckman, *Vice Pres*
Mary Heckman, *Treasurer*
EMP: 17
SQ FT: 33,000
SALES (est): 1.7MM **Privately Held**
WEB: www.customaerosol.com
SIC: 7389 2813 5198 Packaging & labeling services; aerosols; paints

(G-16106)
CAMFIL USA INC
Also Called: Camfil Farr
405 Fox Dr (45356-8237)
PHONE.................................937 773-0866
Matt Caulfield, *Branch Mgr*
EMP: 3
SALES (corp-wide): 864.2MM **Privately Held**
SIC: 3564 3511 Dust or fume collecting equipment, industrial; turbines & turbine generator sets
HQ: Camfil Usa, Inc.
1 N Corporate Dr
Riverdale NJ 07457
973 616-7300

(G-16107)
CRANE PUMPS & SYSTEMS INC
Also Called: Pacific Valve
420 3rd St (45356-3918)
PHONE.................................937 773-2442
Allan Oak, *Branch Mgr*
EMP: 280
SALES (corp-wide): 3.3B **Publicly Held**
SIC: 5085 3494 Valves & fittings; valves & pipe fittings
HQ: Crane Pumps & Systems, Inc.
420 3rd St
Piqua OH 45356
937 773-2442

(G-16108)
CRANE PUMPS & SYSTEMS INC (DH)
420 3rd St (45356-3918)
PHONE.................................937 773-2442
Jim Lavish, *President*
Loius Turner, *Buyer*
Alex Crabtree, *Engineer*
Brock Shepard, *Sales Staff*
Chuck Drake, *Mktg Dir*
▲ **EMP:** 350
SQ FT: 120,000
SALES (est): 193.4MM
SALES (corp-wide): 3.3B **Publicly Held**
WEB: www.cranepumps.com
SIC: 3561 Industrial pumps & parts
HQ: Mcc Holdings, Inc.
4526 Res Frest Dr Ste 400
The Woodlands TX 77381
936 271-6500

(G-16109)
DAN-LOC GROUP LLC
Also Called: Dan-Loc Express
294 Fox Dr (45356-9271)
PHONE.................................937 778-0485
Jerry Jewson, *Opers Mgr*
EMP: 4
SALES (corp-wide): 57.8MM **Privately Held**
SIC: 3053 Gaskets, packing & sealing devices
PA: Dan-Loc Group, Llc
725 N Drennan St
Houston TX 77003
713 356-3500

(G-16110)
DARKE PRECISION INC
291 Fox Dr (45356-9265)
P.O. Box 746, Greenville (45331-0746)
PHONE.................................937 548-2232
Harold Young, *President*
Roger Young, *Principal*
Randy Young, *Corp Secy*
EMP: 18
SQ FT: 4,800
SALES (est): 3.2MM **Privately Held**
SIC: 3544 Special dies, tools, jigs & fixtures

(G-16111)
DENIZEN INC
130 Fox Dr (45356-9269)
PHONE.................................937 615-9561
John H Reynolds, *President*
Shawn Dorsey, *Regl Sales Mgr*
Linda Troy, *Regl Sales Mgr*
Terry Lakin, *Marketing Staff*
Paula Anderson, *Director*
▲ **EMP:** 12
SQ FT: 21,000
SALES (est): 3MM **Privately Held**
WEB: www.denizeninc.com
SIC: 2241 5033 Electric insulating tapes & braids, except plastic; insulation materials

(G-16112)
DYNA VAC PLASTICS INC
921 S Downing St (45356-3823)
P.O. Box 614 (45356-0614)
PHONE.................................937 773-0092
Scott Lade, *President*
Richard Lade, *Principal*
Sandra Lade, *Corp Secy*
EMP: 6
SQ FT: 18,000
SALES (est): 775K **Privately Held**
SIC: 3089 Plastic processing

(G-16113)
EAGLE PRINTING & GRAPHICS LLC
318 N Wayne St (45356-2230)
PHONE.................................937 773-7900
Robert Delaet, *President*
Diane Delaet, *Vice Pres*
Diane De Laet, *Manager*
EMP: 4
SALES (est): 528.2K **Privately Held**
SIC: 2752 Commercial printing, offset

(G-16114)
F & B ENGRAVING TLS & SUP LLC
308 W Statler Rd (45356-9209)
PHONE.................................937 332-7994
Terrance D Blosser, *Owner*
EMP: 3
SQ FT: 1,200
SALES: 148K **Privately Held**
SIC: 3423 5085 Engravers' tools, hand; tools

(G-16115)
FINISHERS INC
1718 Commerce Dr (45356-2602)
PHONE.................................937 773-3177
Jerry Dye, *President*
Jim Schneider, *Vice Pres*
EMP: 5
SQ FT: 1,200
SALES (est): 599.5K **Privately Held**
SIC: 3471 Polishing, metals or formed products

(G-16116)
FORREST ENTERPRISES INC
510 W Statler Rd (45356-8281)
P.O. Box 244 (45356-0244)
PHONE.................................937 773-1714
Staton C Reynolds, *President*
Curtis Reynolds, *Treasurer*
▲ **EMP:** 8 **EST:** 1955
SQ FT: 6,500
SALES (est): 905.4K **Privately Held**
WEB: www.forrestent.net
SIC: 3949 4783 Bowling equipment & supplies; packing & crating

(G-16117)
FRENCH OIL MILL MACHINERY CO (PA)
Also Called: French USA
1035 W Greene St (45356-1855)
P.O. Box 920 (45356-0920)
PHONE.................................937 773-3420
Daniel P French, *CEO*
Jason P McDaniel, *COO*
Dennis D Bratton, *Treasurer*
Brian Robbins, *Human Res Mgr*
Douglas Smith, *Sales Staff*
▲ **EMP:** 60
SQ FT: 210,000
SALES (est): 16MM **Privately Held**
WEB: www.frenchoil.com
SIC: 3559 3542 3556 3554 Rubber working machinery, including tires; presses: hydraulic & pneumatic, mechanical & manual; presses, food: cheese, beet, cider & sugarcane; pulp mill machinery

(G-16118)
GISCO INC
Also Called: General Industrial Supply
308 W Statler Rd (45356-9209)
P.O. Box 463 (45356-0463)
PHONE.................................937 773-7601
Jeffrey Jackson, *President*
Laura Jackson, *Vice Pres*
EMP: 5
SQ FT: 7,500
SALES (est): 1.2MM **Privately Held**
SIC: 3451 Screw machine products

(G-16119)
HAMPSHIRE CO
9225 State Route 66 (45356-8700)
P.O. Box 1195 (45356-1195)
PHONE.................................937 773-3493
Thomas F Hampshire, *President*
Dorothy M Hampshire, *Corp Secy*
Robert Mikolajewski, *Vice Pres*
EMP: 50
SQ FT: 50,000
SALES (est): 5.7MM **Privately Held**
WEB: www.hampshirecabinetry.com
SIC: 2434 Vanities, bathroom: wood

(G-16120)
HANGER PRSTHETCS & ORTHO INC
Also Called: Orpro Prosthetics & Orthotics
9179 N County Road 25a 2b (45356-9521)
PHONE.................................937 773-2441
Vinit Asar, *CEO*
Carrie Melton, *Branch Mgr*
EMP: 3
SALES (corp-wide): 1B **Publicly Held**
SIC: 3842 5999 Limbs, artificial; orthopedic appliances; orthopedic & prosthesis applications
HQ: Hanger Prosthetics & Orthotics, Inc.
10910 Domain Dr Ste 300
Austin TX 78758
512 777-3800

(G-16121)
HARMONY SYSTEMS AND SVC INC
1711 Commerce Dr (45356-2601)
PHONE.................................937 778-1082
Edward Adams, *CEO*
Nellie Adams, *President*
Hugh Wall, *General Counsel*
▲ **EMP:** 70
SQ FT: 110,000
SALES (est): 18.6MM **Privately Held**
WEB: www.harmonysysandsvc.com
SIC: 3089 Injection molding of plastics

GEOGRAPHIC SECTION

Piqua - Miami County (G-16146)

(G-16122)
HARTZELL FAN INC (PA)
910 S Downing St (45356)
PHONE..................................937 773-7411
Jeff Bannister Hartzell, *CEO*
James Robert Hartzell, *Ch of Bd*
George Atkinson, *President*
Thomas Gustafson, *Vice Pres*
Michael Bardo, *CFO*
◆ **EMP:** 145
SQ FT: 196,000
SALES (est): 45MM **Privately Held**
SIC: 3564 3433 Blowers & fans; ventilating fans: industrial or commercial; heating equipment, except electric

(G-16123)
HARTZELL HARDWOODS INC (PA)
1025 S Roosevelt Ave (45356-3713)
P.O. Box 919 (45356-0919)
PHONE..................................937 773-7054
Jeffery Bannister, *CEO*
James Robert Hartzell, *Ch of Bd*
Kelly Hostetter, *President*
Jane Osborn, *Admin Sec*
▼ **EMP:** 90
SQ FT: 275,000
SALES (est): 30.1MM **Privately Held**
WEB: www.hartzellhardwoods.com
SIC: 5031 2421 2426 Lumber: rough, dressed & finished; sawmills & planing mills, general; hardwood dimension & flooring mills

(G-16124)
HARTZELL INDUSTRIES INC (PA)
1025 S Roosevelt Ave (45356-3713)
P.O. Box 919 (45356-0919)
PHONE..................................937 773-6295
Jeff Bannister, *CEO*
James Robert Hartzell, *Ch of Bd*
Michael Bardo, *President*
Chris Oliss, *CFO*
Randi Pearson, *Treasurer*
EMP: 73 **EST:** 1964
SQ FT: 20,000
SALES (est): 12.5MM **Privately Held**
WEB: www.hartzellfan.com
SIC: 2435 6719 Veneer stock, hardwood; personal holding companies, except banks

(G-16125)
HARTZELL PROPELLER INC
Also Called: Hartzell Service Center
1 Propeller Pl (45356-2656)
PHONE..................................937 778-4200
Jim Brown, *President*
Kristy Perkins, *Supervisor*
EMP: 14
SQ FT: 1,500 **Privately Held**
WEB: www.hartzellpropeller.com
SIC: 3728 Governors, aircraft propeller feathering
HQ: Hartzell Propeller Inc.
1 Propeller Pl
Piqua OH 45356
937 778-4200

(G-16126)
HARTZELL PROPELLER INC (HQ)
1 Propeller Pl (45356-2656)
PHONE..................................937 778-4200
Joseph W Brown, *President*
Stephen Reindel, *General Mgr*
James Brown III, *Principal*
Bob Allenbaugh, *COO*
Jj Frigge, *Exec VP*
◆ **EMP:** 250
SQ FT: 175,000
SALES (est): 62.3MM **Privately Held**
WEB: www.hartzellpropeller.com
SIC: 3728 Aircraft propellers & associated equipment

(G-16127)
HOBART BROTHERS COMPANY
8585 Industry Park Dr (45356-9511)
PHONE..................................937 773-5869
Jim Schwepeji, *Principal*
EMP: 20
SALES (corp-wide): 14.7B **Publicly Held**
SIC: 3548 Mfg Weld Equipment
HQ: Hobart Brothers Llc
101 Trade Sq E
Troy OH 45373
937 332-5439

(G-16128)
HOBART CORPORATION
Also Called: P M I Food Equipment Group
8515 Industry Park Dr (45356-9511)
P.O. Box 702 (45356-0702)
PHONE..................................937 332-2797
Dean Ramaeker, *Manager*
EMP: 120
SALES (corp-wide): 14.7B **Publicly Held**
WEB: www.hobartcorp.com
SIC: 3589 3556 3596 3585 Dishwashing machines, commercial; cooking equipment, commercial; commercial cooking & foodwarming equipment; food products machinery; weighing machines & apparatus; refrigeration equipment, complete; gray & ductile iron foundries
HQ: Hobart Llc
701 S Ridge Ave
Troy OH 45374
937 332-3000

(G-16129)
HOLE HUNTER GOLF INC
Also Called: Hole Hunter Golf Driving Range
438 S Downing St (45356-3906)
P.O. Box 731, Troy (45373-0731)
PHONE..................................937 339-5833
William S Brading, *President*
EMP: 3
SQ FT: 4,200
SALES (est): 337.9K **Privately Held**
SIC: 5941 3949 7999 Golf goods & equipment; golf equipment; golf driving range

(G-16130)
INDUSTRY PRODUCTS CO (PA)
500 W Statler Rd (45356-8281)
PHONE..................................937 778-0585
Linda Cleveland, *President*
Bob Axe, *VP Opers*
Tom Craft, *Mfg Mgr*
Tyler Furrow, *Project Mgr*
Joel Roy, *Project Mgr*
▲ **EMP:** 366 **EST:** 1966
SQ FT: 335,000
SALES: 76MM **Privately Held**
WEB: www.industryproductsco.com
SIC: 7692 3053 3714 3544 Automotive welding; gaskets, all materials; motor vehicle parts & accessories; motor vehicle body components & frame; special dies, tools, jigs & fixtures; unsupported plastics film & sheet

(G-16131)
ISAIAH INDUSTRIES INC (PA)
Also Called: Classic Metal Roofing Systems
8510 Industry Park Dr (45356-8535)
P.O. Box 701 (45356-0701)
PHONE..................................937 773-9840
Todd Miller, *CEO*
Karen Gephart, *Purchasing*
Rhonda Morgan, *Human Res Dir*
Tim Price, *VP Sales*
Seth Heckaman, *Sales Mgr*
◆ **EMP:** 40
SQ FT: 5,000
SALES (est): 8.4MM **Privately Held**
WEB: www.classicroof.com
SIC: 3354 3444 2952 Aluminum extruded products; sheet metalwork; asphalt felts & coatings

(G-16132)
J M MOLD INC
1707 Commerce Dr (45356-2601)
PHONE..................................937 778-0077
Kriss Scheer, *President*
Robert P Scheer, *President*
EMP: 8 **EST:** 1966
SQ FT: 9,600
SALES: 1.7MM **Privately Held**
SIC: 3544 Dies & die holders for metal cutting, forming, die casting; industrial molds

(G-16133)
JACKSON TUBE SERVICE INC (PA)
8210 Industry Park Dr (45356-8536)
P.O. Box 1650 (45356-4650)
PHONE..................................937 773-8550
Robert W Jackson, *CEO*
David A Hare, *Vice Pres*
Marcus Sergy, *Vice Pres*
David Linn, *Opers Staff*
James Froning, *Engineer*
▲ **EMP:** 153
SQ FT: 75,000
SALES (est): 47.2MM **Privately Held**
WEB: www.jackson-tube.com
SIC: 3317 Steel pipe & tubes

(G-16134)
JERRY PULFER
Also Called: Piqua Sign
900 S Main St (45356-3858)
PHONE..................................937 778-1861
Jerry Pulfer, *Owner*
EMP: 3
SQ FT: 3,200
SALES (est): 220K **Privately Held**
WEB: www.piquatechnologies.com
SIC: 3993 3953 2796 2671 Signs, not made in custom sign painting shops; marking devices; platemaking services; packaging paper & plastics film, coated & laminated; automotive & apparel trimmings

(G-16135)
K & B STAMPING & MANUFACTURING
9676 Looney Rd (45356-9522)
P.O. Box 405 (45356-0405)
PHONE..................................937 778-8875
Manfried Kirchner, *President*
Brian Kirchner, *Vice Pres*
EMP: 5
SALES: 500K **Privately Held**
SIC: 3469 Stamping metal for the trade

(G-16136)
K B MACHINE & TOOL INC
1500 S Main St (45356-8319)
P.O. Box 426 (45356-0426)
PHONE..................................937 773-1624
Kenneth G Bricker, *President*
Miki Bricker, *Vice Pres*
Joyce K Bricker, *Admin Sec*
EMP: 9
SQ FT: 9,500
SALES (est): 1.2MM **Privately Held**
SIC: 3544 Special dies & tools

(G-16137)
LITTLE PRINTING COMPANY
Also Called: Quality Forms
4317 W Us Route 36 (45356-9334)
P.O. Box 1176 (45356-1176)
PHONE..................................937 773-4595
Tom Kinnison, *President*
Lj Bertke, *CFO*
Dorrell Polhamus, *Human Res Mgr*
L Bertke, *Officer*
EMP: 35
SQ FT: 54,000
SALES (est): 5.5MM **Privately Held**
SIC: 2761 Manifold business forms

(G-16138)
LOSTCREEK TOOL & MACHINE INC
1150 S Main St (45356-9357)
PHONE..................................937 773-6022
Steve Rowe, *President*
Michael Rowe, *President*
Shelby Rowe, *Corp Secy*
Donald Rowe, *Vice Pres*
EMP: 12
SQ FT: 15,500
SALES: 666.8K **Privately Held**
SIC: 3599 7692 3544 Machine shop, jobbing & repair; welding repair; special dies, tools, jigs & fixtures

(G-16139)
LWB/ISE LP
9160 Country Club Rd (45356-8571)
PHONE..................................937 778-3828
Al Baker, *Plant Mgr*
EMP: 12
SALES (corp-wide): 2MM **Privately Held**
SIC: 3465 Body parts, automobile: stamped metal
PA: Lwb-Ise Societe En Commandite
20 Rte De Windsor
Sherbrooke QC J1C 0
819 846-1044

(G-16140)
MAJESTIC SPORTSWEAR COMPANY
2545 Landman Mill Rd (45356-9746)
PHONE..................................937 773-1144
Mike Ivanowicz, *Owner*
EMP: 8
SALES (est): 503.9K **Privately Held**
SIC: 5137 2339 Sweaters, women's & children's; athletic clothing: women's, misses' & juniors'

(G-16141)
MEDICAL EQUIPMENT PROVIDER
102 Fox Dr (45356-9269)
PHONE..................................937 778-2190
Bryan Reed, *Manager*
EMP: 4
SALES (est): 242.9K **Privately Held**
SIC: 3845 Respiratory analysis equipment, electromedical

(G-16142)
MIAMI SPECIALTIES INC
Also Called: M C D Plastics & Manufacturing
172 Robert M Davis Pkwy (45356-8338)
PHONE..................................937 778-1850
Joann Howell, *President*
Robb Howell III, *Vice Pres*
EMP: 7
SQ FT: 10,000
SALES: 524.6K **Privately Held**
WEB: www.mcdplastics.com
SIC: 3599 Machine shop, jobbing & repair

(G-16143)
MIAMI VALLEY POLISHING LLC
170 Fox Dr (45356-9269)
PHONE..................................937 615-9353
Matthew Powers, *Principal*
EMP: 13
SALES (est): 2.1MM **Privately Held**
SIC: 3471 Polishing, metals or formed products

(G-16144)
MOREY WOODWORKING LLC
377 E Loy Rd (45356-9292)
PHONE..................................937 623-5280
Todd Morey, *Owner*
EMP: 4 **EST:** 2010
SALES (est): 447.8K **Privately Held**
SIC: 2431 Millwork

(G-16145)
NICKS PLATING CO INC
6980 Free Rd (45356-9279)
P.O. Box 337 (45356-0337)
PHONE..................................937 773-3175
Duane Penrod, *President*
EMP: 10 **EST:** 1973
SQ FT: 4,500
SALES: 700K **Privately Held**
SIC: 3471 Plating of metals or formed products; polishing, metals or formed products

(G-16146)
NITTO INC
1620 S Main St (45356-8320)
P.O. Box 740 (45356-0740)
PHONE..................................937 773-4820
Katsuhrio Nagase, *Vice Pres*
Vicki Pierre, *Accounting Mgr*
▲ **EMP:** 200
SQ FT: 100,000
SALES: 41MM
SALES (corp-wide): 8B **Privately Held**
WEB: www.nitto.co.jp
SIC: 3053 3296 Motor vehicle parts & accessories
PA: Nitto Denko Corporation
4-20, Ofukacho, Kita-Ku
Osaka OSK 530-0
676 322-101

Piqua - Miami County (G-16147)

(G-16147)
P & R SPECIALTY INC
1835 W High St (45356-9399)
P.O. Box 741 (45356-0741)
PHONE.................................937 773-0263
Greg Blankenship, *President*
Craig Stiefel, *Business Mgr*
Alissa Blankenship, *Vice Pres*
Pat Kiernan, *Vice Pres*
Mike Koon, *Vice Pres*
▲ **EMP:** 35 **EST:** 1982
SQ FT: 47,500
SALES (est): 6.9MM **Privately Held**
WEB: www.prspecialty.com
SIC: 2499 3053 2675 2631 Spools, wood; gaskets, all materials; paper die-cutting; paperboard mills

(G-16148)
PALSTAR INC
9676 Looney Rd (45356-9522)
P.O. Box 1136 (45356-1136)
PHONE.................................937 773-6255
Paul Hrivnak, *President*
Donald Keffler, *Vice Pres*
Eva Hrivnak, *Treasurer*
EMP: 16
SQ FT: 4,000
SALES (est): 3.7MM **Privately Held**
WEB: www.palstar.com
SIC: 3825 Signal generators & averagers

(G-16149)
PERFECTO INDUSTRIES INC
1729 W High St (45356-9300)
PHONE.................................937 778-1900
Ralph Bateman, *Engineer*
Harvey Howard, *Branch Mgr*
EMP: 45
SALES (corp-wide): 18.3MM **Privately Held**
WEB: www.perfectoindustries.com
SIC: 3547 3549 3599 3542 Rolling mill machinery; coiling machinery; custom machinery; industrial trucks & tractors
PA: Perfecto Industries, Inc.
1567 Calkins Dr
Gaylord MI 49735
989 732-2941

(G-16150)
PIQUA CHAMPION FOUNDRY INC
918 S Main St (45356-3858)
P.O. Box 716 (45356-0716)
PHONE.................................937 773-3375
Larry W Pickering, *President*
R P Fite, *Principal*
Renate Pickering, *Vice Pres*
Ken Pickering, *Sales Executive*
EMP: 25
SQ FT: 35,000
SALES (est): 4.7MM **Privately Held**
SIC: 3321 Gray iron castings

(G-16151)
PIQUA CHOCOLATE COMPANY INC (PA)
Also Called: Winans Chocolate and Coffee
310 Spring St (45356-2334)
PHONE.................................937 773-1981
Joe Reiser, *President*
EMP: 9
SQ FT: 2,000
SALES (est): 3.5MM **Privately Held**
SIC: 5441 5947 2064 Candy; greeting cards; candy & other confectionery products

(G-16152)
PIQUA EMERY CUTTER & FNDRY CO
Also Called: Piqua Emery Foundry
821 S Downing St (45356)
PHONE.................................937 773-4134
Stephen Mikolajewski, *President*
Helen Mikolajewski, *Corp Secy*
Roger McLain, *Vice Pres*
EMP: 54 **EST:** 1934
SQ FT: 54,000

SALES (est): 12.7MM **Privately Held**
WEB: www.piquaemery.com
SIC: 3365 3369 3366 Aluminum & aluminum-based alloy castings; nonferrous foundries; castings (except die): bronze; castings (except die): brass

(G-16153)
PIQUA GRANITE & MARBLE CO INC (PA)
Also Called: Classic Monuments
123 N Main St (45356-2311)
P.O. Box 1197 (45356-1197)
PHONE.................................937 773-2000
Pat Obara, *President*
Steve Supinger, *Vice Pres*
EMP: 9
SQ FT: 18,000
SALES (est): 1.7MM **Privately Held**
WEB: www.hmw.com
SIC: 5999 5032 3281 Monuments, finished to custom order; granite building stone; marble, building: cut & shaped

(G-16154)
PIQUA MATERIALS INC
Also Called: Piqua Mineral Division
1750 W Statler Rd (45356-9264)
PHONE.................................937 773-4824
Brent Phillips, *Safety Mgr*
John Harris, *Branch Mgr*
EMP: 30
SQ FT: 16,808
SALES (corp-wide): 10.1MM **Privately Held**
SIC: 1422 3274 Limestones, ground; lime
PA: Piqua Materials Inc
11641 Mostellar Rd Ste 1
Cincinnati OH 45241
513 771-0820

(G-16155)
PIQUA PAPER BOX COMPANY
616 Covington Ave (45356-3205)
P.O. Box 814 (45356-0814)
PHONE.................................937 773-0313
Frank J Gleason Jr, *Ch of Bd*
Brian T Gleason, *President*
Eugene Elsass, *Admin Sec*
▲ **EMP:** 35 **EST:** 1908
SQ FT: 85,000
SALES (est): 7MM **Privately Held**
SIC: 2653 Boxes, corrugated: made from purchased materials

(G-16156)
PRECISE TOOL INC
9676 Looney Rd (45356-9522)
P.O. Box 405 (45356-0405)
PHONE.................................937 778-3441
Brian Kirchner, *President*
Theresa Kirchner, *Vice Pres*
EMP: 5
SQ FT: 10,000
SALES: 690K **Privately Held**
SIC: 3544 Special dies & tools

(G-16157)
PROTO-MOLD PRODUCTS CO INC
1750 Commerce Dr (45356-2699)
PHONE.................................937 778-1959
Graig Flintcraft, *President*
George Reedy, *General Mgr*
Craig Flitcraft, *Vice Pres*
EMP: 25 **EST:** 1979
SQ FT: 50,000
SALES (est): 6.3MM **Privately Held**
WEB: www.protomoldproducts.com
SIC: 3089 Injection molding of plastics

(G-16158)
R DUNN MOLD INC
9055 State Route 66 (45356-9727)
P.O. Box 1805 (45356-4805)
PHONE.................................937 773-3388
EMP: 3
SQ FT: 4,000
SALES: 150K **Privately Held**
SIC: 3089 3545 Mfg Plastic Products Mfg Machine Tool Accessories

(G-16159)
RETTERBUSH FIBERGLASS CORP
719 Long St (45356-9262)
P.O. Box 207 (45356-0207)
PHONE.................................937 778-1936
Bryan Retterbush, *President*
EMP: 25
SQ FT: 32,000
SALES (est): 3.2MM **Privately Held**
WEB: www.retterbushfiberglass.com
SIC: 3089 Injection molding of plastics

(G-16160)
ROTH TRANSIT INC
8590 Industry Park Dr (45356-8535)
P.O. Box 821 (45356-0821)
PHONE.................................937 773-5051
Linda Roth, *President*
EMP: 7 **EST:** 1998
SQ FT: 7,200
SALES (est): 750K **Privately Held**
SIC: 3596 4212 Truck (motor vehicle) scales; local trucking, without storage

(G-16161)
RV XPRESS INC
501 East St (45356-3930)
PHONE.................................937 418-0127
Glenn McKinney, *President*
Michael T McGahan, *Principal*
EMP: 8
SALES (est): 625.3K **Privately Held**
SIC: 3799 Recreational vehicles

(G-16162)
SKINNER POWDER COATING INC
631 Boone St (45356-2043)
PHONE.................................937 606-2188
Jill Middleton, *Principal*
EMP: 3
SALES (est): 274.5K **Privately Held**
SIC: 3479 Coating of metals & formed products

(G-16163)
SRM CONCRETE LLC
Also Called: Piqua Plant
8395 Piqua Lockington Rd (45356-9701)
PHONE.................................937 773-0841
Dick Hoying, *Branch Mgr*
EMP: 77
SALES (corp-wide): 29.4MM **Privately Held**
SIC: 3273 Ready-mixed concrete
PA: Srm Concrete, Llc
1136 2nd Ave N
Nashville TN

(G-16164)
TAILWIND TECHNOLOGIES INC (PA)
1 Propeller Pl (45356-2655)
PHONE.................................937 778-4200
James W Brown III, *President*
Joseph W Brown, *Principal*
Joseph Brown, *Principal*
Michael J Piscatella, *Principal*
Matthew L Jesch, *CFO*
EMP: 20
SALES: 200MM **Privately Held**
SIC: 3356 Titanium

(G-16165)
TEMPO MANUFACTURING COMPANY
Also Called: Tempo Trophy Mfg
727 E Ash St (45356-2411)
P.O. Box 718 (45356-0718)
PHONE.................................937 773-6613
Robert Elrod, *President*
Patricia Elrod, *Vice Pres*
EMP: 8
SQ FT: 30,000
SALES (est): 710.2K **Privately Held**
SIC: 3914 Trophies

(G-16166)
TK HOLDINGS INC
Also Called: T K Holdings
1401 Innovation Pkwy (45356-7524)
PHONE.................................937 778-9713
Monica Bauthn, *Manager*
EMP: 25

SALES (corp-wide): 4B **Privately Held**
SIC: 2399 5013 Seat belts, automobile & aircraft; motor vehicle supplies & new parts
HQ: Tk Holdings Inc.
4611 Wiseman Blvd
San Antonio TX 78251
210 509-0762

(G-16167)
WRIGHTS SAW MILL
9018 Piqua Lockington Rd (45356-9741)
PHONE.................................937 773-2546
James Wright, *Principal*
EMP: 3
SALES (est): 232.5K **Privately Held**
SIC: 2421 Sawmills & planing mills, general

Plain City
Madison County

(G-16168)
ACB THREE INC
9341 Industrial Pkwy (43064-8729)
PHONE.................................614 873-4680
Art Bafchnagel, *Principal*
EMP: 3
SALES (est): 218.4K **Privately Held**
SIC: 3559 Sewing machines & attachments, industrial

(G-16169)
ADVANCED CLEANING TECH LLC
Also Called: Ultimate Cloth
7533 Merchant Rd (43064-9303)
PHONE.................................614 504-2014
Tracy J Stewart,
Tracy Stewart,
EMP: 3
SQ FT: 2,000
SALES (est): 369.1K **Privately Held**
SIC: 2842 Paint & wallpaper cleaners

(G-16170)
ALTRASERV LLC
Also Called: Brio Coffee Co
8350 Industrial Pkwy # 16 (43064-9373)
P.O. Box 355, Dublin (43017-0355)
PHONE.................................614 889-2500
Dorothy Moran, *President*
Tom Moran, *Vice Pres*
EMP: 6
SQ FT: 3,000
SALES (est): 583.7K **Privately Held**
SIC: 2095 Roasted coffee

(G-16171)
AMERICAN APEX CORPORATION
8515 Rausch Dr (43064-8067)
PHONE.................................614 652-2000
Charles R Torson, *President*
Sherry H Torson, *Admin Sec*
▲ **EMP:** 13
SQ FT: 16,000
SALES (est): 2.8MM **Privately Held**
WEB: www.americanapex.com
SIC: 3484 3489 3795 8748 Small arms; ordnance & accessories; tanks & tank components; specialized tank components, military; safety training service

(G-16172)
ASSOCIATED GRAPHICS INC
9021 Heritage Dr Ste I (43064-8757)
PHONE.................................614 873-1273
Adam Wright, *President*
Roger McPeek, *Vice Pres*
EMP: 10
SALES: 365K **Privately Held**
WEB: www.agionline.com
SIC: 2759 Screen printing

(G-16173)
AUTOTOOL INC
7875 Corporate Blvd (43064-8045)
PHONE.................................614 733-0222
Bassam Homsi, *President*
Nicholas Deyhle, *Engineer*
Rilong Jin, *Engineer*
EMP: 38

GEOGRAPHIC SECTION

Plain City - Madison County (G-16203)

SQ FT: 40,000
SALES (est): 10.4MM **Privately Held**
WEB: www.autotoolinc.com
SIC: 3559 Automotive related machinery

(G-16174)
BAHLER MEDICAL INC
Also Called: Venture Medical
8910 Warner Rd (43064-9467)
PHONE.................................614 873-7600
Michael Bahler, *President*
EMP: 36
SALES (est): 3.2MM **Privately Held**
SIC: 3842 Implants, surgical

(G-16175)
BALMAC INC
8205 Estates Pkwy Ste N (43064-8080)
PHONE.................................614 873-8222
Mark Slebodnik, *President*
Steve Crawford, *Vice Pres*
EMP: 10
SQ FT: 6,000
SALES: 1MM **Privately Held**
WEB: www.balmacinc.com
SIC: 3829 Vibration meters, analyzers & calibrators

(G-16176)
BCAST STAINLESS PRODUCTS LLC
9000 Heritage Dr (43064-9493)
PHONE.................................614 873-3945
Lou Castelli,
▲ EMP: 12
SALES (est): 1MM **Privately Held**
SIC: 3312 5075 Stainless steel; furnaces, heating: electric

(G-16177)
BEACHY BARNS LTD
8720 Amish Pike (43064-9538)
PHONE.................................614 873-4193
Dale Beachy, *Partner*
EMP: 10
SQ FT: 7,500
SALES: 1.6MM **Privately Held**
WEB: www.beachybarns.com
SIC: 2452 1542 Prefabricated wood buildings; prefabricated buildings, wood; garage construction

(G-16178)
BINDERY & SPC PRESSWORKS INC
351 W Bigelow Ave (43064-1152)
PHONE.................................614 873-4623
Dick Izzard, *President*
Betty Izzard, *Vice Pres*
Doug Izzard, *Vice Pres*
Mark Izzard, *Vice Pres*
Tami Roberts, *Admin Sec*
EMP: 74
SQ FT: 42,000
SALES (est): 18.1MM **Privately Held**
SIC: 2791 2759 2752 2789 Typesetting; commercial printing; commercial printing, offset; bookbinding & related work; mailing service

(G-16179)
BUILDING BLOCK PERFORMANCE LLC
7920 Corporate Blvd Ste C (43064-9275)
PHONE.................................614 918-7476
Kamyron A White, *Mng Member*
EMP: 6 EST: 2014
SALES: 648K **Privately Held**
SIC: 7999 7372 Physical fitness instruction; application computer software

(G-16180)
CALZUROCOM
8055 Corp Blvd Unit B (43064)
PHONE.................................800 257-9472
Katherine Wesney, *President*
EMP: 3 EST: 2015
SALES (est): 222.3K **Privately Held**
SIC: 3021 Protective footwear, rubber or plastic

(G-16181)
COM-FAB INC
4657 Price Hilliards Rd (43064-8838)
PHONE.................................740 857-1107
Jim Sheehy, *President*
EMP: 22
SQ FT: 20,000
SALES (est): 5MM **Privately Held**
WEB: www.comfab-inc.com
SIC: 3441 Fabricated structural metal

(G-16182)
COPY RIGHT OF OHIO LLC
Also Called: Copy Right Printing
7445 Montgomery Rd B (43064-8612)
PHONE.................................614 431-1303
James Craig Annette, *Mng Member*
EMP: 3
SQ FT: 2,500
SALES (est): 449.3K **Privately Held**
SIC: 2752 Commercial printing, offset

(G-16183)
DABAR INDUSTRIES LLC
8475 Rausch Dr (43064-8064)
PHONE.................................614 873-3949
Cliff Baseler, *President*
EMP: 15 EST: 2015
SQ FT: 12,600
SALES (est): 1.7MM **Privately Held**
SIC: 3443 Tanks, standard or custom fabricated: metal plate

(G-16184)
DAILY NEEDS ASSISTANCE
Also Called: D N A
340 W Main St (43064-1198)
PHONE.................................614 824-8340
Tamara Reed, *Director*
EMP: 12 EST: 2013
SALES (est): 252.2K **Privately Held**
SIC: 2711 Newspapers, publishing & printing

(G-16185)
DARBY CREEK MILLWORK CO
10001 Plain Cy Grgesville (43064)
PHONE.................................614 873-3267
Ivan Beachy, *Owner*
EMP: 7
SQ FT: 8,000
SALES (est): 716.9K **Privately Held**
SIC: 2431 Doors, wood; door frames, wood

(G-16186)
DATA ANALYSIS TECHNOLOGIES
7715 Corporate Blvd (43064-9212)
P.O. Box 3131, Dublin (43016-0063)
PHONE.................................614 873-0710
Ronald K Mitchum, *President*
D Jane Mitchum, *CFO*
Scott Mitchum, *Technician*
EMP: 8
SQ FT: 10,000
SALES (est): 1.4MM **Privately Held**
WEB: www.datlab.com
SIC: 8734 8748 3822 Pollution testing; testing services; systems engineering consultant, ex. computer or professional; auto controls regulating residntl & coml environmt & applncs

(G-16187)
DISTINCTIVE MARBLE & GRAN INC
7635 Commerce Pl (43064-9223)
PHONE.................................614 760-0003
Chris Schnetzler, *President*
Kathy Schnetzler, *Principal*
▲ EMP: 10
SALES (est): 1.5MM **Privately Held**
WEB: www.distinctivemarbleandgranite.com
SIC: 1743 3281 Marble installation, interior; curbing, granite or stone

(G-16188)
DJ BEVERAGE INNOVATIONS INC
Also Called: Beertubes.com
8400 Indl Pkwy Bldg 2 (43064)
PHONE.................................614 769-1569
David J Stein, *President*
Steve Lerner, *Managing Dir*
Jason M Drum, *Vice Pres*
▲ EMP: 3

SALES (est): 427.9K **Privately Held**
SIC: 3585 5078 Soda fountain & beverage dispensing equipment & parts; refrigerated beverage dispensers

(G-16189)
DRIVETRAIN USA INC
Also Called: Cryogenic Technical Services
8445 Rausch Dr (43064-8064)
P.O. Box 3787, Dublin (43016-0406)
PHONE.................................614 733-0940
John Canfield, *President*
EMP: 10
SQ FT: 40,000
SALES (est): 1.2MM **Privately Held**
SIC: 3679 Cryogenic cooling devices for infrared detectors, masers

(G-16190)
EDEN CRYOGENICS LLC
8475 Rausch Dr (43064-8064)
PHONE.................................614 873-3949
Steve L Hensley, *President*
Philip L Korodi, *Manager*
▲ EMP: 45
SALES (est): 11.1MM **Privately Held**
WEB: www.edencryogenics.com
SIC: 3559 Cryogenic machinery, industrial

(G-16191)
FABBERGE LLC
8034 Corporate Blvd Ste B (43064-8001)
PHONE.................................614 365-0056
Stas Makarov, *CEO*
EMP: 4
SQ FT: 5,200
SALES: 500K **Privately Held**
SIC: 3714 Exhaust systems & parts, motor vehicle

(G-16192)
FRIESEN FAB AND EQUIPMENT
Also Called: Friesen Fab & Equipment
10030 Smith Calhoun Rd (43064-9142)
PHONE.................................614 873-4354
Cornelius Friesen, *Owner*
EMP: 4 EST: 1970
SQ FT: 6,000
SALES (est): 419.8K **Privately Held**
WEB: www.friesenfab.com
SIC: 3524 7699 Lawn & garden mowers & accessories; agricultural equipment repair services

(G-16193)
FRIESEN TRANSFER LTD
9280 Iams Rd (43064-9108)
PHONE.................................614 873-5672
Klaas Friesen, *President*
EMP: 6
SALES (est): 460K **Privately Held**
SIC: 3713 0115 0111 Dump truck bodies; corn; wheat

(G-16194)
GK PACKAGING INC (PA)
Also Called: Plain City Molding
7680 Commerce Pl (43064-9222)
PHONE.................................614 873-3900
Gene J Kuzma, *President*
Betty Jo Jerome, *Principal*
Bob Kellerman, *CFO*
Jeff Kuzma, *Treasurer*
Tasshia Lee, *Hum Res Coord*
▲ EMP: 95
SQ FT: 70,000
SALES (est): 24.1MM **Privately Held**
WEB: www.gkpackaging.com
SIC: 3085 Plastics bottles

(G-16195)
GOLD METAL MACHINING INC
Also Called: Union Enterprises Division
216 W Bigelow Ave (43064-1143)
PHONE.................................614 873-5031
Kenneth J Cahill, *President*
Timothy A Goodrich, *Vice Pres*
EMP: 10 EST: 1946
SQ FT: 4,000
SALES (est): 726K **Privately Held**
SIC: 3599 Machine shop, jobbing & repair

(G-16196)
GOLF CAR COMPANY INC
8899 Memorial Dr (43064-8636)
PHONE.................................614 873-1055

William Mead, *President*
Sarah Volker, *General Mgr*
Erik Rogers, *Opers Mgr*
EMP: 12
SALES (est): 1.6MM **Privately Held**
SIC: 3949 7359 5599 Sporting & athletic goods; stores & yards equipment rental; golf cart, powered

(G-16197)
J J POLISHING INC
8520 Rausch Dr (43064-8067)
PHONE.................................614 214-7637
EMP: 3 EST: 2017
SALES (est): 150.9K **Privately Held**
SIC: 3471 Polishing, metals or formed products

(G-16198)
KBI GROUP INC
Also Called: King Mill's Woodworking
7370 Merchant Rd (43064-9301)
PHONE.................................614 873-5825
Norman King, *President*
David King, *Vice Pres*
EMP: 3
SALES: 150K **Privately Held**
SIC: 2541 1751 Counter & sink tops; counters or counter display cases, wood; cabinet & finish carpentry

(G-16199)
KNB TOOLS OF AMERICA INC
8440 Rausch Dr (43064-8047)
PHONE.................................614 733-0400
Toshihiko Kawanobe, *CEO*
▲ EMP: 18
SALES (est): 3.2MM **Privately Held**
SIC: 3545 Cutting tools for machine tools

(G-16200)
KREMA GROUP INC
Also Called: Crazy Richards
7920 Corporate Blvd Ste B (43064-9275)
P.O. Box 715, Dublin (43017-0815)
PHONE.................................614 889-4824
Chris Wernli, *CEO*
Kimberly Wernli, *President*
Craig Sonksen, *President*
Richard Sonksen, *Principal*
Joanna Carroll, *CFO*
EMP: 10
SQ FT: 14,000
SALES: 6.5MM **Privately Held**
SIC: 2099 Peanut butter
PA: Krema Products Inc.
  45 N High St
  Dublin OH 43017
  614 889-4824

(G-16201)
MD SOLUTIONS INC
Also Called: M D Solutions
8225 Estates Pkwy (43064-8408)
PHONE.................................866 637-6588
Nirmal Bajoria, *Principal*
▲ EMP: 3
SALES (est): 658K **Privately Held**
SIC: 3669 3999 Traffic signals, electric; atomizers, toiletry

(G-16202)
MIDWEST MOLDING INC
8245 Estates Pkwy (43064-8408)
PHONE.................................614 873-1572
William Razor, *President*
Dan Stahl, *Plant Engr*
EMP: 40
SQ FT: 40,000
SALES (est): 9.2MM **Privately Held**
SIC: 3089 Molding primary plastic; plastic processing

(G-16203)
MILLER CABINET LTD
6217 Converse Huff Rd (43064-9185)
PHONE.................................614 873-4221
Ken Wilson,
EMP: 35
SALES (est): 4.5MM **Privately Held**
SIC: 5722 2541 2521 2511 Kitchens, complete (sinks, cabinets, etc.); cabinets, except refrigerated: show, display, etc.: wood; wood office furniture; wood household furniture; wood kitchen cabinets

Plain City - Madison County (G-16204)

(G-16204)
OHIO LASER LLC
8260 Estates Pkwy (43064-8409)
PHONE.................................614 873-7030
Gregg P Simpson, *President*
EMP: 20
SQ FT: 30,000
SALES (est): 5.4MM **Privately Held**
WEB: www.ohiolaser.com
SIC: **3499** Welding tips, heat resistant: metal

(G-16205)
OYLAIR SPECIALTY
9029 Heritage Dr (43064-9493)
PHONE.................................614 873-3968
EMP: 6
SALES (est): 987.6K **Privately Held**
SIC: **3592** Mfg Carburetors/Pistons/Rings

(G-16206)
PHOENIX BAT COMPANY
7801 Corp Blvd Unit E (43064)
PHONE.................................614 873-7776
Charles Trudeau, *President*
▲ EMP: 4
SQ FT: 3,000
SALES (est): 475.3K **Privately Held**
WEB: www.phoenixbats.com
SIC: **3949** 5941 5091 Baseball equipment & supplies, general; baseball equipment; sporting & recreation goods

(G-16207)
PREMIERE BUILDING MTLS INC (PA)
Also Called: Orion Lighting Solutions
8200 Memorial Dr Ste A (43064-7013)
PHONE.................................574 293-5800
Kirk Mathews, *CEO*
EMP: 4
SQ FT: 6,000
SALES: 3MM **Privately Held**
SIC: **3646** Commercial indusl & institutional electric lighting fixtures

(G-16208)
PUBLIC SAFETY CONCEPTS LLC
8495 Estates Ct (43064-8015)
PHONE.................................614 733-0200
Tom Parr,
EMP: 6
SALES: 675K **Privately Held**
SIC: **3669** 5531 Intercommunication systems, electric; automotive & home supply stores

(G-16209)
QUILTING INC (PA)
Also Called: Mattress Mart
7600 Industrial Pkwy (43064-9468)
PHONE.................................614 504-5971
Ben Tiburzio, *President*
▲ EMP: 55
SQ FT: 85,000
SALES (est): 13.6MM **Privately Held**
WEB: www.quilting.com
SIC: **2515** Mattresses, innerspring or box spring

(G-16210)
R4 HOLDINGS LLC
7795 Corporate Blvd (43064-9273)
PHONE.................................614 873-6499
John Rucker, *Mng Member*
Meredith Rucker,
EMP: 3
SQ FT: 2,400
SALES (est): 342.7K **Privately Held**
SIC: **5531** 3443 Automotive parts; tanks, standard or custom fabricated: metal plate

(G-16211)
SILVER THREADS INC
7710 Corporate Blvd (43064-9214)
PHONE.................................614 733-0099
Carrie Perini, *President*
Anissa Whalen, *Controller*
EMP: 20 EST: 1979
SQ FT: 6,000
SALES (est): 4MM **Privately Held**
WEB: www.silverthreadsinc.com
SIC: **2211** 7389 2392 2391 Draperies & drapery fabrics, cotton; interior designer; household furnishings; curtains & draperies

(G-16212)
SNAIR CO
8163 Business Way (43064-9216)
PHONE.................................614 873-7020
Masashi J Nagai, *Owner*
Hideta Nagai, *Co-Owner*
EMP: 16
SQ FT: 52,000
SALES (est): 1.1MM **Privately Held**
WEB: www.snair.net
SIC: **3542** 3366 3441 3537 Die casting machines; copper foundries; fabricated structural metal; industrial trucks & tractors; sheet metalwork; fabricated plate work (boiler shop)

(G-16213)
SOMMERS WOOD N DOOR COMPANY
7802 Amish Pike (43064-9317)
PHONE.................................614 873-3506
Edward Sommers, *Owner*
EMP: 4
SALES: 500K **Privately Held**
WEB: www.sommerswood.com
SIC: **2431** Doors, wood

(G-16214)
UNITED ROTARY BRUSH INC
8150 Business Way (43064-9209)
PHONE.................................937 644-3515
Bruce Davis, *Manager*
EMP: 55
SQ FT: 63,820
SALES (corp-wide): 47.1MM **Privately Held**
WEB: www.united-rotary.com
SIC: **3991** Brushes, household or industrial
PA: United Rotary Brush Corporation
15607 W 100th Ter
Lenexa KS 66219
913 888-8450

(G-16215)
VELOCYS INC
7950 Corporate Blvd (43064-9230)
PHONE.................................614 733-3300
David Pummell, *CEO*
Jeff McDaniel, *General Mgr*
Dr Paul F Schubert, *COO*
Brian Blackstone, *Research*
Anthony Detrick, *Research*
EMP: 60
SQ FT: 26,800
SALES (est): 10.3MM
SALES (corp-wide): 1MM **Privately Held**
WEB: www.velocys.com
SIC: **8731** 3559 Commercial physical research; environmental research; electronic research; medical research, commercial; sewing machines & hat & zipper making machinery; refinery, chemical processing & similar machinery
PA: Velocys Plc
173 Curie Avenue
Didcot OXON OX11
123 583-8621

(G-16216)
W OF OHIO INC (PA)
Also Called: Skiff Craft
225 Guy St (43064-1160)
P.O. Box 115 (43064-0115)
PHONE.................................614 873-4664
Gabriel Jabbour, *President*
EMP: 6
SALES (est): 500K **Privately Held**
SIC: **3732** Boat building & repairing

(G-16217)
WHITMER WOODWORKS INC
8490 Carters Mill Rd (43064-9116)
PHONE.................................614 873-1196
Jerry Whitmer, *President*
Don Whitmer, *Treasurer*
Aaron Beachy, *Office Mgr*
EMP: 7
SALES (est): 1MM **Privately Held**
WEB: www.archedcasings.com
SIC: **2431** Millwork

(G-16218)
WHOLESALE FAIRY GARDENSCOM LLC
8400 Industrial Pkwy F (43064-9386)
PHONE.................................614 504-5304
Lori Luke, *Principal*
Patti Kuhlman, *Mng Member*
▲ EMP: 8 EST: 2011
SALES: 2.2MM **Privately Held**
SIC: **5191** 3423 Garden supplies; garden & farm tools, including shovels

(G-16219)
WORLD RESOURCE SOLUTONS CORP
8485 Estates Ct (43064-8015)
PHONE.................................614 733-3737
Thomas Warner, *President*
Noi Sasaki, *Manager*
▲ EMP: 7
SQ FT: 3,750
SALES (est): 2.1MM **Privately Held**
SIC: **3089** Injection molding of plastics

(G-16220)
YASKAWA AMERICA INC
8628 Industrial Pkwy A (43064-8069)
PHONE.................................614 733-3200
Steven Blake, *Engineer*
Jill Hoff, *Branch Mgr*
EMP: 19
SALES (corp-wide): 4B **Privately Held**
SIC: **3699** Electrical equipment & supplies
HQ: Yaskawa America, Inc.
2121 Norman Dr
Waukegan IL 60085
847 887-7000

(G-16221)
YODER CABINETS LTD
9996 Amish Pike (43064-9321)
PHONE.................................614 873-5186
David P Yoder Jr, *President*
EMP: 5
SALES: 520K **Privately Held**
WEB: www.yodercabinets.com
SIC: **2434** Vanities, bathroom: wood

(G-16222)
YONEZAWA USA INC
7920 Corporate Blvd Ste A (43064-9275)
PHONE.................................614 799-2210
Shunichi Aoki, *President*
EMP: 6
SALES (est): 735.5K **Privately Held**
SIC: **3577** Computer peripheral equipment

Pleasant City
Guernsey County

(G-16223)
TIMOTHY SINFIELD
54962 Marietta Rd (43772-9601)
PHONE.................................740 685-3684
Timothy Sinfield, *Director*
EMP: 47
SALES (est): 1MM **Privately Held**
SIC: **1389** Oil & gas field services

Pleasant Hill
Miami County

(G-16224)
CD SOLUTIONS INC
100 W Monument St (45359-9669)
P.O. Box 536 (45359-0536)
PHONE.................................937 676-2376
Jerald Warner, *President*
EMP: 8
SQ FT: 10,000
SALES (est): 970.8K **Privately Held**
SIC: **7374** 3695 5099 Service bureau, computer; magnetic & optical recording media; compact discs

Pleasant Plain
Warren County

(G-16225)
DIESEL RECON SERVICE INC
2641 State Route 28 (45162-9627)
P.O. Box 329, Blanchester (45107-0329)
PHONE.................................513 625-1887
Randy Forbes, *President*
Teresa Forbes, *Vice Pres*
EMP: 4 EST: 1980
SQ FT: 6,000
SALES (est): 80K **Privately Held**
SIC: **2911** 7538 Diesel fuels; general automotive repair shops

(G-16226)
GOODWIN FARMS
10092 State Route 132 (45162-9100)
P.O. Box 190 (45162-0190)
PHONE.................................513 877-2636
Bruce Goodwin, *Partner*
Carole Goodwin, *Partner*
EMP: 5
SALES (est): 497.7K **Privately Held**
SIC: **0115** 0119 0111 3599 Corn; bean (dry field & seed) farm; wheat; machine & other job shop work

(G-16227)
HARTZ MOUNTAIN CORPORATION
Also Called: L M Animal Farms
5374 Long Spurling Rd (45162-9256)
P.O. Box 57 (45162-0057)
PHONE.................................513 877-2131
Chris Bryant, *Prdtn Mgr*
Larry Mohrfield, *Branch Mgr*
Russ Burton, *Manager*
Tracy Miller, *Director*
EMP: 75
SALES (corp-wide): 6.1B **Privately Held**
SIC: **2047** 3999 2048 2011 Cat food; dog food; pet supplies; prepared feeds
HQ: The Hartz Mountain Corporation
400 Plaza Dr Ste 400 # 400
Secaucus NJ 07094
800 275-1414

Pleasantville
Fairfield County

(G-16228)
METALS AND ADDITIVES CORP INC
Ohio Oxide
4850 Elder Rd Ne (43148-9729)
PHONE.................................740 654-6555
EMP: 13
SALES (corp-wide): 17.9MM **Privately Held**
SIC: **2819** Mfg Lead Oxide
PA: Metals And Additives, Llc
5929 Lakeside Blvd
Indianapolis IN 46278
317 290-5007

(G-16229)
OHIO OXIDE CORPORATION DEL
4850 Elder Rd Ne (43148-9729)
P.O. Box 1050, Lancaster (43130-0050)
PHONE.................................740 654-6555
EMP: 13
SQ FT: 15,000
SALES (est): 1.5MM **Privately Held**
SIC: **2819** Mfg Industrial Inorganic Chemicals

(G-16230)
SIGNATURE BEEF LLC
5500 Canal Rd Ne (43148-9752)
PHONE.................................740 468-3579
Brad Berry,
Mary Ann Berry,
EMP: 3
SALES (est): 251.5K **Privately Held**
SIC: **2011** Corned beef from meat slaughtered on site

Plymouth
Huron County

(G-16231)
FIRELANDS MANUFACTURING LLC
500 Industrial Park Dr (44865)
P.O. Box 45 (44865-0045)
PHONE..............................419 687-8237
Shawn Westmeister,
EMP: 15 **EST:** 2011
SALES (est): 2.4MM **Privately Held**
SIC: 3999 3548 Barber & beauty shop equipment; welding & cutting apparatus & accessories

(G-16232)
LESAGE MACHINE INC
5269 State Route 598 (44865-9603)
PHONE..............................419 687-0131
Ronald Lesage, *President*
Rita Lesage, *Manager*
EMP: 4
SQ FT: 6,400
SALES: 500K **Privately Held**
SIC: 3599 Machine shop, jobbing & repair

(G-16233)
POWER SHELF LLC
500 Industrial Park Dr (44865)
PHONE..............................419 775-6125
Lynn K L F Westmeister,
Shawn Westmeister,
EMP: 8
SQ FT: 15,000
SALES: 500K **Privately Held**
SIC: 3644 Noncurrent-carrying wiring services

(G-16234)
SAUDER MACHINE LTD
3071 State Route 603 (44865-9769)
PHONE..............................419 896-3722
Linus H Sauder, *Partner*
Timothy L Sauder,
EMP: 3
SQ FT: 3,000
SALES: 250K **Privately Held**
SIC: 3599 Machine shop, jobbing & repair

(G-16235)
WH FETZER & SONS MFG INC
500 Donnenwirth Dr (44865-1130)
P.O. Box 45 (44865-0045)
PHONE..............................419 687-8237
Fax: 419 687-5185
EMP: 30
SQ FT: 43,800
SALES (est): 6.5MM **Privately Held**
SIC: 3312 3993 3731 3524 Blast Furnace-Steel Work Mfg Signs/Ad Specialties Shipbuilding/Repairing Mfg Lawn/Garden Equip

Poland
Mahoning County

(G-16236)
ACME COMPANY
9495 Harvard Blvd (44514-3369)
PHONE..............................330 758-2313
Carmine Zarlenga Jr, *President*
Adam Lonardo, *Opers Mgr*
John M Newman, *Incorporator*
EMP: 60 **EST:** 1934
SQ FT: 10,000
SALES (est): 13.3MM **Privately Held**
SIC: 5032 3423 1422 3295 Sand, construction; hand & edge tools; crushed & broken limestone; minerals, ground or treated

(G-16237)
AKERS AMERICA INC
58 S Main St (44514-1978)
PHONE..............................330 757-4100
I Lundberg, *CEO*
William Bigley, *President*
Kjell Inestam, *Treasurer*
Tony Ferraro, *Admin Sec*
◆ **EMP:** 3 **EST:** 1975
SQ FT: 1,200
SALES (est): 552.4K
SALES (corp-wide): 419.4MM **Publicly Held**
SIC: 5051 3316 3312 Iron & steel (ferrous) products; cold finishing of steel shapes; blast furnaces & steel mills
HQ: Akers Sweden Ab
Bruksallen 4
Akers Styckebruk 647 5
159 321-00

(G-16238)
POLAND CONCRETE PRODUCTS INC (PA)
70 Poland Mnr (44514-2058)
P.O. Box 5146 (44514-0146)
PHONE..............................330 757-1241
Robert Zedaker Jr, *President*
David Zedaker, *Vice Pres*
Robert Zedeker III, *Vice Pres*
EMP: 3 **EST:** 1946
SQ FT: 25,000
SALES: 3MM **Privately Held**
SIC: 3272 Concrete products, precast; septic tanks, concrete; meter boxes, concrete; manhole covers or frames, concrete

(G-16239)
VIVO BROTHERS LLC
8420 South Ave (44514-3618)
PHONE..............................330 629-8686
Vince Vivo, *Principal*
Nick Vivo, *Vice Pres*
Vincent Vivo, *Vice Pres*
EMP: 10
SALES (est): 1.4MM **Privately Held**
WEB: www.vivobrothers.com
SIC: 2599 Cabinets, factory

Pomeroy
Meigs County

(G-16240)
FACEMYER LUMBER CO INC (PA)
31940 Bailey Run Rd (45769-9301)
P.O. Box 227, Middleport (45760-0227)
PHONE..............................740 992-5965
Eugene Facemyer, *Ch of Bd*
Leslie Facemyer, *Corp Secy*
Dennis Facemyer Jr, *Vice Pres*
▼ **EMP:** 61
SQ FT: 1,500
SALES: 2MM **Privately Held**
SIC: 2421 2411 Custom sawmill; kiln drying of lumber; veneer logs

(G-16241)
SENTINEL DAILY
109 W 2nd St (45769-1035)
PHONE..............................740 992-2155
Charlene Hoeflich, *Principal*
EMP: 6 **EST:** 2009
SALES (est): 204.5K **Privately Held**
SIC: 2711 Commercial printing & newspaper publishing combined; newspapers, publishing & printing

Port Clinton
Ottawa County

(G-16242)
ARES INC
818 Front St (43452)
PHONE..............................419 635-2175
Herb Roder, *President*
Ann Yamrick, *Vice Pres*
Drew Kertis, *Engineer*
Ann L Yamrick, *Financial Exec*
EMP: 56
SQ FT: 60,000
SALES (est): 10.4MM **Privately Held**
WEB: www.ares.com
SIC: 3443 3482 3484 3489 Fabricated plate work (boiler shop); small arms ammunition; small arms; ordnance & accessories; motors & generators

(G-16243)
BAY AREA PRODUCTS INC
4942 W Fremont Rd (43452-9470)
PHONE..............................419 732-2147
Chuck Heiges, *President*
Dawn Mc Nulty, *Director*
EMP: 6
SQ FT: 3,000
SALES: 175K **Privately Held**
SIC: 3949 Fishing equipment; game calls

(G-16244)
CATAWBA ISLAND BREWING CO
2330 East Harbor Rd (43452-1517)
PHONE..............................419 960-7764
Herbert Roder, *President*
Michael J Roder, *President*
Shad Gunderson, *Treasurer*
EMP: 8
SALES (est): 556.7K **Privately Held**
SIC: 2085 Cocktails, alcoholic

(G-16245)
CUSTOM MARINE CANVAS TRAINING
250 Se Catawba Rd Ste C (43452-2674)
PHONE..............................419 732-8362
Roger Griffin,
Russ Griffin,
EMP: 4 **EST:** 2010
SALES: 800K **Privately Held**
SIC: 2211 Canvas

(G-16246)
D & L EXCAVATING LTD
969 N Rymers Rd (43452-9437)
PHONE..............................419 271-0635
Darryl Trent, *Principal*
EMP: 6
SALES (est): 393.2K **Privately Held**
SIC: 3531 Buckets, excavating: clamshell, concrete, dragline, etc.

(G-16247)
FENNER DUNLOP PORT CLINTON INC
5225 W Lakeshore Dr (43452-9285)
PHONE..............................419 635-2191
David Hurd, *President*
Cassandra Pan, *President*
Ben Ficklen, *Corp Secy*
Bill Mooney, *CFO*
▲ **EMP:** 115
SQ FT: 200,000
SALES (est): 35.8MM
SALES (corp-wide): 855.1MM **Privately Held**
SIC: 3069 3535 Medical & laboratory rubber sundries & related products; bucket type conveyor systems
HQ: Fenner Dunlop Americas, Llc
1000 Omega Dr Ste 1400
Pittsburgh PA 15205

(G-16248)
GREAT LAKES POPCORN COMPANY
60 Madison St (43452-1102)
PHONE..............................419 732-3080
Bill Yuhasz, *President*
EMP: 6
SQ FT: 4,000
SALES (est): 370K **Privately Held**
WEB: www.greatlakespopcorn.com
SIC: 2099 2064 5441 Popcorn, packaged: except already popped; nuts, glace; candy, nut & confectionery stores

(G-16249)
LAKECRAFT INC (PA)
1010 W Lakeshore Dr (43452-9564)
PHONE..............................419 734-2828
Samuel J Conte, *President*
Keith Conte, *Manager*
Beth Bieggert, *Administration*
EMP: 9 **EST:** 1940
SQ FT: 15,000
SALES (est): 1.2MM **Privately Held**
WEB: www.lakecraft.com
SIC: 3599 7692 3561 Machine shop, jobbing & repair; welding repair; pumps, domestic: water or sump

(G-16250)
LOADMASTER TRAILER COMPANY
Also Called: Loadmaster Trailers Mfg
2354 East Harbor Rd (43452-1517)
PHONE..............................419 732-3434
Gary Straw, *President*
Diane Straw, *President*
EMP: 13
SQ FT: 12,000
SALES (est): 2.4MM **Privately Held**
WEB: www.loadmastertrailerco.com
SIC: 3799 7699 Boat trailers; nautical repair services

(G-16251)
LUC ICE INC
728 S Railroad St (43452-2063)
PHONE..............................419 734-2201
Michael Luc, *President*
Paul Luc, *Vice Pres*
EMP: 7
SQ FT: 11,000
SALES (est): 892K **Privately Held**
SIC: 2097 Block ice; ice cubes

(G-16252)
MARINEMAX INC
1991 Ne Catawba Rd (43452-3523)
PHONE..............................918 782-3277
Jim Conner, *Branch Mgr*
EMP: 112
SALES (corp-wide): 1.1B **Publicly Held**
SIC: 5551 3732 Motor boat dealers; boat building & repairing
PA: Marinemax, Inc.
2600 Mccormick Dr Ste 200
Clearwater FL 33759
727 531-1700

(G-16253)
MINDERMAN MARINE PRODUCTS INC
129 Buckeye Blvd (43452-1419)
PHONE..............................419 732-2626
Stuart Ghan, *President*
Kenneth J Berger, *Vice Pres*
EMP: 5
SQ FT: 13,100
SALES (est): 704K **Privately Held**
WEB: www.mindermanmarine.com
SIC: 7699 3429 5551 Marine propeller repair; marine hardware; marine supplies & equipment

(G-16254)
NORTH COAST BUSINESS JOURNAL
205 Se Catawba Rd Ste G (43452-2669)
PHONE..............................419 734-4838
John Schaffner, *President*
Dave Kahler, *Director*
EMP: 5
SALES (est): 214.9K **Privately Held**
WEB: www.ncbj.net
SIC: 2711 Newspapers: publishing only, not printed on site

(G-16255)
PORT CLINTON MANUFACTURING LLC
328 W Perry St (43452-1035)
P.O. Box 220 (43452-0220)
PHONE..............................419 734-2141
Daniel Stott, *President*
Jane Stott, *Vice Pres*
David Courtright, *HR Admin*
EMP: 25 **EST:** 1928
SQ FT: 67,000
SALES: 3.1MM **Privately Held**
WEB: www.pcmfg.net
SIC: 3451 Screw machine products

(G-16256)
QUIKSTIR INC
Also Called: Quikspray
2105 W Lakeshore Dr (43452-9485)
P.O. Box 327 (43452-0327)
PHONE..............................419 732-2601
Thomas P Mc Ritchie, *President*
T Park Mc Ritchie, *Admin Sec*
Cindy Riley, *Assistant*
EMP: 12 **EST:** 1954
SQ FT: 6,000

Port Clinton - Ottawa County (G-16257)

SALES (est): 1.2MM *Privately Held*
SIC: 3561 3563 3531 Pumps & pumping equipment; spraying outfits: metals, paints & chemicals (compressor); mixers: ore, plaster, slag, sand, mortar, etc.

(G-16257)
SAFE 4 PEOPLE INC
4661 E Woodland Dr (43452-3142)
PHONE..................................419 797-4087
Carole Fleming, *President*
Thomas Fleming, *Vice Pres*
EMP: 5
SALES (est): 400.8K *Privately Held*
WEB: www.safe4people.com
SIC: 3999 5122 5999 Hair & hair-based products; cosmetics; cosmetics

(G-16258)
SCHAFFNER PUBLICATION INC
Also Called: Beacon, The
205 Se Catawba Rd Ste G (43452-2669)
PHONE..................................419 732-2154
John Schaffner, *President*
Malisha McNabb, *General Mgr*
Mary Alice Schaffner, *Vice Pres*
Tina Britt, *Manager*
EMP: 20
SQ FT: 4,000
SALES (est): 3MM *Privately Held*
WEB: www.thebeacon.net
SIC: 2759 Publication printing

(G-16259)
SCRAMBL-GRAM INC
Also Called: Last Word, The
5225 W Lkshore Dr Ste 340 (43452)
P.O. Box 577 (43452-0577)
PHONE..................................419 635-2321
Scott Bowers, *President*
EMP: 12 EST: 1978
SQ FT: 5,500
SALES (est): 1.2MM *Privately Held*
WEB: www.scrambl-gram.com
SIC: 3944 5945 2741 Board games, puzzles & models, except electronic; hobby, toy & game shops; miscellaneous publishing

(G-16260)
STEVEN NICKEL
3117 E Shore Dr (43452-2748)
PHONE..................................419 732-3377
Steven Nickel, *Principal*
EMP: 3
SALES (est): 213.3K *Privately Held*
SIC: 3356 Nickel

(G-16261)
SURFACE-ALL INC
745 N Hidden Harbor Dr (43452-3744)
PHONE..................................440 428-2233
Richard Duhane, *Principal*
Clair Waid, *Vice Pres*
EMP: 3
SALES (est): 308.6K *Privately Held*
SIC: 2952 Asphalt felts & coatings

(G-16262)
TACK-ANEW INC
Also Called: Brands' Marina
451 W Lakeshore Dr (43452-9478)
PHONE..................................419 734-4212
Dalton Brand, *President*
Darrell A Brand, *President*
EMP: 26
SQ FT: 15,000
SALES (est): 2MM *Privately Held*
WEB: www.brandsmarina.com
SIC: 4493 3731 Boat yards, storage & incidental repair; shipbuilding & repairing

(G-16263)
TIMELY TOURS INC
141 Maple St Ste A (43452-1347)
PHONE..................................419 734-3751
Ralph Burnstine, *Manager*
EMP: 3
SALES (est): 292.2K
SALES (corp-wide): 402.1K *Privately Held*
SIC: 2752 Commercial printing, offset
PA: Timely Tours Inc
  797 Ne Catawba Rd
  Port Clinton OH 43452
  419 797-2569

(G-16264)
WILLIAM J DUPPS
Also Called: Dupps Printing and Supply Co
126 Madison St (43452-1104)
P.O. Box 756 (43452-0756)
PHONE..................................419 734-2126
Fax: 419 732-3256
EMP: 5
SQ FT: 3,000
SALES (est): 360K *Privately Held*
SIC: 2752 5044 5021 5112 Lithographic Coml Print Office Equipment Furniture Stationery/Offc Sup Bookbinding/Related Work

---

Port Jefferson
Shelby County

(G-16265)
MCCRARY METAL POLISHING INC
207 Pasco Montra Rd (45360)
P.O. Box 190 (45360-0190)
PHONE..................................937 492-1979
James P McCrary Jr, *President*
Shirley Mc Crary, *Vice Pres*
▲ EMP: 19
SQ FT: 4,800
SALES (est): 3.3MM *Privately Held*
SIC: 3471 3599 Polishing, metals or formed products; machine shop, jobbing & repair

(G-16266)
TECHNIMOLD PLUS INC
102 Wall St (45360-1105)
PHONE..................................937 492-4077
Greg Jones, *President*
EMP: 3
SQ FT: 1,500
SALES (est): 275K *Privately Held*
SIC: 3089 Injection molding of plastics

Port Washington
Tuscarawas County

(G-16267)
BATES METAL PRODUCTS INC
403 E Mn St (43837)
P.O. Box 68 (43837-0068)
PHONE..................................740 498-8371
James A Bates, *President*
Betty Bates, *Corp Secy*
Terry L Bates, *Vice Pres*
EMP: 60 EST: 1956
SQ FT: 106,500
SALES (est): 15.4MM *Privately Held*
WEB: www.batesmetal.com
SIC: 4783 2542 3993 3469 Packing & crating; racks, merchandise display or storage: except wood; signs & advertising specialties; metal stampings; automotive & apparel trimmings

(G-16268)
DESIGNER STONE CO
303 E Main St (43837-9704)
PHONE..................................740 492-1300
Darren Galbraith, *President*
Dan Armstrong, *Manager*
Lisa Massner, *Admin Sec*
▲ EMP: 8
SALES (est): 1MM *Privately Held*
SIC: 1411 Granite dimension stone

Portage
Wood County

(G-16269)
J D HYDRAULIC INC
Rr 25 (43451)
P.O. Box 188 (43451-0188)
PHONE..................................419 686-5234
James Simon, *President*
EMP: 13
SQ FT: 12,000
SALES (est): 2.1MM *Privately Held*
SIC: 3593 Fluid power cylinders, hydraulic or pneumatic

(G-16270)
LABORIE ENTERPRISES LLC
10892 S Dixie Hwy (43451-9798)
PHONE..................................419 686-6245
Larry C Smith, *Partner*
Douglas Laborie, *Partner*
Edith Laborie, *Partner*
Ronald Laborie, *Partner*
EMP: 7
SQ FT: 10,000
SALES (est): 472.3K *Privately Held*
SIC: 5211 2431 Millwork & lumber; moldings, wood: unfinished & prefinished

(G-16271)
MORLOCK ASPHALT LTD
9362 Merrmill Rd (43451-9729)
PHONE..................................419 686-4601
Tony Morlock, *Mng Member*
EMP: 10
SALES (est): 1.1MM *Privately Held*
SIC: 1611 3541 Surfacing & paving; milling machines

(G-16272)
OGDEN HYDRAULICS LLC
396 W Main St (43451-9788)
P.O. Box 236 (43451-0236)
PHONE..................................419 686-1108
Richard Ogden,
EMP: 3
SALES (est): 500K *Privately Held*
WEB: www.ogdenhydraulics.com
SIC: 3569 Bridge or gate machinery, hydraulic

(G-16273)
PALMER BROS TRANSIT MIX CON
Also Called: Precision Aggregates
12580 Greensburg Pike (43451-9755)
PHONE..................................419 686-2366
Will Smelts, *Manager*
EMP: 10
SALES (corp-wide): 7MM *Privately Held*
SIC: 3273 5032 Ready-mixed concrete; stone, crushed or broken
PA: Palmer Bros Transit Mix Concrete Inc
  12205 E Gypsy Lane Rd
  Bowling Green OH 43402
  419 352-4681

(G-16274)
STONECO INC
11580 S Dixie Hwy (43451-9757)
PHONE..................................419 686-3311
Lee Wehner, *Manager*
EMP: 7
SALES (corp-wide): 29.7B *Privately Held*
WEB: www.stoneco.net
SIC: 1429 Igneous rock, crushed & broken-quarrying
HQ: Stoneco, Inc.
  1700 Fostoria Ave Ste 200
  Findlay OH 45840
  419 422-8854

Portland
Meigs County

(G-16275)
CRAIG SAYLOR
53020 State Route 124 (45770-9768)
PHONE..................................740 352-8363
Craig Saylor, *Principal*
EMP: 3
SALES (est): 144.9K *Privately Held*
SIC: 2411 Logging

Portsmouth
Scioto County

(G-16276)
A SPECIAL TOUCH EMBROIDERY LLC
22326 State Route 73 (45663-6365)
PHONE..................................740 858-2241
Kim Hoyme,
James Hoyme,
Travis Hoyme,
EMP: 4
SALES (est): 400K *Privately Held*
WEB: www.s-t-e.net
SIC: 2759 Screen printing

(G-16277)
APPALACHIAN WOOD FLOORS INC
Also Called: Graf Custom Hardwood
838 Campbell Ave (45662-4561)
PHONE..................................740 354-4572
James W Graf, *President*
John Nichols, *Vice Pres*
Michael Coriell, *CFO*
Heath Chamberlin, *Sales Staff*
Will Pachan, *Sales Staff*
EMP: 80
SQ FT: 175,000
SALES (est): 5.8MM *Privately Held*
WEB: www.appalachianwoodfloors.com
SIC: 2491 Wood preserving

(G-16278)
BICKETT MACHINE AND SUPPLY INC
1411 Robinson Ave (45662-3508)
P.O. Box 698 (45662-0698)
PHONE..................................740 353-5710
Frank M Coburn, *President*
Maureen Coburn, *Vice Pres*
Eric Lewis, *Manager*
EMP: 8 EST: 1948
SQ FT: 7,500
SALES (est): 1.5MM *Privately Held*
WEB: www.bicketts.com
SIC: 5084 3599 Welding machinery & equipment; machine shop, jobbing & repair

(G-16279)
BIG IRON GUNS INC
1712 11th St (45662-4528)
PHONE..................................740 464-0852
Christopher Ponzio, *Principal*
Savanah Whitt, *Admin Sec*
EMP: 3 EST: 2015
SALES (est): 166.5K *Privately Held*
SIC: 3482 Shotgun ammunition: empty, blank or loaded

(G-16280)
COCA-COLA BOTTLING CO CNSLD
5050 Old Scioto Trl (45662-6461)
PHONE..................................740 353-3133
Tony Burns, *Principal*
EMP: 21
SALES (corp-wide): 4.6B *Publicly Held*
WEB: www.colasic.net
SIC: 2086 Bottled & canned soft drinks
PA: Coca-Cola Consolidated, Inc.
  4100 Coca Cola Plz # 100
  Charlotte NC 28211
  704 557-4400

(G-16281)
DELMAR E HICKS (PA)
Also Called: South Shore Gas & Oil
2310 A St (45662)
P.O. Box 1068 (45662-1068)
PHONE..................................740 354-4333
Delmar E Hicks, *Owner*
EMP: 1
SALES (est): 1.5MM *Privately Held*
SIC: 8072 5411 1382 Dental laboratories; convenience stores; oil & gas exploration services

GEOGRAPHIC SECTION

(G-16282)
FANTASTIC SAMS HAIR CARE SALON
4490 Gallia St (45662-5553)
PHONE..................................740 456-4296
Shana Dunn, *Owner*
Dan Brisker, *Owner*
EMP: 7
SALES (est): 38.5K **Privately Held**
SIC: 7231 2844 Unisex hair salons; hair coloring preparations

(G-16283)
GENOA HEALTHCARE
901 Washington St (45662-3944)
PHONE..................................740 370-0759
Ryan Neimeyer, *Controller*
EMP: 5 EST: 2015
SALES (est): 422.7K **Privately Held**
SIC: 2834 Pharmaceutical preparations

(G-16284)
GRACIE PLUM INVESTMENTS INC
609 2nd St Unit 2 (45662-3974)
PHONE..................................740 355-9029
Francesca G Hartop, *CEO*
Aaron Prose, *Vice Pres*
Nancy Prose, *Controller*
▼ EMP: 27
SQ FT: 3,150
SALES (est): 4.3MM **Privately Held**
WEB: www.yostengineering.com
SIC: 7372 7374 7371 Application computer software; data processing & preparation; custom computer programming services

(G-16285)
HANGER PRSTHETCS & ORTHO INC
Also Called: Hanger Clinic
1611 27th St Ste 303 (45662-6932)
PHONE..................................740 354-4775
David Stephens, *Manager*
EMP: 4
SALES (corp-wide): 1B **Publicly Held**
SIC: 8071 3842 Medical laboratories; surgical appliances & supplies
HQ: Hanger Prosthetics & Orthotics, Inc.
10910 Domain Dr Ste 300
Austin TX 78758
512 777-3800

(G-16286)
KEYSTONE PRINTING & COPY CAT
Also Called: Copy Cat Printing
842 4th St (45662-4312)
P.O. Box 174 (45662-0174)
PHONE..................................740 354-6542
John Cooper, *Owner*
Stephanie Howerton, *Director*
EMP: 5
SALES (est): 381.7K **Privately Held**
SIC: 2759 2752 2791 2789 Commercial printing; commercial printing, lithographic; typesetting; bookbinding & related work

(G-16287)
KOPPERS IND INC
400 Harding Ave (45662)
PHONE..................................740 776-2149
Merle Klink, *Principal*
EMP: 3
SALES (est): 243K **Privately Held**
SIC: 2421 Railroad ties, sawed

(G-16288)
KOPPERS INDUSTRIES INC
6501 Pershing Ave (45662-7502)
P.O. Box 4039 (45662-2039)
PHONE..................................740 776-3238
Dick Burke, *Plant Mgr*
EMP: 45
SALES (corp-wide): 1.7B **Publicly Held**
SIC: 3272 2421 Concrete products; sawmills & planing mills, general
HQ: Koppers Industries Of Delaware Inc.
436 7th Ave Ste 2026
Pittsburgh PA 15219

(G-16289)
KSA LIMITED PARTNERSHIP
6501 Pershing Ave (45662-7502)
PHONE..................................740 776-3238
Frank Anderson III, *Partner*
Tom Lodeman, *Partner*
EMP: 40
SALES (est): 4MM **Privately Held**
SIC: 3272 Ties, railroad: concrete

(G-16290)
MCGOVNEY READY MIX INC
Also Called: McGovney River Terminal
55 River Ave (45662-4712)
P.O. Box 510 (45662-0510)
PHONE..................................740 353-4111
Carolyn Kegley, *President*
Debra Coburn, *Corp Secy*
David Kegley, *Vice Pres*
Rhett Hadsell, *Opers Mgr*
EMP: 20
SQ FT: 1,200
SALES (est): 3MM **Privately Held**
WEB: www.mcgovney.com
SIC: 3273 Ready-mixed concrete

(G-16291)
MITCHELLACE INC (PA)
830 Murray St (45662-4515)
P.O. Box 89 (45662-0089)
PHONE..................................740 354-2813
Kerry W Keating, *Ch of Bd*
Steven Keating, *President*
Ryan Bouts, *VP Opers*
Ruth Ann Carter, *Purch Dir*
Tom Keating, *Treasurer*
▲ EMP: 33 EST: 1902
SQ FT: 365,000
SALES (est): 6MM **Privately Held**
WEB: www.mitchellace.com
SIC: 2241 Shoe laces, except leather; braids, textile; cotton narrow fabrics

(G-16292)
MP PRINTING & DESIGN INC
4302 Gallia St (45662-5515)
PHONE..................................740 456-2045
Eddie F Marshall, *President*
EMP: 5
SALES (est): 277K **Privately Held**
SIC: 2752 Commercial printing, lithographic

(G-16293)
OSCO INDUSTRIES INC (PA)
Also Called: Portsmouth Division
734 11th St (45662-3407)
P.O. Box 1388 (45662-1388)
PHONE..................................740 354-3183
William J Burke, *Ch of Bd*
John M Burke, *President*
Tom Brower, *General Mgr*
Jeffrey A Burke, *Senior VP*
Keith Denny, *Vice Pres*
◆ EMP: 285 EST: 1872
SQ FT: 150,000
SALES (est): 90.2MM **Privately Held**
WEB: www.oscoind.com
SIC: 3321 Gray iron castings

(G-16294)
P&M PUBLISHING
2225 8th St (45662-4737)
P.O. Box 248 (45662-0248)
PHONE..................................740 353-3300
Aaron Bennett, *Principal*
EMP: 4
SALES (est): 303.3K **Privately Held**
SIC: 2741 Miscellaneous publishing

(G-16295)
PORTSMOUTH BLOCK INC
Also Called: Portsmouth Block & Brick
2700 Gallia St (45662-4807)
PHONE..................................740 353-4113
Glenn Coriell, *President*
Kevin Coriell, *Vice Pres*
Rob Coriell, *Manager*
Mildred Coriell, *Admin Sec*
EMP: 11
SQ FT: 100,000
SALES (est): 1.6MM **Privately Held**
SIC: 3271 5211 Blocks, concrete or cinder: standard; lumber & other building materials

(G-16296)
PREMIER KITES & DESIGNS INC
1004 Findlay St (45662-3446)
PHONE..................................888 416-0174
EMP: 5 **Privately Held**
SIC: 3944 Kites
HQ: Premier Kites & Designs Inc
5200 Lawrence Pl
Hyattsville MD 20781
301 277-3888

(G-16297)
RUSH WELDING & MACHINE INC
1657 12th St (45662-4535)
P.O. Box 208 (45662-0208)
PHONE..................................740 354-7874
Tim Rush, *President*
EMP: 3
SALES (est): 200K **Privately Held**
SIC: 7692 Welding repair

(G-16298)
SAVORY FOODS INC
2240 6th St (45662-4787)
P.O. Box 1604 (45662-1604)
PHONE..................................740 354-6655
James Speak, *President*
EMP: 58 EST: 1946
SQ FT: 40,000
SALES (est): 13.6MM
SALES (corp-wide): 1.8B **Privately Held**
SIC: 2096 Pork rinds
HQ: Evans Food Group Ltd.
4118 S Halsted St
Chicago IL 60609
773 254-7400

(G-16299)
SIMPSON BROTHERS MACHINE WORKS
2204 Gallia St (45662-4761)
PHONE..................................740 353-6870
George Simpson, *President*
Frank Simpson, *Vice Pres*
EMP: 4
SQ FT: 14,100
SALES (est): 330K **Privately Held**
SIC: 3599 Machine shop, jobbing & repair

(G-16300)
SISSEL LOGGING LLC
69 Pond Lick Rd (45663-8899)
PHONE..................................740 858-4613
Michael Sissel, *Principal*
EMP: 3
SALES (est): 192.3K **Privately Held**
SIC: 2411 Logging

(G-16301)
SNYDER PRINTING LLC
Also Called: Snyder Printing & Signs
1552 Gallia St (45662-4509)
PHONE..................................740 353-3947
Brooks Snyder, *Mng Member*
EMP: 3
SALES (est): 305.9K **Privately Held**
SIC: 2759 5099 Screen printing; signs, except electric

(G-16302)
SOLE CHOICE INC
830 Murray St (45662-4515)
P.O. Box 89 (45662-0089)
PHONE..................................740 354-2813
Nelson K Smith, *Chairman*
Bryan K Davis, *Vice Pres*
Mary Hobstetter, *Opers Mgr*
Ryan B Bouts, *CFO*
Robin Swick, *Controller*
▲ EMP: 30
SALES (est): 4.8MM **Privately Held**
SIC: 2241 Shoe laces, except leather; braids, textile; cotton narrow fabrics

(G-16303)
TOM BARBOUR AUTO PARTS INC (PA)
915 11th St (45662-3410)
PHONE..................................740 354-4654
Josephine Flannery, *President*
Michael Flannery, *Vice Pres*
EMP: 12
SQ FT: 12,000
SALES (est): 8.9MM **Privately Held**
WEB: www.barbourauto.com
SIC: 5531 3599 Automotive parts; machine shop, jobbing & repair

(G-16304)
TRI STATE COUNTERTOP SERVICE
3350 Indian Dr (45662-2409)
PHONE..................................740 354-3663
David Malone, *President*
EMP: 7
SALES: 450K **Privately Held**
SIC: 2511 Kitchen & dining room furniture

(G-16305)
YOST LABS INC
630 2nd St (45662-3902)
PHONE..................................740 876-4936
Greg Merril, *Principal*
Lowell Morrison, *CFO*
Paul Yost, *CTO*
EMP: 16
SALES (est): 855.7K **Privately Held**
SIC: 3812 Search & navigation equipment

Powell
Delaware County

(G-16306)
ACTIS LTD
Also Called: Surgeye
3841b Attucks Dr (43065-6082)
PHONE..................................614 436-0600
Jerry K Mueller Jr, *Principal*
EMP: 4
SALES (est): 22K **Privately Held**
SIC: 3841 Surgical & medical instruments

(G-16307)
ADVANCED INDUS MACHINING INC (PA)
3982 Powell Rd Ste 218 (43065-7662)
PHONE..................................614 596-4183
Morgan Koth, *President*
EMP: 16
SQ FT: 3,600
SALES (est): 1.7MM **Privately Held**
SIC: 1629 3599 Industrial plant construction; amusement park equipment

(G-16308)
ALLERGAN INC
4321 Scioto Pkwy (43065-8056)
PHONE..................................614 623-8140
EMP: 51 **Privately Held**
SIC: 2834 Drugs acting on the central nervous system & sense organs
HQ: Allergan, Inc.
5 Giralda Farms
Madison NJ 07940
862 261-7000

(G-16309)
BUCKEYE VOLLEYBALL CENTER LLC
7824 Maplecreek Ct (43065-9297)
PHONE..................................614 764-1075
Steve Yates, *Principal*
EMP: 3
SALES (est): 287.7K **Privately Held**
SIC: 2273 Carpets & rugs

(G-16310)
BUILDING CTRL INTEGRATORS LLC (PA)
Also Called: B C I
383 N Liberty St (43065-8388)
PHONE..................................614 334-3300
Jim McClintock, *Regional Mgr*
Keith North, *Project Mgr*
Nikki Lawler, *Opers Mgr*
Adam Sleeper, *Engineer*
Kristi Laurent, *Accounting Mgr*
EMP: 31
SQ FT: 20,000
SALES (est): 17.1MM **Privately Held**
WEB: www.bcicontrols.com
SIC: 3822 Temperature controls, automatic

Powell - Delaware County (G-16311)

(G-16311)
CANVAS SALON AND SKIN BAR
3893 Powell Rd (43065-7983)
PHONE 614 336-3942
Stefanie M Fox, *Principal*
EMP: 4
SALES (est): 392.2K **Privately Held**
SIC: 2211 Canvas

(G-16312)
CAPITAL CITY ENERGY GROUP INC
3789 Attucks Dr (43065-6080)
PHONE 614 485-3110
Todd E Crawford, *Ch of Bd*
Timothy S Shear, *President*
William D Faith, *Treasurer*
EMP: 3
SALES (est): 675.2K **Privately Held**
SIC: 1382 Oil & gas exploration services

(G-16313)
CARBONKLEAN LLC
24 Village Pointe Dr (43065-7760)
PHONE 614 980-9515
Daniel Patton, *CEO*
EMP: 7
SQ FT: 5,000
SALES (est): 895.5K **Privately Held**
SIC: 2842 Specialty cleaning preparations

(G-16314)
CARDIAC ANALYTICS LLC
5683 Liberty Rd N (43065-8996)
PHONE 614 314-1332
Dan McFarland, *President*
EMP: 10
SALES: 100K **Privately Held**
SIC: 3845 Electromedical equipment

(G-16315)
CARVED STONE LLC
Also Called: Carved N Stone
505 Village Park Dr (43065-6606)
PHONE 614 778-9855
Kareem Kashmiry, *President*
EMP: 3 EST: 2015
SALES (est): 252.1K **Privately Held**
SIC: 3479 Etching & engraving

(G-16316)
CATALYSIS ADDITIVE TOOLING LLC
35 Clairedan Dr (43065-8064)
PHONE 614 715-3674
Darrell Stafford, *Principal*
EMP: 8
SQ FT: 10,000
SALES: 750K **Privately Held**
SIC: 3544 Forms (molds), for foundry & plastics working machinery

(G-16317)
COLUMBUS OILFIELD EXPLORATION
Also Called: Columbus Oil Field Exploration
80 Grace Dr Ste G (43065-9315)
PHONE 614 895-9520
EMP: 2
SALES: 2.4MM **Privately Held**
SIC: 1381 1382 Oil/Gas Well Drilling Oil/Gas Exploration Services

(G-16318)
CONTINENTAL GL SLS & INV GROUP
Also Called: Continental Group
315 Ashmoore Ct (43065-7486)
P.O. Box 1764 (43065-1764)
PHONE 614 679-1201
Sean Snyder, *Partner*
Chris Snyder, *Partner*
Mark McClain, *Vice Pres*
▲ EMP: 400
SQ FT: 100,000
SALES (est): 33.7MM **Privately Held**
SIC: 3441 7011 3211 Fabricated structural metal; hotels; structural glass

(G-16319)
CRYSTAL CARVERS INC
4040 Essex Ct (43065-7775)
PHONE 800 365-9782
Brad Uhl, *President*
Jennifer Uhl, *Vice Pres*
EMP: 4
SALES (est): 125K **Privately Held**
WEB: www.crystalcarversinc.com
SIC: 3423 Cutters, glass

(G-16320)
D-TERRA SOLUTIONS LLC
35 Clairedan Dr (43065-8064)
PHONE 614 450-1040
Denis Bruncak, *CEO*
▲ EMP: 7 EST: 2012
SALES (est): 1.3MM **Privately Held**
SIC: 3714 Motor vehicle parts & accessories

(G-16321)
EYESCIENCE LABS LLC
493 Village Park Dr (43065-6605)
PHONE 614 885-7100
Jeffrey Northup, *Mng Member*
EMP: 7 EST: 2007
SQ FT: 7,000
SALES: 1.6MM **Privately Held**
SIC: 2834 Vitamin preparations

(G-16322)
GFS CHEMICALS INC (PA)
3041 Home Rd (43065-9710)
P.O. Box 245 (43065-0245)
PHONE 740 881-5501
J Steel Hutchinson, *President*
M Robert Pierron, *Vice Pres*
Rob Pierron, *VP Prdtn*
Walters Jamie, *Purch Agent*
Daniel Ewald, *QC Mgr*
◆ EMP: 20 EST: 1928
SQ FT: 125,000
SALES (est): 23.6MM **Privately Held**
WEB: www.gfschemicals.com
SIC: 2819 2899 2869 2812 Chemicals, reagent grade: refined from technical grade; chemical preparations; industrial organic chemicals; alkalies & chlorine

(G-16323)
HEALTHEDGE SOFTWARE INC
50 S Liberty St Ste 200 (43065-4006)
PHONE 614 431-3711
Nancy Riley, *Principal*
EMP: 5
SALES (est): 207K **Privately Held**
SIC: 7372 Business oriented computer software

(G-16324)
KELLY CABINET COMPANY LLC
525 Thrush Rill Ct (43065-9781)
PHONE 614 563-2971
Christopher J Kelly, *Principal*
EMP: 6
SALES (est): 309.5K **Privately Held**
SIC: 2434 Wood kitchen cabinets

(G-16325)
KRAFT HOUSE NO 5
5 S Liberty St (43065-9301)
PHONE 614 396-9091
EMP: 4
SALES (est): 281.4K **Privately Held**
SIC: 2022 Mfg Cheese

(G-16326)
L E P D INDUSTRIES LTD
2292 Clairborne Dr (43065-8630)
PHONE 614 985-1470
Eric S Delbert, *Principal*
EMP: 3
SALES (est): 248.7K **Privately Held**
SIC: 3999 Manufacturing industries

(G-16327)
LAPCRAFT INC
195 W Olentangy St Unit A (43065-8720)
P.O. Box 389 (43065-0389)
PHONE 614 764-8993
Steve Ussery, *President*
Christina Ussery, *Treasurer*
EMP: 5
SQ FT: 7,500
SALES (est): 663.9K **Privately Held**
WEB: www.lapcraft.com
SIC: 3915 5085 Jewel preparing: instruments, tools, watches & jewelry; industrial supplies

(G-16328)
MICHELE MELLEN
Also Called: Jbm Enterprises
5680 Liberty Rd N (43065-9718)
PHONE 740 369-1422
Michelle Mellen, *Owner*
EMP: 4
SALES (est): 264.2K **Privately Held**
SIC: 3581 Automatic vending machines

(G-16329)
MILLWOOD INC
9743 Fairway Dr (43065-6947)
PHONE 614 717-9099
William Snashall, *Sales Mgr*
EMP: 4 **Privately Held**
SIC: 3565 Packaging machinery
PA: Millwood, Inc.
3708 International Blvd
Vienna OH 44473

(G-16330)
MORGAN WOOD PRODUCTS INC
9761 Fairway Dr (43065-6947)
P.O. Box 177 (43065-0177)
PHONE 614 336-4000
Luke Reinstetle, *President*
Joey Cmehil, *Manager*
◆ EMP: 12
SQ FT: 4,000
SALES: 30MM **Privately Held**
SIC: 2448 Pallets, wood

(G-16331)
NEW PATH INTERNATIONAL LLC
1476 Manning Pkwy Ste A (43065-7295)
PHONE 614 410-3974
Damon Canfield, *Mng Member*
Neil Macivor,
▲ EMP: 50
SQ FT: 13,000
SALES (est): 8.1MM **Privately Held**
WEB: www.npi.com
SIC: 3639 7389 8711 Major kitchen appliances, except refrigerators & stoves; design, commercial & industrial; engineering services

(G-16332)
PHARMCUTICAL DEV SOLUTIONS LLC
7116 Vista Creek Ct (43065-7167)
PHONE 732 766-5222
Krishan Kumar, *Principal*
EMP: 2
SALES (est): 194.8K **Privately Held**
SIC: 2834 Pharmaceutical preparations

(G-16333)
POWELL VILLAGE WINERY LLC
50 S Liberty St (43065-6062)
P.O. Box 246 (43065-0246)
PHONE 614 290-5898
Jeffrey D Kirby, *Principal*
EMP: 3
SALES (est): 331K **Privately Held**
SIC: 2084 Wines

(G-16334)
RANDYS COUNTERTOPS INC
3208 Home Rd (43065-9757)
PHONE 740 881-5831
Randolph Schirtzinger Sr, *President*
Mike Schirtzinger, *Vice Pres*
Reva Schirtzinger, *Admin Sec*
EMP: 13
SQ FT: 72,000
SALES (est): 1.5MM **Privately Held**
SIC: 2541 Counters or counter display cases, wood; sink tops, plastic laminated

(G-16335)
SIGN A RAMA INC
Also Called: Sign-A-Rama
3960 Presidential Pkwy A (43065-9033)
PHONE 614 932-7005
Craig Snider, *Manager*
EMP: 4
SALES (corp-wide): 92.3MM **Privately Held**
WEB: www.franchisemart.com
SIC: 3993 7389 Signs & advertising specialties; lettering & sign painting services
HQ: Sign A Rama Inc.
2121 Vista Pkwy
West Palm Beach FL 33411
561 640-5570

(G-16336)
STELLA LOU LLC
Also Called: Coldstone Creamery
3939 Hickory Rock Dr (43065-7333)
PHONE 937 935-9536
Joshua Klinger, *Mng Member*
EMP: 16 EST: 2014
SQ FT: 1,200
SALES: 3MM **Privately Held**
SIC: 5812 2024 Ice cream stands or dairy bars; ice cream & frozen desserts

(G-16337)
SUCCESS TECHNOLOGIES INC
Also Called: Stronghold Construction
35 Grace Dr (43065-9332)
PHONE 614 761-0008
Doug Kuepfer, *President*
Dori Kuepfer, *Corp Secy*
Paige Barrow, *Director*
EMP: 8
SQ FT: 12,000
SALES (est): 1.4MM **Privately Held**
SIC: 2599 5099 5722 2824 Beds, not household use; tanning salon equipment & supplies; suntanning equipment & supplies; acrylic fibers

(G-16338)
SUMMIT ONLINE PRODUCTS LLC
Also Called: Massageblocks.com
3982 Powell Rd Ste 137 (43065-7662)
PHONE 800 326-1972
Lesa Zoldan, *Sales Staff*
Thomas W Turner, *Mng Member*
EMP: 6
SALES: 190K **Privately Held**
SIC: 3841 Surgical & medical instruments

(G-16339)
TOCCATA TECHNOLOGIES INC
Also Called: Niya Goods
50 E Olentangy St Ste 204 (43065-8467)
PHONE 614 430-9888
Eric Lu, *President*
EMP: 3
SALES: 850K **Privately Held**
SIC: 5961 7372 General merchandise, mail order; application computer software

(G-16340)
VERTEBRATION INC
3982 Powell Rd 220 (43065-7662)
PHONE 614 395-3346
Richard Paul Karr, *President*
EMP: 3
SALES (est): 268.1K **Privately Held**
WEB: www.vertebration.com
SIC: 3841 Surgical & medical instruments

Powhatan Point
Belmont County

(G-16341)
COAL SERVICES INC
Also Called: Coal Services Group
155 Highway 7 S (43942-1033)
PHONE 740 795-5220
Don Gentry, *President*
Michael O McKown, *Principal*
Robert Moore, *Principal*
Bonnie Froehlich, *Manager*
EMP: 90
SALES (est): 12MM
SALES (corp-wide): 4.8B **Publicly Held**
WEB: www.coalservices.com
SIC: 8741 8711 1231 1222 Management services; engineering services; anthracite mining; bituminous coal-underground mining; bituminous coal & lignite-surface mining; coal mining services
HQ: The American Coal Company
9085 Highway 34 N
Galatia IL 62935
618 268-6311

Proctorville
Lawrence County

(G-16342)
AIRTITE MINE PRODUCTS LLC
1279 County Road 411 (45669-9600)
PHONE..................................740 894-8778
Brandon Walters, *Accountant*
James L Earl Jr,
EMP: 10
SQ FT: 21,500
SALES: 3.5MM **Privately Held**
SIC: 1241 Coal mining services

(G-16343)
CANDLES BY JOYCE
343 Township Road 1233 (45669-8416)
P.O. Box 227 (45669-0227)
PHONE..................................740 886-6355
Joyce Snyder, *Owner*
EMP: 5
SALES (est): 223.2K **Privately Held**
SIC: 3999 Candles

(G-16344)
PITTSBURGH WIRE & CABLE
99 Township Road 1248 (45669-8662)
PHONE..................................740 886-0202
Joseph Deton, *Manager*
EMP: 1
SALES: 2MM **Privately Held**
SIC: 3496 Miscellaneous fabricated wire products

(G-16345)
SPECIALTY SYSTEMS ELECTRIC LLC
1853 County Road 411 (45669-9415)
P.O. Box 677 (45669-0677)
PHONE..................................304 529-3861
John Whitfield, *Principal*
EMP: 9
SALES (est): 1.4MM **Privately Held**
SIC: 3648 Lighting fixtures, except electric: residential

(G-16346)
SUPERIOR MARINE WAYS INC
5852 County Rd 1 Suoth Pt (45669)
P.O. Box 519 (45669-0519)
PHONE..................................740 894-6224
Dale Manns, *Manager*
EMP: 120
SALES (corp-wide): 16.3MM **Privately Held**
WEB: www.superiormarine.on.ca
SIC: 3731 7699 Barges, building & repairing; boat repair
PA: Superior Marine Ways, Inc.
  5852 County Road 1
  South Point OH 45680
  740 894-6224

(G-16347)
TRI-STATE MODEL FLYERS INC
358 Township Road 1161 (45669-8762)
PHONE..................................740 886-8429
Billy Lemley Jr, *Principal*
EMP: 84
SALES (est): 5MM **Privately Held**
SIC: 3721 Aircraft

(G-16348)
TRI-STATE PLATING & POLISHING
187 Township Road 1204 (45669-8688)
PHONE..................................304 529-2579
Edison Adkins, *President*
Joseph Adkins, *General Mgr*
Laura L Adkins, *Vice Pres*
EMP: 6
SQ FT: 300
SALES: 300K **Privately Held**
SIC: 3471 7692 Electroplating of metals or formed products; welding repair

Prospect
Marion County

(G-16349)
A S T MACHINE CO
1 N 4th St (43342-9627)
PHONE..................................740 494-2013
Leroy Zent, *Owner*
EMP: 5
SQ FT: 7,500
SALES (est): 377.4K **Privately Held**
SIC: 3599 Machine shop, jobbing & repair

(G-16350)
FLEMING CONSTRUCTION CO
Also Called: Scioto Sand & Gravel
5298 Marion Marysville Rd (43342-9342)
P.O. Box 31, Marion (43301-0031)
PHONE..................................740 494-2177
Gerald E Fleming, *President*
Sonya Fleming, *Vice Pres*
EMP: 35
SQ FT: 2,400
SALES (est): 6.7MM **Privately Held**
SIC: 1542 1541 1623 1442 Commercial & office building, new construction; industrial buildings, new construction; sewer line construction; gravel mining; excavation & grading, building construction

(G-16351)
HERCULES INDUSTRIES INC
7194 Prospect Delaware Rd (43342-7505)
P.O. Box 197 (43342-0197)
PHONE..................................740 494-2620
Keith Popovich, *President*
Jean Meyer, *Vice Pres*
Jennifer Buchanan, *Manager*
▲ **EMP:** 23 **EST:** 1969
SQ FT: 18,380
SALES: 4.2MM **Privately Held**
WEB: www.herculock.com
SIC: 3429 Padlocks
PA: Scientific Forming Technologies Corporation
  2545 Farmers Dr Ste 200
  Columbus OH 43235

Put In Bay
Ottawa County

(G-16352)
GIFT COVE INC
Also Called: Candy Bar
170 Delaware St (43456-6626)
P.O. Box 240 (43456-0240)
PHONE..................................419 285-2920
Linda Mahoney, *Manager*
EMP: 9
SALES (est): 786.5K
SALES (corp-wide): 2MM **Privately Held**
SIC: 2064 Fudge (candy)
PA: Gift Cove, Inc.
  156 Delaware St
  Put In Bay OH 43456
  719 510-9280

Quaker City
Guernsey County

(G-16353)
NY LOGGING & LUMBER
61285 Shannon Run Rd (43773-9552)
PHONE..................................740 679-2085
Noah E Yoder, *Principal*
EMP: 3
SALES (est): 197.3K **Privately Held**
SIC: 2411 Logging

(G-16354)
YODER LOGGING
22144 Oxford Rd (43773-9709)
PHONE..................................740 679-2635
Lester H Yoder, *Owner*
EMP: 3
SALES: 140K **Privately Held**
SIC: 2411 Logging camps & contractors

Quincy
Logan County

(G-16355)
F M SHEET METAL FABRICATION
13019 Shanley Rd (43343-9510)
PHONE..................................937 362-4357
Frank Williamson, *Owner*
EMP: 3
SALES (est): 158.1K **Privately Held**
SIC: 3444 Sheet metalwork

Racine
Meigs County

(G-16356)
J D DRILLING CO
107 S 3rd St (45771-9552)
P.O. Box 369 (45771-0369)
PHONE..................................740 949-2512
James E Diddle, *President*
EMP: 25
SQ FT: 6,000
SALES (est): 3.8MM **Privately Held**
SIC: 1381 Drilling oil & gas wells

Radnor
Delaware County

(G-16357)
CENTRAL OHIO RTRCTABLE SCREENS
6737 Thomas Rd (43066-9618)
PHONE..................................614 868-5080
Marilyn Kulp, *President*
EMP: 5
SALES (est): 583.8K **Privately Held**
SIC: 3442 Screen doors, metal

(G-16358)
SCREENMOBILE INC
6737 Thomas Rd (43066-9618)
PHONE..................................614 868-8663
James Kulp, *President*
EMP: 6
SALES (est): 466.5K **Privately Held**
SIC: 1799 2431 7699 Screening contractor: window, door, etc.; door screens, metal covered wood; window screens, wood frame; door & window repair

(G-16359)
TIM CALVIN ACCESS CONTROLS
Also Called: Tim Calvin Enterprises
7585 Taway Rd (43066-9711)
PHONE..................................740 494-4200
Tim Calvin, *President*
Renee Calvin, *Vice Pres*
Doug Bell, *Associate*
EMP: 8
SQ FT: 240
SALES: 900K **Privately Held**
WEB: www.calvininc.com
SIC: 3446 Architectural metalwork

Randolph
Portage County

(G-16360)
EAST MANUFACTURING CORPORATION (PA)
1871 State Rte 44 (44265)
P.O. Box 277 (44265-0277)
PHONE..................................330 325-9921
Howard D Booher, *CEO*
David De Poincy, *President*
Mark T Tate, *Corp Secy*
Robert J Bruce, *Vice Pres*
Charlie Wells, *Vice Pres*
▼ **EMP:** 267
SQ FT: 350,000
SALES (est): 68.3MM **Privately Held**
WEB: www.eastmfg.com
SIC: 3715 5013 7539 Trailer bodies; truck parts & accessories; automotive repair shops

(G-16361)
EAST MANUFACTURING CORPORATION
3865 Waterloo Rd (44265)
PHONE..................................330 325-9921
Torie Tollman, *Manager*
EMP: 15
SALES (corp-wide): 68.3MM **Privately Held**
SIC: 3715 Trailer bodies
PA: East Manufacturing Corporation
  1871 State Rte 44
  Randolph OH 44265
  330 325-9921

Ravenna
Portage County

(G-16362)
A C WILLIAMS CO INC (PA)
Also Called: Lake Metals
700 N Walnut St (44266-2300)
PHONE..................................330 296-6110
Dale E McCoy, *President*
Barbara Cramer, *Admin Sec*
EMP: 23 **EST:** 1944
SQ FT: 65,000
SALES (est): 8.3MM **Privately Held**
SIC: 3369 3321 Magnesium & magnes.-base alloy castings, exc. die-casting; gray iron castings; ductile iron castings

(G-16363)
ACCESS TO INDEPENDENCE INC
4960 S Prospect St (44266-9016)
PHONE..................................330 296-8111
Tim Spaulding, *Info Tech Dir*
Vince Pelose, *Director*
John Olson, *Director*
EMP: 4
SALES: 1.7MM **Privately Held**
WEB: www.accesstoindependence.com
SIC: 8399 7999 5999 5047 Community development groups; bingo hall; medical apparatus & supplies; hospital equipment & furniture; wheelchair lifts

(G-16364)
AIR CRAFT WHEELS LLC
700 N Walnut St (44266-2372)
PHONE..................................440 937-7903
Dale McCoy, *President*
EMP: 9
SALES (est): 1MM **Privately Held**
WEB: www.aircraftwheels.net
SIC: 3356 3365 3369 Magnesium; aluminum foundries; nonferrous foundries

(G-16365)
ALLEN AIRCRAFT PRODUCTS INC
312 E Lake St (44266-3428)
P.O. Box 951146, Cleveland (44193-0005)
PHONE..................................330 296-9621
Alicia Gonzalez, *Human Resources*
Kevin Barbeck, *Branch Mgr*
Gene Onest, *Supervisor*
EMP: 50
SALES (corp-wide): 28.8MM **Privately Held**
WEB: www.allenaircraft.com
SIC: 3728 3471 Aircraft parts & equipment; plating & polishing
PA: Allen Aircraft Products, Inc.
  6168 Woodbine Rd
  Ravenna OH 44266
  330 296-9621

(G-16366)
ALLEN AIRCRAFT PRODUCTS INC
Also Called: Metal Finishing Divison
4879 Newton Falls Rd (44266-9673)
P.O. Box 1211 (44266-1211)
PHONE..................................330 296-1531

Ravenna - Portage County (G-16367)

Roger Rollison, *Branch Mgr*
EMP: 35
SALES (corp-wide): 28.8MM **Privately Held**
WEB: www.allenaircraft.com
SIC: 3471 Finishing, metals or formed products
PA: Allen Aircraft Products, Inc.
6168 Woodbine Rd
Ravenna OH 44266
330 296-9621

(G-16367)
ASTRA PRODUCTS OF OHIO LTD (PA)
7154 State Route 88 (44266-9189)
PHONE 330 296-0112
Scott Kohl,
◆ **EMP:** 107
SQ FT: 110,000
SALES (est): 29.8MM **Privately Held**
WEB: www.astraproductsltd.com
SIC: 2591 Drapery hardware & blinds & shades

(G-16368)
BECK ENERGY CORP
160 N Chestnut St (44266-2256)
P.O. Box 1070 (44266-1070)
PHONE 330 297-6891
Raymond Beck, *President*
EMP: 15
SQ FT: 4,000
SALES (est): 2.2MM **Privately Held**
SIC: 1382 Oil & gas exploration services

(G-16369)
BECK SAND & GRAVEL INC
2820 Webb Rd (44266-9459)
PHONE 330 626-3863
Rod Wenrich, *President*
Dan Lostoski, *Vice Pres*
EMP: 9
SQ FT: 3,200
SALES (est): 1.5MM **Privately Held**
SIC: 1442 Gravel mining

(G-16370)
BOLLARI/DAVIS INC
5292 S Prospect St (44266-9032)
P.O. Box 609 (44266-0609)
PHONE 330 296-4445
David Stonestreet, *President*
EMP: 10 **EST:** 1958
SQ FT: 13,000
SALES (est): 1.1MM **Privately Held**
SIC: 3599 Machine shop, jobbing & repair

(G-16371)
BUILDING & CONVEYER MAINT LLC
8756 Peck Rd (44266-9775)
PHONE 303 882-0912
George Metcalf, *Mng Member*
Rebecca Metcalf,
EMP: 5 **EST:** 2014
SALES (est): 659K **Privately Held**
SIC: 3535 Conveyors & conveying equipment

(G-16372)
CITY OF RAVENNA
Also Called: Waste Water Plant, The
3722 Hommon Rd (44266-3543)
PHONE 330 296-5214
Michael Lacivita, *Manager*
Bill Bregant, *Manager*
EMP: 9 **Privately Held**
SIC: 4952 3589 Sewerage systems; sewage treatment equipment
PA: City Of Ravenna
210 Park Way
Ravenna OH 44266
330 296-3864

(G-16373)
COLONIAL RUBBER COMPANY (PA)
706 Oakwood St (44266-2138)
P.O. Box 111 (44266-0111)
PHONE 330 296-2831
Dale P Fosnight, *President*
Wayne Slack, *VP Mfg*
Alan D Fosnight, *Controller*
Wayne H Wise, *Admin Sec*
EMP: 90
SQ FT: 55,000
SALES (est): 12.9MM **Privately Held**
SIC: 3061 3069 Mechanical rubber goods; hard rubber & molded rubber products

(G-16374)
DACON INDUSTRIES CO
4839 Washington Ave (44266-9628)
PHONE 330 298-9491
Paula Cayton, *Principal*
EMP: 24 **Privately Held**
SIC: 3069 Hard rubber products
PA: Dacon Industries Co.
10661 N Lombard St
Portland OR 97203

(G-16375)
DIE-NAMIC TOOL & DIE INC
100 Romito St Ste D (44266-2883)
PHONE 330 296-6923
Marie Boyce, *President*
EMP: 5 **EST:** 1997
SQ FT: 6,000
SALES (est): 710.8K **Privately Held**
SIC: 3544 Special dies & tools

(G-16376)
DURACOTE CORPORATION
350 N Diamond St (44266-2155)
P.O. Box 1209 (44266-1209)
PHONE 330 296-9600
Jack Pallay, *President*
▼ **EMP:** 40 **EST:** 1947
SQ FT: 143,000
SALES (est): 11.4MM **Privately Held**
WEB: www.duracote.com
SIC: 3083 2295 3082 2261 Laminated plastics plate & sheet; resin or plastic coated fabrics; unsupported plastics profile shapes; finishing plants, cotton

(G-16377)
DYNA TECH MOLDING & BETA
367 N Freedom St (44266-2444)
PHONE 330 296-2315
EMP: 5
SALES (est): 773.5K **Privately Held**
SIC: 2891 Mfg Adhesives/Sealants

(G-16378)
ECLIPSE BLIND SYSTEMS INC
7154 State Route 88 (44266-9189)
PHONE 330 296-0112
James W Watson, *President*
Dennis Miller, *Purchasing*
EMP: 165
SQ FT: 110,000
SALES (est): 15.2MM **Privately Held**
SIC: 3089 7371 Extruded finished plastic products; custom computer programming services
HQ: Turnils (Uk) Limited
10 Fountain Crescent Inchinnan Business Park
Renfrew PA4 9
141 812-3322

(G-16379)
ENDURO RUBBER COMPANY
685 S Chestnut St (44266-3068)
P.O. Box 752 (44266-0752)
PHONE 330 296-9603
Jerry Stuver, *President*
Luanne Stuver, *Vice Pres*
Neal A Stuver, *Treasurer*
EMP: 9 **EST:** 1946
SQ FT: 24,000
SALES (est): 1.2MM **Privately Held**
WEB: www.endurorubber.com
SIC: 3069 Molded rubber products

(G-16380)
G GRAFTON MACHINE & RUBBER
640 Cleveland Rd (44266-2021)
PHONE 330 297-1062
Montgomery Grafton, *President*
EMP: 10
SQ FT: 17,500
SALES (est): 1.4MM **Privately Held**
SIC: 3599 3069 Machine shop, jobbing & repair; hard rubber & molded rubber products

(G-16381)
GENERAL ALUMINUM MFG COMPANY
5159 S Prospect St (44266-9031)
PHONE 330 297-1020
Craig Schlauch, *Branch Mgr*
EMP: 20
SALES (corp-wide): 1.6B **Publicly Held**
WEB: www.generalaluminum.com
SIC: 3365 3369 Aluminum & aluminum-based alloy castings; nonferrous foundries
HQ: General Aluminum Mfg. Company
6065 Parkland Blvd
Cleveland OH 44124
330 297-1225

(G-16382)
HUGO VGLSANG MASCHINENBAU GMBH
Also Called: Vogelsang Brazil Comercio E
7966 State Route 44 (44266-9781)
P.O. Box 751 (44266-0751)
PHONE 330 296-3820
Russell J Boring, *President*
Gary Haberny, *Engineer*
Monty Gilbert, *Regl Sales Mgr*
Matt Neubauer, *Regl Sales Mgr*
Jon Neuenschwander, *Sales Engr*
▲ **EMP:** 25
SQ FT: 30,000
SALES (est): 7.1MM
SALES (corp-wide): 81.4MM **Privately Held**
WEB: www.vogelsangusa.com
SIC: 3561 Pumps & pumping equipment
PA: Hugo Vogelsang Maschinenbau Gmbh
Holthoge 10-14
Essen (Oldenburg) 49632
543 483-0

(G-16383)
HYTECH SILICONE PRODUCTS INC
6112 Knapp Rd (44266-8876)
PHONE 330 297-1888
John Roberts, *President*
EMP: 16 **EST:** 1987
SQ FT: 2,450
SALES (est): 292.8K **Privately Held**
SIC: 3069 Molded rubber products

(G-16384)
JEFF CALES CUSTOMER AVI LLC
8101 State Route 44 A (44266-8322)
PHONE 330 298-9479
Jeff Cales,
EMP: 3
SALES (est): 283.6K **Privately Held**
WEB: www.customaviation.com
SIC: 3728 Aircraft body assemblies & parts

(G-16385)
JOHNSON MTTHEY PRCESS TECH INC
785 N Freedom St (44266-2469)
PHONE 330 298-7005
EMP: 30
SALES (corp-wide): 19.7B **Privately Held**
SIC: 2819 Catalysts, chemical
HQ: Matthey Johnson Process Technologies Inc
115 Eli Whitney Blvd
Savannah GA 31408
732 223-4644

(G-16386)
KING ENERGY INC
6050 State Route 14 Lot 7 (44266-9340)
PHONE 330 297-5508
Robert Lindsey, *President*
EMP: 5 **EST:** 1992
SQ FT: 5,000
SALES (est): 110K **Privately Held**
WEB: www.playboard.com
SIC: 1381 Drilling oil & gas wells

(G-16387)
LANGSTONS ULTMATE CLG SVCS INC
3764 Summit Rd (44266-3515)
PHONE 330 298-9150
Blake Langston, *President*
EMP: 16 **EST:** 1999
SALES (est): 2.8MM **Privately Held**
SIC: 3354 7699 Aluminum extruded products; cleaning services

(G-16388)
LARIAT MACHINE INC
826 Cleveland Rd (44266-2029)
P.O. Box 649 (44266-0649)
PHONE 330 297-5765
EMP: 6
SQ FT: 3,708
SALES (est): 100K **Privately Held**
SIC: 3599 Machine Shop

(G-16389)
LITE METALS COMPANY
700 N Walnut St (44266-2372)
PHONE 330 296-6110
Dale E Mc Coy, *President*
Barbara Cramer, *Vice Pres*
EMP: 35
SQ FT: 65,000
SALES (est): 8.3MM **Privately Held**
WEB: www.litemetals.com
SIC: 3365 3369 3356 Aluminum foundries; nonferrous foundries; magnesium
PA: A C Williams Co Inc
700 N Walnut St
Ravenna OH 44266
330 296-6110

(G-16390)
MONTGOMERYS PALLET SERVICE
7937 State Route 44 (44266-9781)
PHONE 330 297-6677
Teresa Montgomery, *President*
William Montgomery, *Vice Pres*
EMP: 7
SALES (est): 902.9K **Privately Held**
SIC: 2448 4953 Pallets, wood & wood with metal; refuse collection & disposal services

(G-16391)
NICHOLS MOLD INC
222 W Lake St (44266-3651)
PHONE 330 297-9719
Edward Nichols, *President*
Nancy Nichols, *Corp Secy*
EMP: 6
SQ FT: 4,000
SALES (est): 605K **Privately Held**
SIC: 3544 3599 Industrial molds; machine shop, jobbing & repair

(G-16392)
NOTEWORTHY WOODWORKING
6361 Marchinn Dr (44266-1711)
PHONE 330 297-0509
EMP: 4 **EST:** 2010
SALES (est): 230K **Privately Held**
SIC: 2431 Mfg Millwork

(G-16393)
ORGANIC ROOTS HORTICULTURE LLC
6158 State Route 303 (44266-9123)
PHONE 330 620-1108
Daniel Hickin, *Principal*
Matthew Hickin, *Principal*
EMP: 3
SALES (est): 304K **Privately Held**
SIC: 2824 Organic fibers, noncellulosic

(G-16394)
PARKER-HANNIFIN CORPORATION
Parflex Div
1300 N Freedom St (44266-8405)
PHONE 330 296-2871
Joe Sebera, *Plant Mgr*
Ty Henry, *Engineer*
Craig Mikin, *Engineer*
John Fox, *Marketing Mgr*
Beth Hauser, *Marketing Staff*
EMP: 250
SALES (corp-wide): 14.3B **Publicly Held**
WEB: www.parker.com
SIC: 3052 Rubber & plastics hose & beltings

▲ = Import ▼=Export
◆ =Import/Export

GEOGRAPHIC SECTION

Rawson - Hancock County (G-16421)

PA: Parker-Hannifin Corporation
6035 Parkland Blvd
Cleveland OH 44124
216 896-3000

(G-16395)
PARKER-HANNIFIN CORPORATION
Energy Products Division
1300 N Freedom St (44266-8405)
PHONE..................330 296-2871
John Jansen, *Branch Mgr*
Carla Burgess, *Manager*
EMP: 40
SALES (corp-wide): 12B **Publicly Held**
SIC: 3052 Rubber & plastics hose & beltings
PA: Parker-Hannifin Corporation
6035 Parkland Blvd
Cleveland OH 44124
216 896-3000

(G-16396)
PETTIGREW PUMPING INC
4171 Sandy Lake Rd (44266-9390)
P.O. Box 809 (44266-0809)
PHONE..................330 297-7900
Matthew Pettigrew, *Principal*
EMP: 9 EST: 2007
SALES (est): 1.1MM **Privately Held**
SIC: 1389 Pumping of oil & gas wells

(G-16397)
QUIKRETE COMPANIES LLC
Also Called: Quikrete of Cleveland
2693 Lake Rockwell Rd (44266-8041)
PHONE..................330 296-6080
Tim Ryon, *Manager*
EMP: 30
SQ FT: 48,000 **Privately Held**
WEB: www.quikrete.com
SIC: 3272 5211 3273 3241 Dry mixture concrete; masonry materials & supplies; ready-mixed concrete; cement, hydraulic
HQ: The Quikrete Companies Llc
5 Concourse Pkwy Ste 1900
Atlanta GA 30328
404 634-9100

(G-16398)
R W MACHINE & TOOL INC
7944 State Route 44 (44266-9781)
PHONE..................330 296-5211
Alan Wilbur, *CEO*
Mike Jenkins, *CEO*
Michael Jenkins, *President*
Karen Wilbur, *Corp Secy*
▲ EMP: 40
SQ FT: 17,500
SALES (est): 5.6MM **Privately Held**
WEB: www.rwmachinetool.com
SIC: 3599 Machine shop, jobbing & repair

(G-16399)
ROUTE 14 STORAGE INC
Also Called: Route 14 Promos
7830 State Route 14 (44266-9454)
PHONE..................330 296-0084
Anita Schmitt, *President*
EMP: 4
SALES (est): 597K **Privately Held**
SIC: 4225 5947 2395 Warehousing, self-storage; novelties; embroidery products, except schiffli machine

(G-16400)
SAINT-GOBAIN PRFMCE PLAS CORP
335 N Diamond St (44266-2153)
PHONE..................330 296-9948
Ron Bauer, *General Mgr*
EMP: 130
SALES (corp-wide): 215.9MM **Privately Held**
SIC: 3089 Thermoformed finished plastic products
HQ: Saint-Gobain Performance Plastics Corporation
31500 Solon Rd
Solon OH 44139
440 836-6900

(G-16401)
SANDERS FREDRICK EXCVTG CO INC
5858 State Route 14 (44266-8745)
P.O. Box 668 (44266-0668)
PHONE..................330 297-7980
EMP: 9
SQ FT: 3,200
SALES (est): 1.2MM **Privately Held**
SIC: 1389 1794 Oil/Gas Field Services Excavation Contractor

(G-16402)
SHUR-CO LLC
1100 N Freedom St (44266-2472)
P.O. Box 827 (44266-0827)
PHONE..................330 297-0888
Tim Numbers, *Plant Mgr*
Greg Graff, *Branch Mgr*
EMP: 8 **Privately Held**
WEB: www.shurco.com
SIC: 2394 5531 5199 Canvas & related products; truck equipment & parts; tarpaulins
PA: Shur-Co, Llc
2309 Shurlock St
Yankton SD 57078

(G-16403)
SIX C FABRICATION INC
5245 S Prospect St (44266-9032)
PHONE..................330 296-5594
EMP: 113
SALES (corp-wide): 88.1MM **Privately Held**
SIC: 3495 Wire springs
PA: Six C Fabrication, Inc.
349 Thomas Mill Rd
Winnfield LA 71483
318 628-2764

(G-16404)
SOBER SAND & GRAVEL CO
2908 Tallmadge Rd (44266-9590)
PHONE..................330 325-7088
Tracy Sober, *President*
Waldo A Sober Sr, *President*
Robert Macgregor, *Vice Pres*
EMP: 3 EST: 1940
SALES (est): 244.9K **Privately Held**
SIC: 1442 Construction sand mining; gravel mining

(G-16405)
SPECTRUM DISPERSIONS INC
225 W Lake St (44266-3650)
P.O. Box 805 (44266-0805)
PHONE..................330 296-0600
Gary Klemm, *President*
Gregory Klemm, *Vice Pres*
Mark Grissom, *Opers Mgr*
Timothy Klemm, *Treasurer*
Mark Grissom, *Technology*
▲ EMP: 15
SQ FT: 70,000
SALES (est): 4.4MM **Privately Held**
SIC: 2865 2816 2851 Color pigments, organic; color pigments; paints & paint additives; lacquers, varnishes, enamels & other coatings

(G-16406)
SPORTS EXPRESS
956 E Main St (44266-3326)
PHONE..................330 297-1112
Jim Hunt, *Owner*
EMP: 3
SQ FT: 5,200
SALES (est): 338.9K **Privately Held**
SIC: 5941 5611 5621 2759 Sporting goods & bicycle shops; clothing, sportswear, men's & boys'; women's sportswear; screen printing; sports apparel

(G-16407)
SPRINGSEAL INC
800 Enterprise Pkwy (44266-8061)
PHONE..................330 626-0673
Mark Knapp, *President*
EMP: 12
SQ FT: 10,000
SALES (est): 4.1MM **Privately Held**
SIC: 3089 Thermoformed finished plastic products

(G-16408)
STA-WARM ELECTRIC COMPANY
553 N Chestnut St (44266-2217)
P.O. Box 150 (44266-0150)
PHONE..................330 296-6461
John Snell, *President*
Brian Borthwick, *Vice Pres*
Linda Barns, *Manager*
EMP: 10 EST: 1920
SQ FT: 25,000
SALES (est): 1.3MM **Privately Held**
SIC: 3567 Heating units & devices, industrial: electric

(G-16409)
STAHL FARM MARKET
4560 State Route 14 (44266-8742)
PHONE..................330 325-0640
Charlie Stahl, *Owner*
EMP: 10
SALES (est): 786.3K **Privately Held**
SIC: 2048 Stock feeds, dry

(G-16410)
STAPINS QICK CPY/PRINT CTR LLC
253 W Main St (44266-2742)
PHONE..................330 296-0123
Kenneth Stapin, *Mng Member*
Kenneth A Stapin, *Mng Member*
EMP: 4
SQ FT: 2,800
SALES (est): 330K **Privately Held**
SIC: 2752 Commercial printing, offset

(G-16411)
T&A PALLETS INC
2849 Denny Rd (44266-9419)
PHONE..................330 968-4743
Tony Rodriguez, *Principal*
EMP: 4 EST: 2009
SALES (est): 311.5K **Privately Held**
SIC: 2448 Pallets, wood & wood with metal

(G-16412)
TARPED OUT INC
4442 State Route 14 (44266-8741)
PHONE..................330 325-7722
Marc Campitelli, *Branch Mgr*
EMP: 13
SALES (corp-wide): 574.7MM **Privately Held**
WEB: www.mountaintarp.com
SIC: 2394 Awnings, fabric: made from purchased materials; tarpaulins, fabric: made from purchased materials
HQ: Tarped Out, Inc.
1002 N 15th St
Middlesboro KY 40965
606 248-7717

(G-16413)
TOUCHSTONE WOODWORKS
7820 Cooley Rd (44266-9752)
P.O. Box 112 (44266-0112)
PHONE..................330 297-1313
Tina Walters, *Owner*
Michelle Windhausen, *Purchasing*
EMP: 4
SALES: 300K **Privately Held**
WEB: www.touchstonewoodworks.com
SIC: 2431 Door screens, wood frame

(G-16414)
TREXLER RUBBER CO INC (PA)
503 N Diamond St (44266-2113)
P.O. Box 667 (44266-0667)
PHONE..................330 296-9677
Jack W Schaefer, *President*
Michelle King, *Admin Mgr*
EMP: 25
SQ FT: 26,000
SALES: 2MM **Privately Held**
WEB: www.trexlerballoonwheel.com
SIC: 3069 2851 3544 Latex, foamed; polyurethane coatings; special dies, tools, jigs & fixtures

(G-16415)
TRI-WAY REBAR INC (PA)
Also Called: Clinton Supply
625 S Walnut St (44266-3167)
P.O. Box 750 (44266-0750)
PHONE..................330 296-9662
Gerald Guy, *President*
Bradley, *Principal*
Stanley R Jarosz, *Principal*
William D Simpson, *Principal*
G Way, *Principal*
EMP: 5
SQ FT: 31,000
SALES (est): 1.5MM **Privately Held**
SIC: 3531 1791 Construction machinery; structural steel erection

(G-16416)
TRUE INDUSTRIES INC
Also Called: Cleveland Punch and Die Co
666 Pratt St (44266-3161)
P.O. Box 769 (44266-0769)
PHONE..................330 296-4342
Dan L Brown, *President*
Roger Babb, *Vice Pres*
Ryan Brodie, *Engineer*
Tina Fumich, *Accounting Dir*
Shawn Brodie, *Sales Mgr*
EMP: 50 EST: 1880
SQ FT: 70,000
SALES (est): 8.6MM **Privately Held**
WEB: www.clevelandpunch.com
SIC: 3544 Special dies & tools

(G-16417)
UNITED STATES DEPT OF ARMY
8451 State Route 5 (44266-8569)
PHONE..................330 358-7311
EMP: 3 **Publicly Held**
SIC: 3483 Ammunition, except for small arms
HQ: United States Department Of The Army
101 Army Pentagon
Washington DC 20310

(G-16418)
W POLE CONTRACTING INC
4188 State Route 14 (44266-8739)
PHONE..................330 325-7177
Wade Pol, *President*
Christine Pol, *Treasurer*
EMP: 10
SALES (est): 934.1K **Privately Held**
SIC: 1389 Oil field services

(G-16419)
WESTROCK CP LLC
975 N Freedom St (44266-2465)
P.O. Box 1214 (44266-1214)
PHONE..................330 297-0841
Bill Rich, *General Mgr*
EMP: 108
SALES (corp-wide): 16.2B **Publicly Held**
WEB: www.smurfit-stone.com
SIC: 2653 3412 Boxes, corrugated: made from purchased materials; metal barrels, drums & pails
HQ: Westrock Cp, Llc
1000 Abernathy Rd
Atlanta GA 30328

(G-16420)
WESTROCK RKT COMPANY
Also Called: Rock Tenn
975 N Freedom St (44266-2465)
PHONE..................330 296-5155
EMP: 5
SALES (corp-wide): 16.2B **Publicly Held**
SIC: 2653 Corrugated & solid fiber boxes
HQ: Westrock Rkt, Llc
1000 Abernathy Rd Ste 125
Atlanta GA 30328
770 448-2193

Rawson
Hancock County

(G-16421)
DNC HYDRAULICS LLC
5219 County Road 313 (45881-9650)
PHONE..................419 963-2800
Cody Conaway, *Sales Staff*
David Conaway,
EMP: 12
SALES (est): 1.8MM **Privately Held**
SIC: 7699 3492 Industrial machinery & equipment repair; control valves, fluid power: hydraulic & pneumatic

Ray
Vinton County

(G-16422)
TERRY G SICKLES
2207 Boy Scout Rd (45672-9672)
PHONE 740 286-8880
Terry G Sickles, *Principal*
Terry Sickles, *Principal*
EMP: 3
SALES (est): 213.2K **Privately Held**
SIC: 2411 Logging

Rayland
Jefferson County

(G-16423)
SHELLY AND SANDS INC
Also Called: Tri-State Asphalt Co
1731 Old State Route 7 (43943-7962)
P.O. Box 66 (43943-0066)
PHONE 740 859-2104
Mark Haverty, *General Mgr*
EMP: 60
SALES (corp-wide): 276.3MM **Privately Held**
WEB: www.shellyandsands.com
SIC: 2951 1542 Asphalt paving mixtures & blocks; nonresidential construction
PA: Shelly And Sands, Inc.
  3570 S River Rd
  Zanesville OH 43701
  740 453-0721

Raymond
Union County

(G-16424)
NATURE PURE LLC (PA)
26586 State Route 739 (43067-9763)
PHONE 937 358-2364
Theresa Harris, *General Mgr*
Kurt Lausecker, *Mng Member*
EMP: 24
SALES (est): 3.4MM **Privately Held**
SIC: 0252 2048 Started pullet farm; poultry feeds

Reno
Washington County

(G-16425)
MONDO POLYMER TECHNOLOGIES INC
27620 State Rte 7 (45773)
P.O. Box 250 (45773-0250)
PHONE 740 376-9396
Mark Mondo, *President*
Maggie Ellis, *General Mgr*
Judy Mondo, *Vice Pres*
Rick Hockenberry, *Opers Mgr*
Marc Mondo, *QC Mgr*
EMP: 40
SQ FT: 3,200
SALES (est): 15.2MM **Privately Held**
WEB: www.mondopolymer.com
SIC: 4953 2822 Recycling, waste materials; synthetic rubber

(G-16426)
MUSTANG AERIAL SERVICES INC
27620 State Route 7 (45773)
P.O. Box 250 (45773-0250)
PHONE 740 373-9262
Mark A Mondo, *President*
Judy Mondo, *Admin Sec*
EMP: 8
SALES (est): 949.5K **Privately Held**
SIC: 3089 Plastic boats & other marine equipment

Republic
Seneca County

(G-16427)
JEB MODERN MACHINES LTD
3360 N State Route 19 (44867-9713)
PHONE 419 639-3937
Robert Widman, *Partner*
Eric Widman, *Partner*
James Widman, *Partner*
EMP: 3
SALES (est): 50K **Privately Held**
WEB: www.jebmodernmachine.com
SIC: 3599 Machine shop, jobbing & repair

Reynoldsburg
Franklin County

(G-16428)
AMERICAN AIRLESS INC
7095 Americana Pkwy (43068-4118)
PHONE 614 552-0146
Jimmy Yang, *President*
Lonnie Wells, *General Mgr*
Charles Lee, *Director*
EMP: 50
SALES (est): 4.2MM **Privately Held**
SIC: 3011 Tire & inner tube materials & related products

(G-16429)
B B & H TOOL COMPANY
7719 Taylor Rd Sw (43068-9626)
PHONE 614 868-8634
Mousa Aframian, *Owner*
EMP: 8
SQ FT: 8,000
SALES (est): 889.4K **Privately Held**
WEB: www.bbhtool.com
SIC: 3599 Machine shop, jobbing & repair

(G-16430)
BATH & BODY WORKS LLC (HQ)
7 Limited Pkwy E (43068-5300)
PHONE 614 856-6000
Nicholas Coe, *CEO*
Tony Mendoza, *President*
Michael W Murphy, *General Mgr*
Michelle McKeough, *District Mgr*
Heather Richmond, *District Mgr*
▲ **EMP:** 336
SALES (est): 2.7B
SALES (corp-wide): 13.2B **Publicly Held**
WEB: www.bath-and-body.com
SIC: 5999 2844 Toiletries, cosmetics & perfumes; toilet preparations
PA: L Brands, Inc.
  3 Limited Pkwy
  Columbus OH 43230
  614 415-7000

(G-16431)
BUCKEYE READY-MIX LLC (PA)
Also Called: Buckeye Building Products
7657 Taylor Rd Sw (43068-9626)
P.O. Box 164119, Columbus (43216-4119)
PHONE 614 575-2132
Doug Anderson,
Tom Murphy,
Larry Randles,
EMP: 50
SQ FT: 10,000
SALES (est): 45.1MM **Privately Held**
WEB: www.buckeyereadymix.com
SIC: 3273 Ready-mixed concrete

(G-16432)
COLUMBUS GRAPHICS INC
7295 Rickly St (43068-2513)
PHONE 614 577-9360
William Stewart III, *President*
EMP: 13
SQ FT: 8,000
SALES (est): 1.1MM **Privately Held**
SIC: 3993 Signs & advertising specialties

(G-16433)
CORNERSTONE PRINTING INC
443 Knob Ave (43068-1070)
PHONE 614 861-2138
Tim Kulich, *Principal*
Jill D Kulich, *Principal*
EMP: 3
SALES (est): 330.9K **Privately Held**
SIC: 2752 Commercial printing, offset

(G-16434)
DAIFUKU AMERICA CORPORATION (HQ)
Also Called: Daifuku Co
6700 Tussing Rd (43068-5083)
PHONE 614 863-1888
Nobo Morita, *President*
Mike Conner, *President*
Ken Hamel, *President*
Akihiko Nishimura, *President*
Tetsuya Hibi, *Corp Secy*
◆ **EMP:** 150
SQ FT: 70,000
SALES (est): 152.6MM
SALES (corp-wide): 3.8B **Privately Held**
WEB: www.daifukuamerica.com
SIC: 3535 Conveyors & conveying equipment
PA: Daifuku Co., Ltd.
  3-2-11, Mitejima, Nishiyodogawa-Ku
  Osaka OSK 555-0
  664 721-261

(G-16435)
DIMENSIONAL METALS INC (PA)
Also Called: D M I
58 Klema Dr N (43068-9691)
PHONE 740 927-3633
Stephen C Wissman, *CEO*
Phillip Gastaldo, *President*
Steven Gastaldo, *Vice Pres*
Shawn Walters, *Prdtn Mgr*
Brian Peck, *Purchasing*
EMP: 52
SQ FT: 34,000
SALES (est): 12.7MM **Privately Held**
WEB: www.dmimetals.com
SIC: 1761 3444 3531 Sheet metalwork; sheet metalwork; roofing equipment

(G-16436)
DYNALAB EMS INC
555 Lancaster Ave (43068-1128)
PHONE 614 866-9999
Gary James, *President*
Charles Arbuckle, *Corp Secy*
Brent Ervin, *Engineer*
▲ **EMP:** 107
SALES: 25MM
SALES (corp-wide): 59.5MM **Privately Held**
WEB: www.dynalabems.com
SIC: 3679 Electronic circuits
PA: Dynalab, Inc.
  555 Lancaster Ave
  Reynoldsburg OH 43068
  614 866-9999

(G-16437)
ENVIRONMENTAL CLOSURE SYSTEMS
Also Called: E C S
536 Killin Ct (43068-7100)
PHONE 614 759-9186
Thomas A Sisbarro, *President*
EMP: 19
SQ FT: 4,000
SALES (est): 1.2MM **Privately Held**
SIC: 3589 Commercial cleaning equipment

(G-16438)
FARBER SPECIALTY VEHICLES INC
7052 Americana Pkwy (43068-4117)
PHONE 614 863-6470
Ken Farber, *President*
Patty Jackson, *COO*
Steve Goodyear, *Vice Pres*
Tim Detty, *Purch Mgr*
Craig Farber, *Purchasing*
▼ **EMP:** 110
SQ FT: 60,000
SALES (est): 34.3MM **Privately Held**
WEB: www.farberspecialty.com
SIC: 3711 Automobile assembly, including specialty automobiles

(G-16439)
FEDEX OFFICE & PRINT SVCS INC
2668 Brice Rd (43068-3419)
PHONE 614 575-0800
Greg Mead, *Manager*
EMP: 13
SQ FT: 3,000
SALES (corp-wide): 65.4B **Publicly Held**
WEB: www.kinkos.com
SIC: 7334 2791 2789 Photocopying & duplicating services; typesetting; bookbinding & related work
HQ: Fedex Office And Print Services, Inc.
  7900 Legacy Dr
  Plano TX 75024
  800 463-3339

(G-16440)
FRAME WAREHOUSE
7502 E Main St (43068-1208)
PHONE 614 861-4582
Greg Moulin, *Owner*
EMP: 6 **EST:** 1964
SQ FT: 10,000
SALES (est): 515K **Privately Held**
SIC: 2499 2752 3499 Picture & mirror frames, wood; posters, lithographed; picture frames, metal

(G-16441)
FREDRICK WELDING & MACHINING
6840 Americana Pkwy (43068-4113)
PHONE 614 866-9650
Fred Williams, *President*
Lillian Joyce Williams, *Corp Secy*
John Corriveau, *Vice Pres*
Tammy Corriveau, *Vice Pres*
EMP: 17
SQ FT: 18,750
SALES (est): 2.7MM **Privately Held**
WEB: www.fredrickwelding.com
SIC: 3599 7692 Machine shop, jobbing & repair; welding repair

(G-16442)
GREGOIRE MOULIN
7502 E Main St (43068-1208)
PHONE 614 861-4582
Gregoire Moulin, *Owner*
EMP: 8 **EST:** 2009
SALES (est): 598.2K **Privately Held**
SIC: 2499 Wood products

(G-16443)
HERITAGE INC
Also Called: Heritage Lounge
2087 State Route 256 T (43068-8128)
PHONE 614 860-1185
EMP: 9
SALES (est): 700K **Privately Held**
SIC: 2253 Knit Outerwear Mill

(G-16444)
INTEGRITY GROUP CONSULTING INC
Also Called: Igc Software
6432 E Main St Ste 201 (43068-2369)
PHONE 614 759-9148
Brian Ferguson, *President*
EMP: 10
SALES (est): 1.6MM
SALES (corp-wide): 25.3MM **Privately Held**
WEB: www.igcsoftware.com
SIC: 7372 Business oriented computer software
HQ: Movehq Inc.
  3440 Hollenberg Dr
  Bridgeton MO

(G-16445)
OHIO STATE INSTITUTE OF FIN
Also Called: Ohio Select Imprinted Fabrics
7394 E Main St (43068-2166)
PHONE 614 861-8811
Eleanor J Martin, *CEO*
Robert Martin, *President*
EMP: 8

GEOGRAPHIC SECTION

Richfield - Summit County (G-16473)

SQ FT: 1,600
SALES: 575K **Privately Held**
WEB: www.ohioselect.com
SIC: **2396** 5199 Screen printing on fabric articles; advertising specialties

(G-16446)
PPG INDUSTRIES INC
Also Called: PPG 5538
6585 E Main St (43068-2318)
PHONE..................614 501-7360
Larry Franc, *Branch Mgr*
EMP: 24
SALES (corp-wide): 15.3B **Publicly Held**
WEB: www.ppg.com
SIC: **2851** Paints & allied products
PA: Ppg Industries, Inc.
  1 Ppg Pl
  Pittsburgh PA 15272
  412 434-3131

(G-16447)
PRECAST SERVICES INC
6494 Taylor Rd Sw (43068-9633)
PHONE..................614 428-4541
EMP: 4
SALES (corp-wide): 30MM **Privately Held**
SIC: **1771** 3272 Concrete Contractor Mfg Concrete Products
PA: Precast Services, Inc.
  8200 Boyle Pkwy
  Twinsburg OH 44087
  330 425-2880

(G-16448)
PRECISION POLYMERS INC
6919 Americana Pkwy (43068-4116)
PHONE..................614 322-9951
Andrew Wood, *President*
Nabil Makhoul, *Plant Mgr*
EMP: 8
SQ FT: 17,500
SALES (est): 1.8MM **Privately Held**
WEB: www.precisionpolymers.com
SIC: **3089** Injection molding of plastics

(G-16449)
PRESERVING YOUR MEMORIES
1862 Drugan Ct Sw (43068-8181)
PHONE..................614 861-4283
EMP: 3 EST: 2010
SALES (est): 170K **Privately Held**
SIC: **2491** Wood Preserving

(G-16450)
PROWRITE INC
7644 Slate Ridge Blvd (43068-8159)
PHONE..................614 864-2004
Darlena Kelley, *President*
Kelly Summers, *Vice Pres*
EMP: 4
SALES (est): 329.1K **Privately Held**
WEB: www.prowrite.com
SIC: **8999** 2741 Technical manual preparation; technical manual & paper publishing

(G-16451)
RES Q CLEANING SOLUTIONS INC
638 Klema Dr E (43068)
PHONE..................740 964-9494
Chris Scott, *President*
Steve Scott, *Vice Pres*
EMP: 4
SALES (est): 240K **Privately Held**
SIC: **2841** Detergents, synthetic organic or inorganic alkaline

(G-16452)
SCADATECH LLC
7821 Taylor Rd Sw Ste C (43068-8040)
P.O. Box 250 (43068-0250)
PHONE..................614 552-7726
Robert Cogley, *Mng Member*
Joyce Cogley,
EMP: 4
SQ FT: 1,350
SALES: 1MM **Privately Held**
SIC: **3823** Industrial instrmnts msrmnt display/control process variable

(G-16453)
SNOOK ADVERTISING AL PUBLISHER
Also Called: Snook Al Advertising/Publisher
1567 Alar Ave (43068-2601)
P.O. Box 1 (43068-0001)
PHONE..................614 866-3333
Audrey Iles, *CEO*
Don T Iles, *Owner*
EMP: 10
SQ FT: 1,479
SALES (est): 460K **Privately Held**
SIC: **2741** Directories: publishing only, not printed on site

(G-16454)
SPEEDWAY LLC
Also Called: Speedway Superamerica 4487
7881 E Main St (43068-1233)
PHONE..................614 861-6397
EMP: 10 **Publicly Held**
WEB: www.speedwaynet.com
SIC: **1311** Crude petroleum production
HQ: Speedway Llc
  500 Speedway Dr
  Enon OH 45323
  937 864-3000

(G-16455)
SWAGG PRODUCTIONS2015LLC
Also Called: Gmerecords
2003 Chalfield Ct (43068-5426)
PHONE..................614 815-1173
Travis Maurice McDaniels,
EMP: 12 EST: 2015
SALES (est): 404.4K **Privately Held**
SIC: **2731** 7819 7929 7389 Book music: publishing & printing; sound (effects & music production), motion picture; entertainers & entertainment groups; popular music groups or artists;

(G-16456)
TORTILLA
8134 E Broad St (43068-8037)
PHONE..................614 557-3367
Walter Eguez, *Principal*
EMP: 3 EST: 2014
SALES (est): 238.6K **Privately Held**
SIC: **2099** Tortillas, fresh or refrigerated

(G-16457)
TOWN CNTRY TECHNICAL SVCS INC
Also Called: Keytel Systems
6200 Eastgreen Blvd (43068-3442)
PHONE..................614 866-7700
Kristopher Haley, *President*
Julie Moraine, *Office Admin*
EMP: 10
SQ FT: 4,000
SALES (est): 2MM **Privately Held**
WEB: www.keytelsystems.com
SIC: **7629** 5999 1731 7373 Telecommunication equipment repair (except telephones); telephone equipment & systems; computer installation; local area network (LAN) systems integrator; electronic computers; personal computers (microcomputers); computer storage devices

(G-16458)
TS TECH USA CORPORATION (DH)
8400 E Broad St (43068-9749)
PHONE..................614 577-1088
Kazuhiso Saito, *President*
Rudy Claming, *Vice Pres*
Hideo Mizusawa, *Vice Pres*
Shinya Fukunaga, *Engineer*
Clint Bement, *Senior Engr*
▲ EMP: 138
SQ FT: 244,000
SALES (est): 123.3MM
SALES (corp-wide): 4.5B **Privately Held**
WEB: www.tstna.com
SIC: **3714** Motor vehicle body components & frame
HQ: Ts Tech Americas, Inc.
  8458 E Broad St
  Reynoldsburg OH 43068
  614 575-4100

(G-16459)
TWO GRANDMOTHERS GOURMET KIT
9127 Firstgate Dr (43068-9596)
PHONE..................614 746-0888
Vicky Moore, *Owner*
Ven Jackson, *Owner*
EMP: 6
SALES (est): 210K **Privately Held**
SIC: **2033** Canned fruits & specialties

(G-16460)
VSS STORE OPERATIONS LLC
4 Limited Pkwy E (43068-5300)
PHONE..................800 411-5116
Betsy Hall, *Vice Pres*
EMP: 5
SALES (est): 551.7K **Privately Held**
SIC: **2392** Washcloths & bath mitts: made from purchased materials

Richfield
Summit County

(G-16461)
ACCESS MANUFACTURING SVCS LLC
4807 Hawkins Rd (44286-9538)
PHONE..................330 659-9893
John Ciolkevich, *Principal*
EMP: 3
SALES (est): 119.8K **Privately Held**
SIC: **3999** Manufacturing industries

(G-16462)
BECKER SIGNS INC
4762 Black Rd (44286-9454)
PHONE..................330 659-4504
Brian Becker, *President*
Karen J Becker, *Vice Pres*
EMP: 3
SALES: 350K **Privately Held**
WEB: www.beckersigns.com
SIC: **3993** Signs, not made in custom sign painting shops

(G-16463)
BLUELEVEL TECHNOLOGIES INC
3778 Timberlake Dr (44286-9187)
PHONE..................330 523-5215
Bob Ciulla, *Owner*
▲ EMP: 5
SALES (est): 774.5K **Privately Held**
SIC: **3575** 5085 Computer terminals, monitors & components; industrial tools

(G-16464)
CENTER FOR EXCPTONAL PRACTICES
3404 Brecksville Rd (44286-9662)
PHONE..................330 523-5240
Robyn Reis, *Principal*
EMP: 4
SALES (est): 343.6K **Privately Held**
SIC: **3821** Clinical laboratory instruments, except medical & dental

(G-16465)
CLEVELAND COPPERSMITHING WORKS
4830 Hawkins Rd (44286-9538)
PHONE..................330 607-3998
Leo E Engasser, *President*
Phyllis Engasser, *Vice Pres*
Mike Gill, *Vice Pres*
EMP: 3
SQ FT: 3,600
SALES (est): 360K **Privately Held**
SIC: **3498** Pipe fittings, fabricated from purchased pipe; pipe sections fabricated from purchased pipe; tube fabricating (contract bending & shaping)

(G-16466)
COUNTRY MAID ICE CREAM INC
3252 W Streetsboro Rd (44286-9120)
P.O. Box 151 (44286-0151)
PHONE..................330 659-6830
Mike Torma, *President*
Don Torma, *Corp Secy*
Steve Torma, *Vice Pres*
EMP: 3 EST: 1948
SQ FT: 1,800
SALES (est): 317.2K **Privately Held**
SIC: **2024** 5812 5143 5431 Ice cream, bulk; ice cream stands or dairy bars; ice cream & ices; fruit & vegetable markets

(G-16467)
DENTAL CERAMICS INC
3404 Brecksville Rd (44286-9662)
PHONE..................330 523-5240
John Lavicka, *President*
Jan Bittner, *Office Mgr*
EMP: 37
SALES (est): 4.3MM **Privately Held**
WEB: www.dentalceramics.net
SIC: **8072** 3843 Crown & bridge production; dental equipment & supplies

(G-16468)
EAGLE FAMILY FOODS GROUP LLC (PA)
4020 Kinross Lakes Pkwy # 3 (44286-9084)
PHONE..................330 382-3725
Paul Smucker Wagstaff, *CEO*
Larry Herman, *COO*
Dan Gentile, *VP Finance*
Jeff Boyle,
EMP: 25
SALES (est): 200MM **Privately Held**
SIC: **2023** Condensed milk

(G-16469)
ELEMENT14 US HOLDINGS INC (DH)
4180 Highlander Pkwy (44286-9352)
PHONE..................330 523-4280
Ralf Buehler, *President*
Joseph R Daprile, *Vice Pres*
Paul M Barlak, *Treasurer*
EMP: 3
SALES: 598MM
SALES (corp-wide): 19B **Publicly Held**
SIC: **5065** 3429 Electronic parts & equipment; nozzles, fire fighting
HQ: Premier Farnell Limited
  150 Armley Road
  Leeds
  870 129-8608

(G-16470)
FAWCETT CO INC
3863 Congress Pkwy (44286-9745)
PHONE..................330 659-4187
Jack Grace, *President*
EMP: 7 EST: 1946
SQ FT: 16,000
SALES (est): 1.1MM **Privately Held**
WEB: www.fawcettco.com
SIC: **3559** 7699 Paint making machinery; industrial machinery & equipment repair

(G-16471)
FRONTIER TANK CENTER INC
3800 Congress Pkwy (44286-9745)
P.O. Box 460 (44286-0460)
PHONE..................330 659-3888
James S Hollabaugh, *President*
Mary Hollabaugh, *Admin Sec*
EMP: 25
SQ FT: 25,000
SALES (est): 3.2MM **Privately Held**
WEB: www.frontiertrailer.com
SIC: **7699** 5013 3714 Tank repair; trailer parts & accessories; motor vehicle body components & frame

(G-16472)
GAIL J SHUMAKER ORIGINALS
Also Called: Shu Shop, The
3999 Brush Rd (44286-9580)
PHONE..................330 659-0680
Gail J Shumaker, *President*
EMP: 3
SALES (est): 286.3K **Privately Held**
SIC: **3942** Dolls, except stuffed toy animals

(G-16473)
HAUL-AWAY CONTAINERS INC
3554 Brecksville Rd # 500 (44286-9157)
PHONE..................440 546-1879
Barton F Carmichael, *President*
EMP: 4 EST: 2001

Richfield - Summit County (G-16474)

SALES (est): 656.8K **Privately Held**
WEB: www.haul-away.net
SIC: 2655 4212 Fiber cans, drums & similar products; local trucking, without storage

(G-16474)
ITRAN ELECTRONICS RECYCLING
4100 Congress Pkwy W (44286-9732)
PHONE..................................330 659-0801
EMP: 3
SALES (est): 170K **Privately Held**
SIC: 2611 Operates Electronics Recycling Services

(G-16475)
KINGSCOTE CHEMICALS INC
3778 Timberlake Dr (44286-9187)
PHONE..................................330 523-5300
EMP: 4
SALES (est): 448.1K **Privately Held**
SIC: 2819 Industrial inorganic chemicals

(G-16476)
MOREL LANDSCAPING LLC
3684 Forest Run Dr (44286-9408)
P.O. Box 41420, Brecksville, (44141-0420)
PHONE..................................216 551-4395
Robert Morel,
EMP: 12
SQ FT: 9,000
SALES (est): 218.5K **Privately Held**
SIC: 0782 1771 0783 3645 Mowing services, lawn; seeding services, lawn; patio construction, concrete; planting services, ornamental bush; planting services, ornamental tree; garden, patio, walkway & yard lighting fixtures: electric

(G-16477)
NATIONAL POLISHING SYSTEMS INC
Also Called: NPS
5145 Brecksville Rd # 101 (44286-9250)
PHONE..................................330 659-6547
Robert Tetmayer, *President*
EMP: 28
SALES: 5.4MM **Privately Held**
SIC: 3471 Cleaning, polishing & finishing

(G-16478)
OHIO PRINTED PRODUCTS INC
3920 Congress Pkwy (44286-9745)
PHONE..................................330 659-0909
Fax: 330 659-5884
EMP: 14
SQ FT: 22,000
SALES (est): 950K **Privately Held**
SIC: 2741 Misc Publishing

(G-16479)
PAK MASTER LLC
3778 Timberlake Dr (44286-9187)
PHONE..................................330 523-5319
Peter Biierg, *Mng Member*
EMP: 50
SQ FT: 100,000
SALES: 10MM **Privately Held**
SIC: 3565 Packaging machinery
PA: Switchback Group, Inc.
    3778 Timberlake Dr
    Richfield OH 44286

(G-16480)
PAULER COMMUNICATIONS INC (PA)
Also Called: Town Planner, The
3046 Brecksville Rd Ste B (44286-9252)
PHONE..................................440 243-1229
Larry Paulozzi, *President*
Sam Debona, *Publisher*
Helen Grace, *Publisher*
Brad Lubinger, *Publisher*
Ronald Miller, *Vice Pres*
EMP: 4
SALES (est): 946.5K **Privately Held**
SIC: 2741 Miscellaneous publishing

(G-16481)
POLKA DOT PIN CUSHION INC
3807 Brecksville Rd Ste 8 (44286-9165)
PHONE..................................330 659-0233
Ronelle Rajkovich, *Principal*
EMP: 3
SALES (est): 289.9K **Privately Held**
SIC: 2393 Cushions, except spring & carpet: purchased materials

(G-16482)
PORTER DUMPSTERS LLC
2868 Southern Rd (44286-9521)
PHONE..................................330 659-0043
Russell Porter, *Principal*
EMP: 6
SALES (est): 649.9K **Privately Held**
SIC: 3443 Dumpsters, garbage

(G-16483)
PREMIER FARNELL HOLDING INC (DH)
4180 Highlander Pkwy (44286-9352)
PHONE..................................330 523-4273
Dan Hill, *President*
Joseph R Daprile, *Vice Pres*
Steven Webb, *Vice Pres*
Paul M Barlak, *Treasurer*
◆ EMP: 20
SQ FT: 35,000
SALES: 598MM
SALES (corp-wide): 19B **Publicly Held**
SIC: 5065 3429 Electronic parts & equipment; nozzles, fire fighting
HQ: Element14 Us Holdings Inc
    4180 Highlander Pkwy
    Richfield OH 44286
    330 523-4280

(G-16484)
RAYHAVEN GROUP INC
3842 Congress Pkwy Ste A (44286-9745)
PHONE..................................330 659-3183
Robert Rickenbacker, *Manager*
EMP: 12
SALES (est): 2.2MM
SALES (corp-wide): 20.8MM **Privately Held**
SIC: 3448 5046 5084 Prefabricated metal buildings; commercial equipment; heat exchange equipment, industrial
PA: Rayhaven Group, Inc.
    35901 Schoolcraft Rd
    Livonia MI 48150
    734 744-9260

(G-16485)
SCRIPTYPE PUBLISHING INC
Also Called: Broadview Journal, The
4300 W Streetsboro Rd (44286-9796)
PHONE..................................330 659-0303
Sue Serdinak, *President*
EMP: 25
SQ FT: 5,708
SALES (est): 2.4MM **Privately Held**
WEB: www.scriptype.com
SIC: 2759 Publication printing; magazines: printing; newspapers: printing; periodicals: printing

(G-16486)
SEDLAK
4020 Kinross Lakes Pkwy (44286-9084)
PHONE..................................330 908-2200
Jack Bonanno, *Vice Pres*
EMP: 4
SALES (est): 207.3K **Privately Held**
SIC: 3312 Blast furnaces & steel mills

(G-16487)
SENSIBLE PRODUCTS INC
3857 Brecksville Rd (44286-9634)
PHONE..................................330 659-4212
Philip McLean, *President*
Brittany McLean, *Vice Pres*
EMP: 9
SALES: 100K **Privately Held**
WEB: www.sensible-products.com
SIC: 3429 Nozzles, fire fighting

(G-16488)
SMC CORPORATION OF AMERICA
4160 Highlander Pkwy # 200 (44286-9082)
PHONE..................................330 659-2006
Scott Chonko, *Branch Mgr*
EMP: 50
SALES (corp-wide): 5.5B **Privately Held**
WEB: www.smcusa.com
SIC: 3625 3492 Actuators, industrial; control valves, fluid power: hydraulic & pneumatic

HQ: Smc Corporation Of America
    10100 Smc Blvd
    Noblesville IN 46060
    317 899-4440

(G-16489)
SNAP-ON BUSINESS SOLUTIONS (HQ)
4025 Kinross Lakes Pkwy (44286-9371)
PHONE..................................330 659-1600
Bruce Rhoades, *CEO*
Timothy Chambers, *President*
Joe Gaebelein, *Project Mgr*
Ken Satz, *Project Mgr*
Jeremy Hassar, *Prdtn Mgr*
EMP: 300
SQ FT: 88,000
SALES (est): 126.8MM
SALES (corp-wide): 3.7B **Publicly Held**
WEB: www.pbs.proquest.com
SIC: 2741 Miscellaneous publishing
PA: Snap-On Incorporated
    2801 80th St
    Kenosha WI 53143
    262 656-5200

(G-16490)
SWITCHBACK GROUP INC (PA)
3778 Timberlake Dr (44286-9187)
PHONE..................................330 523-5200
David Shepherd, *President*
Jerry Kennedy, *Engineer*
Liz Anacki, *Sales Staff*
Mark Shimp, *Manager*
EMP: 25
SALES (est): 13.3MM **Privately Held**
SIC: 3565 Packaging machinery

(G-16491)
TAYLOR COMMUNICATIONS INC
4125 Highlander Pkwy # 230 (44286-9085)
PHONE..................................216 265-1800
Ray Taylor, *Manager*
EMP: 53
SALES (corp-wide): 3.2B **Privately Held**
WEB: www.stdreg.com
SIC: 2761 Manifold business forms
HQ: Taylor Communications, Inc.
    1725 Roe Crest Dr
    North Mankato MN 56003
    507 625-2828

(G-16492)
TECUMSEH REDEVELOPMENT INC
4020 Kinross Lakes Pkwy (44286-9084)
PHONE..................................330 659-9100
Rodney Mott, *President*
Bruce Pole, *Vice Pres*
Robert Dalrymple, *Admin Sec*
EMP: 4
SALES (est): 340.6K
SALES (corp-wide): 9.1B **Privately Held**
SIC: 3325 3316 Steel foundries; cold finishing of steel shapes
HQ: Arcelormittal Usa Llc
    1 S Dearborn St Ste 1800
    Chicago IL 60603
    312 346-0300

(G-16493)
VALENTINO INDUSTRIES LLC
3615 Southern Rd (44286-9554)
PHONE..................................330 523-7216
Valentino Camardo, *Principal*
EMP: 3
SALES (est): 186.5K **Privately Held**
SIC: 3999 Manufacturing industries

(G-16494)
W W WILLIAMS COMPANY LLC
Also Called: Williams Carrier Transicold
2920 Brecksville Rd B1 (44286-9395)
PHONE..................................330 659-3084
Alan Gatlin, *President*
Tom Heaton, *Manager*
EMP: 11
SALES (corp-wide): 4.8B **Privately Held**
WEB: www.wwwilliams.com
SIC: 5084 7538 7537 3714 Industrial machinery & equipment; diesel engine repair: automotive; automotive transmission repair shops; motor vehicle engines & parts

HQ: The W W Williams Company Llc
    5025 Bradenton Ave # 130
    Dublin OH 43017
    614 228-5000

(G-16495)
WHITEYS FOOD SYSTEMS INC
3600 Brecksville Rd Ofc (44286-9668)
PHONE..................................330 659-4070
John Bigadza, *President*
Caryl Bigadza, *Corp Secy*
EMP: 4
SQ FT: 20,240
SALES (est): 280K **Privately Held**
SIC: 2032 Chili with or without meat: packaged in cans, jars, etc.

Richmond
Jefferson County

(G-16496)
MC CONNELLS MARKET
Also Called: McConnell's Farm Market
2189 State Route 43 (43944-7980)
PHONE..................................740 765-4300
Kenneth Mc Connell, *Partner*
James Mc Connell, *Partner*
EMP: 6
SALES: 650K **Privately Held**
SIC: 2011 5421 Meat packing plants; meat markets, including freezer provisioners

(G-16497)
OVECO INDUSTRIES ELECTRICA
100 Kragel Rd Ste 4 (43944-6959)
PHONE..................................740 381-3326
Robert Whitaker, *Principal*
EMP: 3
SALES (est): 120K **Privately Held**
SIC: 3999 Manufacturing industries

(G-16498)
SIGN AMERICA INCORPORATED
3887 State Route 43 (43944-7912)
P.O. Box 396 (43944-0396)
PHONE..................................740 765-5555
Judith A Hilty, *President*
Bob Hilty, *Vice Pres*
Scott Hilty Jr, *Vice Pres*
John D Bray, *Executive*
John Bray, *Admin Sec*
EMP: 40
SQ FT: 6,000
SALES (est): 9.6MM **Privately Held**
WEB: www.signamericainc.com
SIC: 5046 3993 Signs, electrical; neon signs; signs & advertising specialties

Richmond Dale
Ross County

(G-16499)
HOWARD & BLAKE EXCAVATING LLC
1030 Main St (45673-9713)
PHONE..................................740 701-7938
Jennifer Blake, *Partner*
EMP: 3
SALES (est): 257.3K **Privately Held**
SIC: 3531 Construction machinery

Richmond Heights
Cuyahoga County

(G-16500)
AJAMI HOLDINGS GROUP LLC
Also Called: Apex Property Management
5247 Wilson Mills Rd # 311 (44143-3016)
PHONE..................................216 396-6089
Mark A Westbrooks, *Mng Member*
Alexander Judah,
EMP: 3
SQ FT: 2,000

GEOGRAPHIC SECTION

SALES: 200K **Privately Held**
SIC: 6719 6799 1389 6531 Investment holding companies, except banks; real estate investors, except property operators; construction, repair & dismantling services; real estate managers

(G-16501)
AVIATION CMPNENT SOLUTIONS INC
26451 Curtiss Wright Pkwy # 106 (44143-4410)
PHONE..................440 295-6590
Joe Klinehamer, *President*
EMP: 15
SALES (est): 3.2MM **Privately Held**
WEB: www.acs-parts.com
SIC: 3728 Aircraft parts & equipment

(G-16502)
JC CARTER LLC
Also Called: JC Carter Nozzles
26451 Curtiss Wright Pkwy # 106 (44143-4400)
PHONE..................440 569-1818
John Glover,
Louis Buchino,
▲ EMP: 4
SALES (est): 677.5K
SALES (corp-wide): 13.8B **Privately Held**
SIC: 3559 Cryogenic machinery, industrial
HQ: Atlas Copco Mafi-Trench Company Llc
3037 Industrial Pkwy
Santa Maria CA 93455
805 352-0112

(G-16503)
MOMENTIVE PERFORMANCE MTLS INC
Also Called: Momentive Performance Mtls
24400 Highland Rd (44143-2503)
PHONE..................440 878-5705
EMP: 532
SALES (corp-wide): 2.7B **Publicly Held**
WEB: www.gewaterford.com
SIC: 2869 3479 Silicones; coating of metals with silicon
HQ: Momentive Performance Materials Inc.
260 Hudson River Rd
Waterford NY 12188

(G-16504)
R & H ENTERPRISES LLC
Also Called: Rh Enterprises
4933 Karen Isle Dr (44143-1412)
PHONE..................216 702-4449
Ryan Hoover, *Mng Member*
EMP: 6
SALES (est): 135.3K **Privately Held**
SIC: 7372 7389 Application computer software;

(G-16505)
TRANZONIC ACQUISITION CORP
Also Called: Tranzonic Companies
26301 Curtiss Wright Pkwy (44143-4413)
PHONE..................216 535-4300
Kenneth Vuylsteke, *Principal*
Thomas S Friedl, *CFO*
Ker Werbeach, *Asst Mgr*
◆ EMP: 1100 EST: 1997
SQ FT: 22,000
SALES (est): 80.7MM **Privately Held**
SIC: 2211 2326 2842 2262 Scrub cloths; work garments, except raincoats: waterproof; sanitation preparations, disinfectants & deodorants; industrial plant disinfectants or deodorants; napping: manmade fiber & silk broadwoven fabrics; napkins, sanitary: made from purchased paper

(G-16506)
TRANZONIC COMPANIES (PA)
Also Called: Ccp Industries
26301 Curtiss Wright Pkwy # 200 (44143-1454)
PHONE..................216 535-4300
Thomas Friedl, *CEO*
Melissa Sims, *Partner*
Rudy Garcia, *District Mgr*
Tim Kline, *Area Mgr*
Paul Lee, *Area Mgr*
◆ EMP: 150

SALES (est): 295.9MM **Privately Held**
SIC: 2842 2273 5087 2676 Sanitation preparations, disinfectants & deodorants; mats & matting; cleaning & maintenance equipment & supplies; napkins, sanitary: made from purchased paper

(G-16507)
TRANZONIC COMPANIES
Also Called: Hospeco
26301 Curtiss Wright Pkwy # 200 (44143-1454)
PHONE..................216 535-4300
Mike Blanchard, *Branch Mgr*
Brett Snow, *Manager*
Nancy Calderone, *MIS Staff*
EMP: 420
SALES (corp-wide): 295.9MM **Privately Held**
SIC: 2676 3581 3842 3586 Napkins, sanitary: made from purchased paper; automatic vending machines; surgical appliances & supplies; measuring & dispensing pumps; women's & children's underwear; men's & boys' underwear & nightwear
PA: The Tranzonic Companies
26301 Curtiss Wright Pkwy # 200
Richmond Heights OH 44143
216 535-4300

Richwood
Union County

(G-16508)
CREATIVE FABRICATION LTD
20110 Predmore Rd (43344-9014)
PHONE..................740 262-5789
John Hughes, *Mng Member*
EMP: 7
SALES (est): 665K **Privately Held**
SIC: 7692 7389 Welding repair;

(G-16509)
WILEY FARMS
29984 State Route 739 (43344-9770)
PHONE..................937 537-0676
David Wiley, *Owner*
Nancy Wiley, *Owner*
EMP: 4
SALES (est): 190K **Privately Held**
SIC: 3523 Driers (farm): grain, hay & seed

Ridgeville Corners
Henry County

(G-16510)
ALEX PRODUCTS INC (PA)
19911 County Rd T (43555)
P.O. Box 326 (43555-0326)
PHONE..................419 267-5240
Dave Von Deylen, *President*
Gary Crider, *CFO*
Sharon Hancock, *Accounting Mgr*
▲ EMP: 300 EST: 1973
SQ FT: 150,000
SALES (est): 110.3MM **Privately Held**
WEB: www.alexproducts.com
SIC: 3599 Machine shop, jobbing & repair

(G-16511)
AP-ALTERNATIVES LLC
20 345 County Road X (43555)
PHONE..................419 267-5280
David Von Deylen, *Ch of Bd*
Kristi Von Deylen, *Business Mgr*
Rick Ely, *Design Engr*
Joshua Von Deylen, *Sales Mgr*
Josh Von Deylen, *Marketing Staff*
EMP: 12
SQ FT: 5,000
SALES (est): 3.1MM **Privately Held**
SIC: 2531 3441 Stadium seating; fabricated structural metal

(G-16512)
MAGNA INTERNATIONAL AMER INC
Also Called: Camslide South
19911 County Rd (43555)
PHONE..................905 853-3604

Phil Holjak, *Principal*
EMP: 45
SALES (corp-wide): 38.9B **Privately Held**
SIC: 2531 Seats, automobile
HQ: Magna International Of America, Inc.
750 Tower Dr 7000
Troy MI 48098

Ripley
Brown County

(G-16513)
G & J PEPSI-COLA BOTTLERS INC
1111 S 2nd St (45167-1535)
P.O. Box 157 (45167-0157)
PHONE..................937 392-4937
Jim Malone, *Branch Mgr*
EMP: 55
SALES (corp-wide): 418.3MM **Privately Held**
WEB: www.gjpepsi.com
SIC: 2086 Soft drinks: packaged in cans, bottles, etc.; carbonated soft drinks, bottled & canned
PA: G & J Pepsi-Cola Bottlers Inc
9435 Waterstone Blvd # 390
Cincinnati OH 45249
513 785-6060

(G-16514)
MERANDA NIXON ESTATE WINE LLC
6517 Laycock Rd (45167-9723)
PHONE..................937 515-8013
Seth Meranda, *Principal*
EMP: 4
SALES (est): 305K **Privately Held**
SIC: 2084 Wines

(G-16515)
ODYSSEY CANVAS WORKS INC
6689 Us Highway 52 (45167-8922)
P.O. Box 280 (45167-0280)
PHONE..................937 392-4422
Bob Blom, *President*
EMP: 5
SALES: 90K **Privately Held**
SIC: 2394 Awnings, fabric: made from purchased materials

(G-16516)
PCP CHAMPION
300 Congress St (45167-1411)
P.O. Box 125 (45167-0125)
PHONE..................937 392-4301
EMP: 3
SALES (est): 338.9K **Privately Held**
SIC: 3842 Surgical appliances & supplies

(G-16517)
RIPLEY METALWORKS LTD
111 Waterworks Rd (45167-1456)
PHONE..................937 392-4992
Michael Walkup, *General Ptnr*
EMP: 45
SQ FT: 75,000
SALES (est): 9.8MM **Privately Held**
WEB: www.ripleymetalworks.com
SIC: 3441 Fabricated structural metal

(G-16518)
SURGICAL APPLIANCE INDS INC
1311 S 2nd St (45167)
PHONE..................937 392-4301
Brian Faught, *Manager*
Randy Bader, *Manager*
EMP: 20
SALES (corp-wide): 64.5MM **Privately Held**
SIC: 3842 Surgical appliances & supplies
PA: Surgical Appliance Industries, Inc.
3960 Rosslyn Dr
Cincinnati OH 45209
513 271-4594

Risingsun
Wood County

(G-16519)
WELLS INC
8176 Us Highway 23 (43457)
P.O. Box 9 (43457-0009)
PHONE..................419 457-2611
Steffen Wellstein, *President*
Steffen R Wellstein, *President*
EMP: 10 EST: 1967
SQ FT: 15,000
SALES (est): 1.4MM **Privately Held**
WEB: www.wells.com
SIC: 3494 Well adapters

Rittman
Wayne County

(G-16520)
FASTFORMINGCOM LLC
300 Morning Star Dr (44270-9644)
PHONE..................330 927-3277
James Reedy, *President*
EMP: 12 EST: 1999
SQ FT: 12,000
SALES: 70K **Privately Held**
WEB: www.fastforming.com
SIC: 3089 Trays, plastic; thermoformed finished plastic products

(G-16521)
IMPERIAL PLASTICS INC
80 Industrial St (44270-1508)
P.O. Box 375 (44270-0375)
PHONE..................330 927-5065
Walter Staiger, *President*
John Klein, *Exec VP*
Eugene Staiger, *Vice Pres*
Genevieve Staiger, *Vice Pres*
Susan Klein, *Treasurer*
EMP: 55 EST: 1960
SQ FT: 60,000
SALES (est): 12.9MM **Privately Held**
WEB: www.ip-inc.com
SIC: 3089 Extruded finished plastic products

(G-16522)
J & O PLASTICS INC
12475 Sheets Rd (44270-9730)
PHONE..................330 927-3169
Oscar Gross, *President*
Christine Gross, *Corp Secy*
Edgar Gross, *Vice Pres*
EMP: 50
SQ FT: 90,000
SALES (est): 14MM **Privately Held**
SIC: 3089 Injection molding of plastics

(G-16523)
J SMOKIN
9797 Benner Rd (44270-9712)
PHONE..................330 466-7087
EMP: 4
SALES (est): 474.3K **Privately Held**
SIC: 2448 Skids, wood & wood with metal

(G-16524)
LIZZIE MAES BIRDSEED & DG CO
11315 Steiner Rd (44270-9735)
PHONE..................330 927-1795
EMP: 5
SALES (est): 820K **Privately Held**
SIC: 2048 Mfg Prepared Feeds

(G-16525)
LUKE ENGINEERING & MFG CORP
11 Pipestone Rd (44270-9729)
PHONE..................330 925-3344
Pam Craig, *Manager*
EMP: 20
SALES (est): 1.7MM
SALES (corp-wide): 7.1MM **Privately Held**
SIC: 3471 Anodizing (plating) of metals or formed products

Rittman - Wayne County (G-16526)

PA: Luke Engineering & Mfg Corp
456 South Blvd
Wadsworth OH 44281
330 335-1501

(G-16526)
MORTON SALT INC
151 Industrial Ave (44270-1593)
PHONE..................................330 925-3015
Mark Wallace, *Branch Mgr*
EMP: 150
SALES (corp-wide): 4.6B **Privately Held**
WEB: www.mortonintl.com
SIC: 5149 2899 Salt, edible; chemical preparations
HQ: Morton Salt, Inc.
444 W Lake St Ste 3000
Chicago IL 60606

(G-16527)
PFI DISPLAYS INC (PA)
Also Called: Promotional Fixtures
40 Industrial St (44270-1525)
P.O. Box 508 (44270-0508)
PHONE..................................330 925-9015
Vincent Tricomi, *Ch of Bd*
Anthony R Tricomi, *President*
Robert J Kapitan, *Principal*
Rose M Tricomi, *Principal*
James Tricomi, *Vice Pres*
EMP: 40
SQ FT: 70,000
SALES (est): 5.8MM **Privately Held**
WEB: www.pfidisplays.com
SIC: 3993 2541 2542 Displays & cutouts, window & lobby; store & office display cases & fixtures; partitions & fixtures, except wood

(G-16528)
RITTMAN INC
Also Called: Mull Iron
10 Mull Dr (44270-9777)
PHONE..................................330 927-6855
Chester Mull Jr, *President*
Robert A O'Neil, *Principal*
Richard J Wendelken, *Principal*
Beth Mull, *Corp Secy*
William Mull, *Vice Pres*
EMP: 60
SQ FT: 34,000
SALES (est): 14.7MM **Privately Held**
SIC: 3441 1791 Fabricated structural metal; structural steel erection

(G-16529)
SWISS WOODCRAFT INC
15 Industrial St (44270-1507)
PHONE..................................330 925-1807
Ken Maibach, *President*
Dave Rufener, *Vice Pres*
Todd Gasser, *Opers Mgr*
Kenneth Maibach, *Executive*
EMP: 30
SQ FT: 45,000
SALES (est): 4.8MM **Privately Held**
WEB: www.swisswoodcraft.com
SIC: 2431 Doors, wood

(G-16530)
WIL-MARK FROYO LLC
124 Joshua Dr (44270-2001)
PHONE..................................330 421-6043
Mark Hotes, *Principal*
EMP: 5
SALES (est): 194.3K **Privately Held**
SIC: 2024 Yogurt desserts, frozen

Rock Creek
Ashtabula County

(G-16531)
4-SURE WIRE PRODUCTS INC
2589 Forman Rd (44084-9666)
P.O. Box 441 (44084-0441)
PHONE..................................440 563-9263
Kathy Stuart, *President*
James Stuart, *Vice Pres*
EMP: 5
SQ FT: 7,500
SALES: 500K **Privately Held**
SIC: 3496 Miscellaneous fabricated wire products

(G-16532)
DAVID BIXEL
Also Called: Hartsgrove Machine
2683 State Route 534 (44084-9340)
PHONE..................................440 474-4410
David Bixel, *Owner*
EMP: 14
SALES (est): 385.4K **Privately Held**
SIC: 3599 Machine shop, jobbing & repair

(G-16533)
REAL ALLOY SPECIALTY PRODUCTS
2639 E Water St (44084-9601)
PHONE..................................440 563-3487
Nancy Kern, *Manager*
EMP: 16
SALES (corp-wide): 1.3B **Publicly Held**
SIC: 3341 Aluminum smelting & refining (secondary)
HQ: Real Alloy Specialty Products, Inc
3700 Park East Dr Ste 300
Beachwood OH 44122

(G-16534)
TRUMBULL LOCKER PLANT INC
3393 State Route 534 (44084-9776)
PHONE..................................440 474-4631
Chris Kovacic, *President*
EMP: 3
SALES (est): 260K **Privately Held**
SIC: 5421 2011 5193 Meat markets, including freezer provisioniers; meat packing plants; plants, potted

(G-16535)
WELDFAB INC
Also Called: J & M Welding & Fabricating
2642 E Water St (44084-9526)
PHONE..................................440 563-3310
Joe Blaha, *President*
Kelly Booth, *Project Mgr*
Mary Blaha, *Treasurer*
EMP: 4
SQ FT: 5,000
SALES (est): 557.6K **Privately Held**
WEB: www.weldfab.com
SIC: 7692 3441 Welding repair; fabricated structural metal

Rockbridge
Hocking County

(G-16536)
ELLINGER MONUMENT INC
27841 Fairview Cmtry Rd (43149-9400)
PHONE..................................740 385-3687
Donald Ellinger, *President*
EMP: 4
SALES: 75K **Privately Held**
SIC: 5999 3272 Monuments, finished to custom order; tombstones, precast terrazzo or concrete

(G-16537)
MANDI A TRIPP
12691 Ovid Rd (43149-9651)
PHONE..................................740 380-1216
Mandi Tripp, *Owner*
EMP: 5 **EST:** 2010
SALES (est): 346K **Privately Held**
SIC: 2431 Woodwork, interior & ornamental

(G-16538)
VORHEES LOGGING LLC
15275 Mount Olive Rd (43149-9738)
PHONE..................................740 385-0216
Todd E Vorhees, *Owner*
EMP: 3
SALES (est): 203.7K **Privately Held**
SIC: 2411 Logging camps & contractors

Rockford
Mercer County

(G-16539)
FREMONT COMPANY
150 Hickory St (45882-9264)
PHONE..................................419 363-2924
George Mc Cracken, *Vice Pres*
James Gibson, *Opers-Prdtn-Mfg*
Philip Reyman, *Assistant*
EMP: 40
SALES (est): 10.3MM
SALES (corp-wide): 59.9MM **Privately Held**
WEB: www.fremontcompany.com
SIC: 2033 2099 2035 Fruit juices: packaged in cans, jars, etc.; food preparations; pickles, sauces & salad dressings
PA: The Fremont Company
802 N Front St
Fremont OH 43420
419 334-8995

(G-16540)
MERCER LANDMARK INC
450 Strable Rd (45882-9748)
PHONE..................................419 363-3391
Alvin Sell, *Branch Mgr*
EMP: 6
SALES (corp-wide): 242.8MM **Privately Held**
SIC: 2879 Agricultural chemicals
PA: Mercer Landmark, Inc.
426 W Market St
Celina OH 45822
419 628-3093

(G-16541)
TRUSS WORX LLC
12412 Frysinger Rd (45882-9520)
PHONE..................................419 363-2100
Kimberly Green, *Principal*
EMP: 5
SALES (est): 465.1K **Privately Held**
SIC: 2439 Trusses, wooden roof

(G-16542)
WORLD CONNECTIONS CORPS
10803 Erastus Durbin Rd (45882-9654)
PHONE..................................419 363-2681
Llloyd Linton, *President*
EMP: 50
SALES (est): 2.7MM **Privately Held**
SIC: 3081 Vinyl film & sheet

Rocky River
Cuyahoga County

(G-16543)
BALBO INDUSTRIES INC (PA)
Also Called: Fitness Serve
20630 Center Ridge Rd (44116-3403)
PHONE..................................440 333-0630
Joseph J Balbo, *President*
EMP: 6 **EST:** 1975
SALES (est): 816.9K **Privately Held**
WEB: www.fitnessserve.com
SIC: 3949 7699 5941 5091 Exercise equipment; recreational sporting equipment repair services; sporting goods & bicycle shops; sporting & recreation goods

(G-16544)
CRUISIN TIMES MAGAZINE
20545 Center Ridge Rd Ll40 (44116-3430)
PHONE..................................440 331-4615
John Shapiro, *Principal*
EMP: 7 **EST:** 2008
SALES (est): 415.1K **Privately Held**
SIC: 5994 2721 Magazine stand; magazines: publishing & printing

(G-16545)
CTB CONSULTING LLC
19056 Old Detroit Rd (44116-1720)
PHONE..................................216 712-7764
Charles T Bartell,
EMP: 14 **EST:** 2010
SALES (est): 832.7K **Privately Held**
SIC: 2024 2052 Ice cream & frozen desserts; cookies

(G-16546)
DDNEWS
19035 Old Detroit Rd (44116-1710)
PHONE..................................440 331-6600
Laurence Doyle, *Exec VP*
EMP: 3
SALES (est): 175.3K **Privately Held**
SIC: 2834 Pharmaceutical preparations

(G-16547)
FINE LINE EMBROIDERY COMPANY (PA)
20525 Detroit Rd Ste 9 (44116-2444)
PHONE..................................440 331-7030
David Michael, *President*
Marilyn Michael, *Vice Pres*
EMP: 6
SALES: 1MM **Privately Held**
SIC: 2395 2759 5137 5136 Embroidery products, except schiffli machine; commercial printing; women's & children's clothing; men's & boys' clothing

(G-16548)
GREAT LAKES MFG GROUP LTD
19035 Old Detroit Rd (44116-1710)
PHONE..................................440 391-8266
Andrew E Drumm, *Partner*
Thomas Mc Neill, *Partner*
EMP: 7
SALES: 1MM **Privately Held**
SIC: 3312 8748 Stainless steel; systems analysis & engineering consulting services

(G-16549)
LUCIO VANNI LLC
Also Called: Vanni Wang Couture
1545 Wooster Rd (44116-1901)
PHONE..................................440 823-6103
Vanni Wang,
EMP: 3
SALES (est): 172.4K **Privately Held**
SIC: 2337 Women's & misses' suits & coats

(G-16550)
OPAL DIAMOND LLC
20033 Detroit Rd (44116-2400)
PHONE..................................330 653-5876
EMP: 7
SQ FT: 2,000
SALES: 200K **Privately Held**
SIC: 2875 Mfg Fertilizers-Mix Only

(G-16551)
ORGANIC SPA MAGAZINE LTD (PA)
19537 Lake Rd 203 (44116-1858)
PHONE..................................440 331-5750
Beverly Maloney-Fischba, *President*
Maryann Javorek, *Director*
EMP: 4
SALES (est): 460K **Privately Held**
SIC: 2721 Magazines: publishing only, not printed on site

(G-16552)
PRIEST SERVICES INC
1127 Linda St (44116-1825)
P.O. Box 16307 (44116-0307)
PHONE..................................440 333-1123
Victor Reichle, *Production*
EMP: 17
SALES (corp-wide): 4.1MM **Privately Held**
WEB: www.floorprep.com
SIC: 3275 Gypsum products
PA: Priest Services, Inc.
1127 Linda St 5885
Mayfield Heights OH 44124
440 333-1123

(G-16553)
PS GRAPHICS INC
20284 Orchard Grove Ave (44116-3527)
PHONE..................................440 356-9656
Nancy Vedda, *President*
Phil Vedda, *Vice Pres*
EMP: 6
SQ FT: 4,000
SALES (est): 400K **Privately Held**
WEB: www.psgraphics.com
SIC: 2759 Commercial printing

(G-16554)
RELIANCE DESIGN INC
3463 Archwood Dr (44116-3703)
PHONE..................................216 267-5450
Irene Kostakis, *President*
Alex Kostakis, *Vice Pres*
Alex Kospakis, *Engineer*
Thomas Kostakis, *Finance*
EMP: 10

SQ FT: 8,000
SALES: 100K **Privately Held**
WEB: www.reliancedesigninc.com
SIC: 8711 3599 Consulting engineer; machine & other job shop work

(G-16555)
ROCKY RIVER BREWING CO
21290 Center Ridge Rd (44116-3204)
PHONE..................................440 895-2739
Gary Cintron, *Owner*
EMP: 50
SQ FT: 4,000
SALES (est): 4.8MM **Privately Held**
SIC: 2082 5813 5812 Malt beverages; drinking places; eating places

(G-16556)
SCRATCH OFF WORKS
19537 Lake Rd (44116-1858)
PHONE..................................440 333-4302
Tony Kozak, *Owner*
Tony Kozack, *Owner*
EMP: 8
SALES: 700K **Privately Held**
SIC: 2752 Commercial printing, offset

(G-16557)
SWEET MELISSAS
19337 Detroit Rd (44116-1801)
PHONE..................................440 333-6357
Jen Graham, *General Mgr*
Raja Lalchand, *Principal*
EMP: 7 EST: 2008
SALES (est): 999.4K **Privately Held**
SIC: 2064 Candy & other confectionery products

(G-16558)
SYNTEC LLC
20525 Center Ridge Rd # 512 (44116-3424)
PHONE..................................440 229-6262
Gary J Fisher,
EMP: 5 EST: 2010
SALES (est): 543.2K **Privately Held**
SIC: 7372 Business oriented computer software

(G-16559)
VITALROCK LLC
19885 Detroit Rd Ste 108 (44116-1815)
PHONE..................................888 596-8892
Ryan Brown, *Mng Member*
Chad Schron,
EMP: 4
SALES (est): 144.3K **Privately Held**
SIC: 7372 Educational computer software

Rogers
Columbiana County

(G-16560)
PAUL R LIPP & SON INC
47563 Pancake Clarkson Rd (44455-9723)
PHONE..................................330 227-9614
Gregory A Lipp, *President*
Paul R Lipp, *Vice Pres*
Lauren Lipp, *Admin Sec*
EMP: 10
SALES: 1.2MM **Privately Held**
WEB: www.prlipp.com
SIC: 1794 3273 Excavation & grading; building construction; ready-mixed concrete

(G-16561)
ROGERS MILL INC (PA)
7431 Depot St (44455-9785)
P.O. Box 297 (44455-0297)
PHONE..................................330 227-3214
Bob Black, *President*
Keith Cope, *President*
Cindy Black, *Admin Sec*
EMP: 5
SQ FT: 20,000
SALES (est): 520.9K **Privately Held**
SIC: 2048 5191 Prepared feeds; farm supplies

Rome
Ashtabula County

(G-16562)
J AARON WEAVER
Also Called: Indian Creek Structures
5759 Us Highway 6 (44085-9634)
PHONE..................................440 474-9185
J Aaron Weaver, *Owner*
EMP: 6
SQ FT: 2,400
SALES (est): 369.8K **Privately Held**
SIC: 2452 Prefabricated wood buildings

(G-16563)
J P DENNIS MACHINE INC
4380 State Route 534 (44085-9540)
PHONE..................................440 474-0247
Jim P Dennis, *President*
EMP: 4
SQ FT: 7,200
SALES: 500K **Privately Held**
SIC: 3599 Machine shop, jobbing & repair

(G-16564)
M S C INDUSTRIES INC
5131 Ireland Rd (44085-9630)
P.O. Box 200, Montville (44064-0200)
PHONE..................................440 474-8788
John M Husek, *President*
Mary C Husek, *Admin Sec*
EMP: 6
SQ FT: 4,000
SALES (est): 726K **Privately Held**
SIC: 3545 3469 Tools & accessories for machine tools; machine parts, stamped or pressed metal

Rootstown
Portage County

(G-16565)
A TO Z PAPER BOX CO
4477 Tallmadge Rd (44272-9610)
P.O. Box 276 (44272-0276)
PHONE..................................330 325-8722
Douglas Eatinger, *President*
EMP: 9
SQ FT: 3,600
SALES (est): 1.5MM **Privately Held**
SIC: 2652 5113 2759 Filing boxes, paperboard: made from purchased materials; bags, paper & disposable plastic; commercial printing

(G-16566)
ADVANTAGE CIRCUITS LTD
3512 Industry Rd (44272-9715)
PHONE..................................330 256-7768
Dawn Miller, *President*
EMP: 3
SALES (est): 338K **Privately Held**
WEB: www.advantagecircuits.com
SIC: 3679 Electronic circuits

(G-16567)
CUSTOM MACHINING SOLUTIONS LLC
5605 Tallmadge Rd (44272-9565)
PHONE..................................330 221-1523
John Morris, *Mng Member*
Michael Morris,
EMP: 4
SALES (est): 147K **Privately Held**
SIC: 3531 7389 Construction machinery;

(G-16568)
EDINBURG FIXTURE & MACHINE
3101 State Route 14 (44272-9791)
PHONE..................................330 947-1700
Terri Tomazin, *President*
EMP: 15
SALES (est): 1.5MM **Privately Held**
SIC: 3599 Machine shop, jobbing & repair

(G-16569)
JET RUBBER COMPANY
4457 Tallmadge Rd (44272-9610)
PHONE..................................330 325-1821
Franklin R Brubaker, *Principal*
Karen Crooks, *Corp Secy*
Ken Beachy, *Sales Mgr*
EMP: 43 EST: 1954
SQ FT: 20,000
SALES (est): 8.5MM **Privately Held**
WEB: www.jetrubber.com
SIC: 3069 3053 3533 5085 Molded rubber products; gaskets, packing & sealing devices; gaskets & sealing devices; gas field machinery & equipment; oil field machinery & equipment; rubber goods, mechanical

(G-16570)
MICHAEL FABRICATING INC
4003 State Route 44 (44272-9633)
PHONE..................................330 325-8636
John Micheal, *President*
EMP: 3
SALES: 500K **Privately Held**
SIC: 3444 Sheet metalwork

(G-16571)
MINERS TRACTOR SALES INC (PA)
Also Called: Miner's Bishop Tractor Sales
6941 Tallmadge Rd (44272-9758)
PHONE..................................330 325-9914
Stephen Miner, *CEO*
Craig M Stephens, *President*
EMP: 11
SALES (est): 3.4MM **Privately Held**
SIC: 3537 5999 Industrial trucks & tractors; farm tractors

(G-16572)
NUEVUE SOLUTIONS INC
4209 State Route 44 D-134 (44272-9698)
PHONE..................................440 836-4772
William McCroskey, *President*
James Sacher, *Principal*
EMP: 6
SALES (est): 377.2K **Privately Held**
SIC: 3841 Surgical & medical instruments

(G-16573)
TRUE DEFENSE SOLUTIONS LLC
3265 State Route 44 (44272-9686)
PHONE..................................330 325-1695
EMP: 3
SALES (est): 153K **Privately Held**
SIC: 3812 Defense systems & equipment

Roseville
Muskingum County

(G-16574)
B & B CAST STONE CO INC
7790 Ransbottom Rd (43777-9506)
PHONE..................................740 697-0008
Richard E Baker, *President*
Rebecca Brydon, *Corp Secy*
EMP: 3 EST: 1966
SQ FT: 5,000
SALES (est): 301.3K **Privately Held**
SIC: 3299 3272 Statuary: gypsum, clay, papier mache, metal, etc.; concrete products

(G-16575)
BOYD SANITATION
5525 4th St (43777-9501)
P.O. Box 73 (43777-0073)
PHONE..................................740 697-7940
Robert Boyd, *Owner*
Robert D Boyd, *Owner*
EMP: 3
SALES (est): 156K **Privately Held**
SIC: 4953 2842 Garbage: collecting, destroying & processing; specialty cleaning, polishes & sanitation goods

(G-16576)
CLAY BURLEY PRODUCTS CO (PA)
455 Gordon St (43777-1110)
P.O. Box 35 (43777-0035)
PHONE..................................740 452-3633
Peter Petratsas, *President*
Emmett Abella, *Traffic Mgr*
Bobbi Bennett, *Sales Executive*
▲ EMP: 50
SQ FT: 180,000
SALES (est): 8.3MM **Privately Held**
WEB: www.burleyclay.com
SIC: 3269 5032 Stoneware pottery products; art & ornamental ware, pottery; ceramic wall & floor tile

(G-16577)
CLAY BURLEY PRODUCTS CO
451 Gordon St (43777-1110)
P.O. Box 35 (43777-0035)
PHONE..................................740 697-0221
Steve McCaan, *President*
EMP: 38
SALES (corp-wide): 8.3MM **Privately Held**
WEB: www.burleyclay.com
SIC: 3269 Stoneware pottery products
PA: Burley Clay Products Co (Inc)
455 Gordon St
Roseville OH 43777
740 452-3633

(G-16578)
LARRY MOORE
6680 Ransbottom Rd (43777-9579)
PHONE..................................740 697-7085
Larry Moore, *Owner*
EMP: 3
SALES (est): 184.5K **Privately Held**
SIC: 3715 Truck trailers

(G-16579)
ROSEVILLE HARDWOOD
103 Church St (43777-1006)
PHONE..................................740 221-8712
Mike Offineer, *Partner*
EMP: 3 EST: 2013
SALES (est): 176.7K **Privately Held**
SIC: 2421 Sawmills & planing mills, general

(G-16580)
TRADEWINDS PRIN TWEAR
35 E Athens Rd (43777-1212)
PHONE..................................740 214-5005
Tom Erdico, *Owner*
Susan Erdico, *Co-Owner*
EMP: 6
SALES: 200K **Privately Held**
SIC: 2752 Commercial printing, offset

Rossburg
Darke County

(G-16581)
CAL-MAINE FOODS INC
3078 Washington Rd (45362-9500)
PHONE..................................937 337-9576
Leonard Kropp, *General Mgr*
EMP: 43
SALES (corp-wide): 1.5B **Publicly Held**
WEB: www.calmainefoods.com
SIC: 0252 2015 Chicken eggs; poultry slaughtering & processing
PA: Cal-Maine Foods, Inc.
3320 W Woodrow Wilson Ave
Jackson MS 39209
601 948-6813

(G-16582)
FORT RECOVERY EQUITY EXCHANGE
Also Called: S & R Egg
13243 Cochran Rd (45362-9753)
PHONE..................................937 338-8901
Lou Daniels, *Manager*
Greag Fortkamp, *Manager*
EMP: 30
SALES (est): 1.7MM **Privately Held**
SIC: 2015 Egg processing

Rossford
Wood County

(G-16583)
ELECTRO PRIME ASSEMBLY INC
63 Dixie Hwy Ste 7 (43460-1264)
PHONE..................................419 476-0100

Rossford - Wood County (G-16584)

Fred Busch, *President*
Kevin Meade, *Vice Pres*
James E Wilson, *VP Mfg*
Tad Cousino, *Engineer*
John Lauffer, *VP Finance*
EMP: 14
SALES: 3.5MM **Privately Held**
SIC: 3471 Plating & polishing

(G-16584)
ELECTRO PRIME GROUP LLC
63 Dixie Hwy Ste 7 (43460-1264)
PHONE.................................419 666-5000
Richard Boehme, *Production*
Kavin Meade, *Branch Mgr*
EMP: 80
SALES (corp-wide): 20MM **Privately Held**
SIC: 3471 Plating & polishing
PA: Electro Prime Group Llc
4510 Lint Ave Ste B
Toledo OH 43612
419 476-0100

(G-16585)
ETCHING CONCEPTS
621 Bruns Dr (43460-1548)
PHONE.................................419 691-9086
Jim Welch, *Partner*
Carolyn Welch, *Partner*
EMP: 3
SQ FT: 1,500
SALES: 200K **Privately Held**
WEB: www.etchingconcepts.com
SIC: 3231 5199 Decorated glassware: chipped, engraved, etched, etc.; glassware, novelty

(G-16586)
HUNGER HYDRAULICS CC LTD
Also Called: Hunger Industrial Complex
63 Dixie Hwy Ste 1 (43460-1270)
P.O. Box 37 (43460-0037)
PHONE.................................419 666-4510
Walter Hunger, *President*
▲ EMP: 12
SALES (est): 2.8MM
SALES (corp-wide): 528.6K **Privately Held**
WEB: www.hunger-group.com
SIC: 3593 7699 Fluid power cylinders, hydraulic or pneumatic; hydraulic equipment repair
HQ: Walter Hunger International Gesellschaft Mit Beschrankter Haftung
Alfred-Nobel-Str. 26
Wurzburg 97080
931 900-970

(G-16587)
NAPTIME PRODUCTIONS LLC
107 Hidden Cove St (43460-1027)
PHONE.................................419 662-9521
Lisa Sattler, *Principal*
Kerri Brimmer,
EMP: 15
SALES (est): 1.6MM **Privately Held**
WEB: www.naptimecards.com
SIC: 2771 5947 Greeting cards; greeting cards

(G-16588)
OBR COOLING TOWERS INC
9665 S Compass Dr (43460-1740)
PHONE.................................419 243-3443
Peter Poll, *President*
John Hall, *Exec VP*
Philip Poll, *Treasurer*
Debra Haas, *Admin Sec*
EMP: 45
SQ FT: 6,000
SALES (est): 7.7MM **Privately Held**
WEB: www.obrcoolingtowers.com
SIC: 7699 3444 Industrial equipment services; cooling towers, sheet metal

(G-16589)
PILKINGTON NORTH AMERICA INC
Also Called: Pilington Libbey-Owens-Ford Co
140 Dixie Hwy (43460-1215)
PHONE.................................419 247-3121
Dick Altman, *Opers-Prdtn-Mfg*
Joe Gyurasics, *Senior Mgr*
Gary Warne, *Technology*
EMP: 360
SQ FT: 3,000,000
SALES (corp-wide): 5.6B **Privately Held**
WEB: www.low-eglass.com
SIC: 3211 3231 Float glass; products of purchased glass
HQ: Pilkington North America, Inc.
811 Madison Ave Fl 3
Toledo OH 43604
419 247-3731

(G-16590)
PRAXAIR INC
Dixie Hwy (43460)
P.O. Box 68 (43460-0068)
PHONE.................................419 666-5206
Randy Lee, *Branch Mgr*
EMP: 55 **Privately Held**
SIC: 2813 Industrial gases
HQ: Praxair, Inc.
10 Riverview Dr
Danbury CT 06810
203 837-2000

(G-16591)
RADOCY INC
30652 E River Rd (43460)
P.O. Box 67 (43460-0067)
PHONE.................................419 666-4400
Thomas Bradley, *President*
Mike Bradley, *Sales Mgr*
Paul F Radocy, *Shareholder*
EMP: 15 EST: 1940
SQ FT: 18,000
SALES (est): 3.8MM **Privately Held**
WEB: www.radocy.com
SIC: 3536 3594 3566 Cranes, industrial plant; fluid power pumps & motors; speed changers, drives & gears

(G-16592)
RSW TECHNOLOGIES LLC
135 Dixie Hwy (43460-1241)
PHONE.................................419 662-8100
Russ Wumer,
▲ EMP: 17
SALES (est): 3.6MM **Privately Held**
SIC: 3823 Industrial instrmnts msrmnt display/control process variable

(G-16593)
SASHA ELECTRONICS INC
Also Called: Digital Technologies
135 Dixie Hwy (43460-1241)
PHONE.................................419 662-8100
William R Wumer Jr, *President*
▲ EMP: 19
SQ FT: 20,000
SALES (est): 1.3MM **Privately Held**
WEB: www.powermiser.com
SIC: 7629 3822 Electronic equipment repair; energy cutoff controls, residential or commercial types

(G-16594)
WELCH PUBLISHING CO
215 Osborne St (43460-1238)
PHONE.................................419 666-5344
John Welch, *Vice Pres*
EMP: 7
SQ FT: 1,167
SALES (corp-wide): 2.2MM **Privately Held**
WEB: www.rossford.com
SIC: 2711 Newspapers: publishing only, not printed on site
PA: Welch Publishing Co
117 E 2nd St
Perrysburg OH 43551
419 874-2528

Rushsylvania
Logan County

(G-16595)
DAYTON SUPERIOR CORPORATION
Also Called: Roberts Screw Products
270 Rush St (43347-2502)
PHONE.................................937 682-4015
Allan Kerns, *Branch Mgr*
EMP: 20 **Publicly Held**
WEB: www.daytonsuperior.com
SIC: 3429 Manufactured hardware (general)
HQ: Dayton Superior Corporation
1125 Byers Rd
Miamisburg OH 45342
937 866-0711

(G-16596)
LEVANS ELECTRIC & HVAC
275 Mill St W (43347-9731)
PHONE.................................937 468-2269
Le Sandy, *Principal*
EMP: 4
SALES (est): 290K **Privately Held**
SIC: 3699 Electrical work

Rushville
Fairfield County

(G-16597)
SOMERSET COMMERCIAL PRTG CO
9050 Pleasantville Rd Ne (43150-9658)
PHONE.................................740 536-7187
Michael John Rutherford, *President*
EMP: 3
SALES (est): 220K **Privately Held**
SIC: 2759 Commercial printing

Russells Point
Logan County

(G-16598)
HONDA TRANSM MFG AMER INC
6964 State Route 235 N (43348-9703)
PHONE.................................937 843-5555
Yuji Takahashi, *President*
Masanori Kato, *President*
Steve Mortimer, *COO*
Gary Hand, *Vice Pres*
Mark Zumberger, *Manager*
▲ EMP: 1200
SQ FT: 900,000
SALES (est): 228.8MM
SALES (corp-wide): 144.1B **Privately Held**
SIC: 3714 Wheels, motor vehicle
HQ: American Honda Motor Co., Inc.
1919 Torrance Blvd
Torrance CA 90501
310 783-2000

(G-16599)
INDIAN LAKE BOAT LIFT
129 Wilgus W (43348)
P.O. Box 1145 (43348-1145)
PHONE.................................937 539-2868
R Steven Snider, *Principal*
EMP: 4 EST: 2013
SALES (est): 317.4K **Privately Held**
SIC: 3536 Boat lifts

(G-16600)
INDIAN LAKE SHOPPERS EDGE
204 1/2 Lincoln Blvd (43348-9681)
P.O. Box 38 (43348-0038)
PHONE.................................937 843-6600
Art Shellenbarger, *Partner*
Miriam Shellenbarger, *Partner*
EMP: 9
SALES (est): 465.8K **Privately Held**
SIC: 2711 Newspapers: publishing only, not printed on site

(G-16601)
STALEY & SONS POWERWASHING LLC
6732 Wisharte (43348)
P.O. Box 161 (43348-0161)
PHONE.................................937 843-2713
Lori L Staley,
Scott L Staley,
EMP: 5
SALES: 530K **Privately Held**
SIC: 3589 Commercial cleaning equipment

(G-16602)
WEST OHIO TOOL COMPANY
7311 World Class Dr (43348-9593)
P.O. Box 1457 (43348-1457)
PHONE.................................937 842-6688
Kerry Buchenroth, *President*
Mike Reigelsperger, *Design Engr*
EMP: 12
SALES (est): 2.3MM **Privately Held**
WEB: www.westohiotool.com
SIC: 3541 Machine tools, metal cutting type

(G-16603)
WORLD CLASS PLASTICS INC
7695 State Route 708 (43348-9506)
PHONE.................................937 843-3003
Steven L Buchenroth, *CEO*
Mark Seeley, *President*
Scott Wisniewski, *Vice Pres*
Wc Wagoner, *Facilities Mgr*
Joe Ferryman, *Engineer*
▲ EMP: 80
SQ FT: 42,000
SALES (est): 27.8MM **Privately Held**
WEB: www.worldclassplastics.com
SIC: 3089 Injection molding of plastics

Russia
Shelby County

(G-16604)
A & M PALLET
3860 Rangeline Rd (45363-9784)
PHONE.................................937 295-3093
Andy Meyer, *Managing Prtnr*
Mike Monnin, *Partner*
EMP: 14 EST: 1984
SQ FT: 700
SALES (est): 1.7MM **Privately Held**
WEB: www.ampallet.com
SIC: 2448 Pallets, wood

(G-16605)
ABRASIVE SOURCE INC
211 W Main St (45363-9678)
P.O. Box 369 (45363-0369)
PHONE.................................937 526-9753
Kenneth W Whetstone, *President*
Diana J Whetstone, *Vice Pres*
EMP: 10
SQ FT: 1,600
SALES (est): 1.2MM **Privately Held**
WEB: www.abrasivesource.com
SIC: 3291 Abrasive products

(G-16606)
CLOPAY BUILDING PDTS CO INC
101 N Liberty St (45363-9810)
PHONE.................................937 526-4301
Steve Lanners, *Branch Mgr*
Paul Poeppelman, *Manager*
EMP: 3
SALES (corp-wide): 1.5B **Publicly Held**
SIC: 2431 3442 2436 Garage doors, overhead: wood; garage doors, overhead: metal; plywood, softwood
HQ: Clopay Building Products Company, Inc.
8585 Duke Blvd
Mason OH 45040

(G-16607)
FRANCIS MANUFACTURING COMPANY
500 E Mn St (45363)
P.O. Box 400 (45363-0400)
PHONE.................................937 526-4551
Thomas V Francis, *Ch of Bd*
William T Francis, *President*
David J Francis, *Vice Pres*
Thomas W Francis, *Vice Pres*
Maryjo High, *Manager*
EMP: 125
SQ FT: 145,000
SALES: 25MM **Privately Held**
WEB: www.francismanufacturing.com
SIC: 3369 3365 Nonferrous foundries; aluminum foundries

GEOGRAPHIC SECTION

Saint Clairsville - Belmont County (G-16633)

(G-16608)
FRANCIS-SCHULZE CO
3880 Rangeline Rd (45363-9711)
P.O. Box 245 (45363-0245)
PHONE...................937 295-3941
Ralph Schulze, *President*
Rita Schulze, *Treasurer*
EMP: 45 **EST:** 1943
SQ FT: 50,000
SALES (est): 7.8MM **Privately Held**
WEB: www.francisschulze.com
SIC: 3442 5031 Metal doors; building materials, exterior

(G-16609)
L & J CABLE INC
102 Industrial Dr (45363-7501)
P.O. Box 61 (45363-0061)
PHONE...................937 526-9445
Doug Francis, *President*
Linda Francis, *Vice Pres*
▲ **EMP:** 20
SALES (est): 3MM **Privately Held**
SIC: 3679 Harness assemblies for electronic use: wire or cable

(G-16610)
OREILLY PRECISION PRODUCTS
Also Called: O'Reilly Precision Tool
560 E Main St (45363-9806)
PHONE...................937 526-4677
Jeffrey O'Reilly, *President*
Craig Martin, *Principal*
Shane Borchers, *Vice Pres*
EMP: 35
SALES: 1.5MM **Privately Held**
SIC: 3312 3599 3541 Tool & die steel; amusement park equipment; grinding machines, metalworking

(G-16611)
PRODUCTION SUPPORT INC
105 Francis St (45363-9692)
P.O. Box 457 (45363-0457)
PHONE...................937 526-3897
Linda Grogean, *President*
EMP: 15
SALES (est): 1.7MM **Privately Held**
SIC: 7389 3441 Packaging & labeling services; fabricated structural metal

(G-16612)
RIGHTWAY FAB & MACHINE INC
4101 Rangeline Rd (45363-9713)
PHONE...................937 295-2200
James L McGuffey, *CEO*
Dennis McMahon, *Vice Pres*
EMP: 4
SALES (est): 550K **Privately Held**
SIC: 3861 Blueprint reproduction machines & equipment

(G-16613)
SAINT PARIS TOOL AND GRINDING
2270 Russia Versailles Rd (45363)
PHONE...................937 526-9800
Jeff Oreilly, *Owner*
EMP: 13
SALES (est): 825.1K **Privately Held**
SIC: 3599 Machine shop, jobbing & repair

(G-16614)
VOISARD TOOL LLC
2700 Russia Versailles Rd (45363-9790)
P.O. Box 276 (45363-0276)
PHONE...................937 526-5451
Douglas Voisard, *Mng Member*
EMP: 30
SQ FT: 25,000
SALES (est): 5.9MM
SALES (corp-wide): 95.8MM **Privately Held**
WEB: www.voisardtool.com
SIC: 3545 3544 Machine tool accessories; special dies & tools
PA: Arch Global Precision Llc
2600 S Telg Rd Ste 180
Bloomfield Hills MI 48302

Sabina
Clinton County

(G-16615)
ACCURATE MACHINING & WELDING
764 N State Route 729 (45169-9440)
PHONE...................937 584-4518
John Meshefki, *Owner*
EMP: 5
SALES (est): 546.4K **Privately Held**
SIC: 3599 3544 3541 3548 Machine shop, jobbing & repair; special dies & tools; diamond dies, metalworking; jigs: inspection, gauging & checking; broaching machines; tapping machines; welding & cutting apparatus & accessories: resistance welders, electric; seam welding apparatus, electric; welding on site

(G-16616)
NEW SABINA INDUSTRIES INC (HQ)
12555 Us Highway 22 And 3 (45169-9463)
P.O. Box 8 (45169-0008)
PHONE...................937 584-2433
Kazu Kishi, *President*
Stuart Lohrum, *Plant Mgr*
Mike Burgess, *Engineer*
Tom Cline, *Engineer*
Chuck Mick, *Engineer*
▲ **EMP:** 205
SQ FT: 150,000
SALES (est): 87.6MM
SALES (corp-wide): 2.1B **Privately Held**
SIC: 3714 Instrument board assemblies, motor vehicle
PA: Nippon Seiki Co.,Ltd.
2-2-34, Higashizao
Nagaoka NIG 940-0
258 243-311

(G-16617)
PENNANT MOLDINGS INC
12381 Route 22 E (45169)
P.O. Box 188 (45169-0188)
PHONE...................937 584-5411
Kurt Walterhouse, *President*
Charles E Foster, *Vice Pres*
Karen Wagoner, *Production*
Larry R Martin, *Treasurer*
Jerri Stanforth, *Human Resources*
EMP: 200 **EST:** 1966
SQ FT: 100,000
SALES (est): 63.6MM **Privately Held**
WEB: www.pennantcompanies.com
SIC: 3469 3444 Stamping metal for the trade; sheet metalwork
PA: Pennant Companies
2000 Bethel Rd Ste D
Columbus OH 43220
614 451-1782

(G-16618)
PREMIER FEEDS LLC (HQ)
292 N Howard St (45169-1110)
PHONE...................937 584-2411
Christopher V Meter, *Corp Secy*
John Surber,
EMP: 7
SQ FT: 60,000
SALES (est): 16.1MM
SALES (corp-wide): 16.2MM **Privately Held**
SIC: 2048 5261 5153 2041 Prepared feeds; fertilizer; grains; flour & other grain mill products
PA: Sabina Farmers Exchange, Inc.
292 N Howard St
Sabina OH 45169
937 584-6528

Sagamore Hills
Summit County

(G-16619)
POLYQUEST INC
762 Valley Brook Cir (44067-2241)
PHONE...................330 888-9448
Matthew Kerns, *President*
Joyce Duvendack, *Administration*
EMP: 23
SQ FT: 12,000
SALES (est): 2.7MM **Privately Held**
SIC: 3089 Injection molding of plastics

Saint Bernard
Hamilton County

(G-16620)
BRIGHTON TECHNOLOGIES LLC
Also Called: Btg Labs
5129 Kieley Pl (45217-1100)
PHONE...................513 469-1800
Giles Dillingham, *Ch of Bd*
Thomas McLean, *President*
Thomas Perazzo, *CFO*
Emily Leporati, *Sales Staff*
EMP: 23
SQ FT: 14,000
SALES: 2MM **Privately Held**
SIC: 3823 Industrial process control instruments

Saint Clairsville
Belmont County

(G-16621)
AUSTIN POWDER COMPANY
74200 Edwards Rd (43950-9510)
PHONE...................740 968-1555
Dave Ferri, *Manager*
EMP: 26
SALES (corp-wide): 567.4MM **Privately Held**
SIC: 2892 Explosives
HQ: Austin Powder Company
25800 Science Park Dr # 300
Cleveland OH 44122
216 464-2400

(G-16622)
B K FABRICATION & MACHINE SHOP
70300 Kagg Hill Rd (43950-9601)
PHONE...................740 695-4164
William Kovachic, *Owner*
EMP: 4
SQ FT: 2,680
SALES (est): 137.7K **Privately Held**
SIC: 7539 3499 Machine shop, automotive; fire- or burglary-resistive products

(G-16623)
BELCO WORKS
68425 Hammond Rd (43950-8783)
PHONE...................740 695-0500
Sally Traversa, *Finance Mgr*
EMP: 3
SALES (est): 131.9K **Privately Held**
SIC: 2448 Wood pallets & skids

(G-16624)
BELCO WORKS INC
340 Fox Shannon Pl (43950)
PHONE...................740 695-0500
Kim Cain, *Opers Staff*
Debbie Alexander, *HR Admin*
Sherri Marlin, *Manager*
Anne Haning, *Director*
EMP: 350 **EST:** 1966
SQ FT: 5,000
SALES: 3.2MM **Privately Held**
WEB: www.belcoworks.com
SIC: 8331 3993 3931 2448 Sheltered workshop; signs & advertising specialties; musical instruments; wood pallets & skids

(G-16625)
BELMONT COUNTY OF OHIO
Also Called: Belmon Coutn Recoder's Office
101 W Main St Ste 205 (43950-1264)
PHONE...................740 699-2140
Mary Catherine Nixon, *Manager*
EMP: 7 **Privately Held**
WEB: www.belmontsheriff.com
SIC: 9211 3931 ; recorders (musical instruments)
PA: Belmont County Of Ohio
101 W Main St
Saint Clairsville OH 43950
740 695-2121

(G-16626)
CATRESS LLC
50482 National Rd (43950-8540)
PHONE...................740 695-0918
Robert Stewart, *Owner*
EMP: 3
SALES (est): 141.5K **Privately Held**
SIC: 1389 Gas field services

(G-16627)
COAL RESOURCES INC
46226 National Rd (43950-8742)
PHONE...................740 338-3100
Robert Murray, *Principal*
Jay C Borkenhagen, *Principal*
Lloyd Boston, *Technology*
EMP: 16
SALES (est): 3.5MM **Privately Held**
SIC: 1241 Coal mining services

(G-16628)
COLEMAN MACHINE INC
Also Called: Coleman Machine Company
49381 Firpoint Maynard Rd (43950-9660)
PHONE...................740 695-3006
James Coleman, *President*
Kristine Melcher, *Nurse*
EMP: 5
SALES (est): 633.9K **Privately Held**
SIC: 3599 1623 5999 Machine shop, jobbing & repair; water main construction; farm equipment & supplies

(G-16629)
CONSOL ENERGY
47355 National Rd (43950-8712)
PHONE...................740 232-2140
EMP: 4
SALES (est): 197.5K **Privately Held**
SIC: 1241 Coal mining services

(G-16630)
D LEWIS INC
Also Called: Bill's Counter Tops
52235 National Rd (43950-9306)
PHONE...................740 695-2615
David Lewis, *President*
EMP: 6
SQ FT: 5,000
SALES (est): 761.2K **Privately Held**
SIC: 2542 2541 2434 Cabinets: show, display or storage: except wood; wood partitions & fixtures; wood kitchen cabinets

(G-16631)
D W TRUAX ENTERPRISE INC
Also Called: E & E Ready Rooms
52499 National Rd (43950-9311)
PHONE...................740 695-2596
David Truax, *President*
EMP: 3
SQ FT: 4,000
SALES: 300K **Privately Held**
SIC: 3792 Travel trailers & campers

(G-16632)
GULFPORT ENERGY CORPORATION
67185 Executive Dr (43950-8494)
PHONE...................740 251-0407
William Sowards, *Facilities Mgr*
Jen Masters, *Engineer*
Cindy Gray, *Branch Mgr*
EMP: 41
SALES (corp-wide): 1.3B **Publicly Held**
SIC: 1311 Crude petroleum production
PA: Gulfport Energy Corporation
3001 Quail Springs Pkwy
Oklahoma City OK 73134
405 252-4600

(G-16633)
HARRISON COUNTY COAL COMPANY (PA)
46226 National Rd (43950-8742)
PHONE...................740 338-3100
Jason D Witt, *Manager*
EMP: 38

Saint Clairsville - Belmont County (G-16634)

SALES (est): 22MM **Privately Held**
SIC: 1241 Coal mining services

(G-16634)
INTERSTATE BATTERIES INC
Also Called: Interstate Battery System Amer
44925 Lafferty Rd (43950-7736)
PHONE 740 968-2211
Michael Sutton, *President*
EMP: 5 Privately Held
SIC: 3691 5013 5063 5531 Storage batteries; automotive supplies & parts; batteries; batteries, automotive & truck
HQ: Interstate Batteries, Inc.
12770 Merit Dr Ste 400
Dallas TX 75251
972 991-1444

(G-16635)
KENAMERICAN RESOURCES INC (HQ)
46226 National Rd (43950-8742)
PHONE 740 338-3100
Bob Sandidge, *President*
Randy L Wiles, *Vice Pres*
James R Turner, *Treasurer*
Robert E Murray, *Director*
Michael O McKown, *Admin Sec*
EMP: 6
SALES (est): 42.3MM
SALES (corp-wide): 4.8B **Publicly Held**
SIC: 1222 Bituminous coal-underground mining
PA: Murray Energy Corporation
46226 National Rd
Saint Clairsville OH 43950
740 338-3100

(G-16636)
LION INDUSTRIES LLC
49068 Reservoir Rd (43950)
PHONE 740 699-0369
David A Humphreys Jr, *Vice Pres*
Audrey Humphreys,
EMP: 20
SALES (est): 4.8MM **Privately Held**
SIC: 3443 3449 Fabricated plate work (boiler shop); custom roll formed products

(G-16637)
MARIETTA COAL CO (PA)
67705 Friends Church Rd (43950-9500)
PHONE 740 695-2197
Paul Gill, *President*
George Nicolozakes, *Chairman*
John Nicolozakes, *Vice Pres*
EMP: 50 EST: 1946
SQ FT: 4,300
SALES (est): 8.2MM **Privately Held**
WEB: www.mcatee.biz
SIC: 1221 Surface mining, bituminous

(G-16638)
MURRAY AMERICAN ENERGY INC
46226 National Rd (43950-8742)
PHONE 740 338-3100
Robert E Murray, *President*
Robert D Moore, *Vice Pres*
Michael D Loiacono, *Treasurer*
Jason D Witt, *Admin Sec*
EMP: 2667 EST: 2013
SALES (est): 443.4K
SALES (corp-wide): 4.8B **Publicly Held**
SIC: 1221 Bituminous coal surface mining
PA: Murray Energy Corporation
46226 National Rd
Saint Clairsville OH 43950
740 338-3100

(G-16639)
MURRAY ENERGY CORPORATION (PA)
46226 National Rd (43950-8742)
PHONE 740 338-3100
Robert E Murray, *CEO*
Paul Piccolini, *Principal*
Robert D Moore, *COO*
Moore Robert D, *Exec VP*
McKown Michael O, *Senior VP*
EMP: 4
SQ FT: 6,000
SALES (corp-wide): 4.8B **Publicly Held**
SIC: 1222 Bituminous coal-underground mining

(G-16640)
MURRAY KENTUCKY ENERGY INC (HQ)
46226 National Rd (43950-8742)
PHONE 740 338-3100
Robert E Murray, *President*
EMP: 3
SALES (est): 10.3MM
SALES (corp-wide): 4.8B **Publicly Held**
SIC: 1222 Bituminous coal-underground mining
PA: Murray Energy Corporation
46226 National Rd
Saint Clairsville OH 43950
740 338-3100

(G-16641)
NOMAC DRILLING LLC
67090 Executive Dr (43950-8473)
PHONE 724 324-2205
Stanley Dean, *Business Mgr*
Mark Hughes, *Branch Mgr*
EMP: 11
SALES (corp-wide): 3.3B **Publicly Held**
SIC: 1381 Drilling oil & gas wells
HQ: Nomac Drilling, L.L.C.
3400 S Radio Rd
El Reno OK 73036
405 422-2754

(G-16642)
OFFICE PRINT N COPY
Also Called: Print-N-Copy
104 N Marietta St (43950-1218)
PHONE 740 695-3616
Gene Sirca, *Owner*
Helen Sirca, *Co-Owner*
EMP: 4
SQ FT: 300
SALES (est): 372.3K **Privately Held**
SIC: 2752 Commercial printing, offset

(G-16643)
OHIO HEAT TRANSFER LTD
66721 Executive Dr (43950-8474)
PHONE 740 695-0635
Mark E Epure, *Mng Member*
Phyliss Epure,
▲ **EMP:** 11
SALES: 2.9MM **Privately Held**
SIC: 3443 Heat exchangers: coolers (after, inter), condensers, etc.; air coolers, metal plate

(G-16644)
OHIO VALLEY COAL COMPANY (DH)
46226 National Rd (43950-8742)
PHONE 740 926-1351
Robert E Murray, *CEO*
Ryan M Murray, *President*
John R Forrelli, *Senior VP*
Michael O McKown, *Senior VP*
Robert D Moore, *Vice Pres*
EMP: 395
SQ FT: 40,380
SALES (est): 218.7MM
SALES (corp-wide): 4.8B **Publicly Held**
SIC: 1221 Bituminous coal & lignite-surface mining
HQ: Ohio Valley Resources, Inc.
29325 Chagrin Blvd # 300
Beachwood OH 44122
216 765-1240

(G-16645)
OHIO VALLEY RESOURCES INC
Also Called: Ohio Valley Coal
46226 National Rd (43950-8742)
PHONE 740 795-5220
Robert E Murray, *CEO*
McKown Michael, *Vice Pres*
Andrew Wentz, *Purchasing*
Bo Putsock, *Accounting Dir*
Colt McVey, *Manager*
EMP: 30
SALES (corp-wide): 4.8B **Publicly Held**
SIC: 1241 Coal mining services
HQ: Ohio Valley Resources, Inc.
29325 Chagrin Blvd # 300
Beachwood OH 44122
216 765-1240

(G-16646)
OHIO VALLEY TRANSLOADING CO
46226 National Rd (43950-8742)
PHONE 740 795-4967
Robert Murray, *CEO*
EMP: 2566
SALES (est): 57.6MM
SALES (corp-wide): 4.8B **Publicly Held**
SIC: 1222 Bituminous coal mining services, contract basis
HQ: Ohio Valley Resources, Inc.
29325 Chagrin Blvd # 300
Beachwood OH 44122
216 765-1240

(G-16647)
PURPLE LAND MANAGEMENT LLC
51461 Jennifer Ln Ste 110 (43950-9378)
PHONE 740 238-4259
Rick Bell, *General Mgr*
Sean Courtney, *Admin Sec*
Patricia Widenmeyer, *Administration*
EMP: 8
SALES (corp-wide): 7.3MM **Privately Held**
SIC: 1389 Cementing oil & gas well casings
PA: Purple Land Management, Llc
210 E 8th St
Fort Worth TX 76102
817 717-3835

(G-16648)
RAYLE COAL CO
67705 Friends Church Rd (43950-9500)
PHONE 740 695-2197
John Nicolozakes, *President*
George Nicolozakes, *Chairman*
EMP: 15
SQ FT: 4,300
SALES (est): 965.5K **Privately Held**
SIC: 1221 4491 Surface mining, bituminous; marine cargo handling

(G-16649)
RIESBECK FOOD MARKETS INC
Also Called: Reisbeck Fd Mkts St Clirsville
104 Plaza Dr (43950-8736)
P.O. Box 707 (43950-0707)
PHONE 740 695-3401
Jay Ropietski, *Vice Pres*
Dennis Kasprowski, *Branch Mgr*
EMP: 200
SALES (corp-wide): 204.1MM **Privately Held**
SIC: 5411 5912 5421 2051 Supermarkets, chain; drug stores & proprietary stores; meat & fish markets; bread, cake & related products
PA: Riesbeck Food Markets, Inc.
48661 National Rd
Saint Clairsville OH 43950
740 695-7050

(G-16650)
SCREEN TECH GRAPHICS
152 Saint Patricks Aly B (43950-1581)
PHONE 740 695-7950
John Jenkins, *Owner*
Joe McNamara, *Manager*
EMP: 4
SALES: 500K **Privately Held**
SIC: 2759 Screen printing

(G-16651)
SIDWELL MATERIALS INC
72607 Gun Club Rd (43950-8637)
PHONE 740 968-4313
Jeffrey Sidwell, *President*
EMP: 15
SALES (est): 1.1MM **Privately Held**
SIC: 3273 Ready-mixed concrete

(G-16652)
ST CLAIRSVILLE DAIRY QUEEN
178 E Main St (43950-1534)
PHONE 740 635-1800
Pat Weisal, *Principal*
Cindy Byrd, *Manager*
EMP: 3
SALES (est): 173.1K **Privately Held**
SIC: 2024 Ice cream & frozen desserts

(G-16653)
STEIN-PALMER PRINTING CO
1 Westwood Dr Unit 202 (43950-1053)
PHONE 740 633-3894
Thomas R Palmer, *Owner*
Melody Palmer, *Owner*
Karen Cook, *Admin Sec*
EMP: 8 EST: 1916
SQ FT: 2,500
SALES: 400K **Privately Held**
SIC: 2752 Commercial printing, offset

(G-16654)
STRATA MINE SERVICES INC
68000 Bayberry Dr Bldg 2 (43950-8102)
PHONE 740 695-6880
Jeff Hamrick, *Vice Pres*
Aaron Wilson, *Director*
EMP: 10
SALES (est): 914.9K **Privately Held**
SIC: 1241 Coal mining services

(G-16655)
THOMAS-WILBERT VAULT CO INC
49132 Randall Dr (43950-9438)
PHONE 740 695-5671
Thomas D James, *Principal*
EMP: 3
SALES (est): 160.8K **Privately Held**
SIC: 3272 Burial vaults, concrete or pre-cast terrazzo

(G-16656)
TROO CLEAN ENVIROMENTAL LLC
47096 Magee Rd (43950-8409)
PHONE 304 215-4501
Owen David, *Mng Member*
Orin David,
Tyler David,
Roy Malone,
EMP: 8
SQ FT: 400
SALES: 2MM **Privately Held**
SIC: 4953 1389 Refuse systems; bailing, cleaning, swabbing & treating of wells

(G-16657)
WEST RIDGE RESOURCES INC (PA)
46226 National Rd (43950-8742)
PHONE 740 338-3100
Bruce Hill, *President*
EMP: 5
SALES: 4.5MM **Privately Held**
SIC: 1222 Bituminous coal-underground mining

(G-16658)
WESTERN KY COAL RESOURCES LLC
46226 National Rd (43950-8742)
PHONE 740 338-3100
Robert E Murray, *President*
EMP: 400
SALES (est): 3.7MM
SALES (corp-wide): 4.8B **Publicly Held**
SIC: 1222 Bituminous coal-underground mining
HQ: Murray Kentucky Energy, Inc.
46226 National Rd
Saint Clairsville OH 43950
740 338-3100

Saint Henry
Mercer County

(G-16659)
BECKMAN & GAST COMPANY (PA)
282 W Kremer Hoying Rd (45883-9617)
P.O. Box 307 (45883-0307)
PHONE 419 678-4195
William C Gast, *President*
Paul Moorman, *Corp Secy*
Karl J Gast, *Vice Pres*
Terri Gast, *Manager*
EMP: 15
SQ FT: 65,000

SALES: 12MM **Privately Held**
WEB: www.beckmangast.com
SIC: **2032** 2033 Beans, without meat: packaged in cans, jars, etc.; tomato products: packaged in cans, jars, etc.

(G-16660)
FUTURE POLY TECH INC
393 N Eastern Ave (45883-9501)
PHONE..................614 942-1209
Ron Anderko, *COO*
EMP: 30
SALES (corp-wide): 3.5MM **Privately Held**
SIC: **3081** Polyethylene film
PA: Future Poly Tech, Inc.
2215 Citygate Dr Ste D
Columbus OH 43219
614 942-1209

(G-16661)
FUTURE POLYTECH INC
393 N Eastern Ave (45883-9501)
PHONE..................419 763-1352
Tony Durieux, *President*
EMP: 23
SALES (est): 4.3MM **Privately Held**
SIC: **2671** Plastic film, coated or laminated for packaging

(G-16662)
HI-TECH WIRE INC
631 E Washington St (45883-9683)
PHONE..................419 678-8376
Bill Hemmelgarn, *President*
Susan Hemmelgarn, *Vice Pres*
EMP: 57
SQ FT: 30,000
SALES (est): 13.9MM **Privately Held**
WEB: www.hi-techwire.com
SIC: **3544** Special dies, tools, jigs & fixtures

(G-16663)
HOMESTRETCH SPORTSWEAR INC
491 S Eastern Ave (45883-9585)
PHONE..................419 678-4282
Don H Hess, *President*
Donna Hess, *Exec VP*
Kelly Hess, *Vice Pres*
Kim Hess, *Treasurer*
EMP: 12
SQ FT: 1,920
SALES (est): 1.4MM **Privately Held**
WEB: www.homestretchsportswear.com
SIC: **2759** Screen printing

(G-16664)
ITR MANUFACTURING LLC
811 Ash St (45883-9826)
PHONE..................419 763-1493
Chris Borgerding, *Mng Member*
EMP: 10
SQ FT: 2,400
SALES: 1.5MM **Privately Held**
SIC: **3553** Furniture makers' machinery, woodworking

(G-16665)
JACOBS & SONS LOGGING LLC
132 N Sycamore St (45883-9673)
PHONE..................419 678-3802
Kenneth Jacobs, *Partner*
Gerald Jacobs, *Partner*
Marjorie Jacobs, *Partner*
Mark Jacobs, *Partner*
EMP: 3
SALES: 547K **Privately Held**
SIC: **2411** Logging

(G-16666)
POLY CONCEPTS LLC
712 Ash St (45883)
P.O. Box 500 (45883-0500)
PHONE..................419 678-3300
Jon Ranly, *Design Engr*
Roger Ranly, *Mng Member*
Shirley Magoteaux,
Karen Ranly,
EMP: 5 EST: 2007
SALES (est): 753.3K **Privately Held**
SIC: **2519** Lawn & garden furniture, except wood & metal; lawn furniture, except wood, metal, stone or concrete

(G-16667)
ST HENRY TILE CO INC (PA)
Also Called: Richmond Builders Supply
281 W Washington St (45883-9663)
P.O. Box 318 (45883-0318)
PHONE..................419 678-4841
Bob Homan, *President*
Robert Homan, *President*
Robert Boeckman, *Principal*
Alfred Homan, *Principal*
Raymond Kremer, *Principal*
EMP: 35 EST: 1960
SQ FT: 7,600
SALES (est): 30MM **Privately Held**
SIC: **3271** 5211 3273 Blocks, concrete or cinder: standard; masonry materials & supplies; ready-mixed concrete

(G-16668)
TRU-EDGE GRINDING INC
752 Jim Lachey Dr (45883)
PHONE..................419 678-4991
Jack Meizlish, *President*
Tim Knapke, *Exec VP*
Rick Meizlish, *Vice Pres*
Mark Stimer, *Vice Pres*
Brent Meizlish, *Treasurer*
EMP: 24
SQ FT: 20,000
SALES: 2.5MM
SALES (corp-wide): 20MM **Privately Held**
WEB: www.tru-edge.com
SIC: **3599** Machine shop, jobbing & repair
PA: Buckeye Industrial Supply Company
3989 Groves Rd
Columbus OH 43232
614 864-8400

(G-16669)
V H COOPER & CO INC
Cooper Processing of St Henry
1 Cooper Farm Dr (45883-9556)
PHONE..................419 678-4853
Diana Kleinhenz, *Marketing Staff*
Dale Hart, *Manager*
Dani Weitzel, *Manager*
EMP: 450
SALES (corp-wide): 256.7MM **Privately Held**
WEB: www.cooperfoods.com
SIC: **2015** 2011 Turkey, processed; meat packing plants
HQ: V. H. Cooper & Co, Inc
2321 State Route 49
Fort Recovery OH 45846

(G-16670)
V H COOPER & CO INC
Also Called: Cooper Farms
1 Cooper Farm Dr (45883-9556)
PHONE..................419 678-4853
Jim Cooper, *Principal*
Dave Garman, *Accounting Mgr*
Ron Pfaff, *Manager*
Doris Siefring, *Manager*
Rene Barton, *Office Admin*
EMP: 46
SALES (corp-wide): 256.7MM **Privately Held**
SIC: **2011** Sausages from meat slaughtered on site
HQ: V. H. Cooper & Co, Inc
2321 State Route 49
Fort Recovery OH 45846

(G-16671)
WEST OHIO TOOL & MFG LLC
Also Called: Oven Windows
3965 Lange Rd (45883-9718)
PHONE..................419 678-4745
Christopher Brackman, *Mng Member*
EMP: 4
SALES: 700K **Privately Held**
SIC: **3541** 3263 Machine tools, metal cutting type; commercial tableware or kitchen articles, fine earthenware

Saint Louisville
Licking County

(G-16672)
KOKOSING MATERIALS INC
9134 Mount Vernon Rd (43071-9637)
PHONE..................740 745-3341
Tom Nethers, *Principal*
EMP: 29
SALES (corp-wide): 19.9MM **Privately Held**
SIC: **2951** Asphalt paving mixtures & blocks
PA: Kokosing Materials, Inc.
17531 Waterford Rd
Fredericktown OH 43019
740 694-9585

(G-16673)
LOWERY INDUSTRIES
10975 Houdeshell Rd (43071-9737)
PHONE..................740 745-5045
Jeff A Lowery, *Owner*
EMP: 3
SALES (est): 197K **Privately Held**
WEB: www.loweryindustries.com
SIC: **3469** Machine parts, stamped or pressed metal

(G-16674)
OLEN CORPORATION
9134 Mount Vernon Rd (43071-9637)
PHONE..................740 745-5865
Michael Miller, *Branch Mgr*
EMP: 4
SALES (corp-wide): 289.1MM **Privately Held**
SIC: **1442** 4212 Construction sand mining; gravel mining; local trucking, without storage
PA: The Olen Corporation
4755 S High St
Columbus OH 43207
614 491-1515

Saint Marys
Auglaize County

(G-16675)
ALLAN A IRISH
Also Called: Irish Electric Motor Service
1600 Celina Rd (45885-1214)
PHONE..................419 394-3284
Kathryn Schneider, *Owner*
EMP: 4
SQ FT: 4,000
SALES: 700K **Privately Held**
SIC: **7694** 5063 5999 Electric motor repair; motors, electric; motors, electric

(G-16676)
BEHRCO INC
Also Called: Unique Awards & Signs
1865 Celina Rd (45885-1219)
PHONE..................419 394-1612
Gerry Schetter, *President*
Tom Crast, *Corp Secy*
Julia Haehn, *Vice Pres*
EMP: 6
SQ FT: 3,000
SALES: 750K **Privately Held**
SIC: **3914** 3993 5094 5046 Trophies, plated (all metals); electric signs; trophies; neon signs; signs, electrical; trophies & plaques

(G-16677)
BEST INC
Hc 116 (45885)
P.O. Box 775 (45885-0775)
PHONE..................419 394-2745
Richard Brock, *President*
Kaye Brock, *Corp Secy*
EMP: 6
SQ FT: 12,050
SALES (est): 568K **Privately Held**
SIC: **3599** Machine shop, jobbing & repair

(G-16678)
BEST PERFORMANCE INC
14381 State Route 116 (45885-9226)
P.O. Box 238 (45885-0238)
PHONE..................419 394-2299
Eric Brock, *President*
EMP: 6
SQ FT: 34,000
SALES (est): 800K **Privately Held**
SIC: **3599** Machine shop, jobbing & repair

(G-16679)
BRW TOOL INC
502 Scott St (45885-1862)
P.O. Box 417 (45885-0417)
PHONE..................419 394-3371
Ray Barber, *President*
EMP: 14
SQ FT: 50,000
SALES (est): 931.7K **Privately Held**
WEB: www.brwtool.com
SIC: **3469** 3544 Metal stampings; special dies & tools

(G-16680)
C O WELDING & FABRICATION INC
850 S Main St (45885-2553)
PHONE..................419 394-3293
Charles E Overley, *President*
Connie Overley, *Treasurer*
EMP: 5
SQ FT: 6,000
SALES (est): 350K **Privately Held**
SIC: **7692** Welding repair

(G-16681)
CARGILL INCORPORATED
1400 Mckinley Rd (45885-1821)
P.O. Box B (45885)
PHONE..................419 394-3374
Brent Marquis, *Manager*
EMP: 40
SALES (corp-wide): 114.7B **Privately Held**
SIC: **2047** 2048 Dog & cat food; prepared feeds
PA: Cargill, Incorporated
15407 Mcginty Rd W
Wayzata MN 55391
952 742-7575

(G-16682)
CLASSIC DELIGHT INC
310 S Park Dr (45885-9688)
P.O. Box 367 (45885-0367)
PHONE..................419 394-7955
Darl Harkleroad, *Owner*
Joni Harkleroad, *Vice Pres*
Michele Laughman, *Production*
Tracy Miley, *Purchasing*
Drl Harkleroad, *Human Res Mgr*
EMP: 50
SQ FT: 18,800
SALES (est): 8.9MM **Privately Held**
WEB: www.classicdelight.com
SIC: **2099** Food preparations

(G-16683)
CONAG INC
Also Called: Con-AG
16672 County Road 66a (45885-9212)
PHONE..................419 394-8870
Robert Hirschfeld, *President*
John Hirschfeld, *President*
Lee Kuck, *Corp Secy*
Johnathan Hirschfeld, *Vice Pres*
EMP: 35
SALES (est): 3.5MM **Privately Held**
WEB: www.conag.com
SIC: **1422** Limestones, ground

(G-16684)
EXPRESS TRADING PINS
105 Marbello Ct (45885-9548)
PHONE..................419 394-2550
Jeff Steininger, *Principal*
EMP: 3
SALES (est): 177K **Privately Held**
SIC: **3452** Pins

(G-16685)
FLUIDPOWER ASSEMBLY INC
313 S Park Dr (45885-9689)
PHONE..................419 394-7486

Saint Marys - Auglaize County (G-16686)

Ronald E Langston, *President*
Mark Langston, *Vice Pres*
Ruth Langston, *Vice Pres*
Eric Langston, *Admin Sec*
EMP: 6
SQ FT: 6,000
SALES (est): 1MM **Privately Held**
SIC: 3542 3511 Riveting machines; turbines & turbine generator sets

(G-16686)
HORIZON OHIO PUBLICATIONS INC (HQ)
Also Called: Evening Leader, The
102 E Spring St (45885-2310)
PHONE 419 394-7414
Todd Boit, *President*
Roland Mc Bride, *Treasurer*
EMP: 17 **EST:** 1905
SQ FT: 8,000
SALES (est): 3.5MM
SALES (corp-wide): 71.5MM **Privately Held**
SIC: 2711 Commercial printing & newspaper publishing combined
PA: Horizon Publications, Inc.
1120 N Carbon St Ste 100
Marion IL 62959
618 993-1711

(G-16687)
KNOUS TOOL & MACHINE INC
14184 State Route 116 (45885-9237)
PHONE 419 394-3541
Paul D Knous, *President*
Patsy Knous, *Corp Secy*
EMP: 5
SQ FT: 10,000
SALES: 400K **Privately Held**
SIC: 3599 3544 Machine & other job shop work; special dies & tools

(G-16688)
KOSEI ST MARYS CORPORATION
Also Called: Aap St. Marys Corp.
1100 Mckinley Rd (45885-1815)
PHONE 419 394-7840
Bruce Sakamoto, *CEO*
Shunkichi Kamiya, *President*
Randy Wendel, *President*
Douglas Kramer, *Treasurer*
Daniel Hosek, *Admin Sec*
▲ **EMP:** 524
SQ FT: 470,000
SALES (est): 203.2MM
SALES (corp-wide): 101.2K **Privately Held**
SIC: 3714 Wheels, motor vehicle
PA: Gyoseishoshi Okuda Tomiko Jimusho
3-5-5, Sayamadai
Sayama STM
429 561-771

(G-16689)
L & S LIETTE EXPRESS
2286 Celina Rd (45885-1226)
P.O. Box 726 (45885-0726)
PHONE 419 394-7077
Gregory D Liette, *Principal*
EMP: 6
SQ FT: 4,910
SALES (est): 702.6K **Privately Held**
SIC: 2741 Miscellaneous publishing

(G-16690)
MUROTECH OHIO CORPORATION
Also Called: M T O
550 Mckinley Rd (45885-1803)
P.O. Box 716 (45885-0716)
PHONE 419 394-6529
Naonobu Kemmoku, *President*
Ralph Wiley, *Manager*
▲ **EMP:** 120
SQ FT: 30,000
SALES: 27.8MM
SALES (corp-wide): 188.5MM **Privately Held**
SIC: 3465 Body parts, automobile: stamped metal
PA: Muro Corporation
7-1, Kiyoharakogyodanchi
Utsunomiya TCG 321-3
286 677-121

(G-16691)
NIDEC MINSTER CORPORATION
Also Called: Nidec Minster
331 S Park Dr (45885-9689)
PHONE 419 394-7504
EMP: 3
SALES (corp-wide): 13.9B **Privately Held**
SIC: 3542 Machine tools, metal forming type
HQ: Nidec Minster Corporation
240 W 5th St
Minster OH 45865
419 628-2331

(G-16692)
OMNI MANUFACTURING
901 Mckinley Rd (45885-1812)
PHONE 419 394-7424
Wayne L Freewalt, *President*
Barbara J Combs, *Corp Secy*
EMP: 3
SALES (est): 290K **Privately Held**
SIC: 3544 Special dies, tools, jigs & fixtures

(G-16693)
OMNI MANUFACTURING INC (PA)
901 Mckinley Rd (45885-1812)
P.O. Box 179 (45885-0179)
PHONE 419 394-7424
Wayne L Freewalt, *President*
Bob Prater, *Plant Mgr*
Mary Klosterman, *Mfg Staff*
Barbara Combs, *Treasurer*
Richard Hines, *Controller*
▲ **EMP:** 100
SQ FT: 190,000
SALES (est): 34MM **Privately Held**
WEB: www.omnimfg.com
SIC: 3469 3479 3544 Stamping metal for the trade; coating of metals & formed products; special dies & tools

(G-16694)
OMNI MANUFACTURING INC
220 Cleveland Ave (45885-1706)
PHONE 419 394-7424
Wayne Freewalt, *Manager*
EMP: 11
SALES (corp-wide): 34MM **Privately Held**
WEB: www.omnimfg.com
SIC: 3469 3479 3544 Stamping metal for the trade; coating of metals & formed products; special dies & tools
PA: Omni Manufacturing, Inc.
901 Mckinley Rd
Saint Marys OH 45885
419 394-7424

(G-16695)
PRO-PET LLC
1601 Mckinley Rd (45885-1864)
P.O. Box 369 (45885-0369)
PHONE 419 394-3374
Jim Wiegmann, *President*
James Flora, *COO*
Melanie Boer, *Marketing Staff*
Lily Lew, *Director*
◆ **EMP:** 7
SQ FT: 5,000
SALES (est): 27MM
SALES (corp-wide): 114.7B **Privately Held**
WEB: www.propet.com
SIC: 2047 2048 4212 7389 Cat food; dog food; prepared feeds; animal & farm product transportation services; packaging & labeling services
PA: Cargill, Incorporated
15407 Mcginty Rd W
Wayzata MN 55391
952 742-7575

(G-16696)
QUALITY READY MIX INC (PA)
16672 County Road 66a (45885-9212)
PHONE 419 394-8870
Robert E Hirschfeld, *President*
Lee Kuck, *Corp Secy*
John Hirschfeld, *Vice Pres*
EMP: 10
SQ FT: 2,000
SALES: 5MM **Privately Held**
SIC: 3273 Ready-mixed concrete

(G-16697)
RELIABLE PRODUCTS CO INC
315 S Park Dr (45885-9689)
PHONE 419 394-5854
Wayne Steineman, *President*
Kristine Ranly, *Corp Secy*
EMP: 8
SQ FT: 10,000
SALES: 350K **Privately Held**
SIC: 3541 Machine tools, metal cutting type

(G-16698)
ROYER TECHNOLOGIES INC
00907 Willies Way (45885-8501)
PHONE 937 743-6114
Marshall Royer, *President*
▲ **EMP:** 9
SQ FT: 10,000
SALES: 966.7K **Privately Held**
SIC: 3544 3545 5251 Special dies & tools; machine tool accessories; tools

(G-16699)
SARAS LITTLE CUPCAKES
321 Sturgeon St (45885-2062)
PHONE 419 305-7914
Sara Little, *Principal*
EMP: 4
SALES (est): 159.2K **Privately Held**
SIC: 2051 Bread, cake & related products

(G-16700)
SETEX INC
1111 Mckinley Rd (45885-1816)
PHONE 419 394-7800
Yamada, *President*
Shinichirou Shirahama, *President*
Robert Bowlin, *CFO*
▲ **EMP:** 470
SQ FT: 168,000
SALES: 35MM **Privately Held**
WEB: www.tachi-s.com
SIC: 2531 Seats, automobile

(G-16701)
ST MARYS FOUNDRY INC (PA)
405 E South St (45885-2540)
PHONE 419 394-3346
Angela Dine Molaskey, *CEO*
Colston L Dine, *Ch of Bd*
Mark Dine, *President*
Ronald S Stumphauzer, *Senior VP*
Terry Lenhart, *Vice Pres*
EMP: 140
SQ FT: 180,000
SALES (est): 29.6MM **Privately Held**
WEB: www.stmfoundry.com
SIC: 3321 3369 3322 Gray iron castings; nonferrous foundries; malleable iron foundries

(G-16702)
ST MARYS IRON WORKS INC
1880 Celina Rd (45885-1218)
PHONE 419 300-6300
Bill Gelhaus, *President*
Dan Gelhaus, *Vice Pres*
EMP: 13
SALES: 1MM **Privately Held**
SIC: 3537 3448 Engine stands & racks, metal; prefabricated metal components

(G-16703)
TAIYO AMERICA INC (DH)
1702 E Spring St (45885-2460)
PHONE 419 300-8811
Matt Konishi, *President*
▲ **EMP:** 10
SQ FT: 50,000
SALES (est): 3.6MM
SALES (corp-wide): 12B **Publicly Held**
SIC: 5084 3492 Industrial machinery & equipment; fluid power valves for aircraft
HQ: Taiyo,Ltd.
2-6-8, Bingomachi, Chuo-Ku
Osaka OSK 541-0
649 671-114

(G-16704)
WEBER READY MIX INC
16672 County Road 66a (45885-9212)
PHONE 419 394-9097
Marc Bader, *Vice Pres*
EMP: 25 **EST:** 2016
SALES (est): 915.3K **Privately Held**
SIC: 3273 Ready-mixed concrete

Saint Paris
Champaign County

(G-16705)
BRYCE HILL INC
8801 State Route 36 (43072-9358)
PHONE 937 663-4152
Bryce Hill, *Manager*
EMP: 47 **Privately Held**
SIC: 3271 Blocks, concrete: landscape or retaining wall
PA: Bryce Hill, Inc.
2301 Sheridan Ave
Springfield OH 45505

(G-16706)
CAM MACHINE INC
513 S Springfield St (43072-9410)
PHONE 937 663-5000
Douglas Macy, *President*
Darla Kunkle, *Vice Pres*
Jeff Macy, *Info Tech Dir*
EMP: 29
SALES (est): 2.7MM **Privately Held**
SIC: 3599 Machine shop, jobbing & repair

(G-16707)
CAM MACHINE INC
3833 State Route 235 N (43072-9536)
PHONE 937 663-0680
Doug Macy, *President*
EMP: 3
SALES (est): 163.6K **Privately Held**
SIC: 3599 Machine shop, jobbing & repair

(G-16708)
ELEMENTS LLC
556 N Heck Hill Rd (43072-9229)
P.O. Box 222 (43072-0222)
PHONE 937 663-5837
James Dickman, *Principal*
EMP: 3 **EST:** 2011
SALES (est): 147.1K **Privately Held**
SIC: 2819 Industrial inorganic chemicals

(G-16709)
KTH PARTS INDUSTRIES INC (PA)
1111 State Route 235 N (43072-9680)
P.O. Box 940 (43072-0940)
PHONE 937 663-5941
Toshio Inoue, *President*
Timothy Harrigan, *General Mgr*
Fumio Takeuchi, *Principal*
Sanichi Kanai, *Exec VP*
Art Liming, *Vice Pres*
▲ **EMP:** 770
SQ FT: 811,500
SALES (est): 209.4MM **Privately Held**
WEB: www.kth.net
SIC: 3714 Motor vehicle parts & accessories

(G-16710)
RIGHT TRACK CORP
11124 Helltown Rd (43072-9520)
PHONE 937 663-0366
Lloyd Lusk, *President*
EMP: 3
SQ FT: 2,400
SALES (est): 367.7K **Privately Held**
SIC: 3566 Speed changers, drives & gears

(G-16711)
RUNKLES SAWMILL LLC
2534 Dialton Rd (43072-9423)
PHONE 937 663-0115
Steve Runkle, *Mng Member*
EMP: 7
SALES: 350K **Privately Held**
SIC: 2421 Sawmills & planing mills, general

(G-16712)
WOODSPIRITS LIMITED INC (PA)
1920 Apple Rd (43072-9783)
P.O. Box 682 (43072-0682)
PHONE 937 663-5025
Barbara Bobo, *President*
EMP: 8

▲ = Import ▼ = Export
◆ = Import/Export

GEOGRAPHIC SECTION

Salem - Columbiana County (G-16739)

SALES (est): 953.4K **Privately Held**
WEB: www.woodspirits.com
SIC: 2841 Soap: granulated, liquid, cake, flaked or chip

Salem
Columbiana County

(G-16713)
ACCU-TEK TOOL & DIE INC
1390 Allen Rd Bldg 1 (44460-1003)
PHONE.................................330 726-1946
James A Kutchel, *President*
Gary Sebrell, *Vice Pres*
EMP: 8
SQ FT: 12,000
SALES (est): 715K **Privately Held**
SIC: 3544 3354 Special dies & tools; aluminum extruded products

(G-16714)
ACCURATE TOOL CO INC
1065 Salem Pkwy (44460-1062)
PHONE.................................330 332-9448
Vincent Cianciola, *President*
Timothy J Cianciola, *Vice Pres*
Jeffrey T Cianciola, *CFO*
Mary Ann Franko, *Admin Sec*
EMP: 4
SQ FT: 20,000
SALES (est): 391.2K **Privately Held**
SIC: 3544 3493 3469 Special dies & tools; jigs & fixtures; steel springs, except wire; stamping metal for the trade

(G-16715)
ADVANTAGE MACHINE SHOP
777 S Ellsworth Ave (44460-3781)
PHONE.................................330 337-8377
Vic Jones, *Owner*
EMP: 6
SALES (est): 430K **Privately Held**
SIC: 3599 Machine shop, jobbing & repair

(G-16716)
ALLIED RETAIL SOLUTIONS
1960 S Lincoln Ave Unit 4 (44460-4304)
PHONE.................................330 332-8141
EMP: 5 EST: 2010
SALES (est): 601.3K **Privately Held**
SIC: 3578 Mfg Calculating Equipment

(G-16717)
AMCAN PRODUCTIONS LTD
3735 Mccracken Rd (44460-9415)
PHONE.................................330 332-9129
Randy Strader, *CEO*
Towanna A Strader, *President*
EMP: 5
SALES: 100K **Privately Held**
SIC: 7929 3599 8711 Entertainers; machine & other job shop work; consulting engineer

(G-16718)
AS AMERICA INC
605 S Ellsworth Ave (44460-3743)
PHONE.................................330 337-2219
Jay Gould, *President*
EMP: 6
SALES (corp-wide): 15.6B **Privately Held**
SIC: 3261 3432 Vitreous plumbing fixtures; plumbing fixture fittings & trim
HQ: As America, Inc.
    1 Centennial Ave Ste 101
    Piscataway NJ 08854

(G-16719)
BARCLAY MACHINE INC
Also Called: Barclay Rolls
650 S Broadway Ave (44460-3795)
PHONE.................................330 337-9541
Jeff Cushman, *President*
John Dance, *CFO*
Kerry Thomas, *Manager*
EMP: 16 EST: 1898
SALES (est): 4.1MM **Privately Held**
WEB: www.barclayrolls.com
SIC: 3542 Machine tools, metal forming type

(G-16720)
BAUMAN CUSTOM WOODWORKING LLC
13650 Green Beaver Rd (44460-9255)
PHONE.................................330 482-4330
Stuart L Bauman,
EMP: 3
SQ FT: 1,176
SALES (est): 419.1K **Privately Held**
SIC: 2434 Wood kitchen cabinets

(G-16721)
BRASS ACCENTS INC
1693 Salem Pkwy W (44460-1082)
PHONE.................................330 332-9500
Alec Pendleton, *CEO*
Tam Pendleton, *Admin Sec*
▲ **EMP:** 12
SQ FT: 8,000
SALES: 1MM **Privately Held**
WEB: www.brassaccents.com
SIC: 3429 Manufactured hardware (general)

(G-16722)
CABINETWORKS UNLIMITED LLC
1725 Salem Pkwy W (44460-1002)
PHONE.................................234 320-4107
Kenneth Bagwell, *Mng Member*
EMP: 4
SALES (est): 135.5K **Privately Held**
SIC: 2517 Wood television & radio cabinets

(G-16723)
CARDINAL PUMPS EXCHANGERS INC (HQ)
Also Called: Unifin Chesapeake
1425 Quaker Ct (44460-1008)
PHONE.................................330 332-8558
Manny A Agostinho, *President*
Ed Shapiro, *General Mgr*
Matthew Flamini, *Vice Pres*
Jeanne R Hernandez, *Treasurer*
▲ **EMP:** 16
SALES (est): 2.6MM
SALES (corp-wide): 4.3B **Publicly Held**
SIC: 3443 Heat exchangers, condensers & components
PA: Westinghouse Air Brake Technologies Corporation
    1001 Airbrake Ave
    Wilmerding PA 15148
    412 825-1000

(G-16724)
CASTRUCTION COMPANY INC
1588 Salem Pkwy (44460-1071)
PHONE.................................330 332-9622
Benjamine R Brown, *President*
Shannon Brown, *Vice Pres*
Jim Gatto, *Opers Mgr*
Benji Brown, *Manager*
EMP: 12
SQ FT: 9,600
SALES (est): 1.8MM **Privately Held**
SIC: 3297 Cement refractories

(G-16725)
CHAPPELL-ZIMMERMAN INC
641 Olive St (44460-4219)
P.O. Box 94 (44460-0094)
PHONE.................................330 337-8711
Chris Chappell, *President*
EMP: 14 EST: 1946
SQ FT: 2,000
SALES: 1.5MM **Privately Held**
SIC: 3273 5999 Ready-mixed concrete; alcoholic beverage making equipment & supplies

(G-16726)
CHURCH BUDGET MONTHLY INC
157 W Pershing St (44460-2745)
P.O. Box 420 (44460-0420)
PHONE.................................330 337-1122
James Pidgeon, *President*
EMP: 60
SALES (est): 9.6MM **Privately Held**
WEB: www.churchbudmail.com
SIC: 2677 Envelopes

(G-16727)
CHURCH-BUDGET ENVELOPE COMPANY
271 S Ellsworth Ave (44460-3071)
P.O. Box 420 (44460-0420)
PHONE.................................800 446-9780
James A Pidgeon Jr, *President*
EMP: 48
SQ FT: 60,000
SALES (est): 13.1MM **Privately Held**
SIC: 2677 Envelopes

(G-16728)
CMI INDUSTRY AMERICAS INC (DH)
435 W Wilson St (44460-2767)
PHONE.................................330 332-4661
Rob Johnson, *Ch of Bd*
Patricia Simonsic, *Treasurer*
▲ **EMP:** 100 EST: 1923
SQ FT: 250,000
SALES (est): 61.7MM
SALES (corp-wide): 417.8K **Privately Held**
SIC: 3567 Metal melting furnaces, industrial: electric; metal melting furnaces, industrial: fuel-fired
HQ: Cockerill Maintenance & Ingenierie Traction Sa
    Avenue Leon Champagne 3
    Tubize 1480
    645 216-31

(G-16729)
COLUMBUS MCKINNON CORPORATION
Also Called: Chester Hoist
240 Pennsylvania Ave (44460-2733)
PHONE.................................330 332-5769
Steve Howell, *Branch Mgr*
EMP: 90
SALES (corp-wide): 839.4MM **Publicly Held**
SIC: 3536 Hoists
PA: Columbus Mckinnon Corporation
    205 Crosspoint Pkwy
    Getzville NY 14068
    716 689-5400

(G-16730)
COMPRHNSIVE BRACE LIMB CTR LLC (PA)
2235 E Pershing St (44460-3478)
PHONE.................................330 337-8333
Stephen Pollak,
Cheryl Pollak,
EMP: 3
SQ FT: 1,200
SALES (est): 450.1K **Privately Held**
SIC: 3842 Limbs, artificial

(G-16731)
CRANE CO
Crane Chemical Pump
1453 Allen Rd (44460-1004)
PHONE.................................330 337-7861
Lucille Karnofel, *Buyer*
Mike Saunders, *Purchasing*
B Mitsch, *Rsch/Dvlpt Dir*
William Dunnavant, *QC Dir*
J Burns, *Personnel*
EMP: 135
SALES (corp-wide): 3.3B **Publicly Held**
WEB: www.craneco.com
SIC: 3561 Industrial pumps & parts
PA: Crane Co.
    100 1st Stamford Pl # 300
    Stamford CT 06902
    203 363-7300

(G-16732)
CTM INTEGRATION INCORPORATED
1318 Quaker Cir (44460-1051)
P.O. Box 589 (44460-0589)
PHONE.................................330 332-1800
Thomas C Rumsey, *President*
Dan Mc Laughlin, *Exec VP*
Dan McLaughlin, *Exec VP*
Kevin Marshall, *Plant Mgr*
Mike Kennedy, *Engineer*
EMP: 36
SQ FT: 30,000

SALES (est): 10.9MM **Privately Held**
WEB: www.ctmint.com
SIC: 3565 5084 3549 Packaging machinery; industrial machinery & equipment; metalworking machinery

(G-16733)
CTM LABELING SYSTEMS
1318 Quaker Cir (44460-1051)
PHONE.................................330 332-1800
Sharon Ryan, *Engineer*
EMP: 10
SALES (est): 1.7MM **Privately Held**
SIC: 3565 Packaging machinery

(G-16734)
DILCO INDUSTRIES INC
300 Benton Rd (44460-2029)
P.O. Box 859 (44460-0859)
PHONE.................................330 337-6732
Robert Dillon Jr, *President*
Kathy Dillion, *Admin Sec*
EMP: 20
SQ FT: 14,000
SALES (est): 1.6MM **Privately Held**
WEB: www.dilcoind.com
SIC: 3599 Machine shop, jobbing & repair

(G-16735)
ETL PERFORMANCE PRODUCTS INC
1717 Pennsylvania Ave (44460-2781)
PHONE.................................234 575-7226
Xiangdong Liu, *President*
EMP: 8
SQ FT: 4,000
SALES: 3MM **Privately Held**
SIC: 3429 Clamps, metal

(G-16736)
EVERFLOW EASTERN PARTNERS LP
Also Called: Strawn Oil Field Service
29093 Salem Alliance Rd (44460-9706)
PHONE.................................330 537-3863
Richard Strawn, *Branch Mgr*
EMP: 6 **Privately Held**
SIC: 1389 Oil field services
PA: Everflow Eastern Partners, L.P.
    585 W Main St
    Canfield OH 44406

(G-16737)
FIRESTONE LASER AND MFG LLC
949 S Broadway Ave (44460-3799)
PHONE.................................330 337-9551
Don Hoover, *Plant Mgr*
EMP: 25
SQ FT: 48,000
SALES (est): 4.2MM **Privately Held**
WEB: www.firestonesheetmetal.com
SIC: 3444 Sheet metalwork

(G-16738)
FLEX N GATE
800 Pennsylvania Ave (44460-2783)
PHONE.................................330 332-6363
Scott Tuel, *General Mgr*
Craig Harbour, *Program Mgr*
Diyaa Qasawa, *Program Mgr*
William Hoffman, *Manager*
Michael Lam, *Manager*
EMP: 3
SALES (est): 105.5K **Privately Held**
SIC: 3714 Motor vehicle parts & accessories

(G-16739)
FOERSTER INSTRUMENTS INC
Foerster Systems Div
1484 Quaker Cir (44460-1053)
PHONE.................................330 332-9100
Dave Smith, *Branch Mgr*
EMP: 13
SALES (corp-wide): 62.6MM **Privately Held**
WEB: www.foerstergroup.com
SIC: 3537 Industrial trucks & tractors
HQ: Foerster Instruments Inc
    140 Industry Dr
    Pittsburgh PA 15275
    412 788-8976

Salem - Columbiana County (G-16740)

(G-16740)
FOERSTER SYSTEMS INC
1484 Quaker Cir (44460)
PHONE................................330 332-9100
Phillip Warga, *President*
EMP: 17
SALES (est): 4.8MM
SALES (corp-wide): 60.6MM **Privately Held**
SIC: 3537 Forklift trucks
HQ: Foerster Instruments Inc
140 Industry Dr
Pittsburgh PA 15275
412 788-8976

(G-16741)
FRESH MARK INC
1735 S Lincoln Ave (44460-4203)
PHONE................................330 332-8508
Steve Smith, *Branch Mgr*
EMP: 650
SQ FT: 125,000
SALES (corp-wide): 1.3B **Privately Held**
WEB: www.freshmark.com
SIC: 2011 2013 Meat packing plants; sausages & other prepared meats
PA: Fresh Mark, Inc.
1888 Southway St Se
Massillon OH 44646
330 834-3669

(G-16742)
GORDON BROTHERS BTLG GROUP INC
776 N Ellsworth Ave (44460-1600)
P.O. Box 63, Lowellville (44436-0063)
PHONE................................330 337-8754
Scott P Jones, *President*
Frank Tombo, *Principal*
Edward P Jones III, *Chairman*
Chris Wood,
EMP: 8
SALES (est): 19.1K **Privately Held**
SIC: 2086 Bottled & canned soft drinks

(G-16743)
GOTTSCHALL TOOL & DIE INC
14028 W Middletown Rd (44460-9184)
PHONE................................330 332-1544
EMP: 30 **EST:** 1950
SQ FT: 24,000
SALES (est): 2.7MM **Privately Held**
SIC: 3544 3469 Mfg Dies/Tools/Jigs/Fixtures Mfg Metal Stampings

(G-16744)
GRAPHIC TOUCH INC
451 E Pershing St (44460-3028)
PHONE................................330 337-3341
Keith Berger, *President*
Beverly Berger, *Corp Secy*
EMP: 3
SQ FT: 3,000
SALES: 158.1K **Privately Held**
SIC: 2752 2759 2791 Commercial printing, offset; letterpress printing; commercial art & graphic design; typesetting

(G-16745)
GRID INDUSTRIAL HEATING INC
1108 Salem Pkwy (44460-1063)
P.O. Box 950 (44460-0950)
PHONE................................330 332-9931
Donald Stamp, *President*
EMP: 7
SQ FT: 20,000
SALES (est): 1MM **Privately Held**
WEB: www.gridheating.com
SIC: 3433 1711 Steam heating apparatus; plumbing, heating, air-conditioning contractors

(G-16746)
HALTEC CORPORATION
32585 N Price Rd (44460-9513)
P.O. Box 1180 (44460-8180)
PHONE................................330 222-1501
Thomas Moyer, *President*
Edward Russell, *Chairman*
Brian Bostick, *Vice Pres*
David Caruso, *Vice Pres*
Mike Russell, *Vice Pres*
◆ **EMP:** 116
SQ FT: 65,000
SALES: 42.8MM **Privately Held**
WEB: www.haltec.com
SIC: 3714 Tire valve cores

(G-16747)
HAZENSTAB MACHINE INC
1575 Salem Pkwy (44460-1072)
PHONE................................330 337-1865
James Hazenstab Jr, *President*
▲ **EMP:** 14
SQ FT: 12,000
SALES (est): 2.3MM **Privately Held**
WEB: www.hazenstabmachine.com
SIC: 3599 Machine shop, jobbing & repair

(G-16748)
HUNT VALVE COMPANY INC
Also Called: Waeco Valve Division
1913 E State St (44460-2491)
PHONE................................330 337-9535
Gerry Bogner, *CEO*
Jennifer Cavanaugh, *Administration*
EMP: 50
SALES (corp-wide): 14MM **Privately Held**
WEB: www.huntvalve.com
SIC: 3491 Automatic regulating & control valves
PA: Hunt Valve Company, Inc.
1913 E State St
Salem OH 44460
330 337-9535

(G-16749)
HUNT VALVE COMPANY INC
Also Called: Union Flonetics
1913 E State St (44460-2491)
PHONE................................330 337-9535
David Huberfield, *President*
EMP: 50
SALES (corp-wide): 14MM **Privately Held**
WEB: www.huntvalve.com
SIC: 3491 Automatic regulating & control valves
PA: Hunt Valve Company, Inc.
1913 E State St
Salem OH 44460
330 337-9535

(G-16750)
JOHN KRIZAY INC
1777 Pennsylvania Ave (44460-2781)
P.O. Box 974 (44460-0974)
PHONE................................330 332-5607
William Stratton, *President*
Linda Horsall, *Admin Sec*
▲ **EMP:** 35
SQ FT: 12,000
SALES (est): 5.6MM **Privately Held**
SIC: 3229 Art, decorative & novelty glassware

(G-16751)
JOSEPH SABATINO
Also Called: Sabatino Cabinet
1834 Depot Rd (44460-4359)
PHONE................................330 332-5879
Joseph Sabatino, *Owner*
EMP: 6
SQ FT: 8,500
SALES: 1MM **Privately Held**
SIC: 1751 2491 Carpentry work; millwork, treated wood

(G-16752)
KORFF HOLDINGS LLC
Also Called: Quaker City Casting
310 E Euclid Ave (44460-3778)
PHONE................................330 332-1566
Geoffrey Korff, *President*
Dave Lordi, *QC Mgr*
Jason Korff,
Ronald H Lasko,
▲ **EMP:** 120
SALES: 20MM **Privately Held**
WEB: www.qccast.com
SIC: 3325 3321 Steel foundries; gray & ductile iron foundries

(G-16753)
KORFF MACHINE LLC
310 E Euclid Ave (44460-3778)
PHONE................................330 332-1566
Penelope Korff, *President*
Geoffrey Korff, *Vice Pres*
EMP: 4 **EST:** 2015
SQ FT: 20,000
SALES (est): 168.3K **Privately Held**
SIC: 3599 Machine shop, jobbing & repair

(G-16754)
L M EQUIPMENT & DESIGN INC
11000 Youngstown Salem Rd (44460-9654)
PHONE................................330 332-9951
Dave Hrovatic, *President*
Sue Lease, *CFO*
EMP: 20
SALES (est): 682.4K **Privately Held**
WEB: www.lmequipment.com
SIC: 7699 3541 Industrial equipment services; milling machines

(G-16755)
LOWRY TOOL & DIE INC
986 Salem Pkwy (44460-1059)
PHONE................................330 332-1722
Robert Lowry, *President*
EMP: 14
SQ FT: 10,000
SALES (est): 2.3MM **Privately Held**
WEB: www.lowrytd.com
SIC: 3544 Special dies & tools

(G-16756)
LYLE PRINTING & PUBLISHING CO (PA)
Also Called: Farm & Dairy
185 E State St (44460-2857)
P.O. Box 38 (44460-0038)
PHONE................................330 337-3419
Scot Darling, *CEO*
Tom Darling, *President*
Sandra Schnader, *Accounting Dir*
Gail Hettrick, *Sales Mgr*
Allison Davis, *Manager*
EMP: 50
SQ FT: 12,500
SALES (est): 6.5MM **Privately Held**
SIC: 2721 2752 2759 Trade journals: publishing only, not printed on site; commercial printing, offset; letterpress printing

(G-16757)
LYLE PRINTING & PUBLISHING CO
193 S Howard Ave (44460-2704)
PHONE................................330 337-7172
Mike Starr, *Branch Mgr*
Michael Ping, *Director*
EMP: 17
SALES (corp-wide): 6.5MM **Privately Held**
SIC: 2721 3555 Trade journals: publishing only, not printed on site; printing presses
PA: Lyle Printing & Publishing Co Inc
185 E State St
Salem OH 44460
330 337-3419

(G-16758)
M M INDUSTRIES INC
Also Called: Vorti-Siv
36135 Salem Grange Rd (44460-9442)
P.O. Box 720 (44460-0720)
PHONE................................330 332-5947
Barbara Maroscher, *President*
Vic Maroscher, *COO*
Victor Maroscher, *Vice Pres*
Kevin Penner, *Prdtn Mgr*
Britt Ortega, *Office Mgr*
▲ **EMP:** 30
SQ FT: 10,000
SALES (est): 6.6MM **Privately Held**
WEB: www.vorti-siv.com
SIC: 3559 Screening equipment, electric

(G-16759)
MAC MANUFACTURING INC
1453 Allen Rd (44460-1004)
PHONE................................330 829-1680
Cora McDonald, *Branch Mgr*
EMP: 104
SALES (est): 36.2MM **Privately Held**
SIC: 3715 5012 Truck trailers; trailers for trucks, new & used; truck bodies
PA: Mac Manufacturing, Inc.
14599 Commerce St Ne
Alliance OH 44601

(G-16760)
METAL & WIRE PRODUCTS COMPANY (PA)
1065 Salem Pkwy (44460-1062)
PHONE................................330 332-9448
Vincent M Cianciola, *President*
Jeffrey T Cianciola, *Vice Pres*
Timothy J Cianciola, *Vice Pres*
Mary Ann Franko, *Admin Sec*
EMP: 70
SQ FT: 62,000
SALES (est): 16.5MM **Privately Held**
SIC: 3469 3542 3544 Stamping metal for the trade; machine tools, metal forming type; special dies, tools, jigs & fixtures

(G-16761)
MIDWEST MINICRANES INC
1350 Pennsylvania Ave (44460-2737)
P.O. Box 466 (44460-0466)
PHONE................................330 332-3700
Margaret Ann Howells, *Owner*
EMP: 3
SALES (est): 355.6K **Privately Held**
SIC: 3625 Crane & hoist controls, including metal mill

(G-16762)
MILSEK FURNITURE POLISH INC
1351 Quaker Cir (44460-1006)
PHONE................................330 542-2700
Chris Ruben, *President*
Dan Bender, *Admin Sec*
EMP: 4
SQ FT: 2,080
SALES (est): 270K **Privately Held**
SIC: 2842 Specialty cleaning, polishes & sanitation goods

(G-16763)
MOORE MR SPECIALTY COMPANY
1050 Pennsylvania Ave (44460)
PHONE................................330 332-1229
Robert N Moore, *President*
Martha Moore, *Treasurer*
EMP: 8
SQ FT: 5,000
SALES: 1MM **Privately Held**
SIC: 3443 Fabricated plate work (boiler shop)

(G-16764)
OGDEN NEWSPAPERS INC
Salem News
161 N Lincoln Ave (44460-2903)
P.O. Box 268 (44460-0268)
PHONE................................330 332-4601
Beth Volosin, *Publisher*
John Celidonio, *Editor*
EMP: 50 **Privately Held**
SIC: 2711 Newspapers: publishing only, not printed on site
HQ: The Ogden Newspapers Inc
1500 Main St
Wheeling WV 26003
304 233-0100

(G-16765)
OVERHEAD DOOR OF SALEM INC
3864 Mccracken Rd (44460-9415)
PHONE................................330 332-9530
Al Kenreigh, *President*
EMP: 3
SALES (est): 366.1K **Privately Held**
SIC: 1542 5211 3699 Garage construction; garage doors, sale & installation; door opening & closing devices, electrical

(G-16766)
PLASTIC PARTNERS LLC
1801 Newgarden Rd (44460-9514)
PHONE................................425 765-2416
John Cote, *President*
EMP: 3 **EST:** 2012
SQ FT: 700
SALES (est): 230.7K **Privately Held**
SIC: 3559 Recycling machinery

▲ = Import ▼ = Export
◆ = Import/Export

GEOGRAPHIC SECTION **Sandusky - Erie County (G-16795)**

(G-16767)
POLLOCK RESEARCH & DESIGN INC
Simmers Crane Design & Svc Co
1134 Salem Pkwy (44460-1063)
PHONE..................330 332-3300
Randy L Stull, *Manager*
EMP: 45
SALES (corp-wide): 73.1MM **Privately Held**
SIC: 8711 7389 7353 3537 Civil engineering; mechanical engineering; structural engineering; crane & aerial lift service; heavy construction equipment rental; industrial trucks & tractors
PA: Pollock Research & Design, Inc.
11 Vanguard Dr
Reading PA 19606
610 582-7203

(G-16768)
QUAKER EXPRESS STAMPING INC
1134 Salem Pkwy (44460-1063)
PHONE..................330 332-9266
EMP: 15
SALES (est): 671.2K **Privately Held**
SIC: 2741 Misc Publishing

(G-16769)
QUALITY FABRICATED METALS INC
14000 W Middletown Rd (44460-9184)
PHONE..................330 332-7008
Danny Beegle, *President*
EMP: 25
SQ FT: 42,000
SALES (est): 4.7MM **Privately Held**
WEB: www.gtd-qfm.com
SIC: 3469 1799 Metal stampings; welding on site

(G-16770)
REDEX INDUSTRIES INC (PA)
Also Called: Udderly Smooth
1176 Salem Pkwy (44460-1063)
P.O. Box 939 (44460-0939)
PHONE..................330 332-9800
William C Kennedy, *President*
Margaret Kennedy, *Corp Secy*
EMP: 17 **EST:** 1976
SQ FT: 24,000
SALES (est): 2.8MM **Privately Held**
WEB: www.uddercream.com
SIC: 2844 Face creams or lotions

(G-16771)
SALEM MILL & CABINET CO
1455 Quaker Cir (44460-1054)
P.O. Box 1072 (44460-8072)
PHONE..................330 337-9568
Steven W Kastenhuber, *President*
EMP: 6
SQ FT: 6,000
SALES: 900K **Privately Held**
SIC: 5211 2431 2434 Lumber products; millwork; wood kitchen cabinets

(G-16772)
SALEM WELDING & SUPPLY COMPANY
475 Prospect St (44460-2618)
P.O. Box 386 (44460-0386)
PHONE..................330 332-4517
Frederick Baker Sr, *President*
Anna Baker, *Corp Secy*
Frederick Baker Jr, *Vice Pres*
EMP: 9 **EST:** 1975
SQ FT: 15,200
SALES (est): 1.8MM **Privately Held**
SIC: 7692 5084 Welding repair; welding machinery & equipment

(G-16773)
SANSCAN INC
Also Called: Instacopy
157 N Ellsworth Ave (44460-2853)
PHONE..................330 332-9365
Jill Harmon, *President*
EMP: 4
SALES (est): 442.3K **Privately Held**
SIC: 2752 Commercial printing, offset

(G-16774)
SEKELY INDUSTRIES INC (PA)
240 Pennsylvania Ave (44460-2733)
PHONE..................248 844-9201
James Sekely, *President*
John Sekely, *Vice Pres*
Earl R Miller, *Admin Sec*
▼ **EMP:** 162 **EST:** 1944
SQ FT: 100,000
SALES (est): 9.2MM **Privately Held**
WEB: www.sekely.com
SIC: 3544 Special dies & tools; jigs & fixtures

(G-16775)
SOLOMONS MINES INC
7219 Salem Unity Rd (44460-9294)
PHONE..................330 337-0123
Jack Solomon, *President*
Shirley Solomon, *Admin Sec*
EMP: 3
SQ FT: 360
SALES (est): 609K **Privately Held**
WEB: www.solomonsmines.com
SIC: 1442 Construction sand & gravel

(G-16776)
THE LABEL TEAM INC
1251 Quaker Cir (44460-1050)
PHONE..................330 332-1067
Dean J McDaniel, *President*
Paula McDaniel, *Vice Pres*
EMP: 15
SQ FT: 11,400
SALES (est): 2.6MM **Privately Held**
SIC: 2759 Labels & seals: printing

(G-16777)
TRI-FAB INC
10372 W South Range Rd (44460-9621)
P.O. Box 310 (44460-0310)
PHONE..................330 337-3425
Samuel Lippiatt, *President*
Wes Weimer, *Engineer*
Sue Sinclair, *Office Mgr*
EMP: 32
SQ FT: 44,000
SALES (est): 4.7MM **Privately Held**
WEB: www.tri-fab.net
SIC: 3644 3441 3444 Fuse boxes, electric; junction boxes, electric; fabricated structural metal; sheet metalwork

(G-16778)
TURNER MACHINE CO
1433 Salem Pkwy (44460-1070)
PHONE..................330 332-5821
Jacob O Kamm, *President*
Patricia Simonsic, *Treasurer*
EMP: 12 **EST:** 1943
SALES (est): 2.2MM **Privately Held**
WEB: www.turnermachineco.com
SIC: 3599 3547 3542 Machine shop, jobbing & repair; rolling mill machinery; machine tools, metal forming type

(G-16779)
VALVECO INC (PA)
1913 E State St (44460-2422)
PHONE..................330 337-9535
Gerald Bagner, *CEO*
EMP: 100
SQ FT: 16,000
SALES (est): 6.3MM **Privately Held**
SIC: 3492 Control valves, fluid power: hydraulic & pneumatic

(G-16780)
VIC MAROSCHER
36135 Salem Grange Rd (44460-9442)
P.O. Box 720 (44460-0720)
PHONE..................330 332-4958
Vic Maroscher, *Owner*
EMP: 10
SALES (est): 432.9K **Privately Held**
SIC: 3999 Manufacturing industries

(G-16781)
WINGS WAY DRIVE THRU INC
Also Called: Wings Way Ice
9194 Salem Warren Rd (44460-7600)
PHONE..................330 533-2788
David Rickard, *President*
Diane Rickard, *Vice Pres*
EMP: 5

SALES (est): 790.4K **Privately Held**
SIC: 5921 2097 Beer (packaged); wine; manufactured ice

(G-16782)
WT TOOL & DIE INC
1300 Pennsylvania Ave (44460-2780)
P.O. Box 7 (44460-0007)
PHONE..................330 332-2254
Fax: 330 332-2889
EMP: 6
SALES: 600K **Privately Held**
SIC: 3599 3544 Mfg Industrial Machinery Mfg Dies/Tools/Jigs/Fixtures

(G-16783)
YOU DOUGH GIRL LLC
12725 Kent Rd (44460-9135)
PHONE..................330 207-5031
Kathy Boswell, *Mng Member*
EMP: 4
SALES (est): 236.4K **Privately Held**
SIC: 2051 Bakery: wholesale or wholesale/retail combined

Salesville
Guernsey County

(G-16784)
VELA
58560 Kennonsburg Rd (43778-9567)
PHONE..................614 500-0150
EMP: 3
SALES (est): 102.6K **Privately Held**
SIC: 2721 7389 Periodicals-Publishing/Printing Business Services At Non-Commercial Site

Salineville
Columbiana County

(G-16785)
A & M LOGGING
8633 Township Road 289 (43945-7721)
PHONE..................740 543-3171
Allen Miller, *Principal*
EMP: 3
SALES (est): 146.4K **Privately Held**
SIC: 2411 Logging

(G-16786)
COLDWELL FAMILY TREE FARM
Also Called: Ohio Woodlands
33320 Hull Rd (43945-9764)
PHONE..................330 506-9012
Jared Coldwell, *Owner*
EMP: 3
SALES: 35K **Privately Held**
SIC: 6531 2411 Real estate brokers & agents; logging

(G-16787)
CREEKSIDE SPRINGS LLC
32 Washington St (43945-1078)
PHONE..................330 679-1010
Michael Mercure, *Branch Mgr*
EMP: 25
SALES (corp-wide): 15MM **Privately Held**
WEB: www.creeksidesprings.com
SIC: 2086 Water, pasteurized: packaged in cans, bottles, etc.
PA: Creekside Springs, Llc
667 Merchant St
Ambridge PA 15003
724 266-9000

(G-16788)
J K LOGGING & CHIPWOOD COMPANY
3218 Oasis Rd Ne (43945-9420)
PHONE..................330 738-3571
John Kruprzak, *Owner*
EMP: 3
SALES (est): 408.3K **Privately Held**
SIC: 2421 Sawmills & planing mills, general

(G-16789)
M3 MIDSTREAM LLC
Also Called: Salineville Office
10 E Main St (43945-1134)
PHONE..................330 679-5580
EMP: 28
SALES (corp-wide): 54.9MM **Privately Held**
SIC: 1311 Natural gas production
PA: M3 Midstream Llc
600 Travis St Ste 5600
Houston TX 77002
713 783-3000

(G-16790)
UTICA E OHIO MIDSTREAM
70 E Main St (43945-1134)
PHONE..................330 679-2295
Carmen Gray, *Human Resources*
EMP: 3
SALES (est): 294.2K **Privately Held**
SIC: 1311 Crude petroleum & natural gas

Sandusky
Erie County

(G-16791)
ACH LLC
Also Called: Ach Sandusky Plastics
3020 Tiffin Ave (44870-5352)
PHONE..................419 621-5748
Andy Short, *Principal*
▲ **EMP:** 8
SALES (est): 680K **Privately Held**
SIC: 3714 Motor vehicle parts & accessories

(G-16792)
ACME PRINTING CO INC
2143 Sherman St (44870-4714)
P.O. Box 2311 (44871-2311)
PHONE..................419 626-4426
Dean Everson, *President*
James Kellam, *Corp Secy*
Fred Everson, *Vice Pres*
EMP: 6 **EST:** 1968
SQ FT: 10,000
SALES (est): 450K **Privately Held**
SIC: 2752 2796 2759 Commercial printing, offset; embossing plates for printing; letterpress printing

(G-16793)
AHNER FABRICATING & SHTMTL INC
2001 E Perkins Ave (44870-5130)
PHONE..................419 626-6641
Mark Ahner, *President*
Timothy Ahner, *President*
Tim Kaser, *Office Mgr*
EMP: 24
SQ FT: 7,000
SALES (est): 6.6MM **Privately Held**
WEB: www.ahner-industrial.com
SIC: 3444 3914 5049 Sheet metal specialties, not stamped; carving sets, stainless steel; precision tools

(G-16794)
AMERICAN QUALITY STRIPPING
1750 5th St (44870-1301)
PHONE..................419 625-6288
Tim Finneran, *President*
Rick Lill, *General Mgr*
Richard Finneran, *Vice Pres*
Matt Swan, *Engineer*
EMP: 30
SQ FT: 16,000
SALES (est): 4.3MM **Privately Held**
WEB: www.americanqualitystripping.com
SIC: 3471 3398 Finishing, metals or formed products; metal heat treating

(G-16795)
AMERICAN RACE CARS
407 E Bogart Rd (44870-6404)
PHONE..................419 836-5070
Mark Horton, *Partner*
Travis Colangelo, *Partner*
EMP: 5

Sandusky - Erie County (G-16796)

SALES (est): 509.8K **Privately Held**
SIC: 3711 Chassis, motor vehicle; automobile assembly, including specialty automobiles

(G-16796)
BAY ELECTRIC CO
2612 Columbus Ave (44870-5596)
PHONE 419 625-1046
Gary Westfall, *President*
EMP: 4
SQ FT: 4,400
SALES (est): 398.8K **Privately Held**
SIC: 7694 5063 Electric motor repair; motors, electric

(G-16797)
BLUE CHIP MACHINE & TOOL LTD
4211 Venice Rd (44870-1649)
PHONE 419 626-9559
Brian S Fiorletta, *Mng Member*
Sherri Fischer,
Timothy C Welfle,
EMP: 5 EST: 1997
SQ FT: 10,000
SALES: 800K **Privately Held**
SIC: 3499 3599 Machine bases, metal; machine shop, jobbing & repair

(G-16798)
BUDERER DRUG CO (PA)
Also Called: Fisher Drug
633 Hancock St (44870-3603)
PHONE 419 626-3429
James Buderer, *Owner*
Mathew Buderer, *Vice Pres*
Joyce Buderer, *Treasurer*
EMP: 6
SALES (est): 759.1K **Privately Held**
SIC: 2834 5122 5912 Medicines, capsuled or ampuled; drugs & drug proprietaries; drug stores & proprietary stores

(G-16799)
BUDERER DRUG COMPANY INC (PA)
633 Hancock St (44870-3603)
PHONE 419 627-2800
James Buderer, *President*
Matthew Buderer, *Vice Pres*
Suzanne Fomich, *Pharmacist*
EMP: 17 EST: 2014
SQ FT: 5,000
SALES (est): 9.5MM **Privately Held**
SIC: 5122 2834 Drugs & drug proprietaries; animal medicines; proprietary (patent) medicines; proprietary drug products

(G-16800)
BUSCH & THIEM INC
1316 Cleveland Rd (44870-4271)
P.O. Box 1088 (44871-1088)
PHONE 419 625-7515
C A Busch, *President*
James R Kellam, *Admin Sec*
EMP: 20 EST: 1926
SQ FT: 45,000
SALES (est): 4.1MM **Privately Held**
WEB: www.buschthiem.com
SIC: 2542 3993 3496 3444 Racks, merchandise display or storage: except wood; signs & advertising specialties; miscellaneous fabricated wire products; sheet metalwork; steel pipe & tubes

(G-16801)
CEDAR POINT LAUNDRY
1 Cedar Point Dr (44870-5259)
PHONE 419 627-2274
EMP: 4
SALES (est): 130K **Privately Held**
SIC: 2842 Laundry cleaning preparations

(G-16802)
D C FILTER & CHEMICAL INC
Also Called: Miracle Core Filters
1517 5th St (44870-3937)
PHONE 419 626-3967
Gary D Morey, *President*
EMP: 7
SQ FT: 60,000

SALES: 900K **Privately Held**
SIC: 3569 2842 Filters, general line: industrial; specialty cleaning, polishes & sanitation goods; drycleaning preparations; industrial plant disinfectants or deodorants; laundry cleaning preparations

(G-16803)
DAVID BUTLER TAX SERVICE
415 Tiffin Ave (44870-2141)
PHONE 419 626-8086
William Butler, *Owner*
EMP: 3 EST: 1953
SALES (est): 116.5K **Privately Held**
SIC: 7291 2752 Tax return preparation services; commercial printing, offset

(G-16804)
DECKO PRODUCTS INC
2105 Superior St (44870-1891)
PHONE 419 626-5757
Bill Niggemyer, *President*
Rob Simonton, *VP Opers*
Mary Galindo, *Purchasing*
Russell Webster, *Engineer*
John Van Dootingh, *Treasurer*
◆ EMP: 65 EST: 1930
SQ FT: 20,000
SALES (est): 19.7MM **Privately Held**
WEB: www.decko.com
SIC: 2064 Cake ornaments, confectionery

(G-16805)
DOUTHIT COMMUNICATIONS INC (PA)
Also Called: Photo Journals
520 Warren St (44870-2958)
P.O. Box 760 (44871-0760)
PHONE 419 625-5825
H Kenneth III, *President*
Harold K Douthit, *Chairman*
Joanne Kraine, *CFO*
EMP: 75
SQ FT: 12,000
SALES (est): 43.4MM **Privately Held**
WEB: www.autosillustrated.com
SIC: 2711 2741 Job printing & newspaper publishing combined; miscellaneous publishing

(G-16806)
EDSAL SANDUSKY CORPORATION
117 E Washington Row (44870-2629)
PHONE 419 626-5465
EMP: 142
SALES (corp-wide): 41.8MM **Privately Held**
SIC: 2522 Cabinets, office: except wood
PA: Edsal Sandusky Llc
4815 Biloxi St
Millington TN 38053
901 872-0188

(G-16807)
ENCORE INDUSTRIES INC (PA)
Also Called: Encore Plastics
319 Howard Dr (44870-8607)
PHONE 419 626-8000
Timothy J Rathbun, *CEO*
Craig Rathbun, *President*
▲ EMP: 225
SQ FT: 250,000
SALES (est): 83.3MM **Privately Held**
WEB: www.e-encore.com
SIC: 3089 Thermoformed finished plastic products

(G-16808)
ENCORE PLASTICS CORPORATION (HQ)
319 Howard Dr (44870-8607)
PHONE 419 626-8000
Timothy Rathbun, *CEO*
Donald Craig Rathbun, *President*
Willard John Rathbun, *Chairman*
Tim Rathbun, *Vice Pres*
Matt Morgan, *CFO*
◆ EMP: 125

SALES (est): 34.2MM
SALES (corp-wide): 83.3MM **Privately Held**
WEB: www.encoreplasticscorporation.com
SIC: 3089 3559 3841 3411 Injection molded finished plastic products; plastics working machinery; surgical & medical instruments; metal cans
PA: Encore Industries, Inc.
319 Howard Dr
Sandusky OH 44870
419 626-8000

(G-16809)
ENTRATECH SYSTEMS LLC (PA)
202 Fox Rd (44870-8363)
PHONE 419 433-7683
Michael Richardson, *President*
EMP: 14
SQ FT: 14,000
SALES (est): 1.3MM **Privately Held**
WEB: www.entratechsystems.com
SIC: 7539 3714 Electrical services; filters: oil, fuel & air, motor vehicle

(G-16810)
EQUINOX ENTERPRISES LLC
Also Called: A & L Metal Processing
1920 George St (44870-1739)
P.O. Box 1367 (44871-1367)
PHONE 419 627-0022
Stephen Kalosis,
Anthony Clark,
EMP: 12
SQ FT: 25,000
SALES (est): 1.1MM **Privately Held**
WEB: www.almetalprocessing.com
SIC: 3471 Finishing, metals or formed products

(G-16811)
FIRELANDS WINERY
Also Called: Mantey Vineyards
917 Bardshar Rd (44870-1507)
PHONE 419 625-5474
Claudio Salvador, *Principal*
Adrian Salvador, *Project Mgr*
Melissa Kadow, *Sales Staff*
Vicki Rogers, *Office Mgr*
▲ EMP: 23
SALES (est): 3.8MM **Privately Held**
SIC: 2084 Wines

(G-16812)
GARY L GAST
Also Called: Ohio Wood Fabrication
2024 Campbell St (44870-4811)
PHONE 419 625-5915
Gary L Gast, *Owner*
EMP: 6
SQ FT: 3,600
SALES: 425K **Privately Held**
SIC: 2541 Cabinets, except refrigerated: show, display, etc.: wood; counter & sink tops

(G-16813)
GENERAL FABRICATIONS CORP
7777 Milan Rd (44870-9705)
P.O. Box 2461 (44871-2461)
PHONE 419 625-6055
Chester Boraski, *President*
Kurt Livingston, *Engineer*
Carol Boraski, *Admin Sec*
EMP: 42 EST: 1982
SQ FT: 10,000
SALES (est): 10.8MM **Privately Held**
WEB: www.gfcfinishing.com
SIC: 3559 3563 Paint making machinery; air & gas compressors

(G-16814)
GUNDLACH SHEET METAL WORKS INC (PA)
Also Called: Honeywell Authorized Dealer
910 Columbus Ave (44870-3594)
PHONE 419 626-4525
Roger M Gundlach, *President*
Terry W Gundlach, *Chairman*
Terry Kette, *Vice Pres*
Andrew Gundluch, *Admin Sec*
EMP: 76
SQ FT: 17,000

SALES (est): 18.7MM **Privately Held**
WEB: www.gundlach-hvac.com
SIC: 1711 3444 Warm air heating & air conditioning contractor; refrigeration contractor; sheet metalwork

(G-16815)
HULL READY MIX CONCRETE INC
Also Called: Hull Builders Supply
4419 Tiffin Ave (44870-9645)
P.O. Box 432, Vermilion (44089-0432)
PHONE 419 625-8070
Jeffery Riddell, *President*
Jim Ebel, *Assistant*
EMP: 10 EST: 1999
SALES (est): 1.1MM **Privately Held**
SIC: 3273 4212 1611 7359 Ready-mixed concrete; truck rental with drivers; highway & street construction; industrial truck rental

(G-16816)
HURON CEMENT PRODUCTS COMPANY
Also Called: H & C Building Supplies
2925 Venice Rd (44870-1839)
PHONE 419 433-4161
Tony Caporini, *Manager*
EMP: 5
SALES (corp-wide): 9.4MM **Privately Held**
SIC: 3273 Ready-mixed concrete
PA: The Huron Cement Products Company
617 Main St
Huron OH 44839
419 433-4161

(G-16817)
INDUSTRIAL NUT CORP
1425 Tiffin Ave (44870-2054)
PHONE 419 625-8543
William Springer, *President*
John E Moffitt, *Vice Pres*
David Springer, *Vice Pres*
James B Springer, *Vice Pres*
John William Springer III, *Vice Pres*
▲ EMP: 100 EST: 1908
SQ FT: 100,000
SALES (est): 21.5MM **Privately Held**
WEB: www.industrialnut.com
SIC: 3452 Nuts, metal

(G-16818)
JAMAC INC
422 Buchanan St (44870-4700)
PHONE 419 625-9790
Mark Mc Gory, *President*
Elaine Mc Gory, *Vice Pres*
James McGory, *Engineer*
James G Mc Gory Jr, *Treasurer*
Tina Wadsworth, *Info Tech Mgr*
▼ EMP: 18
SQ FT: 10,000
SALES (est): 3.8MM **Privately Held**
SIC: 2672 Labels (unprinted), gummed: made from purchased materials

(G-16819)
JOHN BEAN TECHNOLOGIES CORP
Also Called: Jbt Foodtech
1622 1st St (44870-3902)
PHONE 419 627-4349
Susan Beatty, *Buyer*
Larry Martin, *Branch Mgr*
Charlie Rogers, *Manager*
EMP: 260 **Publicly Held**
SIC: 3556 Food products machinery
PA: John Bean Technologies Corporation
70 W Madison St Ste 4400
Chicago IL 60602

(G-16820)
KELLSTONE
201 Putnam St (44870-2171)
PHONE 419 621-8140
Ralph Kunar, *Manager*
EMP: 4
SALES (est): 119.6K **Privately Held**
WEB: www.kellstone.com
SIC: 1499 Asphalt mining & bituminous stone quarrying

▲ = Import ▼ = Export
◆ = Import/Export

GEOGRAPHIC SECTION

Sandusky - Erie County (G-16846)

(G-16821)
LAKESHORE GRAPHIC INDUSTRIES
617 Hancock St (44870-3603)
PHONE..................................419 626-8631
Craig H Stahl, *CEO*
William E Stahl, *Chairman*
EMP: 16
SQ FT: 12,000
SALES (est): 1.8MM **Privately Held**
WEB: www.lakeshoregraphic.com
SIC: 2761 Manifold business forms

(G-16822)
LEWCO INC
706 Lane St (44870-3846)
PHONE..................................419 625-4014
Ronald Guerra, *President*
Gerald Guerra, *Vice Pres*
Jerry Guerra, *Vice Pres*
Blaine Romak, *Purch Mgr*
Sarah Lorcher, *Buyer*
◆ **EMP:** 104
SQ FT: 135,000
SALES (est): 41.1MM **Privately Held**
WEB: www.lewcoinc.com
SIC: 3535 3567 Bulk handling conveyor systems; industrial furnaces & ovens

(G-16823)
LORIS PRINTING INC
Also Called: Loris Printing & Party Center
2111 Cleveland Rd (44870-4412)
PHONE..................................419 626-6648
Joseph Loris, *President*
Kathy Loris, *Corp Secy*
EMP: 7
SALES (est): 1.3MM **Privately Held**
WEB: www.lorisprinting.net
SIC: 2759 2752 7299 Screen printing; commercial printing, lithographic; facility rental & party planning services

(G-16824)
MAAGS AUTOMOTIVE & MACHINE
1640 Columbus Ave (44870-3542)
PHONE..................................419 626-1539
Robert Maag, *President*
EMP: 9
SQ FT: 1,500
SALES (est): 1.5MM **Privately Held**
SIC: 3519 7538 7539 3714 Diesel engine rebuilding; gas engine rebuilding; engine rebuilding: automotive; diesel engine repair: automotive; automotive repair shops; motor vehicle parts & accessories; relays & industrial controls

(G-16825)
MACHINE APPLICATIONS CORP
Also Called: Mac Instruments
3410 Tiffin Ave (44870-9752)
PHONE..................................419 621-2322
James G Weit, *President*
Karen Weit, *Corp Secy*
James Weit, *Engineer*
EMP: 5
SQ FT: 1,672
SALES (est): 1MM **Privately Held**
WEB: www.macinstruments.com
SIC: 3823 Industrial instrmnts msrmnt display/control process variable

(G-16826)
MACK IRON WORKS COMPANY
124 Warren St (44870-2823)
PHONE..................................419 626-3712
John O Bacon, *President*
Peter P Kowalski Jr, *Vice Pres*
Roger Hartley, *Sales Executive*
Jeff Lee, *Manager*
EMP: 40 EST: 1901
SQ FT: 63,000
SALES (est): 9.4MM **Privately Held**
WEB: www.mackiron.com
SIC: 3494 3444 3443 3446 Valves & pipe fittings; sheet metalwork; fabricated plate work (boiler shop); stairs, staircases, stair treads: prefabricated metal

(G-16827)
MARK ADVERTISING AGENCY INC
1600 5th St (44870-1300)
P.O. Box 413 (44871-0413)
PHONE..................................419 626-9000
Joe Wesnitzer, *CEO*
Shelly Cook, *President*
Lori Roth, *COO*
Shirley Wesnitzer, *Vice Pres*
Cody Ward, *Web Dvlpr*
EMP: 15 EST: 1965
SQ FT: 8,000
SALES (est): 2.6MM **Privately Held**
WEB: www.markadvertising.com
SIC: 2752 7311 Commercial printing, offset; advertising agencies

(G-16828)
MASTER LABEL COMPANY INC
1048 Cleveland Rd (44870-4034)
PHONE..................................419 625-8095
Bob Clarkson, *President*
Lee Clarkson, *Admin Sec*
EMP: 5
SQ FT: 3,500
SALES (est): 610K **Privately Held**
WEB: www.masterlabel.com
SIC: 2672 Labels (unprinted), gummed: made from purchased materials

(G-16829)
MH & SON MACHINING & WLDG CO
210 W Perkins Ave Ste 10 (44870-9005)
PHONE..................................419 621-0690
Mark A Howard, *President*
Kim M Howard, *Vice Pres*
EMP: 6
SQ FT: 2,000
SALES (est): 855.6K **Privately Held**
SIC: 3599 1799 Machine shop, jobbing & repair; welding on site

(G-16830)
MIELKE FURNITURE REPAIR INC
3209 Columbus Ave (44805-5595)
PHONE..................................419 625-4572
Daniel H Mielke, *President*
Christine Mielke, *Corp Secy*
Allan R Mielke, *Vice Pres*
EMP: 8 EST: 1947
SQ FT: 2,800
SALES (est): 639.3K **Privately Held**
SIC: 7641 2511 Furniture refinishing; reupholstery; wood household furniture

(G-16831)
NYECO GAS INC
905 Pierce St (44870-4674)
PHONE..................................419 447-2712
Aaron Nye, *Principal*
Juve Guillen, *Manager*
EMP: 9
SALES: 1.2MM **Privately Held**
SIC: 5999 2813 Welding supplies; industrial gases; acetylene; argon

(G-16832)
OKAMOTO SANDUSKY MFG LLC
Also Called: Okamoto USA
3130 W Monroe St (44870-1811)
PHONE..................................419 626-1633
Yoshiyuki Okamoto, *President*
Hirofumi Chiba, *Sales Staff*
▲ **EMP:** 100
SALES (est): 26.4MM **Privately Held**
SIC: 3069 Bibs, vulcanized rubber or rubberized fabric

(G-16833)
ONNYX
3911 Venice Rd (44870-8115)
PHONE..................................419 627-9872
Gina Vincent, *CEO*
Kimberly Stutsman, *Vice Pres*
Mark Tamburrino, *Vice Pres*
Paul Tamburrino Jr, *Vice Pres*
Steve Tamburrino, *Vice Pres*
EMP: 6
SALES (est): 976.8K **Privately Held**
SIC: 2759 Commercial printing

(G-16834)
P & T PRODUCTS INC
472 Industrial Pkwy (44870-5883)
PHONE..................................419 621-1966
Paul Todd, *President*
Mike Alderman, *General Mgr*
Susan K Todd, *Corp Secy*
Jennifer Fildley, *Vice Pres*
Lisa Green, *Office Mgr*
EMP: 20
SQ FT: 20,000
SALES (est): 5.3MM **Privately Held**
WEB: www.p-tproductsinc.com
SIC: 2891 Sealants

(G-16835)
PARK PRESS DIRECT
2143 Sherman St (44870-4714)
PHONE..................................419 626-4426
Slate Kessler, *Principal*
Scott Bowlers, *Principal*
EMP: 9
SALES (est): 364.1K **Privately Held**
SIC: 2759 7389 Commercial printing;

(G-16836)
PEERLESS STOVE & MFG CO INC
Also Called: Peerless Prof Cooking Eqp
334 Harrison St (44870)
PHONE..................................419 625-4514
Brian R Huntley, *President*
EMP: 10
SQ FT: 40,000
SALES (est): 620K **Privately Held**
SIC: 3589 Cooking equipment, commercial

(G-16837)
PEGASUS VANS & TRAILERS INC
4003 Tiffin Ave (44870-9689)
P.O. Box 2308 (44871-2308)
PHONE..................................419 625-8953
Dean Wikel, *President*
Larry McGee, *Vice Pres*
Randy Wikel, *Vice Pres*
EMP: 25
SQ FT: 50,000
SALES (est): 5.2MM **Privately Held**
SIC: 3715 Trailers or vans for transporting horses

(G-16838)
PELZ LETTERING INC
5003 Milan Rd (44870-5845)
PHONE..................................419 623-3567
Maryann Pelz, *President*
Kenneth Pelz, *Corp Secy*
Kevin Pelz, *Vice Pres*
EMP: 5
SQ FT: 5,000
SALES (est): 400K **Privately Held**
WEB: www.barrags.com
SIC: 2395 7299 7336 5699 Emblems, embroidered; stitching, custom; silk screen design; customized clothing & apparel; T-shirts, custom printed; finishing plants

(G-16839)
POLYNT COMPOSITES USA INC
1321 1st St (44870-3901)
PHONE..................................816 391-6000
Michelle Edwards, *Purch Mgr*
Scott Bechtel, *Manager*
EMP: 28
SALES (corp-wide): 1.3B **Privately Held**
WEB: www.ccponline.com
SIC: 2821 2834 2842 2851 Emulsions, pharmaceutical; specialty cleaning, polishes & sanitation goods; paints & allied products; polyesters
HQ: Polynt Composites Usa Inc.
99 E Cottage Ave
Carpentersville IL 60110

(G-16840)
QUANTUM SAILS
207 W Water St (44870-2529)
PHONE..................................567 283-5335
EMP: 3
SALES (est): 110.7K **Privately Held**
SIC: 3572 Computer storage devices

(G-16841)
SANDUSKY DOCK CORPORATION
2705 W Monroe St (44870-1831)
P.O. Box 899 (44871-0899)
PHONE..................................419 626-1214
Jeff Smith, *Superintendent*
EMP: 10
SALES (est): 704.2K
SALES (corp-wide): 11.4B **Publicly Held**
SIC: 1241 Coal Mining Services
HQ: Norfolk Southern Properties Inc
3 Commercial Pl Ste 1a
Norfolk VA 23510
757 629-2600

(G-16842)
SANDUSKY FABRICATING & SLS INC (PA)
Also Called: San-Fab Conveyor and Automtn
2000 Superior St (44870-1824)
PHONE..................................419 626-4465
Timothy H Shenigo, *President*
EMP: 23 EST: 1954
SQ FT: 85,000
SALES (est): 4.4MM **Privately Held**
WEB: www.sanfab.com
SIC: 3535 Conveyors & conveying equipment

(G-16843)
SANDUSKY INTERNATIONAL INC
615 W Market St (44870-2413)
PHONE..................................419 626-5340
Edward R Ryan, *CEO*
Richard A Hargrave, *CFO*
◆ **EMP:** 200 EST: 1904
SQ FT: 500,000
SALES (est): 49.3MM
SALES (corp-wide): 269.8MM **Privately Held**
WEB: www.sanduskyintl.com
SIC: 3325 3369 Alloy steel castings, except investment; castings, except diecastings, precision
PA: Metaltek International, Inc.
905 E Saint Paul Ave
Waukesha WI 53188
262 544-7777

(G-16844)
SANDUSKY MACHINE & TOOL INC
2223 Tiffin Ave (44870-1994)
PHONE..................................419 626-8359
Walter Schaufler, *Ch of Bd*
James Schaufler, *President*
EMP: 13 EST: 1966
SQ FT: 17,600
SALES: 1MM **Privately Held**
SIC: 3599 Machine shop, jobbing & repair

(G-16845)
SANDUSKY NEWSPAPERS INC (PA)
Also Called: Sandusky Newspaper Group
314 W Market St (44870-2410)
PHONE..................................419 625-5500
Dudley A White Jr, *Ch of Bd*
David A Rau, *President*
Kathy Lilje, *Editor*
Aimee Miller, *Vice Pres*
Susan E White, *Admin Sec*
EMP: 140
SQ FT: 45,000
SALES (est): 98.3MM **Privately Held**
WEB: www.sanduskyregister.com
SIC: 4832 2711 2752 Radio broadcasting stations; newspapers; commercial printing, lithographic

(G-16846)
SANDUSKY PACKAGING CORPORATION
2016 George St (44870-1797)
P.O. Box 2217 (44871-2217)
PHONE..................................419 626-8520
Richard M Longer, *President*
Herbert G Hoelzer, *Vice Pres*
Randall A Johnson, *Vice Pres*
William G McRobbie, *Vice Pres*
Lester J Norman, *Treasurer*
EMP: 49 EST: 1965

Sandusky - Erie County (G-16847)

SQ FT: 75,000
SALES: 9MM **Privately Held**
WEB: www.sanduskypackaging.com
SIC: 2652 2657 Setup paperboard boxes; folding paperboard boxes

(G-16847)
SCHWAB MACHINE CO INC
3120 Venice Rd (44870-1886)
PHONE................................419 626-0245
Robert Schwab, *President*
James McMahon, *Vice Pres*
EMP: 6 **EST:** 1946
SQ FT: 9,600
SALES: 800K **Privately Held**
SIC: 3599 Machine shop, jobbing & repair

(G-16848)
SCREEN PRINTING UNLIMITED
3410 Tiffin Ave (44870-9752)
PHONE................................419 621-2335
Karen Weit, *Owner*
EMP: 3
SQ FT: 3,000
SALES: 155K **Privately Held**
WEB: www.promotionsunlimited.net
SIC: 2759 Screen printing

(G-16849)
SHOWCASE CAB MAR RSTORATION LL
5404 Sandy Acres Dr (44870-8626)
PHONE................................419 626-6715
Jeffrey A Witter,
EMP: 3
SALES (est): 460.7K **Privately Held**
SIC: 2434 Wood kitchen cabinets

(G-16850)
SPOERR PRECAST CONCRETE INC
2020 Caldwell St (44870-4874)
PHONE................................419 625-9132
William R Shank, *President*
William Shank, *President*
Thomas Shank, *Manager*
Robert Shank, *Executive*
EMP: 13 **EST:** 1933
SQ FT: 18,000
SALES (est): 1.8MM **Privately Held**
WEB: www.spoerrprecast.com
SIC: 3272 Concrete products, precast; burial vaults, concrete or precast terrazzo; wall & ceiling squares, concrete; septic tanks, concrete

(G-16851)
SURENERGY LLC
319 Howard Dr (44870-8607)
PHONE................................419 626-8000
Timothy Rathbun,
▲ **EMP:** 14
SALES (est): 2.4MM **Privately Held**
SIC: 3621 Windmills, electric generating

(G-16852)
THERMOCOLOR LLC (DH)
Also Called: Rhe-Tech Colors
2901 W Monroe St (44870-1810)
PHONE................................419 626-5677
Tracy Garrison, *Principal*
EMP: 29
SQ FT: 30,000
SALES: 5.4MM
SALES (corp-wide): 1.4B **Privately Held**
SIC: 2865 Cyclic crudes & intermediates
HQ: Hexpol Holding Inc
14330 Kinsman Rd
Burton OH 44021
440 834-4644

(G-16853)
THERMOCOLOR LLC
Also Called: Rhetech Color
2108 Superior St (44870)
PHONE................................419 626-5677
John Levinson, *General Mgr*
EMP: 14
SALES (corp-wide): 1.4B **Privately Held**
SIC: 2865 Cyclic crudes & intermediates
HQ: Thermocolor Llc
2901 W Monroe St
Sandusky OH 44870
419 626-5677

(G-16854)
THORFOOD LLC (HQ)
Also Called: Peanut Roaster, The
2520 Campbell St (44870-5309)
P.O. Box 2218 (44871-2218)
PHONE................................419 626-4375
John Monahan, *President*
Chris Nielsen, *CFO*
David Thorson, *Mng Member*
EMP: 25
SALES (est): 7.8MM
SALES (corp-wide): 89.9MM **Privately Held**
SIC: 2068 Salted & roasted nuts & seeds
PA: Thorworks Industries, Inc.
2520 Campbell St
Sandusky OH 44870
419 626-4375

(G-16855)
THORWORKS INDUSTRIES INC (PA)
Also Called: Sealmaster
2520 Campbell St (44870-5309)
P.O. Box 2218 (44871-2218)
PHONE................................419 626-4375
David Thorson, *President*
Chris Nielsen, *CFO*
◆ **EMP:** 30
SQ FT: 80,000
SALES (corp-wide): 89.9MM **Privately Held**
WEB: www.sealmaster.net
SIC: 2851 3531 2952 2951 Paints & paint additives; construction machinery; asphalt felts & coatings; asphalt paving mixtures & blocks; adhesives & sealants; inorganic pigments

(G-16856)
TOFT DAIRY INC
3717 Venice Rd (44870-1640)
P.O. Box 2558 (44871-2558)
PHONE................................419 625-4376
Eugene H Meisler, *President*
Nicholas Catri, *Principal*
Carl Meisler, *Principal*
Charles M Meisler, *Corp Secy*
Thomas E Meisler, *Vice Pres*
EMP: 52 **EST:** 1900
SQ FT: 94,000
SALES: 20.7MM **Privately Held**
WEB: www.toftdairy.com
SIC: 2026 2024 Milk processing (pasteurizing, homogenizing, bottling); ice cream & ice milk

(G-16857)
TUNE TOWN CAR AUDIO
2345 E Perkins Ave (44870-5198)
PHONE................................419 627-1100
Toll Free:................................877 -
Mark Myers, *Owner*
Kayce Berkey, *CFO*
EMP: 7
SQ FT: 4,800
SALES: 800K **Privately Held**
WEB: www.tune-town.com
SIC: 5731 3651 High fidelity stereo equipment; household audio & video equipment

(G-16858)
UNION FABRICATING & MACHINE CO
3427 Venice Rd (44870-1766)
PHONE................................419 626-5963
Alden V Lake, *CEO*
Daniel Lake, *President*
Jeffrey Lake, *Vice Pres*
Mary Lake, *Admin Sec*
EMP: 7
SALES (est): 604.4K **Privately Held**
SIC: 3441 Fabricated structural metal

(G-16859)
UNIVERSAL DSIGN FBRICATION LLC
5619 Skadden Rd (44870-9651)
PHONE................................419 359-1794
John H Eckhardt,
EMP: 3
SALES: 500K **Privately Held**
SIC: 3499 7389 Fabricated metal products; design services

(G-16860)
US TSUBAKI POWER TRANSM LLC
Also Called: Engineering Chain Div
1010 Edgewater Ave (44870-1601)
PHONE................................419 626-4560
Myron Timmer, *Vice Pres*
Steve Funni, *Mfg Staff*
Chuck Kaman, *Design Engr Mgr*
Vic Hostetter, *Engineer*
Dave Piasecki, *Engineer*
EMP: 180
SALES (corp-wide): 2B **Privately Held**
SIC: 5049 3568 3714 3462 Engineers' equipment & supplies; chain, power transmission; motor vehicle parts & accessories; iron & steel forgings
HQ: U.S. Tsubaki Power Transmission Llc
301 E Marquardt Dr
Wheeling IL 60090
847 459-9500

(G-16861)
VENTRA SANDUSKY LLC
3020 Tiffin Ave (44870-5352)
PHONE................................419 627-3600
Douglas Cellier,
Shaun Tinnel,
▲ **EMP:** 121
SALES (est): 76.7MM
SALES (corp-wide): 3.4B **Privately Held**
SIC: 3714 3822 Motor vehicle parts & accessories; auto controls regulating residntl & coml environmt & applncs
PA: Flex-N-Gate Llc
1306 E University Ave
Urbana IL 61802
217 384-6600

(G-16862)
WAGNER QUARRIES COMPANY
Also Called: Hanson Aggregates
4203 Milan Rd (44870-5880)
PHONE................................419 625-8141
Norman Jacobs, *Plant Mgr*
Chris Kinner, *Plant Mgr*
Bill Hoelzer, *Sales Staff*
Chuck Cashan, *Manager*
Andrew Harper, *Manager*
EMP: 48
SQ FT: 2,400
SALES (est): 4.5MM **Privately Held**
SIC: 1422 Limestones, ground

(G-16863)
WWW BOAT SERVICES INC
2218 River Ave (44870-1303)
PHONE................................419 626-0883
Ryan Kraft, *President*
Debra Kraft, *Corp Secy*
Ray Kraft, *Vice Pres*
EMP: 5 **EST:** 1996
SALES: 142.9K **Privately Held**
SIC: 3732 5551 Boat building & repairing; boat dealers

Sandyville
Tuscarawas County

(G-16864)
VEGGIE VALLEY FARM LLC
3444 Dueber Rd Ne (44671)
P.O. Box 135 (44671-0135)
PHONE................................330 866-2712
Betty Frank,
Edward J Frank,
EMP: 6
SALES (est): 516.3K **Privately Held**
SIC: 2099 Ready-to-eat meals, salads & sandwiches

Sarahsville
Noble County

(G-16865)
BIEDENBACH LOGGING
48443 Seneca Lake Rd (43779-9732)
PHONE................................740 732-6477
John Biedenbach, *Partner*
EMP: 6

SALES (est): 559.4K **Privately Held**
SIC: 2411 1629 Logging camps & contractors; earthmoving contractor

(G-16866)
NED A SHREVE
Also Called: Ben Logging
48398 Seneca Lake Rd (43779-9732)
PHONE................................740 732-6465
Ned A Shreve, *Owner*
EMP: 5
SALES (est): 313.3K **Privately Held**
SIC: 2411 7389 Logging camps & contractors; log & lumber broker

Sardinia
Brown County

(G-16867)
COCA-COLA
136 Fairview Ave (45171-9354)
PHONE................................937 446-4644
EMP: 5 **EST:** 2011
SALES (est): 198.3K **Privately Held**
SIC: 2086 Bottled & canned soft drinks

(G-16868)
COCA-COLA COMPANY
7906 Yochum Rd (45171-8379)
PHONE................................937 446-4644
Kevin Smith, *Manager*
EMP: 18
SALES (corp-wide): 35.4B **Publicly Held**
WEB: www.colasic.net
SIC: 2086 Soft drinks: packaged in cans, bottles, etc.
PA: The Coca-Cola Company
1 Coca Cola Plz Nw
Atlanta GA 30313
404 676-2121

(G-16869)
GREEN BROTHERS ENTERPRISES
516 Sicily Rd (45171)
P.O. Box 1 (45171-0001)
PHONE................................937 444-3323
Fax: 937 444-3323
EMP: 3
SQ FT: 15,000
SALES: 250K **Privately Held**
SIC: 2421 Sawmill/Planing Mill

(G-16870)
MANNINGS PACKING CO
100 College Ave (45171-7500)
P.O. Box 23 (45171-0023)
PHONE................................937 446-3278
Gregory Thomas Manning, *Partner*
Robert Manning, *Partner*
EMP: 8
SQ FT: 5,000
SALES (est): 866.6K **Privately Held**
SIC: 2011 Meat packing plants

(G-16871)
SARDINIA READY MIX INC (PA)
9 Oakdale Ave (45171)
P.O. Box 53 (45171-0053)
PHONE................................937 446-2523
David Taylor, *President*
Cheryl Taylor, *Corp Secy*
Charles Taylor, *Vice Pres*
EMP: 3
SQ FT: 2,000
SALES (est): 2.6MM **Privately Held**
SIC: 3273 Ready-mixed concrete

(G-16872)
SARDINIA READY MIX INC
9 Oakdale Ave (45171)
P.O. Box 53 (45171-0053)
PHONE................................937 446-2523
Cheryle Taylor, *President*
EMP: 12
SALES (est): 826.1K
SALES (corp-wide): 2.6MM **Privately Held**
SIC: 3273 Ready-mixed concrete
PA: Sardinia Ready Mix, Inc.
9 Oakdale Ave
Sardinia OH 45171
937 446-2523

GEOGRAPHIC SECTION

Sebring - Mahoning County (G-16898)

(G-16873)
SCOTT-RANDALL SYSTEMS INC
5815 Tracy Rd (45171-9120)
PHONE..................................937 446-2293
Walter S Prather III, *President*
Janet Prather, *Vice Pres*
EMP: 15
SQ FT: 31,200
SALES (est): 1.3MM Privately Held
WEB: www.scott-randallsystems.com
SIC: 5084 3535 3537 Materials handling machinery; robotic conveyors; industrial trucks & tractors

(G-16874)
TRI-STATE FASTENERS LLC
2875 Gath North Rd (45171-8203)
PHONE..................................937 442-1904
James Herrmann, *Mng Member*
Jayne Burke,
Mark Burke,
EMP: 3
SALES (est): 297.3K Privately Held
SIC: 3965 Fasteners

Sardis
Monroe County

(G-16875)
APPALACHIAN OILFIELD SVCS LLC
34602 State Route 7 (43946-8704)
PHONE..................................337 216-0066
Stuart Lissner,
EMP: 5 EST: 2015
SALES (est): 278.5K Privately Held
SIC: 1389 Oil field services

(G-16876)
MONROE WATER SYSTEM
Also Called: Monroe Water Sys Treatmnt Plnt
35100 State Route 7 (43946-8732)
P.O. Box 15, Laings (43752-0015)
PHONE..................................740 472-1030
Bill Wells, *Manager*
Jim Murray, *Manager*
EMP: 4
SALES (est): 477.5K Privately Held
SIC: 3321 Water pipe, cast iron

Scio
Harrison County

(G-16877)
GINGERBREAD N BOWS
202 W Main St (43988)
PHONE..................................740 945-1027
Jeannie Cagot, *Principal*
EMP: 5
SALES (est): 318.2K Privately Held
SIC: 3944 Craft & hobby kits & sets

(G-16878)
M3 MIDSTREAM LLC
Also Called: Harrison Hub
37950 Crimm Rd (43988)
PHONE..................................740 945-1170
EMP: 57
SALES (corp-wide): 54.9MM Privately Held
SIC: 1311 Crude petroleum & natural gas
PA: M3 Midstream Llc
  600 Travis St Ste 5600
  Houston TX 77002
  713 783-3000

(G-16879)
SCIO LAMINATED PRODUCTS INC
117 Fowler Ave (43988-9779)
P.O. Box 6561, Wheeling WV (26003-0627)
PHONE..................................740 945-1321
W Quay Mull II, *Ch of Bd*
Charles J Kaiser Jr, *Principal*
Terry Call, *Vice Pres*
Michael Piazza, *VP Sales*
Wqm Industries, *Shareholder*
EMP: 28
SQ FT: 70,000
SALES (est): 2.2MM Privately Held
SIC: 2541 Table or counter tops, plastic laminated

(G-16880)
UTICA EAST OHIO MIDSTREAM LLC
117 Fowler Ave (43988-9779)
PHONE..................................740 945-2226
EMP: 6
SALES (est): 471.3K Privately Held
SIC: 1311 Crude petroleum & natural gas

Scottown
Lawrence County

(G-16881)
FOUR JS BLDG COMPONENTS LLC
16435 State Route 217 (45678-9062)
PHONE..................................740 886-6112
Jeff Ramey,
EMP: 15
SALES (est): 682.8K Privately Held
SIC: 1761 2439 Roofing contractor; trusses, wooden roof

Seaman
Adams County

(G-16882)
ALL WAYS GREEN LAWN & TURF LLC
1856 Greenbrier Rd (45679-9552)
PHONE..................................937 763-4766
Jeffrey Mullenix,
EMP: 7
SALES (est): 225K Privately Held
SIC: 2875 0781 Fertilizers, mixing only; landscape services

(G-16883)
M & L MACHINE
17400 State Route 247 (45679-9417)
P.O. Box 227 (45679-0227)
PHONE..................................937 386-2604
Fax: 937 386-2739
EMP: 7
SQ FT: 40,000
SALES (est): 380K Privately Held
SIC: 3599 3728 Mfg Industrial Machinery Mfg Aircraft Parts/ Equipment

(G-16884)
SOUTHERN OHIO MATERIALS
800 Nathan Denton Rd (45679-9554)
PHONE..................................937 386-3200
Nathania Shelton, *Principal*
EMP: 3
SALES (est): 231.5K Privately Held
SIC: 1429 Grits mining (crushed stone)

Sebring
Mahoning County

(G-16885)
CIRCLE MACHINE ROLLS INC
245 W Kentucky Ave (44672-1909)
P.O. Box 9 (44672-0009)
PHONE..................................330 938-9010
Peter Kuhlmann, *President*
Ken Kuhlmann, *Vice Pres*
Ray Muniz, *Buyer*
Brenda Reed, *Admin Sec*
▲ EMP: 27
SQ FT: 15,000
SALES (est): 5MM Privately Held
WEB: www.rollsbycircle.com
SIC: 3599 3547 Machine & other job shop work; rolling mill machinery

(G-16886)
FOUNDRY SAND SERVICE LLC
20455 Lake Park Blvd (44672-1771)
P.O. Box 262 (44672-0262)
PHONE..................................330 823-6152
Jim Budd, *Director*
EMP: 6
SALES (est): 117K Privately Held
SIC: 1442 Construction sand & gravel

(G-16887)
JF MARTT AND ASSOCIATES INC
501 N Johnson Rd (44672-1007)
P.O. Box 10 (44672-0010)
PHONE..................................330 938-4000
Judson Martt, *President*
Frank Tluchowski, *Vice Pres*
Cheryl Tafe, *Human Resources*
David Courtwright, *Manager*
Cheryl K Tafe, *Manager*
EMP: 15
SQ FT: 12,000
SALES (est): 3MM Privately Held
WEB: www.jfmartt.com
SIC: 7699 3599 Industrial machinery & equipment repair; custom machinery

(G-16888)
M PI LABEL SYSTEMS
450 Courtney Rd (44672-1339)
P.O. Box 70 (44672-0070)
PHONE..................................330 938-2134
Randy Kocher, *President*
Carson Mc Neely, *President*
Donald J McDanial, *President*
Joe Skiba, *Treasurer*
EMP: 6 EST: 1991
SALES (est): 695.1K Privately Held
SIC: 2759 2754 3565 Labels & seals: printing; labels: gravure printing; labeling machines, industrial

(G-16889)
MODERN CHINA INC (PA)
550 E Ohio Ave (44672-1642)
P.O. Box 309 (44672-0309)
PHONE..................................330 938-6104
Debbie Grindley, *President*
EMP: 50 EST: 1959
SQ FT: 27,000
SALES (est): 3.3MM Privately Held
SIC: 5947 3229 3263 Souvenirs; greeting cards; glassware, art or decorative; semi-vitreous table & kitchenware

(G-16890)
MPI LABELS OF BALTIMORE INC (HQ)
Also Called: Mpi Label Systems.
450 Courtney Rd (44672-1339)
P.O. Box 70 (44672-0070)
PHONE..................................330 938-2134
Randy L Kocher, *President*
Elvin Barnit, *President*
Carson Mc Neely, *President*
Donald McDanial, *President*
EMP: 17
SQ FT: 110,000
SALES (est): 9MM
SALES (corp-wide): 36.3MM Privately Held
SIC: 2759 2754 3565 Labels & seals: printing; labels: gravure printing; labeling machines, industrial
PA: Miller Products, Inc.
  450 Courtney Rd
  Sebring OH 44672
  330 938-2134

(G-16891)
REFRACTORY SPECIALTIES INC
230 W California Ave (44672-1920)
PHONE..................................330 938-2101
Richard Wilk, *President*
Jim Vaughn, *Corp Secy*
Suhas Patil, *Vice Pres*
▲ EMP: 49
SQ FT: 55,000
SALES (est): 9MM
SALES (corp-wide): 3.1B Privately Held
WEB: www.rsifibre.com
SIC: 3823 3296 3297 Industrial instrmnts msrmnt display/control process variable; mineral wool; graphite refractories: carbon bond or ceramic bond
HQ: Unifrax Holding Co
  55 E 52nd St Fl 35
  New York NY 10055

(G-16892)
S WJ LLCRED
1100 N Johnson Rd (44672-1020)
PHONE..................................330 938-6173
Ted Hines, *Principal*
EMP: 3
SALES (est): 277.5K Privately Held
SIC: 3672 Printed circuit boards

(G-16893)
SALEM-REPUBLIC RUBBER COMPANY
475 W California Ave (44672-1922)
P.O. Box 339 (44672-0339)
PHONE..................................877 425-5079
Drew Ney, *President*
Don McCaughtry, *VP Opers*
Jim Grossi, *Plant Mgr*
Philip Marinucci, *Mfg Staff*
Jason Phillips, *Sales Engr*
▲ EMP: 47
SQ FT: 180,000
SALES (est): 10.3MM Privately Held
WEB: www.salem-republic.com
SIC: 3052 3069 Rubber hose; rubberized fabrics

(G-16894)
SEBRING FLUID POWER CORP
513 N Johnson Rd (44672-1007)
P.O. Box 6 (44672-0006)
PHONE..................................330 938-9984
Paul Mc Guire, *President*
Stan Ware, *Treasurer*
EMP: 7
SQ FT: 10,000
SALES (est): 800K Privately Held
SIC: 3599 3593 Machine shop, jobbing & repair; fluid power cylinders & actuators

(G-16895)
SEBRING INDUSTRIAL PLATING
Also Called: Sebring Plating
546 W Tennessee Ave (44672-1836)
P.O. Box 206 (44672-0206)
PHONE..................................330 938-6666
Richard Sickelsmith, *President*
Eric Sickelsmith, *Vice Pres*
EMP: 8
SQ FT: 10,000
SALES (est): 1.1MM Privately Held
SIC: 3471 Plating of metals or formed products

(G-16896)
TRUCUT INCORPORATED (PA)
1145 Allied Dr (44672-1355)
PHONE..................................330 938-9806
David Gano, *President*
Larry Grossi, *Exec VP*
Carol Darrah, *Materials Mgr*
Michael Geiger, *Opers Staff*
Michael Greenamyer, *Purch Mgr*
▲ EMP: 53
SQ FT: 85,000
SALES (est): 11MM Privately Held
SIC: 3544 3542 3469 3613 Special dies, tools, jigs & fixtures; machine tools, metal forming type; metal stampings; control panels, electric; automotive stampings

(G-16897)
UNITED DIE & MFG CO
100 S 17th St (44672-1914)
P.O. Box 38 (44672-0038)
PHONE..................................330 938-6141
Gary Close, *President*
Dennis Close, *Corp Secy*
EMP: 30
SQ FT: 40,000
SALES (est): 5.4MM Privately Held
WEB: www.uniteddiemfg.com
SIC: 3429 3469 Manufactured hardware (general); stamping metal for the trade

(G-16898)
VACUFORM INC
500 Courtney Rd (44672-1349)
P.O. Box 117 (44672-0117)
PHONE..................................330 938-9674
Michael Hubbs, *Vice Pres*
▲ EMP: 35
SQ FT: 50,000
SALES (est): 5.4MM Publicly Held
WEB: www.vacuforminc.com
SIC: 3297 Nonclay refractories

Senecaville - Guernsey County (G-16899)

HQ: Unifrax I Llc
600 Rverwalk Pkwy Ste 120
Tonawanda NY 14250

Senecaville
Guernsey County

(G-16899)
DWAYNE HALL
57501 Cherry Hill Rd (43780-9772)
PHONE.................................740 685-5270
Dwayne Hall, *Owner*
EMP: 4 EST: 2001
SALES (est): 264.4K **Privately Held**
WEB: www.dwaynehall.com
SIC: 3199 Saddles or parts

(G-16900)
PAUL YODER
13051 Deerfield Rd (43780-9406)
PHONE.................................740 439-5811
Paul Yoder, *Owner*
EMP: 6
SQ FT: 6,500
SALES: 600K **Privately Held**
WEB: www.yoderbuilding.com
SIC: 2542 Cabinets: show, display or storage: except wood

Seven Hills
Cuyahoga County

(G-16901)
ART PRO GRAPHICS
7279 Summitview Dr (44131-4400)
PHONE.................................216 236-6465
Anthony Tomecko, *Owner*
EMP: 5
SALES (est): 368.9K **Privately Held**
SIC: 2752 Commercial printing, lithographic

(G-16902)
CLEANING BY SNDRA MSTERS TOUCH
6516 Gale Dr (44131-3131)
PHONE.................................216 524-6827
Sandra Hines, *Partner*
EMP: 11
SALES (est): 710K **Privately Held**
SIC: 7699 2842 Cleaning services; specialty cleaning preparations

(G-16903)
DUMPSTERS INC
772 Hillside Rd (44131-4416)
PHONE.................................440 241-6927
EMP: 3 EST: 2017
SALES (est): 209.3K **Privately Held**
SIC: 3443 Dumpsters, garbage

(G-16904)
PREFERRED SOLUTIONS INC
7819 Broadview Rd Ste 6 (44131-6150)
PHONE.................................216 642-1200
John A Stahl, *President*
Jack Stahl, *Vice Pres*
EMP: 15
SQ FT: 8,000
SALES (est): 2.8MM **Privately Held**
WEB: www.stayflex.com
SIC: 3089 Plastic processing

(G-16905)
RENT A MOM INC
4531 Hillside Rd (44131-4611)
PHONE.................................216 901-9599
Linda Delaney, *President*
EMP: 12
SALES (est): 1.3MM **Privately Held**
WEB: www.rentamominc.com
SIC: 3635 Household vacuum cleaners

(G-16906)
SEVEN HILLS REPORTER
6817 Parkgate Oval (44131-3642)
PHONE.................................216 524-9515
Timothy Fraundorf, *Principal*
EMP: 4

SALES (est): 196.5K **Privately Held**
SIC: 2711 Newspapers, publishing & printing

Seven Mile
Butler County

(G-16907)
ENCORE PRECAST LLC
416 W Ritter (45062)
P.O. Box 380 (45062-0380)
PHONE.................................513 726-5678
Charles Ehlers, *Principal*
Jeff Meyer, *Project Mgr*
Tim Murray, *QC Mgr*
David Adams, *Sales Staff*
EMP: 15
SALES (est): 2.9MM **Privately Held**
SIC: 3272 5032 5211 Septic tanks, concrete; concrete & cinder building products; concrete & cinder block

(G-16908)
OWEN & SONS
206 S Main St (45062)
PHONE.................................513 726-5406
Thomas Owen, *Owner*
EMP: 3 EST: 1946
SALES (est): 267.2K **Privately Held**
SIC: 3548 Welding apparatus

Seville
Medina County

(G-16909)
4-B WOOD SPECIALTIES INC
Also Called: 4-B Wood Custom Cabinets
255 W Greenwich Rd (44273-8876)
PHONE.................................330 769-2188
Kurt E Grassell, *President*
Tracy Romanotto, *Manager*
EMP: 15
SQ FT: 17,000
SALES (est): 2MM **Privately Held**
WEB: www.4bwood.com
SIC: 2434 Wood kitchen cabinets

(G-16910)
ATLANTIC TOOL & DIE COMPANY
Also Called: Jatdco
4995 Atlantic Dr (44273-8965)
PHONE.................................330 769-4500
Frank Mehwald, *Branch Mgr*
EMP: 200
SALES (corp-wide): 159.9MM **Privately Held**
SIC: 3469 3545 3544 Stamping metal for the trade; machine tool accessories; special dies & tools
PA: Atlantic Tool & Die Company Inc
19963 Progress Dr
Strongsville OH 44149
440 238-6931

(G-16911)
BENCHMARK CRAFTSMAN INC
Also Called: Benchmark Craftsmen
4700 Greenwich Rd (44273-8848)
PHONE.................................330 975-4214
Nathan Sublett, *President*
EMP: 30
SALES (est): 4.1MM **Privately Held**
WEB: www.benchmarkcraftsmen.com
SIC: 7389 3993 Exhibit construction by industrial contractors; displays & cutouts, window & lobby

(G-16912)
BLAIR RUBBER COMPANY
5020 Enterprise Pkwy (44273-8960)
PHONE.................................330 769-5583
John M Glenn, *CEO*
David Jentzsch, *General Mgr*
Tonjua McCullough, *Project Mgr*
Tom Bogart, *Export Mgr*
Gregg Reinmann, *QC Mgr*
◆ EMP: 65
SQ FT: 50,000

SALES (est): 17.7MM
SALES (corp-wide): 54.8MM **Privately Held**
WEB: www.blairrubber.com
SIC: 3069 3535 Linings, vulcanizable rubber; belt conveyor systems, general industrial use
PA: Goldis Enterprises, Inc.
120 Hay Rd
Wilmington DE 19809
302 764-3100

(G-16913)
BLEACHTECH LLC
320 Ryan Rd (44273-9109)
PHONE.................................216 921-1980
Joseph Traylinek, *Maintenance Dir*
William Schaad, *Plant Mgr*
Richard Immerman, *Mng Member*
Bill Shadd, *Manager*
Benjamin Calkins,
EMP: 25
SALES (est): 2MM **Privately Held**
SIC: 7349 5169 2819 Chemical cleaning services; chemicals & allied products; bleaching powder, lime bleaching compounds

(G-16914)
COMDESS COMPANY INC
8733 Wooster Pike Rd (44273-9363)
P.O. Box 91 (44273-0091)
PHONE.................................330 769-2094
Sam Mandich, *President*
▲ EMP: 15
SQ FT: 25,000
SALES (est): 2.3MM **Privately Held**
WEB: www.comdess.com
SIC: 3089 Thermoformed finished plastic products; injection molding of plastics

(G-16915)
DIE CAST DIVISION
271 W Greenwich Rd (44273-8880)
PHONE.................................330 769-2013
EMP: 3
SALES (est): 190.1K **Privately Held**
SIC: 3544 Mfg Dies/Tools/Jigs/Fixtures

(G-16916)
HYLOAD INC (DH)
5020 Enterprise Pkwy (44273-8960)
PHONE.................................330 336-6604
Dave Jentzsch, *President*
David Afanador, *Business Mgr*
▼ EMP: 17 EST: 1982
SQ FT: 40,000
SALES: 9MM
SALES (corp-wide): 54.8MM **Privately Held**
WEB: www.hyload.com
SIC: 3069 2952 Roofing, membrane rubber; asphalt felts & coatings

(G-16917)
ISLAND DELIGHTS INC
Also Called: Birmurco
240 W Greenwich Rd (44273-8878)
P.O. Box 187 (44273-0187)
PHONE.................................866 887-4100
James Murray, *President*
Greg Miller, *Vice Pres*
EMP: 8
SQ FT: 12,000
SALES: 1MM **Privately Held**
SIC: 5441 2064 Candy; candy & other confectionery products

(G-16918)
JJ SEVILLE LLC
Also Called: Seville Bronze
22 Milton St (44273-9316)
P.O. Box 45 (44273-0045)
PHONE.................................330 769-2071
Tim Steele, *President*
EMP: 22
SALES (est): 5MM **Privately Held**
SIC: 3351 Bronze rolling & drawing

(G-16919)
KING DRILLING CO
24 E Main St (44273-9196)
P.O. Box 52 (44273-0052)
PHONE.................................330 769-3434
Andrew King, *President*
Peter King Jr, *Vice Pres*

EMP: 4
SQ FT: 700
SALES (est): 417.6K **Privately Held**
SIC: 1311 Crude petroleum production; natural gas production

(G-16920)
MARTIN RUBBER COMPANY
5020 Panther Pkwy (44273-8960)
PHONE.................................330 336-6604
Fax: 330 336-5512
EMP: 11
SALES (est): 1.4MM **Privately Held**
SIC: 3069 3535 Mfg Fabricated Rubber Products Mfg Conveyors/Equipment

Shade
Athens County

(G-16921)
SHADE TEXT BOOK SERVICE INC
Also Called: Shade Winery
401 Gilkey Ridge Rd (45776-9660)
PHONE.................................740 696-1323
Neal Dix, *President*
EMP: 3 EST: 2002
SALES: 222K **Privately Held**
SIC: 2084 7389 Wines;

Shadyside
Belmont County

(G-16922)
KNIGHT MANUFACTURING CO INC (PA)
399 E 40th St (43947-1206)
P.O. Box 27 (43947-0027)
PHONE.................................740 676-9532
David Knight, *President*
EMP: 10
SQ FT: 140,000
SALES (est): 2.1MM **Privately Held**
SIC: 3599 3469 Machine shop, jobbing & repair; boxes: tool, lunch, mail, etc.: stamped metal

(G-16923)
KNIGHT MANUFACTURING CO INC
Also Called: Belmont Stamping
E 40th St (43947)
P.O. Box 98 (43947-0098)
PHONE.................................740 676-5516
David Knight, *Manager*
EMP: 6
SALES (corp-wide): 2.1MM **Privately Held**
SIC: 3444 3469 3589 Sheet metalwork; metal stampings; garbage disposers & compactors, commercial
PA: Knight Manufacturing Co Inc
399 E 40th St
Shadyside OH 43947
740 676-9532

(G-16924)
NEW CUT TOOL AND MFG CORP
1 New Cut Rd (43947)
PHONE.................................740 676-1666
Michael Koonce, *President*
Cynthia Badia, *Vice Pres*
EMP: 10
SQ FT: 2,700
SALES (est): 2MM **Privately Held**
SIC: 3599 Machine shop, jobbing & repair

Shaker Heights
Cuyahoga County

(G-16925)
ADMIRAL THERAPEUTICS LLC
3101 Warrington Rd (44120-2428)
PHONE.................................410 908-8906
Jeffrey Klein, *President*
EMP: 3

▲ = Import ▼ = Export
◆ = Import/Export

GEOGRAPHIC SECTION

SALES (est): 85.8K **Privately Held**
SIC: 2834 Pharmaceutical preparations

(G-16926)
BULLSEYE LLC
2830 Attleboro Rd (44120-1814)
PHONE..................................216 272-7050
Ryan Cristal, *Mng Member*
EMP: 4
SALES (est): 119.3K **Privately Held**
SIC: 7372 Educational computer software

(G-16927)
CALCOL INC
23425 Bryden Rd (44122-4020)
P.O. Box 22103, Cleveland (44122-0103)
PHONE..................................216 245-6301
Norman Charles Kaplan, *Ch of Bd*
EMP: 21
SQ FT: 1,000
SALES (est): 2.3MM **Privately Held**
WEB: www.calcol.com
SIC: 2834 Pharmaceutical preparations

(G-16928)
CASENTRIC LLC
23700 Fairmount Blvd (44122-2204)
P.O. Box 21101, Cleveland (44121-0101)
PHONE..................................216 233-6300
Steven Washington, *Mng Member*
EMP: 4
SALES: 500K **Privately Held**
SIC: 7372 7379 7389 Business oriented computer software; computer related consulting services;

(G-16929)
CELLULAR TECHNOLOGY LIMITED
Also Called: Ctl Analyzers
20521 Chagrin Blvd # 200 (44122-5350)
PHONE..................................216 791-5084
Paul V Lehmann,
EMP: 40
SQ FT: 30,000
SALES (est): 6MM **Privately Held**
SIC: 8071 3821 Medical laboratories; clinical laboratory instruments, except medical & dental

(G-16930)
CTL ANALYZERS LLC (PA)
Also Called: Cellular Technology Ltd
20521 Chagrin Blvd # 200 (44122-5350)
PHONE..................................216 791-5084
Paul V Lehmann PHD, *President*
George Csatary, *CFO*
Magdalana Terry-Lehmann, *Treasurer*
EMP: 10
SALES (est): 5MM **Privately Held**
WEB: www.immunospot.com
SIC: 3845 Electromedical equipment

(G-16931)
FULLGOSPEL PUBLISHING ✪
16781 Chagrin Blvd # 134 (44120-3721)
P.O. Box 201331 (44120-8105)
PHONE..................................216 339-1973
Kathy Brown, *Owner*
EMP: 10 EST: 2018
SALES: 120K **Privately Held**
SIC: 2741 Miscellaneous publishing

(G-16932)
INSTITUTE MTHMTICAL STATISTICS
Also Called: IMS
3163 Somerset Dr (44122-3812)
P.O. Box 22718 (44122-0718)
PHONE..................................216 295-2340
Terry Steed, *President*
Julia Norton, *Treasurer*
Elyse Gustasfon, *Director*
EMP: 1
SQ FT: 500
SALES (est): 2.3MM **Privately Held**
WEB: www.imstat.org
SIC: 8699 2721 Flying club; periodicals

(G-16933)
LIGHTSTAB LTD CO
3103 Morley Rd (44122-2861)
PHONE..................................216 751-5800
Joseph R Degenfelder, *President*
Theodore Alfred,

Pauline Degenfelder,
EMP: 3
SALES (est): 205.8K **Privately Held**
SIC: 2816 Inorganic pigments

(G-16934)
LUMOPTIK INC
2700 W Park Blvd (44120-1679)
PHONE..................................216 577-3905
Thomas Janicki, *CEO*
George Hillman, *COO*
EMP: 3 EST: 2014
SALES (est): 150.7K **Privately Held**
SIC: 3841 Surgical & medical instruments

(G-16935)
PURUSHEALTH LLC
3558 Lee Rd (44120-5123)
P.O. Box 201727, Cleveland (44120-8112)
PHONE..................................800 601-0580
John Huff, *CEO*
EMP: 11 EST: 2011
SALES (est): 1.7MM **Privately Held**
SIC: 2099 Food preparations

(G-16936)
SHELBURNE CORP (PA)
20001 Shelburne Rd (44118-5013)
PHONE..................................216 321-9177
EMP: 1
SALES (est): 83.4MM **Privately Held**
SIC: 3443 3823 3544 3769 Mfg Industrial Vessels Heat Exchangers Temperature Control Instruments Molds For Plastic Working Machinery Bellows Assembly

(G-16937)
SMS COMMUNICATIONS INC
Also Called: Moto Photo
20116 Chagrin Blvd (44122-4947)
P.O. Box 670514, Northfield (44067-0514)
PHONE..................................216 374-6686
Richard J Santich, *President*
EMP: 23
SQ FT: 2,700
SALES (est): 2.3MM **Privately Held**
SIC: 7384 2759 7221 Film developing & printing; commercial printing; photographer, still or video

(G-16938)
STAR BEVERAGE CORPORATION OHIO
3277 Lee Rd (44120-3451)
PHONE..................................216 991-4799
Arthur Boyd, *President*
Patrick Stafford, *Vice Pres*
Denise Ragland, *Executive Asst*
EMP: 3
SQ FT: 1,600
SALES (est): 346.8K **Privately Held**
SIC: 5149 2086 Soft drinks; soft drinks: packaged in cans, bottles, etc.

(G-16939)
TUNNEL VISION HOOPS LLC
3558 Lee Rd (44120-5123)
PHONE..................................440 487-0939
Carlton W Jackson, *Principal*
EMP: 3 EST: 2016
SALES (est): 298.2K **Privately Held**
SIC: 3999 Manufacturing industries

Shandon
Butler County

(G-16940)
CARTESSA CORPORATION
4825 Cncnnati Brkville Rd (45063-5000)
P.O. Box 190 (45063-0190)
PHONE..................................513 738-4477
Darryl Kristof, *President*
Kathleen Kristof, *Vice Pres*
▼ EMP: 13
SQ FT: 5,000
SALES (est): 2.1MM **Privately Held**
WEB: www.cartessa.com
SIC: 3672 5065 Printed circuit boards; electronic parts & equipment

(G-16941)
DIAMOND TRAILERS INC
Also Called: Diamond Heavy Haul
5045 Cncnnt Brookville Rd (45063)
P.O. Box 146 (45063-0146)
PHONE..................................513 738-4500
Tonya Engel, *President*
Steven J Engel, *President*
EMP: 28
SQ FT: 92,000
SALES (est): 5.4MM **Privately Held**
SIC: 3715 Truck trailers

(G-16942)
TRI STATE EQUIPMENT COMPANY
5009 Cncnnt Brookville Rd (45063)
P.O. Box 155 (45063-0155)
PHONE..................................513 738-7227
Kevin Hughes, *President*
David Hoppel, *Manager*
EMP: 6
SQ FT: 5,000
SALES (est): 960K **Privately Held**
SIC: 5084 7699 7359 3563 Industrial machinery & equipment; aircraft & heavy equipment repair services; equipment rental & leasing; spraying outfits: metals, paints & chemicals (compressor)

Sharon Center
Medina County

(G-16943)
AMERICAN WELDQUIP INC
1375 Wolf Creek Trl (44274)
PHONE..................................330 239-0317
Rex Carper, *President*
Don Aldridge, *Production*
Leslie Saffle, *Purch Mgr*
Marty Voss, *Manager*
Scott Orum, *Technical Staff*
EMP: 16
SQ FT: 10,500
SALES (est): 3.2MM **Privately Held**
WEB: www.weldquip.com
SIC: 3548 Welding apparatus

(G-16944)
ATC LEGACY INC
Also Called: Aerotorque Corporation
1441 Wolf Creek Trl (44274)
P.O. Box 305 (44274-0305)
PHONE..................................330 590-8105
David Heidenreich, *President*
Doug Herr, *General Mgr*
EMP: 6
SALES (est): 848.8K
SALES (corp-wide): 3.5B **Publicly Held**
SIC: 3566 Speed changers, drives & gears
HQ: Ebog Legacy, Inc.
  1441 Wolf Creek Trl
  Sharon Center OH 44274
  330 239-4933

(G-16945)
ATLANTIC TOOL & DIE COMPANY
6965 Ridge Rd (44274)
P.O. Box 586 (44274-0586)
PHONE..................................330 239-3700
Dennis Motil, *Program Mgr*
Ruff Haid, *Manager*
EMP: 200
SALES (corp-wide): 159.9MM **Privately Held**
SIC: 3544 Special dies & tools
PA: Atlantic Tool & Die Company Inc
  19963 Progress Dr
  Strongsville OH 44149
  440 238-6931

(G-16946)
BEAUFORT RFD INC
1420 Wolfcreek Trl (44274)
P.O. Box 359 (44274-0359)
PHONE..................................330 239-4331
David Abbott, *President*
Doug Baxter, *Chairman*
Brian Stringer, *Vice Pres*
Dj Wilman, *Vice Pres*
Graham Robertson, *Technical Mgr*
◆ EMP: 17

SQ FT: 62,000
SALES: 39MM
SALES (corp-wide): 118.7MM **Privately Held**
SIC: 3842 Life preservers, except cork & inflatable
HQ: Survitec Group (Usa), Inc.
  1420 Wolfcreek Trl
  Sharon Center OH 44274
  330 239-4331

(G-16947)
CAREY COLOR INC
6835 Ridge Rd (44274)
PHONE..................................330 239-1835
Gary Moravcik, *President*
Russ Kotalac, *CFO*
Russell Kotalac, *CFO*
Girard J Moravcik, *Sales Executive*
Chad Gray, *Manager*
EMP: 60
SQ FT: 19,000
SALES: 8MM **Privately Held**
WEB: www.careyweb.com
SIC: 2796 Platemaking services

(G-16948)
CELL-O-CORE CO
6935 Ridge Rd (44274)
P.O. Box 342 (44274-0342)
PHONE..................................330 239-4370
Lino Abram, *CEO*
David C Nelson, *CFO*
Craig Cook, *President*
Tom Allen, *Exec VP*
▲ EMP: 50
SQ FT: 50,000
SALES (est): 9.7MM **Privately Held**
WEB: www.cellocore.com
SIC: 3089 Extruded finished plastic products

(G-16949)
EBOG LEGACY INC (HQ)
Also Called: Ebo Group, Inc.
1441 Wolf Creek Trl (44274)
P.O. Box 305 (44274-0305)
PHONE..................................330 239-4933
Keith Nichols, *CEO*
David Given, *Ch of Bd*
EMP: 66
SQ FT: 12,200
SALES (est): 12.2MM
SALES (corp-wide): 3.5B **Publicly Held**
WEB: www.pttech.com
SIC: 3568 3542 3714 3566 Clutches, except vehicular; brakes, metal forming; motor vehicle parts & accessories; speed changers, drives & gears
PA: The Timken Company
  4500 Mount Pleasant St Nw
  North Canton OH 44720
  234 262-3000

(G-16950)
FLAMBEAU INC
1468 Wolfe Creek Trl (44274)
PHONE..................................330 239-0202
Henry Boggs, *Branch Mgr*
EMP: 250
SALES (corp-wide): 320MM **Privately Held**
SIC: 3089 Plastic processing
HQ: Flambeau, Inc.
  801 Lynn Ave
  Baraboo WI 53913
  800 352-6266

(G-16951)
M & G POLYMERS USA LLC
Also Called: Gruppo Mossi & Ghisolfi
6951 Ridge Rd (44274)
PHONE..................................330 239-7400
EMP: 20 **Privately Held**
SIC: 2819 Mfg Industrial Inorganic Chemicals
HQ: M & G Polymers Usa, Llc
  450 Gears Rd Ste 240
  Houston TX 77067
  281 873-5780

(G-16952)
PTT LEGACY INC
Also Called: Pt Tech Inc.
1441 Wolf Creek Trl (44274)
P.O. Box 305 (44274-0305)
PHONE.....................330 239-4933
Keith Nichols, *President*
Gregg W Cullings, *Vice Pres*
Ralph Rogers, *Vice Pres*
EMP: 99
SQ FT: 45,000
SALES (est): 13.2MM
SALES (corp-wide): 3.5B **Publicly Held**
SIC: 3714 Clutches, motor vehicle; motor vehicle brake systems & parts
PA: The Timken Company
4500 Mount Pleasant St Nw
North Canton OH 44720
234 262-3000

(G-16953)
SHARON PRINTING CO INC
Also Called: Jeffrey Weaver
4983 Ridge Rd (44274)
PHONE.....................330 239-1684
Jeffrey Weaver, *Owner*
Bobbi Klish, *Manager*
EMP: 4
SQ FT: 6,000
SALES (est): 495.1K **Privately Held**
SIC: 2752 2759 2791 Commercial printing, offset; thermography; typesetting

(G-16954)
SURVITEC GROUP (USA) INC (HQ)
1420 Wolfcreek Trl (44274)
P.O. Box 359 (44274-0359)
PHONE.....................330 239-4331
David Abbott, *President*
Doug Baxter, *Chairman*
Brian Stringer, *Vice Pres*
Dj Wilman, *Vice Pres*
Gerald Chunat, *Treasurer*
▼ **EMP:** 23
SALES (est): 39MM
SALES (corp-wide): 118.7MM **Privately Held**
SIC: 3069 Pontoons, rubber
PA: Survitec Group Limited
4th Floor
London EC2A
203 744-0105

(G-16955)
TILT 15 INC
1440 Wolf Creek Trl (44274)
PHONE.....................330 239-4192
James Ankoviak, *President*
Kc Corbett-Chaney, *CFO*
Dan Sharpe, *VP Sales*
Tom Lorick, *VP Mktg*
▲ **EMP:** 97
SALES: 14MM **Privately Held**
WEB: www.transmotionmedical.com
SIC: 3842 Surgical appliances & supplies
PA: Winco Mfg., Llc
5516 Sw 1st Ln
Ocala FL 34474

Sharonville
Hamilton County

(G-16956)
DIAMANT COATING SYSTEMS LTD
3495 Mustafa Dr (45241-1668)
PHONE.....................513 515-3078
Larry Grimenstein, *President*
EMP: 4
SALES: 260K **Privately Held**
SIC: 2851 Epoxy coatings

(G-16957)
KUTOL PRODUCTS COMPANY INC
100 Partnership Way (45241-1571)
PHONE.....................513 527-5500
Joseph W Rhodenbaugh, *President*
Tom Rhodenbaugh, *Vice Pres*
Greg Nichols, *Plant Mgr*
Glenn Kolb, *Mfg Mgr*
Kelly Ihle, *Purch Mgr*
◆ **EMP:** 140 **EST:** 1912
SQ FT: 160,000
SALES (est): 43.8MM **Privately Held**
WEB: www.kutol.com
SIC: 2841 Soap: granulated, liquid, cake, flaked or chip

(G-16958)
SAFRAN USA INCORPORATED
300 E Business Way (45241-2384)
PHONE.....................513 247-7000
EMP: 4 **EST:** 2013
SALES (est): 366.4K **Privately Held**
SIC: 3621 Motors & generators

(G-16959)
SCHNEIDER ELECTRIC USA INC
12000 Mosteller Rd (45241-1529)
PHONE.....................513 755-5501
EMP: 145
SALES (corp-wide): 355.8K **Privately Held**
SIC: 3613 Switchgear & switchboard apparatus
HQ: Schneider Electric Usa, Inc.
201 Wshington St Ste 2700
Boston MA 02108
978 975-9600

(G-16960)
USUI INTERNATIONAL CORPORATION
88 Partnership Way (45241-1507)
PHONE.....................513 448-0410
Haruyasu Ito, *President*
EMP: 230
SALES (corp-wide): 776.2MM **Privately Held**
SIC: 3714 Connecting rods, motor vehicle engine
HQ: Usui International Corporation
44780 Helm St
Plymouth MI 48170
734 354-3626

Shawnee
Perry County

(G-16961)
NICOFIBERS INC
9702 Iron Point Rd Se (43782-9723)
PHONE.....................740 394-2491
Robert Ableidinger, *Principal*
EMP: 4
SALES (est): 239.8K **Privately Held**
SIC: 2655 2653 Fiber cans, drums & similar products; corrugated & solid fiber boxes

(G-16962)
SUPERIOR FIBERS INC
9702 Iron Point Rd Se (43782-9723)
P.O. Box 141 (43782-0141)
PHONE.....................740 394-2491
Robert Williams, *Director*
EMP: 434
SALES (corp-wide): 123.3MM **Privately Held**
SIC: 3089 Awnings, fiberglass & plastic combination
PA: Superior Fibers, Inc.
1333 Corporate Dr Ste 350
Irving TX 75038
972 600-9953

Sheffield Lake
Lorain County

(G-16963)
CLEARFLITE INC
5445 E Lake Rd (44054-1902)
PHONE.....................440 281-7368
Terri Zajac, *President*
Bonnie Pohorence, *Manager*
EMP: 3
SQ FT: 2,500
SALES: 1MM **Privately Held**
SIC: 3564 Air purification equipment

Sheffield Village
Lorain County

(G-16964)
ADI MACHINING INC
Also Called: Advanced Design Industries
4686 French Creek Rd (44054-2716)
PHONE.....................440 277-4141
Leonard Jungbluth, *President*
Jerome R Winiasz, *Principal*
EMP: 12
SQ FT: 2,500
SALES (est): 201.6K **Privately Held**
SIC: 3599 Machine shop, jobbing & repair

(G-16965)
ADVANCED DESIGN INDUSTRIES INC
Also Called: ADI
4686 French Creek Rd (44054-2716)
PHONE.....................440 277-4141
Jerome Winiasz, *President*
R G Brooks Jr, *Principal*
Edward J Winiasz, *Principal*
Thomas Winiasz, *Corp Secy*
▲ **EMP:** 25
SQ FT: 27,000
SALES (est): 7.3MM **Privately Held**
SIC: 3569 3599 8711 Robots, assembly line: industrial & commercial; machine shop, jobbing & repair; designing: ship, boat, machine & product

(G-16966)
BENKO PRODUCTS INC
Also Called: Environmental Products Div
5350 Evergreen Pkwy (44054-2446)
PHONE.....................440 934-2180
John Benko, *President*
Robert Benko, *Vice Pres*
Doug Ingram, *Manager*
▼ **EMP:** 23
SQ FT: 30,000
SALES (est): 7.8MM **Privately Held**
WEB: www.benkoproducts.com
SIC: 3534 3567 3448 2542 Elevators & moving stairways; industrial furnaces & ovens; prefabricated metal buildings; partitions & fixtures, except wood

(G-16967)
HKM DRECT MKT CMMNICATIONS INC
Also Called: H K M Drect Mktg Cmmunications
2931 Abbe Rd (44054-2424)
PHONE.....................440 934-3060
Joann Tomasheski, *Manager*
EMP: 20
SALES (corp-wide): 55.8MM **Privately Held**
WEB: www.hkmdirectmarket.com
SIC: 2759 Commercial printing
PA: Hkm Direct Market Communications, Inc.
5501 Cass Ave
Cleveland OH 44102
216 651-9500

(G-16968)
J D INDOOR COMFORT INC
Also Called: J D Indoor Comfort Duct Clg
4040 Colorado Ave (44054-2512)
PHONE.....................440 949-8758
James Sustersic, *President*
EMP: 15
SALES (est): 3.6MM **Privately Held**
WEB: www.jdindoorcomfort.com
SIC: 3585 1711 Air conditioning equipment, complete; plumbing, heating, air-conditioning contractors

(G-16969)
LAPAT SIGNS
4151 E River Rd (44054-2829)
PHONE.....................440 277-6291
Eugene Lapat, *Owner*
EMP: 3
SALES (est): 145.6K **Privately Held**
SIC: 3993 Signs & advertising specialties

(G-16970)
LECTROETCH CO
5342 Evergreen Pkwy (44054-2446)
PHONE.....................440 934-1249
David Badt, *President*
Otis Mahaffey, *Shareholder*
◆ **EMP:** 14
SQ FT: 10,500
SALES (est): 1.1MM **Privately Held**
WEB: www.lectroetch.com
SIC: 3953 Figures (marking devices), metal; letters (marking devices), metal

(G-16971)
METOKOTE CORPORATION
5477 Evergreen Pkwy (44054-2400)
PHONE.....................440 934-4686
John Carnes, *Opers-Prdtn-Mfg*
EMP: 90
SALES (corp-wide): 15.3B **Publicly Held**
WEB: www.metokote.com
SIC: 3479 3471 Coating of metals & formed products; plating & polishing
HQ: Metokote Corporation
1340 Neubrecht Rd
Lima OH 45801
419 996-7800

(G-16972)
NORTHFIELD
5190 Oster Rd (44054-1566)
PHONE.....................440 949-1815
EMP: 3
SALES (est): 196.1K **Privately Held**
SIC: 3821 Laboratory apparatus & furniture

(G-16973)
OLDCASTLE APG MIDWEST INC
Also Called: Sheffield Oldcastle
5190 Oster Rd (44054-1566)
PHONE.....................440 949-1815
Jim Jergins, *Manager*
EMP: 100
SALES (corp-wide): 29.7B **Privately Held**
SIC: 3272 Concrete products, precast
HQ: Oldcastle Apg Midwest, Inc.
901 E Troy Ave
Indianapolis IN 46203
317 786-0971

(G-16974)
ROBBINS FURNACE WORKS INC
3739 Colorado Ave (44054-2505)
PHONE.....................440 949-2292
Michael K Robbins, *President*
EMP: 11
SALES (est): 1.4MM **Privately Held**
SIC: 3567 Industrial furnaces & ovens

(G-16975)
SHEFFIELD METALS CLEVELAND LLC (PA)
Also Called: Sheffield Metals International
5467 Evergreen Pkwy (44054-2400)
PHONE.....................800 283-5262
Michael Blake, *President*
Bryan Yancy, *Project Mgr*
Jill Wilson, *Controller*
Michael Marsh, *Sales Staff*
Tim Murphy, *Technical Staff*
▼ **EMP:** 10
SALES (est): 7.7MM **Privately Held**
SIC: 3444 Sheet metalwork

(G-16976)
VAPEN8R LLC
Also Called: Vapor Cast
5220 Cobblestone Rd (44035-1488)
PHONE.....................440 934-8273
William McCrary, *Administration*
EMP: 6
SALES (est): 550.8K **Privately Held**
SIC: 3911 Cigar & cigarette accessories

Shelby
Richland County

GEOGRAPHIC SECTION

(G-16977)
AMERICAN TOWER ACQUISITION
5085 State Route 39 W (44875-9061)
P.O. Box 29 (44875-0029)
PHONE..................................419 347-1185
Doug Schmidt, *President*
Dave Wagner, *Vice Pres*
EMP: 11 **EST:** 1951
SALES (est): 2.4MM **Privately Held**
WEB: www.amertower.com
SIC: 3441 3448 Tower sections, radio & television transmission; docks: prefabricated metal

(G-16978)
ARCELORMITTAL TUBULAR PRODUCTS
132 W Main St (44875-1475)
PHONE..................................419 347-2424
Edward Vore, *CEO*
Tim Hebauf, *Engineer*
EMP: 631
SALES (est): 127.4MM
SALES (corp-wide): 9.1B **Privately Held**
SIC: 3317 3321 Steel pipe & tubes; gray & ductile iron foundries
HQ: Arcelormittal Holdings Llc
3210 Watling St
East Chicago IN 46312
219 399-1200

(G-16979)
ARCELORMITTAL USA LLC
132 W Main St (44875-1475)
PHONE..................................419 347-2424
Edward Vore, *President*
Loren Kranz, *Superintendent*
Darren Dossi, *Production*
Rhonda Gullett, *Purch Mgr*
Mark Ruffner, *Purch Mgr*
EMP: 63
SALES (corp-wide): 9.1B **Privately Held**
SIC: 3312 Blast furnaces & steel mills
HQ: Arcelormittal Usa Llc
1 S Dearborn St Ste 1800
Chicago IL 60603
312 346-0300

(G-16980)
CARTON SERVICE INCORPORATED (PA)
Also Called: Pharma Packaging Solutions
First Quality Dr (44875)
PHONE..................................419 342-5010
Bob Lederer, *President*
David L Genger, *Principal*
George F Karch Jr, *Principal*
Robert W Lederer, *Principal*
R E Streeter, *Principal*
▲ **EMP:** 300 **EST:** 1926
SQ FT: 135,000
SALES (est): 84.4MM **Privately Held**
WEB: www.cartonservice.com
SIC: 2657 Folding paperboard boxes

(G-16981)
CUSTOM CONTROL TECH LLC
Also Called: CCT
4469 Funk Rd (44875-9701)
PHONE..................................419 342-5593
Brenda Leedy, *Manager*
James Park,
EMP: 9
SALES (est): 2MM **Privately Held**
SIC: 3449 Miscellaneous metalwork

(G-16982)
GB FABRICATION COMPANY
2510 Taylortown Rd (44875-8836)
PHONE..................................419 347-1835
Dave Groff, *Branch Mgr*
EMP: 30
SALES (corp-wide): 55.5MM **Privately Held**
WEB: www.voisard.com
SIC: 3469 3441 Metal stampings; fabricated structural metal

HQ: Gb Fabrication Company
60 Scott St
Shiloh OH 44878
419 896-3191

(G-16983)
LONDON COACH SHOP
2962 London East Rd (44875-9148)
PHONE..................................419 347-4803
Mark Weaver, *Owner*
EMP: 3
SALES (est): 259.5K **Privately Held**
SIC: 3799 Carriages, horse drawn

(G-16984)
MTD PRODUCTS INC
Also Called: M T D Service Division
305 Mansfield Ave (44875-1884)
PHONE..................................419 342-6455
Neal Winslow, *Principal*
Bradford Gray, *Opers Mgr*
Karl Egner, *Maint Spvr*
Chris Gribben, *Info Tech Mgr*
EMP: 250
SALES (corp-wide): 2.4B **Privately Held**
WEB: www.mtdproducts.com
SIC: 3524 Lawn & garden equipment
HQ: Mtd Products Inc
5965 Grafton Rd
Valley City OH 44280
330 225-2600

(G-16985)
PHILLIPS MFG AND TOWER CO (PA)
Also Called: Shelby Welded Tube Div
5578 State Route 61 N (44875-9564)
P.O. Box 125 (44875-0125)
PHONE..................................419 347-1720
Angela Phillip, *CEO*
Theresa Wallace, *CFO*
Lori Metheney, *Administration*
EMP: 85
SQ FT: 90,000
SALES (est): 29.7MM **Privately Held**
WEB: www.shelbytube.com
SIC: 3312 3498 3317 7692 Tubes, steel & iron; fabricated pipe & fittings; steel pipe & tubes; welding repair

(G-16986)
PREMIER TANNING & NUTRITION
35 Mansfield Ave (44875-1322)
PHONE..................................419 342-6259
Jeff Tronewett, *Owner*
EMP: 6
SALES (est): 177.2K **Privately Held**
SIC: 7299 3111 5499 Tanning salon; leather tanning & finishing; health & dietetic food stores

(G-16987)
RICERS RESIDENTIAL SVCS LLC
3526 State Route 314 (44875-8920)
PHONE..................................567 203-7414
Holly Currry, *Owner*
EMP: 3
SALES (est): 103.3K **Privately Held**
SIC: 2493 7299 7389 Insulation & roofing material, reconstituted wood; home improvement & renovation contractor agency;

(G-16988)
SHELBY DAILY GLOBE INC
Also Called: Daily Globe
37 W Main St (44875-1238)
P.O. Box 647 (44875-0647)
PHONE..................................419 342-4276
Scott Gove, *President*
EMP: 35 **EST:** 1900
SQ FT: 6,000
SALES (est): 1.6MM **Privately Held**
SIC: 2711 Newspapers: publishing only, not printed on site

(G-16989)
SHELBY PRINTING PARTNERS LLC
325 S Martin Dr (44875-1761)
P.O. Box 72 (44875-0072)
PHONE..................................419 342-3171
Edward J Miller, *President*

Waye Gurney, *Vice Pres*
Raymond Lynch, *Treasurer*
Art Cooper, *Admin Sec*
EMP: 20 **EST:** 1954
SQ FT: 8,000
SALES (est): 2MM **Privately Held**
SIC: 2752 Commercial printing, offset

Sherrodsville
Carroll County

(G-16990)
ARIELS OAK INC
Also Called: Ariel's Oak
9486 Cutler Rd Ne (44675-9066)
P.O. Box 203 (44675-0203)
PHONE..................................330 343-7453
Jay A Van Natter, *President*
EMP: 25 **EST:** 1993
SQ FT: 1,000
SALES (est): 2.1MM **Privately Held**
SIC: 2511 Wood household furniture

Sherwood
Defiance County

(G-16991)
KEITH GRIMM
100 W Pearl St (43556)
PHONE..................................419 899-2725
Keith Grimm, *Principal*
EMP: 3
SALES (est): 144.7K **Privately Held**
SIC: 2013 Sausages & other prepared meats

(G-16992)
QUALITY MACHINING AND MFG INC
14168 State Route 18 (43556)
PHONE..................................419 899-2543
Amber C Yochum, *President*
▲ **EMP:** 17
SQ FT: 25,000
SALES: 2MM **Privately Held**
SIC: 3599 Machine shop, jobbing & repair

Shiloh
Richland County

(G-16993)
GB FABRICATION COMPANY (HQ)
60 Scott St (44878-8712)
PHONE..................................419 896-3191
EMP: 23
SALES (est): 16.2MM
SALES (corp-wide): 55.5MM **Privately Held**
SIC: 3469 Metal stampings
PA: Gb Manufacturing Company
1120 E Main St
Delta OH 43515
419 822-5323

(G-16994)
HOOVER GROUP
411 Eby Rd (44878-8870)
PHONE..................................419 525-3159
Philip Hoover, *Partner*
Miriam Hoover, *Admin Sec*
EMP: 4
SALES: 200K **Privately Held**
SIC: 2431 Interior & ornamental woodwork & trim

(G-16995)
LAKESIDE CABINS LTD
7389 State Route 13 N (44878-8945)
PHONE..................................419 896-2299
Allis Zim, *Partner*
Ellis Zimmerman, *Principal*
EMP: 7
SALES (est): 1MM **Privately Held**
SIC: 2522 Filing boxes, cabinets & cases: except wood

(G-16996)
LEON NEWSWANGER
Also Called: Newswanger Machine
7828 Planktown North Rd (44878-8906)
PHONE..................................419 896-3336
Leon Newswanger, *Owner*
EMP: 12 **EST:** 1989
SQ FT: 3,500
SALES (est): 522.5K **Privately Held**
SIC: 3599 1799 Machine shop, jobbing & repair; welding on site

(G-16997)
PLYMOUTH LOCOMOTIVE SVC LLC
48 E Main St (44878-8898)
PHONE..................................419 896-2854
David A Shepherd, *Principal*
EMP: 4
SALES (est): 521K **Privately Held**
SIC: 3312 Wheels, locomotive & car: iron & steel

(G-16998)
PLYMOUTH LOCOMOTIVE SVC LLC
8118 Shiloh Norwalk Rd (44878-9022)
PHONE..................................419 896-2854
Dennis Bailey,
David Shepherd,
EMP: 3
SALES (est): 386.7K **Privately Held**
WEB: www.plymouthlocomotiveservice.com
SIC: 3743 Locomotives & parts

(G-16999)
PROLINE TRUSS
29 Free Rd (44878-8939)
PHONE..................................419 895-9980
Paul M Reiff, *Owner*
Anna Reiff, *Co-Owner*
EMP: 17
SALES (est): 1.8MM **Privately Held**
SIC: 2439 Trusses, wooden roof

(G-17000)
SHILOH CARRIAGE SHOP LLC
8465 Shiloh Norwalk Rd (44878-8985)
PHONE..................................419 896-3869
Ebin Shark, *Partner*
Earl Shark, *Mng Member*
EMP: 3 **EST:** 2001
SALES (est): 331.9K **Privately Held**
SIC: 3799 Carriages, horse drawn

Shreve
Wayne County

(G-17001)
GROWERS CHOICE LTD
5505 S Elyria Rd (44676-9567)
PHONE..................................330 262-8754
Charles R Wood, *Partner*
EMP: 6 **EST:** 2007
SALES (est): 602.5K **Privately Held**
SIC: 2499 Wood products

(G-17002)
HYPONEX CORPORATION
Also Called: Scotts- Hyponex
3875 S Elyria Rd (44676-9529)
PHONE..................................330 262-1300
Dennis Tafoya, *Branch Mgr*
EMP: 30
SALES (corp-wide): 2.6B **Publicly Held**
SIC: 2873 2875 Fertilizers: natural (organic), except compost; compost
HQ: Hyponex Corporation
14111 Scottslawn Rd
Marysville OH 43040
937 644-0011

(G-17003)
I CERCO INC (PA)
Also Called: Diamonite Plant
453 W Mcconkey St (44676-9769)
PHONE..................................330 567-2145
Byron Anderson, *President*
Joel Connor, *Engineer*
Susan English, *Finance Mgr*
Charlotte Kelly, *Manager*

Rex Martin, *Manager*
▲ **EMP:** 157
SQ FT: 160,000
SALES (est): 63.9MM **Privately Held**
WEB: www.cercollc.com
SIC: 3567 Ceramic kilns & furnaces

(G-17004)
J & J PERFORMANCE INC
Also Called: J & J Performance Paintball
410 E Wood St (44676-9325)
PHONE..............................330 567-2455
Joseph West, *President*
EMP: 12
SALES (est): 2MM **Privately Held**
SIC: 3499 7699 Nozzles, spray: aerosol, paint or insecticide; gun services

(G-17005)
LENAS AMISH GRANOLA
11051 County Road 329 (44676-9417)
PHONE..............................330 600-1599
Lena Schlabach, *Principal*
EMP: 3
SALES (est): 180.1K **Privately Held**
SIC: 2052 Cookies & crackers

(G-17006)
MIDFLOW SERVICES LLC (PA)
10774 Township Road 506 (44676-9462)
PHONE..............................330 567-3108
Dustin Baker,
EMP: 12
SALES (est): 3.5MM **Privately Held**
SIC: 3533 Oil & gas field machinery

(G-17007)
RED HEAD BRASS INC
643 Legion Dr (44676-9271)
PHONE..............................330 567-2903
Ricardo Leon, *Plant Mgr*
Cathy Wright, *Purch Dir*
Paul Runevitch, *CFO*
Joe Carroll, *Relations*
EMP: 3 **EST:** 1972
SALES (est): 161.2K **Privately Held**
SIC: 3545 3569 Tools & accessories for machine tools; firefighting apparatus & related equipment

(G-17008)
RHBA ACQUISITIONS LLC
Also Called: Red Head Brass
643 Legion Dr (44676-9271)
P.O. Box 566 (44676-0566)
PHONE..............................330 567-2903
Rick Leon, *Plant Mgr*
Kurt Mohn, *Marketing Staff*
Dave Hooper,
Edwin Dumire,
▲ **EMP:** 60
SQ FT: 80,000
SALES (est): 13.9MM **Privately Held**
WEB: www.rhbdist.net
SIC: 3569 Firefighting apparatus & related equipment

(G-17009)
SCOTS
3875 S Elyria Rd (44676-9529)
PHONE..............................215 370-9498
EMP: 4 **EST:** 2017
SALES (est): 185.6K **Privately Held**
SIC: 1499 Miscellaneous nonmetallic minerals

(G-17010)
SHREVE PRINTING LLC
390 E Wood St (44676-9743)
P.O. Box 605 (44676-0605)
PHONE..............................330 567-2341
Maher Wahba,
EMP: 16
SQ FT: 10,000
SALES (est): 3.1MM **Privately Held**
WEB: www.gideonprinting.com
SIC: 2752 2759 Commercial printing, offset; letterpress printing

Sidney
Shelby County

(G-17011)
A & B MACHINE INC
2040 Commerce Dr (45365-9393)
P.O. Box 540 (45365-0540)
PHONE..............................937 492-8662
Marc Gilardi, *President*
Robert L Alexander, *President*
Jimmy Alexander, *Vice Pres*
EMP: 32
SQ FT: 22,500
SALES (est): 5.5MM **Privately Held**
WEB: www.aandbmachine.com
SIC: 3545 Precision tools, machinists'

(G-17012)
ADVANCED COMPOSITES INC
2810 Howard St (45365-7655)
PHONE..............................937 575-9814
Seiji Oshima, *President*
EMP: 7
SALES (corp-wide): 12.4B **Privately Held**
SIC: 3082 3087 Unsupported plastics profile shapes; custom compound purchased resins
HQ: Advanced Composites, Inc.
   1062 S 4th Ave
   Sidney OH 45365
   937 575-9800

(G-17013)
ADVANCED COMPOSITES INC (DH)
Also Called: Sidney Plant
1062 S 4th Ave (45365-8977)
PHONE..............................937 575-9800
Seiji Oshima, *President*
Yoichi Kawai, *President*
Robert Brown, *Principal*
Richard Lake, *Admin Sec*
▲ **EMP:** 220
SQ FT: 128,000
SALES (est): 94.3MM
SALES (corp-wide): 12.4B **Privately Held**
WEB: www.advcmp1.com
SIC: 3082 3087 Unsupported plastics profile shapes; custom compound purchased resins
HQ: Mitsui Chemicals America, Inc.
   800 Westchester Ave N607
   Rye Brook NY 10573
   914 253-0777

(G-17014)
AMERICAN TRIM LLC
1501 Michigan St Ste 1 (45365-3500)
PHONE..............................419 228-1145
Debra Caudill, *President*
Marc Kogge, *Facilities Mgr*
Chris Gallimore, *Opers Spvr*
Michael Campbell, *Engineer*
Russ Fuller, *Engineer*
EMP: 600
SALES (corp-wide): 445.1MM **Privately Held**
SIC: 3469 3465 Metal stampings; moldings or trim, automobile: stamped metal
HQ: American Trim, L.L.C.
   1005 W Grand Ave
   Lima OH 45801

(G-17015)
AMOS MEDIA COMPANY (PA)
Also Called: Coin World
911 S Vandemark Rd (45365-8974)
P.O. Box 4129 (45365-4129)
PHONE..............................937 498-2111
John O Amos, *Ch of Bd*
Bruce Boyd, *President*
William Gibbs, *Editor*
Phyllis Stegemoller, *Sales Associate*
Victoria Hardy, *Marketing Staff*
▲ **EMP:** 200 **EST:** 1876
SQ FT: 90,000
SALES (est): 36.4MM **Privately Held**
SIC: 2721 2711 2796 7389 Magazines: publishing only, not printed on site; newspapers, publishing & printing; platemaking services; appraisers, except real estate; miscellaneous publishing

(G-17016)
ANKIM ENTERPRISES INCORPORATED
2005 Campbell Rd (45365-2474)
PHONE..............................937 599-1121
Stan Wright, *President*
Clara Wright, *Vice Pres*
EMP: 20
SQ FT: 24,000
SALES (est): 2.7MM **Privately Held**
SIC: 3678 3679 Electronic connectors; harness assemblies for electronic use: wire or cable

(G-17017)
AURIA SIDNEY LLC
2000 Schlater Dr (45365-8904)
PHONE..............................937 492-1225
Robert S Miller, *President*
EMP: 262
SALES (corp-wide): 571K **Privately Held**
WEB: www.iaawards.com
SIC: 3714 Motor vehicle parts & accessories
HQ: Auria Sidney, Llc
   2000 Schlater Dr
   Sidney OH 45365

(G-17018)
AURIA SIDNEY LLC (DH)
2000 Schlater Dr (45365-8904)
PHONE..............................937 492-1225
Brian Pour, *President*
Brian K Pour, *President*
Brenda Lamma, *Program Mgr*
EMP: 26
SALES (est): 25.3MM
SALES (corp-wide): 571K **Privately Held**
SIC: 3714 Motor vehicle parts & accessories
HQ: Auria Solutions Usa Inc.
   26999 Central Park Blvd
   Southfield MI 48076
   734 456-2800

(G-17019)
BAUMFOLDER CORPORATION
1660 Campbell Rd (45365-2480)
PHONE..............................937 492-1281
Janice Benanzer, *President*
Jason Muldoon, *President*
Ruth Souder, *Buyer*
Lee Trisler, *Engineer*
Mark Stonerock, *Project Engr*
▲ **EMP:** 45 **EST:** 1917
SQ FT: 125,000
SALES: 10MM
SALES (corp-wide): 3B **Privately Held**
WEB: www.baumfolder.com
SIC: 3579 7389 3554 Binding machines, plastic & adhesive; packaging & labeling services; folding machines, paper
HQ: Heidelberg Americas Inc
   1000 Gutenberg Dr Nw
   Kennesaw GA 30144

(G-17020)
CARGILL INCORPORATED
2400 Industrial Dr (45365-8952)
PHONE..............................937 498-4555
Shane Soloman, *Manager*
EMP: 60
SALES (corp-wide): 114.7B **Privately Held**
WEB: www.cargill.com
SIC: 2075 2077 Soybean oil mills; animal & marine fats & oils
PA: Cargill, Incorporated
   15407 Mcginty Rd W
   Wayzata MN 55391
   952 742-7575

(G-17021)
CARS AND PARTS MAGAZINE
911 S Vandemark Rd (45365-8974)
P.O. Box 4129 (45365-4129)
PHONE..............................937 498-0803
Bruce Boyd, *President*
EMP: 120
SALES (est): 3.9MM
SALES (corp-wide): 36.4MM **Privately Held**
WEB: www.carsandparts.com
SIC: 2721 5521 Magazines: publishing & printing; used car dealers

PA: Amos Media Company
   911 S Vandemark Rd
   Sidney OH 45365
   937 498-2111

(G-17022)
CHERYL HEINTZ
231 Sandpiper Pl (45365-3604)
PHONE..............................937 492-3310
Jean Lescht, *Owner*
EMP: 4 **EST:** 2016
SALES (est): 130.4K **Privately Held**
SIC: 3317 Steel pipe & tubes

(G-17023)
COMPRESSOR TECHNOLOGIES INC
Also Called: Numerics Unlimited North
211 E Russell Rd (45365-1762)
PHONE..............................937 492-3711
Wayne Adkins, *President*
Chad Inman, *Manager*
Wendy Minnich, *Admin Asst*
EMP: 49
SQ FT: 100,000
SALES (est): 8MM **Privately Held**
SIC: 3469 Machine parts, stamped or pressed metal

(G-17024)
CUSTOM POLISHING
559 Plum Ridge Trl (45365-1881)
PHONE..............................937 596-0430
John Kenton, *Owner*
EMP: 5 **EST:** 1970
SALES (est): 303.1K **Privately Held**
SIC: 3471 Polishing, metals or formed products; finishing, metals or formed products

(G-17025)
DAMAR PRODUCTS INC (PA)
17222 State Route 47 E (45365-7242)
PHONE..............................937 492-9023
Don Alexander, *President*
Toinette Alexander, *Corp Secy*
EMP: 15
SALES: 1.6MM **Privately Held**
SIC: 2448 2441 Pallets, wood; boxes, wood; packing cases, wood: nailed or lock corner

(G-17026)
DAMAR PRODUCTS INC
516 Park St (45365-1346)
PHONE..............................937 492-9023
Don Alexander, *President*
EMP: 12
SALES (corp-wide): 1.6MM **Privately Held**
SIC: 2448 2441 Pallets, wood; boxes, wood
PA: Damar Products Inc
   17222 State Route 47 E
   Sidney OH 45365
   937 492-9023

(G-17027)
DERBY FABG SOLUTIONS LLC
570 Lester Ave (45365-7038)
PHONE..............................937 498-4054
Jason Kellams, *COO*
Rose Houser, *Manager*
EMP: 25
SALES (corp-wide): 33.8MM **Privately Held**
WEB: www.derbyfab.com
SIC: 3296 2631 Cutting dies, except metal cutting; motor vehicle parts & accessories; gaskets, packing & sealing devices
HQ: Derby Fabricating Solutions, Llc
   277 Industrial Dr
   Cadiz KY 42211

(G-17028)
DESIGN-N-WOOD LLC
3700 Michigan St (45365-7018)
PHONE..............................937 419-0479
Jason Fogt, *Owner*
Larry Fogt,
EMP: 3
SALES (est): 404.5K **Privately Held**
SIC: 2431 Millwork

GEOGRAPHIC SECTION

Sidney - Shelby County (G-17054)

(G-17029)
DETAILED MACHINING INC
2490 Ross St (45365-8834)
PHONE..................................937 492-1264
John Bertsch, *President*
EMP: 32
SQ FT: 42,000
SALES (est): 6.5MM **Privately Held**
WEB: www.detailedmachining.com
SIC: 3599 Machine shop, jobbing & repair

(G-17030)
DETROIT TECHNOLOGIES INC
1630 Ferguson Ct (45365-9398)
PHONE..................................937 492-2708
Danielle Boisbert, *Controller*
EMP: 30 **Privately Held**
WEB: www.formedfiber.com
SIC: 2396 3429 2221 Automotive trimmings, fabric; manufactured hardware (general); broadwoven fabric mills, man-made
PA: Detroit Technologies, Inc.
32500 Telg Rd Ste 207
Bingham Farms MI 48025

(G-17031)
DRT AEROSPACE LLC
1950 Campbell Rd (45365-2413)
PHONE..................................937 492-6121
Gary Van Gundy, *CEO*
EMP: 85 **Privately Held**
SIC: 3841 Surgical & medical instruments
HQ: Drt Aerospace, Llc
8694 Rite Track Way
West Chester OH 45069
937 298-7391

(G-17032)
DRT PRECISION MFG LLC (HQ)
1985 Campbell Rd (45365-2412)
PHONE..................................937 507-4308
Gary Van Gundy, *CEO*
EMP: 36
SALES (est): 6.5MM **Privately Held**
SIC: 3599 Machine shop, jobbing & repair

(G-17033)
DTI MOLDED PRODUCTS INC
Also Called: Conform Automotive
250 Stolle Ave (45365-8873)
PHONE..................................937 492-5008
Gary Stanis, *CFO*
EMP: 17 **Privately Held**
SIC: 3714 Motor vehicle parts & accessories
HQ: Dti Molded Products, Inc.
32500 Telg Rd Ste 207
Bingham Farms MI 48025
248 647-0400

(G-17034)
EDGEWELL PERSONAL CARE LLC
1810 Progress Way (45365-8961)
PHONE..................................937 492-1057
Eric Simmons, *Branch Mgr*
Terry Ruppert, *Manager*
Kenny Sparks, *Maintence Staff*
Beth Collins, *Associate*
EMP: 147
SALES (corp-wide): 2.3B **Publicly Held**
WEB: www.playtexproductsinc.com
SIC: 2844 Shaving preparations; lotions, shaving; suntan lotions & oils; hair preparations, including shampoos
HQ: Edgewell Personal Care, Llc
1350 Timberlake Mano
Chesterfield MO 63017
314 594-1900

(G-17035)
ELECTRO CONTROLS INC
1625 Ferguson Ct (45365-9398)
P.O. Box 539 (45365-0539)
PHONE..................................866 497-1717
Tim Geise, *President*
Kevin Geise, *Vice Pres*
Ray Lepore, *Sales Engr*
Brett Bender, *Manager*
JAS Fair, *Manager*
EMP: 22
SALES (est): 4.8MM **Privately Held**
SIC: 3613 Control panels, electric

(G-17036)
EMERSON CLIMATE TECH INC (DH)
1675 Campbell Rd (45365-2479)
P.O. Box 4309 (45365-4309)
PHONE..................................937 498-3011
Ed Purvis Jr, *President*
Ken Monnier, *President*
William Ragon, *President*
Jean Caillt, *Vice Pres*
Tom Croone, *Vice Pres*
◆ **EMP:** 1500 **EST:** 2006
SQ FT: 807,000
SALES (est): 1.2B
SALES (corp-wide): 17.4B **Publicly Held**
WEB: www.copeland-corp.com
SIC: 3585 Compressors for refrigeration & air conditioning equipment; condensers, refrigeration

(G-17037)
EMERSON CLIMATE TECH INC
Condensing Unit Division
756 Brooklyn Ave (45365-9401)
P.O. Box 669 (45365-0669)
PHONE..................................937 498-3011
Tom Croone, *Vice Pres*
David Kirk, *Vice Pres*
Norman Grell, *Opers Staff*
Ralph Nietfeld, *Controller*
EMP: 200
SALES (corp-wide): 17.4B **Publicly Held**
WEB: www.copeland-corp.com
SIC: 3585 Condensers, refrigeration
HQ: Emerson Climate Technologies, Inc.
1675 Campbell Rd
Sidney OH 45365
937 498-3011

(G-17038)
EMERSON CLIMATE TECH INC
Design Services Network
1351 N Vandemark Rd (45365-3501)
PHONE..................................937 498-3587
Thomas Crone, *General Mgr*
Keith Brown, *Manager*
Andrew Chavez, *Technology*
Savita Maladkar, *Software Engr*
EMP: 20
SALES (corp-wide): 17.4B **Publicly Held**
WEB: www.copeland-corp.com
SIC: 3585 Condensers, refrigeration; air conditioning units, complete: domestic or industrial
HQ: Emerson Climate Technologies, Inc.
1675 Campbell Rd
Sidney OH 45365
937 498-3011

(G-17039)
FABRICATION UNLIMITED LLC
4343 State Route 29 E (45365-8236)
P.O. Box 126 (45365-0126)
PHONE..................................937 492-3166
Charlene Nichols,
Darrell Nichols Sr,
EMP: 5
SQ FT: 4,300
SALES: 500K **Privately Held**
WEB: www.fabricationunlimited.com
SIC: 3444 7692 Sheet metalwork; welding repair

(G-17040)
FFT SIDNEY LLC
1630 Ferguson Ct (45365-9398)
PHONE..................................937 492-2709
Chuck Hughes, *Branch Mgr*
EMP: 100 **Privately Held**
SIC: 2824 3089 2823 Polyester fibers; fiber, vulcanized; cellulosic manmade fibers
HQ: Fft Sidney, Llc
1630 Ferguson Ct
Sidney MI 48025
248 647-0400

(G-17041)
FRESHWAY FOODS INC (PA)
Also Called: Fresh and Limited
601 Stolle Ave (45365-8895)
PHONE..................................937 498-4664
Frank Gilardi Jr, *Ch of Bd*
Phil Gilardi, *President*
Devon Beer, *CFO*
EMP: 147
SQ FT: 90,000
SALES: 109MM **Privately Held**
SIC: 5148 2099 Vegetables, fresh; food preparations

(G-17042)
H B PRODUCTS INC
Also Called: HB
1661 Saint Marys Rd (45365-9395)
P.O. Box 4098 (45365-4098)
PHONE..................................937 492-7031
Michael L Baker, *President*
Sheryl Bales, *Principal*
Jamie Ellis, *Vice Pres*
▲ **EMP:** 29
SQ FT: 53,000
SALES (est): 6.2MM **Privately Held**
WEB: www.hbproductsinc.com
SIC: 3441 3444 Fabricated structural metal; sheet metalwork

(G-17043)
HEXA AMERICAS INC
1150 S Vandemark Rd (45365-3571)
PHONE..................................937 497-7900
Hideaki Tanaka, *President*
Takuro Miyamoto, *President*
Dale Walters, *Prdtn Mgr*
Kevin Jones, *Department Mgr*
Rachel McBride, *Department Mgr*
▲ **EMP:** 40
SALES (est): 9MM **Privately Held**
SIC: 2821 Protein plastics

(G-17044)
HYDRO ALUMINUM FAYETTEVILLE
401 N Stolle Ave (45365-7806)
PHONE..................................937 492-9194
Eddie Smith, *Principal*
EMP: 6
SALES (est): 887.1K **Privately Held**
SIC: 3354 Aluminum extruded products

(G-17045)
HYDRO EXTRUSION NORTH AMER LLC
401 N Stolle Ave (45365-7806)
PHONE..................................888 935-5759
Brent Taylor, *Branch Mgr*
EMP: 175
SALES (corp-wide): 13.8B **Privately Held**
WEB: www.hydroaluminumna.com
SIC: 3465 3479 Automotive stampings; painting of metal products
HQ: Hydro Extrusion North America, Llc
6250 N River Rd
Rosemont IL 60018
877 710-7272

(G-17046)
IVEX PROTECTIVE PACKAGING INC (HQ)
2600 Campbell Rd (45365-8836)
P.O. Box 4699 (45365-4699)
PHONE..................................937 498-9298
Paul Gaulin, *President*
Tom Trauschst, *Exec VP*
Sean Owen, *Plant Supt*
Kenneth Bruce, *Plant Mgr*
Leslie Hughes, *Manager*
▲ **EMP:** 25
SALES: 15MM
SALES (corp-wide): 119.4MM **Privately Held**
SIC: 3086 2429 Plastics foam products; wrappers, excelsior
PA: Groupe Emballage Specialise S.E.C.
1805 50e Av
Lachine QC H8T 3
514 636-7951

(G-17047)
J AND L MANUFACTURING INC
9401 State Route 29 N (45365-8309)
P.O. Box 253, Botkins (45306-0253)
PHONE..................................937 492-0008
Phil Robenalt, *President*
EMP: 3
SALES (est): 394.8K **Privately Held**
SIC: 3545 Precision tools, machinists'

(G-17048)
KSE MANUFACTURING
175 S Lester Ave (45365-7044)
PHONE..................................937 409-9831
EMP: 7 **EST:** 2012
SALES (est): 1.1MM **Privately Held**
SIC: 3369 Nonferrous foundries

(G-17049)
LANGSTON PALLETS
Also Called: L & H Wood Products
1650 Miami Conservancy Rd (45365-9525)
PHONE..................................937 492-8769
Craig Langston Sr, *Owner*
EMP: 4
SQ FT: 3,200
SALES (est): 170K **Privately Held**
SIC: 7699 2448 Pallet repair; pallets, wood

(G-17050)
MASTIC HOME EXTERIORS INC
Also Called: Ply Gem Siding Group
2405 Campbell Rd (45365-9529)
PHONE..................................937 497-7008
Bob Parker, *Branch Mgr*
Dan Ernst, *Manager*
EMP: 250
SALES (corp-wide): 2B **Publicly Held**
WEB: www.mastic.com
SIC: 3089 Plastic containers, except foam
HQ: Mastic Home Exteriors, Inc.
2600 Grand Blvd Ste 900
Kansas City MO 64108
816 426-8200

(G-17051)
MECHANICAL GALV-PLATING CORP
933 Oak Ave (45365-1374)
P.O. Box 56 (45365-0056)
PHONE..................................937 492-3143
Tim Baker, *President*
John Garmhausen, *Corp Secy*
Susan A Baker, *Exec VP*
Rob Boller, *Vice Pres*
Sandi Freytag, *Buyer*
▲ **EMP:** 45 **EST:** 1981
SQ FT: 40,000
SALES (est): 6.1MM **Privately Held**
WEB: www.mechanicalgalv-plating.com
SIC: 3471 Plating of metals or formed products

(G-17052)
METAL FINISHERS INC
2600 Fair Rd (45365-7532)
P.O. Box 963 (45365-0963)
PHONE..................................937 492-9175
Donald Stephens, *President*
Vicki Stephens, *Vice Pres*
EMP: 16 **EST:** 1975
SQ FT: 9,600
SALES (est): 1.6MM **Privately Held**
SIC: 3471 Finishing, metals or formed products

(G-17053)
MIAMI VALLEY POLISHING LL
1317 Pinetree Ct (45365-3431)
PHONE..................................937 498-1634
EMP: 3
SALES (est): 148.1K **Privately Held**
SIC: 3471 Polishing, metals or formed products

(G-17054)
MITSUBISHI ELC AUTOMTN INC
213 N Ohio Ave (45365-2711)
PHONE..................................937 492-3058
Melynda Rowlett, *President*
EMP: 3
SALES (corp-wide): 41.5B **Privately Held**
SIC: 8742 5084 3699 Automation & robotics consultant; conveyor systems; electrical equipment & supplies
HQ: Mitsubishi Electric Automation, Inc.
500 Corporate Woods Pkwy
Vernon Hills IL 60061
847 478-2100

Sidney - Shelby County (G-17055)

(G-17055)
MK TREMPE CORPORATION
Also Called: Elite Enclosure Company
2349 Industrial Dr
P.O. Box 916 (45365-0916)
PHONE..................................937 492-3548
Michael Trempe, *President*
Karen Trempe, *Corp Secy*
Sherry Potters, *Human Resources*
EMP: 43
SQ FT: 63,000
SALES: 6MM **Privately Held**
SIC: 3441 Fabricated structural metal

(G-17056)
MONARCH LATHES LP
615 Oak Ave (45365-1335)
P.O. Box 4609 (45365-4609)
PHONE..................................937 492-4111
Harold Camp, *Partner*
Lisa Steinke, *Manager*
▲ **EMP:** 20
SQ FT: 40,000
SALES: 3.7MM **Privately Held**
SIC: 3541 Lathes, metal cutting & polishing

(G-17057)
NORCOLD INC (DH)
600 S Kuther Rd (45365-8840)
P.O. Box 180 (45365-0180)
PHONE..................................937 497-3080
Michael Harris, *CEO*
◆ **EMP:** 280
SQ FT: 150,000
SALES (est): 100.9MM
SALES (corp-wide): 465.2MM **Privately Held**
SIC: 3632 Refrigerators, mechanical & absorption: household
HQ: Thetford Corporation
  7101 Jackson Rd
  Ann Arbor MI 48103
  734 769-6000

(G-17058)
PEERLESS FOODS INC
Also Called: Peerless Foods Equipment
500 S Vandemark Rd (45365-8991)
P.O. Box 769 (45365-0769)
PHONE..................................937 492-4158
Robert L Zielsdorf, *CEO*
Dane A Belden, *President*
Robert F Zielsdorf, *Vice Pres*
William D Witten, *Opers Staff*
Thomas Seving, *CFO*
◆ **EMP:** 175 **EST:** 1913
SQ FT: 130,000
SALES (est): 48.2MM **Privately Held**
WEB: www.thepeerlessgroup.us
SIC: 3556 Bakery machinery; dough mixing machinery

(G-17059)
PLAYTEX MANUFACTURING INC
1905 Progress Way (45365-8114)
PHONE..................................937 498-4710
EMP: 60
SALES (corp-wide): 2.3B **Publicly Held**
SIC: 2676 Sanitary paper products
HQ: Playtex Manufacturing, Inc.
  50 N Dupont Hwy
  Dover DE 19901
  302 678-6000

(G-17060)
PLY GEM INDUSTRIES INC
2600 Campbell Rd (45365-8836)
PHONE..................................937 492-1111
EMP: 250
SALES (corp-wide): 2B **Publicly Held**
SIC: 2431 Windows, wood
HQ: Ply Gem Industries, Inc.
  5020 Weston Pkwy Ste 400
  Cary NC 27513
  919 677-3900

(G-17061)
POLYFILL LLC
960 N Vandemark Rd (45365-3508)
PHONE..................................937 493-0041
Andrew Meshew, *President*
Ralph Fearnley, *General Mgr*
Lisa Young, *Materials Mgr*
Mike Clark, *Opers Staff*
Mike Sylvestre, *Sales Staff*
▲ **EMP:** 40
SQ FT: 50,000
SALES (est): 9.6MM **Privately Held**
SIC: 3089 Automotive parts, plastic

(G-17062)
PREFERRED PRINTING (PA)
3700 Michigan St (45365-7018)
PHONE..................................937 492-6961
Gil Bornhorst, *Owner*
EMP: 8
SQ FT: 2,800
SALES (est): 935.9K **Privately Held**
WEB: www.preferredprinting.net
SIC: 2752 Commercial printing, offset

(G-17063)
QUALITY STEEL FABRICATION
2500 Fair Rd (45365-7523)
P.O. Box 905 (45365-0905)
PHONE..................................937 492-9503
Ted Daniel, *Vice Pres*
Robert P Brunswick,
EMP: 15
SQ FT: 25,000
SALES (est): 4.2MM **Privately Held**
SIC: 3441 3444 Fabricated structural metal; sheet metalwork

(G-17064)
REGAL TROPHY & AWARDS COMPANY
1269 Wapakoneta Ave (45365-1415)
PHONE..................................877 492-7531
Jerry Wehrman, *President*
EMP: 4 **EST:** 1967
SQ FT: 3,400
SALES (est): 314.4K **Privately Held**
SIC: 3914 Trophies

(G-17065)
RELIABLE CASTINGS CORPORATION
1521 W Michigan Ave (45365)
P.O. Box 829 (45365-0829)
PHONE..................................937 497-5217
Shirley Branson, *Principal*
Tom Abney, *Opers-Prdtn-Mfg*
Mr Tom Beck, *Sales/Mktg Mgr*
David Allen, *Manager*
Randy Presser, *Maintence Staff*
EMP: 90
SQ FT: 40,000
SALES (corp-wide): 34MM **Privately Held**
WEB: www.reliablecastings.com
SIC: 3363 3369 3365 Aluminum die-castings; nonferrous foundries; aluminum foundries
PA: Reliable Castings Corporation
  3530 Spring Grove Ave
  Cincinnati OH 45223
  513 541-2627

(G-17066)
RING CONTAINER TECH LLC
603 Oak Ave (45365-1335)
PHONE..................................937 492-0961
Dennis W Koerner, *Vice Pres*
Dane Felver, *Plant Mgr*
EMP: 40
SALES (corp-wide): 295MM **Privately Held**
SIC: 3085 Plastics bottles
PA: Ring Container Technologies, Llc.
  1 Industrial Park
  Oakland TN 38060
  800 280-7464

(G-17067)
RIVERSIDE MFG LLC
Also Called: Visionmark
2309 Industrial Dr (45365-8100)
PHONE..................................937 492-3100
Valerie Reinking, *Accounting Mgr*
Carl Branscum, *Comp Spec*
Gary Phlipot, *Maintence Staff*
Lori Lowie,
EMP: 12
SALES (est): 1.3MM
SALES (corp-wide): 76.3MM **Privately Held**
SIC: 2759 Flexographic printing
HQ: Riverside Mfg., Llc
  14510 Lima Rd
  Fort Wayne IN 46818

(G-17068)
ROE TRANSPORTATION ENTPS INC
3680 W Michigan St (45365-9086)
PHONE..................................937 497-7161
Chad Roe, *Principal*
EMP: 7
SQ FT: 7,400
SALES (est): 368K **Privately Held**
SIC: 2875 2499 4212 4953 Potting soil, mixed; mulch or sawdust products, wood; dump truck haulage; recycling, waste materials

(G-17069)
ROSS ALUMINUM CASTINGS LLC
815 Oak Ave (45365-1317)
P.O. Box 609 (45365-0609)
PHONE..................................937 492-4134
Robert Wyehl, *CFO*
Lisa Zumberger, *Human Resources*
Mike Francis, *Mng Member*
Bob Clements,
▲ **EMP:** 165
SQ FT: 250,000
SALES (est): 38.9MM
SALES (corp-wide): 62.8MM **Privately Held**
WEB: www.rossal.com
SIC: 3365 3543 3369 Aluminum & aluminum-based alloy castings; machinery castings, aluminum; industrial patterns; nonferrous foundries
PA: Advanced Metals Group, L.L.C.
  18 Mystic Ln
  Malvern PA 19355
  610 408-8006

(G-17070)
ROSS CASTING & INNOVATION LLC
Also Called: Rci
402 S Kuther Rd (45365)
P.O. Box 89 (45365-0089)
PHONE..................................937 497-4500
Sampath Ramesh, *President*
Brad Hohenstein, *Chief*
Wayne Thompson, *COO*
Dan Coverstone, *Purch Mgr*
Robert Zangri, *CFO*
▲ **EMP:** 350
SQ FT: 120,000
SALES (est): 28.6MM **Privately Held**
SIC: 3363 Aluminum die-castings

(G-17071)
ROTARY COMPRESSION TECH INC
Also Called: Leroi Gas Compressors
211 E Russell Rd (45365-1762)
PHONE..................................937 498-2555
Michael A Toal, *CEO*
Richard Wall, *President*
▲ **EMP:** 25
SALES (est): 9MM
SALES (corp-wide): 2.6B **Publicly Held**
SIC: 3563 Air & gas compressors
PA: Gardner Denver Holdings, Inc.
  222 E Erie St Ste 500
  Milwaukee WI 53202
  414 212-4700

(G-17072)
SCHWANS MAMA ROSASS LLC (DH)
1910 Fair Rd (45365-8906)
PHONE..................................937 498-4511
Dimitrios Smyrnios, *CEO*
Linda McGillivray, *Controller*
EMP: 107
SQ FT: 160,000
SALES: 69.3MM
SALES (corp-wide): 5.3B **Privately Held**
WEB: www.plazabelmont.com
SIC: 2038 Pizza, frozen
HQ: Schwan's Company
  115 W College Dr
  Marshall MN 56258
  507 532-3274

(G-17073)
SCHWARZ PARTNERS PACKAGING LLC
Royal Group, The
2450 Campbell Rd (45365-7533)
PHONE..................................317 290-1140
Jim Freisthler, *Branch Mgr*
EMP: 15
SALES (corp-wide): 702.7MM **Privately Held**
WEB: www.harborpkg.com
SIC: 2653 3412 2671 Boxes, corrugated: made from purchased materials; metal barrels, drums & pails; packaging paper & plastics film, coated & laminated
HQ: Schwarz Partners Packaging, Llc
  3600 Woodview Trce # 300
  Indianapolis IN 46268
  317 290-1140

(G-17074)
SCSRM CONCRETE COMPANY LTD
4723 Hardin Wapakoneta Rd (45365-8056)
PHONE..................................937 533-1001
Gerald Bushelman, *Partner*
Frank Frantz,
Thomas Frantz,
EMP: 50 **EST:** 1996
SALES (est): 6.6MM **Privately Held**
SIC: 3273 Ready-mixed concrete

(G-17075)
SELMCO METAL FABRICATORS INC
1615 Ferguson Ct (45365-9398)
P.O. Box 4368 (45365-4368)
PHONE..................................937 498-1331
Tim Cotterman, *President*
Ron Jones, *Corp Secy*
EMP: 18
SQ FT: 25,000
SALES (est): 3.5MM **Privately Held**
SIC: 3444 Sheet metal specialties, not stamped

(G-17076)
SHAFFER METAL FAB INC
2031 Commerce Dr (45365-9393)
P.O. Box 523 (45365-0523)
PHONE..................................937 492-1384
Michael R Shaffer, *Principal*
Sheryl Scherer, *Controller*
EMP: 34
SQ FT: 45,000
SALES (est): 9.8MM **Privately Held**
WEB: www.shaffermetalfab.com
SIC: 3441 3444 Fabricated structural metal; sheet metalwork

(G-17077)
SIDNEY ALIVE
101 S Ohio Ave (45365-2716)
PHONE..................................937 210-2539
Amy Breinich, *Administration*
EMP: 3 **EST:** 2016
SALES (est): 117.7K **Privately Held**
SIC: 2711 Newspapers: publishing only, not printed on site

(G-17078)
SIDNEY CAN & TOOL LLC
5670 Cecil Rd (45365-8075)
PHONE..................................937 492-0977
Rod Foster, *Principal*
EMP: 5
SALES (est): 343.3K **Privately Held**
SIC: 3411 Aluminum cans

(G-17079)
SIDNEY MANUFACTURING COMPANY
405 N Main Ave (45365-2345)
P.O. Box 380 (45365-0380)
PHONE..................................937 492-4154
Jon F Baker, *President*
Steven Baker, *Vice Pres*
Glenn Yount, *Sales Staff*
▼ **EMP:** 30
SQ FT: 125,000
SALES (est): 7.1MM **Privately Held**
WEB: www.sidneymfg.com
SIC: 3556 3444 Food products machinery; sheet metalwork

▲ = Import ▼ = Export
◆ = Import/Export

(G-17080)
SILVERADO TRUCKS & ACCESSORIES
720 Linden Ave (45365-1322)
PHONE...................................937 492-8862
Scott Dorsey, *Owner*
Eric Mueller, *Manager*
EMP: 3
SQ FT: 1,500
SALES: 150K **Privately Held**
SIC: 3713 5013 7532 4212 Truck bodies & parts; truck parts & accessories; customizing services, non-factory basis; dump truck haulage

(G-17081)
SPONSELLER GROUP INC
808 W Russell Rd Ste A (45365-9063)
PHONE...................................937 492-9949
Ken Hensworth, *Manager*
EMP: 6
SALES (est): 398.4K
SALES (corp-wide): 8.7MM **Privately Held**
SIC: 8711 3599 Consulting engineer; machine shop, jobbing & repair
PA: Sponseller Group, Inc.
    1600 Timber Wolf Dr
    Holland OH 43528
    419 861-3000

(G-17082)
STOLLE MACHINERY COMPANY LLC
Also Called: Stolle Machinery-Sidney
2900 Campbell Rd (45365-8864)
PHONE...................................937 497-5400
Steve Holt, *Engineer*
Greg Butcher, *Manager*
Mike Fitzgerald, *Manager*
EMP: 125
SALES (corp-wide): 262.3MM **Privately Held**
WEB: www.stollemachinery.com
SIC: 3469 2759 3542 Stamping metal for the trade; commercial printing; machine tools, metal forming type
PA: Stolle Machinery Company, Llc
    6949 S Potomac St
    Centennial CO 80112
    303 708-9044

(G-17083)
T & L WELDING LLC
211 E Russell Rd (45365-1762)
PHONE...................................937 498-9170
Lisa Whitt, *Mng Member*
EMP: 3
SALES (est): 120K **Privately Held**
SIC: 7692 Welding repair

(G-17084)
WAPPOO WOOD PRODUCTS INC
Also Called: Interntnl Pckg Pallets Crates
12877 Kirkwood Rd (45365-8102)
PHONE...................................937 492-1166
Thomas G Baker, *Ch of Bd*
T Adam Baker, *President*
Gary O'Connor, *Principal*
Matthew Baker, *Office Mgr*
EMP: 40
SQ FT: 21,800
SALES (est): 19.1MM **Privately Held**
WEB: www.wappoowood.com
SIC: 5031 2435 2436 2421 Lumber: rough, dressed & finished; hardwood veneer & plywood; softwood veneer & plywood; sawmills & planing mills, general; hardwood dimension & flooring mills

(G-17085)
WESTERN OHIO CUT STONE LTD
1130 Dingman Slagle Rd (45365-9102)
P.O. Box 419 (45365-0419)
PHONE...................................937 492-4722
Thomas Milligan, *Mng Member*
EMP: 20
SALES: 1.9MM **Privately Held**
SIC: 3281 Cut stone & stone products

(G-17086)
WIPE OUT ENTERPRISES
6523 Dawson Rd (45365-8672)
PHONE...................................937 497-9473
Dave Waesch, *Owner*
EMP: 7
SALES (est): 846.3K **Privately Held**
WEB: www.wipeoutenterprises.com
SIC: 3599 Machine shop, jobbing & repair

Smithville
Wayne County

(G-17087)
BOVILLE INDUS COATINGS INC
7459 Leichty Rd (44677)
PHONE...................................330 669-8558
Larry Boville Sr, *President*
Larry Boville Jr, *Vice Pres*
EMP: 25
SQ FT: 30,000
SALES: 3MM **Privately Held**
WEB: www.boville.com
SIC: 3471 3479 Sand blasting of metal parts; coating of metals & formed products; coating of metals with plastic or resins; enameling, including porcelain, of metal products; painting of metal products

(G-17088)
FLYING DUTCHMAN INC
6631 Egypt Rd (44677-9774)
PHONE...................................740 694-1734
James Lepley, *CEO*
Gary Lepley, *President*
Kevin Lepley, *Vice Pres*
John Waltman, *Admin Sec*
EMP: 7 EST: 1970
SQ FT: 3,600
SALES (est): 1.2MM **Privately Held**
WEB: www.flyingd.com
SIC: 3523 Silo fillers & unloaders

(G-17089)
IFCO SYSTEMS NORTH AMERICA INC
179 S Gilbert Dr (44677)
PHONE...................................330 669-2726
EMP: 85 **Privately Held**
SIC: 2448 Mfg Wooden Pallets And Skids
HQ: Ifco Systems North America, Inc.
    13100 Nw Fwy Ste 625
    Houston TX 77040

(G-17090)
MAVERICK CORP PARTNERS LLC (PA)
301 W Prospect St (44677-9516)
PHONE...................................330 669-2631
Regan Radzinski, *Principal*
EMP: 5
SALES (est): 6.4MM **Privately Held**
SIC: 3556 Food products machinery

(G-17091)
RIGGENBACH KITCHENS
790 E Main St (44677-9558)
P.O. Box 227 (44677-0227)
PHONE...................................330 669-2113
Glen Riggenbach, *Owner*
EMP: 3
SALES: 500K **Privately Held**
SIC: 2434 Wood kitchen cabinets

(G-17092)
RIVERVIEW INDUS WD PDTS INC
179 S Gilbert Dr (44677)
PHONE...................................330 669-8509
Michael D Meenan, *President*
EMP: 14
SALES (est): 232.8K **Privately Held**
SIC: 2448 Cargo containers, wood; pallets, wood; skids, wood

(G-17093)
S K S MANUFACTURING CORP
212 E Eberly St (44677)
P.O. Box 318 (44677-0318)
PHONE...................................330 669-9133
Allen Namen, *President*
EMP: 4
SQ FT: 8,000
SALES (est): 431.9K **Privately Held**
SIC: 3599 Machine shop, jobbing & repair

(G-17094)
SAIRCORP LTD
6020 N Honeytown Rd (44677-9563)
PHONE...................................330 669-9099
Larry Stanford, *CEO*
EMP: 3
SALES (est): 309.5K **Privately Held**
WEB: www.saircorp.com
SIC: 3812 Aircraft control instruments

(G-17095)
TYLER GRAIN & FERTILIZER CO
3388 Eby Rd (44677-9785)
PHONE...................................330 669-2341
Walter F Tyler Jr, *President*
Nick Franks, *General Mgr*
William A Tyler, *Vice Pres*
Bill Tyler, *Purch Mgr*
Mildred Tyler, *Treasurer*
EMP: 10 EST: 1860
SQ FT: 18,000
SALES: 7.2MM **Privately Held**
SIC: 2875 5191 8748 Fertilizers, mixing only; chemicals, agricultural; agricultural consultant

(G-17096)
VICI DEFENSE LTD
7147 N Honeytown Rd (44677-9771)
PHONE...................................330 669-3735
Matthew Lemmon, *Principal*
EMP: 4 EST: 2017
SALES (est): 284.7K **Privately Held**
SIC: 3812 Mfg Search/Navigation Equipment

Solon
Cuyahoga County

(G-17097)
ABL SCREEN PRINTING
30300 Solon Indus Pkwy (44139-4378)
P.O. Box 429, Brunswick (44212-0429)
PHONE...................................440 914-0093
Kenneth Alexiac, *President*
Lou De Marco, *Principal*
EMP: 5 EST: 2001
SALES (est): 476.8K **Privately Held**
SIC: 2759 Screen printing

(G-17098)
ACLARA TECHNOLOGIES LLC
30400 Solon Rd (44139-3416)
PHONE...................................440 528-7200
Randy Clark, *Prdtn Mgr*
Rich Goetter, *Purch Agent*
Timothy Figura, *Engineer*
Hari Moorthy, *Engineer*
Mark Fredebaugh, *Train & Dev Mgr*
EMP: 120
SALES (corp-wide): 4.4B **Publicly Held**
SIC: 3824 3825 3829 7371 Mechanical & electromechanical counters & devices; instruments to measure electricity; measuring & controlling devices; custom computer programming services; computer integrated systems design
HQ: Aclara Technologies Llc
    77 West Port Plz Ste 500
    Saint Louis MO 63146
    314 895-6400

(G-17099)
ADVANCED LIGHTING TECH LLC (PA)
7905 Cochran Rd Ste 300 (44139-5471)
PHONE...................................888 440-2358
Sabu Krishnan, *President*
Amy Patrick, *Vice Pres*
Ed Enderle, *Safety Mgr*
Bob Branick, *Opers Staff*
Juris Sulcs, *Research*
▲ EMP: 42
SQ FT: 55,000
SALES (est): 70.3MM **Privately Held**
SIC: 3641 3645 3646 3648 Electric lamps & parts for generalized applications; residential lighting fixtures; commercial indusl & institutional electric lighting fixtures; lighting equipment

(G-17100)
ALL PREM CLEANERS INC
Also Called: All Premium Cleaners
33640 Aurora Rd (44139-3708)
PHONE...................................440 349-3649
Kishore Nandbigam, *President*
Prima Mandarn, *Vice Pres*
EMP: 5
SALES (est): 595.4K **Privately Held**
SIC: 2842 Drycleaning preparations

(G-17101)
ALL PRINT LTD
38415 Flanders Dr (44139-4669)
PHONE...................................440 349-6868
Warren Goldenberg, *Principal*
Daniel M Chessin, *Mng Member*
Deborah Chessin,
EMP: 10 EST: 1997
SQ FT: 10,000
SALES (est): 1MM **Privately Held**
SIC: 2752 Commercial printing, lithographic

(G-17102)
ALLEN GRAPHICS INC
Also Called: Printing Partners
27100 Richmond Rd Ste 6 (44139-1030)
PHONE...................................440 349-4100
Donald J Allen, *President*
EMP: 9
SQ FT: 5,000
SALES (est): 1.4MM **Privately Held**
WEB: www.allen-graphics.com
SIC: 2752 2789 Commercial printing, offset; bookbinding & related work

(G-17103)
ALLOY WELDING & FABRICATING
30340 Solon Indtl Pky B (44139-4358)
PHONE...................................440 914-0650
William Kelly, *President*
EMP: 10
SQ FT: 12,000
SALES (est): 2.2MM **Privately Held**
SIC: 3441 Fabricated structural metal

(G-17104)
ALLTECH MED SYSTEMS AMER INC
28900 Fountain Pkwy (44139-4383)
PHONE...................................440 424-2240
Mark Zou, *President*
William Joliat, *Vice Pres*
Don Russell, *Treasurer*
Sandra Ritchie, *Finance Dir*
Leping Zha, *Director*
▼ EMP: 39
SALES (est): 9.3MM **Privately Held**
SIC: 3845 Magnetic resonance imaging device, nuclear

(G-17105)
AMALTECH INC
30670 Bainbridge Rd (44139-2267)
PHONE...................................440 248-7500
Farouk Altahawi, *President*
Khalid Arafah, *Export Mgr*
EMP: 8
SALES (est): 1.1MM **Privately Held**
SIC: 3494 Pipe fittings

(G-17106)
AMERICAN JRNL OF DRMTPATHOLOGY
6554 Dorset Ln (44139-6710)
PHONE...................................440 542-0041
Garry Marquiss, *Principal*
EMP: 3 EST: 2010
SALES (est): 157.3K **Privately Held**
SIC: 2711 Newspapers, publishing & printing

Solon - Cuyahoga County (G-17107)

(G-17107)
AMRESCO LLC
28600 Fountain Pkwy (44139-4314)
P.O. Box 39098 (44139-0098)
PHONE...................................440 349-2805
EMP: 100 Privately Held
SIC: 2833 Mfg Medicinal/Botanical Products
HQ: Amresco, Llc
  28600 Fountain Pkwy
  Solon OH 44139
  440 349-1199

(G-17108)
ARROWHEAD INDUSTRIES
33891 Canterbury Rd (44139-5618)
PHONE...................................440 349-2846
Alan Johnson, *Principal*
EMP: 3 EST: 2010
SALES (est): 174.9K Privately Held
SIC: 3999 Manufacturing industries

(G-17109)
ASPHALT FABRICS & SPECIALTIES
7710 Bond St (44139-5352)
PHONE...................................440 786-1077
Brian Reed, *President*
EMP: 7
SALES (est): 1.2MM Privately Held
SIC: 2951 Asphalt paving mixtures & blocks

(G-17110)
B D G WRAP-TITE INC
6200 Cochran Rd (44139-3308)
PHONE...................................440 349-5400
Suresh Bafna, *CEO*
Sunil Daga, *President*
◆ EMP: 80
SQ FT: 89,000
SALES (est): 11MM Privately Held
WEB: www.jainco.com
SIC: 3069 5199 Film, rubber; leather goods, except footwear, gloves, luggage, belting

(G-17111)
BANKHURST INDUSTRIES LLC
6075 Cochran Rd (44139-3313)
PHONE...................................216 272-5775
EMP: 3 EST: 2017
SALES (est): 245K Privately Held
SIC: 3999 Manufacturing industries

(G-17112)
BARDONS & OLIVER INC (PA)
5800 Harper Rd (44139-1833)
PHONE...................................440 498-5800
William Beattie, *President*
Heath Oliver, *President*
Peter Barrett, *Principal*
Jim Daffinee, *Principal*
Brett Baldi, *Vice Pres*
▲ EMP: 120 EST: 1891
SQ FT: 94,000
SALES (est): 26.7MM Privately Held
WEB: www.bardonsoliver.com
SIC: 3549 3541 3547 3599 Metalworking machinery; lathes, metal cutting & polishing; finishing equipment, rolling mill; machine & other job shop work

(G-17113)
BARUDAN AMERICA INC (HQ)
30901 Carter St Frnt A (44139-4384)
PHONE...................................440 248-8770
Ted Yamaue, *Ch of Bd*
Shin Hasegawa, *President*
David Davidson, *Vice Pres*
Robert Stone, *Vice Pres*
Kevin H Hrabak, *Treasurer*
▲ EMP: 12
SQ FT: 34,970
SALES: 37.3MM
SALES (corp-wide): 86.2MM Privately Held
SIC: 3552 Embroidery machines
PA: Barudan Co., Ltd.
  20, Azatsukakoshi, Josuiji
  Ichinomiya AIC 491-0
  586 766-161

(G-17114)
BCS METAL PREP LLC
31000 Solon Rd (44139-3467)
PHONE...................................440 663-1100
Janet Hamso,
▲ EMP: 50 EST: 2001
SALES (est): 8.8MM Privately Held
SIC: 3316 Cold finishing of steel shapes
PA: Bluff City Steel, Llc
  1175 Harbor Ave
  Memphis TN 38113

(G-17115)
BIRD ELECTRONIC CORPORATION
30303 Aurora Rd (44139-2743)
PHONE...................................440 248-1200
Mark Johnson, *CEO*
Thomas L Kuklo, *Vice Pres*
Karen Scullin, *Buyer*
Dale Jackson, *Research*
Chris Bosler, *Engineer*
▲ EMP: 235 EST: 1942
SQ FT: 80,000
SALES (est): 69.5MM Privately Held
WEB: www.bird-electronic.com
SIC: 3825 Test equipment for electronic & electric measurement
PA: Bird Technologies Group Inc.
  30303 Aurora Rd
  Solon OH 44139

(G-17116)
BIRD TECHNOLOGIES GROUP INC (PA)
30303 Aurora Rd (44139-2743)
PHONE...................................440 248-1200
Mark I Johnson, *President*
Edward J Bartos Jr, *Vice Pres*
Terrence C Grant, *Vice Pres*
Thomas L Kuklo, *Vice Pres*
Michael Simpsoni, *Opers Staff*
EMP: 8
SQ FT: 12,000
SALES (est): 96MM Privately Held
WEB: www.bird-technologies.com
SIC: 3825 3669 Test equipment for electronic & electric measurement; intercommunication systems, electric

(G-17117)
BOWES MANUFACTURING INC
Also Called: Tungsten and Capital
30340 Solon Industrial (44139-4343)
PHONE...................................216 378-2110
Zelda Stutz, *President*
EMP: 19
SQ FT: 30,000
SALES (est): 4MM Privately Held
WEB: www.bowesmfg.com
SIC: 3568 3452 3494 3429 Couplings, shaft: rigid, flexible, universal joint, etc.; bolts, metal; valves & pipe fittings; clamps & couplings, hose

(G-17118)
BRADLEY STONE INDUSTRIES LLC
30801 Carter St (44139-3517)
PHONE...................................440 519-3277
Kevin Macko, *Vice Pres*
Ron Collins, *Project Mgr*
Angela Wake, *Human Res Mgr*
Taylor Novak, *Consultant*
Bradley Disandis,
EMP: 18
SALES (est): 6.2MM Privately Held
SIC: 1423 Crushed & broken granite

(G-17119)
BRAZE SOLUTIONS LLC
6850 Cochran Rd (44139-4336)
PHONE...................................440 349-5100
Gregory Greenspan, *Mng Member*
EMP: 16
SALES (est): 3MM Privately Held
WEB: www.brazesolutions.com
SIC: 8711 7692 Engineering services; brazing

(G-17120)
BREAKER TECHNOLOGY INC
30625 Solon Ind Pkwy (44139-4389)
PHONE...................................440 248-7168
EMP: 22

SALES (corp-wide): 2.7MM Privately Held
SIC: 3532 5084 1629 Mining machinery; hydraulic systems equipment & supplies; trenching contractor
PA: Breaker Technology, Inc.
  3453 Durahart St
  Riverside CA 92507
  951 369-0878

(G-17121)
CAD AUDIO LLC
6573 Cochran Rd Ste I (44139-3972)
PHONE...................................440 349-4900
Carr F Briggs, *Mng Member*
Peter Rutkowski,
▲ EMP: 15
SALES (est): 2.9MM Privately Held
SIC: 3651 Microphones

(G-17122)
CALIFORNIA CREAMERY OPERATORS
30003 Bainbridge Rd (44139-2205)
PHONE...................................440 264-5351
Tim Shirley, *Executive*
EMP: 3 EST: 2014
SALES (est): 76.8K Privately Held
SIC: 2021 Creamery butter

(G-17123)
CARLISLE BRAKE & FRICTION INC
Also Called: Carbon Group, The
29001 Solon Rd (44139-3468)
PHONE...................................440 528-4000
Karl Messmer, *President*
EMP: 14
SALES (corp-wide): 4.4B Publicly Held
SIC: 3714 Motor vehicle brake systems & parts
HQ: Carlisle Brake & Friction, Inc.
  6180 Cochran Rd
  Solon OH 44139
  440 528-4000

(G-17124)
CARLISLE BRAKE & FRICTION INC (HQ)
Also Called: Cbf
6180 Cochran Rd (44139-3306)
PHONE...................................440 528-4000
Karl T Messmer, *President*
Chris Koch, *Principal*
◆ EMP: 239
SALES (est): 388.7MM
SALES (corp-wide): 4.4B Publicly Held
SIC: 3751 Brakes, friction clutch & other: bicycle
PA: Carlisle Companies Incorporated
  16430 N Scottsdale Rd # 400
  Scottsdale AZ 85254
  480 781-5000

(G-17125)
CBG BIOTECH LTD CO
30175 Solon Indus Pkwy (44139-4321)
PHONE...................................440 786-7667
David Camiener, *Manager*
EMP: 32 Privately Held
SIC: 3559 Recycling machinery
PA: Cbg Biotech, Ltd. Co.
  100 Glenview Pl Apt 1003
  Naples FL 34108

(G-17126)
CHANNEL PRODUCTS INC (PA)
30700 Solon Indus Pkwy (44139-4333)
PHONE...................................440 423-0113
Teresa Hack, *President*
Wayne Monaco, *Vice Pres*
Florin Lazar, *Engineer*
Dan Szubra, *Electrical Engi*
Wayne Monoco, *Financial Exec*
▲ EMP: 80
SQ FT: 50,000
SALES (est): 17.2MM Privately Held
WEB: www.channelproducts.com
SIC: 3822 3679 3643 3625 Auto controls regulating residntl & coml environmt & applncs; electronic circuits; current-carrying wiring devices; relays & industrial controls; machine tools, metal cutting type; porcelain electrical supplies

(G-17127)
CLOPAY CORPORATION
7905 Cochran Rd Ste 500 (44139-5469)
PHONE...................................440 542-9215
Matt Laudon, *Branch Mgr*
EMP: 5
SALES (corp-wide): 1.5B Publicly Held
SIC: 3081 Unsupported plastics film & sheet
HQ: Clopay Corporation
  8585 Duke Blvd
  Mason OH 45040
  800 282-2260

(G-17128)
CO- AX TECHNOLOGY INC
30301 Emerald Valley Pkwy (44139-4394)
PHONE...................................440 914-9200
Gholam Hosein Varghai, *President*
Melany Verbiar, *General Mgr*
Hassan Varghai, *Vice Pres*
Randy Rager, *Senior Buyer*
Hamed Varghai, *Purchasing*
EMP: 250
SQ FT: 22,000
SALES: 30MM Privately Held
WEB: www.coaxinc.com
SIC: 3672 3679 Printed circuit boards; harness assemblies for electronic use: wire or cable

(G-17129)
CUSTOM PRODUCTS CORPORATION (PA)
7100 Cochran Rd (44139-4306)
PHONE...................................440 528-7100
Timothy Stepanek, *President*
John Stepanek, *Vice Pres*
William Stepanek Jr, *Vice Pres*
Ashley Cross, *Buyer*
Pam Gall, *Purchasing*
▲ EMP: 78 EST: 1974
SQ FT: 82,000
SALES (est): 14.6MM Privately Held
WEB: www.customproducts.net
SIC: 7389 5131 5199 2761 Packaging & labeling services; labels; packaging materials; manifold business forms; commercial printing; packaging paper & plastics film, coated & laminated

(G-17130)
D D D HAMS INC
34234 Aurora Rd (44139)
PHONE...................................440 487-9572
Dennis D Demshar, *Administration*
EMP: 3 EST: 2010
SALES (est): 202.2K Privately Held
SIC: 2013 Prepared pork products from purchased pork

(G-17131)
DANDI ENTERPRISES INC
Also Called: Dunkin' Donuts
6353 Som Center Rd (44139-2914)
PHONE...................................419 516-9070
Lonnie Weiser, *President*
EMP: 15
SALES (est): 628.5K Privately Held
SIC: 5461 2051 Doughnuts; doughnuts, except frozen

(G-17132)
DEMAG CRANES & COMPONENTS CORP (DH)
Also Called: Terex USA
6675 Parkland Blvd # 200 (44139-4345)
P.O. Box 39245, Cleveland (44139-0245)
PHONE...................................440 248-2400
John Paxton, *President*
Robert Ferry, *District Mgr*
Bill Jepson, *Vice Pres*
Bernhard Barth, *CFO*
Tricia Ater, *Manager*
◆ EMP: 200
SQ FT: 87,000
SALES (est): 169.6MM
SALES (corp-wide): 3.7B Privately Held
WEB: www.demag-us.com
SIC: 3536 Cranes, industrial plant; hoists

(G-17133)
DOCMANN PRINTING & ASSOC INC
5275 Naiman Pkwy Ste E (44139-1033)
PHONE.................................440 975-1775
Todd Brichmann, *President*
James E Docherty, *Vice Pres*
EMP: 7
SQ FT: 14,000
SALES (est): 1.2MM **Privately Held**
WEB: www.docmann.com
SIC: 2752 Commercial printing, lithographic

(G-17134)
DYNAFLOOR SYSTEMS INC
Also Called: Dyna Floor
35079 Quartermane Cir (44139-2467)
PHONE.................................330 467-6005
Jerry Torrelli, *President*
EMP: 18
SQ FT: 10,000
SALES (est): 2MM **Privately Held**
WEB: www.dynafloor.com
SIC: 1752 2851 Floor laying & floor work; epoxy coatings

(G-17135)
EDWARDS VACUUM LLC
7905 Cochran Rd Ste 100 (44139-5470)
PHONE.................................440 248-4453
EMP: 9 **Privately Held**
SIC: 3563 Air & gas compressors
HQ: Edwards Vacuum Llc
  6416 Inducon Dr W
  Sanborn NY 14132
  800 848-9800

(G-17136)
EMERSON ELECTRIC CO
31100 Bainbridge Rd (44139-2229)
PHONE.................................440 248-9400
Michael Erickson, *Manager*
EMP: 23
SALES (corp-wide): 17.4B **Publicly Held**
WEB: www.gotoemerson.com
SIC: 3823 Industrial instrmnts msrmnt display/control process variable
PA: Emerson Electric Co.
  8000 West Florissant Ave
  Saint Louis MO 63136
  314 553-2000

(G-17137)
ENERGY FOCUS INC (PA)
32000 Aurora Rd Ste B (44139-2849)
PHONE.................................440 715-1300
Ronald D Black, *Ch of Bd*
Ted Tewksbury, *President*
Simon Cheng, *Vice Pres*
Jennifer Taylor, *Project Mgr*
Bhaumik Vashi, *Engineer*
EMP: 122
SQ FT: 75,000
SALES: 18.1MM **Publicly Held**
WEB: www.fiberstars.com
SIC: 3641 3648 3674 Lamps, fluorescent, electric; lamps, incandescent filament, electric; lighting equipment; light emitting diodes

(G-17138)
ERICO INC
34600 Solon Rd (44139-2631)
PHONE.................................440 248-0100
George H Vincent, *President*
Peter B Korte, *Vice Pres*
Monica Wilkinson, *Vice Pres*
Steve Greenfield, *Regl Sales Mgr*
Kevin Kobunski, *Regl Sales Mgr*
◆ **EMP:** 27
SALES (est): 63.3MM **Privately Held**
SIC: 3644 Noncurrent-carrying wiring services

(G-17139)
ERICO GLOBAL COMPANY
31700 Solon Rd (44139-3532)
PHONE.................................440 248-0100
EMP: 4
SALES (est): 129.4K **Privately Held**
SIC: 3699 Electrical equipment & supplies
PA: Nvent Electric Public Limited Company
  10 Earlsfort Terrace
  Dublin

(G-17140)
ERICO INTERNATIONAL CORP
34600 Solon Rd (44139-2631)
PHONE.................................440 248-0100
Jim Euske, *Regional Mgr*
George Nahra, *Engineer*
Steve Rohacz, *Branch Mgr*
Ward Judson, *Manager*
Mike Masterson, *Manager*
EMP: 400
SALES (corp-wide): 352.2K **Privately Held**
WEB: www.erico.com
SIC: 3441 3965 Fabricated structural metal; fasteners
HQ: Erico International Corporation
  1665 Utica Ave S Ste 700
  Saint Louis Park MN 55416
  440 349-2630

(G-17141)
ET&F FASTENING SYSTEMS INC
29019 Solon Rd (44139-3440)
PHONE.................................800 248-2376
John C Tillman, *President*
Dave Nolan, *Vice Pres*
David Nolan, *Vice Pres*
▲ **EMP:** 14
SQ FT: 15,000
SALES: 3.8MM **Privately Held**
WEB: www.etf-fastening.com
SIC: 3965 3546 5085 Fasteners; power-driven handtools; fasteners, industrial: nuts, bolts, screws, etc.

(G-17142)
ETCHED METAL COMPANY
30200 Solon Indus Pkwy (44139-4311)
PHONE.................................440 248-0240
Scott Nameth, *Principal*
Mike McDivitt, *Principal*
Jeff Thompson, *CFO*
Don Hunt, *Manager*
Bill Meszaros, *Technology*
▲ **EMP:** 45 **EST:** 1928
SQ FT: 27,500
SALES: 5.1MM **Privately Held**
WEB: www.etched-metal.com
SIC: 3479 3613 3596 3993 Name plates: engraved, etched, etc.; control panels, electric; scales & balances, except laboratory; signs & advertising specialties; plating & polishing; commercial printing, lithographic

(G-17143)
FINDAWAY WORLD LLC
31999 Aurora Rd (44139-2853)
PHONE.................................440 893-0808
Mitch Kroll, *CEO*
▲ **EMP:** 100
SALES (est): 15.4MM **Privately Held**
WEB: www.playawaydigital.com
SIC: 5999 8331 3669 5192 Audio-visual equipment & supplies; job training & vocational rehabilitation services; visual communication systems; periodicals

(G-17144)
FIRE FROM ICE VENTURES LLC
30333 Emerald Valley Pkwy (44139-4394)
PHONE.................................419 944-6705
Timothy Winings,
Lynne Winings,
▲ **EMP:** 11
SQ FT: 13,500
SALES (est): 1.4MM **Privately Held**
WEB: www.airserco.com
SIC: 3585 Refrigeration & heating equipment
PA: The Providence Group Inc
  9290 Metcalf Rd
  Willoughby OH

(G-17145)
FOLIO PHOTONICS LLC
6864 Cochran Rd (44139-4336)
PHONE.................................440 420-4500
Irina Shiyanovskaya, *Vice Pres*
Maria Anzola, *Controller*
Kenneth Singer,
EMP: 6 **EST:** 2012
SQ FT: 9,500
SALES (est): 194.9K **Privately Held**
SIC: 3695 Optical disks & tape, blank

(G-17146)
GE HEALTHCARE INC
34825 Lakeview Dr (44139-2025)
PHONE.................................502 452-4311
EMP: 3
SALES (corp-wide): 121.6B **Publicly Held**
SIC: 2834 Pharmaceutical preparations
HQ: Ge Healthcare Inc.
  100 Results Way
  Marlborough MA 01752
  800 526-3593

(G-17147)
GEARING SOLUTIONS INC
5905 Harper Rd Ste A (44139-1865)
P.O. Box 391703 (44139-8703)
PHONE.................................440 498-9538
Merritt A Osborn, *President*
William Doyle, *Vice Pres*
Arnold Popovitz, *Manager*
EMP: 4
SQ FT: 3,000
SALES (est): 120K **Privately Held**
SIC: 3566 8711 Speed changers, drives & gears; designing: ship, boat, machine & product

(G-17148)
GENESIS PLASTIC TECH LLC
27200 Tinkers Ct (44139-4387)
PHONE.................................440 542-0722
Jim Mayor, *VP Finance*
Mark Urban, *Office Mgr*
Geoffrey C Hanahan,
EMP: 80
SALES (est): 16.1MM **Privately Held**
WEB: www.genesisplastic.com
SIC: 3089 Injection molding of plastics

(G-17149)
GLAVIN INDUSTRIES INC
Also Called: Glavin Specialty Co
6835 Cochran Rd Ste A (44139-3927)
P.O. Box 391316 (44139-8316)
PHONE.................................440 349-0049
Julia S Glavin, *CEO*
David H Glavin, *President*
EMP: 25
SQ FT: 23,000
SALES (est): 15.6MM **Privately Held**
SIC: 5084 3993 2759 Industrial machinery & equipment; signs & advertising specialties; screen printing

(G-17150)
GLENDALE MACHINE INC
30625 Solon Industrial # 1 (44139-4390)
PHONE.................................440 248-8646
Joseph Paterniti Jr, *President*
EMP: 5 **EST:** 1948
SQ FT: 5,500
SALES: 400K **Privately Held**
SIC: 3544 3599 Jigs & fixtures; machine & other job shop work

(G-17151)
GLT FABRICATORS INC (PA)
6810 Cochran Rd (44139-3908)
PHONE.................................713 670-9700
Timothy Scott, *CEO*
EMP: 8
SALES (est): 4.2MM **Privately Held**
SIC: 3644 Insulators & insulation materials, electrical

(G-17152)
GRANEX INDUSTRIES INC (PA)
32400 Aurora Rd Ste 4 (44139-2800)
P.O. Box 391720 (44139-8720)
PHONE.................................440 248-4915
M Corey Obrien, *President*
G Scott Obrien, *Vice Pres*
▲ **EMP:** 12
SALES (est): 2.1MM **Privately Held**
SIC: 3281 Curbing, granite or stone

(G-17153)
GRAPHIC PACKAGING INTL INC
Also Called: Altivity Packaging
6385 Cochran Rd (44139-3961)
PHONE.................................440 248-4370
Jeff Pascarella, *Prdtn Mgr*
Mary Turk, *Branch Mgr*
Keith Haggerty, *Maintence Staff*
EMP: 190 **Publicly Held**
SIC: 2631 2657 Folding boxboard; folding paperboard boxes
HQ: Graphic Packaging International, Llc
  1500 Riveredge Pkwy # 100
  Atlanta GA 30328

(G-17154)
GRAPHICSOURCE INC
30405 Solon Rd Ste 12 (44139-3477)
PHONE.................................440 248-9200
David Scott Eichbaum, *President*
EMP: 3 **EST:** 1978
SQ FT: 600
SALES (est): 445.5K **Privately Held**
WEB: www.graphicsource.net
SIC: 2752 7336 Commercial printing, offset; art design services

(G-17155)
GRAPHITE EQUIPMENT MFG CO
5577 Valley Ln (44139-1501)
PHONE.................................216 271-9500
Thomas O Mulica, *President*
Dale T Lehman, *Vice Pres*
▲ **EMP:** 5
SQ FT: 9,000
SALES (est): 738.8K **Privately Held**
SIC: 3561 Industrial pumps & parts

(G-17156)
GREAT LAKES TEXTILES INC (PA)
Also Called: Glt Products
6810 Cochran Rd (44139-3908)
PHONE.................................440 914-1122
Steven Wake, *President*
Joel Hammer, *Vice Pres*
Jeff Robinson, *Vice Pres*
Patrick Burch, *Plant Mgr*
Marinko Milos, *CFO*
◆ **EMP:** 47
SQ FT: 117,000
SALES (est): 15.8MM **Privately Held**
WEB: www.gltproducts.com
SIC: 2821 5033 5131 5085 Polyvinylidene chloride resins; insulation materials; tape, textile; industrial supplies

(G-17157)
GREENES FENCE CO INC
5250 Naiman Pkwy Ste B (44139-1031)
P.O. Box 22258, Cleveland (44122-0258)
PHONE.................................216 464-3160
Larry Greenes, *President*
▲ **EMP:** 5
SALES (est): 1MM **Privately Held**
SIC: 2499 Fencing, wood

(G-17158)
HAB INC
Also Called: Hab Computer Services
28925 Fountain Pkwy (44139-4356)
PHONE.................................608 785-7650
Michael Juran, *President*
EMP: 25
SALES (est): 2.4MM
SALES (corp-wide): 151.1MM **Privately Held**
WEB: www.habinc.com
SIC: 7371 7372 Computer software development & applications; prepackaged software
PA: Mri Software Llc
  28925 Fountain Pkwy
  Solon OH 44139
  800 321-8770

(G-17159)
HARDWARE EXCHANGE INC
6573 Cochran Rd Ste F (44139-3972)
PHONE.................................440 449-8006
Mark Borlin, *President*
EMP: 5
SQ FT: 7,400
SALES (est): 932.3K **Privately Held**
SIC: 3571 Electronic computers

(G-17160)
HDT EXPEDITIONARY SYSTEMS INC
30500 Aurora Rd Ste 100 (44139-2776)
PHONE.................................216 438-6111
James Maurer, *President*
Mary Geiger, *Principal*
Ryan Benton, *Info Tech Mgr*
EMP: 6 **Privately Held**

Solon - Cuyahoga County (G-17161)

SIC: 3714 3569 Heaters, motor vehicle; filters
HQ: Hdt Expeditionary Systems, Inc.
30500 Aurora Rd Ste 100
Solon OH 44139
216 438-6111

(G-17161)
HDT EXPEDITIONARY SYSTEMS INC (HQ)
30500 Aurora Rd Ste 100 (44139-2776)
PHONE....................216 438-6111
Sean Bond, *President*
Michelle Gawlik, *General Mgr*
Barry Sullivan, *CFO*
Laura Arnold, *Business Anlyst*
Renee Goodbar, *Manager*
▲ EMP: 277
SQ FT: 172,000
SALES (est): 85.9MM **Privately Held**
WEB: www.base-x.com
SIC: 2393 2394 Canvas bags; canvas & related products; tents: made from purchased materials

(G-17162)
HONEYWELL INTERNATIONAL INC
5935 Stephanie Ln (44139-1969)
PHONE....................440 349-7330
EMP: 694
SALES (corp-wide): 41.8B **Publicly Held**
SIC: 3724 Aircraft engines & engine parts
PA: Honeywell International Inc.
115 Tabor Rd
Morris Plains NJ 07950
973 455-2000

(G-17163)
HORIZON GLOBAL AMERICAS INC
29000 Aurora Rd Ste 2 (44139-7202)
PHONE....................440 498-0001
EMP: 85
SALES (corp-wide): 892.9MM **Publicly Held**
SIC: 5531 3714 Ret Auto/Home Supplies Mfg Motor Vehicle Parts/Accessories
HQ: Horizon Global Americas Inc.
47912 Halyard Dr Ste 100
Plymouth MI 48170
734 656-3000

(G-17164)
HUNTER DEFENSE TECH INC (PA)
Also Called: Hdt Engineered Technologies
30500 Aurora Rd Ste 100 (44139-2776)
PHONE....................216 438-6111
Sean Bond, *President*
Frederick Strader, *President*
Robin Carney, *Exec VP*
Greg Miller, *Senior VP*
Bob Demarchi, *Vice Pres*
▲ EMP: 50
SQ FT: 26,000
SALES (est): 261.5MM **Privately Held**
SIC: 3433 3569 3822 8331 Room & wall heaters, including radiators; filters; auto controls regulating residntl & coml environmt & applncs; sheltered workshop; engineering services; assembly machines, including robotic

(G-17165)
HUNTER ENVIRONMENTAL CORP
Also Called: Hunter Manufacturing Company
30525 Aurora Rd (44139-2739)
PHONE....................440 248-6111
Eugene Strine, *CEO*
Denny Weyhe, *Controller*
Deborah Kuivila, *Info Tech Dir*
EMP: 25
SALES (est): 60.2K **Privately Held**
SIC: 3564 Filters, air: furnaces, air conditioning equipment, etc.

(G-17166)
ILLINOIS TOOL WORKS INC
6875 Parkland Blvd (44139-4377)
PHONE....................440 914-3100
Micheal Theise, *Branch Mgr*
EMP: 70
SQ FT: 2,500
SALES (corp-wide): 14.7B **Publicly Held**
WEB: www.notouch.com
SIC: 2819 2992 2899 2891 Industrial inorganic chemicals; lubricating oils & greases; chemical preparations; adhesives & sealants
PA: Illinois Tool Works Inc.
155 Harlem Ave
Glenview IL 60025
847 724-7500

(G-17167)
IMPACTION CO
6100 Cochran Rd (44139-3306)
PHONE....................440 349-5652
Joseph Sarakaitis, *Principal*
EMP: 4 EST: 2011
SALES (est): 425K **Privately Held**
SIC: 3494 Valves & pipe fittings

(G-17168)
INDUSTRIAL METAL FINISHING
7680 Bond St (44139-5351)
PHONE....................440 232-2400
Doug Whitaker, *President*
Glenn Billington, *Corp Secy*
Michael Distaulo, *Vice Pres*
Dennis J Whitaker, *Vice Pres*
EMP: 8
SQ FT: 3,800
SALES (est): 612.9K **Privately Held**
SIC: 3479 Painting, coating & hot dipping

(G-17169)
INFO-GRAPHICS INC
5960 Liberty Rd (44139-2539)
PHONE....................440 498-1640
Susan Haines, *President*
EMP: 5
SQ FT: 1,500
SALES (est): 597.6K **Privately Held**
SIC: 5943 2752 Office forms & supplies; commercial printing, lithographic

(G-17170)
INNOCOMP
33195 Wagon Wheel Dr (44139-2368)
PHONE....................440 248-5104
Jeri Lynn Hoffman, *Partner*
Robert Cecil, *Partner*
Craig Gruber, *Partner*
EMP: 7
SQ FT: 3,500
SALES (est): 590K **Privately Held**
WEB: www.innocomp.com
SIC: 3679 Voice controls

(G-17171)
INNOVATIVE RECYCLING SYSTEMS
31655 Arthur Rd (44139-4551)
PHONE....................440 498-9200
Paul D Popovich, *President*
Barb Popovich, *Corp Secy*
EMP: 3
SALES (est): 340K **Privately Held**
SIC: 3559 Recycling machinery

(G-17172)
INTELLIGENT MOBILE SUPPORT INC
31320 Solon Rd Ste 17 (44139-3572)
PHONE....................440 600-7343
John Steidley, *CEO*
EMP: 13 EST: 2010
SALES (est): 874.2K **Privately Held**
SIC: 7372 Prepackaged software

(G-17173)
J & J SNACK FOODS CORP
5351 Naiman Pkwy Ste B (44139-1014)
PHONE....................440 248-2084
Tim Dorsey, *Plant Mgr*
Timothy Dorsey, *Manager*
EMP: 4
SALES (corp-wide): 1B **Publicly Held**
WEB: www.jjsnack.com
SIC: 5145 2052 Snack foods; pretzels
PA: J & J Snack Foods Corp.
6000 Central Hwy
Pennsauken NJ 08109
856 665-9533

(G-17174)
JAYMAC SYSTEMS INC
34300 Sherbrook Park Dr (44139-2042)
PHONE....................440 498-0810
Fred Koneval, *Principal*
Florian Koneval, *Vice Pres*
Sue Koneval, *Treasurer*
EMP: 4 EST: 1944
SQ FT: 16,500
SALES: 750K **Privately Held**
SIC: 2752 Business forms, lithographed

(G-17175)
JEFFERSON SMURFIT CORPORATION
6385 Cochran Rd (44139-3961)
PHONE....................440 248-4370
Lisa Porter, *General Mgr*
EMP: 8
SALES (est): 1.1MM **Privately Held**
SIC: 2657 Folding paperboard boxes

(G-17176)
JERPBAK-BAYLESS CO
34150 Solon Rd (44139-2623)
P.O. Box 39157 (44139-0157)
PHONE....................440 248-5387
J Scott Jerpbak, *President*
Tim Byrne, *General Mgr*
Jean Hentemann, *Finance Other*
Bonnie Jerpbak, *Director*
EMP: 30 EST: 1944
SQ FT: 40,000
SALES (est): 6.3MM **Privately Held**
WEB: www.jerpbakbayless.com
SIC: 3599 Machine shop, jobbing & repair

(G-17177)
JOY MINING MACHINERY
Also Called: Bedford Gear
6160 Cochran Rd (44139-3306)
PHONE....................440 248-7970
Ed Doheny, *President*
Edward L Doheny II, *President*
▲ EMP: 140
SALES (est): 55.4MM **Privately Held**
SIC: 3532 Mining machinery

(G-17178)
JTM PRODUCTS INC
Also Called: J T M
31025 Carter St (44139-3521)
PHONE....................440 287-2302
Daniel Schodowski, *President*
Brian F Murphy, *Principal*
Greg Myers, *Vice Pres*
EMP: 22
SQ FT: 75,000
SALES (est): 8.6MM **Privately Held**
SIC: 2992 2841 3053 Oils & greases, blending & compounding; soap: granulated, liquid, cake, flaked or chip; packing: steam engines, pipe joints, air compressors, etc.

(G-17179)
KANAN ENTERPRISES INC (PA)
Also Called: King Nut Companies
31900 Solon Rd (44139-3536)
PHONE....................440 248-8484
Martin Kanan, *President*
Michael Kanan, *Chairman*
Matthew Kanan, *Vice Pres*
Kathy Crossgrove, *Purch Mgr*
Justin Rosenberg, *Controller*
◆ EMP: 160
SQ FT: 250,000
SALES (est): 96.1MM **Privately Held**
WEB: www.kingnut.com
SIC: 2068 2034 Nuts: dried, dehydrated, salted or roasted; fruits, dried or dehydrated, except freeze-dried

(G-17180)
KANAN ENTERPRISES INC
Also Called: King Nut Companies, Plant 2
6401 Davis Indus Pkwy (44139-3566)
PHONE....................440 349-0719
Jim Dedario, *Warehouse Mgr*
EMP: 10
SQ FT: 84,130

SALES (corp-wide): 96.1MM **Privately Held**
WEB: www.kingnut.com
SIC: 2068 2034 Nuts: dried, dehydrated, salted or roasted; fruits, dried or dehydrated, except freeze-dried
PA: Kanan Enterprises, Inc.
31900 Solon Rd
Solon OH 44139
440 248-8484

(G-17181)
KATHERINE A STULL INC
Also Called: Crafts For Kids
7079 Navajo Trl (44139-5845)
PHONE....................440 349-3977
Katherine A Stull, *President*
EMP: 4
SALES (est): 374.7K **Privately Held**
SIC: 7922 2731 Television program, including commercial producers; book publishing

(G-17182)
KEITHLEY INSTRUMENTS LLC (DH)
28775 Aurora Rd (44139-1891)
PHONE....................440 248-0400
Joseph P Keithley, *President*
Linda C Rae, *COO*
Philip R Etsler, *Vice Pres*
Mark A Hoersten, *Vice Pres*
Mark Hoersten, *Vice Pres*
▲ EMP: 118 EST: 1946
SQ FT: 125,000
SALES (est): 94.9MM
SALES (corp-wide): 6.4B **Publicly Held**
SIC: 3823 7371 3825 Computer interface equipment for industrial process control; computer software development; test equipment for electronic & electric measurement
HQ: Tektronix, Inc.
14150 Sw Karl Braun Dr
Beaverton OR 97005
800 833-9200

(G-17183)
KENNAMETAL INC
6865 Cochran Rd (44139-4398)
PHONE....................440 349-5151
Brian Maglosky, *Opers-Prdtn-Mfg*
Mark Francis, *Engineer*
Sam Rosenbaum, *Program Mgr*
EMP: 126
SQ FT: 1,500
SALES (corp-wide): 2.3B **Publicly Held**
WEB: www.kennametal.com
SIC: 3545 3532 Tool holders; mining machinery
PA: Kennametal Inc.
600 Grant St Ste 5100
Pittsburgh PA 15219
412 248-8000

(G-17184)
KYNTRONICS INC (HQ)
Also Called: Comptroll
6565 Davis Indus Pkwy (44139-3559)
PHONE....................440 220-5990
Pamela Bregitzer, *HR Admin*
Lori Feldman, *Sales Staff*
Wayne Foley, *Mng Member*
EMP: 9
SALES (est): 1.9MM **Privately Held**
SIC: 3593 Fluid power actuators, hydraulic or pneumatic
PA: Kyntrol Holdings Inc.
34700 Lakeland Blvd
Eastlake OH 44095
440 220-5990

(G-17185)
MAGIC INTERFACE LTD
7295 Popham Pl (44139-5794)
PHONE....................440 498-3700
Edward J Toochak, *President*
Richard J Woodland, *Vice Pres*
Eatriz Woodland, *Treasurer*
Joyce Prochak, *Admin Sec*
EMP: 7
SALES (est): 430K **Privately Held**
WEB: www.magicinterface.com
SIC: 7372 Operating systems computer software

GEOGRAPHIC SECTION

Solon - Cuyahoga County (G-17209)

(G-17186)
MAJESTIC TOOL AND MACHINE INC
30700 Carter St Ste C (44139-3585)
PHONE..........................440 248-5058
Walter Krueger, *President*
Kurt Krueger, *Vice Pres*
Todd Krueger, *Vice Pres*
EMP: 32
SQ FT: 30,000
SALES: 2.5MM **Privately Held**
SIC: 3599 7692 3544 Machine shop, jobbing & repair; welding repair; special dies, tools, jigs & fixtures

(G-17187)
MAMSYS CONSULTING SERVICES
35865 Spatterdock Ln (44139-6503)
PHONE..........................440 287-6824
Madhuri Kumari, *President*
Shiwangni Gupta, *Tech Recruiter*
Deepshikha Sharma,
Yogesh Sharma,
Charles Webb,
EMP: 2
SALES: 1.2MM **Privately Held**
SIC: 8748 7372 7371 7379 Business consulting; application computer software; business oriented computer software; computer software development & applications; data processing consultant;

(G-17188)
MANTUA MANUFACTURING CO (PA)
Also Called: Mantua Bed Frames
31050 Diamond Pkwy (44139-5478)
PHONE..........................800 333-8333
David Jaffe, *CEO*
Charles Bastien, *Vice Pres*
Dirk Smith, *Vice Pres*
Jeff Wick, *Vice Pres*
Frank Barkley, *Plant Mgr*
◆ EMP: 120 EST: 1952
SQ FT: 67,500
SALES (est): 109.4MM **Privately Held**
WEB: www.bedframes.com
SIC: 5021 2514 Bedsprings; frames for box springs or bedsprings; metal

(G-17189)
MEDICAL QUANT USA INC
Also Called: Multi Radiance Medical
6521 Davis Indus Pkwy (44139-3549)
PHONE..........................440 542-0761
Max Kanarsky, *President*
Todd Van Niel, *Vice Pres*
Galina Marqova, *CFO*
Galina Markova, *Accounting Mgr*
Ted Ondrish, *Manager*
EMP: 14
SALES (est): 1.3MM **Privately Held**
SIC: 3845 Laser systems & equipment, medical

(G-17190)
MERCURY IRON AND STEEL CO
Also Called: Misco Refractometer
6275 Cochran Rd (44139-3316)
PHONE..........................440 349-1500
Michael Rainer, *President*
Tom McDaniel, *Manager*
EMP: 14 EST: 1949
SQ FT: 6,000
SALES (est): 2.9MM **Privately Held**
WEB: www.misco.com
SIC: 8711 3827 3443 3441 Industrial engineers; optical instruments & lenses; plate work for the metalworking trade; fabricated structural metal; refractometers, industrial process type; switchgear & switchboard apparatus

(G-17191)
MERCURY MACHINE CO
30250 Carter St (44139-3500)
PHONE..........................440 349-3222
Jonathon Petrenchik, *President*
Mike Stasko, *Safety Mgr*
EMP: 67 EST: 1954
SQ FT: 10,000
SALES (est): 15.7MM **Privately Held**
WEB: www.mercurymachine.com
SIC: 3324 3544 Steel investment foundries; industrial molds

(G-17192)
MFS SUPPLY LLC (PA)
31100 Solon Rd Ste E (44139-3463)
PHONE..........................440 248-5300
Brandon Guzman, *President*
Michael Halpern, *Mng Member*
Jeff Muencz, *Director*
◆ EMP: 14
SALES (est): 5.9MM **Privately Held**
SIC: 2542 Postal lock boxes, mail racks & related products

(G-17193)
MI-LAR FENCE CO INC (PA)
Also Called: Greenes Fence
5250 Naiman Pkwy Ste B (44139-1031)
P.O. Box 22258, Cleveland (44122-0258)
PHONE..........................216 464-3160
Larry A Greenes, *President*
Michael Kalinich, *Vice Pres*
▲ EMP: 1
SQ FT: 12,000
SALES (est): 2.4MM **Privately Held**
SIC: 2499 Fencing, wood

(G-17194)
MICHAEL W HYES DESGR GOLDSMITH
Also Called: Hayes, Michael Designer
28200 Miles Rd Unit F (44139-6915)
PHONE..........................440 519-0889
Michael Hayes, *CEO*
Marcy Hayes, *Vice Pres*
EMP: 7
SQ FT: 1,250
SALES (est): 580K **Privately Held**
SIC: 3911 5944 7631 Jewelry, precious metal; jewelry stores; jewelry repair services

(G-17195)
MILLWOOD INC
30311 Emerald Valley Pkwy (44139)
PHONE..........................440 914-0540
Vern Walker, *Branch Mgr*
Carla Cotter, *Director*
EMP: 138 **Privately Held**
SIC: 2448 Pallets, wood
PA: Millwood, Inc.
 3708 International Blvd
 Vienna OH 44473

(G-17196)
MINIATURE PLASTIC MOLDING LTD
6750 Arnold Miller Pkwy (44139-4363)
PHONE..........................440 564-7210
Willard E Frissell, *Mng Member*
EMP: 4
SALES (est): 355.2K **Privately Held**
SIC: 3089 Injection molding of plastics

(G-17197)
MOLDERS CHOICE INC
5380 Naiman Pkwy Ste E (44139-1032)
PHONE..........................440 248-8500
Ken Berger, *President*
Mark Berger, *Corp Secy*
Robert Dumound, *Vice Pres*
EMP: 5
SQ FT: 6,000
SALES (est): 922.4K **Privately Held**
WEB: www.molderschoice.com
SIC: 3089 Injection molding of plastics

(G-17198)
MOTIONSOURCE INTERNATIONAL LLC
31200 Solon Rd Ste 7 (44139-3583)
PHONE..........................440 287-7037
Charles Hautala, *Principal*
Doug Karpowicz, *Principal*
Lee Shafer, *Sales Staff*
Gary McCormick, *Manager*
EMP: 10 EST: 2012
SQ FT: 4,000
SALES (est): 1.8MM **Privately Held**
SIC: 3569 5084 5013 Lubrication equipment, industrial; pumps & pumping equipment; pumps, oil & gas

(G-17199)
MP BIOMEDICALS LLC
29525 Fountain Pkwy (44139-4351)
PHONE..........................440 337-1200
Dragon Kraojovic, *Branch Mgr*
Viktor Kuzmanov, *Manager*
Randy Mayner, *Manager*
Akshaya Manai, *Executive*
EMP: 130
SALES (corp-wide): 379MM **Privately Held**
WEB: www.mpbio.com
SIC: 8731 2869 2834 8071 Biological research; enzymes; pharmaceutical preparations; medical laboratories; medical research
HQ: Mp Biomedicals, Llc
 3 Hutton Centre Dr # 100
 Santa Ana CA 92707
 949 833-2500

(G-17200)
MULTIPLAST SYSTEMS INC
33355 Station St (44139-2961)
PHONE..........................440 349-0800
Jeff Apisdorf, *President*
EMP: 15
SALES (est): 3MM **Privately Held**
WEB: www.multiplastsystems.com
SIC: 2673 Bags: plastic, laminated & coated

(G-17201)
MUSTARD SEED HEALTH FD MKT INC
6025 Kruse Dr Ste 100 (44139-2378)
PHONE..........................440 519-3663
Margaret Kanfer-Nabors, *Ch of Bd*
Bill Goodwin, *Financial Exec*
EMP: 35
SALES (corp-wide): 59.5MM **Privately Held**
WEB: www.mustardseedmarket.com
SIC: 5499 7299 5812 2051 Gourmet food stores; banquet hall facilities; caterers; bread, cake & related products
PA: Mustard Seed Health Food Market, Inc.
 3885 Medina Rd
 Akron OH 44333
 330 666-7333

(G-17202)
NESTLE BRANDS COMPANY
30000 Bainbridge Rd (44139-2206)
PHONE..........................440 264-6600
Cheryl Lavine, *Principal*
EMP: 12
SALES (est): 2MM **Privately Held**
SIC: 2099 Food preparations

(G-17203)
NESTLE PREPARED FOODS COMPANY (DH)
30003 Bainbridge Rd (44139-2205)
P.O. Box 2178, Wilkes Barre PA (18703-2178)
PHONE..........................440 248-3600
David H Jennings, *Ch of Bd*
C Wayne Partin, *President*
James M Biggar, *Vice Pres*
Charles Werner, *Vice Pres*
James H Ball, *Admin Sec*
▲ EMP: 1910 EST: 1969
SQ FT: 250,000
SALES (est): 1.7B
SALES (corp-wide): 90.8B **Privately Held**
SIC: 2038 5411 2037 Dinners, frozen & packaged; soups, frozen; pizza, frozen; grocery stores; vegetables, quick frozen & cold pack, excl. potato products
HQ: The Stouffer Corporation
 30003 Bainbridge Rd
 Solon OH 44139
 440 349-5757

(G-17204)
NESTLE PREPARED FOODS COMPANY
5750 Harper Rd (44139-1831)
PHONE..........................440 349-5757
C Wayne Partin, *President*
EMP: 68
SALES (corp-wide): 90.8B **Privately Held**
SIC: 2038 5411 2037 Frozen specialties; grocery stores; frozen fruits & vegetables
HQ: Nestle Prepared Foods Company
 30003 Bainbridge Rd
 Solon OH 44139
 440 248-3600

(G-17205)
NESTLE USA INC
Nestle Business Services
30003 Bainbridge Rd (44139-2290)
PHONE..........................440 349-5757
Jim Triskett, *Manager*
EMP: 200
SALES (corp-wide): 90.8B **Privately Held**
WEB: www.nestleusa.com
SIC: 2023 Evaporated milk; canned milk, whole; cream substitutes
HQ: Nestle Usa, Inc.
 1812 N Moore St
 Rosslyn VA 22209
 818 549-6000

(G-17206)
NETSHAPE TECHNOLOGIES MIM INC
31005 Solon Rd (44139-3436)
PHONE..........................440 248-5456
Dax Whitehouse, *CEO*
Ric Wrye, *COO*
▲ EMP: 12
SQ FT: 27,000
SALES (est): 3.4MM
SALES (corp-wide): 185.3MM **Privately Held**
SIC: 3443 Metal parts
HQ: Netshape Technologies Llc
 14670 Cumberland Rd
 Noblesville IN 46060
 812 248-9273

(G-17207)
NETSMART TECHNOLOGIES INC
Also Called: Trend Consulting Services
30775 Bnbridge Rd Ste 200 (44139)
PHONE..........................440 942-4040
Michael Valentine, *CEO*
Kim Schnebelin, *Prgrmr*
EMP: 39
SALES (corp-wide): 219.5MM **Privately Held**
SIC: 7379 7372 Computer related consulting services; business oriented computer software
HQ: Netsmart Technologies, Inc.
 4950 College Blvd
 Overland Park KS 66211

(G-17208)
NOCO COMPANY
30339 Diamond Pkwy # 102 (44139-5473)
PHONE..........................216 464-8131
William K Nook, *President*
Luke Case, *Vice Pres*
Rick Stanfield, *Engineer*
Jeffrey Weiner, *VP Sales*
Lindsey Walters, *Accounts Mgr*
◆ EMP: 500 EST: 1914
SQ FT: 100,000
SALES (est): 32.2MM **Privately Held**
WEB: www.noco-usa.com
SIC: 3694 3714 3315 2899 Battery cable wiring sets for internal combustion engines; booster (jump-start) cables, automotive; filters: oil, fuel & air, motor vehicle; steel wire & related products; chemical preparations; wire & cable; power tools & accessories

(G-17209)
OAKWOOD LABORATORIES LLC
27070 Miles Rd (44139-1162)
PHONE..........................440 505-2011
Gregory Hanzak, *Production*
Jeffrey M Fehn, *CFO*
Shritin Shah, *Branch Mgr*
Jonathan Cook, *Director*
Joe Golombek,
EMP: 17
SALES (est): 2.4MM
SALES (corp-wide): 13.2MM **Privately Held**
SIC: 2834 Vitamin, nutrient & hematinic preparations for human use

Solon - Cuyahoga County (G-17210)

PA: Oakwood Laboratories, L.L.C.
7670 First Pl Ste A
Oakwood Village OH 44146
440 359-0000

(G-17210)
OHIO FLOCK-COTE COMPANY INC
6810 Cochran Rd (44139-3908)
PHONE................................440 914-1122
Steven Wake, *President*
EMP: 50
SQ FT: 44,000
SALES (est): 409.3K **Privately Held**
SIC: 2262 Flock printing: manmade fiber & silk broadwoven fabrics

(G-17211)
OHIO LUMEX CO INC
30350 Bruce Indus Pkwy (44139-3938)
PHONE................................440 264-2500
Joseph Siperstein, *President*
Mike Neyman, *Opers Staff*
EMP: 5
SQ FT: 4,000
SALES (est): 1.5MM **Privately Held**
WEB: www.ohiolumex.com
SIC: 3826 8734 Analytical instruments; testing laboratories

(G-17212)
PACKAGING MATERIAL DIRECT INC
30405 Solon Rd Ste 9 (44139-3477)
PHONE................................989 482-8400
Sunil Daga, *CEO*
Jieesheunemiy Punaniy, *President*
Heresh Vasne, *Chairman*
EMP: 5
SALES (est): 385K **Privately Held**
SIC: 2671 Plastic film, coated or laminated for packaging

(G-17213)
PDI CONSTELLATION LLC
6225 Cochran Rd (44139-3315)
PHONE................................216 271-7344
EMP: 3
SALES (est): 103.9K **Privately Held**
SIC: 3999 Mfg Misc Products

(G-17214)
PDI GROUND SUPPORT SYSTEMS INC
Also Called: PDI GROUP, THE
6225 Cochran Rd (44139-3315)
PHONE................................216 271-7344
Irwin G Haber, *Chairman*
Ida Haber, *Vice Pres*
Lou Kish, *VP Mfg*
Pat Jeffries, *Purch Mgr*
Ron Steiger, *Senior Mgr*
▲ EMP: 60
SQ FT: 110,000
SALES (est): 14.8MM **Privately Held**
WEB: www.pdi-gss.com
SIC: 3714 3715 Axle housings & shafts, motor vehicle; semitrailers for missile transportation

(G-17215)
PENTAIR
34600 Solon Rd (44139-2631)
PHONE................................440 248-0100
Justin Pearce, *Opers Mgr*
Joe Krivich, *Marketing Staff*
Christopher Schmitt, *Director*
Karen Keegans, *Officer*
EMP: 17 EST: 2017
SALES (est): 5.5MM **Privately Held**
SIC: 3561 Pumps & pumping equipment

(G-17216)
PLAS-MAC CORP
30250 Carter St (44139-3506)
PHONE................................440 349-3222
Jonathon Petrenchik, *President*
Marcia Splinter, *Engineer*
Anthony Kaylor, *Manager*
EMP: 100
SQ FT: 33,000
SALES (est): 14.9MM **Privately Held**
WEB: www.plasmaccorp.com
SIC: 3543 3599 Foundry patternmaking; air intake filters, internal combustion engine, except auto

(G-17217)
PLYMOUTH HEALTHCARE PDTS LLC
Also Called: Loma Lux Laboratories
6521 Davis Indus Pkwy (44139-3549)
PHONE................................440 542-0762
EMP: 10
SQ FT: 10,000
SALES (est): 915.1K **Privately Held**
SIC: 2833 Mfg Medicinal/Botanical Products

(G-17218)
PRECISION BRUSH CO
6700 Parkland Blvd (44139-4341)
PHONE................................440 542-9600
James C Benjamin, *President*
Mike Porter, *Sales Executive*
Denise Martin, *Technology*
Barb Ames,
EMP: 14
SQ FT: 11,000
SALES (est): 3.1MM **Privately Held**
WEB: www.precisionbrush.com
SIC: 3991 Brushes, household or industrial

(G-17219)
PRODUCTO DIECO CORPORATION (HQ)
30600 Aurora Rd Ste 160 (44139-2767)
PHONE................................440 542-0000
Newman M Marsilius III, *President*
Glen Collings, *CFO*
EMP: 14 EST: 1998
SQ FT: 37,000
SALES (est): 4.7MM
SALES (corp-wide): 65.8MM **Privately Held**
SIC: 3544 5085 Die sets for metal stamping (presses); bearings, bushings, wheels & gears
PA: Pmt Group, Inc.
800 Union Ave
Bridgeport CT 06607
203 367-8675

(G-17220)
PTMJ ENTERPRISES
32000 Aurora Rd (44139-2875)
P.O. Box 391437 (44139-8437)
PHONE................................440 543-8000
Peter Joyce, *President*
Joe Miller, *Opers Staff*
◆ EMP: 180
SALES (est): 34.4MM **Privately Held**
WEB: www.signum-inc.com
SIC: 2541 1799 Display fixtures, wood; closet organizers, installation & design

(G-17221)
REPLACMENT PRTS SPCIALISTS INC (PA)
Also Called: RPS
30400 Solon Indus Pkwy (44139-4328)
PHONE................................440 248-0731
Gregory Davis, *President*
Chris Davis, *Vice Pres*
EMP: 4
SALES (est): 689.1K **Privately Held**
WEB: www.rps-state.com
SIC: 3536 Hoists, cranes & monorails

(G-17222)
REPUBLIC STEEL WIRE PROC LLC
31000 Solon Rd (44139-3467)
PHONE................................440 996-0740
Larry Braun, *General Mgr*
Jim Phillips, *General Mgr*
▲ EMP: 23
SALES (est): 11.7MM **Privately Held**
SIC: 3315 Steel wire & related products
HQ: Republic Steel
2633 8th St Ne
Canton OH 44704
330 438-5435

(G-17223)
RLS PARTS & EQUIPMENT LLC
33595 Bnbridge Rd Ste 204 (44139)
PHONE................................440 498-1843
Lynn M Vilcheck, *Principal*
EMP: 3
SALES (est): 1MM **Privately Held**
SIC: 3531 Asphalt plant, including gravel-mix type

(G-17224)
ROBBINS COMPANY (DH)
29100 Hall St Ste 100 (44139-3926)
PHONE................................440 248-3303
Lok Home, *President*
Clark Lubaski, *CFO*
◆ EMP: 150
SQ FT: 79,000
SALES (est): 154.3MM
SALES (corp-wide): 14.9MM **Privately Held**
WEB: www.robbinstbm.com
SIC: 3535 3541 3531 Conveyors & conveying equipment; machine tools, metal cutting type; tunnelling machinery
HQ: Northern Heavy Industries Group Co., Ltd.
No.16, Kaifa Avenue, Economic And Technological Development Zone
Shenyang 11014
242 580-2222

(G-17225)
ROHRER CORPORATION
Also Called: Cardpak
29601 Solon Rd (44139-3451)
PHONE................................440 542-3100
Dave Burkhart, *Opers Mgr*
Jay Storm, *Buyer*
Lynn Morrison, *Accounting Mgr*
Jim Joesel, *Sales Mgr*
Sid Hanes, *Sales Staff*
EMP: 130
SALES (corp-wide): 131.7MM **Privately Held**
SIC: 2752 2657 Commercial printing, lithographic; paperboard backs for blister or skin packages
PA: Rohrer Corporation
717 Seville Rd
Wadsworth OH 44281
330 335-1541

(G-17226)
RTSI LLC
6161 Cochran Rd Ste G (44139-3324)
PHONE................................440 542-3066
Vikki Velimesis, *General Mgr*
Donna Ross,
EMP: 7
SALES (est): 890.5K
SALES (corp-wide): 37.2MM **Privately Held**
SIC: 3451 Screw machine products
PA: Kirkwood Holding Inc.
1239 Rockside Rd
Cleveland OH 44134
216 267-6200

(G-17227)
SAINT-GOBAIN PRFMCE PLAS CORP (DH)
31500 Solon Rd (44139-3528)
P.O. Box 2864, Clinton IA (52733-2864)
PHONE................................440 836-6900
Tom Kinisky, *President*
Laurent Guillot, *CFO*
▲ EMP: 200 EST: 1955
SQ FT: 20,000
SALES (est): 1.1B
SALES (corp-wide): 215.9MM **Privately Held**
SIC: 3089 3053 Thermoformed finished plastic products; gaskets, packing & sealing devices
HQ: Saint-Gobain Abrasives, Inc.
1 New Bond St
Worcester MA 01606
508 795-5000

(G-17228)
SCHWEBEL BAKING COMPANY
Also Called: Schwebel Baking Co-Solon Bky
6250 Camp Industrial Rd (44139-2750)
PHONE................................440 248-1500
Grant West, *Manager*
EMP: 150
SALES (corp-wide): 170MM **Privately Held**
WEB: www.schwebels.com
SIC: 5461 5149 2051 Bread; groceries & related products; bread, cake & related products
PA: Schwebel Baking Company
965 E Midlothian Blvd
Youngstown OH 44502
330 783-2860

(G-17229)
SENSICAL INC
Also Called: Unitus
31115 Aurora Rd (44139-2701)
PHONE................................216 641-1141
John F Haas, *Ch of Bd*
Eric Apshago, *Vice Pres*
Denise Trivisonno, *Safety Mgr*
Ann Page, *Purch Mgr*
James Haas, *Treasurer*
▲ EMP: 55
SQ FT: 45,000
SALES (est): 17.8MM **Privately Held**
WEB: www.sensical.net
SIC: 3993 2752 2672 2759 Signs & advertising specialties; commercial printing, lithographic; coated & laminated paper; promotional printing

(G-17230)
SHERWIN SOFTWARE SOLUTIONS
Also Called: Accounting Software Solutions
5380 Naiman Pkwy Ste B (44139-1032)
PHONE................................440 498-8010
Keith Sherwin, *President*
EMP: 6
SALES (est): 570K **Privately Held**
WEB: www.erpsolutions4u.com
SIC: 7372 Prepackaged software

(G-17231)
SIGLENT TECHNOLOGIES AMER INC
6557 Cochran Rd (44139-3901)
PHONE................................440 398-5800
Stephen Barfield, *General Mgr*
EMP: 4
SQ FT: 3,000
SALES (est): 439.2K **Privately Held**
SIC: 3679 5085 Power supplies, all types: static; static power supply converters for electronic applications; power transmission equipment & apparatus

(G-17232)
SKIDMORE-WILHELM MFG COMPANY
Also Called: Columbia Industries
30340 Solon Industrial B (44139-4358)
PHONE................................216 481-4774
John Obrayan, *President*
John Wilhelm, *Shareholder*
Kathleen Wilhelm, *Shareholder*
Joanne Hoffman, *Admin Sec*
▲ EMP: 28 EST: 1944
SQ FT: 15,000
SALES (est): 4.6MM **Privately Held**
WEB: www.skidmore-wilhelm.com
SIC: 3728 3829 3825 3593 Aircraft parts & equipment; torsion testing equipment; instruments to measure electricity; fluid power cylinders & actuators; speed changers, drives & gears; machine tool accessories

(G-17233)
SOLON
38235 Mcdowell Dr (44139-4684)
PHONE................................440 498-1798
Susan A Drucker, *Mayor*
EMP: 6
SALES (est): 677.3K **Privately Held**
SIC: 3089 Plastics products

(G-17234)
SOLON SPECIALTY WIRE CO
Also Called: Solon Specialty 0537
30000 Solon Rd (44139-3408)
PHONE................................440 248-7600
Dave Haffenr, *CEO*
Don Delapa, *Manager*
▲ EMP: 25

SQ FT: 180,000
SALES (est): 6.1MM
SALES (corp-wide): 4.2B Publicly Held
WEB: www.leggett.com
SIC: 3315 Wire, ferrous/iron
PA: Leggett & Platt, Incorporated
    1 Leggett Rd
    Carthage MO 64836
    417 358-8131

(G-17235)
SPECIALIZED BUSINESS SFTWR INC
6240 Som Center Rd # 230 (44139-9711)
PHONE..................................440 542-9145
Steven Wiser, *President*
Ross Pollock, *Project Mgr*
Stuart McKinney, *Software Dev*
Tim Warnky, *Software Dev*
EMP: 20
SALES (est): 2MM Privately Held
WEB: www.specializedbusinesssoftware.com
SIC: 7372 Business oriented computer software

(G-17236)
SPEEDLINE CORPORATION (PA)
6810 Cochran Rd (44139-3908)
PHONE..................................440 914-1122
Steven Wake, *President*
Joel Hammer, *Vice Pres*
Marinko Milos, *CFO*
▲ EMP: 1
SQ FT: 34,000
SALES (est): 4.3MM Privately Held
WEB: www.speedlinepvc.com
SIC: 3089 Fittings for pipe, plastic

(G-17237)
STOUFFER CORPORATION (DH)
30003 Bainbridge Rd (44139-2205)
PHONE..................................440 349-5757
Peter Knox, *Principal*
▲ EMP: 8
SQ FT: 124,000
SALES (est): 1.7B
SALES (corp-wide): 90.8B Privately Held
SIC: 2038 Dinners, frozen & packaged; soups, frozen
HQ: Tsc Holdings, Inc.
    800 N Brand Blvd
    Glendale CA 91203
    818 549-6000

(G-17238)
STRIDE TOOL LLC
30333 Emerald Valley Pkwy (44139-4394)
PHONE..................................440 247-4600
Ron Ortiz, *CEO*
EMP: 150 EST: 2016
SALES (est): 4.5MM Privately Held
SIC: 3423 Hand & edge tools

(G-17239)
SWAGELOK (HQ)
Also Called: Snow Metal Products Co
29500 Solon Rd (44139-3474)
PHONE..................................440 349-5657
Arthur Anton, *CEO*
William Cosgrove, *Ch of Bd*
Lynne Aldridge, *General Mgr*
▲ EMP: 4
SALES (est): 5.5MM
SALES (corp-wide): 940.1MM Privately Held
SIC: 3471 3494 3492 Electroplating & plating; valves & pipe fittings; fluid power valves & hose fittings
PA: Swagelok Company
    29500 Solon Rd
    Solon OH 44139
    440 248-4600

(G-17240)
SWAGELOK COMPANY (PA)
29500 Solon Rd (44139-3474)
PHONE..................................440 248-4600
Arthur F Anton, *President*
Josh McClintock, *COO*
Natalie Baker, *Sr Corp Ofcr*
Frank J Roddy, *Exec VP*
Sylvie A Bon, *Vice Pres*
◆ EMP: 900
SQ FT: 220,000
SALES (est): 940.1MM Privately Held
WEB: www.swagelok.com
SIC: 3494 3491 3599 Pipe fittings; pressure valves & regulators, industrial; machine shop, jobbing & repair

(G-17241)
SWAGELOK COMPANY
6100 Cochran Rd (44139-3306)
PHONE..................................440 349-5652
Nancy Brown, *Branch Mgr*
EMP: 60
SALES (corp-wide): 940.1MM Privately Held
WEB: www.swagelok.com
SIC: 3494 3491 3599 3498 Pipe fittings; pressure valves & regulators, industrial; machine shop, jobbing & repair; fabricated pipe & fittings
PA: Swagelok Company
    29500 Solon Rd
    Solon OH 44139
    440 248-4600

(G-17242)
SWAGELOK COMPANY
31400 Aurora Rd (44139-2764)
PHONE..................................440 349-5934
Bill Ponikvar, *Electrical Engi*
Nick Lubar, *Manager*
EMP: 100
SALES (corp-wide): 940.1MM Privately Held
WEB: www.swagelok.com
SIC: 5051 3593 3498 3494 Tubing, metal; fluid power cylinders & actuators; fabricated pipe & fittings; valves & pipe fittings; fabricated plate work (boiler shop)
PA: Swagelok Company
    29500 Solon Rd
    Solon OH 44139
    440 248-4600

(G-17243)
SWAGELOK COMPANY
Also Called: Crawford Computer Center
6262 Cochran Rd (44139-3308)
PHONE..................................440 349-5836
Arthur Anton, *Principal*
Chris Bryan, *Business Anlyst*
Tom Cichon, *Manager*
Shawn Corey, *Manager*
Janis Davis, *Manager*
EMP: 25
SALES (corp-wide): 940.1MM Privately Held
WEB: www.swagelok.com
SIC: 3494 3491 3599 3594 Pipe fittings; pressure valves & regulators, industrial; machine shop, jobbing & repair; fluid power pumps & motors; fluid power valves & hose fittings; heating equipment, except electric
PA: Swagelok Company
    29500 Solon Rd
    Solon OH 44139
    440 248-4600

(G-17244)
SWAGELOK MANUFACTURING CO LLC
29500 Solon Rd (44139-3474)
PHONE..................................440 248-4600
Chris Gress, *Purchasing*
Jim Novak, *Project Engr*
Greg Wittkopf, *Info Tech Dir*
David B Cathcart,
▲ EMP: 25
SALES (est): 4.9MM Privately Held
SIC: 3599 Hose, flexible metallic

(G-17245)
T J DAVIES COMPANY INC
30745 Solon Rd Ste 1 (44139-3459)
PHONE..................................440 248-5510
Thomas Davies, *President*
EMP: 6
SQ FT: 5,000
SALES: 600K Privately Held
WEB: www.tjdavies.com
SIC: 3535 Belt conveyor systems, general industrial use

(G-17246)
TARKETT INC (DH)
Also Called: Tarkett North America
30000 Aurora Rd (44139-2728)
PHONE..................................800 899-8916
Jeff Buttitta, *CEO*
Jack Lee, *President*
Peter De Bonis, *Corp Secy*
Mike Wagner, *Manager*
Mark Santarelli, *Director*
▲ EMP: 99 EST: 1981
SQ FT: 5,000
SALES (est): 794.4MM
SALES (corp-wide): 589.6K Privately Held
WEB: www.tarkettna.com
SIC: 3069 Flooring, rubber: tile or sheet
HQ: Tarkett Inc
    1001 Rue Yamaska E
    Farnham QC J2N 1
    450 293-3173

(G-17247)
TARKETT USA INC (DH)
Also Called: Johnsonite
30000 Aurora Rd (44139-2728)
PHONE..................................440 543-8916
Jeff Fenwick, *President*
Eric Parada, *Business Mgr*
Michael Rappaport, *Business Mgr*
Pierre Pailheret, *Plant Mgr*
Vince Brown, *Prdtn Mgr*
EMP: 250
SALES (est): 457.3MM
SALES (corp-wide): 589.6K Privately Held
SIC: 3253 Ceramic wall & floor tile

(G-17248)
TECHNOLOGY HOUSE LTD
30555 Solon Indus Pkwy (44139-4329)
PHONE..................................440 248-3025
Dan Stumpf, *Manager*
EMP: 54 Privately Held
SIC: 3369 Nonferrous foundries
PA: The Technology House Ltd
    10036 Aurora Hudson Rd
    Streetsboro OH 44241

(G-17249)
TECHTRON SYSTEMS INC
29500 Fountain Pkwy (44139-4350)
PHONE..................................440 505-2990
Paul Teel Jr, *President*
Pam Teel, *Business Mgr*
Rose Wilcosky, *QC Mgr*
Bill Biscoff, *Engineer*
Jeff Winters, *Info Tech Mgr*
▲ EMP: 50
SQ FT: 38,000
SALES (est): 16.8MM Privately Held
WEB: www.techtronsys.com
SIC: 3672 Printed circuit boards

(G-17250)
TEKTRONIX INC
28775 Aurora Rd (44139-1837)
PHONE..................................440 248-0400
EMP: 26
SALES (corp-wide): 6.4B Publicly Held
SIC: 3825 Instruments to measure electricity
HQ: Tektronix, Inc.
    14150 Sw Karl Braun Dr
    Beaverton OR 97005
    800 833-9200

(G-17251)
TEXAS TILE MANUFACTURING LLC
30000 Aurora Rd (44139-2728)
PHONE..................................713 869-5811
Gilles De Beaumont, *President*
Lee James, *Vice Pres*
Tom Dowling, *Treasurer*
Anthony Matti, *Director*
Jeff Buttitta,
▲ EMP: 20
SALES (est): 3.8MM Privately Held
SIC: 3292 Tile, vinyl asbestos

(G-17252)
THERMACAL INC
30325 Binbridge Rd Ste 2a (44139)
PHONE..................................440 498-1005
Jerry Nickol, *President*
EMP: 5
SQ FT: 5,000
SALES (est): 649.7K Privately Held
WEB: www.thermacal.com
SIC: 3823 Temperature measurement instruments, industrial

(G-17253)
TIMEKEEPING SYSTEMS INC (PA)
30700 Bainbridge Rd Ste H (44139-6403)
PHONE..................................216 595-0890
George Markwitz, *President*
Pete Huber, *Vice Pres*
Barry Markwitz, *Vice Pres*
Jim Gragel, *Accountant*
Jim Huffman, *Regl Sales Mgr*
EMP: 11
SALES (est): 2.5MM Privately Held
SIC: 7371 8711 7372 3577 Custom computer programming services; engineering services; prepackaged software; computer peripheral equipment

(G-17254)
TRITON PRODUCTS LLC
30700 Carter St Ste D (44139-3585)
PHONE..................................440 248-5480
Ronald Accuardi,
Terry C Palermo,
▲ EMP: 18
SQ FT: 38,000
SALES (est): 3.7MM Privately Held
SIC: 3429 Hangers, wall hardware

(G-17255)
TTI FLOOR CARE NORTH AMER INC (DH)
Also Called: Royal Appliance Manufacturing
7005 Cochran Rd (44139-4303)
PHONE..................................440 996-2000
Chris Gurreri, *President*
Mike Ferris, *President*
Nora Covarrubias, *Buyer*
Doug Rukavina, *Engineer*
Steven Kegg, *Senior Engr*
▲ EMP: 350
SQ FT: 450,000
SALES (est): 224.7MM
SALES (corp-wide): 6B Privately Held
SIC: 5072 3825 Power tools & accessories; power measuring equipment, electrical
HQ: Royal Appliance Mfg. Co.
    7005 Cochran Rd
    Cleveland OH 44139
    440 996-2000

(G-17256)
TWINSOURCE LLC
32333 Aurora Rd Ste 50 (44139-2851)
PHONE..................................440 248-6800
Fred Tamjidi, *President*
Dave Gouttiere, *CFO*
EMP: 10
SQ FT: 1,500
SALES (est): 2.1MM Privately Held
WEB: www.twinsource.net
SIC: 3625 Switches, electronic applications

(G-17257)
VALTRONIC TECHNOLOGY INC
29200 Fountain Pkwy (44139-4347)
PHONE..................................440 349-1239
Martin Zimmermann, *CEO*
Clemens J Troche, *President*
Jay Wimer, *President*
Donald Styblo, *Vice Pres*
Nick McPherson, *Project Mgr*
EMP: 68
SQ FT: 26,000
SALES (est): 19.2MM Privately Held
SIC: 3679 Harness assemblies for electronic use: wire or cable
PA: Valtronic Technologies (Holding) Sa
    Route De Bonport 2
    Les CharbonniCres VD
    218 410-111

(G-17258)
VWR CHEMICALS LLC (DH)
28600 Fountain Pkwy (44139-4314)
PHONE..................................800 448-4442
Theodore Pulkownick, *President*
▲ EMP: 30

Solon - Cuyahoga County (G-17259)

SALES (est): 11.9MM **Privately Held**
WEB: www.anachemiachemicals.com
SIC: **2819** Industrial inorganic chemicals
HQ: Vwr Funding, Inc.
100 W Matsonford Rd
Radnor PA 19087
610 386-1700

(G-17259)
W-J INC
34180 Solon Rd (44139-2623)
P.O. Box 39157, Cleveland (44139-0157)
PHONE...............................440 248-8282
Scott Jerpbak, *President*
EMP: 5 EST: 1972
SQ FT: 28,000
SALES (est): 659.5K **Privately Held**
SIC: **3452** Screws, metal

(G-17260)
WATER & WASTE WATER EQP CO
32100 Solon Rd Ste 101a (44139-3584)
PHONE...............................440 542-0972
Walter Senney, *President*
EMP: 7
SALES (est): 1.2MM **Privately Held**
WEB: www.wwe-co.com
SIC: **3589** Water treatment equipment, industrial

(G-17261)
WILLIAM J BERGEN & CO
Also Called: Bergen, W J & Co
32520 Arthur Rd (44139-4503)
PHONE...............................440 248-6132
William J Bergen, *Owner*
EMP: 9
SQ FT: 3,500
SALES (est): 1MM **Privately Held**
SIC: **5112** 2752 2759 Business forms; commercial printing, offset; lithographing on metal; letterpress printing

(G-17262)
WORKSPEED MANAGEMENT LLC
28925 Fountain Pkwy (44139-4356)
PHONE...............................917 369-9025
EMP: 25
SALES (est): 1.8MM **Privately Held**
SIC: **7372** Prepackaged Software Services

(G-17263)
ZIRCOA INC
31501 Solon Rd (44139-3526)
P.O. Box 901150, Cleveland (44190-0003)
PHONE...............................440 349-7237
EMP: 22
SALES (est): 6.3MM
SALES (corp-wide): 27.1MM **Privately Held**
WEB: www.zircoa.com
SIC: **3339** Primary nonferrous metals
PA: Zircoa Inc.
31501 Solon Rd
Cleveland OH 44139
440 248-0500

Somerset
Perry County

(G-17264)
LITZINGER LOGGING
314 S Columbus St (43783)
PHONE...............................740 743-2245
Louis Litzinger, *Principal*
EMP: 3
SALES (est): 245.3K **Privately Held**
SIC: **2411** Logging

(G-17265)
N & N OIL
6111 State Route 13 Ne (43783-9686)
P.O. Box 261 (43783-0261)
PHONE...............................740 743-2848
Amanda Noll, *Principal*
EMP: 3
SALES (est): 315K **Privately Held**
SIC: **3533** Oil & gas field machinery

(G-17266)
RHODES MANUFACTURING CO INC
7045 Buckeye Valley Rd Ne (43783-9709)
PHONE...............................740 743-2614
Douglas L Rhodes, *President*
Brian Rhodes, *Vice Pres*
EMP: 20
SQ FT: 6,000
SALES (est): 5.4MM **Privately Held**
SIC: **3443** Industrial vessels, tanks & containers

(G-17267)
SCHMELZER INDUSTRIES INC
7970 Wesley Chapel Rd Ne (43783-9737)
P.O. Box 249 (43783-0249)
PHONE...............................740 743-2866
Jean Schmelzer, *President*
Monica Schmelzer, *COO*
EMP: 25
SQ FT: 23,700
SALES (est): 4.4MM **Privately Held**
WEB: www.siveils.com
SIC: **2221** 5999 Fiberglass fabrics; fiberglass materials, except insulation

(G-17268)
VILLAGE OF SOMERSET
1672 Big Inch Rd Nw (43783-9768)
P.O. Box 10 (43783-0010)
PHONE...............................740 743-1986
Cindy Grimm, *Principal*
EMP: 4 **Privately Held**
SIC: **3589** Sewage & water treatment equipment
PA: Village Of Somerset
100 Public Sq
Somerset OH 43783
740 743-2963

Somerton
Belmont County

(G-17269)
STUMPTOWN LBR PALLET MILLS LTD
55613 Washington St (43713-9794)
PHONE...............................740 757-2275
Dennis Wilcox,
EMP: 8
SQ FT: 1,300
SALES (est): 400K **Privately Held**
SIC: **2448** Pallets, wood

South Bloomingville
Hocking County

(G-17270)
FRICKCO INC
54660 Pretty Run Rd (43152-9511)
PHONE...............................740 887-2017
Jerry Albright, *President*
EMP: 3
SALES (est): 310K **Privately Held**
SIC: **2421** Sawmills & planing mills, general

South Charleston
Clark County

(G-17271)
BUCKEYE DIAMOND LOGISTICS INC (PA)
Also Called: Bdl Supply
15 Sprague Rd (45368-9644)
PHONE...............................937 462-8361
Samuel J Mc Adow Jr, *President*
John McAdow, *Vice Pres*
David Pennington, *Plant Mgr*
Lester Callahan, *Buyer*
William Hoskins, *VP Sls/Mktg*
EMP: 120
SALES (est): 32MM **Privately Held**
WEB: www.buckeyegroup.com
SIC: **2448** 2441 Pallets, wood; boxes, wood

(G-17272)
GARBER CO
5818 Old State Route 42 (45368-9608)
P.O. Box 698 (45368-0698)
PHONE...............................937 462-8730
Shane Brown, *Manager*
EMP: 3
SALES (est): 347.6K **Privately Held**
WEB: www.garberseeder.com
SIC: **3523** Farm machinery & equipment

(G-17273)
JOHNS JERKY & SNACK MEATS LLC
12499 Clmbus Cncinnati Rd (45368-9307)
PHONE...............................937 207-7008
John Snook, *Mng Member*
EMP: 3 EST: 2011
SALES (est): 182.2K **Privately Held**
SIC: **2013** Snack sticks, including jerky: from purchased meat; bologna from purchased meat

(G-17274)
WOODFORD LOGISTICS
15 Sprague Rd (45368-9644)
PHONE...............................513 417-8453
Steven L Means, *Principal*
EMP: 90
SQ FT: 60,000
SALES (est): 7.9MM **Privately Held**
SIC: **2448** Pallets, wood

(G-17275)
YAMADA NORTH AMERICA INC
Also Called: Yotec
9000 Clmbus Cincinnati Rd (45368-9406)
P.O. Box Y (45368-0825)
PHONE...............................937 462-7111
Kiyoshi Osawa, *President*
John C Beeler, *Principal*
William Mallory, *Vice Pres*
▲ EMP: 350
SQ FT: 110,000
SALES (est): 164.3MM
SALES (corp-wide): 898.1MM **Privately Held**
WEB: www.yna.us
SIC: **3714** 3621 Motor vehicle steering systems & parts; water pump, motor vehicle; rotors, for motors
PA: Yamada Manufacturing Co., Ltd.
2-1296, Kobayashicho
Isesaki GNM 379-2
270 409-111

South Lebanon
Warren County

(G-17276)
GDW WOODWORKING LLC
120 Vista Ridge Dr (45065-8761)
PHONE...............................513 494-3041
Glenn David Williams,
EMP: 4
SALES (est): 322.7K **Privately Held**
SIC: **2431** 7389 Millwork;

(G-17277)
OHIO FLEXIBLE PACKAGING CO
512 S Main St (45065-1441)
PHONE...............................513 494-1800
Larry Lehman, *President*
Juith Lehman, *Corp Secy*
Frank Remmey, *Vice Pres*
EMP: 11
SQ FT: 10,000
SALES (est): 1.8MM **Privately Held**
WEB: www.ohioflex.com
SIC: **2759** Flexographic printing

South Point
Lawrence County

(G-17278)
ALPHA CONTROL LLC
Also Called: Alpha Control Fabg & Mfg
1042 County Road 60 (45680-7465)
P.O. Box 1036 (45680-1036)
PHONE...............................740 377-3400
Greg Joseph, *President*
EMP: 35 EST: 2010
SQ FT: 60,000
SALES (est): 7MM **Privately Held**
SIC: **3449** Bars, concrete reinforcing: fabricated steel

(G-17279)
AMERICAN BOTTLING COMPANY
2531 County Road 1 (45680-7879)
PHONE...............................740 377-4371
Rick Hannon, *Manager*
EMP: 45 **Publicly Held**
WEB: www.cs-americas.com
SIC: **2086** Soft drinks: packaged in cans, bottles, etc.
HQ: The American Bottling Company
5301 Legacy Dr
Plano TX 75024

(G-17280)
BROCK BURIAL VAULT INC
1043 County Road 120 (45680-8823)
PHONE...............................740 894-5246
EMP: 3 EST: 1976
SQ FT: 10,000
SALES (est): 280K **Privately Held**
SIC: **3272** Mfg Burial Vaults

(G-17281)
BROUGHTON FOODS COMPANY
8099 County Road 1 (45680-7825)
PHONE...............................800 598-7545
Jonathan Christian, *Branch Mgr*
EMP: 10 **Publicly Held**
SIC: **2026** Cottage cheese
HQ: Broughton Foods Company
1701 Greene St
Marietta OH 45750
740 373-4121

(G-17282)
DOLIN SUPPLY CO
702 Solida Rd (45680-8953)
PHONE...............................304 529-4171
Mark Sparks,
EMP: 45
SQ FT: 83,000
SALES (est): 6MM **Publicly Held**
WEB: www.mscdirect.com
SIC: **5085** 7353 7694 3496 Industrial supplies; heavy construction equipment rental; armature rewinding shops; miscellaneous fabricated wire products
PA: Msc Industrial Direct Co., Inc.
75 Maxess Rd
Melville NY 11747

(G-17283)
ENGINES INC OF OHIO
101 Commerce Dr (45680-8457)
P.O. Box 428 (45680-0428)
PHONE...............................740 377-9874
Carl C Grover, *President*
David W Sanders, *Vice Pres*
Daniel T Yon, *Director*
EMP: 65
SQ FT: 100,000
SALES (est): 14.3MM **Privately Held**
SIC: **3321** 3325 3743 3532 Railroad car wheels & brake shoes, cast iron; railroad car wheels, cast steel; interurban cars & car equipment; mining machinery

(G-17284)
IV J TELECOMMUNICATIONS LLC
101 Lea St (45680-9685)
PHONE...............................606 694-1762
John Johnson,
EMP: 4
SALES (est): 240.7K **Privately Held**
SIC: **3585** 7699 1623 1711 Compressors for refrigeration & air conditioning equipment; miscellaneous building item repair services; oil & gas pipeline construction; heating & air conditioning contractors

(G-17285)
JENNMAR MCSWEENEY LLC
235 Commerce Dr (45680-8465)
PHONE...............................740 377-3354
Frank Calandra, *President*
Joe McSweeney, *Principal*
Sandra Blackburn, *Vice Pres*

▲ = Import ▼=Export
◆ =Import/Export

▲ EMP: 140 EST: 2013
SQ FT: 30,900
SALES (est): 38.3MM
SALES (corp-wide): 571.6MM Privately Held
SIC: 3532 3531 Bits, except oil & gas field tools, rock; auger mining equipment; blades for graders, scrapers, dozers & snow plows
PA: Calandra Frank Inc
258 Kappa Dr
Pittsburgh PA 15238
412 963-9071

(G-17286)
MCGINNIS INC (HQ)
502 2nd St E (45680-9446)
P.O. Box 534 (45680-0534)
PHONE 740 377-4391
Bruce D McGinnis, *CEO*
Rickey Lee Griffith, *President*
Bill Jessie, *Corp Secy*
D Dwaine Stephens, *Vice Pres*
EMP: 193 EST: 1971
SQ FT: 5,000
SALES (est): 43.9MM
SALES (corp-wide): 152.4MM Privately Held
WEB: www.mcginnisinc.com
SIC: 4491 3731 Marine cargo handling; barges, building & repairing
PA: Mcnational, Inc.
502 2nd St E
South Point OH 45680
740 377-4391

(G-17287)
MCNATIONAL INC (PA)
502 2nd St E (45680-9446)
P.O. Box 534 (45680-0534)
PHONE 740 377-4391
Bruce D McGinnis, *CEO*
Rick Griffith, *President*
C Barry Gipson, *Principal*
Aaron Canfield, *Technology*
C Clayton Johnson, *Admin Sec*
EMP: 26
SQ FT: 5,000
SALES (est): 152.4MM Privately Held
SIC: 3731 7699 4491 Barges, building & repairing; cargo vessels, building & repairing; aircraft & heavy equipment repair services; marine cargo handling

(G-17288)
MICHAEL N WHEELER
Also Called: Phoenix Hydraulics and Contrls
1004 4th St E (45680-9129)
PHONE 740 377-9777
Michael N Wheeler, *Owner*
EMP: 10
SQ FT: 12,500
SALES (est): 800K Privately Held
WEB: www.phoenixhyd.com
SIC: 3592 Valves

(G-17289)
MINOVA USA INC
101 Valley Dr (45680-1300)
P.O. Box 263, Bowerston (44695-0263)
PHONE 740 377-9146
EMP: 52 Privately Held
SIC: 2821 3564 2439 Plastics materials & resins; blowers & fans; structural wood members
HQ: Minova Usa Inc.
150 Summer Ct
Georgetown KY 40324
502 863-6800

(G-17290)
MOTORCARBON ELEMENTS LLC ✪
600 Technology Dr (45680-8062)
P.O. Box 481 (45680-0481)
PHONE 304 617-4047
Don Lee, *Manager*
EMP: 4 EST: 2018
SALES (est): 156.7K
SALES (corp-wide): 196.1K Privately Held
SIC: 2819 Mfg Industrial Inorganic Chemicals

PA: Motorcarbon Llc
1264 Waterfront Dr
Mount Pleasant SC
843 345-3444

(G-17291)
PRECISIONS PAINT SYSTEMS LLC
5852 County Road 1 (45680-7420)
PHONE 740 894-6224
Michael Manns, *CEO*
EMP: 10
SALES (est): 409.5K Privately Held
SIC: 2851 Marine paints

(G-17292)
PYRO-CHEM CORPORATION
Also Called: Better Foam Insulation
2491 County Road 1 (45680-7879)
P.O. Box 884 (45680-0884)
PHONE 740 377-2244
Joseph P Smith, *President*
Gailene M Smith, *Corp Secy*
EMP: 14
SQ FT: 12,000
SALES (est): 4.5MM Privately Held
SIC: 2899 Fire retardant chemicals

(G-17293)
REFRIGERATION INDUSTRIES CORP
719 County Road 1 (45680-8881)
P.O. Box 617 (45680-0617)
PHONE 740 377-9166
John Smith, *President*
EMP: 12
SALES (est): 2.8MM Privately Held
SIC: 3585 Refrigeration equipment, complete

(G-17294)
SAFE RX PHARMACIES INC
503 4th St E (45680-9101)
PHONE 740 377-4162
W Kent Freeman, *Principal*
EMP: 3
SALES (est): 189.3K Privately Held
SIC: 2834 Pharmaceutical Preparations

(G-17295)
SUPERIOR MARINE WAYS INC (PA)
5852 County Road 1 (45680-7420)
P.O. Box 519 (45680-0519)
PHONE 740 894-6224
Robert McCune, *President*
Jeff Irby, *Vice Pres*
Matt Manns, *Vice Pres*
Michael Manns, *CFO*
Brenda McGlone, *Human Res Mgr*
EMP: 3
SQ FT: 10,000
SALES (est): 16.3MM Privately Held
WEB: www.superiormarine.on.ca
SIC: 3731 4492 Tugboats, building & repairing; barges, building & repairing; towing & tugboat service

South Salem
Ross County

(G-17296)
BRETT PURDUM
10989 Cropp St (45681-9784)
PHONE 740 626-2890
Brett Purdum, *Principal*
EMP: 6
SALES (est): 503.3K Privately Held
SIC: 2411 Logging

South Vienna
Clark County

(G-17297)
JOHNSONS LAMP SHOP & ANTQ CO
8518 E National Rd (45369-8772)
PHONE 937 568-4551
Denna L Johnson, *Owner*
EMP: 4

SQ FT: 6,500
SALES (est): 266.2K Privately Held
SIC: 5719 7629 3641 Lighting, lamps & accessories; lamp repair & mounting; lamps, fluorescent, electric; lamps, incandescent filament, electric

South Webster
Scioto County

(G-17298)
MAE MATERIALS LLC
8336 Bennett School House (45682-9029)
PHONE 740 778-2242
Mark Allard, *Mng Member*
Margaret Allard,
EMP: 23 EST: 2012
SQ FT: 108,900
SALES: 5MM Privately Held
SIC: 2951 Asphalt paving mixtures & blocks

(G-17299)
ROGER HALL
Also Called: Hall Trencher Service
429 Railroad Hollow Rd (45682-8910)
P.O. Box 507 (45682-0507)
PHONE 740 778-2861
Roger Hall, *CEO*
EMP: 3
SALES (est): 183.9K Privately Held
SIC: 1442 Construction sand & gravel

(G-17300)
WARNER HILDEBRANT
714 Bear Run Rd (45682-9024)
PHONE 740 286-1903
Warner O Hildebrant, *Partner*
Anthony Wayne Hildebrant, *Partner*
Louise Hildebrant, *Partner*
EMP: 3
SALES (est): 198.5K Privately Held
SIC: 2411 Logging

South Zanesville
Muskingum County

(G-17301)
BAILEYS ASPHALT SEALING
2092 Newark Rd (43701-9635)
PHONE 740 453-9409
EMP: 10
SALES (est): 510K Privately Held
SIC: 1799 2951 1771 1611 Trade Contractor Mfg Asphalt Mixtures/Blocks Concrete Contractor Highway/Street Cnstn

Southington
Trumbull County

(G-17302)
QUALITY MATCH PLATE CO
4211 State Route 534 (44470-9705)
PHONE 330 889-2462
James W Dittrich, *President*
Genevieve Dittrich, *Corp Secy*
Alexis Dittrich, *Treasurer*
EMP: 18
SQ FT: 6,200
SALES (est): 3.3MM Privately Held
WEB: www.qualitymatchplate.com
SIC: 3365 Utensils, cast aluminum

Spencer
Medina County

(G-17303)
ALTA MIRA CORPORATION
Also Called: Spencer Forge & Manufacturing
225 N Main St (44275-9759)
PHONE 330 648-2461
Laurence E Rich, *President*
Deborah Rich, *Corp Secy*
Kirk Jordan, *Manager*
EMP: 86
SQ FT: 83,000

SALES (est): 17.5MM Privately Held
SIC: 3714 3462 Axles, motor vehicle; iron & steel forgings

(G-17304)
GILES LOGGING LLC
7340 Richman Rd (44275-9736)
PHONE 406 855-5284
Wade Giles, *Principal*
EMP: 3 EST: 2016
SALES (est): 96.4K Privately Held
SIC: 2411 Logging

(G-17305)
JOHN BAIRD
Also Called: Temple Architectural Products
12646 Lovers Lane Rd (44275-9509)
PHONE 216 440-3595
John Baird, *Owner*
EMP: 4
SALES: 1.5MM Privately Held
SIC: 3444 Metal roofing & roof drainage equipment

(G-17306)
SPENCER MANUFACTURING COMPANY
Also Called: Spencer Forge & Manufacturing
225 N Main St (44275-9759)
P.O. Box 68 (44275-0068)
PHONE 330 648-2461
Larry E Rich, *President*
EMP: 70
SALES (est): 11.7MM Privately Held
WEB: www.spencer-forge.com
SIC: 3714 3542 Mfg Motor Vehicle Parts/Accessories Mfg Machine Tools-Forming

(G-17307)
TATER TOOL & DIE INC
11145 Old Mill Rd (44275-9536)
PHONE 330 648-1148
John J Raida, *President*
EMP: 8
SALES (est): 667.3K Privately Held
SIC: 3544 Special dies & tools

Spencerville
Allen County

(G-17308)
D&M FENCING LLC
08656 Deep Cut Rd (45887-9315)
PHONE 419 604-0698
Matthew Wirth,
EMP: 3
SALES (est): 249.9K Privately Held
SIC: 3699 3315 5039 2411 Electric fence chargers; chain link fencing; wire fence, gates & accessories; rails, fence: round or split; snow fence lath;

(G-17309)
INNOCOR FOAM TECH - ACP INC
200 E North St (45887-1065)
P.O. Box 124 (45887-0124)
PHONE 419 647-4172
Sonny Raines, *Plant Mgr*
EMP: 17
SALES (corp-wide): 209.9MM Privately Held
SIC: 2515 2392 3069 Mattresses & foundations; cushions & pillows; bathmats, rubber
HQ: Innocor Foam Technologies - Acp, Inc.
200 Schulz Dr Ste 2
Red Bank NJ 07701
732 945-6222

(G-17310)
N BASS BAIT CO
08780 Deep Cut Rd (45887-9315)
PHONE 419 647-4501
Ron Perrine, *President*
Judith Perrine, *Admin Sec*
EMP: 3
SALES (est): 181.5K Privately Held
SIC: 3949 Lures, fishing: artificial

Spencerville - Allen County (G-17311) GEOGRAPHIC SECTION

(G-17311)
OHIO DECORATIVE PRODUCTS LLC (PA)
220 S Elizabeth St (45887-1315)
P.O. Box 126 (45887-0126)
PHONE.................................419 647-9033
Charles D Moeller, *President*
Candace Moeller, *President*
George J Bowers, *Principal*
Charles E Neuman, *Principal*
Donald L Jerwers, *Corp Secy*
◆ EMP: 135
SQ FT: 5,000
SALES (est): 172.5MM **Privately Held**
SIC: 3086 3369 3471 3363 Plastics foam products; zinc & zinc-base alloy castings, except die-castings; plating & polishing; aluminum die-castings

(G-17312)
RELIABLE BUFFING CO INC
Also Called: Reliable Buffing & Polishing
222 N College St (45887-1222)
PHONE.................................419 647-4432
Donald Comer, *President*
Crete Mueller, *President*
Don Comer, *Vice Pres*
Darlene Comer, *Treasurer*
EMP: 6 EST: 1948
SQ FT: 1,050
SALES (est): 601.2K **Privately Held**
SIC: 3471 Buffing for the trade; polishing, metals or formed products

(G-17313)
RURAL IRON WORKS LLC
510 N Saint Marys Rd (45887-9602)
PHONE.................................419 647-4617
Helen Wiechart, *Owner*
John A Wiechart, *Mng Member*
William J Wiechart, *Mng Member*
EMP: 5 EST: 1975
SQ FT: 5,000
SALES (est): 582.3K **Privately Held**
SIC: 3315 3496 3446 Fence gates posts & fittings: steel; miscellaneous fabricated wire products; architectural metalwork

(G-17314)
S I DISTRIBUTING INC
Also Called: Holland Grills Distributing
13540 Spencerville Rd (45887-9525)
PHONE.................................419 647-4909
Dave Durgei, *President*
Todd Keysor, *Principal*
Karen Keysor, *Assistant*
▲ EMP: 13
SQ FT: 22,000
SALES (est): 3.1MM **Privately Held**
WEB: www.sidist.com
SIC: 3523 5083 5023 Cabs, tractors & agricultural machinery; agricultural machinery & equipment; grills, barbecue

Spring Valley
Greene County

(G-17315)
ADVANCED TELEMETRICS INTL
Also Called: A T I
2361 Darnell Dr (45370-8708)
PHONE.................................937 862-6948
Phillip Merrill, *President*
Michael Cartmell, *Purchasing*
EMP: 11
SQ FT: 3,000
SALES (est): 1.2MM **Privately Held**
WEB: www.atitelemetry.com
SIC: 3663 Telemetering equipment, electronic

(G-17316)
EXCELSIOR SOLUTIONS
1742 River Ridge Dr (45370-9777)
PHONE.................................937 848-2569
Timothy J Murphy, *Principal*
EMP: 3 EST: 2010
SALES (est): 149.4K **Privately Held**
SIC: 3053 Packing materials

(G-17317)
MAX MIGHTY INC
Also Called: Advanced Wire and Cable
2434 Darnell Dr (45370-8710)
P.O. Box 98, Xenia (45385-0098)
PHONE.................................937 862-9530
Joann Merrill, *Ch of Bd*
Terry M Merrill, *President*
EMP: 12
SQ FT: 11,500
SALES (est): 1.7MM **Privately Held**
WEB: www.advancedwire.com
SIC: 5063 3355 Wire & cable; aluminum wire & cable

(G-17318)
SAILORS TAILOR INC
Also Called: Bean Bag City
1480 Spg Vly Paintrs Rd (45370-9701)
PHONE.................................937 862-7781
Robert Rowland, *President*
Sandra Rowland, *Manager*
EMP: 9 EST: 1972
SQ FT: 2,400
SALES (est): 750K **Privately Held**
WEB: www.sailorstailor.com
SIC: 2394 2519 5712 5551 Liners & covers, fabric: made from purchased materials; sails: made from purchased materials; household furniture, except wood or metal: upholstered; furniture stores; marine supplies & equipment; sails & equipment; textile bags; furniture & furnishings, mail order

Springboro
Warren County

(G-17319)
ADVANCED ENGRG SOLUTIONS INC
Also Called: Aesi
250 Advanced Dr (45066-1802)
PHONE.................................937 743-6900
Khang Do, *President*
Thomas J Harrington, *Principal*
Pat Croskey, *Program Mgr*
Jim Haws, *Manager*
EMP: 70
SQ FT: 44,000
SALES (est): 12.9MM **Privately Held**
SIC: 8711 3544 Consulting engineer; special dies, tools, jigs & fixtures

(G-17320)
ADVANCED INTR SOLUTIONS INC
250 Advanced Dr (45066-1802)
PHONE.................................937 550-0065
Jeffrey S Senney, *Principal*
▲ EMP: 48
SALES (est): 6.8MM **Privately Held**
SIC: 3544 Special dies, tools, jigs & fixtures

(G-17321)
ALFONS HAAR INC
150 Advanced Dr (45066-1800)
PHONE.................................937 560-2031
Thomas Haar, *President*
Betty Vankerkoerle, *Purchasing*
Bernd Haar, *Treasurer*
Bryan Johnson, *Marketing Staff*
▲ EMP: 31
SQ FT: 5,000
SALES (est): 8MM
SALES (corp-wide): 53.1MM **Privately Held**
WEB: www.alfonshaar.com
SIC: 5084 3599 8711 Packaging machinery & equipment; custom machinery; engineering services
PA: Alfons Haar Maschinenbau Gmbh & Co. Kg
   Fangdieckstr. 67
   Hamburg 22547
   408 339-10

(G-17322)
AMERICAN EXTRUSION SVCS INC (DH)
235 Advanced Dr (45066-1803)
PHONE.................................937 743-1210
David Allison, *President*
EMP: 6
SQ FT: 15,000
SALES (est): 1.6MM
SALES (corp-wide): 1.2B **Publicly Held**
SIC: 3544 Manufacturing Dies/Tools/Jigs/Fixtures

(G-17323)
BUCKEYE FABRICATING CO
245 S Pioneer Blvd (45066-1180)
PHONE.................................937 746-9822
Richard K Macaulay, *President*
Joe Luthman, *Sales Engr*
Teri Macaulay, *Admin Sec*
▼ EMP: 35 EST: 1963
SQ FT: 20,000
SALES (est): 8.3MM **Privately Held**
WEB: www.buckeyefabricating.com
SIC: 3443 Tanks, standard or custom fabricated: metal plate

(G-17324)
CARO MEDICAL LLC
6791 Bunnell Hill Rd (45066-9105)
PHONE.................................937 604-8600
Robert Jarrell, *Principal*
EMP: 4 EST: 2017
SALES (est): 164.1K **Privately Held**
SIC: 3842 Implants, surgical

(G-17325)
DIGILUBE SYSTEMS INC
216 E Mill St (45066-1614)
PHONE.................................937 748-2209
David Hamilton, *President*
Sherri Sutter, *Purchasing*
Lindsay Hamilton, *Corp Comm Staff*
Rocky Willis, *Marketing Staff*
Diane Hursh, *Technology*
EMP: 10
SQ FT: 5,000
SALES (est): 1.8MM **Privately Held**
WEB: www.digilube.com
SIC: 3569 2992 5084 5172 Lubricating equipment; oils & greases, blending & compounding; conveyor systems; lubricating oils & greases

(G-17326)
F & K CONCEPTS INC
Also Called: Fkci
264 Hiawatha Trl (45066-3010)
PHONE.................................937 426-6843
Don Booher, *Vice Pres*
EMP: 4
SALES (est): 350K **Privately Held**
WEB: www.fkci.com
SIC: 3479 5199 Engraving jewelry silverware, or metal; name plates: engraved, etched, etc.; advertising specialties

(G-17327)
FEATHER LITE INNOVATIONS INC (PA)
Also Called: Tuf-N-Lite
650 Pleasant Valley Dr (45066-3026)
PHONE.................................937 743-9008
Dallas Meyers, *President*
Brent Cox, *Vice Pres*
▲ EMP: 20
SALES (est): 6.4MM **Privately Held**
SIC: 3444 5211 Concrete forms, sheet metal; masonry materials & supplies

(G-17328)
GENERAL DYNAMICS-OTS INC
200 S Pioneer Blvd (45066-1179)
PHONE.................................937 746-8500
Adam Stone, *Export Mgr*
Anne-Marie Stanley, *Director*
EMP: 150
SQ FT: 220,000
SALES (corp-wide): 36.1B **Publicly Held**
SIC: 3489 Ordnance & accessories
HQ: General Dynamics-Ots, Inc.
   11399 16th Ct N Ste 200
   Saint Petersburg FL 33716
   727 578-8100

(G-17329)
GRAPHIC SYSTEMS SERVICES INC
Also Called: G S S
400 S Pioneer Blvd (45066-3001)
PHONE.................................937 746-0708
Daniel L Green, *President*
James Copeland, *Corp Secy*
John Sillies, *Exec VP*
John Fillies, *Opers Staff*
Kim Sweet, *Purch Agent*
EMP: 41
SQ FT: 100,000
SALES (est): 6.6MM **Privately Held**
WEB: www.gsspress.com
SIC: 7699 3555 Industrial equipment services; printing presses

(G-17330)
HIGH CONCRETE GROUP LLC
95 Mound Park Dr (45066-2402)
PHONE.................................937 748-2412
Misty Black, *General Mgr*
Dennis Nemenz, *Branch Mgr*
EMP: 158
SALES (corp-wide): 434.6MM **Privately Held**
SIC: 3272 Concrete stuctural support & building material; wall & ceiling squares, concrete; panels & sections, prefabricated concrete
HQ: High Concrete Group Llc
   125 Denver Rd
   Denver PA 17517
   717 336-9300

(G-17331)
JK DIGITAL PUBLISHING LLC
Also Called: Greyden Press
20 Heatherwoode Cir (45066-1500)
P.O. Box 224, Middlebranch (44652-0224)
PHONE.................................937 299-0185
Michael Jarosz,
George R Klein,
EMP: 20
SQ FT: 7,500
SALES (est): 3.5MM **Privately Held**
WEB: www.greydenpress.com
SIC: 2752 3652 Commercial printing, lithographic; compact laser discs, prerecorded

(G-17332)
KASKELL MANUFACTURING INC
240 Hiawatha Trl (45066-3010)
PHONE.................................937 704-9700
Diane W Harris, *President*
Brian Harris, *Vice Pres*
Brent Collinsworth, *Plant Mgr*
EMP: 10
SQ FT: 4,500
SALES (est): 1.8MM **Privately Held**
SIC: 3599 Machine shop, jobbing & repair

(G-17333)
KELCHNER INC (DH)
50 Advanced Dr (45066-1805)
PHONE.................................937 704-9890
Todd Kelchner, *CEO*
Troy Norvell, *President*
Kelly Dawson, *Superintendent*
Jeff Kelchner, *Vice Pres*
Jeremy White, *Project Mgr*
EMP: 134 EST: 1948
SQ FT: 8,600
SALES: 93MM
SALES (corp-wide): 5.3B **Privately Held**
SIC: 1794 1389 Excavation work; mud service, oil field drilling; bailing wells
HQ: Wood Group Uk Limited
   15 Justice Mill Lane
   Aberdeen AB11
   122 437-3772

(G-17334)
KLOSTERMAN BAKING CO
350 S Pioneer Blvd (45066-1181)
PHONE.................................937 743-9021
EMP: 10
SALES (corp-wide): 207.2MM **Privately Held**
SIC: 2051 Bread, cake & related products
PA: Klosterman Baking Co.
   4760 Paddock Rd
   Cincinnati OH 45229
   513 242-5667

(G-17335)
KROGER CO
725 W Central Ave (45066-1113)
PHONE.................................937 743-5900
Daniel Wiley, *Manager*
EMP: 150

SALES (corp-wide): 121.1B **Publicly Held**
WEB: www.kroger.com
SIC: 5411 2051 Supermarkets, chain; bread, cake & related products
PA: The Kroger Co
1014 Vine St Ste 1000
Cincinnati OH 45202
513 762-4000

(G-17336)
MACHINED GLASS SPECIALIST INC
245 Hiawatha Trl (45066-3011)
PHONE..................................937 743-6166
David Behm, *President*
Maurice Vines, *General Mgr*
Melanie Behm, *Admin Sec*
EMP: 16
SQ FT: 9,000
SALES (est): 3.1MM **Privately Held**
WEB: www.mgsquartz.com
SIC: 5039 3211 Glass construction materials; tempered glass

(G-17337)
MOUND STEEL CORP
25 Mound Park Dr (45066-2410)
PHONE..................................937 748-2937
Thomas C Miller, *CEO*
EMP: 40
SALES (est): 7.2MM **Privately Held**
WEB: www.heartlandholdingsinc.com
SIC: 3449 Bars, concrete reinforcing; fabricated steel

(G-17338)
MOUND TECHNOLOGIES INC
25 Mound Park Dr (45066-2402)
PHONE..................................937 748-2937
Thomas Miller, *President*
John Barger, *Vice Pres*
Luke Brongersma, *Project Mgr*
Troy Stevens, *Project Mgr*
Teresa Profitt, *Purch Mgr*
EMP: 45
SQ FT: 40,000
SALES: 20.9MM
SALES (corp-wide): 38.1MM **Privately Held**
WEB: www.moundtechnologies.com
SIC: 3441 1791 3446 Building components, structural steel; structural steel erection; gates, ornamental metal; grillwork, ornamental metal
PA: Heartland, Inc.
1005 N 19th St
Middlesboro KY 40965
606 248-7323

(G-17339)
NO RINSE LABORATORIES LLC
Also Called: Cleanlife Products
868 Pleasant Valley Dr (45066-1159)
PHONE..................................937 746-7357
Cathy Guntle, *Office Mgr*
Greg Davis,
Becky Brock, *Admin Asst*
EMP: 7
SQ FT: 6,000
SALES (est): 1.3MM **Privately Held**
WEB: www.norinse.com
SIC: 2836 Veterinary biological products

(G-17340)
OUR VOICE INITIATIVE INC
Also Called: Ourvoiceusa
237 Creekside Dr (45066-3068)
PHONE..................................740 974-4303
Samuel Ronan, *Principal*
Corey Henderson, *Director*
EMP: 19
SALES (est): 367.6K **Privately Held**
SIC: 7372 8399 Application computer software; social services

(G-17341)
OVONIC ENERGY PRODUCTS INC
50 Ovonic Way (45066-1184)
PHONE..................................937 743-1001
Gary Absher, *Vice Pres*
EMP: 125
SQ FT: 80,000
SALES (est): 10.2MM
SALES (corp-wide): 301.8MM **Privately Held**
WEB: www.cobasys.com
SIC: 3691 Storage batteries
HQ: Robert Bosch Battery Systems Llc
3740 S Lapeer Rd
Orion MI 48359

(G-17342)
PAPER SYSTEMS INCORPORATED (PA)
Also Called: PSI
185 S Pioneer Blvd (45066-3045)
P.O. Box 150 (45066-0150)
PHONE..................................937 746-6841
Larry Curk, *CEO*
Bob Phillips, *President*
Lee Wagoner, *President*
George Tremoulis, *Vice Pres*
Byron Cates, *Plant Mgr*
◆ EMP: 120 EST: 1975
SQ FT: 90,000
SALES (est): 75.1MM **Privately Held**
WEB: www.papersystems.com
SIC: 2679 Paper products, converted; telegraph, teletype & adding machine paper

(G-17343)
PHYMET INC
75 N Pioneer Blvd (45066-3055)
PHONE..................................937 743-8061
Amy Minck Lachman, *President*
Sondra Seay, *Human Res Mgr*
EMP: 17
SQ FT: 12,500
SALES (est): 3.3MM **Privately Held**
WEB: www.phymet.com
SIC: 2992 8734 Oils & greases, blending & compounding; metallurgical testing laboratory

(G-17344)
PIONEER AUTOMOTIVE TECH INC (DH)
100 S Pioneer Blvd (45066-1177)
PHONE..................................937 746-2293
Steven Moerner, *President*
Tina Groves, *Production*
Mike Honda, *Treasurer*
▲ EMP: 175
SQ FT: 155,000
SALES (est): 81.1MM
SALES (corp-wide): 3.4B **Privately Held**
SIC: 5013 3714 3651 Motor vehicle supplies & new parts; motor vehicle parts & accessories; household audio & video equipment
HQ: Pioneer North America, Inc.
2050 W 190th St Ste 100
Torrance CA 90504
310 952-2000

(G-17345)
PRINTING FOR LESS
45 Tahlequah Trl (45066-1154)
PHONE..................................937 743-8268
Steve Atkinson, *Owner*
Lee Ann, *Owner*
EMP: 5
SALES (est): 388.2K **Privately Held**
SIC: 2752 Commercial printing, lithographic

(G-17346)
PROMATCH SOLUTIONS LLC
20 Heatherwoode Cir (45066-1500)
PHONE..................................937 299-0185
Jeffrey R Relick, *President*
EMP: 15
SQ FT: 11,500
SALES (est): 1.6MM **Privately Held**
SIC: 2741 7375 2789 2752 Micropublishing; information retrieval services; bookbinding & related work; commercial printing, lithographic

(G-17347)
QUICK TECH BUSINESS FORMS INC
408 Sharts Dr (45066-3000)
P.O. Box 607 (45066-0607)
PHONE..................................937 743-5952
Chris Felker, *Principal*
Linda Felker, *Principal*
Kevin Gilliam, *Manager*
EMP: 50
SALES (est): 6.2MM **Privately Held**
WEB: www.quicktechgraphics.com
SIC: 2759 3999 Financial note & certificate printing & engraving; barber & beauty shop equipment

(G-17348)
QUICK TECH GRAPHICS INC
408 Sharts Dr Frnt (45066-3021)
P.O. Box 607 (45066-0607)
PHONE..................................937 743-5952
Christopher H Felker, *President*
Linda Felker, *Principal*
EMP: 35
SQ FT: 15,000
SALES: 7MM **Privately Held**
SIC: 2761 5943 2791 2782 Manifold business forms; office forms & supplies; typesetting; blankbooks & looseleaf binders; commercial printing, lithographic

(G-17349)
R L DRAKE HOLDINGS LLC (HQ)
710 Pleasant Valley Dr (45066-1157)
PHONE..................................937 746-4556
Robert Lee, *General Mgr*
Brian Wilkin, *Chief Engr*
Josh Blanton, *Engineer*
Phil Hawkins, *Sales Mgr*
Bob Palle, *Mng Member*
▲ EMP: 13
SALES (est): 2.5MM
SALES (corp-wide): 21.7MM **Publicly Held**
SIC: 3663 Satellites, communications
PA: Blonder Tongue Laboratories, Inc.
1 Jake Brown Rd
Old Bridge NJ 08857
732 679-4000

(G-17350)
R SPORTSWEAR LLC
8068 Forest Glen Dr (45066-9145)
PHONE..................................937 748-3507
Ron Coates, *Mng Member*
EMP: 4 EST: 1994
SALES (est): 325.4K **Privately Held**
SIC: 2395 3552 Embroidery & art needlework; silk screens for textile industry

(G-17351)
RCT INDUSTRIES INC
Also Called: Adcura Mfg
7494 Deep Woods Ct (45066-8554)
PHONE..................................937 602-1100
Russell Thie, *President*
EMP: 10
SQ FT: 4,000
SALES: 500K **Privately Held**
WEB: www.adcuramfg.com
SIC: 3679 Electronic circuits

(G-17352)
ROBERT BOSCH BTRY SYSTEMS LLC
50 Ovonic Way (45066-1184)
PHONE..................................937 743-1001
Matt Jonas, *Branch Mgr*
EMP: 100
SALES (corp-wide): 301.8MM **Privately Held**
WEB: www.cobasys.com
SIC: 3691 Storage batteries
HQ: Robert Bosch Battery Systems Llc
3740 S Lapeer Rd
Orion MI 48359

(G-17353)
SMITTEN ENTERPRISES LLC
205 S Main St (45066-1325)
PHONE..................................937 267-6963
EMP: 5
SALES (est): 351.3K **Privately Held**
SIC: 2331 Women's & misses' blouses & shirts

(G-17354)
SUNSTAR ENGRG AMERICAS INC (HQ)
85 S Pioneer Blvd (45066-3039)
PHONE..................................937 746-8575
Yoshikazu Kuwahara, *President*
David Egge, *Sales Engr*
Jason Kingrey, *Associate*
▲ EMP: 105
SQ FT: 28,000
SALES (est): 26.4MM **Privately Held**
SIC: 3751 2891 Motorcycles & related parts; adhesives
PA: Starlecs Inc.
3-1, Asahimachi
Takatsuki OSK
726 825-552

(G-17355)
THALER MACHINE COMPANY
216 Tahlequah Trl (45066-3052)
P.O. Box 430 (45066-0430)
PHONE..................................937 550-2400
Gregory Donson, *Manager*
EMP: 5
SALES (corp-wide): 14MM **Privately Held**
WEB: www.thalermachine.com
SIC: 3545 Precision measuring tools
PA: The Thaler Machine Company
216 Tahlequah Trl
Springboro OH 45066
937 550-2400

(G-17356)
TOOLING ZONE INC
285 S Pioneer Blvd (45066-1180)
PHONE..................................937 550-4180
Steven D Iiams, *President*
EMP: 30
SQ FT: 9,000
SALES (est): 6.4MM **Privately Held**
SIC: 3544 Special dies & tools

(G-17357)
TOTAL CABLE SOLUTIONS INC
475 Victory Ln (45066-3047)
PHONE..................................513 457-7013
Charles Hoskins, *CEO*
Paul Kirk, *President*
Jim Farrell, *Client Mgr*
Lee Sandy, *Sales Staff*
▲ EMP: 9
SALES (est): 1.8MM **Privately Held**
SIC: 3679 Harness assemblies for electronic use: wire or cable

(G-17358)
TREBNICK SYSTEMS INC
Also Called: Trebnick Tags and Labels
215 S Pioneer Blvd (45066-1180)
PHONE..................................937 743-1550
Gregg Trebnick, *CEO*
Linda Trebnick, *President*
Aaron Trebnick, *Vice Pres*
◆ EMP: 29
SQ FT: 24,480
SALES (est): 5.8MM **Privately Held**
WEB: www.trebnick.com
SIC: 2752 2759 Tags, lithographed; bags, plastic: printing; decals: printing; tags: printing; flexographic printing

Springfield
Clark County

(G-17359)
A & E POWDER COATING LTD
1511 Sheridan Ave (45505-2257)
P.O. Box 1226 (45501-1226)
PHONE..................................937 525-3750
Edward Leventhal, *President*
Mike Casto, *Plant Mgr*
EMP: 7
SALES (est): 943K **Privately Held**
WEB: www.aepowdercoating.com
SIC: 3479 Coating of metals & formed products

(G-17360)
ACE TRANSFER COMPANY
1017 Hometown St (45504-2000)
PHONE..................................937 398-1103
David J Shaw, *President*
EMP: 6 EST: 1994
SALES (est): 716.2K **Privately Held**
SIC: 2759 Screen printing

Springfield - Clark County (G-17361)

(G-17361)
AKZO NOBEL COATINGS INC
1550 Progress Rd (45505-4456)
PHONE.............................937 322-2671
Ron Cecil, *Enginr/R&D Mgr*
Tim Penington, *Maintence Staff*
EMP: 15
SALES (corp-wide): 11.3B **Privately Held**
WEB: www.nam.sikkens.com
SIC: 2851 Paints: oil or alkyd vehicle or water thinned
HQ: Akzo Nobel Coatings Inc.
  8220 Mohawk Dr
  Strongsville OH 44136
  440 297-5100

(G-17362)
AMCAN STAIR & RAIL LLC
20 Zischler St (45504-2853)
PHONE.............................937 781-3084
Mike Edmondson, *Principal*
EMP: 7
SALES (est): 772.4K **Privately Held**
SIC: 2431 Staircases, stairs & railings

(G-17363)
AOT INC
4800 Gateway Blvd (45502-8818)
PHONE.............................937 323-9669
Richard F Dauch, *CEO*
EMP: 21
SQ FT: 136,000
SALES (est): 4.6MM
SALES (corp-wide): 685.5MM **Privately Held**
SIC: 3559 Pack-up assemblies, wheel overhaul
HQ: Accuride Corporation
  7140 Office Cir
  Evansville IN 47715
  812 962-5000

(G-17364)
ARCTECH FABRICATING INC (PA)
1317 Lagonda Ave (45503-4001)
P.O. Box 1447 (45501-1447)
PHONE.............................937 525-9353
Leonard McConnaghey, *CEO*
James C Roberts II, *President*
Len McConnaughey, *Vice Pres*
Tim Bussen, *Sales Mgr*
Joe Wood, *Manager*
EMP: 29
SQ FT: 13,200
SALES (est): 5MM **Privately Held**
WEB: www.arctechfabricating.com
SIC: 7692 3441 Welding repair; fabricated structural metal

(G-17365)
ARMOLOY OF OHIO INC
1950 E Leffel Ln (45505-4623)
P.O. Box 996 (45501-0996)
PHONE.............................937 323-8702
Steven Neely, *President*
Cindy Ray, *Financial Exec*
Chris Neely, *Sales Staff*
EMP: 15
SQ FT: 10,000
SALES (est): 1.9MM **Privately Held**
WEB: www.armoloyofohio.com
SIC: 3479 Coating of metals & formed products

(G-17366)
B O K INC
508 W Main St (45504-2662)
PHONE.............................937 322-9588
Kenneth Klosterman, *CEO*
Chip Klosterman, *CEO*
Ken Klosterman, *CEO*
EMP: 125
SALES (est): 7.7MM
SALES (corp-wide): 207.2MM **Privately Held**
WEB: www.bok.net
SIC: 2045 Bread & bread type roll mixes: from purchased flour
PA: Klosterman Baking Co.
  4760 Paddock Rd
  Cincinnati OH 45229
  513 242-5667

(G-17367)
BAY BUSINESS FORMS INC
1803 W Columbia St (45504-2903)
PHONE.............................937 322-3000
Robert E Troop, *CEO*
Paulette Bay, *President*
EMP: 11
SQ FT: 22,000
SALES (est): 1MM
SALES (corp-wide): 87.9MM **Privately Held**
WEB: www.baybusinessforms.net
SIC: 5112 2752 Business forms; commercial printing, offset
PA: The Shamrock Companies Inc
  24090 Detroit Rd
  Westlake OH 44145
  440 899-9510

(G-17368)
BENJAMIN STEEL COMPANY INC
777 Benjamin Dr (45502-8846)
PHONE.............................937 233-1212
Vincent Demana, *Owner*
Shawn Taylor, *Branch Mgr*
EMP: 40
SQ FT: 36,000
SALES (corp-wide): 86.5MM **Privately Held**
WEB: www.benjaminsteel.com
SIC: 5051 3498 3334 3317 Steel; tube fabricating (contract bending & shaping); primary aluminum; steel pipe & tubes; cold finishing of steel shapes; blast furnaces & steel mills
PA: Benjamin Steel Company, Inc.
  777 Benjamin Dr
  Springfield OH 45502
  937 322-8600

(G-17369)
BRYCE HILL INC (PA)
2301 Sheridan Ave (45505-2515)
P.O. Box 1043 (45501-1043)
PHONE.............................937 325-0651
Deborah L Hill Grimes, *President*
EMP: 2
SALES (est): 7.9MM **Privately Held**
SIC: 3273 Ready-mixed concrete

(G-17370)
CASCADE CORPORATION
2501 Sheridan Ave (45505-2519)
P.O. Box 20187, Portland OR (97294-0187)
PHONE.............................937 327-0300
Rodney Hickman, *Plant Mgr*
Todd Henry, *Purch Agent*
James Taylor, *Engineer*
Shawn Allex, *Sales Engr*
Rodney Hitman, *Branch Mgr*
EMP: 200
SALES (corp-wide): 18.8B **Privately Held**
WEB: www.cascorp.com
SIC: 3537 3713 3593 Trucks, tractors, loaders, carriers & similar equipment; truck & bus bodies; fluid power cylinders & actuators
HQ: Cascade Corporation
  2201 Ne 201st Ave
  Fairview OR 97024
  503 669-6300

(G-17371)
CAVE TOOL & MANUFACTURING INC
20 Walnut St (45505-1145)
PHONE.............................937 324-0662
Gilbert R Cave, *President*
Carrie Cave, *Vice Pres*
EMP: 10
SQ FT: 26,000
SALES (est): 1.3MM **Privately Held**
SIC: 3599 Machine shop, jobbing & repair

(G-17372)
CENTERLINE MACHINE INC
4949 Urbana Rd (45502-8387)
PHONE.............................937 322-4887
EMP: 5
SQ FT: 2,000
SALES (est): 603.4K **Privately Held**
SIC: 3443 Mfg Fabricated Plate Work

(G-17373)
CES NATIONWIDE
567 E Leffel Ln (45505-4748)
PHONE.............................937 322-0771
John Lewis, *Principal*
EMP: 7
SALES (est): 523.1K **Privately Held**
SIC: 3699 3634 5063 Electrical equipment & supplies; electric housewares & fans; electrical supplies

(G-17374)
CHAMPION COMPANY (PA)
400 Harrison St (45505-2067)
P.O. Box 967 (45501-0967)
PHONE.............................937 324-5681
Aristides Gianakopoulos, *President*
Benjamin G Devoe, *Principal*
Bruce Harmison, *Manager*
EMP: 60 **EST:** 1878
SQ FT: 165,000
SALES (est): 12.3MM **Privately Held**
WEB: www.championspd.com
SIC: 2869 3412 Embalming fluids; metal barrels, drums & pails

(G-17375)
CHAMPION COMPANY
1100 Kenton St (45505)
PHONE.............................937 324-5681
Bob Rizer, *General Mgr*
EMP: 68
SALES (corp-wide): 12.3MM **Privately Held**
WEB: www.championspd.com
SIC: 3412 Metal barrels, drums & pails
PA: The Champion Company
  400 Harrison St
  Springfield OH 45505
  937 324-5681

(G-17376)
COFFELT CANDY INC (PA)
6050 Urbana Rd (45502-9544)
PHONE.............................937 399-8772
Dwight W Coffelt, *President*
Betty Coffelt, *Treasurer*
Elizabeth J Coffelt, *Treasurer*
EMP: 5 **EST:** 1941
SQ FT: 10,000
SALES (est): 2.8MM **Privately Held**
WEB: www.coffeltcandy.com
SIC: 5441 2064 Candy; candy & other confectionery products

(G-17377)
COLBY PROPERTIES LLC
2071 N Bechtle Ave (45504-1583)
PHONE.............................937 390-0816
Alan Cowgill,
Julie Cowgill,
EMP: 6
SALES (est): 565.2K **Privately Held**
SIC: 3999 Education aids, devices & supplies

(G-17378)
COMPTONS PRECISION MACHINE
Also Called: Eastern Enterprise
224 Dayton Ave (45506-1206)
P.O. Box 2614 (45501-2614)
PHONE.............................937 325-9139
Fax: 937 325-4541
EMP: 12
SQ FT: 11,000
SALES: 1MM **Privately Held**
SIC: 3599 7692 Mfg Industrial Machinery Welding Repair

(G-17379)
CORROTEC INC
1125 W North St (45504-2713)
PHONE.............................937 325-3585
David A Stratton, *CEO*
Aristides G Gianakopoulos, *President*
Walter A Wildman, *Principal*
John C Stratton, *Vice Pres*
EMP: 35 **EST:** 1981
SQ FT: 28,500
SALES (est): 9.2MM **Privately Held**
WEB: www.corrotec.com
SIC: 3559 7699 3479 3625 Electroplating machinery & equipment; tank repair; coating of metals with plastic or resins; electric controls & control accessories, industrial

(G-17380)
CRANE PRO SERVICES
4401 Gateway Blvd (45502-9339)
PHONE.............................937 525-5555
George Berner, *Engineer*
EMP: 3
SALES (est): 130K **Privately Held**
SIC: 3531 Construction machinery

(G-17381)
CROWNING FOOD COMPANY
Also Called: Wober Muster
1966 Commerce Cir (45504-2012)
P.O. Box 388 (45501-0388)
PHONE.............................937 323-4699
Ray Woeber, *Owner*
◆ **EMP:** 85
SALES (est): 14.3MM **Privately Held**
SIC: 2035 Pickles, sauces & salad dressings

(G-17382)
CSL PLASMA INC
435 E Columbia St (45503-4214)
PHONE.............................937 325-4200
Jason Tate, *Branch Mgr*
Tracy Young, *Manager*
EMP: 44 **Privately Held**
SIC: 2836 Plasmas
HQ: Csl Plasma Inc.
  900 Broken Sound Pkwy Nw # 4
  Boca Raton FL 33487
  561 981-3700

(G-17383)
D L H LOCOMOTIVE WORKS
1528 Mitchell Blvd (45503-3415)
PHONE.............................937 629-0321
David L Hickinbotham, *Owner*
EMP: 6
SALES (est): 418.1K **Privately Held**
SIC: 3944 Railroad models: toy & hobby

(G-17384)
DEARTH RESOURCES INC (PA)
Also Called: Hill Bryce Concrete
2301 Sheridan Ave (45505-2515)
P.O. Box 1043 (45501-1043)
PHONE.............................937 325-0651
Debra Grimes, *Principal*
EMP: 9 **EST:** 1934
SQ FT: 20,000
SALES (est): 1.4MM **Privately Held**
WEB: www.brycehill.com
SIC: 3273 3271 5211 Ready-mixed concrete; blocks, concrete or cinder: standard; lumber & other building materials

(G-17385)
DEARTH RESOURCES INC
8801 State Route 36 (45501)
P.O. Box 1043 (45501-1043)
PHONE.............................937 663-4171
Debra Grimes, *President*
EMP: 8
SALES (corp-wide): 1.4MM **Privately Held**
WEB: www.brycehill.com
SIC: 3273 3271 Ready-mixed concrete; blocks, concrete or cinder: standard
PA: Dearth Resources, Inc.
  2301 Sheridan Ave
  Springfield OH 45505
  937 325-0651

(G-17386)
DELILLE OXYGEN COMPANY
1101 W Columbia St (45504-2846)
PHONE.............................937 325-9595
Mike Lee, *Manager*
EMP: 8
SALES (est): 1.4MM
SALES (corp-wide): 19.8MM **Privately Held**
WEB: www.delille.com
SIC: 2813 5084 Industrial gases; welding machinery & equipment

GEOGRAPHIC SECTION
Springfield - Clark County (G-17411)

PA: Delille Oxygen Company
772 Marion Rd
Columbus OH 43207
614 444-1177

(G-17387)
DELTA CRANE SYSTEMS INC
624 Aberfelda Dr (45504-3973)
PHONE 937 324-7425
Chris McCombs, *President*
Joyce McCombs, *Treasurer*
EMP: 10
SQ FT: 16,600
SALES: 1MM **Privately Held**
SIC: 3536 5084 Cranes, industrial plant; materials handling machinery

(G-17388)
DILLON MANUFACTURING INC
2115 Progress Rd (45505-4470)
PHONE 937 325-8482
Joseph Shouvlin, *President*
Jeremy Hays, *Opers Mgr*
Steve Foley, *Sales Staff*
EMP: 19 **EST:** 1953
SQ FT: 15,000
SALES (est): 2.4MM **Privately Held**
WEB: www.dillonmfg.com
SIC: 3545 Chucks: drill, lathe or magnetic (machine tool accessories)

(G-17389)
DMTCO LLC
302 S Center St (45506-1604)
P.O. Box 958 (45501-0958)
PHONE 937 324-0061
Malcolm Lovelace,
Duane J Newland,
Tony A Stevens,
EMP: 7
SQ FT: 1,100
SALES (est): 730K **Privately Held**
SIC: 3585 Refrigeration & heating equipment

(G-17390)
DOLE FRESH VEGETABLES INC
600 Benjamin Dr (45502-8860)
PHONE 937 525-4300
Elena Jordan, *Opers Mgr*
Melissa Cooley, *Plant Engr*
Michael Locke, *Controller*
Cathleen Entler, *Human Res Mgr*
Lenny Pelifian, *Branch Mgr*
EMP: 190
SALES (corp-wide): 11.5B **Privately Held**
SIC: 5148 2099 Fruits, fresh; food preparations
HQ: Dole Fresh Vegetables, Inc.
2959 Salinas Hwy
Monterey CA 93940
831 422-8871

(G-17391)
DRAKE MONUMENT COMPANY
524 W Mccreight Ave (45504-1606)
PHONE 937 399-7941
Linda Conley, *Partner*
Charles Thrist Jr, *Partner*
EMP: 4
SALES (est): 328.3K **Privately Held**
WEB: www.drakemonumentco.com
SIC: 5999 3281 Monuments, finished to custom order; cut stone & stone products

(G-17392)
DUPLEX MILL & MANUFACTURING CO
Also Called: Kelly Duplex
415 Sigler St (45505-1144)
P.O. Box 1266 (45501-1266)
PHONE 937 325-5555
Eric W Wise, *President*
Frederick Wise, *Vice Pres*
EMP: 20 **EST:** 1908
SQ FT: 50,000
SALES (est): 5.3MM **Privately Held**
WEB: www.dmmc.org
SIC: 3535 3531 Conveyors & conveying equipment; mixers: ore, plaster, slag, sand, mortar, etc.

(G-17393)
E & W ENTERPRISES POWELL INC (HQ)
Also Called: Muncy Co, The
2020 Progress Rd (45505-4472)
PHONE 937 346-0800
Wayne Brumfield, *President*
▲ **EMP:** 80 **EST:** 1946
SQ FT: 60,000
SALES (est): 11.2MM
SALES (corp-wide): 105.6MM **Privately Held**
SIC: 3465 Automotive stampings
PA: Jmac Inc.
200 W Nationwide Blvd # 1
Columbus OH 43215
614 436-2418

(G-17394)
ECHO EMR INC
2755 Columbus Rd (45503-3203)
PHONE 937 322-4972
Ronald K Hill, *President*
Pamela Chiles, *Plant Mgr*
▲ **EMP:** 15
SALES (est): 1.9MM **Privately Held**
SIC: 3229 Tubing, glass

(G-17395)
ELECTRIC EEL MFG CO INC
501 W Leffel Ln (45506-3529)
P.O. Box 419 (45501-0419)
PHONE 937 323-4644
David Hale, *CEO*
Thomas H Hale, *Vice Pres*
Tom Hale, *Officer*
Peggy Barnhart, *Admin Sec*
▲ **EMP:** 38 **EST:** 1968
SQ FT: 21,000
SALES (est): 8.7MM **Privately Held**
SIC: 3423 3589 Hand & edge tools; sewer cleaning equipment, power

(G-17396)
ENTERPRISE / AMERISEAL INC
33 Walnut St (45505-1144)
P.O. Box 88 (45501-0088)
PHONE 937 284-3003
Chuck Falloon, *Managing Dir*
▲ **EMP:** 5
SQ FT: 18,000
SALES (est): 620.9K **Privately Held**
SIC: 3069 Rubber automotive products

(G-17397)
ERNEST INDUSTRIES INC
Also Called: Kelly-Creswell Company
1221 Groop Rd (45504-3829)
PHONE 937 325-9851
Michael T Stute, *President*
Susan Stute, *Treasurer*
EMP: 11
SALES (est): 3.3MM **Privately Held**
WEB: www.ernestindustries.com
SIC: 3563 Air & gas compressors

(G-17398)
ESTERLINE & SONS MFG CO LLC
6508 Old Clifton Rd (45502-8474)
PHONE 937 265-5278
John Maurer, *Mng Member*
▲ **EMP:** 22 **EST:** 1957
SQ FT: 1,500
SALES (est): 4MM **Privately Held**
WEB: www.esterlineandsons.com
SIC: 3599 Machine shop, jobbing & repair

(G-17399)
EVER ROLL SPECIALTIES CO
3988 Lawrenceville Dr (45504-4458)
PHONE 937 964-1302
Edwin J Kohl, *President*
I Scott Wallace, *COO*
Mike Clark, *Engineer*
Rita Rethman, *Accountant*
▲ **EMP:** 50
SQ FT: 43,000
SALES (est): 10.4MM **Privately Held**
WEB: www.ever-roll.com
SIC: 3498 3496 Tube fabricating (contract bending & shaping); miscellaneous fabricated wire products

(G-17400)
F H BONN CO INC
4300 Gateway Blvd (45502-8819)
P.O. Box 12388, Fort Pierce FL (34979-2388)
PHONE 937 323-7024
Neal Bonn, *President*
Allan Bonn, *Corp Secy*
John Townsend, *Materials Mgr*
▲ **EMP:** 61
SQ FT: 43,000
SALES (est): 12.1MM **Privately Held**
WEB: www.fhbonn.com
SIC: 2211 Plushes & piles, broadwoven cotton: including flannels

(G-17401)
FAMILY PACKAGING INC (PA)
504 W Euclid Ave (45506-2010)
PHONE 937 325-4106
Janet Kennedy, *President*
Paul T Miles, *Vice Pres*
Michael A Miles, *VP Prdtn*
James Miles, *Treasurer*
EMP: 6
SQ FT: 47,000
SALES: 2MM **Privately Held**
SIC: 2653 Boxes, corrugated: made from purchased materials

(G-17402)
FINK MEAT COMPANY INC
2475 Troy Rd (45504-4233)
P.O. Box 1281 (45501-1281)
PHONE 937 390-2750
William Craig Minter, *President*
Douglas Minter, *Vice Pres*
EMP: 7
SQ FT: 8,600
SALES: 1.5MM **Privately Held**
SIC: 5147 2013 Meats, fresh; luncheon meat from purchased meat

(G-17403)
FLASHIONS SPORTSWEAR LTD
1002 N Bechtle Ave (45504-2008)
PHONE 937 323-5885
Bethany Turner, *Partner*
Ronald Turner, *General Ptnr*
Beth Turner, *Vice Pres*
EMP: 9
SQ FT: 4,000
SALES (est): 882.6K **Privately Held**
WEB: www.flashions.com
SIC: 5199 2262 Advertising specialties; screen printing: manmade fiber & silk broadwoven fabrics

(G-17404)
FLUID QUIP INC (PA)
1940 S Yellow Spring St # 2 (45506-3048)
PHONE 937 324-0352
Andy Franko, *President*
John McBlane, *Vice Pres*
Dan Rogusky, *Purch Mgr*
Dawn Duncan, *Purchasing*
Robert Patton, *Treasurer*
◆ **EMP:** 38
SQ FT: 50,000
SALES (est): 8MM **Privately Held**
WEB: www.fluidquip.com
SIC: 3554 Pulp mill machinery

(G-17405)
G & R WELDING & MACHINING
4690 E National Rd (45505-1846)
PHONE 937 323-9353
Ralph Rybolt, *Owner*
EMP: 3
SQ FT: 9,500
SALES (est): 500K **Privately Held**
SIC: 1799 3441 Welding on site; fabricated structural metal

(G-17406)
GAIL BERNER
Also Called: Berner Screen Print
514 W Columbia St (45504-2622)
PHONE 937 322-0314
Gail Berner, *Owner*
EMP: 3
SQ FT: 1,800
SALES: 350K **Privately Held**
WEB: www.bernerscreenprint.com
SIC: 2759 2395 5199 3993 Screen printing; embroidery products, except schiffli machine; advertising specialties; signs & advertising specialties; automotive & apparel trimmings

(G-17407)
GRAPHIC PAPER PRODUCTS CORP (HQ)
Also Called: Miller Printing Co
581 W Leffel Ln (45506-3529)
P.O. Box 1666 (45501-1666)
PHONE 937 325-5503
Jeanne Lampe, *President*
Paul Ripplinger, *Controller*
EMP: 82 **EST:** 1891
SQ FT: 50,000
SALES (est): 13MM
SALES (corp-wide): 58.5MM **Privately Held**
WEB: www.miller-printing.com
SIC: 2754 2752 2652 2653 Job printing, gravure; commercial printing, lithographic; setup paperboard boxes; boxes, corrugated: made from purchased materials; packaging paper; miscellaneous publishing
PA: Patented Acquisition Corporation
2490 Cross Pointe Dr
Miamisburg OH 45342
937 353-2299

(G-17408)
GRAPHIC PAPER PRODUCTS CORP
Also Called: Armstrong Printing
222 E Main St (45503-4222)
P.O. Box 166 (45501-0166)
PHONE 937 325-3912
Carol McCoy, *General Mgr*
EMP: 5
SALES (corp-wide): 58.5MM **Privately Held**
WEB: www.miller-printing.com
SIC: 2759 Commercial printing
HQ: Graphic Paper Products Corporation
581 W Leffel Ln
Springfield OH 45506
937 325-5503

(G-17409)
HAIR & NAIL IMPRESSIONS
2330 Northmoor Dr (45503-2344)
PHONE 937 399-0221
Cathy Fent, *Owner*
EMP: 4
SALES (est): 75.8K **Privately Held**
SIC: 7231 2844 Unisex hair salons; manicure preparations

(G-17410)
HALLMARK INDUSTRIES INC (PA)
Also Called: Miller, Jim Furniture
2233 N Limestone St (45503-2635)
P.O. Box 386, Enon (45323-0386)
PHONE 937 864-7378
James Odell Miller, *President*
Diane E Miller, *Vice Pres*
EMP: 25
SQ FT: 54,000
SALES (est): 2.2MM **Privately Held**
SIC: 2512 5712 Living room furniture: upholstered on wood frames; furniture stores

(G-17411)
HANGER PRSTHETCS & ORTHO INC
Also Called: Orpro Prosthetics & Orthotics
30 Warder St Ste 125 (45504-2580)
PHONE 937 325-5404
Randy Daniel, *Branch Mgr*
EMP: 4
SALES (corp-wide): 1B **Publicly Held**
SIC: 3842 Orthopedic & prosthesis applications
HQ: Hanger Prosthetics & Orthotics, Inc.
10910 Domain Dr Ste 300
Austin TX 78758
512 777-3800

Springfield - Clark County (G-17412)

(G-17412)
HAYS FABRICATING & WELDING
633 E Leffel Ln (45505-4750)
PHONE................................937 325-0031
Clayton Hays, *President*
Terry Cadle, *COO*
Jason Esmith, *Engineer*
Richard Shaw, *Sales Mgr*
EMP: 27
SQ FT: 25,000
SALES (est): 7MM **Privately Held**
WEB: www.haysfab.com
SIC: 3441 3555 Fabricated structural metal; plates, metal: engravers'

(G-17413)
HDI LANDING GEAR USA INC (HQ)
663 Montgomery Ave (45506-1847)
PHONE................................937 325-1586
Michael Meshay, *President*
William Michalski, *Treasurer*
Sarah Hendricks, *Manager*
EMP: 100
SALES (est): 37.6MM
SALES (corp-wide): 309.4MM **Privately Held**
SIC: 3728 Alighting (landing gear) assemblies, aircraft
PA: Heroux-Devtek Inc
  1111 Rue Saint-Charles O Bureau 658
  Longueuil QC J4K 5
  450 679-3330

(G-17414)
HEAT TREATING INC (PA)
1762 W Pleasant St (45506-1128)
PHONE................................937 325-3121
Chester L Walthall, *President*
Judith A Walthall, *Corp Secy*
Keith Thue, *Vice Pres*
Michael Trimble, *Vice Pres*
Dan Antrim, *Supervisor*
EMP: 25 **EST:** 1959
SQ FT: 33,000
SALES (est): 3.1MM **Privately Held**
WEB: www.heattreating.com
SIC: 3398 Metal heat treating

(G-17415)
HEAT TREATING INC
1807 W Pleasant St (45506-1199)
PHONE................................937 325-3121
Chester L Walthall, *President*
EMP: 17
SALES (corp-wide): 3.1MM **Privately Held**
WEB: www.heattreating.com
SIC: 3398 Metal heat treating
PA: Heat Treating, Inc
  1762 W Pleasant St
  Springfield OH 45506
  937 325-3121

(G-17416)
HEF USA CORPORATION (PA)
2015 Progress Rd (45505-4472)
PHONE................................937 323-2556
Kenneth Metzgar, *Principal*
▲ **EMP:** 15
SALES (est): 2.9MM **Privately Held**
WEB: www.hefusa.net
SIC: 3826 Surface area analyzers

(G-17417)
HEROUX-DEVTEK INC
Also Called: Heroux-Devtek Springfield
663 Montgomery Ave (45506-1847)
PHONE................................937 325-1586
Gilles Labbe, *President*
EMP: 19
SALES (est): 3MM **Privately Held**
SIC: 3728 Aircraft parts & equipment

(G-17418)
HILLTOP BASIC RESOURCES INC
Enon Washed Sand & Gravel Div
1665 Enon Rd (45502-9102)
PHONE................................937 882-6357
Jack Blair, *Principal*
EMP: 12
SALES (corp-wide): 116.7MM **Privately Held**
WEB: www.hilltopbasicresources.com
SIC: 1771 1442 Concrete work; construction sand & gravel
PA: Hilltop Basic Resources, Inc.
  1 W 4th St Ste 1100
  Cincinnati OH 45202
  513 651-5000

(G-17419)
HOLMES W & SONS PRINTING
Also Called: Holmes Printing
401 E Columbia St (45503-4214)
P.O. Box 2300 (45501-2300)
PHONE................................937 325-1509
William W Holmes, *President*
Carisa Home-Peters, *Executive*
Mike England, *Graphic Designe*
EMP: 14
SQ FT: 2,500
SALES (est): 1.8MM **Privately Held**
WEB: www.holmesprinting.com
SIC: 2752 Commercial printing, offset

(G-17420)
HORIZON INDUSTRIES CORP
1801 W Columbia St (45504-2903)
PHONE................................937 323-0801
John Neiswinger, *President*
Richard Koehler, *Treasurer*
EMP: 9
SQ FT: 15,000
SALES (est): 800K **Privately Held**
WEB: www.horizonindustriescorp.com
SIC: 3544 Special dies & tools

(G-17421)
HORNER INDUSTRIAL SERVICES INC
Also Called: Scherer Industrial Group
5330 Prosperity Dr (45502-9074)
PHONE................................937 390-6667
Michael Harper, *Director*
EMP: 25
SALES (corp-wide): 46.7MM **Privately Held**
SIC: 5063 7694 Motors, electric; electric motor repair
PA: Horner Industrial Services, Inc.
  1521 E Washington St
  Indianapolis IN 46201
  317 639-4261

(G-17422)
HOUSTON MACHINE PRODUCTS INC
1065 W Leffel Ln (45506-3555)
PHONE................................937 322-8022
Sandra White, *President*
Steve Houston, *Vice Pres*
Mark Crider, *Project Mgr*
Sandy White, *Executive*
EMP: 30 **EST:** 1970
SQ FT: 35,000
SALES (est): 5.2MM **Privately Held**
SIC: 3599 3541 3451 Machine shop, jobbing & repair; machine tools, metal cutting type; screw machine products

(G-17423)
HUGO BOSCA COMPANY INC (PA)
Also Called: Bosca Accesories
1905 W Jefferson St (45506-1117)
P.O. Box 777 (45501-0777)
PHONE................................937 323-5523
Christopher B Bosca, *President*
Brian Janetski, *Principal*
Cathy Gainer, *COO*
D'Orsi Bosca, *Vice Pres*
Dick Rabe, *CFO*
▲ **EMP:** 20 **EST:** 1911
SQ FT: 48,000
SALES (est): 6MM **Privately Held**
WEB: www.boscanet.com
SIC: 3171 3172 Handbags, women's; wallets

(G-17424)
HYNES MODERN PATTERN CO INC
2141 Erie Ave (45505-4712)
PHONE................................937 322-3451
Robert L Knox, *President*
EMP: 4 **EST:** 1920
SQ FT: 3,000
SALES: 200K **Privately Held**
SIC: 3543 3469 Industrial patterns; patterns on metal

(G-17425)
INTERTAPE POLYMR WOVEN USA INC
1800 E Pleasant St (45505-3316)
PHONE................................704 279-3011
EMP: 25
SQ FT: 85,000
SALES (corp-wide): 898.1MM **Privately Held**
SIC: 2231 Overcoatings: wool, mohair or similar fibers
HQ: Intertape Polymer Woven Usa Inc.
  100 Paramount Dr Ste 300
  Sarasota FL 34232
  800 474-8273

(G-17426)
JMS INDUSTRIES INC
Also Called: JMS Composites
3240 E National Rd (45505-1524)
P.O. Box 507 (45501-0507)
PHONE................................937 325-3502
Manjit Nagra, *CEO*
Jennifer Nagra, *Vice Pres*
Phil Cremeans, *Engineer*
▲ **EMP:** 21
SQ FT: 27,000
SALES (est): 4.7MM **Privately Held**
WEB: www.glasgoplastics.com
SIC: 2821 Molding compounds, plastics

(G-17427)
JOHN R JURGENSEN CO
1780 Enon Rd (45502-9169)
PHONE................................937 293-3112
Pete Flora, *Branch Mgr*
EMP: 3
SALES (corp-wide): 84MM **Privately Held**
WEB: www.jrjnet.com
SIC: 1622 2951 1611 Bridge, tunnel & elevated highway; asphalt paving mixtures & blocks; surfacing & paving
PA: John R. Jurgensen Co.
  11641 Mosteller Rd
  Cincinnati OH 45241
  513 771-0820

(G-17428)
K K TOOL CO
115 S Center St (45502-1203)
PHONE................................937 325-1373
John Koehler, *President*
Paula Odell, *Corp Secy*
Donald Koehler, *Vice Pres*
Edward Kurt Koehler, *Vice Pres*
Kristopher Kent Koehler, *Vice Pres*
EMP: 22
SALES (est): 4.6MM **Privately Held**
SIC: 3544 Special dies & tools

(G-17429)
K WM BEACH MFG CO INC
4655 Urbana Rd (45502-9503)
PHONE................................937 399-3838
William R Beach, *CEO*
Bret L Beach, *COO*
EMP: 200 **EST:** 1945
SQ FT: 125,000
SALES: 32.2MM **Privately Held**
WEB: www.kwmbeach.com
SIC: 3053 3714 Gaskets, all materials; motor vehicle parts & accessories

(G-17430)
KCI HOLDING USA INC (DH)
4401 Gateway Blvd (45502-9339)
PHONE................................937 525-5533
Bernie D'Ambrosi, *Senior VP*
Guy Shumaker, *Vice Pres*
Amy Corbisier, *Treasurer*
Steve Mayes, *Treasurer*
Todd Robenson, *Admin Sec*
◆ **EMP:** 340
SALES: 176.7MM
SALES (corp-wide): 3.7B **Privately Held**
SIC: 3536 Cranes, industrial plant
HQ: Konecranes Finance Oy
  Koneenkatu 8
  Hyvinkaa 05830
  204 271-1

(G-17431)
KEYAH INTERNATIONAL TRDG LLC (PA)
4655 Urbana Rd (45502-9503)
PHONE................................937 399-3140
Bret L Beach, *President*
Jim Fritts, *General Mgr*
Mark Henson, *Purch Mgr*
Marc Wells, *Director*
Brett L Beach,
▲ **EMP:** 20 **EST:** 2000
SQ FT: 30,000
SALES (est): 7.8MM **Privately Held**
WEB: www.keyahint.com
SIC: 2675 Die-cut paper & board

(G-17432)
KLOSTERMAN BAKING CO
508 W Main St (45504-2662)
PHONE................................937 322-9588
Lewis Banner, *Principal*
EMP: 18
SALES (corp-wide): 207.2MM **Privately Held**
SIC: 2051 Bakery: wholesale or wholesale/retail combined
PA: Klosterman Baking Co.
  4760 Paddock Rd
  Cincinnati OH 45229
  513 242-5667

(G-17433)
KONECRANES INC
Also Called: Americas Components
4505 Gateway Blvd (45502-8863)
PHONE................................937 328-5100
Troy Posts, *Manager*
EMP: 50
SALES (corp-wide): 3.7B **Privately Held**
WEB: www.kciusa.com
SIC: 3536 Cranes, industrial plant
HQ: Konecranes, Inc.
  4401 Gateway Blvd
  Springfield OH 45502

(G-17434)
KONECRANES INC (HQ)
4401 Gateway Blvd (45502-9339)
PHONE................................937 525-5533
Pekka Lundmark, *President*
Brett Lawson, *District Mgr*
Bernard D'Ambrosi Jr, *Vice Pres*
Bernie Dambrosi, *Vice Pres*
Keith Kings, *Vice Pres*
◆ **EMP:** 279
SQ FT: 17,000
SALES (est): 702.5MM
SALES (corp-wide): 3.7B **Privately Held**
WEB: www.kciusa.com
SIC: 3536 Cranes, industrial plant
PA: Konecranes Abp
  Koneenkatu 8
  Hyvinkaa 05800
  204 271-1

(G-17435)
KRAFFT AND ASSOCIATES INC
991 W Leffel Ln (45506-3537)
P.O. Box 1292 (45501-1292)
PHONE................................937 325-4671
William F Krafft, *President*
Gretchen Krafft, *Corp Secy*
EMP: 8
SQ FT: 20,000
SALES (est): 1.1MM **Privately Held**
SIC: 3599 Machine shop, jobbing & repair

(G-17436)
KREIDER CORP
2000 S Yellow Springs St (45506-3398)
PHONE................................937 325-8787
Aristides Gianakopoulas, *President*
John Patton, *Vice Pres*
James Gianakopoulas, *Treasurer*
Walt Wildeman, *Admin Sec*
EMP: 66 **EST:** 1952
SQ FT: 50,000
SALES (est): 13.6MM **Privately Held**
SIC: 3469 3544 Stamping metal for the trade; special dies, tools, jigs & fixtures

GEOGRAPHIC SECTION
Springfield - Clark County (G-17463)

(G-17437)
M & H FABRICATING CO INC (PA)
717 Mound St (45505-1130)
P.O. Box 1248 (45501-1248)
PHONE..................937 325-8708
Michael C De Ramus, *President*
Kathleen J Chapman, *Admin Sec*
EMP: 10 **EST:** 1970
SQ FT: 6,000
SALES (est): 1.2MM **Privately Held**
SIC: 3441 Fabricated structural metal

(G-17438)
M & H FABRICATING CO INC
823 Mound St (45505-1132)
P.O. Box 1248 (45501-1248)
PHONE..................937 325-8708
Michael Duramus, *Manager*
EMP: 6
SALES (corp-wide): 1.2MM **Privately Held**
SIC: 3443 Tanks, standard or custom fabricated; metal plate
PA: M & H Fabricating Co Inc
717 Mound St
Springfield OH 45505
937 325-8708

(G-17439)
M & Y MARKETING
2651 Danbury Rd (45505-3431)
PHONE..................937 322-3423
Karen Matthews, *Owner*
EMP: 3
SALES (est): 92K **Privately Held**
SIC: 2395 Embroidery products, except schiffli machine

(G-17440)
MACRAY CO LLC
100 W North St (45504-2547)
PHONE..................937 325-1726
Robert Yingst, *Mng Member*
EMP: 6
SQ FT: 17,600
SALES (est): 600K **Privately Held**
SIC: 3993 1799 5099 Signs & advertising specialties; sign installation & maintenance; signs, except electric

(G-17441)
MAD RIVER TOPSOIL INC
5625 Lower Valley Pike (45506-4174)
PHONE..................937 882-6115
Richard Renner, *President*
EMP: 8
SQ FT: 8,100
SALES (est): 1.3MM **Privately Held**
SIC: 2499 5261 Mulch, wood & bark; top soil

(G-17442)
MADER ELECTR MOTOR & POWER TRA
205 E Main St (45503-4221)
P.O. Box 626 (45501-0626)
PHONE..................937 325-5576
Bret Eric Mader, *Mng Member*
EMP: 7
SQ FT: 20,000
SALES: 1.9MM **Privately Held**
SIC: 5063 7694 Motors, electric; electric motor repair

(G-17443)
MAINES INC
Also Called: Maine's Sign's & Designs
1718 E Pleasant St (45505-3314)
PHONE..................937 322-2084
Fred Maine, *President*
Kathy Maine, *Vice Pres*
EMP: 3
SALES: 150K **Privately Held**
SIC: 3993 Signs & advertising specialties

(G-17444)
MEAD PAVING
1023 W Perrin Ave (45506-2420)
PHONE..................937 322-7414
Rick Mead, *Mng Member*
EMP: 5
SALES (est): 928.6K **Privately Held**
SIC: 3531 Pavers

(G-17445)
METAL STAMPINGS UNLIMITED
552 W Johnny Lytle Ave (45506-2679)
PHONE..................937 328-0206
Edward Anderson, *President*
Roger Evilsizor, *Vice Pres*
Ed Anderson, *Purchasing*
Chris Clark, *Supervisor*
EMP: 10
SQ FT: 12,000
SALES (est): 1.4MM **Privately Held**
SIC: 3469 Stamping metal for the trade

(G-17446)
METALS USA CRBN FLAT RLLED INC
5750 Lower Valley Pike (45502-9101)
PHONE..................937 882-6354
Jeff Taugh, *Manager*
EMP: 54
SALES (corp-wide): 11.5B **Publicly Held**
SIC: 5051 3312 Steel; blast furnaces & steel mills
HQ: Metals Usa Carbon Flat Rolled, Inc.
1070 W Liberty St
Wooster OH 44691
330 264-8416

(G-17447)
METALTEK INDUSTRIES INC
829 Pauline St (45503-3815)
PHONE..................937 323-4933
Chuck Muscato, *Manager*
EMP: 14
SALES (corp-wide): 1.7MM **Privately Held**
SIC: 2842 3479 7629 3471 Rust removers; bonderizing of metal or metal products; electrical repair shops; plating & polishing
PA: Metaltek Industries Inc
2525 N Limestone St # 203
Springfield OH
937 342-1750

(G-17448)
MILLS LED LLC
845 E High St (45505-1163)
PHONE..................800 690-6403
Michael Hawkins, *Branch Mgr*
EMP: 5
SALES (corp-wide): 1MM **Privately Held**
SIC: 3646 Commercial indusl & institutional electric lighting fixtures
PA: Mills Led, Llc
81 S 5th St Ste 201
Columbus OH 43215
800 690-6403

(G-17449)
MMH AMERICAS INC (DH)
4401 Gateway Blvd (45502-9339)
PHONE..................414 764-6200
Tom Sothard, *President*
Steve Mayes, *Treasurer*
Guy Shumaker, *VP Finance*
Todd Robenson, *Admin Sec*
◆ **EMP:** 5
SALES (est): 32.4MM
SALES (corp-wide): 3.7B **Privately Held**
WEB: www.morriscranes.com
SIC: 5084 6719 3536 Materials handling machinery; cranes, industrial; investment holding companies, except banks; cranes, overhead traveling
HQ: Mmh Holdings, Inc.
4401 Gateway Blvd
Springfield OH 45502
937 525-5533

(G-17450)
MMH HOLDINGS INC (DH)
Also Called: Morris Material Handling
4401 Gateway Blvd (45502-9339)
PHONE..................937 525-5533
Tom Sothard, *President*
Jane H Pronounced Homs, *Purch Agent*
Steve Mayes, *Treasurer*
Guy Shumaker, *VP Finance*
Todd Robenson, *Admin Sec*
◆ **EMP:** 5
SQ FT: 10,500

SALES (est): 48.8MM
SALES (corp-wide): 3.7B **Privately Held**
WEB: www.morriscranes.com
SIC: 5084 3536 Materials handling machinery; cranes, industrial; cranes, overhead traveling

(G-17451)
MORGAL MACHINE TOOL CO
Also Called: McGregor Metalworking
2100 S Yellow Springs St (45506-3369)
P.O. Box 1103 (45501-1103)
PHONE..................937 325-5561
Jamie McGregor, *CEO*
Tom Wright, *President*
Terry Dalton, *COO*
Dwight Kent, *COO*
Andrew Brougher, *Plant Mgr*
▲ **EMP:** 90 **EST:** 1939
SQ FT: 98,000
SALES: 80MM **Privately Held**
WEB: www.morgal.com
SIC: 3568 3544 3451 3429 Power transmission equipment; special dies, tools, jigs & fixtures; screw machine products; manufactured hardware (general); stamping metal for the trade

(G-17452)
MORRIS MATERIAL HANDLING INC (DH)
4401 Gateway Blvd (45502-9339)
PHONE..................937 525-5520
Tom Sothard, *President*
Tom Berringer, *Principal*
Bernard D'Ambrosi Jr, *Vice Pres*
Keith King, *Vice Pres*
Steve Kosir, *Vice Pres*
◆ **EMP:** 5
SQ FT: 25,000
SALES (est): 98.4MM
SALES (corp-wide): 3.7B **Privately Held**
WEB: www.morriscranes.com
SIC: 3625 3443 7699 Crane & hoist controls, including metal mill; crane hooks, laminated plate; construction equipment repair

(G-17453)
MTS ENTERPRISES LLC
1330 Perry St (45504-2347)
PHONE..................937 324-7510
Robert M Corcoran, *President*
Michael Corcoran, *Vice Pres*
Robert Corcoran,
Karen Corcoran,
EMP: 3 **EST:** 2008
SALES: 200K **Privately Held**
SIC: 3499 Fire- or burglary-resistive products

(G-17454)
MULLER ENGINE & MACHINE CO
Also Called: Miller Engine & Machine Co
1414 S Yellow Springs St (45506-2545)
PHONE..................937 322-1861
Ginnie Mullen, *Owner*
EMP: 7 **EST:** 1952
SQ FT: 10,000
SALES (est): 811.3K **Privately Held**
SIC: 3511 3599 Wheels, water; machine shop, jobbing & repair

(G-17455)
NATIONAL STAIR CORP
20 Zischler St (45504-2853)
P.O. Box 1261 (45501-1261)
PHONE..................937 325-1347
John Druckenbroad, *President*
Larry Houck, *Vice Pres*
Mike Earl, *Admin Sec*
EMP: 30
SQ FT: 11,000
SALES (est): 4.7MM **Privately Held**
SIC: 3446 Stairs, staircases, stair treads: prefabricated metal

(G-17456)
NAVISTAR INC
6125 Urbana Rd (45502-9279)
P.O. Box 600 (45501)
PHONE..................937 390-5848
Clarence Richardson, *Research*
Barry Laughlin, *Manager*
Bill Trudo, *Manager*

EMP: 130
SALES (corp-wide): 10.2B **Publicly Held**
WEB: www.internationaldelivers.com
SIC: 3711 Truck & tractor truck assembly
HQ: Navistar, Inc.
2701 Navistar Dr
Lisle IL 60532
331 332-5000

(G-17457)
NAVISTAR INC
349 W County Line Rd (45502-7856)
PHONE..................937 390-5653
Charles Moore, *Branch Mgr*
EMP: 66
SALES (corp-wide): 10.2B **Publicly Held**
WEB: www.internationaldelivers.com
SIC: 3711 3714 Truck & tractor truck assembly; chassis, motor vehicle; motor vehicle parts & accessories
HQ: Navistar, Inc.
2701 Navistar Dr
Lisle IL 60532
331 332-5000

(G-17458)
NAVISTAR INC
811 N Murray St (45503-3733)
PHONE..................937 561-3315
Tom Tullis, *General Mgr*
EMP: 60
SALES (corp-wide): 10.2B **Publicly Held**
WEB: www.internationaldelivers.com
SIC: 3711 Truck & tractor truck assembly
HQ: Navistar, Inc.
2701 Navistar Dr
Lisle IL 60532
331 332-5000

(G-17459)
NAVISTAR INC
4949 Urbana Rd Frnt (45502-9541)
PHONE..................937 390-5704
Ann Hennigan, *Manager*
EMP: 30
SALES (corp-wide): 10.2B **Publicly Held**
WEB: www.internationaldelivers.com
SIC: 3711 3519 3714 Truck tractors for highway use, assembly of; diesel engine rebuilding; motor vehicle parts & accessories
HQ: Navistar, Inc.
2701 Navistar Dr
Lisle IL 60532
331 332-5000

(G-17460)
NEHER BURIAL VAULT COMPANY
Also Called: Burial Vaults By Neher
1903 Saint Paris Pike (45504-1299)
PHONE..................937 399-4494
Doreen Pinney, *President*
Gary W Pinney, *Treasurer*
EMP: 15 **EST:** 1939
SQ FT: 5,500
SALES (est): 2.3MM **Privately Held**
SIC: 3272 Burial vaults, concrete or precast terrazzo

(G-17461)
NEXSTEP COMMERCIAL PDTS LLC
625 Burt St (45505-3266)
PHONE..................937 322-5163
Todd Leventhal, *Principal*
EMP: 3
SALES (est): 364.7K **Privately Held**
SIC: 3999 Manufacturing industries

(G-17462)
NU RISERS STAIR COMPANY
2748 Columbus Rd (45503-3204)
PHONE..................937 322-8100
J Winkleman, *General Mgr*
Christopher Grim,
EMP: 12 **EST:** 1998
SALES (est): 1.3MM **Privately Held**
SIC: 3446 Stairs, staircases, stair treads: prefabricated metal

(G-17463)
OAKES DOOR SERV
5298 Troy Rd (45502-8128)
PHONE..................937 323-6188
Terry Oakes, *President*

Springfield - Clark County (G-17464)

EMP: 4
SALES (est): 486.8K Privately Held
SIC: 3699 Door opening & closing devices, electrical

(G-17464)
OHIO STAMPING & MACHINE LLC
1305 Innisfallen Ave (45506-1899)
P.O. Box 1103 (45501-1103)
PHONE.................................937 322-3880
Dan McGregor, *CEO*
James McGregor, *President*
Tom Wright, *President*
James Doyle, *General Mgr*
Dwight Kent, *COO*
EMP: 120
SQ FT: 140,000
SALES (est): 20.3MM Privately Held
WEB: www.ohiostamping.com
SIC: 3469 Metal stampings

(G-17465)
OS KELLY CORPORATION (DH)
318 E North St (45503-4298)
P.O. Box 1267 (45501-1267)
PHONE.................................937 322-4921
Theodore Golba, *CFO*
▲ EMP: 42
SQ FT: 110,000
SALES (est): 5MM
SALES (corp-wide): 318.4MM Privately Held
WEB: www.oskelly.com
SIC: 3321 Gray & ductile iron foundries
HQ: Steinway, Inc.
1 Steinway Pl
Long Island City NY 11105
718 721-2600

(G-17466)
PALMER ENGINEERED PRODUCTS INC
1310 W Main St (45504-2816)
P.O. Box 1593 (45501-1593)
PHONE.................................937 322-1481
Jack F Palmer, *President*
Ken Strausbaugh, *Engineer*
Kathy Smith, *Manager*
▲ EMP: 3
SALES (est): 499.7K Privately Held
WEB: www.palmereng.com
SIC: 3365 Aluminum & aluminum-based alloy castings

(G-17467)
PALMER KLEIN INC
18 N Bechtle Ave (45504-2841)
PHONE.................................937 323-6339
Jack Palmer, *President*
EMP: 5
SALES (est): 333.2K Privately Held
SIC: 3559 Foundry machinery & equipment

(G-17468)
PALMER MFG AND SUPPLY INC
18 N Bechtle Ave (45504-2841)
P.O. Box 2579 (45501-2579)
PHONE.................................937 323-6339
Jack Palmer, *President*
James Palmer, *Treasurer*
◆ EMP: 25
SQ FT: 60,000
SALES (est): 7.5MM Privately Held
SIC: 3559 Foundry machinery & equipment

(G-17469)
PARKER TRUTEC INCORPORATED (HQ)
4700 Gateway Blvd (45502-8817)
PHONE.................................937 323-8833
Keiko Satomi, *Ch of Bd*
Yutaka Satomi, *President*
Joseph Gummel, *Vice Pres*
▲ EMP: 80
SQ FT: 80,000
SALES: 44.1MM
SALES (corp-wide): 1B Privately Held
SIC: 3398 3479 Metal heat treating; painting, coating & hot dipping; rust proofing (hot dipping) of metals & formed products

PA: Nihon Parkerizing Co., Ltd.
1-15-1, Nihombashi
Chuo-Ku TKY 103-0
332 784-333

(G-17470)
PENTAFLEX INC
4981 Gateway Blvd (45502-8867)
PHONE.................................937 325-5551
Dave Arndt, *President*
Bob Jones, *Vice Pres*
Julie McGregor, *Treasurer*
Mark McClain, *Controller*
Melissa McCrillis, *Human Res Dir*
◆ EMP: 110
SQ FT: 146,000
SALES (est): 28.2MM Privately Held
WEB: www.pentaflex.com
SIC: 3469 7692 Stamping metal for the trade; welding repair

(G-17471)
PHOENIX SAFETY OUTFITTERS LLC
1619 Commerce Rd (45504-2015)
P.O. Box 20445, Upper Arlington (43220-0445)
PHONE.................................614 361-0544
Dennis Grogan, *General Mgr*
Steve Harting, *General Mgr*
Scott Rumple, *Sales Staff*
Jeff Shimel, *Sales Staff*
EMP: 9
SALES (est): 2.5MM Privately Held
SIC: 3569 Assembly machines, non-metalworking

(G-17472)
PIECO INC
Also Called: Superior Trims Springfield Div
5225 Prosperity Dr (45502-9540)
PHONE.................................937 399-5100
Bob Banghle, *Branch Mgr*
EMP: 100
SALES (corp-wide): 37.7MM Privately Held
WEB: www.suptrim.com
SIC: 2396 Automotive trimmings, fabric; furniture trimmings, fabric; trimming, fabric
PA: Pieco, Inc.
2151 Industrial Dr
Findlay OH 45840
419 422-5335

(G-17473)
PRATT (JET CORR) INC
Also Called: Pratt Industries USA
1515 Baker Rd (45504-4501)
PHONE.................................937 390-7100
Michael Day, *General Mgr*
Mark Anderson, *Opers Mgr*
Tami Meeks, *Sales Mgr*
EMP: 20
SALES (corp-wide): 2.5B Privately Held
SIC: 2653 Boxes, corrugated: made from purchased materials
HQ: Pratt (Jet Corr), Inc.
1800 Sarasot Bus Pkwy Ne B
Conyers GA 30013
770 929-1300

(G-17474)
PRAXAIR INC
403 W Columbia St (45504-2619)
PHONE.................................937 323-6408
Bruce Whaley, *Branch Mgr*
EMP: 5 Privately Held
SIC: 2813 Industrial gases
HQ: Praxair, Inc.
10 Riverview Dr
Danbury CT 06810
203 837-2000

(G-17475)
PREFERRED PUMP & EQUIPMENT LP
561 E Leffel Ln (45505-4748)
PHONE.................................937 322-4000
Mike Zvansky, *Branch Mgr*
EMP: 9
SALES (corp-wide): 306.9MM Privately Held
SIC: 3544 5046 Dies & die holders for metal cutting, forming, die casting; commercial equipment

HQ: Preferred Pump & Equipment, L.P.
2201 Scott Ave Ste 100
Fort Worth TX 76103
817 536-9800

(G-17476)
PRESS TECHNOLOGY & MFG INC
1401 Fotler St (45504-2051)
PHONE.................................937 327-0755
George Berner, *President*
▲ EMP: 8
SQ FT: 30,000
SALES: 1.6MM Privately Held
WEB: www.presstechnology.com
SIC: 3554 Paper mill machinery: plating, slitting, waxing, etc.; pulp mill machinery

(G-17477)
PROSYS SAMPLING SYSTEMS LTD
3800 Old Mill Rd (45502-9743)
PHONE.................................937 717-4600
EMP: 3
SALES (est): 176.4K Privately Held
SIC: 3823 Industrial instrmnts msrmnt display/control process variable

(G-17478)
R & L HYDRAULICS INC
109 Tremont City Rd (45502-9506)
PHONE.................................937 399-3407
Ron Randenburg, *President*
Ryan Randenburg, *Vice Pres*
EMP: 5
SQ FT: 4,000
SALES (est): 812.3K Privately Held
WEB: www.r-lhydraulics.com
SIC: 7699 3594 Hydraulic equipment repair; pumps, hydraulic power transfer

(G-17479)
RAINBOW INDUSTRIES INC
Also Called: Rainbow Tarp
5975 E National Rd (45505-1854)
P.O. Box 506, South Vienna (45369-0506)
PHONE.................................937 323-6493
F Vernon McCoy, *CEO*
Joe Schmid, *President*
Evelyn McCoy, *Treasurer*
▲ EMP: 7 EST: 1894
SQ FT: 6,000
SALES (est): 875.9K Privately Held
SIC: 2394 5999 7359 Tarpaulins, fabric: made from purchased materials; awnings, fabric: made from purchased materials; liners & covers, fabric: made from purchased materials; tents; tent & tarpaulin rental

(G-17480)
RAVEN INDUSTRIES INC
2130 Progress Rd (45505-4466)
PHONE.................................937 323-4625
Daniel Sherrock, *Sales/Mktg Mgr*
EMP: 3
SQ FT: 29,000
SALES (corp-wide): 406.6MM Publicly Held
WEB: www.ravenind.com
SIC: 3081 3083 2671 2394 Packing materials, plastic sheet; laminated plastics plate & sheet; packaging paper & plastics film, coated & laminated; canvas & related products
PA: Raven Industries, Inc
205 E 6th St
Sioux Falls SD 57104
605 336-2750

(G-17481)
RAWAC PLATING COMPANY
125 N Bell Ave (45504-2827)
PHONE.................................937 322-7491
Aristides G Gianakopoulos, *President*
Alexandra Gianakopoulos, *Treasurer*
EMP: 33 EST: 1943
SALES (est): 2.8MM Privately Held
WEB: www.rawac.com
SIC: 3471 Plating of metals or formed products

(G-17482)
REED ELVIN BURL II
Also Called: Buckeye Sanitary Service
1236 Villa Rd (45503-1677)
P.O. Box 195 (45501-0195)
PHONE.................................937 399-3242
Elvin Burl Reed II, *Owner*
Twylla Reed, *Treasurer*
Gina Elrod, *Admin Asst*
EMP: 4 EST: 1950
SQ FT: 1,400
SALES: 300K Privately Held
SIC: 7699 3272 Septic tank cleaning service; septic tanks, concrete

(G-17483)
REITER DAIRY OF AKRON INC (DH)
1961 Commerce Cir (45504-2081)
PHONE.................................937 323-5777
Craig McCutcheon, *President*
Bill Riley, *General Mgr*
Tim Rathmell, *Safety Mgr*
David Dungan, *Plant Engr*
Sandra Bethel, *Human Resources*
EMP: 30 EST: 1934
SQ FT: 25,000
SALES (est): 6.9MM Publicly Held
SIC: 2026 Mfg Fluid Milk Mfg Ice Cream/Frozen Desert
HQ: Dean Holding Company
2711 N Haskell Ave
Dallas TX 75204
214 303-3400

(G-17484)
RITTAL CORP
3100 Upper Valley Pike (45504-4518)
PHONE.................................937 399-0500
Jason Tom, *Design Engr*
EMP: 15
SALES (corp-wide): 2.6B Privately Held
WEB: www.ripac.com
SIC: 3469 Metal stampings
HQ: Rittal North America Llc
425 N Martingale Rd # 1540
Schaumburg IL 60173
847 240-4600

(G-17485)
RIVERROCK RECYCL CRUSHING LLC
2484 Lindair Dr (45502-9111)
P.O. Box 341575, Dayton (45434-1575)
PHONE.................................937 325-2052
EMP: 9
SALES (est): 1.2MM Privately Held
SIC: 3532 7389 1429 Mfg Mining Machinery Business Services At Non-Commercial Site Crushed/Broken Stone

(G-17486)
RIWCO CORP
2330 Columbus Rd (45503-3547)
P.O. Box 1204 (45501-1204)
PHONE.................................937 322-6521
David Nelson Funk, *President*
Robert Samosky, *Vice Pres*
EMP: 16 EST: 1925
SQ FT: 40,000
SALES (est): 3MM Privately Held
SIC: 3441 Fabricated structural metal

(G-17487)
ROBBINS & MYERS INC
Also Called: Moyno
1895 W Jefferson St (45506-1115)
P.O. Box 1343, Dayton (45401-1343)
PHONE.................................937 327-3111
Fax: 937 327-3194
EMP: 300
SALES (corp-wide): 7.2B Publicly Held
SIC: 3494 Mfg Motors & Valves
HQ: Robbins & Myers, Inc.
10586 N Highway 75
Willis TX 77378
936 890-1064

(G-17488)
ROBERTSON INCORPORATED (PA)
Also Called: Tower Manufacturing Company
14 N Lowry Ave Ste 200 (45504-2678)
PHONE.................................937 323-3747
Fax: 937 323-9295

EMP: 1
SQ FT: 200,000
SALES (est): 3MM **Privately Held**
SIC: 3315 Mfg Steel Wire/Related Products

(G-17489)
ROSE CITY MANUFACTURING INC
900 W Leffel Ln (45506-3538)
P.O. Box 1103 (45501-1103)
PHONE..................................937 325-5561
Daniel McGregor, *President*
Hugh Barnett, *Principal*
Dane A Belden, *Principal*
▲ **EMP:** 60
SQ FT: 44,000
SALES (est): 9.1MM **Privately Held**
WEB: www.rosecitymfg.com
SIC: 7692 Automotive welding

(G-17490)
SAWMILL ROAD MANAGEMENT CO LLC (PA)
1990 Kingsgate Rd Ste A (45502-8225)
PHONE..................................937 342-9071
Judy Ross, *Mng Member*
EMP: 30
SALES (est): 1.9MM **Privately Held**
SIC: 6531 2421 Buying agent, real estate; sawmills & planing mills, general

(G-17491)
SCHULERS BAKERY INC (PA)
1911 S Limestone St (45505-4045)
PHONE..................................937 323-4154
Theodore Schuler, *President*
Daniel Edward Schuler, *Corp Secy*
Larry Schuler, *Vice Pres*
EMP: 30
SALES (est): 4MM **Privately Held**
SIC: 5461 2052 2051 Doughnuts; cookies & crackers; bread, cake & related products

(G-17492)
SPEEDWAY LLC
Also Called: Speedway Superamerica 4131
2040 N Bechtle Ave (45504-1586)
PHONE..................................937 390-6651
EMP: 10 **Publicly Held**
WEB: www.speedwaynet.com
SIC: 1311 Crude petroleum production
HQ: Speedway Llc
    500 Speedway Dr
    Enon OH 45323
    937 864-3000

(G-17493)
SPRADLIN BROS WELDING CO
2131 Quality Ln (45505-3625)
PHONE..................................800 219-2182
Jeffery Spradlin, *President*
Mike Spradlin, *Vice Pres*
Sim Bowen, *Plant Mgr*
Rhonda Spradlin, *Treasurer*
Tammi Spradlin, *Admin Sec*
EMP: 17
SQ FT: 25,500
SALES: 4MM **Privately Held**
WEB: www.spradlinbros.com
SIC: 1799 7692 3444 3443 Ornamental metal work; welding repair; sheet metalwork; fabricated plate work (boiler shop); fabricated structural metal

(G-17494)
SPRINGFIELD METAL FINISHING
1108 Robin Rd (45503-2351)
PHONE..................................937 324-2353
Tim Wolfe, *President*
Vicki Wolfe, *Admin Sec*
EMP: 4
SALES (est): 248K **Privately Held**
SIC: 3471 Electroplating of metals or formed products; plating of metals or formed products

(G-17495)
SPRINGFIELD NEWSPAPERS INC (HQ)
Also Called: Springfield News Sun
137 E Main St (45502-1363)
PHONE..................................937 323-5533
Ben McLaughlin, *Principal*
Ismail Turay, *Editor*
Robert Mercer, *Sales Staff*
EMP: 23 **EST:** 1904
SQ FT: 76,268
SALES (est): 3.5MM
SALES (corp-wide): 32.5B **Privately Held**
WEB: www.springfieldnewssun.com
SIC: 2711 Job printing & newspaper publishing combined
PA: Cox Enterprises, Inc.
    6205 Pachtree Dunwoody Rd
    Atlanta GA 30328
    678 645-0000

(G-17496)
SPRINGFIELD PLASTICS INC
15 N Bechtle Ave (45504-2897)
PHONE..................................937 322-6071
Frederick B Becker, *President*
Janet Becker, *Treasurer*
EMP: 15
SQ FT: 24,000
SALES (est): 2.2MM **Privately Held**
SIC: 3089 Injection molded finished plastic products; injection molding of plastics

(G-17497)
STAHL CRANESYSTEMS INC
4401 Gateway Blvd (45502-9339)
PHONE..................................843 767-1951
EMP: 3
SALES (corp-wide): 637.1MM **Publicly Held**
SIC: 3536 Mfg Hoists/Cranes/Monorails
HQ: Stahl Cranesystems Inc.
    2284 Clements Ferry Rd E
    Charleston SC 29492

(G-17498)
STALDER SPRING WORKS INC
2345 Springfield Xenia Rd (45506-3994)
PHONE..................................937 322-6120
Damon D Kaufman, *President*
Corella Kaufman, *Corp Secy*
Dana Kaufman, *Vice Pres*
Dennis Kaufman, *Shareholder*
▲ **EMP:** 12 **EST:** 1945
SQ FT: 18,000
SALES (est): 2.5MM **Privately Held**
WEB: www.stalderspring.com
SIC: 3495 Mechanical springs, precision

(G-17499)
STEWART MANUFACTURING CORP
5230 Prosperity Dr (45502-7503)
PHONE..................................937 390-3333
James S Stewart, *President*
Suzanne S Collins, *Vice Pres*
Suzanne Collins, *Vice Pres*
David Everhart, *Prdtn Mgr*
Jeffrey Livingston, *Manager*
EMP: 20
SQ FT: 18,000
SALES (est): 3.3MM **Privately Held**
SIC: 3823 Differential pressure instruments, industrial process type

(G-17500)
SUTPHEN CORPORATION
Also Called: Chassis Division
1701 W County Line Rd (45502)
P.O. Box 2610 (45501-2610)
PHONE..................................937 969-8851
Drew Sutphen, *Opers-Prdtn-Mfg*
EMP: 52
SQ FT: 31,000
SALES (corp-wide): 117.1MM **Privately Held**
WEB: www.sutpheneast.com
SIC: 3711 3714 Chassis, motor vehicle; motor vehicle parts & accessories
PA: The Sutphen Corporation
    6450 Eiterman Rd
    Dublin OH 43016
    800 726-7030

(G-17501)
SWEET MANUFACTURING COMPANY
2000 E Leffel Ln (45505-4625)
P.O. Box 1086 (45501-1086)
PHONE..................................937 325-1511
Alicia Sweet-Hupp, *President*
Chris Smith, *President*
Michael Gannon, *Vice Pres*
Sam Jenkins, *Vice Pres*
Alan D Sweet, *Vice Pres*
◆ **EMP:** 40
SQ FT: 75,000
SALES (est): 16.3MM **Privately Held**
WEB: www.sweetmfg.com
SIC: 3535 3523 3534 3537 Conveyors & conveying equipment; elevators, farm; elevators & equipment; industrial trucks & tractors

(G-17502)
TAC INDUSTRIES INC (PA)
Also Called: TAC Enterprises
2160 Old Selma Rd (45505-4600)
PHONE..................................937 328-5200
Mary Brandstetter, *CEO*
Michael Ahern, *CFO*
Kevin Spriggs, *Manager*
Karol See, *Info Tech Mgr*
EMP: 340
SQ FT: 52,800
SALES (est): 5.2MM **Privately Held**
WEB: www.tacind.com
SIC: 8741 2399 8331 Management services; nets, launderers & dyers; work experience center

(G-17503)
TAYLOR MANUFACTURING COMPANY
1101 W Main St (45504-2899)
PHONE..................................937 322-8622
Robert B Taylor, *President*
Courtney Elliott, *Sales Mgr*
Mildred B Taylor, *Admin Sec*
EMP: 22 **EST:** 1939
SQ FT: 18,000
SALES (est): 4MM **Privately Held**
WEB: www.taylormanufacturing.com
SIC: 3728 Aircraft parts & equipment

(G-17504)
TECHNIQUES SURFACES USA INC
2015 Progress Rd (45505-4472)
PHONE..................................937 323-2556
Alain Charlois, *President*
Kenneth Metzgar, *Director*
EMP: 7
SALES (est): 1.1MM **Privately Held**
SIC: 3398 Metal heat treating
PA: H.E.F. Usa Corporation
    2015 Progress Rd
    Springfield OH 45505

(G-17505)
THOMAS TAPE AND SUPPLY COMPANY
1713 Sheridan Ave (45505-2263)
P.O. Box 207 (45501-0207)
PHONE..................................937 325-6414
David Simonton, *President*
Dee Simonton, *Principal*
Jeanne Simonton, *Vice Pres*
EMP: 11 **EST:** 1891
SQ FT: 17,500
SALES (est): 1.4MM **Privately Held**
SIC: 2672 Gummed paper: made from purchased materials

(G-17506)
TINKER OMEGA MANUFACTURING LLC
2424 Columbus Rd (45503-3549)
P.O. Box 328 (45501-0328)
PHONE..................................937 322-2272
Jared White, *Engineer*
Ben Thomas, *VP Sales*
William F Tinker Jr, *Mng Member*
Jesse Elliott, *Manager*
Jonathan Tinker, *Assistant*
▲ **EMP:** 29
SQ FT: 54,000
SALES (est): 7.7MM **Privately Held**
SIC: 3555 Type casting, founding or melting machines

(G-17507)
TOMCO TOOL INC
203 S Wittenberg Ave (45506-1646)
PHONE..................................937 322-5768
Bryan Stewart, *President*
Mark Stewart, *Corp Secy*
Richard Wheeler, *Vice Pres*
Patfy Stewart, *Manager*
EMP: 7
SQ FT: 18,000
SALES: 270K **Privately Held**
SIC: 3545 3544 Tools & accessories for machine tools; gauges (machine tool accessories); special dies, tools, jigs & fixtures

(G-17508)
TRI CON DISTRIBUTION LLC
776 Deerfield Trl (45503-7444)
PHONE..................................937 399-3312
Constance S Slagle,
EMP: 3
SALES (est): 296.4K **Privately Held**
SIC: 2676 Napkins, paper: made from purchased paper

(G-17509)
TRI STATE PALLET INC
854 Sherman Ave (45503-4308)
PHONE..................................937 323-5210
Mark See, *Branch Mgr*
EMP: 7
SALES (corp-wide): 3.5MM **Privately Held**
SIC: 2448 Pallets, wood
PA: Tri State Pallet, Inc.
    8401 Claude Thomas Rd # 57
    Franklin OH 45005
    937 746-8702

(G-17510)
TURN-ALL MACHINE & GEAR CO
5499 Tremont Ln (45502-7522)
P.O. Box 448 (45501-0448)
PHONE..................................937 342-8710
Carl Power, *President*
Jane Power, *Vice Pres*
EMP: 12
SALES (est): 1.9MM **Privately Held**
SIC: 3599 Machine shop, jobbing & repair

(G-17511)
U-SONICO
543 Cookston Ave (45503-2213)
PHONE..................................423 348-7117
Dean Hazelton, *President*
Loretta Hazelton, *Vice Pres*
EMP: 15
SALES (est): 771.1K **Privately Held**
SIC: 3541 Ultrasonic metal cutting machine tools

(G-17512)
UNITED FIBERGLASS AMERICA INC
2145 Airpark Dr (45502-7931)
PHONE..................................937 325-7305
Greg Gearhart, *President*
EMP: 15
SQ FT: 44,000
SALES (est): 4MM **Privately Held**
WEB: www.unitedfiberglass.com
SIC: 3644 Electric conduits & fittings

(G-17513)
VALCO INDUSTRIES INC
625 Burt St (45505-3266)
PHONE..................................937 399-7400
Edward H Leventhal, *President*
David H Montgomery, *General Mgr*
Edward Leventhal, *Opers Staff*
Gary Lehning, *CFO*
Angie Judy,
EMP: 35 **EST:** 1974
SQ FT: 44,000
SALES (est): 9MM **Privately Held**
WEB: www.valco-ind.com
SIC: 3713 3441 3465 Truck cabs for motor vehicles; fabricated structural metal; body parts, automobile: stamped metal

(G-17514)
W C SIMS CO INC (PA)
3845 W National Rd (45504-3518)
P.O. Box 4 (45501-0004)
PHONE..................................937 325-7035
Brad Sims, *President*
Bill Strader, *Accounts Exec*
Williams C Sims, *Shareholder*
EMP: 2
SQ FT: 17,000

Springfield - Clark County (G-17515)

SALES (est): 1.7MM **Privately Held**
WEB: www.wcsims.com
SIC: 5199 2752 Advertising specialties; commercial printing, lithographic

(G-17515)
WALT MYERS
303 N Greenmount Ave (45503-4050)
PHONE..................................937 325-0313
Myers Walt, *Principal*
EMP: 3
SALES (est): 160K **Privately Held**
SIC: 3599 Machine shop, jobbing & repair

(G-17516)
WESTFIELD STEEL INC
Also Called: Remington Steel
1120 S Burnett Rd (45505-3408)
PHONE..................................937 322-2414
Fritz Prine, *President*
Harry Osborne, *Vice Pres*
Debbie Funderburg, *Treasurer*
Myra Starr, *Human Res Mgr*
Frank Bair, *Branch Mgr*
EMP: 60
SALES (est): 11.5MM
SALES (corp-wide): 140.5MM **Privately Held**
SIC: 5051 3714 Steel; clutches, motor vehicle
PA: Westfield Steel Inc
   530 W State Road 32
   Westfield IN 46074
   317 896-5587

(G-17517)
WETSU GROUP INC
125 W North St (45504-2546)
P.O. Box 1985 (45501-1985)
PHONE..................................937 324-9353
Charles Ingle, *President*
Bob Martineau, *General Mgr*
Jay Greenland, *Vice Pres*
Linda Rice, *Manager*
EMP: 15
SQ FT: 1,200
SALES (est): 2.4MM **Privately Held**
WEB: www.wetsugroup.com
SIC: 3679 Harness assemblies for electronic use: wire or cable

(G-17518)
WINSUPPLY INC
2187 W 1st St (45504-1928)
PHONE..................................937 346-0600
EMP: 10
SALES (corp-wide): 4.9B **Privately Held**
SIC: 5722 5074 3432 1521 Air conditioning room units, self-contained; plumbing fittings & supplies; plumbing fixture fittings & trim; single-family home remodeling, additions & repairs
PA: Winsupply Inc.
   3110 Kettering Blvd
   Moraine OH 45439
   937 294-5331

(G-17519)
WOEBER MUSTARD MFG CO
1966 Commerce Cir (45504-2012)
P.O. Box 388 (45501-0388)
PHONE..................................937 323-6281
Ray Woeber, *President*
Gloria Woeber, *Corp Secy*
D I C K Woeber, *Vice Pres*
Rick Schmidt, *Vice Pres*
Richard E Woeber, *Vice Pres*
◆ EMP: 128 EST: 1905
SQ FT: 40,000
SALES (est): 40.1MM **Privately Held**
WEB: www.woebermustard.com
SIC: 2099 2035 Food preparations; mustard, prepared (wet)

(G-17520)
WOODROW CORP
105 N Thompson Ave (45504-2939)
PHONE..................................937 322-7696
Jeff Clouse, *Principal*
EMP: 3
SALES (est): 408.7K **Privately Held**
SIC: 2759 Commercial printing

(G-17521)
WOODROW MANUFACTURING CO
4300 River Rd (45502-7517)
P.O. Box 1567 (45501-1567)
PHONE..................................937 399-9333
John K Woodrow, *President*
Patrick T McAtee, *Treasurer*
EMP: 40
SQ FT: 26,000
SALES (est): 5MM **Privately Held**
WEB: www.woodrowcorp.com
SIC: 7336 3479 2752 2396 Silk screen design; etching on metals; commercial printing, lithographic; automotive & apparel trimmings

(G-17522)
YOST SUPERIOR CO
300 S Center St Ste 1 (45506-1696)
P.O. Box 1487 (45501-1487)
PHONE..................................937 323-7591
Bert D Barnes, *Ch of Bd*
Gary Dickerhoff, *President*
Dave Deerwester, *Vice Pres*
David Deerwester, *Vice Pres*
Mark Adkins, *Opers Staff*
▼ EMP: 50
SQ FT: 47,000
SALES (est): 11.5MM **Privately Held**
WEB: www.yostsuperior.com
SIC: 3495 3496 Mechanical springs, precision; miscellaneous fabricated wire products; clips & fasteners, made from purchased wire

Sterling
Wayne County

(G-17523)
MJC ENTERPRISES INC
7820 Blough Rd (44276-9734)
P.O. Box 182, Smithville (44677-0182)
PHONE..................................330 669-3744
Matt Carver, *President*
Lynn Carver, *Vice Pres*
EMP: 9
SQ FT: 1,352
SALES: 500K **Privately Held**
SIC: 2448 Pallets, wood

(G-17524)
STOLLER CUSTOM CABINETRY
12573 Frick Rd (44276-9722)
PHONE..................................330 939-6555
Greg Stoller, *Owner*
Rachel Graf, *Admin Asst*
EMP: 4
SALES: 350K **Privately Held**
WEB: www.stollercabinet.com
SIC: 2541 Cabinets, except refrigerated: show, display, etc.: wood

Steubenville
Jefferson County

(G-17525)
ACCESS 2 COMMUNICATIONS INC
Also Called: Bulldogsecurity
225 Technology Way (43952-7079)
PHONE..................................800 561-1110
Brett Barta, *President*
EMP: 2
SQ FT: 15,000
SALES: 10MM **Privately Held**
SIC: 3714 3699 Motor vehicle parts & accessories; security devices

(G-17526)
AMERICAN SUPERIOR LIGHTING
1506 Fernwood Rd (43953-7640)
PHONE..................................740 266-2959
Mike Gill, *President*
EMP: 4
SALES: 700K **Privately Held**
SIC: 3645 Residential lighting fixtures

(G-17527)
ARM (USA) INC
1506 Fernwood Rd (43953-7640)
PHONE..................................740 264-6599
Eric Bates, *Ch of Bd*
Mike Gill, *President*
◆ EMP: 15
SALES (est): 2.9MM **Privately Held**
WEB: www.armusa.com
SIC: 3599 Amusement park equipment

(G-17528)
BLUEFOOT INDUSTRIAL LLC
Also Called: Bluefoot Energy Services
224 N 3rd St (43952-2121)
PHONE..................................740 314-5299
Clyde Larsen,
Peter Urie,
EMP: 25
SQ FT: 7,000
SALES (est): 4MM **Privately Held**
SIC: 7353 2899 7359 1623 Heavy construction equipment rental; fluxes; brazing, soldering, galvanizing & welding; industrial truck rental; oil & gas pipeline construction; crude petroleum pipelines

(G-17529)
BULLY TOOLS INC
14 Technology Way (43952-7079)
PHONE..................................740 282-5834
Mark Gracy, *President*
EMP: 35
SALES (est): 3.9MM **Privately Held**
WEB: www.qpitools.com
SIC: 3545 Machine tool accessories

(G-17530)
DIETRICH VON HILDEBRAND LEGACY
1235 University Blvd (43952-1792)
PHONE..................................703 496-7821
Joseph Rooney, *Manager*
John Crosby, *Director*
EMP: 7
SALES: 440K **Privately Held**
SIC: 2759 8299 Commercial printing; educational services

(G-17531)
DPH DISCOUNT PIN INC
30 Snug Hbr (43953-7615)
P.O. Box 2577 (43953-0577)
PHONE..................................740 264-2450
Tammy Hammer, *President*
Jim Hammer, *Vice Pres*
▲ EMP: 5
SALES (est): 875K **Privately Held**
WEB: www.dphcustompins.com
SIC: 3452 Pins

(G-17532)
EASTERN OHIO INVESTMENTS INC
Also Called: Auto Magic Systems
213 Braybarton Blvd (43952-2337)
PHONE..................................740 266-2228
Dennis Hasak, *General Mgr*
EMP: 4
SALES (est): 363.2K **Privately Held**
SIC: 3589 Car washing machinery

(G-17533)
EXPRESS CARE
Also Called: Ameriwood
197 Main St (43953-3780)
PHONE..................................740 266-2501
Tom Jentil, *Manager*
EMP: 15
SALES (est): 998K **Privately Held**
SIC: 2741 Miscellaneous publishing

(G-17534)
FORT STBEN BURIAL ESTATES ASSN
Also Called: Roberts Brothers
801 Canton Rd (43953-4109)
PHONE..................................740 266-6101
Kirk Roberts, *Partner*
EMP: 6
SALES: 198.9K **Privately Held**
SIC: 6553 3272 Cemeteries, real estate operation; burial vaults, concrete or precast terrazzo

(G-17535)
GENESIS STEEL CORP
6th & Adams St (43952)
P.O. Box 4667 (43952-8667)
PHONE..................................740 282-2300
Duke Rakich, *CEO*
Robert Sagrilla, *President*
EMP: 9
SALES (est): 710K **Privately Held**
SIC: 3315 Steel wire & related products

(G-17536)
HANGER PRSTHETCS & ORTHO INC
2605 Sunset Blvd Unit C (43952-1179)
PHONE..................................740 266-6400
Greg Ekoniak, *Manager*
EMP: 4
SALES (corp-wide): 1B **Publicly Held**
SIC: 3842 5999 Prosthetic appliances; orthopedic & prosthesis applications
HQ: Hanger Prosthetics & Orthotics, Inc.
   10910 Domain Dr Ste 300
   Austin TX 78758
   512 777-3800

(G-17537)
HOLLYWOOD FAMILY EYE CARE
276 S Hollywood Blvd (43952-2422)
PHONE..................................740 264-1220
Maura E Stipanovich, *Principal*
EMP: 7
SALES (est): 751.3K **Privately Held**
SIC: 3851 Eyeglasses, lenses & frames

(G-17538)
J ZAMBERLAN & CO
100 Keagler Dr Bldg 4 (43953-3633)
P.O. Box 2152, Wintersville (43953-0152)
PHONE..................................740 765-9028
Joseph G Zamberlan, *President*
EMP: 3
SQ FT: 3,200
SALES: 110K **Privately Held**
SIC: 3931 Pipes, organ

(G-17539)
JEFFCO SHELTERED WORKSHOP
256 John Scott Hwy (43952-3001)
PHONE..................................740 264-4608
Mikel Michalik, *Exec Dir*
EMP: 20 EST: 1973
SQ FT: 15,000
SALES: 283.9K **Privately Held**
WEB: www.jcmrdd.com
SIC: 8331 8322 2511 Vocational training agency; refugee service; wood household furniture

(G-17540)
KROGER CO
264 S Hollywood Blvd (43952-2422)
PHONE..................................740 264-5057
Robert Orrico, *Manager*
EMP: 250
SALES (corp-wide): 121.1B **Publicly Held**
WEB: www.kroger.com
SIC: 5411 5912 2051 Supermarkets, chain; drug stores & proprietary stores; bread, cake & related products
PA: The Kroger Co
   1014 Vine St Ste 1000
   Cincinnati OH 45202
   513 762-4000

(G-17541)
LT WRIGHT HANDCRAFTED KNIFE CO
130 Warren Ln Unit B (43953-3758)
PHONE..................................740 317-1404
Leonard T Wright, *President*
EMP: 10
SALES (est): 610.8K **Privately Held**
SIC: 3421 Knives: butchers', hunting, pocket, etc.

(G-17542)
MARK NELSON
Also Called: Nelson's Woodcrafts
980 Lincoln Ave (43952-3223)
PHONE..................................740 282-5334
Mark Nelson, *Owner*
Kevin Nelles, *Sales Staff*

EMP: 15 **EST:** 1991
SQ FT: 6,000
SALES (est): 1.7MM **Privately Held**
WEB: www.nelsonwoodcraft.com
SIC: 2499 Carved & turned wood

(G-17543)
MARTIN M HARDIN
Also Called: Williams Grgory Martin Fnrl HM
411 N 7th St (43952-1756)
PHONE 740 282-1234
Hardin M Martin, *Owner*
EMP: 4 **EST:** 2010
SALES (est): 327.8K **Privately Held**
SIC: 2869 7261 Embalming fluids; crematory

(G-17544)
MEYER PRODUCTS LLC
324 N 7th St (43952-2249)
PHONE 216 486-1313
Andrew Outcalt, *President*
◆ **EMP:** 86
SALES (est): 29.1MM
SALES (corp-wide): 75MM **Privately Held**
SIC: 3531 Blades for graders, scrapers, dozers & snow plows
PA: The Louis Berkman Company
600 Grant St Ste 3230
Pittsburgh PA 15219
740 283-3722

(G-17545)
NATIONAL COLLOID COMPANY
906 Adams St (43952-2709)
P.O. Box 309 (43952-5309)
PHONE 740 282-1171
Michael Barber Jr, *President*
▲ **EMP:** 25 **EST:** 1938
SQ FT: 45,000
SALES (est): 11.9MM **Privately Held**
WEB: www.natcoll.com
SIC: 2869 5169 2899 2842 Industrial organic chemicals; caustic soda; calcium chloride; chemical preparations; specialty cleaning, polishes & sanitation goods; industrial inorganic chemicals; alkalies & chlorine

(G-17546)
OGDEN NEWSPAPERS INC
Also Called: Weirton Daily Times, The
401 Herald Sq (43952-2059)
PHONE 304 748-0606
Tammie Macintosh, *Manager*
EMP: 52 **Privately Held**
SIC: 2711 Newspapers: publishing only, not printed on site
HQ: The Ogden Newspapers Inc
1500 Main St
Wheeling WV 26003
304 233-0100

(G-17547)
OGDEN NEWSPAPERS INC
Also Called: Star Printing
401 Herald Sq (43952-2059)
PHONE 740 283-4711
Maggie McGinnis, *Sales Staff*
Monica Yelder, *Advt Staff*
Craih Bartoldeson, *Manager*
John Hale, *Director*
Pat Scheel, *Executive*
EMP: 90 **Privately Held**
SIC: 2711 Newspapers: publishing only, not printed on site
HQ: The Ogden Newspapers Inc
1500 Main St
Wheeling WV 26003
304 233-0100

(G-17548)
OLIVER POOL AND SPA INC
512 Main St (43953-3742)
PHONE 740 264-5368
John Oliver III, *President*
EMP: 3
SQ FT: 5,000
SALES (est): 800K **Privately Held**
SIC: 5999 7694 Swimming pools, above ground; spas & hot tubs; whirlpool baths; motors, electric; electric motor repair

(G-17549)
PUBLIC WORKS DEPT STREET DIV
238 S Lake Erie St (43952-2158)
PHONE 740 283-6013
Dominic Nucci, *Manager*
EMP: 23
SALES (est): 1.2MM **Privately Held**
SIC: 3991 Street sweeping brooms, hand or machine

(G-17550)
RUSSELL HUNT
Also Called: Russel Hunt Total Land Care
175 Detmar Rd (43953-7170)
P.O. Box 126 (43952-5126)
PHONE 740 264-1196
Russell Hunt, *Principal*
EMP: 10
SALES (est): 439.2K **Privately Held**
SIC: 0782 3524 Landscape contractors; snowblowers & throwers, residential

(G-17551)
SIGNS LIMITED LLC
356 Technology Way (43952-7079)
PHONE 740 282-7715
Ed Rice,
EMP: 7
SALES (est): 705.5K **Privately Held**
SIC: 3993 Electric signs

(G-17552)
SPECIAL WAY 2
1592 State Route 213 (43952-7949)
PHONE 740 282-8281
Rick Tallant, *CEO*
EMP: 4
SALES (est): 402.1K **Privately Held**
SIC: 3669 Mfg Communications Equipment

(G-17553)
STEUBENVILLE BAKERY
525 South St (43952-4808)
PHONE 740 282-6851
Louis Tripodi, *Owner*
EMP: 4
SQ FT: 1,200
SALES (est): 100K **Privately Held**
SIC: 2051 Bakery: wholesale or wholesale/retail combined; rolls, bread type: fresh or frozen

(G-17554)
STEUBENVILLE TRUCK CENTER INC
620 South St (43952-2802)
P.O. Box 1741 (43952-7741)
PHONE 740 282-2711
Larry A Remp, *President*
Mary Stead, *Corp Secy*
Marney Remp, *Vice Pres*
EMP: 25
SQ FT: 7,500
SALES (est): 5.7MM **Privately Held**
WEB: www.ohiovolvo.com
SIC: 7538 5511 7692 Truck engine repair, except industrial; trucks, tractors & trailers: new & used; welding repair

(G-17555)
SUPPLY INTERNATIONAL INC
Also Called: Pro Forma Supply International
602 Kingsdale Rd Ste 1 (43952-4356)
PHONE 740 282-8604
Jim Epifano, *President*
Jennie Epifano, *Vice Pres*
EMP: 3
SQ FT: 1,500
SALES (est): 300K **Privately Held**
SIC: 5199 5112 3429 Advertising specialties; office supplies; metal fasteners

(G-17556)
TRI-STATE PUBLISHING COMPANY (PA)
Also Called: Tri-State Printing
157 N 3rd St (43952-2169)
P.O. Box 1119 (43952-6119)
PHONE 740 283-3686
Richard S Pflug, *President*
Dawna L McCabe, *Corp Secy*
EMP: 35
SQ FT: 11,000
SALES (est): 5.1MM **Privately Held**
WEB: www.tristateprintingco.com
SIC: 2752 Commercial printing, offset

(G-17557)
WEIRTON DAILY TIMES
Also Called: Herald Star Newspaper
401 Herald Sq (43952-2059)
PHONE 740 283-4711
Fax: 740 284-7355
EMP: 17
SALES (est): 1.1MM **Privately Held**
SIC: 2711 Newspapers-Publishing/Printing

Stewart
Athens County

(G-17558)
ADVANCED WEB CORPORATION
10999 E Copeland Rd (45778-9538)
PHONE 740 662-6323
Randy Copeland, *President*
Nathan Copeland, *Vice Pres*
EMP: 4
SQ FT: 10,000
SALES (est): 794.1K **Privately Held**
WEB: www.advancedwebcorporation.com
SIC: 3555 Printing presses

Stockport
Morgan County

(G-17559)
C SQUARE LUMBER PRODUCTS
1541 S Elliott Rd (43787-9315)
PHONE 740 557-3129
Carl Wolfe, *Owner*
EMP: 15
SALES (est): 121.4K **Privately Held**
SIC: 2431 Louver doors, wood; windows & window parts & trim, wood

(G-17560)
ROGER L BEST
Also Called: Best Logging
3080 Blind Rd (43787-9201)
PHONE 740 590-9133
Roger L Best, *Principal*
EMP: 3
SALES (est): 150K **Privately Held**
SIC: 2411 Logging

Stone Creek
Tuscarawas County

(G-17561)
M-CO WELDING
10949 Gnther Miller Rd Sw (43840-9448)
PHONE 330 897-1374
Andy Miller, *Owner*
EMP: 4 **EST:** 2010
SALES (est): 190K **Privately Held**
SIC: 3842 Welders' hoods

(G-17562)
MCO WELDING
10949 Gnther Miller Rd Sw (43840-9448)
PHONE 330 401-6130
Andy Miller, *Owner*
EMP: 8
SALES (est): 88.7K **Privately Held**
SIC: 7692 Welding repair

(G-17563)
OXFORD MINING INC
4371 Rice Rd Sw (43840-9478)
P.O. Box 427, Coshocton (43812-0427)
PHONE 330 339-4546
Charles Ungurean, *Principal*
EMP: 3
SALES (est): 143.8K **Privately Held**
SIC: 1241 Coal mining services

(G-17564)
RICHARD A LIMBACHER
Also Called: Ral Robotics Investment Group
7148 Rocky Ridge Rd Sw (43840-9483)
PHONE 330 897-4515
Richard A Limbacher, *Owner*
EMP: 4
SQ FT: 2,000
SALES (est): 295K **Privately Held**
WEB: www.ralrobotics.com
SIC: 3549 Assembly machines, including robotic

Stow
Summit County

(G-17565)
A CUPCAKE A DAY LLC
115 W Liberty St (44224)
PHONE 330 389-1247
Shawna Rollheiser, *Principal*
EMP: 4
SALES (est): 235.4K **Privately Held**
SIC: 2051 Cakes, bakery: except frozen

(G-17566)
ACE PLASTICS CO
122 E Tuscarawas Ave (44224)
PHONE 330 928-7720
Peggy Lyn Assaly, *President*
Joe Vereecken, *President*
EMP: 7 **EST:** 1947
SQ FT: 4,000
SALES (est): 640K **Privately Held**
SIC: 3499 5199 Novelties & giftware, including trophies; advertising specialties

(G-17567)
ADVANCED ENGRG & MFG CO INC
5026 Hudson Dr Ste D (44224-7100)
PHONE 330 686-9911
Bob Hanna, *President*
Paul Christ, *Vice Pres*
EMP: 10
SQ FT: 1,250
SALES (est): 1.1MM **Privately Held**
WEB: www.advancedengineeringmfg.com
SIC: 3599 Machine shop, jobbing & repair

(G-17568)
ANDERSON INTERNATIONAL CORP
4545 Boyce Pkwy (44224-1770)
PHONE 216 641-1112
Len Trocano, *President*
Stephen C Ellis, *President*
Gary Pace, *President*
Jill Marton, *General Mgr*
Paul Kohntopp, *Vice Pres*
◆ **EMP:** 90 **EST:** 1888
SQ FT: 100,000
SALES (est): 38.2MM **Privately Held**
WEB: www.andersonintl.com
SIC: 3559 3556 Rubber working machinery, including tires; meat, poultry & seafood processing machinery
PA: Kimbell Inc
420 Throckmorton St # 710
Fort Worth TX 76102
817 332-6104

(G-17569)
APEX ALLIANCE LLC
Also Called: Summit Arms
2177 Graham Rd (44224-4004)
PHONE 234 200-5930
Nathan Kowalski,
Michael Patacca,
EMP: 3 **EST:** 2017
SALES (est): 90.2K **Privately Held**
SIC: 5941 3484 7389 Firearms; machine guns or machine gun parts, 30 mm. & below;

(G-17570)
AUSTIN TAPE AND LABEL INC
3350 Cavalier Trl (44224-4906)
PHONE 330 928-7999
James Burkle Jr, *President*
Darrell K Floyd, *Vice Pres*
Bill Douglas, *Executive*
EMP: 54

SQ FT: 11,000
SALES (est): 12.3MM Privately Held
WEB: www.austintape.com
SIC: 2672 2759 2671 Tape, pressure sensitive: made from purchased materials; labels (unprinted), gummed: made from purchased materials; commercial printing; packaging paper & plastics film, coated & laminated

(G-17571)
BADIZO LLC
Also Called: Gifted Nutrition
4466 Darrow Rd Ste 3 (44224-1867)
PHONE..................................844 344-3833
John Hillyer, Principal
Michael Walker,
EMP: 5
SALES (est): 252.7K Privately Held
SIC: 2833 Animal based products

(G-17572)
BAKER MCMILLEN CO (PA)
Also Called: Crook Miller Company
3688 Wyoga Lake Rd (44224-4987)
PHONE..................................330 923-8300
William L Kimmerle, President
▲ EMP: 55
SQ FT: 65,000
SALES (est): 9.7MM Privately Held
WEB: www.baker-mcmillen.com
SIC: 2499 Carved & turned wood

(G-17573)
BAKER MCMILLEN CO
Also Called: Waddell Manufacturing Company
3688 Wyoga Lake Rd (44224-4987)
PHONE..................................330 923-3303
Bill Kimmerle, Branch Mgr
EMP: 20
SALES (corp-wide): 9.7MM Privately Held
WEB: www.baker-mcmillen.com
SIC: 2499 3429 2439 Handles, poles, dowels & stakes: wood; manufactured hardware (general); structural wood members
PA: Baker Mcmillen Co.
3688 Wyoga Lake Rd
Stow OH 44224
330 923-8300

(G-17574)
BLAZE TECHNICAL SERVICES INC
1445 Commerce Dr (44224-1709)
PHONE..................................330 923-0409
Ralph Hickman, President
Brian Hickman, Opers Mgr
John Gerbracht, Sales Executive
EMP: 25 EST: 1996
SQ FT: 5,000
SALES (est): 4.7MM Privately Held
WEB: www.blazeprobes.com
SIC: 3829 Thermocouples

(G-17575)
CFC STARTEC LLC
2213 Amdale Rd (44224-1813)
PHONE..................................330 688-8316
Glenn V Tingley Jr,
Glenn Tingley,
EMP: 5
SALES (est): 469.6K Privately Held
SIC: 3585 7389 Refrigeration equipment, complete;

(G-17576)
CHANDLER MACHINE CO INC
Also Called: Chandler Mch & Prod Gear & Bro
4960 Hudson Dr (44224-1789)
PHONE..................................330 688-7615
Jeffery H Capple, President
EMP: 9
SQ FT: 2,400
SALES (est): 880K Privately Held
WEB: www.chandlermachineco.com
SIC: 3599 Machine shop, jobbing & repair

(G-17577)
CHANDLER MACHINE PROD GEAR
4960 Hudson Dr (44224-1789)
PHONE..................................330 688-5585
Jeffery Capple, President
EMP: 7 EST: 1962
SQ FT: 2,400
SALES (est): 861.9K Privately Held
SIC: 3599 Machine shop, jobbing & repair

(G-17578)
CLASSIC TOOL INC
4278 Hudson Dr (44224-2251)
PHONE..................................330 922-1933
Guilford Crocker Jr, President
David Crocker, Vice Pres
Jean Finn, Office Mgr
EMP: 3
SQ FT: 3,600
SALES (est): 492.8K Privately Held
SIC: 3544 Special dies & tools

(G-17579)
CONQUEST INDUSTRIES INC
4488 Allen Rd (44224-1051)
PHONE..................................234 678-5555
Tom Fares, Principal
Harry Frederick, Principal
EMP: 25 EST: 1994
SALES (est): 4.4MM Privately Held
SIC: 3599 Machine shop, jobbing & repair

(G-17580)
DONALDSON COMPANY INC
115 E Steels Corners Rd (44224-4919)
P.O. Box 1459 (44224-0459)
PHONE..................................330 928-4100
Dave Tallarico, Principal
EMP: 80
SALES (corp-wide): 2.7B Publicly Held
SIC: 3599 Air intake filters, internal combustion engine, except auto
PA: Donaldson Company, Inc.
1400 W 94th St
Minneapolis MN 55431
952 887-3131

(G-17581)
ELECTROMOTIVE INC (PA)
4880 Hudson Dr (44224-1708)
PHONE..................................330 688-6494
Michael Piglia, CEO
Jeffrey Bissell, CFO
EMP: 10
SALES (est): 157.9MM Privately Held
WEB: www.electromotive.net
SIC: 3679 3677 Solenoids for electronic applications; electronic coils, transformers & other inductors

(G-17582)
EQUITY OIL & GAS FUNDS INC (PA)
4704 Barrow Ste 1 (44224)
P.O. Box 2230 (44224-1000)
PHONE..................................234 231-1004
Richard Desich, President
Alane King, Admin Sec
EMP: 3
SQ FT: 2,000
SALES: 5.6MM Privately Held
WEB: www.equityoil.com
SIC: 1311 Crude petroleum & natural gas

(G-17583)
ESTERLE MOLD & MACHINE CO INC (PA)
Also Called: Plastics Division
1539 Commerce Dr (44224-1783)
PHONE..................................330 686-1685
Adam Esterle, Ch of Bd
Richard Esterle, President
Carol Esterle, Corp Secy
Kathleen Sawyer, Vice Pres
EMP: 45
SQ FT: 18,100
SALES: 9MM Privately Held
WEB: www.esterle.com
SIC: 3498 3599 3544 Fabricated pipe & fittings; machine shop, jobbing & repair; industrial molds

(G-17584)
ESTERLE MOLD & MACHINE CO INC
1567 Commerce Dr (44224-1711)
PHONE..................................330 686-1685
Richard Esterle, Principal
EMP: 11
SQ FT: 22,920
SALES (corp-wide): 9MM Privately Held
WEB: www.esterle.com
SIC: 3544 Industrial molds
PA: Esterle Mold & Machine Co Inc
1539 Commerce Dr
Stow OH 44224
330 686-1685

(G-17585)
FABRIC SQUARE SHOP
2091 Liberty Rd (44224-3427)
PHONE..................................330 752-3044
Laura Sampsel, Owner
EMP: 4 EST: 2010
SALES (est): 291.3K Privately Held
SIC: 5949 2211 Fabric stores piece goods; apparel & outerwear fabrics, cotton

(G-17586)
FALLS FILTRATION TECH INC
115 E Steels Corners Rd (44224-4919)
PHONE..................................330 928-4100
Tom Page, President
Lou Scalise, Treasurer
EMP: 35
SALES (est): 10MM Privately Held
WEB: www.fallsfti.com
SIC: 3569 Filters, general line: industrial

(G-17587)
FERRY INDUSTRIES INC (PA)
Also Called: Ferry & Quintax
4445 Allen Rd Ste A (44224-1058)
PHONE..................................330 920-9200
W Harry Covington Jr, President
Francis Routh, Vice Pres
Richard Bieterman, CFO
Thomas G Knoll, Admin Sec
▲ EMP: 77 EST: 1927
SQ FT: 70,000
SALES (est): 16.1MM Privately Held
WEB: www.ferryindustries.com
SIC: 3599 3829 Custom machinery; machine shop, jobbing & repair; measuring & controlling devices

(G-17588)
FLEXOTECH GRAPHICS INC (PA)
4830 Hudson Dr (44224-1708)
PHONE..................................330 929-4743
Cris Apley, President
EMP: 12
SQ FT: 6,500
SALES (est): 1.6MM Privately Held
WEB: www.flexotech.com
SIC: 3555 Printing plates

(G-17589)
FORMTECH ENTERPRISES INC (PA)
3924 Clock Pointe Trl # 101 (44224-2952)
PHONE..................................330 688-2171
David Turk, President
Cynthia Turk, Admin Sec
EMP: 44
SQ FT: 35,000
SALES (est): 14MM Privately Held
SIC: 3089 Injection molding of plastics

(G-17590)
FRED MARVIN AND ASSOCIATES INC
Also Called: Fred Marvin Associates
4484 Allen Rd (44224-1051)
PHONE..................................330 784-9211
Jeff Mussay, President
▲ EMP: 6 EST: 1946
SQ FT: 7,000
SALES (est): 1MM Privately Held
WEB: www.pruner.com
SIC: 3421 Cutlery

(G-17591)
GBS CORP
GBS Printed Products & Systems
3658 Wyoga Lake Rd (44224-4944)
PHONE..................................330 929-8050
Jeff Starkey, Vice Pres
Donald Sprowls, Plant Supt
EMP: 48
SALES (corp-wide): 72.8MM Privately Held
SIC: 5999 2759 2672 2679 Art & architectural supplies; commercial printing; coated & laminated paper; labels, paper: made from purchased material
PA: Gbs Corp.
7233 Freedom Ave Nw
North Canton OH 44720
330 494-5330

(G-17592)
GLEBUS ALLOYS LLC
Also Called: G Metal
883 Hampshire Rd Ste E (44224-1120)
PHONE..................................330 867-9999
Michael Stefanidis, Mng Member
EMP: 12
SQ FT: 4,000
SALES (est): 2MM Privately Held
WEB: www.glebusalloys.com
SIC: 3315 Steel wire & related products

(G-17593)
GOJO INDUSTRIES INC
1366 Commerce Dr (44224-1737)
PHONE..................................330 255-6525
EMP: 125
SALES (corp-wide): 373.8MM Privately Held
WEB: www.gojo.com
SIC: 2842 3586 2844 Specialty cleaning, polishes & sanitation goods; measuring & dispensing pumps; toilet preparations
PA: Gojo Industries, Inc.
1 Gojo Plz Ste 500
Akron OH 44311
330 255-6000

(G-17594)
HERFF JONES LLC
4468 Berry Hl (44224-2187)
PHONE..................................330 678-8138
Richard Call, Branch Mgr
EMP: 25
SALES (corp-wide): 1.1B Privately Held
SIC: 2741 Miscellaneous publishing
HQ: Herff Jones, Llc
4501 W 62nd St
Indianapolis IN 46268
800 419-5462

(G-17595)
HUDSON VILLAGE PIZZA INC
3825 Kay Dr (44224-3249)
PHONE..................................330 968-4563
Frank Mc Millen, President
EMP: 5
SQ FT: 3,000
SALES (est): 457.3K Privately Held
SIC: 2038 Pizza, frozen

(G-17596)
INTEGRATED AIRCRAFT SYSTEMS
1337 Commerce Dr Ste 9 (44224-1758)
PHONE..................................330 686-2982
Bill Lipstreu, President
Susan Lipstreu, Vice Pres
EMP: 7
SALES: 1MM Privately Held
WEB: www.integratedaircraftsystems.com
SIC: 3492 5088 Hose & tube fittings & assemblies, hydraulic/pneumatic; aircraft equipment & supplies

(G-17597)
J & S PRODUCTS INC
4534 Berry Hl (44224-2188)
PHONE..................................330 686-5840
Dave Burger, President
EMP: 6
SALES: 300K Privately Held
WEB: www.jsprodinc.com
SIC: 3643 Power line cable

(G-17598)
KILNIT LTD ◆
1625 Graham Rd (44224-3132)
PHONE..................................330 906-0748
Jamee Blair, Owner
EMP: 3 EST: 2018
SALES (est): 180K Privately Held
SIC: 3559 Kilns

GEOGRAPHIC SECTION
Stow - Summit County (G-17623)

(G-17599)
LASPINA TOOL & DIE INC
4282 Hudson Dr (44224-2251)
PHONE..................................330 923-9996
Timothy P Laspina, *Owner*
EMP: 19
SQ FT: 8,500
SALES (est): 1.9MM **Privately Held**
SIC: 3544 3599 Special dies & tools; machine shop, jobbing & repair

(G-17600)
LEAP PUBLISHING SERVICES INC
4301 Darrow Rd Ste 1200a (44224-7600)
P.O. Box 2192 (44224-0192)
PHONE..................................234 738-0082
Shay Carpenter, *Editor*
David Gidorkis, *Opers Staff*
Malvine Litten, *Mng Member*
EMP: 14
SALES (est): 514.8K **Privately Held**
SIC: 2731 7389 Textbooks: publishing only, not printed on site;

(G-17601)
LEVAN ENTERPRISES INC (PA)
Also Called: R F Cook Manufacturing Co
4585 Allen Rd (44224-1035)
PHONE..................................330 923-9797
Peter H Levan, *President*
Steven Levan, *Plant Mgr*
Greg Rowlett, *Sales Staff*
Carolyn G Levan, *Admin Sec*
EMP: 36
SQ FT: 18,000
SALES (est): 4.4MM **Privately Held**
SIC: 3541 3542 3545 3544 Machine tools, metal cutting type; machine tools, metal forming type; precision tools, machinists'; special dies, tools, jigs & fixtures

(G-17602)
LINTEC USA HOLDING INC (HQ)
4560 Darrow Rd (44224-1888)
PHONE..................................781 935-7850
H Kainose, *President*
Hitoshi Asai, *Treasurer*
Paul Moynihan, *Controller*
Kazuya Watanabe, *Clerk*
EMP: 5
SALES (est): 682MM
SALES (corp-wide): 2.3B **Privately Held**
SIC: 3083 2295 Plastic finished products, laminated; window sheeting, plastic; laminating of fabrics
PA: Lintec Corporation
  23-23, Honcho
  Itabashi-Ku TKY 173-0
  352 487-711

(G-17603)
LION MOLD & MACHINE INC
4510 Darrow Rd (44224-1804)
PHONE..................................330 688-4248
William Walton, *President*
EMP: 3
SQ FT: 4,000
SALES (est): 462.7K **Privately Held**
SIC: 3089 3599 Injection molding of plastics; machine shop, jobbing & repair

(G-17604)
MASTER MARKING COMPANY INC
4830 Hudson Dr (44224-1708)
PHONE..................................330 688-6797
Raymond X Heller, *President*
Steve Heller, *Vice Pres*
EMP: 12 **EST:** 1978
SQ FT: 36,000
SALES (est): 1.5MM **Privately Held**
WEB: www.mastermarking.com
SIC: 3479 3953 3544 3545 Etching on metals; marking devices; metalworking machinery; special dies, tools, jigs & fixtures; platemaking services

(G-17605)
MATCO TOOLS CORPORATION (HQ)
Also Called: Nmtc, Inc.
  4403 Allen Rd (44224-1096)
  P.O. Box 1429 (44224-0429)
  PHONE..................................330 929-4949
Timothy J Gilmore, *President*
Rich McKenna, *Regional Mgr*
Mike McCaleb, *District Mgr*
Brian Rose, *District Mgr*
Kelly Smith, *District Mgr*
▲ **EMP:** 400
SALES (est): 150.6MM
SALES (corp-wide): 6.4B **Publicly Held**
WEB: www.matcotools.com
SIC: 5251 5072 3469 3423 Hardware; hardware; metal stampings; hand & edge tools; tools & equipment, automotive
PA: Fortive Corporation
  6920 Seaway Blvd
  Everett WA 98203
  425 446-5000

(G-17606)
MORGAN ADHESIVES COMPANY LLC (DH)
Also Called: Mactac
  4560 Darrow Rd (44224-1898)
  PHONE 330 688-1111
Ingrid V Cluyzen, *General Mgr*
Chad Oney, *VP Opers*
George Matalenas, *Maintenance Dir*
Jeffrey Lipnichan, *Plant Mgr*
Eva Ellis, *Production*
▲ **EMP:** 500
SQ FT: 559,400
SALES (est): 597.2MM
SALES (corp-wide): 2.3B **Privately Held**
WEB: www.mactac.com
SIC: 2891 3565 2672 2823 Adhesives; labeling machines, industrial; adhesive papers, labels or tapes: from purchased material; cellulosic manmade fibers
HQ: Lintec Usa Holding, Inc.
  4560 Darrow Rd
  Stow OH 44224
  781 935-7850

(G-17607)
MOS INTERNATIONAL INC
3213 Peterboro Dr (44224-5913)
PHONE..................................330 329-0905
Jenna Myong OK Song, *President*
EMP: 18
SQ FT: 3,000
SALES (est): 6MM **Privately Held**
SIC: 3089 Automotive parts, plastic

(G-17608)
MULTI FORM MFG
4278 Hudson Dr (44224-2251)
PHONE..................................330 922-1933
David S Crocker, *President*
Guilford M Crocker Jr, *Vice Pres*
Alice Crocker, *Admin Sec*
EMP: 5
SQ FT: 3,600
SALES (est): 540K **Privately Held**
SIC: 3544 Special dies, tools, jigs & fixtures

(G-17609)
MURRUBBER TECHNOLOGIES INC
1350 Commerce Dr (44224-1737)
PHONE..................................330 688-4881
Anthony J Murru, *President*
Tom Rownd, *Principal*
Pamela Fischmann, *Office Mgr*
Lisa A Kuhen,
EMP: 40
SQ FT: 50,000
SALES (est): 15MM **Privately Held**
WEB: www.bedellkraus.com
SIC: 3069 2241 Reclaimed rubber & specialty rubber compounds; custom compounding of rubber materials; rubber & elastic yarns & fabrics

(G-17610)
NATIONAL AVIATION PRODUCTS INC (DH)
4880 Hudson Dr (44224-1708)
PHONE..................................330 688-6494
Peter Piglia, *Ch of Bd*
Thomas G Knoll, *Principal*
EMP: 16
SALES (est): 11MM
SALES (corp-wide): 157.9MM **Privately Held**
SIC: 3599 3492 Machine & other job shop work; machine shop, jobbing & repair; control valves, fluid power: hydraulic & pneumatic
HQ: National Machine Company
  4880 Hudson Dr
  Stow OH 44224
  330 688-6494

(G-17611)
NATIONAL MACHINE COMPANY (HQ)
Also Called: Nmg Aerospace
  4880 Hudson Dr (44224-1799)
  PHONE..................................330 688-6494
Michael Piglia, *CEO*
Bill Anop, *President*
Peter Piglia, *Chairman*
Tracy Konjovic, *Vice Pres*
Richard Mathern, *Prdtn Mgr*
▲ **EMP:** 250
SQ FT: 80,000
SALES (est): 157.9MM **Privately Held**
SIC: 3599 3492 Machine shop, jobbing & repair; control valves, fluid power: hydraulic & pneumatic
PA: Electromotive Inc
  4880 Hudson Dr
  Stow OH 44224
  330 688-6494

(G-17612)
NATIONAL MACHINE COMPANY
1330 Commerce Dr (44224-1737)
PHONE..................................330 688-2584
Tom Huntsman, *Manager*
EMP: 20
SALES (corp-wide): 157.9MM **Privately Held**
SIC: 3545 3599 Sockets (machine tool accessories); machine shop, jobbing & repair
HQ: National Machine Company
  4880 Hudson Dr
  Stow OH 44224
  330 688-6494

(G-17613)
NATIONAL NTWRK EMB PRFSSIONALS
3100 Surrey Hill Ln (44224-4756)
PHONE..................................502 212-7500
Fax: 330 678-8988
EMP: 3 **EST:** 1995
SALES (est): 161.4K **Privately Held**
SIC: 2395 Professional Organization Group For Commercial Embroidery Business Owner

(G-17614)
NEOLA INC (PA)
3914 Clk Pnte Trl Ste 103 (44224)
PHONE..................................330 926-0514
Richard Clapp, *President*
Pat Corbett, *Exec Dir*
Tim Baneck, *Associate*
Jim Conner, *Associate*
Darlene Dongvillo, *Associate*
EMP: 3
SALES (est): 1.9MM **Privately Held**
WEB: www.neola.com
SIC: 2731 Pamphlets: publishing only, not printed on site

(G-17615)
NORDEC INC
900 Hampshire Rd (44224-1113)
PHONE..................................330 940-3700
Christine A Snyder, *President*
Jeffrey L Smith, *Vice Pres*
Jason D Sudbrink, *Vice Pres*
William L Snyder, *Shareholder*
EMP: 60 **EST:** 1962
SQ FT: 50,000
SALES (est): 9.7MM **Privately Held**
WEB: www.nordecinc.com
SIC: 2759 2675 Screen printing; decals: printing; die-cut paper & board

(G-17616)
OSMANS PIES INC
3678 Elm Rd (44224-3954)
PHONE..................................330 607-9083
Ethel Osman, *President*
Terry Osman, *Vice Pres*
Cheryl Osman Crowe, *Admin Sec*
EMP: 30
SQ FT: 3,500
SALES (est): 600K **Privately Held**
SIC: 5461 5149 2052 2051 Bakeries; bakery products; cookies & crackers; bread, cake & related products

(G-17617)
PILAND PARTS
3215 Darrow Rd (44224-4611)
PHONE..................................330 686-3083
Evan Piland, *Owner*
EMP: 4
SALES (est): 257.5K **Privately Held**
SIC: 2241 Fabric tapes

(G-17618)
PNEUMATIC PARTS CO
888 Hampshire Rd (44224-1165)
PHONE..................................330 923-6063
Stephen Biskner, *President*
Elizabeth Biskner, *Vice Pres*
EMP: 12 **EST:** 1958
SQ FT: 7,000
SALES (est): 2.2MM **Privately Held**
SIC: 3532 Mining machinery

(G-17619)
POLAR PRODUCTS INC
3380 Cavalier Trl (44224-4906)
PHONE..................................330 253-9973
William S Graessle, *President*
Maureen Humm, *General Mgr*
Rita Washington, *Opers Mgr*
Rose Graessle, *CFO*
▲ **EMP:** 8
SQ FT: 10,000
SALES (est): 850K **Privately Held**
SIC: 2833 8041 Medicinal chemicals; offices & clinics of chiropractors

(G-17620)
PREMIERE PRINTING & SIGNS INC
778 Mccauley Rd Unit 120 (44224-1067)
PHONE..................................330 688-6244
Craig Evans, *President*
Cheryl Evans, *Vice Pres*
EMP: 3
SQ FT: 1,560
SALES (est): 240K **Privately Held**
SIC: 2759 7389 Screen printing; sign painting & lettering shop

(G-17621)
PRINT-DIGITAL INCORPORATED
Also Called: Print Digital
4688 Darrow Rd (44224-1819)
PHONE..................................330 686-5945
Marvin Weber, *President*
Eric Weber, *Vice Pres*
EMP: 9
SQ FT: 4,500
SALES (est): 1.6MM **Privately Held**
WEB: www.digi-print.com
SIC: 2752 7334 2789 2761 Commercial printing, offset; photocopying & duplicating services; bookbinding & related work; manifold business forms

(G-17622)
PTR DAILY LLC
4501 Eastwicke Blvd (44224-2154)
PHONE..................................330 673-1990
EMP: 3
SALES (est): 125.8K **Privately Held**
SIC: 2711 Newspapers-Publishing/Printing

(G-17623)
RAY COMMUNICATIONS INC
Also Called: Raytec Systems
1337 Commerce Dr Ste 11 (44224-1758)
PHONE..................................330 686-0226
Richard A Yarnell, *President*
EMP: 9
SQ FT: 2,400
SALES (est): 1MM **Privately Held**
SIC: 5065 2542 5999 Communication equipment; telephone booths: except wood; telephone equipment & systems

Stow - Summit County (G-17624)

(G-17624)
SAINT-GOBAIN CERAMICS PLAS INC
Also Called: Saint-Gobain Norpro
3840 Fishcreek Rd (44224-4306)
PHONE..................330 673-5860
EMP: 843
SALES (corp-wide): 215.9MM Privately Held
SIC: 2819 3679 3544 3297 Industrial inorganic chemicals; electronic crystals; special dies & tools; nonclay refractories
HQ: Saint-Gobain Ceramics & Plastics, Inc.
750 E Swedesford Rd
Valley Forge PA 19482

(G-17625)
SAINT-GOBAIN NORPRO (DH)
3840 Fishcreek Rd (44224-4306)
PHONE..................330 673-5860
Antonio Vilela, President
Joseph H Menendez, Chairman
◆ EMP: 126
SALES (est): 67.5MM
SALES (corp-wide): 215.9MM Privately Held
WEB: www.sg-norpro.com
SIC: 3533 5211 Oil & gas field machinery; tile, ceramic
HQ: Saint-Gobain Abrasives, Inc.
1 New Bond St
Worcester MA 01606
508 795-5000

(G-17626)
SCOTT BADER INC
4280 Hudson Dr (44224-2251)
PHONE..................330 920-4410
Nick Padfield, President
Philip Bruce, Managing Dir
Chris Allan, Plant Mgr
Michelle Walker, Opers Mgr
Marie Terrizzi, Purchasing
▲ EMP: 8
SQ FT: 5,500
SALES (est): 1.7MM
SALES (corp-wide): 267.3MM Privately Held
WEB: www.scottbaderinc.com
SIC: 2821 Plastics materials & resins
HQ: Scott Bader Company Limited
Wollaston Hall
Wellingborough NORTHANTS NN29
193 366-3100

(G-17627)
SHANNON WARD
4526 Bunker Ln (44224-5151)
PHONE..................330 592-8177
Ward Shannon, Principal
EMP: 3 EST: 2010
SALES (est): 199.6K Privately Held
SIC: 3645 Residential lighting fixtures

(G-17628)
SIMPLEX-IT LLC
4301 Darrow Rd Ste 1200 (44224-7600)
PHONE..................234 380-1277
Robert L Coppedge, Principal
EMP: 5 EST: 2007
SALES (est): 1MM Privately Held
SIC: 3825 7372 Network analyzers; business oriented computer software

(G-17629)
SPIRAL BRUSHES INC
1355 Commerce Dr (44224-1751)
PHONE..................330 686-2861
Ernest R Preston III, President
Chuck Nichols, Project Mgr
Andy Mercer, Purch Mgr
Richard Harala, Engineer
Laura B Preston, Admin Sec
▲ EMP: 30 EST: 1939
SQ FT: 25,000
SALES (est): 5.5MM Privately Held
WEB: www.spiralbrushes.com
SIC: 3991 Brushes, household or industrial

(G-17630)
SPIROL INTERNATIONAL CORP
Spirol Shim Division
321 Remington Rd (44224-4915)
PHONE..................330 920-3655
Charles Kutchin, President
Anthony Canda, QC Mgr
Kara Mazzola, Engineer
Eric Phillips, Engineer
Jessica Camburako, Sales Engr
EMP: 60
SQ FT: 46,000
SALES (corp-wide): 69.1MM Privately Held
SIC: 3499 Shims, metal
HQ: Spirol International Corporation
30 Rock Ave
Danielson CT 06239
860 774-8571

(G-17631)
STEEL PRODUCTS CORP AKRON
2288 Samira Rd (44224-3404)
PHONE..................330 688-6633
EMP: 22
SQ FT: 100,000
SALES (est): 5MM Privately Held
SIC: 3599 Mfg Industrial Machinery

(G-17632)
STERIS INSTRUMENT MGT SVCS INC
Also Called: Spectrum Surgical Instruments
4575 Hudson Dr (44224-1725)
PHONE..................800 783-9251
Eric Henning, President
Justin Poulin, President
Jim Hoffman, Vice Pres
Matt Rudolph, Vice Pres
Kirk McCallum, Opers Staff
EMP: 30
SALES (corp-wide): 2.6B Privately Held
SIC: 3841 Surgical & medical instruments
HQ: Steris Instrument Management Services, Inc.
3316 2nd Ave N
Birmingham AL 35222

(G-17633)
SUMMIT RESEARCH GROUP
4466 Darrow Rd Ste 15 (44224-1891)
PHONE..................330 689-1778
Ron Antal, Principal
EMP: 4
SALES (est): 203.2K Privately Held
SIC: 2834 Pharmaceutical preparations

(G-17634)
SUP-R-DIE INC
1337 Commerce Dr Ste 3 (44224-1758)
PHONE..................330 688-7600
Jamie Wells, Manager
EMP: 3
SALES (corp-wide): 3.9MM Privately Held
SIC: 3544 Special dies & tools
PA: Sup-R-Die, Inc.
10003 Memphis Ave
Cleveland OH 44144
216 252-3930

(G-17635)
TOTAL REPAIR EXPRESS MICH LLC
Also Called: Dedtru
4575 Hudson Dr (44224-1725)
PHONE..................248 690-9410
Christian Mills,
Kirt Bennett,
EMP: 3 EST: 2011
SALES (est): 396.6K Privately Held
SIC: 3599 Machine shop, jobbing & repair

(G-17636)
TRANSMIT IDENTITY LLC
3916 Clk Pnte Trl Ste 101 (44224)
PHONE..................330 576-4732
Kiel Fleming, Creative Dir
Joseph A Licitri,
EMP: 4
SALES (est): 432.4K Privately Held
SIC: 2621 Printing paper

(G-17637)
TRAXIUM LLC
Also Called: Printing Concepts
4246 Hudson Dr (44224-2251)
PHONE..................330 572-8200
George Schmutz, President
EMP: 49
SQ FT: 45,000
SALES (est): 7.3MM Privately Held
WEB: www.printingconcepts.com
SIC: 2759 2752 7331 2789 Letterpress printing; commercial printing, offset; direct mail advertising services; bookbinding & related work

(G-17638)
TRI-STATE TOOL & DIE INC
1396 Norton Rd (44224-1394)
PHONE..................330 655-2536
Eric Pansegrau, President
▲ EMP: 5
SALES: 900K Privately Held
SIC: 3599 Machine shop, jobbing & repair

(G-17639)
TUFFY PAD COMPANY INC
454 Seasons Rd (44224-1020)
P.O. Box 1302 (44224-0302)
PHONE..................330 688-0043
Joseph M Burks, President
Debbie Burks, Treasurer
Margaret Burks, Admin Sec
EMP: 10
SQ FT: 15,000
SALES (est): 1.1MM Privately Held
WEB: www.tuffypad.com
SIC: 3949 Pads: football, basketball, soccer, lacrosse, etc.; masks: hockey, baseball, football, etc.

(G-17640)
VALV-TROL COMPANY
1340 Commerce Dr (44224-1737)
P.O. Box 2259 (44224-1000)
PHONE..................330 686-2800
Marjorie Ingram, Ch of Bd
Kenneth R Ingram, President
Richard Houck, Vice Pres
Bill Bedilion, Mfg Staff
EMP: 13 EST: 1947
SQ FT: 10,000
SALES: 1.9MM Privately Held
SIC: 3492 5084 Control valves, fluid power: hydraulic & pneumatic; industrial machinery & equipment

(G-17641)
VMI AMERICAS INC (DH)
4670 Allen Rd (44224-1042)
PHONE..................330 929-6800
Auke Diaster, President
▲ EMP: 42
SQ FT: 65,000
SALES (est): 6.6MM
SALES (corp-wide): 183.7K Privately Held
SIC: 3565 3544 Packaging machinery; special dies, tools, jigs & fixtures
HQ: Tkh Group N.V.
Spinnerstraat 15
Haaksbergen 7481
535 732-900

(G-17642)
WAINO SHEET METAL INC
4198 Ellsworth Rd (44224-2204)
P.O. Box 2677 (44224-6677)
PHONE..................330 945-4226
Sandra Waino, Principal
EMP: 4
SALES (est): 569.6K Privately Held
SIC: 3444 Sheet metalwork

(G-17643)
WOLFE GRINDING INC
4582 Allen Rd (44224-1091)
PHONE..................330 929-6677
Larry W Wolfe, President
Phyllis Wolfe, Vice Pres
EMP: 6
SQ FT: 48,750
SALES (est): 780.8K Privately Held
SIC: 3599 Machine shop, jobbing & repair

Strasburg
Tuscarawas County

(G-17644)
ALRON
805 Margo Dr Sw (44680-9792)
PHONE..................330 477-3405
Ron Gritzam, Partner
Allen Knotz, Partner
EMP: 8
SALES (est): 520.1K Privately Held
SIC: 2295 Metallizing of fabrics

(G-17645)
B A MALCUIT RACING INC
Also Called: Malcuit Racing Engines
707 S Wooster Ave (44680-9702)
P.O. Box 166 (44680-0166)
PHONE..................330 878-7111
Mark Malcuit, President
Brad Malcuit, Vice Pres
EMP: 8
SQ FT: 30,000
SALES (est): 580K Privately Held
SIC: 3519 3714 Internal combustion engines; motor vehicle parts & accessories

(G-17646)
BEACH CITY LUMBER LLC
5177 Austin Ln Nw (44680-9109)
PHONE..................330 878-4097
Paul Weaver, Owner
EMP: 7
SQ FT: 5,000
SALES (est): 1MM Privately Held
SIC: 2421 Lumber: rough, sawed or planed

(G-17647)
CASE FARMS OF OHIO INC
Also Called: Hatchery
1225 Hensel Ave Ne (44680-9779)
PHONE..................330 878-7118
Tom David, Manager
EMP: 11
SALES (corp-wide): 455.1MM Privately Held
WEB: www.casefarms.com
SIC: 2015 Poultry slaughtering & processing
HQ: Case Farms Of Ohio, Inc.
1818 County Rd 160
Winesburg OH 44690
330 359-7141

(G-17648)
GREEN RDCED EMSSONS NETWRK LLC
Also Called: Gre'n Disc
5029 Hilltop Dr Nw (44680-9069)
PHONE..................330 340-0941
Marty Lindon,
EMP: 8
SALES (est): 425.1K Privately Held
SIC: 3714 Motor vehicle parts & accessories

(G-17649)
KLEEN TEST PRODUCTS CORP
216 12th St Ne (44680-9752)
PHONE..................330 878-5586
Bill Ahlborn, Branch Mgr
EMP: 12
SALES (corp-wide): 379.3MM Privately Held
SIC: 2842 Cleaning or polishing preparations
HQ: Kleen Test Products Corporation
1611 S Sunset Rd
Port Washington WI 53074
262 284-6600

(G-17650)
NEWTON ASPHALT PAVING INC
8344 Central Rd Nw (44680-9115)
P.O. Box 86 (44680-0086)
PHONE..................330 878-5648
George A Gessner, President
Greg Gessner, Corp Secy
EMP: 15
SALES (est): 2.7MM Privately Held
SIC: 2951 Asphalt paving mixtures & blocks

(G-17651)
OXFORD MINING COMPANY INC
7551 Reed Rd Nw (44680-8902)
P.O. Box 135 (44680-0135)
PHONE..................330 878-5120
Chuck Ungurean, Owner
EMP: 6
SALES (corp-wide): 1.3B Privately Held
SIC: 1241 Coal mining services

GEOGRAPHIC SECTION

Streetsboro - Portage County (G-17678)

HQ: Oxford Mining Company, Inc.
544 Chestnut St
Coshocton OH 43812
740 622-6302

(G-17652)
SCHLUMBERGER LIMITED
211 Zeltman Ave Ne (44680-8983)
PHONE..................330 878-0794
EMP: 7 Publicly Held
SIC: 1389 Oil field services
HQ: Schlumberger Limited
5599 San Felipe St Fl 17
Houston TX 77056
713 513-2000

(G-17653)
STRASBURG PROVISION INC
172 Rosanna Ave (44680-9719)
PHONE..................330 878-1059
EMP: 25
SQ FT: 2,500
SALES (est): 895K Privately Held
SIC: 5421 2091 2013 2011 Meat Packing Plant Ret Meat/Fish

(G-17654)
TREMCAR USA INC
436 12th St Ne (44680-9760)
PHONE..................330 878-7708
William A Kyler, *President*
Jacques Tremblay, *President*
Marie Marquis, *Vice Pres*
Daniel Tremblaym, *Vice Pres*
▲ **EMP:** 57
SQ FT: 35,000
SALES (est): 17.4MM
SALES (corp-wide): 419.3K Privately Held
WEB: www.tremcarusa.com
SIC: 3713 Tank truck bodies
HQ: Tremcar Inc
790 Av Montrichard
Saint-Jean-Sur-Richelieu QC J2X 5
450 347-7822

(G-17655)
UNITED HARDWOODS LTD
5508 Hilltop Dr Nw (44680-9117)
PHONE..................330 878-9510
Norm Shetler, *Principal*
EMP: 9
SALES (est): 1MM Privately Held
SIC: 2421 Custom sawmill

Streetsboro
Portage County

(G-17656)
ACCURATE FAB LLC
1400 Miller Pkwy (44241-4640)
PHONE..................330 562-0566
James Mahallis,
Scott Hollman,
EMP: 6
SALES (est): 1.3MM Privately Held
SIC: 3441 Ship sections, prefabricated metal

(G-17657)
AGRATRONIX LLC
10375 State Route 43 (44241-4992)
PHONE..................330 562-2222
James Falbo, *Vice Pres*
Randy Beck, *Purch Mgr*
Dawn Decker, *Human Res Mgr*
Andrew Laflame, *VP Sales*
Gerald Stephens, *Mng Member*
▲ **EMP:** 30
SALES (est): 10.2MM Privately Held
WEB: www.agratronix.com
SIC: 5039 3699 3446 Wire fence, gates & accessories; electric fence chargers; fences, gates, posts & flagpoles

(G-17658)
ALACRIANT INC (PA)
1760 Miller Pkwy (44241-4633)
PHONE..................330 562-7191
James Berkes, *CEO*
Jeff Berkes, *President*
Zech Paul, *Business Mgr*
Ken Quinn, *Vice Pres*

Tom Nowak, *Controller*
EMP: 55 EST: 1997
SQ FT: 72,000
SALES (est): 27MM Privately Held
WEB: www.artisanindustries.com
SIC: 3499 Strapping, metal

(G-17659)
ALACRIANT INC
1760 Miller Pkwy (44241-4633)
PHONE..................330 562-7191
EMP: 40
SALES (corp-wide): 27MM Privately Held
WEB: www.artisanindustries.com
SIC: 3499 Strapping, metal
PA: Alacriant Inc.
1760 Miller Pkwy
Streetsboro OH 44241
330 562-7191

(G-17660)
AMERICAN HERITAGE BILLD LLC
630 Mondial Pkwy (44241-5211)
PHONE..................330 626-3710
Beth Depompei, *Mktg Dir*
Anthony Pucci, *Manager*
Joseph Pucci,
Michael Bequette,
Garrett Walker,
◆ **EMP:** 70
SQ FT: 64,000
SALES (est): 25.2MM Privately Held
WEB: www.americanheritagebilliards.com
SIC: 3949 Billiard & pool equipment & supplies, general

(G-17661)
ARTISTIC ELEMENTS SALON LLC
8929 State Route 14 Ste C (44241-5687)
PHONE..................330 626-2114
EMP: 3
SALES (est): 90K Privately Held
SIC: 2819 Mfg Industrial Inorganic Chemicals

(G-17662)
AURORA PLASTICS LLC (PA)
9280 Jefferson St (44241-3966)
PHONE..................330 422-0700
Darrell Hughes, *President*
Dan Odonnell, *General Mgr*
Steve Harrigan, *Vice Pres*
Matthew Kuwatch, *Vice Pres*
Matt McDonald, *CFO*
◆ **EMP:** 70
SALES (est): 28.6MM Privately Held
WEB: Www.auroraplastics.com
SIC: 2821 3087 Polyvinyl chloride resins (PVC); custom compound purchased resins

(G-17663)
AUTOMATED PACKG SYSTEMS INC
600 Mondial Pkwy (44241-5211)
PHONE..................330 626-2313
Bernard Lerner, *CEO*
EMP: 120
SQ FT: 173,000
SALES (corp-wide): 225.2MM Privately Held
SIC: 3081 3565 Packing materials, plastic sheet; polyethylene film; packaging machinery
PA: Automated Packaging Systems Inc.
10175 Philipp Pkwy
Streetsboro OH 44241
330 528-2000

(G-17664)
BERRY GLOBAL INC
1275 Ethan Ave (44241-4977)
PHONE..................330 896-6700
Robert Maltarich, *Manager*
EMP: 11 Publicly Held
SIC: 3089 Bottle caps, molded plastic
HQ: Berry Global, Inc.
101 Oakley St
Evansville IN 47710
812 424-2904

(G-17665)
CLEVELAND GAS SYSTEMS LLC
Also Called: Gas Tran Systems
10325 State Route 43 N (44241-4945)
PHONE..................216 391-7780
Matthew Brinn, *President*
▼ **EMP:** 5
SQ FT: 1,500
SALES (est): 857.1K Privately Held
WEB: www.gastransystems.com
SIC: 3556 Food products machinery

(G-17666)
CLEVELAND STEEL CONTAINER CORP
10048 Aurora Hudson Rd (44241-1636)
PHONE..................330 656-5600
Roger Mayle, *General Mgr*
EMP: 50
SALES (corp-wide): 131.9MM Privately Held
SIC: 3412 3411 Pails, shipping: metal; metal cans
PA: Cleveland Steel Container Corporation
30310 Emerald Valley Pkwy
Solon OH 44139
440 349-8000

(G-17667)
COMMERCIAL TURF PRODUCTS LTD
1777 Miller Pkwy (44241-4634)
PHONE..................330 995-7000
Mike Sobera, *General Mgr*
EMP: 240
SQ FT: 177,000
SALES (est): 48.5MM
SALES (corp-wide): 2.4B Privately Held
WEB: www.mtdproducts.com
SIC: 3524 Lawn & garden equipment
HQ: Mtd Products Inc
5965 Grafton Rd
Valley City OH 44280
330 225-2600

(G-17668)
DAVID ROUND COMPANY INC
10200 Wellman Rd (44241-1615)
PHONE..................330 656-1600
Bradley R Young, *President*
▲ **EMP:** 27 EST: 1869
SQ FT: 30,000
SALES (est): 8.3MM Privately Held
WEB: www.davidround.com
SIC: 3536 3531 Hoists; winches; cranes

(G-17669)
DAVIDSON CONVERTING INC
1611 Frost Rd (44241-5005)
PHONE..................330 626-2118
James B Davidson, *President*
Venny R Davidson, *Corp Secy*
Venny Davidson, *Treasurer*
EMP: 5
SQ FT: 10,000
SALES (est): 250K Privately Held
SIC: 2679 Paper products, converted

(G-17670)
DAVIS MACHINE PRODUCTS INC
74 Sapphire Ln (44241-4128)
PHONE..................440 474-0247
William G Davis, *President*
EMP: 6
SQ FT: 7,200
SALES (est): 200K Privately Held
SIC: 3599 Machine shop, jobbing & repair

(G-17671)
DELTA SYSTEMS INC
1734 Frost Rd (44241-5008)
P.O. Box 2459 (44241-0459)
PHONE..................330 626-2811
Elizabeth M Barry, *President*
Mark J Fechtel, *COO*
Kelly Slaw, *Project Mgr*
Tj Pattinson, *Warehouse Mgr*
Greg Schlechter, *Mfg Spvr*
▲ **EMP:** 225 EST: 1971
SQ FT: 137,000
SALES (est): 99.4MM Privately Held
WEB: www.deltasystemsinc.com
SIC: 3613 3625 Switchgear & switchboard apparatus; relays & industrial controls

(G-17672)
DUDICK INC
1818 Miller Pkwy (44241-5067)
PHONE..................330 562-1970
Tom Dudick, *President*
CC Chen, *Vice Pres*
Amy Fazenbaker, *Purchasing*
EMP: 55
SALES (est): 18MM Privately Held
SIC: 2851 Lacquers, varnishes, enamels & other coatings

(G-17673)
EPG INC (DH)
1780 Miller Pkwy (44241-4633)
PHONE..................330 995-9725
Michael Orazen Jr, *President*
Smith McKee, *Vice Pres*
Michael Scanlon, *Vice Pres*
Gabriel Orazen, *CFO*
EMP: 13
SQ FT: 46,000
SALES (est): 12.3MM
SALES (corp-wide): 3.7B Privately Held
WEB: www.epgcando.com
SIC: 3053 3061 Gaskets, all materials; mechanical rubber goods
HQ: Trelleborg Corporation
200 Veterans Blvd Ste 3
South Haven MI 49090
269 639-9891

(G-17674)
FORTEC MEDICAL LITHOTRIPSY LLC
10125 Wellman Rd (44241-1614)
PHONE..................330 656-4301
Todd Hallinan, *Sales Staff*
Drew Forhan, *Mng Member*
Rebecca Atkin, *Technology*
EMP: 50
SQ FT: 1,000
SALES (est): 4.5MM Privately Held
SIC: 3699 Laser systems & equipment

(G-17675)
GORELL ENTERPRISES INC (PA)
Also Called: Gorell Windows & Doors
10250 Philipp Pkwy (44241-4765)
PHONE..................724 465-1800
Wayne C Gorell, *Ch of Bd*
Brian Zimmerman, *President*
Michael A Rempel, *Vice Pres*
Arnold S Levitt, *CFO*
EMP: 370
SQ FT: 240,000
SALES (est): 34.5MM Privately Held
WEB: www.gorell.com
SIC: 3089 5031 Plastic hardware & building products; doors & windows

(G-17676)
GRAPHIC EXPRESSIONS SIGNS
8540 State Route 14 Ste D (44241-4204)
PHONE..................330 422-7446
Ann Landgraf, *President*
EMP: 5
SALES (est): 629K Privately Held
WEB: www.gesignsnmore.com
SIC: 2752 Commercial printing, lithographic

(G-17677)
HORSEMENS PRIDE INC
Also Called: Jolly Pats
10008 State Route 43 (44241-4940)
PHONE..................800 232-7950
Rob Miavitz, *President*
Brenda Miavitz, *Corp Secy*
Kristine Goad, *Manager*
▲ **EMP:** 22
SQ FT: 20,000
SALES (est): 5.2MM Privately Held
WEB: www.horsemenspride.com
SIC: 3089 Extruded finished plastic products

(G-17678)
INTERNATIONAL PAPER COMPANY
700 Mondial Pkwy (44241-4511)
PHONE..................330 626-7300
Chuck Bakaitis, *Branch Mgr*
EMP: 150

Streetsboro - Portage County (G-17679)

SALES (corp-wide): 23.3B **Publicly Held**
WEB: www.tin.com
SIC: 2653 Corrugated boxes, partitions, display items, sheets & pad
PA: International Paper Company
6400 Poplar Ave
Memphis TN 38197
901 419-9000

(G-17679)
JB PRODUCTS CO
Also Called: J B Products
10299 Wellman Rd (44241-1616)
PHONE.....................330 342-0223
Jon Beljon, *Owner*
EMP: 4 EST: 1977
SQ FT: 4,500
SALES: 200K **Privately Held**
SIC: 3544 Special dies & tools

(G-17680)
JOSEPH INDUSTRIES INC
Also Called: BUCKEYE FASTENERS COMPANY
10039 Aurora Hudson Rd (44241-1600)
PHONE.....................330 528-0091
Patrick Finnegan, *President*
Linda Kerekes, *Corp Secy*
Wendy Lovejoy, *Purch Mgr*
Audrey Jackson, *Controller*
Courtney Mahan, *Asst Controller*
▲ EMP: 52
SQ FT: 76,260
SALES: 10.9MM
SALES (corp-wide): 42.3MM **Privately Held**
WEB: www.joseph.com
SIC: 3714 5084 3713 3566 Motor vehicle parts & accessories; lift trucks & parts; truck & bus bodies; speed changers, drives & gears
PA: Fastener Industries, Inc.
1 Berea Cmns Ste 209
Berea OH 44017
440 243-0034

(G-17681)
MICRO-PISE MSRMENT SYSTEMS LLC
555 Mondial Pkwy (44241-4510)
P.O. Box 1869, Akron (44309-1869)
PHONE.....................330 541-9100
Steve Harris, *President*
Chris Price, *Sales Staff*
Kenneth Garvey,
◆ EMP: 250
SALES (est): 105.3MM
SALES (corp-wide): 4.8B **Publicly Held**
SIC: 3559 Automotive maintenance equipment
PA: Ametek, Inc.
1100 Cassatt Rd
Berwyn PA 19312
610 647-2121

(G-17682)
MICROBIOLOGICAL LABS INC
Also Called: Aspery Farms
9593 Page Rd (44241-5571)
P.O. Box 2519 (44241-0519)
PHONE.....................330 626-2264
George Aspery, *President*
Judith Hromi, *Vice Pres*
Joanne Aspery, *Admin Sec*
EMP: 4
SQ FT: 3,000
SALES: 371K **Privately Held**
WEB: www.microbiologicallabs.com
SIC: 8731 8734 2836 Commercial research laboratory; testing laboratories; biological products, except diagnostic

(G-17683)
MM SERVICE
8936 State Route 14 (44241-5605)
PHONE.....................330 474-3098
David Phillips, *Owner*
EMP: 6
SQ FT: 10,000
SALES (est): 694.8K **Privately Held**
SIC: 3524 Lawn & garden equipment

(G-17684)
MOJONNIER USA LLC
10325 State Route 43 N (44241-4945)
PHONE.....................844 665-6664

Matt Brinn, *Manager*
EMP: 7
SALES (est): 184.9K **Privately Held**
SIC: 3556 Beverage machinery

(G-17685)
NORTHCOAST ENVIRONMENTAL LABS
10100 Wellman Rd (44241-1613)
PHONE.....................330 342-3377
Timothy Spevak, *President*
John Lawrence, *Vice Pres*
Dave Morehead, *Vice Pres*
Fred Pratt, *Vice Pres*
David Mitalski, *Lab Dir*
EMP: 8
SQ FT: 3,000
SALES (est): 1.5MM **Privately Held**
SIC: 3826 8731 Environmental testing equipment; commercial physical research

(G-17686)
OHIO CLASSIC STREET RODS INC
Also Called: Stainless Works
10145 Philipp Pkwy (44241-5099)
PHONE.....................440 543-6593
Ronald Fuller, *President*
Geoff Masters, *General Mgr*
Chuck Daff, *Mfg Mgr*
Dave Hinderschied, *Sales Engr*
Barb Clayton, *Admin Asst*
▲ EMP: 3
SALES (est): 792.1K **Privately Held**
SIC: 3714 5013 Exhaust systems & parts, motor vehicle; automotive supplies & parts

(G-17687)
PERMCO INC
1500 Frost Rd (44241-5004)
P.O. Box 2068 (44241-0068)
PHONE.....................330 626-2801
Robert L Shell III, *CEO*
Danny Schiavi, *Regional Mgr*
Bernard Shell, *Exec VP*
Bernie Shell, *Exec VP*
Tim Hill, *Vice Pres*
▲ EMP: 110
SALES (est): 38.9MM **Privately Held**
SIC: 2869 Hydraulic fluids, synthetic base
PA: Guyan International, Inc.
5 Nichols Dr
Barboursville WV 25504
304 733-1029

(G-17688)
PETROX INC
10005 Ellsworth Rd (44241-1608)
PHONE.....................330 653-5526
Benjamin Cart, *President*
Mark Depew, *Vice Pres*
EMP: 10
SALES (est): 1.7MM **Privately Held**
SIC: 1389 5082 Oil field services; oil field equipment

(G-17689)
PM GRAPHICS INC
10170 Philipp Pkwy (44241-4705)
PHONE.....................330 650-0861
Paul W Mc Ghee II, *President*
Christine McGhee, *Corp Secy*
Robert Davis, *CFO*
EMP: 50
SQ FT: 35,000
SALES (est): 9.5MM **Privately Held**
WEB: www.pmgraphics.com
SIC: 2752 Commercial printing, offset

(G-17690)
R R DONNELLEY & SONS COMPANY
Also Called: R R Donnelley
10400 Danner Dr (44241-5070)
PHONE.....................330 562-5250
John Augustiniak, *Manager*
EMP: 100
SALES (corp-wide): 6.8B **Publicly Held**
WEB: www.moore.com
SIC: 2752 Commercial printing, lithographic

PA: R. R. Donnelley & Sons Company
35 W Wacker Dr Ste 3650
Chicago IL 60601
312 326-8000

(G-17691)
RB&W MANUFACTURING LLC (HQ)
10080 Wellman Rd (44241-1611)
PHONE.....................234 380-8540
Craig Cowan, *President*
▲ EMP: 10
SALES (est): 3.1MM
SALES (corp-wide): 1.6B **Publicly Held**
SIC: 5085 3452 3469 Fasteners, industrial: nuts, bolts, screws, etc.; bolts, nuts, rivets & washers; screws, metal; nuts, metal; stamping metal for the trade
PA: Park-Ohio Holdings Corp.
6065 Parkland Blvd Ste 1
Cleveland OH 44124
440 947-2000

(G-17692)
READY FIELD SOLUTIONS LLC
1240 Ethan Ave (44241-4976)
PHONE.....................330 562-0550
Teresa Sondles,
EMP: 4 EST: 2016
SALES (est): 480.1K **Privately Held**
SIC: 3271 Blocks, concrete: landscape or retaining wall

(G-17693)
S TOYS HOLDINGS LLC
10010 Aurora Hudson Rd (44241-1621)
PHONE.....................330 656-0440
Jack Bresics, *CEO*
James Schaefer, *COO*
Jim Smith, *CFO*
Tina Crock, *Marketing Staff*
◆ EMP: 900
SALES: 57MM **Privately Held**
SIC: 3944 3089 Games, toys & children's vehicles; plastic containers, except foam

(G-17694)
SAFEGUARD TECHNOLOGY INC
1460 Miller Pkwy (44241-4640)
PHONE.....................330 995-5200
Mervyn R Litzow, *President*
Rita Rode, *Human Res Mgr*
▲ EMP: 25
SQ FT: 20,510
SALES (est): 5.6MM **Privately Held**
WEB: www.safeguard-technology.com
SIC: 3069 Stair treads, rubber

(G-17695)
SEA AIR SPC MCG AND MLD LLC
10036 Aurora Hudson Rd (44241-1640)
PHONE.....................440 248-3025
Chip Gear,
EMP: 15
SALES: 950K **Privately Held**
SIC: 3721 Aircraft

(G-17696)
SELAS HEAT TECHNOLOGY CO LLC
11012 Aurora Hudson Rd (44241-1629)
PHONE.....................216 662-8800
Christine Orteca, *Branch Mgr*
EMP: 4
SALES (corp-wide): 56.8MM **Privately Held**
SIC: 3433 Gas burners, industrial
HQ: Selas Heat Technology Co Llc
11012 Aurora Hudson Rd
Streetsboro OH 44241
800 523-6500

(G-17697)
SELAS HEAT TECHNOLOGY CO LLC (HQ)
11012 Aurora Hudson Rd (44241-1629)
PHONE.....................800 523-6500
David S Bovenizer, *CEO*
▲ EMP: 28

SALES (est): 21.4MM
SALES (corp-wide): 56.8MM **Privately Held**
SIC: 3433 3255 3823 3564 Heating equipment, except electric; clay refractories; industrial instrmnts msrmnt display/control process variable; blowers & fans; industrial furnaces & ovens
PA: Lionheart Holdings Llc
54 Friends Ln Ste 125
Newtown PA 18940
215 283-8400

(G-17698)
SOFT-LITE LLC (HQ)
Also Called: Soft-Lite Windows
10250 Philipp Pkwy (44241-4765)
PHONE.....................330 528-3400
Roy Anderson, *President*
Kyle Pozek, *CFO*
Jamie Summers, *Controller*
Omayra Cortes, *Asst Controller*
Rachel Boland, *Human Res Mgr*
EMP: 160
SQ FT: 200,000
SALES (est): 126.9MM
SALES (corp-wide): 1.1B **Privately Held**
WEB: www.softlitewindows.com
SIC: 3089 Windows, plastic
PA: Harvey Industries, Inc.
1400 Main St Fl 3
Waltham MA 02451
800 598-5400

(G-17699)
SPECTRUM MACHINE INC (PA)
1668 Frost Rd (44241-5006)
PHONE.....................330 626-3666
Kevin Lamb, *President*
Todd Lamb, *Corp Secy*
Timothy Lamb, *Vice Pres*
EMP: 27
SQ FT: 31,000
SALES (est): 4.1MM **Privately Held**
WEB: www.spectrummachine.com
SIC: 3545 3599 Machine tool accessories; machine parts, stamped or pressed metal; machine shop, jobbing & repair

(G-17700)
STEP2 COMPANY LLC (PA)
Also Called: Step 2
10010 Aurora Hudson Rd (44241-1619)
PHONE.....................866 429-5200
Christopher P Quinn, *CEO*
Mark Collier, *Vice Pres*
Bob Jourdian, *Vice Pres*
Neale Winebrenner, *Project Mgr*
Sara Rector, *Opers Mgr*
◆ EMP: 500
SQ FT: 400,000
SALES (est): 219.9MM **Privately Held**
WEB: www.step2.com
SIC: 3089 3944 3423 Molding primary plastic; games, toys & children's vehicles; hand & edge tools

(G-17701)
TECHNOLOGY HOUSE LTD (PA)
Also Called: North Cape Manufacturing
10036 Aurora Hudson Rd (44241-1640)
PHONE.....................440 248-3025
Chip Gear,
Pamela Gear,
EMP: 46
SQ FT: 14,000
SALES (est): 18.8MM **Privately Held**
SIC: 8711 3544 3369 Industrial engineers; machine tool design; mechanical engineering; special dies, tools, jigs & fixtures; nonferrous foundries

(G-17702)
TELCON LLC
1677 Miller Pkwy (44241-4635)
PHONE.....................330 562-5566
Kevin Kummerlen, *President*
Dan Ferrara, *General Mgr*
Victor Mocarski, *Project Mgr*
EMP: 75
SQ FT: 56,000
SALES (est): 15.6MM **Privately Held**
SIC: 3599 3369 Machine shop, jobbing & repair; nonferrous foundries

GEOGRAPHIC SECTION

Strongsville - Cuyahoga County (G-17729)

(G-17703)
TEXTRON INC
555 Mondial Pkwy (44241-4510)
PHONE...................................330 626-7800
EMP: 10
SALES (corp-wide): 12.1B **Publicly Held**
SIC: 3721 Mfg Aircraft
PA: Textron Inc.
    40 Westminster St
    Providence RI 02903
    401 421-2800

(G-17704)
WYATT INDUSTRIES LLC
1790 Miller Pkwy (44241-4633)
PHONE...................................330 954-1790
Beverly Clemens, *CEO*
EMP: 6
SQ FT: 10,000
SALES (est): 331.4K **Privately Held**
SIC: 3089 Plastic processing

Strongsville
Cuyahoga County

(G-17705)
ACTION INDUSTRIES LTD (PA)
13325 Darice Pkwy (44149-3819)
PHONE...................................216 252-7800
John E Marron, *President*
Guenter Plamper, *Corp Secy*
Jeff Malarik, *Vice Pres*
Michael Simolin, *Plant Mgr*
Joann Lee, *Purchasing*
▲ **EMP:** 15 **EST:** 1980
SQ FT: 25,000
SALES (est): 3.9MM **Privately Held**
WEB: www.action-ind.com
SIC: 3699 2431 Door opening & closing devices, electrical; weather strip, wood

(G-17706)
ADVANCED TECH UTILIZATION CO
12005 Prospect Rd Unit 1 (44149-2935)
P.O. Box 360461 (44136-0008)
PHONE...................................440 238-3770
Terry Yamrick, *Owner*
EMP: 10
SQ FT: 2,500
SALES (est): 560K **Privately Held**
SIC: 3542 5084 Rebuilt machine tools, metal forming types; metalworking machinery

(G-17707)
ALBION INDUSTRIES INC
20246 Progress Dr (44149-3296)
PHONE...................................440 238-1955
Ralph Holstein, *President*
Roman T Keenen, *Principal*
Caroline Holstein, *Corp Secy*
◆ **EMP:** 30
SQ FT: 21,000
SALES (est): 4.3MM **Privately Held**
SIC: 2514 Frames for box springs or bedsprings: metal

(G-17708)
ALPHAGRAPHICS 507 INC
14765 Pearl Rd (44136-5026)
PHONE...................................440 878-9700
Rob Kammer, *President*
EMP: 6
SQ FT: 3,000
SALES (est): 936.8K **Privately Held**
SIC: 2752 Commercial printing, offset

(G-17709)
AMERICAN WATER SERVICES INC
17449 W Sprague Rd (44136-1666)
PHONE...................................440 243-9840
Rick Meloy, *Project Mgr*
EMP: 7
SALES (est): 1.3MM **Privately Held**
SIC: 3823 4941 Water quality monitoring & control systems; water supply

(G-17710)
AMTANK ARMOR
22555 Ascoa Ct (44149-4700)
PHONE...................................440 268-7735
John Mayles, *President*
EMP: 4
SALES (est): 215K **Privately Held**
SIC: 3083 Laminated plastics plate & sheet

(G-17711)
AMTECH INC
Also Called: Amtech Laminating Equipment
11925 Pearl Rd Ste 207 (44136-3343)
P.O. Box 360518, Cleveland (44136-0009)
PHONE...................................440 238-2141
Paul Roache, *President*
Joe Marita, *Vice Pres*
EMP: 4
SALES (est): 932.5K **Privately Held**
SIC: 5084 7699 2759 Industrial machinery & equipment; photographic equipment repair; commercial printing

(G-17712)
ASTRO INSTRUMENTATION LLC
22740 Lunn Rd (44149-4899)
PHONE...................................440 238-2005
Hal Waldman,
Doug Wood,
▲ **EMP:** 85 **EST:** 2000
SQ FT: 40,000
SALES (est): 19.4MM
SALES (corp-wide): 52.3MM **Privately Held**
WEB: www.astroinst.com
SIC: 3826 Laser scientific & engineering instruments
HQ: Sparton Corporation
    425 N Martingale Rd
    Schaumburg IL 60173
    847 762-5800

(G-17713)
ATLANTIC DURANT TECHNOLOGY INC (HQ)
Also Called: Atd
19963 Progress Dr (44149-3211)
PHONE...................................440 238-6931
Frank E Mehwald, *President*
Jamie Brasee, *Engineer*
Jennifer Dumm, *Human Resources*
Bob Kolenda, *Manager*
Michael S Mehwald, *Admin Sec*
▲ **EMP:** 1
SQ FT: 71,500
SALES (est): 6.2MM
SALES (corp-wide): 159.9MM **Privately Held**
SIC: 3469 Metal stampings
PA: Atlantic Tool & Die Company Inc
    19963 Progress Dr
    Strongsville OH 44149
    440 238-6931

(G-17714)
ATLANTIC TOOL & DIE COMPANY (PA)
19963 Progress Dr (44149-3211)
PHONE...................................440 238-6931
Frank Mehwald, *President*
Matt Edmonds, *President*
Richard Dombroski, *General Mgr*
Paul Durant, *General Mgr*
Michael Spenece, *General Mgr*
▲ **EMP:** 240 **EST:** 1947
SQ FT: 110,000
SALES (est): 159.9MM **Privately Held**
SIC: 3469 3544 Stamping metal for the trade; special dies, tools, jigs & fixtures

(G-17715)
AUTO TECHNOLOGY COMPANY
20026 Progress Dr (44149-3214)
PHONE...................................440 572-7800
Kevin A Smith, *President*
Walter Senney, *Vice Pres*
EMP: 15
SQ FT: 50,000
SALES (est): 4.8MM **Privately Held**
SIC: 3826 Environmental testing equipment

(G-17716)
AUTOMATED MFG SOLUTIONS INC
Also Called: AMS
19706 Progress Dr (44149-3208)
PHONE...................................440 878-3711
Thomas P Setele, *President*
Dave Minney, *Engineer*
Mark Ogorzaly, *CFO*
Gary Gembala, *Business Dir*
EMP: 18
SQ FT: 8,000
SALES (est): 5.3MM **Privately Held**
WEB: www.automfgsolutions.com
SIC: 3559 Automotive maintenance equipment

(G-17717)
AUTOWAX INC
15015 Foltz Pkwy (44149-4728)
PHONE...................................440 334-4417
Alina Baron, *CEO*
James Baron, *Vice Pres*
EMP: 6
SALES (est): 1.2MM **Privately Held**
SIC: 3711 Motor vehicles & car bodies

(G-17718)
BEARINGS MANUFACTURING COMPANY (PA)
Also Called: BMC
15157 Foltz Pkwy (44149-4730)
PHONE...................................440 846-5517
Steve Sivo, *President*
Jeff Walls, *Vice Pres*
Paul Milam, *Sales Mgr*
Joe Palladino, *Sales Staff*
Mark West, *Sales Staff*
EMP: 50
SALES (est): 12.1MM **Privately Held**
SIC: 3568 3562 Bearings, bushings & blocks; ball bearings & parts

(G-17719)
BENCO INDUSTRIES INC
19231 Royalton Rd (44149-4944)
P.O. Box 7, Richfield (44286-0007)
PHONE...................................440 572-3555
P Douglas Hatlovic, *President*
Dolores Hatlovic, *Admin Sec*
EMP: 6
SQ FT: 15,000
SALES (est): 756.9K **Privately Held**
WEB: www.bencoindustries.com
SIC: 3479 Painting of metal products

(G-17720)
BLUE CRESCENT ENTERPRISES INC
Also Called: AlphaGraphics
19645 Progress Dr (44149-3205)
P.O. Box 360379 (44136-0036)
PHONE...................................440 878-9700
Saleh Afif Alafifi, *President*
EMP: 7
SQ FT: 3,800
SALES: 550K **Privately Held**
SIC: 2752 Commercial printing, lithographic

(G-17721)
BREW KETTLE INC
Also Called: Ringneck Brewing Company
8377 Pearl Rd (44136-1637)
PHONE...................................440 234-8788
Chris J McKim, *President*
EMP: 11
SQ FT: 3,500
SALES (est): 2MM **Privately Held**
SIC: 2082 5149 Beer (alcoholic beverage); groceries & related products

(G-17722)
CARDINAL MACHINE COMPANY
14459 Foltz Pkwy (44149-4797)
PHONE...................................440 238-7050
Richard Z Kaszei, *CEO*
Greg Kaszei, *President*
EMP: 15
SQ FT: 10,000
SALES: 2MM **Privately Held**
SIC: 3599 Machine shop, jobbing & repair

(G-17723)
CASCADE GROUP OF OHIO LIMITED
Also Called: Budget Blinds
14761 Pearl Rd (44136-5026)
PHONE...................................440 572-2480
Jana Florek, *CEO*
EMP: 4
SQ FT: 1,600
SALES (est): 50K **Privately Held**
SIC: 2591 Window blinds

(G-17724)
CCL LABEL INC
Also Called: CCL Design Electronics
17700 Foltz Pkwy (44149-5536)
PHONE...................................440 878-7277
Patrick Thomas, *Branch Mgr*
Thomas Ravi, *Prgrmr*
EMP: 350
SALES (corp-wide): 3.7B **Privately Held**
WEB: www.avery.com
SIC: 2672 Coated & laminated paper
HQ: Ccl Label, Inc.
    161 Worcester Rd Ste 504
    Framingham MA 01701
    508 872-4511

(G-17725)
CHEMICAL METHODS INC
20338 Progress Dr (44149-3220)
PHONE...................................216 476-8400
Daniel E Richards, *President*
Joe McHenry, *President*
Chris Brunner, *Vice Pres*
EMP: 30
SQ FT: 5,000
SALES (est): 5.4MM **Privately Held**
WEB: www.chemicalmethods.com
SIC: 2842 3471 2992 2899 Cleaning or polishing preparations; plating & polishing; lubricating oils & greases; chemical preparations

(G-17726)
CLARK-RELIANCE CORPORATION (PA)
Also Called: Jerguson
16633 Foltz Pkwy (44149-5597)
PHONE...................................440 572-1500
Matthew P Figgie Jr, *Ch of Bd*
Rick Solon, *President*
Gerry Henwood, *Regional Mgr*
Tom Needham, *Business Mgr*
Jim Karfes, *Plant Mgr*
▲ **EMP:** 155
SQ FT: 93,000
SALES (est): 49.7MM **Privately Held**
WEB: www.clark-reliance.com
SIC: 3823 3491 Industrial process control instruments; process control regulator valves

(G-17727)
CLARK-RELIANCE CORPORATION
Also Called: Jacoby Tarbox Co
16633 Foltz Pkwy (44149-5597)
PHONE...................................440 572-7408
Jeffrey Sawicki, *President*
EMP: 5
SALES (corp-wide): 49.7MM **Privately Held**
WEB: www.clark-reliance.com
SIC: 3491 Industrial valves
PA: Clark-Reliance Corporation
    16633 Foltz Pkwy
    Strongsville OH 44149
    440 572-1500

(G-17728)
CLEVELAND FINISHING INC
16979 Falmouth Dr (44136-7417)
PHONE...................................440 572-5475
Edward Eible, *President*
EMP: 3
SALES (est): 174.6K **Privately Held**
SIC: 3471 Finishing, metals or formed products

(G-17729)
CLEVELAND JSM INC
Also Called: Tenk Machine
11792 Alameda Dr (44149-3011)
PHONE...................................440 876-3050

Strongsville - Cuyahoga County (G-17730)

Dave Holm, *General Mgr*
Ray Knapp, *Principal*
Paul Skidmore, *Plant Mgr*
Brad Shrock, *Manager*
EMP: 65 **EST:** 1942
SALES (est): 393.5K **Privately Held**
SIC: 3599 7699 7692 Custom machinery; industrial machinery & equipment repair; welding repair

(G-17730)
COLOR PROCESS INC
13900 Prospect Rd (44149-3834)
PHONE..................................440 268-7100
Mark Ingham, *President*
Jim Greiner, *Admin Sec*
EMP: 25 **EST:** 1959
SQ FT: 65,000
SALES: 4.8MM **Privately Held**
WEB: www.colorprocess.com
SIC: 2752 Commercial printing, offset

(G-17731)
CONDITION MONITORING SUPPLIES
Also Called: CMS
20338 Progress Dr (44149-3220)
P.O. Box 770804, Cleveland (44107-0037)
PHONE..................................216 941-6868
Dan Richards, *Owner*
EMP: 4
SALES (est): 250.6K **Privately Held**
SIC: 3533 Oil field machinery & equipment

(G-17732)
CONSOLDTED GRNHSE SLUTIONS LLC
14800 Foltz Pkwy (44149-4725)
PHONE..................................330 844-8598
Sylvia Courtney, *Mng Member*
Rebecca Yount, *Mng Member*
John Helline,
EMP: 4
SQ FT: 4,000
SALES (est): 602.9K **Privately Held**
SIC: 1542 3448 Institutional building construction; greenhouses: prefabricated metal

(G-17733)
CRISHTRONICS LLC
15249 Sassafras Dr (44136-1781)
PHONE..................................440 572-8318
James K Roosa, *Mng Member*
EMP: 3
SALES (est): 222.1K **Privately Held**
SIC: 3674 Microcircuits, integrated (semiconductor); microprocessors

(G-17734)
CUSTOM IMPRINT
19573 Progress Dr (44149-3203)
PHONE..................................440 238-4488
Ed Rebish, *Owner*
Scott Walker, *Plant Mgr*
EMP: 10
SALES (est): 565.6K **Privately Held**
WEB: www.customimprint.com
SIC: 2752 Commercial printing, lithographic

(G-17735)
CUSTOM SPEED PARTS INC
Also Called: Harland Sharp
19769 Progress Dr (44149-3207)
PHONE..................................440 238-3260
Randy Becker, *President*
Susan Becker, *Vice Pres*
Micheal Becker, *Production*
Steven Becker, *Marketing Staff*
EMP: 15
SQ FT: 32,000
SALES (est): 3.4MM **Privately Held**
WEB: www.customspeedparts.com
SIC: 3714 Motor vehicle engines & parts

(G-17736)
CYLINDERS & VALVES INC
20811 Westwood Dr (44149-3999)
P.O. Box 360555, Cleveland (44136-0010)
PHONE..................................440 238-7343
James P Gardner III, *President*
Katherine Frederick, *Manager*
EMP: 8 **EST:** 1958
SQ FT: 7,500
SALES (est): 1.2MM **Privately Held**
WEB: www.cylval.com
SIC: 3594 3593 3494 Motors: hydraulic, fluid power or air; fluid power cylinders & actuators; valves & pipe fittings

(G-17737)
DOUGLAS S KUTZ
19395 Knowlton Pkwy # 103 (44149-9056)
P.O. Box 360812, Cleveland (44136-0014)
PHONE..................................440 238-8426
EMP: 3
SALES (est): 160K **Privately Held**
SIC: 3272 Mfg Concrete Products

(G-17738)
DUPLI-SYSTEMS INC
Also Called: Ohio Cut Sheet
8260 Dow Cir (44136-1762)
PHONE..................................440 234-9415
Bud Eldridge, *CEO*
Randy Eldridge, *President*
Todd Eldridge, *Exec VP*
Dave Griffith, *Vice Pres*
Laurie Scalf, *Human Res Mgr*
EMP: 125 **EST:** 1955
SALES (est): 23.6MM **Privately Held**
WEB: www.dupli-systems.com
SIC: 2759 2754 2782 2761 Commercial printing; business forms: gravure printing; blankbooks & looseleaf binders; manifold business forms; commercial printing, lithographic; automotive & apparel trimmings

(G-17739)
DUROX COMPANY
12312 Alameda Dr (44149-3023)
PHONE..................................440 238-5350
Richard A Mathes, *Admin Sec*
▲ **EMP:** 70
SQ FT: 50,000
SALES (est): 23.3MM
SALES (corp-wide): 4.3B **Publicly Held**
WEB: www.durox.com
SIC: 3053 Gaskets, all materials
HQ: Standard Car Truck Company Inc
6400 Shafer Ct Ste 450
Rosemont IL 60018
847 692-6050

(G-17740)
EFFICIENT MACHINE PDTS CORP
12133 Alameda Dr (44149-3018)
PHONE..................................440 268-0205
Ted Imbrogno, *President*
Patrick McGuckin, *Vice Pres*
Paul Klonowski, *QC Mgr*
Jack Waltz, *Manager*
Edward Imbrogno, *Administration*
EMP: 40 **EST:** 1962
SQ FT: 31,000
SALES: 7MM **Privately Held**
WEB: www.efficientmachineprod.com
SIC: 3451 Screw machine products

(G-17741)
ELEGANT EMBROIDERY LLC
11053 Prospect Rd (44149-2839)
PHONE..................................440 878-0904
Peter F Sturtevant,
James Hollingsworth,
EMP: 3 **EST:** 2005
SQ FT: 1,000
SALES: 100K **Privately Held**
SIC: 2395 Embroidery products, except schiffli machine; embroidery & art needlework

(G-17742)
EMCO ELECTRIC INTERNATIONAL
19449 Progress Dr (44149-3201)
P.O. Box 361361 (44136-0023)
PHONE..................................440 878-1199
Richard Tamulewicz Jr, *President*
Michelle Tamulewicz, *Vice Pres*
Sheri Tamulewicz, *Vice Pres*
▲ **EMP:** 5
SQ FT: 22,000
SALES (est): 846.3K **Privately Held**
SIC: 3644 2841 Electric conduits & fittings; soap & other detergents

(G-17743)
ERNST FLOW INDUSTRIES LLC
16633 Foltz Pkwy (44149-5513)
PHONE..................................732 938-5641
Roger Ernst, *President*
John Ernst, *Vice Pres*
Eugene Ernst Jr, *Treasurer*
EMP: 14 **EST:** 1962
SQ FT: 9,000
SALES (est): 3.1MM
SALES (corp-wide): 49.7MM **Privately Held**
WEB: www.tfci.com
SIC: 3823 3824 Flow instruments, industrial process type; water meters
PA: Clark-Reliance Corporation
16633 Foltz Pkwy
Strongsville OH 44149
440 572-1500

(G-17744)
FOUNDATION SOFTWARE INC
17999 Foltz Pkwy (44149-5565)
PHONE..................................330 220-8383
Fred Ode, *CEO*
Thomas Ross, *Project Mgr*
Jason Stypick, *Project Mgr*
Denise Prescott, *Controller*
Mike Ode, *Sales Mgr*
EMP: 92
SQ FT: 16,000
SALES (est): 15.6MM **Privately Held**
SIC: 7372 7371 Prepackaged software; software programming applications; custom computer programming services

(G-17745)
FRANJINHAS INC
17656 Fairfax Ln (44136-7206)
PHONE..................................440 463-1523
Clara Lipszyc-Arroyo, *President*
Steven Aurroyo, *Treasurer*
EMP: 6 **EST:** 1997
SALES (est): 477.9K **Privately Held**
SIC: 2211 Flannels, cotton

(G-17746)
GARETH STEVENS PUBLISHING LP
23221 Morgan Ct (44149-5100)
PHONE..................................800 542-2595
Roger Rosen, *Partner*
Gary Spears, *Partner*
EMP: 150
SALES (est): 5.8MM **Privately Held**
SIC: 2731 Books: publishing only

(G-17747)
GUARANTEE SPECIALTIES INC
Also Called: Garvin Industries Div
21693 Drake Rd (44149-6614)
P.O. Box 360247 (44136-0005)
PHONE..................................216 451-9744
Armando E Pages, *President*
Carol Braunschweig, *Principal*
▲ **EMP:** 57
SQ FT: 75,000
SALES (est): 7.2MM **Privately Held**
WEB: www.gsi-garvin.com
SIC: 3463 3469 3465 Plumbing fixture forgings, nonferrous; stamping metal for the trade; automotive stampings

(G-17748)
HDI LANDING GEAR USA INC
Also Called: Heroux Devtek Landing Gear Div
15900 Foltz Pkwy (44149-5531)
PHONE..................................440 783-5255
Don Benincasa, *Manager*
EMP: 50
SQ FT: 115,000
SALES (corp-wide): 309.4MM **Privately Held**
SIC: 3728 Alighting (landing gear) assemblies, aircraft
HQ: Hdi Landing Gear Usa, Inc.
663 Montgomery Ave
Springfield OH 45506

(G-17749)
HINCHCLIFF LUMBER COMPANY
Also Called: Hinchcliff Products Co
13550 Falling Water Rd # 105 (44136-4360)
PHONE..................................440 238-5200
Jay Philips, *Manager*
EMP: 5
SALES (corp-wide): 9.1MM **Privately Held**
WEB: www.hinchcliffproducts.com
SIC: 2426 2448 Dimension, hardwood; wood pallets & skids
PA: Hinchcliff Lumber Company
Rr 72
Hendricks WV 26271
304 478-2500

(G-17750)
HOUSE SILVA-STRONGSVILLE INC
Al156 Southpark Mall Al (44136)
PHONE..................................330 464-6419
Kelly Silva, *President*
EMP: 3
SQ FT: 1,368
SALES (est): 261.2K **Privately Held**
SIC: 3559 Jewelers' machines

(G-17751)
HUGHES CORPORATION (PA)
Also Called: Weschler Instruments
16900 Foltz Pkwy (44149-5520)
PHONE..................................440 238-2550
David E Hughes, *President*
Esther Carpenter, *Principal*
Michael F Dorman, *Exec VP*
Douglas Hughes, *Vice Pres*
Ryan Hughes, *Vice Pres*
EMP: 30
SQ FT: 11,500
SALES (est): 32.4MM **Privately Held**
WEB: www.weschler.com
SIC: 5063 3825 Electrical apparatus & equipment; instruments to measure electricity

(G-17752)
HUMPHREY POPCORN COMPANY (PA)
11606 Pearl Rd (44136-3320)
PHONE..................................216 662-6629
Micheal Prokop, *President*
Dudley Humphrey, *President*
Betsy Humphrey, *Vice Pres*
Elizabeth Humphrey, *Vice Pres*
Joanne Lynch, *Vice Pres*
EMP: 10
SQ FT: 11,000
SALES: 500K **Privately Held**
SIC: 0191 2064 5145 General farms, primarily crop; popcorn balls or other treated popcorn products; popcorn & supplies

(G-17753)
IMPERIAL DIE & MFG CO
22930 Royalton Rd (44149-3842)
PHONE..................................440 268-9080
Ronald Lapossy, *President*
Kenneth Lapossy, *Treasurer*
EMP: 13 **EST:** 1959
SQ FT: 20,000
SALES (est): 2.3MM **Privately Held**
SIC: 3469 3544 Stamping metal for the trade; special dies & tools

(G-17754)
INFINIUM WALL SYSTEMS INC
22555 Ascoa Ct (44149-4700)
PHONE..................................440 572-5000
Shawn Gaffney, *President*
Kenny Goodwin, *Controller*
Jenny Gaffney, *Comms Mgr*
Jordan Bates, *Comp Tech*
Caryn Gaffney, *Shareholder*
▼ **EMP:** 30
SQ FT: 30,000
SALES: 15MM **Privately Held**
WEB: www.infiniumwalls.com
SIC: 2522 Office furniture, except wood

GEOGRAPHIC SECTION

Strongsville - Cuyahoga County (G-17782)

(G-17755)
INSTRUMENTORS INC
22077 Drake Rd (44149-6606)
PHONE....................440 238-3430
Robert A Heinrich, *President*
Elvera Heinrich, *Corp Secy*
James R Heinrich, *Vice Pres*
James Heinrich, *Vice Pres*
David Wolfs, *Engineer*
EMP: 6 **EST:** 1973
SQ FT: 10,000
SALES (est): 1.2MM **Privately Held**
WEB: www.instrumentorsinc.com
SIC: 3829 7699 5084 Measuring & controlling devices; scientific equipment repair service; instruments & control equipment

(G-17756)
J & J BECHKE INC (PA)
Also Called: Cq Printing
12931 Pearl Rd (44136-3425)
PHONE....................440 238-1441
John Bechke, *President*
Joy Bechke, *Vice Pres*
EMP: 8 **EST:** 1978
SQ FT: 2,200
SALES (est): 1.6MM **Privately Held**
SIC: 2752 Commercial printing, offset

(G-17757)
JATDCO LLC
19963 Progress Dr (44149-3211)
PHONE....................440 238-6570
Louis James,
Michael Mehwald,
EMP: 4
SALES (est): 292.3K **Privately Held**
SIC: 3465 7692 4213 Automotive stampings; automotive welding; automobiles, transport & delivery

(G-17758)
K & M TOOL & MACHINE CO INC
17383 Foltz Pkwy (44149-5527)
PHONE....................440 572-5130
Pete Stojsavljevic, *President*
EMP: 3
SQ FT: 8,800
SALES: 500K **Privately Held**
SIC: 3599 Machine shop, jobbing & repair

(G-17759)
KALINICH FENCE COMPANY INC
12223 Prospect Rd (44149-2994)
PHONE....................440 238-6127
Mike Kalinich Sr, *President*
Erma Kalinich, *Corp Secy*
Mike Kalinich Jr, *Vice Pres*
EMP: 18 **EST:** 1918
SQ FT: 33,000
SALES (est): 3.3MM **Privately Held**
WEB: www.kalinichfenceco.com
SIC: 2499 Fencing, wood; snow fence, wood

(G-17760)
KID CONCOCTIONS COMPANY
18511 Whitemarsh Ln (44149-6863)
PHONE....................440 572-1800
EMP: 4
SALES: 2.1MM **Privately Held**
SIC: 2731 Books Printing & Publishing

(G-17761)
LAKE ERIE RUBBER RECYCLING LLC
19940 Echo Dr (44149-6010)
PHONE....................440 570-6027
Katherine E Miller, *Admin Asst*
EMP: 4
SALES (est): 441.9K **Privately Held**
SIC: 3069 Reclaimed rubber (reworked by manufacturing processes)

(G-17762)
LEES GRINDING INC
15620 Foltz Pkwy (44149-4741)
P.O. Box 360169 (44136-0003)
PHONE....................440 572-4610
Nick D Papanikolaou, *President*
EMP: 30 **EST:** 1961
SQ FT: 20,000
SALES (est): 5.1MM **Privately Held**
WEB: www.leesgrinding.com
SIC: 3599 Machine shop, jobbing & repair

(G-17763)
LUMITEX INC (PA)
8443 Dow Cir (44136-1796)
PHONE....................440 243-8401
Peter W Broer, *President*
Thomas E Walden, *CFO*
Richard D Gridley, *Director*
▲ **EMP:** 90
SQ FT: 19,000
SALES (est): 22MM **Privately Held**
WEB: www.lumitex.com
SIC: 3646 3641 3648 3845 Commercial indusl & institutional electric lighting fixtures; electric lamps; lighting equipment; electromedical equipment

(G-17764)
LUMITEX INC
Poly Optical Pdts & Lumitex
8443 Dow Cir (44136-1796)
PHONE....................949 250-8557
Scott Diestel, *Manager*
EMP: 5
SALES (corp-wide): 22MM **Privately Held**
WEB: www.lumitex.com
SIC: 3641 Electric lamps
PA: Lumitex, Inc.
   8443 Dow Cir
   Strongsville OH 44136
   440 243-8401

(G-17765)
MOMENTIVE PRFMCE MTLS QRTZ INC
22557 Lunn Rd (44149-4871)
PHONE....................440 878-5700
Joseph P Reyes, *President*
Melissa Trout, *Opers Staff*
Kevin Kramer, *Engineer*
Mark Magda, *Manager*
Creighton Tomek, *Technician*
◆ **EMP:** 200
SALES (est): 83.1MM
SALES (corp-wide): 2.7B **Publicly Held**
SIC: 2869 3479 3446 3297 Silicones; coating of metals with silicon; architectural metalwork; nonclay refractories
HQ: Momentive Performance Materials Inc.
   260 Hudson River Rd
   Waterford NY 12188

(G-17766)
MONARCH ENGRAVING INC
8293 Dow Cir (44136-1761)
PHONE....................440 638-1500
William Pfeil Jr, *President*
David Pfeil, *Corp Secy*
Brian Pfeil, *Vice Pres*
EMP: 23 **EST:** 1953
SQ FT: 20,000
SALES (est): 3.5MM **Privately Held**
SIC: 3083 2899 Laminated plastics plate & sheet; chemical preparations

(G-17767)
MTS MEDICATION TECH INC
21550 Drake Rd (44149-6617)
PHONE....................440 238-0840
Gail Baksi, *Branch Mgr*
EMP: 3 **Publicly Held**
WEB: www.mtsp.com
SIC: 3089 3565 Blister or bubble formed packaging, plastic; packaging machinery
HQ: Mts Medication Technologies, Inc.
   2003 Gandy Blvd N Ste 800
   Saint Petersburg FL 33702
   727 576-6311

(G-17768)
MUELLER ART COVER & BINDING CO
12005 Alameda Dr (44149-3016)
P.O. Box 360829 (44136-0014)
PHONE....................440 238-3303
Toll Free:....................888 -
Edmond Mueller, *President*
Bob Mueller, *COO*
Daniel Mack, *Vice Pres*
Robert Mueller, *Manager*
EMP: 45
SQ FT: 38,000
SALES (est): 5.9MM **Privately Held**
WEB: www.muellerartcover.com
SIC: 2782 7336 Looseleaf binders & devices; graphic arts & related design; silk screen design

(G-17769)
NEWBERRY WOOD ENTERPRISES INC (PA)
12223 Prospect Rd (44149-2939)
PHONE....................440 238-6127
Mike Kalinich, *President*
Michael Kalinich Sr, *President*
EMP: 14
SQ FT: 25,000
SALES (est): 1.8MM **Privately Held**
SIC: 2421 Custom sawmill; snow fence lath

(G-17770)
NEXGEN MACHINE COMPANY LLC
19768 Progress Dr (44149-3208)
P.O. Box 361208 (44136-0021)
PHONE....................440 268-2222
Michael Weinrauch, *Principal*
EMP: 9 **EST:** 2014
SALES (est): 1.3MM **Privately Held**
SIC: 3599 Machine shop, jobbing & repair

(G-17771)
NORTH COAST PATTERN INC
10587 Scottsdale Dr (44136-8801)
PHONE....................440 322-5064
Al Ledyard, *President*
EMP: 4
SQ FT: 4,628
SALES (est): 455.2K **Privately Held**
SIC: 3543 Foundry patternmaking

(G-17772)
NUTRO CORPORATION
Also Called: Nutro Machinery
11515 Alameda Dr (44149-3006)
PHONE....................440 572-3800
Mark Rooney, *President*
George Wharton, *Vice Pres*
Dave Wysocki, *Project Mgr*
Richard Sheldon, *Opers Mgr*
Brian Scheuermann, *Purchasing*
EMP: 55
SQ FT: 65,000
SALES (est): 16.7MM **Privately Held**
WEB: www.nutro.com
SIC: 3569 3559 Liquid automation machinery & equipment; paint making machinery

(G-17773)
NUTRO INC
11515 Alameda Dr (44149-3006)
PHONE....................440 572-3800
Mark Rooney, *Principal*
Christian Nuesser, *Vice Pres*
EMP: 31
SALES (est): 6.8MM
SALES (corp-wide): 37MM **Privately Held**
SIC: 3559 3251 Paint making machinery; ceramic glazed brick, clay
PA: Venjakob Maschinenbau Gmbh & Co. Kg
   Augsburger Str. 2-6
   Rheda-Wiedenbruck 33378
   524 296-030

(G-17774)
OAK PRINTING COMPANY
19540 Progress Dr (44149-3284)
PHONE....................440 238-3316
James M Helms, *President*
Alysia Groscost, *General Mgr*
▲ **EMP:** 40
SQ FT: 54,000
SALES (est): 6.9MM **Privately Held**
WEB: www.oakprintingco.com
SIC: 2752 Commercial printing, offset

(G-17775)
OUTOTEC OYJ
Also Called: Outotec North America
11288 Alameda Dr (44149-3037)
PHONE....................440 783-3336
Tim Robinson, *Branch Mgr*
EMP: 20
SALES (corp-wide): 32.7MM **Privately Held**
SIC: 3441 Fabricated structural metal
PA: Outotec Oyj
   Rauhalanpuisto 9
   Espoo 02230
   205 292-11

(G-17776)
PA MA INC
Also Called: Pama Tool & Die
11288 Alameda Dr (44149-3037)
P.O. Box 361459 (44136-0025)
PHONE....................440 846-3799
Ron Pansil, *President*
Donna Pansil, *Vice Pres*
Danuta Pansil, *Treasurer*
EMP: 7
SQ FT: 8,000
SALES (est): 816.5K **Privately Held**
SIC: 3544 Special dies & tools

(G-17777)
PPG INDUSTRIES INC
Also Called: Powder Coatings
19699 Progress Dr (44149-3298)
PHONE....................440 572-2800
William Shaw, *Branch Mgr*
EMP: 100
SALES (corp-wide): 15.3B **Publicly Held**
SIC: 2851 Paints & allied products
PA: Ppg Industries, Inc.
   1 Ppg Pl
   Pittsburgh PA 15272
   412 434-3131

(G-17778)
PRECISION PRODUCTION INC
8250 Dow Cir (44136-1762)
PHONE....................216 252-0372
Craig Cook, *President*
Mathew A Carson, *Treasurer*
▲ **EMP:** 40
SQ FT: 38,000
SALES (est): 8.8MM **Privately Held**
WEB: www.precisionproduction.com
SIC: 3599 Machine shop, jobbing & repair

(G-17779)
PROFESSIONAL PACKAGING COMPANY (PA)
22360 Royalton Rd (44149-3826)
PHONE....................440 238-8850
Scott Gilbert, *President*
Sharon Gilbert, *Corp Secy*
▲ **EMP:** 21
SQ FT: 115,000
SALES (est): 25.5MM **Privately Held**
WEB: www.a-roo.com
SIC: 3081 Packing materials, plastic sheet

(G-17780)
R M TOOL & DIE INC
19768 Progress Dr (44149-3208)
PHONE....................440 238-6459
Mike Regian, *President*
Steven Regian, *General Mgr*
EMP: 12
SQ FT: 25,000
SALES: 3.5MM **Privately Held**
SIC: 3544 Special dies & tools

(G-17781)
RAFTER EQUIPMENT CORPORATION
12430 Alameda Dr (44149-3025)
PHONE....................440 572-3700
Walter Krenz, *President*
Paul Rohde, *Vice Pres*
Paul Herman, *Opers Staff*
Lou Demarco, *Purch Mgr*
Philip Baker, *Electrical Engi*
▲ **EMP:** 30
SQ FT: 22,500
SALES (est): 6.4MM **Privately Held**
WEB: www.rafterequipment.com
SIC: 3542 3549 3547 3541 Machine tools, metal forming type; metalworking machinery; rolling mill machinery; machine tools, metal cutting type; fabricated pipe & fittings

(G-17782)
RITTAL CORP
19541 Winding Trl (44149-8721)
PHONE....................440 572-4999

Strongsville - Cuyahoga County (G-17783)

Dwight Patterson, *Branch Mgr*
EMP: 170
SALES (corp-wide): 2.6B **Privately Held**
SIC: 3469 Electronic enclosures, stamped or pressed metal
HQ: Rittal North America Llc
425 N Martingale Rd # 1540
Schaumburg IL 60173
847 240-4600

(G-17783)
ROBERT E MCGRATH INC
Also Called: Olympia Candies
11606 Pearl Rd (44136-3320)
PHONE....................440 572-7747
Robert McGrath, *President*
Celia McGrath, *Vice Pres*
EMP: 25
SQ FT: 15,000
SALES: 750K **Privately Held**
WEB: www.olympiacandy.com
SIC: 5145 5441 2096 2066 Candy; candy; potato chips & similar snacks; chocolate & cocoa products; ice cream & frozen desserts

(G-17784)
SAFETY SIGN COMPANY
19511 Progress Dr Ste 4 (44149-3262)
P.O. Box 360500 (44136-0009)
PHONE....................440 238-7722
James J Merriman, *President*
Joel G Casas, *Senior VP*
EMP: 50 **EST:** 1952
SQ FT: 42,000
SALES (est): 6.2MM **Privately Held**
WEB: www.safetysignco.com
SIC: 3993 Signs, not made in custom sign painting shops

(G-17785)
SCHWEBEL BAKING COMPANY
22626 Royalton Rd (44149-3838)
PHONE....................440 846-1921
Steve Leach, *Manager*
Tom Siegel, *Manager*
EMP: 154
SALES (corp-wide): 170MM **Privately Held**
SIC: 2051 Bakery: wholesale or wholesale/retail combined
PA: Schwebel Baking Company
965 E Midlothian Blvd
Youngstown OH 44502
330 783-2860

(G-17786)
SGL TECHNIC INC
21945 Drake Rd (44149-6608)
PHONE....................440 572-3600
▲ **EMP:** 30
SQ FT: 52,000
SALES (est): 5.7MM
SALES (corp-wide): 1B **Privately Held**
SIC: 3443 Mfg Fabricated Plate Work
HQ: Sgl Carbon, Llc
10715 David Taylor Dr # 460
Charlotte NC 28262
704 593-5100

(G-17787)
SHEIBAN JEWELRY INC
16938 Pearl Rd (44136-6053)
PHONE....................440 238-0616
Tony Sheiban, *President*
Jason Sheiban, *VP Mktg*
EMP: 10 **EST:** 1976
SQ FT: 3,300
SALES (est): 2.6MM **Privately Held**
SIC: 5094 5944 7631 3911 Jewelry; precious stones (gems); precious metals; jewelry, precious stones & precious metals; watch, clock & jewelry repair; jewelry, precious metal

(G-17788)
SHERWIN-WILLIAMS COMPANY
11410 Alameda Dr (44149-3005)
PHONE....................440 846-4328
Blair Lacour, *President*
Dave Cashin, *Comp Tech*
EMP: 25
SQ FT: 24,150
SALES (corp-wide): 17.5B **Publicly Held**
WEB: www.sherwin.com
SIC: 5231 2851 Paint; wallcoverings; paints & allied products; varnishes; lacquer: bases, dopes, thinner
PA: The Sherwin-Williams Company
101 W Prospect Ave # 1020
Cleveland OH 44115
216 566-2000

(G-17789)
SLY INC (PA)
8300 Dow Cir Ste 600 (44136-6607)
PHONE....................440 891-3200
E D Davis, *Principal*
W C Bruce, *Principal*
W C Sly, *Principal*
W W Sly, *Principal*
Sidney C Vessy, *Principal*
EMP: 13 **EST:** 1874
SQ FT: 36,000
SALES (est): 5MM **Privately Held**
WEB: www.slyinc.com
SIC: 3564 Dust or fume collecting equipment, industrial; purification & dust collection equipment

(G-17790)
SMOOTHIE CREATIONS INC
17137 Misty Lake Dr (44136-7361)
PHONE....................817 313-8212
Samuel Powell II, *Principal*
EMP: 3
SALES (est): 192.8K **Privately Held**
SIC: 2037 Frozen fruits & vegetables

(G-17791)
SPARTON MEDICAL SYSTEMS INC
22740 Lunn Rd (44149-4899)
PHONE....................440 878-4630
Duane Stierhoff, *Principal*
Jerry Szostek, *Mfg Staff*
EMP: 94
SALES (est): 21.4MM
SALES (corp-wide): 52.3MM **Privately Held**
WEB: www.sparton.com
SIC: 3841 Surgical & medical instruments
HQ: Sparton Corporation
425 N Martingale Rd
Schaumburg IL 60173
847 762-5800

(G-17792)
SPIEGELBERG MANUFACTURING INC (PA)
Also Called: Stud Welding Associates
12200 Alameda Dr (44149-3050)
PHONE....................440 324-3042
William Houston, *General Mgr*
Jean L Anderson, *Principal*
Jean Anderson, *Principal*
Terry S Shilling, *Principal*
Matt Kowalski, *Purch Mgr*
▲ **EMP:** 32
SALES (est): 18.7MM **Privately Held**
SIC: 3548 Welding apparatus

(G-17793)
SPS INTERNATIONAL INC
9321 Pheasant Run Pl (44149-1339)
PHONE....................216 671-9911
Daniel J Papcun, *Owner*
EMP: 5
SQ FT: 12,000
SALES (est): 622.5K **Privately Held**
SIC: 3714 Motor vehicle parts & accessories

(G-17794)
SROKA INC
21265 Westwood Dr (44149-2905)
PHONE....................440 572-2811
John Sroka, *President*
▲ **EMP:** 35
SALES (est): 8.3MM **Privately Held**
SIC: 3537 Industrial trucks & tractors

(G-17795)
SROKA INDUSTRIES INC
21265 Westwood Dr (44149-2905)
P.O. Box 360047 (44136-0001)
PHONE....................440 572-2811
John Sroka, *President*
Wieslawa Sroka, *Vice Pres*
Albert Sroka, *Sales Staff*
Gayle Collier, *Office Mgr*
Cynthia Guy, *Office Mgr*
▲ **EMP:** 30
SQ FT: 60,000
SALES (est): 2MM **Privately Held**
SIC: 3599 3544 3498 Machine shop, jobbing & repair; special dies & tools; fabricated pipe & fittings

(G-17796)
STEFRA INC
Also Called: E & E Parts Machining
18021 Cliffside Dr (44136-4256)
PHONE....................440 846-8240
Colleen Ungerer, *CEO*
Frank Ungerer, *President*
Steve Pucha, *Vice Pres*
EMP: 7
SQ FT: 2,900
SALES: 300K **Privately Held**
SIC: 3599 Machine shop, jobbing & repair

(G-17797)
STELFAST INC (DH)
22979 Stelfast Pkwy (44149-5561)
PHONE....................440 879-0077
Surinder Sakhuja, *CEO*
Simmi Sakhuja, *President*
Todd McRoberts, *Vice Pres*
Brandon Mitchell, *Warehouse Mgr*
Jose Roman, *Opers Staff*
▲ **EMP:** 32
SQ FT: 85,000
SALES (est): 23.4MM
SALES (corp-wide): 1.5B **Privately Held**
WEB: www.stelfast.com
SIC: 3452 3965 Bolts, metal; fasteners
HQ: Lindstrom, Llc
2950 100th Ct Ne
Blaine MN 55449
763 780-4200

(G-17798)
SWAGELOK HY-LEVEL COMPANY (PA)
15400 Foltz Pkwy (44149-4737)
PHONE....................440 238-1260
Donald M Rebar, *Ch of Bd*
Peter D Rebar, *President*
Arthur J Fabry, *Principal*
Gerald F Franklin, *Principal*
Carl C Heintel, *Principal*
EMP: 200 **EST:** 1942
SQ FT: 145,000
SALES (est): 31.4MM **Privately Held**
WEB: www.hy-level.com
SIC: 3451 3541 Screw machine products; machine tools, metal cutting type

(G-17799)
TADD SPRING CO INC
15060 Foltz Pkwy (44149-4729)
PHONE....................440 572-1313
Mark Anguilano, *President*
Leslie Naso, *Purch Agent*
Lucy Anguilano, *Admin Asst*
EMP: 20 **EST:** 1962
SQ FT: 5,000
SALES (est): 3.2MM **Privately Held**
WEB: www.taddspring.com
SIC: 3495 3493 Precision springs; steel springs, except wire

(G-17800)
TAKEDA PHARMACEUTICALS USA INC
19495 Trotwood Park (44149-4996)
PHONE....................440 238-0872
Steve Mott, *Principal*
EMP: 3
SALES (corp-wide): 16.6B **Privately Held**
SIC: 2834 Pharmaceutical preparations
HQ: Takeda Pharmaceuticals U.S.A., Inc.
1 Takeda Pkwy
Deerfield IL 60015
224 554-6500

(G-17801)
TRANSCENDIA INC
22889 Lunn Rd (44149-4800)
P.O. Box 368003, Cleveland (44136-9703)
PHONE....................440 638-2000
James Carlin, *Branch Mgr*
EMP: 80
SQ FT: 25,000
SALES (corp-wide): 348.8MM **Privately Held**
WEB: www.transilwrap.com
SIC: 3081 Unsupported plastics film & sheet
PA: Transcendia, Inc.
9201 Belmont Ave
Franklin Park IL 60131
847 678-1800

(G-17802)
TSW INDUSTRIES INC
14960 Foltz Pkwy (44149-4727)
PHONE....................440 572-7200
Tich Wan, *President*
Lee Wan, *Vice Pres*
▲ **EMP:** 30 **EST:** 1981
SQ FT: 41,000
SALES: 2.9MM **Privately Held**
SIC: 3599 Machine shop, jobbing & repair

(G-17803)
WABTEC CORPORATION
12312 Alameda Dr (44149-3023)
PHONE....................440 238-5350
Brian Bode, *Branch Mgr*
EMP: 3
SALES (corp-wide): 4.3B **Publicly Held**
SIC: 3743 Railroad equipment
HQ: Wabtec Corporation
1001 Airbrake Ave
Wilmerding PA 15148

(G-17804)
WALLOVER ENTERPRISES INC (DH)
21845 Drake Rd (44149-6610)
PHONE....................440 238-9250
George M Marquis, *President*
William C Cutri, *Vice Pres*
EMP: 30
SQ FT: 28,000
SALES (est): 25.1MM **Privately Held**
SIC: 2992 8734 Oils & greases, blending & compounding; re-refining lubricating oils & greases; product testing laboratories
HQ: Houghton International Inc.
945 Madison Ave
Norristown PA 19403
888 459-9844

(G-17805)
WALLOVER OIL COMPANY INC
Also Called: Woco
21845 Drake Rd (44149-6610)
PHONE....................440 238-9250
Bill Cutri, *Vice Pres*
EMP: 10 **Privately Held**
SIC: 5172 2992 Petroleum products; lubricating oils & greases
HQ: Wallover Oil Company Incorporated
21845 Drake Rd
Strongsville OH 44149

(G-17806)
WALLOVER OIL COMPANY INC (DH)
Also Called: Woco
21845 Drake Rd (44149-6610)
PHONE....................440 238-9250
James I Wallover, *Ch of Bd*
George Marquis, *President*
William C Cutri, *Vice Pres*
▼ **EMP:** 33
SQ FT: 28,000
SALES (est): 11.3MM **Privately Held**
SIC: 2992 2841 Oils & greases, blending & compounding; re-refining lubricating oils & greases; soap & other detergents
HQ: Wallover Enterprises Inc.
21845 Drake Rd
Strongsville OH 44149
440 238-9250

(G-17807)
WESTERN RESERVE SLEEVE INC
22360 Royalton Rd (44149-3826)
P.O. Box 361310, Cleveland (44136-0022)
PHONE....................440 238-8850
Scott Gilbert, *President*
Sharon Gilbert, *Corp Secy*
Phil Basek, *Controller*
EMP: 35

GEOGRAPHIC SECTION

Stryker - Williams County (G-17833)

SALES (est): 5.3MM **Privately Held**
SIC: 3081 Packing materials, plastic sheet

(G-17808)
WILLOW TOOL & MACHINING LTD
15110 Foltz Pkwy Ste 1 (44149-4765)
PHONE.....................................440 572-2288
Samuel Thomas, *Managing Prtnr*
Teresa Thomas, *Partner*
William A Thomas, *Partner*
EMP: 12 EST: 1972
SQ FT: 7,350
SALES (est): 2.2MM **Privately Held**
WEB: www.willowtool.com
SIC: 3541 3599 Machine tools, metal cutting type; machine shop, jobbing & repair

(G-17809)
YOUR CABINETRY
16488 Pearl Rd (44136-6042)
PHONE.....................................440 638-4925
Matt Howells, *Owner*
EMP: 4
SALES (est): 171.6K **Privately Held**
SIC: 2434 Wood kitchen cabinets

(G-17810)
ZORBX INC
17647 Foltz Pkwy (44149-5535)
PHONE.....................................440 238-1847
Debbie Mabrouk, *CEO*
Issa Mabrouk, *President*
▲ EMP: 25
SQ FT: 30,000
SALES (est): 1.2MM **Privately Held**
WEB: www.zorbx.com
SIC: 2841 Detergents, synthetic organic or inorganic alkaline

Struthers
Mahoning County

(G-17811)
A1 INDUSTRIAL PAINTING INC
635 Dumont Ave Struthers (44471)
P.O. Box 509, Campbell (44405-0509)
PHONE.....................................330 750-9441
Jack Maillis, *President*
EMP: 8
SALES (est): 1MM **Privately Held**
SIC: 1721 1389 Industrial painting; construction, repair & dismantling services

(G-17812)
ADD-A-TRAP LLC
488 Como St (44471-1237)
PHONE.....................................330 750-0417
Robert N Davenport, *CEO*
Ray Hassay, *President*
Allan Stratron, *COO*
EMP: 4
SALES (est): 100K **Privately Held**
SIC: 3088 Plastics plumbing fixtures

(G-17813)
ASTRO ALUMINUM ENTERPRISES INC
65 Main St (44471-1942)
P.O. Box 208 (44471-0208)
PHONE.....................................330 755-1414
Paul Cene, *President*
James Dibacco, *Exec VP*
EMP: 50
SALES (est): 5MM **Privately Held**
SIC: 3354 Aluminum extruded products

(G-17814)
ASTRO SHAPES LLC (PA)
65 Main St (44471-1942)
PHONE.....................................330 755-1414
Paul Cene, *President*
James Dibacco, *Exec VP*
Robert Cene Jr, *Vice Pres*
EMP: 121 EST: 1971
SQ FT: 300,000
SALES (est): 99.6MM **Privately Held**
WEB: www.astroshapes.com
SIC: 3354 3086 Aluminum extruded products; insulation or cushioning material, foamed plastic

(G-17815)
ASTRO SHAPES LLC
65 Main St (44471-1942)
P.O. Box 87 (44471-0087)
PHONE.....................................330 755-1414
EMP: 17
SALES (est): 3.6MM
SALES (corp-wide): 99.6MM **Privately Held**
WEB: www.astroshapes.com
SIC: 3354 Aluminum extruded products
PA: Astro Shapes Llc
65 Main St
Struthers OH 44471
330 755-1414

(G-17816)
ASTRO-COATINGS INC
65 Main St (44471-1942)
P.O. Box 208 (44471-0208)
PHONE.....................................330 755-1414
Paul Cene, *President*
Jim Di Bacco, *Exec VP*
Robert Cene Jr, *Vice Pres*
EMP: 50
SQ FT: 25,000
SALES: 10MM **Privately Held**
SIC: 3479 Painting of metal products

(G-17817)
GIANNIOS CANDY CO INC (PA)
430 Youngstown Poland Rd (44471-1058)
PHONE.....................................330 755-7000
John G Giannios, *President*
EMP: 50
SQ FT: 28,000
SALES (est): 12.2MM **Privately Held**
WEB: www.giannios.com
SIC: 2066 2064 Chocolate candy, solid; candy & other confectionery products

(G-17818)
KITTS HEATING & AC
Also Called: Kitt's Heating & AC Co
289 Elm St Ste 1 (44471-2807)
PHONE.....................................330 755-9242
Michael Kitt Jr, *President*
EMP: 3
SALES (est): 173.2K
SALES (corp-wide): 338.6K **Privately Held**
SIC: 1711 3444 Warm air heating & air conditioning contractor; sheet metalwork
PA: Kitt's Heating & Air Conditioning Inc
1231 Yerian Rd
North Lima OH 44452
330 755-9242

(G-17819)
KURTZ TOOL & DIE CO INC
164 State St (44471-1956)
P.O. Box 116 (44471-0116)
PHONE.....................................330 755-7723
Evelyn Kurtz, *Vice Pres*
Robert Kurtz Sr, *Shareholder*
EMP: 6
SALES (est): 769.4K **Privately Held**
SIC: 3544 Die sets for metal stamping (presses); special dies & tools

(G-17820)
L B INDUSTRIES INC
Also Called: Lally Pipe & Tube
534 Lowellville Rd (44471-2077)
P.O. Box 69 (44471-0069)
PHONE.....................................330 750-1002
Josh Ball, *Asst Controller*
James Mocker, *Branch Mgr*
EMP: 36
SALES (corp-wide): 110MM **Privately Held**
WEB: www.lallypipe.com
SIC: 5051 7692 Pipe & tubing, steel; steel; welding repair
PA: L B Industries, Inc.
8770 Railroad Dr
Taylor Mill KY 41015
859 431-8300

(G-17821)
MUNROE INCORPORATED
Also Called: Youngstown Plant
25 Union St (44471-1964)
PHONE.....................................330 755-7216
Arnie Traud, *Manager*
EMP: 5
SALES (corp-wide): 59.1MM **Privately Held**
SIC: 3325 3443 3317 Steel foundries; fabricated plate work (boiler shop); steel pipe & tubes
HQ: Munroe, Incorporated
1820 N Franklin St
Pittsburgh PA 15233
412 231-0600

(G-17822)
QUALITY BAR INC
17 Union St Ste 7 (44471-1964)
PHONE.....................................330 755-0000
Donald A Casey, *Ch of Bd*
Carrie Casey, *President*
Jim Rugh, *Opers Mgr*
Beverly Kloss, *Admin Asst*
EMP: 17
SALES (est): 3.7MM
SALES (corp-wide): 9.9MM **Privately Held**
WEB: www.qualitybar.com
SIC: 3312 Stainless steel
PA: Casey Equipment Corporation
275 Kappa Dr
Pittsburgh PA 15238
412 963-1111

(G-17823)
R W SIDLEY INCORPORATED
395 Lowellville Rd (44471-2012)
P.O. Box 165 (44471-0165)
PHONE.....................................330 750-1661
EMP: 3
SALES (corp-wide): 148.6MM **Privately Held**
SIC: 3295 Mfg Minerals-Ground/Treated
PA: R. W. Sidley Incorporated
436 Casement Ave
Painesville OH 44077
440 352-9343

(G-17824)
SELAH PAPERIE
130 S Bridge St (44471-1945)
PHONE.....................................330 755-2759
Brian Palumbo, *Owner*
EMP: 4
SALES (est): 200K **Privately Held**
WEB: www.selahrestaurant.com
SIC: 2621 Stationery, envelope & tablet papers

(G-17825)
STEEL VALLEY SIGN
616 Youngstown Poland Rd (44471-1106)
PHONE.....................................330 755-7446
EMP: 3
SALES (est): 190.3K **Privately Held**
SIC: 3993 Mfg Signs/Advertising Specialties

(G-17826)
YOUNGSTOWN DIE DEVELOPMENT
137 Walton Ave (44471-1054)
P.O. Box 237 (44471-0237)
PHONE.....................................330 755-0722
Bob Corll, *President*
Lois Mc Cabe, *President*
Patricia Hynes, *Treasurer*
EMP: 4 EST: 1959
SQ FT: 13,000
SALES (est): 593K **Privately Held**
SIC: 3544 Special dies & tools

Stryker
Williams County

(G-17827)
DALTON CORPORATION
310 Ellis St (43557-9329)
P.O. Box 2600 (43557-2600)
PHONE.....................................419 682-6328
Karen Rich, *Accountant*
Jackie Helberg, *Human Res Dir*
Alan Sheets, *Manager*
Jay Sweatland, *Manager*
EMP: 80
SALES (corp-wide): 76.1MM **Privately Held**
SIC: 3625 Industrial controls: push button, selector switches, pilot
HQ: The Dalton Corporation
1900 E Jefferson St
Warsaw IN 46580
574 267-8111

(G-17828)
DALTON STRYKER MCHINING FCILTY
310 Ellis St (43557-9329)
PHONE.....................................419 682-6328
Joe Derita, *President*
Ron Schmucker, *VP Finance*
EMP: 80
SALES (est): 9.6MM
SALES (corp-wide): 433.9MM **Privately Held**
WEB: www.nfco.com
SIC: 3599 Machine shop, jobbing & repair
HQ: Neenah Foundry Company
2121 Brooks Ave
Neenah WI 54956
920 725-7000

(G-17829)
FRANKS SAWMILL INC
Rr 195 (43557)
P.O. Box 4600 (43557-4600)
PHONE.....................................419 682-3831
Dave Frank, *President*
Mike Meyer, *Corp Secy*
EMP: 10 EST: 1958
SQ FT: 8,000
SALES (est): 1.3MM **Privately Held**
SIC: 2448 Pallets, wood

(G-17830)
JAGGER CONE COMPANY INC
304 Ellis St (43557-9329)
P.O. Box 136 (43557-0136)
PHONE.....................................419 682-1816
Jeff Jagger, *President*
Joe Jagger, *Vice Pres*
Carol Jagger, *Treasurer*
Sherry L Jagger, *Admin Sec*
EMP: 4
SALES (est): 200K **Privately Held**
SIC: 2052 Cones, ice cream

(G-17831)
OHIO TIMBERLAND PRODUCTS
102 Railroad Ave (43557-9533)
P.O. Box 330 (43557-0330)
PHONE.....................................419 682-6322
Mike Burkholder, *President*
Donna Burkholder, *Corp Secy*
Harley Burkholder, *Vice Pres*
EMP: 10 EST: 1996
SQ FT: 15,000
SALES (est): 2.1MM **Privately Held**
SIC: 2411 Poles, posts & pilings: untreated wood

(G-17832)
QUADCO REHABILITATION CTR INC (PA)
Also Called: Northwest Products
427 N Defiance St (43557-9472)
PHONE.....................................419 682-1011
Terry Fruth, *CFO*
Bruce Abell, *Exec Dir*
EMP: 287
SQ FT: 24,000
SALES: 247.7K **Privately Held**
SIC: 8331 2448 2441 Vocational rehabilitation agency; wood pallets & skids; nailed wood boxes & shook

(G-17833)
SAUDER MANUFACTURING CO
Also Called: Stryker Plant
201 Horton St (43557-9310)
PHONE.....................................419 682-3061
Luther Gautsche, *Vice Pres*
Dan Fleming, *Maintence Staff*
EMP: 125
SQ FT: 46,000
SALES (corp-wide): 500MM **Privately Held**
WEB: www.saudermfg.com
SIC: 2531 2521 Chairs, portable folding; wood office furniture

HQ: Sauder Manufacturing Co.
930 W Barre Rd
Archbold OH 43502
419 445-7670

(G-17834)
STRYKER STEEL TUBE LLC (PA)
100 Railroad Ave (43557-9533)
P.O. Box 506 (43557-0506)
PHONE.................419 682-4527
Steve Dominique,
Chris Peterson,
EMP: 10
SALES (est): 1.2MM **Privately Held**
SIC: 3317 Steel pipe & tubes

(G-17835)
STRYKER WELDING
104 W Mulberry St (43557-7757)
P.O. Box 70 (43557-0070)
PHONE.................419 682-2301
Jason Baltosser, *Owner*
EMP: 4
SQ FT: 10,000
SALES (est): 497.1K **Privately Held**
SIC: 7692 Welding repair

(G-17836)
WILLIAMS PORK CO OP
18487 County Road F (43557-9306)
PHONE.................419 682-9022
Paul Kalmbach, *President*
EMP: 9
SALES (est): 458K **Privately Held**
SIC: 2013 Pork, cured: from purchased meat

Sugar Grove
Fairfield County

(G-17837)
COMMERCIAL MUSIC SERVICE CO
Also Called: Chime Master Systems
6312 Goss Rd (43155-9610)
PHONE.................740 746-8500
Jeffrey A Crook, *President*
▼ EMP: 8
SALES (est): 1.2MM **Privately Held**
WEB: www.chimemaster.com
SIC: 3931 Bells (musical instruments); chimes & parts (musical instruments)

(G-17838)
ETCHED IN STONE
5680 Horns Mill Rd (43155-9739)
PHONE.................614 302-8924
Michael McGuire, *Software Dev*
EMP: 3 EST: 2014
SALES (est): 156.9K **Privately Held**
SIC: 3281 Cut stone & stone products

(G-17839)
JAKES SPORTSWEAR LTD
112 Elm St (43155)
P.O. Box 340 (43155-0340)
PHONE.................740 746-8356
Jacob Geiger, *Owner*
EMP: 4
SQ FT: 1,680
SALES: 150K **Privately Held**
WEB: www.jakessportswear.com
SIC: 2396 5611 5999 Screen printing on fabric articles; clothing, sportswear, men's & boys'; trophies & plaques

(G-17840)
WARTHMAN DRILLING INC
7525 Lancaster Logan Rd (43155)
PHONE.................740 746-9950
Steven Warthman, *President*
EMP: 6
SALES (est): 789.5K **Privately Held**
SIC: 1781 1381 Water well servicing; drilling oil & gas wells

Sugarcreek
Tuscarawas County

(G-17841)
ARCHER-DANIELS-MIDLAND COMPANY
Also Called: ADM
554 Pleasant Valley Rd Nw (44681-7800)
P.O. Box 486 (44681-0486)
PHONE.................330 852-3025
Doug Miller, *Branch Mgr*
EMP: 7
SQ FT: 12,000
SALES (corp-wide): 64.3B **Publicly Held**
WEB: www.admalliancenutrition.com
SIC: 2048 Prepared feeds
PA: Archer-Daniels-Midland Company
77 W Wacker Dr Ste 4600
Chicago IL 60601
312 634-8100

(G-17842)
BELDEN BRICK COMPANY
Also Called: Tubar Eureka Industrial Group
750 Edelweiss Dr Ne (44681-9501)
P.O. Box 705 (44681-0705)
PHONE.................330 852-2411
Kenneth L Cook, *Ch of Bd*
Mike Sigman, *General Mgr*
Hemmy Acharya, *Vice Pres*
Hemendra Acharya, *Engineer*
Jeremy Keller, *Engineer*
▲ EMP: 46 EST: 1952
SQ FT: 82,000
SALES (est): 11.9MM **Privately Held**
WEB: www.uhrden.com
SIC: 3535 3561 3537 3536 Conveyors & conveying equipment; pumps & pumping equipment; industrial trucks & tractors; hoists, cranes & monorails; mining machinery; construction machinery

(G-17843)
BELDEN BRICK COMPANY LLC
Also Called: Plant 8
700 Edelweiss Dr Ne (44681-9501)
P.O. Box 430 (44681-0430)
PHONE.................330 456-0031
Doug Mutchelknaus, *Principal*
EMP: 115
SALES (corp-wide): 8.1MM **Privately Held**
WEB: www.beldenbrick.com
SIC: 3251 3271 Structural brick & blocks; brick, concrete
HQ: The Belden Brick Company Llc
700 Tuscarawas St W Up
Canton OH 44702
330 456-0031

(G-17844)
BELDEN BRICK COMPANY LLC
Also Called: Belden Brick Plant 3
690 Dover Rd Ne (44681-7683)
P.O. Box 20910, Canton (44701-0910)
PHONE.................330 265-2030
Doug Mutschelknaus, *VP Opers*
Rick Hicks, *Manager*
EMP: 48
SALES (corp-wide): 8.1MM **Privately Held**
WEB: www.beldenbrick.com
SIC: 3251 3271 Structural brick & blocks; brick, concrete
HQ: The Belden Brick Company Llc
700 Tuscarawas St W Up
Canton OH 44702
330 456-0031

(G-17845)
CARLISLE OAK
3872 Township Road 162 (44681-9621)
PHONE.................330 852-8734
David Miller, *Owner*
EMP: 7
SALES (est): 531.9K **Privately Held**
SIC: 2511 Wood household furniture

(G-17846)
CARLISLE PRTG WALNUT CREEK LTD
2673 Township Road 421 (44681-9486)
PHONE.................330 852-9922
Marcus Wengerd, *President*
Mickey Mayle, *Sales Staff*
Dustin Yoder, *Manager*
EMP: 35
SALES (est): 7.3MM **Privately Held**
SIC: 2621 2791 Catalog, magazine & newsprint papers; typesetting

(G-17847)
CREATIVE WOODWORKS
5209 Evans Creek Rd Sw (44681-8034)
PHONE.................330 897-1432
David Yoder, *Principal*
EMP: 3 EST: 2011
SALES (est): 388K **Privately Held**
SIC: 2431 Millwork

(G-17848)
DUTCH VALLEY WOODWORKING INC
State Rte 39 (44681)
PHONE.................330 852-4319
Dale P Mullet, *President*
Ruth Mullet, *Corp Secy*
EMP: 14
SQ FT: 3,200
SALES (est): 1.8MM **Privately Held**
SIC: 2434 Wood kitchen cabinets

(G-17849)
EAGLE MACHINERY & SUPPLY INC
422 Dutch Valley Dr Ne (44681-7517)
PHONE.................330 852-1300
Kirk Spillman, *President*
Lori Spillman, *Corp Secy*
▲ EMP: 21
SQ FT: 20,000
SALES (est): 5MM **Privately Held**
SIC: 3541 Machine tool replacement & repair parts, metal cutting types

(G-17850)
J & F FURNITURE SHOP
Also Called: Juvenile Furniture Specialties
3521 Township Road 166 (44681-9606)
PHONE.................330 852-2478
James Miller, *Partner*
Freida Miller, *Partner*
EMP: 4
SALES (est): 367K **Privately Held**
SIC: 2511 5021 Wood household furniture; unfinished furniture

(G-17851)
L & M MINERAL CO
2010 County Road 144 (44681-9439)
PHONE.................330 852-3696
John E Ling Jr, *President*
Merle Mullet, *Treasurer*
EMP: 8
SALES (est): 659.5K **Privately Held**
SIC: 1459 1221 Clays (common) quarrying; shale (common) quarrying; bituminous coal & lignite-surface mining

(G-17852)
MIDDAUGH ENTERPRISES INC
Also Called: Idea Works
211 Yoder Ave Nw (44681-9388)
P.O. Box 400 (44681-0400)
PHONE.................330 852-2471
Steven Middaugh, *President*
Jeri Middaugh, *Corp Secy*
L Wade Middaugh, *Vice Pres*
EMP: 15 EST: 1956
SQ FT: 8,500
SALES (est): 1.7MM **Privately Held**
WEB: www.middaughprinters.com
SIC: 2752 2759 Commercial printing, offset; imprinting

(G-17853)
MILLER ENTERPRISES OHIO LLC
1360 County Road 108 (44681-9631)
PHONE.................330 852-4009
Wayne Miller,
Robert Schlabach,
EMP: 5
SQ FT: 5,000
SALES: 229.7K **Privately Held**
SIC: 3061 Automotive rubber goods (mechanical)

(G-17854)
MILLER MANUFACTURING INC
Also Called: Miller Wood Design
2705 Shetler Rd Nw (44681-7604)
P.O. Box 425 (44681-0425)
PHONE.................330 852-0689
Raymond Miller, *President*
▼ EMP: 35
SALES (est): 4.7MM **Privately Held**
SIC: 2493 2499 2435 2431 Particleboard, plastic laminated; decorative wood & woodwork; hardwood veneer & plywood; millwork

(G-17855)
MULLET ENTERPRISES INC (PA)
Also Called: Tmk Farm Service
138 2nd St Nw (44681-7824)
P.O. Box 278 (44681-0278)
PHONE.................330 852-4681
Larry Tietje, *President*
Raymond Mullet, *Vice Pres*
▼ EMP: 8
SQ FT: 34,000
SALES (est): 8.9MM **Privately Held**
WEB: www.tmkvalley.com
SIC: 5153 2041 Grain elevators; flour & other grain mill products

(G-17856)
PALLET DISTRIBUTORS INC
Also Called: Scenic Wood Products
10343 Copperhead Rd Nw (44681)
PHONE.................330 852-3531
Martin Troyer, *General Mgr*
EMP: 55
SALES (est): 5.7MM **Privately Held**
SIC: 2448 Wood pallets & skids
PA: Pallet Distributors, Inc.
14701 Detroit Ave Ste 610
Lakewood OH 44107

(G-17857)
PINE ACRES WOODCRAFT
123 Pleasant Valley Rd Nw (44681-8048)
PHONE.................330 852-0190
Dean Troyer, *Owner*
EMP: 3
SALES: 330K **Privately Held**
SIC: 2514 Metal household furniture

(G-17858)
PLEASANT VALLEY READY MIX INC
559 Pleasant Valley Rd Nw (44681-7800)
P.O. Box 436 (44681-0436)
PHONE.................330 852-2613
Daniel O Miller, *President*
EMP: 10
SQ FT: 3,000
SALES: 2.2MM **Privately Held**
SIC: 3273 5211 Ready-mixed concrete; masonry materials & supplies

(G-17859)
PROVIA HOLDINGS INC (PA)
Also Called: Provia - Heritage Stone
2150 State Route 39 (44681-9201)
PHONE.................330 852-4711
Brian Miller, *President*
Bill Mullet, *Principal*
Willis Schlabach, *Principal*
Phil Wengerd, *Vice Pres*
Mike Yoder, *Plant Mgr*
EMP: 180 EST: 1972
SQ FT: 280,000
SALES: 140.5MM **Privately Held**
WEB: www.precisionentry.com
SIC: 3442 5031 Metal doors; door frames, all materials

(G-17860)
PROVIA LLC
1550 County Road 140 (44681-9204)
PHONE.................330 852-4711
William Mullet, *Ch of Bd*
Brian Miller, *President*
Phil Wengerd, *Vice Pres*
Chris Ross, *Purchasing*
Jason Cunningham, *Engineer*
EMP: 18
SQ FT: 10,000

GEOGRAPHIC SECTION

Sunbury - Delaware County (G-17888)

SALES (est): 3.6MM
SALES (corp-wide): 140.5MM **Privately Held**
SIC: 3272 Building stone, artificial: concrete
PA: Provia Holdings, Inc.
2150 State Route 39
Sugarcreek OH 44681
330 852-4711

(G-17861)
RAINBOW BEDDING
3421 Township Road 166 (44681-9605)
PHONE.................................330 852-3127
Paul Miller,
Edna Miller,
▲ EMP: 4
SALES: 600K **Privately Held**
SIC: 2394 Air cushions & mattresses, canvas

(G-17862)
RNR ENTERPRISES LLC
1361 County Road 108 (44681-9631)
PHONE.................................330 852-3022
Regan R Schlabach,
Robert Schlabach,
EMP: 10
SALES (est): 840K **Privately Held**
SIC: 2511 Wood household furniture

(G-17863)
SCHLABACH PRINTING LTD
Also Called: Schlabach Printers
798 State Route 93 Nw (44681-7726)
PHONE.................................330 852-4687
Dan Miller, *Partner*
Roman Troyer, *Prdtn Mgr*
Luke Yoder, *Marketing Staff*
EMP: 20
SQ FT: 3,500
SALES (est): 2.2MM **Privately Held**
WEB: www.schlabachprinters.com
SIC: 2759 2752 Screen printing; commercial printing, lithographic

(G-17864)
SKYLINE CORPORATION
580 Mill St Nw (44681-9561)
PHONE.................................330 852-2483
Bruce Monteith, *Manager*
EMP: 136
SQ FT: 100,000
SALES (corp-wide): 1.5B **Publicly Held**
WEB: www.skylinecorp.com
SIC: 2451 3448 2452 Mobile homes; prefabricated metal buildings; prefabricated wood buildings
PA: Skyline Champion Corporation
2520 Bypass Rd
Elkhart IN 46514
574 294-6521

(G-17865)
STONY POINT HARDWOODS
Also Called: Pro Hardware 13074
7842 Stony Point Rd Nw (44681-7642)
PHONE.................................330 852-4512
Mark Shrock, *Owner*
EMP: 16
SALES (est): 1.8MM **Privately Held**
SIC: 2448 2435 2431 2426 Pallets, wood; hardwood veneer & plywood; millwork; hardwood dimension & flooring mills; sawmills & planing mills, general

(G-17866)
STONY POINT METALS LLC
7820 Stony Point Rd Nw (44681-7642)
PHONE.................................330 852-7100
Wes Shrock, *Mng Member*
Mark Shrock,
EMP: 4 EST: 2009
SALES (est): 415.7K **Privately Held**
SIC: 3531 5033 5211 Roofing equipment; siding, except wood; roofing material

(G-17867)
SUGARCREEK BUDGET PUBLISHERS
Also Called: Budget Newspaper, The
134 Factory St Ne (44681)
PHONE.................................330 852-4634
Keith Rathbun, *President*
Albert Spector, *Principal*
David Spector, *Vice Pres*

Sonia Cohen, *Shareholder*
Debbie Kloosterman, *Shareholder*
EMP: 16
SQ FT: 4,800
SALES (est): 952.5K **Privately Held**
WEB: www.thebudgetnewspaper.com
SIC: 2711 Newspapers: publishing only, not printed on site

(G-17868)
SUGARCREEK PALLETT
681 Belden Pkwy Ne (44681-7699)
PHONE.................................330 852-9812
Jonas Borntrager, *Principal*
EMP: 4
SALES (est): 314.8K **Privately Held**
SIC: 2448 Wood pallets & skids

(G-17869)
SUGARCREEK SHAVINGS LLC
3121 Winklepleck Rd Nw (44681-7656)
PHONE.................................330 763-4239
Ruth Troyer, *Principal*
EMP: 9
SALES (est): 386.7K **Privately Held**
SIC: 2421 Sawdust & shavings

(G-17870)
SUPERB INDUSTRIES INC
Also Called: Superb Industries Supplier
100 Innovation Plz Nw (44681-9132)
P.O. Box 708 (44681-0708)
PHONE.................................330 852-0500
John Miller, *President*
Adam Demuth, *General Mgr*
Susan Miller, *Treasurer*
▲ EMP: 75
SQ FT: 50,000
SALES (est): 16MM **Privately Held**
WEB: www.superbdesign.com
SIC: 3625 3491 Control equipment, electric; motor controls & accessories; valves, automatic control

(G-17871)
SWP LEGACY LTD
10143 Copperhead Rd Nw (44681-7770)
P.O. Box 396 (44681-0396)
PHONE.................................330 340-9663
Paul Monaco, *CFO*
Martin Troyer,
EMP: 55
SALES (est): 9.9MM **Privately Held**
WEB: www.scenicwood.com
SIC: 2448 Pallets, wood

(G-17872)
TRUPOINT PRODUCTS
Uknown (44681)
P.O. Box 72, Walnut Creek (44687-0072)
PHONE.................................330 204-3302
Myron Miller, *Owner*
EMP: 10
SALES (est): 613.1K **Privately Held**
SIC: 3312 3495 Wire products, steel or iron; wire springs

(G-17873)
TUSCO HARDWOODS LLC
Also Called: M & M Hardwoods
10887 Gerber Valley Rd Nw (44681-7932)
PHONE.................................330 852-4281
Levi P Miller,
EMP: 14
SQ FT: 10,000
SALES (est): 2.5MM **Privately Held**
SIC: 2448 2421 Wood pallets & skids; sawmills & planing mills, general

(G-17874)
VALLEY VIEW WOODCRAFT
Also Called: Valley View Woodcraft & Finshg
1190 Shutt Valley Rd Nw (44681-7743)
PHONE.................................330 852-3000
Bobby Troyer, *Owner*
EMP: 4
SALES: 90K **Privately Held**
SIC: 2519 Lawn & garden furniture, except wood & metal

(G-17875)
WALNUT CREEK WOOD DESIGN
1689 State Route 39 (44681-9666)
PHONE.................................330 852-9663
Scott Troyer, *Owner*
EMP: 3

SALES (est): 208.1K **Privately Held**
SIC: 2499 Decorative wood & woodwork

(G-17876)
WEAVER BARNS LTD
1696 State Route 39 (44681-9666)
PHONE.................................330 852-2103
Mike Weaver, *General Mgr*
Jonathon Beachy, *Controller*
Jay Miller, *Sales Executive*
Michael Troyer, *Manager*
Wayne R Weaver,
EMP: 10
SALES (est): 3.4MM **Privately Held**
WEB: www.weaverbarns.com
SIC: 2452 Prefabricated buildings, wood

(G-17877)
WEAVERS FURNITURE LTD
Also Called: Weaver Craft of Sugarcreek
7011 Old Route 39 Nw (44681-7968)
PHONE.................................330 852-2701
Wayne Weaver, *Owner*
Martha Weaver,
▲ EMP: 16
SQ FT: 42,000
SALES (est): 2.2MM **Privately Held**
WEB: www.weaverfurniture.com
SIC: 2512 5023 Upholstered household furniture; home furnishings

(G-17878)
YODER LUMBER CO INC
3799 County Road 70 (44681-9400)
PHONE.................................330 893-3131
Paul Dow, *Branch Mgr*
EMP: 55
SALES (corp-wide): 30.3MM **Privately Held**
WEB: www.yoderlumber.com
SIC: 5211 2435 2426 2421 Planing mill products & lumber; hardwood veneer & plywood; hardwood dimension & flooring mills; sawmills & planing mills, general
PA: Yoder Lumber Co., Inc.
4515 Township Road 367
Millersburg OH 44654
330 893-3121

Sugarcrk Twp
Greene County

(G-17879)
HORSE HILL WREATH COMPANY
1205 S Alpha Bellbrook Rd (45305-9707)
PHONE.................................937 272-0701
Carla Hunt, *Administration*
EMP: 3
SALES (est): 106.8K **Privately Held**
SIC: 3999 Wreaths, artificial

Sullivan
Ashland County

(G-17880)
BRIARWOOD VALLEY FARMS
502 Us Highway 224 (44880-9771)
P.O. Box 93 (44880-0093)
PHONE.................................419 736-2298
Ladonna Hensen, *Owner*
EMP: 3
SALES (est): 162.2K **Privately Held**
SIC: 2015 Rabbit slaughtering & processing

(G-17881)
EDJEAN TECHNICAL SERVICES INC
Also Called: Edjetech Services
246 Us Highway 224 Ste A (44880-9765)
PHONE.................................440 647-3300
Douglas Heidenreich, *President*
Joseph Insana, *Vice Pres*
EMP: 4
SALES: 610K **Privately Held**
WEB: www.edjetech.com
SIC: 3569 5084 Filters, general line: industrial; industrial machinery & equipment

(G-17882)
US SCREEN CO
462 County Road 40 (44880-9727)
P.O. Box 27, Wellington (44090-0027)
PHONE.................................419 736-2400
Mike Dickason, *CEO*
Joanne Dickason, *President*
Matt Dickason, *CFO*
Doug Dickason, *Sales Mgr*
▲ EMP: 4
SQ FT: 8,000
SALES (est): 351.3K **Privately Held**
SIC: 3496 Screening, woven wire: made from purchased wire

Sunbury
Delaware County

(G-17883)
BRY-AIR INC
10793 E State Route 37 (43074-9311)
PHONE.................................740 965-2974
Mel Meyers, *President*
Doug Howery, *Exec VP*
▲ EMP: 43 EST: 1964
SQ FT: 40,000
SALES (est): 15.3MM **Privately Held**
WEB: www.bryair.com
SIC: 3585 3826 3535 3823 Dehumidifiers electric, except portable; environmental testing equipment; conveyors & conveying equipment; industrial instrmnts msrmnt display/control process variable; auto controls regulating residntl & coml environmt & applncs; blowers & fans

(G-17884)
COUNTER METHOD INC
13767 E State Route 37 (43074-9773)
PHONE.................................614 206-3192
EMP: 3
SALES (est): 165.8K **Privately Held**
SIC: 3131 Mfg Footwear Cut Stock

(G-17885)
DUFFEE FINISHING INC
4860 N County Line Rd (43074-8305)
PHONE.................................740 965-4848
Nancy Duffee, *Vice Pres*
EMP: 8
SQ FT: 20,000
SALES (est): 882.1K **Privately Held**
WEB: www.duffeefinishing.com
SIC: 3479 3399 Painting of metal products; powder, metal

(G-17886)
GERLING AND ASSOCIATES INC
138 Stelzer Ct (43074-8528)
PHONE.................................740 965-6200
Fred Gerling, *President*
Manuel Lopez, *Project Mgr*
Zach Myers, *Opers Mgr*
Jennifer Fenton, *Opers Staff*
Jennifer Myers, *Opers Staff*
◆ EMP: 80
SQ FT: 20,000
SALES (est): 29MM **Privately Held**
WEB: www.gerlinggroup.com
SIC: 3711 Mobile lounges (motor vehicle), assembly of

(G-17887)
GREAT MIDWEST YACHT CO
140 E Granville St (43074-7573)
P.O. Box 364 (43074-0364)
PHONE.................................740 965-4511
Douglas Laber, *President*
EMP: 3
SQ FT: 8,400
SALES: 225K **Privately Held**
SIC: 3732 3429 5551 Sailboats, building & repairing; marine hardware; marine supplies

(G-17888)
HEARTLAND HOME CABINETRY LTD
35 S Galena Rd Unit C (43074-9010)
PHONE.................................740 936-5100
Terry King, *Principal*
EMP: 4 EST: 2009

Sunbury - Delaware County (G-17889)

SALES (est): 532.3K **Privately Held**
SIC: 2434 Wood kitchen cabinets

(G-17889)
ICC SYSTEMS INC
5665 Blue Church Rd # 202 (43074-9695)
PHONE...................................614 524-0299
Harold Arnette, *President*
EMP: 6
SALES (est): 483.1K **Privately Held**
SIC: 7372 Prepackaged software

(G-17890)
INDIAN RIVER INDUSTRIES
Also Called: Village Square Antique Mall
31 E Granville St (43074-9130)
PHONE...................................740 965-4377
Jane Weidner, *Owner*
EMP: 4
SQ FT: 5,184
SALES (est): 41.6K **Privately Held**
SIC: 2541 2732 5099 5932 Showcases, except refrigerated: wood; book music: printing only, not published on site; pamphlets: printing only, not published on site; antiques; antiques

(G-17891)
MINE EQUIPMENT SERVICES LLC (PA)
Also Called: Mes
3958 State Route 3 (43074-9660)
P.O. Box 120 (43074-0120)
PHONE...................................740 936-5427
Christopher Wagner,
Tony Schiavi,
EMP: 25 **EST:** 2012
SQ FT: 10,000
SALES (est): 3.4MM **Privately Held**
SIC: 5084 3535 7699 Industrial machinery & equipment; belt conveyor systems, general industrial use; construction equipment repair; pumps & pumping equipment repair; industrial equipment services; industrial machinery & equipment repair

(G-17892)
NELSON TOOL CORPORATION
388 N County Line Rd (43074-9004)
PHONE...................................740 965-1894
Michael Nelson, *President*
EMP: 14
SQ FT: 18,200
SALES (est): 2.1MM **Privately Held**
SIC: 3544 Special dies, tools, jigs & fixtures

(G-17893)
OBERFIELDS LLC
471 Kintner Pkwy (43074-8978)
PHONE...................................740 369-7644
Bruce Loris, *President*
Robert Fulton, *Vice Pres*
Earl Freeman, *Facilities Mgr*
EMP: 20
SQ FT: 833
SALES (corp-wide): 1.2MM **Privately Held**
SIC: 3272 Concrete products, precast
HQ: Oberfield's, Llc
528 London Rd
Delaware OH 43015
740 369-7644

(G-17894)
OHASHI TECHNICA USA INC (HQ)
111 Burrer Dr (43074-9323)
PHONE...................................740 965-5115
Hikaru Tateiwa, *President*
Mamoru Shibasaki, *Principal*
Masaki Takafuji, *Sales Staff*
Anthony White, *Manager*
▲ **EMP:** 50
SQ FT: 110,000
SALES: 90MM
SALES (corp-wide): 365.8MM **Privately Held**
SIC: 5013 5072 3452 Automotive supplies & parts; automotive supplies; hardware; bolts, nuts, rivets & washers
PA: Ohashi Technica Inc.
4-3-13, Toranomon
Minato-Ku TKY 105-0
354 044-411

(G-17895)
OHASHI TECHNICA USA MFG INC
99 Burrer Dr (43074-9319)
PHONE...................................740 965-9002
Hikaru Tateiwa, *President*
Nobuya Moritani, *Corp Secy*
▲ **EMP:** 20
SQ FT: 60,000
SALES (est): 3MM
SALES (corp-wide): 365.8MM **Privately Held**
SIC: 3965 Fasteners
HQ: Ohashi Technica U.S.A. Inc.
111 Burrer Dr
Sunbury OH 43074
740 965-5115

(G-17896)
OMEGA ENGINEERING INC
Also Called: Omegadyne
149 Stelzer Ct (43074-8528)
PHONE...................................740 965-9340
Mary Larson, *Purchasing*
Jim Novak, *Finance*
Larry Myers, *Sales Mgr*
Dennis Guy, *Branch Mgr*
Ken Gesling, *Info Tech Mgr*
EMP: 50
SALES (corp-wide): 2B **Privately Held**
SIC: 3829 3679 3825 Pressure transducers; loads, electronic; instruments to measure electricity
HQ: Omega Engineering, Inc.
800 Connecticut Ave 5n01
Norwalk CT 06854
203 359-1660

(G-17897)
PRECISION FABRICATIONS INC
272 High St (43074-9457)
PHONE...................................937 297-8606
David Steinberger, *President*
EMP: 4 **EST:** 1968
SQ FT: 3,700
SALES (est): 300K **Privately Held**
SIC: 3082 Rods, unsupported plastic

(G-17898)
PRODUCT TOOLING INC
4290 N 3 Bs And K Rd (43074-9580)
PHONE...................................740 524-2061
Rodney Harp, *President*
Elizabeth Harp, *Corp Secy*
EMP: 7 **EST:** 1968
SQ FT: 3,600
SALES (est): 500K **Privately Held**
SIC: 3599 7692 3544 Machine shop, jobbing & repair; welding repair; special dies, tools, jigs & fixtures

(G-17899)
RICHARD PAULEY
Also Called: Pauley's Machine Shop
3308 N State Route 61 (43074-9404)
P.O. Box 893 (43074-0893)
PHONE...................................740 965-6897
Richard L Pauley, *Owner*
EMP: 3
SQ FT: 1,250
SALES (est): 224.8K **Privately Held**
SIC: 3599 Machine shop, jobbing & repair

(G-17900)
RUSSELL T BUNDY ASSOCIATES INC
Also Called: American Pan Company
601 W Cherry St (43074-9803)
PHONE...................................740 965-3008
Brad Moore, *Manager*
EMP: 14
SALES (corp-wide): 62MM **Privately Held**
SIC: 3479 Coating of metals & formed products
PA: Russell T. Bundy Associates, Inc.
417 E Water St Ste 1
Urbana OH 43078
937 652-2151

(G-17901)
UNIVERSAL COMPOSITE LLC
Also Called: Uc Trailer Co.
200 Kintner Pkwy (43074-9320)
PHONE...................................614 507-1646
Jennifer Myers,
Steven E Hillman,
Kelly Kelley,
EMP: 25
SALES (est): 3.8MM **Privately Held**
SIC: 3711 Automobile assembly, including specialty automobiles

(G-17902)
WHITS FROZEN CUSTARD
101 W Cherry St Unit A (43074-8029)
PHONE...................................740 965-1427
Rick J Dague, *Principal*
EMP: 3 **EST:** 2010
SALES (est): 170.2K **Privately Held**
SIC: 2024 Ice cream, bulk

Swanton
Fulton County

(G-17903)
ABECS COMMUNITY NEWS
13900 Frankfort Rd (43558-6801)
PHONE...................................419 330-9658
Patrick Abec, *Principal*
EMP: 3
SALES (est): 132K **Privately Held**
SIC: 2711 Newspapers, publishing & printing

(G-17904)
AMBROSIA INC (PA)
395 W Airport Hwy (43558-1445)
P.O. Box 299 (43558-0299)
PHONE...................................419 825-1151
Ann M Albright, *President*
William R Albright, *Corp Secy*
EMP: 5
SQ FT: 31,000
SALES (est): 5.5MM **Privately Held**
SIC: 3999 Candles

(G-17905)
AQUABLOK LTD
230 W Airport Hwy (43558-1471)
PHONE...................................419 402-4170
John Collins, *COO*
EMP: 15
SALES (corp-wide): 2.1MM **Privately Held**
SIC: 3299 Non-metallic mineral statuary & other decorative products
PA: Aquablok, Ltd.
175 Woodland Ave
Swanton OH 43558
419 825-1325

(G-17906)
AQUABLOK LTD (PA)
175 Woodland Ave (43558-1026)
PHONE...................................419 825-1325
John Hall, *President*
EMP: 18
SALES (est): 2.1MM **Privately Held**
SIC: 3299 3295 Non-metallic mineral statuary & other decorative products; minerals, ground or treated

(G-17907)
BROKEN SPINNING WHEEL
14230 Monclova Rd (43558-8711)
PHONE...................................419 825-1609
John Kaczor, *Principal*
EMP: 3
SALES (est): 225.6K **Privately Held**
SIC: 2252 Socks

(G-17908)
BYRD PRCUREMENT SPECIALIST INC
12150 Monclova Rd (43558-8706)
PHONE...................................419 936-0019
Jason Byrd, *CEO*
EMP: 4
SALES (est): 300.4K **Privately Held**
SIC: 4813 1522 1389 1521 Telephone communication, except radio; residential construction; construction, repair & dismantling services; patio & deck construction & repair; new construction, single-family houses

(G-17909)
COLUMBUS JACK CORPORATION
Also Called: Columbus Jack Regent
1 Air Cargo Pkwy E (43558-9490)
PHONE...................................614 747-1596
Richard Drexler, *CEO*
Gene Albrecht, *Vice Pres*
TAC Kensler, *CFO*
Karen Hart, *Asst Treas*
▲ **EMP:** 52 **EST:** 1992
SQ FT: 50,000
SALES (est): 8.5MM
SALES (corp-wide): 24MM **Privately Held**
WEB: www.columbusjack.com
SIC: 3728 3542 Aircraft parts & equipment; presses: hydraulic & pneumatic, mechanical & manual
PA: Quality Products, Inc.
1 Air Cargo Pkwy E
Swanton OH 43558
614 228-0185

(G-17910)
COUNTER CREATION PLUS L L C
106 Church St (43558-1014)
PHONE...................................419 826-7449
Jason J Miller, *Principal*
EMP: 3
SALES (est): 277.8K **Privately Held**
SIC: 3131 Counters

(G-17911)
DAE HOLDINGS LLC
Also Called: Dae Industries
1 Air Cargo Pkwy E (43558-9490)
PHONE...................................502 589-1445
Craig Allen, *Production*
Jeff Owen, *Purchasing*
Jason Bruce, *Design Engr*
Dana Oliver, *Controller*
Garrett Hubbard, *Sales Staff*
EMP: 45
SALES (est): 11.6MM **Privately Held**
SIC: 3444 Sheet metalwork

(G-17912)
EAGLE INDUSTRIAL TRUCK MFG LLC
Also Called: Eagle Tugs
1 Air Cargo Pkwy E (43558-9490)
PHONE...................................734 442-1000
Mark Iddon, *President*
Connie Sroufe, *Mktg Dir*
John Morgan,
Jace Morgan,
◆ **EMP:** 30 **EST:** 2000
SQ FT: 70,000
SALES (est): 17.5MM
SALES (corp-wide): 10B **Privately Held**
WEB: www.eaglegse.com
SIC: 5085 3537 Industrial supplies; industrial trucks & tractors
HQ: Tronair, Inc.
1 Air Cargo Pkwy E
Swanton OH 43558
419 866-6301

(G-17913)
GRAND AIRE INC (PA)
11777 W Airport Svc Rd (43558-9387)
PHONE...................................419 861-6700
Zachary Cheema, *CEO*
EMP: 21 **EST:** 1998
SQ FT: 57,000
SALES (est): 10MM **Privately Held**
WEB: www.grandaire.com
SIC: 4522 5172 4512 4581 Air cargo carriers, nonscheduled; petroleum products; air transportation, scheduled; airports, flying fields & services; trucks: freight, baggage, etc.: industrial, except mining; courier services, except by air

(G-17914)
GSE PRODUCTION AND SUPPORT LLC (PA)
Also Called: GSE Spares
1 Air Cargo Pkwy E (43558-9490)
PHONE...................................972 329-2646
Harley Kaplan, *CEO*
▲ **EMP:** 4
SQ FT: 5,000

SALES (est): 1MM **Privately Held**
SIC: 5085 5084 3728 3799 Industrial supplies; safety equipment; aircraft parts & equipment; all terrain vehicles (ATV)

(G-17915)
KELLY MACHINE LTD
7245 County Road 1 3 (43558-9532)
PHONE..............................419 825-2006
Francis Gelske, *President*
EMP: 5
SALES: 500K **Privately Held**
SIC: 3599 Machine shop, jobbing & repair

(G-17916)
M L B MOLDED URETHANE PDTS LLC
1680 Us Highway 20a (43558-8663)
P.O. Box 464, Perrysburg (43552-0464)
PHONE..............................419 825-9140
Donald Bates,
Valdemar Lopez,
James Muir,
EMP: 9
SQ FT: 15,000
SALES (est): 1.6MM **Privately Held**
WEB: www.mlbproducts.net
SIC: 3086 Plastics foam products

(G-17917)
OWENS CORNING SALES LLC
11451 W Airport Svc Rd (43558-9389)
PHONE..............................419 248-5751
Roger G Waddill, *Branch Mgr*
EMP: 13 **Publicly Held**
WEB: www.owenscorning.com
SIC: 3296 Fiberglass insulation
HQ: Owens Corning Sales, Llc
1 Owens Corning Pkwy
Toledo OH 43659
419 248-8000

(G-17918)
PJS CORRUGATED INC
2330 Us Highway 20 (43558-8649)
PHONE..............................419 644-3383
Michael Iozzo, *President*
Priscilla Iozzo, *Corp Secy*
Joseph Iozzo, *Vice Pres*
EMP: 10
SQ FT: 10,000
SALES (est): 2.9MM **Privately Held**
SIC: 2653 Boxes, corrugated: made from purchased materials

(G-17919)
PREFORM TECHNOLOGIES LLC
11362 S Airfield Rd (43558-7900)
P.O. Box 964, Holland (43528-0964)
PHONE..............................419 720-0355
David F Waterman, *Principal*
Jim Sheely, *Officer*
Elizabeth Brady,
L Robert Dearduff,
Dan Durham,
EMP: 4
SQ FT: 7,500
SALES (est): 987.2K **Privately Held**
SIC: 3089 Injection molding of plastics

(G-17920)
QUALITY PRODUCTS INC (PA)
1 Air Cargo Pkwy E (43558-9490)
PHONE..............................614 228-0185
David Somers, *CEO*
Richard Drexler, *Ch of Bd*
Karen Hart, *President*
TAC Kensler, *CFO*
EMP: 67
SQ FT: 45,000
SALES: 24MM **Privately Held**
WEB: www.quality-products.com
SIC: 3542 3569 Presses: hydraulic & pneumatic, mechanical & manual; jacks, hydraulic

(G-17921)
SCOTTDEL CUSHION LLC
400 Church St (43558-1199)
PHONE..............................419 825-0432
Kevin Thornton, *CEO*
Scott Carson,
▲ EMP: 45
SQ FT: 185,000

SALES (est): 15.6MM **Privately Held**
WEB: www.scottdel.com
SIC: 3086 Carpet & rug cushions, foamed plastic; insulation or cushioning material, foamed plastic

(G-17922)
SPINAL BALANCE INC
11360 S Airfield Rd (43558-7900)
PHONE..............................419 530-5935
Anand Agarwal, *CEO*
Marcel Ingels, *Design Engr*
Arthur Karas, *Admin Sec*
EMP: 8
SALES (est): 1.1MM **Privately Held**
SIC: 3842 Implants, surgical

(G-17923)
SWANTON WLDG MACHINING CO INC (PA)
407 Broadway Ave (43558-1341)
PHONE..............................419 826-4816
Norm D Zeiter, *CEO*
Chuck Morgan, *President*
Bill Zeiter, *General Mgr*
Jeff Gyurasics, *COO*
Kessler Kody, *Plant Mgr*
EMP: 80
SQ FT: 314,000
SALES (est): 25.6MM **Privately Held**
WEB: www.swantonweld.com
SIC: 3446 3444 3443 3599 Architectural metalwork; sheet metalwork; fabricated plate work (boiler shop); machine & other job shop work

(G-17924)
TOLEDO JET CENTER LLC (PA)
Also Called: Toledo Express
11591 W Airport Svc Rd (43558-9618)
PHONE..............................419 866-9050
Mindy Leppala, *General Mgr*
Bill Pribe, *General Mgr*
William Pribe, *General Mgr*
Alan R Carsten, *Mng Member*
EMP: 11
SALES (est): 2.7MM **Privately Held**
SIC: 3721 4581 Aircraft; aircraft maintenance & repair services

(G-17925)
TRI-COUNTY BLOCK AND BRICK INC
1628 Us 20 Alternate (43558)
PHONE..............................419 826-7060
Roger L Cooley, *President*
Roberta E Cooley, *Corp Secy*
Donavan Cooley, *Vice Pres*
Karen Cooley, *Vice Pres*
Carl Kuhlman, *Vice Pres*
EMP: 35
SQ FT: 4,160
SALES (est): 11.6MM **Privately Held**
WEB: www.tricountyblock.com
SIC: 5211 3271 Lumber & other building materials; blocks, concrete or cinder: standard

(G-17926)
TRONAIR INC (DH)
1 Air Cargo Pkwy E (43558-9490)
PHONE..............................419 866-6301
Paul Schwarzbaum, *CEO*
Sherry Drake, *President*
Mark Iddon, *President*
Jeffrey Lee, *Corp Secy*
Cliff Langdon, *Vice Pres*
◆ EMP: 100
SQ FT: 80,000
SALES (est): 37.3MM
SALES (corp-wide): 10B **Privately Held**
WEB: www.tronair.com
SIC: 3728 Aircraft parts & equipment
HQ: Tronair Parent, Inc.
1 Air Cargo Pkwy E
Swanton OH 43558
419 866-6301

(G-17927)
TRONAIR PARENT INC (HQ)
1 Air Cargo Pkwy E (43558-9490)
PHONE..............................419 866-6301
Jeffrey Lee, *Corp Secy*
EMP: 0
SQ FT: 110,000

SALES (est): 8.8MM
SALES (corp-wide): 10B **Privately Held**
SIC: 6719 3728 Investment holding companies, except banks; aircraft parts & equipment
PA: Golden Gate Capital Lp
1 Embarcadero Ctr Fl 39
San Francisco CA 94111
415 983-2700

(G-17928)
VAN ORDERS PALLET COMPANY INC
2452 County Road 2 (43558-8894)
PHONE..............................419 875-6932
James Van Order, *Ch of Bd*
Casey Van Order, *President*
Patricia Van Order, *Corp Secy*
EMP: 16 EST: 1971
SQ FT: 11,000
SALES: 898.1K **Privately Held**
SIC: 2448 2441 Pallets, wood; nailed wood boxes & shook

(G-17929)
WILLYS INC
Also Called: Willy's Fresh Salsa
11305 W Airport Svc Rd (43558-9390)
PHONE..............................419 823-3200
Dennis Dickey, *President*
EMP: 16
SQ FT: 6,000
SALES: 400K **Privately Held**
SIC: 2099 Food preparations

Sycamore
Wyandot County

(G-17930)
CREATIVE PLASTIC CONCEPTS LLC (HQ)
206 S Griffith St (44882-9694)
PHONE..............................419 927-9588
Nick Reinhart, *President*
▲ EMP: 56
SALES (est): 21MM
SALES (corp-wide): 35.2MM **Privately Held**
SIC: 2499 5085 Clothes dryers (clothes horses), wood; bins & containers, storage
PA: Jansan Acquisition, Llc
11840 Westline Industrial
Saint Louis MO 63146
314 656-4321

Sylvania
Lucas County

(G-17931)
ADVANCE PRODUCTS
6041 Angleview Dr (43560-1209)
PHONE..............................419 882-8117
David Frantz, *Owner*
James Frantz, *Owner*
EMP: 10
SALES: 1.5MM **Privately Held**
SIC: 3571 3999 Computers, digital, analog or hybrid; models, except toy

(G-17932)
AFFINITY INFORMATION MANAGEMET
3359 Silica Rd (43560-9890)
PHONE..............................419 517-2055
EMP: 4
SALES (est): 288.4K **Privately Held**
SIC: 3559 Tire shredding machinery

(G-17933)
AIR CONVERSION TECHNOLOGY INC
3485 Silica Rd Unit A (43560-8995)
PHONE..............................419 841-1720
Mark E Charpie, *President*
Debra Charpie, *General Mgr*
Scott E Charpie, *Manager*
EMP: 3
SQ FT: 300
SALES: 250K **Privately Held**
SIC: 3592 Pistons & piston rings

(G-17934)
BOBBART INDUSTRIES INC
Also Called: American Custom Industries
5035 Alexis Rd Ste 1 (43560-1637)
PHONE..............................419 350-5477
Bart Lea, *President*
Laura Lea, *Corp Secy*
EMP: 25
SQ FT: 45,000
SALES: 1.7MM **Privately Held**
WEB: www.acivette.com
SIC: 3711 3082 7532 3714 Motor vehicles & car bodies; unsupported plastics profile shapes; top & body repair & paint shops; motor vehicle parts & accessories; plastics plumbing fixtures

(G-17935)
CSW OF NY INC
3545 Silica Rd Unit E (43560-9889)
PHONE..............................413 589-1311
Jeffrey Francis, *Principal*
EMP: 15
SALES (corp-wide): 16.6MM **Privately Held**
SIC: 2796 3544 Platemaking services; dies, steel rule
PA: Csw, Inc.
45 Tyburski Rd
Ludlow MA 01056
413 589-1311

(G-17936)
DON-ELL CORPORATION (PA)
Also Called: X M C Division
8450 Central Ave (43560-9747)
P.O. Box 351480, Toledo (43635-1480)
PHONE..............................419 841-7114
Donald R Sell, *Ch of Bd*
Robert N Sell, *President*
EMP: 35 EST: 1956
SQ FT: 12,000
SALES (est): 5.2MM **Privately Held**
SIC: 3679 3089 Electronic switches; molding primary plastic

(G-17937)
DON-ELL CORPORATION
Also Called: X M C
8456 Central Ave (43560-9747)
PHONE..............................419 841-7114
Jim Krumm, *Manager*
Delores A Krumm, *Manager*
EMP: 8
SALES (corp-wide): 5.2MM **Privately Held**
SIC: 3089 Injection molding of plastics
PA: Don-Ell Corporation
8450 Central Ave
Sylvania OH 43560
419 841-7114

(G-17938)
DRESCH TOLSON DENTAL LABS
8730 Resource Park Dr (43560-8939)
PHONE..............................419 842-6730
Joseph Gerace, *Owner*
EMP: 90
SALES (est): 2MM **Privately Held**
SIC: 8072 3843 Crown & bridge production; dental equipment & supplies

(G-17939)
DURA MAGNETICS INC
5500 Schultz Dr (43560-2384)
PHONE..............................419 882-0591
Donald C Kuchers, *CEO*
Robert M Csortos, *President*
Catherine A Kuchers, *Corp Secy*
▲ EMP: 17
SQ FT: 15,000
SALES (est): 7.2MM **Privately Held**
WEB: www.duramag.com
SIC: 5084 3499 Industrial machinery & equipment; magnets, permanent: metallic

(G-17940)
GALAXY PRODUCTS INC
3403 Silica Rd (43560-9539)
PHONE..............................419 843-7337
Colleen Sanders, *President*
Mark Neeley, *Principal*
EMP: 5

Sylvania - Lucas County (G-17941)

SALES (est): 808.9K **Privately Held**
WEB: www.galaxyproducts.com
SIC: **3544** 3546 3545 Special dies, tools, jigs & fixtures; power-driven handtools; machine tool accessories

(G-17941)
HANSON AGGREGATES LLC
4100 Centennial Rd (43560-9414)
PHONE..................................419 841-3413
Ron Tipton, *Vice Pres*
Dean Harshman, *Safety Mgr*
Michael Ryan, *Sales Mgr*
William Kurtz,
EMP: 20
SALES (corp-wide): 20.6B **Privately Held**
SIC: **1422** Crushed & broken limestone
HQ: Hanson Aggregates Llc
8505 Freport Pkwy Ste 500
Irving TX 75063
469 417-1200

(G-17942)
HANSON AGGREGATES MIDWEST LLC
8130 Brint Rd (43560-9719)
PHONE..................................419 882-0123
William Kurtz, *Facilities Mgr*
Tom Kusmer, *Engineer*
Ron Tipton, *Branch Mgr*
EMP: 10
SALES (corp-wide): 20.6B **Privately Held**
SIC: **1422** Crushed & broken limestone
HQ: Hanson Aggregates Midwest Llc
207 Old Harrods Creek Rd
Louisville KY 40223
502 244-7550

(G-17943)
ICE INDUSTRIES INC (PA)
3810 Herr Rd (43560-8925)
PHONE..................................419 842-3612
Gene Swick, *General Mgr*
Howard Ice, *Principal*
Paul Bishop, *COO*
Jeff Boger, *Exec VP*
Francisco Beltrandelrio, *Opers Staff*
▲ EMP: 26
SQ FT: 10,000
SALES: 100MM **Privately Held**
SIC: **3469** Stamping metal for the trade

(G-17944)
ICE INDUSTRIES COLUMBUS INC
3810 Herr Rd (43560-8925)
PHONE..................................419 842-3600
EMP: 8
SALES (est): 821.7K
SALES (corp-wide): 237.2MM **Privately Held**
SIC: **3469** Mfg Metal Stampings
PA: Ice Industries, Inc.
3810 Herr Rd
Sylvania OH 43560
419 842-3612

(G-17945)
INNOVATIVE HDLG & METALFAB LLC
7755 Sylvania Ave (43560-9518)
PHONE..................................419 882-7480
Alan Meek, *Plant Mgr*
Nick Otersen, *Engineer*
Ken Fashbaugh, *Accounts Mgr*
Earl McHenry, *Accounts Mgr*
Trent Orzechowski, *Accounts Mgr*
EMP: 20
SQ FT: 30,000
SALES: 3MM **Privately Held**
WEB: www.innovativehandling.com
SIC: **3535** 5084 Conveyors & conveying equipment; materials handling machinery

(G-17946)
JASON STULLER PRO SHOP LLC (PA)
5201 Corey Rd (43560-2202)
PHONE..................................419 882-3197
Jason Stuller, *Principal*
EMP: 4
SALES (est): 7.5MM **Privately Held**
SIC: **3949** Golf equipment

(G-17947)
JC AND ASSOCIATES SYLVANIA LLC
5129 Main St (43560-2125)
PHONE..................................419 824-0011
Jerry Cortese, *Manager*
EMP: 3
SALES (est): 347K **Privately Held**
SIC: **3639** Household appliances

(G-17948)
KEVIN K TIDD
Also Called: Arrow Print & Copy
5505 Roan Rd (43560-2306)
PHONE..................................419 885-5603
Kevin K Tidd, *Owner*
EMP: 6
SQ FT: 3,500
SALES (est): 490K **Privately Held**
WEB: www.arrowprint.com
SIC: **2752** 2791 2789 Commercial printing, offset; typesetting; bookbinding & related work

(G-17949)
LUMA ELECTRIC COMPANY
3419 Silica Rd (43560-9539)
PHONE..................................419 843-7842
Daniel Hinds, *President*
Lauren Hinds, *Vice Pres*
EMP: 5
SQ FT: 7,500
SALES (est): 720.7K **Privately Held**
SIC: **3423** Soldering tools

(G-17950)
MAUMEE BAY KITCHEN & BATH CENT
Also Called: Maumee Bay Kitchen & Bath Ctr
5758 Main St Ste 1 (43560-1933)
PHONE..................................419 882-4390
Matt Wingate, *Mng Member*
Dori Wingate,
EMP: 3
SALES (est): 314.7K **Privately Held**
SIC: **2499** Kitchen, bathroom & household ware: wood

(G-17951)
MOLD SHOP INC
8520 Central Ave (43560-9748)
PHONE..................................419 829-2041
Lan Wagner, *President*
Donna Wagner, *Vice Pres*
EMP: 10 EST: 1965
SQ FT: 12,000
SALES (est): 1.2MM **Privately Held**
SIC: **3544** Special dies & tools; forms (molds), for foundry & plastics working machinery

(G-17952)
MOORE CHROME PRODUCTS CO
Also Called: Moore Metal Finishing
3525 Silica Rd (43560-9814)
PHONE..................................419 843-3510
Scott W Backus, *President*
Scott Backus, *President*
Larry Huth, *Vice Pres*
Mary Huth, *Vice Pres*
Bonnie Armistead, *Manager*
EMP: 25 EST: 1930
SQ FT: 24,000
SALES (est): 3.7MM **Privately Held**
WEB: www.mooremetalfinishing.com
SIC: **3471** Plating of metals or formed products

(G-17953)
MUIR GRAPHICS INC
5454 Alger Dr Ste A (43560-2348)
PHONE..................................419 882-7993
Linda Rider, *President*
Karen Garner, *Vice Pres*
Suzanne Emerine, *Admin Sec*
EMP: 13 EST: 1974
SQ FT: 10,000
SALES (est): 2.2MM **Privately Held**
WEB: www.muir-graphics.com
SIC: **2752** Commercial printing, offset

(G-17954)
NABCO ENTRANCES INC
3407 Silica Rd (43560-9539)
PHONE..................................419 842-0484
EMP: 5
SALES (corp-wide): 2.6B **Privately Held**
SIC: **3699** Electrical equipment & supplies
HQ: Nabco Entrances, Inc.
S82w18717 Gemini Dr
Muskego WI 53150
262 679-7532

(G-17955)
NEXT SPECIALTY RESINS INC (PA)
Also Called: Next Resins
3315 Centennial Rd Ste J (43560-9419)
P.O. Box 365, Addison MI (49220-0365)
PHONE..................................419 843-4600
Rajiv H Naik, *President*
Saurabh H Naik, *Vice Pres*
◆ EMP: 35
SALES (est): 7.9MM **Privately Held**
SIC: **2821** Melamine resins, melamine-formaldehyde

(G-17956)
NIGHT LIGHTSCAPES
3303 Herr Rd (43560-9780)
PHONE..................................419 304-2486
Tom Walter, *Principal*
EMP: 3 EST: 2007
SALES (est): 215.2K **Privately Held**
SIC: **3645** Garden, patio, walkway & yard lighting fixtures: electric

(G-17957)
NORTHERN CONCRETE PIPE INC
3756 Centennial Rd (43560-9734)
PHONE..................................419 841-3361
Jeff Levon, *Principal*
EMP: 10
SALES (est): 991K
SALES (corp-wide): 21.3MM **Privately Held**
SIC: **3272** Pipe, concrete or lined with concrete
PA: Northern Concrete Pipe, Inc.
401 Kelton St
Bay City MI 48706
989 892-3545

(G-17958)
OHIO CHAIN COMPANY LLC
7757 Little Rd (43560-3760)
PHONE..................................419 843-9476
Douglas G Shanks,
EMP: 3
SALES (est): 301.9K **Privately Held**
SIC: **3462** Iron & steel forgings

(G-17959)
RESEARCH METRICS LLC
5121 Whiteford Rd (43560-2987)
P.O. Box 809, Norwalk (44857-0809)
PHONE..................................419 464-3333
Robert Bleile, *Mng Member*
EMP: 4
SALES (est): 175.6K **Privately Held**
SIC: **7372** Business oriented computer software

(G-17960)
SHARONCO INC
Also Called: Sylvan Studio
5651 Main St (43560-1929)
PHONE..................................419 882-3443
Scott Stampflmeier, *President*
EMP: 8
SALES (est): 500K **Privately Held**
SIC: **3499** 5094 Novelties & giftware, including trophies; trophies

(G-17961)
SILICA PRESS INC
3545 Silica Rd Unit A2 (43560-9889)
PHONE..................................419 843-8500
Joe Ray, *President*
Rudy Severhof, *Accounts Exec*
EMP: 3
SALES (est): 396K **Privately Held**
WEB: www.silicapress.com
SIC: **2759** Letterpress printing

(G-17962)
STANSLEY MINERAL RESOURCES INC (PA)
3793 Silica Rd B (43560-9814)
PHONE..................................419 843-2813
Rick Stansley, *CEO*
Richard Stansley Jr, *Corp Secy*
Jeff Stansley, *COO*
Mandy Billau, *Manager*
EMP: 35
SQ FT: 10,000
SALES (est): 15MM **Privately Held**
SIC: **1442** Gravel mining

(G-17963)
SYLVAN STUDIO INC
5651 Main St (43560-1929)
P.O. Box 59 (43560-0059)
PHONE..................................419 882-3423
Terry E Crandell, *Owner*
Scott Stampflmeier, *COO*
EMP: 7
SQ FT: 5,000
SALES: 400K **Privately Held**
WEB: www.sylvanstudio.com
SIC: **2396** 7336 Ribbons & bows, cut & sewed; commercial art & graphic design

(G-17964)
SYLVANIA MOOSE LODGE NO
Also Called: Sylvania Moose Lodge 1579
6072 Main St (43560-1266)
PHONE..................................419 885-4953
Gary Muter, *Administration*
EMP: 13
SALES: 300K **Privately Held**
SIC: **8641** 7372 Fraternal associations; application computer software

(G-17965)
TGM HOLDINGS COMPANY
Also Called: Toledo Grmtor Blffton Mtr Wrks
5439 Roan Rd (43560-2304)
PHONE..................................419 885-3769
John Toth, *President*
EMP: 21 EST: 1948
SQ FT: 35,000
SALES (est): 4.8MM **Privately Held**
WEB: www.toledogear.com
SIC: **3566** Reduction gears & gear units for turbines, except automotive

(G-17966)
TOTAL SELF DEFENSE TOLEDO LLC
5921 Therfield Dr (43560-1038)
PHONE..................................419 466-5882
Tyson Coates, *Principal*
EMP: 3
SALES (est): 190.3K **Privately Held**
SIC: **3812** Defense systems & equipment

(G-17967)
V COLLECTION
5630 Main St (43560-1928)
PHONE..................................419 517-0508
Kevin Andrew, *Owner*
EMP: 3
SALES (est): 137.1K **Privately Held**
SIC: **2389** Apparel & accessories

(G-17968)
VAN DELEIGH INDUSTRIES LLC
5611 Bent Oak Rd (43560-1104)
PHONE..................................419 467-2244
Rodney S Brant, *Principal*
EMP: 4
SALES (est): 542.9K **Privately Held**
SIC: **2679** Paper products, converted

(G-17969)
WORLD PREP INC
8432 Central Ave Ste 10 (43560-9700)
PHONE..................................419 843-3869
David T Krueger, *President*
Chip Parsons, *Sales Staff*
▲ EMP: 4
SQ FT: 2,500
SALES (est): 66.5K **Privately Held**
WEB: www.worldprep.com
SIC: **3842** First aid, snake bite & burn kits

▲ = Import ▼ = Export
◆ = Import/Export

Tallmadge
Summit County

(G-17970)
A-A1 MACHINE AND SUPPLY CO
Also Called: AA1 Tool and Tech Supply
3130 Klages Blvd (44278-3323)
PHONE.................................440 346-0698
Russ Busse, *President*
EMP: 5
SQ FT: 19,000
SALES: 1MM Privately Held
SIC: 3599 Machine shop, jobbing & repair

(G-17971)
AKRON GASKET & PACKG ENTPS INC
445 Northeast Ave (44278-1444)
PHONE.................................330 633-3742
Carter Ray, *CEO*
Craig Ray, *President*
Matthew Ray, *Vice Pres*
▲ EMP: 19
SQ FT: 40,000
SALES: 4MM Privately Held
WEB: www.akrongasket.com
SIC: 3053 Gaskets, all materials; packing: steam engines, pipe joints, air compressors, etc.

(G-17972)
ALL-TRA RUBBER PROCESSING
154 Potomac Ave Ste B (44278-2715)
PHONE.................................330 630-1945
Kendell Ashby, *Owner*
EMP: 4
SALES (est): 349.9K Privately Held
SIC: 2822 Synthetic rubber

(G-17973)
AVTEK INTERNATIONAL INC
382 Commerce St (44278-2135)
PHONE.................................330 633-7500
Thomas Milan, *President*
▲ EMP: 6
SQ FT: 6,000
SALES (est): 1MM Privately Held
SIC: 3651 Household audio equipment

(G-17974)
C L S FINISHING INC
409 Munroe Falls Rd (44278-3339)
P.O. Box 239 (44278-0239)
PHONE.................................330 784-4134
Steven Kenneth Geer, *President*
EMP: 10
SALES (est): 990K Privately Held
SIC: 3479 Painting of metal products; coating of metals with plastic or resins

(G-17975)
CHEMIONICS CORPORATION
390 Munroe Falls Rd (44278-3399)
PHONE.................................330 733-8834
John Blackfan, *General Mgr*
Jim Ferguson, *Production*
Mike Schmidt, *Admin Mgr*
▲ EMP: 32 EST: 1978
SQ FT: 80,000
SALES (est): 9.9MM Privately Held
WEB: www.chemionics.com
SIC: 2869 3069 3087 2821 Plasticizers, organic: cyclic & acyclic; reclaimed rubber & specialty rubber compounds; custom compound purchased resins; plastics materials & resins
PA: Protech Powder Coatings, Inc.
    21 Audrey Pl
    Fairfield NJ 07004

(G-17976)
CIRCLE MOLD INCORPORATED
Also Called: Circle Mold & Machine Co
85 S Thomas Rd (44278)
P.O. Box 513 (44278-0513)
PHONE.................................330 633-7017
Edward A Siciliano, *CEO*
Edward T Siciliano, *President*
Agnes Siciliano, *Admin Sec*
EMP: 30
SQ FT: 12,000
SALES (est): 5.4MM Privately Held
WEB: www.circlemold.com
SIC: 3544 Forms (molds), for foundry & plastics working machinery; industrial molds

(G-17977)
COMMAND PLASTIC CORPORATION
124 West Ave (44278-2206)
PHONE.................................800 321-8001
Richard S Ames, *President*
Ron Brengartner, *President*
Robert Acord, *Human Resources*
Ann Ames, *Director*
▲ EMP: 19
SQ FT: 65,000
SALES: 2MM Privately Held
WEB: www.commandplastic.com
SIC: 2671 3081 2673 Plastic film, coated or laminated for packaging; unsupported plastics film & sheet; bags: plastic, laminated & coated

(G-17978)
DES MACHINE SERVICES INC
351 Tacoma Ave (44278-2716)
PHONE.................................330 633-6897
William M Smith, *President*
Debora Smith, *Vice Pres*
Deb Smith, *CFO*
EMP: 9
SQ FT: 5,000
SALES (est): 1.1MM Privately Held
SIC: 3599 Machine shop, jobbing & repair

(G-17979)
DIAMOND MOLD & DIE CO
109 E Garwood Dr (44278-1402)
PHONE.................................330 633-5682
Joseph Speer, *President*
Silvia Schaefer, *Vice Pres*
Helene Speer, *Treasurer*
Corinna Phillips, *Admin Sec*
EMP: 14 EST: 1968
SQ FT: 5,000
SALES (est): 1.2MM Privately Held
SIC: 3544 Forms (molds), for foundry & plastics working machinery

(G-17980)
DIVERSIFIED READY MIX LTD
1680 Southeast Ave (44278-3466)
PHONE.................................330 628-3355
Todd Steinel, *Principal*
EMP: 3
SALES (est): 269.5K Privately Held
SIC: 3273 Ready-mixed concrete

(G-17981)
DOVE CDS INC
290 West Ave Ste J (44278-2143)
PHONE.................................330 928-9160
Larry Adams, *President*
Lisa Ann Adams, *Vice Pres*
Kari Donell, *Graphic Designe*
EMP: 5
SQ FT: 4,800
SALES (est): 1.2MM Privately Held
WEB: www.dovetapes.com
SIC: 5961 2791 Record &/or tape (music or video) club, mail order; typesetting

(G-17982)
DROWNED LURE
3295 Klages Blvd (44278-3367)
PHONE.................................330 548-5873
David Mitchell, *Principal*
EMP: 3
SALES (est): 277.5K Privately Held
SIC: 3949 Lures, fishing: artificial

(G-17983)
FITNESS FUEL TRAINING
1021 Southeast Ave (44278-3156)
PHONE.................................330 807-7353
Terri Pouliot, *Principal*
EMP: 3
SALES (est): 90K Privately Held
SIC: 2869 Physical fitness facilities

(G-17984)
HERMAN MACHINE INC
252 Northeast Ave (44278-1494)
PHONE.................................330 633-3261
Suzanne E Rickards, *President*
EMP: 10
SQ FT: 15,000
SALES (est): 1.6MM Privately Held
SIC: 3599 7389 3429 Machine shop, jobbing & repair; grinding, precision: commercial or industrial; clamps, metal

(G-17985)
HORNING STEEL CO
167 Southwest Ave (44278-2293)
PHONE.................................330 633-0028
Jean Horning, *Owner*
EMP: 5
SQ FT: 7,000
SALES (est): 556.7K Privately Held
SIC: 3441 Fabricated structural metal

(G-17986)
I R B F COMPANY
195 Potomac Ave Ste A (44278-2714)
P.O. Box 29 (44278-0029)
PHONE.................................330 633-5100
Jennifer A Eldridge, *President*
Linda Kerns, *Office Mgr*
Tom Mountain, *Admin Sec*
EMP: 7
SQ FT: 5,000
SALES (est): 847.3K Privately Held
WEB: www.irbf.com
SIC: 3354 3599 Shapes, extruded aluminum; machine shop, jobbing & repair

(G-17987)
INDUSTRIAL CTRL DSGN MINT INC
Also Called: Industrial Ctrl Design & Maint
311 Geneva Ave (44278-2702)
PHONE.................................330 785-9840
David M Brown Jr, *President*
Jon Coles, *Vice Pres*
EMP: 10
SQ FT: 14,000
SALES (est): 2.2MM Privately Held
WEB: www.icdminc.com
SIC: 3613 7699 5063 Control panels, electric; engine repair & replacement, non-automotive; switchboards

(G-17988)
KARG CORPORATION
241 Southwest Ave (44278-2239)
P.O. Box 197 (44278-0197)
PHONE.................................330 633-4916
Michael Karg, *President*
EMP: 15 EST: 1947
SQ FT: 40,000
SALES (est): 4.4MM Privately Held
WEB: www.kargcorp.com
SIC: 3552 Braiding machines, textile

(G-17989)
M & R MANUFACTURING INC
Also Called: Retco Mold & Machine
41 Industry St (44278-2127)
PHONE.................................330 633-5725
Marshall Terry, *Corp Secy*
Marshall T Terry, *Purch Mgr*
EMP: 3
SALES (est): 1.3MM Privately Held
WEB: www.retcomoldandmachine.com
SIC: 3544 Industrial molds

(G-17990)
MANUFACTURING CONCEPTS
409 Munroe Falls Rd (44278-3339)
P.O. Box 493 (44278-0493)
PHONE.................................330 784-9054
Nancy Minne, *Partner*
Sue Brown, *CFO*
Mike Cast, *Manager*
EMP: 12
SQ FT: 14,500
SALES (est): 947.9K Privately Held
WEB: www.manufacturingconcepts.com
SIC: 7692 Welding repair

(G-17991)
MARIK SPRING INC
121 Northeast Ave (44278-1947)
PHONE.................................330 564-0617
Greg A Bedrick, *President*
Debbie Perry, *Bookkeeper*
Dan Young, *Marketing Mgr*
EMP: 19 EST: 1954
SQ FT: 35,000
SALES (est): 4.4MM Privately Held
WEB: www.marikspring.com
SIC: 3493 3496 Flat springs, sheet or strip stock; miscellaneous fabricated wire products

(G-17992)
MARTIN WHEEL CO INC
342 West Ave (44278-2192)
P.O. Box 157 (44278-0157)
PHONE.................................330 633-3278
Jimmy Yang, *CEO*
Thomas J Hartmann, *President*
Chris Jones, *Senior Buyer*
Dolly Yang, *Treasurer*
Nick Williams, *Cust Mgr*
▲ EMP: 100
SQ FT: 125,000
SALES (est): 22.6MM Privately Held
SIC: 3714 3011 Motor vehicle wheels & parts; pneumatic tires, all types
PA: Americana Development, Inc.
    7095 Americana Pkwy
    Reynoldsburg OH 43068

(G-17993)
MIDWEST FABRICATIONS INC
516 Commerce St (44278-2132)
P.O. Box 399 (44278-0399)
PHONE.................................330 633-0191
Robert E Parsons, *President*
Barbara Parsons, *Corp Secy*
Timothy Parsons, *Vice Pres*
EMP: 38 EST: 1979
SQ FT: 9,000
SALES (est): 4.8MM Privately Held
SIC: 3444 Sheet metal specialties, not stamped

(G-17994)
MYERS MOTORS LLC
180 South Ave (44278-2813)
PHONE.................................330 630-7000
Dana S Myers, *President*
▲ EMP: 5
SALES (est): 717.7K Privately Held
SIC: 3711 Cars, electric, assembly of

(G-17995)
NAP ASSET HOLDINGS LTD
North Amer Products
411 Geneva Ave (44278-2704)
PHONE.................................330 633-0599
Glen McLean, *Branch Mgr*
EMP: 15
SALES (corp-wide): 45.7MM Privately Held
WEB: www.naptools.com
SIC: 2819 7699 Carbides; knife, saw & tool sharpening & repair
PA: Nap Asset Holdings Ltd.
    1180 Wernsing Rd
    Jasper IN 47546
    812 482-2000

(G-17996)
NORTHEAST COATINGS INC
415 Munroe Falls Rd (44278-3339)
PHONE.................................330 784-7773
Rod Fisher, *President*
Chad Fisher, *Managing Prtnr*
EMP: 15
SQ FT: 12,000
SALES (est): 880K Privately Held
SIC: 3479 Coating of metals & formed products

(G-17997)
NORTHEAST LASER INC
461 Commerce St (44278-2134)
P.O. Box 295 (44278-0295)
PHONE.................................330 633-2897
Andy Weinsheimer, *President*
EMP: 3
SALES (est): 573K Privately Held
SIC: 3699 Laser systems & equipment

(G-17998)
OWENS CORNING SALES LLC
170 South Ave (44278-2813)
PHONE.................................330 634-0460
Richard W Hooper, *Plant Mgr*
EMP: 140 Publicly Held
WEB: www.owenscorning.com
SIC: 3275 3086 Gypsum products; plastics foam products

Tallmadge - Summit County (G-17999)

HQ: Owens Corning Sales, Llc
1 Owens Corning Pkwy
Toledo OH 43659
419 248-8000

(G-17999)
OWENS CORNING SALES LLC
275 Southwest Ave (44278-2232)
PHONE.................................330 633-6735
Joe Brackman, *Branch Mgr*
EMP: 10
SQ FT: 300 **Publicly Held**
WEB: www.owenscorning.com
SIC: 8711 8731 2821 Engineering services; commercial physical research; plastics materials & resins
HQ: Owens Corning Sales, Llc
1 Owens Corning Pkwy
Toledo OH 43659
419 248-8000

(G-18000)
P & P MOLD & DIE INC
1034 S Munroe Rd (44278-3336)
PHONE.................................330 784-8333
Mary Jean Putra, *President*
William Putra, *Treasurer*
Emil Putra, *Admin Sec*
EMP: 17
SQ FT: 6,000
SALES (est): 2.7MM **Privately Held**
SIC: 3599 Machine shop, jobbing & repair

(G-18001)
PROMOLD INC
Also Called: Promold Gauer
487 Commerce St (44278-2134)
PHONE.................................330 633-3532
Stefan K Schler, *President*
Mary Ann Schler, *Vice Pres*
EMP: 10
SQ FT: 9,000
SALES (est): 1.7MM **Privately Held**
WEB: www.promoldinc.com
SIC: 3544 Mfg Dies/Tools/Jigs/Fixtures

(G-18002)
SATCO INC
59 Industry St (44278-2127)
PHONE.................................330 630-8866
Waffim Farrah, *President*
▲ **EMP:** 4
SQ FT: 50,000
SALES (est): 370K **Privately Held**
SIC: 3714 7389 5013 3694 Motor vehicle engines & parts; motor vehicle transmissions, drive assemblies & parts; transmissions, motor vehicle; packaging & labeling services; automotive supplies & parts; engine electrical equipment; relays & industrial controls; speed changers, drives & gears

(G-18003)
SGB USA INC
180 South Ave (44278-2813)
P.O. Box 188, Golden CO (80402-0188)
PHONE.................................330 472-1187
Robert Ganser Jr, *President*
Asad Jawaid, *Vice Pres*
Denise Morgan, *Admin Sec*
▲ **EMP:** 20
SQ FT: 12,500
SALES (est): 71.4K
SALES (corp-wide): 47.8K **Privately Held**
SIC: 3612 Autotransformers, electric (power transformers)
HQ: Starkstrom - Geratebau Gesellschaft
Mit Beschrankter Haftung
Ohmstr. 10
Regensburg 93055
941 784-10

(G-18004)
SPEELMAN ELECTRIC INC
358 Commerce St (44278-2139)
PHONE.................................330 633-1410
Richard Speelman, *President*
Christeen Parsons, *CFO*
EMP: 80
SQ FT: 7,000
SALES (est): 43.5MM **Privately Held**
WEB: www.speelmanelectric.com
SIC: 3825 1731 Test equipment for electronic & electric measurement; general electrical contractor

(G-18005)
STEERE ENTERPRISES INC
303 Tacoma Ave (44278-2716)
PHONE.................................330 633-4926
Colleen Dillow, *Human Resources*
Mark Stahl, *Branch Mgr*
EMP: 23
SALES (corp-wide): 59.7MM **Privately Held**
SIC: 3089 Blow molded finished plastic products
PA: Steere Enterprises, Inc.
285 Commerce St
Tallmadge OH 44278
330 633-4926

(G-18006)
STORETEK ENGINEERING INC
399 Commerce St (44278-2134)
PHONE.................................330 294-0678
Jim Crews, *President*
James Crews, *Engineer*
John Laguardia, *Project Engr*
Bruce Sandacz, *Controller*
EMP: 22
SALES (est): 5.1MM **Privately Held**
SIC: 8711 3559 Consulting engineer; electronic component making machinery

(G-18007)
SUNSET GOLF LLC
71 West Ave Ste 6 (44278-2236)
PHONE.................................419 994-5563
Bill Whipple,
Dan Dieghan,
▲ **EMP:** 37
SQ FT: 40,000
SALES (est): 3.6MM **Privately Held**
WEB: www.sunsetgolfballs.com
SIC: 3949 5941 Golf equipment; sporting goods & bicycle shops

(G-18008)
TAMARKIN COMPANY
Also Called: Giant Eagle
205 West Ave (44278-2138)
PHONE.................................330 634-0688
EMP: 5
SALES (corp-wide): 6.9B **Privately Held**
SIC: 2836 Vaccines & other immunizing products
HQ: The Tamarkin Company
101 Kappa Dr
Pittsburgh PA 15238
800 553-2324

(G-18009)
TRANS FOAM INC
Also Called: Cutting Edge Roofing Products
281 Southwest Ave (44278-2232)
PHONE.................................330 630-9444
Todd Jordan, *President*
EMP: 9
SALES (est): 1.8MM **Privately Held**
SIC: 3086 Insulation or cushioning material, foamed plastic

(G-18010)
UNITED DENTAL LABORATORIES (PA)
261 South Ave (44278-2819)
P.O. Box 428 (44278-0428)
PHONE.................................330 253-1810
Richard Delapa Jr, *President*
EMP: 35
SQ FT: 15,000
SALES (est): 5.3MM **Privately Held**
WEB: www.uniteddentallab.com
SIC: 8072 3843 Denture production; dental equipment & supplies

(G-18011)
UNIVERSAL POLYMER & RUBBER LTD
Also Called: Universal Rubber & Plastics
165 Northeast Ave (44278-1450)
PHONE.................................330 633-1666
EMP: 22
SALES (est): 1.8MM
SALES (corp-wide): 46.5MM **Privately Held**
SIC: 3061 Mechanical rubber goods
PA: Universal Polymer & Rubber, Ltd.
15730 Madison Rd
Middlefield OH 44062
440 632-1691

(G-18012)
VERSATILE MACHINE
402 Commerce St (44278-2135)
PHONE.................................330 618-9895
Darren George, *Owner*
EMP: 8
SALES (est): 335.4K **Privately Held**
SIC: 3599 Machine shop, jobbing & repair

(G-18013)
WALTCO LIFT CORP (DH)
285 Northeast Ave (44278-1431)
P.O. Box 354 (44278-0354)
PHONE.................................330 633-9191
Bill Chmelik, *Buyer*
Amber Denker, *Accountant*
Anthony Wayne, *Sales Mgr*
Jody Lakins, *Sales Staff*
Kirby Blackert, *Manager*
▲ **EMP:** 120
SQ FT: 70,000
SALES (est): 47.8MM
SALES (corp-wide): 3.8B **Privately Held**
SIC: 3537 3593 Industrial trucks & tractors; fluid power cylinders, hydraulic or pneumatic

(G-18014)
WEB3BOX SOFTWARE LLC
34 Merz Blvd Ste D (44278)
PHONE.................................330 794-7397
EMP: 5
SALES (est): 370K **Privately Held**
SIC: 7372 Prepackaged Software Services

(G-18015)
WHOLE SHOP INC
181 S Thomas Rd (44278-2752)
PHONE.................................330 630-5305
Nancie Scott, *President*
◆ **EMP:** 19
SQ FT: 27,000
SALES (est): 2.4MM **Privately Held**
WEB: www.wholeshopinc.com
SIC: 3441 7389 Fabricated structural metal; metal cutting services

(G-18016)
WOODCRAFT PATTERN WORKS INC
210 Southwest Ave (44278-2233)
PHONE.................................330 630-2158
Don A Kessler, *President*
Brian Kessler, *Vice Pres*
EMP: 4
SQ FT: 5,000
SALES (est): 230K **Privately Held**
SIC: 2499 Decorative wood & woodwork

Terrace Park
Hamilton County

(G-18017)
4ME GROUP LLC
715 Lexington Ave (45174-1217)
PHONE.................................513 898-1083
Chase Shiels, *Marketing Staff*
Nick Trotta, *Director*
EMP: 5
SALES (est): 86K **Privately Held**
SIC: 7372 Business oriented computer software

(G-18018)
CC PALLETS LLC
212 Cambridge Ave (45174-1138)
PHONE.................................513 442-8766
Tamara Fine, *Principal*
EMP: 3
SALES (est): 119.9K **Privately Held**
SIC: 2448 Pallets, wood & wood with metal

The Plains
Athens County

(G-18019)
BIMBO BAKERIES USA INC
33 N Plains Rd (45780-1013)
PHONE.................................740 797-4449
Dave Heiners, *Branch Mgr*
EMP: 24 **Privately Held**
SIC: 2051 Bakery: wholesale or wholesale/retail combined
HQ: Bimbo Bakeries Usa, Inc
255 Business Center Dr # 200
Horsham PA 19044
215 347-5500

(G-18020)
BIMBO BAKERIES USA INC
33 Plains Rd (45780)
PHONE.................................740 797-4449
EMP: 24
SALES (corp-wide): 13.1B **Privately Held**
SIC: 2051 Mfg Bread/Related Products
HQ: Bimbo Bakeries Usa, Inc
255 Business Center Dr
Horsham PA 19044
215 347-5500

(G-18021)
DON GAMERTSFELDER
10416 State Route 682 (45780-1319)
PHONE.................................740 797-4495
Don Gamertsfelder, *Principal*
EMP: 3
SALES (est): 147.4K **Privately Held**
SIC: 1241 Coal mining services

(G-18022)
ELECTRIC MOTOR SVC OF ATHENS
6 E 4th St (45780-1305)
PHONE.................................740 592-1682
Albert W Matters III, *President*
Diane Matters, *Treasurer*
EMP: 10
SALES: 1.4MM **Privately Held**
SIC: 7694 Electric motor repair

(G-18023)
TYJEN INC
Also Called: Slater Builders Supply
8 Slater Dr (45780-1321)
PHONE.................................740 797-4064
Mark Vaughn, *President*
David Vaughn, *Vice Pres*
EMP: 9
SALES (corp-wide): 3.1MM **Privately Held**
SIC: 3271 Blocks, concrete or cinder: standard
PA: Tyjen Inc
35255 Hocking Dr
Logan OH 43138
740 380-3215

(G-18024)
WATTS ANTENNA COMPANY
70 N Plains Rd Ste H (45780-1156)
PHONE.................................740 797-9380
John Johnson, *President*
EMP: 7
SALES (est): 536.3K **Privately Held**
WEB: www.wattsantenna.com
SIC: 3812 3663 Search & navigation equipment; navigational systems & instruments; antennas, transmitting & communications

Thompson
Geauga County

(G-18025)
EDMONDS ELEVATOR COMPANY
6777 Sidley Rd (44086-9715)
PHONE.................................216 781-9135
Tina Schaeffer, *President*
Michael Schaeffer, *Vice Pres*
EMP: 19
SQ FT: 5,000

▲ = Import ▼= Export
◆ = Import/Export

GEOGRAPHIC SECTION

SALES (est): 3.5MM **Privately Held**
SIC: 1796 3534 7699 Installing building equipment; elevators & moving stairways; professional instrument repair services

(G-18026)
PAINE FALLS CENTERPIN LLC
6342 Ledge Rd (44086-9732)
PHONE..............................440 298-3202
Adam N Demarco, *Principal*
EMP: 8
SALES (est): 707.4K **Privately Held**
SIC: 3452 Pins

(G-18027)
QUARTER MILE FABRICATION LLC
7289 Leroy Thompson Rd (44086-9523)
PHONE..............................440 298-1272
Lawrence Gidley, *Principal*
EMP: 3
SALES (est): 199K **Privately Held**
SIC: 3131 Quarters

(G-18028)
R W SIDLEY INCORPORATED
Also Called: Sidley Truck & Equipment
7123 Madison Rd (44086-9775)
P.O. Box 10 (44086-0010)
PHONE..............................440 298-3232
Larry Mc Cune, *Sales Staff*
Rob Sidley, *Manager*
Eric Ludewig, *Manager*
EMP: 30
SALES (corp-wide): 132.6MM **Privately Held**
WEB: www.rwsidleyinc.com
SIC: 3273 Ready-mixed concrete
PA: R. W. Sidley Incorporated
  436 Casement Ave
  Painesville OH 44077
  440 352-9343

Thornville
Perry County

(G-18029)
AMERICAN DREAMS INC
1 Shoreline Dr (43076-8957)
PHONE..............................740 385-4444
David Swain, *President*
EMP: 5 EST: 1996
SALES (est): 392K **Privately Held**
WEB: www.coastalhighway.com
SIC: 7372 6531 Prepackaged software; real estate agents & managers

(G-18030)
BUCKEYE LAKE SHOPPER REPORTER
14886 State Route 13 (43076-8954)
PHONE..............................740 246-4741
Sandy Peters, *Principal*
Twila Rodgers, *Manager*
EMP: 4
SALES (est): 205.3K **Privately Held**
SIC: 2711 Newspapers, publishing & printing

(G-18031)
RE CONNORS CONSTRUCTION LTD
13352 Forrest Rd Ne (43076-9164)
PHONE..............................740 644-0261
Thomas Connors, *Owner*
EMP: 9 EST: 2014
SALES (est): 485.1K **Privately Held**
SIC: 1771 1761 3271 7389 Concrete work; roofing, siding & sheet metal work; concrete block & brick; ; general remodeling, single-family houses

(G-18032)
ROCKS GENERAL MAINTENANCE LLC
10019 Jacksontown Rd (43076-8802)
PHONE..............................740 323-4711
Michael Stonerock,
Twila Stonerock,
EMP: 7

SALES (est): 1.1MM **Privately Held**
SIC: 3498 Piping systems for pulp paper & chemical industries

(G-18033)
SHELLY COMPANY
80 Park Dr (43076-9397)
PHONE..............................740 246-6315
Dave Bathieck, *Manager*
EMP: 7
SALES (corp-wide): 29.7B **Privately Held**
SIC: 3273 2951 1442 Ready-mixed concrete; asphalt paving mixtures & blocks; construction sand & gravel
HQ: Shelly Company
  80 Park Dr
  Thornville OH 43076
  740 246-6315

(G-18034)
SHELLY MATERIALS INC
8775 Blackbird Ln (43076-9515)
PHONE..............................740 246-5009
Larry Shively, *Vice Pres*
EMP: 25
SALES (corp-wide): 29.7B **Privately Held**
SIC: 2951 Asphalt paving mixtures & blocks
HQ: Shelly Materials, Inc.
  80 Park Dr
  Thornville OH 43076
  740 246-6315

(G-18035)
SHELLY MATERIALS INC (DH)
Also Called: Shelly Company, The
80 Park Dr (43076-9397)
P.O. Box 266 (43076-0266)
PHONE..............................740 246-6315
John Power, *President*
Ted Lemon, *Vice Pres*
Doug Radabaugh, *Treasurer*
EMP: 100 EST: 1938
SALES (est): 809.6MM
SALES (corp-wide): 29.7B **Privately Held**
SIC: 1422 1442 2951 4492 Crushed & broken limestone; construction sand & gravel; concrete, asphaltic (not from refineries); tugboat service
HQ: Shelly Company
  80 Park Dr
  Thornville OH 43076
  740 246-6315

(G-18036)
SILK SCREEN SPECIAL TS INC
9075 Boundaries Rd (43076-9400)
P.O. Box 218 (43076-0218)
PHONE..............................740 246-4843
Steven R Dornon, *President*
EMP: 5
SQ FT: 8,500
SALES (est): 643K **Privately Held**
WEB: www.lakesend.com
SIC: 2759 5199 5947 5699 Screen printing; advertising specialties; novelties; sports apparel; T-shirts, custom printed; novelty merchandise, mail order; clothing, mail order (except women's)

Thurman
Gallia County

(G-18037)
CITIZENS DEFENSE LLC
7388 Cora Mill Rd (45685-9302)
PHONE..............................740 645-1101
Floyd Evans, *Principal*
EMP: 3
SALES (est): 141.8K **Privately Held**
SIC: 3812 Defense systems & equipment

(G-18038)
S & J LUMBER CO
3667 Garners Ford Rd (45685-9301)
PHONE..............................740 245-5804
John Smith, *Owner*
Dan Miller, *Manager*
EMP: 30
SQ FT: 3,000
SALES (est): 3.8MM **Privately Held**
SIC: 2421 Building & structural materials, wood

Tiffin
Seneca County

(G-18039)
A & M PRODUCTS
3060 S County Road 591 (44883-9749)
PHONE..............................419 595-2092
Marion A Lucius, *Owner*
EMP: 3
SQ FT: 4,800
SALES (est): 250.6K **Privately Held**
SIC: 2992 2891 Lubricating oils & greases; sealants

(G-18040)
ACT FOR SNECA CNTY OPRTNTY CTR
58 Braden Ct (44883-1407)
PHONE..............................419 447-4362
Joseph Steinr, *President*
James Donaldson, *President*
Joseph Steinger, *President*
Deth Donaldson, *Admin Sec*
EMP: 3
SALES: 8K **Privately Held**
SIC: 2711 Newspapers: publishing only, not printed on site

(G-18041)
AGRATI - TIFFIN LLC
1988 S County Road 593 (44883-9275)
PHONE..............................419 447-2221
Dan Ferguson, *Production*
Bob Lucius, *Marketing Mgr*
Robert S Kaminski,
Betty Hall, *Administration*
EMP: 54
SALES (est): 24.8MM **Privately Held**
SIC: 3452 Screws, metal
HQ: Agrati - Park Forest, Llc
  24000 S Western Ave
  Park Forest IL 60466
  708 228-5193

(G-18042)
AMERICAN FINE SINTER CO LTD
957 N County Road 11 (44883-9415)
PHONE..............................419 443-8880
Toshihiro Nakashima, *President*
Jeremy A Gibson, *Principal*
▲ EMP: 125
SQ FT: 80,000
SALES (est): 30.3MM
SALES (corp-wide): 329.7MM **Privately Held**
SIC: 3519 Parts & accessories, internal combustion engines
PA: Fine Sinter Co., Ltd.
  1189-11, Nishinohora, Akechicho
  Kasugai AIC 480-0
  568 884-355

(G-18043)
AMERICAN SWEET BEAN CO LLC
8133 N Township Road 72a (44883-9335)
PHONE..............................888 995-0007
Charles Fry,
EMP: 5
SALES: 950K **Privately Held**
SIC: 2099 Food preparations

(G-18044)
APEX TARGET SYSTEMS LLC
37 Heilman St (44883-1802)
PHONE..............................877 224-6692
Jamie Chester, *Mng Member*
EMP: 5 EST: 2016
SALES (est): 193.5K **Privately Held**
SIC: 3949 Target shooting equipment

(G-18045)
ARNOLD MACHINE INC
19 Heritage Dr (44883-9503)
PHONE..............................419 443-1818
Zachary W Arnold, *President*
EMP: 13
SQ FT: 22,000
SALES (est): 4MM **Privately Held**
SIC: 3599 Machine shop, jobbing & repair

(G-18046)
ATLAS INDUSTRIES INC
401 Wall St (44883-1369)
PHONE..............................419 637-2117
Donald Rickard, *Manager*
EMP: 302
SALES (corp-wide): 133.9MM **Privately Held**
WEB: www.atlasindustries.com
SIC: 3599 5013 3714 Crankshafts & camshafts, machining; automotive supplies & parts; motor vehicle parts & accessories
PA: Atlas Industries, Inc.
  1750 E State St
  Fremont OH 43420
  419 355-1000

(G-18047)
ATLAS INDUSTRIES INC
401 Wall St (44883-1369)
PHONE..............................419 447-4730
David Noble, *Manager*
EMP: 96
SALES (corp-wide): 133.9MM **Privately Held**
WEB: www.atlasindustries.com
SIC: 3599 3714 Crankshafts & camshafts, machining; manifolds, motor vehicle
PA: Atlas Industries, Inc.
  1750 E State St
  Fremont OH 43420
  419 355-1000

(G-18048)
AUGDON NEWSPAPERS OF OHIO INC
Also Called: Advertiser-Tribune, The
320 Nelson St (44883-8956)
P.O. Box 778 (44883-0778)
PHONE..............................419 448-3200
Nick Dutro, *Editor*
Rob Weaver, *Editor*
Jill Gosche, *Opers Staff*
Jay Sigler, *Production*
Vickie Comer, *Sales Staff*
EMP: 17
SALES (est): 1.1MM **Privately Held**
SIC: 2711 Newspapers, publishing & printing

(G-18049)
B J PALLETT
324 4th Ave (44883-1227)
PHONE..............................419 447-9665
Bernard Breidenbach Jr, *Owner*
EMP: 9
SQ FT: 27,500
SALES (est): 826.6K **Privately Held**
SIC: 2448 Pallets, wood

(G-18050)
BALLREICH BROS INC
Also Called: Ballreichs Potato Chips Snacks
186 Ohio Ave (44883-1746)
PHONE..............................419 447-1814
Brian Reis, *President*
Joseph Weininger, *Controller*
Linda Reis, *Financial Exec*
Haley Thomas, *Sales Dir*
Regina Miller, *Manager*
EMP: 105
SQ FT: 48,000
SALES (est): 10.2MM **Privately Held**
WEB: www.ballreich.com
SIC: 2096 2099 4226 Potato chips & other potato-based snacks; food preparations; special warehousing & storage

(G-18051)
BOOKMYER LLP
144 S Washington St Ste B (44883-2977)
PHONE..............................419 447-3883
Mike Bonham, *Partner*
Mary Hoyda, *Partner*
Barb Patterson, *Partner*
EMP: 5
SALES (est): 431.1K **Privately Held**
SIC: 2759 Visiting cards (including business): printing

(G-18052)
BRADLEYS BEACONS LTD
Also Called: Whitehouse
296 Hedges St (44883-3120)
PHONE..............................419 447-7560

Tiffin - Seneca County (G-18053)

Donna Bradley, *Mng Member*
David Greene,
Heather Greene,
EMP: 3
SALES (est): 124.3K **Privately Held**
SIC: 2759 Promotional printing

(G-18054)
BUTT HUT OF AMERICA INC
1972 W Market St (44883-2556)
PHONE.................................419 443-1997
Wendy Waltermyer, *Manager*
Amy Bridinger, *Manager*
Hal Simon, *Director*
EMP: 4
SALES (est): 416.6K **Privately Held**
SIC: 2111 5194 Cigarettes; tobacco & tobacco products

(G-18054)
C S BELL CO
170 W Davis St (44883-1337)
P.O. Box 291 (44883-0291)
PHONE.................................419 448-0791
Daniel White, *President*
Mary White, *Vice Pres*
▼ **EMP:** 10
SQ FT: 10,000
SALES (est): 1.1MM **Privately Held**
WEB: www.csbellco.com
SIC: 3535 3541 Conveyors & conveying equipment; grinding machines, metalworking

(G-18055)
CARMEUSE LIME INC
1967 W County Rd 42 (44883)
PHONE.................................419 986-2000
Amy Kuhn, *Branch Mgr*
EMP: 4 **Privately Held**
SIC: 1422 Agricultural limestone, ground
HQ: Carmeuse Lime, Inc.
11 Stanwix St Fl 21
Pittsburgh PA 15222
412 995-5500

(G-18056)
CHEMTRANS LOGISTICS INC
281 Hancock St (44883-3115)
PHONE.................................419 447-8041
Kenneth O Stahl, *President*
EMP: 4 **EST:** 2001
SALES (est): 430K **Privately Held**
SIC: 3537 Trucks: freight, baggage, etc.: industrial, except mining

(G-18057)
CUSTOM MACHINE INC
3315 W Township Road 158 (44883-9453)
PHONE.................................419 986-5122
David Hammer, *President*
Jeffery Hammer, *Vice Pres*
Phyllis Hammer, *Treasurer*
EMP: 30
SQ FT: 19,200
SALES: 2.9MM **Privately Held**
WEB: www.custom-machine-inc.com
SIC: 3544 3599 7692 Special dies & tools; machine shop, jobbing & repair; welding repair

(G-18058)
DOREL HOME FURNISHINGS INC
458 2nd Ave (44883-9358)
PHONE.................................419 447-7448
Rick Jackson, *President*
EMP: 250
SALES (corp-wide): 2.5B **Privately Held**
WEB: www.dorel.com
SIC: 2511 Console tables: wood; coffee tables: wood; tea wagons: wood
HQ: Dorel Home Furnishings, Inc.
410 E 1st St S
Wright City MO 63390
636 745-3351

(G-18059)
E SYSTEMS DESIGN & AUTOMTN INC
226 Heritage Dr (44883-9504)
P.O. Box 158 (44883-0158)
PHONE.................................419 443-0220
Don Bagent, *President*
Brenda Bagent, *Treasurer*
EMP: 8

SQ FT: 9,000
SALES (est): 1.5MM **Privately Held**
SIC: 3542 Machine tools, metal forming type

(G-18060)
FIRE TETRAHEDRON JOURNAL
3110 E County Road 50 C (44883-8448)
PHONE.................................567 220-6477
Jennifer Dempsey, *Principal*
EMP: 3
SALES (est): 101.4K **Privately Held**
SIC: 2711 Newspapers

(G-18061)
FRY FOODS INC
99 Maule Rd (44883-9400)
P.O. Box 837 (44883-0837)
PHONE.................................419 448-0831
Norman Fry, *President*
Beverly Fry, *Vice Pres*
David Fry, *Vice Pres*
Philip Fry, *Vice Pres*
Jerry Kaufman, *Vice Pres*
▼ **EMP:** 50
SQ FT: 40,000
SALES (est): 23.9MM **Privately Held**
WEB: www.fryfoods.com
SIC: 2038 2033 Snacks, including onion rings, cheese sticks, etc.; canned fruits & specialties

(G-18062)
J H PLASTICS
4720 W Us Highway 224 (44883-8887)
PHONE.................................419 937-2035
John Defibaugh, *Principal*
EMP: 4
SALES (est): 235.8K **Privately Held**
SIC: 3089 Plastics products

(G-18063)
JOHNS WELDING & TOWING INC
850 N County Road 11 (44883-9415)
PHONE.................................419 447-8937
Joseph Keller, *President*
James Keller, *Vice Pres*
EMP: 14
SQ FT: 20,000
SALES (est): 1.8MM **Privately Held**
SIC: 7549 7692 Towing services; welding repair

(G-18064)
LAMINATE TECHNOLOGIES INC (PA)
Also Called: Lam Tech
161 Maule Rd (44883-9400)
PHONE.................................419 448-0812
Frederick E Zoeller, *President*
Randy Wiser, *General Mgr*
Allan Funkhouser, *CFO*
Spencer Schabel, *Sales Staff*
Belinda Robbins, *Manager*
▲ **EMP:** 55
SQ FT: 80,000
SALES (est): 27.5MM **Privately Held**
WEB: www.lamtech.net
SIC: 2439 2891 2672 Structural wood members; adhesives & sealants; coated & laminated paper

(G-18065)
LIFETIME IRONWORKS LLC
244 Coe St (44883-3158)
PHONE.................................419 443-0567
David Miller, *Mng Member*
EMP: 3
SALES (est): 235K **Privately Held**
SIC: 3446 Architectural metalwork

(G-18066)
M & B ASPHALT COMPANY INC
Also Called: Maple Grove Materials
2100 W Senc County Rd 42 (44883)
P.O. Box 240, Old Fort (44861-0240)
PHONE.................................419 992-4235
R Chesebro, *Corp Secy*
Farley Wood, *Vice Pres*
Chris Harrison, *Manager*
EMP: 5
SALES (corp-wide): 69.4MM **Privately Held**
SIC: 2951 Asphalt paving mixtures & blocks

PA: M & B Asphalt Company, Inc.
1525 W Seneca Cnty Rd 42
Tiffin OH 44883
419 992-4235

(G-18067)
M G Q INC
Also Called: Maple Grove Companies
1525 W County Road 42 (44883-8457)
P.O. Box 130, Old Fort (44861-0130)
PHONE.................................419 992-4236
Lynn Radabaugh, *President*
Tim Bell, *President*
Bruce Chubb, *Principal*
Jeff Murphy, *Principal*
Bob Chesebro, *Corp Secy*
EMP: 45
SALES (est): 3.5MM **Privately Held**
WEB: www.mgq.com
SIC: 4214 1481 Local trucking with storage; mine & quarry services, nonmetallic minerals

(G-18068)
MAPLE GROVE MATERIALS INC
1525 W City Rd Ste 42 (44883)
PHONE.................................419 992-4235
Tim Bell, *President*
Lynn O Radabaugh, *Vice Pres*
Robert Chesebro, *Treasurer*
EMP: 9
SQ FT: 2,000
SALES (est): 926.6K
SALES (corp-wide): 69.4MM **Privately Held**
SIC: 3281 Limestone, cut & shaped
PA: M & B Asphalt Company, Inc.
1525 W Seneca Cnty Rd 42
Tiffin OH 44883
419 992-4235

(G-18069)
ML ADVERTISING & DESIGN LLC
Also Called: Mlad Graphic Design Services
185 Jefferson St (44883-2865)
PHONE.................................419 447-6523
Mark A Levans, *Mng Member*
EMP: 6
SQ FT: 3,000
SALES: 500K **Privately Held**
WEB: www.mlad.com
SIC: 7336 2759 Graphic arts & related design; commercial printing

(G-18070)
NATIONAL MACHINERY LLC (HQ)
161 Greenfield St (44883-2471)
P.O. Box 747 (44883-0747)
PHONE.................................419 447-5211
Andrew Kalnow,
◆ **EMP:** 310
SQ FT: 650,000
SALES (est): 101.1MM
SALES (corp-wide): 125.6MM **Privately Held**
SIC: 3542 Headers; high energy rate metal forming machines; mechanical (pneumatic or hydraulic) metal forming machines
PA: Nm Group Global, Llc
161 Greenfield St
Tiffin OH 44883
419 447-5211

(G-18071)
NM GROUP GLOBAL LLC (PA)
161 Greenfield St (44883-2499)
PHONE.................................419 447-5211
Andrew Kalnow,
EMP: 5 **EST:** 2002
SALES (est): 125.6MM **Privately Held**
SIC: 3542 3599 6799 Forging machinery & hammers; custom machinery; investors

(G-18072)
NMGG CTG LLC (PA)
Also Called: Cleaning Technologies Grp
161 Greenfield St (44883-2499)
PHONE.................................419 447-5211
Andrew H Kalnow, *CEO*
Robert J Foster, *CFO*
EMP: 7

SALES (est): 24.3MM **Privately Held**
SIC: 3569 3541 Blast cleaning equipment, dustless; ultrasonic metal cutting machine tools

(G-18073)
OCECO INC
Also Called: Oceco Co
1616 S County Road 1 (44883-9746)
P.O. Box 159 (44883-0159)
PHONE.................................419 447-0916
Richard Borer, *President*
Julie Morris, *Controller*
Rebecca Mason, *Sales Executive*
EMP: 15
SQ FT: 38,000
SALES (est): 3MM **Privately Held**
SIC: 3494 3589 3599 7692 Valves & pipe fittings; sewage treatment equipment; machine shop, jobbing & repair; welding repair; machine tools, metal cutting type

(G-18074)
OGDEN NEWSPAPERS OF OHIO INC
Also Called: Advertising Tribune
320 Nelson St (44883-8956)
P.O. Box 778 (44883-0778)
PHONE.................................419 448-3200
Fax: 419 447-3274
EMP: 85
SALES (est): 6.4MM
SALES (corp-wide): 683.9MM **Privately Held**
SIC: 2711 Newspapers-Publishing/Printing
PA: The Ogden Newspapers Inc
1500 Main St
Wheeling WV 26003
304 233-0100

(G-18075)
PALMER BROS TRANSIT MIX CON
1900 S County Road 1 (44883-8826)
PHONE.................................419 447-2018
Rick Corbeck, *Manager*
EMP: 8
SALES (est): 899.8K
SALES (corp-wide): 7MM **Privately Held**
SIC: 3273 Ready-mixed concrete
PA: Palmer Bros Transit Mix Concrete Inc
12205 E Gypsy Lane Rd
Bowling Green OH 43402
419 352-4681

(G-18076)
QUICK TAB II INC (PA)
241 Heritage Dr (44883-9504)
P.O. Box 723 (44883-0723)
PHONE.................................419 448-6622
Chuck Daughenbaugh, *CEO*
Mike Daughenbaugh, *Vice Pres*
Marty Ward, *Traffic Mgr*
Charles Eingle, *CFO*
Melissa Chester, *Human Res Mgr*
▼ **EMP:** 64
SQ FT: 30,000
SALES (est): 12.1MM **Privately Held**
WEB: www.qt2.com
SIC: 2752 5112 2791 2789 Business forms, lithographed; stationery & office supplies; typesetting; bookbinding & related work

(G-18077)
RIVERSIDE ENGINES INC
7381 S State Route 231 (44883-8503)
PHONE.................................419 927-6838
Jan Riedel, *President*
Larry Sarka, *Corp Secy*
EMP: 4 **EST:** 1975
SQ FT: 6,500
SALES: 700K **Privately Held**
SIC: 3714 Motor vehicle parts & accessories

(G-18078)
ROBERT NICKEL
125 Minerva St (44883-1559)
PHONE.................................419 448-8256
Robert Nickel, *Principal*
EMP: 3 **EST:** 2010
SALES (est): 166.8K **Privately Held**
SIC: 3356 Nickel

GEOGRAPHIC SECTION

Tipp City - Miami County (G-18104)

(G-18079)
RUSH GRAPHIX LTD
30 Riverside Dr (44883-2332)
P.O. Box 866 (44883-0866)
PHONE 419 448-7874
Bill Franklin, *Owner*
EMP: 3
SALES (est): 273.4K **Privately Held**
SIC: 2759 Screen printing

(G-18080)
SARKA SHTMTL & FABRICATION INC
Also Called: Sarka Conveyor
70 Clinton Ave (44883-1620)
PHONE 419 447-4377
Kendall T Parker, *President*
Larry D Sarka, *Shareholder*
EMP: 22
SQ FT: 11,000
SALES (est): 7MM **Privately Held**
SIC: 3444 Sheet metalwork

(G-18081)
SARVER INDUSTRIES LLC
178 N Sandusky St (44883-1520)
PHONE 419 455-5509
EMP: 3
SALES (est): 137.6K **Privately Held**
SIC: 3999 Manufacturing industries

(G-18082)
SEISLOVE VAULT & SEPTIC TANKS
Also Called: Seislove Brial Vlts Sptic Tnks
2168 S State Route 100 (44883-3699)
PHONE 419 447-5473
P David Seislove, *President*
EMP: 7 **EST:** 1946
SQ FT: 13,000
SALES (est): 752.5K **Privately Held**
SIC: 3272 Burial vaults, concrete or precast terrazzo; septic tanks, concrete

(G-18083)
SENECA SHEET METAL COMPANY
Also Called: Sheet Metal Fabricator
277 Water St (44883-1698)
PHONE 419 447-8434
Robert J Fulton, *President*
George H Wells, *Vice Pres*
John W Hilbert II, *Incorporator*
EMP: 10
SQ FT: 55,000
SALES: 1MM **Privately Held**
SIC: 3444 1761 Sheet metal specialties, not stamped; sheet metalwork

(G-18084)
SONOCO PRODUCTS COMPANY
60 Heritage Dr (44883-9503)
PHONE 419 448-4428
Terry Barfield, *Manager*
EMP: 45
SALES (corp-wide): 5.3B **Publicly Held**
WEB: www.sonoco.com
SIC: 2655 2671 Fiber cans, drums & similar products; packaging paper & plastics film, coated & laminated
PA: Sonoco Products Company
1 N 2nd St
Hartsville SC 29550
843 383-7000

(G-18085)
STACY EQUIPMENT CO
325 Hall St (44883-1419)
PHONE 419 447-6903
Ben Chaffee, *Principal*
EMP: 4
SALES (est): 310.6K **Privately Held**
SIC: 3535 Conveyors & conveying equipment

(G-18086)
TAIHO CORPORATION OF AMERICA
194 Heritage Dr (44883-9503)
PHONE 419 443-1645
Shigeki Awazu, *President*
Karl Kortlandt, *Vice Pres*
Mike Shannaberger, *Vice Pres*
Mark Gibson, *Prdtn Mgr*
Doug Bouillon, *Maint Spvr*
▲ **EMP:** 120
SQ FT: 140
SALES: 27.4MM
SALES (corp-wide): 1B **Privately Held**
SIC: 3714 3585 3568 Air conditioner parts, motor vehicle; motor vehicle transmissions, drive assemblies & parts; refrigeration & heating equipment; power transmission equipment
PA: Taiho Kogyo Co., Ltd.
3-65, Midorigaoka
Toyota AIC 471-0
565 282-225

(G-18087)
TIFFIN FOUNDRY & MACHINE INC
423 W Adams St (44883-9284)
P.O. Box 37 (44883-0037)
PHONE 419 447-3991
Melvin A Jones, *Ch of Bd*
Steven Sobol, *President*
EMP: 35 **EST:** 2004
SQ FT: 45,000
SALES (est): 4.7MM **Privately Held**
SIC: 3592 3321 3599 3325 Carburetors, pistons, rings, valves; gray & ductile iron foundries; machine shop, jobbing & repair; steel foundries; malleable iron foundries

(G-18088)
TIFFIN METAL PRODUCTS CO (PA)
450 Wall St (44883-1366)
PHONE 419 447-8414
Richard S Harrison, *President*
Michael R Reser, *Exec VP*
Ron Myers, *Vice Pres*
Richard M Wyka, *VP Mfg*
Mark Debarbrie, *Purch Mgr*
▼ **EMP:** 110 **EST:** 1903
SQ FT: 120,000
SALES (est): 17.4MM **Privately Held**
WEB: www.tiffinmetal.com
SIC: 2599 2542 2531 2522 Boards: planning, display, notice; factory furniture & fixtures; lockers (not refrigerated): except wood; public building & related furniture; office furniture, except wood; wood office furniture; wood kitchen cabinets

(G-18089)
TIFFIN SCENIC STUDIOS INC (PA)
Also Called: Atlantic and Prfmce Rigging
146 Riverside Dr (44883-1644)
P.O. Box 39 (44883-0039)
PHONE 800 445-1546
Brad Hossler, *President*
Steve Maiberger, *Treasurer*
Steve Everhart, *Admin Sec*
EMP: 66
SQ FT: 24,000
SALES: 9MM **Privately Held**
WEB: www.tiffinscenic.com
SIC: 2391 3999 Draperies, plastic & textile: from purchased materials; stage hardware & equipment, except lighting

(G-18090)
TOLEDO MOLDING & DIE INC
1441 Maule Rd (44883-9130)
PHONE 419 443-9031
Randy Maynard, *Maint Spvr*
Luke Biller, *Engineer*
John Demarsh, *Engineer*
Paul Landers, *Human Res Mgr*
Carl Pastorella, *Human Res Mgr*
EMP: 310
SALES (corp-wide): 309.9MM **Privately Held**
WEB: www.tmdinc.com
SIC: 3089 Automotive parts, plastic; injection molding of plastics
HQ: Toledo Molding & Die, Inc.
1429 Coining Dr
Toledo OH 43612
419 470-3950

(G-18091)
VIEWPOINT GRAPHIC DESIGN
132 S Washington St (44883-2840)
PHONE 419 447-6073
Pete Krupp, *Owner*
EMP: 6
SQ FT: 5,000
SALES (est): 484.5K **Privately Held**
SIC: 2759 Screen printing

(G-18092)
WEBSTER INDUSTRIES INC (PA)
Also Called: Webster Manufacturing Company
325 Hall St (44883-1419)
PHONE 419 447-8232
Andrew J Felter, *President*
Fredric C Spurck, *Chairman*
Dean Bogner, *Vice Pres*
Nicholas D Spurck, *Vice Pres*
Ed Blott, *Opers Mgr*
◆ **EMP:** 295 **EST:** 1876
SQ FT: 250,000
SALES: 55MM **Privately Held**
WEB: www.websterchain.com
SIC: 3535 Bulk handling conveyor systems

Tiltonsville
Jefferson County

(G-18093)
CROFT & SON MFG INC
509 Highland Ave (43963-1110)
P.O. Box 66 (43963-0066)
PHONE 740 859-2200
Samuel E Croft, *President*
Kathy Lester, *Admin Sec*
Shirley Pielech, *Admin Sec*
EMP: 6 **EST:** 1977
SQ FT: 3,600
SALES (est): 856.4K **Privately Held**
SIC: 3599 Machine shop, jobbing & repair

(G-18094)
WALDEN INDUSTRIES INC
Also Called: Belot Concrete Block
101 Walden Ave (43963-1130)
P.O. Box 68 (43963-0068)
PHONE 740 633-5971
John Belot, *President*
Carol Hindman, *Principal*
EMP: 20
SALES (est): 3.7MM **Privately Held**
SIC: 3271 Blocks, concrete or cinder: standard

Tipp City
Miami County

(G-18095)
ACCU TOOL INC
9765 Julie Ct (45371-9000)
PHONE 937 667-5878
Dale Howard, *President*
Patricia Howard, *Vice Pres*
EMP: 8
SQ FT: 7,500
SALES (est): 1.1MM **Privately Held**
WEB: www.accu-tool.com
SIC: 3544 3599 Special dies & tools; machine shop, jobbing & repair

(G-18096)
ACON INC
11408 Dogleg Rd (45371-9516)
PHONE 513 276-2111
Thomas Mescher, *President*
Susan Hoberty, *Vice Pres*
EMP: 7
SQ FT: 12,000
SALES (est): 1MM **Privately Held**
WEB: www.aconinc.net
SIC: 3625 Noise control equipment

(G-18097)
ACTION BLACKTOP SEALCOATING &
7830 Kessler Frederick Rd (45371-9610)
PHONE 937 667-4769
John McGee, *Partner*
EMP: 3
SALES: 300K **Privately Held**
SIC: 1771 1799 2951 1611 Driveway contractor; parking lot maintenance; asphalt paving mixtures & blocks; surfacing & paving

(G-18098)
ADAPT-A-PAK INC
9215 State Route 201 (45371-9768)
PHONE 937 845-0386
Russ Miller, *Branch Mgr*
Terry Wallace,
EMP: 22
SALES (corp-wide): 10.5MM **Privately Held**
SIC: 2653 5113 Boxes, corrugated: made from purchased materials; shipping supplies
PA: Adapt-A-Pak, Inc.
1701 Dalton Dr
New Carlisle OH 45344
937 845-0386

(G-18099)
ALPINE GAGE INC
4325 Lisa Dr (45371-9463)
PHONE 937 669-8665
Dennis Tresslar, *President*
Gene Begley, *Manager*
EMP: 6
SQ FT: 4,400
SALES (est): 947.7K **Privately Held**
SIC: 3825 Instruments for measuring electrical quantities

(G-18100)
B S F INC
320b S 5th St (45371-1625)
PHONE 937 890-6121
Tim Boocher, *Manager*
EMP: 10
SALES (corp-wide): 1.8MM **Privately Held**
SIC: 3498 3568 3599 Couplings, pipe: fabricated from purchased pipe; couplings, shaft: rigid, flexible, universal joint, etc.; machine shop, jobbing & repair
PA: B S F, Inc.
8895 N Dixie Dr
Dayton OH 45414
937 890-6121

(G-18101)
BOOCHERS INC
320 S 5th St (45371-1625)
P.O. Box 25 (45371-0025)
PHONE 937 667-3414
Albert S Boocher, *President*
Tim Boocher, *Vice Pres*
Mary E Boocher, *Admin Sec*
EMP: 4
SQ FT: 4,000
SALES: 600K **Privately Held**
SIC: 3443 Fabricated plate work (boiler shop)

(G-18102)
BR MULCH INC
620 Ginghamsburg Rd (45371-9119)
PHONE 937 667-8288
B G Replogle, *President*
Bartholomew G Replogle, *President*
EMP: 4
SALES (est): 504.1K **Privately Held**
SIC: 2499 Mulch or sawdust products, wood

(G-18103)
BUCKEYE DISTILLERY
130 W Plum St (45371-1843)
PHONE 937 877-1901
Aaron A Lee, *Principal*
EMP: 3
SALES (est): 169.7K **Privately Held**
SIC: 2085 Distillers' dried grains & solubles & alcohol

(G-18104)
C IMPERIAL INC
Also Called: Imperial Castings
1322 Commerce Park Dr (45371-3323)
PHONE 937 669-5620
Larry Haney, *President*
EMP: 6
SQ FT: 9,000

Tipp City - Miami County (G-18105)

SALES (est): 628.2K **Privately Held**
SIC: 3443 Fabricated plate work (boiler shop)

(G-18105)
CANINE CREATIONS
120b W Broadway St A (45371-1638)
PHONE..................937 667-8576
Robert Reidel, *Owner*
Robin Riedel, *Principal*
EMP: 7
SALES (est): 182.4K **Privately Held**
SIC: 0752 3999 Grooming services, pet & animal specialties; pet supplies

(G-18106)
CAPTOR CORPORATION
5040 S County Road 25a (45371-2899)
PHONE..................937 667-8484
Donald Cooper, *Ch of Bd*
D Scott Timms, *President*
Ryan Sollmann, *Design Engr*
Carolyn Kiser, *Treasurer*
Tonya Conley, *Technology*
EMP: 85
SQ FT: 35,000
SALES: 10.7MM **Privately Held**
WEB: www.captorcorp.com
SIC: 3679 Electronic circuits

(G-18107)
CASE CRAFTERS INC
211 S 1st St (45371-1705)
PHONE..................937 667-9473
Dan Paugh, *President*
Steven Paugh, *Vice Pres*
EMP: 8
SQ FT: 9,200
SALES: 650K **Privately Held**
WEB: www.casecrafters.com
SIC: 2541 1751 Cabinets, except refrigerated: show, display, etc.: wood; cabinet & finish carpentry

(G-18108)
CHART TECH TOOL INC
4060 Lisa Dr (45371-9499)
P.O. Box 477 (45371-0477)
PHONE..................937 667-3543
Eugene Crompton, *President*
Lee Scheidweiler, *Vice Pres*
Jeff Crompton, *Mfg Staff*
Mary Ann Crompton, *Controller*
EMP: 20 **EST:** 1965
SQ FT: 30,000
SALES (est): 3.7MM **Privately Held**
WEB: www.ctti-inc.com
SIC: 3541 3545 3544 Machine tools, metal cutting type; gauges (machine tool accessories); special dies, tools, jigs & fixtures

(G-18109)
CONCRETE SEALANTS INC
Also Called: Conseal
9325 State Route 201 (45371-8524)
P.O. Box 176, New Carlisle (45344-0176)
PHONE..................937 845-8776
Howard E Wingert, *President*
Cynthia Wingert, *Treasurer*
◆ **EMP:** 50
SQ FT: 100,000
SALES (est): 21.6MM **Privately Held**
WEB: www.conseal.com
SIC: 3053 2891 2821 2822 Gaskets, packing & sealing devices; sealants; plastics materials & resins; synthetic rubber

(G-18110)
DAP PRODUCTS INC
Also Called: Darusta Woodlife Division
875 N 3rd St (45371-3053)
PHONE..................937 667-4461
Betsy Frappier, *Human Res Mgr*
Gary Williams, *Branch Mgr*
Edie Wiedenheft, *Information Mgr*
EMP: 110
SALES (corp-wide): 5.3B **Publicly Held**
WEB: www.rpm.net
SIC: 2891 2851 Caulking compounds; paints & paint additives
HQ: Dap Products Inc.
2400 Boston St Ste 200
Baltimore MD 21224
800 543-3840

(G-18111)
DUNCAN TOOL INC
9790 Julie Ct (45371-9000)
PHONE..................937 667-9364
Sandra L Duncan, *President*
Dave Duncan, *Vice Pres*
Don Duncan, *Sales Staff*
Chris Duncan, *Director*
▲ **EMP:** 10
SQ FT: 5,500
SALES (est): 1.4MM **Privately Held**
WEB: www.duncantool.com
SIC: 3544 3599 Special dies & tools; machine shop, jobbing & repair

(G-18112)
FIELD STONE INC
2750 Us Route 40 (45371-9230)
PHONE..................937 898-3236
Paul Carmack, *President*
▲ **EMP:** 100 **EST:** 1973
SQ FT: 18,000
SALES (est): 17.4MM **Privately Held**
WEB: www.catlow.com
SIC: 3586 3432 Gasoline pumps, measuring or dispensing; plumbing fixture fittings & trim

(G-18113)
G & M PRECISION MACHINING INC
9785 Wildcat Rd (45371-9421)
PHONE..................937 667-1443
Lori Galovics, *President*
Joe Galovics, *President*
EMP: 6
SQ FT: 10,000
SALES (est): 861K **Privately Held**
SIC: 3599 Machine shop, jobbing & repair

(G-18114)
GRANT SOLUTIONS
7745 Winding Way N (45371-9254)
PHONE..................937 344-5558
Kevin McDonald, *Owner*
EMP: 5
SALES: 1.5K **Privately Held**
SIC: 3999 Manufacturing industries

(G-18115)
HIGH-TEC INDUSTRIAL SERVICES
15 Industry Park Ct (45371-3060)
P.O. Box 533 (45371-0533)
PHONE..................937 667-1772
Brent Black, *President*
William E Oldham, *President*
Christopher Taylor, *Vice Pres*
Chris Taylor, *Manager*
EMP: 139
SQ FT: 18,000
SALES (est): 25.3MM **Privately Held**
WEB: www.hightecindustrial.com
SIC: 3589 7349 Commercial cooking & foodwarming equipment; building & office cleaning services

(G-18116)
INDIAN CREEK FABRICATORS INC
1350 Commerce Park Dr (45371-3323)
PHONE..................937 667-7214
Andrea Dakin, *President*
Chris Dakin, *General Mgr*
Michael Dakin, *Vice Pres*
Richard Hunt, *Design Engr*
Linda Chaney, *Manager*
EMP: 50
SQ FT: 65,000
SALES (est): 11.9MM **Privately Held**
WEB: www.indiancreekfab.com
SIC: 3446 3444 3443 3441 Architectural metalwork; sheet metalwork; fabricated plate work (boiler shop); fabricated structural metal

(G-18117)
IZIT CAIN SHEET METAL CORP
222 N 6th St (45371-1830)
PHONE..................937 667-6521
Clarence Paul Dehus, *President*
Jeanette Dehus, *Corp Secy*
EMP: 5
SQ FT: 4,000

SALES (est): 785.7K **Privately Held**
SIC: 3444 3699 3599 Sheet metal specialties, not stamped; electrical welding equipment; machine & other job shop work

(G-18118)
J & B ROGERS INC
Also Called: Airplane Plastics
9785 Julie Ct (45371-9000)
PHONE..................937 669-2677
Jeffrey Rogers, *President*
Rebecca Rogers, *Vice Pres*
EMP: 5
SQ FT: 5,000
SALES: 600K **Privately Held**
WEB: www.airplaneplastics.com
SIC: 3089 Air mattresses, plastic

(G-18119)
J & L WOOD PRODUCTS INC (PA)
910 Ginghamsburg Rd (45371-9202)
P.O. Box 69 (45371-0069)
PHONE..................937 667-4064
Jeffrey Herzog, *President*
Kevin McClurg, *Vice Pres*
▲ **EMP:** 32
SQ FT: 30,000
SALES (est): 4.4MM **Privately Held**
WEB: www.palletsnskids.com
SIC: 2448 2441 2449 Pallets, wood; skids, wood; nailed wood boxes & shook; rectangular boxes & crates, wood

(G-18120)
JASON WILSON
5575 Ross Rd (45371-9710)
PHONE..................937 604-8209
Jason Wilson, *Mng Member*
Mark Nelson,
EMP: 27
SALES: 1.5MM **Privately Held**
SIC: 3663 7389 3229 Radio & TV communications equipment; ; fiber optics strands

(G-18121)
LEVECK LIGHTING PRODUCTS INC (PA)
8415 S State Route 202 (45371-9074)
P.O. Box 24063, Dayton (45424-0063)
PHONE..................937 667-4421
Mary Leveck, *Owner*
Robert Leveck Jr, *CFO*
EMP: 25 **EST:** 1978
SQ FT: 6,500
SALES (est): 4.7MM **Privately Held**
SIC: 3229 Bulbs for electric lights

(G-18122)
MADERITE LLC
6915 Roberta Dr (45371-2349)
P.O. Box 351 (45371-0351)
PHONE..................937 570-1042
Kevin R Mader,
EMP: 2
SQ FT: 20,000
SALES: 1MM **Privately Held**
SIC: 2679 Labels, paper: made from purchased material

(G-18123)
MORE MANUFACTURING LLC
4025 Lisa Dr Ste A (45371-9462)
PHONE..................937 233-3898
Matt Lovelace, *Mng Member*
EMP: 12 **EST:** 2007
SQ FT: 6,000
SALES (est): 2MM **Privately Held**
SIC: 3599 Machine tool replacement & repair parts, metal cutting types

(G-18124)
MUTUAL TOOL LLC
1350 Commerce Park Dr (45371-3323)
PHONE..................937 667-5818
Bill Baity,
Dean Cooley,
EMP: 80
SQ FT: 31,200
SALES (est): 9.3MM **Privately Held**
WEB: www.mutualtool.com
SIC: 3599 3544 Machine shop, jobbing & repair; special dies, tools, jigs & fixtures

(G-18125)
ODAWARA AUTOMATION INC
4805 S County Road 25a (45371-2900)
PHONE..................937 667-8433
Takayuki Tsugawa, *CEO*
Christopher Spejna, *President*
James Crego, *Sales Engr*
Teresa Douglas, *Office Mgr*
Tom Cartwright, *Manager*
▲ **EMP:** 37
SQ FT: 51,000
SALES (est): 6.9MM
SALES (corp-wide): 114.4MM **Privately Held**
WEB: www.odawara.com
SIC: 3599 Custom machinery
PA: Odawara Engineering Co., Ltd.
1577, Matsudasoryo, Matsuda-Machi
Ashigara Kami-Gun KNG 258-0
465 831-122

(G-18126)
PECO HOLDINGS CORP (PA)
6555 S State Route 202 (45371-9094)
PHONE..................937 667-4451
Michael Van Haaren, *President*
James Zahora, *Vice Pres*
William Rosenberg, *CFO*
EMP: 12
SALES (est): 19.2MM **Privately Held**
SIC: 3599 3548 3549 Machine shop, jobbing & repair; welding apparatus; assembly machines, including robotic

(G-18127)
PRECISION STRIP INC
315 Park Ave (45371-1887)
PHONE..................937 667-6255
Jerry Huber, *Manager*
EMP: 52
SQ FT: 3,080
SALES (corp-wide): 11.5B **Publicly Held**
WEB: www.precision-strip.com
SIC: 4225 3312 General warehousing & storage; blast furnaces & steel mills
HQ: Precision Strip Inc.
86 S Ohio St
Minster OH 45865
419 628-2343

(G-18128)
PROCESS EQUIPMENT CO TIPP CITY (HQ)
Also Called: Process Equipment Company
4754 Us Route 40 (45371-9481)
PHONE..................937 667-4451
Michael V Haaren, *President*
James Zahora, *Vice Pres*
Darren Ostendorf, *Project Mgr*
William Rosenberg, *CFO*
Kurt Baker, *Sales Associate*
▲ **EMP:** 74 **EST:** 1945
SQ FT: 360,000
SALES (est): 10MM **Privately Held**
WEB: www.processeq.com
SIC: 3599 3548 3549 Machine shop, jobbing & repair; welding apparatus; assembly machines, including robotic

(G-18129)
PROTO PLASTICS INC
316 Park Ave (45371-1894)
PHONE..................937 667-8416
Thomas Gagnon, *President*
Thomas A Gagnon, *Owner*
Sue Gagnon, *Vice Pres*
Chad Underwood, *Manager*
▲ **EMP:** 42
SQ FT: 62,000
SALES (est): 10MM **Privately Held**
WEB: www.protoplastics.com
SIC: 3089 3544 Injection molding of plastics; special dies, tools, jigs & fixtures; special dies & tools; jigs: inspection, gauging & checking

(G-18130)
REGAL BELOIT AMERICA INC
531 N 4th St (45371-1857)
PHONE..................937 667-2431
Chuck Albertson, *Opers Mgr*
Bruce Kielgas, *Engineer*
David Wood, *Engineer*
Edward Drye, *Senior Engr*
Shay Geeding, *Design Engr*
EMP: 231

▲ = Import ▼ = Export
◆ = Import/Export

GEOGRAPHIC SECTION

Toledo - Lucas County (G-18157)

SALES (corp-wide): 3.6B **Publicly Held**
SIC: 3621 Motors, electric
HQ: Regal Beloit America, Inc.
200 State St
Beloit WI 53511
608 364-8800

(G-18131)
RPG INDUSTRIES INC
3571 Ginghmsbg Frdrck Rd (45371)
P.O. Box 233, West Milton (45383-0233)
PHONE..................................937 698-9801
Robert Ginsburg, *President*
Ernie Booher, *Engineer*
EMP: 6
SQ FT: 3,600
SALES: 500K **Privately Held**
WEB: www.rpgindustries.com
SIC: 3599 Machine shop, jobbing & repair

(G-18132)
S-K MOLD & TOOL COMPANY (PA)
955 N 3rd St (45371-3055)
PHONE..................................937 339-0299
Samuel K Kingrey, *President*
Keith Kingrey, *Vice Pres*
Vince Hinde, *Admin Sec*
EMP: 45 EST: 1983
SQ FT: 76,500
SALES (est): 15.9MM **Privately Held**
WEB: www.skmold.com
SIC: 3544 3599 Special dies & tools; machine shop, jobbing & repair

(G-18133)
SINBON USA LLC
4265 Gibson Dr (45371-9452)
PHONE..................................937 667-8999
Winnie Chen, *Principal*
Michelle L Cahoon, *Vice Pres*
EMP: 7 EST: 2016
SALES (est): 159.5K **Privately Held**
SIC: 3679 Antennas, receiving

(G-18134)
SP3 CUTTING TOOLS INC (PA)
835 N Hyatt St (45371-1558)
PHONE..................................937 667-4476
Eric Koik, *President*
Dennis Maude, *CFO*
EMP: 2
SALES (est): 6MM **Privately Held**
WEB: www.sp3.com
SIC: 6719 3545 Investment holding companies, except banks; diamond cutting tools for turning, boring, burnishing, etc.

(G-18135)
T & W TOOL & MACHINE INC
467 N 5th St (45371-1872)
PHONE..................................937 667-2039
Tim Owen, *President*
EMP: 4
SQ FT: 11,000
SALES (est): 300K **Privately Held**
SIC: 3544 3599 Special dies & tools; machine shop, jobbing & repair

(G-18136)
TEAM AMITY MOLDS & PLASTIC
1435 Commerce Park Dr (45371-2846)
P.O. Box 309 (45371-0309)
PHONE..................................937 667-7856
Leonard L Dickess, *President*
Leonord Dickess, *Owner*
EMP: 80
SALES: 4.3MM **Privately Held**
WEB: www.amitymold.com
SIC: 3089 Molding primary plastic

(G-18137)
TECH MOLD & TOOL CO INC
4333 Lisa Dr (45371-9463)
PHONE..................................937 667-8851
Dan Isenbarger, *President*
Arlene Isenbarger, *Admin Sec*
EMP: 7 EST: 1975
SQ FT: 5,100
SALES: 800K **Privately Held**
SIC: 3544 Industrial molds

(G-18138)
TIP TOP CANNING CO (PA)
505 S 2nd St (45371-1753)
P.O. Box 126 (45371-0126)
PHONE..................................937 667-3713
George C Timmer, *President*
Scott A Timmer, *Vice Pres*
EMP: 20 EST: 1924
SQ FT: 140,000
SALES (est): 21.9MM **Privately Held**
SIC: 2033 Tomato products: packaged in cans, jars, etc.

(G-18139)
TROPHY NUT CO (PA)
320 N 2nd St (45371-1960)
P.O. Box 199 (45371-0199)
PHONE..................................937 667-8478
Gerald J Allen, *CEO*
Robert J Bollinger, *President*
Robert N Wilke, *Vice Pres*
Robert Loy, *Facilities Mgr*
Ron Weaver, *Opers Staff*
◆ EMP: 59 EST: 1968
SQ FT: 85,000
SALES (est): 25.9MM **Privately Held**
WEB: www.trophynut.com
SIC: 2068 5441 Nuts: dried, dehydrated, salted or roasted; nuts; candy

(G-18140)
TROPHY NUT CO
1567 Harmony Dr (45371-3319)
P.O. Box 199 (45371-0199)
PHONE..................................937 669-5513
Bob Loy, *Manager*
EMP: 6
SALES (corp-wide): 28.8MM **Privately Held**
WEB: www.trophynut.com
SIC: 2068 Nuts: dried, dehydrated, salted or roasted
PA: Trophy Nut Co.
320 N 2nd St
Tipp City OH 45371
937 667-8478

(G-18141)
UDECX LLC
320 N 4th St (45371-1803)
PHONE..................................877 698-3329
John Van Leeuwen, *CEO*
Patrick Bertke, *Director*
EMP: 6
SQ FT: 2,200
SALES (est): 5MM **Privately Held**
SIC: 3089 Floor coverings, plastic

(G-18142)
VISION PROJECTS INC
1350 Commerce Park Dr (45371-3323)
PHONE..................................937 667-8648
George J Minarcek, *CEO*
Chris Dakin, *Treasurer*
EMP: 6
SQ FT: 20,000
SALES (est): 379.1K **Privately Held**
SIC: 3599 Machine shop, jobbing & repair

(G-18143)
VITAL CONNECTIONS INCORPORATED
955 N 3rd St (45371-3055)
PHONE..................................937 667-3880
Samuel Kingrey, *President*
Edward F Hoar, *Vice Pres*
Mark Meister, *Vice Pres*
EMP: 20
SQ FT: 10,000
SALES (est): 3.5MM **Privately Held**
WEB: www.vitalconnections.com
SIC: 3643 Current-carrying wiring devices

(G-18144)
VSCORP LLC
4754 Us Route 40 (45371-9481)
PHONE..................................937 305-3562
Vin Sahni,
EMP: 15
SALES: 4MM **Privately Held**
SIC: 3441 Fabricated structural metal

(G-18145)
WENRICK MACHINE AND TOOL CORP
4685 Us Route 40 (45371-8339)
PHONE..................................937 667-7307
Tom Wenrick, *President*
Betty Wenrick, *Corp Secy*
Corey Wenrick, *Purchasing*
EMP: 10
SQ FT: 8,000
SALES: 425K **Privately Held**
SIC: 3599 7692 Machine shop, jobbing & repair; welding repair

(G-18146)
WRENA LLC
265 Lightner Rd (45371-9228)
PHONE..................................937 667-4403
George J Derr, *Ch of Bd*
Michael R Tanner, *President*
Tom Derr, *Vice Pres*
David Whitehead, *Vice Pres*
Pam Melish, *Purch Mgr*
EMP: 50 EST: 1977
SQ FT: 123,000
SALES (est): 17.8MM **Privately Held**
WEB: www.wrenind.com
SIC: 3465 3544 Body parts, automobile: stamped metal; special dies & tools; jigs & fixtures
HQ: Angstrom Usa Llc
26980 Trolley Indus Dr
Taylor MI 48180
313 295-0100

Tippecanoe
Harrison County

(G-18147)
EXCO RESOURCES LLC
3618 Fallen Timber Rd Se (44699-9650)
PHONE..................................740 254-4061
EMP: 3
SALES (corp-wide): 394MM **Privately Held**
WEB: www.northcoastenergy.com
SIC: 1311 Crude petroleum & natural gas production
HQ: Exco Resources, Llc
13448 State Route 422 # 1
Kittanning PA 16201
724 720-2500

(G-18148)
GARDNER LUMBER CO INC
5805 Laurel Creek Rd Se (44699-9661)
PHONE..................................740 254-4664
Richard Gardner, *President*
Harvey Gardner, *Vice Pres*
EMP: 10 EST: 1938
SALES (est): 1.5MM **Privately Held**
SIC: 2421 2448 5154 Sawmills & planing mills, general; pallets, wood; cattle

(G-18149)
GRAY-EERING LTD
3158 Sandy Ridge Rd Se (44699-9657)
PHONE..................................740 498-8816
Glenn Gray, *Partner*
Jay Gray, *Partner*
Lainard Gray, *Partner*
Sandra K Gray, *Admin Sec*
EMP: 7 EST: 1978
SALES: 600K **Privately Held**
SIC: 3535 3536 3534 Conveyors & conveying equipment; mine hoists; elevators & equipment

---

Toledo
Lucas County

(G-18150)
1 DAY SIGN
4236 Secor Rd (43623-4238)
PHONE..................................419 475-6060
Thomas E Keller, *Owner*
EMP: 3
SQ FT: 2,400
SALES (est): 220K **Privately Held**
SIC: 3993 Signs & advertising specialties

(G-18151)
A & B TOOL & MANUFACTURING
2921 South Ave (43609-1327)
PHONE..................................419 382-0215
Timothy J Adams, *President*
EMP: 7 EST: 1966
SQ FT: 8,000
SALES (est): 734.5K **Privately Held**
SIC: 3544 Special dies & tools

(G-18152)
A & M CHEESE CO
253 Waggoner Blvd (43612-1952)
PHONE..................................419 476-8369
Antonio Sofo, *CEO*
Michael J Sofo, *President*
Joseph J Sofo Jr, *Vice Pres*
EMP: 53
SQ FT: 190,000
SALES (est): 8.5MM **Privately Held**
WEB: www.amcheese.com
SIC: 2022 Processed cheese

(G-18153)
ABBOTT TOOL INC
Also Called: ATI
405 Dura Ave (43612-2619)
PHONE..................................419 476-6742
Karle Stange, *President*
Kevin Webb, *General Mgr*
Arthur Stange, *Vice Pres*
Leonard Livecchi, *Vice Pres*
EMP: 27
SQ FT: 12,000
SALES (est): 5.5MM **Privately Held**
SIC: 3469 7692 Machine parts, stamped or pressed metal; welding repair

(G-18154)
ACCUSHRED LLC
1114 W Central Ave (43610-1061)
PHONE..................................419 244-7473
Nate Segall, *President*
Barry Gudelman, *Vice Pres*
EMP: 11
SALES (est): 1.3MM **Privately Held**
SIC: 3589 Shredders, industrial & commercial

(G-18155)
ACE PRODUCTS CO OF TOLEDO INC
4902 Douglas Rd (43613-3246)
PHONE..................................419 472-1247
Susan Kennedy, *Ch of Bd*
David W Post, *President*
Duane P Post, *Vice Pres*
Robert C Post, *Treasurer*
EMP: 4 EST: 1935
SQ FT: 6,800
SALES: 300K **Privately Held**
SIC: 3728 Aircraft parts & equipment

(G-18156)
ADAMS STREET PUBLISHING CO
Also Called: Toledo City Paper
1120 Adams St (43604-5509)
PHONE..................................419 244-9859
Marck Jacobs, *CEO*
Collette Jacobs, *President*
Mark Jacobs, *CFO*
Robin Armstrong, *Accounting Mgr*
Brittany Stahl, *Accounts Mgr*
EMP: 22
SQ FT: 4,268
SALES (est): 2.6MM **Privately Held**
WEB: www.adamsstreetpublishing.com
SIC: 2721 Magazines: publishing only, not printed on site

(G-18157)
ADVANCED INCENTIVES INC
1732 W Alexis Rd (43613-2349)
PHONE..................................419 471-9088
James Williams, *President*
Brian Williams, *Vice Pres*
Rose Williams, *Admin Sec*
EMP: 6
SQ FT: 1,800
SALES: 400K **Privately Held**
WEB: www.advancedincentives.com
SIC: 2759 Screen printing

Toledo - Lucas County (G-18158)

(G-18158)
ADVANTAGE MOLD INC
525 N Wheeling St (43605-1337)
PHONE..............................419 691-5676
Larry J Bolander, *President*
Betsi Frick, *Office Mgr*
EMP: 8 EST: 1999
SQ FT: 13,000
SALES: 850K **Privately Held**
WEB: www.advantage-mold.com
SIC: **3089** Injection molding of plastics

(G-18159)
AFFORDABLE STUMP REMOVAL LLC
2624 Heysler Rd (43617-1512)
PHONE..............................419 841-8331
Lisa Klebold, *Manager*
Bill Klebold,
EMP: 5
SALES: 230K **Privately Held**
SIC: **2411** 0783 Stumps, wood; removal services, bush & tree

(G-18160)
AIMCO MFG INC
Also Called: Lockrey Manafacturing
203 Matzinger Rd (43612-2624)
PHONE..............................419 476-6572
Mark Makulinski, *President*
Bill Nordolt, *Vice Pres*
EMP: 3
SQ FT: 1,000
SALES (est): 632K **Privately Held**
SIC: **3534** Elevators & equipment

(G-18161)
AIRTECH MECHANICAL INC
4444 Monroe St (43613-4732)
PHONE..............................419 292-0074
EMP: 12
SALES (est): 1.8MM **Privately Held**
SIC: **3433** 3443 Heating equipment, except electric; cooling towers, metal plate

(G-18162)
ALL AMERICAN SCREEN PRINTING
2607 W Central Ave (43606-3548)
PHONE..............................419 475-0696
Jim Schnoering, *Principal*
EMP: 4
SALES (est): 330.6K **Privately Held**
SIC: **2752** Commercial printing, lithographic

(G-18163)
ALLEN ZAHRADNIK INC (PA)
Also Called: Edgewater Canvas Co
5902 Edgewater Dr (43611)
PHONE..............................419 729-1201
Allen Zahradnik, *President*
EMP: 5 EST: 1952
SQ FT: 5,000
SALES (est): 456.5K **Privately Held**
SIC: **2394** Convertible tops, canvas or boat: from purchased materials

(G-18164)
ALLIED MASK AND TOOLING INC
6051 Telegraph Rd Ste 6 (43612-4573)
P.O. Box 639, Temperance MI (48182-0639)
PHONE..............................419 470-2555
Mike Murray, *President*
EMP: 9
SQ FT: 3,600
SALES (est): 1.2MM **Privately Held**
SIC: **3599** 3356 3444 3542 Machine shop, jobbing & repair; nickel; sheet metalwork; forming machine work, sheet metal; electroforming machines

(G-18165)
ALLIED PLASTIC CO INC
3203 South Ave (43609-1103)
PHONE..............................419 389-1688
Jeff W Hood, *President*
Leonard K Pudlicki, *Vice Pres*
EMP: 5
SQ FT: 5,000
SALES: 700K **Privately Held**
SIC: **3089** 2541 2511 Injection molding of plastics; store fixtures, wood; office fixtures, wood; wood household furniture

(G-18166)
ALRO STEEL CORPORATION
3003 Airport Hwy (43609-1405)
P.O. Box 964 (43697-0964)
PHONE..............................419 720-5300
Adam Cristek, *Manager*
EMP: 40
SALES (corp-wide): 1.9B **Privately Held**
WEB: www.alro.com
SIC: **5051** 5085 5162 3444 Steel; aluminum bars, rods, ingots, sheets, pipes, plates, etc.; nonferrous metal sheets, bars, rods, etc.; industrial supplies; plastics materials; sheet metalwork
PA: Alro Steel Corporation
    3100 E High St
    Jackson MI 49203
    517 787-5500

(G-18167)
ALS POLISHING SHOP INC
Also Called: Al's Polsg Pltg Powdr Coating
1615 W Laskey Rd (43612-2915)
PHONE..............................419 476-8857
Albert R Szymanowski, *CEO*
Richard Szymanowski, *President*
Jamie Szymanowski, *Vice Pres*
Sally Pollock, *Admin Sec*
EMP: 8 EST: 1946
SQ FT: 4,800
SALES (est): 964.4K **Privately Held**
SIC: **3471** Polishing, metals or formed products; buffing for the trade; plating of metals or formed products

(G-18168)
ALT CONTROL PRINT
6906 Milrose Ln (43617-1291)
PHONE..............................419 841-2467
Hugh Callahan, *Principal*
EMP: 4
SALES (est): 365.7K **Privately Held**
SIC: **2752** Commercial printing, lithographic

(G-18169)
ALT FUEL LLC
1100 King Rd (43617-2002)
P.O. Box 351330 (43635-1330)
PHONE..............................419 865-4196
Robert C Barry,
EMP: 3
SALES (est): 206.6K **Privately Held**
SIC: **3999** Manufacturing industries

(G-18170)
AMCRAFT INC
Also Called: Amcraft Manufacturing
5144 Enterprise Blvd (43612-3807)
PHONE..............................419 729-7900
David R Frank, *President*
Robin Frank, *Vice Pres*
▼ EMP: 8
SQ FT: 6,000
SALES (est): 1.2MM **Privately Held**
WEB: www.amcraftinc.com
SIC: **3423** 3544 3469 Hand & edge tools; special dies & tools; metal stampings

(G-18171)
AMERICAN BOTTLING COMPANY
7 Up Bottling Co of Toledo
224 N Byrne Rd (43607-2605)
PHONE..............................419 535-0777
Jeff Lark, *Manager*
EMP: 75 **Publicly Held**
WEB: www.cs-americas.com
SIC: **2086** Bottled & canned soft drinks
HQ: The American Bottling Company
    5301 Legacy Dr
    Plano TX 75024

(G-18172)
AMERICAN CANVAS PRODUCTS INC
2925 South Ave (43609-1327)
PHONE..............................419 382-8450
Richard W Jockett, *President*
Andrew Jockett, *Vice Pres*
EMP: 17
SQ FT: 6,000
SALES (est): 1.4MM **Privately Held**
WEB: www.americancanvasproductsinc.com
SIC: **2394** Convertible tops, canvas or boat: from purchased materials

(G-18173)
AMERICAN LASER AND MACHINE LLC
501 Weston St (43609-1128)
PHONE..............................419 214-0880
Rusty Obermyer,
Pat Copeland,
EMP: 3
SALES: 15K **Privately Held**
SIC: **3542** Machine tools, metal forming type

(G-18174)
AMERICAN MANUFACTURING INC (PA)
2375 Dorr St Ste F (43607-3407)
PHONE..............................419 531-9471
Charles P Gotberg, *President*
▲ EMP: 100
SALES (est): 26.2MM **Privately Held**
SIC: **3441** Fabricated structural metal

(G-18175)
AMERICAN METAL CLEANING INC
2512 Albion St (43610-1215)
PHONE..............................419 255-1828
Laura Tobias, *President*
Greg Tobias, *Vice Pres*
EMP: 4
SQ FT: 15,000
SALES (est): 496.3K **Privately Held**
WEB: www.americanmetalcleaninginc.com
SIC: **3471** 5169 Cleaning & descaling metal products; chemicals & allied products

(G-18176)
AMERICAN MNFCTURING OPERATIONS
1931 E Manhattan Blvd (43608-1534)
PHONE..............................419 269-1560
Jonathan R Saul, *President*
EMP: 8
SALES (est): 900K **Privately Held**
SIC: **3715** Truck trailers

(G-18177)
AMERICAN MOBILE FITNESS LLC
2727 N Holland Sylvania Rd (43615-1847)
PHONE..............................419 351-1381
Gregg Schwartz,
EMP: 5
SALES (est): 415.2K **Privately Held**
SIC: **3089** Air mattresses, plastic

(G-18178)
AMERICAN PAPER CONVERTING LLC
6142 American Rd (43612-3902)
PHONE..............................419 729-4782
EMP: 10
SALES (est): 31.8K **Privately Held**
SIC: **2679** Paper Mill

(G-18179)
AMERICAN POSTS LLC
810 Chicago St (43611-3609)
PHONE..............................419 720-0652
David Feniger, *Mng Member*
Andrew Spoering, *Supervisor*
EMP: 30
SALES (est): 7.8MM **Privately Held**
WEB: www.americanposts.com
SIC: **3312** 5051 Rods, iron & steel: made in steel mills; steel

(G-18180)
AMERICAN STEEL ASSOD PDTS INC
2375 Dorr St Ste F (43607-3407)
PHONE..............................419 531-9471
Charles P Gotberg, *President*
EMP: 90
SALES (est): 28.2MM
SALES (corp-wide): 26.2MM **Privately Held**
SIC: **3441** Fabricated structural metal
PA: American Manufacturing, Inc.
    2375 Dorr St Ste F
    Toledo OH 43607
    419 531-9471

(G-18181)
AMERICAN TOOL AND DIE INC
2024 Champlain St (43611-3700)
PHONE..............................419 726-5394
Richard J Russell Jr, *President*
Paul Philabaum, *Vice Pres*
Gerald Russell, *Vice Pres*
Diana West, *Office Mgr*
EMP: 15 EST: 1963
SQ FT: 20,000
SALES (est): 2.9MM **Privately Held**
SIC: **3469** 3544 Stamping metal for the trade; special dies, tools, jigs & fixtures

(G-18182)
AMES DEVELOPMENT GROUP LTD
Also Called: Ceen
2339 Drummond Rd (43606-3126)
PHONE..............................419 704-7812
Ethan Ames, *Principal*
EMP: 3 EST: 2015
SALES (est): 94.6K **Privately Held**
SIC: **7372** Application computer software

(G-18183)
AMES LOCK SPECIALTIES INC
Also Called: Ames Locksmith
2121 W Sylvania Ave (43613-4436)
PHONE..............................419 474-2995
Clair Ames, *President*
Van Baker, *Principal*
EMP: 5
SALES (est): 352.1K **Privately Held**
SIC: **7699** 3089 Locksmith shop; plastic hardware & building products

(G-18184)
ANDERSONS INC
801 S Reynolds Rd (43615-6309)
PHONE..............................419 536-0460
Bill Kale, *Manager*
William Kale, *Manager*
EMP: 7
SALES (corp-wide): 3B **Publicly Held**
SIC: **0723** 5191 2874 4789 Crop preparation services for market; cash grain crops market preparation services; farm supplies; fertilizers & agricultural chemicals; seeds & bulbs; phosphatic fertilizers; plant foods, mixed: from plants making phosphatic fertilizer; railroad car repair; rental of railroad cars; grains
PA: The Andersons Inc
    1947 Briarfield Blvd
    Maumee OH 43537
    419 893-5050

(G-18185)
ANDREW & SONS INC
2401 Consaul St (43605-1367)
PHONE..............................419 693-0292
Andrew Danisouszky, *President*
Mary Danisouszky, *Corp Secy*
Louis Torda, *Vice Pres*
EMP: 4
SQ FT: 4,800
SALES (est): 378.5K **Privately Held**
SIC: **3599** Machine shop, jobbing & repair

(G-18186)
APEX BOLT & MACHINE COMPANY
Also Called: Apex Metal Fabricating & Mch
5324 Enterprise Blvd (43612-3870)
PHONE..............................419 729-3741
William G Foradas, *Ch of Bd*
Michael S Petree, *President*
Luanna M Foradas, *Corp Secy*
Michael Petree, *Sales Mgr*
EMP: 39
SQ FT: 51,000
SALES (est): 8.7MM **Privately Held**
SIC: **3599** Machine shop, jobbing & repair

GEOGRAPHIC SECTION
Toledo - Lucas County (G-18213)

(G-18187)
APEX SOLUTIONS INC
2620 Centennial Rd Ste P (43617-1849)
P.O. Box 8801 (43623-0801)
PHONE..................................419 843-3434
Bruce Turnbull, *President*
Donald Turnbull, *Vice Pres*
EMP: 5
SALES: 1MM **Privately Held**
WEB: www.apexpos.com
SIC: 7372 Prepackaged software

(G-18188)
ARBOR FOODS INC
3332 Saint Lawrence Dr C (43605-1046)
PHONE..................................419 698-4442
Mark S Flegenheimer, *President*
Sheila Severn, *Controller*
EMP: 50
SALES (est): 1.7MM **Privately Held**
SIC: 3556 Mixers, commercial, food

(G-18189)
ARCHER-DANIELS-MIDLAND COMPANY
Also Called: ADM
1308 Miami St (43605-3354)
PHONE..................................419 705-3292
Dan Hines, *Principal*
EMP: 9
SALES (corp-wide): 64.3B **Publicly Held**
SIC: 2041 2048 Flour & other grain mill products; prepared feeds
PA: Archer-Daniels-Midland Company
77 W Wacker Dr Ste 4600
Chicago IL 60601
312 634-8100

(G-18190)
ARCLIN USA LLC
6175 American Rd (43612-3901)
PHONE..................................419 726-5013
Warren Shunk, *Plant Mgr*
Alex Najdek, *Engineer*
EMP: 25
SALES (corp-wide): 23.5MM **Privately Held**
SIC: 2891 2821 Adhesives & sealants; plastics materials & resins
HQ: Arclin Usa Llc
1000 Holcomb Woods Pkwy
Roswell GA 30076
678 999-2100

(G-18191)
ARLINGTON RACK & PACKAGING CO
6120 N Detroit Ave (43612-4810)
PHONE..................................419 476-7700
Michael A Flaum, *President*
Harley Kripke, *Chairman*
Mark Hahm, *Vice Pres*
EMP: 8
SQ FT: 110,000
SALES (est): 1.5MM **Privately Held**
SIC: 3714 3086 Motor vehicle parts & accessories; packaging & shipping materials, foamed plastic

(G-18192)
ART & SIGN CORPORATION
5458 Angola Rd (43615-6326)
PHONE..................................419 865-3336
Michael P Dean, *President*
EMP: 6
SQ FT: 6,400
SALES (est): 657.5K **Privately Held**
SIC: 7336 7389 3993 Silk screen design; sign painting & lettering shop; displays & cutouts, window & lobby

(G-18193)
ASHCO MANUFACTURING INC
5234 Tulane Ave (43611-1573)
PHONE..................................419 838-7157
EMP: 6
SALES: 1MM **Privately Held**
SIC: 3423 3441 Mfg Hand/Edge Tools Structural Metal Fabrication

(G-18194)
AUTOMATED MACHINERY SOLUTIONS
6010 N Summit St (43611-1252)
P.O. Box 5142 (43611-0142)
PHONE..................................419 727-1772
Frank Smith, *Owner*
EMP: 15
SALES (est): 2MM **Privately Held**
SIC: 3549 Assembly machines, including robotic

(G-18195)
AUTOTEC ENGINEERING COMPANY
6155 Brent Dr (43611-1083)
PHONE..................................419 885-2529
Thomas P Ballay, *President*
Paul Sieben, *President*
Jim Proffitt, *Vice Pres*
James Mihaly, *CFO*
EMP: 20
SQ FT: 23,000
SALES: 7MM **Privately Held**
WEB: www.autotecinc.com
SIC: 3544 3599 8711 Designing: ship, boat, machine & product; mechanical engineering; special dies, tools, jigs & fixtures; custom machinery

(G-18196)
B & B BEVERAGE CTR
1901 Broadway St (43609-3203)
PHONE..................................419 243-0752
Abdul Aburiti, *Owner*
EMP: 5
SALES (est): 63.5K **Privately Held**
SIC: 3421 Table & food cutlery, including butchers'

(G-18197)
B & R CUSTOM CHROME
469 Dearborn Ave (43605-1709)
PHONE..................................419 536-7215
Ary Smith, *Principal*
EMP: 3
SALES (est): 146.8K **Privately Held**
SIC: 3471 Chromium plating of metals or formed products

(G-18198)
BANNER MATTRESS CO INC (PA)
Also Called: Banner Mattress & Furniture Co
2544 N Reynolds Rd (43615-2820)
PHONE..................................419 324-7181
Matthew Karp, *President*
George Evanoff, *General Mgr*
Barbara Karp, *Corp Secy*
▲ EMP: 8
SQ FT: 25,000
SALES (est): 12.2MM **Privately Held**
WEB: www.bannermattress.com
SIC: 5712 2515 Mattresses; mattresses & bedsprings

(G-18199)
BASILIUS INC
4338 South Ave (43615-6236)
PHONE..................................419 536-5810
Scott Basilius, *President*
Dave Keiser, *Vice Pres*
Doug Keiser, *Vice Pres*
Mike Nagle, *QC Mgr*
David Tierney, *Supervisor*
▲ EMP: 33 **EST:** 1940
SQ FT: 52,000
SALES (est): 6.6MM **Privately Held**
WEB: www.basilius.com
SIC: 3544 Forms (molds), for foundry & plastics working machinery

(G-18200)
BELL BINDERS LLC
320 21st St (43604-5037)
P.O. Box 313 (43697-0313)
PHONE..................................419 242-3201
Paul Jagielski,
EMP: 15 **EST:** 1954
SALES (est): 2.1MM **Privately Held**
SIC: 2782 3089 Looseleaf binders & devices; laminating of plastic

(G-18201)
BIONIX DEVELOPMENT CORPORATION (PA)
Also Called: Bionix Radiation Therapy
315 Matzinger Rd (43612-2626)
P.O. Box 935 (43697-0935)
PHONE..................................419 727-8421
Andrew J Milligan, *President*
James J Huttner, *Vice Pres*
▲ EMP: 50
SQ FT: 14,000
SALES (est): 12.1MM **Privately Held**
WEB: www.bionix.com
SIC: 3841 3829 Surgical & medical instruments; measuring & controlling devices

(G-18202)
BIONIX SAFETY TECHNOLOGIES LTD (HQ)
5154 Enterprise Blvd (43612-3807)
PHONE..................................419 727-0552
Andrew Milligan, *President*
Dr James Huttner, *Vice Pres*
EMP: 49
SALES (est): 7.7MM
SALES (corp-wide): 12.1MM **Privately Held**
WEB: www.nst-usa.com
SIC: 3825 3826 5084 3829 Test equipment for electronic & electric measurement; analytical instruments; gas testing apparatus; industrial machinery & equipment; measuring & controlling devices
PA: Bionix Development Corporation
315 Matzinger Rd
Toledo OH 43612
419 727-8421

(G-18203)
BISON LEATHER CO
7409 W Central Ave (43617-1122)
PHONE..................................419 517-1737
Barry Cody, *CEO*
EMP: 6
SALES (est): 529.6K **Privately Held**
SIC: 3172 Personal leather goods

(G-18204)
BITUMINOUS PRODUCTS COMPANY
352 George Hardy Dr (43605-1063)
PHONE..................................419 693-3933
John Krups, *Principal*
EMP: 3 **EST:** 2010
SALES (est): 319.4K **Privately Held**
SIC: 2951 Asphalt paving mixtures & blocks

(G-18205)
BLACK CLOISTER BREWING CO LLC
619 Monroe St (43604-1015)
PHONE..................................419 481-3891
Thomas Schaeffer,
EMP: 4
SALES (est): 373.2K **Privately Held**
SIC: 2082 Beer (alcoholic beverage)

(G-18206)
BLOCK COMMUNICATIONS INC (PA)
Also Called: BCI
405 Madison Ave Ste 2100 (43604-1224)
PHONE..................................419 724-6212
Allan J Block, *Ch of Bd*
John R Block, *Vice Ch Bd*
Walter H Carstensen, *President*
T P Brown, *Principal*
J K Hamilton, *Principal*
EMP: 14
SQ FT: 64,100
SALES (est): 921.6MM **Privately Held**
WEB: www.blockcommunications.com
SIC: 4841 4833 2711 Cable television services; television broadcasting stations; newspapers, publishing & printing

(G-18207)
BLUE WATER SATELLITE INC
1510 N Westwood Ave (43606-8202)
PHONE..................................419 372-0160
Milt Baker, *President*
Jim Harpen, *General Mgr*
John Schuller, *Business Mgr*
Charlie Curl, *VP Bus Dvlpt*
Gail Nader, *Administration*
EMP: 8 **EST:** 2009
SALES (est): 862.7K **Privately Held**
SIC: 3826 Environmental testing equipment

(G-18208)
BOBCO ENTERPRISES INC
Also Called: Taylor Mtl Hdlg & Conveyor
2910 Glanzman Rd (43614-3955)
P.O. Box 39, Sylvania (43560-0039)
PHONE..................................419 867-3560
Toll Free:......................................888 -
Robert Cordrey, *President*
Dave Amspoker, *Accounts Mgr*
Pauline Walker, *Accounts Mgr*
EMP: 12
SQ FT: 40,000
SALES (est): 5.8MM **Privately Held**
SIC: 5084 3536 3535 Materials handling machinery; hoists, cranes & monorails; conveyors & conveying equipment

(G-18209)
BOBS CUSTOM STR INTERIORS LLC
5333 Secor Rd Ste 19 (43623-2420)
PHONE..................................567 316-7490
EMP: 3
SALES (est): 191.9K **Privately Held**
SIC: 1751 2542 5046 5712 Carpentry Contractor Mfg Nonwd Partition/Fixt Whol Commercial Equip Ret Furniture

(G-18210)
BOLLIN & SONS INC
Also Called: Bollin Label Systems
6001 Brent Dr (43611-1090)
PHONE..................................419 693-6573
Mark D Bollin, *President*
Chris Younkman, *Vice Pres*
EMP: 40
SQ FT: 21,000
SALES (est): 23.2MM **Privately Held**
WEB: www.bollin.com
SIC: 5084 7389 2851 2759 Packaging machinery & equipment; design services; paints & allied products; commercial printing; packaging paper & plastics film, coated & laminated; adhesive papers, labels or tapes: from purchased material

(G-18211)
BOSTON SCNTFIC NRMDLATION CORP
3130 Executive Pkwy (43606-5529)
PHONE..................................419 720-9510
EMP: 3
SALES (corp-wide): 9.8B **Publicly Held**
SIC: 3841 Surgical & medical instruments
HQ: Boston Scientific Neuromodulation Corporation
25155 Rye Canyon Loop
Valencia CA 91355

(G-18212)
BP PRODUCTS NORTH AMERICA INC
B P Exploration
2450 Hill Ave (43607-3609)
P.O. Box 932 (43697-0932)
PHONE..................................419 537-9540
Jim Brahier, *Branch Mgr*
EMP: 16
SQ FT: 11,485
SALES (corp-wide): 240.2B **Privately Held**
WEB: www.bpproductsnorthamerica.com
SIC: 2911 Petroleum refining
HQ: Bp Products North America Inc.
501 Westlake Park Blvd
Houston TX 77079
281 366-2000

(G-18213)
BPREX PLASTIC PACKAGING INC (DH)
Also Called: Rexam Plastic Packaging
1 Seagate (43604-1558)
PHONE..................................419 247-5000
Joseph Lemieux, *CEO*
Kenneth Hicks, *Principal*
Lisa Hysko, *Principal*
EMP: 10

Toledo - Lucas County (G-18214)   GEOGRAPHIC SECTION

SALES (est): 102.7MM **Publicly Held**
SIC: 3089 3221 Plastic containers, except foam; cases, plastic; jars, plastic; closures, plastic; food containers, glass
HQ: Berry Global, Inc.
  101 Oakley St
  Evansville IN 47710
  812 424-2904

(G-18214)
BRAD SNODERLY
Also Called: ABC Countertops
444 W Laskey Rd Ste K (43612-3467)
PHONE..............................419 476-0184
Brad Snoderly, *Owner*
EMP: 15
SQ FT: 4,400
SALES (est): 1.4MM **Privately Held**
SIC: 2541 1799 Counter & sink tops; counter top installation

(G-18215)
BRAIN CHILD PRODUCTS LLC
146 Main St (43605-2067)
PHONE..............................419 698-4020
Robert Croak,
EMP: 15
SALES (est): 1.3MM **Privately Held**
WEB: www.brainchildproducts.com
SIC: 2822 Silicone rubbers

(G-18216)
BROOKS MANUFACTURING
1102 N Summit St (43604-1816)
PHONE..............................419 244-1777
Michael Brooks, *Owner*
EMP: 9
SQ FT: 5,000
SALES (est): 310K **Privately Held**
SIC: 3931 3592 3824 Brass instruments & parts; valves; water meters

(G-18217)
BTW LLC
2226 Greenlawn Dr (43614-5120)
PHONE..............................419 382-4443
Paul Long, *President*
EMP: 8
SALES (est): 823K **Privately Held**
WEB: www.btw.com
SIC: 2679 5012 Wrappers, paper (unprinted): made from purchased material; automobiles & other motor vehicles

(G-18218)
BUCK EYE PRESSURE WASH
5242 Angola Rd Ste 130 (43615-6334)
P.O. Box 351574 (43635-1574)
PHONE..............................419 385-9274
Robert Moeller, *Owner*
EMP: 7 EST: 2001
SALES (est): 743.5K **Privately Held**
SIC: 3452 Washers

(G-18219)
BUILDER TECH WHOLESALE LLC
Also Called: Builder Tech Windows
2931 South Ave (43609-1327)
PHONE..............................419 535-7606
Brad Montague,
Lynn Burns,
EMP: 8
SQ FT: 6,000
SALES (est): 290K **Privately Held**
SIC: 3089 Windows, plastic

(G-18220)
C M SLICECHIEF CO
3333 Maple St (43608-1147)
P.O. Box 80206 (43608-0206)
PHONE..............................419 241-7647
Susan L Brown, *President*
Barbara Cairl, *Corp Secy*
EMP: 9 EST: 1946
SQ FT: 18,000
SALES (est): 1.2MM **Privately Held**
WEB: www.slicechief.com
SIC: 3556 Slicers, commercial, food

(G-18221)
CAKE ARTS SUPPLIES
Also Called: Cake Arts Supplies & Bakery
2858 W Sylvania Ave (43613-4225)
PHONE..............................419 472-4959
Dorothy Bryan, *Owner*
EMP: 5
SALES: 360K **Privately Held**
WEB: www.cakeartssupply.com
SIC: 5999 2051 Cake decorating supplies; cakes, bakery: except frozen

(G-18222)
CANBERRA CORPORATION
3610 N Hlland Sylvania Rd (43615)
PHONE..............................419 724-4300
R Bruce Yacko, *President*
James C Lower, *Chairman*
William Schneck, *Corp Secy*
Martin Sikula, *Maintenance Dir*
John Hunsinger, *Plant Mgr*
◆ EMP: 205
SQ FT: 220,000
SALES (est): 75.1MM **Privately Held**
WEB: www.canberracorp.com
SIC: 2842 Cleaning or polishing preparations; specialty cleaning preparations

(G-18223)
CAUFFIEL CORPORATION (PA)
3171 N Repub Blvd Ste 102 (43615)
PHONE..............................419 843-7262
EMP: 5 EST: 2012
SALES (est): 6.7MM **Privately Held**
SIC: 3549 Mfg Metalworking Machinery

(G-18224)
CELEBRATIONS
Also Called: JM Gourmet Popcorn
2910 Glanzman Rd Unit 1 (43614-3955)
PHONE..............................419 381-8088
David Poulos, *Owner*
Cathy Poulos, *Co-Owner*
EMP: 5
SQ FT: 8,000
SALES: 350K **Privately Held**
WEB: www.celebrationsfundraising.com
SIC: 2064 Candy & other confectionery products

(G-18225)
CENTAUR INC (PA)
Also Called: Heidtman Steel Products
2401 Front St (43605-1145)
PHONE..............................419 469-8000
Mark Ridenour, *CEO*
John C Bates, *Ch of Bd*
▲ EMP: 5
SQ FT: 100,000
SALES (est): 296.3MM **Privately Held**
SIC: 3312 3316 3999 Sheet or strip, steel, hot-rolled; strip steel, cold-rolled: from purchased hot-rolled; atomizers, toiletry

(G-18226)
CENTRAL COCA-COLA BTLG CO INC
3970 Catawba St (43612-1404)
PHONE..............................419 476-6622
Paul Kenny, *Manager*
EMP: 110
SALES (corp-wide): 35.4B **Publicly Held**
WEB: www.colasic.net
SIC: 2086 2087 5149 Carbonated beverages, nonalcoholic: bottled & canned; soft drinks: packaged in cans, bottles, etc.; fruit drinks (less than 100% juice): packaged in cans, etc.; syrups, drink; concentrates, drink; groceries & related products
HQ: Central Coca-Cola Bottling Company, Inc.
  555 Taxter Rd Ste 550
  Elmsford NY 10523
  914 789-1100

(G-18227)
CHANTILLY DEVELOPMENT CORP
Acme Specialty Mfg Co
3101 Monroe St (43606-4605)
PHONE..............................419 243-8109
Deanna Sifuentes, *General Mgr*
Robert T Skilliter, *Principal*
Thomas Messina, *Plant Mgr*
Tonya Schmitz, *Controller*
EMP: 19
SQ FT: 70,000
SALES (corp-wide): 2MM **Privately Held**
WEB: www.acmespecialty.com
SIC: 3231 3714 3429 3221 Mirrored glass; mirrors, truck & automobile: made from purchased glass; frames, motor vehicle; windshield frames, motor vehicle; manufactured hardware (general); glass containers
PA: Chantilly Development Corp
  Wollaston Rd
  Unionville PA
  419 243-8109

(G-18228)
CHEM-SALES INC
Also Called: C S I
3860 Dorr St (43607-1003)
P.O. Box 351684 (43635-1684)
PHONE..............................419 531-4292
Amos Clay Sr, *CEO*
Amos Clay Jr, *President*
Shirley J Clay, *Corp Secy*
EMP: 12
SQ FT: 1,200
SALES (est): 2.4MM **Privately Held**
WEB: www.chemsalesinc.com
SIC: 2869 5087 5169 Mfg Industrial Organic Chemicals Whol Service Establishment Equipment Whol Chemicals/Products

(G-18229)
CHEMPACE CORPORATION
339 Arco Dr (43607-2908)
PHONE..............................419 535-0101
Richard Shall, *President*
Terry W O'Neill, *Vice Pres*
Terry Oneill, *Vice Pres*
Sue Klotz, *Controller*
Jeff Anderson, *Manager*
▲ EMP: 18 EST: 1968
SQ FT: 12,500
SALES (est): 3.1MM **Privately Held**
WEB: www.chempace.com
SIC: 2842 Cleaning or polishing preparations; degreasing solvent

(G-18230)
CHINA ENTERPRISES INC
Also Called: Chang Audio
5151 Monroe St (43623-3462)
PHONE..............................419 885-1485
Stella Lee, *President*
Michael Chang, *Exec VP*
EMP: 7 EST: 1991
SALES (est): 827.1K **Privately Held**
WEB: www.changlightspeed.com
SIC: 3651 Household audio equipment

(G-18231)
CHIPPEWA INDUSTRIES INC
Also Called: Seaport Mold and Casting Co
1309 W Bancroft St (43606-4634)
PHONE..............................248 880-9193
Jeffrey St Louis, *President*
EMP: 3
SALES: 250K **Privately Held**
SIC: 3599 Machine shop, jobbing & repair

(G-18232)
CLAMPS INC
5960 American Rd E (43612-3966)
PHONE..............................419 729-2141
J D Riker, *CEO*
Anthony Carollo, *President*
Glen Jackson, *Treasurer*
Jeanne E Graham, *Admin Sec*
EMP: 25 EST: 1957
SQ FT: 67,000
SALES (est): 5.4MM **Privately Held**
WEB: www.clampsinc.com
SIC: 3496 Miscellaneous fabricated wire products

(G-18233)
CLEAR IMAGES LLC
121 11th St (43604-5829)
PHONE..............................419 241-9347
Frank Ozanski, *Mng Member*
Marie Micel,
EMP: 13
SALES (est): 1.5MM **Privately Held**
SIC: 2759 Promotional printing

(G-18234)
CLINTON FOUNDRY LTD
1202 W Bancroft St (43606-4631)
PHONE..............................419 243-6885
James D Heninger, *Principal*
Timothy Heninger,
Ronnie L Holbrook,
EMP: 10
SQ FT: 4,500
SALES: 250K **Privately Held**
SIC: 3543 Industrial patterns

(G-18235)
CLINTON PATTERN WORKS INC
1215 W Bancroft St (43606-4632)
PHONE..............................419 243-0855
James D Heninger, *President*
Timothy Heninger, *Vice Pres*
EMP: 11
SQ FT: 25,000
SALES (est): 1.8MM **Privately Held**
SIC: 3543 Industrial patterns

(G-18236)
COMFORT LINE LTD
5500 Enterprise Blvd (43612-3815)
PHONE..............................419 729-8520
Daniel J La Valley, *President*
Richard G La Valley, *President*
Allan Hite, *Engineer*
Dianne Tankoos, *Treasurer*
Rodney Boatright, *Regl Sales Mgr*
▼ EMP: 100 EST: 1959
SQ FT: 200,000
SALES (est): 23.4MM **Privately Held**
WEB: www.comfortlineinc.com
SIC: 3089 Windows, plastic; doors, folding: plastic or plastic coated fabric

(G-18237)
CONCRETE MATERIAL SUPPLY LLC
1 Maritime Plz Fl 4 (43604-1853)
PHONE..............................419 261-6404
Tom Bischoff Jr, *Principal*
EMP: 4
SALES (est): 269.3K **Privately Held**
SIC: 1771 3272 Concrete work; concrete products

(G-18238)
CONFORMING MATRIX CORPORATION
6255 Suder Ave (43611-1022)
PHONE..............................419 729-3777
Albert J Spelker, *President*
Ella Mae Macarthur, *Principal*
H E Macarthur, *Principal*
Chad McComas, *CFO*
EMP: 40
SQ FT: 38,000
SALES (est): 12.1MM **Privately Held**
WEB: www.conformingmatrix.com
SIC: 3559 3544 Metal finishing equipment for plating, etc.; special dies, tools, jigs & fixtures

(G-18239)
CONNECTRONICS CORP (DH)
2745 Avondale Ave (43607-3232)
P.O. Box 3355 (43607-0355)
PHONE..............................419 537-0020
Thomas Ricketts, *CEO*
Thomas L Ricketts, *CEO*
Lex Potter, *President*
Steven Robinson, *General Mgr*
Al Mocek, *Vice Pres*
EMP: 65
SQ FT: 25,000
SALES (est): 11.8MM **Publicly Held**
WEB: www.connectronicscorp.com
SIC: 3678 3643 Electronic connectors; connectors & terminals for electrical devices
HQ: Heico Electronic Technologies Corp.
  3000 Taft St
  Hollywood FL 33021
  954 987-6101

(G-18240)
CONSUMER GUILD FOODS INC
5035 Enterprise Blvd (43612-3839)
PHONE..............................419 726-3406
Wilbur R Ascham, *President*
Ann Ascham, *Vice Pres*

GEOGRAPHIC SECTION
Toledo - Lucas County (G-18268)

Robert J Petrick, *Vice Pres*
EMP: 20 **EST:** 1966
SQ FT: 14,500
SALES (est): 3.4MM **Privately Held**
SIC: 2035 Dressings, salad: raw & cooked (except dry mixes)

(G-18241)
CONTAINER GRAPHICS CORP
305 Ryder Rd (43607-3105)
PHONE..................419 531-5133
Bill Beaker, *Branch Mgr*
EMP: 100
SQ FT: 24,200
SALES (corp-wide): 3MM **Privately Held**
WEB: www.containergraphics.com
SIC: 7336 3545 3944 Graphic arts & related design; cutting tools for machine tools; dice & dice cups
PA: Container Graphics Corp.
  114 Ednbrgh S Dr Ste 104
  Cary NC 27511
  919 481-4200

(G-18242)
CRABAR/GBF INC
Also Called: Printxcel
4444 N Detroit Ave (43612-1978)
P.O. Box 6986 (43612-0986)
PHONE..................419 269-1720
Tom Fiddle, *General Mgr*
Dan Frederick, *Production*
Janice West, *Sales Staff*
EMP: 27
SQ FT: 52,223
SALES (corp-wide): 370.1MM **Publicly Held**
WEB: www.mail-well.com
SIC: 2752 2761 Commercial printing, offset; continuous forms, office & business
HQ: Crabar/Gbf, Inc.
  68 Vine St
  Leipsic OH 45856
  419 943-2141

(G-18243)
CROWN CORK & SEAL USA INC
5201 Enterprise Blvd (43612-3808)
PHONE..................419 727-8201
Willaim Lahner, *Manager*
EMP: 40
SALES (corp-wide): 11.1B **Publicly Held**
WEB: www.crowncork.com
SIC: 3411 Metal cans
HQ: Crown Cork & Seal Usa, Inc.
  770 Township Line Rd # 100
  Yardley PA 19067
  215 698-5100

(G-18244)
CULAINE INC
Also Called: Cpg Printing & Graphics
1036 W Laskey Rd (43612-3030)
PHONE..................419 345-4984
Mike Cutcher, *President*
Elaine R Cutcher, *Vice Pres*
EMP: 6
SQ FT: 4,000
SALES: 500K **Privately Held**
SIC: 2759 2752 Commercial printing; commercial printing, lithographic

(G-18245)
CUSTOM DECO LLC
1345 Miami St (43605)
PHONE..................419 698-2900
EMP: 4
SALES (est): 223.5K **Privately Held**
SIC: 3221 Glass containers

(G-18246)
CUSTOM DECO SOUTH INC
1343 Miami St (43605-3338)
PHONE..................419 698-2900
Dean E Stroh, *President*
Hal Mann, *CFO*
▲ **EMP:** 25
SQ FT: 18,000
SALES (est): 2.5MM **Privately Held**
SIC: 2759 3229 Screen printing; tableware, glass or glass ceramic

(G-18247)
CUSTOMERS CAR CARE CENTER
Also Called: Suzuki of Toleda
5299 Monroe St (43623-3139)
PHONE..................419 841-6646
Robert Fleicher, *Owner*
EMP: 6 **EST:** 2001
SALES (est): 614.5K **Privately Held**
SIC: 3559 Automotive related machinery

(G-18248)
CWM SMOOTHIE LLC
2859 N Hlland Sylvania Rd (43615)
PHONE..................419 283-6387
Chris Markho, *Principal*
EMP: 3
SALES (est): 154.2K **Privately Held**
SIC: 2037 Frozen fruits & vegetables

(G-18249)
D & D NEXT DAY SIGNS INC
2112 N Reynolds Rd (43615-3514)
PHONE..................419 537-9595
Dan Mosher, *President*
EMP: 5
SALES (est): 391.1K **Privately Held**
SIC: 3993 Signs & advertising specialties

(G-18250)
D A L E S CORPORATION
1402 Jackson St (43604-5212)
PHONE..................419 255-5335
Dale Frantz, *President*
Buzz Kutz, *Vice Pres*
Lisa Frantz, *Admin Sec*
EMP: 12
SQ FT: 10,000
SALES: 2.9MM **Privately Held**
WEB: www.dalescorp.com
SIC: 3991 Paint & varnish brushes

(G-18251)
D L SALKIL LLC
Also Called: Toledo Screw Products
8261 W Bancroft St (43617-1804)
PHONE..................419 841-3341
EMP: 6
SALES: 500K **Privately Held**
SIC: 3451 Mfg Screw Machine Products

(G-18252)
DAKKOTA INTEGRATED SYSTEMS LLC
315 Matzinger Rd Unit G (43612-2626)
PHONE..................517 694-6500
James Horwath, *Controller*
EMP: 50
SQ FT: 65,000
SALES (corp-wide): 299MM **Privately Held**
SIC: 3711 Automobile assembly, including specialty automobiles
PA: Dakkota Integrated Systems, Llc
  1875 Holloway Dr
  Holt MI 48842
  517 694-6500

(G-18253)
DANA LIGHT AXLE MFG LLC
Also Called: Toledo Driveline
3044 Jeep Pkwy (43610-1072)
PHONE..................419 887-3000
EMP: 300
SQ FT: 100,000 **Publicly Held**
SIC: 3714 Motor vehicle parts & accessories
HQ: Dana Light Axle Manufacturing, Llc
  3939 Technology Dr
  Maumee OH 43537

(G-18254)
DAY PRE-CAST PRODUCTS CO
801 N Westwood Ave (43607-3561)
PHONE..................419 536-2909
Michele Filipovich, *Owner*
Richard Day, *Co-Owner*
▲ **EMP:** 3
SQ FT: 4,800
SALES (est): 320.5K **Privately Held**
SIC: 3272 Chimney caps, concrete; steps, prefabricated concrete; furniture, garden: concrete

(G-18255)
DEAN FOODS CO
4117 Fitch Rd (43613-4007)
PHONE..................419 473-9621
Randy Bevier, *Principal*
Phil Miller, *Info Tech Mgr*
EMP: 4 **EST:** 2016
SALES (est): 75.4K **Privately Held**
SIC: 2026 Fluid milk

(G-18256)
DECO TOOLS INC
1541 Coining Dr (43612-2978)
PHONE..................419 476-9321
Mike Bollenbacher, *President*
John Schwab, *Project Engr*
Michael Rowley, *Technical Staff*
Brenda Delaney, *Admin Sec*
EMP: 25
SQ FT: 30,000
SALES (est): 6MM **Privately Held**
WEB: www.decotools.com
SIC: 3563 3991 3842 2672 Spraying outfits: metals, paints & chemicals (compressor); brooms & brushes; surgical appliances & supplies; coated & laminated paper

(G-18257)
DECOMA SYSTEMS INTEGRATION GRO
Also Called: Team Systems
1800 Nathan Dr (43611-1091)
PHONE..................419 324-3387
Belinda Stronach, *CEO*
Cosmo Timofeev, *Purchasing*
Pamala Fisher, *Engineer*
Paul Irving, *Engineer*
Ken Wardell, *Design Engr*
EMP: 100
SALES (est): 18.5MM
SALES (corp-wide): 38.9B **Privately Held**
WEB: www.decoma.com
SIC: 3465 Body parts, automobile: stamped metal
PA: Magna International Inc
  337 Magna Dr
  Aurora ON L4G 7
  905 726-2462

(G-18258)
DECOR ARCHITECTURAL PRODUCTS
2375 Dorr St Ste E (43607-3400)
PHONE..................419 537-9493
Terry Creech, *President*
Julie Creech, *Corp Secy*
EMP: 5
SQ FT: 5,000
SALES: 350K **Privately Held**
WEB: www.decorarchitecturalproducts.com
SIC: 3444 3446 Sheet metalwork; architectural metalwork

(G-18259)
DECORATIVE PANELS INTL INC (DH)
Also Called: D P I
2900 Hill Ave (43607-2929)
PHONE..................419 535-5921
Tim Clark, *President*
Allen Steiber, *Controller*
Trish McLaren, *Accountant*
Jim Peloquin, *Sales Dir*
Carolyn Crowell, *Sales Staff*
▼ **EMP:** 75
SQ FT: 225,000
SALES (est): 88.8MM
SALES (corp-wide): 15.6B **Privately Held**
WEB: www.decorativepanelsinternational.com
SIC: 2435 Hardwood plywood, prefinished; panels, hardwood plywood

(G-18260)
DEEP SPRINGS TECHNOLOGY LLC
4750 W Bancroft St Ste 1 (43615-3864)
PHONE..................419 536-5741
Carol Ann Wedding, *President*
Vicky Kurtz, *Managing Prtnr*
▲ **EMP:** 4
SQ FT: 11,000
SALES (est): 686.3K
SALES (corp-wide): 4.3MM **Privately Held**
WEB: www.teamist.com
SIC: 3532 Mining machinery
PA: Imaging Systems Technology Inc.
  4750 W Bancroft St
  Toledo OH 43615
  419 536-5741

(G-18261)
DETROIT TOLEDO FIBER LLC
1245 E Manhattan Blvd (43608-1549)
PHONE..................248 647-0400
Steven Philips, *President*
Gary Stanis, *CFO*
EMP: 10
SALES (est): 1.2MM **Privately Held**
SIC: 3714 Motor vehicle engines & parts
PA: Detroit Technologies, Inc.
  32500 Telg Rd Ste 207
  Bingham Farms MI 48025

(G-18262)
DEVILBISS RANSBURG
320 Phillips Ave (43612-1493)
PHONE..................419 470-2000
Rolan D Kjosen, *Principal*
EMP: 19 **EST:** 2010
SALES (est): 4.7MM **Privately Held**
SIC: 3559 Special industry machinery

(G-18263)
DIGIMATICS INC
Also Called: Architectural Arts
4011 Vermaas Ave (43612-1879)
PHONE..................419 478-0804
Norman Newman, *President*
John Bordner, *Vice Pres*
EMP: 4
SQ FT: 10,000
SALES (est): 450K **Privately Held**
WEB: www.digimaticsinc.com
SIC: 7389 3993 Sign painting & lettering shop; electric signs

(G-18264)
DISMAT CORPORATION
336 N Westwood Ave (43607-3343)
PHONE..................419 531-8963
John A Donofrio, *President*
EMP: 6 **EST:** 1945
SQ FT: 12,000
SALES (est): 875.5K **Privately Held**
SIC: 2034 Soup powders

(G-18265)
DIVERSIFIED WELDING SERVICES
3541 Marine Rd (43609-1017)
PHONE..................419 382-1433
Chris Waite, *Owner*
EMP: 3
SALES (est): 211.7K **Privately Held**
SIC: 7692 Welding repair

(G-18266)
DIVINE PRTG T-SHIRTS & MORE
3433 Monroe St (43606-4140)
PHONE..................419 241-8208
Karen Hoskins, *Principal*
EMP: 3 **EST:** 2008
SALES (est): 262.1K **Privately Held**
SIC: 2759 Commercial printing

(G-18267)
DOLLMAN TECHNICAL SERVICES
2910 Glanzman Rd (43614-3955)
PHONE..................419 877-9404
James M Dollman, *President*
John Dollman, *Engineer*
EMP: 5
SQ FT: 27,084 **Privately Held**
SIC: 3599 Custom machinery
PA: Dollman Technical Services Inc
  5702 Eber Rd
  Whitehouse OH 43571

(G-18268)
DOWNTOWN PRINT SHOP
500 Madison Ave Fl 1 (43604-1230)
PHONE..................419 242-9164
Philip G Cummings, *Partner*
Sharon Cummings, *Partner*

Toledo - Lucas County (G-18269) GEOGRAPHIC SECTION

EMP: 3
SQ FT: 2,500
SALES (est): 220K **Privately Held**
WEB: www.downtownprintshop.com
SIC: 2752 Commercial printing, offset

(G-18269)
DRDC REALTY INC (PA)
4401 Jackman Rd (43612-1529)
PHONE 419 478-7091
Marvin K Himmelein, *President*
Gary L Ames, *Vice Pres*
EMP: 3
SQ FT: 12,000
SALES: 491.5K **Privately Held**
SIC: 3613 6512 7359 Control panels, electric; commercial & industrial building operation; equipment rental & leasing

(G-18270)
DS TECHNOLOGIES GROUP LTD
2537 Wimbledon Park Blvd (43617-2242)
PHONE 419 841-5388
▲ EMP: 5
SQ FT: 14,000
SALES: 5MM **Privately Held**
SIC: 3069 5013 Automotive Driveline And Chassi Components

(G-18271)
DYNAMICS RESEARCH & DEV
Also Called: Dynamics Manufacturing
4401 Jackman Rd (43612-1529)
PHONE 419 478-7091
Marvin K Himmelein, *President*
Gary L Ames, *Vice Pres*
EMP: 3
SQ FT: 6,000
SALES: 192.5K
SALES (corp-wide): 491.5K **Privately Held**
WEB: www.dynamicsresearch.net
SIC: 3613 5084 Control panels, electric; industrial machinery & equipment
PA: D.R.D.C. Realty Inc
4401 Jackman Rd
Toledo OH 43612
419 478-7091

(G-18272)
DYNETECH LLC
916 N Summit St (43604-1812)
PHONE 419 690-4281
Robert Redmond,
EMP: 20 EST: 2005
SALES (est): 2MM **Privately Held**
SIC: 3823 Industrial process control instruments

(G-18273)
E W PERRY SERVICE CO INC
Also Called: Perry Service Co.
4216 W Alexis Rd (43623-1244)
PHONE 419 473-1231
Christopher W Perry, *President*
EMP: 4
SQ FT: 3,300
SALES (est): 709.4K **Privately Held**
SIC: 5023 2391 1799 2591 Window covering parts & accessories; draperies, plastic & textile: from purchased materials; drapery track installation; window blinds

(G-18274)
EARNEST BREW WORKS
4342 S Detroit Ave (43614-5367)
PHONE 419 340-2589
EMP: 4
SALES (est): 204.5K **Privately Held**
SIC: 2082 Malt beverages

(G-18275)
EDCO INC (HQ)
Also Called: Edco Tool & Die
5244 Enterprise Blvd # 5 (43612-3871)
PHONE 419 726-1595
Jai Singh, *President*
Mark Payeff, *QC Mgr*
Paul Riganelli, *Admin Sec*
◆ EMP: 46
SQ FT: 50,000
SALES (est): 9.5MM
SALES (corp-wide): 465.8MM **Privately Held**
WEB: www.edcodie.com
SIC: 3544 Special dies & tools
PA: Exco Technologies Limited
130 Spy Crt
Markham ON L3R 5
905 477-3065

(G-18276)
ELAIRE CORPORATION
7944 W Central Ave Ste 10 (43617-1550)
PHONE 419 843-2192
Mark Neeley, *President*
EMP: 8
SALES (est): 878.5K **Privately Held**
SIC: 3999 Manufacturing industries

(G-18277)
ELDEN DRAPERIES OF TOLEDO INC
1845 N Reynolds Rd (43615-3531)
PHONE 419 535-1909
Betsy Grubb, *President*
Gary Grubb, *Vice Pres*
EMP: 10
SQ FT: 6,000
SALES: 900K **Privately Held**
SIC: 2391 5714 Draperies, plastic & textile: from purchased materials; draperies

(G-18278)
ELECTRO PRIME GROUP LLC (PA)
4510 Lint Ave Ste B (43612-2658)
PHONE 419 476-0100
Brett Grachek, *Vice Pres*
Jim Vellequette, *Plant Mgr*
Don Lublin, *QC Mgr*
Brent Leist, *Accounting Mgr*
John L Lauffer, *Mng Member*
▲ EMP: 70
SQ FT: 20,100
SALES (est): 20MM **Privately Held**
WEB: www.electroprime.com
SIC: 3471 5169 Plating & polishing; anti-corrosion products

(G-18279)
ELEMENT MACHINERY LLC
4801 Bennett Rd (43612-2531)
PHONE 855 447-7648
Benjamin McGilvery, *CEO*
Samuel McGilvery 40, *President*
Joseph Box, *Vice Pres*
EMP: 6
SQ FT: 20,000
SALES (est): 520.8K **Privately Held**
SIC: 3547 Rolling mill machinery

(G-18280)
ELEVATOR CNCEPTS BY WURTEC LLC
6200 Brent Dr (43611-1081)
PHONE 734 246-4700
Douglas Scott, *President*
Leigh Gaither, *Treasurer*
▲ EMP: 10
SQ FT: 10,000
SALES (est): 1.6MM
SALES (corp-wide): 24.5MM **Privately Held**
WEB: www.elevatorconcepts.com
SIC: 3534 Elevators & equipment
PA: Wurtec, Incorporated
6200 Brent Dr
Toledo OH 43611
419 726-1066

(G-18281)
ELKAY PLUMBING PRODUCTS CO
Also Called: Mr Direct, Inc.
7634 New West Rd (43617-4201)
PHONE 419 841-1820
EMP: 3
SALES (corp-wide): 1.3B **Privately Held**
SIC: 2499 Kitchen, bathroom & household ware: wood
HQ: Elkay Plumbing Products Company
2222 Camden Ct
Oak Brook IL 60523
630 574-8484

(G-18282)
ENNIS INC
Tennessee Business Forms
4444 N Detroit Ave (43612-1978)
PHONE 800 537-8648
Tina Furgason, *Branch Mgr*
EMP: 33
SALES (corp-wide): 370.1MM **Publicly Held**
SIC: 2752 Commercial printing, lithographic
PA: Ennis, Inc.
2441 Presidential Pkwy
Midlothian TX 76065
972 775-9801

(G-18283)
ERD SPECIALTY GRAPHICS INC
3250 Monroe St (43606-4550)
PHONE 419 242-9545
Steve Crouse, *President*
Debbie Crouse, *Admin Sec*
EMP: 9 EST: 1934
SQ FT: 19,500
SALES (est): 1.7MM **Privately Held**
WEB: www.erdgraphics.com
SIC: 2759 7389 3554 2396 Screen printing; embossing on paper; printers' services: folding, collating; die cutting & stamping machinery, paper converting; fabric printing & stamping

(G-18284)
ERIE LASER INK LLC
911 Jefferson Ave (43604-5921)
PHONE 419 346-0600
Mike Henry, *Mng Member*
EMP: 3
SALES (est): 320.1K **Privately Held**
SIC: 7389 2893 Printers' services: folding, collating; printing ink

(G-18285)
ERIE STEEL LTD
5540 Jackman Rd (43613-2330)
PHONE 419 478-3743
Pat Flynn, *President*
Michael Mouilleseaux, *General Mgr*
Morgan Little, *Engineer*
EMP: 50
SALES: 10MM **Privately Held**
SIC: 3398 Metal heat treating

(G-18286)
EXOTHERMICS INC
5040 Enterprise Blvd (43612-3880)
PHONE 603 821-5660
Lach Perks, *President*
Rich Lattanzi, *Principal*
Kelly Gonzales, *Corp Secy*
▲ EMP: 25 EST: 1976
SQ FT: 38,000
SALES (est): 4.9MM
SALES (corp-wide): 41.8B **Publicly Held**
WEB: www.exothermics.com
SIC: 3443 Heat exchangers, condensers & components
HQ: Eclipse, Inc.
1665 Elmwood Rd
Rockford IL 61103
815 877-3031

(G-18287)
EXP FUELS INC
3070 Airport Hwy (43609-1406)
PHONE 419 382-7713
Victor Safadi, *Principal*
EMP: 4
SALES (est): 280.2K **Privately Held**
SIC: 2869 Fuels

(G-18288)
FAURECIA AUTOMOTIVE HOLDINGS
543 Matzinger Rd (43612-2638)
PHONE 419 727-5000
Patrick Szaroletta, *Interim Pres*
▲ EMP: 1000
SALES (est): 71.7MM
SALES (corp-wide): 342.9MM **Privately Held**
SIC: 3714 Mufflers (exhaust), motor vehicle
HQ: Faurecia Usa Holdings, Inc.
2800 High Meadow Cir
Auburn Hills MI 48326
248 724-5100

(G-18289)
FAURECIA EMISSIONS CONTROL SYS (DH)
543 Matzinger Rd (43612-2638)
P.O. Box 64010 (43612-0010)
PHONE 812 341-2000
David Degraaf, *President*
Christophe Schmidt,
Mark Stidham,
▲ EMP: 130
SQ FT: 40,000
SALES (est): 1.5B
SALES (corp-wide): 342.9MM **Privately Held**
WEB: www.franklin.faurecia.com
SIC: 3714 5013 Mufflers (exhaust), motor vehicle; motor vehicle supplies & new parts

(G-18290)
FEDEX OFFICE & PRINT SVCS INC
2306 S Reynolds Rd (43614-1417)
PHONE 419 866-5464
EMP: 20
SALES (corp-wide): 65.4B **Publicly Held**
WEB: www.kinkos.com
SIC: 7334 2789 5943 2791 Photocopying & duplicating services; binding only: books, pamphlets, magazines, etc.; stationery stores; typesetting; commercial printing, lithographic
HQ: Fedex Office And Print Services, Inc.
7900 Legacy Dr
Plano TX 75024
800 463-3339

(G-18291)
FENNER DUNLOP (TOLEDO) LLC
146 S Westwood Ave (43607-2948)
P.O. Box 441 (43697-0441)
PHONE 419 531-5300
David Hurd, *President*
Cassandra Pan, *Vice Pres*
Ben Ficklen, *Corp Secy*
Bill Mooney, *CFO*
▲ EMP: 50
SQ FT: 100,000
SALES (est): 10.7MM
SALES (corp-wide): 855.1MM **Privately Held**
SIC: 3052 Rubber belting
HQ: Fenner Dunlop Americas, Llc
1000 Omega Dr Ste 1400
Pittsburgh PA 15205

(G-18292)
FENWICK GALLERY OF FINE ARTS (PA)
Also Called: Fenwick Frame Shppe Art Gllery
3433 W Alexis Rd Frnt (43623-1400)
PHONE 419 475-1651
Beverly A Freshour, *President*
EMP: 6
SQ FT: 3,000
SALES (est): 659.7K **Privately Held**
SIC: 5999 2499 Art dealers; picture & mirror frames, wood

(G-18293)
FERGUSONS FINISHING INC
Also Called: Universal Bindery
126 N Ontario St (43604-5938)
PHONE 419 241-9123
Richard Ferguson, *President*
Janet Ferguson, *Treasurer*
EMP: 20 EST: 1949
SQ FT: 15,000
SALES: 725K **Privately Held**
WEB: www.universalbindery.com
SIC: 2789 Pamphlets, binding; trade binding services

(G-18294)
FIBREBOARD CORPORATION (DH)
1 Owens Corning Pkwy (43659-1000)
PHONE 419 248-8000
David T Brown, *President*

GEOGRAPHIC SECTION
Toledo - Lucas County (G-18321)

Michael Thaman, *CFO*
▲ **EMP:** 200 **EST:** 1917
SALES (est): 25.9MM **Publicly Held**
SIC: 3089 3272 3296 Siding, plastic; cast stone, concrete; mineral wool insulation products
HQ: Owens Corning Sales, Llc
1 Owens Corning Pkwy
Toledo OH 43659
419 248-8000

(G-18295)
FISKE BROTHERS REFINING CO
1500 Oakdale Ave (43605-3843)
P.O. Box 8038 (43605-0038)
PHONE..................419 691-2491
William Kuhlman, *Manager*
EMP: 60
SQ FT: 30,000
SALES (corp-wide): 60.7MM **Privately Held**
SIC: 2992 2077 Re-refining lubricating oils & greases; animal & marine fats & oils
PA: Fiske Brothers Refining Co Inc
129 Lockwood St
Newark NJ 07105
973 589-9150

(G-18296)
FLYNN INC
5540 Jackman Rd (43613-2330)
PHONE..................419 478-3743
Patrick Flynn, *President*
Mary Schira, *Corp Secy*
Doug Kennedy, *Executive*
EMP: 350
SALES (est): 53.8MM **Privately Held**
WEB: www.erie.com
SIC: 3398 Metal heat treating

(G-18297)
FRIGID UNITS INC
5072 Lewis Ave (43612-3257)
PHONE..................419 478-4000
Dawn M Heilman, *President*
Mark S Heilman, *Vice Pres*
EMP: 3
SQ FT: 4,000
SALES: 680K **Privately Held**
WEB: www.frigidunits.com
SIC: 3231 Aquariums & reflectors, glass

(G-18298)
FRITZIE FREEZE INC
5137 N Summit St Unit 1 (43611-2754)
PHONE..................419 727-0818
Chris Schwind, *Principal*
EMP: 3
SALES (est): 201.5K **Privately Held**
SIC: 2024 Ice cream, bulk

(G-18299)
FULTON EQUIPMENT CO (PA)
823 Hamilton St (43607-4477)
PHONE..................419 290-5393
Richard G Paul Jr, *President*
EMP: 35
SQ FT: 8,000
SALES: 3MM **Privately Held**
SIC: 3441 3444 3443 Fabricated structural metal; sheet metalwork; fabricated plate work (boiler shop)

(G-18300)
G H CUTTER SERVICES INC
6203 N Detroit Ave (43612-4818)
PHONE..................419 476-0476
Gene Hodapp, *President*
Mary Hodapp, *Office Mgr*
EMP: 9
SALES: 750K **Privately Held**
WEB: www.ghcutters.com
SIC: 3599 7389 Machine shop, jobbing & repair; grinding, precision: commercial or industrial

(G-18301)
GARDNER SIGNS INC (PA)
3800 Airport Hwy (43615-7106)
PHONE..................419 385-6669
Weston L Gardner Jr, *CEO*
Scott Gardner, *President*
EMP: 25 **EST:** 1945
SQ FT: 13,000
SALES (est): 3.7MM **Privately Held**
WEB: www.gardnrsigns.com
SIC: 3993 Electric signs; neon signs; signs, not made in custom sign painting shops

(G-18302)
GDY INSTALLATIONS INC
302 Arco Dr (43607-2907)
PHONE..................419 467-0036
Gary Young, *President*
Jeff Young, *Manager*
EMP: 30
SQ FT: 8,430
SALES (est): 3.3MM **Privately Held**
WEB: www.gdyinstallations.com
SIC: 3272 Furniture, church: concrete

(G-18303)
GENERAL MILLS INC
1250 W Laskey Rd (43612-2935)
PHONE..................419 269-3100
Ann Bombrys, *Branch Mgr*
EMP: 10
SALES (corp-wide): 15.7B **Publicly Held**
WEB: www.generalmills.com
SIC: 2043 Wheat flakes: prepared as cereal breakfast food; oats, rolled: prepared as cereal breakfast food; corn flakes: prepared as cereal breakfast food; rice: prepared as cereal breakfast food
PA: General Mills, Inc.
1 General Mills Blvd
Minneapolis MN 55426
763 764-7600

(G-18304)
GENOA HEALTHCARE LLC
1832 Adams St (43604-4428)
PHONE..................567 202-8326
Genoa A Qol, *Branch Mgr*
EMP: 3
SALES (corp-wide): 226.2B **Publicly Held**
SIC: 2834 Pharmaceutical preparations
HQ: Genoa Healthcare Llc
707 S Grady Way Ste 700
Renton WA 98057

(G-18305)
GIANT INDUSTRIES INC
900 N Westwood Ave (43607-3261)
PHONE..................419 531-4600
Raymond Simon, *CEO*
Edward Simon, *President*
Wolfgang Drescher, *Admin Sec*
▲ **EMP:** 40
SQ FT: 83,000
SALES (est): 8.6MM **Publicly Held**
WEB: www.giantpumps.com
SIC: 3581 3589 5084 3594 Automatic vending machines; car washing machinery; pumps & pumping equipment; fluid power pumps & motors; pumps & pumping equipment; sanitary paper products
PA: Marathon Petroleum Corporation
539 S Main St
Findlay OH 45840

(G-18306)
GLOBAL CHEMICAL INC
1925 Nebraska Ave (43607-3830)
PHONE..................419 242-1004
EMP: 4
SALES (est): 360K **Privately Held**
SIC: 2899 Mfg Chemical Preparations

(G-18307)
GNRL CHEMICAL L
1661 Campbell St (43607-4322)
PHONE..................419 255-0193
J Poure, *Principal*
EMP: 6
SQ FT: 20,000
SALES (est): 932.3K **Privately Held**
SIC: 2819 Industrial inorganic chemicals

(G-18308)
GOODWILL INDS NW OHIO INC
525 Cherry St (43604-1703)
PHONE..................419 255-0070
Bob Huber, *Branch Mgr*
EMP: 25
SALES (corp-wide): 19.2MM **Privately Held**
SIC: 3999 Barber & beauty shop equipment
PA: Goodwill Industries Of Northwest Ohio, Inc.
1120 Madison Ave
Toledo OH 43604
419 255-0070

(G-18309)
GOTTFRIED MEDICAL INC
2920 Centennial Rd (43617-1833)
P.O. Box 8966 (43623-0966)
PHONE..................419 474-2973
Brent Gottfried, *President*
Pauline Gottfried, *Vice Pres*
Lisa King, *Treasurer*
EMP: 23
SALES (est): 2.9MM **Privately Held**
WEB: www.gottfriedmedical.com
SIC: 3842 Orthopedic appliances

(G-18310)
GRAHAM PACKG PLASTIC PDTS INC (DH)
1 Seagate Ste 10 (43604-1563)
PHONE..................717 849-8500
Joseph H Lemieux, *Ch of Bd*
EMP: 25
SALES (est): 272.7MM
SALES (corp-wide): 11.6B **Publicly Held**
SIC: 3089 Plastic containers, except foam
HQ: Rexam Limited
4 Millbank
London SW1P
158 240-8999

(G-18311)
GREAT AMERICAN COOKIE COMPANY
5001 Monroe St Ste Fc13 (43623-7017)
PHONE..................419 474-9417
Jack Scott, *Owner*
EMP: 12
SQ FT: 400
SALES (est): 264.2K **Privately Held**
SIC: 5461 2052 Cookies; cookies

(G-18312)
GREENWOOD PRINTING & GRAPHICS
3615 Stickney Ave (43608-1307)
PHONE..................419 727-3275
David Stickley, *Owner*
EMP: 12
SQ FT: 5,700
SALES: 800K **Privately Held**
SIC: 2752 Commercial printing, offset

(G-18313)
GREGGS SPECIALTY SERVICES
Also Called: Ch Enterprises
306 Dura Ave (43612-2618)
PHONE..................419 478-0803
Matthew Haocomb, *President*
EMP: 10
SQ FT: 20,000
SALES (est): 860K **Privately Held**
SIC: 7692 7539 7629 Welding repair; trailer repair; electrical repair shops

(G-18314)
GT TECHNOLOGIES INC
Also Called: Gt Technlgies Tledo Operations
99 N Fearing Blvd (43607-3602)
PHONE..................419 324-7300
Daniel Brinker, *President*
EMP: 100
SALES (corp-wide): 101MM **Privately Held**
SIC: 3714 3469 3465 Motor vehicle engines & parts; metal stampings; automotive stampings
PA: Gt Technologies, Inc.
5859 E Executive Dr
Westland MI 48185
734 467-8371

(G-18315)
H P STREICHER INC (PA)
2955 Gradwohl Rd (43617-1507)
PHONE..................419 841-4715
Kurt Smith, *President*
John L Streicher, *Shareholder*
EMP: 2 **EST:** 1860
SQ FT: 3,500
SALES: 5MM **Privately Held**
WEB: www.atlaspaving.com
SIC: 1771 2951 Blacktop (asphalt) work; concrete, asphaltic (not from refineries)

(G-18316)
H&M MACHINE & TOOL LLC
3823 Seiss Ave (43612-1316)
PHONE..................419 776-9220
Mike Whatley, *Vice Pres*
John Miller, *Mng Member*
Dan Harvey,
EMP: 22
SALES (est): 3.1MM **Privately Held**
SIC: 3544 3543 Industrial molds; industrial patterns

(G-18317)
HA-INTERNATIONAL LLC
4243 South Ave (43615-6233)
PHONE..................419 537-0096
Michael Hohol, *Branch Mgr*
EMP: 30
SQ FT: 62,680 **Privately Held**
SIC: 2869 3582 2992 Industrial organic chemicals; commercial laundry equipment; lubricating oils & greases
HQ: Ha-International, Llc
630 Oakmont Ln
Westmont IL 60559
630 575-5700

(G-18318)
HAFNER HARDWOOD CONNECTION LLC
Also Called: Hardwood Connection, The
2845 111th St (43611-2826)
PHONE..................419 726-4828
Todd Hafner, *Mng Member*
EMP: 6
SQ FT: 5,600
SALES: 300K **Privately Held**
WEB: www.woodworkingtools.com
SIC: 3999 7389 Plaques, picture, laminated; engraving service

(G-18319)
HALE PERFORMANCE COATINGS INC
2282 Albion St (43606-4523)
PHONE..................419 244-6451
Frederick M Deye, *President*
R A Jefferies Jr, *Principal*
G C Scharfy, *Principal*
J C Straub, *Principal*
Mike Reese, *Business Mgr*
EMP: 42 **EST:** 1966
SQ FT: 14,700
SALES: 7MM **Privately Held**
WEB: www.halechrome.com
SIC: 3471 3544 Chromium plating of metals or formed products; special dies, tools, jigs & fixtures

(G-18320)
HAMMILL MANUFACTURING CO
Also Called: Co-Op Tool
1517 Coining Dr (43612-2930)
PHONE..................419 724-5702
Dean Johnson, *Plant Mgr*
EMP: 38
SALES (corp-wide): 27.8MM **Privately Held**
WEB: www.hammillmfg.com
SIC: 3841 Surgical & medical instruments
PA: Hammill Manufacturing Co.
360 Tomahawk Dr
Maumee OH 43537
419 476-0789

(G-18321)
HANGER PRSTHETCS & ORTHO INC
3435 N Hlland Sylvania Rd (43615)
PHONE..................419 841-9852
Thomas Sandy, *Manager*
Tom Sandy, *Manager*
EMP: 13
SALES (corp-wide): 1B **Publicly Held**
SIC: 3842 5999 Prosthetic appliances; orthopedic & prosthesis applications

Toledo - Lucas County (G-18322)

HQ: Hanger Prosthetics & Orthotics, Inc.
10910 Domain Dr Ste 300
Austin TX 78758
512 777-3800

(G-18322)
HANSEN-MUELLER CO
1800 N Water St (43611)
P.O. Box 50497 (43605-0497)
PHONE.....................419 729-5535
Mike Burget, *Manager*
EMP: 26
SALES (corp-wide): 85.6MM **Privately Held**
WEB: www.hmgrain.com
SIC: 5153 2041 Grains; flour & other grain mill products
PA: Hansen-Mueller Co.
12231 Emmet St Ste 1
Omaha NE 68164
402 491-3385

(G-18323)
HAPPY TIME ADVENTURES
3434 Secor Rd (43606-1501)
PHONE.....................419 407-6409
Keith Thompson,
EMP: 4
SALES (est): 184.3K **Privately Held**
SIC: 3599 Amusement park equipment

(G-18324)
HAYES BROS ORNAMENTAL IR WORKS
1830 N Reynolds Rd (43615-3530)
PHONE.....................419 531-1491
Gary M Hayes, *President*
Patrick Hayes, *Vice Pres*
Douglas C Hayes, *Treasurer*
Gregory M Hayes, *Admin Sec*
EMP: 10 EST: 1946
SQ FT: 10,000
SALES (est): 1.4MM **Privately Held**
WEB: www.hayesiron.com
SIC: 3446 Railings, prefabricated metal; guards, made from pipe; gates, ornamental metal

(G-18325)
HEARN PLATING CO LTD
3184 Bellevue Rd (43606-1801)
PHONE.....................419 473-9773
John D Drumheller, *Mng Member*
Wallace Friedel, *Manager*
Marcia M Drumheller, *Admin Sec*
EMP: 12 EST: 1902
SQ FT: 6,400
SALES (est): 2MM **Privately Held**
WEB: www.hearnplating.com
SIC: 3471 3599 Electroplating of metals or formed products; amusement park equipment

(G-18326)
HEATHERDOWNS LICENSE BUREAU
4460 Heatherdowns Blvd (43614-3113)
PHONE.....................419 381-1109
Pamela Rupp, *Principal*
EMP: 5
SALES (est): 393.2K **Privately Held**
SIC: 3469 Automobile license tags, stamped metal

(G-18327)
HECKS DIRECT MAIL & PRTG SVC (PA)
417 Main St (43605-2057)
PHONE.....................419 697-3505
Edward Heck, *CEO*
▲ EMP: 40 EST: 1943
SQ FT: 30,000
SALES (est): 4.4MM **Privately Held**
WEB: www.hecksprinting.com
SIC: 7331 2752 2791 2789 Addressing service; commercial printing, offset; typesetting; bookbinding & related work; commercial printing

(G-18328)
HECKS DIRECT MAIL & PRTG SVC
Also Called: Heck's Diamond Printing
202 W Florence Ave (43605-3304)
P.O. Box 8266 (43605-0266)
PHONE.....................419 661-6028
Cosino Trina, *Vice Pres*
EMP: 25
SALES (corp-wide): 4.4MM **Privately Held**
WEB: www.hecksprinting.com
SIC: 2752 7331 5192 Offset & photolithographic printing; direct mail advertising services; books, periodicals & newspapers
PA: Heck's Direct Mail & Printing Service Inc
417 Main St
Toledo OH 43605
419 697-3505

(G-18329)
HEDGES SELECTIVE TOOL & PROD
Also Called: Select Tool & Production
702 W Laskey Rd (43612-3209)
PHONE.....................419 478-8670
Jeff Lachatelle, *President*
Kathy Lachatelle, *Vice Pres*
EMP: 12
SQ FT: 15,048
SALES (est): 1.3MM **Privately Held**
SIC: 3544 Special dies & tools

(G-18330)
HEIDTMAN STEEL PRODUCTS INC (HQ)
2401 Front St (43605-1199)
PHONE.....................419 691-4646
John C Bates, *CEO*
Tim Berra, *President*
F Wm Heidtman, *Principal*
Margery Heidtman, *Principal*
Mark Ridenour, *CFO*
▲ EMP: 45 EST: 1962
SQ FT: 15,000
SALES (est): 287.5MM
SALES (corp-wide): 296.3MM **Privately Held**
WEB: www.heidtman.com
SIC: 3316 3312 Strip steel, cold-rolled: from purchased hot-rolled; sheet or strip, steel, hot-rolled
PA: Centaur, Inc.
2401 Front St
Toledo OH 43605
419 469-8000

(G-18331)
HENLY CORPORATION
520 W Laskey Rd (43612-3207)
PHONE.....................419 476-0851
Steven Henly, *President*
Audrey Henly, *Vice Pres*
Mark Henly, *Admin Sec*
EMP: 3 EST: 1921
SQ FT: 6,500
SALES: 150K **Privately Held**
SIC: 2499 Woodenware, kitchen & household

(G-18332)
HOLLAND ENGRAVING COMPANY
Also Called: Holland Engineering Co
7340 Dorr St (43615-4112)
PHONE.....................419 865-2765
Martin Hartkopf, *President*
EMP: 12 EST: 1939
SQ FT: 15,600
SALES (est): 1.7MM **Privately Held**
WEB: www.holland-eng.com
SIC: 3544 Special dies & tools

(G-18333)
HOMETOWN FOOD COMPANY
1250 W Laskey Rd (43612-2909)
P.O. Box 357 (43697-0357)
PHONE.....................419 470-7914
Wayne Clive, *Branch Mgr*
Lance Allen, *Senior Mgr*
EMP: 4
SALES (corp-wide): 440MM **Privately Held**
WEB: www.smuckers.com
SIC: 2045 2099 Prepared flour mixes & doughs; food preparations
PA: Hometown Food Company
500 W Madison St
Chicago IL 60661
312 500-7710

(G-18334)
HOMEWOOD PRESS INC
400 E State Line Rd (43612-4779)
PHONE.....................419 478-0695
Scott Dubuc, *President*
Mark Dubuc, *Vice Pres*
Dan Curson, *Marketing Staff*
Kyrsten Dubuc, *Marketing Staff*
Linda Rava, *Marketing Staff*
EMP: 30 EST: 1922
SQ FT: 11,000
SALES (est): 7.3MM **Privately Held**
WEB: www.homewoodpress.com
SIC: 2752 2791 2789 2759 Commercial printing, offset; typesetting; bookbinding & related work; commercial printing

(G-18335)
HOOVER & WELLS INC
Also Called: REZ STONE
2011 Seaman St (43605-1908)
PHONE.....................419 691-9220
Margaret Hoover, *Ch of Bd*
Barbara Corsini, *President*
John Corsini, *Vice Pres*
James Mc Collum, *Vice Pres*
Nichole Simon, *Vice Pres*
EMP: 120
SQ FT: 23,448
SALES: 37.3MM **Privately Held**
WEB: www.hooverwells.com
SIC: 1752 2891 2851 Wood floor installation & refinishing; adhesives & sealants; paints & allied products

(G-18336)
HORWITZ & PINTIS CO
1604 Tracy St (43605-3426)
P.O. Box 60257, Rossford (43460-0257)
PHONE.....................419 666-2220
Steve Horwitz, *President*
Phyllis Horwitz, *Corp Secy*
EMP: 15
SQ FT: 20,000
SALES (est): 3.7MM **Privately Held**
SIC: 5085 3412 2655 Drums, new or reconditioned; metal barrels, drums & pails; fiber cans, drums & similar products

(G-18337)
HOT MAMA FOODS INC
5839 Secor Rd (43623-1421)
PHONE.....................419 474-3402
Mike Barone, *President*
◆ EMP: 15
SQ FT: 5,118
SALES (est): 2.1MM **Privately Held**
SIC: 2051 Bread, cake & related products

(G-18338)
I T W AUTOMOTIVE FINISHING
320 Phillips Ave (43612-1467)
PHONE.....................419 470-2000
Roger Cedoz, *Principal*
EMP: 4
SALES (est): 310K **Privately Held**
SIC: 3559 Automotive maintenance equipment

(G-18339)
IBIDLTD-BLUE GREEN ENERGY
1456 N Summit St (43604)
PHONE.....................909 547-5160
Garry Inwood, *Branch Mgr*
EMP: 10
SALES (corp-wide): 1.6MM **Privately Held**
SIC: 2869 Industrial organic chemicals
PA: IbidItd-Blue Green Energy
6659 Schaefer Rd Ste 110
Dearborn MI 48126
909 547-5160

(G-18340)
IGNIO SYSTEMS LLC
444 W Laskey Rd Ste V (43612-3460)
PHONE.....................419 708-0503
Jon Snyder,
Jim Demarest,
EMP: 14 EST: 2013
SALES (est): 2.6MM **Privately Held**
SIC: 3821 3625 3822 5063 Ovens, laboratory; motor controls, electric; temperature controls, automatic; gas burner, automatic controls; boxes & fittings, electrical

(G-18341)
IMPAC HI-PERFORMANCE MACHINING
5515 Enterprise Blvd (43612-3814)
PHONE.....................419 726-7100
Gerald R Nastachowski, *Owner*
Chris Nastachowski, *Manager*
EMP: 6 EST: 1971
SQ FT: 6,000
SALES (est): 300K **Privately Held**
SIC: 3599 Machine shop, jobbing & repair

(G-18342)
IMPACT PRODUCTS LLC (DH)
2840 Centennial Rd (43617-1898)
PHONE.....................419 841-2891
Terry Neal, *CEO*
Jeff Beery, *CFO*
▲ EMP: 155 EST: 2001
SQ FT: 155,000
SALES: 35MM
SALES (corp-wide): 18.7B **Publicly Held**
WEB: www.impact-products.com
SIC: 5084 5087 2392 3089 Safety equipment; janitors' supplies; mops, floor & dust; buckets, plastic; tissue dispensers, plastic
HQ: S. P. Richards Company
6300 Highlands Pkwy Se
Smyrna GA 30082
770 434-4571

(G-18343)
INCEPTOR INC
1301 Progress Ave (43612-3835)
PHONE.....................419 726-8804
Edward F Pavuk, *President*
EMP: 5
SQ FT: 20,000
SALES (est): 750K **Privately Held**
WEB: www.inceptor.net
SIC: 2842 5169 2865 Cleaning or polishing preparations; sanitation preparations, disinfectants & deodorants; chemicals & allied products; dyes, synthetic organic

(G-18344)
INDEPENDENT POWER CONSULTANTS
6051 Telegraph Rd Ste 19 (43612-4560)
PHONE.....................419 476-8383
David Denner, *President*
Patricia M Denner, *Corp Secy*
Michael W Denner, *Vice Pres*
EMP: 7
SALES: 950K **Privately Held**
SIC: 3469 Machine parts, stamped or pressed metal

(G-18345)
INDICATOR ADVISORY CORPORATION
3061 Shoreland Ave (43611-1251)
PHONE.....................419 726-9000
Robert Kneisley, *President*
EMP: 3
SALES (est): 261.3K **Privately Held**
WEB: www.indicatoradvisory.com
SIC: 2721 2731 Periodicals: publishing only; books: publishing only

(G-18346)
INDUSTRIAL SCREEN PROCESS (PA)
Also Called: Isps
17 17th St (43604-6708)
P.O. Box 593 (43697-0593)
PHONE.....................419 255-4900
Thomas V Cutcher Sr, *President*
Sharon Cutcher, *Corp Secy*
Thomas V Cutcher II, *Vice Pres*

GEOGRAPHIC SECTION
Toledo - Lucas County (G-18372)

Teresa House, *Prgrmr*
EMP: 15
SQ FT: 53,000
SALES (est): 2.2MM **Privately Held**
WEB: www.ispsinc.com
SIC: 2759 7373 Screen printing; computer-aided design (CAD) systems service

(G-18347)
INITIAL DESIGNS INC
Also Called: Seaway Enterprises
2453 Tremainsville Rd # 2 (43613-3438)
PHONE.....................................419 475-3900
Robert W Stauffer, *President*
Carole S Stauffer, *Admin Sec*
EMP: 6
SQ FT: 13,000
SALES (est): 206.7K **Privately Held**
WEB: www.seawayenterprises.com
SIC: 2395 Embroidery & art needlework

(G-18348)
INNOVATIVE CONTROLS CORP
1354 E Broadway St (43605-3667)
PHONE.....................................419 691-6684
Louis M Soltis, *President*
Anson F Schultz, *Vice Pres*
Mark Benton, *Engineer*
Bryan Hanthorn, *Engineer*
Walter King, *Info Tech Mgr*
EMP: 63
SQ FT: 20,000
SALES (est): 14.1MM **Privately Held**
WEB: www.innovativecontrolscorp.com
SIC: 3613 3535 8711 3823 Control panels, electric; conveyors & conveying equipment; engineering services; industrial instrmnts msrmnt display/control process variable; relays & industrial controls; food products machinery

(G-18349)
INSTA PLAK INC (PA)
Also Called: Insta-Plak
5025 Dorr St (43615-3855)
PHONE.....................................419 537-1555
Rexford E Hardin DDS, *CEO*
Stephen R Hardin, *President*
James Byrd, *Vice Pres*
Betty Hardin, *Admin Sec*
EMP: 12
SQ FT: 7,800
SALES (est): 1.5MM **Privately Held**
SIC: 2499 3993 Decorative wood & woodwork; signs, not made in custom sign painting shops

(G-18350)
INTERTEC CORPORATION
3400 Executive Pkwy (43606-1396)
PHONE.....................................419 537-9711
George B Seifried, *President*
Scott A Slater, *Vice Pres*
Darrel G Howard, *Admin Sec*
Darrel Howard, *Admin Sec*
◆ **EMP:** 300 EST: 1978
SQ FT: 1,000
SALES (est): 855.3K **Privately Held**
WEB: www.mspro.com
SIC: 3559 1796 3523 Glass making machinery: blowing, molding, forming, etc.; machinery installation; farm machinery & equipment

(G-18351)
IPM INC
1 Owens Corning Pkwy (43659-1000)
PHONE.....................................419 248-8000
EMP: 3
SALES (est): 72.2K **Publicly Held**
SIC: 3296 2952 3229 3089 Mfg Composite & Building Material Systems
PA: Owens Corning
1 Owens Corning Pkwy
Toledo OH 43659

(G-18352)
IPS TREATMENTS INC
3254 Hill Ave (43607-2911)
PHONE.....................................419 241-5955
Fred Pinto, *President*
Manit Vichitchot, *Vice Pres*
EMP: 9
SQ FT: 16,000
SALES (est): 1.1MM **Privately Held**
WEB: www.ipstreatment.com
SIC: 3471 Cleaning, polishing & finishing

(G-18353)
IRON BEAN INC
2269 Ragan Woods Dr (43614-1014)
PHONE.....................................518 641-9917
Chanell Dedrick,
Fredrick Dedrick,
EMP: 5
SALES (est): 92.7K **Privately Held**
SIC: 5812 2095 5149 1541 Coffee shop; roasted coffee; coffee roasting (except by wholesale grocers); coffee, green or roasted; food products manufacturing or packing plant construction; coffee

(G-18354)
IRONHEAD FABG & CONTG INC
2245 Front St (43605-1231)
PHONE.....................................419 690-0000
Anthony Lamantia, *President*
Kathy Lamantia, *CFO*
Nancy Coci, *Manager*
Nancy Williams, *Admin Asst*
EMP: 65
SQ FT: 33,500
SALES (est): 10MM **Privately Held**
SIC: 3441 Fabricated structural metal

(G-18355)
ISHOS BROS FUEL VENTURES INC
2446 W Alexis Rd (43613-2139)
PHONE.....................................419 913-5718
Mahir Isho, *Principal*
EMP: 6
SALES (est): 726.5K **Privately Held**
SIC: 2869 Fuels

(G-18356)
J & S INDUSTRIAL MCH PDTS INC
123 Oakdale Ave (43605-3322)
PHONE.....................................419 691-1380
Nancy Colyer, *Principal*
Elton E Bowland, *Principal*
George Bowland, *Principal*
John Sehr, *Principal*
Donald R Colyer, *Vice Pres*
EMP: 70 EST: 1946
SQ FT: 32,000
SALES (est): 9.2MM **Privately Held**
WEB: www.jsindustrialmach.com
SIC: 3559 7692 Glass making machinery: blowing, molding, forming, etc.; welding repair

(G-18357)
JENSAR MANUFACTURING LLC
1230 S Expressway Dr (43608-1516)
PHONE.....................................419 727-8320
Christopher Jakab, *VP Mfg*
Luis Villaflor,
Tom Villaflor,
EMP: 4
SALES (est): 1,200
SALES (est): 659.2K **Privately Held**
SIC: 3089 Injection molding of plastics

(G-18358)
JENSEN & SONS INC
4481 Monroe St (43613-4708)
PHONE.....................................419 471-1000
David W Jensen, *President*
James Jensen, *Vice Pres*
EMP: 12 EST: 1953
SALES (est): 1.6MM **Privately Held**
SIC: 3911 Jewelry, precious metal

(G-18359)
JOBSKIN DIV OF TORBOT GROUP
5030 Advantage Dr Ste 101 (43612-3861)
PHONE.....................................419 724-1475
Angie Zablocki, *Manager*
EMP: 25
SALES (est): 2.1MM **Privately Held**
SIC: 3842 Bandages & dressings; gauze, surgical

(G-18360)
KAHUNA BAY SPRAY TAN LLC
Also Called: Artesian Tan
757 Warehouse Rd Ste E-F (43615-6467)
PHONE.....................................419 386-2387
A J Licata-Bernath, *Mng Member*
Christopher Bernast,
Andrea J Licata-Bernath,
EMP: 5
SALES (est): 962.9K **Privately Held**
WEB: www.artesiantan.com
SIC: 2844 7299 Face creams or lotions; tanning salon

(G-18361)
KAPIOS LLC
Also Called: Kapios Health
2865 N Reynolds Rd 220d (43615-2068)
PHONE.....................................567 661-0772
Justin Hammerling, *CEO*
EMP: 6
SALES (est): 135.3K **Privately Held**
SIC: 7372 8099 Business oriented computer software; health & allied services

(G-18362)
KASPER ENTERPRISES INC
Also Called: Harmon Sign Company
7844 W Central Ave (43617-1530)
PHONE.....................................419 841-6656
Daniel C Kasper, *Ch of Bd*
Jeff Kasper, *President*
John E Wagoner, *Principal*
Sue Sprouse, *Human Res Dir*
EMP: 7
SQ FT: 55,430
SALES (est): 2MM
SALES (corp-wide): 45MM **Privately Held**
WEB: www.planetharmon.com
SIC: 3993 Neon signs; signs, not made in custom sign painting shops
PA: Allen Industries, Inc.
6434 Burnt Poplar Rd
Greensboro NC 27409
336 668-2791

(G-18363)
KAY TOLEDO TAG INC
6050 Benore Rd (43612-3906)
P.O. Box 5038 (43611-0038)
PHONE.....................................419 729-5479
Dan Kay, *President*
EMP: 96 EST: 1973
SQ FT: 87,000
SALES (est): 16.2MM
SALES (corp-wide): 370.1MM **Publicly Held**
WEB: www.kaytag.com
SIC: 2752 2679 2759 2671 Commercial printing, offset; tags & labels, paper; commercial printing; packaging paper & plastics film, coated & laminated
PA: Ennis, Inc.
2441 Presidential Pkwy
Midlothian TX 76065
972 775-9801

(G-18364)
KENCRAFT CO INC
821 N Westwood Ave (43607-3561)
PHONE.....................................419 536-0333
Ken Spitulski, *President*
Virginia Spitulski, *Corp Secy*
Ginny Spitulski, *Treasurer*
Tracy Spitulski, *Manager*
EMP: 4
SQ FT: 8,000
SALES (est): 575.1K **Privately Held**
WEB: www.kencraftcompany.com
SIC: 5961 5211 2511 Mail order house; millwork & lumber; wood household furniture

(G-18365)
KERN MACHINE TOOL INC
367 E State Line Rd (43612-4709)
P.O. Box 5815 (43613-0815)
PHONE.....................................419 470-1206
Frank Kern, *President*
EMP: 4
SQ FT: 10,000
SALES (est): 399.3K **Privately Held**
WEB: www.kernmachine.com
SIC: 3599 Machine shop, jobbing & repair

(G-18366)
KEURIG DR PEPPER INC
224 N Byrne Rd (43607-2605)
PHONE.....................................419 535-0777
Gladys Cothern, *Branch Mgr*
EMP: 4 **Publicly Held**
SIC: 2086 Bottled & canned soft drinks
PA: Keurig Dr Pepper Inc.
5301 Legacy Dr
Plano TX 01803

(G-18367)
KEYSTONE PRESS INC
1801 Broadway St (43609-3290)
P.O. Box 9183 (43697-9183)
PHONE.....................................419 243-7326
Paul A Schultz, *CEO*
David P Schultz, *President*
Andrew C Schultz, *Vice Pres*
Elizabeth Schultz, *Treasurer*
EMP: 8 EST: 1921
SQ FT: 9,000
SALES (est): 1.4MM **Privately Held**
SIC: 2752 2759 2796 2791 Commercial printing, offset; letterpress printing; platemaking services; typesetting; bookbinding & related work

(G-18368)
KITCHEN DESIGNS PLUS INC
2725 N Reynolds Rd (43615-2031)
PHONE.....................................419 536-6605
Pat McKimmy, *President*
EMP: 20
SQ FT: 6,000
SALES (est): 6.4MM **Privately Held**
SIC: 5031 2434 Kitchen cabinets; wood kitchen cabinets

(G-18369)
KNIGHT INDUSTRIES CORP
5949 Telegraph Rd (43612-4548)
PHONE.....................................419 478-8550
Carrie Ebeid, *Corp Secy*
Kevin Ebeid, *Vice Pres*
EMP: 38
SQ FT: 104,000
SALES (est): 4.1MM **Privately Held**
WEB: www.knightindcorp.com
SIC: 3211 Picture glass; window glass, clear & colored

(G-18370)
KUHLMAN CORPORATION
444 Kuhlman Dr (43609-2629)
PHONE.....................................419 321-1670
Dwayne Palmer, *Branch Mgr*
EMP: 50
SALES (est): 6.9MM
SALES (corp-wide): 50.1MM **Privately Held**
WEB: www.kuhlman-corp.com
SIC: 3273 Ready-mixed concrete
PA: Kuhlman Corporation
1845 Indian Wood Cir
Maumee OH 43537
419 897-6000

(G-18371)
KUHLMAN ENGINEERING CO
840 Champlain St (43604-3643)
PHONE.....................................419 243-2196
Phil Kolling, *President*
Norman Kuhlman, *Vice Pres*
EMP: 10 EST: 1916
SQ FT: 7,500
SALES (est): 1.2MM **Privately Held**
WEB: www.kuhlmanengineering.net
SIC: 3444 Sheet metal specialties, not stamped

(G-18372)
KUKA TOLEDO PRODUCTION
3770 Stickney Ave (43608-1310)
PHONE.....................................419 727-5500
Lawrence A Drake, *CEO*
Cheryl Weller, *Engineer*
Paul Ambros, *CFO*
Brad Crichton, *Manager*
Larry Drake,
EMP: 247
SALES (est): 34MM
SALES (corp-wide): 36.3B **Privately Held**
WEB: www.kukausa.com
SIC: 3713 Truck & bus bodies

Toledo - Lucas County (G-18373)   GEOGRAPHIC SECTION

HQ: Kuka Systems Gmbh
   Blucherstr. 144
   Augsburg 86165
   821 797-0

(G-18373)
KYLE PUBLICATIONS INC
2611 Montebello Rd (43607-1366)
P.O. Box 6469 (43612-0469)
PHONE..................................419 754-4234
Erik R Kyle, *President*
EMP: 6 **EST:** 2001
SALES (est): 491.1K **Privately Held**
SIC: 2721 Magazines: publishing only, not printed on site

(G-18374)
LA PERLA INC (PA)
Also Called: Tortilla Factory
2742 Hill Ave (43607-2926)
PHONE..................................419 534-2074
Santiago Martinez, *President*
EMP: 10
SQ FT: 8,000
SALES (est): 991K **Privately Held**
WEB: www.laperla.com
SIC: 2099 5141 Tortillas, fresh or refrigerated; groceries, general line

(G-18375)
LAFARGE NORTH AMERICA INC
Also Called: Lafargeholcim
840 Water St (43604-1832)
PHONE..................................419 241-5256
Chris Peatty, *Manager*
Chris Peatee, *Manager*
EMP: 3
SQ FT: 13,560
SALES (corp-wide): 26.4B **Privately Held**
WEB: www.lafargenorthamerica.com
SIC: 3241 Cement, hydraulic
HQ: Lafarge North America Inc.
   8700 W Bryn Mawr Ave
   Chicago IL 60631
   773 372-1000

(G-18376)
LED LIGHTING CENTER INC (PA)
Also Called: Optimal Led
6120 N Detroit Ave # 1020 (43612-4810)
PHONE..................................714 271-2633
Steven James, *CEO*
▲ **EMP:** 11
SALES (est): 3.4MM **Privately Held**
SIC: 3646 3645 Commercial indusl & institutional electric lighting fixtures; residential lighting fixtures

(G-18377)
LED LIGHTING CENTER LLC (HQ)
Also Called: Optimalled
6120 N Detroit Ave (43612-4810)
PHONE..................................888 988-6533
Steven James,
Daniel J Lavalley,
EMP: 11
SALES (est): 1.9MM
SALES (corp-wide): 3.4MM **Privately Held**
SIC: 3646 3645 Commercial indusl & institutional electric lighting fixtures; residential lighting fixtures
PA: Led Lighting Center Inc.
   6120 N Detroit Ave # 1020
   Toledo OH 43612
   714 271-2633

(G-18378)
LED LIGHTING CENTER LLC
6120 N Detroit Ave (43612-4810)
PHONE..................................888 988-6533
EMP: 5
SALES (corp-wide): 3.4MM **Privately Held**
SIC: 3648 Lighting equipment
HQ: Led Lighting Center Llc
   6120 N Detroit Ave
   Toledo OH 43612
   888 988-6533

(G-18379)
LEE WILLIAMS MEATS INC (PA)
3002 131st St (43611-2329)
PHONE..................................419 729-3893
Barry L Williams, *President*

Richard W Boldt, *Vice Pres*
Mary Jo Cramer, *Treasurer*
Margaret Williams, *Admin Sec*
EMP: 25 **EST:** 1955
SQ FT: 3,096
SALES (est): 4.2MM **Privately Held**
WEB: www.houseofmeats.com
SIC: 5421 2013 Meat markets, including freezer provisioners; sausages & other prepared meats

(G-18380)
LEEPER PRINTING CO INC
710 S Saint Clair St (43609-2432)
P.O. Box 526 (43697-0526)
PHONE..................................419 243-2604
Susan Brooman, *Vice Pres*
Jeffrey Cunningham, *Admin Sec*
EMP: 3
SQ FT: 3,200
SALES (est): 300K **Privately Held**
SIC: 2759 Commercial printing

(G-18381)
LEMSCO INC
Also Called: Lemsco-Girkins
2056 Canton Ave (43620-1945)
PHONE..................................419 242-4005
Richard J Baldwin, *President*
Richard Baldwin, *President*
Barbara Baldwin, *Corp Secy*
EMP: 8
SQ FT: 11,000
SALES (est): 1.4MM **Privately Held**
SIC: 7694 5999 Electric motor repair; motors, electric

(G-18382)
LIBBEY GLASS INC (HQ)
300 Madison Ave Fl 4 (43604-2634)
P.O. Box 10060 (43699-0060)
PHONE..................................419 325-2100
Richard Reynolds, *Exec VP*
L Frederick Ashton, *Vice Pres*
Daniel P Ibele, *Vice Pres*
Susan A Kovach, *Vice Pres*
Mike Rounds, *Prdtn Mgr*
◆ **EMP:** 200
SALES (est): 775.3MM **Publicly Held**
WEB: www.libbeyglass.com
SIC: 3229 3231 Tableware, glass or glass ceramic; products of purchased glass

(G-18383)
LIBBEY GLASS INC
940 Ash St (43611-3846)
PHONE..................................419 729-7272
Steve Felix, *Plant Mgr*
Michael Kirchner, *Safety Mgr*
John Shaffer, *Technical Staff*
Marvin James, *Maintence Staff*
EMP: 1200 **Publicly Held**
WEB: www.libbeyglass.com
SIC: 3229 3421 3262 Tableware, glass or glass ceramic; cutlery; vitreous china table & kitchenware
HQ: Libbey Glass Inc.
   300 Madison Ave Fl 4
   Toledo OH 43604
   419 325-2100

(G-18384)
LIBBEY INC
Also Called: Libbey Glass Factory Outlet
205 S Erie St (43604-8607)
PHONE..................................419 244-5697
Tom Lower, *Manager*
EMP: 14 **Publicly Held**
WEB: www.libby.com
SIC: 3851 Eyeglasses, lenses & frames
PA: Libbey Inc.
   300 Madison Ave
   Toledo OH 43604

(G-18385)
LIBBEY INC (PA)
300 Madison Ave (43604-1561)
P.O. Box 10060 (43699-0060)
PHONE..................................419 325-2100
William A Foley, *Ch of Bd*
Pat Gans, *Area Mgr*
Brenda Bennett, *Vice Pres*
Brynn Fleig, *Vice Pres*
Terry Hartman, *Vice Pres*
▼ **EMP:** 200

SALES: 801MM **Publicly Held**
WEB: www.libby.com
SIC: 3229 3262 Glass furnishings & accessories; tableware, glass or glass ceramic; bowls, glass; ashtrays, glass; tableware, vitreous china

(G-18386)
LITHIUM INNOVATIONS CO LLC
3171 N Repub Blvd Ste 101 (43615)
PHONE..................................419 843-6051
Ford B Cauffiel, *Principal*
◆ **EMP:** 6
SALES (est): 842.1K **Privately Held**
SIC: 2819 Lithium compounds, inorganic

(G-18387)
LOUISE SWEET LLC
3827 Beechway Blvd (43614-4407)
PHONE..................................419 460-5505
Randa Shallal,
EMP: 3
SALES (est): 220.1K **Privately Held**
SIC: 2099 Sauces: gravy, dressing & dip mixes

(G-18388)
LRBG CHEMICALS USA INC
2112 Sylvan Ave (43606-4767)
PHONE..................................419 244-5856
James Bennett, *Vice Pres*
EMP: 3
SQ FT: 70,000
SALES (est): 107.6K **Privately Held**
SIC: 2821 Plastics materials & resins

(G-18389)
LUCAS COUNTY ASPHALT INC
Also Called: Buckeye Asphalt Paving Co
7540 Hollow Creek Dr (43617-1652)
P.O. Box 353094 (43635-3094)
PHONE..................................419 476-0705
EMP: 25
SQ FT: 4,800
SALES (est): 1.7MM **Privately Held**
SIC: 1771 2951 Asphalt Paving Contractor & Mfg Asphalt Paving Mixtures

(G-18390)
LUCINTECH INC
1510 N Westwood Ave (43606-8202)
PHONE..................................419 265-2641
Alvin Compaan, *President*
David Waterman, *Admin Sec*
EMP: 4
SALES (est): 748.4K **Privately Held**
SIC: 3674 Semiconductors & related devices

(G-18391)
M & B MACHINE INC
4801 Bennett Rd (43612-2531)
PHONE..................................419 476-8836
Patrick Copeland, *President*
EMP: 12
SQ FT: 5,000
SALES (est): 1.5MM **Privately Held**
SIC: 3599 Machine shop, jobbing & repair

(G-18392)
M RUSSELL & ASSOCIATES INC
3250 Monroe St (43606-4550)
PHONE..................................419 478-8795
Melvyn R Russell, *President*
Kim Sherburne, *Treasurer*
Ann M Russell, *Admin Sec*
EMP: 5
SQ FT: 7,000
SALES (est): 574.8K **Privately Held**
SIC: 2796 Plates & cylinders for rotogravure printing

(G-18393)
M&L PLATING WORKS LLC (PA)
425 Jefferson Ave Ste 520 (43604-1073)
PHONE..................................419 255-7701
Glen Matts, *Partner*
Sam Leeviroj, *Partner*
EMP: 3
SALES (est): 570.3K **Privately Held**
SIC: 3471 Plating of metals or formed products

(G-18394)
MAGIC WOK INC (PA)
Also Called: Magic Wok Enterprises
3352 W Laskey Rd (43623-4030)
PHONE..................................419 531-1818
Sutas Pipatjarasgit, *President*
Nucharee Pipatjarasgit, *Admin Sec*
EMP: 7
SQ FT: 580
SALES (est): 1MM **Privately Held**
WEB: www.magicwok.com
SIC: 5812 2032 Chinese restaurant; ethnic foods: canned, jarred, etc.

(G-18395)
MAGNA MODULAR SYSTEMS LLC (DH)
Also Called: Magna Modular Systems, Inc.
1800 Nathan Dr (43611-1091)
PHONE..................................419 324-3387
Grahhame Burrow, *CEO*
Shawn Bentley, *General Mgr*
Keith McMahon, *General Mgr*
Jon Bruning, *Project Mgr*
Jason Alston, *Engineer*
▲ **EMP:** 70
SQ FT: 140,000
SALES (est): 132.8MM
SALES (corp-wide): 38.9B **Privately Held**
SIC: 3714 Motor vehicle body components & frame
HQ: Magna Exteriors Of America, Inc.
   750 Tower Dr
   Troy MI 48098
   248 631-1100

(G-18396)
MAGNETIC PACKAGING LLC
946 Kane St Ste C (43612-1372)
PHONE..................................419 720-4366
Robert Napierala II,
EMP: 2
SQ FT: 62,000
SALES: 2MM **Privately Held**
SIC: 5199 7389 3053 Packaging materials; packaging & labeling services; labeling bottles, cans, cartons, etc.; packing, metallic

(G-18397)
MAGNETNOTES LTD
946 Kane St Ste A (43612-1372)
PHONE..................................419 593-0060
Randall A Boudouris, *CEO*
Tom Stiers, *President*
EMP: 5
SALES (est): 732.5K **Privately Held**
SIC: 3695 Magnetic tape

(G-18398)
MALLORY PATTERN WORKS INC
5340 Enterprise Blvd (43612-3811)
PHONE..................................419 726-8001
Al Antoine, *President*
Janice Mallory, *Treasurer*
Shirley Peschel, *Admin Sec*
EMP: 6 **EST:** 1960
SQ FT: 6,000
SALES (est): 937.9K **Privately Held**
SIC: 3544 3469 Industrial molds; patterns on metal

(G-18399)
MARKEYS AUDIO/VISUAL INC
24 S Saint Clair St (43604-8736)
PHONE..................................419 244-8844
Jason Walton, *Manager*
EMP: 4
SALES (corp-wide): 33.4MM **Privately Held**
WEB: www.markeys.com
SIC: 3651 7819 7622 Household audio & video equipment; video tape or disk reproduction; home entertainment repair services
PA: Markey's Audio/Visual, Inc.
   2365 Enterprise Park Pl
   Indianapolis IN 46218
   317 783-1155

(G-18400)
MARTINEZ FOOD PRODUCTS LLC
1220 Belmont Ave (43607-4105)
PHONE..................................419 720-6973

▲ = Import ▼ = Export
◆ = Import/Export

GEOGRAPHIC SECTION
Toledo - Lucas County (G-18427)

Mark Catko,
Lillian Catko,
Richard Iott,
Ron Teague,
EMP: 6
SALES (est): 435.9K **Privately Held**
SIC: 2035 Pickles, sauces & salad dressings

(G-18401)
MATURE LIVING NEWS MAGAZINE
3601 W Alexis Rd Ste 112 (43623-1347)
P.O. Box 212, Lambertville MI (48144-0212)
PHONE.................................419 241-8880
Diana Calmes, *President*
Lisa Jordan, *Treasurer*
Robin Armstrong, *Accountant*
Veronica Smalley, *Admin Sec*
EMP: 4
SALES (est): 190K **Privately Held**
SIC: 2711 Newspapers

(G-18402)
MAUMEE MACHINE & TOOL CORP
2960 South Ave (43609-1328)
PHONE.................................419 385-2501
Bruce M Denman, *President*
John S Buescher, *Vice Pres*
Patrick T Denman, *Vice Pres*
EMP: 20 **EST:** 1966
SALES (est): 3.3MM **Privately Held**
SIC: 3451 5072 Screw machine products; screws

(G-18403)
MAUMEE PATTERN COMPANY
1019 Hazelwood St (43605-3248)
PHONE.................................419 693-4968
H Jeffrey Neuman, *President*
Alice Neuman, *Corp Secy*
Mark Neuman, *Vice Pres*
EMP: 29
SQ FT: 13,000
SALES (est): 3.6MM **Privately Held**
WEB: www.maumeepattern.com
SIC: 3543 3544 Industrial patterns; industrial molds

(G-18404)
MAUMEE VALLEY FABRICATORS INC
Also Called: Escher Division
4801 Bennett Rd (43612-2531)
PHONE.................................419 476-1411
Patrick Copeland, *President*
Robert N Schuler, *Engineer*
Sue Loucks, *Controller*
Pat Copeland, *Executive*
EMP: 25
SQ FT: 54,000
SALES (est): 8.1MM **Privately Held**
WEB: www.maumeevalleyfab.com
SIC: 3441 Fabricated structural metal

(G-18405)
MECCA REBUILDING & WELDING CO
Also Called: G & J
615 Phillips Ave (43612-1330)
PHONE.................................419 476-8133
George Cole, *President*
Robert Vierling, *Manager*
EMP: 5
SQ FT: 3,536
SALES (est): 182.4K **Privately Held**
SIC: 7692 Welding repair

(G-18406)
MEL STEVENS U-CART CONCRETE
Also Called: Stevens, Mel U-Cart & Rental
6151 Telegraph Rd (43612-4576)
PHONE.................................419 478-2600
Mel Stevens, *CEO*
Timothy Stevens, *President*
David Stevens, *Treasurer*
EMP: 4
SQ FT: 4,000
SALES (est): 607K **Privately Held**
SIC: 3273 7353 5261 Ready-Mix Concrete & Rents Heavy Construction Equipment

(G-18407)
MELDRUM MECHANICAL SERVICES
4455 South Ave (43615-6416)
PHONE.................................419 535-3500
Brent R Meldrum Jr, *President*
Brent Meldrum, *General Mgr*
Debi Meldrum, *Info Tech Mgr*
EMP: 10
SALES (est): 2MM **Privately Held**
SIC: 3599 Machine shop, jobbing & repair

(G-18408)
MELNOR GRAPHICS LLC
5225 Telegraph Rd (43612-3570)
PHONE.................................419 476-8808
Gregory Tremonti,
EMP: 19
SALES (est): 6.3MM **Privately Held**
SIC: 2759 Circulars: printing

(G-18409)
METZGERS
150 Arco Dr (43607-2903)
PHONE.................................419 861-8611
Tom Metzger, *CEO*
Joe Metzger, *Founder*
John Luscombe, *Vice Pres*
John McGaharan, *VP Opers*
Todd Beringer, *VP Sls/Mktg*
EMP: 21
SALES (est): 2.7MM **Privately Held**
SIC: 2752 Commercial printing, offset

(G-18410)
MIDTOWN PALLET & RECYCLING
1987 Hawthorne St (43606)
PHONE.................................419 241-1311
Rita Stang, *President*
EMP: 25
SQ FT: 10,000
SALES (est): 4.1MM **Privately Held**
WEB: www.midtownpallet.com
SIC: 2448 Pallets, wood

(G-18411)
MIDWESTERN BAG CO INC
3230 Monroe St (43606-4519)
PHONE.................................419 241-3112
Toney Oneal, *President*
Paulette Lalor, *Vice Pres*
Brian Hoch, *Admin Sec*
EMP: 23
SQ FT: 43,000
SALES (est): 2.5MM **Privately Held**
SIC: 5199 3069 Bags, baskets & cases; bags, rubber or rubberized fabric

(G-18412)
MMP TOLEDO
5847 Secor Rd (43623-1421)
PHONE.................................419 472-0505
Steven Heaney, *President*
Teresa Heaney, *Principal*
EMP: 15
SQ FT: 1,500
SALES (est): 2.2MM **Privately Held**
WEB: www.mmptoledo.com
SIC: 2752 Commercial printing, offset

(G-18413)
MOBIS NORTH AMERICA LLC
Also Called: Ommc
3900 Stickney Ave (43608-1314)
PHONE.................................419 729-6700
Summer Grindle, *Engineer*
Adam Hanson, *Engineer*
Pamela Law, *Engineer*
Hak Park, *CFO*
Dinny Sullivan, *Human Res Mgr*
EMP: 42
SALES (corp-wide): 18.2B **Privately Held**
SIC: 3711 Chassis, motor vehicle
HQ: Mobis North America, Llc
46501 Commerce Dr
Plymouth MI 48170
248 426-5577

(G-18414)
MODERN BUILDERS SUPPLY INC (PA)
Also Called: Polaris Technologies
3500 Phillips Ave (43608-1070)
P.O. Box 80025 (43608-0025)
PHONE.................................419 241-3961
Kevin Leggett, *CEO*
Larry Leggett, *Ch of Bd*
Eric Leggett, *Vice Pres*
Jack Marstellar, *Vice Pres*
Tony Puntel, *Vice Pres*
EMP: 200
SQ FT: 40,000
SALES (est): 347.7MM **Privately Held**
WEB: www.polaristechnologies.com
SIC: 3089 5032 3446 3442 Windows, plastic; doors, folding: plastic or plastic coated fabric; brick, stone & related material; architectural metalwork; metal doors, sash & trim

(G-18415)
MON-SAY CORP
Also Called: Ergocan
2735 Dorr St (43607-3240)
P.O. Box 8487 (43623-0487)
PHONE.................................419 720-0163
Terry Netterfield, *President*
▲ **EMP:** 7
SQ FT: 22,000
SALES (est): 900K **Privately Held**
SIC: 3089 Bowl covers, plastic

(G-18416)
MONDELEZ GLOBAL LLC
Also Called: Kraft Foods
2221 Front St (43605-1231)
P.O. Box 2208 (43603-2208)
PHONE.................................419 691-5200
William Epperson, *Branch Mgr*
EMP: 100 **Publicly Held**
SIC: 2041 Flour & other grain mill products
HQ: Mondelez Global Llc
3 N Pkwy Ste 300
Deerfield IL 60015
847 943-4000

(G-18417)
MOSSING MACHINE AND TOOL
5225 Telegraph Rd (43612-3570)
PHONE.................................419 476-5657
Dave S Mossing, *President*
EMP: 8
SQ FT: 8,000
SALES (est): 1MM **Privately Held**
SIC: 3599 Machine shop, jobbing & repair

(G-18418)
MR&E LTD
3146 W Lincolnshire Blvd (43606-1219)
PHONE.................................419 872-8180
Deane Horne,
▲ **EMP:** 3
SALES (est): 950K **Privately Held**
SIC: 3823 Mfg Process Control Instruments

(G-18419)
MV GROUP INC
303 Morris St (43604-8874)
PHONE.................................419 776-1133
Hernan Vasquez, *President*
EMP: 4
SALES (est): 1MM **Privately Held**
SIC: 3585 Refrigeration & heating equipment

(G-18420)
MY WAY HOME FINDER MAGAZINE
5215 Monroe St Ste 14 (43623-3190)
PHONE.................................419 841-6201
James Moody, *Partner*
EMP: 6
SQ FT: 2,000
SALES (est): 500K **Privately Held**
WEB: www.iselltoledohomes.com
SIC: 2711 Newspapers

(G-18421)
N-VIRO INTERNATIONAL CORP
2254 Centennial Rd (43617-1870)
P.O. Box 8770 (43623-0770)
PHONE.................................419 535-6374
Timothy R Kasmoch, *Ch of Bd*
Robert W Bohmer, *Exec VP*
James K McHugh, *CFO*
EMP: 10
SALES (est): 1.1MM **Privately Held**
SIC: 3589 4959 Water treatment equipment, industrial; sanitary services

(G-18422)
NEW DIE INC
2828 E Manhattan Blvd (43611-1710)
PHONE.................................419 726-7581
Richard A Pack, *President*
Ken Coss, *Vice Pres*
Donald R Cousino, *Vice Pres*
Terry Cousino, *Vice Pres*
James David, *Vice Pres*
EMP: 22
SQ FT: 7,500
SALES (est): 3.4MM **Privately Held**
SIC: 3544 Special dies & tools

(G-18423)
NEWFAX CORPORATION (PA)
333 W Woodruff Ave (43604-5025)
P.O. Box 656 (43697-0656)
PHONE.................................419 241-5157
Albert J Gossman Jr, *President*
Gregory Scheuerman, *Vice Pres*
Darold Forbes, *Manager*
William Scheuerman, *Shareholder*
EMP: 17
SQ FT: 15,000
SALES (est): 1.5MM **Privately Held**
WEB: www.newfaxcorp.com
SIC: 2752 5084 2791 2789 Photo-offset printing; printing trades machinery, equipment & supplies; typesetting; bookbinding & related work

(G-18424)
NEWFAX CORPORATION
Also Called: Mc Graphix Div of Th Newfax
3333 W Wooddrift (43624)
P.O. Box 656 (43697-0656)
PHONE.................................419 893-4557
EMP: 16
SALES (corp-wide): 1.5MM **Privately Held**
SIC: 5084 2752 Wholesales Photoprinting Equipment & Supplies & Reproduction Services
PA: Newfax Corporation
333 W Woodruff Ave
Toledo OH 43604
419 241-5157

(G-18425)
NEXT DAY SIGN
2112 N Reynolds Rd (43615-3514)
PHONE.................................419 537-9595
Dan Mosher, *President*
EMP: 5
SALES (est): 200K **Privately Held**
SIC: 3993 Signs, not made in custom sign painting shops

(G-18426)
NO BURN NORTH AMERICA INC
2930 Centennial Rd (43617-1833)
PHONE.................................419 841-6055
William Kish, *CEO*
Kenneth Rusk, *CFO*
EMP: 15
SQ FT: 9,000
SALES (est): 1.4MM **Privately Held**
WEB: www.noburnna.com
SIC: 2899 Fire retardant chemicals

(G-18427)
NORTH TOLEDO GRAPHICS LLC
Also Called: Nt
5225 Telegraph Rd (43612-3570)
PHONE.................................419 476-8808
David Tremonti, *COO*
Shirleen Kistner, *Human Res Mgr*
Melanie Tremonti,
EMP: 95
SQ FT: 210,000
SALES (est): 20MM **Privately Held**
WEB: www.northtoledographics.com
SIC: 2752 Commercial printing, offset

Toledo - Lucas County (G-18428)

(G-18428)
NORTHCOAST PMM LLC
Also Called: Blink Print & Mail
4725 Southbridge Rd (43623-3123)
PHONE.................................419 540-8667
Thomas J Pruss, *Mng Member*
EMP: 10
SALES (est): 456K **Privately Held**
SIC: 7331 2752 Mailing service; commercial printing, lithographic

(G-18429)
NSG GLASS NORTH AMERICA INC
811 Madison Ave (43604-5684)
PHONE.................................419 247-4800
Richard A Altman, *President*
Gary J Roser, *Admin Sec*
EMP: 150
SQ FT: 4,000
SALES (est): 4.5MM **Privately Held**
SIC: 3211 Flat glass

(G-18430)
NSS ENTERPRISES INC (PA)
Also Called: National Super Service Co
3115 Frenchmens Rd (43607-2918)
PHONE.................................419 531-2121
Mark J Bevington, *President*
Anthony J Colburn, *Principal*
◆ EMP: 180 EST: 1911
SQ FT: 160,000
SALES (est): 38.6MM **Privately Held**
WEB: www.nss.com
SIC: 3589 Floor washing & polishing machines, commercial; vacuum cleaners & sweepers, electric: industrial

(G-18431)
NTA GRAPHICS INC
5225 Telegraph Rd (43612-3547)
PHONE.................................419 476-8808
Gregory Tremonti, *President*
Gail Shaffer, *Principal*
David Tremonti, *Vice Pres*
John Desellem, *Supervisor*
EMP: 142
SQ FT: 163,000
SALES (est): 16.7MM **Privately Held**
SIC: 2752 Commercial printing, offset

(G-18432)
OASIS MEDITERRANEAN CUISINE
1520 W Laskey Rd (43612-2914)
P.O. Box 8881 (43623-0881)
PHONE.................................419 269-1459
Francois Hashem, *President*
◆ EMP: 32
SQ FT: 30,000
SALES: 4MM **Privately Held**
SIC: 2099 2032 Dips, except cheese & sour cream based; dressings, salad: dry mixes; salads, fresh or refrigerated; canned specialties

(G-18433)
OBARS MACHINE AND TOOL COMPANY (PA)
Also Called: Obars Welding & Fabg Div
115 N Westwood Ave 125 (43607-3341)
PHONE.................................419 535-6307
Alvin R Obarski, *Ch of Bd*
Greg Obarski, *President*
Jeffrey R Obarski, *Exec VP*
Mike Webber, *Vice Pres*
Michael Webber, *VP Opers*
EMP: 45 EST: 1946
SQ FT: 30,000
SALES (est): 4MM **Privately Held**
WEB: www.obarsmachine.com
SIC: 3451 3541 3545 Screw machine products; machine tools, metal cutting type; machine tool accessories

(G-18434)
OFF CONTACT INC
Also Called: Off Contact Productions
4756 W Bancroft St (43615-3902)
PHONE.................................419 255-5546
Allen Schall, *President*
Becky Scott, *Controller*
Seth Grossi, *Sales Staff*
Taylor Clark, *Marketing Staff*
John Brewer, *Manager*
▲ EMP: 15
SQ FT: 9,600
SALES: 900K **Privately Held**
WEB: www.offcontact.com
SIC: 2759 5084 Screen printing; industrial machinery & equipment

(G-18435)
OHIO BLENDERS INC (PA)
Also Called: Alfagreen Supreme
2404 N Summit St (43611-3599)
PHONE.................................419 726-2655
Ken Vaupel, *CEO*
Donald Verhoff, *President*
Becky Lumbrezer-Box, *Corp Secy*
Ronald Yarnell, *Vice Pres*
EMP: 11
SQ FT: 6,000
SALES (est): 2.4MM **Privately Held**
SIC: 2048 2047 Prepared feeds; dog & cat food

(G-18436)
OHIO PICKLING & PROCESSING LLC
Also Called: Opp
1149 Campbell St (43607-4467)
PHONE.................................419 241-9601
Thomas Klein, *President*
Rick Vella, *General Mgr*
Mike Balk, *Vice Pres*
Mike Spencer, *Sales Mgr*
▲ EMP: 70
SALES (est): 14.9MM
SALES (corp-wide): 232.6MM **Privately Held**
WEB: www.mnp.com
SIC: 3312 Blast furnaces & steel mills
PA: Mnp Corporation
44225 Utica Rd
Utica MI 48317
586 254-1320

(G-18437)
OHIO SPECIALTY MFG CO
2008 N Hlland Sylvania Rd (43615)
PHONE.................................419 531-5402
Richard Uhl, *President*
Karen S Taylor, *Admin Sec*
▲ EMP: 3
SALES (est): 510K **Privately Held**
SIC: 5085 2448 Boxes, crates, etc.: other than paper; cargo containers, wood & wood with metal

(G-18438)
OHIO TRANSITIONAL MACHINE & TL
3940 Castener St (43612-1402)
PHONE.................................419 476-0820
Marten Whalen, *President*
EMP: 7
SQ FT: 5,000
SALES: 700K **Privately Held**
SIC: 3599 Machine shop, jobbing & repair

(G-18439)
ONLINE MEGA SELLERS CORP (PA)
Also Called: Distinct Advantage Cabinetry
4236 W Alexis Rd (43623-1255)
PHONE.................................888 384-6468
Timothy Baker, *President*
Craig Poupard, *Vice Pres*
EMP: 53
SQ FT: 250,000
SALES: 7.2MM **Privately Held**
SIC: 2434 7371 7373 Wood kitchen cabinets; computer software systems analysis & design, custom; computer software development; systems software development services

(G-18440)
OPC INC
419 N Reynolds Rd (43615-5221)
PHONE.................................419 531-2222
Anne M Cole, *Principal*
EMP: 4
SALES (est): 332.5K **Privately Held**
SIC: 3842 Braces, orthopedic

(G-18441)
ORTHOTIC PROSTHETIC CENTER
Also Called: OPC Inc
419 N Reynolds Rd (43615-5221)
PHONE.................................419 531-2222
Ann Cole, *President*
Jan Posadny, *Office Mgr*
EMP: 5
SALES (est): 460K **Privately Held**
SIC: 3842 Prosthetic appliances; limbs, artificial; orthopedic appliances; braces, orthopedic

(G-18442)
OSTEONOVUS INC
1510 N Westwood Ave # 1080 (43606-8202)
PHONE.................................617 717-8867
Steven Nemes, *Finance*
Sarit Bhaduri, *Admin Sec*
EMP: 5
SALES (est): 527.2K **Privately Held**
SIC: 3842 Grafts, artificial: for surgery

(G-18443)
OVERHEAD INC
Also Called: Overhead Door Company
340 New Towne Square Dr (43612-4606)
PHONE.................................419 476-0300
Michael Huss, *Manager*
EMP: 7
SQ FT: 11,470
SALES (est): 1MM
SALES (corp-wide): 12.4MM **Privately Held**
WEB: www.overheadinc.com
SIC: 3442 5719 5211 Metal doors, sash & trim; fireplace equipment & accessories; garage doors, sale & installation
PA: Overhead Inc.
340 New Towne Square Dr
Toledo OH 43612
419 476-7811

(G-18444)
OWENS CORNING
1 Corning Pkwy (43659-0001)
PHONE.................................740 964-1727
Ireland Erick, *Branch Mgr*
EMP: 130 **Publicly Held**
SIC: 3296 Fiberglass insulation
PA: Owens Corning
1 Owens Corning Pkwy
Toledo OH 43659

(G-18445)
OWENS CORNING
1 Owens Corning Pkwy (43659-0001)
PHONE.................................419 248-8000
Gwen Lybert, *Principal*
EMP: 4
SALES (est): 75.7K **Privately Held**
SIC: 3296 Mineral wool

(G-18446)
OWENS CORNING (PA)
1 Owens Corning Pkwy (43659-0001)
PHONE.................................419 248-8000
Michael H Thaman, *Ch of Bd*
Brian D Chambers, *President*
Julian Francis, *President*
Marcio Sandri, *President*
Gunner Smith, *President*
◆ EMP: 1000
SQ FT: 400,000
SALES: 7B **Publicly Held**
SIC: 3296 2952 3229 3089 Fiberglass insulation; insulation; rock wool, slag & silica minerals; acoustical board & tile, mineral wool; roofing mats, mineral wool; asphalt felts & coatings; glass fibers, textile; yarn, fiberglass; windows, plastic

(G-18447)
OWENS CORNING HT INC
Owens Corning World (43659-0001)
PHONE.................................419 248-8000
EMP: 3
SALES (est): 75.7K **Publicly Held**
SIC: 3229 Glass fibers, textile
HQ: Owens Corning Sales, Llc
1 Owens Corning Pkwy
Toledo OH 43659
419 248-8000

(G-18448)
OWENS CORNING SALES LLC (HQ)
1 Owens Corning Pkwy (43659-0001)
PHONE.................................419 248-8000
Michael H Thaman, *Ch of Bd*
Rhonda L Brooks, *President*
Carl B Hedlund, *President*
George E Kiemle, *President*
William E Lebaron, *President*
◆ EMP: 1000 EST: 2006
SQ FT: 400,000
SALES (est): 3B **Publicly Held**
WEB: www.owenscorning.com
SIC: 3296 2952 3229 3089 Fiberglass insulation; insulation; rock wool, slag & silica minerals; acoustical board & tile, mineral wool; roofing mats, mineral wool; asphalt felts & coatings; glass fibers, textile; yarn, fiberglass; windows, plastic; roofing, siding & sheet metal work

(G-18449)
OWENS CRNING CMPOSITE MTLS LLC
1 Owens Corning Pkwy (43659-1000)
PHONE.................................419 248-8000
EMP: 25
SALES (est): 2MM **Privately Held**
SIC: 3296 Mfg Mineral Wool

(G-18450)
OWENS-CORNING CAPITAL LLC
1 Owens Corning Pkwy (43659-0001)
PHONE.................................419 248-8000
David T Brown, *CEO*
EMP: 10
SALES (est): 639.9K **Publicly Held**
SIC: 3296 Fiberglass insulation
HQ: Owens Corning Sales, Llc
1 Owens Corning Pkwy
Toledo OH 43659
419 248-8000

(G-18451)
OWENS-ILLINOIS DE PUERTO RICO (PA)
Also Called: O-I
1 Seagate (43604-1558)
PHONE.................................419 874-9708
Steve McCracken, *CEO*
Joseph Lemieux, *President*
▲ EMP: 86
SALES (est): 59.3MM **Privately Held**
SIC: 3221 Glass containers

(G-18452)
P & J INDUSTRIES INC (PA)
4934 Lewis Ave (43612-2825)
P.O. Box 6918 (43612-0918)
PHONE.................................419 726-2675
James E Powers Jr, *President*
James E Powers Sr, *Corp Secy*
Marguerite M Powers, *Vice Pres*
▼ EMP: 120
SALES (est): 11.4MM **Privately Held**
SIC: 3471 Electroplating of metals or formed products; chromium plating of metals or formed products; gold plating

(G-18453)
P & J MANUFACTURING INC
1644 Campbell St (43607-4381)
PHONE.................................419 241-7369
Peter James Harvey, *President*
Elizabeth Harvey, *Corp Secy*
William Harvey, *Vice Pres*
EMP: 10
SQ FT: 14,000
SALES: 700K **Privately Held**
WEB: www.pandjmfginc.com
SIC: 7389 3471 Grinding, precision: commercial or industrial; finishing, metals or formed products

(G-18454)
P B FABRICATION MECH CONTR
750 W Laskey Rd (43612-3209)
PHONE.................................419 478-4869
Charles W Bailey, *President*
Hubert Backes, *Vice Pres*
EMP: 12
SQ FT: 6,000

GEOGRAPHIC SECTION

Toledo - Lucas County (G-18480)

SALES (est): 2.9MM **Privately Held**
SIC: 3535 3444 3443 3441 Conveyors & conveying equipment; sheet metalwork; fabricated plate work (boiler shop); fabricated structural metal; aluminum sheet, plate & foil; plumbing, heating, air-conditioning contractors

(G-18455)
P R RACING ENGINES
1951 W Sylvania Ave (43613-4522)
PHONE..................419 472-2277
Jeffery Snyder, *Owner*
EMP: 5
SQ FT: 2,000
SALES (est): 290K **Privately Held**
SIC: 3541 Machine tools, metal cutting type

(G-18456)
PAGE SLOTTING SAW CO INC
3820 Lagrange St (43612-1425)
PHONE..................419 476-7475
James Bouldin, *President*
EMP: 11
SQ FT: 3,500
SALES (est): 980K **Privately Held**
SIC: 3541 Machine tools, metal cutting type

(G-18457)
PALLET & CONT CORP OF AMER
901 Buckingham St (43607-4410)
PHONE..................419 255-1256
Michael J Burtscher, *President*
Marie J Burtscher, *Vice Pres*
EMP: 5
SQ FT: 39,500
SALES (est): 1.1MM **Privately Held**
SIC: 2448 2653 2449 Pallets, wood; boxes, corrugated: made from purchased materials; containers, plywood & veneer wood

(G-18458)
PATJIM HOLDINGS COMPANY
3444 N Summit St (43611-3242)
PHONE..................419 727-1298
John Weisenberger, *Principal*
EMP: 9
SALES (est): 836.5K **Privately Held**
SIC: 2052 Cookies & crackers

(G-18459)
PBF ENERGY PARTNERS LP
3143 Goddard Rd (43606-1827)
P.O. Box 1014 (43697-1014)
PHONE..................419 698-6724
Jack Parsil, *Principal*
Sean Marko, *Facilities Mgr*
Michael Erwin, *Buyer*
Rod Oliver, *Manager*
EMP: 6
SALES (est): 486.6K **Privately Held**
SIC: 2911 Petroleum refining

(G-18460)
PEAK ELECTRIC INC
320 N Byrne Rd (43607-2607)
PHONE..................419 726-4848
Milton McIntyre, *President*
Rhys Petee, *Principal*
Lenora McIntyre, *Vice Pres*
Mark Weisenburger, *Sales Staff*
EMP: 6
SALES (est): 2.1MM **Privately Held**
SIC: 3612 5063 Transformers, except electric; electrical apparatus & equipment

(G-18461)
PEDESTRIAN PRESS
2233 Robinwood Ave (43620-1020)
PHONE..................419 244-6488
Jeffrey Kent Nelson, *Principal*
EMP: 4
SALES (est): 282.1K **Privately Held**
SIC: 2741 Miscellaneous publishing

(G-18462)
PELHAM PRECIOUS METALS LLC
3105 Pelham Rd (43606-3144)
PHONE..................419 708-7975
Terry Bigioni, *Mng Member*

EMP: 3
SALES (est): 127.2K **Privately Held**
SIC: 3339 Precious metals

(G-18463)
PEPSI-COLA METRO BTLG CO INC
Also Called: Pepsico
3245 Hill Ave (43607-2936)
PHONE..................419 534-2186
Michael Hill, *Branch Mgr*
EMP: 30
SALES (corp-wide): 64.6B **Publicly Held**
WEB: www.whitmancorp.com
SIC: 2086 Carbonated soft drinks, bottled & canned
HQ: Pepsi-Cola Metropolitan Bottling Company, Inc.
1111 Westchester Ave
White Plains NY 10604
914 767-6000

(G-18464)
PERFECT MEASURING TAPE COMPANY (PA)
1116 N Summit St (43604-1870)
PHONE..................419 243-6811
Andrew C Bohnengel, *President*
Barrett Bohnengel, *Vice Pres*
Claire Bohnengel, *Vice Pres*
▲ EMP: 8 EST: 1912
SQ FT: 5,000
SALES (est): 900K **Privately Held**
WEB: www.cintametrica.com
SIC: 3829 5046 Measuring & controlling devices; scales, except laboratory

(G-18465)
PERFORMANCE PACKAGING INC
5219 Telegraph Rd (43612-3570)
PHONE..................419 478-8805
Frank Duval, *President*
Scott Ruetz, *Vice Pres*
▲ EMP: 10
SALES: 700K **Privately Held**
SIC: 7389 7319 4225 2759 Labeling bottles, cans, cartons, etc.; inspection & testing services; display advertising service; general warehousing & storage; labels & seals: printing

(G-18466)
PERFORMANCE SERVICES
828 Warehouse Rd Ste 8 (43615-6480)
PHONE..................419 385-1236
Kirk Moellenberg, *Owner*
EMP: 3
SALES (est): 357.5K **Privately Held**
SIC: 3599 Machine & other job shop work

(G-18467)
PERSTORP POLYOLS INC
600 Matzinger Rd (43612-2695)
PHONE..................419 729-5448
David Wolf, *President*
Larry Fioritto, *Admin Director*
◆ EMP: 109
SQ FT: 3,000
SALES (est): 47.4MM
SALES (corp-wide): 78.8MM **Privately Held**
WEB: www.perstorp.net
SIC: 2819 2851 2821 Elements; paints & allied products; plastics materials & resins
HQ: Perstorp Ab
Perstorp Industripark
Perstorp 284 8
435 380-00

(G-18468)
PEXCO PACKAGING CORP
795 Berdan Ave (43610-1069)
P.O. Box 6540 (43612-0540)
PHONE..................419 470-5935
Bill Buri, *President*
Thomas Jesionowski, *Vice Pres*
Dennis Taylor, *VP Mfg*
Debbie Thomas, *Accounts Exec*
Donna Knaggs, *Clerk*
EMP: 35
SQ FT: 64,000

SALES (est): 9.2MM **Privately Held**
WEB: www.pexcopkg.com
SIC: 2673 3082 3081 2759 Plastic bags: made from purchased materials; unsupported plastics profile shapes; unsupported plastics film & sheet; commercial printing

(G-18469)
PILKINGTON HOLDINGS INC (DH)
Also Called: P H I
811 Madison Ave Fl 1 (43604-5688)
P.O. Box 799 (43697-0799)
PHONE..................419 247-3731
Warren D Knowlton, *CEO*
A R Graham, *President*
G M Gray, *Vice Pres*
S P Harris, *Vice Pres*
J Mc Kenna, *Vice Pres*
◆ EMP: 300
SQ FT: 217,000
SALES (est): 593.3MM
SALES (corp-wide): 5.6B **Privately Held**
SIC: 3211 Flat glass
HQ: Pilkington Group Limited
Pilkington Technology Centre Hall Lane
Ormskirk LANCS L40 5
169 550-0000

(G-18470)
PILKINGTON NORTH AMERICA INC (DH)
811 Madison Ave Fl 3 (43604-5688)
P.O. Box 799 (43697-0799)
PHONE..................419 247-3731
Richard Altman, *President*
Scott Wilson, *Research*
Jeffrey Bowman, *Treasurer*
Garry Roser, *Finance Dir*
Spencer Harris, *VP Human Res*
◆ EMP: 277
SALES (est): 42.8MM
SALES (corp-wide): 5.6B **Privately Held**
WEB: www.low-eglass.com
SIC: 3211 Construction glass
HQ: Pilkington Holdings Inc.
811 Madison Ave Fl 1
Toledo OH 43604
419 247-3731

(G-18471)
PISTON AUTOMOTIVE LLC
Also Called: Piston Group
1212 E Alexis Rd (43612-3974)
PHONE..................419 464-0250
Vincent Johnson, *Branch Mgr*
EMP: 75
SALES (corp-wide): 729MM **Privately Held**
SIC: 3714 Motor vehicle parts & accessories
PA: Piston Automotive, L.L.C.
12723 Telegraph Rd Ste 1
Redford MI 48239
313 541-8674

(G-18472)
PLABELL RUBBER PRODUCTS CORP (PA)
300 S Saint Clair St # 324 (43604)
PHONE..................419 691-5878
John Jaksetic, *President*
Jim Farkas, *Vice Pres*
Randy Reif, *Admin Sec*
EMP: 14
SQ FT: 40,000
SALES (est): 2.7MM **Privately Held**
SIC: 3069 3061 Molded rubber products; mechanical rubber goods

(G-18473)
POLHE TOOL INC
312 W Laskey Rd (43612-3433)
PHONE..................419 476-2433
Jozsef Polhe, *President*
Marianne Polhe, *Treasurer*
Katherina A Arble, *Admin Sec*
EMP: 5
SQ FT: 5,000
SALES (est): 686.4K **Privately Held**
WEB: www.polhetoolinc.com
SIC: 3545 Tools & accessories for machine tools

(G-18474)
POOLES PRINTING & OFFICE SVCS
4036 Monroe St (43606-2144)
PHONE..................419 475-9000
William J Poole Jr, *President*
Scott Poole, *Manager*
EMP: 5 EST: 1965
SQ FT: 5,000
SALES (est): 500K **Privately Held**
SIC: 2752 2791 2789 Commercial printing, offset; typesetting; bookbinding & related work

(G-18475)
POWERBUFF INC
1001 Brown Ave (43607-3942)
PHONE..................419 241-2156
Walter C Anderson, *President*
EMP: 18
SQ FT: 50,000
SALES (est): 2.4MM **Privately Held**
SIC: 3589 Floor washing & polishing machines, commercial

(G-18476)
PRAXAIR INC
6055 Brent Dr (43611-1084)
PHONE..................419 729-7732
EMP: 9 **Privately Held**
SIC: 2813 Industrial gases
HQ: Praxair, Inc.
10 Riverview Dr
Danbury CT 06810
203 837-2000

(G-18477)
PRAXAIR DISTRIBUTION INC
5254 Jackman Rd Ste A (43613-2978)
PHONE..................419 476-0738
Adam Wygast, *Branch Mgr*
EMP: 42 **Privately Held**
SIC: 2813 Industrial gases
HQ: Praxair Distribution, Inc.
10 Riverview Dr
Danbury CT 06810
203 837-2000

(G-18478)
PRECISION GRAPHIC SERVICES
436 Wade St (43604-3856)
PHONE..................419 241-5189
Kenneth P Breier, *President*
EMP: 15
SQ FT: 10,000
SALES (est): 1.9MM **Privately Held**
WEB: www.pgstoledo.com
SIC: 2759 2789 Embossing on paper; binding only: books, pamphlets, magazines, etc.

(G-18479)
PRECISION STEEL SERVICES INC (PA)
31 E Sylvania Ave (43612-1474)
PHONE..................419 476-5702
David L Kelley, *President*
Greg Forrester, *Vice Pres*
Ramin Kalaty, *Vice Pres*
Kathy Zolciak, *Vice Pres*
Jordan Demchyna, *Opers Mgr*
EMP: 60 EST: 1975
SQ FT: 35,000
SALES (est): 62.4MM **Privately Held**
WEB: www.precision-steel.com
SIC: 5051 3441 3444 Steel; fabricated structural metal; sheet metalwork

(G-18480)
PRESTIGE STORE INTERIORS INC
4500 N Detroit Ave (43612-2644)
PHONE..................419 476-2106
Jeffrey Simenski, *President*
Brian Falk, *Sales Mgr*
Mike Bastian, *Manager*
Blain Stobinski, *Executive*
EMP: 60
SQ FT: 50,000
SALES (est): 9.5MM **Privately Held**
WEB: www.prestigestoreinteriors.com
SIC: 2541 Store fixtures, wood

Toledo - Lucas County (G-18481) GEOGRAPHIC SECTION

(G-18481)
PREUSS MOLD & DIE
1010 Matzinger Rd (43612-3823)
PHONE.................................419 729-9100
Jeff Preuss, *Owner*
EMP: 4
SQ FT: 3,700
SALES (est): 300K **Privately Held**
SIC: 3544 Forms (molds), for foundry & plastics working machinery; dies, plastics forming

(G-18482)
PRIDE GAGE ASSOCIATES LLC
7862 W Central Ave Ste D (43617-1549)
PHONE.................................419 318-3793
William Gstalder,
Christopher Grieser,
Janice Gstalder,
EMP: 2
SALES: 1.3MM **Privately Held**
SIC: 3823 Mfg Process Control Instruments

(G-18483)
PRIMARY DEFENSE LLC
3217 Schneider Rd (43614-2432)
PHONE.................................937 673-5703
Joshua Strain, *Owner*
EMP: 3
SALES (est): 242.1K **Privately Held**
SIC: 3812 Defense systems & equipment

(G-18484)
PRINT ALL INC
Also Called: A I M Specialists
380 S Erie St (43604-4634)
PHONE.................................419 534-2880
Ann M Fago, *President*
Irene Fago, *Vice Pres*
EMP: 6
SQ FT: 7,500
SALES (est): 953K **Privately Held**
WEB: www.aimspecialists.com
SIC: 2752 7331 Commercial printing, offset; mailing service

(G-18485)
PRINTPROD INC
6142 American Rd (43612-3902)
PHONE.................................937 228-2181
Robert Flaute Jr, *President*
EMP: 14 **EST:** 1916
SQ FT: 12,000
SALES (est): 1.8MM **Privately Held**
WEB: www.printprodinc.com
SIC: 2752 Tags, lithographed

(G-18486)
PROJECTS DESIGNED & BUILT
Also Called: PD&b
5949 American Rd E (43612-3950)
PHONE.................................419 726-7400
Ken Martin, *President*
▼ **EMP:** 21
SQ FT: 16,000
SALES: 6MM **Privately Held**
WEB: www.pdbinc.com
SIC: 3599 Machine shop, jobbing & repair

(G-18487)
PROPERTY ASSIST INC
Also Called: Floorcraft Designs
1755 W Sylvania Ave (43613-4635)
PHONE.................................419 480-1700
James Mann, *President*
Michael Mann, *Vice Pres*
Sunday Sue Mann, *Admin Sec*
EMP: 3
SALES (est): 401.4K **Privately Held**
SIC: 2426 Flooring, hardwood

(G-18488)
PUCK HOGS PRO SHOP INC
1258 W Alexis Rd (43612-4206)
PHONE.................................419 540-1388
Jeremy Gould, *President*
EMP: 4
SALES: 250K **Privately Held**
SIC: 5941 2329 3949 Hockey equipment, except skates; hockey uniforms: men's, youths' & boys': sticks: hockey, lacrosse, etc.

(G-18489)
Q C PRINTING
Also Called: Qc Prntng By Quality Craft
3650 Upton Ave (43613-5037)
PHONE.................................419 475-4266
Gene Grzymkowski, *Owner*
EMP: 5
SQ FT: 1,200
SALES (est): 300K **Privately Held**
SIC: 2752 Commercial printing, offset

(G-18490)
QUALITY TOOL COMPANY
Also Called: Quality Stamping
577 Mel Simon Dr (43612-4729)
PHONE.................................419 476-8228
James G Pasch, *President*
Michael Pasch, *Vice Pres*
EMP: 20
SQ FT: 48,000
SALES (est): 3.2MM **Privately Held**
SIC: 3469 3312 Stamping metal for the trade; tool & die steel

(G-18491)
QUIKRETE COMPANIES LLC
873 Western Ave (43609-2774)
PHONE.................................419 241-1148
Becky Garner, *Manager*
EMP: 25
SQ FT: 10,700 **Privately Held**
WEB: www.quikrete.com
SIC: 3272 3241 Dry mixture concrete; cement, hydraulic
HQ: The Quikrete Companies Llc
5 Concourse Pkwy Ste 1900
Atlanta GA 30328
404 634-9100

(G-18492)
QUMONT CHEMICAL CO
359 Hamilton St Ste 3 (43604-8548)
PHONE.................................419 241-1057
Donald A Quertinmont, *Owner*
EMP: 3
SALES (est): 299.2K **Privately Held**
SIC: 2899 5169 5113 Water treating compounds; chemicals & allied products; bags, paper & disposable plastic

(G-18493)
R & D CUSTOM MACHINE & TOOL
5961 American Rd E (43612-3950)
PHONE.................................419 727-1700
David Skomer, *President*
Don Loucks, *Vice Pres*
Ron Cline, *Sales Staff*
Don Moscrop, *Manager*
Mary Beth Ross, *Manager*
EMP: 25 **EST:** 1982
SQ FT: 16,800
SALES: 4MM **Privately Held**
SIC: 3599 Machine shop, jobbing & repair

(G-18494)
R J ENGINEERING COMPANY INC
2860 Heysler Rd (43617-1536)
PHONE.................................419 843-8651
Julius A Toth, *President*
Kurt Toth, *Vice Pres*
Rhoda J Toth, *Vice Pres*
EMP: 3 **EST:** 1962
SALES: 40K **Privately Held**
SIC: 3829 3524 Measuring & controlling devices; snowblowers & throwers, residential

(G-18495)
RADCO FIRE PROTECTION INC
444 W Laskey Rd Ste S (43612-3460)
PHONE.................................419 476-0102
Douglas W Ward, *President*
EMP: 7
SQ FT: 1,800
SALES (est): 1MM **Privately Held**
SIC: 3569 Sprinkler systems, fire: automatic

(G-18496)
RADCO INDUSTRIES INC
3226 Frenchmens Rd (43607-2996)
PHONE.................................419 531-4731
Richard Anderson, *President*
Mary Anderson, *Vice Pres*
Doug Michael, *Manager*
▲ **EMP:** 11 **EST:** 1962
SQ FT: 28,000
SALES (est): 1MM **Privately Held**
WEB: www.radcoindustries.com
SIC: 3599 Custom machinery

(G-18497)
RAGMAN INC
1201 N Summit St (43604-1817)
PHONE.................................419 255-8068
Donald F Billings, *President*
Debbie Billings, *Corp Secy*
EMP: 4 **EST:** 1976
SQ FT: 3,000
SALES: 500K **Privately Held**
SIC: 2394 Sails: made from purchased materials; convertible tops, canvas or boat: from purchased materials; tarpaulins, fabric: made from purchased materials

(G-18498)
RAKA CORPORATION
Also Called: Lockrey Manufacturing
203 Matzinger Rd (43612-2624)
PHONE.................................419 476-6572
Don Vollmar, *CEO*
Mark A Makulinski, *Ch of Bd*
EMP: 78 **EST:** 1953
SQ FT: 75,000
SALES (est): 18.2MM **Privately Held**
WEB: www.lockreymanufacturing.com
SIC: 3451 3444 Screw machine products; sheet metalwork

(G-18499)
REA POLISHING INC
1606 W Laskey Rd (43612-2916)
PHONE.................................419 470-0216
Jay REA Sr, *President*
Jay REA Jr, *Treasurer*
Tracy REA, *Manager*
EMP: 61
SQ FT: 19,600
SALES (est): 3MM **Privately Held**
SIC: 3471 Finishing, metals or formed products

(G-18500)
REGAL CABINET INC
315 N Holland Sylvania Rd (43615-4907)
PHONE.................................419 865-3932
Jon Kevin Irwin, *President*
Sonja Irwin, *Corp Secy*
William Irwin, *Vice Pres*
EMP: 3 **EST:** 1955
SQ FT: 4,000
SALES (est): 125K **Privately Held**
SIC: 2434 2511 5211 Wood kitchen cabinets; wood household furniture; lumber products; cabinets, kitchen

(G-18501)
RIKER PRODUCTS INC
4901 Stickney Ave (43612-3716)
P.O. Box 6976 (43612-0976)
PHONE.................................419 729-1626
Gary Frye, *President*
Michael Jaeck, *CFO*
Jeff Stockard, *Info Tech Mgr*
Rollie Bauer, *Admin Sec*
▼ **EMP:** 175
SQ FT: 250,000
SALES (est): 36.7MM **Privately Held**
WEB: www.rikerprod.com
SIC: 3714 3498 Mufflers (exhaust), motor vehicle; exhaust systems & parts, motor vehicle; fabricated pipe & fittings

(G-18502)
RIVER EAST CUSTOM CABINETS
221 S Saint Clair St (43604-8739)
PHONE.................................419 244-3226
Joe Weiser, *President*
John Weiser, *Vice Pres*
Michael McCormick, *Executive Asst*
EMP: 20
SQ FT: 15,000
SALES: 2.5MM **Privately Held**
WEB: www.rivereastcab.net
SIC: 5712 2434 Cabinet work, custom; wood kitchen cabinets

(G-18503)
RLM FABRICATING INC
4801 Bennett Rd (43612-2531)
PHONE.................................419 729-6130
Michael Reser, *President*
Patrick Copeland, *President*
EMP: 30
SALES (est): 5.6MM **Privately Held**
SIC: 3441 Fabricated structural metal

(G-18504)
ROBERT BECKER IMPRESSIONS INC
4646 Angola Rd (43615-6407)
PHONE.................................419 385-5303
Robert O Becker, *President*
Jennie Becker, *Vice Pres*
Rob Becker, *Manager*
EMP: 12
SQ FT: 9,000
SALES (est): 1.2MM **Privately Held**
WEB: www.beckerimpressions.com
SIC: 7334 2752 5044 Blueprinting service; commercial printing, offset; blueprinting equipment

(G-18505)
ROGAR INTERNATIONAL INC
Also Called: N M Hansen Machine and Tool
4015 Dewey St (43612-1415)
P.O. Box 6938 (43612-0938)
PHONE.................................419 476-5500
Ronnie W Clark, *CEO*
Roger Burditt, *Vice Pres*
R Ken Clark, *Treasurer*
James V Schindler, *Admin Sec*
EMP: 15 **EST:** 1909
SQ FT: 30,000
SALES (est): 2.8MM **Privately Held**
SIC: 3599 Machine shop, jobbing & repair

(G-18506)
RONFELDT ASSOCIATES INC
2345 S Byrne Rd (43614-5107)
PHONE.................................419 382-5641
Theodore A Markwood, *President*
Theodore Ronfeld, *Principal*
Howard Ronfeldt, *Principal*
EMP: 96
SQ FT: 57,000
SALES (est): 13.4MM
SALES (corp-wide): 100MM **Privately Held**
WEB: www.ronfeldt.com
SIC: 3469 3544 Stamping metal for the trade; special dies, tools, jigs & fixtures
PA: Ice Industries, Inc.
3810 Herr Rd
Sylvania OH 43560
419 842-3612

(G-18507)
RONFELDT MANUFACTURING LLC (HQ)
Also Called: Ice Industries Ronfeldt
2345 S Byrne Rd (43614-5107)
PHONE.................................419 382-5641
Paul Bishop, *President*
Bill Rawlins, *Purchasing*
Jeff Boger, *CFO*
Howard Ice, *Mng Member*
EMP: 18
SALES (est): 8.7MM
SALES (corp-wide): 100MM **Privately Held**
WEB: www.iceindustries.com
SIC: 3469 Stamping metal for the trade
PA: Ice Industries, Inc.
3810 Herr Rd
Sylvania OH 43560
419 842-3612

(G-18508)
ROULET COMPANY
4221 Lewis Ave (43612-1841)
PHONE.................................419 241-2988
Gary Wahl, *CEO*
Mark Lofgren, *President*
Roger L Bovee, *Vice Pres*
EMP: 5
SQ FT: 7,500

GEOGRAPHIC SECTION

Toledo - Lucas County (G-18538)

SALES (est): 663.4K **Privately Held**
WEB: www.rouletcompany.com
SIC: 3911 5944 7631 Jewelry, precious metal; jewelry, precious stones & precious metals; jewelry repair services

(G-18509)
S F C LTD LLC
110 E Woodruff Ave (43604-5226)
PHONE 419 255-1283
EMP: 3
SALES (est): 92.3K **Privately Held**
SIC: 2752 Catalogs, lithographed

(G-18510)
SABCO INDUSTRIES INC
5242 Angola Rd Ste 150 (43615-6334)
PHONE 419 531-5347
Robert Sulier, *President*
John Pershing, *Vice Pres*
CB M Ash, *Treasurer*
▲ **EMP:** 28 **EST:** 1961
SALES (est): 3.6MM **Privately Held**
WEB: www.kegs.com
SIC: 7699 5085 3993 3412 Tank repair & cleaning services; barrels, new or reconditioned; signs & advertising specialties; metal barrels, drums & pails

(G-18511)
SAN MARCOS SUPERMARKET LLC
Also Called: San Marco Indiana
235 Broadway St (43604-8801)
PHONE 419 469-8963
Oscar Ponce Gomez, *President*
EMP: 4
SALES (est): 360.2K **Privately Held**
SIC: 2032 Mexican foods: packaged in cans, jars, etc.

(G-18512)
SATELYTICS INC
1510 N Westwood Ave # 2070
(43606-8202)
PHONE 419 419-5380
John Schuller, *Business Mgr*
Charlie Curl, *VP Bus Dvlpt*
Allan Adams, *Director*
EMP: 5
SALES (est): 343.7K **Privately Held**
SIC: 7372 7373 Application computer software; systems software development services

(G-18513)
SAXON PRODUCTS INC
2283 Fulton St (43620-1272)
PHONE 419 241-6771
Edward L Poling, *President*
Tony Berezowski, *Vice Pres*
Mary Mazziotti, *Treasurer*
▲ **EMP:** 9 **EST:** 1961
SQ FT: 20,000
SALES: 375K **Privately Held**
WEB: www.inpaksystems.com
SIC: 3496 Miscellaneous fabricated wire products

(G-18514)
SCHUSTER MANUFACTURING INC
1508 W Laskey Rd Ste 2 (43612-2936)
PHONE 419 476-5800
Richard J Schuster, *President*
Matt Schuster, *Engineer*
EMP: 3 **EST:** 1975
SQ FT: 2,600
SALES (est): 371.5K **Privately Held**
SIC: 3544 3599 Jigs & fixtures; machine shop, jobbing & repair

(G-18515)
SEAPORT MOLD & CASTING COMPANY
1309 W Bancroft St (43606-4634)
PHONE 419 243-1422
Michael A Kumor, *President*
Fred Kumor, *Vice Pres*
EMP: 14
SQ FT: 15,000
SALES (est): 1.2MM **Privately Held**
SIC: 3369 3543 Nonferrous foundries; industrial patterns

(G-18516)
SEAWAY PATTERN MFG INC
5749 Angola Rd (43615-6319)
PHONE 419 865-5724
Richard Johnston, *President*
EMP: 26 **EST:** 1962
SQ FT: 30,000
SALES (est): 3.5MM **Privately Held**
WEB: www.seawaypatterninc.com
SIC: 3543 3544 Industrial patterns; industrial molds

(G-18517)
SEM-COM COMPANY INC (PA)
1040 N Westwood Ave (43607-3263)
P.O. Box 8428 (43623-0428)
PHONE 419 537-8813
Michael V Pfaender, *President*
Lawrence V Pfaender, *Chairman*
William Garrett, *Vice Pres*
James Pfaender, *Vice Pres*
Johann Manning, *Admin Sec*
EMP: 18
SQ FT: 22,500
SALES (est): 1.9MM **Privately Held**
WEB: www.sem-com.com
SIC: 3231 2891 3229 Products of purchased glass; adhesives & sealants; fiber optics strands

(G-18518)
SENECA PETROLEUM CO INC
1441 Woodville Rd (43605-3233)
PHONE 419 691-3581
Dean Friend, *Manager*
EMP: 12
SALES (corp-wide): 19.9MM **Privately Held**
SIC: 2951 2911 Asphalt & asphaltic paving mixtures (not from refineries); petroleum refining
PA: Seneca Petroleum Co., Inc.
   13301 Cicero Ave
   Crestwood IL 60418
   708 396-1100

(G-18519)
SENECA PETROLEUM CO INC
2563 Front St (43605)
PHONE 419 691-3581
Dean Friend, *Branch Mgr*
EMP: 12
SALES (corp-wide): 19.9MM **Privately Held**
SIC: 2911 1611 Asphalt or asphaltic materials, made in refineries; highway & street construction
PA: Seneca Petroleum Co., Inc.
   13301 Cicero Ave
   Crestwood IL 60418
   708 396-1100

(G-18520)
SFC GRAPHICS CLEVELAND LTD
Also Called: Sfc Graphic Arts Div
110 E Woodruff Ave (43604-5226)
P.O. Box 877 (43697-0877)
PHONE 419 255-1283
Tom Clark, *CEO*
Paul Clark, *President*
EMP: 40
SQ FT: 15,000
SALES (est): 5.6MM **Privately Held**
WEB: www.sfcgraphics.com
SIC: 2752 Commercial printing, lithographic

(G-18521)
SHELLY MATERIALS INC
Also Called: Shelly Liquid Division
352 George Hardy Dr (43605-1063)
PHONE 740 246-6315
John Power, *President*
EMP: 4
SALES (corp-wide): 29.7B **Privately Held**
SIC: 1422 Crushed & broken limestone
HQ: Shelly Materials, Inc.
   80 Park Dr
   Thornville OH 43076
   740 246-6315

(G-18522)
SIGN LADY INC
5981 Telegraph Rd (43612-4548)
PHONE 419 476-9191
Lynn M Ulrich, *President*
Larry Lemerand, *Vice Pres*
Joshua Bunton, *Production*
EMP: 5
SALES (est): 671.2K **Privately Held**
SIC: 2759 5099 7532 Screen printing; signs, except electric; truck painting & lettering

(G-18523)
SILICONE SOLUTIONS INTL LLC
3441 South Ave (43609-1148)
PHONE 419 720-8709
Eric Tudor, *Mng Member*
EMP: 3
SALES (est): 1MM **Privately Held**
SIC: 5169 2869 Adhesives & sealants; silicones

(G-18524)
SLAP N TICKLE LLC
Also Called: Randys
5645 Angola Rd Ste A (43615-6384)
PHONE 419 349-3226
Brian Nutt, *Mng Member*
▲ **EMP:** 5
SALES (est): 469.7K **Privately Held**
SIC: 3669 Smoke detectors

(G-18525)
SOJOURNERS TRUTH
1811 Adams St (43604-5427)
PHONE 419 243-0007
Fletcher Word, *President*
EMP: 10
SALES (est): 350K **Privately Held**
SIC: 2711 Newspapers, publishing & printing

(G-18526)
SONUS-USA INC
3829 Woodley Rd Bldg B (43606-1171)
PHONE 419 474-9324
Dr Vijay Adappa, *Ch of Bd*
EMP: 20
SALES (corp-wide): 2.6MM **Privately Held**
WEB: www.sonus.com
SIC: 3842 Hearing aids
HQ: Sonus-Usa, Inc.
   5000 Cheshire Pkwy N # 1
   Plymouth MN 55446

(G-18527)
SPC SPECIALTY PRODUCTS LLC
520 E Woodruff Ave (43604-5342)
P.O. Box 370 (43697-0370)
PHONE 844 475-5414
Vicki Rose, *Principal*
EMP: 3 **EST:** 2017
SALES (est): 437.7K **Privately Held**
SIC: 2842 Specialty cleaning, polishes & sanitation goods

(G-18528)
SPRINGTIME MANUFACTURING
1121 Hazelwood St (43605-3211)
PHONE 419 697-3720
George Hazel, *Owner*
EMP: 8
SALES (est): 855.9K **Privately Held**
SIC: 3495 5051 Wire springs; metals service centers & offices

(G-18529)
STEPPING STONE ENTERPRISES INC
Also Called: Minuteman Press
5847 Secor Rd (43623-1421)
PHONE 419 472-0505
Steven Heaney, *President*
Vicki Kimler, *Corp Secy*
Ronald R Kimler, *Vice Pres*
EMP: 13
SQ FT: 3,000
SALES (est): 1.9MM **Privately Held**
SIC: 2752 Commercial printing, lithographic

(G-18530)
STERLING PIPE & TUBE INC (PA)
5335 Enterprise Blvd (43612-3810)
PHONE 419 729-9756
Fred Shelar, *President*
Dennis Krout, *Vice Pres*
▲ **EMP:** 140
SQ FT: 70,000
SALES (est): 27.1MM **Privately Held**
WEB: www.sterlingpipeandtube.com
SIC: 3317 Steel pipe & tubes

(G-18531)
STONECO INC
352 George Hardy Dr (43605-1063)
PHONE 419 693-3933
William Hodges, *Manager*
EMP: 9
SALES (corp-wide): 29.7B **Privately Held**
SIC: 2951 Paving mixtures
HQ: Stoneco, Inc.
   1700 Fostoria Ave Ste 200
   Findlay OH 45840
   419 422-8854

(G-18532)
STRUCTURAL RADAR IMAGING INC
Also Called: SRI
5217 Monroe St Ste A (43623-4604)
PHONE 425 970-3890
Joshua Braunstein, *President*
Rachel Coe, *Finance Mgr*
EMP: 6
SALES (est): 1MM **Privately Held**
WEB: www.srimaging.com
SIC: 3825 Radar testing instruments, electric

(G-18533)
SUNBEAM PRODUCTS CO LLC
623 Main St (43605-1745)
P.O. Box 8097 (43605-0097)
PHONE 419 691-1551
Todd Lincoln, *Managing Prtnr*
George Stoycheff,
EMP: 3 **EST:** 1935
SALES: 370K **Privately Held**
SIC: 2841 7699 Detergents, synthetic organic or inorganic alkaline; industrial equipment services

(G-18534)
SUNFOREST VISION CENTER INC
3915 Sunforest Ct Ste A (43623-4453)
PHONE 419 475-4646
Abraham Sim, *President*
EMP: 3
SALES (est): 326.7K **Privately Held**
SIC: 3851 Eyes, glass & plastic

(G-18535)
SUPERIOR IMPRESSIONS INC
327 12th St (43604-7531)
PHONE 419 244-8676
Douglas A Shelton, *President*
Dawn Freeman, *Director*
EMP: 8
SQ FT: 6,000
SALES (est): 1.1MM **Privately Held**
SIC: 2752 Commercial printing, offset

(G-18536)
SUPERIOR PACKAGING
2930 Airport Hwy (43609-1404)
PHONE 419 380-3335
Steve Davis, *Owner*
EMP: 10
SALES (est): 1.8MM **Privately Held**
SIC: 3629 Electronic generation equipment

(G-18537)
SURFACE ENTERPRISES INC
1465 W Alexis Rd (43612-4044)
PHONE 419 476-5670
Susan Kroma, *President*
Bill Kroma, *Vice Pres*
EMP: 6
SQ FT: 9,000
SALES (est): 2.4MM **Privately Held**
WEB: www.surfaceenterprises.com
SIC: 2434 Wood kitchen cabinets

(G-18538)
SWANSON PROSTHETIC CENTER INC
3102 W Sylvania Ave (43613-4132)
PHONE 419 472-8910

Toledo - Lucas County (G-18539)

Vern Swanson, *President*
Mario Goveia, *Treasurer*
EMP: 6
SQ FT: 5,050
SALES (est): 823.3K **Privately Held**
WEB: www.swansonopcenter.com
SIC: 3842 Prosthetic appliances

(G-18539)
SYRACUSE CHINA COMPANY (DH)
300 Madison Ave (43604-1561)
P.O. Box 10060 (43699-0060)
PHONE 419 727-2100
John F Meier, *Ch of Bd*
Richard Reynolds, *Vice Pres*
George Kuhn, *Art Dir*
◆ **EMP:** 225
SQ FT: 50,000
SALES (est): 17.8MM **Publicly Held**
SIC: 2711 Newspapers, publishing & printing
HQ: Libbey Glass Inc.
  300 Madison Ave Fl 4
  Toledo OH 43604
  419 325-2100

(G-18540)
SYSTEMS SPECIALTY CTRL CO INC
1550 Coining Dr (43612-2905)
PHONE 419 478-4156
Edbert A Karcher, *Principal*
Nancy Coyle, *Business Mgr*
Ken Karcher, *Vice Pres*
Tim Stroshine, *Vice Pres*
EMP: 20
SQ FT: 14,000
SALES (est): 5MM **Privately Held**
SIC: 3613 Control panels, electric

(G-18541)
T E HUBLER INC
Also Called: R & T Microcenters of Ohio
236 New Towne Square Dr 1b (43612-4625)
P.O. Box 12269 (43612-0269)
PHONE 419 476-2552
Rosalina Hubler, *President*
Carrie Lily, *Info Tech Mgr*
EMP: 3
SQ FT: 2,400
SALES (est): 371.9K **Privately Held**
WEB: www.rtmicrocenters.com
SIC: 5734 7378 3577 5045 Computer peripheral equipment; computer maintenance & repair; computer peripheral equipment; computer software

(G-18542)
TAFT TOOL & PRODUCTION CO
756 S Byrne Rd Ste 1 (43609-1088)
PHONE 419 385-2576
Varkes Tavtigian, *President*
Paul Sneider, *General Mgr*
Rose Tavtigian, *Vice Pres*
EMP: 10
SQ FT: 13,000
SALES (est): 1.1MM **Privately Held**
SIC: 3544 3545 7699 Special dies & tools; gauges (machine tool accessories); industrial machinery & equipment repair

(G-18543)
TAPESTRY INC
5001 Monroe St Ste 1743 (43623-3620)
PHONE 419 471-9033
Stephanie Rieck, *Branch Mgr*
EMP: 15
SALES (corp-wide): 5.8B **Publicly Held**
WEB: www.coach.com
SIC: 3171 Handbags, women's
PA: Tapestry, Inc.
  10 Hudson Yards
  New York NY 10001
  212 594-1850

(G-18544)
TECHNOLOGY RESOURCES INC
916 N Summit St (43604-1812)
PHONE 419 241-9248
Robert C Redmond, *President*
Dyne Hoenie, *Vice Pres*
EMP: 5
SQ FT: 6,000
SALES (est): 823.3K **Privately Held**
WEB: www.ohiotechresources.com
SIC: 3823 7371 Computer interface equipment for industrial process control; computer software systems analysis & design, custom

(G-18545)
TELEDYNE BROWN ENGINEERING INC
Teledyne Turbine Engines
1330 W Laskey Rd (43612-2911)
PHONE 419 470-3000
Steve Ryne, *Senior Buyer*
Kimberly Kmit, *Purchasing*
Robert Buss, *Engineer*
Matthew Hames, *Engineer*
James Hoover, *Engineer*
EMP: 100
SALES (corp-wide): 2.9B **Publicly Held**
WEB: www.teledyne.com
SIC: 3364 Nonferrous die-castings except aluminum
HQ: Teledyne Brown Engineering, Inc.
  300 Sparkman Dr Nw
  Huntsville AL 35805
  256 726-1000

(G-18546)
TELEX COMMUNICATIONS INC
Also Called: Toledo Business Journals
5660 Southwyck Blvd # 150 (43614-1504)
PHONE 419 865-0972
Sanford Lubin, *President*
Adam Hintz, *Marketing Mgr*
EMP: 14
SALES (est): 1.1MM **Privately Held**
SIC: 8742 2721 8748 Industry specialist consultants; periodicals; communications consulting

(G-18547)
TEMBEC BTLSR INC
2112 Sylvan Ave (43606-4767)
P.O. Box 2570 (43606-0570)
PHONE 419 244-5856
James M Lopez, *President*
Lawrence Rowley, *General Mgr*
Dan Wozniak, *Admin Sec*
▲ **EMP:** 32
SQ FT: 84,000
SALES (est): 8.8MM **Privately Held**
WEB: www.btlresins.com
SIC: 2821 5169 Plastics materials & resins; industrial chemicals
HQ: Tembec Inc
  4 Place Ville-Marie Bureau 100
  Montreal QC H3B 2
  514 871-0137

(G-18548)
TEX-TYLER CORPORATION
Also Called: Viking Paper
5148 Stickney Ave (43612-3721)
PHONE 419 729-4951
J Anthony Mooter, *President*
Robert L Walker, *Vice Pres*
Kathleen Malosh, *Office Mgr*
Wendy Logan Rogers, *Manager*
EMP: 29
SQ FT: 60,000
SALES (est): 2.5MM **Privately Held**
SIC: 3444 Sheet metalwork

(G-18549)
THE RUBBER STAMP SHOP
4418 Lewis Ave (43612-1846)
PHONE 419 478-4444
Arthur Winzenried, *Owner*
EMP: 3
SQ FT: 7,000
SALES (est): 406.7K **Privately Held**
WEB: www.jillianvillafane.com
SIC: 5112 5999 5943 2672 Marking devices; rubber stamps; stationery stores; coated & laminated paper

(G-18550)
THUNDAWEAR LLC
Also Called: Thundawear Skull Caps
1709 Spielbusch Ave # 100 (43604-5470)
PHONE 419 787-2675
Ronald Roberts, *Mng Member*
EMP: 4
SALES (est): 194.2K **Privately Held**
SIC: 2353 Hats, caps & millinery

(G-18551)
TIMMYS SANDWICH SHOP
5426 Cresthaven Ln (43614-1218)
PHONE 419 350-8267
Timothy Foster, *Owner*
EMP: 6 **EST:** 2014
SALES (est): 160K **Privately Held**
SIC: 2099 7389 Ready-to-eat meals, salads & sandwiches;

(G-18552)
TIMON J REINHART
Also Called: Timon Tool & Die
1560 W Laskey Rd Ste B (43612-2937)
PHONE 419 476-1990
Timon J Reinhart, *Owner*
Tim Reinhart, *Owner*
EMP: 4
SQ FT: 3,800
SALES (est): 225K **Privately Held**
SIC: 3599 Machine shop, jobbing & repair

(G-18553)
TJ METZGERS INC
207 Arco Dr (43607-2906)
PHONE 419 861-8611
Thomas H Metzger, *CEO*
Jackie Klempner, *Accounts Mgr*
Mary Schuck, *Accounts Mgr*
Aaron Meyer, *Manager*
EMP: 100
SQ FT: 63,146
SALES (est): 26.7MM **Privately Held**
WEB: www.metzgers.com
SIC: 2752 2759 2789 2791 Commercial printing, offset; commercial printing; bookbinding & related work; photocomposition, for the printing trade; color separation, photographic & movie film

(G-18554)
TM MACHINE & TOOL INC
521 Mel Simon Dr (43612-4726)
PHONE 419 478-0310
Karyn Weeks, *President*
EMP: 8
SQ FT: 20,000
SALES (est): 1MM **Privately Held**
SIC: 3544 3599 Special dies & tools; machine shop, jobbing & repair

(G-18555)
TOLCO CORPORATION
1920 Linwood Ave (43604-5293)
PHONE 419 241-1113
George L Notarianni, *President*
James Reising, *Regional Mgr*
Tricia Thomas, *Design Engr*
Carole Rayle, *Credit Staff*
Robin Chlebowski, *Sales Staff*
▲ **EMP:** 75
SQ FT: 30,000
SALES (est): 32.6MM **Privately Held**
WEB: www.tolco.com
SIC: 5085 3563 3586 3561 Bottler supplies; spraying outfits; metals, paints & chemicals (compressor); vacuum pumps, except laboratory; measuring & dispensing pumps; pumps & pumping equipment; specialty cleaning, polishes & sanitation goods

(G-18556)
TOLEDO AUTOMATIC SCREW CO
2114 Champlain St (43611-3703)
PHONE 419 726-3441
James R Park, *President*
Steve Sorge, *Corp Secy*
EMP: 5 **EST:** 1946
SQ FT: 3,000
SALES: 400K **Privately Held**
SIC: 3451 Screw machine products

(G-18557)
TOLEDO BLADE COMPANY
541 N Superior St (43660-0002)
P.O. Box 921 (43697-0921)
PHONE 419 724-6000
Joseph H Zerbey IV, *President*
Tommy Gallagher, *Editor*
Matt Swan, *Editor*
Jennifer Mauk, *Advt Staff*
Jeff Pezzano, *Advt Staff*
EMP: 423
SALES (est): 32MM
SALES (corp-wide): 921.6MM **Privately Held**
SIC: 2711 Commercial printing & newspaper publishing combined
PA: Block Communications, Inc.
  405 Madison Ave Ste 2100
  Toledo OH 43604
  419 724-6212

(G-18558)
TOLEDO ENGINEERING CO INC (PA)
Also Called: Teco
3400 Executive Pkwy Ste 4 (43606-1364)
P.O. Box 2927 (43606-0927)
PHONE 419 537-9711
Todd Seifried, *President*
Scott A Slater, *Chairman*
David Black, *Vice Pres*
Christopher J Hoyle, *Vice Pres*
Brian Naveken, *Engineer*
▲ **EMP:** 150
SQ FT: 50,000
SALES (est): 62.6MM **Privately Held**
WEB: www.o2furnace.com
SIC: 3559 Glass making machinery: blowing, molding, forming, etc.

(G-18559)
TOLEDO FIBER PRODUCTS CORP
1245 E Manhattan Blvd (43608-1549)
PHONE 419 720-0303
Mark Connor, *Principal*
EMP: 10
SALES (est): 1.4MM **Privately Held**
SIC: 2221 Textile mills, broadwoven: silk & manmade, also glass

(G-18560)
TOLEDO JOURNAL
3021 Douglas Rd (43606-3504)
P.O. Box 12559 (43606-0159)
PHONE 419 472-4521
Myron A Stewart, *Partner*
EMP: 8
SQ FT: 2,800
SALES (est): 380K **Privately Held**
SIC: 2711 Newspapers: publishing only, not printed on site

(G-18561)
TOLEDO METAL SPINNING COMPANY
1819 Clinton St (43607-1600)
PHONE 419 535-5931
Kenneth F Fankhauser, *President*
Craig B Fankhauser, *Vice Pres*
Eric S Fankhauser, *Treasurer*
▼ **EMP:** 35 **EST:** 1929
SQ FT: 100,000
SALES (est): 10.4MM **Privately Held**
WEB: www.toledometalspinning.com
SIC: 3469 3443 Spinning metal for the trade; stamping metal for the trade; cylinders, pressure: metal plate

(G-18562)
TOLEDO MOBILE MEDIA LLC (PA)
757 Warehouse Rd Ste D (43615-6478)
PHONE 419 389-0687
John S Demitry, *Mng Member*
EMP: 4
SALES (est): 470.4K **Privately Held**
SIC: 3993 3999 Signs & advertising specialties; advertising display products

(G-18563)
TOLEDO MOLDING & DIE INC
4 E Laskey Rd (43612-3517)
PHONE 419 476-0581
Scott Ruskinoff, *Facilities Mgr*
Susan Stang, *Buyer*
Jim Gasser, *Engineer*
Rob Olsen, *Engineer*
Joe Pirrone, *Manager*
EMP: 120
SALES (corp-wide): 309.9MM **Privately Held**
WEB: www.tmdinc.com
SIC: 3089 3544 Injection molded finished plastic products; special dies, tools, jigs & fixtures

▲ = Import ▼ = Export
◆ = Import/Export

GEOGRAPHIC SECTION

Toledo - Lucas County (G-18590)

HQ: Toledo Molding & Die, Inc.
1429 Coining Dr
Toledo OH 43612
419 470-3950

(G-18564)
TOLEDO MOLDING & DIE INC (DH)
Also Called: T M D
1429 Coining Dr (43612-2932)
PHONE.................419 470-3950
Stephen Ciucci, *President*
Wilda Coyle, *Business Mgr*
David Spotts, *COO*
Ernest Samas, *Vice Pres*
Joni Schmidt, *Vice Pres*
▲ EMP: 60
SQ FT: 35,000
SALES (est): 423.1MM
SALES (corp-wide): 309.9MM **Privately Held**
WEB: www.tmdinc.com
SIC: 3544 3089 Special dies, tools, jigs & fixtures; injection molded finished plastic products
HQ: Grammer Ag
Georg-Grammer-Str. 2
Amberg 92224
962 166-0

(G-18565)
TOLEDO OPTICAL LABORATORY INC
1201 Jefferson Ave (43604-5836)
P.O. Box 2028 (43603-2028)
PHONE.................419 248-3384
Irland Tashima, *President*
Jeffrey Seymenski, *Vice Pres*
Mary Johnson, *Manager*
Julie Shook, *Manager*
Jeff Szymanski, *Manager*
EMP: 52
SQ FT: 10,000
SALES (est): 8.1MM **Privately Held**
SIC: 3851 5048 Eyeglasses, lenses & frames; lenses, ophthalmic; frames, ophthalmic

(G-18566)
TOLEDO PAINT & CHEMICAL CO
33 Blucher St (43607-4403)
P.O. Box 324 (43697-0324)
PHONE.................419 244-3726
David C Peters, *President*
Frank D Jacobs, *Admin Sec*
EMP: 6
SQ FT: 20,400
SALES (est): 1MM **Privately Held**
SIC: 2851 Paints & paint additives

(G-18567)
TOLEDO PRO FIBERGLASS INC
210 Wade St (43604-8852)
PHONE.................419 241-9390
Don Jardine, *Vice Pres*
EMP: 8
SQ FT: 24,000
SALES: 500K **Privately Held**
WEB: www.toledopro.com
SIC: 5999 3714 3711 3089 Fiberglass materials, except insulation; motor vehicle parts & accessories; motor vehicles & car bodies; fiberglass doors

(G-18568)
TOLEDO SCREW PRODUCTS INC
8261 W Bancroft St (43617-1804)
PHONE.................419 841-3341
J Warren Ide, *President*
EMP: 7 EST: 1948
SQ FT: 12,500
SALES (est): 510K **Privately Held**
SIC: 3451 Screw machine products

(G-18569)
TOLEDO SIGNS & DESIGNS LTD
6636 W Bancroft St Ste 2 (43615-3188)
PHONE.................419 843-1073
Karrie Lyczkowski, *Branch Mgr*
EMP: 3
SALES (corp-wide): 668.7K **Privately Held**
SIC: 2759 5099 Screen printing; signs, except electric

PA: Toledo Signs & Designs Ltd
1100 N Mccord Rd Ste 1a
Toledo OH 43615
419 843-1073

(G-18570)
TOLEDO STREETS NEWSPAPER
913 Madison Ave (43604-5533)
PHONE.................419 214-3460
Josh Schuyler, *Principal*
Ken Leslie, *Principal*
EMP: 4
SALES (est): 76.2K **Privately Held**
SIC: 2711 Newspapers

(G-18571)
TOLEDO SWORD NEWSPAPER
3332 Stanhope Dr (43606-1249)
PHONE.................419 932-0767
Toledo Sword Newspaper, *Principal*
EMP: 3
SALES (est): 166.4K **Privately Held**
SIC: 2711 Newspapers

(G-18572)
TOLEDO TAPE AND LABEL COMPANY
114 Dulton Dr (43615-9052)
PHONE.................419 536-8316
Norman L Fisher, *Owner*
Harold Browwing, *Manager*
EMP: 5
SALES (est): 382K **Privately Held**
SIC: 2754 Rotary photogravure printing

(G-18573)
TOLEDO TICKET COMPANY
3963 Catawba St (43612-1492)
P.O. Box 6876 (43612-0876)
PHONE.................419 476-5424
Roy L Carter, *Ch of Bd*
Robin G Carter, *Treasurer*
Desiree Deering,
EMP: 50
SQ FT: 50,000
SALES (est): 11.4MM **Privately Held**
WEB: www.toledoticket.com
SIC: 2752 2759 Tickets, lithographed; commercial printing

(G-18574)
TOLEDO TOOL AND DIE CO INC
105 W Alexis Rd (43612-3603)
PHONE.................419 476-4422
John Vanbelle, *President*
▲ EMP: 50 EST: 1941
SQ FT: 60,000
SALES (est): 24.5MM **Privately Held**
WEB: www.toledotool.com
SIC: 3469 3544 Stamping metal for the trade; special dies, tools, jigs & fixtures

(G-18575)
TOLEDO WINDOW & AWNING INC
3035 W Sylvania Ave (43613-4135)
PHONE.................419 474-3396
Dennis Whitaker, *President*
Dawn Whitaker, *Vice Pres*
EMP: 7
SQ FT: 2,600
SALES (est): 1.1MM **Privately Held**
WEB: www.toledowindow.com
SIC: 3444 5031 5211 Awnings, sheet metal; doors & windows; doors, storm: wood or metal; windows, storm: wood or metal

(G-18576)
TOOLING & COMPONENTS CORP
Also Called: Toolcomp
5261 Tractor Rd (43612-3439)
PHONE.................419 478-9122
David Gonzalez, *President*
Ezekiel Gonzalez, *Vice Pres*
EMP: 12
SQ FT: 5,900
SALES (est): 750K **Privately Held**
WEB: www.toolcomp.com
SIC: 3599 3544 Machine shop, jobbing & repair; special dies, tools, jigs & fixtures

(G-18577)
TORBOT GROUP INC
Also Called: Jobskin Division
5030 Advantage Dr Ste 101 (43612-3861)
PHONE.................419 724-1475
Greg Johnson, *Branch Mgr*
EMP: 28
SALES (corp-wide): 7.3MM **Privately Held**
WEB: www.torbot.com
SIC: 3841 Surgical & medical instruments
PA: Torbot Group, Inc.
1367 Elmwood Ave
Cranston RI 02910
401 780-8737

(G-18578)
TOTH INDUSTRIES INC
5102 Enterprise Blvd (43612-3897)
PHONE.................419 729-4669
Richard Toth, *President*
EMP: 70 EST: 1955
SQ FT: 40,000
SALES (est): 13.7MM **Privately Held**
WEB: www.tothindustries.com
SIC: 3599 3594 Machine shop, jobbing & repair; fluid power pumps & motors

(G-18579)
TOUCH OF GLASS
908 Jean Rd (43615-4415)
PHONE.................419 861-2888
Steven Moder, *Owner*
Jean Moder, *Principal*
EMP: 3 EST: 1991
SALES (est): 133.6K **Privately Held**
SIC: 3229 Pressed & blown glass

(G-18580)
TPR PLASMA CENTER
625 Dorr St (43604-8023)
PHONE.................419 244-3910
EMP: 3 EST: 2007
SALES (est): 190K **Privately Held**
SIC: 2836 Plasmas

(G-18581)
TRADITIONS SAUCES LLC
606 Durango Dr (43609-1706)
PHONE.................419 704-4506
Donald Hill, *CEO*
EMP: 5
SALES (est): 60K **Privately Held**
SIC: 2033 Chili sauce, tomato: packaged in cans, jars, etc.

(G-18582)
TRANSCO RAILWAY PRODUCTS INC
4800 Schwartz Rd (43611-1726)
P.O. Box 5009 (43611-0009)
PHONE.................419 726-3383
Jim Smith, *QA Dir*
Antwan Smith, *Branch Mgr*
EMP: 30
SALES (corp-wide): 96.7MM **Privately Held**
SIC: 3537 7699 Industrial trucks & tractors; railroad car customizing
HQ: Transco Railway Products Inc.
200 N La Salle St # 1550
Chicago IL 60601
312 427-2818

(G-18583)
TRU-FORM STEEL & WIRE INC
5509 Telegraph Rd (43612-2662)
PHONE.................765 348-5001
Jeffrey Tuttle, *Branch Mgr*
EMP: 50
SALES (corp-wide): 17.1MM **Privately Held**
SIC: 3315 3441 Steel wire & related products; fabricated structural metal
PA: Tru-Form Steel & Wire, Inc.
1204 Gilkey Ave
Hartford City IN 47348
765 348-5001

(G-18584)
UNITY CABLE TECHNOLOGIES INC
Also Called: Unity Defense Systems
1811 Adams St (43604-5427)
PHONE.................419 322-4118

Annette M Wright, *President*
EMP: 5
SQ FT: 1,500
SALES: 2MM **Privately Held**
SIC: 5063 3612 3299 3694 Insulators, electrical; wire & cable; current limiting reactors, electrical; tubing for electrical purposes, quartz; engine electrical equipment; combat vehicles

(G-18585)
UNIVERSAL URETHANE PDTS INC
410 1st St (43605-2002)
P.O. Box 50617 (43605-0617)
PHONE.................419 693-7400
Harry G Conrad, *CEO*
Jeffrey A Conrad, *President*
Scott Conrad, *Vice Pres*
Monty Coffman, *Purchasing*
EMP: 55
SQ FT: 32,000
SALES (est): 10.1MM **Privately Held**
WEB: www.universalurethane.com
SIC: 3069 3312 3061 2851 Molded rubber products; blast furnaces & steel mills; mechanical rubber goods; paints & allied products; synthetic rubber; platemaking services

(G-18586)
UNLIMITED MACHINE AND TOOL LLC
5139 Tractor Rd Ste C (43612-3432)
PHONE.................419 269-1730
Tom McCloskey, *Mng Member*
Richard Bell,
EMP: 11
SQ FT: 6,000
SALES (est): 1MM **Privately Held**
WEB: www.unlimmachtool.com
SIC: 3544 3312 Special dies & tools; tool & die steel & alloys

(G-18587)
V M SYSTEMS INC
3125 Hill Ave (43607-2987)
PHONE.................419 535-1044
Craig Gabel, *President*
Ronald H Gabel, *President*
Trent Bloomfield, *Vice Pres*
Kevin Phillips, *Project Mgr*
Ron Snyder, *Facilities Mgr*
EMP: 100
SQ FT: 24,000
SALES (est): 26MM **Privately Held**
WEB: www.vmsystemsinc.com
SIC: 1711 3444 Warm air heating & air conditioning contractor; ventilation & duct work contractor; sheet metalwork

(G-18588)
VALLEY PLASTICS COMPANY INC
399 Phillips Ave (43612-1349)
PHONE.................419 666-2349
Walter Norris, *CEO*
EMP: 40
SALES (est): 7.4MM **Privately Held**
WEB: www.valleyplasticsinc.com
SIC: 3089 2542 Plastic processing; partitions & fixtures, except wood

(G-18589)
VANS INC
5001 Monroe St Ste 1560 (43623-7003)
PHONE.................419 471-1541
Tom Ulrich, *Manager*
EMP: 10
SALES (corp-wide): 11.8B **Publicly Held**
SIC: 3021 Canvas shoes, rubber soled
HQ: Vans, Inc.
1588 S Coast Dr
Costa Mesa CA 92626
855 909-8267

(G-18590)
VENTUREMEDGROUP LTD
2865 N Reynolds Rd 220a (43615-2068)
PHONE.................567 661-0768
Gary Smith, *CEO*
EMP: 6
SQ FT: 400
SALES: 175K **Privately Held**
SIC: 3841 Surgical & medical instruments

Toledo - Lucas County (G-18591)

(G-18591)
VERGELINE LLC
1301 N Summit St (43604-1819)
P.O. Box 850, Sylvania (43560-0850)
PHONE..................................419 730-0300
Kristin A Delverne, *Principal*
EMP: 3
SALES (est): 200.9K **Privately Held**
SIC: 3483 Ammunition, except for small arms

(G-18592)
VIKING PAPER COMPANY (PA)
5148 Stickney Ave (43612-3721)
PHONE..................................419 729-4951
J Anthony Mooter, *President*
Robert Walker, *Vice Pres*
EMP: 46 **EST:** 1986
SQ FT: 60,000
SALES (est): 19.9MM **Privately Held**
SIC: 2653 Sheets, corrugated: made from purchased materials

(G-18593)
VILLAGE VOICE PUBLISHING LTD
Also Called: Village Voice of Ottawa Hills
4041 W Central Ave Ste 6 (43606-2213)
PHONE..................................419 537-0286
Yaroslav Kuk, *Managing Prtnr*
YarOslav Kuk, *Managing Prtnr*
Anthony Bassett, *Partner*
Winifred Kuk, *Partner*
Tony Basset, *Editor*
EMP: 3
SQ FT: 275
SALES (est): 207.6K **Privately Held**
SIC: 2711 Newspapers, publishing & printing

(G-18594)
WALL TECHNOLOGY INC
1 Owens Corning Pkwy (43659-1000)
PHONE..................................715 532-5548
Johna Ryan, *Admin Sec*
EMP: 35
SALES (est): 3MM **Publicly Held**
SIC: 3446 3275 Mfg Architectural Metalwork Mfg Gypsum Products
HQ: Owens Corning Sales, Llc
    1 Owens Corning Pkwy
    Toledo OH 43659
    419 248-8000

(G-18595)
WAYNE FRAME PRODUCTS INC
5832 Lakeside Ave (43611-2466)
PHONE..................................419 726-7715
Jack L Bernard, *President*
Margaret Thurber, *Corp Secy*
Gerri Bernard, *Vice Pres*
EMP: 3
SALES (est): 341.3K **Privately Held**
SIC: 3089 Injection molded finished plastic products

(G-18596)
WERSELLS BIKE SHOP CO
Also Called: Wersell's Bike & Ski Shop
2860 W Central Ave (43606-3020)
PHONE..................................419 474-7412
Jill M Wersell, *President*
EMP: 4 **EST:** 1945
SQ FT: 3,000
SALES (est): 489.5K **Privately Held**
SIC: 5941 7699 3751 Bicycle & bicycle parts; skiing equipment; bicycle repair shop; bicycles & related parts

(G-18597)
WEST EQUIPMENT COMPANY INC (PA)
1545 E Broadway St (43605-3852)
PHONE..................................419 698-1601
Bernard Erdmann, *CEO*
Paul Erdmann, *President*
Kristi Erdmann, *Principal*
Chad Erdmann, *Vice Pres*
EMP: 18 **EST:** 1952
SQ FT: 7,200
SALES (est): 12.2MM **Privately Held**
SIC: 5082 7699 7359 3496 General construction machinery & equipment; construction equipment repair; equipment rental & leasing; slings, lifting: made from purchased wire; wire chain

(G-18598)
WESTROCK COMMERCIAL LLC
1635 Coining Dr (43612-2906)
PHONE..................................419 476-9101
EMP: 15
SALES (corp-wide): 16.2B **Publicly Held**
SIC: 2752 5112 Commercial printing, lithographic; stationery & office supplies
HQ: Westrock Commercial, Llc
    501 S 5th St
    Richmond VA 23219
    804 444-1000

(G-18599)
WHITEFORD INDUSTRIES INC
Also Called: Rehn Co
3323 South Ave (43609-1105)
PHONE..................................419 381-1155
Andy Klumb, *President*
EMP: 13
SQ FT: 9,000
SALES (est): 1.8MM **Privately Held**
WEB: www.rehncompany.com
SIC: 3842 3451 Atomizers, medical; screw machine products

(G-18600)
WIFIFACE LLC
5424 Westcastle Dr Apt D (43615-2048)
PHONE..................................419 754-4816
Matthew Howenstein, *CEO*
Hassen Alhandy, *Vice Pres*
Marilyn Howenstein, *Manager*
EMP: 3
SALES (est): 105K **Privately Held**
SIC: 7372 Application computer software

(G-18601)
WIREMAX LTD
705 Wamba Ave (43607-3252)
P.O. Box 3336 (43607-0336)
PHONE..................................419 531-9500
Al Mocek, *President*
Mark Robinson, *Manager*
EMP: 6
SQ FT: 8,000
SALES (est): 1MM **Privately Held**
WEB: www.wiremax.com
SIC: 3643 Current-carrying wiring devices

(G-18602)
WURTEC MANUFACTURING SERVICE
6200 Brent Dr (43611-1081)
PHONE..................................419 726-1066
Steven P Wurth, *President*
Jane A Wurth, *Corp Secy*
▲ **EMP:** 20 **EST:** 1995
SQ FT: 26,000
SALES (est): 3.7MM **Privately Held**
SIC: 3544 3993 Special dies, tools, jigs & fixtures; signs, not made in custom sign painting shops

(G-18603)
YARDER MANUFACTURING COMPANY (PA)
722 Phillips Ave (43612-1333)
P.O. Box 6886 (43612-0886)
PHONE..................................419 476-3933
Richard W Yarder, *President*
Matt Yarder, *Vice Pres*
Amy Conlan, *CFO*
Maryann Bailey, *Admin Sec*
EMP: 53 **EST:** 1930
SQ FT: 55,000
SALES (est): 8.3MM **Privately Held**
WEB: www.yardermfg.com
SIC: 3499 Boxes for packing & shipping, metal

(G-18604)
YARDER MANUFACTURING COMPANY
730 Phillips Ave (43612-1333)
PHONE..................................419 269-3474
EMP: 4

SALES (corp-wide): 8.3MM **Privately Held**
SIC: 3499 Boxes for packing & shipping, metal
PA: The Yarder Manufacturing Company
    722 Phillips Ave
    Toledo OH 43612
    419 476-3933

(G-18605)
ZF NORTH AMERICA INC
5915 Jason St (43611-1088)
PHONE..................................419 726-5599
Dennis Burke, *Branch Mgr*
EMP: 55
SALES (corp-wide): 144.2K **Privately Held**
WEB: www.trw.mediaroom.com
SIC: 3469 Metal stampings
HQ: Trw Automotive U.S. Llc
    12001 Tech Center Dr
    Livonia MI 48150
    734 855-2600

(G-18606)
ZIE BART RHINO LININGS TOLEDO
Also Called: Zie Bart Rhino Linings Toledo
3343 N Hlland Sylvania Rd (43615)
PHONE..................................419 841-2886
Keith Tucker, *Owner*
EMP: 6
SALES (est): 400K **Privately Held**
SIC: 3713 Truck beds

Toronto
Jefferson County

(G-18607)
ESSENTIAL EARTH ELEMENTS LLC
808 Market St (43964-1444)
PHONE..................................740 632-0682
Kimberly Ann Gorney, *Principal*
▲ **EMP:** 3
SALES (est): 182.1K **Privately Held**
SIC: 2819 Mfg Industrial Inorganic Chemicals

(G-18608)
EXPRESS ENERGY SVCS OPER LP
1515 Franklin St (43964-1029)
PHONE..................................740 337-4530
EMP: 42
SALES (corp-wide): 825.2MM **Privately Held**
SIC: 1389 Oil field services
PA: Express Energy Services Operating, Lp
    9800 Richmond Ave Ste 500
    Houston TX 77042
    713 625-7400

(G-18609)
F & M COAL COMPANY
3925 County Road 56 (43964-7927)
PHONE..................................740 544-5203
Edward L Fiala, *Partner*
EMP: 3
SALES (est): 260K **Privately Held**
SIC: 1221 Strip mining, bituminous

(G-18610)
K B ELECTRIC MOTOR SERVICE
Also Called: K B Electric Service
915 Banfield Ave (43964-1103)
PHONE..................................740 537-1346
Sharon Obertance, *President*
Bill Prolago, *Principal*
J B Ash, *Manager*
EMP: 5
SQ FT: 2,000
SALES (est): 75K **Privately Held**
SIC: 7694 Electric motor repair

(G-18611)
RIDGE MACHINE & WELDING CO
1015 Railroad St (43964-1115)
P.O. Box 190 (43964-0190)
PHONE..................................740 537-2821
David Artman, *President*
Debbie Artman, *Corp Secy*
J Curtis Artman, *Vice Pres*
EMP: 6 **EST:** 1950
SQ FT: 27,600
SALES (est): 500K **Privately Held**
SIC: 3599 7692 3398 Machine shop, jobbing & repair; welding repair; metal heat treating

(G-18612)
TITANIUM METALS CORPORATION
Also Called: Timet Toronto
100 Titanium Way (43964-1990)
P.O. Box 309 (43964-0309)
PHONE..................................740 537-1571
Sherri Williams, *Buyer*
Mike Wiggam, *QC Mgr*
Larry Rubin, *Electrical Engi*
Steve Wright, *Branch Mgr*
EMP: 527
SALES (corp-wide): 225.3B **Publicly Held**
WEB: www.timet.com
SIC: 3566 3356 Speed changers, drives & gears; nonferrous rolling & drawing
HQ: Titanium Metals Corporation
    4832 Richmond Rd Ste 100
    Warrensville Heights OH 44128
    610 968-1300

(G-18613)
U S ARMY CORPS OF ENGINEERS
Also Called: New Cumberland Lock & Dam
29501 State Rte 7 (43964)
PHONE..................................740 537-2571
Matt Dillon, *Manager*
David Ciciora, *Network Enginr*
EMP: 16 **Publicly Held**
WEB: www.sac.usace.army.mil
SIC: 3812 8711 Navigational systems & instruments; engineering services
HQ: U S Army Corps Of Engineers
    441 G St Nw
    Washington DC 20314
    202 761-0001

(G-18614)
VALLEY CONVERTING CO INC (PA)
405 Daniels St (43964-1343)
P.O. Box 279 (43964-0279)
PHONE..................................740 537-2152
Gino Biasi, *Ch of Bd*
Michael D Biasi, *President*
Richard Brandt, *Purch Mgr*
▼ **EMP:** 50
SQ FT: 107,500
SALES (est): 11MM **Privately Held**
SIC: 2631 Cardboard

(G-18615)
VALLEY CONVERTING CO INC
310 Loretta Ave (43964-1354)
P.O. Box 279 (43964-0279)
PHONE..................................740 537-2152
Mike Biasi, *Principal*
EMP: 45
SALES (corp-wide): 11MM **Privately Held**
SIC: 2631 Paperboard mills
PA: Valley Converting Co., Inc.
    405 Daniels St
    Toronto OH 43964
    740 537-2152

Tremont City
Clark County

(G-18616)
MIKE LOPPE
Also Called: Kutrite Manufacturing
2 W Main St (45372)
P.O. Box 186 (45372-0186)
PHONE..................................937 969-8102
Mike Loppe, *Owner*
Rose Haggey, *Co-Owner*
EMP: 10
SQ FT: 5,500
SALES (est): 995.2K **Privately Held**
SIC: 3599 7692 3444 Machine shop, jobbing & repair; welding repair; sheet metalwork

Trenton
Butler County

(G-18617)
ELITE MILL SERVICE & CNSTR
5757 Cottonrun Rd (45067-9724)
PHONE..................513 422-4234
John A Edester, *President*
EMP: 5
SQ FT: 3,600
SALES (est): 495.2K **Privately Held**
SIC: 3554 1521 Paper industries machinery; single-family housing construction

(G-18618)
EVERSHARPE DEBURRING TOOL CO
10 Baltimore Ave (45067-1513)
PHONE..................513 988-6240
David Huff, *President*
Bernice Huff, *Corp Secy*
Roger Sprinkle, *Vice Pres*
EMP: 8 EST: 1961
SQ FT: 2,400
SALES: 600K **Privately Held**
WEB: www.eversharpe.com
SIC: 7699 3545 Knife, saw & tool sharpening & repair; machine tool accessories

(G-18619)
GADD LOGGING
823 E Jameson Ct (45067-8621)
PHONE..................513 312-3941
Earl Gadd, *Principal*
EMP: 3
SALES (est): 207.9K **Privately Held**
SIC: 2411 Logging camps & contractors

(G-18620)
GREYFIELD INDUSTRIES INC
3104 Wayne Madison Rd (45067-9746)
PHONE..................513 860-1785
George Estes, *President*
Bob Leslie, *Vice Pres*
EMP: 15
SQ FT: 3,500
SALES (est): 4MM **Privately Held**
WEB: www.greyfieldindustries.com
SIC: 3661 3429 3663 3651 Telephone & telegraph apparatus; locks or lock sets; radio & TV communications equipment; household audio & video equipment

(G-18621)
JUNEBUGS WASH N DRY
6435 E State St (45067)
PHONE..................513 988-5863
Mike Wilson, *Owner*
EMP: 4 EST: 2001
SALES (est): 211.7K **Privately Held**
SIC: 3633 Laundry dryers, household or coin-operated

(G-18622)
MAG ACQUISITIONS LLC
Also Called: Magnode
400 E State St (45067-1549)
PHONE..................513 988-6351
Gary Verplank,
Amy Chase,
EMP: 225
SALES: 60MM **Privately Held**
SIC: 3354 Rods, extruded, aluminum

(G-18623)
MAGNODE CORPORATION (HQ)
400 E State St (45067-1549)
PHONE..................513 988-6351
Arthur W Bidwell, *Ch of Bd*
Martin J Bidwell, *President*
Johnie Adams, *Vice Pres*
Ann F Bidwell, *Vice Pres*
Joseph Bidwell, *Vice Pres*
EMP: 125
SQ FT: 100,000
SALES (est): 44.5MM
SALES (corp-wide): 425MM **Privately Held**
WEB: www.magnode.com
SIC: 3354 Aluminum extruded products

PA: Shape Corp.
1900 Hayes St
Grand Haven MI 49417
616 846-8700

(G-18624)
MAGNODE CORPORATION
Also Called: Awb Metals Division
400 E State St (45067-1549)
PHONE..................317 243-3553
Tony Walter, *Branch Mgr*
EMP: 100
SALES (corp-wide): 425MM **Privately Held**
WEB: www.magnode.com
SIC: 3442 3444 3354 Moldings & trim, except automobile: metal; sheet metalwork; aluminum extruded products
HQ: Magnode Corporation
400 E State St
Trenton OH 45067
513 988-6351

(G-18625)
MIILER BREWING COMPANY
2525 Wayne Madison Rd (45067-9799)
PHONE..................513 896-9200
Wayne McCauley, *Principal*
EMP: 17
SALES (est): 2.4MM **Privately Held**
SIC: 2082 Beer (alcoholic beverage)

(G-18626)
MILLERCOORS LLC
2525 Wayne Madison Rd (45067-9768)
P.O. Box 168 (45067-0168)
PHONE..................513 896-9200
Steve Sharpe, *Purchasing*
Sandra Lewis, *Pub Rel Dir*
Dennis Puffer, *Branch Mgr*
Michael Manning, *Manager*
Wayne Hensley, *Maintence Staff*
EMP: 60
SALES (corp-wide): 10.7B **Publicly Held**
SIC: 2082 Beer (alcoholic beverage)
HQ: Millercoors Llc
250 S Wacker Dr Ste 800
Chicago IL 60606
312 496-2700

Trotwood
Montgomery County

(G-18627)
ALLIANCE MFG SVCS INC
5915 Wolf Creek Pike (45426-2439)
PHONE..................937 222-3394
EMP: 3
SALES (est): 148.7K **Privately Held**
SIC: 3999 Manufacturing industries

(G-18628)
J W DEVERS & SON INC
5 N Broadway St (45426-3555)
P.O. Box 26460 (45426-0460)
PHONE..................937 854-3040
Jerry Haupt, *President*
David Henderson, *Corp Secy*
Steve Wolf, *Vice Pres*
EMP: 13
SALES (est): 3MM **Privately Held**
WEB: www.deverstruck.com
SIC: 5012 3715 Truck bodies; trailer bodies

(G-18629)
KASEL ENGINEERING LLC
5911 Wolf Creek Pike (45426-2439)
PHONE..................937 854-8875
Donald Kasel,
EMP: 8
SQ FT: 8,000
SALES (est): 1MM **Privately Held**
WEB: www.kaselengineering.com
SIC: 3556 Slicers, commercial, food

(G-18630)
STRYVER MFG INC
15 N Broadway St (45426-3555)
PHONE..................937 854-3048
Bruce J Flora, *President*
Lucille Flora, *Corp Secy*
Thomas E Flora, *Vice Pres*

EMP: 30
SQ FT: 30,000
SALES (est): 6.8MM **Privately Held**
SIC: 3599 3548 Machine shop, jobbing & repair; welding apparatus

(G-18631)
TROTWOOD CORPORATION
11 N Broadway St (45426-3594)
PHONE..................937 854-3047
Bruce J Flora, *President*
Lucille Flora, *Corp Secy*
Thomas E Flora, *Vice Pres*
Dainese Flora, *Financial Exec*
Scott Adams, *Administration*
EMP: 40 EST: 1932
SQ FT: 30,000
SALES (est): 5MM **Privately Held**
WEB: www.stryver.com
SIC: 3599 Machine shop, jobbing & repair

Troy
Miami County

(G-18632)
3 SIGMA LLC
1985 W Stanfield Rd (45373-2330)
PHONE..................937 440-3400
Tony Rowley, *President*
Rob Hoffert, *Plant Mgr*
Jon Christopherson, *Sales Staff*
EMP: 75 EST: 2017
SALES (est): 33MM **Privately Held**
SIC: 2672 Coated & laminated paper
PA: Bmc Growth Fund Llc
2991 Newmark Dr
Miamisburg OH 45342
937 291-4110

(G-18633)
AIM MEDIA MIDWEST OPER LLC
Also Called: Troy Daily News
224 S Market St (45373-3327)
PHONE..................937 335-5634
Tom Hutson, *Branch Mgr*
EMP: 19
SALES (corp-wide): 4.3MM **Privately Held**
SIC: 2711 Newspapers
PA: Aim Media Midwest Operating, Llc
4500 Lyons Rd
Miamisburg OH 45342
937 247-2700

(G-18634)
AMERICAN ADVNCED ASSMBLIES LLC
37 Harolds Way (45373-4098)
PHONE..................937 339-6267
Thomas B Fay, *President*
Christopher Hufford, *Manager*
EMP: 28 EST: 2011
SALES: 5.5MM **Privately Held**
SIC: 3679 Harness assemblies for electronic use: wire or cable

(G-18635)
AMERICAN HONDA MOTOR CO INC
Also Called: Honda Mdwest Consolidation Ctr
151 Commerce Center Blvd (45373-9039)
PHONE..................937 339-0157
EMP: 5
SALES (corp-wide): 144.1B **Privately Held**
SIC: 3711 Cars, electric, assembly of
HQ: American Honda Motor Co., Inc.
1919 Torrance Blvd
Torrance CA 90501
310 783-2000

(G-18636)
AMERICAN HONDA MOTOR CO INC
101 S Stanfield Rd (45373-2333)
P.O. Box 1010 (45373-8010)
PHONE..................937 332-6100
Bruce Smith, *Manager*
EMP: 145
SQ FT: 131,000

SALES (corp-wide): 144.1B **Privately Held**
SIC: 5511 3711 Automobiles, new & used; motor vehicles & car bodies
HQ: American Honda Motor Co., Inc.
1919 Torrance Blvd
Torrance CA 90501
310 783-2000

(G-18637)
AMETEK INC
Also Called: Ametek Presto Light Power
66 Industry Ct Ste F (45373-2560)
PHONE..................937 440-0800
Patrick Williams, *Principal*
EMP: 10
SALES (corp-wide): 4.8B **Publicly Held**
SIC: 5063 3699 Batteries; electrical equipment & supplies
PA: Ametek, Inc.
1100 Cassatt Rd
Berwyn PA 19312
610 647-2121

(G-18638)
ARC ABRASIVES INC
Also Called: A R C
2131 Corporate Dr (45373-1067)
P.O. Box 10 (45373-0010)
PHONE..................800 888-4885
Anthony H Stayman, *CEO*
Anthony Stayman, *President*
▲ EMP: 76 EST: 1960
SALES (est): 67.1MM **Privately Held**
WEB: www.arcabrasives.com
SIC: 5085 3291 2296 Abrasives; abrasive products; tire cord & fabrics

(G-18639)
ATI IRRIGATION LLC
4746 W State Route 55 (45373-7538)
PHONE..................937 750-2976
Matt Goodin, *President*
EMP: 3
SALES: 250K **Privately Held**
SIC: 4971 3648 Irrigation systems; outdoor lighting equipment

(G-18640)
CHARACTERS INC
190 Peters Ave Ste A (45373-3995)
PHONE..................937 335-1976
Esther Marko, *President*
Jason Marko, *Vice Pres*
EMP: 9 EST: 1961
SQ FT: 8,000
SALES (est): 700K **Privately Held**
SIC: 2752 Commercial printing, lithographic

(G-18641)
CITY OF TROY
Also Called: Troy Water Treatment Plant
300 E Staunton Rd (45373-2105)
PHONE..................937 339-4826
Tim Ray, *Superintendent*
EMP: 10 **Privately Held**
WEB: www.troyohio.gov
SIC: 3589 4941 Sewage & water treatment equipment; water supply
PA: City Of Troy
100 S Market St Ste 1
Troy OH 45373
937 335-2224

(G-18642)
CLOPAY BUILDING PDTS CO INC
1400 W Market St (45373-3889)
PHONE..................937 440-6403
Tim McNally, *Safety Mgr*
Doug Niekamp, *Financial Analy*
Bernice Weaver, *Cust Mgr*
Mike Kerkman, *Manager*
Brandon Bass, *Manager*
EMP: 3
SALES (corp-wide): 1.5B **Publicly Held**
SIC: 2431 3442 2436 Garage doors, overhead: wood; garage doors, overhead: metal; plywood, softwood
HQ: Clopay Building Products Company, Inc.
8585 Duke Blvd
Mason OH 45040

Troy - Miami County (G-18643)

GEOGRAPHIC SECTION

(G-18643)
CONAGRA FODS PCKAGED FOODS LLC
801 Dye Mill Rd (45373-4223)
PHONE....................................937 440-2800
Scott Adkins, *Branch Mgr*
EMP: 491
SALES (corp-wide): 7.9B **Publicly Held**
SIC: 2099 Food preparations
HQ: Conagra Foods Packaged Foods, Llc
1 Conagra Dr
Omaha NE 68102

(G-18644)
CROWE MANUFACTURING SERVICES
Also Called: King of The Road
2731 Walnut Ridge Dr (45373-4562)
PHONE....................................800 831-1893
Jamie King, *CEO*
Rob Haviland, *President*
Robert King, *Corp Secy*
EMP: 60
SQ FT: 140,000
SALES: 10MM **Privately Held**
WEB: www.crowemanufacturing.com
SIC: 3599 3544 Machine & other job shop work; special dies, tools, jigs & fixtures

(G-18645)
DARE ELECTRONICS INC
3245 S County Road 25a (45373-9384)
P.O. Box 419 (45373-0419)
PHONE....................................937 335-0031
Karen Beagle, *President*
Mark Osman, *Mfg Mgr*
EMP: 50
SQ FT: 28,750
SALES (est): 7.6MM **Privately Held**
WEB: www.dareelectronics.com
SIC: 3679 3651 Power supplies, all types: static; amplifiers: radio, public address or musical instrument

(G-18646)
DAYTON SUPERIOR PDTS CO INC
1370 Lytle Rd (45373-9401)
PHONE....................................937 332-1930
Frank Gleason Jr, *Ch of Bd*
Daniel P Gleason, *President*
EMP: 8
SQ FT: 15,000
SALES: 1.5MM **Privately Held**
SIC: 3714 Motor vehicle transmissions, drive assemblies & parts; clutches, motor vehicle

(G-18647)
DEBRA HARBOUR
Also Called: August Nine Enterprises
251 S Mulberry St # 220 (45373-3585)
P.O. Box 599 (45373-0599)
PHONE....................................937 440-9618
Debra Harbour, *Owner*
EMP: 8
SQ FT: 1,800
SALES (est): 659.1K **Privately Held**
SIC: 3672 3699 Printed circuit boards; electrical equipment & supplies

(G-18648)
DELTECH POLYMERS CORPORATION
1250 S Union St (45373-4118)
PHONE....................................937 339-3150
Robert Elefante, *Ch of Bd*
EMP: 8
SQ FT: 435,600
SALES (est): 2.8MM **Privately Held**
SIC: 3087 2821 Custom compound purchased resins; polystyrene resins

(G-18649)
DESIGN TECHNOLOGIES & MFG CO
Also Called: Des Tech
2000 Corporate Dr (45373-1069)
PHONE....................................937 335-0757
D Jeffrey Meredith, *President*
Marilyn J Freeman, *Principal*
John E Fulker, *Principal*
Debbie Meredith, *Corp Secy*
William Leffel, *Vice Pres*
EMP: 18
SQ FT: 32,000
SALES (est): 4.4MM **Privately Held**
SIC: 3599 Machine shop, jobbing & repair

(G-18650)
DESIGNER AWARDS INC
Also Called: Award One
101 S Market St (45373-3324)
PHONE....................................937 339-4444
Scott Breisch, *Shareholder*
EMP: 3
SQ FT: 6,000
SALES (est): 299.6K **Privately Held**
SIC: 5999 2261 7389 Trophies & plaques; screen printing of cotton broadwoven fabrics; engraving service

(G-18651)
DETRICK DESIGN FABRICATION LLC
425 Wisteria Dr (45373-8850)
PHONE....................................937 620-6736
Eugene Detrick,
EMP: 4 EST: 2014
SALES (est): 114.4K **Privately Held**
SIC: 3499 Novelties & giftware, including trophies; barricades, metal

(G-18652)
ECOTEC LTD LLC
150 Marybill Dr S (45373-1053)
PHONE....................................937 606-2793
Torbjorn Lindgren, *President*
Jim Keyser, *General Mgr*
James Keyser, *Vice Pres*
▲ **EMP: 5 EST:** 2012
SQ FT: 2,000
SALES: 2MM **Privately Held**
SIC: 3629 Battery chargers, rectifying or nonrotating

(G-18653)
ERNST ENTERPRISES INC
Troy Ready Mix
805 S Union St (45373-4109)
PHONE....................................937 339-6249
Dwayne Littlejohn, *Manager*
EMP: 22
SQ FT: 7,446
SALES (corp-wide): 227.2MM **Privately Held**
WEB: www.ernstconcrete.com
SIC: 3273 Ready-mixed concrete
PA: Ernst Enterprises, Inc.
3361 Successful Way
Dayton OH 45414
937 233-5555

(G-18654)
EVENFLO COMPANY INC
1801 W Main St (45373-2303)
PHONE....................................937 773-3971
Rick Frank, *Branch Mgr*
EMP: 100
SALES (corp-wide): 914.5MM **Privately Held**
WEB: www.evenflo.com
SIC: 2519 3944 Fiberglass & plastic furniture; child restraint seats, automotive
HQ: Evenflo Company, Inc.
225 Byers Rd
Miamisburg OH 45342

(G-18655)
F&P AMERICA MFG INC (HQ)
2101 Corporate Dr (45373-1076)
PHONE....................................937 339-0212
Akihide Fukuda, *Ch of Bd*
Masafumi Yamano, *President*
Andrew Kochanek, *Plant Mgr*
David Sutch, *Opers Staff*
Dwane Sloan, *Human Res Dir*
▲ **EMP:** 252
SQ FT: 400,000
SALES: 163.7MM
SALES (corp-wide): 2.1B **Privately Held**
SIC: 3714 Motor vehicle steering systems & parts
PA: F-Tech Inc.
19, Showanuma, Shobucho
Kuki STM 346-0
480 855-211

(G-18656)
FAURECIA EXHAUST SYSTEMS INC
1255 Archer Dr (45373-3841)
PHONE....................................937 339-0551
Bryan Imhoff, *Manager*
EMP: 300
SALES (corp-wide): 342.9MM **Privately Held**
WEB: www.franklin.faurecia.com
SIC: 3714 Exhaust systems & parts, motor vehicle; manifolds, motor vehicle
HQ: Faurecia Emissions Control Systems Na, Llc
543 Matzinger Rd
Toledo OH 43612
812 341-2000

(G-18657)
FEDEX OFFICE & PRINT SVCS INC
1886 W Main St (45373-2304)
PHONE....................................937 335-3816
Charles James, *Manager*
EMP: 11
SALES (corp-wide): 65.4B **Publicly Held**
SIC: 7389 7334 5099 2759 Packaging & labeling services; blueprinting service; firearms & ammunition, except sporting; financial note & certificate printing & engraving
HQ: Fedex Office And Print Services, Inc.
7900 Legacy Dr
Plano TX 75024
800 463-3339

(G-18658)
FREUDENBERG-NOK GENERAL PARTNR
Also Called: Freudenberg-Nok Sealing Tech
1275 Archer Dr (45373-3841)
P.O. Box 844, Spencer IA (51301-0844)
PHONE....................................937 335-3306
Larry Heimilghton, *Manager*
EMP: 30
SALES (corp-wide): 11B **Privately Held**
WEB: www.freudenberg-nok.com
SIC: 3053 Gaskets & sealing devices
HQ: Freudenberg-Nok General Partnership
47774 W Anchor Ct
Plymouth MI 48170
734 451-0020

(G-18659)
FTECH R&D NORTH AMERICA INC (HQ)
1191 Horizon West Ct (45373-7560)
PHONE....................................937 339-2777
Bing Liu, *COO*
EMP: 56
SQ FT: 50,000
SALES (est): 8.4MM
SALES (est): 2.1B **Privately Held**
SIC: 8731 3714 Commercial physical research; motor vehicle parts & accessories
PA: F-Tech Inc.
19, Showanuma, Shobucho
Kuki STM 346-0
480 855-211

(G-18660)
GARY COMPTON
Also Called: Tools Plus
3245 Piqua Troy Rd (45373-7794)
PHONE....................................937 339-6829
Gary Compton, *Owner*
EMP: 4
SQ FT: 3,000
SALES: 1.5MM **Privately Held**
WEB: www.toolsplus1.com
SIC: 5251 3559 Tools, power; automotive related machinery

(G-18661)
GENESIS GRAPHICS
14 N Walnut St Ste 2 (45373-3472)
PHONE....................................937 335-5332
Sam Weiss, *Owner*
EMP: 4
SALES (est): 267.9K **Privately Held**
SIC: 2759 Commercial printing

(G-18662)
GOKOH CORPORATION (HQ)
1280 Archer Dr (45373-3842)
PHONE....................................937 339-4977
Shuji Hioki, *President*
Steve Kershner, *Managing Dir*
Heiju Hashimoto, *Principal*
Parker Bailey, *Vice Pres*
▲ **EMP:** 15
SQ FT: 16,000
SALES (est): 6.4MM
SALES (corp-wide): 76.3MM **Privately Held**
WEB: www.tellthat.com
SIC: 5085 5084 3544 3559 Industrial supplies; industrial machinery & equipment; machine tools & metalworking machinery; special dies & tools; jigs & fixtures; foundry machinery & equipment; fabricated structural metal
PA: Goko Sangyo Co., Ltd.
1-2-2, Higashiryoke
Kawaguchi STM 332-0
482 231-493

(G-18663)
GOODRICH CORPORATION
Also Called: UTC Aerospace Systems
101 Waco St (45373-3872)
P.O. Box 340 (45373-0340)
PHONE....................................937 339-3811
Joel Miller, *General Mgr*
John Perdziola, *VP Opers*
Thad Smith, *Facilities Mgr*
David Little, *Senior Buyer*
Kate Carter, *Buyer*
EMP: 750
SALES (corp-wide): 66.5B **Publicly Held**
WEB: www.bfgoodrich.com
SIC: 3728 3714 3721 Aircraft parts & equipment; wheels, motor vehicle; motor vehicle brake systems & parts; aircraft
HQ: Goodrich Corporation
2730 W Tyvola Rd
Charlotte NC 28217
704 423-7000

(G-18664)
GRICE EQUIPMENT REPAIR INC
518 Garfield Ave (45373-3114)
PHONE....................................937 440-8343
Bruce Grice, *President*
EMP: 4
SQ FT: 5,500
SALES (est): 883.3K **Privately Held**
WEB: www.griceequipment.com
SIC: 3556 Food products machinery

(G-18665)
HINES BUILDERS INC
1587 Lytle Rd (45373-9488)
PHONE....................................937 335-4586
Harold A Hines, *President*
Scherre Mumpower, *Admin Sec*
EMP: 18
SQ FT: 25,000
SALES (est): 2MM **Privately Held**
SIC: 2448 1541 2441 Pallets, wood; cargo containers, wood & wood with metal; industrial buildings, new construction; nailed wood boxes & shook

(G-18666)
HOBART BROS STICK ELECTRODE
101 Trade Sq E (45373-2476)
PHONE....................................937 332-5375
Steve Knostman, *Owner*
EMP: 109
SALES (est): 3.2MM **Privately Held**
SIC: 7692 Welding repair

(G-18667)
HOBART BROTHERS COMPANY
400 Trade Sq E (45373-2463)
PHONE....................................937 332-5338
Dennis Foster, *District Mgr*
John Uhrig, *District Mgr*
Bob Wiscombe, *District Mgr*
Jeff Billett, *Plant Mgr*
Tim Wenrick, *Opers Mgr*
EMP: 6
SALES (corp-wide): 14.7B **Publicly Held**
SIC: 3548 Welding apparatus

GEOGRAPHIC SECTION
Troy - Miami County (G-18692)

HQ: Hobart Brothers Llc
101 Trade Sq E
Troy OH 45373
937 332-5439

(G-18668)
HOBART BROTHERS COMPANY
1260 Bruckner Dr (45373-4354)
PHONE..............................937 332-5023
EMP: 7
SALES (corp-wide): 14.7B Publicly Held
SIC: 3548 Welding apparatus
HQ: Hobart Brothers Llc
101 Trade Sq E
Troy OH 45373
937 332-5439

(G-18669)
HOBART BROTHERS LLC (HQ)
Also Called: ITW Hobart Brothers
101 Trade Sq E (45373-2488)
PHONE..............................937 332-5439
W H Hobart Et Al, *Principal*
S E Hobart, *Principal*
Ron Walker, *District Mgr*
Sundaram Nagarajan, *Vice Pres*
Grant Harvey, *Vice Pres*
◆ EMP: 600 EST: 1917
SQ FT: 1,000,000
SALES (est): 326MM
SALES (corp-wide): 14.7B Publicly Held
SIC: 3548 3537 Welding apparatus; industrial trucks & tractors
PA: Illinois Tool Works Inc.
155 Harlem Ave
Glenview IL 60025
847 724-7500

(G-18670)
HOBART CABINET COMPANY
301 E Water St (45373-3440)
PHONE..............................937 335-4666
Martin E Hobart, *President*
EMP: 9 EST: 1907
SQ FT: 50,000
SALES: 1.1MM Privately Held
WEB: www.hobartcabinet.com
SIC: 2522 Office bookcases, wallcases & partitions, except wood

(G-18671)
HOBART CORPORATION
Also Called: Engineering Dept
401 S Market St (45373)
PHONE..............................937 332-3000
Gary Banks, *Manager*
EMP: 50
SALES (corp-wide): 14.7B Publicly Held
WEB: www.hobartcorp.com
SIC: 3589 3556 3596 3585 Dishwashing machines, commercial; cooking equipment, commercial; commercial cooking & foodwarming equipment; food products machinery; weighing machines & apparatus; refrigeration equipment, complete; gray & ductile iron foundries
HQ: Hobart Llc
701 S Ridge Ave
Troy OH 45374
937 332-3000

(G-18672)
HOBART INTERNATIONAL HOLDINGS
701 S Ridge Ave (45373-3000)
PHONE..............................937 332-3000
Richard Gleitsmann, *President*
Thomas H Rodgers, *Vice Pres*
Sue Flora, *Vice Pres*
Kathy Agenbroad, *Purchasing*
EMP: 250
SQ FT: 500,000
SALES (est): 18.5MM
SALES (corp-wide): 14.7B Publicly Held
SIC: 3556 Food products machinery
PA: Illinois Tool Works Inc.
155 Harlem Ave
Glenview IL 60025
847 724-7500

(G-18673)
ILLINOIS TOOL WORKS INC
Itwfeg
701 S Ridge Ave (45374-0001)
PHONE..............................937 335-7171
John Bieri, *Vice Pres*
Elaine Everman, *Branch Mgr*
EMP: 50
SALES (corp-wide): 14.7B Publicly Held
SIC: 3589 Dishwashing machines, commercial
PA: Illinois Tool Works Inc.
155 Harlem Ave
Glenview IL 60025
847 724-7500

(G-18674)
ILLINOIS TOOL WORKS INC
Also Called: ITW Hobart
750 Lincoln Ave (45373-3137)
PHONE..............................937 332-2839
Bob Freef, *General Mgr*
EMP: 92
SALES (corp-wide): 14.7B Publicly Held
SIC: 3089 Injection molded finished plastic products
PA: Illinois Tool Works Inc.
155 Harlem Ave
Glenview IL 60025
847 724-7500

(G-18675)
ILLINOIS TOOL WORKS INC
Vulcan Food Equipment Group
401 W Market St (45373-3927)
PHONE..............................519 376-8886
Cathy Long, *Branch Mgr*
EMP: 92
SALES (corp-wide): 14.7B Publicly Held
SIC: 3089 Injection molded finished plastic products; closures, plastic; synthetic resin finished products
PA: Illinois Tool Works Inc.
155 Harlem Ave
Glenview IL 60025
847 724-7500

(G-18676)
INDEPENDENT MACHINE & WLDG INC
35 Marybill Dr S (45373-1033)
PHONE..............................937 339-7330
Glenn Reed, *President*
Dale F Deaton, *Vice Pres*
Carol Owens, *Treasurer*
EMP: 6 EST: 2000
SQ FT: 10,000
SALES: 300K Privately Held
SIC: 3599 7692 Machine shop, jobbing & repair; welding repair

(G-18677)
ISHMAEL PRECISION TOOL CORP
Also Called: Iptc
55 Industry Ct (45373-2368)
PHONE..............................937 335-8070
Larry R Ishmael, *President*
Larry Ishmael, *President*
Jackie Mathes, *Principal*
Isaiah Wilmoth, *Principal*
Robert Ishmael, *Vice Pres*
▲ EMP: 20 EST: 1978
SQ FT: 32,000
SALES (est): 4.2MM Privately Held
SIC: 3544 Special dies & tools

(G-18678)
ITW FOOD EQUIPMENT GROUP LLC
Also Called: Ibex Rapid Cooks
401 W Market St (45373-3927)
PHONE..............................937 332-3000
Gary Simpson, *Exec VP*
EMP: 10
SALES (corp-wide): 14.7B Publicly Held
SIC: 3556 Food products machinery
HQ: Itw Food Equipment Group Llc
701 S Ridge Ave
Troy OH 45374

(G-18679)
ITW FOOD EQUIPMENT GROUP LLC (HQ)
Also Called: Hobart
701 S Ridge Ave (45374-0001)
PHONE..............................937 332-2396
Tom Szafranski, *President*
Chris O Herlihy, *Exec VP*
Jennifer Monnin, *Vice Pres*
Jeff CPM, *Manager*
Trudy Tolbert, *Manager*
◆ EMP: 1100
SALES (est): 528.4MM
SALES (corp-wide): 14.7B Publicly Held
SIC: 5046 3556 Restaurant equipment & supplies; food products machinery
PA: Illinois Tool Works Inc.
155 Harlem Ave
Glenview IL 60025
847 724-7500

(G-18680)
JAYNA INC (PA)
15 Marybill Dr S (45373-1033)
PHONE..............................937 335-8922
Damaroo Shah, *President*
Paras Shah, *General Mgr*
Mayank Shah, *Chairman*
Raj Khare, *Vice Pres*
Ruchi Shah, *Vice Pres*
EMP: 43 EST: 1988
SQ FT: 40,000
SALES (est): 10.4MM Privately Held
WEB: www.jayna.com
SIC: 3599 Machine shop, jobbing & repair

(G-18681)
KERBER SHEETMETAL WORKS INC
Also Called: Ksm Metal Fabrications
104 Foss Way (45373-1430)
PHONE..............................937 339-6366
Kathleen Kerber, *President*
Jim Wilmath, *Sales Mgr*
Kathleen Sawchek, *Manager*
EMP: 18
SQ FT: 27,000
SALES (est): 3.9MM Privately Held
WEB: www.kerbersheetmetal.com
SIC: 3444 Ducts, sheet metal

(G-18682)
KISER INDUSTRIES LLC
507 Michigan Ave (45373-2142)
PHONE..............................937 332-6723
EMP: 5 EST: 2012
SALES (est): 280K Privately Held
SIC: 3999 Manufacturing Industries, Nec, Nsk

(G-18683)
KSM METAL FABRICATION
104 Foss Way (45373-1430)
PHONE..............................937 339-6366
Kathy Kerber, *President*
EMP: 4
SALES (est): 286.8K Privately Held
SIC: 3499 Fabricated metal products

(G-18684)
LUKENS INC
1040 S Dorset Rd (45373-4708)
PHONE..............................937 440-2500
Michael Van Haaren, *President*
Greg Sherman, *Superintendent*
Bill Diederich, *Principal*
Michael Burns, *Opers Staff*
Sam Buchman, *Manager*
EMP: 90
SQ FT: 70,000
SALES (est): 15.1MM Privately Held
SIC: 3544 Special dies & tools

(G-18685)
MADER AUTOMOTIVE CENTER INC (PA)
Also Called: Bushong Auto Service
225 S Walnut St (45373-3532)
PHONE..............................937 339-2681
Dan Mader, *President*
EMP: 15
SQ FT: 18,000
SALES (est): 2.6MM Privately Held
SIC: 5013 5531 3599 Automotive supplies & parts; automotive parts; machine shop, jobbing & repair

(G-18686)
MARIETTA MARTIN MATERIALS INC
Also Called: Troy Sand and Gravel
250 Dye Mill Rd (45373-4280)
PHONE..............................937 335-8313
Darrell Sparks, *Manager*
EMP: 7 Publicly Held
WEB: www.martinmarietta.com
SIC: 1442 Sand mining; gravel mining
PA: Martin Marietta Materials Inc
2710 Wycliff Rd
Raleigh NC 27607

(G-18687)
MEDWAY TOOL CORP
2100 Corporate Dr (45373-1085)
PHONE..............................937 335-7717
Tom Drake, *President*
EMP: 23
SQ FT: 15,000
SALES (est): 3MM Privately Held
SIC: 3599 3545 3544 3444 Machine shop, jobbing & repair; machine tool accessories; special dies, tools, jigs & fixtures; sheet metalwork

(G-18688)
NOVACEL INC
421 S Union St (45373-4151)
PHONE..............................937 335-5611
Lora Bridges, *Accountant*
Tim Shank, *Branch Mgr*
EMP: 160
SALES (corp-wide): 4.2MM Privately Held
WEB: www.novacelonline.com
SIC: 2671 Packaging paper & plastics film, coated & laminated
HQ: Novacel, Inc.
21 3rd St
Palmer MA 01069
413 283-3468

(G-18689)
NOVACEL INC
421 Union St (45373-4151)
PHONE..............................413 283-3468
David Neely, *Manager*
EMP: 45
SALES (corp-wide): 4.2MM Privately Held
WEB: www.novacelonline.com
SIC: 2671 Packaging paper & plastics film, coated & laminated
HQ: Novacel, Inc.
21 3rd St
Palmer MA 01069
413 283-3468

(G-18690)
OUTBACK TREE WORKS
808 N Market St (45373-1424)
PHONE..............................937 332-7300
Eric M Anderson, *Principal*
EMP: 3
SALES (est): 273.5K Privately Held
SIC: 3524 Lawn & garden equipment

(G-18691)
PAINTED HILL INV GROUP INC
Also Called: Western Ohio Graphics
402 E Main St (45373-3413)
PHONE..............................937 339-1756
Anthony W Cockerham, *President*
EMP: 10
SQ FT: 13,000
SALES: 800K Privately Held
SIC: 2752 2396 3993 2759 Commercial printing, offset; screen printing on fabric articles; signs & advertising specialties; screen printing; graphic arts & related design

(G-18692)
PEAK FOODS LLC
1903 W Main St Ste B (45373-1153)
PHONE..............................937 440-0707
Brian Adkins, *Opers Mgr*
Debbie Friend, *Prdtn Mgr*
Chris Whipple, *Materials Mgr*
Susan Nunn, *Purchasing*
Debra Driskell, *QC Mgr*
EMP: 65
SQ FT: 5,500
SALES (est): 19.4MM Privately Held
WEB: www.peakfoods.com
SIC: 2026 Whipped topping, except frozen or dry mix

Troy - Miami County (G-18693) GEOGRAPHIC SECTION

(G-18693)
POLYMERS BY DESIGN LLC
2150 Monroe Concord Rd (45373-8208)
P.O. Box 303 (45373-0303)
PHONE.....................................937 361-7398
Janet Zelnick, *CEO*
Mark Zelnick, *General Mgr*
EMP: 4
SALES (est): 689.8K **Privately Held**
SIC: 3087 Custom compound purchased resins

(G-18694)
PREMIER TOOL INC
1333 E Main St (45373-3452)
PHONE.....................................937 332-0996
Brady Wilson, *President*
EMP: 5
SALES: 200K **Privately Held**
SIC: 3599 Machine shop, jobbing & repair

(G-18695)
R T INDUSTRIES INC (PA)
Also Called: CHAMPION INDUSTRIES DIV
110 Foss Way (45373-1430)
PHONE.....................................937 335-5784
Ann Hinkle, *Superintendent*
Karen Mayer, *Superintendent*
EMP: 146
SQ FT: 18,000
SALES: 4.3MM **Privately Held**
SIC: 3579 8331 7349 2789 Paper cutters, trimmers & punches; sheltered workshop; janitorial service, contract basis; bookbinding & related work; home for the mentally handicapped

(G-18696)
R&D MACHINE INC
1204 S Crawford St (45373-4134)
PHONE.....................................937 339-2545
Daniel Daffner, *President*
Pam Daffner, *Owner*
EMP: 15
SALES (est): 3MM **Privately Held**
SIC: 3312 Tool & die steel

(G-18697)
RAYMATH COMPANY
2323 W State Route 55 (45373-9234)
PHONE.....................................937 335-1860
James M Ruef, *President*
Ray Mathieu, *President*
William Moore, *Chairman*
Ward Wildman, *Vice Pres*
Tracy Caudill, *Purch Mgr*
▲ EMP: 109
SQ FT: 50,000
SALES: 9.2MM **Privately Held**
WEB: www.raymath.com
SIC: 3541 3544 Machine tools, metal cutting type; special dies & tools

(G-18698)
RHOMBUS TECHNOLOGIES LTD
755 Barnhart Rd (45373-8704)
PHONE.....................................937 335-1840
Roger Kearney, *President*
Carol Kearney, *Vice Pres*
EMP: 3
SALES (est): 75K **Privately Held**
WEB: www.onthesquare.com
SIC: 7372 Business oriented computer software

(G-18699)
ROCONEX CORPORATION
20 Marybill Dr S (45373-1034)
PHONE.....................................937 339-2616
Ty Spear, *President*
Laura Rudy, *Administration*
EMP: 19
SQ FT: 31,000
SALES (est): 3MM **Privately Held**
WEB: www.roconex.com
SIC: 3555 3444 Printing trades machinery; sheet metalwork

(G-18700)
ROSS SPECIAL PRODUCTS INC
2500 W State Route 55 (45373-9511)
PHONE.....................................937 335-8406
Dave Pollard, *President*
EMP: 17
SQ FT: 13,000
SALES: 900K **Privately Held**
SIC: 3089 3544 Injection molding of plastics; forms (molds), for foundry & plastics working machinery

(G-18701)
S-K MOLD & TOOL COMPANY
2120 Corporate Dr (45373-1085)
P.O. Box 495 (45373-0495)
PHONE.....................................937 339-0299
Vince Hinde, *Branch Mgr*
EMP: 20
SALES (corp-wide): 15.9MM **Privately Held**
WEB: www.skmold.com
SIC: 3544 3599 Special dies & tools; machine shop, jobbing & repair
PA: S-K Mold & Tool Company
955 N 3rd St
Tipp City OH 45371
937 339-0299

(G-18702)
SAN PALLET LLC
1860 State Route 718 (45373-8725)
PHONE.....................................937 271-5308
Richard Sofia, *Mng Member*
Brian Sofia, *Mng Member*
Richard D Sofia, *Mng Member*
EMP: 2
SALES: 2.4MM **Privately Held**
SIC: 2821 5085 Polypropylene resins; plastic pallets

(G-18703)
SCHIFFER GROUP INC
Also Called: Minuteman Press
1602 Marby Dr (45373-9264)
PHONE.....................................937 694-8185
Daniel L Schiffer, *President*
EMP: 3
SQ FT: 2,000
SALES: 120K **Privately Held**
SIC: 2752 7336 7319 Commercial printing, offset; graphic arts & related design; display advertising service

(G-18704)
SEGNA INC
1316 Barnhart Rd (45373-9510)
PHONE.....................................937 335-6700
Junichi Yakahi, *President*
◆ EMP: 15 EST: 2001
SQ FT: 2,100
SALES: 3MM **Privately Held**
SIC: 3559 Automotive maintenance equipment

(G-18705)
SEW-EURODRIVE INC
2001 W Main St (45373-1018)
PHONE.....................................937 335-0036
Mayme Larson, *Safety Mgr*
Pete Johnson, *Engineer*
Gene Hart, *Enginr/R&D Mgr*
Kathy Ward, *Finance Mgr*
Lori Green, *Manager*
EMP: 100
SQ FT: 32,400
SALES (corp-wide): 3.4B **Privately Held**
WEB: www.seweurodrive.com
SIC: 3566 3714 3699 Gears, power transmission, except automotive; motor vehicle parts & accessories; electrical equipment & supplies
HQ: Sew-Eurodrive, Inc.
1295 Old Spartanburg Hwy
Lyman SC 29365
864 439-7537

(G-18706)
SIRIO PANEL INC
1385 Stonycreek Rd Ste E (45373-2584)
P.O. Box 426 (45373-0426)
PHONE.....................................937 238-3607
Tom Kendall, *Principal*
EMP: 3 EST: 2011
SALES (est): 248.3K **Privately Held**
SIC: 3728 Aircraft parts & equipment

(G-18707)
SLIMLINE SURGICAL DEVICES LLC
Also Called: Canyon Run Engineering
1990 W Stanfield Rd (45373-2329)
PHONE.....................................937 335-0496

Gary Ward, *President*
Amy Ward, *Principal*
Carly Witmer, *Principal*
EMP: 7
SALES (est): 344.2K **Privately Held**
SIC: 3599 Machine shop, jobbing & repair

(G-18708)
SOLOMON INDUSTRIES LLC
3365 Peebles Rd (45373-8437)
PHONE.....................................937 558-5334
Jason David Solomon, *Principal*
EMP: 5
SALES (est): 515.9K **Privately Held**
SIC: 3999 Manufacturing industries

(G-18709)
SPECIALTY PRINTING LLC
1202 Archer Dr (45373-3842)
PHONE.....................................937 335-4046
Roger Reed, *Manager*
EMP: 5
SALES (est): 350.5K
SALES (corp-wide): 51.1MM **Privately Held**
SIC: 2752 Commercial printing, offset
PA: Specialty Printing, Llc
4 Thompson Rd
East Windsor CT 06088
860 623-8870

(G-18710)
SPINNAKER COATING LLC
518 E Water St (45373-3400)
PHONE.....................................937 332-6300
Sharon Malone, *Manager*
EMP: 120
SALES (corp-wide): 75.4MM **Privately Held**
SIC: 2672 2891 Labels (unprinted), gummed; made from purchased materials; adhesives & sealants
PA: Spinnaker Coating, Llc
518 E Water St
Troy OH 45373
937 332-6500

(G-18711)
SPINNAKER COATING LLC (PA)
518 E Water St (45373-3400)
PHONE.....................................937 332-6500
Louis A Guzzetti Jr, *CEO*
Chris Hund, *President*
George E Fuehrer, *Exec VP*
Stuart A Postle, *Senior VP*
Perry J Schiller, *Senior VP*
▲ EMP: 100
SQ FT: 298,000
SALES (est): 75.4MM **Privately Held**
SIC: 2672 Labels (unprinted), gummed: made from purchased materials

(G-18712)
SPINNAKER COATINGS
130 Marybill Dr S (45373-1053)
PHONE.....................................937 332-6619
EMP: 3 EST: 2012
SALES (est): 343.2K **Privately Held**
SIC: 2621 Paper mills

(G-18713)
STILLWATER TECHNOLOGIES LLC
1040 S Dorset Rd (45373-4708)
PHONE.....................................937 440-2505
Dennis J Miller, *CEO*
John V Handelsman, *Chairman*
Karen Benanzer, *Accounts Mgr*
Dana Sanders, *Consultant*
Marybeth Roberts, *Agent*
EMP: 90
SQ FT: 1,250
SALES (est): 4.2MM **Privately Held**
SIC: 3599 Machine & other job shop work

(G-18714)
TROY LAMINATING & COATING INC
421 Union St (45373-4151)
PHONE.....................................937 335-5611
David Bullard, *President*
Michael Liu, *General Mgr*
Dave Bullard, *Managing Dir*
Lee Rider, *Research*
Richard Korane, *Finance Mgr*
◆ EMP: 100

SALES (est): 43MM
SALES (corp-wide): 4.2MM **Privately Held**
WEB: www.troylaminatingandcoating.com
SIC: 2672 Coated paper, except photographic, carbon or abrasive
HQ: Novacel
27 Rue Du Docteur Emile Bataille
Deville-Les-Rouen 76250
232 827-222

(G-18715)
TROY WEST LLC
Also Called: West Troy
650 Olympic Dr (45373-2306)
PHONE.....................................937 339-2192
Warren Davidson,
◆ EMP: 3
SQ FT: 45,000
SALES (est): 6.6MM **Privately Held**
WEB: www.westtroy.com
SIC: 5051 3544 Stampings, metal; iron & steel (ferrous) products; special dies, tools, jigs & fixtures
PA: Integral Manufacturing Inc.
650 Olympic Dr
Troy OH 45373
937 339-2192

(G-18716)
TUCKERS MOLD POLISHING
3225 E Peterson Rd (45373-7781)
P.O. Box 922 (45373-0922)
PHONE.....................................937 339-3063
John Tucker, *Owner*
EMP: 5
SALES (est): 319.9K **Privately Held**
SIC: 3471 Polishing, metals or formed products

(G-18717)
VALLEY ASPHALT CORPORATION
250 Dye Mill Rd (45373-4280)
PHONE.....................................937 335-3664
James P Jurgensen, *President*
EMP: 3
SALES (corp-wide): 84MM **Privately Held**
SIC: 2951 Asphalt paving mixtures & blocks
HQ: Valley Asphalt Corporation
11641 Mosteller Rd
Cincinnati OH 45241
513 771-0820

(G-18718)
WELLINGTON WLLAMS WRLDWIDE LLC
Also Called: Simple Living
305 S Market St U871 (45373-6200)
PHONE.....................................423 805-6198
Craig Williams,
EMP: 5
SALES: 300K **Privately Held**
SIC: 6531 7389 5192 7372 Real estate agents & managers; ; books; educational computer software; business training services

(G-18719)
WESTERN OHIO GRAPHICS
Also Called: Quality Quick Print
402 E Main St (45373-3413)
PHONE.....................................937 335-8769
Bob Hephner, *Owner*
EMP: 11
SQ FT: 13,000
SALES (est): 1MM **Privately Held**
SIC: 2759 2752 Commercial printing; commercial printing, offset

---

Tuppers Plains
Meigs County

(G-18720)
REMRAM RECOVERY LLC
49705 E Park Dr (45783)
P.O. Box 189 (45783-0189)
PHONE.....................................740 667-0092
Ray Maxson, *Mng Member*
EMP: 12
SQ FT: 36,000

SALES: 1MM **Privately Held**
SIC: 3089 Panels, building: plastic

(G-18721)
WECAN FABRICATORS LLC
49425 E Park Dr (45783-9000)
P.O. Box 159 (45783-0159)
PHONE..................................740 667-0731
Jeffrey Cox, *Mng Member*
Stephanie Cox,
EMP: 8
SQ FT: 4,000
SALES (est): 1.7MM **Privately Held**
SIC: 3441 Fabricated structural metal

Twinsburg
Summit County

(G-18722)
A E WILSON HOLDINGS INC
Also Called: Quest Service Labs
2307 E Aurora Rd (44087-1958)
PHONE..................................330 405-0316
Al Wilson, *President*
EMP: 8
SALES (est): 661K **Privately Held**
WEB: www.questservicelabs.com
SIC: 2759 Commercial printing

(G-18723)
ACE AMERICAN WIRE DIE CO
9041 Dutton Dr (44087-1930)
PHONE..................................330 425-7269
Linda Hohl, *President*
EMP: 10 **EST:** 1998
SQ FT: 10,000
SALES (est): 1MM **Privately Held**
WEB: www.aawiredie.com
SIC: 3544 Special dies & tools

(G-18724)
ACENSE LLC
8941 Dutton Dr (44087-1939)
PHONE..................................330 242-0046
John Harley, *CEO*
Glenn Mitchell, *President*
EMP: 4
SALES (est): 238.3K **Privately Held**
SIC: 3826 Liquid testing apparatus

(G-18725)
ACHILLES AEROSPACE PDTS INC
2100 Enterprise Pkwy (44087-2212)
PHONE..................................330 425-8444
David L Hoyack, *President*
J Michael Corfias, *Admin Sec*
EMP: 22
SQ FT: 20,000
SALES (est): 4.8MM **Privately Held**
WEB: www.achillesaerospace.com
SIC: 3728 Aircraft body & wing assemblies & parts

(G-18726)
ACTION PRINTING INC
2307 E Aurora Rd Ste 8 (44087-1952)
PHONE..................................330 963-7772
John Dodgson, *President*
EMP: 4
SQ FT: 4,500
SALES (est): 678.2K **Privately Held**
SIC: 2752 Commercial printing, offset

(G-18727)
ADAPTALL AMERICA INC
9047 Dutton Dr (44087-1930)
PHONE..................................330 425-4114
C Lane Wood, *President*
Kevin Moore, *Manager*
Brian Schinkel, *Manager*
Rachel Lilly, *Admin Asst*
EMP: 16
SALES (est): 2.7MM **Privately Held**
WEB: www.adaptall.com
SIC: 3494 Pipe fittings

(G-18728)
AJD HOLDING CO (PA)
2181 Enterprise Pkwy (44087-2211)
PHONE..................................330 405-4477
Frank Defino, *President*
Leonard Defino, *Vice Pres*

EMP: 60
SQ FT: 55,000
SALES (est): 66.4MM **Privately Held**
SIC: 3469 3544 3315 3537 Stamping metal for the trade; special dies, tools, jigs & fixtures; wire & fabricated wire products; tractors, used in plants, docks, terminals, etc.: industrial

(G-18729)
ALBEMARLE CORPORATION
Also Called: Albemarle Sorbent Technologies
1664 Highland Rd (44087-2293)
PHONE..................................330 425-2354
Sid Nelson, *Chief Mktg Ofcr*
John White, *Branch Mgr*
EMP: 7 **Publicly Held**
SIC: 3624 8711 8731 Carbon & graphite products; energy conservation engineering; commercial physical research
PA: Albemarle Corporation
4250 Congress St Ste 900
Charlotte NC 28209

(G-18730)
ALLIED CORPORATION INC (DH)
8920 Canyon Falls Blvd # 120 (44087-1990)
PHONE..................................330 425-7861
Dan Mongomery, *President*
EMP: 2 **EST:** 1948
SQ FT: 500
SALES (est): 1.3MM
SALES (corp-wide): 29.7B **Privately Held**
WEB: www.alliedcorporation.com
SIC: 2951 5032 Asphalt paving mixtures & blocks; sand, construction; gravel
HQ: Shelly Company
80 Park Dr
Thornville OH 43076
740 246-6315

(G-18731)
ALLIED SEPARATION TECH INC (PA)
Also Called: Air Supply Co
2300 E Enterprise Pkwy (44087-2349)
PHONE..................................704 732-8034
Michael E Williams, *President*
Lorrie Williams, *Vice Pres*
▲ **EMP:** 35 **EST:** 2009
SALES (est): 6.1MM **Privately Held**
SIC: 3569 Filters

(G-18732)
ALLIED SEPARATION TECH INC
Also Called: Allied Supplied Company
2300 E Enterprise Pkwy (44087-2349)
PHONE..................................704 736-0420
Mike Williams, *President*
Lori Williams, *Vice Pres*
EMP: 34
SALES (est): 3.6MM **Privately Held**
WEB: www.alliedseparation.com
SIC: 3714 3564 Oil strainers, motor vehicle; air purification equipment

(G-18733)
ANGSTROM CORP
9221 Ravenna Rd Ste 1 (44087-2454)
PHONE..................................330 405-0524
Steven Rasmussen, *President*
EMP: 3
SALES: 500K **Privately Held**
WEB: www.angstromcorp.com
SIC: 3545 Gauges (machine tool accessories)

(G-18734)
ANYTHING PERSONALIZED
9261 Ravenna Rd Ste 10 (44087-2449)
PHONE..................................330 655-0723
Jennie Duecker, *Principal*
EMP: 3
SALES (est): 156.3K **Privately Held**
SIC: 2395 Art goods for embroidering, stamped: purchased materials

(G-18735)
ARGO TOOL CORPORATION
1962 Case Pkwy (44087-4327)
PHONE..................................330 425-2407
Laszlo Repay, *President*
Linda Repay, *Vice Pres*
EMP: 12

SQ FT: 6,723
SALES (est): 1.5MM **Privately Held**
SIC: 3544 Special dies & tools

(G-18736)
AUBURN METAL PROCESSING LLC (PA)
1831 Highland Rd (44087-2222)
PHONE..................................315 253-2565
Steve C Joseph,
▼ **EMP:** 22
SALES (est): 6.4MM **Privately Held**
SIC: 3444 Forming machine work, sheet metal

(G-18737)
AUTOMATION SOFTWARE & ENGRG (PA)
9321 Ravenna Rd Ste A (44087-2461)
PHONE..................................330 405-2990
Kenneth Hutchison, *President*
EMP: 17
SQ FT: 6,000
SALES (est): 2.6MM **Privately Held**
WEB: www.a-s-e.com
SIC: 7372 Prepackaged software

(G-18738)
BAUTEC N TECHNOFORM AMER INC
1755 Entp Pkwy Ste 300 (44087)
PHONE..................................330 487-6600
Albert Stankus, *General Mgr*
▲ **EMP:** 30
SALES: 9.8MM **Privately Held**
SIC: 2431 Windows & window parts & trim, wood

(G-18739)
BAWLS ACQUISITION LLC
8840 Commons Blvd Ste 101 (44087-4100)
PHONE..................................888 731-9708
John Staudt,
Lisa Karell,
EMP: 3
SQ FT: 2,187
SALES (est): 210K **Privately Held**
SIC: 2086 Carbonated beverages, nonalcoholic: bottled & canned

(G-18740)
BESSAMAIRE SALES INC
1869 E Aurora Rd Ste 700 (44087-2500)
PHONE..................................440 439-1200
William Sullivan, *President*
EMP: 23
SQ FT: 50,000
SALES (est): 5.6MM **Privately Held**
SIC: 3585 Refrigeration & heating equipment

(G-18741)
BIRD CONTROL INTERNATIONAL
1393 Highland Rd (44087-2213)
PHONE..................................330 425-2377
Stanley Baker, *President*
Benjamin Baker, *Vice Pres*
Jack Polnick, *Director*
EMP: 25
SALES (est): 1.6MM **Privately Held**
SIC: 2879 2899 Pesticides, agricultural or household; chemical preparations

(G-18742)
BOCK COMPANY LLC
Also Called: Bock Lighting
2476 Edison Blvd (44087-2340)
PHONE..................................216 912-7050
Gretta Albert, *Sales Mgr*
Dana Zakrajsek, *Executive*
Ezra Spero,
▲ **EMP:** 6
SALES (est): 1.1MM **Privately Held**
SIC: 3646 Commercial indusl & institutional electric lighting fixtures

(G-18743)
BONENG TRANSMISSIONS (USA) LLC
1670 Entp Pkwy Unit E (44087)
PHONE..................................330 425-1516
Ashley Lovequiest, *General Mgr*
H Pu, *Marketing Staff*

▲ **EMP:** 4
SQ FT: 15,000
SALES (est): 227.2K
SALES (corp-wide): 36.3MM **Privately Held**
SIC: 3566 7699 Speed changers, drives & gears; industrial machinery & equipment repair
PA: Boneng Transmission (Suzhou) Co., Ltd.
No.100, Ruyuan Rd., Xiangcheng Economic Development Zone
Suzhou 21513
512 661-8960

(G-18744)
BURNER TECH UNLIMITED INC
1499 Enterprise Pkwy (44087-2241)
PHONE..................................440 232-3200
Carl Suchovsky, *President*
EMP: 3
SQ FT: 2,800
SALES (est): 542.8K **Privately Held**
SIC: 3433 3823 Gas burners, industrial; combustion control instruments

(G-18745)
C P ELECTRIC MOTOR REPAIR INC
2212 E Aurora Rd (44087-1926)
PHONE..................................330 425-9593
Michael Chalmers, *President*
Charlotte Papp, *Manager*
EMP: 5
SQ FT: 6,000
SALES (est): 389.7K **Privately Held**
SIC: 7694 5065 5065 Electric motor repair; motors, electric; electronic parts

(G-18746)
CANADUS POWER SYSTEMS LLC
9347 Ravenna Rd Ste A (44087-2463)
PHONE..................................216 831-6600
Jack Scott,
Nelson Mossholder,
EMP: 10
SQ FT: 1,000
SALES (est): 1.6MM **Privately Held**
SIC: 3678 Electronic connectors

(G-18747)
CEIA USA LTD
9155 Dutton Dr (44087-1956)
PHONE..................................330 405-3190
Bruno Carano, *Finance Dir*
Cody Kothera, *Sales Mgr*
Marilyn Thaxton, *Marketing Mgr*
Alessandro Manneschi, *Mng Member*
Marco Manneschi, *Mng Member*
▲ **EMP:** 43
SQ FT: 42,316
SALES: 33.9MM **Privately Held**
WEB: www.ceia-usa.com
SIC: 3669 3812 3829 Metal detectors; magnetic field detection apparatus; magnetometers

(G-18748)
CENTERLESS GRINDING SOLUTIONS
8440 Tower Dr (44087-2000)
PHONE..................................216 520-4612
Rick Keller, *Owner*
EMP: 7
SALES (est): 431.3K **Privately Held**
SIC: 3599 Grinding castings for the trade

(G-18749)
CENTRAL COCA-COLA BTLG CO INC
1882 Highland Rd (44087-2223)
PHONE..................................330 425-4401
Rick Bodzenski, *Manager*
EMP: 73
SALES (corp-wide): 35.4B **Publicly Held**
WEB: www.cokecce.com
SIC: 2086 Bottled & canned soft drinks
HQ: Central Coca-Cola Bottling Company, Inc.
555 Taxter Rd Ste 550
Elmsford NY 10523
914 789-1100

Twinsburg - Summit County (G-18750)

(G-18750)
CERTECH INC
2181 Pinnacle Pkwy (44087-2365)
PHONE..................................330 405-1033
John Stang, *Branch Mgr*
EMP: 4
SALES (corp-wide): 1.3B Privately Held
SIC: 3364 3724 Nonferrous die-castings except aluminum; airfoils, aircraft engine
HQ: Certech Inc
1 Park Pl W
Wood Ridge NJ 07075
201 842-6800

(G-18751)
CHICOPEE ENGINEERING ASSOC INC
2300 E Enterprise Pkwy (44087-2349)
PHONE..................................413 592-2273
David Pieciak, *President*
Roger Fontaine, *Vice Pres*
EMP: 23 EST: 1942
SQ FT: 20,000
SALES (est): 4.4MM Privately Held
WEB: www.chiceng.com
SIC: 3677 Filtration devices, electronic

(G-18752)
CHROMASCAPE INC (PA)
Also Called: Amerimulch
2055 Enterprise Pkwy (44087-2209)
PHONE..................................330 998-7574
George Chase, *Ch of Bd*
Joseph Majewski, *President*
Steve Grudzinski, *CFO*
Chris Spelker, *CFO*
◆ EMP: 33
SQ FT: 48,000
SALES (est): 39.2MM Privately Held
WEB: www.amerimulch.com
SIC: 2499 Mulch or sawdust products, wood

(G-18753)
CHURCHILL STEEL PLATE LTD
7851 Bavaria Rd (44087-2263)
PHONE..................................330 425-9000
Jim Stevenson, *President*
Kirk Mooney, *Vice Pres*
James M Fleming, *Treasurer*
Jim Fleming, *Treasurer*
Steve Fleming, *Administration*
EMP: 48
SQ FT: 120,000
SALES (est): 6.3MM Privately Held
SIC: 3312 Plate, steel

(G-18754)
CLEVELAND ELECTRIC LABS CO (PA)
Also Called: Cleveland Electric Labs
1776 Enterprise Pkwy (44087-2246)
PHONE..................................800 447-2207
Jack Allan Lieske, *President*
C M Lemmon, *Principal*
Val Jean Lieske, *Vice Pres*
Rebecca Lieske, *Admin Sec*
EMP: 50
SQ FT: 30,000
SALES (est): 10.5MM Privately Held
WEB: www.clevelandelectriclabs.com
SIC: 3823 7699 Thermocouples, industrial process type; professional instrument repair services; industrial machinery & equipment repair

(G-18755)
CLEVELAND SYRUP CORP (PA)
2200 Highland Rd (44087-2231)
PHONE..................................330 963-1900
Virginia Chaney, *President*
James Chaney, *Vice Pres*
EMP: 4
SQ FT: 50,000
SALES (est): 1.1MM Privately Held
SIC: 2087 5149 Syrups, flavoring (except drink); flour

(G-18756)
COMTEC INCORPORATED
1800 Enterprise Pkwy (44087-2269)
PHONE..................................330 425-8102
Kenneth Drummond, *President*
EMP: 12
SQ FT: 10,200
SALES: 1.8MM Privately Held
WEB: www.comtecinc.com
SIC: 3823 3625 8711 Computer interface equipment for industrial process control; relays & industrial controls; engineering services

(G-18757)
CONTRACTORS STEEL COMPANY
8383 Boyle Pkwy (44087-2236)
PHONE..................................330 425-3050
Mitch Kubasek, *Manager*
EMP: 49
SQ FT: 58,000
SALES (corp-wide): 250.1MM Privately Held
WEB: www.contractorssteel.com
SIC: 5051 3498 3312 Steel; plates, metal; sheets, metal; strip, metal; fabricated pipe & fittings; blast furnaces & steel mills
HQ: Contractors Steel Company
36555 Amrhein Rd
Livonia MI 48150
734 464-4000

(G-18758)
CROWN BATTERY MANUFACTURING CO
1750 Highland Rd Ste 3 (44087-2244)
PHONE..................................330 425-3308
Jeff Wharton, *Branch Mgr*
EMP: 8
SALES (corp-wide): 179.9MM Privately Held
WEB: www.crownbattery.com
SIC: 3691 Storage batteries
PA: Crown Battery Manufacturing Company
1445 Majestic Dr
Fremont OH 43420
419 334-7181

(G-18759)
CUSTOM SCREEN PRINTING (PA)
Also Called: T Shirts & Soccer Wearhouse
1869 E Aurora Rd Ste 100 (44087-1972)
PHONE..................................330 963-3131
David Tschantz, *Owner*
EMP: 3
SALES (est): 1.1MM Privately Held
SIC: 2759 Screen printing

(G-18760)
DALE ADAMS ENTERPRISES INC
1658 Highland Rd Ste 1 (44087-2274)
PHONE..................................330 524-2800
Dale Adams, *President*
Joanne Adams, *Corp Secy*
▼ EMP: 5
SQ FT: 25,000
SALES (est): 850.7K Privately Held
WEB: www.bonecreeper.com
SIC: 3714 3599 Motor vehicle steering systems & parts; custom machinery

(G-18761)
DAY-GLO COLOR CORP
1570 Highland Rd (44087-2217)
PHONE..................................216 391-7070
Joe Shaw, *Manager*
EMP: 19
SQ FT: 33,500
SALES (corp-wide): 5.3B Publicly Held
WEB: www.dayglo.com
SIC: 2816 Inorganic pigments
HQ: Day-Glo Color Corp.
4515 Saint Clair Ave
Cleveland OH 44103
216 391-7070

(G-18762)
DESCO EQUIPMENT CORP
1903 Case Pkwy (44087-2343)
PHONE..................................330 405-1581
Leo E Henry, *President*
Gene A Gilbert, *Corp Secy*
George Hutchins, *Vice Pres*
Dennis Sweeney, *Purch Mgr*
Gene Gilbert, *Treasurer*
▲ EMP: 26
SQ FT: 50,000
SALES (est): 5.7MM
SALES (corp-wide): 31.9MM Privately Held
WEB: www.descoequipment.com
SIC: 3555 Printing presses
PA: Apex Machine Company
3000 Ne 12th Ter
Oakland Park FL 33334
954 563-0209

(G-18763)
DESIGN AVENUE INC
Also Called: Graphics By Design Avenue
1710 Enterprise Pkwy (44087-2204)
PHONE..................................330 487-5280
Wanda Saltsman, *Admin Sec*
EMP: 6
SQ FT: 5,800
SALES (est): 825.7K Privately Held
SIC: 2731 7336 Pamphlets: publishing & printing; graphic arts & related design

(G-18764)
DIRECT DIGITAL GRAPHICS INC
1716 Enterprise Pkwy (44087-2204)
PHONE..................................330 405-3770
Mike Boswell, *President*
Kimberly Boswell, *Office Mgr*
EMP: 8
SQ FT: 14,000
SALES (est): 1.1MM Privately Held
SIC: 2759 Commercial printing

(G-18765)
DIXON VALVE & COUPLING CO LLC
1900 Enterprise Pkwy (44087-2296)
PHONE..................................330 425-3000
Louis Young, *Manager*
EMP: 15
SALES (corp-wide): 282.2MM Privately Held
SIC: 3492 5085 Fluid power valves & hose fittings; hose, belting & packing
HQ: Dixon Valve & Coupling Company, Llc
800 High St
Chestertown MD 21620

(G-18766)
E S SIGN & DESIGN LLC
Also Called: Es Sign and Design
9478 Ravenna Rd (44087-2104)
PHONE..................................330 405-4799
Mary Ann Serafino, *Area Mgr*
Chris Serafino,
EMP: 5
SQ FT: 1,384
SALES (est): 476.7K Privately Held
SIC: 3993 Electric signs

(G-18767)
EASY CARE PRODUCTS INC
8870 Darrow Rd Ste F106 (44087-2178)
PHONE..................................330 405-1380
Mike Crombie, *President*
▲ EMP: 3
SALES (est): 240K Privately Held
SIC: 2842 Metal polish

(G-18768)
EMERALD TRANSFORMER PPM LLC
1672 Highland Rd (44087-2219)
PHONE..................................800 908-8800
Dan Halling, *Manager*
EMP: 12
SQ FT: 29,322
SALES (corp-wide): 153.8MM Privately Held
SIC: 4953 8734 3341 Hazardous waste collection & disposal; hazardous waste testing; secondary nonferrous metals
HQ: Emerald Transformer Ppm Llc
9820 Westpoint Dr Ste 300
Indianapolis IN 46256

(G-18769)
EPI OF CLEVELAND INC
Also Called: Engineered Products
2224 E Enterprise Pkwy (44087-2393)
PHONE..................................330 468-2872
Robert Knazek, *Vice Pres*
EMP: 8
SALES (corp-wide): 15.9MM Privately Held
WEB: www.engineeredproducts.com
SIC: 3441 5051 Fabricated structural metal; metals service centers & offices
HQ: E.P.I. Of Cleveland, Inc.
1844 Ardmore Blvd
Pittsburgh PA 15221
330 468-2872

(G-18770)
ERIE CHINESE JOURNAL
9810 Ravenna Rd Ste 1 (44087-1761)
PHONE..................................216 324-2959
Ying Tu, *Owner*
EMP: 4
SALES (est): 300.2K Privately Held
SIC: 2711 Newspapers, publishing & printing

(G-18771)
ESSILOR LABORATORIES AMER INC
Also Called: Bell Optical
9221 Ravenna Rd # 3 (44087-2472)
P.O. Box 620 (44087-0620)
PHONE..................................330 425-3003
Ron Sheperd, *Manager*
EMP: 8
SALES (corp-wide): 283.5MM Privately Held
WEB: www.crizal.com
SIC: 3851 Eyeglasses, lenses & frames
HQ: Essilor Laboratories Of America, Inc.
13515 N Stemmons Fwy
Dallas TX 75234
972 241-4141

(G-18772)
EXTREME MARINE
2057 E Aurora Rd Ste Lm (44087-1938)
PHONE..................................330 963-7800
Ellaine Penn, *President*
Lawrence Penn, *Vice Pres*
EMP: 5
SALES (est): 552.7K Privately Held
SIC: 3732 Boat building & repairing

(G-18773)
FABRICATING SOLUTIONS INC
7920 Bavaria Rd (44087-2252)
PHONE..................................330 486-0998
Dewey Lockwood, *Principal*
EMP: 14
SALES (est): 2.3MM Privately Held
SIC: 3499 3444 Fire- or burglary-resistive products; sheet metalwork

(G-18774)
FACIL NORTH AMERICA INC (HQ)
Also Called: Streetsboro Operations
2242 Pinnacle Pkwy # 100 (44087-5301)
PHONE..................................330 487-2500
Rene Achten, *CEO*
Daniel Michiels, *CFO*
◆ EMP: 210
SQ FT: 150,000
SALES (est): 142.6MM
SALES (corp-wide): 5.9MM Privately Held
WEB: www.flexalloy.com
SIC: 5072 3452 5085 Nuts (hardware); bolts; screws; nuts, metal; fasteners, industrial: nuts, bolts, screws, etc.
PA: Facil Corporate
Geleenlaan 20
Genk 3600
894 104-50

(G-18775)
FERRUM INDUSTRIES INC (HQ)
1831 Highland Rd (44087-2222)
P.O. Box 360230, Strongsville (44136-0004)
PHONE..................................440 519-1768
Steve Joseph, *President*
Don Moreno, *Vice Pres*
▲ EMP: 5 EST: 2001
SALES (est): 493.8K
SALES (corp-wide): 6.4MM Privately Held
SIC: 2899 Metal treating compounds

PA: Auburn Metal Processing, Llc
1831 Highland Rd
Twinsburg OH 44087
315 253-2565

(G-18776)
FREEDOM USA INC
Also Called: Avadirect.com
2045 Midway Dr (44087-1933)
PHONE..................................216 503-6374
Alex Sonis, *President*
Gary Muravin, *Vice Pres*
EMP: 10
SQ FT: 8,000
SALES (est): 2.8MM **Privately Held**
WEB: www.avadirect.com
SIC: 7378 3571 Computer maintenance & repair; mainframe computers

(G-18777)
FUCHS LUBRICANTS CO
Also Called: Fuchs Franklin Div
8036 Bavaria Rd (44087-2262)
PHONE..................................330 963-0400
Kipp Kofsky, *Branch Mgr*
EMP: 25
SALES (corp-wide): 2.9B **Privately Held**
WEB: www.fuchs.com
SIC: 4225 2992 2899 2851 General warehousing & storage; lubricating oils & greases; chemical preparations; paints & allied products; specialty cleaning, polishes & sanitation goods
HQ: Fuchs Lubricants Co.
17050 Lathrop Ave
Harvey IL 60426
708 333-8901

(G-18778)
GANZCORP INVESTMENTS INC
Also Called: Mustang Dynamometer
2300 Pinnacle Pkwy (44087-2368)
PHONE..................................330 963-5400
Dean Ganzhorn, *Owner*
Dean K Ganzhorn, *Owner*
Donald W Ganzhorn Jr, *Exec VP*
Paul Bukowski, *Engineer*
Jesse Busby, *Engineer*
◆ **EMP:** 60
SQ FT: 82,000
SALES (est): 24.6MM **Privately Held**
WEB: www.mustangdyne.com
SIC: 3559 Automotive related machinery

(G-18779)
GARMENT SPECIALTIES INC
1885 E Aurora Rd (44087-1917)
PHONE..................................330 425-2928
Lee Pilous, *President*
EMP: 3
SQ FT: 5,000
SALES: 350K **Privately Held**
WEB: www.garmentspecialties.com
SIC: 2395 Embroidery products, except schiffli machine; embroidery & art needlework

(G-18780)
GED HOLDINGS INC
9280 Dutton Dr (44087-1967)
PHONE..................................330 963-5401
William Weaver, *President*
Dave Lewis, *Research*
EMP: 141 **EST:** 2000
SALES (est): 16.5MM **Privately Held**
SIC: 3559 3549 5084 Glass making machinery: blowing, molding, forming, etc.; cutting & slitting machinery; industrial machinery & equipment

(G-18781)
GENERAL DIE CASTERS INC (PA)
2150 Highland Rd (44087-2229)
PHONE..................................330 678-2528
James M Mathias, *CEO*
Thomas J Lennon, *President*
Theresa A Bordelon, *Admin Sec*
▲ **EMP:** 40 **EST:** 1957
SQ FT: 31,000
SALES (est): 31.3MM **Privately Held**
WEB: www.generaldie.com
SIC: 3364 3363 3544 3369 Zinc & zinc-base alloy die-castings; aluminum die-castings; special dies, tools, jigs & fixtures; nonferrous foundries; aluminum foundries

(G-18782)
GENERAL ELECTRIC COMPANY
8499 Darrow Rd (44087-2309)
PHONE..................................330 425-3755
J E Breen, *Principal*
Eric Battiest, *Engineer*
Scott Morneweck, *Engineer*
Claire Marshall, *Human Res Mgr*
Dan Waltermire, *Manager*
EMP: 12
SALES (corp-wide): 121.6B **Publicly Held**
SIC: 1311 Crude petroleum & natural gas
PA: General Electric Company
41 Farnsworth St
Boston MA 02210
617 443-3000

(G-18783)
GENERAL ELECTRIC INTL INC
8941 Dutton Dr (44087-1939)
PHONE..................................330 963-2066
Jeffrey Pack, *Manager*
EMP: 30
SALES (corp-wide): 121.6B **Publicly Held**
SIC: 5084 3561 Compressors, except air conditioning; pumps, oil well & field
HQ: General Electric International, Inc.
191 Rosa Parks St
Cincinnati OH 45202
617 443-3000

(G-18784)
GEORGES DONUTS INC
7995 Darrow Rd (44087-2385)
PHONE..................................330 963-9902
George D Vadaj, *President*
George F Vadaj, *Vice Pres*
EMP: 5
SALES (est): 180K **Privately Held**
SIC: 5461 2051 Doughnuts; doughnuts, except frozen

(G-18785)
GIESECKE & DEVRIENT AMER INC
Also Called: G & D Twinsburg
2020 Enterprise Pkwy (44087-2210)
PHONE..................................330 425-1515
Tina Atwell, *VP Admin*
Randy Gurganus, *Vice Pres*
Dale Ridel, *Plant Mgr*
Ray Daines, *Purch Mgr*
Tina Coleman, *Purch Agent*
EMP: 120
SALES (corp-wide): 308.9K **Privately Held**
SIC: 2672 5044 Coated & laminated paper; office equipment
HQ: Giesecke+Devrient Currency Technology America, Inc.
45925 Horseshoe Dr # 100
Dulles VA 20166
703 480-2000

(G-18786)
GIESECKE & DEVRIENT CAN
2020 Enterprise Pkwy (44087-2210)
PHONE..................................330 425-1515
Fax: 330 425-9105
EMP: 9
SALES (est): 1.1MM **Privately Held**
SIC: 3089 Mfg Plastic Products

(G-18787)
GIESECKE+DEVRIENT
1960 Enterprise Pkwy (44087-2208)
PHONE..................................330 405-8442
Jim Dooley, *Manager*
EMP: 15
SALES (corp-wide): 308.9K **Privately Held**
SIC: 2672 Coated & laminated paper

HQ: Giesecke+Devrient Currency Technology America, Inc.
45925 Horseshoe Dr # 100
Dulles VA 20166
703 480-2000

(G-18788)
GOLF MARKETING GROUP INC
Also Called: Shot Selector
9221 Ravenna Rd Ste 7 (44087-2454)
PHONE..................................330 963-5155
Dave Zabell, *President*
Marc Mascarillo, *Vice Pres*
▲ **EMP:** 8
SQ FT: 2,000
SALES (est): 1.4MM **Privately Held**
WEB: www.shotselector.com
SIC: 2752 2732 3993 Cards, lithographed; book printing; signs & advertising specialties

(G-18789)
GVI MEDICAL DEVICES CORP
Also Called: Gvimd
1470 Enterprise Pkwy (44087-2242)
PHONE..................................330 963-4083
Traci Pack, *Controller*
EMP: 10
SQ FT: 10,000
SALES (est): 947.3K **Privately Held**
SIC: 3845 Magnetic resonance imaging device, nuclear

(G-18790)
HAHS FACTORY OUTLET
1993 Case Pkwy (44087-4328)
PHONE..................................330 405-4227
Gerry Haas, *Owner*
EMP: 50
SALES (est): 3.5MM **Privately Held**
SIC: 1081 Test boring, metal mining

(G-18791)
HANA MICRODISPLAY TECH INC
2061 Case Pkwy S (44087-2361)
PHONE..................................330 405-4600
John Erdmann, *President*
Paul R Brown Jr, *Vice Pres*
Edward M Stiles III, *Vice Pres*
D Scott Worthington, *Vice Pres*
David Tsing, *Admin Sec*
▲ **EMP:** 60
SQ FT: 24,000
SALES (est): 14.2MM **Privately Held**
WEB: www.hanaoh.com
SIC: 3825 Instruments to measure electricity

(G-18792)
HORIZON COMMUNICATIONS INC
Also Called: Dealer Communications
8870 Darrow Rd Ste F106 (44087-2178)
PHONE..................................330 968-6959
Michael Roscoe, *President*
EMP: 7
SALES (est): 689.6K **Privately Held**
WEB: www.horizoncommunications.net
SIC: 2721 Magazines; publishing & printing

(G-18793)
HYDROMOTIVE ENGINEERING CO
9261 Ravenna Rd Bldg B1b2 (44087-2470)
PHONE..................................330 425-4266
Tom Bucknell, *Owner*
EMP: 6
SQ FT: 8,000
SALES (est): 450K **Privately Held**
SIC: 3429 5088 5551 Marine hardware; marine supplies; marine supplies & equipment

(G-18794)
IBYCORP
Also Called: Ibycorp Tool & Die
8968 Dutton Dr (44087-1929)
PHONE..................................330 425-8226
Steven Hamori, *President*
Violet Hamori, *Corp Secy*
EMP: 6 **EST:** 1975
SQ FT: 10,000
SALES: 423.9K **Privately Held**
SIC: 3544 Special dies & tools

(G-18795)
ID CARD SYSTEMS INC
2248 E Enterprise Pkwy (44087-2328)
PHONE..................................330 963-7446
Kenneth Quinn, *President*
Loretta Quinn, *Principal*
Matthew Quinn, *Principal*
Ryan Quinn, *Sales Mgr*
Joanne Tucky, *Sales Staff*
EMP: 5
SALES (est): 552.8K **Privately Held**
WEB: www.idcardsystem.com
SIC: 3999 5043 5943 7378 Identification badges & insignia; photographic equipment & supplies; school supplies; computer maintenance & repair

(G-18796)
INDUSTRIAL MOLD INC
Also Called: Industrial Prfctn Mold & Mch
2057 E Aurora Rd (44087-1938)
PHONE..................................330 425-7374
David Kuhary, *President*
John Ferkul, *Plant Mgr*
Jerry Davis, *Project Mgr*
David Ferkul, *Opers Mgr*
Emily McElfresh, *Human Res Mgr*
EMP: 24
SQ FT: 8,600
SALES (est): 4.7MM **Privately Held**
WEB: www.industrialmold.com
SIC: 3544 5085 3354 Forms (molds), for foundry & plastics working machinery; industrial supplies; aluminum extruded products

(G-18797)
JH INDUSTRIES INC
Also Called: Copperloy
1981 E Aurora Rd (44087-1919)
PHONE..................................330 963-4105
John J Hallack, *President*
Dale Doherty, *Vice Pres*
Jacqueline Hallack, *Vice Pres*
Gina Marrali, *Sales Executive*
EMP: 30 **EST:** 1952
SQ FT: 70,000
SALES: 7MM **Privately Held**
WEB: www.copperloy.com
SIC: 3599 3448 3537 3444 Machine shop, jobbing & repair; ramps: prefabricated metal; docks: prefabricated metal; industrial trucks & tractors; sheet metalwork; fabricated plate work (boiler shop); fabricated structural metal

(G-18798)
KELTEC INC (PA)
Also Called: Keltec-Technolab
2300 E Enterprise Pkwy (44087-2349)
PHONE..................................330 425-3100
Edward Kaiser, *President*
Dolores Kaiser, *Vice Pres*
Bill Castrovinci, *Controller*
Ed Sobieski, *Sales Mgr*
Matthew Bachmann, *Manager*
▲ **EMP:** 74
SQ FT: 100,000
SALES (est): 15.7MM **Privately Held**
WEB: www.keltecinc.com
SIC: 3569 Separators for steam, gas, vapor or air (machinery); gas separators (machinery)

(G-18799)
KES INDUSTRIES LLC (PA)
Also Called: Preform Sealants
8040 Bavaria Rd (44087-2262)
PHONE..................................330 405-2813
Chris Kruty, *General Mgr*
Dan Miller, *QC Mgr*
Guy Swank,
EMP: 5
SQ FT: 18,000
SALES: 1.8MM **Privately Held**
SIC: 3053 Gaskets, packing & sealing devices

(G-18800)
KING-INDIANA FORGE INC
8250 Boyle Pkwy (44087-2234)
PHONE..................................330 425-4250
Raymond W King Jr, *President*
EMP: 17
SQ FT: 250,000

Twinsburg - Summit County (G-18801) — GEOGRAPHIC SECTION

SALES (est): 1.8MM
SALES (corp-wide): 63.2MM **Privately Held**
WEB: www.kingforge.com
SIC: 3462 Iron & steel forgings
PA: Ssp Fittings Corp.
  8250 Boyle Pkwy
  Twinsburg OH 44087
  330 425-4250

(G-18801)
KIWI PROMOTIONAL AP & PRTG CO
Also Called: Inc., K.I.W.I.
2170 E Aurora Rd (44087-1924)
PHONE 330 487-5115
Mark Candle, *President*
Paul Steels, *Principal*
EMP: 37
SQ FT: 28,000
SALES (est): 4.2MM **Privately Held**
SIC: 2396 2395 Screen printing on fabric articles; embroidery products, except schiffli machine

(G-18802)
KRE INC
Also Called: Champion Rivet Company
2181 Enterprise Pkwy (44087-2211)
PHONE 216 883-1600
EMP: 16
SQ FT: 175,000
SALES (est): 2.2MM **Privately Held**
SIC: 3452 Mfg Bolts/Screws/Rivets

(G-18803)
KRISS KREATIONS
Also Called: Edible Arrangement
9224 Darrow Rd (44087-1897)
PHONE 330 405-6102
Kristine Brownfield, *Owner*
James Brownfield, *Co-Owner*
EMP: 6
SALES (est): 931.8K **Privately Held**
SIC: 3523 5999 Shakers, tree: nuts, fruits, etc.; alarm & safety equipment stores

(G-18804)
L J STAR INCORPORATED
2396 Edison Blvd (44087-2376)
P.O. Box 1116 (44087-9116)
PHONE 330 405-3040
David Star, *President*
Leonard J Star, *Chairman*
Eric Steenlandt, *COO*
Christopher Schrantz, *Controller*
Ian Murphy, *Natl Sales Mgr*
▲ **EMP:** 20
SQ FT: 10,000
SALES (est): 5.4MM **Privately Held**
WEB: www.ljstar.com
SIC: 3823 Flow instruments, industrial process type

(G-18805)
LEGACY SUPPLIES INC
8252 Darrow Rd Ste E (44087-2392)
P.O. Box 1173 (44087-9173)
PHONE 330 405-4565
Mike Corcelli, *President*
Frank Corcelli, *Vice Pres*
EMP: 10 **EST:** 1998
SALES (est): 1.4MM **Privately Held**
SIC: 3694 5013 Distributors, motor vehicle engine; motor vehicle supplies & new parts

(G-18806)
LEIDEN CABINET COMPANY LLC (PA)
2385 Edison Blvd (44087-2376)
PHONE 330 425-8555
Thomas Leiden, *CEO*
Chris Rhoa, *COO*
Melissa Hale, *Vice Pres*
Michael Hopp, *Vice Pres*
Mike Hopp, *Vice Pres*
EMP: 110
SQ FT: 210,000
SALES (est): 21.4MM **Privately Held**
SIC: 2541 Store fixtures, wood; cabinets, except refrigerated: show, display, etc.: wood

(G-18807)
LEXINGTON RUBBER GROUP INC (DH)
Also Called: Qsr
1700 Highland Rd (44087-2221)
P.O. Box 1030 (44087-9030)
PHONE 330 425-8472
Randy Ross, *CEO*
Jim Maderitz, *Plant Mgr*
Jeff Salamon, *QC Mgr*
Richard Rybka, *Technical Mgr*
Roger Schulte, *Engineer*
▲ **EMP:** 29
SQ FT: 110,000
SALES (est): 93.8MM
SALES (corp-wide): 1.8B **Privately Held**
SIC: 3069 Hard rubber & molded rubber products
HQ: Q Holding Company
  1700 Highland Rd
  Twinsburg OH 44087
  330 425-8472

(G-18808)
LINDE GAS USA LLC
2045 E Aurora Rd (44087-2280)
PHONE 330 425-3989
Jim Lawrence, *Principal*
EMP: 14
SALES (est): 2.8MM **Privately Held**
SIC: 2813 Industrial gases

(G-18809)
LINEAR ASICS INC
2061 Case Pkwy S (44087-2361)
PHONE 330 474-3920
Mike Ward, *CEO*
EMP: 8
SQ FT: 2,000
SALES (est): 363.7K **Privately Held**
SIC: 3674 Semiconductors & related devices

(G-18810)
MACTEK CORPORATION
2112 Case Pkwy Ste 1 (44087-2378)
PHONE 330 487-5477
EMP: 12
SQ FT: 1,200
SALES (est): 1.1MM **Privately Held**
SIC: 3559 Mfg Electronic Equipment For Process Control Systems

(G-18811)
MARSAM METALFAB INC
1870 Enterprise Pkwy (44087-2206)
PHONE 330 405-1520
Mark Brownfield, *President*
EMP: 25
SQ FT: 30,000
SALES (est): 3.9MM **Privately Held**
SIC: 1799 3441 7692 3444 Welding on site; fabricated structural metal; welding repair; sheet metalwork

(G-18812)
MATHESON TRI-GAS INC
Also Called: Matheson Gas Products
1650 Enterprise Pkwy (44087-2202)
PHONE 330 425-4407
Les Gibson, *Opers-Prdtn-Mfg*
EMP: 18
SQ FT: 7,226 **Privately Held**
WEB: www.matheson-trigas.com
SIC: 2813 5084 Industrial gases; welding machinery & equipment
HQ: Matheson Tri-Gas, Inc.
  150 Allen Rd Ste 302
  Basking Ridge NJ 07920
  908 991-9200

(G-18813)
MAVAL INDUSTRIES LLC
Also Called: Maval Manufacturing
1555 Enterprise Pkwy (44087-2239)
PHONE 330 405-1600
John Dougherty, *President*
Dale Lumby, *Vice Pres*
Steve Summerville, *Plant Mgr*
Ralph Wolanin, *QC Mgr*
Dan Denavich, *Engineer*
▲ **EMP:** 203
SQ FT: 88,000
SALES (est): 30MM
SALES (corp-wide): 10.5B **Publicly Held**
WEB: www.mavalgear.com
SIC: 3714 8711 Power steering equipment, motor vehicle; consulting engineer
HQ: Borgwarner Pds (Indiana) Inc.
  13975 Borg Warner Dr
  Noblesville IN 46060
  800 372-3555

(G-18814)
MCFLUSION INC
2112 Case Pkwy Ste 8 (44087-2378)
PHONE 800 341-8616
Ole Madsen, *President*
Liza Scurr, *Director*
▲ **EMP:** 8
SALES (est): 1.3MM **Privately Held**
SIC: 3559 Pharmaceutical machinery

(G-18815)
MEDICAL ELASTOMER DEV INC
Also Called: Qure Medical
1700 Highland Rd (44087-2221)
P.O. Box 1030 (44087-9030)
PHONE 330 425-8352
Randy Ross, *CEO*
Kray David Alan, *Engineer*
▲ **EMP:** 30
SQ FT: 20,000
SALES (est): 6.9MM
SALES (corp-wide): 1.8B **Privately Held**
WEB: www.medeladev.com
SIC: 2822 Silicone rubbers
HQ: Q Holding Company
  1700 Highland Rd
  Twinsburg OH 44087
  330 425-8472

(G-18816)
MEDINA SUPPLY COMPANY
1516 Highland Rd (44087-2217)
PHONE 330 425-0752
Lowell Perry, *Manager*
EMP: 30
SQ FT: 18,612
SALES (corp-wide): 29.7B **Privately Held**
SIC: 3273 Ready-mixed concrete
HQ: Medina Supply Company
  230 E Smith Rd
  Medina OH 44256
  330 723-3681

(G-18817)
METAL IMPROVEMENT COMPANY LLC
1652 Highland Rd (44087-2219)
PHONE 330 425-1490
Matt Heschel, *Technical Mgr*
Kirk Gray, *Manager*
Jeremy Linamen, *Manager*
Todd Mason, *Maintence Staff*
EMP: 28
SALES (corp-wide): 2.4B **Publicly Held**
WEB: www.mic-houston.com
SIC: 3398 Shot peening (treating steel to reduce fatigue)
HQ: Metal Improvement Company, Llc
  80 E Rte 4 Ste 310
  Paramus NJ 07652
  201 843-7800

(G-18818)
METALDYNE PWRTRAIN CMPNNTS INC
Also Called: Metaldyne Twinsburg
8001 Bavaria Rd (44087-2261)
PHONE 330 486-3200
EMP: 130
SALES (corp-wide): 7.2B **Publicly Held**
WEB: www.metaldyne.com
SIC: 3312 3519 Tool & die steel; parts & accessories, internal combustion engines
HQ: Metaldyne Powertrain Components, Inc.
  1 Dauch Dr
  Detroit MI 48211
  313 758-2000

(G-18819)
METALLIC RESOURCES INC
2368 E Enterprise Pkwy (44087-2349)
P.O. Box 368 (44087-0368)
PHONE 330 425-3155
Stan Rothschild, *President*
Julia Harber, *General Mgr*
William Griffith, *Vice Pres*
▲ **EMP:** 32
SQ FT: 26,000
SALES (est): 10.4MM **Privately Held**
WEB: www.metallicresources.com
SIC: 3356 3339 Solder: wire, bar, acid core, & rosin core; precious metals
PA: Metallic Solders De Mexico, S. De R.L. De C.V.
  Norte 7 No. 35 A
  H. Matamoros TAMPS.

(G-18820)
MILES RUBBER & PACKING COMPANY (PA)
9020 Dutton Dr (44087-1994)
PHONE 330 425-3888
James M Smith, *President*
K J Ertle, *President*
Larry Lempke, *President*
Janet Schickler, *President*
EMP: 25
SQ FT: 27,800
SALES (est): 3.8MM **Privately Held**
WEB: www.milesrubber-ohio.com
SIC: 3053 3069 Gaskets, packing & sealing devices; sponge rubber & sponge rubber products

(G-18821)
MOLD-RITE PLASTICS LLC
2300 Highland Rd (44087-2232)
PHONE 330 405-7739
EMP: 7 **Privately Held**
SIC: 3544 Industrial molds
HQ: Mold-Rite Plastics, Llc
  30 N La Salle St Ste 2425
  Chicago IL 60602
  518 561-1812

(G-18822)
MORGAN ADVANCED CERAMICS INC
Also Called: Morgan Advanced Materials
2181 Pinnacle Pkwy (44087-2365)
PHONE 330 405-1033
EMP: 4
SALES (corp-wide): 1.3B **Privately Held**
SIC: 2899 Chemical preparations
HQ: Morgan Advanced Ceramics, Inc
  2425 Whipple Rd
  Hayward CA 94544

(G-18823)
OLIVER PRINTING & PACKG CO LLC (PA)
1760 Enterprise Pkwy (44087-2291)
PHONE 330 425-7890
George Oliver, *President*
W George Oliver, *Shareholder*
EMP: 77 **EST:** 1952
SQ FT: 21,000
SALES (est): 81.3MM **Privately Held**
SIC: 2752 Commercial printing, offset

(G-18824)
OMA USA INC
9329 Ravenna Rd Ste A (44087-2457)
PHONE 330 487-0602
Mauro Nava, *President*
Antonio Villa, *General Mgr*
Maria Pia Nava, *Vice Pres*
Clara Maria Nava, *Treasurer*
▲ **EMP:** 6
SQ FT: 2,860
SALES (est): 800.4K **Privately Held**
WEB: www.omabraid.com
SIC: 3549 3552 Wiredrawing & fabricating machinery & equipment, ex. die; braiding machines, textile

(G-18825)
OMNITHRUSTER INC
2201 Pinnacle Pkwy Ste A (44087-2479)
PHONE 330 963-6310
John B De Nault, *Ch of Bd*
Kurt Widmer, *President*
EMP: 12
SQ FT: 15,000
SALES (est): 1.8MM **Privately Held**
WEB: www.omnithruster.com
SIC: 3643 Rail bonds, electric: for propulsion & signal circuits

GEOGRAPHIC SECTION
Twinsburg - Summit County (G-18850)

(G-18826)
OMSI TRANSMISSIONS INC
9319 Ravenna Rd Ste A (44087-2462)
PHONE..................................330 405-7350
Renato Soncina, *President*
John Manes, *Admin Sec*
▲ **EMP:** 3
SALES (est): 527.9K Privately Held
WEB: www.omsitrasmissioni.com
SIC: 3714 5088 Axle housings & shafts, motor vehicle; transportation equipment & supplies

(G-18827)
P-AMERICAS LLC
2351 Edison Blvd Ste 2 (44087-2384)
PHONE..................................330 963-0090
Vincent Taddeo, *Accounts Mgr*
William Evans, *Manager*
EMP: 22
SALES (corp-wide): 64.6B Publicly Held
SIC: 2086 Carbonated soft drinks, bottled & canned
HQ: P-Americas Llc
1 Pepsi Way
Somers NY 10589
336 896-5740

(G-18828)
PARO SERVICES CO (PA)
1755 Entp Pkwy Ste 100 (44087)
PHONE..................................330 467-1300
Daniel N Zelman, *President*
Brian McCue, *COO*
Edward J Kubek Jr, *Vice Pres*
Nick La Magna, *Vice Pres*
EMP: 10
SQ FT: 60,000
SALES (est): 31MM Privately Held
SIC: 7349 2842 Cleaning service, industrial or commercial; cleaning or polishing preparations

(G-18829)
PENN MACHINE COMPANY
2182 E Aurora Rd (44087-1924)
PHONE..................................814 288-1547
EMP: 25
SQ FT: 27,000
SALES (corp-wide): 225.3B Publicly Held
WEB: www.pmcgearbox.com
SIC: 3568 3532 3462 Power transmission equipment; mining machinery; iron & steel forgings
HQ: Penn Machine Company
106 Station St
Johnstown PA 15905

(G-18830)
PEPPERL + FUCHS INC (DH)
1600 Enterprise Pkwy (44087-2245)
PHONE..................................330 425-3555
Wolfgang Mueller, *President*
Kishore K Kumble, *General Mgr*
Jessica Mercurio, *General Mgr*
Michael Fuchs, *Managing Dir*
Seitz Juergen, *Managing Dir*
▲ **EMP:** 130
SQ FT: 55,050
SALES (est): 100.4MM
SALES (corp-wide): 744.1MM Privately Held
WEB: www.pepperlfuchs.com
SIC: 5065 3625 3822 3674 Electronic parts & equipment; relays & industrial controls; auto controls regulating residntl & coml environmt & applncs; semiconductors & related devices
HQ: Pepperl + Fuchs Enterprises, Inc.
1600 Enterprise Pkwy
Twinsburg OH 44087
330 425-3555

(G-18831)
PEPPERL + FUCHS ENTPS INC (HQ)
1600 Enterprise Pkwy (44087-2245)
PHONE..................................330 425-3555
Dr Gunther Kegel, *President*
Alexander Gress, *Corp Secy*
James P Bolin Jr, *Vice Pres*
Robert Charles Smith, *Vice Pres*
EMP: 2
SALES (est): 131.7MM
SALES (corp-wide): 744.1MM Privately Held
SIC: 5065 3625 3822 3674 Electronic parts & equipment; relays & industrial controls; auto controls regulating residntl & coml environmt & applncs; semiconductors & related devices
PA: Pepperl + Fuchs Gmbh
Lilienthalstr. 200
Mannheim 68307
621 776-0

(G-18832)
PEPPERL + FUCHS MFG INC
1600 Enterprise Pkwy (44087-2245)
PHONE..................................330 425-3555
Alexander Gress, *President*
EMP: 110
SALES (est): 3MM
SALES (corp-wide): 744.1MM Privately Held
SIC: 3699 Electrical equipment & supplies
HQ: Pepperl + Fuchs Enterprises, Inc.
1600 Enterprise Pkwy
Twinsburg OH 44087
330 425-3555

(G-18833)
PEPSI-COLA METRO BTLG CO INC
1999 Enterprise Pkwy (44087-2253)
PHONE..................................330 963-0426
Joshua Robison, *Prdtn Mgr*
Richard Michaud, *Production*
Michael Gatto, *Sales Staff*
Charlie Powers, *Manager*
Frank O'Neill, *Manager*
EMP: 500
SALES (corp-wide): 64.6B Publicly Held
WEB: www.joy-of-cola.com
SIC: 2086 5149 Bottled & canned soft drinks; groceries & related products
HQ: Pepsi-Cola Metropolitan Bottling Company, Inc.
1111 Westchester Ave
White Plains NY 10604
914 767-6000

(G-18834)
PEPSI-COLA METRO BTLG CO INC
Also Called: Pepsico
1999 Enterprise Pkwy (44087-2253)
PHONE..................................330 963-5300
Amy Rogers, *CPA*
Charlie Powers, *Branch Mgr*
EMP: 30
SALES (corp-wide): 64.6B Publicly Held
WEB: www.whitmancorp.com
SIC: 2086 Carbonated soft drinks, bottled & canned
HQ: Pepsi-Cola Metropolitan Bottling Company, Inc.
1111 Westchester Ave
White Plains NY 10604
914 767-6000

(G-18835)
PERFECTION MOLD & MACHINE CO
2057 E Aurora Rd Ste Hi (44087-1938)
PHONE..................................330 784-5435
Jack Bailey, *President*
EMP: 12
SQ FT: 11,000
SALES (est): 933.7K Privately Held
WEB: www.perfectionmold.com
SIC: 3544 Industrial molds

(G-18836)
PERRY WELDING SERVICE INC
2075 Case Pkwy S (44087-2361)
PHONE..................................330 425-2211
Jerry Perry, *President*
Margo Perry, *Treasurer*
EMP: 14 EST: 1974
SQ FT: 12,000
SALES (est): 2MM Privately Held
SIC: 3599 3469 7692 3544 Custom machinery; machine parts, stamped or pressed metal; welding repair; special dies, tools, jigs & fixtures; fabricated structural metal

(G-18837)
PLATING PERCEPTIONS INC
8815 Herrick Rd (44087-2417)
P.O. Box 81 (44087-0081)
PHONE..................................330 425-4180
Randall Bauer, *President*
James Konicek, *Vice Pres*
EMP: 9
SQ FT: 8,000
SALES (est): 1.1MM Privately Held
SIC: 3471 Plating of metals or formed products

(G-18838)
PREMIER SHOT COMPANY INC
1666 Enterprise Pkwy (44087-2202)
PHONE..................................330 405-0583
Bob Gillespie, *President*
▲ **EMP:** 6
SQ FT: 10,000
SALES (est): 710K Privately Held
WEB: www.premiershot.com
SIC: 3482 Shot, steel (ammunition)

(G-18839)
PRINT MANAGEMENT PARTNERS INC
Also Called: Cable Quest
2265 E Enterprise Pkwy A (44087-2337)
PHONE..................................330 650-5300
Loretta Vaxman, *Opers Staff*
Peter Rubin, *Branch Mgr*
Brando Melgaard, *Manager*
Diane Reish, *Executive Asst*
EMP: 50
SALES (est): 7.2MM Privately Held
WEB: www.ourpartners.com
SIC: 2752 Business forms, lithographed
PA: Print Management Partners, Inc.
701 Lee St Ste 1050
Des Plaines IL 60016

(G-18840)
PROBAKE INC
2057 E Aurora Rd Ste Pq (44087-1938)
PHONE..................................330 425-4427
Kevin Wallace, *President*
Nicki Wallace, *Vice Pres*
◆ **EMP:** 15
SQ FT: 30,000
SALES (est): 9.4MM Privately Held
WEB: www.probake.com
SIC: 3556 Food products machinery

(G-18841)
PRODUCTION TL CO CLEVELAND INC
Also Called: Assembly Tool Specialists
9002 Dutton Dr (44087-1931)
PHONE..................................330 425-4466
EMP: 18
SQ FT: 3,800
SALES (est): 1MM Privately Held
SIC: 3999 Mfg Misc Products

(G-18842)
Q HOLDING COMPANY (HQ)
Also Called: Quality Synthetic Rubber
1700 Highland Rd (44087-2221)
PHONE..................................330 425-8472
Randall Ross, *CEO*
Harald Schliessus, *Business Mgr*
Dennis J Welhouse, *CFO*
Ken Harland, *Sales Engr*
▲ **EMP:** 385
SQ FT: 41,000
SALES (est): 372.7MM
SALES (corp-wide): 1.8B Privately Held
WEB: www.lexingtonprecision.com
SIC: 3061 Mechanical rubber goods
PA: 3i Group Plc
16 Palace Street
London SW1E
207 975-3131

(G-18843)
QUEST SERVICE LABS INC
2307 E Aurora Rd Unit B10 (44087-1958)
PHONE..................................330 405-0316
Al Wilson, *Principal*
EMP: 11
SALES (est): 1.2MM Privately Held
SIC: 2759 Commercial printing

(G-18844)
R A HAMED INTERNATIONAL INC
Also Called: Scott Thomas Furniture
8400 Darrow Rd (44087-2375)
PHONE..................................330 247-0190
Rosemary Hamed, *President*
Scott Hamed, *Vice Pres*
EMP: 12
SQ FT: 19,000
SALES (est): 1.2MM Privately Held
WEB: www.scottthomasfurniture.com
SIC: 2511 Wood household furniture

(G-18845)
REUTER-STOKES LLC
Also Called: Reuter-Stokes, Inc.
8499 Darrow Rd Ste 1 (44087-2398)
PHONE..................................330 425-3755
Leo Zanderschur, *President*
Greg Mellow, *Design Engr*
◆ **EMP:** 260
SQ FT: 110,000
SALES (est): 51.5MM
SALES (corp-wide): 121.6B Publicly Held
SIC: 3829 3826 3823 3812 Nuclear radiation & testing apparatus; environmental testing equipment; industrial instrmnts msrmnt display/control process variable; search & navigation equipment
PA: General Electric Company
41 Farnsworth St
Boston MA 02210
617 443-3000

(G-18846)
RHEACO BUILDERS INC
1941 E Aurora Rd (44087-1919)
PHONE..................................330 425-3090
George Rheaco, *President*
EMP: 6
SALES (est): 745.7K Privately Held
WEB: www.rheacoinc.com
SIC: 2434 Wood kitchen cabinets

(G-18847)
RO-MAI INDUSTRIES INC
1605 Enterprise Pkwy (44087-2201)
PHONE..................................330 425-9090
Robert Maier, *President*
▲ **EMP:** 30
SQ FT: 26,000
SALES (est): 4.4MM Privately Held
SIC: 3089 Injection molding of plastics

(G-18848)
ROCKWELL AUTOMATION INC
8440 Darrow Rd (44087-2310)
P.O. Box 2167, Milwaukee WI (53201-2167)
PHONE..................................330 425-3211
Michael Sparger, *Principal*
Gina Ward, *Opers Mgr*
David Dankelson, *Mfg Staff*
Robb Skruck, *Sales Engr*
Mark Todd, *Branch Mgr*
EMP: 400 Publicly Held
SIC: 3625 Control equipment, electric
PA: Rockwell Automation, Inc.
1201 S 2nd St
Milwaukee WI 53204

(G-18849)
ROONEY OPTICAL INC (PA)
9221 Ravenna Rd Ste 3 (44087-2454)
PHONE..................................216 267-5600
Gerald J Dougher, *Ch of Bd*
Kevin Dougher, *President*
EMP: 50
SQ FT: 20,000
SALES (est): 3.8MM Privately Held
WEB: www.rooneyoptical.com
SIC: 3851 Eyeglasses, lenses & frames

(G-18850)
ROYAL CHEMICAL COMPANY LTD
1755 Entp Pkwy Ste 100 (44087)
PHONE..................................330 467-1300
Eric Cubec, *CFO*
EMP: 15

SALES (corp-wide): 8.9MM **Privately Held**
SIC: **2841** Soap: granulated, liquid, cake, flaked or chip; detergents, synthetic organic or inorganic alkaline; scouring compounds
HQ: Royal Chemical Company, Ltd.
8679 Freeway Dr
Macedonia OH 44056
330 467-1300

(G-18851)
RTD ELECTRONICS INC
1632 Entp Pkwy Ste D (44087)
PHONE..................330 487-0716
Terry L Kellhofer, *President*
EMP: 12
SQ FT: 4,000
SALES (est): 233.5K **Privately Held**
SIC: **3679** Harness assemblies for electronic use: wire or cable

(G-18852)
S & B METAL PRODUCTS INC (PA)
2060 Case Pkwy (44087-2344)
PHONE..................330 487-5790
Stephen Campbell, *CEO*
Brent Cessna, *General Mgr*
Paul Balliette, *Chairman*
Cindy Balliette, *Corp Secy*
Frank Stobierski, *Buyer*
▼ EMP: 50 EST: 1974
SQ FT: 25,000
SALES (est): 10.4MM **Privately Held**
WEB: www.sbmetal.com
SIC: **3444** Sheet metal specialties, not stamped

(G-18853)
SAMUEL STEEL PICKLING COMPANY (PA)
1400 Enterprise Pkwy (44087-2242)
PHONE..................330 963-3777
Rick Snyder, *COO*
William Vason, *Opers Mgr*
Sylvia Herrmann, *Accountant*
EMP: 70
SQ FT: 115,000
SALES: 15MM **Privately Held**
SIC: **7389** 5051 3471 3398 Metal slitting & shearing; metals service centers & offices; plating & polishing; metal heat treating; blast furnaces & steel mills

(G-18854)
SCHAFFER GRINDING CO INC
8470 Chamberlin Rd (44087-2085)
PHONE..................323 724-4476
Chet Schaffer, *General Mgr*
Eric Koleszar, *Plant Mgr*
EMP: 15
SQ FT: 10,000
SALES (corp-wide): 6.5MM **Privately Held**
SIC: **3599** Machine shop, jobbing & repair
PA: Schaffer Grinding Co., Inc.
848 S Maple Ave
Montebello CA
323 724-4476

(G-18855)
SEMATIC USA INC
Also Called: Tyler Elevator Products
7852 Bavaria Rd (44087-2260)
PHONE..................216 524-0100
Roberto Zappa, *President*
Giorgio Scarabello, *Managing Dir*
Stefano Girardi, *COO*
▲ EMP: 35 EST: 1959
SQ FT: 35,000
SALES (est): 13MM **Privately Held**
WEB: www.sematic.com
SIC: **3534** Elevators & equipment
HQ: Sematic Spa
Via Commendatore Francesco Zappa 5
Osio Sotto BG 24046
035 482-4317

(G-18856)
SEMTORQ INC
Also Called: Nucam
1953 Case Pkwy S (44087-2359)
P.O. Box 895 (44087-0895)
PHONE..................330 487-0600
Joseph Seme Jr, *President*
Paul D'Angelo, *Business Mgr*
Greg Lanham, *Opers Staff*
Kirk Stevenson, *Buyer*
Christina Seme, *Admin Sec*
▲ EMP: 12
SQ FT: 40,000
SALES (est): 3.5MM **Privately Held**
WEB: www.semtorq.com
SIC: **3549** 7692 3594 3548 Assembly machines, including robotic; welding repair; fluid power pumps & motors; welding apparatus; machine tools, metal forming type; screw machine products

(G-18857)
SHELLY MATERIALS INC
8920 Canyon Falls Blvd # 120 (44087-1990)
PHONE..................330 425-7861
Matt Moten, *Branch Mgr*
EMP: 4
SALES (corp-wide): 29.7B **Privately Held**
SIC: **1422** Crushed & broken limestone
HQ: Shelly Materials, Inc.
80 Park Dr
Thornville OH 43076
740 246-6315

(G-18858)
SSP FITTINGS CORP (PA)
8250 Boyle Pkwy (44087-2200)
PHONE..................330 425-4250
Jeffrey E King, *CEO*
F B Douglas, *Principal*
O F Douglas, *Principal*
H M Hunter, *Principal*
Jo Soukup, *CFO*
▲ EMP: 150 EST: 1926
SQ FT: 165,000
SALES (est): 63.2MM **Privately Held**
WEB: www.sspfittings.com
SIC: **3494** 5085 3498 3492 Pipe fittings; industrial supplies; fabricated pipe & fittings; fluid power valves & hose fittings

(G-18859)
STANLEY PROCTOR & COMPANY INC
2016 Midway Dr (44087-1960)
P.O. Box 446 (44087-0446)
PHONE..................330 425-7814
John Proctor, *President*
Bill Better, *VP Sales*
EMP: 18 EST: 1983
SALES (est): 2.9MM
SALES (corp-wide): 7.7MM **Privately Held**
WEB: www.stanleyproctor.com
SIC: **3594** Motors: hydraulic, fluid power or air
PA: The Stanley M Proctor Company
2016 Midway Dr
Twinsburg OH 44087
330 425-7814

(G-18860)
STEWART ACQUISITION LLC (PA)
Also Called: Cima Plastics Group
2146 Enterprise Pkwy (44087-2272)
PHONE..................330 963-0322
Bill Brennan, *Purch Mgr*
James M Stewart,
▲ EMP: 45
SQ FT: 44,000
SALES (est): 11.7MM **Privately Held**
WEB: www.cimaplastics.com
SIC: **3089** Injection molding of plastics

(G-18861)
SUMMIT AVIONICS INC
2225 E Entp Pkwy 1a 1 A (44087)
PHONE..................330 425-1440
Michael Tartamella, *President*
Michael Woods, *CFO*
EMP: 18 EST: 2001
SQ FT: 14,000
SALES (est): 1.7MM **Privately Held**
WEB: www.summitavionics.com
SIC: **3728** Aircraft parts & equipment

(G-18862)
SUMMIT PETROLEUM INC
9345 Ravenna Rd (44087-2465)
PHONE..................330 487-5494
William G Kinney, *President*
Sarina Kinney, *Vice Pres*
EMP: 4
SQ FT: 1,500
SALES (est): 988.1K **Privately Held**
SIC: **1311** Crude petroleum production; natural gas production

(G-18863)
TECHNOFORM GL INSUL N AMER INC
1755 Entp Pkwy Ste 300 (44087)
PHONE..................330 487-6600
Albert Stankus, *General Mgr*
▲ EMP: 25
SQ FT: 50,000
SALES (est): 7.1MM
SALES (corp-wide): 356.8MM **Privately Held**
WEB: www.technoform.us
SIC: **3429** Manufactured hardware (general)
HQ: Technoform Bautec Holding Gmbh
Max-Planck-Str. 1-3
Lohfelden 34253
561 510-8822

(G-18864)
TOWER TOOL & MANUFACTURING CO
2057 E Aurora Rd Ste No (44087-1938)
PHONE..................330 425-1623
Fax: 330 425-4757
EMP: 12
SQ FT: 30,000
SALES: 1.3MM **Privately Held**
SIC: **3599** 3544 3444 Mfg Custom Machinery Dies Tools Jigs Or Fixtures & Sheet Metalwork

(G-18865)
TREADSTONE COMPANY
Also Called: Rubber Triangle
1565 Landsdale Cir (44087-3337)
PHONE..................216 410-3435
Thomas Turner, *President*
EMP: 3
SALES (est): 405.9K **Privately Held**
SIC: **3644** 5085 2952 Electric conduits & fittings; rubber goods, mechanical; roofing materials

(G-18866)
TRI COUNTY CONCRETE INC (PA)
9423 Darrow Rd (44087-1415)
P.O. Box 665 (44087-0665)
PHONE..................330 425-4464
Tony Farenacci, *President*
Fred Farenacci, *Vice Pres*
EMP: 30
SQ FT: 62,000
SALES (est): 4.8MM **Privately Held**
SIC: **3273** 3272 1442 Ready-mixed concrete; concrete products; construction sand & gravel

(G-18867)
TRIONIX RESEARCH LABORATORY
8037 Bavaria Rd (44087-2261)
PHONE..................330 425-9055
Dr Chun Bin Lim, *President*
EMP: 6
SQ FT: 150,000
SALES (est): 1.2MM **Privately Held**
SIC: **3844** Nuclear irradiation equipment

(G-18868)
TWIN VENTURES INC
2457 Edison Blvd (44087-2340)
PHONE..................330 405-3838
Dave Potts, *President*
EMP: 15
SALES (est): 1.5MM **Privately Held**
WEB: www.twinsrealm.com
SIC: **3452** 5072 Bolts, nuts, rivets & washers; hardware

(G-18869)
UNIVERSAL ELECTRONICS INC
1864 Entp Pkwy Ste B (44087)
PHONE..................330 487-1110
Jason Etter, *Engineer*
Anne M Frank, *Sales Staff*
Brian Dean, *Manager*
Chhadi Fahd, *Supervisor*
Kevin Meyers, *Supervisor*
EMP: 80
SALES (corp-wide): 680.2MM **Publicly Held**
WEB: www.ezremote.com
SIC: **3651** Video triggers (remote control TV devices)
PA: Universal Electronics Inc.
201 Sandpointe Ave Fl 8
Santa Ana CA 92707
714 918-9500

(G-18870)
UNIVERSAL RACK & EQUIPMENT CO
Also Called: Universal Coatings Division
8511 Tower Dr (44087-2088)
PHONE..................330 963-6776
Ken Palik, *President*
John Palik, *Vice Pres*
EMP: 20
SQ FT: 40,000
SALES (est): 1.6MM **Privately Held**
SIC: **3479** 3559 3443 Coating of metals with plastic or resins; electroplating machinery & equipment; fabricated plate work (boiler shop)

(G-18871)
US FITTINGS INC
2182 E Aurora Rd (44087-1924)
P.O. Box 746 (44087-0746)
PHONE..................234 212-9420
Richard K Raymond, *President*
EMP: 15
SQ FT: 1,500
SALES: 2.5MM **Privately Held**
SIC: **3494** Pipe fittings

(G-18872)
VISIMAX TECHNOLOGIES INC
9177 Dutton Dr (44087-1981)
PHONE..................330 405-8330
Dane Clark, *President*
Melanie Clark, *Vice Pres*
Paul Van Wagenen, *Sales Associate*
EMP: 12
SALES (est): 1.7MM **Privately Held**
WEB: www.visimaxtechnologies.com
SIC: **3479** Coating electrodes

(G-18873)
WEDGE PRODUCTS INC
2181 Enterprise Pkwy (44087-2211)
PHONE..................330 405-4477
Anthony J Defino, *President*
Frank Defino, *Vice Pres*
Leonard Defino, *Vice Pres*
Angie Kerley, *Sales Staff*
Margo Pecnik, *Office Mgr*
▲ EMP: 300 EST: 1925
SQ FT: 55,000
SALES (est): 48.9MM **Privately Held**
WEB: www.wedgeproducts.com
SIC: **3469** 3643 Stamping metal for the trade; current-carrying wiring devices
PA: A.J.D. Holding Co.
2181 Enterprise Pkwy
Twinsburg OH 44087

(G-18874)
WELDON PLASTICS CORPORATION
1962 Case Pkwy (44087-4327)
PHONE..................330 425-9660
Linda Repay, *President*
Laszlo Repay, *Vice Pres*
EMP: 3
SALES (est): 457.4K **Privately Held**
SIC: **3089** Injection molding of plastics; molding primary plastic

(G-18875)
WRWP LLC
Also Called: Western Reserve Wire Products
1920 Case Pkwy S (44087-2358)
PHONE..................330 425-3421
Kelli A Conway, *Vice Pres*
Douglas W Conway, *Plant Mgr*
Tom Dawes, *Plant Mgr*
Eddie Werner, *QC Mgr*
Emily Dizer, *CFO*
EMP: 17 EST: 2014

SALES (est): 3.1MM **Privately Held**
SIC: 3496 Miscellaneous fabricated wire products

(G-18876)
XACT GENOMICS LLC
9022 White Oak Dr (44087-1748)
PHONE..................................216 956-0957
Jerry Wrobel, *Principal*
EMP: 3 EST: 2014
SALES (est): 192K **Privately Held**
SIC: 2835 Microbiology & virology diagnostic products

(G-18877)
ZERUST CONSUMER PRODUCTS LLC
9345 Ravenna Rd Unit E (44087-2452)
PHONE..................................330 405-1965
Elliot Dworkin, *Mng Member*
▲ EMP: 3
SALES (est): 1.5MM **Privately Held**
SIC: 2899 Rust resisting compounds

(G-18878)
ZINKAN ENTERPRISES INC (PA)
1919 Case Pkwy (44087-2343)
PHONE..................................330 487-1500
Thomas W McCrystal, *Principal*
Mr Lou Koenig, *Principal*
◆ EMP: 10
SQ FT: 15,000
SALES (est): 16.1MM **Privately Held**
WEB: www.zinkan.com
SIC: 2899 Chemical preparations

Uhrichsville
Tuscarawas County

(G-18879)
ALERIS ROLLED PRODUCTS INC
7319 Newport Rd Se (44683-6368)
PHONE..................................740 922-2540
EMP: 4 **Privately Held**
SIC: 3341 3353 Secondary nonferrous metals; aluminum sheet, plate & foil
HQ: Aleris Rolled Products, Inc.
  25825 Science Park Dr # 400
  Beachwood OH 44122
  216 910-3400

(G-18880)
ARMSTRONG CUSTOM MOULDING INC
6408 State Route 800 Se (44683-6302)
PHONE..................................740 922-5931
Todd Armstrong, *President*
James B Armstrong Sr, *Admin Sec*
EMP: 6
SALES (est): 637.3K **Privately Held**
SIC: 2431 2426 Moldings & baseboards, ornamental & trim; hardwood dimension & flooring mills

(G-18881)
CAROLINA STAIR SUPPLY INC (PA)
316 Herrick St (44683-2123)
PHONE..................................740 922-3333
Clair Edwards, *President*
▲ EMP: 39
SQ FT: 2,000
SALES (est): 6.4MM **Privately Held**
SIC: 2431 Staircases & stairs, wood

(G-18882)
CF EXTRUSION TECHNOLOGIES LLC
101 E 3rd St (44683-1818)
P.O. Box 272, Cuyahoga Falls (44222-0272)
PHONE..................................844 439-8783
Terrance Hendershot, *President*
EMP: 3
SALES (est): 105.1K **Privately Held**
SIC: 3532 3443 3523 Mine cars, plows, loaders, feeders & similar equipment; mixers, for hot metal; feed grinders, crushers & mixers

(G-18883)
D & A CUSTOM TRAILER INC
6700 Moores Ridge Rd Se (44683-6573)
PHONE..................................740 922-2205
EMP: 3
SALES (est): 200.2K **Privately Held**
SIC: 3799 Mfg Transportation Equipment

(G-18884)
D & B MACHINE WELDING INC
1128 N Main St (44683-1224)
P.O. Box 248 (44683-0248)
PHONE..................................740 922-4930
Bill Brehm, *President*
Linda Brehm, *Treasurer*
EMP: 4 EST: 1946
SQ FT: 4,200
SALES (est): 372.1K **Privately Held**
SIC: 3599 Machine shop, jobbing & repair

(G-18885)
DJ S WELD
424 N Main St (44683-1837)
PHONE..................................330 432-2206
Dwight Jones, *Owner*
EMP: 7
SALES (est): 520.5K **Privately Held**
SIC: 3443 Weldments

(G-18886)
FABOHIO INC
521 E 7th St (44683-1613)
P.O. Box 434 (44683-0434)
PHONE..................................740 922-4233
Kurt Shelley, *CEO*
Joyce Tobin, *Office Mgr*
EMP: 20 EST: 1963
SQ FT: 22,500
SALES: 1.7MM
SALES (corp-wide): 36.8MM **Privately Held**
WEB: www.fabohio.com
SIC: 3089 Plastic containers, except foam
PA: Bowerston Shale Company (Inc)
  515 Main St
  Bowerston OH 44695
  740 269-2921

(G-18887)
HALL SAFETY APPAREL INC
1020 W 1st St (44683-2210)
P.O. Box 392 (44683-0392)
PHONE..................................740 922-3671
Gregory L Schneider, *President*
Delores Schneider, *Vice Pres*
Phillip Schneider, *Admin Sec*
EMP: 14 EST: 1937
SQ FT: 18,000
SALES: 610K **Privately Held**
SIC: 2326 2381 3842 Work apparel, except uniforms; gloves, work: woven or knit, made from purchased materials; radiation shielding aprons, gloves, sheeting, etc.

(G-18888)
IMCO RECYCLING OF OHIO LLC
7335 Newport Rd Se (44683-6368)
PHONE..................................740 922-2373
Sean M Stack, *CEO*
Robert R Holian, *Vice Pres*
▲ EMP: 164
SALES (est): 20.3MM **Privately Held**
WEB: www.imcorecycling.com
SIC: 3341 4953 Aluminum smelting & refining (secondary); recycling, waste materials
HQ: Aleris Rolled Products, Inc.
  25825 Science Park Dr # 400
  Beachwood OH 44122
  216 910-3400

(G-18889)
JOHNSON PRINTING
216 E 5th St (44683-1698)
PHONE..................................740 922-4821
Kevin J Johnson, *Owner*
EMP: 4
SQ FT: 3,000
SALES (est): 245K **Privately Held**
SIC: 2759 2752 Letterpress printing; commercial printing, offset

(G-18890)
K-HILL SIGNAL CO INC
326 W 3rd St (44683-2036)
P.O. Box 432 (44683-0432)
PHONE..................................740 922-0421
William J Hall, *President*
Sally Hall, *Vice Pres*
Kelly Ernandison, *Manager*
Kathy Grandison, *Admin Sec*
EMP: 3 EST: 1935
SQ FT: 4,500
SALES (est): 75K **Privately Held**
WEB: www.khilltrafficounters.com
SIC: 3669 3824 Traffic signals, electric; fluid meters & counting devices

(G-18891)
NORTH STAR METALS MFG CO
6850 Edwards Ridge Rd Se (44683-5602)
P.O. Box 309, Gnadenhutten (44629-0309)
PHONE..................................740 254-4567
Darren Galbraith, *President*
Denny Dewitt, *Sales Staff*
Lisa Messner, *Admin Sec*
EMP: 32
SQ FT: 40,000
SALES (est): 6.5MM **Privately Held**
WEB: www.northstarmetals.com
SIC: 3444 Siding, sheet metal

(G-18892)
ROSEBUD MINING COMPANY
5600 Pleasant Vly Rd Se (44683-9502)
PHONE..................................740 922-9122
Greg Blainer, *Branch Mgr*
EMP: 33
SALES (corp-wide): 605.3MM **Privately Held**
WEB: www.rosebudmining.com
SIC: 1222 1221 Bituminous coal-underground mining; strip mining, bituminous
PA: Rosebud Mining Company
  301 Market St
  Kittanning PA 16201
  724 545-6222

(G-18893)
SEALCO INC
6566 Superior Rd Se (44683-7487)
P.O. Box 307 (44683-0307)
PHONE..................................740 922-4122
Elmer McClave, *President*
Todd McClave, *Vice Pres*
▲ EMP: 6
SALES (est): 480.2K **Privately Held**
SIC: 2499 2448 Plugs, wood; pallets, wood

(G-18894)
SEYEKCUB INC
615 W 4th St (44683-2007)
PHONE..................................330 324-1394
Robert L Drummond Jr, *President*
Dave Markley, *Engineer*
EMP: 8
SQ FT: 10,000
SALES (est): 1.4MM **Privately Held**
SIC: 3363 Aluminum die-castings

(G-18895)
STEBBINS ENGINEERING & MFG CO
Also Called: Semco Ceramics
4778 Belden Dr Se (44683-1078)
P.O. Box 90 (44683-0090)
PHONE..................................740 922-3012
Cliff McPherson, *General Mgr*
EMP: 26
SALES (corp-wide): 178.3MM **Privately Held**
WEB: www.stebbinseng.com
SIC: 3253 3255 3251 Ceramic wall & floor tile; clay refractories; brick & structural clay tile
PA: The Stebbins Engineering And Manufacturing Company
  363 Eastern Blvd
  Watertown NY 13601
  315 782-3000

(G-18896)
SUPERIOR CLAY CORP
6566 Superior Rd Se (44683-7487)
P.O. Box 352 (44683-0352)
PHONE..................................740 922-4122
Elmer W McClave III, *President*
Joe Berni, *Corp Secy*
Tyler McClave, *Vice Pres*
Nan Giumenti, *Technology*
Dana Martini, *Technician*
◆ EMP: 75 EST: 1936
SQ FT: 190,000
SALES (est): 9.9MM **Privately Held**
WEB: www.superiorclay.com
SIC: 3259 8611 Sewer pipe or fittings, clay; flue lining, clay; wall coping, clay; stove lining, clay; business associations

(G-18897)
TOLLOTI PLASTIC PIPE INC
1830 Barbour Dr Se (44683-1084)
P.O. Box 508 (44683-0508)
PHONE..................................740 922-6911
Jack Homman, *Branch Mgr*
EMP: 5
SALES (corp-wide): 3.8MM **Privately Held**
SIC: 3084 Plastics pipe
PA: Tolloti Plastic Pipe Inc.
  102 Barnhill Rd Se
  New Philadelphia OH 44663
  330 364-6627

(G-18898)
TRADING POST
202 N Water St (44683-1845)
PHONE..................................740 922-1199
Richard Sommers, *Owner*
EMP: 5 EST: 2010
SALES (est): 207.6K **Privately Held**
SIC: 2711 Newspapers, publishing & printing

(G-18899)
UHRICHSVILLE CARBIDE INC
410 N Water St (44683-1849)
PHONE..................................740 922-9197
Bob Septer, *President*
Karen Septer, *Corp Secy*
Rhea Septer, *Clerk*
EMP: 17
SALES (est): 1.6MM **Privately Held**
WEB: www.uhrichsvillecarbide.com
SIC: 3545 5072 7699 3546 Cutting tools for machine tools; saw blades; knife, saw & tool sharpening & repair; power-driven handtools; machine tools, metal forming type; saw blades & handsaws

Union
Montgomery County

(G-18900)
CONTINENTAL TESTING INC
104 S Main St (45322-3358)
PHONE..................................937 832-3322
Michael Thee, *President*
Angela Luff, *Sales Associate*
EMP: 11
SQ FT: 800
SALES: 600K **Privately Held**
WEB: www.continentaltesting.com
SIC: 3829 8734 Measuring & controlling devices; calibration & certification

Union City
Darke County

(G-18901)
CAL-MAINE FOODS INC
1039 Zumbrum Rd (45390-8646)
PHONE..................................937 968-4874
Chuck Jenkins, *Branch Mgr*
EMP: 35
SALES (corp-wide): 1.5B **Publicly Held**
WEB: www.calmainefoods.com
SIC: 0252 2015 Chicken eggs; eggs, processed; frozen
PA: Cal-Maine Foods, Inc.
  3320 W Woodrow Wilson Ave
  Jackson MS 39209
  601 948-6813

Union City - Darke County (G-18902)

GEOGRAPHIC SECTION

(G-18902)
CAST METALS TECHNOLOGY INC
305 Se Deerfield Rd (45390-9072)
PHONE..................................937 968-5460
Ryan Olney, *Owner*
Vicky Harris, *Manager*
EMP: 47 **Privately Held**
SIC: 3365 Aluminum foundries
PA: Cast Metals Technology, Inc.
  550 Liberty Rd
  Delaware OH 43015

(G-18903)
CHARLES DANIEL YOUNG
Also Called: Fresh Aire Farms
1324 Wasson Rd (45390-9040)
PHONE..................................937 968-3423
Charles Daniel Young, *Owner*
Michelle Young, *Co-Owner*
EMP: 3
SALES (est): 147K **Privately Held**
SIC: 2875 Compost

(G-18904)
HA-STE MANUFACTURING CO INC
Also Called: Kangaroo Brand Mops
119 E Elm St (45390-1711)
P.O. Box 168 IN (47390-0168)
PHONE..................................937 968-4858
Robin Stewart, *President*
John W Stewart, *Chairman*
Vicky Constable, *Purchasing*
EMP: 25
SQ FT: 5,500
SALES: 16MM **Privately Held**
WEB: www.hastemops.com
SIC: 2392 Mops, floor & dust

(G-18905)
MBM LUMBER
1588 Cox Rd (45390-9036)
PHONE..................................937 459-7448
Craig Mendenhall, *Partner*
Greg Mendenhall, *Partner*
EMP: 5
SALES: 3.2MM **Privately Held**
SIC: 2421 Sawmills & planing mills, general

(G-18906)
WOODBURY WELDING INC
10393 Oh In State Line Rd (45390-9050)
PHONE..................................937 968-3573
Gary Woodbury, *President*
EMP: 3
SALES (est): 376.4K **Privately Held**
SIC: 3441 3523 0191 Fabricated structural metal; farm machinery & equipment; general farms, primarily crop

---

Uniontown
Stark County

(G-18907)
ADVANTAGE TOOL SUPPLY INC
3666 Avanti Ln (44685-8852)
PHONE..................................330 896-8869
Michael Prexta, *President*
Laura Prexta, *Treasurer*
EMP: 3
SALES: 700K **Privately Held**
SIC: 3545 Cutting tools for machine tools

(G-18908)
ALAN L GRANT POLYMER INC
Also Called: Momentum Technologies Intl
1507 Boettler Rd Ste E (44685-7767)
PHONE..................................757 627-4000
Louis Mucciolol, *President*
EMP: 3
SALES (est): 153.1K **Privately Held**
SIC: 2822 Ethylene-propylene rubbers, EPDM polymers

(G-18909)
AMERITECH PUBLISHING INC
Also Called: SBC
1530 Corp Woods Pkwy # 100 (44685-6707)
PHONE..................................330 896-6037
Kim Gergel, *Manager*
EMP: 50
SALES (corp-wide): 170.7B **Publicly Held**
SIC: 2741 Miscellaneous publishing
HQ: Ameritech Publishing, Inc.
  23500 Northwestern Hwy
  Southfield MI 48075
  800 996-4609

(G-18910)
ARATINABOX COMPANIES INC
12910 Cleveland Ave Nw (44685-7207)
PHONE..................................330 699-3421
EMP: 6
SQ FT: 1,200
SALES: 500K **Privately Held**
SIC: 2329 Mfg Men's & Boy's Clothing

(G-18911)
ATLAS GROWTH EAGLE FORD LLC
3500 Massillon Rd (44685-9504)
PHONE..................................330 896-8510
Daniel C Herz, *President*
Freddie M Koteh, *Vice Pres*
Sean P McGrath, *CFO*
James D Toth, *Treasurer*
Lisa Washington, *Admin Sec*
EMP: 3
SALES (est): 149.1K **Privately Held**
SIC: 1389 Building oil & gas well foundations on site

(G-18912)
BOBIT BUSINESS MEDIA INC
Also Called: Modern Time Dealer
3515 Massillon Rd Ste 350 (44685-6217)
PHONE..................................330 899-2200
John Dyal, *Sales Mgr*
Greg Smith, *Branch Mgr*
Joy Kopcha, *Senior Editor*
EMP: 9
SALES (corp-wide): 32.6MM **Privately Held**
WEB: www.bobit.com
SIC: 2721 Magazines: publishing only, not printed on site
PA: Bobit Business Media Inc.
  3520 Challenger St
  Torrance CA 90503
  310 533-2400

(G-18913)
BOMBA S CUSTOM WOODWORKING
3748 Dogwood St Nw (44685-8667)
PHONE..................................330 699-9075
Thomas Bomba, *Principal*
EMP: 4 **EST:** 2008
SALES (est): 461.1K **Privately Held**
SIC: 2431 Millwork

(G-18914)
CHEMSPEC
1559 Corporate Woods Pkwy # 150 (44685-7822)
PHONE..................................330 896-0355
▲ **EMP:** 12
SALES (est): 1MM **Privately Held**
SIC: 2869 Silicones

(G-18915)
CHEMSPEC LTD
Also Called: Chemspec Polymer Additives
1559 Corporate Woods Pkwy (44685-7872)
PHONE..................................330 896-0355
David Moreland, *President*
Richard Dee, *CFO*
◆ **EMP:** 15
SQ FT: 1,500
SALES (est): 5.5MM
SALES (corp-wide): 1.7MM **Privately Held**
WEB: www.chemspecltd.com
SIC: 2891 2952 3011 Adhesives & sealants; mastic roofing composition; automobile tires, pneumatic
HQ: Safic Alcan
  Tour Pacific
  Puteaux 92800
  146 926-464

(G-18916)
CHEVRON AE RESOURCES LLC
3500 Massillon Rd Ste 100 (44685-9575)
PHONE..................................330 896-8510
EMP: 24
SALES (corp-wide): 129.9B **Publicly Held**
SIC: 1311 Petroleum/Natural Gas Production
HQ: Chevron Ae Resources Llc
  1000 Commerce Dr Fl 4
  Pittsburgh PA 15275
  800 251-0171

(G-18917)
CRABWARE LTD
3842 Park Ridge Dr (44685-9010)
PHONE..................................330 699-2305
Anna Gambol, *Mng Member*
Charles Gambol,
Rebecca Habel,
Richard Habel,
EMP: 4
SALES (est): 231.6K **Privately Held**
SIC: 7372 Application computer software

(G-18918)
ENVIRONMENT CHEMICAL CORP
2167 Crestwick Dr (44685)
PHONE..................................330 453-5200
Richard Morena, *President*
Dennis Morena, *Vice Pres*
EMP: 4 **EST:** 2014
SALES (est): 228.3K **Privately Held**
SIC: 2899 Chemical preparations

(G-18919)
FOOT LOGIC INC
2824 Sweitzer Rd (44685-8310)
PHONE..................................330 699-0123
Kathleen Kinsey, *President*
Larry Kinsey, *Vice Pres*
EMP: 6
SALES: 400K **Privately Held**
WEB: www.footlogic-inc.com
SIC: 3069 3842 Orthopedic sundries, molded rubber; surgical appliances & supplies

(G-18920)
GAYDASH ENTERPRISES INC
Also Called: Gaydash Industries
3640 Tabs Dr (44685-9560)
PHONE..................................330 896-4811
Gerald Gaydash, *President*
Joan Gaydash, *Corp Secy*
Joel Gaydash, *Vice Pres*
EMP: 16
SQ FT: 15,000
SALES (est): 1.8MM **Privately Held**
SIC: 3599 Machine shop, jobbing & repair

(G-18921)
HIGH TECH MOLD & MACHINE CO
3771 Tabs Dr (44685-9563)
PHONE..................................330 896-4466
Anthony Klisan Jr, *President*
Connie Klisan, *President*
Stephanie Klisan, *President*
EMP: 15
SQ FT: 15,000
SALES (est): 3MM **Privately Held**
WEB: www.hightechmold.com
SIC: 3544 3599 Industrial molds; machine shop, jobbing & repair

(G-18922)
K2 PURE SOLUTIONS LP (PA)
3515 Massillon Rd Ste 290 (44685-7854)
PHONE..................................925 526-8112
Howard Brodie, *Partner*
David Cynamon, *Chairman*
Penny Hung, *CFO*
EMP: 7 **EST:** 2017
SQ FT: 1,874
SALES (est): 5.8MM **Privately Held**
SIC: 3589 Water purification equipment, household type

(G-18923)
KENDEE CANDLES LLC
4761 Buhl Blvd (44685-9617)
PHONE..................................330 899-9898
Kenneth Belile, *Principal*
EMP: 3
SALES (est): 211.1K **Privately Held**
SIC: 3999 Candles

(G-18924)
KOVATCH CASTINGS INC
3743 Tabs Dr (44685-9563)
PHONE..................................330 896-9944
Douglas Kovatch, *President*
Frank E Lysiak, *Vice Pres*
◆ **EMP:** 195
SQ FT: 65,000
SALES (est): 51MM **Privately Held**
WEB: www.kovatchcastings.com
SIC: 3324 3369 3366 3365 Commercial investment castings, ferrous; aerospace investment castings, ferrous; nonferrous foundries; copper foundries; aluminum foundries; steel foundries

(G-18925)
LIBERTY OUTDOORS LLC
1519 Boettler Rd Ste A (44685-8391)
PHONE..................................330 791-3149
Joe Kicos, *Director*
EMP: 10
SALES (est): 2.3MM **Privately Held**
SIC: 3714 Trailer hitches, motor vehicle

(G-18926)
LOUIS ARTHUR STEEL COMPANY
3700 Massillon Rd Ste 360 (44685-9558)
PHONE..................................440 997-5545
Paul Miller, *Project Engr*
EMP: 3
SALES (corp-wide): 13MM **Privately Held**
SIC: 3441 5051 3444 3443 Fabricated structural metal; steel; sheet metalwork; fabricated plate work (boiler shop)
PA: The Louis Arthur Steel Company
  185 Water St
  Geneva OH 44041
  440 997-5545

(G-18927)
MCAFEE TOOL & DIE INC
1717 Boettler Rd (44685-9588)
PHONE..................................330 896-9555
Gary Mc Afee, *President*
Mike Francek, *General Mgr*
Michael J Francek Jr, *Vice Pres*
Martin Labbe, *Engineer*
Ron Feldner, *Sales Associate*
EMP: 35 **EST:** 1977
SQ FT: 40,000
SALES (est): 6.7MM **Privately Held**
WEB: www.mcafeetool.com
SIC: 3544 3469 Die sets for metal stamping (presses); metal stampings

(G-18928)
MESSER LLC
4179 Meadow Wood Ln (44685-7716)
PHONE..................................330 608-3008
EMP: 23
SALES (corp-wide): 1.4B **Privately Held**
SIC: 2813 Industrial gases
HQ: Messer Llc
  200 Somerset Corporate
  Bridgewater NJ 08807
  908 464-8100

(G-18929)
PLASTIC CARD INC (PA)
Also Called: Rainbow Printing
3711 Boettler Oaks Dr (44685-7733)
PHONE..................................330 896-5555
Kenneth Thompson, *President*
Rich Krauth, *Vice Pres*
Tom Mason, *Vice Pres*
Thomas Thompson, *Vice Pres*
Rose Dunn, *Human Res Mgr*
▼ **EMP:** 60
SQ FT: 24,000
SALES (est): 7.2MM **Privately Held**
WEB: www.plasticcardfactory.com
SIC: 2396 Printing & embossing on plastics fabric articles

GEOGRAPHIC SECTION

(G-18930)
PLASTICARDS INC (PA)
Also Called: Rainbow Printing
3711 Boettler Oaks Dr (44685-7733)
PHONE.................................330 896-5555
Kenneth Thompson, *President*
Rich Crowft, *Vice Pres*
Thomas Thompson, *Vice Pres*
Patty Lou Thompson, *Admin Sec*
EMP: 49
SQ FT: 20,000
SALES (est): 6.4MM **Privately Held**
WEB: www.magnetguys.com
SIC: 3089 Identification cards, plastic

(G-18931)
SMITH INTERNATIONAL INC
2616 Country Squire St Nw (44685-9471)
PHONE.................................330 497-2999
Tom Colston, *Branch Mgr*
EMP: 5 **Publicly Held**
WEB: www.smith-intl.com
SIC: 1389 Oil field services
HQ: Smith International, Inc.
   1310 Rankin Rd
   Houston TX 77073
   281 443-3370

(G-18932)
STEERAMERICA INC
Also Called: Steer America
1525 Corporate Woods Pkwy (44685-7883)
PHONE.................................330 563-4407
Satish Padmanabhan, *CEO*
Babu Padmanabhan, *Managing Dir*
R Padmanabhan, *Chairman*
Mike Millsaps, *COO*
Sue Arthur, *CFO*
▲ EMP: 13
SQ FT: 10,000
SALES (est): 5.4MM
SALES (corp-wide): 19.4MM **Privately Held**
SIC: 3452 Bolts, nuts, rivets & washers
PA: Steer Engineering Private Limited
   No.290, 4th Main, 4th Phase,
   Bengaluru KA 56005
   802 372-3309

(G-18933)
SYNTHETIC RUBBER TECHNOLOGY
11021 Wright Rd Nw (44685-9476)
P.O. Box 639 (44685-0639)
PHONE.................................330 494-2221
Rodney A Rose, *President*
EMP: 5
SQ FT: 1,000
SALES (est): 611.5K **Privately Held**
SIC: 2821 Plastics materials & resins

(G-18934)
TARGET THOMPSON TECHNOLOGY
3651 Apache St Nw (44685-9114)
PHONE.................................330 699-8000
Rick Thompson, *Owner*
EMP: 7
SALES: 450K **Privately Held**
WEB: www.thompsontarget.com
SIC: 3949 Target shooting equipment

(G-18935)
TIN INDIAN PERFORMANCE
2656 Watervale Dr (44685-8354)
PHONE.................................216 214-5485
Kevin Swaney, *Principal*
EMP: 5
SALES (est): 505.3K **Privately Held**
SIC: 3356 Tin

(G-18936)
UNIONTOWN SEPTIC TANKS INC
2781 Raber Rd (44685-8125)
PHONE.................................330 699-3386
James N Kungle, *President*
Jeff Kungle, *Vice Pres*
EMP: 10 EST: 1965
SALES: 750K **Privately Held**
SIC: 3272 Septic tanks, concrete

(G-18937)
UTC AEROSPACE SYSTEMS
1555 Corporate Woods Pkwy (44685-7820)
PHONE.................................330 374-3040
Galdemir Botura, *Principal*
Martin Lei, *Engineer*
Brad Hartzler, *Supervisor*
EMP: 3 EST: 2016
SALES (est): 85.1K **Privately Held**
SIC: 3812 Search & navigation equipment

Unionville Center
Union County

(G-18938)
UNIONVILLE CENTER SIGN CO
Also Called: U C Signs
110 W Main St (43077-8000)
P.O. Box 95 (43077-0095)
PHONE.................................614 873-5834
Drew Youngberg, *Owner*
EMP: 4
SALES: 200K **Privately Held**
WEB: www.ucsigns.com
SIC: 3993 Signs, not made in custom sign painting shops

Uniopolis
Auglaize County

(G-18939)
EAGLE MANUFACTURING INC
88 High St (45888)
P.O. Box 215 (45888-0215)
PHONE.................................419 738-3491
EMP: 4
SQ FT: 10,000
SALES (est): 75K **Privately Held**
SIC: 3599 Machine Shop Jobbing & Repair

University Heights
Cuyahoga County

(G-18940)
CARBOLINE COMPANY
2379 Miramar Blvd (44118-3818)
PHONE.................................800 848-4645
EMP: 3
SALES (corp-wide): 5.3B **Publicly Held**
SIC: 2851 Paints & allied products
HQ: Carboline Company
   2150 Schuetz Rd Fl 1
   Saint Louis MO 63146
   314 644-1000

(G-18941)
DOAN MACHINERY & EQP CO INC
2636 S Belvoir Blvd (44118-4661)
PHONE.................................216 932-6243
Marguerite Levenson, *President*
EMP: 6 EST: 1976
SALES (est): 729.6K **Privately Held**
SIC: 3429 3469 Fireplace equipment, hardware: andirons, grates, screens; bottle openers, stamped metal

(G-18942)
GREAT LAKES DEFENSE SVCS LLC
2319 Miramar Blvd (44118-3818)
PHONE.................................216 272-3450
Erika Rotko, *Vice Pres*
Alicia Cooney, *Mng Member*
Christopher Cooney, *Officer*
Jonathan Rotko, *Officer*
EMP: 4
SALES (est): 193.4K **Privately Held**
SIC: 3451 8742 Screw machine products; industry specialist consultants

Upper Arlington
Franklin County

(G-18943)
AUTO DES SYS INC
3518 Riverside Dr (43221-1735)
PHONE.................................614 488-7984
Chris Yessios, *President*
David Kropp, *Vice Pres*
Alexandra Yessios, *Vice Pres*
Paul Helm, *Technical Staff*
Matthew Holewinski, *Technical Staff*
EMP: 30
SQ FT: 2,000
SALES (est): 3MM **Privately Held**
WEB: www.autodessys.com
SIC: 7371 7372 Computer software development; prepackaged software

(G-18944)
DAILY GROWLER INC
2812 Fishinger Rd (43221-1129)
P.O. Box 218455 (43221-8455)
PHONE.................................614 656-2337
EMP: 5
SALES (est): 310.9K **Privately Held**
SIC: 2711 Newspapers, publishing & printing

Upper Sandusky
Wyandot County

(G-18945)
A-1 PRINTING INC
129 W Wyandot Ave (43351-1348)
PHONE.................................419 294-5247
Becky Lloyd, *Manager*
EMP: 4
SALES (corp-wide): 1.3MM **Privately Held**
SIC: 2752 Commercial printing, offset
PA: A-1 Printing, Inc.
   825 S Sandusky Ave
   Bucyrus OH 44820
   419 562-3111

(G-18946)
BRIDGESTONE APM COMPANY
235 Commerce Way (43351-9079)
P.O. Box 450 (43351-0450)
PHONE.................................419 294-6989
Greg Ickes, *Branch Mgr*
Ray Perry, *Manager*
Mark Brady, *Maintence Staff*
Jeff Overly, *Maintence Staff*
EMP: 100
SALES (corp-wide): 32.4B **Privately Held**
SIC: 3061 Automotive rubber goods (mechanical)
HQ: Bridgestone Apm Company
   2030 Production Dr
   Findlay OH 45840
   419 423-9552

(G-18947)
BRIDGESTONE APM COMPANY
Also Called: Seat Division Bridgestone
245 Commerce Way (43351-9079)
PHONE.................................419 294-6304
Fred Rechtenbach, *Principal*
Jim Lafleur, *Engineer*
EMP: 100
SALES (corp-wide): 32.4B **Privately Held**
SIC: 3061 Automotive rubber goods (mechanical)
HQ: Bridgestone Apm Company
   2030 Production Dr
   Findlay OH 45840
   419 423-9552

(G-18948)
BUCKEYE READY-MIX
6326 County Highway 61 (43351-9749)
PHONE.................................419 294-2389
Chris Mc Carthy, *Principal*
EMP: 3
SALES (est): 315.3K **Privately Held**
SIC: 3273 Ready-mixed concrete

(G-18949)
CUSTOM GLASS SOLUTIONS UPPER S
12688 State Highway 67 (43351-9411)
PHONE.................................419 294-4921
EMP: 500
SALES (est): 65.2MM
SALES (corp-wide): 106.6MM **Privately Held**
SIC: 3231 Laminated glass: made from purchased glass; safety glass: made from purchased glass
PA: Custom Glass Solutions, Llc
   600 Lkview Plz Blvd Ste A
   Worthington OH 43085
   248 340-1800

(G-18950)
DAILY CHIEF UNION
111 W Wyandot Ave (43351-1367)
P.O. Box 180 (43351-0180)
PHONE.................................419 294-2331
Jack L Barnes, *President*
Tom Martin, *Manager*
Charles G Barnes, *Admin Sec*
EMP: 15
SQ FT: 3,000
SALES (est): 856.5K
SALES (corp-wide): 8.7MM **Privately Held**
SIC: 2711 Commercial printing & newspaper publishing combined; newspapers, publishing & printing
HQ: Hardin County Publishing Co Inc
   201 E Columbus St
   Kenton OH 43326
   419 674-4066

(G-18951)
DESIGN & FABRICATION INC
400 Malabar Dr (43351-9747)
P.O. Box 218 (43351-0218)
PHONE.................................419 294-2414
Mike Reamer, *President*
Cathy Reamer, *Admin Sec*
Kathy Reamer,
EMP: 7
SQ FT: 7,200
SALES: 400K **Privately Held**
SIC: 3599 Machine shop, jobbing & repair

(G-18952)
DIAMOND ROLL-UP DOOR INC
295 Commerce Way (43351-9079)
P.O. Box 420 (43351-0420)
PHONE.................................419 294-3373
Ray Van Gunten, *President*
Matthew Baxter, *Corp Secy*
Roger White, *Sales Mgr*
Paul Sleeman, *Director*
◆ EMP: 60
SQ FT: 37,500
SALES (est): 14.4MM **Privately Held**
WEB: www.diamondrollupdoor.com
SIC: 3442 Metal doors

(G-18953)
ENGINEERED WIRE PRODUCTS INC (DH)
1200 N Warpole St (43351-9093)
P.O. Box 313 (43351-0313)
PHONE.................................419 294-3817
Bradley W Evers, *Principal*
Jeff Babcock, *Vice Pres*
Jack Helmer, *VP Mfg*
Grafton Redfren, *VP Sales*
Pam Dyer, *Manager*
▲ EMP: 101
SALES (est): 25.4MM **Privately Held**
WEB: www.keystonesteel.com
SIC: 3496 3315 Miscellaneous fabricated wire products; steel wire & related products
HQ: Keystone Consolidated Industries, Inc.
   5430 Lyndon B Johnson Fwy # 1740
   Dallas TX 75240
   800 441-0308

(G-18954)
FARMERS COMMISSION COMPANY (HQ)
520 W Wyandot Ave (43351-1335)
P.O. Box 59 (43351-0059)
PHONE.................................419 294-2371
Eric Parthemore, *President*

Upper Sandusky - Wyandot County (G-18955)

Lyle Gottfried, *Treasurer*
EMP: 22
SALES (est): 16.1MM **Privately Held**
WEB: www.farmerscommission.com
SIC: 5191 5999 2041 Fertilizer & fertilizer materials; feed & farm supply; flour & other grain mill products

(G-18955)
HANDY TWINE KNIFE CO
5676 County Highway 330 (43351-9772)
P.O. Box 146 (43351-0146)
PHONE 419 294-3424
Lynn L Getz, *President*
John Tschantz, *Vice Pres*
Brian Caldwell, *Treasurer*
EMP: 9
SQ FT: 1,000
SALES: 875K **Privately Held**
WEB: www.handytwineknife.com
SIC: 3423 5719 Knives, agricultural or industrial; cutlery

(G-18956)
HOT SHOT MOTOR WORKS M LLC
555 S Warpole St Rear (43351-1549)
P.O. Box 297 (43351-0297)
PHONE 419 294-1997
Daniel Thompson, *Mng Member*
EMP: 3
SQ FT: 2,600
SALES (est): 220K **Privately Held**
WEB: www.hotshotmotorworks.com
SIC: 3714 5571 Motor vehicle parts & accessories; motorcycle dealers

(G-18957)
KALMBACH FEEDS INC (PA)
7148 State Highway 199 (43351-9359)
PHONE 419 294-3838
Paul M Kalmbach, *President*
Dick Regnier, *CFO*
▲ **EMP:** 110
SALES (est): 30.7MM **Privately Held**
SIC: 2048 Livestock feeds; poultry feeds

(G-18958)
KASAI NORTH AMERICA INC
1111 N Warpole St (43351-9094)
PHONE 419 209-0470
Masaki Sugisawa, *Branch Mgr*
EMP: 29
SALES (corp-wide): 2.1B **Privately Held**
SIC: 3089 3714 Injection molding of plastics; motor vehicle parts & accessories
HQ: Kasai North America, Inc.
1225 Garrison Dr
Murfreesboro TN 37129
615 546-6040

(G-18959)
KIRBY AND SONS INC
Also Called: Kirby Sand & Gravel
4876 County Highway 43 (43351-9155)
PHONE 419 927-2260
Gene Kirby, *President*
Judi Kirby, *Corp Secy*
Franklin Kirby, *Vice Pres*
Minor Kirby, *Webmaster*
Judy Kirby, *Admin Sec*
EMP: 12
SALES (est): 3MM **Privately Held**
SIC: 1442 4212 Common sand mining; gravel mining; dump truck haulage

(G-18960)
LIQUI-BOX CORPORATION
519 Raybestos Dr (43351-9666)
PHONE 419 209-9085
Fax: 419 294-1899
EMP: 120
SQ FT: 42,000
SALES (corp-wide): 429MM **Privately Held**
SIC: 3089 3544 Mfg Plastic Molded Parts
PA: Liqui-Box Corporation
901 E Byrd St Ste 1105
Richmond VA 23219
804 325-1400

(G-18961)
M-TEK INC
1111 N Warpole St (43351-9094)
PHONE 419 209-0399
Sam Kennedy, *Vice Pres*
Tracy Wentling, *Buyer*
Raymond England, *Engineer*
Skyler Hapner, *Engineer*
Linda Meredith, *HR Admin*
EMP: 600
SALES (corp-wide): 2.1B **Privately Held**
WEB: www.m-tek.com
SIC: 3465 3714 Moldings or trim, automobile: stamped metal; motor vehicle parts & accessories
HQ: Kasai North America, Inc.
1225 Garrison Dr
Murfreesboro TN 37129
615 546-6040

(G-18962)
MAR-METAL MFG INC
Also Called: Fanci Forms
420 N Warpole St (43351-9301)
PHONE 419 447-1102
Floyd Marshall, *President*
Craig Marshall, *Vice Pres*
EMP: 27
SQ FT: 28,000
SALES (est): 5.3MM **Privately Held**
SIC: 3544 Special dies, tools, jigs & fixtures

(G-18963)
MIDWEST OHIO TOOL CO
215 Tarhe Trl (43351-8700)
P.O. Box 269 (43351-0269)
PHONE 419 294-1987
Stephanie Kettels, *CEO*
Don Shuster, *General Mgr*
Mark Lewis, *Sales Staff*
EMP: 9
SALES (est): 1.3MM **Privately Held**
SIC: 3541 Machine tools, metal cutting type

(G-18964)
MIDWEST SPRAY DRYING COMPANY
Also Called: Pro-Soy
422 W Guthrie Dr (43351-1154)
PHONE 419 294-4221
Ronald Miller, *President*
Linda Miller, *Corp Secy*
EMP: 5
SQ FT: 44,000
SALES (est): 445K **Privately Held**
SIC: 2099 Seasonings & spices

(G-18965)
NATIONAL LIME AND STONE CO
14407 Township Rd 124 (43351)
PHONE 419 294-3049
Michael Keckler, *Manager*
EMP: 4
SALES (corp-wide): 3.2B **Privately Held**
WEB: www.natlime.com
SIC: 5211 1423 Sand & gravel; crushed & broken granite
PA: The National Lime And Stone Company
551 Lake Cascade Pkwy
Findlay OH 45840
419 422-4341

(G-18966)
NEUMEISTERS CANDY SHOPPE LLC
139 N Sandusky Ave (43351-1253)
PHONE 419 294-3647
Diana Hoover,
EMP: 3
SALES (est): 273.5K **Privately Held**
WEB: www.neumeisterscandyshoppe.com
SIC: 5441 2064 2066 Candy; candy & other confectionery products; chocolate & cocoa products

(G-18967)
NEW EEZY-GRO INC
Also Called: Golden Eagle
9841 County Highway 49 (43351-9662)
PHONE 419 927-6110
Jerry Taylor, *President*
Joseph Fox, *Branch Mgr*
EMP: 17
SALES (corp-wide): 3B **Publicly Held**
WEB: www.eezygro.com
SIC: 2819 5261 Calcium compounds & salts, inorganic; fertilizer
HQ: New Eezy-Gro Inc.
1947 Briarfield Blvd
Maumee OH
419 893-5050

(G-18968)
NJF MANUFACTURING LLC
7387 Township Highway 104 (43351-9353)
PHONE 419 294-0400
Nathan Frey, *Mng Member*
EMP: 9
SALES (est): 450.7K **Privately Held**
SIC: 3999 Manufacturing industries

(G-18969)
OLEN CORPORATION
6326 County Highway 61 (43351-9749)
PHONE 419 294-2611
John Miller, *Branch Mgr*
EMP: 10
SALES (corp-wide): 289.1MM **Privately Held**
SIC: 3273 5032 Ready-mixed concrete; stone, crushed or broken
PA: The Olen Corporation
4755 S High St
Columbus OH 43207
614 491-1515

(G-18970)
OVERHEAD DOOR CORPORATION
Also Called: Todco
781 Rt 30w (43351)
PHONE 419 294-3874
Mike Traxler, *Director*
EMP: 10
SALES (corp-wide): 3.6B **Privately Held**
WEB: www.overheaddoor.com
SIC: 3442 3448 2431 Garage doors, overhead: metal; ramps: prefabricated metal; doors, wood
HQ: Overhead Door Corporation
2501 S State Hwy 121 Ste
Lewisville TX 75067
469 549-7100

(G-18971)
REK ASSOCIATES LLC
11218 County Highway 44 (43351-9056)
PHONE 419 294-3838
Paul Kalmbach,
EMP: 15
SALES (est): 581.4K **Privately Held**
SIC: 2048 Prepared feeds

(G-18972)
SCHMIDT MACHINE COMPANY
Also Called: S M C
7013 State Highway 199 (43351-9347)
PHONE 419 294-3814
Bill, *President*
Randy F Schmidt, *President*
Dorothy M Schmidt, *Principal*
Kevin Schmidt, *Vice Pres*
Darlene Mooney, *Treasurer*
EMP: 50 **EST:** 1935
SQ FT: 2,500
SALES: 17MM **Privately Held**
WEB: www.schmidtmachine.com
SIC: 3599 7692 5083 Machine shop, jobbing & repair; welding repair; farm equipment parts & supplies

(G-18973)
SHOOT A WAY INC
3305 Township Highway 47 (43351-9786)
PHONE 419 294-4654
John Joseph, *President*
EMP: 10
SALES (est): 1.1MM **Privately Held**
WEB: www.shootaway.net
SIC: 5699 3949 7389 Sports apparel; team sports equipment; advertising, promotional & trade show services

(G-18974)
SHOOT-A-WAY INC
8706 State Highway 67 (43351-9150)
PHONE 419 294-4654
John Joseph, *President*
Shane Adams, *Sales Staff*
Troy G Geiser, *Manager*
◆ **EMP:** 14
SALES (est): 1.4MM **Privately Held**
WEB: www.shoot-a-way.com
SIC: 3949 Mfg Sporting/Athletic Goods

(G-18975)
SUPERIOR AG-PATOKA VLLY FEED
7148 State Highway 199 (43351-9346)
PHONE 419 294-3838
EMP: 17
SALES: 13MM **Privately Held**
SIC: 2048 Prepared Feeds, Nec, Nsk

(G-18976)
UPPER MONUMENT
436 N Sandusky Ave (43351-1072)
PHONE 419 310-2387
Douglas Bianchi, *Administration*
EMP: 3
SALES (est): 189.7K **Privately Held**
SIC: 3272 Monuments & grave markers, except terrazo

(G-18977)
WANNEMACHER ENTERPRISES INC
Also Called: Wannemacher Packaging
422 W Guthrie Dr (43351-1154)
PHONE 419 771-1101
Jerry Jackson, *Director*
Sally Buchholz, *Director*
EMP: 10 **EST:** 2012
SALES (est): 414.9K **Privately Held**
SIC: 2099 Food preparations

Urbana
Champaign County

(G-18978)
AMERICAN PAN COMPANY (PA)
Also Called: Durashield
417 E Water St Ste 2 (43078-2178)
P.O. Box 628 (43078-0628)
PHONE 937 652-3232
Gilbert Bundy, *President*
Michael Cornelis, *Vice Pres*
Curt Marino, *Vice Pres*
Jason Tingley, *Vice Pres*
Dennis Dunsdon, *Safety Mgr*
◆ **EMP:** 120
SQ FT: 55,800
SALES (est): 36.6MM **Privately Held**
SIC: 3556 Food products machinery

(G-18979)
BISSON CUSTOM PLASTIC
238 Logan St (43078-1234)
PHONE 937 653-4966
Delin Bolin, *President*
William Adams, *Principal*
Cindy Bolin, *Manager*
EMP: 3
SALES (est): 350.4K **Privately Held**
SIC: 3089 Injection molding of plastics

(G-18980)
BOLDMAN PRINTING LLC
1333 N Main St (43078-1027)
P.O. Box 7 (43078-0007)
PHONE 937 653-3431
Wanda Jones, *Owner*
EMP: 4
SQ FT: 3,100
SALES (est): 578.4K **Privately Held**
SIC: 2752 2759 2791 2789 Commercial printing, offset; letterpress printing; typesetting; bookbinding & related work

(G-18981)
BUCK CREEK PALLET
713 Muzzy Rd (43078-9685)
PHONE 937 653-3098
Steven Grim, *Principal*
EMP: 3
SALES (est): 296.9K **Privately Held**
SIC: 2448 Pallets, wood

(G-18982)
CHRIS HAUGHEY
Also Called: Cupboard Distributing
1463 S Us Highway 68 (43078-8405)
PHONE 937 652-3338
Chris Haughey, *Owner*

GEOGRAPHIC SECTION
Urbana - Champaign County (G-19007)

Lindsey Applegate, *Manager*
EMP: 9
SALES (est): 741K **Privately Held**
WEB: www.cdwood.com
SIC: 2511 Unassembled or unfinished furniture, household: wood

(G-18983)
CMT MACHINING & FABG LLC
1411 Knnard Kingscreek Rd (43078-9505)
P.O. Box 28 (43078-0028)
PHONE.................................937 652-3740
Ted Wallen,
EMP: 14
SQ FT: 22,000
SALES: 650K **Privately Held**
WEB: www.cmt-usa.com
SIC: 1761 7692 3599 3544 Sheet metalwork; welding repair; machine shop, jobbing & repair; jigs & fixtures; industrial supplies; rubber & plastics hose & beltings

(G-18984)
COLE PAK INC
1030 S Edgewood Ave (43078-9694)
P.O. Box 650 (43078-0650)
PHONE.................................937 652-3910
Deborah Cole, *President*
Shannon Hackathorn, *Principal*
Patrick Maurice, *Principal*
Jason Cole, *Vice Pres*
Rick Cole, *Vice Pres*
EMP: 58
SQ FT: 113,000
SALES (est): 14.7MM **Privately Held**
WEB: www.colepak.com
SIC: 2653 2671 Partitions, solid fiber: made from purchased materials; pads, solid fiber: made from purchased materials; packaging paper & plastics film, coated & laminated

(G-18985)
COLLIERS CSTMIZING FABRICATION
1675 W County Line Rd (43078-9107)
PHONE.................................937 523-0420
Dennie Collier Sr, *Branch Mgr*
EMP: 11
SALES (corp-wide): 3.6MM **Privately Held**
SIC: 3399 Metal powders, pastes & flakes
PA: Collier's Customizing And Fabrication
1675 W County Line Rd
Urbana OH 43078
937 450-6480

(G-18986)
CONTAINER KING INC
955 Lippincott Rd (43078-8305)
PHONE.................................937 652-3087
Nolan W King, *President*
EMP: 4
SALES (est): 411.3K **Privately Held**
SIC: 2653 Boxes, corrugated: made from purchased materials

(G-18987)
DANA SIGNS LLC
1052 S Main St Frnt Frnt (43078-2581)
PHONE.................................937 653-3917
James W Dees,
EMP: 3
SALES (est): 389.4K **Privately Held**
SIC: 3993 Signs & advertising specialties

(G-18988)
DAVID BRANDEBERRY
Also Called: U S Graphics
703 Miami St (43078-1909)
P.O. Box 838 (43078-0838)
PHONE.................................937 653-4680
David Brandeberry, *Owner*
EMP: 3
SQ FT: 2,300
SALES (est): 193.4K **Privately Held**
SIC: 2396 2395 Screen printing on fabric articles; pleating & stitching

(G-18989)
DESMOND-STEPHAN MFGCOMPANY
121 W Water St (43078-2048)
P.O. Box 30 (43078-0030)
PHONE.................................937 653-7181
Robert B McConnell, *President*
EMP: 24
SQ FT: 30,000
SALES (est): 5MM **Privately Held**
WEB: www.swirloff.com
SIC: 3423 Hand & edge tools

(G-18990)
GRIMES AEROSPACE COMPANY
Also Called: Honeywell
550 State Route 55 (43078-9482)
PHONE.................................937 484-2001
Bruce Blagg, *Branch Mgr*
EMP: 300
SALES (corp-wide): 41.8B **Publicly Held**
SIC: 5088 7699 3812 3769 Aircraft & parts; aircraft & heavy equipment repair services; search & navigation equipment; guided missile & space vehicle parts & auxiliary equipment; vehicular lighting equipment
HQ: Grimes Aerospace Company
550 State Route 55
Urbana OH 43078
937 484-2000

(G-18991)
GRIMES AEROSPACE COMPANY
Also Called: Honeywell Lightning & Elec
515 N Russell St (43078-1330)
P.O. Box 247 (43078-0247)
PHONE.................................937 484-2000
Ron King, *Manager*
EMP: 150
SALES (corp-wide): 41.8B **Publicly Held**
SIC: 3728 Aircraft parts & equipment
HQ: Grimes Aerospace Company
550 State Route 55
Urbana OH 43078
937 484-2000

(G-18992)
HALL COMPANY
420 E Water St (43078-2163)
PHONE.................................937 652-1376
James A Hall, *Ch of Bd*
Kyle J Hall, *President*
Richard J Walser, *Vice Pres*
Chris Nigh, *Purch Mgr*
Ann Brown, *Draft/Design*
EMP: 47
SQ FT: 38,500
SALES (est): 9.7MM **Privately Held**
WEB: www.hallco.com
SIC: 3679 3993 3471 3444 Electronic switches; signs & advertising specialties; plating & polishing; sheet metalwork; coated & laminated paper; automotive & apparel trimmings

(G-18993)
HEIMANN MANUFACTURING CO
1140 N Main St (43078-1024)
PHONE.................................937 652-1865
Jerrel W Dunham, *President*
EMP: 5 **EST:** 1938
SQ FT: 5,000
SALES (est): 629.3K **Privately Held**
SIC: 3544 3542 Special dies, tools, jigs & fixtures; gear rolling machines

(G-18994)
HONEYWELL AUTOMATION CONTROL
550 State Route 55 (43078-9482)
PHONE.................................937 264-2662
Bill Grilliot, *Principal*
EMP: 11 **EST:** 2008
SALES (est): 2.1MM **Privately Held**
SIC: 3724 Aircraft engines & engine parts

(G-18995)
HONEYWELL INTERNATIONAL INC
550 State Route 55 (43078-9482)
P.O. Box 247 (43078-0247)
PHONE.................................937 484-2000
Randy Marker, *Manager*
EMP: 800
SALES (corp-wide): 41.8B **Publicly Held**
WEB: www.honeywell.com
SIC: 3812 3669 3491 3699 Aircraft control systems, electronic; aircraft/aerospace flight instruments & guidance systems; space vehicle guidance systems & equipment; fire alarm apparatus, electric; gas valves & parts, industrial; security control equipment & systems; auto controls regulating residntl & coml environmt & applncs; energy cutoff controls, residential or commercial types; thermostats, except built-in; humidistats: wall, duct & skeleton; temperature instruments: industrial process type
PA: Honeywell International Inc.
115 Tabor Rd
Morris Plains NJ 07950
973 455-2000

(G-18996)
HUGHEY & PHILLIPS LLC
240 W Twain Ave (43078-1059)
PHONE.................................937 652-3500
Kay Nance, *General Mgr*
Richard Finkbine, *Exec VP*
Jeff Jacobs, *Vice Pres*
Melissa Geuy, *Buyer*
Jerry Ehlers, *Sales Staff*
EMP: 50
SALES (est): 9.2MM **Privately Held**
SIC: 3648 Lighting equipment

(G-18997)
J RETTENMAIER USA LP
1228 Muzzy Rd (43078-9685)
PHONE.................................937 652-2101
Dave McGill, *Branch Mgr*
EMP: 91
SALES (corp-wide): 355.8K **Privately Held**
SIC: 2823 2299 Cellulosic manmade fibers; flock (recovered textile fibers)
HQ: J. Rettenmaier Usa Lp
16369 Us Highway 131 S
Schoolcraft MI 49087
269 679-2340

(G-18998)
J RETTENMAIER USA LP
Also Called: Fiber Sales & Development
1228 Muzzy Rd (43078-9685)
PHONE.................................937 652-2101
Dave McGill, *Branch Mgr*
EMP: 76
SALES (corp-wide): 355.8K **Privately Held**
WEB: www.ifcfiber.com
SIC: 2823 2834 Cellulosic manmade fibers; pharmaceutical preparations
HQ: J. Rettenmaier Usa Lp
16369 Us Highway 131 S
Schoolcraft MI 49087
269 679-2340

(G-18999)
JACK WALTERS & SONS CORP
Also Called: Walters Buildings
5045 N Us Highway 68 (43078-9315)
PHONE.................................937 653-8986
Jerry Kauffman, *Manager*
EMP: 15
SALES (corp-wide): 25.2MM **Privately Held**
WEB: www.waltersbuildings.com
SIC: 3448 Buildings, portable: prefabricated metal
PA: Jack Walters & Sons, Corp.
6600 Midland Ct
Allenton WI 53002
262 629-5521

(G-19000)
JOE REES WELDING
326 W Twain Ave (43078-1061)
PHONE.................................937 652-4067
Joe Rees, *Owner*
EMP: 6
SALES: 440.9K **Privately Held**
SIC: 3441 Fabricated structural metal

(G-19001)
JOHNSON WELDED PRODUCTS INC
Also Called: J W P
625 S Edgewood Ave (43078-8600)
PHONE.................................937 652-1242
Lilli A Johnson, *President*
Clayton W Rose Jr, *Principal*
Melody Lucas, *Director*
▼ **EMP:** 210 **EST:** 1970
SQ FT: 133,000
SALES (est): 57.7MM **Privately Held**
WEB: www.jwp-inc.com
SIC: 3714 Air brakes, motor vehicle

(G-19002)
KOENIG EQUIPMENT INC
Also Called: John Deere Authorized Dealer
3130 E Us Highway 36 (43078-9736)
PHONE.................................937 653-5281
Dale Griest, *Manager*
Gregory Koenig, *Director*
EMP: 15
SALES (corp-wide): 200MM **Privately Held**
WEB: www.koenigequipment.com
SIC: 3524 5082 Lawn & garden equipment; construction & mining machinery
PA: Koenig Equipment, Inc.
15213 State Route 274
Botkins OH 45306
937 693-5000

(G-19003)
LAWNVIEW INDUSTRIES INC
1250 E Us Highway 36 (43078-8002)
P.O. Box 38147 (43078-8147)
PHONE.................................937 653-5217
Micheal Misler, *Director*
EMP: 175
SQ FT: 6,000
SALES: 423.2K **Privately Held**
SIC: 3999 3914 2392 2499 Plaques, picture, laminated; trophies; towels, fabric & nonwoven: made from purchased materials; surveyors' stakes, wood; packaging & labeling services; carwashes

(G-19004)
MARSHALL PLASTICS INC
590 S Edgewood Ave (43078-2603)
P.O. Box 38126 (43078-8126)
PHONE.................................937 653-4740
Henry Taylor, *President*
Richard T Ricketts, *Principal*
EMP: 9
SALES (est): 1.4MM **Privately Held**
SIC: 3089 Blow molded finished plastic products; injection molding of plastics

(G-19005)
MUMFORDS POTATO CHIPS & DELI
325 N Main St (43078-1605)
PHONE.................................937 653-3491
Randy Leopard, *Partner*
Marilyn Leopard, *Partner*
EMP: 9
SQ FT: 12,000
SALES (est): 742.5K **Privately Held**
SIC: 2096 5411 Potato chips & other potato-based snacks; delicatessens

(G-19006)
ORBIS CORPORATION
200 Elm St (43078-1975)
PHONE.................................937 652-1361
Robert G Neff, *Site Mgr*
EMP: 280
SALES (corp-wide): 1.7B **Privately Held**
WEB: www.orbiscorporation.com
SIC: 3089 Synthetic resin finished products
HQ: Orbis Corporation
1055 Corporate Center Dr
Oconomowoc WI 53066
262 560-5000

(G-19007)
PARKER TRUTEC INCORPORATED
Also Called: Nihon Company
4795 Upper Valley Pike (43078-9295)
PHONE.................................937 653-8500
Michael Kleiber, *General Mgr*
EMP: 90

Urbana - Champaign County (G-19008)

SALES (corp-wide): 1B **Privately Held**
SIC: 3479 3471 2899 2851 Painting of metal products; plating & polishing; chemical preparations; paints & allied products
HQ: Parker Trutec Incorporated
4700 Gateway Blvd
Springfield OH 45502
937 323-8833

(G-19008)
PHILLIPS PACKAGING INC
1050 Phoenix Dr Unit B (43078-9547)
PHONE..................................937 484-4702
Fax: 937 484-4449
EMP: 3 **Privately Held**
SIC: 2653 Manufactures Corrugated Products
PA: Phillips Packaging, Inc
120 Fairway Dr
Wilmington OH

(G-19009)
RIBLET PACKAGING CO
955 Lippincott Rd (43078-8305)
PHONE..................................937 652-3087
Nolan King, *President*
EMP: 12
SQ FT: 20,000
SALES (est): 1.1MM **Privately Held**
SIC: 2653 Boxes, corrugated: made from purchased materials

(G-19010)
RITTAL NORTH AMERICA LLC
1 Rittal Pl (43078-5003)
PHONE..................................937 399-0500
Jim Weist, *Vice Pres*
Tami Winnenberg, *Vice Pres*
Randy Schwarz, *Production*
Scott Blumling, *Engineer*
Domenick Cappelli, *Engineer*
EMP: 209
SALES (corp-wide): 2.6B **Privately Held**
SIC: 3469 Metal stampings
HQ: Rittal North America Llc
425 N Martingale Rd # 1540
Schaumburg IL 60173
847 240-4600

(G-19011)
SARICA MANUFACTURING COMPANY
240 W Twain Ave (43078-1059)
PHONE..................................937 484-4030
Corrie Bean, *Purchasing*
Steven M Schneider, *Mng Member*
Lin Giampetro, *Manager*
David Allen, *Maintence Staff*
Constance Schneider,
EMP: 40
SQ FT: 30,000
SALES (est): 10.4MM **Privately Held**
WEB: www.saricamfg.com
SIC: 3629 Electronic generation equipment

(G-19012)
SHAFFER MANUFACTURING CORP
Also Called: Shaffer Mixers & Proc Eqp
720 S Edgewood Ave (43078-9603)
P.O. Box 64 (43078-0064)
PHONE..................................937 652-2151
Mark Geise, *President*
Kirk Lang, *Vice Pres*
Mike Hall, *Engineer*
Jim Blum, *Sales Mgr*
Lonnie Caupp, *Manager*
▼ EMP: 50
SQ FT: 60,000
SALES (est): 18.9MM
SALES (corp-wide): 36.6MM **Privately Held**
SIC: 3556 3531 Bakery machinery; construction machinery
PA: American Pan Company
417 E Water St Ste 2
Urbana OH 43078
937 652-3232

(G-19013)
SPEEDWAY LLC
Also Called: Speedway Superamerica
725 N Main St (43078-1101)
PHONE..................................937 653-6840
Debra Johnson, *Principal*
EMP: 5 **Publicly Held**
WEB: www.speedwaynet.com
SIC: 1311 Crude petroleum production
HQ: Speedway Llc
500 Speedway Dr
Enon OH 45323
937 864-3000

(G-19014)
TECH II INC
1765 W County Line Rd (43078)
PHONE..................................937 969-7000
EMP: 200
SQ FT: 240,500
SALES (corp-wide): 37.6MM **Privately Held**
SIC: 3089 Injection molding of plastics
PA: Tech Ii, Inc.
3100 Upper Valley Pike
Springfield OH 45504

(G-19015)
TECHNOLOGY PRODUCTS INC
2423 Barger Rd (43078-9129)
PHONE..................................937 652-3412
Fax: 937 653-8716
EMP: 4
SALES (est): 285K **Privately Held**
SIC: 3699 3625 3613 Mfg Electrical Equipment/Supplies Mfg Relays/Industrial Controls Mfg Switchgear/Switchboards

(G-19016)
TRIAGE ORTHO GROUP
Also Called: Imperial Orthodontics
132 Lafayette Ave (43078-1420)
P.O. Box 549 (43078-0549)
PHONE..................................937 653-6431
Vincent Gonzalez, *Owner*
Sandra Gonzalez, *Manager*
EMP: 7
SQ FT: 8,900
SALES (est): 490K **Privately Held**
SIC: 5047 2396 Dentists' professional supplies; screen printing on fabric articles

(G-19017)
ULTRA-MET COMPANY
720 N Main St (43078-1102)
PHONE..................................937 653-7133
Brent Sheerer, *President*
Justin Evans, *President*
Jeff Hartshorn, *President*
Jeff Fox, *Principal*
John Potuzko, *Vice Pres*
◆ EMP: 95 EST: 1964
SQ FT: 50,000
SALES (est): 34.9MM **Privately Held**
WEB: www.ultra-met.com
SIC: 3541 Machine tools, metal cutting type

(G-19018)
ULTRA-MET COMPANY
120 Fyffe St (43078-1106)
PHONE..................................937 653-7133
Brent Sheerer, *President*
Brent Streator, *Controller*
Sonny Murphy, *Marketing Staff*
Brian Harrigan, *Maintence Staff*
EMP: 4
SALES (est): 217.6K **Privately Held**
SIC: 1311 5013 5047 8711 Crude petroleum & natural gas; automotive engines & engine parts; instruments, surgical & medical; aviation &/or aeronautical engineering

(G-19019)
WEIDMANN ELECTRICAL TECH INC
700 W Court St (43078-1902)
PHONE..................................937 652-1220
Laura Carneiro, *Principal*
EMP: 60
SALES (corp-wide): 371.2MM **Privately Held**
SIC: 3644 Insulators & insulation materials, electrical
HQ: Weidmann Electrical Technology Inc.
1 Gordon Mills Way
Saint Johnsbury VT 05819
802 748-8106

(G-19020)
WRIGHT JOHN
Also Called: W Productions
935 N Main St (43078-1005)
PHONE..................................937 653-4570
John Wright, *Owner*
EMP: 4 EST: 1992
SALES (est): 312.3K **Privately Held**
SIC: 3993 Signs & advertising specialties

Urbancrest
Franklin County

(G-19021)
HAYDEN VALLEY FOODS INC
3150 Urbancrest Indus (43123-1767)
PHONE..................................614 539-7233
EMP: 19
SALES (corp-wide): 32MM **Privately Held**
SIC: 2032 Canned specialties
PA: Hayden Valley Foods, Inc.
3150 Urbancrest Indus Dr
Urbancrest OH 43123
614 539-7233

(G-19022)
PILKINGTON NORTH AMERICA INC
3440 Centerpoint Dr Ste C (43123-1794)
PHONE..................................419 247-3731
Richard Frampton, *Branch Mgr*
Edward Williams, *Supervisor*
EMP: 223
SALES (corp-wide): 5.6B **Privately Held**
SIC: 3211 Construction glass
HQ: Pilkington North America, Inc.
811 Madison Ave Fl 3
Toledo OH 43604
419 247-3731

Utica
Licking County

(G-19023)
A P PRODUCTION & SERVICE
12546 Pleasant Valley Rd (43080-9714)
PHONE..................................740 745-5317
Karen Ashcraft, *President*
EMP: 3
SALES (est): 416.5K **Privately Held**
SIC: 1311 Crude petroleum production

(G-19024)
CARDINAL CT COMPANY
140 Carey St (43080-9004)
PHONE..................................740 892-2324
EMP: 30
SALES (corp-wide): 1B **Privately Held**
SIC: 3211 Tempered glass
HQ: Cardinal Ct Company
775 Pririe Ctr Dr Ste 200
Eden Prairie MN 55344

(G-19025)
CARDINAL GLASS INDUSTRIES INC
140 Carey St (43080-9004)
PHONE..................................740 892-2324
Roger D O'Shaughnessy, *Branch Mgr*
EMP: 30
SALES (corp-wide): 1B **Privately Held**
SIC: 3211 Tempered glass
PA: Cardinal Glass Industries Inc
775 Pririe Ctr Dr Ste 200
Eden Prairie MN 55344
952 229-2600

(G-19026)
OILER PROCESSING
Also Called: Oiler's Meat Processing
53 S Central Ave (43080-7708)
P.O. Box 501 (43080-0501)
PHONE..................................740 892-2640
Carmel L Oiler, *Partner*
Linda L Oiler, *Partner*
EMP: 4
SQ FT: 3,000
SALES (est): 369.8K **Privately Held**
SIC: 2011 4222 Meat packing plants; storage, frozen or refrigerated goods

(G-19027)
PERMANENT IMPRESSIONS
12182 Bruce Rd (43080-9484)
PHONE..................................740 892-3045
Cathy Grandstaff, *Owner*
EMP: 3
SALES: 500K **Privately Held**
WEB: www.windyhillkennel.com
SIC: 2395 Embroidery & art needlework

(G-19028)
UTICA HERALD
Also Called: Heartland Communications
60 N Main St (43080-7704)
P.O. Box 515 (43080-0515)
PHONE..................................740 892-2771
Randy Almendinger, *Owner*
James Quinif, *Consultant*
EMP: 3 EST: 1878
SQ FT: 3,200
SALES (est): 170K **Privately Held**
SIC: 2711 Job printing & newspaper publishing combined

(G-19029)
VALLEY PETROLEUM INC
25010 Divan Rd (43080-9634)
PHONE..................................740 668-4901
Dennis Dugan, *President*
EMP: 5
SALES (est): 340K **Privately Held**
SIC: 1311 Crude petroleum & natural gas

Valley City
Medina County

(G-19030)
AUTOMATION TOOL & DIE INC
5576 Innovation Dr (44280-9368)
PHONE..................................330 225-8336
William E Bennett, *President*
James R Bennett, *Vice Pres*
Scott Waite, *Supervisor*
EMP: 70
SQ FT: 32,000
SALES (est): 19.2MM **Privately Held**
WEB: www.automationtd.com
SIC: 3544 Special dies & tools

(G-19031)
BOEHM PRESSED STEEL COMPANY
5440 Wegman Dr (44280-9707)
PHONE..................................330 220-8000
Ted McQuade, *President*
William Reis, *Exec VP*
EMP: 50
SQ FT: 41,000
SALES (est): 14.2MM **Privately Held**
WEB: www.boehmstampings.com
SIC: 3469 Stamping metal for the trade

(G-19032)
CON-BELT INC
5656 Innovation Dr (44280-9370)
PHONE..................................330 273-2003
Marc Zeitler, *President*
EMP: 13
SALES (est): 4.1MM **Privately Held**
WEB: www.conbelt.com
SIC: 3535 Conveyors & conveying equipment

(G-19033)
CONSOLIDATED CASEWORK INC
708 Marks Rd Ste 201 (44280-9367)
PHONE..................................330 618-6951
EMP: 7 EST: 2014
SALES (est): 1MM **Privately Held**
SIC: 3523 Farm machinery & equipment

(G-19034)
CUB CADET LLC
5903 Grafton Rd (44280-9329)
PHONE..................................330 273-8669
EMP: 6

GEOGRAPHIC SECTION

Valley City - Medina County (G-19057)

SALES (est): 121.5K **Privately Held**
SIC: 3524 Lawn & garden tractors & equipment

(G-19035)
CUSTOM SURROUNDINGS INC
6450 Grafton Rd (44280-9762)
P.O. Box 461 (44280-0461)
PHONE...........................330 483-9020
Fax: 330 483-0017
EMP: 14
SQ FT: 25,000
SALES: 2.5MM **Privately Held**
SIC: 2541 2599 Mfg Wood Partitions/Fixtures Mfg Furniture/Fixtures

(G-19036)
EMH INC (PA)
Also Called: Engineered Material Handling
550 Crane Dr (44280-9361)
PHONE...........................330 220-8600
Edis Hazne, *President*
Dave Comiono, *Vice Pres*
Barbara Held, *Purchasing*
Don Fenton, *Regl Sales Mgr*
◆ **EMP:** 40
SQ FT: 65,000
SALES (est): 10MM **Privately Held**
WEB: www.emh-inc.com
SIC: 3536 8711 3441 Cranes & monorail systems; hoists; fabricated structural metal

(G-19037)
FMI PRODUCTS LLC
700 Liverpool Dr (44280-9717)
PHONE...........................440 476-8262
John Medas,
▼ **EMP:** 8
SALES (est): 332.4K **Privately Held**
SIC: 3465 Automotive stampings

(G-19038)
FUSERASHI INTL TECH INC
Also Called: F I T
5401 Innovation Dr (44280-9353)
PHONE...........................330 273-0140
Akira Yoshida, *General Mgr*
Mamoru Shimada, *Principal*
Hal Wagoner, *Plant Mgr*
Jennifer Connelly, *Human Resources*
Doug Griesbach, *Cust Mgr*
▲ **EMP:** 22 **EST:** 1996
SQ FT: 200,000
SALES (est): 9.5MM
SALES (corp-wide): 267.4MM **Privately Held**
WEB: www.fitinc.net
SIC: 3465 Body parts, automobile: stamped metal
PA: Fuserashi Co., Ltd.
    11-74, Takaida
    Higashi-Osaka OSK 577-0
    667 897-121

(G-19039)
GOOSEFOOT ACRES INC (PA)
Also Called: Goosefoot Acres Cntr For
5879 Center Rd (44280-9315)
P.O. Box 446 (44280-0446)
PHONE...........................330 225-7184
Peter Gail, *President*
Karin Reale, *Corp Secy*
Dominick Reale, *COO*
Wilma Gail, *Vice Pres*
▲ **EMP:** 4
SALES: 2MM **Privately Held**
WEB: www.dandyblend.com
SIC: 2833 5122 Caffeine & derivatives; medicinals & botanicals

(G-19040)
HY-PRODUCTION INC
6000 Grafton Rd (44280-9330)
PHONE...........................330 273-2400
William Kneebusch, *Ch of Bd*
Mathew Roach, *President*
Keith Koprowski, *Vice Pres*
▲ **EMP:** 124
SQ FT: 60,000
SALES (est): 31.2MM **Privately Held**
WEB: www.hy-production.com
SIC: 3519 3492 3451 3594 Engines, diesel & semi-diesel or dual-fuel; control valves, fluid power: hydraulic & pneumatic; screw machine products; fluid power pumps & motors; machine shop, jobbing & repair

(G-19041)
INDEPENDENT STEEL COMPANY LLC
615 Liverpool Dr (44280-9717)
P.O. Box 472 (44280-0472)
PHONE...........................330 225-7741
Mark Schwertner, *President*
Mark A Schwertner, *Vice Pres*
John F Krupinski, *Mng Member*
James P Bouchard,
Thomas Modrowski,
▲ **EMP:** 50 **EST:** 1957
SQ FT: 110,000
SALES (est): 25.4MM **Privately Held**
WEB: www.independentsteel.com
SIC: 5051 7389 3316 Steel; metal cutting services; cold finishing of steel shapes
PA: Esmark Steel Group, Llc
    2500 Euclid Ave
    Chicago Heights IL 60411

(G-19042)
JOSEPH ADAMS CORP
5740 Grafton Rd (44280-9327)
P.O. Box 583 (44280-0583)
PHONE...........................330 225-9125
Patrick Adams, *President*
▲ **EMP:** 10
SQ FT: 100,000
SALES (est): 1.2MM **Privately Held**
SIC: 2087 2833 Flavoring extracts & syrups; botanical products, medicinal: ground, graded or milled

(G-19043)
KRISDALE INDUSTRIES INC
649 Marks Rd (44280-9774)
PHONE...........................330 225-2392
Glenn D Phelan, *President*
EMP: 6
SALES (est): 758.1K **Privately Held**
WEB: www.krisdale.com
SIC: 3544 Jigs & fixtures; special dies & tools

(G-19044)
MACK CONCRETE INDUSTRIES INC (HQ)
201 Columbia Rd (44280-9706)
P.O. Box 335 (44280-0335)
PHONE...........................330 483-3111
Richard W Mack, *President*
Betsy Mack, *President*
Barbara Mack, *Corp Secy*
Jim Thompson, *Vice Pres*
EMP: 12
SQ FT: 20,000
SALES (est): 5.2MM
SALES (corp-wide): 170.9MM **Privately Held**
SIC: 3273 Ready-mixed concrete
PA: Mack Industries, Inc.
    1321 Industrial Pkwy N # 500
    Brunswick OH 44212
    330 460-7005

(G-19045)
MACK INDUSTRIES PA INC (HQ)
201 Columbia Rd (44280-9706)
P.O. Box 335 (44280-0335)
PHONE...........................330 483-3111
Betsy Mack, *President*
Barbara Mack, *Treasurer*
EMP: 100 **EST:** 1952
SQ FT: 7,000
SALES (est): 25.9MM
SALES (corp-wide): 170.9MM **Privately Held**
SIC: 3272 Concrete products, precast
PA: Mack Industries, Inc.
    1321 Industrial Pkwy N # 500
    Brunswick OH 44212
    330 460-7005

(G-19046)
MACK READY MIX CONCRETE INC
201 Columbia Rd (44280-9706)
P.O. Box 335 (44280-0335)
PHONE...........................330 483-3111
Betsy Nesteca, *President*
Richard W Mack, *President*
Barbara Mack, *Corp Secy*
EMP: 5
SQ FT: 40,000
SALES (est): 409.8K
SALES (corp-wide): 170.9MM **Privately Held**
SIC: 3272 1623 Concrete products used to facilitate drainage; sewer line construction
PA: Mack Industries, Inc.
    1321 Industrial Pkwy N # 500
    Brunswick OH 44212
    330 460-7005

(G-19047)
MARTANS FOODS
6460 Grafton Rd (44280-9762)
PHONE...........................330 483-9009
Stephan Kormoczy, *Principal*
EMP: 3
SALES (est): 151.9K **Privately Held**
SIC: 2051 Bread, cake & related products

(G-19048)
MATTHEW KOSTER
Also Called: Servepro of Parma
720 Marks Rd Ste C (44280-9797)
P.O. Box 30008, Parma (44130-0008)
PHONE...........................440 887-9000
Matthew Koster, *Owner*
EMP: 6
SALES (est): 261.3K **Privately Held**
SIC: 2759 Commercial printing

(G-19049)
MEDINA BLANKING INC (DH)
Also Called: Shiloh Industries, Inc.
5580 Wegman Dr (44280-9321)
PHONE...........................330 558-2300
Ramzi Hermiz, *CEO*
Ray Love, *QC Dir*
David J Hessler, *Admin Sec*
EMP: 150
SQ FT: 200,000
SALES (est): 20MM **Publicly Held**
SIC: 3325 3545 3469 Steel foundries; machine tool accessories; metal stampings
HQ: Shiloh Corporation
    880 Steel Dr
    Valley City OH 44280
    330 558-2600

(G-19050)
MIXED LOGIC LLC
5907 E Law Rd (44280-9770)
PHONE...........................440 826-1676
Kevin Borrowman, *Mng Member*
EMP: 7
SALES (est): 526K **Privately Held**
WEB: www.mixedlogic.com
SIC: 3699 5999 Electric sound equipment; electronic parts & equipment

(G-19051)
MTD CONSUMER GROUP INC (DH)
5965 Grafton Rd (44280-9329)
PHONE...........................330 225-2600
Steven E Pryatel, *Principal*
◆ **EMP:** 12
SALES (est): 204.5MM
SALES (corp-wide): 2.4B **Privately Held**
SIC: 3524 Lawn & garden tractors & equipment
HQ: Mtd Products Inc
    5965 Grafton Rd
    Valley City OH 44280
    330 225-2600

(G-19052)
MTD HOLDINGS INC (PA)
5965 Grafton Rd (44280-9329)
P.O. Box 368022, Cleveland (44136-9722)
PHONE...........................330 225-2600
Curtis E Moll, *Ch of Bd*
Jason Belsito, *Opers Mgr*
Jeff Deuch, *Treasurer*
▼ **EMP:** 500
SALES (est): 2.4B **Privately Held**
SIC: 3524 3544 3469 6141 Lawn & garden equipment; lawnmowers, residential: hand or power; special dies & tools; metal stampings; financing: automobiles, furniture, etc., not a deposit bank

(G-19053)
MTD PRODUCTS INC (HQ)
5965 Grafton Rd (44280-9329)
P.O. Box 368022, Cleveland (44136-9722)
PHONE...........................330 225-2600
Robert T Moll, *CEO*
Jean Hlay, *President*
Josh Harris, *District Mgr*
Mike Abel, *Area Mgr*
Heather Ross, *Counsel*
◆ **EMP:** 500 **EST:** 1932
SQ FT: 180,000
SALES (est): 2.4B
SALES (corp-wide): 2.4B **Privately Held**
WEB: www.mtdproducts.com
SIC: 3524 Lawn & garden equipment; lawnmowers, residential: hand or power
PA: Mtd Holdings Inc.
    5965 Grafton Rd
    Valley City OH 44280
    330 225-2600

(G-19054)
MTD PRODUCTS INC
Industrial Plastics Co Div
680 Liverpool Dr (44280-9717)
P.O. Box 360585, Cleveland (44136-0045)
PHONE...........................330 225-9127
Mark Tyson, *Principal*
Darrel Shepherd, *Facilities Mgr*
Craig Boyd, *Manager*
EMP: 320
SQ FT: 90,000
SALES (corp-wide): 2.4B **Privately Held**
WEB: www.mtdproducts.com
SIC: 3524 Lawnmowers, residential: hand or power
HQ: Mtd Products Inc
    5965 Grafton Rd
    Valley City OH 44280
    330 225-2600

(G-19055)
MTD PRODUCTS INC
Also Called: Mtd Consumer Products Supply
5903 Grafton Rd (44280-9329)
P.O. Box 368022, Cleveland (44136-9722)
PHONE...........................330 225-1940
Mike Abel, *Area Mgr*
Manuel Romero, *Sales Staff*
Annette Anost, *Business Anlyst*
Lee Beckner, *Manager*
EMP: 83
SALES (corp-wide): 2.4B **Privately Held**
WEB: www.mtdproducts.com
SIC: 3524 Lawn & garden equipment
HQ: Mtd Products Inc
    5965 Grafton Rd
    Valley City OH 44280
    330 225-2600

(G-19056)
NORTHLAKE STEEL CORPORATION
5455 Wegman Dr (44280-9707)
PHONE...........................330 220-7717
William K Bissett, *CEO*
Craig O Curie, *President*
Jane Heinz, *Human Res Mgr*
Don Krug, *Sales Staff*
Jason Magyar, *Sales Staff*
▲ **EMP:** 80
SQ FT: 82,000
SALES (est): 24.8MM **Privately Held**
WEB: www.northlakesteelcorp.com
SIC: 3398 3312 Annealing of metal; bar, rod & wire products; bars & bar shapes, steel, cold-finished: own hot-rolled; rods, iron & steel: made in steel mills

(G-19057)
OLIVER SIGNS & GRAPHICS
5880 Myrtle Hill Rd (44280-9724)
P.O. Box 1186, Brunswick (44212-8686)
PHONE...........................330 460-2996
John Oliver, *President*
EMP: 5

Valley City - Medina County (G-19058)

SALES (est): 388.2K *Privately Held*
WEB: www.oliversigns.com
SIC: 3993 Signs & advertising specialties

(G-19058)
RAF ACQUISITION CO
Also Called: Republic Anode Fabricators
5478 Grafton Rd (44280-9719)
PHONE.................................440 572-5999
Mike Horonzy, *President*
Chris Horonzy, *General Mgr*
EMP: 15 EST: 1932
SQ FT: 20,000
SALES (est): 2.1MM *Privately Held*
WEB: www.repanode.com
SIC: 3471 3479 Chromium plating of metals or formed products; coating of metals & formed products

(G-19059)
S K M L INC
Also Called: Stretcher Pad Company, The
580 Liverpool Dr (44280-9335)
PHONE.................................330 220-7565
Susie Lindenmuth, *President*
David Lindenmuth, *Vice Pres*
Mark Lindenmuth, *Vice Pres*
EMP: 6 EST: 1928
SQ FT: 6,000
SALES (est): 960.7K *Privately Held*
WEB: www.stretcherpads.com
SIC: 3842 Surgical appliances & supplies

(G-19060)
SCHAEFFLER GROUP USA INC
5370 Wegman Dr (44280-9700)
PHONE.................................330 273-4383
Bruce G Warmbold, *President*
EMP: 342
SALES (corp-wide): 68.1B *Privately Held*
WEB: www.ina.com
SIC: 3562 Ball & roller bearings
HQ: Schaeffler Group Usa Inc.
308 Springhill Farm Rd
Fort Mill SC 29715
803 548-8500

(G-19061)
SHILOH AUTOMOTIVE INC
Also Called: Liverpool Manufacturing
880 Steel Dr (44280-9736)
PHONE.................................330 558-2600
Ramzi Hermiz, *CEO*
EMP: 23
SALES (est): 3.5MM *Publicly Held*
SIC: 3469 3544 Metal stampings; special dies, tools, jigs & fixtures
PA: Shiloh Industries, Inc.
880 Steel Dr
Valley City OH 44280

(G-19062)
SHILOH CORPORATION (HQ)
Also Called: Mansfield Blanking Div
880 Steel Dr (44280-9736)
PHONE.................................330 558-2600
Ramzi Hermiz, *CEO*
Robert Grissinger, *President*
David J Hessler, *Admin Sec*
EMP: 335 EST: 1950
SQ FT: 275,000
SALES (est): 129.8MM *Publicly Held*
SIC: 3469 3544 Metal stampings; special dies & tools

(G-19063)
SHILOH INDUSTRIES INC
5580 Wegman Dr (44280-9321)
PHONE.................................330 558-2300
Jeff Malik, *Manager*
EMP: 50 *Publicly Held*
SIC: 3465 Automotive stampings
PA: Shiloh Industries, Inc.
880 Steel Dr
Valley City OH 44280

(G-19064)
SHILOH INDUSTRIES INC
Ohio Welded Blank
5569 Innovation Dr (44280-9369)
PHONE.................................330 558-2000
Daniel Brown, *Manager*
EMP: 600 *Publicly Held*
WEB: www.shiloh.com
SIC: 3465 Automotive stampings

PA: Shiloh Industries, Inc.
880 Steel Dr
Valley City OH 44280

(G-19065)
SHILOH INDUSTRIES INC
880 Steel Dr (44280-9736)
PHONE.................................330 558-2600
Richard Greene, *Manager*
EMP: 799 *Publicly Held*
WEB: www.shiloh.com
SIC: 3465 3469 3544 Automotive stampings; metal stampings; special dies & tools
PA: Shiloh Industries, Inc.
880 Steel Dr
Valley City OH 44280

(G-19066)
SHILOH INDUSTRIES INC (PA)
880 Steel Dr (44280-9736)
PHONE.................................330 558-2600
Ramzi Y Hermiz, *President*
Kenton Bednarz, *President*
Gary Dethomas, *Vice Pres*
Thomas M Dugan, *Treasurer*
David J Hessler, *Admin Sec*
◆ EMP: 4
SALES (est): 1B *Publicly Held*
WEB: www.shiloh.com
SIC: 3465 3469 3544 Automotive stampings; metal stampings; special dies & tools

(G-19067)
SUBURBAN ELECTRONICS ASSEMBLY
7877 Grafton Rd (44280-9559)
PHONE.................................330 483-4077
EMP: 3 EST: 2004
SQ FT: 2,327
SALES: 400K *Privately Held*
SIC: 3679 Mfg Electronic Components

(G-19068)
UNITED MEDICAL SUPPLY COMPANY
708 Marks Rd Ste 308 (44280-9112)
PHONE.................................866 678-8633
Ted Walsh, *CEO*
Anthony Fidram, *President*
EMP: 3
SALES (est): 104.8K *Privately Held*
SIC: 3841 5047 Surgical & medical instruments; hospital equipment & supplies; medical equipment & supplies; patient monitoring equipment; industrial safety devices: first aid kits & masks

(G-19069)
WEBB-STILES COMPANY (PA)
Also Called: WEBB-STILES OF ALABAMA
675 Liverpool Dr (44280-9717)
P.O. Box 464 (44280-0464)
PHONE.................................330 225-7761
Donald G Stiles Jr, *President*
Sandra Matthews, *Corp Secy*
Larry Birchler, *Vice Pres*
Matt Weismann, *Vice Pres*
▲ EMP: 90
SQ FT: 140,000
SALES: 29.4MM *Privately Held*
WEB: www.webb-stiles.com
SIC: 3535 3536 3568 3537 Conveyors & conveying equipment; monorail systems; power transmission equipment; industrial trucks & tractors

(G-19070)
ZION INDUSTRIES INC (PA)
6229 Grafton Rd (44280-9312)
PHONE.................................330 225-3246
Bob Puls, *President*
Dorothy Puls, *Corp Secy*
Micheal Laheta, *Vice Pres*
Randy Lane, *Vice Pres*
Cyrena Moskalski, *Purch Mgr*
EMP: 90 EST: 1977
SQ FT: 16,600
SALES: 11MM *Privately Held*
SIC: 3398 Brazing (hardening) of metal

Van Buren
Hancock County

(G-19071)
BENA INC
1390 Township Road 229 (45889-9603)
P.O. Box 77 (45889-0077)
PHONE.................................419 299-3313
Gary Benjamin, *Principal*
Barbara Benjamin, *Corp Secy*
Keith Benjamin, *Vice Pres*
EMP: 9
SQ FT: 5,000
SALES: 1MM *Privately Held*
WEB: www.benainc.com
SIC: 3089 Injection molding of plastics; plastic processing

(G-19072)
NOSTER RUBBER COMPANY INC
1481 Township Road 229 (45889-9603)
P.O. Box 227 (45889-0227)
PHONE.................................419 299-3387
Jeff Wills, *President*
EMP: 12
SQ FT: 20,000
SALES: 2MM *Privately Held*
SIC: 3069 Molded rubber products

Van Wert
Van Wert County

(G-19073)
ADVANCED BIOLOGICAL MKTG INC
375 Bonnewitz Ave (45891-1101)
P.O. Box 222 (45891-0222)
PHONE.................................419 232-2461
Dan Custis, *President*
Leon Bird, *Vice Pres*
Curtis Gordon, *Vice Pres*
Pete Hayes, *Vice Pres*
Terry Roush, *Vice Pres*
▲ EMP: 14 EST: 2000
SQ FT: 3,500
SALES (est): 3.7MM *Privately Held*
WEB: www.abm1st.com
SIC: 2879 0116 Insecticides & pesticides; soybeans

(G-19074)
AEROQUIP CORP
1225 W Main St (45891-9362)
PHONE.................................419 238-1190
Don Waggener, *Principal*
EMP: 8
SALES (est): 834.4K *Privately Held*
SIC: 3052 Rubber & plastics hose & beltings

(G-19075)
ALL PURPOSE MACHINE
1240 E Main St (45891-1826)
PHONE.................................419 238-2794
Paul Workman, *Owner*
Rhonda Stephey, *Admin Sec*
EMP: 5
SQ FT: 4,285
SALES: 500K *Privately Held*
SIC: 3599 Machine shop, jobbing & repair

(G-19076)
ALLIANCE AUTOMATION LLC
560 Bonnewitz Ave (45891-1188)
PHONE.................................419 238-2520
Michael Fiedler, *Mng Member*
Kathleen Fiedler,
Doug Wenninger,
▲ EMP: 13
SALES (est): 4.4MM *Privately Held*
WEB: www.fiedlerelectrical.com
SIC: 3599 Custom machinery

(G-19077)
AT THE READY PUBLICATIONS LLC
308 Pleasant St (45891-1924)
P.O. Box 856 (45891-0856)
PHONE.................................762 822-8549

Dawn Kennedy, *CEO*
Kelsey McIlroy, *COO*
Michelle Dillinger, *Exec VP*
William Dickerson, *Vice Pres*
EMP: 4
SALES (est): 122.6K *Privately Held*
SIC: 7389 2741 2721 Advertising, promotional & trade show services; miscellaneous publishing; ; magazines: publishing only, not printed on site; trade journals: publishing only, not printed on site

(G-19078)
B M DS FISH N MORE LLC
Also Called: Main Street Ice Cream Parlor
121 South Ave (45891-2350)
PHONE.................................419 238-2722
Marvin Vetter, *Principal*
EMP: 12
SALES (est): 1MM *Privately Held*
SIC: 2024 Ice cream & frozen desserts

(G-19079)
BLUE BELL BIO-MEDICAL INC
1260 Industrial Dr (45891-2433)
PHONE.................................419 238-4442
David R Thompson, *President*
EMP: 3
SQ FT: 670,000
SALES: 2MM *Privately Held*
WEB: www.bluebellcarts.com
SIC: 3841 Surgical & medical instruments

(G-19080)
BRAUN INDUSTRIES INC
1170 Production Dr (45891-9391)
PHONE.................................419 232-7020
Kim Braun, *President*
Scott Braun, *Senior VP*
Jill Cilmi, *Vice Pres*
Gary Kohls, *Vice Pres*
Dale A Schroeder, *Vice Pres*
EMP: 270
SQ FT: 160,000
SALES (est): 57.4MM *Privately Held*
WEB: www.braunambulances.com
SIC: 3711 Ambulances (motor vehicles), assembly of

(G-19081)
BUDD CO PLASTICS DIV
1276 Industrial Dr (45891-2466)
PHONE.................................419 238-4332
Frank Macher, *Principal*
EMP: 3
SALES (est): 279.3K *Privately Held*
SIC: 3089 Plastic processing

(G-19082)
CONTINENTAL STRL PLAS INC
Also Called: CSP Van Wert
1276 Industrial Dr (45891-2433)
PHONE.................................419 238-4628
Cindy Schlatter, *Opers Mgr*
Nick Greenland, *Engineer*
Micco Manocchio, *Engineer*
Tom Harth, *Branch Mgr*
Michael Stump, *Manager*
EMP: 285
SALES (corp-wide): 7.8B *Privately Held*
WEB: www.cs-plastics.com
SIC: 3089 3714 Injection molding of plastics; motor vehicle parts & accessories
HQ: Continental Structural Plastics, Inc.
255 Rex Blvd
Auburn Hills MI 48326
248 237-7800

(G-19083)
COOL MACHINES INC
740 Fox Rd (45891-2441)
PHONE.................................419 232-4871
David Krendl, *President*
Andy Schulte, *Plant Mgr*
Carlos Usuda, *Treasurer*
Rebecca Schulte, *Human Res Dir*
Andrew Schulte, *Admin Sec*
EMP: 14
SQ FT: 40,000
SALES (est): 3MM *Privately Held*
WEB: www.coolmachines.com
SIC: 3532 Mining machinery

▲ = Import ▼ = Export
◆ = Import/Export

Van Wert - Van Wert County (G-19109)

(G-19084)
COOPER FOODS
Also Called: Cooper Farms Cooked Meat
6893 Us Route 127 (45891)
PHONE..................................419 232-2440
Eric Ludwig, *General Mgr*
Paula Fleming, *Principal*
Greg Cooper, *Plant Mgr*
Mark Hiegel, *Production*
Terry Johnson, *Accounting Mgr*
EMP: 34 EST: 2009
SALES (est): 6.6MM **Privately Held**
SIC: **2015** Poultry slaughtering & processing

(G-19085)
COOPER HATCHERY INC
Also Called: Cooper Farms Cooked Meats
6793 Us Route 127 (45891-9601)
PHONE..................................419 238-4869
Eric Ludwig, *Branch Mgr*
Duaine Hampton, *Technical Staff*
EMP: 130
SALES (corp-wide): 256.7MM **Privately Held**
WEB: www.cooperfarm.com
SIC: **2015** Poultry slaughtering & processing
PA: Cooper Hatchery, Inc.
22348 Road 140
Oakwood OH 45873
419 594-3325

(G-19086)
CQT KENNEDY LLC
Also Called: CORNWELL QUALITY TOOLS
1260 Industrial Dr (45891-2433)
PHONE..................................419 238-2442
Raymond Moeller, *President*
David Nist, *Treasurer*
Robert Studenic, *Admin Sec*
EMP: 95
SQ FT: 190,000
SALES: 15.9MM
SALES (corp-wide): 173.8MM **Privately Held**
SIC: **3469** 3841 Boxes: tool, lunch, mail, etc.: stamped metal; surgical & medical instruments
PA: The Cornwell Quality Tools Company
667 Seville Rd
Wadsworth OH 44281
330 336-3506

(G-19087)
EATON CORPORATION
Also Called: Mobile Operations
1225 W Main St (45891-9362)
PHONE..................................419 238-1190
Anita Carvajal, *Prdtn Mgr*
Erika Lobsiger, *Mfg Staff*
Mark Hammons, *Buyer*
Rachel Kremer, *Buyer*
Mark Borgmeier, *Engineer*
EMP: 900 **Privately Held**
WEB: www.eaton.com
SIC: **3052** 3429 Rubber hose; clamps & couplings, hose
HQ: Eaton Corporation
1000 Eaton Blvd
Cleveland OH 44122
440 523-5000

(G-19088)
EATON HYDRAULICS LLC
1225 W Main St (45891-9362)
PHONE..................................419 232-7777
Jeffrey Card, *Branch Mgr*
EMP: 21 **Privately Held**
WEB: www.aeroquip-vickers.com
SIC: **3542** 3594 3052 3492 Crimping machinery, metal; fluid power pumps; rubber hose; plastic hose; hose & tube fittings & assemblies, hydraulic/pneumatic; hose & tube couplings, hydraulic/pneumatic; power transmission equipment; aircraft parts & equipment; aircraft assemblies, subassemblies & parts
HQ: Eaton Hydraulics Llc
14615 Lone Oak Rd
Eden Prairie MN 55344
952 937-9800

(G-19089)
EATON-AEROQUIP LLC
Also Called: Eaton Global Hose
1225 W Main St (45891-9362)
PHONE..................................419 238-1190
Steve Brown, *Engineer*
Carey Welker, *Branch Mgr*
EMP: 100 **Privately Held**
SIC: **3052** 3492 3429 Rubber hose; plastic hose; hose & tube fittings & assemblies, hydraulic/pneumatic; clamps & couplings, hose; clamps, metal
HQ: Eaton Aeroquip Llc
1000 Eaton Blvd
Cleveland OH 44122
216 523-5000

(G-19090)
EISENHAUER MFG CO LLC
409 Center St (45891-1135)
P.O. Box 390 (45891-0390)
PHONE..................................419 238-0081
James Russell, *General Ptnr*
Leigh Eisenhauer Jr, *General Ptnr*
Jim Russell, *General Ptnr*
Adam Benner, *Plant Mgr*
Nathan Karcher, *Accounts Mgr*
EMP: 73 EST: 1944
SQ FT: 50,000
SALES: 4MM **Privately Held**
SIC: **3469** 3412 3411 2396 Stamping metal for the trade; metal barrels, drums & pails; metal cans; automotive trimmings, fabric; crowns & closures

(G-19091)
FEDERAL-MOGUL POWERTRAIN LLC
150 Fisher Ave (45891-1409)
PHONE..................................419 238-1053
Terry Offerle, *Branch Mgr*
EMP: 591
SALES (corp-wide): 11.7B **Publicly Held**
SIC: **3053** Gaskets & sealing devices
HQ: Federal-Mogul Powertrain Llc
27300 W 11 Mile Rd # 101
Southfield MI 48034

(G-19092)
GKN SINTER METALS LLC
Also Called: GKN Sinter Metals Mfg Svcs
1180 Kear Rd Rear Bldg250 (45891-8423)
PHONE..................................419 238-8200
Don Powellson, *Branch Mgr*
EMP: 13
SALES (corp-wide): 2.7B **Privately Held**
SIC: **3399** Powder, metal
HQ: Gkn Sinter Metals, Llc
2200 N Opdyke Rd
Auburn Hills MI 48326
248 296-7832

(G-19093)
GLOBAL PRECISION PARTS INC
7600 Us Route 127 (45891-9363)
PHONE..................................260 563-9030
James A Butz, *Principal*
EMP: 6
SALES (est): 1MM **Privately Held**
SIC: **3451** Screw machine products

(G-19094)
GREIF INC
975 Glenn St (45891-2331)
PHONE..................................419 238-0565
Rick Ray, *Plant Mgr*
Doug Benner, *Manager*
EMP: 48
SALES (corp-wide): 3.8B **Publicly Held**
WEB: www.greif.com
SIC: **2655** Drums, fiber: made from purchased material
PA: Greif, Inc.
425 Winter Rd
Delaware OH 43015
740 549-6000

(G-19095)
INK AGAIN
115 N Washington St (45891-1705)
PHONE..................................419 232-4465
Dennis Cummings, *Owner*
EMP: 4
SALES (est): 406.6K **Privately Held**
SIC: **3861** Printing equipment, photographic

(G-19096)
KAM MANUFACTURING INC
1197 Grill Rd (45891-9387)
P.O. Box 407 (45891-0407)
PHONE..................................419 238-6037
Kim Adams, *Owner*
▲ EMP: 150
SQ FT: 5,500
SALES (est): 10.1MM **Privately Held**
WEB: www.kammfg.com
SIC: **2331** 2329 3161 Women's & misses' blouses & shirts; men's & boys' sportswear & athletic clothing; luggage

(G-19097)
KEDAR D ARMY
Also Called: Briarwood Manufacturing
11373 Van Wert Decatur Rd (45891-8401)
PHONE..................................419 238-6929
Kedar D Army, *Owner*
EMP: 4
SALES (est): 323.8K **Privately Held**
SIC: **6512** 6515 3799 7692 Nonresidential building operators; mobile home site operators; recreational vehicles; welding repair; fabricated structural metal

(G-19098)
KENN FELD GROUP LLC
10305 Liberty Union Rd (45891-9178)
PHONE..................................419 238-1299
Bruce Kennedy, *Branch Mgr*
EMP: 12
SALES (est): 2.4MM
SALES (corp-wide): 1.6MM **Privately Held**
SIC: **3531** Aerial work platforms: hydraulic/elec. truck/carrier mounted
PA: Kenn Feld Group Llc
4724 N State Road 101
Woodburn IN 46797
260 632-4242

(G-19099)
LEESBURG LOOMS INCORPORATED
Also Called: Leesburg Loom & Supply
201 N Cherry St (45891-1210)
PHONE..................................419 238-2738
Jim Myers, *President*
EMP: 7
SQ FT: 90,000
SALES (est): 600K **Privately Held**
SIC: **3552** Fabric forming machinery & equipment; looms, textile machinery

(G-19100)
LEY INDUSTRIES INC
121 S Walnut St (45891-1720)
P.O. Box 191 (45891-0191)
PHONE..................................419 238-6742
Watson N Ley, *President*
Esther Ley, *Vice Pres*
EMP: 5
SQ FT: 32,000
SALES (est): 536.8K **Privately Held**
SIC: **3523** Farm machinery & equipment

(G-19101)
LIFE STAR RESCUE INC
1171 Production Dr (45891-9390)
PHONE..................................419 238-2507
Jim Dondlinger, *President*
Dond Linger, *Principal*
Jim Snyder, *Principal*
Lyle Halstead, *Vice Pres*
EMP: 25
SQ FT: 50,000
SALES (est): 6.3MM
SALES (corp-wide): 1.6B **Privately Held**
WEB: www.holmanenterprises.com
SIC: **5521** 5012 3713 Pickups & vans, used; ambulances; ambulance bodies
PA: Holman Enterprises Inc.
244 E Kings Hwy
Maple Shade NJ 08052
856 663-5200

(G-19102)
MEK VAN WERT INC
1265 Industrial Dr (45891-2432)
PHONE..................................419 203-4902
Javier Alcaba Berastegui, *CEO*
▼ EMP: 3
SQ FT: 27,000

SALES (est): 127.2K **Privately Held**
SIC: **3341** Secondary precious metals

(G-19103)
MORRIS MAICO HEARING AID SVC
117 N Washington St (45891-1705)
PHONE..................................419 232-6200
Rick Morris, *President*
EMP: 6
SALES (est): 271.3K **Privately Held**
SIC: **5999** 3842 Hearing aids; hearing aids

(G-19104)
RIDGE TOWNSHIP STONE QUARRY
16905 Middle Point Rd (45891-9771)
PHONE..................................419 968-2222
Roger Davis, *President*
EMP: 7
SALES (est): 1.2MM **Privately Held**
SIC: **1422** 5032 Crushed & broken limestone; stone, crushed or broken

(G-19105)
SHUMAKER RACING COMPONENTS
11037 Van Wert Decatur Rd (45891-9211)
PHONE..................................419 238-0801
John W Shumaker, *Owner*
EMP: 3 EST: 1974
SQ FT: 4,800
SALES (est): 258.6K **Privately Held**
SIC: **3751** 3541 Motorcycles & related parts; machine tools, metal cutting type

(G-19106)
TECUMSEH PACKG SOLUTIONS INC
Also Called: Van Wert Division
1275 Industrial Dr (45891-2432)
PHONE..................................419 238-1122
James Robideau, *Branch Mgr*
EMP: 48
SALES (corp-wide): 8.8MM **Privately Held**
SIC: **2653** Boxes, corrugated: made from purchased materials
PA: Tecumseh Packaging Solutions, Inc.
707 S Evans St
Tecumseh MI 49286
517 423-2126

(G-19107)
TIMES BULLETIN MEDIA
700 Fox Rd (45891-2485)
P.O. Box 271 (45891-0271)
PHONE..................................419 238-2285
Mike Marchek, *Manager*
Tina Byrd, *Director*
EMP: 15 EST: 2012
SALES (est): 580.5K **Privately Held**
SIC: **2711** Newspapers, publishing & printing

(G-19108)
TOOLCO INC
16913 Wren Landeck Rd (45891-8822)
PHONE..................................419 667-3462
Kenneth D Linton, *President*
Matt Linton, *Vice Pres*
EMP: 4
SQ FT: 5,280
SALES: 100K **Privately Held**
WEB: www.toolcoonline.com
SIC: **3599** 3523 Machine shop, jobbing & repair; harrows: disc, spring, tine, etc.

(G-19109)
UNIVERSAL LETTERING INC
Also Called: Universal Lettering Company
1197 Grill Rd B (45891-9387)
P.O. Box 1055 (45891-6055)
PHONE..................................419 238-9320
Mark Hoops, *President*
Scott Geier, *Controller*
▲ EMP: 30
SQ FT: 20,400
SALES (est): 3.1MM **Privately Held**
WEB: www.showjacket.com
SIC: **2339** 2329 Women's & misses' jackets & coats, except sportswear; men's & boys' leather, wool & down-filled outerwear

Van Wert - Van Wert County (G-19110)

(G-19110)
VAN WERT MEMORIALS LLC
625 S Shannon St (45891-2236)
PHONE..................................419 238-9067
Diane R York,
Mike Sellers,
EMP: 3
SALES (est): 112.2K Privately Held
SIC: 7261 3281 Funeral home; tombstones, cut stone (not finishing or lettering only)

(G-19111)
VAN WERT PALLETS LLC
9042 John Brown Rd (45891-8420)
PHONE..................................419 203-1823
Spencer Wise, *Principal*
EMP: 8 EST: 2010
SALES (est): 550K Privately Held
SIC: 2448 Pallets, wood & wood with metal

Vandalia
Montgomery County

(G-19112)
ADAIRS PAVERS
50 Lakin Ct (45377-9400)
PHONE..................................937 454-9302
Lonzo Adair, *Principal*
EMP: 4
SALES (est): 12.3K Privately Held
SIC: 3531 Pavers

(G-19113)
ADARE PHARMACEUTICALS INC (HQ)
845 Center Dr (45377-3129)
PHONE..................................937 898-9669
John Fraher, *CEO*
Shannon Williams, *Human Res Mgr*
▲ EMP: 167 EST: 1980
SQ FT: 870,000
SALES (est): 62.3MM Privately Held
WEB: www.aptalispharma.com
SIC: 2834 Medicines, capsuled or ampuled

(G-19114)
ALL SRVICE PLASTIC MOLDING INC
900 Falls Creek Dr (45377-9685)
PHONE..................................937 890-0322
Joe Minneman, *Branch Mgr*
EMP: 5
SALES (corp-wide): 47.7MM Privately Held
SIC: 3089 Injection molding of plastics
PA: All Service Plastic Molding, Inc.
    900 Fall Creek Dr
    Vandalia OH 45377
    937 890-0322

(G-19115)
ALL SRVICE PLASTIC MOLDING INC (PA)
900 Fall Creek Dr (45377)
P.O. Box 13545, Dayton (45413-0545)
PHONE..................................937 890-0322
Joseph Minneman, *CEO*
Frank Maus, *Principal*
Joe Kavalauskas, *Vice Pres*
Joseph Kavalauskas, *Vice Pres*
Steve Brun, *Materials Mgr*
▲ EMP: 199
SQ FT: 35,500
SALES (est): 59.1MM Privately Held
SIC: 3089 Injection molding of plastics

(G-19116)
AMERICAN QULTY FABRICATION INC
849 Scholz Dr (45377-3121)
PHONE..................................937 742-7001
Joe Beidelschies, *President*
Kevin Nidzorski, *Vice Pres*
EMP: 5
SQ FT: 14,000
SALES (est): 1.2MM Privately Held
SIC: 3441 Building components, structural steel

(G-19117)
BALANCING COMPANY INC (PA)
898 Center Dr (45377-3130)
PHONE..................................937 898-9111
Donald K Belcher, *President*
Michael W Belcher, *President*
Jack Boeke, *Vice Pres*
Jack Pequignot, *Accountant*
Doug Kelchner, *Manager*
EMP: 31 EST: 1967
SQ FT: 53,000
SALES (est): 6.5MM Privately Held
WEB: www.balco.com
SIC: 3599 8734 3544 Machine shop, jobbing & repair; testing laboratories; special dies, tools, jigs & fixtures

(G-19118)
BOSTON STOKER INC (PA)
10855 Engle Rd (45377-9439)
P.O. Box 548 (45377-0548)
PHONE..................................937 890-6401
Donald M Dean, *President*
Sally Dean, *Corp Secy*
EMP: 7
SALES (est): 9.3MM Privately Held
WEB: www.bostonstoker.com
SIC: 2095 5499 5993 Coffee roasting (except by wholesale grocers); coffee; tea; gourmet food stores; tobacco stores & stands

(G-19119)
CHALLENGER AVIATION PRODUCTS
4433 Old Springfield Rd (45377-9739)
P.O. Box 577 (45377-0577)
PHONE..................................937 387-6500
Heather Geissler, *CEO*
Linda Rocco, *President*
Susan Rocco, *CFO*
EMP: 5
SQ FT: 5,000
SALES: 150K Privately Held
SIC: 3724 Aircraft engines & engine parts

(G-19120)
CROSS COMMUNICATIONS INC
Also Called: Christian Citizen USA
250 N Cassel Rd (45377-9451)
P.O. Box 49365, Dayton (45449-0365)
PHONE..................................937 304-0010
Pendra Snyder, *President*
Rick W Snyder, *Vice Pres*
EMP: 4
SALES (est): 247.1K Privately Held
WEB: www.christiancitizen.com
SIC: 2711 Newspapers, publishing & printing

(G-19121)
CROWN EQUIPMENT CORPORATION
Also Called: Crown Lift Trucks
750 Center Dr (45377-3128)
P.O. Box 400 (45377-0400)
PHONE..................................937 454-7545
Lauren Robins, *Branch Mgr*
EMP: 58
SALES (corp-wide): 3.1B Privately Held
SIC: 3537 Lift trucks, industrial: fork, platform, straddle, etc.
PA: Crown Equipment Corporation
    44 S Washington St
    New Bremen OH 45869
    419 629-2311

(G-19122)
DATWYLER SLING SLTIONS USA INC
Also Called: Columbia
875 Center Dr (45377-3129)
PHONE..................................937 387-2800
Mark Bueltel, *Accountant*
Denise Bagaieh, *Human Res Mgr*
Brian Bueltel, *Sales Staff*
◆ EMP: 67
SQ FT: 100,000
SALES (est): 22MM
SALES (corp-wide): 1.3B Privately Held
WEB: www.columbiaerd.com
SIC: 5085 3069 3061 Seals, industrial; gaskets; molded rubber products; mechanical rubber goods

HQ: Keystone Holdings, Inc.
    875 Center Dr
    Vandalia OH 45377

(G-19123)
DOOR FABRICATION SERVICES INC
3250 Old Springfield Rd # 1 (45377-9599)
PHONE..................................937 454-9207
Brian Hakers, *Manager*
▲ EMP: 45
SALES (est): 4.8MM
SALES (corp-wide): 2.1B Publicly Held
WEB: www.masonite.com
SIC: 5046 2431 Partitions; millwork
PA: Masonite International Corporation
    201 N Franklin St Ste 300
    Tampa FL 33602
    800 895-2723

(G-19124)
GE AVIATION SYSTEMS LLC
740 E National Rd (45377-3062)
PHONE..................................937 898-5881
Elizabeth Jacquemin, *General Mgr*
Jennifer Brichacek, *Purch Dir*
Tom Doubts, *Engineer*
Slobodan Gataric, *Engineer*
Joe Jensvold, *Engineer*
EMP: 300
SALES (corp-wide): 121.6B Publicly Held
SIC: 3724 Aircraft engines & engine parts
HQ: Ge Aviation Systems Llc
    1 Neumann Way
    Cincinnati OH 45215
    937 898-9600

(G-19125)
GE AVIATION SYSTEMS LLC
740 E National Rd (45377-3062)
PHONE..................................937 898-5881
Victor Bonneau, *Branch Mgr*
EMP: 300
SALES (corp-wide): 121.6B Publicly Held
SIC: 8711 3643 3625 3624 Aviation &/or aeronautical engineering; current-carrying wiring devices; relays & industrial controls; carbon & graphite products; motors & generators
HQ: Ge Aviation Systems Llc
    1 Neumann Way
    Cincinnati OH 45215
    937 898-9600

(G-19126)
HEPT MACHINE INC
19 E Alkaline Springs Rd (45377-2631)
P.O. Box 486 (45377-0486)
PHONE..................................937 890-5633
Edward W Hept, *President*
Deborah Hept, *Vice Pres*
EMP: 4 EST: 1973
SQ FT: 6,000
SALES: 380K Privately Held
SIC: 3451 3812 Screw machine products; search & navigation equipment

(G-19127)
HERAEUS PRECIOUS METALS NORTH
970 Industrial Park Dr (45377-3116)
PHONE..................................937 264-1000
Jrgen Heraeus, *Chairman*
Alex Christofis, *Manager*
Santosh K Gupta,
Robert Housman,
Ram B Sharma,
▲ EMP: 31
SQ FT: 28,000
SALES (est): 8.8MM
SALES (corp-wide): 96.1K Privately Held
SIC: 2869 2819 8731 Industrial organic chemicals; chemicals, high purity: refined from technical grade; chemical laboratory, except testing
HQ: Heraeus Holding Gesellschaft Mit Beschrankter Haftung
    Heraeusstr. 12-14
    Hanau 63450
    618 135-0

(G-19128)
HIGH TECH ELASTOMERS INC (PA)
885 Scholz Dr (45377-3121)
PHONE..................................937 236-6575
James W Back, *President*
Vicki Back, *Vice Pres*
Russ Thrawford, *Engineer*
▲ EMP: 25
SQ FT: 5,000
SALES (est): 3.3MM Privately Held
WEB: www.htei.com
SIC: 3479 2822 Bonderizing of metal or metal products; synthetic rubber

(G-19129)
INTEVA PRODUCTS LLC
Inteva - Vandalia Engrg Ctr
707 Crossroads Ct (45377-9675)
PHONE..................................937 280-8500
John Salmon, *Buyer*
Jerry Webb, *Buyer*
Christophe Cooley, *Engineer*
Steve Snead, *Engineer*
Stephen Pitrof, *Manager*
EMP: 13
SALES (corp-wide): 3.8B Privately Held
SIC: 3714 Motor vehicle parts & accessories
HQ: Inteva Products, Llc
    1401 Crooks Rd
    Troy MI 48084

(G-19130)
ISKY NORTH AMERICA INC
21 Kenbrook Dr (45377-2103)
PHONE..................................937 823-9595
Delin Hu, *President*
EMP: 5
SALES (est): 705.8K
SALES (corp-wide): 229.3K Privately Held
SIC: 2879 Agricultural chemicals
PA: Isky North America Inc.
    47 W Polk St Ste 208
    Chicago IL 60605
    937 641-1368

(G-19131)
JIMS DONUT SHOP
122 E National Rd (45377-2102)
PHONE..................................937 898-4222
Jim Ashburn, *Owner*
EMP: 3
SALES (est): 115.5K Privately Held
SIC: 5461 2051 Doughnuts; doughnuts, except frozen

(G-19132)
LESLEYS PATTERNS LTD
405 Halifax Dr (45377-2913)
PHONE..................................937 554-4674
Christopher Madden, *Principal*
EMP: 4
SALES (est): 337.9K Privately Held
SIC: 3543 Industrial patterns

(G-19133)
MAC ITS LLC (PA)
1625 Fieldstone Way (45377-9317)
PHONE..................................937 454-0722
EMP: 15
SALES (est): 12.3MM Privately Held
SIC: 3355 Aluminum wire & cable

(G-19134)
MAHLE BEHR DAYTON LLC
250 Northwoods Blvd # 47 (45377-9694)
PHONE..................................937 356-2001
Clayton Brown, *Manager*
EMP: 300
SALES (corp-wide): 336.4K Privately Held
SIC: 3714 Motor vehicle parts & accessories
HQ: Mahle Behr Dayton L.L.C.
    1600 Webster St
    Dayton OH 45404
    937 369-2900

(G-19135)
MAHLE BEHR USA INC
Also Called: Delphi
250 Northwoods Blvd # 47 (45377-9694)
PHONE..................................937 356-2001

Clayton Brown, *Branch Mgr*
EMP: 200
SALES (corp-wide): 336.4K **Privately Held**
SIC: 3714 Motor vehicle parts & accessories
HQ: Mahle Behr Usa Inc.
2700 Daley Dr
Troy MI 48083
248 743-3700

(G-19136)
MASONITE CORPORATION
3250 Old Springfield Rd # 1 (45377-9599)
PHONE 937 454-9207
EMP: 96
SALES (corp-wide): 2.1B **Publicly Held**
SIC: 2431 Doors, wood
HQ: Masonite Corporation
201 N Franklin St Ste 300
Tampa FL 33602
813 877-2726

(G-19137)
MASONITE INTERNATIONAL CORP
875 Center Dr (45377-3129)
PHONE 937 454-9308
Geroge Henderson, *President*
EMP: 3
SALES (corp-wide): 2.1B **Publicly Held**
WEB: www.masoniteinternational.com
SIC: 3441 3442 Fabricated structural metal; metal doors, sash & trim
PA: Masonite International Corporation
201 N Franklin St Ste 300
Tampa FL 33602
800 895-2723

(G-19138)
MICROFINISH INC
865 Scholz Dr (45377-3121)
PHONE 937 264-1598
Dan O'Connor, *President*
Bill J Jernigan, *President*
Mark Marshall, *General Mgr*
EMP: 60
SQ FT: 8,000
SALES (est): 5.7MM **Privately Held**
SIC: 3471 Finishing, metals or formed products

(G-19139)
MISATO COMPUTER PRODUCTS INC
Also Called: Megaform Computer Products
850 Industrial Park Dr (45377-3152)
P.O. Box 667 (45377-0667)
PHONE 937 890-8410
James R Browning, *President*
Jenny Browning-Schiedecker, *Corp Secy*
▲ **EMP:** 5
SQ FT: 10,000
SALES (est): 770.6K **Privately Held**
SIC: 2761 Prints Business Forms

(G-19140)
MURPHY TRACTOR & EQP CO INC
Also Called: John Deere Authorized Dealer
1015 Industrial Park Dr (45377-3117)
PHONE 937 898-4198
Chris Cron, *Manager*
EMP: 8 **Privately Held**
SIC: 3531 5082 Construction machinery; construction & mining machinery
HQ: Murphy Tractor & Equipment Co., Inc.
5375 N Deere Rd
Park City KS 67219
855 246-9124

(G-19141)
NATIONAL STEEL RULE DIE LLC
3580 Lightner Rd (45377-9735)
P.O. Box 74 (45377-0074)
PHONE 937 667-0967
Pete Zelnick, *Managing Prtnr*
David Zelnick, *Partner*
Mark Zelnick, *Partner*
Gregory Crabill, *Manager*
Sue Waldren, *Info Tech Mgr*
EMP: 6
SQ FT: 5,000
SALES (est): 817.4K **Privately Held**
WEB: www.nationalsteelruledie.com
SIC: 3544 Special dies, tools, jigs & fixtures

(G-19142)
PARLEX USA LLC (DH)
801 Scholz Dr (45377-3121)
P.O. Box 427 (45377-0427)
PHONE 937 898-3621
Gary Wright, *President*
William Henson, *Information Mgr*
▲ **EMP:** 92
SQ FT: 130,000
SALES (est): 20.7MM **Privately Held**
WEB: www.parlex.com
SIC: 3672 Wiring boards
HQ: Johnson Electric North America, Inc.
47660 Halyard Dr
Plymouth MI 48170
734 392-5300

(G-19143)
PHILLIPS COMPANIES
555 Old Springfield Rd (45377-9359)
PHONE 937 431-7987
EMP: 23
SALES (corp-wide): 13.3MM **Privately Held**
SIC: 1442 Sand mining
PA: Phillips Companies
620 Phillips Dr
Beavercreek Township OH 45434
937 426-5461

(G-19144)
SAIA-BURGESS LCC
Also Called: Ledex & Dormeyer Products
801 Scholz Dr (45377-3121)
PHONE 937 898-3621
Christopher Hasson, *President*
Gavin Fielden, *Vice Pres*
Rob Brooks, *Engineer*
Luke Vogt, *Engineer*
John Bowden, *Design Engr*
▲ **EMP:** 100
SQ FT: 105,000
SALES (est): 29.9MM **Privately Held**
WEB: www.saia-burgessusa.com
SIC: 3714 3643 Motor vehicle parts & accessories; electric switches
HQ: Johnson Electric North America, Inc.
47660 Halyard Dr
Plymouth MI 48170
734 392-5300

(G-19145)
SRM CONCRETE LLC
555 Old Springfield Rd (45377-9359)
PHONE 937 698-7229
Scott Besecker, *Manager*
EMP: 18
SALES (corp-wide): 29.4MM **Privately Held**
WEB: www.piquaconcrete.com
SIC: 3273 Ready-mixed concrete
PA: Srm Concrete, Llc
1136 2nd Ave N
Nashville TN

(G-19146)
TRIBORO QUILT MFG CORP
303 Corporate Center Dr # 108 (45377-1171)
PHONE 937 222-2132
Mindy Esmond, *Principal*
EMP: 10
SALES (corp-wide): 105MM **Privately Held**
SIC: 3999 Atomizers, toiletry
PA: Triboro Quilt Manufacturing Corporation
172 S Broadway Ste 100
White Plains NY 10605
914 428-7551

(G-19147)
UNIBILT INDUSTRIES INC
8005 Johnson Station Rd (45377-8617)
P.O. Box 373 (45377-0373)
PHONE 937 890-7570
Douglas Scholz, *President*
Sharon Scholz, *Corp Secy*
EMP: 50
SQ FT: 80,000
SALES (est): 9.8MM **Privately Held**
WEB: www.unibilt.com
SIC: 2452 Modular homes, prefabricated, wood

(G-19148)
VANDALIA MACHINING INC
884 Center Dr (45377-3130)
PHONE 937 264-9155
Joe Belcher, *President*
EMP: 4
SQ FT: 6,000
SALES (est): 492.7K **Privately Held**
WEB: www.vandaliamachining.com
SIC: 3599 Machine & other job shop work

(G-19149)
VANDALIA MASSAGE THERAPY
147 W National Rd (45377-1934)
PHONE 937 890-8660
Rick Phillips, *Partner*
EMP: 7
SALES (est): 490.9K **Privately Held**
WEB: www.vandaliamassage.com
SIC: 5087 3999 Service establishment equipment; massage machines, electric: barber & beauty shops

(G-19150)
VEOLIA WATER TECHNOLOGIES INC
945 S Brown School Rd (45377-9632)
PHONE 937 890-4075
Jean De Vauxclairs, *CEO*
Michael Reyes, *Business Mgr*
Arnaud Schalk, *Project Engr*
Robert Pettitt, *Manager*
Graig Rosenberger, *Manager*
▲ **EMP:** 68
SALES (est): 16.8MM
SALES (corp-wide): 600.9MM **Privately Held**
SIC: 3589 Water treatment equipment, industrial
PA: Veolia Environnement
21 Rue La Boetie
Paris 8e Arrondissement 75008
185 577-000

(G-19151)
WENTWORTH MOLD INC ELECTRA
Also Called: Electraform Industries Div
852 Scholz Dr (45377-3122)
PHONE 937 898-8460
Walter T Kuskowski, *CEO*
Tim Bright, *President*
Rick Babington, *Exec VP*
Jeffrey D Barclay, *Vice Pres*
Brian Karns, *Vice Pres*
▲ **EMP:** 60
SQ FT: 65,000
SALES (est): 14.6MM **Privately Held**
WEB: www.electraform.com
SIC: 3544 3559 Forms (molds), for foundry & plastics working machinery; plastics working machinery
PA: Wentworth Technologies Company Limited
156 Adams Blvd
Brantford ON N3S 7
519 754-5400

(G-19152)
ZED INDUSTRIES INC
3580 Lightner Rd (45377-9735)
P.O. Box 458 (45377-0458)
PHONE 937 667-8407
Peter Zelnick, *CEO*
Dave Zelnick, *Chairman*
Ken Johnson, *COO*
Mark Zelnick, *Vice Pres*
Helen Zelnick, *CFO*
EMP: 70 **EST:** 1969
SQ FT: 30,000
SALES (est): 16.4MM **Privately Held**
WEB: www.zedindustries.com
SIC: 3559 Plastics working machinery

Vanlue
Hancock County

(G-19153)
D & H MEATS INC
400 S Blanchard (45890)
PHONE 419 387-7767
Jared Fry, *President*
EMP: 7
SALES (est): 529.4K **Privately Held**
SIC: 2011 5421 Meat packing plants; meat & fish markets

Venedocia
Van Wert County

(G-19154)
KRENDL RACK CO INC
18413 Haver Rd (45894-9420)
PHONE 419 667-4800
Tony Laman, *President*
Chris Koverman, *Vice Pres*
Jeff Koverman, *Treasurer*
Robin Laman, *Admin Sec*
EMP: 8 **EST:** 1953
SQ FT: 12,000
SALES (est): 800K **Privately Held**
SIC: 3471 5051 Electroplating & plating; plates, metal

(G-19155)
OHIO ELECTRO-POLISHING CO INC
15085 Main St (45894-9645)
PHONE 419 667-2281
Marty Koenig, *President*
Randall Koenig, *Vice Pres*
James Koenig, *Admin Sec*
EMP: 6 **EST:** 1963
SQ FT: 15,000
SALES (est): 645.8K **Privately Held**
SIC: 3471 Electroplating of metals or formed products

Vermilion
Erie County

(G-19156)
ARCHITECTURAL AND INDUSTRIAL
Also Called: A & I Metal Finishing
1091 Sunnyside Rd (44089-2759)
PHONE 440 963-0410
Christopher W Morris,
EMP: 15
SALES (est): 2.2MM **Privately Held**
WEB: www.aimetalfinishing.com
SIC: 3479 Coating of metals & formed products

(G-19157)
COLEYS INC
1775 Liberty Ave (44089-2510)
P.O. Box 830 (44089-0830)
PHONE 440 967-5630
Kenneth L Mc Daniel, *President*
Maynard Coleman, *Principal*
Robert J Fetterman, *Principal*
Geraldine Mc Daniel, *Corp Secy*
EMP: 33
SQ FT: 25,000
SALES (est): 7MM **Privately Held**
SIC: 3599 Machine shop, jobbing & repair

(G-19158)
COLEYS INC
1775 Liberty Ave (44089-2510)
PHONE 440 967-5630
Martha Coleman, *Principal*
Brian Kieffer, *Manager*
EMP: 10
SALES (est): 940K **Privately Held**
SIC: 3545 Machine tool accessories

Vermilion - Erie County

(G-19159)
FILTER FACTORY-TTN INC
3409 Liberty Ave Ste 100 (44089-2400)
PHONE..............................440 963-2034
Dave Skodny, *Principal*
EMP: 7
SALES (est): 827.4K **Privately Held**
SIC: 3569 Filters

(G-19160)
GREAT LAKES DIESEL
5148 Concord Dr (44089-1502)
PHONE..............................419 433-9898
Jim Zima, *Owner*
EMP: 3
SALES: 175K **Privately Held**
SIC: 3519 Diesel, semi-diesel or duel-fuel engines, including marine

(G-19161)
HULL BUILDERS SUPPLY INC
685 Main St (44089-1311)
P.O. Box 432 (44089-0432)
PHONE..............................440 967-3159
Steve Holovacs, *President*
EMP: 28
SALES: 1,000K **Privately Held**
SIC: 5032 3273 5211 Limestone; ready-mixed concrete; lumber & other building materials

(G-19162)
INK IT PRESS
13500 W Lake Rd (44089-3135)
PHONE..............................440 967-9062
Dave Reed, *Manager*
EMP: 4
SALES (est): 60.5K **Privately Held**
SIC: 2752 Commercial printing, offset

(G-19163)
IRG OPERATING LLC
Also Called: Cleveland Quarries
850 W River Rd (44089-1530)
PHONE..............................440 963-4008
Jim Penkava, *Facilities Mgr*
Zach Carpenter, *Mng Member*
EMP: 36
SALES: 3.6MM **Privately Held**
SIC: 1411 Sandstone, dimension-quarrying

(G-19164)
KENDRA SCREEN PRINT
3817 Liberty Ave (44089-2335)
PHONE..............................440 967-8820
Ken Roghig, *Owner*
EMP: 3
SALES (est): 169.9K **Privately Held**
SIC: 2759 Screen printing

(G-19165)
KING VINEYARDS
5903 Coen Rd (44089-9524)
PHONE..............................440 967-4191
Joseph King, *Owner*
Joan King, *Co-Owner*
EMP: 3
SALES (est): 125.7K **Privately Held**
SIC: 0172 2084 0191 0175 Grapes; wines; general farms, primarily crop; deciduous tree fruits

(G-19166)
LORAIN ARMATURE & MTR REPR INC
960 Sunnyside Rd (44089-2758)
PHONE..............................440 967-2620
John W Small, *President*
Roy McGlugritch, *Vice Pres*
EMP: 6
SQ FT: 1,200
SALES (est): 967.6K **Privately Held**
SIC: 7694 Electric motor repair

(G-19167)
MCDANIEL PRODUCTS INC (PA)
Also Called: Automatic Parts
1775 Liberty Ave (44089-2510)
PHONE..............................440 967-5630
Kevin L McDaniel, *President*
Ken McDaniel, *Vice Pres*
EMP: 10
SALES (est): 4MM **Privately Held**
SIC: 3451 Screw machine products

(G-19168)
MCQUEEN ADVERTISING INC
Also Called: McQueen Sign Co
2010 Vermilion Rd (44089-2056)
PHONE..............................440 967-1137
Richard McQueen, *President*
Derrick McQueen, *Vice Pres*
EMP: 4
SALES (est): 423.1K **Privately Held**
SIC: 3993 7311 Signs & advertising specialties; advertising agencies

(G-19169)
PAPER MOON WINERY
2008 State Rd (44089-9602)
PHONE..............................440 967-2500
Sheryl Cawrse, *President*
EMP: 5
SALES (est): 467.5K **Privately Held**
SIC: 2084 Wines

(G-19170)
PROMAC INTERNATIONAL INC
1121 Sunnyside Rd (44089-2761)
PHONE..............................440 967-2040
Roger Lewan, *President*
Frank Bobel, *Vice Pres*
▲ EMP: 5
SALES (est): 785.5K **Privately Held**
SIC: 3441 Joists, open web steel: long-span series

(G-19171)
VERMILION DOCK MASTERS
858 Vermilion Rd (44089-1834)
PHONE..............................440 244-5370
Thomas Maccarthy, *Owner*
EMP: 4
SALES (est): 140K **Privately Held**
SIC: 3999 Manufacturing industries

Verona
Preble County

(G-19172)
HARVEST LAND CO-OP INC
Also Called: Verona Agriculture Center
141 S Commerce St (45378-5014)
P.O. Box 682 (45378-0682)
PHONE..............................937 884-5526
Mark Gebhardt, *Manager*
EMP: 8
SALES (corp-wide): 291.2MM **Privately Held**
WEB: www.harvestland.com
SIC: 2873 2879 5261 5153 Nitrogenous fertilizers; nitrogen solutions (fertilizer); urea; agricultural chemicals; fungicides, herbicides, pesticides, agricultural or household; insecticides, agricultural or household; fertilizer; grain elevators; chemicals, agricultural
PA: Harvest Land Co-Op, Inc.
1435 Nw 5th St
Richmond IN 47374
765 962-1527

Versailles
Darke County

(G-19173)
ASPEN MACHINE AND PLASTICS
257 Baker Rd (45380-9317)
PHONE..............................937 526-4644
John Moran, *President*
Mary M Moran, *General Mgr*
Mary Moran, *Corp Secy*
EMP: 7
SALES: 1MM **Privately Held**
WEB: www.mtiplasticmfg.com
SIC: 3599 Machine shop, jobbing & repair

(G-19174)
BEST BITE GRILL LLC
22 N Center St (45380-1201)
PHONE..............................419 344-7462
EMP: 10
SALES (est): 322.9K **Privately Held**
SIC: 5812 2099 Grills (eating places); noodles, fried (Chinese)

(G-19175)
C F POEPPELMAN INC
Also Called: Pepcon Concrete
10175 Old State Route 121 (45380-9586)
PHONE..............................937 526-5137
Dennis Mumaw, *Manager*
EMP: 4
SALES (est): 251.5K
SALES (corp-wide): 11.8MM **Privately Held**
SIC: 3273 Ready-mixed concrete
PA: C F Poeppelman Inc
4755 N State Route 721
Bradford OH 45308
937 448-2191

(G-19176)
CANDLE COTTAGE
732 E Main St (45380-1530)
PHONE..............................937 526-4041
Gary Middendorf, *Owner*
Robin Middendorf, *Co-Owner*
EMP: 3
SALES (est): 215.2K **Privately Held**
SIC: 3499 3999 5947 5999 Novelties & giftware, including trophies; candles; gift, novelty & souvenir shop; candle shops

(G-19177)
COTA INTERNATIONAL INC
67 Industrial Pkwy (45380-9759)
PHONE..............................937 526-5520
Linda Cota, *President*
Sandra Cota, *Vice Pres*
Craig Cota, *Treasurer*
Phillip Cota, *Admin Sec*
▲ EMP: 12
SQ FT: 5,000
SALES (est): 1.5MM **Privately Held**
WEB: www.cotainternational.com
SIC: 3713 5065 Truck bodies & parts; communication equipment

(G-19178)
DIRECT WIRE SERVICE LLP
100 Subler Dr (45380-9788)
PHONE..............................937 526-4447
Eric Barloge, *Managing Prtnr*
Dave Berger, *Managing Prtnr*
EMP: 8
SQ FT: 6,000
SALES (est): 962.3K **Privately Held**
WEB: www.directtoolingconcepts.com
SIC: 3544 Special dies & tools

(G-19179)
ERNST SPORTING GDS MINSTER LLC
32 E Main St (45380-1516)
PHONE..............................937 526-9822
Mike Ernst, *Manager*
EMP: 4
SALES (corp-wide): 915.9K **Privately Held**
SIC: 5941 2395 Sporting goods & bicycle shops; embroidery products, except schiffli machine
PA: Ernst Sporting Goods Of Minster, Llc
334 N Main St
Minster OH 45865
419 628-2602

(G-19180)
EXPERT REGRIND SERVICE INC
20 S Pearl St (45380-1221)
PHONE..............................937 526-5662
Micheal Poling, *President*
Bruce Feltz, *Vice Pres*
Pat Gigandet, *Admin Sec*
EMP: 3 EST: 1981
SALES: 350K **Privately Held**
SIC: 3545 3544 Cutting tools for machine tools; special dies, tools, jigs & fixtures

(G-19181)
G & C RAW LLC
Also Called: G & C Raw Dog Food
225 N West St (45380-1359)
PHONE..............................937 827-0010
Cathy Manning, *Mng Member*
Gary Manning,
EMP: 9
SQ FT: 1,800
SALES: 315K **Privately Held**
SIC: 2047 Dog food

(G-19182)
J & K PALLET INC
30 Subler Dr (45380-9782)
PHONE..............................937 526-5117
John Shardo, *President*
Jerry Shardo, *Vice Pres*
EMP: 6 EST: 1989
SQ FT: 24,000
SALES (est): 1MM **Privately Held**
SIC: 2448 Pallets, wood

(G-19183)
KAMPS INC
Also Called: Pallets-Fam-In-place-packaging
10709 Reed Rd (45380-9701)
PHONE..............................937 526-9333
Nick Schaller, *Branch Mgr*
EMP: 56
SALES (corp-wide): 157.4MM **Privately Held**
SIC: 2448 Pallets, wood
PA: Kamps, Inc.
2900 Peach Ridge Ave Nw
Grand Rapids MI 49534
616 453-9676

(G-19184)
KINGS COMMAND FOODS LLC
770 N Center St (45380-9610)
PHONE..............................937 526-3553
Mack Middendorf, *Branch Mgr*
EMP: 100
SALES (corp-wide): 3B **Privately Held**
SIC: 2015 2013 Poultry slaughtering & processing; sausages & other prepared meats
HQ: King's Command Foods, Llc
7622 S 188th St
Kent WA 98032
425 251-6788

(G-19185)
KNAPKE CUSTOM CABINETRY LTD
9306 Kelch Rd (45380-9679)
PHONE..............................937 459-8866
Bernard Knapke,
Chris Heitkamp,
EMP: 13
SQ FT: 8,800
SALES (est): 1.1MM **Privately Held**
SIC: 2434 Wood kitchen cabinets

(G-19186)
L-K INDUSTRY INC
176 N West St (45380-1210)
PHONE..............................937 526-3000
Karen Stollings, *President*
EMP: 20
SQ FT: 30,000
SALES (est): 2MM **Privately Held**
SIC: 2821 3312 Molding compounds, plastics; tool & die steel & alloys

(G-19187)
MIDMARK CORPORATION
160 Industrial Pkwy (45380-9757)
PHONE..............................937 526-8387
Anne Eiting Klamar, *Principal*
EMP: 8
SALES (corp-wide): 327.4MM **Privately Held**
SIC: 3648 Lighting equipment
PA: Midmark Corporation
1700 S Patterson Blvd # 400
Kettering OH 45409
937 526-3662

(G-19188)
MORAN TOOL INC
261 Baker Rd (45380-9317)
PHONE..............................937 526-5210
John Moran, *President*
Mary Moran, *Corp Secy*
EMP: 4
SQ FT: 12,000
SALES (est): 602.3K **Privately Held**
SIC: 3599 Machine shop, jobbing & repair

GEOGRAPHIC SECTION
Vinton - Gallia County (G-19215)

(G-19189)
PRECISION FAB PRODUCTS INC
10061 Old State Route 121 (45380-9586)
P.O. Box 256 (45380-0256)
PHONE.................................937 526-5681
Eric D Miller, *CEO*
Cindy Miller, *President*
David Miller, *Treasurer*
EMP: 6
SQ FT: 40,000
SALES (est): 1MM **Privately Held**
SIC: 3069 5712 Foam rubber; furniture stores

(G-19190)
SMITH PALLETS
9855 State Route 121 (45380-9512)
PHONE.................................937 564-6492
Joan M Smith, *Principal*
EMP: 4 **EST:** 2009
SALES (est): 298.7K **Privately Held**
SIC: 2448 Pallets, wood & wood with metal

(G-19191)
VERSAILLES BUILDING SUPPLY
741 N Center St (45380-1512)
P.O. Box 236 (45380-0236)
PHONE.................................937 526-3238
Richard P Huelsman, *President*
EMP: 7
SQ FT: 14,000
SALES: 1.5MM **Privately Held**
SIC: 2431 Doors, wood

(G-19192)
VPP INDUSTRIES INC
960 E Main St (45380-1555)
PHONE.................................937 526-3775
Vernon Monnin, *President*
Jane Monnin, *Vice Pres*
EMP: 10 **EST:** 1925
SQ FT: 9,600
SALES (est): 1.1MM **Privately Held**
WEB: www.vppind.com
SIC: 2752 Commercial printing, offset

(G-19193)
WEAVER BROS INC (PA)
Also Called: Tri County Eggs
895 E Main St (45380-1533)
P.O. Box 333 (45380-0333)
PHONE.................................937 526-3907
Timothy John Weaver, *President*
Audrey Weaver, *Principal*
Geo L Weaver, *Principal*
John D Weaver, *Principal*
Kreg Kohli, *Vice Pres*
▲ **EMP:** 60 **EST:** 1931
SQ FT: 20,000
SALES (est): 55MM **Privately Held**
SIC: 0252 5143 2015 Chicken eggs; dairy products, except dried or canned; cheese; butter; poultry slaughtering & processing

Vickery
Sandusky County

(G-19194)
BSE WELDING & FABRICATING LLC
1787 N State Route 510 (43464-9645)
PHONE.................................419 547-1043
Chris Daniel, *Owner*
EMP: 12
SALES (est): 1.5MM **Privately Held**
SIC: 7692 Welding repair

Vienna
Trumbull County

(G-19195)
ADVANCED MICROBEAM INC
4217 King Graves Rd Ste C (44473-9787)
P.O. Box 610 (44473-0610)
PHONE.................................330 394-1255
Donald Lesher, *President*
Pamela Lesher, *Vice Pres*
EMP: 4
SQ FT: 6,300

SALES (est): 566K **Privately Held**
WEB: www.advancedmicrobeam.com
SIC: 3577 8731 Computer peripheral equipment; electronic research

(G-19196)
APTIV SERVICES US LLC
Also Called: Delphi
3400 Aero Park Dr (44473-8704)
P.O. Box 431, Warren (44486-0001)
PHONE.................................330 367-6000
Ken Ellsworth, *Branch Mgr*
EMP: 120
SALES (corp-wide): 16.6B **Privately Held**
SIC: 3714 Motor vehicle parts & accessories
HQ: Aptiv Services Us, Llc
5725 Innovation Dr
Troy MI 48098

(G-19197)
BRAUN MACHINE TECHNOLOGIES LLC
4175 Warren Sharon Rd (44473-9524)
PHONE.................................330 777-5433
Ke Sundvall, *Manager*
EMP: 2
SQ FT: 2,000
SALES: 1.5MM **Privately Held**
SIC: 3291 Abrasive metal & steel products

(G-19198)
DIAMOND OILFIELD TECH LLC
4494 Warren Sharon Rd (44473-9642)
P.O. Box 91 (44473-0091)
PHONE.................................234 806-4185
Matthew Kleese, *Mng Member*
Peter Karousis, *Mng Member*
EMP: 15
SALES: 2MM **Privately Held**
SIC: 1389 Oil consultants

(G-19199)
LATROBE SPCIALTY MTLS DIST INC (HQ)
1551 Vienna Pkwy (44473-8703)
PHONE.................................330 609-5137
Gregory A Pratt, *Ch of Bd*
Timothy R Armstrong, *Vice Pres*
Thomas F Cramsey, *Vice Pres*
James D Dee, *Vice Pres*
Matthew S Enoch, *Vice Pres*
◆ **EMP:** 80
SQ FT: 189,000
SALES: 69.2MM
SALES (corp-wide): 2.1B **Publicly Held**
SIC: 5051 3312 Steel; stainless steel
PA: Carpenter Technology Corporation
1735 Market St Fl 15
Philadelphia PA 19103
610 208-2000

(G-19200)
LIDECO LLC
972 Yngtn Kngs Rd Se (44473-8618)
P.O. Box 596 (44473-0596)
PHONE.................................330 539-9333
Philip Saloom, *Principal*
EMP: 5
SQ FT: 15,000
SALES (est): 240.1K **Privately Held**
SIC: 3544 3441 Dies & die holders for metal cutting, forming, die casting; fabricated structural metal

(G-19201)
LITCO INTERNATIONAL INC (PA)
1 Litco Dr (44473-9600)
P.O. Box 150 (44473-0150)
PHONE.................................330 539-5433
Lionel F Trebilcock, *CEO*
Gary L Trebilcock, *President*
Gary Sharon, *Vice Pres*
Chameika Patterson, *Human Res Mgr*
Pete Snyder, *Human Res Mgr*
◆ **EMP:** 30
SQ FT: 13,000
SALES (est): 4MM **Privately Held**
WEB: www.litco.com
SIC: 2448 5031 Pallets, wood; particleboard

(G-19202)
MACK INDUSTRIES PA INC
2207 Slem Hutchings Rd Ne (44473)
PHONE.................................330 638-7680
Ron Hoover, *Manager*
EMP: 19
SALES (corp-wide): 170.9MM **Privately Held**
SIC: 3589 3272 Sewage treatment equipment; concrete products
HQ: Mack Industries Of Pennsylvania, Inc.
201 Columbia Rd
Valley City OH 44280
330 483-3111

(G-19203)
MILLWOOD INC
Liberty Technologies
3708 International Blvd (44473-9796)
PHONE.................................330 729-2120
Ronald C Ringness, *Senior VP*
EMP: 8 **Privately Held**
WEB: www.millwoodinc.com
SIC: 3565 Packaging machinery
PA: Millwood, Inc.
3708 International Blvd
Vienna OH 44473

(G-19204)
MILLWOOD INC
3708 International Blvd (44473-9796)
PHONE.................................404 629-4811
Dave Scala, *Branch Mgr*
EMP: 17 **Privately Held**
SIC: 3565 5084 Packaging machinery; packaging machinery & equipment
PA: Millwood, Inc.
3708 International Blvd
Vienna OH 44473

(G-19205)
MILLWOOD NATURAL LLC
3708 International Blvd (44473-9796)
PHONE.................................330 393-4400
Lionel Trebilcock, *Partner*
EMP: 105
SALES (est): 11.6MM **Privately Held**
SIC: 3565 4731 Packaging machinery; freight transportation arrangement
PA: Millwood, Inc.
3708 International Blvd
Vienna OH 44473

(G-19206)
NRG SMOOTHIES LLC
1887 Youngstown (44473)
PHONE.................................972 800-1002
Melanie Kmetz, *Administration*
EMP: 3 **EST:** 2016
SALES (est): 158.5K **Privately Held**
SIC: 2037 Frozen fruits & vegetables

(G-19207)
PROCESS INNOVATIONS INC
4219 King Graves Rd (44473-9708)
P.O. Box 25, Fowler (44418-0025)
PHONE.................................330 856-5192
Robert S Crow, *President*
Shane Mealy, *Opers Mgr*
EMP: 6
SQ FT: 6,000
SALES: 790K **Privately Held**
WEB: www.processinnovations.com
SIC: 3569 8711 Robots, assembly line: industrial & commercial; engineering services

(G-19208)
RAMON ROBINSON
Also Called: Robinson Wood Products
475 Niles Vienna Rd (44473-9500)
PHONE.................................330 883-3244
Ramon Robinson, *Owner*
EMP: 3
SALES (est): 76K **Privately Held**
WEB: www.robinsonswoods.com
SIC: 3944 5092 3952 2851 Craft & hobby kits & sets; arts & crafts equipment & supplies; lead pencils & art goods; paints & allied products

(G-19209)
RIVERSIDE STEEL INC
3102 Warren Sharon Rd (44473-9521)
PHONE.................................330 856-5299
John Radu Jr, *President*

John Radu Sr, *Chairman*
Catherine Radu, *Corp Secy*
▼ **EMP:** 11
SQ FT: 38,000
SALES (est): 2.6MM **Privately Held**
WEB: www.riverside-steel.com
SIC: 3441 Fabricated structural metal

(G-19210)
STARR FABRICATING INC
4175 Warren Sharon Rd (44473-9524)
PHONE.................................330 394-9891
Thomas B Smith, *President*
EMP: 77 **EST:** 1965
SALES (est): 13MM **Privately Held**
WEB: www.starrfabricating.com
SIC: 3441 3564 3496 3444 Fabricated structural metal; blowers & fans; miscellaneous fabricated wire products; sheet metalwork; office furniture, except wood

(G-19211)
WATER DROP MEDIA INC
289 Youngstown Kingsvl Se (44473-9601)
PHONE.................................234 600-5817
Dustin Ghizzoni, *Principal*
EMP: 7
SALES (est): 494.8K **Privately Held**
SIC: 4899 5999 5099 2759 Data communication services; banners, flags, decals & posters; signs, except electric; screen printing

Vincent
Washington County

(G-19212)
BLANEY HARDWOODS OHIO INC (PA)
425 Timberline Dr (45784-5615)
PHONE.................................740 678-8288
Randal Blaney, *President*
James Blaney, *Vice Pres*
EMP: 50
SQ FT: 3,000
SALES (est): 4.8MM **Privately Held**
WEB: www.blaneyhardwoods.com
SIC: 2421 Kiln drying of lumber

(G-19213)
DECKER DRILLING INC
11565 State Route 676 (45784-5636)
PHONE.................................740 749-3939
Dean Decker, *President*
Pat Decker, *Vice Pres*
EMP: 42
SALES (est): 6.6MM **Privately Held**
WEB: www.deandecker.com
SIC: 1381 Redrilling oil & gas wells

(G-19214)
MICRO MACHINE WORKS INC
10499 State Route 339 (45784-5429)
P.O. Box 70, Barlow (45712-0070)
PHONE.................................740 678-8471
Linn Yost, *President*
Dan Anstatt, *Sales/Mktg Mgr*
David Yost, *Manager*
EMP: 10
SQ FT: 6,592
SALES: 2MM **Privately Held**
WEB: www.e-mmwi.com
SIC: 3599 Machine shop, jobbing & repair

Vinton
Gallia County

(G-19215)
IVI MINING GROUP LTD
72116 Grey Rd (45686-8410)
P.O. Box 1101, Jackson (45640-7101)
PHONE.................................740 418-7745
Jesse Sizemore, *Ch of Bd*
EMP: 7
SQ FT: 5,000
SALES (est): 205.6K **Privately Held**
SIC: 1041 1221 1222 Placer gold mining; bituminous coal surface mining; bituminous coal-underground mining

Vinton - Gallia County (G-19216)

(G-19216)
STEELIAL WLDG MET FBRCTION INC
Also Called: Steelial Cnstr Met Fabrication
70764 State Route 124 (45686-8545)
PHONE.................................740 669-5300
Larry Allen Hedrick Jr, *President*
Krista Lynnete Hedrick, *Admin Sec*
EMP: 32 EST: 1998
SQ FT: 40,000
SALES (est): 11MM **Privately Held**
WEB: www.steelial.com
SIC: 1623 3441 3444 Pipe laying construction; fabricated structural metal; sheet metalwork

Wadsworth
Medina County

(G-19217)
762MM FIREARMS LLC
Also Called: Elite Tactical Supply
224 High St (44281-1861)
PHONE.................................440 655-8572
Christian J Thomas,
EMP: 5
SQ FT: 500
SALES: 480K **Privately Held**
SIC: 3484 5941 Guns (firearms) or gun parts, 30 mm. & below; firearms

(G-19218)
A & B WOOD DESIGN ASSOC INC
3193 Greenwich Rd (44281-9518)
P.O. Box 88, Oberlin (44074-0088)
PHONE.................................330 721-2789
Brett Arrowood, *President*
EMP: 4
SQ FT: 3,000
SALES (est): 282.9K **Privately Held**
SIC: 7389 2431 5031 5211 Design services; moldings & baseboards, ornamental & trim; molding, all materials; lumber products

(G-19219)
A T TUBE COMPANY INC
188 S Lyman St (44281-1743)
P.O. Box 123 (44282-0123)
PHONE.................................330 336-8706
EMP: 3
SQ FT: 4,000
SALES: 500K **Privately Held**
SIC: 2655 Mfg Fiber Cans/Drums

(G-19220)
ACCEL GROUP INC (PA)
325 Quadral Dr (44281-9571)
PHONE.................................330 336-0317
James Terranova, *President*
Bill Delorm, *VP Opers*
Dana Patterson, *Prdtn Mgr*
Todd Rentsch, *Purchasing*
Mike Nelson, *Engineer*
◆ EMP: 85
SQ FT: 191,000
SALES: 11.7MM **Privately Held**
WEB: www.accelgrp.com
SIC: 2542 Partitions & fixtures, except wood

(G-19221)
ADVANCED ELASTOMER SYSTEMS LP
Also Called: Exxon
1000 Seville Rd (44281-8317)
PHONE.................................330 336-7641
Robert Latham, *Branch Mgr*
EMP: 71
SALES (corp-wide): 290.2B **Publicly Held**
WEB: www.santoprene.com
SIC: 2821 3083 2822 Elastomers, nonvulcanizable (plastics); laminated plastics plate & sheet; synthetic rubber
HQ: Advanced Elastomer Systems Lp
388 S Main St Ste 600
Akron OH 44311
800 352-7866

(G-19222)
ADVANCED PLASTICS INC
307 Water St (44281-1708)
P.O. Box 720 (44282-0720)
PHONE.................................330 336-6681
Phil Nye, *President*
John Davis, *Vice Pres*
EMP: 11 EST: 1999
SQ FT: 12,000
SALES (est): 1.8MM **Privately Held**
WEB: www.advancedplastics.net
SIC: 3089 Injection molded finished plastic products

(G-19223)
AKRON PRODUCTS COMPANY
6600 Ridge Rd (44281-9743)
PHONE.................................330 576-1750
Chester Marshall Jr, *CEO*
EMP: 10
SQ FT: 45,000
SALES: 1MM **Privately Held**
WEB: www.akronproducts.com
SIC: 3446 Fences or posts, ornamental iron or steel

(G-19224)
AL FE HEAT TREATING-OHIO INC
979 Seville Rd (44281-8316)
PHONE.................................330 336-0211
Steve Turner, *Manager*
EMP: 20 **Privately Held**
SIC: 3398 Metal heat treating
PA: Al Fe Heat Treating-Ohio, Inc
6920 Pointe Inverness Way # 140
Fort Wayne IN 46804

(G-19225)
ALTERNATIVE FLASH INC
1734 Wall Rd Ste B (44281-8354)
PHONE.................................330 334-6111
Daniel Broadbent, *President*
Angelo Savakis, *Admin Sec*
EMP: 20
SQ FT: 20,000
SALES (est): 2.4MM **Privately Held**
WEB: www.alternativeflash.com
SIC: 3061 3544 3398 Mechanical rubber goods; special dies, tools, jigs & fixtures; metal heat treating

(G-19226)
AMERICAN PRO-MOLD INC
350 State St 7 (44281-1093)
P.O. Box 325 (44282-0325)
PHONE.................................330 336-4111
Edward F Steinkerchner, *President*
Roberta Steinkerchner, *Corp Secy*
Mark E Steinkerchner, *Vice Pres*
EMP: 25
SQ FT: 10,000
SALES (est): 3.4MM **Privately Held**
SIC: 3069 3061 Molded rubber products; mechanical rubber goods

(G-19227)
APPLIED MATERIALS FINISHING
901 Seville Rd (44281-8316)
PHONE.................................330 336-5645
Faith Ortiz, *Principal*
EMP: 25 EST: 2012
SALES (est): 5.1MM **Privately Held**
SIC: 3341 Secondary nonferrous metals

(G-19228)
BUSSON DIGITAL PRINTING INC
1061 Eastern Rd (44281-9019)
PHONE.................................330 753-8373
Dennis Busson, *President*
EMP: 20
SQ FT: 18,000
SALES (est): 3.2MM **Privately Held**
WEB: www.bussonportraitdirectories.com
SIC: 2752 Commercial printing, lithographic

(G-19229)
CABINET SOURCE
8100 Wadsworth Rd (44281-9527)
PHONE.................................330 336-5600
Paul Ott, *Owner*
Pat Ott, *Owner*
EMP: 4

SALES (est): 177.6K **Privately Held**
SIC: 2434 Wood kitchen cabinets

(G-19230)
CLAMPCO PRODUCTS INC (PA)
1743 Wall Rd (44281-9558)
PHONE.................................330 336-8857
James R Venner, *President*
Jerry Biagini, *General Mgr*
Rich Bobey, *Plant Mgr*
Doug Bases, *Buyer*
Andrew Mackay, *Engineer*
◆ EMP: 200
SQ FT: 54,000
SALES (est): 66MM **Privately Held**
WEB: www.clampco.com
SIC: 3429 Clamps, metal; clamps & couplings, hose

(G-19231)
CUSTOM SPORTSWEAR IMPRINTS LLC
238 High St (44281-1861)
PHONE.................................330 335-8326
Dan Gibbs,
EMP: 9
SQ FT: 3,000
SALES (est): 670K **Privately Held**
SIC: 5199 2759 7389 Advertising specialties; screen printing; embroidering of advertising on shirts, etc.

(G-19232)
D & J ELECTRIC MOTOR REPAIR CO
Also Called: Ohio Belt Control Supply Co
1734 Wall Rd Unit Office (44281-8356)
PHONE.................................330 336-4343
David Zuchniak, *President*
John Zuchniak, *Vice Pres*
EMP: 10
SQ FT: 20,000
SALES (est): 3.2MM **Privately Held**
SIC: 5013 7694 7629 1731 Automotive servicing equipment; electric motor repair; electrical equipment repair services; general electrical contractor

(G-19233)
DAYSON POLYMERS LLC (PA)
9774 Trease Rd (44281-9557)
P.O. Box 372, Rittman (44270-0372)
PHONE.................................330 335-5237
David C Anderson, *CEO*
Michael L Stark, *Principal*
Michael Day,
▲ EMP: 4
SQ FT: 200
SALES (est): 731.1K **Privately Held**
WEB: www.daysonpolymers.com
SIC: 2821 Plastics materials & resins

(G-19234)
DESHEA PRINTING COMPANY
Also Called: Aldridge Folders
924 Seville Rd (44281-8316)
PHONE.................................330 336-7601
Sherri Gasser, *President*
EMP: 6
SALES (est): 491.4K **Privately Held**
SIC: 2752 Photo-offset printing

(G-19235)
DUNHAMS SPORTS
180 Great Oaks Trl Ste C (44281-9407)
PHONE.................................330 334-3257
EMP: 15 EST: 2014
SALES (est): 827.7K **Privately Held**
SIC: 2329 Men's & boys' sportswear & athletic clothing

(G-19236)
DUNKIN DONUTS
809 High St (44281-9420)
PHONE.................................330 336-2500
Tushar Patel, *Principal*
EMP: 6 EST: 2010
SALES (est): 118.3K **Privately Held**
SIC: 5461 2095 Doughnuts; roasted coffee

(G-19237)
EBNER FURNACES INC
Also Called: Ebnerfab
224 Quadral Dr (44281-8327)
PHONE.................................330 335-2311
Robert Ebner, *President*
Darlene Farnsworth, *Partner*
Ralph Myers, *Corp Secy*
Mark Weigand, *Purch Mgr*
Bill Lucas, *Engineer*
▲ EMP: 80
SQ FT: 150,000
SALES (est): 44.4MM
SALES (corp-wide): 247.9MM **Privately Held**
WEB: www.ebnerfurnaces.com
SIC: 3567 3444 3433 3441 Industrial furnaces & ovens; sheet metalwork; heating equipment, except electric; fabricated structural metal; fabricated plate work (boiler shop); fabricated pipe & fittings
HQ: Ebner Verwaltung Gmbh
Ebner-Platz 1
Leonding 4060
732 686-80

(G-19238)
EVANKO WM/BARRINGER RICHD DDS
Also Called: William Evanko Dgs
185 Wadsworth Rd Ste K (44281-9585)
PHONE.................................330 336-6693
William A Evanko, *Manager*
EMP: 5
SALES (est): 465.4K
SALES (corp-wide): 335.6K **Privately Held**
SIC: 3842 Grafts, artificial: for surgery
PA: Evanko, William A & Benninger, Richard M Dds Inc
6101 34th St W Apt 26e
Bradenton FL 34210
330 721-5009

(G-19239)
FILIA
560 Rockglen Dr (44281-8120)
PHONE.................................330 322-1200
Gregory Graham, *Principal*
EMP: 4
SALES (est): 297.3K **Privately Held**
SIC: 2084 Wines

(G-19240)
FIN TUBE PRODUCTS INC
188 S Lyman St Ste 100 (44281-1743)
PHONE.................................330 334-3736
Michael Bandrowsky, *President*
Clare Fahrer, *Principal*
Paul Ankrim, *Vice Pres*
William Collins, *Admin Sec*
EMP: 10
SQ FT: 50,000
SALES (est): 990K **Privately Held**
WEB: www.fintube.com
SIC: 3443 Finned tubes, for heat transfer

(G-19241)
FIVES ST CORP
1 Park Centre Dr Ste 210 (44281-9482)
PHONE.................................234 217-9070
Daniel Balcer, *President*
▲ EMP: 21
SQ FT: 7,000
SALES: 150MM
SALES (corp-wide): 4.5MM **Privately Held**
SIC: 3531 Construction machinery
HQ: Fives Stein
108 A 112
Maisons Alfort 94700
145 186-500

(G-19242)
FLOW LINE OPTIONS CORP
471 E Bergey St (44281-2097)
P.O. Box 1148, Medina (44258-1148)
PHONE.................................330 331-7331
David Grumney, *President*
Kathleen Grumney, *Vice Pres*
EMP: 5
SQ FT: 7,500
SALES (est): 105.3K **Privately Held**
WEB: www.flo-corp.com
SIC: 3824 5084 Fluid meters & counting devices; meters, consumption registering

GEOGRAPHIC SECTION
Wadsworth - Medina County (G-19268)

(G-19243)
GOLDSMITH & EGGLETON LLC
300 1st St (44281-2084)
PHONE.....................203 855-6000
Rob Eggleton, *Vice Pres*
Paul Alic, *Human Res Dir*
Brian Hill, *Marketing Staff*
David Derhagopian, *Mng Member*
Eric Davies, *Manager*
▲ **EMP:** 18
SALES (est): 911.2K
SALES (corp-wide): 1.4MM **Privately Held**
SIC: 2821 3069 5169 Plastics materials & resins; reclaimed rubber (reworked by manufacturing processes); synthetic rubber
HQ: Ravago Holdings America, Inc.
   1900 Summit Tower Blvd
   Orlando FL 32810

(G-19244)
H & S TOOL INC
715 Weber Dr (44281-9550)
P.O. Box 393 (44282-0393)
PHONE.....................330 335-1536
Mark W Hillestad, *President*
Randy Hall, *Manager*
Denise Douglas, *Admin Mgr*
EMP: 19
SQ FT: 12,500
SALES (est): 4.5MM **Privately Held**
WEB: www.handstool.net
SIC: 3545 Tools & accessories for machine tools

(G-19245)
HUBBELL INCORPORATED
8711 Wadsworth Rd (44281-8438)
PHONE.....................330 335-2361
Sabrina Lhatter, *Engineer*
John Breidenbach, *Sales Staff*
Christophe Davis, *Branch Mgr*
EMP: 29
SALES (corp-wide): 4.4B **Publicly Held**
WEB: www.kerite.com
SIC: 3643 Current-carrying wiring devices
PA: Hubbell Incorporated
   40 Waterview Dr
   Shelton CT 06484
   475 882-4000

(G-19246)
HUTNIK COMPANY
Also Called: Ohio Engineering and Mfg Co
350 State St Ste 5 (44281-2417)
PHONE.....................330 336-9700
Victor Hutnik, *President*
Debra Hutnik, *Vice Pres*
EMP: 6
SQ FT: 5,000
SALES: 500K **Privately Held**
SIC: 3599 3443 7389 Machine shop, jobbing & repair; cylinders, pressure: metal plate; design, commercial & industrial

(G-19247)
KEELER ENTERPRISES INC
Also Called: Aldridge Folders
924 Seville Rd (44281-8316)
P.O. Box 269 (44282-0269)
PHONE.....................330 336-7601
Fred Keeler, *President*
Daniel Mills, *Vice Pres*
Sheri Gasser, *Treasurer*
EMP: 8
SQ FT: 10,000
SALES (est): 1.3MM **Privately Held**
WEB: www.aldridgefolders.com
SIC: 2675 2678 Folders, filing, die-cut: made from purchased materials; stationery products

(G-19248)
KEN VENEY INDUSTRIES LLC
690 Weber Dr (44281-9551)
PHONE.....................330 336-5825
Ken Veney,
EMP: 4
SQ FT: 3,800
SALES (est): 503.2K **Privately Held**
SIC: 5531 3089 Automotive parts; automotive parts, plastic

(G-19249)
KLAWHORN INDUSTRIES INC
456 South Blvd (44281-2032)
PHONE.....................330 335-8191
Frank Malec, *President*
Chris Jurey, *Corp Secy*
Fred Hayduk, *Vice Pres*
EMP: 3
SALES (est): 374.7K **Privately Held**
WEB: www.klawhorn.com
SIC: 3423 3524 3634 3541 Hand & edge tools; lawn & garden equipment; housewares, excluding cooking appliances & utensils; machine tools, metal cutting type

(G-19250)
KLEEN POLYMERS INC
145 Rainbow St (44281-1478)
PHONE.....................330 336-4212
John Marefka, *President*
Rick Marefka, *Vice Pres*
EMP: 15
SQ FT: 8,000
SALES (est): 3MM **Privately Held**
WEB: www.kleenpolymers.com
SIC: 3061 Mechanical rubber goods

(G-19251)
KRAMER & KIEFER INC
Also Called: Medina Tool & Die
2662 Valley Side Ave (44281-9233)
PHONE.....................330 336-8742
Clayton Kramer, *President*
Robert Kiefer, *Vice Pres*
EMP: 6
SQ FT: 6,500
SALES: 800K **Privately Held**
SIC: 3544 Special dies, tools, jigs & fixtures

(G-19252)
LUKE ENGINEERING & MFG CORP (PA)
456 South Blvd (44281-2032)
P.O. Box 478 (44282-0478)
PHONE.....................330 335-1501
Fred P Hayduk, *President*
Chris Jurey, *Vice Pres*
Scott Hays, *Administration*
◆ **EMP:** 40 **EST:** 1946
SQ FT: 37,000
SALES (est): 7.4MM **Privately Held**
SIC: 3471 3559 Anodizing (plating) of metals or formed products; metal finishing equipment for plating, etc.

(G-19253)
MICHAEL DAY ENTERPRISES LLC
9774 Trease Rd (44281-9557)
P.O. Box 151 (44282-0151)
PHONE.....................330 335-5100
Michael F Day, *President*
Bill Mitchell, *Plant Mgr*
EMP: 5
SALES (est): 1.2MM **Privately Held**
SIC: 2821 Molding compounds, plastics

(G-19254)
MILLER PRODUCTS INC
Also Called: M P I Labeltek
985 Seville Rd (44281-8316)
PHONE.....................330 335-3110
Ronald Nagy, *Branch Mgr*
EMP: 58
SALES (corp-wide): 36.3MM **Privately Held**
SIC: 2759 Labels & seals: printing
PA: Miller Products, Inc.
   450 Courtney Rd
   Sebring OH 44672
   330 938-2134

(G-19255)
MYERS INDUSTRIES INC
Akro-Mils
250 Seville Rd (44281-1020)
P.O. Box 989, Akron (44309-0989)
PHONE.....................330 336-6621
Gary Taylor, *Manager*
EMP: 120
SQ FT: 10,000
SALES (corp-wide): 566.7MM **Publicly Held**
WEB: www.myersind.com
SIC: 3052 3069 3443 2542 Automobile hose, rubber; rubber automotive products; fabricated plate work (boiler shop); partitions & fixtures, except wood
PA: Myers Industries, Inc.
   1293 S Main St
   Akron OH 44301
   330 253-5592

(G-19256)
NO BURN INC
1392 High St Ste 211 (44281-8262)
PHONE.....................330 336-1500
William Kish, *President*
EMP: 8
SQ FT: 4,000
SALES (est): 1.7MM **Privately Held**
SIC: 2899 Fire retardant chemicals

(G-19257)
NOVEX INC
258 Main St (44281-1446)
PHONE.....................330 335-2371
Charles Lynn, *President*
EMP: 14
SQ FT: 15,000
SALES (est): 3.5MM **Privately Held**
WEB: www.novitane.com
SIC: 3052 3069 Rubber belting; sheets, hard rubber; castings, rubber

(G-19258)
P C M CO (PA)
291 W Bergey St (44281-1334)
PHONE.....................330 336-8040
Duane Coffman, *President*
Paul Bebout, *Vice Pres*
Seng Sisouphanah, *Vice Pres*
Brannon Riley, *Treasurer*
Emma Momchilov, *Shareholder*
EMP: 85 **EST:** 1965
SALES (est): 12MM **Privately Held**
WEB: www.pcm-lw.com
SIC: 3365 Aluminum & aluminum-based alloy castings

(G-19259)
P-AMERICAS LLC
Also Called: Pepsico
904 Seville Rd (44281-8316)
PHONE.....................330 336-3553
Barbara Headley, *Branch Mgr*
EMP: 123
SQ FT: 50,200
SALES (corp-wide): 64.6B **Publicly Held**
SIC: 2086 Carbonated soft drinks, bottled & canned
HQ: P-Americas Llc
   1 Pepsi Way
   Somers NY 10589
   336 896-5740

(G-19260)
PARKER-HANNIFIN CORPORATION
Pneumatic North America
135 Quadral Dr (44281-8326)
PHONE.....................330 336-3511
Deborah Kusmier, *HR Admin*
Dave Flath, *Sales Executive*
Bill Service, *Marketing Mgr*
Bill Treacy, *Branch Mgr*
Devin Jackson, *Info Tech Mgr*
EMP: 130
SALES (corp-wide): 14.3B **Publicly Held**
WEB: www.parker.com
SIC: 3621 3643 3593 Electric motor & generator parts; current-carrying wiring devices; fluid power cylinders & actuators
PA: Parker-Hannifin Corporation
   6035 Parkland Blvd
   Cleveland OH 44124
   216 896-3000

(G-19261)
PARKER-HANNIFIN CORPORATION
Also Called: Ips
135 Quadral Dr (44281-8326)
PHONE.....................330 335-6740
Barbara McCall, *Branch Mgr*
EMP: 19
SALES (corp-wide): 12B **Publicly Held**
SIC: 3569 Lubricating systems, centralized
PA: Parker-Hannifin Corporation
   6035 Parkland Blvd
   Cleveland OH 44124
   216 896-3000

(G-19262)
PARKER-HANNIFIN CORPORATION
Also Called: Electromechanical North Amer
135 Quadral Dr (44281-8326)
PHONE.....................330 336-3511
Kenneth Sweet, *Branch Mgr*
EMP: 15
SALES (corp-wide): 12B **Publicly Held**
WEB: www.parker.com
SIC: 3599 3535 3496 3469 Machine shop, jobbing & repair; conveyors & conveying equipment; miscellaneous fabricated wire products; metal stampings; sheet metalwork; fabricated plate work (boiler shop)
PA: Parker-Hannifin Corporation
   6035 Parkland Blvd
   Cleveland OH 44124
   216 896-3000

(G-19263)
PIN POINT MARKETING LLC
302 Eric Ln (44281-9209)
PHONE.....................330 336-5863
Timothy Davis, *Principal*
EMP: 4
SALES (est): 55.9K **Privately Held**
SIC: 3452 Pins

(G-19264)
PLASTICS R UNIQUE INC
330 Grandview Ave (44281-1161)
PHONE.....................330 334-4820
Kenneth R Boersma, *President*
EMP: 30
SQ FT: 12,300
SALES (est): 5.2MM **Privately Held**
SIC: 3089 5162 Plastic containers, except foam; plastics materials

(G-19265)
PRECISION ALUMINUM INC
733 Weber Dr (44281-9550)
PHONE.....................330 335-2351
Thomas Powell, *President*
EMP: 29
SQ FT: 17,500
SALES (est): 5.7MM **Privately Held**
SIC: 3365 Masts, cast aluminum

(G-19266)
PRECISION ENGINEERED TECH LLC
1785 Wall Rd (44281-9558)
PHONE.....................330 335-3300
Brian K Murray, *President*
Jerry Mullin, *Vice Pres*
EMP: 6
SALES (est): 811.5K **Privately Held**
SIC: 3531 Construction machinery

(G-19267)
PROFILE RUBBER CORPORATION
6784 Ridge Rd (44281-9743)
P.O. Box 299, Sharon Center (44274-0299)
PHONE.....................330 239-1703
Lewis Winland, *CEO*
John Winland, *President*
Jeff Winland, *Vice Pres*
EMP: 17 **EST:** 1961
SQ FT: 12,000
SALES (est): 1.4MM **Privately Held**
WEB: www.profilerubber.com
SIC: 3069 Molded rubber products

(G-19268)
QUALIFORM INC
689 Weber Dr (44281-9550)
PHONE.....................330 336-6777
Andy Antonino, *President*
EMP: 40 **EST:** 1976
SQ FT: 17,000

Wadsworth - Medina County (G-19269)

SALES (est): 6.1MM **Privately Held**
WEB: www.qualforminc.com
SIC: 3069 3544 3061 Molded rubber products; special dies, tools, jigs & fixtures; mechanical rubber goods

(G-19269)
QUALITY REPRODUCTIONS INC
Also Called: Fine Lines
127 Hartman Rd (44281-9402)
PHONE 330 335-5000
Bob Grosser, *President*
EMP: 9
SQ FT: 7,000
SALES (est): 1.5MM **Privately Held**
SIC: 3714 Motor vehicle parts & accessories

(G-19270)
R B MFG CO
Also Called: Akro-Mils
250 Seville Rd (44281-1020)
PHONE 419 626-9464
Tom Roulston Sr, *Chairman*
◆ **EMP:** 18
SQ FT: 54,870
SALES (est): 4.7MM
SALES (corp-wide): 566.7MM **Publicly Held**
WEB: www.rbmfgco.com
SIC: 3444 3443 2522 3537 Sheet metalwork; fabricated plate work (boiler shop); office furniture, except wood; dollies (hand or power trucks), industrial except mining
PA: Myers Industries, Inc.
1293 S Main St
Akron OH 44301
330 253-5592

(G-19271)
RADICI PLASTICS USA INC
960 Seville Rd (44281-8316)
PHONE 330 336-7611
Michael Cain, *CEO*
Danilo Micheletti, *COO*
Mike Cain, *Exec VP*
Mattia Imberti, *CFO*
▲ **EMP:** 95
SQ FT: 235,000
SALES (est): 35.8MM **Privately Held**
WEB: www.radicispandex.com
SIC: 3087 3089 Custom compound purchased resins; plastic processing
HQ: Radici Novacips Spa
Via Bedeschi 20
Chignolo D'isola BG 24040
035 499-7689

(G-19272)
RAYDAR INC OF OHIO
1734 Wall Rd Ste B (44281-8354)
PHONE 330 334-6111
Angelo Savakis, *Corp Secy*
Daniel Broadbent, *Vice Pres*
EMP: 8
SALES (est): 2.9MM **Privately Held**
WEB: www.raydarrubber.com
SIC: 3069 Molded rubber products

(G-19273)
RBA INC
487 College St (44281-1105)
PHONE 330 336-6700
Robert Bault, *President*
Jane Haugh, *Corp Secy*
EMP: 8
SQ FT: 7,000
SALES (est): 800K **Privately Held**
SIC: 2752 7336 Commercial printing, offset; graphic arts & related design

(G-19274)
REMINGTON PRODUCTS CO
961 Seville Rd (44281-8316)
P.O. Box 506 (44282-0506)
PHONE 330 335-1571
Rhonda Newman, *CEO*
Jeff Wert, *Vice Pres*
Ned Goodman, *VP Opers*
C Kevin McComas, *CFO*
John Weisend, *Controller*
▲ **EMP:** 110
SQ FT: 102,000

SALES (est): 31.7MM **Privately Held**
WEB: www.remprod.com
SIC: 3069 3131 Boot or shoe products, rubber; orthopedic sundries, molded rubber; footwear cut stock

(G-19275)
ROHRER CORPORATION (PA)
Also Called: Gateway Printing
717 Seville Rd (44281-1091)
P.O. Box 1009 (44282-1009)
PHONE 330 335-1541
Scot D Adkins, *President*
Troy Eckstine, *General Mgr*
Carmine Lombardi, *General Mgr*
Scott Nagel, *General Mgr*
David Sander, *General Mgr*
▲ **EMP:** 170 **EST:** 1953
SQ FT: 169,000
SALES (est): 131.7MM **Privately Held**
WEB: www.rohrer.com
SIC: 3089 2675 Blister or bubble formed packaging, plastic; die-cut paper & board

(G-19276)
SATTLER COMPANIES INC
Also Called: Sattler Machine Products, Inc.
1455 Wolf Creek Trl (44281)
P.O. Box 306, Sharon Center (44274-0306)
PHONE 330 239-2552
David Sattler, *President*
David F Raynor, *Principal*
Terry Ake, *Purch Mgr*
▲ **EMP:** 20
SQ FT: 22,600
SALES (est): 4.1MM **Privately Held**
WEB: www.sattlercompanies.com
SIC: 3599 Machine shop, jobbing & repair

(G-19277)
SOPREMA USA INC
310 Quadral Dr (44281-9571)
PHONE 330 334-0066
Pierre Bindschedler, *President*
J Bret Treier, *Principal*
Steven P Goetz, *Corp Secy*
Gilbert Lorenzo, *Vice Pres*
Michele Brothers, *Buyer*
EMP: 30
SALES (est): 13.3MM
SALES (corp-wide): 12.3MM **Privately Held**
WEB: www.soprema.us
SIC: 3069 Roofing, membrane rubber
PA: Holding Soprema
14 Rue De Saint Nazaire
Strasbourg 67100
388 798-400

(G-19278)
SROUFE HEALTHCARE PRODUCTS LLC
961 Seville Rd (44281-8316)
PHONE 260 894-4171
Jeff Wells,
Roger L Niles,
Jon W Sroufe,
Cynthia L Wells,
Jeffrey C Wells,
▲ **EMP:** 25 **EST:** 1974
SQ FT: 76,800
SALES (est): 4.1MM **Privately Held**
WEB: www.sroufe.com
SIC: 3842 2396 Orthopedic appliances; screen printing on fabric articles

(G-19279)
WADSWORTH BREWING COMPANY LLC
186 Humbolt Ave (44281-2115)
PHONE 330 475-4935
Brian Joy, *Principal*
EMP: 3 **EST:** 2016
SALES (est): 74.2K **Privately Held**
SIC: 2082 Malt beverages

(G-19280)
WARNER FABRICATING INC
7812 Hartman Rd (44281-8744)
PHONE 330 848-3191
James Warner, *CEO*
Mark Warner, *President*
EMP: 10 **EST:** 1977
SQ FT: 12,000

SALES (est): 722.5K **Privately Held**
WEB: www.warnersummit.com
SIC: 3444 Sheet metalwork

(G-19281)
WESTERN ROTO ENGRAVERS INC
Also Called: Wre Color Tech
668 Seville Rd (44281-1080)
PHONE 330 336-7636
Dean Ellebruch, *Manager*
EMP: 30
SQ FT: 11,000
SALES (corp-wide): 13.8MM **Privately Held**
WEB: www.wrecolor.com
SIC: 2754 2791 2759 Rotogravure printing; typesetting; commercial printing
PA: Western Roto Engravers, Incorporated
533 Banner Ave
Greensboro NC 27401
336 275-9821

Wakeman
Huron County

(G-19282)
CAMMANN INC
7105 State Route 60 (44889-8510)
P.O. Box 219, Birmingham (44816-0219)
PHONE 440 965-4051
Henry Cammann, *CEO*
Fred W Cammann IV, *Vice Pres*
▲ **EMP:** 10 **EST:** 1946
SALES (est): 1.9MM **Privately Held**
WEB: www.cammann.com
SIC: 3559 3823 3624 3549 Chemical machinery & equipment; industrial instrmnts msrmnt display/control process variable; carbon & graphite products; metalworking machinery; machine tools, metal cutting type

(G-19283)
CUSTOM CHASSIS INC
52826 State Route 303 (44889-9537)
PHONE 440 839-5574
Matthew Tipple, *President*
Michael Huhn, *Vice Pres*
Jack Schartman, *Admin Sec*
▲ **EMP:** 9
SQ FT: 13,000
SALES (est): 1.2MM **Privately Held**
WEB: www.customchassisinc.com
SIC: 3711 Chassis, motor vehicle

(G-19284)
DURAFLOW INDUSTRIES INC
15706 Garfield Rd (44889-8439)
P.O. Box 574 (44889-0574)
PHONE 440 965-5047
Mark Sliman, *Principal*
Anne Sliman, *CFO*
EMP: 8
SALES (est): 938.1K **Privately Held**
SIC: 3999 Barber & beauty shop equipment

(G-19285)
KRAUSHER MACHINING INC
4267 Butler Rd (44889-8212)
PHONE 440 839-2828
Dale K Krausher, *President*
Jeffrey Krausher, *Prdtn Mgr*
Barbara Krausher, *CFO*
EMP: 8
SQ FT: 10,000
SALES (est): 1.2MM **Privately Held**
WEB: www.krausher.com
SIC: 3451 Screw machine products

(G-19286)
LAKEWOOD STEEL INC
13616 State Route 113 (44889)
PHONE 440 965-4226
CAM Drennen, *President*
EMP: 10 **EST:** 1973
SQ FT: 12,000
SALES (est): 3.7MM **Privately Held**
SIC: 5051 3498 Steel; fabricated pipe & fittings

(G-19287)
M A HARRISON MFG CO INC
14307 State Route 113 (44889-8320)
PHONE 440 965-4306
Chad A Harrison, *President*
James Harrison, *Chairman*
Keith Harris, *Vice Pres*
Dave Knowles, *Senior Engr*
Walter Denham, *CFO*
EMP: 20
SQ FT: 1,544
SALES (est): 1MM **Privately Held**
WEB: www.maharrisonmfg.com
SIC: 3545 3366 Precision tools, machinists'; castings (except die): copper & copper-base alloy; brass foundry

(G-19288)
PAKK SYSTEMS LLC
39 W Main St (44889-9701)
P.O. Box 22 (44889-0022)
PHONE 440 839-9999
Adam Frey,
EMP: 6
SQ FT: 4,000
SALES (est): 550K **Privately Held**
SIC: 3545 1799 Machine tool accessories; hydraulic equipment, installation & service

(G-19289)
SUNRISE COOPERATIVE INC
1981 Fitchville River Rd (44889-9326)
PHONE 419 929-1568
Jeni Riley, *Opers Mgr*
Pat Fannin, *Manager*
EMP: 12
SALES (corp-wide): 56.3MM **Privately Held**
SIC: 2041 5999 Grain mills (except rice); feed & farm supply
PA: Sunrise Cooperative, Inc.
2025 W State St Ste A
Fremont OH 43420
419 332-6468

(G-19290)
WOODWORKS FOR YOU
465 W River Rd (44889)
PHONE 440 277-8147
Bruce Bales, *Owner*
EMP: 3
SALES (est): 500K **Privately Held**
SIC: 2541 Cabinets, except refrigerated: show, display, etc.: wood

---

Walbridge
Wood County

(G-19291)
AIRTECH
6898 Commodore Dr (43465-9765)
PHONE 419 269-1000
Kurt Lang, *Principal*
EMP: 3
SALES (est): 404.2K **Privately Held**
SIC: 3563 Air & gas compressors

(G-19292)
AK TUBE LLC (DH)
30400 E Broadway St (43465-9568)
PHONE 419 661-4150
Richard Brown, *Safety Dir*
Tom Greco, *Mfg Mgr*
Nathan Goode, *Safety Mgr*
Cheryl Borro, *Purch Mgr*
Stacy Clark, *Purch Agent*
▼ **EMP:** 207 **EST:** 2001
SQ FT: 330,000
SALES (est): 38.7MM **Publicly Held**
WEB: www.aktube.com
SIC: 3317 Steel pipe & tubes
HQ: Ak Steel Corporation
9227 Centre Pointe Dr
West Chester OH 45069
513 425-4200

(G-19293)
FISHER METAL FABRICATING
27953 E Broadway St (43465-9408)
PHONE 419 838-7200
Pam Manuel, *Principal*
EMP: 14

▲ = Import ▼ = Export
◆ = Import/Export

GEOGRAPHIC SECTION — Walton Hills - Cuyahoga County (G-19316)

SALES (est): 2.4MM **Privately Held**
SIC: 3499 Fabricated metal products

(G-19294)
GREAT LAKES WINDOW INC
30499 Tracy Rd (43465-9794)
P.O. Box 1896, Toledo (43603-1896)
PHONE..................................419 666-5555
Lynn Morstadt, *President*
Sharon Maxfield-Weiric, *Manager*
EMP: 600
SQ FT: 170,000
SALES (est): 80.9MM
SALES (corp-wide): 2B **Publicly Held**
WEB: www.greatlakeswindow.com
SIC: 3089 5211 Windows, plastic; doors, folding: plastic or plastic coated fabric; lumber & other building materials
HQ: Ply Gem Industries, Inc.
5020 Weston Pkwy Ste 400
Cary NC 27513
919 677-3900

(G-19295)
JET TOOL AND PROTOTYPE CO
230 W Perry St (43465-1028)
PHONE..................................419 666-1199
Julius Toth, *President*
David Toth, *Vice Pres*
EMP: 4
SQ FT: 4,400
SALES (est): 449.8K **Privately Held**
SIC: 3544 Special dies & tools

(G-19296)
JONES-HAMILTON CO (PA)
30354 Tracy Rd (43465-9792)
PHONE..................................419 666-9838
J Kern Hamilton, *Ch of Bd*
Robert L James, *President*
Ken Jones, *Division Mgr*
Robert Taylor, *Business Mgr*
Charlie Wheeler, *Business Mgr*
◆ EMP: 90
SALES: 85.2MM **Privately Held**
WEB: www.jones-hamilton.com
SIC: 2819 Hydrochloric acid; sodium sulfate, glauber's salt, salt cake; sulfuric acid, oleum

(G-19297)
MSC WALBRIDGE COATINGS INC
Also Called: Walbridge Coatings
30610 E Broadway St (43465-9791)
PHONE..................................419 666-6130
Patrick Murley, *CEO*
EMP: 120
SQ FT: 400,000
SALES (est): 37.6MM **Privately Held**
WEB: www.mscwalbridgecoatings.com
SIC: 3316 3479 Cold finishing of steel shapes; galvanizing of iron, steel or end-formed products
HQ: Material Sciences Corporation
6855 Commerce Blvd
Canton MI 48187
734 207-4444

(G-19298)
RESOURCE MECHANICAL INSUL LLC
6842 Commodore Dr (43465-9765)
PHONE..................................248 577-0200
EMP: 45 EST: 2008
SALES: 6MM
SALES (corp-wide): 567.7MM **Privately Held**
SIC: 3644 Mfg Nonconductive Wiring Devices
HQ: Gem Industrial Inc.
6842 Commodore Dr
Walbridge OH 43465
419 666-6554

(G-19299)
RIVERSIDE MCH & AUTOMTN INC
Also Called: Assembly Division
28701 E Broadway St (43465-9625)
PHONE..................................419 855-8308
Amy Millner, *Branch Mgr*
Denny Meyer, *Manager*
EMP: 7

SALES (corp-wide): 9.7MM **Privately Held**
SIC: 3549 Assembly machines, including robotic
PA: Riverside Machine & Automation, Inc.
1240 N Genoa Clay Ctr Rd
Genoa OH 43430
419 855-8308

(G-19300)
WESTERN STATES ENVELOPE CO
Also Called: Western States Envelope Label
6859 Commodore Dr (43465-9765)
PHONE..................................419 666-7480
Shelly Hinkle, *Manager*
EMP: 70
SALES (corp-wide): 203.2MM **Privately Held**
WEB: www.westernstatesenvelope.com
SIC: 5112 2677 Envelopes; envelopes
PA: Western States Envelope Company
4480 N 132nd St
Butler WI 53007
262 781-5540

(G-19301)
Z3 CONTROLS LLC
27962 E Broadway St (43465-9722)
PHONE..................................419 261-2654
Timothy J Zemenski, *Principal*
EMP: 4
SALES (est): 512.9K **Privately Held**
SIC: 3625 Relays & industrial controls

Waldo
Marion County

(G-19302)
CUSTOM CRETE
6928 Gillette Rd (43356-9117)
PHONE..................................740 726-2433
Terry Lowe, *Owner*
EMP: 5
SALES (est): 280K **Privately Held**
SIC: 3444 Sheet metalwork

(G-19303)
NWP MANUFACTURING INC
Also Called: N W P Manufacturing
2862 County Road 146 (43356-9122)
PHONE..................................419 894-6871
John E Werner III, *President*
John Werner, *President*
Jerry Keiesel, *Vice Pres*
EMP: 10
SQ FT: 36,000
SALES (est): 1.1MM **Privately Held**
SIC: 2842 2448 Sweeping compounds, oil or water absorbent, clay or sawdust; pallets, wood

(G-19304)
OHIGRO INC (PA)
6720 Gillette Rd (43356)
P.O. Box 196 (43356-0196)
PHONE..................................740 726-2429
Jerry Ward, *President*
Jerry A Ward, *President*
James H Ward, *Vice Pres*
David Fierbaugh, *Plant Mgr*
Jeffrey Schweinfurth, *Plant Mgr*
EMP: 36
SQ FT: 9,600
SALES: 12.9MM **Privately Held**
WEB: www.ohigro.com
SIC: 5191 5261 2875 0723 Fertilizer & fertilizer materials; fertilizer; fertilizers, mixing only; crop preparation services for market

Walhonding
Coshocton County

(G-19305)
DUGAN DRILLING INCORPORATED
27238 New Guilford Rd (43843-9612)
P.O. Box 91, Bladensburg (43005-0091)
PHONE..................................740 668-3811

Guy E Dugan, *President*
Linda Dugan, *Admin Sec*
EMP: 9
SALES: 400K **Privately Held**
SIC: 1381 Drilling oil & gas wells

(G-19306)
ELSAAN ENERGY LLC
26100 Township Road 52 (43843-9768)
PHONE..................................740 294-9399
M Dean Ringwalt, *Principal*
EMP: 6
SALES (est): 424.2K **Privately Held**
SIC: 1389 Oil & gas wells: building, repairing & dismantling

Walnut Creek
Holmes County

(G-19307)
MAST FARM SERVICE LTD
3585 State Rte 39 (44687)
P.O. Box 142 (44687-0142)
PHONE..................................330 893-2972
Eli Mast Jr, *Owner*
Joy Yutzy, *Principal*
EMP: 35
SALES (est): 3.7MM **Privately Held**
SIC: 3499 Fire- or burglary-resistive products

(G-19308)
WALNUT CREEK CHOCOLATE COMPANY
Also Called: Coblentz Chocolate Co
4917 State Rte 515 (44687)
PHONE..................................330 893-2995
Jason Coblentz, *President*
Amy Yoder, *Mktg Dir*
EMP: 25
SQ FT: 2,000
SALES (est): 4.6MM **Privately Held**
SIC: 2064 2066 5149 5441 Chocolate covered dates; fruit, chocolate covered (except dates); chocolate candy, solid; chocolate; candy

Walton Hills
Cuyahoga County

(G-19309)
CONTROLLIX CORPORATION
Also Called: Walton Hills
21415 Alexander Rd (44146-5512)
PHONE..................................440 232-8757
John Kelly, *CEO*
Theresa Szalkowski, *Project Mgr*
Cynthia Burry, *Controller*
EMP: 15
SQ FT: 18,000
SALES (est): 4.9MM **Privately Held**
WEB: www.controllix.com
SIC: 3625 5063 Industrial electrical relays & switches; switches, electric power; electric controls & control accessories, industrial; electrical apparatus & equipment

(G-19310)
DUNHAM PRODUCTS INC
7400 Northfield Rd (44146-6108)
PHONE..................................440 232-0885
Joseph F Klukan, *CEO*
Mike Rose, *General Mgr*
Rosemary Klukan, *Corp Secy*
Nick Mann, *Natl Sales Mgr*
Jennifer Somerville, *Sales Mgr*
EMP: 15 EST: 1946
SQ FT: 7,700
SALES (est): 3.6MM **Privately Held**
WEB: www.dunhamproducts.com
SIC: 3451 Screw machine products

(G-19311)
INTIGRAL INC (PA)
Also Called: Est
7850 Northfield Rd (44146-5523)
PHONE..................................440 439-0980
Jason Thomas, *President*
Jim Prete, *Exec VP*
Dick Dietrich, *Vice Pres*
Richard Dietrich, *Vice Pres*

Edmond Leopold, *Vice Pres*
▲ EMP: 200
SQ FT: 158,000
SALES (est): 51.7MM **Privately Held**
WEB: www.edgeseal.com
SIC: 3231 Insulating glass: made from purchased glass

(G-19312)
MASON STRUCTURAL STEEL INC
Also Called: Mason Steel
7500 Northfield Rd (44146-6187)
PHONE..................................440 439-1040
Leonard N Polster, *CEO*
Keith Polster, *President*
J Moldaver, *Principal*
Joseph Patchan, *Principal*
Sol W Wyman, *Principal*
EMP: 100 EST: 1958
SQ FT: 75,000
SALES (est): 30.1MM **Privately Held**
WEB: www.masonsteel.com
SIC: 3441 5031 5074 Fabricated structural metal; doors & windows; window frames, all materials; fireplaces, prefabricated

(G-19313)
POLYMER ADDITIVES INC
7050 Krick Rd (44146-4416)
PHONE..................................216 262-7016
EMP: 4 **Privately Held**
SIC: 5169 2899 Chemicals & allied products; chemical preparations; fire retardant chemicals
HQ: Polymer Additives, Inc.
7500 E Pleasant Valley Rd
Independence OH 44131
216 875-7200

(G-19314)
RAE SYSTEMS INC
7307 Young Dr Ste B (44146-5385)
PHONE..................................440 232-0555
EMP: 3
SALES (corp-wide): 41.8B **Publicly Held**
SIC: 3829 3812 3699 Gas detectors; search & detection systems & instruments; security control equipment & systems
HQ: Rae Systems Inc.
1349 Moffett Park Dr
Sunnyvale CA 94089
408 952-8200

(G-19315)
TRANSTAR HOLDING COMPANY (PA)
7350 Young Dr (44146-5357)
PHONE..................................800 359-3339
Monte Ahuja, *Chairman*
Mark A Kirk, *Vice Pres*
Stephen B Perry, *Vice Pres*
Jeffrey R Marshall, *CFO*
Sharon Ann Milcinovic, *Executive Asst*
EMP: 6
SALES (est): 708.4MM **Privately Held**
SIC: 3444 3281 2952 Metal roofing & roof drainage equipment; cut stone & stone products; asphalt felts & coatings

(G-19316)
VALTRIS SPECIALTY CHEMICALS
7050 Krick Rd (44146-4416)
PHONE..................................216 875-7200
Paul Angus, *CEO*
Richard Catchpole, *President*
Brenda Hollo, *Vice Pres*
Steve Hughes, *Vice Pres*
Jim Mason, *Vice Pres*
EMP: 8
SALES (est): 374K **Privately Held**
SIC: 2899 Chemical preparations

Wapakoneta
Auglaize County

(G-19317)
ADVANCED MACHINE SOLUTIONS LLC
08764 County Road 33a (45895-9577)
PHONE.....................419 733-2537
Jeremy Homan,
Jerry Sawmiller,
Mike Sawmiller,
EMP: 4
SQ FT: 2,000
SALES (est): 575.9K **Privately Held**
SIC: 3599 Machine shop, jobbing & repair

(G-19318)
AMERICAN TRIM LLC
217 Krein Ave (45895)
PHONE.....................419 739-4349
Aaron Art, *Plant Engr*
Randy Fosnaugh, *Branch Mgr*
EMP: 100
SALES (corp-wide): 445.1MM **Privately Held**
SIC: 3469 Porcelain enameled products & utensils
HQ: American Trim, L.L.C.
1005 W Grand Ave
Lima OH 45801

(G-19319)
AMERICAN TRIM LLC
713 Maple St (45895-2323)
PHONE.....................419 738-9664
Mike Staddon, *Branch Mgr*
Dave Stewart, *Supervisor*
EMP: 100
SALES (corp-wide): 445.1MM **Privately Held**
SIC: 3469 Porcelain enameled products & utensils
HQ: American Trim, L.L.C.
1005 W Grand Ave
Lima OH 45801

(G-19320)
AMETEK INC
Westchester Plastics Division
14097 Cemetery Rd (45895)
P.O. Box 385 (45895-0385)
PHONE.....................419 739-3202
Morris Molinero, *Principal*
M Molinero, *Vice Pres*
Scott Trochim, *Prdtn Mgr*
Lew Modice, *Safety Mgr*
David Sigler, *Mfg Staff*
EMP: 150
SALES (corp-wide): 4.8B **Publicly Held**
SIC: 3089 Plastic hardware & building products
PA: Ametek, Inc.
1100 Cassatt Rd
Berwyn PA 19312
610 647-2121

(G-19321)
AMETEK INC
Also Called: Ametek Westchester Plastics
14101 Cemetery Rd (45895)
PHONE.....................419 739-3200
Ron Gasior, *Manager*
EMP: 15
SALES (corp-wide): 4.8B **Publicly Held**
SIC: 2821 Plastics materials & resins
PA: Ametek, Inc.
1100 Cassatt Rd
Berwyn PA 19312
610 647-2121

(G-19322)
ARMIN R JEWETT
607 N Water St (45895-9379)
PHONE.....................419 647-6644
EMP: 3
SALES: 50K **Privately Held**
SIC: 2499 Mfg Wood Products

(G-19323)
AUGLAIZE WELDING COMPANY INC
106 N Water St (45895-1696)
PHONE.....................419 738-4422
D A Rummel, *President*
Marjorie Rummel, *Corp Secy*
EMP: 3
SQ FT: 2,500
SALES: 120K **Privately Held**
SIC: 7692 Welding repair

(G-19324)
BECKERMILLS INC
15286 State Route 67 (45895-9121)
PHONE.....................419 738-3450
Jim L Becker, *Principal*
EMP: 3
SALES (est): 382.2K **Privately Held**
SIC: 3565 Aerating machines, for beverages

(G-19325)
BORNHORST PRINTING COMPANY INC
10139 County Road 25a (45895-8360)
PHONE.....................419 738-5901
Glenn Bornhorst, *President*
Terri Bornhorst, *Corp Secy*
EMP: 7
SQ FT: 5,200
SALES: 500K **Privately Held**
WEB: www.bornhorstprinting.com
SIC: 2752 Commercial printing, offset

(G-19326)
CBR INDUSTRIAL LLC
20086 Wapakoneta Cridersv (45895-7641)
PHONE.....................419 645-6447
Rickie Lotz,
EMP: 4
SALES (est): 47.4K **Privately Held**
SIC: 7349 3443 3444 7389 Building & office cleaning services; office cleaning or charring; chutes & troughs; sheet metalwork;

(G-19327)
CREATIVE CURBING AMERICA LLC
1634 Springfield Ave (45895-9483)
PHONE.....................419 738-7668
Robin William Rosser, *Administration*
EMP: 3
SALES (est): 179K **Privately Held**
SIC: 3272 Well curbing, concrete

(G-19328)
FENIX LLC (HQ)
820 Willipie St (45895-9201)
PHONE.....................419 739-3400
Steven Wray, *President*
Kevin G Shumaker, *CFO*
Douglas Stearns, *VP Sales*
▲ **EMP:** 11
SQ FT: 141,000
SALES (est): 8MM **Privately Held**
WEB: www.Fenixllc.com
SIC: 3315 Wire products, ferrous/iron: made in wiredrawing plants

(G-19329)
G A WINTZER AND SON COMPANY
12279 S Dixey Hwy (45895)
P.O. Box 406 (45895-0406)
PHONE.....................419 739-4913
Jim Keack, *General Mgr*
EMP: 70
SALES (corp-wide): 25.2MM **Privately Held**
WEB: www.gawintzer.com
SIC: 2048 Feeds from meat & from meat & vegetable meals
PA: G. A. Wintzer And Son Company
204 W Auglaize St
Wapakoneta OH 45895
419 739-4900

(G-19330)
GENERAL ALUMINUM MFG COMPANY
Also Called: Wapakoneta Plant
13663 Short Rd (45895-8362)
PHONE.....................419 739-9300
Tina Burd, *Purchasing*
Ken Stakas, *Manager*
John Vandersall, *Manager*
EMP: 170
SALES (corp-wide): 1.6B **Publicly Held**
WEB: www.generalaluminum.com
SIC: 3363 3494 3322 3321 Aluminum die-castings; valves & pipe fittings; plumbing & heating valves; malleable iron foundries; cast iron pipe & fittings; motor vehicle parts & accessories; wheels, motor vehicle; motor vehicle brake systems & parts; motor vehicle body components & frame; aerospace investment castings, ferrous
HQ: General Aluminum Mfg. Company
6065 Parkland Blvd
Cleveland OH 44124
330 297-1225

(G-19331)
HOMESTRETCH INC
203 E Auglaize St (45895)
PHONE.....................419 738-6604
Donna Pest, *President*
EMP: 4
SALES (est): 264.1K **Privately Held**
SIC: 2759 Screen printing

(G-19332)
HORIZON OHIO PUBLICATIONS INC
Also Called: Shelby County Review
520 Industrial Dr (45895-9200)
P.O. Box 389 (45895-0389)
PHONE.....................419 738-2128
Deb Wez, *Branch Mgr*
Melissa Bartlett, *Manager*
EMP: 32
SALES (corp-wide): 71.5MM **Privately Held**
SIC: 2711 2759 2752 Commercial printing & newspaper publishing combined; commercial printing; commercial printing, lithographic
HQ: Horizon Ohio Publications Inc
102 E Spring St
Saint Marys OH 45885
419 394-7414

(G-19333)
HORIZON PUBLICATIONS INC
Also Called: Wapakoneta Daily News
520 Industrial Dr (45895-9200)
PHONE.....................419 738-2128
Deb Zwez, *Branch Mgr*
EMP: 46
SALES (corp-wide): 71.5MM **Privately Held**
WEB: www.malvern-online.com
SIC: 2711 Newspapers, publishing & printing
PA: Horizon Publications, Inc.
1120 N Carbon St Ste 100
Marion IL 62959
618 993-1711

(G-19334)
INGREDIA INC
Also Called: I D I
625 Commerce Rd (45895-8265)
PHONE.....................419 738-4060
Gilles Desgrousilliers, *CEO*
Andrea Hale, *QC Mgr*
Sandrine Delory, *Treasurer*
Kevin Rutter, *Finance Dir*
Sarah Baudry, *Sales Staff*
◆ **EMP:** 23
SQ FT: 39,000
SALES (est): 7.3MM
SALES (corp-wide): 132.4MM **Privately Held**
WEB: www.ingredia.com
SIC: 2023 Dry, condensed, evaporated dairy products
HQ: Ingredia
51 Avenue Fernand Lobbedez
Arras 62000
321 238-000

(G-19335)
JEWETT SUPPLY
Also Called: Barlamy Supply
607 N Water St (45895-9379)
PHONE.....................419 738-9882
Rife Jewett, *Partner*
Lisa Hardeman, *Partner*
Amy Jewett, *Partner*
Lori Jewett, *Partner*
Lynn Jewett, *Partner*
EMP: 12
SQ FT: 768
SALES: 90K **Privately Held**
SIC: 2499 Handles, poles, dowels & stakes: wood

(G-19336)
JUDY DUBOIS
Also Called: Auglaize Embroidery Co
4 N Wood St (45895-1660)
PHONE.....................419 738-6979
Judy Dubois, *Owner*
EMP: 3
SALES (est): 184.2K **Privately Held**
SIC: 2395 Embroidery products, except schiffli machine

(G-19337)
KINSTLE TRUCK & AUTO SVC INC
Also Called: Kinstle Ster/West Star Truck C
1770 Wapak Fisher Rd (45895-9799)
P.O. Box 1986 (45895-0986)
PHONE.....................419 738-7493
Toll Free:.....................888 -
J Michael Kinstle, *President*
Barbara Kinstle, *Corp Secy*
EMP: 14
SQ FT: 10,500
SALES (est): 3.1MM **Privately Held**
SIC: 5012 5511 7538 3519 Truck tractors; trucks, tractors & trailers: new & used; truck engine repair, except industrial; general truck repair; engines, diesel & semi-diesel or dual-fuel; governors, diesel engine

(G-19338)
KN RUBBER LLC (HQ)
Also Called: Koneta Rubber
1400 Lunar Dr (45895-9796)
P.O. Box 150 (45895-0150)
PHONE.....................419 739-4200
Rex Mouland, *Controller*
John B Kepler,
◆ **EMP:** 155
SQ FT: 165,000
SALES (est): 93.8MM
SALES (corp-wide): 275.1MM **Privately Held**
WEB: www.koneta.com
SIC: 3069 Rubber automotive products
PA: Kinderhook Industries, Llc
505 5th Ave Fl 25
New York NY 10017
212 201-6780

(G-19339)
KONETA INC
1400 Lunar Dr (45895-9796)
P.O. Box 150 (45895-0150)
PHONE.....................419 739-4200
Christopher Keogh, *CEO*
Corwynne Carruthers, *Vice Pres*
Thomas Tuttle, *Vice Pres*
Dave Landers, *QC Mgr*
Myra Hanenkratt, *Controller*
▼ **EMP:** 90
SALES: 23MM **Privately Held**
SIC: 3061 Automotive rubber goods (mechanical)

(G-19340)
M B INDUSTRIES INC
310 Commerce Rd (45895-8343)
PHONE.....................419 738-4769
Mike Borges, *Branch Mgr*
EMP: 8
SALES (est): 993.1K **Privately Held**
SIC: 2992 Lubricating oils
PA: M B Industries Inc
11158 Infirmary Rd
Wapakoneta OH 45895

(G-19341)
M B INDUSTRIES INC (PA)
11158 Infirmary Rd (45895-9413)
PHONE.....................419 738-4769
Michael Borges, *President*
EMP: 4
SALES (est): 518.9K **Privately Held**
WEB: www.mbind.com
SIC: 3548 2992 Welding & cutting apparatus & accessories; cutting oils, blending: made from purchased materials

GEOGRAPHIC SECTION
Warren - Trumbull County (G-19370)

(G-19342)
MIDWEST COMPOSITES LLC
302 Krein Ave (45895-2375)
PHONE 419 738-2431
Vern Peak,
EMP: 20
SALES (est): 2.3MM **Privately Held**
SIC: 2231 3229 Upholstery fabrics, wool; glass fiber products

(G-19343)
MIDWEST ELASTOMERS INC
Also Called: MEI
700 Industrial Dr (45895-9200)
P.O. Box 412 (45895-0412)
PHONE 419 738-8844
George Wight, *President*
Ron Clark, *President*
Bill Jacobs, *Principal*
Karen Jacobs, *Principal*
Evan Piland, *Principal*
▲ **EMP:** 65 **EST:** 1986
SQ FT: 56,000
SALES (est): 18MM **Privately Held**
WEB: www.midwestelastomers.com
SIC: 2822 3069 Synthetic rubber; reclaimed rubber (reworked by manufacturing processes)

(G-19344)
MIDWEST METAL FABRICATORS
712 Maple St (45895-2324)
PHONE 419 739-7077
Verne E Peake, *Partner*
Jason Neumann, *Partner*
John Neumann, *Partner*
EMP: 10
SQ FT: 15,500
SALES (est): 1.6MM **Privately Held**
WEB: www.mw-metal.com
SIC: 3444 Sheet metal specialties, not stamped

(G-19345)
MIDWEST METAL FABRICATORS
712 Maple St (45895-2324)
PHONE 419 739-7077
Berne Peake,
EMP: 11
SALES (est): 760K **Privately Held**
SIC: 3444 Sheet metalwork

(G-19346)
MIDWEST SPECIALTIES INC
Also Called: Flexarm
851 Industrial Dr (45895-9243)
PHONE 419 738-8147
Richard D Kennedy, *President*
Penny Kentosh, *Admin Sec*
EMP: 13
SQ FT: 46,000
SALES: 3.5MM **Privately Held**
WEB: www.flexarminc.com
SIC: 3541 3599 3271 Tapping machines; machine shop, jobbing & repair; concrete block & brick

(G-19347)
NATIONAL LIME AND STONE CO
18430 Main Street Rd (45895-9400)
PHONE 419 657-6745
Shaun Place, *Manager*
EMP: 9
SALES (corp-wide): 3.2B **Privately Held**
WEB: www.natlime.com
SIC: 1422 3281 Crushed & broken limestone; limestone, cut & shaped
PA: The National Lime And Stone Company
551 Lake Cascade Pkwy
Findlay OH 45840
419 422-4341

(G-19348)
OEN CUSTOM CABINETS INC
Also Called: Oen Kitchen & Bath Showroom
8 Willipie St (45895-1969)
PHONE 419 738-8115
Ralph J Oen, *President*
Danielle M Oen, *Vice Pres*
EMP: 3
SALES (est): 476.7K **Privately Held**
SIC: 2434 Wood kitchen cabinets

(G-19349)
ROCK LINE PRODUCTS INC
401 Industrial Dr (45895-9234)
PHONE 419 738-4400
Lynn Gerstner, *Branch Mgr*
EMP: 5
SALES (est): 384.1K
SALES (corp-wide): 1.4MM **Privately Held**
SIC: 3715 Truck trailers
PA: Rock Line Products Inc.
1480 Arrow Hwy
La Verne CA 91750
909 392-2170

(G-19350)
ROY HOLTZAPPLE JOHN JOHNS
18526 Williams Rd (45895-7825)
PHONE 419 657-2460
EMP: 4
SALES (est): 260K **Privately Held**
SIC: 2431 Mfg Millwork

(G-19351)
SA-MOR SIGNS
185 Kindle St (45895-8633)
PHONE 937 441-4950
Don Sleven, *Owner*
EMP: 3
SALES (est): 271.9K **Privately Held**
SIC: 3993 Signs & advertising specialties

(G-19352)
SAFE-GRAIN INC
Also Called: Safe Grain Max Tronix
902 N Dixie Hwy (45895-7738)
PHONE 513 398-2500
Greg Stevens, *Director*
EMP: 8
SQ FT: 5,000
SALES (corp-wide): 3.4MM **Privately Held**
SIC: 3523 Farm machinery & equipment
PA: Safe-Grain, Inc.
417 Wards Corner Rd Ste B
Loveland OH 45140
513 398-2500

(G-19353)
SENECA WIRE GROUP INC (PA)
820 Willipie St (45895-9201)
PHONE 419 435-9261
Steven Wray, *President*
Kevin G Shumaker, *CFO*
Douglas Stearns, *VP Sales*
EMP: 3
SALES (est): 11.3MM **Privately Held**
SIC: 3315 Wire products, ferrous/iron: made in wiredrawing plants

(G-19354)
SIMPLY ELEGANT FORMALS INC
708 N Dixie Hwy (45895-7750)
P.O. Box 127 (45895-0127)
PHONE 419 738-7722
Brenda Johns, *Principal*
EMP: 3 **EST:** 2008
SALES (est): 301.7K **Privately Held**
SIC: 2311 Tuxedos: made from purchased materials

(G-19355)
STEVE HENDERSON
1311 Lincoln Hwy (45895-9346)
PHONE 419 738-6999
EMP: 3
SALES (est): 160K **Privately Held**
SIC: 2411 Logging

(G-19356)
T & S MACHINE INC
712 Maple St (45895-2324)
P.O. Box 579, Ottoville (45876-0579)
PHONE 419 453-2101
David Kriegel, *President*
William G Petty, *President*
Todd Kriegel, *Vice Pres*
EMP: 18
SQ FT: 2,129
SALES (est): 2.3MM **Privately Held**
WEB: www.tsmachine.com
SIC: 3599 Machine shop, jobbing & repair

(G-19357)
UNITED BUFF & SUPPLY CO INC
2 E Harrison St (45895-1551)
P.O. Box 373 (45895-0373)
PHONE 419 738-2417
Cora F Slife, *President*
EMP: 8 **EST:** 1958
SQ FT: 17,000
SALES (est): 710.1K **Privately Held**
SIC: 3291 Buffing or polishing wheels, abrasive or nonabrasive

(G-19358)
VMAXX INC
323 Commerce Rd (45895-8373)
P.O. Box 36, Dover (44622-0036)
PHONE 419 738-4044
Darren Meyer, *President*
Mark Meyer, *Vice Pres*
Scott Stiles, *Treasurer*
EMP: 10
SQ FT: 20,000
SALES (est): 1.2MM **Privately Held**
WEB: www.vmaxx.biz
SIC: 3542 Extruding machines (machine tools), metal

(G-19359)
WAPAK TOOL & DIE INC
732 Keller Dr (45895-9341)
PHONE 419 738-6215
Robert H Kantner, *President*
Donald G Kantner, *Corp Secy*
EMP: 4 **EST:** 1964
SALES (est): 300K **Privately Held**
SIC: 3544 Special dies & tools

(G-19360)
WHITE FEATHER FOODS INC
Also Called: Whitefeather Foods
13845 Cemetery Rd (45895-8479)
PHONE 419 738-8975
Stephen L Hengstler, *President*
Dave Jeanneret, *Controller*
EMP: 14
SQ FT: 5,000
SALES: 1MM **Privately Held**
WEB: www.whitefeatherfoods.com
SIC: 2096 2099 Pork rinds; food preparations

(G-19361)
ZIEGLER BROS TOOL & MCH INC
Also Called: Ziegler Brothers Tool & Mch
13790 Infirmary Rd (45895-9358)
PHONE 419 738-6048
Aretha Ziegler, *President*
EMP: 7
SQ FT: 5,000
SALES (est): 266.2K **Privately Held**
SIC: 3599 Machine shop, jobbing & repair

Warren
Trumbull County

(G-19362)
ADS MACHINERY CORP
1201 Vine Ave Ne Ste 1 (44483-3834)
P.O. Box 1027 (44482-1027)
PHONE 330 399-3601
Dale Minton, *President*
K Ramalingham, *Vice Pres*
Patricia S Beil, *CFO*
EMP: 75 **EST:** 1956
SQ FT: 57,000
SALES (est): 16.3MM **Privately Held**
WEB: www.adsmachinery.com
SIC: 3549 3547 Metalworking machinery; rolling mill machinery

(G-19363)
ADVANCED CUSTOM SOUND
1894 Elm Rd Ne (44483-4030)
PHONE 330 372-9900
Daniel Mezbethh, *Owner*
EMP: 8
SALES (est): 1.1MM **Privately Held**
SIC: 3651 Audio electronic systems

(G-19364)
AJAX TOCCO MAGNETHERMIC CORP (HQ)
1745 Overland Ave Ne (44483-2860)
PHONE 330 372-8511
Thomas Illencik, *President*
Chun Lee, *General Mgr*
Scott Tewell, *General Mgr*
Ron Akers, *Vice Pres*
Gerald Jackson, *Vice Pres*
◆ **EMP:** 200
SQ FT: 200,000
SALES (est): 18.8MM
SALES (corp-wide): 1.6B **Publicly Held**
WEB: www.ajaxtocco.com
SIC: 3567 7699 3612 Metal melting furnaces, industrial: electric; industrial machinery & equipment repair; electric furnace transformers
PA: Park-Ohio Holdings Corp.
6065 Parkland Blvd Ste 1
Cleveland OH 44124
440 947-2000

(G-19365)
ALAN BJ COMPANY
3566 Larchmont Ave Ne (44483-2400)
PHONE 330 372-1201
▲ **EMP:** 4
SALES (est): 649.3K **Privately Held**
SIC: 2899 Fireworks

(G-19366)
ALPHABET INC (HQ)
8640 E Market St (44484-2346)
PHONE 330 856-3366
Mark Tervalon, *President*
Cloyd Abruzzo, *Vice Pres*
Michael Jocola, *Vice Pres*
EMP: 100
SALES (est): 68.2MM
SALES (corp-wide): 866.2MM **Publicly Held**
WEB: www.alphabet.com
SIC: 3679 Harness assemblies for electronic use: wire or cable
PA: Stoneridge, Inc.
39675 Mackenzie Dr # 400
Novi MI 48377
248 489-9300

(G-19367)
AM WARREN LLC
Also Called: Arcelormittal Warren
2234 Main Ave Sw (44481)
PHONE 330 841-2800
Lou Schorsch, *CEO*
Joseph Magni, *Engineer*
Jeff Foster, *Manager*
EMP: 6
SALES (est): 139.5K **Privately Held**
SIC: 3312 Blast furnaces & steel mills

(G-19368)
AMERICAN STEEL & ALLOYS LLC
4000 Mahoning Ave Nw (44483-1924)
PHONE 330 847-0487
Mordechai Korf, *Principal*
EMP: 40
SALES (est): 5.7MM **Privately Held**
SIC: 3312 Tool & die steel & alloys

(G-19369)
AMERICAN WAY MANUFACTURING INC
1871 Henn Pkwy Sw (44481-8659)
P.O. Box 189, North Jackson (44451-0189)
PHONE 330 824-2353
Robert E Platt, *President*
▼ **EMP:** 27
SALES (est): 6.3MM **Privately Held**
WEB: www.americanwaymfg.com
SIC: 3089 Mfg Plastic Products

(G-19370)
AML INDUSTRIES INC
520 Pine Ave Se Ste 1 (44483-5763)
P.O. Box 4110 (44482-4110)
PHONE 330 399-5000
Terry L Kartzer, *President*
Robert Hartsough, *Vice Pres*
Joseph O'Toole, *Vice Pres*
▲ **EMP:** 26
SQ FT: 30,000

Warren - Trumbull County (G-19371) GEOGRAPHIC SECTION

SALES: 6.3MM **Privately Held**
WEB: www.amlube.com
SIC: 2992 Lubricating oils

(G-19371)
ANN PRINTING & PROMOTIONS
269 E Market St (44481-1205)
PHONE 330 399-6564
Tom Opalka, *Owner*
EMP: 3
SALES (est): 281.9K **Privately Held**
SIC: 2752 Commercial printing, offset

(G-19372)
APTIV SERVICES US LLC
Also Called: Delphi
4551 Research Prwy (44483)
PHONE 330 306-1000
Dennis Foley, *Senior Engr*
Robert Seidler, *Director*
EMP: 400
SALES (corp-wide): 16.6B **Privately Held**
WEB: www.delphiauto.com
SIC: 3714 Air conditioner parts, motor vehicle
HQ: Aptiv Services Us, Llc
   5725 Innovation Dr
   Troy MI 48098

(G-19373)
APTIV SERVICES US LLC
Also Called: Delphi
Larchmont North River Rd (44483)
PHONE 330 505-3150
Bill Coates, *Branch Mgr*
EMP: 120
SALES (corp-wide): 16.6B **Privately Held**
WEB: www.delphiauto.com
SIC: 3694 Engine electrical equipment
HQ: Aptiv Services Us, Llc
   5725 Innovation Dr
   Troy MI 48098

(G-19374)
BASELINE PRINTING INC
1262 Youngstown Rd Se (44484-4242)
PHONE 330 369-3204
Rey Collazo, *President*
Carolyn Collazo, *Treasurer*
EMP: 3 **EST:** 1970
SQ FT: 3,000
SALES: 320K **Privately Held**
SIC: 2752 Commercial printing, offset

(G-19375)
BEE JAX INC
156 Vermont Ave Sw (44485-2657)
PHONE 330 373-0500
Bill T Jackson Jr, *President*
Bill Jackson, *President*
EMP: 3
SALES (est): 667K **Privately Held**
SIC: 3545 Vises, machine (machine tool accessories)

(G-19376)
BEHLKE DALENE
Also Called: Ram Racewares
958 Tod Ave Nw (44485-2826)
PHONE 330 399-6780
Dalene Behlke, *Owner*
EMP: 3
SALES (est): 171.8K **Privately Held**
SIC: 3751 5013 Motorcycles, bicycles & parts; motorcycle parts

(G-19377)
BLOOM INDUSTRIES INC
Also Called: Incredible Plastics
1052 Mahoney Ave Nw (44483)
PHONE 330 898-3878
Ted E Bloom, *President*
EMP: 60
SQ FT: 95,000
SALES (est): 10.1MM **Privately Held**
SIC: 3089 3544 Injection molding of plastics; special dies, tools, jigs & fixtures

(G-19378)
BOSTON SCNTFIC NRMDLATION CORP
2174 Sarkies Dr Ne (44483-4262)
PHONE 330 372-2652
P A Martof, *Principal*
EMP: 154
SALES (corp-wide): 9.8B **Publicly Held**
SIC: 3841 Surgical & medical instruments
HQ: Boston Scientific Neuromodulation Corporation
   25155 Rye Canyon Loop
   Valencia CA 91355

(G-19379)
BUCKEYE MEDICAL TECH LLC
405 Niles Cortland Rd Se # 202 (44484-2460)
PHONE 330 719-9868
Terry B Philibin,
EMP: 7 **EST:** 2009
SALES (est): 288.9K **Privately Held**
SIC: 3841 Surgical & medical instruments

(G-19380)
BUDDY BACKYARD INC
140 Dana St Ne (44483-3845)
PHONE 330 393-9353
Jan Kiftler, *President*
▲ **EMP:** 25
SALES (est): 4.9MM **Privately Held**
SIC: 3559 Automotive related machinery

(G-19381)
CATTRON HOLDINGS INC (HQ)
655 N River Rd Nw Ste A (44483-2254)
PHONE 234 806-0018
Ryan Wooten, *CEO*
Martin Rapp, *President*
Michael Pearson, *Admin Sec*
EMP: 24
SALES (est): 21.3MM
SALES (corp-wide): 1.5B **Privately Held**
WEB: www.cattron.com
SIC: 3625 7622 5065 5063 Relays & industrial controls; communication equipment repair; communication equipment; closed circuit television; electric alarms & signaling equipment; equipment rental & leasing; hoists, cranes & monorails
PA: Harbour Group Ltd.
   7733 Forsyth Blvd Fl 23
   Saint Louis MO 63105
   314 727-5550

(G-19382)
CATTRON NORTH AMERICA INC (DH)
Also Called: Remtron
655 N River Rd Nw Ste A (44483-2254)
PHONE 234 806-0018
Ryan Wooten, *President*
Brian D'Angelo, *CFO*
Mike Santoni, *Treasurer*
◆ **EMP:** 95
SQ FT: 25,000
SALES (est): 21.3MM
SALES (corp-wide): 1.5B **Privately Held**
WEB: www.cattron-theimeg.com
SIC: 3625 Relays & industrial controls
HQ: Cattron Holdings, Inc
   655 N River Rd Nw Ste A
   Warren OH 44483
   234 806-0018

(G-19383)
CHARLES MFG CO
3021 Sferra Ave Nw (44483-2268)
PHONE 330 395-3490
David Frazier, *President*
Christine M Frazier, *Corp Secy*
EMP: 13
SQ FT: 10,000
SALES (est): 2.4MM **Privately Held**
WEB: www.charlesmfg.com
SIC: 3441 5039 Fabricated structural metal; architectural metalwork

(G-19384)
CLARKWESTERN DIETRICH BUILDING
Also Called: Clark Dietrich Building
1985 N River Rd Ne (44483-2527)
PHONE 330 372-5564
Bill Courtney, *Mng Member*
EMP: 10
SALES (corp-wide): 20.2B **Privately Held**
SIC: 3444 8711 3081 Studs & joists, sheet metal; engineering services; vinyl film & sheet
HQ: Clarkwestern Dietrich Building Systems Llc
   9050 Centre Pointe Dr
   West Chester OH 45069

(G-19385)
COLOR 3 EMBROIDERY INC
387 Chestnut Ave Ne (44483-5856)
P.O. Box 870 (44482-0870)
PHONE 330 652-9495
Traci Miller, *President*
Beth Kane, *General Mgr*
Don Wiley, *Vice Pres*
EMP: 8
SQ FT: 3,600
SALES (est): 412.5K **Privately Held**
WEB: www.color3.com
SIC: 2395 Embroidery products, except schiffli machine

(G-19386)
COMPUTER STITCH DESIGNS INC
1414 Henn Hyde Rd Ne (44484-1227)
PHONE 330 856-7826
Sam Argeras, *President*
Darlene Argeras, *Treasurer*
Donna Mc Guire, *Admin Sec*
EMP: 6
SALES: 350K **Privately Held**
SIC: 2395 Embroidery products, except schiffli machine; embroidery & art needlework

(G-19387)
CONDO INCORPORATED
3869 Niles Rd Se (44484-3548)
PHONE 330 609-6021
John Condoleon, *CEO*
EMP: 55
SQ FT: 40,000
SALES: 4MM **Privately Held**
WEB: www.warrenscrewmachine.com
SIC: 3451 Screw machine products

(G-19388)
CONLEY GROUP INC
Also Called: Concord Steel of Ohio
197 W Market St Ste 202 (44481-1024)
PHONE 330 372-2030
Paul Vessey, *Branch Mgr*
EMP: 9
SALES (est): 1.6MM
SALES (corp-wide): 20.8MM **Privately Held**
WEB: www.ibmoore.com
SIC: 5051 3471 Steel; plating & polishing
PA: Conley Group, Inc.
   21 Powder Hill Rd
   Lincoln RI 02865
   401 334-7756

(G-19389)
CONSOLIDATED CONTAINER CO
2880 Sferra Ave Nw (44483-2272)
PHONE 330 394-0905
EMP: 3
SALES (est): 107.6K **Privately Held**
SIC: 3089 Mfg Plastic Products

(G-19390)
CP METALS INC
2880 Sferra Ave Nw (44483-2272)
PHONE 724 510-4293
Joseph Patrick III, *President*
EMP: 4
SALES: 1MM **Privately Held**
SIC: 3399 Metal fasteners

(G-19391)
CSC LTD
4000 Mahoning Ave Nw (44483-1924)
PHONE 330 841-6011
Butch John, *Manager*
EMP: 4
SALES (est): 546.3K **Privately Held**
SIC: 3312 Blast furnaces & steel mills

(G-19392)
CURRENT INC
455 N River Rd Nw (44483-2250)
PHONE 330 392-5151
Todd Buratti, *CEO*
EMP: 8
SALES (corp-wide): 10.3MM **Privately Held**
WEB: www.currentcomposites.com
SIC: 2821 Thermosetting materials
PA: Current, Inc.
   30 Tyler Street Ext
   East Haven CT 06512
   203 469-1337

(G-19393)
D M V SUPPLY CORPORATION
Also Called: United Safety Authority
3047 Anderson Anthony (44481-9450)
PHONE 330 847-0450
Virginia Chicoine, *President*
David Chicoine, *Vice Pres*
Michael Chicoine, *Vice Pres*
EMP: 3
SQ FT: 2,200
SALES: 800K **Privately Held**
WEB: www.unitedsafetyauthority.com
SIC: 2672 5084 Tape, pressure sensitive: made from purchased materials; safety equipment

(G-19394)
DASHER LAWLESS AUTOMATION LLC
310 Dana St Ne (44483-3850)
PHONE 855 755-7275
Alex Mendikyan, *VP Finance*
Christopher Alan,
EMP: 28
SALES (est): 12MM **Privately Held**
SIC: 7521 7389 3534 Automobile storage garage; design services; automobile elevators

(G-19395)
DIETRICH INDUSTRIES INC
Also Called: Dietrich Metal Framing
1300 Phoenix Rd Ne (44483-2851)
PHONE 330 372-4014
Greg Samsa, *Branch Mgr*
Theresa Naylor, *Manager*
Carrie Probst, *Personnel Assit*
EMP: 180
SALES (corp-wide): 3.5B **Publicly Held**
WEB: www.dietrichmetalframing.com
SIC: 3441 Building components, structural steel
HQ: Dietrich Industries, Inc.
   200 W Old Wlson Bridge Rd
   Worthington OH 43085
   800 873-2604

(G-19396)
DIETRICH INDUSTRIES INC
1985 N River Rd Ne (44483-2527)
PHONE 330 372-2868
Joe Labus, *Manager*
EMP: 162
SALES (corp-wide): 3.5B **Publicly Held**
WEB: www.dietrichmetalframing.com
SIC: 3312 Primary finished or semifinished shapes
HQ: Dietrich Industries, Inc.
   200 W Old Wlson Bridge Rd
   Worthington OH 43085
   800 873-2604

(G-19397)
DRAKE MFG ACQUISITION LLC
4371 N Leavitt Rd Nw (44485-1199)
PHONE 330 847-7291
John Lirong Hu, *President*
David Tang, *Vice Pres*
Stig Mowatt-Larssen, *CTO*
EMP: 55
SALES: 4.1MM **Privately Held**
SIC: 3599 Machine shop, jobbing & repair

(G-19398)
DROP ZONE LTD
3680 N River Rd Ne (44484-1031)
PHONE 234 806-4604
EMP: 4
SALES (est): 272.2K **Privately Held**
SIC: 3949 Shooting equipment & supplies, general

(G-19399)
EMT INC
1201 Vine Ave Ne Ste 2 (44483-3834)
PHONE 330 399-6939
David F Gerback, *President*

▲ = Import ▼ = Export
◆ = Import/Export

GEOGRAPHIC SECTION

Warren - Trumbull County (G-19426)

Wanda S Gerback, *Vice Pres*
Merinda Stephenson, *Office Mgr*
EMP: 4
SQ FT: 7,000
SALES: 250K **Privately Held**
WEB: www.emtinc.biz
SIC: 3613 Control panels, electric

(G-19400)
ENGINEERED WIRE PRODUCTS INC
3121 W Market St (44485-3070)
PHONE 330 469-6958
Dawn Kenney, *Purchasing*
John Bankol, *Manager*
EMP: 48 **Privately Held**
SIC: 3496 Miscellaneous fabricated wire products
HQ: Engineered Wire Products, Inc.
1200 N Warpole St
Upper Sandusky OH 43251

(G-19401)
EVERETT INDUSTRIES LLC
3601 Larchmont Ave Ne (44483-2447)
PHONE 330 372-3700
James Vosmik, *Mng Member*
EMP: 24
SQ FT: 25,000
SALES (est): 671.1K **Privately Held**
SIC: 3291 Abrasive wheels & grindstones, not artificial

(G-19402)
FAURECIA EXHAUST SYSTEMS LLC
1849 Ellsworth Bailey Rd (44481-9234)
PHONE 330 824-2807
Dana Bower, *Branch Mgr*
EMP: 182
SALES (corp-wide): 342.9MM **Privately Held**
WEB: www.franklin.faurecia.com
SIC: 3714 Mufflers (exhaust), motor vehicle
HQ: Faurecia Emissions Control Systems Na, Llc
543 Matzinger Rd
Toledo OH 43612
812 341-2000

(G-19403)
FLEX-STRUT INC
2900 Commonwealth Ave Ne (44483-2831)
PHONE 330 372-9999
Dale H Gebhardt, *President*
Larry Mears, *Vice Pres*
Mark Mirini, *Admin Sec*
EMP: 75
SQ FT: 52,000
SALES (est): 29.1MM **Privately Held**
WEB: www.flexstrut.com
SIC: 3441 3429 Fabricated structural metal; manufactured hardware (general)

(G-19404)
GARBER MACHINE CO
1788 Drexel Ave Nw (44485-2120)
PHONE 330 399-4181
Roger L Garber, *Owner*
EMP: 3
SALES (est): 189.7K **Privately Held**
SIC: 3599 Machine shop, jobbing & repair

(G-19405)
GENERAL MOTORS LLC
2300 Hallock Young Rd Sw (44481-9238)
PHONE 330 824-5000
John Donahoe, *Branch Mgr*
EMP: 1053 **Publicly Held**
SIC: 3711 Automobile assembly, including specialty automobiles
HQ: General Motors Llc
300 Renaissance Ctr L1
Detroit MI 48243

(G-19406)
GENERAL MOTORS LLC
2369 Ellsworth Bailey Rd (44485-9235)
PHONE 330 824-5840
John Donahoe, *Manager*
EMP: 277 **Publicly Held**
SIC: 3465 3714 Automotive stampings; motor vehicle parts & accessories

HQ: General Motors Llc
300 Renaissance Ctr L1
Detroit MI 48243

(G-19407)
GLUNT INDUSTRIES INC
319 N River Rd Nw (44483-2248)
PHONE 330 399-7585
Dennis Glunt, *President*
Mary Ann Patrick, *Principal*
Gary Shells, *Principal*
Harold Glunt, *Vice Pres*
Stuart Gladstone, *CFO*
▲ **EMP:** 125
SQ FT: 150,000
SALES (est): 28.3MM **Privately Held**
SIC: 3599 3549 3444 Machine shop, jobbing & repair; custom machinery; metalworking machinery; sheet metalwork

(G-19408)
HARSCO CORPORATION
Harsco Minerals International
101 Tidewater St Ne (44483-2434)
PHONE 330 372-1781
Brian Conlon, *Branch Mgr*
EMP: 75
SALES (corp-wide): 1.6B **Publicly Held**
SIC: 2816 2899 Metallic & mineral pigments; chemical preparations
PA: Harsco Corporation
350 Poplar Church Rd
Camp Hill PA 17011
717 763-7064

(G-19409)
INCREDIBLE SOLUTIONS INC
1052 Mahoning Ave Nw (44483-4622)
PHONE 330 898-3878
Ted Bloom, *CEO*
▲ **EMP:** 16
SALES (est): 5.9MM **Privately Held**
WEB: www.bloomindustries.com
SIC: 2821 Molding compounds, plastics

(G-19410)
INDUCTION MANAGEMENT SVCS LLC
1745 Overland Ave Ne (44483-2860)
PHONE 440 947-2000
EMP: 4
SALES (est): 305.5K **Privately Held**
SIC: 3398 Metal heat treating

(G-19411)
INTERNATIONAL STEEL GROUP
2234 Main Street Ext Sw (44481-9602)
PHONE 330 841-2800
Rodney Mott, *President*
Jeff Foster, *General Mgr*
EMP: 135
SALES (est): 15.3MM
SALES (corp-wide): 9.1B **Privately Held**
WEB: www.internationalsteelgroup.com
SIC: 3312 1011 Blast furnaces & steel mills; iron ores
HQ: Arcelormittal Usa Llc
1 S Dearborn St Ste 1800
Chicago IL 60603
312 346-0300

(G-19412)
J & L WELDING FABRICATING INC
140 Dana St Ne (44483-3845)
PHONE 330 393-9353
Larry Grossa, *CEO*
Janet Kistler, *President*
EMP: 17
SALES (est): 3.3MM **Privately Held**
SIC: 3449 7692 3444 3441 Bars, concrete reinforcing; fabricated steel; welding repair; sheet metalwork; fabricated structural metal

(G-19413)
J W GOSS CO INC (PA)
Also Called: Reds Auto Glass Shop
410 South St Sw (44483-5737)
P.O. Box 1066 (44482-1066)
PHONE 330 395-0739
Fax: 330 395-0739
EMP: 14
SQ FT: 20,000

SALES (est): 1.6MM **Privately Held**
SIC: 7536 3429 Auto Glass Replacement Mfg Hardware

(G-19414)
JB INDUSTRIES LTD (PA)
160 Clifton Dr Ne Ste 4 (44484-1820)
PHONE 330 856-4587
John E Bancroft,
Bruce O Bancroft,
EMP: 15
SQ FT: 1,800
SALES (est): 2MM **Privately Held**
WEB: www.jb-industries.com
SIC: 8711 3599 Industrial engineers; machine shop, jobbing & repair; custom machinery

(G-19415)
LAFARGE NORTH AMERICA INC
Also Called: Lordstown Cnstr Recovery
6205 Newton Fls Bailey Rd (44481-9763)
PHONE 330 393-5656
Tim Wirtz, *Plant Mgr*
Timothy Wirtz, *Site Mgr*
EMP: 35
SALES (corp-wide): 26.4B **Privately Held**
WEB: www.lafargenorthamerica.com
SIC: 3273 Ready-mixed concrete
HQ: Lafarge North America Inc.
8700 W Bryn Mawr Ave
Chicago IL 60631
773 372-1000

(G-19416)
LAIRD TECHNOLOGIES INC
655 N River Rd Nw (44483-2254)
PHONE 234 806-0105
EMP: 8
SALES (corp-wide): 1.2B **Privately Held**
SIC: 3443 Nuclear shielding, metal plate
HQ: Laird Technologies, Inc.
16401 Swingley
Chesterfield MO 63017
636 898-6000

(G-19417)
LITCO MANUFACTURING LLC
1512 Phoenix Rd Ne (44483-2855)
P.O. Box 150, Vienna (44473-0150)
PHONE 330 539-5433
Lionel F Trebilcock, *CEO*
Raymond W Snider, *Principal*
Gary Tredilcock, *COO*
▲ **EMP:** 17
SALES: 1.2MM
SALES (corp-wide): 4MM **Privately Held**
SIC: 2448 Wood pallets & skids
PA: Litco International, Inc.
1 Litco Dr
Vienna OH 44473
330 539-5433

(G-19418)
LRB TOOL & DIE LTD
3303 Parkman Rd Nw (44481-9142)
PHONE 330 898-5783
Lee Ann Westenselder, *Corp Secy*
George Pearce, *Mng Member*
EMP: 10
SALES: 750K **Privately Held**
SIC: 3544 Special dies & tools

(G-19419)
MACKLAND CO INC
Also Called: Hal Mar Printing
155 North St Nw (44483-3715)
P.O. Box 84 (44482-0084)
PHONE 330 399-5034
Doreen Romack, *President*
Victor A Romack, *Vice Pres*
EMP: 4 **EST:** 1972
SQ FT: 9,000
SALES: 200K **Privately Held**
SIC: 2752 Commercial printing, offset

(G-19420)
MAGNA SEATING AMERICA INC
Also Called: Intier Sting Systems-Lordstown
1702 Henn Pkwy Sw (44481-8656)
PHONE 330 824-3101
Sean Ewing, *Branch Mgr*
Gary Lawson, *Info Tech Mgr*
EMP: 250

SALES (corp-wide): 38.9B **Privately Held**
SIC: 3714 2531 Motor vehicle parts & accessories; seats, automobile
HQ: Magna Seating Of America, Inc.
30020 Cabot Dr
Novi MI 48377

(G-19421)
MAGNEFORCE INC
155 Shaffer Dr Ne (44484-1842)
P.O. Box 8508 (44484-0508)
PHONE 330 856-9300
Richard Miller, *President*
David Miller, *Vice Pres*
EMP: 10
SQ FT: 5,900
SALES (est): 1.7MM **Privately Held**
WEB: www.magneforce.com
SIC: 3567 Induction heating equipment

(G-19422)
MESSER LLC
2000 Pine Ave Se (44483-6550)
PHONE 330 394-4541
Rick Julius, *Manager*
EMP: 6
SALES (corp-wide): 1.4B **Privately Held**
SIC: 2813 Nitrogen
HQ: Messer Llc
200 Somerset Corporate
Bridgewater NJ 08807
908 464-8100

(G-19423)
NOVELIS CORPORATION
390 Griswold St Ne (44483-2738)
P.O. Box 1151 (44482-1151)
PHONE 330 841-3456
Mervyn W Bell, *Branch Mgr*
Jeff Ballyns, *Info Tech Dir*
EMP: 93
SALES (corp-wide): 6.5B **Privately Held**
SIC: 3355 3353 Aluminum rolling & drawing; aluminum sheet, plate & foil
HQ: Novelis Corporation
3560 Lenox Rd Ne Ste 2000
Atlanta GA 30326
404 760-4000

(G-19424)
OAKES FOUNDRY INC
700 Bronze Rd Ne (44483-2720)
PHONE 330 372-4010
Grant Oakes, *President*
Steve Landfried, *Manager*
EMP: 21 **EST:** 1929
SQ FT: 2,000
SALES (est): 5MM **Privately Held**
WEB: www.oakesfoundry.com
SIC: 3366 Castings (except die): bronze; castings (except die): copper & copper-base alloy

(G-19425)
OGDEN NEWSPAPERS INC
Also Called: Town Crier, The
240 Franklin St Se (44483-5711)
PHONE 330 629-6200
Daryl Neve, *Manager*
EMP: 5 **Privately Held**
SIC: 2711 Newspapers: publishing only, not printed on site
HQ: The Ogden Newspapers Inc
1500 Main St
Wheeling WV 26003
304 233-0100

(G-19426)
OGDEN NEWSPAPERS INC
Also Called: Tribune Chronicle
240 Franklin St Se (44483-5711)
PHONE 330 841-1600
Charles Jarvis, *Publisher*
Marly Kosinski, *Editor*
Joseph Landsberger, *Editor*
Brenda Linert, *Editor*
Mark Suter, *Buyer*
EMP: 210 **Privately Held**
SIC: 2711 2752 Newspapers: publishing only, not printed on site; commercial printing, lithographic
HQ: The Ogden Newspapers Inc
1500 Main St
Wheeling WV 26003
304 233-0100

Warren - Trumbull County (G-19427)

(G-19427)
OHIO STAR FORGE CO
4000 Mahoning Ave Nw (44483-1924)
P.O. Box 430 (44482-0430)
PHONE.................................330 847-6360
William J Orbach, *CEO*
David James, *Maint Spvr*
Michael Snider, *Maint Spvr*
Pete Wosotowsky, *Buyer*
Ray Harkins, *QC Mgr*
▲ **EMP:** 84
SQ FT: 150,000
SALES (est): 19.4MM
SALES (corp-wide): 4.7B **Privately Held**
WEB: www.ohiostar.com
SIC: 3462 Iron & steel forgings
PA: Daido Steel Co., Ltd.
   1-1-10, Higashisakura, Higashi-Ku
   Nagoya AIC 461-0
   529 637-501

(G-19428)
OHIO TRAILER INC
1899 Tod Ave Sw (44485-4221)
PHONE.................................330 392-4444
John Miller, *President*
EMP: 18
SQ FT: 20,000
SALES (est): 2MM **Privately Held**
SIC: 5231 7692 7538 3444 Paint, glass & wallpaper; welding repair; general automotive repair shops; sheet metalwork

(G-19429)
ORTHOTICS & PROSTHETICS REHAB
Also Called: Billock, John N Cpo
700 Howland Wilson Rd Se (44484-2512)
PHONE.................................330 856-2553
John N Billock, *Director*
EMP: 11
SQ FT: 9,000
SALES (est): 1.4MM **Privately Held**
WEB: www.oandpcenter.com
SIC: 3842 8011 Braces, orthopedic; limbs, artificial; offices & clinics of medical doctors

(G-19430)
PHOENIX TOOL CO INC
1351 Phoenix Rd Ne (44483-2899)
PHONE.................................330 372-4627
Eric Fredenburg, *President*
Jeff Copeland, *Vice Pres*
Joel Fredenburg, *Treasurer*
Harlan R Fredenburg, *Shareholder*
EMP: 8 **EST:** 1949
SQ FT: 5,000
SALES: 800K **Privately Held**
WEB: www.phoenixtoolco.com
SIC: 3599 Machine shop, jobbing & repair

(G-19431)
PILLAR INDUCTION
1745 Overland Ave Ne (44483-2860)
PHONE.................................262 317-5300
EMP: 5
SALES (est): 706.4K **Privately Held**
SIC: 3567 Industrial furnaces & ovens

(G-19432)
PORTAGE RESOURCES INC
8650 Kimblewick Ln Ne (44484-2068)
PHONE.................................330 856-2622
William R Templeton, *President*
Norman Darl Templeton, *Vice Pres*
Robert P Templeton, *Treasurer*
Eric A Templeton, *Admin Sec*
EMP: 4
SQ FT: 800
SALES (est): 426.4K **Privately Held**
SIC: 1381 Drilling oil & gas wells

(G-19433)
PPG INDUSTRIES INC
2823 Ellsworth Bailey Rd (44481-9201)
PHONE.................................330 824-2537
Charles Bunch, *Branch Mgr*
EMP: 24
SALES (corp-wide): 15.3B **Publicly Held**
WEB: www.ppg.com
SIC: 2851 Paints & allied products
PA: Ppg Industries, Inc.
   1 Ppg Pl
   Pittsburgh PA 15272
   412 434-3131

(G-19434)
PRINTERS EDGE INC
4965 Mahoning Ave Nw (44483-1405)
PHONE.................................330 372-2232
George M Rogers, *President*
Nick Latiano, *General Mgr*
Debbie Freer, *Technology*
Kathy Shirley, *Administration*
▲ **EMP:** 12
SQ FT: 11,000
SALES (est): 1.9MM **Privately Held**
SIC: 2752 Commercial printing, lithographic

(G-19435)
R W SIDLEY INCORPORATED
425 N River Rd Nw (44483-2250)
PHONE.................................330 392-2721
Rich Kaye, *Manager*
EMP: 11
SALES (corp-wide): 132.6MM **Privately Held**
WEB: www.rwsidleyinc.com
SIC: 3273 Ready-mixed concrete
PA: R. W. Sidley Incorporated
   436 Casement Ave
   Painesville OH 44077
   440 352-9343

(G-19436)
RAPTIS COFFEE INC
341 Main Ave Sw (44481-1044)
PHONE.................................330 399-7011
Ilias Raptis, *President*
Marianne Raptis, *Corp Secy*
George Raptis, *Vice Pres*
EMP: 3
SQ FT: 8,000
SALES (est): 291.7K **Privately Held**
WEB: www.raptiscoffee.com
SIC: 2095 Roasted coffee

(G-19437)
RED HOT STUDIOS
728 Shadowood Ln Se (44484-2441)
PHONE.................................330 609-7446
William L Snyder, *Owner*
EMP: 4
SQ FT: 3,000
SALES: 350K **Privately Held**
WEB: www.redhotstudios.com
SIC: 3993 Signs, not made in custom sign painting shops; displays & cutouts, window & lobby

(G-19438)
RESCO PRODUCTS INC
1929 Larchmont Ave Ne (44483-3507)
PHONE.................................330 372-3716
EMP: 30
SALES (corp-wide): 216.3MM **Privately Held**
SIC: 3255 3272 Clay refractories; concrete products, precast
PA: Resco Products, Inc.
   6600 Steubenville Pike # 1
   Pittsburgh PA 15205
   888 283-5505

(G-19439)
RICHMOND CONCRETE PRODUCTS
Also Called: Portage Septic Tank
3640 Kibler Toot Rd Sw (44481-9159)
PHONE.................................330 673-7892
EMP: 5
SALES (est): 598.4K **Privately Held**
SIC: 3272 Mfg Concrete Products

(G-19440)
RINALDI AND PACKARD INDUSTRIES
Also Called: Northeastern Machinery
775 And A Half Nles Rd Se (44483)
PHONE.................................330 395-4942
Kevin Rinaldi, *President*
Barb Rinaldi, *Corp Secy*
EMP: 3
SQ FT: 1,250
SALES (est): 386.1K **Privately Held**
SIC: 3599 Machine shop, jobbing & repair

(G-19441)
SANESE SERVICES INC
Also Called: Sanese Vending Company
2590 Elm Rd Ne (44483-2904)
PHONE.................................330 494-5900
Kris Holzopsel, *Manager*
EMP: 50
SALES (corp-wide): 119.3MM **Privately Held**
WEB: www.sanese.com
SIC: 5962 2099 Sandwich & hot food vending machines; food preparations
PA: Sanese Services, Inc.
   2590 Elm Rd Ne
   Warren OH 44483
   614 436-1234

(G-19442)
SCHAEFER EQUIPMENT INC
1590 Phoenix Rd Ne (44483-2896)
PHONE.................................330 372-4006
Rich Barnhart, *CEO*
Barry Anderson, *Vice Pres*
▲ **EMP:** 80
SQ FT: 101,000
SALES (est): 23.9MM
SALES (corp-wide): 4.3B **Publicly Held**
WEB: www.schaeferequipment.net
SIC: 3462 Railroad wheels, axles, frogs or other equipment: forged
HQ: Wabtec Corporation
   1001 Airbrake Ave
   Wilmerding PA 15148

(G-19443)
SPECIALTIES MDS INDUCTION LTD
762 E Market St (44481-1214)
PHONE.................................330 394-3338
David G Moyer, *President*
John Bevlin, *Partner*
Ron Snyder, *Partner*
EMP: 4
SQ FT: 16,000
SALES (est): 702.4K **Privately Held**
SIC: 3567 Induction heating equipment

(G-19444)
SUMMIT STREET NEWS INC
645 Summit St Nw (44485-2811)
P.O. Box 1270 (44482-1270)
PHONE.................................330 609-5600
Kenneth Heyman, *Principal*
EMP: 5 **EST:** 2009
SALES (est): 242.8K **Privately Held**
SIC: 2711 Newspapers, publishing & printing

(G-19445)
SUPERIOR CUP INC
448 E Market St (44481-1208)
PHONE.................................330 393-6187
Steve Papadimas, *President*
EMP: 27
SQ FT: 24,000
SALES (est): 6.2MM **Privately Held**
SIC: 2656 Cups, paper: made from purchased material

(G-19446)
TECNOCAP LLC
Also Called: Warren Metal Lithography
2100 Griswold St Ne (44483-2750)
PHONE.................................330 392-7222
Brian Bates, *Plant Mgr*
Diana Wilds, *Production*
Harry Kammerer, *Regl Sales Mgr*
Bob Macosko, *Sales Staff*
Ric Smith, *Manager*
EMP: 52
SALES (corp-wide): 71.4MM **Privately Held**
SIC: 3354 2752 Aluminum extruded products; lithographing on metal
HQ: Tecnocap Llc
   1701 Wheeling Ave
   Glen Dale WV 26038
   304 845-3402

(G-19447)
THERM-O-LINK INC
Also Called: Vulkor
621 Dana St Ne Ste 5 (44483-3977)
PHONE.................................330 393-7600
John Mullen, *Manager*
Bryan Crouch, *Supervisor*
EMP: 7
SQ FT: 18,000
SALES (corp-wide): 41.2MM **Privately Held**
WEB: www.tolwire.com
SIC: 3357 Nonferrous wiredrawing & insulating
PA: Therm-O-Link, Inc.
   10513 Freedom St
   Garrettsville OH 44231
   330 527-2124

(G-19448)
THERM-O-LINK OF TEXAS INC
621 Dana St Ne Ste V (44483-3977)
PHONE.................................330 393-4300
Ronald M Krisher, *President*
EMP: 5 **EST:** 2015
SALES (est): 249.5K **Privately Held**
SIC: 3357 Nonferrous wiredrawing & insulating

(G-19449)
TMS INTERNATIONAL LLC
4000 Mahoning Ave Nw (44483-1924)
P.O. Box 1819 (44482-1819)
PHONE.................................330 847-0844
EMP: 28 **Privately Held**
SIC: 3295 Minerals, Ground Or Treated, Nsk

(G-19450)
TRUMBULL CEMENT PRODUCTS CO
2185 Larchmont Ave Ne (44483-2894)
PHONE.................................330 372-4342
Jeffrey Carbone, *President*
Julie Carbone, *Treasurer*
Darla Carbone, *Admin Sec*
EMP: 6
SQ FT: 5,000
SALES: 1MM **Privately Held**
SIC: 3271 5211 5032 Blocks, concrete or cinder: standard; lumber & other building materials; brick, stone & related material

(G-19451)
TRUMBULL COUNTY LEGAL NEWS
108 Main Ave Sw Ste 700 (44481-1010)
P.O. Box 707 (44482-0707)
PHONE.................................330 392-7112
Cheryl Biviano, *President*
EMP: 3
SALES (est): 180K **Privately Held**
SIC: 7313 2711 Newspaper advertising representative; newspapers

(G-19452)
TRUMBULL MANUFACTURING INC
400 Dietz Rd Ne (44483-2749)
P.O. Box 30 (44482-0030)
PHONE.................................330 393-6624
Murray Miller, *President*
Ken Miller, *CFO*
Julian Lehman, *Treasurer*
Chick Haering, *VP Sales*
Curtis Straubhaar, *Sales Staff*
▲ **EMP:** 89
SQ FT: 16,000
SALES (est): 14.8MM **Privately Held**
SIC: 3432 3433 5074 Plumbing fixture fittings & trim; heating equipment, except electric; plumbing & hydronic heating supplies

(G-19453)
TRUMBULL MOBILE MEALS INC
323 E Market St (44481-1207)
PHONE.................................330 394-2538
Sandra Mathews, *Exec Dir*
EMP: 10
SQ FT: 3,567
SALES: 398.7K **Privately Held**
SIC: 8322 2051 Meal delivery program; bakery, for home service delivery

(G-19454)
ULTIMATE PRINTING CO INC
6090 Mahoning Ave Nw C (44481-9495)
PHONE.................................330 847-2941
Richard Wilms, *President*
William Pugh, *Vice Pres*
EMP: 6

GEOGRAPHIC SECTION

SQ FT: 3,000
SALES (est): 665.8K **Privately Held**
SIC: 2752 Commercial printing, lithographic

(G-19455)
VANGUARD DIE & MACHINE INC
2070 Mcmyler St Nw (44485-2615)
PHONE.................................330 394-4170
Fax: 330 395-3505
EMP: 20
SQ FT: 6,000
SALES: 1.5MM **Privately Held**
SIC: 3599 Machine Shop

(G-19456)
VINDICATOR PRINTING COMPANY
Also Called: News Office, Beauro
135 Pine Ave Se Ste 208 (44481-1249)
P.O. Box 780, Youngstown (44501-0780)
PHONE.................................330 392-0176
Tom Wills, *Branch Mgr*
EMP: 4
SALES (corp-wide): 45.5MM **Privately Held**
WEB: www.vindy.com
SIC: 2711 Newspapers, publishing & printing
PA: The Vindicator Printing Company
107 Vindicator Sq
Youngstown OH 44503
330 747-1471

(G-19457)
VULKOR INCORPORATED (PA)
621 Dana St Ne Ste V (44483-3977)
PHONE.................................330 393-7600
David J Campbell, *President*
Ronald M Krisher, *Shareholder*
Richard Thompson, *Shareholder*
EMP: 24
SQ FT: 780
SALES (est): 6.2MM **Privately Held**
SIC: 3357 Nonferrous wiredrawing & insulating

(G-19458)
WARREN CONCRETE AND SUPPLY CO
1113 Parkman Rd Nw (44485-2497)
P.O. Box 1408 (44482-1408)
PHONE.................................330 393-1581
Harry N Hamilton, *President*
David H Hamilton, *President*
James Hamilton, *Vice Pres*
Jim Hamilton, *Vice Pres*
Richard Hamilton, *Vice Pres*
EMP: 18
SQ FT: 2,000
SALES (est): 2.9MM **Privately Held**
SIC: 3273 5211 5032 Ready-mixed concrete; lumber & other building materials; brick, stone & related material

(G-19459)
WARREN FIRE EQUIPMENT INC (PA)
6880 Tod Ave Sw (44481-8628)
PHONE.................................330 824-3523
Robert R Malone, *President*
Lynda L Malone, *COO*
Richard D Garrity, *Vice Pres*
Lemyra Montgomery, *Admin Sec*
EMP: 21 EST: 1920
SQ FT: 8,400
SALES (est): 4.7MM **Privately Held**
WEB: www.warrenfireequip.com
SIC: 5999 2899 Fire extinguishers; fire extinguisher charges

(G-19460)
WARREN SCREW MACHINE INC
3869 Niles Rd Se (44484-3548)
PHONE.................................330 609-6020
John Condoleon, *President*
EMP: 26
SALES (est): 5.7MM **Privately Held**
SIC: 3451 Screw machine products

(G-19461)
WARREN STEEL SPECIALTIES CORP
1309 Niles Rd Se (44484-5106)
P.O. Box 1391 (44482-1391)
PHONE.................................330 399-8360
Christopher Shape, *President*
Frederick Shape, *Vice Pres*
Barbara Shape, *Admin Sec*
EMP: 15 EST: 1931
SQ FT: 21,000
SALES (est): 1.4MM **Privately Held**
WEB: www.warrensteel.com
SIC: 2542 3499 Stands, merchandise display: except wood; strapping, metal

(G-19462)
WATERPRO
2926 Commonwealth Ave Ne (44483-2831)
PHONE.................................330 372-3565
Vern Parker, *Owner*
EMP: 13
SALES (est): 1.2MM **Privately Held**
SIC: 3561 Pumps & pumping equipment

(G-19463)
WELD-ACTION COMPANY INC
2100 N River Rd Ne (44483-2598)
PHONE.................................330 372-1063
Todd Huna, *President*
EMP: 6 EST: 1960
SQ FT: 7,158
SALES (est): 1.6MM **Privately Held**
WEB: www.weldaction.com
SIC: 5084 3548 Welding machinery & equipment; welding & cutting apparatus & accessories

Warrensville Heights
Cuyahoga County

(G-19464)
B & F MANUFACTURING CO
19050 Cranwood Pkwy (44128-4047)
PHONE.................................216 518-0333
Marsha Kutsikovich, *President*
EMP: 10
SQ FT: 10,000
SALES (est): 1.7MM **Privately Held**
SIC: 3599 Machine shop, jobbing & repair

(G-19465)
CHARLES HUFFMAN & ASSOCIATES
19214 Gladstone Rd (44122-6626)
PHONE.................................216 295-0850
Charles Huffman, *Manager*
EMP: 6
SALES (corp-wide): 300K **Privately Held**
SIC: 2759 Commercial printing
PA: Charles Huffman & Associates
17325 Euclid Ave Ste 4002
Cleveland OH 44112
216 295-0850

(G-19466)
CHEM 1 INC
19220 Miles Rd (44128-4106)
PHONE.................................216 475-7443
Sam Zemaitis, *President*
▲ EMP: 5
SQ FT: 42,000
SALES (est): 2.8MM **Privately Held**
SIC: 2842 Cleaning or polishing preparations

(G-19467)
EMBEDDED PLANET INC
4760 Richmond Rd Ste 400 (44128-5979)
PHONE.................................216 245-4180
Mark Lowdermilk, *CEO*
Timothy J Callahan, *Ch of Bd*
Nancy Beatty, *Info Tech Mgr*
EMP: 15
SQ FT: 8,000
SALES (est): 3MM **Privately Held**
WEB: www.embeddedplanet.com
SIC: 7371 3577 Computer software development; computer peripheral equipment

(G-19468)
GE MEDICAL SYSTEMS INFORMATION
18683 S Miles Rd (44128-4239)
PHONE.................................216 663-2110
Ken Koons, *Electrical Engi*
Jason Hisrich, *Branch Mgr*
Kathleen Bradley, *Master*
EMP: 3
SALES (corp-wide): 121.6B **Publicly Held**
SIC: 3845 Patient monitoring apparatus; electrocardiographs; defibrillator; respiratory analysis equipment, electromedical
HQ: Ge Medical Systems Information Technologies, Inc.
9900 W Innovation Dr
Wauwatosa WI 53226
262 544-3011

(G-19469)
GINOS AWARDS INC
Also Called: Gino's Jewelers & Trophy Mfrs
4701 Richmond Rd Ste 200 (44128-5994)
PHONE.................................216 831-6565
Gino Zavarella, *President*
Helen Scanlon, *Accountant*
▲ EMP: 50
SQ FT: 30,000
SALES (est): 7.7MM **Privately Held**
WEB: www.ginosawards.com
SIC: 3911 3993 3914 Jewelry, precious metal; signs & advertising specialties; trophies

(G-19470)
HUMMINGBIRD GRAPHICS LLC
Also Called: Shortstack Printing
4425 Renaissance Pkwy (44128-5754)
PHONE.................................216 595-8835
EMP: 3
SALES (est): 224.5K **Privately Held**
SIC: 2752 Commercial printing, offset

(G-19471)
MICAH SPECIALTY FOODS
18014 Garden Blvd (44128-2621)
PHONE.................................405 320-3325
EMP: 3 EST: 2015
SALES (est): 161.7K **Privately Held**
SIC: 2099 Food preparations

(G-19472)
POLIMEROS USA LLC
Also Called: Roto Systems
26210 Emery Rd Ste 202 (44128-5770)
PHONE.................................216 591-0175
Jose Antonio Chacon,
EMP: 8
SALES (est): 4.3MM **Privately Held**
SIC: 3089 Air mattresses, plastic
PA: Polimeros Mexicanos, S.A. De C.V.
Monte Alto No. 10 Y 21
Cd. Nezahualcoyotl EDOMEX. 57810

(G-19473)
TITANIUM METALS CORPORATION (DH)
Also Called: Timet
4832 Richmond Rd Ste 100 (44128-5993)
PHONE.................................610 968-1300
Steven L Watson, *CEO*
Joan Clark, *President*
Keith R Coogan, *Principal*
Bobby D O'Brien, *Principal*
Glenn R Simmons, *Principal*
◆ EMP: 30 EST: 1950
SALES (est): 768.9MM
SALES (corp-wide): 225.3B **Publicly Held**
WEB: www.timet.com
SIC: 3356 Titanium; titanium & titanium alloy bars, sheets, strip, etc.
HQ: Precision Castparts Corp.
4650 Sw Mcdam Ave Ste 300
Portland OR 97239
503 946-4800

(G-19474)
WHITMORE PRODUCTIONS INC
Also Called: Whitmore's Bbq
20209 Harvard Ave (44122-6808)
PHONE.................................216 752-3960
Virgil Whitmore, *President*
Vance Whitmore, *Vice Pres*
Esther Whitmore, *Treasurer*
Kim Whitmore, *Admin Sec*
EMP: 11
SQ FT: 1,500
SALES (est): 1.3MM **Privately Held**
WEB: www.whitmoreproductions.com
SIC: 2099 Sauces: dry mixes

Warsaw
Coshocton County

(G-19475)
KILLBUCK CREEK DISTILLERY LLC
42879 Us Highway 36 B (43844-9712)
PHONE.................................740 502-2880
EMP: 3
SALES (est): 144.3K **Privately Held**
SIC: 2085 Distilled & blended liquors

Washington Court Hou
Fayette County

(G-19476)
COURTHOUSE MANUFACTURING LLC
Also Called: Chappell Door Company
1730 Wash Ave Solar Ln (43160)
PHONE.................................740 335-2727
Wayne Gooley, *Mng Member*
EMP: 38 EST: 1955
SQ FT: 84,000
SALES (est): 6.7MM **Privately Held**
WEB: www.chappelldoor.net
SIC: 2431 Doors, wood; window frames, wood

(G-19477)
SOUTH CENTRAL INDUSTRIAL LLC
Also Called: Heartland Steel, Inc.
1629 S Fayette St (43160)
PHONE.................................740 333-5401
Thomas Miller, *Principal*
Terry Lee, *Principal*
Lance Miller, *Vice Pres*
EMP: 17
SQ FT: 60,000
SALES: 2.5MM
SALES (corp-wide): 38.1MM **Privately Held**
SIC: 3441 Fabricated structural metal
PA: Heartland, Inc.
1005 N 19th St
Middlesboro KY 40965
606 248-7323

(G-19478)
STARK TRUSS COMPANY INC
2000 Landmark Blvd (43160)
P.O. Box 8, Wshngtn CT Hs (43160-0008)
PHONE.................................740 335-4156
Jeff Coulter, *Branch Mgr*
EMP: 50
SQ FT: 12,000
SALES (corp-wide): 186.7MM **Privately Held**
WEB: www.starktruss.com
SIC: 2439 Trusses, wooden roof
PA: Stark Truss Company, Inc.
109 Miles Ave Sw
Canton OH 44710
330 478-2100

(G-19479)
YUSA CORPORATION (HQ)
151 Jamison Rd Sw (43160)
PHONE.................................740 335-0335
Takeyoshi Usui, *President*
Yoshiji Iwamoto, *Treasurer*
Nobuyuki Tateno, *Admin Sec*
▲ EMP: 1046
SQ FT: 250,000
SALES (est): 228.8MM
SALES (corp-wide): 185.5MM **Privately Held**
SIC: 3069 Rubber covered motor mounting rings (rubber bonded); bushings, rubber; tubing, rubber

Washingtonville - Columbiana County (G-19480)

GEOGRAPHIC SECTION

PA: Yamashita Rubber Co.,Ltd.
1239, Kamekubo
Fujimino STM 356-0
492 622-121

Washingtonville
Columbiana County

(G-19480)
KEEN MANUFACTURING INC
240 High St (44490)
PHONE.................330 427-0045
Terry Turvey, *President*
Tressa Turvey, *Corp Secy*
EMP: 5
SQ FT: 7,000
SALES: 350K **Privately Held**
WEB: www.keenmanufacturing.com
SIC: 3491 Industrial valves

(G-19481)
TURVEY ENGINEERING
Also Called: TS Engineering
240 High St (44490)
P.O. Box 334 (44490-0334)
PHONE.................330 427-0125
Terry Turvey, *President*
EMP: 5
SALES (est): 543K **Privately Held**
WEB: www.tsengineering.com
SIC: 3625 Industrial controls: push button, selector switches, pilot

(G-19482)
W M INC
275 High St (44490)
PHONE.................330 427-6115
EMP: 31 EST: 1952
SQ FT: 30,000
SALES (est): 3.9MM **Privately Held**
SIC: 3469 Metal Stampings, Nec, Nsk

Waterford
Washington County

(G-19483)
AIR HEATER SEAL COMPANY INC
15710 Waterford Rd (45786-5001)
P.O. Box 8 (45786-0008)
PHONE.................740 984-2146
Randy Townsend, *Owner*
Mable Townsend, *Corp Secy*
Janet Farley, *Manager*
EMP: 23
SQ FT: 4,500
SALES (est): 4.9MM **Privately Held**
WEB: www.airheaterseal.com
SIC: 3053 3441 Gaskets, packing & sealing devices; fabricated structural metal

(G-19484)
GLOBE METALLURGICAL INC (DH)
Also Called: Globe Specialty Metals
Co Rd 32 (45786)
P.O. Box 157, Beverly (45715-0157)
PHONE.................740 984-2361
Jeff Bradley, *President*
Alan Kestenbaum, *Chairman*
Marlin Perkins, *Vice Pres*
Joe Ragan, *CFO*
Scott Teters, *Manager*
◆ EMP: 141
SALES (est): 164.4MM
SALES (corp-wide): 1.7B **Privately Held**
WEB: www.globemetallurgical.com
SIC: 3339 3313 2819 Silicon refining (primary, over 99% pure); silicon, epitaxial (silicon alloy); ferrosilicon, not made in blast furnaces; industrial inorganic chemicals

(G-19485)
GYM PRO LLC
50 Washington St (45786-5337)
PHONE.................740 984-4143
Daryl J Van Dyne, *General Mgr*
Karen S Vandyne, *Mng Member*
EMP: 3
SALES: 250K **Privately Held**
SIC: 3949 5999 2759 Sporting & athletic goods; trophies & plaques; screen printing

(G-19486)
LAMINATE SHOP
1145 Klinger Rd (45786-5347)
P.O. Box 1218, Marietta (45750-6218)
PHONE.................740 749-3536
Tim Strahler, *President*
EMP: 10
SQ FT: 25,000
SALES (est): 870K **Privately Held**
SIC: 3083 5211 1799 Laminated plastics plate & sheet; cabinets, kitchen; counter top installation

(G-19487)
LWR ENTERPRISES INC
4310 Sparling Rd (45786-5170)
P.O. Box 245 (45786-0245)
PHONE.................740 984-0036
Jay A Porter, *President*
EMP: 5
SALES (est): 741.6K **Privately Held**
SIC: 3449 Miscellaneous metalwork

(G-19488)
MALTA DYNAMICS LLC (PA)
405 Watertown Rd (45786-5248)
PHONE.................740 749-3512
Damian Lang, *CEO*
Douglas Taylor, *CFO*
Ken Hebert, *Shareholder*
EMP: 14 EST: 2015
SALES (est): 2.9MM **Privately Held**
SIC: 3531 3821 3851 4581 Winches; incubators, laboratory; ophthalmic goods; aircraft maintenance & repair services

Waterville
Lucas County

(G-19489)
ALLSTATES REFR CONTRS LLC
218 Mechanic St B (43566-1438)
P.O. Box 256 (43566-0256)
PHONE.................419 878-4691
David T Boothe, *Mng Member*
EMP: 15
SQ FT: 1,000
SALES: 1MM **Privately Held**
SIC: 3297 Nonclay refractories

(G-19490)
AQUILA PHARMATECH LLC
8225 Farnsworth Rd Ste A7 (43566-9781)
PHONE.................419 386-2527
Han Chen, *Mng Member*
EMP: 3
SALES (est): 227.2K **Privately Held**
WEB: www.aquilapharmatech.com
SIC: 3559 Chemical machinery & equipment

(G-19491)
CARRUTH STUDIO INC (PA)
1178 Farnsworth Rd (43566-1074)
PHONE.................419 878-3060
George Carruth, *President*
Debbie Carruth, *Corp Secy*
EMP: 13
SQ FT: 13,600
SALES (est): 2.5MM **Privately Held**
WEB: www.carruthstudio.com
SIC: 3269 3272 Art & ornamental ware, pottery; concrete products

(G-19492)
CRUM MANUFACTURING INC
1265 Wtrville Monclova Rd (43566-1067)
PHONE.................419 878-9779
Ernest Crum Jr, *President*
Hank Briggs, *Opers Mgr*
Chad Graham, *Opers Mgr*
Brian Loomis, *Project Engr*
Ruth Pochadt, *Office Admin*
EMP: 25
SQ FT: 23,000
SALES (est): 5.7MM **Privately Held**
WEB: www.crummfg.com
SIC: 3544 3599 3462 Special dies, tools, jigs & fixtures; machine & other job shop work; automotive forgings, ferrous: crankshaft, engine, axle, etc.

(G-19493)
DATA MOLD AND TOOL INC
160 Concord St (43566-1417)
PHONE.................419 878-9861
Jeff Suess, *President*
Doris Suess, *Treasurer*
EMP: 7
SQ FT: 7,500
SALES: 580K **Privately Held**
SIC: 3544 Forms (molds), for foundry & plastics working machinery

(G-19494)
DUVALL WOODWORKING INC
Also Called: American Products
7551 Dutch Rd (43566-9732)
PHONE.................419 878-9581
Thomas Duvall, *President*
EMP: 14
SQ FT: 12,000
SALES (est): 1.5MM **Privately Held**
SIC: 2499 Kitchen, bathroom & household ware: wood

(G-19495)
FRANKLIN
Also Called: Rrysburg Sunoco
747 Michigan Ave (43566-1052)
PHONE.................419 699-5757
EMP: 3
SALES (est): 254.5K **Privately Held**
SIC: 2869 Fuels

(G-19496)
FURNACE TECHNOLOGIES INC
Also Called: Furn Tech
1070 Disher Dr (43566-1079)
PHONE.................419 878-2100
Tim Fisher, *President*
EMP: 63
SALES (est): 13MM **Privately Held**
WEB: www.thermeq.com
SIC: 3567 Heating units & devices, industrial: electric

(G-19497)
HANSON AGGREGATES MIDWEST LLC
600 S River Rd (43566-9754)
P.O. Box 49 (43566-0049)
PHONE.................419 878-2006
Paul Carbaugh, *Branch Mgr*
EMP: 9
SALES (corp-wide): 20.6B **Privately Held**
SIC: 2951 Asphalt & asphaltic paving mixtures (not from refineries)
HQ: Hanson Aggregates Midwest Llc
207 Old Harrods Creek Rd
Louisville KY 40223
502 244-7550

(G-19498)
JOHNS MANVILLE CORPORATION
7500 Dutch Rd (43566-9731)
PHONE.................419 878-8111
Rhonda Francis, *Principal*
Mike Sparks, *Buyer*
Mark Beeman, *Engineer*
Marybeth Jones, *Engineer*
Joseph Major, *Engineer*
EMP: 400
SALES (corp-wide): 225.3B **Publicly Held**
WEB: www.jm.com
SIC: 3296 3297 3229 2273 Fiberglass insulation; nonclay refractories; pressed & blown glass; carpets & rugs
HQ: Johns Manville Corporation
717 17th St Ste 800
Denver CO 80202
303 978-2000

(G-19499)
KAUFMAN ENGINEERED SYSTEMS INC
1260 Wtrville Monclova Rd (43566-1066)
PHONE.................419 878-9727
Andrew J Quinn, *President*
Charles R Kaufman, *President*
Robert J Kaufman, *Vice Pres*
Mary Jo Burkert, *Manager*
EMP: 72 EST: 1957
SQ FT: 66,250
SALES (est): 25MM **Privately Held**
WEB: www.kaufmanengsys.com
SIC: 3567 3565 Industrial furnaces & ovens; packaging machinery

(G-19500)
LABCRAFT INC
Also Called: Furn Tech
1070 Disher Dr (43566-1079)
PHONE.................419 878-4400
Timothy J Fisher, *President*
EMP: 20
SALES (est): 859.3K **Privately Held**
WEB: www.labcraft.com
SIC: 3499 Machine bases, metal

(G-19501)
MAUMEE VALLEY MEMORIALS INC (DH)
Also Called: Americraft Bronze Co
111 Anthony Wayne Trl (43566-1373)
PHONE.................419 878-9030
Richard Kimball, *President*
EMP: 12
SQ FT: 2,500
SALES (est): 8.7MM **Privately Held**
SIC: 5999 3281 Monuments, finished to custom order; cut stone & stone products
HQ: Swenson Granite Company Llc
369 N State St
Concord NH 03301
603 225-4322

(G-19502)
PAHL READY MIX CONCRETE INC
600 S River Rd (43566-9754)
P.O. Box 49 (43566-0049)
PHONE.................419 636-4238
Thomas Weber, *Owner*
EMP: 13
SALES (corp-wide): 4.4MM **Privately Held**
SIC: 3273 Ready-mixed concrete
PA: Pahl Ready Mix Concrete, Inc.
14586 Us Highway 127 Ew
Bryan OH 43506
419 636-4238

(G-19503)
REEBAR DIE CASTING INC
1177 Farnsworth Rd (43566-1036)
PHONE.................419 878-7591
Byron G Reed, *President*
Joyce Reed, *Corp Secy*
Byron David Reed, *Vice Pres*
EMP: 15
SQ FT: 22,000
SALES (est): 2.5MM **Privately Held**
SIC: 3364 3089 Zinc & zinc-base alloy die-castings; injection molded finished plastic products

(G-19504)
RIMER ENTERPRISES INC
Also Called: Kelic
916 Rimer Dr (43566-1019)
P.O. Box 27 (43566-0027)
PHONE.................419 878-8156
Chuck Meyers, *President*
Eric Nathe, *Corp Secy*
▲ EMP: 30
SQ FT: 25,000
SALES (est): 7.1MM **Privately Held**
SIC: 3324 Commercial investment castings, ferrous

(G-19505)
SEAGATE PLASTICS COMPANY (PA)
1110 Disher Dr (43566-1256)
PHONE.................419 878-5010
Kevin Fink, *President*
▲ EMP: 39
SQ FT: 50,000
SALES (est): 11.9MM **Privately Held**
WEB: www.seagateplastics.com
SIC: 3089 Extruded finished plastic products; plastic processing

▲ = Import ▼=Export
◆ =Import/Export

GEOGRAPHIC SECTION

(G-19506)
T J F INC
Also Called: Thermeq Co
1070 Disher Dr (43566-1079)
PHONE 419 878-4400
Bill Murry, *Project Mgr*
Ernest Seeman, *Director*
EMP: 18
SALES (est): 5MM **Privately Held**
SIC: 3585 3433 3449 3567 Refrigeration & heating equipment; heating equipment, except electric; miscellaneous metalwork; industrial furnaces & ovens

(G-19507)
TECH SYSTEMS INC
1070 Disher Dr (43566-1079)
PHONE 419 878-2100
Tim Fisher, *President*
EMP: 25 **EST:** 1992
SALES (est): 2.3MM **Privately Held**
SIC: 3441 Fabricated structural metal

(G-19508)
WATERVILLE SHEET METAL COMPANY
1210 Wtrville Monclova Rd (43566-1000)
PHONE 419 878-5050
Ron Kelso, *President*
EMP: 6
SQ FT: 12,000
SALES (est): 3.7MM **Privately Held**
SIC: 3444 Sheet metalwork

Wauseon
Fulton County

(G-19509)
AMERICAN POWER PULL CORP
115 E Linfoot St (43567-1005)
P.O. Box 109 (43567-0109)
PHONE 419 335-7050
Edward S Kraemer, *President*
Gabriella Stover, *Engineer*
Jeff Valiton, *Manager*
▲ **EMP:** 8 **EST:** 1919
SQ FT: 36,600
SALES (est): 1.7MM **Privately Held**
WEB: www.americanpowerpull.com
SIC: 3423 3531 3536 Jacks: lifting, screw or ratchet (hand tools); winches; hoists, cranes & monorails

(G-19510)
BILLS SPORTS CENTER
1495 N Shoop Ave (43567-1824)
PHONE 419 335-2405
Bill Drummer, *Principal*
EMP: 4
SALES (est): 504K **Privately Held**
SIC: 3842 Hearing aids

(G-19511)
BUSSE KNIFE CO
Also Called: Busse Combat Knives
11651 County Road 12 (43567-9622)
PHONE 419 923-6471
Jerry Busse, *President*
EMP: 30
SQ FT: 37,000
SALES (est): 4.2MM **Privately Held**
WEB: www.swampratknives.com
SIC: 3421 Knife blades & blanks

(G-19512)
CONCEPT PRINTING OF WAUSEON
775 N Shoop Ave (43567-1839)
P.O. Box 503 (43567-0503)
PHONE 419 335-6627
Kim M Clark, *President*
Kristene Clark, *Corp Secy*
EMP: 5
SALES: 300K **Privately Held**
SIC: 2752 Lithographing on metal

(G-19513)
E & J DEMARK INC (PA)
1115 N Ottokee St (43567-1911)
P.O. Box 416 (43567-0416)
PHONE 419 337-5866
J Edwin Hecock, *President*

Boonie L Hecock, *Vice Pres*
EMP: 33
SQ FT: 29,000
SALES (est): 6.7MM **Privately Held**
WEB: www.demrk.com
SIC: 3545 3599 Machine tool accessories; machine shop, jobbing & repair

(G-19514)
E & J DEMARK INC
1115 N Ottokee St (43567-1911)
PHONE 419 337-5866
Bonnie Hecock, *Principal*
EMP: 6
SALES (corp-wide): 6.7MM **Privately Held**
WEB: www.demrk.com
SIC: 3545 Machine tool accessories
PA: E & J Demark, Inc.
1115 N Ottokee St
Wauseon OH 43567
419 337-5866

(G-19515)
FINE LINES LASER ENGRAVING
12825 County Road 14 (43567-9660)
PHONE 419 337-6313
James Ballmer, *Principal*
EMP: 3
SALES (est): 275.3K **Privately Held**
SIC: 2796 Platemaking services

(G-19516)
FULTON INDUSTRIES INC (PA)
135 E Linfoot St (43567-1000)
P.O. Box 377 (43567-0377)
PHONE 419 335-3015
John Razzano, *President*
Glenn Badenhop, *President*
Kim Griggs, *Exec VP*
Ned Griggs, *Exec VP*
Robert E Swanson, *Treasurer*
EMP: 70 **EST:** 1979
SQ FT: 170,000
SALES (est): 17.3MM **Privately Held**
WEB: www.fultonindoh.com
SIC: 3469 3648 Stamping metal for the trade; flashlights

(G-19517)
GAZETTE PUBLISHING COMPANY
Also Called: Fulton County Expositor
1270 N Shoop Ave Ste A (43567-2211)
PHONE 419 335-2010
Janice May, *Manager*
EMP: 15
SALES (corp-wide): 6.8MM **Privately Held**
WEB: www.theoberlinnews.com
SIC: 7313 5994 2711 Newspaper advertising representative; newsstand; newspapers
PA: The Gazette Publishing Company
42 S Main St
Oberlin OH 44074
419 483-4190

(G-19518)
GUARDIAN ENGINEERING & MFG CO
965 Fairway Ln (43567-9234)
PHONE 419 335-1784
Michael Christman, *President*
EMP: 2
SALES: 1.2MM **Privately Held**
SIC: 8711 3469 3599 Machine tool design; metal stampings; custom machinery

(G-19519)
HAAS DOOR COMPANY
320 Sycamore St (43567-1100)
PHONE 419 337-9900
Edward Nofziger, *President*
Carol Nofziger, *Corp Secy*
EMP: 200
SQ FT: 150,000
SALES (est): 22.7MM **Privately Held**
SIC: 3442 Garage doors, overhead: metal

(G-19520)
HILL MANUFACTURING INC
318 W Chestnut St (43567-1369)
P.O. Box 241 (43567-0241)
PHONE 419 335-5006
Marion Hill, *President*

Carl T Hill, *Vice Pres*
▲ **EMP:** 50
SQ FT: 55,000
SALES (est): 10.8MM **Privately Held**
WEB: www.hillmfginc.com
SIC: 3469 Stamping metal for the trade

(G-19521)
INTERACTIVE FINCL SOLUTIONS
Also Called: Mrdd Solutions
122 S Fulton St (43567-1350)
PHONE 419 335-1280
Lynn Miller, *President*
Jeff Rutledge, *Vice Pres*
EMP: 15 **EST:** 1997
SALES (est): 1.2MM **Privately Held**
WEB: www.mrddsolutions.com
SIC: 7372 Prepackaged software

(G-19522)
INTERNATIONAL AUTOMOTIVE COMPO
555 W Linfoot St (43567-9558)
PHONE 419 335-1000
EMP: 600 **Privately Held**
WEB: www.iaaawards.com
SIC: 3714 Motor vehicle parts & accessories
HQ: International Automotive Components Group North America, Inc.
28333 Telegraph Rd
Southfield MI 48034

(G-19523)
J & B FEED CO INC
140 S Brunell St (43567-1387)
PHONE 419 335-5821
Kerry Ackerman, *President*
EMP: 4
SQ FT: 1,200
SALES (est): 438K **Privately Held**
SIC: 5999 2048 5191 Feed & farm supply; prepared feeds; animal feeds

(G-19524)
L GARBERS SONS SAWMILLING LLC
6444 County Road 12 (43567-9641)
PHONE 419 335-6362
David Garber,
Kathryn Garber,
Martin Garber,
EMP: 5 **EST:** 1999
SALES (est): 734.9K **Privately Held**
SIC: 2421 Sawmills & planing mills, general

(G-19525)
LATROBE SPECIALTY MTLS CO LLC
14614 County Road H (43567-9796)
PHONE 419 335-8010
Cheryl Bookheimer, *Branch Mgr*
EMP: 76
SALES (corp-wide): 2.1B **Publicly Held**
SIC: 3312 Tool & die steel
HQ: Latrobe Specialty Metals Company, Llc
2626 Ligonier St
Latrobe PA 15650
724 537-7711

(G-19526)
LEAR CORPORATION
Also Called: Sheridan Mfg
447 E Walnut St (43567-1278)
PHONE 419 335-6010
Cary Wood, *Branch Mgr*
EMP: 200
SQ FT: 80,000
SALES (corp-wide): 21.1B **Publicly Held**
SIC: 3714 Motor vehicle parts & accessories
PA: Lear Corporation
21557 Telegraph Rd
Southfield MI 48033
248 447-1500

(G-19527)
MASTER VAC INCORPORATED
741 Parkview St (43567-1241)
PHONE 419 335-7796
D Ross Strayer, *President*
Virgie Strayer, *Vice Pres*
EMP: 3

SALES (est): 184.6K **Privately Held**
SIC: 3479 Coating of metals with plastic or resins

(G-19528)
MULTI CAST LLC
225 E Linfoot St (43567-1007)
PHONE 419 335-0010
Mike Schnipke, *Mng Member*
EMP: 37 **EST:** 1930
SQ FT: 42,500
SALES: 5MM **Privately Held**
WEB: www.multi-cast.com
SIC: 3365 Aluminum & aluminum-based alloy castings

(G-19529)
NEBRASKA INDUSTRIES CORP
447 E Walnut St (43567-1278)
PHONE 419 335-6010
Michael Hemphill, *President*
Ray Cox, *CFO*
Nicholas Cox, *Shareholder*
EMP: 38
SQ FT: 95,000
SALES (est): 5.3MM **Privately Held**
WEB: www.nebraskaindustries.com
SIC: 3469 3089 3714 3465 Stamping metal for the trade; injection molding of plastics; motor vehicle parts & accessories; automotive stampings

(G-19530)
NOFZIGER DOOR SALES INC (PA)
Also Called: Haas Doors
320 Sycamore St (43567-1100)
PHONE 419 337-9900
Edward L Nofziger, *President*
Carol Nofziger, *Corp Secy*
▼ **EMP:** 173
SQ FT: 200,000
SALES (est): 35.1MM **Privately Held**
WEB: www.haasdoor.com
SIC: 3442 1751 5211 Metal doors; garage doors, overhead: metal; garage door, installation or erection; doors, wood or metal, except storm

(G-19531)
PERFECTION FINISHERS INC
1151 N Ottokee St (43567-1911)
PHONE 419 337-8015
Gerald Haack, *CEO*
Sue Krueger, *Office Mgr*
EMP: 25
SQ FT: 80,000
SALES (est): 3.1MM **Privately Held**
WEB: www.perfectionfinishers.com
SIC: 3479 Coating of metals with plastic or resins

(G-19532)
SILVER CREEK LOG HOMES
5350 County Road 16 (43567-8708)
PHONE 419 335-3220
Andrew Davis, *Owner*
Bonnie Davis, *Co-Owner*
EMP: 3
SALES (est): 315.3K **Privately Held**
WEB: www.silvercreekloghomes.com
SIC: 2452 1521 Log cabins, prefabricated, wood; single-family housing construction

(G-19533)
TOMAHAWK PRINTING INC
229 N Fulton St (43567-1171)
P.O. Box 413 (43567-0413)
PHONE 419 335-3161
Jerry Dehnbostel, *President*
Shawn Ferguson, *Opers Mgr*
Lolita Dehnbostel, *Treasurer*
EMP: 12 **EST:** 1938
SQ FT: 3,000
SALES (est): 1.1MM **Privately Held**
WEB: www.tomahawkprinting.com
SIC: 2752 2789 Commercial printing, offset; binding only: books, pamphlets, magazines, etc.

(G-19534)
TOMAHAWK PRINTING LLC (PA)
Also Called: Mustang Printing
229 N Fulton St (43567-1171)
PHONE 419 335-3161
Richard L Elrod, *President*

Shawn Ferguson, *Mng Member*
Amy Ferguson, *Mng Member*
Dylan Leu, *Manager*
Carol Elrod, *Admin Sec*
EMP: 10
SQ FT: 32,000
SALES (est): 1.1MM **Privately Held**
WEB: www.mustangink.com
SIC: 2752 Commercial printing, offset

(G-19535)
TURKEYFOOT CREEK CREAMERY
11313 County Road D (43567-9574)
PHONE..................................419 335-0224
Del Burkholder, *Principal*
EMP: 3
SALES (est): 144.5K **Privately Held**
SIC: 2021 Creamery butter

(G-19536)
VESCO OIL CORPORATION
247 N Brunell St (43567-1102)
P.O. Box 391 (43567-0391)
PHONE..................................419 335-8871
EMP: 3
SALES (est): 99.1K **Privately Held**
SIC: 1311 Crude petroleum & natural gas

(G-19537)
WAUSEON MACHINE & MFG INC (PA)
995 Enterprise Ave (43567-9333)
PHONE..................................419 337-0940
Russell P Dominique, *CEO*
Eric Patty, *President*
Douglas A Weddelman, *Principal*
Chad Desgrange, *Opers Mgr*
Jackie Dominique, *Purch Mgr*
▲ **EMP:** 75
SQ FT: 24,000
SALES (est): 18.4MM **Privately Held**
WEB: www.wauseonmachine.com
SIC: 3599 3441 3559 7629 Machine shop, jobbing & repair; fabricated structural metal; automotive related machinery; electrical repair shops; rolling mill machinery; special dies, tools, jigs & fixtures

(G-19538)
WAUSEON SILO & COAL COMPANY
Also Called: Wauseon Precast
535 Wood St (43567-1248)
PHONE..................................419 335-6041
Barton L Frazier, *President*
EMP: 10
SQ FT: 41,000
SALES: 739.9K **Privately Held**
SIC: 3272 5251 Covers, catch basin: concrete; septic tanks, concrete; steps, prefabricated concrete; builders' hardware

(G-19539)
WYSE INDUSTRIAL CARTS INC
10510 County Road 12 (43567-9237)
PHONE..................................419 923-7353
Gene Wyse, *President*
Randy Wyse, *Vice Pres*
Steve Lauber, *Webmaster*
Wendy Wyse, *Assistant*
EMP: 12
SQ FT: 20,000
SALES (est): 2.2MM **Privately Held**
WEB: www.wyseindustrialcarts.com
SIC: 3448 Ramps: prefabricated metal

(G-19540)
ZIMMERMAN SHTMTL STL & WLDG
1179 N Ottokee St (43567-1911)
PHONE..................................419 335-3806
Dennis M Zimmerman, *Owner*
EMP: 3
SQ FT: 2,100
SALES (est): 242.7K **Privately Held**
SIC: 3441 Fabricated structural metal

Waverly
Pike County

(G-19541)
C & C MOBILE HOMES LLC
Also Called: Colburn Dairy
1580 Valley Rd (45690-9532)
PHONE..................................740 663-5535
Murrell Colburn, *Mng Member*
Imogene Colburn, *Mng Member*
EMP: 4
SALES: 100K **Privately Held**
SIC: 2451 Mobile homes

(G-19542)
CLEARFIELD OHIO HOLDINGS INC
300 E 2nd St (45690-1323)
PHONE..................................740 947-5121
Brian Jonard, *Branch Mgr*
EMP: 67
SALES (corp-wide): 11.4MM **Privately Held**
SIC: 1389 Gas field services
PA: Clearfield Ohio Holdings Inc
Radnor Corp Ctr Bdg5 40
Radnor PA 19087
610 293-0410

(G-19543)
CST ZERO DISCHARGED CAR WASH S
223 Virginia Ln (45690-9639)
PHONE..................................740 947-5480
EMP: 3 **EST:** 1995
SALES (est): 130K **Privately Held**
SIC: 3589 3826 Water And Enviromental Saving

(G-19544)
D & M WELDING & RADIATOR
9093 State Route 220 (45690-9734)
PHONE..................................740 947-9032
Hank Dyke, *Partner*
Chuck Myers, *Partner*
EMP: 4
SQ FT: 2,400
SALES (est): 278.5K **Privately Held**
SIC: 7692 7539 1799 Welding repair; radiator repair shop, automotive; welding on site

(G-19545)
ECHO ENVIRONMENTAL WAVERLY LLC
479 Indl Pk Dr (45690)
PHONE..................................740 286-2810
Alan Stockmeister, *CEO*
EMP: 12
SALES (est): 1.7MM **Privately Held**
SIC: 3341 Copper smelting & refining (secondary)

(G-19546)
GEO-TECH POLYMERS LLC
423 Hopewell Rd Ste 2 (45690-9804)
PHONE..................................614 797-2300
Doug Collins, *President*
▼ **EMP:** 17
SALES (est): 5.2MM **Privately Held**
SIC: 2821 Plastics materials & resins
PA: Wastren Advantage, Inc.
1571 Shyville Rd
Piketon OH 45661

(G-19547)
GRAPHIX NETWORK
122 N High St (45690-1342)
PHONE..................................740 941-3771
Johanna Pixley, *Principal*
EMP: 4
SALES (est): 296.9K **Privately Held**
SIC: 2752 Commercial printing, lithographic

(G-19548)
HOT SPOT
Also Called: Bronze and Beautiful
800 W 2nd St (45690-9191)
PHONE..................................740 947-8888
Jeff Straughtenburger, *Owner*
EMP: 3
SALES (est): 193.2K **Privately Held**
SIC: 3648 Sun tanning equipment, incl. tanning beds

(G-19549)
J&R PALLET LTD
1100 Travis Rd (45690-9086)
PHONE..................................740 226-1112
Ramona Southworth, *Principal*
EMP: 4
SALES (est): 225K **Privately Held**
SIC: 2448 Pallets, wood & wood with metal

(G-19550)
KIRCHHOFF AUTO WAVERLY INC (DH)
Also Called: Vr Waverly Inc.
611 W 2nd St (45690-9701)
PHONE..................................740 947-7763
Dennis Berry, *CEO*
▲ **EMP:** 69
SALES (est): 41.7MM
SALES (corp-wide): 1.8B **Privately Held**
SIC: 3465 Automotive stampings
HQ: Kirchhoff Automotive Gmbh
Stefanstr. 2
Iserlohn 58638
237 182-000

(G-19551)
MILLTREE LUMBER HOLDINGS
535 Coal Dock Rd (45690-9799)
PHONE..................................740 226-2090
Terry Marr, *Principal*
EMP: 7
SALES (est): 809.6K **Privately Held**
SIC: 2448 Pallets, wood

(G-19552)
MILLWOOD INC
535 Coal Dock Rd (45690-9799)
PHONE..................................740 226-2090
Terry Robbins, *Branch Mgr*
EMP: 75 **Privately Held**
SIC: 2448 Pallets, wood
PA: Millwood, Inc.
3708 International Blvd
Vienna OH 44473

(G-19553)
NEWS WATCHMAN & PAPER
Also Called: Acm Ohio
860 W Emmitt Ave Ste 5 (45690-1080)
P.O. Box 151 (45690-0151)
PHONE..................................740 947-2149
Norman Guilliland, *Principal*
Carrie Humble, *Principal*
EMP: 10
SALES (est): 461.2K **Privately Held**
WEB: www.newswatchman.com
SIC: 2711 7313 Newspapers, publishing & printing; newspaper advertising representative

(G-19554)
OAK CHIPS INC
Also Called: O C I
9329 State Route 220 A (45690-9190)
PHONE..................................740 947-4159
Edward Todd Nathan, *President*
◆ **EMP:** 49 **EST:** 2014
SALES (est): 924.9K **Privately Held**
SIC: 2448 2861 Wood pallets & skids; wood extract products

(G-19555)
OHIO CANDLE CO INC
7040 Us Rte 23 (45690)
P.O. Box 103, Piketon (45661-0103)
PHONE..................................740 289-8000
William Purpeco, *President*
Ed Purpeco, *Vice Pres*
Melinda Purpeco, *Treasurer*
Rebecca Purpeco, *Admin Sec*
EMP: 3
SALES: 350K **Privately Held**
SIC: 3999 Candles

(G-19556)
PERFORMANX SPECIALTY CHEM LLC
423 Hopewell Rd (45690-9801)
PHONE..................................614 300-7001
Kim Pellock, *Branch Mgr*
EMP: 6
SALES (corp-wide): 1MM **Privately Held**
SIC: 2834 Pharmaceutical preparations
PA: Performanx Specialty Chemicals, Llc
300 Westdale Ave
Westerville OH 43082
614 300-7001

(G-19557)
PIKE COUNTY PAPER INC
14572 Us Highway 23 Ste C (45690-9448)
PHONE..................................740 947-5522
EMP: 14
SQ FT: 800
SALES (est): 670K **Privately Held**
SIC: 2741 Newsletter Publishing

(G-19558)
PIKE TOOL & MANUFACTURING CO
754 W 2nd St (45690-9701)
PHONE..................................740 947-7462
James E Hambrick, *President*
Dal Hambrick, *Admin Sec*
EMP: 3
SQ FT: 4,800
SALES (est): 75K **Privately Held**
SIC: 3545 Machine tool accessories

(G-19559)
PRINTEX INCORPORATED
Also Called: Fomerly Daniels Printing Den
101 Victory Dr (45690-1062)
PHONE..................................740 947-8800
Todd Schobelock, *Manager*
EMP: 3
SALES (corp-wide): 1.6MM **Privately Held**
SIC: 2752 Commercial printing, offset
PA: Printex, Incorporated
185 E Main St
Chillicothe OH 45601
740 773-0088

Wayne
Wood County

(G-19560)
BRADNER OIL COMPANY INC
Wayne Rd (43466)
PHONE..................................419 288-2945
Robert Harstter, *President*
Carla Harstter, *Vice Pres*
EMP: 3
SALES: 500K **Privately Held**
SIC: 1389 5172 Oil & gas field services; petroleum products

Waynesburg
Stark County

(G-19561)
ACE ASSEMBLY PACKAGING INC
133 N Mill St (44688-9124)
P.O. Box 55 (44688-0055)
PHONE..................................330 866-9117
Dency S Cilona, *President*
EMP: 30
SALES (est): 2.4MM **Privately Held**
SIC: 7389 3999 Packaging & labeling services; manufacturing industries

(G-19562)
BAUGHMANS MACHINE & WELD SHOP
6498 June Rd Nw (44688-9433)
PHONE..................................330 866-9243
Paul Baughman, *President*
John Baughaman, *Vice Pres*
Kathy Miller, *Treasurer*
EMP: 8
SQ FT: 960
SALES (est): 632.4K **Privately Held**
SIC: 7692 Welding repair

(G-19563)
E & M LIBERTY WELDING INC
141 James St (44688)
PHONE..................................330 866-2338
Mark Crowe, *President*

Earl Ecenbarger, *Vice Pres*
EMP: 8
SALES (est): 50K **Privately Held**
SIC: 7692 1711 Welding repair; boiler & furnace contractors

(G-19564)
OS POWER TONG INC
7330 Minerva Rd Se (44688-9340)
P.O. Box 694 (44688-0694)
PHONE..................................330 866-3815
Thomas R Orlando, *President*
Steven Nicholson, *Vice Pres*
EMP: 4
SALES (est): 410K **Privately Held**
SIC: 1389 Gas field services

(G-19565)
PETROS CONCRETE INC (PA)
7105 Lardon Rd Nw (44688-9604)
PHONE..................................330 868-6130
EMP: 6
SALES (est): 626.5K **Privately Held**
SIC: 3273 Mfg Ready-Mixed Concrete

(G-19566)
TERRA STAR INC
111 N Main St (44688)
PHONE..................................405 200-1336
Bradley Wittrock, *CEO*
Tommy Peck, *Foreman/Supr*
EMP: 29
SALES (corp-wide): 12.6MM **Privately Held**
SIC: 1389 Cementing oil & gas well casings
PA: Terra Star Inc
1515 S 7th St Ste 300
Kingfisher OK 73750
405 200-1336

Waynesfield
Auglaize County

(G-19567)
INDUSTRIAL PAINT & STRIP INC
1000 Commerce Ct (45896-8415)
P.O. Box 967, Logan (43138-0967)
PHONE..................................419 568-2222
Richard W Libby, *President*
Donna J Libby, *Treasurer*
EMP: 35
SQ FT: 13,500
SALES (est): 340.7K **Privately Held**
SIC: 3471 Plating & polishing

Waynesville
Warren County

(G-19568)
INDICATOR SHOP
8875 Bellbrook Rd (45068-9741)
PHONE..................................513 897-0055
Mary Conley, *Owner*
EMP: 3
SALES: 140K **Privately Held**
SIC: 3829 Measuring & controlling devices

(G-19569)
JOHN PURDUM
Also Called: Brass Lantern Antiques
100 S Main St (45068-8954)
P.O. Box 597 (45068-0597)
PHONE..................................513 897-9686
John Purdum, *Owner*
EMP: 6
SQ FT: 3,720
SALES (est): 307.3K **Privately Held**
WEB: www.purdumantiques.com
SIC: 5932 5399 2519 7011 Antiques; country general stores; household furniture, except wood or metal: upholstered; hotels & motels; eating places

(G-19570)
OUTHOUSE PAPER ETC INC
319 Collett Rd (45068-9306)
P.O. Box 101, Cuba (45177-0101)
PHONE..................................937 382-2800
Shelley Taylor, *President*
EMP: 6

SQ FT: 3,250
SALES (est): 498.3K **Privately Held**
SIC: 2679 Paperboard products, converted

(G-19571)
PATRICK M DAVIDSON
Also Called: Davidson Meat Processing Plant
6490 Corwin Ave (45068-9722)
PHONE..................................513 897-2971
Patrick M Davidson, *Owner*
EMP: 6
SQ FT: 3,000
SALES (est): 80K **Privately Held**
SIC: 0751 2013 2011 Slaughtering: custom livestock services; sausages & other prepared meats; meat packing plants

(G-19572)
ROSE OF SHARON ENTERPRISES
9243 Old Stage Rd (45068-8831)
P.O. Box 984 (45068-0984)
PHONE..................................937 862-4543
Sharon Willard, *Owner*
James Willard, *Co-Owner*
EMP: 3
SALES: 250K **Privately Held**
SIC: 3999 Potpourri

Wellington
Lorain County

(G-19573)
BOOS MAKE & TAKE
676 N Main St (44090-1040)
PHONE..................................440 647-0000
Terry Jenkins, *Manager*
EMP: 4
SALES (est): 378.5K **Privately Held**
SIC: 3911 Cigar & cigarette accessories

(G-19574)
CLEVELAND CITY FORGE INC
46950 State Route 18 (44090-9791)
PHONE..................................440 647-5400
Richard Kovach, *President*
Kenneth Kovach, *Treasurer*
Drew Maddock, *Admin Sec*
EMP: 40
SQ FT: 200,000
SALES (est): 10.2MM **Privately Held**
WEB: www.clevelandcityforge.com
SIC: 3441 Fabricated structural metal

(G-19575)
E D M STAR-ONE INC
745 Shiloh Ave (44090-1190)
PHONE..................................440 647-0600
Howard White, *President*
Samuel White, *Vice Pres*
Michael White, *Treasurer*
Timothy White, *Admin Sec*
EMP: 10
SQ FT: 6,500
SALES (est): 880K **Privately Held**
WEB: www.star-one-edm.com
SIC: 3599 Machine shop, jobbing & repair

(G-19576)
ECO MECHANICAL LLC
47559 Hughes Rd (44090-9717)
PHONE..................................440 610-9253
James McKnight, *President*
EMP: 3
SQ FT: 1,000
SALES: 414.8K **Privately Held**
SIC: 3569 Testing chambers for altitude, temperature, ordnance, power

(G-19577)
EDWARD W DANIEL LLC
46950 State Route 18 S (44090-9791)
PHONE..................................440 647-1960
Ken Wrona, *CFO*
Robert Oriti,
Stuart W Cordell,
EMP: 36 EST: 1922
SQ FT: 75,000

SALES (est): 5.8MM **Privately Held**
WEB: www.ewdaniel.com
SIC: 3429 5085 3494 3463 Manufactured hardware (general); industrial supplies; valves & pipe fittings; nonferrous forgings; iron & steel forgings; bolts, nuts, rivets & washers

(G-19578)
FOREST CITY TECHNOLOGIES INC (PA)
299 Clay St (44090-1128)
P.O. Box 86 (44090-0086)
PHONE..................................440 647-2115
John D Cloud Sr, *President*
Amy Martin, *President*
Charles Schillig, *Vice Pres*
David Snowball, *Vice Pres*
Fran Stack, *Vice Pres*
▲ EMP: 430 EST: 1955
SQ FT: 50,000
SALES (est): 291.7MM **Privately Held**
SIC: 3053 Gaskets, all materials

(G-19579)
FOREST CITY TECHNOLOGIES INC
232 Maple St (44090-1164)
P.O. Box 86 (44090-0086)
PHONE..................................440 647-2115
Chuck Shilleg, *Manager*
EMP: 500
SALES (corp-wide): 291.7MM **Privately Held**
SIC: 3053 Gaskets & sealing devices; gaskets, all materials
PA: Forest City Technologies, Inc.
299 Clay St
Wellington OH 44090
440 647-2115

(G-19580)
FOREST CITY TECHNOLOGIES INC
Also Called: Forest City Tech Plant 4
401 Magyar St (44090-1278)
P.O. Box 86 (44090-0086)
PHONE..................................440 647-2115
Bob Nelson, *General Mgr*
Bud Brasee, *Engineer*
EMP: 150
SALES (corp-wide): 291.7MM **Privately Held**
SIC: 3053 Gasket materials
PA: Forest City Technologies, Inc.
299 Clay St
Wellington OH 44090
440 647-2115

(G-19581)
FOREST CITY TECHNOLOGIES INC
Also Called: Adelphia
299 Clay St (44090-1128)
P.O. Box 86 (44090-0086)
PHONE..................................440 647-2115
Buzz Bernning, *Manager*
EMP: 120
SALES (corp-wide): 291.7MM **Privately Held**
SIC: 3053 Gasket materials
PA: Forest City Technologies, Inc.
299 Clay St
Wellington OH 44090
440 647-2115

(G-19582)
FOREST CITY TECHNOLOGIES INC
Also Called: Technofab
234 Maple St (44090-1164)
P.O. Box 86 (44090-0086)
PHONE..................................440 647-2115
EMP: 4
SALES (corp-wide): 291.7MM **Privately Held**
SIC: 3053 Gaskets & sealing devices
PA: Forest City Technologies, Inc.
299 Clay St
Wellington OH 44090
440 647-2115

(G-19583)
HUNTINGTON HARDWOOD LBR CO INC
28211 Baker Rd (44090-9349)
P.O. Box 5, Spencer (44275-0005)
PHONE..................................440 647-2283
EMP: 7
SALES (est): 625.4K **Privately Held**
SIC: 2411 2431 Logging Mfg Millwork

(G-19584)
KALRON LLC
143 Erie St (44090-1206)
P.O. Box 156 (44090-0156)
PHONE..................................440 647-3039
Todd Markus, *Principal*
EMP: 20
SALES (est): 4.5MM **Privately Held**
SIC: 3444 Sheet metalwork

(G-19585)
L & L FABRICATING LLC
46419 Whitney Rd (44090-9846)
PHONE..................................440 647-6649
Larry Gilles, *Owner*
Linda Gilles, *Owner*
EMP: 4
SALES: 350K **Privately Held**
WEB: www.llfab.com
SIC: 3999 Education aids, devices & supplies

(G-19586)
MD TOOL & DIE INC
755 Industrial Ave (44090-1193)
P.O. Box 298 (44090-0298)
PHONE..................................440 647-6456
Michael Donovan, *President*
Linda Donovan, *Office Mgr*
EMP: 4
SQ FT: 2,400
SALES (est): 478.4K **Privately Held**
SIC: 3544 Special dies & tools

(G-19587)
NN INC
125 Bennett St (44090-1202)
PHONE..................................440 647-4711
EMP: 203
SALES (corp-wide): 770.6MM **Publicly Held**
SIC: 3562 Ball bearings & parts
PA: Nn, Inc.
6210 Ardrey Kell Rd
Charlotte NC 28277
980 264-4300

(G-19588)
NN AUTOCAM PRECISION COMPONENT
720 Shiloh Ave (44090-1190)
PHONE..................................440 647-4711
EMP: 3
SALES (est): 298.7K **Privately Held**
SIC: 3599 Machine shop, jobbing & repair

(G-19589)
PRECISION FITTINGS LLC
709 N Main St (44090-1089)
PHONE..................................440 647-4143
Christopher H Lake, *President*
▲ EMP: 49
SQ FT: 65,000
SALES (est): 10.9MM **Privately Held**
WEB: www.precisionfittings.com
SIC: 3452 3451 3498 3494 Bolts, nuts, rivets & washers; screw machine products; fabricated pipe & fittings; valves & pipe fittings

(G-19590)
ROCHESTER MANUFACTURING INC
Also Called: ELECTROBURR
24765 Quarry Rd (44090-9293)
PHONE..................................440 647-2463
David Younglas, *CEO*
Scott Frombaugh, *President*
EMP: 16
SQ FT: 14,000
SALES: 1.2MM **Privately Held**
WEB: www.rochestermfg.com
SIC: 3599 Machine shop, jobbing & repair

Wellington - Lorain County (G-19591)

(G-19591)
SECTIONAL STAMPING INC
Also Called: Wellington Stamping
350 Maple St (44090-1171)
PHONE...............................440 647-2100
Ramzi Hermiz, *CEO*
Jack Falcon, *President*
James Fanello, *Vice Pres*
David J Hessler, *Admin Sec*
EMP: 280
SQ FT: 200,000
SALES (est): 53.3MM **Publicly Held**
SIC: 3469 Stamping metal for the trade
HQ: Shiloh Corporation
    880 Steel Dr
    Valley City OH 44280
    330 558-2600

(G-19592)
SHILOH INDUSTRIES INC
350 Maple St (44090-1171)
PHONE...............................440 647-2100
SRI Perumal, *Plant Mgr*
EMP: 799 **Publicly Held**
SIC: 3469 Metal stampings
PA: Shiloh Industries, Inc.
    880 Steel Dr
    Valley City OH 44280

(G-19593)
TITE SEAL CASE COMPANY INC
Also Called: Forest City Tech
299 Clay St (44090-1128)
P.O. Box 86 (44090-0086)
PHONE...............................440 647-2371
John Cloud, *President*
Dave Snowball, *Vice Pres*
EMP: 4 **EST:** 1948
SQ FT: 1,000
SALES (est): 117.1K **Privately Held**
WEB: www.forestcitytech.com
SIC: 3053 Gaskets, packing & sealing devices

(G-19594)
WELLINGTON MANUFACTURING
200 Erie St (44090-1268)
PHONE...............................440 647-1162
Gary Petshe, *Principal*
EMP: 3
SALES (est): 267.7K **Privately Held**
SIC: 3999 Manufacturing industries

(G-19595)
WHIRLAWAY CORPORATION (HQ)
720 Shiloh Ave (44090-1190)
PHONE...............................440 647-4711
Roderick R Baty, *CEO*
James R Widders, *Vice Pres*
▲ **EMP:** 175
SALES (est): 54.1MM
SALES (corp-wide): 770.6MM **Publicly Held**
WEB: www.whirlawaycorporation.com
SIC: 3714 3451 3469 Motor vehicle brake systems & parts; screw machine products; appliance parts, porcelain enameled
PA: Nn, Inc.
    6210 Ardrey Kell Rd
    Charlotte NC 28277
    980 264-4300

(G-19596)
WHIRLAWAY CORPORATION
125 Bennett St (44090-1202)
PHONE...............................440 647-4711
Thomas G Zupan, *Principal*
EMP: 150
SALES (corp-wide): 770.6MM **Publicly Held**
WEB: www.whirlawaycorporation.com
SIC: 3714 3451 Motor vehicle parts & accessories; screw machine products
HQ: Whirlaway Corporation
    720 Shiloh Ave
    Wellington OH 44090
    440 647-4711

(G-19597)
WHIRLAWAY CORPORATION
Whirlaway Cincinnatti, A Div Nn
720 Shiloh Ave (44090-1190)
PHONE...............................440 647-4711
Richard Eichmann, *Branch Mgr*
EMP: 20
SALES (corp-wide): 770.6MM **Publicly Held**
WEB: www.whirlawaycorporation.com
SIC: 3714 3451 Motor vehicle parts & accessories; screw machine products
HQ: Whirlaway Corporation
    720 Shiloh Ave
    Wellington OH 44090
    440 647-4711

Wellston
Jackson County

(G-19598)
BROWN-FORMAN CORPORATION
Also Called: Blue Grass Cooperage - Jackson
468 Salem Church Rd (45692)
P.O. Box 528, Jackson (45640-0528)
PHONE...............................740 384-3027
James Gulley, *Branch Mgr*
Miguel Jimenez, *Manager*
Jo E Boggs, *Admin Asst*
EMP: 27
SALES (corp-wide): 3.2B **Publicly Held**
WEB: www.brown-forman.com
SIC: 2429 2449 Cooperage stock products: staves, headings, hoops, etc.; wood containers
PA: Brown-Forman Corporation
    850 Dixie Hwy
    Louisville KY 40210
    502 585-1100

(G-19599)
DAVIS CAULKING & SEALANT LLC
199 Garfield Rd (45692-9746)
PHONE...............................740 286-3825
Arnold Davis, *Principal*
EMP: 4 **EST:** 2008
SALES (est): 433.5K **Privately Held**
SIC: 2891 Sealants

(G-19600)
GEM BEVERAGES INC
106 E 11th St (45692-1713)
PHONE...............................740 384-2411
Rex Holzapfel, *President*
EMP: 12 **EST:** 1995
SALES (est): 1.5MM **Privately Held**
SIC: 2086 Soft drinks: packaged in cans, bottles, etc.

(G-19601)
GENERAL MILLS INC
2403 S Pennsylvania Ave (45692-9503)
PHONE...............................740 286-2170
John Komor, *Plant Mgr*
Sam Stover, *Manager*
Bill Stowe, *Manager*
Byron Walters, *Director*
Tim Dill, *Director*
EMP: 28
SALES (corp-wide): 15.7B **Publicly Held**
SIC: 2043 Cereal breakfast foods
PA: General Mills, Inc.
    1 General Mills Blvd
    Minneapolis MN 55426
    763 764-7600

(G-19602)
J-FAB
21 N Wisconsin Ave (45692-1149)
P.O. Box 622 (45692-0622)
PHONE...............................740 384-2649
Nick Rypert Sr, *Partner*
Bryan Rypert, *Partner*
EMP: 5
SALES (est): 258.1K **Privately Held**
SIC: 3999 Manufacturing industries

(G-19603)
J-VAC INDUSTRIES INC
202 S Pennsylvania Ave (45692-1797)
PHONE...............................740 384-2155
Frank Declemente, *President*
Richard Moore, *Director*
Ann Ogletree, *Director*
EMP: 74
SQ FT: 8,300
SALES: 28.4K **Privately Held**
SIC: 8331 3269 Sheltered workshop; art & ornamental ware, pottery

(G-19604)
JACK HUFFMAN
1210 Hiram West Rd (45692-9536)
PHONE...............................740 384-5178
ADM Jack Huffman, *Owner*
Jack Huffman, *Owner*
EMP: 3
SALES (est): 113.7K **Privately Held**
SIC: 3281 Cut stone & stone products

(G-19605)
PILLSBURY COMPANY LLC
2403 S Pennsylvania Ave (45692-9503)
P.O. Box 151 (45692-0151)
PHONE...............................740 286-2170
Gary Deinert, *VP Human Res*
Tim Dill, *Manager*
EMP: 15
SALES (corp-wide): 15.7B **Publicly Held**
WEB: www.pillsbury.com
SIC: 2041 2033 Flour & other grain mill products; canned fruits & specialties
HQ: The Pillsbury Company Llc
    1 General Mills Blvd
    Minneapolis MN 55426

(G-19606)
SEYMOURS LOGGING
1085 Loop Rd (45692-9768)
PHONE...............................740 288-1825
Ralph Seymour, *Partner*
EMP: 12
SALES (est): 1MM **Privately Held**
SIC: 2411 Wood chips, produced in the field; pole cutting contractors

(G-19607)
SOUTHERN OHIO WOOD
1085 Loop Rd (45692-9768)
P.O. Box 452, Hamden (45634-0452)
PHONE...............................740 288-1825
Ralph Seymour, *Owner*
EMP: 7
SALES (est): 378.7K **Privately Held**
SIC: 2421 Sawmills & planing mills, general

(G-19608)
SUPERIOR HARDWOODS OHIO INC (PA)
134 Wellston Indus Pk Rd (45692)
P.O. Box 606 (45692-0606)
PHONE...............................740 384-5677
Emmett Conway Jr, *President*
EMP: 60
SALES (est): 9.1MM **Privately Held**
SIC: 2421 2426 Sawmills & planing mills, general; hardwood dimension & flooring mills

(G-19609)
T&R LOGGING LLC
1085 Loop Rd (45692-9768)
P.O. Box 452, Hamden (45634-0452)
PHONE...............................740 288-1825
Ralph Seymour, *Principal*
EMP: 3
SALES (est): 182.6K **Privately Held**
SIC: 2411 Logging camps & contractors

(G-19610)
WELLSTON AEROSOL MFG CO INC
105 W A St (45692-1113)
P.O. Box 326 (45692-0326)
PHONE...............................740 384-2320
Norma Lockard, *President*
Dan Lockard Jr, *Vice Pres*
EMP: 25 **EST:** 1957
SALES (est): 4.9MM **Privately Held**
SIC: 2813 Aerosols

(G-19611)
WILKETT ENTERPRISES LLC
Also Called: Dirt Works Excavating
109 Mitchell Dr 4 (45692-9204)
PHONE...............................740 384-2890
Gregory Wilkett, *Principal*
EMP: 6
SALES: 350K **Privately Held**
SIC: 3531 Construction machinery

Wellsville
Columbiana County

(G-19612)
CIMBAR PERFORMANCE MNRL WV LLC
2400 Clark Ave (43968-1070)
PHONE...............................330 532-2034
John H Waters, *President*
EMP: 24
SALES (est): 3.5MM
SALES (corp-wide): 29.3MM **Privately Held**
WEB: www.cimbar.com
SIC: 3295 Minerals, ground or otherwise treated
PA: United Minerals And Properties, Inc.
    49 Jackson Lake Rd Ste O
    Chatsworth GA 30705
    770 387-0319

(G-19613)
QUALITY LIQUID FEEDS INC
2402 Clark Ave (43968-1070)
PHONE...............................330 532-4635
Darin Porter, *Manager*
Tim Halfhill, *Manager*
EMP: 10
SALES (corp-wide): 148.2MM **Privately Held**
WEB: www.qlf.com
SIC: 2048 Prepared feeds
PA: Quality Liquid Feeds, Inc.
    3586 State Road 23
    Dodgeville WI 53533
    608 935-2345

(G-19614)
STEVENSON MFG CO
Also Called: Stevco
1 1st St (43968)
PHONE...............................330 532-1581
Timothy Lynch, *President*
Todd Lynch, *Vice Pres*
Lisa De Ardo, *Controller*
EMP: 8 **EST:** 1800
SQ FT: 115,000
SALES (est): 1.3MM **Privately Held**
WEB: www.stevensonmfg.com
SIC: 3541 3599 Grinding machines, metalworking; machine shop, jobbing & repair

(G-19615)
YELLOW CREEK CASTING COMPANY
18141 Fife Coal Rd (43968-9760)
PHONE...............................330 532-4608
Ron Kelly, *President*
Erin Kelly, *Prdtn Mgr*
Jeanne Kelly, *Treasurer*
Lois Kelly, *Treasurer*
Gerald Kelly, *Sales Staff*
EMP: 20
SQ FT: 4,500
SALES (est): 3.1MM **Privately Held**
WEB: www.yellowcreekcasting.com
SIC: 3321 3322 Gray iron castings; malleable iron foundries

West Alexandria
Preble County

(G-19616)
AMS GLOBAL LTD
119 E Dayton St (45381-1209)
P.O. Box 746, Verona (45378-0746)
PHONE...............................937 620-1036
Terrence Brennan, *Partner*
Anna Matthews, *Partner*
EMP: 14
SQ FT: 10,000
SALES (est): 700K **Privately Held**
SIC: 3089 Plastic processing

(G-19617)
CLEARY MACHINE COMPANY INC
4858 Us Route 35 E (45381-8316)
PHONE...............................937 839-4278
Paul Kasperski, *President*

Angela Salazar, *Executive*
EMP: 21
SQ FT: 24,000
SALES (est): 3.9MM **Privately Held**
SIC: 3599 Machine shop, jobbing & repair

(G-19618)
DOW CHEMICAL COMPANY
10 Electric St (45381-1212)
PHONE..................937 839-4612
David Kistner, *Director*
EMP: 76
SALES (corp-wide): 85.9B **Publicly Held**
SIC: 2869 Industrial organic chemicals
HQ: The Dow Chemical Company
2211 H H Dow Way
Midland MI 48642
989 636-1000

(G-19619)
JOHN M HAND
Also Called: Treasured Times Enterprises
6417 Enterprise Rd (45381-9500)
PHONE..................937 902-1327
John M Hand, *Principal*
EMP: 4
SALES (est): 256.9K **Privately Held**
SIC: 2431 Millwork

(G-19620)
REXARC INTERNATIONAL INC
35 E 3rd St (45381-1231)
P.O. Box 7 (45381-0007)
PHONE..................937 839-4604
Robert Moyer, *CEO*
James P Bowman, *President*
Ann C Smith, *Principal*
Joseph R Smith, *Chairman*
Gretchen Jones, *COO*
◆ **EMP:** 25 **EST:** 1916
SQ FT: 96,000
SALES (est): 6MM **Privately Held**
SIC: 3498 3548 3569 Manifolds, pipe: fabricated from purchased pipe; gas welding equipment; gas generators

(G-19621)
ROGUE MANUFACTURING INC
304 Stotler Rd (45381-1261)
PHONE..................937 839-4026
Paul Kasperski, *President*
EMP: 5
SALES (est): 437.7K **Privately Held**
SIC: 3531 Cranes

(G-19622)
TWIN VALLEY METALCRAFT ASM LLC
4739 Enterprise Rd (45381-9518)
PHONE..................937 787-4634
Debra L Purdy,
David R Purdy,
EMP: 6
SQ FT: 7,000
SALES: 340K **Privately Held**
SIC: 3451 3429 3599 Screw machine products; aircraft hardware; machine shop, jobbing & repair

(G-19623)
VILLAGE OF WEST ALEXANDRIA (PA)
16 N Main St Unit 2 (45381-1191)
P.O. Box 265 (45381-0265)
PHONE..................937 839-4168
Carol Lunssord, *Mayor*
Mitchell Suggs, *Mayor*
EMP: 4 **EST:** 1985
SALES (est): 1.7MM **Privately Held**
WEB: www.walexpreb.org
SIC: 3589 Sewage & water treatment equipment

(G-19624)
WEBERS BODY & FRAME
2017 State Route 503 N (45381-9701)
PHONE..................937 839-5946
David P Weber, *President*
EMP: 9
SALES (est): 875.3K **Privately Held**
SIC: 7532 7536 7692 Body shop, automotive; automotive glass replacement shops; welding repair

(G-19625)
WOEBKENBERG STARTING GATES
8011 Kinsey Rd (45381-9517)
PHONE..................937 696-2446
Mike Woebkenburg, *Owner*
EMP: 5
SALES (est): 115.5K **Privately Held**
SIC: 2399 Horse harnesses & riding crops, etc.: non-leather

(G-19626)
WYSONG GRAVEL CO INC (PA)
Also Called: Camden Ready Mix
2332 State Route 503 N (45381)
PHONE..................937 456-4539
John D Wysong, *President*
Carroll Wysong, *Vice Pres*
EMP: 10
SQ FT: 1,500
SALES (est): 3.1MM **Privately Held**
SIC: 1442 Gravel mining

(G-19627)
WYSONG GRAVEL CO INC
2032 State Route 503 N (45381-9701)
PHONE..................937 839-5497
Carroll Wysong, *Vice Pres*
EMP: 9
SALES (corp-wide): 3.1MM **Privately Held**
SIC: 1442 Gravel mining
PA: Wysong Gravel Co Inc
2332 State Route 503 N
West Alexandria OH 45381
937 456-4539

West Carrollton
Montgomery County

(G-19628)
AERO JET WASH LLC
440 Fame Rd (45449-2315)
PHONE..................866 381-7955
Shawn Tadayon, *Mng Member*
Mike Vahedy, *Mng Member*
Maggy Bahramian, *Manager*
EMP: 10
SQ FT: 4,400
SALES (est): 1.3MM **Privately Held**
WEB: www.aerojetwash.com
SIC: 3724 4581 Aircraft engines & engine parts; aircraft cleaning & janitorial service

(G-19629)
APPVION OPERATIONS INC
1030 W Alex Bell Rd (45449-1923)
PHONE..................937 859-8261
Mark Ferguson, *Manager*
EMP: 400
SALES (corp-wide): 6.3B **Publicly Held**
WEB: www.appletonpapers.com
SIC: 2672 2621 Coated paper, except photographic, carbon or abrasive; paper mills
HQ: Appvion Operations, Inc.
825 E Wisconsin Ave
Appleton WI 54911
920 734-9841

(G-19630)
BARTLEY LAWN SERVICE LLC
Also Called: Bartleys Lawn Services
69 W Alex Bell Rd (45449-1912)
PHONE..................937 435-8884
Todd Bartley, *Mng Member*
EMP: 4
SALES (est): 30K **Privately Held**
SIC: 0782 0783 3711 Lawn services; ornamental shrub & tree services; motor vehicles & car bodies

(G-19631)
FOURTEEN VENTURES GROUP LLC
3131 W Alex Bell Rd (45449-2832)
PHONE..................937 866-2341
Richard Dobson, *Mng Member*
EMP: 8 **EST:** 2014
SALES (est): 776.5K **Privately Held**
SIC: 3993 Signs & advertising specialties

(G-19632)
GITI TECH GROUP LTD
440 Fame Rd (45449-2315)
PHONE..................866 381-7955
Shahin Tadayon, *Managing Dir*
EMP: 5 **EST:** 2011
SALES: 500K **Privately Held**
SIC: 3563 Air & gas compressors

(G-19633)
WEST CARROLLTON CONVERTING INC
400 E Dixie Dr (45449-1827)
PHONE..................937 859-3621
Pierce J Lonergan, *President*
Alan P Berens, *Vice Pres*
◆ **EMP:** 80
SALES (est): 13.5MM **Privately Held**
WEB: www.friendgrp.com
SIC: 2621 Paper mills

(G-19634)
WEST CARROLLTON PARCHMENT
400 E Dixie Dr (45449-1827)
PHONE..................513 594-3341
Cameron Lonergan, *President*
EMP: 28
SALES (est): 7MM **Privately Held**
SIC: 2759 Flexographic printing

West Chester
Butler County

(G-19635)
ABRA AUTO BODY & GLASS LP
8445 Cncnnati Columbus Rd (45069-3523)
PHONE..................513 755-7709
John Webb, *Branch Mgr*
EMP: 6
SALES (corp-wide): 1.8B **Privately Held**
SIC: 5013 2851 Body repair or paint shop supplies, automotive; paint removers
HQ: Abra Auto Body & Glass Lp
7225 Northland Dr N # 110
Brooklyn Park MN 55428
888 872-2272

(G-19636)
ACCUFAB INC
9059 Sutton Pl (45011-9316)
P.O. Box 62433, Cincinnati (45262-0433)
PHONE..................513 942-1929
Geneva Morgan, *President*
James Morgan, *Vice Pres*
Kerry Ward, *CFO*
EMP: 7
SQ FT: 6,500
SALES (est): 1.2MM **Privately Held**
WEB: www.cincy-accufab.com
SIC: 3444 Sheet metalwork

(G-19637)
ADDIS GLASS FABRICATING INC
9418 Sutton Pl (45011-9698)
PHONE..................513 860-3340
Kevin Addis, *President*
Kevin J Addis, *Principal*
Penni Addis, *Corp Secy*
Kevin Ingram, *Sales Mgr*
Kally Addis, *Office Mgr*
▲ **EMP:** 19
SQ FT: 39,000
SALES (est): 1.6MM **Privately Held**
SIC: 3211 3231 Flat glass; products of purchased glass

(G-19638)
ADVANCED TECHNICAL PDTS SUP CO
6186 Centre Park Dr (45069-3868)
PHONE..................513 851-6858
Ben Conner, *President*
Timothy Conner, *Vice Pres*
EMP: 10
SQ FT: 15,000
SALES (est): 1.8MM **Privately Held**
SIC: 3479 Coating of metals & formed products; painting, coating & hot dipping

(G-19639)
AGENT TECHNOLOGIES INC (PA)
8216 Princeton Glendale (45069-1675)
PHONE..................513 942-9444
Ben Moore, *President*
Benjamin E Moore, *President*
EMP: 4
SALES (est): 324K **Privately Held**
WEB: www.agenttech.com
SIC: 7371 3613 Computer software development; control panels, electric

(G-19640)
AK STEEL CORPORATION (HQ)
9227 Centre Pointe Dr (45069-4822)
PHONE..................513 425-4200
James Wainscott, *President*
Roger K Newport, *COO*
Kirk W Reich, *Exec VP*
Keith J Howell, *Senior VP*
Joseph C Alter, *Vice Pres*
◆ **EMP:** 277
SQ FT: 136,000
SALES (est): 2.2B **Publicly Held**
WEB: www.ketnar.org
SIC: 3312 Sheet or strip, steel, hot-rolled

(G-19641)
AK STEEL HOLDING CORPORATION (PA)
9227 Centre Pointe Dr (45069-4822)
PHONE..................513 425-5000
Roger K Newport, *CEO*
James A Thomson, *Ch of Bd*
Kirk W Reich, *President*
Dan Nix, *General Mgr*
Mark Lambert, *District Mgr*
◆ **EMP:** 300
SALES: 6.8B **Publicly Held**
WEB: www.aksteel.com
SIC: 3312 Sheet or strip, steel, hot-rolled

(G-19642)
ALMO PROCESS TECHNOLOGY INC
8849 Brookside Ave # 101 (45069-7114)
PHONE..................513 402-2566
Tom Schroeder, *President*
Dixon F Miller, *Principal*
Jodi Lex, *Business Mgr*
Scott McMaster, *Regl Sales Mgr*
Xander Williams, *Sales Staff*
▲ **EMP:** 6
SALES: 5MM **Privately Held**
SIC: 3443 3535 Separators, industrial process: metal plate; belt conveyor systems, general industrial use

(G-19643)
AMYLIN OHIO
8814 Trade Port Dr (45011-8661)
PHONE..................512 592-8710
EMP: 13
SALES (est): 2.7MM **Privately Held**
SIC: 2834 Pharmaceutical preparations

(G-19644)
ANEST IWATA AIR ENGRG INC
9525 Glades Dr (45011-9410)
PHONE..................513 755-3100
Atsuo Shiria, *President*
▲ **EMP:** 10
SALES (est): 2.4MM **Privately Held**
SIC: 3563 Spraying & dusting equipment

(G-19645)
ANOTEX INDUSTRIES INC
4914 Rialto Rd (45069-2927)
PHONE..................513 860-1165
Diem Pham, *President*
Vinh Pham, *Vice Pres*
Dominic Pham, *Admin Mgr*
Thao Pham, *Shareholder*
EMP: 7
SQ FT: 6,000
SALES: 1MM **Privately Held**
SIC: 3479 Coating, rust preventive

(G-19646)
AP TECH GROUP INC
5130 Rialto Rd (45069-2923)
PHONE..................513 761-8111
James Heimert, *President*
Albert C Heimert, *Vice Pres*

West Chester - Butler County (G-19647) — GEOGRAPHIC SECTION

▼ EMP: 15
SALES (est): 4.1MM Privately Held
SIC: 2499 Food handling & processing products, wood

(G-19647)
APEX CIRCUITS INC
Also Called: Apex Crcits Elctrnic Dsign Man
5100 Excello Ct (45069-3090)
P.O. Box 1190 (45071-1190)
PHONE 513 942-4400
Ken Rensing, *President*
Rob Troescher, *Corp Secy*
JC Privett, *Sales Staff*
EMP: 5
SQ FT: 10,900
SALES (est): 3MM Privately Held
WEB: www.apexcircuits.com
SIC: 3613 3625 Control panels, electric; industrial controls: push button, selector switches, pilot

(G-19648)
AQUA TECHNOLOGY GROUP LLC
8104 Beckett Center Dr (45069-5015)
PHONE 513 298-1183
Chris Davis, *Info Tech Mgr*
Greg Davis,
Joe Davis,
EMP: 8
SQ FT: 15,428
SALES (est): 250K Privately Held
SIC: 7363 5085 3823 3824 Industrial help service; industrial supplies; industrial process control instruments; fluid meters & counting devices; indicating instruments, electric

(G-19649)
AQUAPRO SYSTEMS LLC
Also Called: Aqua Pro Systems
4438 Muhlhauser Rd # 600 (45011-9775)
PHONE 513 315-3647
Charles Murphy, *Mng Member*
Barry Handwerker,
EMP: 40 EST: 2009
SQ FT: 50,000
SALES (est): 927.1K Privately Held
SIC: 3949 Swimming pools, plastic

(G-19650)
AQUAPRO SYSTEMS LLC
4438 Muhlhauser Rd # 500 (45011-9775)
PHONE 877 278-2797
Gary Tamburri, *Natl Sales Mgr*
Zack Lowe, *Technical Staff*
Barry Handwerker,
EMP: 15 EST: 2004
SALES (est): 2MM Privately Held
SIC: 3585 Heating & air conditioning combination units

(G-19651)
ARTH LLC
6680 Burlington Dr (45069-4350)
PHONE 513 293-1646
Mital Patel, *Principal*
EMP: 3
SALES (est): 172.6K Privately Held
SIC: 2834 Pharmaceutical preparations

(G-19652)
ASHLAND LLC
Also Called: Valvoline
9451 Meridian Way (45069-6525)
PHONE 513 682-2405
EMP: 7
SALES (corp-wide): 3.7B Publicly Held
SIC: 2899 Chemical preparations
HQ: Ashland Llc
50 E Rivercenter Blvd # 1600
Covington KY 41011
859 815-3333

(G-19653)
ASLAN WORLDWIDE
8583 Rupp Farm Dr (45069-4526)
PHONE 513 671-0671
Josh Stebbins, *Principal*
EMP: 10
SALES (est): 1MM Privately Held
SIC: 2441 Boxes, wood

(G-19654)
B L ANDERSON CO INC
8887 Eagle Ridge Ct (45069-4544)
PHONE 765 463-1518
Cindy Sell, *Business Mgr*
EMP: 4
SALES (corp-wide): 9.5MM Privately Held
SIC: 3589 Sewage & water treatment equipment
PA: B L Anderson Co Inc
4801 Tazer Dr
Lafayette IN 47905
765 463-1518

(G-19655)
BARNES GROUP INC
9826 Crescent Park Dr (45069-3800)
PHONE 513 759-3528
Rick Dehner, *Branch Mgr*
EMP: 1388
SALES (corp-wide): 1.5B Publicly Held
SIC: 3724 Aircraft engines & engine parts
PA: Barnes Group Inc.
123 Main St
Bristol CT 06010
860 583-7070

(G-19656)
BARNES GROUP INC
Also Called: Windsor Airmotive
9826 Crescent Park Dr (45069-3800)
PHONE 513 779-6888
Jerry Bach, *Branch Mgr*
EMP: 1434
SALES (corp-wide): 1.5B Publicly Held
WEB: www.barnesgroupinc.com
SIC: 3724 Aircraft engines & engine parts
PA: Barnes Group Inc.
123 Main St
Bristol CT 06010
860 583-7070

(G-19657)
BELLWYCK PACKG SOLUTIONS INC
Also Called: Bellwyck Clinical Services
8946 Global Way (45069-7071)
PHONE 513 874-1200
Bruce Wells, *CFO*
EMP: 4
SALES (est): 549.1K Privately Held
SIC: 2834 Pharmaceutical preparations

(G-19658)
BENCHMARK LAND MANAGEMENT LLC
9431 Butler Warren Rd (45069-3765)
PHONE 513 310-7850
Diana E Honerlaw, *Principal*
EMP: 8 EST: 2012
SALES (est): 410.3K Privately Held
SIC: 0781 3271 0782 Landscape planning services; landscape services; blocks, concrete: landscape or retaining wall; landscape contractors

(G-19659)
BESI MANUFACTURING INC (PA)
9087 Sutton Pl (45011-9316)
PHONE 513 874-0232
William Moore, *President*
Sue Weaver, *Vice Pres*
Tom Moore, *Traffic Mgr*
Dave Moore, *Production*
▲ EMP: 24
SQ FT: 17,500
SALES (est): 11.9MM Privately Held
WEB: www.besi-inc.com
SIC: 2399 Seat covers, automobile; seat belts, automobile & aircraft

(G-19660)
BETHART ENTERPRISES INC
Also Called: Bethart Printing Services
8548 Lakota Dr W Ste B (45069-4805)
PHONE 513 777-8707
Dan Hingsbergen, *Manager*
EMP: 4
SALES (est): 331.9K
SALES (corp-wide): 1.5MM Privately Held
SIC: 2752 Commercial printing, lithographic

PA: Bethart Enterprises, Inc
531 Main St
Hamilton OH 45013
513 863-6161

(G-19661)
BMA METALS GROUP INC
7770 W Chester Rd Ste 120 (45069-4157)
PHONE 513 874-5152
Jeanne Beebe, *President*
EMP: 3
SALES (est): 950K Privately Held
SIC: 3449 Miscellaneous metalwork

(G-19662)
BORKE MOLD SPECIALIST INC
9541 Glades Dr (45011-9410)
PHONE 513 870-8000
Fritz Borke, *President*
Patty Borke, *Admin Sec*
EMP: 20
SQ FT: 14,000
SALES (est): 3.3MM Privately Held
WEB: www.borkemold.com
SIC: 3544 Industrial molds

(G-19663)
BRAININ-ADVANCE INDUSTRIES LLC
Also Called: Pep Brainin Fairfield Division
4348 Le Saint Ct (45014-5486)
PHONE 513 874-9760
Carl Dearman, *Manager*
EMP: 25
SALES (corp-wide): 770.6MM Publicly Held
WEB: www.brainin.com
SIC: 3469 3544 Stamping metal for the trade; special dies & tools
HQ: Brainin-Advance Industries Llc
48 Frank Mossberg Dr
Attleboro MA 02703
508 226-1200

(G-19664)
CARDINAL HEALTH 414 LLC
9866 Windisch Rd Bldg 3 (45069-3806)
PHONE 513 759-1900
Tommy Ward, *Branch Mgr*
EMP: 9
SALES (corp-wide): 136.8B Publicly Held
SIC: 2834 2835 Pharmaceutical preparations; radioactive diagnostic substances
HQ: Cardinal Health 414, Llc
7000 Cardinal Pl
Dublin OH 43017
614 757-5000

(G-19665)
CDS TECHNOLOGIES INC
9025 Centre Pointe Dr (45069-4984)
PHONE 800 338-1122
Ronald Keating, *Principal*
EMP: 4 EST: 2008
SALES (est): 276.8K Privately Held
SIC: 3443 Fabricated plate work (boiler shop)

(G-19666)
CEDAR ELEC HOLDINGS CORP
5440 W Chester Rd (45069-2950)
PHONE 773 804-6288
Chris Cowger, *CEO*
Manuel Jaime, *Chief Engr*
Gail Babitt, *CFO*
Dave Smidebush, *Branch Mgr*
Jonas Forsberg, *Officer*
EMP: 70
SALES (corp-wide): 139.2MM Privately Held
SIC: 3812 5013 5015 Navigational systems & instruments; tools & equipment, automotive; automotive supplies, used
PA: Cedar Electronics Holdings Corp.
6500 W Cortland St
Chicago IL 60707
630 862-7282

(G-19667)
CFM INTERNATIONAL INC (PA)
6440 Aviation Way (45069-4546)
P.O. Box 15514, Cincinnati (45215-0514)
PHONE 513 552-2787
Gael Meheust, *President*
Cedric Goubet, *Exec VP*

Sebastien Imbourg, *Exec VP*
Allen Paxson, *Exec VP*
Pierre Bry, *Vice Pres*
EMP: 64
SALES (est): 16.8MM Privately Held
WEB: www.cfm56.com
SIC: 3724 Aircraft engines & engine parts

(G-19668)
CHEMINSTRUMENTS INC (PA)
510 Commercial Dr (45014-7593)
PHONE 513 860-1598
Richard Muny, *President*
Keith Muny, *Vice Pres*
Matt Johnson, *Prdtn Mgr*
Bonnie Cole, *VP Finance*
▲ EMP: 10
SQ FT: 15,000
SALES (est): 2.5MM Privately Held
WEB: www.cheminstruments.com
SIC: 3821 Laboratory equipment: fume hoods, distillation racks, etc.

(G-19669)
CHEMINSTRUMENTS INC
Also Called: Chemical Instruments
510 Commercial Dr (45014-7593)
PHONE 513 860-1598
Keith Muny, *Manager*
EMP: 7 Privately Held
WEB: www.cheminstruments.com
SIC: 3821 Chemical laboratory apparatus
PA: Cheminstruments, Inc
510 Commercial Dr
West Chester OH 45014

(G-19670)
CHEMSULTANTS INTERNATIONAL INC
Also Called: Chem Instruments
510 Commercial Dr (45014-7593)
PHONE 513 860-1598
Keith Muny, *Manager*
EMP: 7
SALES (est): 1.1MM
SALES (corp-wide): 5.4MM Privately Held
SIC: 3821 Laboratory apparatus & furniture
PA: Chemsultants International, Inc.
9079 Tyler Blvd
Mentor OH 44060
440 974-3080

(G-19671)
CINCINNATI COLD DRAWN INC
9108 Sutton Pl (45011-9317)
PHONE 513 874-3296
William H Ward, *President*
Terry Bien, *Exec VP*
EMP: 4
SQ FT: 30,000
SALES (est): 1.2MM
SALES (corp-wide): 46.5MM Privately Held
WEB: www.cincinnaticolddrawn.com
SIC: 3316 Cold finishing of steel shapes
PA: Ashley F. Ward, Inc.
7490 Easy St
Mason OH 45040
513 398-1414

(G-19672)
CINCINNATI GUTTER SUPPLY INC
9345 Prnceton Glendale Rd (45011-9707)
PHONE 513 825-0500
Clarence Mollett, *Principal*
EMP: 5
SQ FT: 12,000
SALES (est): 447.2K Privately Held
SIC: 1761 3444 5082 Gutter & downspout contractor; metal roofing & roof drainage equipment; contractors' materials

(G-19673)
CINCINNATI PRECISION MCHY INC
9083 Sutton Pl (45011-9316)
PHONE 513 860-4133
Pam Ison, *President*
Kathy Nevels, *Marketing Staff*
Dina Schnitzer, *Admin Sec*
EMP: 9
SQ FT: 4,800

GEOGRAPHIC SECTION

West Chester - Butler County (G-19698)

SALES (est): 1.8MM **Privately Held**
WEB: www.cincinnatiprecisionmachinery.com
SIC: 3599 Machine shop, jobbing & repair

(G-19674)
CINCINNATI PRINTERS CO INC
9053 Le Saint Dr (45014-2242)
PHONE.................................513 860-9053
A James Yockey, *President*
Chuck King, *Purchasing*
EMP: 13
SQ FT: 25,000
SALES (est): 2.2MM **Privately Held**
WEB: www.cintiprinters.com
SIC: 2752 Commercial printing, offset

(G-19675)
CIP INTERNATIONAL INC
Also Called: Commercial Interior Products
9575 Le Saint Dr (45014-5447)
PHONE.................................513 874-9925
Thomas Huff, *Ch of Bd*
Kathleen Huff, *President*
Mark Elmlinger, *Vice Pres*
Jay Voss, *CFO*
EMP: 83 **EST:** 1975
SQ FT: 140,000
SALES: 33MM **Privately Held**
WEB: www.cipinternational.net
SIC: 7389 2541 Interior designer; lettering & sign painting services; store fixtures, wood; cabinets, except refrigerated: show, display, etc.: wood

(G-19676)
CLARKWESTERN DIETRICH BUILDING
9050 Centre Pointe Dr (45069-4874)
PHONE.................................513 870-1100
Angelo Gentile, *Exec VP*
Mike Gaskins, *Maint Spvr*
Mike Collins, *Opers Staff*
Chris Ernst, *Manager*
Ryan Mitchell, *Manager*
EMP: 113
SALES (corp-wide): 20.2B **Privately Held**
WEB: www.clarksteel.com
SIC: 3444 Studs & joists, sheet metal
HQ: Clarkwestern Dietrich Building Systems Llc
9050 Centre Pointe Dr
West Chester OH 45069

(G-19677)
CLARKWESTERN DIETRICH BUILDING (DH)
9050 Centre Pointe Dr (45069-4874)
PHONE.................................513 870-1100
Bill Courtney, *CEO*
Greg Ralph, *President*
Clifton Melcher, *General Mgr*
Jay Parr, *General Mgr*
Todd Fischer, *Vice Pres*
▼ **EMP:** 13
SQ FT: 80,000
SALES: 113.9MM
SALES (corp-wide): 20.2B **Privately Held**
SIC: 3444 8711 3081 Studs & joists, sheet metal; engineering services; vinyl film & sheet
HQ: Marubeni-Itochu Steel America Inc.
150 E 42nd St Fl 7
New York NY 10017
212 660-6000

(G-19678)
CONTECH BRIDGE SOLUTIONS LLC (DH)
Also Called: Bridgetek
9025 Cntrpinte Dr Ste 400 (45069)
PHONE.................................513 645-7000
Michael M Rafi, *Principal*
EMP: 15
SQ FT: 1,440
SALES (est): 16.8MM **Privately Held**
SIC: 3443 Fabricated plate work (boiler shop)
HQ: Contech Engineered Solutions Llc
9025 Centre Pointe Dr
West Chester OH 45069
513 645-7000

(G-19679)
CONTECH CNSTR PDTS HLDINGS INC
9025 Centre Pointe Dr # 400 (45069-9700)
PHONE.................................513 645-7000
Ronald Keating, *Principal*
Larry Asbury, *Vice Pres*
Lori Arnold, *Plant Mgr*
Jacob Waugh, *Mfg Staff*
Jim Feltner, *Production*
EMP: 2000 **EST:** 2012
SALES (est): 6.4MM **Privately Held**
SIC: 3443 Fabricated plate work (boiler shop)
HQ: Apax Partners, L.P.
601 Lexington Ave Fl 53
New York NY 10022

(G-19680)
CONTECH ENGNERED SOLUTIONS INC (PA)
9025 Ctr Pinte Dr Ste 400 (45069)
PHONE.................................513 645-7000
Michael Rafi, *President*
Dan Priest, *General Mgr*
Curt Kruger, *District Mgr*
J Paul Allen, *Vice Pres*
Hugh Mickel, *Vice Pres*
EMP: 12
SALES (est): 119.2MM **Privately Held**
SIC: 3084 3317 3441 3443 Plastics pipe; steel pipe & tubes; fabricated structural metal; fabricated plate work (boiler shop); culverts, sheet metal

(G-19681)
CONTECH ENGNERED SOLUTIONS LLC (HQ)
9025 Centre Pointe Dr # 400 (45069-9700)
PHONE.................................513 645-7000
Mike Rafi, *President*
Vernon B Cameron, *President*
MO Heshmati, *President*
Thomas P Slabe, *President*
Steve R Spangel, *President*
◆ **EMP:** 150
SQ FT: 75,000
SALES (est): 616.7MM **Privately Held**
WEB: www.conteches.com
SIC: 3444 3084 3317 3441 Sheet metalwork; culverts, sheet metal; plastics pipe; steel pipe & tubes; fabricated structural metal; fabricated plate work (boiler shop)

(G-19682)
CONTECH STRMWTER SOLUTIONS LLC
9025 Centre Pointe Dr # 400 (45069-9700)
PHONE.................................513 645-7000
Rick Stepien, *President*
James Lenhart, *CTO*
Rebecca H Appenzeller, *Admin Sec*
EMP: 8
SALES (est): 1.3MM **Privately Held**
SIC: 3677 Filtration devices, electronic
HQ: Contech Engineered Solutions Llc
9025 Centre Pointe Dr # 400
West Chester OH 45069
513 645-7000

(G-19683)
CONTROL INTERFACE INC
517 Commercial Dr (45014-7594)
PHONE.................................513 874-2062
Tom Osborn, *President*
Ryan Osborn, *Project Mgr*
Chris Ingram, *Engineer*
Chris Fox, *Project Engr*
▲ **EMP:** 8
SQ FT: 5,000
SALES (est): 1.4MM **Privately Held**
WEB: www.controlinterface.com
SIC: 3613 Control panels, electric

(G-19684)
CORNERSTONE BRANDS INC
Also Called: Grandinroad Catalog
5568 W Chester Rd (45069-2914)
PHONE.................................866 668-5962
Steve Sweeney, *Opers Staff*
David Cleavinger, *Branch Mgr*
EMP: 7 **Publicly Held**
SIC: 3199 Dog furnishings: collars, leashes, muzzles, etc.: leather
HQ: Cornerstone Brands, Inc.
5568 W Chester Rd
West Chester OH 45069
513 603-1000

(G-19685)
CORNERSTONE INDUSTRIES LCC
Also Called: Adam Printing
10132 Mosteller Ln (45069-3872)
PHONE.................................513 871-4546
Andy Werth,
Amy Werth,
EMP: 3 **EST:** 1963
SQ FT: 4,200
SALES (est): 455.5K **Privately Held**
WEB: www.adamprinting.com
SIC: 2752 2791 2759 Commercial printing, offset; typesetting; letterpress printing

(G-19686)
CR BRANDS INC (DH)
8790 Beckett Rd (45069-2904)
PHONE.................................513 860-5039
Richard Owen, *CEO*
John Samoya, *CFO*
Joe Cilurzo, *Sales Dir*
Elli Frasier, *Director*
▼ **EMP:** 82
SQ FT: 5,000
SALES (est): 27.5MM **Publicly Held**
WEB: www.redoxbrands.com
SIC: 2841 5169 3999 Soap & other detergents; detergents & soaps, except specialty cleaning; atomizers, toiletry

(G-19687)
CR HOLDING INC (HQ)
9100 Centre Pointe Dr (45069-4846)
PHONE.................................513 860-5039
Richard Owen, *CEO*
John Samoya, *VP Finance*
EMP: 8
SQ FT: 5,000
SALES (est): 27.5MM **Publicly Held**
SIC: 2841 Soap: granulated, liquid, cake, flaked or chip; detergents, synthetic organic or inorganic alkaline

(G-19688)
CRANE TRAINING USA INC
7908 Cincinnati Dayton Rd H (45069-6629)
PHONE.................................513 755-2177
Alan Stein, *President*
Sandy Stein, *Vice Pres*
EMP: 6
SALES: 520K **Privately Held**
WEB: www.cranetraining.com
SIC: 3536 Hoists, cranes & monorails

(G-19689)
CRYOVAC INC
7410 Union Centre Blvd (45014-2286)
PHONE.................................513 771-7770
Sharon Drysdale, *Opers-Prdtn-Mfg*
EMP: 10
SALES (corp-wide): 4.7B **Publicly Held**
WEB: www.cryovac.com
SIC: 3086 Packaging & shipping materials, foamed plastic
HQ: Cryovac, Inc.
2415 Cascade Pointe Blvd
Charlotte NC 28208
980 430-7000

(G-19690)
CUSTOM MILLCRAFT CORP
9092 Le Saint Dr (45014-2241)
PHONE.................................513 874-7080
Jody Corbett, *Owner*
EMP: 25
SQ FT: 56,000
SALES (est): 5.3MM **Privately Held**
WEB: www.custommillcraft.com
SIC: 2521 2522 2542 Cabinets, office: wood; office furniture, except wood; partitions & fixtures, except wood

(G-19691)
DEE SIGN CO (PA)
Also Called: Diversified Sign
6163 Allen Rd (45069-3855)
PHONE.................................513 779-3333
Braden R Huenefeld, *Ch of Bd*
Craig Dixon, *Vice Pres*
Joe Kolks, *CFO*
Tim Korte, *Controller*
◆ **EMP:** 40 **EST:** 1967
SQ FT: 125,000
SALES (est): 8.6MM **Privately Held**
WEB: www.dee-sign.com
SIC: 3993 Signs, not made in custom sign painting shops

(G-19692)
DEE SIGN USA LLC
6163 Allen Rd (45069-3855)
PHONE.................................513 779-3333
Braden R Huenefeld, *Mng Member*
EMP: 7
SALES (est): 753.9K **Privately Held**
SIC: 3993 Signs & advertising specialties

(G-19693)
DELL INC
9701 Windisch Rd (45069-3827)
PHONE.................................513 644-1700
Kevin Rollins, *Branch Mgr*
EMP: 9
SALES (corp-wide): 90.6B **Publicly Held**
WEB: www.dell.com
SIC: 3571 Electronic computers
HQ: Dell Inc.
1 Dell Way
Round Rock TX 78682
800 289-3355

(G-19694)
DOVER CORPORATION
9393 Prnceton Glendale Rd (45011-9707)
PHONE.................................513 870-3206
EMP: 11
SALES (corp-wide): 6.9B **Publicly Held**
SIC: 3632 Household refrigerators & freezers
PA: Dover Corporation
3005 Highland Pkwy # 200
Downers Grove IL 60515
630 541-1540

(G-19695)
DRT AEROSPACE LLC (HQ)
8694 Rite Track Way (45069-7022)
PHONE.................................937 298-7391
Steve Smith, *Controller*
Gary Van Gundy,
EMP: 25
SQ FT: 36,000
SALES (est): 116.4MM **Privately Held**
SIC: 3728 Research & dev by manuf., aircraft parts & auxiliary equip

(G-19696)
EATON CORPORATION
9902 Windisch Rd (45069-3804)
PHONE.................................513 387-2000
Chris Kuzak, *Administration*
EMP: 35 **Privately Held**
SIC: 3613 Power circuit breakers
HQ: Eaton Corporation
1000 Eaton Blvd
Cleveland OH 44122
440 523-5000

(G-19697)
EMS/HOOPTECH (PA)
9185 Le Saint Dr (45014-5467)
PHONE.................................513 829-7768
Mark Mason, *Owner*
EMP: 3
SALES (est): 530.2K **Privately Held**
WEB: www.hooptechproducts.com
SIC: 2395 Embroidery products, except schiffli machine

(G-19698)
ENERSYS
9436 Meridian Way (45069-6527)
PHONE.................................513 737-2268
Karyl McKnight, *Manager*
EMP: 92
SALES (corp-wide): 2.5B **Publicly Held**
SIC: 3691 Lead acid batteries (storage batteries)
PA: Enersys
2366 Bernville Rd
Reading PA 19605
610 208-1991

West Chester - Butler County (G-19699)

(G-19699)
ESCORT INC
5440 W Chester Rd (45069-9004)
PHONE.................513 870-8500
Chris Cowger, *CEO*
Mark Carrm, *President*
John A Malone, *Senior VP*
Gail Babirr, *CFO*
Manuel Jaime, *CTO*
▲ **EMP:** 90 **EST:** 1997
SQ FT: 32,000
SALES (est): 35.3MM
SALES (corp-wide): 139.2MM **Privately Held**
WEB: www.escortradar.com
SIC: 3812 Radar systems & equipment
PA: Cedar Electronics Holdings Corp.
6500 W Cortland St
Chicago IL 60707
630 862-7282

(G-19700)
ESTECH INC
6217 Centre Park Dr (45069-3866)
PHONE.................805 895-1263
Tamer Ibrahim, *Principal*
EMP: 4
SALES (est): 390K **Privately Held**
SIC: 3841 Surgical & medical instruments

(G-19701)
F A TECH CORP
9065 Sutton Pl (45011-9316)
PHONE.................513 942-1920
Michael Michimi, *President*
EMP: 35
SALES (est): 5.4MM **Privately Held**
WEB: www.brazer.com
SIC: 3599 Machine shop, jobbing & repair; machine & other job shop work

(G-19702)
FEINBLANKING LIMITED INC
9461 Le Saint Dr (45014-5447)
PHONE.................513 860-2100
EMP: 8
SQ FT: 25,000
SALES (est): 860K **Privately Held**
SIC: 3469 Mfg Metal Stampings

(G-19703)
FISHER CONTROLS INTL LLC
5453 W Chester Rd (45069-2963)
PHONE.................513 285-6000
EMP: 4
SALES (corp-wide): 17.4B **Publicly Held**
SIC: 3491 Valves, automatic control
HQ: Fisher Controls International Llc
205 S Center St
Marshalltown IA 50158
641 754-3011

(G-19704)
FLOTURN INC (PA)
4236 Thunderbird Ln (45014-5482)
PHONE.................513 860-8040
R V Glutting, *President*
Don Spillane, *CFO*
Linda Dietz, *Human Res Mgr*
Sonya Finley, *HR Admin*
Michael Finn, *Manager*
◆ **EMP:** 184 **EST:** 1962
SQ FT: 75,000
SALES (est): 61MM **Privately Held**
WEB: www.floturn.com
SIC: 3599 Machine shop, jobbing & repair

(G-19705)
FLUID-BAG LLC
9078 Union Cntre Blvd 3 (45069)
PHONE.................513 310-9550
Mark Evans, *Director*
EMP: 5 **EST:** 2015
SALES (est): 157.4K
SALES (corp-wide): 13.4MM **Privately Held**
SIC: 3412 Milk (fluid) shipping containers, metal
HQ: Oy Fluid-Bag Ab
Bottenviksv 54
Pietarsaari 68600
207 790-444

(G-19706)
FOAM CONCEPTS & DESIGN INC
4602 Muhlhauser Rd (45011-9708)
PHONE.................513 860-5589
Jeff Labermeier, *President*
EMP: 19
SQ FT: 40,500
SALES (est): 2.4MM **Privately Held**
SIC: 3086 Packaging & shipping materials, foamed plastic

(G-19707)
FRECON ENGINEERING
Also Called: Frecon Technologies
9319 Prnceton Glendale Rd (45011-9707)
PHONE.................513 874-8981
Fred J Pfirrmann, *Owner*
Edwin A Pfirrmann, *Co-Owner*
EMP: 5 **EST:** 1963
SQ FT: 500
SALES: 400K **Privately Held**
WEB: www.frecontechnologies.com
SIC: 3545 Machine tool attachments & accessories

(G-19708)
FRECON TECHNOLOGIES INC
9319 Prnceton Glendale Rd (45011-9707)
PHONE.................513 874-8981
Fred J Pfirrmann, *CEO*
Judy Hummer, *Office Mgr*
▲ **EMP:** 12
SQ FT: 6,000
SALES: 15MM **Privately Held**
SIC: 3545 Machine tool attachments & accessories; tools & accessories for machine tools

(G-19709)
G F FRANK AND SONS INC
9075 Le Saint Dr (45014-2242)
PHONE.................513 870-9075
George P Frank, *President*
John Frank, *Vice Pres*
Mark Frank, *Vice Pres*
Donna Chitwood, *Office Mgr*
EMP: 15
SQ FT: 40,000
SALES (est): 3.6MM **Privately Held**
SIC: 3556 3599 Food products machinery; machine shop, jobbing & repair

(G-19710)
GE AVIATION SYSTEMS LLC
Also Called: Rapid Quality Manufacturing
5223 Muhlhauser Rd (45011-9327)
PHONE.................513 889-5150
James C Taylor, *Branch Mgr*
EMP: 15
SALES (corp-wide): 121.6B **Publicly Held**
SIC: 3313 Alloys, additive, except copper: not made in blast furnaces
HQ: Ge Aviation Systems Llc
1 Neumann Way
Cincinnati OH 45215
937 898-9600

(G-19711)
GE AVIATION SYSTEMS LLC
9100 Centre Pointe Dr (45069-4846)
PHONE.................513 552-4278
Dave Daniels, *Manager*
EMP: 7
SALES (corp-wide): 121.6B **Publicly Held**
SIC: 3812 Aircraft control systems, electronic
HQ: Ge Aviation Systems Llc
1 Neumann Way
Cincinnati OH 45215
937 898-9600

(G-19712)
GENERAL ELECTRIC COMPANY
9050 Centre Pointe Dr (45069-4874)
PHONE.................513 243-9317
CHI Tang, *Branch Mgr*
EMP: 10
SALES (corp-wide): 121.6B **Publicly Held**
SIC: 3511 Turbines & turbine generator sets

PA: General Electric Company
41 Farnsworth St
Boston MA 02210
617 443-3000

(G-19713)
GENERAL ELECTRIC COMPANY
9100 Centre Pointe Dr # 4 (45069-4846)
PHONE.................513 552-5364
Paul Kemme, *Senior Engr*
Michael Gilloon, *Manager*
Dave Hartshorne, *Manager*
EMP: 4
SALES (est): 104.1K **Privately Held**
SIC: 3724 Aircraft engines & engine parts

(G-19714)
GENERAL ELECTRIC COMPANY
Also Called: GE Additive
6380 Aviation Way (45069)
PHONE.................513 341-0214
Chris Schuppe, *Branch Mgr*
EMP: 300
SALES (corp-wide): 121.6B **Publicly Held**
SIC: 3541 Machine tools, metal cutting type
PA: General Electric Company
41 Farnsworth St
Boston MA 02210
617 443-3000

(G-19715)
GEORGIA-PACIFIC LLC
9048 Port Union Rialto Rd (45069-2937)
PHONE.................513 942-4800
Jeff Holsom, *Manager*
EMP: 25
SALES (corp-wide): 42.4B **Privately Held**
WEB: www.gp.com
SIC: 2621 Paper mills
HQ: Georgia-Pacific Llc
133 Peachtree St Nw
Atlanta GA 30303
404 652-4000

(G-19716)
GLOBAL PACKAGING & EXPORTS INC (PA)
9166 Sutton Pl (45011-9317)
P.O. Box 62687, Cincinnati (45262-0687)
PHONE.................513 454-2020
Lori Jordan, *President*
EMP: 6
SQ FT: 19,000
SALES (est): 1.9MM **Privately Held**
WEB: www.globalpkg.com
SIC: 4783 2448 2441 Packing goods for shipping; crating goods for shipping; skids, wood; cases, wood

(G-19717)
GLOBAL PARTNERS USA CO INC
7544 Bermuda Trce (45069-6324)
PHONE.................513 276-4981
Rudy Shephard, *Principal*
EMP: 3
SALES (est): 186K **Privately Held**
SIC: 3953 Stationery embossers, personal

(G-19718)
GRAPHEL CORPORATION
Also Called: Carbon Products
6115 Centre Park Dr (45069-3869)
P.O. Box 369 (45071-0369)
PHONE.................513 779-6166
Cliff Kersker, *President*
Mark Grammer, *CFO*
EMP: 140 **EST:** 1965
SQ FT: 35,000
SALES (est): 64.2MM
SALES (corp-wide): 36MM **Privately Held**
WEB: www.graphel.com
SIC: 5052 3599 3624 Coal & other minerals & ores; machine shop, jobbing & repair; electrodes, thermal & electrolytic uses: carbon, graphite
PA: Graphite Metallizing Corp
1050 Nepperhan Ave
Yonkers NY 10703
914 968-8400

(G-19719)
HATFIELD INDUSTRIES LLC
9717 Flagstone Way (45069-7042)
PHONE.................513 225-0456
Raymond Carl Hatfield, *Principal*
EMP: 3
SALES (est): 281.5K **Privately Held**
SIC: 3585 Heating equipment, complete

(G-19720)
HERITAGE BAG COMPANY
4255 Thunderbird Ln (45014-5483)
PHONE.................513 874-3311
John Wurmlinger, *Sales Staff*
Gary Munsch, *Manager*
Margo Coley, *Executive*
Jim Collett, *Maintence Staff*
EMP: 100
SALES (corp-wide): 3B **Privately Held**
WEB: www.heritage-bag.com
SIC: 2673 Trash bags (plastic film): made from purchased materials
HQ: Heritage Bag Company
501 Gateway Pkwy
Roanoke TX 76262
972 241-5525

(G-19721)
HI TECH AERO SPARES
9436 Meridian Way (45069-6527)
PHONE.................513 942-4150
Tom Wahl, *Principal*
EMP: 3
SALES (est): 248.2K **Privately Held**
SIC: 3812 Aircraft/aerospace flight instruments & guidance systems

(G-19722)
INSTRUMENT & VALVE SERVICES CO
4400 Muhlhauser Rd (45011-9708)
PHONE.................513 942-1118
Tom Spector, *Manager*
EMP: 9
SALES (corp-wide): 17.4B **Publicly Held**
SIC: 3823 Industrial instrmnts msrmnt display/control process variable
HQ: Instrument & Valve Services Company
205 S Center St
Marshalltown IA 50158

(G-19723)
INTEL CORPORATION
5785 Woodbridge Ln (45069-4517)
PHONE.................513 860-9686
J Gruber, *Principal*
EMP: 4
SALES (corp-wide): 70.8B **Publicly Held**
WEB: www.intel.com
SIC: 3674 Semiconductors & related devices
PA: Intel Corporation
2200 Mission College Blvd
Santa Clara CA 95054
408 765-8080

(G-19724)
INTERMEC INC
9290 Le Saint Dr (45014-5454)
PHONE.................513 874-5882
Robert Young, *Manager*
EMP: 9
SALES (corp-wide): 41.8B **Publicly Held**
WEB: www.unova.com
SIC: 3577 Computer peripheral equipment
HQ: Intermec, Inc.
16201 25th Ave W
Lynnwood WA 98087

(G-19725)
INTERMEC TECHNOLOGIES CORP
9290 Le Saint Dr (45014-5454)
P.O. Box 630250, Cincinnati (45263-0250)
PHONE.................513 874-5882
EMP: 9
SALES (corp-wide): 41.8B **Publicly Held**
WEB: www.intermec.net
SIC: 3577 Computer peripheral equipment
HQ: Intermec Technologies Corporation
16201 25th Ave W
Lynnwood WA 98087
425 348-2600

West Chester - Butler County

(G-19726)
INTERMEC TECHNOLOGIES CORP
9290 Le Saint Dr (45014-5454)
PHONE 513 874-5882
Gerald Witte, *Branch Mgr*
EMP: 13
SALES (corp-wide): 41.8B **Publicly Held**
WEB: www.intermec.net
SIC: 3577 2759 7372 Computer peripheral equipment; commercial printing; prepackaged software
HQ: Intermec Technologies Corporation
16201 25th Ave W
Lynnwood WA 98087
425 348-2600

(G-19727)
INTERMEC ULTRA PRINT INC
Also Called: Intermec Media Products
9290 Le Saint Dr (45014-5454)
PHONE 513 874-5882
Al Fettes, *Info Tech Mgr*
EMP: 250 **EST:** 1973
SQ FT: 65,000
SALES (est): 34.4MM
SALES (corp-wide): 41.8B **Publicly Held**
WEB: www.intermec.net
SIC: 2759 Flexographic printing
HQ: Intermec Technologies Corporation
16201 25th Ave W
Lynnwood WA 98087
425 348-2600

(G-19728)
IT XCEL CONSULTING LLC
Also Called: Xgs.it
7112 Office Park Dr (45069-2261)
PHONE 513 847-8261
Dennis Hollstegge, *Mng Member*
Mark Hollstegge,
EMP: 15
SQ FT: 1,880
SALES (est): 5.2MM **Privately Held**
WEB: www.xgsit.com
SIC: 2752 7379 Commercial printing, lithographic; computer related consulting services

(G-19729)
KC ROBOTICS INC
9000 Le Saint Dr (45014-2241)
PHONE 513 860-4442
Kenneth P Carrier Jr, *President*
Constance M Carrier, *Corp Secy*
Gregory Davis, *Project Mgr*
Jason Jamiel, *Accounts Mgr*
Nancy Smith, *Sales Staff*
◆ **EMP:** 18
SQ FT: 18,000
SALES: 6MM **Privately Held**
WEB: www.kcrobotics.com
SIC: 5084 3569 7373 Robots, industrial; filters; systems integration services

(G-19730)
KIMBERLY-CLARK CORPORATION
9277 Centre Pointe Dr # 200 (45069-4963)
PHONE 513 794-1005
Woody Bowling, *Manager*
EMP: 209
SALES (corp-wide): 18.4B **Publicly Held**
WEB: www.kimberly-clark.com
SIC: 2621 2676 Sanitary tissue paper; infant & baby paper products
PA: Kimberly-Clark Corporation
351 Phelps Dr
Irving TX 75038
972 281-1200

(G-19731)
KNAPPCO CORPORATION
Also Called: Civacon
9393 Prnceton Glendale Rd (45011-9707)
PHONE 816 741-0786
John F Anderson, *CEO*
Pat Gerard, *President*
Dan Taylor, *CFO*
▲ **EMP:** 140
SQ FT: 110,000
SALES (est): 39.7MM
SALES (corp-wide): 6.9B **Publicly Held**
WEB: www.civacon.net
SIC: 3321 3643 3494 Manhole covers, metal; caps & plugs, electric: attachment; valves & pipe fittings
PA: Dover Corporation
3005 Highland Pkwy # 200
Downers Grove IL 60515
630 541-1540

(G-19732)
KONECRANES INC
Also Called: Crane Pro Services
9879 Crescent Park Dr (45069-3867)
PHONE 513 755-2800
Barb Rothert, *Administration*
EMP: 30
SALES (corp-wide): 3.7B **Privately Held**
WEB: www.kciusa.com
SIC: 3536 Hoists, cranes & monorails
HQ: Konecranes, Inc.
4401 Gateway Blvd
Springfield OH 45502

(G-19733)
KZ SOLUTIONS INC
9440 Sutton Pl (45011-9698)
PHONE 513 942-9378
Mike Lichon, *President*
EMP: 6 **EST:** 2008
SALES: 2.5MM **Privately Held**
SIC: 3625 Actuators, industrial

(G-19734)
LAKOTA PRINTING INC
7967 Cincinnati Dayton Rd J (45069-3578)
P.O. Box 876 (45071-0876)
PHONE 513 755-3666
Fax: 513 755-3667
EMP: 3
SQ FT: 10,000
SALES (est): 230K **Privately Held**
SIC: 7334 2752 Photocopying & Offset Printing

(G-19735)
LAURA DAWSON
7827 Plantation Dr (45069-2266)
PHONE 513 777-2513
Laura Dawson, *Owner*
EMP: 5
SQ FT: 1,000
SALES (est): 180K **Privately Held**
SIC: 2342 7389 Foundation garments, women's; design services

(G-19736)
LEM PRODUCTS HOLDING LLC
Also Called: L.E.M. Products
4440 Muhlhauser Rd # 300 (45011-9767)
PHONE 513 202-1188
Hill Kohnen, *CEO*
▲ **EMP:** 20
SALES (est): 7.9MM **Privately Held**
WEB: www.lemproducts.com
SIC: 3556 3949 Cutting, chopping, grinding, mixing & similar machinery; hunting equipment

(G-19737)
LIGHTING CONCEPTS & CONTROL
9753 Crescent Park Dr (45069-3893)
PHONE 513 761-6360
Dave Robinson, *Owner*
EMP: 6
SALES (est): 907.8K **Privately Held**
WEB: www.lightingconcepts.net
SIC: 3645 Residential lighting fixtures

(G-19738)
LONG-STANTON MFG COMPANY
9388 Sutton Pl (45011-9702)
PHONE 513 874-8020
Daniel B Cunningham, *President*
Richard Hassinger, *General Mgr*
Tom Kachovec, *COO*
Tim Hershey, *CFO*
Lisa Wetterich, *Human Res Mgr*
▲ **EMP:** 50
SQ FT: 66,000
SALES (est): 11.7MM **Privately Held**
WEB: www.longstanton.com
SIC: 3444 7692 3469 3544 Sheet metalwork; welding repair; metal stampings; special dies, tools, jigs & fixtures; fabricated plate work (boiler shop)

(G-19739)
LOST TECHNOLOGY LLP
9501 Woodland Hills Dr (45011-9300)
P.O. Box 8257 (45069-8257)
PHONE 513 685-0054
Larry Hansonsmith, *Partner*
EMP: 7
SALES: 500K **Privately Held**
WEB: www.losttech.com
SIC: 7372 Educational computer software

(G-19740)
MARTIN MARIETTA MATERIALS INC
Also Called: Martin Marietta Aggregate
9277 Centre Pointe Dr # 250 (45069-4844)
P.O. Box 30013, Raleigh NC (27622-0013)
PHONE 513 701-1140
Harry Charles, *Manager*
EMP: 40 **Publicly Held**
WEB: www.martinmarietta.com
SIC: 1423 1422 3295 3297 Crushed & broken granite; crushed & broken limestone; magnesite, crude: ground, calcined or dead-burned; nonclay refractories; construction sand & gravel
PA: Martin Marietta Materials Inc
2710 Wycliff Rd
Raleigh NC 27607

(G-19741)
MARTIN-BROWER COMPANY LLC
Also Called: Distribution Center
4260 Port Union Rd (45011-9768)
PHONE 513 773-2301
Ryan Rozen, *General Mgr*
Jeanne Malone, *Manager*
EMP: 275 **Privately Held**
SIC: 2013 2015 5087 Frozen meats from purchased meat; poultry, processed: frozen; restaurant supplies
HQ: The Martin-Brower Company L L C
6250 N River Rd Ste 9000
Rosemont IL 60018
847 227-6500

(G-19742)
MECC-USA LLC (PA)
Also Called: Umecc
9468 Meridian Way (45069-6527)
PHONE 513 891-0301
George He, *President*
Bernhard Schiefer, *Treasurer*
▲ **EMP:** 7
SALES (est): 1.5MM **Privately Held**
WEB: www.mecc-usa.com
SIC: 3429 Manufactured hardware (general)

(G-19743)
MERCHANTS METALS LLC
Also Called: Meadow Burke Products
8760 Global Way Bldg 1 (45069-7066)
PHONE 513 942-0268
Debbie Humbert, *General Mgr*
EMP: 15
SALES (corp-wide): 2.4B **Privately Held**
SIC: 3315 Wire & fabricated wire products
HQ: Merchants Metals Llc
211 Perimeter Center Pkwy
Atlanta GA 30346
770 741-0306

(G-19744)
MILLWOOD INC
4438 Muhlhauser Rd # 100 (45011-9776)
PHONE 513 860-4567
Antonio Delgado, *Branch Mgr*
EMP: 17 **Privately Held**
SIC: 3565 5084 Packaging machinery; packaging machinery & equipment
PA: Millwood, Inc.
3708 International Blvd
Vienna OH 44473

(G-19745)
MITEL (DELAWARE) INC
Also Called: Inter Tel
9100 W Chester Towne Ctr (45069-3106)
PHONE 513 733-8000
Dan Ziezerink, *Branch Mgr*
EMP: 25
SALES (corp-wide): 987.6MM **Privately Held**
WEB: www.inter-tel.com
SIC: 3661 5045 4813 5065 Telephone & telegraph apparatus; computer software; long distance telephone communications; telephone equipment; telephone & telephone equipment installation; equipment rental & leasing
HQ: Mitel (Delaware). Inc.
1146 N Alma School Rd
Mesa AZ 85201
480 449-8900

(G-19746)
MODEL GRAPHICS & MEDIA INC
2614 Crescentville Rd (45069-3819)
PHONE 513 541-2355
Steve Fleissner, *President*
Barb Fleissner, *Vice Pres*
EMP: 48
SQ FT: 38,000
SALES (est): 13.8MM **Privately Held**
WEB: www.modelgraphicsinc.com
SIC: 2679 Labels, paper: made from purchased material

(G-19747)
NEASE CO LLC (DH)
Also Called: Nease Performance Chemicals
9774 Windisch Rd (45069-3808)
PHONE 513 587-2800
Mike Biehle, *Business Mgr*
Terry Herdemann, *Maint Spvr*
Cathy Lefevers, *HR Admin*
Byron Alipio, *Accounts Mgr*
Gwen Schnieder, *Office Mgr*
▲ **EMP:** 10
SALES (est): 18.4MM
SALES (corp-wide): 14.9MM **Privately Held**
SIC: 2869 Industrial organic chemicals
HQ: Wp Mannheim Gmbh
Sandhofer Str. 96
Mannheim 68305
621 765-40

(G-19748)
NEPTUNE CHEMICAL PUMP COMPANY
9393 Princetone Glendale (45011-9707)
PHONE 513 870-3239
Michael Dowse, *CEO*
EMP: 6
SALES (corp-wide): 6.9B **Publicly Held**
SIC: 3586 3561 Measuring & dispensing pumps; pumps & pumping equipment
HQ: Neptune Chemical Pump Company
1809 Century Ave Sw
Grand Rapids MI 49503
215 699-8700

(G-19749)
NORCAL SIGNS INC
6163 Allen Rd (45069-3855)
PHONE 513 779-6982
Braden R Huenefeld, *Principal*
EMP: 3
SALES (est): 154.7K **Privately Held**
SIC: 3993 Signs & advertising specialties

(G-19750)
NUTRITIONAL MEDICINALS LLC
Also Called: Functional Formularies
9277 Centre Pointe Dr # 220 (45069-4844)
PHONE 937 433-4673
Robin McGee, *CEO*
Brian McGee, *COO*
Namrata Maquire, *CFO*
EMP: 12 **EST:** 2006
SALES (est): 2.5MM **Privately Held**
SIC: 2833 8011 Organic medicinal chemicals: bulk, uncompounded; offices & clinics of medical doctors

(G-19751)
OGARA HESS EISENHARDT
9113 Le Saint Dr (45014-5453)
PHONE 513 346-1300

West Chester - Butler County (G-19752) — GEOGRAPHIC SECTION

N Carpinello, *Principal*
▲ **EMP:** 7
SALES (est): 1.7MM **Privately Held**
SIC: 3711 Motor vehicles & car bodies

(G-19752)
OHIO ALUMINUM CHEMICALS LLC
4544 Muhlhauser Rd (45011-9708)
PHONE.................513 860-3842
Richard Rosen,
EMP: 6
SALES (est): 430K **Privately Held**
SIC: 2899 Chemical preparations

(G-19753)
OHIO EAGLE DISTRIBUTING LLC
9300 Allen Rd (45069-3847)
PHONE.................513 539-8483
John W Saputo, *Principal*
EMP: 21
SALES (est): 3.8MM **Privately Held**
SIC: 2086 5921 Tea, iced: packaged in cans, bottles, etc.; water, pasteurized: packaged in cans, bottles, etc.; wine & beer; beer (packaged)

(G-19754)
OMER J SMITH INC
Also Called: Paper Products Company
9112 Le Saint Dr (45014-5452)
PHONE.................513 921-4717
Dennis J Smith II, *President*
Denny J Smith II, *Vice Pres*
Mary Smith, *Vice Pres*
James Davis, *Sales Mgr*
Mary C Smith, *Admin Sec*
▲ **EMP:** 30
SQ FT: 80,000
SALES (est): 7.3MM **Privately Held**
WEB: www.paperproductscompany.com
SIC: 2653 Boxes, corrugated: made from purchased materials

(G-19755)
OPW INC
Also Called: Opw Engineering Systems
9393 Prnceton Glendale Rd (45011-9707)
PHONE.................800 422-2525
David Crouse, *President*
Richard Jones, *Vice Pres*
James Walton, *Vice Pres*
Fred Wilking, *Vice Pres*
Parrish Evans, *Director*
▲ **EMP:** 559
SQ FT: 250,000
SALES (est): 73.4K
SALES (corp-wide): 6.9B **Publicly Held**
SIC: 3594 Fluid power pumps
PA: Dover Corporation
    3005 Highland Pkwy # 200
    Downers Grove IL 60515
    630 541-1540

(G-19756)
OPW FUELING COMPONENTS INC (HQ)
Also Called: Opw Engineered Systems
9393 Prnceton Glendale Rd (45011-9707)
PHONE.................800 422-2525
David Crouse, *President*
◆ **EMP:** 47
SALES (est): 84.4MM
SALES (corp-wide): 6.9B **Publicly Held**
WEB: www.dovercorporation.com
SIC: 2899 Fuel treating compounds
PA: Dover Corporation
    3005 Highland Pkwy # 200
    Downers Grove IL 60515
    630 541-1540

(G-19757)
PARKER-HANNIFIN CORPORATION
9050 Centre Pointe Dr # 310 (45069-4874)
PHONE.................513 847-1758
Rick Stumpf, *Branch Mgr*
EMP: 123
SALES (corp-wide): 14.3B **Publicly Held**
SIC: 3594 Fluid power pumps & motors
PA: Parker-Hannifin Corporation
    6035 Parkland Blvd
    Cleveland OH 44124
    216 896-3000

(G-19758)
PFIZER INC
9878 Windisch Rd (45069-3806)
PHONE.................513 342-9056
EMP: 6
SALES (corp-wide): 52.5B **Publicly Held**
SIC: 2834 Mfg Pharmaceutical Preparations
PA: Pfizer Inc.
    235 E 42nd St
    New York NY 10017
    212 733-2323

(G-19759)
PHASE ARRAY COMPANY LLC
9365 Allen Rd (45069-3846)
PHONE.................513 785-0801
Dominique Braconnier, *Mng Member*
EMP: 7
SALES (est): 271.1K **Privately Held**
SIC: 3577 7379 Computer peripheral equipment; computer related consulting services

(G-19760)
PLASTRX INC
7682 Wetherington Dr (45069-4609)
PHONE.................513 847-4032
Greg Boyd, *President*
◆ **EMP:** 3
SQ FT: 3,000
SALES (est): 233.1K **Privately Held**
SIC: 2821 Plastics materials & resins

(G-19761)
PMCO LLC
Also Called: PM Company
9220 Glades Dr (45011-8821)
PHONE.................513 825-7626
Mike Webster,
▲ **EMP:** 88 **EST:** 1905
SQ FT: 85,000
SALES (est): 65.2MM
SALES (corp-wide): 2.4B **Privately Held**
WEB: www.pmcompany.com
SIC: 2679 Paper products, converted
HQ: Iconex, Llc
    3237 Satellite Blvd # 550
    Duluth GA 30096
    800 543-8130

(G-19762)
POLE/ZERO ACQUISITION INC
5558 Union Centre Dr (45069-4821)
PHONE.................513 870-9060
Larry Ochs, *Vice Pres*
EMP: 180
SQ FT: 50,000
SALES (est): 59.1MM
SALES (corp-wide): 6.9B **Publicly Held**
WEB: www.emxo.com
SIC: 3663 Radio & television switching equipment
PA: Dover Corporation
    3005 Highland Pkwy # 200
    Downers Grove IL 60515
    630 541-1540

(G-19763)
POLYMET CORPORATION
7397 Union Centre Blvd (45014-2288)
PHONE.................513 874-3586
Bill Mosier, *President*
Thomas J Dagenback, *Vice Pres*
▲ **EMP:** 45
SQ FT: 47,000
SALES (est): 11.2MM **Privately Held**
WEB: www.polymetcorp.com
SIC: 3496 3548 3341 3315 Miscellaneous fabricated wire products; welding apparatus; secondary nonferrous metals; steel wire & related products

(G-19764)
PRECISION DIE & STAMPING INC
9800 Harwood Ct (45014-7589)
PHONE.................513 942-8220
Greg Johnson, *President*
Mike Stephens, *Principal*
Trina Johnson, *Office Mgr*
EMP: 8
SQ FT: 6,500
SALES (est): 1.2MM **Privately Held**
WEB: www.precisiondie.com
SIC: 3469 Metal stampings

(G-19765)
PRECISION ENVIRONMENTS INC
Also Called: Precison Clean Rooms
9830 Windisch Rd (45069-3806)
P.O. Box 325, Shrewsbury PA (17361-0325)
PHONE.................513 847-1510
Douglas J Cooper, *President*
Beth Clark, *Treasurer*
EMP: 23 **EST:** 2009
SQ FT: 8,000
SALES (est): 10.6MM **Privately Held**
SIC: 3829 5085 Measuring & controlling devices; clean room supplies

(G-19766)
PREMIER COATINGS LTD
9390 Le Saint Dr (45014-5446)
PHONE.................513 942-1070
Brandon Stock, *General Mgr*
EMP: 14
SQ FT: 20,000
SALES (est): 775.6K **Privately Held**
WEB: www.premiercoatings.com
SIC: 3291 1721 Coated abrasive products; painting & paper hanging

(G-19767)
PROCTER & GAMBLE COMPANY
8868 Beckett Rd (45069-2902)
PHONE.................513 672-4044
Carlos Lange, *Opers Mgr*
EMP: 417
SALES (corp-wide): 66.8B **Publicly Held**
SIC: 2844 2676 3421 2842 Deodorants, personal; towels, napkins & tissue paper products; razor blades & razors; specialty cleaning preparations; soap: granulated, liquid, cake, flaked or chip
PA: The Procter & Gamble Company
    1 Procter And Gamble Plz
    Cincinnati OH 45202
    513 983-1100

(G-19768)
PROCTER & GAMBLE COMPANY
8256 Union Centre Blvd (45069-7056)
PHONE.................513 634-9600
Luke Walker, *Senior Engr*
Pam Dunnon, *Branch Mgr*
M Mattingly, *Senior Mgr*
James Boesken, *Technology*
Eric Goudy, *Technology*
EMP: 205
SALES (corp-wide): 66.8B **Publicly Held**
WEB: www.pg.com
SIC: 2844 2676 3421 2842 Deodorants, personal; towels, napkins & tissue paper products; razor blades & razors; specialty cleaning preparations; soap: granulated, liquid, cake, flaked or chip
PA: The Procter & Gamble Company
    1 Procter And Gamble Plz
    Cincinnati OH 45202
    513 983-1100

(G-19769)
PROCTER & GAMBLE COMPANY
8611 Beckett Rd (45069-4868)
PHONE.................513 634-9110
Jerry Hammond, *Opers Staff*
Dimitris Collias, *Research*
Leroy Kocher, *Research*
Jon Calderas, *Engineer*
Nancy Jackson, *Engineer*
EMP: 205
SALES (corp-wide): 66.8B **Publicly Held**
WEB: www.pg.com
SIC: 2844 2676 3421 2842 Deodorants, personal; bath salts; towels, napkins & tissue paper products; diapers, paper (disposable): made from purchased paper; razor blades & razors; specialty cleaning preparations; soap: granulated, liquid, cake, flaked or chip
PA: The Procter & Gamble Company
    1 Procter And Gamble Plz
    Cincinnati OH 45202
    513 983-1100

(G-19770)
PROTECTION DEVICES INC
9113 Le Saint Dr (45014-5453)
PHONE.................210 399-2273
Dominic Hunter, *Treasurer*

EMP: 3
SALES (est): 264.5K **Privately Held**
SIC: 3711 Motor vehicles & car bodies

(G-19771)
PTS PRFSSNAL TECHNICAL SVC INC (PA)
Also Called: Est Analytical
503 Commercial Dr (45014-7594)
PHONE.................513 642-0111
James R Murphy, *CEO*
Justin Murphy, *President*
Kelly Cravenor, *General Mgr*
Lindsey Pyron, *Vice Pres*
Cindy Lewis, *Purch Mgr*
EMP: 52
SQ FT: 12,000
SALES (est): 7.6MM **Privately Held**
WEB: www.ptsltd.com
SIC: 3826 Analytical instruments

(G-19772)
QPI CINCINNATI LLC
6455 Gano Rd (45069-4830)
PHONE.................513 755-2670
Eduardo Rosado, *Owner*
EMP: 3
SQ FT: 50,000
SALES (est): 28.7MM **Privately Held**
SIC: 2676 Infant & baby paper products

(G-19773)
QUALITURN INC
9081 Le Saint Dr (45014-2242)
PHONE.................513 868-3333
Mike Barber, *President*
Ron Lucas, *Supervisor*
EMP: 24
SQ FT: 1,500
SALES (est): 5.1MM **Privately Held**
SIC: 3599 Machine shop, jobbing & repair

(G-19774)
QUANTUM COMMERCE LLC
6748 Dimmick Rd (45069-3931)
P.O. Box 1640 (45071-1640)
PHONE.................513 777-0737
Gregory Workman II, *Principal*
EMP: 4
SALES (est): 277.4K **Privately Held**
SIC: 3572 Computer storage devices

(G-19775)
QUASONIX INC (PA)
6025 Schumacher Park Dr (45069-4812)
PHONE.................513 942-1287
Terrance Hill, *President*
Norman Eichenberger, *Engineer*
Tim O'Connell, *Engineer*
Sean Wilson, *Engineer*
Pamela S Hill, *Treasurer*
EMP: 28
SQ FT: 15,000
SALES (est): 15MM **Privately Held**
WEB: www.quasonix.com
SIC: 5065 3663 3812 3669 Communication equipment; airborne radio communications equipment; antennas, radar or communications; intercommunication systems, electric; physical research, non-commercial

(G-19776)
QUEEN CITY POLYMERS INC (PA)
6101 Schumacher Park Dr (45069-3818)
PHONE.................513 779-0990
James M Powers, *President*
James L Powers, *Principal*
EMP: 42
SQ FT: 33,000
SALES (est): 11.2MM **Privately Held**
WEB: www.qcpinc.net
SIC: 3089 5162 Injection molding of plastics; plastics products

(G-19777)
R L INDUSTRIES INC
9355 Le Saint Dr (45014-5458)
PHONE.................513 874-2800
John R Gierl, *Principal*
EMP: 75 **EST:** 1962
SALES (est): 7.5MM
SALES (corp-wide): 17.2MM **Privately Held**
SIC: 3089 Plastic & fiberglass tanks

GEOGRAPHIC SECTION
West Chester - Butler County (G-19805)

PA: R L Holdings, Inc.
9355 Le Saint Dr
West Chester OH 45014
513 874-2800

(G-19778)
R R DONNELLEY & SONS COMPANY
Also Called: RR Donnelley
8720 Global Way (45069-7066)
PHONE.................513 552-1512
Brad Hull, *Manager*
EMP: 7
SALES (corp-wide): 6.8B Publicly Held
WEB: www.rrdonnelley.com
SIC: 2759 Commercial printing
PA: R. R. Donnelley & Sons Company
35 W Wacker Dr Ste 3650
Chicago IL 60601
312 326-8000

(G-19779)
REPUBLIC WIRE INC
5525 Union Centre Dr (45069-4820)
PHONE.................513 860-1800
Ron Rosenbeck, *Principal*
Mark Huelsebusch, *CFO*
▲ EMP: 75
SQ FT: 175,000
SALES (est): 53.2MM Privately Held
WEB: www.republicwire.com
SIC: 3351 3315 Wire, copper & copper alloy; steel wire & related products

(G-19780)
RETTERBUSH GRAPHIC AND PACKG
6187 Schumacher Park Dr (45069-3818)
PHONE.................513 779-4466
Joseph Retterbush, *President*
Denny Meador, *Vice Pres*
EMP: 20
SQ FT: 5,000
SALES (est): 4.5MM Privately Held
SIC: 2671 2754 Paper coated or laminated for packaging; labels: gravure printing

(G-19781)
REV38 LLC
8888 Beckett Rd (45069)
PHONE.................937 572-4000
Erick Carlson, *Branch Mgr*
EMP: 6
SALES (corp-wide): 905.9K Privately Held
SIC: 3663 Radio & TV communications equipment
PA: Rev38 Llc
131 Waterstone Dr
Franklin OH 45005
937 269-9641

(G-19782)
RIOTECH INTERNATIONAL LTD (PA)
Also Called: Queen City Polymers
6101 Schumacher Park Dr (45069-3818)
PHONE.................513 779-0990
James M Powers, *Partner*
Jerry Pavone, *COO*
EMP: 70
SQ FT: 40,000
SALES (est): 9.8MM Privately Held
SIC: 3089 Plastic kitchenware, tableware & houseware

(G-19783)
RIVERCITY WOODWORKING INC
9837 Harwood Ct (45014-7588)
PHONE.................513 860-1900
Richard Neubauer Jr, *President*
EMP: 6
SQ FT: 10,000
SALES (est): 1.1MM Privately Held
SIC: 2541 Store fixtures, wood

(G-19784)
ROBOWORLD MOLDED PRODUCTS LLC
Also Called: Pendant Armor
8216 Princeton Glendale (45069-1675)
PHONE.................513 720-6900
Christian Tur, *President*
EMP: 4 EST: 2016

SALES (est): 329.4K Privately Held
SIC: 3061 7389 Mechanical rubber goods;

(G-19785)
ROCKWELL AUTOMATION INC
9355 Allen Rd (45069-3846)
PHONE.................513 942-9828
Jim Sell, *District Mgr*
Scott Thomas, *Consultant*
EMP: 80
SQ FT: 16,000 Publicly Held
SIC: 3625 Relays & industrial controls
PA: Rockwell Automation, Inc.
1201 S 2nd St
Milwaukee WI 53204

(G-19786)
ROSEMOUNT INC
4400 Muhlhauser Rd (45011-9708)
PHONE.................513 851-5555
Nelson Schroeder, *Branch Mgr*
EMP: 17
SALES (corp-wide): 17.4B Publicly Held
WEB: www.rosemount.com
SIC: 3823 Manometers, industrial process type
HQ: Rosemount Inc.
8200 Market Blvd
Chanhassen MN 55317
952 906-8888

(G-19787)
ROTO-DIE COMPANY INC
Also Called: Roto Met Rice
4430 Muhlhauser Rd (45011-9708)
PHONE.................513 942-3500
Mike Frazer, *Manager*
EMP: 6
SALES (corp-wide): 195.5MM Privately Held
WEB: www.rotometrics.com
SIC: 3544 Special dies, tools, jigs & fixtures
PA: Roto-Die Company, Inc.
800 Howerton Ln
Eureka MO 63025
636 587-3600

(G-19788)
RPS AMERICA INC (PA)
8808 Beckett Center Dr (45069)
PHONE.................937 231-9339
Roberto Facci, *President*
Edward Kwiatkowski, *Vice Pres*
EMP: 2
SQ FT: 18,800
SALES: 5MM Privately Held
SIC: 3699 Electrical equipment & supplies

(G-19789)
RR DONNELLEY & SONS COMPANY
8740 Global Way (45069-7066)
PHONE.................513 870-4040
EMP: 8
SALES (corp-wide): 6.8B Publicly Held
SIC: 2657 Folding paperboard boxes
PA: R. R. Donnelley & Sons Company
35 W Wacker Dr Ste 3650
Chicago IL 60601
312 326-8000

(G-19790)
RSA CONTROLS INC
6422 Fountains Blvd (45069-2101)
PHONE.................513 476-6277
Ruth McWilliams, *Principal*
EMP: 4
SALES (est): 356.8K Privately Held
SIC: 3823 Thermal conductivity instruments, industrial process type

(G-19791)
SAFEWAY SAFETY STEP LLC
Also Called: Cleancut
5242 Rialto Rd (45069-2921)
PHONE.................513 942-7837
Chris Stafford,
EMP: 10 EST: 2000
SALES (est): 476.7K Privately Held
SIC: 3088 Tubs (bath, shower & laundry), plastic

(G-19792)
SCHNEIDER ELECTRIC USA INC
9870 Crescent Park Dr (45069-3800)
PHONE.................513 755-5000
Regis Ganley, *Partner*
Alexander Gorski, *Partner*
Darren Meiser, *District Mgr*
CAM Slaughter, *District Mgr*
Todd Gilliam, *Business Mgr*
EMP: 75
SALES (corp-wide): 355.8K Privately Held
WEB: www.squared.com
SIC: 3613 3643 3612 3823 Mfg Electrical Distribution & Industrial Products Systems & Services
HQ: Schneider Electric Usa, Inc.
201 Wshington St Ste 2700
Boston MA 02108
978 975-9600

(G-19793)
SCHNEIDER ELECTRIC USA INC
9928 Windisch Rd (45069-3804)
PHONE.................513 398-9800
David Lovitz, *Sales Mgr*
Char Buchanan, *Office Mgr*
Eric Everman, *Manager*
Roger Manus, *Manager*
EMP: 20
SALES (corp-wide): 355.8K Privately Held
WEB: www.squared.com
SIC: 3699 Electrical work
HQ: Schneider Electric Usa, Inc.
201 Wshington St Ste 2700
Boston MA 02108
978 975-9600

(G-19794)
SENTRILOCK LLC
7701 Service Center Dr (45069-2440)
PHONE.................513 618-5800
Scott R Fisher, *President*
John G Wenker, *Vice Pres*
Chris Hunt, *Electrical Engi*
Geri Morgan, *Human Res Mgr*
Toni Clark, *Train & Dev Mgr*
EMP: 83
SQ FT: 7,000
SALES: 16.5MM Privately Held
WEB: www.sentrilock.com
SIC: 2542 Electronic circuits

(G-19795)
SHAW INDUSTRIES INC
4436 Muhlhauser Rd # 100 (45011-9774)
PHONE.................513 942-3692
Jim Brown, *Branch Mgr*
EMP: 7
SALES (corp-wide): 225.3B Publicly Held
WEB: www.shawinc.com
SIC: 3999 Barber & beauty shop equipment
HQ: Shaw Industries, Inc.
616 E Walnut Ave
Dalton GA 30721

(G-19796)
SINE WALL LLC
7162 Liberty (45069)
PHONE.................919 453-2011
Heather Hardwick, *Credit Mgr*
Timothy Brereton, *Mng Member*
EMP: 5 EST: 2009
SALES (est): 50.8K Privately Held
SIC: 3446 Architectural metalwork

(G-19797)
SPICY OLIVE LLC (PA)
7671 Cox Ln (45069-6546)
PHONE.................513 847-4397
Theresa A Banks, *Principal*
EMP: 12
SALES (est): 22.4MM Privately Held
SIC: 2079 Olive oil

(G-19798)
STABLE STEP LLC
Also Called: Powersteps
8930 Global Way (45069-7071)
PHONE.................513 825-1888
Rhonda Newman, *CEO*
EMP: 23

SALES (est): 830.8K Privately Held
SIC: 3842 5047 5999 Foot appliances, orthopedic; orthopedic equipment & supplies; orthopedic & prosthesis applications

(G-19799)
STERLING COATING
9048 Port Union Rialto Rd (45069-2937)
PHONE.................513 942-4900
Craig Lowe, *General Mgr*
EMP: 4
SALES (est): 356.9K Privately Held
SIC: 3479 Etching & engraving

(G-19800)
SUGAR CREEK PACKING CO
4235 Thunderbird Ln (45014-5483)
PHONE.................513 874-4422
Jeff Shutte, *Branch Mgr*
EMP: 140
SALES (corp-wide): 700MM Privately Held
SIC: 2013 2011 Bacon, side & sliced: from purchased meat; meat packing plants
PA: Sugar Creek Packing Co.
2101 Kenskill Ave
Wshngtn Ct Hs OH 43160
740 335-3586

(G-19801)
SUGAR CREEK PACKING CO
4585 Muhlhauser Rd (45011-9788)
PHONE.................513 874-4422
John Richardson, *Ch of Bd*
EMP: 5
SALES (corp-wide): 700MM Privately Held
SIC: 2013 2011 Sausages & other prepared meats; meat packing plants
PA: Sugar Creek Packing Co.
2101 Kenskill Ave
Wshngtn Ct Hs OH 43160
740 335-3586

(G-19802)
SUMMIT CONTAINER CORPORATION (PA)
8080 Beckett Center Dr # 203 (45069-5036)
PHONE.................719 481-8400
Adam C Walker, *CEO*
Dave Johnson, *Vice Pres*
EMP: 29
SALES (est): 12.5MM Privately Held
WEB: www.summitcontainer.com
SIC: 2653 Boxes, corrugated: made from purchased materials

(G-19803)
SUMMIT PACKAGING SOLUTIONS LLC (PA)
8080 Beckett Center Dr # 203 (45069-5036)
PHONE.................719 481-8400
Patrick Ton, *Director*
EMP: 12
SALES (est): 14.5MM Privately Held
SIC: 2631 Container, packaging & boxboard

(G-19804)
SYNDICATE PRINTERS INC
7291 Saint Ives Pl (45069-4647)
PHONE.................513 779-3625
Ambrish K Bansal, *Principal*
EMP: 3
SALES (est): 34.1K Privately Held
SIC: 2752 Commercial printing, lithographic

(G-19805)
SYSTECON LLC
6121 Schumacher Park Dr (45069-3818)
PHONE.................513 777-7222
Martin P Tierney, *President*
EMP: 85
SQ FT: 60,000
SALES (est): 70MM
SALES (corp-wide): 31.8B Privately Held
WEB: www.systecon.com
SIC: 3561 Pumps & pumping equipment
HQ: Engie North America Inc.
1990 Post Oak Blvd # 1900
Houston TX 77056
713 636-0000

West Chester - Butler County (G-19806)

(G-19806)
TEMPAC LLC
7370 Avenel Ct (45069-4649)
PHONE..................513 505-9700
Heidi Temming, *Psychologist*
Dave R Temming,
EMP: 2
SQ FT: 1,500
SALES (est): 2.4MM **Privately Held**
SIC: 2011 5131 Meat packing plants; labels

(G-19807)
TENACITY MANUFACTURING COMPANY
4455 Muhlhauser Rd (45011-9788)
PHONE..................513 821-0201
Layne Meader, *President*
Jerry Crowder, *Vice Pres*
Tim Baumgardner, *Treasurer*
EMP: 28 EST: 1905
SQ FT: 36,500
SALES (est): 2.9MM
SALES (corp-wide): 18.1MM **Privately Held**
SIC: 3469 2782 Machine parts, stamped or pressed metal; looseleaf binders & devices
PA: Enduro Binders, Inc.
  6480 Enduro Dr
  Washington MO 63090
  636 239-0140

(G-19808)
THREE BOND INTERNATIONAL INC (DH)
6184 Schumacher Park Dr (45069-4802)
PHONE..................513 779-7300
Kazunori Shibayama, *President*
Lee A Wittich, *Accounts Exec*
▲ **EMP:** 60
SALES: 39.5MM **Privately Held**
SIC: 2891 Adhesives
HQ: Threebond Co., Ltd.
  4-3-3, Minamiosawa
  Hachioji TKY 192-0
  426 705-333

(G-19809)
THYSSENKRUPP BILSTEIN AMER INC
4440 Muhlhauser Rd (45011-9767)
PHONE..................513 881-7600
Jimmy Brentle, *Manager*
EMP: 25
SALES (corp-wide): 39.8B **Privately Held**
SIC: 5013 3714 Automotive supplies & parts; motor vehicle parts & accessories
HQ: Thyssenkrupp Bilstein Of America, Inc.
  8685 Bilstein Blvd
  Hamilton OH 45015
  513 881-7600

(G-19810)
TOKIN AMERICA CORPORATION
9844 Windisch Rd (45069-3806)
PHONE..................513 644-9743
Motoaki Suzuki, *President*
EMP: 4
SQ FT: 8,500
SALES: 1.6MM
SALES (corp-wide): 23.8MM **Privately Held**
SIC: 3548 Welding apparatus
PA: Tokin Corporation
  1509, Okubocho, Nishi-Ku
  Hamamatsu SZO 432-8
  534 855-555

(G-19811)
TREY CORRUGATED INC
9048 Port Union Rialto Rd (45069-2937)
PHONE..................513 942-4800
Tim Cossey, *President*
Jeff Altom, *Manager*
EMP: 98
SALES: 48MM
SALES (corp-wide): 42.4B **Privately Held**
SIC: 2653 Sheets, corrugated: made from purchased materials
HQ: Georgia-Pacific Corrugated Iii Llc
  5645 W 82nd St
  Indianapolis IN 46278

(G-19812)
TRIANGLE LABEL INC
6392 Gano Rd (45069-4809)
PHONE..................513 242-2822
Scott Kenner, *President*
EMP: 9
SQ FT: 5,000
SALES (est): 156.2K **Privately Held**
SIC: 2759 Labels & seals: printing; tags: printing

(G-19813)
TVH PARTS CO
Also Called: C-Tech Industries
8756 Global Way (45069-7066)
PHONE..................877 755-7311
EMP: 18
SALES (corp-wide): 182.8MM **Privately Held**
SIC: 3625 Relays & industrial controls
PA: Tvh Parts Co.
  16355 S Lone Elm Rd
  Olathe KS 66062
  913 829-1000

(G-19814)
U S THERMAL INC
9846 Crescent Park Dr (45069-3800)
PHONE..................513 777-7763
Dan Reagan, *President*
EMP: 3
SQ FT: 4,000
SALES: 600K **Privately Held**
SIC: 3639 Hot water heaters, household

(G-19815)
UNIVERSAL MACHINE PRODUCTS
9060 Goldpark Dr (45011-9764)
PHONE..................513 860-4530
Brian Bogan, *President*
EMP: 4
SQ FT: 6,400
SALES (est): 554.1K **Privately Held**
SIC: 3599 Machine shop, jobbing & repair

(G-19816)
UPA TECHNOLOGY INC
8963 Cncnnati Columbus Rd (45069-3513)
P.O. Box 8172 (45069-8172)
PHONE..................513 755-1380
Michael Justice, *President*
Susan Justice, *Vice Pres*
◆ **EMP:** 11
SQ FT: 4,500
SALES (est): 1.9MM **Privately Held**
WEB: www.upa.com
SIC: 3829 7699 Measuring & controlling devices; professional instrument repair services

(G-19817)
USUI INTERNATIONAL CORPORATION
Also Called: UIC West Chester Plant
8748 Jacquemin Dr Ste 100 (45069-4859)
PHONE..................734 354-3626
Devon Thompson, *Manager*
EMP: 100
SALES (corp-wide): 776.2MM **Privately Held**
SIC: 3714 Motor vehicle parts & accessories
HQ: Usui International Corporation
  44780 Helm St
  Plymouth MI 48170
  734 354-3626

(G-19818)
VIP-SUPPLY CHAIN SOLUTIONS LLC (PA)
Also Called: VIP-Scs
9166 Sutton Pl (45011-9317)
PHONE..................513 454-2020
Stephanie Burnside, *Office Mgr*
Lori Jordan,
Mike Francis,
EMP: 4 EST: 2012
SQ FT: 30,000
SALES (est): 2.1MM **Privately Held**
SIC: 7389 5085 4731 2449 Packaging & labeling services; inventory computing service; boxes, crates, etc., other than paper; freight transportation arrangement; rectangular boxes & crates, wood

(G-19819)
WEST CHESTER LOCK CO LLC
6847 Lakota Plaza Dr (45069-6006)
P.O. Box 8052 (45069-8052)
PHONE..................513 777-6486
Rod Herdman,
EMP: 8
SQ FT: 2,000
SALES (est): 571K **Privately Held**
SIC: 3429 Door locks, bolts & checks

(G-19820)
WESTROCK CONVERTING COMPANY
9266 Meridian Way (45069-6521)
PHONE..................513 860-0225
EMP: 117
SALES (corp-wide): 16.2B **Publicly Held**
SIC: 2631 Container board
HQ: Westrock Converting, Llc
  1000 Abernathy Rd Ste 125
  Atlanta GA 30328
  770 448-2193

(G-19821)
WESTROCK RKT LLC
Also Called: Rocktenn Merchandising Display
9245 Meridian Way (45069-6523)
PHONE..................513 860-5546
Bob Akers, *Ltd Ptnr*
EMP: 35
SALES (corp-wide): 16.2B **Publicly Held**
WEB: www.rocktenn.com
SIC: 2653 Boxes, corrugated: made from purchased materials
HQ: Westrock Rkt, Llc
  1000 Abernathy Rd Ste 125
  Atlanta GA 30328
  770 448-2193

(G-19822)
WRR CREATIVE CONCEPTS LLC
Also Called: Walton, Rego and Roy
6082 Ash Hill Ct (45069-6663)
PHONE..................513 659-2284
Randall James Walton,
EMP: 4
SALES: 1,000K **Privately Held**
SIC: 3089 Plastics products

(G-19823)
YKK AP AMERICA INC
Also Called: YKK USA
8748 Jacquemin Dr Ste 400 (45069-4999)
PHONE..................513 942-7200
Phil Blizzard, *Manager*
EMP: 13
SALES (corp-wide): 7B **Privately Held**
WEB: www.ykkap.com
SIC: 3442 3449 Sash, door or window: metal; metal doors; curtain wall, metal
HQ: Ykk Ap America Inc.
  270 Riverside Pkwy Sw # 100
  Austell GA 30168

(G-19824)
YOCKEY GROUP INC
9053 Le Saint Dr (45014-2242)
PHONE..................513 860-9053
A James Yockey, *President*
EMP: 30
SALES (est): 1.4MM **Privately Held**
SIC: 2759 Commercial printing

West Chester
Hamilton County

(G-19825)
ACE MANUFACTURING COMPANY
Also Called: Ace Sanitary
5452 Spellmire Dr (45246-4842)
PHONE..................513 541-2490
Charles H Tobias Jr, *Principal*
M R Fredwest, *Principal*
Donald A Schenck, *Principal*
Greg Evans, *Regl Sales Mgr*
Scott Brown, *Sales Staff*
▲ **EMP:** 32
SQ FT: 27,500
SALES (est): 6MM **Privately Held**
WEB: www.acemanco.com
SIC: 3599 3492 Hose, flexible metallic; hose & tube fittings & assemblies, hydraulic/pneumatic

(G-19826)
ADVANCEPIERRE FOODS INC (DH)
Also Called: Advance Pierre Foods
9990 Prnceton Glendale Rd (45246-1116)
PHONE..................513 874-8741
John Tyson, *Ch of Bd*
Tom Hayes, *President*
Steve Booker, *President*
Tom Lavan, *President*
Walt Thurn, *President*
▲ **EMP:** 300
SALES (est): 1.2B
SALES (corp-wide): 40B **Publicly Held**
WEB: www.pierrefoods.com
SIC: 2013 2015 Prepared beef products from purchased beef; prepared pork products from purchased pork; chicken, processed

(G-19827)
ADVANCEPIERRE FOODS INC
9990 Prnceton Glendale Rd (45246-1116)
PHONE..................513 874-8741
Brian Bauman, *Business Mgr*
Steve Clyne, *Business Mgr*
Susan Cohen, *Business Mgr*
Sally Feeney, *Business Mgr*
Joyce Podojil, *Business Mgr*
EMP: 5
SALES (corp-wide): 40B **Publicly Held**
SIC: 2013 Sausages & other prepared meats
HQ: Advancepierre Foods, Inc.
  9990 Prnceton Glendale Rd
  West Chester OH 45246
  513 874-8741

(G-19828)
ADVANCPERRE FOODS HOLDINGS INC (HQ)
9990 Prnceton Glendale Rd (45246-1116)
PHONE..................800 969-2747
Tom Hayes, *CEO*
John Corr, *Business Mgr*
Doug Santschi, *Vice Pres*
Michael Doeden, *Plant Mgr*
Stephan Jennings, *Materials Mgr*
EMP: 37
SALES: 1.5B
SALES (corp-wide): 40B **Publicly Held**
SIC: 2099 2013 Sandwiches, assembled & packaged: for wholesale market; sausages & other prepared meats
PA: Tyson Foods, Inc.
  2200 W Don Tyson Pkwy
  Springdale AR 72762
  479 290-4000

(G-19829)
AGEAN MARBLE MANUFACTURING
9756 Prnceton Glendale Rd (45246-1015)
PHONE..................513 874-1475
Gary Bolte, *Chairman*
Lois Bolte, *Corp Secy*
Chris Bolte, *Vice Pres*
EMP: 15
SQ FT: 26,000
SALES (est): 2.2MM **Privately Held**
SIC: 3272 5211 5091 3431 Art marble, concrete; bathroom fixtures, equipment & supplies; spa equipment & supplies; hot tubs; metal sanitary ware; cut stone & stone products; wood kitchen cabinets

(G-19830)
AJJ ENTERPRISES LLC
10073 Commerce Park Dr (45246-1333)
PHONE..................513 755-9562
Jason Wahl, *Master*
Jonathan Back,
Shane Back,
Adam Brinkman,
▲ **EMP:** 10
SALES (est): 1.7MM **Privately Held**
SIC: 3944 Games, toys & children's vehicles

GEOGRAPHIC SECTION
West Chester - Hamilton County (G-19855)

(G-19831)
AMANO MCGANN INC
10162 International Blvd (45246-4846)
PHONE..................513 683-2906
Jordan Vierling, *Branch Mgr*
EMP: 15
SALES (corp-wide): 1.1B Privately Held
SIC: 3873 Watches, clocks, watchcases & parts
HQ: Amano Mcgann, Inc.
 2699 Patton Rd
 Saint Paul MN 55113
 612 331-2020

(G-19832)
ANEST IWATA USA INC
10148 Commerce Park Dr (45246-1336)
PHONE..................513 755-3100
Hiroki Nishida, *President*
▲ EMP: 8
SQ FT: 4,800
SALES (est): 1.7MM
SALES (corp-wide): 308MM Privately Held
WEB: www.anestiwata.com
SIC: 3479 5013 Painting, coating & hot dipping; motor vehicle supplies & new parts; automotive supplies & parts
PA: Anest Iwata Corporation
 3176, Shin-Yoshidacho, Kohoku-Ku
 Yokohama KNG 223-0
 455 911-111

(G-19833)
APF LEGACY SUBS LLC (DH)
9990 Prnceton Glendale Rd (45246-1116)
PHONE..................513 682-7173
Norbert E Woodhams,
EMP: 5
SALES (est): 4MM
SALES (corp-wide): 40B Publicly Held
WEB: www.pierrefoods.com
SIC: 2099 Food preparations
HQ: Advancepierre Foods, Inc.
 9990 Prnceton Glendale Rd
 West Chester OH 45246
 513 874-8741

(G-19834)
ATLAS MACHINE AND SUPPLY INC
4985 Provident Dr (45246-1020)
PHONE..................502 584-7262
Kurt Colwell, *Div Sub Head*
Sonny Welker, *Manager*
EMP: 32
SALES (corp-wide): 43.5MM Privately Held
WEB: www.atlasmachine.com
SIC: 5084 3599 Compressors, except air conditioning; machine shop, jobbing & repair
PA: Atlas Machine And Supply, Inc.
 7000 Global Dr
 Louisville KY 40258
 502 584-7262

(G-19835)
BEIERSDORF INC
5232 E Provident Dr (45246-1040)
PHONE..................513 682-7300
Gayle Gao, *President*
Dan Heil, *Opers Mgr*
Aneesa Khan, *Human Res Dir*
Melanie Peck, *Human Res Mgr*
Jim Kenton, *Branch Mgr*
EMP: 168
SALES (corp-wide): 12.1B Privately Held
WEB: www.bdfusa.com
SIC: 2844 5122 3842 2841 Face creams or lotions; antiseptics; bandages & dressings; stockinette, surgical; soap: granulated, liquid, cake, flaked or chip; tape, pressure sensitive: made from purchased materials
HQ: Beiersdorf, Inc.
 45 Danbury Rd
 Wilton CT 06897
 203 563-5200

(G-19836)
BUILDING CTRL INTEGRATORS LLC
10174 International Blvd (45246-4846)
PHONE..................513 860-9600
David Milar, *General Mgr*
EMP: 7
SALES (corp-wide): 17.1MM Privately Held
SIC: 3822 Temperature controls, automatic
PA: Building Control Integrators, Llc
 383 N Liberty St
 Powell OH 43065
 614 334-3300

(G-19837)
CAE RANSOHOFF INC
4933 Provident Dr (45246-1020)
PHONE..................513 870-0100
EMP: 7
SALES (est): 470K Privately Held
SIC: 3569 General Industrial Machinery, Nec, Nsk

(G-19838)
CECO ENVIRONMENTAL CORP
Effox-Flextor
9759 Inter Ocean Dr (45246-1027)
PHONE..................513 874-8915
Jack Neiser, *Branch Mgr*
EMP: 25
SALES (corp-wide): 337.3MM Publicly Held
SIC: 3443 3441 Fabricated plate work (boiler shop); fabricated structural metal
PA: Ceco Environmental Corp.
 14651 Dallas Pkwy
 Dallas TX 75254
 513 458-2600

(G-19839)
CEPHAS ENTERPRISES LLC
4740 Dues Dr Unit F (45246-1087)
PHONE..................513 317-5685
Doug Waever,
EMP: 5 EST: 2007
SQ FT: 7,000
SALES: 500K Privately Held
SIC: 2822 Ethylene-propylene rubbers, EPDM polymers

(G-19840)
CHASE DOORS ACQUISITION CORP
10021 Commerce Park Dr (45246-1333)
PHONE..................513 860-5565
Oliver Ewald, *President*
Daniel Weintraub, *President*
Michael Fondo, *Asst Treas*
Iveshu Bhatia, *Director*
Jay Jester, *Director*
EMP: 2
SALES (est): 12.4MM
SALES (corp-wide): 7MM Privately Held
SIC: 3442 Metal doors, sash & trim
PA: Chase Doors Group Holdings, Llc
 10021 Commerce Park Dr
 West Chester OH 45246
 513 860-4455

(G-19841)
CHASE INDUSTRIES INC (DH)
Also Called: Chase Doors
10021 Commerce Park Dr (45246-1333)
PHONE..................513 860-5565
Tony Bartelson, *General Mgr*
Charles Chapter, *Regional Mgr*
Alan D Baker, *Corp Secy*
Todd Ray, *Exec VP*
Jason Di Leo, *Vice Pres*
◆ EMP: 80 EST: 1996
SQ FT: 280,000
SALES (est): 92.9MM
SALES (corp-wide): 6.3B Privately Held
WEB: www.restaurantdoors.com
SIC: 3442 Metal doors, sash & trim
HQ: Senneca Holdings, Inc.
 11502 Century Blvd
 Cincinnati OH 45246
 800 543-4455

(G-19842)
CLEANING TECH GROUP LLC (HQ)
Also Called: Ransohoff
4933 Provident Dr (45246-1020)
PHONE..................877 933-8278
Jim McEachen, *CEO*
Helene Buse, *CFO*
▲ EMP: 127
SQ FT: 32,780
SALES (est): 24.3MM Privately Held
SIC: 3699 Cleaning equipment, ultrasonic, except medical & dental

(G-19843)
CLEANING TECH GROUP LLC
Ransohoff Division
4933 Provident Dr (45246-1020)
PHONE..................513 870-0100
Jeff Mills, *Vice Pres*
Steven Stivers, *Engineer*
Rob McCulley, *Project Engr*
Lisa Finley, *Regl Sales Mgr*
Barney Bosse, *Manager*
EMP: 50 Privately Held
SIC: 3569 3599 Blast cleaning equipment, dustless; custom machinery
HQ: Cleaning Technologies Group, Llc
 4933 Provident Dr
 West Chester OH 45246

(G-19844)
CMA SUPPLY COMPANY INC
Also Called: C M A Supply Company
9984 Commerce Park Dr (45246-1332)
PHONE..................513 942-6663
Alan Monnin, *Branch Mgr*
EMP: 12
SALES (est): 907.4K
SALES (corp-wide): 6.7MM Privately Held
SIC: 5032 3444 Concrete building products; concrete forms, sheet metal
PA: C.M.A. Supply Company, Inc.
 3201 Roosevelt Ave
 Indianapolis IN 46218
 317 545-4446

(G-19845)
CTL-AEROSPACE INC (PA)
Also Called: OEM
5616 Spellmire Dr (45246-4898)
PHONE..................513 874-7900
James T Irwin, *President*
Robert W Buechner, *Principal*
Vicki Osborne, *Principal*
John Irwin, *Vice Pres*
Steve Kennedy, *Vice Pres*
EMP: 245 EST: 1946
SQ FT: 100,000
SALES (est): 65.8MM Privately Held
WEB: www.ctlaerospace.com
SIC: 3728 Aircraft assemblies, subassemblies & parts; aircraft body & wing assemblies & parts; airframe assemblies, except for guided missiles; aircraft propellers & associated equipment

(G-19846)
CTL-AEROSPACE INC
9970 International Blvd (45246-4852)
PHONE..................513 874-7900
JC Owen, *President*
EMP: 60
SALES (corp-wide): 65.8MM Privately Held
WEB: www.ctlaerospace.com
SIC: 3728 Aircraft parts & equipment
PA: Ctl-Aerospace, Inc.
 5616 Spellmire Dr
 West Chester OH 45246
 513 874-7900

(G-19847)
CUSTOM CARBIDE CUTTER INC
133 Circle Freeway Dr (45246-1203)
PHONE..................513 851-6363
Steven Long, *President*
Nancy Long, *Admin Sec*
EMP: 15
SQ FT: 5,000
SALES (est): 3.1MM Privately Held
WEB: www.customcarbidecutter.com
SIC: 3545 Drill bits, metalworking; cutting tools for machine tools

(G-19848)
D C CONTROLS LLC
Also Called: Coffey and Associates
4836 Duff Dr Ste E (45246-1194)
PHONE..................513 225-0813
David A Coffey, *Mng Member*
Linda D Coffey,
EMP: 7
SALES (est): 975.9K Privately Held
SIC: 3315 Wire & fabricated wire products

(G-19849)
E2 MERCHANDISING INC
9706 Inter Ocean Dr (45246-1028)
PHONE..................513 860-5444
Chris Kin, *President*
Henry Kin, *Managing Prtnr*
Chuck Snyder, *Senior Engr*
Michelle Heywood, *Manager*
▼ EMP: 20 EST: 2010
SALES (est): 3.1MM Privately Held
SIC: 2542 Racks, merchandise display or storage: except wood

(G-19850)
ECKEL INDUSTRIES INC
Rubbair Door
10021 Commerce Park Dr (45246-1333)
PHONE..................978 772-0480
Scott Salem, *Sales Staff*
Alex Eckel, *Branch Mgr*
EMP: 30
SALES (corp-wide): 9.6MM Privately Held
WEB: www.eckelacoustic.com
SIC: 3089 3069 Doors, folding: plastic or plastic coated fabric; hard rubber & molded rubber products
PA: Eckel Industries, Inc.
 100 Groton Shirley Rd
 Ayer MA 01432
 978 772-0840

(G-19851)
ELIASON CORPORATION
10021 Commerce Park Dr (45246-1333)
PHONE..................800 828-3655
EMP: 5
SALES (corp-wide): 6.3B Privately Held
SIC: 3442 3089 Metal doors; plastic containers, except foam
HQ: Eliason Corporation
 9229 Shaver Rd
 Portage MI 49024
 269 327-7003

(G-19852)
FIRE-END & CROKER CORP
4690 Interstate Dr Ste P (45246-1142)
PHONE..................513 870-0517
Bob Orth, *General Mgr*
EMP: 9
SALES (corp-wide): 18MM Privately Held
SIC: 3699 Fire control or bombing equipment, electronic
PA: Fire End & Croker Corp.
 7 Westchester Plz Ste 267
 Elmsford NY 10523
 914 592-3640

(G-19853)
FLAVOR SYSTEMS INTERNATIONAL
9930 Commerce Park Dr (45246-1332)
PHONE..................513 870-0420
Thomas L Cuni, *Principal*
Maria Burns, *Representative*
EMP: 5
SALES (est): 421.7K Privately Held
SIC: 2087 Extracts, flavoring

(G-19854)
FLAVOR SYSTEMS INTL INC (HQ)
5404 Duff Dr (45246-1323)
PHONE..................513 870-4900
William W Wasz, *President*
William Baker, *Vice Pres*
John Disebastian, *Vice Pres*
▲ EMP: 32
SQ FT: 50,000
SALES (est): 7MM
SALES (corp-wide): 1.3B Privately Held
WEB: www.flavorsystems.com
SIC: 2087 Flavoring extracts & syrups
PA: Frutarom Industries Ltd
 2 Hamanofim, Entrance
 Herzliya 46725
 996 038-00

(G-19855)
FRUTAROM USA HOLDING INC (DH)
5404 Duff Dr (45246-1323)
PHONE..................201 861-9500

West Chester - Hamilton County (G-19856) GEOGRAPHIC SECTION

Ori Yehudai, *CEO*
Amos Anatot, *Exec VP*
Alon Granot, *CFO*
EMP: 6
SALES (est): 2.5MM
SALES (corp-wide): 1.3B Privately Held
SIC: 2869 Flavors or flavoring materials, synthetic
HQ: Frutarom Usa Inc.
5404 Duff Dr
West Chester OH 45246
513 870-4900

(G-19856)
FRUTAROM USA INC (HQ)
5404 Duff Dr (45246-1323)
PHONE 513 870-4900
Ori Yehudai, *President*
Alon Granot, *Senior VP*
Luis Gayo, *Vice Pres*
Michael J Gill, *Treasurer*
◆ **EMP:** 120 EST: 1933
SQ FT: 360,000
SALES (est): 39.5MM
SALES (corp-wide): 1.3B Privately Held
WEB: www.frutarommeer.com
SIC: 2099 2833 2087 Spices, including grinding; botanical products, medicinal: ground, graded or milled; extracts, flavoring
PA: Frutarom Industries Ltd
2 Hamanofim, Entrance
Herzliya 46725
996 038-00

(G-19857)
FRUTAROM USA INC
9950 Commerce Park Dr (45246-1332)
PHONE 513 870-4900
Reed Lynn, *General Mgr*
EMP: 13
SALES (corp-wide): 1.3B Privately Held
SIC: 2099 Spices, including grinding
HQ: Frutarom Usa Inc.
5404 Duff Dr
West Chester OH 45246
513 870-4900

(G-19858)
FRUTAROM USA INC
9930 Commerce Park Dr (45246-1332)
PHONE 513 870-4900
EMP: 4
SALES (corp-wide): 1.3B Privately Held
SIC: 2099 Spices, including grinding
HQ: Frutarom Usa Inc.
5404 Duff Dr
West Chester OH 45246
513 870-4900

(G-19859)
FRUTAROM USA INC
10139 Commerce Park Dr (45246-1335)
PHONE 513 870-4900
Ori Yehudai, *CEO*
EMP: 6
SALES (corp-wide): 1.3B Privately Held
SIC: 2833 Medicinals & botanicals
HQ: Frutarom Usa Inc.
5404 Duff Dr
West Chester OH 45246
513 870-4900

(G-19860)
GOYAL ENTERPRISES INC
Also Called: Bharat Trading
4836 Business Center Way (45246-1318)
P.O. Box 1728 (45071-1728)
PHONE 513 874-9303
Kavita Goyal, *President*
Arun Goyal, *General Mgr*
EMP: 10
SQ FT: 4,500
SALES (est): 1.2MM Privately Held
WEB: www.gemini-jewelers.com
SIC: 5094 5944 3911 Jewelry & precious stones; jewelry, precious stones & precious metals; bracelets, precious metal

(G-19861)
GRAHAM PACKAGING COMPANY LP
290 Circle Freeway Dr (45246-1206)
PHONE 513 874-1770
Kevin George, *Manager*
Russ Stegman, *Administration*
EMP: 43
SALES (corp-wide): 1MM Privately Held
WEB: www.grahampackaging.com
SIC: 3089 3085 Plastic containers, except foam; plastics bottles
HQ: Graham Packaging Company, L.P.
700 Indian Springs Dr # 100
Lancaster PA 17601
717 849-8500

(G-19862)
GREENWORLD ENTERPRISES INC
Also Called: Focal Point Communications
61 Circle Freeway Dr (45246-1201)
PHONE 800 525-6999
Joe Shooner, *CEO*
Renee Langefeld, *COO*
Ben Shooner, *Program Mgr*
EMP: 6 EST: 1982
SQ FT: 3,600
SALES (est): 1MM Privately Held
SIC: 2741 Newsletter publishing

(G-19863)
HANSEN SCAFFOLDING LLC (PA)
193 Circle Freeway Dr (45246-1203)
PHONE 513 574-9000
Aaron Hansen, *President*
Jennifer McDonald, *Principal*
EMP: 15
SQ FT: 22,000
SALES (est): 3.1MM Privately Held
WEB: www.hiloclimbers.com
SIC: 7359 3446 Equipment rental & leasing; scaffolds, mobile or stationary: metal

(G-19864)
HANSER MUSIC GROUP INC (PA)
9615 Inter Ocean Dr (45246-1029)
PHONE 859 817-7100
John F Hanser III, *President*
Timothy J Hanser, *Corp Secy*
Gary Hanser, *Vice Pres*
David F Rasfeld, *CFO*
Carlos Vargas, *Sales Mgr*
◆ **EMP:** 80 EST: 1924
SQ FT: 121,000
SALES (est): 21.7MM Privately Held
WEB: www.powerwerks.com
SIC: 5099 3931 Musical instruments; musical instruments

(G-19865)
HORNER INDUSTRIAL SERVICES INC
4721 Interstate Dr (45246-1111)
PHONE 513 874-8722
Mark Wolma, *Vice Pres*
EMP: 15
SALES (corp-wide): 46.7MM Privately Held
SIC: 7694 Armature rewinding shops
PA: Horner Industrial Services, Inc.
1521 E Washington St
Indianapolis IN 46201
317 639-4261

(G-19866)
ICEE USA
44 Carnegie Way (45246-1224)
PHONE 513 771-0630
Bob Keegan, *Principal*
EMP: 6
SALES (est): 284.8K Privately Held
SIC: 2024 Ice cream & frozen desserts

(G-19867)
INDRA HOLDINGS CORP (PA)
9655 International Blvd (45246-4861)
PHONE 513 682-8200
Daniel S Rajczak, *President*
Ronald P Spogli, *Principal*
EMP: 3
SALES (est): 11.9MM Privately Held
SIC: 5632 2396 5699 2389 Apparel accessories; apparel & other linings, except millinery; customized clothing & apparel; men's miscellaneous accessories; women's & misses' accessories; investment holding companies, except banks

(G-19868)
INTELLIGRATED INC
10045 International Blvd (45246-4845)
PHONE 513 874-0788
Cindy Lynies, *Branch Mgr*
EMP: 21
SALES (corp-wide): 41.8B Publicly Held
SIC: 3535 5084 7371 Conveyors & conveying equipment; industrial machinery & equipment; custom computer programming services
HQ: Intelligrated, Inc.
7901 Innovation Way
Mason OH 45040
866 936-7300

(G-19869)
INTELLIGRATED SYSTEMS OHIO LLC
Also Called: Fki Logistex
10045 International Blvd (45246-4845)
PHONE 513 682-6600
Doug Westman, *Dir Ops-Prd-Mfg*
EMP: 8
SALES (corp-wide): 41.8B Publicly Held
WEB: www.fkilogistex.com
SIC: 3535 Conveyors & conveying equipment
HQ: Intelligrated Systems Of Ohio, Llc
7901 Innovation Way
Mason OH 45040
513 701-7300

(G-19870)
J & K CABINETRY INCORPORATED
9920 Prnceton Glendale Rd (45246-1116)
PHONE 513 860-3461
Zhi WEI Huang, *Administration*
EMP: 5 EST: 2014
SALES (est): 534.1K Privately Held
SIC: 2434 Wood kitchen cabinets

(G-19871)
JOHNNY CHIN INSURANCE AGENCY
Also Called: State Farm Insurance
9676 Cncnnati Columbus Rd (45241-1071)
PHONE 513 777-8695
Johnny Chin, *Owner*
Angela Chin, *Office Mgr*
EMP: 3
SALES: 3MM Privately Held
SIC: 6411 2741 Insurance agents; miscellaneous publishing

(G-19872)
LASTING FIRST IMPRESSIONS INC
Also Called: Heartland Thermography
36 Carnegie Way (45246-1224)
PHONE 513 870-6900
Douglas Rodenfels, *President*
Laurie Rodenfels, *Admin Sec*
EMP: 19
SQ FT: 10,000
SALES (est): 2.3MM Privately Held
SIC: 2752 Commercial printing, offset

(G-19873)
LOUIS TRAUTH DAIRY LLC (HQ)
9991 Commerce Park Dr (45246-1331)
P.O. Box 721770, Newport KY (41072-1770)
PHONE 859 431-7553
Greg Engles, *CEO*
Rachael A Gonzalez, *Principal*
Steven J Kemps, *Principal*
Gary Sparks, *Senior VP*
Dan Smith, *Vice Pres*
EMP: 260 EST: 1920
SQ FT: 160,000
SALES (est): 39.2MM Publicly Held
WEB: www.trauthdairy.com
SIC: 5149 2033 2026 2024 Beverages, except coffee & tea; mineral or spring water bottling; tea; canned fruits & specialties; fluid milk; ice cream & frozen desserts; milk & cream, fluid

(G-19874)
MAGNUM PIERING INC
156 Circle Freeway Dr (45246-1204)
PHONE 513 759-3348
Brian Dwyer, *President*
Bill Bonekemper, *Vice Pres*
Jason Woodward, *Opers Mgr*
Sharon Appelman, *Admin Sec*
EMP: 30
SALES (est): 8.4MM
SALES (corp-wide): 15MM Privately Held
WEB: www.magnumpiering.com
SIC: 3441 3561 Fabricated structural metal; pumps & pumping equipment
PA: Dwyer Companies, Inc.
156 Circle Freeway Dr
West Chester OH 45246
513 759-3349

(G-19875)
MAI MEDIA GROUP LLC
Also Called: Eye3data
9624 Cincinnati Columbus (45241-4123)
PHONE 513 779-0604
Erum Ansari,
EMP: 5
SALES (est): 791.2K
SALES (corp-wide): 2.7B Privately Held
SIC: 3699 5065 Security control equipment & systems; security control equipment & systems
HQ: Point Blank Enterprises, Inc.
2102 Sw 2nd St
Pompano Beach FL 33069
954 630-0900

(G-19876)
MCCC SPORTSWEAR INC
9944 Prnceton Glendale Rd (45246-1116)
PHONE 513 583-9210
Marta Callahan, *President*
Sue Kollstedt, *Vice Pres*
Debbie Johnson, *Art Dir*
Pam Bedell,
▲ **EMP:** 30
SQ FT: 45,000
SALES: 8MM Privately Held
WEB: www.mccc-sportswear.com
SIC: 5137 2395 5136 Women's & children's clothing; embroidery & art needlework; men's & boys' clothing

(G-19877)
MED CENTER SYSTEMS LLC
10179 Commerce Park Dr (45246-1335)
PHONE 513 942-6066
Mandy Engel, *Vice Pres*
Linda Pipkins, *Sales Staff*
David Cooper,
Martin Cooper,
EMP: 3
SALES: 750K Privately Held
SIC: 3089 Plastic containers, except foam

(G-19878)
MEKA SIGNS ENTERPRISES INC
Also Called: Signs By Tomorrow
10126 Prncton Glendale Rd (45246-1200)
PHONE 513 942-5494
Kevin Moe, *President*
EMP: 3
SALES: 150K Privately Held
SIC: 3993 Signs & advertising specialties

(G-19879)
MICROTEK FINISHING LLC
5579 Spellmire Dr (45246-4841)
PHONE 513 766-5600
Tim Bell, *Vice Pres*
▲ **EMP:** 22
SQ FT: 5,000
SALES (est): 3.2MM Privately Held
WEB: www.MicroTekFinishing.com
SIC: 3471 Polishing, metals or formed products

(G-19880)
MIDWEST FILTRATION LLC
9775 International Blvd (45246-4855)
PHONE 513 874-6510
Chris Noe, *Business Mgr*
Jim Valentine, *Plant Mgr*
Gary Caudill, *Production*
Troy Mastern, *Purch Mgr*
Gary Staggs, *Purchasing*
◆ **EMP:** 50
SQ FT: 110,000

GEOGRAPHIC SECTION

SALES (est): 19MM **Privately Held**
WEB: www.midwestfiltration.com
SIC: **3569** 2653 Filters, general line: industrial; corrugated & solid fiber boxes

(G-19881)
NORTHROP GRUMMAN SYSTEMS CORP
460 W Crescentville Rd (45246-1221)
PHONE.................................513 881-3296
Michael Feverston, *General Mgr*
David Hutchison, *Project Mgr*
Allen McEwen, *Project Mgr*
Tod Ostrander, *Project Mgr*
Michael Chapman, *Facilities Mgr*
EMP: 270 **Publicly Held**
WEB: www.sperry.ngc.com
SIC: **3812** Search & navigation equipment
HQ: Northrop Grumman Systems Corporation
2980 Fairview Park Dr
Falls Church VA 22042
703 280-2900

(G-19882)
OCTAL EXTRUSION CORP
5399 E Provident Dr (45246-1044)
PHONE.................................513 881-6100
Joe Barenberg, *CEO*
Cameron Warren, *Controller*
EMP: 50
SQ FT: 130,000
SALES: 18MM **Privately Held**
SIC: **2631** Paper coated or laminated for packaging
PA: Octal Holding
Al Rawaq Building Next To Nissan Showroom
Muscat
220 307-00

(G-19883)
OMNI BUSINESS FORMS INC
4747 Devitt Dr (45246-1105)
PHONE.................................513 860-0111
Louis Silverberg, *President*
Colleen Silverberg, *Admin Sec*
EMP: 5
SQ FT: 500
SALES: 1MM **Privately Held**
SIC: **2752** Commercial printing, lithographic

(G-19884)
PERFECTION BAKERIES INC
374 Circle Freeway Dr C (45246-1260)
PHONE.................................513 942-1442
Jeri Meinking, *Principal*
EMP: 37
SALES (corp-wide): 515.3MM **Privately Held**
SIC: **2051** Bread, all types (white, wheat, rye, etc): fresh or frozen
PA: Perfection Bakeries, Inc.
350 Pearl St
Fort Wayne IN 46802
260 424-8245

(G-19885)
PF MANAGEMENT INC
Also Called: Pfmi
9990 Prnceton Glendale Rd (45246-1116)
PHONE.................................513 874-8741
Norbert E Woodhams, *President*
EMP: 7
SQ FT: 220,000
SALES (est): 424K
SALES (corp-wide): 533.9MM **Privately Held**
SIC: **8741** 2015 2051 Management services; chicken slaughtering & processing; bread, cake & related products
HQ: Pierre Holding Corp
9990 Prnceton Glendale Rd
West Chester OH 45246

(G-19886)
PIERRE HOLDING CORP (HQ)
9990 Prnceton Glendale Rd (45246-1116)
PHONE.................................513 874-8741
Norbert E Wooadhams, *President*
Robert C Naylor, *Senior VP*
Joseph W Meyers, *CFO*
EMP: 7
SQ FT: 220,000

SALES (est): 227.1MM
SALES (corp-wide): 533.9MM **Privately Held**
SIC: **2013** 2015 2051 Prepared beef products from purchased beef; prepared pork products from purchased pork; chicken slaughtering & processing; bread, cake & related products
PA: Madison Dearborn Partners Iv Lp
70 W Madison St Ste 3800
Chicago IL 60602
312 895-1000

(G-19887)
POWERSONIC INDUSTRIES LLC
5406 Spellmire Dr (45246-4842)
PHONE.................................513 429-2329
Jason Rampersand, *President*
EMP: 25
SALES (est): 1.9MM **Privately Held**
SIC: **3571** Electronic computers

(G-19888)
PPG INDUSTRIES INC
Also Called: PPG 4341
9304 Cincinnati Columbus (45241-6101)
PHONE.................................513 779-2727
EMP: 24
SALES (corp-wide): 15.3B **Publicly Held**
WEB: www.ppg.com
SIC: **2851** Paints & allied products
PA: Ppg Industries, Inc.
1 Ppg Pl
Pittsburgh PA 15272
412 434-3131

(G-19889)
PRINT ZONE
9588 Cncnnati Columbus Rd (45241-1112)
PHONE.................................513 733-0067
B Ariapad, *Principal*
EMP: 4
SALES (est): 452.5K **Privately Held**
SIC: **2752** Commercial printing, lithographic

(G-19890)
PROFESSIONAL CASE INC
Also Called: PCI
9790 Inter Ocean Dr (45246-1028)
PHONE.................................513 682-2520
Thomas Brown, *President*
Erin Biel, *Vice Pres*
EMP: 10 EST: 1978
SQ FT: 7,000
SALES (est): 1.5MM **Privately Held**
WEB: www.professionalcase.com
SIC: **3161** Cases, carrying

(G-19891)
QUALITY ENVELOPE INC
9792 Inter Ocean Dr (45246-1028)
PHONE.................................513 942-7578
Robert Lester, *President*
Rick Doxtator, *Vice Pres*
Jeffery Leatherwood Sr, *Vice Pres*
EMP: 6
SALES (est): 1.2MM **Privately Held**
WEB: www.qenvelopes.com
SIC: **2677** Envelopes

(G-19892)
QUEEN CITY TECHNOLOGIES
34 W Crescentville Rd (45246)
PHONE.................................513 253-1312
Aaron Hoffman, *Officer*
EMP: 10
SALES (est): 446.8K **Privately Held**
SIC: **7371** 7372 Computer software development; business oriented computer software

(G-19893)
READING ROCK INC (PA)
4600 Devitt Dr (45246-1104)
P.O. Box 46387, Cincinnati (45246-0387)
PHONE.................................513 874-2345
Gordon Rich, *President*
Mark Swortwood, *Vice Pres*
Brian Campbell, *CFO*
▲ EMP: 150
SQ FT: 64,000

SALES (est): 33.7MM **Privately Held**
WEB: www.readingrock.com
SIC: **3271** 2951 Blocks, concrete or cinder: standard; paving blocks, concrete; asphalt paving mixtures & blocks

(G-19894)
REITER DAIRY OF AKRON INC
9991 Commerce Park Dr (45246-1331)
PHONE.................................513 795-6962
EMP: 9 **Publicly Held**
SIC: **2026** Mfg Fluid Milk
HQ: Reiter Dairy Of Akron, Inc.
1961 Commerce Cir
Springfield OH 45504
937 323-5777

(G-19895)
ROOFING ANNEX LLC
4866 Duff Dr Ste D (45246-1151)
PHONE.................................513 942-0555
Chad Janisch, *CEO*
Stephen Michels, *Corp Secy*
Joey Michels, *Vice Pres*
Valerie Wiley, *Manager*
Ryan Kaz, *Art Dir*
EMP: 7
SQ FT: 4,000
SALES: 8MM **Privately Held**
SIC: **5031** 1761 3444 Windows; roofing, siding & sheet metal work; roof repair; gutters, sheet metal

(G-19896)
SAF-HOLLAND INC
246 Circle Freeway Dr (45246-1206)
PHONE.................................513 874-7888
EMP: 8 **Privately Held**
SIC: **3715** 3568 3537 3452 Truck trailers; power transmission equipment; industrial trucks & tractors; bolts, nuts, rivets & washers; trailer hitches, motor vehicle
HQ: Saf-Holland, Inc.
1950 Industrial Blvd
Muskegon MI 49442
231 773-3271

(G-19897)
SEI INC
10004 International Blvd (45246-4839)
PHONE.................................513 942-6170
EMP: 10 **Privately Held**
SIC: **2741** Miscellaneous publishing
PA: Sei, Inc.
3854 Broadmoor Ave Se # 101
Grand Rapids MI 49512

(G-19898)
SEXTON INDUSTRIAL INC
366 Circle Freeway Dr (45246-1208)
PHONE.................................513 530-5555
Abbe Sexton, *President*
Dan Towne, *Corp Secy*
Ron Sexton, *Vice Pres*
EMP: 150
SQ FT: 85,000
SALES (est): 39.2MM **Privately Held**
WEB: www.artisanmechanical.com
SIC: **1711** 3443 Mechanical contractor; industrial vessels, tanks & containers

(G-19899)
SLUSH PUPPIE
44 Carnegie Way (45246-1224)
PHONE.................................513 771-0940
Will Radcliff, *Ch of Bd*
Dan Keating, *President*
Robert Schwartz, *Admin Sec*
EMP: 90
SQ FT: 40,000
SALES (est): 7.6MM **Privately Held**
WEB: www.slushpuppie.net
SIC: **2087** 5078 Syrups, drink; cocktail mixes, nonalcoholic; soda fountain equipment, refrigerated

(G-19900)
SONOCO PRODUCTS COMPANY
Sonoco Consumer Products
4633 Dues Rd (45246-1008)
PHONE.................................513 870-3985
Lowern Laster, *Manager*
EMP: 45

SALES (corp-wide): 5.3B **Publicly Held**
WEB: www.sonoco.com
SIC: **2655** 2656 Cans, composite: foil-fiber & other: from purchased fiber; sanitary food containers
PA: Sonoco Products Company
1 N 2nd St
Hartsville SC 29550
843 383-7000

(G-19901)
SPLICENET INC
9624 Cincinnati Columbus (45241-4100)
PHONE.................................513 563-3533
James B Lisk, *CEO*
James Gast, *President*
EMP: 4
SALES (est): 612K **Privately Held**
WEB: www.splice.net
SIC: **7372** 7373 Prepackaged software; systems integration services

(G-19902)
SSI MANUFACTURING INC
9615 Inter Ocean Dr (45246-1029)
PHONE.................................513 761-7757
John R Monday, *President*
Carl Thiem, *Vice Pres*
EMP: 15
SQ FT: 13,500
SALES: 1MM **Privately Held**
WEB: www.ssimfg.com
SIC: **1751** 2522 Cabinet building & installation; filing boxes, cabinets & cases: except wood

(G-19903)
STOLLE MILK BIOLOGICS INC
4735 Devitt Dr (45246-1105)
PHONE.................................513 489-7997
Con F Sterling Jr, *CEO*
Dr Robert Stohrer, *Vice Pres*
Jada Eley, *Associate*
▲ EMP: 176
SQ FT: 1,000
SALES (est): 7.8MM **Privately Held**
WEB: www.smbimilk.com
SIC: **2023** Powdered milk

(G-19904)
STOROPACK INC (DH)
Also Called: Foam Pac Materials Company
4758 Devitt Dr (45246-1106)
PHONE.................................513 874-0314
Hans Reichenecker, *Ch of Bd*
Daniel Wachter, *President*
Thomas G Eckel, *Vice Pres*
Joe Lagrasta, *Vice Pres*
Lester Whisnant, *Vice Pres*
▲ EMP: 50
SQ FT: 35,000
SALES: 110MM
SALES (corp-wide): 443.7MM **Privately Held**
WEB: www.storopack.com
SIC: **5199** 3086 2671 Packaging materials; packaging & shipping materials, foamed plastic; packaging paper & plastics film, coated & laminated
HQ: Storopack Deutschland Gmbh + Co. Kg
Untere Rietstr. 30
Metzingen 72555
712 316-40

(G-19905)
SWISHER HYGIENE INC
5579 Spellmire Dr (45246-4841)
PHONE.................................513 870-4830
EMP: 3 **Privately Held**
SIC: **3582** Commercial laundry equipment
PA: Swisher Hygiene Inc.
350 E Las Olas Blvd
Fort Lauderdale FL 33301

(G-19906)
TEKTRONIX INC
9639 Inter Ocean Dr Dr2 (45246-1029)
PHONE.................................513 870-4729
EMP: 23
SALES (corp-wide): 6.4B **Publicly Held**
SIC: **3825** Instruments to measure electricity

West Chester - Hamilton County (G-19907)

HQ: Tektronix, Inc.
14150 Sw Karl Braun Dr
Beaverton OR 97005
800 833-9200

(G-19907)
TOTES ISOTONER CORPORATION (HQ)
9655 International Blvd (45246-4861)
PHONE 513 682-8200
Daniel S Rajczak, *President*
Jason Herr, *Vice Pres*
James Thatcher, *Export Mgr*
Ryan Delp, *Engineer*
Donna Deye, *CFO*
▲ **EMP:** 18 **EST:** 1924
SQ FT: 450,000
SALES (est): 12.8MM
SALES (corp-wide): 11.9MM **Privately Held**
WEB: www.isotoner.com
SIC: 2381 3151 2211 3021 Gloves, woven or knit: made from purchased materials; leather gloves & mittens; umbrella cloth, cotton; rubber & plastics footwear; umbrellas; stockings: men's, women's & children's; raincoats; leather garments; men's & boys' clothing
PA: Indra Holdings Corp.
9655 International Blvd
West Chester OH 45246
513 682-8200

(G-19908)
TOTES ISOTONER HOLDINGS CORP (PA)
9655 International Blvd (45246-4861)
PHONE 513 682-8200
Daniel S Rajczak, *CEO*
Doug Baker, *Principal*
Joshua Beckenstein, *Vice Pres*
Donna Deye, *CFO*
Bob Mills, *Manager*
▲ **EMP:** 200
SALES (est): 118.6MM **Privately Held**
SIC: 2381 3151 2211 3021 Gloves, woven or knit: made from purchased materials; leather gloves & mittens; umbrella cloth, cotton; rubber & plastics footwear; umbrellas; stockings: men's, women's & children's; raincoats; leather garments

(G-19909)
TSK AMERICA CO LTD
9668 Inter Ocean Dr (45246-1030)
PHONE 513 942-4002
Takeshi Takeuchi, *President*
▲ **EMP:** 10
SALES: 3MM **Privately Held**
SIC: 3568 5051 3562 Bearings, bushings & blocks; joints & couplings; metals service centers & offices; iron & steel (ferrous) products; ball bearings & parts

(G-19910)
UNITED GROUP SERVICES INC (PA)
9740 Near Dr (45246-1013)
PHONE 800 633-9690
Daniel Freese, *President*
Clarence Evenson, *Vice Pres*
Kevin Sell, *Vice Pres*
John Long, *Project Mgr*
Matt Mofield, *Project Mgr*
EMP: 200
SQ FT: 45,500
SALES: 50.4MM **Privately Held**
WEB: www.united-gs.com
SIC: 3498 1711 Fabricated pipe & fittings; process piping contractor; mechanical contractor

(G-19911)
UNIVAR USA INC
4600 Dues Dr (45246-1009)
PHONE 513 714-5264
Charles Miller, *Accounts Mgr*
Gary Southern, *Branch Mgr*
EMP: 150
SQ FT: 129,100
SALES (corp-wide): 8.6B **Publicly Held**
SIC: 5169 2819 2869 2899 Industrial chemicals; industrial inorganic chemicals; industrial organic chemicals; chemical preparations; specialty cleaning, polishes & sanitation goods

HQ: Univar Usa Inc.
3075 Highland Pkwy # 200
Downers Grove IL 60515
331 777-6000

(G-19912)
UPSIDE INNOVATIONS LLC
5470 Spellmire Dr (45246-4842)
PHONE 513 889-2492
Kevin Sharp, *President*
Chris Gormley, *Opers Staff*
Sean Faller, *Design Engr*
Amy Langford, *Accounting Mgr*
Rick Hofer, *Accounts Mgr*
EMP: 5
SALES (est): 850.5K **Privately Held**
SIC: 3448 3444 3446 Ramps: prefabricated metal; canopies, sheet metal; stairs, staircases, stair treads: prefabricated metal

(G-19913)
V I P PRINTING & DESIGN
4836 Duff Dr Ste A (45246-1194)
PHONE 513 777-7468
Douglas Rinnert, *Owner*
EMP: 4
SQ FT: 3,000
SALES: 200K **Privately Held**
SIC: 2752 3544 3555 2759 Commercial printing, offset; punches, forming & stamping; engraving machinery & equipment, except plates; laser printing

(G-19914)
VALCO CINCINNATI INC (PA)
Also Called: Valco Melton
497 Circle Freeway Dr # 490 (45246-1257)
P.O. Box 465619, Cincinnati (45246-5619)
PHONE 513 874-6550
Richard Santefort, *President*
David Huang, *General Mgr*
Sergio Contreras, *Project Mgr*
William Schlensker, *Buyer*
Mark Lickert, *Purchasing*
▲ **EMP:** 180
SQ FT: 43,000
SALES (est): 47.7MM **Privately Held**
WEB: www.valco-cp.com
SIC: 3586 3561 Measuring & dispensing pumps; industrial pumps & parts

(G-19915)
VALCO CINCINNATI INC
411 Circle Freeway Dr (45246-1284)
PHONE 513 874-6550
EMP: 4
SALES (corp-wide): 47.7MM **Privately Held**
SIC: 3586 Measuring & dispensing pumps
PA: Valco Cincinnati, Inc.
497 Circle Freeway Dr # 490
West Chester OH 45246
513 874-6550

(G-19916)
VALCO MELTON INC
411 Circle Freeway Dr (45246-1213)
PHONE 513 874-6550
Austin Koehler, *Principal*
▲ **EMP:** 34
SALES (est): 8MM **Privately Held**
SIC: 3663 Radio & TV communications equipment

(G-19917)
XPEDX NATIONAL ACCOUNTS
4225 Dues Dr (45246-1001)
PHONE 513 870-0711
Gary Burkert, *Principal*
EMP: 6 **EST:** 2010
SALES (est): 227.4K **Privately Held**
SIC: 2621 Paper mills

West Farmington
Trumbull County

(G-19918)
ACRYLIC ARTS
3698 G P Easterly Rd (44491-8700)
PHONE 440 537-0300
Justine Conklin, *Owner*
Shannon Conklin, *Owner*

EMP: 4
SALES (est): 327.7K **Privately Held**
SIC: 3089 Aquarium accessories, plastic

(G-19919)
ALPHA MACHINING LLC
394 E Main St (44491-8726)
P.O. Box 195 (44491-0195)
PHONE 330 889-2207
Connie Blair, *CFO*
Gary Blair, *Manager*
EMP: 3
SALES: 200K **Privately Held**
SIC: 3599 Amusement park equipment

(G-19920)
REYNOLDS INDUSTRIES INC
380 W Main St (44491-9712)
P.O. Box 6 (44491-0006)
PHONE 330 889-9466
Gregory A Reynolds, *President*
EMP: 25
SQ FT: 3,500
SALES (est): 2.6MM **Privately Held**
SIC: 3069 4783 Rubber hardware; packing goods for shipping

West Jefferson
Madison County

(G-19921)
BUCKEYE READY-MIX LLC
6600 State Route 29 (43162-9746)
PHONE 614 879-6316
Don Harsh, *Branch Mgr*
EMP: 7
SALES (corp-wide): 45.1MM **Privately Held**
SIC: 3273 Ready-mixed concrete
PA: Buckeye Ready-Mix, Llc
7657 Taylor Rd Sw
Reynoldsburg OH 43068
614 575-2132

(G-19922)
CONDUIT PIPE PRODUCTS COMPANY
1501 W Main St (43162-9627)
PHONE 614 879-9114
John Rodgers, *President*
Tim McGhee, *Principal*
Tom Costello, *Opers Mgr*
Brenda Somar, *Accountant*
Mark McIntosh, *Chief Mktg Ofcr*
EMP: 60
SALES (est): 15.7MM
SALES (corp-wide): 156.1MM **Privately Held**
WEB: www.conduitpipe.com
SIC: 3317 Steel pipe & tubes
PA: The Phoenix Forge Group Llc
1020 Macarthur Rd
Reading PA 19605
800 234-8665

(G-19923)
JEFFERSON INDUSTRIES CORP (HQ)
Also Called: J I C
6670 State Route 29 (43162-9677)
PHONE 614 879-5300
Shiro Shimokagi, *President*
Curtis A Loveland, *Principal*
Steve Yoder, *Senior VP*
Kazuhiko Hara, *Vice Pres*
Hassan Saadat, *Vice Pres*
▲ **EMP:** 149
SQ FT: 370,000
SALES (est): 320MM
SALES (corp-wide): 2B **Privately Held**
WEB: www.jic-ohio.com
SIC: 3711 Chassis, motor vehicle
PA: G-Tekt Corporation
1-9-4, Sakuragicho, Omiya-Ku
Saitama STM 330-0
486 463-400

(G-19924)
KELLOGG COMPANY
125 Enterprise Pkwy (43162-9414)
PHONE 614 879-9659
Richard Emerson, *Principal*
EMP: 385

SALES (corp-wide): 13.5B **Publicly Held**
SIC: 2043 Cereal breakfast foods
PA: Kellogg Company
1 Kellogg Sq
Battle Creek MI 49017
269 961-2000

(G-19925)
M H EBY INC
4435 State Route 29 (43162-9544)
P.O. Box 137 (43162-0137)
PHONE 614 879-6901
Fax: 614 879-6904
EMP: 50 **Privately Held**
SIC: 5012 3444 Whol Autos/Motor Vehicles Mfg Sheet Metalwork

(G-19926)
PHOENIX FORGE GROUP LLC
Capitol Manufacturing Division
1501 W Main St (43162-9627)
PHONE 800 848-6125
Anita Woods, *Sales Associate*
David R Halman, *Branch Mgr*
EMP: 220
SALES (corp-wide): 156.1MM **Privately Held**
SIC: 3498 Pipe fittings, fabricated from purchased pipe
PA: The Phoenix Forge Group Llc
1020 Macarthur Rd
Reading PA 19605
800 234-8665

(G-19927)
R L PARSONS & SON EQUIPMENT CO
Also Called: Micro Mower
7155 State Route 142 Se (43162-9591)
P.O. Box 28 (43162-0028)
PHONE 614 879-7601
Ralph L Parsons Jr, *President*
Ralph L Parsons III, *Vice Pres*
Julie Walker, *Vice Pres*
Mary Parsons, *Treasurer*
▲ **EMP:** 4
SQ FT: 11,000
SALES (est): 1MM **Privately Held**
WEB: www.bomfordcenter.com
SIC: 5083 3523 Farm implements; grounds mowing equipment

(G-19928)
TOAGOSEI AMERICA INC
Also Called: Krazy Glue
1450 W Main St (43162-9730)
PHONE 614 718-3855
Tonio Kambayashi, *President*
Kenichi Ohashi, *Plant Mgr*
Toshio Nakao, *Incorporator*
▲ **EMP:** 100
SQ FT: 64,000
SALES (est): 25.3MM
SALES (corp-wide): 1.2B **Privately Held**
WEB: www.toagosei.net
SIC: 2891 Adhesives
PA: Toagosei Co., Ltd.
1-14-1, Nishishimbashi
Minato-Ku TKY 105-0
335 977-215

West Lafayette
Coshocton County

(G-19929)
CABOT LUMBER INC
304 E Union Ave (43845-1250)
P.O. Box 101 (43845-0101)
PHONE 740 545-7109
Donald Cabot, *President*
Dennis E Cabot, *Treasurer*
Kenneth Cabot, *Admin Sec*
EMP: 9
SQ FT: 14,000
SALES (est): 1.3MM **Privately Held**
SIC: 5031 2448 Lumber: rough, dressed & finished; pallets, wood

(G-19930)
GLENN RAVENS WINERY
56183 County Road 143 (43845)
PHONE 740 545-1000
Bob Guilliams, *Principal*

▲ = Import ▼ = Export
◆ = Import/Export

Traci Dennis, *Finance Mgr*
EMP: 25
SALES (est): 3.4MM **Privately Held**
WEB: www.ravensglenn.com
SIC: 2084 5812 Wines; Italian restaurant

(G-19931)
JONES METAL PRODUCTS COMPANY (PA)
200 N Center St (43845-1270)
P.O. Box 179 (43845-0179)
PHONE 740 545-6381
Marion M Sutton, *Ch of Bd*
Daniel P Erb III, *President*
Mike Baker, *Vice Pres*
Harold R Howell, *Vice Pres*
Carole M Loos, *Vice Pres*
EMP: 124
SQ FT: 140,000
SALES: 9.5MM **Privately Held**
WEB: www.joneszylon.com
SIC: 3842 3444 3469 Surgical appliances & supplies; forming machine work, sheet metal; metal stampings

(G-19932)
JONES METAL PRODUCTS COMPANY
Jones-Zylon Company
305 N Center St (43845-1001)
PHONE 740 545-6341
Todd Kohl, *Manager*
EMP: 40
SALES (est): 2.3MM
SALES (corp-wide): 9.5MM **Privately Held**
WEB: www.joneszylon.com
SIC: 5047 3842 Hospital equipment & supplies; surgical appliances & supplies
PA: Jones Metal Products Company
200 N Center St
West Lafayette OH 43845
740 545-6381

(G-19933)
JONESZYLON COMPANY LLC
300 N Center St (43845-1002)
P.O. Box 149 (43845-0149)
PHONE 740 545-6341
Robert Zachrich, *President*
Tracey Zachrich, *Principal*
EMP: 9
SQ FT: 20,000
SALES (est): 1.5MM **Privately Held**
SIC: 3089 5046 Plastic kitchenware, tableware & houseware; food warming equipment

(G-19934)
YANKEE WIRE CLOTH PRODUCTS INC
221 W Main St (43845-1103)
P.O. Box 58 (43845-0058)
PHONE 740 545-9129
William D Timmons, *President*
Mary Timmons, *Exec VP*
EMP: 45 **EST:** 1963
SQ FT: 35,000
SALES (est): 8.7MM **Privately Held**
WEB: www.yankeewire.com
SIC: 3496 Screening, woven wire: made from purchased wire

West Liberty
Logan County

(G-19935)
BAC TECHNOLOGIES LTD
Also Called: Burkett Advnced Composite Tech
8115 Calland Rd (43357-9604)
PHONE 937 465-2228
Jerald S Burkett,
EMP: 5
SALES (est): 913.3K **Privately Held**
WEB: www.bactechnologies.com
SIC: 5031 3542 Composite board products, woodboard; spinning, spline rolling & winding machines

(G-19936)
HOLDREN BROTHERS INC
301 Runkle St (43357-9476)
P.O. Box 459 (43357-0459)
PHONE 937 465-7050
Shirley Holdren, *President*
Dennis Watkins, *Plant Mgr*
Gerald Huxley, *Purch Dir*
Ronda Deleon, *Admin Mgr*
Shirley Dunaway, *Admin Sec*
EMP: 10
SQ FT: 4,800
SALES: 1.3MM **Privately Held**
WEB: www.holdrenbrothers.com
SIC: 3599 3589 7692 3549 Machine & other job shop work; commercial cleaning equipment; welding repair; metalworking machinery

(G-19937)
MARIES CANDIES LLC
311 Zanesfield Rd (43357-9563)
P.O. Box 766 (43357-0766)
PHONE 937 465-3061
Rebecca Craig,
EMP: 30
SQ FT: 4,100
SALES (est): 3.3MM **Privately Held**
WEB: www.mariescandies.com
SIC: 2064 5441 Candy bars, including chocolate covered bars; candy

(G-19938)
TIGER SUL PRODUCTS LLC
7361 Township Road 163 (43357-9694)
PHONE 203 451-3305
EMP: 3
SALES (est): 169.8K **Privately Held**
SIC: 2819 Industrial inorganic chemicals

(G-19939)
WILGUSS AUTOMOTIVE MACHINE
216 Runkle St (43357-9442)
PHONE 937 465-0043
John R Wilgus, *Owner*
EMP: 4
SQ FT: 2,600
SALES: 81K **Privately Held**
SIC: 7699 3599 7538 Lawn mower repair shop; machine shop, jobbing & repair; general automotive repair shops

West Manchester
Preble County

(G-19940)
BEEVINWOOD INC
5748 Clark Rd (45382-9608)
PHONE 937 678-9910
Contance Pitts, *President*
EMP: 3
SALES (est): 206.8K **Privately Held**
SIC: 2731 Books: publishing only

(G-19941)
ROWE PREMIX INC
10107 Us Rr 127 Box N (45382)
P.O. Box 205 (45382-0205)
PHONE 937 678-9015
Gene Rowe, *President*
Sharon Rowe, *Vice Pres*
EMP: 12 **EST:** 1979
SQ FT: 5,000
SALES: 1.7MM **Privately Held**
SIC: 2048 Feed premixes; feed supplements

West Mansfield
Logan County

(G-19942)
INDUSTRIAL PULLEY & MACHINE CO
151 E Center St (43358-9730)
P.O. Box 35 (43358-0035)
PHONE 937 355-4910
Steve Oliver, *President*
Cindy Bettinger, *Corp Secy*
Tim Oliver, *Vice Pres*
Raleigh Oliver, *Shareholder*
EMP: 8
SQ FT: 12,000
SALES: 850K **Privately Held**
SIC: 3429 Pulleys metal

(G-19943)
M & M CONCEPTS INC
Also Called: Cmg Company Plant 2
2633 State Route 292 (43358-9523)
PHONE 937 355-1115
Thomas P McGrady, *President*
Larry Vermillion, *Vice Pres*
Kris Carpenter, *Treasurer*
Alexa McGrady, *Admin Sec*
EMP: 8
SQ FT: 14,000
SALES (est): 1.2MM **Privately Held**
SIC: 7692 Welding repair

(G-19944)
M J S OIL INC
Also Called: Smith Marathon Distributing
23296 Treaty Line Rd (43358-9624)
PHONE 937 982-3519
Mark Smith, *President*
Julia Smith, *Admin Sec*
EMP: 3
SALES (est): 459.2K **Privately Held**
SIC: 2869 Fuels

(G-19945)
NATURE PURE LLC
26560 Storms Rd (43358)
PHONE 937 358-2364
Kurt Lausecker, *CEO*
Sandra Lausecker, *CEO*
EMP: 14 **Privately Held**
SIC: 0252 2015 Chicken eggs; egg processing
PA: Nature Pure Llc
26586 State Route 739
Raymond OH 43067

West Millgrove
Wood County

(G-19946)
MAC RITCHIE MATERIALS INC
6126 S Main St (43467)
PHONE 419 288-2790
Donald B Mac Ritchie, *President*
Ronald Mac Ritchie, *Vice Pres*
EMP: 12 **EST:** 1911
SQ FT: 4,000
SALES (est): 1MM **Privately Held**
SIC: 1422 Crushed & broken limestone

West Milton
Miami County

(G-19947)
BOYDS MACHINE AND MET FINSHG
7650 S Kssler Frderick Rd (45383-8790)
PHONE 937 698-5623
Larry E Boyd, *President*
Stephen Boyd, *Vice Pres*
EMP: 17
SQ FT: 1,800
SALES (est): 1.3MM **Privately Held**
SIC: 3599 Machine shop, jobbing & repair

(G-19948)
COATE CONCRETE PRODUCTS INC (PA)
7330 W State Route 571 (45383-9741)
P.O. Box 159 (45383-0159)
PHONE 937 698-4181
Craig Coate, *President*
Travis Coate, *Office Mgr*
EMP: 5 **EST:** 1925
SQ FT: 22,500
SALES (est): 3.1MM **Privately Held**
SIC: 3272 Burial vaults, concrete or precast terrazzo; septic tanks, concrete

(G-19949)
MIAMI CONTROL SYSTEMS INC
955 S Main St (45383-1364)
P.O. Box 96 (45383-0096)
PHONE 937 698-5725
Andy Minniear, *President*
Aaron Levy, *Design Engr*
EMP: 9
SQ FT: 7,500
SALES (est): 2.1MM **Privately Held**
WEB: www.miamicontrol.com
SIC: 3625 Electric controls & control accessories, industrial

(G-19950)
MIAMI GRAPHICS SERVICES INC
225 N Jay St (45383-1706)
P.O. Box 194 (45383-0194)
PHONE 937 698-4013
Norma Parmenter, *President*
Charles Parmenter, *Vice Pres*
EMP: 10
SQ FT: 8,500
SALES (est): 576.5K **Privately Held**
SIC: 2759 Commercial printing

(G-19951)
OLD MASON WINERY INC
4199 S Iddings Rd (45383-8741)
PHONE 937 698-1122
Jeff Clark, *President*
Donna Clarke, *Vice Pres*
EMP: 9 **EST:** 2013
SALES (est): 751K **Privately Held**
SIC: 2084 Wines

(G-19952)
ROBERTSON CABINETS INC
1090 S Main St (45383-1365)
PHONE 937 698-3755
William Robertson Sr, *Ch of Bd*
Jeff Yantis, *President*
Judith Robertson, *Vice Pres*
Brian Smith, *Draft/Design*
EMP: 20
SQ FT: 22,000
SALES: 1.5MM **Privately Held**
WEB: www.about-rci.com
SIC: 2541 2431 Cabinets, except refrigerated: show, display, etc.: wood; bar fixtures, wood; millwork

West Salem
Wayne County

(G-19953)
CENSTAR COATINGS INC
11829 Jeffrey Rd (44287-9219)
PHONE 330 723-8000
Jim Feterle, *President*
EMP: 6
SQ FT: 6,000
SALES (est): 678.6K **Privately Held**
SIC: 3069 Sheeting, rubber or rubberized fabric

(G-19954)
HAYNN CONSTRUCTION CO INC
14866 N Elyria Rd (44287-8958)
P.O. Box 346 (44287-0346)
PHONE 419 853-4747
EMP: 6
SALES (est): 1MM **Privately Held**
SIC: 3567 Fab Industrial Equip

(G-19955)
JOHNSON BROS RUBBER CO INC (PA)
42 W Buckeye St (44287-9747)
P.O. Box 812 (44287-0812)
PHONE 419 853-4122
Lawrence G Cooke, *President*
Eric Vail, *Vice Pres*
Michelle Green, *Materials Mgr*
Jill Lifer, *Train & Dev Mgr*
Tom Fisher, *Sales Mgr*
▲ **EMP:** 100 **EST:** 1947
SQ FT: 70,000
SALES (est): 54.4MM **Privately Held**
SIC: 5199 3061 Foams & rubber; mechanical rubber goods

West Salem - Wayne County (G-19956)

(G-19956)
LATTASBURG LUMBERWORKS CO LLC
9399 Lattasburg Rd (44287-9725)
PHONE..................330 202-7671
Pascal King-Smith, *Principal*
EMP: 6 EST: 1997
SQ FT: 1,500
SALES (est): 1MM **Privately Held**
WEB: www.lattasburglumberworks.com
SIC: 2435 Hardwood veneer & plywood

(G-19957)
PAROBEK TRUCKING CO
192 State Route 42 (44287-9130)
PHONE..................419 869-7500
Keigm Parobek, *Owner*
EMP: 6
SALES (est): 467.8K **Privately Held**
SIC: 3537 4213 4212 Industrial trucks & tractors; trucking, except local; local trucking, without storage

(G-19958)
SUNNY SIDE FEEDS LLC
6371 W Pleasant Home Rd (44287-9573)
PHONE..................330 635-1455
Wade Mahoney, *Principal*
Randy Tegtmeier, *Principal*
EMP: 5
SQ FT: 12,000
SALES: 500K **Privately Held**
SIC: 2048 Bird food, prepared

West Union
Adams County

(G-19959)
BROWN PUBLISHING CO
Also Called: People's Defender
229 N Cross St (45693-1266)
P.O. Box 308 (45693-0308)
PHONE..................937 544-2391
Roy Brown, *CEO*
EMP: 12
SQ FT: 5,000
SALES (est): 666.7K **Privately Held**
SIC: 2711 Commercial printing & newspaper publishing combined; newspapers: publishing only, not printed on site

(G-19960)
COLUMBUS INDUSTRIES INC
11545 State Route 41 (45693-9434)
PHONE..................937 544-6896
Harold Pontius, *Branch Mgr*
EMP: 11
SALES (corp-wide): 228.8MM **Privately Held**
SIC: 3999 Barber & beauty shop equipment
PA: Columbus Industries, Inc.
2938 State Route 752
Ashville OH 43103
740 983-2552

(G-19961)
DINSMORE INC
Also Called: Purvis Milling Co
11780 State Route 41 (45693-8025)
PHONE..................937 544-3332
Ron Dinsmore, *President*
Diane Dinsmore, *Corp Secy*
EMP: 8
SQ FT: 12,000
SALES (est): 1.2MM **Privately Held**
SIC: 3524 5999 Lawn & garden equipment; feed & farm supply

(G-19962)
J MCCOY LUMBER CO LTD
733 Vaughn Ridge Rd (45693-9620)
P.O. Box 306, Peebles (45660-0306)
PHONE..................937 544-2968
Jack McCoy, *Owner*
EMP: 3
SALES (est): 257.2K
SALES (corp-wide): 4.4MM **Privately Held**
SIC: 5031 2426 2431 Lumber: rough, dressed & finished; dimension, hardwood; moldings, wood: unfinished & prefinished

PA: J. Mccoy Lumber Co. Ltd
6 N Main St
Peebles OH 45660
937 587-3423

(G-19963)
JERRY TADLOCK
Also Called: Tadlock Trailer Sales
5645 State Route 125 (45693-9332)
PHONE..................937 544-2851
Jerry Tadlock, *Owner*
EMP: 5
SALES: 400K **Privately Held**
WEB: www.tadlocktrailersales.com
SIC: 5599 5531 3715 Utility trailers; truck equipment & parts; truck trailers

(G-19964)
KENNETH SCHROCK
Also Called: Ridgeway Lumber
3735 Wheat Ridge Rd (45693-9428)
PHONE..................937 544-7566
Kenneth Schrock, *Owner*
Carol Schrock, *Owner*
EMP: 5
SALES: 280K **Privately Held**
SIC: 7389 2448 Log & lumber broker; pallets, wood

(G-19965)
LS2 PRINTING
111 E Main St (45693-1301)
PHONE..................937 544-1000
Tyler Sheeley, *Owner*
EMP: 5
SALES (est): 107.2K **Privately Held**
SIC: 2759 2711 Commercial printing; newspapers

(G-19966)
SCHROCK JOHN
Also Called: Wheat Ridge Pallet & Lumber
61 Poole Rd (45693-9736)
PHONE..................937 544-8457
John Schrock, *Owner*
Melissa Black, *Accountant*
EMP: 9
SALES (est): 1MM **Privately Held**
SIC: 2448 Pallets, wood

West Unity
Williams County

(G-19967)
CONVERSION TECH INTL INC
700 Oak St (43570-9457)
P.O. Box 707 (43570-0707)
PHONE..................419 924-5566
Chester Cromwell, *President*
Jason Cromwell, *Principal*
▲ EMP: 33
SQ FT: 130,000
SALES (est): 8.9MM **Privately Held**
WEB: www.conversiontechnologies.com
SIC: 2891 7389 Adhesives; laminating service

(G-19968)
H K K MACHINING CO
1201 Oak St (43570-9435)
PHONE..................419 924-5116
Duane E King, *President*
Sharon King, *Vice Pres*
EMP: 20 EST: 1966
SQ FT: 23,500
SALES (est): 3.7MM **Privately Held**
WEB: www.hkkmach.com
SIC: 3544 Special dies & tools

(G-19969)
HARDLINE INTERNATIONAL INC
Also Called: Rimm Kleen Systems
1107 Oak St (43570-9429)
PHONE..................419 924-9556
Robert Warmingham, *President*
EMP: 10
SQ FT: 12,000
SALES (est): 1.4MM **Privately Held**
WEB: www.rimmkleensystems.com
SIC: 3479 Aluminum coating of metal products

(G-19970)
JACOBY PACKING CO
Also Called: Jacoby Old Smokehouse
505 S Main St (43570-9734)
P.O. Box 466 (43570-0466)
PHONE..................419 924-2684
James Kieffer, *Owner*
Jim Keifer, *Partner*
EMP: 8
SALES: 750K **Privately Held**
SIC: 2011 Meat packing plants

(G-19971)
KAMCO INDUSTRIES INC (HQ)
1001 E Jackson St (43570-9414)
PHONE..................419 924-5511
Bryan Barshel, *Assistant VP*
Joe Tubbs, *Vice Pres*
Allan Benien, *VP Opers*
Dave Lotz, *Prdtn Mgr*
Shun Sasaki, *Purchasing*
▲ EMP: 370
SQ FT: 160,000
SALES (est): 82.7MM
SALES (corp-wide): 136.5MM **Privately Held**
WEB: www.kamcoind.com
SIC: 3089 Injection molded finished plastic products; thermoformed finished plastic products
PA: Kumi Kasei Co., Ltd.
47-1, Kandahigashimatsushitacho
Chiyoda-Ku TKY 101-0
352 981-511

(G-19972)
MIDWEST PRODUCTION MACHINING
Also Called: Midwest Machine
10484 State Route 191 (43570-9506)
P.O. Box 464 (43570-0464)
PHONE..................419 924-5616
Fax: 419 924-5610
EMP: 3
SQ FT: 6,000
SALES (est): 500K **Privately Held**
SIC: 3599 Contract Production Machining

(G-19973)
RAVAGO AMERICAS LLC
Trinity Specialty Compounding
600 Oak St (43570-9545)
PHONE..................419 924-9090
Timothy L Walkowski, *General Mgr*
EMP: 19
SALES (corp-wide): 1.4MM **Privately Held**
SIC: 2821 Plastics materials & resins
HQ: Ravago Americas Llc
1900 Summit Tower Blvd
Orlando FL 32810
407 875-9595

(G-19974)
RUPCOL INC
509 Parkway St (43570-9575)
PHONE..................419 924-5215
Burdel Colon, *President*
EMP: 4
SQ FT: 24,000
SALES: 750K **Privately Held**
SIC: 3448 1541 Prefabricated metal buildings; prefabricated building erection, industrial

(G-19975)
VISION COLOR LLC
214 S Defiance St (43570-9620)
P.O. Box 264 (43570-0264)
PHONE..................419 924-9450
Richard Bacon, *President*
Adam Bacon, *Comp Lab Dir*
Gary Watts, *Technical Staff*
EMP: 8
SALES (est): 1.7MM **Privately Held**
WEB: www.visioncolorllc.com
SIC: 3089 Injection molding of plastics

Westerville
Delaware County

(G-19976)
1984 PRINTING
7817 Silver Lake Ct (43082-8288)
PHONE..................510 435-8338
EMP: 4 EST: 2010
SALES (est): 390.2K **Privately Held**
SIC: 2752 Commercial printing, offset

(G-19977)
AMERICAN CERAMIC SOCIETY (PA)
Also Called: Pottery Making Illustrate
550 Polaris Pkwy Ste 510 (43082-7132)
PHONE..................614 890-4700
Michael Johnson, *CFO*
Scott Steen, *Exec Dir*
EMP: 35
SQ FT: 10,126
SALES: 7.5MM **Privately Held**
WEB: www.ceramics.org
SIC: 8621 2721 Medical field-related associations; engineering association; scientific membership association; periodicals: publishing & printing

(G-19978)
ANRO LOGISTICS INC
7473 Bentley Pl (43082-8662)
PHONE..................614 428-7490
William Anderson, *Principal*
EMP: 4
SALES (est): 247.3K **Privately Held**
SIC: 4789 3444 Transportation services; sheet metalwork

(G-19979)
BAKERWELL INC
6295 Maxtown Rd Ste 300 (43082-8885)
P.O. Box 1678 (43086-1678)
PHONE..................614 898-7590
Rex Baker, *President*
Jeff Baker, *Corp Secy*
EMP: 51 EST: 1981
SALES (est): 2.9MM **Privately Held**
WEB: www.bakerwell.com
SIC: 1382 Oil & gas exploration services

(G-19980)
BASS INTERNATIONAL SFTWR LLC (PA)
Also Called: Onevuex
752 N State St (43082-9066)
PHONE..................877 227-0155
Darrel F Bass, *President*
EMP: 5
SQ FT: 400
SALES (est): 1.6MM **Privately Held**
SIC: 7372 Business oriented computer software

(G-19981)
BRIGHTSTAR PROPANE & FUELS
Also Called: Guttman Oil
6190 Frost Rd (43082-9027)
PHONE..................614 891-8395
Richard Guttman, *President*
EMP: 7
SALES (est): 286.4K **Privately Held**
SIC: 5984 1389 2869 Propane gas, bottled; construction, repair & dismantling services; fuels

(G-19982)
BUCKEYE BUSINESS FORMS INC
Also Called: Proforma Buckeye
7307 Red Bank Rd (43082-8241)
PHONE..................614 882-1890
Ann Kaylor Patton, *President*
James Patton, *Admin Sec*
EMP: 6 EST: 1966
SQ FT: 13,500
SALES (est): 1.4MM **Privately Held**
WEB: bbf.cc
SIC: 7311 2752 7331 Advertising agencies; commercial printing, offset; mailing service

GEOGRAPHIC SECTION
Westerville - Delaware County (G-20010)

(G-19983)
CENTURY GRAPHICS INC
9101 Hawthorne Pt (43082-9231)
PHONE..................................614 895-7698
Richard Bonham, *President*
EMP: 40
SQ FT: 26,000
SALES (est): 4.3MM **Privately Held**
WEB: www.centurygr.com
SIC: **2796** 2789 2759 2752 Platemaking services; bookbinding & related work; commercial printing; commercial printing, offset

(G-19984)
CHARISMA PRODUCTS INC
6342 Worthington Rd (43082-9446)
PHONE..................................614 846-8888
Gary L Chiero, *President*
Kathleen A Chiero, *Treasurer*
EMP: 3 EST: 1977
SQ FT: 3,400
SALES (est): 276.6K **Privately Held**
SIC: **2396** Screen printing on fabric articles; apparel & other linings, except millinery; millinery materials & supplies

(G-19985)
CHERYL & CO (HQ)
646 Mccorkle Blvd (43082-8778)
PHONE..................................614 776-1500
Cheryl L Krueger, *President*
Bob Happle, *General Mgr*
Jeff Krauss, *Exec VP*
Bob Happel, *Vice Pres*
Lisa Henry, *Vice Pres*
▲ EMP: 225 EST: 1981
SALES (est): 106.2MM **Publicly Held**
WEB: www.cherylandco.com
SIC: **2052** Cookies

(G-19986)
COLD CONTROL LLC
470 Olde Worthington Rd # 200 (43082-9127)
PHONE..................................614 564-7011
Brian A Oconnor, *Mng Member*
EMP: 3
SALES: 550K **Privately Held**
SIC: **8221** 3585 Colleges universities & professional schools; refrigeration & heating equipment

(G-19987)
DERN TROPHIES CORP
Also Called: Dern Trophy Mfg
6225 Frost Rd (43082-9027)
PHONE..................................614 895-3260
Ronald M Spohn, *President*
B Thomas Dern, *Vice Pres*
▲ EMP: 12
SQ FT: 20,000
SALES (est): 1.7MM **Privately Held**
WEB: www.dern-trophy.com
SIC: **3499** 5094 3993 Trophies, metal, except silver; trophies; signs & advertising specialties

(G-19988)
E - I CORP
214 Hoff Rd Unit M (43082-7157)
PHONE..................................614 899-2282
Glenn Meek, *Principal*
Glen Fox, *Manager*
▲ EMP: 11
SALES (est): 2.1MM **Privately Held**
SIC: **3589** Sewage treatment equipment

(G-19989)
E STAR AEROSPACE CORPORATION
470 Olde Worthington Rd # 200 (43082-8985)
PHONE..................................614 396-6868
Ely Bachir, *CEO*
EMP: 3
SALES: 500K **Privately Held**
SIC: **3721** Research & development on aircraft by the manufacturer

(G-19990)
ERIC NICKEL
5563 Covington Meadows Ct (43082-8371)
PHONE..................................614 818-2488
Eric Nickel, *Principal*
EMP: 3
SALES (est): 183.7K **Privately Held**
SIC: **3356** Nickel

(G-19991)
EXELON ENERGY COMPANY
470 Olde Worthington Rd # 375 (43082-7907)
PHONE..................................614 797-4377
EMP: 14
SALES (corp-wide): 31.3B **Publicly Held**
SIC: **1389** Oil/Gas Field Services
HQ: Exelon Energy Company
300 Exelon Way
Kennett Square PA 19348
312 394-7158

(G-19992)
GAIN LLC
8475 Fallgold Ln (43082-9745)
PHONE..................................440 396-6613
Greg Miller, *Co-Owner*
Nugeen Aftab, *Co-Owner*
Alex Chudik, *Co-Owner*
EMP: 4
SALES (est): 187.2K **Privately Held**
SIC: **7372** Application computer software

(G-19993)
GANGER ENTERPRISES INC
Also Called: Northwest Printing
214 Hoff Rd Unit D (43082-7156)
PHONE..................................614 776-3985
William E Ganger Jr, *President*
EMP: 3
SQ FT: 3,000
SALES (est): 260K **Privately Held**
WEB: www.geography.uwo.ca
SIC: **2752** 2789 Commercial printing, offset; bookbinding & related work

(G-19994)
GLASS MEDIC INC
Also Called: Glass Medic America
6996 Four Seasons Dr (43082-8533)
PHONE..................................800 356-4009
John Robinson, *President*
▲ EMP: 3
SQ FT: 2,200
SALES: 1MM
SALES (corp-wide): 3.7B **Privately Held**
WEB: www.glassmedic.com
SIC: **3423** Cutters, glass
PA: D'ieteren
Rue Du Mail 50
Bruxelles 1050
322 536-5111

(G-19995)
GUITAMMER COMPANY
Also Called: Buttkicker
6117 Maxtown Rd (43082-9051)
P.O. Box 82 (43086-0082)
PHONE..................................614 898-9370
Mark A Luden, *Ch of Bd*
Rich Conn, *General Mgr*
Lawrence L Lemoine, *COO*
Marvin Clamme, *VP Engrg*
▲ EMP: 7
SQ FT: 15,000
SALES: 1.5MM **Privately Held**
WEB: www.thebuttkicker.com
SIC: **3679** Transducers, electrical

(G-19996)
HARRIS MACKESSY & BRENNAN
Also Called: Hmb Information Sys Developers
570 Polaris Pkwy Ste 125 (43082-7924)
PHONE..................................614 221-6831
Thomas Harris, *President*
Tom Harris, *President*
Mark Buchy, *Vice Pres*
John Mackessy, *Admin Sec*
EMP: 150
SQ FT: 9,000
SALES (est): 36.4MM **Privately Held**
WEB: www.hmbnet.com
SIC: **8742** 3577 Management consulting services; decoders, computer peripheral equipment

(G-19997)
IMAGE PRINT INC
214 Hoff Rd Unit D (43082-7156)
PHONE..................................614 776-3985
Alan Lang, *General Mgr*
EMP: 6 EST: 2009
SALES (est): 933.5K **Privately Held**
SIC: **2752** Commercial printing, offset

(G-19998)
IMT DEFENSE CORP
5386 Club Dr (43082-8312)
PHONE..................................614 891-8812
James Hacking, *Ch of Bd*
Remo Assini, *President*
EMP: 7
SALES (est): 590K **Privately Held**
SIC: **3812** Defense systems & equipment

(G-19999)
INTEK INC
751 Intek Way (43082-9057)
PHONE..................................614 895-0301
Joseph W Harpster, *President*
Marilyn Y C Harpster, *Exec VP*
Mitch Morrison, *Accounts Mgr*
Jocelyn Curry, *Shareholder*
▼ EMP: 22
SQ FT: 12,800
SALES: 2.7MM **Privately Held**
WEB: www.intekflow.com
SIC: **3823** 8732 Industrial flow & liquid measuring instruments; commercial non-physical research

(G-20000)
JBW SYSTEMS INC
5840 Chandler Ct (43082-9049)
P.O. Box 1530 (43086-1530)
PHONE..................................614 882-5008
James Watkins, *President*
Billie L Watkins, *Vice Pres*
EMP: 10
SQ FT: 5,000
SALES (est): 1.2MM **Privately Held**
WEB: www.jbwsystems.com
SIC: **3559** 3531 Chemical machinery & equipment; construction machinery

(G-20001)
JOHNSTONS BANKS INC
6927 Sherbrook Dr (43082-8568)
PHONE..................................614 499-4374
Mary J Johnston, *Principal*
EMP: 5
SALES (est): 567.6K **Privately Held**
SIC: **3961** Costume jewelry

(G-20002)
JST LLC
6240 Frost Rd Ste C (43082-6928)
PHONE..................................614 423-7815
Susan Testaguzza, *Mng Member*
James Testaguzza, *Mng Member*
EMP: 7
SALES (est): 246K **Privately Held**
SIC: **7372** Educational computer software

(G-20003)
LAKE SHORE CRYOTRONICS INC (PA)
575 Mccorkle Blvd (43082-8888)
PHONE..................................614 891-2243
Michael S Swartz, *President*
John M Swartz, *Chairman*
Karen Lint, *COO*
Brad Dodrill, *Vice Pres*
Ed Maloof, *Vice Pres*
EMP: 110
SQ FT: 60,000
SALES (est): 17.7MM **Privately Held**
WEB: www.lakeshore.com
SIC: **3679** 3823 3825 3812 Cryogenic cooling devices for infrared detectors, masers; industrial instrmnts msrmnt display/control process variable; measuring instruments & meters, electric; search & navigation equipment; tachometer, centrifugal; temperature sensors, except industrial process & aircraft

(G-20004)
LANCASTER COLONY CORPORATION (PA)
380 Polaris Pkwy Ste 400 (43082-8069)
PHONE..................................614 224-7141
John B Gerlach Jr, *Ch of Bd*
David A Ciesinski, *President*
Carl Stealey, *President*
Douglas A Fell, *CFO*
William Carter, *Bd of Directors*
◆ EMP: 25 EST: 1961
SALES: 1.2B **Publicly Held**
WEB: www.lancastercolony.com
SIC: **2035** 2038 Dressings, salad: raw & cooked (except dry mixes); seasonings & sauces, except tomato & dry; frozen specialties

(G-20005)
LANCASTER COLONY CORPORATION
Also Called: Lancaster Colony Design Group
380 Polaris Pkwy Ste 400 (43082-8069)
PHONE..................................614 792-9774
Doug Covell, *Manager*
EMP: 13
SALES (corp-wide): 1.2B **Publicly Held**
WEB: www.lancastercolony.com
SIC: **2035** Dressings, salad: raw & cooked (except dry mixes)
PA: Lancaster Colony Corporation
380 Polaris Pkwy Ste 400
Westerville OH 43082
614 224-7141

(G-20006)
LANCASTER COLONY CORPORATION
380 Polaris Pkwy Ste 400 (43082-8069)
PHONE..................................614 224-7141
Wendell Gingrich, *Counsel*
Robyn Eramo, *Controller*
David Fallis, *Tax Mgr*
Christine Wallen, *Accountant*
David M Segal, *Corp Counsel*
EMP: 55
SALES (corp-wide): 1.2B **Publicly Held**
SIC: **2035** Dressings, salad: raw & cooked (except dry mixes)
PA: Lancaster Colony Corporation
380 Polaris Pkwy Ste 400
Westerville OH 43082
614 224-7141

(G-20007)
LIEBERT FIELD SERVICES INC
Also Called: Emerson Network Power System
610 Executive Campus Dr (43082-8870)
PHONE..................................614 841-5763
Lisa Hunt, *Manager*
EMP: 53 EST: 2001
SALES (est): 13.1MM
SALES (corp-wide): 2.1B **Privately Held**
SIC: **3629** Electronic generation equipment
HQ: Vertiv Corporation
1050 Dearborn Dr
Columbus OH 43085
614 888-0246

(G-20008)
M&M GREAT ADVENTURES LLC
586 Deer Trl (43082-6410)
PHONE..................................937 344-1415
Michael Pennington, *Mng Member*
Mary Ellen Pennington, *Mng Member*
▼ EMP: 3 EST: 2009
SALES (est): 233.1K **Privately Held**
SIC: **3949** 5199 7389 Camping equipment & supplies; general merchandise, non-durable;

(G-20009)
MARK RASCHE
Also Called: Rasche Cabinetmakers
6962 Harlem Rd (43082-9247)
PHONE..................................614 882-1810
Fax: 614 882-1810
EMP: 3
SQ FT: 6,000
SALES: 100K **Privately Held**
SIC: **2511** 7641 2522 2521 Mfg Wood Household Furn Reupholstery/Furn Repair Mfg Nonwood Office Furn Mfg Wood Office Furn

(G-20010)
MCNISH CORPORATION
Also Called: E & I
214 Hoff Rd Unit M (43082-7157)
PHONE..................................614 899-2282
Glenn E Meek, *Branch Mgr*
EMP: 7

Westerville - Delaware County (G-20011)

SALES (est): 1.1MM
SALES (corp-wide): 33.2MM **Privately Held**
WEB: www.walker-process.com
SIC: **3589** Sewage treatment equipment
PA: Mcnish Corporation
   840 N Russell Ave
   Aurora IL 60506
   630 892-7921

(G-20011)
NEW YORK FROZEN FOODS
380 Polaris Pkwy Ste 400 (43082-8069)
P.O. Box 297737, Columbus (43229-7737)
PHONE..................................614 846-2232
Thomas E Moloney, *Principal*
Dick Anderson, *Vice Pres*
Tim Tate, *Sales Staff*
EMP: 11
SALES (est): 2.7MM **Privately Held**
SIC: **3421** Table & food cutlery, including butchers'

(G-20012)
NOLAN MANUFACTURING LLC
Also Called: Nolan Mfg Co - Electronics Div
493 Blue Heron Ct (43082-7448)
PHONE..................................614 859-2302
Andrew Nolan, *President*
EMP: 3
SALES (est): 191.4K **Privately Held**
SIC: **3613** Power connectors, electric

(G-20013)
ONEVISION CORPORATION (PA)
5805 Chandler Ct Ste A (43082-9076)
PHONE..................................614 794-1144
Neil E Morris, *President*
EMP: 8
SQ FT: 3,200
SALES (est): 1MM **Privately Held**
WEB: www.onevisioncorp.com
SIC: **3823** Industrial instrmnts msrmnt display/control process variable

(G-20014)
ORTON EDWARD JR CRMIC FNDATION
6991 S Old 3c Hwy (43082-9026)
P.O. Box 2760 (43086-2760)
PHONE..................................614 895-2663
Jonathan Hinton, *Ch of Bd*
J Gary Childress, *General Mgr*
Dr Stephen Freiman, *Trustee*
Dr John Morral, *Trustee*
Dr James Williams, *Trustee*
▼ EMP: 31
SQ FT: 34,260
SALES: 5MM **Privately Held**
WEB: www.ortonceramic.com
SIC: **3269** 3826 3825 8748 Cones, pyrometric: earthenware; analytical instruments; instruments to measure electricity; testing services

(G-20015)
OSTEO SOLUTION
117 Commerce Park Dr (43082-6063)
PHONE..................................614 485-9790
Tom Meyer, *Principal*
EMP: 4
SALES (est): 498.2K **Privately Held**
SIC: **3842** Orthopedic appliances

(G-20016)
PERFORMANX SPECIALTY CHEM LLC (PA)
300 Westdale Ave (43082-8962)
PHONE..................................614 300-7001
Michael Suver, *President*
EMP: 6 EST: 2014
SQ FT: 2,500
SALES (est): 1MM **Privately Held**
SIC: **2834** Emulsions, pharmaceutical

(G-20017)
PHOTON LABS LLC
752 N State St (43082-9066)
PHONE..................................214 455-0727
Amit Chandna, *Owner*
EMP: 4
SALES (est): 409K **Privately Held**
SIC: **3648** Lighting equipment

(G-20018)
QUADRIGA AMERICAS LLC (DH)
480 Olde Worthington Rd # 350 (43082-7067)
PHONE..................................614 890-6090
Roger Taylor, *CEO*
Candice Deluca, *Vice Pres*
Eric Wilder, *Director*
▼ EMP: 6
SQ FT: 5,000
SALES (est): 2.4MM
SALES (corp-wide): 66.1MM **Privately Held**
SIC: **2741**
HQ: Quadriga Worldwide Limited
   Forum 1
   Reading BERKS RG7 4
   118 930-6030

(G-20019)
QUALITY BAKERY COMPANY INC (DH)
380 Polaris Pkwy Ste 400 (43082-8069)
PHONE..................................614 846-2232
Bruce Rosa, *President*
Dawna Hopkins, *Administration*
EMP: 5
SALES (est): 10.8MM
SALES (corp-wide): 1.2B **Publicly Held**
WEB: www.marzetti.com
SIC: **2051** Bread, cake & related products
HQ: T.Marzetti Company
   380 Polaris Pkwy Ste 400
   Westerville OH 43082
   614 846-2232

(G-20020)
REVOLUTION GROUP INC
600 N Cleveland Ave # 110 (43082-6921)
PHONE..................................614 212-1111
Richard Snide, *President*
Polly Clavijo, *Vice Pres*
Carlos Clavijo, *CFO*
Cindy Snide, *Mktg Dir*
Amit Joshi, *Manager*
EMP: 80
SALES (est): 7.6MM **Privately Held**
SIC: **7379** 7372 4813 8741 Computer related consulting services; prepackaged software; ; ; management services

(G-20021)
RKE TRUCKING CO
6305 Frost Rd (43082-9027)
PHONE..................................614 891-1786
Ed Deim, *President*
Michael Hrabcak, *President*
EMP: 15
SALES (est): 3.5MM **Privately Held**
SIC: **3713** Automobile wrecker truck bodies

(G-20022)
ROCKWELL AUTOMATION INC
350 Worthington Rd Ste A (43082-8327)
PHONE..................................614 776-3021
John Fossen, *Manager*
Paul Burgan, *Technology*
EMP: 80 **Publicly Held**
SIC: **3625** Relays & industrial controls
PA: Rockwell Automation, Inc.
   1201 S 2nd St
   Milwaukee WI 53204

(G-20023)
SKLADANY ENTERPRISES INC
Also Called: Skladany Printing Center
695 Mccorkle Blvd (43082-8790)
PHONE..................................614 823-6883
Thomas Skladany, *President*
Debbie Skladany, *Vice Pres*
Michael Niezgoda, *VP Sales*
EMP: 8
SALES: 1.1MM **Privately Held**
WEB: www.skladany.com
SIC: **2752** Commercial printing, offset

(G-20024)
STANLEY INDUSTRIAL & AUTO LLC
Also Called: Mac Tools
505 N Cleveland Ave # 200 (43082-7130)
PHONE..................................614 755-7089
Paul North, *Manager*
EMP: 150
SALES (corp-wide): 13.9B **Publicly Held**
WEB: www.stanleyworks.com
SIC: **3469** 3423 5251 2542 Boxes: tool, lunch, mail, etc.: stamped metal; hand & edge tools; tools; partitions & fixtures, except wood
HQ: Stanley Industrial & Automotive, Llc
   505 N Cleveland Ave
   Westerville OH 43082
   614 755-7000

(G-20025)
STANLEY INDUSTRIAL & AUTO LLC (HQ)
505 N Cleveland Ave (43082-7130)
PHONE..................................614 755-7000
Joanna Sohovich, *President*
Joe McCormack, *President*
James Ray, *President*
Brett Shaw, *President*
Christine Yingli Yan, *President*
▲ EMP: 72
SALES (est): 373MM
SALES (corp-wide): 13.9B **Publicly Held**
SIC: **3429** 3546 3423 3452 Builders' hardware; power-driven handtools; hand & edge tools; bolts, nuts, rivets & washers
PA: Stanley Black & Decker, Inc.
   1000 Stanley Dr
   New Britain CT 06053
   860 225-5111

(G-20026)
STEELES DISPLAY CASES
5665 State Route 605 S (43082-9647)
PHONE..................................740 965-6426
Mike Steele, *Owner*
Sherrie Steele, *Co-Owner*
EMP: 4
SALES (est): 200K **Privately Held**
SIC: **2541** Store & office display cases & fixtures

(G-20027)
SUPERMEDIA LLC
470 Olde Worthington Rd (43082-8985)
PHONE..................................614 216-6566
Adrienne Wilson, *Principal*
EMP: 4 EST: 2011
SALES (est): 209K **Privately Held**
SIC: **2741** Directories, telephone: publishing only, not printed on site

(G-20028)
TMARZETTI COMPANY
380 Polaris Pkwy Ste 400 (43082-8069)
PHONE..................................614 268-3722
Doug Fell, *Vice Pres*
Tom Kellett, *Vice Pres*
Tim Tate, *Vice Pres*
Mark Wilder, *Vice Pres*
Cara Stamm, *VP Opers*
EMP: 180
SALES (corp-wide): 1.2B **Publicly Held**
SIC: **2035** Dressings, salad: raw & cooked (except dry mixes)
HQ: T.Marzetti Company
   380 Polaris Pkwy Ste 400
   Westerville OH 43082
   614 846-2232

(G-20029)
TMARZETTI COMPANY (HQ)
Also Called: Inn Maid Products
380 Polaris Pkwy Ste 400 (43082-8069)
PHONE..................................614 846-2232
David Ciesinski, *President*
◆ EMP: 147 EST: 1927
SQ FT: 28,000
SALES (est): 588.8MM
SALES (corp-wide): 1.2B **Publicly Held**
SIC: **2035** 2098 Dressings, salad: raw & cooked (except dry mixes); noodles (e.g. egg, plain & water), dry
PA: Lancaster Colony Corporation
   380 Polaris Pkwy Ste 400
   Westerville OH 43082
   614 224-7141

(G-20030)
WESTERVILLE ENDOSCOPY CTR LLC
300 Polaris Pkwy Ste 1500 (43082-7990)
PHONE..................................614 568-1666
Tammy Blankenship, *Principal*
EMP: 12

SALES (est): 1.8MM **Privately Held**
SIC: **3845** 8011 Gastroscopes, electromedical; internal medicine, physician/surgeon

(G-20031)
WORTHINGTON CYLINDER CORP
333 Maxtown Rd (43082-8757)
PHONE..................................614 840-3800
Craig Breedlove, *Vice Pres*
Mark Braniger, *Engineer*
Robert Kotarba, *Branch Mgr*
EMP: 200
SQ FT: 12,880
SALES (corp-wide): 3.5B **Publicly Held**
SIC: **3443** Cylinders, pressure: metal plate
HQ: Worthington Cylinder Corporation
   200 W Old Wlson Bridge Rd
   Worthington OH 43085
   614 840-3210

Westerville
Franklin County

(G-20032)
A TWIST ON OLIVES LLC
44 N State St (43081-2124)
PHONE..................................614 823-8800
EMP: 3
SALES (est): 242.3K **Privately Held**
SIC: **2079** Olive oil

(G-20033)
ALLEN PRESS
6132 Batavia Rd (43081-3515)
PHONE..................................614 891-4413
James Tiedt, *President*
EMP: 3
SQ FT: 6,000
SALES: 130K **Privately Held**
SIC: **2752** Commercial printing, offset

(G-20034)
ANDERSON PRINTING & SUPPLY LLC
237 E Broadway Ave (43081-1646)
P.O. Box 2125 (43086-2125)
PHONE..................................614 891-1100
Nicole Lynn Anderson, *Mng Member*
EMP: 5
SALES (est): 370K **Privately Held**
SIC: **2752** Commercial printing, lithographic

(G-20035)
AVCOM SMT INC
213 E Broadway Ave (43081-1656)
P.O. Box 1516 (43086-1516)
PHONE..................................614 882-8176
Paul Wiese, *President*
Barbara Wiese, *Vice Pres*
Scott Wiese, *Marketing Staff*
EMP: 12 EST: 1970
SQ FT: 10,000
SALES (est): 2.5MM **Privately Held**
WEB: www.avcomsmt.com
SIC: **3672** Printed circuit boards

(G-20036)
B L F ENTERPRISES INC
Also Called: Great Harvest Bread
445 S State St (43081-2956)
PHONE..................................937 642-6425
Bruce Fowler, *President*
Linda Fowler, *Corp Secy*
EMP: 10
SQ FT: 2,000
SALES (est): 490.1K **Privately Held**
SIC: **5461** 2052 2051 Bread; cookies & crackers; bread, cake & related products

(G-20037)
BLIND OUTLET (PA)
574 W Schrock Rd (43081-8996)
PHONE..................................614 895-2002
David Bornhorst, *President*
Diane Bornhorst, *Vice Pres*
Stephanie Bornhorst, *Vice Pres*
Roger Bornhorst, *Treasurer*
EMP: 9
SQ FT: 2,400

▲ = Import ▼ = Export
◆ = Import/Export

SALES: 1.5MM **Privately Held**
SIC: 2591 5719 5023 Blinds vertical; vertical blinds; vertical blinds

(G-20038)
BLUELOGOS INC
Also Called: Sullivan Company, The
130 Graphic Way (43081-2360)
PHONE.................................614 898-9971
David Duhl, *CEO*
EMP: 17
SQ FT: 5,760
SALES (est): 2.3MM **Privately Held**
WEB: www.wearbarndmatters.com
SIC: 2759 5699 5199 Screen printing; customized clothing & apparel; advertising specialties

(G-20039)
BUFFALO ABRASIVES INC
1093 Smoke Burr Dr (43081-4542)
PHONE.................................614 891-6450
Timothy J Wagner, *Principal*
EMP: 3
SALES (corp-wide): 11.9MM **Privately Held**
SIC: 3291 Abrasive products
HQ: Buffalo Abrasives, Inc.
    960 Erie Ave
    North Tonawanda NY 14120
    716 693-3856

(G-20040)
COLUMBUS PRESCR REHABILITATION
Also Called: The Mobility Store
975 Eastwind Dr Ste 155 (43081-3344)
PHONE.................................614 294-1600
Mark A Witchey, *President*
Jack A Witchey, *Admin Sec*
EMP: 6
SQ FT: 50,000
SALES (est): 1.7MM **Privately Held**
WEB: www.themobilitystore.com
SIC: 3842 7352 Wheelchairs; medical equipment rental

(G-20041)
COLUMBUS VSCLAR INTRVNTION LLC
895 S State St (43081-3345)
PHONE.................................614 917-0696
Raj Pannu, *Surgeon*
Rajmony Pannu,
EMP: 26
SALES (est): 4.3MM **Privately Held**
SIC: 3841 Surgical & medical instruments

(G-20042)
CREATIVE PRINT SOLUTIONS LLC
71 Granby Pl W (43081-1205)
PHONE.................................614 989-1747
Jay Broyles,
EMP: 3
SALES: 252K **Privately Held**
SIC: 2759 Commercial printing

(G-20043)
CRUISE QUARTERS AND TOURS
730 Mohican Way (43081-3048)
PHONE.................................614 891-6089
EMP: 3
SALES (est): 153K **Privately Held**
SIC: 3131 Mfg Footwear Cut Stock

(G-20044)
CURV IMAGING LLC
841 Green Crest Dr (43081-2838)
P.O. Box 360641, Columbus (43236-0641)
PHONE.................................614 890-2878
Bernie Sigal, *President*
Reta Sigal, *Vice Pres*
Gary Shaw, *Opers Staff*
EMP: 6
SALES: 1MM **Privately Held**
SIC: 2752 Commercial printing, offset

(G-20045)
DAIKIN APPLIED AMERICAS INC
192 Heatherdown Dr (43081-2868)
PHONE.................................614 351-9862
Dale Matheny, *Branch Mgr*
EMP: 9

SALES (corp-wide): 21.5B **Privately Held**
SIC: 3585 5075 Refrigeration & heating equipment; warm air heating & air conditioning
HQ: Daikin Applied Americas Inc.
    13600 Industrial Pk Blvd
    Minneapolis MN 55441
    763 553-5330

(G-20046)
DARIFILL INC
750 Green Crest Dr (43081-2837)
PHONE.................................614 890-3274
Steve Aspery, *President*
Eric Rousculp, *Vice Pres*
Jack Spencer, *Vice Pres*
▲ EMP: 18
SALES (est): 6.2MM **Privately Held**
WEB: www.darifill.com
SIC: 3565 Packaging machinery

(G-20047)
DEVRIES & ASSOCIATES INC
Also Called: Fastsigns
654 Brooksedge Blvd Ste A (43081-2962)
PHONE.................................614 890-3821
Mary Devries, *President*
Scott Oliphant, *Accounts Exec*
EMP: 14
SALES (est): 1.2MM **Privately Held**
SIC: 3993 Signs & advertising specialties

(G-20048)
DEVRIES & ASSOCIATES INC (PA)
Also Called: Fastsigns
5117 E Main St (43081)
PHONE.................................614 860-0103
Thomas R De Vries, *President*
Mary L De Vries, *CFO*
EMP: 7
SALES (est): 1MM **Privately Held**
SIC: 3993 Signs & advertising specialties

(G-20049)
DSC SUPPLY COMPANY LLC
237 E Broadway Ave Ste A (43081-1646)
P.O. Box 2125 (43086-2125)
PHONE.................................614 891-1100
Nikki Anderson, *President*
EMP: 7
SALES (est): 817K **Privately Held**
SIC: 2759 Commercial printing

(G-20050)
ELAN DESIGNS INC
10 E Schrock Rd 110 (43081-2915)
PHONE.................................614 985-5600
Nelia Anderson, *President*
Neilia Anderson, *President*
▲ EMP: 6
SALES (est): 581.2K **Privately Held**
WEB: www.elandesigns.com
SIC: 3524 Lawn & garden equipment

(G-20051)
EMROID ME
6065 Shreven Dr (43081-8261)
PHONE.................................614 789-1898
Joe Vulpio, *Owner*
EMP: 6
SALES (est): 448.2K **Privately Held**
SIC: 2395 Embroidery & art needlework

(G-20052)
EN-HANCED PRODUCTS INC
229 E Broadway Ave (43081-1656)
PHONE.................................614 882-7400
James M Hance, *President*
EMP: 7
SALES (est): 1.3MM **Privately Held**
SIC: 3443 Fabricated plate work (boiler shop)

(G-20053)
FASTSIGNS WESTERVILLE
654 Brooksedge Blvd Ste A (43081-2962)
PHONE.................................614 890-3821
Tom Devries, *President*
Mary Devries, *Vice Pres*
EMP: 20
SALES (est): 1.8MM **Privately Held**
SIC: 3993 Signs & advertising specialties

(G-20054)
FEDEX OFFICE & PRINT SVCS INC
604 W Schrock Rd (43081-8996)
PHONE.................................614 898-0000
EMP: 40
SALES (corp-wide): 65.4B **Publicly Held**
WEB: www.kinkos.com
SIC: 7334 2759 2396 Photocopying & duplicating services; commercial printing; automotive & apparel trimmings
HQ: Fedex Office And Print Services, Inc.
    7900 Legacy Dr
    Plano TX 75024
    800 463-3339

(G-20055)
GENERAL PARTS INC
Also Called: Carquest Auto Parts
24 E Schrock Rd (43081-2915)
PHONE.................................614 891-6014
Sherrie Rowlison, *Branch Mgr*
EMP: 4
SALES (corp-wide): 9.3B **Publicly Held**
WEB: www.carquest.com
SIC: 5013 5531 3599 Automotive supplies & parts; automotive parts; machine shop, jobbing & repair
HQ: General Parts, Inc.
    2635 E Millbrook Rd Ste C
    Raleigh NC 27604
    919 573-3000

(G-20056)
H G SCHNEIDER COMPANY
291 Broad St (43081-1603)
PHONE.................................614 882-6944
Constance Schneider, *President*
Harold Schneider, *Vice Pres*
EMP: 6
SALES: 200K **Privately Held**
WEB: www.unikix.net
SIC: 3544 Special dies, tools, jigs & fixtures

(G-20057)
HEARTBEAT COMPANY LLC
895 S State St (43081-3345)
PHONE.................................614 423-5646
Rajmony Pannu, *Mng Member*
EMP: 1
SQ FT: 300
SALES: 1MM **Privately Held**
SIC: 3841 Surgical instruments & apparatus

(G-20058)
HOMMATI FRANCHISE NETWORK INC
6264 S Sunbury Rd Ste 100 (43081-2972)
PHONE.................................833 466-6284
Jerry Clum, *President*
EMP: 4
SALES (est): 98.3K **Privately Held**
SIC: 7372 Application computer software

(G-20059)
INDUSTRIAL FABRICATORS INC
265 E Broadway Ave (43081-1646)
PHONE.................................614 882-7423
Frederick R Landig Jr, *President*
Frederick Landig Sr, *President*
EMP: 38 EST: 1964
SQ FT: 98,000
SALES (est): 8.1MM **Privately Held**
WEB: www.ifab.com
SIC: 3444 Sheet metalwork

(G-20060)
JEFFREY REEDY
Also Called: Computer Forms Printing
237 E Broadway Ave Ste D (43081-1646)
PHONE.................................614 794-9292
Jeffrey Reedy, *Owner*
EMP: 3
SQ FT: 2,500
SALES (est): 260.6K **Privately Held**
SIC: 2759 2752 Commercial printing; commercial printing, lithographic

(G-20061)
KOKOSING MATERIALS INC
6189 Westerville Rd (43081-4057)
P.O. Box 334, Fredericktown (43019-0334)
PHONE.................................614 891-5090

Josh Bartlett, *Manager*
EMP: 4
SALES (corp-wide): 19.9MM **Privately Held**
WEB: www.kokosingmaterials.biz
SIC: 2951 Asphalt & asphaltic paving mixtures (not from refineries)
PA: Kokosing Materials, Inc.
    17531 Waterford Rd
    Fredericktown OH 43019
    740 694-9585

(G-20062)
KUFBAG INC
1333 Cobblestone Ave (43081-4581)
PHONE.................................614 589-8687
Glenda L Hill-Foster, *CEO*
John Foster, *CFO*
EMP: 4
SQ FT: 2,400
SALES (est): 350.4K **Privately Held**
WEB: www.kufbag.com
SIC: 3842 Limbs, artificial

(G-20063)
LABELDATA
275 Old County Line Rd I (43081-1081)
PHONE.................................614 891-5858
Scott Bendger, *Owner*
EMP: 3 EST: 2007
SALES: 600K **Privately Held**
SIC: 3565 Packing & wrapping machinery

(G-20064)
MC VAY VENTURES INC
Also Called: Wm Caxton Printing
40 W College Ave (43081-2104)
PHONE.................................614 890-1516
Larry Mc Vay, *President*
EMP: 4
SQ FT: 1,200
SALES (est): 597.6K **Privately Held**
WEB: www.caxtonprinting.com
SIC: 2752 Commercial printing, offset

(G-20065)
MICRO INDUSTRIES CORPORATION (PA)
8399 Green Meadows Dr N (43081)
PHONE.................................740 548-7878
John Curran, *CEO*
Michael Curran, *President*
Amanda Curran, *Vice Pres*
William Jackson, *Vice Pres*
EMP: 67
SQ FT: 52,000
SALES (est): 11.9MM **Privately Held**
WEB: www.microindustries.com
SIC: 8711 3674 Engineering services; semiconductor circuit networks; microcircuits, integrated (semiconductor)

(G-20066)
NAIL ART
Also Called: Nail Artist
5470 Westerville Rd (43081-9361)
PHONE.................................614 899-7155
H Meadows, *Owner*
EMP: 3
SALES (est): 130K **Privately Held**
SIC: 3999 7231 Fingernails, artificial; manicurist, pedicurist

(G-20067)
NANAK BAKERY
895 S State St (43081-3345)
PHONE.................................614 882-0882
EMP: 8
SALES (est): 280K **Privately Held**
SIC: 2051 Mfg Bread/Related Products

(G-20068)
OHIO SHELTERALL INC
Also Called: Moore Outdoor Sign Craftsman
6060 Westerville Rd (43081-4048)
PHONE.................................614 882-1110
Steve P Moore, *President*
Tom Moore, *Vice Pres*
Ellen Moore, *Treasurer*
Riley Moore, *Executive*
Dave Moore, *Admin Sec*
EMP: 10

Westerville - Franklin County (G-20069)

SALES (est): 880K **Privately Held**
WEB: www.ohioagriculture.gov
SIC: 7312 7389 7338 3993 Outdoor advertising services; sign painting & lettering shop; secretarial & typing service; signs & advertising specialties

(G-20069)
OPTIMUM SYSTEM PRODUCTS INC (PA)
Also Called: Optimum Graphics
921 Eastwind Dr Ste 133 (43081-3363)
PHONE.................................614 885-4464
John Martin, *CEO*
Dorothy Martin, *President*
EMP: 40
SQ FT: 75,000
SALES (est): 10.5MM **Privately Held**
WEB: www.optimumsystem.com
SIC: 2752 5112 Business form & card printing, lithographic; business forms

(G-20070)
PRECISION Q SYSTEMS LLC
285 Old County Line Rd B (43081-1886)
PHONE.................................614 286-5142
J R Gaines, *Director*
EMP: 3
SALES (est): 182.7K **Privately Held**
WEB: www.low-nox.com
SIC: 3491 Valves, automatic control

(G-20071)
PRINT SOLUTIONS TODAY LLC
657 Collingwood Dr (43081-2461)
PHONE.................................614 848-4500
David D Dinning, *Mng Member*
EMP: 4
SQ FT: 1,200
SALES: 4MM **Privately Held**
SIC: 2752 Commercial printing, lithographic

(G-20072)
RISING MOON CUSTOM APPAREL
19 E College Ave (43081-2101)
PHONE.................................614 882-1336
Sue M Swihart, *Owner*
Robert Swihart, *Co-Owner*
EMP: 4
SALES: 400K **Privately Held**
SIC: 2759 Screen printing

(G-20073)
ROBIN ENTERPRISES COMPANY
111 N Otterbein Ave (43081-5703)
P.O. Box 6180 (43086-6180)
PHONE.................................614 891-0250
Brad Hance, *President*
Julie Stewart, *General Mgr*
Mike Barker, *Project Mgr*
John Kaufman, *Mfg Staff*
Shane Gruber, *Accounting Dir*
EMP: 120
SQ FT: 90,000
SALES: 22MM **Privately Held**
WEB: www.robinent.com
SIC: 2752 2789 2791 Commercial printing, offset; bookbinding & related work; typesetting

(G-20074)
SHOWERLINE PRODUCTS LLC
1143 Lori Ln (43081-1179)
PHONE.................................614 794-3476
Robert W Wesley, *Principal*
EMP: 3
SALES (est): 204.7K **Privately Held**
SIC: 3089 Plastics products

(G-20075)
SYMMETRY OES
4528 Ravine Dr (43081-9335)
PHONE.................................614 890-1758
Karen Fischbach, *Principal*
EMP: 3 EST: 2017
SALES (est): 277.5K **Privately Held**
SIC: 3369 Nonferrous foundries

(G-20076)
TAHOE INTERACTIVE SYSTEMS INC
60 Nadine Pl N (43081-2518)
P.O. Box 820 (43086-0820)
PHONE.................................614 891-2323
Paul Coleman, *President*
EMP: 18
SQ FT: 12,000
SALES: 1MM **Privately Held**
SIC: 7372 7375 7371 Prepackaged software; information retrieval services; custom computer programming services

(G-20077)
TECHNOPRINT INC
Also Called: Inkwell, The
515 S State St (43081-2921)
PHONE.................................614 899-1403
Pat Patel, *President*
Diane L Burchetp-Patel, *Admin Sec*
EMP: 10
SQ FT: 1,800
SALES: 620K **Privately Held**
SIC: 2752 7334 Commercial printing, lithographic; photocopying & duplicating services

(G-20078)
THOMAS TOOL & MOLD COMPANY
271 Broad St (43081-1603)
PHONE.................................614 890-4978
James W Thomas, *President*
James P Thomas, *Vice Pres*
EMP: 11
SQ FT: 7,500
SALES: 1.3MM **Privately Held**
WEB: www.ttmco.com
SIC: 3089 Injection molding of plastics

(G-20079)
TOP HAT DESIGNS
776 Autumn Branch Rd (43081-3104)
PHONE.................................614 898-1962
Mary Jo Lee, *Owner*
EMP: 5
SALES (est): 180K **Privately Held**
SIC: 2389 Theatrical costumes

(G-20080)
TRACEWELL POWER INC
567 Enterprise Dr (43081-8883)
PHONE.................................614 846-6175
Larry Tracewell, *President*
EMP: 25
SQ FT: 100,000
SALES (est): 3.9MM
SALES (corp-wide): 26.3MM **Privately Held**
SIC: 3679 Power supplies, all types: static
PA: Tracewell Systems, Inc.
567 Enterprise Dr
Lewis Center OH 43035
614 846-6175

(G-20081)
WES-GARDE COMPONENTS GROUP INC
300 Enterprise Dr (43081)
PHONE.................................614 885-0319
Joe Jeenan, *General Mgr*
EMP: 6
SALES (corp-wide): 61.4MM **Privately Held**
SIC: 5065 3625 5063 Electronic parts; switches, electric power; switches, except electronic
PA: Wes-Garde Components Group, Inc.
2820 Drane Field Rd
Lakeland FL 33811
863 644-7564

(G-20082)
WEST-CAMP PRESS INC (PA)
39 Collegeview Rd (43081-1463)
PHONE.................................614 882-2378
Ed Evina, *Principal*
Dave Mars, *Principal*
Chip Hilleary, *Exec VP*
David Gundelfinger, *Prdtn Mgr*
Steve Chappelear, *Engineer*
▲ EMP: 75 EST: 1961
SQ FT: 55,000

SALES (est): 26.9MM **Privately Held**
WEB: www.westcamp.com
SIC: 2752 2796 2791 2789 Commercial printing, offset; platemaking services; typesetting; bookbinding & related work; commercial printing

(G-20083)
WORLD DEVELOPMENT & CONSLT LLC
Also Called: Vicrobiz
855 S Sunbury Rd (43081-9553)
PHONE.................................614 805-4450
Ron Paul, *President*
▼ EMP: 3
SALES (est): 143.1K **Privately Held**
SIC: 1442 Construction sand & gravel

(G-20084)
YESPRESS GRAPHICS LLC
515 S State St (43081-2921)
PHONE.................................614 899-1403
Sunir Patel, *Principal*
EMP: 7
SALES (est): 1MM **Privately Held**
SIC: 2752 Commercial printing, offset

Westfield Center
Medina County

(G-20085)
J WILLIAMS & ASSOCIATES INC
8761 Virginia Dr (44251-9755)
P.O. Box 727 (44251-0727)
PHONE.................................330 887-1392
Jeffery Williams, *President*
EMP: 4
SALES (est): 504.7K **Privately Held**
SIC: 3469 Metal stampings

Westlake
Cuyahoga County

(G-20086)
ACME DUPLICATING CO
Also Called: Acme Printing
1565 Greenleaf Cir (44145-2609)
PHONE.................................216 241-1241
Donald Sebold, *Owner*
EMP: 7
SQ FT: 3,300
SALES (est): 579.3K **Privately Held**
WEB: www.namepads.com
SIC: 2752 Photolithographic printing

(G-20087)
ADVANCED TRANSLATION/CNSLTNG
Also Called: Spanish Portugese Translation
3751 Willow Run (44145-5720)
PHONE.................................440 716-0820
Hugo R Urizar, *Owner*
EMP: 30
SALES (est): 1.4MM **Privately Held**
SIC: 7389 2791 Translation services; typesetting

(G-20088)
AEROCASE INCORPORATED
Also Called: Odell Electronic Cleaning Stns
1061 Bradley Rd (44145-1044)
PHONE.................................440 617-9294
John Koniarczyk, *President*
Deborah Koniarczyk, *Vice Pres*
Aaron Nix, *Sales Staff*
EMP: 10
SALES (est): 1.8MM **Privately Held**
WEB: www.aerocaseinc.com
SIC: 3089 2441 Cases, plastic; cases, wood

(G-20089)
ALL AMERICAN ENERGY COOP ASSN
28901 Clemens Rd Ste 119 (44145-1166)
P.O. Box 640, Malvern (44644-0640)
PHONE.................................440 772-4340
Robert Smith, *President*
EMP: 4

SALES: 126.7K **Privately Held**
SIC: 1311 Natural gas production

(G-20090)
ALLEGRA PRINTING & IMAGING LLC
Also Called: Allegra Print & Imaging
1486 Barclay Blvd (44145-6822)
PHONE.................................440 449-6989
EMP: 7
SALES (est): 610K **Privately Held**
SIC: 2752 Lithographic Commercial Printing

(G-20091)
ALUMINUM LINE PRODUCTS COMPANY (PA)
Also Called: Alpco
24460 Sperry Cir (44145-1591)
PHONE.................................440 835-8880
Edward Murray, *Principal*
Chris Harrington, *Vice Pres*
Richard Daniel, *CFO*
Wendy L Wilson-Kieding, *Treasurer*
▲ EMP: 100 EST: 1960
SQ FT: 100,000
SALES: 100MM **Privately Held**
WEB: www.aluminumline.com
SIC: 5051 3365 3999 Metals service centers & offices; aluminum foundries; barber & beauty shop equipment

(G-20092)
AMERICAN LAWYERS CO INC (PA)
Also Called: American Lawyers Quarterly
853 Westpoint Pkwy # 710 (44145-1546)
PHONE.................................440 333-5190
Edward D Familo, *President*
Thomas W Hamilton, *Exec VP*
Jeremy Brown, *Manager*
EMP: 11
SQ FT: 4,000 **Privately Held**
WEB: www.alqlist.com
SIC: 2721 Periodicals: publishing only

(G-20093)
AMERICAN MERCHANT SERVIC
3076 Waterfall Way (44145-6811)
PHONE.................................216 598-3100
Ramzy Assad, *Owner*
Mike Assad, *Office Mgr*
EMP: 4 EST: 2010
SALES: 400K **Privately Held**
SIC: 3578 7699 Automatic teller machines (ATM); automated teller machine (ATM) repair

(G-20094)
AMERICAN MFG & ENGRG CO
910 Cahoon Rd (44145-1228)
PHONE.................................440 899-9400
Mike Perkins, *Branch Mgr*
EMP: 3 **Privately Held**
SIC: 3441 Fabricated structural metal
PA: American Manufacturing And Engineering Company
4600 W 160th St
Cleveland OH 44135

(G-20095)
AMERICAN OFFICE SERVICES INC
30257 Clemens Rd Ste C (44145-1004)
PHONE.................................440 899-6888
Scott C Ashbrook, *President*
Margo L Ashbrook, *Vice Pres*
Kristen M Ashbrook, *Treasurer*
Marilyn Smith, *Administration*
EMP: 6
SQ FT: 8,000
SALES: 1.7MM **Privately Held**
SIC: 7641 2531 Office furniture repair & maintenance; stadium seating

(G-20096)
AMERICAN TCHNICAL COATINGS INC
Also Called: A T C
28045 Ranney Pkwy Ste H (44145-1144)
PHONE.................................440 401-2270
Charles Inglefield, *President*
Mark Hawthorne, *Research*
Brian Barry, *Info Tech Mgr*
EMP: 6

GEOGRAPHIC SECTION

Westlake - Cuyahoga County (G-20124)

SALES (est): 966.6K Privately Held
SIC: 3479 Coating of metals & formed products

(G-20097)
ANCHOR CHEMICAL CO INC (PA)
777 Canterbury Rd (44145-1499)
PHONE..................................440 871-1660
Diana Firth, *Ch of Bd*
Mark Atzel, *Vice Pres*
▼ EMP: 3
SQ FT: 6,000
SALES (est): 454.8K Privately Held
WEB: www.anchorlube.com
SIC: 2992 Cutting oils, blending: made from purchased materials

(G-20098)
APPLIED MARKETING SERVICES (HQ)
Also Called: Medical & Home Health
28825 Ranney Pkwy (44145-1173)
PHONE..................................440 716-9962
David J Marquard II, *President*
Sandi Kinley, *Purch Agent*
C V Guggenviller, *CFO*
Cathy Marquard, *Controller*
Jane Binzer, *Sales Staff*
▲ EMP: 28
SQ FT: 20,000
SALES (est): 5.8MM Privately Held
WEB: www.applied-inc.com
SIC: 3569 8742 Gas producers, generators & other gas related equipment; marketing consulting services; new products & services consultants
PA: Oxygo Hq Florida Llc
    7380 W Sand Lake Rd # 500
    Orlando FL 32819
    440 716-9962

(G-20099)
ARCHER CUSTOM CHROME LLC
25703 Rustic Ln (44145-5476)
PHONE..................................216 441-2795
Roy Ansen, *Principal*
EMP: 3
SALES (est): 122.7K Privately Held
SIC: 3471 Chromium plating of metals or formed products

(G-20100)
ASSOC TALENTS INC
3700 Greenbriar Cir (44145-5436)
PHONE..................................440 716-1265
Carol Gantz, *President*
EMP: 3
SALES (est): 150K Privately Held
SIC: 2395 5099 Embroidery & art needlework; durable goods

(G-20101)
BLACK BOX CORPORATION
26100 1st St (44145-1478)
PHONE..................................800 837-7777
EMP: 3
SALES (corp-wide): 1.8MM Privately Held
SIC: 3577 Computer peripheral equipment
HQ: Black Box Corporation
    1000 Park Dr
    Lawrence PA 15055
    724 746-5500

(G-20102)
BONNE BELL LLC (PA)
1006 Crocker Rd (44145-1094)
PHONE..................................440 835-2440
Jess A Bell Jr, *Mng Member*
James G Bell,
Robert A Sigmund,
Scott Sumser,
Janet W Thompson,
▲ EMP: 8 EST: 1927
SQ FT: 40,000
SALES (est): 36MM Privately Held
SIC: 2844 Cosmetic preparations; toilet preparations; colognes; face creams or lotions

(G-20103)
BORCHERS AMERICAS INC (HQ)
Also Called: Om Group
811 Sharon Dr (44145-1522)
PHONE..................................440 899-2950
Joseph Scaminace, *CEO*
◆ EMP: 60
SQ FT: 30,000
SALES (est): 41.4MM
SALES (corp-wide): 1.4B Privately Held
SIC: 8731 2819 2899 2992 Commercial physical research; industrial inorganic chemicals; chemical preparations; lubricating oils & greases; industrial organic chemicals
PA: The Jordan Company L P
    399 Park Ave Fl 30
    New York NY 10022
    212 572-0800

(G-20104)
BRAZING SERVICE INC
24480 Sperry Cir (44145-1593)
PHONE..................................440 871-1120
Robert Deucher, *President*
Robert Doucher, *President*
EMP: 5
SQ FT: 4,000
SALES (est): 390K Privately Held
SIC: 3398 Brazing (hardening) of metal

(G-20105)
CLEAR IMAGE TECHNOLOGY LLC
26202 Detroit Rd Ste 340 (44145-2480)
PHONE..................................440 366-4330
▲ EMP: 5
SALES (est): 538.3K Privately Held
SIC: 3845 Mfg Electromedical Equipment

(G-20106)
CLOROX SALES COMPANY
24500 Center Ridge Rd # 240 (44145-5601)
PHONE..................................440 892-1700
EMP: 25
SALES (corp-wide): 5.5B Publicly Held
SIC: 2812 Mfg Alkalies/Chlorine
HQ: The Clorox Sales Company
    1221 Broadway Ste 13
    Oakland CA 94612
    510 271-7000

(G-20107)
COMROD INC
909 Canterbury Rd Ste A (44145-7212)
PHONE..................................440 455-9186
William Convery, *Managing Dir*
EMP: 5
SQ FT: 12,000
SALES (est): 441.7K
SALES (corp-wide): 44.7MM Privately Held
SIC: 3663 Radio & TV communications equipment
HQ: Comrod As
    Fiskavegen 1
    Tau 4120
    669 072-00

(G-20108)
DIAMOND RESERVE INC
Also Called: National Diamond Tl & Coating
801 Sharon Dr (44145-1522)
PHONE..................................440 892-7877
William Pastis, *CEO*
Tom Abersold, *President*
EMP: 10
SQ FT: 2,000
SALES (est): 1.6MM Privately Held
WEB: www.diamondreserve.com
SIC: 3545 Diamond cutting tools for turning, boring, burnishing, etc.

(G-20109)
DOME DRILLING CO (PA)
Also Called: Dome Resources
2001 Crocker Rd Ste 420 (44145-6967)
PHONE..................................440 892-9434
Jon O Newton, *President*
James E Gessel, *Vice Pres*
Noreen C Mc Kinney, *Vice Pres*
James A Carney, *Treasurer*
John James Carney, *Admin Sec*
EMP: 6 EST: 1981
SQ FT: 1,200
SALES (est): 1.6MM Privately Held
SIC: 1311 1382 Crude petroleum production; natural gas production; oil & gas exploration services

(G-20110)
DOME ENERGICORP
2001 Crocker Rd Ste 420 (44145-6967)
PHONE..................................440 892-4900
John J Carney, *Ch of Bd*
Jon O Newton, *President*
James A Carney, *Admin Sec*
EMP: 4
SQ FT: 1,500
SALES: 224.3K Privately Held
SIC: 1382 8741 Oil & gas exploration services; financial management for business

(G-20111)
EDGEWELL PER CARE BRANDS LLC
25225 Detroit Rd (44145-2536)
P.O. Box 450777 (44145-0616)
PHONE..................................440 835-7500
Claire Marie Langkau, *Principal*
EMP: 98
SALES (corp-wide): 2.3B Publicly Held
WEB: www.eveready.com
SIC: 3421 Razor blades & razors
HQ: Edgewell Personal Care Brands, Llc
    6 Research Dr
    Shelton CT 06484
    203 944-5500

(G-20112)
ENERGIZER MANUFACTURING INC
25225 Detroit Rd (44145-2536)
PHONE..................................440 835-7866
EMP: 58
SALES (corp-wide): 1.7B Publicly Held
WEB: www.eveready.com
SIC: 3691 Alkaline cell storage batteries
HQ: Energizer Manufacturing, Inc.
    533 Maryville Univ Dr
    Saint Louis MO 63141
    314 985-2000

(G-20113)
FENIX MAGNETICS INC
909 Canterbury Rd Ste K (44145-7212)
PHONE..................................440 455-1142
Douglas Kirkpatrick, *CEO*
David Matthiesen, *Chief Engr*
Joshua Silber, *Treasurer*
EMP: 5
SQ FT: 1,000
SALES (est): 166.8K Privately Held
SIC: 3499 8731 Magnets, permanent: metallic; commercial physical research; energy research

(G-20114)
FRANKIES GRAPHICS INC
3770 Windsong Ct (44145-5483)
PHONE..................................440 979-0824
Frank Fusco, *President*
EMP: 3
SALES: 100K Privately Held
SIC: 2752 Commercial printing, lithographic

(G-20115)
FUEL G USA LLC
1457 Mendelssohn Dr (44145-2346)
PHONE..................................440 617-0950
Azdiher Abuhamdeh, *Principal*
EMP: 3 EST: 2011
SALES (est): 173.3K Privately Held
SIC: 2869 Fuels

(G-20116)
G I PLASTEK INC
24700 Center Ridge Rd # 8 (44145-5636)
PHONE..................................440 230-1942
Charles Lagasse Jr, *CEO*
Graham Gund, *Principal*
James Lyman, *Principal*
Shelly Trochemenko, *Treasurer*
EMP: 7
SQ FT: 3,000
SALES (est): 854.4K Privately Held
SIC: 3089 Plastic processing

(G-20117)
GENERAL BAR INC
25000 Center Ridge Rd # 3 (44145-4108)
PHONE..................................440 835-2000
Charles Sonnhalter, *President*
Michael Sonnhalter, *Vice Pres*
EMP: 18
SQ FT: 1,500
SALES (est): 1.4MM Privately Held
WEB: www.generalbar.com
SIC: 2741 8111 Directories: publishing only, not printed on site; legal services

(G-20118)
GIBRALTAR INDUSTRIES INC
26314 Center Ridge Rd (44145-4070)
PHONE..................................440 617-9230
Alan W Douglas, *Principal*
EMP: 4
SALES (corp-wide): 1B Publicly Held
SIC: 3999 Barber & beauty shop equipment
PA: Gibraltar Industries, Inc.
    3556 Lake Shore Rd # 100
    Buffalo NY 14219
    716 826-6500

(G-20119)
GILLZ LLC (PA)
28915 Clemens Rd Ste 20 (44145-1122)
P.O. Box 45495 (44145-0495)
PHONE..................................904 330-1094
James Phelan, *Mng Member*
EMP: 4
SALES (est): 518.4K Privately Held
SIC: 2211 Apparel & outerwear fabrics, cotton

(G-20120)
GRIFFIN CIDER WORKS LLC
2165 Elmwood Dr (44145-3128)
PHONE..................................440 785-7418
EMP: 7
SALES (est): 510.4K Privately Held
SIC: 2037 Fruit juices

(G-20121)
HANGER PRSTHETCS & ORTHO INC
29101 Health Campus Dr # 104 (44145-5268)
PHONE..................................440 892-6665
Terri Woolf, *Manager*
Teresa Kole,
EMP: 6
SALES (corp-wide): 1B Publicly Held
SIC: 3842 Surgical appliances & supplies
HQ: Hanger Prosthetics & Orthotics, Inc.
    10910 Domain Dr Ste 300
    Austin TX 78758
    512 777-3800

(G-20122)
HENKEL US OPERATIONS CORP
Also Called: Loctite
26235 1st St (44145-1439)
PHONE..................................440 250-7700
James Heginbotham, *Branch Mgr*
Anna Mulgrew, *Manager*
Thomas Harris, *Technology*
Jace Stampfer, *Technical Staff*
EMP: 202
SALES (corp-wide): 22.7B Privately Held
SIC: 2891 Adhesives & sealants
HQ: Henkel Us Operations Corporation
    1 Henkel Way
    Rocky Hill CT 06067
    860 571-5100

(G-20123)
HIGH PERFORMANCE SERVO LLC
1477 E Crossings Pl (44145-6247)
PHONE..................................440 541-3529
Peter Ganczarski, *President*
EMP: 5 EST: 2012
SALES (est): 315K Privately Held
SIC: 3621 Coils, for electric motors or generators

(G-20124)
HMS INDUSTRIES LLC
27995 Ranney Pkwy (44145-1178)
PHONE..................................440 899-0001
Rick Kucinski, *Engineer*

Westlake - Cuyahoga County (G-20125)   GEOGRAPHIC SECTION

Neal Saluja, *Sales Staff*
Biri Saluja, *Mng Member*
▲ **EMP:** 8
SQ FT: 10,000
SALES (est): 1.7MM **Privately Held**
WEB: www.wanxiang.com
SIC: 3562 5085 Roller bearings & parts; industrial supplies

(G-20125)
HYLAND SOFTWARE INC (HQ)
28500 Clemens Rd (44145-1145)
PHONE.....................440 788-5000
Bill Priemer, *CEO*
Christopher J Hyland, *Ch of Bd*
Tom Vongunden, *Editor*
Noreen Kilbane, *Senior VP*
Brenda Kirk, *Senior VP*
EMP: 1800
SQ FT: 150,000
SALES (est): 496.8MM
SALES (corp-wide): 492.6MM **Privately Held**
WEB: www.onbase.com
SIC: 7372 Application computer software
PA: Thoma Cressey Bravo, Inc.
   300 N La Salle Dr # 4350
   Chicago IL 60654
   312 254-3300

(G-20126)
INNOVTIVE CNFCTION SLTIONS LLC
Also Called: Phillips Syrup
28025 Ranney Pkwy (44145-1159)
PHONE.....................440 835-8001
Mark E Krohn,
EMP: 4
SALES (est): 74.6K **Privately Held**
SIC: 2087 Syrups, drink; concentrates, drink

(G-20127)
KAEDEN CORPORATION
Also Called: Kaeden Books
806 Sharon Dr Ste F (44145-7701)
P.O. Box 16190, Rocky River (44116-0190)
PHONE.....................440 617-1400
Craig Urmston, *President*
Kathleen Urmston, *Vice Pres*
Christian Neuzil, *Warehouse Mgr*
Grant Urmston, *Director*
▲ **EMP:** 6
SQ FT: 5,000
SALES (est): 1.1MM **Privately Held**
WEB: www.kaeden.com
SIC: 2731 Books: publishing only

(G-20128)
LAMOR CORPORATION
841 Hamlet Ln Apt A2 (44145-1673)
PHONE.....................440 871-8000
Thomas Mackey, *CEO*
James Mackey, *President*
Jamie Roehm, *CFO*
▲ **EMP:** 15
SQ FT: 3,600
SALES (est): 2MM **Privately Held**
WEB: www.lamor.com
SIC: 2899 Oil absorption equipment

(G-20129)
LS STARRETT COMPANY
Webber Gage Div
24500 Detroit Rd (44145-2580)
PHONE.....................440 835-0005
Carl Stearns, *Engineer*
Diane Gabryszewski, *Human Res Mgr*
EMP: 80
SQ FT: 35,000
SALES (corp-wide): 216.3MM **Publicly Held**
WEB: www.starrett.com
SIC: 3545 3829 3823 Gauge blocks; measuring tools & machines, machinists' metalworking type; measuring & controlling devices; industrial instrmnts msrmnt display/control process variable
PA: The L S Starrett Company
   121 Crescent St
   Athol MA 01331
   978 249-3551

(G-20130)
METAL EQUIPMENT CO
1985 Savannah Pkwy (44145-1851)
PHONE.....................440 835-3100
Walter W Walzer, *CEO*
William G Walzer, *President*
Tracey A Strehle, *Admin Sec*
EMP: 20 **EST:** 1922
SQ FT: 55,000
SALES (est): 232.7K **Privately Held**
SIC: 3599 3589 3535 Machine shop, jobbing & repair; commercial cleaning equipment; unit handling conveying systems

(G-20131)
MMI TEXTILES INC
Also Called: Ndw Textiles
29260 Clemens Rd Bldg Ii (44145-1020)
PHONE.....................440 899-8050
Amy Hammond, *President*
Joshua Slack,
▲ **EMP:** 10
SQ FT: 5,000
SALES (est): 4.8MM **Privately Held**
WEB: www.mmitextiles.com
SIC: 2211 2221 2262 5131 Duck, cotton; manmade & synthetic broadwoven fabrics; chemical coating or treating: manmade broadwoven fabrics; broadwoven fabrics

(G-20132)
NORDSON CORPORATION (PA)
28601 Clemens Rd (44145-1119)
PHONE.....................440 892-1580
Joseph P Keithley, *Ch of Bd*
Michael F Hilton, *President*
Chris Tsai, *General Mgr*
Charlie Case, *Regional Mgr*
John J Keane, *Senior VP*
EMP: 58 **EST:** 1935
SQ FT: 28,000
SALES: 2.2B **Publicly Held**
WEB: www.nordson.com
SIC: 3563 Spraying outfits: metals, paints & chemicals (compressor); robots for industrial spraying, painting, etc.

(G-20133)
NOVO FOAM PRODUCTS LLC
1991 Crocker Rd Ste 600 (44145-6976)
PHONE.....................440 892-3325
EMP: 4
SALES (est): 310K **Privately Held**
SIC: 2821 Mfg Plastic Materials/Resins

(G-20134)
OAKMOOR PALLET
795 Sharon Dr Ste 210 (44145-1542)
PHONE.....................216 926-1858
Michael Keating, *Owner*
EMP: 3 **EST:** 2011
SALES (est): 423.5K **Privately Held**
SIC: 2448 Pallets, wood

(G-20135)
OAKMOOR PALLET
795 Sharon Dr (44145-1542)
PHONE.....................440 385-7340
EMP: 4
SALES (est): 301.5K **Privately Held**
SIC: 2448 Pallets, wood & wood with metal

(G-20136)
ODORTECH DISTRIBUTING LLC
35 Ashbourne Dr (44145-8123)
PHONE.....................216 339-0773
Michael Daugstrup,
EMP: 4
SALES (est): 348.1K **Privately Held**
SIC: 2842 Specialty cleaning, polishes & sanitation goods

(G-20137)
OMAR MCDOWELL CO
25109 Detroit Rd Ste 320 (44145-2544)
PHONE.....................440 808-2280
O'Mar McDowell, *Principal*
Erin McDowell, *Treasurer*
EMP: 4
SALES (est): 580.5K **Privately Held**
SIC: 3559 Sewing machines & attachments, industrial

(G-20138)
OPEN SIDED MRI CLEVELAND LLC
30400 Detroit Rd Ste 30 (44145-1872)
PHONE.....................804 217-7114
Sharon Keeling, *Principal*
EMP: 3 **EST:** 2000
SALES (est): 330K **Privately Held**
SIC: 3845 Ultrasonic scanning devices, medical

(G-20139)
PARTY ANIMAL INC
909 Crocker Rd (44145-1030)
PHONE.....................440 471-1030
Jim Cantrall, *President*
Phyllis Cantrall, *Vice Pres*
Danielle Stark, *Opers Staff*
Ian Rockwood, *Sales Staff*
Stuart Dudukovich, *Director*
▲ **EMP:** 7
SQ FT: 3,800
SALES (est): 1.1MM **Privately Held**
WEB: www.metronet.net
SIC: 2399 Banners, made from fabric

(G-20140)
PENGUIN ENTERPRISES INC
Also Called: PS Copy
869 Canterbury Rd Ste 2 (44145-1492)
PHONE.....................440 899-5112
Phil Seman, *President*
EMP: 35
SALES (est): 4.1MM **Privately Held**
WEB: www.ncsports.com
SIC: 2796 2791 2789 2759 Platemaking services; typesetting; bookbinding & related work; commercial printing; commercial printing, offset

(G-20141)
PINES MANUFACTURING INC (PA)
Also Called: Pines Technology
29100 Lakeland Blvd (44145)
PHONE.....................440 835-5553
Donald Rebar, *Ch of Bd*
Ian Williamson, *President*
Dan Wilczynski, *Plant Mgr*
Tom Wright, *Manager*
Bob Nosky, *Real Est Agnt*
▲ **EMP:** 43
SQ FT: 48,000
SALES (est): 13.6MM **Privately Held**
WEB: www.pines-mfg.com
SIC: 5084 3542 3549 3547 Industrial machinery & equipment; bending machines; metalworking machinery; rolling mill machinery

(G-20142)
PINES MANUFACTURING INC
Also Called: H & H Tooling
30505 Clemens Rd (44145-1011)
PHONE.....................440 835-5553
Lonnie Smiley, *Branch Mgr*
EMP: 45 **Privately Held**
WEB: www.pines-mfg.com
SIC: 3544 8661 3547 3498 Special dies, tools, jigs & fixtures; religious organizations; rolling mill machinery; fabricated pipe & fittings
PA: Pines Manufacturing, Inc.
   29100 Lakeland Blvd
   Westlake OH 44145

(G-20143)
PINNACLE SALES INC
159 Crocker Park Blvd # 400 (44145-8131)
PHONE.....................440 734-9195
James G Loparich, *President*
EMP: 4
SALES (est): 467.7K **Privately Held**
SIC: 5044 5085 3999 Office equipment; industrial supplies; barber & beauty shop equipment

(G-20144)
PIPE LINE DEVELOPMENT COMPANY
Also Called: Plidco Ppline Repr Ppline Mint
870 Canterbury Rd (44145-1490)
PHONE.....................440 871-5700
Kimberly Smith, *President*
Ben Sweeney, *General Mgr*
Rachael Lauer, *Export Mgr*
Rachael Nagy, *Export Mgr*
Bill Wilkinson, *Production*
▲ **EMP:** 90 **EST:** 1949
SQ FT: 70,000
SALES (est): 26.7MM **Privately Held**
WEB: www.plidco.com
SIC: 3498 Pipe fittings, fabricated from purchased pipe

(G-20145)
PREMAR MANUFACTURING LTD
803 Sharon Dr (44145-1522)
PHONE.....................440 250-0373
Jonathan Krapf, *Partner*
Janet Krapf, *Partner*
EMP: 3 **EST:** 1999
SALES (est): 468.6K **Privately Held**
WEB: www.premar.com
SIC: 3399 Flakes, metal

(G-20146)
Q-LAB CORPORATION (PA)
800 Canterbury Rd (44145-1419)
PHONE.....................440 835-8700
Douglas M Grossman, *President*
Brad Reis, *Vice Pres*
Ron Roberts, *Vice Pres*
Gary Simecek, *Vice Pres*
Kirk Wilhelm, *CFO*
▲ **EMP:** 53 **EST:** 1956
SQ FT: 40,000
SALES (est): 18.8MM **Privately Held**
WEB: www.q-lab.com
SIC: 3823 3829 3826 Industrial instrmnts msrmnt display/control process variable; measuring & controlling devices; analytical instruments

(G-20147)
R AND J CORPORATION
Also Called: Haynes Manufacturing Company
24142 Detroit Rd (44145-1515)
PHONE.....................440 871-6009
Beth Kloos, *President*
Timothy Kloos, *Vice Pres*
Sheri Bohning, *Purchasing*
Ric Thornton, *Project Engr*
Matt Rogan, *Sales Engr*
EMP: 42
SQ FT: 23,000
SALES (est): 15.8MM **Privately Held**
WEB: www.haynesmfg.com
SIC: 3556 5084 7389 3053 Food products machinery; food industry machinery; design, commercial & industrial; gaskets, packing & sealing devices; lubricating oils & greases

(G-20148)
RAM SENSORS INC
875 Canterbury Rd Ste 875 # 875 (44145-1488)
PHONE.....................440 835-3540
Connie Field, *Manager*
EMP: 8
SALES (corp-wide): 1.4MM **Privately Held**
WEB: www.ramsensors.com
SIC: 3315 Wire, steel: insulated or armored
PA: Ram Sensors Inc
   875 Canterbury Rd
   Cleveland OH 44145
   440 835-3540

(G-20149)
RECTOR INC
Also Called: Profiles In Diversity Journal
1991 Crocker Rd Ste 320 (44145-6971)
P.O. Box 45605, Cleveland (44145-0605)
PHONE.....................440 892-0444
Jim Rector, *President*
James Gorman, *Info Tech Dir*
EMP: 7
SQ FT: 1,000
SALES (est): 680K **Privately Held**
WEB: www.diversityjournal.com
SIC: 2721 Magazines: publishing only, not printed on site

(G-20150)
REVOLAZE LLC
31000 Viking Pkwy (44145-1019)
PHONE.....................440 617-0502
Darryl Costin Jr, *President*

Kimberly Ripley, *Vice Pres*
Ryan Ripley, *Vice Pres*
Rick King, *Director*
EMP: 5
SALES (est): 250.1K **Privately Held**
SIC: 3699 Laser systems & equipment

(G-20151)
ROBERT A REICH COMPANY
24930 Detroit Rd D (44145-2528)
P.O. Box 45490 (44145-0490)
PHONE..................................440 808-0033
Robert A Reich III, *President*
Page Reich, *Corp Secy*
Adam J Reich, *Vice Pres*
EMP: 4
SQ FT: 6,000
SALES (est): 310K **Privately Held**
SIC: 3399 Metal fasteners

(G-20152)
ROMARK INDUSTRIES INC
24500 Center Ridge Rd # 250 (44145-5602)
PHONE..................................440 333-5480
Sheryl P Greenleaf, *President*
Alan R Greenleaf, *Vice Pres*
▲ **EMP:** 5
SQ FT: 1,200
SALES: 2MM **Privately Held**
SIC: 3462 Railroad, construction & mining forgings

(G-20153)
S J T ENTERPRISES INC
28045 Ranney Pkwy Ste B (44145-1144)
PHONE..................................440 617-1100
Timothy J Smith, *President*
Rikki Ludwig, *Cust Mgr*
Tami Haggerty, *Graphic Designe*
▲ **EMP:** 22
SQ FT: 17,000
SALES (est): 2.2MM **Privately Held**
WEB: www.sjtent.com
SIC: 2741 Miscellaneous publishing

(G-20154)
SANGRAF INTERNATIONAL INC
159 Crocker Park Blvd # 100 (44145-8137)
PHONE..................................216 543-3288
Xiu Qin Hou, *Principal*
Lesley Inderrieden, *Business Mgr*
▲ **EMP:** 11 **EST:** 2012
SALES (est): 1.6MM
SALES (corp-wide): 3.1MM **Privately Held**
SIC: 3624 Electrodes, thermal & electrolytic uses: carbon, graphite
HQ: Henan Sanli Carbon Products Co., Ltd.
North Side Of Xiaotun Village, Baiquan Town, Xijiao Development
Xinxiang 45363
373 621-3819

(G-20155)
SARASOTA QUALITY PRODUCTS
27330 Center Ridge Rd (44145-3957)
PHONE..................................440 899-9820
James Schilens, *President*
▲ **EMP:** 8
SALES (est): 937.7K **Privately Held**
WEB: www.sarasotaqp.com
SIC: 3429 Manufactured hardware (general)

(G-20156)
SCOTT FETZER COMPANY (DH)
28800 Clemens Rd (44145-1197)
PHONE..................................440 892-3000
Robert McBride, *CEO*
William Stephans, *Treasurer*
John Gretta, *Asst Treas*
Trish Scanlon, *Admin Sec*
EMP: 15
SQ FT: 2,000
SALES (est): 2.7MM
SALES (corp-wide): 225.3B **Publicly Held**
SIC: 2731 2741 5961 Textbooks: publishing only, not printed on site; atlases: publishing only, not printed on site; books, mail order (except book clubs)

(G-20157)
SEST INC
24509 Annie Ln (44145-4144)
PHONE..................................440 777-9777
Ashwin Shah, *President*
EMP: 10 **EST:** 1997
SQ FT: 1,000
SALES (est): 891.8K **Privately Held**
WEB: www.sest.com
SIC: 8711 7373 7372 7371 Consulting engineer; computer-aided engineering (CAE) systems service; application computer software; computer software development & applications; computer software development

(G-20158)
SHAMROCK COMPANIES INC (PA)
Also Called: Shamrock Acquisition Company
24090 Detroit Rd (44145-1513)
P.O. Box 450980 (44145-0623)
PHONE..................................440 899-9510
Tim Connor, *CEO*
Robert E Troop, *Ch of Bd*
Dave Fechter, *COO*
Gary A Lesjak, *CFO*
Jen Barnhart, *Sales Staff*
▲ **EMP:** 65
SQ FT: 42,500
SALES (est): 87.9MM **Privately Held**
WEB: www.shamrockcompanies.net
SIC: 5112 5199 7336 7389 Business forms; advertising specialties; art design services; brokers services; commercial printing, gravure; pleating & stitching

(G-20159)
SONORAN SALSA COMPANY LLC
25456 Hilliard Blvd (44145-3549)
PHONE..................................216 513-3596
Gina Cole, *Principal*
EMP: 3 **EST:** 2013
SALES (est): 167.7K **Privately Held**
SIC: 2099 Dips, except cheese & sour cream based

(G-20160)
SPECTRE SENSORS INC (PA)
2392 Georgia Dr (44145-5806)
PHONE..................................440 250-0372
Glen Keller, *Ch of Bd*
John Keller, *President*
EMP: 7
SALES: 4MM **Privately Held**
WEB: www.spectresensors.com
SIC: 3612 Electronic meter transformers

(G-20161)
STAR METAL PRODUCTS CO INC (PA)
30405 Clemens Rd (44145-1018)
PHONE..................................440 899-7000
John C Murray, *CEO*
Rita A Dunham, *Principal*
Mary C Reidy, *Principal*
Arthur Stenzel, *Principal*
Allen Luznar, *Engineer*
EMP: 60 **EST:** 1958
SQ FT: 24,000
SALES (est): 12MM **Privately Held**
WEB: www.starmetal.com
SIC: 3545 Machine tool attachments & accessories

(G-20162)
STARBRINGER MEDIA GROUP LTD
871 Canterbury Rd Ste B (44145-1482)
PHONE..................................440 871-5448
Sharon Klingler, *President*
EMP: 4
SALES (est): 368.6K **Privately Held**
WEB: www.starbringermedia.com
SIC: 2741 Miscellaneous publishing

(G-20163)
STRUERS INC (DH)
24766 Detroit Rd (44145-2525)
PHONE..................................440 871-0071
Bente Freiberg, *President*
Christopher Sopko, *President*
Bill Thompson, *General Mgr*
Roland Zale, *Warehouse Mgr*
Steen Jensen, *Treasurer*
◆ **EMP:** 58 **EST:** 1875
SALES (est): 12.7MM
SALES (corp-wide): 5.1B **Publicly Held**
WEB: www.logitech-us.com
SIC: 3829 Measuring & controlling devices
HQ: Struers Aps
Pederstrupvej 84
Ballerup 2750
446 008-00

(G-20164)
SURILI COUTURE LLC
29961 Persimmon Dr (44145-5103)
PHONE..................................440 600-1456
Anuja Katyal,
EMP: 14
SALES: 250K **Privately Held**
SIC: 2335 Bridal & formal gowns

(G-20165)
SWORD FURS
25112 Center Ridge Rd (44145-4115)
PHONE..................................440 249-5001
Jim Sword, *Owner*
EMP: 3
SALES (est): 199.5K **Privately Held**
SIC: 3999 Furs

(G-20166)
SYNERGY GRINDING INC
1994 Coes Post Run (44145-2059)
PHONE..................................216 447-4000
Barbara Bissett Kitchen, *Owner*
EMP: 10
SALES (est): 1.1MM **Privately Held**
WEB: www.synergygrinding.com
SIC: 3541 Grinding machines, metalworking

(G-20167)
THE SHELBY CO
865 Canterbury Rd (44145-1420)
PHONE..................................440 871-9901
Richard J Rapacz, *President*
EMP: 33 **EST:** 1923
SQ FT: 50,000
SALES (est): 8.8MM **Privately Held**
WEB: www.shelbycompany.com
SIC: 2657 2653 Folding paperboard boxes; display items, corrugated: made from purchased materials

(G-20168)
VISIBLE SOLUTIONS INC (PA)
1991 Crocker Rd Ste 222 (44145-6971)
PHONE..................................440 925-2810
Sandra L Haftl, *President*
Lyle Storey, *Vice Pres*
EMP: 4
SQ FT: 850 **Privately Held**
WEB: www.visi-sol.com
SIC: 2899 3714 Deicing or defrosting fluid; windshield wiper systems, motor vehicle

(G-20169)
VISION GRAPHIX INC
Also Called: AlphaGraphics Westlake
29260 Clemens Rd Ste A (44145-1076)
PHONE..................................440 835-6540
Jeff Brant Jr, *President*
Benjamin Brant, *Manager*
EMP: 6
SQ FT: 4,000
SALES (est): 660K **Privately Held**
WEB: www.visiongraphixinc.com
SIC: 2752 3993 Commercial printing, offset; advertising artwork

(G-20170)
WESTERN/SCOTT FETZER COMPANY
Also Called: Western Enterprises
875 Bassett Rd (44145-1142)
PHONE..................................440 871-2160
Gary Heeman, *Branch Mgr*
EMP: 250
SALES (corp-wide): 225.3B **Publicly Held**
SIC: 3635 Household vacuum cleaners
HQ: Western/Scott Fetzer Company
28800 Clemens Rd
Westlake OH 44145

(G-20171)
WESTERN/SCOTT FETZER COMPANY (DH)
28800 Clemens Rd (44145-1134)
PHONE..................................440 892-3000
Robert D McBride, *CEO*
Kenneth Semelsberger, *Ch of Bd*
John Gretta, *Treasurer*
◆ **EMP:** 45
SALES (est): 44.1MM
SALES (corp-wide): 225.3B **Publicly Held**
SIC: 3635 Household vacuum cleaners
HQ: The Scott Fetzer Company
28800 Clemens Rd
Westlake OH 44145
440 892-3000

(G-20172)
WIDE AREA MEDIA LLC
24500 Center Ridge Rd # 205 (44145-5602)
P.O. Box 45285 (44145-0285)
PHONE..................................440 356-3133
Roger Vichill, *Vice Pres*
Brian Clancy,
EMP: 3
SALES (est): 421K **Privately Held**
WEB: www.wideareamedia.com
SIC: 8742 3993 Management consulting services; electric signs; scoreboards, electric

(G-20173)
WOODBURY VINEYARDS INC (PA)
2001 Crocker Rd Ste 440 (44145-6968)
PHONE..................................440 835-2828
Joseph D Carney, *CEO*
Gary F Woodbury, *COO*
EMP: 2
SALES (est): 1.7MM **Privately Held**
WEB: www.woodburyvineyards.com
SIC: 2084 Wines

(G-20174)
XIM PRODUCTS INC
1169 Bassett Rd (44145-1112)
P.O. Box 45516 (44145-0516)
PHONE..................................440 871-4737
Richard Hardy, *President*
▲ **EMP:** 21
SQ FT: 30,000
SALES (est): 4.1MM **Privately Held**
WEB: www.ximbonder.com
SIC: 2851 Mfg Paints/Allied Products

Weston
Wood County

(G-20175)
CRESSET CHEMICAL CO INC (PA)
13255 Main St (43569-9544)
P.O. Box 367 (43569-0367)
PHONE..................................419 669-2041
George F Baty, *Ch of Bd*
Mike Baty, *President*
Robert Criner, *Purchasing*
▼ **EMP:** 10 **EST:** 1946
SQ FT: 2,000
SALES (est): 2MM **Privately Held**
WEB: www.cresset.com
SIC: 2899 2841 Chemical preparations; soap & other detergents

(G-20176)
CRESSET CHEMICAL CO INC
13490 Silver St (43569-9522)
PHONE..................................419 669-2041
George Baty, *Manager*
EMP: 10
SALES (corp-wide): 2MM **Privately Held**
WEB: www.cresset.com
SIC: 2899 Chemical preparations
PA: Cresset Chemical Co Inc
13255 Main St
Weston OH 43569
419 669-2041

Weston - Wood County (G-20177)

(G-20177)
MCM PRECISION CASTINGS INC
13133 Beech St (43569-9516)
PHONE.....................419 669-3226
Donald Marion, *President*
Doug Marion, *Plant Mgr*
EMP: 20
SQ FT: 7,896
SALES: 1.2MM **Privately Held**
SIC: 3369 Castings, except die-castings, precision

(G-20178)
VITAKRAFT SUN SEED INC
20584 Long Judson Rd (43569-9639)
P.O. Box 33, Bowling Green (43402-0033)
PHONE.....................419 832-1641
Brent Weinmann, *President*
Nate Brinkman, *COO*
Andy Messinger, *Exec VP*
Tim Norsen, *Natl Sales Mgr*
▲ EMP: 60
SQ FT: 50,000
SALES (est): 12.8MM **Privately Held**
WEB: www.sunseed.com
SIC: 2048 2047 Bird food, prepared; feeds, specialty: mice, guinea pig, etc.; dog & cat food

Wheelersburg
Scioto County

(G-20179)
CONNIES CANDLES
9103 Ohio River Rd (45694-1927)
P.O. Box 97 (45694-0097)
PHONE.....................740 574-1224
Connie Potters, *Owner*
William Potters, *Co-Owner*
EMP: 6
SALES: 300K **Privately Held**
WEB: www.conniescandles.com
SIC: 3999 Candles

(G-20180)
FORREST RAWLINS
Also Called: Rawlins Pallet & Lumber
902 Great Meadow Rd (45694-8465)
PHONE.....................740 778-3366
Forrest Rawlins, *Owner*
Debra Rawlins, *Co-Owner*
EMP: 4
SQ FT: 5,000
SALES: 150K **Privately Held**
SIC: 2448 Pallets, wood

(G-20181)
FUHRMANN ORCHARDS LLC
510 Hansgen Morgan Rd (45694-8839)
PHONE.....................740 776-6406
Susan Fuhrmann, *Partner*
Paul William Fuhrmann,
EMP: 5 EST: 1958
SALES (est): 380.4K **Privately Held**
SIC: 0175 0161 2099 Peach orchard; apple orchard; nectarine orchard; cantaloupe farm; pepper farm, sweet & hot (vegetables); cider, nonalcoholic

(G-20182)
GREG BLUME
Also Called: Copyrite Printing
7459 Ohio River Rd (45694)
P.O. Box 388 (45694-0388)
PHONE.....................740 574-2308
Greg Blume, *Owner*
EMP: 6
SALES: 330K **Privately Held**
SIC: 5999 2791 2789 2752 Trophies & plaques; typesetting; bookbinding & related work; commercial printing, offset

(G-20183)
PATRIOT HOLDINGS UNLIMITED LLC
Also Called: Patriot Building Solutions
956 Patriot Ridge Dr (45694-7822)
P.O. Box 58 (45694-0058)
PHONE.....................740 574-2112
Michael Russell, *Mng Member*
Kimberly Russell,
EMP: 4

SQ FT: 4,400
SALES: 50K **Privately Held**
SIC: 6553 3272 Real property subdividers & developers, cemetery lots only; building materials, except block or brick: concrete

(G-20184)
SCIOTO VOICE
1280 Dogwood Ridge Rd (45694-9322)
PHONE.....................740 574-5400
EMP: 3
SALES (est): 107K **Privately Held**
SIC: 2711 Newspapers

(G-20185)
SHIRT STOP LLC
11769 Gallia Pike Rd (45694-9540)
PHONE.....................740 574-4774
Peggy Ruggles, *Partner*
Terri Laxton, *Partner*
EMP: 4
SALES (est): 542.9K **Privately Held**
SIC: 2261 Screen printing of cotton broad-woven fabrics

(G-20186)
TRI-AMERICA CONTRACTORS INC (PA)
1664 State Route 522 (45694-7828)
PHONE.....................740 574-0148
Teresa Smith, *CEO*
Scott Taylor, *President*
John Mauk, *General Mgr*
Gregory Stanley, *General Mgr*
Paul Montgomery, *Superintendent*
EMP: 37
SQ FT: 34,000
SALES: 12MM **Privately Held**
WEB: www.triaminc.com
SIC: 3498 3441 1629 Fabricated pipe & fittings; fabricated structural metal; industrial plant construction

(G-20187)
TRI-AMERICA CONTRACTORS INC
1664 State Route 522 (45694-7828)
PHONE.....................740 574-0148
Teresa Smith, *Branch Mgr*
Nelson Smith, *Technology*
EMP: 8
SALES (est): 1.3MM
SALES (corp-wide): 12MM **Privately Held**
SIC: 3498 Fabricated pipe & fittings
PA: Tri-America Contractors, Inc.
1664 State Route 522
Wheelersburg OH 45694
740 574-0148

Whitehouse
Lucas County

(G-20188)
BASF CORPORATION
Coatings & Colorants Division
6125 Industrial Pkwy (43571-9595)
P.O. Box 2757 (43571-0757)
PHONE.....................419 877-5308
Kenneth Terry, *Engrg Dir*
EMP: 136
SQ FT: 20,000
SALES (corp-wide): 71.7B **Privately Held**
WEB: www.basf.com
SIC: 2869 Industrial organic chemicals
HQ: Basf Corporation
100 Park Ave
Florham Park NJ 07932
973 245-6000

(G-20189)
BITTERSWEET INC (PA)
Also Called: BITTERSWEET FARMS
12660 Archbold Whthuse Rd (43571-9566)
PHONE.....................419 875-6986
Vicki Obee-Hilty, *Exec Dir*
EMP: 62
SQ FT: 20,000
SALES: 6.7MM **Privately Held**
WEB: www.bittersweetfarms.org
SIC: 8361 2032 8052 Home for the mentally handicapped; canned specialties; intermediate care facilities

(G-20190)
G L HELLER CO INC
6246 Industrial Pkwy (43571-9594)
PHONE.....................419 877-5122
Gary Lee Heller, *President*
M Jean Heller, *Corp Secy*
Brian Heller, *Sales Associate*
Todd Heller, *Manager*
EMP: 14
SQ FT: 17,000
SALES (est): 2.4MM **Privately Held**
SIC: 3599 Machine shop, jobbing & repair; machine & other job shop work

(G-20191)
GENERAL INTL PWR PDTS LLC
6243 Industrial Pkwy (43571-9594)
PHONE.....................419 877-5234
Craig Valentine, *President*
EMP: 7
SALES (est): 1MM
SALES (corp-wide): 9.3MM **Privately Held**
SIC: 3553 Woodworking machinery
PA: Dmt Holdings, Inc.
33400 9th Ave S Ste 104
Federal Way WA 98003
253 545-0015

(G-20192)
KENNAMETAL INC
6325 Industrial Pkwy (43571-9792)
PHONE.....................419 877-5358
Mike Riley, *Purch Mgr*
Jerry Natter, *Engineer*
Rich Heban, *Senior Engr*
Gary Hankins, *Design Engr*
Fred Morgan, *Manager*
EMP: 118
SALES (corp-wide): 2.3B **Publicly Held**
SIC: 3545 Cutting tools for machine tools
PA: Kennametal Inc.
600 Grant St Ste 5100
Pittsburgh PA 15219
412 248-8000

(G-20193)
PROHOS INC
10755 Logan St (43571-9698)
PHONE.....................419 877-0153
William A Green, *President*
Joan Green, *Corp Secy*
Kevin Green, *Vice Pres*
EMP: 9
SQ FT: 18,000
SALES (est): 1.3MM **Privately Held**
WEB: www.prohos-inc.com
SIC: 3599 Machine shop, jobbing & repair

(G-20194)
PROHOS MANUFACTURING CO INC
10755 Logan St (43571-9698)
PHONE.....................419 877-0153
William Green, *President*
Joan Green, *Corp Secy*
EMP: 8
SQ FT: 18,000
SALES: 600K **Privately Held**
SIC: 3599 Machine shop, jobbing & repair; machine & other job shop work

Wickliffe
Lake County

(G-20195)
ACCURATE PLASMA CUTTING INC
1271 E 289th St (44092-2358)
P.O. Box 310 (44092-0310)
PHONE.....................440 943-1655
Gary Smith, *President*
EMP: 12
SALES (est): 2MM **Privately Held**
SIC: 3541 Plasma process metal cutting machines

(G-20196)
AJAX MANUFACTURING COMPANY
Also Called: Ajax - Ceco
29100 Lakeland Blvd (44092-2323)
PHONE.....................440 295-0244
Charlie Crout, *President*
Barry Yost, *Purch Mgr*
Wayne Byers, *Sales Staff*
Johanna Markko, *Sales Staff*
Margaret Hodakievic, *Technology*
▲ EMP: 21
SALES: 4.8MM
SALES (corp-wide): 1.6B **Publicly Held**
WEB: www.ajax-ceco.com
SIC: 3542 Forging machinery & hammers
HQ: Park-Ohio Industries, Inc.
6065 Parkland Blvd Ste 1
Cleveland OH 44124
440 947-2000

(G-20197)
AJAX TOCCO MAGNETHERMIC CORP
Also Called: Pines Engineering
29100 Lakeland Blvd (44092-2323)
PHONE.....................440 278-7200
Thomas Illencik, *President*
Kile F Snyder, *General Mgr*
EMP: 193
SALES (corp-wide): 1.6B **Publicly Held**
SIC: 3567 Industrial furnaces & ovens
HQ: Ajax Tocco Magnethermic Corporation
1745 Overland Ave Ne
Warren OH 44483
330 372-8511

(G-20198)
ANDY RUSSO JR INC
Also Called: A R J
29200 Anderson Rd (44092-2312)
PHONE.....................440 585-1456
Andy Russo Jr, *President*
Richard J Silvestro, *Principal*
EMP: 15
SQ FT: 30,000
SALES (est): 2MM **Privately Held**
WEB: www.arjinc.net
SIC: 1761 3444 Ceilings, metal: erection & repair; sheet metalwork

(G-20199)
BACO MANUFACTURING CORP
29175 Anderson Rd (44092-2357)
P.O. Box 329 (44092-0329)
PHONE.....................440 585-5858
John Garron, *President*
Marion Gulic, *President*
Robert A Gulic, *President*
EMP: 4
SQ FT: 4,000
SALES: 600K **Privately Held**
SIC: 3599 Machine shop, jobbing & repair

(G-20200)
BAR PROCESSING CORP
1271 E 289th St (44092-2358)
PHONE.....................440 943-0094
EMP: 3 EST: 2016
SALES (est): 505.9K **Privately Held**
SIC: 3599 Machine shop, jobbing & repair

(G-20201)
BAR TECH SERVICE INC
30012 Lakeland Blvd (44092-1745)
PHONE.....................440 943-5286
Randy Demell, *President*
EMP: 5
SALES (est): 591.3K **Privately Held**
WEB: www.bartechdesign.com
SIC: 3541 Machine tool replacement & repair parts, metal cutting types

(G-20202)
BERTIN STEEL PROCESSING INC
1271 E 289th St Ste 1 (44092-2358)
PHONE.....................440 943-0094
Bernard D'Ambrosi, *President*
Denny Perrino, *Vice Pres*
▲ EMP: 47
SQ FT: 300,000

SALES (est): 7.8MM **Privately Held**
WEB: www.bertinsteel.com
SIC: **3312** Bars & bar shapes, steel, cold-finished: own hot-rolled

(G-20203)
BEST PLATING RACK CORP
1321 E 289th St (44092-2350)
PHONE..................................440 944-3270
Robert Evatz, *Owner*
Barbara Evatz, *Co-Owner*
William Evatz, *Co-Owner*
EMP: 12
SALES (est): 1.4MM **Privately Held**
SIC: **3471** Plating of metals or formed products; electroplating of metals or formed products

(G-20204)
BICKFORD LABORATORIES INC
Also Called: Bickford Flavors
1197 E 305th St (44092-1520)
PHONE..................................440 354-7747
Barbara Sofer, *President*
EMP: 5
SQ FT: 2,000
SALES (est): 100K **Privately Held**
WEB: www.bickfordflavors.com
SIC: **2087** Extracts, flavoring

(G-20205)
BISON WLDG & FABRICATION INC
29301 Clayton Ave (44092-1907)
PHONE..................................440 944-4770
Theresa Bice, *President*
Lloyd Bice, *Vice Pres*
EMP: 5
SQ FT: 15,000
SALES (est): 675.1K **Privately Held**
SIC: **3441** Fabricated structural metal

(G-20206)
BREWER COMPANY
30060 Lakeland Blvd (44092-1745)
PHONE..................................440 944-3800
S Choromanski, *General Mgr*
EMP: 25
SQ FT: 73,188
SALES (corp-wide): 50MM **Privately Held**
WEB: www.thebrewerco.com
SIC: **2952** Coating compounds, tar
PA: The Brewer Company
1354 Us Route 50
Milford OH 45150
800 394-0017

(G-20207)
CLEVELAND SPECIAL TOOL INC
1351 E 286th St (44092-2505)
PHONE..................................440 944-1600
Jim Treblas, *President*
EMP: 13 EST: 1966
SQ FT: 6,000
SALES (est): 2.2MM **Privately Held**
SIC: **3599** Machine shop, jobbing & repair

(G-20208)
CP CHEMICALS GROUP LP
Also Called: CP Trading Group
28960 Lakeland Blvd (44092-2321)
PHONE..................................440 833-3000
Joseph Patrick III, *President*
EMP: 54
SALES (est): 7.6MM **Privately Held**
SIC: **2899** Chemical preparations

(G-20209)
DSM INDUSTRIES INC
1340 E 289th St (44092-2304)
PHONE..................................440 585-1100
Scott Soble, *President*
▲ EMP: 16 EST: 1944
SQ FT: 106,000
SALES (est): 3.7MM **Privately Held**
WEB: www.diamondshine.com
SIC: **2841** Soap: granulated, liquid, cake, flaked or chip; detergents, synthetic organic or inorganic alkaline

(G-20210)
EUCLID SPRING COMPANY INC
30006 Lakeland Blvd (44092-1745)
PHONE..................................440 943-3213
James L Marsey, *President*
Donald Seaburn, *Principal*
William J Marsey, *Vice Pres*
EMP: 22 EST: 1950
SQ FT: 7,000
SALES (est): 4.3MM **Privately Held**
WEB: www.euclidspring.com
SIC: **3493** Steel springs, except wire

(G-20211)
GREAT LAKES CRUSHING LTD
30831 Euclid Ave (44092-1042)
PHONE..................................440 944-5500
Mark M Belich, *General Ptnr*
EMP: 47 EST: 1996
SQ FT: 10,000
SALES (est): 23.9MM **Privately Held**
SIC: **1429** 7359 1623 1629 Igneous rock, crushed & broken-quarrying; equipment rental & leasing; office machine rental, except computers; underground utilities contractor; land clearing contractor; grading

(G-20212)
HAWTHORNE TOOL LLC
1340 Lloyd Rd Ste C (44092-2381)
PHONE..................................440 516-1891
Dominic Rega, *President*
Don G Nettis,
EMP: 10
SALES (est): 860K **Privately Held**
SIC: **3544** Dies & die holders for metal cutting, forming, die casting; die springs

(G-20213)
HI TECMETAL GROUP INC
Also Called: Brite Brazing
28910 Lakeland Blvd (44092-2321)
PHONE..................................440 373-5101
Duane Heinrich, *Manager*
EMP: 40
SALES (corp-wide): 25.2MM **Privately Held**
SIC: **3398** 7692 Metal heat treating; welding repair
PA: Hi Tecmetal Group Inc
1101 E 55th St
Cleveland OH 44103
216 881-8100

(G-20214)
KINETIC TECHNOLOGIES INC
1350 Rockefeller Rd (44092-1930)
PHONE..................................440 943-4111
Larry Tyler, *President*
John Neumann, *Vice Pres*
EMP: 17
SQ FT: 1,000
SALES (est): 5.3MM **Privately Held**
WEB: www.ktecinc.com
SIC: **3537** Industrial trucks & tractors

(G-20215)
LUBRIZOL CORPORATION (HQ)
Also Called: Lubricant Additives
29400 Lakeland Blvd (44092-2298)
PHONE..................................440 943-4200
James L Hambrick, *President*
Mark Wilson, *Business Mgr*
Stephen F Kirk, *COO*
David Borcas, *Vice Pres*
Tesham Gor, *Vice Pres*
◆ EMP: 1300 EST: 1928
SALES (est): 4.9B
SALES (corp-wide): 225.3B **Publicly Held**
WEB: www.lubrizol.com
SIC: **2899** 2869 Oil treating compounds; industrial organic chemicals
PA: Berkshire Hathaway Inc.
3555 Farnam St Ste 1140
Omaha NE 68131
402 346-1400

(G-20216)
MASTER GRINDING COMPANY INC
28917 Anderson Rd (44092-2307)
PHONE..................................440 944-3680
Brad Brown, *President*
Joy Brown, *Vice Pres*
Rich Fairbanks, *Manager*
EMP: 3
SQ FT: 3,000
SALES (est): 300K **Privately Held**
SIC: **3541** Grinding machines, metalworking

(G-20217)
MATTEO ALUMINUM INC
1261 E 289th St (44092-2367)
PHONE..................................440 585-5213
Steve Matteo, *President*
EMP: 20
SQ FT: 25,444
SALES: 13MM **Privately Held**
SIC: **3444** 3449 Gutters, sheet metal; miscellaneous metalwork

(G-20218)
MULTI LAPPING SERVICE INC
30032 Lakeland Blvd (44092)
PHONE..................................440 944-7592
Donna Wohr, *President*
Enos Adkins III, *Vice Pres*
Michael Adkins, *Vice Pres*
EMP: 12
SQ FT: 72,000
SALES (est): 1.2MM **Privately Held**
SIC: **3829** Whole body counters, nuclear

(G-20219)
NOVEON FCC INC
29400 Lakeland Blvd (44092-2201)
PHONE..................................440 943-4200
Charles P Cooley III, *Senior VP*
▼ EMP: 4
SALES (est): 718.9K
SALES (corp-wide): 225.3B **Publicly Held**
SIC: **2869** 2899 Industrial organic chemicals; chemical preparations
HQ: The Lubrizol Corporation
29400 Lakeland Blvd
Wickliffe OH 44092
440 943-4200

(G-20220)
OMCO HOLDINGS INC (PA)
30396 Lakeland Blvd (44092-1748)
PHONE..................................440 944-2100
Ben Yorks, *Ch of Bd*
Gary Schuster, *President*
Nathan Schuster, *Business Mgr*
Clark Lichtinger, *Purch Agent*
Clint Cassese, *CFO*
EMP: 30
SALES (est): 52.7MM **Privately Held**
SIC: **3449** Miscellaneous metalwork

(G-20221)
P O MCINTIRE COMPANY (PA)
29191 Anderson Rd (44092-2357)
PHONE..................................440 269-1848
James Goglin, *President*
Scott Goglin, *Vice Pres*
EMP: 27 EST: 1938
SQ FT: 12,000
SALES (est): 1.8MM **Privately Held**
WEB: www.pomcintire.com
SIC: **3545** 3544 Cutting tools for machine tools; reamers, machine tool; jigs & fixtures

(G-20222)
P R W TOOL INC
30036 Lakeland Blvd (44092-1745)
PHONE..................................440 585-3373
Bill Satyshur, *President*
David Satyshur, *Vice Pres*
EMP: 3
SQ FT: 3,000
SALES: 60K **Privately Held**
SIC: **3599** Machine shop, jobbing & repair

(G-20223)
PANELTECH LLC
1430 Lloyd Rd (44092-2320)
PHONE..................................440 516-1300
Andrea Christensen,
EMP: 11
SALES (est): 2.2MM **Privately Held**
SIC: **3825** Test equipment for electronic & electric measurement

(G-20224)
PARKER-HANNIFIN CORPORATION
Hose Products Div
30240 Lakeland Blvd (44092-1797)
PHONE..................................440 943-5700
James Blaha, *Principal*
Robert Kennedy, *Project Engr*
Paul Sirko, *Human Res Mgr*
Lonnie Gallup, *Branch Mgr*
Becki Ramsay, *Senior Mgr*
EMP: 271
SQ FT: 145,000
SALES (corp-wide): 14.3B **Publicly Held**
WEB: www.parker.com
SIC: **3714** 3492 Motor vehicle parts & accessories; fluid power valves & hose fittings
PA: Parker-Hannifin Corporation
6035 Parkland Blvd
Cleveland OH 44124
216 896-3000

(G-20225)
PARKER-HANNIFIN CORPORATION
Also Called: Industrial Hose Product Div
30242 Lakeland Blvd (44092-1747)
PHONE..................................440 943-5700
Dan Barrett, *Branch Mgr*
EMP: 36
SALES (corp-wide): 14.3B **Publicly Held**
WEB: www.parker.com
SIC: **3492** Hose & tube fittings & assemblies, hydraulic/pneumatic; hose & tube couplings, hydraulic/pneumatic
PA: Parker-Hannifin Corporation
6035 Parkland Blvd
Cleveland OH 44124
216 896-3000

(G-20226)
PCC CERAMIC GROUP 1
1470 E 289th St (44092-2306)
PHONE..................................440 516-3672
Daren Kennedy, *Vice Pres*
EMP: 9
SALES (est): 450K **Privately Held**
SIC: **3253** Floor tile, ceramic

(G-20227)
PMC INDUSTRIES CORP
Also Called: A Park Ohio Company
29100 Lakeland Blvd (44092-2323)
PHONE..................................440 943-3300
Edward K Novak, *Vice Pres*
Christine Hope, *Production*
Tim Jackson, *Purch Mgr*
Paul Znidar, *Sales Staff*
▲ EMP: 85 EST: 1912
SQ FT: 125,000
SALES (est): 19MM
SALES (corp-wide): 1.6B **Publicly Held**
WEB: www.pmcindustries.com
SIC: **3317** Steel pipe & tubes
HQ: Park-Ohio Industries, Inc.
6065 Parkland Blvd Ste 1
Cleveland OH 44124
440 947-2000

(G-20228)
PRECIOUS METAL PLATING CO
30335 Palisades Pkwy (44092-1598)
PHONE..................................440 585-7117
Thomas Talty III, *President*
EMP: 22
SQ FT: 14,000
SALES (est): 2.8MM **Privately Held**
WEB: www.preciousmetalplating.com
SIC: **3471** Electroplating of metals or formed products; gold plating

(G-20229)
REGAL DIAMOND PRODUCTS CORP
1405 E 286th St (44092-2506)
P.O. Box 198 (44092-0198)
PHONE..................................440 944-7700
Steve Brewer, *President*
Robert Simcic, *Plant Mgr*
Bob Gray, *Sales Mgr*
▼ EMP: 22 EST: 1958
SQ FT: 16,500

Wickliffe - Lake County (G-20230)

SALES (est): 3.1MM **Privately Held**
SIC: 3291 3545 3425 Abrasive wheels & grindstones, not artificial; cutting tools for machine tools; saw blades & handsaws

(G-20230)
RESEARCH ABRASIVE PRODUCTS INC
1400 E 286th St (44092-2507)
PHONE.....................................440 944-3200
Ken Dixon Sr, *President*
Ken Dixon Jr, *Vice Pres*
Kathy Matt, *Vice Pres*
Margaret Tripp, *Executive*
EMP: 40
SQ FT: 32,000
SALES (est): 5.1MM **Privately Held**
WEB: www.researchabrasive.com
SIC: 3291 Wheels, abrasive

(G-20231)
SPEEDWAY LLC
Also Called: Speedway Superamerica 3027
29201 Euclid Ave (44092-2359)
PHONE.....................................440 943-0044
EMP: 10
SALES (corp-wide): 82.4B **Publicly Held**
SIC: 1311 Crude Petroleum & Natural Gas
HQ: Speedway Llc
    500 Speedway Dr
    Enon OH 45323
    937 864-3000

(G-20232)
THERMAL TREATMENT CENTER INC
Nettleton Steel Treating Div
28910 Lakeland Blvd (44092-2321)
PHONE.....................................440 943-4555
Rodney Holstein, *Manager*
EMP: 47
SQ FT: 13,000
SALES (corp-wide): 25.2MM **Privately Held**
WEB: www.htg.cc
SIC: 3398 Brazing (hardening) of metal
HQ: Thermal Treatment Center Inc
    1101 E 55th St
    Cleveland OH 44103
    216 881-8100

(G-20233)
UMICORE SPCLTY MTLS RECYCL LLC
28960 Lakeland Blvd (44092-2321)
PHONE.....................................440 833-3000
Ben Gilliams, *CEO*
Galen Jones, *President*
Jesse Ferreira, *Controller*
Gretchen Nystrand, *Human Res Mgr*
▲ EMP: 60
SALES (est): 11.5MM
SALES (corp-wide): 3.3B **Privately Held**
SIC: 3341 Recovery & refining of nonferrous metals
HQ: Umicore Usa Inc.
    3600 Glenwood Ave Ste 250
    Raleigh NC 27612

(G-20234)
UNITED HYDRAULICS
29627 Lakeland Blvd (44092-2203)
PHONE.....................................440 585-0906
John Birkic, *President*
EMP: 15
SALES (est): 1.3MM **Privately Held**
WEB: www.unitedhydraulics.com
SIC: 3593 5084 Fluid power cylinders, hydraulic or pneumatic; industrial machinery & equipment

(G-20235)
UNIVERSAL METAL PRODUCTS INC (PA)
Also Called: Hercules
29980 Lakeland Blvd (44092-1744)
P.O. Box 130 (44092-0130)
PHONE.....................................440 943-3040
Hugh S Seaholm, *CEO*
Ken Bateman, *Vice Pres*
Jaime Martinez, *Plant Mgr*
Keith Shadle, *Mfg Mgr*
Michelle Hudd, *Accountant*
▲ EMP: 250
SQ FT: 15,000
SALES: 60MM **Privately Held**
WEB: www.ump-inc.com
SIC: 3469 Stamping metal for the trade

(G-20236)
USM PRECISION PRODUCTS INC
Also Called: U S M
1340 Lloyd Rd Ste D (44092-2381)
PHONE.....................................440 975-8600
Donald R Nettis, *President*
Ken Marvar, *Vice Pres*
Derek West, *VP Sales*
Miroslav Nadinic, *Supervisor*
EMP: 100 EST: 1979
SQ FT: 55,000
SALES (est): 15.9MM
SALES (corp-wide): 9.5MM **Privately Held**
WEB: www.usmonline.com
SIC: 3451 Screw machine products
PA: Usm Acquisition Corporation
    2002 Joseph Lloyd Pkwy
    Willoughby OH 44094
    440 975-8600

Wilberforce
Greene County

(G-20237)
SPEEDWAY LLC
Also Called: Speedway Superamerica 5839
1455 Brush Row Rd (45384-1300)
PHONE.....................................937 372-7129
Timothy Gosnell, *President*
EMP: 10 **Publicly Held**
WEB: www.speedwaynet.com
SIC: 1311 Crude petroleum production
HQ: Speedway Llc
    500 Speedway Dr
    Enon OH 45323
    937 864-3000

Willard
Huron County

(G-20238)
CAROLS ULTRA STITCH & VARIETY
122 S Myrtle Ave (44890-1425)
PHONE.....................................419 935-8991
Carol Barnett, *Owner*
EMP: 8
SQ FT: 4,000
SALES (est): 547.7K **Privately Held**
SIC: 5699 2395 Customized clothing & apparel; T-shirts, custom printed; embroidery products, except schiffli machine

(G-20239)
DONALD SCHLOEMER
Also Called: Schloemer, Don Masonry
2441 Niver Rd (44890-9669)
PHONE.....................................419 933-2002
Donald Schloemer, *Owner*
EMP: 4
SALES: 350K **Privately Held**
SIC: 1741 3272 Chimney construction & maintenance; concrete products, precast

(G-20240)
GUARDIAN MANUFACTURING CO LLC
Also Called: Guardian Gloves
302 S Conwell Ave (44890-9525)
PHONE.....................................419 933-2711
Gene Lamoreaux, *President*
Ron Vanderpool, *Treasurer*
Cynthia Showman, *Human Res Mgr*
Doug Boyer, *Manager*
Brian Sebastian, *Manager*
▲ EMP: 25
SQ FT: 100,000
SALES (est): 5.8MM **Privately Held**
WEB: www.guardian-mfg.com
SIC: 3069 3842 Medical & laboratory rubber sundries & related products; surgical appliances & supplies

(G-20241)
LSC COMMUNICATIONS INC
Also Called: Manufacturing Division
1145 S Conwell Ave (44890-9392)
PHONE.....................................419 935-0111
Robert Gospodarek, *Opers-Prdtn-Mfg*
EMP: 980
SALES (corp-wide): 3.8B **Publicly Held**
WEB: www.rrdonnelley.com
SIC: 2741 2732 2759 2752 Directories: publishing & printing; books: printing only; commercial printing; commercial printing, lithographic
PA: Lsc Communications, Inc.
    191 N Wacker Dr Ste 1400
    Chicago IL 60606
    773 272-9200

(G-20242)
MTD PRODUCTS INC
Midwest Industries
979 S Conwell Ave (44890-9301)
PHONE.....................................419 935-6611
Rob Fox, *General Mgr*
Jerry Shepherd, *General Mgr*
Matt Bahleda, *Opers Mgr*
Jeff Diamond, *Safety Mgr*
Smith Keviin, *Engineer*
EMP: 800
SQ FT: 480,000
SALES (corp-wide): 2.4B **Privately Held**
WEB: www.mtdproducts.com
SIC: 3524 Lawn & garden mowers & accessories
HQ: Mtd Products Inc
    5965 Grafton Rd
    Valley City OH 44280
    330 225-2600

(G-20243)
NUTRIFRESH EGGS
342 Plymouth East Rd (44890-9579)
PHONE.....................................567 224-7676
Dean Steiner, *Managing Prtnr*
EMP: 5 EST: 2011
SALES: 500K **Privately Held**
SIC: 2015 Chicken, processed: fresh

(G-20244)
PEPPERIDGE FARM INCORPORATED
3320 State Route 103 E (44890-9777)
PHONE.....................................419 933-2611
George Litvak, *Branch Mgr*
EMP: 9
SALES (corp-wide): 8.6B **Publicly Held**
WEB: www.pepperidgefarm.com
SIC: 5145 2052 2099 2053 Snack foods; cookies; bread crumbs, not made in bakeries; frozen bakery products, except bread
HQ: Pepperidge Farm, Incorporated
    595 Westport Ave
    Norwalk CT 06851
    203 846-7000

(G-20245)
SNEAKY PETE BAND
4418 N Greenfield Rd (44890-9527)
PHONE.....................................419 933-6251
EMP: 3
SALES (est): 140K **Privately Held**
SIC: 2836 Mfg Biological Products

(G-20246)
TIN SHED LLC
6 S Myrtle Ave (44890-1423)
PHONE.....................................330 636-2524
EMP: 4
SALES (est): 370.9K **Privately Held**
SIC: 3356 Tin

(G-20247)
V & R MOLDED PRODUCTS INC
181 Us Highway 224 W (44890-9788)
PHONE.....................................419 752-4171
EMP: 10
SQ FT: 23,000
SALES (est): 82.3K **Privately Held**
SIC: 3089 Mfg Plastic Products

(G-20248)
WEAVER BOOS CONSULTANTS INC
1145 S Conwell Ave (44890-9392)
PHONE.....................................419 933-5216
Dirk Hiler, *Manager*
EMP: 14
SALES (corp-wide): 29.1MM **Privately Held**
SIC: 2731 Book publishing
PA: Weaver Boos Consultants, Inc.
    35 E Wacker Dr Ste 1250
    Chicago IL 60601
    312 922-1030

(G-20249)
WILLARD TIMES JUNCTION
211 S Myrtle Ave (44890-1407)
P.O. Box 368 (44890-0368)
PHONE.....................................419 935-0184
Scott Gove, *Owner*
EMP: 13
SALES (est): 414.4K **Privately Held**
SIC: 2711 Newspapers: publishing only, not printed on site

Williamsburg
Clermont County

(G-20250)
AEC BREWS LLC DBA OLD FRHUSE B
Also Called: Old Firehouse Brewery
237 W Main St (45176-1342)
PHONE.....................................513 536-9071
Adam Cowan,
Lori Ward,
▲ EMP: 6
SALES: 750K **Privately Held**
SIC: 2082 Malt liquors

(G-20251)
G & L MACHINING INC
299 N 3rd St (45176-8101)
PHONE.....................................513 724-2600
Gary Abrams, *President*
Leslie Abrams, *President*
EMP: 8
SQ FT: 4,000
SALES (est): 1.1MM **Privately Held**
SIC: 3599 Machine shop, jobbing & repair

(G-20252)
IV M TOOL & DIE
3227 Us Highway 50 (45176-6202)
PHONE.....................................513 625-6464
Patti Mallaley, *Owner*
EMP: 4
SQ FT: 15,000
SALES (est): 411.7K **Privately Held**
SIC: 3599 3544 Machine shop, jobbing & repair; special dies, tools, jigs & fixtures

(G-20253)
PATCHES LLC
1696 Pin Oak Ln (45176-9106)
PHONE.....................................513 304-4882
Jeff Clock, *Principal*
EMP: 3
SALES (est): 240K **Privately Held**
SIC: 2298 Cargo nets

(G-20254)
R & L WOOD PRODUCTS
16137 Eastwood Rd (45176-9338)
PHONE.....................................937 444-2496
Robert L Lodwick, *Owner*
EMP: 7
SALES (est): 678.4K **Privately Held**
SIC: 2421 Lumber: rough, sawed or planed; kiln drying of lumber

(G-20255)
STEPHEN J PAGE
143 Winding Trails Dr (45176-1475)
PHONE.....................................865 951-3316
Stephen Page, *Owner*
EMP: 3
SALES (est): 102.6K **Privately Held**
SIC: 2511 2521 2541 7389 Wood household furniture; wood office furniture; store & office display cases & fixtures;

GEOGRAPHIC SECTION

Willoughby - Lake County (G-20284)

(G-20256)
W&W ROCK SAND AND GRAVEL
1451 Maple Grove Rd (45176-9636)
P.O. Box 640 (45176-0640)
PHONE..................513 266-3708
Rick A Wuebold, *Principal*
EMP: 6
SALES (est): 366.5K **Privately Held**
SIC: 1442 Construction sand & gravel

(G-20257)
WOLFE OIL COMPANY LLC
2944 Quitter Rd (45176-8211)
PHONE..................513 732-6220
Lance Wolfe, *Principal*
EMP: 3
SALES (est): 222.7K **Privately Held**
SIC: 3559 Petroleum refinery equipment

(G-20258)
ZIPPER MANUFACTURING LLC
16698 Edgington Rd (45176-6531)
PHONE..................937 444-0904
William A Dunn, *Principal*
EMP: 6 **EST:** 2008
SALES (est): 517.4K **Privately Held**
SIC: 3965 Zipper

Williamsfield
Ashtabula County

(G-20259)
PREMIER STAMPING AND ASSEMBLY
Also Called: Premiere Stamping
7924 Mill St (44093-9757)
PHONE..................440 293-8961
Christopher Mott, *President*
Nikki Mott, *Corp Secy*
EMP: 3
SQ FT: 9,000
SALES (est): 220K **Privately Held**
SIC: 3469 3444 Stamping metal for the trade; sheet metalwork

Williamsport
Pickaway County

(G-20260)
R GORDON JONES INC
Also Called: Jet Electric
20849 Five Points Pike (43164-9708)
PHONE..................740 986-8381
R Gordon Jones, *President*
Marcia Eyre, *Manager*
EMP: 5
SQ FT: 5,000
SALES (est): 1MM **Privately Held**
WEB: www.jetelectric.com
SIC: 3621 Motors & generators

(G-20261)
ROOF TO ROAD LLC
27910 Chillicothe Pike (43164-9654)
PHONE..................740 986-6923
Stephen Johnson, *Mng Member*
Slyvia Johnson, *Agent*
Alfred Johnson,
EMP: 7
SALES (est): 1.2MM **Privately Held**
SIC: 2951 Road materials, bituminous (not from refineries)

Williston
Ottawa County

(G-20262)
DURIVAGE PATTERN & MFG CO
20522 State Route 579 W (43468)
P.O. Box 337 (43468-0337)
PHONE..................419 836-8655
Gary Durivage, *President*
Gretchen Durivage, *Corp Secy*
Larry Durivage, *Vice Pres*
Ron Miller, *Vice Pres*
EMP: 30
SQ FT: 24,000
SALES (est): 4.9MM **Privately Held**
WEB: www.durivagepattern.com
SIC: 3469 3544 3369 3365 Patterns on metal; industrial molds; nonferrous foundries; aluminum foundries; steel foundries; laminated plastics plate & sheet

Willoughby
Lake County

(G-20263)
A & D PRINTING CO
Also Called: Sterling Media
38287 Airport Pkwy Ste A (44094-8066)
PHONE..................440 975-8001
Dean Sterling, *President*
EMP: 5
SQ FT: 2,000
SALES (est): 400K **Privately Held**
SIC: 2752 Commercial printing, offset

(G-20264)
A M D
4580 Beidler Rd (44094-4602)
PHONE..................440 918-8930
Mike Bollas, *Manager*
EMP: 3
SALES (est): 348.9K **Privately Held**
SIC: 3674 Integrated circuits, semiconductor networks, etc.

(G-20265)
A&S MACHINE
38363 Western Pkwy Unit 1 (44094-8843)
PHONE..................440 946-3976
Allan Bockhoff, *Owner*
EMP: 4
SALES (est): 412.8K **Privately Held**
SIC: 3599 Machine shop, jobbing & repair

(G-20266)
ACE GRINDING CO
37518 N Industrial Pkwy (44094-6279)
PHONE..................440 951-6760
Brian Danolfo, *President*
EMP: 6 **EST:** 1956
SQ FT: 12,000
SALES (est): 657.7K **Privately Held**
SIC: 3999 Custom pulverizing & grinding of plastic materials; education aids, devices & supplies

(G-20267)
ADVANCED RV LLC
4590 Hamann Pkwy (44094-5630)
PHONE..................440 283-0405
Mike Neundorfer, *President*
EMP: 5 **EST:** 2012
SALES (est): 610.3K **Privately Held**
SIC: 3716 7519 7532 Motor homes; motor home rental; mobile home & trailer repair

(G-20268)
AIRCRAFT WELDING INC
38335 Apollo Pkwy Unit 1 (44094-7795)
PHONE..................440 951-3863
Michael Horvath, *President*
Patricia Horvath, *Admin Sec*
EMP: 8 **EST:** 1990
SQ FT: 6,500
SALES (est): 1MM **Privately Held**
WEB: www.aircraftweldinginc.com
SIC: 7692 Welding repair

(G-20269)
ALD GROUP LLC
34201 Melinz Pkwy Unit A (44095-4018)
P.O. Box 435, Cleveland (44107-0435)
PHONE..................440 942-9800
Don Defonzo, *General Mgr*
Don Difonzo, *Mng Member*
EMP: 6
SQ FT: 10,000
SALES (est): 900.6K **Privately Held**
WEB: www.aldgroup.net
SIC: 3541 Machine tool replacement & repair parts, metal cutting types

(G-20270)
AMD FABRICATORS INC
4580 Beidler Rd (44094-4602)
PHONE..................440 946-8855
Michael Watts, *President*
EMP: 20
SQ FT: 50,000
SALES (est): 3.3MM **Privately Held**
SIC: 3444 Sheet metalwork

(G-20271)
AMETCO MANUFACTURING CORP
4326 Hamann Pkwy (44094-5626)
P.O. Box 1210 (44096-1210)
PHONE..................440 951-4300
Steve G Mitrovich, *President*
Greg Mitrovich, *Vice Pres*
Rona Mitrovich, *Vice Pres*
Brad Pelt, *Project Mgr*
Jack Stapleton, *Purch Mgr*
▲ **EMP:** 38 **EST:** 1966
SQ FT: 85,000
SALES (est): 9.8MM **Privately Held**
WEB: www.ametco.com
SIC: 3441 Fabricated structural metal

(G-20272)
AMFM INC
Also Called: Omega One
38373 Pelton Rd (44094-7719)
PHONE..................440 953-4545
Morgun McIntosh, *President*
John Drcar, *General Mgr*
▲ **EMP:** 37
SALES (est): 6MM **Privately Held**
SIC: 2241 Braids, textile

(G-20273)
ANDERSON BROTHERS ENTPS INC
38180 Airport Pkwy (44094-8021)
PHONE..................440 269-3920
H W Domeck, *President*
Tenneth Anderson, *President*
Theresa Inman, *Controller*
EMP: 20 **EST:** 1945
SQ FT: 52,000
SALES (est): 4.2MM
SALES (corp-wide): 59.9MM **Privately Held**
SIC: 2035 Pickles, sauces & salad dressings
PA: The Fremont Company
802 N Front St
Fremont OH 43420
419 334-8995

(G-20274)
API PATTERN WORKS INC
4456 Hamann Pkwy (44094-5628)
PHONE..................440 269-1766
Jesse Baden, *President*
Michael Scanlon, *Corp Secy*
EMP: 45
SQ FT: 20,000
SALES (est): 3MM **Privately Held**
SIC: 3543 Industrial patterns

(G-20275)
APOLLO PRODUCTS INC
4456 Hamann Pkwy (44094-5628)
PHONE..................440 269-8551
Jess Baden, *President*
Michael Scanlon, *Corp Secy*
EMP: 15
SQ FT: 5,000
SALES (est): 2.4MM **Privately Held**
SIC: 3544 3545 Special dies & tools; machine tool accessories

(G-20276)
APOLLO WELDING & FABG INC (PA)
35600 Curtis Blvd (44095-4109)
PHONE..................440 942-0227
John Turkalj, *President*
Mary Turkalj, *Corp Secy*
Doug Barth, *Vice Pres*
EMP: 20
SQ FT: 25,000
SALES (est): 2.8MM **Privately Held**
SIC: 7692 Welding repair

(G-20277)
APPLIED CONCEPTS INC
Also Called: Applied Bingo Mate
36445 Biltmore Pl Ste E (44094-8228)
PHONE..................440 229-5033
John Adams, *President*
John Q Adams, *Corp Secy*
Tom Marzella, *Vice Pres*
Robert Koopman, *Sales Staff*
EMP: 11
SQ FT: 3,000
SALES (est): 1.5MM **Privately Held**
SIC: 3944 Electronic game machines, except coin-operated

(G-20278)
APR TOOL INC
4712 Beidler Rd Ste A (44094-4604)
PHONE..................440 946-0393
Robert Zietz, *President*
John Zeitz, *Vice Pres*
EMP: 9 **EST:** 1974
SQ FT: 3,200
SALES (est): 977.5K **Privately Held**
SIC: 3599 3544 Machine shop, jobbing & repair; dies & die holders for metal cutting, forming, die casting

(G-20279)
AQUA LILY PRODUCTS LLC (PA)
4485 Glenbrook Rd (44094-8219)
PHONE..................951 246-9610
Craig Cushman, *Principal*
Brian Cannon,
Donna Cannon,
EMP: 14
SALES: 3.3MM **Privately Held**
SIC: 3086 7389 Padding, foamed plastic;

(G-20280)
AQUENT STUDIOS
33433 Curtis Blvd (44095-4457)
PHONE..................216 266-7551
Dave Puette, *Manager*
EMP: 5
SALES (est): 55K **Privately Held**
SIC: 2741 Miscellaneous publishing

(G-20281)
ARTISTIC FINISHES INC
38357 Apollo Pkwy (44094-7723)
PHONE..................440 951-7850
Michael Credico, *President*
Bonnie Credico, *Corp Secy*
Robert Fine, *Vice Pres*
EMP: 18
SALES (est): 1.7MM **Privately Held**
WEB: www.artisticfinishes.net
SIC: 2541 2511 Store fixtures, wood; wood household furniture

(G-20282)
ASCENDTECH INC
4772 E 355th St (44094-4632)
PHONE..................216 458-1101
Igor Lapinskiy, *President*
Gary Lapinskiy, *General Mgr*
EMP: 35
SALES (est): 8.3MM **Privately Held**
SIC: 5045 7379 3571 7378 Computer peripheral equipment; computer related maintenance services; electronic computers; computer peripheral equipment repair & maintenance; electrical repair shops; scrap & waste materials

(G-20283)
B V GRINDING MACHINING INC
1438 E 363rd St (44095-4136)
PHONE..................440 918-1884
Ivica Begovic, *President*
EMP: 8
SALES (est): 1.2MM **Privately Held**
WEB: www.bvgrinding.com
SIC: 3541 Grinding machines, metalworking

(G-20284)
BENDER CYCLE & MACHINE CORP
1476 E 359th St (44095-4123)
PHONE..................440 946-0681
Ronald Bender, *President*
EMP: 5

Willoughby - Lake County (G-20285)

SQ FT: 3,500
SALES (est): 430K **Privately Held**
SIC: 3599 Machine shop, jobbing & repair

(G-20285)
BESCAST INC
4600 E 355th St (44094-4699)
PHONE..................440 946-5300
David M Brown, *Principal*
John W Gallagher, *Principal*
Russ Gallagher, *Vice Pres*
John Gallagher, *Vice Pres*
Scott Sutch, *Facilities Mgr*
▲ EMP: 170 EST: 1945
SQ FT: 85,000
SALES (est): 40.9MM **Privately Held**
WEB: www.bescast.com
SIC: 3324 Aerospace investment castings, ferrous

(G-20286)
BRANDTS CANDIES
1238 Lost Nation Rd (44094-7325)
PHONE..................440 942-1016
Theodore Prindle, *President*
Barbara Tabernick, *Manager*
EMP: 7 EST: 1948
SQ FT: 3,000
SALES: 700K **Privately Held**
WEB: www.brandts-candies.com
SIC: 5441 2066 Candy; chocolate & cocoa products

(G-20287)
BRIGHTGUY INC
38205b Stevens Blvd (44094-6239)
PHONE..................440 942-8318
Gregory Atwell, *President*
Tina Fram, *VP Sales*
Stephanie Fram, *Marketing Staff*
EMP: 6
SALES (est): 945.2K **Privately Held**
SIC: 3648 Lighting equipment

(G-20288)
BRONCO MACHINE INC
38411 Apollo Pkwy (44094-7725)
PHONE..................440 951-5015
Michael Bronaka, *President*
Ann Turpin, *Vice Pres*
Diana Bronaka, *Treasurer*
EMP: 10 EST: 1962
SQ FT: 6,000
SALES (est): 1.6MM **Privately Held**
WEB: www.broncomachine.com
SIC: 3451 Screw machine products

(G-20289)
BUD INDUSTRIES INC (PA)
4605 E 355th St (44094-4600)
PHONE..................440 946-3200
Blair K Haas, *President*
Stephen H Haas, *President*
Stephen Haas, *Exec VP*
Greg A Haas, *Vice Pres*
Ravi Jain, *Engineer*
▲ EMP: 4 EST: 1928
SQ FT: 170,000
SALES (est): 17.4MM **Privately Held**
WEB: www.budind.com
SIC: 3469 3672 3644 3643 Electronic enclosures, stamped or pressed metal; printed circuit boards; noncurrent-carrying wiring services; current-carrying wiring devices; switchgear & switchboard apparatus; partitions & fixtures, except wood

(G-20290)
BULLSEYE DART SHOPPE INC
950c Erie Rd (44095-1811)
PHONE..................440 951-9277
Thomas Nazarak, *President*
▲ EMP: 8
SQ FT: 14,000
SALES (est): 679.5K **Privately Held**
WEB: www.bullseyetcnaz.com
SIC: 3949 Billiard & pool equipment & supplies, general

(G-20291)
BV THERMAL SYSTEMS LLC
38241 Willoughby Pkwy (44094-7582)
PHONE..................209 522-3701
EMP: 10
SALES (est): 1.3MM **Privately Held**
SIC: 3625 Mfg Relays/Industrial Controls

(G-20292)
CARBIDE SPECIALIST INC
36430 Reading Ave Ste 10 (44094-8220)
PHONE..................440 951-4027
Ray Northern, *President*
Naomi Northern, *Corp Secy*
EMP: 12
SALES: 200K **Privately Held**
SIC: 3544 Wire drawing & straightening dies

(G-20293)
CASTMOR PRODUCTS INC
4708 Beidler Rd (44094-4604)
P.O. Box 70 (44096-0070)
PHONE..................440 953-1103
Edward A Marvin, *President*
Craig Marvin, *Vice Pres*
EMP: 4
SQ FT: 4,800
SALES: 1MM **Privately Held**
SIC: 3369 Zinc & zinc-base alloy castings, except die-castings

(G-20294)
CENTER LINE DRILLING INC
33000 Lakeland Blvd (44095-5203)
PHONE..................440 951-5920
Mike Burgess, *President*
David Rockefeller, *Vice Pres*
EMP: 3
SALES: 370K **Privately Held**
WEB: www.centerlinedrilling.com
SIC: 3599 Machine shop, jobbing & repair

(G-20295)
CENTRAL COCA-COLA BTLG CO INC
4800 E 355th St (44094-4634)
PHONE..................440 269-1433
Valerie Nobacco, *Manager*
EMP: 60
SALES (corp-wide): 35.4B **Publicly Held**
WEB: www.colasic.net
SIC: 2086 Bottled & canned soft drinks
HQ: Central Coca-Cola Bottling Company, Inc.
555 Taxter Rd Ste 550
Elmsford NY 10523
914 789-1100

(G-20296)
CHIPS MANUFACTURING INC
35720 Lakeland Blvd (44095-5307)
PHONE..................440 946-3666
Frank Cipriano, *President*
EMP: 8
SQ FT: 7,200
SALES (est): 1.2MM **Privately Held**
SIC: 3599 Machine shop, jobbing & repair

(G-20297)
COIT TOOL COMPANY INC
38134 Western Pkwy Unit 3 (44094-7588)
PHONE..................440 946-3377
Russell P Bliss, *President*
Judy Arnold, *Office Mgr*
EMP: 10
SQ FT: 6,400
SALES (est): 1.8MM **Privately Held**
SIC: 3599 Machine shop, jobbing & repair

(G-20298)
COMMERCIAL ANODIZING CO
38387 Apollo Pkwy (44094-7791)
PHONE..................440 942-8384
Mark S Swetel, *President*
Shirley Swetel, *Corp Secy*
EMP: 20
SQ FT: 20,000
SALES (est): 2.3MM **Privately Held**
SIC: 3471 Anodizing (plating) of metals or formed products; coloring & finishing of aluminum or formed products

(G-20299)
CONCORDE CASTINGS INC
34000 Lakeland Blvd (44095-5213)
PHONE..................440 953-0053
Joe Weber, *President*
EMP: 4 EST: 2015
SALES (est): 334.6K **Privately Held**
SIC: 3369 Nonferrous foundries

(G-20300)
CONN-SELMER INC
Also Called: Eastlake Mfg Facility
34199 Curtis Blvd (44095-4008)
PHONE..................440 946-6100
Robert Stone, *Manager*
EMP: 300
SQ FT: 140,000
SALES (corp-wide): 318.4MM **Privately Held**
WEB: www.conn-selmer.com
SIC: 3931 Guitars & parts, electric & non-electric
HQ: Conn-Selmer, Inc.
600 Industrial Pkwy
Elkhart IN 46516
574 522-1675

(G-20301)
CORTEST INC
38322 Apollo Pkwy (44094-7724)
PHONE..................440 942-1235
Allen F Denzine, *President*
Genti Cini, *Engineer*
Stephen Kubiak, *Project Engr*
Marsha Denzine, *Admin Sec*
EMP: 14
SQ FT: 10,000
SALES (est): 3.1MM **Privately Held**
SIC: 3821 5084 Laboratory apparatus & furniture; industrial machinery & equipment

(G-20302)
COUNTY OF LAKE
Also Called: Lake Cnty Deptmntl Retrdtn/Dvl
2100 Joseph Lloyd Pkwy (44094-8032)
PHONE..................440 269-2193
Gary Metelko, *Director*
EMP: 72 **Privately Held**
WEB: www.lakecountyohio.gov
SIC: 8322 8331 3441 Individual & family services; job training & vocational rehabilitation services; fabricated structural metal
PA: County Of Lake
8 N State St Ste 215
Painesville OH 44077
440 350-2500

(G-20303)
CREST AWNING & HOME IMPRV CO
1571 E 361st St Bldg 1 (44095-5328)
PHONE..................440 942-3092
EMP: 3
SALES: 300K **Privately Held**
SIC: 3444 Mfg Alluminum Awnings

(G-20304)
D & D QUALITY MACHINING CO INC
36495 Reading Ave Ste 1 (44094-8243)
PHONE..................440 942-2772
Zarko Duvnjak, *President*
EMP: 15
SALES (est): 2.3MM **Privately Held**
SIC: 3599 Machine shop, jobbing & repair

(G-20305)
D S H MACHINE CO
36255 Reading Ave Ste A (44094-8236)
PHONE..................440 946-4311
Kenneth Lekes, *President*
Diane P Sustar, *Corp Secy*
EMP: 4
SQ FT: 6,000
SALES (est): 412.2K **Privately Held**
SIC: 3599 Machine shop, jobbing & repair

(G-20306)
DAI CERAMICS INC
38240 Airport Pkwy (44094-8023)
PHONE..................440 946-6964
Richard Ruggerio, *President*
Carole Coughlin, *Purch Mgr*
EMP: 65
SQ FT: 40,000
SALES (est): 11.1MM
SALES (corp-wide): 179.8K **Privately Held**
WEB: www.daiceramics.com
SIC: 3253 Ceramic wall & floor tile
HQ: Ceramtec North America Llc
1 Technology Pl
Laurens SC 29360
864 682-3215

(G-20307)
DE MILTA SAND AND GRAVEL INC
921 Erie Rd (44095-1812)
PHONE..................440 942-2015
Nick De Milta, *President*
Joe De Milta, *Vice Pres*
EMP: 15
SQ FT: 1,800
SALES (est): 2.1MM **Privately Held**
SIC: 1442 4212 Common sand mining; gravel mining; local trucking, without storage

(G-20308)
DE-KO INC
38334 Willoughby Pkwy (44094-7584)
PHONE..................440 951-2585
Dennis Kog, *President*
EMP: 5 EST: 1979
SQ FT: 10,400
SALES (est): 1.5MM **Privately Held**
SIC: 5084 1796 3441 Cranes, industrial; machinery installation; fabricated structural metal

(G-20309)
DESIGNER CNTEMPORARY LAMINATES
37105 Code Ave (44094-6337)
PHONE..................440 946-8207
Robert Krauss, *President*
EMP: 8
SQ FT: 5,600
SALES: 480K **Privately Held**
WEB: www.dclweb.net
SIC: 3083 2541 Plastic finished products, laminated; cabinets, except refrigerated: show, display, etc.: wood

(G-20310)
DUKE GRAPHICS INC
Also Called: Duke Printing
33212 Lakeland Blvd (44095-5205)
PHONE..................440 946-0606
Blake A Leduc, *President*
Thomas Chubb, *Vice Pres*
Cindy Ruck, *Marketing Staff*
Lynette Cogley, *Office Mgr*
Mark Williamson, *Manager*
EMP: 33
SQ FT: 24,000
SALES (est): 8.1MM **Privately Held**
WEB: www.dukeprint.com
SIC: 2752 Commercial printing, offset

(G-20311)
DURA BILT DRAPERY & UPHOLSTERY
4041 Erie St (44094-7871)
PHONE..................440 269-8438
Helen T Luskin, *President*
James F Luskin, *Treasurer*
Gerard M Luskin, *Admin Sec*
EMP: 12
SQ FT: 4,000
SALES (est): 1MM **Privately Held**
SIC: 2512 7641 Upholstered household furniture; furniture refinishing; reupholstery

(G-20312)
DYOUNG ENTERPRISE INC
38241 Willoughby Pkwy (44094-7582)
PHONE..................440 918-0505
Edward S Young, *Ch of Bd*
David F Young, *President*
▲ EMP: 63
SQ FT: 50,000
SALES (est): 26.6MM **Privately Held**
WEB: www.budzar.com
SIC: 3585 3822 3823 3634 Refrigeration & heating equipment; auto controls regulating residntl & coml environmt & applncs; temperature instruments: industrial process type; electric housewares & fans

GEOGRAPHIC SECTION

Willoughby - Lake County (G-20339)

(G-20313)
EAGLE WLDG & FABRICATION INC
1766 Joseph Lloyd Pkwy (44094-8028)
PHONE................440 946-0692
Mareo Paulic, *President*
Nick Paulic, *Vice Pres*
Milan Paulic, *Treasurer*
William Schwenner, *Admin Sec*
EMP: 20
SQ FT: 15,500
SALES (est): 4.4MM **Privately Held**
WEB: www.eagle-welding.com
SIC: 3443 3699 7692 3444 Fabricated plate work (boiler shop); laser systems & equipment; welding repair; sheet metalwork

(G-20314)
EASTLAKE MACHINE PRODUCTS INC
1956 Joseph Lloyd Pkwy (44094-8030)
PHONE................440 953-1014
Ivan Saric, *President*
Richard Moroscak, *Principal*
EMP: 43 **EST:** 1980
SQ FT: 14,000
SALES (est): 5.1MM **Privately Held**
SIC: 3599 3451 Machine shop, jobbing & repair; screw machine products

(G-20315)
ERICSON MANUFACTURING CO
4323 Hamann Pkwy (44094-5625)
PHONE................440 951-8000
John Ericson III, *President*
Diane Contreraz, *General Mgr*
William Murphy, *Foreman/Supr*
Ann GE, *Purchasing*
Jeff Angle, *Engineer*
◆ **EMP:** 80
SQ FT: 25,000
SALES (est): 32.5MM **Privately Held**
WEB: www.ericson.com
SIC: 3643 3648 Electric connectors; plugs, electric; connectors, electric cord; lighting equipment

(G-20316)
EUCLID DESIGN & MANUFACTURING
38333 Willoughby Pkwy (44094-7585)
PHONE................440 942-0066
Don Nemeth, *President*
EMP: 10 **EST:** 1972
SQ FT: 8,000
SALES (est): 1.3MM **Privately Held**
SIC: 3544 Special dies & tools

(G-20317)
EUCLID PRODUCTS CO INC
Also Called: Main Fare Box Division
38341 Western Pkwy Unit A (44094-7528)
PHONE................440 942-7310
Bruce T Finke, *President*
EMP: 9
SALES: 1MM **Privately Held**
WEB: www.epco-mfb.com
SIC: 3567 3829 3565 3365 Heating units & devices, industrial; electric; fare registers for street cars, buses, etc.; packaging machinery; aluminum foundries; packaging paper & plastics film, coated & laminated

(G-20318)
F & J GRINDING INC
36495 Reading Ave Ste 2 (44094-8243)
PHONE................440 942-4430
Joe Faraguna, *President*
EMP: 4
SQ FT: 3,600
SALES (est): 504.3K **Privately Held**
SIC: 3599 Grinding castings for the trade

(G-20319)
FABTECH OHIO
38311 Apollo Pkwy Ste 3 (44094-7760)
PHONE................440 942-0811
Ron Beech, *President*
EMP: 3
SQ FT: 5,000
SALES (est): 260K **Privately Held**
SIC: 3444 Sheet metalwork

(G-20320)
FAITH TOOL & MANUFACTURING
36575 Reading Ave (44094-8210)
PHONE................440 951-5934
Robert Levak, *Principal*
Donna Levak, *Vice Pres*
EMP: 8
SALES: 910K **Privately Held**
SIC: 3544 Industrial molds

(G-20321)
FEEDALL INC
38379 Pelton Rd (44094-7719)
PHONE................440 942-8100
Roger W Winslow Jr, *President*
Roger Winslow, *Vice Pres*
Jackie Nagle, *Office Mgr*
Michael J O'Brien, *Admin Sec*
EMP: 12
SQ FT: 15,300
SALES (est): 3.7MM **Privately Held**
WEB: www.feedall.com
SIC: 3535 3545 Conveyors & conveying equipment; hopper feed devices

(G-20322)
FIONAS FINERIES
Also Called: Fellow's
9077 Billings Rd (44094-9573)
PHONE................440 796-7426
Christine Fellows, *Owner*
Thomas Overhausen, *Owner*
EMP: 3
SALES: 950K **Privately Held**
SIC: 2386 Garments, leather

(G-20323)
FIRST MACHINE & TOOL CORP
38181 Airport Pkwy (44094-8038)
PHONE................440 269-8644
Mladen Laush, *President*
Herman Lackner, *Vice Pres*
EMP: 12
SQ FT: 5,600
SALES (est): 1.2MM **Privately Held**
WEB: www.firstmachinegages.com
SIC: 3544 Jigs: inspection, gauging & checking

(G-20324)
FLORLINE DISPLAY PRODUCTS CORP
38160 Western Pkwy (44094-7588)
PHONE................440 975-9449
Patricia Primozic, *President*
Randy Primozic, *Corp Secy*
James Primozic, *Vice Pres*
EMP: 3
SQ FT: 60,000
SALES (est): 413.2K **Privately Held**
WEB: www.floralinedisplay.com
SIC: 3585 Counters & counter display cases, refrigerated

(G-20325)
FOCUS MANUFACTURING INC
Also Called: Libra Industries
38127 Willoughby Pkwy (44094-7581)
PHONE................440 946-8766
Ronald K Brehm, *President*
Jeff Waterman, *Vice Pres*
Peter Snitzer, *Engineer*
Richard Scebbi, *Treasurer*
Bruce Vanek, *Admin Sec*
EMP: 16
SQ FT: 6,000
SALES (est): 1.3MM **Privately Held**
SIC: 3599 Machine shop, jobbing & repair

(G-20326)
FUSION AUTOMATION INC (HQ)
4658 E 355th St (44094-4630)
PHONE................440 602-5595
Kent Williams, *President*
Bruce Williams, *Vice Pres*
Roger Barker, *Technical Staff*
EMP: 2
SALES: 10MM
SALES (corp-wide): 22.1MM **Privately Held**
SIC: 3548 3356 3423 3398 Soldering equipment, except hand soldering irons; solder: wire, bar, acid core, & rosin core; hand & edge tools; metal heat treating; secondary nonferrous metals; chemical preparations
PA: Fusion Incorporated
4658 E 355th St
Willoughby OH 44094
440 946-3300

(G-20327)
FUSION INCORPORATED
4658 E 355th St (44094-4630)
PHONE................440 946-3300
Christopher T Turner, *President*
Deke Morrow, *Vice Pres*
▲ **EMP:** 44
SALES (est): 8.7MM **Privately Held**
SIC: 3511 Hydraulic turbines

(G-20328)
FUSION INCORPORATED
4711 Topps Indus Pkwy (44094-4635)
PHONE................440 946-3300
Kent Williams, *President*
Dick Lamb, *CTO*
EMP: 30
SALES (corp-wide): 22.1MM **Privately Held**
WEB: www.fai-uk.com
SIC: 3356 3548 Nonferrous rolling & drawing; welding apparatus
PA: Fusion Incorporated
4658 E 355th St
Willoughby OH 44094
440 946-3300

(G-20329)
G-M-I INC
4822 E 355th St (44094-4634)
PHONE................440 953-8811
Donald J Restly, *President*
Carol L Restly, *Treasurer*
EMP: 9
SQ FT: 9,200
SALES (est): 1.5MM **Privately Held**
WEB: www.gmiincusa.com
SIC: 3053 Gaskets & sealing devices

(G-20330)
GEARTEC INC
4245 Hamann Pkwy (44094-5623)
PHONE................440 953-3900
John Grazia, *President*
Betty Masitto, *Controller*
Dick Zeleznak, *Planning*
▲ **EMP:** 26
SQ FT: 35,000
SALES (est): 2.2MM
SALES (corp-wide): 0 **Privately Held**
SIC: 3566 Gears, power transmission, except automotive
HQ: The Electric Materials Company
50 S Washington St
North East PA 16428
814 725-9621

(G-20331)
GENERAL PRECISION CORPORATION
4553 Beidler Rd (44094-4646)
PHONE................440 951-9380
Allen Ernst, *President*
EMP: 7
SALES: 600K **Privately Held**
WEB: www.generalprecisioncorp.com
SIC: 8711 3365 Engineering services; machinery castings, aluminum

(G-20332)
GLENRIDGE MACHINE CO
4610 Beidler Rd (44094-4603)
PHONE................440 975-1055
Mark Negrelli Jr, *Ch of Bd*
Jerry Negrelli, *President*
Mark Negrelli III, *Vice Pres*
Michael Genzen, *Engineer*
Phil Zendarski, *Senior Engr*
▲ **EMP:** 33
SQ FT: 66,000
SALES (est): 7.8MM **Privately Held**
WEB: www.glenridgemachine.com
SIC: 3599 7692 Machine shop, jobbing & repair; welding repair

(G-20333)
GOOD FORTUNES INC
1486 E 361st St (44095-3174)
P.O. Box 43419, Cleveland (44143-0419)
PHONE................440 942-2888
Gene Yee, *President*
Yuet Yee, *Principal*
EMP: 12
SQ FT: 5,000
SALES (est): 1.4MM **Privately Held**
WEB: www.goodfortunecookies.com
SIC: 2052 Bakery products, dry; cookies

(G-20334)
GRADEWORKS
10655 Hickory Hill Ct (44094-9418)
PHONE................440 487-4201
Matthew Clem, *Principal*
EMP: 6
SALES (est): 599.1K **Privately Held**
SIC: 3531 Road construction & maintenance machinery

(G-20335)
H & R METAL FINISHING INC
1650 E 361st St Unit L (44095-5334)
PHONE................440 942-6656
Rosemarie Cruz, *President*
Hermes C Cruz, *Managing Dir*
Rose Espendez, *Corp Secy*
EMP: 6
SQ FT: 3,600
SALES (est): 731.2K **Privately Held**
WEB: www.hrmetal.com
SIC: 3471 Finishing, metals or formed products

(G-20336)
HEISLER TOOL COMPANY
38228 Western Pkwy (44094-7590)
PHONE................440 951-2424
Timothy M McCord, *President*
Susan McCord, *Vice Pres*
EMP: 15
SQ FT: 22,000
SALES (est): 2.5MM **Privately Held**
WEB: www.heislertool.com
SIC: 3599 3549 Custom machinery; metalworking machinery

(G-20337)
HI TECMETAL GROUP INC
HI Tech Aero
34800 Lakeland Blvd (44095-5224)
PHONE................440 946-2280
Scott St Claire, *Branch Mgr*
EMP: 27
SQ FT: 17,433
SALES (corp-wide): 25.2MM **Privately Held**
SIC: 7692 3398 Welding repair; brazing (hardening) of metal
PA: Hi Tecmetal Group Inc
1101 E 55th St
Cleveland OH 44103
216 881-8100

(G-20338)
HUDCO MANUFACTURING INC
38250 Western Pkwy (44094-7590)
PHONE................440 951-4040
Donald M Hudak, *President*
Joan L Hudak, *Corp Secy*
Joan Hudak, *Treasurer*
◆ **EMP:** 8
SQ FT: 6,000
SALES (est): 1.4MM **Privately Held**
WEB: www.hudcomfg.com
SIC: 3531 Rock crushing machinery, portable

(G-20339)
HYDRAULIC PRODUCTS INC
4540 Beidler Rd (44094-4602)
PHONE................440 946-4575
Joseph Focareto, *President*
▲ **EMP:** 8 **EST:** 1972

Willoughby - Lake County (G-20340)

SALES (est): 939.4K **Privately Held**
SIC: 3593 7699 3594 Fluid power cylinders, hydraulic or pneumatic; hydraulic equipment repair; fluid power pumps & motors

(G-20340)
HYLUN MACHINE CO INC
9220 Woods Way Dr (44094-9370)
PHONE.................................440 256-8755
Kim Hyder, *President*
Bonnie Hyder, *Corp Secy*
EMP: 4 **EST:** 1974
SQ FT: 5,000
SALES (est): 362.5K **Privately Held**
SIC: 3599 Machine shop, jobbing & repair

(G-20341)
IDA CONTROLS
38593 Bell Rd (44094-7519)
PHONE.................................440 785-8457
Vince Difranco, *Owner*
EMP: 9
SALES (est): 1.4MM **Privately Held**
SIC: 3613 Switchgear & switchboard apparatus

(G-20342)
IMAGING SCIENCES LLC
38174 Willoughby Pkwy (44094-7580)
PHONE.................................440 975-9640
Geoffrey R Brown, *President*
Geoffrey Brown, *President*
Brenda Brown,
Charles Vendeville,
EMP: 9
SQ FT: 18,000
SALES (est): 1.7MM **Privately Held**
WEB: www.imaging-sciences.com
SIC: 3211 Construction glass

(G-20343)
INTEGRA ENCLOSURES INC (PA)
7750 Pyler Blvd (44094)
P.O. Box 1870, Mentor (44061-1870)
PHONE.................................440 269-4966
Jim McWilliams, *President*
EMP: 6
SQ FT: 30,000
SALES: 3.4MM **Privately Held**
WEB: www.integraenclosures.com
SIC: 3089 Injection molding of plastics; thermoformed finished plastic products

(G-20344)
INTELITOOL MANUFACTURING SVCS
36335 Reading Ave Ste 4 (44094-8200)
PHONE.................................440 953-1071
Gary Struna, *President*
Collen Mocz, *Principal*
William Tulloch, *Senior VP*
EMP: 6
SQ FT: 10,500
SALES (est): 802.3K **Privately Held**
WEB: www.intelitoolinc.com
SIC: 2542 Partitions & fixtures, except wood

(G-20345)
INTERLAKE INDUSTRIES INC (PA)
4732 E 355th St (44094-4632)
PHONE.................................440 942-0800
Lisa M Habe, *Ch of Bd*
Dan Valentino, *Vice Pres*
John Ellis, *Controller*
Liz Tolbert, *Director*
EMP: 3
SQ FT: 3,000
SALES (est): 23.4MM **Privately Held**
WEB: www.interlakestamping.com
SIC: 3469 Stamping metal for the trade

(G-20346)
INTERLAKE STAMPING OHIO INC
4732 E 355th St (44094-4632)
PHONE.................................440 942-0800
Lisa M Habe, *President*
Mark Groenstein, *General Mgr*
Dan Valentino, *Vice Pres*
Liz Tolbert, *Director*
EMP: 40 **EST:** 1957

SQ FT: 36,000
SALES (est): 12.4MM
SALES (corp-wide): 23.4MM **Privately Held**
WEB: www.interlakestamping.com
SIC: 3469 Stamping metal for the trade
PA: Interlake Industries, Inc.
 4732 E 355th St
 Willoughby OH 44094
 440 942-0800

(G-20347)
JAMES L WEREB
Also Called: Wereb Metal Fabricating
38005 Apollo Pkwy Ste 2 (44094-7759)
PHONE.................................440 942-2405
James L Wereb, *Owner*
EMP: 3
SQ FT: 2,400
SALES (est): 323K **Privately Held**
SIC: 3446 3599 Railings, bannisters, guards, etc.: made from metal pipe; stairs, staircases, stair treads: prefabricated metal; machine shop, jobbing & repair

(G-20348)
JOHN WOLF & CO INC
36420 Biltmore Pl Ste 1 (44094-8232)
PHONE.................................440 942-0083
John R Wolf, *President*
EMP: 3
SQ FT: 1,600
SALES (est): 277.9K **Privately Held**
SIC: 3812 Airspeed instrumentation (aeronautical instruments)

(G-20349)
JOURNAL REGISTER COMPANY
Journal, The
7085 Mentor Ave (44094-7948)
PHONE.................................440 951-0000
Stephen Roszczyk, *Principal*
Michael Beckwith, *Manager*
Kim Cencula, *Supervisor*
EMP: 225
SALES (corp-wide): 661.2MM **Privately Held**
WEB: www.journalregister.com
SIC: 2711 Newspapers, publishing & printing
PA: Journal Register Company
 5 Hanover Sq Fl 25
 New York NY 10004
 212 257-7212

(G-20350)
KALCOR COATINGS COMPANY
37721 Stevens Blvd (44094-6231)
PHONE.................................440 946-4700
Cori Zucker, *President*
Don Mihalik, *Vice Pres*
Cory Zucker, *Vice Pres*
Carol McGee, *Traffic Mgr*
Roger Lafrance, *Research*
▲ **EMP:** 25 **EST:** 1961
SQ FT: 55,000
SALES (est): 7MM **Privately Held**
SIC: 2851 Paints & paint additives; lacquers, varnishes, enamels & other coatings

(G-20351)
KEB INDUSTRIES INC
2166 Joseph Lloyd Pkwy (44094-8032)
PHONE.................................440 953-4623
Brad Butler, *President*
EMP: 8
SQ FT: 6,500
SALES (est): 1.2MM **Privately Held**
WEB: www.kebkollets.com
SIC: 3545 Precision tools, machinists'; cutting tools for machine tools

(G-20352)
KENNEDY GROUP INCORPORATED (PA)
38601 Kennedy Pkwy (44094-7395)
PHONE.................................440 951-7660
Bertram Kennedy, *CEO*
Michael R Kennedy, *President*
Todd Kennedy, *COO*
Mary Lou Kennedy, *Vice Pres*
Patrick Kennedy, *Vice Pres*
▲ **EMP:** 83
SQ FT: 80,000

SALES (est): 30.2MM **Privately Held**
WEB: www.kennedygrp.com
SIC: 2679 2673 3089 3565 Tags & labels, paper; bags: plastic, laminated & coated; garment bags (plastic film): made from purchased materials; plastic containers, except foam; boxes, plastic; cases, plastic; packaging machinery; nailed wood boxes & shook

(G-20353)
KJ MACHINING SYSTEMS INC
38254 Airport Pkwy Unit C (44094-8023)
PHONE.................................440 975-8624
Jonathan Deblasi, *President*
EMP: 5
SQ FT: 2,500
SALES (est): 292.8K **Privately Held**
WEB: www.kjmsinc.com
SIC: 3599 Machine shop, jobbing & repair

(G-20354)
KOPACHKO MACHINING INC
38341 Western Pkwy (44094-7528)
PHONE.................................440 953-3988
Robert Kopachko, *President*
Lois Kopachko, *Vice Pres*
EMP: 5
SQ FT: 4,800
SALES (est): 300K **Privately Held**
SIC: 3599 Machine shop, jobbing & repair

(G-20355)
KOTTLER METAL PRODUCTS CO INC
1595 Lost Nation Rd (44094-7329)
PHONE.................................440 946-7473
Barry Feldman, *President*
Harold Feldman, *Vice Pres*
Mike Mangan, *Mfg Staff*
Ron McCloud, *Mfg Staff*
Pat Garrett, *Sales Mgr*
▲ **EMP:** 25
SALES: 7.4MM **Privately Held**
WEB: www.kottlermetal.com
SIC: 3498 3441 7692 3547 Pipe sections fabricated from purchased pipe; tube fabricating (contract bending & shaping); fabricated structural metal; welding repair; rolling mill machinery

(G-20356)
LABEL TECHNIQUE SOUTHEAST LLC
38601 Kennedy Pkwy (44094-7395)
PHONE.................................440 951-7660
Bertram Kennedy,
David Ard,
Michael Kennedy,
Patrick Kennedy,
Todd Kennedy,
EMP: 29
SQ FT: 12,000
SALES (est): 3.6MM
SALES (corp-wide): 30.2MM **Privately Held**
WEB: www.labeltechnique.com
SIC: 2759 2672 2679 Labels & seals: printing; coated & laminated paper; labels, paper: made from purchased material
PA: The Kennedy Group Incorporated
 38601 Kennedy Pkwy
 Willoughby OH 44094
 440 951-7660

(G-20357)
LAKE COMMUNITY NEWS
Also Called: Painesville Pride
36081 Lake Shore Blvd # 5 (44095-1578)
P.O. Box 814, Mantua (44255-0814)
PHONE.................................440 946-2577
Deanne Nelisse, *President*
Gordon Moser, *Finance*
EMP: 7
SALES (est): 310K **Privately Held**
SIC: 2711 Newspapers, publishing & printing

(G-20358)
LANDERWOOD INDUSTRIES INC
4245 Hamann Pkwy (44094-5623)
PHONE.................................440 233-4234
James H Weaver III, *President*

EMP: 30
SQ FT: 30,000
SALES (est): 2.9MM **Privately Held**
WEB: www.geartecinc.com
SIC: 3462 Gears, forged steel

(G-20359)
LANGA TOOL & MACHINE INC
36430 Reading Ave Ste 1 (44094-8220)
PHONE.................................440 953-1138
William Langa, *President*
EMP: 20 **EST:** 1979
SQ FT: 7,000
SALES (est): 3MM **Privately Held**
SIC: 3599 Machine shop, jobbing & repair

(G-20360)
LAPA LOWE ENTERPRISES LLC
Also Called: Gas & Grills
5900 Som Center Rd Ste 16 (44094-3044)
PHONE.................................440 944-9410
Lacy Lowe, *Mng Member*
EMP: 3
SALES (est): 260K **Privately Held**
SIC: 3631 Barbecues, grills & braziers (outdoor cooking)

(G-20361)
LOKRING TECHNOLOGY LLC
38376 Apollo Pkwy (44094-7724)
PHONE.................................440 942-0880
Bill Lennon, *President*
Brad Shepard, *Area Mgr*
Jeff Vasenda, *Office Mgr*
Dario Rampersad, *Info Tech Dir*
▲ **EMP:** 54
SALES (est): 28.8MM **Privately Held**
SIC: 3312 Pipes & tubes

(G-20362)
LOST NATION FUEL
3525 Lost Nation Rd (44094-7753)
PHONE.................................440 951-9088
Dan Triplett, *Principal*
EMP: 4
SALES (est): 432.6K **Privately Held**
SIC: 2869 Fuels

(G-20363)
LURE INC
38040 3rd St (44094-6139)
PHONE.................................440 951-8862
EMP: 20
SALES (est): 1.3MM **Privately Held**
SIC: 3949 Mfg Sporting/Athletic Goods

(G-20364)
M L GRINDING CO
34620 Lakeland Blvd (44095-5222)
PHONE.................................440 975-9111
Fred Lazar, *Owner*
EMP: 3 **EST:** 1975
SQ FT: 4,000
SALES (est): 204.8K **Privately Held**
SIC: 3599 Grinding castings for the trade

(G-20365)
MAGNETIC RESONANCE TECH
4261 Hamann Pkwy (44094-5623)
PHONE.................................440 942-2922
Michael Profeta, *President*
Kathleen Profeta, *Vice Pres*
Tim Paradise, *Foreman/Supr*
EMP: 5
SQ FT: 20,000
SALES: 1.5MM **Privately Held**
WEB: www.mritechnologies.com
SIC: 3845 Magnetic resonance imaging device, nuclear

(G-20366)
MAGNUS ENGINEERED EQP LLC
4500 Beidler Rd (44094-4602)
PHONE.................................440 942-8488
William Martin, *President*
Bill Martin, *COO*
Jeffrey Mendrala, *CFO*
EMP: 26
SQ FT: 38,000
SALES: 4MM **Privately Held**
SIC: 3699 Cleaning equipment, ultrasonic, except medical & dental

GEOGRAPHIC SECTION
Willoughby - Lake County (G-20394)

(G-20367)
MANICO INC
37105 Code Ave (44094-6337)
P.O. Box 509 (44096-0509)
PHONE 440 946-5333
Nicholas Manta, *President*
EMP: 6
SQ FT: 12,000
SALES: 500K **Privately Held**
WEB: www.manico.com
SIC: 3491 3823 Pressure valves & regulators, industrial; regulators (steam fittings); water works valves; flow instruments, industrial process type

(G-20368)
MAR-BAL PULTRUSION INC
38310 Apollo Pkwy (44094-7724)
PHONE 440 953-0456
Allen J Goryance, *President*
James Gortance, *Vice Pres*
EMP: 10 **EST:** 1974
SQ FT: 10,000
SALES: 1MM **Privately Held**
SIC: 2519 Furniture, household: glass, fiberglass & plastic

(G-20369)
MARC INDUSTRIES INC
Also Called: Best Snow Plow
35140 Lakeland Blvd (44095-5228)
PHONE 440 944-9305
Howard Hren, *President*
Salvatore Lazzano, *Vice Pres*
EMP: 8 **EST:** 1979
SQ FT: 8,000
SALES: 630K **Privately Held**
WEB: www.bestsnowplow.com
SIC: 3441 3711 Fabricated structural metal; snow plows (motor vehicles), assembly of

(G-20370)
MARK-N-MEND INC
38151 Airport Pkwy Ste 54 (44094-8050)
PHONE 440 951-2003
Melvin L March, *General Mgr*
Todd March, *Admin Sec*
EMP: 3
SQ FT: 5,000
SALES (est): 200K **Privately Held**
WEB: www.marknmend.com
SIC: 2752 Transfers, decalcomania or dry: lithographed

(G-20371)
MARKETING COMM RESOURCE INC
4800 E 345th St (44094-4607)
PHONE 440 484-3010
Dominic Tiunno, *CEO*
Frank Tiunno, *Exec VP*
EMP: 57
SALES (est): 6.9MM **Privately Held**
SIC: 4961 2759 Steam/Air-Conditioning Supply Commercial Printing

(G-20372)
MARTIN MACHINE CO INC
37151 Ben Hur Ave Ste D (44094-6349)
P.O. Box 136 (44096-0136)
PHONE 440 946-5174
James Martin, *President*
EMP: 5
SQ FT: 3,000
SALES: 600K **Privately Held**
SIC: 3599 Machine shop, jobbing & repair

(G-20373)
MAY THREAD GRINDING CO
38401 Apollo Pkwy Ste F (44094-7757)
PHONE 440 953-0678
Richard May, *President*
Shelby May, *President*
EMP: 4
SQ FT: 1,200
SALES: 500K **Privately Held**
SIC: 3599 Machine shop, jobbing & repair

(G-20374)
MCATTACK MACHINE LLC
38338 Apollo Pkwy Bldg 2 (44094-7796)
PHONE 440 946-3855
Sharon McIntire,
EMP: 3

SALES (est): 496.4K **Privately Held**
SIC: 3599 Machine shop, jobbing & repair

(G-20375)
MCTT MACHINE TOOL INC
Also Called: T T Machine Tool
38131 Arprpt Pkwy Unit 207 (44094)
PHONE 440 946-9559
Tadija Erceg, *President*
Tom Erceg, *Vice Pres*
Milka Erceg, *Treasurer*
EMP: 3
SQ FT: 1,700
SALES (est): 412K **Privately Held**
SIC: 3599 Machine shop, jobbing & repair

(G-20376)
MEIBUHR CO INC
38301 Apollo Pkwy Ste 1 (44094-7758)
P.O. Box 317 (44096-0317)
PHONE 440 942-9375
A Scott Lining, *Vice Pres*
Jeannie Lining, *Vice Pres*
Kurt Lining, *Vice Pres*
Jason Salaty, *Vice Pres*
Timothy Lining, *VP Mfg*
EMP: 4
SALES: 200K **Privately Held**
WEB: www.meibuhr.com
SIC: 3599 Mfg Industrial Machinery

(G-20377)
MEISTER MEDIA WORLDWIDE INC (PA)
37733 Euclid Ave (44094-5992)
PHONE 440 942-2000
Gary T Fitzgerald, *Ch of Bd*
Eric Davis, *Publisher*
Rosemary Gordon, *Publisher*
Homero Ontiveros, *Publisher*
Frank Giles, *Editor*
EMP: 100
SQ FT: 29,000
SALES (est): 20.4MM **Privately Held**
WEB: www.meistermedia.com
SIC: 2721 Magazines: publishing only, not printed on site

(G-20378)
MELINZ INDUSTRIES INC (PA)
Also Called: Riverview Raquetball Club
34099 Melinz Pkwy Unit D (44095-4001)
PHONE 440 946-3512
Adolph Melinz, *President*
Jeff Sloat, *Treasurer*
Nancy Sloat, *Admin Sec*
EMP: 10
SQ FT: 11,000
SALES (est): 1.3MM **Privately Held**
SIC: 7999 3599 Racquetball club, non-membership; machine & other job shop work

(G-20379)
MENTOR TOOL INC
990 Erie Rd Unit D (44095-1813)
PHONE 440 942-5273
John Elersich, *President*
Skip Schwab, *Corp Secy*
EMP: 4
SQ FT: 2,000
SALES: 250K **Privately Held**
SIC: 3599 Machine shop, jobbing & repair

(G-20380)
METAL SEAL PRECISION LTD
4369 Hamann Pkwy (44094-5625)
PHONE 440 255-8888
John L Habe, *Branch Mgr*
EMP: 125
SALES (corp-wide): 34.3MM **Privately Held**
SIC: 3444 Sheet metalwork
PA: Metal Seal Precision, Ltd.
8687 Tyler Blvd
Mentor OH 44060
440 255-8888

(G-20381)
MICONVI PROPERTIES INC
Also Called: Bevcorp Properties
4711 E 355th St (44094-4631)
PHONE 440 954-3500
Michael Connelly, *President*
Vicki Connelly, *Corp Secy*
Pete Wills, *Info Tech Mgr*

◆ **EMP:** 40
SQ FT: 25,000
SALES (est): 8.2MM **Privately Held**
SIC: 3565 Bottling machinery: filling, capping, labeling

(G-20382)
MIKA METAL FABRICATING CO
4530 Hamann Pkwy (44094-5630)
PHONE 440 951-5500
Fred J G Mika, *President*
Jack W Grootegoed, *General Mgr*
Fred G Mika, *Vice Pres*
Scott M Mika, *Vice Pres*
EMP: 45
SQ FT: 78,000
SALES (est): 12.9MM **Privately Held**
SIC: 3444 Sheet metal specialties, not stamped

(G-20383)
MILLENNIUM MCH TECHLONLOGY LLC
38323 Apollo Pkwy Ste 7 (44094-7761)
PHONE 440 269-8080
Jeffrey J Downs, *Mng Member*
EMP: 11
SALES (est): 1.7MM **Privately Held**
SIC: 3599 Machine shop, jobbing & repair

(G-20384)
MILLWORK DESIGN SOLUTIONS INC
4547 Beidler Rd (44094-4646)
PHONE 440 946-8837
Ray Wojtasik, *President*
EMP: 3
SQ FT: 6,000
SALES: 200K **Privately Held**
WEB: www.millworkdesign.com
SIC: 2434 Wood kitchen cabinets

(G-20385)
MIRMAT CNC MACHINING INC
4550 Hamann Pkwy (44094-5630)
PHONE 440 951-2410
Miroslav Vujovic, *President*
EMP: 5
SALES (est): 621.3K **Privately Held**
SIC: 3599 Machine shop, jobbing & repair; machine & other job shop work

(G-20386)
NATIONAL ROLLER DIE INC
4750 Beidler Rd Unit 4 (44094-4663)
PHONE 440 951-3850
Kelly Johnson, *CEO*
Will Corral, *President*
Jeff Watt, *Superintendent*
EMP: 10
SALES (est): 1.2MM **Privately Held**
WEB: www.nrdi.net
SIC: 3544 Special dies & tools

(G-20387)
NEUNDORFER INC
Also Called: Neundorfer Engineering Service
4590 Hamann Pkwy (44094-5691)
PHONE 440 942-8990
Michael Neundorfer, *CEO*
EMP: 42
SQ FT: 38,000
SALES (est): 8.4MM **Privately Held**
WEB: www.neundorfer.com
SIC: 8711 3564 Pollution control engineering; precipitators, electrostatic

(G-20388)
NEWAY STAMPING & MFG INC
4820 E 345th St (44094-4607)
P.O. Box 1023 (44096-1023)
PHONE 440 951-8500
Adam Bowden, *President*
Jason H Bowden, *Vice Pres*
Matthew J Bowden, *Vice Pres*
EMP: 85
SQ FT: 15,000
SALES (est): 22.8MM **Privately Held**
WEB: www.newaystamping.com
SIC: 3469 3544 Stamping metal for the trade; special dies, tools, jigs & fixtures

(G-20389)
NORBAR TORQUE TOOLS INC
36400 Biltmore Pl (44094-8221)
PHONE 440 953-1175
Keith Daiber, *President*
Bernice Daiber, *Corp Secy*
Terry Daiber, *Vice Pres*
▲ **EMP:** 12
SQ FT: 5,000
SALES (est): 4.2MM
SALES (corp-wide): 3.7B **Publicly Held**
WEB: www.norbar.com
SIC: 5072 3423 Hand tools; wrenches, hand tools
PA: Snap-On Incorporated
2801 80th St
Kenosha WI 53143
262 656-5200

(G-20390)
NORTHEASTERN RFRGN CORP
38274 Western Pkwy (44094-7590)
PHONE 440 942-7676
Carol A Primozic, *President*
James A Primozic, *Vice Pres*
Fern Peters, *Info Tech Mgr*
EMP: 20
SQ FT: 11,000
SALES (est): 5MM **Privately Held**
WEB: www.nrcinc.net
SIC: 3585 1711 7623 Refrigeration equipment, complete; heating & air conditioning contractors; refrigeration repair service

(G-20391)
NRC INC
Also Called: Northeastern Process Cooling
38160 Western Pkwy (44094-7588)
PHONE 440 975-9449
Randolph J Primozic, *President*
Patricia A Primozic, *Corp Secy*
Randy Primozic, *Exec VP*
Thomas Galon, *Project Mgr*
EMP: 30
SALES (est): 5.4MM **Privately Held**
SIC: 3585 Refrigeration equipment, complete

(G-20392)
NUPRO COMPANY
4800 E 345th St (44094-4607)
PHONE 440 951-9729
F J Callahan Jr, *Ch of Bd*
William Cosgrove, *President*
Roy Dick, *Engineer*
EMP: 250
SQ FT: 60,000
SALES (est): 18.4MM
SALES (corp-wide): 940.1MM **Privately Held**
WEB: www.swagelok.com
SIC: 3494 3569 3564 3491 Valves & pipe fittings; filters, general line: industrial; blowers & fans; industrial valves
PA: Swagelok Company
29500 Solon Rd
Solon OH 44139
440 248-4600

(G-20393)
OHIO BROACH & MACHINE COMPANY
35264 Topps Indus Pkwy (44094-4684)
PHONE 440 946-1040
Charles P Van De Motter, *CEO*
Christopher C Van De Motter, *President*
Neil Van De Motter, *Vice Pres*
Richard Van De Motter, *Vice Pres*
James L Lutz, *Treasurer*
▼ **EMP:** 34 **EST:** 1956
SQ FT: 52,000
SALES (est): 6.2MM **Privately Held**
WEB: www.ohiobroach.com
SIC: 3541 7699 3545 3599 Broaching machines; knife, saw & tool sharpening & repair; machine tool accessories; machine shop, jobbing & repair

(G-20394)
OHIO CARBON BLANK INC
38403 Pelton Rd (44094-7721)
PHONE 440 953-9302
Scott Boncha, *President*
Dale McCartney, *President*
Susan Furman, *Mfg Staff*
Jeff Hutchinson, *Manager*

Willoughby - Lake County (G-20395)   GEOGRAPHIC SECTION

EMP: 20 **EST:** 1980
SQ FT: 2,000
SALES (est): 3.8MM **Privately Held**
WEB: www.ohiocarbonblank.com
SIC: 3624 Carbon & graphite products

(G-20395)
P M MACHINE INC
38205 Western Pkwy (44094-7591)
PHONE...............................440 942-6537
Tom Decumbe, *President*
EMP: 15
SQ FT: 10,000
SALES (est): 1.3MM **Privately Held**
SIC: 3089 Injection molding of plastics

(G-20396)
PACE CONSOLIDATED INC (PA)
Also Called: Pace Engineering
4800 Beidler Rd (44094-4605)
PHONE...............................440 942-1234
Craig Wallace, *CEO*
Randy Murphy, *Vice Pres*
Stephen Sherbondy, *Vice Pres*
◆ **EMP:** 95
SQ FT: 120,000
SALES (est): 30.2MM **Privately Held**
SIC: 3531 Construction machinery

(G-20397)
PACE ENGINEERING INC
4800 Beidler Rd (44094-4605)
PHONE...............................440 942-1234
Craig R Wallace, *CEO*
EMP: 105 **EST:** 1963
SQ FT: 120,000
SALES: 8.5MM
SALES (corp-wide): 30.2MM **Privately Held**
WEB: www.paceparts.net
SIC: 3531 Construction machinery
PA: Pace Consolidated, Inc.
    4800 Beidler Rd
    Willoughby OH 44094
    440 942-1234

(G-20398)
PALESH & ASSOCIATES INC
3659 Lost Nation Rd (44094-7756)
PHONE...............................440 942-9168
Frank G Palesh III, *CEO*
EMP: 5 **EST:** 1979
SQ FT: 12,000
SALES (est): 794.4K **Privately Held**
WEB: www.palesh.com
SIC: 7629 3621 5063 7699 Electrical equipment repair services; motors, electric; motors, electric; industrial machinery & equipment repair

(G-20399)
PAULO PRODUCTS COMPANY
Also Called: American Brzing Div Paulo Pdts
4428 Hamann Pkwy (44094-5628)
PHONE...............................440 942-0153
Bob Muto, *Branch Mgr*
Jim Loveland, *Manager*
EMP: 38
SALES (corp-wide): 98.4MM **Privately Held**
WEB: www.paulo.com
SIC: 7692 1799 Brazing; coating of concrete structures with plastic
PA: Paulo Products Company
    5711 W Park Ave
    Saint Louis MO 63110
    314 647-7500

(G-20400)
PHIL MATIC SCREW PRODUCTS INC
1457 E 357th St (44095-4127)
P.O. Box 1178 (44096-1178)
PHONE...............................440 942-7290
Larry E Phillis, *President*
Richard Phillis, *Vice Pres*
Fraser Young, *Vice Pres*
EMP: 14
SQ FT: 11,300
SALES (est): 2.2MM **Privately Held**
WEB: www.philmatic.com
SIC: 3599 Machine shop, jobbing & repair

(G-20401)
PIP PRINTING
35401 Euclid Ave Ste 109 (44094-4561)
PHONE...............................440 951-2606
Tom Jones, *Owner*
EMP: 3
SALES (est): 203.7K **Privately Held**
SIC: 2752 Commercial printing, offset

(G-20402)
PLASTIC FABRICATION SVCS INC
Also Called: Pierce Ohio
38167 Airport Pkwy Unit 1 (44094-8020)
P.O. Box 242, Grand River (44045-0242)
PHONE...............................440 953-9990
Richard Pierce, *President*
EMP: 3
SALES (est): 381.3K **Privately Held**
WEB: www.plastictanks.com
SIC: 3089 Air mattresses, plastic

(G-20403)
PM COAL COMPANY LLC
9717 Chillicothe Rd (44094-9200)
PHONE...............................440 256-7624
Scott Brown, *President*
Jack M Grinwis, *Partner*
EMP: 5
SALES (est): 231K **Privately Held**
SIC: 1221 Bituminous coal surface mining

(G-20404)
PMC GAGE INC (PA)
Also Called: PMC Lonestar
38383 Willoughby Pkwy (44094-7585)
PHONE...............................440 953-1672
Nicholas Bosworth, *CEO*
Mike McWilliams, *Managing Dir*
Teri Feldmann, *QC Mgr*
Dave Maisch, *Treasurer*
Ann Gross, *Controller*
EMP: 50
SALES (est): 13.1MM **Privately Held**
WEB: www.pmclonestar.com
SIC: 3545 3826 3829 Measuring tools & machines, machinists' metalworking type; analytical instruments; measuring & controlling devices

(G-20405)
PMC MERCURY (PA)
38383 Willoughby Pkwy (44094-7585)
PHONE...............................440 953-3300
Nick Boxworth, *President*
John Selesky, *Sales Associate*
EMP: 7
SQ FT: 38,000
SALES (est): 2.1MM **Privately Held**
WEB: www.mercurygage.com
SIC: 3545 Gauges (machine tool accessories)

(G-20406)
POLYFLEX LLC
4803 E 345th St (44094-4606)
PHONE...............................440 946-0758
Timothy Reed,
Scott Janda,
EMP: 10
SALES (est): 1.6MM **Privately Held**
SIC: 2297 Nonwoven fabrics

(G-20407)
POSITIVE SAFETY MFR CO
34099 Melinz Pkwy Unit A (44095-4001)
PHONE...............................440 951-2130
EMP: 15
SQ FT: 11,000
SALES (est): 2MM **Privately Held**
SIC: 3625 Mfg Safety Control Devices Used On Punch Presses

(G-20408)
POWER-PACK CONVEYOR COMPANY
38363 Airport Pkwy (44094-7562)
PHONE...............................440 975-9955
Kevin Ensinger, *President*
James L Ensinger, *President*
Donnell Ensinger, *Exec VP*
Harry Cook, *VP Mfg*
Eric Ensinger, *CFO*
EMP: 25 **EST:** 1929
SQ FT: 48,000
SALES: 5.6MM **Privately Held**
WEB: www.power-packconveyor.com
SIC: 5084 3531 3535 Industrial machinery & equipment; road construction & maintenance machinery; unit handling conveying systems

(G-20409)
PRECISE TOOL & DIE COMPANY
38128 Willoughby Pkwy (44094-7580)
P.O. Box 1055 (44096-1055)
PHONE...............................440 951-9173
Steve Hunyadi, *CEO*
Eva Pinkerton, *President*
Al Large, *Prdtn Mgr*
Elizabeth Hunyadi, *Treasurer*
Frank Corrao, *Sales Executive*
▲ **EMP:** 35
SQ FT: 22,000
SALES (est): 9.9MM **Privately Held**
WEB: www.precisetoolanddie.com
SIC: 3599 Machine shop, jobbing & repair

(G-20410)
PRECISION HONING INC
33000 Lakeland Blvd (44095-5203)
PHONE...............................440 942-7339
Don Bard, *President*
EMP: 4
SQ FT: 10,000
SALES (est): 488.4K **Privately Held**
SIC: 3541 Honing & lapping machines

(G-20411)
PRIME TIME MACHINE INC
38302 Arprt Pkwy Unit 10 (44094)
PHONE...............................440 942-7410
James R Vaughn, *President*
EMP: 3
SQ FT: 5,000
SALES (est): 260K **Privately Held**
SIC: 3544 Special dies & tools; jigs & fixtures

(G-20412)
PROGRESSIVE LABELS LLC
38601 Kennedy Pkwy (44094-7395)
PHONE...............................570 688-9636
Albert C Walck III,
EMP: 12
SQ FT: 10,000
SALES (est): 1.8MM **Privately Held**
WEB: www.progressivelabels.com
SIC: 2672 Tape, pressure sensitive: made from purchased materials

(G-20413)
QUALITY CNC MACHINING INC
38195 Airport Pkwy (44094-8038)
PHONE...............................440 942-0542
Joseph Katic, *President*
EMP: 12
SQ FT: 8,000
SALES (est): 2.2MM **Privately Held**
SIC: 3599 Machine shop, jobbing & repair

(G-20414)
QUALITY FRP FABRICATIONS
1450 E 363rd St (44095-4136)
PHONE...............................440 942-9067
Robert Archbold, *Owner*
EMP: 7
SQ FT: 3,000
SALES (est): 675.2K **Privately Held**
SIC: 3089 Pallets, plastic

(G-20415)
QUALITY SCREW PRODUCTS INC
38302 Arprt Pkwy Unit 15 (44094)
PHONE...............................440 975-1828
Frank Fiorta, *President*
Michele Fiorta, *Vice Pres*
Edward Krukowski, *Treasurer*
EMP: 3
SQ FT: 3,100
SALES: 300K **Privately Held**
SIC: 3599 Machine shop, jobbing & repair

(G-20416)
QUALTECH TECHNOLOGIES INC
1685b Joseph Lloyd Pkwy (44094-8044)
PHONE...............................440 946-8081
Dave Vance, *President*
Joel Wolnik, *Prdtn Mgr*
Mike Trebuchon, *Purch Mgr*
Doug Pohly, *QC Mgr*
Carlina Card, *Program Mgr*
▲ **EMP:** 50 **EST:** 2002
SQ FT: 18,000
SALES (est): 11.5MM **Privately Held**
WEB: www.qualtechinc.com
SIC: 3672 Electrical equipment & supplies; printed circuit boards

(G-20417)
RACEDIRECTOR LLC
38613 Andrews Ridge Way (44094-7830)
PHONE...............................440 940-6675
Craig Rowe, *Administration*
EMP: 3 **EST:** 2017
SALES (est): 94.6K **Privately Held**
SIC: 7372 Application computer software

(G-20418)
RAPID BLANKET RESTORER CORP
8735 Palomino Trl (44094-5144)
PHONE...............................330 821-6326
Walter Tornstrom, *President*
EMP: 4
SALES (est): 625.2K **Privately Held**
SIC: 2819 8748 Chemicals, reagent grade: refined from technical grade; business consulting

(G-20419)
REID ASSET MANAGEMENT COMPANY
Also Called: Magnus Equipment
4500 Beidler Rd (44094-4602)
PHONE...............................440 942-8488
Scott Miller, *Branch Mgr*
EMP: 30
SALES: 3MM
SALES (corp-wide): 9.9MM **Privately Held**
WEB: www.magnusequipment.com
SIC: 2842 Specialty cleaning, polishes & sanitation goods
PA: Reid Asset Management Company
    9555 Rockside Rd Ste 350
    Cleveland OH 44125
    216 642-3223

(G-20420)
RIMECO PRODUCTS INC
2002 Joseph Lloyd Pkwy (44094-8032)
PHONE...............................440 918-1220
Valentine Ribic, *President*
John Ribic, *Vice Pres*
EMP: 7
SQ FT: 12,000
SALES (est): 1.3MM **Privately Held**
WEB: www.rimecoproducts.com
SIC: 3599 Machine shop, jobbing & repair

(G-20421)
RINOS WOODWORKING SHOP INC
36475 Biltmore Pl (44094-8222)
PHONE...............................440 946-1718
Rino Ritosa, *President*
David Osborne, *Manager*
▲ **EMP:** 19 **EST:** 1982
SQ FT: 15,000
SALES (est): 2MM **Privately Held**
WEB: www.rinoswoodworking.com
SIC: 2541 2431 Cabinets, except refrigerated: show, display, etc.: wood; millwork

(G-20422)
RISE HOLDINGS LLC
Also Called: All-Craft Wellman Products
4839 E 345th St (44094-4606)
PHONE...............................440 946-9646
Gil Wellman, *President*
Rick Serio, *Manager*
EMP: 15
SQ FT: 8,000
SALES: 500K **Privately Held**
SIC: 3953 3499 Letters (marking devices), metal; tablets, bronze or other metal

(G-20423)
RONSON MANUFACTURING INC
9933 Chillicothe Rd (44094-9733)
PHONE...............................440 256-1463
Ronald J Ducca, *President*

Bonnie Webb, *Vice Pres*
EMP: 5 **EST:** 1978
SQ FT: 10,000
SALES (est): 817K **Privately Held**
SIC: 3452 Bolts, metal; nuts, metal; screws, metal

(G-20424)
SAWYER TECHNICAL MATERIALS LLC (HQ)
Also Called: Sawyer Crystal Systems
35400 Lakeland Blvd (44095-5304)
PHONE.................................440 951-8770
Kelly Scott, *Mng Member*
Fred Taylor, *Mng Member*
▲ **EMP:** 35
SQ FT: 100,000
SALES (est): 9.5MM **Privately Held**
WEB: www.sawyerresearch.com
SIC: 3679 3471 Quartz crystals, for electronic application; plating & polishing
PA: Forter Corporation

    Taipei City TAP
    223 817-122

(G-20425)
SCHEEL PUBLISHING LLC
5900 Som Center Rd (44094-3086)
PHONE.................................216 731-8616
J Scheel, *Principal*
Nicholas Vonderau, *Marketing Mgr*
Kat Chesbrough, *Marketing Staff*
Katherine Turner, *Marketing Staff*
EMP: 8
SALES (est): 790.6K **Privately Held**
SIC: 2741 Miscellaneous publishing

(G-20426)
SCHUPP ADVANCED MATERIALS LLC
10770 Chillicothe Rd (44094-5102)
PHONE.................................440 488-6416
John Schupp,
EMP: 3
SALES (est): 169.1K **Privately Held**
SIC: 3679 Quartz crystals, for electronic application

(G-20427)
SERVICE STAMPINGS INC
4700 Hamann Pkwy (44094-5616)
PHONE.................................440 946-2330
Thurston Reid, *Ch of Bd*
Christopher T Reid, *President*
Robert A Stohlman, *Vice Pres*
Donald Bowen, *VP Mfg*
Jefferey J Campbell, *Treasurer*
EMP: 31 **EST:** 1956
SQ FT: 28,000
SALES: 4MM **Privately Held**
WEB: www.servicestampings.com
SIC: 3469 Stamping metal for the trade

(G-20428)
SHAFTS MFG
1585 E 361st St Unit G1 (44095-5329)
PHONE.................................440 942-6012
Berndy Heckelmann, *Principal*
EMP: 8
SALES (est): 573.4K **Privately Held**
SIC: 3999 Manufacturing industries

(G-20429)
SHERBROOKE METALS
36490 Reading Ave (44094-8207)
P.O. Box 689 (44096-0689)
PHONE.................................440 942-3520
Randy Spoth, *President*
Nancy Spoth, *Treasurer*
Laura Krus, *Admin Sec*
EMP: 22
SQ FT: 9,000
SALES (est): 6.8MM **Privately Held**
WEB: www.sherbrookemetals.com
SIC: 3624 3823 3548 Electrodes, thermal & electrolytic uses: carbon, graphite; industrial instrmnts msrmnt display/control process variable; welding apparatus

(G-20430)
SIGNS PDQ INC
35160 Topps Industrial Pk (44094-4675)
PHONE.................................440 951-6651
Brenda O'Toole, *President*
Don O'Toole, *Vice Pres*

Marge Mackey, *CFO*
EMP: 4
SALES (est): 599K **Privately Held**
WEB: www.signspdq.com
SIC: 3993 Signs, not made in custom sign painting shops

(G-20431)
SKRL DIE CASTING INC
34580 Lakeland Blvd (44095-5221)
PHONE.................................440 946-7200
Sandra Szuch, *President*
EMP: 75 **EST:** 1967
SQ FT: 30,000
SALES (est): 12.8MM **Privately Held**
SIC: 3544 Special dies & tools

(G-20432)
SLABE MACHINE PRODUCTS CO
4659 Hamann Pkwy (44094-5631)
PHONE.................................440 946-6555
Edward Slabe Jr, *President*
Brendan Slabe, *Vice Pres*
Judith Slabe, *Treasurer*
Christopher Slabe, *Admin Sec*
▲ **EMP:** 100
SQ FT: 58,000
SALES (est): 25.1MM **Privately Held**
WEB: www.slabemachine.com
SIC: 3599 Machine shop, jobbing & repair

(G-20433)
SLOAT INC
34099 Melinz Pkwy Unit A (44095-4001)
PHONE.................................440 951-9554
Jeff Sloat, *President*
EMP: 6
SALES (est): 750K **Privately Held**
SIC: 2892 Primary explosives, fuses & detonators

(G-20434)
SMOLIC MACHINE CO
37127 Ben Hur Ave (44094-6333)
PHONE.................................440 946-1747
Joseph Smolic Sr, *President*
Emil Smolic, *General Mgr*
EMP: 4
SQ FT: 10,500
SALES: 1.5MM **Privately Held**
SIC: 3599 Machine shop, jobbing & repair

(G-20435)
SONOMA GRINDING MACHINING INC
37195 Ben Hur Ave Ste E (44094-6348)
PHONE.................................440 918-7990
Josip Filipovic, *President*
EMP: 6
SQ FT: 6,000
SALES (est): 417.8K **Privately Held**
SIC: 3599 Machine shop, jobbing & repair

(G-20436)
SPENCE TECHNOLOGIES INC
Also Called: R.W.
4752 Topps Indus Pkwy (44094-4636)
PHONE.................................440 946-3035
William Spence, *President*
EMP: 18
SQ FT: 10,320
SALES (est): 2.9MM **Privately Held**
SIC: 3599 Machine shop, jobbing & repair

(G-20437)
STEEL TECHNOLOGIES LLC
Steel Technologies Ohio
220 Joseph Lloyd Pkwy (44094)
PHONE.................................440 946-8666
Rick Furber, *Vice Pres*
EMP: 70 **Privately Held**
WEB: www.steeltechnologies.com
SIC: 3316 Cold finishing of steel shapes
HQ: Steel Technologies Llc
    700 N Hurstbourne Pkwy # 400
    Louisville KY 40222
    502 245-2110

(G-20438)
STICKER CORPORATION (PA)
Also Called: Reighart Steel Products
37877 Elm St (44094-6243)
PHONE.................................440 946-2100
Douglas Reighart, *President*

Lori Harrison, *Accountant*
Laura Schwarz, *Bookkeeper*
EMP: 18 **EST:** 1947
SQ FT: 18,000
SALES (est): 3.8MM **Privately Held**
WEB: www.stickercorp.com
SIC: 3585 3549 3547 3443 Heating equipment, complete; metalworking machinery; rolling mill machinery; fabricated plate work (boiler shop); heating equipment, except electric

(G-20439)
T & S DISCOUNT TIRES INC
Also Called: Gear Products Co
36525 Reading Ave (44094-8210)
PHONE.................................440 951-9084
David Takacs, *President*
EMP: 4
SQ FT: 14,000
SALES (est): 708.2K **Privately Held**
SIC: 3462 Iron & steel forgings

(G-20440)
TABLOX INC
4821 E 345th St (44094-4606)
PHONE.................................440 953-1951
Dana Talcott, *President*
Pam Cleverly, *Vice Pres*
Aaron Talcott, *QC Mgr*
EMP: 9
SQ FT: 16,000
SALES (est): 955K **Privately Held**
WEB: www.tablox.com
SIC: 3471 Finishing, metals or formed products

(G-20441)
TC SERVICE CO
Also Called: Top Cat Air Tools
38285 Pelton Rd (44094-7740)
PHONE.................................440 954-7500
Edgar G Henry, *President*
Gerald J Henry, *Principal*
Valeria S Henry, *Principal*
Andrew K Henry, *Engineer*
M Anne Henry, *Admin Sec*
EMP: 40
SQ FT: 60,000
SALES (est): 7.6MM **Privately Held**
WEB: www.tcservice.com
SIC: 3546 Power-driven handtools

(G-20442)
TDC SYSTEMS INC
38296 Western Pkwy (44094-7590)
PHONE.................................440 953-5918
Tony Kalar, *President*
Diana Kalar, *Vice Pres*
EMP: 5
SQ FT: 2,500
SALES: 700K **Privately Held**
SIC: 3721 Research & development on aircraft by the manufacturer

(G-20443)
TECHNICAL TRANSLATION SERVICES (PA)
37841 Euclid Ave Ste 7 (44094-5981)
PHONE.................................440 942-3130
J M Crouvisier, *President*
EMP: 11 **EST:** 1976
SQ FT: 10,000
SALES (est): 1.1MM **Privately Held**
WEB: www.onelap.com
SIC: 7389 7819 7812 2791 Translation services; film processing, editing & titling: motion picture; audio-visual program production; typesetting

(G-20444)
TELLING INDUSTRIES LLC (PA)
4420 Sherwin Rd (44094-7994)
PHONE.................................440 974-3370
Brian Nunes, *Controller*
Harbour Garrett, *Accounting Mgr*
Edward Slish, *Mng Member*
Troy Frank,
Tom Gallagher,
◆ **EMP:** 10
SQ FT: 400,000
SALES (est): 29.1MM **Privately Held**
WEB: www.tellingindustries.com
SIC: 3316 Bars, steel, cold finished, from purchased hot-rolled

(G-20445)
TELLING INDUSTRIES LLC
4420 Sherwin Rd Ste 3 (44094-7995)
PHONE.................................928 681-2010
EMP: 10
SALES (corp-wide): 31.5MM **Privately Held**
SIC: 3316 Mfg Cold-Rolled Steel Sheet
PA: Telling Industries, Llc
    4420 Sherwin Rd
    Willoughby OH 44094
    440 974-3370

(G-20446)
TETRAD ELECTRONICS INC (PA)
2048 Joseph Lloyd Pkwy (44094-8032)
PHONE.................................440 946-6443
Ronald K Brehm, *President*
Jeffrey Waterman, *Vice Pres*
Richard Scebbi, *Treasurer*
Bruce Vanek, *Admin Sec*
EMP: 61
SQ FT: 14,000
SALES (est): 9.7MM **Privately Held**
WEB: www.tetradelec.com
SIC: 3672 Printed circuit boards

(G-20447)
TITAN MANUFACTURING LLC
4730 Beidler Rd (44094-4604)
PHONE.................................440 942-2258
Marcel Uhrich, *Principal*
EMP: 4 **EST:** 2000
SQ FT: 1,680
SALES (est): 580.3K **Privately Held**
WEB: www.titansoap.com
SIC: 3599 Machine shop, jobbing & repair

(G-20448)
TKR METAL FABRICATING LLC
Also Called: T-Fab
37552 N Industrial Pkwy (44094-6214)
PHONE.................................440 221-2770
Kevin Humphreys, *Vice Pres*
Timothy Herbert, *Vice Pres*
Mark Humphreys, *Engineer*
EMP: 5 **EST:** 2010
SQ FT: 7,000
SALES (est): 260K **Privately Held**
SIC: 3444 Machine guards, sheet metal

(G-20449)
TOKU AMERICA INC
Also Called: Striker Hydraulic Breakers
3900 Ben Hur Ave Ste 3 (44094-6398)
PHONE.................................440 954-9923
David Nakamura, *President*
Akinori Kihara, *Admin Sec*
▲ **EMP:** 13
SQ FT: 15,000
SALES: 3.8MM
SALES (corp-wide): 75.7MM **Privately Held**
SIC: 3531 Crushers, portable
PA: Toku Pneumatic Co.,Ltd.
    4-3-4, Katakasu, Hakata-Ku
    Fukuoka FUK 812-0
    924 720-275

(G-20450)
TOM THUMB CLIP CO INC
36300 Lkeland Blvd Unit 2 (44095)
P.O. Box 709 (44096-0709)
PHONE.................................440 953-9606
Jennifer Baxter, *President*
June Baxter, *Vice Pres*
EMP: 10 **EST:** 1947
SALES (est): 650K **Privately Held**
WEB: www.tomthumbclip.com
SIC: 3496 Clips & fasteners, made from purchased wire

(G-20451)
TRU-FAB TECHNOLOGY INC
34820 Lakeland Blvd (44095-5224)
PHONE.................................440 954-9760
John J Stegh, *President*
Connie Stegh, *Treasurer*
EMP: 10
SQ FT: 15,000
SALES (est): 1.8MM **Privately Held**
SIC: 3599 7692 Custom machinery; welding repair

Willoughby - Lake County (G-20452)

(G-20452)
TRUCAST INC
4382 Hamann Pkwy (44094-5683)
PHONE...................440 942-4923
Jesse Baden, *President*
Ray Newcomb, *Financial Exec*
EMP: 60
SQ FT: 20,000
SALES (est): 3.6MM **Privately Held**
SIC: 3599 Machine shop, jobbing & repair

(G-20453)
TRV INCORPORATED
4860 E 345th St (44094-4607)
PHONE...................440 951-7722
Peter Kolaric, *President*
Tom Kolaric, *Vice Pres*
Victoria Kolaric, *Treasurer*
EMP: 30
SALES (est): 6.9MM **Privately Held**
SIC: 3599 Machine shop, jobbing & repair

(G-20454)
TWO M PRECISION CO INC
Also Called: United Hydraulics
1747 Joseph Lloyd Pkwy # 3 (44094-8067)
PHONE...................440 946-2120
Mate Brkic, *President*
Nate Brkic, *Vice Pres*
Frank Bortnick, *Purchasing*
Doris Brkic, *Treasurer*
EMP: 45
SQ FT: 35,000
SALES (est): 7.2MM **Privately Held**
WEB: www.twomprecision.com
SIC: 3599 3569 7692 Machine shop, jobbing & repair; grinding castings for the trade; filter elements, fluid, hydraulic line; welding repair

(G-20455)
UNIVERSAL J&Z MACHINE LLC
4781 E 355th St (44094-4631)
PHONE...................216 486-2220
Marina Grman, *President*
Joseph Grman, *Vice Pres*
Jose Padilla, *Prdtn Mgr*
EMP: 24
SQ FT: 5,000
SALES (est): 450K **Privately Held**
SIC: 3599 Machine shop, jobbing & repair

(G-20456)
US MOLDING MACHINERY CO INC
38294 Pelton Rd (44094-7765)
PHONE...................440 918-1701
Zac Cohen, *President*
Jerry Harper, *Vice Pres*
Robert Luck, *Vice Pres*
Bill Sprowls, *Vice Pres*
Roger Anderson, *Plant Engr*
EMP: 28
SQ FT: 12,500
SALES (est): 5.2MM **Privately Held**
WEB: www.usmolding.com
SIC: 3089 7699 Injection molding of plastics; industrial equipment services

(G-20457)
USM ACQUISITION CORPORATION (PA)
Also Called: Universal Machine
2002 Joseph Lloyd Pkwy (44094-8032)
PHONE...................440 975-8600
Lisa Netiss, *President*
EMP: 100
SALES (est): 9.5MM **Privately Held**
WEB: www.usmonline.com
SIC: 3599 3541 Machine shop, jobbing & repair; machine tools, metal cutting type

(G-20458)
WILLOUGHBY BREWING COMPANY
4057 Erie St (44094-7804)
P.O. Box 946 (44096-0946)
PHONE...................440 975-0202
Jeremy Vanhorn, *Managing Prtnr*
Jeremy Banhoron, *Mng Member*
Rick Seibt, *Director*
EMP: 80
SQ FT: 1,200
SALES (est): 10.5MM **Privately Held**
WEB: www.willoughbybrewing.com
SIC: 2082 5812 Beer (alcoholic beverage); eating places

(G-20459)
WILLOW HILL INDUSTRIES LLC
37611 Euclid Ave (44094-5923)
PHONE...................440 942-3003
Ronald A Bone,
EMP: 80
SALES (est): 8.1MM **Privately Held**
WEB: www.whindustries.com
SIC: 3469 Metal stampings

(G-20460)
WIRED INC
38849 Courtland Dr (44094-7509)
PHONE...................440 567-8379
David Allen, *Principal*
EMP: 5
SALES (est): 481.7K **Privately Held**
SIC: 3629 Electrical industrial apparatus

(G-20461)
X PRESS PRINTING SERVICES INC
4405 Glenbrook Rd (44094-8219)
PHONE...................440 951-8848
John Platko, *President*
EMP: 11
SALES (est): 1.5MM **Privately Held**
SIC: 2752 Commercial printing, offset

(G-20462)
Z & Z MANUFACTURING INC
4765 E 355th St (44094-4631)
PHONE...................440 953-2800
Tom Zovko, *President*
EMP: 18
SQ FT: 20,000
SALES: 2.5MM **Privately Held**
WEB: www.z-zmfg.com
SIC: 3599 Machine shop, jobbing & repair

(G-20463)
ZERO-D PRODUCTS INC (PA)
Also Called: Akron Jewelry Rubber
37939 Stevens Blvd (44094-6235)
PHONE...................440 417-1843
William W Mull, *President*
James R Dillhoefer, *Corp Secy*
Robert J Beausoleil, *Vice Pres*
John Holliday, *Branch Mgr*
EMP: 5
SALES (est): 671K **Privately Held**
WEB: www.zerodproducts.com
SIC: 3915 Jewelers' findings & materials

(G-20464)
ZITNIK ENTERPRISES INC
Also Called: D M Z Machine Co
35530 Lakeland Blvd (44095-5305)
PHONE...................440 951-0089
Dusan Mark Zitnik, *Owner*
Bill Hufgard, *Controller*
EMP: 4
SQ FT: 5,000
SALES (est): 417K **Privately Held**
SIC: 3599 Machine shop, jobbing & repair

(G-20465)
ZUKOWSKI RACK CO
1647 E 361st St (44095-5331)
PHONE...................440 942-5889
Dan Zukowski, *President*
Francis Zukowski, *President*
EMP: 5
SQ FT: 6,000
SALES (est): 250K **Privately Held**
SIC: 2542 Racks, merchandise display or storage: except wood

Willoughby Hills
Lake County

(G-20466)
ATLANTIC CO
26651 Curtiss Wright Pkwy (44092-2832)
PHONE...................440 944-8988
F Joseph Callahan, *Ch of Bd*
William Cosgrove, *President*
Thomas Janock, *Treasurer*
EMP: 50
SQ FT: 30,000
SALES (est): 4.9MM
SALES (corp-wide): 940.1MM **Privately Held**
WEB: www.swagelok.com
SIC: 3432 Plumbing fixture fittings & trim
PA: Swagelok Company
29500 Solon Rd
Solon OH 44139
440 248-4600

(G-20467)
BUTERA MANUFACTURING INC
2935 Lynn Dr (44092-1419)
P.O. Box 349, Wickliffe (44092-0349)
PHONE...................440 516-3698
Richard E Butera, *CEO*
Brian Butera, *President*
Kim Butera, *Corp Secy*
EMP: 18
SQ FT: 50,000
SALES (est): 1.8MM **Privately Held**
SIC: 3429 5941 Animal traps, iron or steel; hunting equipment

(G-20468)
CHAGRIN VLY STL ERECTORS INC
Also Called: Ruple Trucking
2278 River Rd (44094-9685)
PHONE...................440 975-1556
Victoria Ruple, *President*
John Ruple, *President*
EMP: 13
SQ FT: 10,040
SALES: 4MM **Privately Held**
SIC: 3441 1791 4213 1796 Fabricated structural metal; structural steel erection; trucking, except local; machine moving & rigging

(G-20469)
IDCOMM LLC
32315 White Rd (44092-1339)
PHONE...................661 250-4081
Gary Marsh, *Principal*
Karen Marsh, *Principal*
EMP: 5
SALES (est): 423.5K **Privately Held**
SIC: 3679 Microwave components

(G-20470)
KIRTLAND CPITL PARTNERS III LP (PA)
2550 Som Center Rd # 105 (44094-9655)
PHONE...................440 585-9010
Fax: 440 585-9699
EMP: 1
SALES (est): 41.2MM **Privately Held**
SIC: 3085 2821 Mfg Plastic Bottles Mfg Plastic Materials/Resins

(G-20471)
MICRO PRODUCTS CO INC
26653 Curtiss Wright Pkwy (44092-2832)
PHONE...................440 943-0258
Arthur Anton, *President*
Reese Armstrong, *Safety Mgr*
Frank Roddy, *CFO*
Ernie Mansour, *Admin Sec*
EMP: 70 EST: 1981
SQ FT: 10,000
SALES (est): 3.7MM
SALES (corp-wide): 940.1MM **Privately Held**
WEB: www.swagelok.com
SIC: 3471 7389 Plating & polishing; grinding, precision: commercial or industrial
PA: Swagelok Company
29500 Solon Rd
Solon OH 44139
440 248-4600

(G-20472)
NEUROS MEDICAL INC
35010 Chardon Rd Ste 210 (44094-9011)
PHONE...................440 951-2565
Alan Kaganov, *Ch of Bd*
Tom Wilder, *President*
Mark Teague, *CFO*
Zi-Ping Fang, *CTO*
EMP: 8
SQ FT: 4,275
SALES (est): 1MM **Privately Held**
SIC: 3845 Electromedical equipment

(G-20473)
NIKLEE CO
2959 Canterbury Ct (44092-1467)
PHONE...................440 944-0082
Linda Motuza, *President*
Rick Motuza, *Vice Pres*
EMP: 5
SALES (est): 380K **Privately Held**
WEB: www.niklee.com
SIC: 2759 Screen printing

(G-20474)
QUAD INDUSTRIES INC
37151 Rogers Rd (44094-9480)
PHONE...................440 951-4849
Fred Zupancic, *President*
EMP: 4
SQ FT: 3,000
SALES (est): 30.4K **Privately Held**
SIC: 3599 Machine shop, jobbing & repair

(G-20475)
SWAGELOK COMPANY
26653 Curtiss Wright Pkwy (44092-2832)
P.O. Box 31300, Independence (44131-0300)
PHONE...................440 248-4600
EMP: 72
SALES (corp-wide): 940.1MM **Privately Held**
SIC: 3491 3599 Pressure valves & regulators, industrial; machine shop, jobbing & repair
PA: Swagelok Company
29500 Solon Rd
Solon OH 44139
440 248-4600

(G-20476)
SWAGELOK COMPANY
Also Called: Swagelok Biopharm Services Co
26651 Curtiss Wright Pkwy (44092-2832)
PHONE...................440 944-8988
Chuck Pereksta, *Manager*
Brian Muckenthaler, *Manager*
EMP: 20
SALES (corp-wide): 940.1MM **Privately Held**
WEB: www.swagelok.com
SIC: 3494 Valves & pipe fittings
PA: Swagelok Company
29500 Solon Rd
Solon OH 44139
440 248-4600

Willowick
Lake County

(G-20477)
E E CONTROLS INC
30301 Fairway Blvd (44095-4647)
P.O. Box 5098, Willoughby (44095-0098)
PHONE...................440 585-5554
Rollin Randolph, *President*
EMP: 3
SQ FT: 3,500
SALES (est): 263.4K **Privately Held**
SIC: 7699 3823 Industrial equipment services; industrial process control instruments

(G-20478)
EMES SUPPLY LLC
35622 Vine St (44095-3150)
PHONE...................216 400-8025
Elie Koval,
EMP: 7
SALES (est): 1.5MM **Privately Held**
SIC: 2842 Cleaning or polishing preparations

(G-20479)
JAKPRINTS INC
34440 Vine St (44095-5114)
PHONE...................877 246-3132
Jacob Edwards, *President*
Bill Rupnik, *President*
Dameon Guess, *Vice Pres*
Brad Fishbaugh, *Facilities Mgr*
Ashley Edmonson, *Accounts Mgr*
EMP: 127
SQ FT: 32,000

GEOGRAPHIC SECTION

Wilmington - Clinton County (G-20507)

SALES (est): 30.6MM **Privately Held**
WEB: www.jakprints.com
SIC: 2752 Commercial printing, offset

(G-20480)
PEER PANTRY LLC
30901 Lake Shore Blvd (44095-3609)
PHONE..................................216 236-4087
Marcus Allen Coleman,
EMP: 5
SALES (est): 152.6K **Privately Held**
SIC: 2099 Food preparations

(G-20481)
PUBLIC SAFETY OHIO DEPARTMENT
Also Called: Ross County License Bureau
31517 Vine St (44095-3561)
PHONE..................................440 943-5545
Cynthia Marfisi, *General Mgr*
EMP: 6 **Privately Held**
SIC: 3469 9221 Automobile license tags, stamped metal; police protection;
HQ: Ohio Department Of Public Safety
1970 W Broad St Fl 5
Columbus OH 43223

Willshire
Van Wert County

(G-20482)
PHOTO STAR
307 State St (45898)
PHONE..................................419 495-2696
Judith E Bunner, *Owner*
EMP: 3 EST: 1895
SQ FT: 1,500
SALES: 200K **Privately Held**
SIC: 2711 Newspapers, publishing & printing

Wilmington
Clinton County

(G-20483)
ABBOT IMAGE SOLUTIONS LLC
185 Park Dr (45177-2891)
PHONE..................................937 382-6677
Greg Abbott, *Owner*
Mackenzie Cinnamon, *Marketing Staff*
EMP: 5 EST: 2012
SALES: 9MM **Privately Held**
SIC: 3993 Signs & advertising specialties

(G-20484)
AHRESTY WILMINGTON CORPORATION
2627 S South St (45177-2926)
PHONE..................................937 382-6112
Kenichi Nonaka, *President*
Justin Rummer, *Vice Pres*
Brent West, *Purch Agent*
Jeffrey Fliegel, *Purchasing*
Robin Carpenter, *Engineer*
▲ EMP: 378
SQ FT: 334,000
SALES: 29MM
SALES (corp-wide): 1.3B **Privately Held**
WEB: www.ahresty.com
SIC: 3363 Aluminum die-castings
PA: Ahresty Corporation
1-2, Nakahara, Mitsuyacho
Toyohashi AIC 441-3
532 652-170

(G-20485)
ALKERMES INC
265 Olinger Cir (45177-2484)
PHONE..................................937 382-5642
Brandon Baird, *Mfg Spvr*
Beth Clark, *Buyer*
Nick Steege, *Research*
Robert Adkins, *Engineer*
Justin McCurdy, *Engineer*
EMP: 40
SQ FT: 12,000 **Privately Held**
WEB: www.alkermes.com
SIC: 2834 Pharmaceutical preparations

HQ: Alkermes, Inc.
852 Winter St
Waltham MA 02451
781 609-6000

(G-20486)
ATEC DIVERSFD WLDG FABRICATION
Also Called: A T E C Diversified
466 Dehan Rd (45177-9771)
PHONE..................................937 546-4399
David Sanford, *Owner*
EMP: 5 EST: 2001
SALES (est): 304.7K **Privately Held**
WEB: www.atecdiversified.com
SIC: 1389 Oil field services

(G-20487)
BUSH SPECIALTY VEHICLES INC
80 Park Dr (45177-2038)
PHONE..................................937 382-5502
Larry Vanover, *Vice Pres*
EMP: 15
SALES (est): 3.8MM **Privately Held**
WEB: www.bushinteriors.com
SIC: 3713 Specialty motor vehicle bodies

(G-20488)
CHAMPION BRIDGE COMPANY
261 E Sugartree St (45177-2316)
PHONE..................................937 382-2521
Randy Dell, *President*
Gale Gerard, *Vice Pres*
Debbie Laufer, *Administration*
EMP: 20 EST: 1934
SQ FT: 30,000
SALES (est): 5.7MM **Privately Held**
SIC: 3441 Fabricated structural metal

(G-20489)
CLIFFCO STANDS INC
Also Called: Wilmington Precision Machining
397 Starbuck Rd (45177-8875)
PHONE..................................937 382-3700
Steve Garrison, *Principal*
David D Clay, *Principal*
Clifton Hamilton, *Principal*
EMP: 24 EST: 1996
SQ FT: 9,000
SALES (est): 5.7MM **Privately Held**
SIC: 3544 Special dies & tools

(G-20490)
COMPTON METAL PRODUCTS INC
416 Steele Rd (45177-9332)
PHONE..................................937 382-2403
James Compton, *President*
EMP: 82
SQ FT: 2,000
SALES (est): 2.4MM **Privately Held**
SIC: 7699 3599 7692 Engine repair & replacement, non-automotive; machine shop, jobbing & repair; welding repair

(G-20491)
COX PRINTING CO
Also Called: Cox Painting
1087 Wayne Rd (45177-2024)
P.O. Box 263, Maineville (45039-0263)
PHONE..................................937 382-2312
Pamela Olds, *President*
Ramona Cox, *President*
Frank A Cox, *Consultant*
EMP: 7
SQ FT: 2,600
SALES (est): 784K **Privately Held**
SIC: 2752 2759 2789 Commercial printing, offset; letterpress printing; bookbinding & related work

(G-20492)
CPG INTERNATIONAL LLC
Also Called: Timbertech
894 Prairie Rd (45177-8847)
PHONE..................................937 655-8766
EMP: 260
SALES (corp-wide): 958.4MM **Publicly Held**
SIC: 3089 Plastic hardware & building products

HQ: Cpg International Llc
1330 W Fulton St Ste 350
Chicago IL 60607
570 558-8000

(G-20493)
CUSTOM MOLDED PRODUCTS LLC
92 Grant St (45177-2362)
PHONE..................................937 382-1070
Marsha Leigh, *Manager*
Norman Allen Jr,
▲ EMP: 84
SQ FT: 11,000
SALES (est): 17.1MM **Privately Held**
WEB: www.custommolded.com
SIC: 3089 Injection molding of plastics

(G-20494)
EDWARD KEITER & SONS
1235 Stone Rd (45177-9680)
PHONE..................................937 382-3249
Edward Keiter, *Owner*
Steve Keiter, *Co-Owner*
EMP: 4
SALES (est): 310K **Privately Held**
SIC: 2048 Livestock feeds

(G-20495)
GRANDPAS POTTERY
3558 W State Route 73 (45177-9292)
PHONE..................................937 382-6442
Ray Storer, *Owner*
Betty Storer, *Co-Owner*
EMP: 4
SALES: 50K **Privately Held**
SIC: 3269 Pottery cooking & kitchen articles

(G-20496)
GRAPHICS TO GO LLC
761 S Nelson Ave (45177-2517)
PHONE..................................937 382-4100
Tracy L Addison, *Mng Member*
EMP: 5
SALES (est): 486.8K **Privately Held**
SIC: 2759 Screen printing

(G-20497)
HALE MANUFACTURING LLC
1065 Wayne Rd (45177-2024)
PHONE..................................937 382-2127
David Hale, *President*
EMP: 10 EST: 1947
SQ FT: 10,000
SALES (est): 1.4MM **Privately Held**
SIC: 3599 Machine shop, jobbing & repair

(G-20498)
HOOD PACKAGING CORPORATION
Also Called: Southern Bag
1961 Rombach Ave (45177-1997)
P.O. Box 745 (45177-0745)
PHONE..................................937 382-6681
Bill Terrill, *Branch Mgr*
EMP: 200
SQ FT: 150,000 **Privately Held**
WEB: www.hoodpkg.com
SIC: 2674 2673 Shipping bags or sacks, including multiwall & heavy duty; bags: plastic, laminated & coated
HQ: Hood Packaging Corporation
25 Woodgreen Pl
Madison MS 39110
601 853-7260

(G-20499)
MELVIN GRAIN CO
413 Melvin Rd (45177-9675)
PHONE..................................937 382-1249
Mike Keither, *Owner*
Ed Keither, *Partner*
Jim Keither, *Partner*
Steve Keithers, *Partner*
EMP: 4 EST: 1944
SALES: 30K **Privately Held**
SIC: 3999 Custom pulverizing & grinding of plastic materials

(G-20500)
MONEY JEWELRY VAULTS
236 E Sugartree St (45177-2317)
PHONE..................................937 366-6391
EMP: 3

SALES (est): 140K **Privately Held**
SIC: 3272 Mfg Concrete Products

(G-20501)
ORANGE FRAZER PRESS INC
37 1/2 W Main St (45177-2236)
P.O. Box 214 (45177-0214)
PHONE..................................937 382-3196
Marcy Hawley, *President*
John Baskin, *Vice Pres*
Sarah Hawley, *Mktg Dir*
Janice Ellis, *Office Mgr*
Alyson Rua, *Graphic Designe*
EMP: 7
SQ FT: 2,000
SALES (est): 1MM **Privately Held**
WEB: www.orangefrazer.com
SIC: 2731 Books: publishing only

(G-20502)
POLARIS INDUSTRIES INC
3435 Airborne Rd Ste A (45177-8951)
PHONE..................................937 283-1200
Dan Smith, *Branch Mgr*
EMP: 40
SALES (corp-wide): 6B **Publicly Held**
SIC: 3799 All terrain vehicles (ATV)
PA: Polaris Industries Inc.
2100 Highway 55
Medina MN 55340
763 542-0500

(G-20503)
PORTER HYBRIDS INC
1683 N State Route 134 (45177-9651)
PHONE..................................937 382-2324
Larry Kirk, *Manager*
EMP: 3
SALES (est): 317.3K **Privately Held**
SIC: 2841 Soap & other detergents

(G-20504)
PRAXAIR DISTRIBUTION INC
105 Praxair Way (45177-7189)
PHONE..................................937 283-3400
Chris Lawson, *Branch Mgr*
EMP: 11 **Privately Held**
SIC: 5084 2813 Welding machinery & equipment; carbon dioxide
HQ: Praxair Distribution, Inc.
10 Riverview Dr
Danbury CT 06810
203 837-2000

(G-20505)
QUALI-TEE DESIGN SPORTS
Also Called: Quali-Tee Design Sportswear
50 W Sugartree St (45177-2226)
PHONE..................................937 382-7997
James Evans, *President*
Todd Evans, *Vice Pres*
Terri Gehlbach, *Manager*
EMP: 18
SALES (est): 910.7K **Privately Held**
SIC: 7336 2395 5699 5999 Silk screen design; swiss loom embroideries; sports apparel; trophies & plaques; screen printing

(G-20506)
R & B MACHINING INC (PA)
2695 Progress Way (45177-7702)
PHONE..................................937 698-3528
Randy Workman, *President*
Betty Workman, *President*
Ethan Long, *Sales Staff*
John Wiget, *Manager*
Randy W Workman, *Manager*
EMP: 4
SQ FT: 4,000
SALES (est): 7.8MM **Privately Held**
WEB: www.rbmachining.com
SIC: 3599 Machine shop, jobbing & repair

(G-20507)
R & B MACHINING INC
2695 Progress Way (45177-7702)
PHONE..................................937 382-6710
Joe Eramo, *CEO*
EMP: 35
SALES (corp-wide): 7.8MM **Privately Held**
SIC: 3599 3542 Machine shop, jobbing & repair; bending machines

Wilmington - Clinton County (G-20508) GEOGRAPHIC SECTION

PA: R & B Machining, Inc.
2695 Progress Way
Wilmington OH 45177
937 698-3528

(G-20508)
RTPROCESS LLC
311 Davids Dr (45177-2431)
PHONE..................................937 366-6215
Ali Kerr, *General Mgr*
EMP: 4
SQ FT: 8,000
SALES (est): 554.6K **Privately Held**
SIC: 2819 Industrial inorganic chemicals

(G-20509)
TRI STATE MEDIA LLC
325 Davids Dr (45177-2431)
PHONE..................................513 933-0101
John Clary, *President*
EMP: 15 **EST:** 2001
SQ FT: 10,500
SALES: 5MM **Privately Held**
SIC: 2679 Labels, paper: made from purchased material

(G-20510)
W L AREHART COMPUTING SYSTEMS
555 Fife Rd (45177-8901)
PHONE..................................937 383-4710
William Arehart Jr, *Owner*
Anita Hobart, *Director*
EMP: 5
SALES (est): 368.2K **Privately Held**
SIC: 7379 7372 Data processing consultant; prepackaged software

(G-20511)
WELLSGROUP
1481 S Us Highway 68 (45177-8929)
PHONE..................................937 382-4003
Scott Wells, *Owner*
EMP: 3
SALES (est): 214.5K **Privately Held**
SIC: 3273 Ready-mixed concrete

(G-20512)
WILMINGTON FOREST PRODUCTS
5562 S Us Highway 68 (45177-7112)
PHONE..................................937 382-5013
Thomas D Driscoll, *President*
Mary B Driscoll, *Vice Pres*
EMP: 6
SQ FT: 7,500
SALES (est): 739.8K **Privately Held**
SIC: 2421 Sawmills & planing mills, general

Wilmot
Stark County

(G-20513)
AMISH DOOR INC (PA)
Also Called: Amish Door Restaurant
1210 Winesburg St (44689)
P.O. Box 215 (44689-0215)
PHONE..................................330 359-5464
Milo Miller, *President*
Eric Gerber, *Vice Pres*
Yvonne Torrence, *Treasurer*
Katherine Miller, *Shareholder*
EMP: 294
SQ FT: 7,500
SALES (est): 17.4MM **Privately Held**
WEB: www.amishdoor.com
SIC: 5947 5812 7011 2051 Gift shop; restaurant, family: independent; hotels & motels; bread, cake & related products

(G-20514)
COSMO CORPORATION
Also Called: Cosmo Plastics Co
211 Winesburg St (44689-9616)
PHONE..................................330 359-5429
Vicky Wartcentruber, *Manager*
EMP: 100
SQ FT: 12,000
SALES (corp-wide): 45.5K **Privately Held**
SIC: 3089 Injection molding of plastics
HQ: Cosmo Plastics Company
30201 Aurora Rd
Cleveland OH 44139
440 498-7500

(G-20515)
DAVID E EASTERDAY AND CO INC
Also Called: Easterday & Co
1225 Us Route 62 Unit C (44689-9628)
PHONE..................................330 359-0700
David E Easterday, *President*
Valeria Easterday, *Corp Secy*
EMP: 12
SQ FT: 40,000
SALES (est): 3.3MM **Privately Held**
SIC: 2851 Varnishes

(G-20516)
HARDWOOD SOLUTIONS
112 E Main St (44689)
PHONE..................................330 359-5755
Brian Kyle, *Principal*
EMP: 6
SALES (est): 787K **Privately Held**
SIC: 2499 Decorative wood & woodwork

(G-20517)
WEAVER LUMBER CO
1925 Us Route 62 (44689-9604)
PHONE..................................330 359-5091
Robert Weaver, *Owner*
EMP: 6
SALES (est): 575K **Privately Held**
SIC: 2421 Custom sawmill

Winchester
Adams County

(G-20518)
BETTER BUILT BARNS (PA)
10628 Russellville Winchs (45697-9636)
PHONE..................................606 348-6146
Lyndon Yoder, *Owner*
EMP: 4
SQ FT: 4,000
SALES (est): 886.5K **Privately Held**
SIC: 3448 Prefabricated metal buildings

(G-20519)
CANTRELL RFINERY SLS TRNSP INC
18856 State Route 136 (45697-9793)
P.O. Box 175 (45697-0175)
PHONE..................................937 695-0318
Robert Cantrell, *President*
EMP: 15 **EST:** 2008
SALES (est): 1.9MM **Privately Held**
SIC: 3559 Petroleum refinery equipment

(G-20520)
FOX HOLLOW PALLET
3519 Graces Run Rd (45697-9763)
PHONE..................................937 386-2872
Freeman Yutzy, *Owner*
EMP: 3
SALES (est): 106.4K **Privately Held**
SIC: 2448 Pallets, wood

(G-20521)
HANSON AGGREGATES EAST LLC
13526 Overstake Rd (45697-9644)
PHONE..................................937 442-6009
Bob Roades, *Plant Mgr*
Bobby Roades, *Branch Mgr*
EMP: 30
SALES (corp-wide): 20.6B **Privately Held**
SIC: 1422 Crushed & broken limestone
HQ: Hanson Aggregates East Llc
3131 Rdu Center Dr
Morrisville NC 27560
919 380-2500

(G-20522)
LEROY YUTZY
Also Called: Fox Hollow Pallet
191 Russellville Rd (45697-9635)
PHONE..................................937 386-2872
EMP: 4
SALES (est): 170K **Privately Held**
SIC: 2448 Mfg Wood Pallets/Skids

(G-20523)
N & W MACHINING & FABRICATING
8 Mathias Rd (45697-9727)
PHONE..................................937 695-5582
Junior Nesbitt, *President*
Julene Nesbitt, *Corp Secy*
EMP: 9 **EST:** 1996
SQ FT: 10,000
SALES (est): 1.1MM **Privately Held**
SIC: 3599 Machine shop, jobbing & repair

Windham
Portage County

(G-20524)
HARBISONWALKER INTL INC
9686 E Center St (44288-1050)
P.O. Box 490 (44288-0490)
PHONE..................................330 326-2010
John Stock, *Branch Mgr*
EMP: 22
SQ FT: 300,000
SALES (corp-wide): 703.8MM **Privately Held**
WEB: www.hwr.com
SIC: 3255 Clay refractories
HQ: Harbisonwalker International, Inc.
1305 Cherrington Pkwy # 100
Moon Township PA 15108

(G-20525)
KNUKONCEPTZCOM LTD
7227 Anderson Rd (44288-9702)
PHONE..................................216 310-6555
William Greenberg, *Mng Member*
▲ **EMP:** 5
SQ FT: 5,000
SALES (est): 848K **Privately Held**
SIC: 3651 Household audio & video equipment

Windsor
Ashtabula County

(G-20526)
HERSHBERGER MANUFACTURING
Also Called: Eagle Hardwoods
7584 Rockwood Rd (44099-9741)
P.O. Box 336 (44099-0336)
PHONE..................................440 272-5555
John Hershberger, *Owner*
EMP: 20
SQ FT: 6,500
SALES: 4.1MM **Privately Held**
SIC: 2448 4212 Pallets, wood; local trucking, without storage

(G-20527)
HILLSIDE PALLET
8552 Cox Rd (44099-9729)
PHONE..................................440 272-5425
Norman Byler, *Partner*
Timothy Miller, *Partner*
EMP: 7
SALES (est): 450K **Privately Held**
SIC: 2448 Pallets, wood

(G-20528)
SES FABRACATING LLC
17217 Huntley Rd (44099-9604)
PHONE..................................440 636-5853
Daniel Stutzman, *Mng Member*
EMP: 4
SALES (est): 318.3K **Privately Held**
SIC: 3499 Fabricated metal products

Winesburg
Holmes County

(G-20529)
9444 OHIO HOLDING CO
1658 Us Route 62 E (44690)
P.O. Box 181 (44690-0181)
PHONE..................................330 359-6291
Robert Ramseyer, *President*
▲ **EMP:** 45 **EST:** 1997
SQ FT: 5,500
SALES (est): 18.6MM **Privately Held**
WEB: www.alpinelace.com
SIC: 2022 Cheese, natural & processed

(G-20530)
CASE FARMS OF OHIO INC (HQ)
Also Called: Case Farms Chicken
1818 County Rd 160 (44690)
P.O. Box 185 (44690-0185)
PHONE..................................330 359-7141
Thomas Shelton, *President*
James Witt, *Safety Mgr*
Mike Popowycz, *CFO*
EMP: 200 **EST:** 1947
SQ FT: 8,000
SALES (est): 40.8MM
SALES (corp-wide): 455.1MM **Privately Held**
WEB: www.casefarms.com
SIC: 2015 2011 Poultry slaughtering & processing; meat packing plants
PA: Case Foods, Inc.
385 Pilch Rd
Troutman NC 28166
704 528-4501

(G-20531)
H & S OPERATING COMPANY INC
2581 County Rd 160 (44690)
P.O. Box 82 (44690-0082)
PHONE..................................330 830-8178
Eric Smith, *President*
Ervin Hostetler, *Corp Secy*
EMP: 3
SALES (est): 262.6K **Privately Held**
SIC: 1321 Natural gas liquids

(G-20532)
MARIC DRILLING COMPANY INC
2581 County Rd 160 (44690)
P.O. Box 82 (44690-0082)
PHONE..................................330 830-8178
Eric Smith, *President*
Martha Smith, *Corp Secy*
EMP: 12
SALES (est): 955.1K **Privately Held**
SIC: 1381 Drilling oil & gas wells

(G-20533)
MERIDIAN INDUSTRIES INC
Also Called: Kent Elastomer Products
7369 Peabody Kent Rd (44690)
P.O. Box 186 (44690-0186)
PHONE..................................330 359-5447
Robert Oborn, *Branch Mgr*
EMP: 75
SALES (corp-wide): 379.3MM **Privately Held**
WEB: www.meridiancompanies.com
SIC: 3069 3949 Tubing, rubber; sporting & athletic goods
PA: Meridian Industries, Inc.
735 N Water St Ste 630
Milwaukee WI 53202
414 224-0610

(G-20534)
ROBIN INDUSTRIES INC
Also Called: Holmco Division
7227 State Route 515 (44690)
P.O. Box 188 (44690-0188)
PHONE..................................330 359-5418
Paul Rogers, *Principal*
Missy Bahler, *Safety Mgr*
Patty Frazier, *Production*
Tina Loibl, *Manager*
Rahul Patil, *Manager*
EMP: 120
SALES (corp-wide): 81.6MM **Privately Held**
WEB: www.robin-industries.com
SIC: 3069 3061 Molded rubber products; mechanical rubber goods
PA: Robin Industries, Inc.
6500 Rockside Rd Ste 230
Independence OH 44131
216 631-7000

(G-20535)
WINESBURG MEATS INC
2181 Us Rte 62 (44690)
P.O. Box 202 (44690-0202)
PHONE..................................330 359-5092

Marion Pacula, *President*
EMP: 8
SQ FT: 5,500
SALES: 750K **Privately Held**
SIC: 2011 5421 Meat packing plants; meat markets, including freezer provisioners

Wingett Run
Washington County

(G-20536)
JAMES L WILLIAMS
Also Called: Gas Enterprise Company
52 Tr 12 (45789)
PHONE.................................740 865-3382
James L Williams, *Owner*
EMP: 4
SALES: 234.8K **Privately Held**
SIC: 1389 Gas field services

Wintersville
Jefferson County

(G-20537)
ANTHONY MINING CO INC
72 Airport Rd (43953-9204)
PHONE.................................740 266-8100
Mike Carapellotti, *President*
EMP: 6
SALES (est): 425.7K **Privately Held**
SIC: 1241 Coal mining services

(G-20538)
COLONIAL HEIGHTS MHP LLC
917 Two Ridge Rd (43953-9688)
PHONE.................................740 314-5182
Daniel Williamson, *Mng Member*
EMP: 3
SALES (est): 203.9K **Privately Held**
SIC: 2451 Mobile homes

(G-20539)
JOHNDAVID D JONES
Also Called: Ssk Industries
590 Woodvue Ln (43953-9029)
PHONE.................................740 264-0176
Johndavid D Jones, *Owner*
EMP: 4
SALES: 400K **Privately Held**
SIC: 3482 5941 Pellets & BB's, pistol & air rifle ammunition; sporting goods & bicycle shops

(G-20540)
P-AMERICAS LLC
450 Luray Dr (43953-3971)
PHONE.................................740 266-6121
Mark Heil, *Manager*
EMP: 24
SQ FT: 8,000
SALES (corp-wide): 64.6B **Publicly Held**
SIC: 2086 Carbonated soft drinks, bottled & canned
HQ: P-Americas Llc
 1 Pepsi Way
 Somers NY 10589
 336 896-5740

(G-20541)
ROBS CREATIVE SCREEN PRINTING
Also Called: Rob's Specialties
350 Cadiz Rd (43953-3926)
PHONE.................................740 264-6383
Kathy Jo Barker, *President*
Kathy Barker, *President*
Robert Barker, *Vice Pres*
EMP: 5
SALES: 400K **Privately Held**
WEB: www.robsts.com
SIC: 2741 5699 5661 2791 Miscellaneous publishing; T-shirts, custom printed; bathing suits; women's shoes; typesetting; commercial printing, lithographic; pleating & stitching

Woodsfield
Monroe County

(G-20542)
CHRISTMAN SUPPLY CO INC
239 Oaklawn Ave (43793-9066)
PHONE.................................740 472-0046
Charles Christman, *President*
Mark Christman, *Corp Secy*
Paul Christman, *Vice Pres*
EMP: 4
SQ FT: 2,700
SALES (est): 812.6K **Privately Held**
WEB: www.chrismansearch.com
SIC: 5031 3273 Building materials, exterior; building materials, interior; ready-mixed concrete

(G-20543)
COUNTRY CLIPPINS
237 S Main St (43793-1024)
PHONE.................................740 472-5228
Leslie Cisler, *Principal*
EMP: 3
SALES (est): 140K **Privately Held**
SIC: 3999 Barber & beauty shop equipment

(G-20544)
D&D LOGGING
52759 State Route 379 (43793-9222)
PHONE.................................740 679-2573
Bruce Stephen, *Owner*
EMP: 3
SALES (est): 138.9K **Privately Held**
SIC: 2411 Logging camps & contractors

(G-20545)
J C L S ENTERPRISES LLC
Also Called: Sew It Seams
742 Lewisville Rd (43793-9061)
P.O. Box 150 (43793-0150)
PHONE.................................740 472-0314
Christina Seawash,
EMP: 7
SALES: 100K **Privately Held**
SIC: 2331 2321 Blouses, women's & juniors': made from purchased material; sport shirts, men's & boys': from purchased materials

(G-20546)
MEDI HOME HEALTH AGENCY INC
117 S Main St (43793-1022)
PHONE.................................740 472-3220
Kim Warner, *Branch Mgr*
EMP: 4
SALES (corp-wide): 180.5MM **Privately Held**
SIC: 2086 Bottled & canned soft drinks
HQ: Medi Home Health Agency Inc
 105 Main St
 Steubenville OH 43953
 740 266-3977

(G-20547)
MONROE COUNTY BEACON INC
103 E Court St (43793-1110)
P.O. Box 70 (43793-0070)
PHONE.................................740 472-0734
Murray Cohen, *President*
EMP: 13
SQ FT: 3,500
SALES: 577.9K
SALES (corp-wide): 1.1MM **Privately Held**
WEB: www.delphosherald.com
SIC: 2711 Newspapers, publishing & printing; newspapers: publishing only, not printed on site
PA: Herald Delphos Inc
 405 N Main St
 Delphos OH 45833
 419 695-0015

(G-20548)
MONROE DRILLING OPERATIONS
46886 Moore Ridge Rd (43793-9483)
PHONE.................................740 472-0866
Kerry Brown, *Owner*
EMP: 8
SALES (est): 1.4MM **Privately Held**
SIC: 3533 Oil & gas drilling rigs & equipment

(G-20549)
WARD MOLD & MACHINE
317 Fairground Rd (43793-9308)
PHONE.................................740 472-5303
Gary Ward, *Owner*
EMP: 4
SALES (est): 220K **Privately Held**
SIC: 3544 Forms (molds), for foundry & plastics working machinery

(G-20550)
WOODSFELD TRUE VLUE HM CTR INC
218 State Rte 78 (43793)
P.O. Box 30 (43793-0030)
PHONE.................................740 472-1651
Walter L Kemp, *President*
Charles Orum, *Corp Secy*
Sally Kemp, *Vice Pres*
EMP: 15
SQ FT: 12,000
SALES (est): 4MM **Privately Held**
SIC: 5251 2421 Hardware; lumber: rough, sawed or planed

Woodville
Sandusky County

(G-20551)
CHIPPEWA TOOL & MFG CO
1101 Oak St (43469-9792)
P.O. Box 158 (43469-0158)
PHONE.................................419 849-2790
Jim Kusian, *President*
EMP: 10 EST: 1965
SQ FT: 8,600
SALES (est): 1MM **Privately Held**
SIC: 3545 3544 Precision tools, machinists'; special dies & tools

Wooster
Wayne County

(G-20552)
7&7 WOODWORKING
11080 Ashland Rd (44691-9339)
PHONE.................................330 347-6574
Jake S Cassady, *Principal*
EMP: 4
SALES (est): 260K **Privately Held**
SIC: 2431 Millwork

(G-20553)
ABS MATERIALS INC
Also Called: AMC
1909 Old Mansfield Rd (44691-9359)
PHONE.................................330 234-7999
J Gary McDaniel, *CEO*
Stephen Spoonamore, *President*
Glenn Johnso, *COO*
Steve Jolly, *Vice Pres*
Graham Evans, *CFO*
EMP: 69
SALES: 35.6K **Privately Held**
SIC: 2869 Industrial organic chemicals

(G-20554)
ADVANCED DRAINAGE SYSTEMS INC
3113 W Old Lincoln Way (44691-3262)
PHONE.................................330 264-4949
Barry Girvin, *Manager*
EMP: 52
SALES (corp-wide): 1.3B **Publicly Held**
WEB: www.ads-pipe.com
SIC: 3084 3083 Plastics pipe; laminated plastics plate & sheet
PA: Advanced Drainage Systems, Inc.
 4640 Trueman Blvd
 Hilliard OH 43026
 614 658-0050

(G-20555)
AIRGAS
115 N Smyser Rd (44691-3230)
PHONE.................................330 345-1257
Ryan Joyce, *Manager*
EMP: 4
SALES (est): 327.4K **Privately Held**
SIC: 3548 5084 Welding & cutting apparatus & accessories; instruments & control equipment

(G-20556)
AKRON BRASS COMPANY
343 Venture Blvd (44691-7564)
PHONE.................................309 444-4440
Dan Peters, *President*
Thomas H Hudak, *President*
Joseph R Daprile, *Admin Sec*
▲ EMP: 25
SALES (est): 5MM **Privately Held**
WEB: www.akronbrass.com
SIC: 3364 3569 Brass & bronze die-castings; firefighting apparatus & related equipment; firefighting apparatus

(G-20557)
AKRON BRASS COMPANY
1615 Old Mansfield Rd (44691-7211)
PHONE.................................330 264-5678
Dan Peters, *Superintendent*
Tim Van Fleet, *Sales Dir*
EMP: 300
SALES (corp-wide): 2.4B **Publicly Held**
WEB: www.v-mux.com
SIC: 3647 3569 Vehicular lighting equipment; firefighting apparatus & related equipment
HQ: Akron Brass Company
 343 Venture Blvd
 Wooster OH 44691

(G-20558)
AKRON BRASS COMPANY (DH)
343 Venture Blvd (44691-7564)
P.O. Box 86 (44691-0086)
PHONE.................................330 264-5678
Sean Tillinghast, *President*
Joseph R Daprile, *Vice Pres*
Steven Webb, *Vice Pres*
Mark Whiteling, *Vice Pres*
Richard Wuescher, *Vice Pres*
▲ EMP: 325
SQ FT: 20,000
SALES (est): 115.1MM
SALES (corp-wide): 2.4B **Publicly Held**
WEB: www.v-mux.com
SIC: 3647 3699 Vehicular lighting equipment; electrical equipment & supplies
HQ: Akron Brass Holding Corp.
 343 Venture Blvd
 Wooster OH 44691
 330 264-5678

(G-20559)
AKRON BRASS HOLDING CORP (HQ)
343 Venture Blvd (44691-7564)
PHONE.................................330 264-5678
Sean Tillinghast, *President*
EMP: 3
SALES (est): 115.1MM
SALES (corp-wide): 2.4B **Publicly Held**
SIC: 3647 3699 6719 Vehicular lighting equipment; electrical equipment & supplies; investment holding companies, except banks
PA: Idex Corporation
 1925 W Field Ct Ste 200
 Lake Forest IL 60045
 847 498-7070

(G-20560)
ALAN MANUFACTURING INC
3927 E Lincoln Way (44691-8997)
P.O. Box 24875, Cleveland (44124-0875)
PHONE.................................330 262-1555
Richard Bluestone, *President*
Dean Weidner, *Manager*
▲ EMP: 36 EST: 1993
SQ FT: 110,000
SALES (est): 3.9MM **Privately Held**
SIC: 3444 3822 1711 1761 Sheet metalwork; auto controls regulating residntl & coml environmt & applncs; plumbing, heating, air-conditioning contractors; roofing, siding & sheet metal work

Wooster - Wayne County (G-20561) GEOGRAPHIC SECTION

(G-20561)
ALBRIGHT RADIATOR INC
331 N Hillcrest Dr (44691-3722)
P.O. Box 214 (44691-0214)
PHONE..................................330 264-8886
Dave Albright, *President*
Scott Albright, *Corp Secy*
EMP: 6 **EST:** 1928
SQ FT: 4,000
SALES (est): 919.8K **Privately Held**
SIC: 7539 7692 3714 Radiator repair shop, automotive; welding repair; radiators & radiator shells & cores, motor vehicle

(G-20562)
APPALACHIAN EQUIPMENT CO LLC
2054 Great Trails Dr (44691-3740)
PHONE..................................330 345-2251
John Collier, *Mng Member*
Joshua Collier, *Mng Member*
EMP: 3
SALES (est): 380K **Privately Held**
SIC: 3533 Oil & gas field machinery

(G-20563)
ARTFINDERS
Also Called: Artfind Tile
143 S Market St (44691-4838)
PHONE..................................330 264-7706
Brigid O'Connor, *President*
EMP: 3
SQ FT: 10,000
SALES (est): 125K **Privately Held**
SIC: 3253 5032 5211 Ceramic wall & floor tile; ceramic wall & floor tile; tile, ceramic

(G-20564)
ARTIFLEX MANUFACTURING LLC (PA)
Also Called: Gerstco Division
1425 E Bowman St (44691-3185)
P.O. Box 6011 (44691-6011)
PHONE..................................330 262-2015
Erin Hoffmann, *President*
Randy Zeigler, *President*
Vince Cover, *Plant Mgr*
Steve Radford, *Project Mgr*
Jim Hammel, *Opers Mgr*
▲ **EMP:** 428 **EST:** 2011
SQ FT: 1,200,000
SALES (est): 210.9MM **Privately Held**
WEB: www.artiflexmfg.com
SIC: 3465 3469 Body parts, automobile: stamped metal; metal stampings

(G-20565)
AT PALLET
4224 E Messner Rd (44691-9406)
PHONE..................................330 264-3903
Armando Pacheco, *Principal*
EMP: 3 **EST:** 2008
SALES (est): 173.5K **Privately Held**
SIC: 2448 Pallets, wood & wood with metal

(G-20566)
ATKINSON PRINTING INC
2876 N Applecreek Rd (44691-7942)
PHONE..................................330 669-3515
James Atkinson, *President*
James D Atkinson Jr, *Corp Secy*
EMP: 5 **EST:** 1970
SQ FT: 5,200
SALES (est): 703.2K **Privately Held**
SIC: 2752 Commercial printing, offset

(G-20567)
AUTOMATION WELDING SYSTEM
3132 E Lincoln Way (44691-3757)
P.O. Box 35 (44691-0035)
PHONE..................................330 263-1176
Jim Horst, *Partner*
EMP: 3
SALES (est): 221.2K **Privately Held**
SIC: 7692 Welding repair

(G-20568)
BAARON ABRASIVES INC
Also Called: Easton-Mccarthy Division
2015 Great Trails Dr (44691-3741)
P.O. Box 194 (44691-0194)
PHONE..................................330 263-7737
Terry Perrine, *President*
Daryl Perrine, *Treasurer*
EMP: 4 **EST:** 1972
SQ FT: 10,000
SALES (est): 400K **Privately Held**
WEB: www.baaronabrasives.com
SIC: 3291 5085 Abrasive products; industrial supplies

(G-20569)
BAUER CORPORATION (PA)
Also Called: Bauer Ladder
2540 Progress Dr (44691-7970)
PHONE..................................800 321-4760
Mark McConnell, *President*
Richard Stoner, *General Mgr*
Ward McConnel, *Chairman*
John Vasichko, *Vice Pres*
Bruce Worstell, *Plant Mgr*
EMP: 30
SQ FT: 71,500
SALES (est): 17.1MM **Privately Held**
WEB: www.bauerladder.com
SIC: 5082 3499 3446 3441 Ladders; metal ladders; architectural metalwork; fabricated structural metal

(G-20570)
BC INVESTMENT CORPORATION (PA)
1505 E Bowman St (44691-3128)
P.O. Box 165 (44691-0165)
PHONE..................................330 262-3070
Norman L Miller Jr, *President*
EMP: 6
SQ FT: 72,500
SALES (est): 10.1MM **Privately Held**
SIC: 2499 3499 4213 3089 Ladders & stepladders, wood; ladders, wood; metal ladders; trucking, except local; plastic processing

(G-20571)
BISHOP WELL SERVICE CORP
416 N Bauer Rd (44691-8626)
P.O. Box 511 (44691-0511)
PHONE..................................330 264-2023
David Bishop, *President*
Tom Patton, *Principal*
EMP: 9
SQ FT: 6,000
SALES (est): 814.2K **Privately Held**
SIC: 1389 Oil field services

(G-20572)
BLAZE OIL & GAS INC
1699 Nupp Dr (44691-1113)
P.O. Box 1407 (44691-7087)
PHONE..................................330 345-6700
EMP: 3 **EST:** 1967
SALES (est): 84K **Privately Held**
SIC: 1311 Crude Petroleum/Natural Gas Production

(G-20573)
BOSCH REXROTH CORPORATION
Mannesmann Rexroth
1683 Enterprise Pkwy (44691-7967)
PHONE..................................330 263-3300
Mike Gerhart, *Engineer*
Glenn Schaal, *Engineer*
Jim Skeels, *Engineer*
Mike Bickel, *Branch Mgr*
Charles Back, *Manager*
EMP: 500
SQ FT: 225,000
SALES (corp-wide): 301.8MM **Privately Held**
WEB: www.us.rexroth.com
SIC: 3594 3494 3491 Pumps, hydraulic power transfer; expansion joints pipe; industrial valves
HQ: Bosch Rexroth Corporation
14001 S Lakes Dr
Charlotte NC 28273
704 583-4338

(G-20574)
BOXES & SUCH
1118 Mindy Ln (44691-5427)
PHONE..................................440 237-7122
Ed Allen, *President*
Roberta Allen, *CFO*
EMP: 3
SALES (est): 258.1K **Privately Held**
SIC: 2441 Boxes, wood

(G-20575)
BUCKEYE CORRUGATED INC
Also Called: Buckeye Container Division
3350 Long Rd (44691-7953)
PHONE..................................330 264-6336
Jack Nebesky, *Vice Pres*
Terry Pine, *Project Mgr*
Bill Burkhart, *Design Engr*
John Powell, *Controller*
EMP: 100
SALES (corp-wide): 188.4MM **Privately Held**
WEB: www.buckeyecorrugated.com
SIC: 2653 Boxes, corrugated: made from purchased materials
PA: Buckeye Corrugated, Inc
822 Kumho Dr Ste 400
Fairlawn OH 44333
330 576-0590

(G-20576)
BUCKEYE OIL PRODUCING CO
544 E Liberty St (44691-3602)
P.O. Box 129 (44691-0129)
PHONE..................................330 264-8847
Mark Lytle, *President*
Steve Sigler, *Vice Pres*
EMP: 15
SQ FT: 10,000
SALES (est): 2.9MM **Privately Held**
WEB: www.buckeyeoilinc.com
SIC: 1311 1381 Crude petroleum production; natural gas production; drilling oil & gas wells

(G-20577)
BUILT-RITE BOX & CRATE INC
608 Freedlander Rd (44691)
P.O. Box 1051 (44691-7051)
PHONE..................................330 263-0936
John C Meenan, *President*
Jodie L Meenan, *Corp Secy*
Dave Schaeufele, *Vice Pres*
EMP: 20
SQ FT: 10,000
SALES (est): 3.9MM **Privately Held**
WEB: www.builtritebox.com
SIC: 2441 2448 Boxes, wood; cases, wood; skids, wood

(G-20578)
CLARK-FOWLER ENTERPRISES INC
Also Called: Clark-Fowler Elc Mtr & Sups
510 W Henry St (44691-4773)
P.O. Box 310, Westerville (43086-0310)
PHONE..................................330 262-0906
Don Clark, *President*
Doug Fowler, *Vice Pres*
Douglas Fowler, *Vice Pres*
Dave Garan, *Sales Mgr*
Jerry L Clark, *Admin Sec*
EMP: 24 **EST:** 1995
SQ FT: 5,000
SALES (est): 6.4MM **Privately Held**
SIC: 7694 5063 Electric motor repair; rewinding stators; motors, electric; power transmission equipment, electric

(G-20579)
COIL TECHNOLOGY INC
Also Called: Coil Tek
2109 Great Trails Dr (44691-3738)
P.O. Box 540 (44691-0540)
PHONE..................................330 601-1350
Andrew Cary, *President*
Annette Cary, *CFO*
▼ **EMP:** 3
SQ FT: 1,500
SALES (est): 600K **Privately Held**
WEB: www.coiltek.com
SIC: 3541 Machine tools, metal cutting type

(G-20580)
COLLIER WELL EQP & SUP INC (PA)
3310 Columbus Rd (44691-9134)
PHONE..................................330 345-3968
Doug Drughal, *President*
Bill Stanton, *Shareholder*
EMP: 16
SQ FT: 14,000
SALES (est): 5.8MM **Privately Held**
SIC: 1389 3444 4212 Construction, repair & dismantling services; sheet metalwork; local trucking, without storage

(G-20581)
CRYOPLUS INC
2429 N Millborne Rd (44691-9539)
PHONE..................................330 683-3375
Kathi Bond, *President*
Hobart Bond, *Vice Pres*
Ross Miller, *Treasurer*
EMP: 4
SALES (est): 69.2K **Privately Held**
WEB: www.cryoplus.com
SIC: 3399 Cryogenic treatment of metal

(G-20582)
DAISY BRAND LLC
3600 N Geyers Chapel Rd (44691-9641)
PHONE..................................330 202-4376
David M Sokolsky, *Mng Member*
Tammy Myers, *Admin Asst*
EMP: 18
SALES (est): 3.3MM
SALES (corp-wide): 197.7MM **Privately Held**
SIC: 2026 Milk processing (pasteurizing, homogenizing, bottling)
PA: Daisy Brand, Llc
12750 Merit Dr Ste 600
Dallas TX 75251
972 726-0800

(G-20583)
DAVID A WALDRON & ASSOCIATES (PA)
2285 Eagle Pass Ste A (44691-5349)
P.O. Box 766 (44691-0766)
PHONE..................................330 264-7275
David A Waldron, *President*
EMP: 8
SQ FT: 2,000
SALES (est): 911.4K **Privately Held**
SIC: 1311 8999 6512 Crude Petroleum/Natural Gas Production Services-Misc Nonresidential Building Operator

(G-20584)
DINOS DRIVE THRU LLC
1541 Jones Ave (44691-4523)
PHONE..................................330 263-1111
Mary Spencer, *Administration*
EMP: 5
SALES (est): 273.5K **Privately Held**
SIC: 2082 Beer (alcoholic beverage)

(G-20585)
DOME DRILLING CO
4489 E Lincoln Way (44691-8602)
PHONE..................................330 262-5113
James Gessel, *Branch Mgr*
EMP: 3
SALES (corp-wide): 1.6MM **Privately Held**
SIC: 1311 1382 Crude petroleum production; oil & gas exploration services
PA: Dome Drilling Co
2001 Crocker Rd Ste 420
Westlake OH 44145
440 892-9434

(G-20586)
DRAGON PRODUCTS LLC
3310 Columbus Rd (44691-9134)
PHONE..................................330 345-3968
Charles Baker, *Branch Mgr*
EMP: 40 **Privately Held**
SIC: 3531 3537 Construction machinery; industrial trucks & tractors
HQ: Dragon Products, Llc
1655 Louisiana St
Beaumont TX 77701
409 833-2665

(G-20587)
E S H INC
Also Called: Mc Products
390 W South St (44691-4762)
P.O. Box 1524 (44691-7089)
PHONE..................................330 345-1010
Bill Barnes, *President*
EMP: 4

GEOGRAPHIC SECTION

Wooster - Wayne County (G-20617)

SALES (est): 338.9K Privately Held
SIC: 3569 Firefighting apparatus & related equipment

(G-20588)
E-PAK MANUFACTURING LLC
1109 Pittsburg Ave (44691-3805)
P.O. Box 269 (44691-0269)
PHONE..................................800 235-1632
Bryan Mullet, *Mng Member*
▼ EMP: 75 EST: 1975
SQ FT: 12,000
SALES (est): 19.1MM Privately Held
SIC: 3443 3441 Dumpsters, garbage; fabricated structural metal

(G-20589)
EXPERT TS
Also Called: Expertise
221 Beall Ave (44691-3674)
PHONE..................................330 263-4588
Anna Gerig, *President*
EMP: 5
SALES (est): 200K Privately Held
SIC: 2759 2395 Screen printing; embroidery & art needlework

(G-20590)
F J DESIGNS INC
Also Called: Cat's Meow Village, The
2163 Great Trails Dr (44691-3738)
PHONE..................................330 264-1377
Faline Jones, *CEO*
Emily Pajak-Stenger, *Principal*
EMP: 20
SQ FT: 7,000
SALES (est): 4.2MM Privately Held
WEB: www.fjdesign.com
SIC: 2499 2759 3993 Novelties, wood fiber; commercial printing; signs & advertising specialties

(G-20591)
FEW ATMTIVE GL APPLCATIONS INC
1660 Enterprise Pkwy (44691-7968)
PHONE..................................234 249-1880
Andre Jenrich, *President*
Jesse King, *General Mgr*
▲ EMP: 3
SQ FT: 12,000
SALES (est): 350K Privately Held
SIC: 3089 Windshields, plastic

(G-20592)
FOUGHT SIGNS
514 E South St (44691-4322)
PHONE..................................330 262-5901
Rod Fought, *Owner*
Dan Fought, *Co-Owner*
EMP: 4
SQ FT: 2,900
SALES (est): 297.5K Privately Held
SIC: 3993 Signs & advertising specialties

(G-20593)
FRANKLIN GAS & OIL COMPANY LLC
1615 W Old Lincoln Way (44691-3329)
P.O. Box 1005 (44691-7005)
PHONE..................................330 264-8739
James C Morgan, *Mng Member*
James Morgan III,
John J Morgan,
EMP: 7
SQ FT: 4,000
SALES (est): 881.3K Privately Held
SIC: 1311 Crude petroleum production

(G-20594)
FRITO-LAY NORTH AMERICA INC
1626 Old Mansfield Rd (44691-9056)
PHONE..................................972 334-7000
Amanda Peretti, *Human Res Mgr*
Mark Vantrease, *Manager*
EMP: 234
SALES (corp-wide): 64.6B Publicly Held
WEB: www.fritolay.com
SIC: 2099 2096 Food preparations; potato chips & similar snacks
HQ: Frito-Lay North America, Inc.
    7701 Legacy Dr
    Plano TX 75024

(G-20595)
G & S BAR AND WIRE LLC
4000 E Lincoln Way (44691-8600)
PHONE..................................260 747-4154
Troy Linder,
EMP: 45
SALES (est): 1.9MM Privately Held
SIC: 3315 Steel wire & related products

(G-20596)
GDC INC
1700 Old Mansfield Rd (44691-7212)
PHONE..................................574 533-3128
Lonnie Abney, *COO*
EMP: 10
SALES (corp-wide): 50.4MM Privately Held
SIC: 2822 2869 2891 3069 Synthetic rubber; perfumes, flavorings & food additives; adhesives & sealants; medical & laboratory rubber sundries & related products; plastics foam products
PA: Gdc, Inc.
    815 Logan St
    Goshen IN 46528
    574 533-3128

(G-20597)
GLOBAL BODY & EQUIPMENT CO
Also Called: C & C Metal Products
2061 Sylvan Rd (44691-3849)
P.O. Box 857 (44691-0857)
PHONE..................................330 264-6640
Robert Lapsley, *President*
Bob Lapsley, *President*
EMP: 100
SALES (est): 17MM Privately Held
WEB: www.cncmetalproducts.com
SIC: 3444 Sheet metalwork

(G-20598)
GLORIAS
2023 Portage Rd (44691-1909)
PHONE..................................330 264-8963
Gloria Cantleberry, *Owner*
EMP: 6
SALES (est): 200K Privately Held
SIC: 2395 Emblems, embroidered

(G-20599)
GREEN ENERGY INC
4489 E Lincoln Way (44691-8602)
PHONE..................................330 262-5112
Stephen R Gessel, *President*
Debra J Falde, *Corp Secy*
James E Gessel, *Vice Pres*
Carl Robert Gessel, *Treasurer*
EMP: 7
SQ FT: 3,700
SALES (est): 1MM Privately Held
SIC: 1311 Crude petroleum production

(G-20600)
GRT UTILICORP INC
9268 Ashland Rd (44691-9235)
PHONE..................................330 264-8444
Rod Zimmermen, *President*
Rod Zimmerman, *President*
Thomas Funk, *Vice Pres*
Tom Funk, *Treasurer*
Lisa Kerr, *Persnl Dir*
◆ EMP: 20
SQ FT: 7,840
SALES (est): 4.7MM Privately Held
WEB: www.grtutilicorp.com
SIC: 3541 5084 Drilling & boring machines; industrial machine parts

(G-20601)
H & H EQUIPMENT INC
Also Called: Snyder Hot Shot
6247 Ashland Rd (44691-9233)
PHONE..................................330 264-5400
Gerald Snyder, *President*
EMP: 6
SQ FT: 8,400
SALES (est): 610K Privately Held
SIC: 3715 Truck trailers

(G-20602)
HACKWORTH ELECTRIC MOTORS INC
4952 Cleveland Rd (44691-1195)
PHONE..................................330 345-6049
Jeffery K Hackworth, *President*
Brenda K Hackworth, *Vice Pres*
Jeff Hackworth, *Legal Staff*
EMP: 7
SQ FT: 5,000
SALES (est): 1.5MM Privately Held
SIC: 7694 5063 Electric motor repair; motors, electric

(G-20603)
HACKWORTH OIL FIELD ELECTRIC
Also Called: Hackworth Electrical Contrs In
4931 Cleveland Rd (44691-1161)
PHONE..................................330 345-6504
Jerry Hackworth, *President*
Brenda S Hackworth, *Corp Secy*
EMP: 4
SQ FT: 40,000
SALES (est): 541.7K Privately Held
SIC: 1389 Servicing oil & gas wells

(G-20604)
HORIZONTAL EQP MANUFACTORING
3310 Columbus Rd (44691-9134)
P.O. Box 145, Southern Pines NC (28388-0145)
PHONE..................................330 264-2229
Leo Barbera, *President*
EMP: 4
SQ FT: 40,000
SALES (est): 439.8K Privately Held
SIC: 3532 Auger mining equipment

(G-20605)
ILLUSIONS SCREENPRINTING
214 N Bever St (44691-3526)
PHONE..................................330 263-7770
Charles Steinman, *Owner*
EMP: 4
SQ FT: 4,500
SALES (est): 190K Privately Held
SIC: 2759 Screen printing

(G-20606)
INGREDIENT INNOVATIONS INTL CO
Also Called: 3i Solutions
146 S Bever St (44691-4326)
PHONE..................................330 262-4440
Charles Brain, *President*
Brett Wright, *QC Mgr*
EMP: 7
SQ FT: 12,000
SALES (est): 9MM Privately Held
SIC: 2099 Food preparations

(G-20607)
INTERNATIONAL PAPER COMPANY
689 Palmer St (44691-3197)
P.O. Box 1047 (44691-7045)
PHONE..................................330 264-1322
Jim Gracey, *General Mgr*
EMP: 109
SALES (corp-wide): 23.3B Publicly Held
WEB: www.internationalpaper.com
SIC: 2653 Boxes, corrugated: made from purchased materials
PA: International Paper Company
    6400 Poplar Ave
    Memphis TN 38197
    901 419-9000

(G-20608)
IRON GATE INDUSTRIES LLC
Also Called: Morrison Custom Welding
1435 S Honeytown Rd (44691-8914)
PHONE..................................330 264-0626
Michael Goren, *President*
Dave Samerdak, *Project Mgr*
EMP: 24
SQ FT: 37,000
SALES: 15MM Privately Held
WEB: www.morrisonwelding.com
SIC: 3441 Fabricated structural metal for bridges

(G-20609)
JAMES R BERNHARDT PRODUCING
6717 Cleveland Rd (44691-9619)
P.O. Box 638 (44691-0638)
PHONE..................................330 345-5306
John Bernhardt, *Owner*
EMP: 3
SALES (est): 225.7K Privately Held
SIC: 1311 Crude petroleum & natural gas

(G-20610)
JAMES R SMAIL INC
2285 Eagle Pass Ste B (44691-5322)
P.O. Box 1157 (44691-7082)
PHONE..................................330 264-7500
James R Smail, *President*
Mark A Sparr, *Vice Pres*
EMP: 7
SALES (est): 780K Privately Held
SIC: 1381 Drilling oil & gas wells

(G-20611)
JUST BASIC SPORTS INC
Also Called: Pizzazz
1615 N Geyers Chapel Rd (44691-9563)
PHONE..................................330 264-7771
Bill Older, *President*
Freddick Older, *Vice Pres*
EMP: 3 EST: 1999
SQ FT: 4,500
SALES: 518.4K
SALES (corp-wide): 50.4K Privately Held
SIC: 5091 3949 Sporting & recreation goods; sporting & athletic goods
PA: Older Bros, Inc
    408 N Bever St
    Wooster OH 44691
    330 262-1065

(G-20612)
KENOIL INC
1537 Blachleyville Rd (44691-9752)
P.O. Box 1085 (44691-7081)
PHONE..................................330 262-1144
Steve Fleisher, *Vice Pres*
EMP: 50 EST: 1982
SALES (est): 2.7MM Privately Held
SIC: 1311 Crude petroleum & natural gas production

(G-20613)
KETMAN CORPORATION
Also Called: Wooster Book Company, The
205 W Liberty St (44691-4831)
PHONE..................................330 262-1688
David Wiesenberg, *President*
Carol A Rueger, *Corp Secy*
EMP: 8
SQ FT: 7,500
SALES: 750K Privately Held
WEB: www.woosterbook.com
SIC: 5942 2731 8742 Comic books; books: publishing only; industry specialist consultants

(G-20614)
KILLBUCK CREEK OIL CO
2538 Columbus Rd (44691-4466)
PHONE..................................330 601-0921
Jim Shoots, *Owner*
EMP: 4
SALES (est): 310.7K Privately Held
SIC: 1311 Crude petroleum & natural gas

(G-20615)
KORDA MANUFACTURING INC
3927 E Lincoln Way (44691-8997)
PHONE..................................330 262-1555
Dan Korda, *President*
EMP: 61
SALES (est): 8.8MM Privately Held
SIC: 3444 Sheet metalwork

(G-20616)
LETTERMANS LLC
344 Beall Ave (44691-3520)
PHONE..................................330 345-2628
Jodi Kennedy, *Principal*
EMP: 3
SALES (est): 136.5K Privately Held
SIC: 2329 2339 Men's & boys' sportswear & athletic clothing; women's & misses' accessories

(G-20617)
LUK CLUTCH SYSTEMS LLC (DH)
3401 Old Airport Rd (44691-9544)
PHONE..................................330 264-4383
Kris Rouch, *Purchasing*
Steven Magers, *Engineer*

Darlene John, *Controller*
Richard Wallace, *Supervisor*
Hans Peter Seiter, *MIS Mgr*
▲ **EMP:** 41
SQ FT: 400,000
SALES (est): 110.7MM
SALES (corp-wide): 68.1B **Privately Held**
WEB: www.luk-us.com
SIC: 3568 3566 3714 Power transmission equipment; speed changers, drives & gears; clutches, motor vehicle
HQ: Schaeffler Transmission, Llc
3401 Old Airport Rd
Wooster OH 44691
330 264-4383

(G-20618)
MAINTENANCE + INC
1051 W Liberty St (44691-3307)
P.O. Box 408 (44691-0408)
PHONE.................................330 264-6262
William Neckermann, *President*
Robert Huebner, *Opers Staff*
◆ **EMP:** 12
SQ FT: 10,000
SALES (est): 1.9MM **Privately Held**
SIC: 2951 Asphalt & asphaltic paving mixtures (not from refineries)

(G-20619)
MARCUM DEVELOPMENT LLC
2245 Flickinger Hill Rd (44691-9064)
PHONE.................................330 466-8231
Howard Marcum Jr, *Mng Member*
Sonny Marcum, *Manager*
EMP: 5
SALES: 250K **Privately Held**
SIC: 3089 Pallets, plastic

(G-20620)
MCCANN TOOL & DIE INC
Also Called: J R Tool & Die
3230 Columbus Rd (44691-8430)
PHONE.................................330 264-8820
Jess R McCann Sr, *President*
Nellie McCann, *Corp Secy*
J R McCann Jr, *Vice Pres*
EMP: 11 **EST:** 1982
SQ FT: 6,500
SALES: 500K **Privately Held**
SIC: 3599 3089 Machine shop, jobbing & repair; injection molding of plastics

(G-20621)
MCELROY CONTRACT PACKAGING
249 S Bauer Rd (44691-3803)
P.O. Box 608, Orrville (44667-0608)
PHONE.................................330 262-0855
Larry McElroy, *President*
Steve McElroy, *Vice Pres*
Lorrie Mendenhall, *Manager*
Judie McElroy, *Admin Sec*
EMP: 15 **EST:** 1978
SQ FT: 14,500
SALES (est): 3.5MM **Privately Held**
WEB: www.mcelroypackaging.com
SIC: 4783 2675 2653 Packing goods for shipping; crating goods for shipping; die-cut paper & board; pads, corrugated: made from purchased materials

(G-20622)
METAL DYNAMICS CO
4047 Unit A Lincoln Way (44691)
P.O. Box 1348 (44691-7086)
PHONE.................................330 601-0748
Wendy K Bowman, *Principal*
EMP: 4
SALES (est): 460K **Privately Held**
SIC: 3441 Fabricated structural metal

(G-20623)
METALS USA CRBN FLAT RLLED INC (DH)
1070 W Liberty St (44691-3308)
P.O. Box 999 (44691-0999)
PHONE.................................330 264-8416
James C Hernoon, *President*
▲ **EMP:** 96
SQ FT: 140,000
SALES (est): 119.4MM
SALES (corp-wide): 11.5B **Publicly Held**
SIC: 3312 Blast furnaces & steel mills

HQ: Metals Usa, Inc.
4901 Nw 17th Way Ste 405
Fort Lauderdale FL 33309
954 202-4000

(G-20624)
METROMEDIA TECHNOLOGIES INC
1061 Venture Blvd (44691-9358)
PHONE.................................330 264-2501
Dan Schmidt, *Production*
Ralph Degliotta, *Manager*
EMP: 80
SALES (corp-wide): 63.7MM **Privately Held**
WEB: www.mmt.com
SIC: 3993 Signs, not made in custom sign painting shops
PA: Metromedia Technologies, Inc.
810 7th Ave Fl 29
New York NY 10019
212 273-2100

(G-20625)
MIDWAY SWISS TURN INC
2160 Great Trails Dr (44691-3711)
PHONE.................................330 264-4300
Jim Rahz, *President*
Jaymie Rahz, *Admin Sec*
EMP: 5
SALES (est): 558.6K **Privately Held**
SIC: 3599 Machine shop, jobbing & repair

(G-20626)
MILITARY RESOURCES LLC
1036 Burbank Rd (44691)
PHONE.................................330 263-1040
EMP: 50
SALES (corp-wide): 3MM **Privately Held**
SIC: 3559 7389 Mfg Misc Industry Machinery Business Services
PA: Military Resources, Llc
1834 Cleveland Rd Ste 301
Wooster OH 44691
330 309-9970

(G-20627)
MILITARY RESOURCES LLC (PA)
1834 Cleveland Rd Ste 301 (44691-2206)
PHONE.................................330 309-9970
William D Johnson, *CEO*
Arthur Summerville,
Roger Williams,
▼ **EMP:** 59
SQ FT: 3,000
SALES: 3MM **Privately Held**
WEB: www.militaryresources.com
SIC: 3559 7389 Business Services Mfg Misc Industry Machinery

(G-20628)
MORTON BUILDINGS INC
1055 Columbus Avenue Ext (44691-9701)
PHONE.................................330 345-6188
Gary Schodorf, *Manager*
EMP: 14
SALES (corp-wide): 463.7MM **Privately Held**
WEB: www.mortonbuildings.com
SIC: 3448 5039 Buildings, portable: prefabricated metal; prefabricated structures
PA: Morton Buildings, Inc.
252 W Adams St
Morton IL 61550
800 447-7436

(G-20629)
MOTTS OILS & MORE
137 W Liberty St (44691-4801)
PHONE.................................330 601-1645
EMP: 3 **EST:** 2016
SALES (est): 158K **Privately Held**
SIC: 2079 Olive oil

(G-20630)
MURR CORPORATION
Also Called: Murr Printing and Graphics
201 N Buckeye St (44691-3501)
PHONE.................................330 264-2223
Joseph F Murr, *President*
Barbara Speelman, *Technology*
EMP: 14
SQ FT: 5,800

SALES (est): 2.2MM **Privately Held**
WEB: www.murrprinting.com
SIC: 2752 5943 Commercial printing, offset; office forms & supplies

(G-20631)
NATIONAL LIME AND STONE CO
Also Called: National Lime Stone
1455 Timken Rd (44691-8346)
P.O. Box 1154 (44691-7082)
PHONE.................................330 262-1317
Dave Webber, *Manager*
EMP: 3
SALES (corp-wide): 3.2B **Privately Held**
WEB: www.natlime.com
SIC: 1422 Limestones, ground
PA: The National Lime And Stone Company
551 Lake Cascade Pkwy
Findlay OH 45840
419 422-4341

(G-20632)
NORTH CENTRAL CONCRETE DESIGN
Also Called: Nccd
3331 E Lincoln Way (44691-3762)
PHONE.................................419 606-1908
Daniel Zawacki, *President*
Mike Wiseman, *Vice Pres*
Lori Crum, *Treasurer*
EMP: 13
SALES (est): 2.5MM **Privately Held**
SIC: 3271 1741 Blocks, concrete: insulating; concrete block masonry laying

(G-20633)
NORTH EAST FUEL INC
3927 Cleveland Rd (44691-1223)
PHONE.................................330 264-4454
Timothy E Miller, *Principal*
EMP: 3
SALES (est): 219.4K **Privately Held**
SIC: 2869 Fuels

(G-20634)
NORTHEAST TUBULAR SERVICE INC
Also Called: Northeast Piping Supply
6740 E Lincoln Way (44691-8643)
PHONE.................................330 262-1881
Rick Casper, *President*
William Meismer, *Vice Pres*
EMP: 3
SALES (est): 310K **Privately Held**
SIC: 3312 5541 Primary finished or semi-finished shapes; gasoline service stations

(G-20635)
OLEN CORPORATION
3001 Prairie Ln (44691-9441)
PHONE.................................330 262-6821
EMP: 5
SALES (corp-wide): 289.1MM **Privately Held**
SIC: 1442 Construction sand & gravel
PA: The Olen Corporation
4755 S High St
Columbus OH 43207
614 491-1515

(G-20636)
PETRO EVALUATION SERVICES INC
3927 Cleveland Rd (44691-1223)
PHONE.................................330 264-4454
Jay G Henthorne Jr, *President*
Lisa Milazzo, *Office Mgr*
EMP: 4
SQ FT: 3,000
SALES (est): 704K **Privately Held**
SIC: 1311 8748 Crude petroleum production; business consulting

(G-20637)
PONDEROSA CONSULTING SERVICES (PA)
4060 Millbrook Rd (44691-8400)
P.O. Box 357 (44691-0357)
PHONE.................................330 264-2298
Robert Breneman, *President*
EMP: 4
SALES (est): 860K **Privately Held**
SIC: 1381 8748 Drilling oil & gas wells; business consulting

(G-20638)
PPG INDUSTRIES INC
Also Called: PPG 5414
239 W Liberty St (44691-4831)
PHONE.................................330 262-9741
Tim Miles, *Manager*
EMP: 24
SALES (corp-wide): 15.3B **Publicly Held**
WEB: www.ppg.com
SIC: 2851 Paints & allied products
PA: Ppg Industries, Inc.
1 Ppg Pl
Pittsburgh PA 15272
412 434-3131

(G-20639)
PRAIRIE LANE CORPORATION
Also Called: Prairie Lane Gravel Co
4489 Prairie Ln (44691-9442)
P.O. Box 233 (44691-0233)
PHONE.................................330 262-3322
Ralph Miller, *President*
James Lanham, *Admin Sec*
EMP: 7 **EST:** 1954
SQ FT: 2,400
SALES (est): 1.1MM **Privately Held**
SIC: 1442 7032 6519 Construction sand & gravel; sporting & recreational camps; farm land leasing

(G-20640)
PRAXAIR INC
4265 E Lincoln Way Unit A (44691-8666)
PHONE.................................330 264-6633
Larry Sauriol, *Business Mgr*
Gerry Parker, *Manager*
EMP: 19 **Privately Held**
SIC: 2813 Industrial gases
HQ: Praxair, Inc.
10 Riverview Dr
Danbury CT 06810
203 837-2000

(G-20641)
PRENTKE ROMICH COMPANY (PA)
1022 Heyl Rd (44691-9744)
P.O. Box 76079, Cleveland (44101-4203)
PHONE.................................330 262-1984
Dave Hershberger, *CEO*
Barry Romich, *Ch of Bd*
Jo Donofrio, *Vice Pres*
Lisa Maynard, *Plant Mgr*
April Topovski, *Purch Agent*
EMP: 190
SQ FT: 8,000
SALES (est): 45.7MM **Privately Held**
WEB: www.prentrom.com
SIC: 3822 3663 3577 3841 Auto controls regulating residntl & coml environmt & applncs; radio & TV communications equipment; computer peripheral equipment; surgical & medical instruments; measuring & controlling devices; telephone & telegraph apparatus

(G-20642)
RAYCO MANUFACTURING LLC
4255 E Lincoln Way (44691-8601)
PHONE.................................330 264-8699
Erika Harwood, *Vice Pres*
Kim Vantol, *Purch Agent*
Ryan McCollough, *Engineer*
Seth Brokaw, *Design Engr*
Loran Smucker, *Design Engr*
EMP: 7 **EST:** 2017
SALES (est): 235.2K
SALES (corp-wide): 110.1MM **Privately Held**
SIC: 3531 Forestry related equipment
PA: Morbark, Llc
8507 S Winn Rd
Winn MI 48896
989 866-2381

(G-20643)
RBB SYSTEMS INC
1909 Old Mansfield Rd (44691-9359)
PHONE.................................330 263-4502
Bruce Hendrick, *President*
Richard L Beery, *Principal*
Michele Hendrick, *Treasurer*
EMP: 65
SQ FT: 20,000

SALES: 7.7MM Privately Held
WEB: www.rbbsystems.com
SIC: 3625 Relays & industrial controls

(G-20644)
RICELAND CABINET INC
326 N Hillcrest Dr Ste A (44691-3745)
PHONE..................330 601-1071
Leroy Miller, *President*
David A Miller, *Principal*
Paul A Miller, *Principal*
Wanda Mullet, *Principal*
Myron Miller, *Corp Secy*
EMP: 92 EST: 1979
SQ FT: 24,220
SALES (est): 13MM Privately Held
WEB: www.rricelandcabinet.com
SIC: 2434 3281 2541 Wood kitchen cabinets; cut stone & stone products; wood partitions & fixtures

(G-20645)
RICELAND CABINET CORPORATION
326 N Hillcrest Dr Ste A (44691-3745)
PHONE..................330 601-1071
Kit Carin, *Principal*
EMP: 16
SALES (est): 2MM Privately Held
SIC: 2434 Wood kitchen cabinets

(G-20646)
RIVERVIEW INDUS WD PDTS INC
646 Industrial Blvd (44691-8926)
P.O. Box 408, Smithville (44677-0408)
PHONE..................330 669-8509
Michael Meenan, *President*
EMP: 60
SQ FT: 17,000
SALES (est): 8.9MM Privately Held
WEB: www.riverviewpallet.com
SIC: 2448 Cargo containers, wood; pallets, wood; skids, wood

(G-20647)
SANTMYER COML FLING NETWRK LLC
2829 Cleveland Rd (44691-1737)
PHONE..................330 262-2334
Dave First, *Treasurer*
EMP: 3
SALES (est): 177.7K Privately Held
SIC: 2869 Fuels

(G-20648)
SANTMYER OIL CO OF ASHLAND (HQ)
1055 W Old Lincoln Way (44691-3317)
PHONE..................330 262-6501
Terry Santmyer, *President*
Joe Miller, *Vice Pres*
Randy Ruggles, *Vice Pres*
Dave First, *Treasurer*
EMP: 1
SQ FT: 1,000
SALES (est): 1.4MM
SALES (corp-wide): 93.8MM Privately Held
SIC: 5172 5983 1382 Fuel oil; fuel oil dealers; oil & gas exploration services
PA: Santmyer Oil Co., Inc.
3000 Old Airport Rd
Wooster OH 44691
330 262-6501

(G-20649)
SCHAEFFLER TRANSM SYSTEMS LLC
3401 Old Airport Rd (44691-9581)
PHONE..................330 264-4383
Marc McGrath,
◆ EMP: 925
SALES (est): 228.8MM
SALES (corp-wide): 68.1B Privately Held
SIC: 3714 3566 Motor vehicle parts & accessories; speed changers, drives & gears
HQ: Schaeffler Transmission, Llc
3401 Old Airport Rd
Wooster OH 44691
330 264-4383

(G-20650)
SCHAEFFLER TRANSMISSION LLC (DH)
Also Called: Luk USA LLC
3401 Old Airport Rd (44691-9581)
PHONE..................330 264-4383
Klaus Rosenfeld, *CEO*
Marc McGrath, *President*
Ashi Uppal, *Vice Pres*
Prasanna Gurumurthy, *Mfg Staff*
Paul Dougall, *Engineer*
◆ EMP: 171
SALES (est): 339.5MM
SALES (corp-wide): 68.1B Privately Held
SIC: 3714 Motor vehicle engines & parts
HQ: Schaeffler Group Usa Inc.
308 Springhill Farm Rd
Fort Mill SC 29715
803 548-8500

(G-20651)
SCOT INDUSTRIES INC
6578 Ashland Rd (44691-9233)
P.O. Box 1106 (44691-7081)
PHONE..................330 262-7585
Mike Bannert, *Plant Mgr*
Cody Wesson, *Prdtn Mgr*
Tammy Myers, *Human Resources*
Robert G Gralinski, *Manager*
Keith Hodkinson, *Manager*
EMP: 40
SQ FT: 2,018
SALES (corp-wide): 155.5MM Privately Held
WEB: www.scotindustries.com
SIC: 5051 7389 3498 3471 Steel; pipe & tubing, steel; metal cutting services; fabricated pipe & fittings; plating & polishing
PA: Scot Industries, Inc.
3756 Fm 250 N
Lone Star TX 75668
903 639-2551

(G-20652)
SEAMAN CORPORATION (PA)
1000 Venture Blvd (44691-9358)
PHONE..................330 262-1111
Richard N Seaman, *Ch of Bd*
John Crum, *President*
James E Dye, *COO*
James Dye, *COO*
Stephen Bodnar, *Vice Pres*
◆ EMP: 130 EST: 1951
SQ FT: 90,000
SALES (est): 119.4MM Privately Held
WEB: www.seamancorp.com
SIC: 2221 Nylon broadwoven fabrics; polyester broadwoven fabrics

(G-20653)
SHEARER FARM INC (PA)
Also Called: John Deere Authorized Dealer
7762 Cleveland Rd (44691-7700)
PHONE..................330 345-9023
Brian Giauque, *President*
Gerald Shearer, *Principal*
EMP: 45 EST: 1937
SQ FT: 9,400
SALES (est): 59.5MM Privately Held
WEB: www.shearerequipment.com
SIC: 3523 5082 Fertilizing machinery, farm; construction & mining machinery

(G-20654)
SIGN DESIGN WOOSTER INC
1537 W Old Lincoln Way (44691-3327)
PHONE..................330 262-8838
Ken Stiffler, *President*
Stephanie Stiffler, *Corp Secy*
EMP: 8
SQ FT: 2,000
SALES (est): 741.8K Privately Held
WEB: www.signdesignwooster.com
SIC: 3993 Signs, not made in custom sign painting shops

(G-20655)
SMITHVILLE MFG CO
6563 Cleveland Rd (44691-9690)
P.O. Box 258, Smithville (44677-0258)
PHONE..................330 345-5818
Allen Nayman, *President*
Dennis Vaughn, *Manager*
EMP: 30
SQ FT: 624
SALES (est): 3.8MM Privately Held
SIC: 3469 3544 Metal stampings; special dies & tools

(G-20656)
SOL-FLY TECHNOLOGIES LLC
3098 Tamarack Ln (44691-9023)
PHONE..................330 465-8883
Austin Doerr, *Owner*
EMP: 8
SALES (est): 625K Privately Held
SIC: 3679 Mfg Electronic Components

(G-20657)
SPEED NORTH AMERICA INC
1700a Old Mansfield Rd (44691-7212)
PHONE..................330 202-7775
Emmanuel Legrand, *President*
Alexis Taylor, *Admin Asst*
◆ EMP: 38
SALES (est): 9.2MM
SALES (corp-wide): 40K Privately Held
SIC: 3524 Hedge trimmers, electric
HQ: Tecomec Srl
Strada Della Mirandola 11
Reggio Emilia RE 42124
052 295-9001

(G-20658)
STAHL/SCOTT FETZER COMPANY (DH)
Also Called: Arbortech
3201 W Old Lincoln Way (44691-3298)
PHONE..................800 277-8245
Craig Aszkler, *President*
Bob Businger, *Vice Pres*
W W T Stephens, *Treasurer*
EMP: 115
SQ FT: 70,000
SALES (est): 25.9MM
SALES (corp-wide): 225.3B Publicly Held
SIC: 3715 Trailer bodies
HQ: The Scott Fetzer Company
28800 Clemens Rd
Westlake OH 44145
440 892-3000

(G-20659)
TEKFOR INC
Also Called: Tekfor USA
3690 Long Rd (44691-7962)
PHONE..................330 202-7420
Kevin Weldi, *President*
Mitch Kelly, *Engineer*
▲ EMP: 265 EST: 2001
SQ FT: 100,000
SALES (est): 88.9MM
SALES (corp-wide): 453.1K Privately Held
WEB: www.tekfor.com
SIC: 3462 Automotive forgings, ferrous: crankshaft, engine, axle, etc.
HQ: Neumayer Tekfor Holding Gmbh
Hauptstr. 115
Offenburg 77652

(G-20660)
TRICOR INDUSTRIAL INC (PA)
Also Called: Tricor Metals
3225 W Old Lincoln Way (44691-3258)
P.O. Box 752 (44691-0752)
PHONE..................330 264-3299
Nancy A Stitzlein, *CEO*
Michael D Stitzlein, *President*
◆ EMP: 77
SQ FT: 140,000
SALES: 50MM Privately Held
WEB: www.tricormetals.com
SIC: 5051 5169 3444 5085 Metals service centers & offices; chemicals & allied products; sheet metalwork; fasteners, industrial: nuts, bolts, screws, etc.

(G-20661)
UNITED TITANIUM INC (PA)
3450 Old Airport Rd (44691-9581)
PHONE..................330 264-2111
C Michael Reardon, *President*
Charlie Gray, *Vice Pres*
◆ EMP: 120
SQ FT: 150,000
SALES (est): 31.2MM Privately Held
WEB: www.unitedtitanium.com
SIC: 3452 Bolts, nuts, rivets & washers

(G-20662)
VERTICAL RUNNER
148 W Liberty St (44691-4802)
PHONE..................330 262-3000
Adam Johnson, *Principal*
EMP: 4
SALES (est): 439.9K Privately Held
SIC: 2591 Blinds vertical

(G-20663)
WASTE WATER POLLUTION CONTROL
Also Called: Wooster
1123 Columbus Rd (44691-4617)
PHONE..................330 263-5290
Jim Borton, *Managing Prtnr*
Michael Hunter, *Manager*
EMP: 12
SALES (est): 1.5MM Privately Held
SIC: 3589 4953 Water treatment equipment, industrial; refuse systems

(G-20664)
WAYNE COUNTY RUBBER INC
1205 E Bowman St (44691-3182)
PHONE..................330 264-5553
Laurie Schang, *President*
Arnie Berkowitz, *General Mgr*
EMP: 30
SQ FT: 170,000
SALES (est): 10.2MM Privately Held
SIC: 2822 3069 Synthetic rubber; custom compounding of rubber materials

(G-20665)
WESTERMAN INC
Also Called: Wooster Tool and Supply Co
899 Venture Blvd (44691-7521)
PHONE..................330 262-6946
Brian Householder, *Branch Mgr*
EMP: 65
SALES (corp-wide): 3.5B Publicly Held
WEB: www.westermancompanies.com
SIC: 3566 3443 3533 3823 Reduction gears & gear units for turbines, except automotive; industrial vessels, tanks & containers; gas field machinery & equipment; oil field machinery & equipment; flow instruments, industrial process type; boat lifts; pumps, oil well & field
HQ: Westerman, Inc.
245 N Broad St
Bremen OH 43107
740 569-4143

(G-20666)
WESTERMAN ACQUISITION CO LLC
Also Called: Woosco
776 Kemrow Ave (44691-4857)
P.O. Box 915 (44691-0915)
PHONE..................330 264-2447
Terry McGhee, *President*
Scott Carpenter, *Exec VP*
Judith Van Buren, *Admin Sec*
EMP: 23 EST: 1924
SQ FT: 31,000
SALES (est): 2.9MM
SALES (corp-wide): 3.5B Publicly Held
WEB: www.westermancompanies.com
SIC: 3599 7692 Machine & other job shop work; welding repair
HQ: Westerman, Inc.
245 N Broad St
Bremen OH 43107
740 569-4143

(G-20667)
WHITE JEWELERS
211 E Liberty St (44691-4347)
PHONE..................330 264-3324
Heather Maxwell, *Owner*
EMP: 6 EST: 1928
SQ FT: 500
SALES (est): 547.1K Privately Held
SIC: 5944 7631 3911 Jewelry, precious stones & precious metals; watch repair; jewelry repair services; jewelry, precious metal

(G-20668)
WOOSTER DAILY RECORD INC LLC (HQ)
212 E Liberty St (44691-4348)
PHONE..................330 264-1125

Wooster - Wayne County (G-20669)

Charles Dix, *President*
David E Dix, *Vice Pres*
Robert C Dix Jr, *Vice Pres*
G Charles Dix II, *Treasurer*
Timothy V Dix, *Admin Sec*
EMP: 120
SQ FT: 25,000
SALES (est): 69.9MM
SALES (corp-wide): 528.2MM **Privately Held**
SIC: 2711 Commercial printing & newspaper publishing combined
PA: Dix 1898, Inc.
 212 E Liberty St
 Wooster OH
 330 264-3511

(G-20669)
WOOSTER PRODUCTS INC (PA)
1000 Spruce St (44691-4682)
P.O. Box 6005 (44691-6005)
PHONE................................330 264-2844
G K Arora, *President*
Poonam A Harvey, *COO*
Dr Urmil Arora, *Vice Pres*
Wayne Kasserman, *Prdtn Mgr*
Rashmi Jeirath, *VP Finance*
▼ **EMP:** 70
SQ FT: 100,000
SALES (est): 13.1MM **Privately Held**
WEB: www.wooster-products.com
SIC: 3446 2851 Stairs, staircases, stair treads: prefabricated metal; paints & allied products; lacquers, varnishes, enamels & other coatings

(G-20670)
WOOSTER PRODUCTS INC
3503 Old Airport Rd (44691)
PHONE................................330 264-2844
Poonam Harvey, *COO*
Rashmi Jeirath, *Controller*
EMP: 45
SALES (est): 3MM **Privately Held**
SIC: 3446 Stairs, staircases, stair treads: prefabricated metal

(G-20671)
WOOSTER PRODUCTS INC
Also Called: Plant 2
1000 Spruce St (44691-4682)
P.O. Box 6005 (44691-6005)
PHONE................................330 264-2854
Adrienne Rodgers, *Branch Mgr*
EMP: 3
SALES (est): 244.4K
SALES (corp-wide): 13.1MM **Privately Held**
WEB: www.wooster-products.com
SIC: 3446 Stairs, staircases, stair treads: prefabricated metal
PA: Wooster Products Inc
 1000 Spruce St
 Wooster OH 44691
 330 264-2844

(G-20672)
WORTHINGTON CYLINDER CORP
899 Venture Blvd (44691-7521)
PHONE................................330 262-1762
EMP: 191
SALES (corp-wide): 3.5B **Publicly Held**
SIC: 3443 Cylinders, pressure: metal plate
HQ: Worthington Cylinder Corporation
 200 W Old Wlson Bridge Rd
 Worthington OH 43085
 614 840-3210

Worthington
Franklin County

(G-20673)
AERO TUBE & CONNECTOR COMPANY
7100 N High St (43085-2316)
PHONE................................614 885-2514
Richard O Chakroff, *President*
Barbara M Chakroff, *Corp Secy*
Christopher Norman, *Vice Pres*
EMP: 7 EST: 1954
SQ FT: 4,000
SALES (est): 664.9K **Privately Held**
SIC: 3728 Aircraft parts & equipment

(G-20674)
ALBRIGHT ALBRIGHT & SCHN
89 E Wilson Bridge Rd D (43085-2379)
PHONE................................614 825-4829
James B Albright, *President*
EMP: 4
SALES (est): 439.8K **Privately Held**
SIC: 3851 Contact lenses

(G-20675)
ALL A CART MANUFACTURING INC
870 High St Ste 15 (43085-4139)
PHONE................................614 443-5544
Jeff Morris, *President*
▼ **EMP:** 15
SALES (est): 4.7MM **Privately Held**
WEB: www.allacart.com
SIC: 3715 Truck trailers

(G-20676)
ALVITO CUSTOM IMPRINTS
7469 Wrthington Galena Rd (43085)
PHONE................................614 846-8986
Dominique Romanilli, *Owner*
EMP: 4
SALES (est): 308.7K **Privately Held**
SIC: 2752 Commercial printing, lithographic

(G-20677)
AMERICAN IMPRSSIONS SPORTSWEAR
Also Called: American Imprssions Sportswear
6969 Wrthington Galena Rd (43085-2322)
PHONE................................614 848-6677
Robert Midkiff, *President*
Jason Jamison, *Prdtn Mgr*
EMP: 9
SALES: 1MM **Privately Held**
SIC: 2396 2759 Screen printing on fabric articles; promotional printing

(G-20678)
AMETEK INC
530 Lakeview Plaza Blvd C (43085-4710)
PHONE................................302 636-5401
EMP: 9 EST: 1986
SALES (est): 1MM **Privately Held**
SIC: 3621 Motors & generators

(G-20679)
CGAS EXPLORATION INC (HQ)
110 E Wilson Bridge Rd # 250 (43085-2317)
PHONE................................614 436-4631
Kenneth Kirk, *President*
William Grubaugh, *Exec VP*
John Erwin, *CFO*
EMP: 6
SQ FT: 27,500
SALES: 20MM
SALES (corp-wide): 21.8MM **Privately Held**
WEB: www.cgasinc.com
SIC: 1311 1382 Crude petroleum production; natural gas production; oil & gas exploration services
PA: Cgas Inc
 110 E Wilson Bridge Rd # 250
 Worthington OH 43085
 614 975-4697

(G-20680)
CGAS INC (PA)
110 E Wilson Bridge Rd # 250 (43085-2317)
PHONE................................614 975-4697
Kenneth Kirk, *President*
William Grubaugh, *Exec VP*
John O Erwin, *CFO*
EMP: 5
SQ FT: 36,000
SALES (est): 21.8MM **Privately Held**
SIC: 1311 Crude petroleum production; natural gas production

(G-20681)
COLUMBUS MOBILITY SPECIALIST
6330 Proprietors Rd Ste F (43085-3296)
PHONE................................614 825-8996
Brian Marcun, *President*
Scott Grassette, *Vice Pres*
EMP: 3
SQ FT: 5,000
SALES (est): 407.1K **Privately Held**
SIC: 3713 Specialty motor vehicle bodies

(G-20682)
CUSTOM GLASS SOLUTIONS LLC (PA)
600 Lkview Plz Blvd Ste A (43085)
PHONE................................248 340-1800
Jeff Knight, *President*
Gary Greene, *Treasurer*
David B Jaffe, *Admin Sec*
EMP: 10 EST: 2006
SALES (est): 106.6MM **Privately Held**
SIC: 3211 Flat glass

(G-20683)
DIETRICH INDUSTRIES INC
200 W Old Wlson Bridge Rd (43085-2247)
PHONE................................614 438-3210
Richard Berdik, *President*
Dave Cunkelman, *Purchasing*
John Meyers, *Sales Staff*
Lisa Churma, *Executive Asst*
Debra Merritt, *Admin Asst*
EMP: 19
SALES (corp-wide): 3.5B **Publicly Held**
WEB: www.dietrichmetalframing.com
SIC: 3441 Building components, structural steel
HQ: Dietrich Industries, Inc.
 200 W Old Wlson Bridge Rd
 Worthington OH 43085
 800 873-2604

(G-20684)
DIETRICH INDUSTRIES INC
200 W Old Wlson Bridge Rd (43085-2247)
PHONE................................614 438-3210
Bill Wick, *Manager*
EMP: 30
SQ FT: 66,613
SALES (corp-wide): 3.5B **Publicly Held**
WEB: www.dietrichmetalframing.com
SIC: 3316 3441 Cold finishing of steel shapes; building components, structural steel
HQ: Dietrich Industries, Inc.
 200 W Old Wlson Bridge Rd
 Worthington OH 43085
 800 873-2604

(G-20685)
FIBERTECH NETWORKS
720 Lakeview Plaza Blvd (43085-4733)
PHONE................................614 436-3565
David Burch, *Principal*
EMP: 3
SALES (est): 216.9K **Privately Held**
SIC: 3089 Plastics products

(G-20686)
GEOPETRO LLC
7100 N High St Ste 303 (43085-2316)
PHONE................................614 885-9350
Ron Ullman, *Opers Staff*
Paul L Archer, *Mng Member*
Paul Archer,
EMP: 2
SQ FT: 1,000
SALES (est): 1MM **Privately Held**
SIC: 1311 Crude petroleum production; natural gas production

(G-20687)
GEORGE R SILCOTT RAILWAY EQUIP
564 E Dublin Granville Rd (43085-3166)
PHONE................................614 885-7224
George R Silcot, *Principal*
EMP: 4
SALES (est): 295.6K **Privately Held**
SIC: 3743 Railroad equipment

(G-20688)
GUARDIAN INDUSTRIES LLC
600 Lkview Plz Blvd Ste A (43085)
PHONE................................614 431-6309
Paul Janisse, *Branch Mgr*
EMP: 40
SALES (corp-wide): 42.4B **Privately Held**
SIC: 3211 Flat glass
HQ: Guardian Industries, Llc
 2300 Harmon Rd
 Auburn Hills MI 48326
 248 340-1800

(G-20689)
HAMAN ENTERPRISES INC
Also Called: Haman Midwest
7525 Pingue Dr (43085-1715)
PHONE................................614 888-7574
Tod Haman, *Owner*
Paul Baronda, *Production*
Jon Ankrom, *Account Dir*
Mike Biro,
▲ **EMP:** 19
SQ FT: 24,000
SALES (est): 4.1MM **Privately Held**
WEB: www.southprint.net
SIC: 2752 2759 Commercial printing, offset; calendars: printing

(G-20690)
HANNIBAL CO INC
Also Called: Heartland Bread & Roll
6536 Proprietors Rd (43085-3233)
PHONE................................614 846-5060
Rebecca Henderson, *President*
EMP: 10
SALES (est): 888.3K **Privately Held**
SIC: 2051 Breads, rolls & buns

(G-20691)
INPACO CORPORATION
6950 Wrthington Galena Rd (43085-2360)
PHONE................................614 888-9288
Ken J Swanson, *CEO*
◆ **EMP:** 13
SALES (est): 29.3MM
SALES (corp-wide): 377.1MM **Privately Held**
SIC: 2673 Plastic bags: made from purchased materials
PA: Liqui-Box Corporation
 901 E Byrd St Ste 1105
 Richmond VA 23219
 804 325-1400

(G-20692)
INSLEY PRINTING INC
666 High St Ste 400 (43085-4135)
P.O. Box 387 (43085-0387)
PHONE................................614 885-5973
Paul Insley, *President*
EMP: 5
SQ FT: 2,500
SALES (est): 629.5K **Privately Held**
SIC: 2752 Commercial printing, offset

(G-20693)
KNAPE INDUSTRIES INC
6592 Proprietors Rd (43085-3233)
PHONE................................614 885-3016
John Knape, *President*
Elcy Dunwoody, *General Mgr*
Joyce Knape, *Vice Pres*
Carl Roth, *Purchasing*
Adam Russell, *Manager*
EMP: 22
SQ FT: 14,000
SALES (est): 4.1MM **Privately Held**
WEB: www.knapeindustries.com
SIC: 3599 Machine shop, jobbing & repair

(G-20694)
L S MANUFACTURING INC
480 E Wilson Bridge Rd C (43085-2372)
PHONE................................614 885-7988
Glenn Liebert, *President*
Mary P Liebert, *Admin Sec*
EMP: 3
SALES: 100K **Privately Held**
SIC: 2499 5999 Trophy bases, wood; trophies & plaques

(G-20695)
METTLER-TOLEDO LLC
Also Called: Toledo Scales & Systems
720 Dearborn Park Ln (43085-5703)
PHONE................................614 438-4511
Todd Manifold, *Opers Mgr*
Jeff Hatfield, *Purch Mgr*
Jeff Siefker, *Human Res Mgr*
Gary Wilkins, *Manager*
Dave Piechotte, *Manager*
EMP: 81

GEOGRAPHIC SECTION

Wshngtn CT Hs - Fayette County (G-20719)

SALES (corp-wide): 2.9B **Publicly Held**
WEB: www.mtnw.com
SIC: 3596 Industrial scales
HQ: Mettler-Toledo, Llc
    1900 Polaris Pkwy Fl 6
    Columbus OH 43240
    614 438-4511

(G-20696)
METTLER-TOLEDO LLC
Toledo Scales & Systems
1150 Dearborn Dr (43085-4766)
PHONE..................614 438-4390
Todd Manifold, *General Mgr*
William Miller, *Engineer*
Bud Wagstaff, *Engineer*
Doug Johnson, *Marketing Staff*
Richard Sliwinski, *Manager*
EMP: 200
SALES (corp-wide): 2.9B **Publicly Held**
WEB: www.mtnw.com
SIC: 3596 Industrial scales
HQ: Mettler-Toledo, Llc
    1900 Polaris Pkwy Fl 6
    Columbus OH 43240
    614 438-4511

(G-20697)
MICROWELD ENGINEERING INC
7451 Oakmeadows Dr (43085-1713)
PHONE..................614 847-9410
Robert Lloyd, *President*
Daniel Mitchell, *Vice Pres*
EMP: 11
SALES (est): 1.5MM **Privately Held**
WEB: www.microweldengineering.com
SIC: 3369 8731 7692 3728 Aerospace castings, nonferrous: except aluminum; commercial physical research; welding repair; aircraft parts & equipment

(G-20698)
MORK PROCESS INC
400 W Wilson Bridge Rd # 130 (43085-2259)
PHONE..................330 928-3700
Christopher Yessayan, *CEO*
Ole Madsen, *Vice Pres*
Michael Port, *Vice Pres*
▲ EMP: 20
SALES (est): 2.9MM **Privately Held**
WEB: www.morkusa.com
SIC: 3589 High pressure cleaning equipment

(G-20699)
PENGUIN SERV ICE
530 Lakeview Plaza Blvd (43085-4710)
PHONE..................614 848-6511
Pete Bahill, *Principal*
EMP: 3
SALES (est): 193.6K **Privately Held**
SIC: 2097 Manufactured ice

(G-20700)
PRECISION SPECIALTY METALS INC
Also Called: Worthington Steel
200 W Old Wlson Bridge Rd (43085-2247)
PHONE..................800 944-2255
Mark A Russell, *President*
Ronald Archibetue, *General Mgr*
Pat Clark, *Principal*
Perry Madison, *Principal*
Tony Gallegos, *Vice Pres*
▲ EMP: 65
SQ FT: 369,750
SALES: 60MM
SALES (corp-wide): 3.5B **Publicly Held**
WEB: www.psm-inc.com
SIC: 3312 Blast furnaces & steel mills; sheet or strip, steel, cold-rolled: own hot-rolled; stainless steel
HQ: The Worthington Steel Company
    200 W Old Wlson Bridge Rd
    Worthington OH 43085
    614 438-3210

(G-20701)
RECYCLED SYSTEMS FURNITURE INC
Also Called: Rsfi Office Furniture
401 E Wilson Bridge Rd (43085-2320)
PHONE..................614 880-9110
Ron Morris, *President*
Jim Ellison, *Vice Pres*
EMP: 25
SQ FT: 100,000
SALES (est): 4.4MM **Privately Held**
WEB: www.rsfi.com
SIC: 7641 5712 2522 Office furniture repair & maintenance; furniture upholstery repair; office furniture; office furniture, except wood

(G-20702)
S O S GRAPHICS & PRINTING INC
445 E Wilson Bridge Rd (43085-2320)
PHONE..................614 846-8229
Maryann Ondecko, *President*
EMP: 4
SQ FT: 3,400
SALES (est): 390K **Privately Held**
SIC: 2752 2791 5112 Commercial printing, offset; typesetting; albums, scrapbooks & binders; office supplies

(G-20703)
SEVEN-OGUN INTERNATIONAL LLC
670 Lkview Plz Blvd Ste K (43085)
PHONE..................614 888-8939
Fernanda Aler, *Mng Member*
Antonio Machado,
EMP: 5
SQ FT: 1,700
SALES (est): 614.6K **Privately Held**
SIC: 3496 3411 Conveyor belts; food & beverage containers

(G-20704)
TATUM PETROLEUM CORPORATION
667 Lkview Plz Blvd Ste E (43085)
P.O. Box 2607, Zanesville (43702-2607)
PHONE..................740 819-6810
Zachary Thomas Tatum, *President*
EMP: 4
SQ FT: 2,400
SALES (est): 721K **Privately Held**
SIC: 1311 Crude petroleum production

(G-20705)
TECSIS LP
771 Dearborn Park Ln F (43085-5720)
PHONE..................614 430-0683
Bruce Yohr, *President*
Mark Jones, *Engineer*
Vera Dubrovsky, *Financial Exec*
Rob Turner, *Sales Mgr*
EMP: 50
SALES (est): 11.5MM
SALES (corp-wide): 51.9MM **Privately Held**
SIC: 3823 Industrial instrmnts msrmnt display/control process variable
PA: Tecsis Gmbh
    Carl-Legien-Str. 40-44
    Offenbach Am Main 63073
    695 806-0

(G-20706)
UNITED STATE PLTG BUMPER SVC
1937 W Dblin Granville Rd (43085-3346)
PHONE..................614 403-4666
EMP: 3
SALES (est): 128.1K **Privately Held**
SIC: 3471 Plating of metals or formed products

(G-20707)
WHEMPYS CORP
6969 Worth Galena Rd P (43085-2322)
PHONE..................614 888-6670
David Reed, *President*
Kathy Reed, *Corp Secy*
Eugene Reed, *Manager*
EMP: 9
SQ FT: 2,000
SALES: 500K **Privately Held**
WEB: www.whempys.com
SIC: 5719 1711 7349 1741 Fireplace equipment & accessories; heating systems repair & maintenance; chimney cleaning; chimney construction & maintenance; chimney caps, concrete

(G-20708)
WHITNEY HOUSE
666 High St Ste 102 (43085-4135)
PHONE..................614 396-7846
Ian F Brown, *Principal*
EMP: 7
SALES (est): 237.6K **Privately Held**
SIC: 2711 Newspapers

(G-20709)
WORTHINGTON CYLINDER CORP (HQ)
200 W Old Wlson Bridge Rd (43085-2247)
PHONE..................614 840-3210
Carol L Barnum, *Principal*
Theodore Armbruster, *Vice Pres*
Jim Knox, *Vice Pres*
Emanuelle Galvan, *Project Mgr*
Kurt Vogel, *Purchasing*
◆ EMP: 185
SQ FT: 125,000
SALES (est): 441.7MM
SALES (corp-wide): 3.5B **Publicly Held**
SIC: 3443 Cylinders, pressure: metal plate
PA: Worthington Industries, Inc.
    200 W Old Wlson Bridge Rd
    Worthington OH 43085
    614 438-3210

(G-20710)
WORTHINGTON INDUSTRIES INC (PA)
200 W Old Wlson Bridge Rd (43085-2247)
PHONE..................614 438-3210
John P McConnell, *Ch of Bd*
Geoffrey G Gilmore, *President*
Andy Rose, *President*
Mark A Russell, *President*
Geoff Gilmore, *COO*
EMP: 250
SALES: 3.5B **Publicly Held**
WEB: www.worthingtonindustries.com
SIC: 3316 3449 3443 3325 Strip steel, cold-rolled: from purchased hot-rolled; fabricated bar joists & concrete reinforcing bars; cylinders, pressure: metal plate; alloy steel castings, except investment

(G-20711)
WORTHINGTON INDUSTRIES INC
200 W Old Wlson Bridge Rd (43085-2247)
PHONE..................937 556-6111
EMP: 23
SALES (corp-wide): 3.5B **Publicly Held**
SIC: 2899 Fluxes: brazing, soldering, galvanizing & welding
PA: Worthington Industries, Inc.
    200 W Old Wlson Bridge Rd
    Worthington OH 43085
    614 438-3210

(G-20712)
WORTHINGTON INDUSTRIES INC (HQ)
200 W Old Wlson Bridge Rd (43085-2247)
PHONE..................614 438-3077
John P McConnell, *CEO*
John H McConnell, *Ch of Bd*
Edward A Ferkany, *Vice Pres*
Cathy Lyttle, *Vice Pres*
Greg Shakley, *Mfg Staff*
EMP: 1200
SALES (est): 562.6MM
SALES (corp-wide): 3.5B **Publicly Held**
WEB: www.worthingtonindustries.com
SIC: 3312 Blast furnaces & steel mills
PA: Worthington Industries, Inc.
    200 W Old Wlson Bridge Rd
    Worthington OH 43085
    614 438-3210

(G-20713)
WORTHINGTON INDUSTRIES LSG LLC
200 W Old Wlson Bridge Rd (43085-2247)
PHONE..................614 438-3210
EMP: 4
SALES (est): 313.1K
SALES (corp-wide): 3.5B **Publicly Held**
SIC: 3316 Cold finishing of steel shapes
PA: Worthington Industries, Inc.
    200 W Old Wlson Bridge Rd
    Worthington OH 43085
    614 438-3210

(G-20714)
WORTHINGTON PALLET
160 Tucker Dr (43085-3064)
PHONE..................614 888-1573
Lynn Lazorik-Tucker, *Owner*
EMP: 3
SALES (est): 179.3K **Privately Held**
SIC: 2448 Pallets, wood & wood with metal

(G-20715)
WORTHINGTON STEEL COMPANY (HQ)
200 W Old Wlson Bridge Rd (43085-2247)
PHONE..................614 438-3210
John H Mc Connell, *Ch of Bd*
Donal H Malenick, *President*
Mark A Russell, *President*
Eric Smolenski, *General Mgr*
Tim Adams, *Vice Pres*
◆ EMP: 177
SALES (est): 115.9MM
SALES (corp-wide): 3.5B **Publicly Held**
SIC: 3316 3471 3312 Cold-rolled strip or wire; plating & polishing; blast furnaces & steel mills
PA: Worthington Industries, Inc.
    200 W Old Wlson Bridge Rd
    Worthington OH 43085
    614 438-3210

Wright Patterson Afb
Greene County

(G-20716)
AIR FORCE US DEPT OF
5465 Arnold Rd (45433-5100)
PHONE..................937 245-1962
EMP: 9 **Publicly Held**
SIC: 3728 Military aircraft equipment & armament
HQ: United States Department Of The Air Force
    1000 Air Force Pentagon
    Washington DC 20330

(G-20717)
BOEING COMPANY
5200 Vincent Ave (45433-5127)
PHONE..................937 431-3503
EMP: 275
SALES (corp-wide): 101.1B **Publicly Held**
SIC: 3721 Aircraft
PA: The Boeing Company
    100 N Riverside Plz
    Chicago IL 60606
    312 544-2000

Wshngtn CT Hs
Fayette County

(G-20718)
ALL-AMERICAN FIRE EQP INC
Also Called: All American Fire Equiptment
5101 Us Highway 22 Sw (43160-9695)
PHONE..................800 972-6035
Jeff Vossler, *President*
EMP: 10
SALES (corp-wide): 5.8MM **Privately Held**
WEB: www.all-americanfire.com
SIC: 5099 3569 Safety equipment & supplies; firefighting apparatus & related equipment
PA: All-American Fire Equipment, Inc.
    3253 Us Route 60
    Ona WV 25545
    304 733-3581

(G-20719)
BONHAM ENTERPRSISES
Also Called: Bonham Doors & Openers
2555 Us Highway 62 Ne (43160-9073)
PHONE..................740 333-0501
Barry Bonham, *Owner*
EMP: 3
SALES: 200K **Privately Held**
SIC: 5211 3699 Garage doors, sale & installation; door opening & closing devices, electrical

(G-20720)
BRASS BULL 1 LLC
Also Called: Print Shop, The
1020 Leesburg Ave (43160-1272)
PHONE.................................740 335-8030
James Davis,
EMP: 6
SQ FT: 6,500
SALES (est): 532.5K Privately Held
SIC: 2752 2791 2759 2396 Commercial printing, offset; typesetting; commercial printing; automotive & apparel trimmings

(G-20721)
C H WASHINGTON WATER PLAN
220 Park Ave (43160-1181)
PHONE.................................740 636-2382
Joe Burbage, Director
EMP: 4
SALES (est): 421.2K Privately Held
SIC: 3823 Water quality monitoring & control systems

(G-20722)
CRESTAR CRUSTS INC
Also Called: Crestar Foods
1104 Clinton Ave (43160-1215)
PHONE.................................740 335-4813
Richard Hayward, President
Dan Walsh, Controller
EMP: 400 EST: 1998
SQ FT: 120,000
SALES (est): 36.3MM
SALES (corp-wide): 851.2K Privately Held
WEB: www.richelieufoods.com
SIC: 2041 Pizza dough, prepared
HQ: Richelieu Foods, Inc.
 222 Forbes Rd Ste 401
 Braintree MA 02184
 781 786-6800

(G-20723)
DOMTAR PAPER COMPANY LLC
1803 Lowes Blvd (43160-8611)
PHONE.................................740 333-0003
Sue Wiggins, Branch Mgr
Jim Fink, Manager
EMP: 85
SALES (corp-wide): 301.1MM Privately Held
SIC: 2621 Paper mills
HQ: Domtar Paper Company, Llc
 234 Kingsley Park Dr
 Fort Mill SC 29715

(G-20724)
DOUG MARINE MOTORS INC
1120 Clinton Ave (43160-1215)
PHONE.................................740 335-3700
Doug Marine, President
Bill D Marine, Admin Sec
EMP: 31
SQ FT: 8,000
SALES (est): 10.4MM Privately Held
WEB: www.dougmarinemotors.com
SIC: 5511 7538 5531 5012 Automobiles, new & used; general automotive repair shops; automotive & home supply stores; automobiles & other motor vehicles; motor vehicle parts & accessories

(G-20725)
FIBER -TECH INDUSTRIES INC
2000 Kenskill Ave (43160-9311)
PHONE.................................740 335-9400
Harris Armstrong, CEO
Robert Pfeifer, Principal
Wayne Durnin, Vice Pres
Mike Caskey, Plant Mgr
Jerry Kroll, CFO
EMP: 75
SQ FT: 180,000
SALES (est): 17.6MM
SALES (corp-wide): 28.4MM Privately Held
WEB: www.fiber-tech.net
SIC: 3089 Air mattresses, plastic
PA: Celstar Group Inc
 40 N Main St Ste 1730
 Dayton OH 45423
 937 224-1730

(G-20726)
FIBERGLASS TECHNOLOGY INDS INC
2000 Kenskill Ave (43160-9311)
PHONE.................................740 335-9400
Bob Pfeifer, President
EMP: 4
SALES (corp-wide): 28.4MM Privately Held
SIC: 3089 Panels, building: plastic
HQ: Fiberglass Technology Industries, Inc.
 3808 N Sullivan Rd 29c
 Spokane Valley WA 99216
 509 928-8880

(G-20727)
HALLIDAY HOLDINGS INC
1544 Old Us 35 Se (43160-8624)
P.O. Box 700 (43160-0700)
PHONE.................................740 335-1430
John Halliday, President
William Halliday II, Vice Pres
EMP: 40
SQ FT: 50,000
SALES (est): 6.8MM Privately Held
WEB: www.hallidaylumber.com
SIC: 2448 2426 Pallets, wood; dimension, hardwood

(G-20728)
IHEARTCOMMUNICATIONS INC
Also Called: Wcho AM
1535 N North St (43160-1111)
P.O. Box 94, Chillicothe (45601-0094)
PHONE.................................740 335-0941
Josh Coch, Branch Mgr
Kim Vance, Director
EMP: 5 Publicly Held
SIC: 4832 2711 Radio broadcasting stations; newspapers
HQ: Iheartcommunications, Inc.
 20880 Stone Oak Pkwy
 San Antonio TX 78258
 210 822-2828

(G-20729)
J K PRECAST LLC
1001 Armbrust Ave (43160-2457)
PHONE.................................740 335-2188
James E Kimmey, Owner
EMP: 8 EST: 2000
SQ FT: 20,500
SALES (est): 900K Privately Held
SIC: 3272 3089 Septic tanks, concrete; septic tanks, plastic

(G-20730)
JAMES KIMMEY
Also Called: J K Precast
1000 Armbrust Ave (43160-1392)
PHONE.................................740 335-5746
James Kimmey, Owner
EMP: 13
SALES (est): 100.2K Privately Held
SIC: 3272 Septic tanks, concrete

(G-20731)
KROGER CO
548 Clinton Ave (43160-1299)
PHONE.................................740 335-4030
William Drum, Manager
EMP: 110
SALES (corp-wide): 121.1B Publicly Held
WEB: www.kroger.com
SIC: 5411 5122 2051 Supermarkets, chain; drugs, proprietaries & sundries; bread, cake & related products
PA: The Kroger Co
 1014 Vine St Ste 1000
 Cincinnati OH 45202
 513 762-4000

(G-20732)
MELVIN STONE COMPANY LLC
3333 Plano Rd (43160-9105)
PHONE.................................740 998-5016
Randy Grooms, Principal
EMP: 6
SALES (corp-wide): 84MM Privately Held
SIC: 5211 1422 Sand & gravel; crushed & broken limestone
HQ: The Melvin Stone Company Llc
 228 Melvin Rd
 Wilmington OH
 937 584-2486

(G-20733)
MILLWORK DESIGNS INC
230 Topaz Ln (43160-1745)
PHONE.................................740 335-5203
Stephen Willis, President
Marsha Willis, Vice Pres
EMP: 3
SALES: 120K Privately Held
SIC: 2431 2499 Millwork; decorative wood & woodwork

(G-20734)
NORWESCO INC
2424 Kenskill Ave (43160-9309)
PHONE.................................740 335-6236
Jeff Pauley, Executive
EMP: 17
SQ FT: 14,000
SALES (corp-wide): 44.1MM Privately Held
WEB: www.ncmmolding.com
SIC: 3089 Plastic & fiberglass tanks
PA: Norwesco, Inc.
 4365 Steiner St
 Saint Bonifacius MN 55375
 952 446-1945

(G-20735)
PHILIP ARMBRUST
Also Called: Armbrust Concrete
4939 Branen Dr (43160-9716)
PHONE.................................740 335-7285
Philip Armbrust, Owner
EMP: 4
SQ FT: 6,000
SALES (est): 280K Privately Held
SIC: 3273 Ready-mixed concrete

(G-20736)
PROEPO SOFTWARE LTD
609 E Paint St (43160-1509)
PHONE.................................937 243-3825
EMP: 3
SALES (est): 112.2K Privately Held
SIC: 7372 Prepackaged software

(G-20737)
PURINA ANIMAL NUTRITION LLC
767 Old Chillicothe Rd Se (43160-9308)
PHONE.................................740 335-0207
Mark Harm, Branch Mgr
EMP: 18
SALES (corp-wide): 10.4B Privately Held
WEB: www.landolakes.com
SIC: 2048 Prepared feeds
HQ: Purina Animal Nutrition Llc
 100 Danforth Dr
 Gray Summit MO 63039

(G-20738)
QUALI TEE DESIGN
1270 Us Highway 22 Nw # 9 (43160-9187)
PHONE.................................740 335-8497
Jim Evans, CEO
James Evans, CEO
Todd Evans, President
EMP: 3
SALES (est): 235.9K Privately Held
SIC: 2759 Screen printing

(G-20739)
QUALITEE DESIGN SPORTSWEAR CO (PA)
1270 Us Highway 22 Nw # 9 (43160-9187)
PHONE.................................740 333-8337
Jim Evans, CEO
Todd Evans, President
Monica Matthews, Sales Staff
EMP: 20
SQ FT: 6,500
SALES (est): 2.1MM Privately Held
SIC: 7336 2395 5999 2759 Silk screen design; embroidery & art needlework; trophies & plaques; screen printing

(G-20740)
RAM MACHINING INC
806 Delaware St (43160-1552)
PHONE.................................740 333-5522
Rick Miller, President
Barb Massie, Admin Sec
EMP: 6
SALES: 100K Privately Held
WEB: www.rammachining.com
SIC: 3599 Machine shop, jobbing & repair

(G-20741)
RICHELIEU FOODS INC
1104 Clinton Ave (43160-1278)
PHONE.................................740 335-4813
Richard Hayward, Principal
EMP: 10
SALES (est): 1.3MM Privately Held
SIC: 2038 Breakfasts, frozen & packaged

(G-20742)
RITEN INDUSTRIES INCORPORATED
1100 Lakeview Ave (43160-1037)
P.O. Box 340 (43160-0340)
PHONE.................................740 335-5353
Andrew Lachelt, President
Mitchell Kirby, VP Mfg
Misty Depugh, Purch Mgr
Don Spangler, Purch Mgr
Scott Robinson, Purch Agent
EMP: 40
SQ FT: 28,500
SALES (est): 11.8MM Privately Held
WEB: www.riten.com
SIC: 3545 Machine tool attachments & accessories

(G-20743)
ROSS CO REDI MIX CO INC
1865 Old Us 35 Se (43160-8687)
PHONE.................................740 333-6833
Mark Crabtree, Principal
EMP: 3
SALES (est): 205.5K Privately Held
SIC: 3273 Ready-mixed concrete

(G-20744)
SHOWA ALUMINUM CORP AMERICA
210 Washington Sq (43160-1750)
P.O. Box 280 (43160-0280)
PHONE.................................740 895-6422
Yasushi Munakata, President
Dan Butler, General Mgr
◆ EMP: 3
SQ FT: 210,000
SALES: 2MM
SALES (corp-wide): 8.8B Privately Held
WEB: www.sdk.co.jp
SIC: 3714 Motor vehicle electrical equipment
PA: Showa Denko K.K.
 1-13-9, Shibadaimon
 Minato-Ku TKY 105-0
 354 703-235

(G-20745)
SUGAR CREEK PACKING CO (PA)
2101 Kenskill Ave (43160-9404)
PHONE.................................740 335-3586
John Richardson, CEO
Michael Richardson, COO
Allan Riney, Exec VP
Jim Coughlin, Vice Pres
Thomas Schurig, Vice Pres
◆ EMP: 360 EST: 1966
SQ FT: 80,000
SALES: 700MM Privately Held
WEB: www.sugarcreek.com
SIC: 2013 Bacon, side & sliced; from purchased meat

(G-20746)
TONYS WLDG & FABRICATION LLC
2305 Robinson Rd Se (43160-8675)
PHONE.................................740 333-4000
Linda Borland, Principal
EMP: 24
SALES (est): 3.2MM Privately Held
SIC: 7692 Welding repair

(G-20747)
VALUTEX REINFORCEMENTS INC
2000 Kenskill Ave (43160-9311)
PHONE.................................800 251-2507
EMP: 9 EST: 2011

SALES (est): 1.4MM **Privately Held**
SIC: 3089 Plastics products

(G-20748)
WCH MOLDING LLC
1850 Lowes Blvd (43160-8611)
PHONE 740 335-6320
Gene J Kuzma, *President*
Jeff Kuzma, *Treasurer*
EMP: 20
SALES (est): 3.5MM
SALES (corp-wide): 24.1MM **Privately Held**
WEB: www.gkpackaging.com
SIC: 3089 Molding primary plastic
PA: Gk Packaging, Inc.
7680 Commerce Pl
Plain City OH 43064
614 873-3900

(G-20749)
WCR INCORPORATED
809 Delaware St (43160-1551)
PHONE 740 333-3448
Mattias Olsson, *COO*
EMP: 21
SALES (corp-wide): 39.9MM **Privately Held**
SIC: 3443 Heat exchangers, plate type
PA: Wcr Inc
2377 Commerce Center Blvd B
Fairborn OH 45324
937 223-0703

(G-20750)
WESTROCK CP LLC
1010 Mead St (43160-9310)
PHONE 770 448-2193
Mark Badgley, *Branch Mgr*
EMP: 93
SALES (corp-wide): 16.2B **Publicly Held**
WEB: www.smurfit-stone.com
SIC: 2653 5113 3412 Boxes, corrugated: made from purchased materials; corrugated & solid fiber boxes; metal barrels, drums & pails
HQ: Westrock Cp, Llc
1000 Abernathy Rd
Atlanta GA 30328

(G-20751)
WEYERHAEUSER COMPANY
Also Called: Washington Crt Hse Converting
1803 Lowes Blvd (43160-8611)
PHONE 740 335-4480
Jim Fink, *Manager*
EMP: 61
SALES (corp-wide): 7.4B **Publicly Held**
SIC: 2653 Boxes, corrugated: made from purchased materials
PA: Weyerhaeuser Company
220 Occidental Ave S
Seattle WA 98104
206 539-3000

Wyoming
Hamilton County

(G-20752)
JOHN MCHAEL PRIESTER ASSOC INC
Also Called: Power Engineering Technology
266 Elm Ave (45215-4328)
PHONE 513 761-8605
John E Priester, *President*
Jayne Priester, *Corp Secy*
EMP: 3
SQ FT: 2,800
SALES (est): 343.7K
SALES (corp-wide): 135.8MM **Privately Held**
SIC: 1796 3823 Power generating equipment installation; industrial process control instruments
PA: G-A-I Consultants, Inc.
385 E Waterfront Dr Fl 1
Homestead PA 15120
412 476-2000

Xenia
Greene County

(G-20753)
ACTION AIR & HYDRAULICS INC
1087 Bellbrook Ave (45385-4011)
P.O. Box 655 (45385-0655)
PHONE 937 372-8614
Peter J Pacier, *CEO*
Pat Minnela, *Corp Secy*
EMP: 6
SQ FT: 2,500
SALES (est): 822.1K **Privately Held**
SIC: 3822 Energy cutoff controls, residential or commercial types

(G-20754)
ADELPHI ENTERPRISES
1340 Gultice Rd (45385-9628)
PHONE 937 372-3791
Barbara Klawonn, *Owner*
EMP: 3
SALES (est): 78.7K **Privately Held**
SIC: 2741 Misc Publishing

(G-20755)
ALPHABET EMBROIDERY STUDIOS
Also Called: Americas Best Cstm Digitizing
1291 Bellbrook Ave (45385-4015)
PHONE 937 372-6557
Dee Thompson, *President*
Mark Thompson, *Vice Pres*
EMP: 17
SQ FT: 10,000
SALES (est): 530K **Privately Held**
WEB: www.alphabetembroidery.com
SIC: 2395 Embroidery products, except schiffli machine

(G-20756)
AMERICAN METAL TECH LLC
Also Called: Destin Die Casting, LLC
851 Bellbrook Ave (45385-4057)
PHONE 937 347-1111
Bob Trieber, *Branch Mgr*
EMP: 60
SALES (corp-wide): 65.1MM **Privately Held**
SIC: 3542 Die casting & extruding machines
PA: American Metal Technologies Llc
8213 Durand Ave
Sturtevant WI 53177
262 633-1756

(G-20757)
B5 SYSTEMS INC
1463 Bellbrook Ave (45385-4019)
PHONE 937 372-4768
Philip Burke, *President*
Phil Burke, *General Mgr*
Judd Burke, *Vice Pres*
Mark Keller, *Vice Pres*
Mike Martin, *Prdtn Mgr*
EMP: 8
SALES (est): 1.9MM **Privately Held**
SIC: 3679 Electronic circuits

(G-20758)
BOB EVANS FARMS INC
640 Birch Rd (45385-7600)
P.O. Box 44 (45385-0044)
PHONE 937 372-4493
Tom Sefton, *Manager*
EMP: 85
SQ FT: 3,000 **Publicly Held**
SIC: 2011 Sausages from meat slaughtered on site
HQ: Bob Evans Farms, Inc.
8111 Smiths Mill Rd
New Albany OH 43054
614 491-2225

(G-20759)
BURKE PRODUCTS INC
1355 Enterprise Ln (45385-6504)
PHONE 937 372-3516
Shiv Bakhshi, *President*
Katie Scott, *General Mgr*
Aaron Bakshi, *Vice Pres*
Kewal Salwan, *Vice Pres*
Angela Copsey, *Purch Mgr*

▲ EMP: 20 EST: 1966
SQ FT: 10,000
SALES (est): 4.5MM **Privately Held**
WEB: www.burkeproducts.com
SIC: 3674 3599 Solid state electronic devices; machine shop, jobbing & repair

(G-20760)
CEMEX CNSTR MTLS ATL LLC
Also Called: Cem - Fairborn Plant
3250 Linebaugh Rd (45385-8567)
PHONE 937 878-8651
John Cass, *Manager*
EMP: 78 **Privately Held**
SIC: 3273 Ready-mixed concrete
HQ: Cemex Construction Materials Atlantic, Llc
1501 Belvedere Rd
West Palm Beach FL 33406
561 833-5555

(G-20761)
CIL ISOTOPE SEPARATIONS LLC
1689 Burnett Dr (45385-5691)
PHONE 937 376-5413
Joel Bradley, *CEO*
Peter Dodwell, *President*
Maureen Duffy, *Vice Pres*
Steve Igo, *Vice Pres*
▲ EMP: 10
SQ FT: 8,000
SALES (est): 2MM **Privately Held**
WEB: www.isotope.com
SIC: 2819 Industrial inorganic chemicals
HQ: Cambridge Isotope Laboratories, Inc.
3 Highwood Dr
Tewksbury MA 01876
978 749-8000

(G-20762)
CITY OF XENIA
Also Called: Xenia City Water Treatment Div
1831 Us Route 68 N (45385-9547)
PHONE 937 376-7269
Roger Beehler, *Branch Mgr*
EMP: 16 **Privately Held**
SIC: 3589 Water treatment equipment, industrial
PA: City Of Xenia
101 N Detroit St
Xenia OH 45385
937 376-7231

(G-20763)
CLARKSVILLE STAVE & LUMBER CO
2808 Jasper Rd (45385-9425)
PHONE 937 376-4618
Martha Valentine, *President*
Charles Valentine, *Vice Pres*
Chuck Valentine, *Vice Pres*
EMP: 9
SQ FT: 10,800
SALES (est): 1.2MM **Privately Held**
SIC: 2421 5031 5211 Lumber: rough, sawed or planed; lumber: rough, dressed & finished; lumber products

(G-20764)
DAILY GAZETTE
1836 W Park Sq (45385-2668)
PHONE 937 372-4444
Fred Gibson, *Publisher*
Jeffery Lewis, *Superintendent*
EMP: 36
SALES (est): 1.4MM
SALES (corp-wide): 763.9MM **Privately Held**
WEB: www.brownpublishing.com
SIC: 2711 2791 2752 Newspapers, publishing & printing; typesetting; commercial printing, lithographic
HQ: Ocm, Llc
4500 Lyons Rd
Miamisburg OH 45342
937 247-2700

(G-20765)
DAYTON TRACTOR & CRANE
1861 Us Route 42 S (45385-7350)
PHONE 937 317-5014
Dave Younkin, *Principal*
EMP: 3

SALES (est): 719.8K **Privately Held**
SIC: 5082 3469 General construction machinery & equipment; metal stampings

(G-20766)
DESTIN DIE CASTING LLC
851 Bellbrook Ave (45385-4057)
PHONE 937 347-1111
San Santharum,
EMP: 45
SALES (est): 6.8MM
SALES (corp-wide): 65.1MM **Privately Held**
SIC: 3363 Aluminum die-castings
PA: American Metal Technologies Llc
8213 Durand Ave
Sturtevant WI 53177
262 633-1756

(G-20767)
DODDS MONUMENT INC (PA)
123 W Main St (45385-2914)
PHONE 937 372-2736
Eric Fogarty, *President*
Rebecca Fogarty, *Corp Secy*
Neil Fogarty, *Exec VP*
Larry Morrison, *Vice Pres*
▲ EMP: 17
SQ FT: 7,500
SALES (est): 2.9MM **Privately Held**
WEB: www.doddsmonuments.com
SIC: 5999 3281 Monuments, finished to custom order; gravestones, finished; monuments, cut stone (not finishing or lettering only); tombstones, cut stone (not finishing or lettering only)

(G-20768)
EDGE CYCLING TECHNOLOGIES LLC
1549 Woodside Way (45385-7619)
PHONE 937 532-3891
Shane Page, *President*
John Massengale, *CFO*
EMP: 4
SALES (est): 500K **Privately Held**
SIC: 3751 Bicycles & related parts

(G-20769)
ELEVATED INDUSTRIES LLC
1835 Wlberforce Switch Rd (45385-7822)
P.O. Box 340, Wilberforce (45384-0340)
PHONE 937 608-3325
Theresa White, *Principal*
Michael Dawson, *Principal*
Jeremiah Johnston, *Principal*
Eric Welsh, *Principal*
EMP: 4
SALES (est): 125.1K **Privately Held**
SIC: 3999 Manufacturing industries

(G-20770)
ESTERLINE GEORGIA US LLC (DH)
600 Bellbrook Ave (45385-4053)
PHONE 937 372-7579
Mark Saturno, *Vice Pres*
EMP: 45 EST: 2014
SQ FT: 200,000
SALES: 30MM
SALES (corp-wide): 3.8B **Publicly Held**
SIC: 3577 Computer peripheral equipment
HQ: Esterline Belgium
President Kennedypark 35a
Kortrijk 8500
562 720-00

(G-20771)
FAIRBORN CEMENT COMPANY LLC
3250 Linebaugh Rd (45385-8567)
PHONE 937 879-8393
Gerald Essl, *President*
Ray Meier, *Vice Pres*
EMP: 110
SALES (est): 3.7MM
SALES (corp-wide): 1.3B **Publicly Held**
SIC: 3241 Natural cement
PA: Eagle Materials Inc.
5960 Berkshire Ln Ste 900
Dallas TX 75225
214 432-2000

Xenia - Greene County (G-20772)

(G-20772)
FILE SHARPENING COMPANY INC
Also Called: Save Edge USA
360 W Church St (45385-2900)
PHONE.................................937 376-8268
George Whyde, *President*
▲ **EMP:** 25
SALES (est): 7.8MM **Privately Held**
SIC: 5085 7699 3423 3315 Industrial tools; knife, saw & tool sharpening & repair; hand & edge tools; steel wire & related products

(G-20773)
FIVEPOINT LLC
825 Bellbrook Ave Unit B (45385-4076)
PHONE.................................937 374-3193
John Caldwell,
Edward Crowley,
Gregory Robinson,
EMP: 12
SQ FT: 70,000
SALES (est): 1.7MM **Privately Held**
WEB: www.5point.com
SIC: 3575 Computer terminals

(G-20774)
G2 DIGITAL SOLUTIONS
1841 Trebein Rd (45385-9558)
PHONE.................................937 951-1530
Vincent W Cowie, *Owner*
EMP: 10
SQ FT: 1,200
SALES: 1.7MM **Privately Held**
SIC: 7335 3571 Aerial photography, except mapmaking; minicomputers

(G-20775)
GRAPHIC PACKAGING INTL INC
Also Called: Gpi
1439 Lavelle Dr (45385-5679)
PHONE.................................937 372-8001
Wayne Soutter, *Branch Mgr*
EMP: 53 **Publicly Held**
SIC: 2631 Packaging board
HQ: Graphic Packaging International, Llc
1500 Riveredge Pkwy # 100
Atlanta GA 30328

(G-20776)
H & K PALLET SERVICES
1039 Jasper Ave (45385-3303)
PHONE.................................937 608-1140
Jonathon Holley, *Administration*
EMP: 4
SALES (est): 209.3K **Privately Held**
SIC: 2448 Pallets, wood & wood with metal

(G-20777)
IDIALOGS LLC
121 Pawleys Plantation Ct (45385-9120)
PHONE.................................937 372-2890
Lea Goldstein, *Manager*
Ian Goldstein, *CTO*
Warrington Bloomfield, *Software Dev*
Ira Goldstein,
EMP: 8
SALES (est): 531.7K **Privately Held**
SIC: 7372 Application computer software

(G-20778)
JADE TOOL CO INC
1280 Burnett Dr (45385-5687)
PHONE.................................937 376-4740
Jeff Sakalaskas, *President*
Dan Baker, *Corp Secy*
EMP: 9
SQ FT: 3,600
SALES: 490K **Privately Held**
SIC: 3599 Machine shop, jobbing & repair

(G-20779)
JCL EQUIPMENT CO INC
915 Trumbull St (45385-3644)
P.O. Box 396 (45385-0396)
PHONE.................................937 374-1010
Jim Lunay, *President*
EMP: 9
SQ FT: 23,000
SALES (est): 1.9MM **Privately Held**
WEB: www.jclequipment.com
SIC: 3531 5084 Road construction & maintenance machinery; industrial machinery & equipment

(G-20780)
KEY MOBILITY SERVICES LTD
1944 Us Route 68 N (45385-9552)
PHONE.................................937 374-3226
Deborah Patrick, *CEO*
Cecil Patrick, *President*
Angela Adams, *General Mgr*
EMP: 4
SALES (est): 604K **Privately Held**
WEB: www.keymobility.com
SIC: 7532 3999 Van conversion; wheelchair lifts

(G-20781)
LAKOTA INDUSTRIES INC
Also Called: Lakota Archery
1463 Bellbrook Ave (45385-4019)
PHONE.................................937 532-6394
Richard Williamson, *CEO*
Daniel Obrovac, *CFO*
EMP: 3
SQ FT: 5,000
SALES (est): 225.8K **Privately Held**
WEB: www.lakota-industries.com
SIC: 3949 Bows, archery

(G-20782)
LIMING PRINTING INC
Also Called: Screenplay Printing
1450 S Patton St (45385-7406)
PHONE.................................937 374-2646
Brian Liming, *President*
Alan Liming, *Treasurer*
EMP: 10
SQ FT: 6,700
SALES (est): 1.6MM **Privately Held**
WEB: www.screenplayprinting.com
SIC: 2752 2759 7336 2791 Commercial printing, offset; commercial printing; silk screen design; typesetting

(G-20783)
MAHLE BEHR SERVICE AMERICA LLC
1003 Bellbrook Ave (45385-4011)
PHONE.................................937 369-2610
Ricardo Studebaker, *Manager*
EMP: 3
SALES (corp-wide): 336.4K **Privately Held**
SIC: 3714 Radiators & radiator shells & cores, motor vehicle
HQ: Mahle Behr Service America L.L.C.
5020 Augusta Dr
Fort Worth TX 76106
817 740-3791

(G-20784)
MARMAC CO
1231 Bellbrook Ave (45385-4015)
P.O. Box 157 (45385-0157)
PHONE.................................937 372-8093
Gary Walthall, *President*
Sharon L Walthall, *Exec VP*
EMP: 6 **EST:** 1954
SQ FT: 17,060
SALES (est): 2.6MM **Privately Held**
WEB: www.marmacco.com
SIC: 3569 Jacks, hydraulic

(G-20785)
OHTA PRESS US INC
1125 S Patton St (45385-5671)
PHONE.................................937 374-3382
Shigeki Ikuta, *President*
▲ **EMP:** 15
SQ FT: 12,000
SALES (est): 2.6MM **Privately Held**
SIC: 3714 Motor vehicle parts & accessories

(G-20786)
PRINTING CENTER OF XENIA
402 W Church St (45385-2908)
PHONE.................................937 372-1687
Sandra Smittkamp, *Owner*
EMP: 4
SALES (est): 330.6K **Privately Held**
SIC: 2752 Commercial printing, offset

(G-20787)
PROIMAGE PRINTING & DESIGN LLC
1803 Roxbury Dr (45385-4932)
PHONE.................................937 312-9544
Carol A Hurt, *Principal*
EMP: 9
SALES (est): 1MM **Privately Held**
SIC: 2752 Commercial printing, lithographic

(G-20788)
SANDY SMITTCAMP
Also Called: Printing Center, The
402 W Church St (45385-2908)
PHONE.................................937 372-1687
Sandy Smittcamp, *Owner*
EMP: 3
SQ FT: 3,200
SALES (est): 270K **Privately Held**
SIC: 2752 2791 2789 2759 Business form & card printing, lithographic; typesetting; bookbinding & related work; commercial printing

(G-20789)
SAS AUTOMATION LLC
1200 S Patton St (45385-5672)
PHONE.................................937 372-5255
Trent P Fisher, *President*
EMP: 18
SQ FT: 16,000
SALES (est): 5.3MM **Privately Held**
WEB: www.sas-automation.com
SIC: 3569 Robots, assembly line: industrial & commercial

(G-20790)
SPI INC
Also Called: S P I
1170 S Patton St (45385-5670)
PHONE.................................937 374-2700
William J Shannon Jr, *President*
Donna L Shannon, *Corp Secy*
Thomas R Heffernan, *Vice Pres*
Thomas Heffernan, *Vice Pres*
Michael Rosenberger, *Manager*
▲ **EMP:** 9
SQ FT: 28,000
SALES (est): 3.3MM **Privately Held**
WEB: www.spi-connects.com
SIC: 5065 5063 3678 3679 Connectors, electronic; electrical apparatus & equipment; electronic connectors; harness assemblies for electronic use: wire or cable

(G-20791)
SPINTECH LLC
Also Called: Smart Tooling
1150 S Patton St (45385-5670)
PHONE.................................937 912-3250
Patrick J Hood, *Mng Member*
Craig J Jennings, *Info Tech Mgr*
Craig Jennings,
EMP: 13
SALES (est): 2.6MM **Privately Held**
SIC: 3544 Special dies, tools, jigs & fixtures

(G-20792)
STEINBARGER PRECISION CNC INC
634 Cincinnati Ave (45385-5013)
PHONE.................................937 376-0322
Steve Steinbarger, *President*
EMP: 6
SQ FT: 1,000
SALES (est): 500K **Privately Held**
SIC: 3549 Drawing machinery

(G-20793)
SUPERION INC
1285 S Patton St (45385-5673)
PHONE.................................937 374-0033
Alton Choiniere, *President*
Masaru Yokokawa, *Treasurer*
▲ **EMP:** 40
SQ FT: 12,000
SALES (est): 6.2MM
SALES (corp-wide): 21.7MM **Privately Held**
WEB: www.superioninc.com
SIC: 3423 3541 3545 3425 Knives, agricultural or industrial; machine tools, metal cutting type; machine tool accessories; saw blades & handsaws
PA: Sanyo Tool Mfg,Co, Ltd.
3-6-21, Osaki
Shinagawa-Ku TKY 141-0
334 906-821

(G-20794)
TDL TOOL INC
1296 S Patton St (45385-5672)
PHONE.................................937 374-0055
Steve Mangan, *President*
Dan Mangan, *Vice Pres*
Dave Galpin, *Manager*
Dave G Galpin, *Manager*
EMP: 15
SQ FT: 2,000
SALES (est): 3.6MM **Privately Held**
WEB: www.tdltool.com
SIC: 3599 Machine & other job shop work

(G-20795)
THE WOOD SHED
Also Called: Cdracks.com
2665 Trebein Rd (45385-9563)
PHONE.................................937 429-3355
James Rusch, *Owner*
EMP: 4
SALES (est): 404.8K **Privately Held**
WEB: www.cdracks.com
SIC: 2599 Cabinets, factory

(G-20796)
TIMAC MANUFACTURING COMPANY
825 Bellbrook Ave (45385-4075)
P.O. Box 329 (45385-0329)
PHONE.................................937 372-3305
Tim McIntire, *President*
EMP: 12
SQ FT: 5,000
SALES (est): 2MM **Privately Held**
WEB: www.timacspring.com
SIC: 3493 Coiled flat springs

(G-20797)
TJAR INNOVATIONS LLC
1004 Cincinnati Ave (45385-9353)
P.O. Box 357 (45385-0357)
PHONE.................................937 347-1999
Tony Arsenault, *Vice Pres*
Anthony Arsenault,
EMP: 12
SALES (est): 2.4MM **Privately Held**
WEB: www.tjarinnovations.com
SIC: 3089 Injection molding of plastics

(G-20798)
TREMAC CORPORATION
550 Bellbrook Ave (45385-4051)
P.O. Box 34 (45385-0034)
PHONE.................................937 372-8662
Scott McIntire, *President*
Scott Mc Intire, *President*
Brenda Day, *Admin Sec*
EMP: 28 **EST:** 1960
SQ FT: 37,000
SALES (est): 5.2MM **Privately Held**
SIC: 3493 Steel springs, except wire

(G-20799)
TRIAD GOVERNMENTAL SYSTEMS
358 S Monroe St (45385-3442)
PHONE.................................937 376-5446
Tod A Rapp, *President*
EMP: 27
SALES (est): 2.6MM **Privately Held**
WEB: www.triadgsi.com
SIC: 7371 7372 Computer software development; prepackaged software

(G-20800)
VALLEY ASPHALT CORPORATION
782 N Valley Rd (45385)
PHONE.................................937 426-7682
Jim Jurgenson, *Manager*
EMP: 3
SALES (corp-wide): 84MM **Privately Held**
SIC: 2951 Asphalt & asphaltic paving mixtures (not from refineries)
HQ: Valley Asphalt Corporation
11641 Mosteller Rd
Cincinnati OH 45241
513 771-0820

GEOGRAPHIC SECTION

Yorkshire - Darke County (G-20826)

(G-20801)
VISUAL INFORMATION INSTITUTE
Also Called: V I I Craft
1065 Lower Bellbrook Rd (45385-7308)
PHONE..................937 376-4361
John H Harshbarger Jr, *President*
June S Harshbarger, *Vice Pres*
Karen S Pellerin, *Vice Pres*
EMP: 18 EST: 1964
SQ FT: 18,000
SALES (est): 2.2MM Privately Held
WEB: www.videoinstruments.com
SIC: 3444 3672 2759 3825 Sheet metal specialties, not stamped; printed circuit boards; commercial printing; instruments to measure electricity

(G-20802)
W H K COMPANY
1720 State Route 380 (45385-8788)
PHONE..................937 372-3368
William H Kingsolver, *Owner*
EMP: 3
SALES (est): 116.6K Privately Held
SIC: 2499 Decorative wood & woodwork

(G-20803)
WA HAMMOND DRIERITE CO LTD
138 Dayton Ave (45385-2830)
P.O. Box 460 (45385-0460)
PHONE..................937 376-2927
Joan L Hammond, *Partner*
James F Hammond, *Partner*
Travis Linton, *Sales Staff*
Dave Schock, *Supervisor*
EMP: 21 EST: 1932
SQ FT: 80,000
SALES: 5.9MM Privately Held
WEB: www.drierite.com
SIC: 2819 Industrial inorganic chemicals

(G-20804)
WADES WOODWORKING INC
1427 Bellbrook Ave (45385-4064)
PHONE..................937 374-6470
Wade A Smith, *President*
EMP: 10
SQ FT: 13,000
SALES: 1MM Privately Held
WEB: www.wadeswoodworking.com
SIC: 1751 2599 Cabinet building & installation; cabinets, factory

Yellow Springs
Greene County

(G-20805)
BUSHWORKS INCORPORATED
144 Cliff St Ste A (45387-2099)
PHONE..................937 767-1713
John Bush, *President*
EMP: 8
SQ FT: 8,000
SALES (est): 520K Privately Held
SIC: 2499 Woodenware, kitchen & household

(G-20806)
GRAPHICOM PRESS INC
302 Orton Rd (45387-1321)
PHONE..................937 767-1916
Phyllis D Schmidt, *President*
Eric K Schmidt, *Corp Secy*
Ronald G Schmidt, *Vice Pres*
EMP: 5
SALES (est): 470K Privately Held
SIC: 2721 Periodicals

(G-20807)
HAMILTON ARTS INC
750 Union St (45387-1740)
P.O. Box 293 (45387-0293)
PHONE..................937 767-1834
Arnold Adoff, *President*
Virginia Hamilton, *Webmaster*
EMP: 3
SALES (est): 250K Privately Held
WEB: www.virginiahamilton.com
SIC: 2731 Books: publishing & printing

(G-20808)
HUNTINGTON INSTRUMENTS INC
303 N Walnut St (45387-2041)
P.O. Box 718 (45387-0718)
PHONE..................937 767-7001
Jeffrey Huntington, *President*
Lee C Huntington, *Treasurer*
EMP: 4
SALES (est): 390K Privately Held
WEB: www.huntingtoninstruments.com
SIC: 3823 Industrial instrmnts msrmnt display/control process variable

(G-20809)
KENWAY CORP
Also Called: Oak Heritage
504 Xenia Ave (45387-1838)
PHONE..................937 767-1660
Linda Greenway, *President*
Keeth Kinney, *Vice Pres*
EMP: 3
SALES (est): 222.6K Privately Held
SIC: 2511 Wood household furniture

(G-20810)
MASSMATRIX INC
302 Corry St (45387-1813)
PHONE..................614 321-9730
George Johnson, *CEO*
EMP: 5
SALES (est): 126.7K Privately Held
SIC: 7372 Business oriented computer software; application computer software

(G-20811)
MIAMI VALLEY EDUCTL CMPT ASSN
Also Called: Mveca
330 E Enon Rd (45387-1415)
PHONE..................937 767-1468
Beth Justice, *Superintendent*
Brian Hoehner, *Info Tech Dir*
Kelly Kilbarger, *Comp Spec*
Thor Sage, *Exec Dir*
Norma Stewart, *Director*
EMP: 13
SQ FT: 2,900
SALES (est): 2MM Privately Held
WEB: www.mveca.com
SIC: 7372 7374 Prepackaged software; computer time-sharing

(G-20812)
MORRIS BEAN & COMPANY
777 E Hyde Rd (45387-9726)
PHONE..................937 767-7301
Edward Myers, *President*
Debbie Whitt, *Opers Mgr*
Dennis Cloyd, *Engineer*
Christopher Hastings, *Engineer*
Beth Umina, *Engineer*
EMP: 175 EST: 1932
SQ FT: 185,000
SALES (est): 35.8MM Privately Held
WEB: www.morrisbean.com
SIC: 3365 3769 3369 Aluminum & aluminum-based alloy castings; guided missile & space vehicle parts & auxiliary equipment; nonferrous foundries

(G-20813)
OHIO SILVER CO
245 Xenia Ave (45387-1832)
PHONE..................937 767-8261
Marcia Wallgren, *Owner*
EMP: 4 EST: 1971
SQ FT: 1,500
SALES (est): 320.8K Privately Held
SIC: 5944 3911 5094 Jewelry, precious stones & precious metals; jewelry, precious metal; jewelry

(G-20814)
RITA CAZ JWLY STUDIO & GALLERY
220 Xenia Ave Ste 2 (45387-1865)
P.O. Box 487 (45387-0487)
PHONE..................937 767-7713
Fax: 937 767-2766
EMP: 5
SALES (est): 471.9K Privately Held
SIC: 3911 5944 Mfr & Ret Jewelry

(G-20815)
SALTBOX ILLUSTRATIONS
120 Kenneth Hamilton Way (45387-1767)
PHONE..................937 319-6434
Deborah Strain, *Owner*
EMP: 3
SALES: 500K Privately Held
SIC: 2679 Paper products, converted

(G-20816)
SILVER MAPLE PUBLICATIONS
1308 Corry St (45387-1312)
P.O. Box 846 (45387-0846)
PHONE..................937 767-1259
Barbara Fleming, *President*
EMP: 3
SALES (est): 104.7K Privately Held
WEB: www.silvermaplepublications.com
SIC: 2741 Miscellaneous publishing

(G-20817)
SONTEK CORPORATION
Also Called: Sontek / Ysi
1725 Brannum Ln (45387-1107)
PHONE..................937 767-7241
Roosey Khawly, *President*
Ron Geis, *General Mgr*
Oscar Ruiz, *Vice Pres*
David Misonznick, *Treasurer*
Jeff Winters, *Cust Svc Dir*
EMP: 5 EST: 2012
SALES (est): 549K Privately Held
SIC: 3825 Waveform measuring and/or analyzing equipment

(G-20818)
VERNAY MANUFACTURING INC (HQ)
120 E South College St (45387-1623)
PHONE..................937 767-7261
Thomas Allen, *President*
Andy Woodward, *Vice Pres*
Hugh Barnett, *Admin Sec*
▲ EMP: 22
SQ FT: 40,000
SALES (est): 13.5MM
SALES (corp-wide): 124.9MM Privately Held
SIC: 3069 Molded rubber products
PA: Vernay Laboratories, Inc.
    2077 Cnvntion Ctr Cncurse
    Atlanta GA 30337
    404 994-2000

(G-20819)
XYLEM INC
Also Called: Ysi
1700 Brannum Ln 1725 (45387-1106)
PHONE..................937 767-7241
Darrin Honious, *General Mgr*
Tom Moeggenberg, *General Mgr*
Russel Meinka, *Principal*
Jennifer Bishop, *Engineer*
Barry Gebhart, *Engineer*
EMP: 54 EST: 1999
SALES (est): 13.5MM Privately Held
SIC: 3823 Industrial instrmnts msrmnt display/control process variable

(G-20820)
YELLOW SPRINGS BREWERY LLC
305 N Walnut St Ste B (45387-2059)
PHONE..................937 767-0222
Nathaniel Cornett, *Owner*
Lisa Wolters,
EMP: 40
SQ FT: 6,700
SALES (est): 1.2MM Privately Held
SIC: 2082 Malt beverages

(G-20821)
YELLOW SPRINGS NEWS INC
253 And A Half Xenia Ave (45387)
PHONE..................937 767-7373
Robert Hasek, *Adv Mgr*
Diane Chiddister, *Office Mgr*
EMP: 11 EST: 1880
SQ FT: 4,000
SALES (est): 817.2K Privately Held
WEB: www.ysnews.com
SIC: 2711 Job printing & newspaper publishing combined

(G-20822)
YELLOW SPRINGS POTTERY
222 Xenia Ave Ste 1 (45387-1866)
PHONE..................937 767-1666
Janet Murie, *Principal*
Eliza Bush, *Principal*
Marcia Cochran, *Principal*
Jerry Davis, *Principal*
Kim Kramer, *Principal*
EMP: 10
SALES (est): 633.2K Privately Held
SIC: 5023 3269 Pottery; pottery products

(G-20823)
YOUNGS JERSEY DAIRY INC
Also Called: Golden Jersey Inn
6880 Springfield Xenia Rd (45387-9610)
PHONE..................937 325-0629
C Daniel Young, *President*
C Robert Young, *President*
Brian Patterson, *General Mgr*
William H Young, *Vice Pres*
Debra Whittaker, *Treasurer*
EMP: 300
SQ FT: 35,000
SALES (est): 12.1MM Privately Held
SIC: 5812 5451 5947 7999 Ice cream stands or dairy bars; family restaurants; dairy products stores; gift shop; golf driving range; miniature golf course operation; dairy farms; ice cream & frozen desserts

(G-20824)
YSI ENVIRONMENTAL INC
Also Called: Ysie
1725 Brannum Ln (45387-1107)
PHONE..................937 767-7241
Richard Omlor, *President*
EMP: 200
SALES: 58K Privately Held
SIC: 3823 Water quality monitoring & control systems

(G-20825)
YSI INCORPORATED (DH)
Also Called: Yellow Springs International
1700 Brannum Ln 1725 (45387-1106)
PHONE..................937 767-7241
Richard J Omlor, *President*
Ron Geis, *General Mgr*
Darrin Honious, *General Mgr*
Sham Chaudhari, *Regional Mgr*
Gayle Rominger, *Senior VP*
◆ EMP: 100 EST: 1948
SQ FT: 120,000
SALES (est): 34.9MM Publicly Held
SIC: 3826 3823 3841 Water testing apparatus; industrial instrmnts msrmnt display/control process variable; temperature measurement instruments, industrial; diagnostic apparatus, medical
HQ: O.I. Corporation
    151 Graham Rd
    College Station TX 77845
    979 690-1711

Yorkshire
Darke County

(G-20826)
ROBERT WINNER SONS INC (PA)
Also Called: Winner's Meat Service
8544 State Route 705 (45388-9784)
P.O. Box 39, Osgood (45351-0039)
PHONE..................419 582-4321
Brian K Winner, *President*
Alan Winner, *Senior VP*
Ted Winner, *Vice Pres*
Terrance Winner, *Vice Pres*
Steven Winner, *Treasurer*
EMP: 40 EST: 1928
SQ FT: 6,500
SALES: 33.9MM Privately Held
SIC: 0213 0751 5154 5147 Hog feedlot; slaughtering: custom livestock services; hogs; meats & meat products; sausages & other prepared meats; meat packing plants

Yorkville
Jefferson County

(G-20827)
OHIO COATINGS COMPANY
2100 Tin Plate Pl (43971-1053)
PHONE..................740 859-5500
James Tennant, *President*
Yong Sig Bin, *Exec VP*
Paul Conaway, *Production*
EMP: 73
SQ FT: 134,000
SALES (est): 16.2MM **Privately Held**
WEB: www.ohiocoatingscompany.com
SIC: **3479** 2819 3312 3398 Coating of metals & formed products; tin (stannic/stannous) compounds or salts, inorganic; coated or plated products; annealing of metal; surface burner controls, temperature

Youngstown
Mahoning County

(G-20828)
1ST CHOICE WEB SOLUTION INC
3000 Belmont Ave (44505-1846)
PHONE..................330 503-1591
Bill Arfaras, *CEO*
EMP: 3 EST: 2013
SALES (est): 201.1K **Privately Held**
SIC: **3555** Printing presses

(G-20829)
4S COMPANY
3730 Mahoning Ave (44515-3020)
PHONE..................330 792-5518
Debra Woodford, *President*
EMP: 10
SALES: 350K **Privately Held**
SIC: **3999** Manufacturing industries

(G-20830)
A A S AMELS SHEET METAL INC
222 Steel St (44509-2547)
P.O. Box 2407 (44509-0407)
PHONE..................330 793-9326
Andrew A Samuels Jr, *President*
George Timar, *Admin Sec*
EMP: 40
SQ FT: 12,000
SALES (est): 6.7MM **Privately Held**
SIC: **1711** 3585 3564 3444 Ventilation & duct work contractor; warm air heating & air conditioning contractor; refrigeration & heating equipment; blowers & fans; sheet metalwork; fabricated plate work (boiler shop)

(G-20831)
A UNITED
Also Called: AM & PM United
5234 Southern Blvd Ste D (44512-2245)
PHONE..................330 782-6005
Tony Mark, *Owner*
EMP: 4 EST: 1997
SALES (est): 387.5K **Privately Held**
SIC: **2951** Asphalt paving mixtures & blocks

(G-20832)
AARDVARK SPORTSWEAR INC
5329 Mahoning Ave (44515-2417)
PHONE..................330 793-9428
Linda Davies, *President*
EMP: 5 EST: 1982
SALES: 303.8K **Privately Held**
SIC: **2759** 2395 5699 Screen printing; embroidery products, except schiffli machine; sports apparel

(G-20833)
ABI ORTHTC/PROSTHETIC LABS LTD (HQ)
930 Trailwood Dr (44512-5007)
PHONE..................330 758-1143
William W De Toro,
Kevin Hawkins,
Richard A Riffle,
Joseph W Whiteside,
EMP: 20
SALES (est): 1.4MM
SALES (corp-wide): 1B **Publicly Held**
SIC: **3842** Braces, orthopedic; prosthetic appliances
PA: Hanger, Inc.
10910 Domain Dr Ste 300
Austin TX 78758
512 777-3800

(G-20834)
ACCUFORM MANUFACTURING INC
2750 Intertech Dr (44509-4023)
PHONE..................330 797-9291
Bob Hockenberry, *President*
Jeff Hockenberry, *QC Mgr*
Thomas Manos, *Treasurer*
Rob Kovach, *Supervisor*
EMP: 32
SQ FT: 1,056
SALES (est): 5.3MM **Privately Held**
WEB: www.accuformmfg.com
SIC: **3599** 3543 3544 Machine shop, jobbing & repair; foundry patternmaking; special dies, tools, jigs & fixtures

(G-20835)
ACE LUMBER COMPANY
1039 Poland Ave (44502-2138)
P.O. Box 508 (44501-0508)
PHONE..................330 744-3167
Herbert Soss, *President*
Julie Soss, *Shareholder*
Susan Soss, *Shareholder*
Diann Zenda, *Shareholder*
EMP: 13
SQ FT: 300,000
SALES (est): 2.1MM **Privately Held**
WEB: www.acelumberco.com
SIC: **2431** 5211 Millwork; lumber products

(G-20836)
ACME STEAK & SEAFOOD INC
31 Bissell Ave (44505-2707)
P.O. Box 688 (44501-0688)
PHONE..................330 270-8000
Michael A Mike III, *President*
EMP: 10
SALES (est): 6.7MM **Privately Held**
WEB: www.acmesteak.com
SIC: **5146** 5113 5149 5147 Seafoods; disposable plates, cups, napkins & eating utensils; canned goods: fruit, vegetables, seafood, meats, etc.; meats, fresh; dairy products, except dried or canned; meat packing plants

(G-20837)
ADVANCED MARKING SYSTEMS INC (PA)
Also Called: Advanced Printing
6000 Mahoning Ave Ste 50 (44515-2248)
PHONE..................330 792-8239
Fred Fye, *Ch of Bd*
Carol L Fye, *President*
EMP: 5 EST: 1979
SQ FT: 3,000
SALES (est): 401.6K **Privately Held**
WEB: www.advancedmarkingsystems.com
SIC: **2752** 5112 Commercial printing, offset; marking devices

(G-20838)
AEROLITE EXTRUSION COMPANY
4605 Lake Park Rd (44512-1891)
PHONE..................330 782-1127
Thomas E Hutch Jr, *President*
John D Hutch, *Principal*
Paul J Hutch, *Principal*
Thomas E Hutch, *Principal*
David Camacci, *CFO*
EMP: 90
SQ FT: 200,000
SALES (est): 23.1MM **Privately Held**
WEB: www.aeroext.com
SIC: **3354** 3444 Shapes, extruded aluminum; sheet metalwork

(G-20839)
AGC FLAT GLASS NORTH AMER INC
365 Mcclurg Rd Ste E (44512-6452)
PHONE..................330 965-1000
Caryn Mills, *Branch Mgr*
EMP: 4
SALES (corp-wide): 13.5B **Privately Held**
SIC: **3211** Flat glass
HQ: Agc Flat Glass North America, Inc.
11175 Cicero Dr Ste 400
Alpharetta GA 30022
404 446-4200

(G-20840)
AIRMACHINESCOM INC
4705 Belmont Ave (44505-1013)
PHONE..................330 759-1620
Donald R Taylor, *President*
William A Taylor, *Vice Pres*
EMP: 5
SQ FT: 5,000
SALES: 500K **Privately Held**
SIC: **3546** Drills, portable, except rock: electric or pneumatic

(G-20841)
ALLIED CONSOLIDATED INDUSTRIES (PA)
2100 Poland Ave (44502-2751)
PHONE..................330 744-0808
John Ramun, *President*
Louise Ramun, *Admin Sec*
EMP: 104
SQ FT: 24,000
SALES (est): 29MM **Privately Held**
SIC: **3535** 3531 Conveyors & conveying equipment; construction machinery

(G-20842)
AM GRAPHICS
20 S Maryland Ave (44509-2807)
PHONE..................330 799-7319
Alfred Eusanio, *Owner*
EMP: 3
SQ FT: 3,500
SALES (est): 200K **Privately Held**
SIC: **2759** 7336 3993 2396 Screen printing; commercial art & graphic design; signs & advertising specialties; automotive & apparel trimmings

(G-20843)
AMERICAN ROLL FORMED PDTS CORP (HQ)
Also Called: Arf
3805 Hendricks Rd Ste A (44515-1536)
PHONE..................440 352-0753
Rob Touzalin, *President*
Ken Obermiyer, *Project Mgr*
Rob Irvine, *Production*
Scott McLaughlin, *Production*
Jeff Laturell, *CFO*
▼ EMP: 105 EST: 1960
SQ FT: 70,000
SALES (est): 21.5MM
SALES (corp-wide): 75MM **Privately Held**
WEB: www.arfpcorp.com
SIC: **3498** 3449 Fabricated pipe & fittings; custom roll formed products
PA: Hynes Industries, Inc.
3805 Hendricks Rd Ste A
Youngstown OH 44515
330 799-3221

(G-20844)
AMTECH TOOL AND MACHINE INC
100 Mcclurg Rd (44512-6738)
PHONE..................330 758-8215
Fred Coss, *President*
EMP: 13
SQ FT: 6,200
SALES (est): 2.1MM **Privately Held**
SIC: **3544** 3599 3441 Special dies & tools; machine shop, jobbing & repair; fabricated structural metal

(G-20845)
AMTHOR STEEL INC
5019 Belmont Ave (44505-1019)
PHONE..................330 759-0200
Raymond G Makara, *Project Engr*
Michael Guzzo, *Sales Staff*
George Ohlin, *Manager*
EMP: 7
SALES (corp-wide): 900MM **Privately Held**
SIC: **3312** Blast furnaces & steel mills
PA: Amthor Steel, Inc.
1717 Gaskell Ave
Erie PA 16503
814 452-4700

(G-20846)
ANATOMICAL CONCEPTS INC
1399 E Western Reserve Rd (44514-5224)
PHONE..................330 757-3569
William W De Toro, *President*
William W Detoro, *President*
Richard A Riffle, *Vice Pres*
EMP: 15
SQ FT: 1,600
SALES (est): 2.1MM **Privately Held**
WEB: www.prafo.com
SIC: **3842** Braces, orthopedic

(G-20847)
ARMADA FORTRESS LLC
Also Called: Pennslyvania Hill
8061 Market St (44512-6242)
PHONE..................330 953-2185
Danny Chew, *President*
EMP: 6
SALES (est): 572.1K
SALES (corp-wide): 4.1MM **Privately Held**
SIC: **2511** Wood household furniture
PA: Amish Furniture Mart, Inc.
401 E County Road 200n
Arcola IL 61910
217 268-4504

(G-20848)
AUSTINTOWN METAL WORKS INC
45 Victoria Rd (44515-2023)
PHONE..................330 259-4673
Jim Myers, *President*
EMP: 19
SALES (est): 3MM **Privately Held**
SIC: **3444** 3449 Sheet metalwork; bars, concrete reinforcing: fabricated steel

(G-20849)
AUSTINTOWN PRINTING INC
Also Called: Kwik Kopy Printing
5015 Mahoning Ave Ste 3 (44515-1701)
P.O. Box 312, North Lima (44452-0312)
PHONE..................330 797-0099
Sue Roberts, *President*
EMP: 5
SQ FT: 1,620
SALES (est): 538.7K **Privately Held**
WEB: www.austintownprinting.com
SIC: **2759** Thermography

(G-20850)
AZTEC MANUFACTURING INC
4325 Simon Rd (44512-1327)
PHONE..................330 783-9747
Jim Rutana, *Owner*
EMP: 20
SQ FT: 6,000
SALES (est): 2.4MM **Privately Held**
WEB: www.aztecmetalfab.com
SIC: **3365** 3444 Aluminum foundries; sheet metalwork

(G-20851)
BAKER PLASTICS INC
900 Mahoning Ave (44502-1488)
PHONE..................330 743-3142
Bonnie Baker, *President*
Robert E Baker, *Chairman*
Ruth Luarde, *Admin Sec*
EMP: 7 EST: 1946
SQ FT: 15,000
SALES (est): 1.3MM **Privately Held**
WEB: www.bakerplastics.com
SIC: **3089** 3993 5099 5046 Novelties, plastic; signs & advertising specialties; displays & cutouts, window & lobby; signs, not made in custom sign painting shops; advertising novelties; novelties, durable; store fixtures & display equipment; advertising specialties

GEOGRAPHIC SECTION

Youngstown - Mahoning County (G-20876)

(G-20852)
BERLIN INDUSTRIES INC
Also Called: Berlin Inds Protector Pdts
1275 Boardman Poland Rd # 1
(44514-3911)
PHONE..................................330 549-2100
Scott Gorley, *President*
EMP: 19
SQ FT: 35,000
SALES (est): 4.4MM
SALES (corp-wide): 1.4B **Privately Held**
SIC: 2834 5047 Veterinary pharmaceutical preparations; veterinarians' equipment & supplies
PA: Kobayashi Pharmaceutical Co., Ltd.
4-4-10, Doshomachi, Chuo-Ku
Osaka OSK 541-0
662 311-144

(G-20853)
BOARDMAN MOLDED INTL LLC
1110 Thalia Ave (44512-1825)
PHONE..................................330 788-2400
EMP: 120
SALES (est): 13.7MM
SALES (corp-wide): 25MM **Privately Held**
SIC: 3089 Injection molding of plastics
PA: Boardman Molded Products, Inc.
1110 Thalia Ave
Youngstown OH 44512
330 788-2400

(G-20854)
BOARDMAN MOLDED PRODUCTS INC (PA)
1110 Thalia Ave (44512-1825)
P.O. Box 1858 (44501-1858)
PHONE..................................330 788-2400
Ronald N Kessler, *President*
Daniel A Kessler, *Vice Pres*
▲ **EMP:** 80 **EST:** 1978
SQ FT: 85,000
SALES: 25MM **Privately Held**
SIC: 3089 3466 3429 2273 Injection molding of plastics; crowns & closures; manufactured hardware (general); carpets & rugs

(G-20855)
BOLTECH INCORPORATED
1201 Crescent St (44502-1303)
P.O. Box 749 (44501-0749)
PHONE..................................330 746-6881
Alex Benyo, *President*
C R Pallante, *Principal*
Brian Benyo, *Vice Pres*
Lucas Bacon, *Webmaster*
EMP: 9
SQ FT: 6,500
SALES (est): 1.5MM **Privately Held**
WEB: www.boltechinc.com
SIC: 3537 Trucks, tractors, loaders, carriers & similar equipment

(G-20856)
BRENTWOOD ORIGINALS INC
1309 N Meridian Rd (44509-1099)
PHONE..................................330 793-2255
Beth Foley, *Safety Dir*
Monica Wills, *Design Engr*
Kenji Onishi, *Controller*
Tim Domer, *Branch Mgr*
Mark Zarlengo, *Manager*
EMP: 330
SQ FT: 130,000
SALES (corp-wide): 145.3MM **Privately Held**
WEB: www.brentwoodoriginals.com
SIC: 2392 Pillows, bed: made from purchased materials
PA: Brentwood Originals, Inc.
20639 S Fordyce Ave
Carson CA 90745
310 637-6804

(G-20857)
BRIER HILL SLAG COMPANY (PA)
18 Hogue St (44502-1425)
PHONE..................................330 743-8170
Scott Marucci, *President*
William Gaffney, *Corp Secy*
John Ridel, *Sales Staff*
Nicki Williams, *Admin Sec*
EMP: 10
SQ FT: 700
SALES (est): 725.3K **Privately Held**
SIC: 3295 Slag, crushed or ground

(G-20858)
BRILEX INDUSTRIES INC
101 Andrews Ave (44503-1607)
PHONE..................................330 744-1114
Jessica Llyod, *Branch Mgr*
EMP: 100 **Privately Held**
SIC: 3542 3549 3441 Machine tools, metal forming type; metalworking machinery; fabricated structural metal
PA: Brilex Industries, Inc.
1201 Crescent St
Youngstown OH 44502

(G-20859)
BRILEX INDUSTRIES INC (PA)
Also Called: Brilex Tech Services
1201 Crescent St (44502-1303)
P.O. Box 749 (44501-0749)
PHONE..................................330 744-1114
Brian Benyo, *President*
Alex M Benyo, *Vice Pres*
Ryan Engelhardt, *Plant Mgr*
Dan Hennen, *Project Mgr*
Eleanor Seidel, *Purchasing*
▲ **EMP:** 160
SQ FT: 54,000
SALES (est): 37.2MM **Privately Held**
WEB: www.brilex.com
SIC: 3441 3542 3549 Fabricated structural metal; machine tools, metal forming type; metalworking machinery

(G-20860)
BROCKER MACHINE INC
1530 Poland Ave (44502-2188)
PHONE..................................330 744-5858
Brad Brocker, *President*
EMP: 11
SQ FT: 10,000
SALES (est): 1.4MM **Privately Held**
SIC: 3599 Machine shop, jobbing & repair

(G-20861)
BUDS SIGN SHOP INC
892 Mahoning Ave (44502-1414)
PHONE..................................330 744-5555
Robert Perkins, *President*
Barbara Perkins, *Vice Pres*
EMP: 10
SQ FT: 10,000
SALES: 1.1MM **Privately Held**
WEB: www.budsignshop.com
SIC: 3993 Signs, not made in custom sign painting shops

(G-20862)
BUSINESS JOURNAL
Also Called: Business Journal, The
25 E Boardman St Ste 306 (44503-1803)
P.O. Box 714 (44501-0714)
PHONE..................................330 744-5023
Andrea Wood, *President*
Spencer Percival, *Production*
EMP: 15
SQ FT: 2,700
SALES (est): 1.6MM **Privately Held**
WEB: www.business-journal.com
SIC: 2711 Newspapers, publishing & printing

(G-20863)
C M L CONCRETE CONSTRUCTION
482 Garden Valley Ct (44512-6503)
PHONE..................................330 758-8314
Carman Lofaro, *President*
EMP: 4
SALES (est): 566.3K **Privately Held**
SIC: 3444 Concrete forms, sheet metal

(G-20864)
CANFIELD INDUSTRIES INC (PA)
8510 Foxwood Ct (44514-4301)
PHONE..................................800 554-5071
John R Rasmussen, *President*
John Simon, *President*
Charles P Henderson, *Principal*
Ruth Smedley, *Principal*
Nancy M Williard, *Principal*
▲ **EMP:** 2 **EST:** 1965
SQ FT: 35,000
SALES (est): 27.5MM **Privately Held**
WEB: www.canfieldconnector.com
SIC: 7389 3491 3678 3677 Purchasing service; industrial valves; electronic connectors; electronic coils, transformers & other inductors; fluid power valves & hose fittings

(G-20865)
CARDIAC ARRHYTHMIA ASSOCIATES
3622 Belmont Ave Ste 1112 (44505-1450)
PHONE..................................330 759-8169
Mita Raheja, *President*
EMP: 3
SALES (est): 343.7K **Privately Held**
SIC: 8011 3845 Cardiologist & cardio-vascular specialist; pacemaker, cardiac

(G-20866)
CARNEY PLASTICS INC
1010 W Rayen Ave (44502-1317)
PHONE..................................330 746-8273
Sean Carney, *President*
▲ **EMP:** 9
SALES (est): 1.5MM **Privately Held**
WEB: www.carneyplastics.com
SIC: 3089 5162 Injection molding of plastics; plastics products

(G-20867)
CENTRAL COCA-COLA BTLG CO INC
531 E Indianola Ave (44502-2319)
PHONE..................................330 783-1982
John Flynt, *Branch Mgr*
EMP: 60
SALES (corp-wide): 35.4B **Publicly Held**
WEB: www.colasic.net
SIC: 2086 Bottled & canned soft drinks
HQ: Central Coca-Cola Bottling Company, Inc.
555 Taxter Rd Ste 550
Elmsford NY 10523
914 789-1100

(G-20868)
CENTRAL HEATING & COOLING INC
5626 South Ave Ste 1 (44512-2461)
PHONE..................................330 782-7100
Joseph Del Fraino, *President*
EMP: 5
SALES (est): 891.1K **Privately Held**
SIC: 3585 1711 Refrigeration & heating equipment; plumbing, heating, air-conditioning contractors

(G-20869)
CENTRAL OPTICAL INC
6981 Southern Blvd Ste B (44512-4657)
PHONE..................................330 783-9660
Lloyd Yazbek, *President*
Richard J Thomas, *Co-President*
Pamela A Thomas, *Treasurer*
Linda B Yazbek, *Admin Sec*
Joyce Fiersdorf, *Administration*
▲ **EMP:** 28
SQ FT: 10,000
SALES (est): 4.8MM **Privately Held**
WEB: www.centraloptical.com
SIC: 3851 5995 Eyeglasses, lenses & frames; optical goods stores

(G-20870)
CITY MACHINE TECHNOLOGIES INC (PA)
773 W Rayen Ave (44502-1112)
P.O. Box 1466 (44501-1466)
PHONE..................................330 747-2639
Michael J Kovach, *President*
Terry Herzberger, *Opers Mgr*
Doug Meek, *Finance Mgr*
Sam Farsco, *Officer*
Claudia Kovach, *Admin Sec*
EMP: 18 **EST:** 1986
SQ FT: 17,000
SALES (est): 13.7MM **Privately Held**
WEB: www.cmtcompanies.com
SIC: 3621 7694 3599 7692 Motors & generators; armature rewinding shops; machine shop, jobbing & repair; welding repair; industrial trucks & tractors

(G-20871)
CITY MACHINE TECHNOLOGIES INC
Electric Machinery Division
825 Martin Luther King Jr (44502-1105)
P.O. Box 1466 (44501-1466)
PHONE..................................330 740-8186
Michael J Kovach, *President*
Natalie Jenyk, *Office Mgr*
EMP: 40
SALES (corp-wide): 13.7MM **Privately Held**
WEB: www.cmtcompanies.com
SIC: 3599 7694 3621 3568 Machine shop, jobbing & repair; armature rewinding shops; motors & generators; power transmission equipment
PA: City Machine Technologies, Inc.
773 W Rayen Ave
Youngstown OH 44502
330 747-2639

(G-20872)
CITY MACHINE TECHNOLOGIES INC
Electric Machinery Division
773 W Rayen Ave (44502-1112)
P.O. Box 1466 (44501-1466)
PHONE..................................330 747-2639
Michael Kovach, *Manager*
EMP: 50
SALES (corp-wide): 13.7MM **Privately Held**
WEB: www.cmtcompanies.com
SIC: 3599 3613 Machine shop, jobbing & repair; control panels, electric
PA: City Machine Technologies, Inc.
773 W Rayen Ave
Youngstown OH 44502
330 747-2639

(G-20873)
CITY MACHINE TECHNOLOGIES INC
Lifting Magnet Division
448 Andrews Ave (44505-3063)
P.O. Box 1466 (44501-1466)
PHONE..................................330 747-2639
Doug Meek, *Manager*
EMP: 7
SALES (corp-wide): 13.7MM **Privately Held**
WEB: www.cmtcompanies.com
SIC: 3599 3613 Machine shop, jobbing & repair; control panels, electric
PA: City Machine Technologies, Inc.
773 W Rayen Ave
Youngstown OH 44502
330 747-2639

(G-20874)
CITY PRINTING CO INC
122 Oak Hill Ave (44502-1428)
PHONE..................................330 747-5691
Joseph A Valentini, *President*
EMP: 20 **EST:** 1920
SQ FT: 11,000
SALES: 92.7K **Privately Held**
WEB: www.cityprinting.com
SIC: 2752 Commercial printing, offset

(G-20875)
CLASSIC OPTICAL LABS INC
3710 Belmont Ave (44505-1406)
P.O. Box 1341 (44501-1341)
PHONE..................................330 759-8245
Dawn Friedkin, *President*
▲ **EMP:** 195
SQ FT: 30,000
SALES (est): 13.2MM **Privately Held**
WEB: www.classicoptical.com
SIC: 3851 Ophthalmic goods

(G-20876)
COMMERCIAL BAR & CABINETRY
Also Called: Commercial Cabinets
12 S Worthington St (44502-1336)
PHONE..................................330 743-1420
James Pupino, *Owner*
EMP: 6
SQ FT: 5,000
SALES: 450K **Privately Held**
SIC: 2434 Wood kitchen cabinets

Youngstown - Mahoning County (G-20877)

(G-20877)
COMPREHENSIVE LOGISTICS CO INC
365 Victoria Rd (44515-2027)
PHONE...................................330 793-0504
Doug Caswell, *Branch Mgr*
EMP: 50 **Privately Held**
SIC: 8742 4226 3714 3711 Mgmt Consulting Svcs Special Warehse/Storage Mfg Motor Vehicle Parts Mfg Motor Vehicle Bodies
PA: Comprehensive Logistics, Co., Inc.
  4944 Belmont Ave Ste 202
  Youngstown OH 44505

(G-20878)
CONISON TOOL AND DIE INC
8100 Southern Blvd (44512-6307)
PHONE...................................330 758-1574
Edward Straub, *President*
Michelle Straub, *President*
EMP: 9
SQ FT: 3,500
SALES (est): 1.1MM **Privately Held**
SIC: 3544 Special dies & tools

(G-20879)
CONSTRUCTION BULLETIN INC
4178 Market St Lowr (44512-1116)
PHONE...................................330 782-3733
Fax: 330 782-8110
EMP: 6
SQ FT: 2,000
SALES (est): 280K **Privately Held**
SIC: 2711 Newspapers-Publishing/Printing

(G-20880)
CRAFCO INC
912 Salt Springs Rd (44509-1171)
PHONE...................................330 270-3034
John Perry, *Branch Mgr*
EMP: 17
SALES (corp-wide): 1B **Privately Held**
SIC: 2951 Asphalt paving mixtures & blocks
HQ: Crafco, Inc.
  6165 W Detroit St
  Chandler AZ 85226
  602 276-0406

(G-20881)
CROWES CABINETS INC
590 E West Reserve Bldg 8 (44514)
PHONE...................................330 729-9911
Diane Crowe, *President*
EMP: 20
SQ FT: 6,000
SALES (est): 1.4MM **Privately Held**
WEB: www.crowescabinets.com
SIC: 2434 Wood kitchen cabinets

(G-20882)
CUBBISON COMPANY (PA)
380 Victoria Rd (44515-2054)
PHONE...................................330 793-2481
Timothy Merrifield, *President*
Heather Haywood, *Purch Mgr*
Ken Baytosh, *Purchasing*
Sean Danks, *Manager*
Greg Lamica, *Info Tech Mgr*
EMP: 67
SQ FT: 27,000
SALES: 7.6MM **Privately Held**
WEB: www.cubbison.com
SIC: 3469 3993 3479 Metal stampings; name plates: except engraved, etched, etc.: metal; etching & engraving

(G-20883)
CUSTOM TARPAULIN PRODUCTS INC
8095 Southern Blvd (44512-6336)
PHONE...................................330 758-1801
Beth Robinson, *Corp Secy*
Brian Robinson, *Vice Pres*
EMP: 19
SALES (est): 2.2MM **Privately Held**
WEB: www.customtarpaulin.com
SIC: 2394 Tarpaulins, fabric: made from purchased materials

(G-20884)
CUSTOMER PRINTING INC
Also Called: Pegasus Printing Group
592 Industrial Rd (44509-2917)
PHONE...................................330 629-8676
EMP: 15
SALES (est): 2.9MM **Privately Held**
SIC: 2752 Commercial Printing, Lithographic

(G-20885)
DAILY LEGAL NEWS INC
100 E Federal St Ste 126 (44503-1834)
PHONE...................................330 747-7777
John Burleson, *President*
Kimberly Durgala, *General Mgr*
Kim Pearson, *Manager*
EMP: 5
SALES (est): 270.8K **Privately Held**
WEB: www.dlnnews.com
SIC: 2711 Newspapers, publishing & printing

(G-20886)
DATCO MFG COMPANY INC
4605 Lake Park Rd (44512-1814)
PHONE...................................330 787-1127
John Kerns, *Principal*
EMP: 45
SALES (corp-wide): 18.9MM **Privately Held**
SIC: 3999 Atomizers, toiletry
PA: Datco Mfg. Company, Inc.
  4605 Lake Park Rd
  Youngstown OH 44512
  330 781-6100

(G-20887)
DATCO MFG COMPANY INC (PA)
4605 Lake Park Rd (44512-1814)
PHONE...................................330 781-6100
Thomas E Hutch Jr, *President*
EMP: 90
SQ FT: 32,000
SALES (est): 18.9MM **Privately Held**
SIC: 3354 3444 Aluminum extruded products; sheet metalwork

(G-20888)
DEKAY FABRICATORS INC
295 S Meridian Rd (44509-2924)
PHONE...................................330 793-0826
Bryan Kennedy, *President*
EMP: 8
SQ FT: 10,000
SALES: 100K **Privately Held**
SIC: 3498 Tube fabricating (contract bending & shaping)

(G-20889)
DESIGN TRAC INC
4136 Logan Way (44505-5703)
PHONE...................................330 759-3131
Gary Gasser, *CEO*
Mark Gasser, *President*
Cindy Gasser, *Treasurer*
Cathy Gasser, *Admin Sec*
EMP: 5
SQ FT: 3,000
SALES (est): 390K **Privately Held**
SIC: 2522 Office furniture, except wood

(G-20890)
DIAMOND SPARKLER MFG CO (PA)
555 Martin Luther King Jr (44502-1102)
PHONE...................................330 746-1064
Bruce J Zoldan, *President*
John Reiss, *Plant Mgr*
EMP: 1
SQ FT: 30,000
SALES (est): 8.1MM **Privately Held**
SIC: 2899 Fireworks

(G-20891)
DIGITAL GRAPHICS
4589 Dobbins Rd (44514-2398)
PHONE...................................330 707-1720
Tom Donegan, *Owner*
EMP: 4 **EST:** 1989
SALES (est): 226.4K **Privately Held**
SIC: 2759 Commercial printing

(G-20892)
DIRUSSOS SAUSAGE INC
1035 W Rayen Ave (44502-1316)
PHONE...................................330 744-1208
Robert Dirusso, *President*
Kevin Vrabel, *Opers Mgr*
Michael Testa, *Prdtn Mgr*
Brenda Gioppo, *Manager*
EMP: 30
SQ FT: 8,000
SALES (est): 4.9MM **Privately Held**
SIC: 2013 Sausages from purchased meat

(G-20893)
DON WALTER KITCHEN DISTRS INC
260 Victoria Rd (44515-2024)
PHONE...................................330 793-9338
Betty Kern, *Manager*
EMP: 5
SALES (corp-wide): 19.6MM **Privately Held**
SIC: 2599 5211 Cabinets, factory; cabinets, kitchen
PA: Don Walter Kitchen Distributors Inc
  260 Victoria Rd
  Youngstown OH 44515
  330 793-9338

(G-20894)
DR PEPPER BOTTLERS ASSOCIATES
500 Pepsi Pl (44502-1432)
PHONE...................................330 746-7651
Danny Rittenberry, *Principal*
EMP: 3
SALES (est): 137.6K **Privately Held**
SIC: 2086 Soft drinks: packaged in cans, bottles, etc.

(G-20895)
EASTERDAYS PRINTING CENTER
86 Boardman Poland Rd (44512-4602)
PHONE...................................330 726-1182
John Easterday, *President*
Sharlene Easterday, *Treasurer*
EMP: 4
SALES (est): 500K **Privately Held**
SIC: 5112 2752 2791 2789 Stationery & office supplies; commercial printing, offset; typesetting; bookbinding & related work

(G-20896)
EINSTRUCTION CORP
255 W Federal St (44503-1207)
PHONE...................................940 565-0004
EMP: 11
SALES (est): 308.6K
SALES (corp-wide): 125.9MM **Privately Held**
SIC: 7372 Prepackaged software
PA: Turning Technologies, Llc
  255 W Federal St
  Youngstown OH 44503
  330 746-3015

(G-20897)
EINSTRUCTION CORPORATION (HQ)
255 W Federal St (44503-1207)
PHONE...................................330 746-3015
Rich Fennessy, *CEO*
Tim Torno, *CFO*
▼ **EMP:** 100
SQ FT: 8,000
SALES (est): 35.8MM
SALES (corp-wide): 125.9MM **Privately Held**
WEB: www.einstruction.com
SIC: 7371 7379 5045 7372 Computer software development; computer related consulting services; computers, peripherals & software; prepackaged software
PA: Turning Technologies, Llc
  255 W Federal St
  Youngstown OH 44503
  330 746-3015

(G-20898)
EJ USA INC
4150 Simon Rd (44512-1322)
PHONE...................................330 782-3900
Mark Duvall, *Plant Mgr*
Bill Denidovich, *Manager*
EMP: 16 **Privately Held**
WEB: www.ejiw.com
SIC: 3449 3321 Custom roll formed products; manhole covers, metal
HQ: Ej Usa, Inc.
  301 Spring St
  East Jordan MI 49727
  800 874-4100

(G-20899)
EPCO EXTRUSION PAINTING CO
4605 Lake Park Rd (44512-1814)
PHONE...................................330 781-6100
Thomas E Hutch Jr, *President*
EMP: 45
SALES (est): 7.3MM **Privately Held**
SIC: 3479 Aluminum coating of metal products

(G-20900)
ESSENTIAL PATHWAYS OHIO LLC
726 E Boston Ave (44502-2420)
PHONE...................................330 518-3091
Andrea Dawson,
EMP: 3
SALES (est): 108K **Privately Held**
SIC: 5699 5661 7389 5044 Sports apparel; customized clothing & apparel; men's shoes; women's shoes; ; typewriters; radio & TV communications equipment

(G-20901)
EXAL CORPORATION (PA)
1 Performance Pl (44502-2099)
PHONE...................................330 744-9505
Michael Mapes, *CEO*
Delfin Gibert, *President*
Robert Huffman, *Vice Pres*
Brenda Oman, *Vice Pres*
Matthew Futkos, *Plant Engr Mgr*
◆ **EMP:** 35
SQ FT: 476,000
SALES (est): 113.9MM **Privately Held**
WEB: www.exal.com
SIC: 3411 3354 Aluminum cans; aluminum extruded products

(G-20902)
EXTENDIT COMPANY
601 Jones St (44502-2161)
PHONE...................................330 743-4343
Henry M Garlick, *President*
EMP: 6
SQ FT: 50,000
SALES (est): 1MM **Privately Held**
WEB: www.extenditco.com
SIC: 2891 Sealants

(G-20903)
FALMER SCREW PDTS & MFG INC
690 Mcclurg Rd (44512-6407)
PHONE...................................330 758-0593
Rick Dravecky, *President*
George Dravecky, *Corp Secy*
Joseph Dravecky, *Vice Pres*
EMP: 15
SQ FT: 30,000
SALES (est): 3MM **Privately Held**
WEB: www.falmerinc.com
SIC: 3599 3451 Machine shop, jobbing & repair; screw machine products

(G-20904)
FINE LINE EMBROIDERY COMPANY
4660 Lake Park Rd (44512-1813)
PHONE...................................330 788-9070
Michael David, *Owner*
EMP: 5
SALES (est): 238.8K **Privately Held**
WEB: www.fineline-emb.com
SIC: 2395 Embroidery & art needlework
PA: Fine Line Embroidery Company, Inc
  20525 Detroit Rd Ste 9
  Rocky River OH 44116

(G-20905)
FIRELINE INC
8560 Foxwood Ct (44514-4301)
PHONE...................................330 259-0647
Barbara Burley, *Branch Mgr*

GEOGRAPHIC SECTION

Youngstown - Mahoning County (G-20930)

EMP: 20
SALES (corp-wide): 23.2MM **Privately Held**
SIC: 3299 Non-metallic mineral statuary & other decorative products; ceramic fiber
PA: Fireline, Inc.
300 Andrews Ave
Youngstown OH 44505
330 743-1164

(G-20906)
FIRELINE INC (PA)
Also Called: Fireline Tcon
300 Andrews Ave (44505-3061)
PHONE...................................330 743-1164
Barbara Burley, *President*
Edward Ress, *General Mgr*
Ed Ress, *Exec VP*
John Austin, *Opers Staff*
Gloria Jones, *Treasurer*
▼ EMP: 125
SQ FT: 85,000
SALES: 23.2MM **Privately Held**
SIC: 3299 Non-metallic mineral statuary & other decorative products; insulsleeves (foundry materials); ceramic fiber

(G-20907)
FITHIAN-WILBERT BURIAL VLT CO
6234 Market St (44512-3329)
PHONE...................................330 758-2327
Heather Davis, *President*
EMP: 14 EST: 1924
SALES (est): 1.3MM **Privately Held**
SIC: 3272 Burial vaults, concrete or pre-cast terrazzo

(G-20908)
FOOD 4 YOUR SOUL
3957 S Schenley Ave (44511-3428)
PHONE...................................330 402-4073
Michelle White, *Owner*
EMP: 10
SALES (est): 327.5K **Privately Held**
SIC: 2099 Food preparations

(G-20909)
FORGE INDUSTRIES INC (PA)
4450 Market St (44512-1512)
PHONE...................................330 782-8301
William T James II, *Ch of Bd*
Carl G James, *President*
W Thomas James III, *Vice Pres*
Dan Maisonville, *CFO*
Gary Davis, *Asst Sec*
▲ EMP: 1250 EST: 1900
SQ FT: 1,500
SALES (est): 549.3MM **Privately Held**
WEB: www.forgeindustries.com
SIC: 5085 3566 3599 3531 Bearings; power transmission equipment & apparatus; gears, power transmission, except automotive; machine shop, jobbing & repair; road construction & maintenance machinery; insurance brokers; industrial equipment services

(G-20910)
FRANCIS INDUSTRIES LLC
1424 Albert St (44505-3222)
PHONE...................................330 333-3352
EMP: 3 EST: 2016
SALES (est): 200.1K **Privately Held**
SIC: 3999 Barber & beauty shop equipment

(G-20911)
GARVEY CORPORATION
Also Called: M7 Technologies
1019 Ohio Works Dr (44510-1078)
PHONE...................................330 779-0700
Michael S Garvey, *President*
William Heid, *Project Engr*
Jeanette Garvey, *Treasurer*
EMP: 25
SQ FT: 20,000
SALES (est): 6MM **Privately Held**
SIC: 3599 Machine shop, jobbing & repair

(G-20912)
GASSER CHAIR CO INC (PA)
4136 Logan Way (44505-1797)
PHONE...................................330 534-2234
Gary L Gasser, *CEO*
Mark E Gasser, *President*
Diane Hughes, *Opers Mgr*
Rick Williams, *Opers Mgr*
April Kerchak, *Purch Mgr*
◆ EMP: 25
SQ FT: 22,000
SALES (est): 24.7MM **Privately Held**
WEB: www.gasserchair.com
SIC: 2531 2521 Chairs, table & arm; chairs, office: padded, upholstered or plain: wood

(G-20913)
GASSER CHAIR CO INC
4136 Logan Way (44505-1797)
PHONE...................................330 534-2234
Scott Gasser, *Manager*
EMP: 15
SQ FT: 8,900
SALES (corp-wide): 24.7MM **Privately Held**
WEB: www.gasserchair.com
SIC: 5021 2522 2512 2531 Chairs; chairs, office: padded or plain, except wood; chairs: upholstered on wood frames; chairs, portable folding; chairs, table & arm
PA: Gasser Chair Co., Inc.
4136 Logan Way
Youngstown OH 44505
330 534-2234

(G-20914)
GASSER CHAIR CO INC
Also Called: Production Div
2457 Logan Ave (44505-2550)
PHONE...................................330 759-2234
Frank Joy, *Vice Pres*
Evelyn McCabe, *Controller*
EMP: 100
SALES (corp-wide): 24.7MM **Privately Held**
WEB: www.gasserchair.com
SIC: 2531 2522 2521 2511 Chairs, table & arm; office furniture, except wood; wood office furniture; wood household furniture
PA: Gasser Chair Co., Inc.
4136 Logan Way
Youngstown OH 44505
330 534-2234

(G-20915)
GEI OF COLUMBIANA INC
4040 Lake Park Rd (44512-1801)
PHONE...................................330 783-0270
Michael C Schuler, *President*
EMP: 62 EST: 2000
SALES (est): 7.2MM **Privately Held**
SIC: 3354 3471 Shapes, extruded aluminum; polishing, metals or formed products; finishing, metals or formed products; anodizing (plating) of metals or formed products

(G-20916)
GENERAL ELECTRIC COMPANY
280 N Meridian Rd (44509-1858)
PHONE...................................330 793-3911
George Lopuchovsky, *Opers Mgr*
George Lupuzhovky, *Branch Mgr*
EMP: 230
SALES (corp-wide): 121.6B **Publicly Held**
SIC: 3641 3356 Filaments, for electric lamps; nonferrous rolling & drawing
PA: General Electric Company
41 Farnsworth St
Boston MA 02210
617 443-3000

(G-20917)
GENERAL EXTRUSIONS INC
Also Called: Gei
4040 Lake Park Rd (44512-1801)
P.O. Box 3488 (44513-3488)
PHONE...................................330 783-0270
Herbert F Schuler, *President*
EMP: 58
SQ FT: 220,000
SALES (est): 21.1MM **Privately Held**
WEB: www.genext.com
SIC: 3354 3471 Shapes, extruded aluminum; polishing, metals or formed products

(G-20918)
GENEVA LIBERTY STEEL LTD (PA)
Also Called: GENMAK GENEVA LIBERTY
947 Martin Luther King Jr (44502-1106)
P.O. Box 6124 (44501-6124)
PHONE...................................330 740-0103
David T McLeroy, *President*
EMP: 47
SQ FT: 85,000
SALES: 43.2MM **Privately Held**
SIC: 3316 7389 Strip steel, flat bright, cold-rolled: purchased hot-rolled; scrap steel cutting

(G-20919)
GENEX TOOL & DIE INC
4000 Lake Park Rd (44512)
PHONE...................................330 788-2466
Herbert F Schuler, *President*
Michael Schuler, *Admin Sec*
EMP: 11
SQ FT: 23,000
SALES (est): 1MM **Privately Held**
WEB: www.genext.com
SIC: 3541 Machine tools, metal cutting type

(G-20920)
GEORGE A MITCHELL COMPANY
557 Mcclurg Rd (44512-6443)
P.O. Box 3727 (44513-3727)
PHONE...................................330 758-5777
George A Mitchell, *President*
Patricia Jasinski, *Corp Secy*
Mark A Mitchell, *Vice Pres*
Paul F Russo, *Vice Pres*
Gary Sansenbaugher, *Engineer*
▼ EMP: 20
SQ FT: 22,000
SALES (est): 4.8MM **Privately Held**
WEB: www.mitchellmachinery.com
SIC: 3542 3541 3547 Extruding machines (machine tools), metal; machine tools, metal cutting type; rolling mill machinery

(G-20921)
GIA RUSSA (PA)
Also Called: John Zidian Company
574 Mcclurg Rd (44512-6405)
PHONE...................................330 743-6050
Loren Grossman, *Warehouse Mgr*
Doug Koller, *Regl Sales Mgr*
▲ EMP: 15 EST: 2011
SALES (est): 2.7MM **Privately Held**
SIC: 2032 Italian foods: packaged in cans, jars, etc.

(G-20922)
GL INTERNATIONAL LLC
Also Called: Gli Pool Products
215 Sinter Ct (44510-1076)
PHONE...................................330 744-8812
Mike Loccisano, *VP Opers*
Scott Grdina, *Opers Mgr*
Rich Garbee, *VP Sls/Mktg*
Ron Garland, *CFO*
Brian Frost, *Sales Staff*
▲ EMP: 130
SALES (est): 18.6MM **Privately Held**
SIC: 3949 Swimming pools, plastic

(G-20923)
GRALE TECHNOLOGIES INC
1019 Ohio Works Dr (44510-1078)
P.O. Box 1001, Aliquippa PA (15001-0801)
PHONE...................................724 683-8141
Fred Persi, *Partner*
Michael Garvey, *Partner*
James Osterloh, *Partner*
EMP: 3
SALES (est): 153.9K **Privately Held**
SIC: 3829 Measuring & controlling devices

(G-20924)
GREAT LAKES TELCOM LTD
Also Called: Broadband Hospitality
590 E Western Reserve Rd (44514-3354)
PHONE...................................330 629-8848
Vincent Lucci, *Partner*
EMP: 30
SQ FT: 9,200
SALES (est): 8.7MM **Privately Held**
WEB: www.broadbandhospitality.com
SIC: 4813 3663 ; satellites, communications

(G-20925)
GRENGA MACHINE & WELDING
56 Wayne Ave (44502-1938)
PHONE...................................330 743-1113
Joe Grenga, *Owner*
EMP: 10
SQ FT: 30,000
SALES (est): 2.1MM **Privately Held**
SIC: 5051 5084 3599 3443 Steel; industrial machinery & equipment; machine shop, jobbing & repair; fabricated plate work (boiler shop); fabricated structural metal; blast furnaces & steel mills

(G-20926)
GRINDING EQUIPMENT & MCHY LLC
15 S Worthington St (44502-1335)
PHONE...................................330 747-2313
James Johnson, *President*
Tracy Gross, *Office Mgr*
Fredrick Houston, *Mng Member*
EMP: 13 EST: 1982
SQ FT: 10,000
SALES (est): 1.7MM **Privately Held**
WEB: www.gem-usa.com
SIC: 3599 Custom machinery

(G-20927)
GUNDERSON RAIL SERVICES LLC
Also Called: Greenbrier Rail Services
3710 Hendricks Rd Bldg 2a (44515-1537)
PHONE...................................330 792-6521
Adam Strysseler, *Manager*
EMP: 20
SALES (corp-wide): 2.5B **Publicly Held**
SIC: 3743 3444 3441 Railroad equipment; sheet metalwork; fabricated structural metal
HQ: Gunderson Rail Services Llc
1 Centerpointe Dr Ste 200
Lake Oswego OR 97035
503 684-7000

(G-20928)
HANGER PRSTHETCS & ORTHO INC
Also Called: Hanger Clinic
930 Trailwood Dr (44512-5007)
PHONE...................................330 758-1143
Sam Liang, *CEO*
William Detoro, *Branch Mgr*
EMP: 7
SALES (corp-wide): 1B **Publicly Held**
SIC: 3842 Limbs, artificial
HQ: Hanger Prosthetics & Orthotics, Inc.
10910 Domain Dr Ste 300
Austin TX 78758
512 777-3800

(G-20929)
HATTENBACH COMPANY
52 E Myrtle Ave (44507-1268)
PHONE...................................330 744-2732
Roy Guerrieri, *Branch Mgr*
EMP: 20
SALES (corp-wide): 15MM **Privately Held**
WEB: www.hattenbach.com
SIC: 5078 1711 2434 2541 Commercial refrigeration equipment; refrigeration contractor; wood kitchen cabinets; cabinets, except refrigerated: show, display, etc.: wood
PA: The Hattenbach Company
5309 Hamilton Ave
Cleveland OH 44114
216 881-5200

(G-20930)
HIGH TECH MOLDING & DESIGN INC
27 W Indianola Ave (44507-1462)
PHONE...................................330 726-1676
Doug Bieber, *President*
Mary Ann Bieber, *Vice Pres*
Gary Graham, *Manager*
EMP: 5
SQ FT: 500,000

Youngstown - Mahoning County (G-20931)

SALES (est): 1.7MM **Privately Held**
SIC: 3089 Injection molding of plastics

(G-20931)
HILLSHIRE BRANDS COMPANY
Also Called: Superior Coffee & Foods
95 Karago Ave (44512-5951)
PHONE.................330 758-8885
Bob Clyde, *Branch Mgr*
EMP: 3
SALES (corp-wide): 40B **Publicly Held**
SIC: 2013 Sausages & other prepared meats
HQ: The Hillshire Brands Company
400 S Jefferson St Fl 1
Chicago IL 60607
312 614-6000

(G-20932)
HOWARD GRANT CORP
Also Called: Vector Chemicals
316 Alexander St (44502-2117)
P.O. Box 47, Lowellville (44436-0047)
PHONE.................330 743-3151
Claudia Hirschochs, *President*
Patty Meehan, *Sales Mgr*
Michael Kortan, *Admin Sec*
EMP: 3
SQ FT: 8,000
SALES: 400K **Privately Held**
WEB: www.vectorchemicals.com
SIC: 2841 Detergents, synthetic organic or inorganic alkaline

(G-20933)
HUDSON FASTENERS INC
241 W Federal St 512 (44503-1207)
PHONE.................330 270-9500
Lisa Kleinhandler, *President*
Cris Young, *Exec VP*
Laura Yarab, *Accounting Mgr*
EMP: 4
SQ FT: 3,000
SALES (est): 590K **Privately Held**
WEB: www.hudsonfasteners.com
SIC: 5072 3452 3429 Bolts; nuts (hardware); screws; washers (hardware); wood screws; metal fasteners

(G-20934)
HYNES INDUSTRIES INC (PA)
Also Called: Roll Formed Products Co Div
3805 Hendricks Rd Ste A (44515-3046)
PHONE.................330 799-3221
William W Bresnahan, *Ch of Bd*
William J Bresnahan, *President*
D R Golding, *President*
C A Covington Jr, *Principal*
Joseph S Donchess, *Principal*
▲ **EMP:** 124
SQ FT: 154,000
SALES (est): 75MM **Privately Held**
WEB: www.hynesind.com
SIC: 5051 3449 3316 3441 Steel; strip, metal; custom roll formed products; wire, flat, cold-rolled strip: not made in hot-rolled mills; fabricated structural metal

(G-20935)
I-DEE-X INC
Also Called: Idx Supply Division
4302 Lake Park Rd (44512-1830)
PHONE.................330 788-2186
Martin Mayer Jr, *President*
EMP: 4
SQ FT: 5,400
SALES: 388.6K **Privately Held**
SIC: 5085 3544 Industrial supplies; special dies & tools

(G-20936)
ICTM INC
Also Called: United Wood Products
7204 Glenwood Ave (44512-4852)
P.O. Box 3964 (44513-3964)
PHONE.................330 629-6060
Scott Wood, *President*
EMP: 3
SQ FT: 300
SALES: 1.5MM **Privately Held**
SIC: 2448 Pallets, wood

(G-20937)
IMDS CORPORATION
935 Augusta Dr (44512-7923)
PHONE.................330 747-4637
Robert A Hill Jr, *President*
EMP: 10
SQ FT: 18,600
SALES (est): 1.3MM **Privately Held**
WEB: www.imds-ohio.com
SIC: 3599 8711 Machine shop, jobbing & repair; industrial engineers

(G-20938)
INDUCTION IRON INCORPORATED
3710 Hendricks Rd Bldg 1 (44515-1537)
PHONE.................330 501-8852
Robert Macklin, *Manager*
EMP: 5
SALES (corp-wide): 6.7MM **Privately Held**
SIC: 5093 3444 Ferrous metal scrap & waste; sheet metalwork
PA: Induction Iron Incorporated
13909 N Dale Mabry Hwy # 203
Tampa FL 33618
813 969-3300

(G-20939)
INDUSTRIAL MILL MAINTENANCE
1609 Wilson Ave Ste 2 (44506-1838)
P.O. Box 1465 (44501-1465)
PHONE.................330 746-1155
Michael McCarthy Sr, *President*
Kathy McCarthy, *Vice Pres*
EMP: 50
SQ FT: 5,600
SALES: 4MM **Privately Held**
SIC: 3471 1721 3444 3441 Sand blasting of metal parts; industrial painting; sheet metalwork; fabricated structural metal

(G-20940)
INK FACTORY INC
2750 Salt Springs Rd (44509-1034)
PHONE.................330 799-0888
Charles Nannicola, *President*
Kevin McHenry, *Vice Pres*
Frank Nannicola, *Vice Pres*
EMP: 4
SQ FT: 12,000
SALES (est): 437.4K **Privately Held**
WEB: www.nannicola.com
SIC: 2893 3944 2899 Printing ink; games, toys & children's vehicles; chemical preparations

(G-20941)
INNOVATION EXHIBITS INC
85 Karago Ave Ste 1&2 (44512-5969)
P.O. Box 3198 (44513-3198)
PHONE.................330 726-1324
Monica Gable, *President*
EMP: 5
SALES (corp-wide): 1.2MM **Privately Held**
WEB: www.innovationexhibits.com
SIC: 3993 Signs & advertising specialties
PA: Innovation Exhibits, Inc.
850 Mcclurg Rd
Youngstown OH 44512
330 726-1324

(G-20942)
INTIGRAL INC
45 Karago Ave (44512-5950)
PHONE.................440 439-0980
Michael McHugh, *Manager*
EMP: 27
SALES (corp-wide): 51.7MM **Privately Held**
WEB: www.edgeseal.com
SIC: 3231 Insulating glass: made from purchased glass
PA: Intigral, Inc.
7850 Northfield Rd
Walton Hills OH 44146
440 439-0980

(G-20943)
IRON CITY WOOD PRODUCTS INC
900 Albert St (44505-2968)
PHONE.................330 755-2772
David S Muslovski, *President*
Denise Muslovski, *Vice Pres*
Dj Yanssens, *Opers Mgr*
EMP: 48
SQ FT: 2,560
SALES (est): 8.5MM **Privately Held**
WEB: www.ironcitywoodproducts.com
SIC: 2448 Pallets, wood

(G-20944)
J TYLER ENTERPRISE LLC
66 Parkgate Ave (44515-3236)
PHONE.................330 774-4490
Jeffrey Duzzny, *Principal*
EMP: 3 **EST:** 2013
SALES (est): 181.6K **Privately Held**
SIC: 3751 Motorcycle accessories

(G-20945)
JAMEN TOOL & DIE CO (PA)
Also Called: Truex Tool & Die Div
4450 Lake Park Rd (44512-1809)
PHONE.................330 788-6521
Carmen P Chicone Sr, *President*
Antonette Chicone, *Vice Pres*
Carmen Chicone Jr, *Shareholder*
Paul Chicone, *Admin Sec*
EMP: 19 **EST:** 1965
SQ FT: 5,000
SALES (est): 7.7MM **Privately Held**
SIC: 3544 Extrusion dies

(G-20946)
JAMEN TOOL & DIE CO
Also Called: Mor-X Plastics
914 E Indianola Ave (44502-2674)
PHONE.................330 782-6731
Bob Marcum, *Manager*
EMP: 22
SALES (corp-wide): 7.7MM **Privately Held**
SIC: 3544 Industrial molds
PA: Jamen Tool & Die Co.
4450 Lake Park Rd
Youngstown OH 44512
330 788-6521

(G-20947)
JAMESTOWN INDUSTRIES INC
650 N Meridian Rd Ste 3 (44509-1233)
PHONE.................330 779-0670
Clark Babb, *Manager*
EMP: 60
SQ FT: 32,000
SALES (corp-wide): 12.1MM **Privately Held**
SIC: 3493 Steel springs, except wire
PA: Jamestown Industries, Inc.
2210 Arbor Blvd Ste 99
Moraine OH

(G-20948)
JEWISH JOURNAL MONTHLY MAG
505 Gypsy Ln (44504-1314)
PHONE.................330 746-3251
Sherry Weinblatt, *Principal*
Sam Cooperman, *Exec Dir*
Cristal Vincent, *Asst Admin*
EMP: 4
SALES: 150K **Privately Held**
WEB: www.jewishyoungstown.org
SIC: 2711 Newspapers, publishing & printing

(G-20949)
JONES & ASSOC ADVG & DESIGN
5015 Mahoning Ave Ste 1 (44515-1701)
PHONE.................330 799-6876
Diane Jones, *Owner*
EMP: 3
SALES: 100K **Privately Held**
SIC: 5949 5099 3993 2759 Sewing, needlework & piece goods; signs, except electric; signs & advertising specialties; screen printing; T-shirts, custom printed

(G-20950)
JUGGERBOT 3D LLC
241 W Federal St (44503-1207)
PHONE.................330 406-6900
Daniel Joseph Fernback Jr, *CEO*
EMP: 3
SALES (est): 146.7K **Privately Held**
SIC: 3699 Electrical equipment & supplies

(G-20951)
K & J HOLDINGS INC
Also Called: Trolios Silk Screening & EMB
8060 Southern Blvd (44512-6083)
PHONE.................330 726-0828
Judy Schenkler, *President*
Ken Schenkler, *Principal*
EMP: 3
SALES (est): 50K **Privately Held**
SIC: 2759 Screen printing

(G-20952)
KIM BRAUER & COMPANY LLC
7465 Huntington Dr Apt 6 (44512-4057)
PHONE.................330 540-9152
Kim Brauer, *Principal*
EMP: 3 **EST:** 2010
SALES (est): 211.7K **Privately Held**
SIC: 2771 Greeting cards

(G-20953)
KIND SPECIAL ALLOYS US LLC
1221 Velma Ct (44512-1829)
PHONE.................330 788-2437
Susanne Wildner,
EMP: 4
SALES (est): 195.1K **Privately Held**
SIC: 3312 Tool & die steel & alloys

(G-20954)
KIRALY TOOL AND DIE INC
1250 Crescent St (44502-1303)
PHONE.................330 744-5773
Steve Kiraly, *President*
Shari Kiraly, *Vice Pres*
EMP: 10
SQ FT: 9,500
SALES: 750K **Privately Held**
WEB: www.kiralytool.com
SIC: 3542 3544 Machine tools, metal forming type; special dies, tools, jigs & fixtures

(G-20955)
L M ENGINEERING INC
2720 Intertech Dr (44509-4023)
PHONE.................330 270-2400
Joann Laguardia, *President*
William Laguardia, *Corp Secy*
David Hendrick, *Engineer*
Don Dipiero,
EMP: 25
SQ FT: 40,000
SALES (est): 5.4MM **Privately Held**
SIC: 3161 Musical instrument cases; cases, carrying

(G-20956)
LAKE PARK TOOL & MACHINE LLC
1221 Velma Ct (44512-1829)
PHONE.................330 788-2437
Oscar Lund, *President*
Dave Cornelius, *Principal*
Susanne Wildner, *Principal*
EMP: 13
SALES (est): 762.2K **Privately Held**
SIC: 3429 Manufactured hardware (general)

(G-20957)
LARICCIAS ITALIAN FOODS
7438 Southern Blvd (44512-5629)
PHONE.................330 729-0222
Tessa Lariccia, *President*
Michael Allegretto, *Vice Pres*
EMP: 10 **EST:** 1910
SQ FT: 4,000
SALES (est): 1.1MM **Privately Held**
SIC: 5411 2098 2035 Grocery stores, independent; macaroni & spaghetti; pickles, sauces & salad dressings

(G-20958)
LARRYS DRIVE THRU & MINI MART
3305 Center Rd (44514-2204)
PHONE.................330 953-0512
Diana M Ornelas, *Principal*
EMP: 3 **EST:** 2011
SALES (est): 247.9K **Privately Held**
SIC: 5411 2082 2084 Convenience stores, independent; beer (alcoholic beverage); wines

GEOGRAPHIC SECTION

Youngstown - Mahoning County (G-20985)

(G-20959)
LIBERTY PATTERN AND MOLD INC
1131 Meadowbrook Ave (44512-1822)
PHONE..................330 788-9463
John Plaskett, *President*
EMP: 7
SQ FT: 4,800
SALES: 400K **Privately Held**
WEB: www.libpattern.com
SIC: 3543 Industrial patterns

(G-20960)
LION BLACK PRODUCTS LLC
3710 Hendricks Rd (44515-1537)
PHONE..................412 400-6980
Don Fuchs,
Edward Hallsky,
Felix Hallsky Jr,
EMP: 12
SQ FT: 250,000
SALES: 2MM **Privately Held**
SIC: 3441 Fabricated structural metal

(G-20961)
LUBE DEPOT
6122 Market St (44512-3326)
PHONE..................330 758-0570
Rex McMasters, *General Mgr*
EMP: 5
SALES (est): 378.4K **Privately Held**
SIC: 3559 Automotive maintenance equipment

(G-20962)
M A K FABRICATING INC
1609 Wilson Ave (44506-1838)
P.O. Box 212 (44501-0212)
PHONE..................330 747-0040
Dan Maccarthy, *President*
EMP: 10
SQ FT: 54,000
SALES (est): 1.3MM **Privately Held**
SIC: 3499 Fire- or burglary-resistive products

(G-20963)
M F Y INC
Also Called: Youngstown Metal Fabricating
1640 Wilson Ave (44506-1839)
PHONE..................330 747-1334
Andrew Weaver Jr, *President*
EMP: 15
SQ FT: 35,000
SALES (est): 3.1MM **Privately Held**
SIC: 3446 Stairs, staircases, stair treads: prefabricated metal

(G-20964)
M I P INC
701 Jones St (44502-2160)
PHONE..................330 744-0215
Richard B Weaver Jr, *President*
Leigh Marsden, *President*
Melvin Weaver Jr, *President*
Russel W Brown, *Vice Pres*
Judy W Milton, *Vice Pres*
EMP: 19
SQ FT: 50,000
SALES: 2.1MM **Privately Held**
SIC: 3471 Finishing, metals or formed products; electroplating of metals or formed products

(G-20965)
MAGNETIC ANALYSIS CORPORATION
Also Called: Mac Mfg and Test Facilities
675 Mcclurg Rd (44512-6408)
PHONE..................330 758-1367
Manual Morales, *Mfg Staff*
Manuel Morales, *Manager*
Clifford Guarino, *Info Tech Mgr*
EMP: 15
SQ FT: 19,000
SALES (corp-wide): 25MM **Privately Held**
WEB: www.mac-ndt.com
SIC: 3829 Testing equipment: abrasion, shearing strength, etc.
PA: Magnetic Analysis Corporation
103 Fairview Pk Dr Ste 2
Elmsford NY 10523
914 530-2000

(G-20966)
MARK RITE CO
206 Evergreen Dr (44514-3706)
PHONE..................330 757-7229
Margaret Broadwater, *Principal*
EMP: 4
SALES (est): 152.9K **Privately Held**
SIC: 3953 Textile marking stamps, hand: rubber or metal

(G-20967)
MASTERCRAFT MFG INC
4136 Logan Way (44505-5703)
PHONE..................330 893-3366
Les Yoder, *President*
EMP: 30
SQ FT: 25,000
SALES (est): 3.7MM **Privately Held**
SIC: 2512 Upholstered household furniture

(G-20968)
MCHENRY INDUSTRIES INC
85 Victoria Rd (44515-2023)
PHONE..................330 799-8930
Robert P Willison, *President*
Ron Musilli Sr, *President*
Ronald Musilli, *Vice Pres*
Mark Wollet, *Purchasing*
Ronald Kovach, *Human Res Dir*
EMP: 24 EST: 1964
SQ FT: 20,000
SALES (est): 6.1MM **Privately Held**
WEB: www.mchenryindustries.com
SIC: 3083 3315 Thermoplastic laminates: rods, tubes, plates & sheet; steel wire & related products

(G-20969)
MERIDIAN ARTS AND GRAPHICS
16 Belgrade St (44505-1818)
PHONE..................330 759-9099
Ted Webb, *President*
Robert Millham, *Vice Pres*
Cheryl Millham, *Admin Sec*
EMP: 11
SQ FT: 10,000
SALES (est): 1.1MM **Privately Held**
WEB: www.meridianarts.com
SIC: 7336 2752 Art design services; lithographing on metal

(G-20970)
MERIDIAN MANUFACTURING COMPANY
1191 N Meridian Rd (44509-1018)
PHONE..................330 793-9632
James Povhe, *President*
EMP: 3 EST: 1979
SQ FT: 687
SALES (est): 323K **Privately Held**
SIC: 3599 Machine shop, jobbing & repair

(G-20971)
MID-STATE SALES INC
Also Called: Youngstown Rubber Products
854 Mahoning Ave (44502-1408)
PHONE..................330 744-2158
James B Tomaino, *Manager*
EMP: 8
SALES (corp-wide): 18MM **Privately Held**
WEB: www.midstate-sales.com
SIC: 5085 3492 Rubber goods, mechanical; hose & tube fittings & assemblies, hydraulic/pneumatic
PA: Mid-State Sales, Inc.
1101 Gahanna Pkwy
Columbus OH 43230
614 864-1811

(G-20972)
MILLER CURBER COMPANY LLC
4020 Simon Rd (44512-1320)
PHONE..................330 782-8081
James B Rochette, *President*
Randall Best, *Vice Pres*
Hank Rochette,
▲ EMP: 10
SQ FT: 20,000
SALES (est): 2.2MM **Privately Held**
WEB: www.millerspreader.com
SIC: 3531 Road construction & maintenance machinery

(G-20973)
NATIONAL TOOL & EQUIPMENT INC
60 Karago Ave (44512-5949)
PHONE..................330 629-8665
James Simon Jr, *CEO*
Anthony Vross, *President*
Alex Simon, *Admin Sec*
EMP: 10
SQ FT: 8,000
SALES (est): 822.4K **Privately Held**
SIC: 7699 5084 5072 5251 Engine repair & replacement, non-automotive; tool repair services; fans, industrial; hand tools; power tools & accessories; tools; asphalt felts & coatings

(G-20974)
NELIS PRINTING CO
5146 Sterling Ave (44515-3952)
PHONE..................330 757-4114
David Nelis, *Owner*
EMP: 3 EST: 1953
SALES (est): 224K **Privately Held**
SIC: 2752 2759 Commercial printing, offset; letterpress printing

(G-20975)
NEW CASTLE INDUSTRIES INC (DH)
375 Victoria Rd Ste 1 (44515-2053)
PHONE..................724 654-2603
Walter Cox, *President*
EMP: 140 EST: 1968
SQ FT: 7,200
SALES (est): 33.2MM
SALES (corp-wide): 2.2B **Publicly Held**
WEB: www.newcas.com
SIC: 3451 3471 Screw machine products; chromium plating of metals or formed products
HQ: Nordson Xaloy Incorporated
375 Victoria Rd Ste 1
Youngstown OH 44515
724 656-5600

(G-20976)
NOMIS PUBLICATIONS INC
Also Called: Boardman Printing
8570 Foxwood Ct (44514-4301)
P.O. Box 5159 (44514-0159)
PHONE..................330 965-2380
Lucille Mc Guire, *President*
Margaret Rouzzo, *Corp Secy*
Kim Graham, *Vice Pres*
Dana Depillo, *Sales Staff*
EMP: 15
SQ FT: 7,000
SALES: 1.6MM **Privately Held**
WEB: www.yelobk.com
SIC: 2741 2711 2752 2759 Directories: publishing only, not printed on site; newspapers: publishing only, not printed on site; commercial printing, offset; commercial printing

(G-20977)
NORDSON XALOY INCORPORATED (HQ)
375 Victoria Rd Ste 1 (44515-2053)
PHONE..................724 656-5600
Michael F Hilton, *CEO*
Keith E Young, *Treasurer*
Mary Goclano, *Director*
▲ EMP: 190 EST: 1929
SALES (est): 173.5MM
SALES (corp-wide): 2.2B **Publicly Held**
WEB: www.xaloy.com
SIC: 3544 Forms (molds), for foundry & plastics working machinery
PA: Nordson Corporation
28601 Clemens Rd
Westlake OH 44145
440 892-1580

(G-20978)
NORTHERN STATES METALS COMPANY
3207 Innovation Pl (44509-4025)
PHONE..................860 521-6001
Robert Voytilla, *Branch Mgr*
EMP: 60
SQ FT: 4,000
SALES (corp-wide): 23.7MM **Privately Held**
WEB: www.extrusions.com
SIC: 3354 Aluminum extruded products
PA: Northern States Metals Company
3207 Innovation Pl
Youngstown OH 44509
330 799-1855

(G-20979)
NUTECH COMPANY LLC
4496 Mahoning Ave Ste 919 (44515-1601)
PHONE..................440 867-8900
Dennis Spittler, *Mng Member*
◆ EMP: 5
SALES: 250K **Privately Held**
SIC: 2992 Lubricating oils & greases

(G-20980)
ODYSSEY CELLARS INC
4033 Hopkins Rd (44511-3442)
PHONE..................330 782-0177
Ed Goist, *President*
EMP: 3
SALES (est): 163.8K **Privately Held**
SIC: 2084 Wines

(G-20981)
OHIO FLAME
7655 Spring Park Dr (44512-5328)
P.O. Box 3368 (44513-3368)
PHONE..................330 953-0863
EMP: 3 EST: 2011
SALES (est): 199.7K **Privately Held**
SIC: 3272 Fireplace & chimney material: concrete

(G-20982)
OHIO FOAM CORPORATION
1201 Ameritech Blvd (44509-4022)
PHONE..................330 799-4553
Pete Kesler, *Sales Mgr*
Jerry Mouser, *Branch Mgr*
EMP: 25
SALES (corp-wide): 11.7MM **Privately Held**
WEB: www.ohiofoam.com
SIC: 3069 Foam rubber
PA: Ohio Foam Corporation
820 Plymouth St
Bucyrus OH 44820
419 563-0399

(G-20983)
OHIO RESTORATION GROUP LLC
557 S Meridian Rd Ste 4 (44509-2960)
PHONE..................330 568-5815
EMP: 8 EST: 2015
SALES (est): 149.1K **Privately Held**
SIC: 3531 1521 Mfg Construction Machinery Single-Family House Construction

(G-20984)
OHIO VALLEY ENERGY SYSTEMS
200 Victoria Rd Bldg 4 (44515-2093)
PHONE..................330 799-2268
Charles W Masters, *President*
EMP: 2
SQ FT: 9,000
SALES: 2MM **Privately Held**
SIC: 1381 1382 Drilling oil & gas wells; oil & gas exploration services

(G-20985)
ONEALS TARPAULIN & AWNING CO
Also Called: Air Locke Dock Seal Division
549 W Indianola Ave (44511-2460)
PHONE..................330 788-6504
Greg O'Neal, *President*
Dan O'Neal, *Vice Pres*
Larry O'Neal, *Admin Sec*
EMP: 17 EST: 1935
SQ FT: 32,000
SALES: 800K **Privately Held**
WEB: www.onealawnings.com
SIC: 3448 2394 Prefabricated metal buildings; awnings, fabric: made from purchased materials

Youngstown - Mahoning County (G-20986)

(G-20986)
P & L HEAT TRTING GRINDING INC
313 E Wood St (44503-1691)
PHONE..................330 746-1339
William H Pociask, *President*
Helen Premec, *Admin Sec*
EMP: 28
SQ FT: 16,000
SALES (est): 6.3MM **Privately Held**
WEB: www.plheattreatinggrinding.com
SIC: 3398 3599 3471 Metal heat treating; grinding castings for the trade; plating & polishing

(G-20987)
P & L METALCRAFTS LLC
1050 Ohio Works Dr (44510-1077)
PHONE..................330 793-2178
Mary Ann Troy, *Office Mgr*
John Lyras, *Mng Member*
▲ EMP: 12 EST: 1959
SALES (est): 3.1MM
SALES (corp-wide): 18.4MM **Privately Held**
WEB: www.metalcrafts.com
SIC: 3446 3444 3441 Ornamental metalwork; sheet metalwork; fabricated structural metal
PA: Jolley Industrial Supply Co., Inc.
  105 Agate Way 109
  Sharon PA 16146
  724 981-5400

(G-20988)
P & L PRECISION GRINDING LLC
948 Poland Ave (44502-2137)
PHONE..................330 746-8081
David Maxwell Jr,
EMP: 11 EST: 2009
SQ FT: 15,000
SALES: 1MM **Privately Held**
SIC: 7699 7389 3398 Knife, saw & tool sharpening & repair; grinding, precision: commercial or industrial; metal heat treating

(G-20989)
P&S BAKERY INC
3279 E Western Reserve Rd (44514-2844)
PHONE..................330 707-4141
David George, *President*
Bonnie George, *Treasurer*
EMP: 50
SQ FT: 20,000
SALES: 3MM **Privately Held**
SIC: 2051 Bread, cake & related products

(G-20990)
P-AMERICAS LLC
Also Called: Pepsico
500 Pepsi Pl (44502-1432)
PHONE..................330 746-7652
Richard Dripps, *Plant Mgr*
Kennneth Kemmer, *Warehouse Mgr*
Kathryn Frantz, *Buyer*
Richard Plant, *Manager*
EMP: 105
SALES (corp-wide): 64.6B **Publicly Held**
SIC: 2086 5149 4225 Carbonated soft drinks, bottled & canned; groceries & related products; general warehousing & storage
HQ: P-Americas Llc
  1 Pepsi Way
  Somers NY 10589
  336 896-5740

(G-20991)
PANELMATIC INC
Also Called: Panelmatic Youngstown
1125 Meadowbrook Ave (44512-1884)
PHONE..................330 782-8007
Rod Fellows, *General Mgr*
Gary M Urso, *Branch Mgr*
EMP: 29
SALES (corp-wide): 38MM **Privately Held**
WEB: www.panelmatic.com
SIC: 3613 8711 Control panels, electric; cubicles (electric switchboard equipment); designing: ship, boat, machine & product
PA: Panelmatic, Inc.
  258 Donald Dr
  Fairfield OH 45014
  513 829-3666

(G-20992)
PANELMATIC YOUNGSTOWN INC
1125 Meadowbrook Ave (44512-1884)
PHONE..................330 782-8007
Richard Leach, *President*
David D Adamson, *CFO*
▼ EMP: 40
SQ FT: 44,000
SALES (est): 8MM
SALES (corp-wide): 38MM **Privately Held**
WEB: www.panelmatic.com
SIC: 3613 Control panels, electric; cubicles (electric switchboard equipment)
PA: Panelmatic, Inc.
  258 Donald Dr
  Fairfield OH 45014
  513 829-3666

(G-20993)
PARK PLC PRNTG CPYG & DGTL IMG
3410 Canfield Rd Ste B (44511-2713)
PHONE..................330 799-1739
Kay F Probst, *President*
EMP: 6
SALES (est): 459.6K **Privately Held**
SIC: 2759 Commercial printing

(G-20994)
PARKER-HANNIFIN CORPORATION
1911 Logan Ave (44505-2673)
PHONE..................330 740-8366
Michael Wood, *Principal*
EMP: 126
SALES (corp-wide): 14.3B **Publicly Held**
SIC: 3594 Fluid power pumps
PA: Parker-Hannifin Corporation
  6035 Parkland Blvd
  Cleveland OH 44124
  216 896-3000

(G-20995)
PARKER-HANNIFIN CORPORATION
Mobile Cylinder Division
58 Hubbard Rd (44505-3117)
PHONE..................330 743-6893
Dave Olson, *General Mgr*
EMP: 11
SALES (corp-wide): 14.3B **Publicly Held**
WEB: www.parker.com
SIC: 3594 Fluid power pumps & motors
PA: Parker-Hannifin Corporation
  6035 Parkland Blvd
  Cleveland OH 44124
  216 896-3000

(G-20996)
PATRICIAN FURNITURE BUILDERS
1097 Wick Ave (44505-2860)
PHONE..................330 746-6354
Kenneth Mason, *President*
Louis Loverde, *Admin Sec*
EMP: 4
SQ FT: 15,000
SALES: 400K **Privately Held**
SIC: 2511 Wood household furniture

(G-20997)
PATRIOT SEATING INC
1584 Tamarisk Trl (44514-3632)
PHONE..................330 779-0768
Kenneth Altiero, *President*
Sam Marocco, *Vice Pres*
EMP: 13
SALES (est): 1.2MM **Privately Held**
SIC: 2522 Office furniture, except wood

(G-20998)
PERFETTES SAUSAGE LLC
1264 S Schenley Ave (44511-1255)
PHONE..................330 792-0775
Chris Burton,
Joe Perfette,
EMP: 3
SALES (est): 207.2K **Privately Held**
SIC: 2013 5812 Sausages & other prepared meats; sandwiches & submarines shop

(G-20999)
PESCE BAKING COMPANY LTD
45 N Hine St (44506-1203)
PHONE..................330 746-6537
Gary Cellone, *Partner*
Dean Cellone,
EMP: 25
SALES (est): 2.3MM **Privately Held**
SIC: 2051 Bread, cake & related products

(G-21000)
PLASTIC PRODUCTS AND SUPPLY
1305 Lilac St (44502-1309)
PHONE..................330 744-5076
Craig Wylie, *President*
Sidney Wiley, *Corp Secy*
EMP: 3 EST: 1945
SQ FT: 9,000
SALES: 286K **Privately Held**
SIC: 7389 3089 Engraving service; plastic processing

(G-21001)
POLYTECH COMPONENT CORP
8469 Southern Blvd (44512-6709)
PHONE..................330 726-3235
Paul Colby, *President*
Robert Barber, *Vice Pres*
Michael Durina, *Vice Pres*
William White, *Treasurer*
Illene Colby, *Admin Sec*
EMP: 25
SQ FT: 6,000
SALES (est): 2.5MM **Privately Held**
SIC: 3599 Machine shop, jobbing & repair

(G-21002)
PRAXAIR INC
2211 Poland Ave (44502-2773)
PHONE..................330 747-4126
Jim Thomas, *Branch Mgr*
EMP: 3 **Privately Held**
SIC: 2813 Industrial gases
HQ: Praxair, Inc.
  10 Riverview Dr
  Danbury CT 06810
  203 837-2000

(G-21003)
PRECISION FOAM FABRICATION INC
2716 Intertech Dr (44509-4023)
PHONE..................330 270-2440
Joann Laguargia, *President*
Paula Rich, *Manager*
EMP: 15
SALES (est): 2.8MM **Privately Held**
WEB: www.precisionfoam.com
SIC: 3086 Packaging & shipping materials, foamed plastic

(G-21004)
PRECISION OF OHIO INC
3850 Hendricks Rd (44515-1528)
PHONE..................330 793-0900
Mike Pallotta, *Manager*
▲ EMP: 18 EST: 2000
SALES (est): 3.6MM **Privately Held**
SIC: 3354 Aluminum extruded products

(G-21005)
PRESSED COFFEE BAR & EATERY
215 Lincoln Ave (44503-1013)
PHONE..................330 746-8030
EMP: 4
SALES (est): 163.8K **Privately Held**
SIC: 2741 Miscellaneous publishing

(G-21006)
PRINTING 3D PARTS INC
16 Belgrade St (44505-1818)
PHONE..................330 759-9099
Paul Palovich, *President*
Theodore Webb, *President*
EMP: 4
SALES (est): 211.8K **Privately Held**
SIC: 3089 Synthetic resin finished products

(G-21007)
PRINTING DEPOT INC
3828 Southern Blvd (44507-2078)
PHONE..................330 783-5341
Sandy Parker, *President*
Kevin Farr, *Vice Pres*
EMP: 3
SALES: 150K **Privately Held**
SIC: 2759 Commercial printing

(G-21008)
PROUT BOILER HTG & WLDG INC
3124 Temple St (44510-1048)
PHONE..................330 744-0293
Wes Prout, *President*
Richard Dalleske, *Vice Pres*
Linda Prout, *Shareholder*
Donald Raybuck, *Admin Sec*
EMP: 50 EST: 1945
SQ FT: 3,000
SALES (est): 10.1MM **Privately Held**
WEB: www.proutboiler.com
SIC: 1711 7692 3443 Boiler maintenance contractor; heating & air conditioning contractors; plumbing contractors; mechanical contractor; welding repair; fabricated plate work (boiler shop)

(G-21009)
QUALITY SEATING COMPANY INC
4136 Logan Way (44505-5703)
PHONE..................330 747-0181
Frank J Joy, *President*
Roger E Gasser, *Vice Pres*
Jay Buttermore, *Natl Sales Mgr*
EMP: 35 EST: 1978
SQ FT: 45,000
SALES (est): 3MM **Privately Held**
SIC: 2599 2531 Restaurant furniture, wood or metal; public building & related furniture

(G-21010)
R & M FLUID POWER INC
7953 Southern Blvd (44512-6091)
PHONE..................330 758-2766
Robert Gustafson Sr, *Ch of Bd*
Robert Gustafson II, *Vice Pres*
Jennifer Kenetz, *Treasurer*
Melissa Ricciardi, *Admin Sec*
EMP: 25
SQ FT: 40,000
SALES (est): 5.6MM **Privately Held**
WEB: www.rmfluidpower.com
SIC: 3593 5084 Fluid power cylinders, hydraulic or pneumatic; hydraulic systems equipment & supplies

(G-21011)
R T COMMUNICATIONS INC
Also Called: Sprint Signs & Graphics
6031 Applecrest Dr (44512-3143)
PHONE..................330 726-7892
David Touvelle, *President*
Rick Rush, *Corp Secy*
EMP: 4 EST: 1991
SALES: 125K **Privately Held**
SIC: 2499 7374 Signboards, wood; computer graphics service

(G-21012)
R W SIDLEY INCORPORATED
3424 Oregon Ave (44509-1075)
PHONE..................330 793-7374
Gary Hawkins, *Manager*
EMP: 25
SALES (corp-wide): 132.6MM **Privately Held**
WEB: www.rwsidleyinc.com
SIC: 5032 3273 Brick, stone & related material; ready-mixed concrete
PA: R. W. Sidley Incorporated
  436 Casement Ave
  Painesville OH 44077
  440 352-9343

(G-21013)
RAM Z NEON
1227 E Indianola Ave (44502-2645)
PHONE..................330 788-5121
Greg Ramsey, *Partner*
Jeff Ramsey, *Partner*
Walt Woznak, *Partner*

GEOGRAPHIC SECTION

Youngstown - Mahoning County (G-21041)

EMP: 4
SALES: 180K Privately Held
SIC: 3993 Neon signs

(G-21014)
RB FABRICATORS INC
4021 Mahoning Ave (44515-2904)
PHONE.................................330 779-0263
James E Sullivan, *President*
EMP: 15
SQ FT: 72,000
SALES: 1.5MM Privately Held
WEB: www.rbfabricators.com
SIC: 3441 Fabricated structural metal

(G-21015)
RICCI ANTHONY
Also Called: Rich Print
755 Boardman Canfield Rd (44512-4300)
PHONE.................................330 758-5761
Anthony Ricci, *President*
EMP: 4
SALES (est): 280K Privately Held
SIC: 2752 2334 2791 2789 Commercial printing, lithographic; photocopying & duplicating services; typesetting; bookbinding & related work

(G-21016)
RL SMITH GRAPHICS LLC
Also Called: Rl Smith Graphics
493 Bev Rd Bldg 7b (44512-6459)
PHONE.................................330 629-8616
Ronald L Smith, *Owner*
Keri Johnson, *Manager*
Tonya Hammer, *Graphic Designe*
EMP: 8
SALES: 397.7K Privately Held
SIC: 2752 Commercial printing, lithographic

(G-21017)
RL SMITH PRINTING CO
4030 Simon Rd (44512-1320)
PHONE.................................330 747-9590
EMP: 10
SALES (est): 1.2MM Privately Held
SIC: 2759 Commercial Printing

(G-21018)
RNW HOLDINGS INC
200 Division Street Ext (44510-1000)
P.O. Box 478 (44501-0478)
PHONE.................................330 792-0600
Major Hammond, *Branch Mgr*
EMP: 40
SALES (corp-wide): 64.4MM Privately Held
SIC: 5093 1795 3341 Scrap & waste materials; wrecking & demolition work; secondary nonferrous metals
HQ: Rnw Holdings, Inc.
26949 Chagrin Blvd # 305
Cleveland OH 44122
216 831-0510

(G-21019)
ROBERTS GRAPHIC CENTER
5375 Market St (44512-2252)
PHONE.................................330 788-4642
Robert Patrick, *Owner*
EMP: 5
SQ FT: 1,500
SALES (est): 504K Privately Held
SIC: 2752 7336 Commercial printing, offset; graphic arts & related design

(G-21020)
ROCKNSTARR HOLDINGS LLC
112 S Meridian Rd (44509-2640)
PHONE.................................330 509-9086
Ray Starr,
EMP: 28
SQ FT: 52,000
SALES: 12MM Privately Held
SIC: 5013 3312 Wheels, motor vehicle; wheels

(G-21021)
ROMAN CTHLIC DOCESE YOUNGSTOWN
Also Called: Catholic Exponent
144 W Wood St Fl 1 (44503-1030)
P.O. Box 6787 (44501-6787)
PHONE.................................330 744-8451
Lou Jacquet, *Manager*

EMP: 8
SALES (corp-wide): 23.6MM Privately Held
WEB: www.stjosephmantua.com
SIC: 2711 Newspapers, publishing & printing
PA: Roman Catholic Diocese Of Youngstown
144 W Wood St
Youngstown OH 44503
330 744-8451

(G-21022)
RUST BELT BREWING LLC
1744 Overlook Ave (44509-2101)
PHONE.................................330 423-3818
Kenneth Blair, *Principal*
EMP: 4
SALES (est): 308.5K Privately Held
SIC: 2082 Malt beverages

(G-21023)
S & W CUSTOM TOPS INC
4300 Simon Rd Ste 2 (44512-1365)
PHONE.................................330 788-2525
Edward Sullivan, *President*
Phyllis Sullivan, *Vice Pres*
EMP: 6
SQ FT: 3,500
SALES: 550K Privately Held
SIC: 2434 1751 Wood kitchen cabinets; cabinet building & installation

(G-21024)
SAMMARTINO WELDING & AUTO SLS
155 W Indianola Ave (44507-1460)
PHONE.................................330 782-6086
Dayne C Sammartino, *Owner*
Dayne Sammartino, *Owner*
EMP: 4
SQ FT: 3,200
SALES (est): 244.7K Privately Held
SIC: 7538 7692 5521 General automotive repair shops; automotive welding; automobiles, used cars only

(G-21025)
SCHWEBEL BAKING COMPANY (PA)
965 E Midlothian Blvd (44502-2869)
P.O. Box 6013 (44501-6013)
PHONE.................................330 783-2860
Paul Schwebel, *President*
Fred Ciarniello, *Division Mgr*
Bruce Raber, *District Mgr*
Barry Solomon, *Senior VP*
Lonnie Howard, *Vice Pres*
EMP: 450 EST: 1906
SQ FT: 125,000
SALES (est): 170MM Privately Held
WEB: www.schwebels.com
SIC: 2051 Bakery: wholesale or wholesale/retail combined

(G-21026)
SDS NATIONAL LLC
Also Called: SDS Logistics Services
19 Colonial Dr Ste 27 (44505-2162)
PHONE.................................330 759-8066
Andrew Weiss, *CEO*
Tom Shapiro, *COO*
Ryan Clausen, *Accounts Exec*
Angela Ward, *Manager*
Samuel Shapiro,
EMP: 6
SALES (est): 1.8MM Privately Held
WEB: www.sdslogistics.com
SIC: 3559 4731 Recycling machinery; freight transportation arrangement

(G-21027)
SEIFERT PRINTING COMPANY
Also Called: Minuteman Press
3200 Belmont Ave Ste 11 (44505-1862)
PHONE.................................330 759-7414
Dean W Seifert Sr, *President*
EMP: 4
SQ FT: 2,000
SALES (est): 555.7K Privately Held
SIC: 2752 Commercial printing, lithographic

(G-21028)
SHADE YOUNGSTOWN & ALUMINUM CO
Also Called: Richards Intrors Bldg Cmpnents
3335 South Ave (44502-2407)
P.O. Box 8627, Warren (44484-0627)
PHONE.................................330 782-2373
Richard Gula, *Owner*
EMP: 8
SQ FT: 15,000
SALES: 1.6MM Privately Held
SIC: 1542 2591 3444 3442 Commercial & office buildings, renovation & repair; venetian blinds; awnings, sheet metal; metal doors, sash & trim; millwork; canvas & related products

(G-21029)
SHELLY AND SANDS INC
Also Called: Mar Zane
2800 Center Rd (44514)
PHONE.................................330 743-8850
Bill Castle, *Manager*
EMP: 3
SALES (corp-wide): 276.3MM Privately Held
WEB: www.shellyandsands.com
SIC: 2951 Asphalt paving mixtures & blocks
PA: Shelly And Sands, Inc.
3570 S River Rd
Zanesville OH 43701
740 453-0721

(G-21030)
SHENANGO VALLEY SAND AND GRAV (PA)
7240 Glenwood Ave (44512-4800)
PHONE.................................330 758-9100
John Cernica, *President*
EMP: 4
SQ FT: 900
SALES (est): 930.7K Privately Held
WEB: www.pymatuning.com
SIC: 1442 Common sand mining; gravel mining

(G-21031)
SIFTED SWEET SHOP LLC
4496 Mahoning Ave Ste 905 (44515-1601)
PHONE.................................216 901-7100
Nichelle Hall, *Principal*
EMP: 4
SALES (est): 149.8K Privately Held
SIC: 2051 Cakes, bakery: except frozen

(G-21032)
SIMON ROOFING AND SHTMTL CORP (PA)
70 Karago Ave (44512-5949)
P.O. Box 951109, Cleveland (44193-0005)
PHONE.................................330 629-7392
Stephen Manser, *President*
Roberto Morales, *Regional Mgr*
Rocco Augustine, *Vice Pres*
Alex J Simon Jr, *CFO*
Marian Vross, *Regl Sales Mgr*
EMP: 105
SQ FT: 30,000
SALES (est): 86.2MM Privately Held
WEB: www.simonroofing.com
SIC: 1761 2952 Roofing contractor; asphalt felts & coatings

(G-21033)
SOLAR ARTS GRAPHIC DESIGNS
824 Tod Ave (44502-1326)
PHONE.................................330 744-0535
Daniel Klingensmith, *President*
Catherine Klingensmith, *Vice Pres*
EMP: 6
SALES: 250K Privately Held
WEB: www.solar-arts.com
SIC: 2396 5199 Printing & embossing on plastics fabric articles; advertising specialties

(G-21034)
SPACE-LINKS INC
1110 Thalia Ave (44512-1825)
PHONE.................................330 788-2401
Ronald N Kessler, *President*
EMP: 20
SQ FT: 15,000

SALES (est): 2.8MM Privately Held
WEB: www.spacelinks1.com
SIC: 3069 Mats or matting, rubber

(G-21035)
SPACELINKS ENTERPRISES INC
1110 Thalia Ave (44512-1825)
PHONE.................................330 788-2401
Daniel Kessler, *President*
EMP: 60
SQ FT: 90,000
SALES: 7MM Privately Held
SIC: 2273 Mats & matting

(G-21036)
SPARTAN FABRICATION
230 Mcclurg Rd (44512-6740)
PHONE.................................330 758-3512
Joe Steppo, *Owner*
EMP: 4
SALES (est): 457K Privately Held
SIC: 3599 Machine & other job shop work

(G-21037)
SPECIALTY SWITCH CO
525 Mcclurg Rd (44512-6406)
PHONE.................................330 427-3000
Terry Turvey, *President*
Piotr Blaszczyk, *General Mgr*
Steve Davis, *General Mgr*
▲ EMP: 15
SQ FT: 7,000
SALES: 700K Privately Held
WEB: www.specialtyswitch.com
SIC: 3679 5063 Electronic switches; electrical apparatus & equipment

(G-21038)
SPECTRUM METAL FINISHING INC
535 Bev Rd (44512-6490)
PHONE.................................330 758-8358
Neil Chrisman, *President*
Debbie Baez, *Human Resources*
Thomas Hutch, *Admin Sec*
▼ EMP: 57
SQ FT: 60,000
SALES (est): 14.1MM Privately Held
WEB: www.spectrummetal.com
SIC: 3479 Painting of metal products

(G-21039)
STAR FORMING MANUFACTURING LL
Also Called: Commercial Metal Forming
1775 Logan Ave (44505-2622)
PHONE.................................330 740-8300
Bob Messaros, *CEO*
Thomas Depinto, *Vice Pres*
Michael Conglose, *Opers Dir*
Jim Petrides, *CFO*
Ken Ross, *Sales Mgr*
EMP: 148
SALES: 28.6MM
SALES (corp-wide): 8.1MM Privately Held
SIC: 3272 Tanks, concrete
PA: Ce Star Holdings, Llc
1775 Logan Ave
Youngstown OH 44505
800 826-5867

(G-21040)
SUGAR SHOWCASE
1725 S Raccoon Rd (44515-4588)
PHONE.................................330 792-9154
Cheryl Bair, *Principal*
EMP: 4
SQ FT: 2,000
SALES (est): 130K Privately Held
SIC: 5461 3089 7999 Cakes; molding primary plastic; cake or pastry decorating instruction

(G-21041)
SUMMCO INC
Also Called: Fastsigns
6981 Southern Blvd Ste D (44512-4657)
PHONE.................................330 965-7446
Jay Summer, *President*
EMP: 7 EST: 1999
SALES (est): 550K Privately Held
SIC: 3993 Signs & advertising specialties

(PA)=Parent Co (HQ)=Headquarters (DH)=Div Headquarters
✪ = New Business established in last 2 years

2019 Harris Ohio
Industrial Directory

Youngstown - Mahoning County (G-21042)

(G-21042)
T C REDI MIX YOUNGSTOWN INC (PA)
2400 Poland Ave (44502-2782)
PHONE..................330 755-2143
Sherry Andrews, *President*
Susan Kirkwood, *Corp Secy*
Sandra Raider, *Vice Pres*
EMP: 20
SQ FT: 3,000
SALES (est): 4.4MM **Privately Held**
SIC: 3273 5211 Ready-mixed concrete; lumber & other building materials

(G-21043)
TAYLOR-WINFIELD TECH INC (HQ)
Also Called: Taylor Winfield Indus Wldg Eqp
3200 Innovation Pl (44509-4025)
P.O. Box 779 (44501-0779)
PHONE..................330 259-8500
Alex Benyo, *President*
Brian Benyo, *Vice Pres*
Frank Deley, *Vice Pres*
Scott Stewart, *Project Mgr*
Tom Solich, *Engineer*
EMP: 50
SQ FT: 25,000
SALES (est): 13.7MM **Privately Held**
SIC: 3548 Welding apparatus

(G-21044)
THE FLORAND COMPANY
1776 Cherry St Ste A (44506-1859)
PHONE..................330 747-8986
Andrew Hirt, *President*
Kevin Carney, *Vice Pres*
Florence Hirt, *Treasurer*
EMP: 20 **EST:** 1967
SALES (est): 3.9MM **Privately Held**
WEB: www.florand.com
SIC: 3312 Plate, sheet & strip, except coated products

(G-21045)
TIMEKAP INC
Also Called: Timekap Indus Sls Svc & Mch
2315 Belmont Ave (44505-2404)
PHONE..................330 747-2122
Patrick Chrystal, *President*
Scott Lawrence, *Vice Pres*
EMP: 6
SQ FT: 15,000
SALES (est): 941.8K **Privately Held**
SIC: 3599 Machine shop, jobbing & repair

(G-21046)
TMI INC
6475 Victoria East Rd (44515-2051)
P.O. Box 4596 (44515-0596)
PHONE..................330 270-9780
Michael J Myhal Jr, *President*
Dean Ciccone, *Plant Mgr*
Bob Hurst, *Project Mgr*
Brittany Fenstermaker, *Director*
Rebecca Myhal, *Admin Sec*
▼ **EMP:** 28
SQ FT: 30,000
SALES (est): 5.5MM **Privately Held**
SIC: 3069 Molded rubber products

(G-21047)
TOROK SUPPLY COMPANY
52 S Meridian Rd (44509-2638)
PHONE..................330 799-6677
Victor Torok Jr, *President*
Jean Torok, *Vice Pres*
EMP: 3
SQ FT: 12,000
SALES: 450K **Privately Held**
SIC: 3444 5075 Sheet metalwork; elbows, for air ducts, stovepipes, etc.; sheet metal; electrical heating equipment

(G-21048)
TRAFFIC DETECTORS & SIGNS INC
7521 Forest Hill Ave (44514-2635)
PHONE..................330 707-9060
Leila M Meris, *Principal*
EMP: 6
SALES (est): 645K **Privately Held**
SIC: 1611 3993 Highway signs & guardrails; signs & advertising specialties

(G-21049)
TRANSIT SITTINGS OF NA
295 S Meridian Rd (44509-2924)
PHONE..................330 797-2516
Wayne Donitzen, *Office Mgr*
EMP: 6
SALES (est): 350K **Privately Held**
SIC: 3498 Fabricated pipe & fittings

(G-21050)
TRANSUE & WILLIAMS STAMPG CORP
207 N Four Mile Run Rd (44515-3008)
PHONE..................330 270-0891
EMP: 18
SALES (corp-wide): 5MM **Privately Held**
SIC: 3469 Stamping metal for the trade
PA: Transue & Williams Stampings Corporation
930 W Ely St
Alliance OH 44601
330 821-5777

(G-21051)
TRESCO INTERNATIONAL LTD CO
1637 Bluebell Trl (44514-5215)
PHONE..................330 757-8131
▲ **EMP:** 5
SQ FT: 5,400
SALES (est): 390K **Privately Held**
SIC: 3645 Mfg Residential Lighting Fixtures

(G-21052)
TRI COUNTY ASPHALT MATERIALS
405 Andrews Ave (44505-3062)
P.O. Box 338, North Lima (44452-0338)
PHONE..................330 549-2852
Jo Anne Vernal, *President*
Richard Vernal, *Treasurer*
EMP: 2
SALES: 2.7MM
SALES (corp-wide): 8.8MM **Privately Held**
SIC: 2951 Asphalt paving mixtures & blocks
PA: R T Vernal Paving Inc
11299 South Ave
North Lima OH 44452
330 549-2852

(G-21053)
TRI-R DIES INC
556 Bev Rd (44512-6420)
PHONE..................330 758-8050
Benjamin Morucci, *President*
Mary Morucci, *Admin Sec*
EMP: 30 **EST:** 1978
SQ FT: 6,000
SALES (est): 4.3MM **Privately Held**
WEB: www.trirdies.com
SIC: 3544 Extrusion dies; special dies & tools

(G-21054)
TRUNK SHOW
339 Imperial St (44509-1161)
PHONE..................330 565-5326
Marisa Ronci, *Principal*
EMP: 3
SALES (est): 145.3K **Privately Held**
SIC: 3161 Trunks

(G-21055)
TURNING TECHNOLOGIES LLC (PA)
255 W Federal St (44503-1207)
PHONE..................330 746-3015
Mike Broderick, *CEO*
Dave Kauer, *President*
Ethan Cohen, *COO*
Sheila Hura, *Vice Pres*
Kevin Owens, *Vice Pres*
◆ **EMP:** 140
SQ FT: 26,200
SALES (est): 125.9MM **Privately Held**
WEB: www.turningtechnologies.com
SIC: 7372 Business oriented computer software; educational computer software

(G-21056)
U S WEATHERFORD L P
1100 Performance Pl (44502-4001)
PHONE..................330 746-2502
EMP: 250 **Privately Held**
SIC: 1389 Oil field services
HQ: U S Weatherford L P
179 Weatherford Dr
Schriever LA 70395
985 493-6100

(G-21057)
V & M STAR LP
2669 Mrtn Luthr Kg Jr Bld (44510)
PHONE..................330 742-6300
Brian R Colquhoun, *Principal*
▲ **EMP:** 41 **EST:** 2012
SALES (est): 9.6MM **Privately Held**
SIC: 3061 Oil & gas field machinery rubber goods (mechanical)

(G-21058)
VALLOUREC STAR LP (HQ)
2669 M L K J Blvd (44510)
PHONE..................330 742-6300
Judson Wallace, *President*
Danielle Williamson, *Buyer*
Frank Kowalczyk, *Engineer*
Philippe Lesage, *CFO*
Josh Ploch, *Human Res Mgr*
▲ **EMP:** 257
SALES (est): 204.2MM
SALES (corp-wide): 2.6MM **Privately Held**
SIC: 3317 Pipes, seamless steel
PA: Vallourec
27 Avenue Du General Leclerc
Boulogne Billancourt 92100
149 093-500

(G-21059)
VAM USA LLC
1053 Ohio Works Dr (44510-1078)
PHONE..................330 742-3130
EMP: 5
SALES (est): 551.8K **Privately Held**
SIC: 1389 Oil field services

(G-21060)
VEIN CENTER AND MEDSPA
Also Called: Vein Center, The
965 Windham Ct Ste 2 (44512-5088)
PHONE..................330 629-9400
Richard A Michaels MD, *Owner*
EMP: 4
SALES (est): 483.3K **Privately Held**
WEB: www.the-vein-center.com
SIC: 8011 2844 Dermatologist; cosmetic preparations

(G-21061)
VETERANS REPRESENTATIVE CO LLC
1584 Tamarisk Trl (44514-3632)
PHONE..................330 779-0768
James Altiero Jr,
Kenneth Altiero,
Gerald Ragozine,
EMP: 10
SQ FT: 800
SALES: 500K **Privately Held**
SIC: 2522 Chairs, office: padded or plain, except wood

(G-21062)
VICTOR ORGAN COMPANY
5340 Mahoning Ave (44515-2415)
PHONE..................330 792-1321
Victor Marsilo, *Owner*
EMP: 8
SQ FT: 6,500
SALES (est): 781.5K **Privately Held**
SIC: 3931 7699 Organs, all types: pipe, reed, hand, electronic, etc.; organ tuning & repair

(G-21063)
VICTORIA VENTURES INC (PA)
425 Victoria Rd Ste 427 (44515-2029)
PHONE..................330 793-9321
John M Antonucci, *President*
Eileen Rinehart, *Principal*
Daniel Simms, *Purch Agent*
EMP: 22
SALES (est): 1.7MM **Privately Held**
SIC: 6799 5182 5181 2082 Venture capital companies; wine & distilled beverages; beer & ale; malt beverages

(G-21064)
VINDICATOR BOARDMAN OFFICE
8075 Southern Blvd (44512-6306)
PHONE..................330 259-1732
EMP: 3
SALES (est): 128.3K **Privately Held**
SIC: 2711 Newspapers

(G-21065)
VINDICATOR PRINTING COMPANY
Also Called: Wfmj-Tv21
101 W Boardman St (44503-1305)
P.O. Box 689 (44501-0689)
PHONE..................330 744-8611
John Grdic, *Manager*
EMP: 85
SALES (corp-wide): 45.5MM **Privately Held**
WEB: www.vindy.com
SIC: 2711 Newspapers, publishing & printing
PA: The Vindicator Printing Company
107 Vindicator Sq
Youngstown OH 44503
330 747-1471

(G-21066)
VINYL TOOL & DIE COMPANY INC
1144 Meadowbrook Ave (44512-1821)
PHONE..................330 782-0254
Paul Chicone, *President*
Carmen Chicone Jr, *Corp Secy*
Carmen Chicone Sr, *Vice Pres*
EMP: 12
SALES (est): 1.2MM **Privately Held**
SIC: 3544 Extrusion dies

(G-21067)
VINYLUME PRODUCTS INC
3745 Hendricks Rd (44515-1506)
PHONE..................330 799-2000
Jack M White, *CEO*
Orlando White, *President*
Kathy Simpson, *Data Proc Staff*
Helen White, *Admin Sec*
EMP: 70
SQ FT: 200,000
SALES (est): 14.9MM **Privately Held**
WEB: www.vinylume.com
SIC: 3089 3442 3211 Window frames & sash, plastic; metal doors, sash & trim; flat glass

(G-21068)
W B BECHERER INC
Also Called: Modernfold
7905 Southern Blvd (44512-6025)
P.O. Box 3186 (44513-3186)
PHONE..................330 758-6616
William B Becherer Sr, *President*
William B Becherer Jr, *Treasurer*
Bruce Becherer, *Admin Sec*
EMP: 9 **EST:** 1950
SQ FT: 4,000
SALES: 2.5MM **Privately Held**
WEB: www.modernfold.com
SIC: 2542 Partitions & fixtures, except wood

(G-21069)
YELLOW TANG INTERIORS LLC
1255 Barbie Dr (44512-3702)
PHONE..................330 629-9279
John R Boris Jr,
EMP: 8
SALES (est): 830.5K **Privately Held**
SIC: 2521 Wood office furniture

(G-21070)
YOUNGSTOWN ARC ENGRAVING CO
Also Called: Youngstown Lithographing Co
380 Victoria Rd (44515-2026)
PHONE..................330 793-2471
E Craig Olsen, *President*
Tim Merrifield, *Exec VP*
George B Snyder, *Vice Pres*

Ken Baytosh, *Purchasing*
EMP: 26 **EST:** 1900
SQ FT: 30,000
SALES (est): 2.6MM **Privately Held**
WEB: www.youngstownwholesale.com
SIC: 2796 7335 2791 2789 Photoengraving plates, linecuts or halftones; commercial photography; typesetting; bookbinding & related work; commercial printing; commercial printing, offset

(G-21071)
YOUNGSTOWN BENDING ROLLING
3710 Hendricks Rd Bldg 2b (44515-1537)
PHONE..................................330 799-2227
Daniel Kish, *Principal*
EMP: 16
SALES (est): 3.2MM **Privately Held**
SIC: 3531 Railroad related equipment

(G-21072)
YOUNGSTOWN BOLT & SUPPLY CO
340 N Meridian Rd (44509-1246)
PHONE..................................330 799-3201
Al Fedorisin, *President*
Lorraine Fedorisin, *Vice Pres*
EMP: 6
SQ FT: 20,000
SALES (est): 1.1MM **Privately Held**
SIC: 5085 3965 Fasteners, industrial: nuts, bolts, screws, etc.; fasteners

(G-21073)
YOUNGSTOWN BURIAL VAULT CO
546 E Indianola Ave (44502-2320)
PHONE..................................330 782-0015
Charles Phillips, *President*
EMP: 9 **EST:** 1945
SQ FT: 4,000
SALES (est): 1.2MM **Privately Held**
SIC: 3272 Burial vaults, concrete or precast terrazzo

(G-21074)
YOUNGSTOWN CASKET CO INC
450 Melbourne Ave (44512-4410)
PHONE..................................330 758-2008
John R Kiefer, *President*
Robert Kiefer, *Corp Secy*
EMP: 6 **EST:** 1951
SQ FT: 7,500
SALES (est): 508.9K **Privately Held**
SIC: 3995 Burial caskets

(G-21075)
YOUNGSTOWN CURVE FORM INC
1102 Rigby St (44506-1500)
PHONE..................................330 744-3028
Frank Laskay, *President*
EMP: 10 **EST:** 1964
SQ FT: 7,800
SALES (est): 1.4MM **Privately Held**
SIC: 5031 2541 Building materials, interior; table or counter tops, plastic laminated

(G-21076)
YOUNGSTOWN FENCE INC
235 E Indianola Ave (44507-1546)
PHONE..................................330 788-8110
Frank J Mikitaw, *President*
Suzanne Mikitaw, *Vice Pres*
EMP: 6
SQ FT: 34,000
SALES (est): 800K **Privately Held**
SIC: 1799 5211 2499 Fence construction; fencing; fencing, wood

(G-21077)
YOUNGSTOWN HARD CHROME PLATING
8451 Southern Blvd (44512-6709)
P.O. Box 3508 (44513-3508)
PHONE..................................330 758-9721
Richard S McCarthy, *President*
Daniel J McCarthy, *Vice Pres*
EMP: 28 **EST:** 1962
SQ FT: 35,000
SALES (est): 2.9MM **Privately Held**
WEB: www.youngstownhardchrome.com
SIC: 3471 3599 Chromium plating of metals or formed products; grinding castings for the trade

(G-21078)
YOUNGSTOWN HEAT TREATING
1118 Meadowbrook Ave (44512-1821)
PHONE..................................330 788-3025
Carmen P Chicone Sr, *President*
EMP: 6
SQ FT: 5,000
SALES (est): 830K **Privately Held**
SIC: 3398 Annealing of metal

(G-21079)
YOUNGSTOWN LETTER SHOP INC
615 N Meridian Rd (44509-1229)
PHONE..................................330 793-4935
Jean Tuscano, *President*
Kathy Cressman, *Manager*
EMP: 9
SQ FT: 5,000
SALES (est): 1.7MM **Privately Held**
SIC: 7331 2752 7521 Mailing service; commercial printing, offset; parking garage

(G-21080)
YOUNGSTOWN PLASTIC TOOLING (PA)
1209 Velma Ct (44512-1829)
PHONE..................................330 782-7222
Donald J Liga, *President*
Janet Liga, *Admin Sec*
EMP: 35
SQ FT: 20,000
SALES (est): 6.8MM **Privately Held**
WEB: www.yptm.com
SIC: 3559 8711 Plastics working machinery; machine tool design; mechanical engineering

(G-21081)
YOUNGSTOWN PRE-PRESS INC
3691 Leharps Dr (44515-1437)
P.O. Box 2375 (44509-0375)
PHONE..................................330 793-3690
Kenneth Slater, *President*
Gary P Dobrindt, *Vice Pres*
Brian Dickens, *Admin Sec*
EMP: 14
SQ FT: 4,000
SALES (est): 1.5MM **Privately Held**
SIC: 7336 2752 Art design services; lithographing on metal

(G-21082)
YOUNGSTOWN SPECIALTY MTLS INC
571 Andrews Ave (44505-3064)
PHONE..................................330 259-1110
Frank Wadlinger, *CEO*
Michael Miklus, *Vice Pres*
Richard Wadlinger, *CFO*
EMP: 8
SQ FT: 20,000
SALES (est): 1.8MM **Privately Held**
WEB: www.yngspecmetals.com
SIC: 3499 3053 Strapping, metal; gaskets, packing & sealing devices

(G-21083)
YOUNGSTOWN TOOL & DIE COMPANY
1261 Poland Ave (44502-2192)
PHONE..................................330 747-4464
Fred Fisher, *President*
Allison Martinco, *Office Mgr*
Eric Houck, *Data Proc Staff*
EMP: 62 **EST:** 1961
SQ FT: 12,800
SALES (est): 9.6MM **Privately Held**
WEB: www.youngstowntool.com
SIC: 3544 3354 Special dies & tools; extrusion dies; aluminum extruded products

(G-21084)
YOUNGSTOWN TUBE CO
401 Andrews Ave (44505-3062)
PHONE..................................330 743-7414
William Veri, *President*
EMP: 30
SQ FT: 93,000
SALES (est): 6.9MM **Privately Held**
WEB: www.youngstowntube.com
SIC: 3312 Pipes, iron & steel; tubes, steel & iron

(G-21085)
YRP INDUSTRIES INC
854 Mahoning Ave (44502-1408)
P.O. Box 444 (44501-0444)
PHONE..................................330 533-2524
James Tomaino, *CEO*
EMP: 4
SALES (est): 296.1K **Privately Held**
SIC: 3011 Tire & inner tube materials & related products

(G-21086)
YSD INDUSTRIES INC
3710 Henricks Rd (44515)
PHONE..................................330 792-6521
Jerome D Hines, *President*
Bruce Wylie, *Vice Pres*
Michael Feschak, *CFO*
Karen Flavell, *Human Resources*
Ralph Boland, *Director*
▲ **EMP:** 100
SQ FT: 30,000
SALES (est): 20.3MM **Privately Held**
SIC: 5088 3444 3441 Railroad equipment & supplies; sheet metalwork; fabricated structural metal

(G-21087)
ZITELLO FINE ART LLC
Also Called: Fresh Prints
1221 N Meridian Rd Ste 16 (44509-1065)
PHONE..................................330 792-8894
Lisa Zitello, *Mng Member*
EMP: 3
SALES (est): 129.4K **Privately Held**
SIC: 3953 Screens, textile printing

Zaleski
Vinton County

(G-21088)
LMP MACHINE LLC
115 E Chestnut St (45698)
P.O. Box 255 (45698-0255)
PHONE..................................740 596-4559
Mark Peters,
Lawrence M Peters,
EMP: 9
SQ FT: 4,800
SALES (est): 760K **Privately Held**
SIC: 3599 Machine shop, jobbing & repair

Zanesfield
Logan County

(G-21089)
QUANTUM WORLD TECHNOLOGIES
6973 Township Road 177 (43360-9717)
PHONE..................................937 747-3018
Hollis L Smith, *Principal*
EMP: 3
SALES (est): 186.1K **Privately Held**
SIC: 3572 Computer storage devices

Zanesville
Muskingum County

(G-21090)
5 BS INC (PA)
Also Called: B-Wear Sportswear
1000 5 Bs Dr (43701-7630)
P.O. Box 520 (43702-0520)
PHONE..................................740 454-8453
Todd Biles, *President*
Steven R Baldwin, *Principal*
Leland Biles, *Principal*
Larry R King, *Principal*
John Klies, *Vice Pres*
▲ **EMP:** 250
SQ FT: 170,000
SALES (est): 54.1MM **Privately Held**
WEB: www.5bs.com
SIC: 2339 2395 Athletic clothing: women's, misses' & juniors'; embroidery products, except schiffli machine

(G-21091)
ACE TRUCK EQUIPMENT CO
1130 Newark Rd (43701-2619)
P.O. Box 2605 (43702-2605)
PHONE..................................740 453-0551
Robert D Beitzel, *CEO*
David Beitzel, *President*
Darren Founds, *Sales Staff*
Shawn Hampp, *Sales Staff*
Dora Beitzel, *Admin Sec*
EMP: 21
SQ FT: 30,500
SALES (est): 4MM **Privately Held**
WEB: www.acetruck.net
SIC: 5531 5012 3713 Truck equipment & parts; truck bodies; trucks, commercial; truck tractors; trailers for trucks, new & used; truck & bus bodies

(G-21092)
ADAMS BROS CONCRETE PDTS LTD
3401 East Pike (43701-8419)
PHONE..................................740 452-7566
Scott M Zemba, *Administration*
EMP: 10
SALES (est): 1.2MM **Privately Held**
SIC: 3273 Ready-mixed concrete

(G-21093)
ADAMS BROTHERS INC
1501 Woodlawn Ave (43701-5955)
P.O. Box 27 (43702-0027)
PHONE..................................740 819-0323
William Adams IV, *President*
William H Adams III, *President*
Nancy Adams, *Vice Pres*
Katie Brown, *Treasurer*
Cortney Clewell, *Manager*
EMP: 12 **EST:** 1908
SALES (est): 1.4MM **Privately Held**
SIC: 3273 5211 Ready-mixed concrete; lumber & other building materials

(G-21094)
ADKEL CORP (PA)
Also Called: Custom Bobbin Winding
2920 Newark Rd (43701-7759)
P.O. Box 2369 (43702-2369)
PHONE..................................740 452-6973
Doral S Mills Jr, *President*
Dale Young, *General Mgr*
EMP: 6
SQ FT: 15,000
SALES (est): 528.9K **Privately Held**
SIC: 3677 Coil windings, electronic; electronic transformers

(G-21095)
AK STEEL CORPORATION
1724 Linden Ave (43701-2307)
P.O. Box 1520 (43702-1520)
PHONE..................................740 450-5600
Douglas C Garvin, *General Mgr*
Michael McKee, *Opers Mgr*
Bill Adams, *Safety Mgr*
Chad Neighbor, *Safety Mgr*
Jim Bridge, *Consultant*
EMP: 315 **Publicly Held**
WEB: www.ketnar.org
SIC: 3312 3316 Blast furnaces & steel mills; cold finishing of steel shapes
HQ: Ak Steel Corporation
 9227 Centre Pointe Dr
 West Chester OH 45069
 513 425-4200

(G-21096)
ALFRED NICKLES BAKERY INC
Also Called: Nickles Bakery 45
1147 Newark Rd (43701-2618)
PHONE..................................740 453-6522
Les Bell, *General Mgr*
EMP: 30
SALES (corp-wide): 205MM **Privately Held**
WEB: www.nicklesbakery.com
SIC: 2051 5461 Bakery: wholesale or wholesale/retail combined; bakeries

Zanesville - Muskingum County (G-21097)

PA: Alfred Nickles Bakery, Inc.
26 Main St N
Navarre OH 44662
330 879-5635

(G-21097)
ALLIED MACHINE WORKS INC
120 Graham St (43701-3100)
P.O. Box 2743 (43702-2743)
PHONE..................................740 454-2534
Richard J Straker, *President*
Patricia Folden, *Principal*
EMP: 8
SQ FT: 56,058
SALES: 750K Privately Held
WEB: www.allliedmachineworks.com
SIC: 3599 7629 3533 Machine shop, jobbing & repair; machine & other job shop work; electrical repair shops; oil & gas field machinery

(G-21098)
AMERICAN BAND SAW CO
4049 Newark Rd (43701-8727)
PHONE..................................740 452-8168
Bob Holbein, *Owner*
EMP: 5
SALES: 300K Privately Held
WEB: www.americanbandsawcompany.com
SIC: 2221 Textile mills, broadwoven: silk & manmade, also glass

(G-21099)
ANCHOR GLASS CONTAINER CORP
Zanesville Mould Division
1206 Brandywine Blvd C (43701-1731)
PHONE..................................740 452-2743
Steve Brock, *Superintendent*
Kyle Ferguson, *Controller*
Harry Burnell, *Supervisor*
Charles Hogg, *Administration*
EMP: 202
SALES (corp-wide): 264.1K Privately Held
WEB: www.anchorglass.com
SIC: 3321 3221 3544 Gray iron ingot molds, cast; glass containers; special dies, tools, jigs & fixtures
HQ: Anchor Glass Container Corporation
401 E Jackson St Ste 1100
Tampa FL 33602

(G-21100)
AXION STRL INNOVATIONS LLC (PA)
1100 Brandywine Blvd H (43701-7303)
PHONE..................................740 452-2500
Claude Brown, *President*
Dave Crane, *Exec VP*
Matt Elli, *Exec VP*
Donald Fallon, *CFO*
Allen Kronstadt,
EMP: 17 EST: 2016
SALES (est): 16.3MM Privately Held
SIC: 3089 Extruded finished plastic products

(G-21101)
BAKER CRANE SERVICE LTD
2820 S River Rd (43701-7184)
PHONE..................................740 453-5868
Heidi Fox, *Principal*
EMP: 3
SALES (est): 227.6K Privately Held
SIC: 7692 Welding repair

(G-21102)
BALLAS EGG PRODUCTS CORP
40 N 2nd St (43701-3402)
P.O. Box 2217 (43702-2217)
PHONE..................................614 453-0386
Leonard Ballas, *President*
Joseph G Saliba, *Vice Pres*
Craig Ballas, *Admin Sec*
▼ **EMP:** 100 EST: 1961
SQ FT: 200,000
SALES (est): 14.5MM Privately Held
SIC: 2015 5144 Egg processing; eggs, processed: desiccated (dried); eggs, processed: frozen; eggs

(G-21103)
BARNES ADVERTISING CORP
1580 Fairview Rd (43701-0934)
P.O. Box 277 (43702-0277)
PHONE..................................740 453-6836
Maryjane Shackelford, *President*
Roderick W Barnes, *President*
John Barnes, *Vice Pres*
Joe Panzica, *Sales Mgr*
EMP: 13
SALES (est): 1.6MM Privately Held
SIC: 7312 3993 Billboard advertising; signs & advertising specialties

(G-21104)
BATTERY UNLIMITED
1080 Linden Ave (43701-2952)
PHONE..................................740 452-5030
Kent Curry, *Owner*
EMP: 6
SALES: 900K Privately Held
WEB: www.batteryunlimited.com
SIC: 5063 5531 5999 7699 Batteries; batteries, dry cell; batteries, automotive & truck; batteries, non-automotive; battery service & repair; battery testers, electrical

(G-21105)
BE PRODUCTS INC
Also Called: Ballas Egg Products
40 N 2nd St (43701-3402)
P.O. Box 2217 (43702-2217)
PHONE..................................740 453-0386
Criag Ballas, *President*
Craig Ballas, *President*
Leonard Ballas, *Vice Pres*
EMP: 100
SQ FT: 125,000
SALES (est): 15.1MM Privately Held
SIC: 2015 Egg processing

(G-21106)
BIGGYS AUTO BUFFET
806 W Main St (43701-3142)
PHONE..................................740 455-4663
Zack Wagner, *Principal*
EMP: 7
SALES (est): 350K Privately Held
SIC: 3711 Automobile bodies, passenger car, not including engine, etc.

(G-21107)
BILCO COMPANY
3400 Jim Granger Dr (43701-7231)
PHONE..................................740 455-9020
Charles Chirdon, *President*
EMP: 50
SALES (corp-wide): 690.6MM Privately Held
WEB: www.bilco.com
SIC: 3442 3272 Metal doors; areaways, basement window: concrete
HQ: The Bilco Company
37 Water St
West Haven CT 06516
203 934-6363

(G-21108)
BIMBO QSR OHIO LLC (DH)
3005 E Pointe Dr (43701-7263)
P.O. Box 256, Dublin (43017-0256)
PHONE..................................740 454-6876
Mark Bendix, *CEO*
▼ **EMP:** 10 EST: 1975
SQ FT: 200,000
SALES (est): 84.8MM Privately Held
SIC: 2051 Buns, bread type: fresh or frozen

(G-21109)
BIMBO QSR OHIO LLC
3005 E Pointe Dr (43701-7263)
PHONE..................................740 454-6876
Dan Augburgur, *General Mgr*
EMP: 5 Privately Held
SIC: 2051 Buns, bread type: fresh or frozen
HQ: Bimbo Qsr Ohio, Llc
3005 E Pointe Dr
Zanesville OH 43701
740 454-6876

(G-21110)
BISHOP MACHINE TOOL & DIE
Also Called: Bishop Machine Shop
2304 Hoge Ave (43701-2166)
PHONE..................................740 453-8818
Robert L Bishop, *Partner*
John R Bishop, *Partner*
Alva Bishop Jr, *Manager*
EMP: 10 EST: 1964
SQ FT: 2,000
SALES (est): 1.2MM Privately Held
SIC: 3599 3953 Machine shop, jobbing & repair; marking devices

(G-21111)
BROCKS WELDING & REPAIR SVC
3985 East Pike (43701-8008)
PHONE..................................740 453-3943
Charles Brock, *President*
Myrtle Ann Brock, *Corp Secy*
Marsha Brock, *Vice Pres*
EMP: 4
SALES (est): 501.3K Privately Held
SIC: 7692 7629 Welding repair; electrical repair shops

(G-21112)
BUCKEYE COMPANIES (PA)
999 Zane St (43701-3863)
P.O. Box 1480 (43702-1480)
PHONE..................................740 452-3641
C E Straker, *President*
Stephen R Straker, *President*
M Dean Cole, *Corp Secy*
EMP: 31
SALES (est): 15.5MM Privately Held
SIC: 3533 5083 Drill rigs; agricultural machinery & equipment

(G-21113)
BUCKEYE ENERGY RESOURCES INC
Also Called: Seth Enterprises
999 Zane St (43701-3863)
PHONE..................................740 452-9506
Charles E Straker, *CEO*
Stephen Straker, *President*
C E Staker, *Chairman*
M Dean Cole, *Corp Secy*
EMP: 6
SALES (est): 914K
SALES (corp-wide): 15.5MM Privately Held
WEB: www.buckeyedrill.com
SIC: 4213 1311 Trucking, except local; crude petroleum & natural gas
PA: Buckeye Companies
999 Zane St
Zanesville OH 43701
740 452-3641

(G-21114)
CAMERON DRILLING CO INC
3636 Adamsville Rd (43701-6954)
PHONE..................................740 453-3300
James H Cameron, *President*
Richard M Cameron, *Vice Pres*
EMP: 12 EST: 1966
SQ FT: 3,000
SALES (est): 219.6K Privately Held
SIC: 1311 Crude petroleum production; natural gas production

(G-21115)
CAPITAL PROSTHETIC &
4035 Northpointe Dr A (43701-7647)
PHONE..................................740 453-9545
Lisa Crawford, *Branch Mgr*
EMP: 3
SALES (corp-wide): 2.9MM Privately Held
SIC: 3842 Limbs, artificial; braces, orthopedic
PA: Capital Prosthetic And Orthotic Center, Inc.
4678 Larwell Dr
Columbus OH 43220
614 451-0446

(G-21116)
CARL RITTBERGER SR INC
1900 Lutz Ln (43701-9260)
PHONE..................................740 452-2767
Andrew Rittberger, *President*
Pauline Butler, *Corp Secy*
EMP: 32
SQ FT: 100,000
SALES (est): 4.4MM Privately Held
SIC: 2011 2013 Beef products from beef slaughtered on site; pork products from pork slaughtered on site; sausages & other prepared meats

(G-21117)
CASTING SOLUTIONS LLC
2345 Licking Rd (43701-2728)
P.O. Box 3148 (43702-3148)
PHONE..................................740 452-9371
Jeremiah Clegg, *President*
Susan Stotts, *Purch Mgr*
David King, *Data Proc Exec*
EMP: 106
SALES (est): 23MM
SALES (corp-wide): 172.4MM Publicly Held
WEB: www.burnhamfoundry.com
SIC: 3321 Gray iron castings
PA: Burnham Holdings, Inc.
1241 Harrisburg Ave
Lancaster PA 17603
717 390-7800

(G-21118)
CENTRAL COCA-COLA BTLG CO INC
154 S 7th St (43701-4332)
PHONE..................................740 452-3608
Dave Llewellen, *Manager*
EMP: 30
SALES (corp-wide): 35.4B Publicly Held
WEB: www.colasic.net
SIC: 2086 Bottled & canned soft drinks
HQ: Central Coca-Cola Bottling Company, Inc.
555 Taxter Rd Ste 550
Elmsford NY 10523
914 789-1100

(G-21119)
CLEARPATH UTLITY SOLUTIONS LLC
8155 Ridge Rd (43701-8283)
PHONE..................................740 661-4240
Maureen E Riley, *Principal*
Rodney Riley, *Principal*
EMP: 10
SALES (est): 2.9MM Privately Held
SIC: 1381 Directional drilling oil & gas wells

(G-21120)
CLOSETS BY MIKE
517 Winton Ave (43701-1918)
PHONE..................................740 607-2212
Michael Lmills, *Principal*
EMP: 3 EST: 2011
SALES (est): 175.8K Privately Held
SIC: 3088 Shower stalls, fiberglass & plastic

(G-21121)
COLUMBIA MACHINE COMPANY
961 Hughes St (43701-4388)
PHONE..................................740 452-1736
John Mc Cutcheon, *President*
EMP: 4 EST: 1906
SQ FT: 5,500
SALES: 250K Privately Held
SIC: 3599 Machine shop, jobbing & repair

(G-21122)
COLUMBUS EQUIPMENT COMPANY
818 Lee St (43701-3375)
PHONE..................................740 455-4036
Dan Minnis, *Branch Mgr*
EMP: 4
SALES (corp-wide): 84.2MM Privately Held
SIC: 1442 Construction sand mining
PA: The Columbus Equipment Company
2323 Performance Way
Columbus OH 43207
614 437-0352

GEOGRAPHIC SECTION

Zanesville - Muskingum County (G-21149)

(G-21123)
CONNS POTATO CHIP CO INC (PA)
1805 Kemper Ct (43701-4634)
PHONE.................................740 452-4615
Monte Hunter, *President*
Thomas George Sr, *Vice Pres*
John George, *Site Mgr*
EMP: 30
SQ FT: 100,000
SALES (est): 8.1MM **Privately Held**
SIC: 2096 5963 Potato chips & other potato-based snacks; snacks, direct sales

(G-21124)
CREATIVE PACKAGING LLC
1781 Kemper Ct (43701-4606)
P.O. Box 305 (43702-0305)
PHONE.................................740 452-8497
Jim Theisen, *Sales Mgr*
Keith Imhoff, *Mng Member*
EMP: 48
SQ FT: 125,000
SALES (est): 19.4MM **Privately Held**
WEB: www.creativepkg.net
SIC: 2653 2671 Boxes, corrugated: made from purchased materials; packaging paper & plastics film, coated & laminated

(G-21125)
CRUDE OIL COMPANY
1819 Newark Rd (43701-2631)
PHONE.................................740 452-3335
Sharp Ellen P, *Owner*
EMP: 3 **EST:** 1943
SALES (est): 243.5K **Privately Held**
SIC: 1311 Crude petroleum production

(G-21126)
CUSTOM COIL & TRANSFORMER CO
2900 Newark Rd (43701-7759)
P.O. Box 8063 (43702-8063)
PHONE.................................740 452-5211
Marty Lucas, *President*
Martin C Lucas, *President*
Pam Lucas, *Admin Sec*
EMP: 50
SQ FT: 9,000
SALES: 1MM **Privately Held**
SIC: 3621 3677 3612 Coils, for electric motors or generators; electronic coils, transformers & other inductors; transformers, except electric

(G-21127)
DEBOLT MACHINE INC
4208 West Pike (43701-8289)
PHONE.................................740 454-8082
Paul W Debolt, *President*
EMP: 5
SQ FT: 3,600
SALES: 250K **Privately Held**
SIC: 3999 7539 3519 Models, general, except toy; machine shop, automotive; internal combustion engines

(G-21128)
DMV CORPORATION
1024 Military Rd (43701-1343)
P.O. Box 878 (43702-0878)
PHONE.................................740 452-4787
Allan Patterson, *President*
EMP: 9
SQ FT: 1,500
SALES: 1MM **Privately Held**
WEB: www.dmvcorp.com
SIC: 3851 Ophthalmic goods

(G-21129)
DOW CAMERON OIL & GAS LLC
5555 Eden Park Dr (43701-7052)
PHONE.................................740 452-1568
Dow Cameron,
EMP: 8
SALES (est): 1.3MM **Privately Held**
SIC: 1389 Oil & gas wells: building, repairing & dismantling

(G-21130)
DR PEPPER BOTTLING COMPANY
335 N 6th St (43701-3636)
PHONE.................................740 452-2721
Rick Stone, *Principal*

EMP: 4
SALES (est): 171.7K **Privately Held**
SIC: 2086 Soft drinks: packaged in cans, bottles, etc.

(G-21131)
DRESDEN SPECIALTIES INC
Also Called: Tom's Print Shop
710 Main St (43701-3732)
P.O. Box 146 (43702-0146)
PHONE.................................740 452-7100
Dean Cole, *Manager*
EMP: 5
SALES (corp-wide): 558.2K **Privately Held**
WEB: www.socialsupper.com
SIC: 2752 2759 Commercial printing, offset; letterpress printing
PA: Dresden Specialties Inc
 305 Main St
 Dresden OH 43821
 740 754-2451

(G-21132)
ECLIPSE RESOURCES - OHIO LLC
4900 Boggs Rd (43701-9491)
P.O. Box 910 (43702-0910)
PHONE.................................740 452-4503
Kristen Heavilin, *Buyer*
Tj Blizzard, *Engineer*
Drew Gray, *Engineer*
Benjamin W Hulburt, *Mng Member*
Bruce Carpenter, *Manager*
EMP: 42
SALES (est): 8.9MM
SALES (corp-wide): 515.1MM **Publicly Held**
SIC: 1381 Drilling oil & gas wells
HQ: Eclipse Resources I, Lp
 2121 Old Gatesburg Rd # 110
 State College PA 16803
 814 308-9754

(G-21133)
EMCO USA LLC
1000 Linden Ave (43701-3098)
PHONE.................................740 588-1722
Teresa Reef, *Principal*
▲ **EMP:** 15
SALES (est): 2.3MM **Privately Held**
SIC: 3559 Ammunition & explosives, loading machinery

(G-21134)
EMEGA TECHNOLOGIES LLC
205 N 5th St (43701-3507)
PHONE.................................740 407-3712
Donald E Duffy, *CEO*
EMP: 4
SQ FT: 1,000
SALES: 1MM **Privately Held**
SIC: 3699 Electrical equipment & supplies

(G-21135)
FINELINE IMPRINTS INC
516 State St (43701-3237)
P.O. Box 2688 (43702-2688)
PHONE.................................740 453-1083
Robert Kessler, *President*
Matt McCandlish, *Supervisor*
Jeff Buck, *Graphic Designe*
EMP: 20
SQ FT: 12,000
SALES (est): 1.9MM **Privately Held**
WEB: www.finelineimprints.com
SIC: 5999 2396 3993 2395 Trophies & plaques; screen printing on fabric articles; signs & advertising specialties; pleating & stitching

(G-21136)
FLOW-LINER SYSTEMS LTD
4830 Northpointe Dr (43701-7273)
PHONE................................800 348-0020
Jeff Tanner, *CEO*
Rick Boles, *Superintendent*
Pam Davis, *Sales Staff*
Brent Musselman, *Manager*
▲ **EMP:** 28 **EST:** 2000
SQ FT: 30,000
SALES (est): 5.8MM **Privately Held**
WEB: www.flow-liner.com
SIC: 3589 1799 Sewage & water treatment equipment; epoxy application

(G-21137)
FORMATION CEMENTING INC
1800 Timber Port Dr (43701)
P.O. Box 2667 (43702-2667)
PHONE.................................740 453-6926
Brian G Jasper, *President*
Rae Anne Jasper, *Admin Sec*
EMP: 7
SQ FT: 500
SALES: 2MM **Privately Held**
SIC: 1389 Oil & gas wells: building, repairing & dismantling; servicing oil & gas wells

(G-21138)
FRANKLINS PRINTING COMPANY
984 Beverly Ave (43701-1413)
PHONE.................................740 452-6375
Everett Jackson Jr, *President*
Alice Lucille Jackson, *Corp Secy*
EMP: 10 **EST:** 1949
SQ FT: 7,000
SALES (est): 1.4MM **Privately Held**
SIC: 2752 7331 2791 2789 Commercial printing, offset; addressing service; mailing service; typesetting; bookbinding & related work

(G-21139)
FRIESINGERS INC
120 Graham St (43701-4393)
PHONE.................................740 452-9480
Michael F La Plante, *President*
EMP: 3
SQ FT: 18,000
SALES (est): 399.3K **Privately Held**
SIC: 3449 Miscellaneous metalwork

(G-21140)
G & J PEPSI-COLA BOTTLERS INC
Also Called: Pepsico
335 N 6th St (43701-3636)
PHONE.................................740 452-2721
Rick Stone, *Branch Mgr*
EMP: 85
SALES (corp-wide): 418.3MM **Privately Held**
WEB: www.gjpepsi.com
SIC: 2086 5149 Soft drinks: packaged in cans, bottles, etc.; groceries & related products
PA: G & J Pepsi-Cola Bottlers Inc
 9435 Waterstone Blvd # 390
 Cincinnati OH 45249
 513 785-6060

(G-21141)
GANNETT CO INC
Also Called: Times Recorder, The
3871 Gorsky Dr (43701-6429)
PHONE.................................740 452-4561
Tom Claybaugh, *Manager*
EMP: 60
SALES (corp-wide): 2.9B **Publicly Held**
WEB: www.gannett.com
SIC: 2711 Newspapers, publishing & printing
PA: Gannett Co., Inc.
 7950 Jones Branch Dr
 Mc Lean VA 22102
 703 854-6000

(G-21142)
GENERAL MACHINE & SUPPLY CO
Also Called: GM Management
3135 Lookout Dr (43701-1690)
PHONE.................................740 453-4804
Lynne A Sprague, *President*
Robert T Sprague, *Vice Pres*
EMP: 5
SALES: 150K **Privately Held**
SIC: 3599 5085 Machine shop, jobbing & repair; industrial supplies

(G-21143)
H & R TOOL & MACHINE CO INC
Also Called: Zanesville Bearing Div
18 Jefferson St (43701-4904)
P.O. Box 1444 (43702-1444)
PHONE.................................740 452-0784
William Hill, *President*
Charlene Hill, *Corp Secy*

EMP: 8 **EST:** 1967
SALES (est): 660K **Privately Held**
SIC: 3599 5013 7538 3544 Machine shop, jobbing & repair; automotive supplies & parts; engine rebuilding: automotive; special dies, tools, jigs & fixtures

(G-21144)
HALLIBURTON ENERGY SVCS INC
4999 E Pointe Dr (43701-7680)
PHONE.................................740 617-2917
EMP: 101 **Publicly Held**
SIC: 1389 Oil field services
HQ: Halliburton Energy Services, Inc.
 3000 N Sam Houston Pkwy E
 Houston TX 77032
 281 871-4000

(G-21145)
HANGER PRSTHETCS & ORTHO INC
930 Orchard Hill Rd (43701-7311)
PHONE.................................740 454-6215
Vern Hostetler, *Manager*
EMP: 5
SALES (corp-wide): 1B **Publicly Held**
SIC: 8071 5999 3842 Medical laboratories; artificial limbs; limbs, artificial
HQ: Hanger Prosthetics & Orthotics, Inc.
 10910 Domain Dr Ste 300
 Austin TX 78758
 512 777-3800

(G-21146)
HANNON COMPANY
Electric Motor & Service Co
218 Adams St (43701-4902)
P.O. Box 667 (43702-0667)
PHONE.................................740 453-0527
Todd Wagoner, *Engineer/R&D Asst*
Michael Arrasmith, *Branch Mgr*
EMP: 24
SALES (corp-wide): 25.8MM **Privately Held**
WEB: www.hanco.com
SIC: 7694 7699 5063 Electric motor repair; welding equipment repair; motors, electric
PA: The Hannon Company
 1605 Waynesburg Dr Se
 Canton OH 44707
 330 456-4728

(G-21147)
HYDRO SUPPLY CO
3112 East Pike (43701-8975)
PHONE.................................740 454-3842
Charles William Kimble, *President*
Judy K Kimble, *Corp Secy*
Judy Kimble, *Finance*
Tim Hampp, *Sales Mgr*
EMP: 12
SQ FT: 6,500
SALES (est): 3.7MM **Privately Held**
WEB: www.hydrosupply.com
SIC: 5084 7699 3599 Hydraulic systems equipment & supplies; industrial machinery & equipment repair; machine shop, jobbing & repair

(G-21148)
IG WATTEEUW USA LLC
1000 Linden Ave (43701-3098)
PHONE.................................740 588-1722
Dan Bucur, *CEO*
▲ **EMP:** 11
SQ FT: 51,946
SALES: 5MM **Privately Held**
SIC: 3714 5085 Gears, motor vehicle; gears
HQ: Ig Watteeuw International
 Kampveldstraat 51
 Oostkamp 8020
 508 269-07

(G-21149)
IGW USA
1000 Linden Ave (43701-3098)
PHONE.................................740 588-1722
EMP: 4
SALES (est): 492.8K **Privately Held**
SIC: 3714 Motor vehicle parts & accessories

Zanesville - Muskingum County (G-21150)

(G-21150)
J A B WELDING SERVICE INC
Also Called: Bakers Welding
2820 S River Rd (43701-7184)
PHONE..................................740 453-5868
Jeffrey A Baker, *President*
Cyndy Baker, *Vice Pres*
EMP: 12
SQ FT: 20,000
SALES (est): 2MM Privately Held
SIC: 7692 Welding repair

(G-21151)
JOE MCCLELLAND INC (PA)
Also Called: O K Coal & Concrete
98 E La Salle St (43701-6281)
P.O. Box 1815 (43702-1815)
PHONE..................................740 452-3036
Joe Mc Clelland, *President*
Jack Mc Clelland, *Vice Pres*
Michael McClelland, *Vice Pres*
Richard Mc Clelland, *Treasurer*
Gala Lemon, *Admin Sec*
EMP: 25 EST: 1934
SQ FT: 1,500
SALES (est): 6.7MM Privately Held
WEB: www.okcoalandconcrete.com
SIC: 3273 7992 1442 Ready-mixed concrete; public golf courses; construction sand & gravel

(G-21152)
KELLOGG COMPANY
1675 Fairview Rd (43701-5168)
PHONE..................................740 453-5501
Gary Pilnick, *Owner*
Dean Rinehart, *Manager*
EMP: 125
SALES (corp-wide): 13.5B Publicly Held
WEB: www.kelloggs.com
SIC: 2043 Cereal breakfast foods
PA: Kellogg Company
    1 Kellogg Sq
    Battle Creek MI 49017
    269 961-2000

(G-21153)
KESSLER SIGN COMPANY (PA)
Also Called: Kessler Outdoor Advertising
2669 National Rd (43701-8257)
P.O. Box 785 (43702-0785)
PHONE..................................740 453-0668
Robert Kessler, *President*
Rodger Kessler, *Vice Pres*
Dave Kessler, *VP Opers*
Elaine Kessler, *Treasurer*
Elaine Kessler-Kuntz, *Treasurer*
EMP: 50
SQ FT: 25,000
SALES (est): 7.4MM Privately Held
WEB: www.kesslersignco.com
SIC: 3993 7312 Signs, not made in custom sign painting shops; outdoor advertising services

(G-21154)
MANSFIELD ASPHALT PAVING INC
Also Called: Shelly and Shells
3570 S River Rd (43701-7731)
P.O. Box 1585 (43702-1585)
PHONE..................................740 453-0721
Richard Mc Clelland, *President*
EMP: 12
SALES (est): 826.2K
SALES (corp-wide): 276.3MM Privately Held
WEB: www.shellyandsands.com
SIC: 2951 Asphalt paving mixtures & blocks
PA: Shelly And Sands, Inc.
    3570 S River Rd
    Zanesville OH 43701
    740 453-0721

(G-21155)
MAR-ZANE INC (HQ)
Also Called: Mar-Zane Materials
3570 S River Rd (43701-7731)
P.O. Box 1585 (43702-1585)
PHONE..................................740 453-0721
Gerald N Little, *President*
Wade Hamm, *Vice Pres*
Mike Cline, *Controller*
EMP: 12
SQ FT: 5,000
SALES (est): 9.5MM
SALES (corp-wide): 276.3MM Privately Held
SIC: 2951 Asphalt paving mixtures & blocks
PA: Shelly And Sands, Inc.
    3570 S River Rd
    Zanesville OH 43701
    740 453-0721

(G-21156)
MICHAEL ZAKANY LLC
Also Called: Jose Madrid Salsa
601 Putnam Ave (43701-5504)
PHONE..................................740 221-3934
Michael Zakany, *President*
EMP: 8
SQ FT: 300
SALES: 600K Privately Held
WEB: www.josemadridsalsa.com
SIC: 2035 5149 Pickles, sauces & salad dressings; seasonings, sauces & extracts
PA: Unique Pizza And Subs Corp
    302 W Otterman St
    Greensburg PA

(G-21157)
MOCK WOODWORKING COMPANY LLC
4400 West Pike (43701-9208)
PHONE..................................740 452-2701
Douglas F Mock, *Mng Member*
EMP: 44 EST: 1954
SQ FT: 46,000
SALES (est): 7.2MM Privately Held
WEB: www.mockwoodworking.com
SIC: 2434 2541 2531 Wood kitchen cabinets; office fixtures, wood; store fixtures, wood; public building & related furniture

(G-21158)
MOMENTIVE SPECIALTY CHEM INC
Borden
2055 Grief Rd (43701-2759)
PHONE..................................740 452-5451
Fax: 740 452-4706
EMP: 12
SALES (corp-wide): 2.6B Privately Held
SIC: 2869 Mfg Industrial Organic Chemicals
HQ: Momentive Specialty Chemicals Inc.
    180 E Broad St Fl 26
    Columbus OH 43215
    614 225-4000

(G-21159)
NEFF MACHINERY AND SUPPLIES
Also Called: Neff Parts
112 S Shawnee Ave (43701-6221)
P.O. Box 1822 (43702-1822)
PHONE..................................740 454-0128
Robert Neff, *President*
EMP: 30
SQ FT: 20,000
SALES (est): 3.8MM Privately Held
SIC: 3599 5084 5013 Machine & other job shop work; machine tools & accessories; motor vehicle supplies & new parts

(G-21160)
NESTLE PURINA PETCARE COMPANY
5 N 2nd St (43701-3402)
P.O. Box 38 (43702-0038)
PHONE..................................740 454-8575
Dante Benincasa, *Manager*
EMP: 100
SALES (corp-wide): 90.8B Privately Held
WEB: www.purina.com
SIC: 2047 Dog & cat food
HQ: Nestle Purina Petcare Company
    1 Checkerboard Sq
    Saint Louis MO 63164
    314 982-1000

(G-21161)
NEW BLOOMER CANDY COMPANY LLC
1445 Deercreek Dr (43701-7233)
PHONE..................................740 452-7501
Tom Barry, *Sales Staff*
Jerry Nolder,
EMP: 40
SALES (est): 6.5MM Privately Held
SIC: 2064 Chocolate candy, except solid chocolate

(G-21162)
NEW WAYNE INC
Also Called: Wayne Manufacturing
1555 Ritchey Pkwy (43701-7050)
PHONE..................................740 453-3454
Michael Higgins, *President*
Kurt Paul, *Vice Pres*
Mike Paul, *CFO*
EMP: 8 EST: 1953
SQ FT: 40,000
SALES: 1.8MM Privately Held
SIC: 3441 3443 Fabricated structural metal; fabricated plate work (boiler shop)

(G-21163)
NORTHPOINTE CABINETRY LLC
4800 Frazeysburg Rd (43701-8928)
PHONE..................................740 455-4045
Robert Corbett, *Mng Member*
Nancy Corbett, *Manager*
EMP: 5 EST: 2011
SALES (est): 712K Privately Held
SIC: 2434 1522 Wood kitchen cabinets; hotel/motel & multi-family home renovation & remodeling

(G-21164)
O E M HYDRAULICS INC
1150 Newark Rd (43701-2619)
P.O. Box 2969 (43702-2969)
PHONE..................................740 454-1201
Daniel Perone, *President*
EMP: 3
SQ FT: 10,000
SALES (est): 432.1K Privately Held
SIC: 3494 Valves & pipe fittings

(G-21165)
OHIO NATURAL GAS SERVICES INC
5600 East Pike (43701-8013)
PHONE..................................740 796-3305
John Busch, *President*
EMP: 4
SALES (est): 200K Privately Held
SIC: 1389 Oil field services

(G-21166)
OXFORD MINING COMPANY INC
1855 Kemper Ct (43701-4634)
PHONE..................................740 588-0190
Joe Douglas, *Branch Mgr*
EMP: 11
SALES (corp-wide): 1.3B Privately Held
SIC: 1221 Bituminous coal surface mining
HQ: Oxford Mining Company, Inc.
    544 Chestnut St
    Coshocton OH 43812
    740 622-6302

(G-21167)
PEABODY COAL COMPANY
2810 East Pike Apt 3 (43701-9197)
PHONE..................................740 450-2420
J T Kneen, *Principal*
EMP: 312
SALES (corp-wide): 5.5B Publicly Held
SIC: 1241 Coal mining services
HQ: Peabody Coal Company
    701 Market St
    Saint Louis MO 63101
    314 342-3400

(G-21168)
PLASKOLITE LLC
1175 5 Bs Dr (43701-7376)
PHONE..................................740 450-1109
Mark Gringley, *Branch Mgr*
EMP: 100
SALES (corp-wide): 243.4MM Privately Held
WEB: www.plaskolite.com
SIC: 2821 3083 Acrylic resins; laminated plastic sheets
PA: Plaskolite, Llc
    400 W Nationwide Blvd # 400
    Columbus OH 43215
    614 294-3281

(G-21169)
PORTERS WELDING INC (PA)
601 Linden Ave (43701-3397)
PHONE..................................740 452-4181
Virginia Porter, *President*
Daryl Porter, *Vice Pres*
Kimberly Browning, *Admin Sec*
EMP: 10
SQ FT: 70,000
SALES (est): 1.6MM Privately Held
SIC: 3441 Fabricated structural metal

(G-21170)
PORTO PUMP INC
Also Called: Zanesville Terminal Warehouse
8th And South St (43702)
P.O. Box 1003 (43702-1003)
PHONE..................................740 454-2576
Clarence Goss, *President*
Dorothy Goss, *Corp Secy*
David Goss, *Vice Pres*
Terry Goss, *Vice Pres*
EMP: 4
SALES (est): 533.7K Privately Held
SIC: 3586 Measuring & dispensing pumps

(G-21171)
PRAXAIR INC
130 N 3rd St (43701-3406)
PHONE..................................740 453-0346
Scott Sills, *Manager*
EMP: 3 Privately Held
SIC: 2813 Industrial gases
HQ: Praxair, Inc.
    10 Riverview Dr
    Danbury CT 06810
    203 837-2000

(G-21172)
PRECISION FABG & STAMPING
1755 Kemper Ct (43701-4606)
P.O. Box 2065 (43702-2065)
PHONE..................................740 453-7310
Charlie Sode, *President*
Christine Sode, *Corp Secy*
EMP: 9
SQ FT: 10,000
SALES (est): 1.7MM Privately Held
WEB: www.precisionfabricating.com
SIC: 3441 Fabricated structural metal

(G-21173)
PRINT MASTERS LTD
941 W Main St (43701-3143)
PHONE..................................740 450-2885
Tom Bughman, *President*
Monica Bughman, *Partner*
EMP: 5
SALES: 300K Privately Held
SIC: 2752 Commercial printing, offset

(G-21174)
PSC HOLDINGS INC (PA)
109 Graham St (43701-3103)
P.O. Box 2277 (43702-2277)
PHONE..................................740 454-6253
Dan Pottmeyer, *Principal*
Kelly Hartman, *Principal*
Jim Rose, *Principal*
Cathy Brown, *Manager*
Debbie Armstrong, *Admin Sec*
EMP: 6
SALES: 83.5MM Privately Held
SIC: 1389 Hydraulic fracturing wells

(G-21175)
S & S AGGREGATES INC (HQ)
3570 S River Rd (43701-7731)
P.O. Box 1585 (43702-1585)
PHONE..................................740 453-0721
Gerald Little, *President*
Wade Hamm, *Exec VP*
EMP: 2 EST: 1923
SQ FT: 15,000
SALES: 50MM
SALES (corp-wide): 276.3MM Privately Held
SIC: 1442 3272 3271 Sand mining; gravel mining; concrete products; concrete block & brick
PA: Shelly And Sands, Inc.
    3570 S River Rd
    Zanesville OH 43701
    740 453-0721

(G-21176)
SHELLY AND SANDS INC (PA)
3570 S River Rd (43701-9052)
P.O. Box 1585 (43702-1585)
PHONE.................................740 453-0721
Richard H McClelland, *President*
Gerald N Little, *President*
Larry E Young, *Vice Pres*
EMP: 12 **EST:** 1942
SQ FT: 5,000
SALES (est): 276.3MM **Privately Held**
WEB: www.shellyandsands.com
SIC: 1611 1442 2951 Highway & street paving contractor; construction sand mining; asphalt & asphaltic paving mixtures (not from refineries)

(G-21177)
SHELLY AND SANDS INC
3570 S River Rd (43701-9052)
PHONE.................................740 453-0721
Matt Kelley, *Vice Pres*
EMP: 35
SALES (corp-wide): 276.3MM **Privately Held**
WEB: www.shellyandsands.com
SIC: 1611 2951 1442 1771 Highway & street paving contractor; asphalt & asphaltic paving mixtures (not from refineries); construction sand & gravel; concrete work
PA: Shelly And Sands, Inc.
  3570 S River Rd
  Zanesville OH 43701
  740 453-0721

(G-21178)
SHIRLEY KS STORAGE TRAYS LLC
1150 Newark Rd (43701-2619)
P.O. Box 2519 (43702-2519)
PHONE.................................740 868-8140
Carrie Matheney, *President*
Amanda Huber, *Office Mgr*
EMP: 8
SALES (est): 1.8MM **Privately Held**
SIC: 3089 Plastic containers, except foam

(G-21179)
SIDNEY STIERS
Also Called: Stiers Countertop Sales
620 Moxahala Ave (43701-5528)
PHONE.................................740 454-7368
Sidney Stiers, *Owner*
EMP: 4
SQ FT: 4,200
SALES (est): 344.3K **Privately Held**
SIC: 2541 2434 Counter & sink tops; wood kitchen cabinets

(G-21180)
SIDWELL MATERIALS INC
4200 Maysville Pike (43701-9372)
P.O. Box 192, White Cottage (43791-0192)
PHONE.................................740 849-2394
Jeffrey R Sidwell, *President*
EMP: 130
SALES (est): 21.3MM **Privately Held**
SIC: 1795 4953 2951 1422 Demolition, buildings & other structures; rubbish collection & disposal; asphalt paving mixtures & blocks; crushed & broken limestone; brick, stone & related material

(G-21181)
SOUTHEAST OHIO TIMBER PDTS CO
Also Called: Industrial Crate & Lumber Div
67 Beech Rock Dr (43701-6348)
PHONE.................................740 344-2570
Thomas H York, *President*
George Fouch, *Vice Pres*
EMP: 8
SQ FT: 15,000
SALES (est): 870K **Privately Held**
SIC: 2435 2448 Veneer stock, hardwood; pallets, wood

(G-21182)
SPRINTER MARKING INC
1805 Chandlersville Rd (43701-4644)
PHONE.................................740 453-1000
Bob Bishop, *President*
John Bishop, *Treasurer*
Al Bishop, *Admin Sec*
EMP: 15
SQ FT: 6,000
SALES (est): 1.9MM **Privately Held**
WEB: www.sprintermarking.com
SIC: 3953 Date stamps, hand: rubber or metal

(G-21183)
STEVEN L LONES
3275 Carnation Rd (43701-9815)
PHONE.................................740 452-8851
Steven L Lones, *Owner*
EMP: 4
SALES (est): 263.6K **Privately Held**
SIC: 3494 7389 Pipe fittings;

(G-21184)
T & K HEINS CORPORATION
Also Called: American Speedy Printing
1326 Brandywine Blvd (43701-1089)
PHONE.................................740 452-6006
Thomas Heins, *President*
Katherin Heins, *President*
Alex Abernethy, *Marketing Staff*
Brad Richert, *Marketing Staff*
James Heins, *Representative*
EMP: 5
SQ FT: 1,250
SALES (est): 751.8K **Privately Held**
SIC: 2752 Commercial printing, offset

(G-21185)
UNIQUE STRAIGHT LINE & SFETY S
2776 Coopermill Rd (43701-7041)
PHONE.................................740 452-2724
Lori Wickham, *Principal*
EMP: 3
SALES (est): 275.8K **Privately Held**
SIC: 3993 Signs & advertising specialties

(G-21186)
US WATER COMPANY LLC
Also Called: Culligan
1115 Newark Rd (43701-2618)
PHONE.................................740 453-0604
Richard Dovenbarger, *Manager*
EMP: 9
SALES (corp-wide): 9.6MM **Privately Held**
WEB: www.culliganmiami.com
SIC: 5999 7389 2899 5074 Water purification equipment; water softener service; water treating compounds; plumbing & hydronic heating supplies
PA: U.S. Water Company, Llc
  270 W Palatine Rd
  Wheeling IL 60090
  815 526-3375

(G-21187)
VICTOR MCKENZIE DRILLING CO
3596 Maple Ave Ste A (43701-1686)
P.O. Box 3323 (43702-3323)
PHONE.................................740 453-0834
Victor McKenzie, *President*
Sandy McKenzie, *Corp Secy*
EMP: 27
SALES (est): 1.5MM **Privately Held**
SIC: 1381 Drilling oil & gas wells

(G-21188)
WHITE MACHINE & MFG CO (PA)
120 Graham St (43701-3100)
PHONE.................................740 453-3444
Kenneth F Vlah, *President*
EMP: 18 **EST:** 1955
SQ FT: 20,000
SALES (est): 2.3MM **Privately Held**
SIC: 3599 3441 Mfg Industrial Machinery Structural Metal Fabrication

(G-21189)
WORTHINGTON FOODS INC
1675 Fairview Rd (43701-5168)
PHONE.................................740 453-5501
Jackie Minarik, *Principal*
▲ **EMP:** 87
SALES (est): 7.4MM
SALES (corp-wide): 13.5B **Publicly Held**
SIC: 2038 Frozen specialties
PA: Kellogg Company
  1 Kellogg Sq
  Battle Creek MI 49017
  269 961-2000

(G-21190)
Y CITY RECYCLING LLC
4005 All American Way (43701-7306)
PHONE.................................740 452-2500
Brian Coll, *CEO*
Matt Elli, *Vice Pres*
EMP: 70
SALES (est): 7.6MM **Privately Held**
SIC: 3089 Plastic processing

(G-21191)
ZANE CASKET COMPANY INC
1201 Hall Ave (43701-3859)
P.O. Box 2113 (43702-2113)
PHONE.................................740 452-4680
Robert C Dougherty, *President*
William L Dougherty, *Vice Pres*
EMP: 20 **EST:** 1946
SALES (est): 1.4MM **Privately Held**
SIC: 3995 Burial caskets

(G-21192)
ZANESVILLE NEWSPAPER
34 S 4th St (43701-3417)
PHONE.................................740 452-4561
Dan Shaw, *Principal*
EMP: 3
SALES (est): 128.4K **Privately Held**
SIC: 2711 Newspapers, publishing & printing

(G-21193)
ZANESVILLE PALLET CO INC
2235 Licking Rd (43701-2728)
P.O. Box 2757 (43702-2757)
PHONE.................................740 454-3700
Lee Gunnels, *President*
Zane Lambert, *Vice Pres*
EMP: 19
SALES (est): 2.5MM **Privately Held**
SIC: 2448 Pallets, wood

(G-21194)
ZANESVILLE TOOL GRINDING
624 Main St (43701-3625)
PHONE.................................740 453-9356
Jerry Richardson, *Owner*
EMP: 3 **EST:** 1971
SALES (est): 165.4K **Privately Held**
SIC: 7699 3599 Knife, saw & tool sharpening & repair; machine shop, jobbing & repair

Zoarville
Tuscarawas County

(G-21195)
BUCKEYE FRANKLIN CO
3471 New Zoarville Rd Ne (44656-9707)
P.O. Box 117 (44656-0117)
PHONE.................................330 859-2465
R Dean Smith, *President*
Hazel Yockey, *Asst Sec*
EMP: 12
SQ FT: 15,000
SALES (est): 659.5K **Privately Held**
SIC: 1311 Natural gas production

(G-21196)
LEGACY OAK AND HARDWOODS LLC
7138 Mount Pleasant Rd Ne (44656-8992)
PHONE.................................330 859-2656
Renee Kirtley,
EMP: 12
SALES: 800K **Privately Held**
SIC: 2511 Wood household furniture

SIC INDEX

Standard Industrial Classification Alphabetical Index

SIC NO	PRODUCT

A

3291 Abrasive Prdts
2891 Adhesives & Sealants
3563 Air & Gas Compressors
3585 Air Conditioning & Heating Eqpt
3721 Aircraft
3724 Aircraft Engines & Engine Parts
3728 Aircraft Parts & Eqpt, NEC
2812 Alkalies & Chlorine
3363 Aluminum Die Castings
3354 Aluminum Extruded Prdts
3365 Aluminum Foundries
3355 Aluminum Rolling & Drawing, NEC
3353 Aluminum Sheet, Plate & Foil
3483 Ammunition, Large
3826 Analytical Instruments
2077 Animal, Marine Fats & Oils
1231 Anthracite Mining
2389 Apparel & Accessories, NEC
2387 Apparel Belts
3446 Architectural & Ornamental Metal Work
7694 Armature Rewinding Shops
3292 Asbestos products
2952 Asphalt Felts & Coatings
3822 Automatic Temperature Controls
3581 Automatic Vending Machines
3465 Automotive Stampings
2396 Automotive Trimmings, Apparel Findings, Related Prdts

B

2673 Bags: Plastics, Laminated & Coated
2674 Bags: Uncoated Paper & Multiwall
3562 Ball & Roller Bearings
2836 Biological Prdts, Exc Diagnostic Substances
1221 Bituminous Coal & Lignite: Surface Mining
1222 Bituminous Coal: Underground Mining
2782 Blankbooks & Looseleaf Binders
3312 Blast Furnaces, Coke Ovens, Steel & Rolling Mills
3564 Blowers & Fans
3732 Boat Building & Repairing
3452 Bolts, Nuts, Screws, Rivets & Washers
2732 Book Printing, Not Publishing
2789 Bookbinding
2731 Books: Publishing & Printing
3131 Boot & Shoe Cut Stock & Findings
2342 Brassieres, Girdles & Garments
2051 Bread, Bakery Prdts Exc Cookies & Crackers
3251 Brick & Structural Clay Tile
3991 Brooms & Brushes
3995 Burial Caskets
2021 Butter

C

3578 Calculating & Accounting Eqpt
2064 Candy & Confectionery Prdts
2033 Canned Fruits, Vegetables & Preserves
2032 Canned Specialties
2394 Canvas Prdts
3624 Carbon & Graphite Prdts
2895 Carbon Black
3955 Carbon Paper & Inked Ribbons
3592 Carburetors, Pistons, Rings & Valves
2273 Carpets & Rugs
2823 Cellulosic Man-Made Fibers
3241 Cement, Hydraulic
3253 Ceramic Tile
2043 Cereal Breakfast Foods
2022 Cheese
1479 Chemical & Fertilizer Mining
2899 Chemical Preparations, NEC
2361 Children's & Infants' Dresses & Blouses
3261 China Plumbing Fixtures & Fittings
3262 China, Table & Kitchen Articles
2066 Chocolate & Cocoa Prdts
2111 Cigarettes
2121 Cigars
3255 Clay Refractories
1459 Clay, Ceramic & Refractory Minerals, NEC
1241 Coal Mining Svcs
3479 Coating & Engraving, NEC
2095 Coffee
3316 Cold Rolled Steel Sheet, Strip & Bars
3582 Commercial Laundry, Dry Clean & Pressing Mchs

2759 Commercial Printing
2754 Commercial Printing: Gravure
2752 Commercial Printing: Lithographic
3646 Commercial, Indl & Institutional Lighting Fixtures
3669 Communications Eqpt, NEC
3577 Computer Peripheral Eqpt, NEC
3572 Computer Storage Devices
3575 Computer Terminals
3271 Concrete Block & Brick
3272 Concrete Prdts
3531 Construction Machinery & Eqpt
1442 Construction Sand & Gravel
2679 Converted Paper Prdts, NEC
3535 Conveyors & Eqpt
2052 Cookies & Crackers
3366 Copper Foundries
1021 Copper Ores
2298 Cordage & Twine
2653 Corrugated & Solid Fiber Boxes
3961 Costume Jewelry & Novelties
2261 Cotton Fabric Finishers
2211 Cotton, Woven Fabric
3466 Crowns & Closures
1311 Crude Petroleum & Natural Gas
1423 Crushed & Broken Granite
1422 Crushed & Broken Limestone
1429 Crushed & Broken Stone, NEC
3643 Current-Carrying Wiring Devices
2391 Curtains & Draperies
3087 Custom Compounding Of Purchased Plastic Resins
3281 Cut Stone Prdts
3421 Cutlery
2865 Cyclic-Crudes, Intermediates, Dyes & Org Pigments

D

3843 Dental Eqpt & Splys
2835 Diagnostic Substances
2675 Die-Cut Paper & Board
3544 Dies, Tools, Jigs, Fixtures & Indl Molds
1411 Dimension Stone
2047 Dog & Cat Food
3942 Dolls & Stuffed Toys
2591 Drapery Hardware, Window Blinds & Shades
2381 Dress & Work Gloves
2034 Dried Fruits, Vegetables & Soup
1381 Drilling Oil & Gas Wells

E

3263 Earthenware, Whiteware, Table & Kitchen Articles
3634 Electric Household Appliances
3641 Electric Lamps
3694 Electrical Eqpt For Internal Combustion Engines
3629 Electrical Indl Apparatus, NEC
3699 Electrical Machinery, Eqpt & Splys, NEC
3845 Electromedical & Electrotherapeutic Apparatus
3313 Electrometallurgical Prdts
3675 Electronic Capacitors
3677 Electronic Coils & Transformers
3679 Electronic Components, NEC
3571 Electronic Computers
3678 Electronic Connectors
3676 Electronic Resistors
3471 Electroplating, Plating, Polishing, Anodizing & Coloring
3534 Elevators & Moving Stairways
3431 Enameled Iron & Metal Sanitary Ware
2677 Envelopes
2892 Explosives

F

2241 Fabric Mills, Cotton, Wool, Silk & Man-Made
3499 Fabricated Metal Prdts, NEC
3498 Fabricated Pipe & Pipe Fittings
3443 Fabricated Plate Work
3069 Fabricated Rubber Prdts, NEC
3441 Fabricated Structural Steel
2399 Fabricated Textile Prdts, NEC
2295 Fabrics Coated Not Rubberized
2297 Fabrics, Nonwoven
3523 Farm Machinery & Eqpt
3965 Fasteners, Buttons, Needles & Pins
1061 Ferroalloy Ores, Except Vanadium
2875 Fertilizers, Mixing Only
2655 Fiber Cans, Tubes & Drums
2091 Fish & Seafoods, Canned & Cured

3211 Flat Glass
2087 Flavoring Extracts & Syrups
2045 Flour, Blended & Prepared
2041 Flour, Grain Milling
3824 Fluid Meters & Counters
3593 Fluid Power Cylinders & Actuators
3594 Fluid Power Pumps & Motors
3492 Fluid Power Valves & Hose Fittings
2657 Folding Paperboard Boxes
3556 Food Prdts Machinery
2099 Food Preparations, NEC
3149 Footwear, NEC
2053 Frozen Bakery Prdts
2037 Frozen Fruits, Juices & Vegetables
2038 Frozen Specialties
2371 Fur Goods
2599 Furniture & Fixtures, NEC

G

3944 Games, Toys & Children's Vehicles
3524 Garden, Lawn Tractors & Eqpt
3053 Gaskets, Packing & Sealing Devices
3221 Glass Containers
3231 Glass Prdts Made Of Purchased Glass
1041 Gold Ores
3321 Gray Iron Foundries
2771 Greeting Card Publishing
3769 Guided Missile/Space Vehicle Parts & Eqpt, NEC
3761 Guided Missiles & Space Vehicles
2861 Gum & Wood Chemicals
3275 Gypsum Prdts

H

3423 Hand & Edge Tools
3425 Hand Saws & Saw Blades
3171 Handbags & Purses
3429 Hardware, NEC
2426 Hardwood Dimension & Flooring Mills
2435 Hardwood Veneer & Plywood
2353 Hats, Caps & Millinery
3433 Heating Eqpt
3536 Hoists, Cranes & Monorails
2252 Hosiery, Except Women's
2392 House furnishings: Textile
3142 House Slippers
3639 Household Appliances, NEC
3651 Household Audio & Video Eqpt
3631 Household Cooking Eqpt
2519 Household Furniture, NEC
3633 Household Laundry Eqpt
3632 Household Refrigerators & Freezers
3635 Household Vacuum Cleaners

I

2097 Ice
2024 Ice Cream
2819 Indl Inorganic Chemicals, NEC
3823 Indl Instruments For Meas, Display & Control
3569 Indl Machinery & Eqpt, NEC
3567 Indl Process Furnaces & Ovens
3537 Indl Trucks, Tractors, Trailers & Stackers
2813 Industrial Gases
2869 Industrial Organic Chemicals, NEC
3543 Industrial Patterns
1446 Industrial Sand
3491 Industrial Valves
2816 Inorganic Pigments
3825 Instrs For Measuring & Testing Electricity
3519 Internal Combustion Engines, NEC
3462 Iron & Steel Forgings
1011 Iron Ores

J

3915 Jewelers Findings & Lapidary Work
3911 Jewelry: Precious Metal

K

2253 Knit Outerwear Mills

L

3821 Laboratory Apparatus & Furniture
2258 Lace & Warp Knit Fabric Mills
3952 Lead Pencils, Crayons & Artist's Mtrls
2386 Leather & Sheep Lined Clothing
3151 Leather Gloves & Mittens

SIC INDEX

SIC NO	PRODUCT
3199	Leather Goods, NEC
3111	Leather Tanning & Finishing
3648	Lighting Eqpt, NEC
3274	Lime
3996	Linoleum & Hard Surface Floor Coverings, NEC
2085	Liquors, Distilled, Rectified & Blended
2411	Logging
2992	Lubricating Oils & Greases
3161	Luggage

M

SIC NO	PRODUCT
2098	Macaroni, Spaghetti & Noodles
3545	Machine Tool Access
3541	Machine Tools: Cutting
3542	Machine Tools: Forming
3599	Machinery & Eqpt, Indl & Commercial, NEC
3322	Malleable Iron Foundries
2082	Malt Beverages
2761	Manifold Business Forms
3999	Manufacturing Industries, NEC
3953	Marking Devices
2515	Mattresses & Bedsprings
3829	Measuring & Controlling Devices, NEC
3586	Measuring & Dispensing Pumps
2011	Meat Packing Plants
3568	Mechanical Power Transmission Eqpt, NEC
2833	Medicinal Chemicals & Botanical Prdts
2329	Men's & Boys' Clothing, NEC
2325	Men's & Boys' Separate Trousers & Casual Slacks
2321	Men's & Boys' Shirts
2311	Men's & Boys' Suits, Coats & Overcoats
2322	Men's & Boys' Underwear & Nightwear
2326	Men's & Boys' Work Clothing
3143	Men's Footwear, Exc Athletic
3412	Metal Barrels, Drums, Kegs & Pails
3411	Metal Cans
3442	Metal Doors, Sash, Frames, Molding & Trim
3497	Metal Foil & Leaf
3398	Metal Heat Treating
2514	Metal Household Furniture
1081	Metal Mining Svcs
3469	Metal Stampings, NEC
3549	Metalworking Machinery, NEC
2026	Milk
2023	Milk, Condensed & Evaporated
2431	Millwork
3296	Mineral Wool
3295	Minerals & Earths: Ground Or Treated
3532	Mining Machinery & Eqpt
3496	Misc Fabricated Wire Prdts
2741	Misc Publishing
3449	Misc Structural Metal Work
1499	Miscellaneous Nonmetallic Mining
2451	Mobile Homes
3061	Molded, Extruded & Lathe-Cut Rubber Mechanical Goods
3716	Motor Homes
3714	Motor Vehicle Parts & Access
3711	Motor Vehicles & Car Bodies
3751	Motorcycles, Bicycles & Parts
3621	Motors & Generators
3931	Musical Instruments

N

SIC NO	PRODUCT
1321	Natural Gas Liquids
2711	Newspapers: Publishing & Printing
2873	Nitrogenous Fertilizers
3297	Nonclay Refractories
3644	Noncurrent-Carrying Wiring Devices
3364	Nonferrous Die Castings, Exc Aluminum
3463	Nonferrous Forgings
3369	Nonferrous Foundries: Castings, NEC
3357	Nonferrous Wire Drawing
3299	Nonmetallic Mineral Prdts, NEC
1481	Nonmetallic Minerals Svcs, Except Fuels

O

SIC NO	PRODUCT
2522	Office Furniture, Except Wood
3579	Office Machines, NEC
1382	Oil & Gas Field Exploration Svcs
1389	Oil & Gas Field Svcs, NEC
3533	Oil Field Machinery & Eqpt
3851	Ophthalmic Goods
3827	Optical Instruments
3489	Ordnance & Access, NEC
3842	Orthopedic, Prosthetic & Surgical Appliances/Splys

P

SIC NO	PRODUCT
3565	Packaging Machinery
2851	Paints, Varnishes, Lacquers, Enamels
2671	Paper Coating & Laminating for Packaging
2672	Paper Coating & Laminating, Exc for Packaging
3554	Paper Inds Machinery
2621	Paper Mills
2631	Paperboard Mills
2542	Partitions & Fixtures, Except Wood
2951	Paving Mixtures & Blocks
3951	Pens & Mechanical Pencils
2844	Perfumes, Cosmetics & Toilet Preparations
2721	Periodicals: Publishing & Printing
3172	Personal Leather Goods
2879	Pesticides & Agricultural Chemicals, NEC
2911	Petroleum Refining
2834	Pharmaceuticals
3652	Phonograph Records & Magnetic Tape
2874	Phosphatic Fertilizers
3861	Photographic Eqpt & Splys
2035	Pickled Fruits, Vegetables, Sauces & Dressings
3085	Plastic Bottles
3086	Plastic Foam Prdts
3083	Plastic Laminated Plate & Sheet
3084	Plastic Pipe
3088	Plastic Plumbing Fixtures
3089	Plastic Prdts
3082	Plastic Unsupported Profile Shapes
3081	Plastic Unsupported Sheet & Film
2821	Plastics, Mtrls & Nonvulcanizable Elastomers
2796	Platemaking & Related Svcs
2395	Pleating & Stitching For The Trade
3432	Plumbing Fixture Fittings & Trim, Brass
3264	Porcelain Electrical Splys
2096	Potato Chips & Similar Prdts
3269	Pottery Prdts, NEC
2015	Poultry Slaughtering, Dressing & Processing
3546	Power Hand Tools
3612	Power, Distribution & Specialty Transformers
3448	Prefabricated Metal Buildings & Cmpnts
2452	Prefabricated Wood Buildings & Cmpnts
7372	Prepackaged Software
2048	Prepared Feeds For Animals & Fowls
3229	Pressed & Blown Glassware, NEC
3692	Primary Batteries: Dry & Wet
3399	Primary Metal Prdts, NEC
3339	Primary Nonferrous Metals, NEC
3334	Primary Production Of Aluminum
3331	Primary Smelting & Refining Of Copper
3672	Printed Circuit Boards
2893	Printing Ink
3555	Printing Trades Machinery & Eqpt
2999	Products Of Petroleum & Coal, NEC
2531	Public Building & Related Furniture
2611	Pulp Mills
3561	Pumps & Pumping Eqpt

R

SIC NO	PRODUCT
3663	Radio & T V Communications, Systs & Eqpt, Broadcast/Studio
3671	Radio & T V Receiving Electron Tubes
3743	Railroad Eqpt
3273	Ready-Mixed Concrete
2493	Reconstituted Wood Prdts
3695	Recording Media
3625	Relays & Indl Controls
3645	Residential Lighting Fixtures
2384	Robes & Dressing Gowns
3547	Rolling Mill Machinery & Eqpt
3351	Rolling, Drawing & Extruding Of Copper
3356	Rolling, Drawing-Extruding Of Nonferrous Metals
3021	Rubber & Plastic Footwear
3052	Rubber & Plastic Hose & Belting

S

SIC NO	PRODUCT
2068	Salted & Roasted Nuts & Seeds
2656	Sanitary Food Containers
2676	Sanitary Paper Prdts
2013	Sausages & Meat Prdts
2421	Saw & Planing Mills
3596	Scales & Balances, Exc Laboratory
3451	Screw Machine Prdts
3812	Search, Detection, Navigation & Guidance Systs & Instrs
3341	Secondary Smelting & Refining Of Nonferrous Metals
3674	Semiconductors
3589	Service Ind Machines, NEC
2652	Set-Up Paperboard Boxes
3444	Sheet Metal Work
3731	Shipbuilding & Repairing
2079	Shortening, Oils & Margarine
3993	Signs & Advertising Displays
2262	Silk & Man-Made Fabric Finishers
2221	Silk & Man-Made Fiber
3914	Silverware, Plated & Stainless Steel Ware
3484	Small Arms
3482	Small Arms Ammunition
2841	Soap & Detergents
2086	Soft Drinks
2436	Softwood Veneer & Plywood
2075	Soybean Oil Mills
2842	Spec Cleaning, Polishing & Sanitation Preparations
3559	Special Ind Machinery, NEC
2429	Special Prdt Sawmills, NEC
3566	Speed Changers, Drives & Gears
3949	Sporting & Athletic Goods, NEC
2678	Stationery Prdts
3511	Steam, Gas & Hydraulic Turbines & Engines
3325	Steel Foundries, NEC
3324	Steel Investment Foundries
3317	Steel Pipe & Tubes
3493	Steel Springs, Except Wire
3315	Steel Wire Drawing & Nails & Spikes
3691	Storage Batteries
3259	Structural Clay Prdts, NEC
2439	Structural Wood Members, NEC
2063	Sugar, Beet
2843	Surface Active & Finishing Agents, Sulfonated Oils
3841	Surgical & Medical Instrs & Apparatus
3613	Switchgear & Switchboard Apparatus
2824	Synthetic Organic Fibers, Exc Cellulosic
2822	Synthetic Rubber (Vulcanizable Elastomers)

T

SIC NO	PRODUCT
3795	Tanks & Tank Components
3661	Telephone & Telegraph Apparatus
2393	Textile Bags
2269	Textile Finishers, NEC
2299	Textile Goods, NEC
3552	Textile Machinery
2284	Thread Mills
2296	Tire Cord & Fabric
3011	Tires & Inner Tubes
2131	Tobacco, Chewing & Snuff
3799	Transportation Eqpt, NEC
3792	Travel Trailers & Campers
3713	Truck & Bus Bodies
3715	Truck Trailers
2791	Typesetting

U

SIC NO	PRODUCT
1094	Uranium, Radium & Vanadium Ores

V

SIC NO	PRODUCT
3494	Valves & Pipe Fittings, NEC
3647	Vehicular Lighting Eqpt

W

SIC NO	PRODUCT
3873	Watch & Clock Devices & Parts
2385	Waterproof Outerwear
3548	Welding Apparatus
7692	Welding Repair
2046	Wet Corn Milling
2084	Wine & Brandy
3495	Wire Springs
2331	Women's & Misses' Blouses
2335	Women's & Misses' Dresses
2339	Women's & Misses' Outerwear, NEC
2337	Women's & Misses' Suits, Coats & Skirts
3144	Women's Footwear, Exc Athletic
2341	Women's, Misses' & Children's Underwear & Nightwear
2441	Wood Boxes
2449	Wood Containers, NEC
2511	Wood Household Furniture
2512	Wood Household Furniture, Upholstered
2434	Wood Kitchen Cabinets
2521	Wood Office Furniture
2448	Wood Pallets & Skids
2499	Wood Prdts, NEC
2491	Wood Preserving
2517	Wood T V, Radio, Phono & Sewing Cabinets
2541	Wood, Office & Store Fixtures
3553	Woodworking Machinery
2231	Wool, Woven Fabric

X

SIC NO	PRODUCT
3844	X-ray Apparatus & Tubes

Y

SIC NO	PRODUCT
2281	Yarn Spinning Mills
2282	Yarn Texturizing, Throwing, Twisting & Winding Mills

SIC INDEX

Standard Industrial Classification Numerical Index

SIC NO	PRODUCT

10 metal mining
1011 Iron Ores
1021 Copper Ores
1041 Gold Ores
1061 Ferroalloy Ores, Except Vanadium
1081 Metal Mining Svcs
1094 Uranium, Radium & Vanadium Ores

12 coal mining
1221 Bituminous Coal & Lignite: Surface Mining
1222 Bituminous Coal: Underground Mining
1231 Anthracite Mining
1241 Coal Mining Svcs

13 oil and gas extraction
1311 Crude Petroleum & Natural Gas
1321 Natural Gas Liquids
1381 Drilling Oil & Gas Wells
1382 Oil & Gas Field Exploration Svcs
1389 Oil & Gas Field Svcs, NEC

14 mining and quarrying of nonmetallic minerals, except fuels
1411 Dimension Stone
1422 Crushed & Broken Limestone
1423 Crushed & Broken Granite
1429 Crushed & Broken Stone, NEC
1442 Construction Sand & Gravel
1446 Industrial Sand
1459 Clay, Ceramic & Refractory Minerals, NEC
1479 Chemical & Fertilizer Mining
1481 Nonmetallic Minerals Svcs, Except Fuels
1499 Miscellaneous Nonmetallic Mining

20 food and kindred products
2011 Meat Packing Plants
2013 Sausages & Meat Prdts
2015 Poultry Slaughtering, Dressing & Processing
2021 Butter
2022 Cheese
2023 Milk, Condensed & Evaporated
2024 Ice Cream
2026 Milk
2032 Canned Specialties
2033 Canned Fruits, Vegetables & Preserves
2034 Dried Fruits, Vegetables & Soup
2035 Pickled Fruits, Vegetables, Sauces & Dressings
2037 Frozen Fruits, Juices & Vegetables
2038 Frozen Specialties
2041 Flour, Grain Milling
2043 Cereal Breakfast Foods
2045 Flour, Blended & Prepared
2046 Wet Corn Milling
2047 Dog & Cat Food
2048 Prepared Feeds For Animals & Fowls
2051 Bread, Bakery Prdts Exc Cookies & Crackers
2052 Cookies & Crackers
2053 Frozen Bakery Prdts
2063 Sugar, Beet
2064 Candy & Confectionery Prdts
2066 Chocolate & Cocoa Prdts
2068 Salted & Roasted Nuts & Seeds
2075 Soybean Oil Mills
2077 Animal, Marine Fats & Oils
2079 Shortening, Oils & Margarine
2082 Malt Beverages
2084 Wine & Brandy
2085 Liquors, Distilled, Rectified & Blended
2086 Soft Drinks
2087 Flavoring Extracts & Syrups
2091 Fish & Seafoods, Canned & Cured
2095 Coffee
2096 Potato Chips & Similar Prdts
2097 Ice
2098 Macaroni, Spaghetti & Noodles
2099 Food Preparations, NEC

21 tobacco products
2111 Cigarettes
2121 Cigars
2131 Tobacco, Chewing & Snuff

22 textile mill products
2211 Cotton, Woven Fabric
2221 Silk & Man-Made Fiber
2231 Wool, Woven Fabric
2241 Fabric Mills, Cotton, Wool, Silk & Man-Made
2252 Hosiery, Except Women's
2253 Knit Outerwear Mills
2258 Lace & Warp Knit Fabric Mills
2261 Cotton Fabric Finishers
2262 Silk & Man-Made Fabric Finishers
2269 Textile Finishers, NEC
2273 Carpets & Rugs
2281 Yarn Spinning Mills
2282 Yarn Texturizing, Throwing, Twisting & Winding Mills
2284 Thread Mills
2295 Fabrics Coated Not Rubberized
2296 Tire Cord & Fabric
2297 Fabrics, Nonwoven
2298 Cordage & Twine
2299 Textile Goods, NEC

23 apparel and other finished products made from fabrics and similar material
2311 Men's & Boys' Suits, Coats & Overcoats
2321 Men's & Boys' Shirts
2322 Men's & Boys' Underwear & Nightwear
2325 Men's & Boys' Separate Trousers & Casual Slacks
2326 Men's & Boys' Work Clothing
2329 Men's & Boys' Clothing, NEC
2331 Women's & Misses' Blouses
2335 Women's & Misses' Dresses
2337 Women's & Misses' Suits, Coats & Skirts
2339 Women's & Misses' Outerwear, NEC
2341 Women's, Misses' & Children's Underwear & Nightwear
2342 Brassieres, Girdles & Garments
2353 Hats, Caps & Millinery
2361 Children's & Infants' Dresses & Blouses
2371 Fur Goods
2381 Dress & Work Gloves
2384 Robes & Dressing Gowns
2385 Waterproof Outerwear
2386 Leather & Sheep Lined Clothing
2387 Apparel Belts
2389 Apparel & Accessories, NEC
2391 Curtains & Draperies
2392 House furnishings: Textile
2393 Textile Bags
2394 Canvas Prdts
2395 Pleating & Stitching For The Trade
2396 Automotive Trimmings, Apparel Findings, Related Prdts
2399 Fabricated Textile Prdts, NEC

24 lumber and wood products, except furniture
2411 Logging
2421 Saw & Planing Mills
2426 Hardwood Dimension & Flooring Mills
2429 Special Prdt Sawmills, NEC
2431 Millwork
2434 Wood Kitchen Cabinets
2435 Hardwood Veneer & Plywood
2436 Softwood Veneer & Plywood
2439 Structural Wood Members, NEC
2441 Wood Boxes
2448 Wood Pallets & Skids
2449 Wood Containers, NEC
2451 Mobile Homes
2452 Prefabricated Wood Buildings & Cmpnts
2491 Wood Preserving
2493 Reconstituted Wood Prdts
2499 Wood Prdts, NEC

25 furniture and fixtures
2511 Wood Household Furniture
2512 Wood Household Furniture, Upholstered
2514 Metal Household Furniture
2515 Mattresses & Bedsprings
2517 Wood T V, Radio, Phono & Sewing Cabinets
2519 Household Furniture, NEC
2521 Wood Office Furniture
2522 Office Furniture, Except Wood
2531 Public Building & Related Furniture
2541 Wood, Office & Store Fixtures
2542 Partitions & Fixtures, Except Wood
2591 Drapery Hardware, Window Blinds & Shades
2599 Furniture & Fixtures, NEC

26 paper and allied products
2611 Pulp Mills
2621 Paper Mills
2631 Paperboard Mills
2652 Set-Up Paperboard Boxes
2653 Corrugated & Solid Fiber Boxes
2655 Fiber Cans, Tubes & Drums
2656 Sanitary Food Containers
2657 Folding Paperboard Boxes
2671 Paper Coating & Laminating for Packaging
2672 Paper Coating & Laminating, Exc for Packaging
2673 Bags: Plastics, Laminated & Coated
2674 Bags: Uncoated Paper & Multiwall
2675 Die-Cut Paper & Board
2676 Sanitary Paper Prdts
2677 Envelopes
2678 Stationery Prdts
2679 Converted Paper Prdts, NEC

27 printing, publishing, and allied industries
2711 Newspapers: Publishing & Printing
2721 Periodicals: Publishing & Printing
2731 Books: Publishing & Printing
2732 Book Printing, Not Publishing
2741 Misc Publishing
2752 Commercial Printing: Lithographic
2754 Commercial Printing: Gravure
2759 Commercial Printing
2761 Manifold Business Forms
2771 Greeting Card Publishing
2782 Blankbooks & Looseleaf Binders
2789 Bookbinding
2791 Typesetting
2796 Platemaking & Related Svcs

28 chemicals and allied products
2812 Alkalies & Chlorine
2813 Industrial Gases
2816 Inorganic Pigments
2819 Indl Inorganic Chemicals, NEC
2821 Plastics, Mtrls & Nonvulcanizable Elastomers
2822 Synthetic Rubber (Vulcanizable Elastomers)
2823 Cellulosic Man-Made Fibers
2824 Synthetic Organic Fibers, Exc Cellulosic
2833 Medicinal Chemicals & Botanical Prdts
2834 Pharmaceuticals
2835 Diagnostic Substances
2836 Biological Prdts, Exc Diagnostic Substances
2841 Soap & Detergents
2842 Spec Cleaning, Polishing & Sanitation Preparations
2843 Surface Active & Finishing Agents, Sulfonated Oils
2844 Perfumes, Cosmetics & Toilet Preparations
2851 Paints, Varnishes, Lacquers, Enamels
2861 Gum & Wood Chemicals
2865 Cyclic-Crudes, Intermediates, Dyes & Org Pigments
2869 Industrial Organic Chemicals, NEC
2873 Nitrogenous Fertilizers
2874 Phosphatic Fertilizers
2875 Fertilizers, Mixing Only
2879 Pesticides & Agricultural Chemicals, NEC
2891 Adhesives & Sealants
2892 Explosives
2893 Printing Ink
2895 Carbon Black
2899 Chemical Preparations, NEC

29 petroleum refining and related industries
2911 Petroleum Refining
2951 Paving Mixtures & Blocks
2952 Asphalt Felts & Coatings
2992 Lubricating Oils & Greases
2999 Products Of Petroleum & Coal, NEC

30 rubber and miscellaneous plastics products
3011 Tires & Inner Tubes
3021 Rubber & Plastic Footwear
3052 Rubber & Plastic Hose & Belting
3053 Gaskets, Packing & Sealing Devices
3061 Molded, Extruded & Lathe-Cut Rubber Mechanical Goods
3069 Fabricated Rubber Prdts, NEC
3081 Plastic Unsupported Sheet & Film
3082 Plastic Unsupported Profile Shapes
3083 Plastic Laminated Plate & Sheet
3084 Plastic Pipe
3085 Plastic Bottles
3086 Plastic Foam Prdts
3087 Custom Compounding Of Purchased Plastic Resins
3088 Plastic Plumbing Fixtures
3089 Plastic Prdts

31 leather and leather products
3111 Leather Tanning & Finishing

SIC INDEX

SIC NO	PRODUCT
3131	Boot & Shoe Cut Stock & Findings
3142	House Slippers
3143	Men's Footwear, Exc Athletic
3144	Women's Footwear, Exc Athletic
3149	Footwear, NEC
3151	Leather Gloves & Mittens
3161	Luggage
3171	Handbags & Purses
3172	Personal Leather Goods
3199	Leather Goods, NEC

32 stone, clay, glass, and concrete products

SIC NO	PRODUCT
3211	Flat Glass
3221	Glass Containers
3229	Pressed & Blown Glassware, NEC
3231	Glass Prdts Made Of Purchased Glass
3241	Cement, Hydraulic
3251	Brick & Structural Clay Tile
3253	Ceramic Tile
3255	Clay Refractories
3259	Structural Clay Prdts, NEC
3261	China Plumbing Fixtures & Fittings
3262	China, Table & Kitchen Articles
3263	Earthenware, Whiteware, Table & Kitchen Articles
3264	Porcelain Electrical Splys
3269	Pottery Prdts, NEC
3271	Concrete Block & Brick
3272	Concrete Prdts
3273	Ready-Mixed Concrete
3274	Lime
3275	Gypsum Prdts
3281	Cut Stone Prdts
3291	Abrasive Prdts
3292	Asbestos products
3295	Minerals & Earths: Ground Or Treated
3296	Mineral Wool
3297	Nonclay Refractories
3299	Nonmetallic Mineral Prdts, NEC

33 primary metal industries

SIC NO	PRODUCT
3312	Blast Furnaces, Coke Ovens, Steel & Rolling Mills
3313	Electrometallurgical Prdts
3315	Steel Wire Drawing & Nails & Spikes
3316	Cold Rolled Steel Sheet, Strip & Bars
3317	Steel Pipe & Tubes
3321	Gray Iron Foundries
3322	Malleable Iron Foundries
3324	Steel Investment Foundries
3325	Steel Foundries, NEC
3331	Primary Smelting & Refining Of Copper
3334	Primary Production Of Aluminum
3339	Primary Nonferrous Metals, NEC
3341	Secondary Smelting & Refining Of Nonferrous Metals
3351	Rolling, Drawing & Extruding Of Copper
3353	Aluminum Sheet, Plate & Foil
3354	Aluminum Extruded Prdts
3355	Aluminum Rolling & Drawing, NEC
3356	Rolling, Drawing-Extruding Of Nonferrous Metals
3357	Nonferrous Wire Drawing
3363	Aluminum Die Castings
3364	Nonferrous Die Castings, Exc Aluminum
3365	Aluminum Foundries
3366	Copper Foundries
3369	Nonferrous Foundries: Castings, NEC
3398	Metal Heat Treating
3399	Primary Metal Prdts, NEC

34 fabricated metal products, except machinery and transportation equipment

SIC NO	PRODUCT
3411	Metal Cans
3412	Metal Barrels, Drums, Kegs & Pails
3421	Cutlery
3423	Hand & Edge Tools
3425	Hand Saws & Saw Blades
3429	Hardware, NEC
3431	Enameled Iron & Metal Sanitary Ware
3432	Plumbing Fixture Fittings & Trim, Brass
3433	Heating Eqpt
3441	Fabricated Structural Steel
3442	Metal Doors, Sash, Frames, Molding & Trim
3443	Fabricated Plate Work
3444	Sheet Metal Work
3446	Architectural & Ornamental Metal Work
3448	Prefabricated Metal Buildings & Cmpnts
3449	Misc Structural Metal Work
3451	Screw Machine Prdts
3452	Bolts, Nuts, Screws, Rivets & Washers
3462	Iron & Steel Forgings
3463	Nonferrous Forgings
3465	Automotive Stampings
3466	Crowns & Closures
3469	Metal Stampings, NEC
3471	Electroplating, Plating, Polishing, Anodizing & Coloring
3479	Coating & Engraving, NEC
3482	Small Arms Ammunition
3483	Ammunition, Large
3484	Small Arms
3489	Ordnance & Access, NEC
3491	Industrial Valves
3492	Fluid Power Valves & Hose Fittings
3493	Steel Springs, Except Wire
3494	Valves & Pipe Fittings, NEC
3495	Wire Springs
3496	Misc Fabricated Wire Prdts
3497	Metal Foil & Leaf
3498	Fabricated Pipe & Pipe Fittings
3499	Fabricated Metal Prdts, NEC

35 industrial and commercial machinery and computer equipment

SIC NO	PRODUCT
3511	Steam, Gas & Hydraulic Turbines & Engines
3519	Internal Combustion Engines, NEC
3523	Farm Machinery & Eqpt
3524	Garden, Lawn Tractors & Eqpt
3531	Construction Machinery & Eqpt
3532	Mining Machinery & Eqpt
3533	Oil Field Machinery & Eqpt
3534	Elevators & Moving Stairways
3535	Conveyors & Eqpt
3536	Hoists, Cranes & Monorails
3537	Indl Trucks, Tractors, Trailers & Stackers
3541	Machine Tools: Cutting
3542	Machine Tools: Forming
3543	Industrial Patterns
3544	Dies, Tools, Jigs, Fixtures & Indl Molds
3545	Machine Tool Access
3546	Power Hand Tools
3547	Rolling Mill Machinery & Eqpt
3548	Welding Apparatus
3549	Metalworking Machinery, NEC
3552	Textile Machinery
3553	Woodworking Machinery
3554	Paper Inds Machinery
3555	Printing Trades Machinery & Eqpt
3556	Food Prdts Machinery
3559	Special Ind Machinery, NEC
3561	Pumps & Pumping Eqpt
3562	Ball & Roller Bearings
3563	Air & Gas Compressors
3564	Blowers & Fans
3565	Packaging Machinery
3566	Speed Changers, Drives & Gears
3567	Indl Process Furnaces & Ovens
3568	Mechanical Power Transmission Eqpt, NEC
3569	Indl Machinery & Eqpt, NEC
3571	Electronic Computers
3572	Computer Storage Devices
3575	Computer Terminals
3577	Computer Peripheral Eqpt, NEC
3578	Calculating & Accounting Eqpt
3579	Office Machines, NEC
3581	Automatic Vending Machines
3582	Commercial Laundry, Dry Clean & Pressing Mchs
3585	Air Conditioning & Heating Eqpt
3586	Measuring & Dispensing Pumps
3589	Service Ind Machines, NEC
3592	Carburetors, Pistons, Rings & Valves
3593	Fluid Power Cylinders & Actuators
3594	Fluid Power Pumps & Motors
3596	Scales & Balances, Exc Laboratory
3599	Machinery & Eqpt, Indl & Commercial, NEC

36 electronic and other electrical equipment and components, except computer

SIC NO	PRODUCT
3612	Power, Distribution & Specialty Transformers
3613	Switchgear & Switchboard Apparatus
3621	Motors & Generators
3624	Carbon & Graphite Prdts
3625	Relays & Indl Controls
3629	Electrical Indl Apparatus, NEC
3631	Household Cooking Eqpt
3632	Household Refrigerators & Freezers
3633	Household Laundry Eqpt
3634	Electric Household Appliances
3635	Household Vacuum Cleaners
3639	Household Appliances, NEC
3641	Electric Lamps
3643	Current-Carrying Wiring Devices
3644	Noncurrent-Carrying Wiring Devices
3645	Residential Lighting Fixtures
3646	Commercial, Indl & Institutional Lighting Fixtures
3647	Vehicular Lighting Eqpt
3648	Lighting Eqpt, NEC
3651	Household Audio & Video Eqpt
3652	Phonograph Records & Magnetic Tape
3661	Telephone & Telegraph Apparatus
3663	Radio & T V Communications, Systs & Eqpt, Broadcast/Studio
3669	Communications Eqpt, NEC
3671	Radio & T V Receiving Electron Tubes
3672	Printed Circuit Boards
3674	Semiconductors
3675	Electronic Capacitors
3676	Electronic Resistors
3677	Electronic Coils & Transformers
3678	Electronic Connectors
3679	Electronic Components, NEC
3691	Storage Batteries
3692	Primary Batteries: Dry & Wet
3694	Electrical Eqpt For Internal Combustion Engines
3695	Recording Media
3699	Electrical Machinery, Eqpt & Splys, NEC

37 transportation equipment

SIC NO	PRODUCT
3711	Motor Vehicles & Car Bodies
3713	Truck & Bus Bodies
3714	Motor Vehicle Parts & Access
3715	Truck Trailers
3716	Motor Homes
3721	Aircraft
3724	Aircraft Engines & Engine Parts
3728	Aircraft Parts & Eqpt, NEC
3731	Shipbuilding & Repairing
3732	Boat Building & Repairing
3743	Railroad Eqpt
3751	Motorcycles, Bicycles & Parts
3761	Guided Missiles & Space Vehicles
3769	Guided Missile/Space Vehicle Parts & Eqpt, NEC
3792	Travel Trailers & Campers
3795	Tanks & Tank Components
3799	Transportation Eqpt, NEC

38 measuring, analyzing and controlling instruments; photographic, medical an

SIC NO	PRODUCT
3812	Search, Detection, Navigation & Guidance Systs & Instrs
3821	Laboratory Apparatus & Furniture
3822	Automatic Temperature Controls
3823	Indl Instruments For Meas, Display & Control
3824	Fluid Meters & Counters
3825	Instrs For Measuring & Testing Electricity
3826	Analytical Instruments
3827	Optical Instruments
3829	Measuring & Controlling Devices, NEC
3841	Surgical & Medical Instrs & Apparatus
3842	Orthopedic, Prosthetic & Surgical Appliances/Splys
3843	Dental Eqpt & Splys
3844	X-ray Apparatus & Tubes
3845	Electromedical & Electrotherapeutic Apparatus
3851	Ophthalmic Goods
3861	Photographic Eqpt & Splys
3873	Watch & Clock Devices & Parts

39 miscellaneous manufacturing industries

SIC NO	PRODUCT
3911	Jewelry: Precious Metal
3914	Silverware, Plated & Stainless Steel Ware
3915	Jewelers Findings & Lapidary Work
3931	Musical Instruments
3942	Dolls & Stuffed Toys
3944	Games, Toys & Children's Vehicles
3949	Sporting & Athletic Goods, NEC
3951	Pens & Mechanical Pencils
3952	Lead Pencils, Crayons & Artist's Mtrls
3953	Marking Devices
3955	Carbon Paper & Inked Ribbons
3961	Costume Jewelry & Novelties
3965	Fasteners, Buttons, Needles & Pins
3991	Brooms & Brushes
3993	Signs & Advertising Displays
3995	Burial Caskets
3996	Linoleum & Hard Surface Floor Coverings, NEC
3999	Manufacturing Industries, NEC

73 business services

SIC NO	PRODUCT
7372	Prepackaged Software

76 miscellaneous repair services

SIC NO	PRODUCT
7692	Welding Repair
7694	Armature Rewinding Shops

SIC SECTION

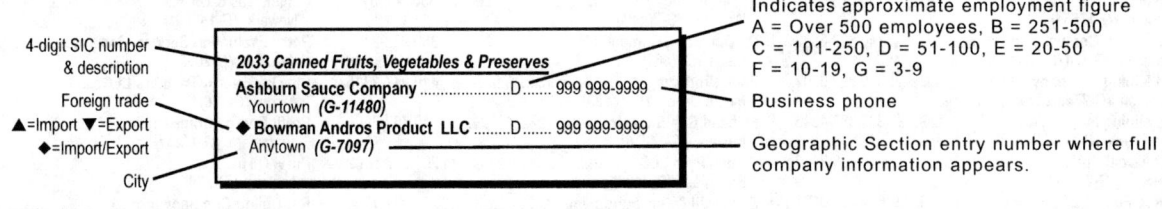

- 4-digit SIC number & description
- Foreign trade ▲=Import ▼=Export ◆=Import/Export
- City
- Indicates approximate employment figure
  A = Over 500 employees, B = 251-500
  C = 101-250, D = 51-100, E = 20-50
  F = 10-19, G = 3-9
- Business phone
- Geographic Section entry number where full company information appears.

See footnotes for symbols and codes identification.

- The SIC codes in this section are from the latest Standard Industrial Classification manual published by the U.S. Government's Office of Management and Budget. For more information regarding SICs, see the Explanatory Notes.
- Companies may be listed under multiple classifications.

10 METAL MINING

1011 Iron Ores

Bloom Lake Iron Ore Mine Ltd	G	216 694-5700
Cleveland *(G-4822)*		
Cleveland-Cliffs Inc	D	216 694-5700
Cleveland *(G-4986)*		
Cliffs & Associates Ltd	G	216 694-5700
Cleveland *(G-4988)*		
Cliffs Michigan Operation	E	216 694-5303
Cleveland *(G-4990)*		
Cliffs Mining Company	F	216 694-5700
Cleveland *(G-4991)*		
Cliffs Minnesota Minerals Co	A	216 694-5700
Cleveland *(G-4992)*		
Empire Iron Mining Partnership	G	216 694-5700
Cleveland *(G-5174)*		
▲ Hibbing Taconite A Joint Ventr	G	216 694-5700
Cleveland *(G-5406)*		
International Steel Group	C	330 841-2800
Warren *(G-19411)*		
▼ Northshore Mining Company	G	216 694-5700
Cleveland *(G-5785)*		
The Cleveland-Cliffs Iron Co	C	216 694-5700
Cleveland *(G-6162)*		
Tilden Mining Company LC	A	216 694-5700
Cleveland *(G-6175)*		
▼ United Taconite LLC	G	218 744-7800
Cleveland *(G-6237)*		
Wabush Mines Cliffs Mining Co	A	216 694-5700
Cleveland *(G-6281)*		

1021 Copper Ores

◆ Warrenton Copper LLC	E	636 456-3488
Cleveland *(G-6290)*		

1041 Gold Ores

Ivi Mining Group Ltd	G	740 418-7745
Vinton *(G-19215)*		

1061 Ferroalloy Ores, Except Vanadium

▲ Rhenium Alloys Inc	D	440 365-7388
North Ridgeville *(G-15251)*		

1081 Metal Mining Svcs

Alloy Metal Exchange LLC	E	216 478-0200
Bedford Heights *(G-1459)*		
Hahs Factory Outlet	E	330 405-4227
Twinsburg *(G-18790)*		
Hopedale Mining LLC	E	740 937-2225
Hopedale *(G-10991)*		
Metokote Corporation	G	419 996-7800
Lima *(G-11907)*		
Mining Reclamation Inc	F	740 327-5555
Dresden *(G-8869)*		
Omega Cementing Co	G	330 695-7147
Apple Creek *(G-616)*		

1094 Uranium, Radium & Vanadium Ores

◆ AMG Vanadium LLC	G	740 435-4600
Cambridge *(G-2423)*		

12 COAL MINING

1221 Bituminous Coal & Lignite: Surface Mining

B&N Coal Inc	D	740 783-3575
Dexter City *(G-8792)*		
CAM Co Inc	G	740 922-4533
Dennison *(G-8783)*		
▼ Cliffs Logan County Coal LLC	G	216 694-5700
Cleveland *(G-4989)*		
Coal Services Inc	D	740 795-5220
Powhatan Point *(G-16341)*		
Commercial Minerals Inc	G	330 549-2165
North Lima *(G-15168)*		
East Fairfield Coal Co	E	330 542-1010
Petersburg *(G-16033)*		
F & M Coal Company	G	740 544-5203
Toronto *(G-18609)*		
Holmes Limestone Co	G	330 893-2721
Berlin *(G-1642)*		
Ivi Mining Group Ltd	G	740 418-7745
Vinton *(G-19215)*		
J & D Mining Inc	E	330 339-4935
New Philadelphia *(G-14776)*		
Kenneth Mc Beth	G	740 922-9494
Dennison *(G-8784)*		
King Quarries Inc	G	740 732-2923
Caldwell *(G-2408)*		
L & M Mineral Co	G	330 852-3696
Sugarcreek *(G-17851)*		
Marietta Coal Co	E	740 695-2197
Saint Clairsville *(G-16637)*		
Morning Sun Technologies Inc	G	513 461-1417
Oxford *(G-15698)*		
Murray American Energy Inc	A	740 338-3100
Saint Clairsville *(G-16638)*		
Nacco Industries Inc	E	440 229-5151
Cleveland *(G-5719)*		
Ohio Valley Coal Company	B	740 926-1351
Saint Clairsville *(G-16644)*		
Oxford Mining Company Inc	D	740 342-7666
New Lexington *(G-14719)*		
Oxford Mining Company Inc	F	740 588-0190
Zanesville *(G-21166)*		
Oxford Mining Company - KY LLC		740 622-6302
Coshocton *(G-7749)*		
PM Coal Company LLC		440 256-7624
Willoughby *(G-20403)*		
Rayle Coal Co	F	740 695-2197
Saint Clairsville *(G-16648)*		
Rosebud Mining Company	E	740 768-2097
Bergholz *(G-1635)*		
Rosebud Mining Company	E	740 922-9122
Uhrichsville *(G-18892)*		
Sands Hill Coal Hauling Co Inc	C	740 384-4211
Hamden *(G-10524)*		
Straight Creek Bushman LLC	G	513 732-1698
Batavia *(G-1187)*		
Subtropolis Mining Co	G	330 549-2165
North Lima *(G-15179)*		
Ted Tipple	G	740 432-3263
Cambridge *(G-2459)*		
Thompson Brothers Mining Co	F	330 549-3979
New Springfield *(G-14821)*		
Westmoreland Resources Gp LLC	F	740 622-6302
Coshocton *(G-7756)*		

1222 Bituminous Coal: Underground Mining

American Energy Corporation	F	740 926-9152
Beallsville *(G-1289)*		
Coal Services Inc	D	740 795-5220
Powhatan Point *(G-16341)*		
Ivi Mining Group Ltd	G	740 418-7745
Vinton *(G-19215)*		
Kenamerican Resources Inc	G	740 338-3100
Saint Clairsville *(G-16635)*		
Maple Creek Mining Inc	G	740 926-9205
Alledonia *(G-446)*		
Murray Energy Corporation	G	740 338-3100
Saint Clairsville *(G-16639)*		
Murray Kentucky Energy Inc	G	740 338-3100
Saint Clairsville *(G-16640)*		
Rosebud Mining Company	E	740 658-4217
Freeport *(G-9985)*		
Rosebud Mining Company	E	740 768-2097
Bergholz *(G-1635)*		
Rosebud Mining Company	E	740 922-9122
Uhrichsville *(G-18892)*		
Sterling Mining Corporation	F	330 549-2165
North Lima *(G-15178)*		
West Ridge Resources Inc	G	740 338-3100
Saint Clairsville *(G-16657)*		
Western KY Coal Resources LLC	B	740 338-3100
Saint Clairsville *(G-16658)*		

1231 Anthracite Mining

Coal Services Inc	D	740 795-5220
Powhatan Point *(G-16341)*		

1241 Coal Mining Svcs

Airtite Mine Products LLC	F	740 894-8778
Proctorville *(G-16342)*		
American Energy Corporation	F	740 926-9152
Beallsville *(G-1289)*		
Anthony Mining Co Inc	G	740 266-8100
Wintersville *(G-20537)*		
Appalachian Fuels LLC	G	606 928-0460
Dublin *(G-8880)*		
Boich Companies LLC	G	614 221-0101
Columbus *(G-6685)*		
Coal Resources Inc	F	740 338-3100
Saint Clairsville *(G-16627)*		
Coal Services Inc	D	740 795-5220
Powhatan Point *(G-16341)*		
Consol Energy	G	740 232-2140
Saint Clairsville *(G-16629)*		
D & D Mining Co Inc	F	330 549-3127
New Springfield *(G-14819)*		
Don Gamertsfelder	G	740 797-4495
The Plains *(G-18021)*		
Duncan Brothers Drilling Inc	F	330 426-9507
East Palestine *(G-9074)*		
Duncan Brothers Drilling Inc	F	330 426-9507
East Palestine *(G-9075)*		
▼ Global Coal Sales Group LLC	G	614 221-0101
Columbus *(G-6956)*		
Global Mining Holding Co LLC	G	614 221-0101
Columbus *(G-6957)*		
Harrison County Coal Company	E	740 338-3100
Saint Clairsville *(G-16633)*		
Kurtz Bros Inc	E	614 491-0868
Groveport *(G-10500)*		
North American Auger Mining	G	740 622-8782
Coshocton *(G-7744)*		
Ohio Valley Resources Inc	E	740 795-5220
Saint Clairsville *(G-16645)*		

12 COAL MINING

Ohio Valley Transloading Co ....A 740 795-4967
  Saint Clairsville *(G-16646)*
Oxford Mining Company Inc ....G 330 878-5120
  Strasburg *(G-17651)*
Oxford Mining Company Inc ....G 740 622-6302
  Coshocton *(G-7747)*
Oxford Mining Company LLC ....E 740 622-6302
  Coshocton *(G-7748)*
Oxford Mining Inc ....G 330 339-4546
  Stone Creek *(G-17563)*
Peabody Coal Company ....B 740 450-2420
  Zanesville *(G-21167)*
Resource Fuels LLC ....G 614 221-0101
  Columbus *(G-7389)*
Sandusky Dock Corporation ....F 419 626-1214
  Sandusky *(G-16841)*
Strata Mine Services Inc ....F 740 695-6880
  Saint Clairsville *(G-16654)*
Suncoke Energy Nc ....E 513 727-5571
  Middletown *(G-13955)*

13 OIL AND GAS EXTRACTION

1311 Crude Petroleum & Natural Gas

A P Production & Service ....G 740 745-5317
  Utica *(G-19023)*
A S Nf Producing Inc ....G 330 933-0622
  Hartville *(G-10682)*
AB Resources LLC ....E 440 922-1098
  Brecksville *(G-2017)*
All American Energy Coop Assn ....G 440 772-4340
  Westlake *(G-20089)*
Alliance Petroleum Corporation ....D 330 493-0440
  Canton *(G-2569)*
American Rodpump Ltd ....G 440 987-9457
  Dublin *(G-8879)*
B & J Drilling Company Inc ....G 740 599-6700
  Danville *(G-7956)*
Bakerwell Inc ....E 330 276-2161
  Killbuck *(G-11448)*
Belden & Blake Corporation ....E 330 602-5551
  Dover *(G-8808)*
Beucler Brothers Inc ....G 330 735-2267
  Dellroy *(G-8733)*
Blaze Oil & Gas Inc ....G 330 345-6700
  Wooster *(G-20572)*
Brendel Producing Company ....G 330 854-4151
  Canton *(G-2598)*
Broad Street Financial Company ....G 614 228-0326
  Columbus *(G-6704)*
BT Energy Corporation ....G 740 373-6134
  Fleming *(G-9779)*
Buckeye Energy Resources Inc ....G 740 452-9506
  Zanesville *(G-21113)*
Buckeye Franklin Co ....F 330 859-2465
  Zoarville *(G-21195)*
Buckeye Oil Producing Co ....F 330 264-8847
  Wooster *(G-20576)*
Cac Energy Ltd ....G 937 867-5593
  Dayton *(G-8072)*
Cameron Drilling Co Inc ....G 740 453-3300
  Zanesville *(G-21114)*
Carlton Oil Corp ....G 740 473-2629
  Newport *(G-14983)*
▲ Carol Mickley ....G 740 599-7870
  Danville *(G-7960)*
Cgas Exploration Inc ....G 614 436-4631
  Worthington *(G-20679)*
Cgas Inc ....G 614 975-4697
  Worthington *(G-20680)*
Chevron Ae Resources LLC ....E 330 896-8510
  Uniontown *(G-18916)*
Chevron Ae Resources LLC ....G 330 654-4343
  Deerfield *(G-8607)*
City of Lancaster ....G 740 687-6670
  Lancaster *(G-11554)*
Columbia Energy Group ....A 614 460-4683
  Columbus *(G-6781)*
Columbia Gas Meter Shop ....F 614 460-5519
  Columbus *(G-6782)*
Columbia Midstream Group LLC ....F 330 542-1095
  New Middletown *(G-14748)*
Crude Oil Company ....G 740 452-3335
  Zanesville *(G-21125)*
D & L Energy Inc ....E 330 270-1201
  Canton *(G-2645)*
David A Waldron & Associates ....G 330 264-7275
  Wooster *(G-20583)*
Derrick Petroleum Inc ....G 740 668-5711
  Bladensburg *(G-1696)*

Dome Drilling Co ....G 440 892-9434
  Westlake *(G-20109)*
Dome Drilling Co ....G 330 262-5113
  Wooster *(G-20585)*
Dp Operating Company Inc ....G 330 938-2172
  Beloit *(G-1569)*
Edco Producing ....G 419 947-2515
  Mount Gilead *(G-14423)*
Elkhead Gas & Oil Co ....G 740 763-3966
  Newark *(G-14870)*
Enrevo Pyro LLC ....G 203 517-5002
  Brookfield *(G-2106)*
Equity Oil & Gas Funds Inc ....G 234 231-1004
  Stow *(G-17582)*
Everflow Eastern Partners LP ....G 330 533-2692
  Canfield *(G-2528)*
Excalibur Exploration Inc ....G 330 966-7003
  Greentown *(G-10358)*
Exco Resources LLC ....G 740 254-4061
  Tippecanoe *(G-18147)*
Franklin Gas & Oil Company LLC ....G 330 264-8739
  Wooster *(G-20593)*
General Electric Company ....F 330 425-3755
  Twinsburg *(G-18782)*
Geopetro LLC ....G 614 885-9350
  Worthington *(G-20686)*
Green Energy Inc ....G 330 262-5112
  Wooster *(G-20599)*
Gulfport Energy Corporation ....E 740 251-0407
  Saint Clairsville *(G-16632)*
H & S Drilling Co Inc ....G 740 828-2411
  Frazeysburg *(G-9940)*
H I Smith Oil & Gas Inc ....G 330 279-2361
  Holmesville *(G-10975)*
Hanini Seven Oil ....G 216 857-0172
  Cleveland *(G-5370)*
Hopco Resources Inc ....G 614 882-8533
  Columbus *(G-7008)*
Hunter Eureka Pipeline LLC ....G 740 374-2940
  Marietta *(G-12633)*
Interstate Gas Supply Inc ....D 614 659-5000
  Dublin *(G-8930)*
James R Bernhardt Producing ....G 330 345-5306
  Wooster *(G-20609)*
Jerry Moore Inc ....G 330 877-1155
  Hartville *(G-10697)*
John D Oil and Gas Company ....G 440 255-6325
  Mentor *(G-13486)*
Kenoil Inc ....E 330 262-1144
  Wooster *(G-20612)*
Kilbarger Investments Inc ....G 740 385-6019
  Logan *(G-12031)*
Killbuck Creek Oil Co ....G 330 601-0921
  Wooster *(G-20614)*
King Drilling Co ....G 330 769-3434
  Seville *(G-16919)*
◆ Koch Knight LLC ....D 330 488-1651
  East Canton *(G-9041)*
Konoil Inc ....G 330 499-9811
  Canton *(G-2729)*
Lagc Ltd ....G 419 886-2141
  Fredericktown *(G-9972)*
Lake Region Oil Inc ....G 330 828-8420
  Dalton *(G-7946)*
Lee A Williams Jr ....G 419 225-6751
  Lima *(G-11886)*
M3 Midstream LLC ....D 740 945-1170
  Scio *(G-16878)*
M3 Midstream LLC ....G 330 679-5580
  Salineville *(G-16789)*
M3 Midstream LLC ....E 330 223-2220
  Kensington *(G-11285)*
M3 Midstream LLC ....E 740 431-4168
  Dennison *(G-8785)*
Marietta Resources Corporation ....F 740 373-6305
  Marietta *(G-12643)*
Mason Producing Inc ....G 740 913-0686
  Galena *(G-10115)*
MFC Drilling Inc ....G 740 622-5600
  Coshocton *(G-7740)*
Midland Oil Co ....G 740 787-2557
  Brownsville *(G-2184)*
MRC Global (us) Inc ....F 614 475-4033
  Gahanna *(G-10092)*
National Gas & Oil Company ....G 740 344-2102
  Newark *(G-14899)*
Northwood Energy Corporation ....E 614 457-1024
  Columbus *(G-7230)*
Oil & Go LLC ....G 330 854-6345
  Canal Fulton *(G-2488)*

P & S Energy Inc ....G 330 652-2525
  Mineral Ridge *(G-14170)*
Penick Gas & Oil ....G 740 323-3040
  Newark *(G-14909)*
Petro Evaluation Services Inc ....G 330 264-4454
  Wooster *(G-20636)*
Pin Oak Energy Partners LLC ....G 888 748-0763
  Akron *(G-320)*
Profit Energy Company Inc ....G 740 472-1018
  Jerusalem *(G-11251)*
Purvi Oil Inc ....G 419 207-8234
  Ashland *(G-739)*
R C Poling Company Inc ....G 740 939-0023
  Junction City *(G-11275)*
R D Holder Oil Co Inc ....G 740 522-3136
  Heath *(G-10728)*
RCM Engineering Company ....G 330 666-0575
  Akron *(G-345)*
Robert Barr ....F 740 826-7325
  New Concord *(G-14686)*
Rodco Petroleum Inc ....G 330 477-9823
  Canton *(G-2810)*
Saint Croix Ltd ....G 330 666-1544
  Akron *(G-371)*
Sheridan One Stop Carryout ....G 740 687-1300
  Lancaster *(G-11607)*
Speedway LLC ....F 330 874-4616
  Bolivar *(G-1928)*
Speedway LLC ....F 440 943-0044
  Wickliffe *(G-20231)*
Speedway LLC ....G 937 653-6840
  Urbana *(G-19013)*
Speedway LLC ....F 614 418-9325
  Columbus *(G-7475)*
Speedway LLC ....G 937 390-6651
  Springfield *(G-17492)*
Speedway LLC ....F 614 861-6397
  Reynoldsburg *(G-16454)*
Speedway LLC ....G 330 339-7770
  New Philadelphia *(G-14800)*
Speedway LLC ....G 937 372-7129
  Wilberforce *(G-20237)*
Speedway LLC ....F 513 683-2034
  Cincinnati *(G-4358)*
Speedway LLC ....G 330 468-3320
  Macedonia *(G-12328)*
Speedway LLC ....F 330 343-9469
  Dover *(G-8857)*
Speedway LLC ....F 419 468-9773
  Galion *(G-10156)*
Speedway LLC ....F 440 988-8014
  Amherst *(G-575)*
Standard Energy Company ....G 614 885-1901
  Columbus *(G-7484)*
Stocker & Sitler Oil Company ....G 614 888-9588
  Columbus *(G-7491)*
Stonebridge Operating Co LLC ....G 740 373-6134
  Fleming *(G-9781)*
Summit Petroleum Inc ....G 330 487-5494
  Twinsburg *(G-18862)*
T JS Oil & Gas Inc ....G 740 623-0192
  Coshocton *(G-7754)*
Tatum Petroleum Corporation ....G 740 819-6810
  Worthington *(G-20704)*
Temple Oil & Gas Company ....G 740 452-7878
  Crooksville *(G-7820)*
Triad Hunter LLC ....F 740 374-2940
  Marietta *(G-12684)*
Triad Hunter LLC ....G 740 374-2940
  Marietta *(G-12685)*
U S Fuel Development Co ....G 614 486-0614
  Columbus *(G-7553)*
Ultra-Met Company ....G 937 653-7133
  Urbana *(G-19018)*
Utica E Ohio Midstream ....G 330 679-2295
  Salineville *(G-16790)*
Utica East Ohio Midstream LLC ....G 740 945-2226
  Scio *(G-16880)*
Valley Petroleum Inc ....G 740 668-4901
  Utica *(G-19029)*
Vesco Oil Corporation ....G 419 335-8871
  Wauseon *(G-19536)*
Viking Intl Resources Co Inc ....G 304 628-3878
  Marietta *(G-12688)*
W H Patten Drilling Co Inc ....G 330 674-3046
  Millersburg *(G-14144)*
W P Brown Enterprises Inc ....G 740 685-2594
  Byesville *(G-2396)*
William S Miller Inc ....G 330 223-1794
  Kensington *(G-11287)*

Williams Partners LP ....C 330 966-3674
North Canton *(G-15137)*
Xto Energy Inc ....D 740 671-9901
Bellaire *(G-1489)*

1321 Natural Gas Liquids

A Plus Propane LLC ....G 419 399-4445
Paulding *(G-15854)*
Consolidated Gas Coop Inc ....G 419 946-6600
Mount Gilead *(G-14422)*
H & S Operating Company Inc ....G 330 830-8178
Winesburg *(G-20531)*
Husky Marketing and Supply Co ....E 614 210-2300
Dublin *(G-8927)*
Markwest Energy Partners LP ....G 740 942-0463
Cadiz *(G-2399)*
Markwest Utica Emg LLC ....G 740 942-4810
Jewett *(G-11252)*
Nimco Inc ....G 740 596-4477
Mc Arthur *(G-13182)*
RCM Engineering Company ....G 330 666-0575
Akron *(G-345)*

1381 Drilling Oil & Gas Wells

Anderson Energy Inc ....G 740 678-8608
Fleming *(G-9777)*
Artex Oil Company ....E 740 373-3313
Marietta *(G-12605)*
Bakerwell Service Rigs Inc ....F 330 276-2161
Killbuck *(G-11449)*
Bancequity Petroleum Corp ....G 330 468-5935
Macedonia *(G-12278)*
Brendel Producing Company ....G 330 854-4151
Canton *(G-2598)*
Buckeye Oil Producing Co ....F 330 264-8847
Wooster *(G-20576)*
Camphire Drilling Inc ....G 740 599-6928
Danville *(G-7959)*
Clarence Tussel Jr ....G 440 576-3415
Jefferson *(G-11228)*
Clearpath Utility Solutions LLC ....F 740 661-4240
Zanesville *(G-21119)*
Columbus Oilfield Exploration ....G 614 895-9520
Powell *(G-16317)*
D Anderson Corp ....G 330 433-0606
Canton *(G-2646)*
Decker Drilling Inc ....E 740 749-3939
Vincent *(G-19213)*
Directional One Svcs Inc USA ....G 740 371-5031
Marietta *(G-12620)*
Dnl Oil Corp ....G 740 342-4970
New Lexington *(G-14715)*
Domestic Oil & Gas Co Inc ....G 440 232-3150
Cleveland *(G-5104)*
Doris Kimble ....E 330 343-1226
Dover *(G-8817)*
Dugan Drilling Incorporated ....G 740 668-3811
Walhonding *(G-19305)*
Echo Drilling Inc ....G 740 254-4127
Gnadenhutten *(G-10278)*
Eclipse Resources - Ohio LLC ....E 740 452-4503
Zanesville *(G-21132)*
Frank Csapo ....G 330 435-4458
Creston *(G-7805)*
Future Productions Inc ....G 330 478-0477
Canton *(G-2677)*
G & H Drilling Inc ....E 330 674-4868
Millersburg *(G-14083)*
Geocore Drilling Inc ....G 419 864-4011
Cardington *(G-2872)*
Gills Petroleum LLC ....G 740 702-2600
Chillicothe *(G-3189)*
Groundhogs 2000 LLC ....G 440 653-1647
Bedford *(G-1407)*
H & D Drilling Co Inc ....G 740 745-2236
Frazeysburg *(G-9939)*
Hocking Hills Energy & Well SE ....G 740 385-6690
Logan *(G-12026)*
Interden Industries Inc ....G 419 368-9011
Lakeville *(G-11506)*
J D Drilling Co ....E 740 949-2512
Racine *(G-16356)*
J Valtier Gas and Oil Co Inc ....G 740 342-2839
Malta *(G-12383)*
JAC Construction Ohio Llc ....G 440 564-5005
Newbury *(G-14958)*
Jackson Wells Services ....G 419 886-2017
Bellville *(G-1558)*
James R Smail Inc ....G 330 264-7500
Wooster *(G-20610)*
Kilbarger Construction Inc ....C 740 385-6019
Logan *(G-12030)*
King Energy Inc ....G 330 297-5508
Ravenna *(G-16386)*
Kirk Excavating & Construction ....E 614 444-4008
Columbus *(G-7095)*
Lee Oil & Gas Inc ....G 937 223-8891
Oakwood *(G-15463)*
Maric Drilling Company Inc ....F 330 830-8178
Winesburg *(G-20532)*
Moore Well Services Inc ....E 330 650-4443
Mogadore *(G-14244)*
▲ **Ngo Development Corporation** ....F 740 344-3790
Newark *(G-14903)*
Nomac Drilling LLC ....G 330 476-7040
Carrollton *(G-2926)*
Nomac Drilling LLC ....F 724 324-2205
Saint Clairsville *(G-16641)*
Oak Dale Drilling Inc ....G 740 385-5888
Logan *(G-12037)*
Ohio Valley Energy Systems ....G 330 799-2268
Youngstown *(G-20984)*
Oogeep ....G 740 587-0410
Granville *(G-10335)*
Osair Inc ....G 440 974-6500
Mentor *(G-13537)*
P & S Energy Inc ....G 330 652-2525
Mineral Ridge *(G-14170)*
PAC Drilling O & G LLC ....G 330 874-3781
Bolivar *(G-1921)*
Parrot Energy Company ....G 330 637-0151
Cortland *(G-7714)*
Paul A Grim Inc ....G 740 385-9637
Logan *(G-12040)*
Petro Quest Inc ....G 740 593-3800
Athens *(G-844)*
Ponderosa Consulting Services ....G 330 264-2298
Wooster *(G-20637)*
Portage Resources Inc ....G 330 856-2622
Warren *(G-19432)*
Professional Oilfield Services ....G 740 685-5168
Byesville *(G-2392)*
Qes Pressure Control LLC ....E 740 489-5721
Lore City *(G-12139)*
R & J Drilling Company Inc ....G 740 763-3991
Frazeysburg *(G-9941)*
Rj Drilling Company Inc ....G 740 763-3991
Nashport *(G-14570)*
Rockbottom Oil & Gas ....G 740 374-2478
Marietta *(G-12664)*
Sabre Energy Corporation ....G 740 685-8266
Lore City *(G-12140)*
Smith Smith & Deyarman ....G 330 866-5521
Magnolia *(G-12363)*
Stratagraph Ne Inc ....E 740 373-3091
Marietta *(G-12677)*
Summit Drilling Company Inc ....F 800 775-5537
Akron *(G-390)*
Temple Oil & Gas Company ....G 740 452-7878
Crooksville *(G-7820)*
Tiger Oil Inc ....G 614 837-5552
Canal Winchester *(G-2513)*
Timco Inc ....F 740 685-2594
Byesville *(G-2393)*
Top Drilling Corporation ....F 304 477-3333
Marietta *(G-12682)*
Transcontinental Oil & Gas ....G 330 995-0777
Aurora *(G-909)*
U S Fuel Development Co ....G 614 486-0614
Columbus *(G-7553)*
Victor McKenzie Drilling Co ....E 740 453-0834
Zanesville *(G-21187)*
Warren Drilling Co Inc ....C 740 783-2775
Dexter City *(G-8796)*
Warthman Drilling Inc ....G 740 746-9950
Sugar Grove *(G-17840)*
Well Service Group Inc ....F 330 308-0880
New Philadelphia *(G-14808)*

1382 Oil & Gas Field Exploration Svcs

Alliance Petroleum Corporation ....D 330 493-0440
Canton *(G-2569)*
Alteirs Oil Inc ....G 740 347-4335
Corning *(G-7699)*
Antero Resources Corporation ....D 740 760-1000
Marietta *(G-12603)*
Atlas America Inc ....E 330 339-3155
New Philadelphia *(G-14759)*
Bakerwell Inc ....D 614 898-7590
Westerville *(G-19979)*
Bands Company Inc ....G 330 674-0446
Millersburg *(G-14062)*
Beck Energy Corp ....F 330 297-6891
Ravenna *(G-16368)*
Belden & Blake Corporation ....E 330 602-5551
Dover *(G-8808)*
Bergstein Oil & Gas Partnr ....G 513 771-6220
Cincinnati *(G-3390)*
Blue Racer Midstream LLC ....F 740 630-7556
Cambridge *(G-2428)*
Bocor Holdings LLC ....G 330 494-1221
Canton *(G-2594)*
Canton Oil Well Service Inc ....F 330 494-1221
Canton *(G-2613)*
Capital City Energy Group Inc ....G 614 485-3110
Powell *(G-16312)*
Capital Oil & Gas Inc ....G 330 533-1828
Austintown *(G-931)*
Cgas Exploration Inc ....G 614 436-4631
Worthington *(G-20679)*
Chevron Ae Resources LLC ....E 330 654-4343
Deerfield *(G-8607)*
Clarence Tussel Jr ....G 440 576-3415
Jefferson *(G-11228)*
Columbus Oilfield Exploration ....G 614 895-9520
Powell *(G-16317)*
David R Hill Inc ....G 740 685-5168
Byesville *(G-2381)*
Delmar E Hicks ....G 740 354-4333
Portsmouth *(G-16281)*
Dlz Ohio Inc ....C 614 888-0040
Columbus *(G-6871)*
Dome Drilling Co ....G 440 892-9434
Westlake *(G-20109)*
Dome Drilling Co ....G 330 262-5113
Wooster *(G-20585)*
Dome Energicorp ....G 440 892-4900
Westlake *(G-20110)*
Dunn S Tank Service Inc ....G 330 863-2200
Malvern *(G-12388)*
Eastern Reserve Development ....G 614 319-3179
Columbus *(G-6883)*
Elkhead Gas & Oil Co ....G 740 763-3966
Newark *(G-14870)*
Enervest Ltd ....D 330 877-6747
Hartville *(G-10690)*
Everflow Eastern Partners LP ....E 330 533-2692
Canfield *(G-2528)*
Global Oil & Gas Services LLC ....G 330 807-1490
Mc Donald *(G-13200)*
Gonzoil Inc ....G 330 497-5888
Canton *(G-2686)*
H & S Drilling Co Inc ....G 740 828-2411
Frazeysburg *(G-9940)*
Hocking Hills Energy & Well SE ....G 740 385-6690
Logan *(G-12026)*
Husky Marketing and Supply Co ....E 614 210-2300
Dublin *(G-8927)*
John D Oil and Gas Company ....G 440 255-6325
Mentor *(G-13486)*
K Petroleum Inc ....F 614 532-5420
Gahanna *(G-10086)*
Mori Shuji ....G 614 459-1296
Columbus *(G-7196)*
New World Energy Resources ....B 740 344-4087
Newark *(G-14901)*
Ngo Development Corporation ....F 740 622-9560
Coshocton *(G-7743)*
Ohio Valley Energy Systems ....G 330 799-2268
Youngstown *(G-20984)*
Precision Geophysical Inc ....E 330 674-2198
Millersburg *(G-14120)*
Precision Geophysical Inc ....F 740 849-3044
Mount Perry *(G-14457)*
Quantum Energy LLC ....F 440 285-7381
Chardon *(G-3133)*
Range Rsurces - Appalachia LLC ....E 330 866-3301
Dover *(G-8848)*
Reserve Energy Exploration Co ....G 440 543-0770
Chagrin Falls *(G-3072)*
Santmyer Oil Co of Ashland ....G 330 262-6501
Wooster *(G-20648)*
Standard Energy Company ....G 614 885-1901
Columbus *(G-7484)*
Standard Oil Company ....G 419 691-2460
Oregon *(G-15569)*
Summit Well Services Inc ....G 330 223-1074
East Rochester *(G-9091)*
Triad Energy Corporation ....E 740 374-2940
Marietta *(G-12683)*

Employee Codes: A=Over 500 employees, B=251-500
C=101-250, D=51-100, E=20-50, F=10-19, G=3-9
2019 Harris Ohio
Industrial Directory
811

True North Energy LLC E 440 442-0060
Mayfield Heights *(G-13172)*

Utica East Ohio Midstream G 330 223-1766
Kensington *(G-11286)*

Whitacre Enterprises Inc F 740 934-2331
Graysville *(G-10342)*

Wilkes Energy Inc G 330 252-4560
Akron *(G-436)*

Wrp Energy Inc G 330 533-1921
Canfield *(G-2553)*

1389 Oil & Gas Field Svcs, NEC

A W Tipka Oil & Gas Inc G 330 364-4333
Dover *(G-8802)*

A1 Industrial Painting Inc G 330 750-9441
Struthers *(G-17811)*

Acer Contracting LLC G 702 236-5917
Columbus *(G-6537)*

Acuren Inspection Inc D 937 228-9729
Dayton *(G-8006)*

Ajami Holdings Group LLC G 216 396-6089
Richmond Heights *(G-16500)*

Altheirs Oil Inc G 740 347-4335
Corning *(G-7700)*

Altier Brothers Inc F 740 347-4329
Corning *(G-7701)*

Appalachian Oilfield Svcs LLC G 337 216-0066
Sardis *(G-16875)*

Appalachian Well Surveys Inc G 740 255-7652
Cambridge *(G-2425)*

Atec Diversfd Wldg Fabrication G 937 546-4399
Wilmington *(G-20486)*

Atlas Growth Eagle Ford LLC G 330 896-8510
Uniontown *(G-18911)*

Bakerwell Inc E 330 276-2161
Killbuck *(G-11448)*

Barnes Services LLC G 440 319-2088
Maple Heights *(G-12565)*

▲ **Bdi Inc** C 216 642-9100
Cleveland *(G-4796)*

Bearcat Construction Inc G 513 314-0867
Mason *(G-12832)*

Belden & Blake Corporation E 330 602-5551
Dover *(G-8808)*

Bill Hall Well Service G 330 695-4671
Fredericksburg *(G-9943)*

Bishop Well Service Corp G 330 264-2023
Wooster *(G-20571)*

BJ Oilfield Services Ltd G 419 768-2408
Cardington *(G-2870)*

Boyce Ltd G 614 236-8901
Columbus *(G-6690)*

Bradner Oil Company Inc G 419 288-2945
Wayne *(G-19560)*

Brightstar Propane & Fuels G 614 891-8395
Westerville *(G-19981)*

Buckeye Brine LLC F 740 575-4482
Coshocton *(G-7724)*

Byrd Prcurement Specialist Inc G 419 936-0019
Swanton *(G-17908)*

Carper Well Service Inc F 740 374-2567
Marietta *(G-12613)*

Catress LLC G 740 695-0918
Saint Clairsville *(G-16626)*

Cgh-Global Emerg Mngmt Strateg E 800 376-0655
Cincinnati *(G-3242)*

Circleville Oil Co G 740 477-3341
Circleville *(G-4539)*

Clearfield Ohio Holdings Inc D 740 947-5121
Waverly *(G-19542)*

Collier Well Eqp & Sup Inc F 330 345-3968
Wooster *(G-20580)*

Complete Energy Services Inc G 440 577-1070
Pierpont *(G-16064)*

Countryside Pumping Inc G 330 628-0058
Mogadore *(G-14233)*

Crescent Services LLC G 405 603-1200
Cambridge *(G-2433)*

D & D Energy Co G 330 495-1631
Canton *(G-2644)*

Dansco Mfg & Pmpg Unit Svc LP G 330 452-3677
Canton *(G-2648)*

Darin Jordan G 740 819-3525
Nashport *(G-14566)*

Diamond Oilfield Tech LLC F 234 806-4185
Vienna *(G-19198)*

Diesel Fltrtion Spcialists LLC G 740 698-0255
New Marshfield *(G-14743)*

Dover Atwood Corp G 330 809-0630
Massillon *(G-12975)*

Dow Cameron Oil & Gas LLC G 740 452-1568
Zanesville *(G-21129)*

Dp2 Energy LLC G 330 376-5068
Akron *(G-146)*

Echo Drilling Inc G 740 498-8560
Newcomerstown *(G-14973)*

Elite Property Group LLC F 216 356-7469
Elyria *(G-9250)*

Elsaan Energy LLC G 740 294-9399
Walhonding *(G-19306)*

EP Ferris & Associates Inc G 614 299-2999
Columbus *(G-6902)*

Erodetech Inc G 330 725-9181
Medina *(G-13258)*

Everflow Eastern Partners LP G 330 537-3863
Salem *(G-16736)*

Exelon Energy Company F 614 797-4377
Westerville *(G-19991)*

Express Energy Svcs Oper LP E 740 337-4530
Toronto *(G-18608)*

Fishburn Tank Truck Service D 419 253-6031
Marengo *(G-12591)*

Formation Cementing Inc G 740 453-6926
Zanesville *(G-21137)*

Franks Casing G 330 236-4264
Massillon *(G-12982)*

Fts International Inc A 330 754-2375
East Canton *(G-9040)*

Full Circle Oil Field Svcs Inc G 740 371-5422
Marietta *(G-12625)*

Gas Analytical Services Inc G 330 539-4267
Girard *(G-10260)*

Global Oilfield Services LLC G 419 756-8027
Mansfield *(G-12446)*

Granger Pipeline Corporation G 330 454-8095
Canton *(G-2687)*

Greer & Whitehead Cnstr Inc E 513 202-1757
Harrison *(G-10644)*

Hackworth Oil Field Electric G 330 345-6504
Wooster *(G-20603)*

Halliburton Energy Svcs Inc C 740 617-2917
Zanesville *(G-21144)*

Harmon John G 740 934-2032
Graysville *(G-10341)*

Heckmann Wtr Resources Cvr Inc G 740 844-0045
Norwich *(G-15420)*

Hill & Associates Inc G 740 685-5168
Byesville *(G-2386)*

HI Oilfield Services LLC G 740 783-1156
Caldwell *(G-2406)*

Homestead Landscapers G 740 435-8480
Cambridge *(G-2443)*

Ingle-Barr Inc C 740 702-6117
Chillicothe *(G-3195)*

Interden Industries Inc G 419 368-9011
Lakeville *(G-11506)*

J Valtier Gas and Oil Co Inc G 740 342-2839
Malta *(G-12383)*

James Engineering Inc G 740 373-9521
Marietta *(G-12636)*

James L Williams G 740 865-3382
Wingett Run *(G-20536)*

Joseph G Pappas G 330 383-2917
East Liverpool *(G-9061)*

Karlco Oilfield Services Inc F 440 576-3415
Jefferson *(G-11231)*

Kbc Services F 513 693-3743
Loveland *(G-12203)*

Kelchner Inc C 937 704-9890
Springboro *(G-17333)*

Killbuck Oilfield Services G 330 276-6706
Killbuck *(G-11453)*

Ksn Clearing LLC F 304 269-3306
Gallipolis *(G-10170)*

Lakeside Sport Shop Inc G 330 637-2862
Cortland *(G-7711)*

Loken Oil Field Services LLC G 740 749-3495
Marietta *(G-12639)*

Mac Oil Field Service Inc F 330 674-7371
Millersburg *(G-14109)*

Martz Well Service G 330 323-7417
Canton *(G-2744)*

MGM Construction Inc F 440 234-7660
Berea *(G-1617)*

Natural Gas Construction Inc G 330 364-9240
Dover *(G-8844)*

Naw Petroleum Service G 740 464-7988
Chillicothe *(G-3202)*

Northeastern Oilfield Svcs LLC G 330 581-3304
Canton *(G-2767)*

Oaktree Wireline LLC G 330 352-7250
New Philadelphia *(G-14791)*

Ohio Natural Gas Services Inc G 740 796-3305
Zanesville *(G-21165)*

Omega Cementing Co G 330 695-7147
Apple Creek *(G-616)*

OS Power Tong Inc G 330 866-3815
Waynesburg *(G-19564)*

Ottawa Oil Co Inc F 419 425-3301
Findlay *(G-9737)*

P & M Enterprises Group Inc G 330 316-0387
Canton *(G-2777)*

Performance Technologies LLC G 330 875-1216
Louisville *(G-12164)*

Personnel Selection Services F 440 835-3255
Cleveland *(G-5865)*

Petrox Inc F 330 653-5526
Streetsboro *(G-17688)*

Pettigrew Pumping Inc G 330 297-7900
Ravenna *(G-16396)*

Pluggers Inc G 330 383-7692
Niles *(G-15027)*

Predict Inc F 216 642-3223
Cleveland *(G-5914)*

PSC Holdings Inc G 740 454-6253
Zanesville *(G-21174)*

Purple Land Management LLC G 740 238-4259
Saint Clairsville *(G-16647)*

Pyramid Treating Inc G 330 325-2811
Atwater *(G-863)*

R & B Enterprises USA Inc G 330 674-2227
Millersburg *(G-14121)*

R & J Drilling Company Inc G 740 763-3991
Frazeysburg *(G-9941)*

R Anthony Enterprises LLC F 419 341-0961
Marion *(G-12729)*

Ralph Robinson Inc G 740 385-2747
Logan *(G-12042)*

Ream and Haager Laboratory F 330 343-3711
Dover *(G-8849)*

Red Bone Services LLC G 330 364-0022
New Philadelphia *(G-14795)*

Renegade Well Services LLC G 330 488-6055
Canton *(G-2803)*

Ruscilli Real Estate Services F 614 923-6400
Dublin *(G-8976)*

Sanders Fredrick Excvtg Co Inc G 330 297-7980
Ravenna *(G-16401)*

Scassa Asphalt Inc F 330 830-2039
Massillon *(G-13046)*

Schlumberger Limited G 330 878-0794
Strasburg *(G-17652)*

Siler Excavation Services E 513 400-8628
Milford *(G-14041)*

Smith International Inc G 330 497-2999
Uniontown *(G-18931)*

Stallion Oilfield Cnstr LLC E 330 868-2083
Paris *(G-15809)*

Standard Oil Company G 419 691-2460
Oregon *(G-15569)*

Stevens Oil & Gas LLC G 740 374-4542
Marietta *(G-12675)*

▲ **Stingray Pressure Pumping LLC** E 405 648-4177
Belmont *(G-1567)*

Stocker & Sitler Oil Company G 614 888-9588
Columbus *(G-7491)*

Stratagraph Ne Inc E 740 373-3091
Marietta *(G-12677)*

Surveying Cannon Land G 740 342-2835
New Lexington *(G-14725)*

Terra Star Inc E 405 200-1336
Waynesburg *(G-19566)*

Timothy Sinfield E 740 685-3684
Pleasant City *(G-16223)*

Tk Gas Services Inc E 740 826-0303
New Concord *(G-14687)*

Tkn Oilfield Services LLC F 740 516-2583
Marietta *(G-12681)*

Trico Corporation E 216 642-3223
Cleveland *(G-6211)*

Triple J Oilfield Services LLC G 740 483-9030
Hannibal *(G-10625)*

Troo Clean Enviromental LLC G 304 215-4501
Saint Clairsville *(G-16656)*

Tuboscope Pipeline Svcs Inc G 530 695-3569
Lorain *(G-12130)*

U S Weatherford L P C 330 746-2502
Youngstown *(G-21056)*

United Chart Processors Inc G 740 373-5801
Marietta *(G-12686)*

Universal Well Services Inc ....E.... 814 333-2656
Millersburg *(G-14140)*
Vam Usa Llc ....G.... 330 742-3130
Youngstown *(G-21059)*
Vanguard Oil & Gas ....G.... 330 223-1074
East Rochester *(G-9092)*
Varco LP ....E.... 440 277-8696
Lorain *(G-12133)*
W Pole Contracting Inc ....F.... 330 325-7177
Ravenna *(G-16418)*
Washita Valley Enterprises Inc ....F.... 330 510-1568
Louisville *(G-12171)*
Williams John F Oil Field Svcs ....G.... 740 622-7692
Jackson *(G-11201)*
Wolfe Creek Farms ....G.... 740 962-4563
Malta *(G-12384)*
Wrights Well Service ....G.... 740 380-9602
Logan *(G-12046)*
Wyoming Casing Service Inc ....E.... 330 479-8785
Canton *(G-2866)*

14 MINING AND QUARRYING OF NONMETALLIC MINERALS, EXCEPT FUELS

1411 Dimension Stone

C F Poeppelman Inc ....E.... 937 448-2191
Bradford *(G-2010)*
Connolly Construction Co Inc ....G.... 937 644-8831
Marysville *(G-12775)*
▲ **Designer Stone Co** ....G.... 740 492-1300
Port Washington *(G-16268)*
Gerald Christman ....G.... 740 838-2475
Lewisville *(G-11803)*
Glens Bedford Garden Center ....G.... 330 305-1971
North Canton *(G-15087)*
Gregory Stone Co Inc ....G.... 937 275-7455
Dayton *(G-8239)*
Helmart Company Inc ....G.... 513 941-3095
Cincinnati *(G-3806)*
Heritage Marble of Ohio Inc ....E.... 614 436-1464
Columbus *(G-6990)*
Irg Operating LLC ....E.... 440 963-4008
Vermilion *(G-19163)*
Jim Nier Construction Inc ....F.... 740 289-2629
Piketon *(G-16071)*
Marble Cliff Limestone Inc ....G.... 614 488-3030
Hilliard *(G-10838)*
National Lime and Stone Co ....D.... 419 562-0771
Bucyrus *(G-2339)*
North Hill Marble & Granite Co ....F.... 330 253-2179
Akron *(G-301)*
North Shore Stone Inc ....F.... 614 870-7531
Columbus *(G-7228)*
Ohio Beauty Inc ....G.... 330 644-2241
Akron *(G-305)*
S E Johnson Companies Inc ....F.... 419 893-8731
Maumee *(G-13142)*
▲ **Stone Statements Incorporated** ....G.... 513 489-7866
Cincinnati *(G-4384)*
Stoneco Inc ....D.... 419 422-8854
Findlay *(G-9762)*

1422 Crushed & Broken Limestone

Acme Company ....D.... 330 758-2313
Poland *(G-16236)*
Allgeier & Son Inc ....E.... 513 574-3735
Cincinnati *(G-3324)*
Ayers Limestone Quarry Inc ....F.... 740 633-2958
Martins Ferry *(G-12757)*
Bluffton Stone Co ....E.... 419 358-6941
Bluffton *(G-1886)*
Carmeuse Lime Inc ....E.... 419 638-2511
Millersville *(G-14163)*
Carmeuse Lime Inc ....G.... 419 986-2000
Tiffin *(G-18055)*
Carmeuse Lime Inc ....E.... 419 986-5200
Bettsville *(G-1660)*
Chalk Outline Pictures ....G.... 216 291-3944
Cleveland *(G-4908)*
Chesterhill Stone Co ....E.... 740 849-2338
East Fultonham *(G-9045)*
Conag Inc ....E.... 419 394-8870
Saint Marys *(G-16683)*
◆ **Covia Holdings Corporation** ....D.... 440 214-3284
Independence *(G-11123)*
Drummond Dolomite Inc ....F.... 440 942-7000
Mentor *(G-13432)*
Duff Quarry Inc ....E.... 937 686-2811
Huntsville *(G-11085)*
Duff Quarry Inc ....F.... 419 273-2518
Forest *(G-9787)*
Feikert Sand & Gravel Co Inc ....E.... 330 674-0038
Millersburg *(G-14082)*
Gerald Christman ....G.... 740 838-2475
Lewisville *(G-11803)*
Hanson Aggregates East LLC ....E.... 937 587-2671
Peebles *(G-15878)*
Hanson Aggregates East LLC ....D.... 419 483-4390
Castalia *(G-2939)*
Hanson Aggregates East LLC ....E.... 937 442-6009
Winchester *(G-20521)*
Hanson Aggregates LLC ....E.... 419 841-3413
Sylvania *(G-17941)*
Hanson Aggregates Midwest LLC ....F.... 419 882-0123
Sylvania *(G-17942)*
Hanson Aggregates Midwest LLC ....G.... 419 983-2211
Bloomville *(G-1715)*
King Limestone Inc ....F.... 740 638-3942
Cumberland *(G-7824)*
▲ **Lang Stone Company Inc** ....D.... 614 235-4099
Columbus *(G-7114)*
Latham Limestone LLC ....G.... 740 493-2677
Latham *(G-11622)*
Mac Ritchie Materials Inc ....F.... 419 288-2790
West Millgrove *(G-19946)*
Marietta Martin Materials Inc ....F.... 919 781-4550
Brookville *(G-2175)*
Marietta Martin Materials Inc ....E.... 937 766-2351
Cedarville *(G-2944)*
Marietta Martin Materials Inc ....F.... 937 884-5814
Brookville *(G-2176)*
Martin Marietta Materials Inc ....G.... 513 200-2303
Harrison *(G-10657)*
Martin Marietta Materials Inc ....D.... 513 353-1400
North Bend *(G-15052)*
Martin Marietta Materials Inc ....E.... 513 871-7152
Cincinnati *(G-3983)*
Martin Marietta Materials Inc ....E.... 513 701-1140
West Chester *(G-19740)*
Maysville Materials LLC ....G.... 740 849-0474
Mount Perry *(G-14455)*
Melvin Stone Company LLC ....G.... 740 998-5016
Wshngtn CT Hs *(G-20732)*
National Lime and Stone Co ....C.... 419 396-7671
Carey *(G-2884)*
National Lime and Stone Co ....G.... 419 657-6745
Wapakoneta *(G-19347)*
National Lime and Stone Co ....G.... 330 262-1317
Wooster *(G-20631)*
National Lime and Stone Co ....E.... 740 548-4206
Delaware *(G-8708)*
National Lime and Stone Co ....E.... 740 387-3485
Marion *(G-12724)*
National Lime and Stone Co ....E.... 419 228-3434
Lima *(G-11910)*
National Lime and Stone Co ....G.... 419 642-6690
Columbus Grove *(G-7636)*
National Lime and Stone Co ....G.... 216 883-9840
Cleveland *(G-5726)*
National Lime and Stone Co ....E.... 419 423-3400
Findlay *(G-9729)*
National Lime and Stone Co ....D.... 419 562-0771
Bucyrus *(G-2339)*
Ohio Asphaltic Limestone Corp ....F.... 937 364-2191
Hillsboro *(G-10886)*
◆ **Omya Industries Inc** ....D.... 513 387-4600
Blue Ash *(G-1828)*
Oster Sand and Gravel Inc ....G.... 330 833-2649
Massillon *(G-13035)*
Piqua Materials Inc ....E.... 937 773-4824
Piqua *(G-16154)*
Piqua Materials Inc ....D.... 513 771-0820
Cincinnati *(G-4163)*
Quarries LLC ....G.... 513 306-2924
Cincinnati *(G-4231)*
R W Sidley Incorporated ....E.... 440 352-9343
Painesville *(G-15778)*
Ridge Township Stone Quarry ....G.... 419 968-2222
Van Wert *(G-19104)*
Sergeant Stone Inc ....G.... 740 452-7434
Corning *(G-7702)*
Sharon Stone Inc ....G.... 740 732-7100
Caldwell *(G-2411)*
Shelly Materials Inc ....G.... 419 229-2741
Lima *(G-11938)*
Shelly Materials Inc ....G.... 740 246-6315
Toledo *(G-18521)*
Shelly Materials Inc ....G.... 330 274-0802
Mantua *(G-12558)*
Shelly Materials Inc ....G.... 330 722-2190
Medina *(G-13341)*
Shelly Materials Inc ....G.... 330 364-4411
Dover *(G-8853)*
Shelly Materials Inc ....G.... 330 425-7861
Twinsburg *(G-18857)*
Shelly Materials Inc ....G.... 330 673-3646
Kent *(G-11385)*
Shelly Materials Inc ....E.... 740 666-5841
Ostrander *(G-15646)*
Shelly Materials Inc ....G.... 740 745-5965
Newark *(G-14918)*
Shelly Materials Inc ....D.... 740 246-6315
Thornville *(G-18035)*
Sidwell Materials Inc ....C.... 740 849-2394
Zanesville *(G-21180)*
Stoneco Inc ....E.... 419 393-2555
Oakwood *(G-15474)*
Stoneco Inc ....F.... 419 893-7645
Maumee *(G-13149)*
Suever Stone Company ....F.... 419 331-1945
Lima *(G-11945)*
The National Lime and Stone Co ....G.... 330 455-5722
North Canton *(G-15124)*
Wagner Quarries Company ....E.... 419 625-8141
Sandusky *(G-16862)*
White Rock Quarry L P ....A.... 419 855-8388
Clay Center *(G-4570)*
Wysong Stone Co ....F.... 937 962-2559
Lewisburg *(G-11799)*

1423 Crushed & Broken Granite

Bradley Stone Industries LLC ....F.... 440 519-3277
Solon *(G-17118)*
Martin Marietta Materials Inc ....F.... 513 701-1120
Mason *(G-12907)*
Martin Marietta Materials Inc ....E.... 513 701-1140
West Chester *(G-19740)*
Martin Marietta Materials Inc ....E.... 937 766-2351
Cedarville *(G-2945)*
National Lime and Stone Co ....G.... 419 294-3049
Upper Sandusky *(G-18965)*
National Lime and Stone Co ....G.... 330 339-2144
New Philadelphia *(G-14790)*
National Lime and Stone Co ....G.... 216 883-9840
Cleveland *(G-5726)*

1429 Crushed & Broken Stone, NEC

Great Lakes Crushing Ltd ....E.... 440 944-5500
Wickliffe *(G-20211)*
Riverrock Recycl Crushing LLC ....G.... 937 325-2052
Springfield *(G-17485)*
Sands Hill Mining LLC ....F.... 740 384-4211
Hamden *(G-10525)*
Southern Ohio Materials ....G.... 937 386-3200
Seaman *(G-16884)*
Stoneco Inc ....G.... 419 686-3311
Portage *(G-16274)*

1442 Construction Sand & Gravel

Alden Sand & Gravel Co Inc ....F.... 330 928-3249
Cuyahoga Falls *(G-7832)*
Allen Harper ....G.... 740 543-3919
Amsterdam *(G-576)*
Arden J Neer Sr ....F.... 937 585-6733
Bellefontaine *(G-1504)*
Barrett Paving Materials Inc ....C.... 513 271-6200
Middletown *(G-13970)*
Beck Sand & Gravel Inc ....G.... 330 626-3863
Ravenna *(G-16369)*
Beldex Land Company LLC ....G.... 740 783-3575
Dexter City *(G-8793)*
Big Bills Trucking LLC ....G.... 614 850-0626
Hilliard *(G-10813)*
Bonsal American Inc ....E.... 513 398-7300
Cincinnati *(G-3403)*
C F Poeppelman Inc ....E.... 937 448-2191
Bradford *(G-2010)*
Carl E Oeder Sons Sand & Grav ....E.... 513 494-1555
Lebanon *(G-11640)*
Central Allied Enterprises Inc ....G.... 330 879-2132
Navarre *(G-14573)*
Central Ready Mix LLC ....E.... 513 402-5001
Cincinnati *(G-3457)*
Clay LBC Co ....G.... 740 492-5055
Newcomerstown *(G-14972)*
Columbus Equipment Company ....G.... 740 455-4036
Zanesville *(G-21122)*

S I C

Employee Codes: A=Over 500 employees, B=251-500
C=101-250, D=51-100, E=20-50, F=10-19, G=3-9
2019 Harris Ohio
Industrial Directory
813

◆ **Covia Holdings Corporation**.............D....... 440 214-3284
Independence *(G-11123)*
De Milta Sand and Gravel Inc.................F....... 440 942-2015
Willoughby *(G-20307)*
Feikert Sand & Gravel Co Inc.................E....... 330 674-0038
Millersburg *(G-14082)*
Fisher Sand & Gravel Inc.......................G....... 330 745-9239
Norton *(G-15368)*
Fleming Construction Co.......................E....... 740 494-2177
Prospect *(G-16350)*
FML Resin LLC.......................................E....... 440 214-3200
Independence *(G-11129)*
FML Sand LLC..G....... 440 214-3200
Independence *(G-11130)*
FML Terminal Logistics LLC..................G....... 440 214-3200
Independence *(G-11131)*
Foundry Sand Service LLC....................G....... 330 823-6152
Sebring *(G-16886)*
Fouremans Sand & Gravel Inc...............G....... 937 547-1005
Greenville *(G-10368)*
Gravel Doctor of Ohio LLC....................G....... 844 472-8353
Millersport *(G-14159)*
Gravel-Tech..G....... 513 703-3672
Morrow *(G-14410)*
Grimes Sand & Gravel.............................G....... 740 865-3990
New Matamoras *(G-14746)*
Hanson Aggregates East........................G....... 513 353-1100
Cleves *(G-6363)*
Hanson Aggregates East LLC................E....... 740 773-2172
Chillicothe *(G-3191)*
Haueter Construction Co........................G....... 440 834-8220
Newbury *(G-14956)*
Hilltop Basic Resources Inc...................F....... 513 651-5000
Cincinnati *(G-3813)*
Hilltop Basic Resources Inc...................F....... 937 882-6357
Springfield *(G-17418)*
Hilltop Basic Resources Inc...................F....... 937 859-3616
Miamisburg *(G-13676)*
Hilltop Basic Resources Inc...................E....... 513 621-1500
Cincinnati *(G-3814)*
Hocking Valley Concrete Inc..................E....... 740 385-2165
Logan *(G-12027)*
Holmes Redimix Inc................................F....... 330 674-0865
Millersburg *(G-14099)*
Holmes Supply Corp................................G....... 330 279-2634
Holmesville *(G-10980)*
Hugo Sand Company................................G....... 216 570-1212
Kent *(G-11333)*
J P Sand & Gravel Company...................E....... 614 497-0083
Lockbourne *(G-11995)*
James Bunnell Inc....................................F....... 513 353-1100
Cleves *(G-6365)*
James Ryan Soloman...............................G....... 740 659-2304
Glenford *(G-10270)*
Joe McClelland Inc..................................E....... 740 452-3036
Zanesville *(G-21151)*
John L Garber Materials Corp................F....... 419 884-1567
Mansfield *(G-12463)*
Keeney Sand & Stone Inc........................G....... 440 254-4582
Painesville *(G-15752)*
Kenmore Construction Co Inc................E....... 330 832-8888
Massillon *(G-13009)*
Kipps Gravel Company Inc......................F....... 513 732-1024
Batavia *(G-1160)*
Kirby and Sons Inc..................................F....... 419 927-2260
Upper Sandusky *(G-18959)*
L & I Natural Resources Inc....................G....... 513 683-2045
Loveland *(G-12208)*
Lakeside Sand & Gravel Inc....................E....... 330 274-2569
Mantua *(G-12550)*
M J Coates Construction Co....................G....... 937 886-9546
Dayton *(G-8318)*
Marietta Martin Materials Inc..................G....... 937 335-8313
Troy *(G-18686)*
Martin Marietta Materials Inc..................E....... 513 701-1140
West Chester *(G-19740)*
Masons Sand and Gravel Co...................G....... 614 491-3611
Obetz *(G-15510)*
Massillon Materials Inc............................E....... 330 837-4767
Dalton *(G-7947)*
Mecco Inc..E....... 513 422-3651
Middletown *(G-13926)*
Mechanicsburg Sand & Gravel................F....... 937 834-2606
Mechanicsburg *(G-13211)*
Medina Supply Company..........................E....... 330 723-3681
Medina *(G-13298)*
Morrow Gravel Company Inc...................F....... 513 899-2000
Morrow *(G-14413)*
Morrow Gravel Company Inc...................E....... 513 771-0820
Cincinnati *(G-4048)*
National Lime and Stone Co....................G....... 330 339-2144
New Philadelphia *(G-14790)*
National Lime and Stone Co....................E....... 614 497-0083
Lockbourne *(G-11998)*
National Lime and Stone Co....................G....... 216 883-9840
Cleveland *(G-5726)*
National Lime and Stone Co....................C....... 419 396-7671
Carey *(G-2884)*
Nelson Sand & Gravel Inc.......................F....... 440 224-0198
Kingsville *(G-11461)*
Oeder Carl E Sons Sand & Grav.............E....... 513 494-1238
Lebanon *(G-11677)*
Olen Corporation......................................G....... 330 262-6821
Wooster *(G-20635)*
Olen Corporation......................................G....... 740 745-5865
Saint Louisville *(G-16674)*
▼ **Osborne Materials Company**................E....... 440 357-7026
Grand River *(G-10325)*
Oscar Brugmann Sand & Gravel.............F....... 330 274-8224
Mantua *(G-12556)*
Oster Sand and Gravel Inc......................G....... 330 494-5472
Canton *(G-2776)*
Oster Sand and Gravel Inc......................G....... 330 874-3322
Bolivar *(G-1920)*
Oster Sand and Gravel Inc......................G....... 330 833-2649
Massillon *(G-13035)*
Phillips Companies..................................E....... 937 426-5461
Beavercreek Township *(G-1370)*
Phillips Companies..................................E....... 937 431-7987
Vandalia *(G-19143)*
Phillips Ready Mix Co..............................D....... 937 426-5151
Beavercreek Township *(G-1372)*
Phoenix Asphalt Company Inc................G....... 330 339-4935
Magnolia *(G-12362)*
Pioneer Sands LLC...................................E....... 740 599-7773
Howard *(G-10997)*
Prairie Lane Corporation.........................G....... 330 262-3322
Wooster *(G-20639)*
R W Sidley Incorporated.........................E....... 440 564-2221
Newbury *(G-14962)*
Rjw Trucking Company Ltd.....................E....... 740 363-5343
Delaware *(G-8720)*
Robert Perez Carpentry...........................G....... 330 497-0043
Canton *(G-2808)*
Roger Hall...G....... 740 778-2861
South Webster *(G-17299)*
Rupp Construction Inc............................F....... 330 855-2781
Marshallville *(G-12755)*
S & S Aggregates Inc...............................G....... 740 453-0721
Zanesville *(G-21175)*
S & S Aggregates Inc...............................F....... 419 938-5604
Perrysville *(G-16031)*
Sant Sand & Gravel Co............................G....... 740 397-0000
Mount Vernon *(G-14506)*
Shelly and Sands Inc...............................F....... 740 453-0721
Zanesville *(G-21176)*
Shelly and Sands Inc...............................E....... 740 453-0721
Zanesville *(G-21177)*
Shelly Company..F....... 740 687-4420
Lancaster *(G-11606)*
Shelly Company..G....... 740 246-6315
Thornville *(G-18033)*
Shelly Materials Inc.................................F....... 740 775-4567
Chillicothe *(G-3222)*
Shelly Materials Inc.................................G....... 330 673-3646
Kent *(G-11385)*
Shelly Materials Inc.................................D....... 740 246-6315
Thornville *(G-18035)*
Shenango Valley Sand and Grav............G....... 330 758-9100
Youngstown *(G-21030)*
Small Sand & Gravel Inc..........................E....... 740 427-3130
Gambier *(G-10183)*
Smith Concrete Co....................................E....... 740 373-7441
Dover *(G-8854)*
Sober Sand & Gravel Co..........................G....... 330 325-7088
Ravenna *(G-16404)*
Solomons Mines Inc.................................G....... 330 337-0123
Salem *(G-16775)*
Stafford Gravel Inc...................................G....... 419 298-2440
Edgerton *(G-9180)*
Stansley Mineral Resources Inc..............E....... 419 843-2813
Sylvania *(G-17962)*
Stocker Concrete Company.....................F....... 740 254-4626
Gnadenhutten *(G-10283)*
Stocker Sand & Gravel Co.......................E....... 740 254-4635
Gnadenhutten *(G-10284)*
Streamside Materials Llc..........................G....... 419 423-1290
Findlay *(G-9763)*
▲ **Technisand Inc**.......................................G....... 440 285-3132
Chardon *(G-3138)*
Tiger Sand & Gravel LLC.........................F....... 330 833-6325
Massillon *(G-13052)*
Tipp Stone Inc...G....... 937 890-4051
Dayton *(G-8559)*
Tri County Concrete Inc...........................E....... 330 425-4464
Twinsburg *(G-18866)*
Turkeyfoot Hill Sand & Gravel................G....... 330 899-1997
Akron *(G-415)*
Twinsburg Development Corp.................G....... 440 357-5562
Cleveland *(G-6224)*
W&W Rock Sand and Gravel...................G....... 513 266-3708
Williamsburg *(G-20256)*
Ward Construction Co.............................F....... 419 943-2450
Leipsic *(G-11739)*
Watson Gravel Inc....................................E....... 513 422-3781
Middletown *(G-13964)*
Watson Gravel Inc....................................D....... 513 863-0070
Hamilton *(G-10621)*
Wayne Concrete Company.......................F....... 937 545-9919
Medway *(G-13367)*
Weber Sand & Gravel Inc........................F....... 419 298-2388
Edgerton *(G-9182)*
Weber Sand & Gravel Inc........................G....... 419 636-7920
Bryan *(G-2312)*
Welch Holdings Inc...................................E....... 513 353-3220
Cincinnati *(G-4497)*
▼ **World Development & Conslt LLC**....G....... 614 805-4450
Westerville *(G-20083)*
Wysong Gravel Co Inc..............................F....... 937 456-4539
West Alexandria *(G-19626)*
Wysong Gravel Co Inc..............................G....... 937 452-1523
Camden *(G-2467)*
Wysong Gravel Co Inc..............................G....... 937 839-5497
West Alexandria *(G-19627)*
X L Sand and Gravel Co...........................F....... 330 426-9876
Negley *(G-14592)*
Young Sand & Gravel Co Inc....................F....... 419 994-3040
Loudonville *(G-12150)*

1446 Industrial Sand

▼ **C E D Process Minerals Inc**....................F....... 330 666-5500
Akron *(G-101)*
◆ **Covia Holdings Corporation**..................D....... 440 214-3284
Independence *(G-11123)*
Fairmount Minerals LLC..........................C....... 269 926-9450
Independence *(G-11126)*
Farsight Management Inc.........................G....... 330 602-8338
Dover *(G-8826)*
Jim Nier Construction Inc........................F....... 740 289-2629
Piketon *(G-16071)*
Kistler Instrument Corp............................G....... 937 268-5920
Dayton *(G-8298)*
Parry Co...G....... 740 884-4893
Chillicothe *(G-3206)*
Patriarch Trucking LLC.............................G....... 877 875-5402
Flushing *(G-9784)*
Pioneer Sands LLC....................................E....... 740 659-2241
Glenford *(G-10271)*
Pioneer Sands LLC....................................E....... 740 599-7773
Howard *(G-10997)*

1459 Clay, Ceramic & Refractory Minerals, NEC

American Colloid Company......................G....... 419 445-9085
Archbold *(G-635)*
Blue Jay Entps of Tscrwas Cnty..............G....... 330 874-2048
Bolivar *(G-1907)*
◆ **Covia Holdings Corporation**..................D....... 440 214-3284
Independence *(G-11123)*
E J Bognar Inc..F....... 330 426-9292
East Palestine *(G-9076)*
L & M Mineral Co.......................................G....... 330 852-3696
Sugarcreek *(G-17851)*

1479 Chemical & Fertilizer Mining

Cargill Incorporated...................................C....... 216 651-7200
Cleveland *(G-4877)*
◆ **Everris NA Inc**...E....... 614 726-7100
Dublin *(G-8914)*
Glf International Inc...................................F....... 216 621-6901
Cleveland *(G-5324)*
Morton International LLC..........................G....... 513 941-1578
Cincinnati *(G-4049)*

1481 Nonmetallic Minerals Svcs, Except Fuels

Barr Engineering Incorporated................F....... 614 892-0162
Columbus *(G-6649)*

Barr Engineering Incorporated....E.... 614 714-0299
Columbus (G-6650)
Fgb International LLC....G.... 440 359-0000
Cleveland (G-5235)
Longyear Company....E.... 740 373-2190
Marietta (G-12640)
M G Q Inc....E.... 419 992-4236
Tiffin (G-18067)
Masters Group Inc....G.... 440 893-1900
Chagrin Falls (G-3059)
Robin Industries Inc....E.... 330 893-3501
Berlin (G-1644)
▲ **Sandy Creek Mining Co Inc**....G.... 419 435-5891
Fostoria (G-9857)
Stoepfel Drilling Co....G.... 419 532-3307
Ottawa (G-15667)
Tresslers Plumbing LLC....G.... 419 784-2142
Defiance (G-8646)

1499 Miscellaneous Nonmetallic Mining

◆ **Covia Holdings Corporation**....D.... 440 214-3284
Independence (G-11123)
Graftech Holdings Inc....B.... 216 676-2000
Independence (G-11134)
Kellstone....G.... 419 621-8140
Sandusky (G-16820)
Mar-Zane Inc....G.... 419 529-2086
Ontario (G-15543)
Massillon Metaphysics....G.... 330 837-1653
Massillon (G-13021)
National Lime and Stone Co....G.... 330 339-2144
New Philadelphia (G-14790)
National Lime and Stone Co....G.... 216 883-9840
Cleveland (G-5726)
Scots....G.... 215 370-9498
Shreve (G-17009)
Shelly Liquid Division....G.... 216 781-9264
Cleveland (G-6051)

20 FOOD AND KINDRED PRODUCTS

2011 Meat Packing Plants

Acme Steak & Seafood Inc....F.... 330 270-8000
Youngstown (G-20836)
American Foods Group LLC....E.... 513 733-8898
Cincinnati (G-3332)
Atlantic Veal & Lamb LLC....G.... 330 435-6400
Creston (G-7803)
Baltic Country Meats....G.... 330 897-7025
Baltic (G-1023)
Bob Evans Farms Inc....D.... 937 372-4493
Xenia (G-20758)
Bob Evans Farms Inc....F.... 740 245-5305
Bidwell (G-1664)
Bob Evans Farms Inc....B.... 614 491-2225
New Albany (G-14609)
C J Kraft Enterprises Inc....E.... 740 653-9606
Lancaster (G-11551)
Canaan Country Meats....G.... 330 435-4778
Creston (G-7804)
Carl Rittberger Sr Inc....E.... 740 452-2767
Zanesville (G-21116)
Case Farms of Ohio Inc....C.... 330 359-7141
Winesburg (G-20530)
Caven and Sons Meat Packing Co....F.... 937 368-3841
Conover (G-7662)
D & H Meats Inc....G.... 419 387-7767
Vanlue (G-19153)
Dalton Veal....G.... 330 828-8337
Dalton (G-7939)
Dee-Jays Custom Butchering....F.... 740 694-7492
Fredericktown (G-9965)
Duma Deer Processing LLC....G.... 330 805-3429
Mogadore (G-14234)
Empire Packing Company LP....A.... 901 948-4788
Mason (G-12865)
Fresh Mark Inc....A.... 330 332-8508
Salem (G-16741)
◆ **Fresh Mark Inc**....B.... 330 834-3669
Massillon (G-12983)
Gortons Inc....E.... 216 362-1050
Cleveland (G-5333)
Hartville Locker Service Inc....G.... 330 877-9547
Hartville (G-10693)
Heffelfingers Meats Inc....E.... 419 368-7131
Jeromesville (G-11250)
Horst Packing Inc....G.... 330 482-2997
Columbiana (G-6469)
Industrial Packaging Products....G.... 440 734-2663
Cleveland (G-5454)
J M Meat Processing....G.... 740 259-3030
Mc Dermott (G-13193)
Jacoby Packing Co....G.... 419 924-2684
West Unity (G-19970)
John Stehlin & Sons Co Inc....F.... 513 385-6164
Cincinnati (G-3881)
Jones Processing....G.... 330 772-2193
Hartford (G-10681)
Karn Meats Inc....E.... 614 252-3712
Columbus (G-7083)
King Kold Inc....E.... 937 836-2731
Englewood (G-9366)
Links Country Meats....G.... 419 683-2195
Crestline (G-7796)
Mahan Packing Co Inc....E.... 330 889-2454
Bristolville (G-2083)
Mannings Packing Co....G.... 937 446-3278
Sardinia (G-16870)
Marshallville Packing Co Inc....E.... 330 855-2871
Marshallville (G-12753)
Mc Connells Market....G.... 740 765-4300
Richmond (G-16496)
New Riegel Cafe Inc....E.... 419 595-2255
New Riegel (G-14816)
Northside Meat Co Inc....G.... 513 681-4111
Cincinnati (G-4088)
Ohio Farms Packing Co Ltd....G.... 330 435-6400
Creston (G-7808)
Ohio Packing Company....D.... 614 445-0627
Columbus (G-7254)
Oiler Processing....G.... 740 892-2640
Utica (G-19026)
Patrick M Davidson....G.... 513 897-2971
Waynesville (G-19571)
Pine Ridge Processing....G.... 740 749-3166
Fleming (G-9780)
Presslers Meats Inc....F.... 330 644-5636
Akron (G-329)
R&C Packing & Custom Butcher....G.... 740 245-9440
Bidwell (G-1668)
Robert Winner Sons Inc....G.... 937 548-7513
Greenville (G-10393)
Robert Winner Sons Inc....E.... 419 582-4321
Yorkshire (G-20826)
Rxpert Consultants LLC....G.... 614 579-9384
Columbus (G-7409)
Shaker Valley Foods Inc....E.... 216 961-8600
Cleveland (G-6046)
Shirer Brothers Meats....G.... 740 796-3214
Adamsville (G-10)
Signature Beef LLC....G.... 740 468-3579
Pleasantville (G-16230)
◆ **Smithfield Packaged Meats Corp**....C.... 513 782-3800
Cincinnati (G-4348)
Smithfield Packaged Meats Corp....B.... 513 782-3805
Cincinnati (G-4349)
Smokin TS Smokehouse....G.... 440 577-1117
Jefferson (G-11238)
Strasburg Provision Inc....E.... 330 878-1059
Strasburg (G-17653)
Sugar Creek Packing Co....B.... 937 268-6601
Dayton (G-8528)
Sugar Creek Packing Co....C.... 513 874-4422
West Chester (G-19800)
Sugar Creek Packing Co....G.... 513 874-4422
West Chester (G-19801)
Tempac LLC....G.... 513 505-9700
West Chester (G-19806)
Tri-State Beef Co Inc....E.... 513 579-1722
Cincinnati (G-4433)
Troyers Trail Bologna Inc....E.... 330 893-2414
Dundee (G-9029)
Trumbull Locker Plant Inc....G.... 440 474-4631
Rock Creek (G-16534)
V H Cooper & Co Inc....E.... 419 678-4853
Saint Henry (G-16670)
V H Cooper & Co Inc....B.... 419 678-4853
Saint Henry (G-16669)
V H Cooper & Co Inc....C.... 419 375-4116
Fort Recovery (G-9829)
Werling and Sons Inc....F.... 937 338-3281
Burkettsville (G-2356)
Winesburg Meats Inc....G.... 330 359-5092
Winesburg (G-20535)
Youngs Locker Service Inc....F.... 740 599-6833
Danville (G-7967)

2013 Sausages & Meat Prdts

A To Z Portion Ctrl Meats Inc....E.... 419 358-2926
Bluffton (G-1883)
▲ **Advancepierre Foods Inc**....B.... 513 874-8741
West Chester (G-19826)
Advancepierre Foods Inc....G.... 513 874-8741
West Chester (G-19827)
Advancepierre Foods Inc....G.... 580 616-4403
Amherst (G-552)
Advancperre Foods Holdings Inc....E.... 800 969-2747
West Chester (G-19828)
American Foods Group LLC....E.... 513 733-8898
Cincinnati (G-3332)
Amish Wedding Foods Inc....E.... 330 674-9199
Millersburg (G-14060)
Brentmoor Hams LLC....G.... 513 677-0813
Loveland (G-12181)
Brinkman Turkey Farms Inc....F.... 419 365-5127
Findlay (G-9662)
Carl Rittberger Sr Inc....E.... 740 452-2767
Zanesville (G-21116)
Caven and Sons Meat Packing Co....F.... 937 368-3841
Conover (G-7662)
D D D Hams Inc....G.... 440 487-9572
Solon (G-17130)
Dirussos Sausage Inc....E.... 330 744-1208
Youngstown (G-20892)
Dumas Meats Inc....G.... 330 628-3438
Mogadore (G-14235)
Edelmann Provision Company....D.... 513 881-5800
Harrison (G-10639)
Fink Meat Company Inc....G.... 937 390-2750
Springfield (G-17402)
Frank Brunckhorst Company LLC....G.... 614 662-5300
Groveport (G-10491)
◆ **Fresh Mark Inc**....B.... 330 834-3669
Massillon (G-12983)
Fresh Mark Inc....B.... 330 832-7491
Massillon (G-12984)
Fresh Mark Inc....A.... 330 332-8508
Salem (G-16741)
Hillshire Brands Company....G.... 330 758-8885
Youngstown (G-20931)
Hoffman Meat Processing....G.... 419 864-3994
Cardington (G-2873)
Honeybaked Ham Company....E.... 513 583-9700
Cincinnati (G-3824)
John Krusinski....F.... 216 441-0100
Cleveland (G-5502)
John Stehlin & Sons Co Inc....F.... 513 385-6164
Cincinnati (G-3881)
Johns Jerky & Snack Meats LLC....G.... 937 207-7008
South Charleston (G-17273)
Jtm Provisions Company Inc....B.... 513 367-4900
Harrison (G-10653)
Karn Meats Inc....E.... 614 252-3712
Columbus (G-7083)
Katies Snack Foods LLC....G.... 614 440-0780
Hilliard (G-10836)
Keith Grimm....G.... 419 899-2725
Sherwood (G-16991)
Kenosha Beef International Ltd....C.... 614 771-1330
Columbus (G-7087)
Keystone Foods LLC....C.... 419 257-2341
North Baltimore (G-15044)
King Kold Inc....E.... 937 836-2731
Englewood (G-9366)
Kings Command Foods LLC....D.... 937 526-3553
Versailles (G-19184)
Kraft Heinz Foods Company....B.... 740 622-0523
Coshocton (G-7738)
Lee Williams Meats Inc....E.... 419 729-3893
Toledo (G-18379)
Lous Sausage Ltd....F.... 216 752-5060
Cleveland (G-5585)
Mama Mias Foods Inc....G.... 216 281-2188
Cleveland (G-5610)
Marshallville Packing Co Inc....E.... 330 855-2871
Marshallville (G-12753)
Martin-Brower Company LLC....B.... 513 773-2301
West Chester (G-19741)
Medina Foods Inc....E.... 330 725-1390
Litchfield (G-11985)
Old Country Sausage Kitchen....G.... 216 662-5988
Cleveland (G-5809)
Patrick M Davidson....G.... 513 897-2971
Waynesville (G-19571)
Peggys Pride....G.... 614 464-2511
Columbus (G-7307)
Perfettes Sausage LLC....G.... 330 792-0775
Youngstown (G-20998)
Pettisville Meats Inc....F.... 419 445-0921
Pettisville (G-16036)

S I C

20 FOOD AND KINDRED PRODUCTS SIC SECTION

Pierre Holding Corp.....G..... 513 874-8741
West Chester *(G-19886)*
Queen City Sausage & Provision.....E..... 513 541-5581
Cincinnati *(G-4241)*
Raddells Sausage.....G..... 216 486-1944
Cleveland *(G-5954)*
Rays Sausage Inc.....G..... 216 921-8782
Cleveland *(G-5963)*
Robert Winner Sons Inc.....E..... 419 582-4321
Yorkshire *(G-20826)*
Sara Lee Foods.....G..... 513 204-4941
Mason *(G-12935)*
Sausage Shoppe.....G..... 216 351-5213
Brunswick *(G-2237)*
Simply Unique Snacks LLC.....G..... 513 223-7736
Cincinnati *(G-4339)*
Steven Yant.....G..... 937 596-0497
Jackson Center *(G-11216)*
Strasburg Provision Inc.....E..... 330 878-1059
Strasburg *(G-17653)*
◆ **Sugar Creek Packing Co**.....B..... 740 335-3586
Wshngtn CT Hs *(G-20745)*
Sugar Creek Packing Co.....B..... 937 268-6601
Dayton *(G-8528)*
Sugar Creek Packing Co.....C..... 513 874-4422
West Chester *(G-19800)*
Sugar Creek Packing Co.....G..... 513 874-4422
West Chester *(G-19801)*
Sunrise Foods Inc.....E..... 614 276-2880
Columbus *(G-7500)*
Tri-State Beef Co Inc.....E..... 513 579-1722
Cincinnati *(G-4433)*
◆ **White Castle System Inc**.....B..... 614 228-5781
Columbus *(G-7603)*
▲ **Wild Joes Inc**.....G..... 513 681-9200
Cincinnati *(G-4508)*
Williams Pork Co Op.....G..... 419 682-9022
Stryker *(G-17836)*
Youngs Locker Service Inc.....F..... 740 599-6833
Danville *(G-7967)*

2015 Poultry Slaughtering, Dressing & Processing

▲ **Advancepierre Foods Inc**.....B..... 513 874-8741
West Chester *(G-19826)*
▼ **Ballas Egg Products Corp**.....D..... 614 453-0386
Zanesville *(G-21102)*
BE Products Inc.....D..... 740 453-0386
Zanesville *(G-21105)*
Briarwood Valley Farms.....G..... 419 736-2298
Sullivan *(G-17880)*
Brinkman Turkey Farms Inc.....F..... 419 365-5127
Findlay *(G-9662)*
Cal-Maine Foods Inc.....E..... 937 337-9576
Rossburg *(G-16581)*
Cal-Maine Foods Inc.....E..... 937 968-4874
Union City *(G-18901)*
Case Farms of Ohio Inc.....C..... 330 359-7141
Winesburg *(G-20530)*
Case Farms of Ohio Inc.....F..... 330 878-7118
Strasburg *(G-17647)*
Cooper Foods.....E..... 419 232-2440
Van Wert *(G-19084)*
Cooper Hatchery Inc.....C..... 419 238-4869
Van Wert *(G-19085)*
Cooper Hatchery Inc.....C..... 419 594-3325
Oakwood *(G-15469)*
Fort Recovery Equity Inc.....C..... 419 375-4119
Fort Recovery *(G-9817)*
Fort Recovery Equity Exchange.....E..... 937 338-8901
Rossburg *(G-16582)*
Freak-N-Fries Inc.....G..... 440 453-1877
Lagrange *(G-11480)*
Gerber Farm Division Inc.....G..... 800 362-7381
Kidron *(G-11446)*
Hemmelgarn & Sons Inc.....D..... 419 678-2351
Coldwater *(G-6412)*
Just Natural Provision Company.....G..... 216 431-7922
Cleveland *(G-5510)*
Kings Command Foods LLC.....D..... 937 526-3553
Versailles *(G-19184)*
Koch Meat Co Inc.....B..... 513 874-3500
Fairfield *(G-9519)*
Martin-Brower Company LLC.....B..... 513 773-2301
West Chester *(G-19741)*
Nature Pure LLC.....F..... 937 358-2364
West Mansfield *(G-19945)*
Nutrifresh Eggs.....G..... 567 224-7676
Willard *(G-20243)*
▲ **Ohio Fresh Eggs LLC**.....C..... 740 893-7200
Croton *(G-7822)*
Ohio Fresh Eggs LLC.....E..... 937 354-2233
Mount Victory *(G-14520)*
Pf Management Inc.....G..... 513 874-8741
West Chester *(G-19885)*
Pierre Holding Corp.....G..... 513 874-8741
West Chester *(G-19886)*
Rcf Kitchens Indiana LLC.....C..... 765 478-6600
Beavercreek *(G-1361)*
Roots Poultry Inc.....F..... 419 332-0041
Fremont *(G-10048)*
V H Cooper & Co Inc.....B..... 419 678-4853
Saint Henry *(G-16669)*
V H Cooper & Co Inc.....C..... 419 375-4116
Fort Recovery *(G-9829)*
▲ **Weaver Bros Inc**.....D..... 937 526-3907
Versailles *(G-19193)*
Whitewater Processing Co.....D..... 513 367-4133
Harrison *(G-10680)*

2021 Butter

Black Radish Creamery Ltd.....G..... 614 323-6016
New Albany *(G-14608)*
California Creamery Operators.....G..... 440 264-5351
Solon *(G-17122)*
Dairy Farmers America Inc.....E..... 330 670-7800
Medina *(G-13249)*
Fairmont Creamery LLC.....G..... 216 357-2560
Cleveland *(G-5216)*
Minerva Dairy Inc.....D..... 330 868-4196
Minerva *(G-14193)*
Turkeyfoot Creek Creamery.....G..... 419 335-0224
Wauseon *(G-19535)*

2022 Cheese

▲ **9444 Ohio Holding Co**.....E..... 330 359-6291
Winesburg *(G-20529)*
A & M Cheese Co.....D..... 419 476-8369
Toledo *(G-18152)*
Amish Wedding Foods Inc.....E..... 330 674-9199
Millersburg *(G-14060)*
▲ **Biery Cheese Co**.....C..... 330 875-3381
Louisville *(G-12152)*
Brewster Cheese Company.....C..... 330 767-3492
Brewster *(G-2067)*
Bunker Hill Cheese Co Inc.....D..... 330 893-2131
Millersburg *(G-14073)*
Christina A Kraft PHD.....G..... 330 375-7474
Akron *(G-115)*
Dairy Farmers America Inc.....E..... 330 670-7800
Medina *(G-13249)*
Es Steiner Dairy LLC.....F..... 330 897-5555
Baltic *(G-1027)*
◆ **Great Lakes Cheese Co Inc**.....B..... 440 834-2500
Hiram *(G-10910)*
Guggisberg Cheese Inc.....E..... 330 893-2550
Millersburg *(G-14086)*
▲ **Hans Rothenbuhler & Son Inc**.....E..... 440 632-6000
Middlefield *(G-13802)*
▲ **Holmes Cheese Co**.....E..... 330 674-6451
Millersburg *(G-14096)*
Inter American Products Inc.....E..... 800 645-2233
Cincinnati *(G-3853)*
Kathys Krafts and Kollectibles.....G..... 423 787-3709
Medina *(G-13284)*
Kraft House No 5.....G..... 614 396-9091
Powell *(G-16325)*
Kraft of Writing.....G..... 614 620-2476
Columbus *(G-7100)*
▲ **Lake Erie Frozen Foods Mfg Co**.....E..... 419 289-9204
Ashland *(G-720)*
Lakeview Farms LLC.....E..... 419 695-9925
Delphos *(G-8749)*
Lakeview Farms LLC.....C..... 419 695-9925
Delphos *(G-8750)*
Land OLakes Inc.....C..... 330 678-1578
Kent *(G-11346)*
▲ **Miceli Dairy Products Co**.....D..... 216 791-6222
Cleveland *(G-5666)*
Middlefield Cheese House Inc.....E..... 440 632-5228
Middlefield *(G-13822)*
Middlefield Mix Inc.....F..... 440 632-0157
Middlefield *(G-13824)*
Middlfeld Original Cheese Coop.....E..... 440 632-5567
Middlefield *(G-13828)*
Minerva Dairy Inc.....D..... 330 868-4196
Minerva *(G-14193)*
Oakvale Farm Cheese Inc.....G..... 740 857-1230
London *(G-12067)*
Pearl Valley Cheese Inc.....E..... 740 545-6002
Fresno *(G-10068)*
Schindlers Broad Run Chese Hse.....F..... 330 343-4108
Dover *(G-8850)*
Tri State Dairy LLC.....G..... 419 542-8788
Hicksville *(G-10784)*
Tri State Dairy LLC.....F..... 330 897-5555
Baltic *(G-1034)*
Wood Kraft.....G..... 440 487-4634
Garrettsville *(G-10205)*

2023 Milk, Condensed & Evaporated

Aggregate Tersornance LLC.....G..... 330 418-4751
Canton *(G-2560)*
Alifet USA Inc.....G..... 513 793-8033
Blue Ash *(G-1726)*
Eagle Family Foods Group LLC.....E..... 330 382-3725
Richfield *(G-16468)*
▲ **Freedom Health LLC**.....E..... 330 562-0888
Aurora *(G-880)*
▲ **Hans Rothenbuhler & Son Inc**.....E..... 440 632-6000
Middlefield *(G-13802)*
Healthy Living.....G..... 937 962-4705
Lewisburg *(G-11792)*
▲ **Infinit Nutrition LLC**.....F..... 513 791-3500
Blue Ash *(G-1793)*
◆ **Ingredia Inc**.....E..... 419 738-4060
Wapakoneta *(G-19334)*
Innovated Health LLC.....G..... 330 858-0651
Cuyahoga Falls *(G-7881)*
Instantwhip-Columbus Inc.....E..... 614 871-9447
Grove City *(G-10435)*
▲ **Instantwhip-Dayton Inc**.....F..... 937 235-5930
Dayton *(G-8269)*
Instantwhip-Dayton Inc.....G..... 937 435-4371
Dayton *(G-8270)*
▼ **J M Smucker Company**.....A..... 330 682-3000
Orrville *(G-15596)*
L & F Lauch LLC.....G..... 513 732-5805
Batavia *(G-1161)*
Lifestyle Nutraceuticals Ltd.....F..... 513 376-7218
Cincinnati *(G-3941)*
▼ **Milnot Company**.....G..... 888 656-3245
Gahanna *(G-10091)*
Minerva Dairy Inc.....D..... 330 868-4196
Minerva *(G-14193)*
Moo Technologies Inc.....G..... 513 732-5805
Batavia *(G-1169)*
▲ **Muscle Feast LLC**.....F..... 740 877-8808
Nashport *(G-14568)*
Nestle Usa Inc.....C..... 216 524-7738
Cleveland *(G-5742)*
Nestle Usa Inc.....C..... 216 524-3397
Cleveland *(G-5743)*
Nestle Usa Inc.....C..... 440 349-5757
Solon *(G-17205)*
Nestle Usa Inc.....D..... 216 861-8350
Cleveland *(G-5744)*
Nu Pet Company.....C..... 330 682-3000
Orrville *(G-15606)*
Rich Products Corporation.....C..... 614 771-1117
Hilliard *(G-10858)*
▲ **Stolle Milk Biologics Inc**.....C..... 513 489-7997
West Chester *(G-19903)*
Tmarzetti Company.....C..... 614 279-8673
Columbus *(G-7532)*
Toomey Inc.....G..... 513 831-4771
Milford *(G-14044)*
Wileys Finest LLC.....C..... 740 622-1072
Coshocton *(G-7759)*
▲ **Yoders Cider Barn**.....F..... 740 668-4961
Gambier *(G-10186)*

2024 Ice Cream

Archies Too.....D..... 419 427-2663
Findlay *(G-9651)*
Awesome Yogurt LLC.....G..... 937 643-0879
Dayton *(G-8047)*
B M DS Fish N More LLC.....F..... 419 238-2722
Van Wert *(G-19078)*
Bacconis Lickety Split.....G..... 330 924-0418
Cortland *(G-7703)*
Better Than Sex Ice Cream LLC.....G..... 614 444-5505
Columbus *(G-6664)*
Bojos Cream.....G..... 330 270-3332
Austintown *(G-930)*
Broughton Foods Company.....C..... 740 373-4121
Marietta *(G-12610)*
Country Caterers Inc.....G..... 740 389-1013
Marion *(G-12700)*

20 FOOD AND KINDRED PRODUCTS

Country Maid Ice Cream Inc................G...... 330 659-6830
  Richfield (G-16466)
Country Parlour Ice Cream Co..............F...... 440 237-4040
  Cleveland (G-5032)
CTB Consulting LLC.........................F...... 216 712-7764
  Rocky River (G-16545)
Dairy Shed.................................... 937 848-3504
  Bellbrook (G-1492)
Danone Us LLC............................B...... 513 229-0092
  Mason (G-12854)
Danone Us LLC............................B...... 419 628-3861
  Minster (G-14211)
Dietsch Brothers Incorporated..........D...... 419 422-4474
  Findlay (G-9677)
Double Dippin Inc.........................G...... 937 847-2572
  Miamisburg (G-13660)
Fritzie Freeze Inc..........................G...... 419 727-0818
  Toledo (G-18298)
Gibson Bros Inc............................E...... 440 774-2401
  Oberlin (G-15496)
Graeters Manufacturing Co.............D...... 513 721-3323
  Cincinnati (G-3774)
Home City Ice Company................F...... 419 562-4953
  Delaware (G-8694)
Honeybaked Ham Company............E...... 513 583-9700
  Cincinnati (G-3824)
ICEE USA......................................G...... 513 771-0630
  West Chester (G-19866)
International Brand Services...........F...... 513 376-8209
  Cincinnati (G-3856)
Jim H Niemeyer............................F...... 419 422-2465
  Findlay (G-9709)
Johnsons Real Ice Cream Co...........E...... 614 231-0014
  Columbus (G-7074)
Joshua Leigh Enterprises Inc...........G...... 330 244-9200
  Canton (G-2720)
Louis Trauth Dairy LLC....................B...... 859 431-7553
  West Chester (G-19873)
▲ Malleys Candies..........................C...... 216 362-8700
  Lakewood (G-11528)
Mitchell Bros Ice Cream Inc.............F...... 216 861-2799
  Cleveland (G-5697)
▲ Pierres French Ice Cream Inc.........E...... 216 431-2555
  Cleveland (G-5876)
R D Lucky LLC...............................F...... 614 570-8005
  Columbus (G-7373)
Reiter Dairy of Akron Inc................E...... 419 424-5060
  Findlay (G-9746)
Robert E McGrath Inc....................E...... 440 572-7747
  Strongsville (G-17783)
◆ Royal Ice Cream Co....................D...... 216 432-1144
  Cleveland (G-6012)
Schwans Home Service Inc............F...... 419 222-9977
  Lima (G-11936)
Smithfoods Inc..............................G...... 330 683-8710
  Orrville (G-15620)
Springdale Ice Cream Beverage......E...... 513 699-4984
  Cincinnati (G-4364)
St Clairsville Dairy Queen................G...... 740 635-1800
  Saint Clairsville (G-16652)
Stella Lou LLC...............................F...... 937 935-9536
  Powell (G-16336)
Superior Tasting Products Inc..........E...... 614 442-0622
  Columbus (G-7502)
Tmarzetti Company........................C...... 614 279-8673
  Columbus (G-7532)
Toft Dairy Inc...............................D...... 419 625-4376
  Sandusky (G-16856)
United Dairy Inc............................C...... 740 633-1451
  Martins Ferry (G-12763)
United Dairy Farmers Inc................C...... 513 396-8700
  Cincinnati (G-4447)
Weldon Ice Cream Company...........G...... 740 467-2400
  Millersport (G-14162)
Welsh Farms LLC..........................G...... 513 723-4487
  Cincinnati (G-4498)
Whits Frozen Custard....................G...... 740 965-1427
  Sunbury (G-17902)
Wil-Mark Froyo LLC.......................G...... 330 421-6043
  Rittman (G-16530)
Yagoot... 513 791-6600
  Cincinnati (G-4531)
Youngs Jersey Dairy Inc..................B...... 937 325-0629
  Yellow Springs (G-20823)
ZS Cream & Bean.........................G...... 440 652-6369
  Hinckley (G-10908)

2026 Milk

American Confections Co LLC...........G...... 614 888-8838
  Coventry Township (G-7765)

Auburn Dairy Products Inc..............E...... 614 488-2536
  Columbus (G-6628)
Borden Dairy Co Cincinnati LLC.......C...... 513 948-8811
  Cincinnati (G-3404)
Borden Dairy Company Ohio LLC....C...... 216 671-2300
  Cleveland (G-4832)
Broughton Foods Company............G...... 740 373-4121
  Marietta (G-12610)
Broughton Foods Company............F...... 800 598-7545
  South Point (G-17281)
Consun Food Industries Inc............D...... 440 322-6301
  Elyria (G-9238)
Dairy Farmers America Inc.............E...... 330 670-7800
  Medina (G-13249)
Daisy Brand LLC............................F...... 330 202-4376
  Wooster (G-20582)
Dallas Instantwhip Inc....................F...... 614 488-2536
  Columbus (G-6847)
Dean Foods Co.............................G...... 419 473-9621
  Toledo (G-18255)
Instantwhip Connecticut Inc...........F...... 614 488-2536
  Columbus (G-7031)
Instantwhip Detroit Inc..................F...... 614 488-2536
  Columbus (G-7032)
Instantwhip Detroit Inc..................F...... 800 544-9447
  Columbus (G-7033)
Instantwhip Foods Inc...................F...... 614 488-2536
  Columbus (G-7034)
Instantwhip of Buffalo Inc.............F...... 614 488-2536
  Columbus (G-7035)
Instantwhip Products Co PA...........F...... 614 488-2536
  Columbus (G-7036)
Instantwhip-Chicago Inc................F...... 614 488-2536
  Columbus (G-7037)
Instantwhip-Columbus Inc..............E...... 614 871-9447
  Grove City (G-10435)
▲ Instantwhip-Dayton Inc..............F...... 937 235-5930
  Dayton (G-8269)
Instantwhip-Dayton Inc..................F...... 937 435-4371
  Dayton (G-8270)
Instantwhip-Syracuse Inc...............F...... 614 488-2536
  Columbus (G-7038)
Lakeview Farms Inc......................D...... 419 695-9925
  Delphos (G-8748)
Lakeview Farms LLC......................F...... 419 695-9925
  Delphos (G-8749)
Lakeview Farms LLC......................C...... 419 695-9925
  Delphos (G-8750)
Louis Instantwhip-St Inc................F...... 614 488-2536
  Columbus (G-7138)
Louis Trauth Dairy LLC...................B...... 859 431-7553
  West Chester (G-19873)
Ohio Processors Inc......................G...... 740 852-9243
  Columbus (G-7255)
Peak Foods Llc.............................D...... 937 440-0707
  Troy (G-18692)
Philadelphia Instantwhip Inc...........F...... 614 488-2536
  Columbus (G-7314)
Reiter Dairy of Akron Inc................E...... 937 323-5777
  Springfield (G-17483)
Reiter Dairy of Akron Inc................C...... 513 795-6962
  West Chester (G-19894)
Reiter Dairy of Akron Inc................E...... 419 424-5060
  Findlay (G-9746)
Smithfoods Inc.............................G...... 330 683-8710
  Orrville (G-15620)
Toft Dairy Inc...............................D...... 419 625-4376
  Sandusky (G-16856)
United Dairy Inc............................C...... 740 633-1451
  Martins Ferry (G-12763)
United Dairy Farmers Inc................C...... 513 396-8700
  Cincinnati (G-4447)

2032 Canned Specialties

Abbott Laboratories......................A...... 614 624-3191
  Columbus (G-6519)
Beckman & Gast Company.............F...... 419 678-4195
  Saint Henry (G-16659)
Bittersweet Inc.............................D...... 419 875-6986
  Whitehouse (G-20189)
Campbell Soup Company...............D...... 419 592-1010
  Napoleon (G-14534)
Clovervale Farms Inc....................D...... 440 960-0146
  Amherst (G-558)
Conagra Brands Inc......................B...... 419 445-8015
  Archbold (G-642)
D & A Rofael Enterprises Inc..........G...... 513 751-4929
  Cincinnati (G-3567)
Disalvos Deli & Italian Store...........G...... 937 298-5053
  Dayton (G-8163)

Elizabeths Closet..........................G...... 513 646-5025
  Maineville (G-12367)
Food Designs Inc..........................F...... 216 651-9221
  Cleveland (G-5259)
▲ Gia Russa..................................F...... 330 743-6050
  Youngstown (G-20921)
Gold Star Chili Inc........................C...... 513 231-4541
  Cincinnati (G-3767)
Hayden Valley Foods Inc...............F...... 614 539-7233
  Urbancrest (G-19021)
JES Foods/Celina Inc...................E...... 419 586-7446
  Celina (G-2971)
Kick Salsa LLC..............................F...... 614 330-2499
  Columbus (G-7094)
L J Minor Corp..............................G...... 216 861-8350
  Cleveland (G-5550)
Lifo Enterprises Inc......................E...... 513 225-8801
  Loveland (G-12210)
Magic Wok Inc.............................G...... 419 531-1818
  Toledo (G-18394)
▼ Milnot Company........................G...... 888 656-3245
  Gahanna (G-10091)
▲ More Than Gourmet Inc............E...... 330 762-6652
  Akron (G-286)
◆ Oasis Mediterranean Cuisine......E...... 419 269-1459
  Toledo (G-18432)
P3 Secure LLC.............................E...... 937 610-5500
  Dayton (G-8415)
Randall Foods Inc.........................G...... 513 793-6525
  Cincinnati (G-4247)
▲ Robert Rothschild Farm LLC......F...... 937 653-7397
  Cincinnati (G-4279)
San Marcos Supermarket LLC........G...... 419 469-8963
  Toledo (G-18511)
▲ Skyline Chili Inc........................C...... 513 874-1188
  Fairfield (G-9565)
Troyer Cheese Inc........................E...... 330 893-2479
  Millersburg (G-14139)
Whiteys Food Systems Inc............G...... 330 659-4070
  Richfield (G-16495)
▼ Wornick Company.....................B...... 800 860-4555
  Blue Ash (G-1876)
Wornick Company........................A...... 513 552-7463
  Blue Ash (G-1877)
Wornick Holding Company Inc......A...... 513 794-9800
  Blue Ash (G-1878)
Worthmore Food Products Co.......F...... 513 559-1473
  Cincinnati (G-4519)

2033 Canned Fruits, Vegetables & Preserves

Amys Beauty Jams LLC..................G...... 330 869-8317
  Akron (G-66)
Beckman & Gast Company.............F...... 419 678-4195
  Saint Henry (G-16659)
Bellisio Foods Inc..........................C...... 740 286-5505
  Jackson (G-11182)
Campbell Soup Company...............D...... 419 592-1010
  Napoleon (G-14534)
▲ Cincinnati Preserving Company...F...... 513 771-2000
  Cincinnati (G-3504)
Clovervale Farms Inc....................D...... 440 960-0146
  Amherst (G-558)
Coopers Mill Inc...........................F...... 419 562-4215
  Bucyrus (G-2322)
◆ Country Pure Foods Inc............C...... 330 848-6875
  Akron (G-123)
Dominion Liquid Tech LLC..............E...... 513 272-2824
  Cincinnati (G-3600)
▼ Fremont Company.....................C...... 419 334-8995
  Fremont (G-10015)
Fremont Company........................E...... 419 334-8995
  Fremont (G-10016)
Fremont Company........................E...... 419 363-2924
  Rockford (G-16539)
▼ Fry Foods Inc............................E...... 419 448-0831
  Tiffin (G-18061)
Garden of Flavor LLC....................G...... 216 702-7991
  Cleveland (G-5290)
Gofast LLC...................................F...... 419 562-8027
  Bucyrus (G-2332)
Great Western Juice Company......F...... 216 475-5770
  Cleveland (G-5352)
Guys Barbeque Inc......................G...... 330 872-7256
  Newton Falls (G-14987)
Hirzel Canning Company...............E...... 419 287-3288
  Pemberville (G-15885)
▲ Hirzel Canning Company............D...... 419 693-0531
  Northwood (G-15338)
Hirzel Canning Company...............F...... 419 523-3225
  Ottawa (G-15654)

Employee Codes: A=Over 500 employees, B=251-500
C=101-250, D=51-100, E=20-50, F=10-19, G=3-9

20 FOOD AND KINDRED PRODUCTS

Inter American Products Inc .... E 800 645-2233
  Cincinnati *(G-3853)*
▼ J M Smucker Company .... A 330 682-3000
  Orrville *(G-15596)*
J M Smucker Company .... F 330 684-1500
  Orrville *(G-15597)*
J M Smucker Company .... G 330 497-0073
  Canton *(G-2714)*
JES Foods/Celina Inc .... E 419 586-7446
  Celina *(G-2971)*
Kraft Heinz Company .... A 330 837-8331
  Massillon *(G-13012)*
Kraft Heinz Foods Company .... E 419 332-7357
  Fremont *(G-10032)*
Landec Corporation .... C 419 931-1095
  Bowling Green *(G-1980)*
Louis Trauth Dairy LLC .... B 859 431-7553
  West Chester *(G-19873)*
▲ Meiers Wine Cellars Inc .... E 513 891-2900
  Cincinnati *(G-4003)*
Milos Whole World Gourmet LLC .... G 740 589-6456
  Athens *(G-840)*
▲ Natural Country Farms Inc .... G 330 753-2293
  Akron *(G-294)*
Nu Pet Company .... C 330 682-3000
  Orrville *(G-15606)*
Ocean Spray Cranberries Inc .... G 513 455-5770
  Loveland *(G-12219)*
▲ Ohio Pure Foods Inc .... G 330 753-2293
  Akron *(G-309)*
OSister Jams & Jellies .... G 419 968-2505
  Delphos *(G-8753)*
Pillsbury Company LLC .... F 740 286-2170
  Wellston *(G-19605)*
Pillsbury Company LLC .... D 419 845-3751
  Caledonia *(G-2420)*
▼ Portion Pac Inc .... B 513 398-0400
  Mason *(G-12922)*
RC Industries Inc .... E 330 879-5486
  Navarre *(G-14586)*
▲ Robert Rothschild Farm LLC .... F 937 653-7397
  Cincinnati *(G-4279)*
▼ Smucker International Inc .... G 330 682-3000
  Orrville *(G-15621)*
Smucker Manufacturing Inc .... G 888 550-9555
  Orrville *(G-15622)*
The Fremont Kraut Company .... D 419 332-6481
  Fremont *(G-10055)*
Tip Top Canning Co .... E 937 667-3713
  Tipp City *(G-18138)*
Traditions Sauces LLC .... G 419 704-4506
  Toledo *(G-18581)*
Two Grandmothers Gourmet Kit .... G 614 746-0888
  Reynoldsburg *(G-16459)*
Uncle Jesters Fine Foods LLC .... G 937 550-1025
  Miamisburg *(G-13729)*
Welch Foods Inc A Cooperative 513 632-5610
  Cincinnati *(G-4496)*
Worthmore Food Products Co .... F 513 559-1473
  Cincinnati *(G-4519)*
▲ Yoders Cider Barn .... F 740 668-4961
  Gambier *(G-10186)*

2034 Dried Fruits, Vegetables & Soup

Dismat Corporation .... G 419 531-8963
  Toledo *(G-18264)*
Green Gourmet Foods LLC .... E 740 400-4212
  Baltimore *(G-1038)*
▲ Hirzel Canning Company .... D 419 693-0531
  Northwood *(G-15338)*
◆ Kanan Enterprises Inc .... C 440 248-8484
  Solon *(G-17179)*
Kanan Enterprises Inc .... G 440 349-0719
  Solon *(G-17180)*

2035 Pickled Fruits, Vegetables, Sauces & Dressings

Anderson Brothers Entps Inc .... E 440 269-3920
  Willoughby *(G-20273)*
Belton Foods .... E 937 890-7768
  Dayton *(G-8053)*
Blue Point Capitl Partners LLC .... F 216 535-4700
  Cleveland *(G-4824)*
Bob Evans Farms Inc .... B 614 491-2225
  New Albany *(G-14609)*
Consumer Guild Foods Inc .... E 419 726-3406
  Toledo *(G-18240)*
◆ Crowning Food Company .... D 937 323-4699
  Springfield *(G-17381)*

Food Specialties Co .... G 513 761-1242
  Cincinnati *(G-3701)*
Fremont Company .... E 419 363-2924
  Rockford *(G-16539)*
Hermann Pickle Company .... E 330 527-2696
  Garrettsville *(G-10192)*
Hinkle Fine Foods Inc .... G 937 836-3665
  Dayton *(G-8250)*
▼ J M Smucker Company .... A 330 682-3000
  Orrville *(G-15596)*
JES Foods/Celina Inc .... E 419 586-7446
  Celina *(G-2971)*
Kaiser Foods Inc .... F 513 241-6833
  Cincinnati *(G-3895)*
▲ Kaiser Foods Inc .... E 513 621-2053
  Cincinnati *(G-3894)*
Kaiser Pickles LLC .... E 513 621-2053
  Cincinnati *(G-3896)*
◆ Lancaster Colony Corporation .... E 614 224-7141
  Westerville *(G-20004)*
Lancaster Colony Corporation .... F 614 792-9774
  Westerville *(G-20005)*
Lancaster Colony Corporation .... D 614 224-7141
  Westerville *(G-20006)*
Lariccias Italian Foods .... F 330 729-0222
  Youngstown *(G-20957)*
Mark Grzianis St Treats Ex Inc .... F 330 414-6266
  Kent *(G-11349)*
Martinez Food Products LLC .... A 419 720-6973
  Toledo *(G-18400)*
Michael Zakany LLC .... G 740 221-3934
  Zanesville *(G-21156)*
Nu Pet Company .... C 330 682-3000
  Orrville *(G-15606)*
▼ Portion Pac Inc .... B 513 398-0400
  Mason *(G-12922)*
Randys Pickles LLC .... G 440 864-6611
  Cleveland *(G-5960)*
RC Industries Inc .... E 330 879-5486
  Navarre *(G-14586)*
Ribs King Inc .... G 513 791-1942
  Cincinnati *(G-4265)*
▲ Robert Rothschild Farm LLC .... F 937 653-7397
  Cincinnati *(G-4279)*
Sunrise Foods Inc .... E 614 276-2880
  Columbus *(G-7500)*
Tmarzetti Company .... E 614 268-3722
  Westerville *(G-20028)*
◆ Tmarzetti Company .... C 614 846-2232
  Westerville *(G-20029)*
Tmarzetti Company .... G 216 292-5655
  Bedford *(G-1450)*
Tmarzetti Company .... A 614 277-3577
  Grove City *(G-10474)*
Trixies Pickles Inc .... E 817 658-6648
  Findlay *(G-9771)*
Uncle Jesters Fine Foods LLC .... G 937 550-1025
  Miamisburg *(G-13729)*
Waymakers Inc .... G 330 352-1096
  Akron *(G-432)*
◆ Woeber Mustard Mfg Co .... C 937 323-6281
  Springfield *(G-17519)*

2037 Frozen Fruits, Juices & Vegetables

Big Gus Onion Rings Inc .... E 216 883-9045
  Cleveland *(G-4812)*
◆ Country Pure Foods Inc .... C 330 848-6875
  Akron *(G-123)*
Creek Smoothies LLC .... G 937 429-1519
  Beavercreek *(G-1309)*
Cwm Smoothie LLC .... G 419 283-6387
  Toledo *(G-18248)*
Griffin Cider Works LLC .... G 440 785-7418
  Westlake *(G-20120)*
Heinz Foreign Investment Co .... F 330 837-8331
  Massillon *(G-12994)*
▲ HJ Heinz Company LP .... A 330 837-8331
  Massillon *(G-12997)*
▲ Lake Erie Frozen Foods Mfg Co .... E 419 289-9204
  Ashland *(G-720)*
National Fruit Vegetable Tech .... E 740 400-4055
  Columbus *(G-7210)*
▲ Natural Country Farms Inc .... G 330 753-2293
  Akron *(G-294)*
▲ Nestle Prepared Foods Company .... A 440 248-3600
  Solon *(G-17203)*
Nestle Prepared Foods Company .... D 440 349-5757
  Solon *(G-17204)*
NRG Smoothies LLC .... G 972 800-1002
  Vienna *(G-19206)*

Old World Foods Inc .... G 216 341-5665
  Cleveland *(G-5810)*
Schwans Home Service Inc .... E 419 222-9977
  Lima *(G-11936)*
Simply Unique Snacks LLC .... G 513 223-7736
  Cincinnati *(G-4339)*
Smoothie Creations Inc 817 313-8212
  Strongsville *(G-17790)*
Smoothie-Licious .... E 513 742-2260
  Batavia *(G-1184)*
Tri-State Special Events Inc .... G 513 221-2962
  Cincinnati *(G-4435)*
Tropical Ohio Smoothie Inc .... E 937 673-6218
  Centerville *(G-3006)*

2038 Frozen Specialties

Ascot Valley Foods LLC .... G 330 376-9411
  Cuyahoga Falls *(G-7840)*
Athens Foods Inc .... C 216 676-8500
  Cleveland *(G-4758)*
◆ Bellisio .... G 740 286-5505
  Jackson *(G-11181)*
Bellisio Foods Inc .... C 740 286-5505
  Jackson *(G-11182)*
Brilista Foods Company Inc .... G 614 299-4132
  Columbus *(G-6700)*
Campbell Soup Company .... D 419 592-1010
  Napoleon *(G-14534)*
Chef 2 Chef Foods .... G 216 696-0080
  Cleveland *(G-4918)*
Chieffos Frozen Foods Inc .... G 330 652-1222
  Niles *(G-15002)*
Classic Recipe Chili Inc .... E 513 771-1441
  Cincinnati *(G-3525)*
Clovervale Farms Inc .... D 440 960-0146
  Amherst *(G-558)*
Frozen Specialties Inc .... C 419 445-9015
  Archbold *(G-647)*
▼ Frozen Specialties Inc .... E 419 445-9015
  Perrysburg *(G-15956)*
▼ Fry Foods Inc .... E 419 448-0831
  Tiffin *(G-18061)*
FSI/Mfp Inc .... G 419 445-9015
  Archbold *(G-648)*
Hudson Village Pizza Inc .... G 330 968-4563
  Stow *(G-17595)*
▲ Kahiki Foods Inc .... C 614 322-3180
  Gahanna *(G-10087)*
King Kold Inc .... E 937 836-2731
  Englewood *(G-9366)*
▲ Lake Erie Frozen Foods Mfg Co .... E 419 289-9204
  Ashland *(G-720)*
◆ Lancaster Colony Corporation .... E 614 224-7141
  Westerville *(G-20004)*
Lopaus Point Inc .... G 614 302-7242
  Columbus *(G-7137)*
▲ Nestle Prepared Foods Company .... A 440 248-3600
  Solon *(G-17203)*
Nestle Prepared Foods Company .... D 440 349-5757
  Solon *(G-17204)*
Paleomd LLC .... G 248 854-0031
  Bedford *(G-1435)*
Richelieu Foods Inc .... F 740 335-4813
  Wshngtn CT Hs *(G-20741)*
Rsw Distributors LLC .... G 502 587-8877
  Blue Ash *(G-1841)*
Schwans Mama Rosass LLC .... C 937 498-4511
  Sidney *(G-17072)*
▲ Skyline Chili Inc .... C 513 874-1188
  Fairfield *(G-9565)*
▲ Stouffer Corporation .... G 440 349-5757
  Solon *(G-17237)*
Sunrise Foods Inc .... E 614 276-2880
  Columbus *(G-7500)*
▲ Worthington Foods Inc .... D 740 453-5501
  Zanesville *(G-21189)*

2041 Flour, Grain Milling

1-2-3 Gluten Free Inc .... G 216 378-9233
  Chagrin Falls *(G-3007)*
Archer-Daniels-Midland Company .... G 419 705-3292
  Toledo *(G-18189)*
Archer-Daniels-Midland Company .... E 419 435-6633
  Fostoria *(G-9833)*
Archer-Daniels-Midland Company .... F 740 702-6179
  Chillicothe *(G-3175)*
Bunge North America Foundation .... G 419 483-5340
  Bellevue *(G-1533)*
Cargill Incorporated .... E 937 236-1971
  Dayton *(G-8075)*

Company	Code	Phone
Countyline Co-Op Inc Pemberville (G-15883)	F	419 287-3241
Crestar Crusts Inc Wshngtn CT Hs (G-20722)	B	740 335-4813
Dik Jaxon Products Co Dayton (G-8162)	G	937 890-7350
Farmers Commission Company Upper Sandusky (G-18954)	E	419 294-2371
Fowlers Milling Co Inc Chardon (G-3112)		440 286-2024
Friends of Bears Mill Inc Greenville (G-10370)	D	937 548-5112
General Mills Inc Mason (G-12876)	D	513 770-0558
Grain Craft Inc Cleveland (G-5338)	E	216 621-3206
H Nagel & Son Co Cincinnati (G-3791)	F	513 665-4550
Hansen-Mueller Co Toledo (G-18322)	E	419 729-5535
I Dream of Cakes Eaton (G-9153)	G	937 533-6024
Indie-Peasant Enterprises Athens (G-835)	G	740 590-8240
◆ International Multifoods Corp Orrville (G-15595)	G	330 682-3000
Jaz Foods Inc Canton (G-2717)		800 456-7115
Legacy Farmers Cooperative Findlay (G-9713)	F	419 423-2611
Mennel Milling Company Fostoria (G-9848)	D	419 436-5130
Mennel Milling Company Logan (G-12036)	D	740 385-6824
Mennel Milling Company Logan (G-12035)	E	740 385-6824
Mondelez Global LLC Toledo (G-18416)	D	419 691-5200
▼ Mullet Enterprises Inc Sugarcreek (G-17855)	G	330 852-4681
Mullet Enterprises Inc Bakersville (G-1021)	G	330 897-3911
Pettisville Grain Co Pettisville (G-16035)	E	419 446-2547
Pillsbury Company LLC Wellston (G-19605)	F	740 286-2170
Pillsbury Company LLC Caledonia (G-2420)	D	419 845-3751
Pioneer Hi-Bred Intl Inc Grand Rapids (G-10318)	E	419 748-8051
Premier Feeds LLC Sabina (G-16618)	G	937 584-2411
Sunrise Cooperative Inc Wakeman (G-19289)	F	419 929-1568
Sunrise Cooperative Inc Minster (G-14225)	F	419 628-4705

2043 Cereal Breakfast Foods

Company	Code	Phone
General Mills Inc Cincinnati (G-3745)	D	513 771-8200
General Mills Inc Toledo (G-18303)	F	419 269-3100
General Mills Inc Wellston (G-19601)	E	740 286-2170
Kellogg Company West Jefferson (G-19924)	B	614 879-9659
Kellogg Company Cincinnati (G-3903)	B	513 792-2700
Kellogg Company Delaware (G-8699)	A	614 855-3437
Kellogg Company Zanesville (G-21152)	C	740 453-5501
Niese Farms Crestline (G-7797)	G	419 347-1204
Olde Man Granola LLC Findlay (G-9735)	F	419 819-9576
Treehouse Private Brands Inc Lancaster (G-11615)	B	740 654-8880
Treehouse Private Brands Inc Lancaster (G-11616)	G	740 654-8880

2045 Flour, Blended & Prepared

Company	Code	Phone
◆ Abitec Corporation Columbus (G-6527)	E	614 429-6464
Athens Foods Inc Cleveland (G-4758)	C	216 676-8500
B & D Commissary LLC Mount Perry (G-14454)	F	740 743-3890
B O K Inc Springfield (G-17366)	C	937 322-9588

Company	Code	Phone
Bigmouth Donut Company LLC Cleveland (G-4813)	G	216 264-0250
Fleetchem LLC Monroe (G-14262)	F	513 539-1111
Hometown Food Company Toledo (G-18333)	G	419 470-7914
J M Smucker Company Elyria (G-9280)	E	440 323-5100
Mid American Ventures Inc Cleveland (G-5673)	F	216 524-0974
▼ Procter & Gamble Mfg Co Cincinnati (G-4212)		513 983-1100
Rich Products Corporation Hilliard (G-10858)	C	614 771-1117

2046 Wet Corn Milling

Company	Code	Phone
Cargill Incorporated Dayton (G-8075)	E	937 236-1971
Marion Ethanol LLC Marion (G-12717)	E	740 383-4400
Tate Lyle Ingrdnts Amricas LLC Dayton (G-8542)	D	937 235-4074

2047 Dog & Cat Food

Company	Code	Phone
About Cats & Dogs LLC Hudson (G-11025)	G	440 263-8989
Bil-Jac Foods Inc Medina (G-13229)	E	330 722-7888
Cargill Incorporated Saint Marys (G-16681)		419 394-3374
G & C Raw LLC Versailles (G-19181)	G	937 827-0010
Hartz Mountain Corporation Pleasant Plain (G-16227)	D	513 877-2131
▲ IAMS Company Mason (G-12887)	B	800 675-3849
IAMS Company Leipsic (G-11726)	C	419 943-4267
IAMS Company Lewisburg (G-11793)	D	937 962-7782
In Good Hlth & Animal Wellness Northfield (G-15319)	G	330 908-1234
▼ Kelly Foods Corporation Medina (G-13285)		330 722-8855
Lakeshore Feed & Seed Inc Cleveland (G-5555)	G	216 961-5729
Land OLakes Inc Massillon (G-13013)	E	330 879-2158
Lucky Paws LLC Cincinnati (G-3954)	G	859 620-2525
Mars Petcare Us Inc Columbus (G-7153)	E	614 878-7242
Nestle Purina Petcare Company Zanesville (G-21160)	D	740 454-8575
Nom Nom Nom Columbus (G-7222)	G	614 302-4815
Ohio Blenders Inc Toledo (G-18435)	F	419 726-2655
◆ Ohio Pet Foods Inc Lisbon (G-11977)	E	330 424-1431
◆ Pro-Pet LLC Saint Marys (G-16695)	G	419 394-3374
▲ Vitakraft Sun Seed Inc Weston (G-20178)	D	419 832-1641

2048 Prepared Feeds For Animals & Fowls

Company	Code	Phone
2nd Roe LLC Monroeville (G-14285)	G	419 499-3031
Agri-Products Inc Cleveland (G-4642)	G	216 831-5890
Archer-Daniels-Midland Company Sugarcreek (G-17841)	G	330 852-3025
Archer-Daniels-Midland Company Toledo (G-18189)	G	419 705-3292
Cargill Incorporated Akron (G-104)	C	330 745-0031
Cargill Incorporated Saint Marys (G-16681)	E	419 394-3374
Centerra Co-Op Jefferson (G-11226)	E	800 362-9598
Centerra Co-Op Ashland (G-690)	E	419 281-2153
Cooper Farms Inc Fort Recovery (G-9813)	D	419 375-4116
Cooper Farms Inc Fort Recovery (G-9814)	D	419 375-4119
Cooper Farms Inc Fort Recovery (G-9815)	D	419 375-4619
Cooper Hatchery Inc Oakwood (G-15469)	F	419 594-3325

Company	Code	Phone
Csa Nutrition Services Inc Brookville (G-2164)	F	800 257-3788
Direct Action Co Inc Dover (G-8816)	D	330 364-3219
Edward Keiter & Sons Wilmington (G-20494)	G	937 382-3249
Four Natures Keepers Inc Delaware (G-8679)	F	740 363-8007
G A Wintzer and Son Company Wapakoneta (G-19329)	D	419 739-4913
Geauga Feed and Grain Supply Newbury (G-14953)	G	440 564-5000
Gerber & Sons Inc Baltic (G-1030)	E	330 897-6201
Granville Milling Co Newark (G-14881)	G	740 345-1305
▼ Hamlet Protein Inc Findlay (G-9698)		567 525-5627
Hanby Farms Inc Nashport (G-14567)	E	740 763-3554
Hartz Mountain Corporation Pleasant Plain (G-16227)	D	513 877-2131
▲ IAMS Company Mason (G-12887)	B	800 675-3849
◆ International Multifoods Corp Orrville (G-15595)	G	330 682-3000
J & B Feed Co Inc Wauseon (G-19523)	G	419 335-5821
Jroll LLC Medina (G-13283)	F	330 661-0600
▲ Kalmbach Feeds Inc Upper Sandusky (G-18957)	C	419 294-3838
▼ Kelly Foods Corporation Medina (G-13285)	E	330 722-8855
Lakeshore Feed & Seed Inc Cleveland (G-5555)	G	216 961-5729
Land OLakes Inc Massillon (G-13013)	E	330 879-2158
Le Summer Kidron Inc Apple Creek (G-610)	E	330 857-2031
Legacy Farmers Cooperative Findlay (G-9713)	F	419 423-2611
Lizzie Maes Birdseed & Dg Co Rittman (G-16524)	G	330 927-1795
▲ Magnus International Group Inc Chagrin Falls (G-3056)	G	216 592-8355
Manco Inc Lewisburg (G-11795)	G	937 962-2661
Mid-Wood Inc North Baltimore (G-15046)	F	419 257-3331
Nature Pure LLC Raymond (G-16424)	E	937 358-2364
Occidental Chemical Corp Cincinnati (G-4097)	E	513 242-2900
Ocean Providence Columbus LLC Columbus (G-7238)	G	614 272-5973
Ohio Blenders Inc Toledo (G-18435)	F	419 726-2655
◆ Ohio Pet Foods Inc Lisbon (G-11977)	E	330 424-1431
Pettisville Grain Co Pettisville (G-16035)	E	419 446-2547
Premier Feeds LLC Sabina (G-16618)	G	937 584-2411
◆ Pro-Pet LLC Saint Marys (G-16695)	G	419 394-3374
Provimi North America Inc Lewisburg (G-11798)	D	937 770-2400
◆ Provimi North America Inc Brookville (G-2182)	B	937 770-2400
Psd Partners LLC Carey (G-2888)	E	419 294-3838
Purina Animal Nutrition LLC Wshngtn CT Hs (G-20737)	F	740 335-0207
Purina Animal Nutrition LLC Lima (G-11923)	E	419 224-2015
Purina Animal Nutrition LLC Orrville (G-15611)	E	330 682-1951
Purina Animal Nutrition LLC Massillon (G-13043)	E	330 879-2158
Purina Mills LLC Orrville (G-15612)	G	330 682-1951
Quality Liquid Feeds Inc Wellsville (G-19613)	F	330 532-4635
Rek Associates LLC Upper Sandusky (G-18971)	F	419 294-3838
▼ Republic Mills Inc Okolona (G-15523)	F	419 758-3511
Ridley USA Inc Botkins (G-1936)	F	800 837-8222

Employee Codes: A=Over 500 employees, B=251-500
C=101-250, D=51-100, E=20-50, F=10-19, G=3-9

20 FOOD AND KINDRED PRODUCTS SIC SECTION

Ridley USA Inc ....E.... 937 693-6393
Botkins *(G-1937)*

Rogers Mill Inc ....G.... 330 227-3214
Rogers *(G-16561)*

Rowe Premix Inc ....F.... 937 678-9015
West Manchester *(G-19941)*

Stahl Farm Market ....F.... 330 325-0640
Ravenna *(G-16409)*

Sunny Side Feeds LLC ....G.... 330 635-1455
West Salem *(G-19958)*

Superior Ag-Patoka Vlly Feed ....F.... 419 294-3838
Upper Sandusky *(G-18975)*

Tenda Horse Products LLC ....G.... 740 694-8836
Fredericktown *(G-9979)*

Terry A Johnson ....G.... 614 561-0706
Etna *(G-9389)*

Toledo Alfalfa Mills Inc ....G.... 419 836-3705
Oregon *(G-15571)*

Verhoff Alfalfa Mills Inc ....G.... 419 653-4161
New Bavaria *(G-14643)*

▼ Verhoff Alfalfa Mills Inc ....G.... 419 523-4767
Ottawa *(G-15670)*

▲ Vitakraft Sun Seed Inc ....D.... 419 832-1641
Weston *(G-20178)*

Woodstock Products Inc ....G.... 216 641-3811
Cleveland *(G-6323)*

Yarnell Bros Inc ....G.... 419 278-2831
Deshler *(G-8790)*

2051 Bread, Bakery Prdts Exc Cookies & Crackers

614 Cupcakes LLC ....G.... 614 245-8800
New Albany *(G-14602)*

7 Little Cupcakes ....G.... 419 252-0858
Perrysburg *(G-15915)*

A Bun In Oven ....G.... 419 559-3056
Fremont *(G-9987)*

A Cupcake A Day LLC ....G.... 330 389-1247
Stow *(G-17565)*

▲ Alfred Nickles Bakery Inc ....B.... 330 879-5635
Navarre *(G-14571)*

Alfred Nickles Bakery Inc ....E.... 740 453-6522
Zanesville *(G-21096)*

Alfred Nickles Bakery Inc ....F.... 937 256-3762
Dayton *(G-8015)*

Amish Door Inc ....B.... 330 359-5464
Wilmot *(G-20513)*

An Baiceir Bakery ....G.... 740 739-0501
Etna *(G-9391)*

Angry Cupcakes Productions LLC ....G.... 216 229-2394
Cleveland *(G-4715)*

Atlas Produce LLC ....G.... 937 223-1446
Dayton *(G-8042)*

Auntie Annes ....G.... 330 652-1939
Niles *(G-15000)*

B & J Baking Company Inc ....F.... 513 541-2386
Cincinnati *(G-3374)*

B L F Enterprises Inc ....F.... 937 642-6425
Westerville *(G-20036)*

Bake ME Happy LLC ....G.... 614 477-3642
Columbus *(G-6643)*

Beckers Bakeshop Inc ....F.... 216 752-4161
Cleveland *(G-4800)*

◆ Berlin Natural Bakery Inc ....E.... 330 893-2734
Berlin *(G-1638)*

Bimbo Bakeries Usa Inc ....E.... 740 797-4449
The Plains *(G-18019)*

Bimbo Bakeries Usa Inc ....E.... 740 797-4449
The Plains *(G-18020)*

Bimbo Bakeries USA Cleveland ....F.... 216 641-5700
Cleveland *(G-4814)*

▼ Bimbo Qsr Ohio LLC ....F.... 740 454-6876
Zanesville *(G-21108)*

Bimbo Qsr Ohio LLC ....G.... 740 454-6876
Zanesville *(G-21109)*

Bites Baking Company LLC ....G.... 614 457-6092
Dublin *(G-8889)*

Blue Cottage Bakery LLC ....G.... 216 221-9733
Lakewood *(G-11513)*

Bonbonneri Inc ....F.... 513 321-3399
Cincinnati *(G-3401)*

Borden Bakers Inc ....G.... 614 457-9800
Columbus *(G-6687)*

Bread Kneads Inc ....G.... 419 422-3863
Findlay *(G-9661)*

Breaking Bread Pizza Company ....E.... 614 754-4777
Lewis Center *(G-11752)*

Buns of Delaware Inc ....E.... 740 363-2867
Delaware *(G-8659)*

Cake Arts Supplies ....G.... 419 472-4959
Toledo *(G-18221)*

Calvary Christian Ch of Ohio ....E.... 740 828-9000
Frazeysburg *(G-9937)*

Campbell Soup Company ....D.... 419 592-1010
Napoleon *(G-14534)*

Caryns Cuisine ....G.... 614 237-4143
Columbus *(G-6749)*

Champa Ventures LLC ....G.... 614 726-1801
Dublin *(G-8900)*

Cjr Desserts ....G.... 513 549-6403
Maineville *(G-12365)*

Cora Cupcakes ....G.... 440 227-7145
Painesville *(G-15726)*

Country Crust Bakery ....G.... 888 860-2940
Bainbridge *(G-1015)*

Crispie Creme of Chillicothe ....E.... 740 774-3770
Chillicothe *(G-3183)*

Crumbs Inc ....F.... 740 592-3803
Athens *(G-826)*

Cupcake Divaz ....G.... 216 509-3850
North Ridgeville *(G-15217)*

Cupcake Wishes ....G.... 440 315-3856
North Ridgeville *(G-15218)*

Cupcakes For A Cure ....G.... 419 764-1719
Perrysburg *(G-15936)*

Dandi Enterprises Inc ....F.... 419 516-9070
Solon *(G-17131)*

Danis Sweet Cupcakes ....G.... 614 581-8978
Centerburg *(G-2993)*

Desserts By Sandy LLC ....G.... 513 385-8755
Cincinnati *(G-3585)*

Destination Donuts LLC ....G.... 614 370-0754
Columbus *(G-6861)*

Dulcelicious Cupcakes and More ....G.... 440 385-7706
Cleveland *(G-5118)*

DUrso Bakery Inc ....F.... 330 652-4741
Niles *(G-15006)*

Eat Moore Cupcakes ....G.... 513 713-8139
Batavia *(G-1138)*

Empire Bakery Commissary LLC ....G.... 513 793-6241
Blue Ash *(G-1764)*

Evans Bakery Inc ....G.... 937 228-4151
Dayton *(G-8190)*

Fields Associates Inc ....G.... 513 426-8652
Cincinnati *(G-3688)*

Flowers Bakeries LLC ....E.... 330 724-1604
Akron *(G-174)*

Four Generations Inc ....G.... 330 784-2243
Lakemore *(G-11499)*

Fragapane Bakeries Inc ....G.... 440 779-6050
North Olmsted *(G-15190)*

Garys Chesecakes Fine Desserts ....G.... 513 574-1700
Cincinnati *(G-3728)*

George Weston Co ....G.... 614 868-7565
Columbus *(G-6948)*

Georges Donuts Inc ....G.... 330 963-9902
Twinsburg *(G-18784)*

Geyers Markets Inc ....D.... 419 468-9477
Galion *(G-10141)*

Gibson Bros Inc ....E.... 440 774-2401
Oberlin *(G-15496)*

Giminetti Baking Company ....E.... 513 751-7655
Cincinnati *(G-3753)*

Glorious Cupcakes ....G.... 216 544-2325
Medina *(G-13268)*

Gluten-Free Expressions ....G.... 740 928-0338
Hebron *(G-10746)*

Go Cupcake ....G.... 937 299-4985
Dayton *(G-8232)*

Graeters Manufacturing Co ....D.... 513 721-3323
Cincinnati *(G-3774)*

Hannibal Co Inc ....F.... 614 846-5060
Worthington *(G-20690)*

Hazel and Rye Artisan Bkg Co ....G.... 330 454-6658
Canton *(G-2695)*

Heinens Inc ....D.... 330 562-5297
Aurora *(G-882)*

Home Bakery ....F.... 419 678-3018
Coldwater *(G-6413)*

◆ Hot Mama Foods Inc ....F.... 419 474-3402
Toledo *(G-18337)*

I Heart Cupcakes ....G.... 614 787-3896
Columbus *(G-7017)*

International Multifoods Corp ....G.... 440 323-5100
Elyria *(G-9268)*

J M Smucker Company ....E.... 440 323-5100
Elyria *(G-9280)*

▲ Jasmine Distributing Ltd ....E.... 216 251-9420
Cleveland *(G-5494)*

Jeffs Bakery ....G.... 937 890-9703
Dayton *(G-8284)*

Jims Donut Shop ....G.... 937 898-4222
Vandalia *(G-19131)*

Jtm Provisions Company Inc ....B.... 513 367-4900
Harrison *(G-10653)*

K & B Acquisitions Inc ....F.... 937 253-1163
Dayton *(G-8288)*

K Cupcakes ....G.... 440 576-3464
Jefferson *(G-11230)*

Kellogg Company ....B.... 513 271-3500
Cincinnati *(G-3902)*

Kennedys Bakery Inc ....E.... 740 432-2301
Cambridge *(G-2444)*

Killer Brownie Ltd ....F.... 937 535-5690
Dayton *(G-8296)*

Klosterman Baking Co ....E.... 513 242-5667
Cincinnati *(G-3916)*

Klosterman Baking Co ....F.... 937 322-9588
Springfield *(G-17432)*

Klosterman Baking Co ....F.... 937 743-9021
Springboro *(G-17334)*

Klosterman Baking Co ....F.... 513 398-2707
Mason *(G-12899)*

Klosterman Baking Co ....G.... 614 338-8111
Columbus *(G-7097)*

Klosterman Baking Co ....D.... 513 242-1004
Cincinnati *(G-3917)*

Kneading Dough LLC ....G.... 719 310-5774
Mason *(G-12900)*

Krispy Kreme Doughnut Corp ....F.... 614 798-0812
Columbus *(G-7101)*

Kroger Co ....C.... 513 742-9500
Cincinnati *(G-3924)*

Kroger Co ....C.... 937 743-5900
Springboro *(G-17335)*

Kroger Co ....C.... 740 335-4030
Wshngtn CT Hs *(G-20731)*

Kroger Co ....C.... 740 264-5057
Steubenville *(G-17540)*

Kroger Co ....D.... 419 423-2065
Findlay *(G-9711)*

Kroger Co ....C.... 614 263-1766
Columbus *(G-7103)*

Kroger Co ....C.... 614 575-3742
Columbus *(G-7104)*

Kroger Co ....C.... 740 671-5164
Bellaire *(G-1487)*

Kroger Co ....D.... 513 683-4001
Maineville *(G-12372)*

Kroger Co ....C.... 937 277-0950
Dayton *(G-8302)*

Kroger Co ....D.... 740 374-2523
Marietta *(G-12638)*

Kustom Cases LLC ....G.... 240 380-6275
Dayton *(G-8303)*

M Mazzone & Sons Bakery Inc ....G.... 216 631-6511
Cleveland *(G-5593)*

Main Street Gourmet LLC ....C.... 330 929-0000
Cuyahoga Falls *(G-7895)*

Martans Foods ....G.... 330 483-9009
Valley City *(G-19047)*

Mary Ann Donut Shoppe Inc ....E.... 330 478-1655
Canton *(G-2745)*

McHappys Donuts of Parkersburg ....G.... 740 593-8744
Athens *(G-838)*

McL Inc ....D.... 614 861-6259
Columbus *(G-7167)*

Meeks Pastry Shop ....G.... 419 782-4871
Defiance *(G-8637)*

Morselicious Cupcakes ....G.... 216 408-7508
Brookpark *(G-2152)*

Mustard Seed Health Fd Mkt Inc ....E.... 440 519-3663
Solon *(G-17201)*

My Lady Muffins LLC ....G.... 937 854-5317
Dayton *(G-8374)*

Nanak Bakery ....G.... 614 882-0882
Westerville *(G-20067)*

Nanbrands LLC ....G.... 513 313-9581
Cincinnati *(G-4057)*

New Bakery of Zanesville LLC ....B.... 614 764-3100
Dublin *(G-8955)*

New Horizons Baking Company ....B.... 419 668-8226
Norwalk *(G-15407)*

New York Frozen Foods Inc ....B.... 216 292-5655
Bedford *(G-1430)*

Nikkicakes ....G.... 330 606-5745
Cuyahoga Falls *(G-7901)*

Norcia Bakery ....E.... 330 454-1077
Canton *(G-2763)*

SIC SECTION

20 FOOD AND KINDRED PRODUCTS

Olde Home Market LLC .... G 614 738-3975
  Grove City *(G-10454)*
▲ Orlando Baking Company .... C 216 361-1872
  Cleveland *(G-5820)*
Osmans Pies Inc .... E 330 607-9083
  Stow *(G-17616)*
P&S Bakery Inc .... E 330 707-4141
  Youngstown *(G-20989)*
Perfection Bakeries Inc .... D 614 866-8171
  Blacklick *(G-1691)*
Perfection Bakeries Inc .... D 419 221-2359
  Lima *(G-11916)*
Perfection Bakeries Inc .... E 513 942-1442
  West Chester *(G-19884)*
Perkins & Marie Callenders LLC ...... C 513 881-7900
  Fairfield *(G-9548)*
Pesce Baking Company Ltd .... E 330 746-6537
  Youngstown *(G-20999)*
Pf Management Inc .... G 513 874-8741
  West Chester *(G-19885)*
Pierre Holding Corp .... G 513 874-8741
  West Chester *(G-19886)*
Quality Bakery Company Inc .... G 614 846-2232
  Westerville *(G-20019)*
Quality Bakery Company Inc .... E 614 224-1424
  Columbus *(G-7364)*
Reineckers Bakery Ltd .... G 330 467-2221
  Macedonia *(G-12323)*
Rich Products Corporation .... C 614 771-1117
  Hilliard *(G-10858)*
Riesbeck Food Markets Inc .... C 740 695-3401
  Saint Clairsville *(G-16649)*
Royal Gateau .... G 216 351-3553
  Cleveland *(G-6011)*
Rudys Strudel Shop .... G 440 886-4430
  Cleveland *(G-6016)*
Saras Little Cupcakes .... G 419 305-7914
  Saint Marys *(G-16699)*
Schulers Bakery Inc .... E 937 323-4154
  Springfield *(G-17491)*
Schwebel Baking Company .... B 330 783-2860
  Youngstown *(G-21025)*
Schwebel Baking Company .... C 440 846-1921
  Strongsville *(G-17785)*
Schwebel Baking Company .... E 216 481-1880
  Euclid *(G-9442)*
Schwebel Baking Company .... D 330 783-2860
  Hebron *(G-10762)*
Schwebel Baking Company .... C 440 248-1500
  Solon *(G-17228)*
Servatii Inc .... F 513 231-4455
  Cincinnati *(G-4324)*
Servatii Inc .... F 513 271-5040
  Cincinnati *(G-4325)*
Sifted Sweet Shop LLC .... G 216 901-7100
  Youngstown *(G-21031)*
Sinful Sweets LLC .... G 330 721-0916
  Medina *(G-13343)*
Skyliner .... G 740 738-0874
  Bridgeport *(G-2078)*
Slice of Heaven Bakery .... G 419 656-6606
  Clyde *(G-6396)*
Smashing Events and Baking .... G 513 415-9693
  Cincinnati *(G-3264)*
Squire Shoppe Bakery .... G 440 964-3303
  Ashtabula *(G-805)*
Steubenville Bakery .... G 740 282-6851
  Steubenville *(G-17553)*
Sugar Shack .... G 419 961-4016
  Mansfield *(G-12522)*
Sweet GS Cupcakery Ltd .... G 419 610-8507
  Columbus *(G-7505)*
Sweet Mobile Cupcakery .... G 440 465-7333
  Bay Village *(G-1210)*
Sweet Persuasions LLC .... G 614 216-9052
  Pickerington *(G-16061)*
Ta Die For Gourmet Cupcakes .... G 740 751-4586
  Marion *(G-12739)*
▲ Taste of Belgium LLC .... G 513 381-3280
  Cincinnati *(G-4406)*
Thurns Bakery & Deli .... E 614 221-9246
  Columbus *(G-7527)*
Trumbull Mobile Meals Inc .... F 330 394-2538
  Warren *(G-19453)*
Turbos FBC LLC .... G 614 245-4840
  Columbus *(G-7550)*
Unger Kosher Bakery Inc .... E 216 321-7176
  Cleveland Heights *(G-6352)*
Wal-Bon of Ohio Inc .... F 740 423-6351
  Belpre *(G-1585)*

Wal-Bon of Ohio Inc .... D 740 423-8178
  Belpre *(G-1586)*
Were Rolling Pretzel Company .... G 419 784-0762
  Alliance *(G-514)*
◆ White Castle System Inc .... B 614 228-5781
  Columbus *(G-7603)*
You Dough Girl LLC .... G 330 207-5031
  Salem *(G-16783)*

2052 Cookies & Crackers

Annes Auntie Pretzels .... E 614 418-7021
  Columbus *(G-6605)*
B L F Enterprises Inc .... F 937 642-6425
  Westerville *(G-20036)*
Basic Grain Products Inc .... D 419 678-2304
  Coldwater *(G-6402)*
Beckers Bakeshop Inc .... F 216 752-4161
  Cleveland *(G-4800)*
◆ Brand Castle LLC .... F 216 292-7700
  Bedford Heights *(G-1462)*
Campbell Soup Company .... D 419 592-1010
  Napoleon *(G-14534)*
▲ Cheryl & Co .... C 614 776-1500
  Westerville *(G-19985)*
Cheryl & Co .... G 614 776-1500
  Obetz *(G-15509)*
Cleveland Bean Sprout Inc .... F 216 881-2112
  Cleveland *(G-4947)*
Consolidated Biscuit Company .... F 419 293-2911
  Mc Comb *(G-13187)*
Cookie Bouquets Inc .... G 614 888-2171
  Columbus *(G-6817)*
CTB Consulting LLC .... F 216 712-7764
  Rocky River *(G-16545)*
Ditsch Usa LLC .... E 513 782-8888
  Cincinnati *(G-3591)*
Frischco Inc .... G 740 363-7537
  Delaware *(G-8680)*
Good Fortunes Inc .... F 440 942-2888
  Willoughby *(G-20333)*
Great American Cookie Company .... F 419 474-9417
  Toledo *(G-18311)*
Hearthside Food Solutions LLC ..... A 419 293-2911
  Mc Comb *(G-13189)*
Hen of Woods LLC .... G 513 833-7357
  Cincinnati *(G-3807)*
J & J Snack Foods Corp .... G 440 248-2084
  Solon *(G-17173)*
Jagger Cone Company Inc .... G 419 682-1816
  Stryker *(G-17830)*
K & R Pretzel Co .... G 937 299-2231
  Dayton *(G-8289)*
Keebler Company .... E 513 271-3500
  Cincinnati *(G-3901)*
Kellogg Company .... B 513 271-3500
  Cincinnati *(G-3902)*
Kennedys Bakery Inc .... E 740 432-2301
  Cambridge *(G-2444)*
Kroger Co .... C 740 671-5164
  Bellaire *(G-1487)*
Kroger Co .... D 513 683-4001
  Maineville *(G-12372)*
Kroger Co .... C 937 277-0950
  Dayton *(G-8302)*
Kroger Co .... D 740 374-2523
  Marietta *(G-12638)*
Lenas Amish Granola .... G 330 600-1599
  Shreve *(G-17005)*
Main Street Gourmet LLC .... C 330 929-0000
  Cuyahoga Falls *(G-7895)*
Mar Chele Inc .... F 937 429-2300
  Beavercreek *(G-1330)*
Mar Chele Inc .... G 937 833-3400
  Brookville *(G-2174)*
Norcia Bakery .... E 330 454-1077
  Canton *(G-2763)*
◆ Norse Dairy Systems LP .... B 614 421-5297
  Columbus *(G-7225)*
Osmans Pies Inc .... E 330 607-9083
  Stow *(G-17616)*
Patjim Holdings Company .... G 419 727-1298
  Toledo *(G-18458)*
Pepperidge Farm Incorporated .... G 614 457-4800
  Columbus *(G-7309)*
Pepperidge Farm Incorporated .... G 419 933-2611
  Willard *(G-20244)*
Rudys Strudel Shop .... G 440 886-4430
  Cleveland *(G-6016)*
Rykrisp Llc .... G 843 338-0750
  Cincinnati *(G-4293)*

Schulers Bakery Inc .... E 937 323-4154
  Springfield *(G-17491)*
Snyders-Lance Inc .... G 614 856-4616
  Grove City *(G-10469)*
Y Z Enterprises Inc .... E 419 893-8777
  Maumee *(G-13161)*

2053 Frozen Bakery Prdts

Atk2 Inc .... G 513 661-5869
  Cincinnati *(G-3366)*
Bartells Cupcakery .... G 330 957-1793
  Austintown *(G-929)*
Chefs Pantry Inc .... G 440 288-0146
  Amherst *(G-557)*
Cleveland Bagel Company LLC .... G 216 385-7723
  Cleveland *(G-4946)*
Kissicakes - N-Sweets LLC .... G 614 940-2779
  Columbus *(G-7096)*
Main Street Gourmet LLC .... C 330 929-0000
  Cuyahoga Falls *(G-7895)*
Mammas Mandel .... G 513 827-2457
  Mason *(G-12906)*
Pepperidge Farm Incorporated .... G 614 457-4800
  Columbus *(G-7309)*
Pepperidge Farm Incorporated .... G 419 933-2611
  Willard *(G-20244)*

2063 Sugar, Beet

Michigan Sugar Company .... F 419 332-9931
  Fremont *(G-10040)*
Michigan Sugar Company .... G 419 423-1666
  Findlay *(G-9724)*

2064 Candy & Confectionery Prdts

69 Taps .... G 330 253-4554
  Akron *(G-16)*
Al Meda Chocolates Inc .... G 419 446-2676
  Archbold *(G-634)*
Albanese Concessions LLC .... G 614 402-4937
  Canal Winchester *(G-2498)*
Amerisource Health Svcs LLC .... D 614 492-8177
  Columbus *(G-6590)*
▲ Anthony-Thomas Candy Company .. C .. 614 274-8405
  Columbus *(G-6606)*
Anthony-Thomas Candy Company .. G 614 870-8899
  Columbus *(G-6607)*
Arnolds Candies Inc .... G 330 733-4022
  Akron *(G-70)*
Becky Knapp .... G 330 854-4400
  Canal Fulton *(G-2476)*
Cake Decor .... G 614 836-5533
  Groveport *(G-10487)*
Celebrations .... G 419 381-8088
  Toledo *(G-18224)*
Chocolate Pig Inc .... E 440 461-4511
  Cleveland *(G-4923)*
Cincinnati Premier Candy LLC .... E 513 253-0079
  Cincinnati *(G-3513)*
Coffelt Candy Inc .... G 937 399-8772
  Springfield *(G-17376)*
Coons Homemade Candies .... G 740 496-4141
  Harpster *(G-10626)*
Crawford Acquisition Corp .... F 216 486-0702
  Cleveland *(G-5038)*
Daffins Candies .... G 330 545-0325
  Girard *(G-10256)*
◆ Decko Products Inc .... D 419 626-5757
  Sandusky *(G-16804)*
Doschers Candies LLC .... F 513 381-8656
  Cincinnati *(G-3603)*
E R B Enterprises Inc .... G 740 948-9174
  Jeffersonville *(G-11246)*
Ervan Guttman Co .... G 513 791-0767
  Cincinnati *(G-3653)*
Fawn Confectionery .... F 513 574-9612
  Cincinnati *(G-3675)*
Giannios Candy Co Inc .... E 330 755-7000
  Struthers *(G-17817)*
Gibson Bros Inc .... E 440 774-2401
  Oberlin *(G-15496)*
Gift Cove Inc .... G 419 285-2920
  Put In Bay *(G-16352)*
Good Nutrition LLC .... F 216 534-6617
  Oakwood Village *(G-15480)*
Graeters Manufacturing Co .... D 513 721-3323
  Cincinnati *(G-3774)*
Great Lakes Popcorn Company .... G 419 732-3080
  Port Clinton *(G-16248)*
Gwen Rosenberg Enterprises LLC .. G 330 678-1893
  Kent *(G-11328)*

Employee Codes: A=Over 500 employees, B=251-500
C=101-250, D=51-100, E=20-50, F=10-19, G=3-9

20 FOOD AND KINDRED PRODUCTS

▲ Hake Head LLC .... E 614 291-2244
  Columbus *(G-6976)*
Humphrey Popcorn Company .... F 216 662-6629
  Strongsville *(G-17752)*
Island Delights Inc .... G 866 887-4100
  Seville *(G-16917)*
▲ Jml Holdings Inc .... F 419 866-7500
  Holland *(G-10937)*
Kevin G Ryba Inc .... G 419 627-2010
  Huron *(G-11101)*
Light Vision .... E 513 351-9444
  Cincinnati *(G-3942)*
Lollipop Stop .... G 614 991-5192
  Grove City *(G-10442)*
Mageros Candies .... G 330 534-1146
  Hubbard *(G-11005)*
▲ Malleys Candies .... C 216 362-8700
  Lakewood *(G-11528)*
Malleys Candies Inc .... E 216 529-6262
  Cleveland *(G-5609)*
Maries Candies LLC .... E 937 465-3061
  West Liberty *(G-19937)*
Marshas Buckeyes LLC .... E 419 872-7666
  Perrysburg *(G-15975)*
▲ McJak Candy Company LLC .... G 330 722-3531
  Medina *(G-13292)*
Milk & Honey .... F 330 492-5884
  Canton *(G-2755)*
Nestle Usa Inc .... E 513 576-4930
  Loveland *(G-12217)*
Neumeisters Candy Shoppe LLC .... G 419 294-3647
  Upper Sandusky *(G-18966)*
New Bloomer Candy Company LLC ..... E 740 452-7501
  Zanesville *(G-21161)*
Normant Candy Co .... F 419 886-4214
  Mansfield *(G-12494)*
Piqua Chocolate Company Inc .... G 937 773-1981
  Piqua *(G-16151)*
Popped .... F 330 678-1893
  Kent *(G-11365)*
Rcs Brewhouse .... G 440 984-3103
  Amherst *(G-572)*
Richards Maple Products Inc .... G 440 286-4160
  Chardon *(G-3134)*
Snyders-Lance Inc .... G 614 856-4616
  Grove City *(G-10469)*
Sugar Memories LLC .... G 216 472-0206
  Cleveland *(G-6115)*
Suzin L Chocolatiers .... F 440 323-3372
  Elyria *(G-9332)*
Sweet Melissas .... G 440 333-6357
  Rocky River *(G-16557)*
Walnut Creek Chocolate Company ...... E 330 893-2995
  Walnut Creek *(G-19308)*
Wittichs Candies Inc .... G 740 474-3313
  Circleville *(G-4564)*
Yost Candy Co .... G 330 828-2777
  Dalton *(G-7954)*

2066 Chocolate & Cocoa Prdts

American Confections Co LLC .... G 614 888-8838
  Coventry Township *(G-7765)*
▲ Anthony-Thomas Candy Company ... C 614 274-8405
  Columbus *(G-6606)*
Becky Knapp .... G 330 854-4400
  Canal Fulton *(G-2476)*
▲ Benjamin P Forbes Company .... F 440 838-4400
  Broadview Heights *(G-2088)*
Brandts Candies .... G 440 942-1016
  Willoughby *(G-20286)*
Brownie Points Inc .... G 614 860-8470
  Columbus *(G-6705)*
Campbells Candies .... G 330 493-1805
  Canton *(G-2606)*
Cheryl & Co .... G 614 776-1500
  Obetz *(G-15509)*
Chocolate Pig Inc .... E 440 461-4511
  Cleveland *(G-4923)*
Dietsch Brothers Incorporated .... D 419 422-4474
  Findlay *(G-9677)*
E R B Enterprises Inc .... G 740 948-9174
  Jeffersonville *(G-11246)*
Fannie May Confections Inc .... A 330 494-0833
  North Canton *(G-15082)*
Fawn Confectionery .... F 513 574-9612
  Cincinnati *(G-3675)*
Giannios Candy Co Inc .... G 330 755-7000
  Struthers *(G-17817)*
Golden Turtle Chocolate Fctry .... G 513 932-1990
  Lebanon *(G-11658)*
Gorant Chocolatier LLC .... C 330 726-8821
  Boardman *(G-1899)*
Graeters Manufacturing Co .... D 513 721-3323
  Cincinnati *(G-3774)*
▲ Harry London Candies Inc .... D 330 494-0833
  North Canton *(G-15092)*
Hartville Chocolates Inc .... F 330 877-1999
  Hartville *(G-10692)*
Haute Chocolate Inc .... G 513 793-9999
  Montgomery *(G-14294)*
▼ L C F Inc .... F 330 877-3322
  Hartville *(G-10700)*
▲ Malleys Candies .... C 216 362-8700
  Lakewood *(G-11528)*
Malleys Candies Inc .... E 216 529-6262
  Cleveland *(G-5609)*
Milk & Honey .... F 330 492-5884
  Canton *(G-2755)*
Neumeisters Candy Shoppe LLC .... G 419 294-3647
  Upper Sandusky *(G-18966)*
Robert E McGrath Inc .... E 440 572-7747
  Strongsville *(G-17783)*
Walnut Creek Chocolate Company ...... E 330 893-2995
  Walnut Creek *(G-19308)*

2068 Salted & Roasted Nuts & Seeds

▲ Anthony-Thomas Candy Company ... C 614 274-8405
  Columbus *(G-6606)*
Back Development LLC .... G 937 671-7896
  Cleveland *(G-4787)*
♦ Kanan Enterprises Inc .... C 440 248-8484
  Solon *(G-17179)*
Kanan Enterprises Inc .... F 440 349-0719
  Solon *(G-17180)*
▲ Malleys Candies .... C 216 362-8700
  Lakewood *(G-11528)*
Nuts Are Good Inc .... F 586 619-2400
  Columbus *(G-7233)*
Simply Unique Snacks LLC .... G 513 223-7736
  Cincinnati *(G-4339)*
Southside Wolfies .... G 419 422-5450
  Findlay *(G-9760)*
Thorfood LLC .... E 419 626-4375
  Sandusky *(G-16854)*
♦ Trophy Nut Co .... D 937 667-8478
  Tipp City *(G-18139)*
Trophy Nut Co .... G 937 669-5513
  Tipp City *(G-18140)*

2075 Soybean Oil Mills

Archer-Daniels-Midland Company .... E 419 435-6633
  Fostoria *(G-9833)*
Bunge North America Foundation .... D 740 383-1181
  Marion *(G-12697)*
Bunge North America Foundation .... G 419 483-5340
  Bellevue *(G-1533)*
Bunge North America Foundation .... G 740 426-6332
  Jeffersonville *(G-11245)*
Cargill Incorporated .... D 937 498-4555
  Sidney *(G-17020)*
Pioneer Hi-Bred Intl Inc .... E 419 748-8051
  Grand Rapids *(G-10318)*
Schlessman Seed Co .... E 419 499-2572
  Milan *(G-13988)*
Solae LLC .... C 419 483-0400
  Bellevue *(G-1546)*

2077 Animal, Marine Fats & Oils

Archer-Daniels-Midland Company .... E 419 435-6633
  Fostoria *(G-9833)*
Cargill Incorporated .... D 937 498-4555
  Sidney *(G-17020)*
Darling Ingredients Inc .... G 972 717-0300
  Cincinnati *(G-3576)*
Darling Ingredients Inc .... G 216 351-3440
  Cleveland *(G-5065)*
Darling International Inc .... F 216 651-9300
  Cleveland *(G-5066)*
Fiske Brothers Refining Co .... D 419 691-2491
  Toledo *(G-18295)*
▲ Holmes By Products Co .... E 330 893-2322
  Millersburg *(G-14095)*
Inland Products Inc .... E 614 443-3425
  Columbus *(G-7027)*
Wileys Finest LLC .... C 740 622-1072
  Coshocton *(G-7759)*

2079 Shortening, Oils & Margarine

A Twist On Olives LLC .... G 614 823-8800
  Westerville *(G-20032)*
Cincinnati Biorefining Corp .... G 513 482-8800
  Cincinnati *(G-3485)*
♦ Cincinnati Renewable Fuels LLC ...... D 513 482-8800
  Cincinnati *(G-3506)*
Garden of Delight LLC .... G 513 300-7205
  Cincinnati *(G-3725)*
Ill Olive LLC Spicy .... G 937 247-5969
  Miamisburg *(G-13678)*
Inter American Products Inc .... E 800 645-2233
  Cincinnati *(G-3853)*
Motts Oils & More .... G 330 601-1645
  Wooster *(G-20629)*
▲ Olivamed LLC .... F 937 401-0821
  Franklin *(G-9906)*
Olive Branch .... G 614 563-3139
  London *(G-12068)*
Olive Smuckers Oil .... G 513 646-7103
  Cincinnati *(G-4109)*
Olive Tap .... G 330 721-6500
  Medina *(G-13311)*
▼ Procter & Gamble Mfg Co .... F 513 983-1100
  Cincinnati *(G-4212)*
Spicy Olive LLC .... G 513 847-4397
  West Chester *(G-19797)*
Spicy Olive LLC .... G 513 376-9061
  Cincinnati *(G-4359)*
Sunny Olive LLC .... G 513 996-4091
  Cincinnati *(G-4396)*
Wileys Finest LLC .... C 740 622-1072
  Coshocton *(G-7759)*

2082 Malt Beverages

Actual Brewing Company LLC .... F 614 636-3825
  Columbus *(G-6540)*
▲ AEC Brews LLC DBA Old Frhuse B . G 513 536-9071
  Williamsburg *(G-20250)*
Anheuser-Busch LLC .... B 614 847-6213
  Columbus *(G-6604)*
Bar 25 LLC .... G 216 621-4000
  Cleveland *(G-4789)*
Barnstorm Brewing Company LLC ...... G 419 852-9366
  Coldwater *(G-6400)*
Birdfish Brewing Company LLC .... G 330 397-4010
  Columbiana *(G-6454)*
Black Cloister Brewing Co LLC .... G 419 481-3891
  Toledo *(G-18205)*
Brew Kettle Inc .... F 440 234-8788
  Strongsville *(G-17721)*
Brew Kettle Strongsville LLC .... G 440 915-7074
  Medina *(G-13233)*
Brew Monkeys LLC .... G 513 330-8806
  Cincinnati *(G-3413)*
Brewery Real Estate Partnr .... G 614 224-9023
  Columbus *(G-6695)*
Brewpub Restaurant Corp .... D 614 228-2537
  Columbus *(G-6696)*
Brick and Barrel .... G 503 927-0629
  Cleveland *(G-4837)*
Brufist LLC .... G 330 221-4472
  Bowling Green *(G-1957)*
Burgie Brauerei Inc .... G 740 344-1620
  Newark *(G-14858)*
Carry Grandview Out .... G 614 487-0305
  Columbus *(G-6748)*
Columbus Kombucha Company LLC ... G 614 262-0000
  Columbus *(G-6795)*
Commissary Brewing .... G 614 636-3164
  Columbus *(G-6807)*
Dayton Heidelberg Distrg Co .... D 440 989-1027
  Lorain *(G-12088)*
Dinos Drive Thru LLC .... G 330 263-1111
  Wooster *(G-20584)*
▲ District Brewing Co Inc .... G 614 224-3626
  Columbus *(G-6870)*
Eagles Club .... G 740 962-6490
  McConnelsville *(G-13203)*
Earnest Brew Works .... G 419 340-2589
  Toledo *(G-18274)*
Fifty West Brewing Company .... D 513 834-8789
  Cincinnati *(G-3689)*
Flat Rocks Brewing Company .... G 419 270-3582
  Napoleon *(G-14538)*
Georgetown Vineyards Inc .... E 740 435-3222
  Cambridge *(G-2440)*
Green Room Brewing LLC .... G 614 596-3655
  Columbus *(G-6970)*

SIC SECTION — 20 FOOD AND KINDRED PRODUCTS

Guys Brewing Gear .... G 330 554-9362
Kent *(G-11327)*
Hansa Bewery LLC .... G 216 631-6585
Cleveland *(G-5372)*
Hill James R & Hill Earley W .... G 740 591-4203
Albany *(G-442)*
Homestead Beer Company .... G 740 522-8018
Heath *(G-10720)*
Jackie Os Pub Brewery LLC .... D 740 274-0777
Athens *(G-836)*
Larrys Drive Thru & Mini Mart .... G 330 953-0512
Youngstown *(G-20958)*
Marios Drive Thru .... G 330 452-8793
Canton *(G-2743)*
Marks Brew Thru .... G 330 699-1755
Akron *(G-271)*
McKinleys Meadery LLC .... G 740 928-0229
Hebron *(G-10751)*
Miiler Brewing Company .... F 513 896-9200
Trenton *(G-18625)*
Millercoors LLC .... D 513 896-9200
Trenton *(G-18626)*
Minnicks Drive-Thru .... G 513 868-6126
Hamilton *(G-10587)*
Moeller Brew Barn LLC .... G 419 925-3005
Maria Stein *(G-12600)*
Municipal Brew Works LLC .... G 513 889-8369
Hamilton *(G-10588)*
Nine Giant Brewing LLC .... G 510 220-5104
Cincinnati *(G-4081)*
▲ North High Brewing LLC .... F 614 407-5278
Columbus *(G-7227)*
Platform Beers LLC .... F 440 539-3245
Cleveland *(G-5889)*
Pop A Top Cruise Thru .... G 419 947-5855
Mount Gilead *(G-14430)*
▲ Rivertown Brewing Company LLC .... E 513 827-9280
Monroe *(G-14275)*
Rocky River Brewing Co .... E 440 895-2739
Rocky River *(G-16555)*
Rust Belt Brewing LLC .... G 330 423-3818
Youngstown *(G-21022)*
Seventh Son Brewing Co .... G 614 783-4217
Columbus *(G-7442)*
Snyder Intl Brewing Group LLC .... E 216 619-7424
Cleveland *(G-6076)*
South Side Drive Thru .... G 937 295-2927
Fort Loramie *(G-9807)*
Tailspin Brewing Company .... G 419 852-9366
Coldwater *(G-6421)*
▲ The Great Lakes Brewing Co .... D 216 771-4404
Cleveland *(G-6164)*
Thirsty Dog Brewing Co .... G 330 252-8740
Akron *(G-404)*
Tom Bad Brewing LLC .... F 513 871-4677
Cincinnati *(G-4425)*
Two Bandits Brewing Co LLC .... G 419 636-4045
Bryan *(G-2310)*
Unbridled Brewing Company LLC .... F 937 361-2573
Middletown *(G-13961)*
Victoria Ventures Inc .... E 330 793-9321
Youngstown *(G-21063)*
Wadsworth Brewing Company LLC .... G 330 475-4935
Wadsworth *(G-19279)*
Warped Wing Brewing Co LLC .... F 937 222-7003
Dayton *(G-8583)*
Wedco LLC .... G 513 309-0781
Mount Orab *(G-14452)*
Westend Brewing LLC .... G 513 922-0289
Cincinnati *(G-4501)*
Willoughby Brewing Company .... D 440 975-0202
Willoughby *(G-20458)*
Wright Designs Inc .... G 216 524-6662
Cleveland *(G-6329)*
Yellow Springs Brewery LLC .... E 937 767-0222
Yellow Springs *(G-20820)*

2084 Wine & Brandy

Autumn Rush Vineyard LLC .... G 614 312-5748
Johnstown *(G-11258)*
▲ Belvino LLC .... G 440 715-0076
Chagrin Falls *(G-3010)*
Breitenbach Wine Cellar Inc .... G 330 343-3603
Dover *(G-8810)*
Camelot Cellars Winery .... G 614 441-8860
Columbus *(G-6726)*
Chalet Debonne Vineyards Inc .... F 440 466-3485
Madison *(G-12343)*
Creekside Cottage Winery LLC .... G 330 694-1013
Magnolia *(G-12359)*
CWC Partners LLC .... G 567 208-1573
Findlay *(G-9676)*
Deluca Vineyards .... G 440 685-4242
North Bloomfield *(G-15064)*
Deodora Vineyards & Winery LLC .... G 513 238-1167
Cincinnati *(G-3582)*
Drake Brothers Ltd .... G 415 819-4941
Columbus *(G-6874)*
E & J Gallo Winery .... E 513 381-4050
Cincinnati *(G-3615)*
Emerine Estates Inc .... G 440 293-8199
Jefferson *(G-11229)*
Ferrante Wine Farm Inc .... E 440 466-8466
Geneva *(G-10219)*
Filia .... G 330 322-1200
Wadsworth *(G-19239)*
▲ Firelands Winery .... E 419 625-5474
Sandusky *(G-16811)*
Flint Ridge Vineyard LLC .... G 740 787-2116
Hopewell *(G-10992)*
Four Fires Meadery LLC .... G 419 704-9573
Maumee *(G-13110)*
Georgetown Vineyards Inc .... E 740 435-3222
Cambridge *(G-2440)*
Gillig Custom Winery Inc .... G 419 202-6057
Findlay *(G-9693)*
Glenn Ravens Winery .... E 740 545-1000
West Lafayette *(G-19930)*
Hanover Winery Inc .... G 513 304-9702
Hamilton *(G-10569)*
High Low Winery .... G 844 466-4456
Medina *(G-13273)*
Hillside Winery .... G 419 456-3108
Gilboa *(G-10250)*
Hundley Cellars LLC .... G 843 368-5016
Geneva *(G-10223)*
John Christ Winery Inc .... G 440 933-9672
Avon Lake *(G-991)*
Kelleys Island Wine Co .... G 419 746-2678
Kelleys Island *(G-11283)*
King Vineyards .... G 440 967-4191
Vermilion *(G-19165)*
Klingshirn Winery Inc .... G 440 933-6666
Avon Lake *(G-992)*
Larrys Drive Thru & Mini Mart .... G 330 953-0512
Youngstown *(G-20958)*
Laurentia Winery .... G 440 296-9170
Madison *(G-12353)*
Markko Vineyard .... G 440 593-3197
Conneaut *(G-7655)*
Mastropietro Winery Inc .... G 330 547-2151
Berlin Center *(G-1647)*
▲ Meiers Wine Cellars Inc .... E 513 891-2900
Cincinnati *(G-4003)*
Meranda Nixon Estate Wine LLC .... G 937 515-8013
Ripley *(G-16514)*
Mio Vino .... G 513 407-0486
Cincinnati *(G-4033)*
Moyer Vineyards Inc .... E 937 549-2957
Manchester *(G-12395)*
Mt Carmel Brewing Company .... G 513 519-7161
Cincinnati *(G-4052)*
Muirfield Wine Company LLC .... G 614 799-9222
Dublin *(G-8949)*
Odyssey Cellars Inc .... G 330 782-0177
Youngstown *(G-20980)*
Old Mason Winery Inc .... G 937 698-1122
West Milton *(G-19951)*
Old Mill Winery Inc .... F 440 466-5560
Geneva *(G-10227)*
Olde Schlhuse Vnyrd Winery LLC .... G 937 273-6023
Eldorado *(G-9190)*
Paper Moon Winery .... G 440 967-2500
Vermilion *(G-19169)*
Powell Village Winery LLC .... G 614 290-5898
Powell *(G-16333)*
Rainbow Hills Vineyards Inc .... G 740 545-9305
Newcomerstown *(G-14980)*
Renee Barrett Winery .... G 513 471-1340
Cincinnati *(G-4259)*
Rockside Winery & Vineyards LL .... G 740 687-4414
Lancaster *(G-11605)*
Sand Hollow Winery .... G 740 323-3959
Heath *(G-10732)*
Sandra Weddington .... G 740 417-4286
Delaware *(G-8722)*
SCC Wine Company LLC .... G 216 374-3740
Madison *(G-12356)*
School House Winery LLC .... G 330 602-9463
Dover *(G-8851)*
Shade Text Book Service Inc .... G 740 696-1323
Shade *(G-16921)*
Sharon James Cellers .... G 440 739-4065
Newbury *(G-14965)*
Shawne Springs Winery .... G 740 623-0744
Coshocton *(G-7751)*
Stoney Ridge Winery Ltd .... G 419 636-3500
Bryan *(G-2307)*
Thorncreek Winery & Garden .... G 330 562-9245
Aurora *(G-908)*
Vervasi Vineyard & Itln Bistro .... E 330 497-1000
Canton *(G-2860)*
Virant Family Winery Inc .... G 440 466-6279
Geneva *(G-10230)*
Winery At Spring Hill Inc .... F 440 466-0626
Geneva *(G-10231)*
Winery At Wolf Creek .... F 330 666-9285
Barberton *(G-1113)*
Wines For You .... G 440 946-1420
Mentor *(G-13627)*
Woodbury Vineyards Inc .... G 440 835-2828
Westlake *(G-20173)*
Wyandotte Wine Cellar Inc .... G 614 476-3624
Columbus *(G-7618)*

2085 Liquors, Distilled, Rectified & Blended

Black Swamp Distillery .... G 419 344-4347
Fremont *(G-9999)*
Buckeye Distillery .... G 937 877-1901
Tipp City *(G-18103)*
Catawba Island Brewing Co .... G 419 960-7764
Port Clinton *(G-16244)*
Cleveland Whiskey LLC .... G 216 881-8481
Cleveland *(G-4984)*
Doc Howards Distillery .... G 440 488-9463
Mentor *(G-13430)*
Five Points Distillery LLC .... G 937 776-4634
Dayton *(G-8197)*
Indian Creek Distillery .... G 937 846-1443
New Carlisle *(G-14668)*
Iron Vault Distillery LLC .... G 419 747-7560
Ontario *(G-15542)*
John McCulloch Distillery .... G 937 725-5588
Martinsville *(G-12766)*
Killbuck Creek Distillery LLC .... G 740 502-2880
Warsaw *(G-19475)*
Klivlend Cask Distilling LLC .... G 216 926-1682
Painesville *(G-15754)*
Luxco Inc .... E 216 671-6300
Cleveland *(G-5588)*
Smedleys Bar and Grill .... G 216 941-0124
Cleveland *(G-6073)*
Stillwrights Distillery .... G 937 879-4447
Fairborn *(G-9469)*
Veriano Fine Foods Spirits Ltd .... F 614 745-7705
New Albany *(G-14641)*
Western Reserve Distillers LLC .... G 330 780-9599
Lakewood *(G-11537)*

2086 Soft Drinks

7 Up of Marietta Inc .... E 740 423-9230
Little Hocking *(G-11988)*
Abbott Laboratories .... A 614 624-3191
Columbus *(G-6519)*
American Bottling Company .... D 614 237-4201
Columbus *(G-6580)*
American Bottling Company .... D 937 236-0333
Dayton *(G-8023)*
American Bottling Company .... E 740 922-5253
Midvale *(G-13974)*
American Bottling Company .... E 740 377-4371
South Point *(G-17279)*
American Bottling Company .... D 740 423-9230
Little Hocking *(G-11990)*
American Bottling Company .... D 614 237-4201
Columbus *(G-6581)*
American Bottling Company .... E 419 229-7777
Lima *(G-11836)*
American Bottling Company .... D 419 535-0777
Toledo *(G-18171)*
American Bottling Company .... D 513 381-4891
Cincinnati *(G-3329)*
American Bottling Company .... C 513 242-5151
Cincinnati *(G-3330)*
Bawls Acquisition LLC .... G 888 731-9708
Twinsburg *(G-18739)*
Belton Foods .... E 937 890-7768
Dayton *(G-8053)*
Borden Dairy Co Cincinnati LLC .... C 513 948-8811
Cincinnati *(G-3404)*

SIC

Employee Codes: A=Over 500 employees, B=251-500
C=101-250, D=51-100, E=20-50, F=10-19, G=3-9
2019 Harris Ohio
Industrial Directory
823

20 FOOD AND KINDRED PRODUCTS

Cadbury Schweppes Bottling ....G...... 614 238-0469
  Columbus (G-6722)
Central Coca-Cola Btlg Co Inc ....C...... 419 476-6622
  Toledo (G-18226)
Central Coca-Cola Btlg Co Inc ....D...... 330 783-1982
  Youngstown (G-20867)
Central Coca-Cola Btlg Co Inc ....D...... 614 863-7200
  Columbus (G-6751)
Central Coca-Cola Btlg Co Inc ....E...... 419 522-2653
  Mansfield (G-12424)
Central Coca-Cola Btlg Co Inc ....D...... 440 324-3335
  Elyria (G-9235)
Central Coca-Cola Btlg Co Inc 740 452-3608
  Zanesville (G-21118)
Central Coca-Cola Btlg Co Inc ....D...... 330 425-4401
  Twinsburg (G-18749)
Central Coca-Cola Btlg Co Inc 440 269-1433
  Willoughby (G-20295)
Central Coca-Cola Btlg Co Inc ....G...... 740 474-2180
  Circleville (G-4538)
Central Coca-Cola Btlg Co Inc ....G...... 330 875-1487
  Akron (G-110)
Central Coca-Cola Btlg Co Inc ....G...... 330 487-0212
  Macedonia (G-12282)
Cincinnati Marlins Inc 513 761-3320
  Cincinnati (G-3500)
Cleveland Coca-Cola Btlg Inc ....C...... 216 690-2653
  Bedford Heights (G-1465)
Coca-Cola 937 446-4644
  Sardinia (G-16867)
Coca-Cola Bottling Co Cnsld 419 422-3743
  Lima (G-11849)
Coca-Cola Bottling Co Cnsld ....E...... 740 353-3133
  Portsmouth (G-16280)
Coca-Cola Bottling Co Cnsld ....B...... 513 527-6600
  Cincinnati (G-3535)
Coca-Cola Bottling Co Cnsld ....D...... 937 878-5000
  Dayton (G-8096)
Coca-Cola Company ....C...... 614 491-6305
  Columbus (G-6779)
Coca-Cola Company ....F...... 937 446-4644
  Sardinia (G-16868)
◆ Country Pure Foods Inc ....C...... 330 848-6675
  Akron (G-123)
Creekside Springs LLC ....E...... 330 679-1010
  Salineville (G-16787)
Csv Inc ....F...... 937 438-1142
  Dayton (G-8115)
Currier Richard & James ....G...... 440 988-4132
  Amherst (G-559)
Delite Fruit Juices 614 470-4333
  Columbus (G-6858)
Dominion Liquid Tech LLC ....E...... 513 272-2824
  Cincinnati (G-3600)
Dr Pepper Bottlers Associates ....G...... 330 746-7651
  Youngstown (G-20894)
Dr Pepper Bottling Company ....G...... 740 452-2721
  Zanesville (G-21130)
Dr Pepper Snapple Group ....G...... 419 223-0072
  Lima (G-11856)
Dr Pepper Snapple Group ....G...... 513 242-5151
  Cincinnati (G-3608)
Dr Pepper/Seven Up Inc ....D...... 419 229-7777
  Lima (G-11857)
Dragon Beverage Inc 614 506-5592
  Columbus (G-6873)
Fbg Bottling Group LLC ....F...... 614 554-4646
  Columbus (G-6914)
G & J Pepsi-Cola Bottlers Inc ....B...... 740 354-9191
  Franklin Furnace (G-9934)
G & J Pepsi-Cola Bottlers Inc ....F...... 513 785-6060
  Cincinnati (G-3718)
G & J Pepsi-Cola Bottlers Inc ....D...... 937 392-4937
  Ripley (G-16513)
G & J Pepsi-Cola Bottlers Inc 513 896-3700
  Hamilton (G-10560)
G & J Pepsi-Cola Bottlers Inc ....A...... 614 253-8771
  Columbus (G-6942)
G & J Pepsi-Cola Bottlers Inc ....D...... 740 452-2721
  Zanesville (G-21140)
G & J Pepsi-Cola Bottlers Inc ....E...... 740 774-2148
  Chillicothe (G-3187)
G & J Pepsi-Cola Bottlers Inc ....D...... 740 593-3366
  Athens (G-831)
Gehm & Sons Limited ....G...... 330 724-8423
  Akron (G-185)
Gem Beverages Inc ....F...... 740 384-2411
  Wellston (G-19600)
Gordon Brothers Btlg Group Inc .....G...... 330 337-8754
  Salem (G-16742)

Haus Mathias ....G...... 330 533-5305
  Canfield (G-2529)
Hornell Brewing Co Inc ....G...... 516 812-0384
  Cincinnati (G-3827)
Keurig Dr Pepper Inc ....D...... 614 237-4201
  Columbus (G-7089)
Keurig Dr Pepper Inc ....G...... 419 535-0777
  Toledo (G-18366)
Keurig Dr Pepper Inc ....D...... 614 237-4201
  Columbus (G-7090)
L & F Lauch LLC ....G...... 513 732-5805
  Batavia (G-1161)
L & J Drive Thru ....G...... 330 767-2185
  Brewster (G-2069)
Life Support Development Ltd ....G...... 614 221-1765
  Columbus (G-7126)
Medi Home Health Agency Inc ......G...... 740 472-3220
  Woodsfield (G-20546)
▲ Meiers Wine Cellars Inc ....E...... 513 891-2900
  Cincinnati (G-4003)
National Beverage Corp ....E...... 614 491-5415
  Obetz (G-15512)
▲ Natural Country Farms Inc ....G...... 330 753-2293
  Akron (G-294)
▲ Niagara Bottling LLC ....F...... 614 751-7420
  Gahanna (G-10096)
Nurture Brands LLC ....G...... 513 307-2338
  Cincinnati (G-4093)
Ohio Beverage Systems Inc ....F...... 216 475-3900
  Cleveland (G-5800)
Ohio Eagle Distributing LLC ....E...... 513 539-8483
  West Chester (G-19753)
▲ Ohio Pure Foods Inc ....D...... 330 753-2293
  Akron (G-309)
Our Heart Health Care Svcs LLC ....G...... 614 943-5216
  Columbus (G-7279)
P-Americas LLC ....E...... 740 266-6121
  Wintersville (G-20540)
P-Americas LLC ....B...... 513 948-5100
  Cincinnati (G-4129)
P-Americas LLC ....C...... 614 253-8771
  Columbus (G-7283)
P-Americas LLC ....C...... 440 323-5524
  Elyria (G-9307)
P-Americas LLC ....C...... 330 336-3553
  Wadsworth (G-19259)
P-Americas LLC ....C...... 330 837-4224
  Massillon (G-13036)
P-Americas LLC ....G...... 330 963-0090
  Twinsburg (G-18827)
P-Americas LLC ....C...... 330 746-7652
  Youngstown (G-20990)
P-Americas LLC ....E...... 419 227-3541
  Lima (G-11913)
Pepsi-Cola Metro Btlg Co Inc ....B...... 937 461-4664
  Dayton (G-8421)
Pepsi-Cola Metro Btlg Co Inc ....C...... 614 261-8193
  Columbus (G-7310)
Pepsi-Cola Metro Btlg Co Inc ....B...... 330 963-0426
  Twinsburg (G-18833)
Pepsi-Cola Metro Btlg Co Inc 330 963-5300
  Twinsburg (G-18834)
Pepsi-Cola Metro Btlg Co Inc ....E...... 419 534-2186
  Toledo (G-18463)
Recov Beverages LLC ....G...... 513 518-9794
  Cincinnati (G-4255)
SD Ip Holdings Company ....G...... 513 483-3300
  Blue Ash (G-1844)
Shasta Beverages Inc ....E...... 614 491-5415
  Obetz (G-15513)
Skinny Piggy Kombucha LLC ....G...... 513 646-5753
  Cincinnati (G-4342)
▼ Smucker International Inc ....G...... 330 682-3000
  Orrville (G-15621)
Smucker Natural Foods Inc ....E...... 330 682-3000
  Orrville (G-15623)
Star Beverage Corporation Ohio ....G...... 216 991-4799
  Shaker Heights (G-16938)
▼ Sunny Delight Beverage Co ....D...... 513 483-3300
  Blue Ash (G-1853)
Vinnies Drive Thru ....G...... 419 225-5872
  Lima (G-11956)

2087 Flavoring Extracts & Syrups

Abbott Laboratories ....A...... 614 624-3191
  Columbus (G-6519)
Agrana Fruit Us LLC ....C...... 937 693-3821
  Botkins (G-1932)
Ancient Infusions LLC ....G...... 419 659-5110
  Columbus Grove (G-7630)

▲ Bayswater Beverages LLC ....G...... 312 224-8012
  Cincinnati (G-3383)
Belton Foods ....E...... 937 890-7768
  Dayton (G-8053)
◆ Berghausen Corporation ....E...... 513 541-5631
  Cincinnati (G-3389)
Bickford Laboratories Inc ....G...... 440 354-7747
  Wickliffe (G-20204)
Cargill Incorporated ....E...... 937 236-1971
  Dayton (G-8075)
Central Coca-Cola Btlg Co Inc ....E...... 419 476-6622
  Toledo (G-18226)
Cleveland Syrup Corp ....G...... 330 963-1900
  Twinsburg (G-18755)
Dominion Liquid Tech LLC ....E...... 513 272-2824
  Cincinnati (G-3600)
Flavor Systems International ....G...... 513 870-0420
  West Chester (G-19853)
▲ Flavor Systems Intl Inc ....E...... 513 870-4900
  West Chester (G-19854)
◆ Frutarom USA Inc ....G...... 513 870-4900
  West Chester (G-19856)
Givaudan Flavors Corporation ....G...... 513 948-8000
  Cincinnati (G-3756)
Givaudan Flavors Corporation ....B...... 513 948-4933
  Cincinnati (G-3755)
Givaudan Flvors Fragrances Inc ....G...... 513 948-8000
  Cincinnati (G-3757)
Givaudan Fragrances Corp ....B...... 513 948-3428
  Cincinnati (G-3759)
◆ Givaudan Roure US Inc ....G...... 513 948-8000
  Cincinnati (G-3760)
Great Western Juice Company ....F...... 216 475-5770
  Cleveland (G-5352)
Innovtive Cnfction Sltions LLC ....G...... 440 835-8001
  Westlake (G-20126)
Inter American Products Inc ....E...... 800 645-2233
  Cincinnati (G-3853)
▼ J M Smucker Company ....A...... 330 682-3000
  Orrville (G-15596)
▲ Joseph Adams Corp ....F...... 330 225-9125
  Valley City (G-19042)
◆ Mane Inc ....D...... 513 248-9876
  Lebanon (G-11671)
Mane Inc ....E...... 513 248-9876
  Lebanon (G-11672)
Mapledale Farm Inc ....G...... 440 286-3389
  Chardon (G-3125)
Nu Pet Company ....G...... 330 682-3000
  Orrville (G-15606)
Roare-Q LLC ....G...... 419 801-4040
  Bowling Green (G-1997)
Sensoryeffects Flavor Company ....E...... 419 782-5010
  Defiance (G-8642)
▲ Sensus LLC ....F...... 513 892-7100
  Fairfield Township (G-9585)
Slush Puppie ....D...... 513 771-0940
  West Chester (G-19899)
Synergy Flavors (oh) LLC ....G...... 513 892-7100
  Fairfield Township (G-9587)
Tate Lyle Ingrdnts Amricas LLC .....D...... 937 236-5906
  Dayton (G-8541)
Third Wave Water LLC ....G...... 855 590-4500
  Cedarville (G-2947)
Wiley Organics Inc ....C...... 740 622-0755
  Coshocton (G-7758)

2091 Fish & Seafoods, Canned & Cured

Strasburg Provision Inc ....E...... 330 878-1059
  Strasburg (G-17653)

2095 Coffee

Altraserv LLC ....G...... 614 889-2500
  Plain City (G-16170)
Boston Stoker Inc ....G...... 937 890-6401
  Vandalia (G-19118)
Crooked River Coffee Co ....G...... 440 442-8330
  Cleveland (G-5039)
Dunkin Donuts ....G...... 330 336-2500
  Wadsworth (G-19236)
Essential Wonders Inc ....G...... 888 525-5282
  Cuyahoga Falls (G-7863)
Euclid Coffee Co Inc ....G...... 216 481-3333
  Cleveland (G-5195)
▲ Folger Coffee Company ....F...... 800 937-9745
  Orrville (G-15591)
Generations Coffee Company LLC ....G...... 440 546-0901
  Brecksville (G-2038)
Good Beans Coffee Roasters LLC ....G...... 513 310-9516
  Milford (G-14012)

Inter American Products Inc.................E....... 800 645-2233
Cincinnati *(G-3853)*
Iron Bean Inc.................G....... 518 641-9917
Toledo *(G-18353)*
Little Ghost Roasters.................G....... 614 325-2065
Columbus *(G-7132)*
Mc Concepts Llc.................G....... 330 933-6402
Canton *(G-2748)*
▲ **Millstone Coffee Inc**.................D....... 513 983-1100
Cincinnati *(G-4029)*
▲ **Pmd Enterprises Inc**.................F....... 440 546-0901
Brecksville *(G-2055)*
Raptis Coffee Inc.................G....... 330 399-7011
Warren *(G-19436)*
Rezas Roast LLC.................G....... 937 823-1193
Fairborn *(G-9467)*
▲ **Stonefruit Coffee Co**.................G....... 330 509-2787
Canfield *(G-2548)*
▼ **Wallingford Coffee Mills Inc**.................D....... 513 771-3131
Cincinnati *(G-4489)*

2096 Potato Chips & Similar Prdts

Ballreich Bros Inc.................C....... 419 447-1814
Tiffin *(G-18050)*
Basic Grain Products Inc.................E....... 614 408-3091
Coldwater *(G-6401)*
Basic Grain Products Inc.................D....... 419 678-2304
Coldwater *(G-6402)*
Birds Eye Foods Inc.................E....... 330 854-0818
Canal Fulton *(G-2477)*
Campbell Soup Company.................D....... 419 592-1010
Napoleon *(G-14534)*
Conns Potato Chip Co Inc.................E....... 740 452-4615
Zanesville *(G-21123)*
Daniel Meenan.................G....... 330 756-2818
Beach City *(G-1211)*
Frito-Lay North America Inc.................D....... 330 477-7009
Canton *(G-2676)*
Frito-Lay North America Inc.................C....... 614 508-3004
Columbus *(G-6940)*
Frito-Lay North America Inc.................C....... 513 229-3000
Mason *(G-12872)*
Frito-Lay North America Inc.................C....... 972 334-7000
Wooster *(G-20594)*
Gold N Krisp Chips & Pretzels.................G....... 330 832-8395
Massillon *(G-12988)*
Grippo Potato Chip Co Inc.................D....... 513 923-1900
Cincinnati *(G-3786)*
Herr Foods Incorporated.................E....... 740 773-8282
Chillicothe *(G-3192)*
Jones Potato Chip Co.................E....... 419 529-9424
Mansfield *(G-12464)*
Mike-Sells Potato Chip Co.................E....... 937 228-9400
Dayton *(G-8357)*
Mumfords Potato Chips & Deli.................G....... 937 653-3491
Urbana *(G-19005)*
Pats Delicious LLC.................G....... 614 441-7047
Columbus *(G-7298)*
Poppees Popcorn Inc.................E....... 440 327-0775
North Ridgeville *(G-15245)*
Robert E McGrath Inc.................E....... 440 572-7747
Strongsville *(G-17783)*
◆ **Rudolph Foods Company Inc**.................C....... 909 383-7463
Lima *(G-11935)*
Savory Foods Inc.................D....... 740 354-6655
Portsmouth *(G-16298)*
◆ **Shearers Foods LLC**.................A....... 330 834-4030
Massillon *(G-13047)*
◆ **Snack Alliance Inc**.................E....... 330 767-3426
Massillon *(G-13049)*
Waffle House Inc.................E....... 937 746-6830
Franklin *(G-9929)*
Waffle House Inc.................F....... 513 539-8372
Monroe *(G-14281)*
White Feather Foods Inc.................F....... 419 738-8975
Wapakoneta *(G-19360)*
▲ **Wyandot Inc**.................B....... 740 383-4031
Marion *(G-12751)*

2097 Ice

Brady A Lantz Enterprises.................G....... 513 742-4921
Cincinnati *(G-3408)*
Donahues Hilltop Ice Company.................F....... 740 432-3348
Cambridge *(G-2435)*
Haller Enterprises Inc.................F....... 330 733-9693
Akron *(G-195)*
Home City Ice Company.................F....... 513 353-9346
Harrison *(G-10647)*
Home City Ice Company.................G....... 513 941-0340
Cincinnati *(G-3822)*
Home City Ice Company.................E....... 513 851-4040
Cincinnati *(G-3823)*
Home City Ice Company.................E....... 937 461-6028
Dayton *(G-8252)*
Home City Ice Company.................F....... 419 562-4953
Delaware *(G-8694)*
Home City Ice Company.................F....... 440 439-5001
Bedford *(G-1413)*
Home City Ice Company.................E....... 614 836-2877
Groveport *(G-10493)*
Lori Holding Co.................E....... 740 342-3230
New Lexington *(G-14717)*
Luc Ice Inc.................G....... 419 734-2201
Port Clinton *(G-16251)*
Millersburg Ice Co.................E....... 330 674-3016
Millersburg *(G-14114)*
Olmsted Ice Inc.................E....... 440 235-8411
Olmsted Twp *(G-15535)*
Penguin Serv Ice.................G....... 614 848-6511
Worthington *(G-20699)*
Velvet Ice Cream Company.................F....... 419 562-2009
Bucyrus *(G-2348)*
Wings Way Drive Thru Inc.................G....... 330 533-2788
Salem *(G-16781)*
Zygo Inc.................G....... 513 281-0888
Cincinnati *(G-4535)*

2098 Macaroni, Spaghetti & Noodles

Big Noodle LLC.................G....... 614 558-7170
Columbus *(G-6668)*
Fusion Noodle Co.................G....... 740 589-5511
Athens *(G-830)*
▲ **International Noodle Company**.................F....... 614 888-0665
Lewis Center *(G-11764)*
Lariccias Italian Foods.................F....... 330 729-0222
Youngstown *(G-20957)*
▲ **Mrs Mllers Hmmade Noodles Ltd**.................F....... 330 694-5814
Fredericksburg *(G-9954)*
Pho & Rice LLC.................G....... 216 563-1122
Cleveland Heights *(G-6350)*
T & R Noodles LLC.................G....... 614 537-4710
New Lexington *(G-14726)*
Tmarzetti Company.................F....... 330 674-2993
Millersburg *(G-14136)*
◆ **Tmarzetti Company**.................C....... 614 846-2232
Westerville *(G-20029)*
Twg Noodle Company LLC.................G....... 419 560-2033
Marengo *(G-12596)*
YAR Corporation.................G....... 330 652-1222
Niles *(G-15041)*

2099 Food Preparations, NEC

Advancperre Foods Holdings Inc.................E....... 800 969-2747
West Chester *(G-19828)*
Agrana Fruit Us Inc.................C....... 937 693-3821
Botkins *(G-1932)*
Alacwin Nutrition Corporation.................G....... 614 961-6479
Columbus *(G-6561)*
Alamarra Inc.................G....... 800 336-3007
Mentor *(G-13381)*
Allenbaugh Foods LLC.................G....... 216 952-3984
Lakewood *(G-11509)*
American Sweet Bean Co LLC.................G....... 888 995-0007
Tiffin *(G-18043)*
Amir International Foods Inc.................G....... 614 332-1742
Grove City *(G-10415)*
Amish Wedding Foods Inc.................E....... 330 674-9199
Millersburg *(G-14060)*
Ancient Infusions LLC.................G....... 419 659-5110
Columbus Grove *(G-7630)*
▲ **Andys Mdterranean Fd Pdts LLC**.................G....... 513 281-9791
Cincinnati *(G-3347)*
Apf Legacy Subs LLC.................G....... 513 682-7173
West Chester *(G-19833)*
Artistic Foods Incorporated.................G....... 330 401-1313
Lodi *(G-12006)*
Atlantic Investment.................G....... 440 567-5054
Lorain *(G-12079)*
Ballreich Bros Inc.................C....... 419 447-1814
Tiffin *(G-18050)*
Barkett Fruit Co Inc.................E....... 330 364-6645
Dover *(G-8807)*
Basic Grain Products Inc.................D....... 419 678-2304
Coldwater *(G-6402)*
Beatty Foods LLC.................G....... 330 327-2442
Canton *(G-2588)*
Beckwith Orchards Inc.................F....... 330 673-6433
Kent *(G-11299)*
Bellissimo Distribution LLC.................F....... 216 431-3344
Cleveland *(G-4803)*
Best Bite Grill LLC.................F....... 419 344-7462
Versailles *(G-19174)*
Big Gus Onion Rings Inc.................E....... 216 883-9045
Cleveland *(G-4812)*
Blue Point Capitl Partners LLC.................F....... 216 535-4700
Cleveland *(G-4824)*
Bob Evans Farms Inc.................B....... 614 491-2225
New Albany *(G-14609)*
Bread Kneads Inc.................G....... 419 422-3863
Findlay *(G-9661)*
Chez Rama Restaurant.................G....... 614 237-9315
Columbus *(G-6763)*
Cincinnati Premier Candy LLC.................E....... 513 253-0079
Cincinnati *(G-3513)*
Classic Delight Inc.................E....... 419 394-7955
Saint Marys *(G-16682)*
Clovervale Farms Inc.................D....... 440 960-0146
Amherst *(G-558)*
▲ **Coalescence LLC**.................E....... 614 861-3639
Columbus *(G-6778)*
Conagra Brands Inc.................C....... 513 229-0305
Mason *(G-12853)*
Conagra Brands Inc.................F....... 740 465-3912
Morral *(G-14403)*
Conagra Brands Inc.................B....... 419 445-8015
Archbold *(G-642)*
Conagra Fods Pckaged Foods LLC.................B....... 937 440-2800
Troy *(G-18643)*
Country Parlour Ice Cream Co.................F....... 440 237-4040
Cleveland *(G-5032)*
Curation Foods Inc.................G....... 419 931-1029
Bowling Green *(G-1967)*
Cuyahoga Vending Co Inc.................F....... 440 353-9595
North Ridgeville *(G-15219)*
Daniel Meenan.................G....... 330 756-2818
Beach City *(G-1211)*
Deer Creek Honey Farms Ltd.................G....... 740 852-0899
London *(G-12057)*
Dno Inc.................D....... 614 231-3601
Columbus *(G-6872)*
Dole Fresh Vegetables Inc.................C....... 937 525-4300
Springfield *(G-17390)*
Domino Foods Inc.................D....... 216 432-3222
Cleveland *(G-5106)*
Feinkost Ingredient Co U S A.................G....... 330 948-3006
Lodi *(G-12011)*
Food 4 Your Soul.................F....... 330 402-4073
Youngstown *(G-20908)*
Food Designs Inc.................F....... 216 651-9221
Cleveland *(G-5259)*
Frank L Harter & Son Inc.................G....... 513 574-1330
Cincinnati *(G-3709)*
Fremont Company.................E....... 419 363-2924
Rockford *(G-16539)*
Fresh Table LLC.................G....... 513 381-3774
Cincinnati *(G-3713)*
Freshway Foods Inc.................C....... 937 498-4664
Sidney *(G-17041)*
Frito-Lay North America Inc.................C....... 972 334-7000
Wooster *(G-20594)*
Frito-Lay North America Inc.................D....... 330 477-7009
Canton *(G-2676)*
Frog Ranch Foods Ltd.................F....... 740 767-3705
Glouster *(G-10276)*
◆ **Frutarom USA Inc**.................C....... 513 870-4900
West Chester *(G-19856)*
Frutarom USA Inc.................F....... 513 870-4900
West Chester *(G-19857)*
Frutarom USA Inc.................G....... 513 870-4900
West Chester *(G-19858)*
Fuhrmann Orchards LLC.................G....... 740 776-6406
Wheelersburg *(G-20181)*
Gaslamp Popcorn Company.................G....... 951 684-6767
Lima *(G-11868)*
General Mills Inc.................D....... 513 771-8200
Cincinnati *(G-3745)*
Gold Star Chili Inc.................E....... 513 231-4541
Cincinnati *(G-3767)*
Gold Star Chili Inc.................E....... 513 631-1990
Cincinnati *(G-3768)*
Gomez Salsa LLC.................F....... 513 314-1978
Cincinnati *(G-3769)*
Goodell Farms.................G....... 330 274-2161
Mantua *(G-12547)*
Graffiti Foods Limited.................F....... 614 759-1921
Columbus *(G-6963)*
Great Lakes Popcorn Company.................G....... 419 732-3080
Port Clinton *(G-16248)*
Grippo Potato Chip Co Inc.................D....... 513 923-1900
Cincinnati *(G-3786)*

S I C

Employee Codes: A=Over 500 employees, B=251-500
C=101-250, D=51-100, E=20-50, F=10-19, G=3-9
2019 Harris Ohio
Industrial Directory
825

20 FOOD AND KINDRED PRODUCTS

Haus Mathias .... G 330 533-5305
  Canfield *(G-2529)*
Hays Orchard & Cider Mill LLC .... F 330 482-2924
  Columbiana *(G-6468)*
Herold Salads Inc .... E 216 991-7500
  Cleveland *(G-5399)*
Hiland Group Incorporated .... D 330 499-8404
  Canton *(G-2699)*
Homestat Farm Ltd .... E 614 718-3060
  Dublin *(G-8924)*
Hometown Food Company .... G 419 470-7914
  Toledo *(G-18333)*
Honeybaked Ham Company .... G 513 583-9700
  Cincinnati *(G-3824)*
Hydrofresh Ltd .... G 419 785-3221
  Delphos *(G-8745)*
Indie-Peasant Enterprises .... G 740 590-8240
  Athens *(G-835)*
Infant Food Project Inc .... G 614 239-5763
  Columbus *(G-7025)*
Ingredient Innovations Intl Co .... G 330 262-4440
  Wooster *(G-20606)*
Inter American Products Inc .... E 800 645-2233
  Cincinnati *(G-3853)*
J M Smucker Company .... D 513 482-8000
  Cincinnati *(G-3865)*
▼ J M Smucker Company .... A 330 682-3000
  Orrville *(G-15596)*
J M Smucker Company .... E 440 323-5100
  Elyria *(G-9280)*
JM Smucker Co .... G 330 684-8274
  Orrville *(G-15600)*
John Krusinski .... F 216 441-0100
  Cleveland *(G-5502)*
▲ Koch Foods of Cincinnati LLC .... C 513 874-3500
  Fairfield *(G-9518)*
Kraft Heinz Company .... A 330 837-8331
  Massillon *(G-13012)*
Krema Group Inc .... F 614 889-4824
  Plain City *(G-16200)*
Krema Products Inc .... G 614 889-4824
  Dublin *(G-8939)*
La Perla Inc .... F 419 534-2074
  Toledo *(G-18374)*
Lakeview Farms LLC .... C 419 695-9925
  Delphos *(G-8750)*
Lanxess Solutions US Inc .... E 440 324-6060
  Elyria *(G-9284)*
Louise Sweet LLC .... G 419 460-5505
  Toledo *(G-18387)*
Main Street Gourmet LLC .... C 330 929-0000
  Cuyahoga Falls *(G-7895)*
◆ Mane Inc .... D 513 248-9876
  Lebanon *(G-11671)*
Miami Valley Pizza Hut Inc .... E 419 586-5900
  Celina *(G-2976)*
Micah Specialty Foods .... G 405 320-3325
  Warrensville Heights *(G-19471)*
Mid American Ventures Inc .... F 216 524-0974
  Cleveland *(G-5673)*
Midwest Spray Drying Company .... G 419 294-4221
  Upper Sandusky *(G-18964)*
Minnie Hanmons Catering Inc .... G 216 815-7744
  Cleveland *(G-5694)*
▲ National Foods Packaging Inc .... F 216 415-7102
  Cleveland *(G-5725)*
Nestle Brands Company .... F 440 264-6600
  Solon *(G-17202)*
Nija Foods LLC .... G 513 377-7495
  Cincinnati *(G-4079)*
Nu Pet Company .... G 330 682-3000
  Orrville *(G-15606)*
◆ Oasis Mediterranean Cuisine .... E 419 269-1459
  Toledo *(G-18432)*
Oceanside Foods .... G 440 554-7810
  Avon Lake *(G-999)*
Ohio Hickory Harvest Brand Pro .... E 330 644-6266
  Coventry Township *(G-7775)*
Peer Pantry LLC .... G 216 236-4087
  Willowick *(G-20480)*
Pepperidge Farm Incorporated .... G 614 457-4800
  Columbus *(G-7309)*
Pepperidge Farm Incorporated .... G 419 933-2611
  Willard *(G-20244)*
Perez Foods LLC .... G 419 264-0303
  Holgate *(G-10912)*
Pfizer Inc .... G 937 746-3603
  Franklin *(G-9908)*
Pita Wrap LLC .... G 330 886-8091
  Boardman *(G-1900)*

▼ Procter & Gamble Mfg Co .... F 513 983-1100
  Cincinnati *(G-4212)*
Pure Foods LLC .... G 303 358-8375
  Highland Heights *(G-10799)*
Purushealth LLC .... F 800 601-0580
  Shaker Heights *(G-16935)*
Rich Products Corporation .... G 614 771-1117
  Hilliard *(G-10858)*
Ritchie Foods LLC .... G 440 354-7474
  Fairport Harbor *(G-9630)*
Roare-Q LLC .... G 419 801-4040
  Bowling Green *(G-1997)*
Rossi Pasta Factory Inc .... F 740 376-2065
  Marietta *(G-12665)*
◆ Rudolph Foods Company Inc .... C 909 383-7463
  Lima *(G-11935)*
▲ Sandridge Food Corporation .... G 330 725-2348
  Medina *(G-13334)*
Sandridge Food Corporation .... G 330 725-8883
  Medina *(G-13335)*
Sanese Services Inc .... E 330 494-5900
  Warren *(G-19441)*
Savor Seasonings LLC .... G 513 732-2333
  Batavia *(G-1183)*
SC Campana Inc .... G 440 390-8854
  Amherst *(G-573)*
◆ Sensoryffcts Powdr Systems Inc ... D 419 783-5518
  Defiance *(G-8643)*
Sharpys Food Systems LLC .... G 440 232-9601
  Oakwood Village *(G-15483)*
Simple Products LLC .... G 330 674-2448
  Millersburg *(G-14129)*
▼ Smucker International Inc .... G 330 682-3000
  Orrville *(G-15621)*
Solae LLC .... G 419 483-5340
  Bellevue *(G-1547)*
Sonoran Salsa Company LLC .... G 216 513-3596
  Westlake *(G-20159)*
Special t Foods LLC .... G 330 533-9493
  Canfield *(G-2545)*
Staceys Kitchen Limited .... G 614 921-1290
  Hilliard *(G-10863)*
Sticky Petes Maple Syrup .... G 740 662-2726
  Athens *(G-850)*
Sugarbush Creek Farm .... G 440 636-5371
  Middlefield *(G-13856)*
Sunrise Foods Inc .... E 614 276-2880
  Columbus *(G-7500)*
Tarrier Foods Corp .... E 614 876-8594
  Columbus *(G-7513)*
Three Peaks Wellness LLC .... G 216 438-3334
  Cleveland *(G-6173)*
Timmys Sandwich Shop .... G 419 350-8267
  Toledo *(G-18551)*
Toms Country Place Inc .... E 440 934-4553
  Avon *(G-971)*
Tortilla .... G 614 557-3367
  Reynoldsburg *(G-16456)*
Tortilleria El Maizal LLP .... G 330 209-9344
  Massillon *(G-13053)*
▼ Tortilleria La Bamba LLC .... G 216 469-0410
  Cleveland *(G-6190)*
Tortilleria La Bamba LLC .... E 216 515-1600
  Cleveland *(G-6191)*
Twenty Second Cntury Foods LLC .... G 419 866-6343
  Maumee *(G-13157)*
Umami Seasonings LLC .... G 614 687-0315
  Columbus *(G-7555)*
Unger Kosher Bakery Inc .... E 216 321-7176
  Cleveland Heights *(G-6352)*
Veggie Valley Farm LLC .... G 330 866-2712
  Sandyville *(G-16864)*
Wake Robin Fermented Foods LLC ... G 216 961-9944
  Cleveland *(G-6285)*
Wal-Bon of Ohio Inc .... D 740 423-8178
  Belpre *(G-1586)*
▼ Wallingford Coffee Mills Inc .... D 513 771-3131
  Cincinnati *(G-4489)*
Wannemacher Enterprises Inc .... F 419 771-1101
  Upper Sandusky *(G-18977)*
Western Reserve Foods LLC .... G 330 770-0885
  Chagrin Falls *(G-3032)*
White Castle System Inc .... E 513 563-2290
  Cincinnati *(G-4506)*
White Feather Foods Inc .... F 419 738-8975
  Wapakoneta *(G-19360)*
Whitmore Productions Inc .... F 216 752-3960
  Warrensville Heights *(G-19474)*
Wildcat Creek Farms Inc .... F 419 263-2549
  Payne *(G-15876)*

Willys Inc .... F 419 823-3200
  Swanton *(G-17929)*
◆ Woeber Mustard Mfg Co .... C 937 323-6281
  Springfield *(G-17519)*
Yost Foods Inc .... G 330 273-4420
  Brunswick *(G-2255)*
▲ Zidian Manufacturing Inc .... G 330 965-8455
  Boardman *(G-1905)*

21 TOBACCO PRODUCTS

2111 Cigarettes

Butt Hut of America Inc .... G 419 443-1997
  Tiffin *(G-18053)*
Itg Brands LLC 614 431-0044
  Columbus *(G-7053)*

2121 Cigars

Cigars of Cincy .... G 513 931-5926
  Cincinnati *(G-3475)*
Guari Inc .... G 330 733-4005
  Akron *(G-192)*
Moosehead Cigar Company Llc .... G 513 266-7207
  Fairfield *(G-9530)*

2131 Tobacco, Chewing & Snuff

Great Midwest Tobacco Inc .... G 513 745-0450
  Cincinnati *(G-3779)*
Hookah Rush .... G 614 267-6463
  Columbus *(G-7007)*
Smoke Rings Inc .... G 419 420-9966
  Findlay *(G-9757)*

22 TEXTILE MILL PRODUCTS

2211 Cotton, Woven Fabric

Akron Cotton Products Inc .... G 330 434-7171
  Akron *(G-36)*
Associated Hygienic Pdts LLC .... B 770 497-9800
  Delaware *(G-8655)*
Canton Sterilized Wiping Cloth .... G 330 455-5179
  Canton *(G-2618)*
Canvas Salon and Skin Bar .... G 614 336-3942
  Powell *(G-16311)*
Carmens Installation Co .... F 216 321-4040
  Cleveland *(G-4879)*
Cleveland Drapery Stitch Inc .... F 216 252-3857
  Cleveland *(G-4957)*
Compass Energy LLC .... D 866 665-2225
  Cleveland *(G-5009)*
Custom Craft Drap Inc .... G 330 929-5728
  Cuyahoga Falls *(G-7856)*
Custom Marine Canvas Training 419 732-8362
  Port Clinton *(G-16245)*
▲ F H Bonn Co Inc 937 323-7024
  Springfield *(G-17400)*
Fabric Square Shop .... G 330 752-3044
  Stow *(G-17585)*
Franjinhas Inc 440 463-1523
  Strongsville *(G-17745)*
Gillz LLC .... G 904 330-1094
  Westlake *(G-20119)*
Grow With Me- Creations 800 850-1889
  Hartville *(G-10691)*
I-Group Technologies LLC .... G 877 622-3377
  New Philadelphia *(G-14775)*
Linsalata Capital Partners Fun .... G 440 684-1400
  Cleveland *(G-5579)*
Lumenomics Inc .... E 614 798-3500
  Lewis Center *(G-11766)*
Mary James Inc .... E 419 599-2941
  Napoleon *(G-14550)*
▲ Mmi Textiles Inc .... F 440 899-8050
  Westlake *(G-20131)*
Moleman .... G 513 662-3017
  Cincinnati *(G-4041)*
Nancys Draperies 330 855-7751
  Marshallville *(G-12754)*
Noble Denim Workshop .... G 513 560-5640
  Cincinnati *(G-4084)*
Omnova Solutions Inc .... C 216 682-7000
  Beachwood *(G-1257)*
Osnaburg Quilt Fibr Art Guild .... G 330 488-2591
  East Canton *(G-9042)*
Silver Threads Inc .... E 614 733-0099
  Plain City *(G-16211)*
▲ Sk Textile Inc .... C 323 581-8986
  Cincinnati *(G-4341)*

◆ Standard Textile Co Inc ....B 513 761-9256
  Cincinnati (G-4372)
▲ Star Wipers Inc ....G 724 695-2721
  Newark (G-14922)
Struggle Grind Success LLC ....G 330 834-6738
  Boardman (G-1903)
The Max ....G 440 357-0036
  Painesville (G-15789)
▲ Totes Isotoner Corporation ....F 513 682-8200
  West Chester (G-19907)
▲ Totes Isotoner Holdings Corp ....C 513 682-8200
  West Chester (G-19908)
◆ Tranzonic Acquisition Corp ....A 216 535-4300
  Richmond Heights (G-16505)
Tranzonic Companies ....C 440 446-0643
  Cleveland (G-6198)
Twin Design AP Promotions Ltd ......G 937 732-6798
  Dayton (G-8573)
Weiskopf Industries Corp ....E 440 442-4400
  Cleveland (G-6297)
Winspec Inc ....G 440 834-9068
  Middlefield (G-13867)
Wonder-Shirts Inc ....G 917 679-2336
  Dublin (G-9012)

2221 Silk & Man-Made Fiber

American Band Saw Co ....G 740 452-8168
  Zanesville (G-21098)
▲ Architectural Fiberglass Inc ....E 216 641-8300
  Cleveland (G-4727)
C S A Enterprises ....G 740 342-9367
  New Lexington (G-14713)
Chautauqua Fiberglass & Plasti ....G 513 423-8840
  Middletown (G-13892)
Cleveland Drapery Stitch Inc ....F 216 252-3857
  Cleveland (G-4957)
Detroit Technologies Inc ....E 937 492-2708
  Sidney (G-17030)
▲ King Bag and Manufacturing Co .....E 513 541-5440
  Cincinnati (G-3910)
Lumenomics Inc ....E 614 798-3500
  Lewis Center (G-11766)
M C L Window Coverings Inc ....G 513 868-6000
  Fairfield Township (G-9584)
Mini Graphics Inc ....G 513 563-8600
  Cincinnati (G-4030)
▲ Mmi Textiles Inc ....F 440 899-8050
  Westlake (G-20131)
Old Es LLC ....E 330 468-6600
  Macedonia (G-12312)
Owens Corning Sales LLC ....B 740 587-3562
  Granville (G-10336)
P C R Restorations Inc ....E 419 747-7957
  Mansfield (G-12501)
Schmelzer Industries Inc ....E 740 743-2866
  Somerset (G-17267)
◆ Seaman Corporation ....C 330 262-1111
  Wooster (G-20652)
Snyder Manufacturing Co Ltd ....G 330 343-4456
  Dover (G-8856)
Toledo Fiber Products Corp ....F 419 720-0303
  Toledo (G-18559)
Yoders Nylon Halter Shop ....G 330 893-3479
  Millersburg (G-14155)

2231 Wool, Woven Fabric

Intertape Polymr Woven USA Inc .....E 704 279-3011
  Springfield (G-17425)
Midwest Composites LLC ....E 419 738-2431
  Wapakoneta (G-19342)

2241 Fabric Mills, Cotton, Wool, Silk & Man-Made

A & P Technology Inc ....E 513 688-3200
  Cincinnati (G-3234)
A & P Technology Inc ....D 513 688-3200
  Cincinnati (G-3235)
A & P Technology Inc ....D 513 688-3200
  Cincinnati (G-3236)
A & P Technology Inc ....E 513 688-3200
  Cincinnati (G-3237)
▲ A & P Technology Inc ....E 513 688-3200
  Cincinnati (G-3238)
▲ Amfm Inc ....E 440 953-4545
  Willoughby (G-20272)
Champion Webbing Company Inc ....G 330 920-1007
  Cuyahoga Falls (G-7848)
Community Action Program Corp ....F 740 374-8501
  Marietta (G-12617)

◆ Db Rediheat Inc ....E 216 361-0530
  Cleveland (G-5075)
▲ Denizen Inc ....F 937 615-9561
  Piqua (G-16111)
▲ Grove Engineered Products Inc .....G 419 659-5939
  Columbus Grove (G-7635)
Joe Busby ....G 513 821-1716
  Cincinnati (G-3876)
◆ Keuchel & Associates Inc ....E 330 945-9455
  Cuyahoga Falls (G-7888)
▲ Mitchellace Inc ....E 740 354-2813
  Portsmouth (G-16291)
Murrubber Technologies Inc ....G 330 688-4881
  Stow (G-17609)
Paxar Corporation ....F 937 681-4541
  Dayton (G-8418)
Piland Parts ....G 330 686-3083
  Stow (G-17617)
Ransom & Randolph ....G 419 794-1210
  Maumee (G-13141)
▲ Samsel Rope & Marine Supply Co ..E 216 241-0333
  Cleveland (G-6029)
▲ Shore To Shore Inc ....D 937 866-1908
  Dayton (G-8505)
Shurtape Technologies LLC ....B 440 937-7000
  Avon (G-966)
▲ Sole Choice Inc ....E 740 354-2813
  Portsmouth (G-16302)
◆ Spunfab Ltd ....E 330 945-9455
  Cuyahoga Falls (G-7922)
US Cotton LLC ....B 216 676-6400
  Cleveland (G-6244)
Vacuflo Factory ....G 330 875-2450
  Louisville (G-12170)

2252 Hosiery, Except Women's

Agile Socks LLC ....G 614 440-2812
  Columbus (G-6550)
Broken Spinning Wheel ....G 419 825-1609
  Swanton (G-17907)
Disante Socks ....G 614 481-3243
  Columbus (G-6866)
Forepleasure ....G 330 821-1293
  Alliance (G-468)
Hype Socks LLC ....F 855 497-3769
  Columbus (G-6497)
Next Step Socks LLC ....G 216 534-8077
  Lakewood (G-11531)

2253 Knit Outerwear Mills

Digitek Corp ....F 513 794-3190
  Blue Ash (G-1758)
E Retailing Associates LLC ....D 614 300-5785
  Columbus (G-6880)
Fine Points Inc ....F 216 229-6644
  Cleveland (G-5239)
Gibbs E & Associates LLC ....G 614 939-1672
  New Albany (G-14625)
Heritage Inc ....G 614 860-1185
  Reynoldsburg (G-16443)
Okm LLC ....G 216 272-6375
  Cleveland (G-5808)
▲ Pjs Wholesale Inc ....G 614 402-9363
  Columbus (G-7318)
Wonder-Shirts Inc ....G 917 679-2336
  Dublin (G-9012)

2258 Lace & Warp Knit Fabric Mills

Murray Fabrics Inc ....F 216 881-4041
  Cleveland (G-5713)

2261 Cotton Fabric Finishers

◆ Air Waves LLC ....C 740 548-1200
  Lewis Center (G-11743)
Apparel Screen Printing Inc ....G 513 733-9495
  Cincinnati (G-3352)
▲ Atlantis Sportswear Inc ....E 937 773-0680
  Piqua (G-16101)
Designer Awards Inc ....G 937 339-4444
  Troy (G-18650)
▼ Duracote Corporation ....E 330 296-9600
  Ravenna (G-16376)
Fryes Soccer Shoppe ....G 937 832-2230
  Englewood (G-9359)
◆ Image Group of Toledo Inc ....E 419 866-3300
  Holland (G-10935)
Phantasm Designs ....G 419 538-6737
  Ottawa (G-15662)

Precision Imprint ....G 740 592-5916
  Athens (G-846)
Rapid Signs & More Inc ....G 513 553-4040
  New Richmond (G-14814)
Shirt Stop LLC ....G 740 574-4774
  Wheelersburg (G-20185)
Three Cord LLC ....G 419 445-2673
  Archbold (G-671)
Uptown Dog The Inc ....G 740 592-4600
  Athens (G-853)
West-Camp Press Inc ....D 216 426-2660
  Cleveland (G-6301)
Zenos Activewear Inc ....G 614 443-0070
  Columbus (G-7626)

2262 Silk & Man-Made Fabric Finishers

717 Inc ....G 440 925-0402
  Lakewood (G-11507)
B Richardson Inc ....F 330 724-2122
  Akron (G-76)
Cincinnati Advg Pdts LLC ....E 513 346-7310
  Cincinnati (G-3479)
Creatia Inc ....G 937 368-3100
  Fletcher (G-9782)
E & E Screen Prtg & Cstm EMB ....E 614 235-2177
  Columbus (G-6878)
Evolution Crtive Solutions LLC ....E 513 681-4450
  Cincinnati (G-3660)
Fcs Graphics Inc ....G 216 771-5177
  Cleveland (G-5225)
Flashions Sportswear Ltd ....G 937 323-5885
  Springfield (G-17403)
Great Oppurtunities Inc ....G 614 868-1899
  Columbus (G-6969)
▲ Mmi Textiles Inc ....F 440 899-8050
  Westlake (G-20131)
Ohio Flock-Cote Company Inc ....E 440 914-1122
  Solon (G-17210)
Phantasm Designs ....G 419 538-6737
  Ottawa (G-15662)
Scenic Screen ....G 419 468-3110
  Galion (G-10153)
Sportsco Imprinting ....G 513 641-5111
  Cincinnati (G-4360)
◆ Tranzonic Acquisition Corp ....A 216 535-4300
  Richmond Heights (G-16505)
Tranzonic Companies ....C 440 446-0643
  Cleveland (G-6198)
Wayne Sporting Goods ....G 937 236-6665
  Dayton (G-8586)
Wizard Graphics Inc ....G 419 354-3098
  Bowling Green (G-2006)

2269 Textile Finishers, NEC

Creative Commercial Finishing ....G 513 722-9393
  Loveland (G-12184)
◆ Paxar Corporation ....E 845 398-3229
  Mentor (G-13544)
Pelz Lettering Inc ....G 419 625-3567
  Sandusky (G-16838)
Southern Adhesive Coatings ....G 513 561-8440
  Cincinnati (G-4355)

2273 Carpets & Rugs

Absorbcore LLC ....G 440 614-0457
  North Olmsted (G-15180)
Alliance Carpet Cushion Co ....D 740 966-5001
  Johnstown (G-11254)
B and L Sales Inc ....G 330 279-2007
  Millersburg (G-14061)
▲ Boardman Molded Products Inc ....D 330 788-2400
  Youngstown (G-20854)
Buckeye Volleyball Center LLC ....G 614 764-1075
  Powell (G-16309)
Crown Dielectric Inds Inc ....C 614 224-5161
  Columbus (G-6839)
Davies Since 1900 ....G 419 756-4212
  Mansfield (G-12432)
◆ Durable Corporation ....D 800 537-1603
  Norwalk (G-15389)
Johns Manville Corporation ....B 419 878-8111
  Waterville (G-19498)
Kadee Industries Newco Inc ....F 440 439-8650
  Bedford (G-1420)
Lapchi LLC ....G 216 360-0104
  Cleveland (G-5561)
Mat Basics Incorporated ....G 513 793-0313
  Blue Ash (G-1814)
Mini Graphics Inc ....G 513 563-8600
  Cincinnati (G-4030)

Employee Codes: A=Over 500 employees, B=251-500
C=101-250, D=51-100, E=20-50, F=10-19, G=3-9

22 TEXTILE MILL PRODUCTS

Mohawk Industries Inc .... C 800 837-3812
  Grove City *(G-10447)*
Remnant Room .... G 937 938-7350
  Dayton *(G-8471)*
Spacelinks Enterprises Inc .... D 330 788-2401
  Youngstown *(G-21035)*
◆ Tranzonic Companies .... C 216 535-4300
  Richmond Heights *(G-16506)*
Tranzonic Companies .... C 440 446-0643
  Cleveland *(G-6198)*
Xt Innovations Ltd .... G 419 562-1989
  Bucyrus *(G-2352)*

2281 Yarn Spinning Mills

▲ Specilty Fbrics Converting Inc .... E 706 637-3000
  Fairlawn *(G-9618)*
Yarn Shop Inc .... G 614 457-7836
  Columbus *(G-7621)*

2282 Yarn Texturizing, Throwing, Twisting & Winding Mills

Alliance Carpet Cushion Co .... D 740 966-5001
  Johnstown *(G-11254)*
US Greentech .... G 513 371-5520
  Cincinnati *(G-4457)*

2284 Thread Mills

Alvin L Roepke .... F 419 862-3891
  Elmore *(G-9203)*

2295 Fabrics Coated Not Rubberized

Alron .... G 330 477-3405
  Strasburg *(G-17644)*
Bexley Fabrics Inc .... G 614 231-7272
  Columbus *(G-6666)*
▲ Biothane Coated Webbing Corp .... E 440 327-0485
  North Ridgeville *(G-15212)*
▲ Buschman Corporation .... F 216 431-6633
  Cleveland *(G-4853)*
▼ Duracote Corporation .... E 330 296-9600
  Ravenna *(G-16376)*
Durez Corporation .... C 567 295-6400
  Kenton *(G-11404)*
Excello Fabric Finishers Inc .... G 740 622-7444
  Coshocton *(G-7732)*
Gvc Plastics & Metals LLC .... G 440 232-9360
  Bedford *(G-1409)*
Laserflex Corporation .... D 614 850-9600
  Hilliard *(G-10837)*
Lintec USA Holding Inc .... G 781 935-7850
  Stow *(G-17602)*
Ohio Metalizing LLC .... G 330 830-1092
  Massillon *(G-13030)*
Omnova Overseas Inc .... C 330 869-4200
  Fairlawn *(G-9614)*
Petfiber LLC .... F 216 767-4482
  Cleveland *(G-5866)*
Prints & Paints Flr Cvg Co Inc .... E 419 462-5663
  Galion *(G-10151)*
▲ Schneller LLC .... C 330 676-7183
  Kent *(G-11380)*
Shaheen Oriental Rug Co Inc .... F 330 493-9000
  Canton *(G-2813)*
Spectroglass Corp .... G 614 297-0412
  Columbus *(G-7471)*
Trim Systems Operating Corp ...... C 614 289-5360
  New Albany *(G-14639)*

2296 Tire Cord & Fabric

▲ Akro Polychem Inc .... G 330 864-0360
  Fairlawn *(G-9592)*
▲ ARC Abrasives Inc .... D 800 888-4885
  Troy *(G-18638)*
Cleveland Canvas Goods Mfg Co .. D 216 361-4567
  Cleveland *(G-4948)*
Mfh Partners Inc .... F 440 461-4100
  Cleveland *(G-5664)*
Midwest Precision Products .... F 440 237-9500
  Cleveland *(G-5683)*

2297 Fabrics, Nonwoven

Autoneum North America Inc .... B 419 693-0511
  Oregon *(G-15556)*
Intrusion-Prepakt Inc .... G 440 238-6950
  Cleveland *(G-5472)*
Polyflex LLC .... F 440 946-0758
  Willoughby *(G-20406)*

▲ Toyobo Kureha America Co Ltd ... E 513 771-6788
  Cincinnati *(G-4427)*

2298 Cordage & Twine

Connect Television .... G 614 876-4402
  Hilliard *(G-10820)*
Patches LLC .... G 513 304-4882
  Williamsburg *(G-20253)*
Phoenix/Electrotek LLC .... E 740 681-1412
  Lancaster *(G-11597)*
▲ R C Packaging Systems .... F 248 684-6363
  Mentor *(G-13568)*
Radix Wire & Cable LLC .... G 216 731-9191
  Cleveland *(G-5955)*

2299 Textile Goods, NEC

Big Productions Inc .... G 440 775-0015
  Oberlin *(G-15491)*
Construction Techniques Inc .... F 216 267-7310
  Cleveland *(G-5019)*
▲ Cusc International Ltd .... G 513 881-2000
  Hamilton *(G-10549)*
Dayton Bag & Burlap Co .... F 937 253-1722
  Dayton *(G-8128)*
J Rettenmaier USA LP .... G 440 385-6701
  Oberlin *(G-15500)*
J Rettenmaier USA LP .... D 937 652-2101
  Urbana *(G-18997)*
Johnston-Morehouse-Dickey Co ... G 614 866-0452
  Columbus *(G-7075)*
Johnston-Morehouse-Dickey Co ... G 330 405-6050
  Macedonia *(G-12308)*
Meridian Industries Inc .... E 330 359-5809
  Beach City *(G-1212)*
Nanomeld LLC .... G 740 477-5900
  Circleville *(G-4549)*
▲ NC Works Inc .... E 937 514-7781
  Franklin *(G-9903)*
▲ Ohio Table Pad Company .... D 419 872-6400
  Perrysburg *(G-15986)*
▲ Ohio Table Pad of Indiana .... E 419 872-6400
  Perrysburg *(G-15987)*
Tops Inc .... G 440 954-9451
  Mentor *(G-13609)*

23 APPAREL AND OTHER FINISHED PRODUCTS MADE FROM FABRICS AND SIMILAR MATERIAL

2311 Men's & Boys' Suits, Coats & Overcoats

American Commodore Tuxedos ... G 440 324-2889
  Elyria *(G-9214)*
Bea-Ecc Apparels Inc .... G 216 650-6336
  Cleveland *(G-4797)*
Cinderella .... G 937 312-9969
  Dayton *(G-8089)*
Contingncy Prcrement Group LLC ... G 513 204-9590
  Maineville *(G-12366)*
▲ Fechheimer Brothers Company .... C 513 793-5400
  Blue Ash *(G-1772)*
Global Gear LLC .... G 941 830-0531
  Chagrin Falls *(G-3048)*
Government Specialty Pdts LLC ... G 937 672-9473
  Dayton *(G-8233)*
Hugo Boss Usa Inc .... B 216 671-8100
  Cleveland *(G-5425)*
◆ Lion Apparel Inc .... G 937 898-1949
  Dayton *(G-8313)*
Simply Elegant Formals Inc .... G 419 738-7722
  Wapakoneta *(G-19354)*
Tom James Company .... G 614 488-8400
  Columbus *(G-7533)*
Vgs Inc .... C 216 431-7800
  Cleveland *(G-6256)*
Wahconah Group Inc .... F 216 923-0570
  Cleveland *(G-6284)*

2321 Men's & Boys' Shirts

▲ Fun-In-Games Inc .... G 866 587-1004
  Mason *(G-12874)*
J C L S Enterprises LLC .... G 740 472-0314
  Woodsfield *(G-20545)*
Pvh Corp .... G 330 562-4440
  Aurora *(G-900)*

2322 Men's & Boys' Underwear & Nightwear

Tranzonic Companies .... B 216 535-4300
  Richmond Heights *(G-16507)*

2325 Men's & Boys' Separate Trousers & Casual Slacks

Levi Strauss & Co .... F 513 539-7822
  Monroe *(G-14273)*
Whip Appeal Inc .... G 216 288-6201
  Cleveland *(G-6304)*

2326 Men's & Boys' Work Clothing

3n1 Mens Fashion .... G 513 851-3610
  Cincinnati *(G-3272)*
All-Bilt Uniform Corp .... E 513 793-5400
  Blue Ash *(G-1728)*
▲ Alsico Usa Inc .... D 330 673-7413
  Kent *(G-11292)*
Ansell Healthcare Products LLC ... C 740 295-5414
  Coshocton *(G-7720)*
Barton-Carey Medical Products ... E 419 887-1285
  Maumee *(G-13078)*
Bello Verde LLC .... G 614 365-3000
  Columbus *(G-6661)*
Carhartt Inc .... E 513 657-7130
  Cincinnati *(G-3444)*
Cintas Corporation .... D 513 631-5750
  Cincinnati *(G-3519)*
◆ Cintas Corporation .... A 513 459-1200
  Cincinnati *(G-3518)*
Cintas Corporation No 2 .... D 330 966-7800
  Canton *(G-2624)*
Cintas Sales Corporation .... E 513 459-1200
  Cincinnati *(G-3520)*
Cleveland Canvas Goods Mfg Co .. D 216 361-4567
  Cleveland *(G-4948)*
DCW Acquisition Inc .... F 216 451-0666
  Cleveland *(G-5079)*
Epluno LLC .... F 800 249-5275
  Miamisburg *(G-13664)*
Geauga Group LLC .... G 440 543-8797
  Chagrin Falls *(G-3047)*
Hall Safety Apparel Inc .... F 740 922-3671
  Uhrichsville *(G-18887)*
▲ Hands On International LLC .... G 513 502-9000
  Mason *(G-12884)*
Kip-Craft Incorporated .... D 216 898-5500
  Cleveland *(G-5537)*
Lawft .... G 419 422-5293
  Findlay *(G-9712)*
Linsalata Capital Partners Fun ..... G 440 684-1400
  Cleveland *(G-5579)*
▲ Morning Pride Mfg LLC .... A 937 264-2662
  Dayton *(G-8367)*
Pearl Healthwear Inc .... G 440 446-0265
  Cleveland *(G-5859)*
Pvh Corp .... G 330 562-4440
  Aurora *(G-900)*
▲ Rich Industries Inc .... E 330 339-4113
  New Philadelphia *(G-14797)*
Rons Texstyles LLC .... G 513 936-9975
  Columbus *(G-7400)*
Samson .... G 614 504-8038
  Columbus *(G-7419)*
Seven Mile Creek Corporation ..... F 937 456-3320
  Eaton *(G-9165)*
◆ Standard Textile Co Inc .... B 513 761-9256
  Cincinnati *(G-4372)*
◆ Tranzonic Acquisition Corp .... A 216 535-4300
  Richmond Heights *(G-16505)*
Tranzonic Companies .... C 440 446-0643
  Cleveland *(G-6198)*
Vgs Inc .... C 216 431-7800
  Cleveland *(G-6256)*
▲ Wagoner Stores Inc .... G 937 836-3636
  Englewood *(G-9383)*
Whip Appeal Inc .... G 216 288-6201
  Cleveland *(G-6304)*

2329 Men's & Boys' Clothing, NEC

Adidas North America Inc .... G 330 562-4689
  Aurora *(G-866)*
Afi Brands LLC .... G 614 999-6426
  Dublin *(G-8875)*
Aratinabox Companies Inc .... G 330 699-3421
  Uniontown *(G-18910)*
Carrera Holdings Inc .... G 216 687-1311
  Cleveland *(G-4883)*

Dunhams Sports .... F 330 334-3257
  Wadsworth *(G-19235)*
Fanz Stop .... G 937 310-1436
  Bellbrook *(G-1494)*
Gametime Apparel & Dezigns LLC .... G 740 255-5254
  Cambridge *(G-2439)*
Hilliard Cat Shack LLC .... G 614 527-9711
  Hilliard *(G-10829)*
Inner Fire Sports LLC .... G 719 244-6622
  Cincinnati *(G-3849)*
J America LLC .... G 614 914-2091
  Columbus *(G-7054)*
▲ Kam Manufacturing Inc .... C 419 238-6037
  Van Wert *(G-19096)*
Lettermans LLC .... G 330 345-2628
  Wooster *(G-20616)*
Noxgear LLC .... G 937 248-1860
  Columbus *(G-7231)*
Outdoor Army Store of Ashtabula .... F 440 992-8791
  Ashtabula *(G-794)*
Pantac Usa Ltd .... G 614 423-6743
  Columbus *(G-7289)*
Promotions Plus Inc .... G 440 582-2855
  Broadview Heights *(G-2098)*
Puck Hogs Pro Shop Inc .... G 419 540-1388
  Toledo *(G-18488)*
Quality Sewing Inc .... G 216 475-0411
  Cleveland *(G-5944)*
Riegle Colors .... G 937 548-8444
  Greenville *(G-10392)*
Rocky Brands Inc .... B 740 753-1951
  Nelsonville *(G-14595)*
Sacks Bruce & Associates .... G 419 537-0623
  Ottawa Hills *(G-15677)*
Torso .... G 614 421-7663
  Columbus *(G-7534)*
Under Armour Inc .... G 330 995-9557
  Aurora *(G-912)*
▲ Universal Lettering Inc .... E 419 238-9320
  Van Wert *(G-19109)*
▲ Vesi Incorporated .... E 513 563-6002
  Cincinnati *(G-4479)*
Whip Appeal Inc .... G 216 288-6201
  Cleveland *(G-6304)*

2331 Women's & Misses' Blouses

Afi Brands LLC .... G 614 999-6426
  Dublin *(G-8875)*
J C L S Enterprises LLC .... G 740 472-0314
  Woodsfield *(G-20545)*
▲ Kam Manufacturing Inc .... C 419 238-6037
  Van Wert *(G-19096)*
Quality Sewing Inc .... G 216 475-0411
  Cleveland *(G-5944)*
Rocky Brands Inc .... B 740 753-1951
  Nelsonville *(G-14595)*
Smitten Enterprises LLC .... G 937 267-6963
  Springboro *(G-17353)*

2335 Women's & Misses' Dresses

Finishing Touch .... F 440 263-9264
  Cleveland *(G-5241)*
Lavander Bridal Salon .... F 330 602-0333
  Dover *(G-8836)*
Polished Pearl LLP .... G 513 659-8824
  Montgomery *(G-14298)*
Quality Sewing Inc .... G 216 475-0411
  Cleveland *(G-5944)*
Surili Couture LLC .... F 440 600-1456
  Westlake *(G-20164)*

2337 Women's & Misses' Suits, Coats & Skirts

◆ Cintas Corporation .... A 513 459-1200
  Cincinnati *(G-3518)*
Cintas Corporation .... D 513 631-5750
  Cincinnati *(G-3519)*
Cintas Corporation No 2 .... D 330 966-7800
  Canton *(G-2624)*
▲ Fechheimer Brothers Company .... C 513 793-5400
  Blue Ash *(G-1772)*
Lucio Vanni LLC .... G 440 823-6103
  Rocky River *(G-16549)*
Pearl Healthwear Inc .... G 440 446-0265
  Cleveland *(G-5859)*
◆ Standard Textile Co Inc .... B 513 761-9256
  Cincinnati *(G-4372)*

2339 Women's & Misses' Outerwear, NEC

▲ 5 BS Inc .... C 740 454-8453
  Zanesville *(G-21090)*
Barton-Carey Medical Products .... E 419 887-1285
  Maumee *(G-13078)*
Carrera Holdings Inc .... G 216 687-1311
  Cleveland *(G-4883)*
Fanz Stop .... G 937 310-1436
  Bellbrook *(G-1494)*
▲ Fechheimer Brothers Company .... C 513 793-5400
  Blue Ash *(G-1772)*
Geauga Group LLC .... G 440 543-8797
  Chagrin Falls *(G-3047)*
Hipsy LLC .... G 513 403-5333
  Fairfield *(G-9504)*
Indra Holdings Corp .... G 513 682-8200
  West Chester *(G-19867)*
Inner Fire Sports LLC .... G 719 244-6622
  Cincinnati *(G-3849)*
Kip-Craft Incorporated .... D 216 898-5500
  Cleveland *(G-5537)*
Lena Fiore Inc .... F 330 659-0020
  Akron *(G-252)*
Lettermans LLC .... G 330 345-2628
  Wooster *(G-20616)*
Majestic Sportswear Company .... G 937 773-1144
  Piqua *(G-16140)*
Owl Be Sweatin .... G 513 260-2026
  Cincinnati *(G-4127)*
Rocky Brands Inc .... B 740 753-1951
  Nelsonville *(G-14595)*
▲ Universal Lettering Inc .... E 419 238-9320
  Van Wert *(G-19109)*
▲ Vesi Incorporated .... E 513 563-6002
  Cincinnati *(G-4479)*
Whip Appeal Inc .... G 216 288-6201
  Cleveland *(G-6304)*

2341 Women's, Misses' & Children's Underwear & Nightwear

Tranzonic Companies .... B 216 535-4300
  Richmond Heights *(G-16507)*

2342 Brassieres, Girdles & Garments

◆ Golda Inc .... B 216 464-5490
  Cleveland *(G-5328)*
Laura Dawson .... G 513 777-2513
  West Chester *(G-19735)*

2353 Hats, Caps & Millinery

▲ Barbs Graffiti Inc .... E 216 881-5550
  Cleveland *(G-4790)*
Blonde Swan .... F 419 307-8591
  Fremont *(G-10000)*
Bows Barrettes & Baubles .... F 440 247-2697
  Moreland Hills *(G-14401)*
Genesco Inc .... G 330 633-8179
  Akron *(G-187)*
◆ Pukka Inc .... D 419 429-7808
  Findlay *(G-9743)*
Thomas Creative Apparel Inc .... E 419 929-1506
  New London *(G-14739)*
Thundawear LLC .... G 419 787-2675
  Toledo *(G-18550)*
▲ Wagoner Stores Inc .... G 937 836-3636
  Englewood *(G-9383)*

2361 Children's & Infants' Dresses & Blouses

Tween Brands Inc .... F 937 435-6928
  Dayton *(G-8572)*

2371 Fur Goods

Blonde Swan .... F 419 307-8591
  Fremont *(G-10000)*

2381 Dress & Work Gloves

C & G Associates Inc .... G 419 756-6583
  Mansfield *(G-12418)*
Hall Safety Apparel Inc .... F 740 922-3671
  Uhrichsville *(G-18887)*
Hillman Group Inc .... G 440 248-7000
  Cleveland *(G-5409)*
Independent Protection Systems .... G 330 832-7992
  Massillon *(G-13003)*
Pristine Exteriors .... G 330 957-5664
  New Franklin *(G-14697)*
▲ Totes Isotoner Corporation .... F 513 682-8200
  West Chester *(G-19907)*
▲ Totes Isotoner Holdings Corp .... C 513 682-8200
  West Chester *(G-19908)*
▲ Wcm Holdings Inc .... C 513 705-2100
  Cincinnati *(G-4493)*
▲ West Chester Holdings LLC .... C 800 647-1900
  Cincinnati *(G-4499)*

2384 Robes & Dressing Gowns

Thomas Creative Apparel Inc .... E 419 929-1506
  New London *(G-14739)*

2385 Waterproof Outerwear

Grow With Me- Creations .... G 800 850-1889
  Hartville *(G-10691)*
Paradigm International Inc .... G 740 370-2428
  Piketon *(G-16078)*

2386 Leather & Sheep Lined Clothing

Fionas Fineries .... G 440 796-7426
  Willoughby *(G-20322)*

2387 Apparel Belts

Peregrine Outdoor Products LLC .... G 800 595-3850
  Lebanon *(G-11683)*

2389 Apparel & Accessories, NEC

Akron Design & Costume Co .... G 330 644-4849
  Coventry Township *(G-7762)*
Alma Mater Sportswear LLC .... G 614 260-8222
  Columbus *(G-6576)*
Costume Specialists Inc .... E 614 464-2115
  Columbus *(G-6825)*
Costume Specialists Inc .... E 614 464-2115
  Columbus *(G-6826)*
Direct Disposables LLC .... G 440 717-3335
  Brecksville *(G-2029)*
◆ Fire-Dex LLC .... D 330 723-0000
  Medina *(G-13262)*
◆ Golda Inc .... B 216 464-5490
  Cleveland *(G-5328)*
Indra Holdings Corp .... G 513 682-8200
  West Chester *(G-19867)*
Inner Fire Sports LLC .... G 719 244-6622
  Cincinnati *(G-3849)*
L Brands Inc .... C 614 479-2000
  Columbus *(G-7106)*
New London Regalia Mfg Co .... F 419 929-1516
  New London *(G-14734)*
Novak Supply LLC .... G 216 741-5112
  Cleveland *(G-5791)*
Promo Costumes Inc .... G 740 383-5176
  Marion *(G-12728)*
Rageon Inc .... E 617 633-0544
  Cleveland *(G-5958)*
Ralphie Gianni Mfg & Co .... F 216 507-3873
  Euclid *(G-9439)*
▲ Rich Industries Inc .... E 330 339-4113
  New Philadelphia *(G-14797)*
Rocky Brands Inc .... B 740 753-1951
  Nelsonville *(G-14595)*
Salindia LLC .... G 614 501-4799
  Columbus *(G-7416)*
Schenz Theatrical Supply Inc .... F 513 542-6100
  Cincinnati *(G-4306)*
Snaps Inc .... G 419 477-5100
  Mount Cory *(G-14418)*
Stagecraft Costuming Inc .... F 513 541-7150
  Cincinnati *(G-4369)*
◆ Standard Textile Co Inc .... B 513 761-9256
  Cincinnati *(G-4372)*
▲ Status Mens Accessories .... G 440 232-6700
  Cleveland *(G-6100)*
Tactical Revolution LLC .... G 419 348-9526
  Ottawa *(G-15668)*
Thomas Creative Apparel Inc .... E 419 929-1506
  New London *(G-14739)*
Top Hat Designs .... G 614 898-1962
  Westerville *(G-20079)*
V Collection .... G 419 517-0508
  Sylvania *(G-17967)*
Walter F Stephens Jr Inc .... E 937 746-0521
  Franklin *(G-9930)*

2391 Curtains & Draperies

A Designers Workroom .... G 513 251-7396
  Cincinnati *(G-3280)*
Accent Drapery Co Inc .... E 614 488-0741
  Columbus *(G-6531)*

23 APPAREL AND OTHER FINISHED PRODUCTS MADE FROM FABRICS AND SIMILAR MATERIAL — SIC SECTION

Anthony Decorative Fabrics and ....G...... 937 299-4637
  Moraine (G-14331)
Biaginis Draperies ....G...... 614 876-1706
  Hilliard (G-10812)
Carter Drapery Service Inc................G...... 419 289-2530
  Ashland (G-689)
Drapery Stitch Cincinnati Inc.............F...... 513 561-2443
  Cincinnati (G-3609)
Drapery Stitch of Delphos ....E...... 419 692-3921
  Delphos (G-8741)
E W Perry Service Co Inc..................G...... 419 473-1231
  Toledo (G-18273)
Elden Draperies of Toledo Inc ....F...... 419 535-1909
  Toledo (G-18277)
Janson Industries ....D...... 330 455-7029
  Canton (G-2716)
Silver Threads Inc...........................E...... 614 733-0099
  Plain City (G-16211)
▲ Sk Textile Inc.............................G...... 323 581-8986
  Cincinnati (G-4341)
Specialty Drapery Workroom ....G...... 330 864-4190
  Akron (G-383)
Stan Rileys Custom Draperies.............G...... 513 821-3732
  Cincinnati (G-4370)
◆ Standard Textile Co Inc.................B...... 513 761-9256
  Cincinnati (G-4372)
Style-Line Incorporated ....G...... 614 291-0600
  Columbus (G-7497)
Tiffin Scenic Studios Inc....................D...... 800 445-1546
  Tiffin (G-18089)
Vocational Services Inc.....................C...... 216 431-8085
  Cleveland (G-6267)
Wahlies Cstm Cft Drapery Uphl............G...... 419 229-1731
  Lima (G-11958)
Wise Window Treatment Inc ....F...... 216 676-4080
  Berea (G-1633)

2392 House furnishings: Textile

A & W Table Pad Co ....F...... 800 541-0271
  Cleveland (G-4582)
Aunties Attic ....E...... 740 548-5059
  Lewis Center (G-11748)
Brentwood Originals Inc ....B...... 330 793-2255
  Youngstown (G-20856)
▲ Casco Mfg Solutions Inc ....D...... 513 681-0003
  Cincinnati (G-3447)
Columbus Canvas Products Inc ....F...... 614 375-1397
  Columbus (G-6785)
▲ Cvg National Seating Co LLC ....D...... 219 872-7295
  New Albany (G-14621)
◆ Db Rediheat Inc ....E...... 216 361-0530
  Cleveland (G-5075)
DCW Acquisition Inc........................F...... 216 451-0666
  Cleveland (G-5079)
▲ Down-Lite International Inc............C...... 513 229-3696
  Mason (G-12858)
▲ Downhome Inc...........................E...... 513 921-3373
  Cincinnati (G-3607)
Eastern Slipcover Company Inc ....G...... 440 951-2310
  Mentor (G-13436)
◆ Easy Way Leisure Corporation ....E...... 513 731-5640
  Cincinnati (G-3627)
Fluvitex USA Inc.............................G...... 614 610-1199
  Groveport (G-10490)
▲ Greendale Home Fashions LLC......D...... 859 916-5475
  Cincinnati (G-3782)
Guardian Co Inc ....G...... 216 721-2262
  Cleveland (G-5359)
Ha-Ste Manufacturing Co Inc.............E...... 937 968-4858
  Union City (G-18904)
▲ Henty USA ....F...... 513 984-5590
  Cincinnati (G-3809)
▲ Impact Products LLC...................C...... 419 841-2891
  Toledo (G-18342)
Innocor Foam Tech - Acp Inc ....F...... 419 647-4172
  Spencerville (G-17309)
Lawnview Industries Inc....................C...... 937 653-5217
  Urbana (G-19003)
▲ Master Mfg Co Inc ....G...... 216 641-0500
  Cleveland (G-5632)
Ohio Table Pad Company ....E...... 419 872-6400
  Perrysburg (G-15985)
▲ Ohio Table Pad Company ....D...... 419 872-6400
  Perrysburg (G-15986)
Pen Brands LLC ....E...... 216 674-1430
  Brooklyn Heights (G-2129)
◆ Saturday Knight Ltd ....D...... 513 641-1400
  Cincinnati (G-4300)
Seven Mile Creek Corporation ....F...... 937 456-3320
  Eaton (G-9165)

Sewline Products Inc........................F...... 419 929-1114
  New London (G-14738)
Silver Threads Inc...........................E...... 614 733-0099
  Plain City (G-16211)
Stan Rileys Custom Draperies.............G...... 513 821-3732
  Cincinnati (G-4370)
Vss Store Operations LLC ....G...... 800 411-5116
  Reynoldsburg (G-16460)
Wise Window Treatment Inc ....F...... 216 676-4080
  Berea (G-1633)

2393 Textile Bags

American Made Bags LLC..................F...... 330 475-1385
  Akron (G-62)
▼ Baggallini Inc.............................G...... 800 628-0321
  Pickerington (G-16040)
Capital City Awning Company ....E...... 614 221-5404
  Columbus (G-6731)
Cleveland Canvas Goods Mfg Co ....D...... 216 361-4567
  Cleveland (G-4948)
Columbus Canvas Products Inc ....F...... 614 375-1397
  Columbus (G-6785)
DCW Acquisition Inc........................F...... 216 451-0666
  Cleveland (G-5079)
▲ Hdt Expeditionary Systems Inc ......B...... 216 438-6111
  Solon (G-17161)
Jordan E Armour ....E...... 330 252-0290
  Akron (G-226)
▲ King Bag and Manufacturing Co .....E...... 513 541-5440
  Cincinnati (G-3910)
Lamports Filter Media Inc ....F...... 216 881-2050
  Cleveland (G-5557)
Loctote LLC ....G...... 614 407-0882
  Blacklick (G-1688)
Luxaire Cushion Co ....F...... 330 872-0995
  Newton Falls (G-14989)
Nyp Corp (frmr Ny-Pters Corp) ....G...... 440 428-0129
  Madison (G-12354)
Polka DOT Pin Cushion Inc................G...... 330 659-0233
  Richfield (G-16481)
Queen City Carpets LLC ....F...... 513 823-8238
  Cincinnati (G-4235)
▲ Rich Industries Inc.....................G...... 330 339-4113
  New Philadelphia (G-14797)
Sailors Tailor Inc.............................G...... 937 862-7781
  Spring Valley (G-17318)
Seven Mile Creek Corporation ....F...... 937 456-3320
  Eaton (G-9165)

2394 Canvas Prdts

A B C Sign Inc ....F...... 513 241-8884
  Cincinnati (G-3278)
▼ Advantage Tent Fittings Inc ....F...... 740 773-3015
  Chillicothe (G-3173)
Allen Zahradnik Inc..........................G...... 419 729-1201
  Toledo (G-18163)
American Canvas Products Inc...........F...... 419 382-8450
  Toledo (G-18172)
Awning Fabri Caters Inc ....G...... 216 476-4888
  Cleveland (G-4781)
Berlin Boat Covers...........................G...... 330 547-7600
  Berlin Center (G-1645)
Canvas Exchange Inc ....G...... 216 749-2233
  Cleveland (G-4868)
Canvas Specialty Mfg Co ....G...... 216 881-0647
  Cleveland (G-4868)
Capital City Awning Company ....E...... 614 221-5404
  Columbus (G-6731)
▼ Celina Tent Inc..........................E...... 419 586-3610
  Celina (G-2954)
▼ Chalfant Sew Fabricators Inc.........E...... 216 521-7922
  Cleveland (G-4907)
Cleveland Canvas Goods Mfg Co ....D...... 216 361-4567
  Cleveland (G-4948)
Columbus Canvas Products Inc ....F...... 614 375-1397
  Columbus (G-6785)
Crown Dielectric Inds Inc ....C...... 614 224-5161
  Columbus (G-6839)
Custom Canvas & Boat Repair ....F...... 419 732-3314
  Lakeside (G-11501)
Custom Tarpaulin Products Inc ....F...... 330 758-1801
  Youngstown (G-20883)
DCW Acquisition Inc........................F...... 216 451-0666
  Cleveland (G-5079)
Deer Creek Custom Canvas LLC ....G...... 740 495-9239
  New Holland (G-14701)
Delphos Tent and Awning Inc ....E...... 419 692-5776
  Delphos (G-8740)
Electra Tarp Inc..............................F...... 330 477-7168
  Canton (G-2667)

Embedee LLC ....G...... 419 678-7007
  Coldwater (G-6407)
Forest City Companies Inc ....E...... 216 586-5279
  Cleveland (G-5261)
Galion Canvas Products ....F...... 419 468-5333
  Galion (G-10139)
Glawe Manufacturing Co Inc..............G...... 937 754-0064
  Fairborn (G-9460)
Griffin Fisher Co Inc ....G...... 513 961-2110
  Cincinnati (G-3785)
▲ Hdt Expeditionary Systems Inc ......B...... 216 438-6111
  Solon (G-17161)
Independent Awning & Canvas Co......G...... 937 223-9661
  Dayton (G-8261)
J & W Canvas Company ....G...... 330 652-7678
  Mineral Ridge (G-14167)
Lesch Boat Cover Canvas Co LLC ......G...... 419 668-6374
  Norwalk (G-15404)
Lumenomics Inc..............................E...... 614 798-3500
  Lewis Center (G-11766)
◆ Main Awning & Tent Inc ....G...... 513 621-6947
  Cincinnati (G-3974)
National Bias Fabric Co ....E...... 216 361-0530
  Cleveland (G-5722)
Odyssey Canvas Works Inc ....G...... 937 392-4422
  Ripley (G-16515)
▲ Ohio Awning & Manufacturing Co ...E...... 216 861-2400
  Cleveland (G-5799)
ONeals Tarpaulin & Awning Co ....F...... 330 788-6504
  Youngstown (G-20985)
P C R Restorations Inc ....F...... 419 747-7957
  Mansfield (G-12501)
Phillips Awning Co..........................G...... 740 653-2433
  Lancaster (G-11596)
Queen City Awning & Tent Co ....E...... 513 530-9660
  Cincinnati (G-4234)
R F W Holdings Inc ....G...... 440 331-8300
  Cleveland (G-5951)
Ragman Inc ....G...... 419 255-8068
  Toledo (G-18497)
▲ Rainbow Bedding ....G...... 330 852-3127
  Sugarcreek (G-17861)
▲ Rainbow Industries Inc................G...... 937 323-6493
  Springfield (G-17479)
Raven Industries Inc........................G...... 937 323-4625
  Springfield (G-17480)
Rex Manufacturing Co ....F...... 419 224-5751
  Lima (G-11931)
Sailors Tailor Inc.............................G...... 937 862-7781
  Spring Valley (G-17318)
▲ Samsel Rope & Marine Supply Co ...E...... 216 241-0333
  Cleveland (G-6029)
Schaaf Co Inc ....G...... 513 241-7044
  Cincinnati (G-4304)
▲ Scherba Industries Inc ....D...... 330 273-3200
  Brunswick (G-2238)
Shade Youngstown & Aluminum Co ....G...... 330 782-2373
  Youngstown (G-21028)
Shur-Co LLC ....G...... 330 297-0888
  Ravenna (G-16402)
South Akron Awning Co ....F...... 330 848-7611
  Akron (G-382)
Stan Rileys Custom Draperies.............G...... 513 821-3732
  Cincinnati (G-4370)
Tarpco Inc ....G...... 330 677-8277
  Kent (G-11392)
Tarped Out Inc...............................G...... 330 325-7722
  Ravenna (G-16412)
Tri County Tarp LLC ....E...... 419 288-3350
  Bradner (G-2016)
William Thompson ....G...... 440 232-4363
  Aurora (G-916)
Wolf G T Awning & Tent Co ....F...... 937 548-4161
  Greenville (G-10402)

2395 Pleating & Stitching For The Trade

▲ 5 BS Inc...................................C...... 740 454-8453
  Zanesville (G-21090)
A & S Inc ....G...... 866 209-1574
  Arcanum (G-627)
A Graphic Solution ....F...... 216 228-7223
  Cleveland (G-4587)
A To Z Wear Ltd ....G...... 513 923-4662
  Cincinnati (G-3281)
Aardvark Sportswear Inc...................G...... 330 793-9428
  Youngstown (G-20832)
Action Sports Apparel Inc ....G...... 330 848-9300
  Norton (G-15358)
All For Show Inc..............................G...... 440 729-7186
  Chesterland (G-3152)

SIC SECTION — 23 APPAREL AND OTHER FINISHED PRODUCTS MADE FROM FABRICS AND SIMILAR MATERIAL

Alley Cat Designs Inc ....G....... 937 291-8803
  Dayton *(G-8017)*
Alphabet Embroidery Studios ....F....... 937 372-6557
  Xenia *(G-20755)*
Alphabet Soup Inc ....G....... 330 467-4418
  Macedonia *(G-12276)*
Angelics A Quilters Haven ....G....... 330 484-5480
  Canton *(G-2573)*
Anything Personalized ....G....... 330 655-0723
  Twinsburg *(G-18734)*
Apparel Impressions Inc ....G....... 513 247-0555
  Cincinnati *(G-3351)*
Appleheart ....G....... 937 384-0430
  Miamisburg *(G-13641)*
Assoc Talents Inc ....G....... 440 716-1265
  Westlake *(G-20100)*
▲ Atlantis Sportswear Inc ....E....... 937 773-0680
  Piqua *(G-16101)*
Aubrey Rose Apparel LLC ....G....... 513 728-2681
  Cincinnati *(G-3370)*
Avina Specialties Inc ....G....... 419 592-5646
  Napoleon *(G-14533)*
B D P Services Inc ....D....... 740 828-9685
  Nashport *(G-14564)*
Barbs Custom Embroidery ....G....... 419 393-2226
  Defiance *(G-8616)*
Barbs Embroidery............................G....... 614 875-9933
  Grove City *(G-10416)*
▲ Barbs Graffiti Inc ....E....... 216 881-5550
  Cleveland *(G-4790)*
Big Kahuna Graphics LLC ....G....... 330 455-2625
  Canton *(G-2591)*
Cal Sales Embroidery ....G....... 440 236-3820
  Columbia Station *(G-6431)*
Campbell Signs & Apparel LLC ....F....... 330 386-4768
  East Liverpool *(G-9052)*
Carols Ultra Stitch & Variety ....G....... 419 935-8991
  Willard *(G-20238)*
Carter Evans Enterprises Inc ....G....... 614 920-2276
  Granville *(G-10327)*
▲ Catania Medallic Specialty ....E....... 440 933-9595
  Avon Lake *(G-981)*
Charles Wisvari ....F....... 740 671-9960
  Bellaire *(G-1484)*
Cheryl A Lucas ....G....... 614 755-2100
  Columbus *(G-6762)*
Chris Stepp ....G....... 513 248-0822
  Milford *(G-14002)*
CNG Business Group ....G....... 614 771-0877
  Hilliard *(G-10818)*
Color 3 Embroidery Inc ....G....... 330 652-9495
  Warren *(G-19385)*
Computer Stitch Designs Inc ....G....... 330 856-7826
  Warren *(G-19386)*
Craco Embroidery Inc ....G....... 513 563-6999
  Cincinnati *(G-3556)*
Creative Stitches Monogramming ....G....... 740 667-3592
  Little Hocking *(G-11991)*
David Brandeberry ....G....... 937 653-4680
  Urbana *(G-18988)*
Design Original Inc ....F....... 937 596-5121
  Jackson Center *(G-11207)*
Dimensions Three Inc ....G....... 614 539-5180
  Grove City *(G-10426)*
Eastgate Custom Graphics Ltd ....G....... 513 528-7922
  Cincinnati *(G-3625)*
Elegant Embroidery Llc ....G....... 440 878-0904
  Strongsville *(G-17741)*
Embroid ME ....G....... 216 459-9250
  Cleveland *(G-5171)*
Embroidered ID Inc ....G....... 440 974-8113
  Mentor *(G-13439)*
Embroidery Design Group LLC ....F....... 614 798-8152
  Columbus *(G-6894)*
Embroidme ....G....... 330 484-8484
  Canton *(G-2668)*
Emroid ME ....G....... 614 789-1898
  Westerville *(G-20051)*
Ems/Hooptech ....G....... 513 829-5768
  West Chester *(G-19697)*
Ernst Sporting Gds Minster LLC ......G....... 937 526-9822
  Versailles *(G-19179)*
Expert TS ....G....... 330 263-4588
  Wooster *(G-20589)*
Fastpatch Ltd ....F....... 513 367-1838
  Harrison *(G-10640)*
Fcs Graphics Inc ....G....... 216 771-5177
  Cleveland *(G-5225)*
Fine Line Embroidery Company ......G....... 330 788-9070
  Youngstown *(G-20904)*

Fine Line Embroidery Company ......G....... 440 331-7030
  Rocky River *(G-16547)*
Fineline Imprints Inc ....E....... 740 453-1083
  Zanesville *(G-21135)*
Finn Graphics Inc ....E....... 513 941-6161
  Cincinnati *(G-3690)*
Gail Berner ....G....... 937 322-0314
  Springfield *(G-17406)*
Garment Specialties Inc ....G....... 330 425-2928
  Twinsburg *(G-18779)*
Glorias ....G....... 330 264-8963
  Wooster *(G-20598)*
Good JP ....G....... 419 207-8484
  Ashland *(G-706)*
Got Graphix Llc ....F....... 330 703-9047
  Fairlawn *(G-9606)*
Graphic Stitch Inc ....G....... 937 642-6707
  Marysville *(G-12784)*
Graphix Junction ....G....... 234 284-8392
  Hudson *(G-11049)*
Great Oppurtunities Inc ....G....... 614 868-1899
  Columbus *(G-6969)*
H & H Screen Process Inc ....G....... 937 253-7520
  Dayton *(G-8240)*
Hang Time Group Inc ....G....... 216 771-5885
  Cleveland *(G-5369)*
Heller Acquisitions Inc ....G....... 937 833-2676
  Brookville *(G-2171)*
Hometown Threads ....G....... 440 779-6053
  North Olmsted *(G-15193)*
Initial Designs Inc ....G....... 419 475-3900
  Toledo *(G-18347)*
Initially Yours ....G....... 216 228-4478
  Lakewood *(G-11521)*
J America LLC ....G....... 614 914-2091
  Columbus *(G-7054)*
Jane Valentine ....G....... 330 452-3154
  North Canton *(G-15094)*
Jaquas Monogramming & Design ....G....... 419 422-2244
  Findlay *(G-9708)*
Jetts Embroideries ....G....... 937 981-3716
  Greenfield *(G-10353)*
Judy Dubois ....G....... 419 738-6979
  Wapakoneta *(G-19336)*
Just Name It Inc ....G....... 614 626-8662
  Pickerington *(G-16052)*
K Ventures Inc ....F....... 419 678-2308
  Coldwater *(G-6415)*
Kathy Simecek ....G....... 440 886-2468
  Cleveland *(G-5518)*
Kens His & Hers Shop Inc ....G....... 330 872-3190
  Newton Falls *(G-14988)*
Kiwi Promotional AP & Prtg Co ....E....... 330 487-5115
  Twinsburg *(G-18801)*
Kts Cstm Lgs/Xclsvely You Inc ....G....... 440 285-9803
  Chardon *(G-3120)*
Kts Custom Logos ....G....... 440 285-9803
  Chardon *(G-3121)*
Kuhls Hot Sportspot ....F....... 513 474-2282
  Cincinnati *(G-3926)*
Lion Clothing Inc ....G....... 419 692-9981
  Delphos *(G-8751)*
Locker Room Lettering Ltd ....G....... 419 359-1761
  Castalia *(G-2940)*
Logan Screen Printing ....G....... 740 385-3303
  Logan *(G-12033)*
Logo This ....G....... 419 445-1355
  Archbold *(G-657)*
Lynns Logos Inc ....G....... 440 786-1156
  Cleveland *(G-5589)*
M & Y Marketing ....G....... 937 322-3423
  Springfield *(G-17439)*
Markt ....G....... 740 397-5900
  Mount Vernon *(G-14490)*
▲ McCc Sportswear Inc ....E....... 513 583-9210
  West Chester *(G-19876)*
Mr Emblem Inc ....G....... 419 697-1888
  Oregon *(G-15561)*
National Ntwrk EMB Prfssionals .....G....... 502 212-7500
  Stow *(G-17613)*
Novak J F Manufacturing Co LLC ...G....... 216 741-5112
  Cleveland *(G-5790)*
Oasis Embroidery ....G....... 614 785-7266
  Columbus *(G-7235)*
Our Family Mall ....G....... 216 761-8669
  Cleveland *(G-5827)*
Pelz Lettering Inc ....G....... 419 625-3567
  Sandusky *(G-16838)*
Permanent Impressions ....G....... 740 892-3045
  Utica *(G-19027)*

Personal Stitch Monogramming ....G....... 440 282-7707
  Amherst *(G-570)*
Phantasm Designs ....G....... 419 538-6737
  Ottawa *(G-15662)*
Precision Imprint ....G....... 740 592-5916
  Athens *(G-846)*
Quali-Tee Design Sports ....F....... 937 382-7997
  Wilmington *(G-20505)*
Qualitee Design Sportswear Co ......E....... 740 333-8337
  Wshngtn CT Hs *(G-20739)*
Quality Image Embroidery & AP .....G....... 440 230-1109
  Broadview Heights *(G-2099)*
Quality Rubber Stamp Inc ....G....... 614 235-2700
  Columbus *(G-7365)*
Quality Stitch Embroidery Inc ....G....... 614 237-0480
  Columbus *(G-7366)*
Quickstitch Plus LLC ....G....... 614 476-3186
  Columbus *(G-7368)*
R Sportswear LLC ....G....... 937 748-3507
  Springboro *(G-17350)*
Randy Gray ....G....... 513 533-3200
  Cincinnati *(G-4248)*
Red Barn Screen Printing & EMB ....F....... 740 474-6657
  Circleville *(G-4556)*
Robs Creative Screen Printing ....G....... 740 264-6383
  Wintersville *(G-20541)*
Route 14 Storage Inc ....G....... 330 296-0084
  Ravenna *(G-16399)*
▲ Shamrock Companies Inc ....D....... 440 899-9510
  Westlake *(G-20158)*
Sovereign Stitch ....G....... 440 829-0678
  Avon Lake *(G-1010)*
Spectrum Embroidery Inc ....G....... 937 847-9905
  Dayton *(G-8518)*
Sportsco Imprinting ....G....... 513 641-5111
  Cincinnati *(G-4360)*
Stitches & Stuff ....G....... 330 426-9500
  East Palestine *(G-9084)*
Sun Shine Awards ....F....... 740 425-2504
  Barnesville *(G-1119)*
T & L Custom Screening Inc ....G....... 937 237-3121
  Dayton *(G-8534)*
Tag Sportswear LLC ....G....... 330 456-8867
  Canton *(G-2832)*
Tech Wear Embroidery Company ....G....... 740 344-1276
  Newark *(G-14928)*
Thompson Assoc Hudson Ohio ....G....... 330 655-2142
  Hudson *(G-11079)*
▲ Thread Works Custom Embroidery..G....... 937 478-5231
  Beavercreek *(G-1344)*
Top Shelf Embroidery ....G....... 440 209-8566
  Mentor *(G-13608)*
Truck Stop Embroidery ....G....... 419 257-2860
  North Baltimore *(G-15049)*
Twin Design AP Promotions Ltd .....G....... 937 732-6798
  Dayton *(G-8573)*
Unisport Inc ....F....... 419 529-4727
  Ontario *(G-15549)*
United Sport Apparel ....F....... 330 722-0818
  Medina *(G-13357)*
Vasil Co Inc ....G....... 419 562-2901
  Bucyrus *(G-2347)*
Vector International Corp ....G....... 440 942-2002
  Mentor *(G-13623)*
Walnut Hill Shop ....G....... 740 828-3346
  Frazeysburg *(G-9942)*
Wholesale Imprints Inc ....E....... 440 224-3527
  North Kingsville *(G-15161)*
Wizard Graphics Inc ....G....... 419 354-3098
  Bowling Green *(G-2006)*
Writely Sew LLC ....G....... 513 728-2682
  Cincinnati *(G-4523)*
▲ Zimmer Enterprises Inc ....E....... 937 428-1057
  Dayton *(G-8604)*

2396 Automotive Trimmings, Apparel Findings, Related Prdts

A C Hadley - Printing Inc ....G....... 937 426-0952
  Beavercreek *(G-1296)*
Aardvark Graphic Enterprises L ......F....... 419 352-3197
  Bowling Green *(G-1947)*
ABC Inoac Exterior Systems LLC ....C....... 419 334-8951
  Fremont *(G-9988)*
ABC Lettering & Embroidery ....G....... 216 321-8338
  Lakewood *(G-11508)*
Action Sports Apparel Inc ....G....... 330 848-9300
  Norton *(G-15358)*
Adcraft Decals Inc ....E....... 216 524-2934
  Cleveland *(G-4615)*

23 APPAREL AND OTHER FINISHED PRODUCTS MADE FROM FABRICS AND SIMILAR MATERIAL

Akron Felt & Chenille Mfg Co .... F 330 733-7778
  Akron *(G-39)*
Am Graphics .... G 330 799-7319
  Youngstown *(G-20842)*
American Imprssions Sportswear ..... G 614 848-6677
  Worthington *(G-20677)*
▲ Anomatic Corporation .... B 740 522-2203
  Johnstown *(G-11255)*
Art Tees Inc .... G 614 338-8337
  Columbus *(G-6617)*
Art Works .... G 740 425-5765
  Barnesville *(G-1115)*
▲ Atlantis Sportswear Inc .... E 937 773-0680
  Piqua *(G-16101)*
B D P Services Inc .... D 740 828-9685
  Nashport *(G-14564)*
Bates Metal Products Inc .... G 740 498-8371
  Port Washington *(G-16267)*
Big Kahuna Graphics LLC .... G 330 455-2625
  Canton *(G-2591)*
Brandon Screen Printing .... F 419 229-9837
  Lima *(G-11845)*
Brass Bull 1 LLC .... G 740 335-8030
  Wshngtn CT Hs *(G-20720)*
Brown Cnty Bd Mntal Rtardation ..... G 937 378-4891
  Georgetown *(G-10237)*
Cal Sales Embroidery .... G 440 236-3820
  Columbia Station *(G-6431)*
Camela Nitschke Ribbonry .... G 419 872-0073
  Perrysburg *(G-15929)*
Charisma Products Inc .... G 614 846-8888
  Westerville *(G-19984)*
Charizma Corp .... G 216 621-2220
  Cleveland *(G-4909)*
Charles Wisvari .... F 740 671-9960
  Bellaire *(G-1484)*
Crabar/Gbf Inc .... F 419 943-2141
  Leipsic *(G-11724)*
David Brandeberry .... G 937 653-4680
  Urbana *(G-18988)*
Design Original Inc .... F 937 596-5121
  Jackson Center *(G-11207)*
Detroit Technologies Inc .... E 937 492-2708
  Sidney *(G-17030)*
Dresden Specialties Inc .... G 740 754-2451
  Dresden *(G-8868)*
Dupli-Systems Inc .... C 440 234-9415
  Strongsville *(G-17738)*
Eisenhauer Mfg Co LLC .... D 419 238-0081
  Van Wert *(G-19090)*
Elken Co .... G 513 459-7207
  Maineville *(G-12368)*
Erd Specialty Graphics Inc .... G 419 242-9545
  Toledo *(G-18283)*
Fedex Office & Print Svcs Inc .... E 614 898-0000
  Westerville *(G-20054)*
Fineline Imprints Inc .... E 740 453-1083
  Zanesville *(G-21135)*
Fried Daddy .... G 937 854-4542
  Dayton *(G-8207)*
Gail Berner .... G 937 322-0314
  Springfield *(G-17406)*
Gail Zeilmann .... G 440 888-4858
  Cleveland *(G-5286)*
General Theming Contrs LLC .... C 614 252-6342
  Columbus *(G-6945)*
Gotcha Covered .... G 513 829-7555
  Fairfield *(G-9500)*
▼ Greenfield Research Inc .... C 937 981-7763
  Greenfield *(G-10350)*
Greenfield Research Inc .... G 937 876-9224
  Greenfield *(G-10351)*
Griffin Fisher Co Inc .... G 513 961-2110
  Cincinnati *(G-3785)*
H & H Screen Process Inc .... G 937 253-7520
  Dayton *(G-8240)*
Hall Company .... E 937 652-1376
  Urbana *(G-18992)*
Hayes Reconditioning Group .... G 937 299-8013
  Dayton *(G-8246)*
▲ Hfi LLC .... B 614 491-0700
  Columbus *(G-6995)*
Hollywood Imprints LLC .... F 614 501-6040
  Gahanna *(G-10083)*
Hunt Products Inc .... E 440 667-2457
  Newburgh Heights *(G-14940)*
Indra Holdings Corp .... G 513 682-8200
  West Chester *(G-19867)*
J America LLC .... G 614 914-2091
  Columbus *(G-7054)*

Jakes Sportswear Ltd .... G 740 746-8356
  Sugar Grove *(G-17839)*
Jerry Pulfer .... G 937 778-1861
  Piqua *(G-16134)*
Jetts Embroideries .... G 937 981-3716
  Greenfield *(G-10353)*
Jls Funeral Home .... G 614 625-1220
  Columbus *(G-7068)*
Johnson Brothers Holdings LLC ..... G 614 868-5273
  Columbus *(G-7073)*
Kemper Automotive .... G 800 783-8004
  Franklin *(G-9892)*
Kent Stow Screen Printing Inc .... F 330 923-5118
  Akron *(G-235)*
Kiwi Promotional AP & Prtg Co ...... G 330 487-5115
  Twinsburg *(G-18801)*
Lesch Boat Cover Canvas Co LLC . G 419 668-6374
  Norwalk *(G-15404)*
Logan Screen Printing .... G 740 385-3303
  Logan *(G-12033)*
Lund Printing Co .... G 330 628-4047
  Akron *(G-262)*
M & H Screen Printing .... G 740 522-1957
  Newark *(G-14894)*
Madison Group Inc .... G 216 362-9000
  Cleveland *(G-5602)*
Mr Emblem Inc .... G 419 697-1888
  Oregon *(G-15561)*
National Bias Fabric Co .... E 216 361-0530
  Cleveland *(G-5722)*
Nicholas Ray Enterprises LLC .... G 330 454-4811
  Canton *(G-2761)*
Northeastern Plastics Inc .... G 330 453-5925
  Canton *(G-2768)*
Ohio State Institute of Fin .... E 614 861-8811
  Reynoldsburg *(G-16445)*
Painted Hill Inv Group Inc .... F 937 339-1756
  Troy *(G-18691)*
Peska Inc .... F 440 998-4664
  Ashtabula *(G-797)*
Pieco Inc .... E 419 422-5335
  Findlay *(G-9741)*
Pieco Inc .... D 937 399-5100
  Springfield *(G-17472)*
Pinky & Thumb LLC .... G 614 939-5216
  New Albany *(G-14634)*
▼ Plastic Card Inc .... D 330 896-5555
  Uniontown *(G-18929)*
▲ Plus Mark LLC .... E 216 252-6770
  Cleveland *(G-5891)*
Pro Companies Inc .... G 614 738-1222
  Pickerington *(G-16057)*
Puttco Inc .... G 937 299-1527
  Dayton *(G-8453)*
Quality Rubber Stamp Inc .... G 614 235-2700
  Columbus *(G-7365)*
Quality Spt & Silk Screen Sp .... G 513 769-8300
  Cincinnati *(G-4229)*
R & A Sports Inc .... E 216 289-2254
  Euclid *(G-9438)*
Randy Gray .... G 513 533-3200
  Cincinnati *(G-4248)*
Schilling Graphics Inc .... E 419 468-1037
  Galion *(G-10154)*
Screen Works Inc .... E 937 264-9111
  Dayton *(G-8499)*
Simply Canvas Inc .... E 330 436-6500
  Akron *(G-376)*
Solar Arts Graphic Designs .... G 330 744-0535
  Youngstown *(G-21033)*
Spirit Avionics Ltd .... F 614 237-4271
  Columbus *(G-7477)*
▲ Sroufe Healthcare Products LLC .. E 260 894-4171
  Wadsworth *(G-19278)*
Standard Prototyping Ideals .... G 614 837-9180
  Pickerington *(G-16060)*
Sweaty Bands LLC .... E 513 871-1222
  Cincinnati *(G-4402)*
Swocat Design Inc .... G 440 282-4700
  Lorain *(G-12127)*
Sylvan Studio Inc .... G 419 882-3423
  Sylvania *(G-17963)*
T & L Custom Screening Inc .... G 937 237-3121
  Dayton *(G-8534)*
Tee Creations .... G 937 878-2822
  Fairborn *(G-9472)*
Telempu N Hayashi Amer Corp ...... G 513 932-9319
  Lebanon *(G-11700)*
Tendon Manufacturing Inc .... E 216 663-3200
  Cleveland *(G-6159)*

Tim L Humbert .... F 330 497-4944
  Canton *(G-2836)*
Triage Ortho Group .... G 937 653-6431
  Urbana *(G-19016)*
Trim Systems Operating Corp .... C 740 772-5998
  Chillicothe *(G-3228)*
▲ Universal Drect FIfllment Corp ..... C 330 650-5000
  Hudson *(G-11081)*
Vasil Co Inc .... G 419 562-2901
  Bucyrus *(G-2347)*
Vector International Corp .... G 440 942-2002
  Mentor *(G-13623)*
▲ Vgu Industries Inc .... E 216 676-9093
  Cleveland *(G-512)*
▼ W J Egli Company Inc .... F 330 823-3666
  Alliance *(G-512)*
West & Barker Inc .... E 330 652-9923
  Niles *(G-15040)*
Wholesale Imprints Inc .... E 440 224-3527
  North Kingsville *(G-15161)*
Wizard Graphics Inc .... G 419 354-3098
  Bowling Green *(G-2006)*
Woodrow Manufacturing Co .... E 937 399-9333
  Springfield *(G-17521)*
Yi Xing Inc .... G 614 785-9631
  Columbus *(G-7623)*
Zenos Activewear Inc .... G 614 443-0070
  Columbus *(G-7626)*
Zide Sport Shop of Ohio Inc .... F 740 373-8199
  Marietta *(G-12690)*

2399 Fabricated Textile Prdts, NEC

Akron Felt & Chenille Mfg Co .... F 330 733-7778
  Akron *(G-39)*
Annin & Co .... D 740 622-4447
  Coshocton *(G-7718)*
▲ Besi Manufacturing Inc .... E 513 874-0232
  West Chester *(G-19659)*
Buckeye Seating LLC .... F 330 473-2379
  Millersburg *(G-14071)*
C H R Industries Inc .... G 440 361-0744
  Geneva *(G-10215)*
Crown Dielectric Inds Inc .... C 614 224-5161
  Columbus *(G-6839)*
▲ Drifter Marine Inc .... G 419 666-8144
  Perrysburg *(G-15941)*
Exochem Corporation .... F 330 426-9898
  East Palestine *(G-9079)*
Flag Lady Inc .... G 614 263-1776
  Columbus *(G-6927)*
Griffin Fisher Co Inc .... G 513 961-2110
  Cincinnati *(G-3785)*
Kanel Brothers Supply .... G 330 499-4802
  Canton *(G-2721)*
Kolhfab Cstm Plstic Fbrication .... G 937 237-2098
  Dayton *(G-8299)*
Markers Inc .... G 440 933-5927
  Avon Lake *(G-995)*
▲ Party Animal Inc .... G 440 471-1030
  Westlake *(G-20139)*
Rex Manufacturing Co .... G 419 224-5751
  Lima *(G-11931)*
Scenic Ridge Manufacturing LLC ... G 330 674-0557
  Millersburg *(G-14127)*
School Maintenance Supply Inc ..... G 513 376-8670
  Blue Ash *(G-1843)*
School Pride Limited .... E 614 568-0697
  Columbus *(G-7428)*
Seven Mile Creek Corporation .... F 937 456-3320
  Eaton *(G-9165)*
Sewline Products Inc .... F 419 929-1114
  New London *(G-14738)*
▲ Specilty Fbrics Converting Inc ..... E 706 637-3000
  Fairlawn *(G-9618)*
TAC Industries Inc .... B 937 328-5200
  Springfield *(G-17502)*
Tk Holdings Inc .... G 937 778-9713
  Piqua *(G-16166)*
TS Trim Industries Inc .... B 740 593-5958
  Athens *(G-852)*
Ver Mich Ltd .... G 330 493-7330
  Canton *(G-2858)*
Vitamin Lac .... F 440 548-5294
  Middlefield *(G-13865)*
Watershed Mangement LLC .... F 740 852-5607
  Mount Sterling *(G-14466)*
Woebkenberg Starting Gates .... G 937 696-2446
  West Alexandria *(G-19625)*

24 LUMBER AND WOOD PRODUCTS, EXCEPT FURNITURE

2411 Logging

A & M Logging.....G..... 740 543-3171
Salineville (G-16785)
A & P Wood Products Inc.....G..... 419 673-1196
Kenton (G-11400)
Affordable Stump Removal LLC.....G..... 419 841-8331
Toledo (G-18159)
Alfman Logging LLC.....G..... 740 982-6227
Crooksville (G-7814)
Appalachia Wood Inc.....E..... 740 596-2551
Mc Arthur (G-13178)
Art Saylor Logging.....F..... 740 682-6188
Oak Hill (G-15449)
B Hogenkamp & R Harlamert.....G..... 419 925-0526
Celina (G-2950)
Baker Logging.....G..... 740 686-2817
Belmont (G-1565)
Beachs Trees Selective Harvest.....F..... 513 289-5976
Cincinnati (G-3241)
Beekman Logging.....G..... 740 493-2763
Piketon (G-16067)
Biedenbach Logging.....G..... 740 732-6477
Sarahsville (G-16865)
Blair Logging.....G..... 740 934-2730
Lower Salem (G-12258)
Blankenship Logging LLC.....G..... 740 372-3833
Otway (G-15684)
Bolon Timber LLC.....G..... 740 567-4102
Lewisville (G-11802)
Brett Purdum.....G..... 740 626-2890
South Salem (G-17296)
Broty Enterprises Inc.....G..... 330 674-6900
Millersburg (G-14069)
Brown Forest Products.....G..... 937 544-1515
Otway (G-15686)
Busy Bee Lumber.....G..... 330 674-1305
Millersburg (G-14075)
C & B Logging Inc.....G..... 740 347-4844
Glouster (G-10275)
C & L Erectors & Riggers Inc.....E..... 740 332-7185
Laurelville (G-11626)
Chester F Hale.....G..... 740 379-2437
Patriot (G-15849)
Chili Logging Ltd.....G..... 740 545-9502
Fresno (G-10067)
Chipmunk Logging & Lumber LLC.....G..... 440 537-5124
Middlefield (G-13785)
Chub Gibsons Logging.....G..... 740 884-4079
Chillicothe (G-3181)
Coldwell Family Tree Farm.....G..... 330 506-9012
Salineville (G-16786)
Craig Saylor.....G..... 740 352-8363
Portland (G-16275)
Crisenbery Logging LLC.....G..... 740 256-1439
Patriot (G-15850)
Custom Material Hdlg Eqp LLC.....G..... 513 235-5336
Cincinnati (G-3565)
D&D Logging.....G..... 740 679-2573
Woodsfield (G-20544)
D&M Fencing LLC.....G..... 419 604-0698
Spencerville (G-17308)
David Adkins Logging.....G..... 740 533-0297
Kitts Hill (G-11474)
Denver Adkins.....F..... 740 682-3123
Oak Hill (G-15450)
Dunagan Logging.....G..... 740 599-9368
Danville (G-7962)
Erichar Inc.....G..... 216 402-2628
Cleveland (G-5188)
Ervin Lee Logging.....G..... 330 771-0039
Minerva (G-14179)
▼ Facemyer Lumber Co Inc.....D..... 740 992-5965
Pomeroy (G-16240)
For Every Home.....G..... 740 710-1253
Jackson (G-11185)
Gadd Logging.....G..... 513 312-3941
Trenton (G-18619)
Gerald D Damron.....G..... 740 894-3680
Chesapeake (G-3146)
Giles Logging LLC.....G..... 406 855-5284
Spencer (G-17304)
GM Logging.....G..... 740 501-0819
Johnstown (G-11267)
H & H Tree Service LLC.....G..... 440 632-0551
Middlefield (G-13801)
Haessly Lumber Sales Co.....D..... 740 373-6681
Marietta (G-12630)
HK Logging & Lumber Ltd.....G..... 440 632-1997
Middlefield (G-13806)
Huntington Hardwood Lbr Co Inc.....G..... 440 647-2283
Wellington (G-19583)
Ingles Logging.....G..... 740 379-2909
Patriot (G-15851)
Ingles Logging.....G..... 740 379-2760
Patriot (G-15852)
J & J Logging.....G..... 740 896-2827
Lowell (G-12246)
J D Knisley Logging.....G..... 740 634-3207
Bainbridge (G-1016)
Jacobs & Sons Logging LLC.....G..... 419 678-3802
Saint Henry (G-16665)
Jason C Gibson.....F..... 740 663-4520
Chillicothe (G-3196)
Jeffrey Adams Logging Inc.....G..... 740 634-2286
Bainbridge (G-1017)
Jlm Logging LLC.....G..... 330 340-4863
Millersburg (G-14102)
JM Logging Inc.....G..... 740 441-0941
Gallipolis (G-10168)
John Byler.....G..... 330 627-7635
Carrollton (G-2921)
John J Yoder Logging.....G..... 330 749-6324
Apple Creek (G-609)
Knauff Bros Logging & Lumber.....F..... 740 634-2432
Bainbridge (G-1018)
L&L Excavating & Land Clearing.....G..... 740 682-7823
Oak Hill (G-15454)
Lee Saylor Logging LLC.....G..... 740 682-0479
Oak Hill (G-15455)
Litzinger Logging.....G..... 740 743-2245
Somerset (G-17264)
M H Logging & Lumber.....G..... 740 694-1988
Fredericktown (G-9973)
McFadden Logging.....G..... 740 599-6902
Danville (G-7964)
Michael D Strickland.....G..... 740 682-6902
Oak Hill (G-15456)
▼ Milestone Ventures LLC.....G..... 317 908-2093
Granville (G-10334)
Miller & Son Logging.....G..... 330 738-2031
Mechanicstown (G-13213)
Miller Logging.....G..... 440 693-4001
Middlefield (G-13829)
Miller Logging Inc.....E..... 330 279-4721
Holmesville (G-10983)
Ned A Shreve.....G..... 740 732-6465
Sarahsville (G-16866)
NY Logging & Lumber.....G..... 740 679-2085
Quaker City (G-16353)
Oakbridge Timber Framing.....G..... 419 994-1052
Loudonville (G-12145)
Ohio Timberland Products.....F..... 419 682-6322
Stryker (G-17831)
Omega Logging Inc.....F..... 330 534-0378
Hubbard (G-11008)
Perkins Logging LLC.....G..... 740 288-7311
Chillicothe (G-3209)
Perkins Wood Products.....G..... 740 884-4046
Chillicothe (G-3210)
Powell Logging.....G..... 740 372-6131
Otway (G-15689)
Randy Carter Logging Inc.....G..... 740 634-2604
Bainbridge (G-1020)
Ray L Lute LL.....G..... 740 372-7703
Lucasville (G-12267)
Robert Ashcraft.....G..... 740 667-3690
Guysville (G-10520)
Roger L Best.....G..... 740 590-9133
Stockport (G-17560)
Ross Tmber Harvstg For MGT Inc.....G..... 513 383-6933
Batavia (G-1181)
Select Logging.....G..... 419 564-0361
Marengo (G-12594)
Seymours Logging.....F..... 740 288-1825
Wellston (G-19606)
Shellenbarger Excavating & Log.....G..... 740 397-9949
Mount Vernon (G-14509)
Sissel Logging LLC.....G..... 740 858-4613
Portsmouth (G-16300)
Stark Truss Company Inc.....D..... 419 298-3777
Edgerton (G-9181)
Steve Henderson.....G..... 419 738-6999
Wapakoneta (G-19355)
Superior Hardwoods of Ohio.....D..... 740 384-6862
Jackson (G-11196)
T J Ellis Enterprises Inc.....G..... 419 224-1969
Lima (G-11948)
T&R Logging LLC.....G..... 740 288-1825
Wellston (G-19609)
Terry G Sickles.....G..... 740 286-8880
Ray (G-16422)
Top Notch Logging.....G..... 330 466-1780
Apple Creek (G-621)
Vorhees Logging LLC.....G..... 740 385-0216
Rockbridge (G-16538)
Warner Hildebrant.....G..... 740 286-1903
South Webster (G-17300)
Y&B Logging.....G..... 440 437-1053
Orwell (G-15641)
Yoder Logging.....G..... 740 679-2635
Quaker City (G-16354)

2421 Saw & Planing Mills

5874 Sawmill LLC.....G..... 614 795-1818
Dublin (G-8870)
Appalachia Wood Inc.....E..... 740 596-2551
Mc Arthur (G-13178)
Automated Bldg Components Inc.....E..... 419 257-2152
North Baltimore (G-15042)
Baillie Lumber Co LP.....E..... 419 462-2000
Galion (G-10123)
Beach City Lumber LLC.....G..... 330 878-4097
Strasburg (G-17646)
Beaver Wood Products.....E..... 740 226-6211
Beaver (G-1292)
Blaney Hardwoods Ohio Inc.....E..... 740 678-8288
Vincent (G-19212)
Blankenship Lumber Inc.....G..... 740 372-0191
Otway (G-15685)
▲ Bruewer Woodwork Mfg Co.....D..... 513 353-3505
Cleves (G-6355)
Cherokee Hardwoods Inc.....F..... 440 632-0322
Middlefield (G-13784)
Clarksville Stave & Lumber Co.....G..... 937 376-4618
Xenia (G-20763)
Clear Run Lumber Co.....G..... 740 747-2665
Marengo (G-12589)
Coblentz Brothers Inc.....E..... 330 857-7211
Apple Creek (G-602)
Conover Lumber Company Inc.....F..... 937 368-3010
Conover (G-7663)
Contract Lumber Inc.....D..... 614 751-1109
Columbus (G-6814)
Crownover Lumber Co Inc.....D..... 740 596-5229
Mc Arthur (G-13180)
D&M Fencing LLC.....G..... 419 604-0698
Spencerville (G-17308)
Del Holdash.....G..... 440 427-0611
North Olmsted (G-15185)
Denoon Lumber Company LLC.....D..... 740 768-2220
Bergholz (G-1634)
Dexter Hardwoods Inc.....G..... 740 783-4141
Dexter City (G-8794)
DIA Enterprises Inc.....G..... 740 802-7075
New Bloomington (G-14644)
Don Puckett Lumber Inc.....F..... 740 887-4191
Londonderry (G-12075)
Dues Jersey Farm.....G..... 419 678-2102
Coldwater (G-6406)
Facemyer Forest Products Inc.....F..... 740 992-7425
Middleport (G-13872)
▼ Facemyer Lumber Co Inc.....D..... 740 992-5965
Pomeroy (G-16240)
Fivecoat Lumber Inc.....F..... 740 254-4681
Gnadenhutten (G-10279)
Frickco Inc.....G..... 740 887-2017
South Bloomingville (G-17270)
Gardner Lumber Co Inc.....F..... 740 254-4664
Tippecanoe (G-18148)
Gary Brown Farm & Sawmill.....G..... 740 372-5022
Otway (G-15688)
Green Brothers Enterprises.....G..... 937 444-3323
Sardinia (G-16869)
Gross Lumber Inc.....E..... 330 683-2055
Apple Creek (G-606)
Haessly Lumber Sales Co.....D..... 740 373-6681
Marietta (G-12630)
▼ Hartzell Hardwoods Inc.....D..... 937 773-7054
Piqua (G-16123)
▲ Hess & Gault Lumber Co.....G..... 419 281-3105
Ashland (G-710)
Hillcrest Lumber Ltd.....G..... 330 359-5721
Apple Creek (G-607)
Industrial Timber & Land Co.....G..... 740 596-5294
Hamden (G-10523)

SIC

Employee Codes: A=Over 500 employees, B=251-500
C=101-250, D=51-100, E=20-50, F=10-19, G=3-9
2019 Harris Ohio
Industrial Directory
833

Industrial Timber & Lumber Co G 800 829-9663
Beachwood *(G-1241)*

▼ Itl Corp E 216 831-3140
Cleveland *(G-5478)*

J K Logging & Chipwood Company G 330 738-3571
Salineville *(G-16788)*

Kaufman Mulch Inc G 330 893-3676
Millersburg *(G-14103)*

Knisley Lumber F 740 634-2935
Bainbridge *(G-1019)*

Koppers Ind Inc G 740 776-2149
Portsmouth *(G-16287)*

Koppers Industries Inc E 740 776-3238
Portsmouth *(G-16288)*

L Garbers Sons Sawmilling LLC G 419 335-6362
Wauseon *(G-19524)*

Lansing Bros Sawmill G 937 588-4291
Piketon *(G-16073)*

Lantz Lumber & Saw Shop G 740 286-5658
Jackson *(G-11189)*

Leppert Companies Inc G 614 889-2818
Dublin *(G-8941)*

Marathon At Sawmill F 614 734-0836
Columbus *(G-7149)*

MB Manufacturing Corp G 513 682-1461
Fairfield *(G-9527)*

Mbm Lumber G 937 459-7448
Union City *(G-18905)*

McMillion Lock & Key G 937 473-5342
Covington *(G-7790)*

Miller Logging Inc E 330 279-4721
Holmesville *(G-10983)*

Miller Lumber Co Inc E 330 674-0273
Millersburg *(G-14112)*

Millwood Lumber Inc E 740 254-4681
Gnadenhutten *(G-10280)*

Mohler Lumber Company E 330 499-5461
North Canton *(G-15102)*

Mowhawk Lumber Ltd E 330 698-5333
Apple Creek *(G-615)*

Newberry Wood Enterprises Inc F 440 238-6127
Strongsville *(G-17769)*

No Name Lumber LLC G 740 289-3722
Piketon *(G-16075)*

▼ Ohio Valley Veneer Inc E 740 493-2901
Piketon *(G-16076)*

Omega Logging Inc F 330 534-0378
Hubbard *(G-11008)*

Plaza At Sawmill Pl G 614 889-6121
Columbus *(G-7326)*

R & D Hilltop Lumber Inc E 740 342-3051
New Lexington *(G-14721)*

R & L Wood Products G 937 444-2496
Williamsburg *(G-20254)*

R J Dobay Enterprises Inc G 440 227-1005
Burton *(G-2367)*

R M Wood Co G 419 845-2661
Mount Gilead *(G-14431)*

Raber Lumber Co G 330 893-2797
Charm *(G-3142)*

Ramona Southworth G 740 226-8202
Beaver *(G-1293)*

Residents of Sawmill Park G 614 659-6678
Dublin *(G-8973)*

Roseville Hardwood G 740 221-8712
Roseville *(G-16579)*

Runkles Sawmill LLC G 937 663-0115
Saint Paris *(G-16711)*

S & J Lumber Co E 740 245-5804
Thurman *(G-18038)*

S&R Lumber LLC F 740 352-6135
Piketon *(G-16079)*

Salt Creek Lumber Company Inc G 330 695-3500
Fredericksburg *(G-9959)*

Sawmill Crossing G 614 766-1685
Columbus *(G-7423)*

Sawmill Eye Associates Inc G 440 724-0396
Broadview Heights *(G-2100)*

Sawmill Eye Associates Inc G 614 734-2685
Columbus *(G-7424)*

Sawmill Road Management Co LLC E 937 342-9071
Springfield *(G-17490)*

Sawmill Station G 614 434-6147
Dublin *(G-8980)*

Siefker Sawmill G 419 339-1956
Elida *(G-9201)*

Southern Ohio Wood G 740 288-1825
Wellston *(G-19607)*

Sphon Associates Inc G 614 741-4002
Gahanna *(G-10107)*

Stark Truss Company Inc E 330 756-3050
Beach City *(G-1215)*

▲ Stephen M Trudick E 440 834-1891
Burton *(G-2371)*

Stony Point Hardwoods F 330 852-4512
Sugarcreek *(G-17865)*

Stutzman Brothers Sawmill G 440 272-5179
Middlefield *(G-13854)*

Sugarcreek Shavings LLC G 330 763-4239
Sugarcreek *(G-17869)*

Summit Valley Lumber G 330 698-7781
Apple Creek *(G-620)*

Superior Hardwoods of Ohio E 740 596-2561
Mc Arthur *(G-13184)*

Superior Hardwoods of Ohio D 740 384-6862
Jackson *(G-11196)*

Superior Hardwoods Ohio Inc D 740 384-5677
Wellston *(G-19608)*

Superior Hardwoods Ohio Inc E 740 439-2727
Cambridge *(G-2457)*

Supply Dynamics Inc E 513 965-2000
Loveland *(G-12238)*

T & D Thompson Inc E 740 332-8515
Laurelville *(G-11627)*

◆ Taylor Lumber Worldwide Inc C 740 259-6222
Mc Dermott *(G-13194)*

Timbermill Ltd G 740 862-3426
Baltimore *(G-1044)*

▼ Trumbull County Hardwoods E 440 632-0555
Middlefield *(G-13861)*

Tusco Hardwoods LLC F 330 852-4281
Sugarcreek *(G-17873)*

United Hardwoods Ltd G 330 878-9510
Strasburg *(G-17655)*

W O Hardwoods Inc G 740 425-1588
Barnesville *(G-1120)*

Wagner Farms & Sawmill LLC F 419 653-4126
Leipsic *(G-11738)*

Walnut Creek Lumber Co Ltd E 330 852-4559
Dundee *(G-9031)*

◆ Walnut Creek Planing Ltd D 330 893-3244
Millersburg *(G-14146)*

Wappoo Wood Products Inc E 937 492-1166
Sidney *(G-17084)*

Weaver Lumber Co G 330 359-5091
Wilmot *(G-20517)*

Whitewater Forest Products LLC G 513 673-7596
Batavia *(G-1196)*

Wilmington Forest Products G 937 382-5013
Wilmington *(G-20512)*

Woodsfeld True Vlue HM Ctr Inc F 740 472-1651
Woodsfield *(G-20550)*

Wooldridge Lumber Co D 740 289-4912
Piketon *(G-16082)*

Wrights Saw Mill G 937 773-2546
Piqua *(G-16167)*

▼ Yoder Lumber Co Inc D 330 893-3121
Millersburg *(G-14153)*

Yoder Lumber Co Inc E 330 674-1435
Millersburg *(G-14154)*

Yoder Lumber Co Inc D 330 893-3131
Sugarcreek *(G-17878)*

2426 Hardwood Dimension & Flooring Mills

Armstrong Custom Moulding Inc G 740 922-5931
Uhrichsville *(G-18880)*

Baillie Lumber Co LP E 419 462-2000
Galion *(G-10123)*

Beaver Wood Products E 740 226-6211
Beaver *(G-1292)*

Canfield Manufacturing Co Inc G 330 533-3333
North Jackson *(G-15143)*

Cardinal Building Supply LLC G 614 706-4499
Columbus *(G-6740)*

Carter-Jones Lumber Company C 330 674-9060
Millersburg *(G-14077)*

Cherokee Hardwoods Inc F 440 632-0322
Middlefield *(G-13784)*

Creative Concepts G 216 513-6463
Medina *(G-13246)*

Crownover Lumber Co Inc D 740 596-5229
Mc Arthur *(G-13180)*

Denoon Lumber Company LLC D 740 768-2220
Bergholz *(G-1634)*

Dutch Heritage Woodcraft E 330 893-2211
Berlin *(G-1641)*

Gross Lumber Inc E 330 683-2055
Apple Creek *(G-606)*

Haessly Lumber Sales Co D 740 373-6681
Marietta *(G-12630)*

Halliday Holdings Inc E 740 335-1430
Wshngtn CT Hs *(G-20727)*

▼ Hardwood Flrg & Paneling Inc D 440 834-1710
Middlefield *(G-13803)*

▼ Hartzell Hardwoods Inc D 937 773-7054
Piqua *(G-16123)*

Hillcrest G 740 824-4849
Brinkhaven *(G-2081)*

Hillside Wood Ltd E 330 359-5991
Millersburg *(G-14092)*

Hinchcliff Lumber Company G 440 238-5200
Strongsville *(G-17749)*

Hochstetler Wood F 330 893-2384
Millersburg *(G-14093)*

Holmes Lumber & Bldg Ctr Inc C 330 674-9060
Millersburg *(G-14098)*

Itl LLC B 216 831-3140
Beachwood *(G-1242)*

▼ Itl Corp E 216 831-3140
Cleveland *(G-5478)*

J McCoy Lumber Co Ltd E 937 587-3423
Peebles *(G-15879)*

J McCoy Lumber Co Ltd G 937 544-2968
West Union *(G-19962)*

Kelco Hardwood Floors Inc G 440 354-0974
Painesville *(G-15753)*

Knisley Lumber F 740 634-2935
Bainbridge *(G-1019)*

Marsh Valley Forest Pdts Ltd G 440 632-1889
Middlefield *(G-13816)*

McKay-Gross Div G 330 683-2055
Apple Creek *(G-613)*

Mid Ohio Wood Products Inc E 740 323-0427
Newark *(G-14897)*

Mohler Lumber Company E 330 499-5461
North Canton *(G-15102)*

▼ Ohio Valley Veneer Inc E 740 493-2901
Piketon *(G-16076)*

Plank and Hide Co F 888 462-6852
Cincinnati *(G-4165)*

◆ Prestige Enterprise Intl Inc D 513 469-6044
Blue Ash *(G-1835)*

Property Assist Inc G 419 480-1700
Toledo *(G-18487)*

◆ Robbins Inc E 513 871-8988
Cincinnati *(G-4276)*

Siefker Sawmill G 419 339-1956
Elida *(G-9201)*

Silk Road Sourcing LLC G 814 571-5533
Amherst *(G-574)*

▲ Stephen M Trudick E 440 834-1891
Burton *(G-2371)*

Stony Point Hardwoods F 330 852-4512
Sugarcreek *(G-17865)*

Superior Hardwoods of Ohio E 740 596-2561
Mc Arthur *(G-13184)*

Superior Hardwoods Ohio Inc D 740 384-5677
Wellston *(G-19608)*

Superior Hardwoods Ohio Inc E 740 439-2727
Cambridge *(G-2457)*

T & D Thompson Inc E 740 332-8515
Laurelville *(G-11627)*

▼ Trumbull County Hardwoods E 440 632-0555
Middlefield *(G-13861)*

Urbn Timber LLC G 614 981-3043
Columbus *(G-7565)*

Valleyview Wood Turning Co F 330 763-0407
Millersburg *(G-14142)*

Wagner Farms & Sawmill LLC F 419 653-4126
Leipsic *(G-11738)*

◆ Walnut Creek Planing Ltd D 330 893-3244
Millersburg *(G-14146)*

Wappoo Wood Products Inc E 937 492-1166
Sidney *(G-17084)*

Woodcraft Industries Inc D 440 437-7811
Orwell *(G-15640)*

Woodcraft Industries Inc C 440 632-9655
Middlefield *(G-13868)*

Wooden Horse G 740 503-5243
Baltimore *(G-1046)*

Yoder Lumber Co Inc D 330 893-3131
Sugarcreek *(G-17878)*

▼ Yoder Lumber Co Inc D 330 893-3121
Millersburg *(G-14153)*

2429 Special Prdt Sawmills, NEC

Brown-Forman Corporation E 740 384-3027
Wellston *(G-19598)*

▲ IVEX Protective Packaging Inc E 937 498-9298
Sidney *(G-17046)*

2431 Millwork

7&7 Woodworking G 330 347-6574 Wooster *(G-20552)*
7d Marketing Inc F 330 721-8822 Medina *(G-13215)*
A & B Wood Design Assoc Inc G 330 721-2789 Wadsworth *(G-19218)*
A & J Woodworking Inc G 419 695-5655 Delphos *(G-8734)*
A & M Woodworking G 330 893-1331 Millersburg *(G-14054)*
A C Shutters Inc G 216 429-2424 Cleveland *(G-4584)*
A W S Incorporated G 419 352-5397 Bowling Green *(G-1944)*
A&M Country Woodworking LLC G 330 674-1011 Holmesville *(G-10971)*
A&M Woodworking G 513 722-5415 Loveland *(G-12173)*
Ace Lumber Company F 330 744-3167 Youngstown *(G-20835)*
▲ Action Industries Ltd F 216 252-7800 Strongsville *(G-17705)*
Adams Custom Woodworking F 513 761-1395 Cincinnati *(G-3297)*
▼ Advantage Tent Fittings Inc F 740 773-3015 Chillicothe *(G-3173)*
Ailes Millwork Inc F 330 678-4300 Kent *(G-11290)*
Aj Stineburg Wdwkg Studio LLC G 614 526-9480 Columbus *(G-6555)*
All Around Garage Door Inc G 440 759-5079 North Ridgeville *(G-15207)*
All Pro Ovrhd Door Systems LLC G 614 444-3667 Columbus *(G-6567)*
Amarr Company G 216 573-7100 Independence *(G-11119)*
Amcan Stair & Rail LLC G 937 781-3084 Springfield *(G-17362)*
American Plastech LLC G 330 538-0576 North Jackson *(G-15140)*
American Woodwork Specialty Co E 937 263-1053 Dayton *(G-8029)*
Anderson Door Co E 216 475-5700 Cleveland *(G-4712)*
Architectural Door Systems LLC G 513 808-9900 Norwood *(G-15422)*
Armstrong Custom Moulding Inc G 740 922-5931 Uhrichsville *(G-18880)*
Art Woodworking & Mfg Co E 513 681-2986 Cincinnati *(G-3359)*
Automated Bldg Components Inc E 419 257-2152 North Baltimore *(G-15042)*
Baird Brothers Sawmill Inc C 330 533-3122 Canfield *(G-2523)*
▲ Bautec N Technoform Amer Inc E 330 487-6600 Twinsburg *(G-18738)*
Bay World International Inc E 419 525-2222 Mansfield *(G-12410)*
Beechvale Laminating F 330 674-2804 Millersburg *(G-14064)*
Berlin Woodworking G 330 893-3234 Millersburg *(G-14068)*
Berry Woodworking F 513 734-6133 Amelia *(G-533)*
Bomba S Custom Woodworking G 330 699-9075 Uniontown *(G-18913)*
Brogan Machine Shop G 513 683-9054 Loveland *(G-12182)*
▲ Bruewer Woodwork Mfg Co D 513 353-3505 Cleves *(G-6355)*
Buckeye Products G 740 969-4718 Amanda *(G-523)*
C & W Custom Wdwkg Co Inc E 513 891-6340 Cincinnati *(G-3435)*
C Square Lumber Products F 740 557-3129 Stockport *(G-17559)*
Capital City Millwork Inc F 614 939-0670 New Albany *(G-14613)*
Carden Door Company LLC G 513 459-2233 Mason *(G-12837)*
▲ Carolina Stair Supply Inc E 740 922-3333 Uhrichsville *(G-18881)*
Carter-Jones Lumber Company C 330 674-9060 Millersburg *(G-14077)*
▲ Cascade Ohio Inc B 440 593-5800 Conneaut *(G-7642)*
Cassady Woodworks Inc E 937 256-7948 Dayton *(G-7974)*
Cincinnati Wood Products Co G 513 542-0569 Cincinnati *(G-3511)*
Cincinnati Woodworks Inc G 513 241-6412 Cincinnati *(G-3512)*
Cindoco Wood Products Co G 937 444-2504 Mount Orab *(G-14440)*
Clark Wood Specialties Inc G 330 499-8711 Clinton *(G-6384)*
◆ Clopay Building Pdts Co Inc E 513 770-4800 Mason *(G-12846)*
Clopay Building Pdts Co Inc G 937 526-4301 Russia *(G-16606)*
Clopay Building Pdts Co Inc G 937 440-6403 Troy *(G-18642)*
▲ Clopay Corporation C 800 282-2260 Mason *(G-12847)*
Complete Expressions WD Works G 614 245-4152 New Albany *(G-14616)*
Corns Quality Woodworking LLC G 419 589-4899 Mansfield *(G-12428)*
Cortland Hardwood Products LLC E 330 638-3232 Cortland *(G-7707)*
Country Comfort Woodworking G 330 695-4408 Fredericksburg *(G-9946)*
Courthouse Manufacturing LLC E 740 335-2727 Washington Court Hou *(G-19476)*
Cox Interior Inc F 270 789-3129 Norwood *(G-15425)*
Creative Millwork Ohio Inc E 440 992-3566 Ashtabula *(G-768)*
Creative Woodworks G 330 897-1432 Sugarcreek *(G-17847)*
Curves and More Woodworking G 614 239-7837 Columbus *(G-6842)*
Custom Carving Source LLC G 513 407-1008 Cincinnati *(G-3563)*
Darby Creek Millwork Co G 614 873-3267 Plain City *(G-16185)*
Decker Custom Wood Llc G 419 332-3464 Fremont *(G-10011)*
Dendratec Ltd G 330 473-4878 Dalton *(G-7940)*
Denoon Lumber Company LLC D 740 768-2220 Bergholz *(G-1634)*
Design-N-Wood LLC G 937 419-0479 Sidney *(G-17028)*
◆ Designer Doors Inc E 330 772-6391 Burghill *(G-2354)*
Display Dynamics Inc F 937 832-2830 Englewood *(G-9355)*
Division Overhead Door Inc F 513 872-0888 Cincinnati *(G-3597)*
Dlwoodworking G 740 927-2693 Pataskala *(G-15829)*
▲ Door Fabrication Services Inc E 937 454-9207 Vandalia *(G-19123)*
Dublin Millwork Co Inc E 614 889-7776 Dublin *(G-8908)*
Dutch Heritage Woodcraft E 330 893-2211 Berlin *(G-1641)*
Fairfield Woodworks Ltd G 740 689-1953 Lancaster *(G-11571)*
Farmstead Acres Woodworking G 330 695-6492 Fredericksburg *(G-9951)*
Fdi Cabinetry LLC G 513 353-4500 Cleves *(G-6362)*
Fifth Avenue Lumber Co D 614 833-6655 Canal Winchester *(G-2503)*
▼ Fixture Dimensions Inc E 513 360-7512 Middletown *(G-13908)*
Flottemesch Anthony & Son F 513 561-1212 Cincinnati *(G-3696)*
Forum III Inc F 513 961-5123 Cincinnati *(G-3706)*
▼ Gateway Industrial Pdts Inc F 440 324-4112 Elyria *(G-9263)*
Gdw Woodworking LLC G 513 494-3041 South Lebanon *(G-17276)*
Gerstenslager Construction G 330 832-3604 Massillon *(G-12987)*
Great Lakes Stair & Mllwk Co G 330 225-2005 Hinckley *(G-10900)*
Gross & Sons Custom Millwork G 419 227-0214 Lima *(G-11871)*
Hawk Engine & Machine G 440 582-0900 North Royalton *(G-15276)*
Heartland Stairway Ltd G 330 279-2554 Millersburg *(G-14087)*
Heartland Stairways Inc G 330 279-2554 Holmesville *(G-10976)*
Hinckley Wood Products F 330 220-9999 Hinckley *(G-10902)*
Hj Systems Inc F 614 351-9777 Columbus *(G-7004)*
Hoehnes Custom Woodworking G 937 693-8008 Anna *(G-590)*
Holes Custom Woodworking G 419 586-8171 Celina *(G-2968)*
Holmes Lumber & Bldg Ctr Inc C 330 674-9060 Millersburg *(G-14098)*
Hoover Group G 419 525-3159 Shiloh *(G-16994)*
Hrh Door Corp D 440 593-5226 Conneaut *(G-7649)*
◆ Hrh Door Corp A 850 208-3400 Mount Hope *(G-14438)*
Huntington Hardwood Lbr Co Inc G 440 647-2283 Wellington *(G-19583)*
Hyde Park Lumber Company E 513 271-1500 Cincinnati *(G-3830)*
Idx Corporation C 937 401-3225 Dayton *(G-8259)*
Inter Cab Corporation G 216 351-0770 Cleveland *(G-5464)*
J A H Woodworking LLC G 740 266-6949 Bloomingdale *(G-1711)*
J McCoy Lumber Co Ltd E 937 587-3423 Peebles *(G-15879)*
J McCoy Lumber Co Ltd G 937 544-2968 West Union *(G-19962)*
Jaco Inc G 513 722-3947 Loveland *(G-12202)*
Jeld-Wen Inc B 740 397-1144 Mount Vernon *(G-14485)*
Jeld-Wen Inc C 740 964-1431 Etna *(G-9394)*
Jeld-Wen Inc E 740 397-3403 Mount Vernon *(G-14486)*
Jh Woodworking LLC G 330 276-7600 Killbuck *(G-11452)*
Joe P Fischer Woodcraft G 513 530-9600 Blue Ash *(G-1796)*
John M Hand G 937 902-1327 West Alexandria *(G-19619)*
Judy Mills Company Inc E 513 271-4241 Cincinnati *(G-3887)*
K D Hardwoods Inc G 440 834-1772 Burton *(G-2364)*
Kacy Stairs F 740 599-5201 Howard *(G-10996)*
Khempco Bldg Sup Co Ltd Partnr D 740 549-0465 Delaware *(G-8700)*
L & L Ornamental Iron Co F 513 353-1930 Cleves *(G-6369)*
L and J Woodworking F 330 359-3216 Dundee *(G-9020)*
▲ L J Smith Inc C 740 269-2221 Bowerston *(G-1940)*
Laborie Enterprises LLC G 419 686-6245 Portage *(G-16270)*
LAtelier Custom Woodworking G 234 759-3359 North Lima *(G-15175)*
▲ LE Smith Company D 419 636-4555 Bryan *(G-2295)*
Lehman & Sons G 330 857-7404 Orrville *(G-15601)*
Liechty Specialties Inc G 419 445-6696 Archbold *(G-655)*
Lima Millwork Inc E 419 331-3303 Elida *(G-9195)*
Longs Custom Doors G 419 339-2331 Lima *(G-11895)*
M H Woodworking LLC G 330 893-3929 Millersburg *(G-14108)*
M21 Industries LLC D 937 781-1377 Dayton *(G-8319)*
▲ Mag Resources LLC G 330 294-0494 Barberton *(G-1083)*
Mandi A Tripp G 740 380-1216 Rockbridge *(G-16537)*
Maple Hill Woodworking G 330 674-2500 Millersburg *(G-14110)*
Marsh Industries Inc E 330 308-8667 New Philadelphia *(G-14784)*
Martin Bauder Woodworking LLC G 513 735-0659 Milford *(G-14025)*
Masco Cbinetry Middlefield LLC B 440 437-8537 Orwell *(G-15634)*
Masonite Corporation D 937 454-9207 Vandalia *(G-19136)*

Employee Codes: A=Over 500 employees, B=251-500 C=101-250, D=51-100, E=20-50, F=10-19, G=3-9
2019 Harris Ohio Industrial Directory
835

Menard Inc F 513 250-4566
Cincinnati *(G-4005)*
Menard Inc C 513 583-1444
Loveland *(G-12214)*
Menard Inc E 419 998-4348
Lima *(G-11899)*
Midwest Woodworking Co Inc E 513 631-6684
Cincinnati *(G-4028)*
Miller and Slay Wdwkg LLC G 513 265-3816
Mason *(G-12910)*
▼ Miller Manufacturing Inc E 330 852-0689
Sugarcreek *(G-17854)*
Mills Customs Woodworks G 216 407-3600
Cleveland *(G-5691)*
Millwood Wholesale Inc F 330 359-6109
Dundee *(G-9023)*
Millwork Designs Inc G 740 335-5203
Wshngtn CT Hs *(G-20733)*
Millwork Fabricators Inc G 937 299-5452
Moraine *(G-14371)*
Mohican Wood Products G 740 599-5655
Butler *(G-2377)*
Morey Woodworking LLC G 937 623-5280
Piqua *(G-16144)*
Mount Hope Planing F 330 359-0538
Millersburg *(G-14115)*
Nauvoo Custom Woodworking G 440 632-9502
Middlefield *(G-13838)*
North View Woodworking G 330 359-6286
Dundee *(G-9024)*
Noteworthy Woodworking G 330 297-0509
Ravenna *(G-16392)*
Oak Front Inc G 330 948-4500
Lodi *(G-12017)*
Oak Pointe Stair Systems Inc E 740 498-9820
Newcomerstown *(G-14979)*
Ohio Woodworking Co Inc G 513 631-0870
Cincinnati *(G-4107)*
Overhead Door Corporation D 740 383-6376
Marion *(G-12727)*
Overhead Door Corporation F 419 294-3874
Upper Sandusky *(G-18970)*
P & T Millwork Inc E 440 543-2151
Chagrin Falls *(G-3064)*
Paragon Woodworking LLC G 614 402-1459
Columbus *(G-7293)*
Pease Industies Inc B 513 870-3600
Fairfield *(G-9546)*
Pete Emmert Co G 740 455-3924
Nashport *(G-14569)*
Pickens Window Service Inc F 513 931-4432
Cincinnati *(G-4157)*
Pj Woodwork LLC G 419 886-0008
Bellville *(G-1562)*
Pleasant Valley Wdwkg LLC G 440 636-5860
Middlefield *(G-13847)*
Ply Gem Industries Inc C 937 492-1111
Sidney *(G-17060)*
Precision Wood Products Inc E 937 787-3523
Camden *(G-2466)*
Precision Woodwork Ltd G 440 257-3002
Mentor *(G-13553)*
Premium Panel & Tread G 330 695-9979
Fredericksburg *(G-9955)*
▲ Profac Inc C 440 942-0205
Mentor *(G-13555)*
R C Moore Lumber Co F 740 732-4950
Caldwell *(G-2410)*
R Carney Thomas G 740 342-3388
New Lexington *(G-14722)*
Rebsco Inc F 937 548-2246
Greenville *(G-10390)*
Renewal By Andersen LLC G 614 781-9600
Columbus *(G-6506)*
Reserve Millwork Inc E 216 531-6982
Bedford *(G-1441)*
Richardson Woodworking G 614 893-8850
Blacklick *(G-1693)*
▲ Rinos Woodworking Shop Inc F 440 946-1718
Willoughby *(G-20421)*
Riverside Cnstr Svcs Inc E 513 723-0900
Cincinnati *(G-4273)*
Robertson Cabinets Inc E 937 698-3755
West Milton *(G-19952)*
Rockwood Products Ltd F 330 893-2392
Millersburg *(G-14124)*
Roettger Hardwood Inc F 937 693-6811
Kettlersville *(G-11445)*
Roy Holtzapple John Johns G 419 657-2460
Wapakoneta *(G-19350)*
S & S Panel G 330 412-6735
Orrville *(G-15617)*
S R Door Inc C 740 927-3558
Hebron *(G-10761)*
Salem Mill & Cabinet Co G 330 337-9568
Salem *(G-16771)*
Sauder Wdwkg Co Welfare Tr G 419 446-2711
Archbold *(G-667)*
Sawdust G 740 862-0612
Baltimore *(G-1043)*
Scarred Hands Wood Creations G 740 975-2835
Etna *(G-9399)*
Schreiner Cstm Stairs & Mllwk G 419 435-8935
Fostoria *(G-9858)*
Screenmobile Inc G 614 868-8663
Radnor *(G-16358)*
Select Woodworking Inc G 513 948-9901
Cincinnati *(G-4319)*
▲ Seneca Millwork Inc E 419 435-6671
Fostoria *(G-9859)*
Shade Youngstown & Aluminum Co G 330 782-2373
Youngstown *(G-21028)*
Shawnee Wood Products Inc G 440 632-1771
Middlefield *(G-13852)*
Sheridan Woodworks Inc F 216 663-9333
Cleveland *(G-6052)*
Sommers Wood N Door Company G 614 873-3506
Plain City *(G-16213)*
Stainwood Products F 440 244-1352
Lorain *(G-12124)*
Star Door & Sash Co Inc F 419 841-3396
Berkey *(G-1636)*
Stein Inc F 419 747-2611
Mansfield *(G-12519)*
▲ Stephen M Trudick E 440 834-1891
Burton *(G-2371)*
Stoney Acres Woodworking Llc G 440 834-0717
Burton *(G-2372)*
Stony Point Hardwoods F 330 852-4512
Sugarcreek *(G-17865)*
Stratton Creek Wood Works LLC F 330 876-0005
Kinsman *(G-11466)*
Summit Millwork LLC G 330 920-4000
Cuyahoga Falls *(G-7924)*
Swartz Woodworking G 330 359-6359
Millersburg *(G-14132)*
Swiss Woodcraft Inc E 330 925-1807
Rittman *(G-16529)*
Sylvan Forge Inc G 440 237-3626
North Royalton *(G-15303)*
T & D Thompson Inc E 740 332-8515
Laurelville *(G-11627)*
Teledoor LLC G 419 227-3000
Lima *(G-11949)*
Todco F 740 223-2542
Marion *(G-12742)*
Touchstone Woodworks G 330 297-1313
Ravenna *(G-16413)*
▲ Turnwood Industries Inc E 330 278-2421
Hinckley *(G-10907)*
Ufp Hamilton LLC F 513 285-7190
Hamilton *(G-10616)*
V & W Woodcraft G 330 674-0073
Millersburg *(G-14141)*
Versailles Building Supply G 937 526-3238
Versailles *(G-19191)*
Vinylmax Corporation D 800 847-3736
Hamilton *(G-10618)*
Volpe Millwork Inc G 216 581-0200
Cleveland *(G-6270)*
Walnut Creek Woodworking LLC G 513 504-3520
Bethel *(G-1656)*
Wedge Hardwood Products G 330 525-7775
Alliance *(G-513)*
Whitmer Woodworks Inc G 614 873-1196
Plain City *(G-16217)*
▲ Wittrock Wdwkg & Mfg Co Inc D 513 891-5800
Blue Ash *(G-1873)*
Woodcraft Industries Inc C 440 632-9655
Middlefield *(G-13868)*
Woodcraft Industries Inc D 440 437-7811
Orwell *(G-15640)*
Woodland Woodworking G 330 897-7282
Baltic *(G-1035)*
Woodworks Design G 440 693-4414
Middlefield *(G-13869)*
Woodworks Unlimited G 740 574-4523
Franklin Furnace *(G-9936)*
Wyman Woodworking G 614 338-0615
Columbus *(G-7619)*
▼ Yoder Lumber Co Inc D 330 893-3121
Millersburg *(G-14153)*
Yoder Window & Siding Ltd F 330 695-6960
Fredericksburg *(G-9962)*
Yoder Woodworking G 740 399-9400
Butler *(G-2378)*
▲ Yutzy Woodworking Ltd C 330 359-6166
Millersburg *(G-14157)*

2434 Wood Kitchen Cabinets

4-B Wood Specialties Inc F 330 769-2188
Seville *(G-16909)*
A & J Woodworking Inc G 419 695-5655
Delphos *(G-8734)*
▲ Affordable Cabinet Doors G 513 734-9663
Bethel *(G-1655)*
Agean Marble Manufacturing F 513 874-1475
West Chester *(G-19829)*
Ailes Millwork Inc F 330 678-4300
Kent *(G-11290)*
Al-Co Products Inc F 419 399-3867
Latty *(G-11624)*
Alpine Cabinets Inc G 330 273-2131
Hinckley *(G-10897)*
Apex Cabinetry G 859 581-5300
Cincinnati *(G-3350)*
Approved Plumbing Co F 216 663-5063
Cleveland *(G-4722)*
As America Inc E 419 522-4211
Mansfield *(G-12408)*
Bauman Custom Woodworking LLC G 330 482-4330
Salem *(G-16720)*
Bear Cabinetry LLC G 216 481-9282
Euclid *(G-9404)*
Benchmark Cabinets E 740 397-4615
Mount Vernon *(G-14470)*
Benchmark Cabinets E 740 694-1144
Fredericktown *(G-9963)*
Bestway Cabinets LLC G 614 306-3518
Hilliard *(G-10811)*
Bowes Mill and Cabinet LLC G 440 236-3255
Columbia Station *(G-6430)*
Bowman Cabinet Shop G 419 331-8209
Elida *(G-9194)*
Breits Inc G 216 651-5800
Cleveland *(G-4836)*
Bricolage Inc F 614 853-6789
Grove City *(G-10418)*
Brower Products Inc D 937 563-1111
Cincinnati *(G-3426)*
▲ Bruewer Woodwork Mfg Co D 513 353-3505
Cleves *(G-6355)*
Cabinet Source G 330 336-5600
Wadsworth *(G-19229)*
Cabinet Specialties Inc E 330 695-3463
Fredericksburg *(G-9944)*
Cabinet Systems Inc G 440 237-1924
Cleveland *(G-4861)*
Cabinetry By Ebbing G 419 678-2191
Celina *(G-2952)*
Canton Cabinet Co G 330 455-2585
Canton *(G-2607)*
Cardinal Custom Cabinets Ltd G 216 281-1570
Cleveland *(G-4876)*
Care Cabinetry Inc G 216 481-7445
Euclid *(G-9407)*
Carnegie Plas Cabinetry Inc G 216 451-3300
Cleveland *(G-4880)*
Carter-Jones Lumber Company C 330 674-9060
Millersburg *(G-14077)*
Cedee Cedar Inc F 740 363-3148
Delaware *(G-8662)*
Chesterland Cabinet Company G 440 564-1157
Newbury *(G-14947)*
Clancys Cabinet Shop E 419 445-4455
Archbold *(G-641)*
▼ Clark Son Actn Liquidation Inc G 330 866-9330
East Sparta *(G-9094)*
Cleveland Custom Cabinets LLC G 213 663-0606
Cleveland *(G-4955)*
Colonial Cabinets Inc F 440 355-9663
Lagrange *(G-11478)*
Commercial Bar & Cabinetry G 330 743-1420
Youngstown *(G-20876)*
Creative Cabinets Ltd F 740 689-0603
Lancaster *(G-11557)*
Crowes Cabinets Inc E 330 729-9911
Youngstown *(G-20881)*
Custom Woodworking Inc G 419 456-3330
Ottawa *(G-15649)*

D Lewis Inc .... G 740 695-2615
Saint Clairsville *(G-16630)*
Danny Cabinet Co .... G 440 667-6635
Cleveland *(G-5062)*
Distinct Cbntry Innvations LLC .... G 937 661-1051
New Lebanon *(G-14708)*
Distinctive Surfaces LLC .... F 614 431-0898
Columbus *(G-6869)*
Dover Cabinet Inc .... F 330 343-9074
Dover *(G-8818)*
Dutch Valley Woodworking Inc .... F 330 852-4319
Sugarcreek *(G-17848)*
E J Skok Industries .... E 216 292-7533
Bedford *(G-1403)*
East Oberlin Cabinets .... G 440 775-1166
Oberlin *(G-15493)*
Easyfit Products Inc .... G 740 362-9900
Delaware *(G-8674)*
Ernst Custom Cabinets LLC .... G 513 376-9554
Cincinnati *(G-3652)*
Fairfield Woodworks Ltd .... G 740 689-1953
Lancaster *(G-11571)*
Fdi Cabinetry LLC .... G 513 353-4500
Cleves *(G-6362)*
Fine Wood Design Inc .... G 440 327-0751
North Ridgeville *(G-15225)*
Fleetwood Custom Countertops .... F 740 965-9833
Johnstown *(G-11265)*
Flottemesch Anthony & Son .... F 513 561-1212
Cincinnati *(G-3696)*
Formware Inc .... G 614 231-9387
Columbus *(G-6930)*
Forum III Inc .... F 513 961-5123
Cincinnati *(G-3706)*
Franklin Cabinet Company Inc .... E 937 743-9606
Franklin *(G-9884)*
Gillard Construction Inc .... F 740 376-9744
Marietta *(G-12627)*
Gross & Sons Custom Millwork .... G 419 227-0214
Lima *(G-11871)*
Hampshire Co .... E 937 773-3493
Piqua *(G-16119)*
Harold Flory .... G 937 473-3030
Covington *(G-7787)*
Hattenbach Company .... E 330 744-2732
Youngstown *(G-20929)*
Hattenbach Company .... D 216 881-5200
Cleveland *(G-5380)*
Heartland Home Cabinetry Ltd .... G 740 936-5100
Sunbury *(G-17888)*
Holmes Lumber & Bldg Ctr Inc .... C 330 674-9060
Millersburg *(G-14098)*
Idx Corporation .... C 937 401-3225
Dayton *(G-8259)*
Inter Cab Corporation .... G 216 351-0770
Cleveland *(G-5464)*
J & K Cabinetry Incorporated .... G 513 860-3461
West Chester *(G-19870)*
J & L Door .... G 330 684-1496
Dalton *(G-7944)*
James F Seme .... G 440 759-6455
Berea *(G-1614)*
Johannings Inc .... G 330 875-1706
Louisville *(G-12159)*
◆ Kellogg Cabinets Inc .... G 614 833-9596
Canal Winchester *(G-2504)*
Kelly Cabinet Company LLC .... G 614 563-2971
Powell *(G-16324)*
Kinnemyers Cornerstone Cab Inc .... G 513 353-3030
Cleves *(G-6367)*
Kinsella Manufacturing Co Inc .... F 513 561-5285
Cincinnati *(G-3911)*
Kitchen Designs Plus Inc .... E 419 536-6605
Toledo *(G-18368)*
Kitchen Works Inc .... G 440 353-0939
North Ridgeville *(G-15236)*
▲ Kitchens By Rutenschroer Inc .... F 513 251-8333
Cincinnati *(G-3914)*
Knapke Custom Cabinetry Ltd .... F 937 459-8866
Versailles *(G-19185)*
Lima Millwork Inc .... E 419 331-3303
Elida *(G-9195)*
M A Miller .... G 440 636-5697
Middlefield *(G-13814)*
Malco Laminated Inc .... G 513 541-8300
Cincinnati *(G-3975)*
Marsh Industries Inc .... E 330 308-8667
New Philadelphia *(G-14784)*
Masco Cabinetry LLC .... A 440 632-2547
Middlefield *(G-13817)*
◆ Masco Cbinetry Middlefield LLC .... A 440 632-5333
Middlefield *(G-13818)*
Masco Cbinetry Middlefield LLC .... D 440 632-5058
Middlefield *(G-13819)*
Masco Cbinetry Middlefield LLC .... B 440 437-8537
Orwell *(G-15634)*
Midwest Woodworking Co Inc .... E 513 631-6684
Cincinnati *(G-4028)*
Miller Cabinet Ltd .... E 614 873-4221
Plain City *(G-16203)*
Millwork Design Solutions Inc .... G 440 946-8837
Willoughby *(G-20384)*
Mock Woodworking Company LLC .... E 740 452-2701
Zanesville *(G-21157)*
Mro Built Inc .... D 330 526-0555
North Canton *(G-15104)*
N C W Nicoloff Cab Works LLC .... G 513 821-1400
Fairfield *(G-9534)*
Navigator Construction LLC .... G 330 244-0221
North Canton *(G-15106)*
Northeast Cabinet Co LLC .... G 614 759-0800
Columbus *(G-7229)*
Northpointe Cabinetry LLC .... G 740 455-4045
Zanesville *(G-21163)*
Oakwood Furniture Inc .... G 740 896-3162
Lowell *(G-12247)*
Oen Custom Cabinets Inc .... G 419 738-8115
Wapakoneta *(G-19348)*
Ohio River Valley Cabinet .... G 740 975-8846
Newark *(G-14906)*
Old Mill Custom Cabinetry Co .... G 419 423-8897
Findlay *(G-9734)*
Online Mega Sellers Corp .... D 888 384-6468
Toledo *(G-18439)*
Peters Cabinetry .... G 937 884-7514
Brookville *(G-2181)*
Phil D De Mint .... G 740 474-7777
Circleville *(G-4551)*
Pleasant Valley Wdwkg LLC .... G 440 636-5860
Middlefield *(G-13847)*
Profiles In Design Inc .... F 513 751-2212
Cincinnati *(G-4217)*
R Carney Thomas .... G 740 342-3388
New Lexington *(G-14722)*
Red Barn Cabinet Co .... G 937 884-9800
Arcanum *(G-632)*
Regal Cabinet Inc .... G 419 865-3932
Toledo *(G-18500)*
Reserve Millwork Inc .... E 216 531-6982
Bedford *(G-1441)*
Rheaco Builders Inc .... G 330 425-3090
Twinsburg *(G-18846)*
Riceland Cabinet Inc .... D 330 601-1071
Wooster *(G-20644)*
Riceland Cabinet Corporation .... F 330 601-1071
Wooster *(G-20645)*
Richard Benhase & Associates .... F 513 772-1896
Cincinnati *(G-4267)*
Riggenbach Kitchens .... G 330 669-2113
Smithville *(G-17091)*
River East Custom Cabinets .... E 419 244-3226
Toledo *(G-18502)*
Riverside Cnstr Svcs Inc .... E 513 723-0900
Cincinnati *(G-4273)*
Rn Cabinets & More Ltd .... G 330 275-0203
Fredericksburg *(G-9957)*
Roettger Hardwood Inc .... F 937 693-6811
Kettlersville *(G-11445)*
Royal Cabinet Design Co Inc .... F 216 267-5330
Cleveland *(G-6010)*
S & G Manufacturing Group LLC .... C 614 529-0100
Hilliard *(G-10859)*
S & W Custom Tops Inc .... G 330 788-2525
Youngstown *(G-21023)*
Salem Mill & Cabinet Co .... G 330 337-9568
Salem *(G-16771)*
Schrock Woodworking .... G 740 489-5229
Freeport *(G-9986)*
Shawnee Wood Products Inc .... G 440 632-1771
Middlefield *(G-13852)*
Showcase Cab Mar Rstoration LL .... G 419 626-6715
Sandusky *(G-16849)*
Sidney Stiers .... G 740 454-7368
Zanesville *(G-21179)*
Signature Cabinetry Inc .... F 614 252-2227
Columbus *(G-7450)*
Snows Wood Shop Inc .... E 419 836-3805
Oregon *(G-15567)*
Specified Structures Inc .... G 330 753-0693
Barberton *(G-1106)*
Summit Custom Cabinets .... G 740 345-1734
Newark *(G-14927)*
Surface Enterprises Inc .... G 419 476-5670
Toledo *(G-18537)*
TDS Custom Cabinets LLC .... G 614 517-2220
Columbus *(G-7516)*
Tenkotte Tops Inc .... G 513 738-7300
Harrison *(G-10677)*
Thomas Cabinet Shop Inc .... F 937 847-8239
Dayton *(G-8554)*
▼ Tiffin Metal Products Co .... C 419 447-8414
Tiffin *(G-18088)*
Timberlane Woodworking .... G 419 895-9945
Greenwich *(G-10409)*
Trail Cabinet .... G 330 893-3791
Dundee *(G-9027)*
Trutech Cabinetry .... G 614 338-0680
Columbus *(G-7549)*
▲ Turnwood Industries Inc .... E 330 278-2421
Hinckley *(G-10907)*
Unique Woodmasters LLC .... G 419 268-9663
Celina *(G-2990)*
Virgils Kitchens Inc .... G 440 355-5058
Lagrange *(G-11497)*
Wengerd Cabinets .... G 330 231-0879
Millersburg *(G-14150)*
Westgerdes Cabinets .... G 419 375-2113
Fort Recovery *(G-9831)*
Wilson Cabinet Co .... E 330 276-8711
Killbuck *(G-11455)*
Woodcraft Industries Inc .... D 440 437-7811
Orwell *(G-15640)*
Woodcraft Industries Inc .... C 440 632-9655
Middlefield *(G-13868)*
Wurms Woodworking Company .... E 419 492-2184
New Washington *(G-14834)*
Xxx Intrntional Amusements Inc .... E 216 671-6900
Cleveland *(G-6332)*
Yoder Cabinets Ltd .... G 614 873-5186
Plain City *(G-16221)*
Your Cabinetry .... G 440 638-4925
Strongsville *(G-17809)*

2435 Hardwood Veneer & Plywood

A & M Kiln Dry Ltd .... F 330 852-0505
Dundee *(G-9017)*
▲ American Vneer Edgebanding Inc .... G 740 928-2700
Heath *(G-10716)*
▲ Arkansas Face Veneer Co Inc .... E 937 773-6295
Piqua *(G-16100)*
Automated Bldg Components Inc .... E 419 257-2152
North Baltimore *(G-15042)*
Beaver Wood Products .... E 740 226-6211
Beaver *(G-1292)*
▲ Bruewer Woodwork Mfg Co .... D 513 353-3505
Cleves *(G-6355)*
Carl C Andre Inc .... G 614 864-0123
Brice *(G-2071)*
▼ Decorative Panels Intl Inc .... D 419 535-5921
Toledo *(G-18259)*
▲ Dimension Hardwood Veneers Inc .... E 419 272-2245
Edon *(G-9184)*
◆ Erath Veneer Corp Virginia .... F 540 483-5223
Granville *(G-10330)*
Fifth Avenue Lumber Co .... D 614 833-6655
Canal Winchester *(G-2503)*
Haessly Lumber Sales Co .... D 740 373-6681
Marietta *(G-12630)*
Hartzell Industries Inc .... D 937 773-6295
Piqua *(G-16124)*
Knisley Lumber .... F 740 634-2935
Bainbridge *(G-1019)*
Lattasburg Lumberworks Co LLC .... G 330 202-7671
West Salem *(G-19956)*
Miller Crist .... F 330 359-7877
Fredericksburg *(G-9953)*
▼ Miller Manufacturing Inc .... E 330 852-0689
Sugarcreek *(G-17854)*
Mohler Lumber Company .... E 330 499-5461
North Canton *(G-15102)*
▼ Ohio Valley Veneer Inc .... E 740 493-2901
Piketon *(G-16076)*
S & G Manufacturing Group LLC .... C 614 529-0100
Hilliard *(G-10859)*
▲ Sims-Lohman Inc .... E 513 651-3510
Cincinnati *(G-4340)*
Southeast Ohio Timber Pdts Co .... G 740 344-2570
Zanesville *(G-21181)*
Starecasing Systems Inc .... G 312 203-5632
Columbus *(G-7488)*

S
I
C

Employee Codes: A=Over 500 employees, B=251-500
C=101-250, D=51-100, E=20-50, F=10-19, G=3-9
2019 Harris Ohio
Industrial Directory
837

Stony Point Hardwoods ....F 330 852-4512
Sugarcreek (G-17865)
◆ Universal Veneer Sales Corp ....C 740 522-1147
Newark (G-14932)
Wappoo Wood Products Inc ....E 937 492-1166
Sidney (G-17084)
Yoder Lumber Co Inc ....D 330 893-3131
Sugarcreek (G-17878)

2436 Softwood Veneer & Plywood

▲ American Vneer Edgebanding Inc ....G 740 928-2700
Heath (G-10716)
Beaver Wood Products ....E 740 226-6211
Beaver (G-1292)
◆ Clopay Building Pdts Co Inc ....E 513 770-4800
Mason (G-12846)
Clopay Building Pdts Co Inc ....G 937 526-4301
Russia (G-16606)
Clopay Building Pdts Co Inc ....G 937 440-6403
Troy (G-18642)
S & G Manufacturing Group LLC ....C 614 529-0100
Hilliard (G-10859)
Ufp Hamilton LLC ....F 513 285-7190
Hamilton (G-10616)
▼ Universal Veneer Production ....C 740 522-1147
Newark (G-14931)
Wappoo Wood Products Inc ....E 937 492-1166
Sidney (G-17084)

2439 Structural Wood Members, NEC

Automated Bldg Components Inc ....E 419 257-2152
North Baltimore (G-15042)
Baker McMillen Co ....E 330 923-3303
Stow (G-17573)
Buckeye Components LLC ....E 330 482-5163
Columbiana (G-6456)
Building Concepts Inc ....F 419 298-2371
Edgerton (G-9169)
Byler Truss ....G 330 465-5412
Ashland (G-688)
Carter-Jones Lumber Company ....C 330 674-9060
Millersburg (G-14077)
Columbus Roof Trusses Inc ....E 614 272-6464
Columbus (G-6800)
Columbus Roof Trusses Inc ....F 740 763-3000
Newark (G-14862)
Contract Building Components ....E 937 644-0739
Marysville (G-12777)
Dutchcraft Truss Component Inc ....F 330 862-2220
Minerva (G-14178)
Fifth Avenue Lumber Co ....D 614 833-6655
Canal Winchester (G-2503)
Four Js Bldg Components LLC ....F 740 886-6112
Scottown (G-16881)
Holmes Lumber & Bldg Ctr Inc ....C 330 674-9060
Millersburg (G-14098)
Khempco Bldg Sup Co Ltd Partnr ....D 740 549-0465
Delaware (G-8700)
▲ Laminate Technologies Inc ....D 419 448-0812
Tiffin (G-18064)
M & G Truss Rafters ....G 740 667-3166
Coolville (G-7673)
Miller Truss LLC ....G 440 321-0126
Middlefield (G-13830)
Minova USA Inc ....D 740 377-9146
South Point (G-17289)
Ohio Valley Truss Co ....E 937 393-3995
Hillsboro (G-10887)
Ohio Valley Truss Co ....G 937 393-3995
Hillsboro (G-10888)
Pioneer Homes Inc ....G 419 737-2371
Pioneer (G-16089)
Proline Truss ....F 419 895-9980
Shiloh (G-16999)
R & L Truss Inc ....F 419 587-3440
Grover Hill (G-10519)
Redbuilt LLC ....E 740 363-0870
Delaware (G-8719)
Richland Laminated Columns LLC ....F 419 895-0036
Greenwich (G-10407)
Schilling Truss Inc ....F 740 984-2396
Beverly (G-1662)
Socar of Ohio Inc ....D 419 596-3100
Continental (G-7668)
Stark Truss Company Inc ....D 330 478-2100
Canton (G-2825)
Stark Truss Company Inc ....E 740 335-4156
Washington Court Hou (G-19478)
Stark Truss Company Inc ....D 419 298-3777
Edgerton (G-9181)
Stark Truss Company Inc ....E 330 756-3050
Beach City (G-1215)
Stark Truss Company Inc ....F 330 478-2100
Canton (G-2824)
▲ Thomas Do-It Center Inc ....D 740 446-2002
Gallipolis (G-10176)
Truss Worx LLC ....G 419 363-2100
Rockford (G-16541)
Waynedale Truss & Panel Co ....G 330 683-4471
Dalton (G-7953)
Waynedale Truss and Panel Co ....E 330 698-7373
Apple Creek (G-622)

2441 Wood Boxes

Aerocase Incorporated ....F 440 617-9294
Westlake (G-20088)
Aslan Worldwide ....F 513 671-0671
West Chester (G-19653)
Boxes & Such ....G 440 237-7122
Wooster (G-20574)
Buckeye Diamond Logistics Inc ....C 937 462-8361
South Charleston (G-17271)
Built-Rite Box & Crate Inc ....E 330 263-0936
Wooster (G-20577)
Caravan Packaging Inc ....F 440 243-4100
Cleveland (G-4875)
Cassady Woodworks Inc ....E 937 256-7948
Dayton (G-7974)
Cedar Craft Products Inc ....E 614 759-1600
Blacklick (G-1681)
Clark Rm Inc ....E 419 425-9889
Findlay (G-9669)
Custom Displays LLC ....G 330 454-8850
Bolivar (G-1910)
Damar Products Inc ....F 937 492-9023
Sidney (G-17025)
Damar Products Inc ....F 937 492-9023
Sidney (G-17026)
Dp Products LLC ....G 440 834-9663
Burton (G-2357)
Fca LLC ....F 309 644-2424
Clayton (G-4573)
Forest City Companies Inc ....E 216 586-5279
Cleveland (G-5261)
Global Packaging & Exports Inc ....G 513 454-2020
West Chester (G-19716)
▲ H Gerstner & Sons Inc ....E 937 228-1662
Dayton (G-8241)
Hann Manufacturing Inc ....E 740 962-3752
McConnelsville (G-13206)
Hines Builders Inc ....F 937 335-4586
Troy (G-18665)
▲ J & L Wood Products Inc ....E 937 667-4064
Tipp City (G-18119)
▲ Kennedy Group Incorporated ....D 440 951-7660
Willoughby (G-20352)
Lefco Worthington LLC ....E 216 432-4422
Cleveland (G-5571)
Lima Pallet Company Inc ....E 419 229-5736
Lima (G-11889)
Ohio Box & Crate Inc ....F 440 526-3133
Burton (G-2366)
Quadco Rehabilitation Ctr Inc ....B 419 682-1011
Stryker (G-17832)
Schaefer Box & Pallet Co ....E 513 738-2500
Hamilton (G-10603)
Scorpion Case Mfg LLC ....F 614 274-7246
Dublin (G-8981)
Sterling Industries Inc ....F 419 523-3788
Ottawa (G-15666)
Thomas J Weaver Inc ....F 740 622-2040
Coshocton (G-7755)
Traveling & Recycle Wood Pdts ....F 419 968-2649
Middle Point (G-13757)
Van Orders Pallet Company Inc ....F 419 875-6932
Swanton (G-17928)
World Express Packaging Corp ....G 216 634-9000
Cleveland (G-6324)
Zak Box Co Inc ....G 216 961-5636
Cleveland (G-6337)

2448 Wood Pallets & Skids

A & D Wood Products Inc ....F 419 331-8859
Elida (G-9192)
A & M Pallet ....F 937 295-3093
Russia (G-16604)
A & M Pallet Shop Inc ....F 440 632-1941
Middlefield (G-13772)
A W Taylor Lumber Incorporated ....F 440 577-1889
Pierpont (G-16063)
A-Z Packaging Company ....F 614 444-8441
Columbus (G-6518)
A2z Pallets LLC ....G 513 652-9026
Cincinnati (G-3284)
AA Pallets LLC ....G 216 856-2614
Cleveland (G-4595)
AAA Plastics and Pallets Ltd ....G 330 844-2556
Orrville (G-15580)
Able Pallet Mfg & Repr ....F 614 444-2115
Columbus (G-6529)
Akron Crate and Pallet LLC ....G 330 524-8955
Kent (G-11291)
American Built Custom Pallets ....G 330 532-4780
Lisbon (G-11963)
Anderson Pallet & Packg Inc ....E 937 962-2614
Lewisburg (G-11789)
Arrowhead Pallets LLC ....F 440 693-4241
Middlefield (G-13778)
At Pallet ....G 330 264-3903
Wooster (G-20565)
B & B Pallet Co ....G 419 435-4530
Fostoria (G-9834)
B J Pallett ....G 419 447-9665
Tiffin (G-18049)
Belco Works ....G 740 695-0500
Saint Clairsville (G-16623)
Belco Works Inc ....B 740 695-0500
Saint Clairsville (G-16624)
Bonded Pallets ....G 513 541-1855
Cincinnati (G-3402)
Brookhill Center Industries ....C 419 876-3932
Ottawa (G-15648)
Buck Creek Pallet ....G 937 653-3098
Urbana (G-18981)
Buckeye Diamond Logistics Inc ....C 937 462-8361
South Charleston (G-17271)
Buckeye Pallett ....G 330 359-5919
Millersburg (G-14070)
Built-Rite Box & Crate Inc ....E 330 263-0936
Wooster (G-20577)
Cabot Lumber Inc ....G 740 545-7109
West Lafayette (G-19929)
Caesarcreek Pallets Ltd ....F 937 416-4447
Jamestown (G-11219)
Carrillo Pallets LLC ....G 513 942-2210
Cincinnati (G-3446)
CC Pallets LLC ....G 513 442-8766
Terrace Park (G-18018)
Chep (usa) Inc ....E 614 497-9448
Columbus (G-6761)
Cima Inc ....E 513 382-8976
Hamilton (G-10545)
Cimino Box Inc ....G 216 961-7377
Cleveland (G-4928)
Clark Rm Inc ....E 419 425-9889
Findlay (G-9669)
Cleveland Cstm Pllet Crate Inc ....E 216 881-1414
Cleveland (G-4954)
Clover Pallet LLC ....G 330 454-5592
Canton (G-2629)
Coblentz Brothers Inc ....E 330 857-7211
Apple Creek (G-602)
Coshocton Pallet & Door Bldg ....G 740 622-9766
Coshocton (G-7729)
Cottonwood Pallet Inc ....G 419 468-9703
Galion (G-10129)
Cox Wood Product Inc ....F 740 372-4735
Otway (G-15687)
Crosscreek Pallet Co ....G 440 632-1940
Middlefield (G-13788)
Cs Products ....G 330 452-8566
Canton (G-2640)
Custom Palet Manufacturing ....G 440 693-4603
Middlefield (G-13789)
D M Pallet Service Inc ....F 614 491-0881
Columbus (G-6845)
D P Products Inc ....G 440 834-9663
Middlefield (G-13791)
Damar Products Inc ....F 937 492-9023
Sidney (G-17025)
Damar Products Inc ....F 937 492-9023
Sidney (G-17026)
Dan S Miller & David S Miller ....G 937 464-9061
Belle Center (G-1498)
Daves Pallets ....G 740 525-4938
Belpre (G-1573)
David J Fisher ....G 440 636-2256
Middlefield (G-13793)
Diamond Pallets LLC ....G 419 281-2908
Ashland (G-701)

Dj Pallets G 216 701-9183
Columbia Station *(G-6436)*
▲ **Emergency Products & RES Inc** G 330 673-5003
Kent *(G-11319)*
Findlay Pallet Inc G 419 423-0511
Findlay *(G-9685)*
Findlay Pallett Inc G 419 423-0511
Findlay *(G-9686)*
Fisher Pallet G 440 632-0863
Middlefield *(G-13798)*
Forrest Rawlins G 740 778-3366
Wheelersburg *(G-20180)*
Fox Hollow Pallet G 937 386-2872
Winchester *(G-20520)*
Frankes Wood Products LLC E 937 642-0706
Marysville *(G-12783)*
Franks Sawmill Inc F 419 682-3831
Stryker *(G-17829)*
Gallagher Lumber Co G 330 274-2333
Mantua *(G-12546)*
Gardner Lumber Co Inc F 740 254-4664
Tippecanoe *(G-18148)*
Global Packaging & Exports Inc G 513 454-2020
West Chester *(G-19716)*
Grant Street Pallet Inc G 330 424-0355
Lisbon *(G-11967)*
Gross Lumber Inc E 330 683-2055
Apple Creek *(G-606)*
H & K Pallet Services G 937 608-1140
Xenia *(G-20776)*
Hacker Wood Products Inc G 513 737-4462
Hamilton *(G-10566)*
Haessly Lumber Sales Co D 740 373-6681
Marietta *(G-12630)*
Halliday Holdings Inc E 740 335-1430
Wshngtn CT Hs *(G-20727)*
Hann Box Works E 740 962-3752
McConnelsville *(G-13205)*
Hann Manufacturing Inc E 740 962-3752
McConnelsville *(G-13206)*
Harrys Pallets LLC G 330 704-1056
Navarre *(G-14576)*
Hershberger Manufacturing E 440 272-5555
Windsor *(G-20526)*
Hillside Pallet G 440 272-5425
Windsor *(G-20527)*
Hinchcliff Lumber Company G 440 238-5200
Strongsville *(G-17749)*
Hines Builders Inc F 937 335-4586
Troy *(G-18665)*
Hope Timber & Marketing Group F 740 344-1788
Newark *(G-14884)*
▼ **Hope Timber Pallet Recycl Inc** E 740 344-1788
Newark *(G-14886)*
Ictm Inc G 330 629-6060
Youngstown *(G-20936)*
Ifco Systems North America Inc D 330 669-2726
Smithville *(G-17089)*
Ifco Systems Us LLC E 513 769-0377
Cincinnati *(G-3836)*
▲ **Inca Presswood-Pallets Ltd** E 330 343-3361
Dover *(G-8831)*
Industrial Hardwood Inc G 419 666-2503
Perrysburg *(G-15966)*
Inland Hardwood Corporation D 740 373-7187
Marietta *(G-12635)*
Iron City Wood Products Inc E 330 755-2772
Youngstown *(G-20943)*
Ironhouse Pallets G 330 635-5218
North Ridgeville *(G-15233)*
Iroquois Pallet G 513 677-0048
Cincinnati *(G-3860)*
J & K Pallet Inc G 937 526-5117
Versailles *(G-19182)*
▲ **J & L Wood Products Inc** E 937 667-4064
Tipp City *(G-18119)*
J D L Hardwoods G 440 272-5630
Middlefield *(G-13807)*
J E Johnson Pallett Inc G 614 424-9663
Columbus *(G-7055)*
J I T Pallets Inc G 330 424-0355
Lisbon *(G-11971)*
J Smokin G 330 466-7087
Rittman *(G-16523)*
J&R Pallet Ltd G 740 226-1112
Waverly *(G-19549)*
JIT Packaging Inc E 330 562-8080
Aurora *(G-885)*
Joe Barrett G 216 385-2384
East Liverpool *(G-9060)*
Joe Gonda Company Inc F 440 458-6000
Grafton *(G-10305)*
Kamps Inc D 937 526-9333
Versailles *(G-19183)*
Ken Harper C 740 439-4452
Byesville *(G-2388)*
Kenneth Schrock G 937 544-7566
West Union *(G-19964)*
Kmak Group LLC F 937 308-1023
London *(G-12064)*
Kountry Pride Enterprises G 330 868-3345
Minerva *(G-14189)*
L N S Pallets G 330 936-7507
Navarre *(G-14579)*
Lake Wood Product Inc G 419 832-0150
Grand Rapids *(G-10316)*
Langston Pallets G 937 492-8769
Sidney *(G-17049)*
Lawrence Pallets & Solutions G 740 259-4283
Lucasville *(G-12265)*
Leroy Yutzy G 937 386-2872
Winchester *(G-20522)*
Lima Pallet Company Inc E 419 229-5736
Lima *(G-11889)*
◆ **Litco International Inc** E 330 539-5433
Vienna *(G-19201)*
▲ **Litco Manufacturing LLC** F 330 539-5433
Warren *(G-19417)*
Lumberjack Pallet Recycl LLC G 513 821-7543
Cincinnati *(G-3956)*
Martin Pallet Inc E 330 832-5309
Massillon *(G-13018)*
Mec G 419 483-4852
Bellevue *(G-1539)*
Melt Inc G 330 426-3545
Negley *(G-14591)*
Mid Ohio Wood Products Inc E 740 323-0427
Newark *(G-14897)*
Mid Ohio Wood Recycling Inc G 419 673-8470
Kenton *(G-11413)*
Middlefield Pallet Inc E 440 632-0553
Middlefield *(G-13825)*
Midtown Pallet & Recycling E 419 241-1311
Toledo *(G-18410)*
Miller Pallet Company G 937 464-4483
Belle Center *(G-1500)*
Milltree Lumber Holdings G 740 226-2090
Waverly *(G-19551)*
Millwood Inc E 330 359-5220
Dundee *(G-9022)*
Millwood Inc D 330 857-3075
Apple Creek *(G-614)*
Millwood Inc D 740 226-2090
Waverly *(G-19552)*
Millwood Inc C 440 914-0540
Solon *(G-17195)*
Mjc Enterprises Inc G 330 669-3744
Sterling *(G-17523)*
Montgomerys Pallet Service G 330 297-6677
Ravenna *(G-16390)*
◆ **Morgan Wood Products Inc** F 614 336-4000
Powell *(G-16330)*
Mt Eaton Pallet Ltd E 330 893-2986
Millersburg *(G-14116)*
Mulch World G 419 873-6852
Perrysburg *(G-15978)*
Nwp Manufacturing Inc F 419 894-6871
Waldo *(G-19303)*
◆ **Oak Chips Inc** E 740 947-4159
Waverly *(G-19554)*
Oakmoor Pallet G 216 926-1858
Westlake *(G-20134)*
Oakmoor Pallet G 440 385-7340
Westlake *(G-20135)*
Ohio Box & Crate Inc F 440 526-3133
Burton *(G-2366)*
▲ **Ohio Specialty Mfg Co** G 419 531-5402
Toledo *(G-18437)*
Ohio State Pallet Corp G 614 332-3961
Homer *(G-10985)*
Ohio Wood Recycling Inc E 614 491-0881
Columbus *(G-7265)*
Olympic Forest Products Co F 216 421-2775
Cleveland *(G-5812)*
P R U Industries Inc F 937 746-8702
Franklin *(G-9907)*
Pallet & Cont Corp of Amer G 419 255-1256
Toledo *(G-18457)*
Pallet Distributors Inc D 330 852-3531
Sugarcreek *(G-17856)*
Pallet Guys G 440 897-3001
North Royalton *(G-15292)*
Pallet Pros G 440 537-9087
Grafton *(G-10308)*
Pallet Specs Plus LLC F 513 351-3200
Norwood *(G-15427)*
Pallet World Inc E 419 874-9333
Perrysburg *(G-16000)*
Parks West Pallet Llc G 440 693-4651
Middlefield *(G-13843)*
Paul E Cekovich G 330 424-3213
Lisbon *(G-11979)*
Pettits Pallets Inc G 614 351-4920
Orient *(G-15576)*
Plains Precut Ltd G 330 893-3300
Millersburg *(G-14119)*
Plastic Pallet & Container Inc G 330 650-6700
Hudson *(G-11067)*
Precise Pallets LLC G 513 560-8236
Batavia *(G-1178)*
Precision Pallet Inc G 419 381-8191
Ottawa Hills *(G-15676)*
Premier Pallet & Recycling F 330 767-2221
Navarre *(G-14585)*
Price Management Services Ltd G 419 298-5423
Paulding *(G-15870)*
▲ **Prime Wood Craft Inc** E 216 738-2222
Brunswick *(G-2229)*
Pymatning Spcialty Pallets LLC G 440 293-3306
Andover *(G-586)*
Quadco Rehabilitation Center D 419 445-1950
Archbold *(G-665)*
Quadco Rehabilitation Ctr Inc B 419 682-1011
Stryker *(G-17832)*
Quality Pllets Recyclables LLC G 419 396-3244
Carey *(G-2889)*
Queen City Pallets Inc E 513 821-6700
Cincinnati *(G-4239)*
R C Family Wood Products G 937 295-2393
Fort Loramie *(G-9802)*
Raber Lumber Co G 330 893-2797
Charm *(G-3142)*
Rettig Family Pallets Inc F 419 264-1540
Napoleon *(G-14560)*
Richland Newhope Industries C 419 774-4400
Mansfield *(G-12506)*
Riverview Indus WD Pdts Inc D 330 669-8509
Wooster *(G-20646)*
Riverview Indus WD Pdts Inc F 330 669-8509
Smithville *(G-17092)*
Russell L Garber F 937 548-6224
Greenville *(G-10394)*
S & M Products G 419 272-2054
Blakeslee *(G-1697)*
S & S Pallets G 513 967-7432
Milford *(G-14038)*
Schaefer Box & Pallet Co E 513 738-2500
Hamilton *(G-10603)*
Schnider Pallet LLC G 440 632-5346
Middlefield *(G-13850)*
Schrock John G 937 544-8457
West Union *(G-19966)*
Schutz Container Systems Inc D 419 872-2477
Perrysburg *(G-16005)*
▲ **Sealco Inc** G 740 922-4122
Uhrichsville *(G-18893)*
Shaw Pallets & Specialties G 740 498-7892
Newcomerstown *(G-14981)*
Silvesco Inc F 740 373-6661
Marietta *(G-12669)*
Slats and Nails Inc G 330 866-1008
East Sparta *(G-9095)*
Smith Pallets G 937 564-6492
Versailles *(G-19190)*
Southeast Ohio Timber Pdts Co G 740 344-2570
Zanesville *(G-21181)*
Southern Ohio Lumber LLC E 614 436-4472
Peebles *(G-15882)*
Specialty Pallet & Design Ltd E 330 857-0257
Orrville *(G-15624)*
Specialty Pallet Entps LLC G 419 673-0247
Kenton *(G-11423)*
Sterling Industries Inc F 419 523-3788
Ottawa *(G-15666)*
Stony Point Hardwoods F 330 852-4512
Sugarcreek *(G-17865)*
Stumptown Lbr Pallet Mills Ltd G 740 757-2275
Somerton *(G-17269)*
Sugarcreek Pallett G 330 852-9812
Sugarcreek *(G-17868)*

S I C

Employee Codes: A=Over 500 employees, B=251-500
C=101-250, D=51-100, E=20-50, F=10-19, G=3-9
2019 Harris Ohio
Industrial Directory
839

24 LUMBER AND WOOD PRODUCTS, EXCEPT FURNITURE

Swp Legacy Ltd .... D 330 340-9663
 Sugarcreek *(G-17871)*
T & D Thompson Inc .... E 740 332-8515
 Laurelville *(G-11627)*
T&A Pallets Inc .... G 330 968-4743
 Ravenna *(G-16411)*
Terry Lumber and Supply Co .... G 330 659-6800
 Peninsula *(G-15899)*
Thomas J Weaver Inc .... F 740 622-2040
 Coshocton *(G-7755)*
Three AS Inc .... G 419 227-4240
 Lima *(G-11951)*
Timber Products Inc .... G 440 693-4098
 Middlefield *(G-13858)*
Tolson Pallet Mfg Inc .... F 937 787-3511
 Gratis *(G-10340)*
Traveling & Recycle Wood Pdts .... F 419 968-2649
 Middle Point *(G-13757)*
Tri State Pallet Inc .... G 937 323-5210
 Springfield *(G-17509)*
Tri State Pallet Inc .... G 937 746-8702
 Franklin *(G-9927)*
Troyers Pallet Shop .... G 330 897-1038
 Fresno *(G-10072)*
Troymill Manufacturing Inc .... F 440 632-5580
 Middlefield *(G-13860)*
Tusco Hardwoods LLC .... G 330 852-4281
 Sugarcreek *(G-17873)*
Ultimate Pallet & Trucking LLC .... G 440 693-4090
 Middlefield *(G-13862)*
Universal Pallets Inc .... G 614 444-1095
 Columbus *(G-7562)*
Universal Pallets Inc .... G 614 444-1095
 Columbus *(G-7563)*
Valley View Pallets LLC .... G 740 599-0010
 Danville *(G-7966)*
Van Orders Pallet Company Inc .... F 419 875-6932
 Swanton *(G-17928)*
Van Wert Pallets LLC .... G 419 203-1823
 Van Wert *(G-19111)*
Weaver Pallet Ltd .... G 330 682-4022
 Apple Creek *(G-623)*
Winesburg Hardwood Lumber Co .... E 330 893-2705
 Dundee *(G-9033)*
Wjf Enterprises LLC .... F 513 871-7320
 Cincinnati *(G-4514)*
Woodford Logistics .... D 513 417-8453
 South Charleston *(G-17274)*
Worthington Pallet .... G 614 888-1573
 Worthington *(G-20714)*
▼ Yoder Lumber Co Inc .... D 330 893-3121
 Millersburg *(G-14153)*
Yoder Lumber Co Inc .... E 330 674-1435
 Millersburg *(G-14154)*
Zak Box Co Inc .... G 216 961-5636
 Cleveland *(G-6337)*
Zanesville Pallet Co Inc .... F 740 454-3700
 Zanesville *(G-21193)*

2449 Wood Containers, NEC

A-Z Packaging Company .... G 614 444-8441
 Columbus *(G-6518)*
Brown-Forman Corporation .... E 740 384-3027
 Wellston *(G-19598)*
Cima Inc .... E 513 382-8976
 Hamilton *(G-10545)*
▲ Cima Inc .... E 513 382-8976
 Hamilton *(G-10546)*
Clark Rm Inc .... E 419 425-9889
 Findlay *(G-9669)*
Custom Built Crates Inc .... E 513 248-4422
 Milford *(G-14006)*
Denoon Lumber Company LLC .... D 740 768-2220
 Bergholz *(G-1634)*
Dp Products LLC .... G 440 834-9663
 Burton *(G-2357)*
Frankes Wood Products LLC .... E 937 642-0706
 Marysville *(G-12783)*
◆ Greif Inc .... E 740 549-6000
 Delaware *(G-8681)*
Greif Inc .... E 740 657-6500
 Delaware *(G-8682)*
Haessly Lumber Sales Co .... D 740 373-6681
 Marietta *(G-12630)*
Hann Box Works .... E 740 962-3752
 McConnelsville *(G-13205)*
▲ J & L Wood Products Inc .... E 937 667-4064
 Tipp City *(G-18119)*
Joe Gonda Company Inc .... F 440 458-6000
 Grafton *(G-10305)*

Ohio Plywood Box .... G 513 242-9125
 Cincinnati *(G-4104)*
Overseas Packing LLC .... F 440 232-2917
 Bedford *(G-1434)*
Pallet & Cont Corp of Amer .... G 419 255-1256
 Toledo *(G-18457)*
Patriotic Buildings LLC .... G 740 853-3970
 Patriot *(G-15853)*
Schaefer Box & Pallet Co .... E 513 738-2500
 Hamilton *(G-10603)*
Silvesco Inc .... F 513 373-6661
 Marietta *(G-12669)*
T & D Thompson Inc .... E 740 332-8515
 Laurelville *(G-11627)*
Terry Lumber and Supply Co .... G 330 659-6800
 Peninsula *(G-15899)*
Traveling & Recycle Wood Pdts .... F 419 968-2649
 Middle Point *(G-13757)*
VIP-Supply Chain Solutions LLC .... G 513 454-2020
 West Chester *(G-19818)*

2451 Mobile Homes

C & C Mobile Homes LLC .... G 740 663-5535
 Waverly *(G-19541)*
Colonial Heights Mhp LLC .... G 740 314-5182
 Wintersville *(G-20538)*
▲ Ellis & Watts Intl LLC .... G 513 752-9000
 Batavia *(G-1143)*
Holiday Homes Inc .... F 513 353-9777
 Harrison *(G-10646)*
Manufactured Housing Entps Inc .... C 419 636-4511
 Bryan *(G-2298)*
Mobile Conversions Inc .... F 513 797-1991
 Amelia *(G-544)*
Skyline Corporation .... C 330 852-2483
 Sugarcreek *(G-17864)*
Sun Communities Inc .... G 740 548-1942
 Lewis Center *(G-11782)*

2452 Prefabricated Wood Buildings & Cmpnts

Al Yoder Construction Company .... G 330 359-5726
 Millersburg *(G-14056)*
Americraft Stor Buildings Ltd .... G 330 877-6900
 Hartville *(G-10684)*
Beachy Barns Ltd .... F 614 873-4193
 Plain City *(G-16177)*
Carter-Jones Lumber Company .... F 440 834-8164
 Middlefield *(G-13782)*
Consolidatd Analytical Sys Inc .... F 513 542-1200
 Cleves *(G-6359)*
Duffy Family Partner .... G 330 650-6716
 Peninsula *(G-15892)*
Everything In America .... G 347 871-6872
 Cleveland *(G-5203)*
Fifth Avenue Lumber Co .... D 614 833-6655
 Canal Winchester *(G-2503)*
Gillard Construction Inc .... F 740 376-9744
 Marietta *(G-12627)*
Hershbergers Dutch Market LLP .... E 740 489-5322
 Old Washington *(G-15526)*
Hochstetler Milling LLC .... E 419 368-0004
 Loudonville *(G-12143)*
J Aaron Weaver .... G 440 474-9185
 Rome *(G-16562)*
J L Wannemacher Sales & Svc .... F 419 453-3445
 Ottoville *(G-15681)*
Millers Storage Barns LLC .... E 330 893-3293
 Millersburg *(G-14113)*
Mohican Log Homes Inc .... G 419 994-4088
 Loudonville *(G-12144)*
Morton Buildings Inc .... D 419 675-2311
 Kenton *(G-11415)*
Nef Ltd .... F 419 445-6696
 Archbold *(G-661)*
Patio Enclosures .... F 513 733-4646
 Cincinnati *(G-4135)*
Premier Construction Company .... E 513 874-2611
 Fairfield *(G-9550)*
Rona Enterprises Inc .... G 740 927-9971
 Pataskala *(G-15841)*
Silver Creek Log Homes .... E 419 335-3220
 Wauseon *(G-19532)*
Skyline Corporation .... C 330 852-2483
 Sugarcreek *(G-17864)*
Smiths Sawdust Studio .... G 740 484-4656
 Bethesda *(G-1658)*
Twin Oaks Barn .... F 330 893-3126
 Dundee *(G-9030)*

Unibilt Industries Inc .... E 937 890-7570
 Vandalia *(G-19147)*
Vinyl Design Corporation .... F 419 283-4009
 Holland *(G-10965)*
Weaver Barns Ltd .... F 330 852-2103
 Sugarcreek *(G-17876)*

2491 Wood Preserving

Appalachia Wood Inc .... E 740 596-2551
 Mc Arthur *(G-13178)*
Appalachian Wood Floors Inc .... D 740 354-4572
 Portsmouth *(G-16277)*
Clark Rm Inc .... E 419 425-9889
 Findlay *(G-9669)*
Couch Business Development Inc .... F 937 253-1099
 Dayton *(G-8104)*
ISK Americas Incorporated .... E 440 357-4600
 Painesville *(G-15750)*
Joseph Sabatino .... G 330 332-5879
 Salem *(G-16751)*
Luxus Products LLC .... G 937 444-6500
 Mount Orab *(G-14446)*
Preserving Your Memories .... G 614 861-4283
 Reynoldsburg *(G-16449)*
Ufp Blanchester LLC .... E 937 783-2443
 Blanchester *(G-1707)*
Ufp Hamilton LLC .... E 513 285-7190
 Hamilton *(G-10616)*
Urbn Timber LLC .... G 614 981-3043
 Columbus *(G-7565)*

2493 Reconstituted Wood Prdts

Amerilam Laminating .... G 440 235-4687
 Cleveland *(G-4700)*
Celcore Inc .... F 440 234-7888
 Cleveland *(G-4897)*
Commercial Innovations Inc .... G 216 641-7500
 Cleveland *(G-5003)*
Frankes Wood Products LLC .... E 937 642-0706
 Marysville *(G-12783)*
▲ GMI Companies Inc .... C 513 932-3445
 Lebanon *(G-11657)*
GMI Companies Inc .... G 937 981-0244
 Greenfield *(G-10348)*
◆ Michael Kaufman Companies Inc .... F 330 673-4881
 Kent *(G-11353)*
Michael Kaufman Companies Inc .... F 330 673-4881
 Kent *(G-11354)*
▼ Miller Manufacturing Inc .... E 330 852-0689
 Sugarcreek *(G-17854)*
Mpc Inc .... F 440 835-1405
 Cleveland *(G-5707)*
Profile Products LLC .... F 330 452-2630
 Canton *(G-2795)*
Ricers Residential Svcs LLC .... G 567 203-7414
 Shelby *(G-16987)*
▼ Tectum Inc .... C 740 345-9691
 Newark *(G-14929)*
Tri-State Supply Co Inc .... F 614 272-6767
 Columbus *(G-7543)*
Wico Products Inc .... G 937 783-0000
 Blanchester *(G-1708)*

2499 Wood Prdts, NEC

77 Coach Supply Ltd .... E 330 674-1454
 Millersburg *(G-14053)*
Adroit Thinking Inc .... F 419 542-9363
 Hicksville *(G-10774)*
American Wood Fibers Inc .... E 740 420-3233
 Circleville *(G-4537)*
▼ AP Tech Group Inc .... F 513 761-8111
 West Chester *(G-19646)*
Armin R Jewett .... G 419 647-6644
 Wapakoneta *(G-19322)*
Attractive Kitchens & Flrg LLC .... G 440 406-9299
 Elyria *(G-9220)*
▲ Baker McMillen Co .... D 330 923-8300
 Stow *(G-17572)*
Baker McMillen Co .... E 330 923-3303
 Stow *(G-17573)*
Barkman Products LLC .... G 330 893-2520
 Millersburg *(G-14063)*
Bc Investment Corporation .... E 330 262-3070
 Wooster *(G-20570)*
Berlin Wood Products Inc .... E 330 893-3281
 Berlin *(G-1639)*
Blang Acquisition LLC .... F 937 223-2155
 Dayton *(G-8058)*
Bonfoey Co .... F 216 621-0178
 Cleveland *(G-4831)*

25 FURNITURE AND FIXTURES

BR Mulch Inc .... G 937 667-8288
  Tipp City (G-18102)
Brown Wood Products Company .... G 330 339-8000
  New Philadelphia (G-14761)
Buckeye Dimensions LLC .... G 330 857-0223
  Dalton (G-7936)
▲ Buhi Imports .... G 440 224-0013
  North Kingsville (G-15159)
Bushworks Incorporated .... G 937 767-1713
  Yellow Springs (G-20805)
Cado Door & Design Inc .... G 330 343-4288
  New Philadelphia (G-14763)
Canfield Manufacturing Co Inc .... G 330 533-3333
  North Jackson (G-15143)
Cass Frames Inc .... G 419 468-2863
  Galion (G-10126)
Cedar Chest .... G 937 878-9097
  Fairborn (G-9454)
◆ Cedar Products LLC .... G 937 892-0070
  Peebles (G-15877)
◆ Chromascape Inc .... E 330 998-7574
  Twinsburg (G-18752)
◆ Cincinnati Dowel & WD Pdts Co .... E 937 444-2502
  Mount Orab (G-14439)
◆ CM Paula Company .... E 513 759-7473
  Mason (G-12849)
Colby Woodworking Inc .... G 937 224-7676
  Dayton (G-8097)
▲ Columbus Washboard Company Ltd .... G
740 380-3828
  Logan (G-12023)
Company Front Awards .... G 440 636-5493
  Middlefield (G-13786)
Cornerstone Spclty WD Pdts LLC .... D 513 772-5560
  Cincinnati (G-3550)
County Line Wood Working LLC .... G 330 316-3057
  Baltic (G-1025)
▲ Creative Plastic Concepts LLC .... D 419 927-9588
  Sycamore (G-17930)
Crosco Wood Products .... G 330 857-0228
  Dalton (G-7938)
Dalton Wood Products Inc .... G 330 682-0727
  Orrville (G-15589)
Decorative Veneer Inc .... G 216 741-5511
  Cleveland (G-5080)
Duvall Woodworking Inc .... F 419 878-9581
  Waterville (G-19494)
Elkay Plumbing Products Co .... G 419 841-1820
  Toledo (G-18281)
Ely Road Reel Company Ltd .... G 330 683-1818
  Apple Creek (G-604)
F J Designs Inc .... E 330 264-1477
  Wooster (G-20590)
Family Woodworks LLC .... G 740 289-4071
  Piketon (G-16070)
Fenwick Gallery of Fine Arts .... G 419 475-1651
  Toledo (G-18292)
Frame Depot Inc .... G 330 652-7865
  Niles (G-15009)
◆ Frame USA .... E 513 577-7107
  Cincinnati (G-3708)
Frame Warehouse .... G 614 861-4582
  Reynoldsburg (G-16440)
▲ G R K Manufacturing Co Inc .... E 513 863-3131
  Hamilton (G-10563)
Garick LLC .... E 216 581-0100
  Cleveland (G-5293)
◆ Gayston Corporation .... C 937 743-6050
  Miamisburg (G-13672)
George & Underwood LLP .... G 513 409-5631
  Lebanon (G-11653)
Ginnys Custom Framing Gallery .... G 419 468-7240
  Galion (G-10142)
Global Wood Products LLC .... G 440 442-5859
  Highland Heights (G-10791)
▲ Good Wood Inc .... G 740 484-1500
  Belmont (G-1566)
▲ Greenes Fence Co Inc .... G 216 464-3160
  Solon (G-17157)
Gregoire Moulin .... G 614 861-4582
  Reynoldsburg (G-16442)
Growers Choice Ltd .... G 330 262-8754
  Shreve (G-17001)
Hackman Frames LLC .... F 614 841-0007
  Columbus (G-6975)
▼ Handicraft LLC .... G 216 295-1950
  Bedford (G-1410)
Hardwood Solutions .... G 330 359-5755
  Wilmot (G-20516)
Hardwood Store Inc .... G 937 864-2899
  Enon (G-9384)

Hauser Services Llc .... E 440 632-5126
  Middlefield (G-13804)
Heartland Design Concepts .... G 419 774-0199
  Mansfield (G-12456)
Henly Corporation .... G 419 476-0851
  Toledo (G-18331)
Herbert Wood Products Inc .... G 440 834-1410
  Middlefield (G-13805)
Hit Trophy Inc .... G 419 445-5356
  Archbold (G-653)
▲ Holmes Wheel Shop Inc .... G 330 279-2891
  Holmesville (G-10981)
Homestead Collections .... G 419 422-8286
  Findlay (G-9705)
Hope Timber & Marketing Group .... F 740 344-1788
  Newark (G-14884)
Hope Timber Mulch Inc .... G 740 344-1788
  Newark (G-14885)
House of 10000 Picture Frames .... G 937 254-5541
  Dayton (G-8253)
Insta Plak Inc .... G 419 537-1555
  Toledo (G-18349)
Irvine Wood Recovery Inc .... E 513 831-0060
  Miamiville (G-13752)
J & R Woodworking .... G 330 893-0713
  Millersburg (G-14101)
J R Custom Unlimited .... F 513 894-9800
  Hamilton (G-10575)
Jewett Supply .... F 419 738-9882
  Wapakoneta (G-19335)
Judith C Zell .... G 740 385-0386
  Logan (G-12029)
Kalinich Fence Company Inc .... F 440 238-6127
  Strongsville (G-17759)
Kaufman Mulch Inc .... G 330 893-3676
  Millersburg (G-14103)
Kennewegs Wood Products .... G 330 832-1540
  Massillon (G-13010)
L S Manufacturing Inc .... G 614 885-7988
  Worthington (G-20694)
Latham Lumber & Pallet Co Inc .... F 740 493-2707
  Latham (G-11623)
Lawnview Industries Inc .... G 937 653-5217
  Urbana (G-19003)
Lazars Art Gllery Crtive Frmng .... G 330 477-8351
  Canton (G-2731)
Lehner Signs Inc .... G 614 258-0500
  Columbus (G-7122)
Lucius Fence Decking Irrigat .... G 419 450-9907
  New Riegel (G-14815)
Mad River Topsoil Inc .... G 937 882-6115
  Springfield (G-17441)
Marcum Crew Cut Inc .... G 740 862-3400
  Baltimore (G-1039)
Mark Nelson .... F 740 282-5334
  Steubenville (G-17542)
Maumee Bay Kitchen & Bath Cent ..... G 419 882-4390
  Sylvania (G-17950)
▲ Mi-Lar Fence Co Inc .... G 216 464-3160
  Solon (G-17193)
Mikes Mill Shop Inc .... G 419 538-6091
  Ottawa (G-15659)
▼ Miller Manufacturing Inc .... E 330 852-0689
  Sugarcreek (G-17854)
Millwork Designs Inc .... G 740 335-5203
  Wshngtn CT Hs (G-20733)
Minotas Trophies & Awards .... G 440 720-1288
  Cleveland (G-5696)
Mollard Conducting Batons Inc .... F 330 659-7081
  Bath (G-1202)
Mt Perry Foods Inc .... D 740 743-3890
  Mount Perry (G-14456)
Mulch Madness LLC .... F 330 920-9900
  Aurora (G-893)
Mulch Man .... E 937 866-5370
  Dayton (G-7987)
National Pallet & Mulch LLC .... F 937 237-1643
  Dayton (G-8378)
Newboury Woodworks .... G 440 564-5273
  Newbury (G-14960)
▲ P & R Specialty Inc .... E 937 773-0263
  Piqua (G-16147)
P & T Millwork Inc .... G 440 543-2151
  Chagrin Falls (G-3064)
▲ Puttmann Industries Inc .... F 513 202-9444
  Harrison (G-10665)
R M Wood Co .... G 419 845-2661
  Mount Gilead (G-14431)
R T Communications Inc .... G 330 726-7892
  Youngstown (G-21011)

Randy Lewis Inc .... F 330 784-0456
  Akron (G-342)
Red Lion Nursery Inc .... G 937 704-9840
  Lebanon (G-11689)
Revonoc Inc .... G 440 548-3491
  Parkman (G-15813)
Rework Furnishings LLC .... F 614 300-5021
  Columbus (G-7390)
Rightway Food Service .... G 419 223-4075
  Lima (G-11932)
Roe Transportation Entps Inc .... G 937 497-7161
  Sidney (G-17068)
Ryanworks Inc .... F 937 438-1282
  Dayton (G-8488)
◆ Scotts Company LLC .... B 937 644-0011
  Marysville (G-12809)
▲ Sealco Inc .... G 740 922-4122
  Uhrichsville (G-18893)
Signature Sign Co Inc .... F 216 426-1234
  Cleveland (G-6065)
Singleton Reels Inc .... E 330 274-2961
  Mantua (G-12559)
Smith P K Woodcarving LLC .... G 513 271-7077
  Louisville (G-12167)
▲ Solid Dimensions Inc .... G 419 663-1134
  Norwalk (G-15415)
Sonoco Products Company .... E 614 759-8470
  Columbus (G-7462)
Steeles 5 Acre Mill Inc .... F 419 542-9363
  Hicksville (G-10782)
Todd W Goings .... G 740 389-5842
  Marion (G-12743)
W H K Company .... G 937 372-3368
  Xenia (G-20802)
◆ Walnut Creek Planing Ltd .... D 330 893-3244
  Millersburg (G-14146)
Walnut Creek Wood Design .... G 330 852-9663
  Sugarcreek (G-17875)
Wengerd Wood Inc .... G 330 359-4300
  Dundee (G-9032)
▲ Woodcor America Inc .... G 614 277-2930
  Columbus (G-7611)
Woodcraft Pattern Works Inc .... G 330 630-2158
  Tallmadge (G-18016)
Wurms Woodworking Company .... E 419 492-2184
  New Washington (G-14834)
▼ Yoder Lumber Co Inc .... D 330 893-3121
  Millersburg (G-14153)
Youngstown Fence Inc .... G 330 788-8110
  Youngstown (G-21076)
Zaenkert Surveying Essentials .... G 513 738-2917
  Okeana (G-15522)

25 FURNITURE AND FIXTURES

2511 Wood Household Furniture

Allied Plastic Co Inc .... G 419 389-1688
  Toledo (G-18165)
Andal Woodworking .... F 330 897-8059
  Baltic (G-1022)
Andy Raber .... G 740 622-1386
  Fresno (G-10066)
◆ Archbold Furniture Co .... E 567 444-4666
  Archbold (G-638)
Ariels Oak Inc .... E 330 343-7453
  Sherrodsville (G-16990)
Armada Fortress LLC .... G 330 953-2185
  Youngstown (G-20847)
Artistic Finishes Inc .... G 440 951-7850
  Willoughby (G-20281)
Basic Cases Inc .... G 216 662-3900
  Cleveland (G-4795)
Battershell Cabinets .... G 419 542-6448
  Hicksville (G-10777)
Benners Custom Woodworking .... G 513 932-9159
  Lebanon (G-11636)
Berlin Gardens Gazebos Ltd .... E 330 893-3411
  Berlin (G-1637)
Briar Hill Furniture .... G 330 223-2109
  Kensington (G-11284)
Cabinet Systems Inc .... G 440 237-1924
  Cleveland (G-4861)
▼ Canal Dover Furniture LLC .... D 330 359-5375
  Millersburg (G-14076)
Carlisle Oak .... G 330 852-8734
  Sugarcreek (G-17845)
Cedar Outdoor Furniture Inc .... G 330 863-2580
  Malvern (G-12386)
Chris Haughey .... G 937 652-3338
  Urbana (G-18982)

▲ **Clearwater Wood Group LLC**..........G....... 567 644-9951
Hebron *(G-10739)*
Colonial Woodcraft Inc..........F....... 513 779-8088
Lebanon *(G-11642)*
Criswell Furniture LLC..........F....... 330 695-2082
Fredericksburg *(G-9947)*
Diversified Products & Svcs..........C....... 740 393-6202
Mount Vernon *(G-14478)*
Dorel Home Furnishings Inc..........C....... 419 447-7448
Tiffin *(G-18058)*
Dutch Heritage Woodcraft..........E....... 330 893-2211
Berlin *(G-1641)*
Dutch Legacy LLC..........G....... 330 359-0270
Dundee *(G-9018)*
Dutch Valley Woodcraft Ltd..........G....... 330 695-2364
Fredericksburg *(G-9949)*
East Oberlin Cabinets..........G....... 440 775-1166
Oberlin *(G-15493)*
Farmside Wood..........G....... 330 695-5100
Apple Creek *(G-605)*
Feslers Refinishing..........G....... 740 622-4849
Coshocton *(G-7733)*
Fleetwood Custom Countertops..........F....... 740 965-9833
Johnstown *(G-11265)*
Flottemesch Anthony & Son..........F....... 513 561-1212
Cincinnati *(G-3696)*
◆ **Foundations Worldwide Inc**..........E....... 330 722-5033
Medina *(G-13264)*
Furniture By Otmar Inc..........F....... 937 435-2039
Dayton *(G-8211)*
Furniture By Otmar Inc..........G....... 513 891-5141
Cincinnati *(G-3717)*
▲ **G R K Manufacturing Co Inc**..........E....... 513 863-3131
Hamilton *(G-10563)*
Gasser Chair Co Inc..........D....... 330 759-2234
Youngstown *(G-20914)*
Grabo Interiors Inc..........G....... 216 391-6677
Cleveland *(G-5335)*
Green Acres Furniture Ltd..........F....... 330 359-6251
Navarre *(G-14574)*
▲ **Hen House Inc**..........E....... 419 663-3377
Norwalk *(G-15398)*
Hill Finishing..........G....... 740 623-0650
Millersburg *(G-14091)*
Hochstetler Wood..........F....... 330 893-2384
Millersburg *(G-14093)*
Hochstetler Wood Ltd..........F....... 330 893-1601
Millersburg *(G-14094)*
Holmes Panel..........G....... 330 897-5040
Baltic *(G-1031)*
Hopewood Inc..........E....... 330 359-5656
Millersburg *(G-14100)*
Idx Corporation..........C....... 937 401-3225
Dayton *(G-8259)*
Installed Building Pdts LLC..........E....... 614 308-9900
Columbus *(G-7029)*
Integral Design Inc..........F....... 216 524-0555
Cleveland *(G-5462)*
J & F Furniture Shop..........G....... 330 852-2478
Sugarcreek *(G-17850)*
J-J Berlin Woodcraft Inc..........G....... 330 893-9171
Berlin *(G-1643)*
Jeffco Sheltered Workshop..........E....... 740 264-4608
Steubenville *(G-17539)*
Joe P Fischer Woodcraft..........G....... 513 474-4316
Cincinnati *(G-3877)*
Ken Harper..........C....... 740 439-4452
Byesville *(G-2388)*
Kencraft Co Inc..........G....... 419 536-0333
Toledo *(G-18364)*
Kenway Corp..........G....... 937 767-1660
Yellow Springs *(G-20809)*
▲ **Kitchens By Rutenschroer Inc**..........F....... 513 251-8333
Cincinnati *(G-3914)*
Lauber Manufacturing Co..........G....... 419 446-2450
Archbold *(G-654)*
Legacy Oak and Hardwoods LLC..........F....... 330 859-2656
Zoarville *(G-21196)*
Lima Millwork Inc..........E....... 419 331-3303
Elida *(G-9195)*
Mark Rasche..........G....... 614 882-1810
Westerville *(G-20009)*
Masco Cbinetry Middlefield LLC..........D....... 440 632-5058
Middlefield *(G-13819)*
Michaels Pre-Cast Con Pdts..........F....... 513 683-1292
Loveland *(G-12215)*
Mielke Furniture Repair Inc..........G....... 419 625-4572
Sandusky *(G-16830)*
Miller Cabinet Ltd..........E....... 614 873-4221
Plain City *(G-16203)*
Millwood Wholesale Inc..........F....... 330 359-6109
Dundee *(G-9023)*
Mini Graphics Inc..........G....... 513 563-8600
Cincinnati *(G-4030)*
N Wasserstrom & Sons Inc..........D....... 614 737-5410
Columbus *(G-7207)*
◆ **P Graham Dunn Inc**..........D....... 330 828-2105
Dalton *(G-7949)*
Paradise Inc..........G....... 330 928-3789
Cuyahoga Falls *(G-7902)*
Patrician Furniture Builders..........G....... 330 746-6354
Youngstown *(G-20996)*
Penwood Mfg..........G....... 330 359-5600
Fresno *(G-10069)*
▲ **Progressive Furniture Inc**..........E....... 419 446-4500
Archbold *(G-664)*
R A Hamed International Inc..........F....... 330 247-0190
Twinsburg *(G-18844)*
▲ **R D Cook Company LLC**..........G....... 614 262-0550
Columbus *(G-7372)*
Regal Cabinet Inc..........G....... 419 865-3932
Toledo *(G-18500)*
Richard Benhase & Associates..........F....... 513 772-1896
Cincinnati *(G-4267)*
Richmonds Woodworks Inc..........F....... 330 343-8184
New Philadelphia *(G-14798)*
Rnr Enterprises LLC..........F....... 330 852-3022
Sugarcreek *(G-17862)*
Simmons Company..........G....... 614 871-8088
Grove City *(G-10468)*
Specialty Services Inc..........G....... 614 421-1599
Columbus *(G-7469)*
Stark Truss Company Inc..........D....... 330 478-2100
Canton *(G-2825)*
Stark Truss Company Inc..........D....... 419 298-3777
Edgerton *(G-9181)*
Stephen J Page..........G....... 865 951-3316
Williamsburg *(G-20255)*
▲ **Textiles Inc**..........C....... 740 852-0782
London *(G-12070)*
Textiles Inc..........G....... 614 529-8642
Hilliard *(G-10869)*
Trailway Wood..........F....... 330 893-9966
Dundee *(G-9028)*
Tri State Countertop Service..........G....... 740 354-3663
Portsmouth *(G-16304)*
Vocational Services Inc..........C....... 216 431-8085
Cleveland *(G-6267)*
Waller Brothers Stone Company..........E....... 740 858-1948
Mc Dermott *(G-13195)*
Weaver Woodcraft L L C..........G....... 330 695-2150
Apple Creek *(G-624)*
Western & Southern Lf Insur Co..........A....... 513 629-1800
Cincinnati *(G-4503)*
Western Reserve Furniture Co..........G....... 440 235-6216
North Olmsted *(G-15203)*
◆ **Wine Cellar Innovations LLC**..........C....... 513 321-3733
Cincinnati *(G-4513)*
Yoders Woodworking..........G....... 888 818-0568
Millersburg *(G-14156)*

2512 Wood Household Furniture, Upholstered

Central Design Services..........G....... 513 829-7027
Fairfield *(G-9489)*
Dura Bilt Drapery & Upholstery..........F....... 440 269-8438
Willoughby *(G-20311)*
▲ **Fortner Upholstering Inc**..........F....... 614 475-8282
Columbus *(G-6933)*
Franklin Cabinet Company Inc..........E....... 937 743-9606
Franklin *(G-9884)*
▲ **G R K Manufacturing Co Inc**..........E....... 513 863-3131
Hamilton *(G-10563)*
Gasser Chair Co Inc..........F....... 330 534-2234
Youngstown *(G-20913)*
▲ **H Goodman Inc**..........D....... 216 341-0200
Newburgh Heights *(G-14936)*
Hallmark Industries Inc..........E....... 937 864-7378
Springfield *(G-17410)*
Hopewood Inc..........E....... 330 359-5656
Millersburg *(G-14100)*
Joseph G Betz & Sons..........G....... 513 481-0322
Cincinnati *(G-3884)*
Kenneth Shannon..........G....... 513 777-8888
Liberty Twp *(G-11826)*
▲ **Kroehler Furniture Mfg Co Inc**..........B....... 828 459-9865
Columbus *(G-7102)*
LAtelier Custom Woodworking..........G....... 234 759-3359
North Lima *(G-15175)*
Mastercraft Mfg Inc..........E....... 330 893-3366
Youngstown *(G-20967)*
Njm Furniture Outlet Inc..........F....... 330 893-3514
Millersburg *(G-14118)*
Quality Fabrications LLC..........G....... 330 695-2478
Fredericksburg *(G-9956)*
Robert Mayo Industries..........G....... 330 426-2587
East Palestine *(G-9083)*
◆ **Sauder Woodworking Co**..........A....... 419 446-2711
Archbold *(G-668)*
Stiglers Woodworks..........G....... 513 733-3009
Blue Ash *(G-1851)*
▲ **Weavers Furniture Ltd**..........F....... 330 852-2701
Sugarcreek *(G-17877)*

2514 Metal Household Furniture

◆ **Albion Industries Inc**..........E....... 440 238-1955
Strongsville *(G-17707)*
▲ **Angels Landing Inc**..........G....... 513 687-3681
Moraine *(G-14330)*
Bailey & Jensen Inc..........F....... 937 272-1784
Centerville *(G-2998)*
C-Link Enterprises LLC..........F....... 937 222-2829
Dayton *(G-8071)*
Cabintpak Kitchens of Columbus..........G....... 614 294-4646
Columbus *(G-6721)*
Installed Building Pdts LLC..........E....... 614 308-9900
Columbus *(G-7029)*
◆ **Invacare Corporation**..........A....... 440 329-6000
Elyria *(G-9272)*
Invacare Corporation..........D....... 800 333-6900
Elyria *(G-9273)*
▲ **Invacare Holdings Corporation**..........G....... 440 329-6000
Elyria *(G-9276)*
Invacare International Corp..........G....... 440 329-6000
Elyria *(G-9277)*
◆ **Mantua Manufacturing Co**..........C....... 800 333-8333
Solon *(G-17188)*
◆ **Medallion Lighting Corporation**..........E....... 440 255-8383
Mentor *(G-13514)*
Metal Fabricating Corporation..........D....... 216 631-8121
Cleveland *(G-5658)*
Pine Acres Woodcraft..........G....... 330 852-0190
Sugarcreek *(G-17857)*

2515 Mattresses & Bedsprings

Ahmf Inc..........E....... 614 921-1223
Columbus *(G-6553)*
▲ **Banner Mattress Co Inc**..........G....... 419 324-7181
Toledo *(G-18198)*
▲ **Casco Mfg Solutions Inc**..........D....... 513 681-0003
Cincinnati *(G-3447)*
▲ **H Goodman Inc**..........D....... 216 341-0200
Newburgh Heights *(G-14936)*
Heritage Sleep Products LLC..........E....... 440 437-4425
Orwell *(G-15631)*
Homecare Mattress Inc..........F....... 937 746-2556
Franklin *(G-9889)*
Innocor Foam Tech - Acp Inc..........F....... 419 647-4172
Spencerville *(G-17309)*
J C Logan Barie LLC..........G....... 567 336-6523
Perrysburg *(G-15968)*
Midwest Quality Bedding Inc..........G....... 614 504-5971
Columbus *(G-7182)*
National Bedding Company LLC..........G....... 513 825-4172
Cincinnati *(G-4060)*
Ohio Mattress..........G....... 740 739-8219
Lancaster *(G-11593)*
Original Mattress Factory Inc..........G....... 216 661-8388
Cleveland *(G-5819)*
Original Mattress Factory Inc..........G....... 513 752-6600
Cincinnati *(G-3260)*
Protective Industrial Polymers..........F....... 440 327-0015
North Ridgeville *(G-15246)*
▲ **Quilting Inc**..........D....... 614 504-5971
Plain City *(G-16209)*
Sealy Mattress Company..........C....... 330 725-4146
Medina *(G-13337)*
Sealy Mattress Mfg Co Inc..........D....... 800 697-3259
Medina *(G-13338)*
SSP Tennessee LLC..........G....... 614 279-8850
Columbus *(G-7483)*
Tep Bedding Grp Inc..........E....... 440 437-7700
Orwell *(G-15635)*
Timken Foundation..........G....... 330 452-1144
Canton *(G-2840)*
Tru Comfort Mattress..........G....... 614 595-8600
Dublin *(G-9006)*
Walter F Stephens Jr Inc..........E....... 937 746-0521
Franklin *(G-9930)*

▲ White Dove Mattress Ltd .... E 216 341-0200
Newburgh Heights **(G-14945)**

2517 Wood T V, Radio, Phono & Sewing Cabinets

Cabinetworks Unlimited LLC .... G 234 320-4107
Salem **(G-16722)**
Innerwood & Company .... F 513 677-2229
Loveland **(G-12199)**
Kraftmaid Trucking Inc .... D 440 632-2531
Middlefield **(G-13812)**
▲ Progressive Furniture Inc .... E 419 446-4500
Archbold **(G-664)**
Xxx Intrntional Amusements Inc .... E 216 671-6900
Cleveland **(G-6332)**

2519 Household Furniture, NEC

Bulk Carrier Trnsp Eqp Co .... E 330 339-3333
New Philadelphia **(G-14762)**
Daniels Amish Collection LLC .... C 330 276-0110
Killbuck **(G-11451)**
Entertainment Junction .... D 513 326-1100
Cincinnati **(G-3644)**
Evenflo Company Inc .... D 937 773-3971
Troy **(G-18654)**
◆ Evenflo Company Inc .... C 937 415-3300
Miamisburg **(G-13666)**
G Keener & Co .... G 937 846-1210
New Carlisle **(G-14666)**
Hershy Way Ltd .... G 330 893-2809
Millersburg **(G-14090)**
John Purdum .... G 513 897-9686
Waynesville **(G-19569)**
▲ Kitchens By Rutenschroer Inc .... F 513 251-8333
Cincinnati **(G-3914)**
Mar-Bal Pultrusion Inc .... F 440 953-0456
Willoughby **(G-20368)**
Office Magic Inc .... F 510 782-6100
Medina **(G-13310)**
Poly Concepts LLC .... G 419 678-3300
Saint Henry **(G-16666)**
Sailors Tailor Inc .... G 937 862-7781
Spring Valley **(G-17318)**
Sauder Woodworking Co .... G 419 446-2711
Archbold **(G-669)**
Valley View Woodcraft .... G 330 852-3000
Sugarcreek **(G-17874)**

2521 Wood Office Furniture

Basic Cases Inc .... G 216 662-3900
Cleveland **(G-4795)**
▲ Buzz Seating Inc .... F 877 263-5737
Cincinnati **(G-3432)**
Cabinet Systems Inc .... G 440 237-1924
Cleveland **(G-4861)**
Creative Woodworks .... G 440 355-8155
Grafton **(G-10295)**
Crow Works LLC .... E 888 811-2769
Killbuck **(G-11450)**
Custom Millcraft Corp .... E 513 874-7080
West Chester **(G-19690)**
Dlng Products .... G 440 442-7777
Cleveland **(G-5096)**
Dutch Design Products LLC .... E 330 674-1167
Fredericksburg **(G-9948)**
▼ Dvuv LLC .... F 216 741-5511
Cleveland **(G-5124)**
East Woodworking Company .... G 216 791-5950
Cleveland **(G-5140)**
Frontier Signs & Displays Inc .... G 513 367-0813
Harrison **(G-10642)**
◆ Gasser Chair Co Inc .... E 330 534-2234
Youngstown **(G-20912)**
Gasser Chair Co Inc .... D 330 759-2234
Youngstown **(G-20914)**
Geograph Industries Inc .... E 513 202-9200
Harrison **(G-10643)**
Global Design Factory LLC .... G 330 322-8775
Hudson **(G-11047)**
▲ GMI Companies Inc .... C 513 932-3445
Lebanon **(G-11657)**
GMI Companies Inc .... G 937 981-0244
Greenfield **(G-10348)**
H S Morgan Limited Partnership .... G 513 870-4400
Fairfield **(G-9502)**
▲ Hoge Lumber Company .... E 419 753-2263
New Knoxville **(G-14703)**
Idx Corporation .... C 937 401-3225
Dayton **(G-8259)**

Innerwood & Company .... F 513 677-2229
Loveland **(G-12199)**
Innovative Woodworking Inc .... G 513 531-1940
Cincinnati **(G-3850)**
Interior Products Co Inc .... F 216 641-1919
Cleveland **(G-5466)**
LAtelier Custom Woodworking .... G 234 759-3359
North Lima **(G-15175)**
Lima Millwork Inc .... E 419 331-3303
Elida **(G-9195)**
Macwood Inc .... G 614 279-7676
Columbus **(G-7143)**
Mark Rasche .... G 614 882-1810
Westerville **(G-20009)**
Mel Heitkamp Builders Ltd .... G 419 375-0405
Fort Recovery **(G-9825)**
Miller Cabinet Ltd .... E 614 873-4221
Plain City **(G-16203)**
▲ National Electro-Coatings Inc .... D 216 898-0080
Cleveland **(G-5724)**
R Carney Thomas .... G 740 342-3388
New Lexington **(G-14722)**
Richard Benhase & Associates .... F 513 772-1896
Cincinnati **(G-4267)**
Sauder Manufacturing Co .... C 419 682-3061
Stryker **(G-17833)**
▲ Senator International Inc .... E 419 887-5806
Maumee **(G-13143)**
Specialty Services Inc .... G 614 421-1599
Columbus **(G-7469)**
Stephen J Page .... G 865 951-3316
Williamsburg **(G-20255)**
Symatic Inc .... E 330 225-1510
Brunswick **(G-2243)**
▼ Tiffin Metal Products Co .... C 419 447-8414
Tiffin **(G-18088)**
▼ Workstream Inc .... D 513 870-4400
Fairfield **(G-9577)**
Yellow Tang Interiors LLC .... G 330 629-9279
Youngstown **(G-21069)**

2522 Office Furniture, Except Wood

Axess International LLC .... G 330 460-4840
Brunswick **(G-2189)**
▲ Casco Mfg Solutions Inc .... D 513 681-0003
Cincinnati **(G-3447)**
Custom Millcraft Corp .... E 513 874-7080
West Chester **(G-19690)**
Design Trac Inc .... G 330 759-3131
Youngstown **(G-20889)**
East Woodworking Company .... G 216 791-5950
Cleveland **(G-5140)**
Edsal Sandusky Corporation .... C 419 626-5465
Sandusky **(G-16806)**
▲ Ergo Desktop LLC .... E 567 890-3746
Celina **(G-2960)**
Frontier Signs & Displays Inc .... G 513 367-0813
Harrison **(G-10642)**
Furniture Concepts Inc .... F 216 292-9100
Cleveland **(G-5280)**
Gasser Chair Co Inc .... F 330 534-2234
Youngstown **(G-20913)**
Gasser Chair Co Inc .... D 330 759-2234
Youngstown **(G-20914)**
Geograph Industries Inc .... E 513 202-9200
Harrison **(G-10643)**
▲ GMI Companies Inc .... C 513 932-3445
Lebanon **(G-11657)**
GMI Companies Inc .... G 937 981-0244
Greenfield **(G-10348)**
H S Morgan Limited Partnership .... G 513 870-4400
Fairfield **(G-9502)**
Hobart Cabinet Company .... G 937 335-4666
Troy **(G-18670)**
▼ Infinium Wall Systems Inc .... E 440 572-5000
Strongsville **(G-17754)**
Innovative Woodworking Inc .... G 513 531-1940
Cincinnati **(G-3850)**
Jsc Employee Leasing Corp .... F 330 773-8971
Akron **(G-228)**
Kitchen Works Inc .... G 440 353-0939
North Ridgeville **(G-15236)**
Lakeside Cabins Ltd .... G 419 896-2299
Shiloh **(G-16995)**
▲ M/W International Inc .... F 440 526-6900
Broadview Heights **(G-2094)**
Mark Rasche .... G 614 882-1810
Westerville **(G-20009)**
Marsh Industries Inc .... E 330 308-8667
New Philadelphia **(G-14784)**

Metal Fabricating Corporation .... D 216 631-8121
Cleveland **(G-5658)**
▲ National Electro-Coatings Inc .... D 216 898-0080
Cleveland **(G-5724)**
Office Magic Inc .... F 510 782-6100
Medina **(G-13310)**
Patriot Seating Inc .... F 330 779-0768
Youngstown **(G-20997)**
Pucel Enterprises Inc .... D 216 881-4604
Cleveland **(G-5933)**
◆ R B Mfg Co .... F 419 626-9464
Wadsworth **(G-19270)**
Recycled Systems Furniture Inc .... E 614 880-9110
Worthington **(G-20701)**
▲ Senator International Inc .... E 419 887-5806
Maumee **(G-13143)**
Ssi Manufacturing Inc .... F 513 761-7757
West Chester **(G-19902)**
Starr Fabricating Inc .... D 330 394-9891
Vienna **(G-19210)**
▼ Tiffin Metal Products Co .... C 419 447-8414
Tiffin **(G-18088)**
Veterans Representative Co LLC .... F 330 779-0768
Youngstown **(G-21061)**
▼ Workstream Inc .... D 513 870-4400
Fairfield **(G-9577)**

2531 Public Building & Related Furniture

Absolutely Paper Established .... G 216 932-4822
Cleveland **(G-4602)**
American Office Services Inc .... G 440 899-6888
Westlake **(G-20095)**
Ap-Alternatives LLC .... F 419 267-5280
Ridgeville Corners **(G-16511)**
Bell Vault & Monument Works .... E 937 866-2444
Miamisburg **(G-13643)**
Brocar Products Inc .... E 513 922-2888
Cincinnati **(G-3421)**
▲ C E White Co .... E 419 492-2157
New Washington **(G-14827)**
City of Conneaut .... G 440 599-7071
Conneaut **(G-7643)**
City of Kent .... F 330 673-8897
Kent **(G-11304)**
County of Summit .... G 330 865-8065
Akron **(G-124)**
Franklin Cabinet Company Inc .... E 937 743-9606
Franklin **(G-9884)**
◆ Gasser Chair Co Inc .... E 330 534-2234
Youngstown **(G-20912)**
Gasser Chair Co Inc .... D 330 759-2234
Youngstown **(G-20914)**
Gasser Chair Co Inc .... F 330 534-2234
Youngstown **(G-20913)**
General Motors LLC .... A 216 265-5000
Cleveland **(G-5312)**
Global Furnishings Inc .... G 216 595-0901
Cleveland **(G-5325)**
▲ GMI Companies Inc .... C 513 932-3445
Lebanon **(G-11657)**
GMI Companies Inc .... G 937 981-0244
Greenfield **(G-10348)**
▲ Gra-Mag Truck Intr Systems LLC .... E 740 490-1000
London **(G-12061)**
Gramag LLC .... E 614 875-8435
Grove City **(G-10431)**
▲ Grand-Rock Company Inc .... E 440 639-2000
Painesville **(G-15742)**
◆ Granite Industries Inc .... D 419 445-4733
Archbold **(G-651)**
Hann Manufacturing Inc .... E 740 962-3752
McConnelsville **(G-13206)**
▲ Jay Industries Inc .... A 419 747-4161
Mansfield **(G-12461)**
Johnson Controls Inc .... D 419 636-4211
Bryan **(G-2292)**
Johnson Controls Inc .... D 216 587-0100
Cleveland **(G-5504)**
Johnson Controls Inc .... F 513 671-6338
Cincinnati **(G-3882)**
Magna International Amer Inc .... E 905 853-3604
Ridgeville Corners **(G-16512)**
Magna Seating America Inc .... C 330 824-3101
Warren **(G-19420)**
Mayflower Vehicle Systems LLC .... G 419 668-8132
New Albany **(G-14630)**
McGill Septic Tank Co .... E 330 876-2171
Kinsman **(G-11465)**
Michaels Pre-Cast Con Pdts .... F 513 683-1292
Loveland **(G-12215)**

SIC

Employee Codes: A=Over 500 employees, B=251-500
C=101-250, D=51-100, E=20-50, F=10-19, G=3-9
2019 Harris Ohio
Industrial Directory
843

25 FURNITURE AND FIXTURES

Mock Woodworking Company LLC ....E 740 452-2701
  Zanesville (G-21157)
Modern Manufacturing Inc ....F 513 251-3600
  Cincinnati (G-4039)
N Wasserstrom & Sons Inc ....D 614 737-5410
  Columbus (G-7207)
Oberfields LLC ....F 614 252-0955
  Columbus (G-7237)
Quality Seating Company Inc ....E 330 747-0181
  Youngstown (G-21009)
◆ Sauder Manufacturing Co ....E 419 445-7670
  Archbold (G-666)
Sauder Manufacturing Co ....E 419 682-3061
  Stryker (G-17833)
▲ Setex Inc ....B 419 394-7800
  Saint Marys (G-16700)
▲ Shiffler Equipment Sales Inc ....E 440 285-9175
  Chardon (G-3136)
Soft Touch Wood LLC ....E 330 545-4204
  Girard (G-10266)
▼ Tiffin Metal Products Co ....E 419 447-8414
  Tiffin (G-18088)
Tri-State Supply Co Inc ....F 614 272-6767
  Columbus (G-7543)
Trim Systems Operating Corp ....C 614 289-5360
  New Albany (G-14639)
W C Heller & Co Inc ....F 419 485-3176
  Montpelier (G-14321)
Wurms Woodworking Company ....E 419 492-2184
  New Washington (G-14834)
Yanfeng US Automotive ....D 419 662-4905
  Northwood (G-15354)

2541 Wood, Office & Store Fixtures

119c Landis Display Co ....G 937 307-9499
  Franklin (G-9865)
▲ 3jd Inc ....F 513 324-9655
  Moraine (G-14327)
7d Marketing Inc ....F 330 721-8822
  Medina (G-13215)
A & J Woodworking Inc ....G 419 695-5655
  Delphos (G-8734)
A J Construction Co ....G 330 539-9544
  Girard (G-10251)
A-Display Service Corp ....F 614 469-1230
  Columbus (G-6517)
Accent Manufacturing Inc ....F 330 724-7704
  Norton (G-15355)
Action Group Inc ....D 614 868-8868
  Blacklick (G-1676)
Allied Plastic Co Inc ....G 419 389-1688
  Toledo (G-18165)
American Countertops Inc ....G 330 877-0343
  Hartville (G-10683)
American Interior Design Inc ....F 216 663-0606
  Cleveland (G-4689)
Amtekco Industries LLC ....D 614 228-6590
  Columbus (G-6596)
Amtekco Industries Inc ....G 614 228-6525
  Columbus (G-6597)
Andy Raber ....G 740 622-1386
  Fresno (G-10066)
▲ Archer Counter Design Inc ....G 513 396-7526
  Cincinnati (G-3354)
Artistic Finishes Inc ....F 440 951-7850
  Willoughby (G-20281)
As America Inc ....E 419 522-4211
  Mansfield (G-12408)
Automated Bldg Components Inc ....E 419 257-2152
  North Baltimore (G-15042)
Benchmark Cabinets ....E 740 694-1144
  Fredericktown (G-9963)
Brad Snoderly ....F 419 476-0184
  Toledo (G-18214)
Brower Products Inc ....D 937 563-1111
  Cincinnati (G-3426)
▲ Bruewer Woodwork Mfg Co ....D 513 353-3505
  Cleves (G-6355)
C & D Counters ....G 740 259-5529
  Lucasville (G-12260)
Cameo Countertops Inc ....G 419 865-6371
  Holland (G-10918)
▲ Cap & Associates Incorporated ....C 614 863-3463
  Columbus (G-6728)
Case Crafters Inc ....G 937 667-9473
  Tipp City (G-18107)
Cassady Woodworks Inc ....G 937 256-7948
  Dayton (G-7974)
CIP International Inc ....D 513 874-9925
  West Chester (G-19675)

Couch Business Development Inc ....F 937 253-1099
  Dayton (G-8104)
Counter Concepts Inc ....F 330 848-4848
  Doylestown (G-8864)
Counter- Advice Inc ....F 937 291-1600
  Franklin (G-9876)
Countertop Sales ....G 614 626-4476
  Columbus (G-6830)
Countertop Xpress ....G 440 358-0500
  Painesville (G-15727)
Crafted Surface and Stone LLC ....E 440 658-3799
  Bedford Heights (G-1467)
Creative Products Inc ....E 419 866-5501
  Holland (G-10920)
Custom Counter Tops & Spc Co ....G 330 637-4856
  Cortland (G-7709)
Custom Design Cabinets & Tops ....E 440 639-9900
  Painesville (G-15728)
Custom Surroundings Inc ....F 330 483-9020
  Valley City (G-19035)
D Lewis Inc ....G 740 695-2615
  Saint Clairsville (G-16630)
▲ Darko Inc ....E 330 425-9805
  Bedford (G-1398)
▲ Dell Fixtures Inc ....E 614 449-1750
  Columbus (G-6859)
Designer Cntemporary Laminates ....G 440 946-8207
  Willoughby (G-20309)
Display Dynamics Inc ....F 937 832-2830
  Englewood (G-9355)
Diversified Products & Svcs ....C 740 393-6202
  Mount Vernon (G-14478)
Dovetail Dimensions ....G 330 674-9533
  Millersburg (G-14078)
E J Skok Industries ....E 216 292-7533
  Bedford (G-1403)
▼ Fixture Dimensions Inc ....E 513 360-7512
  Middletown (G-13908)
Fleetwood Custom Countertops ....F 740 965-9833
  Johnstown (G-11265)
Form-A-Top Products Inc ....G 440 779-9452
  North Olmsted (G-15189)
▲ Formatech Inc ....E 330 273-2800
  Brunswick (G-2205)
◆ Formica Corporation ....E 513 786-3400
  Cincinnati (G-3705)
Formware Inc ....G 614 231-9387
  Columbus (G-6930)
Forum III Inc ....F 513 961-5123
  Cincinnati (G-3706)
Franklin Cabinet Company Inc ....E 937 743-9606
  Franklin (G-9884)
▲ G & W Products LLC ....C 513 860-4050
  Fairfield (G-9499)
▲ Gabriel Logan LLC ....D 740 380-6809
  Logan (G-12024)
Gary L Gast ....E 419 626-5915
  Sandusky (G-16812)
Geograph Industries Inc ....E 513 202-9200
  Harrison (G-10643)
GMI Companies Inc ....F 937 981-7724
  Greenfield (G-10349)
▲ GMI Companies Inc ....C 513 932-3445
  Lebanon (G-11657)
GMI Companies Inc ....G 937 981-0244
  Greenfield (G-10348)
Gross & Sons Custom Millwork ....G 419 227-0214
  Lima (G-11871)
Hattenbach Company ....D 216 881-5200
  Cleveland (G-5380)
Hattenbach Company ....E 330 744-2732
  Youngstown (G-20929)
Helmart Company Inc ....G 513 941-3095
  Cincinnati (G-3806)
Home Stor & Off Solutions Inc ....F 216 362-4660
  Cleveland (G-5414)
▲ Idx Dayton LLC ....C 937 401-3460
  Dayton (G-8260)
Imperial Countertops ....E 216 851-0888
  Cleveland (G-5443)
Indian River Industries ....G 740 965-4377
  Sunbury (G-17890)
▲ Innovative Retail Displays Inc ....F 937 237-7908
  Dayton (G-8266)
Kbi Group Inc ....G 614 873-5825
  Plain City (G-16198)
Kdm Signs Inc ....E 513 769-3900
  Cincinnati (G-3899)
◆ Kellogg Cabinets Inc ....G 614 833-9596
  Canal Winchester (G-2504)

Kinsella Manufacturing Co Inc ....F 513 561-5285
  Cincinnati (G-3911)
Kitchen & Bath Factory Inc ....G 440 510-8111
  Mentor (G-13490)
▲ Kitchens By Rutenschroer Inc ....F 513 251-8333
  Cincinnati (G-3914)
▲ LE Smith Company ....D 419 636-4555
  Bryan (G-2295)
Leiden Cabinet Company LLC ....C 330 425-8555
  Twinsburg (G-18806)
Lima Millwork Inc ....E 419 331-3303
  Elida (G-9195)
M21 Industries LLC ....D 937 781-1377
  Dayton (G-8319)
Macwood Inc ....G 614 279-7676
  Columbus (G-7143)
Malco Laminated Inc ....E 513 541-8300
  Cincinnati (G-3975)
Mespo Woodworking ....G 440 693-4041
  Middlefield (G-13821)
Miami Valley Counters & Spc ....G 937 865-0562
  Miamisburg (G-13690)
◆ Michael Kaufman Companies Inc ....F 330 673-4881
  Kent (G-11353)
Michael Kaufman Companies Inc ....F 330 673-4881
  Kent (G-11354)
Midwest Woodworking Co Inc ....E 513 631-6684
  Cincinnati (G-4028)
Miller Cabinet Ltd ....E 614 873-4221
  Plain City (G-16203)
Mock Woodworking Company LLC ....E 740 452-2701
  Zanesville (G-21157)
Modern Designs Inc ....G 330 644-1771
  Coventry Township (G-7773)
Murray Display Fixtures Ltd ....F 614 875-1594
  Grove City (G-10448)
Norton Industries Inc ....E 888 357-2345
  Lakewood (G-11532)
Ohio Woodworking Co Inc ....E 513 631-0870
  Cincinnati (G-4107)
Partitions Plus LLC ....F 419 422-2600
  Findlay (G-9740)
Pfi Displays Inc ....G 330 925-9015
  Rittman (G-16527)
Prestige Store Interiors Inc ....D 419 476-2106
  Toledo (G-18480)
◆ Ptmj Enterprises ....C 440 543-8000
  Solon (G-17220)
▲ R D Cook Company LLC ....G 614 262-0550
  Columbus (G-7372)
Randys Countertops Inc ....F 740 881-5831
  Powell (G-16334)
Regalia Products Inc ....G 614 579-8399
  Columbus (G-7384)
Reserve Millwork Inc ....E 216 531-6982
  Bedford (G-1441)
Riceland Cabinet Inc ....D 330 601-1071
  Wooster (G-20644)
Richard B Linneman ....G 513 922-5537
  Cincinnati (G-4266)
▲ Rinos Woodworking Shop Inc ....F 440 946-1718
  Willoughby (G-20421)
Rivercity Woodworking Inc ....G 513 860-1900
  West Chester (G-19783)
Robertson Cabinets Inc ....E 937 698-3755
  West Milton (G-19952)
Roy L Bayes ....G 614 274-6729
  Columbus (G-7404)
Scio Laminated Products Inc ....E 740 945-1321
  Scio (G-16879)
Shur Fit Distributors Inc ....E 937 746-0567
  Franklin (G-9919)
Sidney Stiers ....G 740 454-7368
  Zanesville (G-21179)
Skeeles Manufacturing Corp ....F 614 274-4700
  Columbus (G-7457)
Steeles Display Cases ....G 740 965-6426
  Westerville (G-20026)
Stephen J Page 865 951-3316
  Williamsburg (G-20255)
Stephen R Lilley ....G 513 899-4400
  Morrow (G-14415)
Stoller Custom Cabinetry ....G 330 939-6555
  Sterling (G-17524)
Summit Custom Cabinets ....G 740 345-1734
  Newark (G-14927)
Symatic Inc ....G 330 225-1510
  Brunswick (G-2243)
Tenkotte Tops Inc ....G 513 738-7300
  Harrison (G-10677)

Thiels Replacement Systems Inc ....D.... 419 289-6139
Ashland *(G-751)*
Thomas Cabinet Shop Inc ....F.... 937 847-8239
Dayton *(G-8554)*
Tim Crabtree ....G.... 740 286-4535
Jackson *(G-11198)*
Tri-Co Industries ....G.... 740 927-1928
Pataskala *(G-15847)*
Trumbull Industries Inc ....E.... 330 434-6174
Akron *(G-413)*
Ultrabuilt Play Systems Inc ....F.... 419 652-2294
Nova *(G-15436)*
Vances Department Store ....G.... 937 549-2188
Manchester *(G-12397)*
Vances Department Store ....F.... 937 549-3033
Manchester *(G-12398)*
Village Cabinet Shop Inc ....G.... 704 966-0801
Cincinnati *(G-4481)*
▼ **W J Egli Company Inc** ....F.... 330 823-3666
Alliance *(G-512)*
Wilsonart LLC ....E.... 614 876-1515
Columbus *(G-7605)*
◆ **Wine Cellar Innovations LLC** ....C.... 513 321-3733
Cincinnati *(G-4513)*
Witt-Gor Inc ....G.... 419 659-2151
Columbus Grove *(G-7639)*
Wood Specialists ....G.... 440 639-9797
Mentor *(G-13629)*
Woodworks For You ....G.... 440 277-8147
Wakeman *(G-19290)*
Xxx Intrntional Amusements Inc ....E.... 216 671-6900
Cleveland *(G-6332)*
Youngstown Curve Form Inc ....F.... 330 744-3028
Youngstown *(G-21075)*

2542 Partitions & Fixtures, Except Wood

3-D Technical Services Company ....E.... 937 746-2901
Franklin *(G-9866)*
◆ **Accel Group Inc** ....D.... 330 336-0317
Wadsworth *(G-19220)*
Acrylicon Inc ....G.... 614 263-2086
Columbus *(G-6539)*
American Truck Equipment Inc ....G.... 216 362-0400
Cleveland *(G-4699)*
Arsco Custom Metals LLC ....D.... 513 563-8822
Cincinnati *(G-3357)*
▲ **B-R-O-T Incorporated** ....E.... 216 267-5335
Cleveland *(G-4786)*
Bates Metal Products Inc ....D.... 740 498-8371
Port Washington *(G-16267)*
Bedford Cabinet Inc ....G.... 440 439-4830
Cleveland *(G-4802)*
▼ **Benko Products Inc** ....E.... 440 934-2180
Sheffield Village *(G-16966)*
Bobs Custom Str Interiors LLC ....G.... 567 316-7490
Toledo *(G-18209)*
▲ **Bud Industries Inc** ....G.... 440 946-3200
Willoughby *(G-20289)*
Busch & Thiem Inc ....E.... 419 625-7515
Sandusky *(G-16800)*
▲ **Cap & Associates Incorporated** ....C.... 614 863-3363
Columbus *(G-6728)*
▲ **Cdc Corporation** ....D.... 715 532-5548
Maumee *(G-13081)*
Component Systems Inc ....E.... 216 252-9292
Cleveland *(G-5012)*
Control Electric Co ....E.... 216 671-8010
Columbia Station *(G-6434)*
▲ **Conwed Designscape** ....F.... 715 532-5548
Maumee *(G-13083)*
▲ **Crescent Metal Products Inc** ....C.... 440 350-1100
Mentor *(G-13426)*
Custom Millcraft Corp ....E.... 513 874-7080
West Chester *(G-19690)*
D Lewis Inc ....G.... 740 695-2615
Saint Clairsville *(G-16630)*
▲ **Darko Inc** ....E.... 330 425-9805
Bedford *(G-1398)*
▲ **Dell Fixtures Inc** ....E.... 614 449-1750
Columbus *(G-6859)*
Display Dynamics Inc ....F.... 937 832-2830
Englewood *(G-9355)*
Dwayne Bennett Industries ....G.... 440 466-5724
Geneva *(G-10217)*
▼ **E2 Merchandising Inc** ....E.... 513 860-5444
West Chester *(G-19849)*
Easy Board Inc ....G.... 440 205-8836
Mentor *(G-13437)*
Environmental Wall Systems ....G.... 440 542-6600
Hudson *(G-11043)*
▲ **Formatech Inc** ....E.... 330 273-2800
Brunswick *(G-2205)*
◆ **Gallo Displays Inc** ....E.... 216 431-9500
Cleveland *(G-5288)*
GMR Furniture Services Ltd ....F.... 216 244-5072
Parma *(G-15820)*
▲ **Gwp Holdings Inc** ....D.... 513 860-4050
Fairfield *(G-9501)*
◆ **Heat Seal LLC** ....C.... 216 341-2022
Cleveland *(G-5386)*
HP Manufacturing Company Inc ....D.... 216 361-6500
Cleveland *(G-5421)*
▲ **Idx Dayton LLC** ....C.... 937 401-3460
Dayton *(G-8260)*
◆ **Industrial Mfg Co LLC** ....F.... 440 838-4700
Brecksville *(G-2041)*
Integral Design Inc ....F.... 216 524-0555
Cleveland *(G-5462)*
Intelitool Manufacturing Svcs ....G.... 440 953-1071
Willoughby *(G-20344)*
Jhg Retail Services LLC ....F.... 216 447-0831
Cincinnati *(G-3872)*
◆ **Kellogg Cabinets Inc** ....G.... 614 833-9596
Canal Winchester *(G-2504)*
Marlite Inc ....C.... 330 343-6621
Dover *(G-8837)*
◆ **Marlite Inc** ....C.... 330 343-6621
Dover *(G-8838)*
Metal Fabricating Corporation ....D.... 216 631-8121
Cleveland *(G-5658)*
Metrodeck Inc ....F.... 513 541-4370
Cincinnati *(G-4018)*
◆ **Mfs Supply LLC** ....F.... 440 248-5300
Solon *(G-17192)*
◆ **Midmark Corporation** ....A.... 937 526-3662
Kettering *(G-11434)*
▲ **Mills Company** ....E.... 740 375-0770
Marion *(G-12720)*
▼ **Modern Retail Solutions LLC** ....E.... 330 527-4308
Garrettsville *(G-10199)*
Mro Built Inc ....D.... 330 526-0555
North Canton *(G-15104)*
Myers Industries Inc ....C.... 330 336-6621
Wadsworth *(G-19255)*
Ohio Displays Inc ....F.... 216 961-5600
Elyria *(G-9303)*
▲ **Organized Living Inc** ....E.... 513 489-9300
Cincinnati *(G-4118)*
◆ **Panacea Products Corporation** ....E.... 614 850-7000
Columbus *(G-7287)*
Panacea Products Corporation ....D.... 614 429-6320
Columbus *(G-7288)*
Paul Yoder ....G.... 740 439-5811
Senecaville *(G-16900)*
▲ **Pete Gaietto & Associates Inc** ....D.... 513 771-0903
Cincinnati *(G-4152)*
Pfi Displays Inc ....E.... 330 925-9015
Rittman *(G-16527)*
Pucel Enterprises Inc ....D.... 216 881-4604
Cleveland *(G-5933)*
Qualco LLC ....G.... 614 257-7408
Columbus *(G-7363)*
Rack Processing Company Inc ....E.... 937 294-1911
Moraine *(G-14387)*
Rack Processing Company Inc ....E.... 937 294-1911
Moraine *(G-14388)*
Ray Communications Inc ....G.... 330 686-0226
Stow *(G-17623)*
Richard B Linneman ....G.... 513 922-5537
Cincinnati *(G-4266)*
Sentrilock LLC ....D.... 513 618-5800
West Chester *(G-19794)*
Stanley Industrial & Auto LLC ....C.... 614 755-7089
Westerville *(G-20024)*
◆ **Summa Holdings Inc** ....G.... 440 838-4700
Cleveland *(G-6116)*
Sunrise Cooperative Inc ....E.... 419 683-4600
Crestline *(G-7801)*
◆ **Ternion Inc** ....E.... 216 642-6180
Cleveland *(G-6161)*
▼ **Tiffin Metal Products Co** ....C.... 419 447-8414
Tiffin *(G-18088)*
Tri County Tarp LLC ....E.... 419 288-3350
Bradner *(G-2016)*
Unarco Material Handling Inc ....G.... 419 384-3211
Pandora *(G-15807)*
Valley Plastics Company Inc ....E.... 419 666-2349
Toledo *(G-18588)*
W B Becherer Inc ....G.... 330 758-6616
Youngstown *(G-21068)*
▼ **W J Egli Company Inc** ....F.... 330 823-3666
Alliance *(G-512)*
Warren Steel Specialties Corp ....F.... 330 399-8360
Warren *(G-19461)*
Witt-Gor Inc ....G.... 419 659-2151
Columbus Grove *(G-7639)*
Zak Box Co Inc ....G.... 216 961-5636
Cleveland *(G-6337)*
Zukowski Rack Co ....G.... 440 942-5889
Willoughby *(G-20465)*

2591 Drapery Hardware, Window Blinds & Shades

11 92 Holdings LLC ....E.... 216 920-7790
Chagrin Falls *(G-3008)*
ARC Blinds Inc ....G.... 513 889-4864
Mason *(G-12825)*
◆ **Astra Products of Ohio Ltd** ....C.... 330 296-0112
Ravenna *(G-16367)*
Blind Factory Showroom ....E.... 614 771-6549
Hilliard *(G-10814)*
Blind Outlet ....G.... 614 895-2002
Westerville *(G-20037)*
Cascade Group of Ohio Limited ....G.... 440 572-2480
Strongsville *(G-17723)*
Cincinnati Window Shade Inc ....G.... 513 398-8510
Mason *(G-12844)*
Cincinnati Window Shade Inc ....F.... 513 631-7200
Cincinnati *(G-3510)*
Desinger Window Treatment Inc ....G.... 419 822-4967
Delta *(G-8768)*
E W Perry Service Co Inc ....G.... 419 473-1231
Toledo *(G-18273)*
Gannons Discount Blinds ....G.... 216 398-2761
Cleveland *(G-5289)*
Hang-UPS Instllation Group Inc ....G.... 614 239-7004
Columbus *(G-6978)*
Lumenomics Inc ....E.... 614 798-3500
Lewis Center *(G-11766)*
M C L Window Coverings Inc ....G.... 513 868-6000
Fairfield Township *(G-9584)*
▲ **Mag Resources LLC** ....G.... 330 294-0494
Barberton *(G-1083)*
Miles Pk Vntian Blind Shds Mfg ....G.... 216 239-0850
Beachwood *(G-1248)*
Optimun Blinds Inc ....G.... 740 598-5808
Brilliant *(G-2079)*
Shade Youngstown & Aluminum Co ....G.... 330 782-2373
Youngstown *(G-21028)*
Simex Inc ....G.... 304 665-1104
Columbus *(G-7452)*
Vertical Runner ....G.... 330 262-3000
Wooster *(G-20662)*

2599 Furniture & Fixtures, NEC

Adkins Marlena ....G.... 216 704-2751
Cleveland *(G-4617)*
After Werk ....G.... 513 661-9375
Cincinnati *(G-3308)*
Aster Industries Inc ....F.... 330 762-7965
Akron *(G-72)*
Belmont Community Hospital ....B.... 740 671-1216
Bellaire *(G-1483)*
Bolons Custom Kitchens Inc ....F.... 330 499-0092
Canton *(G-2595)*
Brodwill LLC ....G.... 513 258-2716
Cincinnati *(G-3423)*
Cateringstone ....G.... 513 410-1064
Cincinnati *(G-3448)*
Columbia Cabinets Inc ....G.... 440 748-1010
Columbia Station *(G-6432)*
Crow Works LLC ....E.... 888 811-2769
Killbuck *(G-11450)*
Custom Sink Top Mfg ....F.... 440 245-6220
Lorain *(G-12087)*
Custom Surroundings Inc ....F.... 330 483-9020
Valley City *(G-19035)*
Don Walter Kitchen Distrs Inc ....G.... 330 793-9338
Youngstown *(G-20893)*
Epix Tube Co Inc ....D.... 937 529-4858
Dayton *(G-8184)*
Flipside Inc ....G.... 440 600-7274
Chagrin Falls *(G-3020)*
Franklin Cabinet Company Inc ....E.... 937 743-9606
Franklin *(G-9884)*
▲ **GMI Companies Inc** ....C.... 513 932-3445
Lebanon *(G-11657)*
GMI Companies Inc ....G.... 937 981-0244
Greenfield *(G-10348)*

S I C

Employee Codes: A=Over 500 employees, B=251-500
C=101-250, D=51-100, E=20-50, F=10-19, G=3-9
2019 Harris Ohio
Industrial Directory
845

25 FURNITURE AND FIXTURES SIC SECTION

Home Idea Center Inc ....F 419 375-4951
Fort Recovery *(G-9821)*
Howard B Claflin Co ....G....... 330 928-1704
Cuyahoga Falls *(G-7880)*
Joseph Knapp ....F 330 832-3515
Massillon *(G-13006)*
Kinnemyers Cornerstone Cab Inc ....G....... 513 353-3030
Cleves *(G-6367)*
Lasting Impression Llc ....G....... 614 806-1186
Columbus *(G-7117)*
▲ Master Mfg Co Inc ....E....... 216 641-0500
Cleveland *(G-5632)*
McLeod Bar Group LLC ....F 614 299-2099
Columbus *(G-7168)*
◆ Michael Kaufman Companies Inc .....F 330 673-4881
Kent *(G-11353)*
Michael Kaufman Companies Inc ....F 330 673-4881
Kent *(G-11354)*
Modroto ....G....... 800 772-7659
Ashtabula *(G-787)*
Moorchild LLC ....F 513 649-8867
Middletown *(G-13931)*
Mro Built Inc ....D....... 330 526-0555
North Canton *(G-15104)*
Pegasus Products Company Inc ....G....... 330 677-1123
Kent *(G-11361)*
Quadra - Tech Inc ....D....... 614 445-0690
Columbus *(G-7362)*
Quality Seating Company Inc ....E....... 330 747-0181
Youngstown *(G-21009)*
Rightway Food Service ....G....... 419 223-4075
Lima *(G-11932)*
Sotto ....G....... 513 977-6886
Cincinnati *(G-4354)*
Success Technologies Inc ....G....... 614 761-0008
Powell *(G-16337)*
Suds ....G....... 937 273-6007
Eldorado *(G-9191)*
Textiles Inc ....G....... 614 529-8642
Hilliard *(G-10869)*
The Wood Shed ....G....... 937 429-3355
Xenia *(G-20795)*
▼ Tiffin Metal Products Co ....C....... 419 447-8414
Tiffin *(G-18088)*
Tri-Co Industries ....G....... 740 927-1928
Pataskala *(G-15847)*
Venu On 3rd ....G....... 937 222-2891
Dayton *(G-8578)*
Vivo Brothers LLC ....F 330 629-8686
Poland *(G-16239)*
Wades Woodworking Inc ....F 937 374-6470
Xenia *(G-20804)*
Wood Works ....G....... 330 674-0333
Millersburg *(G-14152)*

26 PAPER AND ALLIED PRODUCTS

2611 Pulp Mills

Caraustar Industries Inc ....F 216 961-5060
Cleveland *(G-4873)*
Caraustar Industries Inc ....D....... 740 862-4167
Baltimore *(G-1037)*
Flegal Brothers Inc ....F 419 298-3539
Edgerton *(G-9175)*
Green Recycling Works LLC ....G 513 278-7111
Cincinnati *(G-3781)*
Greif Packaging LLC ....C....... 330 879-2101
Massillon *(G-12992)*
Itran Electronics Recycling ....G....... 330 659-0801
Richfield *(G-16474)*
◆ Newpage Holding Corporation ....G....... 877 855-7243
Miamisburg *(G-13699)*
Polymer Tech & Svcs Inc ....E 740 929-5500
Heath *(G-10727)*
Riverview Productions Inc ....G 740 441-1150
Gallipolis *(G-10174)*
Rumpke Transportation Co LLC ....C 513 242-4600
Cincinnati *(G-4289)*
SMA Plastics LLC ....G....... 330 627-1377
Carrollton *(G-2929)*
Verso Corporation ....D....... 901 369-4105
Miamisburg *(G-13733)*
◆ Verso Paper Holding LLC ....B....... 877 855-7243
Miamisburg *(G-13735)*
Waste Parchment Inc ....E 330 674-6868
Millersburg *(G-14147)*
World Wide Recyclers Inc ....F 614 554-3296
Columbus *(G-7613)*

2621 Paper Mills

▲ Ahlstrom West Carrollton LLC ....C....... 937 859-3621
Dayton *(G-8011)*
▲ Ampac Plastics LLC ....B....... 513 671-1777
Cincinnati *(G-3342)*
Appvion Operations Inc ....B....... 937 859-8261
West Carrollton *(G-19629)*
B & B Paper Converters Inc ....F 216 941-8100
Cleveland *(G-4782)*
Blue Ridge Paper Products Inc ....C....... 440 235-7200
Olmsted Falls *(G-15529)*
Byedak Construction Ltd ....G....... 937 414-6153
New Paris *(G-14752)*
Carlisle Prtg Walnut Creek Ltd ....E....... 330 852-9922
Sugarcreek *(G-17846)*
▲ Cheney Pulp and Paper Company ...E....... 937 746-9991
Franklin *(G-9874)*
Domtar Paper Company LLC ....D....... 740 333-0003
Wshngtn CT Hs *(G-20723)*
▼ Duracorp LLC ....D....... 740 549-3336
Lewis Center *(G-11758)*
Eagle Wright Innovations Inc ....G....... 937 640-8093
Moraine *(G-14348)*
Essity Prof Hygiene N Amer LLC ....G....... 513 217-3644
Middletown *(G-13906)*
Evergreen Packaging Inc ....G....... 440 235-7200
Olmsted Falls *(G-15530)*
Georgia-Pacific LLC ....F 513 336-4200
Mason *(G-12877)*
Georgia-Pacific LLC ....E....... 614 491-9100
Columbus *(G-6949)*
Georgia-Pacific LLC ....C....... 330 794-4444
Mogadore *(G-14238)*
Georgia-Pacific LLC ....E....... 513 942-4800
West Chester *(G-19715)*
Graphic Packaging Intl LLC ....B 419 673-0711
Kenton *(G-11407)*
Graphic Paper Products Corp ....D....... 937 325-5503
Springfield *(G-17407)*
Gvs Industries Inc ....G....... 513 851-3606
Hamilton *(G-10565)*
Hanchett Paper Company ....D....... 513 782-4440
Cincinnati *(G-3796)*
Honey Cell Inc Mid West ....E....... 513 360-0280
Monroe *(G-14267)*
Honeycomb Midwest ....E....... 513 360-0280
Monroe *(G-14268)*
International Paper Company ....C....... 937 456-4131
Eaton *(G-9154)*
International Paper Company ....C....... 740 397-5215
Mount Vernon *(G-14483)*
International Paper Company ....G....... 937 578-7718
Marysville *(G-12796)*
International Paper Company ....C....... 800 473-0830
Middletown *(G-13916)*
International Paper Company ....B....... 877 447-2737
Milford *(G-14018)*
International Paper Company ....G....... 440 428-5116
Madison *(G-12351)*
International Paper Company ....E....... 740 439-3527
Byesville *(G-2387)*
International Paper Company ....G....... 513 248-6000
Loveland *(G-12201)*
JMJ Paper Inc ....F 216 941-8100
Avon Lake *(G-990)*
JMJ Paper Inc ....F 419 332-6675
Fremont *(G-10029)*
▲ Ken AG Inc ....E....... 419 281-1204
Ashland *(G-718)*
Kimberly-Clark Corporation ....C....... 513 864-3780
Cincinnati *(G-3909)*
Kimberly-Clark Corporation ....C....... 513 794-1005
West Chester *(G-19730)*
Kn8designs LLC ....G....... 859 380-5926
Cincinnati *(G-3918)*
Metro Recycling Company ....G....... 513 251-1800
Cincinnati *(G-4017)*
Millcraft Paper Company ....G....... 216 429-9860
Cleveland *(G-5690)*
Mini Graphics Inc ....G....... 513 563-8600
Cincinnati *(G-4030)*
Mohawk Fine Papers Inc ....E....... 440 969-2000
Ashtabula *(G-788)*
Newpage Group Inc ....A....... 937 242-9500
Miamisburg *(G-13698)*
◆ Newpage Holding Corporation ....G....... 877 855-7243
Miamisburg *(G-13699)*
Novolex Holdings Inc ....D....... 740 397-2555
Mount Vernon *(G-14496)*
Novolex Holdings Inc ....B....... 937 746-1933
Franklin *(G-9905)*
Owens Corning Sales LLC ....D....... 614 399-3915
Mount Vernon *(G-14497)*
P H Glatfelter Company ....D 740 772-3111
Chillicothe *(G-3204)*
▲ Plus Mark LLC ....E 216 252-6770
Cleveland *(G-5891)*
▲ Polymer Packaging Inc ....D....... 330 832-2000
Massillon *(G-13040)*
Quest Solutions Group LLC ....G....... 513 703-4520
Liberty Township *(G-11818)*
Resolute FP US Inc ....B....... 216 961-3900
Cleveland *(G-5980)*
Resolute FP US Inc ....B....... 614 443-6300
Columbus *(G-7388)*
Resolute FP US Inc ....B....... 513 242-3671
Cincinnati *(G-4260)*
Rumford Paper Company ....G....... 937 242-9230
Miamisburg *(G-13713)*
Selah Paperie ....G....... 330 755-2759
Struthers *(G-17824)*
Smart Papers Holdings LLC ....C....... 513 869-5583
Hamilton *(G-10606)*
Spinnaker Coatings ....G....... 937 332-6619
Troy *(G-18712)*
T J Target ....G....... 330 658-3057
Doylestown *(G-8867)*
Transmit Identity LLC ....G....... 330 576-4732
Stow *(G-17636)*
Verso Corporation ....B....... 877 855-7243
Miamisburg *(G-13732)*
Verso Corporation ....B....... 901 369-4100
Miamisburg *(G-13734)*
Verso Corporation ....D....... 901 369-4105
Miamisburg *(G-13733)*
◆ Verso Paper Holding LLC ....B....... 877 855-7243
Miamisburg *(G-13735)*
Wausau Paper Corp ....C....... 513 217-3623
Middletown *(G-13965)*
Wausau Ppr Towel & Tissue LLC ....C....... 513 424-2999
Middletown *(G-13966)*
Welch Packaging Group Inc ....C....... 614 870-2000
Columbus *(G-7597)*
◆ West Carrollton Converting Inc.........D....... 937 859-3621
West Carrollton *(G-19633)*
Westrock Cp LLC ....C....... 937 898-2115
Dayton *(G-8589)*
Westrock Cp LLC ....B....... 513 745-2586
Cincinnati *(G-4504)*
Westrock Cp LLC ....B....... 740 622-0581
Coshocton *(G-7757)*
Xpedx National Accounts ....G....... 513 870-0711
West Chester *(G-19917)*

2631 Paperboard Mills

Ball Corporation ....D....... 330 244-2800
Canton *(G-2584)*
▲ Buckeye Boxes Inc ....C....... 614 274-8484
Columbus *(G-6707)*
Caraustar Industries Inc ....E....... 614 529-5535
Columbus *(G-6737)*
Caraustar Industries Inc ....E 513 871-7112
Cincinnati *(G-3441)*
Caraustar Industries Inc ....F....... 216 939-3001
Cleveland *(G-4874)*
Caraustar Industries Inc ....D....... 740 862-4167
Baltimore *(G-1037)*
Caraustar Industries Inc ....E....... 330 665-7700
Copley *(G-7679)*
Centor Inc ....F....... 567 336-8094
Perrysburg *(G-15932)*
Centor Inc ....C....... 800 321-3391
Berlin *(G-1640)*
Churmac Industries Inc ....E....... 740 773-5800
Chillicothe *(G-3182)*
Coburn Inc ....D....... 419 368-4051
Hayesville *(G-10714)*
Corpad Company Inc ....D....... 419 522-7818
Mansfield *(G-12429)*
Custom Aluminum Boxes ....G....... 440 864-2664
Amherst *(G-560)*
Derby Fabg Solutions LLC ....E....... 937 498-4054
Sidney *(G-17027)*
Diversipak Inc ....C....... 513 321-7884
Cincinnati *(G-3596)*
▲ Fibercorr Mills LLC ....D....... 330 837-5151
Massillon *(G-12981)*
Folding Carton Service Inc ....F 419 281-4099
Ashland *(G-705)*

SIC SECTION 26 PAPER AND ALLIED PRODUCTS

G S K Inc....G.... 937 547-1611
Greenville *(G-10371)*
Galion Packaging Co Inc....G.... 419 468-2548
Galion *(G-10140)*
Georgia-Pacific LLC....C.... 740 477-3347
Circleville *(G-4546)*
Graphic Packaging Intl Inc....C.... 513 424-4200
Middletown *(G-13911)*
Graphic Packaging Intl Inc....C.... 440 248-4370
Solon *(G-17153)*
Graphic Packaging Intl Inc....D.... 937 372-8001
Xenia *(G-20775)*
Greif Paper Packg & Svcs LLC....D.... 740 549-6000
Delaware *(G-8689)*
International Cont Systems LLC....F.... 216 481-8219
Cleveland *(G-5468)*
International Paper Company....C.... 740 383-4061
Marion *(G-12713)*
International Paper Company....C.... 740 363-9882
Delaware *(G-8696)*
◆ **Loroco Industries Inc**....E.... 513 891-9544
Blue Ash *(G-1807)*
Martin Paper Products Inc....E.... 740 756-9271
Carroll *(G-2907)*
Miami Valley Paper LLC....F.... 937 746-6451
Franklin *(G-9900)*
National Bias Fabric Co....E.... 216 361-0530
Cleveland *(G-5722)*
Norse Dairy Systems Inc....C.... 614 294-4931
Columbus *(G-7224)*
Octal Extrusion Corp....E.... 513 881-6100
West Chester *(G-19882)*
▲ **P & R Specialty Inc**....E.... 937 773-0263
Piqua *(G-16147)*
Pactiv LLC....C.... 614 771-5400
Columbus *(G-7285)*
Planet Display & Packaging Inc....G.... 216 251-9641
Cleveland *(G-5884)*
Quilting Creations Intl....E.... 330 874-4741
Bolivar *(G-1926)*
Safeway Packaging Inc....D.... 419 629-3200
New Bremen *(G-14660)*
▲ **Smith-Lustig Paper Box Mfg Co**....E.... 216 621-0453
Bedford *(G-1446)*
Sonoco Products Company....C.... 330 688-8247
Munroe Falls *(G-14527)*
Sonoco Products Company....D.... 740 927-2525
Johnstown *(G-11271)*
Sonoco Products Company....E.... 614 759-8470
Columbus *(G-7462)*
Summit Packaging Solutions LLC....F.... 719 481-8400
West Chester *(G-19803)*
Third Party Service Ltd....F.... 419 872-2312
Perrysburg *(G-16015)*
Thorwald Holdings Inc....E.... 740 756-9271
Lancaster *(G-11613)*
▼ **Valley Converting Co Inc**....E.... 740 537-2152
Toronto *(G-18614)*
Valley Converting Co Inc....E.... 740 537-2152
Toronto *(G-18615)*
Verso Corporation....D.... 901 369-4105
Miamisburg *(G-13733)*
Wayne Signer Enterprises Inc....E.... 513 841-1351
Cincinnati *(G-4492)*
Westrock Converting Company....C.... 513 860-0225
West Chester *(G-19820)*
Westrock Cp LLC....B.... 740 622-0581
Coshocton *(G-7757)*
Westrock Cp LLC....E.... 614 445-6850
Columbus *(G-7601)*
Westrock Mwv LLC....C.... 937 495-6323
Kettering *(G-11443)*

2652 Set-Up Paperboard Boxes

A To Z Paper Box Co....G.... 330 325-8722
Rootstown *(G-16565)*
Boxit Corporation....D.... 216 631-6900
Cleveland *(G-4834)*
Boxit Corporation....G.... 216 416-9475
Cleveland *(G-4835)*
◆ **Chilcote Company**....C.... 216 781-6000
Cleveland *(G-4922)*
Clarke-Boxit Corporation....G.... 716 487-1950
Cleveland *(G-4938)*
Graphic Paper Products Corp....D.... 937 325-5503
Springfield *(G-17407)*
R and D Incorporated....E.... 216 581-6328
Maple Heights *(G-12577)*
Sandusky Packaging Corporation....E.... 419 626-8520
Sandusky *(G-16846)*

2653 Corrugated & Solid Fiber Boxes

1923 W 25th St Inc....G.... 216 696-7529
Cleveland *(G-4579)*
3d Corrugated LLC....G.... 513 241-8126
Cincinnati *(G-3270)*
A-Kobak Container Company....F.... 330 225-7791
Hinckley *(G-10896)*
Acrylicon Inc....G.... 614 263-2086
Columbus *(G-6539)*
Adapt-A-Pak Inc....E.... 937 845-0386
Tipp City *(G-18098)*
▲ **Akers Packaging Service Inc**....C.... 513 422-6312
Middletown *(G-13879)*
Akers Packaging Solutions Inc....D.... 513 422-6312
Middletown *(G-13880)*
Akers Packaging Solutions Inc....E.... 304 525-0342
Middletown *(G-13881)*
▲ **Alpha Container Co Inc**....F.... 937 644-5511
Marysville *(G-12769)*
American Made Corrugated Packg....F.... 937 981-2111
Greenfield *(G-10346)*
Archbold Container Corp....C.... 800 446-2520
Archbold *(G-637)*
Argrov Box Co....F.... 937 898-1700
Dayton *(G-8036)*
B & B Box Company Inc....F.... 419 872-5600
Perrysburg *(G-15922)*
Basic Packaging Ltd....F.... 330 634-9665
Lima *(G-11961)*
BDS Packaging Inc....D.... 937 643-0530
Moraine *(G-14333)*
Bruce Box Co Inc....G.... 740 533-0670
Ironton *(G-11162)*
Bryan Packaging Inc....F.... 419 636-2600
Bryan *(G-2273)*
▲ **Buckeye Boxes Inc**....C.... 614 274-8484
Columbus *(G-6707)*
Buckeye Boxes Inc....G.... 937 599-2551
Bellefontaine *(G-1508)*
Buckeye Boxes Inc....E.... 614 274-8484
Columbus *(G-6708)*
Buckeye Corrugated Inc....G.... 330 576-0590
Fairlawn *(G-9599)*
Buckeye Corrugated Inc....D.... 330 264-6336
Wooster *(G-20575)*
Cambridge Packaging Inc....E.... 740 432-3351
Cambridge *(G-2430)*
▲ **Cameron Packaging Inc**....G.... 419 222-9404
Lima *(G-11848)*
Cardinal Container Corporation....E.... 614 497-3033
Columbus *(G-6741)*
Charles Messina....D.... 216 663-3344
Cleveland *(G-4911)*
Chillicothe Packaging Corp....E.... 740 773-5800
Chillicothe *(G-3180)*
Clecorr Inc....E.... 216 961-5500
Cleveland *(G-4944)*
Cole Pak Inc....D.... 937 652-3910
Urbana *(G-18984)*
Combined Container Board....D.... 513 530-5700
Cincinnati *(G-3536)*
Container King Inc....G.... 937 652-3087
Urbana *(G-18986)*
Creative Packaging LLC....E.... 740 452-8497
Zanesville *(G-21124)*
Digital Color Intl LLC....E.... 330 762-6959
Akron *(G-143)*
Family Packaging Inc....G.... 937 325-4106
Springfield *(G-17401)*
Gatton Packaging Inc....G.... 419 886-2577
Bellville *(G-1556)*
Gbc International LLC....G.... 513 943-7283
Cincinnati *(G-3251)*
Georgia-Pacific LLC....C.... 740 477-3347
Circleville *(G-4546)*
Georgia-Pacific LLC....C.... 513 536-3020
Batavia *(G-1149)*
Graphic Paper Products Corp....D.... 937 325-5503
Springfield *(G-17407)*
Green Bay Packaging Inc....C.... 419 332-5593
Fremont *(G-10027)*
Green Bay Packaging Inc....D.... 513 228-5560
Lebanon *(G-11660)*
Greif Inc....E.... 740 657-6500
Delaware *(G-8682)*
◆ **Greif Inc**....E.... 740 549-6000
Delaware *(G-8681)*
Honeymoon Paper Products Inc....D.... 513 755-7200
Fairfield *(G-9505)*
International Paper Company....C.... 330 264-1322
Wooster *(G-20607)*
International Paper Company....C.... 740 363-9882
Delaware *(G-8696)*
International Paper Company....C.... 740 369-7691
Delaware *(G-8697)*
International Paper Company....D.... 740 522-3123
Newark *(G-14888)*
International Paper Company....C.... 330 626-7300
Streetsboro *(G-17678)*
Jamestown Cont Cleveland Inc....B.... 216 831-3700
Cleveland *(G-5493)*
Jet Container Company....E.... 614 444-2133
Columbus *(G-7066)*
JIT Packaging Inc....G.... 513 934-0905
Lebanon *(G-11665)*
JIT Packaging Inc....E.... 330 562-8080
Aurora *(G-885)*
Jordon Auto Service & Tire Inc....G.... 216 214-6528
Cleveland *(G-5505)*
Joseph T Snyder Industries....G.... 216 883-6900
Cleveland *(G-5506)*
Kennedy Mint Inc....D.... 440 572-3222
Cleveland *(G-5528)*
▲ **Lewisburg Container Company**....C.... 937 962-2681
Lewisburg *(G-11794)*
▲ **Marshalltown Packaging Inc**....G.... 641 753-5272
Columbus *(G-7154)*
Martin Paper Products Inc....E.... 740 756-9271
Carroll *(G-2907)*
McElroy Contract Packaging....F.... 330 262-0855
Wooster *(G-20621)*
Menasha Packaging Company LLC....F.... 740 773-8204
Groveport *(G-10505)*
▲ **Miami Vly Packg Solutions Inc**....F.... 937 224-1800
Dayton *(G-8348)*
Mid Ohio Packaging LLC....E.... 740 383-9200
Marion *(G-12719)*
Midwest Box Company....E.... 216 281-9021
Cleveland *(G-5678)*
Midwest Container Corporation....E.... 513 870-3000
Fairfield *(G-9529)*
◆ **Midwest Filtration LLC**....E.... 513 874-6510
West Chester *(G-19880)*
Mount Vernon Packaging Inc....F.... 740 397-3221
Mount Vernon *(G-14494)*
N-Stock Box Inc....E.... 513 423-0319
Middletown *(G-13934)*
Nicofibers Inc....G.... 740 394-2491
Shawnee *(G-16961)*
Northeast Box Company....D.... 440 992-5500
Ashtabula *(G-793)*
Novolex Holdings Inc....B.... 937 746-1933
Franklin *(G-9905)*
▲ **Omer J Smith Inc**....E.... 513 921-4717
West Chester *(G-19754)*
Orbis Corporation....D.... 262 560-5000
Perrysburg *(G-15994)*
Orora Packaging Solutions....G.... 513 539-8274
Monroe *(G-14274)*
Packaging Corporation America....D.... 513 424-3542
Middletown *(G-13939)*
Packaging Corporation America....C.... 419 282-5809
Ashland *(G-733)*
Packaging Corporation America....G.... 513 860-1145
Fairfield *(G-9543)*
Packaging Corporation America....G.... 513 582-0690
Cincinnati *(G-4130)*
Packaging Corporation America....C.... 740 344-1126
Newark *(G-14908)*
Packaging Corporation America....E.... 330 644-9542
Coventry Township *(G-7776)*
Packaging Tech LLC....E.... 216 374-7308
Cleveland *(G-5836)*
Pactiv LLC....E.... 330 644-9542
Coventry Township *(G-7777)*
Pallet & Cont Corp of Amer....G.... 419 255-1256
Toledo *(G-18457)*
Pax Corrugated Products Inc....D.... 513 932-9855
Lebanon *(G-11682)*
Phillips Packaging Inc....G.... 937 484-4702
Urbana *(G-19008)*
▲ **Piqua Paper Box Company**....E.... 937 773-0313
Piqua *(G-16155)*
Pjs Corrugated Inc....F.... 419 644-3383
Swanton *(G-17918)*
Pratt (jet Corr) Inc....E.... 937 390-7100
Springfield *(G-17473)*
Pratt Industries Inc....D.... 513 770-0851
Mason *(G-12924)*

S I C

Employee Codes: A=Over 500 employees, B=251-500
C=101-250, D=51-100, E=20-50, F=10-19, G=3-9
2019 Harris Ohio
Industrial Directory
847

▲ **Prestige Display and Packg LLC** ......F 513 285-1040
Fairfield *(G-9551)*
Pro-Pak Industries Inc ......C 419 729-0751
Maumee *(G-13139)*
R and D Incorporated ......E 216 581-6328
Maple Heights *(G-12577)*
Riblet Packaging Co ......F 937 652-3087
Urbana *(G-19009)*
Riverview Packaging Inc ......E 937 743-9530
Franklin *(G-9915)*
Safeway Packaging Inc ......D 419 629-3200
New Bremen *(G-14660)*
Schwarz Partners Packaging LLC ......F 317 290-1140
Sidney *(G-17073)*
Skybox Investments Inc ......E 419 525-6013
Mansfield *(G-12514)*
▲ **Smith-Lustig Paper Box Mfg Co** ......E 216 621-0453
Bedford *(G-1446)*
Sonoco Products Company ......E 614 759-8470
Columbus *(G-7462)*
Square One Solutions LLC ......F 419 425-5445
Findlay *(G-9761)*
Summit Container Corporation ......E 719 481-8400
West Chester *(G-19802)*
Systems Pack Inc ......E 330 467-5729
Macedonia *(G-12336)*
Tavens Container Inc ......D 216 883-3333
Bedford *(G-1448)*
Tecumseh Packg Solutions Inc ......E 419 238-1122
Van Wert *(G-19106)*
Temple Inland ......G 513 425-0830
Middletown *(G-13956)*
Temple-Inland Inc ......G 614 221-1522
Marion *(G-12740)*
The Shelby Co ......E 440 871-9901
Westlake *(G-20167)*
Trey Corrugated Inc ......D 513 942-4800
West Chester *(G-19811)*
Unipac Inc ......E 740 929-2000
Hebron *(G-10769)*
US Corrugated of Massillon ......F 216 663-3344
Maple Heights *(G-12583)*
Valley Containers Inc ......F 330 544-2244
Mineral Ridge *(G-14173)*
▲ **Value Added Packaging Inc** ......F 937 832-9595
Englewood *(G-9381)*
Verso Corporation ......D 901 369-4105
Miamisburg *(G-13733)*
Viking Paper Company ......E 419 729-4951
Toledo *(G-18592)*
▼ **Warwick Products Company** ......E 216 334-1200
Cleveland *(G-6291)*
Westrock Cp LLC ......B 513 745-2400
Blue Ash *(G-1868)*
Westrock Cp LLC ......D 770 448-2193
Wshngtn CT Hs *(G-20750)*
Westrock Cp LLC ......C 330 297-0841
Ravenna *(G-16419)*
Westrock Rkt LLC ......E 513 860-5546
West Chester *(G-19821)*
Westrock Rkt Company ......G 330 296-5155
Ravenna *(G-16420)*
Westrock Usc Inc ......C 740 681-1600
Lancaster *(G-11618)*
Westrock Usc Inc ......G 740 484-1000
Bethesda *(G-1659)*
Weyerhaeuser Co Containeerboar ......G 740 397-5215
Mount Vernon *(G-14518)*
Weyerhaeuser Company ......D 740 335-4480
Wshngtn CT Hs *(G-20751)*
Wood Specialists ......G 440 639-9797
Mentor *(G-13629)*

2655 Fiber Cans, Tubes & Drums

A T Tube Company Inc ......G 330 336-8706
Wadsworth *(G-19219)*
Acme Spirally Wound Paper Pdts ......F 216 267-2950
Cleveland *(G-4607)*
Advanced Paper Tube Inc ......F 216 281-5691
Cleveland *(G-4630)*
Artistic Composite & Mold Co ......G 330 352-6632
Litchfield *(G-11984)*
Caraustar Industrial and Con ......E 330 868-4111
Minerva *(G-14177)*
Caraustar Industries Inc ......E 330 665-7700
Copley *(G-7679)*
Companies of North Coast LLC ......G 216 398-8550
Cleveland *(G-5008)*
Dayton Industrial Drum Inc ......E 937 253-8933
Dayton *(G-7977)*
Erdie Industries Inc ......E 440 288-0166
Lorain *(G-12090)*
Greif Inc ......D 740 657-6500
Delaware *(G-8683)*
Greif Inc ......E 419 238-0565
Van Wert *(G-19094)*
Greif Inc ......F 740 549-6000
Delaware *(G-8684)*
Greif Inc ......D 740 549-6000
Delaware *(G-8685)*
Greif Inc ......D 330 879-2101
Navarre *(G-14575)*
Greif Inc ......D 937 548-4111
Delaware *(G-8686)*
Greif Inc ......C 330 879-2936
Massillon *(G-12991)*
◆ **Greif Inc** ......E 740 549-6000
Delaware *(G-8681)*
Greif Inc ......E 740 657-6500
Delaware *(G-8682)*
Greif Bros Corp Ohio Inc ......F 740 549-6000
Delaware *(G-8687)*
Greif USA LLC ......G 740 549-6000
Delaware *(G-8690)*
Haul-Away Containers Inc ......G 440 546-1879
Richfield *(G-16473)*
Horwitz & Pintis Co ......F 419 666-2220
Toledo *(G-18336)*
Howard B Claflin Co ......G 330 928-1704
Cuyahoga Falls *(G-7880)*
Hpc Holdings LLC ......F 330 666-3751
Fairlawn *(G-9608)*
Modroto ......G 800 772-7659
Ashtabula *(G-787)*
Newkor Inc ......E 216 631-7800
Cleveland *(G-5750)*
Nicofibers Inc ......G 740 394-2491
Shawnee *(G-16961)*
▲ **North Coast Composites Inc** ......G 216 398-8550
Cleveland *(G-5762)*
Ohio Paper Tube Co ......F 330 478-5171
Canton *(G-2774)*
Operational Support Svcs LLC ......F 419 425-0889
Findlay *(G-9736)*
Shockakhan Express LLC ......G 614 432-3133
Groveport *(G-10511)*
Sonoco Products Company ......D 937 429-0040
Beavercreek Township *(G-1374)*
Sonoco Products Company ......E 513 870-3985
West Chester *(G-19900)*
Sonoco Products Company ......E 419 448-4428
Tiffin *(G-18084)*
Sonoco Products Company ......C 330 688-8247
Munroe Falls *(G-14527)*
Sonoco Products Company ......E 614 759-8470
Columbus *(G-7462)*
Transport Container Corp ......G 614 459-8140
Columbus *(G-7540)*

2656 Sanitary Food Containers

◆ **American Greetings Corporation** ......A 216 252-7300
Cleveland *(G-4688)*
Clovernook Center For The Bli ......C 513 522-3860
Cincinnati *(G-3530)*
▼ **Duracorp LLC** ......D 740 549-3336
Lewis Center *(G-11758)*
Graphic Packaging Intl LLC ......B 419 673-0711
Kenton *(G-11407)*
Huhtamaki Inc ......B 937 746-9700
Franklin *(G-9890)*
Huhtamaki Inc ......B 513 201-1525
Batavia *(G-1153)*
International Paper Company ......C 800 422-4657
Kenton *(G-11410)*
Kerry Inc ......G 760 685-2548
Byesville *(G-2389)*
◆ **Norse Dairy Systems LP** ......B 614 421-5297
Columbus *(G-7225)*
Novolex Holdings Inc ......B 937 746-1933
Franklin *(G-9905)*
Ohio State Plastics ......F 614 299-5618
Columbus *(G-7258)*
Pactiv LLC ......D 815 547-1200
Columbus *(G-7284)*
Premier Industries Inc ......E 513 271-2550
Cincinnati *(G-4187)*
Ricking Paper and Specialty Co ......E 513 825-3551
Cincinnati *(G-4269)*
Sonoco Products Company ......E 513 870-3985
West Chester *(G-19900)*
▲ **Sunamericaconverting LLC** ......D 330 821-6300
Alliance *(G-504)*
Superior Cup Inc ......E 330 393-6187
Warren *(G-19445)*
Taylor Company ......G 513 271-2550
Cincinnati *(G-4408)*
Verso Corporation ......D 901 369-4105
Miamisburg *(G-13733)*
Washington Products Inc ......F 330 837-5101
Massillon *(G-13057)*

2657 Folding Paperboard Boxes

Americraft Carton Inc ......E 419 668-1006
Norwalk *(G-15380)*
Ample Industries Inc ......C 937 746-9700
Franklin *(G-9869)*
B & L Labels and Packg Co Inc ......G 937 773-9080
Piqua *(G-16103)*
Bell Ohio Inc ......F 605 332-6721
Groveport *(G-10485)*
Boxit Corporation ......G 216 416-9475
Cleveland *(G-4835)*
Boxit Corporation ......D 216 631-6900
Cleveland *(G-4834)*
▲ **Carton Service Incorporated** ......B 419 342-5010
Shelby *(G-16980)*
◆ **Chilcote Company** ......C 216 781-6000
Cleveland *(G-4922)*
Graphic Packaging Intl Inc ......C 513 424-4200
Middletown *(G-13911)*
Graphic Packaging Intl Inc ......C 440 248-4370
Solon *(G-17153)*
Graphic Packaging Intl LLC ......C 740 387-6543
Marion *(G-12707)*
Jefferson Smurfit Corporation ......G 440 248-4370
Solon *(G-17175)*
Oak Hills Carton Co ......E 513 948-4200
Cincinnati *(G-4095)*
Rohrer Corporation ......C 440 542-3100
Solon *(G-17225)*
RR Donnelley & Sons Company ......G 513 870-4040
West Chester *(G-19789)*
Sandusky Packaging Corporation ......E 419 626-8520
Sandusky *(G-16846)*
The Shelby Co ......E 440 871-9901
Westlake *(G-20167)*
Therm-O-Packaging Suppliers ......F 440 543-5188
Chagrin Falls *(G-3082)*
Unipac Inc ......E 740 929-2000
Hebron *(G-10769)*
Yuckon International Corp ......G 216 361-2103
Cleveland *(G-6334)*

2671 Paper Coating & Laminating for Packaging

Adaptive Data Inc ......F 937 436-2343
Dayton *(G-8007)*
Amatech Inc ......E 614 252-2506
Columbus *(G-6579)*
Austin Tape and Label Inc ......D 330 928-7999
Stow *(G-17570)*
Bemis Company Inc ......E 419 334-9465
Fremont *(G-9996)*
Bollin & Sons Inc ......E 419 693-6573
Toledo *(G-18210)*
▲ **Central Coated Products Inc** ......D 330 821-9830
Alliance *(G-462)*
Central Ohio Paper & Packg Inc ......F 419 621-9239
Huron *(G-11092)*
Cole Pak Inc ......D 937 652-3910
Urbana *(G-18984)*
▲ **Command Plastic Corporation** ......F 800 321-8001
Tallmadge *(G-17977)*
Cpg - Ohio LLC ......D 513 825-4800
Cincinnati *(G-3555)*
Crabar/Gbf Inc ......F 419 943-2141
Leipsic *(G-11724)*
Creative Packaging LLC ......E 740 452-8497
Zanesville *(G-21124)*
▲ **Custom Products Corporation** ......D 440 528-7100
Solon *(G-17129)*
▲ **Dayton Fruit Tree Label Co** ......G 937 223-4650
Dayton *(G-8133)*
E-Z Stop Service Center ......D 330 448-2236
Brookfield *(G-2105)*
Esperia Holdings LLC ......G 714 249-7888
Oak Harbor *(G-15444)*
Euclid Products Co Inc ......G 440 942-7310
Willoughby *(G-20317)*

Future Polytech Inc ... E ... 419 763-1352
Saint Henry *(G-16661)*
Gauntlet Awards & Engraving ... G ... 937 890-5811
Dayton *(G-8214)*
Georgia-Pacific LLC ... C ... 740 477-3347
Circleville *(G-4546)*
Greenrock Ltd ... G ... 646 388-4281
Cincinnati *(G-3783)*
Gt Industrial Supply Inc ... F ... 513 771-7000
Blue Ash *(G-1783)*
▲ Hooven - Dayton Corp ... D ... 937 233-4473
Miamisburg *(G-13677)*
Hunt Products Inc ... E ... 440 667-2457
Newburgh Heights *(G-14940)*
Hygient Corporation ... G ... 440 796-7964
Cleveland *(G-5431)*
▲ Inno-Pak Holding Inc ... G ... 740 363-0090
Delaware *(G-8695)*
International Paper Company ... C ... 740 363-9882
Delaware *(G-8696)*
Jerry Pulfer ... G ... 937 778-1861
Piqua *(G-16134)*
Johnson Energy Company ... G ... 937 435-5401
Oakwood *(G-15462)*
Joseph T Snyder Industries ... G ... 216 883-6900
Cleveland *(G-5506)*
Kapstone Container Corporation ... C ... 330 562-6111
Aurora *(G-886)*
Kay Toledo Tag Inc ... D ... 419 729-5479
Toledo *(G-18363)*
▲ Kroy LLC ... C ... 216 426-5600
Cleveland *(G-5544)*
Level Packaging LLC ... G ... 614 392-2412
Findlay *(G-9714)*
Liqui-Box Corporation ... C ... 419 289-9696
Ashland *(G-721)*
◆ Loroco Industries Inc ... E ... 513 891-9544
Blue Ash *(G-1807)*
Marlen Manufacturing & Dev Co ... E ... 216 292-7546
Bedford *(G-1425)*
Multi-Color Corporation ... D ... 513 943-0080
Batavia *(G-1172)*
National Glass Svc Group LLC ... F ... 614 652-3699
Dublin *(G-8951)*
Next Design & Build LLC ... G ... 330 907-3042
Green *(G-10343)*
Next Generation Films Inc ... B ... 419 884-8150
Mansfield *(G-12493)*
▲ Next Generation Films Inc ... C ... 419 884-8150
Lexington *(G-11805)*
◆ Nilpeter Usa Inc ... C ... 513 489-4400
Cincinnati *(G-4080)*
Norse Dairy Systems Inc ... C ... 614 294-4931
Columbus *(G-7224)*
North American Plas Chem Inc ... D ... 216 531-3400
Euclid *(G-9430)*
Novacel Inc ... C ... 937 335-5611
Troy *(G-18688)*
Novacel Inc ... E ... 413 283-3468
Troy *(G-18689)*
Novolex Holdings Inc ... D ... 740 397-2555
Mount Vernon *(G-14496)*
Packaging Material Direct Inc ... G ... 989 482-8400
Solon *(G-17212)*
Packaging Tech LLC ... E ... 216 374-7308
Cleveland *(G-5836)*
Paxar Corporation ... F ... 937 681-4541
Dayton *(G-8418)*
Perfection Packaging Inc ... G ... 614 866-8558
Gahanna *(G-10098)*
Plastic Works Inc ... F ... 440 331-5575
Cleveland *(G-5887)*
Plastipak Packaging Inc ... B ... 937 596-6142
Jackson Center *(G-11212)*
◆ Polychem Corporation ... C ... 440 357-1500
Mentor *(G-13549)*
Polychem Corporation ... G ... 440 357-1500
Mentor *(G-13550)*
Prime Industries Inc ... E ... 440 288-3626
Lorain *(G-12113)*
Proampac Pg Borrower LLC ... G ... 513 671-1777
Cincinnati *(G-4195)*
Raven Industries Inc ... G ... 937 323-4625
Springfield *(G-17480)*
Retterbush Graphic and Packg ... E ... 513 779-4466
West Chester *(G-19780)*
Richards and Simmons Inc ... G ... 614 268-3909
Columbus *(G-7392)*
Safeway Packaging Inc ... D ... 419 629-3200
New Bremen *(G-14660)*
Schilling Graphics Inc ... E ... 419 468-1037
Galion *(G-10154)*
Schwarz Partners Packaging LLC ... F ... 317 290-1140
Sidney *(G-17073)*
Shurtape Technologies LLC ... B ... 440 937-7000
Avon *(G-966)*
◆ Shurtech Brands LLC ... C ... 440 937-7000
Avon *(G-967)*
Signode Industrial Group LLC ... E ... 513 248-2990
Loveland *(G-12232)*
Sonoco Products Company ... E ... 419 448-4428
Tiffin *(G-18084)*
Sonoco Products Company ... E ... 614 759-8470
Columbus *(G-7462)*
Sonoco Prtective Solutions Inc ... G ... 419 420-0029
Findlay *(G-9758)*
Springdot Inc ... D ... 513 542-4000
Cincinnati *(G-4365)*
▲ Storopack Inc ... E ... 513 874-0314
West Chester *(G-19904)*
▲ Stretchtape Inc ... E ... 216 486-9400
Cleveland *(G-6107)*
Superior Label Systems Inc ... B ... 513 336-0825
Mason *(G-12944)*
▼ Tce International Ltd ... F ... 800 962-2376
Perry *(G-15914)*
Tcp Inc ... G ... 330 836-4239
Fairlawn *(G-9622)*
Tech/III Inc ... E ... 513 482-7500
Cincinnati *(G-4409)*
Therm-O-Packaging Suppliers ... F ... 440 543-5188
Chagrin Falls *(G-3082)*
Thomas Products Co Inc ... E ... 513 756-9009
Cincinnati *(G-4420)*
Universal Packg Systems Inc ... B ... 513 732-2000
Batavia *(G-1193)*
Universal Packg Systems Inc ... B ... 513 674-9400
Cincinnati *(G-4452)*
Universal Packg Systems Inc ... E ... 513 735-4777
Batavia *(G-1194)*
Verso Paper Holding LLC ... A ... 901 369-4100
Miamisburg *(G-13736)*
▲ Virgail Industries Inc ... G ... 740 928-6001
Hebron *(G-10770)*
Westrock Cp LLC ... B ... 513 745-2400
Blue Ash *(G-1868)*
Zebco Industries Inc ... F ... 740 654-4510
Lancaster *(G-11620)*
Zech Printing Industries Inc ... E ... 937 748-2776
Cincinnati *(G-4532)*

2672 Paper Coating & Laminating, Exc for Packaging

21st Century Printers Inc ... G ... 513 771-4150
Cincinnati *(G-3268)*
3 Sigma LLC ... D ... 937 440-3400
Troy *(G-18632)*
3M Company ... D ... 330 725-1444
Medina *(G-13214)*
Adcraft Decals Inc ... E ... 216 524-2934
Cleveland *(G-4615)*
Admiral Products Company Inc ... E ... 216 671-0600
Cleveland *(G-4619)*
▲ Ahlstrom West Carrollton LLC ... C ... 937 859-3621
Dayton *(G-8011)*
All-Seasons Paper Company ... E ... 440 826-1700
Cleveland *(G-4668)*
▲ Ameri-Cal Corporation ... F ... 330 725-7735
Medina *(G-13223)*
Appvion Operations Inc ... B ... 937 859-8261
West Carrollton *(G-19629)*
Austin Tape and Label Inc ... D ... 330 928-7999
Stow *(G-17570)*
Avery Dennison ... F ... 937 865-2439
Miamisburg *(G-13642)*
Avery Dennison Corporation ... E ... 440 358-3466
Painesville *(G-15714)*
Avery Dennison Corporation ... C ... 440 358-4691
Painesville *(G-15715)*
Avery Dennison Corporation ... B ... 440 358-3700
Painesville *(G-15716)*
Avery Dennison Corporation ... G ... 216 267-8700
Cleveland *(G-4775)*
Avery Dennison Corporation ... G ... 440 534-6527
Mentor *(G-13396)*
Avery Dennison Corporation ... D ... 440 358-3408
Painesville *(G-15717)*
Avery Dennison Corporation ... F ... 513 682-7500
Cincinnati *(G-3372)*
Avery Dennison Corporation ... C ... 614 418-7740
New Albany *(G-14607)*
Avery Dennison Corporation ... C ... 440 358-2828
Mentor *(G-13397)*
Avery Dennison Corporation ... C ... 440 266-2500
Mentor *(G-13398)*
Avery Dennison Corporation ... C ... 440 358-2930
Mentor *(G-13399)*
B & L Labels and Packg Co Inc ... G ... 937 773-9080
Piqua *(G-16103)*
Beiersdorf Inc ... C ... 513 682-7300
West Chester *(G-19835)*
Bemis Company Inc ... E ... 419 334-9465
Fremont *(G-9996)*
Bemis Company Inc ... E ... 330 923-5281
Akron *(G-83)*
Boehm Inc ... E ... 614 875-9010
Grove City *(G-10417)*
Bollin & Sons Inc ... E ... 419 693-6573
Toledo *(G-18210)*
CCL Label Inc ... C ... 216 676-2703
Cleveland *(G-4894)*
CCL Label Inc ... E ... 440 878-7000
Brunswick *(G-2194)*
CCL Label Inc ... B ... 440 878-7277
Strongsville *(G-17724)*
▲ Central Coated Products Inc ... D ... 330 821-9830
Alliance *(G-462)*
Coating Applications Intl LLC ... G ... 513 956-5222
Cincinnati *(G-3534)*
◆ Cortape Inc ... F ... 330 929-6700
Cuyahoga Falls *(G-7853)*
D M V Supply Corporation ... G ... 330 847-0450
Warren *(G-19393)*
Deco Tools Inc ... E ... 419 476-9321
Toledo *(G-18256)*
▲ Dermamed Coatin ... G ... 330 474-3786
Kent *(G-11313)*
Gary I Teach Jr ... G ... 614 582-7483
London *(G-12060)*
GBS Corp ... E ... 330 929-8050
Stow *(G-17591)*
GBS Corp ... C ... 330 863-1828
Malvern *(G-12391)*
▲ GBS Corp ... C ... 330 494-5330
North Canton *(G-15085)*
Giesecke & Devrient Amer Inc ... C ... 330 425-1515
Twinsburg *(G-18785)*
Giesecke+devrient ... F ... 330 405-8442
Twinsburg *(G-18787)*
Hall Company ... E ... 937 652-1376
Urbana *(G-18992)*
▲ Hooven - Dayton Corp ... D ... 937 233-4473
Miamisburg *(G-13677)*
▲ ID Images LLC ... D ... 330 220-7300
Brunswick *(G-2215)*
▼ Jamac Inc ... F ... 419 625-9790
Sandusky *(G-16818)*
▼ Kardol Quality Products LLC ... E ... 513 933-8206
Blue Ash *(G-1800)*
▼ Kent Adhesive Products Co ... D ... 330 678-1626
Kent *(G-11338)*
Label Technique Southeast LLC ... E ... 440 951-7660
Willoughby *(G-20356)*
Lam Pro Inc ... F ... 216 426-0661
Cleveland *(G-5556)*
▲ Laminate Technologies Inc ... D ... 419 448-0812
Tiffin *(G-18064)*
◆ Loroco Industries Inc ... E ... 513 891-9544
Blue Ash *(G-1807)*
Marlen Manufacturing & Dev Co ... E ... 216 292-7546
Bedford *(G-1425)*
Master Label Company Inc ... G ... 419 625-8095
Sandusky *(G-16828)*
▲ Miller Studio Inc ... D ... 330 339-1100
New Philadelphia *(G-14787)*
▲ Morgan Adhesives Company LLC ... B ... 330 688-1111
Stow *(G-17606)*
Mr Label Inc ... E ... 513 681-2088
Cincinnati *(G-4051)*
Multi-Color Corporation ... G ... 513 459-3283
Mason *(G-12913)*
▲ Multi-Color Corporation ... F ... 513 381-1480
Batavia *(G-1171)*
◆ Newpage Holding Corporation ... G ... 877 855-7243
Miamisburg *(G-13699)*
◆ Nilpeter Usa Inc ... C ... 513 489-4400
Cincinnati *(G-4080)*
▲ Northcoast Tape & Label Inc ... G ... 440 439-3200
Cleveland *(G-5772)*

Employee Codes: A=Over 500 employees, B=251-500
C=101-250, D=51-100, E=20-50, F=10-19, G=3-9
2019 Harris Ohio
Industrial Directory
849

26 PAPER AND ALLIED PRODUCTS

Novolex Holdings Inc ....D...... 740 397-2555
 Mount Vernon (G-14496)
Ohio Label Inc ....F...... 614 777-0180
 Columbus (G-7249)
▲ Ohio Laminating & Binding Inc ......E...... 614 771-4868
 Hilliard (G-10846)
Oliver Products Company ....F...... 513 860-6880
 Hamilton (G-10593)
P H Glatfelter Company ....D...... 419 333-6700
 Fremont (G-10043)
Paxar Corporation ....F...... 937 681-4541
 Dayton (G-8418)
Pilot Production Solutions LLC .....G...... 513 602-1467
 Mason (G-12921)
Progressive Labels LLC ....F...... 570 688-9636
 Willoughby (G-20412)
R R Donnelley & Sons Company ...E...... 440 774-2101
 Oberlin (G-15504)
Roemer Industries Inc ....D...... 330 448-2000
 Masury (G-13062)
▲ Sensical Inc ....D...... 216 641-1141
 Solon (G-17229)
Shurtape Technologies LLC ....B...... 440 937-7000
 Avon (G-966)
Specialty Adhesive Film Co ....G...... 513 353-1885
 Cleves (G-6375)
Spinnaker Coating LLC ....C...... 937 332-6300
 Troy (G-18710)
▲ Spinnaker Coating LLC ....E...... 937 332-6500
 Troy (G-18711)
◆ SRC Liquidation LLC ....A...... 937 221-1000
 Dayton (G-8521)
Storad Label Co ....F...... 740 382-6440
 Marion (G-12738)
▲ Stretchtape Inc ....E...... 216 486-9400
 Cleveland (G-6107)
Superior Label Systems Inc ....B...... 513 336-0825
 Mason (G-12944)
◆ Technicote Inc ....E...... 800 358-4448
 Miamisburg (G-13724)
Technicote Westfield Inc ....D...... 937 859-4448
 Miamisburg (G-13725)
Tekni-Plex Inc ....E...... 419 491-2399
 Holland (G-10960)
The Rubber Stamp Shop ....G...... 419 478-4444
 Toledo (G-18549)
Thomas Products Co Inc ....E...... 513 756-9009
 Cincinnati (G-4420)
Thomas Tape and Supply Company ...F...... 937 325-6414
 Springfield (G-17505)
◆ Troy Laminating & Coating Inc ...D...... 937 335-5611
 Troy (G-18714)
Unitherm Inc ....G...... 937 278-1900
 Lebanon (G-11705)
USA Label Express Inc ....E...... 330 874-1001
 Bolivar (G-1930)
▲ Waytek Corporation ....E...... 937 743-6142
 Franklin (G-9932)

2673 Bags: Plastics, Laminated & Coated

Accutech Films Inc ....F...... 419 678-8700
 Coldwater (G-6398)
Advanced Poly-Packaging Inc ....G...... 330 785-4000
 Akron (G-32)
American Plastics LLC ....C...... 419 423-1213
 Findlay (G-9650)
◆ Ampac Holdings LLC ....A...... 513 671-1777
 Cincinnati (G-3340)
◆ Ampac Packaging LLC ....G...... 513 671-1777
 Cincinnati (G-3341)
▲ Atlapac Corp ....D...... 614 252-2121
 Columbus (G-6625)
Automated Packg Systems Inc .....D...... 330 342-2000
 Bedford (G-1386)
Automated Packg Systems Inc .....C...... 216 663-2000
 Cleveland (G-4770)
B K Plastics Inc ....G...... 937 473-2087
 Covington (G-7783)
▲ Buckeye Boxes Inc ....C...... 614 274-8484
 Columbus (G-6707)
Charter Nex Films - Del OH Inc ....E...... 740 369-2770
 Delaware (G-8663)
Charter Nex Holding Company .....E...... 740 369-2770
 Delaware (G-8664)
▲ Command Plastic Corporation ...F...... 800 321-8001
 Tallmadge (G-17977)
Cpg - Ohio LLC ....D...... 513 825-4800
 Cincinnati (G-3555)
Dayton Industrial Drum Inc ....E...... 937 253-8933
 Dayton (G-7977)

◆ Flavorseal LLC ....D...... 440 937-3900
 Avon (G-949)
General Films Inc ....D...... 888 436-3456
 Covington (G-7786)
Global Plastic Tech Inc ....G...... 440 879-6045
 Lorain (G-11093)
Heritage Bag Company ....D...... 513 874-3311
 West Chester (G-19720)
Hood Packaging Corporation ....C...... 937 382-6681
 Wilmington (G-20498)
◆ Inpaco Corporation ....E...... 614 888-9288
 Worthington (G-20691)
▲ Kennedy Group Incorporated ...D...... 440 951-7660
 Willoughby (G-20352)
L & C Plastic Bags Inc ....F...... 937 473-2968
 Covington (G-7789)
Liqui-Box Corporation ....D...... 419 289-9696
 Ashland (G-721)
▲ Mid-West Poly Pak Inc ....E...... 330 658-2921
 Doylestown (G-8865)
Multiplast Systems Inc ....F...... 440 349-0800
 Solon (G-17200)
Next Generation Bag Inc ....B...... 419 884-1327
 Mansfield (G-12492)
▲ Next Generation Films Inc ....C...... 419 884-8150
 Lexington (G-11805)
North American Plas Chem Inc ....D...... 216 531-3400
 Euclid (G-9430)
▼ Packaging Materials Inc ....E...... 740 432-6337
 Cambridge (G-2452)
Pexco Packaging Corp ....E...... 419 470-5935
 Toledo (G-18468)
Pitt Plastics Inc ....D...... 614 868-8660
 Columbus (G-7317)
◆ Poly Works ....G...... 419 678-3758
 Coldwater (G-6418)
Primary Packaging Incorporated ...D...... 330 874-3131
 Bolivar (G-1924)
Safeway Packaging Inc ....D...... 419 629-3200
 New Bremen (G-14660)
Vee Gee Enterprise Corporation ...G...... 330 493-9780
 Canton (G-2857)

2674 Bags: Uncoated Paper & Multiwall

◆ Ampac Holdings LLC ....A...... 513 671-1777
 Cincinnati (G-3340)
Cleveland Canvas Goods Mfg Co ...D...... 216 361-4567
 Cleveland (G-4948)
◆ Greif Inc ....E...... 740 549-6000
 Delaware (G-6681)
Greif Inc ....E...... 740 657-6500
 Delaware (G-6682)
Home Care Products LLC ....F...... 919 693-1002
 Chagrin Falls (G-3050)
Hood Packaging Corporation ....C...... 937 382-6681
 Wilmington (G-20498)

2675 Die-Cut Paper & Board

A G Ruff Paper Specialties Co ......G...... 513 891-7990
 Blue Ash (G-1718)
A H Pelz Co ....G...... 216 861-1882
 Cleveland (G-4589)
Alliance Indus Masking Inc ....G...... 937 681-5569
 Dayton (G-8018)
Art Guild Binders Inc ....E...... 513 242-3000
 Cincinnati (G-3358)
▲ Buckeye Boxes Inc ....C...... 614 274-8484
 Columbus (G-6707)
◆ Chilcote Company ....C...... 216 781-6000
 Cleveland (G-4922)
Commercial Cutng Graphics LLC ...D...... 419 526-4800
 Mansfield (G-12427)
Consuetudo Abscisum Inc ....D...... 419 281-8002
 Ashland (G-697)
Cornerstone Indus Holdings ....G...... 440 893-9144
 Chagrin Falls (G-3014)
D A Stirling Inc ....G...... 330 923-3195
 Cuyahoga Falls (G-7857)
Forest Converting Company Inc ...G...... 513 631-4190
 Cincinnati (G-3703)
GBS Corp ....C...... 330 863-1828
 Malvern (G-12391)
▲ GBS Corp ....C...... 330 494-5330
 North Canton (G-15085)
Georgia-Pacific LLC ....C...... 740 477-3347
 Circleville (G-4546)
Harris Paper Crafts Inc ....F...... 614 299-2141
 Columbus (G-6983)
Honeymoon Paper Products Inc ...D...... 513 755-7200
 Fairfield (G-9505)

SIC SECTION

Hunt Products Inc ....E...... 440 667-2457
 Newburgh Heights (G-14940)
Keeler Enterprises Inc ....G...... 330 336-7601
 Wadsworth (G-19247)
▼ Kent Adhesive Products Co .....D...... 330 678-1626
 Kent (G-11338)
▲ Keyah International Trdg LLC ...E...... 937 399-3140
 Springfield (G-17431)
Lam Pro Inc ....E...... 216 426-0661
 Cleveland (G-5556)
◆ Loroco Industries Inc ....E...... 513 891-9544
 Blue Ash (G-1807)
McElroy Contract Packaging ....G...... 330 262-0855
 Wooster (G-20621)
Multi-Craft Litho Inc ....E...... 859 581-2754
 Blue Ash (G-1824)
Nordec Inc ....D...... 330 940-3700
 Stow (G-17615)
▲ P & R Specialty Inc ....E...... 937 773-0263
 Piqua (G-16147)
Paxar Corporation ....F...... 937 681-4541
 Dayton (G-8418)
Paycard USA Inc ....F...... 702 216-6801
 Dublin (G-8959)
▲ Printers Bindery Services Inc ...D...... 513 821-8039
 Cincinnati (G-4192)
R D Thompson Paper Pdts Co Inc ...E...... 419 994-3614
 Loudonville (G-12147)
R W Michael Printing Co ....G...... 330 923-9277
 Akron (G-340)
▲ Rohrer Corporation ....C...... 330 335-1541
 Wadsworth (G-19275)
Smead Manufacturing Company ...C...... 740 385-5601
 Logan (G-12044)
Spencer-Walker Press Inc ....F...... 740 344-6110
 Newark (G-14920)
Springdot Inc ....D...... 513 542-4000
 Cincinnati (G-4365)
Stat Industries Inc ....G...... 513 860-4482
 Hamilton (G-10608)
Stat Industries Inc ....G...... 740 779-6561
 Chillicothe (G-3224)
Stat Industries Inc ....G...... 740 779-6561
 Chillicothe (G-3225)
Stuart Company ....F...... 513 621-9462
 Cincinnati (G-4386)
Vya Inc ....E...... 513 772-5400
 Cincinnati (G-4485)
Williams Steel Rule Die Co ....F...... 216 431-3232
 Cleveland (G-6311)

2676 Sanitary Paper Prdts

◆ Absorbent Products Company Inc ...E...... 419 352-5353
 Bowling Green (G-1949)
◆ Aci Industries Converting Ltd ...E...... 740 368-4160
 Delaware (G-8649)
Cbl Products ....G...... 216 321-2599
 Cleveland (G-4893)
Fox Supply LLC ....G...... 419 628-3051
 Minster (G-14214)
▲ Giant Industries Inc ....E...... 419 531-4600
 Toledo (G-18305)
▲ Health Care Products Inc ....E...... 419 678-9620
 Coldwater (G-6411)
Hygient Corporation ....E...... 440 796-7964
 Cleveland (G-5431)
Kimberly-Clark Corporation ....C...... 513 864-3780
 Cincinnati (G-3909)
Kimberly-Clark Corporation ....C...... 513 794-1005
 West Chester (G-19730)
Linsalata Capital Partners Fun .....G...... 440 684-1400
 Cleveland (G-5579)
▲ Little Busy Bodies LLC ....E...... 513 351-5700
 Cincinnati (G-3948)
▲ Novex Products Incorporated ...E...... 440 244-3330
 Lorain (G-12109)
PGT Healthcare LLP ....G...... 513 983-1100
 Cincinnati (G-4156)
Playtex Manufacturing Inc ....D...... 937 498-4710
 Sidney (G-17059)
▲ Principle Business Entps Inc ...C...... 419 352-1551
 Bowling Green (G-1992)
◆ Procter & Gamble Company .....C...... 513 983-1100
 Cincinnati (G-4198)
Procter & Gamble Company ....C...... 513 983-1100
 Cincinnati (G-4199)
Procter & Gamble Company ....E...... 513 266-4375
 Cincinnati (G-4200)
Procter & Gamble Company ....E...... 513 871-7557
 Cincinnati (G-4201)

Procter & Gamble Company ......B 419 998-5891
Lima *(G-11920)*

Procter & Gamble Company ......F 513 482-6789
Cincinnati *(G-4203)*

Procter & Gamble Company ......B 513 672-4044
West Chester *(G-19767)*

Procter & Gamble Company ......B 513 627-7115
Cincinnati *(G-4205)*

Procter & Gamble Company ......C 513 634-9600
West Chester *(G-19768)*

Procter & Gamble Company ......C 513 634-9110
West Chester *(G-19769)*

Procter & Gamble Company ......C 513 934-3406
Oregonia *(G-15573)*

Procter & Gamble Company ......G 513 627-7779
Cincinnati *(G-4207)*

Procter & Gamble Company ......B 513 945-0340
Cincinnati *(G-4208)*

Procter & Gamble Company ......C 513 622-1000
Mason *(G-12926)*

Procter & Gamble Far East Inc ......C 513 983-1100
Cincinnati *(G-4210)*

▼ Procter & Gamble Paper Pdts Co ......F 513 983-1100
Cincinnati *(G-4213)*

Procter & Gamble Paper Pdts Co ......E 513 983-2222
Cincinnati *(G-4214)*

Procter Gamble Co ......G 513 698-7675
Hamilton *(G-10598)*

Qpi Cincinnati LLC ......G 513 755-2670
West Chester *(G-19772)*

Sposie LLC ......F 888 977-2229
Maumee *(G-13148)*

▲ Tambrands Sales Corp ......C 513 983-1100
Cincinnati *(G-4405)*

◆ Tranzonic Acquisition Corp ......A 216 535-4300
Richmond Heights *(G-16505)*

Tranzonic Companies ......B 216 535-4300
Richmond Heights *(G-16507)*

◆ Tranzonic Companies ......C 216 535-4300
Richmond Heights *(G-16506)*

Tranzonic Companies ......C 440 446-0643
Cleveland *(G-6198)*

Tri Con Distribution LLC ......G 937 399-3312
Springfield *(G-17508)*

Wausau Ppr Towel & Tissue LLC ......C 513 424-2999
Middletown *(G-13966)*

2677 Envelopes

Access Envelope Inc ......F 513 889-0888
Hamilton *(G-10528)*

◆ Ampac Holdings LLC ......A 513 671-1777
Cincinnati *(G-3340)*

Bayley Envelope Inc ......G 330 821-2150
Alliance *(G-457)*

Church Budget Monthly Inc ......D 330 337-1122
Salem *(G-16726)*

Church-Budget Envelope Company ......E 800 446-9780
Salem *(G-16727)*

▲ Envelope 1 Inc ......D 330 482-3900
Columbiana *(G-6464)*

Envelope Mart of Ohio Inc ......E 440 365-8177
Elyria *(G-9259)*

Ohio Envelope Manufacturing Co ......E 216 267-2920
Cleveland *(G-5805)*

Pac Worldwide Corporation ......D 800 610-9367
Middletown *(G-13938)*

Quality Envelope Inc ......G 513 942-7578
West Chester *(G-19891)*

◆ SRC Liquidation LLC ......A 937 221-1000
Dayton *(G-8521)*

Tcp Inc ......G 330 836-4239
Fairlawn *(G-9622)*

United Envelope LLC ......B 513 542-4700
Cincinnati *(G-4448)*

Western States Envelope Co ......D 419 666-7480
Walbridge *(G-19300)*

2678 Stationery Prdts

◆ American Greetings Corporation ......A 216 252-7300
Cleveland *(G-4688)*

▼ Bookfactory LLC ......E 937 226-7100
Dayton *(G-8059)*

CCL Label Inc ......C 216 676-2703
Cleveland *(G-4894)*

CCL Label Inc ......E 440 878-7000
Brunswick *(G-2194)*

◆ CM Paula Company ......E 513 759-7473
Mason *(G-12849)*

Keeler Enterprises Inc ......G 330 336-7601
Wadsworth *(G-19247)*

▲ Nature Friendly Products LLC ......G 216 464-5490
Cleveland *(G-5730)*

▲ Primary Colors Design Corp ......G 419 903-0403
Ashland *(G-738)*

Selco Industries Inc ......C 419 861-0336
Holland *(G-10957)*

◆ Steel City Corporation ......E 330 792-7663
Ashland *(G-749)*

Westrock Mwv LLC ......A 937 495-6323
Dayton *(G-8590)*

2679 Converted Paper Prdts, NEC

4 Walls Com LLC ......F 216 432-1400
Cleveland *(G-4581)*

Adaptive Data Inc ......F 937 436-2343
Dayton *(G-8007)*

Aloterra Packaging LLC ......G 281 547-0568
Andover *(G-578)*

◆ American Greetings Corporation ......A 216 252-7300
Cleveland *(G-4688)*

American Paper Converting LLC ......F 419 729-4782
Toledo *(G-18178)*

Avery Dennison Corporation ......C 440 358-4691
Painesville *(G-15715)*

Blue Ash Paper Sales LLC ......G 513 891-9544
Blue Ash *(G-1736)*

Btw LLC ......G 419 382-4443
Toledo *(G-18217)*

▼ Buckeye Paper Co Inc ......E 330 477-5925
Canton *(G-2600)*

▲ Buschman Corporation ......F 216 431-6633
Cleveland *(G-4853)*

Caraustar Industries Inc ......F 216 961-5060
Cleveland *(G-4873)*

Caraustar Industries Inc ......E 330 665-7700
Copley *(G-7679)*

CCL Label Inc ......C 216 676-2703
Cleveland *(G-4894)*

▼ Century Marketing Corporation ......C 419 354-2591
Bowling Green *(G-1961)*

▲ CMC Daymark Corporation ......C 419 354-2591
Bowling Green *(G-1963)*

▲ Corrchoice Inc ......D 330 833-5705
Massillon *(G-12970)*

Davidson Converting Inc ......G 330 626-2118
Streetsboro *(G-17669)*

E-Z Grader Company ......G 440 247-7511
Chagrin Falls *(G-3017)*

Federal Barcode Label Systems ......G 440 748-8060
North Ridgeville *(G-15224)*

▲ Fibercorr Mills LLC ......D 330 837-5151
Massillon *(G-12981)*

◆ Formica Corporation ......E 513 786-3400
Cincinnati *(G-3705)*

GBS Corp ......E 330 929-8050
Stow *(G-17591)*

▲ Gemini Fiber Corporation ......F 330 874-4131
Bolivar *(G-1915)*

▲ General Data Company Inc ......C 513 752-7978
Cincinnati *(G-3252)*

Harris Paper Crafts Inc ......F 614 299-2141
Columbus *(G-6983)*

▲ Hooven - Dayton Corp ......D 937 233-4473
Miamisburg *(G-13677)*

Inline Label Company ......F 513 217-5662
Middletown *(G-13915)*

J and N Inc ......F 234 759-3741
North Lima *(G-15172)*

Joshua Enterprises Inc ......G 419 872-9699
Perrysburg *(G-15970)*

Jr Kennel Mfg ......G 937 780-6104
Leesburg *(G-11711)*

Kay Toledo Tag Inc ......D 419 729-5479
Toledo *(G-18363)*

Keithley Enterprises Inc ......G 937 890-1878
Dayton *(G-8290)*

▲ Kennedy Group Incorporated ......D 440 951-7660
Willoughby *(G-20352)*

▼ Kent Adhesive Products Co ......D 330 678-1626
Kent *(G-11338)*

▲ Label Aid Inc ......F 419 433-2888
Huron *(G-11102)*

Label Technique Southeast LLC ......E 440 951-7660
Willoughby *(G-20356)*

Maderite LLC ......G 937 570-1042
Tipp City *(G-18122)*

Media Procurement Services Inc ......G 513 977-3000
Cincinnati *(G-3996)*

▲ Millcraft Group LLC ......D 216 441-5500
Cleveland *(G-5689)*

Model Graphics & Media Inc ......E 513 541-2355
West Chester *(G-19746)*

Multi-Color Corporation ......G 513 459-3283
Mason *(G-12913)*

▲ Multi-Color Corporation ......F 513 381-1480
Batavia *(G-1171)*

Multicorr Corp ......G 502 935-1000
Delaware *(G-8707)*

Oak Hills Carton Co ......E 513 948-4200
Cincinnati *(G-4095)*

▲ Ohio Packaging ......E 330 833-2884
Massillon *(G-13031)*

Orbytel Print and Packg Inc ......G 216 267-8734
Cleveland *(G-5818)*

Outhouse Paper Etc Inc ......G 937 382-2800
Waynesville *(G-19570)*

Paper Service Inc ......F 330 227-3546
Lisbon *(G-11978)*

◆ Paper Systems Incorporated ......C 937 746-6841
Springboro *(G-17342)*

Paxar Corporation ......F 937 681-4541
Dayton *(G-8418)*

▲ Pmco LLC ......D 513 825-7626
West Chester *(G-19761)*

Rivercor LLC ......E 330 784-1113
Akron *(G-350)*

Roberds Converting Co Inc ......E 513 683-6667
Loveland *(G-12227)*

Saltbox Illustrations ......G 937 319-6434
Yellow Springs *(G-20815)*

▼ Scratch-Off Systems Inc ......E 216 649-7800
Brecksville *(G-2056)*

▲ Shore To Shore Inc ......D 937 866-1908
Dayton *(G-8505)*

Signode Industrial Group LLC ......E 513 248-2990
Loveland *(G-12232)*

Stumps Converting Inc ......F 419 492-2542
New Washington *(G-14833)*

Tekni-Plex Inc ......E 419 491-2399
Holland *(G-10960)*

Tri State Media LLC ......F 513 933-0101
Wilmington *(G-20509)*

Unique Covers ......G 419 925-9600
Maria Stein *(G-12601)*

Van Deleigh Industries LLC ......G 419 467-2244
Sylvania *(G-17968)*

▲ Vemuri International LLC ......G 513 483-6300
Cincinnati *(G-4471)*

Verstraete In Mold Lab ......F 513 943-0080
Batavia *(G-1195)*

Vista Industrial Packaging LLC ......D 800 454-6117
Columbus *(G-7586)*

W/S Packaging Group Inc ......F 740 929-2210
Heath *(G-10734)*

W/S Packaging Group Inc ......C 513 459-2400
Mason *(G-12953)*

Warren Printing & Off Pdts Inc ......F 419 523-3635
Ottawa *(G-15671)*

Wolff House Art Papers Inc ......G 740 501-3766
Mount Vernon *(G-14519)*

27 PRINTING, PUBLISHING, AND ALLIED INDUSTRIES

2711 Newspapers: Publishing & Printing

Abecs Community News ......G 419 330-9658
Swanton *(G-17903)*

Act For Sneca Cnty Oprtnty Ctr ......G 419 447-4362
Tiffin *(G-18040)*

Active Daily Living LLC ......G 513 607-6769
Cincinnati *(G-3295)*

Ada Herald ......G 419 634-6055
Ada *(G-2)*

Adams Publishing Group LLC ......F 740 592-6612
Athens *(G-821)*

Adult Daily Living LLC ......G 330 612-7941
Coventry Township *(G-7761)*

Advance Reporter ......G 419 485-4851
Montpelier *(G-14301)*

Aim Media Midwest Oper LLC ......F 937 335-5634
Troy *(G-18633)*

Akron Legal News Inc ......F 330 296-7578
Akron *(G-42)*

Alliance Publishing Co Inc ......C 330 453-1304
Alliance *(G-454)*

American City Bus Journals Inc ......E 513 337-9450
Cincinnati *(G-3331)*

American City Bus Journals Inc ......E 937 528-4400
Dayton *(G-8024)*

S I C

Employee Codes: A=Over 500 employees, B=251-500
C=101-250, D=51-100, E=20-50, F=10-19, G=3-9

2019 Harris Ohio
Industrial Directory

851

American Community Newspapers.......G....... 614 888-4567
Columbus (G-6582)
American Israelite Co.......G....... 513 621-3145
Cincinnati (G-3334)
American Jrnl of Drmtpathology.......G....... 440 542-0041
Solon (G-17106)
American Lithuanian Press.......G....... 216 531-8150
Cleveland (G-4691)
▲ Amos Media Company.......C....... 937 498-2111
Sidney (G-17015)
Antwerp Bee-Argus.......G....... 419 258-8161
Antwerp (G-595)
Archbold Buckeye Inc.......F....... 419 445-4466
Archbold (G-636)
Arens Corporation.......E....... 937 473-2028
Covington (G-7781)
Arens Corporation.......G....... 937 473-2028
Covington (G-7782)
Ashland Publishing Co.......A....... 419 281-0581
Ashland (G-680)
Atrium At Anna Maria Inc.......G....... 330 562-7777
Aurora (G-870)
Augdon Newspapers of Ohio Inc.......F....... 419 448-3200
Tiffin (G-18048)
B G News.......E....... 419 372-2601
Bowling Green (G-1952)
Barbara A Eisenhardt.......G....... 614 436-9690
Columbus (G-6647)
Becky Brisker.......G....... 614 266-6575
Columbus (G-6659)
Bellefontaine Examiner.......G....... 937 592-3060
Bellefontaine (G-1507)
Block Communications Inc.......F....... 419 724-6212
Toledo (G-18206)
Bloomville Gazette Inc.......G....... 419 426-3491
Attica (G-855)
Bluffton News Pubg & Prtg Co.......E....... 419 358-8010
Bluffton (G-1884)
Boardman News.......G....... 330 758-6397
Boardman (G-1898)
Box Seat Publishing LLC.......G....... 513 519-2812
Cincinnati (G-3406)
Brecksville Broadview Gazette.......E....... 440 526-7977
Brecksville (G-2024)
Brookville Star.......G....... 937 833-2545
Brookville (G-2163)
Brothers Publishing Co LLC.......E....... 937 548-3330
Greenville (G-10361)
Brown Publishing Co.......F....... 937 544-2391
West Union (G-19959)
Brown Publishing Co Inc.......G....... 740 286-2187
Jackson (G-11184)
Brown Publishing Inc LLC.......G....... 513 794-5040
Blue Ash (G-1742)
Brv Inc.......F....... 513 977-3000
Cincinnati (G-3427)
Bryan Publishing Company.......D....... 419 636-1111
Bryan (G-2274)
Bryan Publishing Company.......G....... 419 485-3113
Montpelier (G-14302)
Buckeye Lake Shopper Reporter.......G....... 740 246-4741
Thornville (G-18030)
Buckeye Post.......G....... 330 724-2800
Akron (G-97)
Business First Columbus Inc.......E....... 614 461-4040
Columbus (G-6715)
Business Journal.......F....... 330 744-5023
Youngstown (G-20862)
Cameco Communications.......G....... 937 840-9490
Hillsboro (G-10877)
Carrollton Publishing Company.......F....... 330 627-5591
Carrollton (G-2918)
Cathie D Hubbard.......E....... 937 593-0316
Bellefontaine (G-1509)
Catholic Diocese of Columbus.......G....... 614 224-5195
Columbus (G-6750)
Central Ohio Printing Corp.......D....... 740 852-1616
London (G-12052)
Chagrin Valley Publishing Co.......C....... 440 247-5335
Chagrin Falls (G-3012)
Chesterland News Inc.......F....... 440 729-7667
Chesterland (G-3154)
Chronicle Telegram.......G....... 330 725-4166
Medina (G-13236)
Chronicle Your Life Story.......G....... 614 456-7576
Columbus (G-6765)
Cincinnati Crt Index Press Inc.......F....... 513 241-1450
Cincinnati (G-3488)
Cincinnati Enquirer.......E....... 513 721-2700
Cincinnati (G-3491)

Cincinnati Ftn Sq News Inc.......F....... 513 421-4049
Mason (G-12841)
Citizens USA.......G....... 937 280-2001
Dayton (G-8092)
Clair Zeits.......G....... 419 643-8980
Columbus Grove (G-7633)
Clermont Sun Publishing Co.......G....... 937 444-3441
Mount Orab (G-14441)
Cleveland Citizen Pubg Co.......G....... 216 861-4283
Cleveland (G-4951)
Cleveland East Ed Wns Jurnl.......G....... 216 228-1379
Cleveland (G-4958)
Cleveland Jewish Publ Co.......E....... 216 454-8300
Cleveland (G-4966)
Cleveland Jewish Publ Co Fdn.......G....... 216 454-8300
Beachwood (G-1227)
Clevelandcom.......G....... 216 862-7159
Cleveland (G-4987)
Columbus Alive Inc.......F....... 614 221-2449
Columbus (G-6783)
Columbus Messenger Company.......E....... 614 272-5422
Columbus (G-6797)
Columbus Messenger Company.......G....... 740 852-0809
London (G-12055)
Columbus-Sports Publications.......F....... 614 486-2202
Columbus (G-6804)
Comcorp Inc.......B....... 718 981-1234
Cleveland (G-5000)
Construction Bulletin Inc.......G....... 330 782-3733
Youngstown (G-20879)
Consumers News Services Inc.......C....... 740 888-6000
Columbus (G-6811)
Consumers News Services Inc.......G....... 614 875-2307
Grove City (G-10422)
Copley Ohio Newspapers Inc.......D....... 585 598-0030
Canton (G-2636)
Copley Ohio Newspapers Inc.......C....... 330 364-5577
New Philadelphia (G-14765)
Copley Ohio Newspapers Inc.......D....... 330 833-2631
Massillon (G-12969)
Coshocton Community Choir.......G....... 740 623-0554
Coshocton (G-7725)
Coshocton Community Choir Inc.......G....... 740 622-8571
Coshocton (G-7726)
County Classifieds.......G....... 937 592-8847
Bellefontaine (G-1510)
Cox Media Group Ohio Inc.......A....... 937 225-2000
Dayton (G-8105)
Cox Media Group Ohio Inc.......G....... 937 743-6700
Dayton (G-8106)
Cox Newspapers LLC.......E....... 513 696-4500
Liberty Township (G-11812)
Cox Newspapers LLC.......F....... 937 866-3331
Miamisburg (G-13652)
Cox Newspapers LLC.......D....... 937 225-2000
Dayton (G-8107)
Cox Newspapers LLC.......D....... 513 863-8200
Liberty Township (G-11813)
Cox Newspapers LLC.......G....... 513 523-4139
Oxford (G-15692)
Crain Communications Inc.......D....... 330 836-9180
Akron (G-125)
Crain Communications Inc.......E....... 216 522-1383
Cleveland (G-5037)
Cross Communications Inc.......G....... 937 304-0010
Vandalia (G-19120)
Cuyahoga Co Med Examiner S Off.......G....... 216 721-5610
Cleveland (G-5053)
Daily Agency Inc.......F....... 937 456-9808
Eaton (G-9147)
Daily Chief Union.......F....... 419 294-2331
Upper Sandusky (G-18950)
Daily Dog.......G....... 419 708-4923
Holland (G-10924)
Daily Fostoria Review Co.......C....... 419 435-6641
Fostoria (G-9836)
Daily Gazette.......E....... 937 372-4444
Xenia (G-20764)
Daily Growler Inc.......G....... 614 656-2337
Upper Arlington (G-18944)
Daily Legal News Inc.......G....... 330 747-7777
Youngstown (G-20885)
Daily Needs Assistance.......F....... 614 824-8340
Plain City (G-16184)
Daily Needs Personal Care LLC.......G....... 614 598-8383
Ashville (G-817)
Daily Reporter.......E....... 614 224-4835
Columbus (G-6846)
Daily Squawk LLC.......G....... 937 426-6247
Dayton (G-7976)

Dayton City Paper New LLC.......F....... 937 222-8855
Dayton (G-8129)
Dayton Dailey News.......F....... 937 743-2387
Franklin (G-9878)
Dayton Weekly News.......G....... 937 223-8060
Dayton (G-8147)
Delaware Gazette Company.......D....... 740 363-1161
Delaware (G-8670)
Delphos Herald Inc.......D....... 419 695-0015
Delphos (G-8738)
Delphos Herald Inc.......G....... 419 399-4015
Paulding (G-15859)
Delphos Herald Inc.......D....... 419 695-0015
Delphos (G-8739)
Digicom Inc.......G....... 216 642-3838
Brooklyn Heights (G-2120)
Dispatch Printing Company.......C....... 740 548-5331
Lewis Center (G-11757)
Dispatch Printing Company.......E....... 614 885-6020
Columbus (G-6868)
Dog Daily.......G....... 216 624-0735
Cleveland (G-5103)
Douthit Communications Inc.......D....... 419 625-5825
Sandusky (G-16805)
Dow Jones & Company Inc.......E....... 419 352-4696
Bowling Green (G-1970)
Dragonflies and Angels Press.......G....... 740 964-9149
Pataskala (G-15830)
Eastern Ohio Newspapers Inc.......G....... 740 633-1131
Martins Ferry (G-12760)
Easy Side Publishing Co Inc.......G....... 216 721-1674
Cleveland (G-5142)
Erie Chinese Journal.......G....... 216 324-2959
Twinsburg (G-18770)
Euclid Media Group LLC.......E....... 216 241-7550
Cleveland (G-5197)
EW Scripps Company.......E....... 513 977-3000
Cincinnati (G-3663)
Farmland News LLC.......F....... 419 445-9456
Archbold (G-645)
Fire Tetrahedron Journal.......G....... 567 220-6477
Tiffin (G-18060)
First Catholc Slovak Union U S.......F....... 216 642-9406
Cleveland (G-5242)
Fostoria Focus Inc.......F....... 419 435-6397
Fostoria (G-9842)
Franklin Communications Inc.......D....... 614 459-9769
Columbus (G-6936)
Fremont Discover Ltd.......G....... 419 332-8696
Fremont (G-10018)
Fresh Press LLC.......G....... 513 378-1402
Loveland (G-12189)
Full Gospel Baptist Times.......G....... 614 279-3307
Columbus (G-6941)
Funny Times Inc.......G....... 216 371-8600
Cleveland (G-5277)
Gannett Co Inc.......C....... 740 345-4053
Newark (G-14876)
Gannett Co Inc.......D....... 513 721-2700
Cincinnati (G-3723)
Gannett Co Inc.......E....... 740 654-1321
Lancaster (G-11574)
Gannett Co Inc.......C....... 740 773-2111
Chillicothe (G-3188)
Gannett Co Inc.......E....... 419 521-7341
Marion (G-12703)
Gannett Co Inc.......D....... 740 452-4561
Zanesville (G-21141)
Gannett Co Inc.......F....... 419 332-5511
Fremont (G-10020)
Gannett Co Inc.......C....... 419 522-3311
Mansfield (G-12443)
Gannett Co Inc.......F....... 740 349-1100
Newark (G-14877)
Gannett Publishing Svcs LLC.......G....... 419 522-3311
Mansfield (G-12444)
Gannett Stllite Info Ntwrk Inc.......D....... 513 721-2700
Cincinnati (G-3724)
Gannett Stllite Info Ntwrk LLC.......D....... 419 334-1012
Fremont (G-10021)
Gate West Coast Ventures LLC.......F....... 513 891-1000
Blue Ash (G-1781)
Gazette Publishing Company.......C....... 419 483-4190
Oberlin (G-15495)
Gazette Publishing Company.......F....... 419 335-2010
Wauseon (G-19517)
Graphic Publications Inc.......D....... 330 343-4377
Dover (G-8828)
Hamilton Journal News Inc.......D....... 513 863-8200
Liberty Township (G-11815)

Hardin County Publishing Co ....E 419 674-4066
Kenton *(G-11408)*
Harrison News Herald Inc ....F 740 942-2118
Cadiz *(G-2398)*
Heartland Education Community ....F 330 684-3034
Orrville *(G-15593)*
Heartland Publications LLC ....F 740 446-2342
Gallipolis *(G-10167)*
Herald Looms ....G 330 948-1080
Lodi *(G-12012)*
Herald Reflector Inc ....D 419 668-3771
Norwalk *(G-15399)*
Highschoolball Inc ....G 330 321-8536
Hinckley *(G-10901)*
Hirt Publishing Co Inc ....E 419 946-3010
Mount Gilead *(G-14426)*
Hirt Publishing Co Inc ....G 419 523-5709
Ottawa *(G-15652)*
Hirt Publishing Co Inc ....F 419 523-5709
Ottawa *(G-15653)*
Holland Springfield Journal ....G 419 874-2528
Perrysburg *(G-15963)*
Holmes County Hub Inc ....G 330 674-1811
Millersburg *(G-14097)*
Horizon Ohio Publications Inc ....F 419 394-7414
Saint Marys *(G-16686)*
Horizon Ohio Publications Inc ....E 419 738-2128
Wapakoneta *(G-19332)*
Horizon Publications Inc ....G 419 628-2369
Minster *(G-14217)*
Horizon Publications Inc ....E 419 738-2128
Wapakoneta *(G-19333)*
Hubbard Publishing Co ....E 937 592-3060
Bellefontaine *(G-1518)*
Huron Hometown News ....G 419 433-1401
Huron *(G-11097)*
Iheartcommunications Inc ....G 740 335-0941
Wshngtn CT Hs *(G-20728)*
Iheartcommunications Inc ....D 419 223-2060
Lima *(G-11876)*
Impact Publications ....G 740 928-5541
Buckeye Lake *(G-2315)*
Indian Lake Shoppers Edge ....G 937 843-6600
Russells Point *(G-16600)*
Ironton Publications Inc ....A 740 532-1441
Ironton *(G-11166)*
James Oshea ....G 614 262-3188
Columbus *(G-7062)*
Jewish Journal Monthly Mag ....G 330 746-3251
Youngstown *(G-20948)*
Job News ....G 513 984-5724
Blue Ash *(G-1795)*
Job News USA ....F 614 310-1700
Columbus *(G-7070)*
Journal News ....G 513 829-7900
Fairfield *(G-9515)*
Journal Register Company ....C 440 951-0000
Willoughby *(G-20349)*
Journal Register Company ....C 440 245-6901
Lorain *(G-12096)*
Kent State University ....G 330 672-2586
Kent *(G-11345)*
King Media Enterprises Inc ....E 216 588-6700
Cleveland *(G-5535)*
Knowles Press Inc ....G 330 877-9345
Hartville *(G-10699)*
Knox County Printing Co ....G 740 848-4032
Galion *(G-10147)*
Kroner Publications Inc ....E 330 544-5500
Niles *(G-15020)*
La Voz Hispania Newspaper ....G 614 274-5505
Columbus *(G-7109)*
Lake Community News ....G 440 946-2577
Willoughby *(G-20357)*
Lakewood Observer Inc ....G 216 712-7070
Lakewood *(G-11526)*
Leader Publications Inc ....E 330 665-9595
Fairlawn *(G-9612)*
Leaf & Thorn Press ....G 614 396-6055
Columbus *(G-6498)*
Legal News Publishing Co ....E 216 696-3322
Cleveland *(G-5572)*
Lets Golf Daily Inc ....G 330 966-3373
North Canton *(G-15097)*
Lisa Arters ....G 330 435-1804
Creston *(G-7806)*
Lore Inc ....G 513 969-8481
Milford *(G-14024)*
Louisville Herald Inc ....G 330 875-5610
Louisville *(G-12160)*
Ls2 Printing ....G 937 544-1000
West Union *(G-19965)*
Mansfield Journal Co ....G 330 364-8641
New Philadelphia *(G-14782)*
Mark Daily ....G 937 369-5358
Eaton *(G-9161)*
Marketing Essentials LLC ....F 419 629-0080
New Bremen *(G-14656)*
Marrow County Sentinel ....G 419 946-3010
Mount Gilead *(G-14428)*
Marysville Monument Company ....G 937 642-7039
Marysville *(G-12798)*
Marysville Newspaper Inc ....E 937 644-9111
Marysville *(G-12799)*
Mature Living News Magazine ....G 419 241-8880
Toledo *(G-18401)*
Medina County Publications Inc ....G 330 721-4040
Medina *(G-13293)*
Merrill Corporation ....C 614 801-4700
Grove City *(G-10444)*
Messenger Publishing Company ....C 740 592-6612
Athens *(G-839)*
Mickens Inc ....G 419 533-2401
Liberty Center *(G-11809)*
Mickens Inc ....G 419 943-2590
Leipsic *(G-11729)*
Middletownusacom ....G 513 594-2831
Middletown *(G-13971)*
Mirror ....E 419 893-8135
Maumee *(G-13134)*
Mirror Publishing Co Inc ....E 419 893-8135
Maumee *(G-13135)*
Monroe County Beacon Inc ....F 740 472-0734
Woodsfield *(G-20547)*
Morgan County Publishing Co ....G 740 962-3377
McConnelsville *(G-13209)*
My Way Home Finder Magazine ....G 419 841-6201
Toledo *(G-18420)*
Napoleon Inc ....E 419 592-5055
Napoleon *(G-14552)*
Neighborhood News Pubg Co ....G 216 441-2141
Cleveland *(G-5734)*
New Urban Distributors LLC ....G 216 373-2349
Cleveland *(G-5749)*
Newark Downtown Center Inc ....G 740 403-5454
Newark *(G-14902)*
News Watchman & Paper ....F 740 947-2149
Waverly *(G-19553)*
Newspaper Holding Inc ....D 440 998-2323
Ashtabula *(G-792)*
Newspaper Network Central OH ....G 419 524-3545
Mansfield *(G-12491)*
Newspaper Solutions LLC ....G 937 694-9370
Englewood *(G-9371)*
Nomis Publications Inc ....F 330 965-2380
Youngstown *(G-20976)*
North Coast Business Journal ....G 419 734-4838
Port Clinton *(G-16254)*
North Coast Voice Mag ....G 440 415-0999
Geneva *(G-10226)*
Northeast Scene Inc ....E 216 241-7550
Cleveland *(G-5776)*
Northeast Suburban Life ....E 513 248-8600
Cincinnati *(G-4087)*
Ocm LLC ....E 937 247-2700
Miamisburg *(G-13701)*
Ogden Newspapers Inc ....D 304 748-0606
Steubenville *(G-17546)*
Ogden Newspapers Inc ....G 330 629-6200
Warren *(G-19425)*
Ogden Newspapers Inc ....E 330 332-4601
Salem *(G-16764)*
Ogden Newspapers Inc ....D 740 283-4711
Steubenville *(G-17547)*
Ogden Newspapers Inc ....C 330 841-1600
Warren *(G-19426)*
Ogden Newspapers of Ohio Inc ....D 419 448-3200
Tiffin *(G-18074)*
Ogden Newspapers Ohio Inc ....E 330 424-9541
Lisbon *(G-11976)*
Ohio City Power ....G 216 651-6250
Cleveland *(G-5804)*
Ohio Community Media ....G 740 848-4064
Fredericktown *(G-9974)*
Ohio News Network ....D 614 460-3700
Columbus *(G-7251)*
Ohio Newspaper Services Inc ....G 614 486-6677
Columbus *(G-7252)*
Ohio Newspapers Foundation ....G 614 486-6677
Columbus *(G-7253)*
Ohio Rights Group ....G 614 300-0529
Columbus *(G-7257)*
Ohio University ....C 740 593-4010
Athens *(G-843)*
Pataskala Post ....F 740 964-6226
Pataskala *(G-15837)*
Patriot ....G 419 864-8411
Cardington *(G-2875)*
Peebles Messenger Newspaper ....G 937 587-1451
Peebles *(G-15880)*
Perry County Tribune ....F 740 342-4121
New Lexington *(G-14720)*
Photo Star ....G 419 495-2696
Willshire *(G-20482)*
Pickaway News Journal ....G 740 851-3072
Circleville *(G-4552)*
Plain Dealer Publishing Co ....F 216 999-5000
Cleveland *(G-5882)*
Plain Dealer Publishing Co ....G 614 228-8200
Columbus *(G-7319)*
Plain Dealer Publishing Co ....A 216 999-5000
Cleveland *(G-5883)*
Post ....G 513 768-8000
Lockland *(G-12001)*
Post Newspapers ....G 330 721-7678
Medina *(G-13321)*
Pride of Geneva ....G 440 466-5695
Chagrin Falls *(G-3069)*
Progressive Communications ....D 740 397-5333
Mount Vernon *(G-14503)*
Progressor Times ....G 419 396-7567
Carey *(G-2887)*
Ptr Daily LLC ....G 330 673-1990
Stow *(G-17622)*
Pulse Journal ....E 513 829-7900
Liberty Township *(G-11817)*
Ray Barnes Newspaper Inc ....G 419 674-4066
Kenton *(G-11420)*
Register Herald Office ....F 937 456-5553
Eaton *(G-9164)*
Reporter Newspaper Inc ....F 330 535-7061
Akron *(G-346)*
Richardson Publishing Company ....F 330 753-1068
Barberton *(G-1102)*
Robert Tuneberg ....G 440 899-9277
Bay Village *(G-1209)*
Roman Cthlic Docese Youngstown ....G 330 744-8451
Youngstown *(G-21021)*
Royalton Recorder ....G 440 237-2235
North Royalton *(G-15300)*
Rural Urban Record Inc ....G 440 236-8982
Columbia Station *(G-6447)*
Sandusky Newspapers Inc ....C 419 625-5500
Sandusky *(G-16845)*
Scenic Valley Surplus LLC ....G 330 359-0555
Fredericksburg *(G-9960)*
Scioto Voice ....G 740 574-5400
Wheelersburg *(G-20184)*
Scripps Media Inc ....D 513 977-3000
Cincinnati *(G-4310)*
Sdg News Group Inc ....F 419 929-3411
New London *(G-14737)*
Sentinel Daily ....G 740 992-2155
Pomeroy *(G-16241)*
Sesh Communications ....F 513 851-1693
Cincinnati *(G-4326)*
Seven Hills Reporter ....G 216 524-9515
Seven Hills *(G-16906)*
Shelby Daily Globe Inc ....E 419 342-4276
Shelby *(G-16988)*
Sidney Alive ....G 937 210-2539
Sidney *(G-17077)*
Smart Business Network Inc ....E 440 250-7000
Cleveland *(G-6071)*
Sojourners Truth ....F 419 243-0007
Toledo *(G-18525)*
Southeast Publications Inc ....F 740 732-2341
Caldwell *(G-2412)*
Springfield Newspapers Inc ....E 937 323-5533
Springfield *(G-17495)*
Standard Printing Co Inc ....E 419 586-2371
Celina *(G-2985)*
Star Newspaper ....G 614 622-5930
Columbus *(G-7486)*
Stumbo Publishing Co ....G 419 529-2847
Ontario *(G-15548)*
Sugarcreek Budget Publishers ....F 330 852-4634
Sugarcreek *(G-17867)*
Summit Street News Inc ....G 330 609-5600
Warren *(G-19444)*

Employee Codes: A=Over 500 employees, B=251-500
C=101-250, D=51-100, E=20-50, F=10-19, G=3-9
2019 Harris Ohio
Industrial Directory
853

27 PRINTING, PUBLISHING, AND ALLIED INDUSTRIES SIC SECTION

◆ **Syracuse China Company** C 419 727-2100 Toledo *(G-18539)*
Telegram F 740 286-3604 Jackson *(G-11197)*
The Beacon Journal Pubg Co C 330 996-3000 Akron *(G-400)*
The Cleveland Jewish Publ Co F 216 454-8300 Beachwood *(G-1280)*
The Defiance Publishing Co A 419 784-5441 Defiance *(G-8645)*
The Gazette Printing Co Inc D 440 576-9125 Jefferson *(G-11240)*
The Gazette Printing Co Inc G 440 593-6030 Conneaut *(G-7660)*
Time 4 You G 614 593-2695 Columbus *(G-7530)*
Times Bulletin Media F 419 238-2285 Van Wert *(G-19107)*
Timothy C Georges G 330 933-9114 North Canton *(G-15129)*
Toledo Blade Company B 419 724-6000 Toledo *(G-18557)*
Toledo Journal G 419 472-4521 Toledo *(G-18560)*
Toledo Streets Newspaper G 419 214-3460 Toledo *(G-18570)*
Toledo Sword Newspaper G 419 932-0767 Toledo *(G-18571)*
Trading Post G 740 922-1199 Uhrichsville *(G-18898)*
Travelers Vacation Guide G 440 582-4949 North Royalton *(G-15306)*
Tribune Printing Inc G 419 542-7764 Hicksville *(G-10785)*
Trogdon Publishing Inc E 330 721-7678 Medina *(G-13355)*
Truax Printing Inc E 419 994-4166 Loudonville *(G-12149)*
Trumbull County Legal News G 330 392-7112 Warren *(G-19451)*
University Sports Publications E 614 291-6416 Columbus *(G-7564)*
Utica Herald G 740 892-2771 Utica *(G-19028)*
Venice Cornerstone Newspaper G 513 738-7151 Hamilton *(G-10617)*
Village Reporter G 419 485-4851 Montpelier *(G-14320)*
Village Voice Publishing Ltd G 419 537-0286 Toledo *(G-18593)*
Vindicator G 330 755-0135 Campbell *(G-2471)*
Vindicator Boardman Office G 330 259-1732 Youngstown *(G-21064)*
Vindicator Printing Company D 330 744-8611 Youngstown *(G-21065)*
Vindicator Printing Company G 330 392-0176 Warren *(G-19456)*
Voice Media Group Inc D 216 241-7550 Cleveland *(G-6268)*
Weekly Brothers Cnty Line Far G 330 674-4195 Millersburg *(G-14149)*
Weekly Chatter G 740 336-4704 Belpre *(G-1587)*
Weekly Juicery G 513 321-0680 Cincinnati *(G-4494)*
Weekly Villager Inc G 330 527-5761 Garrettsville *(G-10204)*
Weirton Daily Times F 740 283-4711 Steubenville *(G-17557)*
Welch Publishing Co E 419 874-2528 Perrysburg *(G-16025)*
Welch Publishing Co G 419 666-5344 Rossford *(G-16594)*
Whitney House G 614 396-7846 Worthington *(G-20708)*
Willard Times Junction F 419 935-0184 Willard *(G-20249)*
Winkler Co Inc G 937 294-2662 Dayton *(G-8596)*
Wooster Daily Record Inc LLC C 330 264-1125 Wooster *(G-20668)*
World Journal G 216 458-0988 Cleveland *(G-6325)*
Yellow Springs News Inc F 937 767-7373 Yellow Springs *(G-20821)*
Your Daily Motivation Ydm Fitn G 440 954-1038 Painesville *(G-15804)*
Zanesville Newspaper G 740 452-4561 Zanesville *(G-21192)*

2721 Periodicals: Publishing & Printing

614 Media Group LLC D 614 488-4400 Columbus *(G-6513)*
A R Harding Publishing Co F 614 231-5735 Columbus *(G-6516)*
Acoustical Publications Inc G 440 835-0101 Bay Village *(G-1204)*
Adams Street Publishing Co E 419 244-9859 Toledo *(G-18156)*
Advanced Media Corporation F 440 260-9910 Cleveland *(G-4629)*
Agri Communicators Inc E 614 273-0465 Columbus *(G-6551)*
AGS Custom Graphics Inc D 330 963-7770 Macedonia *(G-12275)*
Alcohol & Drug Addiction Svcs E 216 348-4830 Cleveland *(G-4652)*
Alternative Press Magazine Inc E 216 631-1510 Cleveland *(G-4678)*
American Ceramic Society E 614 890-4700 Westerville *(G-19977)*
American Heart Association Inc F 419 740-6180 Maumee *(G-13070)*
American Lawyers Co Inc F 440 333-5190 Westlake *(G-20092)*
▲ **Amos Media Company** C 937 498-2111 Sidney *(G-17015)*
▼ **Angstrom Graphics Inc** C 216 271-5300 Cleveland *(G-4716)*
Arens Corporation E 937 473-2028 Covington *(G-7781)*
Arens Corporation G 937 473-2028 Covington *(G-7782)*
▲ **Asm International** D 440 338-5151 Novelty *(G-15438)*
At The Ready Publications LLC G 762 822-8549 Van Wert *(G-19077)*
Baker Media Group LLC F 330 253-0056 Akron *(G-78)*
▲ **Benjamin Media Inc** E 330 467-7588 Brecksville *(G-2022)*
Bluffton News Pubg & Prtg Co E 419 358-8010 Bluffton *(G-1884)*
Bobit Business Media Inc G 330 899-2200 Uniontown *(G-18912)*
Buckeye Prep Report Magazine G 614 855-6977 New Albany *(G-14612)*
C & S Associates Inc E 440 461-9661 Highland Heights *(G-10786)*
Camargo Publications Inc G 513 779-7177 Cincinnati *(G-3438)*
Carmel Trader Publishing Inc E 330 478-9200 Canton *(G-2620)*
Cars and Parts Magazine C 937 498-0803 Sidney *(G-17021)*
Center For Inquiry Inc G 330 671-7192 Peninsula *(G-15890)*
CFM Religion Pubg Group LLC E 513 931-4050 Cincinnati *(G-3461)*
Charlotte M Peters G 216 798-8997 Cleveland *(G-4912)*
Cincinnati Magazine G 513 421-4300 Cincinnati *(G-3499)*
City Girl Magazine LLC G 216 481-4110 Cleveland *(G-4929)*
City of Parma G 440 885-8816 Cleveland *(G-4932)*
City Visitor Inc G 216 661-6666 Cleveland *(G-4934)*
Clipper Magazine LLC G 937 534-0470 Moraine *(G-14338)*
Columbus Bride D 614 888-4567 Columbus *(G-6784)*
Communication Resources Inc E 800 992-2144 Canton *(G-2633)*
Crain Communications Inc E 216 522-1383 Cleveland *(G-5037)*
Crain Communications Inc D 330 836-9180 Akron *(G-125)*
Cruisin Times Magazine G 440 331-4615 Rocky River *(G-16544)*
Curt Harler Inc G 440 238-4556 Cleveland *(G-5044)*
Dispatch Printing Company E 614 885-6020 Columbus *(G-6868)*
Dominion Enterprises E 216 472-1870 Cleveland *(G-5105)*
Downey Enterprises Inc G 740 587-4258 Granville *(G-10329)*
▲ **F+w Media Inc** B 513 531-2690 Blue Ash *(G-1770)*
Family Motor Coach Assn Inc C 513 474-3622 Cincinnati *(G-3671)*
Family Motor Coaching Inc D 513 474-3622 Cincinnati *(G-3672)*
Family Values Magazine G 419 566-1102 Mansfield *(G-12438)*
Fontanelle Group Inc G 440 834-8900 Burton *(G-2358)*
Gardner Business Media Inc E 513 527-8800 Cincinnati *(G-3727)*
Generals Books G 614 870-1861 Columbus *(G-6946)*
Gie Media Inc E 800 456-0707 Cleveland *(G-5322)*
Gongwer News Service Inc F 614 221-1992 Columbus *(G-6960)*
Gongwer News Service Inc G 614 221-1992 Columbus *(G-6961)*
▲ **Graphic Publications Inc** E 330 674-2300 Millersburg *(G-14085)*
Graphicom Press Inc G 937 767-1916 Yellow Springs *(G-20806)*
Great Lakes Publishing Company D 216 771-2833 Cleveland *(G-5350)*
Greater Cincinnati Bowl Assn E 513 761-7387 Cincinnati *(G-3780)*
Guitar Digest Inc F 740 592-4614 Athens *(G-834)*
Hacienda Publications LLC G 216 202-5440 Euclid *(G-9419)*
Harvey Whitney Books Company G 513 793-3555 Cincinnati *(G-3801)*
Highlights For Children Inc C 614 486-0631 Hilliard *(G-10828)*
Horizon Communications Inc G 330 968-6959 Twinsburg *(G-18792)*
Housetrends G 513 794-4103 Blue Ash *(G-1789)*
In Box Publications LLC G 330 592-4288 Akron *(G-215)*
Incorporated Trst Gspl Wk Scty D 216 749-2100 Cleveland *(G-5448)*
Indicator Advisory Corporation G 419 726-9000 Toledo *(G-18345)*
Institute Mthmtical Statistics G 216 295-2340 Shaker Heights *(G-16932)*
Jadlyn Inc G 330 670-9545 Akron *(G-221)*
Kaleidoscope Magazine LLC E 216 566-5500 Cleveland *(G-5515)*
Kent Information Services Inc G 330 672-2110 Kent *(G-11342)*
Kenyon Review G 740 427-5208 Gambier *(G-10182)*
Kyle Publications Inc G 419 754-4234 Toledo *(G-18373)*
Lavish Lyfe Magazine G 937 938-5816 Dayton *(G-8307)*
Legal News Publishing Co E 216 696-3322 Cleveland *(G-5572)*
Lippincott & Peto Inc F 330 864-2122 Akron *(G-254)*
▲ **Lorenz Corporation** D 937 228-6118 Dayton *(G-8316)*
Lyle Printing & Publishing Co E 330 337-3419 Salem *(G-16756)*
Lyle Printing & Publishing Co F 330 337-7172 Salem *(G-16757)*
Marketing Directions Inc G 440 835-5550 Cleveland *(G-5621)*
Marketing Essentials LLC F 419 629-0080 New Bremen *(G-14656)*
Marula Publishing LLC G 513 549-5218 Cincinnati *(G-3984)*
Matthew Bender & Company Inc C 518 487-3000 Miamisburg *(G-13686)*
Meister Media Worldwide Inc D 440 942-2000 Willoughby *(G-20377)*
◆ **Midwest Exposure Magazine** G 937 626-6738 Dayton *(G-8352)*
Miller Publishing Company G 937 866-3331 Miamisburg *(G-13695)*
Morrison Media Group-Cmj LLP G 216 973-4005 Cleveland *(G-5706)*
▲ **New Track Media LLC** F 513 421-6500 Blue Ash *(G-1825)*
North Coast Minority Media LLC E 216 407-4327 Cleveland *(G-5769)*

Northeast Scene Inc ....E 216 241-7550
Cleveland *(G-5776)*
Ohio Association Realtors Inc ....E 614 228-6675
Columbus *(G-7241)*
Ohio Designer Craftsmen Entps ....F 614 486-7119
Columbus *(G-7245)*
Ohio State University ....F 614 292-1462
Columbus *(G-7262)*
Open House Magazine Inc ....G 614 523-7775
Columbus *(G-7272)*
Organic Spa Magazine Ltd ....G 440 331-5750
Rocky River *(G-16551)*
Pardson Inc ....F 740 373-5285
Marietta *(G-12651)*
Pearson Education Inc ....F 614 876-0371
Columbus *(G-7303)*
Pearson Education Inc ....F 614 841-3700
Columbus *(G-7304)*
Peninsula Publishing LLC ....G 330 524-3359
Akron *(G-316)*
Pink Corner Office Inc ....G 614 547-9350
Lewis Center *(G-11772)*
Pjl Enterprise Inc ....D 937 293-1415
Moraine *(G-14377)*
Pjl Enterprise Inc ....E 937 293-1415
Moraine *(G-14378)*
Plus Publications Inc ....G 740 345-5542
Newark *(G-14911)*
Prehistoric Antiquities ....G 937 747-2225
North Lewisburg *(G-15164)*
Province of St John The Baptis ....D 513 241-5615
Cincinnati *(G-4219)*
Publishing Group Ltd ....F 614 572-1240
Columbus *(G-7356)*
Quad/Graphics Inc ....A 513 932-1064
Lebanon *(G-11687)*
Rector Inc ....G 440 892-0444
Westlake *(G-20149)*
Reel Image ....G 937 296-9036
Dayton *(G-8468)*
Relx Inc ....E 937 865-6800
Miamisburg *(G-13708)*
Relx Inc ....F 937 865-6800
Miamisburg *(G-13709)*
Rubber World Magazine Inc ....F 330 864-2122
Akron *(G-357)*
Sabre Publishing ....G 440 243-4300
Berea *(G-1624)*
SC Solutions Inc ....G 614 317-7119
Grove City *(G-10465)*
Sesh Communications ....F 513 851-1693
Cincinnati *(G-4326)*
Sheep & Farm Life Inc ....G 419 492-2364
New Washington *(G-14832)*
▲ St Media Group Intl Inc ....D 513 421-2050
Blue Ash *(G-1849)*
▲ Standard Publishing LLC ....C 513 931-4050
Cincinnati *(G-4371)*
Sterling Associates Inc ....G 330 630-3500
Akron *(G-389)*
Suburban Communications Inc ....E 440 632-0130
Middlefield *(G-13855)*
Target Printing & Graphics ....G 937 228-0170
Dayton *(G-8539)*
Telex Communications Inc ....F 419 865-0972
Toledo *(G-18546)*
Toastmasters International ....F 937 429-2680
Dayton *(G-7991)*
University Sports Publications ....E 614 291-6416
Columbus *(G-7564)*
Upcreek Productions Inc ....G 740 208-8124
Bidwell *(G-1672)*
Vela ....G 614 500-0150
Salesville *(G-16784)*
Venue Lifestyle & Event Guide ....F 513 405-6822
Cincinnati *(G-4475)*
Virtus Stunts LLC ....G 440 543-0472
Chagrin Falls *(G-3089)*
Welch Publishing Co ....E 419 874-2528
Perrysburg *(G-16025)*
Wordcross Enterprises Inc ....F 614 410-4140
Columbus *(G-7612)*
Xray Media Ltd ....G 513 751-9641
Cincinnati *(G-4528)*
Youngs Publishing Inc ....F 937 259-6575
Beavercreek *(G-1347)*
Z Track Magazine ....G 614 764-1703
Dublin *(G-9013)*

2731 Books: Publishing & Printing

American Academic Press ....G 216 906-2518
Bedford *(G-1382)*
American Legal Publishing Corp ....E 513 421-4248
Cincinnati *(G-3335)*
Americanhort Services Inc ....F 614 884-1203
Columbus *(G-6588)*
Anderson Publishing Co ....D 513 474-9305
Miamisburg *(G-13640)*
▲ Asm International ....D 440 338-5151
Novelty *(G-15438)*
B & S Transport Inc ....F 330 767-4319
Navarre *(G-14572)*
▼ Bearing Precious Seed ....G 513 575-1706
Milford *(G-13996)*
Beevinwood Inc ....G 937 678-9910
West Manchester *(G-19940)*
▲ Bendon Inc ....D 419 207-3600
Ashland *(G-685)*
▼ Bookfactory LLC ....E 937 226-7100
Dayton *(G-8059)*
◆ Bookmasters Inc ....C 419 281-1802
Ashland *(G-686)*
Carmel Trader Publishing Inc ....E 330 478-9200
Canton *(G-2620)*
Cengage Learning Inc ....C 513 234-5967
Mason *(G-12840)*
Communication Resources Inc ....E 800 992-2144
Canton *(G-2633)*
Conway Greene Co Inc ....G 216 619-8091
Cleveland *(G-5026)*
CSS Publishing Co Inc ....E 419 227-1818
Lima *(G-11850)*
▲ Dalmatian Press LLC ....E 419 207-3600
Ashland *(G-700)*
Decent Hill Publishers LLC ....G 216 548-1255
Hilliard *(G-10824)*
Design Avenue Inc ....G 330 487-5280
Twinsburg *(G-18763)*
Dialogue House Associates Inc ....G 216 342-5170
Beachwood *(G-1232)*
Dreamscape Media LLC ....G 877 983-7326
Holland *(G-10927)*
Eastword Publications Dev ....G 216 781-9594
Cleveland *(G-5141)*
Elloras Cave Publishing Inc ....E 330 253-3521
Akron *(G-151)*
F+w Media Inc ....G 603 253-8148
Blue Ash *(G-1771)*
▲ F+w Media Inc ....B 513 531-2690
Blue Ash *(G-1770)*
Frasernet Inc ....G 216 691-6686
Cleveland *(G-5273)*
Gardner Business Media Inc ....E 513 527-8800
Cincinnati *(G-3727)*
Gareth Stevens Publishing LP ....C 800 542-2595
Strongsville *(G-17746)*
Gie Media Inc ....E 800 456-0707
Cleveland *(G-5322)*
▲ Golf Galaxy Golfworks Inc ....C 740 328-4193
Newark *(G-14880)*
Grand Unification Press Inc ....G 330 683-1187
Orrville *(G-15592)*
Hamilton Arts Inc ....G 937 767-1834
Yellow Springs *(G-20807)*
Harvey Whitney Books Company ....G 513 793-3555
Cincinnati *(G-3801)*
Highlights Press Inc ....G 614 487-2767
Columbus *(G-6998)*
Hubbard Company ....E 419 784-4455
Defiance *(G-8627)*
Indicator Advisory Corporation ....G 419 726-9000
Toledo *(G-18345)*
Instruction & Design Concepts ....G 937 439-2698
Dayton *(G-8271)*
J S C Publishing ....G 614 424-6911
Columbus *(G-7056)*
Just Business Inc ....F 866 577-3303
Dayton *(G-8287)*
▲ Kaeden Corporation ....G 440 617-1400
Westlake *(G-20127)*
Katherine A Stull Inc ....G 440 349-3977
Solon *(G-17181)*
Kelley Communication Dev ....G 937 298-6132
Dayton *(G-8291)*
Kendall/Hunt Publishing Co ....D 877 275-4725
Cincinnati *(G-3904)*
Kent State University ....F 330 672-7913
Kent *(G-11344)*

Ketman Corporation ....G 330 262-1688
Wooster *(G-20613)*
Kid Concoctions Company ....G 440 572-1800
Strongsville *(G-17760)*
Lachina Creative Inc ....D 216 292-7959
Cleveland *(G-5552)*
Leap Publishing Services Inc ....F 234 738-0082
Stow *(G-17600)*
Lloyd Library & Museum ....G 513 721-3707
Cincinnati *(G-3949)*
Manifest Productions LLC ....G 614 806-3054
Columbus *(G-7147)*
Marysville Newspaper Inc ....E 937 644-9111
Marysville *(G-12799)*
▲ Master Communications Inc ....G 208 821-3473
Blue Ash *(G-1813)*
Matthew Bender & Company Inc ....C 518 487-3000
Miamisburg *(G-13686)*
McDonald & Woodward Pubg Co ....G 740 321-1140
Granville *(G-10332)*
McGraw-Hill Global Educatn LLC ....B 614 755-4151
Blacklick *(G-1690)*
McGraw-Hill School Education H ....B 419 207-7400
Ashland *(G-724)*
McGraw-Hill School Education H ....B 614 430-4000
Columbus *(G-6499)*
McNamaras Pub Inc ....G 216 671-8820
Cleveland *(G-5647)*
Micropress America LLC ....G 513 746-0689
Cincinnati *(G-4024)*
National Dirctry of Morts Inc ....G 440 247-3561
Chagrin Falls *(G-3025)*
Neal Publications Inc ....G 419 874-4787
Perrysburg *(G-15980)*
Neola Inc ....G 330 926-0514
Stow *(G-17614)*
Neola Inc ....F 740 622-5341
Coshocton *(G-7742)*
North Coast Media LLC ....E 216 706-3700
Cleveland *(G-5768)*
Northstar Publishing ....G 330 721-9126
Medina *(G-13307)*
Nurdcon LLC ....G 614 208-5898
Canal Winchester *(G-2509)*
Ohio Psychlogy Pblications Inc ....G 614 861-1999
Columbus *(G-7256)*
One Liberty Street ....G 419 352-6298
Bowling Green *(G-1987)*
Orange Frazer Press Inc ....G 937 382-3196
Wilmington *(G-20501)*
Pardson Inc ....F 740 373-5285
Marietta *(G-12651)*
▲ Precision Metalforming Assn ....E 216 241-1482
Independence *(G-11148)*
Province of St John The Baptis ....D 513 241-5615
Cincinnati *(G-4219)*
Relx Inc ....C 937 865-6800
Miamisburg *(G-13710)*
Relx Inc ....E 937 865-6800
Miamisburg *(G-13708)*
Reynolds Industries Group LLC ....E 614 864-6199
Blacklick *(G-1692)*
River Corp ....G 513 641-3355
Cincinnati *(G-4272)*
SC Solutions Inc ....G 614 317-7119
Grove City *(G-10465)*
Scott Fetzer Company ....F 440 892-3000
Westlake *(G-20156)*
Simon & Schuster Inc ....C 614 876-0371
Columbus *(G-7453)*
Spanish Lngage Productions Inc ....G 614 737-3424
Alexandria *(G-443)*
▲ St Media Group Intl Inc ....D 513 421-2050
Blue Ash *(G-1849)*
Swagg Productions2015llc ....F 614 815-1173
Reynoldsburg *(G-16455)*
Talbot Drake Incorporated ....G 216 441-5600
Cleveland *(G-6148)*
Teachers Publishing Group ....F 614 486-0631
Hilliard *(G-10868)*
Tgs International Inc ....E 330 893-4828
Millersburg *(G-14134)*
Tomahawk Entertainment Group ....G 216 505-0548
Cleveland *(G-6180)*
Vista Research Group LLC ....G 419 281-3927
Ashland *(G-753)*
Weaver Boos Consultants Inc ....F 419 933-5216
Willard *(G-20248)*
Wolters Kluwer Clinical Drug ....D 330 650-6506
Hudson *(G-11083)*

Employee Codes: A=Over 500 employees, B=251-500
C=101-250, D=51-100, E=20-50, F=10-19, G=3-9
2019 Harris Ohio
Industrial Directory
855

Woodburn Press LLC G 937 293-9245
Dayton *(G-8599)*

World Harvest Church Inc B 614 837-1990
Canal Winchester *(G-2516)*

Zaner-Bloser Inc D 614 486-0221
Columbus *(G-7624)*

Zaner-Bloser Inc G 608 441-5555
Columbus *(G-7625)*

2732 Book Printing, Not Publishing

All Systems Colour Inc G 937 859-9701
Dayton *(G-8016)*

Amerilam Laminating G 440 235-4687
Cleveland *(G-4700)*

Bip Printing Solutions LLC F 216 832-5673
Beachwood *(G-1225)*

▼ C J Krehbiel Company D 513 271-6035
Cincinnati *(G-3436)*

Digicom Inc G 216 642-3838
Brooklyn Heights *(G-2120)*

▲ Golf Marketing Group Inc G 330 963-5155
Twinsburg *(G-18788)*

Hf Group LLC A 440 729-9411
Chesterland *(G-3160)*

Hf Group LLC D 440 729-9411
Chesterland *(G-3161)*

Hubbard Company E 419 784-4455
Defiance *(G-8627)*

Indian River Industries G 740 965-4377
Sunbury *(G-17890)*

J & L Management Corporation G 440 205-1199
Mentor *(G-13479)*

Lsc Communications Inc A 419 935-0111
Willard *(G-20241)*

Morse Enterprises Inc G 513 229-3600
Mason *(G-12912)*

Multi-Craft Litho Inc E 859 581-2754
Blue Ash *(G-1824)*

Naomi Kight G 937 278-0040
Dayton *(G-8375)*

Printex Incorporated F 740 773-0088
Chillicothe *(G-3217)*

Quebecor World Johnson Hardin A 614 326-0299
Cincinnati *(G-4233)*

Society of The Precious Blood E 419 925-4516
Celina *(G-2984)*

2741 Misc Publishing

360 Communications LLC G 330 329-2013
Akron *(G-14)*

3dnsew LLC G 740 618-8005
Newark *(G-14846)*

▼ 48 Hr Books Inc E 330 374-6917
Akron *(G-15)*

Aaronyx Publishing G 419 747-2400
Mansfield *(G-12400)*

Adelphi Enterprises G 937 372-3791
Xenia *(G-20754)*

Ahalogy E 314 974-5599
Cincinnati *(G-3311)*

Albert Bickel G 513 530-5700
Cincinnati *(G-3317)*

Align Assess Achieve LLC G 614 505-6820
Columbus *(G-6563)*

All County Phone Directories G 419 865-2464
Holland *(G-10915)*

Alonovus Corp D 330 674-2300
Millersburg *(G-14057)*

American City Bus Journals Inc E 513 337-9450
Cincinnati *(G-3331)*

American Guild of English Hand G 937 438-0085
Cincinnati *(G-3333)*

American Legal Publishing Corp E 513 421-4248
Cincinnati *(G-3335)*

Ameritech Publishing Inc D 614 895-6123
Columbus *(G-6591)*

Ameritech Publishing Inc E 330 896-6037
Uniontown *(G-18909)*

▲ Amos Media Company C 937 498-2111
Sidney *(G-17015)*

Anadem Inc G 614 262-2539
Columbus *(G-6598)*

Anderson Publishing Co D 513 474-9305
Miamisburg *(G-13640)*

Aquent Studios G 216 266-7551
Willoughby *(G-20280)*

At The Ready Publications LLC G 762 822-8549
Van Wert *(G-19077)*

AT&T Corp A 614 223-8236
Columbus *(G-6623)*

B G News E 419 372-2601
Bowling Green *(G-1952)*

Bcmr Publications LLC G 740 441-7778
Gallipolis *(G-10160)*

Beaver Productions G 330 352-4603
Akron *(G-82)*

Beckenhorst Press Inc G 614 451-6461
Columbus *(G-6657)*

Becker Gallagher Legal Pubg F 513 677-5044
Cincinnati *(G-3385)*

Berry Company G 513 768-7800
Cincinnati *(G-3392)*

Blue Line Painting LLC G 440 951-2583
Cleveland *(G-4823)*

Cbd Media Holdings LLC G 513 217-9483
Cincinnati *(G-3449)*

Ceja Publishing G 216 319-0268
Cleveland *(G-4896)*

Checkered Express Inc F 330 530-8169
Girard *(G-10255)*

Christian Blue Pages F 937 847-2583
Miamisburg *(G-13650)*

Clark Optimization LLC E 330 417-2164
Canton *(G-2627)*

▲ Competitive Press Inc G 330 289-1968
Copley *(G-7680)*

Computer Workshop Inc E 614 798-9505
Dublin *(G-8902)*

Computercrafts G 614 231-7559
Columbus *(G-6809)*

Conquest Maps G 614 654-1627
Columbus *(G-6810)*

Consumer Source Inc G 513 621-7300
Cincinnati *(G-3543)*

Copy Source Inc G 937 642-7140
Marysville *(G-12778)*

County Classifieds G 937 592-8847
Bellefontaine *(G-1510)*

Cox Publishing Hq G 937 225-2000
Dayton *(G-8108)*

Deemsys Inc D 614 322-9928
Gahanna *(G-10079)*

Deward Publishing Co Ltd G 800 300-9778
Chillicothe *(G-3184)*

Dickman Directories Inc G 740 548-6130
Lewis Center *(G-11755)*

Diocesan Publications Inc Ohio E 614 718-9500
Dublin *(G-8907)*

Discover Publications G 614 785-1111
Columbus *(G-6867)*

Dodge Data & Analytics LLC E 513 763-3660
Cincinnati *(G-3598)*

Dotcentral LLC F 330 809-0112
Massillon *(G-12974)*

Douthit Communications Inc D 419 625-5825
Sandusky *(G-16805)*

Ebsco Industries Inc F 513 398-3695
Mason *(G-12860)*

Educational Publisher Inc G 614 485-0721
Columbus *(G-6884)*

Elbern Publications G 614 235-2643
Columbus *(G-6889)*

Elloras Cave Publishing Inc E 330 253-3521
Akron *(G-151)*

Evans Creative Group LLC G 614 657-9439
Columbus *(G-6909)*

Express Care F 740 266-2501
Steubenville *(G-17533)*

F and W Publications Inc G 513 531-2690
Cincinnati *(G-3668)*

Fax Medley Group Inc G 513 272-1932
Cincinnati *(G-3676)*

Fgm Media Inc G 440 376-0487
North Royalton *(G-15272)*

Fire Ball Press G 614 280-0100
Columbus *(G-6925)*

Fish Express G 513 661-3000
Cincinnati *(G-3692)*

Fleetmaster Express Inc C 419 425-0666
Findlay *(G-9688)*

Franklin Covey Co G 513 792-0099
Cincinnati *(G-3710)*

Free Bird Publications Ltd G 216 673-0229
Brunswick *(G-2206)*

Fullgospel Publishing F 216 339-1973
Shaker Heights *(G-16931)*

Gb Liquidating Company Inc E 513 248-7600
Milford *(G-14010)*

General Bar Inc F 440 835-2000
Westlake *(G-20117)*

Gordon Bernard Company LLC E 513 248-7600
Milford *(G-14013)*

Gospel Trumpet Publishing G 937 548-9876
Greenville *(G-10373)*

Graphic Paper Products Corp D 937 325-5503
Springfield *(G-17407)*

Gray & Company Publishers G 216 431-2665
Cleveland *(G-5343)*

Great Works Publishing Inc F 440 926-1100
Grafton *(G-10303)*

Greenworld Enterprises Inc G 800 525-6999
West Chester *(G-19862)*

Guadalupe Publishing Inc G 614 450-2474
Etna *(G-9393)*

▲ Haines & Company Inc C 330 494-9111
North Canton *(G-15090)*

Haines Criss Cross G 330 494-9111
North Canton *(G-15091)*

Haines Publishing Inc D 330 494-9111
Canton *(G-2691)*

Hampton Publishing Company G 513 777-9543
Liberty Township *(G-11816)*

Hanover Publishing Co G 440 838-0911
Brecksville *(G-2040)*

Hebraic Way Press Company G 330 614-4872
Alliance *(G-472)*

Herff Jones LLC E 330 678-8138
Stow *(G-17594)*

Holistic Measures G 216 261-0329
Euclid *(G-9420)*

Immigration Law Systems Inc G 614 252-3078
Columbus *(G-7023)*

Incorporated Trustees Gospel W D 216 749-1428
Cleveland *(G-5449)*

Interweave Press LLC G 513 531-2690
Blue Ash *(G-1794)*

IPA Ltd F 614 523-3974
Columbus *(G-7048)*

Johnny Chin Insurance Agency G 513 777-8695
West Chester *(G-19871)*

Kennedy Catalogs LLC G 513 753-1518
Batavia *(G-1157)*

L & S Liette Express G 419 394-7077
Saint Marys *(G-16689)*

L M Berry and Company A 937 296-2121
Moraine *(G-14364)*

Lake Publishing Inc G 440 299-8500
Mentor *(G-13495)*

Lanier & Associates Inc G 216 391-7735
Cleveland *(G-5559)*

Latte Living G 440 364-2201
Cleveland *(G-5564)*

▲ Lexisnexis Group C 937 865-6800
Miamisburg *(G-13684)*

Lily Tiger Press E 513 591-0817
Cincinnati *(G-3944)*

Local Insight Yellow Pages Inc C 330 650-7100
Hudson *(G-11061)*

▲ Lorenz Corporation D 937 228-6118
Dayton *(G-8316)*

LPC Publishing Co G 216 721-1800
Cleveland *(G-5586)*

Lsc Communications Inc A 419 935-0111
Willard *(G-20241)*

Ludwig Music Publishing Co F 440 926-1100
Grafton *(G-10307)*

M Grafix LLC F 419 528-8665
Mansfield *(G-12471)*

M R I Education Foundation C 513 281-3400
Cincinnati *(G-3964)*

Marketing Essentials LLC F 419 629-0080
New Bremen *(G-14656)*

Masterpiece Publisher L P G 513 948-1000
Cincinnati *(G-3985)*

Matly Digital Solutions LLC G 513 860-3435
Fairfield *(G-9526)*

Matthew R Copp G 614 276-8959
Columbus *(G-7159)*

McDonald & Woodward Publishing G 740 641-2691
Newark *(G-14896)*

Mia Express Inc G 330 896-8180
Akron *(G-281)*

Nature Trek G 513 314-3916
Cincinnati *(G-4063)*

Network Communications Inc C 614 934-1919
Gahanna *(G-10095)*

New Century Sales LLC G 513 422-3631
Middletown *(G-13937)*

Nomis Publications Inc F 330 965-2380
Youngstown *(G-20976)*

North Bend Express....G....513 481-4623
Cincinnati *(G-4086)*
Ogr Publishing Inc....G....330 757-3020
Hilliard *(G-10845)*
Ohio Printed Products Inc....F....330 659-0909
Richfield *(G-16478)*
Ohlinger Publishing Svcs Inc....F....614 261-5360
Columbus *(G-7267)*
ONeil & Associates Inc....B....937 865-0800
Miamisburg *(G-13704)*
P&M Publishing....G....740 353-3300
Portsmouth *(G-16294)*
Paula and Julies Cookbooks LLC....G....614 863-1193
Columbus *(G-7301)*
Pauler Communications Inc....G....440 243-1229
Richfield *(G-16480)*
Pedestrian Press....G....419 244-6488
Toledo *(G-18461)*
Peebles Creative Group Inc....G....614 487-2011
Dublin *(G-8961)*
Permaguide....E....330 456-8519
Canton *(G-2783)*
Pflaum Publishing Group....G....937 293-1415
Moraine *(G-14376)*
Pike County Paper Inc....F....740 947-5522
Waverly *(G-19557)*
Pixslap Inc....G....937 559-2671
Middletown *(G-13942)*
▲ Posterservice Incorporated....E....513 577-7100
Cincinnati *(G-4176)*
Powerhouse Factories Inc....F....513 719-6417
Cincinnati *(G-4178)*
Pressed Coffee Bar & Eatery....G....330 746-8030
Youngstown *(G-21005)*
Promatch Solutions LLC....F....937 299-0185
Springboro *(G-17346)*
Propress Inc....F....216 631-8200
Cleveland *(G-5929)*
Province of St John The Baptis....D....513 241-5615
Cincinnati *(G-4219)*
Prowrite Inc....G....614 864-2004
Reynoldsburg *(G-16450)*
Psa Consulting Inc....G....513 382-4315
Cincinnati *(G-4220)*
Publishing Group Ltd....F....614 572-1240
Columbus *(G-7356)*
Puhd....G....216 244-3336
Bedford *(G-1439)*
Purebred Publishing Inc....G....614 339-5393
Columbus *(G-7357)*
▼ Quadriga Americas LLC....G....614 890-6090
Westerville *(G-20018)*
Quaker Express Stamping Inc....F....330 332-9266
Salem *(G-16768)*
Questline Inc....E....614 255-3166
Dublin *(G-8971)*
Rawhide Software Inc....G....419 878-0857
Bowling Green *(G-1993)*
▼ Rcl Publishing Group LLC....G....972 390-6400
Cincinnati *(G-4252)*
Recob Great Lakes Express Inc....G....216 265-7940
Cleveland *(G-5966)*
Research and Development Group....G....614 261-0454
Columbus *(G-7386)*
Robs Creative Screen Printing....G....740 264-6383
Wintersville *(G-20541)*
▲ S J T Enterprises Inc....E....440 617-1100
Westlake *(G-20153)*
SC Solutions Inc....G....614 317-7119
Grove City *(G-10465)*
Scheel Publishing LLC....G....216 731-8616
Willoughby *(G-20425)*
Scott Fetzer Company....F....440 892-3000
Westlake *(G-20156)*
Scrambl-Gram Inc....F....419 635-2321
Port Clinton *(G-16259)*
Sea Bird Publications Inc....G....513 869-2200
Fairfield *(G-9562)*
See Ya There Inc....G....614 856-9037
Millersport *(G-14161)*
Sei Inc....F....513 942-6170
West Chester *(G-19897)*
Senior Impact Publication....F....513 791-8800
Cincinnati *(G-4321)*
Sentinel USA Inc....F....740 345-6412
Newark *(G-14917)*
Sevell + Sevell Inc....G....614 341-9700
Columbus *(G-7441)*
Shoppers Compass....G....419 947-9234
Mount Gilead *(G-14432)*
Silver Maple Publications....G....937 767-1259
Yellow Springs *(G-20816)*
Simon & Schuster Inc....C....614 876-0371
Columbus *(G-7453)*
Singer Press....G....216 595-9400
Beachwood *(G-1279)*
Snap-On Business Solutions....B....330 659-1600
Richfield *(G-16489)*
Snook Advertising Al Publisher....F....614 866-3333
Reynoldsburg *(G-16453)*
Specialty Gas Publishing Inc....G....216 226-3796
Cleveland *(G-6084)*
Star Brite Express Car WA....G....330 674-0062
Millersburg *(G-14130)*
Starbringer Media Group Ltd....G....440 871-5448
Westlake *(G-20162)*
Suburban Communications Inc....E....440 632-0130
Middlefield *(G-13855)*
Success Pro Publications....G....614 886-9922
Columbus *(G-7499)*
Supermedia LLC....G....614 216-6566
Westerville *(G-20027)*
Terewell Inc....G....216 334-6897
Cleveland *(G-6160)*
Thickemz Entertainment LLC....G....404 399-4255
Cuyahoga Falls *(G-7928)*
Thunder Dreamer Publishing....G....419 424-2004
Findlay *(G-9770)*
Tiny Lion Music Groups....G....419 874-7353
Perrysburg *(G-16017)*
Trogdon Publishing Inc....E....330 721-7678
Medina *(G-13355)*
▲ Universal Drect Flfllment Corp....C....330 650-5000
Hudson *(G-11081)*
User Friendly Phone Book LLC....E....216 674-6500
Independence *(G-11154)*
Van-Griner LLC....G....419 733-7951
Cincinnati *(G-4465)*
Walter H Drane Co Inc....G....216 514-1022
Beachwood *(G-1285)*
Willis Music Company....F....513 671-3288
Cincinnati *(G-4511)*
Wizard Publications Inc....F....808 821-1214
Lancaster *(G-11619)*
Woodburn Press LLC....G....937 293-9245
Dayton *(G-8599)*
▲ Zoo Publishing Inc....E....513 824-8297
Blue Ash *(G-1882)*

2752 Commercial Printing: Lithographic

1455 Group LLC....G....330 494-9074
Canton *(G-2554)*
1984 Printing....G....510 435-8338
Westerville *(G-19976)*
21st Century Printers Inc....G....513 771-4150
Cincinnati *(G-3268)*
A & D Printing Co....G....440 975-8001
Willoughby *(G-20263)*
A F Krainz Co....G....216 431-4341
Cleveland *(G-4586)*
A Grade Notes Inc....G....614 766-9999
Dublin *(G-8871)*
A Z Printing Inc....G....513 733-3900
Cincinnati *(G-3282)*
A-1 Printing Inc....G....419 294-5247
Upper Sandusky *(G-18945)*
A-1 Printing Inc....G....419 562-3111
Bucyrus *(G-2316)*
A-1 Printing Inc....G....419 468-5422
Galion *(G-10121)*
A-A Blueprint Co Inc....E....330 794-8803
Akron *(G-23)*
Able Printing Company....G....614 294-4547
Columbus *(G-6530)*
Academy Graphic Comm Inc....E....216 661-2550
Cleveland *(G-4603)*
Ace Printing LLC....G....614 855-7227
New Albany *(G-14603)*
Acme Duplicating Co....G....216 241-1241
Westlake *(G-20086)*
Acme Printing Co Inc....G....419 626-4426
Sandusky *(G-16792)*
Action Printing & Photography....G....419 332-9615
Fremont *(G-9989)*
Action Printing Inc....G....330 963-7772
Twinsburg *(G-18726)*
▲ Activities Press Inc....E....440 953-1200
Mentor *(G-13374)*
Adcraft Decals Inc....E....216 524-2934
Cleveland *(G-4615)*
Adkins & Co Inc....G....216 521-6323
Cleveland *(G-4618)*
Admark Printing Inc....G....937 833-5111
Brookville *(G-2160)*
Admiral Products Company Inc....E....216 671-0600
Cleveland *(G-4619)*
Advanatage Print Solut....G....614 519-2392
Columbus *(G-6543)*
Advanced Marking Systems Inc....G....330 792-8239
Youngstown *(G-20837)*
Advantage Printing Inc....G....614 272-8259
Columbus *(G-6546)*
Aero Printing Inc....G....419 695-2931
Delphos *(G-8735)*
Affordable Bus Support LLC....G....440 543-5547
Chagrin Falls *(G-3036)*
AGS Custom Graphics Inc....D....330 963-7770
Macedonia *(G-12275)*
Akron Litho-Print Company Inc....F....330 434-3145
Akron *(G-43)*
Akron Thermography Inc....E....330 896-9712
Akron *(G-54)*
Albert Bramkamp Printing Co....G....513 641-1069
Cincinnati *(G-3318)*
▲ Alberts Screen Print Inc....C....330 753-7559
Norton *(G-15360)*
All American Screen Printing....G....419 475-0696
Toledo *(G-18162)*
All Print Ltd....F....440 349-6868
Solon *(G-17101)*
All Systems Colour Inc....G....937 859-9701
Dayton *(G-8016)*
Allegra Print & Imaging....F....419 427-8095
Findlay *(G-9649)*
Allegra Printing & Imaging LLC....G....440 449-6989
Westlake *(G-20090)*
Allen Graphics Inc....G....440 349-4100
Solon *(G-17102)*
Allen Kenard Printing Inc....F....440 323-7405
Elyria *(G-9213)*
Allen Press....G....614 891-4413
Westerville *(G-20033)*
Alliance Printing & Publishing....F....513 422-7611
Middletown *(G-13883)*
Alliance Publishing Co Inc....C....330 453-1304
Alliance *(G-454)*
AlphaGraphics 507 Inc....G....440 878-9700
Strongsville *(G-17708)*
Alt Control Print....G....419 841-2467
Toledo *(G-18168)*
Alvito Custom Imprints....G....614 846-8986
Worthington *(G-20676)*
American Printing Inc....F....330 630-1121
Akron *(G-64)*
Anderson Graphics Inc....E....330 745-2165
Barberton *(G-1052)*
Anderson Printing & Supply LLC....G....614 891-1100
Westerville *(G-20034)*
Angel Prtg & Reproduction Co....F....216 631-5225
Cleveland *(G-4714)*
▼ Angstrom Graphics Inc....C....216 271-5300
Cleveland *(G-4716)*
Angstrom Graphics Inc Midwest....B....216 271-5300
Cleveland *(G-4717)*
◆ Angstrom Graphics Southeast....G....216 271-5300
Cleveland *(G-4718)*
Ann Printing & Promotions....G....330 399-6564
Warren *(G-19371)*
Anthony Business Forms Inc....F....937 253-0072
Dayton *(G-7971)*
Arch Parent Inc....A....440 701-7420
Mentor *(G-13392)*
Arens Corporation....E....937 473-2028
Covington *(G-7781)*
Arens Corporation....G....937 473-2028
Covington *(G-7782)*
Armstrong S Printing Ex LLC....G....937 276-7794
Dayton *(G-8037)*
Arnold Printing Inc....G....330 494-1191
Canton *(G-2576)*
Art Printing Co Inc....G....419 281-4371
Ashland *(G-677)*
Art Pro Graphics....G....216 236-6465
Seven Hills *(G-16901)*
Atkinson Printing Inc....G....330 669-3515
Wooster *(G-20566)*
Avon Lake Printing....G....440 933-2078
Avon Lake *(G-979)*
Avondale Printing Inc....G....330 477-1180
Canton *(G-2579)*

S I C

Employee Codes: A=Over 500 employees, B=251-500
C=101-250, D=51-100, E=20-50, F=10-19, G=3-9
2019 Harris Ohio
Industrial Directory
857

B & B Printing Graphics Inc..........F....... 419 893-7068
Maumee *(G-13076)*
B2 Incorporated..........G....... 330 244-9510
North Canton *(G-15071)*
Baise Enterprises Inc..........G....... 614 444-3171
Columbus *(G-6642)*
Bang Printing of Ohio Inc..........F....... 800 678-1222
Kent *(G-11298)*
Bansal Enterprises Inc..........F....... 330 633-9355
Akron *(G-79)*
Barberton Magic Press Printing..........G....... 330 753-9578
Barberton *(G-1062)*
Barberton Printcraft..........G....... 330 848-3000
Barberton *(G-1064)*
Barnhart Printing Corp..........F....... 330 456-2279
Canton *(G-2585)*
Baseline Printing Inc..........G....... 330 369-3204
Warren *(G-19374)*
Bates Printing Inc..........F....... 330 833-5830
Massillon *(G-12962)*
Bay Business Forms Inc..........F....... 937 322-3000
Springfield *(G-17367)*
BCT Alarm Services Inc..........G....... 440 669-8153
Amherst *(G-554)*
Beach Company..........F....... 740 622-0905
Coshocton *(G-7722)*
Beckman Xmo..........F....... 614 864-2232
Columbus *(G-6658)*
Belle Printing..........G....... 937 592-5161
Bellefontaine *(G-1506)*
Bemis Company Inc..........E....... 330 923-5281
Akron *(G-83)*
Berea Printing Company..........G....... 440 243-1080
Berea *(G-1594)*
Bethart Enterprises Inc..........F....... 513 863-6161
Hamilton *(G-10540)*
Bethart Enterprises Inc..........G....... 513 777-8707
West Chester *(G-19660)*
Betley Printing Co..........G....... 216 206-5600
Cleveland *(G-4810)*
Bill Wyatt Inc..........G....... 330 535-1113
Mentor *(G-13403)*
Bindery & Spc Pressworks Inc..........D....... 614 873-4623
Plain City *(G-16178)*
Bizzy Bee Printing Inc..........G....... 614 771-1222
Columbus *(G-6672)*
Black River Group Inc..........D....... 419 524-6699
Mansfield *(G-12411)*
Bloch Printing Company..........G....... 330 576-6760
Copley *(G-7678)*
Blooms Printing Inc..........F....... 740 922-1765
Dennison *(G-8782)*
Blt Inc..........F....... 513 631-5050
Norwood *(G-15424)*
Blue Crescent Enterprises Inc..........G....... 440 878-9700
Strongsville *(G-17720)*
Blue Streak Services Inc..........G....... 216 223-3282
Cleveland *(G-4825)*
Blueserv Reprograhics LLC..........G....... 937 426-6410
Beavercreek *(G-1351)*
Bock & Pierce Enterprises..........G....... 513 474-9500
Cincinnati *(G-3398)*
Bodnar Printing Co Inc..........F....... 440 277-8295
Lorain *(G-12080)*
Boehr Print..........G....... 419 358-1350
Findlay *(G-9659)*
Bohlender Engraving Company..........F....... 513 621-4095
Cincinnati *(G-3400)*
Boldman Printing LLC..........G....... 937 653-3431
Urbana *(G-18980)*
◆ Bookmasters Inc..........C....... 419 281-1802
Ashland *(G-686)*
Bornhorst Printing Company Inc..........G....... 419 738-5901
Wapakoneta *(G-19325)*
Bpm Realty Inc..........E....... 614 221-6811
Columbus *(G-6692)*
Bramkamp Printing Company Inc..........E....... 513 241-1865
Blue Ash *(G-1740)*
Brandon Screen Printing..........F....... 419 229-9837
Lima *(G-11845)*
Brass Bull 1 LLC..........G....... 740 335-8030
Wshngtn CT Hs *(G-20720)*
Brent Carter Enterprises Inc..........G....... 513 731-1440
Cincinnati *(G-3411)*
Brentwood Printing & Sty..........G....... 513 522-2679
Cincinnati *(G-3412)*
Bricolage Inc..........F....... 614 853-6789
Grove City *(G-10418)*
Brooke Printers Inc..........G....... 614 235-6800
Lancaster *(G-11548)*
Brookville Star..........G....... 937 833-2545
Brookville *(G-2163)*
Brothers Printing Co Inc..........F....... 216 621-6050
Cleveland *(G-4844)*
Brune Printing Co..........G....... 419 399-2756
Paulding *(G-15858)*
Buckeye Business Forms Inc..........G....... 614 882-1890
Westerville *(G-19982)*
Buckeye Cstm Screen Print EMB..........F....... 614 237-0196
Columbus *(G-6709)*
Bucyrus Graphics Inc..........F....... 419 562-2906
Bucyrus *(G-2319)*
Busson Digital Printing Inc..........E....... 330 753-8373
Wadsworth *(G-19228)*
C Massouh Printing Co Inc..........F....... 330 408-7330
Canal Fulton *(G-2478)*
C Massouh Printing Co Inc..........G....... 330 832-6334
Massillon *(G-12964)*
Canton Graphic Arts Service..........G....... 330 456-9868
Canton *(G-2611)*
Capehart Enterprises LLC..........F....... 614 769-7746
Columbus *(G-6730)*
Capitol Square Printing Inc..........G....... 614 221-2850
Columbus *(G-6736)*
Capozzolo Printers Inc..........G....... 513 542-7874
Cincinnati *(G-3440)*
Carbonless On Demandcom..........F....... 330 837-8611
Massillon *(G-12967)*
Cardinal Printing Inc..........G....... 330 773-7300
Akron *(G-103)*
Carriage House Printery LLC..........G....... 740 243-7493
Carroll *(G-2900)*
Cats Printing Inc..........G....... 216 381-8181
Cleveland *(G-4892)*
Central Ohio Printing Corp..........D....... 740 852-1616
London *(G-12052)*
Century Graphics Inc..........E....... 614 895-7698
Westerville *(G-19983)*
▼ Century Marketing Corporation..........C....... 419 354-2591
Bowling Green *(G-1961)*
Characters Inc..........G....... 937 335-1976
Troy *(G-18640)*
Charger Press Inc..........F....... 513 542-3113
Miamitown *(G-13745)*
Child Evngelism Fellowship Inc..........E....... 440 218-4982
Cuyahoga Falls *(G-7849)*
Child Evngelism Fellowship Inc..........E....... 419 756-7799
Ontario *(G-15538)*
Cincinnati Print Solutions LLC..........G....... 513 943-9500
Amelia *(G-534)*
Cincinnati Printers Co Inc..........F....... 513 860-9053
West Chester *(G-19674)*
City of Cleveland..........F....... 216 664-3013
Cleveland *(G-4930)*
City Printing Co Inc..........E....... 330 747-5691
Youngstown *(G-20874)*
Clark Associates Inc..........G....... 419 334-3838
Fremont *(G-10008)*
Cleveland Letter Service Inc..........E....... 216 781-8300
Chagrin Falls *(G-3013)*
Clints Printing Inc..........G....... 937 426-2771
Beavercreek *(G-1354)*
Cnb LLC..........G....... 419 528-3109
Ontario *(G-15539)*
Cns Inc..........G....... 513 631-7073
Cincinnati *(G-3533)*
Cold Duck Screen Prtg & EMB Co..........G....... 330 426-1900
East Palestine *(G-9071)*
Color Bar Printing Centers Inc..........E....... 216 595-3939
Cleveland *(G-4997)*
Color Process Inc..........E....... 440 268-7100
Strongsville *(G-17730)*
Coloramic Process Inc..........F....... 440 275-1199
Austinburg *(G-919)*
Commercial Prtg of Greenvill..........G....... 937 548-3835
Greenville *(G-10365)*
Concept Printing of Wauseon..........G....... 419 335-6627
Wauseon *(G-19512)*
▲ Consoldated Graphics Group Inc..........C....... 216 881-9191
Cleveland *(G-5015)*
Copley Ohio Newspapers Inc..........C....... 330 364-5577
New Philadelphia *(G-14765)*
Copley Ohio Newspapers Inc..........D....... 330 833-2631
Massillon *(G-12969)*
Copy Cats Printing LLC..........G....... 440 345-5966
Cleveland *(G-5030)*
Copy Right of Ohio LLC..........G....... 614 431-1303
Plain City *(G-16182)*
Cornerstone Industries Lcc..........G....... 513 871-4546
West Chester *(G-19685)*
Cornerstone Printing Inc..........G....... 614 861-2138
Reynoldsburg *(G-16433)*
Corporate Dcment Solutions Inc..........F....... 513 595-8200
Cincinnati *(G-3552)*
COS Blueprint Inc..........F....... 330 376-0022
Akron *(G-122)*
County Classifieds..........G....... 937 592-8847
Bellefontaine *(G-1510)*
Covap Inc..........F....... 513 793-1855
Blue Ash *(G-1753)*
Cowgill Printing Co..........G....... 216 741-2076
Parma *(G-15815)*
Cox Printing Co..........G....... 937 382-2312
Wilmington *(G-20491)*
Cpmm Services Group Inc..........F....... 614 447-0165
Columbus *(G-6834)*
Crabar/Gbf Inc..........E....... 419 269-1720
Toledo *(G-18242)*
Crabar/Gbf Inc..........D....... 419 943-2141
Leipsic *(G-11723)*
Crabar/Gbf Inc..........E....... 740 622-0222
Coshocton *(G-7730)*
Crabar/Gbf Inc..........F....... 419 943-2141
Leipsic *(G-11724)*
Crain-Tharp Printing Inc..........G....... 740 345-9823
Newark *(G-14866)*
Creative Impressions Inc..........F....... 937 435-5296
Dayton *(G-8112)*
Crest Craft Company..........F....... 513 271-4858
Blue Ash *(G-1754)*
Crest Graphics Inc..........F....... 513 271-2200
Blue Ash *(G-1755)*
Crown Printing Inc..........G....... 740 477-2511
Circleville *(G-4541)*
Culaine Inc..........G....... 419 345-4984
Toledo *(G-18244)*
Curless Printing Company..........E....... 937 783-2403
Blanchester *(G-1702)*
Curv Imaging LLC..........G....... 614 890-2878
Westerville *(G-20044)*
Custom Graphics Inc..........C....... 330 963-7770
Macedonia *(G-12287)*
Custom Imprint..........F....... 440 238-4488
Strongsville *(G-17734)*
Customer Printing Inc..........F....... 330 629-8676
Youngstown *(G-20884)*
Customer Service Systems Inc..........G....... 330 677-2877
Kent *(G-11308)*
Cwh Graphics LLC..........G....... 866 241-8515
Bedford Heights *(G-1468)*
D M J F Inc..........G....... 440 845-1155
Cleveland *(G-5057)*
Daily Gazette..........E....... 937 372-4444
Xenia *(G-20764)*
▲ Dana Graphics Inc..........G....... 513 351-4400
Cincinnati *(G-3575)*
Danner Press Corp..........G....... 330 454-5692
Canton *(G-2647)*
Dansizen Printing Co Inc..........G....... 330 966-4962
North Canton *(G-15077)*
Daubenmires Printing..........G....... 513 425-7223
Middletown *(G-13899)*
David A and Mary A Mathis..........G....... 330 837-8611
Massillon *(G-12973)*
David Butler Tax Service..........G....... 419 626-8086
Sandusky *(G-16803)*
DC Reprographics Co..........G....... 614 297-1200
Columbus *(G-6854)*
Debandale Printing Inc..........G....... 330 725-5122
Medina *(G-13251)*
Deerfield Ventures Inc..........G....... 614 875-0688
Grove City *(G-10425)*
Delores E OBeirn..........G....... 440 582-3610
Cleveland *(G-5082)*
Delphos Herald Inc..........D....... 419 695-0015
Delphos *(G-8738)*
Delphos Herald Inc..........D....... 419 695-0015
Delphos *(G-8739)*
Deshea Printing Company..........G....... 330 336-7601
Wadsworth *(G-19234)*
Dewitt Group Inc..........F....... 614 847-5919
Columbus *(G-6862)*
Digital Color Intl LLC..........E....... 330 762-6959
Akron *(G-143)*
Directconnectgroup Ltd..........A....... 216 281-2866
Cleveland *(G-5097)*
Dispatch Printing Company..........E....... 614 885-6020
Columbus *(G-6868)*
Distributor Graphics Inc..........G....... 440 260-0024
Cleveland *(G-5099)*

27 PRINTING, PUBLISHING, AND ALLIED INDUSTRIES

Dixie Flyer & Printing Co .... G 937 687-0088
  New Lebanon (G-14709)
Dla Document Services .... G 216 522-3535
  Cleveland (G-5101)
Dla Document Services .... E 937 257-6014
  Dayton (G-7978)
Docmann Printing & Assoc Inc .... G 440 975-1775
  Solon (G-17133)
Doll Inc .... G 419 586-7880
  Celina (G-2957)
Domicone Printing Inc .... G 937 878-3080
  Fairborn (G-9457)
Donnelley Financial LLC .... F 216 621-8384
  Cleveland (G-5108)
Dorothy Crooker .... G 513 385-0888
  Cincinnati (G-3602)
Double b Printing LLC .... G 740 593-7393
  Athens (G-829)
Doug Smith .... G 740 345-1398
  Newark (G-14868)
DOV Graphics Inc .... E 513 241-5150
  Cincinnati (G-3605)
Dove Graphics Inc .... G 440 238-1800
  Cleveland (G-5110)
Downtown Print Shop .... G 419 242-9164
  Toledo (G-18268)
Dresden Specialties Inc .... G 740 452-7100
  Zanesville (G-21131)
Dresden Specialties Inc .... G 740 754-2451
  Dresden (G-8868)
Dsk Imaging LLC .... F 513 554-1797
  Blue Ash (G-1759)
Duke Graphics Inc .... E 440 946-0606
  Willoughby (G-20310)
Duncan Press Corporation .... E 330 477-4529
  Canton (G-2664)
Dupli-Systems Inc .... C 440 234-9415
  Strongsville (G-17738)
Durbin Minuteman Press .... G 513 791-9171
  Blue Ash (G-1760)
◆ Dynamic Design & Systems Inc .... G 440 708-1010
  Chagrin Falls (G-3044)
E Bee Printing Inc .... G 614 224-0416
  Columbus (G-6879)
E T & K Inc .... G 440 777-7375
  North Olmsted (G-15186)
E T & K Inc .... G 440 888-4780
  Cleveland (G-5131)
Eagle Advertising .... G 216 881-0800
  Cleveland (G-5134)
Eagle Printing & Graphics LLC .... G 937 773-7900
  Piqua (G-16113)
Earl D Arnold Printing Company .... E 513 533-6900
  Cincinnati (G-3624)
Easterdays Printing Center .... G 330 726-1182
  Youngstown (G-20895)
▲ Echographics Inc .... G 440 846-2330
  North Ridgeville (G-15222)
Edwards Electrical & Mech .... E 614 485-2003
  Columbus (G-6885)
Eg Enterprise Services Inc .... F 216 431-3300
  Cleveland (G-5158)
Elyria Copy Center Inc .... G 440 323-4145
  Elyria (G-9251)
Emta Inc .... G 440 734-6464
  North Olmsted (G-15187)
Engler Printing Co .... G 419 332-2181
  Fremont (G-10013)
Enlarging Arts Inc .... G 330 434-3433
  Akron (G-156)
Ennis Inc .... E 800 537-8648
  Toledo (G-18282)
Enquirer Printing Co Inc .... F 513 241-1956
  Cincinnati (G-3642)
Enquirer Printing Company .... G 513 241-1956
  Cincinnati (G-3643)
Envoi Design Inc .... G 513 651-4229
  Cincinnati (G-3645)
▲ Etched Metal Company .... E 440 248-0240
  Solon (G-17142)
Eugene Stewart .... G 937 898-1117
  Dayton (G-8189)
▲ Eurostampa North America Inc .... D 513 821-2275
  Cincinnati (G-3656)
Eveready Printing Inc .... E 216 587-2389
  Cleveland (G-5200)
Evolution Crtive Solutions Inc .... G 513 681-4450
  Cincinnati (G-3659)
Excelsior Printing Co .... G 740 927-2934
  Pataskala (G-15831)

Exchange Printing Company .... G 330 773-7842
  Akron (G-161)
Express Graphic Prtg & Design .... G 513 728-3344
  Cincinnati (G-3666)
F P C Printing Inc .... G 937 743-8136
  Franklin (G-9881)
Fair Publishing House Inc .... F 419 668-3746
  Norwalk (G-15394)
Fairchild Printing Co .... G 216 641-4192
  Cleveland (G-5214)
Fedex Corporation .... G 740 687-0334
  Lancaster (G-11572)
Fedex Office & Print Svcs Inc .... F 330 376-6002
  Akron (G-167)
Fedex Office & Print Svcs Inc .... E 419 866-5464
  Toledo (G-18290)
Feld Printing Co .... G 513 271-6806
  Cincinnati (G-3682)
Fine Line Graphics Inc .... G 330 920-6096
  Akron (G-170)
▲ Fine Line Graphics Corp .... C 614 486-0276
  Columbus (G-6923)
Fine Print LLC .... G 419 702-7087
  Lakeside Marblehead (G-11502)
Finn Graphics Inc .... E 513 941-6161
  Cincinnati (G-3690)
Fleet Graphics Inc .... G 937 252-2552
  Dayton (G-8198)
Flowers Print Inc .... G 937 429-3823
  Beavercreek (G-1315)
Folks Creative Printers Inc .... E 740 383-6326
  Marion (G-12702)
Follow Print Club On Facebook .... G 216 707-2579
  Cleveland (G-5258)
Foote Printing Company Inc .... F 216 431-1757
  Cleveland (G-5260)
Fortec Litho Central LLC .... G 330 463-1265
  Hudson (G-11044)
Fourjays Inc .... G 216 741-8258
  Parma (G-15819)
Frame Warehouse .... G 614 861-4582
  Reynoldsburg (G-16440)
Frank J Prucha & Associates .... G 216 642-3838
  Cleveland (G-5272)
Frankies Graphics Inc .... G 440 979-0824
  Westlake (G-9605)
Franklins Printing Company .... F 740 452-6375
  Zanesville (G-21138)
Freeport Press Inc .... G 330 308-3300
  New Philadelphia (G-14770)
Fremont Quick Print .... G 419 334-8808
  Helena (G-10771)
Friends Service Co Inc .... G 800 427-1704
  Dayton (G-8208)
Friends Service Co Inc .... G 800 427-1704
  Kent (G-11322)
Friends Service Co Inc .... E 419 427-1704
  Findlay (G-9690)
Frisby Printing Company .... G 330 665-4565
  Fairlawn (G-9605)
▲ Fun-In-Games Inc .... G 866 587-1004
  Mason (G-12874)
Fx Digital Media Inc .... E 216 241-4040
  Cleveland (G-5283)
G A Spring Advertising .... G 330 343-9030
  Dover (G-8827)
G S Link & Associates .... G 513 722-2457
  Goshen (G-10287)
▲ Galaxy Balloons Incorporated ...... C 216 476-3360
  Cleveland (G-5287)
Galley Printing Inc .... G 330 220-5577
  Brunswick (G-2208)
Ganger Enterprises Inc .... G 614 776-3985
  Westerville (G-19993)
Gannett Co Inc .... C 740 773-2111
  Chillicothe (G-3188)
Gannett Stllite Info Ntwrk LLC .... D 419 334-1012
  Fremont (G-10021)
Gaspar Services LLC .... G 330 467-8292
  Macedonia (G-12299)
Gazette Publishing Company .... C 419 483-4190
  Oberlin (G-15495)
Gb Liquidating Company Inc .... G 513 248-7600
  Milford (G-14010)
GBS Corp .... C 330 863-1828
  Malvern (G-12391)
Genesis Quality Printing Inc .... G 440 975-5700
  Mentor (G-13457)
Genie Repros Inc .... E 216 965-0213
  Cleveland (G-5315)

Gerald L Hermann Co Inc .... F 513 661-1818
  Cincinnati (G-3750)
Gergel-Kellem Company Inc .... D 216 398-2000
  Cleveland (G-5318)
Geygan Enterprises Inc .... F 513 932-4222
  Lebanon (G-11656)
Globus Printing & Packg Co Inc .... D 419 628-2381
  Minster (G-14216)
Golden Graphics Ltd .... F 419 673-6260
  Kenton (G-11406)
▲ Golf Marketing Group Inc .... G 330 963-5155
  Twinsburg (G-18788)
Good Impressions LLC .... G 740 392-4327
  Mount Vernon (G-14482)
Gordon Bernard Company LLC .... E 513 248-7600
  Milford (G-14013)
Gordons Graphics Inc .... G 330 863-2322
  Malvern (G-12392)
Grant John .... G 937 298-0633
  Dayton (G-8234)
Graphic Expressions Signs .... G 330 422-7446
  Streetsboro (G-17676)
Graphic Paper Products Corp .... D 937 325-5503
  Springfield (G-17407)
Graphic Print Solutions Inc .... G 513 948-3344
  Cincinnati (G-3777)
Graphic Solutions Company .... F 513 484-3067
  Cincinnati (G-3778)
Graphic Touch Inc .... G 330 337-3341
  Salem (G-16744)
Graphicsource Inc .... G 440 248-9200
  Solon (G-17154)
Graphix Network .... G 740 941-3771
  Waverly (G-19547)
Graphtech Communications Inc .... F 216 676-1020
  Cleveland (G-5342)
Great Lakes Engraving Corp .... G 419 867-1607
  Maumee (G-13113)
▲ Great Lakes Integrated Inc .... D 216 651-1500
  Cleveland (G-5347)
Great Lakes Lithograph .... F 216 651-1500
  Cleveland (G-5348)
Great Lakes Printing Inc .... D 440 993-8781
  Ashtabula (G-779)
Green Leaf Printing and Design .... G 937 222-3634
  Dayton (G-8236)
Greenwood Printing & Graphics .... F 419 727-3275
  Toledo (G-18312)
Greg Blume .... G 740 574-2308
  Wheelersburg (G-20182)
Gregg Macmillan .... G 513 248-2121
  Milford (G-14014)
Gtlp Holdings LLC .... E 513 489-6700
  Cincinnati (G-3788)
H & An LLC .... G 740 435-0200
  Cambridge (G-2442)
▲ Haines & Company Inc .... C 330 494-9111
  North Canton (G-15090)
▲ Haman Enterprises Inc .... F 614 888-7574
  Worthington (G-20689)
Harper Engraving & Printing Co .... D 614 276-0700
  Columbus (G-6982)
Harris Hawk .... G 800 459-4295
  Mason (G-12885)
Hartco Printing Company .... G 614 761-1292
  Dublin (G-8921)
Hartman Printing Co .... G 419 946-2854
  Mount Gilead (G-14425)
Hartmann Incorporated .... F 513 276-7318
  Blue Ash (G-1785)
Hawks & Associates Inc .... E 513 752-4311
  Cincinnati (G-3254)
Headlee Enterprises Ltd .... G 614 785-0011
  Columbus (G-6496)
Hecks Direct Mail & Prtg Svc .... E 419 661-6028
  Toledo (G-18328)
▲ Hecks Direct Mail & Prtg Svc .... E 419 697-3505
  Toledo (G-18327)
Hedges Printing Co .... G 740 422-8500
  Lancaster (G-11579)
Heitkamp & Kremer Printing .... G 419 925-4121
  Celina (G-2967)
Henry Bussman .... G 614 224-0417
  Columbus (G-6988)
Herald Inc .... E 419 492-2133
  New Washington (G-14829)
Herff Jones LLC .... G 740 357-2160
  Lucasville (G-12264)
Heritage Press Inc .... E 419 289-9209
  Ashland (G-709)

Employee Codes: A=Over 500 employees, B=251-500
C=101-250, D=51-100, E=20-50, F=10-19, G=3-9

2019 Harris Ohio
Industrial Directory

Heskamp Printing Co Inc .... G 513 871-6770
Cincinnati *(G-3811)*
Hilleary-Whitaker Inc .... G 614 766-4694
Columbus *(G-7001)*
Hkm Drect Mkt Cmmnications Inc .... C 216 651-9500
Cleveland *(G-5412)*
Hollys Custom Print Inc .... E 740 928-2697
Hebron *(G-10748)*
Holmes Printing Solutions LLC .... G 330 234-9699
Fredericksburg *(G-9952)*
Holmes W & Sons Printing .... F 937 325-1509
Springfield *(G-17419)*
Homewood Press Inc .... E 419 478-0695
Toledo *(G-18334)*
Horizon Ohio Publications Inc .... E 419 738-2128
Wapakoneta *(G-19332)*
Hoster Graphics Company Inc .... F 614 299-9770
Columbus *(G-7009)*
HOT Graphic Services Inc .... E 419 242-7000
Northwood *(G-15339)*
Howland Printing Inc .... G 330 637-8255
Cortland *(G-7710)*
Hubbard Company .... E 419 784-4455
Defiance *(G-8627)*
Hubbard Publishing Co .... E 937 592-3060
Bellefontaine *(G-1518)*
Hudson Printing of Medina LLC .... G 330 591-4800
Medina *(G-13276)*
Hummingbird Graphics LLC .... G 216 595-8835
Warrensville Heights *(G-19470)*
Icandi Graphics LLC .... G 330 723-8337
Medina *(G-13277)*
Ideas & Ad Ventures Inc .... G 513 542-7154
Cincinnati *(G-3835)*
Image Concepts Inc .... F 216 524-9000
Cleveland *(G-5437)*
Image Print Inc .... G 614 776-3985
Westerville *(G-19997)*
Image Print Inc .... G 614 430-8470
Columbus *(G-7021)*
◆ **In-Touch Corp** .... G 440 268-0881
Cleveland *(G-5447)*
Info-Graphics Inc .... G 440 498-1640
Solon *(G-17169)*
Ink Inc .... G 330 875-4789
Louisville *(G-12157)*
Ink It Press .... G 440 967-9062
Vermilion *(G-19162)*
Ink Well .... G 614 861-7113
Gahanna *(G-10084)*
Innomark Communications LLC .... E 937 454-5555
Miamisburg *(G-13679)*
Inskeep Brothers Inc .... F 614 898-6620
Columbus *(G-7028)*
Insley Printing Inc .... G 614 885-5973
Worthington *(G-20692)*
Insta-Print Inc .... G 216 741-6500
Cleveland *(G-5461)*
Instant Replay .... G 937 592-0534
Bellefontaine *(G-1520)*
Integrity Print Solutions Inc .... G 330 818-0161
Akron *(G-216)*
International Cntr Artfcial or .... G 440 358-1102
Painesville *(G-15749)*
Irwin Engraving & Printing Co .... G 216 391-7300
Cleveland *(G-5477)*
It XCEL Consulting LLC .... F 513 847-8261
West Chester *(G-19728)*
J & J Bechke Inc .... G 440 238-1441
Strongsville *(G-17756)*
J & K Printing .... G 330 456-5306
Canton *(G-2713)*
J & L Management Corporation .... G 440 205-1199
Mentor *(G-13479)*
J & P Investments Inc .... F 513 821-2299
Cincinnati *(G-3861)*
J D B Partners Inc .... G 513 874-3056
Fairfield *(G-9513)*
J P Quality Printing Inc .... G 216 791-6303
Cleveland *(G-5485)*
J&B Postal and Print Svcs LLC .... G 740 363-7653
Delaware *(G-8698)*
▲ **Jack Walker Printing Co** .... F 440 352-4222
Mentor *(G-13483)*
Jakprints Inc .... C 877 246-3132
Willowick *(G-20479)*
Jarman Printing Company LLC .... G 330 823-8585
Alliance *(G-479)*
Jaymac Systems Inc .... G 440 498-0810
Solon *(G-17174)*
Jeffrey Reedy .... G 614 794-9292
Westerville *(G-20060)*
Jk Digital Publishing LLC .... E 937 299-0185
Springboro *(G-17331)*
JM Printing .... G 740 412-8666
Circleville *(G-4547)*
Joe The Printer Guy LLC .... G 216 651-3880
Lakewood *(G-11523)*
John Kolesar and Sons Inc .... G 216 221-7117
Cleveland *(G-5501)*
John S Swift Company Inc .... F 513 721-4147
Cincinnati *(G-3880)*
Johnson Printing .... G 740 922-4821
Uhrichsville *(G-18889)*
Jones Printing Services Inc .... G 440 946-7300
Eastlake *(G-9116)*
Joseph Berning Printing Co .... F 513 721-0781
Cincinnati *(G-3883)*
JPS Print .... G 614 235-8947
Columbus *(G-7078)*
Jt Premier Printing Corp .... G 216 831-8785
Cleveland *(G-5509)*
K B Printing .... G 614 771-1222
Columbus *(G-7081)*
Kad Holdings Inc .... G 614 792-3399
Dublin *(G-8935)*
Kahny Printing Inc .... E 513 251-2911
Cincinnati *(G-3893)*
Kay Toledo Tag Inc .... D 419 729-5479
Toledo *(G-18363)*
Kee Printing Inc .... G 937 456-6851
Eaton *(G-9156)*
Keener Printing Inc .... F 216 531-7595
Cleveland *(G-5523)*
▲ **Kehl-Kolor Inc** .... E 419 281-3107
Ashland *(G-717)*
Kehoe Brothers Printing Inc .... G 216 351-4100
Cleveland *(G-5524)*
Keithley Enterprises Inc .... G 937 890-1878
Dayton *(G-8290)*
Kelly Prints LLC .... G 440 356-6361
North Olmsted *(G-15194)*
Kem Advertising and Prtg LLC .... G 330 818-5061
Barberton *(G-1080)*
Kendall & Sons Company .... G 937 222-6996
Dayton *(G-8292)*
Kennedy Graphics Inc .... G 419 223-9825
Lima *(G-11883)*
Kennedy Mint Inc .... D 440 572-3222
Cleveland *(G-5528)*
Kenwel Printers Inc .... E 614 261-1011
Columbus *(G-7088)*
Kever Incorporated .... G 614 552-9000
Columbus *(G-7091)*
Kevin K Tidd .... G 419 885-5603
Sylvania *(G-17948)*
Key Maneuvers Inc .... F 440 285-0774
Chardon *(G-3119)*
Key Press Inc .... G 513 721-1203
Cincinnati *(G-3907)*
Keystone Press Inc .... G 419 243-7326
Toledo *(G-18367)*
Keystone Printing & Copy Cat .... G 740 354-6542
Portsmouth *(G-16286)*
Keystone Printing Co .... G 330 385-9519
East Liverpool *(G-9065)*
Kimpton Printing & Spc Co .... F 330 467-1640
Macedonia *(G-12310)*
Klingstedt Brothers Company .... F 330 456-8319
Canton *(G-2726)*
KMS 2000 Inc .... F 330 454-9444
Canton *(G-2727)*
Knowles Press Inc .... G 330 877-9345
Hartville *(G-10699)*
Knox County Printing Co .... G 740 848-4032
Galion *(G-10147)*
Kovacevic Printing Inc .... G 440 887-1000
Cleveland *(G-5542)*
Kuwatch Printing LLC .... G 513 759-5850
Liberty Twp *(G-11827)*
L & H Printing .... G 937 855-4512
Germantown *(G-10243)*
L & T Collins Inc .... G 740 345-4494
Newark *(G-14892)*
L B L Lithographers Inc .... F 440 350-0106
Painesville *(G-15755)*
Lake Erie Graphics Inc .... E 216 575-1333
Brookpark *(G-2151)*
Lakota Printing Inc .... G 513 755-3666
West Chester *(G-19734)*
Lamar Proforma .... G 440 285-2277
Chardon *(G-3122)*
Landen Desktop Pubg Ctr Inc .... G 513 683-5181
Loveland *(G-12209)*
Lanz Printing Co Inc .... G 614 221-1724
Columbus *(G-7115)*
Laser Images Inc .... G 419 668-8348
Norwalk *(G-15403)*
Lasting First Impressions Inc .... F 513 870-6900
West Chester *(G-19872)*
Lasting Impression Direct .... G 216 464-1960
Beachwood *(G-1245)*
Laurenee Ltd LLC .... G 513 662-2225
Cincinnati *(G-3934)*
Lee Corporation .... G 513 771-3602
Cincinnati *(G-3937)*
Legal News Publishing Co .... E 216 696-3322
Cleveland *(G-5572)*
Legalcraft Inc .... F 330 494-1261
Canton *(G-2732)*
Letter Shop .... G 937 981-3117
Greenfield *(G-10354)*
Letterman Printing Inc .... G 513 523-1111
Oxford *(G-15696)*
Lilienthal Southeastern Inc .... F 740 439-1640
Cambridge *(G-2446)*
Liming Printing Inc .... F 937 374-2646
Xenia *(G-20782)*
Lindsey Graphics Inc .... G 330 995-9241
Aurora *(G-891)*
Lobo Awrds Screen Prtg Graphix .... G 740 972-9087
Marion *(G-12716)*
Lorain Printing Company .... E 440 288-6000
Lorain *(G-12103)*
Loris Printing Inc .... G 419 626-6648
Sandusky *(G-16823)*
Lsc Communications Inc .... A 419 935-0111
Willard *(G-20241)*
Lund Printing Co .... G 330 628-4047
Akron *(G-262)*
Lyle Printing & Publishing Co .... E 330 337-3419
Salem *(G-16756)*
M D M Graphics Inc .... G 859 816-7375
Cincinnati *(G-3962)*
M-Fischer Enterprises LLC .... G 419 782-5309
Defiance *(G-8634)*
Mabar Printing Service .... G 419 257-3659
North Baltimore *(G-15045)*
Mac Printing Company .... G 937 393-1101
Hillsboro *(G-10884)*
Mackland Co Inc .... G 330 399-5034
Warren *(G-19419)*
Mansfield Journal Co .... G 330 364-8641
New Philadelphia *(G-14782)*
Marbee Inc .... G 419 422-9441
Findlay *(G-9722)*
Marco Printed Products Co .... E 937 433-7030
Dayton *(G-8332)*
Marco Printed Products Co Inc .... G 937 433-5680
Dayton *(G-8333)*
Margaret Trentman .... G 513 948-1700
Cincinnati *(G-3980)*
Mariotti Printing Co LLC .... G 440 245-4120
Lorain *(G-12104)*
Mark Advertising Agency Inc .... F 419 626-9000
Sandusky *(G-16827)*
Mark-N-Mend Inc .... G 440 951-2003
Willoughby *(G-20370)*
Martin Printing Co .... G 419 224-9176
Lima *(G-11897)*
Martys Print Shop .... G 740 373-3454
Marietta *(G-12644)*
Marysville Printing Company .... G 937 644-4959
Marysville *(G-12800)*
◆ **Mass-Marketing Inc** .... C 513 860-6200
Fairfield *(G-9523)*
Master Printing Company .... E 216 351-2246
Cleveland *(G-5633)*
Mathews Printing Company .... F 614 444-1010
Columbus *(G-7158)*
Maumee Quick Print Inc .... G 419 893-4321
Maumee *(G-13131)*
Maximum Graphix Inc .... G 440 353-3301
North Ridgeville *(G-15240)*
Mc Vay Ventures Inc .... G 614 890-1516
Westerville *(G-20064)*
McMath & Sheets Unlimited Inc .... G 216 381-0010
Cleveland *(G-5646)*
◆ **McNerney & Associates LLC** .... E 513 241-9951
Cincinnati *(G-3989)*

SIC SECTION
27 PRINTING, PUBLISHING, AND ALLIED INDUSTRIES

Mercer Color Corporation ....G ....419 678-8273 Coldwater *(G-6417)*
Meridian Arts and Graphics ....F ....330 759-9099 Youngstown *(G-20969)*
Messenger Publishing Company ....C ....740 592-6612 Athens *(G-839)*
Metzgers ....E ....419 861-8611 Toledo *(G-18409)*
Miami Valley Press Inc ....G ....937 547-0771 Greenville *(G-10381)*
Michael R Kelly ....G ....614 491-1745 Obetz *(G-15511)*
Middaugh Enterprises Inc ....F ....330 852-2471 Sugarcreek *(G-17852)*
Middaugh Printers ....G ....330 852-2471 Dover *(G-8841)*
Middleton Printing Co Inc ....G ....614 294-7277 Gahanna *(G-10090)*
Mike B Crawford ....G ....330 673-7944 Kent *(G-11355)*
Milford Printers ....E ....513 831-6630 Milford *(G-14027)*
Milford Printers ....G ....513 831-6630 Milford *(G-14028)*
Milo Bennett Corp ....G ....419 874-1492 Perrysburg *(G-15977)*
Minuteman Press ....G ....440 946-3311 Mentor *(G-13521)*
Minuteman Press ....G ....419 782-8002 Defiance *(G-8639)*
Minuteman Press ....G ....513 772-0500 Cincinnati *(G-4031)*
Minuteman Press ....G ....614 337-2334 Columbus *(G-7185)*
Minuteman Press ....G ....937 429-8610 Beavercreek *(G-1332)*
Minuteman Press ....G ....330 725-4121 Medina *(G-13302)*
Minuteman Press Inc ....G ....513 741-9056 Cincinnati *(G-4032)*
Minuteman Press of Athens LLC ....G ....740 593-7393 Athens *(G-841)*
Minuteman Press of Elyria ....G ....440 365-9377 Elyria *(G-9296)*
Minutman Press Frfeld Cnty LLC ....G ....740 689-1992 Lancaster *(G-11589)*
Mizer Printing & Graphics ....G ....740 942-3343 Cadiz *(G-2400)*
Mmp Printing Inc ....E ....513 381-0990 Cincinnati *(G-4035)*
Mmp Toledo ....F ....419 472-0505 Toledo *(G-18412)*
Montview Corporation ....G ....330 723-3409 Medina *(G-13304)*
Morse Enterprises Inc ....G ....513 229-3600 Mason *(G-12912)*
Mp Printing & Design Inc ....G ....740 456-2045 Portsmouth *(G-16292)*
Muir Graphics Inc ....F ....419 882-7993 Sylvania *(G-17953)*
Mullin Print Solutions ....G ....216 383-2901 Euclid *(G-9428)*
Multi-Color Australia LLC ....B ....513 381-1480 Batavia *(G-1170)*
Multi-Craft Litho Inc ....E ....859 581-2754 Blue Ash *(G-1824)*
Murr Corporation ....F ....330 264-2223 Wooster *(G-20630)*
Mustang Printing ....F ....419 592-2746 Napoleon *(G-14551)*
Nari Inc ....G ....440 960-2280 Monroeville *(G-14289)*
National Bank Note Company ....G ....216 281-7792 Cleveland *(G-5721)*
Nelis Printing Co ....G ....330 757-4114 Youngstown *(G-20974)*
Network Printing & Graphics ....F ....614 230-2084 Columbus *(G-7214)*
Newfax Corporation ....F ....419 241-5157 Toledo *(G-18423)*
Newfax Corporation ....F ....419 893-4557 Toledo *(G-18424)*
Newhouse & Faulkner Inc ....G ....513 721-1660 Cincinnati *(G-4073)*
Newmast Mktg & Communications ....E ....614 837-1200 Columbus *(G-7217)*
News Gazette Printing Company ....F ....419 227-2527 Lima *(G-11911)*
Newspaper Holding Inc ....D ....440 998-2323 Ashtabula *(G-792)*
Newton Falls Printing ....G ....330 872-3532 Newton Falls *(G-14990)*
Nickum Enterprises Inc ....G ....513 561-2292 Cincinnati *(G-4077)*
Nomis Publications Inc ....F ....330 965-2380 Youngstown *(G-20976)*
North Coast Litho Inc ....E ....216 881-1952 Cleveland *(G-5767)*
North Toledo Graphics LLC ....D ....419 476-8808 Toledo *(G-18427)*
Northcoast Pmm LLC ....F ....419 540-8667 Toledo *(G-18428)*
Northeast Blueprint & Sup Co ....G ....216 261-7500 Cleveland *(G-5773)*
Northern Ohio Printing Inc ....E ....216 398-0000 Cleveland *(G-5781)*
Northwest Print Inc ....G ....419 385-3375 Perrysburg *(G-15982)*
Nova Creative Group Inc ....F ....937 291-8653 Dayton *(G-8388)*
◆ **Novelty Advertising Co Inc** ....E ....740 622-3113 Coshocton *(G-7745)*
Nta Graphics Inc ....C ....419 476-8808 Toledo *(G-18431)*
O Connor Office Pdts & Prtg ....G ....740 852-2209 London *(G-12066)*
▲ **Oak Printing Company** ....E ....440 238-3316 Strongsville *(G-17774)*
Odyssey Press Inc ....F ....614 410-0356 Huron *(G-11107)*
Office Print N Copy ....G ....740 695-3616 Saint Clairsville *(G-16642)*
Ogden Newspapers Inc ....C ....330 841-1600 Warren *(G-19426)*
▲ **Ohio Art Company** ....D ....419 636-3141 Bryan *(G-2301)*
Old Trail Printing Company ....C ....614 443-4852 Columbus *(G-7269)*
Oliver Printing & Packg Co LLC ....D ....330 425-7890 Twinsburg *(G-18823)*
Olmsted Printing Inc ....G ....440 234-2600 Berea *(G-1621)*
Omni Business Forms Inc ....G ....513 860-0111 West Chester *(G-19883)*
▼ **One-Write Company** ....E ....740 654-2128 Lancaster *(G-11594)*
Onetouchpoint East Corp ....D ....513 421-1600 Cincinnati *(G-4113)*
Optimum System Products Inc ....E ....614 885-4464 Westerville *(G-20069)*
Oregon Village Print Shoppe ....F ....937 222-9418 Dayton *(G-8407)*
Orrville Printing Co Inc ....G ....330 682-5066 Orrville *(G-15608)*
Orwell Printing ....G ....440 285-2233 Chardon *(G-3131)*
Oscar Hicks ....G ....937 435-4350 Dayton *(G-8409)*
Our Nine LLC ....G ....614 844-6655 Columbus *(G-7280)*
Page One Group ....G ....740 397-4240 Mount Vernon *(G-14499)*
Painesville Publishing Co ....G ....440 354-4142 Austinburg *(G-924)*
Painted Hill Inv Group Inc ....F ....937 339-1756 Troy *(G-18691)*
Papworth Prints ....G ....614 428-6137 Columbus *(G-7292)*
Paragon Press ....G ....513 281-9911 Cincinnati *(G-4133)*
▲ **Paragraphics Inc** ....E ....330 493-1074 Canton *(G-2778)*
Patio Printing Inc ....G ....614 785-9553 Columbus *(G-7295)*
Patterson-Britton Printing ....G ....216 781-7997 Cleveland *(G-5855)*
Paul Stipkovich ....G ....330 499-7391 North Canton *(G-15110)*
Paul/Jay Associates ....G ....740 676-8776 Bellaire *(G-1488)*
◆ **Paxar Corporation** ....E ....845 398-3229 Mentor *(G-13544)*
Paxar Corporation ....F ....937 681-4541 Dayton *(G-8418)*
PDQ Printing Service ....F ....216 241-5443 Cleveland *(G-5858)*
Peck Engraving Co ....E ....216 221-1556 Cleveland *(G-5860)*
Peerless Printing Company ....F ....513 721-4657 Cincinnati *(G-4145)*
Penguin Enterprises Inc ....E ....440 899-5112 Westlake *(G-20140)*
Penny Printing Inc ....G ....330 645-2955 Coventry Township *(G-7778)*
Performa La Mar Printing Inc ....G ....440 632-9800 Middlefield *(G-13845)*
Perrons Printing Company ....E ....440 236-8870 Columbia Station *(G-6442)*
Phil Vedda & Sons Inc ....G ....216 671-2222 Cleveland *(G-5870)*
Pinnacle Press Inc ....F ....330 453-7060 Canton *(G-2785)*
PIP and Huds LLC ....G ....740 208-5519 Gallipolis *(G-10173)*
PIP Enterprises LLC ....G ....740 373-5276 Marietta *(G-12654)*
PIP Printing ....G ....440 951-2606 Willoughby *(G-20401)*
Plain Dealer Publishing Co ....A ....216 999-5000 Cleveland *(G-5883)*
PM Graphics Inc ....E ....330 650-0861 Streetsboro *(G-17689)*
Pooles Printing & Office Svcs ....G ....419 475-9000 Toledo *(G-18474)*
Porath Business Services Inc ....F ....216 626-0060 Cleveland *(G-5896)*
Post Printing Co ....D ....859 254-7714 Minster *(G-14222)*
POv Print Communication Inc ....G ....440 591-5443 Chagrin Falls *(G-3068)*
Power Management Inc ....E ....937 222-2909 Dayton *(G-8430)*
Preferred Printing ....G ....937 492-6961 Sidney *(G-17062)*
Preisser Inc ....E ....614 345-0199 Columbus *(G-7344)*
Premier Printing and Packg Inc ....G ....937 436-5290 Dayton *(G-8436)*
Premier Printing Corporation ....F ....216 478-9720 Cleveland *(G-5917)*
Premier Printing Solutions ....G ....740 374-2836 Marietta *(G-12658)*
Press For Less Printing Firm I ....G ....931 912-4606 Lebanon *(G-11686)*
Pressmark Inc ....G ....740 373-6005 Marietta *(G-12659)*
Priesman Printery ....G ....419 898-2526 Oak Harbor *(G-15447)*
Prime Printing Inc ....E ....937 438-3707 Dayton *(G-8442)*
Print All Inc ....G ....419 534-2880 Toledo *(G-18484)*
Print Craft Inc ....G ....513 931-6828 Cincinnati *(G-4191)*
▼ **Print Direct For Less 2 Inc** ....E ....440 236-8870 Columbia Station *(G-6444)*
Print Factory Pll ....G ....330 549-9640 North Lima *(G-15176)*
Print Management Partners Inc ....E ....330 650-5300 Twinsburg *(G-18839)*
▲ **Print Marketing Inc** ....E ....330 625-1500 Homerville *(G-10986)*
Print Masters Ltd ....G ....740 450-2885 Zanesville *(G-21173)*
Print Shop Design and Print ....G ....440 232-2391 Bedford *(G-1438)*
Print Shop of Canton Inc ....G ....330 497-3212 Canton *(G-2792)*
Print Solutions Today LLC ....G ....614 848-4500 Westerville *(G-20071)*
Print Syndicate Inc ....G ....614 657-8318 Columbus *(G-7348)*
Print Syndicate LLC ....F ....614 519-0341 Columbus *(G-7349)*
Print Zone ....G ....513 733-0067 West Chester *(G-19889)*
Print-Digital Incorporated ....G ....330 686-5945 Stow *(G-17621)*
Printcraft Inc ....G ....440 599-8903 Conneaut *(G-7657)*
Printed Image ....F ....614 221-1412 Columbus *(G-7350)*
Printers Devil Inc ....F ....330 650-1218 Hudson *(G-11068)*
▲ **Printers Edge Inc** ....F ....330 372-2232 Warren *(G-19434)*
Printers Emergency Service LLC ....G ....513 421-7799 Cincinnati *(G-4193)*
Printex Incorporated ....G ....740 947-8800 Waverly *(G-19559)*

S I C

Employee Codes: A=Over 500 employees, B=251-500 C=101-250, D=51-100, E=20-50, F=10-19, G=3-9
2019 Harris Ohio Industrial Directory
861

27 PRINTING, PUBLISHING, AND ALLIED INDUSTRIES SIC SECTION

Printex Incorporated......F 740 773-0088
Chillicothe *(G-3217)*

Printing Arts Press......F 740 397-6106
Mount Vernon *(G-14502)*

Printing Center of Xenia......G 937 372-1687
Xenia *(G-20786)*

Printing Connection Inc......G 216 898-4878
Brookpark *(G-2154)*

Printing Express......G 937 276-7794
Moraine *(G-14383)*

Printing Express Inc......G 740 532-7003
Ironton *(G-11171)*

Printing For Less......G 937 743-8268
Springboro *(G-17345)*

Printing Service Company......D 937 425-6100
Miamisburg *(G-13705)*

Printing Services......E 440 708-1999
Chagrin Falls *(G-3070)*

Printing System Inc......F 330 375-9128
Akron *(G-331)*

Printpoint Printing Inc......G 937 223-9041
Dayton *(G-8443)*

Printprod Inc......F 937 228-2181
Toledo *(G-18485)*

Printzone......G 513 733-0067
Cincinnati *(G-4194)*

Pro Companies Inc......G 614 738-1222
Pickerington *(G-16057)*

Pro Printing Inc......G 614 276-8366
Columbus *(G-7351)*

Pro-Decal Inc......G 330 484-0089
Canton *(G-2793)*

Professional Screen Printing......G 740 687-0760
Lancaster *(G-11600)*

Profile Digital Printing LLC......E 937 866-4241
Dayton *(G-8448)*

Proforma Print & Imaging......G 216 520-8400
Dublin *(G-8969)*

Progressive Communications......D 740 397-5333
Mount Vernon *(G-14503)*

Progressive Printers Inc......D 937 222-1267
Dayton *(G-8450)*

Proimage Printing & Design LLC......G 937 312-9544
Xenia *(G-20787)*

Promatch Solutions LLC......F 937 299-0185
Springboro *(G-17346)*

Province of St John The Baptis......D 513 241-5615
Cincinnati *(G-4219)*

Q C Printing......G 419 475-4266
Toledo *(G-18489)*

Quad/Graphics Inc......A 513 932-1064
Lebanon *(G-11687)*

Quality Publishing Co......F 513 863-8210
Hamilton *(G-10600)*

Quebecor World Johnson Hardin......A 614 326-0299
Cincinnati *(G-4233)*

Queen City Reprographics......C 513 326-2300
Cincinnati *(G-4240)*

Quez Media Marketing Inc......F 216 910-0202
Independence *(G-11149)*

Quick As A Wink Printing Co......F 419 224-9786
Lima *(G-11926)*

▼ Quick Tab II Inc......D 419 448-6622
Tiffin *(G-18076)*

Quick Tech Graphics Inc......E 937 743-5952
Springboro *(G-17348)*

R & J Bardon Inc......G 614 457-5500
Columbus *(G-7370)*

R & J Printing Enterprises Inc......F 330 343-1242
Dover *(G-8847)*

R & W Printing Company......G 513 575-0131
Loveland *(G-12224)*

R Design & Printing Co......G 614 299-1420
Columbus *(G-7374)*

R R Donnelley & Sons Company......D 330 562-5250
Streetsboro *(G-17690)*

R R Donnelley & Sons Company......E 440 774-2101
Oberlin *(G-15504)*

▲ R S C Sales Company......E 423 581-4916
Dayton *(G-8460)*

R S Imprints......F 330 872-5905
Newton Falls *(G-14992)*

R W Michael Printing Co......G 330 923-9277
Akron *(G-340)*

R&D Marketing Group Inc......G 216 398-9100
Brooklyn Heights *(G-2130)*

Randd Assoc Prtg & Promotions......G 937 294-1874
Dayton *(G-8464)*

Rba Inc......G 330 336-6700
Wadsworth *(G-19273)*

Red Vette Printing Company......G 740 364-1766
Granville *(G-10337)*

Renco Printing Inc......G 216 267-5585
Cleveland *(G-5973)*

▲ Repro Acquisition Company LLC......E 216 738-3800
Cleveland *(G-5977)*

Resilient Holdings Inc......F 614 847-5600
Columbus *(G-7387)*

Reynolds and Reynolds Company......F 419 584-7000
Celina *(G-2983)*

Rhoads Printing Center Inc......G 330 678-2042
Kent *(G-11375)*

Ricci Anthony......G 330 758-5761
Youngstown *(G-21015)*

▲ Richardson Printing Corp......D 740 373-5362
Marietta *(G-12663)*

Rl Smith Graphics LLC......G 330 629-8616
Youngstown *(G-21016)*

Robert Becker Impressions Inc......F 419 385-5303
Toledo *(G-18504)*

Robert H Shackelford......G 330 364-2221
New Philadelphia *(G-14799)*

Roberts Graphic Center......G 330 788-4642
Youngstown *(G-21019)*

Robin Enterprises Company......C 614 891-0250
Westerville *(G-20073)*

Robs Creative Screen Printing......G 740 264-6383
Wintersville *(G-20541)*

Rohrer Corporation......C 440 542-3100
Solon *(G-17225)*

Rotary Forms Press Inc......E 937 393-3426
Hillsboro *(G-10890)*

RPI Color Service Inc......D 513 471-4040
Cincinnati *(G-4285)*

Ruda Print & Graphics......G 419 331-7832
Lima *(G-11934)*

Rutobo Inc......G 614 236-2948
Columbus *(G-7408)*

Ryans Newark Leader Ex Prtg......F 740 522-2149
Newark *(G-14916)*

S & S Printing Service Inc......G 937 228-9411
Dayton *(G-8490)*

S and K Painting......G 330 505-1910
Niles *(G-15036)*

S Beckman Print & G......E 614 864-2232
Columbus *(G-7410)*

S F C Ltd LLC......G 419 255-1283
Toledo *(G-18509)*

S O S Graphics & Printing Inc......G 614 846-8229
Worthington *(G-20702)*

Sandusky Newspapers Inc......C 419 625-5500
Sandusky *(G-16845)*

Sandy Smittcamp......G 937 372-1687
Xenia *(G-20788)*

Sanscan Inc......G 330 332-9365
Salem *(G-16773)*

Saturn Press Inc......G 440 232-3344
Bedford *(G-1444)*

Schiffer Group Inc......G 937 694-8185
Troy *(G-18703)*

Schilling Graphics Inc......E 419 468-1037
Galion *(G-10154)*

Schlabach Printing Ltd......E 330 852-4687
Sugarcreek *(G-17863)*

Schuerholz Printing Inc......G 937 294-5218
Dayton *(G-8496)*

Scorecards Unlimited LLC......G 614 885-0796
Columbus *(G-7432)*

Scratch Off Works......G 440 333-4302
Rocky River *(G-16556)*

▼ Scrip-Safe Security Products......E 513 697-7789
Loveland *(G-12230)*

Sdg News Group Inc......F 419 929-3411
New London *(G-14737)*

Seemless Design & Printing LLC......G 513 871-2366
Cincinnati *(G-4315)*

Seifert Printing Company......G 330 759-7414
Youngstown *(G-21027)*

Selby Service/Roxy Press Inc......G 513 241-3445
Cincinnati *(G-4318)*

▲ Sensical Inc......D 216 641-1141
Solon *(G-17229)*

Sentry Graphics Inc......G 440 735-0850
Northfield *(G-15324)*

Serv All Graphics LLC......G 513 681-8883
Blue Ash *(G-1846)*

Sfc Graphics Cleveland Ltd......E 419 255-1283
Toledo *(G-18520)*

Shallow Lake Corp......G 614 883-6350
Lewis Center *(G-11779)*

Sharon Printing Co Inc......G 330 239-1684
Sharon Center *(G-16953)*

Sharp Enterprises Inc......F 937 295-2965
Fort Loramie *(G-9806)*

▲ Shawnee Systems Inc......D 513 561-9932
Cincinnati *(G-4330)*

Shelby Printing Partners LLC......E 419 342-3171
Shelby *(G-16989)*

Ship Print E Sell......G 614 459-1205
Columbus *(G-7446)*

Shreve Printing LLC......F 330 567-2341
Shreve *(G-17010)*

Sidney Printing Works Inc......G 513 542-4000
Cincinnati *(G-4333)*

Sitler Printer Inc......G 330 482-4463
Columbiana *(G-6480)*

Six-3......G 614 260-5610
Columbus *(G-7456)*

Sjpm Inc......G 614 475-4571
Gahanna *(G-10104)*

Skladany Enterprises Inc......G 614 823-6883
Westerville *(G-20023)*

Slimans Printery Inc......F 330 454-9141
Canton *(G-2818)*

Slutzkers Quickprint Center......G 440 244-0330
Lorain *(G-12123)*

Snow Printing Co Inc......F 419 229-7669
Lima *(G-11941)*

Soondook LLC......E 614 389-5757
Columbus *(G-7463)*

◆ Source3media Inc......E 330 467-9003
Macedonia *(G-12326)*

Sourcelink Ohio LLC......C 937 885-8000
Miamisburg *(G-13718)*

South End Printing Co......G 216 341-0669
Cleveland *(G-6081)*

Southeast Publications Inc......F 740 732-2341
Caldwell *(G-2412)*

SP Mount Printing Company......E 216 881-3316
Cleveland *(G-6082)*

SPAOS Inc......F 937 890-0783
Dayton *(G-8515)*

Specialty Lithographing Co......F 513 621-0222
Cincinnati *(G-4357)*

Specialty Printing LLC......G 937 335-4046
Troy *(G-18709)*

Spectrum Image LLC......G 614 954-0102
Columbus *(G-7473)*

Spencer-Walker Press Inc......F 740 344-6110
Newark *(G-14920)*

Sportsartcom......G 330 903-0895
Copley *(G-7697)*

Springdot Inc......D 513 542-4000
Cincinnati *(G-4365)*

Sprint Print Inc......G 740 622-4429
Coshocton *(G-7752)*

Sro Prints LLC......G 865 604-0420
Cincinnati *(G-4366)*

Stapins Qick Cpy/Print Ctr LLC......G 330 296-0123
Ravenna *(G-16410)*

Star Calendar & Printing Co......G 216 741-3223
Cleveland *(G-6095)*

Star Printing Company Inc......E 330 376-0514
Akron *(G-386)*

Starr Printing Services Inc......G 513 241-7708
Cincinnati *(G-4375)*

Start Printing......G 513 424-2121
Middletown *(G-13954)*

Stationery Shop Inc......G 330 376-2033
Akron *(G-387)*

Stein-Palmer Printing Co......G 740 633-3894
Saint Clairsville *(G-16653)*

Stephen Andrews Inc......G 330 725-2672
Lodi *(G-12020)*

Stepping Stone Enterprises Inc......F 419 472-0505
Toledo *(G-18529)*

Stevenson Color Inc......C 513 321-7500
Cincinnati *(G-4381)*

Stick-It Graphics LLC......G 330 407-0142
New Philadelphia *(G-14801)*

Streichers Enterprises Inc......G 419 423-8606
Findlay *(G-9764)*

Suburban Press Inc......E 216 961-0766
Cleveland *(G-6114)*

Summit Printing & Graphics......G 330 645-7644
Akron *(G-391)*

Sun Art Decals Inc......G 440 234-9045
Berea *(G-1626)*

Superior Impressions Inc......G 419 244-8676
Toledo *(G-18535)*

Superprinter Inc....G....440 277-0787
Lorain (G-12125)
Superprinter Ltd....G....440 277-0787
Lorain (G-12126)
Swimmer Printing Inc....G....216 623-1005
Cleveland (G-6138)
Syndicate Printers Inc....G....513 779-3625
West Chester (G-19804)
T & K Heins Corporation....G....740 452-6006
Zanesville (G-21184)
T D Dynamics Inc....F....216 881-0800
Cleveland (G-6143)
T H E B Inc....G....216 391-4800
Cleveland (G-6145)
Target Printing & Graphics....G....937 228-0170
Dayton (G-8539)
Taylor Communications Inc....G....614 351-6868
Columbus (G-7515)
Taylor Communications Inc....E....937 221-1000
Dayton (G-8543)
Taylor Communications Inc....G....937 228-5800
Dayton (G-8545)
Taylor Quick Print....G....740 439-2208
Cambridge (G-2458)
▼ Tce International Ltd....F....800 962-2376
Perry (G-15914)
Tcp Inc....G....330 836-4239
Fairlawn (G-9622)
Technoprint Inc....F....614 899-1403
Westerville (G-20077)
Tecnocap LLC....D....330 392-7222
Warren (G-19446)
The Gazette Printing Co Inc....G....440 593-6030
Conneaut (G-7660)
Timely Tours Inc....G....419 734-3751
Port Clinton (G-16263)
Tj Metzgers Inc....D....419 861-8611
Toledo (G-18553)
TL Krieg Offset Inc....E....513 542-1522
Cincinnati (G-4424)
Toledo Ticket Company....E....419 476-5424
Toledo (G-18573)
Tomahawk Printing Inc....F....419 335-3161
Wauseon (G-19533)
Tomahawk Printing LLC....F....419 335-3161
Wauseon (G-19534)
Tope Printing Inc....G....330 674-4993
Millersburg (G-14137)
Tradewinds Prin Twear....G....740 214-5005
Roseville (G-16580)
◆ Transfer Express Inc....D....440 918-1900
Mentor (G-13613)
Traxium LLC....E....330 572-8200
Stow (G-17637)
Traxler Printing....G....614 593-1270
Columbus (G-7541)
◆ Trebnick Systems Inc....E....937 743-1550
Springboro (G-17358)
Tri-State Publishing Company....E....740 283-3686
Steubenville (G-17556)
Tribune Printing Inc....G....419 542-7764
Hicksville (G-10785)
True Dinero Records & Tech LLC....G....513 428-4610
Cincinnati (G-4443)
Ultimate Printing Co Inc....G....330 847-2941
Warren (G-19454)
Ultra Impressions Inc....G....440 951-4777
Mentor (G-13617)
Ultra Printing & Design Inc....G....440 887-0393
Cleveland (G-6228)
United Prtrs & Lithographers....G....216 771-2759
Cleveland (G-6235)
University of Cincinnati....G....513 556-5042
Cincinnati (G-4454)
USA Quickprint Inc....E....330 455-5119
Canton (G-2854)
V & C Enterprises Co....G....614 221-1412
Columbus (G-7568)
V I P Printing & Design....G....513 777-7468
West Chester (G-19913)
Valley Graphics....G....330 652-0484
Niles (G-15038)
Variety Printing....G....216 676-9815
Brookpark (G-2157)
Victory Direct LLC....G....614 626-0000
Gahanna (G-10110)
Vision Graphics....G....330 665-4451
Copley (G-7698)
Vision Graphix Inc....G....440 835-6540
Westlake (G-20169)
Visual Art Graphic Services....E....330 274-2775
Mantua (G-12562)
Vpp Industries Inc....F....937 526-3775
Versailles (G-19192)
Vya Inc....E....513 772-5400
Cincinnati (G-4485)
W B Mason Co Inc....E....888 926-2766
Cleveland (G-6277)
W C Sims Co Inc....G....937 325-7035
Springfield (G-17514)
W/S Packaging Group Inc....F....740 929-2210
Heath (G-10734)
Walter Graphics Inc....G....419 522-5261
Mansfield (G-12536)
Warren Printing & Off Pdts Inc....F....419 523-3635
Ottawa (G-15671)
Wasserstrom Company....F....614 228-2233
Columbus (G-7592)
Watkins Printing Company....E....614 297-8270
Columbus (G-7593)
Weekly Villager Inc....G....330 527-5761
Garrettsville (G-10204)
Welch Publishing Co....E....419 874-2528
Perrysburg (G-16025)
West Bend Printing & Pubg Inc....G....419 258-2000
Antwerp (G-600)
▲ West-Camp Press Inc....D....614 882-2378
Westerville (G-20082)
West-Camp Press Inc....E....614 895-0233
Columbus (G-7600)
Western Ohio Graphics....F....937 335-8769
Troy (G-18719)
Western Reserve Graphics....G....440 729-9527
Chesterland (G-3172)
Westrock Commercial LLC....F....419 476-9101
Toledo (G-18598)
▲ Wfsr Holdings LLC....A....877 735-4966
Dayton (G-8592)
Whiskey Fox Corporation....F....440 779-6767
Berea (G-1632)
Wholesale Printers Ltd....G....440 354-5788
Painesville (G-15799)
William J Bergen & Co....G....440 248-6132
Solon (G-17261)
William J Dupps....G....419 734-2126
Port Clinton (G-16264)
Williams Executive Entps Inc....G....440 887-1000
Cleveland (G-6310)
Wilson Prtg Graphics of London....G....740 852-5934
London (G-12072)
Wirick Press Inc....G....330 273-3488
Brunswick (G-2252)
Woodrow Manufacturing Co....E....937 399-9333
Springfield (G-17521)
X Press Printing Services Inc....F....440 951-8848
Willoughby (G-20461)
Xpress Print Inc....F....330 494-7246
Louisville (G-12172)
Yes Press Printing Co....G....330 535-8398
Akron (G-440)
Yespress Graphics LLC....G....614 899-1403
Westerville (G-20084)
Youngstown ARC Engraving Co....E....330 793-2471
Youngstown (G-21070)
Youngstown Letter Shop Inc....G....330 793-4935
Youngstown (G-21079)
Youngstown Pre-Press Inc....F....330 793-3690
Youngstown (G-21081)
Yuckon International Corp....G....216 361-2103
Cleveland (G-6334)
Zip Laser Systems Inc....G....740 286-6613
Jackson (G-11203)
Zippitycom Print LLC....F....216 438-0001
Cleveland (G-6344)

2754 Commercial Printing: Gravure

Admiral Products Company Inc....E....216 671-0600
Cleveland (G-4619)
▼ Angstrom Graphics Inc....C....216 271-5300
Cleveland (G-4716)
Anthony Business Forms Inc....F....937 253-0072
Dayton (G-7971)
Barberton Magic Press Printing....G....330 753-9578
Barberton (G-1062)
Business Fnctnality Forms Svcs....G....614 557-9420
Gahanna (G-10077)
Cham Cor Industries Inc....G....740 967-9015
Johnstown (G-11262)
Clipper Magazine LLC....G....937 534-0470
Moraine (G-14338)
Dulle Associates....G....513 723-9600
Cincinnati (G-3612)
Dupli-Systems Inc....C....440 234-9415
Strongsville (G-17738)
E-Z Stop Service Center....D....330 448-2236
Brookfield (G-2105)
Fx Digital Media Inc....E....216 241-4040
Cleveland (G-5282)
Graphic Paper Products Corp....D....937 325-5503
Springfield (G-17407)
Klingstedt Brothers Company....F....330 456-8319
Canton (G-2726)
▲ Label Print Technologies LLC....F....800 475-4030
Mogadore (G-14243)
Lloyd F Helber....E....740 756-9607
Carroll (G-2906)
M PI Label Systems....G....330 938-2134
Sebring (G-16888)
Miami Valley Press Inc....G....937 547-0771
Greenville (G-10381)
Mpi Labels of Baltimore Inc....F....330 938-2134
Sebring (G-16890)
Multi-Color Australia LLC....B....513 381-1480
Batavia (G-1170)
Multi-Color Corporation....D....513 943-0080
Batavia (G-1172)
Ohio Envelope Manufacturing Co....E....216 267-2920
Cleveland (G-5805)
▲ Ohio Gravure Technologies Inc....E....937 439-1582
Miamisburg (G-13703)
Quad/Graphics Inc....A....513 932-1064
Lebanon (G-11687)
R R Donnelley & Sons Company....G....740 376-9276
Marietta (G-12661)
Retterbush Graphic and Packg....E....513 779-4466
West Chester (G-19780)
Revenue Management Group LLC....G....419 993-2200
Lima (G-11930)
▼ Scratch-Off Systems Inc....E....216 649-7800
Brecksville (G-2056)
▲ Shamrock Companies Inc....D....440 899-9510
Westlake (G-20158)
Taylor Communications Inc....G....866 541-0937
Dayton (G-8546)
Taylor Communications Inc....G....937 228-5800
Dayton (G-8545)
Toledo Tape and Label Company....G....419 536-8316
Toledo (G-18572)
Veritrack Inc....F....513 202-0790
Harrison (G-10678)
W L Beck Printing & Design....G....330 762-3020
Akron (G-430)
Western Roto Engravers Inc....E....330 336-7636
Wadsworth (G-19281)
▲ Wfsr Holdings LLC....A....877 735-4966
Dayton (G-8592)
Wilmer....G....419 678-6000
Coldwater (G-6424)

2759 Commercial Printing

3dlt LLC....F....513 452-3358
Cincinnati (G-3271)
4 Over LLC....F....937 610-0629
Dayton (G-7995)
4d Screenprinting Ltd....G....513 353-1070
Cleves (G-6353)
A C Hadley - Printing Inc....G....937 426-0952
Beavercreek (G-1296)
A E Wilson Holdings Inc....G....330 405-0316
Twinsburg (G-18722)
A Screen Printed Products....G....419 352-1535
Bowling Green (G-1943)
A Sign For The Times Inc....G....216 297-2977
Cleveland (G-4593)
A Special Touch Embroidery LLC....G....740 858-2241
Portsmouth (G-16276)
A To Z Paper Box Co....G....330 325-8722
Rootstown (G-16565)
A Z Printing Inc....G....513 745-0700
Cincinnati (G-3283)
A-A Blueprint Co Inc....E....330 794-8803
Akron (G-23)
Aardvark Screen Prtg & EMB LLC....F....419 354-6686
Bowling Green (G-1948)
Aardvark Sportswear Inc....G....330 793-9428
Youngstown (G-20832)
Abl Screen Printing....G....440 914-0093
Solon (G-17097)
Absolute Impressions Inc....F....614 840-0599
Lewis Center (G-11742)

SIC

Employee Codes: A=Over 500 employees, B=251-500
C=101-250, D=51-100, E=20-50, F=10-19, G=3-9
2019 Harris Ohio
Industrial Directory
863

Ace Transfer Company G 937 398-1103
Springfield *(G-17360)*
Acme Printing Co Inc G 419 626-4426
Sandusky *(G-16792)*
Adcraft Decals Inc E 216 524-2934
Cleveland *(G-4615)*
Admiral Products Company Inc E 216 671-0600
Cleveland *(G-4619)*
Advanced Incentives Inc G 419 471-9088
Toledo *(G-18157)*
▼ Advanced Specialty Products D 419 882-6528
Bowling Green *(G-1950)*
Adyl Inc G 330 797-8700
Austintown *(G-928)*
Aero Fulfillment Services Corp D 800 225-7145
Mason *(G-12820)*
Agnone-Kelly Enterprises Inc G 800 634-6503
Cincinnati *(G-3310)*
AGS Custom Graphics Inc D 330 963-7770
Macedonia *(G-12275)*
Akos Promotions Inc G 513 398-6324
Mason *(G-12822)*
Akron Litho-Print Company Inc F 330 434-3145
Akron *(G-43)*
▲ Alberts Screen Print Inc C 330 753-7559
Norton *(G-15360)*
Alfacomp Inc G 216 459-1790
Cleveland *(G-4659)*
Allied Silk Screen Inc G 937 223-4921
Dayton *(G-8020)*
Alpha Bus Forms & Prtg LLC G 419 999-5138
Lima *(G-11835)*
Alvin L Roepke F 419 862-3891
Elmore *(G-9203)*
Am Graphics G 330 799-7319
Youngstown *(G-20842)*
American Imprssions Sportswear G 614 848-6677
Worthington *(G-20677)*
Amerigraph Llc G 614 278-8000
Columbus *(G-6589)*
Ameriprint G 440 235-6094
Olmsted Falls *(G-15528)*
Amtech Inc G 440 238-2141
Strongsville *(G-17711)*
Anderson Graphics Inc E 330 745-2165
Barberton *(G-1052)*
Anthony Business Forms Inc F 937 253-0072
Dayton *(G-7971)*
Anthony-Lee Screen Prtg Inc F 419 683-1861
Crestline *(G-7793)*
Appleheart G 937 384-0430
Miamisburg *(G-13641)*
▲ Ares Sportswear Ltd D 614 767-1950
Hilliard *(G-10805)*
Art Brands LLC E 614 755-4278
Blacklick *(G-1677)*
Art Printing Co Inc G 419 281-4371
Ashland *(G-677)*
Art Tees Inc G 614 338-8337
Columbus *(G-6617)*
Ashton LLC F 614 833-4165
Pickerington *(G-16039)*
Associated Graphics Inc F 614 873-1273
Plain City *(G-16172)*
Assocted Vsual Cmmncations Inc E 330 452-4449
Canton *(G-2577)*
Atlas Printing and Embroidery G 440 882-3537
Cleveland *(G-4761)*
Austin Tape and Label Inc D 330 928-7999
Stow *(G-17570)*
Austintown Printing Inc G 330 797-0099
Youngstown *(G-20849)*
Axent Graphics LLC G 216 362-7560
Brookpark *(G-2137)*
Baise Enterprises Inc G 614 444-3171
Columbus *(G-6642)*
Bar Codes Unlimited Inc G 937 434-2633
Dayton *(G-8051)*
Barnhart Printing Corp F 330 456-2279
Canton *(G-2585)*
Basinger Inc G 614 771-8300
Columbus *(G-6654)*
Bates Printing Inc F 330 833-5830
Massillon *(G-12962)*
Bayard Inc F 937 293-1415
Moraine *(G-14332)*
Bemis Company Inc E 330 923-5281
Akron *(G-83)*
Benchmark Prints F 419 332-7640
Fremont *(G-9997)*
Berea Printing Company G 440 243-1080
Berea *(G-1594)*
Betley Printing Co G 216 206-5600
Cleveland *(G-4810)*
Better Living Concepts Inc F 330 494-2213
Canton *(G-2590)*
Big Kahuna Graphics LLC G 330 455-2625
Canton *(G-2591)*
Bindery & Spc Pressworks Inc D 614 873-4623
Plain City *(G-16178)*
Blue Ribbon Screen Graphics G 216 226-6200
Avon *(G-942)*
Bluelogos Inc F 614 898-9971
Westerville *(G-20038)*
Bob King Sign Company Inc G 330 753-2679
Akron *(G-90)*
Bob Smith G 513 242-7700
Blue Ash *(G-1738)*
Bock & Pierce Enterprises G 513 474-9500
Cincinnati *(G-3398)*
Boehm Inc E 614 875-9010
Grove City *(G-10417)*
Bohlender Engraving Company F 513 621-4095
Cincinnati *(G-3400)*
Boldman Printing LLC G 937 653-3431
Urbana *(G-18980)*
Bollin & Sons Inc E 419 693-6573
Toledo *(G-18210)*
Bookmyer LLP G 419 447-3883
Tiffin *(G-18051)*
▲ Bottomline Ink Corporation E 419 897-8000
Perrysburg *(G-15923)*
Bradleys Beacons Ltd G 419 447-7560
Tiffin *(G-18052)*
Brahler Inc G 330 966-7730
Canton *(G-2597)*
Brakers Publishing & Prtg Svc G 440 576-0136
Jefferson *(G-11225)*
Bramkamp Printing Company Inc E 513 241-1865
Blue Ash *(G-1740)*
Brass Bull 1 LLC G 740 335-8030
Wshngtn CT Hs *(G-20720)*
Broadway Printing LLC G 513 621-3429
Cincinnati *(G-3419)*
Brothers Printing Co Inc F 216 621-6050
Cleveland *(G-4844)*
Buckeye Cstm Screen Print EMB F 614 237-0196
Columbus *(G-6709)*
Bullseye Activewear Inc G 330 220-1720
Brunswick *(G-2193)*
Burns & Rink Enterprises LLC G 513 421-7799
Cincinnati *(G-3431)*
Bush Inc E 216 362-6700
Cleveland *(G-4854)*
C A I R Ohio G 513 281-8200
Blue Ash *(G-1743)*
C P S Enterprises Inc F 216 441-7969
Cleveland *(G-4858)*
Campbell Signs & Apparel LLC F 330 386-4768
East Liverpool *(G-9052)*
Canvas 123 Inc G 312 805-0563
Coventry Township *(G-7766)*
Cap City Direct LLC F 614 252-6245
Columbus *(G-6729)*
Carbonless & Cut Sheet Forms F 740 826-1700
New Concord *(G-14683)*
Carey Color Llc/Cincinnati G 513 241-5210
Cincinnati *(G-3442)*
Carnegie Promotions Inc G 440 442-2099
Cleveland *(G-4881)*
Carroll Exhibit and Print Svcs G 216 361-2325
Cleveland *(G-4884)*
▲ Casad Company Inc F 419 586-9457
Coldwater *(G-6404)*
Centennial Screen Printing G 419 422-5548
Findlay *(G-9665)*
Century Graphics Inc E 614 895-7698
Westerville *(G-19983)*
Century Marketing Corporation G 419 354-2591
Bowling Green *(G-1960)*
▼ Century Marketing Corporation C 419 354-2591
Bowling Green *(G-1961)*
Charles Huffman & Associates G 216 295-0850
Warrensville Heights *(G-19465)*
Cincinnati Convertors Inc F 513 731-6600
Cincinnati *(G-3487)*
Cincinnati Print Solutions LLC G 513 943-9500
Amelia *(G-534)*
Ckm Ventures LLC G 216 623-0370
Cleveland *(G-4935)*
Clear Images LLC F 419 241-9347
Toledo *(G-18233)*
Cleveland Copy & Prtg Svc LLC G 216 861-0324
Cleveland *(G-4953)*
▼ Cleveland Menu Printing Inc E 216 241-5256
Cleveland *(G-4967)*
Cleveland Printwear Inc G 216 521-5500
Cleveland *(G-4970)*
Cloverleaf Office Slutions LLC G 614 219-9050
Hilliard *(G-10817)*
Club 513 LLC G 800 530-2574
Cincinnati *(G-3531)*
▲ CMC Group Inc C 419 354-2591
Bowling Green *(G-1964)*
Cnr Marketing Ltd G 937 293-1030
Dayton *(G-8094)*
Cns Inc G 513 631-7073
Cincinnati *(G-3533)*
Cold Duck Screen Prtg & EMB Co G 330 426-1900
East Palestine *(G-9071)*
Collotype Labels Usa Inc D 513 381-1480
Batavia *(G-1132)*
▲ Coloring Book Solutions LLC F 419 281-9641
Ashland *(G-695)*
Columbus Humungous Apparel LLC G 614 824-2657
Columbus *(G-6791)*
Comdoc Inc G 330 899-8000
Columbus *(G-6805)*
Commercial Decal of Ohio Inc E 330 385-7178
East Liverpool *(G-9053)*
▲ Consoldated Graphics Group Inc C 216 881-9191
Cleveland *(G-5015)*
Consolidated Graphics Inc C 740 654-2112
Lancaster *(G-11556)*
Consolidated Web G 216 881-7816
Cleveland *(G-5018)*
Contemprary Image Labeling Inc G 513 583-5699
Lebanon *(G-11644)*
Copy Source Inc G 937 642-7140
Marysville *(G-12778)*
Cornerstone Industries Lcc G 513 871-4546
West Chester *(G-19685)*
Corporate Dcment Solutions Inc F 513 595-8200
Cincinnati *(G-3552)*
Corporate Supply LLC G 614 876-8400
Columbus *(G-6824)*
Coso Media LLC G 330 904-5889
Hudson *(G-11039)*
Cotton Pickin Tees & Caps G 419 636-3595
Bryan *(G-2277)*
Cox Printing Co G 937 382-2312
Wilmington *(G-20491)*
Crabar/Gbf Inc F 419 943-2141
Leipsic *(G-11724)*
Crabro Printing Inc G 740 533-3404
Ironton *(G-11163)*
Creative Documents Solutions G 740 389-4252
Marion *(G-12701)*
Creative Print Solutions LLC G 614 989-1747
Westerville *(G-20042)*
Culaine Inc G 419 345-4984
Toledo *(G-18244)*
Custom Apparel LLC G 330 633-2626
Akron *(G-127)*
▲ Custom Deco South Inc E 419 698-2900
Toledo *(G-18246)*
▲ Custom Products Corporation D 440 528-7100
Solon *(G-17129)*
Custom Screen Printing G 330 963-3131
Twinsburg *(G-18759)*
Custom Sportswear Imprints LLC G 330 335-8326
Wadsworth *(G-19231)*
Customer Service Systems Inc G 330 677-2877
Kent *(G-11308)*
D & J Printing Inc D 330 678-5868
Kent *(G-11309)*
D&D Design Concepts Inc F 513 752-2191
Batavia *(G-1135)*
▲ Dana Graphics Inc G 513 351-4400
Cincinnati *(G-3575)*
Danner Press Corp G 330 454-5692
Canton *(G-2647)*
Dayton Mailing Services Inc E 937 222-5056
Dayton *(G-8138)*
DCS Technologies Corporation E 937 743-4060
Franklin *(G-9879)*
Ddg Incorporated G 440 343-5060
Medina *(G-13250)*
Debandale Printing Inc G 330 725-5122
Medina *(G-13251)*

Company	Code	Phone
Dee Printing Inc, Columbus (G-6856)	F	614 777-8700
Dietrich Von Hildebrand Legacy, Steubenville (G-17530)	G	703 496-7821
Digital Graphics, Youngstown (G-20891)	G	330 707-1720
Digital Shorts Inc, Dayton (G-8161)	G	937 228-1700
Digital Visuals Inc, Middletown (G-13900)	G	513 420-9466
Diocesan Publications Inc Ohio, Dublin (G-8907)	E	614 718-9500
Direct Digital Graphics Inc, Twinsburg (G-18764)	G	330 405-3770
Divine Prtg T-Shirts & More, Toledo (G-18266)	G	419 241-8208
Domicone Printing Inc, Fairborn (G-9457)	G	937 878-3080
Dominion Labels & Forms, Defiance (G-8622)	G	419 784-1041
Doug Smith, Newark (G-14868)	G	740 345-1398
DOV Graphics Inc, Cincinnati (G-3605)	E	513 241-5150
Dresden Specialties Inc, Zanesville (G-21131)	G	740 452-7100
Dresden Specialties Inc, Dresden (G-8868)	G	740 754-2451
Drycal Inc, Mentor (G-13433)	G	440 974-1999
DSC Supply Company LLC, Westerville (G-20049)	G	614 891-1100
Dupli-Systems Inc, Strongsville (G-17738)	C	440 234-9415
Durbin Minuteman Press, Blue Ash (G-1760)	G	513 791-9171
Dyenamo Distributing, Galion (G-10133)	F	419 462-9474
◆ Dynamic Design & Systems Inc, Chagrin Falls (G-3044)	G	440 708-1010
E & E Nameplates Inc, Galion (G-10134)	F	419 468-3617
Eagle Image Inc, Cincinnati (G-3621)	F	513 662-3000
Earl D Arnold Printing Company, Cincinnati (G-3624)	E	513 533-6900
Eastern Graphic Arts, Loudonville (G-12141)	G	419 994-5815
Ebel-Binder Printing Co, Cincinnati (G-3628)	G	513 471-1067
▲ Echographics Inc, North Ridgeville (G-15222)	G	440 846-2330
Eci Macola/Max LLC, Dublin (G-8911)	C	978 539-6186
Electronic Imaging Svcs Inc, Lewis Center (G-11759)	G	740 549-2487
Emta Inc, North Olmsted (G-15187)	G	440 734-6464
Erd Specialty Graphics Inc, Toledo (G-18283)	G	419 242-9545
Everythings Image Inc, Blue Ash (G-1768)	F	513 469-6727
Evolution Crtive Solutions LLC, Cincinnati (G-3660)	E	513 681-4450
Exchange Printing Company, Akron (G-161)	G	330 773-7842
Expert TS, Wooster (G-20589)	G	330 263-4588
Exxcite Marketing Inc, Cincinnati (G-3667)	G	513 271-4550
F J Designs Inc, Wooster (G-20590)	G	330 264-1377
Fair Publishing House Inc, Norwalk (G-15394)	E	419 668-3746
Federal Barcode Label Systems, North Ridgeville (G-15224)	G	440 748-8060
Fedex Office & Print Svcs Inc, Westerville (G-20054)	E	614 898-0000
Fedex Office & Print Svcs Inc, Troy (G-18657)	F	937 335-3816
Fine Line Embroidery Company, Rocky River (G-16547)	G	440 331-7030
Firelands Fas-Print LLC, Norwalk (G-15395)	G	419 668-3045
First Impression Wear, Eaton (G-9149)	G	937 456-3900
First Stop Signs and Decals, New Philadelphia (G-14769)	G	330 343-1859
Five Star Graphics Inc, Girard (G-10259)	G	330 545-5077
Flex Pro Label Inc, Blue Ash (G-1775)	G	513 489-4417
Folks Creative Printers Inc, Marion (G-12702)	E	740 383-6326
Foote Printing Company Inc, Cleveland (G-5260)	F	216 431-1757
▲ Forward Movement Publications, Cincinnati (G-3707)	G	513 721-6659
Four Ambition, Dayton (G-8205)	G	937 239-4479
Freeport Press Inc, New Philadelphia (G-14771)	F	740 658-4000
Functional Imaging Ltd, Lancaster (G-11573)	G	740 689-2466
Future Screen Inc, Cleveland (G-5281)	G	440 838-5055
G Q Business Products, Blue Ash (G-1780)	G	513 792-4750
G2 Print Plus, Columbus (G-6943)	F	614 276-0500
Gail Berner, Springfield (G-17406)	G	937 322-0314
Gail Zeilmann, Cleveland (G-5286)	G	440 888-4858
Gb Liquidating Company Inc, Milford (G-14010)	E	513 248-7600
GBS Corp, Stow (G-17591)	E	330 929-8050
▲ GBS Corp, North Canton (G-15085)	G	330 494-5330
▲ GCI Digital Imaging Inc, Cincinnati (G-3730)	F	513 521-7446
▲ General Data Company Inc, Cincinnati (G-3252)	C	513 752-7978
General Theming Contrs LLC, Columbus (G-6945)	G	614 252-6342
Genesis Graphics, Troy (G-18661)	G	937 335-5332
Genesis Quality Printing Inc, Mentor (G-13457)	G	440 975-5700
Geygan Enterprises Inc, Lebanon (G-11656)	F	513 932-4222
Glauners Wholesale Inc, Cleveland (G-5323)	G	216 398-7088
Glavin Industries Inc, Solon (G-17149)	E	440 349-0049
Glen D Lala, Dayton (G-8224)	G	937 274-7770
Golden Graphics Ltd, Kenton (G-11406)	F	419 673-6260
Good JP, Ashland (G-706)	G	419 207-8484
Gordons Graphics Inc, Malvern (G-12392)	G	330 863-2322
Got Graphix Llc, Fairlawn (G-9606)	F	330 703-9047
Grace Imaging LLC, Perrysburg (G-15960)	G	419 874-2127
Grady McCauley Inc, North Canton (G-15089)	D	330 494-9444
▲ Grafisk Msknfabrik-America LLC, Lebanon (G-11659)	G	630 432-4370
Grant John, Dayton (G-8234)	G	937 298-0633
Graphic Info Systems Inc, Cincinnati (G-3776)	F	513 948-1300
Graphic Paper Products Corp, Springfield (G-17408)	G	937 325-3912
Graphic Plus, Chillicothe (G-3190)	G	740 701-1860
Graphic Stitch Inc, Marysville (G-12784)	G	937 642-6707
Graphic Touch Inc, Salem (G-16744)	G	330 337-3341
Graphics To Go LLC, Wilmington (G-20496)	G	937 382-4100
Graphix Junction, Hudson (G-11049)	G	234 284-8392
Great Lakes Printing Inc, Ashtabula (G-779)	D	440 993-8781
Green Willow Inc, Dayton (G-8238)	G	937 436-5290
Gym Pro LLC, Waterford (G-19485)	G	740 984-4143
H & H Screen Process Inc, Dayton (G-8240)	G	937 253-7520
▲ Haines & Company Inc, North Canton (G-15090)	C	330 494-9111
▲ Haman Enterprises Inc, Worthington (G-20689)	F	614 888-7574
Handcrafted Jewelry Inc, Hudson (G-11051)	G	330 650-9011
Harper Engraving & Printing Co, Columbus (G-6982)	D	614 276-0700
Hartman Distributing LLC, Heath (G-10719)	D	740 616-7764
Hawks & Associates Inc, Cincinnati (G-3254)	E	513 752-4311
Heartland Publications LLC, Miamisburg (G-13675)	F	860 664-1075
Heartland Publications LLC, Gallipolis (G-10167)	F	740 446-2342
▲ Hecks Direct Mail & Prtg Svc, Toledo (G-18327)	E	419 697-3505
Heskamp Printing Co Inc, Cincinnati (G-3811)	G	513 871-6770
Hilltop Printing, Defiance (G-8626)	G	419 782-9898
Hkm Drect Mkt Cmmnications Inc, Sheffield Village (G-16967)	E	440 934-3060
Hkm Drect Mkt Cmmnications Inc, Cleveland (G-5412)	C	216 651-9500
Hoffee John, Minerva (G-14183)	G	330 868-3553
Hollys Custom Print Inc, Hebron (G-10748)	E	740 928-2697
Holmes Prcut/Troyer Imprinting, Dundee (G-9019)	G	330 359-0000
Homestretch Inc, Wapakoneta (G-19331)	G	419 738-6604
Homestretch Sportswear Inc, Saint Henry (G-16663)	F	419 678-4282
Homewood Press Inc, Toledo (G-18334)	E	419 478-0695
▲ Hooven - Dayton Corp, Miamisburg (G-13677)	D	937 233-4473
Horizon Ohio Publications Inc, Wapakoneta (G-19332)	E	419 738-2128
Humtown Pattern Company, Columbiana (G-6470)	D	330 482-5555
Hyde Brothers Prtg & Mktg LLC, Marietta (G-12634)	G	740 373-2054
ID Images LLC, Fairfield (G-9509)	F	513 874-5325
Illusions Screenprinting, Wooster (G-20605)	G	330 263-7770
Imagemart Inc, Cleveland (G-5439)	G	216 486-4767
Imagine This Renovations, Navarre (G-14577)	G	330 833-6739
Impressions - A Print Shop, Cleveland (G-5446)	G	440 449-6966
Industrial Screen Process, Toledo (G-18346)	F	419 255-4900
Informa Media Inc, Cleveland (G-5457)	A	216 696-7000
Innomark Communications LLC, Fairfield (G-9510)	C	513 285-1040
Innovtive Crtive Solutions LLC, Groveport (G-10494)	E	614 491-9638
Instant Impressions Inc, Columbus (G-7030)	G	614 538-9844
Intermec Technologies Corp, West Chester (G-19726)	F	513 874-5882
Intermec Ultra Print Inc, West Chester (G-19727)	C	513 874-5882
International Advg Concepts, Cleveland (G-5467)	G	440 331-4733
Irwin Engraving & Printing Co, Cleveland (G-5477)	G	216 391-7300
J & K Printing, Canton (G-2713)	G	330 456-5306
J D B Partners Inc, Fairfield (G-9513)	G	513 874-3056
J P Quality Printing Inc, Cleveland (G-5485)	G	216 791-6303
J-M Designs LLC, Maumee (G-13120)	G	419 794-2114
▲ Jack Walker Printing Co, Mentor (G-13483)	F	440 352-4222
Jarman Printing Company LLC, Alliance (G-479)	G	330 823-8585
Jazz Textile Impressions, Maumee (G-13121)	G	419 242-5940
Jeffrey Reedy, Westerville (G-20060)	G	614 794-9292
Jjkb Enterprises LLC, Cincinnati (G-3873)	G	513 731-4332
Joe Paxton, Columbus (G-7071)	G	614 424-9000

Employee Codes: A=Over 500 employees, B=251-500 C=101-250, D=51-100, E=20-50, F=10-19, G=3-9

Joe Sestito G 614 871-7778
Grove City *(G-10437)*
John C Starr G 740 852-5592
London *(G-12063)*
Johnson Printing G 740 922-4821
Uhrichsville *(G-18889)*
Jones & Assoc Advg & Design G 330 799-6876
Youngstown *(G-20949)*
Jscs Group Inc G 513 563-4900
Cincinnati *(G-3886)*
K & J Holdings Inc G 330 726-0828
Youngstown *(G-20951)*
▲ **Kaufman Container Company** C 216 898-2000
Cleveland *(G-5519)*
Kay Toledo Tag Inc D 419 729-5479
Toledo *(G-18363)*
▲ **Kdm Signs Inc** C 513 769-1932
Cincinnati *(G-3900)*
Kee Printing Inc G 937 456-6851
Eaton *(G-9156)*
Kehoe Brothers Printing Inc G 216 351-4100
Cleveland *(G-5524)*
Keithley Enterprises Inc G 937 890-1878
Dayton *(G-8290)*
Kendra Screen Print G 440 967-8820
Vermilion *(G-19164)*
Kens His & Hers Shop Inc G 330 872-3190
Newton Falls *(G-14988)*
Kenwel Printers Inc E 614 261-1011
Columbus *(G-7088)*
Keteli Teamwear LLC G 740 373-7969
Marietta *(G-12637)*
Key Marketing Group G 440 748-3479
Grafton *(G-10306)*
Key Press Inc G 513 721-1203
Cincinnati *(G-3907)*
Keystone Press Inc G 419 243-7326
Toledo *(G-18367)*
Keystone Printing & Copy Cat G 740 354-6542
Portsmouth *(G-16286)*
KMS 2000 Inc F 330 454-9444
Canton *(G-2727)*
▲ **Kramer Graphics Inc** E 937 296-9600
Moraine *(G-14363)*
KS Designs Inc G 513 241-5953
Cincinnati *(G-3925)*
Label Technique Southeast LLC E 440 951-7660
Willoughby *(G-20356)*
Lake Screen Printing Inc G 440 244-5707
Lorain *(G-12099)*
Lamar D Steiner G 330 466-1479
Millersburg *(G-14105)*
Landen Desktop Pubg Ctr Inc G 513 683-5181
Loveland *(G-12209)*
Larmax Inc G 513 984-0783
Blue Ash *(G-1803)*
Laser Printing Solutions Inc F 216 351-4444
Cleveland *(G-5563)*
Laughing Star Montessory G 513 683-5682
Maineville *(G-12373)*
Lazer Systems Inc F 513 641-4002
Cincinnati *(G-3935)*
Lee Corporation G 513 771-3602
Cincinnati *(G-3937)*
Leeper Printing Co Inc G 419 243-2604
Toledo *(G-18380)*
Legendary Ink Inc G 614 766-5101
Columbus *(G-7120)*
Lesher Printers Inc E 419 332-8253
Fremont *(G-10033)*
Letterman Printing Inc G 513 523-1111
Oxford *(G-15696)*
Lilienthal Southeastern Inc F 740 439-1640
Cambridge *(G-2446)*
Lima Sporting Goods Inc E 419 222-1036
Lima *(G-11894)*
Liming Printing Inc F 937 374-2646
Xenia *(G-20782)*
Locker Room Inc G 419 445-9600
Archbold *(G-656)*
Locker Room Lettering Ltd G 419 359-1761
Castalia *(G-2940)*
Logan Screen Printing G 740 385-3303
Logan *(G-12033)*
Logos On Lee G 216 862-5226
Cleveland *(G-5583)*
▲ **Lorenz Corporation** D 937 228-6118
Dayton *(G-8316)*
Loris Printing Inc G 419 626-6648
Sandusky *(G-16823)*

Ls2 Printing G 937 544-1000
West Union *(G-19965)*
Lsc Communications Inc A 419 935-0111
Willard *(G-20241)*
LSI Industries Inc E 513 793-3200
Blue Ash *(G-1808)*
Lund Printing Co G 330 628-4047
Akron *(G-262)*
Lyle Printing & Publishing Co E 330 337-3419
Salem *(G-16756)*
M PI Label Systems G 330 938-2134
Sebring *(G-16888)*
Mac Printing Company G 937 393-1101
Hillsboro *(G-10884)*
Madison Graphics G 216 226-5770
Cleveland *(G-5601)*
Madison Press Inc G 216 521-3789
Lakewood *(G-11527)*
Magnetic Mktg Solutions LLC G 513 721-3801
Cincinnati *(G-3973)*
Marazita Graphics Inc G 330 773-6462
Akron *(G-267)*
Marbee Inc G 419 422-9441
Findlay *(G-9722)*
Marcus Uppe Inc D 216 263-4000
Cleveland *(G-5616)*
Margaret Trentman G 513 948-1700
Cincinnati *(G-3980)*
Mariotti Printing Co LLC G 440 245-4120
Lorain *(G-12104)*
Marketing Comm Resource Inc D 440 484-3010
Willoughby *(G-20371)*
Markt G 740 397-5900
Mount Vernon *(G-14490)*
Martin Printing Co G 419 224-9176
Lima *(G-11897)*
Marysville Printing Company G 937 644-4959
Marysville *(G-12800)*
Matthew Koster G 440 887-9000
Valley City *(G-19048)*
McDaniel Envelope Co Inc F 330 868-5929
Minerva *(G-14191)*
Meders Special Tees G 513 921-3800
Cincinnati *(G-3995)*
Melnor Graphics LLC F 419 476-8808
Toledo *(G-18408)*
Metro Flex Inc G 937 299-5360
Moraine *(G-14369)*
Meyers Printing & Design Inc G 937 461-6000
Dayton *(G-8344)*
Miami Graphics Services Inc F 937 698-4013
West Milton *(G-19950)*
Miami Valley Press Inc G 937 547-0771
Greenville *(G-10381)*
▲ **Microplex Printware Corp** F 440 374-2424
Bedford *(G-1426)*
Mid Ohio Screen Print Inc G 614 875-1774
Grove City *(G-10446)*
Middaugh Enterprises Inc F 330 852-2471
Sugarcreek *(G-17852)*
Middleton Printing Co Inc G 614 294-7277
Gahanna *(G-10090)*
Mike B Crawford G 330 673-7944
Kent *(G-11355)*
Miller Products Inc D 330 335-3110
Wadsworth *(G-19254)*
Minuteman Press of Athens LLC G 740 593-7393
Athens *(G-841)*
Mlp Interent Enterprises LLC E 614 917-8705
Mansfield *(G-12483)*
Miracle Custom Awards & Gifts G 330 376-8335
Akron *(G-283)*
Miracle Documents G 513 651-2222
Cincinnati *(G-4034)*
ML Advertising & Design LLC G 419 447-6523
Tiffin *(G-18069)*
ML Erectors LLC G 440 328-3227
Elyria *(G-9297)*
Mmp Printing Inc E 513 381-0990
Cincinnati *(G-4035)*
Modern Displays Inc G 513 471-1639
Cincinnati *(G-4037)*
Moonshine Screen Printing Inc F 513 523-7775
Oxford *(G-15697)*
Morrison Sign Company Inc E 614 276-1181
Columbus *(G-7198)*
Morse Enterprises Inc G 513 229-3600
Mason *(G-12912)*
Mound Printing Company Inc E 937 866-2872
Miamisburg *(G-13696)*

Mpi Labels of Baltimore Inc F 330 938-2134
Sebring *(G-16890)*
Mr Label Inc E 513 681-2088
Cincinnati *(G-4051)*
Multi-Color Australia LLC B 513 381-1480
Batavia *(G-1170)*
Multi-Color Corporation G 513 459-3283
Mason *(G-12913)*
Multi-Color Corporation C 513 396-5600
Cincinnati *(G-4054)*
▲ **Multi-Color Corporation** F 513 381-1480
Batavia *(G-1171)*
Multi-Color Corporation D 513 943-0080
Batavia *(G-1172)*
Multi-Craft Litho Inc E 859 581-2754
Blue Ash *(G-1824)*
Nelis Printing Co G 330 757-4114
Youngstown *(G-20974)*
Network Printing & Graphics F 614 230-2084
Columbus *(G-7214)*
New Dawn Designs G 330 759-3500
Girard *(G-10263)*
Newton Falls Printing G 330 872-3532
Newton Falls *(G-14990)*
Niklee Co G 440 944-0082
Willoughby Hills *(G-20473)*
◆ **Nilpeter Usa Inc** C 513 489-4400
Cincinnati *(G-4080)*
Nomis Publications Inc F 330 965-2380
Youngstown *(G-20976)*
Nordec Inc D 330 940-3700
Stow *(G-17615)*
Northeastern Plastics Inc G 330 453-5925
Canton *(G-2768)*
▲ **Novavision Inc** D 419 354-1427
Bowling Green *(G-1986)*
Odyssey Press Inc F 614 410-0356
Huron *(G-11107)*
Odyssey Spirits Inc F 330 562-1523
Aurora *(G-896)*
▲ **Off Contact Inc** F 419 255-5546
Toledo *(G-18434)*
Ohio Envelope Manufacturing Co E 216 267-2920
Cleveland *(G-5805)*
Ohio Flexible Packaging Co F 513 494-1800
South Lebanon *(G-17277)*
Ohio Legal Blank Co G 216 281-7792
Cleveland *(G-5806)*
Old Salt Tees G 440 463-0628
Mentor *(G-13533)*
Old Trail Printing Company C 614 443-4852
Columbus *(G-7269)*
Onetouchpoint East Corp D 513 421-1600
Cincinnati *(G-4113)*
Onnyx G 419 627-9872
Sandusky *(G-16833)*
▼ **Packaging Materials Inc** E 740 432-6337
Cambridge *(G-2452)*
Painted Hill Inv Group Inc F 937 339-1756
Troy *(G-18691)*
Papel Couture G 614 848-5700
Columbus *(G-7290)*
Paragon Press G 513 281-9911
Cincinnati *(G-4133)*
Park PLC Prntg Cpyg & Dgtl IMG G 330 799-1739
Youngstown *(G-20993)*
Park Press Direct G 419 626-4426
Sandusky *(G-16835)*
Patio Printing Inc G 614 785-9553
Columbus *(G-7295)*
Peebles Creative Group Inc G 614 487-2011
Dublin *(G-8961)*
Penca Design Group Ltd G 440 210-4422
Painesville *(G-15774)*
Penguin Enterprises Inc E 440 899-5112
Westlake *(G-20140)*
Perfection Printing F 513 874-2173
Fairfield *(G-9547)*
▲ **Performance Packaging Inc** F 419 478-8805
Toledo *(G-18465)*
Pexco Packaging Corp E 419 470-5935
Toledo *(G-18468)*
PJ Bush Associates Inc E 216 362-6700
Cleveland *(G-5881)*
Pops Printed Apparel LLC G 614 372-5651
Columbus *(G-7332)*
Post Printing Co D 859 254-7714
Minster *(G-14222)*
Powell Prints LLC G 614 771-4830
Hilliard *(G-10853)*

Precision Business Solutions ....G 419 661-8700
Perrysburg *(G-16001)*
Precision Graphic Services ....F 419 241-5189
Toledo *(G-18478)*
Precision Imprint ....G 740 592-5916
Athens *(G-846)*
▲ **Premier Southern Ticket Co Inc** ....E 513 489-6700
Cincinnati *(G-4188)*
Premiere Printing & Signs Inc ....G 330 688-6244
Stow *(G-17620)*
Press of Ohio Inc ....E 330 678-5868
Kent *(G-11367)*
Prestige Printing ....G 937 236-8468
Dayton *(G-8438)*
Primal Screen Inc ....E 330 677-1766
Kent *(G-11368)*
Printex Incorporated ....F 740 773-0088
Chillicothe *(G-3217)*
Printing Depot Inc ....G 330 783-5341
Youngstown *(G-21007)*
Profile Digital Printing LLC ....E 937 866-4241
Dayton *(G-8448)*
Proforma Advantage ....G 440 781-5255
Mayfield Village *(G-13175)*
Proforma Steinbacher & Assoc ....G 330 241-5370
Medina *(G-13322)*
Proforma Systems Advantage ....G 419 224-8747
Lima *(G-11922)*
Progressive Printers Inc ....D 937 222-1267
Dayton *(G-8450)*
Proline Screenwear ....G 440 205-3700
Mentor *(G-13560)*
Promo Sparks ....G 513 844-2211
Fairfield *(G-9552)*
Promospark Inc ....G 513 844-2211
Fairfield *(G-9553)*
PS Graphics Inc ....G 440 356-9656
Rocky River *(G-16553)*
Quali Tee Design ....G 740 335-8497
Wshngtn CT Hs *(G-20738)*
Quali-Tee Design Sports ....F 937 382-7997
Wilmington *(G-20505)*
Qualitee Design Sportswear Co ....E 740 333-8337
Wshngtn CT Hs *(G-20739)*
Quality Print Shop Inc ....G 740 992-3345
Middleport *(G-13873)*
Quebecor World Johnson Hardin ....A 614 326-0299
Cincinnati *(G-4233)*
Queen City Office Machine ....F 513 251-7200
Cincinnati *(G-4238)*
Quest Service Labs Inc ....F 330 405-0316
Twinsburg *(G-18843)*
Quick As A Wink Printing Co ....F 419 224-9786
Lima *(G-11926)*
Quick Tech Business Forms Inc ....E 937 743-5952
Springboro *(G-17347)*
R R Donnelley & Sons Company ....G 513 552-1512
West Chester *(G-19778)*
R R Donnelley & Sons Company ....E 440 774-2101
Oberlin *(G-15504)*
R W Michael Printing Co ....G 330 923-9277
Akron *(G-340)*
R&D Marketing Group Inc ....G 216 398-9100
Brooklyn Heights *(G-2130)*
Research and Development Group ....G 614 261-0454
Columbus *(G-7386)*
Reynolds and Reynolds Company ....G 937 485-4771
Dayton *(G-8475)*
Reynolds and Reynolds Company ....F 419 584-7000
Celina *(G-2983)*
Richardson Supply Ltd ....G 614 539-3033
Grove City *(G-10462)*
Richland Blue Printcom Inc ....G 419 524-2781
Mansfield *(G-12505)*
Rising Moon Custom Apparel ....G 614 882-1336
Westerville *(G-20072)*
Riverside Mfg LLC ....F 937 492-3100
Sidney *(G-17067)*
Rl Smith Printing Co ....F 330 747-9590
Youngstown *(G-21017)*
Robert Esterman ....G 513 541-3311
Cincinnati *(G-4277)*
Robert H Shackelford ....G 330 364-2221
New Philadelphia *(G-14799)*
Robloc Inc ....G 330 723-5853
Medina *(G-13329)*
Rotary Printing Company ....G 419 668-4821
Norwalk *(G-15414)*
RR Donnelley & Sons Company ....B 740 928-6110
Hebron *(G-10760)*

Rush Graphix Ltd ....G 419 448-7874
Tiffin *(G-18079)*
▲ **Ruthie Ann Inc** ....F 800 231-3567
New Paris *(G-14755)*
Rutland Plastic Tech Inc ....G 614 846-3055
Columbus *(G-7407)*
Ryans Newark Leader Ex Prtg ....F 740 522-2149
Newark *(G-14916)*
S F Mock & Associates LLC ....F 937 438-0196
Dayton *(G-8491)*
Sams Graphic Industries ....F 330 821-4710
Alliance *(G-498)*
Samuels Products Inc ....E 513 891-4456
Blue Ash *(G-1842)*
Sandy Smittcamp ....G 937 372-1687
Xenia *(G-20788)*
Schaffner Publication Inc ....E 419 732-2154
Port Clinton *(G-16258)*
Schilling Graphics Inc ....E 419 468-1037
Galion *(G-10154)*
Schlabach Printing Ltd ....E 330 852-4687
Sugarcreek *(G-17863)*
▼ **Scratch-Off Systems Inc** ....E 216 649-7800
Brecksville *(G-2056)*
Screen Craft Plastics ....G 440 286-4060
Chardon *(G-3135)*
Screen Printing Show House ....G 614 252-2202
Columbus *(G-7433)*
Screen Printing Unlimited ....G 419 621-2335
Sandusky *(G-16848)*
Screen Tech Graphics ....G 740 695-7950
Saint Clairsville *(G-16650)*
Scriptype Publishing Inc ....E 330 659-0303
Richfield *(G-16485)*
Selby Service/Roxy Press Inc ....G 513 241-3445
Cincinnati *(G-4318)*
Seneca Label Inc ....E 440 237-1600
Cleveland *(G-6044)*
▲ **Sensical Inc** ....D 216 641-1141
Solon *(G-17229)*
Sevell + Sevell Inc ....G 614 341-9700
Columbus *(G-7441)*
Sharon Printing Co Inc ....G 330 239-1684
Sharon Center *(G-16953)*
Shirt Family ....G 740 706-1284
Marietta *(G-12668)*
Shops By Todd Inc ....G 937 458-3192
Beavercreek *(G-1340)*
Shreve Printing LLC ....F 330 567-2341
Shreve *(G-17010)*
Sign Lady Inc ....G 419 476-9191
Toledo *(G-18522)*
Signs By George ....G 216 394-2095
Brookfield *(G-2109)*
Silica Press Inc ....G 419 843-8500
Sylvania *(G-17961)*
Silk Screen Special TS Inc ....G 740 246-4843
Thornville *(G-18036)*
Sitler Printer Inc ....G 330 482-4463
Columbiana *(G-6480)*
Slater Silk Screen ....G 419 755-8337
Mansfield *(G-12516)*
Slimans Printery Inc ....F 330 454-9141
Canton *(G-2818)*
Slutzkers Quickprint Center ....G 440 244-0330
Lorain *(G-12123)*
Small Dog Printing ....G 614 777-7620
Hilliard *(G-10862)*
Smartbill Ltd ....F 740 928-6909
Hebron *(G-10763)*
SMS Communications Inc ....E 216 374-6686
Shaker Heights *(G-16937)*
Snow Printing Co Inc ....F 419 229-7669
Lima *(G-11941)*
Snyder Printing LLC ....G 740 353-3947
Portsmouth *(G-16301)*
Solution Ventures Inc ....G 440 242-1658
Avon Lake *(G-1008)*
Somerset Commercial Prtg Co ....G 740 536-7187
Rushville *(G-16597)*
South End Printing Co ....G 216 341-0669
Cleveland *(G-6081)*
▲ **Spear USA Inc** ....C 513 459-1100
Mason *(G-12941)*
Specialtee Sportswear & Design ....G 614 877-0976
Orient *(G-15578)*
Specialty Printing and Proc ....F 614 322-9035
Columbus *(G-7468)*
Spectrum Embroidery Inc ....G 937 847-9905
Dayton *(G-8518)*

Spencer-Walker Press Inc ....G 740 345-4494
Newark *(G-14921)*
Spencer-Walker Press Inc ....F 740 344-6110
Newark *(G-14920)*
Sports Express ....G 330 297-1112
Ravenna *(G-16406)*
Springdot Inc ....D 513 542-4000
Cincinnati *(G-4365)*
◆ **SRC Liquidation LLC** ....A 937 221-1000
Dayton *(G-8521)*
▲ **SRI Ohio Inc** ....D 740 653-5800
Lancaster *(G-11611)*
Srm Graphics Inc ....G 614 263-4433
Columbus *(G-7482)*
Sro Prints LLC ....G 865 604-0420
Cincinnati *(G-4366)*
Stadvec Inc ....G 330 644-7724
Barberton *(G-1107)*
Standout Stickers Inc ....G 877 449-7703
Medina *(G-13347)*
Star Calendar & Printing Co ....G 216 741-3223
Cleveland *(G-6095)*
Star Printing Company Inc ....E 330 376-0514
Akron *(G-386)*
Starr Printing Services Inc ....G 513 241-7708
Cincinnati *(G-4375)*
Stationery Shop Inc ....G 330 376-2033
Akron *(G-387)*
Stephen Andrews Inc ....G 330 725-2672
Lodi *(G-12020)*
Steves Sports Inc ....G 440 735-0044
Northfield *(G-15326)*
Stolle Machinery Company LLC ....C 937 497-5400
Sidney *(G-17082)*
▲ **Studio Eleven Inc** ....E 937 295-2225
Fort Loramie *(G-9808)*
Studs N Hip Hop ....G 614 477-0786
Columbus *(G-7496)*
Suburban Press Inc ....E 216 961-0766
Cleveland *(G-6114)*
▲ **Suntwist Corp** ....E 800 935-3534
Maple Heights *(G-12581)*
Superior Label Systems Inc ....B 513 336-0825
Mason *(G-12944)*
T & L Custom Screening Inc ....G 937 237-3121
Dayton *(G-8534)*
T K L Lettering ....G 937 832-2091
Englewood *(G-9376)*
Tag ....G 614 921-1732
Columbus *(G-7508)*
Taylor Communications Inc ....C 419 678-6000
Coldwater *(G-6422)*
Taylor Communications Inc ....C 614 277-7500
Grove City *(G-10471)*
Taylor Communications Inc ....E 937 221-1000
Dayton *(G-8543)*
Tech/III Inc ....E 513 482-7500
Cincinnati *(G-4409)*
Tewell & Associates ....G 440 543-5190
Chagrin Falls *(G-3081)*
The Label Team Inc ....F 330 332-1067
Salem *(G-16776)*
Thomas Allen Co ....G 330 823-8487
Alliance *(G-506)*
Thomas Products Co Inc ....E 513 756-9009
Cincinnati *(G-4420)*
Tj Metzgers Inc ....D 419 861-8611
Toledo *(G-18553)*
Toledo Signs & Designs Ltd ....G 419 843-1073
Toledo *(G-18569)*
Toledo Ticket Company ....E 419 476-5424
Toledo *(G-18573)*
Tope Printing Inc ....G 330 674-4993
Millersburg *(G-14137)*
◆ **Transfer Express Inc** ....D 440 918-1900
Mentor *(G-13613)*
Traxium LLC ....E 330 572-8200
Stow *(G-17637)*
◆ **Trebnick Systems Inc** ....E 937 743-1550
Springboro *(G-17358)*
Tree Free Resources LLC ....F 740 751-4844
Marion *(G-12744)*
Triangle Label Inc ....G 513 242-2822
West Chester *(G-19812)*
Trinity Printing Co ....F 513 469-1000
Cincinnati *(G-4439)*
True Dinero Records & Tech LLC ....G 513 428-4610
Cincinnati *(G-4443)*
▲ **Underground Sport Shop Inc** ....F 513 751-1662
Cincinnati *(G-4446)*

SIC

Employee Codes: A=Over 500 employees, B=251-500
C=101-250, D=51-100, E=20-50, F=10-19, G=3-9

2019 Harris Ohio
Industrial Directory

867

Unisport Inc ...F ... 419 529-4727
Ontario (G-15549)
United Sport Apparel ...F ... 330 722-0818
Medina (G-13357)
Uptown Dog The Inc ...G ... 740 592-4600
Athens (G-853)
US Government Publishing Off ...G ... 614 469-5657
Columbus (G-7566)
V I P Printing & Design ...G ... 513 777-7468
West Chester (G-19913)
Value Added Business Svcs Co ...G ... 614 854-9755
Jackson (G-11200)
Verstraete In Mold Lab ...F ... 513 943-0080
Batavia (G-1195)
▲ Vgu Industries Inc ...E ... 216 676-9093
Cleveland (G-6257)
Victory Postcards Inc ...G ... 614 764-8975
Columbus (G-7583)
Viewpoint Graphic Design ...G ... 419 447-6073
Tiffin (G-18091)
Vision Press Inc ...G ... 440 357-6362
Painesville (G-15796)
Visual Information Institute ...F ... 937 376-4361
Xenia (G-20801)
Vya Inc ...E ... 513 772-5400
Cincinnati (G-4485)
Ward/Kraft Forms of Ohio Inc ...D ... 740 694-0015
Fredericktown (G-9983)
Warren Printing & Off Pdts Inc ...F ... 419 523-3635
Ottawa (G-15671)
Water Drop Media Inc ...G ... 234 600-5817
Vienna (G-19211)
Watson Haran & Company Inc ...G ... 937 436-1414
Dayton (G-8585)
West Carrollton Parchment ...E ... 513 594-3341
West Carrollton (G-19634)
▲ West-Camp Press Inc ...D ... 614 882-2378
Westerville (G-20082)
Western Ohio Graphics ...F ... 937 335-8769
Troy (G-18719)
Western Roto Engravers Inc ...E ... 330 336-7636
Wadsworth (G-19281)
▲ Wfsr Holdings LLC ...A ... 877 735-4966
Dayton (G-8592)
William J Bergen & Co ...G ... 440 248-6132
Solon (G-17261)
William J Dupps ...G ... 419 734-2126
Port Clinton (G-16264)
Williams Steel Rule Die Co ...F ... 216 431-3232
Cleveland (G-6311)
Wingate Packaging Inc ...E ... 513 745-8600
Blue Ash (G-1871)
Wirick Press Inc ...G ... 330 273-3488
Brunswick (G-2252)
Wolfe Associates Inc ...G ... 614 461-5000
Columbus (G-7610)
Woodrow Corp ...G ... 937 322-7696
Springfield (G-17520)
Yi Xing Inc ...G ... 614 785-9631
Columbus (G-7623)
Yockey Group Inc ...E ... 513 860-9053
West Chester (G-19824)
Youngs Screenprinting & Embro ...G ... 330 922-5777
Cuyahoga Falls (G-7935)
Youngstown ARC Engraving Co ...E ... 330 793-2471
Youngstown (G-21070)
Zech Printing Industries Inc ...E ... 937 748-2776
Cincinnati (G-4532)
Zenos Activewear Inc ...G ... 614 443-0070
Columbus (G-7626)

2761 Manifold Business Forms

Anderson Graphics Inc ...E ... 330 745-2165
Barberton (G-1052)
Anthony Business Forms Inc ...F ... 937 253-0072
Dayton (G-7971)
Crabar/Gbf Inc ...E ... 419 269-1720
Toledo (G-18242)
Crabar/Gbf Inc ...F ... 419 943-2141
Leipsic (G-11724)
▲ Custom Products Corporation ...D ... 440 528-7100
Solon (G-17129)
Delores E OBeirn ...G ... 440 582-3610
Cleveland (G-5082)
Dupli-Systems Inc ...C ... 440 234-9415
Strongsville (G-17738)
▲ Eleet Cryogenics Inc ...E ... 330 874-4009
Bolivar (G-1913)
GBS Corp ...C ... 330 863-1828
Malvern (G-12391)
▲ GBS Corp ...C ... 330 494-5330
North Canton (G-15085)
Geygan Enterprises Inc ...F ... 513 932-4222
Lebanon (G-11656)
Highland Computer Forms Inc ...C ... 937 393-4215
Hillsboro (G-10879)
Hubert Enterprises Inc ...G ... 513 367-8600
Harrison (G-10648)
▲ Kroy LLC ...C ... 216 426-5600
Cleveland (G-5544)
Lakeshore Graphic Industries ...F ... 419 626-8631
Sandusky (G-16821)
Little Printing Company ...E ... 937 773-4595
Piqua (G-16137)
▲ Misato Computer Products Inc ...G ... 937 890-8410
Vandalia (G-19139)
P H Glatfelter Company ...D ... 419 333-6700
Fremont (G-10043)
Print-Digital Incorporated ...G ... 330 686-5945
Stow (G-17621)
Quick Tech Graphics Inc ...E ... 937 743-5952
Springboro (G-17348)
R R Donnelley & Sons Company ...E ... 440 774-2101
Oberlin (G-15504)
Reynolds and Reynolds Company ...F ... 419 584-7000
Celina (G-2983)
Reynolds and Reynolds Company ...E ... 937 449-4039
Dayton (G-8476)
Reynolds and Reynolds Company ...F ... 937 485-2805
Beavercreek (G-1362)
Rotary Forms Press Inc ...E ... 937 393-3426
Hillsboro (G-10890)
S F Mock & Associates LLC ...F ... 937 438-0196
Dayton (G-8491)
▲ Shawnee Systems Inc ...D ... 513 561-9932
Cincinnati (G-4330)
◆ SRC Liquidation LLC ...A ... 937 221-1000
Dayton (G-8521)
Taylor Communications Inc ...G ... 440 974-1611
Mentor (G-13600)
Taylor Communications Inc ...E ... 937 221-1000
Dayton (G-8543)
Taylor Communications Inc ...D ... 216 265-1800
Richfield (G-16491)
Taylor Communications Inc ...F ... 732 356-0081
Dayton (G-8544)
Taylor Communications Inc ...D ... 937 221-3347
Grove City (G-10472)
Taylor Communications Inc ...G ... 937 228-5800
Dayton (G-8545)
Tcp Inc ...G ... 330 836-4239
Fairlawn (G-9622)
Thomas Products Co Inc ...E ... 513 756-9009
Cincinnati (G-4420)
Unit Sets Inc ...E ... 937 840-6123
Hillsboro (G-10892)
▲ Wfsr Holdings LLC ...A ... 877 735-4966
Dayton (G-8592)

2771 Greeting Card Publishing

◆ American Greetings Corporation ...A ... 216 252-7300
Cleveland (G-4688)
Frogs In Bloom ...G ... 330 678-9508
Kent (G-11323)
Kim Brauer & Company LLC ...G ... 330 540-9152
Youngstown (G-20952)
Naptime Productions LLC ...F ... 419 662-9521
Rossford (G-16587)
▲ Plus Mark LLC ...E ... 216 252-6770
Cleveland (G-5891)
Those Charc From Cleve Inc ...F ... 216 252-7300
Cleveland (G-6172)

2782 Blankbooks & Looseleaf Binders

A H Pelz Co ...G ... 216 861-1882
Cleveland (G-4589)
▲ Art Guild Binders Inc ...E ... 513 242-3000
Cincinnati (G-3358)
Bell Binders LLC ...F ... 419 242-3201
Toledo (G-18200)
Deluxe Corporation ...C ... 330 342-1500
Hudson (G-11041)
Dupli-Systems Inc ...C ... 440 234-9415
Strongsville (G-17738)
Elken Co ...G ... 513 459-7207
Maineville (G-12368)
Gotta Groove Records Inc ...E ... 216 431-7373
Cleveland (G-5334)
Lilienthal Southeastern Inc ...F ... 740 439-1640
Cambridge (G-2446)
M & R Phillips Enterprises ...F ... 740 323-0580
Newark (G-14895)
Mueller Art Cover & Binding Co ...E ... 440 238-3303
Strongsville (G-17768)
Quick Tech Graphics Inc ...E ... 937 743-5952
Springboro (G-17348)
Tenacity Manufacturing Company ...E ... 513 821-0201
West Chester (G-19807)
W N Albums and Frames Inc ...G ... 800 325-5179
Cleveland (G-6278)
William Exline Inc ...E ... 216 941-0800
Cleveland (G-6309)

2789 Bookbinding

21st Century Printers Inc ...G ... 513 771-4150
Cincinnati (G-3268)
A-A Blueprint Co Inc ...E ... 330 794-8803
Akron (G-23)
AAA Laminating and Bindery Inc ...G ... 513 860-2680
Fairfield (G-9477)
▲ Activities Press Inc ...E ... 440 953-1200
Mentor (G-13374)
AGS Custom Graphics Inc ...D ... 330 963-7770
Macedonia (G-12275)
Allen Graphics Inc ...G ... 440 349-4100
Solon (G-17102)
Anderson Graphics Inc ...E ... 330 745-2165
Barberton (G-1052)
▲ Art Guild Binders Inc ...E ... 513 242-3000
Cincinnati (G-3358)
B & B Bindery Inc ...G ... 330 722-5430
Medina (G-13227)
Baise Enterprises Inc ...G ... 614 444-3171
Columbus (G-6642)
Barnhart Printing Corp ...F ... 330 456-2279
Canton (G-2585)
Beck & Orr Inc ...G ... 614 276-8809
Columbus (G-6656)
Bernard Specialty Co ...G ... 216 881-2200
Cleveland (G-4807)
Bill Wyatt Inc ...G ... 330 535-1113
Mentor (G-13403)
Bindery & Spc Pressworks Inc ...D ... 614 873-4623
Plain City (G-16178)
Bindery Tech Inc ...F ... 440 934-3247
North Ridgeville (G-15211)
Bindtech LLC ...D ... 615 834-0404
Cleveland (G-4815)
Bip Printing Solutions LLC ...F ... 216 832-5673
Beachwood (G-1225)
Black River Group Inc ...D ... 419 524-6699
Mansfield (G-12411)
Blains Folding Service Inc ...G ... 216 631-4700
Cleveland (G-4817)
Bock & Pierce Enterprises ...G ... 513 474-9500
Cincinnati (G-3398)
Boldman Printing LLC ...G ... 937 653-3431
Urbana (G-18980)
Bookbinders Incorporated ...G ... 330 848-4980
Barberton (G-1066)
Bookcolor Bindery Services ...E ... 614 252-2941
Columbus (G-6686)
▼ Bookfactory LLC ...E ... 937 226-7100
Dayton (G-8059)
Century Graphics Inc ...E ... 614 895-7698
Westerville (G-19983)
Cincinnati Bindery & Packg Inc ...G ... 859 816-0282
Cincinnati (G-3484)
Classic Laminations Inc ...E ... 440 735-1333
Cleveland (G-4939)
Cleveland Letter Service Inc ...E ... 216 781-8300
Chagrin Falls (G-3013)
Clints Printing Inc ...G ... 937 426-2771
Beavercreek (G-1354)
▲ Consoldated Graphics Group Inc ...C ... 216 881-9191
Cleveland (G-5015)
Copley Ohio Newspapers Inc ...C ... 330 364-5577
New Philadelphia (G-14765)
COS Blueprint Inc ...F ... 330 376-0022
Akron (G-122)
Cott Systems Inc ...D ... 614 847-4405
Columbus (G-6827)
Cox Printing Co ...G ... 937 382-2312
Wilmington (G-20491)
Customformed Products Inc ...F ... 937 388-0480
Miamisburg (G-13653)
D and D Business Equipment Inc ...G ... 440 777-5441
Cleveland (G-5056)
Debandale Printing Inc ...G ... 330 725-5122
Medina (G-13251)

SIC SECTION 27 PRINTING, PUBLISHING, AND ALLIED INDUSTRIES

Delphos Herald Inc ..... D 419 695-0015
   Delphos *(G-8739)*
Durbin Minuteman Press ..... G 513 791-9171
   Blue Ash *(G-1760)*
E Z Binderys ..... G 513 733-0005
   Cincinnati *(G-3619)*
Earl D Arnold Printing Company ..... E 513 533-6900
   Cincinnati *(G-3624)*
Easterdays Printing Center ..... G 330 726-1182
   Youngstown *(G-20895)*
Eugene Stewart ..... G 937 898-1117
   Dayton *(G-8189)*
Fedex Office & Print Svcs Inc ..... E 419 866-5464
   Toledo *(G-18290)*
Fedex Office & Print Svcs Inc ..... E 937 436-0677
   Dayton *(G-8192)*
Fedex Office & Print Svcs Inc ..... E 614 575-0800
   Reynoldsburg *(G-16439)*
Fedex Office & Print Svcs Inc ..... E 216 573-1511
   Cleveland *(G-5228)*
Fergusons Finishing Inc ..... E 419 241-9123
   Toledo *(G-18293)*
Folks Creative Printers Inc ..... E 740 383-6326
   Marion *(G-12702)*
Frank J Prucha & Associates ..... G 216 642-3838
   Cleveland *(G-5272)*
Franklins Printing Company ..... F 740 452-6375
   Zanesville *(G-21138)*
G W Steffen Bookbinders Inc ..... E 330 963-0300
   Macedonia *(G-12298)*
Ganger Enterprises Inc ..... G 614 776-3985
   Westerville *(G-19993)*
Golden Graphics Ltd ..... F 419 673-6260
   Kenton *(G-11406)*
Grant John ..... G 937 298-0633
   Dayton *(G-8234)*
▲ Great Lakes Integrated Inc ..... D 216 651-1500
   Cleveland *(G-5347)*
Greg Blume ..... G 740 574-2308
   Wheelersburg *(G-20182)*
Harris Paper Crafts Inc ..... F 614 299-2141
   Columbus *(G-6983)*
▲ Hecks Direct Mail & Prtg Svc ..... E 419 697-3505
   Toledo *(G-18327)*
Henry Bussman ..... G 614 224-0417
   Columbus *(G-6988)*
Hf Group ..... E 440 729-9411
   Chesterland *(G-3158)*
Hf Group LLC ..... F 440 729-2445
   Chesterland *(G-3159)*
Homewood Press Inc ..... E 419 478-0695
   Toledo *(G-18334)*
Hopewell Industries Inc ..... D 740 622-3563
   Coshocton *(G-7737)*
Icibinding Corporation ..... E 440 729-2445
   Chesterland *(G-3162)*
Innomark Communications LLC ..... E 937 454-5555
   Miamisburg *(G-13679)*
Irvin Oslin Inc ..... G 216 361-7555
   Cleveland *(G-5476)*
▲ Jack Walker Printing Co ..... F 440 352-4222
   Mentor *(G-13483)*
Kad Holdings Inc ..... G 614 792-3399
   Dublin *(G-8935)*
▲ Kehl-Kolor Inc ..... E 419 281-3107
   Ashland *(G-717)*
Kenwel Printers Inc ..... E 614 261-1011
   Columbus *(G-7088)*
Kevin K Tidd ..... G 419 885-5603
   Sylvania *(G-17948)*
Keystone Press Inc ..... G 419 243-7326
   Toledo *(G-18367)*
Keystone Printing & Copy Cat ..... G 740 354-6542
   Portsmouth *(G-16286)*
L B Folding Co Inc ..... E 216 961-0888
   North Royalton *(G-15282)*
Laipplys Prtg Mktg Sltions Inc ..... G 740 387-9282
   Marion *(G-12715)*
Lam Pro Inc ..... F 216 426-0661
   Cleveland *(G-5556)*
Lee Corporation ..... G 513 771-3602
   Cincinnati *(G-3937)*
Legal News Publishing Co ..... G 216 696-3322
   Cleveland *(G-5572)*
Lilienthal Southeastern Inc ..... F 740 439-1640
   Cambridge *(G-2446)*
Lund Printing Co ..... G 330 628-4047
   Akron *(G-262)*
Macke Brothers Inc ..... D 513 771-7500
   Cincinnati *(G-3969)*

Mmp Printing Inc ..... E 513 381-0990
   Cincinnati *(G-4035)*
Monco Enterprises Inc ..... A 937 461-0034
   Dayton *(G-8366)*
Montview Corporation ..... G 330 723-3409
   Medina *(G-13304)*
Multi-Craft Litho Inc ..... E 859 581-2754
   Blue Ash *(G-1824)*
Nari Inc ..... G 440 960-2280
   Monroeville *(G-14289)*
Network Printing & Graphics ..... F 614 230-2084
   Columbus *(G-7214)*
Newfax Corporation ..... F 419 241-5157
   Toledo *(G-18423)*
North End Press Incorporated ..... E 740 653-6514
   Lancaster *(G-11591)*
▲ Ohio Laminating & Binding Inc ..... E 614 771-4868
   Hilliard *(G-10846)*
Old Trail Printing Company ..... C 614 443-4852
   Columbus *(G-7269)*
Onetouchpoint East Corp ..... D 513 421-1600
   Cincinnati *(G-4113)*
Orrville Printing Co Inc ..... G 330 682-5066
   Orrville *(G-15608)*
Painesville Publishing Co ..... G 440 354-4142
   Austinburg *(G-924)*
Patricia Lee Burd ..... G 513 302-4860
   Cincinnati *(G-4136)*
Penguin Enterprises Inc ..... E 440 899-5112
   Westlake *(G-20140)*
Pooles Printing & Office Svcs ..... G 419 475-9000
   Toledo *(G-18474)*
Precision Graphic Services ..... F 419 241-5189
   Toledo *(G-18478)*
Prime Printing Inc ..... E 937 438-3707
   Dayton *(G-8442)*
Print-Digital Incorporated ..... G 330 686-5945
   Stow *(G-17621)*
Printed Image ..... F 614 221-1412
   Columbus *(G-7350)*
▲ Printers Bindery Services Inc ..... D 513 821-8039
   Cincinnati *(G-4192)*
Progressive Folding Binding Co ..... G 216 621-1893
   Northfield *(G-15322)*
Promatch Solutions LLC ..... F 937 299-0185
   Springboro *(G-17346)*
▼ Quick Tab II Inc ..... D 419 448-6622
   Tiffin *(G-18076)*
R T Industries Inc ..... C 937 335-5784
   Troy *(G-18695)*
R W Michael Printing Co ..... G 330 923-9277
   Akron *(G-340)*
▲ Repro Acquisition Company LLC ..... E 216 738-3800
   Cleveland *(G-5977)*
Ricci Anthony ..... G 330 758-5761
   Youngstown *(G-21015)*
Riverside Mfg Acquisition LLC ..... C 585 458-2090
   Cleveland *(G-5989)*
Rmt Holdings Inc ..... F 419 221-1168
   Lima *(G-11933)*
Robert Esterman ..... G 513 541-3311
   Cincinnati *(G-4277)*
Robert H Shackelford ..... G 330 364-2221
   New Philadelphia *(G-14799)*
Robin Enterprises Company ..... C 614 891-0250
   Westerville *(G-20073)*
Ryans Newark Leader Ex Prtg ..... F 740 522-2149
   Newark *(G-14916)*
Sandy Smittcamp ..... G 937 372-1687
   Xenia *(G-20788)*
Slutzkers Quickprint Center ..... G 440 244-0330
   Lorain *(G-12123)*
Spencer-Walker Press Inc ..... E 740 344-6110
   Newark *(G-14920)*
Spring Grove Manufacturing ..... F 513 542-6900
   Cincinnati *(G-4362)*
Springdale Bindery LLC ..... G 513 772-8500
   Cincinnati *(G-4363)*
Star Printing Company Inc ..... E 330 376-0514
   Akron *(G-386)*
Strong Bindery ..... G 216 231-0001
   Cleveland *(G-6112)*
Suburban Press Inc ..... E 216 961-0766
   Cleveland *(G-6114)*
Target Printing & Graphics ..... F 937 228-0170
   Dayton *(G-8539)*
Taylor Communications Inc ..... G 937 228-5800
   Dayton *(G-8545)*
The Bookseller Inc ..... G 330 865-5831
   Akron *(G-401)*

Tj Metzgers Inc ..... D 419 861-8611
   Toledo *(G-18553)*
TL Krieg Offset Inc ..... E 513 542-1522
   Cincinnati *(G-4424)*
Tomahawk Printing Inc ..... F 419 335-3161
   Wauseon *(G-19533)*
Traxium LLC ..... E 330 572-8200
   Stow *(G-17637)*
Watkins Printing Company ..... E 614 297-8270
   Columbus *(G-7593)*
▲ West-Camp Press Inc ..... D 614 882-2378
   Westerville *(G-20082)*
▲ Wfsr Holdings LLC ..... A 877 735-4966
   Dayton *(G-8592)*
William J Dupps ..... G 419 734-2126
   Port Clinton *(G-16264)*
Youngstown ARC Engraving Co ..... E 330 793-2471
   Youngstown *(G-21070)*

2791 Typesetting

21st Century Printers Inc ..... G 513 771-4150
   Cincinnati *(G-3268)*
A-A Blueprint Co Inc ..... E 330 794-8803
   Akron *(G-23)*
▲ Activities Press Inc ..... E 440 953-1200
   Mentor *(G-13374)*
Advanced Translation/Cnsltng ..... E 440 716-0820
   Westlake *(G-20087)*
AGS Custom Graphics Inc ..... D 330 963-7770
   Macedonia *(G-12275)*
Alfacomp Inc ..... G 216 459-1790
   Cleveland *(G-4659)*
Anderson Graphics Inc ..... E 330 745-2165
   Barberton *(G-1052)*
Anthony Business Forms Inc ..... F 937 253-0072
   Dayton *(G-7971)*
Applied Graphics Ltd ..... G 419 756-6882
   Mansfield *(G-12407)*
Art Printing Co Inc ..... F 419 281-4371
   Ashland *(G-677)*
Art Tees Inc ..... G 614 338-8337
   Columbus *(G-6617)*
Asist Translation Services ..... F 614 451-6744
   Columbus *(G-6620)*
Baise Enterprises Inc ..... G 614 444-3171
   Columbus *(G-6642)*
Bill Wyatt Inc ..... G 330 535-1113
   Mentor *(G-13403)*
Bindery & Spc Pressworks Inc ..... D 614 873-4623
   Plain City *(G-16178)*
Black River Group Inc ..... D 419 524-6699
   Mansfield *(G-12411)*
Blt Inc ..... F 513 631-5050
   Norwood *(G-15424)*
Bock & Pierce Enterprises ..... G 513 474-9500
   Cincinnati *(G-3398)*
Boldman Printing LLC ..... G 937 653-3431
   Urbana *(G-18980)*
◆ Bookmasters Inc ..... C 419 281-1802
   Ashland *(G-686)*
Brass Bull 1 LLC ..... G 740 335-8030
   Wshngtn CT Hs *(G-20720)*
Brothers Publishing Co LLC ..... E 937 548-3330
   Greenville *(G-10361)*
Camelot Typesetting Company ..... G 216 574-8973
   Cleveland *(G-4864)*
Canton Graphic Arts Service ..... G 330 456-9868
   Canton *(G-2611)*
Capozzolo Printers Inc ..... G 513 542-7874
   Cincinnati *(G-3440)*
Carlisle Prtg Walnut Creek Ltd ..... E 330 852-9922
   Sugarcreek *(G-17846)*
Clints Printing Inc ..... G 937 426-2771
   Beavercreek *(G-1354)*
Cold Duck Screen Prtg & EMB Co ..... G 330 426-1900
   East Palestine *(G-9071)*
Colortech Graphics & Printing ..... F 614 766-2400
   Columbus *(G-6780)*
▲ Consolidated Graphics Group Inc ..... C 216 881-9191
   Cleveland *(G-5015)*
Copley Ohio Newspapers Inc ..... C 330 364-5577
   New Philadelphia *(G-14765)*
Cornerstone Industries Lcc ..... G 513 871-4546
   West Chester *(G-19685)*
COS Blueprint Inc ..... F 330 376-0022
   Akron *(G-122)*
Crabar/Gbf Inc ..... F 419 943-2141
   Leipsic *(G-11724)*
Customer Service Systems Inc ..... G 330 677-2877
   Kent *(G-11308)*

27 PRINTING, PUBLISHING, AND ALLIED INDUSTRIES

Daily Gazette .....E..... 937 372-4444
Xenia *(G-20764)*
Daubenmires Printing .....G..... 513 425-7223
Middletown *(G-13899)*
Debandale Printing Inc .....G..... 330 725-5122
Medina *(G-13251)*
Dorothy Crooker .....G..... 513 385-0888
Cincinnati *(G-3602)*
DOV Graphics Inc .....E..... 513 241-5150
Cincinnati *(G-3605)*
Dove Cds Inc .....G..... 330 928-9160
Tallmadge *(G-17981)*
Earl D Arnold Printing Company .....E..... 513 533-6900
Cincinnati *(G-3624)*
Easterdays Printing Center .....G..... 330 726-1182
Youngstown *(G-20895)*
Emta Inc .....G..... 440 734-6464
North Olmsted *(G-15187)*
Eugene Stewart .....G..... 937 898-1117
Dayton *(G-8189)*
Fedex Office & Print Svcs Inc .....E..... 937 436-0677
Dayton *(G-8192)*
Fedex Office & Print Svcs Inc .....E..... 614 621-1100
Columbus *(G-6917)*
Fedex Office & Print Svcs Inc .....F..... 614 575-0800
Reynoldsburg *(G-16439)*
Fedex Office & Print Svcs Inc .....E..... 216 573-1511
Cleveland *(G-5228)*
Fedex Office & Print Svcs Inc .....E..... 419 866-5464
Toledo *(G-18290)*
Flexoplate Inc .....E..... 513 489-0433
Blue Ash *(G-1776)*
Frank J Prucha & Associates .....G..... 216 642-3838
Cleveland *(G-5272)*
Franklins Printing Company .....F..... 740 452-6375
Zanesville *(G-21138)*
Gazette Publishing Company .....C..... 419 483-4190
Oberlin *(G-15495)*
Genesis Quality Printing Inc .....G..... 440 975-5700
Mentor *(G-13457)*
Geygan Enterprises Inc .....F..... 513 932-4222
Lebanon *(G-11656)*
Graphic Image .....G..... 937 320-0302
Beavercreek *(G-1318)*
Graphic Touch Inc .....G..... 330 337-3341
Salem *(G-16744)*
Greg Blume .....G..... 740 574-2308
Wheelersburg *(G-20182)*
Harlan Graphic Arts Svcs Inc .....E..... 513 251-5700
Cincinnati *(G-3798)*
▲ Hecks Direct Mail & Prtg Svc .....E..... 419 697-3505
Toledo *(G-18327)*
Henderson Builders Inc .....E..... 419 665-2684
Gibsonburg *(G-10248)*
Heritage Press Inc .....E..... 419 289-9209
Ashland *(G-709)*
Hilleary-Whitaker Inc .....G..... 614 766-4694
Columbus *(G-7001)*
Hkm Drect Mkt Cmmnications Inc .....C..... 216 651-9500
Cleveland *(G-5412)*
Homewood Press Inc .....E..... 419 478-0695
Toledo *(G-18334)*
HOT Graphic Services Inc .....E..... 419 242-7000
Northwood *(G-15339)*
Hubbard Publishing Co .....F..... 419 592-3060
Bellefontaine *(G-1518)*
Image Industries Inc .....G..... 937 832-7969
Clayton *(G-4575)*
Imprints .....F..... 330 650-0467
Hudson *(G-11054)*
▲ Jack Walker Printing Co .....F..... 440 352-4222
Mentor *(G-13483)*
Kad Holdings Inc .....G..... 614 792-3399
Dublin *(G-8935)*
Keener Printing Inc .....E..... 216 531-7595
Cleveland *(G-5523)*
▲ Kehl-Kolor Inc .....E..... 419 281-3107
Ashland *(G-717)*
Kevin K Tidd .....G..... 419 885-5603
Sylvania *(G-17948)*
Keystone Press Inc .....G..... 419 243-7326
Toledo *(G-18367)*
Keystone Printing & Copy Cat .....G..... 740 354-6542
Portsmouth *(G-16286)*
La Dua Inc .....G..... 440 243-9600
Lakewood *(G-11524)*
Landen Desktop Pubg Ctr Inc .....G..... 513 683-5181
Loveland *(G-12209)*
Laurenee Ltd LLC .....G..... 513 662-2225
Cincinnati *(G-3934)*

Lee Corporation .....G..... 513 771-3602
Cincinnati *(G-3937)*
Legal News Publishing Co .....E..... 216 696-3322
Cleveland *(G-5572)*
Liming Printing Inc .....F..... 937 374-2646
Xenia *(G-20782)*
Lund Printing Co .....G..... 330 628-4047
Akron *(G-262)*
M Web Type Inc .....G..... 614 272-8973
Columbus *(G-7141)*
Margaret Trentman .....G..... 513 948-1700
Cincinnati *(G-3980)*
Middleton Printing Co Inc .....G..... 614 294-7277
Gahanna *(G-10090)*
Mmp Printing Inc .....E..... 513 381-0990
Cincinnati *(G-4035)*
Montview Corporation .....G..... 330 723-3409
Medina *(G-13304)*
Multi-Craft Litho Inc .....E..... 859 581-2754
Blue Ash *(G-1824)*
Nari Inc .....G..... 440 960-2280
Monroeville *(G-14289)*
Network Printing & Graphics .....F..... 614 230-2084
Columbus *(G-7214)*
Newfax Corporation .....F..... 419 241-5157
Toledo *(G-18423)*
Newspaper Holding Inc .....D..... 440 998-2323
Ashtabula *(G-792)*
Old Trail Printing Company .....C..... 614 443-4852
Columbus *(G-7269)*
Onetouchpoint East Corp .....D..... 513 421-1600
Cincinnati *(G-4113)*
Orrville Printing Co Inc .....G..... 330 682-5066
Orrville *(G-15608)*
Our Fifth Street LLC .....G..... 614 866-4065
Pickerington *(G-16055)*
Painesville Publishing Co .....G..... 440 354-4142
Austinburg *(G-924)*
Paul/Jay Associates .....G..... 740 676-8776
Bellaire *(G-1488)*
Penguin Enterprises Inc .....E..... 440 899-5112
Westlake *(G-20140)*
Performa La Mar Printing Inc .....G..... 440 632-9800
Middlefield *(G-13845)*
Photo-Type Engraving Company .....F..... 614 308-1900
Columbus *(G-7315)*
Photo-Type Engraving Company .....F..... 614 308-7914
Columbus *(G-7316)*
Plott Graphic Directions Inc .....G..... 614 475-0217
Columbus *(G-7329)*
Pooles Printing & Office Svcs .....G..... 419 475-9000
Toledo *(G-18474)*
Preisser Inc .....E..... 614 345-0199
Columbus *(G-7344)*
Prime Printing Inc .....E..... 937 438-3707
Dayton *(G-8442)*
Printed Image .....F..... 614 221-1412
Columbus *(G-7350)*
Printing Arts Press .....F..... 740 397-6106
Mount Vernon *(G-14502)*
Progressive Communications .....D..... 740 397-5333
Mount Vernon *(G-14503)*
Quick As A Wink Printing Co .....F..... 419 224-9786
Lima *(G-11926)*
▼ Quick Tab II Inc .....D..... 419 448-6622
Tiffin *(G-18076)*
Quick Tech Graphics Inc .....E..... 937 743-5952
Springboro *(G-17348)*
R & W Printing Company .....G..... 513 575-0131
Loveland *(G-12224)*
R W Michael Printing Co .....G..... 330 923-9277
Akron *(G-340)*
Registered Images Inc .....G..... 859 781-9200
Cincinnati *(G-4257)*
Ricci Anthony .....G..... 330 758-5761
Youngstown *(G-21015)*
River Corp .....G..... 513 641-3355
Cincinnati *(G-4272)*
Robert Esterman .....G..... 513 541-3311
Cincinnati *(G-4277)*
Robin Enterprises Company .....C..... 614 891-0250
Westerville *(G-20073)*
Robs Creative Screen Printing .....G..... 740 264-6383
Wintersville *(G-20541)*
▲ Royal Acme Corporation .....E..... 216 241-1477
Cleveland *(G-6009)*
Ryans Newark Leader Ex Prtg .....F..... 740 522-2149
Newark *(G-14916)*
S O S Graphics & Printing Inc .....G..... 614 846-8229
Worthington *(G-20702)*

Sandy Smittcamp .....G..... 937 372-1687
Xenia *(G-20788)*
Sharon Printing Co Inc .....G..... 330 239-1684
Sharon Center *(G-16953)*
Sjpm Inc .....G..... 614 475-4571
Gahanna *(G-10104)*
South End Printing Co .....E..... 216 341-0669
Cleveland *(G-6081)*
Spencer-Walker Press Inc .....F..... 740 344-6110
Newark *(G-14920)*
▲ St Media Group Intl Inc .....D..... 513 421-2050
Blue Ash *(G-1849)*
Stationery Shop Inc .....G..... 330 376-2033
Akron *(G-387)*
Stumbo Publishing Co .....E..... 419 529-2847
Ontario *(G-15548)*
Suburban Press Inc .....G..... 216 961-0766
Cleveland *(G-6114)*
Target Printing & Graphics .....G..... 937 228-0170
Dayton *(G-8539)*
Technical Translation Services .....F..... 440 942-3130
Willoughby *(G-20443)*
Tim L Humbert .....F..... 330 497-4944
Canton *(G-2836)*
Tj Metzgers Inc .....D..... 419 861-8611
Toledo *(G-18553)*
Ulrich Rubber Stamp Company .....G..... 419 339-9939
Elida *(G-9202)*
W L Beck Printing & Design .....G..... 330 762-3020
Akron *(G-430)*
Watkins Printing Company .....E..... 614 297-8270
Columbus *(G-7593)*
▲ West-Camp Press Inc .....D..... 614 882-2378
Westerville *(G-20082)*
Western Roto Engravers Inc .....G..... 330 336-7636
Wadsworth *(G-19281)*
▲ Wfsr Holdings LLC .....A..... 877 735-4966
Dayton *(G-8592)*
Winkler Co Inc .....G..... 937 294-2662
Dayton *(G-8596)*
Wolters Kluwer Clinical Drug .....D..... 330 650-6506
Hudson *(G-11083)*
Youngstown ARC Engraving Co .....E..... 330 793-2471
Youngstown *(G-21070)*

2796 Platemaking & Related Svcs

Acme Printing Co Inc .....G..... 419 626-4426
Sandusky *(G-16792)*
American Hvy Plate Sltions LLC .....G..... 740 331-4620
Clarington *(G-4566)*
▲ Amos Media Company .....C..... 937 498-2111
Sidney *(G-17015)*
Anderson & Vreeland Inc .....D..... 419 636-5002
Bryan *(G-2264)*
Art-American Printing Plates .....E..... 216 241-4420
Cleveland *(G-4738)*
B & B Trophies & Awards .....G..... 330 225-6193
Brunswick *(G-2190)*
Bock & Pierce Enterprises .....G..... 513 474-9500
Cincinnati *(G-3398)*
Bomen Marking Products Inc .....G..... 440 582-0053
Cleveland *(G-4829)*
Capital Engraving Company .....G..... 440 237-7760
Cleveland *(G-4870)*
Carey Color Inc .....D..... 330 239-1835
Sharon Center *(G-16947)*
Century Graphics Inc .....E..... 614 895-7698
Westerville *(G-19983)*
Converters/Prepress Inc .....F..... 937 743-0935
Carlisle *(G-2891)*
Csw of Ny Inc .....F..... 413 589-1311
Sylvania *(G-17935)*
Custom Cntrwght Plate Proc Inc .....G..... 330 448-2347
Masury *(G-13060)*
Customer Service Systems Inc .....G..... 330 677-2877
Kent *(G-11308)*
Dorothy Crooker .....G..... 513 385-0888
Cincinnati *(G-3602)*
E C Shaw Co .....E..... 513 721-6334
Cincinnati *(G-3616)*
Earl D Arnold Printing Company .....E..... 513 533-6900
Cincinnati *(G-3624)*
Econo Products Inc .....F..... 330 923-4101
Cuyahoga Falls *(G-7862)*
Fine Lines Laser Engraving .....G..... 419 337-6313
Wauseon *(G-19515)*
Flexoplate Inc .....E..... 513 489-0433
Blue Ash *(G-1776)*
FT Group Inc .....E..... 937 746-6439
Cincinnati *(G-3716)*

Grant John .... G 937 298-0633
Dayton *(G-8234)*

▲ Great Lakes Integrated Inc .... D 216 651-1500
Cleveland *(G-5347)*

Hadronics Inc .... D 513 321-9350
Cincinnati *(G-3792)*

Harris Paper Crafts Inc .... F 614 299-2141
Columbus *(G-6983)*

Jerry Pulfer .... G 937 778-1861
Piqua *(G-16134)*

▲ Kehl-Kolor Inc .... E 419 281-3107
Ashland *(G-717)*

Keystone Press Inc .... G 419 243-7326
Toledo *(G-18367)*

Lazer Systems Inc .... F 513 641-4002
Cincinnati *(G-3935)*

Linger Photo Engraving Corp .... G 513 579-1380
Cincinnati *(G-3945)*

Litho-Craft Lithography Inc .... G 513 542-6404
Cincinnati *(G-3947)*

M Russell & Associates Inc .... G 419 478-8795
Toledo *(G-18392)*

▲ Mark-All Enterprises LLC .... E 800 433-3615
Akron *(G-268)*

Master Marking Company Inc .... F 330 688-6797
Stow *(G-17604)*

Northmont Sign Co Inc .... G 937 890-0372
Dayton *(G-8384)*

Peck Engraving Co .... E 216 221-1556
Cleveland *(G-5860)*

Penguin Enterprises Inc .... E 440 899-5112
Westlake *(G-20140)*

Pinnacle Graphics & Imaging .... F 216 781-1800
Cleveland *(G-5878)*

Plate Engraving Corporation .... F 330 239-2155
Medina *(G-13320)*

Precision Reflex Inc .... F 419 629-2603
New Bremen *(G-14659)*

Prime Printing Inc .... E 937 438-3707
Dayton *(G-8442)*

Quality Rubber Stamp Inc .... G 614 235-2700
Columbus *(G-7365)*

R E May Inc .... F 216 771-6332
Cleveland *(G-5950)*

R W Michael Printing Co .... G 330 923-9277
Akron *(G-340)*

Registered Images Inc .... G 859 781-9200
Cincinnati *(G-4257)*

Roban Inc .... G 330 794-1059
Lakemore *(G-11500)*

Robert H Shackelford .... G 330 364-2221
New Philadelphia *(G-14799)*

Sams Graphic Industries .... F 330 821-4710
Alliance *(G-498)*

Shamrock Plastics Inc .... F 740 392-5555
Mount Vernon *(G-14508)*

South End Printing Co .... G 216 341-0669
Cleveland *(G-6081)*

Stevenson Color Inc .... C 513 321-7500
Cincinnati *(G-4381)*

Summit Finishing Technologies .... G 937 424-5512
Moraine *(G-14396)*

Universal Urethane Pdts Inc .... D 419 693-7400
Toledo *(G-18585)*

▲ West-Camp Press Inc .... D 614 882-2378
Westerville *(G-20082)*

Westrock Cp LLC .... C 937 898-2115
Dayton *(G-8589)*

Williams Steel Rule Die Co .... F 216 431-3232
Cleveland *(G-6311)*

◆ Wood Graphics Inc .... E 513 771-6300
Cincinnati *(G-4516)*

Youngstown ARC Engraving Co .... E 330 793-2471
Youngstown *(G-21070)*

28 CHEMICALS AND ALLIED PRODUCTS

2812 Alkalies & Chlorine

▲ Ashta Chemicals Inc .... D 440 997-5221
Ashtabula *(G-762)*

Church & Dwight Co Inc .... D 740 852-3621
London *(G-12053)*

Church & Dwight Co Inc .... F 419 992-4244
Old Fort *(G-15524)*

Clorox Company .... F 513 445-1840
Mason *(G-12848)*

Clorox Sales Company .... E 440 892-1700
Westlake *(G-20106)*

Gbc Metals LLC .... E 330 823-1700
Alliance *(G-469)*

◆ GFS Chemicals Inc .... E 740 881-5501
Powell *(G-16322)*

Jci Jones Chemicals Inc .... F 330 825-2531
New Franklin *(G-14692)*

▲ National Colloid Company .... E 740 282-1171
Steubenville *(G-17545)*

National Lime and Stone Co .... C 419 396-7671
Carey *(G-2884)*

Occidental Chemical Corp .... E 513 242-2900
Cincinnati *(G-4097)*

Occidental Chemical Corp .... E 330 764-3441
Medina *(G-13309)*

PPG Industries Inc .... E 419 683-2400
Crestline *(G-7799)*

▲ Valvsys LLC .... G 513 539-1234
Monroe *(G-14279)*

2813 Industrial Gases

Air Products and Chemicals Inc .... D 513 420-3663
Middletown *(G-13876)*

Air Products and Chemicals Inc .... F 216 781-2801
Cleveland *(G-4644)*

Air Products and Chemicals Inc .... G 513 242-9215
Cincinnati *(G-3312)*

Airgas Usa LLC .... F 419 228-2828
Lima *(G-11831)*

Airgas Usa LLC .... G 937 237-0621
Dayton *(G-8014)*

Airgas Usa LLC .... E 330 454-1330
Canton *(G-2563)*

Airgas Usa LLC .... E 937 228-8594
Dayton *(G-8013)*

Airgas Usa LLC .... G 440 232-6397
Oakwood Village *(G-15477)*

C A P Industries Inc .... F 937 773-1824
Piqua *(G-16105)*

Delille Oxygen Company .... E 614 444-1177
Columbus *(G-6857)*

Delille Oxygen Company .... G 937 325-9595
Springfield *(G-17386)*

Endurance Manufacturing Inc .... G 330 628-2600
Mogadore *(G-14236)*

Eveready Products Corporation .... F 216 661-2755
Cleveland *(G-5201)*

GSC Neon .... G 216 310-6243
Mayfield Hts *(G-13173)*

Gsf Energy LLC .... G 513 825-0504
Cincinnati *(G-3787)*

Hydrogen Energy Systems LLC .... G 330 236-0358
Akron *(G-211)*

Ihod USA LLC .... G 216 459-7179
Cleveland *(G-5436)*

◆ Invacare Corporation .... A 440 329-6000
Elyria *(G-9272)*

Invacare Corporation .... D 800 333-6900
Elyria *(G-9273)*

Linde Gas North America LLC .... F 614 846-7048
Columbus *(G-7129)*

Linde Gas USA LLC .... F 330 425-3989
Twinsburg *(G-18808)*

Matheson Tri-Gas Inc .... F 330 425-4407
Twinsburg *(G-18812)*

Matheson Tri-Gas Inc .... F 513 727-9638
Middletown *(G-13925)*

Matheson Tri-Gas Inc .... F 419 865-8881
Holland *(G-10943)*

Messer LLC .... E 330 608-3008
Uniontown *(G-18928)*

Messer LLC .... E 513 831-4742
Miamiville *(G-13753)*

Messer LLC .... E 419 227-9585
Lima *(G-11900)*

Messer LLC .... E 216 533-7256
Cleveland *(G-5657)*

Messer LLC .... G 614 539-2259
Grove City *(G-10445)*

Messer LLC .... G 330 394-4541
Warren *(G-19422)*

Messer LLC .... E 419 221-5043
Lima *(G-11901)*

Messer LLC .... G 419 822-3909
Delta *(G-8776)*

National Gas & Oil Corporation .... E 740 344-2102
Newark *(G-14900)*

Neo Tech .... G 937 845-0999
New Carlisle *(G-14674)*

Neon .... G 216 761-4782
Cleveland *(G-5735)*

Neon Beach Tan .... G 440 933-3051
Amherst *(G-565)*

Neon By Deon LLC .... G 440 292-5626
Cleveland *(G-5736)*

Neon City .... G 440 301-2000
Cleveland *(G-5737)*

Neon Goldfish Mktg Solutions .... G 419 842-4462
Holland *(G-10946)*

Neon Health Services Inc .... E 216 231-7700
Cleveland *(G-5738)*

Neon Hussy LLC .... G 513 374-7644
Columbus *(G-7213)*

Neon Paintbrush .... G 419 436-1202
Fostoria *(G-9851)*

Northeast OH Neighborhood Heal .... D 216 751-3100
Cleveland *(G-5774)*

Nyeco Gas Inc .... G 419 447-2712
Sandusky *(G-16831)*

Osair Inc .... G 440 974-6500
Mentor *(G-13537)*

Praxair Inc .... D 440 994-1000
Ashtabula *(G-800)*

Praxair Inc .... E 216 778-5555
Cleveland *(G-5903)*

Praxair Inc .... E 440 237-8690
Cleveland *(G-5904)*

Praxair Inc .... G 419 698-8005
Oregon *(G-15564)*

Praxair Inc .... G 419 729-7732
Toledo *(G-18476)*

Praxair Inc .... G 740 453-0346
Zanesville *(G-21171)*

Praxair Inc .... G 937 323-6408
Springfield *(G-17474)*

Praxair Inc .... G 740 373-6449
Marietta *(G-12656)*

Praxair Inc .... G 419 422-1353
Lima *(G-11917)*

Praxair Inc .... F 330 264-6633
Wooster *(G-20640)*

Praxair Inc .... E 419 652-3562
Cleveland *(G-5905)*

Praxair Inc .... G 440 944-8844
Cleveland *(G-5906)*

Praxair Inc .... F 740 374-5525
Marietta *(G-12657)*

Praxair Inc .... E 330 453-9904
Canton *(G-2789)*

Praxair Inc .... D 419 666-5206
Rossford *(G-16590)*

Praxair Inc .... G 330 747-4126
Youngstown *(G-21002)*

Praxair Inc .... G 330 825-4449
Barberton *(G-1098)*

Praxair Distribution Inc .... F 614 443-7687
Columbus *(G-7341)*

Praxair Distribution Inc .... G 419 422-1353
Lima *(G-11918)*

Praxair Distribution Inc .... G 513 821-2192
Cincinnati *(G-4184)*

Praxair Distribution Inc .... E 419 476-0738
Toledo *(G-18477)*

Praxair Distribution Inc .... F 937 283-3400
Wilmington *(G-20504)*

Reliable Mfg Co LLC .... G 740 756-9373
Carroll *(G-2908)*

Welders Supply Inc .... F 216 241-1696
Cleveland *(G-6299)*

Wellston Aerosol Mfg Co Inc .... E 740 384-2320
Wellston *(G-19610)*

William Harding .... G 513 738-3344
Hamilton *(G-10622)*

Wright Brothers Inc .... E 513 731-2222
Cincinnati *(G-4520)*

Wright Brothers Global Gas LLC .... G 513 731-2222
Cincinnati *(G-4521)*

▲ Zenex International .... E 440 232-4155
Bedford *(G-1457)*

2816 Inorganic Pigments

Americhem Inc .... E 330 926-3185
Cuyahoga Falls *(G-7834)*

▲ Americhem Inc .... A 330 929-4213
Cuyahoga Falls *(G-7835)*

Ampacet Corporation .... C 740 929-5521
Newark *(G-14850)*

BASF Corporation .... G 440 329-2525
Elyria *(G-9223)*

▲ Chromaflo Technologies Corp .... C 440 997-0081
Ashtabula *(G-764)*

S I C

28 CHEMICALS AND ALLIED PRODUCTS

Chromaflo Technologies Corp...............C 513 733-5111
  Cincinnati (G-3474)
Chromaflo Technologies Corp...............C 440 997-5137
  Ashtabula (G-765)
Colormatrix Group Inc..........................G 216 622-0100
  Berea (G-1598)
Colormatrix Holdings Inc.......................C 440 930-3162
  Berea (G-1599)
▲ Day-Glo Color Corp...........................C 216 391-7070
  Cleveland (G-5073)
Day-Glo Color Corp..............................C 216 391-7070
  Cleveland (G-5074)
Day-Glo Color Corp..............................F 216 391-7070
  Twinsburg (G-18761)
▲ Degussa Incorporated.......................G 513 733-5111
  Cincinnati (G-3580)
◆ Eckart America Corporation................E 440 954-7600
  Painesville (G-15734)
▲ Ferro Corporation..............................D 216 875-5600
  Mayfield Heights (G-13163)
Ferro International Svcs Inc..................E 216 875-5600
  Mayfield Heights (G-13164)
General Color Investments Inc..............D 330 868-4161
  Minerva (G-14180)
Harsco Corporation..............................D 330 372-1781
  Warren (G-19408)
Ironics Inc...G 330 652-0583
  Niles (G-15016)
ISK Americas Incorporated...................E 440 357-4600
  Painesville (G-15750)
Leonhardt Plating Company.................E 513 242-1410
  Cincinnati (G-3938)
Lightstab Ltd Co..................................G 216 751-5800
  Shaker Heights (G-16933)
Obron Atlantic Corporation...................D 440 954-7600
  Painesville (G-15767)
▲ PMC Specialties Group Inc...............E 513 242-3300
  Cincinnati (G-4169)
PMC Specialties Group Inc..................G 513 242-3300
  Cincinnati (G-4170)
Polyone Corporation.............................C 419 668-4844
  Norwalk (G-15412)
Revlis Corporation................................E 330 535-2108
  Barberton (G-1101)
Rti Niles...G 330 455-4010
  Niles (G-15034)
▲ Spectrum Dispersions Inc.................F 330 296-0600
  Ravenna (G-16405)
Sun Chemical Corporation....................C 513 681-5950
  Cincinnati (G-4391)
◆ Thorworks Industries Inc...................E 419 626-4375
  Sandusky (G-16855)
Vwm-Republic Inc................................F 216 271-1400
  Cleveland (G-6276)
Whiterock Pigments Inc.......................G 216 391-7765
  Cleveland (G-6305)

2819 Indl Inorganic Chemicals, NEC

Adna Inc..G 614 397-4974
  Dublin (G-8873)
Airgas Usa LLC....................................G 440 232-6397
  Oakwood Village (G-15477)
▲ Akron Dispersions Inc.......................E 330 666-0045
  Copley (G-7676)
▲ Alchem Corporation..........................G 330 725-2436
  Medina (G-13221)
Aldrich Chemical..................................D 937 859-1808
  Miamisburg (G-13638)
Allyn Corp..G 614 442-3900
  Columbus (G-6575)
Alpha Zeta Holdings Inc.......................G 216 271-1601
  Cleveland (G-4677)
◆ Aluchem Inc......................................E 513 733-8519
  Cincinnati (G-3327)
Aluchem of Jackson Inc.......................E 740 286-2455
  Jackson (G-11180)
▲ Americhem Inc..................................A 330 929-4213
  Cuyahoga Falls (G-7835)
Amresco LLC.......................................D 440 349-2805
  Cleveland (G-4701)
Arboris LLC..E 740 522-9350
  Newark (G-14852)
Arizona Chemical Company LLC..........C 330 343-7701
  Dover (G-8804)
Artistic Elements Salon LLC.................G 330 626-2114
  Streetsboro (G-17661)
◆ Baerlocher Production Usa LLC........E 513 482-6300
  Cincinnati (G-3377)
▲ Baerlocher Usa LLC..........................F 330 364-6000
  Dover (G-8805)

BASF Catalysts LLC..............................B 440 322-3741
  Elyria (G-9222)
BASF Catalysts LLC..............................D 216 360-5005
  Cleveland (G-4794)
Bio-Systems Corporation.......................D 608 365-9550
  Bowling Green (G-1956)
BLaster Corporation..............................E 216 901-5800
  Cleveland (G-4819)
Bleachtech LLC....................................E 216 921-1980
  Seville (G-16913)
Blue Cube Operations LLC...................G 440 248-1223
  Macedonia (G-12280)
Bond Chemicals Inc.............................F 330 725-5935
  Medina (G-13230)
◆ Borchers Americas Inc......................D 440 899-2950
  Westlake (G-20103)
C Soltesz Co..G 614 529-5494
  Columbus (G-6720)
C T Chemicals Inc................................G 513 459-9744
  Lebanon (G-11638)
Calgon Carbon Corporation..................G 614 258-9501
  Columbus (G-6723)
▲ Calvary Industries Inc.......................D 513 874-1113
  Fairfield (G-9487)
▲ Capital Resin Corporation.................G 614 445-7177
  Columbus (G-6733)
Chem Technologies Ltd.......................E 440 632-9311
  Middlefield (G-13783)
Chemtrade Chemicals US LLC.............G 513 422-6319
  Middletown (G-13893)
Chemtrade Refinery Svcs Inc...............F 419 641-4151
  Cairo (G-2402)
▲ Cil Isotope Separations LLC.............F 937 376-5413
  Xenia (G-20761)
Cincinnati Specialties LLC....................C 513 242-3300
  Cincinnati (G-3507)
◆ Columbia Chemical Corporation........E 330 225-3200
  Brunswick (G-2196)
▲ Coolant Control Inc..........................G 513 471-8770
  Cincinnati (G-3548)
Cristal USA Inc....................................C 440 994-1400
  Ashtabula (G-769)
Curtis Chemical Inc..............................G 330 656-2514
  Hudson (G-11040)
Custom Metal Shearing Inc..................F 937 233-6950
  Dayton (G-8120)
Db Parent Inc......................................G 513 475-3265
  Cincinnati (G-3578)
◆ Detrex Corporation...........................F 216 749-2605
  Cleveland (G-5087)
Distinctive Building Elem.....................G 419 420-5528
  Findlay (G-9678)
Diverseylever Inc.................................G 513 554-4200
  Cincinnati (G-3593)
Diversified Brands................................G 216 595-8777
  Bedford (G-1401)
◆ Dover Chemical Corporation.............C 330 343-7711
  Dover (G-8819)
Dpa Investments Inc............................G 440 992-3377
  Ashtabula (G-771)
Dpa Investments Inc............................F 513 737-7100
  Fairfield (G-9495)
Dpa Investments Inc............................F 440 992-7039
  Ashtabula (G-772)
Drs Industries Inc................................D 419 861-0334
  Holland (G-10928)
Earthganic Elements LLC.....................G 513 430-0503
  Batavia (G-1137)
Elco Corporation..................................G 440 997-6131
  Ashtabula (G-773)
Element One Home Staging................G 740 972-4714
  Dublin (G-8913)
Elements LLC......................................G 937 663-5837
  Saint Paris (G-16708)
Enerchem Incorporated........................G 513 745-0580
  Cincinnati (G-3639)
▲ Engelhard Corp.................................G 440 322-3741
  Elyria (G-9258)
▲ Essential Earth Elements LLC..........G 740 632-0682
  Toronto (G-18607)
Evonik Corporation..............................D 513 554-8969
  Cincinnati (G-3661)
Ferro Corporation................................D 216 577-7144
  Bedford (G-1405)
Four Elements Integratve Cnsel..........G 216 381-8584
  Cleveland Heights (G-6348)
▲ Gabriel Performance Pdts LLC.........F 866 800-2436
  Akron (G-180)
Gabriel Performance Pdts LLC.............G 440 992-3200
  Ashtabula (G-778)

◆ Gayston Corporation.........................C 937 743-6050
  Miamisburg (G-13672)
General Electric Company...................D 216 268-3846
  Cleveland (G-5310)
◆ GFS Chemicals Inc...........................E 740 881-5501
  Powell (G-16322)
GFS Chemicals Inc..............................C 614 224-5345
  Columbus (G-6950)
GFS Chemicals Inc..............................D 614 351-5347
  Columbus (G-6951)
◆ Globe Metallurgical Inc......................C 740 984-2361
  Waterford (G-19484)
Gnrl Chemical L...................................G 419 255-0193
  Toledo (G-18307)
Graphite Sales Inc...............................G 419 652-3388
  Nova (G-15434)
Helena Agri-Enterprises LLC................C 419 596-3806
  Continental (G-7666)
Helena Agri-Enterprises LLC................C 614 275-4200
  Columbus (G-6986)
▲ Heraeus Precious Metals North.......E 937 264-1000
  Vandalia (G-19127)
Hilltop Energy Inc................................E 330 859-2108
  Mineral City (G-14164)
Illinois Tool Works Inc..........................D 440 914-3100
  Solon (G-17166)
Johnson Mtthey Prcess Tech Inc.........E 330 298-7005
  Ravenna (G-16385)
◆ Jones-Hamilton Co............................G 419 666-9838
  Walbridge (G-19296)
Kerry Flavor Systems Us LLC..............E 513 539-7373
  Monroe (G-14270)
Kingscote Chemicals Inc......................G 330 523-5300
  Richfield (G-16475)
◆ Lithium Innovations Co LLC..............G 419 843-6051
  Toledo (G-18386)
Littlern Corporation..............................G 330 848-8847
  Barberton (G-1081)
M & G Polymers Usa LLC....................C 330 239-7400
  Sharon Center (G-16951)
McGean-Rohco Inc..............................D 216 441-4900
  Newburgh Heights (G-14941)
Metals and Additives Corp Inc..............F 740 654-6555
  Pleasantville (G-16228)
▲ Molecular Research Center..............F 513 841-0900
  Cincinnati (G-4040)
Motorcarbon Elements LLC..................G 304 617-4047
  South Point (G-17290)
◆ Nachurs Alpine Solutions Corp.........E 740 382-5701
  Marion (G-12723)
Nap Asset Holdings Ltd.......................F 330 633-0599
  Tallmadge (G-17995)
▲ National Colloid Company................E 740 282-1171
  Steubenville (G-17545)
New Eezy-Gro Inc................................F 419 927-6110
  Upper Sandusky (G-18967)
Nutrien AG Solutions Inc.....................C 513 941-4100
  North Bend (G-15053)
Occidental Chemical Corp....................E 513 242-2900
  Cincinnati (G-4097)
▲ Occidental Chemical Durez..............G 419 675-5300
  Kenton (G-11417)
Ohio Coatings Company......................D 740 859-5500
  Yorkville (G-20827)
Ohio Metal Working Products..............E 330 455-2009
  Canton (G-2773)
Ohio Oxide Corporation Del.................F 740 654-6555
  Pleasantville (G-16229)
Omnova Solutions Inc..........................D 330 734-1237
  Akron (G-311)
Omnova Solutions Inc..........................C 216 682-7000
  Beachwood (G-1257)
Omnova Wallcovering USA Inc............G 216 682-7000
  Beachwood (G-1258)
Omya Distribution LLC.........................G 513 387-4600
  Blue Ash (G-1827)
Pcs Phosphate Company Inc...............E 513 738-1261
  Harrison (G-10662)
Pennex Aluminum................................D 330 427-6704
  Leetonia (G-11719)
◆ Perstorp Polyols Inc..........................C 419 729-5448
  Toledo (G-18467)
Pickett Enterprises Inc.........................G 937 428-6747
  Dayton (G-8425)
▲ PMC Specialties Group Inc..............E 513 242-3300
  Cincinnati (G-4169)
PMC Specialties Group Inc..................G 513 242-3300
  Cincinnati (G-4170)
▲ Polymerics Inc..................................E 330 434-6665
  Cuyahoga Falls (G-7906)

SIC SECTION
28 CHEMICALS AND ALLIED PRODUCTS

◆ Porocel Industries LLC ....G..... 513 733-8519
  Cincinnati *(G-4172)*
PQ Corporation ....G..... 216 341-2578
  Newburgh Heights *(G-14943)*
Press Chemical & Phrm Lab ....G..... 614 863-2802
  Columbus *(G-7345)*
Process Sltions For Indust Inc ....G..... 330 702-1685
  Canfield *(G-2541)*
PVS Chemical Solutions Inc ....F..... 330 666-0888
  Copley *(G-7693)*
Rapid Blanket Restorer Corp ....G..... 330 821-6326
  Willoughby *(G-20418)*
Rtprocess LLC ....G..... 937 366-6215
  Wilmington *(G-20508)*
Saint-Gobain Ceramics Plas Inc .....A..... 330 673-5860
  Stow *(G-17624)*
Saint-Gobain Ceramics Plas Inc .....C..... 440 834-5600
  Hiram *(G-10911)*
Selective Micro Tech LLC ....G..... 614 551-5974
  Dublin *(G-8982)*
Shepherd Chemical Company ....F..... 513 200-6987
  Cincinnati *(G-4331)*
Shepherd Chemical Company ....F..... 513 731-1110
  Cincinnati *(G-4332)*
Shepherd Chemical Company ....F..... 513 424-7276
  Middletown *(G-13952)*
Shepherd Material Science Co ....F..... 513 731-1110
  Norwood *(G-15428)*
Solvay Advanced Polymers LLC ....G..... 740 373-9242
  Marietta *(G-12672)*
Solvay USA Inc ....E..... 513 482-5700
  Cincinnati *(G-4353)*
Tate Lyle Ingrdnts Amricas LLC ......D..... 937 236-5906
  Dayton *(G-8541)*
TEC Line Inc ....G..... 740 881-5948
  Lewis Center *(G-11783)*
▲ Three Leaf Inc ....G..... 888 308-1007
  Fairfield Township *(G-9588)*
Tiger Sul Products LLC ....G..... 203 451-3305
  West Liberty *(G-19938)*
Tru-Chem Company Inc ....F..... 614 888-2436
  Columbus *(G-7547)*
▲ Union Camp Corp ....G..... 330 343-7701
  Dover *(G-8862)*
◆ United Initiators Inc ....D..... 440 326-2416
  Elyria *(G-9341)*
Univar USA Inc ....C..... 513 714-5264
  West Chester *(G-19911)*
Veolia NA Regeneration Srvcs ....F..... 513 941-4121
  North Bend *(G-15057)*
▲ VWR Chemicals LLC ....E..... 800 448-4442
  Solon *(G-17258)*
WA Hammond Drierite Co Ltd ....E..... 937 376-2927
  Xenia *(G-20803)*
▲ Zaclon LLC ....E..... 216 271-1601
  Cleveland *(G-6335)*

2821 Plastics, Mtrls & Nonvulcanizable Elastomers

◆ A Schulman Inc ....D..... 330 666-3751
  Fairlawn *(G-9589)*
A Schulman Inc ....E..... 330 498-4840
  North Canton *(G-15066)*
A Schulman Inc ....G..... 440 224-7544
  Geneva *(G-10210)*
A Schulman Inc ....C..... 330 773-2700
  Akron *(G-20)*
A Schulman Inc ....G..... 419 872-1408
  Perrysburg *(G-15916)*
A Schulman Inc ....G..... 909 356-8091
  Fairlawn *(G-9590)*
A Schulman Inc ....C..... 330 630-0308
  Akron *(G-21)*
A Schulman Inc ....F..... 330 630-3315
  Akron *(G-22)*
A Schulman International Inc ....G..... 330 666-3751
  Fairlawn *(G-9591)*
▼ Ada Solutions Inc ....E..... 440 576-0423
  Jefferson *(G-11223)*
Advanced Elastomer Systems LP ..D..... 330 336-7641
  Wadsworth *(G-19221)*
Advanced Fiber LLC ....E..... 419 562-1337
  Bucyrus *(G-2317)*
Al-Co Products Inc ....F..... 419 399-3867
  Latty *(G-11624)*
Altera Polymers LLC ....G..... 864 973-7000
  Jefferson *(G-11224)*
American Polymer Standards ....G..... 440 255-2211
  Mentor *(G-13386)*

Ametek Inc ....F..... 419 739-3200
  Wapakoneta *(G-19321)*
Ampacet Corp ....E..... 513 247-5403
  Mason *(G-12823)*
Amros Industries Inc ....E..... 216 433-0010
  Cleveland *(G-4702)*
Anchor Hocking Glass Company ...G..... 740 681-6025
  Lancaster *(G-11544)*
Arclin USA LLC ....E..... 419 726-5013
  Toledo *(G-18190)*
Arizona Chemical Company LLC ....C..... 330 343-7701
  Dover *(G-8804)*
Ashland LLC ....G..... 513 557-3100
  Cincinnati *(G-3361)*
Asi Investment Holding Co ....D..... 330 666-3751
  Fairlawn *(G-9593)*
◆ Aurora Plastics LLC ....D..... 330 422-0700
  Streetsboro *(G-17662)*
Aviles Construction Company ....E..... 216 939-1084
  Cleveland *(G-4777)*
BCi and V Investments Inc ....D..... 330 538-0660
  North Jackson *(G-15141)*
Biobent Holdings LLC ....G..... 513 658-5560
  Columbus *(G-6670)*
▲ Biothane Coated Webbing Corp ...E..... 440 327-0485
  North Ridgeville *(G-15212)*
Bricolage Inc ....F..... 614 853-6789
  Grove City *(G-10418)*
▲ Buckeye Polymers Inc ....E..... 330 948-3007
  Lodi *(G-12008)*
Cameo Countertops Inc ....G..... 419 865-6371
  Holland *(G-10918)*
▲ Capital Resin Corporation ....D..... 614 445-7177
  Columbus *(G-6733)*
Carolina Color Corp Ohio ....E..... 740 363-6622
  Delaware *(G-8660)*
▲ Chemionics Corporation ....E..... 330 733-8834
  Tallmadge *(G-17975)*
Chroma Color Corporation ....E..... 740 363-6622
  Delaware *(G-8666)*
Clyde Tool & Die Inc ....F..... 419 547-9574
  Clyde *(G-6387)*
Colormatrix ....G..... 440 930-1000
  Avon Lake *(G-982)*
Composite Technical Svcs LLC ......G..... 937 660-3783
  Kettering *(G-11430)*
◆ Concrete Sealants Inc ....E..... 937 845-8776
  Tipp City *(G-18109)*
Cornerstone Indus Holdings ....G..... 440 893-9144
  Chagrin Falls *(G-3014)*
Covestro LLC ....C..... 740 929-2015
  Hebron *(G-10740)*
Crane Blending Center ....E..... 614 542-1199
  Columbus *(G-6835)*
Crane Plastics Mfg Ltd ....G..... 614 754-3700
  Columbus *(G-6836)*
▲ Crg Plastics Inc ....F..... 937 298-2025
  Dayton *(G-8113)*
▲ Crown Plastics Co ....D..... 513 367-0238
  Harrison *(G-10638)*
Current Inc ....G..... 330 392-5151
  Warren *(G-19392)*
▲ Dayson Polymers LLC ....G..... 330 335-5237
  Wadsworth *(G-19233)*
Deltech Polymers Corporation ....F..... 937 339-3150
  Troy *(G-18648)*
Denney Plastics Machining LLC ....F..... 330 308-5300
  New Philadelphia *(G-14766)*
Dentsply Sirona Inc ....D..... 419 865-9497
  Maumee *(G-13108)*
Dlhbowles Inc ....F..... 330 478-2503
  Canton *(G-2662)*
Dow Chemical Company ....G..... 419 423-6500
  Findlay *(G-9680)*
Dow Chemical Company ....G..... 740 929-5100
  Hebron *(G-10742)*
Dow Chemical Company ....F..... 937 254-1550
  Dayton *(G-8166)*
Dupont Specialty Pdts USA LLC ....E..... 740 474-0220
  Circleville *(G-4543)*
Dupont Specialty Pdts USA LLC ....D..... 740 474-0635
  Circleville *(G-4544)*
Durez Corporation ....C..... 567 295-6400
  Kenton *(G-11404)*
E C Shaw Co ....E..... 513 721-6334
  Cincinnati *(G-3616)*
E P S Specialists Ltd Inc ....F..... 513 489-3676
  Cincinnati *(G-3618)*
Eagle Elastomer Inc ....E..... 330 923-7070
  Peninsula *(G-15893)*

Emerald Performance Mtls LLC .....D..... 330 374-2418
  Akron *(G-152)*
Emerald Specialty Polymers LLC ...E..... 330 374-2424
  Akron *(G-154)*
Engineered Polymer Systems LLC ...G..... 216 255-2116
  Medina *(G-13255)*
Ep Bollinger LLC ....A..... 513 941-1101
  Cincinnati *(G-3646)*
◆ Etna Products Incorporated ....E..... 440 543-9845
  Chagrin Falls *(G-3046)*
Farmed Materials Inc ....G..... 513 680-4046
  Cincinnati *(G-3673)*
▲ Ferro Corporation ....D..... 216 875-5600
  Mayfield Heights *(G-13163)*
Fibretuff Med Biopolymers LLC .....G..... 419 346-8728
  Perrysburg *(G-15950)*
Flex Technologies Inc ....E..... 330 897-6311
  Baltic *(G-1029)*
◆ Flexsys America LP ....D..... 330 666-4111
  Akron *(G-173)*
Freeman Manufacturing & Sup Co ...E..... 440 934-1902
  Avon *(G-950)*
▼ Geo-Tech Polymers LLC ....F..... 614 797-2300
  Waverly *(G-19546)*
▲ Global Biochem ....G..... 513 792-2218
  Cincinnati *(G-3762)*
▲ Goldsmith & Eggleton LLC ....F..... 203 855-6000
  Wadsworth *(G-19243)*
◆ Great Lakes Textiles Inc ....E..... 440 914-1122
  Solon *(G-17156)*
Grit Guard Inc ....G..... 937 592-9003
  Bellefontaine *(G-1516)*
Hancor Inc ....D..... 419 424-8225
  Findlay *(G-9701)*
▲ Hexa Americas Inc ....E..... 937 497-7900
  Sidney *(G-17043)*
Hexion Inc ....B..... 614 225-4000
  Columbus *(G-6992)*
◆ Hexion LLC ....E..... 614 225-4000
  Columbus *(G-6993)*
▼ Hexion US Finance Corp ....F..... 614 225-4000
  Columbus *(G-6994)*
Hexpol Compounding LLC ....G..... 440 682-4038
  Mogadore *(G-14239)*
▲ Hexpol Compounding LLC ....E..... 440 834-4644
  Burton *(G-2361)*
Hexpol Holding Inc ....F..... 440 834-4644
  Burton *(G-2362)*
▲ Hfi LLC ....B..... 614 491-0700
  Columbus *(G-6995)*
Hggc Citadel Plas Holdings Inc .....G..... 330 666-3751
  Fairlawn *(G-9607)*
Hpc Holdings LLC ....F..... 330 666-3751
  Fairlawn *(G-9608)*
Huntsman ....G..... 614 659-0155
  Dublin *(G-8925)*
Ic3d Inc ....F..... 614 344-0414
  Columbus *(G-7019)*
ICO Holdings LLC ....G..... 330 666-3751
  Fairlawn *(G-9609)*
▲ ICP Adhesives and Sealants Inc ...F..... 330 753-4585
  Norton *(G-15369)*
▲ Ier Fujikura Inc ....C..... 330 425-7121
  Macedonia *(G-12300)*
Illinois Tool Works Inc ....C..... 513 489-7600
  Blue Ash *(G-1791)*
▲ Incredible Solutions Inc ....F..... 330 898-3878
  Warren *(G-19409)*
Industrial Thermoset Plas Inc ....F..... 440 975-0411
  Mentor *(G-13471)*
◆ Ineos ABS (usa) LLC ....C..... 513 467-2400
  Addyston *(G-11)*
Integra Enclosures Limited ....D..... 440 269-4966
  Mentor *(G-13472)*
Integrated Chem Concepts Inc .....G..... 440 838-5666
  Brecksville *(G-2042)*
Intergroup International Ltd ....D..... 216 965-0257
  Akron *(G-218)*
▲ International Technical ....E..... 330 505-1218
  Niles *(G-15015)*
▲ Isochem Incorporated ....G..... 614 775-9328
  New Albany *(G-14627)*
▲ J P Industrial Products Inc ....G..... 330 424-1110
  Lisbon *(G-11972)*
▲ Jain America Foods Inc ....G..... 614 850-9400
  Columbus *(G-7058)*
◆ Jain America Holdings Inc ....D..... 614 850-9400
  Columbus *(G-7059)*
JB Polymers Inc ....G..... 216 941-7041
  Oberlin *(G-15501)*

28 CHEMICALS AND ALLIED PRODUCTS

Jerico Plastic Industries Inc ....E 330 868-4600
  Minerva *(G-14185)*
Jjc Plastics Ltd ....G 330 334-3637
  Norton *(G-15372)*
▲ JMS Industries Inc ....E 937 325-3502
  Springfield *(G-17426)*
▼ Kardol Quality Products LLC .....E 513 933-8206
  Blue Ash *(G-1800)*
Kathom Manufacturing Co Inc ....E 513 868-8890
  Hamilton *(G-10579)*
◆ Key Resin Company ....F 513 943-4225
  Batavia *(G-1159)*
Kiley Mold Company LLC ....G 513 875-3223
  Fayetteville *(G-9641)*
Kirtland Cpitl Partners III LP ....G 440 585-9010
  Willoughby Hills *(G-20470)*
Kraton Polymers US LLC ....B 740 423-7571
  Belpre *(G-1578)*
L-K Industry Inc ....E 937 526-3000
  Versailles *(G-19186)*
Louisville Molded Products ....G 330 877-9740
  Hartville *(G-10701)*
Lrbg Chemicals USA Inc ....G 419 244-5856
  Toledo *(G-18388)*
Ltg Polymers Limited ....G 330 854-5609
  Massillon *(G-13015)*
Lubrizol Advanced Mtls Inc ....E 440 933-0400
  Avon Lake *(G-993)*
▲ Maintenance Repair Supply Inc ...E 740 922-3006
  Midvale *(G-13980)*
▲ Mar-Bal Inc ....D 440 543-7526
  Chagrin Falls *(G-3057)*
Mar-Bal Inc ....D 440 543-7526
  Chagrin Falls *(G-3058)*
Materion Brush Inc ....E 440 960-5660
  Lorain *(G-12105)*
Meggitt (erlanger) LLC ....D 513 851-5550
  Cincinnati *(G-4000)*
◆ Mexichem Specialty Resins Inc ...F 440 930-1435
  Avon Lake *(G-996)*
Michael Day Enterprises LLC ....G 330 335-5100
  Wadsworth *(G-19253)*
Minova USA Inc ....D 740 377-9146
  South Point *(G-17289)*
Mitsubishi Chls Perf Plyrs Inc ....D 419 483-2931
  Bellevue *(G-1540)*
Mjs Plastics ....E 937 548-1000
  Greenville *(G-10383)*
Modern Plastics Recovery Inc ......F 419 622-4611
  Haviland *(G-10713)*
Momentive Performance Mtls Inc ..G 614 986-2495
  Columbus *(G-7193)*
◆ Multibase Inc ....D 330 666-0505
  Copley *(G-7689)*
▲ Mum Industries Inc ....E 440 269-4966
  Mentor *(G-13525)*
Nano Innovations LLC ....G 614 203-5706
  Columbus *(G-7208)*
▼ Nanosperse LLC ....G 937 296-5030
  Kettering *(G-11435)*
National Polymer Dev Co Inc ....F 440 708-1245
  Chagrin Falls *(G-3061)*
Nexeo Solutions LLC ....F 800 531-7106
  Dublin *(G-8956)*
Next Generation Plastics LLC ....G 330 668-1200
  Fairlawn *(G-9613)*
◆ Next Specialty Resins Inc ....E 419 843-4600
  Sylvania *(G-17955)*
Nona Composites LLC ....G 937 490-4814
  Miamisburg *(G-13700)*
Nova Chemicals Inc ....D 440 352-3381
  Painesville *(G-15766)*
Novo Foam Products LLC ....G 440 892-3325
  Westlake *(G-20133)*
Oak View Enterprises Inc ....E 513 860-4446
  Bucyrus *(G-2340)*
Occidental Chemical Corp ....E 513 242-2900
  Cincinnati *(G-4097)*
Ohio Foam Corporation ....F 419 492-2151
  New Washington *(G-14831)*
Ohio Plastics Belting Co ....G 330 882-6764
  New Franklin *(G-14695)*
OK Industries Inc ....E 419 435-2361
  Fostoria *(G-9854)*
Optem Inc ....G 330 723-5686
  Medina *(G-13312)*
▲ OSI Global Sourcing LLC ....G 614 471-4800
  Columbus *(G-7277)*
▲ Ovation Polymer Technology and ...E 330 723-5686
  Medina *(G-13314)*

Owens Corning Sales LLC ....F 330 633-6735
  Tallmadge *(G-17999)*
Pace Mold & Machine LLC ....E 330 879-1777
  Massillon *(G-13037)*
Pahuja Inc ....D 614 864-3989
  Gahanna *(G-10097)*
Performnce Plymr Solutions Inc ....F 937 298-3713
  Moraine *(G-14375)*
◆ Perstorp Polyols Inc ....C 419 729-5448
  Toledo *(G-18467)*
◆ Pet Processors LLc ....E 440 354-4321
  Painesville *(G-15775)*
Pitt Plastics Inc ....D 614 868-8660
  Columbus *(G-7317)*
◆ Plaskolite LLC ....C 614 294-3281
  Columbus *(G-7320)*
Plaskolite LLC ....D 740 450-1109
  Zanesville *(G-21168)*
Plaskolite LLC ....C 614 294-3281
  Columbus *(G-7321)*
Plasti-Kemm Inc ....G 330 239-1555
  Medina *(G-13318)*
Plastic Compounders Inc ....E 740 432-7371
  Cambridge *(G-2453)*
Plastic Regrinders Inc ....G 740 659-2346
  Glenford *(G-10272)*
▼ Plastic Selection Group Inc ....G 614 464-2008
  Columbus *(G-7322)*
◆ Plastrx Inc ....E 513 847-4032
  West Chester *(G-19760)*
Poly Green Technologies LLC ....G 419 529-9909
  Ontario *(G-15547)*
▲ Poly-Carb Inc ....E 440 248-1223
  Macedonia *(G-12318)*
▲ Polygroup Inc ....E 877 476-5972
  Loveland *(G-12222)*
▼ Polymer Concepts Inc ....E 440 953-9605
  Mentor *(G-13551)*
◆ Polymer Packaging Inc ....D 330 832-2000
  Massillon *(G-13040)*
Polymerics Inc ....E 330 677-1131
  Kent *(G-11364)*
▲ Polymerics Inc ....E 330 434-6665
  Cuyahoga Falls *(G-7906)*
Polynew Inc ....G 330 897-3202
  Baltic *(G-1032)*
Polynt Composites USA Inc ....E 816 391-6000
  Sandusky *(G-16839)*
Polyone Corporation ....F 740 423-7571
  Belpre *(G-1583)*
Polyone Corporation ....G 216 622-0100
  Berea *(G-1622)*
Polyone Corporation ....D 440 930-1000
  North Baltimore *(G-15047)*
Polyone Corporation ....C 800 727-4338
  Greenville *(G-10387)*
Polyone Corporation ....E 937 548-2133
  Greenville *(G-10388)*
Polyone Corporation ....D 330 834-3812
  Massillon *(G-13041)*
◆ Polyone Corporation ....G 440 930-1000
  Avon Lake *(G-1001)*
Polyone Corporation ....F 440 930-3817
  Avon Lake *(G-1002)*
Polyone Funding Corporation ....G 440 930-1000
  Avon Lake *(G-1003)*
Polyone LLC ....G 440 930-1000
  Avon Lake *(G-1004)*
PPG Industries Inc ....E 419 683-2400
  Crestline *(G-7799)*
Ppl Holding Company ....E 216 514-1840
  Cleveland *(G-5902)*
▼ Premix Inc ....C 440 224-2181
  North Kingsville *(G-15160)*
◆ Prime Conduit Inc ....F 216 464-3400
  Beachwood *(G-1269)*
Prime Industries Inc ....E 440 288-3626
  Lorain *(G-12113)*
Pro Mold Design Inc ....G 440 352-1212
  Mentor *(G-13554)*
▲ Progressive Foam Tech Inc ....C 330 756-3200
  Beach City *(G-1214)*
Queen City Foam Inc ....G 513 741-7722
  Cincinnati *(G-4236)*
▲ Rauh Polymers Inc ....F 330 376-1120
  Akron *(G-344)*
Ravago Americas LLC ....F 419 924-9090
  West Unity *(G-19973)*
Ray Fogg Construction Inc ....F 216 351-7976
  Cleveland *(G-5962)*

▲ Renegade Materials Corporation ....E 508 579-7888
  Miamisburg *(G-13711)*
▲ Resinoid Engineering Corp ....D 740 928-6115
  Hebron *(G-10759)*
◆ Rochling Glastic Composites LP ....C 216 486-0100
  Cleveland *(G-5996)*
Rotopolymers ....G 216 645-0333
  Cleveland *(G-6008)*
Saco Aei Polymers Inc ....F 330 995-1600
  Aurora *(G-906)*
San Pallet LLC ....G 937 271-5308
  Troy *(G-18702)*
▲ Scott Bader Inc ....E 330 920-4410
  Stow *(G-17626)*
Scott Molders Incorporated ....E 330 673-5777
  Kent *(G-11382)*
Sherwood Rtm Corp ....E 330 875-7151
  Louisville *(G-12166)*
Solvay Spclty Polymers USA LLC ....E 740 373-9242
  Marietta *(G-12673)*
Sonoco Prtective Solutions Inc ......D 419 420-0029
  Findlay *(G-9759)*
Sorbothane Inc ....E 330 678-9444
  Kent *(G-11388)*
STC International Co Ltd ....E 561 308-6002
  Lebanon *(G-11699)*
Stopol Equipment Sales LLC ....G 440 499-0030
  Brunswick *(G-2240)*
Sun Color Corporation ....G 330 499-7010
  North Canton *(G-15123)*
Sunprene Company ....C 330 666-3751
  Fairlawn *(G-9621)*
Synthetic Rubber Technology ....G 330 494-2221
  Uniontown *(G-18933)*
▲ Tembec Btlsr Inc ....E 419 244-5856
  Toledo *(G-18547)*
Tribotech Composites Inc ....E 216 901-1300
  Cleveland *(G-6210)*
◆ Triple Arrow Industries Inc ....G 614 437-5588
  Marysville *(G-12818)*
Ultratech Polymers Inc ....F 330 945-9410
  Cuyahoga Falls *(G-7932)*
◆ Uniloy Milacron Inc ....E 513 487-5000
  Batavia *(G-1192)*
V & A Process Inc ....F 440 288-8137
  Lorain *(G-12132)*
Vinyl Profiles Acquisition LLC ....C 330 538-0660
  North Jackson *(G-15157)*
Wilsonart LLC ....E 614 876-1515
  Columbus *(G-7605)*
Winsell Incorporated ....G 330 836-7421
  Akron *(G-437)*

2822 Synthetic Rubber (Vulcanizable Elastomers)

Advanced Elastomer Systems LP ....D 330 336-7641
  Wadsworth *(G-19221)*
Alan L Grant Polymer Inc ....G 757 627-4000
  Uniontown *(G-18908)*
All-Tra Rubber Processing ....G 330 630-1945
  Tallmadge *(G-17972)*
Brain Child Products LLC ....F 419 698-4020
  Toledo *(G-18215)*
Bridgestone Americas Center Fo ...G 330 379-7575
  Akron *(G-94)*
Bridgestone Procurement Holdin ...A 337 882-1200
  Akron *(G-95)*
◆ Brp Manufacturing Company ......E 800 858-0482
  Lima *(G-11847)*
Canton OH Rubber Speclty Prods ....G 330 454-3847
  Canton *(G-2612)*
▲ Cardinal Rubber Company Inc ....E 330 745-2191
  Barberton *(G-1069)*
Cephas Enterprises LLC ....E 513 317-5685
  West Chester *(G-19839)*
◆ Concrete Sealants Inc ....E 937 845-8776
  Tipp City *(G-18109)*
Covestro LLC ....C 740 929-2015
  Hebron *(G-10740)*
East West Copolymer & Rbr LLC ....F 225 267-3713
  Cleveland *(G-5138)*
▲ East West Copolymer LLC ....C 225 267-3400
  Cleveland *(G-5139)*
Eliokem Inc ....E 330 734-1100
  Fairlawn *(G-9604)*
◆ Flexsys America LP ....D 330 666-4111
  Akron *(G-173)*
Gdc Inc ....F 574 533-3128
  Wooster *(G-20596)*

SIC SECTION
28 CHEMICALS AND ALLIED PRODUCTS

▲ High Tech Elastomers Inc ....E 937 236-6575
  Vandalia (G-19128)
◆ Key Resin Company ....F 513 943-4225
  Batavia (G-1159)
Kraton Emplyees Recreation CLB.......G 740 423-7571
  Belpre (G-1577)
Kraton Polymers US LLC ....B 740 423-7571
  Belpre (G-1578)
Lyondell Chemical Company ....D 513 530-4000
  Cincinnati (G-3960)
Lyondellbasell 513 530-4000
  Cincinnati (G-3961)
Matterworks 740 200-0071
  Heath (G-10726)
▲ Medical Elastomer Dev Inc ....E 330 425-8352
  Twinsburg (G-18815)
Meggitt (erlanger) LLC 513 851-5550
  Cincinnati (G-4000)
◆ Mexichem Specialty Resins Inc ....E 440 930-1435
  Avon Lake (G-996)
▲ Midwest Elastomers Inc ....D 419 738-8844
  Wapakoneta (G-19343)
Mohican Industries Inc ....F 330 869-0500
  Akron (G-284)
Mondo Polymer Technologies Inc ....E 740 376-9396
  Reno (G-16425)
Nova Polymers Inc ....G 888 484-6682
  Bryan (G-2300)
Polyshield Corporation ....F 614 755-7674
  Pickerington (G-16056)
Protective Industrial Polymers ....F 440 327-0015
  North Ridgeville (G-15246)
Toyo Seiki Usa Inc ....G 513 546-9657
  Blue Ash (G-1860)
Universal Urethane Pdts Inc ....D 419 693-7400
  Toledo (G-18585)
Vibronic..F 937 274-1114
  Dayton (G-8579)
Wayne County Rubber Inc ....E 330 264-5553
  Wooster (G-20664)

2823 Cellulosic Man-Made Fibers

Advanced Fiber LLC ....E 419 562-1337
  Bucyrus (G-2317)
Fft Sidney LLC...................................D 937 492-2709
  Sidney (G-17040)
◆ Flexsys America LP ....D 330 666-4111
  Akron (G-173)
J Rettenmaier USA LP ....G 440 385-6701
  Oberlin (G-15500)
J Rettenmaier USA LP ....G 937 652-2101
  Urbana (G-18997)
J Rettenmaier USA LP ....G 937 652-2101
  Urbana (G-18998)
Laser Horizons ....G 330 208-0575
  Norton (G-15373)
▼ Mfg Composite Systems Company..B 440 997-5851
  Ashtabula (G-786)
▲ Morgan Adhesives Company LLC..B 330 688-1111
  Stow (G-17606)

2824 Synthetic Organic Fibers, Exc Cellulosic

Bridge Components Incorporated........G 614 873-0777
  Columbus (G-6697)
▲ Buckeye Polymers Inc ....E 330 948-3007
  Lodi (G-12008)
▲ Dowco LLC ....E 330 773-6654
  Akron (G-145)
Ecm Biofilms Inc ....G 440 350-1400
  Painesville (G-15735)
Fft Sidney LLC...................................D 937 492-2709
  Sidney (G-17040)
Ineos Nitriles USA LLC ....C 419 226-1200
  Lima (G-11878)
▲ Mytee Products Inc ....F 440 591-4301
  Aurora (G-894)
Omnova Solutions Inc 330 628-6550
  Mogadore (G-14246)
Organic Roots Horticulture LLC..........G 330 620-1108
  Ravenna (G-16393)
Success Technologies Inc ....G 614 761-0008
  Powell (G-16337)

2833 Medicinal Chemicals & Botanical Prdts

Amresco LLC.....................................D 440 349-2805
  Solon (G-17107)
Amresco LLC.....................................C 440 349-2805
  Cleveland (G-4701)

B & A Holistic Fd & Herbs LLC ....F 614 747-2200
  Columbus (G-6639)
Badizo LLC 844 344-3833
  Stow (G-17571)
Frutarom USA Inc ....G 513 870-4900
  West Chester (G-19859)
◆ Frutarom USA Inc ....C 513 870-4900
  West Chester (G-19856)
Galapagos Inc ....G 937 890-3068
  Dayton (G-8213)
▲ Goosefoot Acres Inc ....G 330 225-7184
  Valley City (G-19039)
Graminex LLC ....F 419 278-1023
  Deshler (G-8789)
▲ Joseph Adams Corp ....F 330 225-9125
  Valley City (G-19042)
Natural Options Aromatherapy ....G 419 886-3736
  Bellville (G-1560)
Nutritional Medicinals LLC ....F 937 433-4673
  West Chester (G-19750)
Odacs Inc ....G 513 761-0539
  Cincinnati (G-4098)
Ohio Valley Herbal Products...............G 330 382-1229
  East Liverpool (G-9067)
Patenthealth LLC 330 208-1111
  North Canton (G-15109)
Pfizer Inc ....C 937 746-3603
  Franklin (G-9908)
Pharmacia Hepar LLC ....D 937 746-3603
  Franklin (G-9909)
Plymouth Healthcare Pdts LLC ....F 440 542-0762
  Solon (G-17217)
▲ Polar Products Inc ....G 330 253-9973
  Stow (G-17619)
Press Chemical & Phrm Lab ....G 614 863-2802
  Columbus (G-7345)
Proctoer & Gamble ....G 513 983-1100
  Blue Ash (G-1837)
Satellite Gear Inc............................... ...... 216 514-8668
  Aurora (G-907)
USB Corporation ....D 216 765-5000
  Cleveland (G-6246)
Valley Vitamins II Inc 330 533-0051
  Columbus (G-7570)

2834 Pharmaceuticals

Abbott Laboratories............................F 614 624-3192
  Columbus (G-6520)
Abbott Laboratories............................A 614 624-7677
  Columbus (G-6521)
Abbott Laboratories............................D 614 624-6627
  Columbus (G-6522)
Abbott Laboratories............................ ...... 614 624-6627
  Columbus (G-6523)
Abbott Laboratories............................ ...... 800 551-5838
  Columbus (G-6524)
Abbott Laboratories............................F 614 624-6088
  Columbus (G-6525)
Abbott Laboratories............................A 614 624-3191
  Columbus (G-6519)
Abbott Nutrition Mfg Inc ....F 614 624-7485
  Columbus (G-6526)
◆ Abitec Corporation ....E 614 429-6464
  Columbus (G-6527)
▲ Adare Pharmaceuticals Inc ....C 937 898-9669
  Vandalia (G-19113)
Admiral Therapeutics LLC ....G 410 908-8906
  Shaker Heights (G-16925)
Advanced Medical Solutions Inc........G 937 291-0069
  Centerville (G-2995)
Aerpio Pharmaceuticals Inc...............G 513 985-1920
  Blue Ash (G-1723)
Affinity Therapeutics LLC ....G 216 224-9364
  Cleveland (G-4639)
Alkermes Inc......................................E 937 382-5642
  Wilmington (G-20485)
Allergan Inc ....D 614 623-8140
  Powell (G-16308)
Allergan Sales LLC ....C 513 271-6800
  Cincinnati (G-3323)
American Regent Inc ....F 614 436-2222
  New Albany (G-14604)
American Regent Inc 614 436-2222
  Columbus (G-6586)
American Regent Inc 614 436-2222
  Hilliard (G-10804)
Amerisourcebergen Corporation ....D 614 497-3665
  Lockbourne (G-11992)
Amerix Nutra-Pharma......................... ...... 567 204-7756
  Lima (G-11841)

▼ Amish Country Essentials LLC.........G 330 674-3088
  Millersburg (G-14059)
Amylin Ohio 512 592-8710
  West Chester (G-19643)
Analiza Inc ....F 216 432-9050
  Cleveland (G-4704)
Andrew M Farnham............................ ...... 419 298-4300
  Edgerton (G-9168)
Aprecia Pharmaceuticals LLC ....F 513 864-4107
  Blue Ash (G-1729)
Arth LLC..G 513 293-1646
  West Chester (G-19651)
Athersys Inc......................................D 216 431-9900
  Cleveland (G-4759)
Aultwrks Occupational Medicine.........F 330 491-9675
  Canton (G-2578)
Barr Laboratories Inc........................B 513 731-9900
  Cincinnati (G-3380)
Baxters LLC......................................G 234 678-5484
  Akron (G-81)
Bellwyck Packg Solutions Inc 513 874-1200
  West Chester (G-19657)
Berlin Industries Inc ....F 330 549-2100
  Youngstown (G-20852)
Bigmar Inc ....E 740 966-5800
  Johnstown (G-11259)
Biorx LLC..C 866 442-4679
  Cincinnati (G-3394)
Bnoat Oncology ....G 330 285-2537
  Akron (G-89)
Bodyvega Nutrition LLC ....G 708 712-5743
  Akron (G-91)
▲ Boehringer Ingelheim USA Corp ....F 440 232-3320
  Bedford (G-1390)
Boehrnger Inglheim Phrmcctcals.......G 440 286-5667
  Chardon (G-3100)
Bristol-Myers Squibb Company ....E 800 321-1335
  Columbus (G-6489)
Buderer Drug Co 419 626-3429
  Sandusky (G-16798)
Buderer Drug Company Inc ....F 419 627-2800
  Sandusky (G-16799)
Buderer Drug Company Inc ....F 419 873-2800
  Perrysburg (G-15925)
Buderer Drug Company Inc ....G 440 934-3100
  Avon (G-943)
Bulk Molding Compounds Inc ....D 419 874-7941
  Perrysburg (G-15926)
Cabell Huntington.............................G 740 867-2665
  Chesapeake (G-3143)
Calcol Inc ....E 216 245-6301
  Shaker Heights (G-16927)
Camargo Phrm Svcs LLC ....F 513 561-3329
  Blue Ash (G-1746)
Caps ....G 216 524-0418
  Cleveland (G-4872)
▲ Cardinal Health 414 LLC ....C 614 757-5000
  Dublin (G-8895)
Cardinal Health 414 LLC ....G 513 759-1900
  West Chester (G-19664)
Cardinal Health 414 LLC 614 473-0786
  Columbus (G-6742)
Casselberry Clinic Inc ....G 440 995-0555
  Cleveland (G-4887)
Catalent Pharma Solutions LLC ....G 614 757-4757
  Dublin (G-8897)
Chester Labs Inc...............................E 513 458-3871
  Cincinnati (G-3468)
◆ Chester Packaging LLC...................C 513 458-3840
  Cincinnati (G-3469)
Clearwater One LLC..........................F 216 554-4747
  Cleveland (G-4943)
Clinical Specialties Inc ....D 888 873-7888
  Brecksville (G-2027)
Cloud 9 Naturally Inc ....G 403 348-9704
  Bridgeport (G-2073)
CMC Pharmaceuticals Inc ....G 216 600-9430
  Cleveland (G-4993)
Dayton Laser & Aesthetic Medic ....G 937 208-8282
  Dayton (G-8137)
Ddnews ....G 440 331-6600
  Rocky River (G-16546)
Diasome Pharmaceuticals Inc............G 216 444-7110
  Cleveland (G-5092)
Dow Chemical Company ....F 937 254-1550
  Dayton (G-8166)
Dr Hess Products LLC ....G 800 718-8022
  Ashland (G-702)
Eli Lilly and Company........................G 937 855-3300
  Germantown (G-10241)

Employee Codes: A=Over 500 employees, B=251-500
C=101-250, D=51-100, E=20-50, F=10-19, G=3-9

Ennovea LLC .... E 814 838-6664
Columbus (G-6898)
Essence Maker .... G 440 729-3894
Chesterland (G-3157)
Exonanorna LLC .... G 614 928-3512
Columbus (G-6910)
Eyescience Labs LLC .... G 614 885-7100
Powell (G-16321)
Family Medical Clinic & Laser .... G 740 345-2767
Newark (G-14874)
▲ Ferro Corporation .... D 216 875-5600
Mayfield Heights (G-13163)
▲ Flow Dry Technology Inc .... C 937 833-2161
Brookville (G-2168)
Fluence Therapeutics .... G 216 780-5220
Akron (G-175)
Forest Pharmaceuticals Inc .... C 513 271-6800
Cincinnati (G-3704)
Forrest Pharmaceuticals .... G 513 791-1701
Blue Ash (G-1778)
Ftd Investments LLC .... C 937 833-2161
Brookville (G-2169)
GE Healthcare Inc .... G 502 452-4311
Solon (G-17146)
▲ Gebauer Company .... E 216 581-3030
Cleveland (G-5299)
Genoa Healthcare .... G 740 370-0759
Portsmouth (G-16283)
Genoa Healthcare LLC .... G 513 727-0471
Middletown (G-13909)
Genoa Healthcare LLC .... G 567 202-8326
Toledo (G-18304)
Genoa Healthcare LLC .... G 513 541-0164
Cincinnati (G-3749)
Glaxosmithkline LLC .... E 937 623-2680
Columbus (G-6953)
Glaxosmithkline LLC .... E 440 552-2895
North Ridgeville (G-15227)
Glaxosmithkline LLC .... E 330 608-2365
Copley (G-7685)
Glaxosmithkline LLC .... E 614 570-5970
Columbus (G-6954)
Glaxosmithkline LLC .... E 330 241-4447
Medina (G-13267)
Graminex LLC .... F 419 278-1023
Deshler (G-8789)
▲ Hikma Labs Inc .... C 614 276-4000
Columbus (G-6999)
Hikma Pharmaceuticals USA Inc .... G 732 542-1191
Lockbourne (G-11994)
Hikma Pharmaceuticals USA Inc .... F 732 542-1191
Bedford (G-1412)
Hikma Pharmaceuticals USA Inc .... E 614 276-4000
Columbus (G-7000)
Independent Particle Labs .... G 330 477-2016
Canton (G-2707)
Isp Chemicals LLC .... D 614 876-3637
Columbus (G-7052)
J Rettenmaier USA LP .... D 937 652-2101
Urbana (G-18998)
Kdc US Holdings Inc .... G 740 927-2817
Johnstown (G-11269)
Kerry Inc .... E 440 229-5200
Mayfield Heights (G-13166)
Lib Therapeutics LLC .... G 859 240-7764
Cincinnati (G-3940)
Libido Edge Labs LLC .... G 740 344-1401
Newark (G-14893)
◆ Lubrizol Global Management .... F 216 447-5000
Brecksville (G-2048)
M Pharmaceutical USA .... G 859 868-3131
Cincinnati (G-3963)
Mallinckrodt LLC .... F 513 948-5751
Cincinnati (G-3976)
Masters Pharmaceutical Inc .... G 513 290-2969
Fairfield (G-9525)
Medpace Holdings Inc .... F 513 579-9911
Cincinnati (G-3998)
Medpace Research Inc .... G 513 579-9911
Cincinnati (G-3999)
Meridian Bioscience Inc .... B 513 271-3700
Cincinnati (G-4006)
Middletown Pharmacy Inc .... G 513 705-6252
Middletown (G-13929)
Migraine Proof LLC .... G 330 635-7874
Medina (G-13301)
Millers Liniments LLC .... G 440 548-5800
Middlefield (G-13831)
Molorokalin Inc .... F 330 629-1332
Canfield (G-2537)
Mp Biomedicals LLC .... C 440 337-1200
Solon (G-17199)
Mvp Pharmacy .... G 614 449-8000
Columbus (G-7204)
N M R Inc .... G 513 530-9075
Cincinnati (G-4056)
N-Molecular Inc .... F 440 439-5356
Oakwood Village (G-15481)
N8 Medical Inc .... G 614 537-7246
Dublin (G-8950)
Nanofiber Solutions Inc .... G 614 453-5877
Hilliard (G-10843)
Navidea Biopharmaceuticals Inc .... E 614 793-7500
Dublin (G-8952)
Nigerian Assn Pharmacists & PH .... G 513 861-2329
Cincinnati (G-4078)
Nitto Denko Avecia Inc .... F 513 679-3000
Cincinnati (G-4082)
Nnodum Pharmaceuticals Corp .... F 513 861-2329
Cincinnati (G-4083)
▲ Norwich Overseas Inc .... F 513 983-1100
Mason (G-12916)
Nostrum Laboratories Inc .... E 419 636-1168
Bryan (G-2299)
Novartis Corporation .... D 919 577-5000
Cincinnati (G-4090)
Nutrimir LLC .... G 614 600-2478
Delaware (G-8711)
Oak Tree Intl Holdings Inc .... G 702 462-7295
Elyria (G-9302)
Oakwood Laboratories LLC .... E 440 359-0000
Oakwood Village (G-15482)
Oakwood Laboratories LLC .... F 440 505-2011
Solon (G-17209)
Ohio Lab Pharma LLC .... G 484 522-2601
Kettering (G-11439)
Omnicare Phrm of Midwest LLC .... D 513 719-2600
Cincinnati (G-4111)
Organon Inc .... G 440 729-2290
Chesterland (G-3167)
Patenthealth LLC .... G 330 208-1111
North Canton (G-15109)
Patheon Pharmaceuticals Inc .... B 513 948-9111
Cincinnati (G-4134)
PBM Covington LLC .... F 937 473-2050
Covington (G-7791)
Performanx Specialty Chem LLC .... G 614 300-7001
Westerville (G-20016)
Performanx Specialty Chem LLC .... G 614 300-7001
Waverly (G-19556)
Perrigo .... G 937 473-2050
Covington (G-7792)
Pfizer Inc .... G 513 342-9056
West Chester (G-19758)
Pfizer Inc .... C 614 496-0990
Dublin (G-8965)
Pfizer Inc .... D 216 591-0642
Beachwood (G-1265)
Pfizer Inc .... C 937 746-3603
Franklin (G-9908)
Pharma Tegix LLC .... G 740 879-4015
Lewis Center (G-11771)
Pharmacia Hepar LLC .... D 937 746-3603
Franklin (G-9909)
Pharmcutical Dev Solutions LLC .... G 732 766-5222
Powell (G-16332)
Polgenix Inc .... G 440 537-9691
Cleveland (G-5892)
Polynt Composites USA Inc .... E 816 391-6000
Sandusky (G-16839)
▲ Prasco LLC .... C 513 204-1100
Mason (G-12923)
Principled Dynamics Inc .... G 419 351-6303
Holland (G-10951)
Propharma Sales LLC .... G 513 486-3353
Mason (G-12927)
Protein Express Inc .... G 513 769-9654
Blue Ash (G-1838)
Quality Care Products LLC .... E 734 847-2704
Holland (G-10952)
Ranir Dcp .... G 616 698-8880
Bay Village (G-1207)
RC Outsourcing LLC .... G 330 536-8500
Lowellville (G-12255)
River City Pharma .... D 513 870-1680
Fairfield (G-9558)
Roxane Laboratories .... G 614 276-4000
Columbus (G-7403)
Safe Rx Pharmacies Inc .... G 740 377-4162
South Point (G-17294)
Safecor Health LLC .... F 781 933-8780
Columbus (G-7412)
Sara Wood Pharmaceuticals LLC .... G 513 833-5502
Mason (G-12936)
Scicompro - LLC .... G 513 680-8686
Mason (G-12937)
Sermonix Pharmaceuticals .... G 614 864-4919
Columbus (G-7439)
Soleo Health Inc .... F 844 467-8200
Dublin (G-8993)
Specialized Pharmaceuticals .... G 419 371-2081
Lima (G-11943)
Suarez Corporation Industries .... D 330 494-4282
Canton (G-2827)
Summit Research Group .... G 330 689-1778
Stow (G-17633)
Takeda Pharmaceuticals USA Inc .... G 440 238-0872
Strongsville (G-17800)
Tersus Pharmaceuticals .... F 440 951-2451
Mentor (G-13604)
Teva Pharmaceuticals Inc .... G 800 225-6878
Cincinnati (G-4415)
Teva Womens Health Inc .... C 513 731-9900
Cincinnati (G-4416)
Tri-Tech Laboratories Inc .... G 614 656-1130
New Albany (G-14637)
USB Corporation .... D 216 765-5000
Cleveland (G-6246)
Venture Therapeutics Inc .... G 614 430-3300
New Albany (G-14640)
Warner Chlcott Phrmcticals Inc .... F 513 983-1100
Cincinnati (G-4490)
West Pharmaceutical Svcs Inc .... G 513 741-3004
Cincinnati (G-4500)
Xellia Pharmaceuticals USA LLC .... E 847 986-7984
Bedford (G-1455)
Z M O Company Inc .... G 614 875-0230
Grove City (G-10480)

2835 Diagnostic Substances

Apollo Medical Devices LLC .... G 440 935-5027
Cleveland (G-4721)
Cardinal Health 414 LLC .... G 614 473-0786
Columbus (G-6742)
▲ Cardinal Health 414 LLC .... C 614 757-5000
Dublin (G-8895)
Cardinal Health 414 LLC .... G 513 759-1900
West Chester (G-19664)
Cleveland AEC West LLC .... G 216 362-6000
Cleveland (G-4945)
Core Quantum Technologies Inc .... G 614 214-7210
Columbus (G-6821)
Diagnostic Hybrids Inc .... C 740 593-1784
Athens (G-828)
Diramed LLC .... F 614 487-3660
Columbus (G-6864)
Enlyton Ltd .... G 614 888-9220
Columbus (G-6897)
Filament LLC .... G 614 732-0754
Columbus (G-6921)
GE Healthcare Inc .... F 513 241-5955
Cincinnati (G-3737)
John P Ellis Clinic Podiatry .... G 440 460-0444
Cleveland (G-5503)
Meridian Bioscience Inc .... B 513 271-3700
Cincinnati (G-4006)
Meridian Life Science Inc .... D 513 271-3700
Cincinnati (G-4007)
Molecular Theranostics LLC .... G 216 595-1968
Cleveland (G-5701)
Nanofiber Solutions Inc .... G 614 453-5877
Hilliard (G-10843)
Perkinelmer Hlth Sciences Inc .... E 330 825-4525
Akron (G-318)
Petnet Solutions Inc .... G 865 218-2000
Cincinnati (G-4154)
Petnet Solutions Inc .... G 865 218-2000
Cleveland (G-5867)
Quidel Corporation .... D 740 589-3300
Athens (G-847)
Sarcokinetics LLC .... G 414 477-9585
Cleveland (G-6031)
Thermo Fisher Scientific Inc .... C 800 871-8909
Oakwood Village (G-15486)
USB Corporation .... D 216 765-5000
Cleveland (G-6246)
Vetgraft LLC .... G 614 203-0603
New Albany (G-14642)
Xact Genomics LLC .... G 216 956-0957
Twinsburg (G-18876)

2836 Biological Prdts, Exc Diagnostic Substances

ABI Inc........F....... 216 378-1336
Bedford *(G-1378)*
Bio-Blood Components Inc........E....... 614 294-3183
Columbus *(G-6669)*
Carbogene USA LLC........G....... 215 378-4306
Columbus *(G-6738)*
Columbus Serum Co........G....... 614 793-0615
Columbus *(G-6801)*
Copernicus Therapeutics Inc........F....... 216 707-1776
Cleveland *(G-5029)*
Csl Plasma Inc........E....... 937 325-4200
Springfield *(G-17382)*
Decaria Brothers Inc........G....... 330 385-0825
East Liverpool *(G-9055)*
EMD Millipore Corporation........C....... 513 631-0445
Norwood *(G-15426)*
Envirozyme LLC........G....... 800 232-2847
Bowling Green *(G-1972)*
Ferro Corporation........D....... 216 577-7144
Bedford *(G-1405)*
General Environmental Science........G....... 216 464-0680
Beachwood *(G-1239)*
Global Health Services Inc........G....... 513 777-8111
Hamilton *(G-10564)*
Microbiological Labs Inc........G....... 330 626-2264
Streetsboro *(G-17682)*
No Rinse Laboratories LLC........G....... 937 746-7357
Springboro *(G-17339)*
Perkinelmer Hlth Sciences Inc........E....... 330 825-4525
Akron *(G-318)*
Phagevax Inc........G....... 740 502-9010
Newark *(G-14910)*
Protein Express Laboratories........G....... 513 769-9654
Blue Ash *(G-1839)*
Safewhite Inc........G....... 614 340-1450
Columbus *(G-7414)*
Sneaky Pete Band........G....... 419 933-6251
Willard *(G-20245)*
Star Spangled Spectacular Inc........G....... 419 879-3502
Lima *(G-11944)*
Supply Dynamics Inc........E....... 513 965-2000
Loveland *(G-12238)*
Tamarkin Company........G....... 330 634-0688
Tallmadge *(G-18008)*
Tamarkin Company........G....... 614 878-8942
Columbus *(G-7510)*
Tpr Plasma Center........G....... 419 244-3910
Toledo *(G-18580)*
Venom Exterminating LLC........G....... 330 637-3366
Cortland *(G-7716)*

2841 Soap & Detergents

AIN Industries Inc........G....... 440 781-0950
Cleveland *(G-4643)*
▼ Amish Country Essentials LLC........G....... 330 674-3088
Millersburg *(G-14059)*
Beiersdorf Inc........C....... 513 682-7300
West Chester *(G-19835)*
◆ Chester Packaging LLC........C....... 513 458-3840
Cincinnati *(G-3469)*
Cincinnati - Vulcan Company........D....... 513 242-5300
Cincinnati *(G-3477)*
Cleaning Lady Inc........F....... 419 589-5566
Mansfield *(G-12426)*
▼ Cr Brands Inc........D....... 513 860-5039
West Chester *(G-19686)*
Cr Holding Inc........G....... 513 860-5039
West Chester *(G-19687)*
▼ Cresset Chemical Co Inc........F....... 419 669-2041
Weston *(G-20175)*
▲ DSM Industries Inc........F....... 440 585-1100
Wickliffe *(G-20209)*
Edmar Chemical Company........G....... 440 247-9560
Chagrin Falls *(G-3018)*
▲ Emco Electric International........G....... 440 878-1199
Strongsville *(G-17742)*
Equipment Spcalists Dayton LLC........G....... 937 415-2151
Dayton *(G-8185)*
EZ Brite Brands Inc........F....... 440 871-7817
Cleveland *(G-5211)*
▲ Fairy Dust Ltd Inc........F....... 513 251-0065
Cincinnati *(G-3669)*
▲ Foam-Tex Solutions Corp........G....... 216 889-2702
Cleveland *(G-5257)*
Guardian Co Inc........G....... 216 721-2262
Cleveland *(G-5359)*
Henkel Corporation........E....... 740 363-1351
Delaware *(G-8693)*
Howard Grant Corp........G....... 330 743-3151
Youngstown *(G-20932)*
Jabco & Associates Inc........G....... 513 752-0600
Amelia *(G-542)*
Jtm Products Inc........E....... 440 287-2302
Solon *(G-17178)*
◆ KAO USA Inc........B....... 513 421-1400
Cincinnati *(G-3897)*
▼ Kardol Quality Products LLC........E....... 513 933-8206
Blue Ash *(G-1800)*
◆ Kutol Products Company Inc........C....... 513 527-5500
Sharonville *(G-16957)*
Mix-Masters Inc........F....... 513 228-2800
Lebanon *(G-11673)*
New Vulco Mfg & Sales Co LLC........D....... 513 242-2672
Cincinnati *(G-4072)*
◆ Noveon Incorporated........G....... 216 447-5000
Brecksville *(G-2052)*
Oliver Chemical Co Inc........G....... 513 541-4540
Cincinnati *(G-4110)*
Our Detergent Inc........G....... 419 589-5571
Mansfield *(G-12500)*
◆ Pilot Chemical Company Ohio........E....... 513 326-0600
Cincinnati *(G-4159)*
Pilot Chemical Company Ohio........E....... 513 733-4880
Cincinnati *(G-4160)*
◆ Pilot Chemical Corp........F....... 513 326-0600
Cincinnati *(G-4161)*
Pilot Chemical Corp........E....... 513 424-9700
Middletown *(G-13941)*
▼ Polar Inc........F....... 937 297-0911
Moraine *(G-14380)*
Porter Hybrids Inc........G....... 937 382-2324
Wilmington *(G-20503)*
Procter & Gamble........G....... 513 207-8931
Cincinnati *(G-4197)*
◆ Procter & Gamble Company........B....... 513 983-1100
Cincinnati *(G-4198)*
Procter & Gamble Company........C....... 513 983-1100
Cincinnati *(G-4199)*
Procter & Gamble Company........E....... 513 266-4375
Cincinnati *(G-4200)*
Procter & Gamble Company........E....... 513 871-7557
Cincinnati *(G-4201)*
Procter & Gamble Company........B....... 419 998-5891
Lima *(G-11920)*
Procter & Gamble Company........F....... 513 482-6789
Cincinnati *(G-4203)*
Procter & Gamble Company........B....... 513 672-4044
West Chester *(G-19767)*
Procter & Gamble Company........B....... 513 627-7115
Cincinnati *(G-4205)*
Procter & Gamble Company........C....... 513 634-9600
West Chester *(G-19768)*
Procter & Gamble Company........C....... 513 634-9110
West Chester *(G-19769)*
Procter & Gamble Company........C....... 513 934-3406
Oregonia *(G-15573)*
Procter & Gamble Company........G....... 513 627-7779
Cincinnati *(G-4207)*
Procter & Gamble Company........B....... 513 945-0340
Cincinnati *(G-4208)*
Procter & Gamble Company........C....... 513 622-1000
Mason *(G-12926)*
▼ Procter & Gamble Mfg Co........F....... 513 983-1100
Cincinnati *(G-4212)*
Renegade Brands LLC........G....... 216 342-4347
Cleveland *(G-5974)*
RES Q Cleaning Solutions Inc........G....... 740 964-9494
Reynoldsburg *(G-16451)*
Royal Chemical Company Ltd........F....... 330 467-1300
Twinsburg *(G-18850)*
▲ St Bernard Soap Company........B....... 513 242-2227
Cincinnati *(G-4368)*
▼ State Industrial Products Corp........B....... 877 747-6986
Cleveland *(G-6097)*
Sunbeam Products Co LLC........G....... 419 691-1551
Toledo *(G-18533)*
Trillium Health Care Products........G....... 513 242-2227
Cincinnati *(G-4438)*
US Industrial Lubricants Inc........E....... 513 541-2225
Cincinnati *(G-4458)*
▼ Wallover Oil Company Inc........E....... 440 238-9250
Strongsville *(G-17806)*
▼ Washing Systems LLC........C....... 800 272-1974
Loveland *(G-12244)*
Woodspirits Limited Inc........G....... 937 663-5025
Saint Paris *(G-16712)*
▲ Zorbx Inc........E....... 440 238-1847
Strongsville *(G-17810)*

2842 Spec Cleaning, Polishing & Sanitation Preparations

Advanced Cleaning Tech LLC........G....... 614 504-2014
Plain City *(G-16169)*
▲ Alco-Chem Inc........E....... 330 253-3535
Akron *(G-56)*
All Prem Cleaners Inc........G....... 440 349-3649
Solon *(G-17100)*
Aman & Co Inc........G....... 330 854-1122
Canal Fulton *(G-2473)*
American Chemical Products........F....... 216 267-7722
Cleveland *(G-4685)*
Aromair Fine Fragrance Company........B....... 614 984-2896
New Albany *(G-14605)*
◆ Betco Corporation Ltd........C....... 419 241-2156
Bowling Green *(G-1955)*
BLaster Corporation........E....... 216 901-5800
Cleveland *(G-4819)*
Boyd Sanitation........G....... 740 697-7940
Roseville *(G-16575)*
◆ Canberra Corporation........C....... 419 724-4300
Toledo *(G-18222)*
Capital Chemical Co........E....... 330 494-9535
Canton *(G-2619)*
Carbonklean Llc........G....... 614 980-9515
Powell *(G-16313)*
Carolyn Chemical Company........F....... 614 252-5000
Columbus *(G-6746)*
Cedar Point Laundry........G....... 419 627-2274
Sandusky *(G-16801)*
▲ Chem 1 Inc........G....... 216 475-7443
Warrensville Heights *(G-19466)*
Chemical Methods Inc........E....... 216 476-8400
Strongsville *(G-17725)*
▲ Chempace Corporation........F....... 419 535-0101
Toledo *(G-18229)*
◆ Chester Packaging LLC........C....... 513 458-3840
Cincinnati *(G-3469)*
Cincinnati - Vulcan Company........D....... 513 242-5300
Cincinnati *(G-3477)*
Clayton Manufacturing Company........F....... 513 563-1300
Cincinnati *(G-3526)*
Cleaning By Sndra Msters Touch........F....... 216 524-6827
Seven Hills *(G-16902)*
Clorox Company........F....... 513 445-1840
Mason *(G-12848)*
Consolidated Coatings Corp........E....... 216 514-7596
Cleveland *(G-5017)*
Custom Chemical Packaging LLC........E....... 330 331-7416
Medina *(G-13247)*
◆ D & J Distributing & Mfg........E....... 419 865-2552
Holland *(G-10923)*
D C Filter & Chemical Inc........G....... 419 626-3967
Sandusky *(G-16802)*
Dem Technology LLC........G....... 937 223-1317
Dayton *(G-8155)*
Diversey Inc........F....... 513 326-8300
Cincinnati *(G-3592)*
Durr Megtec LLC........C....... 614 258-9501
Columbus *(G-6876)*
▲ Easy Care Products Inc........G....... 330 405-1380
Twinsburg *(G-18767)*
Ecolab Inc........G....... 513 932-0830
Lebanon *(G-11649)*
Edmar Chemical Company........G....... 440 247-9560
Chagrin Falls *(G-3018)*
EMD Millipore Corporation........C....... 513 631-0445
Norwood *(G-15426)*
Emes Supply LLC........G....... 216 400-8025
Willowick *(G-20478)*
EZ Brite Brands Inc........F....... 440 871-7817
Cleveland *(G-5211)*
Ferro Corporation........D....... 216 577-7144
Bedford *(G-1405)*
◆ Fresh Products LLC........D....... 419 531-9741
Perrysburg *(G-15955)*
Fuchs Lubricants Co........E....... 330 963-0400
Twinsburg *(G-18777)*
Glister Inc........G....... 614 252-6400
Columbus *(G-6955)*
◆ Gojo Industries Inc........C....... 330 255-6000
Akron *(G-189)*
Gojo Industries Inc........E....... 330 255-6000
Cuyahoga Falls *(G-7873)*
Gojo Industries Inc........C....... 330 255-6525
Stow *(G-17593)*
Gojo Industries Inc........C....... 330 922-4522
Cuyahoga Falls *(G-7874)*
Guardian Co Inc........G....... 216 721-2262
Cleveland *(G-5359)*

S I C

Employee Codes: A=Over 500 employees, B=251-500
C=101-250, D=51-100, E=20-50, F=10-19, G=3-9

Henkel Corporation E 740 363-1351
Delaware *(G-8693)*
Henkel Corporation C 216 475-3600
Cleveland *(G-5392)*
Inceptor Inc G 419 726-8804
Toledo *(G-18343)*
Intercontinental Chemical Corp E 513 541-7100
Cincinnati *(G-3854)*
Jackson Deluxe Cleaners Ltd G 419 592-2826
Napoleon *(G-14547)*
James C Robinson G 513 969-7482
Cincinnati *(G-3869)*
Jason Incorporated F 513 860-3400
Hamilton *(G-10576)*
Jax Wax Inc F 614 476-6769
Columbus *(G-7064)*
▼ Kardol Quality Products LLC E 513 933-8206
Blue Ash *(G-1800)*
Kcs Cleaning Service F 740 418-5479
Oak Hill *(G-15453)*
Kinzua Environmental Inc E 216 881-4040
Cleveland *(G-5536)*
Klc Brands Inc G 201 456-4115
Cincinnati *(G-3915)*
Kleen Test Products Corp F 330 878-5586
Strasburg *(G-17649)*
L-Mor Inc F 216 541-2224
Cleveland *(G-5551)*
Leesburg Modern Sales Inc G 937 780-2613
Leesburg *(G-11712)*
Leonhardt Plating Company E 513 242-1410
Cincinnati *(G-3938)*
Malco Products Inc E 330 753-0361
Alliance *(G-487)*
Malco Products Inc E 330 753-0361
Akron *(G-266)*
McGean-Rohco Inc D 216 441-4900
Newburgh Heights *(G-14941)*
Metaltek Industries Inc F 937 323-4933
Springfield *(G-17447)*
Milsek Furniture Polish Inc G 330 542-2700
Salem *(G-16762)*
Mix-Masters Inc F 513 228-2800
Lebanon *(G-11673)*
Mold Masters Intl Inc C 440 953-0220
Eastlake *(G-9123)*
Morris Clean It N Sweep Clean G 513 200-8222
Cincinnati *(G-4046)*
▲ National Colloid Company E 740 282-1171
Steubenville *(G-17545)*
New Vulco Mfg & Sales Co LLC D 513 242-2672
Cincinnati *(G-4072)*
New Waste Concepts Inc F 877 736-6924
Perrysburg *(G-15981)*
◆ Nilodor Inc E 800 443-4321
Bolivar *(G-1919)*
Nwp Manufacturing Inc F 419 894-6871
Waldo *(G-19303)*
Odortech Distributing LLC G 216 339-0773
Westlake *(G-20136)*
Ohio Auto Supply Company E 330 454-5105
Canton *(G-2771)*
Ohio Mills Corporation G 216 431-3979
Cleveland *(G-5807)*
Oliver Chemical Co Inc G 513 541-4540
Cincinnati *(G-4110)*
Orchem Corporation E 513 874-9700
Dayton *(G-8406)*
Paro Services Co F 330 467-1300
Twinsburg *(G-18828)*
Pats Nu-Style Cleaners Inc G 216 676-4855
Cleveland *(G-5854)*
Pen Brands LLC E 216 674-1430
Brooklyn Heights *(G-2129)*
Personal Plumber Service Corp F 440 324-4321
Elyria *(G-9311)*
Pilot Chemical Company Ohio E 513 733-4880
Cincinnati *(G-4160)*
Pilot Chemical Corp E 513 424-9700
Middletown *(G-13941)*
Polynt Composites USA Inc E 816 391-6000
Sandusky *(G-16839)*
◆ Procter & Gamble Company B 513 983-1100
Cincinnati *(G-4198)*
Procter & Gamble Company C 513 983-1100
Cincinnati *(G-4199)*
Procter & Gamble Company E 513 266-4375
Cincinnati *(G-4200)*
Procter & Gamble Company E 513 871-7557
Cincinnati *(G-4201)*
Procter & Gamble Company B 419 998-5891
Lima *(G-11920)*
Procter & Gamble Company F 513 482-6789
Cincinnati *(G-4203)*
Procter & Gamble Company B 513 672-4044
West Chester *(G-19767)*
Procter & Gamble Company B 513 627-7115
Cincinnati *(G-4205)*
Procter & Gamble Company C 513 634-9600
West Chester *(G-19768)*
Procter & Gamble Company C 513 634-9110
West Chester *(G-19769)*
Procter & Gamble Company C 513 934-3406
Oregonia *(G-15573)*
Procter & Gamble Company G 513 627-7779
Cincinnati *(G-4207)*
Procter & Gamble Company B 513 945-0340
Cincinnati *(G-4208)*
Procter & Gamble Company C 513 622-1000
Mason *(G-12926)*
Procter & Gamble Far East Inc C 513 983-1100
Cincinnati *(G-4210)*
Reid Asset Management Company E 440 942-8488
Willoughby *(G-20419)*
◆ Republic Powdered Metals Inc D 330 225-3192
Medina *(G-13327)*
Rose Products and Services Inc E 614 443-7647
Columbus *(G-7402)*
◆ RPM International Inc D 330 273-5090
Medina *(G-13331)*
S C Johnson & Son Inc E 513 665-3600
Cincinnati *(G-4294)*
Saint Ctherines Metalworks Inc G 216 409-0576
Cleveland *(G-6026)*
Sara Hudson G 850 890-1455
Dayton *(G-8493)*
Sevan At-Ndustrial Pnt Abr Ltd G 614 258-4747
Columbus *(G-7440)*
Sherwin-Williams Company C 330 830-6000
Massillon *(G-13048)*
Shur Clean Usa LLC G 513 341-5486
Liberty Township *(G-11820)*
Skybryte Company Inc G 216 771-1590
Cleveland *(G-6070)*
Smart Sonic Corporation G 818 610-7900
Cleveland *(G-6072)*
Solutions Plus Inc E 513 943-9600
Amelia *(G-547)*
◆ Spartan Chemical Company Inc E 419 897-5551
Maumee *(G-13147)*
Spc Specialty Products LLC G 844 475-5414
Toledo *(G-18527)*
▼ State Industrial Products Corp B 877 747-6986
Cleveland *(G-6097)*
▼ Strib Industries Inc E 216 281-1155
Cleveland *(G-6108)*
Sun Cleaners & Laundry Inc G 740 756-4749
Carroll *(G-2912)*
▲ Tolco Corporation D 419 241-1113
Toledo *(G-18555)*
◆ Tranzonic Acquisition Corp A 216 535-4300
Richmond Heights *(G-16505)*
◆ Tranzonic Companies C 216 535-4300
Richmond Heights *(G-16506)*
Tranzonic Companies C 440 446-0643
Cleveland *(G-6198)*
◆ Tremco Incorporated B 216 292-5000
Beachwood *(G-1283)*
Trigon Industries Inc G 937 299-1350
Oakwood *(G-15467)*
Univar USA Inc C 513 714-5264
West Chester *(G-19911)*
US Industrial Lubricants Inc E 513 541-2225
Cincinnati *(G-4458)*
▼ Ventco Inc F 440 834-8888
Chagrin Falls *(G-3088)*
Vitex Corporation F 216 883-0920
Cleveland *(G-6266)*
Wilkshire Dry Cleaners LLC G 330 674-7696
Millersburg *(G-14151)*
Wise Consumer Products Company G 513 484-6530
Blue Ash *(G-1872)*
▲ Woodbine Products Company F 330 725-0165
Medina *(G-13363)*

2843 Surface Active & Finishing Agents, Sulfonated Oils

◆ Berghausen Corporation E 513 541-5631
Cincinnati *(G-3389)*
▲ Peter Cremer North America LP D 513 471-7200
Cincinnati *(G-4153)*
◆ Pilot Chemical Company Ohio E 513 326-0600
Cincinnati *(G-4159)*
Pilot Chemical Company Ohio E 513 733-4880
Cincinnati *(G-4160)*
◆ Pilot Chemical Corp F 513 326-0600
Cincinnati *(G-4161)*

2844 Perfumes, Cosmetics & Toilet Preparations

◆ Abitec Corporation E 614 429-6464
Columbus *(G-6527)*
Aeroscena LLC F 800 671-1890
Cleveland *(G-4634)*
▼ Amish Country Essentials LLC G 330 674-3088
Millersburg *(G-14059)*
Argentifex LLC G 440 990-1108
Ashtabula *(G-761)*
◆ Art of Beauty Company Inc F 216 438-6363
Bedford *(G-1385)*
▲ Ashland Specialty Ingredients E 302 594-5000
Dublin *(G-8884)*
Ashland Specialty Ingredients D 614 529-3311
Columbus *(G-6619)*
B & P Company Inc G 937 298-0265
Dayton *(G-8048)*
▲ Barbasol LLC E 419 903-0738
Ashland *(G-684)*
▲ Bath & Body Works LLC B 614 856-6000
Reynoldsburg *(G-16430)*
Beiersdorf Inc C 513 682-7300
West Chester *(G-19835)*
Biocurv Medical Instruments G 330 454-6621
Canton *(G-2592)*
Bocchi Laboratories Ohio LLC B 614 741-7458
New Albany *(G-14610)*
▲ Bonne Bell LLC G 440 835-2440
Westlake *(G-20102)*
▲ Cameo Inc E 419 661-9611
Perrysburg *(G-15930)*
Cashmere & Twig LLC F 740 404-8468
New Concord *(G-14684)*
▲ Cellera LLC G 513 539-1500
Monroe *(G-14256)*
Colgate-Palmolive Company C 212 310-2000
Cambridge *(G-2432)*
Columbus Kdc F 614 656-1130
New Albany *(G-14614)*
Dover Wipes Company G 513 983-1100
Cincinnati *(G-3606)*
Edgewell Per Care Brands LLC D 937 228-0105
Dayton *(G-8177)*
Edgewell Personal Care LLC C 937 492-1057
Sidney *(G-17034)*
Eileen Musser Shiela G 937 295-4212
Fort Loramie *(G-9796)*
Erik V Lamb G 330 962-1540
Copley *(G-7684)*
Estee Lauder Companies Inc G 310 994-9651
Loveland *(G-12186)*
Facial Sensation Products G 937 293-2280
Oakwood *(G-15461)*
Fantastic Sams Hair Care Salon G 740 456-4296
Portsmouth *(G-16282)*
Galleria Co G 513 983-1490
Cincinnati *(G-3722)*
Garden Art Innovations LLC G 330 697-0007
Barberton *(G-1072)*
◆ Gojo Industries Inc C 330 255-6000
Akron *(G-189)*
Gojo Industries Inc C 330 255-6525
Stow *(G-17593)*
Gojo Industries Inc C 330 922-4522
Cuyahoga Falls *(G-7874)*
Good Earth Good Eating LLC G 513 256-5935
Cincinnati *(G-3771)*
Hair & Nail Impressions G 937 399-0221
Springfield *(G-17409)*
Honey Sweetie Acres LLC G 513 456-6090
Goshen *(G-10288)*
House of Delara Fragrances G 216 651-5803
Cleveland *(G-5420)*
John Frieda Prof Hair Care Inc E 800 521-3189
Cincinnati *(G-3879)*
Kahuna Bay Spray Tan LLC G 419 386-2387
Toledo *(G-18360)*
◆ KAO USA Inc B 513 421-1400
Cincinnati *(G-3897)*

KAO USA Inc ....G 513 421-1400
Hamilton *(G-10578)*
LOreal Usa Inc ....A 440 248-3700
Cleveland *(G-5584)*
LS Bombshelles ....G 513 254-6898
Cincinnati *(G-3953)*
Luminex Home Decor ....A 513 563-1113
Blue Ash *(G-1812)*
▲ Madaen Natural Products Inc ....G 800 600-1445
Cuyahoga Falls *(G-7894)*
Mantra Haircare LLC ....F 440 526-3304
Broadview Heights *(G-2095)*
Meridian Industries Inc ....E 330 359-5809
Beach City *(G-1212)*
Natural Beauty Products Inc ....F 513 420-9400
Middletown *(G-13935)*
◆ Natural Essentials Inc ....E 330 562-8022
Aurora *(G-895)*
Naturally Smart Labs LLC ....G 216 503-9398
Independence *(G-11143)*
▲ Nehemiah Manufacturing Co LLC ....E 513 351-5700
Cincinnati *(G-4066)*
Oasis Consumer Healthcare LLC ....G 216 394-0544
Cleveland *(G-5794)*
Oil Bar LLC ....F 614 880-3950
Columbus *(G-6504)*
◆ Oils By Nature Incorporated ....G 330 468-8897
Hudson *(G-11064)*
Olay LLC ....G 787 535-2191
Blue Ash *(G-1826)*
Olfactorium Corp Inc ....G 216 663-8831
Cleveland *(G-5811)*
Pfizer Inc ....C 937 746-3603
Franklin *(G-9908)*
Primal Life Organics LLC ....G 419 356-3843
Akron *(G-330)*
Procter & Gamble Company ....C 513 983-1100
Cincinnati *(G-4199)*
Procter & Gamble Company ....E 513 266-4375
Cincinnati *(G-4200)*
Procter & Gamble Company ....E 513 871-7557
Cincinnati *(G-4201)*
Procter & Gamble Company ....E 513 983-1100
Cincinnati *(G-4202)*
Procter & Gamble Company ....B 419 998-5891
Lima *(G-11920)*
Procter & Gamble Company ....F 513 482-6789
Cincinnati *(G-4203)*
Procter & Gamble Company ....B 513 672-4044
West Chester *(G-19767)*
Procter & Gamble Company ....B 513 634-5069
Cincinnati *(G-4204)*
Procter & Gamble Company ....B 513 627-7115
Cincinnati *(G-4205)*
Procter & Gamble Company ....C 513 634-9600
West Chester *(G-19768)*
Procter & Gamble Company ....C 513 634-9110
West Chester *(G-19769)*
Procter & Gamble Company ....B 513 983-1100
Cincinnati *(G-4206)*
Procter & Gamble Company ....C 513 934-3406
Oregonia *(G-15573)*
Procter & Gamble Company ....G 513 627-7779
Cincinnati *(G-4207)*
Procter & Gamble Company ....B 513 945-0340
Cincinnati *(G-4208)*
Procter & Gamble Company ....C 513 626-2500
Blue Ash *(G-1836)*
Procter & Gamble Company ....C 513 622-1000
Mason *(G-12926)*
Procter & Gamble Company ....F 513 242-5752
Cincinnati *(G-4209)*
Procter & Gamble Company ....C 410 527-5735
Grove City *(G-10460)*
◆ Procter & Gamble Company ....B 513 983-1100
Cincinnati *(G-4198)*
Procter & Gamble Far East Inc ....C 513 983-1100
Cincinnati *(G-4210)*
Procter & Gamble Hair Care LLC ....G 513 983-4502
Cincinnati *(G-4211)*
Procter & Gamble Mfg Co ....C 419 226-5500
Lima *(G-11921)*
▼ Procter & Gamble Mfg Co ....F 513 983-1100
Cincinnati *(G-4212)*
▲ Proft & Gamble ....G 513 945-0340
Cincinnati *(G-4218)*
Redex Industries Inc ....F 330 332-9800
Salem *(G-16770)*
Sally Beauty Supply LLC ....G 330 823-7476
Alliance *(G-497)*
Sentinel Consumer Products Inc ....D 801 825-5671
Mentor *(G-13579)*
Skin ....G 937 222-0222
Dayton *(G-8510)*
Sysco Guest Supply LLC ....F 440 960-2515
Lorain *(G-12128)*
Universal Packg Systems Inc ....B 513 732-2000
Batavia *(G-1193)*
Universal Packg Systems Inc ....B 513 674-9400
Cincinnati *(G-4452)*
Universal Packg Systems Inc ....E 513 735-4777
Batavia *(G-1194)*
US Cotton LLC ....B 216 676-6400
Cleveland *(G-6244)*
Vein Center and Medspa ....G 330 629-9400
Youngstown *(G-21060)*
Vellus Products Inc ....G 614 889-2391
Columbus *(G-7572)*
▲ Woodbine Products Company ....F 330 725-0165
Medina *(G-13363)*

2851 Paints, Varnishes, Lacquers, Enamels

ABRA Auto Body & Glass LP ....G 513 367-9200
Harrison *(G-10627)*
ABRA Auto Body & Glass LP ....G 513 247-3400
Cincinnati *(G-3289)*
ABRA Auto Body & Glass LP ....G 513 755-7709
West Chester *(G-19635)*
◆ Akron Paint & Varnish Inc ....D 330 773-8911
Akron *(G-46)*
Akzo Nobel Coatings Inc ....C 614 294-3361
Columbus *(G-6558)*
Akzo Nobel Coatings Inc ....F 937 322-2671
Springfield *(G-17361)*
Akzo Nobel Coatings Inc ....C 614 294-3361
Columbus *(G-6559)*
Akzo Nobel Inc ....E 614 294-3361
Columbus *(G-6560)*
All Coatings Co Inc ....G 330 821-3806
Alliance *(G-451)*
Aluminum Coating Manufacturers ....E 216 341-2000
Cleveland *(G-4680)*
American Paint Recyclers LLC ....G 888 978-6558
Middle Point *(G-13755)*
▲ Americhem Inc ....A 330 929-4213
Cuyahoga Falls *(G-7835)*
▲ Aps-Materials Inc ....D 937 278-6547
Dayton *(G-8034)*
Avion Manufacturing Company ....G 330 220-1989
Brunswick *(G-2188)*
Axalt Powde Coati Syste Usa I ....F 614 600-4104
Hilliard *(G-10808)*
Baker Built Products Inc ....G 419 965-2646
Ohio City *(G-15514)*
Basic Coatings LLC ....E 419 241-2156
Bowling Green *(G-1954)*
Bollin & Sons Inc ....E 419 693-6573
Toledo *(G-18210)*
Brinkman LLC ....F 419 204-5934
Lima *(G-11846)*
Cahill Services Inc ....G 216 410-5595
Lakewood *(G-11514)*
Cansto Coatings Ltd ....F 216 231-6115
Cleveland *(G-4865)*
Cansto Paint and Varnish Co ....G 216 231-6115
Cleveland *(G-4866)*
Carboline Company ....G 800 848-4645
University Heights *(G-18940)*
Certon Technologies Inc ....F 440 786-7185
Bedford *(G-1395)*
Cetek Ltd ....E 216 362-3900
Cleveland *(G-4905)*
◆ Chemmasters Inc ....E 440 428-2105
Madison *(G-12344)*
▼ Chemspec Usa LLC ....D 330 669-8512
Orrville *(G-15587)*
◆ Coloramics LLC ....E 614 876-1171
Hilliard *(G-10819)*
◆ Comex North America Inc ....D 303 307-2100
Cleveland *(G-5001)*
Consolidated Coatings Corp ....E 216 514-7596
Cleveland *(G-5017)*
Continental Products Company ....E 216 383-3932
Cleveland *(G-5023)*
Continental Products Company ....E 216 531-0710
Cleveland *(G-5024)*
CPI Industrial Co ....E 614 445-0800
Columbus *(G-6833)*
Creative Commercial Finishing ....G 513 722-9393
Loveland *(G-12184)*
Custom Powdercoating LLC ....G 937 972-3516
Dayton *(G-8122)*
Dap Products Inc ....C 937 667-4461
Tipp City *(G-18110)*
David E Easterday and Co Inc ....F 330 359-0700
Wilmot *(G-20515)*
▲ Day-Glo Color Corp ....C 216 391-7070
Cleveland *(G-5073)*
Day-Glo Color Corp ....C 216 391-7070
Cleveland *(G-5074)*
Deco Plas Properties LLC ....E 419 485-0632
Montpelier *(G-14306)*
Diamant Coating Systems Ltd ....G 513 515-3078
Sharonville *(G-16956)*
Dolgencorp LLC ....G 740 289-4790
Piketon *(G-16069)*
Dudick Inc ....D 330 562-1970
Streetsboro *(G-17672)*
Dynafloor Systems Inc ....F 330 467-6005
Solon *(G-17134)*
Envirnmntal Prtctive Ctngs LLC ....G 740 363-6180
Ostrander *(G-15643)*
Epoxy Systems Blstg Cating Inc ....G 513 924-1800
Cleves *(G-6361)*
Ferro Corporation ....D 216 577-7144
Bedford *(G-1405)*
Ferro Corporation ....C 216 875-6178
Cleveland *(G-5231)*
▲ Ferro Corporation ....D 216 875-5600
Mayfield Heights *(G-13163)*
Filament LLC ....G 614 732-0754
Columbus *(G-6921)*
Fuchs Lubricants Co ....E 330 963-0400
Twinsburg *(G-18777)*
General Electric Company ....D 216 268-3846
Cleveland *(G-5310)*
Genvac Aerospace Corp ....F 440 646-9986
Cleveland *(G-5317)*
▼ Harrison Paint Company ....E 330 455-5120
Canton *(G-2694)*
Henkel Corporation ....C 216 475-3600
Cleveland *(G-5392)*
Hess Advanced Technology Inc ....G 937 268-4377
Huber Heights *(G-11020)*
Hexpol Compounding LLC ....C 440 834-4644
Burton *(G-2360)*
Hoover & Wells Inc ....C 419 691-9220
Toledo *(G-18335)*
Hytek Coatings Inc ....G 513 424-0131
Middletown *(G-13913)*
Janet Sullivan ....G 419 658-2333
Ney *(G-14997)*
▲ Kalcor Coatings Company ....E 440 946-4700
Willoughby *(G-20350)*
▼ Kardol Quality Products LLC ....E 513 933-8206
Blue Ash *(G-1800)*
Kars Ohio LLC ....G 614 655-1099
Pataskala *(G-15834)*
Karyall-Telday Inc ....E 216 281-4063
Cleveland *(G-5516)*
Leonhardt Plating Company ....E 513 242-1410
Cincinnati *(G-3938)*
Mameco International Inc ....F 216 752-4400
Cleveland *(G-5611)*
Mansfield Paint Co Inc ....G 330 725-2436
Medina *(G-13289)*
◆ Master Builders LLC ....E 216 831-5500
Beachwood *(G-1247)*
Matrix Sys Auto Finishes LLC ....D 248 668-8135
Massillon *(G-13023)*
Meggitt (erlanger) LLC ....D 513 851-5550
Cincinnati *(G-4000)*
Mid America Chemical Corp ....G 216 749-0100
Cleveland *(G-5672)*
Myko Industries ....G 216 431-0900
Cleveland *(G-5717)*
▼ Nanosperse LLC ....G 937 296-5030
Kettering *(G-11435)*
Nextgen Materials LLC ....G 513 858-2365
Fairfield *(G-9535)*
▲ North Shore Strapping Inc ....D 216 661-5200
Brooklyn Heights *(G-2128)*
▲ Npa Coatings Inc ....C 216 651-5900
Cleveland *(G-5792)*
Parker Trutec Incorporated ....D 937 653-8500
Urbana *(G-19007)*
Parkins Asphalt Sealing ....G 419 422-2399
Findlay *(G-9739)*
◆ Perstorp Polyols Inc ....C 419 729-5448
Toledo *(G-18467)*

S I C

Employee Codes: A=Over 500 employees, B=251-500
C=101-250, D=51-100, E=20-50, F=10-19, G=3-9
2019 Harris Ohio
Industrial Directory
879

28 CHEMICALS AND ALLIED PRODUCTS SIC SECTION

▲ Polymerics Inc ....E 330 434-6665
   Cuyahoga Falls (G-7906)
Polynt Composites USA Inc ....E 816 391-6000
   Sandusky (G-16839)
Polyone Corporation ....C 419 668-4844
   Norwalk (G-15412)
▲ Postle Industries Inc ....E 216 265-9000
   Cleveland (G-5897)
PPG Architectural Coatings LLC ......F 419 433-5664
   Huron (G-11109)
PPG Architectural Finishes Inc ....G 330 477-8165
   Canton (G-2788)
PPG Industries Inc 330 825-0831
   Barberton (G-1096)
PPG Industries Inc ....G 513 737-1893
   Hamilton (G-10597)
PPG Industries Inc 440 572-2800
   Strongsville (G-17777)
PPG Industries Inc ....G 740 774-8734
   Chillicothe (G-3212)
PPG Industries Inc ....F 440 232-1260
   Bedford (G-1437)
PPG Industries Inc ....E 216 671-7793
   Cleveland (G-5900)
PPG Industries Inc 740 363-9610
   Delaware (G-8715)
PPG Industries Inc ....E 513 576-0360
   Milford (G-14033)
PPG Industries Inc 614 252-6384
   Columbus (G-7336)
PPG Industries Inc 330 825-6328
   Barberton (G-1097)
PPG Industries Inc ....C 740 474-3161
   Circleville (G-4553)
PPG Industries Inc ....E 740 774-7600
   Chillicothe (G-3213)
PPG Industries Inc ....F 740 774-7600
   Chillicothe (G-3214)
PPG Industries Inc 740 774-7600
   Chillicothe (G-3215)
PPG Industries Inc ....E 513 231-3200
   Cincinnati (G-4179)
PPG Industries Inc 740 474-3945
   Circleville (G-4554)
PPG Industries Inc ....E 513 829-6006
   Fairfield (G-9549)
PPG Industries Inc 513 661-5220
   Cincinnati (G-4180)
PPG Industries Inc ....G 614 277-0620
   Grove City (G-10458)
PPG Industries Inc 614 921-9228
   Hilliard (G-10854)
PPG Industries Inc 513 424-1241
   Middletown (G-13943)
PPG Industries Inc 513 984-6761
   Cincinnati (G-4181)
PPG Industries Inc 614 939-2365
   Columbus (G-7337)
PPG Industries Inc 614 268-2609
   Columbus (G-7338)
PPG Industries Inc ....E 513 779-2727
   West Chester (G-19888)
PPG Industries Inc ....E 513 242-3050
   Cincinnati (G-4182)
PPG Industries Inc 614 501-7360
   Reynoldsburg (G-16446)
PPG Industries Inc 330 262-9741
   Wooster (G-20638)
PPG Industries Inc 513 576-3100
   Milford (G-14034)
PPG Industries Inc 330 824-2537
   Warren (G-19433)
PPG Industries Inc ....E 614 846-3128
   Columbus (G-7339)
PPG Industries Inc 419 683-2400
   Crestline (G-7799)
PPG Industries Ohio Inc 740 363-9610
   Delaware (G-8716)
PPG Industries Ohio Inc ....D 216 486-5300
   Euclid (G-9436)
◆ PPG Industries Ohio Inc ....A 216 671-0050
   Cleveland (G-5901)
Precisions Paint Systems LLC ....F 740 894-6224
   South Point (G-17291)
Premier Ink Systems Inc ....F 513 367-2300
   Harrison (G-10664)
Priest Services Inc ....E 440 333-1123
   Mayfield Heights (G-13170)
▲ Prism Powder Coatings Ltd 330 225-5626
   Brunswick (G-2230)

Quality Durable Indus Floors ....F 937 696-2833
   Farmersville (G-9631)
Ramon Robinson ....G 330 883-3244
   Vienna (G-19208)
◆ Republic Powdered Metals Inc ....D 330 225-3192
   Medina (G-13327)
Robert Raack ....G 216 932-6127
   Cleveland Heights (G-6351)
Roger Hoover ....G 330 857-1815
   Orrville (G-15616)
RPM Consumer Holding Company ...G 330 273-5090
   Medina (G-13330)
◆ RPM International Inc ....D 330 273-5090
   Medina (G-13331)
Ruscoe Company ....E 330 253-8148
   Akron (G-358)
Sheffield Bronze Paint Corp ....E 216 481-8330
   Cleveland (G-6050)
Sherwin-Williams Company ....A 216 566-2000
   Cleveland (G-6053)
Sherwin-Williams Company ....G 440 282-2310
   Lorain (G-12120)
Sherwin-Williams Company ....C 330 830-6000
   Massillon (G-13048)
Sherwin-Williams Company 330 253-6625
   North Canton (G-15117)
Sherwin-Williams Company ....E 614 539-8456
   Grove City (G-10467)
Sherwin-Williams Company 440 846-4328
   Strongsville (G-17788)
Sherwin-Williams Company ....G 216 662-3300
   Cleveland (G-6054)
Sherwin-Williams Company 330 528-0124
   Hudson (G-11072)
Sherwin-Williams Mfg Co ....F 216 566-2000
   Cleveland (G-6055)
◆ Sherwn-WIlams Auto Fnshes Corp ..C 216 332-8330
   Cleveland (G-6056)
Sherwn-WIlams Intl Hldings Inc 216 566-2000
   Medina (G-13342)
▲ Spectrum Dispersions Inc ....F 330 296-0600
   Ravenna (G-16405)
Stronghold Coating Ltd 937 704-4020
   Cincinnati (G-4385)
Sun Color Corporation ....G 330 499-7010
   North Canton (G-15123)
Superior Printing Ink Co Inc ....G 216 328-1720
   Cleveland (G-6124)
▲ Teknol Inc ....D 937 264-0190
   Dayton (G-8550)
◆ Thorworks Industries Inc ....E 419 626-4375
   Sandusky (G-16855)
Toledo Paint & Chemical Co ....G 419 244-3726
   Toledo (G-18566)
◆ Tremco Incorporated ....B 216 292-5000
   Beachwood (G-1283)
Treved Exteriors ....G 513 771-3888
   Cincinnati (G-4432)
Trexler Rubber Co Inc ....E 330 296-9677
   Ravenna (G-16414)
Universal Urethane Pdts Inc ....D 419 693-7400
   Toledo (G-18585)
▼ Waterlox Coatings Corporation ......F 216 641-4877
   Cleveland (G-6293)
▼ Wooster Products Inc ....D 330 264-2844
   Wooster (G-20669)
X-Treme Finishes Inc ....F 330 474-0614
   Medina (G-13364)
▲ Xim Products Inc ....E 440 871-4737
   Westlake (G-20174)
▲ Zircoa Inc ....C 440 248-0500
   Cleveland (G-6345)

2861 Gum & Wood Chemicals

Arizona Chemical Company LLC .....C 330 343-7701
   Dover (G-8804)
Kingsford Ink LLC ....E 216 507-4032
   Cleveland Heights (G-6349)
◆ Oak Chips Inc ....E 740 947-4159
   Waverly (G-19554)
Tanning ....G 937 233-4554
   Dayton (G-8538)

2865 Cyclic-Crudes, Intermediates, Dyes & Org Pigments

Accel Corporation ....F 440 327-7418
   Avon (G-937)
Altivia Petrochemicals LLC ....E 740 532-3420
   Haverhill (G-10707)

Americhem Inc ....E 330 926-3185
   Cuyahoga Falls (G-7834)
▲ Americhem Inc ....A 330 929-4213
   Cuyahoga Falls (G-7835)
◆ Berghausen Corporation ....E 513 541-5631
   Cincinnati (G-3389)
Chromaflo Technologies Corp ....C 513 733-5111
   Cincinnati (G-3474)
▲ Chromaflo Technologies Corp ....C 440 997-0081
   Ashtabula (G-764)
◆ Cleveland FP Inc ....D 216 249-4900
   Cleveland (G-4959)
Colormatrix Group Inc ....G 216 622-0100
   Berea (G-1598)
Colormatrix Holdings Inc ....C 440 930-3162
   Berea (G-1599)
Dorum Color Co Inc ....G 330 773-1900
   Coventry Township (G-7768)
Ferro Corporation ....F 330 682-8015
   Orrville (G-15590)
Ferro Corporation ....C 216 875-6178
   Cleveland (G-5231)
Flint Group US LLC ....D 513 771-1900
   Cincinnati (G-3695)
Hexpol Compounding LLC ....C 440 834-4644
   Burton (G-2360)
Inceptor Inc ....G 419 726-8804
   Toledo (G-18343)
Kingscote Chemicals Inc ....G 937 886-9100
   Miamisburg (G-13683)
◆ Marathon Petroleum Company LP ..F 419 422-2121
   Findlay (G-9719)
Norlab Inc ....G 440 282-5265
   Lorain (G-12107)
▲ Polymerics Inc ....E 330 434-6665
   Cuyahoga Falls (G-7906)
Polyone Corporation ....C 419 668-4844
   Norwalk (G-15412)
◆ Republic Powdered Metals Inc ....D 330 225-3192
   Medina (G-13327)
◆ RPM International Inc ....D 330 273-5090
   Medina (G-13331)
Ruscoe Company ....E 330 253-8148
   Akron (G-359)
▲ Spectrum Dispersions Inc ....F 330 296-0600
   Ravenna (G-16405)
Sun Chemical Corporation ....C 513 681-5950
   Cincinnati (G-4391)
Sun Chemical Corporation ....D 513 753-9550
   Amelia (G-549)
Sun Chemical Corporation ....E 513 830-8667
   Cincinnati (G-4395)
Thermocolor LLC 419 626-5677
   Sandusky (G-16852)
Thermocolor LLC ....F 419 626-5677
   Sandusky (G-16853)

2869 Industrial Organic Chemicals, NEC

1803 Bacon Ltd ....G 740 398-7644
   Columbus (G-6510)
A-Gas US Holdings Inc ....F 419 867-8990
   Bowling Green (G-1945)
A-Gas US Inc ....G 800 372-1301
   Bowling Green (G-1946)
◆ Abitec Corporation ....E 614 429-6464
   Columbus (G-6527)
ABS Materials Inc ....D 330 234-7999
   Wooster (G-20553)
Adr Fuel Inc 419 872-2178
   Perrysburg (G-15917)
Akzo Nobel Chemicals LLC ....G 419 229-0088
   Lima (G-11833)
▲ Alco-Chem Inc ....E 330 253-3535
   Akron (G-56)
Aldrich Chemical ....D 937 859-1808
   Miamisburg (G-13638)
Alpha Zeta Holdings Inc ....G 216 271-1601
   Cleveland (G-4677)
AMA Fuel Services LLC ....E 513 836-3800
   Lebanon (G-11633)
Ampacet Corporation ....C 740 929-5521
   Newark (G-14850)
Andersons Clymers Ethanol LLC ......E 574 722-2627
   Maumee (G-13074)
Ashland LLC ....C 614 529-3318
   Columbus (G-6618)
B P Oil Company 513 671-4107
   Cincinnati (G-3376)
Bam Fuel Inc ....G 740 397-6674
   Howard (G-10995)

SIC SECTION

28 CHEMICALS AND ALLIED PRODUCTS

BASF Corporation ....C....... 937 547-6700
   Greenville *(G-10360)*
BASF Corporation ....C....... 419 877-5308
   Whitehouse *(G-20188)*
BASF Corporation ....C....... 513 482-3000
   Cincinnati *(G-3381)*
Beloit Fuel LLC ....G....... 330 584-1915
   North Benton *(G-15060)*
▲ Biowish Technologies Inc ....G....... 312 572-6700
   Cincinnati *(G-3395)*
◆ Borchers Americas Inc ....D....... 440 899-2950
   Westlake *(G-20103)*
Brightstar Propane & Fuels ....G....... 614 891-8395
   Westerville *(G-19981)*
Canton Fuel ....G....... 330 455-3400
   Canton *(G-2609)*
Canton OH Rubber Speclty Prods ....G....... 330 454-3847
   Canton *(G-2612)*
Cargill Incorporated ....F....... 513 941-7400
   Cincinnati *(G-3443)*
▲ Carson-Saeks Inc ....D....... 937 278-5311
   Dayton *(G-8078)*
Catholic Charity Hispanic Off ....F....... 216 696-2197
   Cleveland *(G-4891)*
Champion Company ....D....... 937 324-5681
   Springfield *(G-17374)*
Chem-Sales Inc ....F....... 419 531-4292
   Toledo *(G-18228)*
Chemcore Inc ....F....... 937 228-6118
   Dayton *(G-8088)*
▲ Chemionics Corporation ....E....... 330 733-8834
   Tallmadge *(G-17975)*
◆ Chempak International LLC ....G....... 440 543-8511
   Chagrin Falls *(G-3039)*
▲ Chemspec ....F....... 330 896-0355
   Uniontown *(G-18914)*
Clariant Corporation ....G....... 513 791-2964
   Blue Ash *(G-1751)*
Coil Specialty Chemicals LLC ......G....... 740 236-2407
   Marietta *(G-12616)*
Controlled Release Society Inc ....G....... 513 948-8000
   Cincinnati *(G-3545)*
Corrugated Chemicals Inc ....G....... 513 561-7773
   Cincinnati *(G-3553)*
Coshocton Ethanol LLC ....E....... 740 623-3046
   Coshocton *(G-7727)*
Creative Fuels LLC ....F....... 330 923-2222
   Cuyahoga Falls *(G-7854)*
Custom Fresheners ....G....... 888 241-9109
   Fremont *(G-10010)*
Dnd Emulsions Inc ....G....... 419 525-4988
   Mansfield *(G-12433)*
◆ Dover Chemical Corporation .....C....... 330 343-7711
   Dover *(G-8339)*
Dow Chemical Company ....D....... 937 839-4612
   West Alexandria *(G-19618)*
Dow Silicones Corporation ....C....... 330 319-1127
   Copley *(G-7682)*
East Side Fuel Plus Operations ....G....... 419 563-0777
   Bucyrus *(G-2327)*
Eco Chem Alternative Fuels LLC ....G....... 614 764-3835
   Dublin *(G-8912)*
Eco Fuel Solution LLC ....G....... 440 282-8592
   Amherst *(G-562)*
Elco Corporation ....E....... 440 997-6131
   Ashtabula *(G-773)*
▼ Elco Corporation ....D....... 800 321-0467
   Cleveland *(G-5160)*
Emerald Polymer Additives LLC ...D....... 330 374-2424
   Akron *(G-153)*
Enzyme Catalyzed Polymers LLC ....G....... 330 310-1072
   Akron *(G-158)*
Enzyme Industries of The U S A ....G....... 740 929-4975
   Newark *(G-14871)*
Eqm Technologies & Energy Inc ....F....... 513 825-7500
   Cincinnati *(G-3650)*
Equistar Chemicals LP ....F....... 513 530-4000
   Cincinnati *(G-3651)*
Es Manufacturing Inc ....G....... 888 331-3443
   Newark *(G-14873)*
Exp Fuels Inc ....G....... 419 382-7713
   Toledo *(G-18287)*
Ferro Corporation ....D....... 216 577-7144
   Bedford *(G-1405)*
Fitness Fuel Training ....G....... 330 807-7353
   Tallmadge *(G-17983)*
Fly Race Fuels LLC ....G....... 419 744-9402
   North Fairfield *(G-15138)*
Fostoria Ethanol LLC ....E....... 419 436-0954
   Fostoria *(G-9841)*

Franklin ....G....... 419 699-5757
   Waterville *(G-19495)*
Frutarom USA Holding Inc ....G....... 201 861-9500
   West Chester *(G-19855)*
Fuel America ....G....... 419 586-5609
   Celina *(G-2963)*
Fuel G USA LLC ....G....... 440 617-0950
   Westlake *(G-20115)*
Gdc Inc ....F....... 574 533-3128
   Wooster *(G-20596)*
Geo Specialty Chemical ....G....... 330 650-0237
   Hudson *(G-11045)*
◆ GFS Chemicals Inc ....E....... 740 881-5501
   Powell *(G-16322)*
GFS Chemicals Inc ....D....... 614 224-5345
   Columbus *(G-6950)*
Givaudan ....F....... 513 482-2536
   Cincinnati *(G-3754)*
Givaudan Flavors Corporation ......B....... 513 948-4933
   Cincinnati *(G-3755)*
Givaudan Flvors Fragrances Inc ....G....... 513 948-8000
   Cincinnati *(G-3757)*
◆ Givaudan Fragrances Corp ....B....... 513 948-3428
   Cincinnati *(G-3758)*
Givaudan Fragrances Corp ....B....... 513 948-3428
   Cincinnati *(G-3759)*
◆ Givaudan Roure US Inc ....G....... 513 948-8000
   Cincinnati *(G-3760)*
▲ Global Biochem ....G....... 513 792-2218
   Cincinnati *(G-3762)*
Greater Ohio Ethanol LLC ....G....... 567 940-9500
   Lima *(G-11870)*
Green Harvest Energy LLC ....F....... 330 716-3068
   Columbiana *(G-6467)*
Greene Fuel Plaza Inc ....G....... 937 532-4826
   Kettering *(G-11432)*
Guardian Lima LLC ....E....... 567 940-9500
   Lima *(G-11872)*
Ha-International LLC ....E....... 419 537-0096
   Toledo *(G-18317)*
▲ Hardy Industrial Tech LLC ....D....... 440 350-6300
   Painesville *(G-15745)*
Harrison 20 Mtd Borefinery LLC ...G....... 740 796-4797
   Adamsville *(G-9)*
▲ Heraeus Precious Metals North ....E....... 937 264-1000
   Vandalia *(G-19127)*
Hill & Griffith Company ....G....... 513 921-1075
   Cincinnati *(G-3812)*
Homeland AG Fuels LLC ....G....... 216 763-1004
   Cleveland *(G-5415)*
▲ Hunt Imaging LLC ....E....... 440 826-0433
   Berea *(G-1611)*
Ibidltd-Blue Green Energy ....F....... 909 547-5160
   Toledo *(G-18339)*
◆ Image Armor LLC ....G....... 877 673-4377
   Midvale *(G-13979)*
Ineos Nitriles USA LLC ....C....... 419 226-1200
   Lima *(G-11878)*
Insightfuel LLC ....F....... 330 998-7380
   Macedonia *(G-12304)*
Ishos Bros Fuel Ventures Inc ....G....... 586 634-0187
   Maumee *(G-13119)*
Ishos Bros Fuel Ventures Inc ....G....... 419 913-5718
   Toledo *(G-18355)*
▲ J R M Chemical Inc ....F....... 216 475-8488
   Cleveland *(G-5487)*
▼ Jatrodiesel Inc ....F....... 937 847-8050
   Miamisburg *(G-13681)*
K & E Chemical Co Inc ....F....... 216 341-0500
   Cleveland *(G-5511)*
Karl Industries Inc ....G....... 330 562-4100
   Aurora *(G-887)*
Kerry Flavor Systems Us LLC ......E....... 513 539-7373
   Monroe *(G-14270)*
L and S Express Fuel Center ....G....... 330 549-9566
   North Lima *(G-15174)*
Leaf Lono Earth Alterntv Fuels ......G....... 614 829-7159
   Canal Winchester *(G-2505)*
Littlern Corporation ....G....... 330 848-8847
   Barberton *(G-1081)*
Lost Nation Fuel ....G....... 440 951-9088
   Willoughby *(G-20362)*
◆ Lubrizol Corporation ....A....... 440 943-4200
   Wickliffe *(G-20215)*
Lyondell Chemical Company ....E....... 440 352-9393
   Fairport Harbor *(G-9625)*
Lyondell Chemical Company ....D....... 513 530-4000
   Cincinnati *(G-3960)*
M J S Oil Inc ....G....... 937 982-3519
   West Mansfield *(G-19944)*

Marion Ethanol LLC ....E....... 740 383-4400
   Marion *(G-12717)*
Mart Plus Fuel ....G....... 216 261-0420
   Euclid *(G-9425)*
Martin M Hardin ....G....... 740 282-1234
   Steubenville *(G-17543)*
Mid America Chemical Corp ....G....... 216 749-0100
   Cleveland *(G-5672)*
Momentive Performance Mtls Inc ....C....... 740 928-7010
   Hebron *(G-10753)*
Momentive Performance Mtls Inc ....A....... 440 878-5705
   Richmond Heights *(G-16503)*
Momentive Performance Mtls Inc ....G....... 614 986-2495
   Columbus *(G-7193)*
◆ Momentive Prfmce Mtls Qrtz Inc ....C....... 440 878-5700
   Strongsville *(G-17765)*
Momentive Specialty Chem Inc ....F....... 740 452-5451
   Zanesville *(G-21158)*
Mp Biomedicals LLC ....C....... 440 337-1200
   Solon *(G-17199)*
◆ Nachurs Alpine Solutions Corp ....E....... 740 382-5701
   Marion *(G-12723)*
▲ National Colloid Company ....E....... 740 282-1171
   Steubenville *(G-17545)*
Nationwide Chemical Products .....G....... 419 714-7075
   Perrysburg *(G-15979)*
▲ Nease Co LLC ....F....... 513 587-2800
   West Chester *(G-19747)*
Nease Co LLC ....D....... 513 738-1255
   Harrison *(G-10661)*
New Mulch In A Bottle Limited ......G....... 724 290-2341
   Marietta *(G-12648)*
North East Fuel Inc ....G....... 330 264-4454
   Wooster *(G-20633)*
Novation Solutions LLC ....G....... 330 620-1189
   Barberton *(G-1090)*
▼ Noveon Fcc Inc ....G....... 440 943-4200
   Wickliffe *(G-20219)*
Occidental Chemical Corp ....E....... 513 242-2900
   Cincinnati *(G-4097)*
Ohio Biosystems Coop Inc ....G....... 419 980-7663
   Loudonville *(G-12146)*
Ohio Chemical Two ....G....... 614 482-8073
   Columbus *(G-7243)*
Ohio State University ....E....... 614 292-7656
   Columbus *(G-7259)*
Orion Engineered Carbons LLC ....D....... 740 423-9571
   Belpre *(G-1581)*
Oxyrase Inc ....F....... 419 589-8800
   Ontario *(G-15545)*
P S P Inc ....E....... 330 283-5635
   Kent *(G-11359)*
Patriot Energy LLC ....D....... 330 923-4442
   Cuyahoga Falls *(G-7903)*
Pen Brands LLC ....E....... 216 674-1430
   Brooklyn Heights *(G-2129)*
▲ Permco Inc ....C....... 330 626-2801
   Streetsboro *(G-17687)*
Polychem Dispersions Inc ....E....... 800 545-3530
   Middlefield *(G-13848)*
Polymer Additives Inc ....G....... 216 875-7273
   Cleveland *(G-5894)*
▲ Reclamation Technologies Inc ....E....... 800 372-1301
   Bowling Green *(G-1994)*
Reclamation Technologies Inc .....F....... 419 867-8990
   Bowling Green *(G-1995)*
▲ Research Organics LLC ....D....... 216 883-8025
   Cleveland *(G-5978)*
Rex American Resources Corp ....C....... 937 276-3931
   Dayton *(G-8474)*
▲ Rezkem Chemicals LLC ....F....... 330 653-9104
   Hudson *(G-11070)*
Ronald T Dodge Co ....F....... 937 439-4497
   Dayton *(G-8484)*
Santmyer Coml Fling Netwrk LLC ....G....... 330 262-2334
   Wooster *(G-20647)*
Shepherd Chemical Company ......F....... 513 200-6987
   Cincinnati *(G-4331)*
Shepherd Material Science Co .....F....... 513 731-1110
   Norwood *(G-15428)*
Silicone Solutions Inc ....F....... 330 920-3125
   Cuyahoga Falls *(G-7917)*
Silicone Solutions Intl LLC ....G....... 419 720-8709
   Toledo *(G-18523)*
Speedway LLC ....A....... 937 864-3000
   Enon *(G-9387)*
Sugar Foods Corporation ....G....... 513 336-9748
   Mason *(G-12943)*
Summit Ethanol LLC ....E....... 419 943-7447
   Leipsic *(G-11737)*

Employee Codes: A=Over 500 employees, B=251-500
C=101-250, D=51-100, E=20-50, F=10-19, G=3-9

Symrise Inc...C... 440 324-6060
Elyria *(G-9334)*
◆ **Systech Environmental Corp**...E... 800 888-8011
Dayton *(G-8532)*
◆ **Tedia Company Inc**...D... 513 874-5340
Fairfield *(G-9567)*
Trugreen Cleaners LLC...G... 740 703-1063
Chillicothe *(G-3229)*
Twin Rvers Tech - Pnsville LLC...D... 440 350-6300
Painesville *(G-15793)*
Ultimate Chem Solutions Inc...E... 440 998-6751
Ashtabula *(G-809)*
Union Carbide Corporation...D... 216 529-3784
Cleveland *(G-6231)*
◆ **United Initiators Inc**...D... 440 326-2416
Elyria *(G-9341)*
Univar USA Inc...C... 513 714-5264
West Chester *(G-19911)*
Vadose Syn Fuels Inc...G... 330 564-0545
Munroe Falls *(G-14529)*
▲ **Vantage Specialty Ingredients**...E... 937 264-1222
Englewood *(G-9382)*
Wacker Chemical Corporation...E... 330 899-0847
Canton *(G-2862)*
West Erie Fuel...G... 440 282-3493
Lorain *(G-12137)*
▲ **Zaclon LLC**...E... 216 271-1601
Cleveland *(G-6335)*

2873 Nitrogenous Fertilizers

Advancing Eco-Agriculture LLC...G... 800 495-6603
Middlefield *(G-13773)*
Agrium Advanced Tech US Inc...G... 614 276-5103
Columbus *(G-6552)*
Alpha Omega Bioremediation LLC...F... 614 287-2600
Columbus *(G-6577)*
Amsoil Inc...G... 614 274-9851
Columbus *(G-6593)*
Andersons Plant Nutrient LLC...G... 419 396-3501
Carey *(G-2878)*
Deerfield Farms Service Inc...D... 800 589-8606
Deerfield *(G-8608)*
Harvest Land Co-Op Inc...G... 937 884-5526
Verona *(G-19172)*
Hawthorne Hydroponics LLC...G... 800 221-1760
Marysville *(G-12788)*
Hyponex Corporation...D... 937 644-0011
Marysville *(G-12794)*
Hyponex Corporation...E... 330 262-1300
Shreve *(G-17002)*
Naturym LLC...G... 614 284-3068
Gahanna *(G-10093)*
Nutrien AG Solutions Inc...E... 513 941-4100
North Bend *(G-15053)*
Pcs Nitrogen Inc...B... 419 226-1200
Lima *(G-11914)*
Pcs Nitrogen Ohio LP...G... 419 879-8989
Lima *(G-11915)*
R & J AG Manufacturing Inc...F... 419 962-4707
Ashland *(G-741)*
Scotts Company LLC...E... 614 863-3920
Gahanna *(G-10102)*
Scotts Company LLC...F... 937 454-2782
Dayton *(G-8498)*
◆ **Scotts Company LLC**...B... 937 644-0011
Marysville *(G-12809)*
Scotts Miracle-Gro Company...D... 330 684-0421
Orrville *(G-15619)*
Scotts Miracle-Gro Company...E... 937 578-5065
Marysville *(G-12811)*
Scotts Miracle-Gro Products...E... 937 644-0011
Marysville *(G-12812)*
Synagro Midwest Inc...F... 937 384-0669
Miamisburg *(G-13722)*
▼ **Turf Care Supply Corp**...B... 877 220-1014
Brunswick *(G-2247)*

2874 Phosphatic Fertilizers

Andersons Inc...C... 419 893-5050
Maumee *(G-13072)*
Andersons Inc...G... 419 536-0460
Toledo *(G-18184)*
Occidental Chemical Corp...E... 513 242-2900
Cincinnati *(G-4097)*
◆ **Scotts Company LLC**...B... 937 644-0011
Marysville *(G-12809)*

2875 Fertilizers, Mixing Only

All Ways Green Lawn & Turf LLC...G... 937 763-4766
Seaman *(G-16882)*
Charles Daniel Young...G... 937 968-3423
Union City *(G-18903)*
City of Columbus...E... 614 645-3152
Lockbourne *(G-11993)*
Compost Cincy...G... 513 278-8178
Cincinnati *(G-3540)*
Countyline Co-Op Inc...F... 419 287-3241
Pemberville *(G-15883)*
Garick LLC...E... 216 581-0100
Cleveland *(G-5293)*
Growmark Fs LLC...F... 330 386-7626
East Liverpool *(G-9057)*
Hoopes Fertilizer Works Inc...G... 330 894-2121
East Rochester *(G-9090)*
Hoopes Fertilizer Works Inc...G... 330 821-3550
Alliance *(G-476)*
Hyponex Corporation...D... 937 644-0011
Marysville *(G-12794)*
Hyponex Corporation...E... 330 262-1300
Shreve *(G-17002)*
Insta-Gro Manufacturing Inc...G... 419 845-3046
Caledonia *(G-2417)*
Kurtz Bros Compost Services...E... 330 864-2621
Akron *(G-242)*
Legacy Farmers Cooperative...F... 419 423-2611
Findlay *(G-9713)*
Lesco Inc...F... 740 633-6366
Martins Ferry *(G-12761)*
LLC Kurtz Bros Central Ohio...G... 614 733-3074
Dublin *(G-8943)*
Luckey Farmers Inc...G... 419 287-3275
Bradner *(G-2013)*
Midwest Compost Inc...F... 419 547-7979
Clyde *(G-6391)*
◆ **Nachurs Alpine Solutions Corp**...E... 740 382-5701
Marion *(G-12723)*
Nutrien AG Solutions Inc...E... 513 941-4100
North Bend *(G-15053)*
Nutrien AG Solutions Inc...G... 614 873-4253
Milford Center *(G-14047)*
Ohigro Inc...E... 740 726-2429
Waldo *(G-19304)*
Opal Diamond LLC...G... 330 653-5876
Rocky River *(G-16550)*
Ottokee Group Inc...G... 419 636-1932
Bryan *(G-2302)*
Price Farms Organics Ltd...F... 740 369-1000
Delaware *(G-8717)*
Roe Transportation Entps Inc...G... 937 497-7161
Sidney *(G-17068)*
Rural Farm Distributors Co...G... 419 747-6807
Mansfield *(G-12508)*
Tri-State Garden Supply Inc...E... 419 445-6561
Archbold *(G-672)*
Tyler Grain & Fertilizer Co...F... 330 669-2341
Smithville *(G-17095)*
Werlor Inc...E... 419 784-4285
Defiance *(G-8647)*

2879 Pesticides & Agricultural Chemicals, NEC

A Best Trmt & Pest Ctrl Sups...G... 330 434-5555
Akron *(G-18)*
▲ **Advanced Biological Mktg Inc**...F... 419 232-2461
Van Wert *(G-19073)*
Bird Control International...E... 330 425-2377
Twinsburg *(G-18741)*
Dow Chemical Company...F... 937 254-1550
Dayton *(G-8166)*
Harvest Land Co-Op Inc...G... 937 884-5526
Verona *(G-19172)*
▲ **Hawthorne Hydroponics LLC**...D... 480 777-2000
Marysville *(G-12787)*
Isky North America Inc...G... 937 823-9595
Vandalia *(G-19130)*
Mercer Landmark Inc...G... 419 363-3391
Rockford *(G-16540)*
Modern AG Supply Inc...G... 419 753-3484
New Knoxville *(G-14705)*
Monsanto Company...F... 937 548-7858
Greenville *(G-10384)*
Mystic Chemical Products Co...G... 216 251-4416
Cleveland *(G-5718)*
▲ **Quality Borate Co LLC**...F... 216 896-1949
Cleveland *(G-5940)*
◆ **Scotts Company LLC**...B... 937 644-0011
Marysville *(G-12809)*
Scotts Miracle-Gro Company...E... 937 578-5065
Marysville *(G-12811)*
▲ **Scotts Miracle-Gro Company**...B... 937 644-0011
Marysville *(G-12810)*
Village of Dupont...G... 419 596-3061
Dupont *(G-9037)*
▲ **Waldo & Associates Inc**...E... 419 666-3662
Perrysburg *(G-16023)*

2891 Adhesives & Sealants

A & M Products...G... 419 595-2092
Tiffin *(G-18039)*
▲ **Adchem Adhesives Inc**...F... 440 526-1976
Cleveland *(G-4614)*
Akron Coating & Adhesives Inc...F... 330 724-4716
Akron *(G-35)*
◆ **Akron Paint & Varnish Inc**...D... 330 773-8911
Akron *(G-46)*
Akzo Nobel Paints LLC...G... 513 242-0530
Cincinnati *(G-3316)*
Alpha Coatings Inc...C... 419 435-5111
Fostoria *(G-9832)*
Aluminum Coating Manufacturers...E... 216 341-2000
Cleveland *(G-4680)*
Arclin USA LLC...E... 419 726-5013
Toledo *(G-18190)*
Avery Dennison Corporation...B... 440 358-3700
Painesville *(G-15716)*
Besten Equipment Inc...E... 216 581-1166
Akron *(G-87)*
▲ **Boltaron Inc**...D... 740 498-5900
Newcomerstown *(G-14970)*
Brewer Company...G... 513 576-6300
Cincinnati *(G-3414)*
Brewer Company...E... 614 279-8688
Columbus *(G-6694)*
▲ **Cardinal Rubber Company Inc**...E... 330 745-2191
Barberton *(G-1069)*
Cemedine North America LLC...G... 513 618-4652
Cincinnati *(G-3454)*
Century Industries Corporation...E... 330 457-2367
New Waterford *(G-14838)*
Certon Technologies Inc...F... 440 786-7185
Bedford *(G-1395)*
◆ **Chemmasters Inc**...E... 440 428-2105
Madison *(G-12344)*
◆ **Chemspec Ltd**...F... 330 896-0355
Uniontown *(G-18915)*
Choice Brands Adhesives Ltd...G... 800 330-5566
Cincinnati *(G-3472)*
▲ **Cincinnati Assn For The Blind**...C... 513 221-8558
Cincinnati *(G-3481)*
◆ **Concrete Sealants Inc**...E... 937 845-8776
Tipp City *(G-18109)*
Consolidated Coatings Corp...E... 216 514-7596
Cleveland *(G-5017)*
Continental Products Company...E... 216 531-0710
Cleveland *(G-5024)*
▲ **Conversion Tech Intl Inc**...E... 419 924-5566
West Unity *(G-19967)*
Cornerstone Indus Holdings...G... 440 893-9144
Chagrin Falls *(G-3014)*
▲ **CP Industries Inc**...F... 740 763-2886
Newark *(G-14865)*
Dap Products Inc...C... 937 667-4461
Tipp City *(G-18110)*
Davis Caulking & Sealant LLC...G... 740 286-3825
Wellston *(G-19599)*
Dental Sealants...G... 440 582-3466
North Royalton *(G-15269)*
Durez Corporation...C... 567 295-6400
Kenton *(G-11404)*
Dyna Tech Molding & Beta...G... 330 296-2315
Ravenna *(G-16377)*
Econo Products Inc...F... 330 923-4101
Cuyahoga Falls *(G-7862)*
▲ **Egc Enterprises Inc**...E... 440 285-5835
Chardon *(G-3110)*
Elaston Company...F... 330 863-2865
Malvern *(G-12389)*
Elmer S Inc...G... 614 225-4000
Columbus *(G-6892)*
Engineered Conductive Mtl LLC...G... 740 362-4444
Delaware *(G-8676)*
▲ **Engineered Mtls Systems Inc**...E... 740 362-4444
Delaware *(G-8677)*
Entrochem Inc...F... 614 946-7602
Columbus *(G-6900)*
Evans Adhesive Corporation...E... 614 451-2665
Columbus *(G-6908)*
Extendit Company...G... 330 743-4343
Youngstown *(G-20902)*

▼ **Fairmount Santrol Inc**..................G....... 440 214-3200
Independence *(G-11127)*
▲ **Federal Process Corporation**............E....... 216 464-6440
Cleveland *(G-5227)*
Foam Seal Inc..................D....... 216 881-8111
Cleveland *(G-5256)*
Freedom Asphalt Sealant & Line...........G....... 937 416-1053
Miamisburg *(G-13671)*
Gdc Inc..................F....... 574 533-3128
Wooster *(G-20596)*
▲ **Gold Key Processing Inc**..................C....... 440 632-0901
Middlefield *(G-13800)*
Har Equipment Sales Inc..................G....... 440 786-7189
Bedford *(G-1411)*
Hartline Products Coinc..................G....... 216 291-2303
Cleveland *(G-5377)*
Hartline Products Coinc..................G....... 216 851-7189
Cleveland *(G-5378)*
HB Fuller Company..................E....... 513 719-3600
Blue Ash *(G-1786)*
HB Fuller Company..................G....... 513 719-3600
Blue Ash *(G-1787)*
Henkel Adhesive Corporation..................G....... 513 677-5800
Maineville *(G-12370)*
Henkel Corporation..................C....... 216 475-3600
Cleveland *(G-5392)*
Henkel US Operations Corp..................E....... 440 255-8900
Mentor *(G-13464)*
Henkel US Operations Corp..................C....... 440 250-7700
Westlake *(G-20122)*
Henkel US Operations Corp..................D....... 513 830-0260
Cincinnati *(G-3808)*
Hexpol Compounding LLC..................C....... 440 834-4644
Burton *(G-2360)*
Hoover & Wells Inc..................C....... 419 691-9220
Toledo *(G-18335)*
Hydratech Engineered Pdts LLC..................F....... 513 827-9169
Cincinnati *(G-3831)*
▲ **ICP Adhesives and Sealants Inc**..................F....... 330 753-4585
Norton *(G-15369)*
Illinois Tool Works Inc..................C....... 513 489-7600
Blue Ash *(G-1791)*
Illinois Tool Works Inc..................D....... 440 914-3100
Solon *(G-17166)*
Imperial Adhesives..................G....... 513 351-1300
Cincinnati *(G-3841)*
Invisible Repair Products Inc..................G....... 330 798-0441
Akron *(G-219)*
Jetcoat LLC..................E....... 800 394-0047
Columbus *(G-7067)*
Kcg Inc..................G....... 614 238-9450
Columbus *(G-7084)*
Laird Technologies Inc..................D....... 216 939-2300
Cleveland *(G-5554)*
▲ **Laminate Technologies Inc**..................D....... 419 448-0812
Tiffin *(G-18064)*
Leesburg Modern Sales Inc..................G....... 937 780-2613
Leesburg *(G-11712)*
▲ **LMI Custom Mixing LLC**..................D....... 740 435-0444
Cambridge *(G-2447)*
◆ **Lubrizol Global Management**..................F....... 216 447-5000
Brecksville *(G-2048)*
Mameco International Inc..................F....... 216 752-4400
Cleveland *(G-5611)*
Marlen Manufacturing & Dev Co..................E....... 216 292-7546
Bedford *(G-1425)*
Millennium Adhesive Pdts Inc..................F....... 440 708-1212
Chagrin Falls *(G-3024)*
Millennium Adhesive Products..................G....... 440 708-1212
Chagrin Falls *(G-3060)*
Mitsubishi Chls Perf Plyrs Inc..................D....... 419 483-2931
Bellevue *(G-1540)*
▲ **Morgan Adhesives Company LLC**...B....... 330 688-1111
Stow *(G-17606)*
Nac Products..................G....... 330 644-3117
Coventry Township *(G-7774)*
▼ **Nanosperse LLC**..................G....... 937 296-5030
Kettering *(G-11435)*
National Adhesives Inc..................F....... 513 683-8650
Cincinnati *(G-4059)*
National Polymer Inc..................F....... 440 708-1245
Chagrin Falls *(G-3062)*
National Starch Chemical..................G....... 513 830-0260
Cincinnati *(G-4062)*
▲ **Nova Films and Foils Inc**..................F....... 440 201-1300
Bedford *(G-1431)*
Novagard Solutions Inc..................F....... 216 881-3890
Cleveland *(G-5789)*
Ohio Valley Adhesives..................G....... 513 454-1800
Cincinnati *(G-4106)*

P & T Products Inc..................E....... 419 621-1966
Sandusky *(G-16834)*
▲ **Paramelt Argueso Kindt Inc**..................G....... 216 252-4122
Cleveland *(G-5839)*
▲ **Polymerics Inc**..................E....... 330 434-6665
Cuyahoga Falls *(G-7906)*
PRC - Desoto International Inc..................E....... 800 772-9378
Chillicothe *(G-3216)*
◆ **Premier Building Solutions Inc**..................D....... 330 244-2907
Massillon *(G-13042)*
▼ **Premier Seals Mfg LLC**..................G....... 330 861-1060
Akron *(G-328)*
Priest Services Inc..................E....... 440 333-1123
Mayfield Heights *(G-13170)*
Quest Solutions Group LLC..................G....... 513 703-4520
Liberty Township *(G-11818)*
▲ **Renegade Materials Corporation**......E....... 508 579-7888
Miamisburg *(G-13711)*
◆ **Republic Powdered Metals Inc**..................D....... 330 225-3192
Medina *(G-13327)*
Royal Adhesives & Sealants LLC..................F....... 440 708-1212
Chagrin Falls *(G-3073)*
RPM Consumer Holding Company..................G....... 330 273-5090
Medina *(G-13330)*
◆ **RPM International Inc**..................D....... 330 273-5090
Medina *(G-13331)*
▼ **Rubex Inc**..................F....... 614 875-6343
Grove City *(G-10463)*
Ruscoe Company..................E....... 330 253-8148
Akron *(G-358)*
◆ **Savare Specialty Adhesives LLC**......E....... 614 255-2648
Delaware *(G-8723)*
Sealant Solutions..................G....... 614 599-8000
Columbus *(G-7435)*
Sem-Com Company Inc..................F....... 419 537-8813
Toledo *(G-18517)*
Shelli R McMurray..................G....... 614 275-4381
Columbus *(G-7444)*
Sherwin-Williams Company..................C....... 330 830-6000
Massillon *(G-13048)*
Silicone Solutions Inc..................F....... 330 920-3125
Cuyahoga Falls *(G-7917)*
▲ **Sirrus Inc**..................E....... 513 448-0308
Loveland *(G-12233)*
Sivon Manufacturing LLC..................G....... 440 259-5505
Perry *(G-15912)*
Sonoco Products Company..................D....... 937 429-0040
Beavercreek Township *(G-1374)*
Southern Adhesive Coatings..................G....... 513 561-8440
Cincinnati *(G-4355)*
Specialty Adhesive Film Co..................G....... 513 353-1885
Cleves *(G-6375)*
Spectra Group Limited Inc..................G....... 419 837-9783
Millbury *(G-14052)*
Spectrum Adhesives Inc..................F....... 740 763-2886
Newark *(G-14919)*
Spinnaker Coating LLC..................C....... 937 332-6300
Troy *(G-18710)*
Sportsmaster..................F....... 440 257-3900
Mentor *(G-13586)*
Summitville Tiles Inc..................E....... 330 868-6463
Minerva *(G-14203)*
▲ **Sunstar Engrg Americas Inc**..................C....... 937 746-8575
Springboro *(G-17354)*
Tech-Bond Solutions..................G....... 614 327-8884
Carroll *(G-2913)*
◆ **Technical Rubber Company Inc**.......B....... 740 967-9015
Johnstown *(G-11272)*
Technicote Inc..................E....... 330 928-1476
Cuyahoga Falls *(G-7926)*
▲ **Teknol Inc**..................D....... 937 264-0190
Dayton *(G-8550)*
◆ **Thorworks Industries Inc**..................E....... 419 626-4375
Sandusky *(G-16855)*
Three Bond International Inc..................E....... 937 610-3000
Dayton *(G-8556)*
▲ **Three Bond International Inc**..................D....... 513 779-7300
West Chester *(G-19808)*
▲ **Toagosei America Inc**..................D....... 614 718-3855
West Jefferson *(G-19928)*
Tremco Inc..................G....... 216 514-7783
Beachwood *(G-1282)*
Tremco Incorporated..................C....... 216 752-4401
Cleveland *(G-6202)*
◆ **Tremco Incorporated**..................B....... 216 292-5000
Beachwood *(G-1283)*
Tremco Incorporated..................D....... 419 289-2050
Ashland *(G-752)*
Triangle Adhesives LLC..................G....... 330 670-9722
Akron *(G-412)*

◆ **Truseal Technologies Inc**..................E....... 216 910-1500
Akron *(G-414)*
▲ **United McGill Corporation**..................E....... 614 829-1200
Groveport *(G-10516)*
▲ **Waytek Corporation**..................E....... 937 743-6142
Franklin *(G-9932)*
Weatherproofing Tech Inc..................G....... 281 480-7900
Beachwood *(G-1286)*

2892 Explosives

▲ **Austin Powder Company**..................D....... 216 464-2400
Cleveland *(G-4765)*
Austin Powder Company..................C....... 740 596-5286
Mc Arthur *(G-13179)*
Austin Powder Company..................G....... 419 299-3347
Findlay *(G-9652)*
Austin Powder Company..................E....... 740 968-1555
Saint Clairsville *(G-16621)*
◆ **Austin Powder Holdings Company**...D....... 216 464-2400
Cleveland *(G-4766)*
Hilltop Energy Inc..................E....... 330 859-2108
Mineral City *(G-14164)*
Sloat Inc..................G....... 440 951-9554
Willoughby *(G-20433)*
Viking Explosives LLC..................E....... 218 263-8845
Cleveland *(G-6262)*

2893 Printing Ink

Actega North America Inc..................G....... 800 426-4657
Blue Ash *(G-1720)*
American Inks and Coatings Co..................F....... 513 552-7200
Fairfield *(G-9481)*
◆ **Eckart America Corporation**..................D....... 440 954-7600
Painesville *(G-15734)*
Erie Laser Ink LLC..................G....... 419 346-0600
Toledo *(G-18284)*
Ferro Corporation..................C....... 216 875-6178
Cleveland *(G-5231)*
Flint Group US LLC..................G....... 513 934-6500
Lebanon *(G-11652)*
Flint Group US LLC..................D....... 513 771-1900
Cincinnati *(G-3695)*
▲ **Glass Coatings & Concepts LLC**......E....... 513 539-5300
Monroe *(G-14264)*
Grand Rapids Printing Ink Co..................G....... 859 261-4530
Cincinnati *(G-3775)*
Ink Factory Inc..................G....... 330 799-0888
Youngstown *(G-20940)*
Ink Production Services Inc..................F....... 513 733-9338
Cincinnati *(G-3848)*
▲ **Ink Technology Corporation**..................E....... 216 486-6720
Cleveland *(G-5458)*
INX International Ink Co..................F....... 707 693-2990
Lebanon *(G-11663)*
INX International Ink Co..................F....... 513 282-2920
Lebanon *(G-11664)*
INX International Ink Co..................F....... 440 239-1766
Cleveland *(G-5473)*
Kennedy Ink Company Inc..................F....... 513 871-2515
Cincinnati *(G-3905)*
Kennedy Ink Company Inc..................G....... 937 461-5600
Dayton *(G-8293)*
L A Machine..................G....... 216 651-1712
Cleveland *(G-5549)*
Magnum Magnetics Corporation..................F....... 740 516-6237
Caldwell *(G-2409)*
Premier Ink Systems Inc..................F....... 513 367-2300
Harrison *(G-10664)*
▲ **Red Tie Group Inc**..................C....... 216 271-2300
Cleveland *(G-5968)*
Red Tie Group Inc..................G....... 614 443-9100
Columbus *(G-7381)*
Sun Chemical Corporation..................D....... 513 671-0407
Cincinnati *(G-4390)*
Sun Chemical Corporation..................D....... 419 891-3514
Maumee *(G-13150)*
Sun Chemical Corporation..................D....... 513 753-9550
Amelia *(G-549)*
Sun Chemical Corporation..................E....... 513 681-5950
Cincinnati *(G-4392)*
Sun Chemical Corporation..................E....... 937 743-8055
Franklin *(G-9922)*
Sun Chemical Corporation..................E....... 513 771-4030
Cincinnati *(G-4393)*
Sun Chemical Corporation..................B....... 513 681-5950
Cincinnati *(G-4394)*
Sun Chemical Corporation..................E....... 513 830-8667
Cincinnati *(G-4395)*
Superior Printing Ink Co Inc..................F....... 513 221-4707
Blue Ash *(G-1855)*

SIC

28 CHEMICALS AND ALLIED PRODUCTS

Superior Printing Ink Co Inc .... G 216 328-1720
  Cleveland (G-6124)
Wikoff Color Corporation .... D 216 271-2300
  Cleveland (G-6307)
Wikoff Color Corporation .... G 513 423-0727
  Middletown (G-13968)

2895 Carbon Black

◆ Jacobi Carbons Inc .... E 215 546-3900
  Columbus (G-7057)
North Central Processing Inc .... G 216 623-1090
  Cleveland (G-5760)

2899 Chemical Preparations, NEC

Abraxus Salt Inc .... G 440 743-7669
  Cleveland (G-4601)
Ace Gasket Manufacturing Co .... G 513 271-6321
  Cincinnati (G-3292)
▲ Additive Technology Inc .... G 419 968-2777
  Middle Point (G-13754)
Advanced Chem Solutions Inc .... G 216 692-3005
  Orrville (G-15582)
Advanced Chemical Solutions .... G 330 283-5157
  Medina (G-13217)
▲ Akron Dispersions Inc .... E 330 666-0045
  Copley (G-7676)
Akzo Nobel Chemicals LLC .... G 419 229-0088
  Lima (G-11833)
▲ Alan BJ Company .... G 330 372-1201
  Warren (G-19365)
Aldrich Chemical .... D 937 859-1808
  Miamisburg (G-13638)
Allyn Corp .... G 614 442-3900
  Columbus (G-6575)
American Metal Chemical Corp .... G 440 244-1800
  Lorain (G-12078)
Amresco LLC .... C 440 349-2805
  Cleveland (G-4701)
Anchor Corporation .... G 614 836-9590
  Columbus (G-6600)
▲ Apex Advanced Technologies LLC ... G 216 898-1595
  Cleveland (G-4720)
▲ Aps-Materials Inc .... D 937 278-6547
  Dayton (G-8034)
Aqua Science Inc .... E 614 252-5000
  Columbus (G-6611)
Aquablue Inc .... G 330 343-0220
  New Philadelphia (G-14758)
Ashland LLC .... C 614 790-3333
  Dublin (G-8883)
Ashland LLC .... G 513 682-2405
  West Chester (G-19652)
Ashland LLC .... E 419 998-8728
  Lima (G-11844)
Ask Chemicals .... F 216 961-4690
  Cleveland (G-4751)
◆ Ask Chemicals LLC .... C 800 848-7485
  Dublin (G-8885)
Atotech USA Inc .... D 216 398-0550
  Cleveland (G-4762)
Attia Applied Sciences Inc .... G 740 369-1891
  Delaware (G-8656)
Aufbackgroundscreeningcom .... G 216 831-4113
  Beachwood (G-1224)
▲ Bernard Laboratories Inc .... E 513 681-7373
  Cincinnati (G-3391)
Bird Control International .... E 330 425-2377
  Twinsburg (G-18741)
Blackthorn LLC .... F 937 836-9296
  Clayton (G-4572)
BLaster Corporation .... E 216 901-5800
  Cleveland (G-4819)
Bluefoot Industrial LLC .... E 740 314-5299
  Steubenville (G-17528)
Bond Chemicals Inc .... G 330 725-5935
  Medina (G-13230)
Bond Distributing LLC .... G 440 461-7920
  Cleveland (G-4830)
◆ Borchers Americas Inc .... G 440 899-2950
  Westlake (G-20103)
Brewer Industries LLC .... G 216 469-0808
  Chagrin Falls (G-3011)
Broco Products Inc .... G 216 531-0880
  Cleveland (G-4839)
Bulk Molding Compounds Inc .... D 419 874-7941
  Perrysburg (G-15926)
Capital Chemical Co .... E 330 494-9535
  Canton (G-2619)
Cargill Incorporated .... F 513 941-7400
  Cincinnati (G-3443)

Cargill Incorporated .... C 216 651-7200
  Cleveland (G-4877)
Chem Technologies Ltd .... E 440 632-9311
  Middlefield (G-13783)
Chemical Methods Inc .... E 216 476-8400
  Strongsville (G-17725)
◆ Chemmasters Inc .... E 440 428-2105
  Madison (G-12344)
Cinchempro Inc .... C 513 724-6111
  Batavia (G-1129)
Cincinnati - Vulcan Company .... D 513 242-5300
  Cincinnati (G-3477)
City of Mount Vernon .... G 740 393-9508
  Mount Vernon (G-14475)
▲ Coolant Control Inc .... E 513 471-8770
  Cincinnati (G-3548)
CP Chemicals Group LP .... D 440 833-3000
  Wickliffe (G-20208)
Creative Commercial Finishing .... G 513 722-9393
  Loveland (G-12184)
▼ Cresset Chemical Co Inc .... F 419 669-2041
  Weston (G-20175)
Cresset Chemical Co Inc .... F 419 669-2041
  Weston (G-20176)
Dayton Superior Corporation .... E 815 732-3136
  Miamisburg (G-13656)
◆ Dayton Superior Corporation .... C 937 866-0711
  Miamisburg (G-13655)
Diamond Sparkler Mfg Co .... G 330 746-1064
  Youngstown (G-20890)
Dinol US Inc .... G 740 548-1656
  Lewis Center (G-11756)
Distillata Company .... D 216 771-2900
  Cleveland (G-5098)
◆ Dover Chemical Corporation .... C 330 343-7711
  Dover (G-8819)
Durr Megtec LLC .... C 614 258-9501
  Columbus (G-6876)
▲ Eagle Fireworks Co .... G 740 373-3357
  Marietta (G-12622)
Elco Corporation .... E 440 997-6131
  Ashtabula (G-773)
EMD Millipore Corporation .... C 513 631-0445
  Norwood (G-15426)
Emerald Performance Mtls LLC .... D 513 841-4000
  Cincinnati (G-3634)
Emerald Performance Mtls LLC .... D 330 374-2418
  Akron (G-152)
◆ Emery Oleochemicals LLC .... B 513 762-2500
  Cincinnati (G-3636)
Ensign Product Company Inc .... G 216 341-5911
  Cleveland (G-5180)
Envirnmntal Prtctive Ctngs LLC .... G 740 363-6180
  Ostrander (G-15643)
Enviro Polymers & Chemicals .... G 937 427-1315
  Beavercreek (G-1314)
Environment Chemical Corp .... G 330 453-5200
  Uniontown (G-18918)
◆ Etna Products Incorporated .... E 440 543-9845
  Chagrin Falls (G-3046)
◆ Euclid Chemical Company .... E 800 321-7628
  Cleveland (G-5193)
Euclid Chemical Company .... F 216 292-5000
  Beachwood (G-1238)
Euclid Chemical Company .... D 216 531-9222
  Cleveland (G-5194)
Ferro Corporation .... C 216 875-6178
  Cleveland (G-5231)
Ferro Corporation .... D 216 875-5600
  Cleveland (G-5232)
▲ Ferrum Industries Inc .... E 440 519-1768
  Twinsburg (G-18775)
◆ Flexsys America LP .... D 330 666-4111
  Akron (G-173)
Formlabs Ohio Inc .... E 419 837-9783
  Millbury (G-14049)
▲ Fort Amanda Specialties LLC .... D 419 229-0088
  Lima (G-11865)
▲ Foseco Inc .... E 440 826-4548
  Cleveland (G-5267)
Fuchs Lubricants Co .... E 330 963-0400
  Twinsburg (G-18777)
Fusion Automation Inc .... G 440 602-5595
  Willoughby (G-20326)
◆ Fusion Ceramics Inc .... E 330 627-5821
  Carrollton (G-2920)
Galapagos Inc .... G 937 890-3068
  Dayton (G-8213)
◆ Gasflux Company .... G 440 365-1941
  Elyria (G-9262)

General Electric Company .... D 216 268-3846
  Cleveland (G-5310)
◆ GFS Chemicals Inc .... E 740 881-5501
  Powell (G-16322)
GFS Chemicals Inc .... D 614 224-5345
  Columbus (G-6950)
Global Bioprotect LLC .... F 336 861-0162
  Columbus (G-6495)
Global Chemical Inc .... G 419 242-1004
  Toledo (G-18306)
Grean Technologies LLC .... G 513 510-7116
  Monroe (G-14265)
Harsco Corporation .... G 330 372-1781
  Warren (G-19408)
◆ Hexion LLC .... D 614 225-4000
  Columbus (G-6993)
Hexpol Compounding LLC .... C 440 834-4644
  Burton (G-2360)
Hill & Griffith Company .... G 513 921-1075
  Cincinnati (G-3812)
▲ Hunt Imaging LLC .... E 440 826-0433
  Berea (G-1611)
▲ I P Specrete Inc .... G 216 721-2050
  Cleveland (G-5434)
Illinois Tool Works Inc .... G 440 914-3100
  Solon (G-17166)
▲ Ineos LLC .... D 419 226-1200
  Lima (G-11877)
Ink Factory Inc .... G 330 799-0888
  Youngstown (G-20940)
International Paper Company .... C 740 363-9882
  Delaware (G-8696)
Jay Tackett .... G 740 779-1715
  Frankfort (G-9862)
Jeff Pendergrass .... G 513 575-1226
  Milford (G-14021)
Joules Angstrom UV Printing .... E 740 964-9113
  Etna (G-9395)
K2 Petroleum & Supply LLC .... G 937 503-2614
  Cincinnati (G-3891)
▲ Lamor Corporation .... F 440 871-8000
  Westlake (G-20128)
Leonhardt Plating Company .... E 513 242-1410
  Cincinnati (G-3938)
Lfg Specialties LLC .... E 419 424-4999
  Findlay (G-9715)
▲ Liquid Development Company .... G 216 641-9366
  Independence (G-11141)
Lubrizol Advanced Mtls Inc .... E 419 352-5565
  Bowling Green (G-1982)
Lubrizol Advanced Mtls Inc .... E 440 933-0400
  Avon Lake (G-993)
◆ Lubrizol Corporation .... A 440 943-4200
  Wickliffe (G-20215)
Lubrizol Corporation .... E 440 357-7064
  Painesville (G-15758)
Lubrizol Corporation .... G 216 447-6212
  Akron (G-261)
◆ Lubrizol Global Management .... F 216 447-5000
  Brecksville (G-2048)
Luxfer Magtech Inc .... E 513 772-3066
  Cincinnati (G-3958)
Lynx Chemical .... G 513 856-9161
  Franklin (G-9896)
◆ Master Builders LLC .... E 216 831-5500
  Beachwood (G-1247)
McGean-Rohco Inc .... D 216 441-4900
  Newburgh Heights (G-14941)
Merry X-Ray Chemical Corp .... G 614 219-2011
  Hilliard (G-10839)
Midwest Fireworks Mfg Co II .... G 330 584-7000
  Deerfield (G-8610)
◆ Milacron LLC .... E 513 487-5000
  Blue Ash (G-1822)
Momentive Performance .... G 281 325-3536
  Columbus (G-7192)
Momentive Performance Mtls Inc .... G 614 986-2495
  Columbus (G-7193)
Monarch Engraving Inc .... E 440 638-1500
  Strongsville (G-17766)
Morgan Advanced Ceramics Inc .... C 440 232-8604
  Bedford (G-1428)
Morgan Advanced Ceramics Inc .... G 330 405-1033
  Twinsburg (G-18822)
Morton Salt Inc .... F 440 354-9901
  Painesville (G-15764)
Morton Salt Inc .... C 330 925-3015
  Rittman (G-16526)
▲ National Colloid Company .... E 740 282-1171
  Steubenville (G-17545)

29 PETROLEUM REFINING AND RELATED INDUSTRIES

◆ Natural Essentials Inc .... E 330 562-8022
   Aurora *(G-895)*
Natures Own Source LLC .... G 440 838-5135
   Brecksville *(G-2050)*
New Vulco Mfg & Sales Co LLC .... D 513 242-2672
   Cincinnati *(G-4072)*
No Burn Inc .... G 330 336-1500
   Wadsworth *(G-19256)*
No Burn North America Inc .... F 419 841-6055
   Toledo *(G-18426)*
◆ Noco Company .... B 216 464-8131
   Solon *(G-17208)*
▲ Nof Metal Coatings N Amer Inc 440 285-2231
   Chardon *(G-3128)*
▲ Northern Chem Blnding Corp Inc .. G ... 216 781-7799
   Cleveland *(G-5778)*
▼ Noveon Fcc Inc .... G 440 943-4200
   Wickliffe *(G-20219)*
Obersons Nurs & Landscapes Inc ... F 513 894-0669
   Fairfield *(G-9538)*
Ohio Aluminum Chemicals LLC .... G 513 860-3842
   West Chester *(G-19752)*
Oil Bar LLC .... G 614 501-9815
   Columbus *(G-7268)*
Oliver Chemical Co Inc .... G 513 541-4540
   Cincinnati *(G-4110)*
▲ Opta Minerals (usa) Inc .... G 330 659-3003
   Independence *(G-11145)*
◆ Opw Fueling Components Inc .... E 800 422-2525
   West Chester *(G-19756)*
Parker Trutec Incorporated .... G 937 653-8500
   Urbana *(G-19007)*
Pemro Corporation .... F 800 440-5441
   Cleveland *(G-5863)*
Phantom Fireworks Inc .... G 419 237-2185
   Fayette *(G-9635)*
▼ Plating Process Systems Inc .... G 440 951-9667
   Mentor *(G-13548)*
◆ Polymer Additives Inc .... D 216 875-7200
   Independence *(G-11146)*
Polymer Additives Inc .... G 216 875-5840
   Cleveland *(G-5895)*
Polymer Additives Inc .... G 216 262-7016
   Walton Hills *(G-19313)*
Polymer Additives Holdings Inc .... C 216 875-7200
   Independence *(G-11147)*
Polymerics Inc .... E 330 677-1131
   Kent *(G-11364)*
Premier Ink Systems Inc .... F 513 367-2300
   Harrison *(G-10664)*
Prestige Fireworks LLC .... F 513 492-7726
   Mason *(G-12925)*
Pyro-Chem Corporation .... F 740 377-2244
   South Point *(G-17292)*
▲ Quaker Chemical Corporation .... D 513 422-9600
   Middletown *(G-13947)*
Qualico Inc .... G 216 271-2550
   Cleveland *(G-5938)*
▲ Ques Industries Inc .... F 216 267-8989
   Cleveland *(G-5946)*
Quikrete Companies Inc .... E 614 885-4406
   Columbus *(G-7369)*
Qumont Chemical Co .... G 419 241-1057
   Toledo *(G-18492)*
Railtech Matweld Inc .... G 419 592-5050
   Napoleon *(G-14558)*
Railtech Matweld Inc .... G 419 591-3770
   Napoleon *(G-14559)*
◆ Republic Powdered Metals Inc ... D 330 225-3192
   Medina *(G-13327)*
▲ Research Organics LLC .... D 216 883-8025
   Cleveland *(G-5978)*
▲ Rhenium Alloys Inc .... D 440 365-7388
   North Ridgeville *(G-15251)*
Rotech Products Incorporated .... G 216 476-3722
   Cleveland *(G-6006)*
▲ Rozzi Company Inc .... E 513 683-0620
   Loveland *(G-12228)*
Rozzi Company Inc .... F 513 683-0620
   Martinsville *(G-12767)*
◆ RPM International Inc .... D 330 273-5090
   Medina *(G-13331)*
Sam Abdallah .... E 330 532-3900
   Hammondsville *(G-10623)*
▲ SC Fire Protection Ltd .... G 330 468-3300
   Macedonia *(G-12324)*
Sika Corporation .... D 740 387-9224
   Marion *(G-12735)*
◆ Smithfield Bioscience Inc .... E 513 772-8130
   Cincinnati *(G-4347)*

Solvay USA Inc .... E 513 482-5700
   Cincinnati *(G-4353)*
Sports Care Products Inc .... G 216 663-8110
   Cleveland *(G-6086)*
▲ SRC Worldwide Inc .... F 216 941-6115
   Cleveland *(G-6088)*
St Bernard Insulation LLC .... F 513 266-2158
   Cincinnati *(G-4367)*
▼ State Industrial Products Corp .... B 877 747-6986
   Cleveland *(G-6097)*
Suez Wts Usa Inc .... E 330 339-2292
   New Philadelphia *(G-14802)*
Summitville Tiles Inc .... E 330 868-6463
   Minerva *(G-14203)*
Sun & Soil LLC .... G 513 575-5900
   Loveland *(G-12237)*
Sun Chemical Corporation .... D 513 671-0407
   Cincinnati *(G-4390)*
◆ Superior Flux & Mfg Co .... F 440 349-3000
   Cleveland *(G-6120)*
▲ Surtec Inc .... G 440 239-9710
   Brunswick *(G-2242)*
Tate Lyle Ingrdnts Amricas LLC .... D 937 236-5906
   Dayton *(G-8541)*
▲ Teknol Inc .... D 937 264-0190
   Dayton *(G-8550)*
Tidewater Products Inc .... G 419 873-0223
   Perrysburg *(G-16016)*
Tidewater Products Inc .... G 419 534-9870
   Ottawa Hills *(G-15678)*
Truco Inc .... B 216 631-1000
   Cleveland *(G-6219)*
◆ U S Chemical & Plastics .... G 740 254-4311
   Massillon *(G-13055)*
Univar USA Inc .... C 513 714-5264
   West Chester *(G-19911)*
University of Cincinnati .... F 513 558-1243
   Cincinnati *(G-4453)*
US Water Company LLC .... G 740 453-0604
   Zanesville *(G-21186)*
Usalco Fairfield Plant LLC .... E 513 737-7100
   Fairfield *(G-9571)*
Valtris Specialty Chemicals .... G 216 875-7200
   Walton Hills *(G-19316)*
Vesuvius U S A Corporation .... E 440 593-1161
   Conneaut *(G-7661)*
Vesuvius U S A Corporation .... E 440 816-3051
   Cleveland *(G-6254)*
Viking Group Inc .... G 937 443-0433
   Dayton *(G-8580)*
Visible Solutions Inc .... G 440 925-2810
   Westlake *(G-20168)*
Wagers Inc .... G 513 825-6300
   Okeana *(G-15520)*
Warren Fire Equipment Inc .... E 330 824-3523
   Warren *(G-19459)*
Water Warriors Inc .... G 513 288-5669
   Cincinnati *(G-4491)*
▲ Wild Berry Incense Inc .... F 513 523-8583
   Oxford *(G-15703)*
Worthington Industries Inc .... E 937 556-6111
   Worthington *(G-20711)*
▲ Zerust Consumer Products LLC ... G 330 405-1965
   Twinsburg *(G-18877)*
◆ Zinkan Enterprises Inc .... F 330 487-1500
   Twinsburg *(G-18878)*
Zircon Industries Inc .... G 216 595-0200
   Cleveland *(G-6346)*

29 PETROLEUM REFINING AND RELATED INDUSTRIES

2911 Petroleum Refining

Aecom Energy & Cnstr Inc .... C 419 698-6277
   Oregon *(G-15553)*
Appal Energy .... G 740 448-4605
   Amesville *(G-551)*
Appalachian Solvents LLC .... G 740 680-3649
   Cambridge *(G-2424)*
Arizona Chemical Company LLC ... C 330 343-7701
   Dover *(G-8804)*
Ashland LLC .... G 513 557-3100
   Cincinnati *(G-3361)*
Blanchard Refining Company LLC ... G 419 422-2121
   Findlay *(G-9657)*
Blanchard Terminal Company LLC ... G 419 422-2121
   Findlay *(G-9658)*
Blaster Chemical Co Inc .... G 216 901-5800
   Cleveland *(G-4818)*

BLaster Corporation .... E 216 901-5800
   Cleveland *(G-4819)*
Bloom Center Biodiesel LLC .... G 937 585-6412
   Lewistown *(G-11800)*
BP Products North America Inc ..... G 937 461-3621
   Dayton *(G-8060)*
BP Products North America Inc ...... F 419 537-9540
   Toledo *(G-18212)*
BP Products North America Inc ..... G 419 636-2249
   Bryan *(G-2270)*
Capital City Oil Inc .... G 740 397-4483
   Mount Vernon *(G-14473)*
Certified Oil Company Inc .... C 614 421-7500
   Columbus *(G-6755)*
Citgo Petroleum Corporation .... G 419 698-8055
   Oregon *(G-15558)*
Cyberutility LLC .... G 216 291-8723
   Cleveland *(G-5055)*
Diesel Recon Service Inc .... G 513 625-1887
   Pleasant Plain *(G-16225)*
Durr Megtec LLC .... G 614 340-4154
   Columbus *(G-6877)*
Enrevo Pyro LLC .... G 203 517-5002
   Brookfield *(G-2106)*
Foam Seal Inc .... D 216 881-8111
   Cleveland *(G-5256)*
Husky Energy .... F 614 766-5633
   Dublin *(G-8926)*
Husky Lima Refinery .... D 419 226-2300
   Lima *(G-11875)*
Hydrodec Inc .... G 330 454-8202
   Canton *(G-2702)*
▼ Hydrodec of North America LLC ... E 330 454-8202
   Canton *(G-2703)*
▲ Isp Lima LLC .... E 419 998-8700
   Lima *(G-11880)*
Jetfuel Sports Inc .... G 614 327-3300
   New Albany *(G-14629)*
K2 Petroleum & Supply LLC .... G 937 503-2614
   Cincinnati *(G-3891)*
Knox Energy Inc .... F 740 927-6731
   Pataskala *(G-15835)*
◆ Koch Knight LLC .... D 330 488-1651
   East Canton *(G-9041)*
Lavy Inc .... G 937 692-8189
   Arcanum *(G-630)*
▲ Lima Refining Company .... B 419 226-2300
   Lima *(G-11890)*
Lima Refining Company .... D 419 226-2300
   Lima *(G-11891)*
Lube Depot .... G 330 854-6345
   Canal Fulton *(G-2484)*
Marathon Oil Company .... E 419 422-2121
   Findlay *(G-9718)*
Marathon Petroleum Coporation .... G 419 422-2121
   Findlay *(G-9720)*
Marathon Petroleum Corporation ... B 419 422-2121
   Findlay *(G-9721)*
National Hwy Maint Systems LLC ... G 330 922-3649
   Peninsula *(G-15896)*
Novagard Solutions Inc .... F 216 881-3890
   Cleveland *(G-5789)*
Ohio Biofuels .... G 614 886-6518
   Cincinnati *(G-4099)*
Pbf Energy Partners LP .... G 419 698-6724
   Toledo *(G-18459)*
Road Maintenance Products .... G 740 465-7181
   Morral *(G-14405)*
Santmyer Oil Co of Ashland .... G 419 289-8815
   Ashland *(G-746)*
Seneca Petroleum Co Inc .... F 419 691-3581
   Toledo *(G-18519)*
Seneca Petroleum Co Inc .... F 419 691-3581
   Toledo *(G-18518)*
Sports Care Products Inc .... G 216 663-8110
   Cleveland *(G-6086)*
Standard Oil Company .... E 419 698-6200
   Oregon *(G-15568)*
Stark Materials Inc .... E 330 497-1648
   Canton *(G-2822)*
Sunoco Inc .... E 216 912-2579
   Akron *(G-393)*
Troy Valley Petroleum .... G 937 604-0012
   Dayton *(G-8570)*
Usalco LLC .... G 440 993-2721
   Ashtabula *(G-810)*
Vertex Refining OH LLC .... E 614 441-4001
   Columbus *(G-7574)*
Vertex Refining OH LLC .... E 281 486-4182
   Norwalk *(G-15416)*

2951 Paving Mixtures & Blocks

A United .... G 330 782-6005
  Youngstown (G-20831)
Action Blacktop Sealcoating & .... G 937 667-4769
  Tipp City (G-18097)
Advanced Fiber LLC .... E 419 562-1337
  Bucyrus (G-2317)
All Coatings Co Inc .... G 330 821-3806
  Alliance (G-451)
Allied Corporation Inc .... G 330 425-7861
  Twinsburg (G-18730)
Aluminum Coating Manufacturers ..... E 216 341-2000
  Cleveland (G-4680)
Ashland LLC .... G 513 557-3100
  Cincinnati (G-3361)
Asphalt Fabrics & Specialties .... G 440 786-1077
  Solon (G-17109)
Asphalt Materials Inc .... G 740 373-3040
  Marietta (G-12606)
Asphalt Materials Inc .... F 419 693-0626
  Oregon (G-15554)
Asphalt Materials Inc .... G 740 374-5100
  Marietta (G-12607)
Atlas Roofing Corporation .... C 937 746-9941
  Franklin (G-9870)
B & S Blacktop .... G 513 797-5759
  New Richmond (G-14810)
Baileys Asphalt Sealing .... F 740 453-9409
  South Zanesville (G-17301)
Barrett Paving Materials Inc .... C 513 271-6200
  Middletown (G-13970)
Bituminous Products Company .... G 419 693-3933
  Toledo (G-18204)
Bluffton Stone Co .... E 419 358-6941
  Bluffton (G-1886)
Bowerston Shale Company .... E 740 269-2921
  Bowerston (G-1939)
Brewer Company .... E 614 279-8688
  Columbus (G-6694)
▲ Brewer Company .... G 800 394-0017
  Milford (G-13999)
Central Oil Asphalt Corp .... G 614 224-8111
  Columbus (G-6754)
Crafco Inc .... F 330 270-3034
  Youngstown (G-20880)
D & R Supply Inc .... G 330 855-3781
  Marshallville (G-12752)
D and D Asp Sealcoating LLC .... G 614 288-3597
  Pickerington (G-16044)
Erie Materials Inc .... G 419 483-4648
  Castalia (G-2938)
Full Circle Technologies LLC .... G 216 650-0007
  Cleveland (G-5276)
Glenn O Hawbaker Inc .... G 330 308-0533
  New Philadelphia (G-14772)
Grand River Asphalt .... G 440 352-2254
  Grand River (G-10322)
H P Streicher Inc .... G 419 841-4715
  Toledo (G-18315)
Hanson Aggregates Midwest LLC ..... G 419 983-2211
  Bloomville (G-1715)
Hanson Aggregates Midwest LLC ..... G 419 878-2006
  Waterville (G-19497)
Holmes Supply Corp .... G 330 279-2634
  Holmesville (G-10980)
Husac Paving .... G 513 200-2818
  Harrison (G-10650)
Hy-Grade Corporation .... E 216 341-7711
  Cleveland (G-5429)
Image Pavement Maintenance .... G 937 833-9200
  Brookville (G-2172)
John R Jurgensen Co .... G 937 293-3112
  Springfield (G-17427)
Kokosing Materials Inc .... F 419 522-2715
  Mansfield (G-12467)
Kokosing Materials Inc .... E 740 745-3341
  Saint Louisville (G-16672)
Kokosing Materials Inc .... G 614 891-5090
  Westerville (G-20061)
Kokosing Materials Inc .... E 614 491-1199
  Columbus (G-7098)
Koski Construction Co .... G 440 997-5337
  Ashtabula (G-782)
La Rose Paving Co Inc .... G 440 632-0330
  Middlefield (G-13813)
Lake Erie Asphalt Paving Inc .... G 440 526-5191
  Brecksville (G-2047)
Lucas County Asphalt Inc .... E 419 476-0705
  Toledo (G-18389)

Lynn James Contracting LLC .... G 419 467-4505
  Delta (G-8775)
M & B Asphalt Company Inc .... G 419 992-4235
  Tiffin (G-18066)
M & B Asphalt Company Inc .... G 419 992-4236
  Old Fort (G-15525)
Mae Materials LLC .... G 740 778-2242
  South Webster (G-17298)
◆ Maintenance + Inc .... F 330 264-6262
  Wooster (G-20618)
Mansfield Asphalt Paving Inc .... F 740 453-0721
  Zanesville (G-21154)
Mar-Zane Inc .... F 740 453-0721
  Zanesville (G-21155)
Mar-Zane Inc .... G 740 782-1240
  Bethesda (G-1657)
Mar-Zane Inc .... G 740 685-5178
  Byesville (G-2390)
Mar-Zane Inc .... G 330 626-2079
  Mantua (G-12552)
◆ Marathon Petroleum Company LP .... F 419 422-2121
  Findlay (G-9719)
Massillon Asphalt Co .... G 330 833-6330
  Massillon (G-13019)
Miller Bros Paving Inc .... F 419 445-1015
  Archbold (G-659)
Morrow Gravel Company Inc .... E 513 771-0820
  Cincinnati (G-4048)
Mplx Terminals LLC .... B 330 479-5539
  Canton (G-2757)
Mt Pleasant Blacktopping Inc .... G 513 874-3777
  Fairfield (G-9532)
Newton Asphalt Paving Inc .... F 330 878-5648
  Strasburg (G-17650)
▲ Reading Rock Inc .... C 513 874-2345
  West Chester (G-19893)
Road Maintenance Products .... G 740 465-7181
  Morral (G-14405)
Robert Gorey .... G 330 725-7272
  Medina (G-13328)
Roof To Road LLC .... G 740 986-6923
  Williamsport (G-20261)
Rub-R-Road Inc .... G 330 678-7050
  Kent (G-11379)
Russell Standard Corporation .... G 330 733-9400
  Akron (G-363)
Rutland Township .... G 740 742-2805
  Bidwell (G-1669)
S E Johnson Companies Inc .... F 419 893-8731
  Maumee (G-13142)
Seal Master Corporation .... E 330 673-8410
  Kent (G-11383)
Seneca Petroleum Co Inc .... F 419 691-3581
  Toledo (G-18518)
Shalersville Asphalt Co .... E 440 834-4294
  Burton (G-2370)
Shelly and Sands Inc .... G 330 743-8850
  Youngstown (G-21029)
Shelly and Sands Inc .... F 740 373-6495
  Marietta (G-12667)
Shelly and Sands Inc .... D 740 859-2104
  Rayland (G-16423)
Shelly and Sands Inc .... E 740 453-0721
  Zanesville (G-21177)
Shelly and Sands Inc .... F 740 453-0721
  Zanesville (G-21176)
Shelly Company .... D 419 422-8854
  Findlay (G-9753)
Shelly Company .... G 740 474-6255
  Circleville (G-4557)
Shelly Company .... G 740 246-6315
  Thornville (G-18033)
Shelly Materials Inc .... E 740 246-5009
  Thornville (G-18034)
Shelly Materials Inc .... G 740 446-7789
  Gallipolis (G-10175)
Shelly Materials Inc .... G 419 622-2101
  Convoy (G-7671)
Shelly Materials Inc .... E 740 666-5841
  Ostrander (G-15646)
Shelly Materials Inc .... G 330 673-3646
  Kent (G-11385)
Shelly Materials Inc .... G 419 273-2510
  Forest (G-9788)
Shelly Materials Inc .... D 740 246-6315
  Thornville (G-18035)
Sidwell Materials Inc .... C 740 849-2394
  Zanesville (G-21180)
Smalls Asphalt Paving Inc .... E 740 427-4096
  Gambier (G-10184)

▼ Specialty Technology & Res .... G 614 870-0744
  Columbus (G-7470)
Star Seal of Ohio Inc .... G 614 870-1590
  Columbus (G-7487)
Stark Materials Inc .... E 330 497-1648
  Canton (G-2822)
Stoneco Inc .... D 419 422-8854
  Findlay (G-9762)
Stoneco Inc .... G 419 693-3933
  Toledo (G-18531)
Stoneco Inc .... G 419 393-2555
  Oakwood (G-15474)
T-N-T Concrete Inc .... G 540 480-4040
  Mentor (G-13599)
◆ Thorworks Industries Inc .... E 419 626-4375
  Sandusky (G-16855)
Tri County Asphalt Materials .... G 330 549-2852
  Youngstown (G-21052)
Unique Paving Materials Corp .... E 216 341-7711
  Cleveland (G-6232)
Valley Asphalt Corporation .... G 513 381-0652
  Morrow (G-14416)
Valley Asphalt Corporation .... G 937 426-7682
  Xenia (G-20800)
Valley Asphalt Corporation .... G 937 335-3664
  Troy (G-18717)
Valley Asphalt Corporation .... G 513 353-2171
  Cleves (G-6381)
Valley Asphalt Corporation .... G 513 784-1476
  Cincinnati (G-4463)
Valley Asphalt Corporation .... G 513 561-1551
  Cincinnati (G-4462)
Walls Bros Asphalt Co Inc .... G 937 548-7158
  Greenville (G-10399)
Wilson Blacktop Corporation .... E 740 635-3566
  Martins Ferry (G-12764)
York Paving Co .... F 740 594-3600
  Athens (G-854)

2952 Asphalt Felts & Coatings

Aluminum Coating Manufacturers ..... E 216 341-2000
  Cleveland (G-4680)
American Orginal Bldg Pdts LLC .... F 330 786-3000
  Akron (G-63)
Atlas Roofing Corporation .... C 937 746-9941
  Franklin (G-9870)
▲ Brewer Company .... G 800 394-0017
  Milford (G-13999)
Brewer Company .... E 440 944-3800
  Wickliffe (G-20206)
Brewer Company .... E 614 279-8688
  Columbus (G-6694)
Brewer Company .... G 513 576-6300
  Cincinnati (G-3414)
Century Industries Corporation .... E 330 457-2367
  New Waterford (G-14838)
Certainteed Corporation .... C 419 499-2581
  Milan (G-13981)
◆ Chemspec Ltd .... F 330 896-0355
  Uniontown (G-18915)
Classic Metals Ltd .... G 330 763-1162
  Holmesville (G-10974)
Commercial Innovations Inc .... G 216 641-7500
  Cleveland (G-5000)
Consolidated Coatings Corp .... E 216 514-7596
  Cleveland (G-5017)
Dnd Emulsions Inc .... G 419 525-4988
  Mansfield (G-12433)
Garland Industries Inc .... G 216 641-7500
  Cleveland (G-5294)
Garland/Dbs Inc .... C 216 641-7500
  Cleveland (G-5295)
Hy-Grade Corporation .... E 216 341-7711
  Cleveland (G-5429)
▼ Hyload Inc .... F 330 336-6604
  Seville (G-16916)
Iko Production Inc .... E 937 746-4561
  Franklin (G-9891)
Ipm Inc .... G 419 248-8000
  Toledo (G-18351)
◆ Isaiah Industries Inc .... E 937 773-9840
  Piqua (G-16131)
Johns Manville Corporation .... D 419 499-1400
  Milan (G-13986)
Kettering Roofing & Shtmtl .... F 513 281-6413
  Cincinnati (G-3906)
Metal Sales Manufacturing Corp .... E 440 319-3779
  Jefferson (G-11234)
Midwest Industrial Products .... G 216 771-8555
  Cleveland (G-5681)

National Tool & Equipment Inc..........F....... 330 629-8665
Youngstown *(G-20973)*
◆ **Owens Corning**..........A....... 419 248-8000
Toledo *(G-18446)*
◆ **Owens Corning Sales LLC**..........A....... 419 248-8000
Toledo *(G-18448)*
P C R Inc..........F....... 330 945-7721
Akron *(G-313)*
Qualico Inc..........G....... 216 271-2550
Cleveland *(G-5938)*
Simon Roofing and Shtmtl Corp..........C....... 330 629-7392
Youngstown *(G-21032)*
Sr Products..........G....... 330 998-6500
Macedonia *(G-12329)*
▼ **State Industrial Products Corp**..........B....... 877 747-6986
Cleveland *(G-6097)*
Surface-All Inc..........G....... 440 428-2233
Port Clinton *(G-16261)*
Terry Asphalt Materials Inc..........E....... 513 874-6192
Hamilton *(G-10609)*
◆ **Thorworks Industries Inc**..........E....... 419 626-4375
Sandusky *(G-16855)*
Topps Products Inc..........G....... 216 271-2550
Cleveland *(G-6188)*
Transtar Holding Company..........G....... 800 359-3339
Walton Hills *(G-19315)*
Treadstone Company..........G....... 216 410-3435
Twinsburg *(G-18865)*
◆ **Tremco Incorporated**..........B....... 216 292-5000
Beachwood *(G-1283)*
Truco Inc..........B....... 216 631-1000
Cleveland *(G-6219)*

2992 Lubricating Oils & Greases

A & M Products..........G....... 419 595-2092
Tiffin *(G-18039)*
Advanced Fluids Inc..........G....... 216 692-3050
Cleveland *(G-4626)*
▲ **Aerospace Lubricants Inc**..........F....... 614 878-3600
Columbus *(G-6549)*
American Ultra Specialties Inc..........F....... 330 656-5000
Hudson *(G-11030)*
▲ **Aml Industries Inc**..........E....... 330 399-5000
Warren *(G-19370)*
Amsoil Inc..........G....... 614 274-9851
Columbus *(G-6593)*
▼ **Anchor Chemical Co Inc**..........G....... 440 871-1660
Westlake *(G-20097)*
▲ **Bechem Lubrication Tech LLC**..........G....... 440 543-9845
Chagrin Falls *(G-3037)*
BLaster Corporation..........E....... 216 901-5800
Cleveland *(G-4819)*
Blendzall Inc..........G....... 740 633-1333
Martins Ferry *(G-12758)*
◆ **Borchers Americas Inc**..........D....... 440 899-2950
Westlake *(G-20103)*
Cambridge Mill Products Inc..........G....... 330 863-1121
Malvern *(G-12385)*
Chemical Methods Inc..........E....... 216 476-8400
Strongsville *(G-17725)*
▲ **Chemical Solvents Inc**..........E....... 216 741-9310
Cleveland *(G-4919)*
Cincinnati - Vulcan Company..........D....... 513 242-5300
Cincinnati *(G-3477)*
Commercial Lubricants Inc..........G....... 614 475-5952
Columbus *(G-6806)*
Digilube Systems Inc..........F....... 937 748-2209
Springboro *(G-17325)*
Diversified Technology Inc..........G....... 330 722-4995
Medina *(G-13253)*
Dnd Emulsions Inc..........G....... 419 525-4988
Mansfield *(G-12433)*
Douglas W & B C Richardson..........G....... 440 247-5262
Chagrin Falls *(G-3015)*
Eni USA R & M Co Inc..........F....... 330 723-6457
Medina *(G-13256)*
Ensign Product Company Inc..........G....... 216 341-5911
Cleveland *(G-5180)*
◆ **Etna Products Incorporated**..........E....... 440 543-9845
Chagrin Falls *(G-3046)*
Fiske Brothers Refining Co..........D....... 419 691-2491
Toledo *(G-18295)*
Fuchs Lubricants Co..........E....... 330 963-0400
Twinsburg *(G-18777)*
▲ **Functional Products Inc**..........E....... 330 963-3060
Macedonia *(G-12296)*
▲ **G W Smith and Sons Inc**..........E....... 937 253-5114
Dayton *(G-7979)*
Ha-International LLC..........E....... 419 537-0096
Toledo *(G-18317)*
Illinois Tool Works Inc..........D....... 440 914-3100
Solon *(G-17166)*
Interlube Corporation..........F....... 513 531-1777
Cincinnati *(G-3855)*
▼ **Into Great Brands Inc**..........F....... 888 771-5656
Gahanna *(G-10085)*
J J Merlin Systems Inc..........G....... 330 666-8609
Copley *(G-7686)*
Jtm Products Inc..........E....... 440 287-2302
Solon *(G-17178)*
Koki Laboratories Inc..........E....... 330 773-7669
Akron *(G-241)*
Lcp Tech Inc..........G....... 513 271-1389
Cincinnati *(G-3936)*
Lubrizol Corporation..........E....... 440 357-7064
Painesville *(G-15758)*
M B Industries Inc..........G....... 419 738-4769
Wapakoneta *(G-19340)*
M B Industries Inc..........G....... 419 738-4769
Wapakoneta *(G-19341)*
▲ **Magnus International Group Inc**..........G....... 216 592-8355
Chagrin Falls *(G-3056)*
Mar Mor Inc..........G....... 216 961-6900
Cleveland *(G-5614)*
◆ **Master Chemical Corporation**..........B....... 419 874-7902
Perrysburg *(G-15976)*
McGlaughln Oil Compny/Fas Lube..........E....... 614 231-2518
Columbus *(G-7165)*
McO Inc..........E....... 216 341-8914
Cleveland *(G-5648)*
Melanda Inc..........G....... 330 833-0517
Massillon *(G-13025)*
New Vulco Mfg & Sales Co LLC..........D....... 513 242-2672
Cincinnati *(G-4072)*
▲ **North Shore Strapping Inc**..........D....... 216 661-5200
Brooklyn Heights *(G-2128)*
◆ **Nutech Company LLC**..........G....... 440 867-8900
Youngstown *(G-20979)*
Oliver Chemical Co Inc..........G....... 513 541-4540
Cincinnati *(G-4110)*
Paramount Products..........G....... 419 832-0235
Grand Rapids *(G-10317)*
Perma-Fix of Dayton Inc..........F....... 937 268-6501
Dayton *(G-8422)*
Petroliance..........G....... 614 475-5952
Columbus *(G-7313)*
Petroliance LLC..........C....... 216 441-7200
Cleveland *(G-5869)*
Phymet Inc..........F....... 937 743-8061
Springboro *(G-17343)*
▲ **Quaker Chemical Corporation**..........D....... 513 422-9600
Middletown *(G-13947)*
R and J Corporation..........E....... 440 871-6009
Westlake *(G-20147)*
Reladyne Inc..........D....... 513 489-6000
Cincinnati *(G-4258)*
Renite Company..........F....... 800 883-7876
Columbus *(G-7385)*
Shooters Choice LLC..........G....... 440 834-8888
Chagrin Falls *(G-3076)*
Spec Mask Ohio LLC..........G....... 440 522-3055
Kirtland *(G-11470)*
Starchem Inc..........G....... 513 458-8262
Cincinnati *(G-4373)*
▼ **State Industrial Products Corp**..........B....... 877 747-6986
Cleveland *(G-6097)*
Triad Energy Corporation..........E....... 740 374-2940
Marietta *(G-12683)*
Universal Oil Inc..........E....... 216 771-4300
Cleveland *(G-6239)*
US Industrial Lubricants Inc..........E....... 513 541-2225
Cincinnati *(G-4458)*
▼ **Ventco Inc**..........F....... 440 834-8888
Chagrin Falls *(G-3088)*
Wallover Enterprises Inc..........E....... 440 238-9250
Strongsville *(G-17804)*
▼ **Wallover Oil Company Inc**..........E....... 440 238-9250
Strongsville *(G-17806)*
Wallover Oil Company Inc..........F....... 440 238-9250
Strongsville *(G-17805)*
Wallover Oil Hamilton Inc..........F....... 513 896-6692
Hamilton *(G-10620)*
Western Reserve Lubricants..........G....... 440 951-5700
Painesville *(G-15798)*

2999 Products Of Petroleum & Coal, NEC

Citi 2 Citi Logistics..........E....... 614 306-4109
Columbus *(G-6766)*

30 RUBBER AND MISCELLANEOUS PLASTICS PRODUCTS

3011 Tires & Inner Tubes

◆ **31 Inc**..........D....... 740 498-8324
Newcomerstown *(G-14968)*
American Airless Inc..........E....... 614 552-0146
Reynoldsburg *(G-16428)*
B & S Transport Inc..........F....... 330 767-4319
Navarre *(G-14572)*
▲ **Bkt USA Inc**..........F....... 330 836-1090
Fairlawn *(G-9598)*
Buckman Machine Works Inc..........G....... 330 525-7665
Homeworth *(G-10987)*
◆ **Chemspec Ltd**..........F....... 330 896-0355
Uniontown *(G-18915)*
Continental Tire Americas LLC..........G....... 419 633-4221
Bryan *(G-2276)*
◆ **Cooper Tire & Rubber Company**..........A....... 419 423-1321
Findlay *(G-9672)*
Cooper Tire & Rubber Company..........E....... 419 424-4202
Findlay *(G-9673)*
Cooper Tire & Rubber Company..........D....... 419 424-4384
Findlay *(G-9674)*
▲ **Cooper Tire Vhcl Test Ctr Inc**..........E....... 419 423-1321
Findlay *(G-9675)*
Goodrich Corporation..........G....... 216 429-4655
Brooklyn Heights *(G-2122)*
Goodyear Tire & Rubber Company..........C....... 216 265-1800
Cleveland *(G-5332)*
◆ **Goodyear Tire & Rubber Company**...A....... 330 796-2121
Akron *(G-191)*
Gregs Eagle Tire Co Inc..........G....... 330 837-1983
Massillon *(G-12990)*
▲ **Grove Engineered Products Inc**..........G....... 419 659-5939
Columbus Grove *(G-7635)*
H & H Industries Inc..........G....... 740 682-7721
Oak Hill *(G-15451)*
Intertex World Resources Inc..........G....... 770 214-5551
Canton *(G-2710)*
▲ **Martin Wheel Co Inc**..........D....... 330 633-3278
Tallmadge *(G-17992)*
PPG Industries Inc..........G....... 614 921-9228
Hilliard *(G-10854)*
◆ **Technical Rubber Company Inc**..........B....... 740 967-9015
Johnstown *(G-11272)*
Titan Tire Corporation..........B....... 419 633-4221
Bryan *(G-2309)*
◆ **Trelleborg Wheel Systems Ameri**..........E....... 866 633-8473
Akron *(G-409)*
Troy Engineered Components and..........G....... 937 335-8070
Dayton *(G-8569)*
Truflex Rubber Products Co..........C....... 740 967-9015
Johnstown *(G-11273)*
Umd Contractors Inc..........F....... 740 694-8614
Fredericktown *(G-9982)*
Ws Trading LLC..........G....... 800 830-4547
Galena *(G-10118)*
Yrp Industries Inc..........G....... 330 533-2524
Youngstown *(G-21085)*

3021 Rubber & Plastic Footwear

Advantage Products Corporation..........F....... 513 489-2283
Blue Ash *(G-1722)*
American Doll Accessories..........G....... 740 590-8458
Coolville *(G-7672)*
Calzurocom..........G....... 800 257-9472
Plain City *(G-16180)*
Cobblers Corner LLC..........F....... 330 482-4005
Columbiana *(G-6458)*
Georgia-Boot Inc..........D....... 740 753-1951
Nelsonville *(G-14593)*
Mulhern Belting Inc..........E....... 201 337-5700
Fairfield *(G-9533)*
Nwc HUD Corp II..........G....... 419 228-8400
Lima *(G-11912)*
▲ **Totes Isotoner Corporation**..........F....... 513 682-8200
West Chester *(G-19907)*
▲ **Totes Isotoner Holdings Corp**..........C....... 513 682-8200
West Chester *(G-19908)*
Vans Inc..........F....... 419 471-1541
Toledo *(G-18589)*

3052 Rubber & Plastic Hose & Belting

Aeroquip Corp..........G....... 419 238-1190
Van Wert *(G-19074)*
Aeroquip-Vickers Inc..........G....... 216 523-5000
Cleveland *(G-4633)*

S I C

Employee Codes: A=Over 500 employees, B=251-500
C=101-250, D=51-100, E=20-50, F=10-19, G=3-9
2019 Harris Ohio
Industrial Directory
887

Allied Fabricating & Wldg Co ... E ... 614 751-6664
Columbus (G-6572)
Cmt Machining & Fabg LLC ... F ... 937 652-3740
Urbana (G-18983)
Cooper-Standard Automotive Inc ... B ... 419 352-3533
Bowling Green (G-1965)
Crushproof Tubing Co ... E ... 419 293-2111
Mc Comb (G-13188)
◆ Eaton Aeroquip LLC ... C ... 216 523-5000
Cleveland (G-5143)
Eaton Corporation ... A ... 419 238-1190
Van Wert (G-19087)
Eaton Corporation ... C ... 330 274-0743
Aurora (G-877)
Eaton Hydraulics LLC ... E ... 419 232-7777
Van Wert (G-19088)
Eaton-Aeroquip Llc ... D ... 419 238-1190
Van Wert (G-19089)
Eaton-Aeroquip Llc ... D ... 419 891-7775
Maumee (G-13109)
▲ Engineered Plastics Corp ... E ... 330 376-7700
Akron (G-155)
▲ Fenner Dunlop (toledo) LLC ... E ... 419 531-5300
Toledo (G-18291)
◆ Goodyear Tire & Rubber Company ... A ... 330 796-2121
Akron (G-191)
Hbd/Thermoid Inc ... G ... 937 593-5010
Bellefontaine (G-1517)
▼ Hbd/Thermoid Inc ... C ... 614 526-7000
Dublin (G-8922)
Kent Elastomer Products Inc ... G ... 800 331-4762
Mogadore (G-14242)
▲ Kent Elastomer Products Inc ... C ... 330 673-1011
Kent (G-11341)
Kentak Products Company ... D ... 330 386-3700
East Liverpool (G-9062)
▲ Kentak Products Company ... E ... 330 382-2000
East Liverpool (G-9063)
Kentak Products Company ... G ... 330 532-6211
East Liverpool (G-9064)
Klockner Pentaplast Amer Inc ... G ... 937 743-8040
Franklin (G-9893)
Mechanical Elastomerics Inc ... G ... 330 863-1014
Malvern (G-12393)
Mm Outsourcing LLC ... F ... 937 661-4300
Leesburg (G-11714)
Myers Industries Inc ... C ... 330 336-6621
Wadsworth (G-19255)
Myers Industries Inc ... E ... 330 253-5592
Akron (G-292)
Novex Inc ... F ... 330 335-2371
Wadsworth (G-19257)
Parker-Hannifin Corporation ... C ... 330 296-2871
Ravenna (G-16394)
Parker-Hannifin Corporation ... E ... 330 296-2871
Ravenna (G-16395)
Polychem Corporation ... D ... 419 547-1400
Clyde (G-6392)
Roller Source Inc ... F ... 440 748-4033
Columbia Station (G-6445)
▲ Salem-Republic Rubber Company ... E ... 877 425-5079
Sebring (G-16893)
▲ Sumiriko Ohio Inc ... C ... 419 358-2121
Bluffton (G-1893)
Summers Acquisition Corp ... G ... 740 373-0303
Marietta (G-12678)
Summers Acquisition Corp ... G ... 419 526-5800
Mansfield (G-12523)
Summers Acquisition Corp ... G ... 419 423-5800
Findlay (G-9765)
◆ Watteredge LLC ... D ... 440 933-6110
Avon Lake (G-1013)

3053 Gaskets, Packing & Sealing Devices

▲ Accel Performance Group LLC ... C ... 216 658-6413
Independence (G-11117)
Ace Gasket Manufacturing Co ... G ... 513 271-6321
Cincinnati (G-3292)
Air Heater Seal Company Inc ... E ... 740 984-2146
Waterford (G-19483)
▲ Akron Gasket & Packg Entps Inc ... F ... 330 633-3742
Tallmadge (G-17971)
▲ Ashtabula Rubber Co ... C ... 440 992-2195
Ashtabula (G-763)
Blackthorn LLC ... F ... 937 836-9296
Clayton (G-4572)
▲ Chestnut Holdings Inc ... G ... 330 849-6503
Akron (G-114)
▲ Cincinnati Gasket Pkg Mfg Inc ... E ... 513 761-3458
Cincinnati (G-3492)
▲ Columbus Gasket Co Inc ... G ... 614 878-6041
Columbus (G-6789)
◆ Concrete Sealants Inc ... E ... 937 845-8776
Tipp City (G-18109)
Cornerstone Indus Holdings ... G ... 440 893-9144
Chagrin Falls (G-3014)
Dan-Loc Group LLC ... G ... 937 778-0485
Piqua (G-16109)
▲ Dana Limited ... B ... 419 887-3000
Maumee (G-13099)
Die-Cut Products Co ... E ... 216 771-6994
Cleveland (G-5094)
▲ Durox Company ... D ... 440 238-5350
Strongsville (G-17739)
Eagleburgmann Industries LP ... G ... 513 563-7325
Cincinnati (G-3622)
▲ Egc Enterprises Inc ... E ... 440 285-5835
Chardon (G-3110)
Epg Inc ... D ... 330 995-5125
Aurora (G-879)
Epg Inc ... F ... 330 995-9725
Streetsboro (G-17673)
Essential Sealing Products Inc ... F ... 440 543-8108
Chagrin Falls (G-3045)
Excelsior Solutions ... G ... 937 848-2569
Spring Valley (G-17316)
Expert Gasket & Seal LLC ... G ... 330 468-0066
Macedonia (G-12293)
Faurecia Exhaust Systems Inc ... B ... 937 743-0551
Franklin (G-9882)
Federal-Mogul Powertrain LLC ... C ... 740 432-2393
Cambridge (G-2437)
Federal-Mogul Powertrain LLC ... A ... 419 238-1053
Van Wert (G-19091)
▲ Ferrotherm Corporation ... C ... 216 883-9350
Cleveland (G-5233)
▲ Flow Dry Technology Inc ... C ... 937 833-2161
Brookville (G-2168)
Foam Seal Inc ... D ... 216 881-8111
Cleveland (G-5256)
▲ Forest City Technologies Inc ... B ... 440 647-2115
Wellington (G-19578)
Forest City Technologies Inc ... B ... 440 647-2115
Wellington (G-19579)
Forest City Technologies Inc ... C ... 440 647-2115
Wellington (G-19580)
Forest City Technologies Inc ... C ... 440 647-2115
Wellington (G-19581)
Forest City Technologies Inc ... G ... 440 647-2115
Wellington (G-19582)
▲ Fouty & Company Inc ... E ... 419 693-0017
Oregon (G-15560)
Freudenberg-Nok General Partnr ... E ... 937 335-3306
Troy (G-18658)
Freudenberg-Nok General Partnr ... C ... 419 427-5221
Findlay (G-9689)
G-M-I Inc ... G ... 440 953-8811
Willoughby (G-20329)
Gasko Fabricated Products LLC ... E ... 330 239-1781
Medina (G-13266)
High Quality Plastics ... G ... 419 422-8290
Findlay (G-9703)
Hunt Products Inc ... E ... 440 667-2457
Newburgh Heights (G-14940)
▲ Ier Fujikura Inc ... C ... 330 425-7121
Macedonia (G-12302)
▲ Industry Products Co ... B ... 937 778-0585
Piqua (G-16130)
▲ Ishikawa Gasket America Inc ... F ... 419 353-7300
Bowling Green (G-1975)
Ishikawa Gasket America Inc ... C ... 419 353-7300
Bowling Green (G-1976)
Jbm Technologies Inc ... G ... 419 368-4362
Hayesville (G-10715)
Jet Rubber Company ... E ... 330 325-1821
Rootstown (G-16569)
Johnson Bros Rubber Co Inc ... E ... 419 752-4814
Greenwich (G-10404)
Jtm Products Inc ... E ... 440 287-2302
Solon (G-17178)
K Wm Beach Mfg Co Inc ... C ... 937 399-3838
Springfield (G-17429)
Kes Industries LLC ... G ... 330 405-2813
Twinsburg (G-18799)
Magnetic Packaging LLC ... G ... 419 720-4366
Toledo (G-18396)
May Lin Silicone Products Inc ... G ... 330 825-9019
Barberton (G-1085)
Mechanical Dynamics Analis Ltd ... E ... 440 946-0082
Euclid (G-9426)
Miami Valley Gasket Co Inc ... E ... 937 228-0781
Dayton (G-8346)
Middlefield Plastics Inc ... E ... 440 834-4638
Middlefield (G-13826)
Midwest Industrial Rubber Inc ... F ... 614 876-3110
Hilliard (G-10841)
Miles Rubber & Packing Company ... E ... 330 425-3888
Twinsburg (G-18820)
Neff-Perkins Company ... C ... 440 632-1658
Middlefield (G-13839)
Netherland Rubber Company ... F ... 513 733-0883
Cincinnati (G-4068)
▲ Newman International Inc ... D ... 513 932-7379
Lebanon (G-11674)
Newman Sanitary Gasket Company ... E ... 513 932-7379
Lebanon (G-11675)
▲ Nitto Inc ... C ... 937 773-4820
Piqua (G-16146)
Novagard Solutions Inc ... F ... 216 881-3890
Cleveland (G-5789)
▲ Ohio Gasket and Shim Co Inc ... E ... 330 630-0626
Akron (G-307)
P & E Sales Ltd ... G ... 330 829-0100
Alliance (G-495)
▲ P & R Specialty Inc ... E ... 937 773-0263
Piqua (G-16147)
Paramont Machine Company LLC ... E ... 330 339-3489
New Philadelphia (G-14792)
▲ Parker-Hannifin Corporation ... B ... 216 896-3000
Cleveland (G-5848)
Parker-Hannifin Corporation ... F ... 216 896-3000
Cleveland (G-5850)
Paul J Tatulinski Ltd ... F ... 330 584-8251
North Benton (G-15061)
Phoenix Associates ... E ... 440 543-9701
Chagrin Falls (G-3066)
Produce Packaging Inc ... C ... 216 391-6129
Cleveland (G-5925)
Quanex Ig Systems Inc ... C ... 740 439-2338
Cambridge (G-2454)
◆ Quanex Ig Systems Inc ... C ... 216 910-1519
Akron (G-336)
R and J Corporation ... E ... 440 871-6009
Westlake (G-20147)
▲ Royal Acme Corporation ... E ... 216 241-1477
Cleveland (G-6009)
Rubbertec Industrial Pdts Co ... G ... 740 657-3345
Lewis Center (G-11778)
▲ Saint-Gobain Prfmce Plas Corp ... C ... 440 836-6900
Solon (G-17227)
▲ SKF Usa Inc ... F ... 800 589-5563
Cleveland (G-6068)
Smith Quarter Horses ... G ... 419 420-0112
Findlay (G-9756)
▲ Soffseal Inc ... E ... 513 934-0815
Lebanon (G-11697)
▲ Sur-Seal LLC ... C ... 513 574-8500
Cincinnati (G-4398)
Sur-Seal Corporation ... G ... 513 574-8500
Harrison (G-10675)
Thermodyn Corporation ... G ... 419 874-5100
Perrysburg (G-16014)
Tite Seal Case Company Inc ... G ... 440 647-2371
Wellington (G-19593)
Treaty City Industries Inc ... F ... 937 548-9000
Greenville (G-10398)
Trellborg Sling Prfiles US Inc ... E ... 330 995-5125
Aurora (G-910)
Tri-Seal LLC ... G ... 330 821-1166
Alliance (G-510)
▲ Vertex Inc ... E ... 330 628-6230
Mogadore (G-14252)
Youngstown Specialty Mtls Inc ... G ... 330 259-1110
Youngstown (G-21082)

3061 Molded, Extruded & Lathe-Cut Rubber Mechanical Goods

Alternative Flash Inc ... E ... 330 334-6111
Wadsworth (G-19225)
American Pro-Mold Inc ... E ... 330 336-4111
Wadsworth (G-19226)
ARC Rubber Inc ... F ... 440 466-4555
Geneva (G-10214)
▲ Ashtabula Rubber Co ... C ... 440 992-2195
Ashtabula (G-763)
Bridgestone APM Company ... D ... 419 294-6989
Upper Sandusky (G-18946)
Bridgestone APM Company ... D ... 419 294-6304
Upper Sandusky (G-18947)

SIC SECTION
30 RUBBER AND MISCELLANEOUS PLASTICS PRODUCTS

◆ Brp Manufacturing Company ....E 800 858-0482
Lima *(G-11847)*
C & M Rubber Co Inc ....F 937 299-2782
Dayton *(G-8069)*
Canton OH Rubber Speclty Prods ....G 330 454-3847
Canton *(G-2612)*
▲ Cardinal Rubber Company Inc ....E 330 745-2191
Barberton *(G-1069)*
Chardon Custom Polymers LLC ....F 440 285-2161
Chardon *(G-3101)*
Clark Rbr Plastic Intl Sls Inc ....D 440 255-9793
Mentor *(G-13413)*
Colonial Rubber Company ....D 330 296-2831
Ravenna *(G-16373)*
▲ Contitech North America Inc ....F 330 664-7180
Fairlawn *(G-9602)*
◆ Datwyler Sling Sltions USA Inc ....D 937 387-2800
Vandalia *(G-19122)*
Duramax Global Corp ....D 440 834-5400
Hiram *(G-10909)*
Elbex Corporation ....D 330 673-3233
Kent *(G-11318)*
Epg Inc ....D 330 995-5125
Aurora *(G-879)*
Epg Inc ....F 330 995-9725
Streetsboro *(G-17673)*
Extruded Silicon Products Inc ....E 330 733-0101
Mogadore *(G-14237)*
Frankes Wood Products LLC ....E 937 642-0706
Marysville *(G-12783)*
◆ Goodyear International Corp ....E 330 796-2121
Akron *(G-190)*
Harwood Rubber Products Inc ....E 330 923-3256
Cuyahoga Falls *(G-7878)*
Hygenic Acquisition Co ....C 330 633-8460
Akron *(G-212)*
◆ Hygenic Corporation ....C 330 633-8460
Akron *(G-213)*
▲ Ier Fujikura Inc ....C 330 425-7121
Macedonia *(G-12302)*
Jakmar Incorporated ....F 513 631-4303
Cincinnati *(G-3867)*
▲ Johnson Bros Rubber Co Inc ....D 419 853-4122
West Salem *(G-19955)*
Karman Rubber Company ....E 330 864-2161
Akron *(G-232)*
Kleen Polymers Inc ....F 330 336-4212
Wadsworth *(G-19250)*
▼ Koneta Inc ....D 419 739-4200
Wapakoneta *(G-19339)*
▲ Lauren Manufacturing LLC ....B 330 339-3373
New Philadelphia *(G-14781)*
Lexington Rubber Group Inc ....E 330 425-8352
Canton *(G-2733)*
Macdivitt Rubber Company LLC ....E 440 259-5937
Perry *(G-15909)*
Mantaline Corporation ....D 330 274-2264
Mantua *(G-12551)*
Martin Industries Inc ....E 419 862-2694
Elmore *(G-9207)*
Meridian Industries Inc ....D 330 673-1011
Kent *(G-11351)*
▲ Midlands Millroom Supply Inc ....E 330 453-9100
Canton *(G-2753)*
Midwest Industrial Rubber Inc ....F 614 876-3110
Hilliard *(G-10841)*
Miller Enterprises Ohio LLC ....G 330 852-4009
Sugarcreek *(G-17853)*
Mm Outsourcing LLC ....F 937 661-4300
Leesburg *(G-11714)*
Neff-Perkins Company ....C 440 632-1658
Middlefield *(G-13839)*
Ohio Elastomers ....G 440 354-9750
Perry *(G-15910)*
Ottawa Rubber Company ....F 419 865-1378
Holland *(G-10947)*
Plabell Rubber Products Corp ....F 419 691-5878
Toledo *(G-18472)*
Polycraft Products Inc ....G 513 353-3334
Cleves *(G-6373)*
▲ Q Holding Company ....B 330 425-8472
Twinsburg *(G-18842)*
Qualiform Inc ....E 330 336-6777
Wadsworth *(G-19268)*
Quanex Ig Systems Inc ....C 740 439-2338
Cambridge *(G-2454)*
◆ Quanex Ig Systems Inc ....C 216 910-1519
Akron *(G-336)*
Robin Industries Inc ....E 330 893-3501
Berlin *(G-1644)*
Robin Industries Inc ....C 330 359-5418
Winesburg *(G-20534)*
Robin Industries Inc ....C 330 695-9300
Fredericksburg *(G-9958)*
Roboworld Molded Products LLC ....G 513 720-6900
West Chester *(G-19784)*
Rubber-Tech Inc ....F 937 274-1114
Dayton *(G-8487)*
Saint-Gobain Prfmce Plas Corp ....C 330 798-6981
Akron *(G-372)*
Saint-Gobain Prfmce Plas Corp ....B 614 889-2220
Dublin *(G-8978)*
▲ Shreiner Sole Co Inc ....F 330 276-6135
Killbuck *(G-11454)*
▲ Soffseal Inc ....E 513 934-0815
Lebanon *(G-11697)*
▲ Tigerpoly Manufacturing Inc ....B 614 871-0045
Grove City *(G-10473)*
◆ Trelleborg Wheel Systems Ameri ....E 866 633-8473
Akron *(G-409)*
▲ United Feed Screws Ltd ....F 330 798-5532
Akron *(G-420)*
Universal Polymer & Rubber Ltd ....E 330 633-1666
Tallmadge *(G-18011)*
Universal Urethane Pdts Inc ....D 419 693-7400
Toledo *(G-18585)*
▲ V & M Star LP ....E 330 742-6300
Youngstown *(G-21057)*
▲ Vertex Inc ....E 330 628-6230
Mogadore *(G-14252)*
Woodlawn Rubber Co ....F 513 489-1718
Blue Ash *(G-1875)*
Yokohama Tire Corporation ....C 440 352-3321
Painesville *(G-15803)*

3069 Fabricated Rubber Prdts, NEC

Abeon Medical Corporation ....G 440 262-6000
Brecksville *(G-2018)*
Action Rubber Co Inc ....F 937 866-5975
Dayton *(G-8005)*
Aeroquip-Vickers Inc ....G 216 523-5000
Cleveland *(G-4633)*
American Pro-Mold Inc ....E 330 336-4111
Wadsworth *(G-19226)*
Ansell Healthcare Products LLC ....D 740 622-4311
Coshocton *(G-7719)*
Ansell Healthcare Products LLC ....C 740 295-5414
Coshocton *(G-7720)*
ARC Rubber Inc ....F 440 466-4555
Geneva *(G-10214)*
▲ Ashtabula Rubber Co ....C 440 992-2195
Ashtabula *(G-763)*
◆ B D G Wrap-Tite Inc ....D 440 349-5400
Solon *(G-17110)*
◆ Blair Rubber Company ....D 330 769-5583
Seville *(G-16912)*
Boomerang Rubber Inc ....E 937 693-4611
Botkins *(G-1933)*
◆ Brp Manufacturing Company ....E 800 858-0482
Lima *(G-11847)*
Canton OH Rubber Speclty Prods ....G 330 454-3847
Canton *(G-2612)*
▲ Cardinal Rubber Company Inc ....E 330 745-2191
Barberton *(G-1069)*
Censtar Coatings Inc ....G 330 723-8000
West Salem *(G-19953)*
Cep Holdings LLC ....G 330 665-2900
Fairlawn *(G-9600)*
▼ Chalfant Sew Fabricators Inc ....E 216 521-7922
Cleveland *(G-4907)*
Champion Manufacturing Inc ....G 419 253-7930
Marengo *(G-12588)*
Chardon Custom Polymers LLC ....F 440 285-2161
Chardon *(G-3101)*
▲ Chemionics Corporation ....E 330 733-8834
Tallmadge *(G-17975)*
Clark Rbr Plastic Intl Sls Inc ....D 440 255-9793
Mentor *(G-13413)*
Clearly Visible Mobile Wash ....G 440 543-9299
Chagrin Falls *(G-3040)*
Colonial Rubber Company ....D 330 296-2831
Ravenna *(G-16373)*
▲ Columbus Gasket Co Inc ....G 614 878-6041
Columbus *(G-6789)*
◆ Contitech Usa Inc ....F 330 664-7000
Fairlawn *(G-9603)*
◆ Custom Rubber Corporation ....D 216 391-2928
Cleveland *(G-5048)*
Custom Stamp Makers Inc ....G 216 351-1470
Cleveland *(G-5049)*
Dacon Industries Co ....E 330 298-9491
Ravenna *(G-16374)*
Dandy Products Inc ....F 513 625-3000
Goshen *(G-10286)*
◆ Datwyler Sling Sltions USA Inc ....D 937 387-2800
Vandalia *(G-19122)*
◆ Deruijter Intl USA Inc ....F 419 678-3909
Coldwater *(G-6405)*
Die-Cut Products Co ....E 216 771-6994
Cleveland *(G-5094)*
▲ Ds Technologies Group Ltd ....G 419 841-5388
Toledo *(G-18270)*
▲ DTR Equipment Inc ....F 419 692-3000
Delphos *(G-8742)*
◆ Durable Corporation ....D 800 537-1603
Norwalk *(G-15389)*
Eagle Elastomer Inc ....E 330 923-7070
Peninsula *(G-15893)*
◆ Eaton Aeroquip LLC ....C 216 523-5000
Cleveland *(G-5143)*
Eckel Industries Inc ....E 978 772-0480
West Chester *(G-19850)*
Econo Products Inc ....F 330 923-4101
Cuyahoga Falls *(G-7862)*
Elastostar Rubber Corp ....E 614 841-4400
Columbus *(G-6888)*
Enduro Rubber Company ....G 330 296-9603
Ravenna *(G-16379)*
▲ Enterprise / Ameriseal Inc ....G 937 284-3003
Springfield *(G-17396)*
Farmed Materials Inc ....G 513 680-4046
Cincinnati *(G-3673)*
▲ Fenner Dunlop Port Clinton Inc ....C 419 635-2191
Port Clinton *(G-16247)*
◆ Firestone Polymers LLC ....D 330 379-7000
Akron *(G-171)*
◆ Flexsys America LP ....D 330 666-4111
Akron *(G-173)*
Foot Logic Inc ....G 330 699-0123
Uniontown *(G-18919)*
Formco Inc ....G 330 966-2111
Canton *(G-2674)*
Foxtronix Inc ....G 937 866-2112
Miamisburg *(G-13670)*
G Grafton Machine & Rubber ....F 330 297-1062
Ravenna *(G-16380)*
Garro Tread Corporation ....G 330 376-3125
Akron *(G-181)*
Gdc Inc ....F 574 533-3128
Wooster *(G-20596)*
▲ Gold Key Processing Inc ....C 440 632-0901
Middlefield *(G-13800)*
▲ Goldsmith & Eggleton LLC ....F 203 855-6000
Wadsworth *(G-19243)*
◆ Green Tokai Co Ltd ....A 937 833-5444
Brookville *(G-2170)*
Grypmat Inc ....G 419 953-7607
Celina *(G-2964)*
▲ Guardian Manufacturing Co LLC ....E 419 933-2711
Willard *(G-20240)*
Hhi Company Inc ....G 330 455-3983
Canton *(G-2698)*
Hygenic Acquisition Co ....C 330 633-8460
Akron *(G-212)*
◆ Hygenic Corporation ....C 330 633-8460
Akron *(G-213)*
▼ Hyload Inc ....F 330 336-6604
Seville *(G-16916)*
Hytech Silicone Products Inc ....G 330 297-1888
Ravenna *(G-16383)*
▲ Ier Fujikura Inc ....C 330 425-7121
Macedonia *(G-12302)*
Innocor Foam Tech - Acp Inc ....F 419 647-4172
Spencerville *(G-17309)*
International Automotive ....F 330 279-6557
Holmesville *(G-10982)*
▲ International Sources Inc ....G 440 735-9890
Bedford *(G-1417)*
ISO Technologies Inc ....E 740 344-9554
Hebron *(G-10749)*
Jet Rubber Company ....E 330 325-1821
Rootstown *(G-16569)*
K F D Inc ....G 330 773-4300
Coventry Township *(G-7771)*
Karman Rubber Company ....E 330 864-2161
Akron *(G-232)*
Keener Rubber Company ....E 330 821-1880
Alliance *(G-481)*
Killian Latex Inc ....F 330 644-6746
Akron *(G-236)*

Employee Codes: A=Over 500 employees, B=251-500
C=101-250, D=51-100, E=20-50, F=10-19, G=3-9
2019 Harris Ohio
Industrial Directory
889

Kiltex Corporation....E....330 644-6746
Akron (G-237)
◆ Kn Rubber LLC....C....419 739-4200
Wapakoneta (G-19338)
▲ Koroseal Interior Products LLC....C....330 668-7600
Fairlawn (G-9611)
Lake Erie Rubber Recycling LLC....G....440 570-6027
Strongsville (G-17761)
Lanxess Corporation....C....440 279-2367
Chardon (G-3123)
▲ Lauren International Ltd....C....330 339-3373
New Philadelphia (G-14780)
▲ Lauren Manufacturing LLC....B....330 339-3373
New Philadelphia (G-14781)
▲ Lexington Rubber Group Inc....E....330 425-8472
Twinsburg (G-18807)
◆ Ludlow Composites Corporation....C....419 332-5531
Fremont (G-10038)
Luxx Ultra-Tech Inc....G....330 483-6051
Medina (G-13288)
Macdivitt Rubber Company LLC....E....440 259-5937
Perry (G-15909)
Maine Rubber Preforms LLC....G....216 210-2094
Middlefield (G-13815)
Mameco International Inc....F....216 752-4400
Cleveland (G-5611)
▲ Maple City Rubber Company....E....419 668-8261
Norwalk (G-15405)
Martin Industries Inc....E....419 862-2694
Elmore (G-9207)
Martin Rubber Company....F....330 336-6604
Seville (G-16920)
▲ Master Mfg Co Inc....E....216 641-0500
Cleveland (G-5632)
May Lin Silicone Products Inc....G....330 825-9019
Barberton (G-1085)
Meridian Industries Inc....D....330 359-5447
Winesburg (G-20533)
Meridian Industries Inc....D....330 673-1011
Kent (G-11351)
Merrico Inc....G....419 525-2711
Mansfield (G-12479)
▲ Meteor Sealing Systems LLC....C....330 343-9595
Dover (G-8840)
▲ Midwest Elastomers Inc....D....419 738-8844
Wapakoneta (G-19343)
Midwestern Bag Co Inc....E....419 241-3112
Toledo (G-18411)
Miles Rubber & Packing Company....E....330 425-3888
Twinsburg (G-18820)
Mitchell Plastics Inc....E....330 825-2461
Barberton (G-1086)
MPS Manufacturing Company LLC....G....330 343-1435
New Philadelphia (G-14788)
Mullins Rubber Products Inc....D....937 233-4211
Dayton (G-8372)
Murrubber Technologies Inc....E....330 688-4881
Stow (G-17609)
Myers Industries Inc....C....330 336-6621
Wadsworth (G-19255)
Myers Industries Inc....E....330 253-5592
Akron (G-292)
Neff-Perkins Company....C....440 632-1658
Middlefield (G-13839)
Newact Inc....F....513 321-5177
Batavia (G-1173)
Newell Brands Inc....F....330 733-1184
Kent (G-11358)
Niles Roll Service Inc....F....330 544-0026
Niles (G-15025)
Noster Rubber Company Inc....F....419 299-3387
Van Buren (G-19072)
▲ Novatex North America Inc....D....419 282-4264
Ashland (G-728)
Novex Inc....F....330 335-2371
Wadsworth (G-19257)
Ohio Foam Corporation....G....614 252-4877
Columbus (G-7248)
Ohio Foam Corporation....E....330 799-4553
Youngstown (G-20982)
Ohio Foam Corporation....F....419 492-2151
New Washington (G-14831)
▲ Okamoto Sandusky Mfg LLC....D....419 626-1633
Sandusky (G-16832)
Omnova Solutions Inc....C....216 682-7000
Beachwood (G-1257)
◆ Park-Ohio Holdings Corp....F....440 947-2000
Cleveland (G-5842)
Park-Ohio Industries Inc....C....440 947-2000
Cleveland (G-5843)
▲ Park-Ohio Products Inc....D....216 961-7200
Cleveland (G-5844)
◆ Performance Additives Amer LLC....G....330 365-9256
New Philadelphia (G-14793)
▲ Philpott Rubber LLC....E....330 225-3344
Brunswick (G-2225)
Philpott Rubber LLC....G....330 225-3344
Aurora (G-899)
Pinnacle Roller Co....F....513 369-4830
Cincinnati (G-4162)
▲ Pioneer National Latex Inc....D....419 289-3300
Ashland (G-736)
Plabell Rubber Products Corp....F....419 691-5878
Toledo (G-18472)
Plan B Toys Ltd....G....614 751-6605
Groveport (G-10510)
▲ Polymerics Inc....E....330 434-6665
Cuyahoga Falls (G-7906)
Ppafco Inc....F....614 488-7259
Columbus (G-7335)
Prcc Holdings Inc....C....330 798-4790
Copley (G-7691)
Precision Component & Mch Inc....E....740 867-6366
Chesapeake (G-3147)
Precision Fab Products Inc....G....937 526-5681
Versailles (G-19189)
▲ Preferred Compounding Corp....C....330 798-4790
Copley (G-7692)
Premiere Medical Resources Inc....F....330 923-5899
Cuyahoga Falls (G-7908)
Profile Rubber Corporation....F....330 239-1703
Wadsworth (G-19267)
Q Model Inc....E....330 673-0473
Barberton (G-1100)
Qualiform Inc....E....330 336-6777
Wadsworth (G-19268)
▼ R C A Rubber Company....D....330 784-1291
Akron (G-338)
R C Musson Rubber Co....E....330 773-7651
Akron (G-339)
◆ R T H Processing Inc....D....419 692-3000
Delphos (G-8754)
Raydar Inc of Ohio....G....330 334-6111
Wadsworth (G-19272)
▲ Remington Products Co....C....330 335-1571
Wadsworth (G-19274)
◆ Republic Powdered Metals Inc....D....330 225-3192
Medina (G-13327)
Reynolds Industries Inc....E....330 889-9466
West Farmington (G-19920)
Robin Industries Inc....C....330 359-5418
Winesburg (G-20534)
Robin Industries Inc....C....330 695-9300
Fredericksburg (G-9958)
Robin Industries Inc....E....330 893-3501
Berlin (G-1644)
◆ Roppe Corporation....B....419 435-8546
Fostoria (G-9855)
Roppe Holding Company....G....419 435-6601
Fostoria (G-9856)
◆ RPM International Inc....D....330 273-5090
Medina (G-13331)
▲ Rubber Associates Inc....D....330 745-2186
New Franklin (G-14698)
Rubber-Tech Inc....F....937 274-1114
Dayton (G-8487)
Rubberite Corp....G....832 457-0654
Columbus (G-7406)
▲ Safeguard Technology Inc....E....330 995-5200
Streetsboro (G-17694)
▲ Salem-Republic Rubber Company....E....877 425-5079
Sebring (G-16893)
▲ Scherba Industries Inc....D....330 273-3200
Brunswick (G-2238)
▲ Shreiner Sole Co Inc....F....330 276-6135
Killbuck (G-11454)
▲ Sml Inc....G....330 668-6555
Akron (G-380)
▲ Soffseal Inc....E....513 934-0815
Lebanon (G-11697)
Soprema USA Inc....E....330 334-0066
Wadsworth (G-19277)
Sorbothane Inc....E....330 678-9444
Kent (G-11388)
Space-Links Inc....E....330 788-2401
Youngstown (G-21034)
▲ Sparton Enterprises Inc....E....330 745-6088
Norton (G-15375)
Spiralcool Company....G....419 483-2510
Bellevue (G-1548)
▲ Starpoint Extrusions LLC....E....330 825-2373
Norton (G-15376)
▲ Sumiriko Ohio Inc....C....419 358-2121
Bluffton (G-1893)
Sunsong North America Inc....G....919 365-3825
Moraine (G-14397)
▲ Sur-Seal LLC....C....513 574-8500
Cincinnati (G-4398)
▼ Survitec Group (usa) Inc....E....330 239-4331
Sharon Center (G-16954)
Tahoma Enterprises Inc....D....330 745-9016
Barberton (G-1108)
▼ Tahoma Rubber & Plastics Inc....D....330 745-9016
Barberton (G-1109)
Tallmadge Finishing Co Inc....E....330 633-7466
Akron (G-394)
Tarkett Inc....G....440 708-9366
Chagrin Falls (G-3080)
▲ Tarkett Inc....D....800 899-8916
Solon (G-17246)
Timco Rubber Products Inc....E....216 267-6242
Berea (G-1629)
Tmac Machine Inc....G....330 673-0621
Kent (G-11394)
▼ TMI Inc....E....330 270-9780
Youngstown (G-21046)
Trexler Rubber Co Inc....E....330 296-9677
Ravenna (G-16414)
Trico Group LLC....G....216 589-0198
Cleveland (G-6212)
Trico Group Holdings LLC....G....216 274-9027
Cleveland (G-6213)
Tristan Rubber Molding Inc....E....330 499-4055
North Canton (G-15132)
Truflex Rubber Products Co....C....740 967-9015
Johnstown (G-11273)
Ultimate Rb Inc....E....419 692-3000
Delphos (G-8760)
▲ Universal Polymer & Rubber Ltd....C....440 632-1691
Middlefield (G-13864)
Universal Urethane Pdts Inc....D....419 693-7400
Toledo (G-18585)
US 261 Corp....G....216 531-7143
Cleveland (G-6243)
Usui International Corporation....E....513 448-0410
Cincinnati (G-4459)
Valley Rubber Mixing Inc....F....330 434-4442
Akron (G-424)
▲ Vernay Manufacturing Inc....E....937 767-7261
Yellow Springs (G-20818)
▲ Vertex Inc....E....330 628-6230
Mogadore (G-14252)
Vulcan International Corp....G....513 621-2850
Cincinnati (G-4484)
Wayne County Rubber Inc....E....330 264-5553
Wooster (G-20664)
West & Barker Inc....E....330 652-9923
Niles (G-15040)
Woodbridge Group....C....419 334-3666
Fremont (G-10064)
Woodlawn Rubber Co....F....513 489-1718
Blue Ash (G-1875)
▲ Yokohama Inds Amricas Ohio Inc....D....440 352-3321
Painesville (G-15802)
▲ Yusa Corporation....A....740 335-0335
Washington Court Hou (G-19479)

3081 Plastic Unsupported Sheet & Film

▲ Advanced Polymer Coatings Ltd....E....440 937-6218
Avon (G-939)
American Insulation Tech LLC....F....513 733-4248
Milford (G-13993)
◆ Ampac Holdings LLC....A....513 671-1777
Cincinnati (G-3340)
Automated Packg Systems Inc....C....330 626-2313
Streetsboro (G-17663)
Automated Packg Systems Inc....C....216 663-2000
Cleveland (G-4770)
Avery Dennison Corporation....D....440 358-3408
Painesville (G-15717)
◆ Berry Film Products Co Inc....D....800 225-6729
Mason (G-12835)
Berry Global Inc....F....419 887-1602
Maumee (G-13080)
▲ Berry Plastics Filmco Inc....D....330 562-6111
Aurora (G-873)
Blako Industries Inc....E....419 246-6172
Dunbridge (G-9014)
▲ Boltaron Inc....D....740 498-5900
Newcomerstown (G-14970)

SIC SECTION 30 RUBBER AND MISCELLANEOUS PLASTICS PRODUCTS

Buckeye Diamond Logistics Inc............G....... 937 644-2194
Marysville (G-12772)
CCL Label Inc.......................................C....... 216 676-2703
Cleveland (G-4894)
CCL Label Inc.......................................E....... 440 878-7000
Brunswick (G-2194)
◆ Champion Win Co Cleveland LLC.....E....... 440 899-2562
Macedonia (G-12283)
Charter Nex Films - Del OH Inc.............E....... 740 369-2770
Delaware (G-8663)
Charter Nex Holding Company..............E....... 740 369-2770
Delaware (G-8664)
Clarkwestern Dietrich Building.............F....... 330 372-5564
Warren (G-19384)
▼ Clarkwestern Dietrich Building.........F....... 513 870-1100
West Chester (G-19677)
▲ Clopay Corporation ....C....... 800 282-2260
Mason (G-12847)
Clopay Corporation ....G....... 440 542-9215
Solon (G-17127)
Clopay Corporation ....G....... 513 742-1984
Cincinnati (G-3529)
▲ Command Plastic Corporation ....F....... 800 321-8001
Tallmadge (G-17977)
Cool Seal Usa LLC................................F....... 419 666-1111
Perrysburg (G-15935)
▲ Crown Plastics Co ....D....... 513 367-0238
Harrison (G-10638)
◆ DJM Plastics Ltd...............................F....... 419 424-5250
Findlay (G-9679)
Dow Chemical Company ....F....... 937 254-1550
Dayton (G-8166)
Dupont Specialty Pdts USA LLC ....E....... 740 474-0220
Circleville (G-4543)
▲ Entrotech Inc.....................................F....... 614 946-7602
Columbus (G-6901)
Future Poly Tech Inc..............................E....... 614 942-1209
Saint Henry (G-16660)
▲ General Data Company Inc ....C....... 513 752-7978
Cincinnati (G-3252)
General Films Inc..................................D....... 888 436-3456
Covington (G-7786)
▲ Graphic Art Systems Inc ....E....... 216 581-9050
Cleveland (G-5341)
▲ Industry Products Co ....B....... 937 778-0585
Piqua (G-16130)
▲ Jain America Foods Inc....................G....... 614 850-9400
Columbus (G-7058)
◆ Jain America Holdings Inc.................D....... 614 850-9400
Columbus (G-7059)
James McGuire ....G....... 614 483-9825
Columbus (G-7061)
Kapstone Container Corporation ....C 330 562-6111
Aurora (G-886)
▲ Koroseal Interior Products LLC........C....... 330 668-7600
Fairlawn (G-9611)
Liqui-Box Corporation...........................C....... 419 289-9696
Ashland (G-721)
◆ Ludlow Composites Corporation......C....... 419 332-5531
Fremont (G-10038)
▲ Mar-Bal Inc...D....... 440 543-7526
Chagrin Falls (G-3057)
Mar-Bal Inc...D....... 440 543-7526
Chagrin Falls (G-3058)
▲ North Shore Strapping Inc ....D....... 216 661-5200
Brooklyn Heights (G-2128)
North Shore Strapping Inc ....D....... 216 661-5200
Cleveland (G-5770)
Omnova Solutions Inc............................C....... 216 682-7000
Beachwood (G-1257)
Orbis Rpm LLC.......................................G....... 419 307-8511
Columbus (G-7276)
Orbis Rpm LLC.......................................G....... 740 772-6355
Chillicothe (G-3203)
Orbis Rpm LLC.......................................F 419 355-8310
Fremont (G-10042)
▼ Packaging Materials Inc ....E....... 740 432-6337
Cambridge (G-2452)
Pexco Packaging Corp ....E....... 419 470-5935
Toledo (G-18468)
◆ Plastic Suppliers Inc ....E....... 614 471-9100
Columbus (G-7323)
Plastic Suppliers Inc...............................E....... 214 467-3700
Columbus (G-7324)
Plastic Suppliers Inc...............................D....... 614 475-8010
Columbus (G-7325)
Plastic Works Inc ....F 419 433-6576
Huron (G-11108)
PMC Acquisitions Inc ....D....... 419 429-0042
Findlay (G-9742)
◆ Polyone Corporation..........................D....... 440 930-1000
Avon Lake (G-1001)
▲ Priority Custom Molding Inc.............F 937 431-8770
Beavercreek Township (G-1373)
▲ Professional Packaging Company ...E....... 440 238-8850
Strongsville (G-17779)
Profusion Industries LLC.......................G....... 800 938-2858
Fairlawn (G-9615)
Profusion Industries LLC.......................E....... 740 374-6400
Marietta (G-12660)
Putnam Plastics Inc...............................G....... 937 866-6261
Dayton (G-8452)
Quality Poly Corp...................................F 330 453-9559
Canton (G-2796)
Raven Industries Inc...............................G....... 937 323-4625
Springfield (G-17480)
▲ Renegade Materials Corporation......E....... 508 579-7888
Miamisburg (G-13711)
Rotary Products Inc................................F 740 747-2623
Ashley (G-759)
Rotary Products Inc................................F 740 747-2623
Ashley (G-760)
▲ Scherba Industries Inc ....D....... 330 273-3200
Brunswick (G-2238)
Simona PMC LLC...................................D....... 419 429-0042
Findlay (G-9755)
Snyder Manufacturing Co Ltd...............G....... 330 343-4456
Dover (G-8856)
Spartech LLC..D....... 937 548-1395
Greenville (G-10395)
Spartech LLC..C....... 419 399-4050
Paulding (G-15871)
Specialty Films Inc.................................E....... 614 471-9100
Columbus (G-7467)
▲ Summit Plastic Company..................D....... 330 633-3668
Mogadore (G-14251)
Team Plastics Inc...................................F 216 251-8270
Cleveland (G-6150)
Transcendia Inc......................................C....... 740 929-5100
Hebron (G-10768)
Transcendia Inc......................................D....... 440 638-2000
Strongsville (G-17801)
Tsp Inc...E....... 513 732-8900
Batavia (G-1191)
▲ United Converting Inc........................G....... 614 863-9972
Columbus (G-7556)
Valfilm LLC ....D....... 419 423-6500
Findlay (G-9772)
Vinyl Building Products LLC ....B....... 513 539-4444
Monroe (G-14280)
▲ Walton Plastics Inc ....E....... 440 786-7711
Bedford (G-1454)
Western Reserve Sleeve Inc ....E....... 440 238-8850
Strongsville (G-17807)
World Connections Corps......................E....... 419 363-2681
Rockford (G-16542)

3082 Plastic Unsupported Profile Shapes

Advanced Composites Inc.....................G....... 937 575-9814
Sidney (G-17012)
▲ Advanced Composites Inc ....C....... 937 575-9800
Sidney (G-17013)
▲ Akron Polymer Products Inc............D....... 330 628-5551
Akron (G-48)
▲ Alkon Corporation.............................D 419 355-9111
Fremont (G-9990)
Alkon Corporation ....E....... 614 799-6650
Dublin (G-8876)
Bobbart Industries Inc............................E....... 419 350-5477
Sylvania (G-17934)
Dayton Technologies..............................F 513 539-5474
Monroe (G-14259)
▲ Deceuninck North America LLC ......B....... 513 539-4444
Monroe (G-14260)
Dlhbowles Inc...D....... 330 488-0716
East Canton (G-9039)
◆ Dlhbowles Inc ....B....... 330 478-2503
Canton (G-2661)
▼ Duracote Corporation.......................E....... 330 296-9600
Ravenna (G-16376)
Global Manufacturing Solutions...........F 937 236-8315
Dayton (G-8225)
HP Manufacturing Company Inc...........D....... 216 361-6500
Cleveland (G-5421)
Inventive Extrusions Corp ....E....... 330 874-3000
Bolivar (G-1917)
Kentak Products Company....................D....... 330 386-3700
East Liverpool (G-9062)
▲ Kentak Products Company...............E....... 330 382-2000
East Liverpool (G-9063)
Kentak Products Company....................G....... 330 532-6211
East Liverpool (G-9064)
▲ Machining Technologies Inc ....E....... 419 862-3110
Elmore (G-9206)
Meridian Industries Inc..........................D....... 330 673-1011
Kent (G-11351)
New Image Plastics Mfg Co ....G....... 330 854-3010
Canal Fulton (G-2487)
Normandy Products Company ....D....... 440 632-5050
Middlefield (G-13840)
Pexco Packaging Corp...........................E....... 419 470-5935
Toledo (G-18468)
Plasto-Tech Corporation ....F 440 323-6300
Elyria (G-9314)
Precision Fabrications Inc.....................G....... 937 297-8606
Sunbury (G-17897)
Quality Poly Corp...................................F 330 453-9559
Canton (G-2796)
Roach Wood Products & Plas Inc ....G....... 740 532-4855
Ironton (G-11172)
Wurms Woodworking Company.............E....... 419 492-2184
New Washington (G-14834)

3083 Plastic Laminated Plate & Sheet

Advanced Drainage Systems Inc ....D....... 330 264-4949
Wooster (G-20554)
Advanced Drainage Systems Inc ....E....... 419 599-9565
Napoleon (G-14530)
Advanced Drainage Systems Inc ....E....... 419 424-8324
Findlay (G-9648)
Advanced Elastomer Systems LP ....D....... 330 336-7641
Wadsworth (G-19221)
Aetna Plastics Corp................................G....... 330 274-2855
Mantua (G-12541)
Amtank Armor ....G....... 440 268-7735
Strongsville (G-17710)
Applied Medical Technology Inc ....E....... 440 717-4000
Brecksville (G-2020)
Arthur Corporation ....D....... 419 433-7202
Huron (G-11089)
▲ Biothane Coated Webbing Corp.......E....... 440 327-0485
North Ridgeville (G-15212)
Blt Inc..F 513 631-5050
Norwood (G-15424)
▲ Bruewer Woodwork Mfg Co ....D....... 513 353-3505
Cleves (G-6355)
Bulk Molding Compounds Inc ....D....... 419 874-7941
Perrysburg (G-15926)
Cool Seal Usa LLC.................................F 419 666-1111
Perrysburg (G-15935)
Counter Concepts Inc.............................F 330 848-4848
Doylestown (G-8864)
Cuda Composites LLC ....G....... 937 499-0360
Dayton (G-8117)
Custom Powdercoating LLC...................G....... 937 972-3516
Dayton (G-8122)
Designer Cntemporary Laminates ....G....... 440 946-8207
Willoughby (G-20309)
▼ Duracote Corporation.......................E....... 330 296-9600
Ravenna (G-16376)
Durivage Pattern & Mfg Co ....E....... 419 836-8655
Williston (G-20262)
◆ Elster Perfection Corporation ....D....... 440 428-1171
Geneva (G-10218)
Fdi Cabinetry LLC ....G....... 513 353-4500
Cleves (G-6362)
▲ Fowler Products Inc..........................F 419 683-4057
Crestline (G-7794)
Franklin Cabinet Company Inc ....E....... 937 743-9606
Franklin (G-9884)
General Electric Company ....D....... 740 623-5379
Coshocton (G-7735)
Great Lakes Textiles Inc ....E....... 440 201-1300
Bedford (G-1406)
◆ Hancor Inc..B....... 614 658-0050
Hilliard (G-10827)
Hrh Door Corp..D....... 440 593-5226
Conneaut (G-7649)
Idx Corporation ....C....... 937 401-3225
Dayton (G-8259)
Iko Production Inc...................................E....... 937 746-4561
Franklin (G-9891)
Ilpea Industries Inc ....C....... 330 562-2916
Aurora (G-884)
Industrial Molded Plastics.......................E....... 330 673-1464
Kent (G-11334)
International Laminating Corp................E....... 937 254-8181
Dayton (G-8274)
◆ Interntnal Cnvrter Cldwell Inc ....C....... 740 732-5665
Caldwell (G-2407)

SIC

Employee Codes: A=Over 500 employees, B=251-500
C=101-250, D=51-100, E=20-50, F=10-19, G=3-9
2019 Harris Ohio
Industrial Directory
891

30 RUBBER AND MISCELLANEOUS PLASTICS PRODUCTS

Laminate Shop .... F 740 749-3536
 Waterford (G-19486)
Lintec USA Holding Inc .... G 781 935-7850
 Stow (G-17602)
McHenry Industries Inc .... E 330 799-8930
 Youngstown (G-20968)
Meridian Industries Inc .... D 330 673-1011
 Kent (G-11351)
◆ Meridienne International Inc .... G 330 274-8317
 Mantua (G-12554)
Monarch Engraving Inc .... E 440 638-1500
 Strongsville (G-17766)
▲ Organized Living Inc .... E 513 489-9300
 Cincinnati (G-4118)
Plaskolite LLC .... D 740 450-1109
 Zanesville (G-21168)
Plaskolite LLC .... B 614 294-3281
 Columbus (G-7321)
Plextrusions Inc .... G 330 668-2587
 North Ridgeville (G-15244)
Quality Rubber Stamp Inc .... G 614 235-2700
 Columbus (G-7365)
Raven Industries Inc .... G 937 323-4625
 Springfield (G-17480)
Recto Molded Products Inc .... D 513 871-5544
 Cincinnati (G-4256)
▲ Resinoid Engineering Corp .... G 740 928-6115
 Hebron (G-10759)
◆ Rochling Glastic Composites LP ...... C 216 486-0100
 Cleveland (G-5996)
◆ Rowmark LLC .... F 419 425-8974
 Findlay (G-9748)
Saint-Gobain Prfmce Plas Corp .... C 330 798-6981
 Akron (G-372)
Schneller LLC .... D 330 673-1299
 Kent (G-11381)
Shamrock Plastics Inc .... F 740 392-5555
 Mount Vernon (G-14508)
Shurtape Technologies LLC .... G 440 937-7000
 Avon (G-966)
▲ Snyder Manufacturing Inc .... D 330 343-4456
 Dover (G-8855)
Snyder Manufacturing Co Ltd .... G 330 343-4456
 Dover (G-8856)
Somerset Galleries Inc .... G 614 443-0003
 Columbus (G-7461)
Southern Cabinetry Inc .... E 740 245-5992
 Bidwell (G-1670)
Spartech LLC .... F 419 399-4050
 Paulding (G-15871)
Specialty Adhesive Film Co .... G 513 353-1885
 Cleves (G-6375)
Spring Grove Manufacturing .... F 513 542-0185
 Cincinnati (G-4361)
Techniform Industries Inc .... E 419 332-8484
 Fremont (G-10054)
Trim Systems Operating Corp .... C 614 289-5360
 New Albany (G-14639)
▲ United Converting Inc .... G 614 863-9972
 Columbus (G-7556)
Victory Store Fixtures Inc .... F 740 499-3494
 La Rue (G-11477)
Wurms Woodworking Company .... E 419 492-2184
 New Washington (G-14834)

3084 Plastic Pipe

ADS .... G 419 422-6521
 Findlay (G-9645)
ADS Ventures Inc .... G 614 658-0050
 Hilliard (G-10801)
Advanced Drainage of Ohio Inc .... D 614 658-0050
 Hilliard (G-10802)
Advanced Drainage Systems Inc .... E 740 852-9554
 London (G-12047)
Advanced Drainage Systems Inc .... D 513 863-1384
 Hamilton (G-10529)
Advanced Drainage Systems Inc .... F 419 384-3140
 Pandora (G-15806)
Advanced Drainage Systems Inc .... D 330 264-4949
 Wooster (G-20554)
▼ Advanced Drainage Systems Inc ..... D 614 658-0050
 Hilliard (G-10803)
Advanced Drainage Systems Inc .... E 419 599-9565
 Napoleon (G-14530)
Advanced Drainage Systems Inc .... D 740 852-2980
 London (G-12048)
Advanced Drainage Systems Inc .... E 419 424-8324
 Findlay (G-9648)
Aetna Plastics Corp .... G 330 274-2855
 Mantua (G-12541)

Baughman Tile Company .... D 800 837-3160
 Paulding (G-15856)
Cantex Inc .... D 330 995-3665
 Aurora (G-874)
Contech Engnered Solutions Inc .... F 513 645-7000
 West Chester (G-19680)
Contech Engnered Solutions LLC .... D 513 645-7000
 Middletown (G-13896)
◆ Contech Engnered Solutions LLC ... C 513 645-7000
 West Chester (G-19681)
Drain Products LLC .... G 419 230-4549
 Lakeview (G-11504)
Drainage Products Inc .... E 419 622-6951
 Haviland (G-10709)
Dura-Line Corporation .... E 440 322-1000
 Elyria (G-9245)
◆ Elster Perfection Corporation .... D 440 428-1771
 Geneva (G-10218)
▲ Fowler Products Inc .... F 419 683-4057
 Crestline (G-7794)
◆ Hancor Holding Corporation .... B 419 422-6521
 Findlay (G-9700)
◆ Hancor Inc .... B 614 658-0050
 Hilliard (G-10827)
Hancor Inc .... D 419 424-8222
 Findlay (G-9702)
Hancor Inc .... D 419 424-8225
 Findlay (G-9701)
Harrison Mch & Plastic Corp .... E 330 527-5641
 Garrettsville (G-10191)
Ipex USA LLC .... G 513 942-9910
 Fairfield (G-9511)
Nupco Inc .... G 419 629-2259
 New Bremen (G-14658)
Plas-Tanks Industries Inc .... G 513 942-3800
 Hamilton (G-10596)
Savko Plastic Pipe & Fittings .... F 614 885-8420
 Columbus (G-7422)
Tolloti Pipe LLC .... F 330 364-6627
 New Philadelphia (G-14805)
Tolloti Plastic Pipe Inc .... E 330 364-6627
 New Philadelphia (G-14806)
Tolloti Plastic Pipe Inc .... G 740 922-6911
 Uhrichsville (G-18897)
Utility Solutions Inc .... G 740 369-4300
 Delaware (G-8729)

3085 Plastic Bottles

▲ AI Root Company .... C 330 723-4359
 Medina (G-13219)
AI Root Company .... G 330 725-6677
 Medina (G-13220)
Alpha Packaging Holdings Inc .... B 216 252-5595
 Cleveland (G-4675)
▲ Alpla Inc .... F 419 991-9484
 Lima (G-11960)
Eco-Groupe Inc .... F 937 898-2603
 Dayton (G-8176)
▲ GK Packaging Inc .... D 614 873-3900
 Plain City (G-16194)
Graham Packaging Company LP .... E 419 334-4197
 Fremont (G-10024)
Graham Packaging Company LP .... E 513 874-1770
 West Chester (G-19861)
Graham Packaging Pet Tech Inc .... C 419 334-4197
 Fremont (G-10025)
Graham Packg Plastic Pdts Inc .... C 419 421-8037
 Findlay (G-9695)
Kirtland Cpitl Partners III LP .... G 440 585-9010
 Willoughby Hills (G-20470)
▲ Novatex North America Inc .... D 419 282-4264
 Ashland (G-728)
▲ Phoenix Technologies Intl LLC .... E 419 353-7738
 Bowling Green (G-1990)
Plastipak Packaging Inc .... B 937 596-6142
 Jackson Center (G-11212)
Plastipak Packaging Inc .... C 937 596-5166
 Jackson Center (G-11213)
Plastipak Packaging Inc .... C 740 928-4435
 Hebron (G-10757)
Pure Water Global Inc .... G 419 737-2352
 Pioneer (G-16093)
Quality-Service Products Inc .... F 614 447-9522
 Columbus (G-7367)
Rexam PLC .... G 330 893-2451
 Millersburg (G-14122)
Ring Container Tech LLC .... E 937 492-0961
 Sidney (G-17066)
Southeastern Container Inc .... D 419 352-6300
 Bowling Green (G-2000)

3086 Plastic Foam Prdts

A K Athletic Equipment Inc .... E 614 920-3069
 Canal Winchester (G-2497)
ADS Ventures Inc .... G 614 658-0050
 Hilliard (G-10801)
▼ Advanced Drainage Systems Inc ..... D 614 658-0050
 Hilliard (G-10803)
All Foam Products Co .... G 330 849-3636
 Middlefield (G-13775)
All Foam Products Co .... G 330 849-3636
 Middlefield (G-13776)
Amatech Inc .... E 614 252-2506
 Columbus (G-6579)
American Foam Products Inc .... G 440 352-3434
 Painesville (G-15710)
Aqua Lily Products LLC .... F 951 246-9610
 Willoughby (G-20279)
Archbold Container Corp .... C 800 446-2520
 Archbold (G-637)
Arlington Rack & Packaging Co .... G 419 476-7700
 Toledo (G-18191)
▼ Armaly LLC .... F 740 852-3621
 London (G-12049)
Astro Shapes LLC .... C 330 755-1414
 Struthers (G-17814)
Atlas Roofing Corporation .... C 937 746-9941
 Franklin (G-9870)
Austin Foam Plastics Inc .... E 614 921-0824
 Columbus (G-6632)
B B Bradley Company Inc .... E 440 354-2005
 Painesville (G-15718)
B B Bradley Company Inc .... E 614 777-5600
 Columbus (G-6641)
Concept Manufacturing LLC .... G 812 677-2043
 Johnstown (G-11263)
Creative Foam Dayton Mold .... G 937 279-9987
 Dayton (G-8111)
Cryovac Inc .... F 513 771-7770
 West Chester (G-19689)
Custom Foam Products Inc .... E 937 295-2700
 Fort Loramie (G-9794)
Dayton Molded Urethanes LLC .... D 937 279-9987
 Dayton (G-8139)
Dayton Polymeric Products Inc .... D 937 279-9987
 Dayton (G-8141)
Deufol Worldwide Packaging LLC ...... E 440 232-1100
 Bedford (G-1400)
Dow Chemical Company .... F 937 254-1550
 Dayton (G-8166)
Energy Storage Technologies .... E 937 312-0114
 Dayton (G-8183)
▲ Eps Specialties Ltd Inc .... F 513 489-3676
 Cincinnati (G-3649)
Extol of Ohio Inc .... E 419 668-2072
 Norwalk (G-15392)
Fabricated Packaging Mtls Inc .... G 740 681-1750
 Lancaster (G-11569)
▲ Fabricated Packaging Mtls Inc .... F 740 654-3492
 Lancaster (G-11570)
Foam Concepts & Design Inc .... F 513 860-5589
 West Chester (G-19706)
Gdc Inc .... F 574 533-3128
 Wooster (G-20596)
▲ Greif Packaging LLC .... D 740 549-6000
 Delaware (G-8688)
▲ Hfi LLC .... B 614 491-0700
 Columbus (G-6995)
Hitti Enterprises Inc .... F 440 243-4100
 Cleveland (G-5410)
▲ ICP Adhesives and Sealants Inc .... F 330 753-4585
 Norton (G-15369)
Interior Dnnage Spcialites Inc .... F 614 291-0900
 Columbus (G-7042)
ISO Technologies Inc .... G 740 928-0084
 Heath (G-10722)
▲ IVEX Protective Packaging Inc ...... E 937 498-9298
 Sidney (G-17046)
J P Industrial Products Inc .... E 330 424-3388
 Lisbon (G-11973)
▲ Jain America Foods Inc .... G 614 850-9400
 Columbus (G-7058)
◆ Jain America Holdings Inc .... D 614 850-9400
 Columbus (G-7059)
Jason Incorporated .... D 419 668-4474
 Milan (G-13985)
▲ Johnsonite Inc .... B 440 632-3441
 Middlefield (G-13811)
M L B Molded Urethane Pdts LLC ..... G 419 825-9140
 Swanton (G-17916)

SIC SECTION

30 RUBBER AND MISCELLANEOUS PLASTICS PRODUCTS

Myers Industries Inc ....E 330 253-5592
  Akron *(G-292)*
◆ Ohio Decorative Products LLC ....C 419 647-9033
  Spencerville *(G-17311)*
Ohio Foam Corporation ....G 419 563-0399
  Bucyrus *(G-2341)*
Ohio Foam Corporation ....G 614 252-4877
  Columbus *(G-7248)*
Orbis Corporation ....D 262 560-5000
  Perrysburg *(G-15994)*
Owens Corning Sales LLC ....G 330 634-0460
  Tallmadge *(G-17998)*
Palpac Industries Inc ....F 419 523-3230
  Ottawa *(G-15661)*
Paragon Custom Plastics Inc ....E 419 636-6060
  Bryan *(G-2304)*
Paratus Supply Inc ....G 330 745-3600
  Barberton *(G-1093)*
Plastic Forming Company Inc ....E 330 830-5167
  Massillon *(G-13039)*
Plastic Works Inc ....F 440 331-5575
  Cleveland *(G-5887)*
Plymouth Foam LLC ....E 740 254-1188
  Gnadenhutten *(G-10282)*
Polycel Incorporated ....G 614 252-2400
  Columbus *(G-7331)*
Precision Foam Fabrication Inc ....F 330 270-2440
  Youngstown *(G-21003)*
Prime Industries Inc ....E 440 288-3626
  Lorain *(G-12113)*
▲ S & A Industries Corporation ....D 330 733-6040
  Akron *(G-364)*
Sash Foam Works Inc ....E 419 522-4074
  Mansfield *(G-12511)*
▲ Scott Port-A-Fold Inc ....E 419 748-8880
  Napoleon *(G-14561)*
▲ Scottdel Cushion LLC ....E 419 825-0432
  Swanton *(G-17921)*
Skybox Packaging LLC ....E 419 525-7209
  Mansfield *(G-12515)*
▼ Smithers-Oasis Company ....F 330 945-5100
  Kent *(G-11386)*
Smithers-Oasis Company ....F 330 673-5831
  Kent *(G-11387)*
Solo Products Inc ....F 513 321-7884
  Cincinnati *(G-4352)*
Sonoco Prtective Solutions Inc ....G 419 420-0029
  Findlay *(G-9759)*
Special Design Products Inc ....E 614 272-6700
  Columbus *(G-7466)*
▲ Storopack Inc ....E 513 874-0314
  West Chester *(G-19904)*
Surface Dynamics Inc ....F 513 772-6635
  Cincinnati *(G-4399)*
▲ Team Wendy LLC ....D 216 738-2518
  Cleveland *(G-6151)*
Technifab Inc ....E 440 934-8324
  Avon *(G-968)*
Technifab Inc ....D 440 934-8324
  Avon *(G-969)*
◆ Technifab Inc ....E 440 934-8324
  Avon *(G-970)*
▲ Thermal Visions Inc ....G 740 587-4025
  Granville *(G-10339)*
Toy & Sport Trends Inc ....E 419 748-8880
  Napoleon *(G-14562)*
Trans Foam Inc ....G 330 630-9444
  Tallmadge *(G-18009)*
Truechoicepack Corp ....E 937 630-3832
  Mason *(G-12951)*
Unique-Chardan Inc ....E 419 636-6900
  Bryan *(G-2311)*
US Foam Corporation ....G 513 528-9800
  Cincinnati *(G-4456)*
Zebco Industries Inc ....F 740 654-4510
  Lancaster *(G-11620)*
Zing Pac Inc ....G 440 248-7997
  Cleveland *(G-6342)*

3087 Custom Compounding Of Purchased Plastic Resins

▲ Accel Corporation ....D 440 934-7711
  Avon *(G-938)*
Advanced Composites Inc ....G 937 575-9814
  Sidney *(G-17012)*
▲ Advanced Composites Inc ....G 937 575-9800
  Sidney *(G-17013)*
◆ Aurora Plastics LLC ....D 330 422-0700
  Streetsboro *(G-17662)*
▲ Chemionics Corporation ....E 330 733-8834
  Tallmadge *(G-17975)*
▲ Chromaflo Technologies Corp ....G 440 997-0081
  Ashtabula *(G-764)*
Chromaflo Technologies Corp ....C 513 733-5111
  Cincinnati *(G-3474)*
Deltech Polymers Corporation ....G 937 339-3150
  Troy *(G-18648)*
Dyneon LLC ....E 859 334-4500
  Cincinnati *(G-3614)*
Flex Technologies Inc ....G 330 897-6311
  Baltic *(G-1029)*
Freeman Manufacturing & Sup Co ....E 440 934-1902
  Avon *(G-950)*
General Color Investments Inc ....D 330 868-4161
  Minerva *(G-14180)*
Hexpol Compounding LLC ....E 440 834-4644
  Burton *(G-2360)*
▲ Hexpol Compounding LLC ....E 440 834-4644
  Burton *(G-2361)*
Hexpol Holding Inc ....F 440 834-4644
  Burton *(G-2362)*
Killian Latex Inc ....F 330 644-6746
  Akron *(G-236)*
McCann Plastics Inc ....E 330 499-1515
  Canton *(G-2750)*
▼ Nanosperse LLC ....E 937 296-5030
  Kettering *(G-11435)*
Omnova Solutions Inc ....C 330 628-6550
  Mogadore *(G-14246)*
Polymera Inc ....E 740 527-2069
  Hebron *(G-10758)*
Polymers By Design LLC ....E 937 361-7398
  Troy *(G-18693)*
Polyone Corporation ....C 419 668-4844
  Norwalk *(G-15412)*
◆ Polyone Corporation ....D 440 930-1000
  Avon Lake *(G-1001)*
Polyone Corporation ....D 440 930-1000
  North Baltimore *(G-15047)*
▲ Radici Plastics Usa Inc ....D 330 336-7611
  Wadsworth *(G-19271)*
Rutland Plastic Tech Inc ....G 614 846-3055
  Columbus *(G-7407)*
Sherwin-Williams Company ....C 330 830-6000
  Massillon *(G-13048)*
Thermafab Alloy Inc ....E 216 861-0540
  Olmsted Falls *(G-15531)*
Tymex Plastics Inc ....E 216 429-8950
  Cleveland *(G-6226)*

3088 Plastic Plumbing Fixtures

Add-A-Trap LLC ....G 330 750-0417
  Struthers *(G-17812)*
Bobbart Industries Inc ....E 419 350-5477
  Sylvania *(G-17934)*
Certified Walk In Tubs ....F 614 436-4848
  Columbus *(G-6756)*
Cfrc Wtr & Enrgy Solutions Inc ....G 216 479-0290
  Cleveland *(G-4906)*
▲ Cincinnati Machines Inc ....A 513 536-2432
  Batavia *(G-1130)*
Closets By Mike ....G 740 607-2212
  Zanesville *(G-21120)*
Cultured Marble Inc ....G 330 549-2282
  North Lima *(G-15169)*
▲ Dbhl Inc ....F 216 267-7100
  Cleveland *(G-5076)*
◆ E L Mustee & Sons Inc ....D 216 267-3100
  Brookpark *(G-2145)*
◆ Hancor Inc ....B 614 658-0050
  Hilliard *(G-10827)*
◆ Lubrizol Global Management ....F 216 447-5000
  Brecksville *(G-2048)*
Mansfield Plumbing Pdts LLC ....E 330 496-2301
  Big Prairie *(G-1675)*
◆ Mansfield Plumbing Pdts LLC ....A 419 938-5211
  Perrysville *(G-16030)*
Marble Arch Products Inc ....F 937 746-8388
  Franklin *(G-9897)*
Meese Inc ....D 440 998-1202
  Ashtabula *(G-785)*
Nibco Inc ....E 513 228-1426
  Lebanon *(G-11676)*
Pro-Kleen Industrial Svcs Inc ....E 740 689-1886
  Lancaster *(G-11599)*
Righter Plumbing ....G 614 604-7197
  Pataskala *(G-15840)*
Safeway Safety Step LLC ....F 513 942-7837
  West Chester *(G-19791)*
Tower Industries Ltd ....E 330 837-2216
  Massillon *(G-13054)*

3089 Plastic Prdts

1 888 U Pitch It ....G 440 796-9028
  Mentor *(G-13368)*
20/20 Custom Molded Plast ....D 419 485-2020
  Montpelier *(G-14300)*
6s Products LLC ....G 937 394-7440
  Anna *(G-587)*
7 Rowe Court Properties LLC ....G 513 874-7236
  Hamilton *(G-10526)*
A & A Discount Tire ....G 330 863-1936
  Carrollton *(G-2914)*
A Aabaco Plastics Inc ....F 216 663-9494
  Cleveland *(G-4583)*
A C Shutters Inc ....G 216 429-2424
  Cleveland *(G-4584)*
AB Plastics Inc ....G 513 576-6333
  Milford *(G-13992)*
ABC Plastics Inc ....E 330 948-3322
  Lodi *(G-12002)*
Acco Brands USA LLC ....A 937 495-6323
  Kettering *(G-11426)*
Accurate Plastics LLC ....F 330 346-0048
  Kent *(G-11288)*
Accutech Plastic Molding Inc ....G 937 233-0017
  Dayton *(G-8004)*
Achill Island Composites LLC ....G 440 838-1746
  Brecksville *(G-2019)*
◆ Aco Polymer Products Inc ....E 440 285-7000
  Mentor *(G-13373)*
Acrylic Arts ....G 440 537-0300
  West Farmington *(G-19918)*
Advanced Plastic Systems Inc ....F 614 759-6550
  Gahanna *(G-10073)*
Advanced Plastics Inc ....F 330 336-6681
  Wadsworth *(G-19222)*
Advantage Mold Inc ....G 419 691-5676
  Toledo *(G-18158)*
Aerocase Incorporated ....F 440 617-9294
  Westlake *(G-20088)*
Aetna Plastics Corp ....G 330 274-2855
  Mantua *(G-12541)*
▲ Akron Polymer Products Inc ....D 330 628-5551
  Akron *(G-48)*
▲ Akron Porcelain & Plastics Co ....C 330 745-2159
  Akron *(G-49)*
All Around Garage Door Inc ....G 440 759-5079
  North Ridgeville *(G-15207)*
All Srvice Plastic Molding Inc ....E 937 415-3674
  Fairborn *(G-9451)*
All Srvice Plastic Molding Inc ....G 937 890-0322
  Vandalia *(G-19114)*
▲ All Srvice Plastic Molding Inc ....C 937 890-0322
  Vandalia *(G-19115)*
▲ Alliance Equipment Company Inc ...F 330 821-2291
  Alliance *(G-453)*
Allied Custom Molded Products ....G 614 291-0629
  Columbus *(G-6571)*
◆ Allied Moulded Products Inc ....C 419 636-4217
  Bryan *(G-2259)*
Allied Moulded Products Inc ....G 419 636-4217
  Bryan *(G-2260)*
Allied Moulded Products Inc ....G 419 636-4217
  Bryan *(G-2261)*
Allied Plastic Co Inc ....G 419 389-1688
  Toledo *(G-18165)*
Alpha Omega Import Export LLC .....G 740 885-9155
  Marietta *(G-12602)*
Alpha Packaging Holdings Inc ....B 216 252-5595
  Cleveland *(G-4675)*
◆ Alsco Metals Corporation ....E 740 983-2571
  Dennison *(G-8781)*
Amclo Group Inc ....C 216 791-8400
  North Royalton *(G-15259)*
Amcor Rigid Plastics Usa LLC ....D 419 483-4343
  Bellevue *(G-1527)*
Amcor Rigid Plastics Usa LLC ....E 419 592-1998
  Napoleon *(G-14531)*
▲ AMD Plastics LLC ....F 216 289-4862
  Euclid *(G-9401)*
Amelia Plastics ....G 513 386-4926
  Amelia *(G-530)*
American Mobile Fitness LLC ....G 419 351-1381
  Toledo *(G-18177)*
American Molded Plastics Inc ....F 330 872-3838
  Newton Falls *(G-14984)*
American Molding Company Inc .....G 330 620-6799
  Barberton *(G-1051)*

Employee Codes: A=Over 500 employees, B=251-500
C=101-250, D=51-100, E=20-50, F=10-19, G=3-9

30 RUBBER AND MISCELLANEOUS PLASTICS PRODUCTS SIC SECTION

▲ **American Plastic Tech Inc** ....C....... 440 632-5203
Middlefield *(G-13777)*
▼ **American Way Manufacturing Inc** .....E....... 330 824-2353
Warren *(G-19369)*
Ames Lock Specialties Inc ....G....... 419 474-2995
Toledo *(G-18183)*
Ametek Inc ....C....... 419 739-3202
Wapakoneta *(G-19320)*
Ampacet Corporation ....E....... 513 247-5400
Cincinnati *(G-3343)*
Amrex Inc ....G....... 330 678-7050
Kent *(G-11295)*
AMS Global Ltd ....F....... 937 620-1036
West Alexandria *(G-19616)*
◆ **Anchor Hocking LLC** ....A....... 740 681-6478
Lancaster *(G-11541)*
Anchor Hocking LLC ....G....... 740 687-2500
Lancaster *(G-11542)*
Apollo Plastics Inc ....F....... 440 951-7774
Mentor *(G-13391)*
▼ **Armaly LLC** ....E....... 740 852-3621
London *(G-12049)*
Armeton US Co ....F....... 419 660-9296
Norwalk *(G-15381)*
Arthur Corporation ....D....... 419 433-7202
Huron *(G-11089)*
Artisan Mold Co Inc ....G....... 440 926-4511
Grafton *(G-10292)*
Aspec Inc ....G....... 513 561-9922
Cincinnati *(G-3363)*
▲ **Associated Materials LLC** ....B....... 330 929-1811
Cuyahoga Falls *(G-7841)*
Associated Materials Group Inc ....E....... 330 929-1811
Cuyahoga Falls *(G-7842)*
Associated Mtls Holdings LLC ....A....... 330 929-1811
Cuyahoga Falls *(G-7843)*
▲ **Associated Plastics Corp** ....D....... 419 634-3910
Ada *(G-5)*
▲ **Atc Group Inc** ....D....... 440 293-4064
Andover *(G-579)*
Atc Nymold Corporation ....G....... 440 293-4064
Andover *(G-581)*
Atc Nymold Corporation ....G....... 440 293-4064
Andover *(G-582)*
Auld Company ....E....... 614 454-1010
Columbus *(G-6629)*
Automation Plastics Corp ....D....... 330 562-5148
Aurora *(G-871)*
Axion Strl Innovations LLC ....F....... 740 452-2500
Zanesville *(G-21100)*
▲ **B & B Molded Products Inc** ....E....... 419 592-8700
Defiance *(G-8614)*
Bakelite N Sumitomo Amer Inc ....G....... 419 675-1282
Kenton *(G-11403)*
Baker Plastics Inc ....G....... 330 743-3142
Youngstown *(G-20851)*
▲ **Baldie Corporation** ....G....... 513 503-0953
Cincinnati *(G-3378)*
◆ **Ball Bounce and Sport Inc** ....B....... 419 289-9310
Ashland *(G-682)*
Ball Corp ....G....... 419 483-4343
Bellevue *(G-1530)*
Bc Investment Corporation ....G....... 330 262-3070
Wooster *(G-20570)*
Beach Mfg Plastic Molding Div ....D....... 937 882-6400
New Carlisle *(G-14663)*
Beast Carbon Corporation ....G....... 800 909-9051
Cincinnati *(G-3384)*
Bell Binders LLC ....F....... 419 242-3201
Toledo *(G-18200)*
Bena Inc ....G....... 419 299-3313
Van Buren *(G-19071)*
Bennett Plastics Inc ....E....... 740 432-2209
Cambridge *(G-2427)*
Berlekamp Plastics Inc ....F....... 419 334-4481
Fremont *(G-9998)*
Berry Global Inc ....F....... 419 887-1602
Maumee *(G-13080)*
Berry Global Inc ....F....... 330 896-6700
Streetsboro *(G-17664)*
Bisson Custom Plastic ....G....... 937 653-4966
Urbana *(G-18979)*
Bkhn Inc ....D....... 513 831-4402
Milford *(G-13998)*
Blackthorn LLC ....F....... 937 836-9296
Clayton *(G-4572)*
Bloom Industries Inc ....D....... 330 898-3878
Warren *(G-19377)*
Boardman Molded Intl LLC ....C....... 330 788-2400
Youngstown *(G-20853)*

▲ **Boardman Molded Products Inc** ......D....... 330 788-2400
Youngstown *(G-20854)*
▲ **Bprex Halthcare Brookville Inc** ....C....... 847 541-9700
Perrysburg *(G-15924)*
Bprex Plastic Packaging Inc ....F....... 419 247-5000
Toledo *(G-18213)*
Brighteye Innovations LLC ....F....... 800 573-0052
Akron *(G-96)*
Brown Company of Findlay Ltd ....E....... 419 425-3002
Findlay *(G-9663)*
Bta Enterprises Inc ....E....... 937 277-0881
Dayton *(G-8067)*
Bu E Comp Inc ....G....... 419 284-3381
Bloomville *(G-1712)*
Buckeye Design & Engr Svc LLC ....G....... 419 375-4241
Fort Recovery *(G-9812)*
Buckeye Stamping Company ....D....... 614 445-0059
Columbus *(G-6712)*
◆ **Buckhorn Inc** ....E....... 513 831-4402
Milford *(G-14000)*
▼ **Buckhorn Material Hdlg Group** ....D....... 513 831-4402
Milford *(G-14001)*
Budd Co Plastics Div ....G....... 419 238-4332
Van Wert *(G-19081)*
Buecomp Inc ....E....... 419 284-3840
Bloomville *(G-1713)*
Bugh Vinyl Products Inc ....G....... 330 305-0978
Canton *(G-2601)*
Builder Tech Wholesale LLC ....G....... 419 535-7606
Toledo *(G-18219)*
▲ **C A Joseph Co** ....G....... 330 385-6869
East Liverpool *(G-9051)*
C B & S Spouting Inc ....G....... 937 866-1600
Miamisburg *(G-13646)*
Cantex Inc ....D....... 330 995-3665
Aurora *(G-874)*
Caraustar Industries Inc ....E....... 330 665-7700
Copley *(G-7679)*
Cardinal Products Inc ....G....... 440 237-8280
North Royalton *(G-15265)*
Carlisle Plastics Company Inc ....G....... 937 845-9411
New Carlisle *(G-14664)*
▲ **Carney Plastics Inc** ....G....... 330 746-8273
Youngstown *(G-20866)*
Carson Industries LLC ....G....... 419 592-2309
Napoleon *(G-14535)*
▲ **Cell-O-Core Co** ....E....... 330 239-4370
Sharon Center *(G-16948)*
Centrex Plastics LLC ....C....... 419 423-1213
Findlay *(G-9666)*
Century Container LLC ....E....... 330 457-2367
New Waterford *(G-14837)*
Century Container LLC ....G....... 330 457-2367
Columbiana *(G-6457)*
Century Mold Company Inc ....D....... 513 539-9283
Middletown *(G-13891)*
Cep Holdings LLC ....G....... 330 665-2900
Fairlawn *(G-9600)*
▲ **Champion Opco LLC** ....B....... 513 327-7338
Cincinnati *(G-3463)*
Chatelain Plastics Inc ....G....... 419 422-4323
Findlay *(G-9667)*
Checkpoint Systems Inc ....C....... 330 456-7776
Canton *(G-2622)*
Chemigon LLC ....G....... 330 592-1875
Akron *(G-113)*
Chica Bands LLC ....G....... 513 871-4300
Cincinnati *(G-3470)*
Chuck Meadors Plastics Co ....F....... 440 813-4466
Jefferson *(G-11227)*
▲ **CK Technologies LLC** ....B....... 419 485-1110
Montpelier *(G-14305)*
Claflin Company Inc ....G....... 330 650-0582
Hudson *(G-11036)*
Clark Prfmce Fabrication LLC ....G....... 701 721-1378
Dayton *(G-8093)*
Clark Rbr Plastic Intl Sls Inc ....D....... 440 255-9793
Mentor *(G-13413)*
Classic Laminations Inc ....E....... 440 735-1333
Cleveland *(G-4939)*
Clear Fold Door Inc ....G....... 440 735-1351
Cleveland *(G-4942)*
Clear One LLC ....G....... 800 279-3724
Columbus *(G-6772)*
▲ **Clearsonic Manufacturing Inc** ....G....... 828 772-9809
Hudson *(G-11037)*
Cleveland Plastic Fabricat ....F....... 216 797-7300
Euclid *(G-9409)*
Cleveland Specialty Pdts Inc ....E....... 216 281-8300
Cleveland *(G-4977)*

◆ **CM Paula Company** ....E....... 513 759-7473
Mason *(G-12849)*
◆ **Cobra Plastics Inc** ....D....... 330 425-3669
Macedonia *(G-12284)*
▲ **Comdess Company Inc** ....F....... 330 769-2094
Seville *(G-16914)*
▼ **Comfort Line Ltd** ....D....... 419 729-8520
Toledo *(G-18236)*
Composite Technologies Co LLC ....D....... 937 228-2880
Dayton *(G-8101)*
Consolidated Container Co ....G....... 330 394-0905
Warren *(G-19389)*
Continental Strl Plas Inc ....C....... 440 945-4800
Conneaut *(G-7644)*
Continental Strl Plas Inc ....B....... 419 396-1980
Carey *(G-2880)*
Continental Strl Plas Inc ....C....... 419 257-2231
North Baltimore *(G-15043)*
Continental Strl Plas Inc ....B....... 419 238-4628
Van Wert *(G-19082)*
Converge Group Inc ....F....... 419 281-0000
Ashland *(G-698)*
Core Composites Cincinnati LLC ....E....... 513 724-6111
Batavia *(G-1133)*
Core Molding Technologies Inc ....B....... 614 870-5000
Columbus *(G-6820)*
Corvac Composites LLC ....F....... 248 807-0969
Greenfield *(G-10347)*
Cosmo Corporation ....D....... 330 359-5429
Wilmot *(G-20514)*
Country Molding ....G....... 440 564-5235
Newbury *(G-14948)*
▲ **CP Technologies Company** ....E....... 614 866-9200
Blacklick *(G-1682)*
Cpca Manufacturing LLC ....D....... 937 723-9031
Dayton *(G-8109)*
Cpg International LLC ....B....... 937 655-8766
Wilmington *(G-20492)*
Creative Plastics Intl ....F....... 937 596-6769
Jackson Center *(G-11206)*
▲ **Crg Plastics Inc** ....F....... 937 298-2025
Dayton *(G-8113)*
Crown Cork & Seal Usa Inc ....D....... 740 681-3000
Lancaster *(G-11560)*
Ctc Plastics ....B....... 937 228-9184
Dayton *(G-8116)*
▲ **Custom Molded Products LLC** ....D....... 937 382-1070
Wilmington *(G-20493)*
Custom Pultrusions Inc ....E....... 330 562-5201
Aurora *(G-876)*
Customized Vinyl Sales ....G....... 330 518-3238
East Palestine *(G-9072)*
D & D Plastics Inc ....F....... 330 376-0668
Akron *(G-131)*
D J Metro Mold & Die Inc ....G....... 440 237-1130
North Royalton *(G-15268)*
D K Manufacturing ....D....... 740 654-5566
Lancaster *(G-11562)*
D M Tool & Plastics Inc ....F....... 937 962-4140
Brookville *(G-2166)*
D M Tool & Plastics Inc ....F....... 937 962-4140
Lewisburg *(G-11790)*
D Martone Industries Inc ....E....... 440 632-5800
Middlefield *(G-13790)*
Dadco Inc ....F....... 513 489-2244
Cincinnati *(G-3573)*
Dadco Inc ....F....... 513 489-2244
Cincinnati *(G-3572)*
Daddy Katz LLC ....G....... 937 296-0347
Moraine *(G-14341)*
Dak Enterprises Inc ....C....... 740 828-3291
Marysville *(G-12780)*
David Wolfe Design Inc ....F....... 330 633-6124
Akron *(G-134)*
▲ **Dawn Enterprises Inc** ....E....... 216 642-5506
Cleveland *(G-5072)*
◆ **Dayton Superior Corporation** ....C....... 937 866-0711
Miamisburg *(G-13655)*
Deflecto LLC ....E....... 330 602-0840
Dover *(G-8815)*
▲ **Deimling/Jeliho Plastics Inc** ....D....... 513 752-6653
Amelia *(G-536)*
▲ **Design Molded Plastics Inc** ....C....... 330 963-4400
Macedonia *(G-12288)*
◆ **Dester Corporation** ....F....... 419 362-8020
Lima *(G-11854)*
Dester Corporation ....F....... 419 362-8020
Lima *(G-11855)*
Diamond Plastics Inc ....D....... 419 759-3838
Dunkirk *(G-9034)*

30 RUBBER AND MISCELLANEOUS PLASTICS PRODUCTS

▲ Dimcgray Corporation .... D 937 433-7600
  Centerville (G-3001)
◆ Dimex LLC .... C 740 374-3100
  Marietta (G-12619)
▲ Dinesol Plastics Inc .... C 330 544-7171
  Niles (G-15005)
Diskin Enterprises LLC .... E 330 527-4308
  Garrettsville (G-10187)
Diversity-Vuteq LLC .... G 614 490-5034
  Gahanna (G-10080)
◆ DJM Plastics Ltd .... F 419 424-5250
  Findlay (G-9679)
DK Manfcturing Frazeysburg Inc ...... C 740 828-3291
  Frazeysburg (G-9938)
DK Manufacturing Lancaster Inc ...... D 740 654-5566
  Lancaster (G-11568)
Dlhbowles Inc .... E 330 479-7595
  Canton (G-2663)
Dlhbowles Inc .... D 330 488-0716
  East Canton (G-9039)
◆ Dlhbowles Inc .... B 330 478-2503
  Canton (G-2661)
Doglok Inc .... G 440 223-1836
  Perry (G-15904)
▲ Dometic Sanitation Corporation ... D 330 439-5550
  Big Prairie (G-1673)
Don-Ell Corporation .... C 419 841-7114
  Sylvania (G-17937)
Don-Ell Corporation .... E 419 841-7114
  Sylvania (G-17936)
Dover High Prfmce Plas Inc .... C 330 343-3477
  Dover (G-8821)
Doyle Manufacturing Inc .... D 419 865-2548
  Holland (G-10926)
▲ Dreco Inc .... C 440 327-6021
  North Ridgeville (G-15221)
Drs Industries Inc .... D 419 861-0334
  Holland (G-10928)
Drummond Corp .... F 440 834-9660
  Middlefield (G-13794)
Dublin Plastics Inc .... G 216 641-5904
  Cleveland (G-5115)
Duo-Corp .... E 330 549-2149
  North Lima (G-15170)
Dyna Vac Plastics Inc .... G 937 773-0092
  Piqua (G-16112)
Dynamic Plastics Inc .... G 937 437-7261
  New Paris (G-14753)
Eaton Corporation .... C 330 274-0743
  Aurora (G-877)
Eckel Industries Inc .... E 978 772-0480
  West Chester (G-19850)
Eclipse Blind Systems Inc .... C 330 296-0112
  Ravenna (G-16378)
▲ Edge Plastics Inc .... C 419 522-6696
  Mansfield (G-12435)
Eger Products Inc .... E 513 735-1400
  Batavia (G-1139)
Electr-Gnral Plas Corp Clumbus ...... G 614 871-2915
  Grove City (G-10429)
Electro-Cap International Inc .... F 937 456-6099
  Eaton (G-9148)
Eliason Corporation .... C 800 828-3655
  West Chester (G-19851)
Elra Industries Inc .... G 513 868-6228
  Hamilton (G-10554)
◆ Elster Perfection Corporation .... D 440 428-1171
  Geneva (G-10218)
▲ Encore Industries Inc .... C 419 626-8000
  Sandusky (G-16807)
Encore Plastics Corporation .... D 740 432-1652
  Cambridge (G-2436)
◆ Encore Plastics Corporation .... C 419 626-8000
  Sandusky (G-16808)
Endura Plastics Inc .... D 440 951-4466
  Kirtland (G-11467)
Engineered Profiles LLC .... C 614 754-3700
  Columbus (G-6896)
Enginred Plstic Components Inc ...... C 513 228-0298
  Lebanon (G-11650)
◆ Enpac LLC .... E 440 975-0070
  Eastlake (G-9108)
▼ Enpress LLC .... E 440 510-0108
  Eastlake (G-9109)
▲ Enterprise Plastics Inc .... E 330 346-0496
  Kent (G-11320)
▲ Environmental Sampling Sup Inc E 330 497-9396
  North Canton (G-15080)
Erie Lake Plastic Inc .... F 440 333-4880
  Cleveland (G-5189)

▲ Ernie Green Industries Inc .... G 614 219-1423
  Columbus (G-6903)
Evans Industries Inc .... F 330 453-1122
  Canton (G-2669)
Extrudex Limited Partnership .... E 440 352-7101
  Painesville (G-15737)
Fabohio Inc .... E 740 922-4233
  Uhrichsville (G-18886)
Fastformingcom LLC .... F 330 927-3277
  Rittman (G-16520)
Fci Inc .... D 216 251-5200
  Cleveland (G-5224)
Fdi Enterprises .... E 440 269-8282
  Cleveland (G-5226)
Felicity Plastics Machinery .... E 513 876-7003
  Felicity (G-9643)
▲ Ferriot Inc .... C 330 786-3000
  Akron (G-169)
▲ Few Atmtive GL Applcations Inc . G 234 249-1880
  Wooster (G-20591)
Fft Sidney LLC .... G 937 492-2709
  Sidney (G-17040)
Fiber-Tech Industries Inc .... D 740 335-9400
  Wshngtn CT Hs (G-20725)
Fiberglass Technology Inds Inc .... G 740 335-9400
  Wshngtn CT Hs (G-20726)
Fibertech Networks .... G 614 436-3565
  Worthington (G-20685)
▲ Fibreboard Corporation .... C 419 248-8000
  Toledo (G-18294)
▲ First Choice Packaging Inc .... C 419 333-4100
  Fremont (G-10014)
Flambeau Inc .... D 440 632-6131
  Middlefield (G-13799)
Flambeau Inc .... G 330 239-0202
  Sharon Center (G-16950)
Flex Technologies Inc .... D 330 359-5415
  Mount Eaton (G-14420)
Florida Production Engrg Inc .... C 740 420-5252
  Circleville (G-4545)
Formtech Enterprises Inc .... E 330 688-2171
  Stow (G-17589)
▼ Foundation Industries Inc .... D 330 564-1250
  Akron (G-176)
Fountain Specialists Inc .... C 513 831-5717
  Milford (G-14009)
▲ Fowler Products Inc .... F 419 683-4057
  Crestline (G-7794)
▼ Fox Lite Inc .... E 937 864-1966
  Fairborn (G-9459)
Frantz Medical Development Ltd .... C 440 255-1155
  Mentor (G-13447)
▲ Fukuvi Usa Inc .... D 937 236-7288
  Dayton (G-8210)
▲ Fypon Ltd .... C 800 446-3040
  Maumee (G-13112)
G & J Extrusions Inc .... G 330 753-0162
  New Franklin (G-14690)
G I Plastek Inc .... G 440 230-1942
  Westlake (G-20116)
▲ G M R Technology Inc .... E 440 992-6003
  Ashtabula (G-777)
G S K Inc .... G 937 547-1611
  Greenville (G-10371)
Gad-Jets Inc .... G 937 274-2111
  Franklin (G-9885)
Garner Industries Inc .... E 740 349-0238
  Newark (G-14878)
▼ Gateway Industrial Pdts Inc .... F 440 324-4112
  Elyria (G-9263)
Genesis Plastic Tech LLC .... D 440 542-0722
  Solon (G-17148)
Genpak LLC .... E 614 276-5156
  Columbus (G-6947)
▲ Gentek Building Products Inc ..... F 800 548-4542
  Cuyahoga Falls (G-7872)
▼ Ghp II LLC .... C 740 687-2500
  Lancaster (G-11575)
Giesecke & Devrient Can .... G 330 425-1515
  Twinsburg (G-18786)
Gilkey Window Company Inc .... E 513 769-9663
  Cincinnati (G-3751)
▲ Gilkey Window Company Inc ..... D 513 769-4527
  Cincinnati (G-3752)
Gorell Enterprises Inc .... B 724 465-1800
  Streetsboro (G-17675)
Graham Packaging Co Europe LLC C 513 398-5000
  Mason (G-12882)
Graham Packaging Company LP .... E 740 439-4242
  Cambridge (G-2441)

Graham Packaging Company LP .... E 513 874-1770
  West Chester (G-19861)
Graham Packaging Company LP .... E 419 334-4197
  Fremont (G-10024)
Graham Packg Plastic Pdts Inc .... E 717 849-8500
  Toledo (G-18310)
Granger Plastic Company .... E 513 424-1955
  Middletown (G-13910)
Great Lakes McHy & Automtn LLC . G 419 208-2004
  Fremont (G-10026)
Great Lakes Window Inc .... A 419 666-5555
  Walbridge (G-19294)
Greenlight Optics LLC .... E 513 247-9777
  Loveland (G-12193)
Greenville Technology Inc .... G 937 642-6744
  Marysville (G-12785)
▲ Greenville Technology Inc .... A 937 548-3217
  Greenville (G-10374)
◆ Greif Inc .... E 740 549-6000
  Delaware (G-8681)
Greif Inc .... E 740 657-6500
  Delaware (G-8682)
H & H Engineered Molded Pdts ...... D 440 415-1814
  Geneva (G-10220)
H P Manufacturing Co .... D 216 361-6500
  Cleveland (G-5363)
▲ Hadlock Plastics LLC .... C 440 466-4876
  Geneva (G-10221)
Hamilton Custom Molding Inc .... G 513 844-6643
  Hamilton (G-10568)
Hancor Inc .... D 419 424-8225
  Findlay (G-9701)
◆ Hancor Inc .... B 614 658-0050
  Hilliard (G-10827)
Hanlon Industries Inc .... F 216 261-7056
  Cleveland (G-5371)
Harbor Industrial Corp .... F 440 599-8366
  Conneaut (G-7647)
▲ Harmony Systems and Svc Inc .. D 937 778-1082
  Piqua (G-16121)
Harrison Mch & Plastic Corp .... E 330 527-5641
  Garrettsville (G-10191)
Hartville Plastics Inc .... G 330 877-9090
  Hartville (G-10694)
Hathaway Stamp Co .... F 513 621-1052
  Cincinnati (G-3803)
▼ Haviland Plastic Products Co ..... E 419 622-3110
  Haviland (G-10712)
Hematite Inc .... G 937 540-9889
  Englewood (G-9362)
Hendrickson International Corp ...... D 740 929-5600
  Hebron (G-10747)
HI Lite Plastic Products .... G 614 235-9050
  Columbus (G-6996)
HI Tek Mold .... G 440 942-4090
  Mentor (G-13465)
Hi-Tech Extrusions Ltd .... E 440 286-4000
  Chardon (G-3116)
High Tech Molding & Design Inc .... G 330 726-1676
  Youngstown (G-20930)
Hinkle Manufacturing LLC .... F 313 584-0400
  Perrysburg (G-15962)
Hkb Enterprises Inc .... G 330 733-3200
  Akron (G-208)
Holm Industries Inc .... G 330 562-2900
  Aurora (G-883)
▲ Horsemens Pride Inc .... E 800 232-7950
  Streetsboro (G-17677)
HP Manufacturing Company Inc ..... D 216 361-6500
  Cleveland (G-5421)
Hrh Door Corp .... D 440 593-5226
  Conneaut (G-7649)
Hub Plastics Inc .... D 614 861-1791
  Blacklick (G-1686)
Hudson Extrusions Inc .... D 330 653-6015
  Hudson (G-11053)
Huhtamaki Inc .... B 937 987-3078
  New Vienna (G-14824)
Hydrant Hat LLC .... G 440 224-1007
  Kingsville (G-11459)
ICO Mold LLC .... G 419 867-3900
  Holland (G-10934)
ICO Technology Inc .... G 330 666-3751
  Fairlawn (G-9610)
Ieg Plastics LLC .... F 937 565-4211
  Bellefontaine (G-1519)
Illinois Tool Works Inc .... D 937 332-2839
  Troy (G-18674)
Illinois Tool Works Inc .... E 419 633-3236
  Bryan (G-2287)

Employee Codes: A=Over 500 employees, B=251-500
C=101-250, D=51-100, E=20-50, F=10-19, G=3-9

30 RUBBER AND MISCELLANEOUS PLASTICS PRODUCTS SIC SECTION

Illinois Tool Works Inc ....B 419 636-3161
Bryan *(G-2288)*
Illinois Tool Works Inc ....D 519 376-8886
Troy *(G-18675)*
Ilpea Industries Inc ....C 330 562-2916
Aurora *(G-884)*
Iml Containers Ohio Inc ....F 330 754-1066
Canton *(G-2705)*
▲ Impact Products LLC ....C 419 841-2891
Toledo *(G-18342)*
Imperial Plastics Inc ....D 330 927-5065
Rittman *(G-16521)*
Industrial Container Svcs LLC ....E 513 921-2056
Cincinnati *(G-3843)*
Inhance Technologies LLC ....F 614 846-6400
Columbus *(G-7026)*
Injection Molding Specialist ....G 440 639-7896
Painesville *(G-15748)*
Innovations In Plastic Inc ....G 216 541-6060
Cleveland *(G-5460)*
Innovative Plastic Molders LLC ....E 937 898-3775
Dayton *(G-8265)*
Integra Enclosures Inc ....G 440 269-4966
Willoughby *(G-20343)*
Integral Design Inc ....F 216 524-0555
Cleveland *(G-5462)*
International Automotive Compo ....A 419 433-5653
Huron *(G-11099)*
International Supply Corp ....G 513 793-0393
Cincinnati *(G-3858)*
◆ Interntnal Cnvrter Cldwell Inc ....C 740 732-5665
Caldwell *(G-2407)*
Interntnal Plstic Cmpnents Inc ....F 330 744-0625
Campbell *(G-2468)*
▼ Interpak Inc ....E 440 974-8999
Mentor *(G-13475)*
Inventive Extrusions Corp ....E 330 874-3000
Bolivar *(G-1917)*
Ipm Inc ....G 419 248-8000
Toledo *(G-18351)*
▲ Iten Industries Inc ....C 440 997-6134
Ashtabula *(G-780)*
J & B Rogers Inc ....G 937 669-2677
Tipp City *(G-18118)*
J & M Construction LLP ....G 740 454-8986
Hopewell *(G-10993)*
J & O Plastics Inc ....E 330 927-3169
Rittman *(G-16522)*
J H Plastics ....G 419 937-2035
Tiffin *(G-18062)*
J K Precast LLC ....G 740 335-2188
Wshngtn CT Hs *(G-20729)*
Jack Gruber ....G 740 408-2718
Cardington *(G-2874)*
Jaco Manufacturing Company ....D 440 234-4000
Berea *(G-1612)*
Jaco Manufacturing Company ....F 440 234-4000
Berea *(G-1613)*
▲ Janorpot LLC ....E 330 564-0232
Mogadore *(G-14241)*
▲ Jay Industries Inc ....A 419 747-4161
Mansfield *(G-12461)*
Jeffrey Brandewie ....G 937 726-7765
Fort Loramie *(G-9800)*
Jensar Manufacturing LLC ....G 419 727-8320
Toledo *(G-18357)*
Jjc Products Inc ....G 330 666-4582
Akron *(G-224)*
Johnston-Morehouse-Dickey Co ....G 614 866-0452
Columbus *(G-7075)*
Johnston-Morehouse-Dickey Co ....G 330 405-6050
Macedonia *(G-12308)*
Joneszylon Company LLC ....G 740 545-6341
West Lafayette *(G-19933)*
Jos-Tech Inc ....E 330 678-3260
Kent *(G-11337)*
▲ Joslyn Manufacturing Company ....E 330 467-8111
Macedonia *(G-12309)*
JPS Technologies Inc ....F 513 984-6400
Blue Ash *(G-1797)*
JPS Technologies Inc ....F 513 984-6400
Blue Ash *(G-1798)*
Jr Larry Knight ....G 216 762-3141
Maple Heights *(G-12574)*
Just Plastics Inc ....E 419 468-5506
Galion *(G-10146)*
▲ Kamco Industries Inc ....B 419 924-5511
West Unity *(G-19971)*
Kar-Del Plastics Inc ....G 419 289-9739
Ashland *(G-715)*

Kasai North America Inc ....E 419 209-0470
Upper Sandusky *(G-18958)*
Kasai North America Inc ....F 614 356-1494
Dublin *(G-8936)*
Kathom Manufacturing Co Inc ....E 513 868-8890
Hamilton *(G-10579)*
Ken Veney Industries LLC ....G 330 336-5825
Wadsworth *(G-19248)*
▲ Kennedy Group Incorporated ....D 440 951-7660
Willoughby *(G-20352)*
Kennick Mold & Die Inc ....G 216 631-3535
Cleveland *(G-5529)*
Kittyhawk Molding Company Inc ....E 937 746-3663
Carlisle *(G-2894)*
Klockner Pentaplast Amer Inc ....D 937 548-7272
Greenville *(G-10378)*
Klw Plastics Inc ....G 678 674-2990
Monroe *(G-14271)*
▲ Klw Plastics Inc ....G 513 539-2673
Monroe *(G-14272)*
▲ Koroseal Interior Products LLC ....C 330 668-7600
Fairlawn *(G-9611)*
Kurz-Kasch Inc ....C 740 498-8343
Newcomerstown *(G-14976)*
▲ Kurz-Kasch Inc ....D 740 498-8343
Newcomerstown *(G-14977)*
▲ Kurzkasch Inc Wilm Div ....F 740 498-8345
Newcomerstown *(G-14978)*
L C Liming & Sons Inc ....G 513 876-2555
Felicity *(G-9644)*
Laird Plastics Inc ....F 614 272-0777
Columbus *(G-7110)*
Lam Pro Inc ....F 216 426-0661
Cleveland *(G-5556)*
◆ Lancaster Commercial Pdts LLC ....E 740 286-5081
Columbus *(G-7112)*
◆ Landmark Plastic Corporation ....C 330 785-2200
Akron *(G-248)*
Larmco Windows Inc ....E 216 502-2832
Cleveland *(G-5562)*
▲ Laszeray Technology LLC ....D 440 582-8430
North Royalton *(G-15283)*
Lee Plastic Company LLC ....G 937 456-5720
Eaton *(G-9160)*
Lenz Inc ....E 937 277-9364
Dayton *(G-8311)*
Lion Mold & Machine Inc ....G 330 688-4248
Stow *(G-17603)*
Liqui-Box Corporation ....C 419 209-9085
Upper Sandusky *(G-18960)*
Liqui-Box Corporation ....C 419 289-9696
Ashland *(G-721)*
Louis G Freeman Co ....G 513 263-1720
Batavia *(G-1163)*
M L C Technologies Inc ....G 513 874-7792
Hamilton *(G-10583)*
M W Solutions LLC ....F 419 782-1611
Defiance *(G-8633)*
▲ Mag-Nif Inc ....D 440 255-9366
Mentor *(G-13508)*
Magnum Molding Inc ....G 937 368-3040
Conover *(G-7665)*
▲ Mahar Spar Industries Inc ....G 216 249-7143
Cleveland *(G-5606)*
Majestic Plastics Inc ....G 937 593-9500
Bellefontaine *(G-1522)*
◆ Malish Corporation ....C 440 951-5356
Mentor *(G-13509)*
▲ Mar-Bal Inc ....D 440 543-7526
Chagrin Falls *(G-3057)*
Mar-Bal Inc ....D 440 543-7526
Chagrin Falls *(G-3058)*
Marcum Development LLC ....G 330 466-8231
Wooster *(G-20619)*
Marne Plastics LLC ....G 614 732-4666
Columbus *(G-7152)*
Marshall Plastics Inc ....G 937 653-4740
Urbana *(G-19004)*
Mastic Home Exteriors Inc ....C 937 497-7008
Sidney *(G-17050)*
Matrix Cable and Mould ....G 513 832-2577
Cincinnati *(G-3987)*
Matrix Plastics Co Inc ....G 330 666-7730
Medina *(G-13290)*
Matrix Plastics Co Inc ....G 330 666-2395
Medina *(G-13291)*
Maverick Corporation ....F 513 469-9919
Blue Ash *(G-1816)*
McCann Tool & Die Inc ....F 330 264-8820
Wooster *(G-20620)*

MCS Midwest LLC ....F 513 217-0805
Franklin *(G-9898)*
Mdi of Ohio Inc ....E 937 866-2345
Miamisburg *(G-13688)*
Med Center Systems LLC ....G 513 942-6066
West Chester *(G-19877)*
Meese Inc ....D 440 998-1202
Ashtabula *(G-785)*
Mega Plastics Co ....E 330 527-2211
Garrettsville *(G-10198)*
Meggitt (erlanger) LLC ....D 513 851-5550
Cincinnati *(G-4000)*
Mercury Plastics LLC ....G 440 632-5281
Middlefield *(G-13820)*
Metro Recycling Company ....G 513 251-1800
Cincinnati *(G-4017)*
▲ Miami Valley Plastics Inc ....E 937 273-3200
Eldorado *(G-9189)*
Mibtach Enterprises Inc ....G 513 941-0387
Cincinnati *(G-4021)*
Middlefield Plastics Inc ....E 440 834-4638
Middlefield *(G-13826)*
Midwest Molding Inc ....E 614 873-1572
Plain City *(G-16202)*
Midwest Plastic Systems Inc ....G 513 553-4380
New Richmond *(G-14813)*
▲ Milacron LLC ....E 513 536-2000
Batavia *(G-1166)*
Milkmen Design LLC ....G 440 590-5788
Cleveland *(G-5687)*
Miniature Plastic Molding Ltd ....G 440 564-7210
Solon *(G-17196)*
Minotas Trophies & Awards ....G 440 720-1288
Cleveland *(G-5696)*
Modern Builders Supply Inc ....C 419 241-3961
Toledo *(G-18414)*
Modern Builders Supply Inc ....F 419 526-0002
Mansfield *(G-12485)*
Modern Mold Corporation ....G 440 236-9600
Columbia Station *(G-6440)*
Molded Extruded ....G 216 475-5491
Bedford Heights *(G-1475)*
▼ Molded Fiber Glass Companies ....A 440 997-5851
Ashtabula *(G-789)*
Molded Fiber Glass Companies ....B 440 997-5851
Ashtabula *(G-790)*
Molders Choice Inc ....G 440 248-8500
Solon *(G-17197)*
Molders World Inc ....G 513 469-6653
Blue Ash *(G-1823)*
Molding Dynamics Inc ....F 440 786-8100
Bedford *(G-1427)*
Molding Technologies Ltd ....F 740 929-2065
Hebron *(G-10752)*
Moldmakers Inc ....F 419 673-0902
Kenton *(G-11414)*
▲ Molten North America Corp ....C 419 425-2700
Findlay *(G-9728)*
▲ Mon-Say Corp ....G 419 720-0163
Toledo *(G-18415)*
Montville Plastics & Rbr LLC ....D 440 548-3211
Parkman *(G-15812)*
▲ Moore Industries Inc ....D 419 485-5572
Montpelier *(G-14313)*
Mor-Lite Co Inc ....G 513 661-8587
Cincinnati *(G-4045)*
Mos International Inc ....F 330 329-0905
Stow *(G-17607)*
MTI Acquisition LLC ....E 740 929-2065
Hebron *(G-10755)*
MTS Medication Tech Inc ....G 440 238-0840
Strongsville *(G-17767)*
Mustang Aerial Services Inc ....G 740 373-9262
Reno *(G-16426)*
Mvp Plastics Inc ....F 440 834-1790
Middlefield *(G-13835)*
Mye Automotive Inc ....G 330 253-5592
Akron *(G-291)*
Myers Industries Inc ....E 330 253-5592
Akron *(G-292)*
Myers Industries Inc ....E 440 632-1006
Middlefield *(G-13836)*
Myers Industries Inc ....E 330 253-5592
Akron *(G-293)*
National Access Design LLC ....F 513 351-3400
Cincinnati *(G-4058)*
National Fleet Svcs Ohio LLC ....F 440 930-5177
Avon Lake *(G-997)*
National Molded Products Inc ....E 440 365-3400
Elyria *(G-9299)*

NBC Industries Inc F 216 651-9800
Cleveland *(G-5731)*
Nebraska Industries Corp E 419 335-6010
Wauseon *(G-19529)*
Newell Brands Inc F 330 733-7771
Mogadore *(G-14245)*
▲ Next Generation Films Inc C 419 884-8150
Lexington *(G-11805)*
▲ Nifco America Corporation B 614 920-6800
Canal Winchester *(G-2507)*
Nifco America Corporation C 614 836-3808
Canal Winchester *(G-2508)*
Nifco America Corporation C 614 836-8691
Groveport *(G-10507)*
▲ Nissen Chemitec America Inc C 740 852-3200
London *(G-12065)*
Nitrojection G 440 834-8790
Chesterland *(G-3166)*
North Canton Plastics Inc E 330 497-0071
Canton *(G-2765)*
North Coast Custom Molding Inc F 419 905-6447
Dunkirk *(G-9035)*
Northshore Mold Inc G 440 838-8212
Cleveland *(G-5786)*
Northwest Molded Plastics G 419 459-4414
Edon *(G-9186)*
Norwesco Inc F 740 335-6236
Wshngtn CT Hs *(G-20734)*
Norwesco Inc E 740 654-6402
Lancaster *(G-11592)*
▲ Novatex North America Inc D 419 282-4264
Ashland *(G-728)*
O A R Vinyl Windows & Siding G 440 636-5573
Middlefield *(G-13842)*
Octsys Security Corp G 614 470-4510
Columbus *(G-7239)*
Ohio Plastics Company G 740 828-3291
Newark *(G-14905)*
▲ Ohio Precision Molding Inc E 330 745-9393
Barberton *(G-1091)*
Olan Plastics Inc E 614 834-6526
Canal Winchester *(G-2510)*
Oldcastle Precast Inc E 419 592-2309
Napoleon *(G-14554)*
Omega Polymer Technologies Inc G 330 562-5201
Aurora *(G-897)*
Omega Pultrusions Incorporated C 330 562-5201
Aurora *(G-898)*
Oneida Group Inc C 740 687-2500
Lancaster *(G-11595)*
Orbis Corporation B 937 652-1361
Urbana *(G-19006)*
Orbis Corporation C 440 974-3857
Mentor *(G-13535)*
Orbis Corporation G 513 737-9489
Hamilton *(G-10595)*
Orbit Manufacturing Inc E 513 732-6097
Batavia *(G-1175)*
▲ Osburn Associates Inc E 740 385-5732
Logan *(G-12038)*
◆ Owens Corning A 419 248-8000
Toledo *(G-18446)*
◆ Owens Corning Sales LLC A 419 248-8000
Toledo *(G-18448)*
P & S Welding Co G 330 274-2850
Mantua *(G-12557)*
P C R Restorations Inc F 419 747-7957
Mansfield *(G-12501)*
P M Machine Inc F 440 942-6537
Willoughby *(G-20395)*
▲ P P E Inc D 440 322-8577
Elyria *(G-9306)*
P S Plastics Inc F 614 262-7070
Columbus *(G-7282)*
▲ P T I Inc E 419 445-2800
Archbold *(G-663)*
Pace Mold & Machine LLC G 330 879-1777
Massillon *(G-13037)*
Pahuja Inc D 614 864-3989
Gahanna *(G-10097)*
Palpac Industries Inc F 419 523-3230
Ottawa *(G-15661)*
Paragon Plastics F 330 542-9825
New Middletown *(G-14751)*
Parker-Hannifin Corporation D 330 673-2700
Kent *(G-11360)*
▲ Patrick Products Inc C 419 943-4137
Leipsic *(G-11730)*
Pave Technology Co E 937 890-1100
Dayton *(G-8417)*

Pease Industies Inc B 513 870-3600
Fairfield *(G-9546)*
Pendaform Company C 740 826-5000
New Concord *(G-14685)*
Performance Plastics Ltd E 513 321-8404
Cincinnati *(G-4150)*
Philpott Indus Plas Entps Ltd G 330 225-3344
Brunswick *(G-2224)*
Pilot Plastics Inc E 330 920-1718
Peninsula *(G-15897)*
▲ Pinnacle Industrial Entps Inc C 419 352-8688
Bowling Green *(G-1991)*
Pioneer Custom Molding Inc E 419 737-3252
Pioneer *(G-16088)*
Pioneer Plastics Corporation C 330 896-2356
Akron *(G-321)*
Plas-Tanks Industries Inc E 513 942-3800
Hamilton *(G-10596)*
Plas-TEC Corp D 419 272-2731
Edon *(G-9187)*
▲ Plastex Industries Inc E 419 531-0189
Maumee *(G-13138)*
▲ Plastic Enterprises Inc E 440 324-3240
Elyria *(G-9312)*
Plastic Enterprises Inc G 440 366-0220
Elyria *(G-9313)*
▼ Plastic Extrusion Tech Ltd E 440 632-5611
Middlefield *(G-13846)*
Plastic Fabrication Svcs Inc G 440 953-9990
Willoughby *(G-20402)*
Plastic Forming Company Inc E 330 830-5167
Massillon *(G-13039)*
Plastic Materials Inc E 330 468-5706
Macedonia *(G-12315)*
Plastic Materials Inc E 330 468-0184
Macedonia *(G-12316)*
▲ Plastic Moldings Company Llc D 513 921-5040
Blue Ash *(G-1830)*
Plastic Products and Supply G 330 744-5076
Youngstown *(G-21000)*
Plastic Works Inc F 419 433-6576
Huron *(G-11108)*
Plasticards Inc E 330 896-5555
Uniontown *(G-18930)*
Plastics Converting Solutions G 330 722-2537
Medina *(G-13319)*
Plastics R Unique Inc E 330 334-4820
Wadsworth *(G-19264)*
Plastikos Corporation E 513 732-0961
Batavia *(G-1176)*
Plastipak Packaging Inc C 740 928-4435
Hebron *(G-10757)*
Plate Engraving Corporation F 330 239-2155
Medina *(G-13320)*
Podnar Plastics Inc E 330 673-2255
Kent *(G-11362)*
Podnar Plastics Inc E 330 673-2255
Kent *(G-11363)*
Polimeros Usa LLC G 216 591-0175
Warrensville Heights *(G-19472)*
▲ Polyfill LLC E 937 493-0041
Sidney *(G-17061)*
▼ Polymer & Steel Tech Inc E 440 510-0108
Eastlake *(G-9128)*
Polymer Tech & Svcs Inc E 740 929-5500
Heath *(G-10727)*
Polyquest Inc E 330 888-9448
Sagamore Hills *(G-16619)*
Positool Technologies Inc G 330 220-4002
Brunswick *(G-2227)*
Possible Plastics Inc G 614 277-2100
Grove City *(G-10457)*
Ppafco Inc F 614 488-7259
Columbus *(G-7335)*
Precision Custom Products Inc E 937 585-4011
De Graff *(G-8605)*
Precision Polymers Inc G 614 322-9951
Reynoldsburg *(G-16448)*
◆ Precision Thrmplstc Componts D 419 227-4500
Lima *(G-11962)*
Preferred Solutions Inc F 216 642-1200
Seven Hills *(G-16904)*
Preform Technologies LLC G 419 720-0355
Swanton *(G-17919)*
▼ Premix Inc C 440 224-2181
North Kingsville *(G-15160)*
Pretium Packaging LLC C 419 943-3733
Leipsic *(G-11732)*
Prime Engineered Plastics Corp F 330 452-5110
Canton *(G-2791)*

Printing 3d Parts Inc G 330 759-9099
Youngstown *(G-21006)*
▲ Priority Custom Molding Inc F 937 431-8770
Beavercreek Township *(G-1373)*
Professional Plastics Corp G 614 336-2498
Dublin *(G-8968)*
Proficient Plastics Inc F 440 205-9700
Mentor *(G-13557)*
Profile Plastics Inc E 330 452-7000
Canton *(G-2794)*
Profusion Industries LLC G 800 938-2858
Fairlawn *(G-9615)*
Progressive Molding Tech G 330 220-7030
Medina *(G-13323)*
Progrssive Molding Bolivar Inc C 330 874-3000
Bolivar *(G-1925)*
Protec Industries Incorporated G 440 937-4142
Avon *(G-959)*
▲ Proto Plastics Inc E 937 667-8416
Tipp City *(G-18129)*
Proto-Mold Products Co Inc E 937 778-1959
Piqua *(G-16157)*
▲ Ptc Enterprises Inc E 419 272-2524
Edon *(G-9188)*
▲ PVS Plastics Technology Corp E 937 233-4376
Huber Heights *(G-11023)*
Pyramid Plastics Inc E 216 641-5904
Cleveland *(G-5936)*
Quality Blow Molding Inc D 440 458-6550
Elyria *(G-9315)*
Quality Frp Fabrications G 440 942-9067
Willoughby *(G-20414)*
Quality Innovative Pdts LLC G 330 990-9888
Akron *(G-335)*
Qube Corporation F 440 543-2393
Chagrin Falls *(G-3071)*
Queen City Polymers Inc E 513 779-0990
West Chester *(G-19776)*
Queen City Polymers Inc G 937 236-2710
Dayton *(G-8456)*
R A M Plastics Co Inc E 330 549-3107
North Lima *(G-15177)*
R and S Technologies Inc F 419 483-3691
Bellevue *(G-1542)*
R Dunn Mold Inc G 937 773-3388
Piqua *(G-16158)*
R L Industries Inc D 513 874-2800
West Chester *(G-19777)*
Radar Love Co F 419 951-4750
Findlay *(G-9744)*
▲ Radici Plastics Usa Inc D 330 336-7611
Wadsworth *(G-19271)*
▲ Rage Corporation D 614 771-4771
Hilliard *(G-10857)*
Randy Lewis Inc F 330 784-0456
Akron *(G-342)*
Raven Concealment Systems LLC F 440 508-9000
North Ridgeville *(G-15249)*
▲ Reactive Resin Products Co E 419 666-6119
Perrysburg *(G-16003)*
Recto Molded Products Inc D 513 871-5544
Cincinnati *(G-4256)*
Reebar Die Casting Inc F 419 878-7591
Waterville *(G-19503)*
Remram Recovery LLC F 740 667-0092
Tuppers Plains *(G-18720)*
◆ Replex Mirror Company E 740 397-5535
Mount Vernon *(G-14504)*
Reserve Industries Inc E 440 871-2796
Bay Village *(G-1208)*
Resinoid Engineering Corp E 740 928-2220
Heath *(G-10730)*
▲ Resinoid Engineering Corp D 740 928-6115
Hebron *(G-10759)*
▼ Resource Mtl Hdlg & Recycl Inc E 440 834-0727
Middlefield *(G-13849)*
Retterbush Fiberglass Corp E 937 778-1936
Piqua *(G-16159)*
Revere Plas Systems Group LLC B 419 547-6918
Clyde *(G-6393)*
▲ Revere Plastics Systems LLC B 419 547-6918
Clyde *(G-6394)*
▲ Rez-Tech Corporation E 330 673-4009
Kent *(G-11374)*
▲ Rhino Rubber LLC F 877 744-6603
North Canton *(G-15115)*
Riotech International Ltd D 513 779-0990
West Chester *(G-19782)*
Rlr Industries Inc E 440 951-9501
Mentor *(G-13574)*

S I C

30 RUBBER AND MISCELLANEOUS PLASTICS PRODUCTS — SIC SECTION

▲ Ro-MAI Industries Inc .... E 330 425-9090
  Twinsburg *(G-18847)*
◆ Rochling Glastic Composites LP ...... C 216 486-0100
  Cleveland *(G-5996)*
▲ Rohrer Corporation .... C 330 335-1541
  Wadsworth *(G-19275)*
Roppe Holding Company .... C 419 435-6601
  Fostoria *(G-9856)*
Ross Special Products Inc .... F 937 335-8406
  Troy *(G-18700)*
Roswell Inc .... G 419 433-4709
  Huron *(G-11111)*
Roto Solutions Inc .... D 330 279-2424
  Holmesville *(G-10984)*
Rotosolutions Inc. .... F 419 903-0800
  Ashland *(G-745)*
◆ Rowmark LLC .... C 419 425-8974
  Findlay *(G-9748)*
Rowmark LLC .... D 419 429-0042
  Findlay *(G-9749)*
▲ Royal Plastics Inc .... C 440 352-1357
  Mentor *(G-13575)*
RPM Consumer Holding Company ...... G 330 273-5090
  Medina *(G-13330)*
▲ RTS Companies (us) Inc .... C 440 275-3077
  Austinburg *(G-925)*
Rubbermaid Incorporated .... C 330 733-7771
  Mogadore *(G-14247)*
Rubys Country Store .... G 330 359-0406
  Dundee *(G-9026)*
Rutland Plastic Tech Inc .... D 614 846-3055
  Columbus *(G-7407)*
Ryan Development Corp .... E 937 587-2266
  Peebles *(G-15881)*
◆ S Toys Holdings LLC .... A 330 656-0440
  Streetsboro *(G-17693)*
▲ S&T Automotive America LLC .... G 614 782-9041
  Grove City *(G-10464)*
▲ S&V Industries Inc .... E 330 666-1986
  Medina *(G-13333)*
Saint-Gobain Hycomp LLC .... C 440 234-2002
  Cleveland *(G-6027)*
Saint-Gobain Prfmce Plas Corp .... C 330 296-9948
  Ravenna *(G-16400)*
▲ Saint-Gobain Prfmce Plas Corp ..... C 440 836-6900
  Solon *(G-17227)*
Samuel Strapping Systems Inc .... D 740 522-2500
  Heath *(G-10731)*
Schmidt Progressive LLC .... E 513 934-2600
  Lebanon *(G-11693)*
Scott Molders Incorporated .... D 330 673-5777
  Kent *(G-11382)*
▲ Seagate Plastics Company .... D 419 878-5010
  Waterville *(G-19505)*
▼ Sentry Protection LLC .... G 216 228-3200
  Lakewood *(G-11535)*
Shelly Fisher .... D 419 522-6696
  Mansfield *(G-12512)*
Shiloh Industries Inc .... F 937 236-5100
  Dayton *(G-8504)*
Shirley KS Storage Trays LLC .... G 740 868-8140
  Zanesville *(G-21178)*
Showerline Products LLC .... G 614 794-3476
  Westerville *(G-20074)*
Silgan Plastics LLC .... C 419 523-3737
  Ottawa *(G-15664)*
Skribs Tool and Die Inc .... E 440 951-7774
  Mentor *(G-13583)*
Soft-Lite LLC .... C 330 528-3400
  Streetsboro *(G-17698)*
Solon .... G 440 498-1798
  Solon *(G-17233)*
Solutions In Polycarbonate LLC .... G 330 572-2860
  Medina *(G-13345)*
Sonoco Products Company .... E 614 759-8470
  Columbus *(G-7462)*
Sonoco Prtective Solutions Inc .... D 419 420-0029
  Findlay *(G-9759)*
Southeastern Container Inc .... D 419 352-6300
  Bowling Green *(G-2000)*
Spartech LLC .... D 937 548-1395
  Greenville *(G-10395)*
Spartech LLC .... C 419 399-4050
  Paulding *(G-15871)*
▲ Specialty Plas Fabrications .... G 513 856-9475
  Hamilton *(G-10607)*
▲ Spectrum Plastics Corporation ...... G 330 926-9766
  Cuyahoga Falls *(G-7921)*
Speed City LLC .... G 440 975-1969
  Newbury *(G-14966)*

▲ Speedline Corporation .... G 440 914-1122
  Solon *(G-17236)*
Springfield Plastics Inc .... F 937 322-6071
  Springfield *(G-17496)*
Springseal Inc .... F 330 626-0673
  Ravenna *(G-16407)*
Stanek E F and Assoc Inc .... G 216 341-7700
  Macedonia *(G-12333)*
▲ Stanley Electric US Co Inc .... B 740 852-5200
  London *(G-12069)*
Starks Plastics LLC .... G 513 541-4591
  Cincinnati *(G-4374)*
State Tool and Die Inc .... G 216 267-6030
  Cleveland *(G-6099)*
Steere Enterprises Inc .... E 330 633-4926
  Tallmadge *(G-18005)*
▲ Step2 Company LLC .... G 866 429-5200
  Streetsboro *(G-17700)*
Step2 Company LLC .... B 419 938-6343
  Perrysville *(G-16032)*
Sterilite Corporation .... B 330 830-2204
  Massillon *(G-13051)*
Stewart Acquisition LLC .... E 800 376-4466
  Kirtland *(G-11471)*
▲ Stewart Acquisition LLC .... E 330 963-0322
  Twinsburg *(G-18860)*
Stopol Equipment Sales LLC .... G 440 499-0030
  Brunswick *(G-2240)*
Stuchell Products LLC .... E 330 821-4299
  Alliance *(G-503)*
◆ Style Crest Inc .... B 419 332-7369
  Fremont *(G-10052)*
Style Crest Enterprises Inc .... D 419 355-8586
  Fremont *(G-10053)*
Sugar Showcase .... G 330 792-9154
  Youngstown *(G-21040)*
Sun State Plastics Inc .... E 330 494-5220
  Canton *(G-2829)*
Superior Fibers Inc .... B 740 394-2491
  Shawnee *(G-16962)*
T&M Plastics Co Inc .... G 216 651-7700
  Cleveland *(G-6146)*
Tahoma Enterprises Inc .... D 330 745-9016
  Barberton *(G-1108)*
▼ Tahoma Rubber & Plastics Inc ...... D 330 745-9016
  Barberton *(G-1109)*
Takeya USA Corporation .... F 714 374-9900
  Columbus *(G-7509)*
Tapco Holdings Inc .... F 800 771-4486
  Franklin *(G-9924)*
Team Amity Molds & Plastic .... D 937 667-7856
  Tipp City *(G-18136)*
Tech II Inc .... C 937 969-7000
  Urbana *(G-19014)*
Tech-Way Industries Inc .... D 937 746-1004
  Franklin *(G-9925)*
Technimold Plus Inc .... F 937 492-4077
  Port Jefferson *(G-16266)*
▲ Tema Isenmann Inc .... G 859 252-0613
  Cincinnati *(G-4412)*
Tetra Mold & Tool Inc .... F 937 845-1651
  New Carlisle *(G-14679)*
Tez Tool & Fabrication Inc .... G 440 323-2300
  Elyria *(G-9337)*
Th Plastics Inc .... C 419 352-2770
  Bowling Green *(G-2001)*
Th Plastics Inc .... F 419 425-5825
  Findlay *(G-9768)*
Th Plastics Inc .... C 419 425-5825
  Findlay *(G-9769)*
▲ The Hc Companies Inc .... E 440 632-3333
  Middlefield *(G-13857)*
Therma-Tru Corp .... D 419 740-5193
  Maumee *(G-13152)*
Thermoplastic Accessories Corp .... E 614 771-4777
  Hilliard *(G-10870)*
▲ Thogus Products Company .... D 440 933-8850
  Avon Lake *(G-1011)*
Thomas Tool & Mold Company .... F 614 890-4978
  Westerville *(G-20078)*
Three AS Inc .... G 419 227-4240
  Lima *(G-11951)*
▲ Tigerpoly Manufacturing Inc .... B 614 871-0045
  Grove City *(G-10473)*
Timbertech Limited .... F 614 443-4891
  Columbus *(G-7529)*
Tjar Innovations LLC .... F 937 347-1999
  Xenia *(G-20797)*
Tmd Wek North LLC .... C 440 576-6940
  Jefferson *(G-11241)*

Toledo Molding & Die Inc .... D 419 354-6050
  Bowling Green *(G-2002)*
Toledo Molding & Die Inc .... D 419 476-0581
  Toledo *(G-18563)*
Toledo Molding & Die Inc .... B 419 443-9031
  Tiffin *(G-18090)*
Toledo Molding & Die Inc .... C 419 692-6022
  Delphos *(G-8756)*
▲ Toledo Molding & Die Inc .... D 419 470-3950
  Toledo *(G-18564)*
Toledo Pro Fiberglass Inc .... G 419 241-9390
  Toledo *(G-18567)*
▲ Tom Smith Industries Inc .... A 937 832-1555
  Englewood *(G-9378)*
Tooling Tech Holdings LLC .... G 937 295-3672
  Fort Loramie *(G-9809)*
Torsion Plastics .... G 812 453-9645
  Kent *(G-11395)*
Total Plastics Resources LLC .... G 440 891-1140
  Cleveland *(G-6192)*
Toth Mold & Die Inc .... F 440 232-8530
  Cleveland *(G-6193)*
Treemen Industries Inc .... E 330 965-3777
  Boardman *(G-1904)*
Trellborg Sling Prfiles US Inc .... E 330 995-9725
  Aurora *(G-911)*
Tri-Craft Inc .... E 440 826-1050
  Cleveland *(G-6206)*
Triaxis Machine & Tool LLC .... G 440 230-0303
  North Royalton *(G-15308)*
▲ Trifecta Tool & Engrg LLC .... G 937 291-0933
  Dayton *(G-8565)*
Trilogy Plastics Inc .... D 330 821-4700
  Alliance *(G-511)*
Trilogy Plastics Inc .... G 440 893-5522
  Chagrin Falls *(G-3085)*
Trimold LLC .... B 740 474-7591
  Circleville *(G-4563)*
Triple Diamond Plastics LLC .... D 419 533-0085
  Liberty Center *(G-11810)*
Truechoicepack Corp .... E 937 630-3832
  Mason *(G-12951)*
Tsp Inc .... C 513 732-8900
  Batavia *(G-1191)*
Turbo Machine & Tool Inc .... G 216 651-1940
  Cleveland *(G-6223)*
U S Development Corp .... E 570 966-5990
  Kent *(G-11397)*
U S Development Corp .... E 330 673-6900
  Kent *(G-11398)*
Udecx LLC .... G 877 698-3329
  Tipp City *(G-18141)*
Unique Plastics LLC .... E 419 352-0066
  Bowling Green *(G-2003)*
Unique-Chardan Inc .... E 419 636-6900
  Bryan *(G-2311)*
▲ United Security Seals Inc .... E 614 443-7633
  Columbus *(G-7558)*
Universal Plastics - Sajar .... G 440 632-5203
  Middlefield *(G-13863)*
▲ Universal Polymer & Rubber Ltd ... C 440 632-1691
  Middlefield *(G-13864)*
Upl International Inc .... E 330 433-2860
  North Canton *(G-15134)*
▲ US Coexcell Inc .... E 419 897-9110
  Maumee *(G-13158)*
US Molding Machinery Co Inc .... E 440 918-1701
  Willoughby *(G-20456)*
V & R Molded Products Inc .... F 419 752-4171
  Willard *(G-20247)*
Valley Plastics Company Inc .... E 419 666-2349
  Toledo *(G-18588)*
Valutex Reinforcements Inc .... G 800 251-2507
  Wshngtn CT Hs *(G-20747)*
Vast Mold & Tool Co Inc .... D 440 942-7585
  Mentor *(G-13622)*
Venture Packaging Inc .... B 419 465-2534
  Monroeville *(G-14292)*
Venture Packaging Midwest Inc .... G 419 465-2534
  Monroeville *(G-14293)*
▲ Venture Plastics Inc .... C 330 872-5774
  Newton Falls *(G-14995)*
Venture Plastics Inc .... E 330 872-6262
  Newton Falls *(G-14996)*
Versa-Pak Ltd .... E 419 586-5466
  Celina *(G-2991)*
Vicas Manufacturing Co Inc .... E 513 791-7741
  Cincinnati *(G-4480)*
Vinyl Design Corporation .... E 419 283-4009
  Holland *(G-10965)*

Vinylmax Corporation....D....800 847-3736
Hamilton *(G-10618)*
Vinylume Products Inc....D....330 799-2000
Youngstown *(G-21067)*
Vision Color LLC....G....419 924-9450
West Unity *(G-19975)*
Vlchek Plastics....G....440 632-1631
Middlefield *(G-13866)*
Vts Co Ltd....G....419 273-4010
Forest *(G-9790)*
▼W T Inc....F....419 224-6942
Lima *(G-11957)*
▼Warwick Products Company....E....216 334-1200
Cleveland *(G-6291)*
Waugs Inc....G....440 315-4851
Ashland *(G-754)*
Wayne Frame Products Inc....G....419 726-7715
Toledo *(G-18595)*
Wayne Pak Ltd....F....440 323-8744
Elyria *(G-9345)*
Wch Molding LLC....E....740 335-6320
Wshngtn CT Hs *(G-20748)*
Weldon Plastics Corporation....G....330 425-9660
Twinsburg *(G-18874)*
West & Barker Inc....E....330 652-9923
Niles *(G-15040)*
West Extrusion LLC....G....330 744-0625
Campbell *(G-2472)*
Westar Plastics Llc....G....419 636-1333
Bryan *(G-2313)*
White Co David....G....440 247-2920
Novelty *(G-15440)*
Wilbert Inc....D....419 483-2300
Bellevue *(G-1551)*
▼William J Minneman Family LP....E....937 890-7461
Dayton *(G-8593)*
Win Cd Inc....F....330 929-1999
Cuyahoga Falls *(G-7934)*
Windsor Mold Inc....E....419 484-2400
Bellevue *(G-1552)*
▲Windsor Mold USA Inc....E....419 483-0653
Bellevue *(G-1553)*
Wisco Products Incorporated....E....937 228-2101
Dayton *(G-8598)*
▲World Class Plastics Inc....D....937 843-3003
Russells Point *(G-16603)*
▲World Resource Solutons Corp....G....614 733-3737
Plain City *(G-16219)*
▲Worthignton Products Inc....G....330 452-7400
Canton *(G-2865)*
Wrr Creative Concepts LLC....G....513 659-2284
West Chester *(G-19822)*
Wyatt Industries LLC....G....330 954-1790
Streetsboro *(G-17704)*
◆XYZ Plastics Inc....C....440 632-5281
Middlefield *(G-13870)*
Y City Recycling LLC....D....740 452-2500
Zanesville *(G-21190)*
▲Yachiyo of America Inc....C....614 876-3220
Columbus *(G-7620)*
Yanfeng US Automotive....B....419 636-4211
Bryan *(G-2314)*
▲Zehrco-Giancola Composites Inc....C....440 994-6317
Ashtabula *(G-813)*
Zehrco-Giancola Composites Inc....G....440 576-9941
Jefferson *(G-11244)*

31 LEATHER AND LEATHER PRODUCTS

3111 Leather Tanning & Finishing

▲Old West Industries Inc....G....513 889-0500
Hamilton *(G-10592)*
Premier Tanning & Nutrition....G....419 342-6259
Shelby *(G-16986)*

3131 Boot & Shoe Cut Stock & Findings

Bean Counter LLC....G....419 636-0705
Bryan *(G-2268)*
Bond Quarters Horses....G....614 354-4028
Freeport *(G-9984)*
Buckeye Counters....G....330 682-0902
Orrville *(G-15585)*
Classic Countertops LLC....G....330 882-4220
Akron *(G-119)*
Colonels Quarters....G....740 385-3374
Circleville *(G-4540)*
Counter Creation Plus L L C....G....419 826-7449
Swanton *(G-17910)*
Counter Method Inc....G....614 206-3192
Sunbury *(G-17884)*
Counter Rhythm Group....G....513 379-6587
Columbus *(G-6829)*
Cruise Quarters....G....614 777-6022
Hilliard *(G-10821)*
Cruise Quarters and Tours....G....614 891-6089
Westerville *(G-20043)*
Custom Floaters LLC....G....216 536-8979
Brookpark *(G-2141)*
Dewey Smith Quarter Horses....G....682 597-2424
Bellefontaine *(G-1513)*
Dicks Counter D M....G....440 322-3312
Elyria *(G-9243)*
Halvey Quarter Horses....G....614 648-0483
Blacklick *(G-1685)*
Home Quarters North Canto....G....330 806-5336
Hartville *(G-10696)*
Hudson Leather Ltd....G....419 485-8531
Pioneer *(G-16085)*
Ingersoll-Rand Co....G....704 655-4000
Hillsboro *(G-10881)*
Latin Quarter....G....513 271-5400
Cincinnati *(G-3933)*
McClellan Rand L....G....614 462-4782
Columbus *(G-7162)*
Perfume Counter....G....513 885-5989
Cincinnati *(G-4151)*
Quarter Bistro....G....513 271-5400
Cincinnati *(G-4232)*
Quarter Mile Fabrication LLC....G....440 298-1272
Thompson *(G-18027)*
Randy R Wilson....G....740 454-4440
Findlay *(G-9745)*
▲Remington Products Co....C....330 335-1571
Wadsworth *(G-19274)*
Scioto Darby Quarter Horses....G....614 464-7290
Orient *(G-15577)*
Sentinel Consumer Products Inc....D....801 825-5671
Mentor *(G-13579)*
Upper Echelon Bar LLC....G....513 531-2814
Cincinnati *(G-4455)*
Upper Sarahsville LLC....G....740 732-2071
Caldwell *(G-2413)*

3142 House Slippers

▲Principle Business Entps Inc....C....419 352-1551
Bowling Green *(G-1992)*

3143 Men's Footwear, Exc Athletic

▲Acor Orthopaedic Inc....D....216 662-4500
Cleveland *(G-4608)*
Georgia-Boot Inc....D....740 753-1951
Nelsonville *(G-14593)*
Rocky Brands Inc....B....740 753-1951
Nelsonville *(G-14595)*
Rocky Brands Inc....D....740 753-1951
Nelsonville *(G-14596)*

3144 Women's Footwear, Exc Athletic

▲Acor Orthopaedic Inc....D....216 662-4500
Cleveland *(G-4608)*
Foot Petals Inc....G....614 729-7205
Pickerington *(G-16048)*
Georgia-Boot Inc....D....740 753-1951
Nelsonville *(G-14593)*
Rocky Brands Inc....B....740 753-1951
Nelsonville *(G-14595)*

3149 Footwear, NEC

NTS Enterprises Ltd....G....513 531-1166
Cincinnati *(G-4092)*

3151 Leather Gloves & Mittens

Hillman Group Inc....G....440 248-7000
Cleveland *(G-5409)*
▲Totes Isotoner Corporation....F....513 682-8200
West Chester *(G-19907)*
▲Totes Isotoner Holdings Corp....C....513 682-8200
West Chester *(G-19908)*

3161 Luggage

Buckeye Stamping Company....D....614 445-0059
Columbus *(G-6712)*
Cleveland Canvas Goods Mfg Co....D....216 361-4567
Cleveland *(G-4948)*
Clipper Products Inc....G....513 688-7300
Cincinnati *(G-3243)*
Eagle Creek Inc....D....513 385-4442
Cincinnati *(G-3620)*
▲Kam Manufacturing Inc....C....419 238-6037
Van Wert *(G-19096)*
L M Engineering Inc....E....330 270-2400
Youngstown *(G-20955)*
Plastic Forming Company Inc....E....330 830-5167
Massillon *(G-13039)*
Professional Case Inc....F....513 682-2520
West Chester *(G-19890)*
▲Tia Marie & Company....G....513 521-8694
Cincinnati *(G-4421)*
Travelers Custom Case Inc....F....216 621-8447
Cleveland *(G-6199)*
Trunk Show....G....330 565-5326
Youngstown *(G-21054)*
Whitman Corporation....G....513 541-3223
Okeana *(G-15521)*

3171 Handbags & Purses

Gro2 Bags & Accessories LLC....G....740 622-0928
Coshocton *(G-7736)*
▲Hugo Bosca Company Inc....E....937 323-5523
Springfield *(G-17423)*
Judith Leiber LLC....D....614 449-4217
Columbus *(G-7080)*
Ravenworks Deer Skin....G....937 354-5151
Mount Victory *(G-14521)*
Tapestry Inc....F....419 471-9033
Toledo *(G-18543)*

3172 Personal Leather Goods

Bison Leather Co....G....419 517-1737
Toledo *(G-18203)*
Down Home....G....740 393-1186
Mount Vernon *(G-14479)*
Fount....G....540 810-0594
Cleveland *(G-5269)*
▲Hamilton Manufacturing Corp....E....419 867-4858
Holland *(G-10933)*
▲Hugo Bosca Company Inc....E....937 323-5523
Springfield *(G-17423)*
Nelson Constantinelli Ltd....G....800 680-1029
Dublin *(G-8954)*
Ravenworks Deer Skin....G....937 354-5151
Mount Victory *(G-14521)*
Williams Leather Products Inc....G....740 223-1604
Marion *(G-12749)*

3199 Leather Goods, NEC

AM Retail Group Inc....G....513 539-7837
Monroe *(G-14254)*
Berlin Custom Leather Ltd....G....330 674-3768
Millersburg *(G-14066)*
Brighton Collectibles LLC....E....614 418-7561
Columbus *(G-6699)*
Charm Harness and Boot Ltd....F....330 893-0402
Charm *(G-3141)*
Cornerstone Brands Inc....G....866 668-5962
West Chester *(G-19684)*
Cromwell Aleene....G....937 547-2281
Greenville *(G-10366)*
Diy Holster LLC....G....419 921-2168
Elyria *(G-9244)*
Dnd Products Inc....G....440 286-7275
Chardon *(G-3109)*
Dog Depot....G....513 771-9274
Cincinnati *(G-3599)*
Dpi Inc....G....419 273-1400
Forest *(G-9786)*
Dwayne Hall....G....740 685-5270
Senecaville *(G-16899)*
Ervin Yoder....G....330 359-5862
Mount Hope *(G-14436)*
▲Hamilton Animal Products LLC....E....937 293-9994
Moraine *(G-14357)*
▲Holmes Wheel Shop Inc....E....330 279-2891
Holmesville *(G-10981)*
In Good Hlth & Animal Wellness....G....330 908-1234
Northfield *(G-15319)*
LLC Bowman Leather....G....330 893-1954
Millersburg *(G-14107)*
Lockbourne AG Center Inc....G....614 491-0635
Lockbourne *(G-11996)*
Maysville Harness Shop Ltd....G....330 695-9977
Apple Creek *(G-612)*
Rantek Products LLC....G....419 485-2421
Montpelier *(G-14315)*
Straight Razor Designes....G....330 598-1414
Medina *(G-13348)*

31 LEATHER AND LEATHER PRODUCTS

◆ Tarahill Inc .... E 706 864-0808
   Columbus (G-7511)
▼ Trd Leathers .... G 216 631-6233
   Cleveland (G-6200)
Whitman Corporation .... G 513 541-3223
   Okeana (G-15521)
Wright Leather Works .... G 567 314-0019
   Fremont (G-10065)
Yoders Harness Shop .... G 440 632-1505
   Middlefield (G-13871)

32 STONE, CLAY, GLASS, AND CONCRETE PRODUCTS

3211 Flat Glass

3-G Incorporated .... G 513 921-4515
   Cincinnati (G-3269)
▲ Addis Glass Fabricating Inc .... F 513 860-3340
   West Chester (G-19637)
AGC Flat Glass North Amer Inc ...... F 937 292-7784
   Bellefontaine (G-1502)
AGC Flat Glass North Amer Inc ...... G 330 965-1000
   Youngstown (G-20839)
AGC Flat Glass North Amer Inc ...... G 330 965-1000
   Boardman (G-1897)
AGC Flat Glass North Amer Inc ...... G 937 599-3131
   Bellefontaine (G-1503)
Cardinal CT Company .... E 740 892-2324
   Utica (G-19024)
Cardinal Glass Industries Inc .... E 740 892-2324
   Utica (G-19025)
▲ Continental GL Sls & Inv Group ... B 614 679-1201
   Powell (G-16318)
Custom GL Sltions Millbury LLC ..... C 419 855-7706
   Millbury (G-14048)
Custom Glass Solutions LLC .... F 248 340-1800
   Worthington (G-20682)
Dela-Glassware Ltd LLC .... G 740 369-6737
   Delaware (G-8669)
Glass Fabricators Inc .... G 216 529-1919
   Lakewood (G-11518)
◆ Glasstech Inc .... C 419 661-9500
   Perrysburg (G-15959)
Guardian Industries LLC .... E 614 431-6309
   Worthington (G-20688)
Imaging Sciences LLC .... G 440 975-9640
   Willoughby (G-20342)
Kaaa/Hamilton Enterprises Inc .... E 513 874-5874
   Fairfield (G-9516)
Knight Industries Corp .... E 419 478-8550
   Toledo (G-18369)
Machined Glass Specialist Inc .... F 937 743-6166
   Springboro (G-17336)
Mentor Glass Supplies and Repr .... G 440 255-9444
   Mentor (G-13515)
Nsg Glass North America Inc .... C 419 247-4800
   Toledo (G-18429)
◆ Pilkington Holdings Inc .... B 419 247-3731
   Toledo (G-18469)
Pilkington North America Inc .... C 800 547-9280
   Northwood (G-15344)
Pilkington North America Inc .... B 419 247-3211
   Rossford (G-16589)
Pilkington North America Inc .... C 419 247-3731
   Urbancrest (G-19022)
◆ Pilkington North America Inc ...... C 419 247-3731
   Toledo (G-18470)
Pittsburgh Glass Works LLC .... F 740 774-8762
   Chillicothe (G-3211)
Poma GL Specialty Windows Inc .... G 330 965-1000
   Boardman (G-1901)
PPG Industries Inc .... E 419 683-2400
   Crestline (G-7799)
S R Door Inc .... C 740 927-3558
   Hebron (G-10761)
Schodorf Truck Body & Eqp Co ...... E 614 228-6793
   Columbus (G-7426)
Sonalysts Inc .... E 937 429-9711
   Beavercreek (G-1342)
Taylor Products Inc .... E 419 263-2313
   Payne (G-15875)
Therm-All Inc .... E 440 779-9494
   North Olmsted (G-15201)
Vinylume Products Inc .... D 330 799-2000
   Youngstown (G-21067)
Yoder Window & Siding Ltd .... G 330 857-4530
   Fredericksburg (G-9961)

3221 Glass Containers

Anchor Glass Container Corp .... C 740 452-2743
   Zanesville (G-21099)
◆ Anchor Hocking LLC .... A 740 681-6478
   Lancaster (G-11541)
Anchor Hocking LLC .... G 740 687-2500
   Lancaster (G-11542)
Bprex Plastic Packaging Inc .... F 419 247-5000
   Toledo (G-18213)
Chantilly Development Corp .... F 419 243-8109
   Toledo (G-18227)
Custom Deco LLC .... E 419 698-2900
   Toledo (G-18245)
Dura Temp Corporation .... F 419 866-4348
   Holland (G-10929)
▲ G&M Media Packaging Inc .... F 419 636-5461
   Bryan (G-2282)
▼ Ghp II LLC .... C 740 687-2500
   Lancaster (G-11575)
◆ Owens-Brockway Glass Cont Inc ... C 567 336-8449
   Perrysburg (G-15995)
◆ Owens-Brockway Packaging Inc ... G 567 336-5000
   Perrysburg (G-15996)
Owens-Illinois Inc .... B 567 336-5000
   Perrysburg (G-15997)
▲ Owens-Illinois De Puerto Rico ...... D 419 874-9708
   Toledo (G-18451)
◆ Owens-Illinois General Inc .... B 567 336-5000
   Perrysburg (G-15998)
◆ Owens-Illinois Group Inc .... G 567 336-5000
   Perrysburg (G-15999)
Pyromatics Corp .... F 440 352-3500
   Mentor (G-13561)
Tiama Americas Inc .... E 269 274-3107
   Maumee (G-13153)

3229 Pressed & Blown Glassware, NEC

All State GL Block Fctry Inc .... G 440 205-8410
   Mentor (G-13384)
◆ Anchor Hocking LLC .... A 740 681-6478
   Lancaster (G-11541)
Anchor Hocking LLC .... G 740 687-2500
   Lancaster (G-11542)
▼ Anchor Hocking Consmr GL Corp ... G 740 653-2527
   Lancaster (G-11543)
Anderson Glass Co Inc .... E 614 476-4877
   Columbus (G-6603)
Angel Glass Lost .... E 419 353-2831
   Bowling Green (G-1951)
Blockamerica Corporation .... G 614 274-0700
   Columbus (G-6680)
Brubaker Metalcrafts Inc .... F 937 456-5834
   Eaton (G-9143)
Celstar Group Inc .... G 937 224-1730
   Dayton (G-8080)
▲ Cincinnati Gasket Pkg Mfg Inc ..... E 513 761-3458
   Cincinnati (G-3492)
▲ Custom Deco South Inc .... E 419 698-2900
   Toledo (G-18246)
Dal-Little Fabricating Inc .... G 216 883-3323
   Cleveland (G-5059)
Eagle Laboratory Glass Co LLC ..... G 440 354-8350
   Painesville (G-15733)
◆ Echo EMR Inc .... F 937 322-4972
   Springfield (G-17394)
▲ Eye Lighting Intl N Amer Inc .... C 440 350-7000
   Mentor (G-13442)
General Electric Company .... D 740 385-2114
   Logan (G-12025)
General Electric Company .... A 330 373-1400
   Mc Donald (G-13199)
▼ Ghp II LLC .... C 740 687-2500
   Lancaster (G-11575)
Glass Axis .... G 614 291-4250
   Columbus (G-6952)
◆ Glasstech Inc .... C 419 661-9500
   Perrysburg (G-15959)
▲ Global Glass Block Inc .... G 216 731-2333
   Euclid (G-9414)
Industrial Fiberglass Spc Inc .... E 937 222-9000
   Dayton (G-8263)
International Automotive Compo ... A 419 433-5653
   Huron (G-11099)
Ipm Inc .... G 419 248-8000
   Toledo (G-18351)
Jason Wilson .... E 937 604-8209
   Tipp City (G-18120)
Jjs3 Foundation .... E 513 751-3292
   Cincinnati (G-3874)

▲ John Krizay Inc .... E 330 332-5607
   Salem (G-16750)
Johns Manville Corporation .... B 419 878-8111
   Waterville (G-19498)
Katies Light House LLC .... E 419 645-5451
   Cridersville (G-7811)
Knoble Glass & Metal Inc .... G 513 753-1246
   Cincinnati (G-3919)
Leveck Lighting Products Inc .... E 937 667-4421
   Tipp City (G-18121)
◆ Libbey Glass Inc .... C 419 325-2100
   Toledo (G-18382)
Libbey Glass Inc .... A 419 729-7272
   Toledo (G-18383)
▼ Libbey Inc .... C 419 325-2100
   Toledo (G-18385)
Matthews Art Glass .... E 419 335-2448
   Archbold (G-658)
▼ Mfg Composite Systems Company .. B 440 997-5851
   Ashtabula (G-786)
Midwest Composites LLC .... E 419 738-2431
   Wapakoneta (G-19342)
Modern China Inc .... E 330 938-6104
   Sebring (G-16889)
Molded Fiber Glass Research .... G 440 994-5100
   Ashtabula (G-791)
▲ Mosser Glass Incorporated .... E 740 439-1827
   Cambridge (G-2449)
Nextgen Fiber Optics LLC .... D 513 549-4691
   Cincinnati (G-4075)
◆ Owens Corning .... A 419 248-8000
   Toledo (G-18446)
Owens Corning Ht Inc .... G 419 248-8000
   Toledo (G-18447)
◆ Owens Corning Sales LLC .... A 419 248-8000
   Toledo (G-18448)
Pierce GL Inc .... G 513 772-7202
   Cincinnati (G-4158)
◆ PLC Connections LLC .... F 614 279-1796
   Columbus (G-7327)
PPG Industries Inc .... E 419 683-2400
   Crestline (G-7799)
R G C Inc .... F 513 683-3110
   Loveland (G-12225)
Scottrods LLC .... G 419 499-2705
   Monroeville (G-14290)
Sem-Com Company Inc .... F 419 537-8813
   Toledo (G-18517)
Srico Inc .... F 614 799-0664
   Columbus (G-7481)
Techneglas Inc .... F 419 873-2000
   Perrysburg (G-16012)
Technical Glass Products Inc .... C 425 396-8420
   Perrysburg (G-16013)
Tencate Advanced Armor USA Inc .. D 740 928-0326
   Hebron (G-10765)
Touch of Glass .... F 419 861-2888
   Toledo (G-18579)
Variety Glass Inc .... F 740 432-3643
   Cambridge (G-2461)
Wilson Optical Laboratory Inc .... E 440 357-7000
   Mentor (G-13626)

3231 Glass Prdts Made Of Purchased Glass

A & B Iron & Metal Company .... F 937 228-1561
   Dayton (G-7997)
A Service Glass Inc .... F 937 426-4920
   Beavercreek (G-1297)
▲ Addis Glass Fabricating Inc .... F 513 860-3340
   West Chester (G-19637)
Adria Scientific GL Works Co .... G 440 474-6691
   Geneva (G-10211)
▲ AGC Automotive Americas .... D 937 599-3131
   Bellefontaine (G-1501)
AGC Flat Glass North Amer Inc .... G 937 599-3131
   Bellefontaine (G-1503)
American Woodwork Specialty Co .. E 937 263-1053
   Dayton (G-8029)
◆ Amerihua Intl Entps Inc .... G 740 549-0300
   Lewis Center (G-11744)
◆ Anchi Inc .... A 740 653-2527
   Lancaster (G-11540)
Anderson Glass Co Inc .... E 614 476-4877
   Columbus (G-6603)
Architectural Art Glass Studio .... G 513 731-7336
   Cincinnati (G-3355)
▲ Atc Lighting & Plastics Inc .... C 440 466-7670
   Andover (G-580)
◆ Auto Temp Inc .... C 513 732-6969
   Batavia (G-1123)

◆ **Basco Manufacturing Company**........C....... 513 573-1900
Mason *(G-12831)*
Beach Manufacturing Co........................C....... 937 882-6372
Donnelsville *(G-8800)*
Bruening Glass Works Inc.......................G....... 440 333-4768
Cleveland *(G-4846)*
Cadenza Enterprises LLC........................G....... 937 428-6058
Dayton *(G-8073)*
Champion Window Co of Toledo...........E....... 419 841-0154
Perrysburg *(G-15933)*
Chantilly Development Corp..................F....... 419 243-8109
Toledo *(G-18227)*
Colleen D Turner.....................................G....... 419 886-4810
Bellville *(G-1555)*
Commercial Vehicle Group Inc.............A....... 614 289-5360
New Albany *(G-14615)*
▲ **Crystal Art Imports Inc**........................F....... 614 430-8180
Columbus *(G-6840)*
Custom GL Sltions Millbury LLC...........C....... 419 855-7706
Millbury *(G-14048)*
Custom Glass Solutions Upper S..........B....... 419 294-4921
Upper Sandusky *(G-18949)*
Dresden Specialties Inc..........................G....... 740 754-2451
Dresden *(G-8868)*
▲ **East Palestine Decorating LLC**.........F....... 330 426-9600
East Palestine *(G-9078)*
▲ **Enclosure Suppliers LLC**....................E....... 513 782-3900
Cincinnati *(G-3637)*
▲ **Environmental Sampling Sup Inc**.....E....... 330 497-9396
North Canton *(G-15080)*
Etching Concepts.....................................G....... 419 691-9086
Rossford *(G-16585)*
Fergusons Cut Glass Works...................G....... 419 734-0808
Marblehead *(G-12585)*
▲ **Franklin Art Glass Studios**..................E....... 614 221-2972
Columbus *(G-6935)*
Frigid Units Inc...G....... 419 478-4000
Toledo *(G-18297)*
Fuyao Glass America Inc........................C....... 937 496-5777
Dayton *(G-8212)*
General Electric Company.....................D....... 740 385-2114
Logan *(G-12025)*
General Glass & Screen Inc...................G....... 440 350-9033
Mentor *(G-13456)*
Ghp II LLC...B....... 740 681-6825
Lancaster *(G-11576)*
Glass Seale Ltd..G....... 513 733-1464
Cincinnati *(G-3761)*
Glass Surface Systems Inc....................D....... 330 745-8500
Barberton *(G-1075)*
◆ **Glasstech Inc**...C....... 419 661-9500
Perrysburg *(G-15959)*
Great Day Improvements LLC...............G....... 330 468-0700
Macedonia *(G-12300)*
Installed Building Pdts LLC...................E....... 614 308-9900
Columbus *(G-7029)*
▲ **Intigral Inc**..C....... 440 439-0980
Walton Hills *(G-19311)*
Intigral Inc..E....... 440 439-0980
Youngstown *(G-20942)*
Jafe Decorating Co Inc...........................E....... 937 547-1888
Greenville *(G-10375)*
Kessler Studios Inc...................................G....... 513 683-7500
Loveland *(G-12204)*
Kimmatt Corp...G....... 937 228-3811
Dayton *(G-8297)*
◆ **Libbey Glass Inc**.....................................C....... 419 325-2100
Toledo *(G-18382)*
Macpherson Engineering Inc................E....... 440 243-6565
Berea *(G-1616)*
Marchione Studio Inc...............................G....... 330 454-7408
Canton *(G-2742)*
Middlefield Glass Incorporated............E....... 440 632-5699
Middlefield *(G-13823)*
▲ **North Central Insulation Inc**...............F....... 419 886-2030
Bellville *(G-1561)*
Ohio Mirror Technologies Inc................F....... 419 399-5903
Paulding *(G-15867)*
Ohio Mirror Technologies Inc................F....... 419 399-5903
Paulding *(G-15868)*
Oldcastle Buildingenvelope Inc.............D....... 419 661-5079
Perrysburg *(G-15988)*
Pilkington North America Inc...............B....... 419 247-3211
Rossford *(G-16589)*
Potters Industries LLC............................E....... 216 621-0840
Cleveland *(G-5898)*
PPG Industries Inc...................................E....... 419 683-2400
Crestline *(G-7799)*
Pyromatics Corp.......................................F....... 440 352-3500
Mentor *(G-13561)*
R G C Inc..F....... 513 683-3110
Loveland *(G-12225)*
R M Yates Co Inc.......................................G....... 216 441-0900
Cleveland *(G-5953)*
Rumpke Transportation Co LLC............C....... 513 242-4600
Cincinnati *(G-4289)*
▲ **Safelite Group Inc**.................................A....... 614 210-9000
Columbus *(G-7413)*
Scs Construction Services Inc..............E....... 513 929-0260
Cincinnati *(G-4311)*
Sem-Com Company Inc............................F....... 419 537-8813
Toledo *(G-18517)*
Solon Glass Center Inc............................F....... 440 248-5018
Cleveland *(G-6078)*
Standing Rock Designery.......................G....... 330 650-9089
Hudson *(G-11077)*
Strategic Materials Inc............................G....... 740 349-9523
Newark *(G-14925)*
Studio Arts & Glass Inc...........................F....... 330 494-9779
Canton *(G-2826)*
Taylor Products Inc..................................E....... 419 263-2313
Payne *(G-15874)*
Taylor Products Inc..................................E....... 419 263-2313
Payne *(G-15875)*
Technicolor Usa Inc..................................A....... 614 474-8821
Circleville *(G-4561)*
Tiger Mirror Corporation.........................G....... 419 855-3146
Clay Center *(G-4569)*
Trio Insulated Glass Inc...........................G....... 614 276-1647
Columbus *(G-7544)*
Tyseka...G....... 419 860-9585
Lima *(G-11954)*
Vidonish Studios..G....... 419 884-1119
Mansfield *(G-12535)*
Whitney Stained Glass Studio...............G....... 216 348-1616
Cleveland *(G-6306)*
XS Smith Inc...E....... 252 940-5060
Cincinnati *(G-4529)*

3241 Cement, Hydraulic

Asphalt Services Ohio Inc.......................G....... 614 864-4600
Columbus *(G-6621)*
Cincinnati Blacktop Company................F....... 513 681-0952
Cincinnati *(G-3486)*
Fairborn Cement Company LLC............C....... 937 879-8393
Xenia *(G-20771)*
Hartline Products Coinc...........................G....... 216 851-7189
Cleveland *(G-5378)*
Huron Cement Products Company........E....... 419 433-4161
Huron *(G-11096)*
Lafarge North America Inc.....................C....... 419 399-4861
Paulding *(G-15864)*
Lafarge North America Inc.....................G....... 216 781-9330
Cleveland *(G-5553)*
Lafarge North America Inc.....................G....... 419 241-5256
Toledo *(G-18375)*
Lafarge North America Inc.....................F....... 419 897-7656
Maumee *(G-13125)*
Lafarge North America Inc.....................G....... 740 423-5900
Belpre *(G-1579)*
Lehigh Hanson Ecc Inc.............................G....... 614 497-2001
Columbus *(G-7121)*
Lozinak & Sons Inc...................................G....... 440 877-1819
North Royalton *(G-15284)*
Murphy James Construction LLC..........E....... 740 667-3626
Coolville *(G-7675)*
Myko Industries...G....... 216 431-0900
Cleveland *(G-5717)*
Quikrete Companies Inc..........................E....... 614 885-4406
Columbus *(G-7369)*
Quikrete Companies LLC........................E....... 419 241-1148
Toledo *(G-18491)*
Quikrete Companies LLC........................E....... 330 296-6080
Ravenna *(G-16397)*
RC Lonestar Inc...G....... 513 467-0430
Cincinnati *(G-4251)*
St Marys Cement Inc (us).......................G....... 937 642-4573
Marysville *(G-12814)*
Wallseye Concrete Corp..........................F....... 440 235-1800
Cleveland *(G-6287)*
Wallseye Concrete Corp..........................F....... 419 483-2738
Castalia *(G-2941)*

3251 Brick & Structural Clay Tile

Afc Company..F....... 330 533-5581
Canfield *(G-2519)*
Armstrong World Industries Inc............D....... 614 771-9307
Hilliard *(G-10806)*
Belden Brick Company LLC....................C....... 330 456-0031
Sugarcreek *(G-17843)*
Belden Brick Company LLC....................E....... 330 265-2030
Sugarcreek *(G-17844)*
Bowerston Shale Company.....................E....... 740 763-3921
Newark *(G-14856)*
Bowerston Shale Company.....................E....... 740 269-2921
Bowerston *(G-1939)*
Glen-Gery Corporation............................D....... 419 845-3321
Caledonia *(G-2416)*
Glen-Gery Corporation............................E....... 419 468-5002
Iberia *(G-11113)*
Kepcor Inc..F....... 330 868-6434
Minerva *(G-14186)*
LBC Clay Co LLC......................................G....... 330 674-0674
Millersburg *(G-14106)*
Meridian Brick LLC...................................G....... 937 294-1548
Franklin *(G-9899)*
Minteq International Inc..........................E....... 330 343-8821
Dover *(G-8843)*
Morgan Advanced Ceramics Inc............C....... 440 232-8604
Bedford *(G-1428)*
Nutro Inc..E....... 440 572-3800
Strongsville *(G-17773)*
Resco Products Inc..................................E....... 740 682-7794
Oak Hill *(G-15459)*
Stebbins Engineering & Mfg Co............E....... 740 922-3012
Uhrichsville *(G-18895)*
Whitacre Greer Company.......................E....... 330 823-1610
Alliance *(G-515)*
Wk Brick Company..................................G....... 614 416-6700
Columbus *(G-7607)*

3253 Ceramic Tile

Artfinders...G....... 330 264-7706
Wooster *(G-20563)*
Dai Ceramics Inc.......................................D....... 440 946-6964
Willoughby *(G-20306)*
Epro Inc..E....... 419 426-5053
Bloomville *(G-1714)*
Florida Tile Inc..G....... 513 891-1122
Blue Ash *(G-1777)*
Florida Tile Inc..G....... 614 436-2511
Columbus *(G-6928)*
Florida Tile Inc..G....... 937 293-5151
Miamisburg *(G-13669)*
▲ **Ironrock Capital Incorporated**...........D....... 330 484-4887
Canton *(G-2712)*
Kepcor Inc..F....... 330 868-6434
Minerva *(G-14186)*
Mohawk Industries Inc............................C....... 800 837-3812
Grove City *(G-10447)*
▲ **Ohio Tile & Marble Co**..........................E....... 513 541-4211
Cincinnati *(G-4105)*
PCC Ceramic Group 1..............................G....... 440 516-3672
Wickliffe *(G-20226)*
◆ **Seneca Tiles Inc**.....................................D....... 419 426-3561
Attica *(G-859)*
Stebbins Engineering & Mfg Co............E....... 740 922-3012
Uhrichsville *(G-18895)*
▲ **Studio Vertu Inc**.....................................E....... 513 241-9038
Cincinnati *(G-4387)*
Summitville Tiles Inc................................C....... 330 868-6771
Minerva *(G-14202)*
Tarkett USA Inc..C....... 440 543-8916
Solon *(G-17247)*
Wccv Floor Coverings LLC......................E....... 330 688-0114
Peninsula *(G-15901)*

3255 Clay Refractories

A N H..G....... 513 576-6240
Batavia *(G-1121)*
Afc Company..F....... 330 533-5581
Canfield *(G-2519)*
Bowerston Shale Company.....................E....... 740 269-2921
Bowerston *(G-1939)*
Glen-Gery Corporation............................E....... 419 468-5002
Iberia *(G-11113)*
Glen-Gery Corporation............................D....... 419 845-3321
Caledonia *(G-2416)*
Harbisonwalker Intl Inc............................E....... 330 326-2010
Windham *(G-20524)*
Harbisonwalker Intl Inc............................G....... 440 234-8002
Cleveland *(G-5373)*
Harbisonwalker Intl Inc............................E....... 513 576-6240
Batavia *(G-1152)*
Harbisonwalker Intl Inc............................F....... 330 868-4141
Minerva *(G-14181)*
I Cerco Inc..D....... 740 982-2050
Crooksville *(G-7816)*
Lakeway Mfg Inc.......................................E....... 419 433-3030
Huron *(G-11103)*

S I C

Employee Codes: A=Over 500 employees, B=251-500
C=101-250, D=51-100, E=20-50, F=10-19, G=3-9
2019 Harris Ohio
Industrial Directory
901

Magneco/Metrel Inc ... E ... 330 426-9468
Negley *(G-14590)*

Minteq International Inc ... E ... 330 343-8821
Dover *(G-8843)*

▲ Nock and Son Company ... F ... 440 871-5525
Cleveland *(G-5754)*

Nock and Son Company ... F ... 740 682-7741
Oak Hill *(G-15457)*

Resco Products Inc ... E ... 330 372-3716
Warren *(G-19438)*

Resco Products Inc ... D ... 330 488-1226
East Canton *(G-9044)*

Resco Products Inc ... E ... 740 682-7794
Oak Hill *(G-15459)*

▲ Selas Heat Technology Co LLC ... E ... 800 523-6500
Streetsboro *(G-17697)*

Specialty Ceramics Inc ... D ... 330 482-0800
Columbiana *(G-6481)*

Stebbins Engineering & Mfg Co ... E ... 740 922-3012
Uhrichsville *(G-18895)*

Summitville Tiles Inc ... E ... 330 868-6463
Minerva *(G-14203)*

▲ Wahl Refractory Solutions LLC ... D ... 419 334-2658
Fremont *(G-10063)*

Whitacre Greer Company ... E ... 330 823-1610
Alliance *(G-515)*

3259 Structural Clay Prdts, NEC

Baughman Tile Company ... D ... 800 837-3160
Paulding *(G-15856)*

Clay Logan Products Company ... D ... 740 385-2184
Logan *(G-12022)*

Haviland Drainage Products Co ... F ... 419 622-4611
Haviland *(G-10711)*

◆ Ludowici Roof Tile Inc ... D ... 740 342-1995
New Lexington *(G-14718)*

Nr Lee Restoration Ltd ... G ... 419 692-2233
Delphos *(G-8752)*

◆ Superior Clay Corp ... D ... 740 922-4122
Uhrichsville *(G-18896)*

Terreal North America LLC ... C ... 888 582-9052
New Lexington *(G-14727)*

3261 China Plumbing Fixtures & Fittings

▼ A C Products Co ... D ... 330 698-1105
Apple Creek *(G-601)*

Aabel Plumbing Inc ... E ... 937 434-4343
Dayton *(G-7999)*

Accent Manufacturing Inc ... F ... 330 724-7704
Norton *(G-15355)*

As America Inc ... G ... 330 337-2219
Salem *(G-16718)*

As America Inc ... E ... 419 522-4211
Mansfield *(G-12408)*

Bridgits Bath LLC ... G ... 937 259-1960
Dayton *(G-8061)*

Dittmar Sales and Service ... G ... 740 653-7933
Lancaster *(G-11567)*

East Woodworking Company ... G ... 216 791-5950
Cleveland *(G-5140)*

◆ Mansfield Plumbing Pdts LLC ... A ... 419 938-5211
Perrysville *(G-16030)*

Watersource LLC ... G ... 419 747-9552
Mansfield *(G-12538)*

3262 China, Table & Kitchen Articles

Libbey Glass Inc ... A ... 419 729-7272
Toledo *(G-18383)*

▼ Libbey Inc ... C ... 419 325-2100
Toledo *(G-18385)*

3263 Earthenware, Whiteware, Table & Kitchen Articles

Added Touch Decorating Gallery ... G ... 419 747-3146
Ontario *(G-15537)*

Anchor Hocking Glass Company ... G ... 740 681-6025
Lancaster *(G-11544)*

Modern China Inc ... E ... 330 938-6104
Sebring *(G-16889)*

Us Inc ... G ... 513 791-1162
Blue Ash *(G-1863)*

West Ohio Tool & Mfg LLC ... G ... 419 678-4745
Saint Henry *(G-16671)*

3264 Porcelain Electrical Splys

▲ Akron Porcelain & Plastics Co ... C ... 330 745-2159
Akron *(G-49)*

CAM-Lem Inc ... G ... 216 391-7750
Cleveland *(G-4863)*

▲ Channel Products Inc ... D ... 440 423-0113
Solon *(G-17126)*

▲ Electrodyne Company Inc ... F ... 513 732-2822
Batavia *(G-1140)*

Ferro Corporation ... C ... 216 875-6178
Cleveland *(G-5231)*

Fram Group Operations LLC ... G ... 937 316-3000
Greenville *(G-10369)*

Fram Group Operations LLC ... A ... 419 436-5827
Fostoria *(G-9845)*

▲ Materion Brush Inc ... D ... 216 486-4200
Mayfield Heights *(G-13167)*

Petro Ware Inc ... D ... 740 982-1302
Crooksville *(G-7819)*

3269 Pottery Prdts, NEC

All Fired Up Pnt Your Own Pot ... G ... 330 865-5858
Copley *(G-7677)*

Annies Mud Pie Shop LLC ... G ... 513 871-2529
Cincinnati *(G-3348)*

Beaumont Brothers Stoneware ... G ... 740 982-0055
Crooksville *(G-7815)*

Bodycote Imt Inc ... E ... 740 852-5000
London *(G-12050)*

Bosco Pup Co LLC ... G ... 614 833-0349
Pickerington *(G-16042)*

Carruth Studio Inc ... F ... 419 878-3060
Waterville *(G-19491)*

▲ Clay Burley Products Co ... E ... 740 452-3633
Roseville *(G-16576)*

Clay Burley Products Co ... E ... 740 697-0221
Roseville *(G-16577)*

◆ E R Advanced Ceramics Inc ... E ... 330 426-9433
East Palestine *(G-9077)*

Grandpas Pottery ... G ... 937 382-6442
Wilmington *(G-20495)*

J-Vac Industries Inc ... D ... 740 384-2155
Wellston *(G-19603)*

Javanation ... F ... 419 584-1705
Celina *(G-2970)*

Kiln of Hyde Park Inc ... F ... 513 321-3307
Cincinnati *(G-3908)*

Larose Industries LLC ... E ... 419 237-1600
Fayette *(G-9634)*

Marchione Studio Inc ... G ... 330 454-7408
Canton *(G-2742)*

▼ Orton Edward Jr Crmic Fndation ... E ... 614 895-2663
Westerville *(G-20014)*

Potter House ... G ... 419 584-1705
Celina *(G-2981)*

Stoneware Palace Ltd ... G ... 614 529-6974
Columbus *(G-7492)*

Strictly Stitchery Inc ... F ... 440 543-7128
Cleveland *(G-6110)*

Yellow Springs Pottery ... F ... 937 767-1666
Yellow Springs *(G-20822)*

3271 Concrete Block & Brick

American Concrete Products ... F ... 937 224-1433
Dayton *(G-8025)*

B & S Blacktop Co ... G ... 513 797-5759
New Richmond *(G-14810)*

Belden Brick Company LLC ... C ... 330 456-0031
Sugarcreek *(G-17843)*

Belden Brick Company LLC ... E ... 330 265-2030
Sugarcreek *(G-17844)*

Benchmark Land Management LLC ... G ... 513 310-7850
West Chester *(G-19658)*

Bryce Hill Inc ... E ... 937 663-4152
Saint Paris *(G-16705)*

Cantelli Block and Brick Inc ... E ... 419 433-0102
Huron *(G-11091)*

Cement Products Inc ... E ... 419 524-4342
Mansfield *(G-12423)*

Charles Svec Inc ... E ... 216 662-5200
Maple Heights *(G-12568)*

Dearth Resources Inc ... G ... 937 325-0651
Springfield *(G-17384)*

Dearth Resources Inc ... G ... 937 663-4171
Springfield *(G-17385)*

E C S Corp ... F ... 440 323-1707
Elyria *(G-9247)*

Frankie Tatum ... G ... 614 216-1556
Columbus *(G-6934)*

Gennaro Pavers ... G ... 330 536-6825
Lowellville *(G-12252)*

Green Vision Materials Inc ... F ... 440 564-5500
Newbury *(G-14954)*

Hanson Aggregates East LLC ... E ... 740 773-2172
Chillicothe *(G-3191)*

Hazelbaker Industries Ltd ... E ... 614 276-2631
Columbus *(G-6984)*

ICC Safety Service Inc ... G ... 614 261-4557
Columbus *(G-7020)*

J P Sand & Gravel Company ... E ... 614 497-0083
Lockbourne *(G-11995)*

K & L Ready Mix Inc ... F ... 419 532-3585
Kalida *(G-11277)*

Kathy Edie ... G ... 740 763-4887
Newark *(G-14890)*

Koltcz Concrete Block Co ... E ... 440 232-3630
Bedford *(G-1421)*

Mapes Concrete Construction ... G ... 513 245-2631
Cincinnati *(G-3978)*

Martin Block Company ... G ... 740 286-7507
Jackson *(G-11190)*

◆ Meridienne International Inc ... G ... 330 274-8317
Mantua *(G-12554)*

Midwest Specialties Inc ... F ... 419 738-8147
Wapakoneta *(G-19346)*

National Lime and Stone Co ... E ... 614 497-0083
Lockbourne *(G-11998)*

North Central Concrete Design ... F ... 419 606-1908
Wooster *(G-20632)*

Oberfields LLC ... E ... 614 491-7643
Columbus *(G-7236)*

Oberfields LLC ... F ... 614 252-0955
Columbus *(G-7237)*

▲ Osborne Inc ... E ... 440 942-7000
Mentor *(G-13539)*

Portsmouth Block Inc ... F ... 740 353-4113
Portsmouth *(G-16295)*

Quality Block & Supply Inc ... E ... 330 364-4411
Mount Eaton *(G-14421)*

R W Sidley Incorporated ... E ... 440 564-2221
Newbury *(G-14962)*

RE Connors Construction Ltd ... G ... 740 644-0261
Thornville *(G-18031)*

▲ Reading Rock Inc ... C ... 513 874-2345
West Chester *(G-19893)*

Ready Field Solutions LLC ... G ... 330 562-0550
Streetsboro *(G-17692)*

S & S Aggregates Inc ... G ... 740 453-0721
Zanesville *(G-21175)*

Simon & Simon Blue Pond Inc ... G ... 330 928-2298
Cuyahoga Falls *(G-7918)*

▲ Snyder Concrete Products Inc ... E ... 937 885-5176
Moraine *(G-14394)*

Snyder Concrete Products Inc ... G ... 937 224-1433
Dayton *(G-8511)*

St Henry Tile Co Inc ... E ... 419 678-4841
Saint Henry *(G-16667)*

St Henry Tile Co Inc ... F ... 937 548-1101
Greenville *(G-10396)*

Stiger Pre Cast Inc ... G ... 740 482-2313
Nevada *(G-14601)*

Stocker Concrete Company ... F ... 740 254-4626
Gnadenhutten *(G-10283)*

Stocker Sand & Gravel Co ... E ... 740 254-4635
Gnadenhutten *(G-10284)*

Sunny Brook Pressed Con Co ... G ... 330 673-7667
Kent *(G-11391)*

T-N-T Concrete Inc ... G ... 540 480-4040
Mentor *(G-13599)*

Tri-County Block and Brick Inc ... E ... 419 826-7060
Swanton *(G-17925)*

Trumbull Cement Products Co ... G ... 330 372-4342
Warren *(G-19450)*

Tyjen Inc ... G ... 740 380-3215
Logan *(G-12045)*

Tyjen Inc ... G ... 740 797-4064
The Plains *(G-18023)*

Walden Industries Inc ... E ... 740 633-5971
Tiltonsville *(G-18094)*

William Dauch Concrete Company ... F ... 419 668-4458
Norwalk *(G-15418)*

3272 Concrete Prdts

9/10 Castings Inc ... G ... 216 406-8907
Chardon *(G-3094)*

◆ Aco Polymer Products Inc ... E ... 440 285-7000
Mentor *(G-13373)*

Adler & Company Inc ... F ... 513 248-1500
Cincinnati *(G-3298)*

Advantic LLC ... G ... 937 490-4712
Dayton *(G-8010)*

Aetna Plastics Corp ... G ... 330 274-2855
Mantua *(G-12541)*

Agean Marble Manufacturing ... F ... 513 874-1475
West Chester *(G-19829)*

Akron Vault Company Inc ....F 330 784-5475
Akron (G-55)
Ald Precast Corp ....G 614 449-3366
Columbus (G-6562)
Alexander Wilbert Vault Co ....F 419 468-3477
Galion (G-10122)
Allen Enterprises Inc ....E 740 532-5913
Ironton (G-11159)
▲ American Spring Wire Corp ....C 216 292-4620
Bedford Heights (G-1460)
Andras Corp ....G 440 323-2528
Elyria (G-9217)
Armstrong World Industries Inc ....E 740 967-1063
Johnstown (G-11257)
Art Columbus Memorial Inc ....G 614 221-9333
Columbus (G-6616)
Artistic Rock LLC ....G 216 291-8856
Cleveland (G-4742)
Ash Sewer & Drain Service ....G 330 376-9714
Akron (G-71)
Ashland Monument Company Inc ....G 419 281-2688
Ashland (G-678)
B & B Cast Stone Co Inc ....G 740 697-0008
Roseville (G-16574)
Babbert Real Estate Inv Co Ltd ....D 614 837-8444
Canal Winchester (G-2499)
▲ Baswa Acoustics North Amer LLC ...F 216 475-7197
Bedford (G-1388)
Baxter Burial Vault Service ....E 513 641-1010
Cincinnati (G-3382)
Baxter Holdings Inc ....E 513 860-3593
Hamilton (G-10538)
Bell Burial Vault Co ....G 513 896-9044
Hamilton (G-10539)
Bell Vault & Monument Works ....E 937 866-2444
Miamisburg (G-13643)
Bilco Company ....E 740 455-9020
Zanesville (G-21107)
Bluffton Precast Concrete Co ....F 419 358-6946
Bluffton (G-1885)
Brock Burial Vault Inc ....G 740 894-5246
South Point (G-17280)
Buckeye Vault Service Inc ....G 419 747-1976
Mansfield (G-12416)
Carey Precast Concrete Company ....G 419 396-7142
Carey (G-2879)
Carruth Studio Inc ....F 419 878-3060
Waterville (G-19491)
Cement Products Inc ....E 419 524-4342
Mansfield (G-12423)
Cemex Materials LLC ....D 937 268-6706
Dayton (G-8081)
Charles Svec Inc ....E 216 662-5200
Maple Heights (G-12568)
Coate Concrete Products Inc ....G 937 698-4181
West Milton (G-19948)
Complete Cylinder Service Inc ....G 513 772-1500
Cincinnati (G-3538)
Concrete Material Supply LLC ....G 419 261-6404
Toledo (G-18237)
Contech Bridge Solutions LLC ....F 937 878-2170
Dayton (G-8103)
Cox Inc ....F 740 858-4400
Lucasville (G-12261)
Creative Curbing America LLC ....G 419 738-7668
Wapakoneta (G-19327)
Crummitt & Son Vault Corp ....G 304 281-2420
Martins Ferry (G-12759)
Dalaco Materials LLC ....F 513 893-5483
Liberty Twp (G-11824)
▲ Day Pre-Cast Products Co ....G 419 536-2909
Toledo (G-18254)
Donald Schloemer ....G 419 933-2002
Willard (G-20239)
Douglas Industries LLC ....E 740 775-2400
Chillicothe (G-3185)
Douglas S Kutz ....G 440 238-8426
Strongsville (G-17737)
E A Cox Inc ....G 740 858-4400
Lucasville (G-12262)
E C Babbert Inc ....D 614 837-8444
Canal Winchester (G-2502)
E C S Corp ....F 440 323-1707
Elyria (G-9247)
E Pompili & Sons Inc ....G 216 581-8080
Cleveland (G-5130)
Ellinger Monument Inc ....G 740 385-3687
Rockbridge (G-16536)
Encore Precast LLC ....F 513 726-5678
Seven Mile (G-16907)
Evan Ragouzis Co ....G 513 242-5900
Hamilton (G-10555)
Everly Concrete Products ....G 740 635-1415
Bridgeport (G-2074)
Fabcon Companies LLC ....D 614 875-8601
Grove City (G-10430)
▲ Fibreboard Corporation ....C 419 248-8000
Toledo (G-18294)
▲ Fin Pan Inc ....F 513 870-9200
Hamilton (G-10558)
Fithian-Wilbert Burial Vlt Co ....F 330 758-2327
Youngstown (G-20907)
Flowers & Monuments R US ....G 937 813-8496
Dayton (G-8199)
Fort Loramie Cast Stone Pdts ....G 937 420-2257
Fort Loramie (G-9798)
Fort Stben Burial Estates Assn ....G 740 266-6101
Steubenville (G-17534)
Forterra Pipe & Precast LLC ....F 614 445-3830
Columbus (G-6931)
Forterra Pipe & Precast LLC ....G 330 467-7890
Macedonia (G-12295)
Forterra Pipe & Precast LLC ....E 937 268-6707
Dayton (G-8204)
Forterra Pipe & Precast LLC ....G 937 268-6707
Dayton (G-8203)
Fountain Specialists Inc ....G 513 831-5717
Milford (G-14009)
Galena Vault Ltd ....G 740 965-2200
Galena (G-10112)
Gdy Installations Inc ....E 419 467-0036
Toledo (G-18302)
Growco Inc ....G 419 886-4628
Mansfield (G-12454)
Hanson Aggregates East LLC ....E 330 467-7890
Macedonia (G-12301)
Hanson Aggregates East LLC ....E 740 773-2172
Chillicothe (G-3191)
Hanson Concrete Products Ohio ....E 614 443-4846
Columbus (G-6980)
Harn Vault Service Inc ....F 330 832-1995
Minerva (G-14182)
Haviland Culvert Company ....G 419 622-6951
Haviland (G-10710)
Hazelbaker Industries Ltd ....E 614 276-2631
Columbus (G-6984)
Headwaters Incorporated ....F 989 671-1500
Manchester (G-12394)
High Concrete Group LLC ....C 937 748-2412
Springboro (G-17330)
Hilles Burial Vaults Inc ....G 330 823-2251
Alliance (G-473)
Hilltop Basic Resources Inc ....E 513 621-1500
Cincinnati (G-3814)
Hilltop Stone Llc ....G 513 651-5000
Cincinnati (G-3816)
Huron Cement Products Company ....E 419 433-4161
Huron (G-11096)
J K Precast LLC ....G 740 335-2188
Wshngtn CT Hs (G-20729)
Jackson Monument Inc ....G 740 286-1590
Jackson (G-11187)
James Kimmey ....F 740 335-5746
Wshngtn CT Hs (G-20730)
Janell Inc ....G 740 532-9111
Ironton (G-11168)
▲ Jet Stream International Inc ....E 330 505-9988
Niles (G-15018)
Jim Bumen Construction Company ....G 740 663-2659
Chillicothe (G-3197)
K M B Inc ....E 330 889-3451
Bristolville (G-2082)
Kcg Inc ....G 614 238-9450
Columbus (G-7084)
Koppers Industries Inc ....E 740 776-3238
Portsmouth (G-16288)
KSA Limited Partnership ....E 740 776-3238
Portsmouth (G-16289)
L B Weiss Construction Inc ....G 440 205-1774
Mentor (G-13492)
Landon Vault Company ....F 614 443-5505
Columbus (G-7113)
▲ Lang Stone Company Inc ....D 614 235-4099
Columbus (G-7114)
Lindsay Package Systems Inc ....G 330 854-4511
Canal Fulton (G-2482)
▼ Lindsay Precast Inc ....E 800 837-7788
Canal Fulton (G-2483)
Mack Industries ....C 419 353-7081
Bowling Green (G-1983)
Mack Industries Inc ....G 330 460-7005
Brunswick (G-2219)
Mack Industries PA Inc ....D 330 483-3111
Valley City (G-19045)
Mack Industries PA Inc ....F 330 638-7680
Vienna (G-19202)
Mack Ready Mix Concrete Inc ....G 330 483-3111
Valley City (G-19046)
Mansfield Brick & Supply Co ....G 419 526-1191
Mansfield (G-12475)
Marblelife of Central Ohio ....G 614 837-6146
Pickerington (G-16053)
McGill Septic Tank Co ....E 330 876-2171
Kinsman (G-11465)
Metro Mech Inc ....G 216 641-6262
Cleveland (G-5662)
Michaels Pre-Cast Con Pdts ....F 513 683-1292
Loveland (G-12215)
Money Jewelry Vaults ....G 937 366-6391
Wilmington (G-20500)
Motz Mobile Containers Inc ....G 513 772-6689
Cincinnati (G-4050)
Neher Burial Vault Company ....F 937 399-4494
Springfield (G-17460)
Next Dimension Components Inc ....E 440 576-0194
Jefferson (G-11235)
North American Cast Stone Inc ....G 440 286-1999
Chardon (G-3129)
Northern Concrete Pipe Inc ....F 419 841-3361
Sylvania (G-17957)
▲ Norwalk Concrete Inds Inc ....E 419 668-8167
Norwalk (G-15408)
Norwalk Concrete Inds Inc ....E 419 668-8167
Norwalk (G-15409)
O K Brugmann Jr & Sons Inc ....F 330 274-2106
Mantua (G-12555)
Oberfields LLC ....D 740 369-7644
Delaware (G-8712)
Oberfields LLC ....E 740 369-7644
Sunbury (G-17893)
Oberfields LLC ....F 614 252-0955
Columbus (G-7237)
Oberfields LLC ....G 937 885-3711
Dayton (G-8393)
Oberfields LLC ....E 614 491-7643
Columbus (G-7236)
Oberfields Holdings LLC ....G 740 369-7644
Delaware (G-8713)
Ohio Cast Stone Co LLC ....G 614 444-2278
Columbus (G-7242)
Ohio Flame ....G 330 953-0863
Youngstown (G-20981)
Oldcastle Apg Midwest Inc ....D 440 949-1815
Sheffield Village (G-16973)
Oldcastle Companies ....G 800 899-8455
Oakwood (G-15472)
Olde Wood Ltd ....E 330 866-1441
Magnolia (G-12361)
One Wish LLC ....F 800 505-6883
Beachwood (G-1259)
Orrville Trucking & Grading Co ....E 330 682-4010
Orrville (G-15609)
P L M Corporation ....G 216 341-8008
Cleveland (G-5831)
Paper Vault ....G 614 859-5538
Columbus (G-7291)
Patriot Holdings Unlimited LLC ....G 740 574-2112
Wheelersburg (G-20183)
Pavestone LLC ....D 513 474-3783
Cincinnati (G-4142)
Pawnee Maintenance Inc ....D 740 373-6861
Marietta (G-12652)
Paws & Remember Nwo ....G 419 662-9000
Northwood (G-15343)
Poland Concrete Products Inc ....G 330 757-1241
Poland (G-16238)
Precast Services Inc ....G 614 428-4541
Reynoldsburg (G-16447)
Premere Precast Products ....F 740 533-3333
Ironton (G-11170)
Premiere Con Solutions LLC ....F 419 737-9808
Pioneer (G-16092)
Prestress Services Inds LLC ....C 859 299-0461
Columbus (G-7346)
Prestress Services Inds LLC ....E 614 871-2900
Grove City (G-10459)
Provia LLC ....F 330 852-4711
Sugarcreek (G-17860)
Quaker City Septic Tanks LLC ....G 330 427-2239
Leetonia (G-11720)

S I C

Employee Codes: A=Over 500 employees, B=251-500
C=101-250, D=51-100, E=20-50, F=10-19, G=3-9
2019 Harris Ohio
Industrial Directory
903

Quikrete Companies Inc........E....... 614 885-4406
Columbus *(G-7369)*

Quikrete Companies Inc........E....... 513 367-6135
Harrison *(G-10666)*

Quikrete Companies LLC........E....... 419 241-1148
Toledo *(G-18491)*

Quikrete Companies LLC........E....... 330 296-6080
Ravenna *(G-16397)*

R W Sidley Incorporated........E....... 440 564-2221
Newbury *(G-14962)*

Ramp Creek III Ltd........G....... 740 522-0660
Heath *(G-10729)*

Redi Rock Structures Oki LLC........G....... 513 965-9221
Milford *(G-14036)*

Reed Elvin Burl II........G....... 937 399-3242
Springfield *(G-17482)*

Resco Products Inc........E....... 330 372-3716
Warren *(G-19438)*

Richmond Concrete Products........G....... 330 673-7892
Warren *(G-19439)*

Rock Decor Company........G....... 330 857-7625
Orrville *(G-15615)*

S & S Aggregates Inc........G....... 740 453-0721
Zanesville *(G-21175)*

Seislove Vault & Septic Tanks........G....... 419 447-5473
Tiffin *(G-18082)*

Septic Products Inc........G....... 419 282-5933
Ashland *(G-748)*

Shaw Wilbert Vaults LLC........G....... 740 498-7438
Newcomerstown *(G-14982)*

Smith Concrete Co........E....... 740 373-7441
Dover *(G-8854)*

▲ **Snyder Concrete Products Inc**........E....... 937 885-5176
Moraine *(G-14394)*

Snyder Concrete Products Inc........F....... 513 539-7686
Monroe *(G-14276)*

Spoerr Precast Concrete Inc........F....... 419 625-9132
Sandusky *(G-16850)*

St Henry Tile Co Inc........F....... 937 548-1101
Greenville *(G-10396)*

Star Forming Manufacturing LL........C....... 330 740-8300
Youngstown *(G-21039)*

Stiger Pre Cast Inc........G....... 740 482-2313
Nevada *(G-14601)*

Stress Con Industries Inc........G....... 586 731-1628
Brunswick *(G-2241)*

Stuart Burial Vault Company........F....... 740 569-4158
Bremen *(G-2064)*

Tamarron Technology Inc........F....... 800 277-3207
Cincinnati *(G-4404)*

Thomas-Wilbert Vault Co Inc........G....... 740 695-5671
Saint Clairsville *(G-16655)*

Tri County Concrete Inc........E....... 330 425-4464
Twinsburg *(G-18866)*

Turner Vault Co........E....... 419 537-1133
Northwood *(G-15349)*

Uniontown Septic Tanks Inc........F....... 330 699-3386
Uniontown *(G-18936)*

United Precast Inc........C....... 740 393-1121
Mount Vernon *(G-14516)*

Upper Monument........G....... 419 310-2387
Upper Sandusky *(G-18976)*

USA Precast Concrete Limited........G....... 330 854-9600
Canal Fulton *(G-2495)*

Vapor Vault........G....... 513 400-8089
Cincinnati *(G-4466)*

Vintage Vault........G....... 330 607-0136
Akron *(G-426)*

Wauseon Silo & Coal Company........F....... 419 335-6041
Wauseon *(G-19538)*

Whempys Corp........G....... 614 888-6670
Worthington *(G-20707)*

William Dauch Concrete Company........F....... 419 668-4458
Norwalk *(G-15418)*

Wilson Concrete Products Inc........E....... 937 885-7965
Dayton *(G-8594)*

Wilsons Country Creations........F....... 330 377-4190
Killbuck *(G-11456)*

Wysong Concrete Products LLC........G....... 513 874-3109
Fairfield *(G-9578)*

Youngstown Burial Vault Co........G....... 330 782-0015
Youngstown *(G-21073)*

3273 Ready-Mixed Concrete

A K Ready Mix LLC........F....... 740 286-8900
Jackson *(G-11179)*

ACE Ready Mix LLC........G....... 330 745-8125
Norton *(G-15356)*

Ace Ready Mix Concrete Co Inc........F....... 330 745-8125
Norton *(G-15357)*

Adams Bros Concrete Pdts Ltd........F....... 740 452-7566
Zanesville *(G-21092)*

Adams Brothers Inc........F....... 740 819-0323
Zanesville *(G-21093)*

Alexis Concrete Enterprise Inc........F....... 440 366-0031
Elyria *(G-9211)*

All Ohio Ready Mix Concrete........G....... 419 841-3838
Perrysburg *(G-15918)*

All-Rite Rdymx Miami Vly LLC........G....... 513 738-1933
Harrison *(G-10630)*

Allega Concrete Corp........E....... 216 447-0814
Cleveland *(G-4670)*

Anderson Concrete Corp........C....... 614 443-0123
Columbus *(G-6602)*

Arrow Coal Grove Inc........F....... 740 532-6143
Ironton *(G-11160)*

ASAP Ready Mix Inc........G....... 513 797-1774
Amelia *(G-532)*

Associated Associates Inc........E....... 330 626-3300
Mantua *(G-12542)*

Avon Concrete Corporation........G....... 440 937-6264
Avon *(G-941)*

Baird Concrete Products Inc........F....... 740 623-8600
Coshocton *(G-7721)*

Baker-Shindler Contracting Co........G....... 419 399-4841
Cecil *(G-2942)*

Baker-Shindler Contracting Co........E....... 419 782-5080
Defiance *(G-8615)*

▼ **Bellbrook Transport Inc**........G....... 937 233-5555
Dayton *(G-8052)*

Bryce Hill Inc........G....... 937 325-0651
Springfield *(G-17369)*

Buckeye Ready-Mix........G....... 419 294-2389
Upper Sandusky *(G-18948)*

Buckeye Ready-Mix LLC........G....... 740 967-4801
Johnstown *(G-11260)*

Buckeye Ready-Mix LLC........G....... 614 879-6316
West Jefferson *(G-19921)*

Buckeye Ready-Mix LLC........F....... 740 387-8846
Marion *(G-12696)*

Buckeye Ready-Mix LLC........E....... 614 575-2132
Reynoldsburg *(G-16431)*

Buckeye Ready-Mix LLC........E....... 937 642-2951
Marysville *(G-12773)*

Buckeye Ready-Mix LLC........F....... 740 654-4423
Lancaster *(G-11549)*

C F Poeppelman Inc........G....... 937 526-5137
Versailles *(G-19175)*

C F Poeppelman Inc........E....... 937 448-2191
Bradford *(G-2010)*

Caldwell Lumber & Supply Co........E....... 740 732-2306
Caldwell *(G-2404)*

Caldwell Redi Mix Company........G....... 740 732-2906
Caldwell *(G-2405)*

Caldwell Redi Mix Company........G....... 740 685-6554
Byesville *(G-2379)*

Camden Ready Mix Co........F....... 937 456-4539
Camden *(G-2464)*

Car Bros Inc........G....... 440 232-1840
Bedford *(G-1393)*

Carr Bros Inc........E....... 440 232-3700
Bedford *(G-1394)*

Carr Bros Bldrs Sup & Coal Co........E....... 440 232-3700
Cleveland *(G-4882)*

Castalia Trenching & Ready Mix........F....... 419 684-5502
Castalia *(G-2936)*

Cement Products Inc........E....... 419 524-4342
Mansfield *(G-12423)*

Cemex Cnstr Mtls ATL LLC........D....... 937 878-8651
Xenia *(G-20760)*

Cemex Construction Corporation........G....... 440 449-0872
Mentor *(G-13411)*

Cemex Construction Mtls Inc........G....... 440 449-0872
Cleveland *(G-4898)*

Cemex Materials LLC........E....... 937 268-6706
Dayton *(G-8082)*

Cemex USA Inc........F....... 937 879-8350
Fairborn *(G-9455)*

Center Concrete Inc........F....... 800 453-4224
Edgerton *(G-9170)*

Central Ready Mix LLC........E....... 513 402-5001
Cincinnati *(G-3457)*

Central Ready Mix LLC........G....... 513 367-1939
Cleves *(G-6356)*

Central Ready-Mix of Ohio LLC........E....... 614 252-3452
Cincinnati *(G-3458)*

Chappell-Zimmerman Inc........F....... 330 337-8711
Salem *(G-16725)*

Christman Supply Co Inc........G....... 740 472-0046
Woodsfield *(G-20542)*

Citywide Materials Inc........E....... 513 533-1111
Cincinnati *(G-3522)*

Cleveland Ready Mix........G....... 216 399-6688
Cleveland *(G-4973)*

Consumeracq Inc........C....... 440 277-9305
Lorain *(G-12084)*

Consumers Builders Supply Co........E....... 440 277-9306
Lorain *(G-12085)*

Cremeans Concrete and Sup Co........G....... 740 446-1142
Gallipolis *(G-10162)*

D W Dickey and Son Inc........D....... 330 424-1441
Lisbon *(G-11966)*

Dan K Williams Inc........E....... 419 893-3251
Maumee *(G-13085)*

Dan Shrock Cement........G....... 440 548-2498
Parkman *(G-15811)*

Dearth Resources Inc........G....... 937 325-0651
Springfield *(G-17384)*

Dearth Resources Inc........G....... 937 663-4171
Springfield *(G-17385)*

Diano Construction and Sup Co........E....... 330 456-7229
Canton *(G-2658)*

Diversified Ready Mix Ltd........G....... 330 628-3355
Tallmadge *(G-17980)*

Eci........G....... 419 483-2738
Castalia *(G-2937)*

Ernst Enterprises Inc........F....... 937 878-9378
Fairborn *(G-9458)*

Ernst Enterprises Inc........E....... 937 233-5555
Dayton *(G-8186)*

Ernst Enterprises Inc........E....... 513 874-8300
Lebanon *(G-11651)*

Ernst Enterprises Inc........E....... 937 848-6811
Bellbrook *(G-1493)*

Ernst Enterprises Inc........E....... 937 866-9441
Carrollton *(G-2919)*

Ernst Enterprises Inc........G....... 614 308-0063
Columbus *(G-6905)*

Ernst Enterprises Inc........E....... 937 339-6249
Troy *(G-18653)*

Ernst Enterprises Inc........F....... 513 422-3651
Middletown *(G-13905)*

Ernst Enterprises Inc........E....... 614 443-9456
Columbus *(G-6904)*

Feikert Sand & Gravel Co Inc........E....... 330 674-0038
Millersburg *(G-14082)*

G Big Inc........E....... 740 867-5758
Chesapeake *(G-3145)*

G Big Inc........G....... 740 532-9123
Ironton *(G-11165)*

Geauga Concrete Inc........F....... 440 338-4915
Newbury *(G-14952)*

Grafton Ready Mix Concret Inc........E....... 440 926-2911
Grafton *(G-10302)*

Hanson Aggregates East LLC........E....... 740 773-2172
Chillicothe *(G-3191)*

Hanson Aggregates East LLC........E....... 937 587-2671
Peebles *(G-15878)*

Hanson Ready Mix Inc........D....... 614 221-5345
Columbus *(G-6981)*

Hensel Ready Mix........G....... 419 253-9200
Marengo *(G-12592)*

Hensel Ready Mix Inc........F....... 419 675-1808
Kenton *(G-11409)*

Hensel Ready Mix Inc........G....... 614 755-6365
Columbus *(G-6989)*

Hilltop Basic Resources Inc........F....... 937 795-2020
Aberdeen *(G-1)*

Hilltop Basic Resources Inc........E....... 513 621-1500
Cincinnati *(G-3814)*

Hilltop Basic Resources Inc........F....... 513 651-5000
Cincinnati *(G-3813)*

Hilltop Big Bend Quarry LLC........G....... 513 651-5000
Cincinnati *(G-3815)*

Hocking Valley Concrete Inc........E....... 740 385-2165
Logan *(G-12027)*

Hocking Valley Concrete Inc........G....... 740 342-1948
New Lexington *(G-14716)*

Hocking Valley Concrete Inc........G....... 740 385-2165
Logan *(G-12028)*

Hull Builders Supply Inc........E....... 440 967-3159
Vermilion *(G-19161)*

Hull Ready Mix Concrete Inc........F....... 419 625-8070
Sandusky *(G-16815)*

Huron Cement Products Company........G....... 419 433-4161
Sandusky *(G-16816)*

Huron Cement Products Company........E....... 419 433-4161
Huron *(G-11096)*

Huron Products........G....... 419 483-5608
Bellevue *(G-1536)*

SIC SECTION — 32 STONE, CLAY, GLASS, AND CONCRETE PRODUCTS

Huth Ready Mix & Supply Co .... F 330 833-4191
  Massillon *(G-12999)*
IMI-Irving Materials Inc .... G 513 844-8444
  Hamilton *(G-10571)*
Ioppolo Concrete Corporation .... E 440 439-6606
  Bedford *(G-1418)*
Irving Materials Inc .... F 513 523-7127
  Oxford *(G-15695)*
Irving Materials Inc .... F 513 844-8444
  Hamilton *(G-10573)*
Joe McClelland Inc .... E 740 452-3036
  Zanesville *(G-21151)*
K & L Ready Mix Inc .... G 419 943-2200
  Leipsic *(G-11727)*
K & L Ready Mix Inc .... F 419 523-4376
  Ottawa *(G-15656)*
K & L Ready Mix Inc .... F 419 532-3585
  Kalida *(G-11277)*
K & L Ready Mix Inc .... F 419 293-2937
  Mc Comb *(G-13190)*
K M B Inc .... E 330 889-3451
  Bristolville *(G-2082)*
Kuhlman Corporation .... E 419 321-1670
  Toledo *(G-18370)*
▲ Kuhlman Corporation .... C 419 897-6000
  Maumee *(G-13124)*
Lafarge North America Inc .... D 419 798-4486
  Marblehead *(G-12586)*
Lafarge North America Inc .... E 330 393-5656
  Warren *(G-19415)*
Lancaster West Side Coal Co .... F 740 862-4713
  Lancaster *(G-11582)*
Lehigh Cement Company LLC ...... E 330 499-9100
  Middlebranch *(G-13759)*
Lehigh Hanson Ecc Inc .... E 330 499-9100
  Middlebranch *(G-13760)*
M & R Redi Mix Inc .... E 419 445-7771
  Pettisville *(G-16034)*
M & R Redi Mix Inc .... G 419 748-8442
  Mc Clure *(G-13186)*
Mack Concrete Industries Inc .... F 330 483-3111
  Valley City *(G-19044)*
Mack Concrete Industries Inc .... F 330 784-7008
  Akron *(G-264)*
Market Ready .... G 513 289-9231
  Maineville *(G-12374)*
Marvin Mix .... G 614 774-9337
  Columbus *(G-7156)*
McConnell Ready Mix .... G 440 458-4325
  Elyria *(G-9292)*
McGovney Ready Mix Inc .... E 740 353-4111
  Portsmouth *(G-16290)*
Mecco Inc .... E 513 422-3651
  Middletown *(G-13926)*
Medina Supply Company .... E 330 425-0752
  Twinsburg *(G-18816)*
Medina Supply Company .... E 330 723-3681
  Medina *(G-13298)*
Mel Stevens U-Cart Concrete .... G 419 478-2600
  Toledo *(G-18406)*
Miami Valley Ready Mix Inc .... E 513 738-2616
  Harrison *(G-10659)*
▲ Mini Mix Inc .... F 513 353-3811
  Cleves *(G-6371)*
Moritz Concrete Inc .... E 419 529-3232
  Mansfield *(G-12486)*
Moritz Materials Inc .... E 419 281-0575
  Ashland *(G-726)*
Nalcon Ready Mix Inc .... G 419 422-4341
  Kenton *(G-11416)*
National Lime and Stone Co .... E 419 423-3400
  Findlay *(G-9729)*
National Lime and Stone Co .... G 330 339-2144
  New Philadelphia *(G-14790)*
National Lime and Stone Co .... G 216 883-9840
  Cleveland *(G-5726)*
Nissen Lumber & Coal Co Inc .... G 419 836-8035
  Oregon *(G-15562)*
O K Brugmann Jr & Sons Inc .... F 330 274-2106
  Mantua *(G-12555)*
Olen Corporation .... F 419 294-2611
  Upper Sandusky *(G-18969)*
Orrville Trucking & Grading Co ..... E 330 682-4010
  Orrville *(G-15609)*
Osborne Inc .... F 440 232-1440
  Cleveland *(G-5822)*
▲ Osborne Inc .... E 440 942-7000
  Mentor *(G-13539)*
Osborne Inc .... E 216 771-0010
  Cleveland *(G-5821)*

Pahl Ready Mix Concrete Inc .... F 419 636-4238
  Bryan *(G-2303)*
Pahl Ready Mix Concrete Inc .... F 419 636-4238
  Waterville *(G-19502)*
Palmer Bros Transit Mix Con .... F 419 332-6363
  Fremont *(G-10044)*
Palmer Bros Transit Mix Con .... F 419 352-4681
  Bowling Green *(G-1989)*
Palmer Bros Transit Mix Con .... G 419 447-2018
  Tiffin *(G-18075)*
Palmer Bros Transit Mix Con .... F 419 686-2366
  Portage *(G-16273)*
Paul H Rohe Company Inc .... E 513 326-6789
  Cincinnati *(G-4140)*
Paul R Lipp & Son Inc .... F 330 227-9614
  Rogers *(G-16560)*
Petros Concrete Inc .... G 330 868-6130
  Waynesburg *(G-19565)*
Philip Armbrust .... G 740 335-7285
  Wshngtn CT Hs *(G-20735)*
Phillips Companies .... E 937 426-5461
  Beavercreek Township *(G-1371)*
Phillips Ready Mix Co .... D 937 426-5151
  Beavercreek Township *(G-1372)*
Placecrete Inc .... F 937 298-2121
  Moraine *(G-14379)*
Pleasant Valley Ready Mix Inc ...... F 330 852-2613
  Sugarcreek *(G-17858)*
Quadcast .... G 330 854-4511
  Canal Fulton *(G-2490)*
Quality Block & Supply Inc .... E 330 364-4411
  Mount Eaton *(G-14421)*
Quality Ready Mix Inc .... F 419 394-8870
  Saint Marys *(G-16696)*
Quikrete Companies Inc .... E 513 367-6135
  Harrison *(G-10666)*
Quikrete Companies LLC .... E 330 296-6080
  Ravenna *(G-16397)*
R W Sidley Inc .... F 440 224-2664
  Kingsville *(G-11462)*
R W Sidley Incorporated .... E 440 298-3232
  Thompson *(G-18028)*
R W Sidley Incorporated .... E 440 564-2221
  Newbury *(G-14962)*
R W Sidley Incorporated .... F 330 499-5616
  Canton *(G-2801)*
R W Sidley Incorporated .... F 330 392-2721
  Warren *(G-19435)*
R W Sidley Incorporated .... E 330 793-7374
  Youngstown *(G-21012)*
Ready To Go LLC .... G 216 862-8572
  Cleveland *(G-5964)*
Rinker Materials .... G 330 654-2511
  Diamond *(G-8799)*
Rockport Cnstr & Mtls Inc .... E 216 432-9465
  Cleveland *(G-5997)*
Ross Co Redi Mix Co Inc .... G 740 333-6833
  Wshngtn CT Hs *(G-20743)*
Ross-Co Redi-Mix Co Inc .... E 740 775-4466
  Chillicothe *(G-3221)*
S J Roth Enterprises Inc .... E 513 242-8400
  Cincinnati *(G-4296)*
Sakrete Inc .... E 513 242-3644
  Cincinnati *(G-4299)*
Sardinia Concrete Company .... E 513 248-0090
  Milford *(G-14039)*
Sardinia Ready Mix Inc .... G 937 446-2523
  Sardinia *(G-16871)*
Sardinia Ready Mix Inc .... F 937 446-2523
  Sardinia *(G-16872)*
Schwab Industries Inc .... F 330 364-4411
  Dover *(G-8852)*
Scioto Ready Mix LLC .... D 740 924-9273
  Pataskala *(G-15843)*
Scioto Readymix Co .... G 614 491-0773
  Columbus *(G-7431)*
Scsrm Concrete Company Ltd ...... E 937 533-1001
  Sidney *(G-17074)*
Shelly Company .... G 740 246-6315
  Thornville *(G-18033)*
Shelly Materials Inc .... G 614 871-6704
  Grove City *(G-10466)*
Sidwell Materials Inc .... F 740 968-4313
  Saint Clairsville *(G-16651)*
Smalls Inc .... F 740 427-3633
  Gambier *(G-10185)*
Smith Concrete Co .... E 740 373-7441
  Dover *(G-8854)*
Spurlino Materials LLC .... E 513 705-0111
  Middletown *(G-13953)*

Spurlino Materials LLC .... G 513 202-1111
  Cleves *(G-6376)*
Srm Concrete LLC .... D 937 773-0841
  Piqua *(G-16163)*
Srm Concrete LLC .... F 937 698-7229
  Vandalia *(G-19145)*
St Henry Tile Co Inc .... E 419 678-4841
  Saint Henry *(G-16667)*
Stamm Contracting Co Inc .... E 330 274-8230
  Mantua *(G-12560)*
Stark Ready Mix & Supply Co .... E 330 580-4307
  Canton *(G-2823)*
Stocker Concrete Company .... F 740 254-4626
  Gnadenhutten *(G-10283)*
T C Redi Mix Youngstown Inc .... E 330 755-2143
  Youngstown *(G-21042)*
Tech Ready Mix Inc .... E 216 361-5000
  Cleveland *(G-6154)*
Ten Mfg LLC .... F 440 487-1100
  Mentor *(G-13603)*
▲ Terminal Ready-Mix Inc .... E 440 288-0181
  Lorain *(G-12129)*
Tow Path Ready Mix .... F 740 286-2131
  Jackson *(G-11199)*
Tow Path Ready Mix .... G 740 259-3222
  Lucasville *(G-12268)*
Trail Mix .... G 330 657-2277
  Peninsula *(G-15900)*
Tri County Concrete Inc .... E 330 425-4464
  Twinsburg *(G-18866)*
Tri County Concrete Inc .... F 330 425-4464
  Cleveland *(G-6205)*
Twin Cities Concrete Co .... F 330 343-4491
  Dover *(G-8861)*
Twin Cities Concrete Co .... G 330 627-2158
  Carrollton *(G-2931)*
United Ready Mix Inc .... E 216 696-1600
  Cleveland *(G-6236)*
W G Lockhart Construction Co .... D 330 745-6520
  Akron *(G-429)*
W M Dauch Concrete Inc .... G 419 562-6917
  Bucyrus *(G-2349)*
Warren Concrete and Supply Co .. F 330 393-1581
  Warren *(G-19458)*
Weber Ready Mix Inc .... E 419 394-9097
  Saint Marys *(G-16704)*
Wells Group LLC .... F 740 532-9240
  Ironton *(G-11176)*
Wellsgroup .... G 740 289-1000
  Piketon *(G-16081)*
Wellsgroup .... G 937 382-4003
  Wilmington *(G-20511)*
Westview Concrete Corp .... E 440 458-5800
  Elyria *(G-9346)*
William Dauch Concrete Company ... F 419 562-6917
  Bucyrus *(G-2350)*
William Dauch Concrete Company ... F 419 668-4458
  Norwalk *(G-15418)*
William Oeder Ready Mix Inc .... E 513 899-3901
  Martinsville *(G-12768)*
Williams Concrete Inc .... F 419 893-3251
  Maumee *(G-13160)*
Winters Products Inc .... F 740 286-4149
  Jackson *(G-11202)*

3274 Lime

Ayers Limestone Quarry Inc .... F 740 633-2958
  Martins Ferry *(G-12757)*
Bluffton Stone Co .... E 419 358-6941
  Bluffton *(G-1886)*
▼ Graymont Dolime (oh) Inc .... D 419 855-8682
  Genoa *(G-10232)*
Hanson Aggregates East LLC ...... E 937 587-2671
  Peebles *(G-15878)*
Hanson Aggregates East LLC ...... D 419 483-4390
  Castalia *(G-2939)*
Mineral Processing Company ...... G 419 396-3501
  Carey *(G-2883)*
Naked Lime .... D 937 485-1932
  Beavercreek *(G-1359)*
National Lime and Stone Co .... C 419 396-7671
  Carey *(G-2884)*
Piqua Materials Inc .... E 937 773-4824
  Piqua *(G-16154)*
Shelly Materials Inc .... E 740 666-5841
  Ostrander *(G-15646)*
Sugarcreek Lime Service .... G 330 364-4460
  Dover *(G-8858)*

32 STONE, CLAY, GLASS, AND CONCRETE PRODUCTS

3275 Gypsum Prdts

California Ceramic Supply Co .... G 216 531-9185
   Euclid *(G-9406)*
Caraustar Industries Inc .... E 330 665-7700
   Copley *(G-7679)*
Ernst Enterprises Inc .... F 419 222-2015
   Lima *(G-11861)*
Mineral Processing Company .... G 419 396-3501
   Carey *(G-2883)*
Next Sales LLC .... G 330 704-4126
   Dover *(G-8845)*
Owens Corning Sales LLC .... C 330 634-0460
   Tallmadge *(G-17998)*
Priest Services Inc .... E 440 333-1123
   Mayfield Heights *(G-13170)*
Priest Services Inc .... F 440 333-1123
   Rocky River *(G-16552)*
United States Gypsum Company .... B 419 734-3161
   Gypsum *(G-10521)*
Wall Technology Inc .... E 715 532-5548
   Toledo *(G-18594)*

3281 Cut Stone Prdts

Accent Manufacturing Inc .... F 330 724-7704
   Norton *(G-15355)*
Agean Marble Manufacturing .... F 513 874-1475
   West Chester *(G-19829)*
Akron Cultured Marble Pdts LLC .... G 330 628-6757
   Mogadore *(G-14228)*
Al-Co Products Inc .... G 419 399-3867
   Latty *(G-11624)*
Angelina Stone & Marble Ltd .... G 740 633-3360
   Bridgeport *(G-2072)*
Artistic Memorials Ltd .... G 419 873-0433
   Perrysburg *(G-15921)*
As America Inc .... E 419 522-4211
   Mansfield *(G-12408)*
Barta Viorel .... G 440 735-1699
   Bedford *(G-1387)*
Bartan Design Inc .... G 216 267-6474
   North Royalton *(G-15262)*
Bell Burial Vault Co .... G 513 896-9044
   Hamilton *(G-10539)*
Bell Vault & Monument Works .... E 937 866-2444
   Miamisburg *(G-13643)*
Bella Stone Cincinnati .... G 513 772-3552
   Cincinnati *(G-3387)*
Briar Hill Stone Company .... E 330 377-5100
   Glenmont *(G-10274)*
Brocks Chimney .... G 740 819-2489
   Nashport *(G-14565)*
Brower Products Inc .... D 937 563-1111
   Cincinnati *(G-3426)*
Cardinal Aggregate .... F 419 872-4380
   Perrysburg *(G-15931)*
Cascade Cut Stone .... G 419 422-4341
   Findlay *(G-9664)*
▲ Castelli Marble Inc .... G 216 361-2410
   Cleveland *(G-4890)*
Classic Stone Company Inc .... F 614 833-3946
   Columbus *(G-6770)*
▲ Cleveland Granite & Marble LLC .... E 216 291-7637
   Cleveland *(G-4961)*
Creative Countertops Ohio LLC .... G 937 540-9450
   Englewood *(G-9352)*
Creative Design Marble Inc .... G 937 434-8892
   Dayton *(G-8110)*
Cumberland Limestone LLC .... F 740 638-3942
   Cumberland *(G-7823)*
Custar Stone Co .... G 419 669-4327
   Napoleon *(G-14536)*
▲ Custom Cast Marbleworks Inc .... E 513 769-6505
   Cincinnati *(G-3564)*
▼ Cutting Edge Countertops Inc .... E 419 873-9500
   Perrysburg *(G-15937)*
D J Decorative Stone Inc .... G 937 848-6462
   Bellbrook *(G-1491)*
Davids Stone Company LLC .... G 740 373-1996
   Marietta *(G-12618)*
▲ Distinctive Marble & Gran Inc .... F 614 760-0003
   Plain City *(G-16187)*
▲ Dodds Monument Inc .... F 937 372-2736
   Xenia *(G-20767)*
Drake Monument Company .... G 937 399-7941
   Springfield *(G-17391)*
▲ Dutch Quality Stone Inc .... E 877 359-7866
   Mount Eaton *(G-14419)*
Earth Anatomy Fabrication LLC .... G 740 244-5316
   Norton *(G-15366)*

Engineered Marble Inc .... G 614 308-0041
   Columbus *(G-6895)*
Etched In Stone .... G 614 302-8924
   Sugar Grove *(G-17838)*
Fostoria Monument Co .... G 419 435-0373
   Fostoria *(G-9844)*
▲ Granex Industries Inc .... F 440 248-4915
   Solon *(G-17152)*
▲ Granite Fabricators Inc .... G 216 228-3669
   Cleveland *(G-5340)*
HBK Stoneworks .... G 740 817-2244
   Johnstown *(G-11268)*
Heritage Marble of Ohio Inc .... E 614 436-1464
   Columbus *(G-6990)*
Jack Huffman .... G 740 384-5178
   Wellston *(G-19604)*
Jalco Industries Inc .... G 740 286-3808
   Jackson *(G-11188)*
▲ Lang Stone Company Inc .... F 614 235-4099
   Columbus *(G-7114)*
Lima Millwork Inc .... E 419 331-3303
   Elida *(G-9195)*
▲ Lind Stoneworks Ltd .... F 614 866-9733
   Columbus *(G-7128)*
Linden Monuments .... G 419 468-4130
   Galion *(G-10148)*
Maple Grove Materials Inc .... G 419 992-4235
   Tiffin *(G-18068)*
Marble Works .... G 216 496-7745
   Cleveland *(G-5615)*
Marsh Industries Inc .... E 330 308-8667
   New Philadelphia *(G-14784)*
Maumee Valley Memorials Inc .... F 419 878-9030
   Waterville *(G-19501)*
Medina Supply Company .... G 330 723-3681
   Medina *(G-13298)*
Melvin Stone Co LLC .... G 513 771-0820
   Cincinnati *(G-4004)*
◆ Michael Kaufman Companies Inc ... F 330 673-4881
   Kent *(G-11353)*
Michael Kaufman Companies Inc ...... F 330 673-4881
   Kent *(G-11354)*
National Lime and Stone Co .... G 419 657-6745
   Wapakoneta *(G-19347)*
National Lime and Stone Co .... D 419 562-0771
   Bucyrus *(G-2339)*
National Lime and Stone Co .... C 419 396-7671
   Carey *(G-2884)*
North Hill Marble & Granite Co .... F 330 253-2179
   Akron *(G-301)*
▲ OBrien Cut Stone Company .... E 216 663-7800
   Cleveland *(G-5796)*
OBrien Cut Stone Company .... E 216 663-7800
   Cleveland *(G-5797)*
Ohio Beauty Inc .... G 330 644-2241
   Akron *(G-305)*
Ohio Centech .... G 513 477-8779
   Cincinnati *(G-4100)*
▲ Ohio Tile & Marble Co .... E 513 541-4211
   Cincinnati *(G-4105)*
Pavestone LLC .... D 513 474-3783
   Cincinnati *(G-4142)*
Pietra Naturale Inc .... F 937 438-8882
   Franklin *(G-9911)*
Piqua Granite & Marble Co Inc .... F 937 773-2000
   Piqua *(G-16153)*
▲ Quarrymasters Inc .... G 330 612-0474
   Canton *(G-2797)*
Rainbow Cultured Marble .... F 330 225-3400
   Brunswick *(G-2232)*
Riceland Cabinet Inc .... D 330 601-1071
   Wooster *(G-20644)*
Schena Company Ltd .... G 419 868-5207
   Holland *(G-10955)*
Sims-Lohman Inc .... E 440 799-8285
   Brooklyn Heights *(G-2131)*
Sims-Lohman Inc .... G 330 456-8408
   North Canton *(G-15119)*
▲ Studio Vertu Inc .... E 513 241-9038
   Cincinnati *(G-4387)*
Suburban Marble and Granite Co .... G 216 281-5557
   Cleveland *(G-6113)*
▲ Take It For Granite LLC .... E 513 735-0555
   Cincinnati *(G-3265)*
▲ Traditional Marble & Gran Ltd .... F 419 625-3966
   Milan *(G-13990)*
Transtar Holding Company .... G 800 359-3339
   Walton Hills *(G-19315)*
Van Wert Memorials LLC .... G 419 238-9067
   Van Wert *(G-19110)*

Waller Brothers Stone Company .... E 740 858-1948
   Mc Dermott *(G-13195)*
Western Ohio Cut Stone Ltd .... E 937 492-4722
   Sidney *(G-17085)*

3291 Abrasive Prdts

Abrasive Source Inc .... G 937 526-9753
   Russia *(G-16605)*
▲ Abrasive Supply Company Inc .... F 330 894-2818
   Minerva *(G-14175)*
▲ Abrasive Technology Inc .... C 740 548-4100
   Lewis Center *(G-11740)*
Action Super Abrasive Pdts Inc .... E 330 673-7333
   Kent *(G-11289)*
◆ Ali Industries Inc .... C 937 878-3946
   Fairborn *(G-9450)*
▲ ARC Abrasives Inc .... D 800 888-4885
   Troy *(G-18638)*
▲ B & P Polishing Inc .... F 330 753-4202
   Barberton *(G-1057)*
Baaron Abrasives Inc .... G 330 263-7737
   Wooster *(G-20568)*
Braun Machine Technologies LLC ..... G 330 777-5433
   Vienna *(G-19197)*
Buckeye Abrasive Inc .... G 330 753-1041
   Barberton *(G-1067)*
Buffalo Abrasives Inc .... G 614 891-6450
   Westerville *(G-20039)*
▲ Cleveland Granite & Marble LLC .... E 216 291-7637
   Cleveland *(G-4961)*
Coastal Diamond Incorporated .... G 440 946-7171
   Mentor *(G-13417)*
▲ Diamond Innovations Inc .... B 614 438-2000
   Columbus *(G-6863)*
Everett Industries LLC .... E 330 372-3700
   Warren *(G-19401)*
▲ Golden Dynamic Inc .... G 614 575-1222
   Columbus *(G-6959)*
▲ Hec Investments Inc .... C 937 278-9123
   Dayton *(G-8247)*
Inner City Abrasives LLC .... G 216 391-4402
   Cleveland *(G-5459)*
Innovation Sales LLC .... G 330 239-0400
   Medina *(G-13279)*
Jason Incorporated .... F 513 860-3400
   Hamilton *(G-10576)*
◆ Lawrence Industries Inc .... C 216 518-7000
   Cleveland *(G-5566)*
▲ Lexington Abrasives Inc .... D 330 821-1166
   Alliance *(G-482)*
▲ Mill-Rose Company .... C 440 255-9171
   Mentor *(G-13520)*
Nanolap Technologies LLC .... E 877 658-4949
   Englewood *(G-9370)*
National Lime and Stone Co .... C 419 396-7671
   Carey *(G-2884)*
Noritake Co Inc .... E 513 234-0770
   Mason *(G-12915)*
Ohio Slitting & Storage .... E 937 452-1108
   Camden *(G-2465)*
Park-Hio Frged McHned Pdts LLC ..... F 216 692-7200
   Euclid *(G-9432)*
▲ Performance Abrasives Inc .... G 513 733-9283
   Cincinnati *(G-4147)*
Performance Superabrasives LLC ...... G 440 946-7171
   Mentor *(G-13547)*
Premier Coatings Ltd .... F 513 942-1070
   West Chester *(G-19766)*
▲ Qibco Buffing Pads Inc .... F 937 743-0805
   Carlisle *(G-2897)*
▼ Regal Diamond Products Corp .... E 440 944-7700
   Wickliffe *(G-20229)*
Research Abrasive Products Inc .... E 440 944-3200
   Wickliffe *(G-20230)*
Schumann Enterprises Inc .... E 216 267-6850
   Cleveland *(G-6033)*
▲ Sure-Foot Industries Corp .... E 440 234-4446
   Cleveland *(G-6131)*
Tomson Steel Company .... E 513 420-8600
   Middletown *(G-13960)*
▲ Unisand Incorporated .... E 330 722-0222
   Medina *(G-13356)*
United Buff & Supply Co Inc .... G 419 738-2417
   Wapakoneta *(G-19357)*
◆ US Technology Corporation .... E 330 455-1181
   Canton *(G-2853)*
US Technology Media Inc .... F 330 874-3094
   Bolivar *(G-1929)*
Vibra Finish Co .... E 513 870-6300
   Fairfield *(G-9572)*

SIC SECTION
32 STONE, CLAY, GLASS, AND CONCRETE PRODUCTS

Wright Buffing Wheel Company ....G....... 330 424-7887
 Lisbon *(G-11983)*

3292 Asbestos products

American Way Exteriors LLC ....G....... 855 766-3293
 Dayton *(G-8028)*
Pop/Pos Advantage ....G....... 440 543-9452
 Chagrin Falls *(G-3067)*
▲ Texas Tile Manufacturing LLC ....E....... 713 869-5811
 Solon *(G-17251)*

3295 Minerals & Earths: Ground Or Treated

6062 Holdings LLC ....G....... 216 359-9005
 Beachwood *(G-1216)*
Acme Company ....D....... 330 758-2313
 Poland *(G-16236)*
▲ Alteo Na LLC ....G....... 440 460-4600
 Hudson *(G-11028)*
Aquablok Ltd ....F....... 419 825-1325
 Swanton *(G-17906)*
Brier Hill Slag Company ....F....... 330 743-8170
 Youngstown *(G-20857)*
Cimbar Performance Mnrl WV LLC ....E....... 330 532-2034
 Wellsville *(G-19612)*
Edw C Levy Co ....E....... 330 484-6328
 Canton *(G-2665)*
Edw C Levy Co ....F....... 419 822-8286
 Delta *(G-8769)*
EMD Millipore Corporation ....C....... 513 631-0445
 Norwood *(G-15426)*
GRB Holdings Inc ....D....... 937 236-3250
 Dayton *(G-8235)*
Harsco Corporation ....F....... 740 367-7322
 Cheshire *(G-3148)*
▲ Industrial Quartz Corp ....F....... 440 942-0909
 Mentor *(G-13469)*
Ironics Inc ....G....... 330 652-0583
 Niles *(G-15016)*
J R Goslee Co ....F....... 330 723-4904
 Medina *(G-13282)*
Martin Marietta Materials Inc ....E....... 513 701-1140
 West Chester *(G-19740)*
Pioneer Sands LLC ....F....... 740 659-2241
 Glenford *(G-10271)*
Pioneer Sands LLC ....E....... 740 599-7773
 Howard *(G-10997)*
Pyrotek Incorporated ....F....... 440 349-8800
 Aurora *(G-901)*
R W Sidley Incorporated ....F....... 330 750-1661
 Struthers *(G-17823)*
▲ Seaforth Mineral & Ore Co Inc ....F....... 216 292-5820
 Cleveland *(G-6042)*
Sharon Stone Co ....G....... 740 374-3236
 Dexter City *(G-8795)*
Stein Steel Mill Services Inc ....F....... 440 526-9301
 Broadview Heights *(G-2102)*
Tms International LLC ....G....... 330 847-0844
 Warren *(G-19449)*
Trans Ash Inc ....F....... 859 341-1528
 Cincinnati *(G-4430)*

3296 Mineral Wool

American Insulation Tech LLC ....F....... 513 733-4248
 Milford *(G-13993)*
Autoneum North America Inc ....B....... 419 693-0511
 Oregon *(G-15556)*
Blackthorn LLC ....F....... 937 836-9296
 Clayton *(G-4572)*
Brendons Fiber Works ....G....... 614 353-6599
 Columbus *(G-6693)*
Corrosion Resistant Technology ....G....... 800 245-3769
 Aurora *(G-875)*
Cpic Automotive Inc ....G....... 740 587-3262
 Granville *(G-10328)*
Derby Fabg Solutions LLC ....E....... 937 498-4054
 Sidney *(G-17027)*
Essi Acoustical Products ....F....... 216 251-7888
 Cleveland *(G-5192)*
▼ Extol of Ohio Inc ....E....... 419 668-2072
 Norwalk *(G-15391)*
▲ Fibreboard Corporation ....C....... 419 248-8000
 Toledo *(G-18294)*
▲ ICP Adhesives and Sealants Inc .....F....... 330 753-4585
 Norton *(G-15369)*
Ipm Inc ....G....... 419 248-8000
 Toledo *(G-18351)*
Johns Manville Corporation ....F....... 419 782-0180
 Defiance *(G-8628)*
Johns Manville Corporation ....B....... 419 878-8111
 Waterville *(G-19498)*
Johns Manville Corporation ....A....... 419 784-7000
 Defiance *(G-8629)*
Johns Manville Corporation ....F....... 419 784-7000
 Defiance *(G-8630)*
Johns Manville Corporation ....C....... 419 467-8189
 Maumee *(G-13122)*
Johns Manville Corporation ....C....... 419 878-8111
 Defiance *(G-8631)*
Metal Building Intr Pdts Co ....F....... 440 322-6500
 Elyria *(G-9294)*
◆ Mid-Continent Minerals Corp ....F....... 216 283-5700
 Cleveland *(G-5676)*
Midwest Acoust-A-Fiber Inc ....C....... 740 369-3624
 Delaware *(G-8705)*
Midwest Acoust-A-Fiber Inc ....F....... 740 363-6247
 Delaware *(G-8706)*
Mpc Inc ....F....... 440 835-1405
 Cleveland *(G-5707)*
▲ Nitto Inc ....C....... 937 773-4820
 Piqua *(G-16146)*
Owens Corning ....F....... 419 248-8000
 Navarre *(G-14584)*
Owens Corning ....C....... 740 964-1727
 Toledo *(G-18444)*
Owens Corning ....G....... 614 754-4098
 Columbus *(G-7281)*
Owens Corning ....F....... 419 248-8000
 Toledo *(G-18445)*
◆ Owens Corning ....A....... 419 248-8000
 Toledo *(G-18446)*
◆ Owens Corning Sales LLC ....A....... 419 248-8000
 Toledo *(G-18448)*
Owens Corning Sales LLC ....C....... 740 328-2300
 Newark *(G-14907)*
Owens Corning Sales LLC ....C....... 330 764-7800
 Medina *(G-13315)*
Owens Corning Sales LLC ....F....... 419 248-5751
 Swanton *(G-17917)*
Owens Corning Sales LLC ....E....... 614 539-0830
 Grove City *(G-10455)*
Owens Corning Sales LLC ....D....... 614 399-3915
 Mount Vernon *(G-14497)*
Owens Crning Cmposite Mtls LLC ....E....... 419 248-8000
 Toledo *(G-18449)*
Owens-Corning Capital LLC ....F....... 419 248-8000
 Toledo *(G-18450)*
◆ Premier Manufacturing Corp ....D....... 216 941-9700
 Cleveland *(G-5916)*
▲ Refractory Specialties Inc ....E....... 330 938-2101
 Sebring *(G-16891)*
Silvercote LLC ....G....... 330 748-8500
 Macedonia *(G-12325)*
Sorbothane Inc ....E....... 330 678-9444
 Kent *(G-11388)*
▼ Tectum Inc ....C....... 740 345-9691
 Newark *(G-14929)*

3297 Nonclay Refractories

A & M Refractories Inc ....E....... 740 456-8020
 New Boston *(G-14645)*
◆ Allied Mineral Products Inc ....B....... 614 876-0244
 Columbus *(G-6573)*
Allstates Refr Contrs LLC ....F....... 419 878-4691
 Waterville *(G-19489)*
Castruction Company Inc ....F....... 330 332-9622
 Salem *(G-16724)*
▲ E I Ceramics LLC ....D....... 513 772-7001
 Cincinnati *(G-3617)*
Ets Schaefer LLC ....G....... 330 468-6600
 Macedonia *(G-12292)*
Ets Schaefer LLC ....G....... 330 468-6600
 Beachwood *(G-1237)*
General Electric Company ....G....... 740 928-7010
 Hebron *(G-10745)*
Global Graphite Group LLC ....G....... 216 538-0362
 Independence *(G-11132)*
I Cerco Inc ....D....... 740 982-2050
 Crooksville *(G-7816)*
Impact Armor Technologies LLC ....F....... 216 706-2024
 Cleveland *(G-5442)*
Johns Manville Corporation ....B....... 419 878-8111
 Waterville *(G-19498)*
Magneco/Metrel Inc ....E....... 330 426-9468
 Negley *(G-14590)*
Martin Marietta Materials Inc ....E....... 513 701-1140
 West Chester *(G-19740)*
Minteq International Inc ....E....... 330 343-8821
 Dover *(G-8843)*
◆ Momentive Prfmce Mtls Qrtz Inc ......C....... 440 878-5700
 Strongsville *(G-17765)*
▲ Nock and Son Company ....F....... 440 871-5525
 Cleveland *(G-5754)*
Ohio Vly Stmpng-Assemblies Inc ....E....... 419 522-0983
 Mansfield *(G-12498)*
Old Es LLC ....E....... 330 468-6600
 Macedonia *(G-12312)*
Plibrico Company LLC ....E....... 740 682-7755
 Oak Hill *(G-15458)*
Pyromatics Corp ....F....... 440 352-3500
 Mentor *(G-13561)*
Refractory Coating Tech Inc ....E....... 330 683-2200
 Orrville *(G-15614)*
▲ Refractory Specialties Inc ....E....... 330 938-2101
 Sebring *(G-16891)*
Resco Products Inc ....E....... 740 682-7794
 Oak Hill *(G-15459)*
Ruscoe Company ....E....... 330 253-8148
 Akron *(G-358)*
Saint-Gobain Ceramics Plas Inc ....A....... 330 673-5860
 Stow *(G-17624)*
▲ US Refractory Products LLC ....E....... 440 386-4580
 North Ridgeville *(G-15258)*
▲ Vacuform Inc ....E....... 330 938-9674
 Sebring *(G-16898)*
Veitsch-Radex America LLC ....D....... 440 969-2300
 Ashtabula *(G-811)*
▲ Wahl Refractory Solutions LLC ....D....... 419 334-2658
 Fremont *(G-10063)*
▲ Zircoa Inc ....C....... 440 248-0500
 Cleveland *(G-6345)*

3299 Nonmetallic Mineral Prdts, NEC

Aquablok Ltd ....F....... 419 402-4170
 Swanton *(G-17905)*
Aquablok Ltd ....F....... 419 825-1325
 Swanton *(G-17906)*
Architectural Products Dev ....G....... 216 631-6260
 Cleveland *(G-4728)*
Astro Met Inc ....E....... 513 772-1242
 Cincinnati *(G-3364)*
B & B Cast Stone Co Inc ....G....... 740 697-0008
 Roseville *(G-16574)*
Brady A Lantz Enterprises Inc ....G....... 513 742-4921
 Cincinnati *(G-3409)*
Cultured Marble Inc ....G....... 330 549-2282
 North Lima *(G-15169)*
Dayton Wright Composite ....G....... 937 469-3962
 Dayton *(G-8150)*
▲ Exochem Corporation ....D....... 800 807-7464
 Lorain *(G-12091)*
Fillous & Ruppel Inc ....G....... 216 431-0470
 Cleveland *(G-5237)*
Fireline Inc ....E....... 330 259-0647
 Youngstown *(G-20905)*
▼ Fireline Inc ....C....... 330 743-1164
 Youngstown *(G-20906)*
Functional Imaging Ltd ....G....... 740 689-2466
 Lancaster *(G-11573)*
Holmes Supply Corp ....G....... 330 279-2634
 Holmesville *(G-10980)*
Kent Paverbrick LLC ....G....... 330 995-7000
 Aurora *(G-888)*
Maverick Corporation ....F....... 513 469-9919
 Blue Ash *(G-1816)*
▲ Mazzolini Artcraft Co Inc ....F....... 216 431-7529
 Cleveland *(G-5640)*
▲ Miller Studio Inc ....D....... 330 339-1100
 New Philadelphia *(G-14787)*
▲ R W Sidley Incorporated ....E....... 440 352-9343
 Painesville *(G-15777)*
Richtech Industries Inc ....G....... 440 937-4401
 Avon *(G-964)*
Scioto Ceramic Products Inc ....E....... 614 436-0405
 Columbus *(G-7430)*
◆ Seves Glass Block Inc ....G....... 440 627-6257
 Broadview Heights *(G-2101)*
Southwest Greens Ohio LLC ....F....... 614 389-6042
 Columbus *(G-7465)*
Stephen R Lilley ....G....... 513 899-4400
 Morrow *(G-14415)*
The Fischer & Jirouch Company ....G....... 216 361-3840
 Cleveland *(G-6163)*
Unity Cable Technologies Inc ....G....... 419 322-4118
 Toledo *(G-18584)*

Employee Codes: A=Over 500 employees, B=251-500
C=101-250, D=51-100, E=20-50, F=10-19, G=3-9

33 PRIMARY METAL INDUSTRIES

3312 Blast Furnaces, Coke Ovens, Steel & Rolling Mills

A-1 Welding & Fabrication.....F..... 440 233-8474
Lorain *(G-12077)*
Acme Surface Dynamics Inc.....G..... 330 821-3900
Alliance *(G-450)*
◆ Aco Polymer Products Inc.....E..... 440 285-7000
Mentor *(G-13373)*
Adams Fabricating Inc.....G..... 330 866-2986
East Sparta *(G-9093)*
AK Steel Corporation.....B..... 419 755-3011
Mansfield *(G-12402)*
AK Steel Corporation.....B..... 740 450-5600
Zanesville *(G-21095)*
AK Steel Corporation.....A..... 740 829-2206
Coshocton *(G-7717)*
AK Steel Corporation.....B..... 513 425-3694
Middletown *(G-13877)*
AK Steel Corporation.....F..... 513 425-3593
Middletown *(G-13878)*
AK Steel Corporation.....G..... 513 231-2552
Cincinnati *(G-3315)*
◆ AK Steel Corporation.....B..... 513 425-4200
West Chester *(G-19640)*
◆ AK Steel Holding Corporation.....B..... 513 425-5000
West Chester *(G-19641)*
◆ Akers America Inc.....G..... 330 757-4100
Poland *(G-16237)*
Alba Manufacturing Inc.....D..... 513 874-0551
Fairfield *(G-9480)*
▲ All Ohio Threaded Rod Co Inc.....E..... 216 426-1800
Cleveland *(G-4665)*
Allegheny Ludlum LLC.....E..... 330 875-2244
Louisville *(G-12151)*
Alro Steel Corporation.....E..... 937 253-6121
Dayton *(G-8021)*
AM Warren LLC.....G..... 330 841-2800
Warren *(G-19367)*
American Culvert & Fabg Co.....F..... 740 432-6334
Cambridge *(G-2422)*
American Posts LLC.....E..... 419 720-0652
Toledo *(G-18179)*
American Processing LLC.....E..... 216 486-4600
Cleveland *(G-4695)*
American Steel & Alloys LLC.....E..... 330 847-0487
Warren *(G-19368)*
Amthor Steel Inc.....G..... 330 759-0200
Youngstown *(G-20845)*
Applied Innovations.....G..... 330 837-5694
Massillon *(G-12960)*
▲ Arcelormittal Cleveland LLC.....C..... 216 429-6000
Cleveland *(G-4725)*
Arcelormittal Cleveland LLC.....E..... 216 429-6000
Cleveland *(G-4726)*
Arcelormittal Obetz LLC.....E..... 614 492-8287
Columbus *(G-6614)*
Arcelormittal USA LLC.....F..... 740 375-2299
Marion *(G-12694)*
Arcelormittal USA LLC.....D..... 419 347-2424
Shelby *(G-16979)*
▼ Arrowstrip Inc.....E..... 740 633-2609
Martins Ferry *(G-12756)*
B & G Tool Company.....G..... 614 451-2538
Columbus *(G-6640)*
▲ Bcast Stainless Products LLC.....F..... 614 873-3945
Plain City *(G-16176)*
Benjamin Steel Company Inc.....E..... 937 233-1212
Springfield *(G-17368)*
▲ Bertin Steel Processing Inc.....E..... 440 943-0094
Wickliffe *(G-20202)*
Brenmar Construction Inc.....D..... 740 286-2151
Jackson *(G-11183)*
Bridge Components Inds Inc.....G..... 614 873-0777
Columbus *(G-6698)*
Burn-Rite Mold & Machine Inc.....G..... 330 956-4143
Canton *(G-2602)*
▲ Buschman Corporation.....F..... 216 431-6633
Cleveland *(G-4853)*
C & R Inc.....E..... 614 497-1130
Groveport *(G-10486)*
◆ Canton Drop Forge Inc.....B..... 330 477-4511
Canton *(G-2608)*
Carter Scott-Browne.....E..... 513 398-3970
Mason *(G-12839)*
▲ Centaur Inc.....G..... 419 469-8000
Toledo *(G-18225)*
▲ Challenger Hardware Company.....F..... 216 591-1141
Independence *(G-11122)*
Charles C Lewis Company.....F..... 440 439-3150
Cleveland *(G-4910)*
Charter Manufacturing Co Inc.....A..... 216 883-3800
Cleveland *(G-4916)*
Chemwise.....G..... 419 425-3604
Findlay *(G-9668)*
Churchill Steel Plate Ltd.....E..... 330 425-9000
Twinsburg *(G-18753)*
Cincinnati Barge Rail Trml LLC.....G..... 513 227-3611
Cincinnati *(G-3482)*
▲ Cleveland Track Material Inc.....D..... 216 641-4000
Cleveland *(G-4980)*
Cleveland Track Material Inc.....F..... 216 641-4000
Cleveland *(G-4981)*
Cohen Brothers Inc.....G..... 513 422-3696
Middletown *(G-13895)*
Columbus Processing Co LLC.....G..... 614 492-8287
Columbus *(G-6799)*
Community Care On Wheels.....F..... 330 882-5506
Clinton *(G-6385)*
Contractors Steel Company.....E..... 330 425-3050
Twinsburg *(G-18757)*
Crest Bending Inc.....E..... 419 492-2108
New Washington *(G-14828)*
Csc Ltd.....G..... 330 841-6011
Warren *(G-19391)*
Custom Blast & Coat Inc.....G..... 419 225-6024
Lima *(G-11851)*
Deaks Form Tools Inc.....G..... 440 286-2353
Chardon *(G-3108)*
Die Services Ltd.....G..... 216 883-5800
Cleveland *(G-5093)*
Dietrich Industries Inc.....C..... 330 372-2868
Warren *(G-19396)*
▲ Diversifd OH Vlly Eqpt & Srvcs.....F..... 740 458-9881
Clarington *(G-4567)*
▼ Eastern Automated Piping.....G..... 740 535-8184
Mingo Junction *(G-14208)*
Egypt Structural Steel Proc.....E..... 419 628-2375
Minster *(G-14213)*
◆ Elster Perfection Corporation.....D..... 440 428-1171
Geneva *(G-10218)*
Emt Trading Company LLC.....G..... 888 352-8000
Chagrin Falls *(G-3019)*
▲ Ernst Metal Technologies LLC.....E..... 937 434-3133
Moraine *(G-14351)*
Esm Products Inc.....G..... 937 492-4644
Celina *(G-2961)*
Falcon Fab and Finishes LLC.....G..... 740 820-4458
Lucasville *(G-12263)*
Famous Industries Inc.....C..... 740 397-8842
Mount Vernon *(G-14481)*
FBC Chemical Corporation.....G..... 216 341-2000
Cleveland *(G-5223)*
Ferguson Fire Fabrication Inc.....F..... 614 299-2070
Columbus *(G-6918)*
Forge Products Corporation.....D..... 216 231-2600
Cleveland *(G-5262)*
▲ Franklin Iron & Metal Corp.....C..... 937 253-8184
Dayton *(G-8206)*
▲ Fulton County Processing Ltd.....D..... 419 822-9266
Delta *(G-8771)*
▲ Garden Street Iron & Metal.....E..... 513 853-3700
Cincinnati *(G-3726)*
Geauga Coatings LLC.....G..... 440 286-5571
Chardon *(G-3113)*
General Machine & Saw Company.....D..... 740 382-1104
Marion *(G-12704)*
George Manufacturing Inc.....E..... 513 932-1067
Lebanon *(G-11654)*
GKN Sinter Metals LLC.....C..... 740 441-3203
Gallipolis *(G-10166)*
Grace Metals Ltd.....G..... 234 380-1433
Hudson *(G-11048)*
Great Lakes Mfg Group Ltd.....G..... 440 391-8266
Rocky River *(G-16548)*
Gregory Roll Form Inc.....D..... 330 477-4800
Canton *(G-2689)*
Grenga Machine & Welding.....F..... 330 743-1113
Youngstown *(G-20925)*
Hadronics Inc.....D..... 513 321-9350
Cincinnati *(G-3792)*
Harvard Coil Processing Inc.....E..... 216 883-6366
Cleveland *(G-5379)*
▲ Heidtman Steel Products Inc.....E..... 419 691-4646
Toledo *(G-18330)*
Holgate Metal Fab Inc.....F..... 419 599-2000
Napoleon *(G-14543)*
Humble Construction Co.....E..... 614 888-8960
Columbus *(G-7010)*
International Steel Group.....C..... 330 841-2800
Warren *(G-19411)*
J & L Steel Bar LLC.....G..... 440 526-0050
Broadview Heights *(G-2093)*
Jck Industries.....E..... 419 433-6277
Huron *(G-11100)*
John Maneely Company.....E..... 724 342-6851
Niles *(G-15019)*
Kind Special Alloys Us LLC.....G..... 330 788-2437
Youngstown *(G-20953)*
◆ Kirtland Capital Partners LP.....E..... 216 593-0100
Beachwood *(G-1244)*
▲ L&H Threaded Rods Corp.....C..... 937 294-6666
Moraine *(G-14365)*
L-K Industry Inc.....E..... 937 526-3000
Versailles *(G-19186)*
Lapham-Hickey Steel Corp.....E..... 614 443-4881
Columbus *(G-7116)*
◆ Latrobe Specialty Mtls Dist Inc.....D..... 330 609-5137
Vienna *(G-19199)*
Latrobe Specialty Mtls Co LLC.....D..... 419 335-8010
Wauseon *(G-19525)*
▲ Lokring Technology LLC.....D..... 440 942-0880
Willoughby *(G-20361)*
Long View Steel Corp.....F..... 419 747-1108
Mansfield *(G-12470)*
Louis G Freeman Co.....E..... 419 334-9709
Fremont *(G-10037)*
Lukjan Metal Products Inc.....C..... 440 599-8127
Conneaut *(G-7654)*
Major Metals Company.....E..... 419 886-4600
Mansfield *(G-12472)*
Matandy Steel & Metal Pdts LLC.....D..... 513 844-2277
Hamilton *(G-10585)*
Maull Tool & Die Supply Llc.....G..... 513 646-4229
Loveland *(G-12213)*
Mc Cully Supply & Sales Inc.....G..... 330 497-2211
Canton *(G-2749)*
▲ McDonald Steel Corporation.....C..... 330 530-9118
Mc Donald *(G-13201)*
McWane Inc.....B..... 740 622-6651
Coshocton *(G-7739)*
Metaldyne Pwrtrain Cmpnnts Inc.....C..... 330 486-3200
Twinsburg *(G-18818)*
▲ Metals USA Crbn Flat Rlled Inc.....D..... 330 264-8416
Wooster *(G-20623)*
Metals USA Crbn Flat Rlled Inc.....D..... 937 882-6354
Springfield *(G-17446)*
▲ Miba Sinter USA LLC.....F..... 740 962-4242
McConnelsville *(G-13208)*
Mid-America Steel Corp.....E..... 800 282-3466
Cleveland *(G-5674)*
Mid-Continent Coal and Coke Co.....G..... 216 283-5700
Cleveland *(G-5675)*
Middletown Tube Works Inc.....D..... 513 727-0080
Middletown *(G-13930)*
Msls Group LLC.....E..... 330 723-4431
Medina *(G-13305)*
▼ Mtr Martco LLC.....D..... 513 424-5307
Middletown *(G-13932)*
New Age Design & Tool Inc.....F..... 440 355-5400
Lagrange *(G-11490)*
Nichidai America Corporation.....E..... 419 423-7511
Findlay *(G-9730)*
North American Steel Company.....E..... 216 475-7300
Cleveland *(G-5759)*
North Jckson Specialty Stl LLC.....F..... 330 538-9621
North Jackson *(G-15150)*
▲ North Shore Strapping Inc.....D..... 216 661-5200
Brooklyn Heights *(G-2128)*
◆ North Star Bluescope Steel LLC.....B..... 419 822-2200
Delta *(G-8777)*
Northeast Tubular Service Inc.....G..... 330 262-1881
Wooster *(G-20634)*
▲ Northlake Steel Corporation.....D..... 330 220-7717
Valley City *(G-19056)*
Nova Structural Steel Inc.....F..... 216 938-7476
Cleveland *(G-5788)*
Nuflux LLC.....G..... 330 399-1122
Cortland *(G-7713)*
Ohio Coatings Company.....D..... 740 859-5500
Yorkville *(G-20827)*
◆ Ohio Gratings Inc.....B..... 330 477-6707
Canton *(G-2772)*
▲ Ohio Pickling & Processing LLC.....D..... 419 241-9601
Toledo *(G-18436)*
Ohio Steel Sheet & Plate Inc.....E..... 800 827-2401
Hubbard *(G-11007)*
▲ Ohio Valley Alloy Services Inc.....E..... 740 373-1900
Marietta *(G-12649)*

OReilly Precision Products ....E 937 526-4677
Russia *(G-16610)*
Pelletier Brothers Mfg ....F 740 774-4704
Chillicothe *(G-3208)*
Pendleton Mold & Machine LLC ....G 440 998-0041
Ashtabula *(G-796)*
Phillips Mfg and Tower Co ....D 419 347-1720
Shelby *(G-16985)*
▲ Pilgrim-Harp Co ....G 440 249-4185
Avon *(G-957)*
◆ Pioneer Equipment Company ....F 330 857-6340
Dalton *(G-7951)*
▲ Pioneer Pipe Inc ....A 740 376-2400
Marietta *(G-12653)*
Plymouth Locomotive Svc LLC ....G 419 896-2854
Shiloh *(G-16997)*
Precision Laser & Forming ....F 419 943-4350
Leipsic *(G-11731)*
▲ Precision Specialty Metals Inc ....D 800 944-2255
Worthington *(G-20700)*
Precision Strip Inc ....D 937 667-6255
Tipp City *(G-18127)*
Precision Wood & Metal Co ....G 419 221-1512
Lima *(G-11919)*
Premier Metal Trading LLC ....G 440 247-9494
Beachwood *(G-1267)*
◆ Prime Conduit Inc ....F 216 464-3400
Beachwood *(G-1269)*
▼ Qual-Fab Inc ....E 440 327-5000
Avon *(G-960)*
Quality Bar Inc ....F 330 755-0000
Struthers *(G-17822)*
Quality Tool Company ....E 419 476-8228
Toledo *(G-18490)*
R&D Machine Inc ....F 937 339-2545
Troy *(G-18696)*
Racelite South Coast Inc ....F 216 581-4600
Maple Heights *(G-12578)*
Radix Wire & Cable LLC ....G 216 731-9191
Cleveland *(G-5955)*
Republic Engineered Products ....E 440 277-2000
Lorain *(G-12116)*
▲ Republic Steel ....B 330 438-5435
Canton *(G-2804)*
Republic Steel ....F 330 837-7024
Massillon *(G-13045)*
Republic Steel Inc ....C 330 438-5533
Canton *(G-2805)*
Republic Steel Inc ....E 440 277-2000
Lorain *(G-12117)*
Rmi Titanium Company LLC ....D 330 471-1844
Canton *(G-2807)*
Robs Welding Technologies Ltd ....G 937 890-4963
Dayton *(G-8483)*
Rocknstarr Holdings LLC ....E 330 509-9086
Youngstown *(G-21020)*
▲ Rti Alloys ....G 330 652-9952
Niles *(G-15032)*
S & J Precision Inc ....G 937 296-0068
Moraine *(G-14391)*
▲ S&V Industries Inc ....E 330 666-1986
Medina *(G-13333)*
Samuel Steel Pickling Company ....D 330 963-3777
Twinsburg *(G-18853)*
Schaefer Group Inc ....G 419 897-2883
Perrysburg *(G-16004)*
Sedlak ....G 330 908-2200
Richfield *(G-16486)*
Seilkop Industries Inc ....E 513 353-3090
Miamitown *(G-13751)*
Seneca Railroad & Mining Co ....F 419 483-7764
Bellevue *(G-1545)*
Sertek LLC ....D 614 504-5828
Dublin *(G-8984)*
Shear Service Inc ....G 216 341-2700
Cleveland *(G-6049)*
Stainless Specialties Inc ....E 440 942-4242
Eastlake *(G-9130)*
Steel Technologies LLC ....E 419 523-5199
Ottawa *(G-15665)*
Steve Vore Welding and Steel ....F 419 375-4087
Fort Recovery *(G-9827)*
◆ Superior Forge & Steel Corp ....D 419 222-4412
Lima *(G-11946)*
Systems Jay LLC Nanogate ....E 419 747-1096
Mansfield *(G-12524)*
The Florand Company ....E 330 747-8986
Youngstown *(G-21044)*
Thrift Tool Inc ....G 937 275-3600
Dayton *(G-8557)*
Timken Receivables Corporation ....G 234 262-3000
North Canton *(G-15128)*
◆ Timkensteel Corporation ....B 330 471-7000
Canton *(G-2841)*
Tms International LLC ....G 513 425-6462
Middletown *(G-13958)*
Tms International LLC ....G 419 747-5500
Mansfield *(G-12532)*
Tms International LLC ....G 513 422-4572
Middletown *(G-13959)*
Tms International LLC ....F 216 441-9702
Cleveland *(G-6178)*
Tms International Corporation ....F 740 223-0091
Marion *(G-12741)*
Trupoint Products ....F 330 204-3302
Sugarcreek *(G-17872)*
▲ United Security Seals Inc ....E 614 443-7633
Columbus *(G-7558)*
United States Steel Corp ....A 440 240-2500
Lorain *(G-12131)*
Universal Metals Cutting Inc ....G 330 580-5192
Canton *(G-2852)*
Universal Urethane Pdts Inc ....D 419 693-7400
Toledo *(G-18585)*
Unlimited Machine and Tool LLC ....F 419 269-1730
Toledo *(G-18586)*
West Motorsports Inc ....G 330 350-0375
Akron *(G-434)*
Western Reserve Metals Inc ....E 330 448-4092
Masury *(G-13064)*
WH Fetzer & Sons Mfg Inc ....E 419 687-8237
Plymouth *(G-16235)*
▼ Witt Industries Inc ....D 513 871-5700
Mason *(G-12955)*
Wodin Inc ....E 440 439-4222
Cleveland *(G-6320)*
Worthington Industries Inc ....D 419 822-2500
Delta *(G-8780)*
Worthington Industries Inc ....C 513 539-9291
Monroe *(G-14282)*
Worthington Industries Inc ....A 614 438-3077
Worthington *(G-20712)*
◆ Worthington Steel Company ....C 614 438-3210
Worthington *(G-20715)*
◆ Xtek Inc ....B 513 733-7800
Cincinnati *(G-4530)*
Youngstown Tube Co ....E 330 743-7414
Youngstown *(G-21084)*
Zekelman Industries Inc ....C 740 432-2146
Cambridge *(G-2463)*

3313 Electrometallurgical Prdts

Castlebar Corporation ....G 330 451-6511
Canton *(G-2621)*
GE Aviation Systems LLC ....C 513 733-1611
Cincinnati *(G-3734)*
GE Aviation Systems LLC ....F 513 889-5150
West Chester *(G-19710)*
GE Aviation Systems LLC ....G 513 552-5663
Cincinnati *(G-3735)*
◆ Globe Metallurgical Inc ....C 740 984-2361
Waterford *(G-19484)*
H C Starck Inc ....B 216 692-3990
Euclid *(G-9418)*
International Metal Supply LLC ....F 330 764-1004
Medina *(G-13281)*
▲ Marietta Eramet Inc ....C 740 374-1000
Marietta *(G-12642)*
Morris Technologies Inc ....C 513 733-1611
Cincinnati *(G-4047)*
Real Alloy Specialty Pdts LLC ....A 216 755-8836
Beachwood *(G-1273)*
Real Alloy Specification LLC ....G 216 755-8900
Beachwood *(G-1275)*
▲ Rhenium Alloys Inc ....D 440 365-7388
North Ridgeville *(G-15251)*
Slice Mfg LLC ....G 330 733-7600
Akron *(G-378)*
Tungsten Sltons Group Intl Inc ....G 440 708-3096
Chagrin Falls *(G-3086)*

3315 Steel Wire Drawing & Nails & Spikes

Advance Industries Group LLC ....E 216 741-1800
Cleveland *(G-4621)*
Advance Wire Forming Inc ....F 216 432-3250
Cleveland *(G-4624)*
AJD Holding Co ....D 330 405-4477
Twinsburg *(G-18728)*
Aluminum Fence & Mfg Co ....G 330 755-3323
Aurora *(G-868)*
▲ American Spring Wire Corp ....C 216 292-4620
Bedford Heights *(G-1460)*
▲ American Wire & Cable Company ....E 440 235-1140
Olmsted Twp *(G-15532)*
Bayloff Stmped Pdts Knsman Inc ....D 330 876-4511
Kinsman *(G-11463)*
Bekaert Corporation ....C 330 683-5060
Orrville *(G-15583)*
Bekaert Corporation ....F 330 683-5060
Orrville *(G-15584)*
Bekaert Corporation ....E 330 835-5124
Fairlawn *(G-9595)*
Bekaert Corporation ....G 330 867-3325
Fairlawn *(G-9596)*
◆ Bekaert North America MGT Corp ....E 330 867-3325
Fairlawn *(G-9597)*
▲ Brushes Inc ....E 216 267-8084
Cleveland *(G-4848)*
Cambridge Cable Service Co ....G 740 685-5775
Byesville *(G-2380)*
Contour Forming Inc ....E 740 345-9777
Newark *(G-14864)*
Custom Cltch Jint Hydrlics Inc ....F 216 431-1630
Cleveland *(G-5046)*
D C Controls LLC ....G 513 225-0813
West Chester *(G-19848)*
D M L Steel Tech ....F 513 737-9911
Liberty Twp *(G-11823)*
D&M Fencing LLC ....G 419 604-0698
Spencerville *(G-17308)*
◆ Dayton Superior Corporation ....C 937 866-0711
Miamisburg *(G-13655)*
Electroduct LLC ....E 330 220-9300
Brunswick *(G-2202)*
▲ Engineered Wire Products Inc ....C 419 294-3817
Upper Sandusky *(G-18953)*
Euclid Steel & Wire Inc ....F 216 731-6744
Lakewood *(G-11516)*
Falcon Fab and Finishes LLC ....G 740 820-4458
Lucasville *(G-12263)*
▲ Fenix LLC ....F 419 739-3400
Wapakoneta *(G-19328)*
▲ File Sharpening Company Inc ....E 937 376-8268
Xenia *(G-20772)*
Freudenberg-Nok Sealing Tech ....F 877 331-8427
Milan *(G-13983)*
G & S Bar and Wire LLC ....E 260 747-4154
Wooster *(G-20595)*
Genesis Steel Corp ....G 740 282-2300
Steubenville *(G-17535)*
Glebus Alloys LLC ....F 330 867-9999
Stow *(G-17592)*
Hawthorne Wire Ltd ....F 216 712-4747
Lakewood *(G-11519)*
Hawthorne Wire Services Ltd ....G 216 712-4747
Lakewood *(G-11520)*
Hsm Wire International Inc ....G 330 244-8501
North Canton *(G-15093)*
▲ Injection Alloys Incorporated ....F 513 422-8819
Middletown *(G-13914)*
▲ JR Manufacturing Inc ....C 419 375-8021
Fort Recovery *(G-9823)*
▲ Madsen Wire Products Inc ....E 937 829-6561
Dayton *(G-8322)*
▲ Marlin Thermocouple Wire Inc ....E 440 835-1950
Cleveland *(G-5624)*
Master-Halco Inc ....E 513 869-7600
Fairfield *(G-9524)*
McHenry Industries Inc ....E 330 799-8930
Youngstown *(G-20968)*
Merchants Metals LLC ....F 513 942-0268
West Chester *(G-19743)*
▼ Midwestern Industries Inc ....C 330 837-4203
Massillon *(G-13026)*
▲ Murphy Industries Inc ....E 740 387-7890
Marion *(G-12722)*
◆ Noco Company ....B 216 464-8131
Solon *(G-17208)*
Partners Manufacturing Group ....G 419 468-8516
Galion *(G-10149)*
▲ Polymet Corporation ....E 513 874-3586
West Chester *(G-19763)*
Radix Wire & Cable LLC ....G 216 731-9191
Cleveland *(G-5955)*
Ram Sensors Inc ....G 440 835-3540
Westlake *(G-20148)*
Ram Sensors Inc ....F 440 835-3540
Cleveland *(G-5959)*
Randy Lewis Inc ....F 330 784-0456
Akron *(G-342)*

Employee Codes: A=Over 500 employees, B=251-500
C=101-250, D=51-100, E=20-50, F=10-19, G=3-9

2019 Harris Ohio
Industrial Directory

909

33 PRIMARY METAL INDUSTRIES

▲ Republic Steel Wire Proc LLC .... E 440 996-0740
  Solon *(G-17222)*
▲ Republic Wire Inc .... D 513 860-1800
  West Chester *(G-19779)*
▲ Richards Whl Fence Co Inc .... E 330 773-0423
  Akron *(G-348)*
Robertson Incorporated .... G 937 323-3747
  Springfield *(G-17488)*
Rural Iron Works LLC .... G 419 647-4617
  Spencerville *(G-17313)*
S & S Wldg Fabg Machining Inc .... E 330 392-7878
  Newton Falls *(G-14993)*
Seneca Wire Group Inc .... G 419 435-9261
  Wapakoneta *(G-19353)*
▲ Solon Specialty Wire Co .... E 440 248-7600
  Solon *(G-17234)*
Stephens Pipe & Steel LLC .... C 740 869-2257
  Mount Sterling *(G-14465)*
▲ Stop Stick Ltd .... E 513 202-5500
  Harrison *(G-10673)*
Summit Engineered Products .... F 330 854-5388
  Canal Fulton *(G-2493)*
Sunrise Cooperative Inc .... E 419 683-4600
  Crestline *(G-7801)*
Tru-Form Steel & Wire Inc .... E 765 348-5001
  Toledo *(G-18583)*
Unison Industries LLC .... F 937 426-0621
  Alpha *(G-517)*
Wire Products Company Inc .... C 216 267-0777
  Cleveland *(G-6316)*

3316 Cold Rolled Steel Sheet, Strip & Bars

AK Steel Corporation .... B 740 450-5600
  Zanesville *(G-21095)*
AK Steel Corporation .... A 740 829-2206
  Coshocton *(G-7717)*
◆ Akers America Inc .... G 330 757-4100
  Poland *(G-16237)*
▲ All Ohio Threaded Rod Co Inc .... E 216 426-1800
  Cleveland *(G-4665)*
Allegheny Ludlum LLC .... E 330 875-2244
  Louisville *(G-12151)*
Alro Steel Corporation .... E 937 253-6121
  Dayton *(G-8021)*
▲ American Spring Wire Corp .... C 216 292-4620
  Bedford Heights *(G-1460)*
Bar Processing Corporation .... D 330 872-0914
  Newton Falls *(G-14985)*
▲ Bcs Metal Prep LLC .... E 440 663-1100
  Solon *(G-17114)*
Bekaert Corporation .... C 330 683-5060
  Orrville *(G-15583)*
Benjamin Steel Company Inc .... E 937 233-1212
  Springfield *(G-17368)*
▲ Centaur Inc .... G 419 469-8000
  Toledo *(G-18225)*
Cincinnati Cold Drawn Inc .... G 513 874-3296
  West Chester *(G-19671)*
Clark Grave Vault Company .... C 614 294-3761
  Columbus *(G-6769)*
▲ Clouth Sprenger LLC .... G 937 642-8390
  Marysville *(G-12774)*
Columbia Steel and Wire Inc .... G 330 468-2709
  Northfield *(G-15315)*
Consolidated Metal Pdts Inc .... C 513 251-2624
  Cincinnati *(G-3542)*
Dietrich Industries Inc .... E 614 438-3210
  Worthington *(G-20684)*
Elgin Fastener Group LLC .... E 216 481-4400
  Cleveland *(G-5168)*
Formetal Inc .... F 419 898-2211
  Oak Harbor *(G-15445)*
Geneva Liberty Steel Ltd .... E 330 740-0103
  Youngstown *(G-20918)*
H S Processing LP .... G 216 641-6995
  Cleveland *(G-5364)*
▲ Heidtman Steel Products Inc .... E 419 691-4646
  Toledo *(G-18330)*
▲ Hynes Industries Inc .... G 330 799-3221
  Youngstown *(G-20934)*
▲ Independent Steel Company LLC .... E 330 225-7741
  Valley City *(G-19041)*
Lakeway Mfg Inc .... G 419 433-3030
  Huron *(G-11103)*
Lapham-Hickey Steel Corp .... D 419 399-4803
  Paulding *(G-15865)*
LLC Ring Masters .... E 330 832-1511
  Massillon *(G-13014)*
Mid-America Steel Corp .... E 800 282-3466
  Cleveland *(G-5674)*

MSC Walbridge Coatings Inc .... C 419 666-6930
  Walbridge *(G-19297)*
▲ New Dimension Metals Corp .... E 937 299-2233
  Moraine *(G-14373)*
Nucor Bright Bar Orville LLC .... F 330 682-5555
  Orrville *(G-15607)*
Raco Cutting Inc .... G 937 293-1228
  Moraine *(G-14389)*
Sandvik Inc .... F 614 438-6579
  Columbus *(G-7420)*
Steel Technologies LLC .... D 440 946-8666
  Willoughby *(G-20437)*
◆ Superior Forge & Steel Corp .... D 419 222-4412
  Lima *(G-11946)*
Tecumseh Redevelopment Inc .... G 330 659-9100
  Richfield *(G-16492)*
◆ Telling Industries LLC .... F 440 974-3370
  Willoughby *(G-20444)*
Telling Industries LLC .... F 928 681-2010
  Willoughby *(G-20445)*
Telling Industries LLC .... F 740 435-8900
  Cambridge *(G-2460)*
Western Reserve Metals Inc .... E 330 448-4092
  Masury *(G-13064)*
Worthington Industries Inc .... C 614 438-3210
  Worthington *(G-20710)*
Worthington Industries Inc .... F 614 438-3113
  Columbus *(G-7615)*
Worthington Industries Inc .... F 614 438-3190
  Columbus *(G-7616)*
Worthington Industries Lsg LLC .... E 614 438-3210
  Worthington *(G-20713)*
◆ Worthington Steel Company .... C 614 438-3210
  Worthington *(G-20715)*
Worthington Steel Company .... C 216 441-8300
  Cleveland *(G-6328)*

3317 Steel Pipe & Tubes

▼ AK Tube LLC .... C 419 661-4150
  Walbridge *(G-19292)*
All Steel Structures Inc .... G 330 312-3131
  Carrollton *(G-2915)*
Alro Steel Corporation .... E 937 253-6121
  Dayton *(G-8021)*
▲ Arcelormittal Tubular .... D 740 382-3979
  Marion *(G-12693)*
Arcelormittal Tubular Products .... A 419 347-2424
  Shelby *(G-16978)*
Benjamin Steel Company Inc .... E 937 233-1212
  Springfield *(G-17368)*
Bull Moose Tube Company .... G 330 448-4878
  Masury *(G-13059)*
Busch & Thiem Inc .... E 419 625-7515
  Sandusky *(G-16800)*
Chart International Inc .... E 440 753-1490
  Cleveland *(G-4915)*
Cheryl Heintz .... F 937 492-3310
  Sidney *(G-17022)*
▲ Commercial Honing LLC .... D 330 343-8896
  Dover *(G-8811)*
Conduit Pipe Products Company .... D 614 879-9114
  West Jefferson *(G-19922)*
Contech Engnered Solutions Inc .... F 513 645-7000
  West Chester *(G-19680)*
Contech Engnered Solutions LLC .... D 513 645-7000
  Middletown *(G-13896)*
◆ Contech Engnered Solutions LLC .... C 513 645-7000
  West Chester *(G-19681)*
Crest Bending Inc .... E 419 492-2108
  New Washington *(G-14828)*
Fd Rolls Corp .... G 216 536-1433
  Highland Heights *(G-10789)*
▲ Jackson Tube Service Inc .... C 937 773-8550
  Piqua *(G-16133)*
James O Emert Jr .... G 330 650-6990
  Hudson *(G-11059)*
Jmc Steel Group .... E 216 910-3700
  Beachwood *(G-1243)*
John Maneely Company .... E 724 342-6851
  Niles *(G-15019)*
◆ Kirtland Capital Partners LP .... E 216 593-0100
  Beachwood *(G-1244)*
Major Metals Company .... E 419 886-4600
  Mansfield *(G-12472)*
Metal Matic .... G 513 422-6007
  Middletown *(G-13927)*
Mid-Ohio Tubing LLC .... D 419 883-2066
  Butler *(G-2376)*
Mid-Ohio Tubing LLC .... G 419 886-0220
  Bellville *(G-1559)*

Munroe Incorporated .... G 330 755-7216
  Struthers *(G-17821)*
Phillips Mfg and Tower Co .... F 419 347-1720
  Shelby *(G-16985)*
▲ PMC Industries Corp .... D 440 943-3300
  Wickliffe *(G-20227)*
Precision Cutoff LLC .... C 419 866-8000
  Holland *(G-10950)*
▲ Reliacheck Manufacturing Inc .... E 440 933-6162
  Avon Lake *(G-1005)*
Shawcor Inc .... E 513 683-7800
  Loveland *(G-12231)*
◆ Specialty Pipe & Tube Inc .... F 330 505-8262
  Mineral Ridge *(G-14171)*
▲ Sterling Pipe & Tube Inc .... C 419 729-9756
  Toledo *(G-18530)*
Stryker Steel Tube LLC .... F 419 682-4527
  Stryker *(G-17834)*
T & D Fabricating Inc .... E 440 951-5646
  Eastlake *(G-9135)*
TI Group Auto Systems LLC .... C 740 929-2049
  Hebron *(G-10767)*
Timkensteel Corporation .... F 330 471-7000
  Canton *(G-2842)*
Tubetech Inc .... E 330 426-9476
  East Palestine *(G-9087)*
Unison Industries LLC .... B 904 667-9904
  Dayton *(G-7994)*
United Tube Corporation .... D 330 725-4196
  Medina *(G-13358)*
▲ Vallourec Star LP .... B 330 742-6300
  Youngstown *(G-21058)*
Vallourec Star LP .... F 330 742-6227
  Girard *(G-10268)*
▲ Welded Tubes Inc .... E 216 378-2092
  Orwell *(G-15637)*
Welded Tubes Inc .... F 440 437-5144
  Orwell *(G-15638)*
Welded Tubes LLC .... E 210 278-3757
  Orwell *(G-15639)*
Woodsage LLC .... C 419 866-8000
  Holland *(G-10969)*
Zekelman Industries Inc .... C 740 432-2146
  Cambridge *(G-2463)*

3321 Gray Iron Foundries

A C Williams Co Inc .... E 330 296-6110
  Ravenna *(G-16362)*
Akron Gear & Engineering Inc .... E 330 773-6608
  Akron *(G-41)*
Amsted Industries Incorporated .... C 614 836-2323
  Groveport *(G-10481)*
Anchor Glass Container Corp .... C 740 452-2743
  Zanesville *(G-21099)*
Arcelormittal Tubular Products .... A 419 347-2424
  Shelby *(G-16978)*
Arconic Inc .... A 216 641-3600
  Newburgh Heights *(G-14934)*
Barberton Steel Industries Inc .... E 330 745-6837
  Barberton *(G-1065)*
Blanchester Foundry Co Inc .... F 937 783-2091
  Blanchester *(G-1700)*
Cast Metals Incorporated .... F 419 278-2010
  Deshler *(G-8787)*
Castco Inc .... E 440 365-2333
  Elyria *(G-9233)*
Casting Solutions LLC .... C 740 452-9371
  Zanesville *(G-21117)*
Castings Usa Inc .... G 330 339-3611
  New Philadelphia *(G-14764)*
Chris Erhart Foundry & Mch Co .... E 513 421-6550
  Cincinnati *(G-3473)*
Col-Pump Company Inc .... D 330 482-1029
  Columbiana *(G-6459)*
D Picking & Co .... E 419 562-5016
  Bucyrus *(G-2324)*
▲ Dd Foundry Inc .... D 216 362-4100
  Brookpark *(G-2143)*
Domestic Casting Company LLC .... C 717 532-6615
  Delaware *(G-8673)*
Ej Usa Inc .... E 216 692-3001
  Cleveland *(G-5159)*
Ej Usa Inc .... G 614 871-2436
  Grove City *(G-10428)*
Ej Usa Inc .... F 330 782-3900
  Youngstown *(G-20898)*
◆ Ellwood Engineered Castings Co .... C 330 568-3000
  Hubbard *(G-11001)*
Engines Inc of Ohio .... D 740 377-9874
  South Point *(G-17283)*

Foote Foundry LLC .... D 740 694-1595
Fredericktown *(G-9969)*

Ford Motor Company .... A 216 676-7918
Brookpark *(G-2147)*

General Aluminum Mfg Company .... C 419 739-9300
Wapakoneta *(G-19330)*

General Motors LLC .... A 419 782-7010
Defiance *(G-8623)*

Hamilton Brass & Alum Castings .... E 513 867-0400
Hamilton *(G-10567)*

Hobart Corporation .... E 937 332-3000
Troy *(G-18671)*

Hobart Corporation .... C 937 332-2797
Piqua *(G-16128)*

Kenton Iron Products Inc .... D 419 674-4178
Kenton *(G-11411)*

Knapp Foundry Co Inc .... F 330 434-0916
Akron *(G-240)*

▲ **Knappco Corporation** .... C 816 741-0786
West Chester *(G-19731)*

▲ **Korff Holdings LLC** .... C 330 332-1566
Salem *(G-16752)*

▲ **Liberty Casting Company LLC** .... C 740 363-1941
Delaware *(G-8702)*

McWane Inc .... B 740 622-6651
Coshocton *(G-7739)*

Miami-Cast Inc .... E 937 866-2951
Miamisburg *(G-13692)*

Monroe Water System .... G 740 472-1030
Sardis *(G-16876)*

▲ **OS Kelly Corporation** .... E 937 322-4921
Springfield *(G-17465)*

◆ **Osco Industries Inc** .... B 740 354-3183
Portsmouth *(G-16293)*

Osco Industries Inc .... C 740 286-5004
Jackson *(G-11193)*

Pioneer City Casting Company .... E 740 423-7533
Belpre *(G-1582)*

Piqua Champion Foundry Inc .... E 937 773-3375
Piqua *(G-16150)*

Quality Castings Company .... B 330 682-6871
Orrville *(G-15613)*

▲ **Rotek Incorporated** .... C 330 562-4000
Aurora *(G-904)*

Sancast Inc .... E 740 622-8660
Coshocton *(G-7750)*

Skuld LLC .... G 330 423-7339
Groveport *(G-10512)*

St Marys Foundry Inc .... C 419 394-3346
Saint Marys *(G-16701)*

T & B Foundry Company .... D 216 391-4200
Cleveland *(G-6141)*

Tangent Air Inc .... E 740 474-1114
Circleville *(G-4560)*

Tiffin Foundry & Machine Inc .... E 419 447-3991
Tiffin *(G-18087)*

Tri Cast Limited Partnership .... E 330 733-8718
Akron *(G-410)*

Tri-Cast Inc .... E 330 733-8718
Akron *(G-411)*

▲ **Wallace Forge Company** .... D 330 488-1203
Canton *(G-2863)*

Whemco-Ohio Foundry Inc .... C 419 222-2111
Lima *(G-11959)*

Yellow Creek Casting Company .... E 330 532-4608
Wellsville *(G-19615)*

3322 Malleable Iron Foundries

Ej Usa Inc .... E 216 692-3001
Cleveland *(G-5159)*

◆ **Ellwood Engineered Castings Co** .... C 330 568-3000
Hubbard *(G-11001)*

General Aluminum Mfg Company .... C 419 739-9300
Wapakoneta *(G-19330)*

General Motors LLC .... A 419 782-7010
Defiance *(G-8623)*

Kenton Iron Products Inc .... D 419 674-4178
Kenton *(G-11411)*

Osco Industries Inc .... C 740 286-5004
Jackson *(G-11193)*

Pioneer City Casting Company .... E 740 423-7533
Belpre *(G-1582)*

Sancast Inc .... E 740 622-8660
Coshocton *(G-7750)*

St Marys Foundry Inc .... C 419 394-3346
Saint Marys *(G-16701)*

T & B Foundry Company .... D 216 391-4200
Cleveland *(G-6141)*

Tiffin Foundry & Machine Inc .... E 419 447-3991
Tiffin *(G-18087)*

Tooling Technology LLC .... D 937 295-3672
Fort Loramie *(G-9810)*

Whemco-Ohio Foundry Inc .... C 419 222-2111
Lima *(G-11959)*

Yellow Creek Casting Company .... E 330 532-4608
Wellsville *(G-19615)*

3324 Steel Investment Foundries

B W Grinding Co .... E 419 923-1376
Lyons *(G-12273)*

▲ **Bescast Inc** .... C 440 946-5300
Willoughby *(G-20285)*

Brost Foundry Company .... E 216 641-1131
Cleveland *(G-4842)*

Caspa Home Page Inc .... G 216 781-0748
Cleveland *(G-4886)*

▲ **Castalloy Inc** .... D 216 961-7990
Cleveland *(G-4889)*

▲ **Consoldted Precision Pdts Corp** .... C 216 453-4800
Cleveland *(G-5016)*

▲ **Dd Foundry Inc** .... D 216 362-4100
Brookpark *(G-2143)*

General Aluminum Mfg Company .... C 419 739-9300
Wapakoneta *(G-19330)*

Harbor Castings Inc .... E 330 499-7178
Cuyahoga Falls *(G-7877)*

Howmet Castings & Services Inc .... B 216 641-4400
Newburgh Heights *(G-14938)*

◆ **Howmet Corporation** .... E 757 825-7086
Newburgh Heights *(G-14939)*

▲ **International Precision** .... G 330 342-0407
Hudson *(G-11056)*

◆ **Kovatch Castings Inc** .... C 330 896-9944
Uniontown *(G-18924)*

Mercury Machine Co .... D 440 349-3222
Solon *(G-17191)*

Mold Masters Intl Inc .... C 440 953-0220
Eastlake *(G-9123)*

PCC Airfoils LLC .... C 330 868-6441
Minerva *(G-14196)*

PCC Airfoils LLC .... C 440 255-9770
Mentor *(G-13545)*

Premier Inv Cast Group LLC .... E 413 727-2860
Moraine *(G-14382)*

▲ **Rimer Enterprises Inc** .... E 419 878-8156
Waterville *(G-19504)*

Skuld LLC .... G 330 423-7339
Groveport *(G-10512)*

Summit Resources Group Inc .... G 330 653-3992
Hudson *(G-11078)*

▲ **Xapc Co** .... D 216 362-4100
Cleveland *(G-6331)*

3325 Steel Foundries, NEC

▲ **Alcon Industries Inc** .... D 216 961-1100
Cleveland *(G-4653)*

Anointed Design & Technologies .... G 330 826-1493
Massillon *(G-12959)*

Aza Enterprises LLC .... G 740 678-8482
Fleming *(G-9778)*

◆ **B-Tek Scales LLC** .... E 330 471-8900
Canton *(G-2582)*

Brost Foundry Company .... E 216 641-1131
Cleveland *(G-4842)*

Castings Usa Inc .... G 330 339-3611
New Philadelphia *(G-14764)*

▲ **Dd Foundry Inc** .... D 216 362-4100
Brookpark *(G-2143)*

Durivage Pattern & Mfg Co .... E 419 836-8655
Williston *(G-20262)*

Engines Inc of Ohio .... D 740 377-9874
South Point *(G-17283)*

▲ **Evertz Technology Service Usa** .... E 513 422-8400
Middletown *(G-13907)*

Harbor Castings Inc .... E 330 499-7178
Cuyahoga Falls *(G-7877)*

▲ **Jmac Inc** .... E 614 436-2418
Columbus *(G-7069)*

▲ **Korff Holdings LLC** .... C 330 332-1566
Salem *(G-16752)*

◆ **Kovatch Castings Inc** .... C 330 896-9944
Uniontown *(G-18924)*

Lakeway Mfg Inc .... E 419 433-3030
Huron *(G-11103)*

Medina Blanking Inc .... C 330 558-2300
Valley City *(G-19049)*

Munroe Incorporated .... G 330 755-7216
Struthers *(G-17821)*

Precision Polymer Casting LLC .... G 440 343-0461
Moreland Hills *(G-14402)*

Premier Inv Cast Group LLC .... E 937 299-7333
Moraine *(G-14381)*

Rampp Company .... E 740 373-7886
Marietta *(G-12662)*

◆ **Sandusky International Inc** .... C 419 626-5340
Sandusky *(G-16843)*

▲ **Sawbrook Steel Castings Co** .... D 513 554-1700
Cincinnati *(G-4302)*

Sns Nano Fiber Technology LLC .... G 330 655-0030
Hudson *(G-11074)*

Steel Service Plus Ltd .... F 216 391-9000
Cleveland *(G-6102)*

Tecumseh Redevelopment Inc .... G 330 659-9100
Richfield *(G-16492)*

Tiffin Foundry & Machine Inc .... E 419 447-3991
Tiffin *(G-18087)*

United Engineering & Fndry Co .... F 330 456-2761
Canton *(G-2847)*

Whemco-Ohio Foundry Inc .... C 419 222-2111
Lima *(G-11959)*

Worthington Industries Inc .... C 513 539-9291
Monroe *(G-14282)*

Worthington Industries Inc .... C 614 438-3210
Worthington *(G-20710)*

Worthngton Stelpac Systems LLC .... C 614 438-3205
Columbus *(G-7617)*

3331 Primary Smelting & Refining Of Copper

▲ **Bryan Metals LLC** .... G 419 636-4571
Bryan *(G-2272)*

Hildreth Mfg LLC .... E 740 375-5832
Marion *(G-12712)*

▲ **Sam Dong Ohio Inc** .... D 740 363-1985
Delaware *(G-8721)*

3334 Primary Production Of Aluminum

Arconic Inc .... G 216 391-3885
Cleveland *(G-4730)*

Benjamin Steel Company Inc .... E 937 233-1212
Springfield *(G-17368)*

Boggs Recycling Inc .... G 800 837-8101
Newbury *(G-14946)*

Fabrication Group LLC .... E 216 251-1125
Cleveland *(G-5213)*

Homan Metals LLC .... G 513 721-5010
Cincinnati *(G-3821)*

Imperial Alum - Minerva LLC .... D 330 868-7765
Minerva *(G-14184)*

Kaiser Aluminum Fab Pdts LLC .... C 740 522-1151
Heath *(G-10723)*

Real Alloy Specialty Pdts LLC .... A 216 755-8836
Beachwood *(G-1273)*

Real Alloy Specification LLC .... G 216 755-8900
Beachwood *(G-1275)*

Wagner Rustproofing Co Inc .... F 216 361-4930
Cleveland *(G-6283)*

3339 Primary Nonferrous Metals, NEC

◆ **Aci Industries Ltd** .... E 740 368-4160
Delaware *(G-8648)*

▲ **Advanced Materials Products** .... G 330 650-4000
Hudson *(G-11026)*

▲ **American Friction Tech LLC** .... D 216 823-0861
Cleveland *(G-4687)*

▲ **American Spring Wire Corp** .... C 216 292-4620
Bedford Heights *(G-1460)*

Galt Alloys Inc Main Ofc .... G 330 453-4678
Canton *(G-2678)*

Gdc Industries LLC .... G 937 367-7229
Beavercreek *(G-1316)*

◆ **Globe Metallurgical Inc** .... C 740 984-2361
Waterford *(G-19484)*

H C Starck Inc .... F 216 692-6990
Euclid *(G-9417)*

H C Starck Inc .... B 216 692-3990
Euclid *(G-9418)*

Hamilton Rti Inc .... G 330 652-9951
Niles *(G-15011)*

▲ **Magnesium Refining Tech Inc** .... E 419 483-9199
Cleveland *(G-5604)*

Magnesium Refining Tech Inc .... E 419 483-9199
Bellevue *(G-1538)*

Materion Brush Inc .... A 419 862-2745
Elmore *(G-9208)*

▲ **Materion Brush Inc** .... D 216 486-4200
Mayfield Heights *(G-13167)*

◆ **Materion Corporation** .... C 216 486-4200
Mayfield Heights *(G-13168)*

▲ **Metallic Resources Inc** .... E 330 425-3155
Twinsburg *(G-18819)*

S I C

Employee Codes: A=Over 500 employees, B=251-500
C=101-250, D=51-100, E=20-50, F=10-19, G=3-9

2019 Harris Ohio
Industrial Directory

911

Ohio Valley Specialty Company F 740 373-2276
Marietta *(G-12650)*
Pelham Precious Metals LLC G 419 708-7975
Toledo *(G-18462)*
▲ Quality Gold Inc B 513 942-7659
Fairfield *(G-9554)*
▲ Rhenium Alloys Inc D 440 365-7388
North Ridgeville *(G-15251)*
Rml Tool Inc G 216 941-1615
Cleveland *(G-5991)*
Rti Finance Corp G 330 652-9952
Niles *(G-15033)*
Swift Manufacturing Co Inc G 740 237-4405
Ironton *(G-11173)*
▲ Zircoa Inc C 440 248-0500
Cleveland *(G-6345)*
Zircoa Inc E 440 349-7237
Solon *(G-17263)*

3341 Secondary Smelting & Refining Of Nonferrous Metals

A & B Iron & Metal Company F 937 228-1561
Dayton *(G-7997)*
▲ A J Oster Foils LLC D 330 823-1700
Alliance *(G-447)*
Able Alloy Inc F 216 251-6110
Cleveland *(G-4599)*
◆ Aci Industries Ltd E 740 368-4160
Delaware *(G-8648)*
Agmet LLC F 216 663-8200
Cleveland *(G-4641)*
Aleris Rolled Pdts Sls Corp G 216 910-3400
Cleveland *(G-4656)*
Aleris Rolled Products Inc B 216 910-3400
Beachwood *(G-1221)*
Aleris Rolled Products Inc D 740 983-2571
Ashville *(G-814)*
Aleris Rolled Products Inc G 740 922-2540
Uhrichsville *(G-18879)*
Applied Materials Finishing E 330 336-5645
Wadsworth *(G-19227)*
Auris Noble LLC F 330 321-6649
Fairlawn *(G-9594)*
Auris Noble LLC G 330 685-3748
Akron *(G-73)*
City Scrap & Salvage Co E 330 753-5051
Akron *(G-118)*
Cohen Brothers Inc G 513 422-3696
Middletown *(G-13895)*
Continental Metal Proc Co F 216 268-0000
Cleveland *(G-5021)*
Continental Metal Proc Co E 216 268-0000
Cleveland *(G-5022)*
Echo Environmental Waverly LLC F 740 286-2810
Waverly *(G-19545)*
Emerald Transformer Ppm LLC F 800 908-8800
Twinsburg *(G-18768)*
▲ Fpt Cleveland LLC C 216 441-3800
Cleveland *(G-5270)*
▲ Franklin Iron & Metal Corp C 937 253-8184
Dayton *(G-8206)*
Fusion Automation Inc G 440 602-5595
Willoughby *(G-20326)*
G A Avril Company F 513 641-0566
Cincinnati *(G-3719)*
▲ Garden Street Iron & Metal E 513 853-3700
Cincinnati *(G-3726)*
Gold 2 Green Ltd G 304 551-1172
Bridgeport *(G-2075)*
▲ Grandview Materials Inc G 614 488-6998
Lewis Center *(G-11761)*
HC Starck Inc B 216 692-3990
Cleveland *(G-5382)*
I H Schlezinger Inc E 614 252-1188
Columbus *(G-7016)*
◆ I Schumann & Co LLC C 440 439-2300
Bedford *(G-1414)*
▲ Imco Recycling of Ohio LLC C 740 922-2373
Uhrichsville *(G-18888)*
Lake County Auto Recyclers G 440 428-2886
Painesville *(G-15757)*
Masters Group Inc G 440 893-1900
Chagrin Falls *(G-3059)*
Materion Brush Inc A 419 862-2745
Elmore *(G-9208)*
▲ Materion Brush Inc D 216 486-4200
Mayfield Heights *(G-13167)*
◆ Materion Corporation C 216 486-4200
Mayfield Heights *(G-13168)*
▼ Mek Van Wert Inc G 419 203-4902
Van Wert *(G-19102)*
Metal Shredders Inc E 937 866-0777
Miamisburg *(G-13689)*
Metalico Akron Inc E 330 376-1400
Akron *(G-279)*
Metals Recovery Services LLC G 614 870-0364
Columbus *(G-7173)*
Midwest Iron and Metal Co D 937 222-5992
Dayton *(G-8353)*
▲ National Bronze Mtls Ohio Inc E 440 277-1226
Lorain *(G-12106)*
◆ Oakwood Industries Inc D 440 232-8700
Bedford *(G-1433)*
▲ Ohio Valley Alloy Services Inc E 740 373-1900
Marietta *(G-12649)*
Old Rar Inc E 216 910-3400
Beachwood *(G-1256)*
Panama Jewelers LLC G 440 376-6987
Painesville *(G-15771)*
▲ Polymet Corporation E 513 874-3586
West Chester *(G-19763)*
Precision Strip Inc C 419 674-4186
Kenton *(G-11418)*
R L S Corporation E 740 773-1440
Chillicothe *(G-3219)*
Real Alloy Holding LLC G 216 755-8900
Beachwood *(G-1270)*
Real Alloy Recycling LLC E 346 444-8540
Beachwood *(G-1271)*
▲ Real Alloy Recycling LLC D 216 755-8900
Beachwood *(G-1272)*
Real Alloy Specialty Pdts LLC A 216 755-8836
Beachwood *(G-1273)*
Real Alloy Specialty Products F 440 563-3487
Rock Creek *(G-16533)*
Real Alloy Specialty Products E 440 322-0072
Elyria *(G-9318)*
Real Alloy Specification LLC G 216 755-8900
Beachwood *(G-1275)*
River Smelting & Ref Mfg Co E 216 459-2100
Cleveland *(G-5987)*
Rm Advisory Group Inc E 513 242-2100
Cincinnati *(G-4274)*
Rmi Titanium Company LLC D 330 471-1844
Canton *(G-2807)*
Rnw Holdings Inc E 330 792-0600
Youngstown *(G-21018)*
Rumpke Transportation Co LLC C 513 242-4600
Cincinnati *(G-4289)*
▲ Sawbrook Steel Castings Co D 513 554-1700
Cincinnati *(G-4302)*
Shaneway Inc G 330 868-2220
Minerva *(G-14201)*
Thyssenkrupp Materials NA Inc D 216 883-8100
Independence *(G-11152)*
▲ Umicore Spclty Mtls Recycl LLC D 440 833-3000
Wickliffe *(G-20233)*
Victory White Metal Company E 216 271-1400
Cleveland *(G-6261)*
W R G Inc E 216 351-8494
Cleveland *(G-6279)*
Wall Colmonoy Corporation F 937 278-9111
Cincinnati *(G-4487)*

3351 Rolling, Drawing & Extruding Of Copper

◆ Alcan Corporation E 440 460-3307
Cleveland *(G-4650)*
▲ American Wire & Cable Company E 440 235-1140
Olmsted Twp *(G-15532)*
Arem Co F 440 974-6740
Mentor *(G-13393)*
Avtron Aerospace Inc C 216 750-5152
Cleveland *(G-4778)*
▲ Bryan Metals LLC G 419 636-4571
Bryan *(G-2272)*
◆ Chase Brass and Copper Co LLC B 419 485-3193
Montpelier *(G-14304)*
Commconnect G 937 414-0505
Dayton *(G-8099)*
Federal Metal Company D 440 232-8700
Bedford *(G-1404)*
Jj Seville LLC E 330 769-2071
Seville *(G-16918)*
▲ Materion Brush Inc D 216 486-4200
Mayfield Heights *(G-13167)*
◆ Materion Corporation C 216 486-4200
Mayfield Heights *(G-13168)*
▲ Republic Wire Inc D 513 860-1800
West Chester *(G-19779)*
T & D Fabricating Inc E 440 951-5646
Eastlake *(G-9135)*

3353 Aluminum Sheet, Plate & Foil

▲ A J Oster Foils LLC D 330 823-1700
Alliance *(G-447)*
Aleris Rolled Products Inc G 740 922-2540
Uhrichsville *(G-18879)*
Arconic Inc C 330 835-6000
Mogadore *(G-14230)*
Arconic Inc C 330 848-4000
Barberton *(G-1053)*
Arconic Inc G 330 544-7633
Niles *(G-14998)*
B&B Distributors LLC F 440 324-1293
Elyria *(G-9221)*
◆ Interntnal Cnvrter Cldwell Inc C 740 732-5665
Caldwell *(G-2407)*
▲ Monarch Steel Company Inc E 216 587-8000
Cleveland *(G-5703)*
Nichols Aluminum-Alabama LLC C 256 353-1550
Beachwood *(G-1253)*
Novelis G 440 392-6150
Concord Township *(G-7640)*
Novelis Corporation D 330 841-3456
Warren *(G-19423)*
P B Fabrication Mech Contr F 419 478-4869
Toledo *(G-18454)*

3354 Aluminum Extruded Prdts

Accu-Tek Tool & Die Inc G 330 726-1946
Salem *(G-16713)*
Aerolite Extrusion Company D 330 782-1127
Youngstown *(G-20838)*
◆ Alanod Westlake Metal Ind Inc E 440 327-8184
North Ridgeville *(G-15206)*
Aleris Corporation G 216 910-3400
Cleveland *(G-4654)*
Allen Morgan Trucking & Repair G 330 336-5192
Norton *(G-15361)*
Aluminum Extruded Shapes Inc C 513 563-2205
Cincinnati *(G-3328)*
▲ American Aluminum Extrusions C 330 458-0300
Canton *(G-2572)*
Arem Co F 440 974-6740
Mentor *(G-13393)*
Astro Aluminum Enterprises Inc E 330 755-1414
Struthers *(G-17813)*
Astro Shapes LLC C 330 755-1414
Struthers *(G-17814)*
Astro Shapes LLC F 330 755-1414
Struthers *(G-17815)*
BRT Extrusions Inc C 330 544-0177
Niles *(G-15001)*
Central Aluminum Company LLC E 614 491-5700
Obetz *(G-15508)*
Compliant Access Products LLC G 513 518-4525
Cleves *(G-6358)*
Datco Mfg Company Inc D 330 781-6100
Youngstown *(G-20887)*
◆ Exal Corporation E 330 744-9505
Youngstown *(G-20901)*
▲ Extrudex Aluminum Inc C 330 538-4444
North Jackson *(G-15146)*
Gdic Group LLC G 330 468-0700
Cleveland *(G-5297)*
Gei of Columbiana Inc D 330 783-0270
Youngstown *(G-20915)*
General Extrusions Inc D 330 783-0270
Youngstown *(G-20917)*
Hydro Aluminum Fayetteville G 937 492-9194
Sidney *(G-17044)*
I R B F Company G 330 633-5100
Tallmadge *(G-17986)*
Industrial Mold Inc E 330 425-7374
Twinsburg *(G-18796)*
◆ Isaiah Industries Inc E 937 773-9840
Piqua *(G-16131)*
▲ Kit MB Systems Inc E 330 945-4500
Akron *(G-239)*
▲ Klb Industries Inc E 937 592-9010
Bellefontaine *(G-1521)*
Knoble Glass & Metal Inc G 513 753-1246
Cincinnati *(G-3919)*
L & L Ornamental Iron Co F 513 353-1930
Cleves *(G-6369)*
Langstons Ultmate Clg Svcs Inc F 330 298-9150
Ravenna *(G-16387)*
Loxcreen Company Inc F 513 539-2255
Middletown *(G-13921)*

Mag Acquisitions LLC .... C 513 988-6351
Trenton (G-18622)
Magnode Corporation............................ C 513 988-6351
Trenton (G-18623)
Magnode Corporation............................ D 317 243-3553
Trenton (G-18624)
▲ National Metal Shapes Inc .... E 740 363-9559
Delaware (G-8709)
Navarre Industries Inc .... E 330 767-3003
Navarre (G-14582)
Northern States Metals Company .... D 860 521-6001
Youngstown (G-20978)
▲ Orrvilon Inc .... C 330 684-9400
Orrville (G-15610)
Owens Corning Sales LLC .... G 740 983-1300
Ashville (G-819)
Patton Aluminum Products Inc .... F 937 845-9404
New Carlisle (G-14676)
▲ Precision of Ohio Inc .... F 330 793-0900
Youngstown (G-21004)
Star Extruded Shapes Inc .... B 330 533-9863
Canfield (G-2546)
▲ Star Fab Inc .... C 330 533-9863
Canfield (G-2547)
Star Fab Inc .... E 330 482-1601
Columbiana (G-6482)
T & D Fabricating Inc .... E 440 951-5646
Eastlake (G-9135)
Tecnocap LLC .... D 330 392-7222
Warren (G-19446)
Tri County Tarp LLC .... E 419 288-3350
Bradner (G-2016)
▲ Vari-Wall Tube Specialists Inc........... D 330 482-0000
Columbiana (G-6485)
Youngstown Tool & Die Company .... D 330 747-4464
Youngstown (G-21083)
Zarbana Alum Extrusions LLC .... E 330 482-5092
Columbiana (G-6487)

3355 Aluminum Rolling & Drawing, NEC

◆ Alcan Corporation .... E 440 460-3307
Cleveland (G-4650)
Aleris Corporation .... G 216 910-3400
Cleveland (G-4654)
▲ Aleris International Inc .... C 216 910-3400
Beachwood (G-1218)
Aleris Rm Inc .... C 216 910-3400
Beachwood (G-1220)
▲ Aleris Rolled Products LLC............... E 216 910-3400
Cleveland (G-4657)
Aluminum Extrusion Tech LLC .... G 330 533-3994
Canfield (G-2522)
Amh Holdings LLC .... A 330 929-1811
Cuyahoga Falls (G-7836)
Amh Holdings II Inc .... B 330 929-1811
Cuyahoga Falls (G-7837)
Arconic Inc .... G 330 544-7633
Niles (G-14998)
Eastman Kodak Company .... E 937 259-3000
Dayton (G-8175)
Homan Metals LLC .... G 513 721-5010
Cincinnati (G-3821)
Kaiser Aluminum Fab Pdts LLC .... C 740 522-1151
Heath (G-10723)
Mac Its LLC .... F 937 454-0722
Vandalia (G-19133)
Max Mighty Inc .... F 937 862-9530
Spring Valley (G-17317)
Novelis Corporation .... D 330 841-3456
Warren (G-19423)
Nuvox .... G 614 232-9115
Columbus (G-7234)
◆ Pandrol Inc .... E 419 592-5050
Napoleon (G-14555)
Powermount Systems Inc .... G 740 499-4330
La Rue (G-11476)
Real Alloy Specialty Pdts LLC .... G 440 322-0072
Elyria (G-9317)
Real Alloy Specialty Products .... C 216 755-8836
Beachwood (G-1274)
Southwire Company LLC .... G 440 933-6110
Avon Lake (G-1009)
Waxco International Inc .... F 937 746-4845
Miamisburg (G-13740)

3356 Rolling, Drawing-Extruding Of Nonferrous Metals

Air Craft Wheels LLC .... G 440 937-7903
Ravenna (G-16364)

Allied Mask and Tooling Inc .... G 419 470-2555
Toledo (G-18164)
API Machining Fabrication Inc .... G 740 369-0455
Delaware (G-8654)
Arconic Titanium.................................... G 330 544-7633
Niles (G-14999)
Artistic Composite & Mold Co .... G 330 352-6632
Litchfield (G-11984)
BCi and V Investments Inc .... D 330 538-0660
North Jackson (G-15141)
Bunting Bearings LLC .... E 419 522-3323
Mansfield (G-12417)
◆ Canton Drop Forge Inc .... B 330 477-4511
Canton (G-2608)
Castlebar Corporation .... G 330 451-6511
Canton (G-2621)
Chris Nckel Cstm Ltherwork LLC .... G 614 262-2672
Columbus (G-6764)
▲ Cleanlife Energy LLC .... F 800 316-2532
Cleveland (G-4941)
Consolidated Metal Pdts Inc .... E 513 251-2624
Cincinnati (G-3542)
Contour Forming Inc .... E 740 345-9777
Newark (G-14864)
Curtiss-Wright Flow Ctrl Corp .... D 216 267-3200
Cleveland (G-5045)
Economy Straightening Service .... G 216 432-4410
Cleveland (G-5155)
Eric Nickel... G 614 818-2488
Westerville (G-19990)
ESAB Group Incorporated .... G 440 813-2506
Ashtabula (G-774)
Fusion Automation Inc .... G 440 602-5595
Willoughby (G-20326)
Fusion Incorporated .... E 440 946-3300
Willoughby (G-20328)
G A Avril Company................................ F 513 731-5133
Cincinnati (G-3720)
G A Avril Company................................ F 513 641-0566
Cincinnati (G-3719)
Gem City Metal Tech LLC .... E 937 252-8998
Dayton (G-8220)
General Electric Company .... C 330 793-3911
Youngstown (G-20916)
H C Starck Inc.. B 216 692-3990
Euclid (G-9418)
Kilroy Company .... D 440 951-8700
Eastlake (G-9117)
Lite Metals Company .... E 330 296-6110
Ravenna (G-16389)
▲ Materion Brush Inc .... D 216 486-4200
Mayfield Heights (G-13167)
▲ Materion Corporation .... C 216 486-4200
Mayfield Heights (G-13168)
Mestek Inc... D 419 288-2703
Bradner (G-2015)
Metal Merchants Usa Inc .... G 330 723-3228
Medina (G-13300)
▲ Metallic Resources Inc .... E 330 425-3155
Twinsburg (G-18819)
▲ Nova Machine Products Inc .... D 216 267-3200
Middleburg Heights (G-13767)
▲ Patriot Special Metals Inc .... G 330 538-9621
North Jackson (G-15152)
Patriot Special Metals Inc..................... D 330 580-9600
Canton (G-2781)
▲ Rhenium Alloys Inc .... D 440 365-7388
North Ridgeville (G-15251)
Rmi Titanium Company LLC .... E 330 544-7633
Niles (G-15030)
Rmi Titanium Company LLC .... G 330 652-9955
Niles (G-15031)
◆ Rmi Titanium Company LLC .... G 330 652-9952
Niles (G-15028)
Robert Nickel.. G 419 448-8256
Tiffin (G-18078)
Steven Nickel.. G 419 732-3377
Port Clinton (G-16260)
Tailwind Technologies Inc.................... E 937 778-4200
Piqua (G-16164)
Th Magnesium Inc................................ G 513 285-7568
Cincinnati (G-4417)
Tin Indian Performance .... G 216 214-5485
Uniontown (G-18935)
Tin Shed LLC .... G 330 636-2524
Willard (G-20246)
Tin Wizard Heating and Cooling .... G 330 468-7884
Macedonia (G-12337)
Tin-Sau LLC... G 419 586-8886
Celina (G-2989)

Titanium Contractors Ltd .... G 513 256-2152
Cincinnati (G-4422)
Titanium Lacrosse LLC .... F 614 562-8082
Lewis Center (G-11786)
◆ Titanium Metals Corporation .... E 610 968-1300
Warrensville Heights (G-19473)
Titanium Metals Corporation .... A 740 537-1571
Toronto (G-18612)
Titanium Sales Group LLC .... G 614 204-6098
Dublin (G-9004)
Titanium Trout LLC............................... G 440 543-3187
Chagrin Falls (G-3083)
Victory White Metal Company .... F 216 641-2575
Cleveland (G-6259)
▲ Victory White Metal Company......... D 216 271-1400
Cleveland (G-6260)
▲ Water Star Inc .... F 440 996-0800
Painesville (G-15797)

3357 Nonferrous Wire Drawing

◆ Alcan Corporation .... E 440 460-3307
Cleveland (G-4650)
▲ American Wire & Cable Company ....E 440 235-1140
Olmsted Twp (G-15532)
▲ Arnco Corporation .... C 800 847-7661
Elyria (G-9219)
Astro Industries Inc .... E 937 429-5900
Beavercreek (G-1301)
AT&T Corp .... G 513 792-9300
Cincinnati (G-3365)
Calvert Wire & Cable Corp .... G 330 494-3248
North Canton (G-15075)
Composite Concepts Inc .... G 440 247-3844
Mason (G-12852)
▲ Connectors Unlimited Inc .... E 440 357-1161
Painesville (G-15724)
Cory Electronics .... G 440 951-9424
Mentor (G-13424)
▲ Electra - Cord Inc .... D 330 832-8124
Massillon (G-12979)
Electrovations Inc .... E 330 274-3558
Aurora (G-878)
▲ HM Wire International Inc .... G 330 244-8501
Canton (G-2700)
Integrated Systems Professiona .... G 614 875-0104
Grove City (G-10436)
Legrand North America LLC .... B 937 224-0639
Dayton (G-8309)
Master Magnetics Inc............................ F 740 373-0909
Marietta (G-12645)
▲ Mueller Electric Company Inc .... E 216 771-5225
Akron (G-290)
▲ Murphy Industries Inc .... G 740 387-7890
Marion (G-12722)
Ohio Associated Entps LLC .... E 440 354-3148
Painesville (G-15770)
Radix Wire Co.. D 216 731-9191
Cleveland (G-5956)
Radix Wire Co.. D 216 731-9191
Cleveland (G-5957)
Radix Wire Company .... E 330 995-3677
Aurora (G-902)
◆ Ribbon Technology Corporation........ F 614 864-5444
Gahanna (G-10100)
Schneider Electric Usa Inc .... B 513 523-4171
Oxford (G-15700)
Scott Fetzer Company .... C 216 267-9000
Cleveland (G-6035)
Syscom Advanced Materials Inc .... F 614 487-3626
Columbus (G-7506)
▲ Therm-O-Link Inc .... D 330 527-2124
Garrettsville (G-10203)
Therm-O-Link Inc .... G 330 393-7600
Warren (G-19447)
Therm-O-Link of Texas Inc .... G 330 393-4300
Warren (G-19448)
Veteran Industries LLC......................... G 937 751-2133
Columbus (G-7581)
Vulkor Incorporated .... E 330 393-7600
Warren (G-19457)
Xponet Inc... E 440 354-6617
Painesville (G-15801)

3363 Aluminum Die Castings

▲ Ahresty Wilmington Corporation....... B 937 382-6112
Wilmington (G-20484)
Akron Foundry Co .... C 330 745-3101
Akron (G-40)
▲ Alliance Castings Company LLC ..... E 330 829-5600
Alliance (G-452)

33 PRIMARY METAL INDUSTRIES

Alumacast LLC .... G 419 584-1473
  Celina (G-2949)
American Light Metals LLC .... C 330 908-3065
  Macedonia (G-12277)
Apex Aluminum Die Cast Co Inc .... E 937 773-0432
  Piqua (G-16099)
Cast Specialties Inc .... E 216 292-7393
  Cleveland (G-4888)
CSM Horvath Ledgebrook .... G 419 522-1133
  Mansfield (G-12430)
Custom Industries Inc .... G 216 251-2804
  Cleveland (G-5047)
Destin Die Casting LLC .... E 937 347-1111
  Xenia (G-20766)
◆ Fort Recovery Industries Inc .... B 419 375-4121
  Fort Recovery (G-9818)
General Aluminum Mfg Company ..... C 419 739-9300
  Wapakoneta (G-19330)
General Die Casters Inc .... D 330 467-6700
  Northfield (G-15318)
▲ General Die Casters Inc .... E 330 678-2528
  Twinsburg (G-18781)
Krengel Equipment LLC .... C 440 946-3570
  Eastlake (G-9118)
▲ Matalco (us) Inc .... G 330 452-4760
  Canton (G-2746)
Model Pattern & Foundry Co .... E 513 542-2322
  Cincinnati (G-4036)
▲ Ohio Aluminum Industries Inc ...... C 216 641-8865
  Cleveland (G-5798)
◆ Ohio Decorative Products LLC ..... E 419 647-9033
  Spencerville (G-17311)
▼ Omni Die Casting Inc .... E 330 830-5500
  Massillon (G-13033)
◆ Park-Ohio Holdings Corp .... F 440 947-2000
  Cleveland (G-5842)
Park-Ohio Industries Inc .... E 440 947-2000
  Cleveland (G-5843)
Plaster Process Castings Co .... E 216 663-1814
  Cleveland (G-5885)
Ramco Electric Motors Inc .... D 937 548-2525
  Greenville (G-10389)
Ravana Industries Inc .... G 330 536-4015
  Lowellville (G-12254)
Reliable Castings Corporation .... D 937 497-5217
  Sidney (G-17065)
▲ Ross Casting & Innovation LLC ... B 937 497-4500
  Sidney (G-17070)
Seilkop Industries Inc .... E 513 761-1035
  Cincinnati (G-4316)
Seilkop Industries Inc .... F 513 679-5680
  Cincinnati (G-4317)
Seyekcub Inc .... G 330 324-1394
  Uhrichsville (G-18894)
SRS Die Casting Holdings LLC .... G 330 467-0750
  Macedonia (G-12330)
SRS Light Metals Inc .... G 330 467-0750
  Macedonia (G-12331)
▲ Thompson Aluminum Casting Co D 216 206-2781
  Cleveland (G-6171)
Tooling Technology LLC .... D 937 295-3672
  Fort Loramie (G-9810)
United States Drill Head Co .... E 513 941-0300
  Cincinnati (G-4450)
Yoder Industries Inc .... C 937 278-5769
  Dayton (G-8602)

3364 Nonferrous Die Castings, Exc Aluminum

▲ Akron Brass Company .... E 309 444-4440
  Wooster (G-20556)
American Light Metals LLC .... C 330 908-3065
  Macedonia (G-12277)
Cast Specialties Inc .... E 216 292-7393
  Cleveland (G-4888)
Certech Inc .... G 330 405-1033
  Twinsburg (G-18750)
Custom Industries Inc .... G 216 251-2804
  Cleveland (G-5047)
D Picking & Co .... G 419 562-5016
  Bucyrus (G-2324)
▲ Dd Foundry Inc .... D 216 362-4100
  Brookpark (G-2143)
▲ Empire Brass Co .... E 216 431-6565
  Cleveland (G-5173)
Federal Metal Company .... D 440 232-8700
  Bedford (G-1404)
▲ General Die Casters Inc .... E 330 678-2528
  Twinsburg (G-18781)

General Die Casters Inc .... D 330 467-6700
  Northfield (G-15318)
Hamilton Brass & Alum Castings .... E 513 867-0400
  Hamilton (G-10567)
M & M Dies Inc .... G 216 883-6628
  Cleveland (G-5590)
Magnesium Elektron North Amer .... E 419 424-8878
  Findlay (G-9716)
Martina Metal UC .... E 614 291-9700
  Columbus (G-7155)
Model Pattern & Foundry Co .... E 513 542-2322
  Cincinnati (G-4036)
◆ Oakwood Industries Inc .... D 440 232-8700
  Bedford (G-1433)
Omni USA Inc .... D 330 830-5500
  Massillon (G-13034)
Plaster Process Castings Co .... E 216 663-1814
  Cleveland (G-5885)
Ray Lewis & Son Incorporated .... E 937 644-4015
  Marysville (G-12807)
Reebar Die Casting Inc .... F 419 878-7591
  Waterville (G-19503)
Ryder-Heil Bronze Inc .... E 419 562-2841
  Bucyrus (G-2343)
SRS Die Casting Holdings LLC .... G 330 467-0750
  Macedonia (G-12330)
SRS Light Metals Inc .... G 330 467-0750
  Macedonia (G-12331)
Support Svc LLC .... G 419 617-0660
  Lexington (G-11808)
Teledyne Brown Engineering Inc .... D 419 470-3000
  Toledo (G-18545)
Tessec LLC .... E 937 985-3552
  Dayton (G-8552)
▲ Thompson Aluminum Casting Co D 216 206-2781
  Cleveland (G-6171)
Yoder Industries Inc .... E 937 890-4322
  Dayton (G-8603)
Yoder Industries Inc .... C 937 278-5769
  Dayton (G-8602)

3365 Aluminum Foundries

Accro-Cast Corporation .... F 937 228-0497
  Dayton (G-8001)
Acuity Brands Lighting Inc .... B 740 349-4343
  Newark (G-14848)
Air Craft Wheels LLC .... G 440 937-7903
  Ravenna (G-16364)
Akron Foundry Co .... C 330 745-3101
  Akron (G-40)
Akron Foundry Co .... C 330 745-3101
  Barberton (G-1050)
▲ Aluminum Line Products Company D 440 835-8880
  Westlake (G-20091)
Aztec Manufacturing Inc .... E 330 783-9747
  Youngstown (G-20850)
Boscott Metals Inc .... F 937 448-2018
  Bradford (G-2009)
Brost Foundry Company .... E 216 641-1131
  Cleveland (G-4842)
C M M S - Re LLC .... E 513 489-5111
  Blue Ash (G-1745)
▲ Calphalon Corporation .... D 770 418-7100
  Perrysburg (G-15927)
Calphalon Corporation .... E 419 666-8700
  Perrysburg (G-15928)
Cast Metals Technology Inc .... E 937 968-5460
  Union City (G-18902)
Cast Metals Technology Inc .... G 740 363-1690
  Delaware (G-8661)
Castek Aluminum Inc .... E 440 365-2333
  Elyria (G-9234)
▲ Consolidated Precision Pdts Corp C 216 453-4800
  Cleveland (G-5016)
Cushman Foundry LLC .... F 513 984-5570
  Blue Ash (G-1757)
▲ Dd Foundry Inc .... D 216 362-4100
  Brookpark (G-2143)
Durivage Pattern & Mfg Co .... E 419 836-8655
  Williston (G-20262)
▲ Enprotech Industrial Tech LLC .... C 216 883-3220
  Cleveland (G-5179)
Euclid Products Co Inc .... G 440 942-7310
  Willoughby (G-20317)
Francis Manufacturing Company ..... C 937 526-4551
  Russia (G-16607)
▲ General Aluminum Mfg Company B 330 297-1225
  Cleveland (G-5304)
General Aluminum Mfg Company .... E 330 297-1020
  Ravenna (G-16381)

General Aluminum Mfg Company ... B 440 593-6225
  Conneaut (G-7646)
▲ General Die Casters Inc .... E 330 678-2528
  Twinsburg (G-18781)
General Motors LLC .... A 419 782-7010
  Defiance (G-8623)
General Precision Corporation .... G 440 951-9380
  Willoughby (G-20331)
Globe Motors Inc .... G 937 228-3171
  Dayton (G-8227)
Howmet Aluminum Casting Inc ...... E 216 641-4340
  Newburgh Heights (G-14937)
Htci Co .... F 937 845-1204
  New Carlisle (G-14667)
Iabf Inc .... G 614 279-4498
  Columbus (G-7018)
◆ Kovatch Castings Inc .... G 330 896-9944
  Uniontown (G-18924)
Lite Metals Company .... E 330 296-6110
  Ravenna (G-16389)
Lockheed Martin Investments .... F 937 429-0100
  Beavercreek (G-1329)
Lodi Foundry Co Inc .... E 330 948-1516
  Lodi (G-12014)
Merit Foundry Co Inc .... G 216 741-4282
  Cleveland (G-5656)
Metal-Mation Inc .... F 216 651-1083
  Cleveland (G-5660)
Miller Casting Inc .... F 330 482-2923
  Columbiana (G-6473)
Model Pattern & Foundry Co .... E 513 542-2322
  Cincinnati (G-4036)
Morris Bean & Company .... C 937 767-7301
  Yellow Springs (G-20812)
Mpe Aeroengines Inc .... G 937 878-3800
  Huber Heights (G-11022)
Multi Cast LLC .... E 419 335-0010
  Wauseon (G-19528)
Myron D Budd .... G 330 682-5866
  Orrville (G-15604)
Nelson Aluminum Foundry Inc .... G 440 543-1941
  Chagrin Falls (G-3063)
New London Foundry Inc .... F 419 929-2073
  New London (G-14733)
New Mansfield Brass & Alum Co ... E 419 492-2166
  New Washington (G-14830)
Non-Ferrous Casting Co .... G 937 228-1162
  Dayton (G-8382)
OKeefe Casting Co .... G 440 277-5427
  Lorain (G-12110)
P C M Co .... D 330 336-8040
  Wadsworth (G-19258)
▲ Palmer Engineered Products Inc E 937 322-1481
  Springfield (G-17466)
Piqua Emery Cutter & Fndry Co ..... D 937 773-4134
  Piqua (G-16152)
Precision Aluminum Inc .... E 330 335-2351
  Wadsworth (G-19265)
▲ Pride Cast Metals Inc .... D 513 541-1295
  Cincinnati (G-4189)
Quality Match Plate Co .... F 330 889-2462
  Southington (G-17302)
▲ Range Kleen Mfg Inc .... B 419 331-8000
  Elida (G-9199)
Reliable Castings Corporation .... D 937 497-5217
  Sidney (G-17065)
▲ Ross Aluminum Castings LLC ... C 937 492-4134
  Sidney (G-17069)
Rotocast Technologies Inc .... G 330 798-9091
  Akron (G-354)
▲ Sawbrook Steel Castings Co ..... D 513 554-1700
  Cincinnati (G-4302)
Seilkop Industries Inc .... F 513 679-5680
  Cincinnati (G-4317)
Skuld LLC .... G 330 423-7339
  Groveport (G-10512)
▲ Stripmatic Products Inc .... E 216 241-7143
  Cleveland (G-6111)
▲ Thompson Aluminum Casting Co D 216 206-2781
  Cleveland (G-6171)
Tooling Technology LLC .... D 937 295-3672
  Fort Loramie (G-9810)
Tri - Flex of Ohio Inc .... F 330 705-7084
  North Canton (G-15131)
TW Corporation .... E 440 461-3234
  Akron (G-416)
◆ US Metalcraft Inc .... G 419 692-4962
  Delphos (G-8762)
Yoder Industries Inc .... E 937 890-4322
  Dayton (G-8603)

Yoder Industries Inc....C....937 278-5769
Dayton (G-8602)
Zephyr Industries Inc....G....419 281-4485
Ashland (G-756)

3366 Copper Foundries

A & H Automotive Industries....G....614 235-1759
Columbus (G-6514)
Accurate Products Company....G....740 498-7202
Newcomerstown (G-14969)
▲ Advance Bronze Inc....D....330 948-1231
Lodi (G-12003)
Advance Bronzehubco Div....E....304 232-4414
Lodi (G-12004)
Advanced Propeller Systems....G....937 409-1038
Dayton (G-7968)
American Bronze Corporation....E....216 341-7800
Cleveland (G-4684)
Anchor Bronze and Metals Inc....E....440 549-5653
Cleveland (G-4705)
Brost Foundry Company....E....216 641-1131
Cleveland (G-4842)
Brost Foundry Company....F....419 522-1133
Mansfield (G-12415)
Buckeye Aluminum Foundry Inc....G....440 428-7180
Madison (G-12340)
Bunting Bearings LLC....E....419 522-3323
Mansfield (G-12417)
▲ Bunting Bearings LLC....D....419 866-7000
Holland (G-10917)
Calmego Specialized Pdts LLC....F....937 669-5620
Greenville (G-10362)
▲ Climax Metal Products Company....D....440 943-8898
Mentor (G-13416)
Connell Limited Partnership....D....877 534-8986
Northfield (G-15316)
D Picking & Co....G....419 562-5016
Bucyrus (G-2324)
▲ Daido Metal Bellefontaine LLC....C....937 592-5010
Bellefontaine (G-1511)
Dupont Specialty Pdts USA LLC....C....216 901-3600
Cleveland (G-5120)
◆ Falcon Foundry Company....D....330 536-6221
Lowellville (G-12250)
Foundry Artist Inc....G....216 391-9030
Cleveland (G-5268)
Hadronics Inc....D....513 321-9350
Cincinnati (G-3792)
◆ Kovatch Castings Inc....C....330 896-9944
Uniontown (G-18924)
M A Harrison Mfg Co Inc....E....440 965-4306
Wakeman (G-19287)
Maass Midwest Mfg Inc....G....419 894-6424
Arcadia (G-625)
▲ McNeil Industries Inc....E....440 951-7756
Painesville (G-15762)
▲ Meierjohan-Wengler Inc....F....513 771-6074
Cincinnati (G-4002)
Model Pattern & Foundry Co....E....513 542-2322
Cincinnati (G-4036)
National Brass Company Inc....G....216 651-8530
Cleveland (G-5723)
▲ National Bronze Mtls Ohio Inc....E....440 277-1226
Lorain (G-12106)
Non-Ferrous Casting Co....G....937 228-1162
Dayton (G-8382)
Oakes Foundry Inc....E....330 372-4010
Warren (G-19424)
OKeefe Casting Co....G....440 277-5427
Lorain (G-12110)
Piqua Emery Cutter & Fndry Co....D....937 773-4134
Piqua (G-16152)
▲ Pride Cast Metals Inc....D....513 541-1295
Cincinnati (G-4189)
▲ Randall Bearings Inc....D....419 223-1075
Lima (G-11927)
Randall Bearings Inc....F....419 678-2486
Coldwater (G-6419)
▲ S C Industries Inc....E....216 732-9000
Euclid (G-9441)
Santos Industrial Ltd....E....937 299-7333
Moraine (G-14392)
▲ Semco....D....800 848-5764
Marion (G-12734)
Snair Co....F....614 873-7020
Plain City (G-16212)
▲ Stripmatic Products Inc....E....216 241-7143
Cleveland (G-6111)
Whip Guide Co....F....440 543-5151
Chagrin Falls (G-3090)

3369 Nonferrous Foundries: Castings, NEC

A C Williams Co Inc....E....330 296-6110
Ravenna (G-16362)
Air Craft Wheels LLC....G....440 937-7903
Ravenna (G-16364)
Akron Foundry Co....C....330 745-3101
Akron (G-40)
▲ Alcon Industries Inc....D....216 961-1100
Cleveland (G-4653)
Apex Aluminum Die Cast Co Inc....E....937 773-0432
Piqua (G-16099)
Auld Company....E....614 454-1010
Columbus (G-6629)
Brost Foundry Company....E....216 641-1131
Cleveland (G-4842)
Bunting Bearings LLC....E....419 522-3323
Mansfield (G-12417)
Castmor Products Inc....G....440 953-1103
Willoughby (G-20293)
▲ Catania Medallic Specialty....E....440 933-9595
Avon Lake (G-981)
Computational Engineering Svcs....G....513 745-0313
Blue Ash (G-1752)
Concorde Castings Inc....G....440 953-0053
Willoughby (G-20299)
Consoldted Precision Pdts Corp....D....440 953-0053
Eastlake (G-9102)
Curtiss-Wright Flow Ctrl Corp....D....216 267-3200
Cleveland (G-5045)
Custom Industries Inc....G....216 251-2804
Cleveland (G-5047)
▲ Dd Foundry Inc....D....216 362-4100
Brookpark (G-2143)
Dmk Industries Inc....F....513 727-4549
Middletown (G-13901)
Durivage Pattern & Mfg Co....E....419 836-8655
Williston (G-20262)
◆ Ellwood Engineered Castings Co....C....330 568-3000
Hubbard (G-11001)
Francis Manufacturing Company....C....937 526-4551
Russia (G-16607)
▼ Garfield Alloys Inc....F....216 587-4843
Cleveland (G-5292)
▲ General Aluminum Mfg Company....B....330 297-1225
Cleveland (G-5304)
General Aluminum Mfg Company....E....330 297-1020
Ravenna (G-16381)
General Aluminum Mfg Company....B....440 593-6225
Conneaut (G-7646)
▲ General Die Casters Inc....E....330 678-2528
Twinsburg (G-18781)
General Motors LLC....A....419 782-7010
Defiance (G-8623)
Globe Motors Inc....C....937 228-3171
Dayton (G-8227)
Harbor Castings Inc....E....330 499-7178
Cuyahoga Falls (G-7877)
Iabf Inc....G....614 279-4498
Columbus (G-7018)
◆ Kovatch Castings Inc....C....330 896-9944
Uniontown (G-18924)
Kse Manufacturing....G....937 409-9831
Sidney (G-17048)
Liberty Die Casting Company....G....419 636-3971
Bryan (G-2297)
Lite Metals Company....E....330 296-6110
Ravenna (G-16389)
Materion Brush Inc....A....419 862-2745
Elmore (G-9208)
McM Precision Castings Inc....E....419 669-3226
Weston (G-20177)
Microweld Engineering Inc....F....614 847-9410
Worthington (G-20697)
Morris Bean & Company....C....937 767-7301
Yellow Springs (G-20812)
Nelson Aluminum Foundry Inc....G....440 543-1941
Chagrin Falls (G-3063)
New London Foundry Inc....F....419 929-2073
New London (G-14733)
▲ Nova Machine Products Inc....D....216 267-3200
Middleburg Heights (G-13767)
◆ Ohio Decorative Products LLC....C....419 647-9033
Spencerville (G-17311)
PCC Airfoils LLC....C....330 868-6441
Minerva (G-14196)
PCC Airfoils LLC....B....740 982-6025
Crooksville (G-7818)
PCC Airfoils LLC....F....440 350-6150
Painesville (G-15773)
PCC Airfoils LLC....F....216 766-6206
Beachwood (G-1263)
◆ PCC Airfoils LLC....E....216 831-3590
Cleveland (G-5856)
PCC Airfoils LLC....C....216 692-7900
Cleveland (G-5857)
PCC Airfoils LLC....C....440 255-9770
Mentor (G-13545)
Piqua Emery Cutter & Fndry Co....D....937 773-4134
Piqua (G-16152)
Ray Lewis & Son Incorporated....E....937 644-4015
Marysville (G-12807)
Reliable Castings Corporation....D....937 497-5217
Sidney (G-17065)
▲ Ross Aluminum Castings LLC....C....937 492-4134
Sidney (G-17069)
Rossborough Supply Co....G....216 941-6115
Cleveland (G-6005)
Sam Americas Inc....E....330 628-1118
Mogadore (G-14248)
◆ Sandusky International Inc....C....419 626-5340
Sandusky (G-16843)
▲ Sawbrook Steel Castings Co....D....513 554-1700
Cincinnati (G-4302)
Seaport Mold & Casting Company....F....419 243-1422
Toledo (G-18515)
Seilkop Industries Inc....F....513 679-5680
Cincinnati (G-4317)
St Marys Foundry Inc....C....419 394-3346
Saint Marys (G-16701)
Symmetry Oes....G....614 890-1758
Westerville (G-20075)
T & B Foundry Company....D....216 391-4200
Cleveland (G-6141)
Technology House Ltd....D....440 248-3025
Solon (G-17248)
Technology House Ltd....E....440 248-3025
Streetsboro (G-17701)
Telcon LLC....D....330 562-5566
Streetsboro (G-17702)
▲ Thompson Aluminum Casting Co....D....216 206-2781
Cleveland (G-6171)
▲ Voss Industries LLC....C....216 771-7655
Cleveland (G-6273)
Warren Castings Inc....F....216 883-2520
Cleveland (G-6289)
Yoder Industries Inc....C....937 278-5769
Dayton (G-8602)

3398 Metal Heat Treating

Accuphase Metal Treating LLC....G....937 610-5934
Moraine (G-14328)
Advanced Flame Hardening Inc....G....216 431-0370
Cleveland (G-4625)
Akron Steel Treating Co....E....330 773-8211
Akron (G-53)
Al Fe Heat Treating-Ohio Inc....E....330 336-0211
Wadsworth (G-19224)
Al-Fe Heat Treating Inc....E....419 782-7200
Defiance (G-8612)
Allegheny Ludlum LLC....E....330 875-2244
Louisville (G-12151)
Alternative Flash Inc....E....330 334-6111
Wadsworth (G-19225)
AM Castle & Co....D....330 425-7000
Bedford (G-1381)
▲ Amac Enterprises Inc....C....216 362-1880
Parma (G-15814)
▲ American Metal Treating Co....E....216 431-4492
Cleveland (G-4692)
American Quality Stripping....E....419 625-6288
Sandusky (G-16794)
American Steel Treating Inc....E....419 874-2044
Perrysburg (G-15919)
Analytic Stress Relieving Inc....G....804 271-7198
Northwood (G-15332)
▲ Arcelormittal Columbus LLC....C....614 492-6800
Columbus (G-6613)
Atmosphere Annealing LLC....D....330 478-0314
Kenton (G-11402)
B&C Machine Co LLC....B....330 745-4013
Barberton (G-1058)
Bekaert Corporation....C....330 683-5060
Orrville (G-15583)
Bob Lanes Welding Inc....F....740 373-3567
Marietta (G-12609)
Bodycote Imt Inc....E....740 852-5000
London (G-12050)
Bodycote Thermal Proc Inc....E....614 444-1181
Columbus (G-6683)

33 PRIMARY METAL INDUSTRIES

Bodycote Thermal Proc Inc .... E 513 921-2300
Cincinnati (G-3399)
Bodycote Thermal Proc Inc .... F 440 473-2020
Cleveland (G-4827)
Bodycote Thermal Proc Inc .... E 216 475-0400
Cleveland (G-4828)
Bodycote Thermal Proc Inc .... G 740 852-4955
London (G-12051)
Bowdil Company .... F 800 356-8663
Canton (G-2596)
Brazing Service Inc .... G 440 871-1120
Westlake (G-20104)
Carpe Diem Industries LLC .... E 419 358-0129
Bluffton (G-1887)
Carpe Diem Industries LLC .... D 419 659-5639
Columbus Grove (G-7632)
Certified Heat Treating Inc .... E 937 866-0245
Dayton (G-8084)
Cincinnati Gearing Systems Inc .... D 513 527-8600
Cincinnati (G-3493)
Cincinnati Gearing Systems Inc .... D 513 527-8600
Cincinnati (G-3495)
Cleveland Hollow Boring Inc .... G 216 883-1926
Cleveland (G-4963)
▲ Clifton Steel Company .... D 216 662-6111
Maple Heights (G-12569)
Columbus Coatings Company .... D 614 492-6800
Columbus (G-6786)
Commercial Steel Treating Co .... F 216 431-8204
Cleveland (G-5004)
Dayton Forging Heat Treating .... D 937 253-4126
Dayton (G-8132)
Derrick Company Inc .... E 513 321-8122
Cincinnati (G-3583)
Detroit Flame Hardening Co .... D 216 531-4273
Euclid (G-9410)
Detroit Flame Hardening Co .... F 513 942-1400
Fairfield (G-9494)
Dewitt Inc .... G 216 662-0800
Maple Heights (G-12570)
▲ Die Co Inc .... E 440 942-8856
Eastlake (G-9104)
▲ Dowa Tht America Inc .... E 419 354-4144
Bowling Green (G-1971)
Erie Steel Ltd .... E 419 478-3743
Toledo (G-18285)
Euclid Heat Treating Co .... D 216 481-8444
Euclid (G-9413)
Fbf Limited .... E 513 541-6300
Cincinnati (G-3679)
Flynn Inc .... B 419 478-3743
Toledo (G-18296)
Franklin Field Service .... G 614 885-1779
Columbus (G-6937)
Fusion Automation Inc .... G 440 602-5595
Willoughby (G-20326)
General Steel Corporation .... F 216 883-4200
Cleveland (G-5314)
Gerdau Macsteel Atmosphere Ann .... D 330 478-0314
Canton (G-2683)
Gt Technologies Inc .... C 419 782-8955
Defiance (G-8625)
H & M Metal Processing Co .... E 330 745-3075
Akron (G-194)
H & S Steel Treating Inc .... F 330 678-5245
Kent (G-11329)
Heat Treating Inc .... E 937 325-3121
Springfield (G-17414)
Heat Treating Inc .... F 937 325-3121
Springfield (G-17415)
Heat Treating Inc .... G 614 759-9963
Gahanna (G-10082)
Heat Treating Technologies .... E 419 224-8324
Lima (G-11873)
HI Tecmetal Group Inc .... E 216 881-8100
Cleveland (G-5402)
HI Tecmetal Group Inc .... E 440 373-5101
Wickliffe (G-20213)
HI Tecmetal Group Inc .... F 216 941-0440
Cleveland (G-5403)
HI Tecmetal Group Inc .... F 216 881-8100
Cleveland (G-5404)
HI Tecmetal Group Inc .... G 440 946-2280
Willoughby (G-20337)
Hmt Inc .... G 440 599-7005
Conneaut (G-7648)
Induction Hrdning Spclists Inc .... G 234 678-6820
Peninsula (G-15894)
Induction Management Svcs LLC .... G 440 947-2000
Warren (G-19410)

Isostatic Pressing Svcs LLC .... G 614 370-2140
Columbus (G-7051)
▲ J W Harris Co Inc .... F 216 481-8100
Euclid (G-9421)
Kando of Cincinnati Inc .... E 513 459-7782
Lebanon (G-11668)
Kowalski Heat Treating Co .... F 216 631-4411
Cleveland (G-5543)
Lapham-Hickey Steel Corp .... D 419 399-4803
Paulding (G-15865)
Lapham-Hickey Steel Corp .... D 614 443-4881
Columbus (G-7116)
Mannings USA .... G 614 836-0021
Groveport (G-10502)
Metal Improvement Company LLC .... E 513 489-6484
Blue Ash (G-1819)
Metal Improvement Company LLC .... E 330 425-1490
Twinsburg (G-18817)
Metallurgical Service Inc .... E 937 294-2681
Moraine (G-14368)
Miller Consolidated Industries .... C 937 294-2681
Moraine (G-14370)
Moore Mc Millen Holdings .... D 330 745-3075
Cuyahoga Falls (G-7899)
National Peening .... G 216 342-9155
Bedford Heights (G-1476)
▲ Neturen America Corporation .... F 513 863-1900
Hamilton (G-10589)
▲ Northlake Steel Corporation .... D 330 220-7717
Valley City (G-19056)
Northwind Industries Inc .... E 216 433-0666
Cleveland (G-5787)
Ohio Coatings Company .... D 740 859-5500
Yorkville (G-20827)
Ohio Flame Hardening Company .... E 513 336-6160
Lebanon (G-11678)
Ohio Flame Hardening Company .... E 513 733-5162
Cincinnati (G-4102)
Ohio Metallurgical Service Inc .... D 440 365-4104
Elyria (G-9304)
P & L Heat Trting Grinding Inc .... E 330 746-1339
Youngstown (G-20986)
P & L Precision Grinding LLC .... F 330 746-8081
Youngstown (G-20988)
▲ Parker Trutec Incorporated .... D 937 323-8833
Springfield (G-17469)
Pike Machine Products Co .... E 216 731-1880
Euclid (G-9433)
Pressure Technology Ohio Inc .... E 215 628-1975
Painesville (G-15776)
Pride Investments LLC .... F 937 461-1121
Dayton (G-8439)
Pro-TEC Coating Company LLC .... D 419 943-1100
Leipsic (G-11733)
Quality Metal Treating Company .... G 931 432-7467
Cincinnati (G-4227)
Ridge Machine & Welding Co .... G 740 537-2821
Toronto (G-18611)
Ropama Inc .... F 440 358-1304
Painesville (G-15781)
Samuel Steel Pickling Company .... D 330 963-3777
Twinsburg (G-18853)
Surface Enhancement Tech LLC .... F 513 561-1520
Cincinnati (G-4400)
Team Inc .... F 614 263-1808
Columbus (G-7517)
Team Cooperheat Mqs .... G 614 501-7304
Columbus (G-7518)
Techniques Surfaces Usa Inc .... G 937 323-2556
Springfield (G-17504)
Thermal Solutions Inc .... G 614 263-1808
Columbus (G-7526)
Thermal Treatment Center Inc .... E 216 881-8100
Cleveland (G-6167)
Thermal Treatment Center Inc .... E 216 883-4820
Cleveland (G-6168)
Thermal Treatment Center Inc .... E 440 943-4555
Wickliffe (G-20232)
Thermal Treatment Center Inc .... F 216 941-0440
Cleveland (G-6169)
Universal Heat Treating Inc .... E 216 641-2000
Cleveland (G-6238)
USA Heat Treating Inc .... E 216 587-4700
Cleveland (G-6245)
Vicon Fabricating Company Ltd .... E 440 205-6700
Mentor (G-13624)
Wall Colmonoy Corporation .... F 937 278-9111
Cincinnati (G-4487)
Weiss Industries Inc .... E 419 526-2480
Mansfield (G-12539)

Winston Heat Treating Inc .... E 937 226-0110
Dayton (G-8597)
◆ Xtek Inc .... B 513 733-7800
Cincinnati (G-4530)
Youngstown Heat Treating .... G 330 788-3025
Youngstown (G-21078)
Zion Industries Inc .... D 330 225-3246
Valley City (G-19070)

3399 Primary Metal Prdts, NEC

A-Gas US Holdings Inc .... F 419 867-8990
Bowling Green (G-1945)
Additive Metal Alloys Ltd .... G 800 687-6110
Holland (G-10914)
Aerotech Industries Inc .... E 216 881-6660
Cleveland (G-4636)
Altana .... G 440 954-7600
Painesville (G-15709)
Bogie Industries Inc Ltd .... E 330 745-3105
Akron (G-92)
Bricolage Inc .... F 614 853-6789
Grove City (G-10418)
Colliers Cstmizing Fabrication .... F 937 523-0420
Urbana (G-18985)
CP Metals Inc .... G 724 510-4293
Warren (G-19390)
Cryoplus Inc .... G 330 683-3375
Wooster (G-20581)
▼ Destiny Manufacturing Inc .... E 330 273-9000
Brunswick (G-2199)
Duffee Finishing Inc .... G 740 965-4848
Sunbury (G-17885)
◆ Eckart America Corporation .... D 440 954-7600
Painesville (G-15734)
Elgin Fastener Group LLC .... F 812 689-8990
Brecksville (G-2032)
▲ Ferro Corporation .... D 216 875-5600
Mayfield Heights (G-13163)
GKN Sinter Metals LLC .... F 419 238-8200
Van Wert (G-19092)
J & K Powder Coating .... G 330 540-6145
Mineral Ridge (G-14166)
▲ Key Finishes LLC .... G 614 351-8393
Columbus (G-7093)
Legacy Finishing Inc .... G 937 743-7278
Franklin (G-9895)
Liberty Steel Pressed Pdts LLC .... G 330 538-2236
North Jackson (G-15149)
Masters Group Inc .... G 440 893-1900
Chagrin Falls (G-3059)
Matandy Steel & Metal Pdts LLC .... D 513 844-2277
Hamilton (G-10585)
Materion Technical Mtls Inc .... D 216 486-4200
Cleveland (G-5635)
▲ Midwest Motor Supply Co .... C 800 233-1294
Columbus (G-7181)
National Fasteners Inc .... G 216 771-6473
Brooklyn Heights (G-2127)
Nuflux LLC .... G 330 399-1122
Cortland (G-7713)
Obron Atlantic Corporation .... G 440 954-7600
Painesville (G-15767)
Ohio Valley Manufacturing Inc .... D 419 522-5818
Mansfield (G-12497)
Payne Family LLC II .... G 513 861-7600
Blue Ash (G-1829)
▲ Powder Alloy Corporation .... E 513 984-4016
Loveland (G-12223)
Powdermet Inc .... E 216 404-0053
Euclid (G-9434)
Premar Manufacturing Ltd .... G 440 250-0373
Westlake (G-20145)
◆ Rmi Titanium Company LLC .... E 330 652-9952
Niles (G-15028)
Robert A Reich Company .... G 440 808-0033
Westlake (G-20151)
Royal Powder Corporation .... G 216 898-0074
Cleveland (G-6013)
◆ Shinagawa Advanced Materials A .... E 330 628-1118
Mogadore (G-14249)
▲ Stein Inc .... F 440 526-9301
Cleveland (G-6104)
Stein Inc .... D 216 883-7444
Cleveland (G-6105)
Stonebrook Machine .... G 440 951-5013
Eastlake (G-9132)
Topkote Inc .... G 440 428-0525
Madison (G-12357)
▼ Transmet Corporation .... G 614 276-5522
Columbus (G-7539)

34 FABRICATED METAL PRODUCTS, EXCEPT MACHINERY AND TRANSPORTATION EQUIPMENT

Tru-Har Products................................G....... 330 338-6826
  Hudson *(G-11080)*
◆ Truck Fax Inc...................................G....... 216 921-8866
  Cleveland *(G-6218)*
Veelo Technologies LLC................F....... 513 309-5947
  Cincinnati *(G-4469)*
▲ Waterford Tank Fabrication Ltd........D....... 740 984-4100
  Beverly *(G-1663)*

34 FABRICATED METAL PRODUCTS, EXCEPT MACHINERY AND TRANSPORTATION EQUIPMENT

3411 Metal Cans

Amcor Rigid Plastics Usa LLC..........G....... 419 483-4343
  Bellevue *(G-1528)*
◆ Anchor Hocking LLC.....................A....... 740 681-6478
  Lancaster *(G-11541)*
Anchor Hocking LLC.........................G....... 740 687-2500
  Lancaster *(G-11542)*
Ball Corporation.................................C....... 419 423-3071
  Findlay *(G-9653)*
Ball Corporation.................................F....... 330 244-2313
  North Canton *(G-15072)*
Ball Corporation................................D....... 614 771-9112
  Columbus *(G-6645)*
Ball Metal Beverage Cont Corp.........C....... 419 423-3071
  Findlay *(G-9654)*
Broodle Brands LLC..........................F....... 855 276-6353
  Cincinnati *(G-3424)*
Buckeye Stamping Company............G....... 614 445-0059
  Columbus *(G-6712)*
Busch Properties Inc........................G....... 614 888-0946
  Columbus *(G-6714)*
BWAY Corporation.............................E....... 513 388-2200
  Cincinnati *(G-3433)*
Cardinal Welding Inc.........................G....... 330 426-2404
  East Palestine *(G-9069)*
Cleveland Steel Container Corp........E....... 330 656-5600
  Streetsboro *(G-17666)*
Container Manufacturing Ltd............G....... 937 264-2370
  Dayton *(G-8102)*
Crown Cork & Seal Usa Inc..............E....... 419 727-8201
  Toledo *(G-18243)*
Crown Cork & Seal Usa Inc..............B....... 330 833-1011
  Massillon *(G-12971)*
Crown Cork & Seal Usa Inc..............C....... 937 299-2027
  Moraine *(G-14339)*
Crown Cork & Seal Usa Inc..............E....... 740 681-6593
  Lancaster *(G-11561)*
Crown Cork & Seal Usa Inc..............D....... 740 681-3000
  Lancaster *(G-11560)*
Eisenhauer Mfg Co LLC...................D....... 419 238-0081
  Van Wert *(G-19090)*
◆ Encore Plastics Corporation..........C....... 419 626-8000
  Sandusky *(G-16808)*
◆ Exal Corporation.............................E....... 330 744-9505
  Youngstown *(G-20901)*
G W Cobb Co......................................F....... 216 341-0100
  Cleveland *(G-5285)*
▲ G&M Media Packaging Inc..........F....... 419 636-5461
  Bryan *(G-2282)*
▼ Ghp II LLC.......................................C....... 740 687-2500
  Lancaster *(G-11575)*
Independent Can Company...............E....... 440 593-5300
  Conneaut *(G-7650)*
Industrial Container Svcs LLC...........E....... 513 921-8811
  Cincinnati *(G-3844)*
Industrial Container Svcs LLC..........D....... 614 864-1900
  Blacklick *(G-1687)*
▲ Organized Living Inc....................E....... 513 489-9300
  Cincinnati *(G-4118)*
▲ Packaging Specialties Inc...........E....... 330 723-6000
  Medina *(G-13316)*
Seven-Ogun International LLC..........G....... 614 888-8939
  Worthington *(G-20703)*
Sidney Can & Tool LLC.....................G....... 937 492-0977
  Sidney *(G-17078)*
▲ SSP Industrial Group Inc............G....... 330 665-2900
  Fairlawn *(G-9619)*
Two Tin Cans LLC..............................G....... 419 692-2027
  Delphos *(G-8759)*
▼ Witt Industries Inc........................D....... 513 871-5700
  Mason *(G-12955)*

3412 Metal Barrels, Drums, Kegs & Pails

Champion Company..........................D....... 937 324-5681
  Springfield *(G-17375)*

Champion Company..........................D....... 937 324-5681
  Springfield *(G-17374)*
Cleveland Steel Container Corp........E....... 330 656-5600
  Streetsboro *(G-17666)*
Cleveland Steel Container Corp........E....... 330 544-2271
  Niles *(G-15003)*
Deufol Worldwide Packaging LLC....E....... 440 232-1100
  Bedford *(G-1400)*
Eisenhauer Mfg Co LLC...................D....... 419 238-0081
  Van Wert *(G-19090)*
Fluid-Bag LLC...................................G....... 513 310-9550
  West Chester *(G-19705)*
Georgia-Pacific LLC..........................C....... 740 477-3347
  Circleville *(G-4546)*
Green Bay Packaging Inc.................C....... 419 332-5593
  Fremont *(G-10027)*
Green Bay Packaging Inc.................D....... 513 228-5560
  Lebanon *(G-11660)*
◆ Greif Inc..E....... 740 549-6000
  Delaware *(G-8681)*
Greif Inc..E....... 740 657-6500
  Delaware *(G-8682)*
Horwitz & Pintis Co.............................F....... 419 666-2220
  Toledo *(G-18336)*
Industrial Container Svcs LLC...........E....... 513 921-8811
  Cincinnati *(G-3844)*
Industrial Container Svcs LLC..........D....... 614 864-1900
  Blacklick *(G-1687)*
Mauser Usa LLC................................D....... 513 398-1300
  Mason *(G-12908)*
Mauser Usa LLC................................E....... 614 856-5982
  Mount Vernon *(G-14491)*
Mauser USA LLC................................E....... 614 856-5982
  Mount Vernon *(G-14492)*
Mobile Mini Inc....................................F....... 614 449-8655
  Columbus *(G-7188)*
North Coast Container Corp.............D....... 216 441-6214
  Cleveland *(G-5763)*
Overseas Packing LLC......................F....... 440 232-2917
  Bedford *(G-1434)*
▲ Packaging Specialties Inc...........E....... 330 723-6000
  Medina *(G-13316)*
▲ Sabco Industries Inc...................E....... 419 531-5347
  Toledo *(G-18510)*
Schwarz Partners Packaging LLC.....F....... 317 290-1140
  Sidney *(G-17073)*
▲ SSP Industrial Group Inc............G....... 330 665-2900
  Fairlawn *(G-9619)*
Syme Inc...E....... 330 723-6000
  Medina *(G-13350)*
Tavens Container Inc.........................D....... 216 883-3333
  Bedford *(G-1448)*
▲ Unican Ohio LLC..........................G....... 419 636-5461
  Fremont *(G-10059)*
▲ Werk-Brau Company...................D....... 419 422-2912
  Findlay *(G-9775)*
Westrock Cp LLC...............................C....... 330 297-0841
  Ravenna *(G-16419)*
Westrock Cp LLC...............................B....... 513 745-2400
  Blue Ash *(G-1868)*
Westrock Cp LLC...............................D....... 770 448-2193
  Wshngtn CT Hs *(G-20750)*
▼ Witt Industries Inc........................D....... 513 871-5700
  Mason *(G-12955)*

3421 Cutlery

1967..G....... 216 882-4228
  Bedford *(G-1377)*
A & P Tech Services Inc....................G....... 330 535-1700
  Akron *(G-17)*
Advetech Inc.......................................E....... 330 533-2227
  Canfield *(G-2517)*
◆ Air Technical Industries Inc.........E....... 440 951-5191
  Mentor *(G-13378)*
American Punch Co Inc.....................E....... 216 731-4501
  Euclid *(G-9403)*
▲ American Quicksilver Co.............G....... 513 871-4517
  Cincinnati *(G-3337)*
B & B Beverage Ctr...........................D....... 419 243-0752
  Toledo *(G-18196)*
Busse Knife Co...................................E....... 419 923-6471
  Wauseon *(G-19511)*
Cut Off Blades Inc..............................D....... 440 543-2947
  Chagrin Falls *(G-3043)*
Dan Wilzynski.....................................G....... 800 531-3343
  Columbus *(G-6848)*
Edgewell Per Care Brands LLC........D....... 440 835-7500
  Westlake *(G-20111)*
El Nuevo Naranjo................................G....... 614 863-4212
  Galloway *(G-10177)*

▲ Evolution Resources LLC............G....... 937 438-2390
  Centerville *(G-3002)*
▲ Fred Marvin and Associates Inc....G....... 330 784-9211
  Stow *(G-17590)*
General Cutlery Inc............................E....... 419 332-2316
  Fremont *(G-10023)*
Klenk Industries Inc...........................D....... 330 453-7857
  Canton *(G-2725)*
Kne LLC...G....... 859 356-1690
  Fairfield *(G-9517)*
Libbey Glass Inc.................................A....... 419 729-7272
  Toledo *(G-18383)*
Lt Wright Handcrafted Knife Co........F....... 740 317-1404
  Steubenville *(G-17541)*
New York Frozen Foods.....................F....... 614 846-2232
  Westerville *(G-20011)*
◆ Npk Construction Equipment Inc....D....... 440 232-7900
  Bedford *(G-1432)*
◆ Procter & Gamble Company........B....... 513 983-1100
  Cincinnati *(G-4198)*
Procter & Gamble Company..............C....... 513 983-1100
  Cincinnati *(G-4199)*
Procter & Gamble Company..............E....... 513 266-4375
  Cincinnati *(G-4200)*
Procter & Gamble Company..............E....... 513 871-7557
  Cincinnati *(G-4201)*
Procter & Gamble Company..............B....... 419 998-5891
  Lima *(G-11920)*
Procter & Gamble Company..............E....... 513 482-6789
  Cincinnati *(G-4203)*
Procter & Gamble Company..............E....... 513 672-4044
  West Chester *(G-19767)*
Procter & Gamble Company..............B....... 513 627-7115
  Cincinnati *(G-4205)*
Procter & Gamble Company..............E....... 513 634-9600
  West Chester *(G-19768)*
Procter & Gamble Company..............C....... 513 634-9110
  West Chester *(G-19769)*
Procter & Gamble Company..............C....... 513 934-3406
  Oregonia *(G-15573)*
Procter & Gamble Company..............G....... 513 627-7779
  Cincinnati *(G-4207)*
Procter & Gamble Company..............B....... 513 945-0340
  Cincinnati *(G-4208)*
Procter & Gamble Company..............C....... 513 622-1000
  Mason *(G-12926)*
Tom Fucito Inc....................................E....... 513 273-2092
  Oxford *(G-15701)*

3423 Hand & Edge Tools

▲ Abhushan LLC...............................G....... 614 789-0632
  Dublin *(G-8872)*
Acme Company..................................D....... 330 758-2313
  Poland *(G-16236)*
Advetech Inc.......................................E....... 330 533-2227
  Canfield *(G-2518)*
Advetech Inc.......................................E....... 330 533-2227
  Canfield *(G-2517)*
▼ Amcraft Inc......................................G....... 419 729-7900
  Toledo *(G-18170)*
◆ American Agritech LLC................E....... 480 777-2000
  Marysville *(G-12770)*
▲ American Power Pull Corp..........G....... 419 335-7050
  Wauseon *(G-19509)*
Ames Companies Inc........................E....... 740 783-2535
  Dexter City *(G-8791)*
ASG...F....... 216 486-6163
  Cleveland *(G-4748)*
Asg Division Jergens Inc..................G....... 888 486-6163
  Cleveland *(G-4749)*
Ashco Manufacturing Inc..................E....... 419 838-7157
  Toledo *(G-18193)*
Bartter & Sons....................................G....... 419 651-0374
  Jeromesville *(G-11249)*
Bergman Safety Spanner Co Inc......G....... 419 691-1462
  Northwood *(G-15334)*
Buckeye Gear Co................................F....... 216 292-7998
  Chagrin Falls *(G-3038)*
▲ C B Mfg & Sls Co Inc..................D....... 937 866-5986
  Miamisburg *(G-13647)*
C-H Tool & Die....................................G....... 740 397-7214
  Mount Vernon *(G-14471)*
Calvin Lanier.......................................E....... 937 952-4221
  Dayton *(G-8074)*
Cannon Salt and Supply Inc.............G....... 440 232-1700
  Bedford *(G-1392)*
CB Manufacturing & Sls Co Inc........D....... 937 866-5986
  Dayton *(G-8079)*
Chrisnik Inc...G....... 513 738-2920
  Okeana *(G-15516)*

34 FABRICATED METAL PRODUCTS, EXCEPT MACHINERY AND TRANSPORTATION EQUIPMENT

Cleveland Iron Workers Members ....G...... 216 687-2290
   Cleveland *(G-4965)*
Cornwell Quality Tools Company ....D...... 330 628-2627
   Mogadore *(G-14232)*
Crystal Carvers Inc ....G...... 800 365-9782
   Powell *(G-16319)*
D & M Saw & Tool Inc ....G...... 513 871-5433
   Cincinnati *(G-3568)*
Desmond-Stephan Mfgcompany ....E...... 937 653-7181
   Urbana *(G-18989)*
▲ E Z Grout Corporation ....E...... 740 749-3512
   Malta *(G-12381)*
E Z Rout Inc ....G...... 330 467-4814
   Northfield *(G-15317)*
▲ Eaton Electric Holdings LLC ....B...... 440 523-5000
   Cleveland *(G-5151)*
Edgerton Forge Inc ....E...... 419 298-2333
   Edgerton *(G-9171)*
▲ Electric Eel Mfg Co Inc ....E...... 937 323-4644
   Springfield *(G-17395)*
Empire Plow Company Inc ....E...... 216 641-2290
   Cleveland *(G-5175)*
Eric Mondene ....G...... 740 965-2842
   Galena *(G-10111)*
▲ Everhard Products Inc ....G...... 330 453-7786
   Canton *(G-2670)*
F & B Engraving Tls & Sup LLC ....G...... 937 332-7994
   Piqua *(G-16114)*
Falcon Industries Inc ....G...... 330 723-0099
   Medina *(G-13260)*
▲ File Sharpening Company Inc ....E...... 937 376-8268
   Xenia *(G-20772)*
▼ Furukawa Rock Drill USA Co Ltd ....E...... 330 673-5826
   Kent *(G-11325)*
Fusion Automation Inc ....G...... 440 602-5595
   Willoughby *(G-20326)*
▲ Glass Medic Inc ....G...... 800 356-4009
   Westerville *(G-19994)*
Handy Twine Knife Co ....G...... 419 294-3424
   Upper Sandusky *(G-18955)*
Harbor Freight Tools Usa Inc ....E...... 937 415-0770
   Dayton *(G-8244)*
Hutchinson-Stevens Inc ....G...... 216 281-8585
   Cleveland *(G-5428)*
J and S Tool Incorporated ....E...... 216 676-8330
   Cleveland *(G-5482)*
▲ Jbc Technologies Inc ....D...... 440 327-4522
   North Ridgeville *(G-15234)*
Klawhorn Industries Inc ....G...... 330 335-8191
   Wadsworth *(G-19249)*
Knight Ergonomics Inc ....F...... 440 746-0044
   Brecksville *(G-2045)*
♦ Komar Industries Inc ....E...... 614 836-2366
   Groveport *(G-10497)*
Luma Electric Company ....G...... 419 843-7842
   Sylvania *(G-17949)*
Martin Sprocket & Gear Inc ....D...... 419 485-5515
   Montpelier *(G-14312)*
▲ Matco Tools Corporation ....B...... 330 929-4949
   Stow *(G-17605)*
Midwest Knife Grinding Inc ....G...... 330 854-1030
   Canal Fulton *(G-2486)*
Myers Industries Inc ....E...... 440 632-1006
   Middlefield *(G-13836)*
▲ Norbar Torque Tools Inc ....F...... 440 953-1175
   Willoughby *(G-20389)*
North Coast Holdings Inc ....G...... 330 535-7177
   Akron *(G-299)*
Oldforge Tools Inc ....G...... 330 535-7177
   Akron *(G-310)*
Panacea Products Corporation ....D...... 614 429-6320
   Columbus *(G-7288)*
Randolph Tool Company Inc ....F...... 330 877-4923
   Hartville *(G-10703)*
▲ Rex International USA Inc ....E...... 800 321-7950
   Ashtabula *(G-803)*
♦ Ridge Tool Company ....A...... 440 323-5581
   Elyria *(G-9320)*
Ridge Tool Manufacturing Co ....A...... 440 323-5581
   Elyria *(G-9322)*
▲ S & H Industries Inc ....E...... 216 831-0550
   Cleveland *(G-6018)*
S & H Industries Inc ....G...... 216 831-0550
   Bedford *(G-1442)*
Sewer Rodding Equipment Co ....E...... 419 991-2065
   Lima *(G-11937)*
Silver Expressions ....G...... 740 687-0144
   Lancaster *(G-11608)*
Simon Ellis Superabrasives ....G...... 937 226-0683
   Dayton *(G-8508)*

Simonds International LLC ....E...... 978 424-0100
   Kimbolton *(G-11457)*
Spa Pool Covers Inc ....G...... 440 235-9981
   North Royalton *(G-15302)*
Stanley Access Tech LLC ....C...... 440 461-5500
   Cleveland *(G-6093)*
Stanley Industrial & Auto LLC ....C...... 614 755-7089
   Westerville *(G-20024)*
▲ Stanley Industrial & Auto LLC ....D...... 614 755-7000
   Westerville *(G-20025)*
♦ Step2 Company LLC ....B...... 866 429-5200
   Streetsboro *(G-17700)*
Step2 Company LLC ....D...... 419 938-6343
   Perrysville *(G-16032)*
Sterling Jewelers Inc ....G...... 614 799-8000
   Dublin *(G-8995)*
Stride Tool LLC ....C...... 440 247-4600
   Solon *(G-17238)*
Sumitomo Elc Carbide Mfg Inc ....F...... 440 354-0600
   Grand River *(G-10326)*
▲ Summit Tool Company ....D...... 330 535-7177
   Akron *(G-392)*
▲ Superion Inc ....E...... 937 374-0033
   Xenia *(G-20793)*
Toolovation LLC ....G...... 216 514-3022
   Cleveland *(G-6185)*
Tribus Innovations LLC ....G...... 509 992-4743
   Englewood *(G-9379)*
▲ Wholesale Fairy Gardenscom LLC ....G...... 614 504-5304
   Plain City *(G-16218)*
▲ Wright Tool Company ....C...... 330 848-0600
   Barberton *(G-1114)*
Your Carpenter Inc ....G...... 216 241-6434
   Cleveland *(G-6333)*

3425 Hand Saws & Saw Blades

▲ Blade Manufacturing Co Inc ....F...... 614 294-1649
   Columbus *(G-6679)*
♦ Callahan Cutting Tools Inc ....G...... 614 294-1649
   Columbus *(G-6724)*
Cammel Saw Company Inc ....F...... 330 477-3764
   Canton *(G-2605)*
Dynatech Systems Inc ....E...... 440 365-1774
   Elyria *(G-9246)*
Form-A-Chip Inc ....G...... 937 223-4135
   Dayton *(G-8201)*
J and S Tool Incorporated ....E...... 216 676-8330
   Cleveland *(G-5482)*
Joes Saw Shop ....G...... 440 834-1196
   Burton *(G-2363)*
♦ M K Morse Company ....B...... 330 453-8187
   Canton *(G-2737)*
Martindale Electric Company ....E...... 216 521-8567
   Cleveland *(G-5628)*
♦ Peerless Saw Company ....C...... 614 836-5790
   Groveport *(G-10509)*
▼ Regal Diamond Products Corp ....E...... 440 944-7700
   Wickliffe *(G-20229)*
▲ Superion Inc ....E...... 937 374-0033
   Xenia *(G-20793)*
Uhrichsville Carbide Inc ....F...... 740 922-9197
   Uhrichsville *(G-18899)*

3429 Hardware, NEC

AB Bonded Locksmiths Inc ....G...... 513 531-7334
   Cincinnati *(G-3286)*
Acorn Technology Corporation ....E...... 216 663-1244
   Cleveland *(G-4610)*
▲ Action Coupling & Eqp Inc ....D...... 330 279-4242
   Holmesville *(G-10972)*
Aeroquip-Vickers Inc ....G...... 216 523-5000
   Cleveland *(G-4633)*
▲ Allfasteners Usa LLC ....E...... 440 232-6060
   Medina *(G-13222)*
Aluminum Bearing Co of America ....G...... 216 267-8560
   Cleveland *(G-4679)*
Ampex Metal Products Company ....E...... 216 267-9242
   Brookpark *(G-2136)*
Annin & Co ....D...... 740 622-4447
   Coshocton *(G-7718)*
Architectural Door Systems LLC ....G...... 513 808-9900
   Norwood *(G-15422)*
▲ Arnco Corporation ....C...... 800 847-7661
   Elyria *(G-9219)*
Arrow Tru-Line Inc ....D...... 419 636-7013
   Bryan *(G-2265)*
Baker McMillen Co ....E...... 330 923-3303
   Stow *(G-17573)*
▲ Boardman Molded Products Inc ....D...... 330 788-2400
   Youngstown *(G-20854)*

Bowes Manufacturing Inc ....F...... 216 378-2110
   Solon *(G-17117)*
▲ Brass Accents Inc ....F...... 330 332-9500
   Salem *(G-16721)*
Butera Manufacturing Inc ....F...... 440 516-3698
   Willoughby Hills *(G-20467)*
Butera Manufacturing Inds ....G...... 216 761-8800
   Cleveland *(G-4855)*
▲ Case-Maul Clamps Inc ....E...... 419 668-6563
   Norwalk *(G-15384)*
Chantilly Development Corp ....F...... 419 243-8109
   Toledo *(G-18227)*
♦ Clampco Products Inc ....G...... 330 336-8857
   Wadsworth *(G-19230)*
▲ Cleveland Hdwr & Forging Co ....E...... 216 641-5200
   Cleveland *(G-4962)*
Cleveland Steel Specialty Co ....F...... 216 464-9400
   Bedford Heights *(G-1466)*
Curtiss-Wright Flow Ctrl Corp ....D...... 216 267-3200
   Cleveland *(G-5045)*
Custom Metal Works Inc ....F...... 419 668-7831
   Norwalk *(G-15385)*
Dayton Superior Corporation ....E...... 937 682-4015
   Rushsylvania *(G-16595)*
Desco Corporation ....G...... 614 888-8855
   New Albany *(G-14622)*
Design Magnetics Ltd ....G...... 234 380-5500
   Hudson *(G-11042)*
Detroit Technologies Inc ....E...... 937 492-2708
   Sidney *(G-17030)*
▲ Die Co Inc ....E...... 440 942-8856
   Eastlake *(G-9104)*
Doan Machinery & Eqp Co Inc ....G...... 216 932-6243
   University Heights *(G-18941)*
♦ Eaton Aeroquip LLC ....E...... 216 523-5000
   Cleveland *(G-5143)*
Eaton Corporation ....A...... 419 238-1190
   Van Wert *(G-19087)*
Eaton Corporation ....C...... 330 274-0743
   Aurora *(G-877)*
Eaton-Aeroquip Llc ....D...... 419 238-1190
   Van Wert *(G-19089)*
Edward W Daniel LLC ....E...... 440 647-1960
   Wellington *(G-19577)*
Element14 US Holdings Inc ....G...... 330 523-4280
   Richfield *(G-16469)*
♦ Elster Perfection Corporation ....D...... 440 428-1171
   Geneva *(G-10218)*
Etl Performance Products Inc ....G...... 234 575-7226
   Salem *(G-16735)*
Exact Pipe Tools ....G...... 330 922-8150
   Cuyahoga Falls *(G-7865)*
Fastenal Company ....E...... 419 629-3024
   New Bremen *(G-14654)*
Faull & Son LLC ....F...... 330 652-4341
   Niles *(G-15008)*
▲ Federal Equipment Company ....D...... 513 621-5260
   Cincinnati *(G-3680)*
First Francis Company Inc ....E...... 440 352-8927
   Painesville *(G-15739)*
Flex-Strut Inc ....E...... 330 372-9999
   Warren *(G-19403)*
Florida Production Engrg Inc ....D...... 937 996-4361
   New Madison *(G-14741)*
♦ Fort Recovery Industries Inc ....B...... 419 375-4121
   Fort Recovery *(G-9818)*
▲ Fortner Upholstering Inc ....F...... 614 475-8282
   Columbus *(G-6933)*
Gateway Concrete Forming Svcs ....D...... 513 353-2000
   Miamitown *(G-13746)*
Great Midwest Yacht Co ....G...... 740 965-4511
   Sunbury *(G-17887)*
Greyfield Industries Inc ....F...... 513 860-1785
   Trenton *(G-18620)*
▲ Group Industries Inc ....E...... 216 271-0702
   Cleveland *(G-5355)*
Hawthorne Bolt Works Corp ....G...... 330 723-0555
   Medina *(G-13270)*
Hbd/Thermoid Inc ....F...... 937 593-5010
   Bellefontaine *(G-1517)*
▼ Hbd/Thermoid Inc ....C...... 614 526-7000
   Dublin *(G-8922)*
Hebco Products Inc ....A...... 419 562-7987
   Bucyrus *(G-2333)*
Heller Machine Products Inc ....G...... 216 281-2951
   Cleveland *(G-5390)*
▲ Hercules Industries Inc ....E...... 740 494-2620
   Prospect *(G-16351)*
Herman Machine Inc ....F...... 330 633-3261
   Tallmadge *(G-17984)*

SIC SECTION
34 FABRICATED METAL PRODUCTS, EXCEPT MACHINERY AND TRANSPORTATION EQUIPMENT

▲ **Hfi LLC** ....B 614 491-0700
Columbus *(G-6995)*
Hillman Group Inc ....G 800 800-4900
Parma *(G-15822)*
Hillman Group Inc ....G 440 248-7000
Cleveland *(G-5409)*
Hoffman Hinge and Hardware LLC ....G 330 935-2240
Alliance *(G-474)*
Hudson Fasteners Inc ....G 330 270-9500
Youngstown *(G-20933)*
Hydromotive Engineering Co ....G 330 425-4266
Twinsburg *(G-18793)*
▲ **Independence 2 LLC** ....F 800 414-0545
Hubbard *(G-11002)*
Industrial Pulley & Machine Co ....G 937 355-4910
West Mansfield *(G-19942)*
International Automotive Compo ....A 419 433-5653
Huron *(G-11099)*
J B Kepple Sheet Metal ....G 740 393-2971
Mount Vernon *(G-14484)*
J L R Products Inc ....F 330 832-9557
Massillon *(G-13004)*
J W Goss Co Inc ....F 330 395-0739
Warren *(G-19413)*
John Stieg & Associates ....G 614 889-7954
Dublin *(G-8933)*
Kasai North America Inc ....F 614 356-1494
Dublin *(G-8936)*
▲ **Kirk Key Interlock Company LLC** ....E 330 833-8223
North Canton *(G-15096)*
L & W Inc ....D 734 397-6300
Avon *(G-953)*
Lake Park Tool & Machine LLC ....F 330 788-2437
Youngstown *(G-20956)*
Langenau Manufacturing Company ....F 216 651-3400
Cleveland *(G-5558)*
Leetonia Tool Company ....F 330 427-6944
Leetonia *(G-11718)*
▲ **Marlboro Manufacturing Inc** ....E 330 935-2221
Alliance *(G-488)*
▲ **Master Mfg Co Inc** ....E 216 641-0500
Cleveland *(G-5632)*
▲ **Matdan Corporation** ....E 513 794-0500
Blue Ash *(G-1815)*
Maumee Hose & Fitting Inc ....G 419 893-7252
Maumee *(G-13130)*
▲ **Mecc-Usa LLC** ....G 513 891-0301
West Chester *(G-19742)*
Meese Inc ....D 440 998-1202
Ashtabula *(G-785)*
Midlake Products & Mfg Co ....D 330 875-4202
Louisville *(G-12161)*
▲ **Miller Studio Inc** ....D 330 339-1100
New Philadelphia *(G-14787)*
Minderman Marine Products Inc ....G 419 732-2626
Port Clinton *(G-16253)*
▲ **Morgal Machine Tool Co** ....D 937 325-5561
Springfield *(G-17451)*
◆ **Napoleon Spring Works Inc** ....C 419 445-1010
Archbold *(G-660)*
Netherland Rubber Company ....F 513 733-0883
Cincinnati *(G-4068)*
▲ **Nova Machine Products Inc** ....D 216 267-3200
Middleburg Heights *(G-13767)*
Ohio Hydraulics Inc ....E 513 771-2590
Cincinnati *(G-4103)*
Ottawa Products Co ....E 419 836-5115
Curtice *(G-7826)*
PA Stratton & Co Inc ....G 419 660-9979
Collins *(G-6425)*
◆ **Premier Farnell Holding Inc** ....E 330 523-4273
Richfield *(G-16483)*
Progressive Machine Die Inc ....E 330 405-6600
Macedonia *(G-12321)*
▲ **R & R Tool Inc** ....E 937 783-8665
Blanchester *(G-1705)*
R H Industries Inc ....E 216 281-5210
Cleveland *(G-5952)*
Racelite South Coast Inc ....F 216 581-4600
Maple Heights *(G-12578)*
▲ **Samsel Rope & Marine Supply Co** ....E 216 241-0333
Cleveland *(G-6029)*
▲ **Sarasota Quality Products** ....G 440 899-9820
Westlake *(G-20155)*
Sensible Products Inc ....G 330 659-4212
Richfield *(G-16487)*
Sheet Metal Products Co Inc ....E 440 392-9000
Mentor *(G-13581)*
Sky Climber Fasteners LLC ....G 740 816-9830
Delaware *(G-8726)*
▲ **Stanley Industrial & Auto LLC** ....D 614 755-7000
Westerville *(G-20025)*
Strutt Products LLC ....G 330 889-2727
Bristolville *(G-2084)*
▲ **Summers Acquisition Corp** ....E 216 941-7700
Cleveland *(G-6117)*
Summers Acquisition Corp ....G 419 526-5800
Mansfield *(G-12523)*
Summers Acquisition Corp ....G 440 946-5611
Eastlake *(G-9134)*
Summers Acquisition Corp ....G 419 423-5800
Findlay *(G-9765)*
◆ **Superior Metal Products Inc** ....E 419 228-1145
Lima *(G-11947)*
Supply International Inc ....G 740 282-8604
Steubenville *(G-17555)*
▲ **Te-Co Manufacturing LLC** ....D 937 836-0961
Englewood *(G-9377)*
▲ **Technoform GL Insul N Amer Inc** ....E 330 487-6600
Twinsburg *(G-18863)*
▲ **Texmaster Tools Inc** ....F 740 965-8778
Fredericktown *(G-9980)*
Thermo-Rite Mfg Company ....E 330 633-8680
Akron *(G-403)*
Three Sons Minerva Hardware ....F 330 868-7709
Minerva *(G-14204)*
▲ **Trim Parts Inc** ....E 513 934-0815
Lebanon *(G-11702)*
Trim Systems Operating Corp ....C 614 289-5360
New Albany *(G-14639)*
▲ **Triton Products LLC** ....F 440 248-5480
Solon *(G-17254)*
Trust Manufacturing LLC ....F 216 531-8787
Euclid *(G-9449)*
Tungsten Capital Partners LLC ....G 216 481-4774
Cleveland *(G-6221)*
Twin Valley Metalcraft Asm LLC ....G 937 787-4634
West Alexandria *(G-19622)*
United Die & Mfg Co ....E 330 938-6141
Sebring *(G-16897)*
▲ **Universal Industrial Pdts Inc** ....F 419 737-9584
Pioneer *(G-16097)*
Verhoff Machine & Welding Inc ....C 419 596-3202
Continental *(G-7669)*
Voss Industries Inc ....D 216 771-7655
Cleveland *(G-6272)*
▲ **Voss Industries LLC** ....C 216 771-7655
Cleveland *(G-6273)*
Wallen Commercial Hardware ....G 937 426-5711
Beavercreek Township *(G-1376)*
Washington Products Inc ....F 330 837-5101
Massillon *(G-13057)*
Wecall Inc ....G 440 437-8202
Orwell *(G-15636)*
West Chester Lock Co LLC ....G 513 777-6486
West Chester *(G-19819)*
◆ **Whiteside Manufacturing Co** ....E 740 363-1179
Delaware *(G-8732)*
Wilson Bohannan Company ....D 740 382-3639
Marion *(G-12750)*
Winzeler Stamping Co ....D 419 485-3147
Montpelier *(G-14322)*
▲ **Worthignton Products Inc** ....G 330 452-7400
Canton *(G-2865)*

3431 Enameled Iron & Metal Sanitary Ware

Accent Manufacturing Inc ....F 330 724-7704
Norton *(G-15355)*
Agean Marble Manufacturing ....F 513 874-1475
West Chester *(G-19829)*
As America Inc ....E 419 522-4211
Mansfield *(G-12408)*
BJ Equipment Ltd ....F 614 497-1776
Columbus *(G-6673)*
Extrudex Limited Partnership ....E 440 352-7101
Painesville *(G-15737)*
◆ **Mansfield Plumbing Pdts LLC** ....A 419 938-5211
Perrysville *(G-16030)*
Murdock Inc ....F 513 471-7700
Cincinnati *(G-4055)*
Zurn Industries LLC ....F 814 455-0921
Hilliard *(G-10875)*

3432 Plumbing Fixture Fittings & Trim, Brass

▲ **American Brass Manufacturing** ....E 216 431-6565
Cleveland *(G-4683)*
As America Inc ....C 614 497-9384
Groveport *(G-10483)*
As America Inc ....G 330 337-2219
Salem *(G-16718)*
Atlantic Co ....E 440 944-8988
Willoughby Hills *(G-20466)*
Carr Supply Co ....G 937 316-6300
Greenville *(G-10363)*
Carr Supply Co ....G 937 276-2555
Dayton *(G-8076)*
Cfrc Wtr & Enrgy Solutions Inc ....G 216 479-0290
Cleveland *(G-4906)*
◆ **CMI Holding Company Crawford** ....D 419 468-9122
Galion *(G-10128)*
Dittmar Sales and Service ....G 740 653-7933
Lancaster *(G-11567)*
▲ **Empire Brass Co** ....E 216 431-6565
Cleveland *(G-5173)*
▲ **Field Stone Inc** ....D 937 898-3236
Tipp City *(G-18112)*
◆ **Fort Recovery Industries Inc** ....B 419 375-4121
Fort Recovery *(G-9818)*
Fort Recovery Industries Inc ....E 419 375-3005
Fort Recovery *(G-9819)*
▼ **Krendl Machine Company** ....D 419 692-3060
Delphos *(G-8747)*
Langenau Manufacturing Company ....F 216 651-3400
Cleveland *(G-5558)*
Lsq Manufacturing Inc ....F 330 725-4905
Medina *(G-13287)*
Maass Midwest Mfg Inc ....G 419 894-6424
Arcadia *(G-625)*
◆ **Mansfield Plumbing Pdts LLC** ....A 419 938-5211
Perrysville *(G-16030)*
National Brass Company Inc ....G 216 651-8530
Cleveland *(G-5723)*
Next Gerenation Crimping ....G 440 237-6300
North Royalton *(G-15288)*
Scotts Miracle-Gro Products ....E 937 644-0011
Marysville *(G-12812)*
Toolbold Corporation ....E 440 543-1660
Cleveland *(G-6184)*
▲ **Trumbull Manufacturing Inc** ....D 330 393-6624
Warren *(G-19452)*
W A S P Inc ....G 740 439-2398
Cambridge *(G-2462)*
◆ **Waxman Industries Inc** ....C 440 439-1830
Cleveland *(G-6295)*
Winsupply Inc ....F 937 346-0600
Springfield *(G-17518)*
Zekelman Industries Inc ....C 740 432-2146
Cambridge *(G-2463)*

3433 Heating Eqpt

Abbott Mechanical Services LLC ....G 419 460-4315
Maumee *(G-13065)*
Accent Manufacturing Inc ....F 330 724-7704
Norton *(G-15355)*
Airtech Mechanical Inc ....F 419 292-0074
Toledo *(G-18161)*
Aitken Products Inc ....G 440 466-5711
Geneva *(G-10213)*
▲ **Beckett Air Incorporated** ....D 440 327-9999
North Ridgeville *(G-15209)*
◆ **Beckett Gas Inc** ....C 440 327-3141
North Ridgeville *(G-15210)*
BMC Holdings Inc ....G 419 636-1194
Bryan *(G-2269)*
Burner Tech Unlimited Inc ....G 440 232-3200
Twinsburg *(G-18744)*
Dalton Combustion Systems Inc ....G 216 447-0647
Cleveland *(G-5060)*
Data Cooling Technologies LLC ....C 330 954-3800
Cleveland Heights *(G-6347)*
◆ **Dcm Manufacturing Inc** ....E 216 265-8006
Cleveland *(G-5078)*
▲ **Duro Dyne Midwest Corp** ....B 513 870-6000
Hamilton *(G-10551)*
▲ **Ebner Furnaces Inc** ....D 330 335-2311
Wadsworth *(G-19237)*
▲ **Enerco Group Inc** ....C 216 916-3000
Cleveland *(G-5177)*
▲ **Enerco Technical Products Inc** ....C 216 916-3000
Cleveland *(G-5178)*
Es Thermal Inc ....E 440 323-3291
Elyria *(G-9260)*
Ets Schaefer LLC ....G 330 468-6600
Macedonia *(G-12292)*
Ets Schaefer LLC ....G 330 468-6600
Beachwood *(G-1237)*
Famous Industries Inc ....D 740 685-2592
Byesville *(G-2384)*
First Solar Inc ....B 419 661-1478
Perrysburg *(G-15952)*

S I C

Employee Codes: A=Over 500 employees, B=251-500
C=101-250, D=51-100, E=20-50, F=10-19, G=3-9
2019 Harris Ohio
Industrial Directory
919

◆ **Fives N Amercn Combustn Inc** .... C 216 271-6000
Cleveland *(G-5244)*
Fives N Amercn Combustn Inc .... G 734 207-7008
Cleveland *(G-5245)*
Fives N Amercn Combustn Inc .... G 412 655-0101
Cleveland *(G-5246)*
Glo-Quartz Electric Heater Co .... E 440 255-9701
Mentor *(G-13459)*
Grid Industrial Heating Inc .... G 330 332-9931
Salem *(G-16745)*
◆ **Hartzell Fan Inc** .... C 937 773-7411
Piqua *(G-16122)*
Hdt Expeditionary Systems Inc .... E 440 466-6640
Geneva *(G-10222)*
▲ **Hunter Defense Tech Inc** .... E 216 438-6111
Solon *(G-17164)*
Iosil Energy Corporation .... F 614 295-8680
Groveport *(G-10495)*
Lakeway Mfg Inc .... E 419 433-3030
Huron *(G-11103)*
Mid-Ohio Regional Plg Comm .... E 614 351-9210
Columbus *(G-7179)*
▲ **Mr Heater Inc** .... E 216 916-3000
Cleveland *(G-5711)*
Nbbi .... G 614 888-8320
Columbus *(G-7212)*
North Amrcn Sstnable Enrgy Ltd .... G 440 539-7133
Parma *(G-15824)*
Old Es LLC .... E 330 468-6600
Macedonia *(G-12312)*
▲ **Onix Corporation** .... E 800 844-0076
Perrysburg *(G-15990)*
Panelbloc Inc .... G 440 974-8877
Mentor *(G-13541)*
▼ **Qual-Fab Inc** .... E 440 327-5000
Avon *(G-960)*
◆ **Rbi Solar Inc** .... G 513 242-2051
Cincinnati *(G-4250)*
◆ **RW Beckett Corporation** .... C 440 327-1060
North Ridgeville *(G-15252)*
Selas Heat Technology Co LLC .... G 216 662-8800
Streetsboro *(G-17696)*
▲ **Selas Heat Technology Co LLC** .... E 800 523-6500
Streetsboro *(G-17697)*
Sgm Co Inc .... E 440 255-1190
Mentor *(G-13580)*
Shark Solar LLC .... G 216 630-7395
Medina *(G-13340)*
Specialty Ceramics Inc .... D 330 482-0800
Columbiana *(G-6481)*
▲ **Spectrum Inc** .... F 440 951-6061
Brooklyn Heights *(G-2132)*
Stelter and Brinck Inc .... E 513 367-9300
Harrison *(G-10672)*
Sticker Corporation .... F 440 946-2100
Willoughby *(G-20438)*
Suarez Corporation Industries .... E 330 494-5504
Canton *(G-2828)*
Swagelok Company .... E 440 349-5836
Solon *(G-17243)*
T J F Inc .... F 419 878-4400
Waterville *(G-19506)*
Thermo Systems Technology .... E 216 292-8250
Cleveland *(G-6170)*
▲ **Trumbull Manufacturing Inc** .... D 330 393-6624
Warren *(G-19452)*
▼ **Willard Kelsey Solar Group LLC** .... E 419 931-2001
Perrysburg *(G-16028)*
Wood Stove Shed .... G 419 562-1545
Bucyrus *(G-2351)*
Ws Thermal Process Tech Inc .... G 440 385-6829
Lorain *(G-12138)*

3441 Fabricated Structural Steel

A & E Butscha Co .... G 513 761-1919
Cincinnati *(G-3275)*
▲ **A & G Manufacturing Co Inc** .... E 419 468-7433
Galion *(G-10119)*
A+ Engineering Fabrication Inc .... F 419 832-0748
Grand Rapids *(G-10314)*
A-1 Fabricators Finishers LLC .... D 513 724-0383
Batavia *(G-1122)*
Accu-Tech Manufacturing Co .... F 330 848-8100
Coventry Township *(G-7760)*
Accurate Fab LLC .... G 330 562-0566
Streetsboro *(G-17656)*
Ace Boiler & Welding Co Inc .... G 330 745-4443
Barberton *(G-1048)*
Advance Industrial Mfg Inc .... E 614 871-3333
Grove City *(G-10411)*
Advance Industries Group LLC .... E 216 741-1800
Cleveland *(G-4621)*
Advanced Onsight Welding Svcs .... G 513 924-1400
Cincinnati *(G-3302)*
Air Heater Seal Company Inc .... E 740 984-2146
Waterford *(G-19483)*
▲ **Akron Rebar Co** .... E 330 745-7100
Akron *(G-50)*
Akron Rebar Co .... F 216 433-0000
Cleveland *(G-4648)*
Albert Freytag Inc .... E 419 628-2018
Minster *(G-14209)*
▲ **Alcon Industries Inc** .... D 216 961-1100
Cleveland *(G-4653)*
Allied Fabricating & Wldg Co .... E 614 751-6664
Columbus *(G-6572)*
Alloy Fabricators Inc .... E 330 948-3535
Lodi *(G-12005)*
Alloy Welding & Fabricating .... F 440 914-0650
Solon *(G-17103)*
Alro Steel Corporation .... E 937 253-6121
Dayton *(G-8021)*
Alron Inc .... G 330 477-3405
Canton *(G-2570)*
▲ **Alufab Inc** .... G 513 528-7281
Cincinnati *(G-3240)*
Ambassador Steel Corporation .... F 740 382-9969
Marion *(G-12692)*
Ameco USA Metal Fabrication .... G 440 899-9400
Cleveland *(G-4682)*
▼ **American Ir Met Cleveland LLC** .... E 216 266-0509
Cleveland *(G-4690)*
▲ **American Manufacturing Inc** .... D 419 531-9471
Toledo *(G-18174)*
American Metal Stamping Co LLC .... F 216 531-3100
Euclid *(G-9402)*
American Mfg & Engrg Co .... G 440 899-9400
Westlake *(G-20094)*
American Mfg & Engrg Co .... G 440 899-9400
Cleveland *(G-4693)*
American Qulty Fabrication Inc .... G 937 742-7001
Vandalia *(G-19116)*
American Steel Assod Pdts Inc .... D 419 531-9471
Toledo *(G-18180)*
American Tower Acquisition .... F 419 347-1185
Shelby *(G-16977)*
Ameridian Specialty Services .... E 513 769-0150
Cincinnati *(G-3339)*
▲ **Ametco Manufacturing Corp** .... E 440 951-4300
Willoughby *(G-20271)*
Amrod Bridge & Iron LLC .... E 330 530-8230
Mc Donald *(G-13196)*
Amtank Armor LLC .... G 216 252-1500
Cleveland *(G-4703)*
Amtech Tool and Machine Inc .... F 330 758-8215
Youngstown *(G-20844)*
Anstine Machining Corp .... F 330 821-4365
Alliance *(G-455)*
Ap-Alternatives LLC .... F 419 267-5280
Ridgeville Corners *(G-16511)*
▲ **Appian Manufacturing Corp** .... E 614 445-2230
Columbus *(G-6608)*
Applied Energy Tech Inc .... E 419 537-9052
Maumee *(G-13075)*
Applied Engneered Surfaces Inc .... F 440 366-0440
Elyria *(G-9218)*
Arctech Fabricating Inc .... E 937 525-9353
Springfield *(G-17364)*
Armor Consolidated Inc .... G 513 923-5260
Mason *(G-12826)*
▲ **Armor Group Inc** .... C 513 923-5260
Mason *(G-12827)*
▲ **Armor Metal Group Mason Inc** .... C 513 769-0700
Mason *(G-12828)*
Arrow Fabricating Co .... E 216 641-0490
Novelty *(G-15437)*
Ashco Manufacturing Inc .... G 419 838-7157
Toledo *(G-18193)*
Aster Elements Inc .... E 440 942-2799
Cleveland *(G-4754)*
◆ **Astro-TEC Mfg Inc** .... E 330 854-2209
Canal Fulton *(G-2475)*
Avenue Fabricating Inc .... E 513 752-1911
Batavia *(G-1124)*
Banks Manufacturing Company .... F 440 458-8661
Grafton *(G-10293)*
Bauer Corporation .... E 800 321-4760
Wooster *(G-20569)*
Bcfab Inc .... G 419 532-2899
Fort Jennings *(G-9791)*
Beauty Cft Met Fabricators Inc .... F 440 439-0710
Bedford *(G-1389)*
Berran Industrial Group Inc .... E 330 253-5800
Akron *(G-85)*
Best Process Solutions Inc .... E 330 220-1440
Brunswick *(G-2192)*
Bethel Engineering and Eqp Inc .... E 419 568-1100
New Hampshire *(G-14699)*
Bickers Metal Products Inc .... E 513 353-4000
Miamitown *(G-13743)*
Bird Equipment LLC .... E 330 549-1004
North Lima *(G-15166)*
Bison Wldg & Fabrication Inc .... G 440 944-4770
Wickliffe *(G-20205)*
Black McCuskey Souers .... G 330 456-8341
Canton *(G-2593)*
Blackburns Fabrication Inc .... E 614 875-0784
Columbus *(G-6677)*
Blevins Metal Fabrication Inc .... E 419 522-6082
Mansfield *(G-12412)*
Boardman Steel Inc .... D 330 758-0951
Columbiana *(G-6455)*
Breitinger Company .... C 419 526-4255
Mansfield *(G-12414)*
▲ **Brilex Industries Inc** .... C 330 744-1114
Youngstown *(G-20859)*
Brilex Industries Inc .... D 330 744-1114
Youngstown *(G-20858)*
▲ **Buck Equipment Inc** .... E 614 539-3039
Grove City *(G-10419)*
Buckeye Fbricators of Leetonia .... G 330 427-0330
Leetonia *(G-11716)*
Buckeye Steel Inc .... F 740 425-2306
Barnesville *(G-1116)*
Burghardt Manufacturing Inc .... G 330 253-7590
Akron *(G-98)*
Burghardt Metal Fabg Inc .... F 330 794-1830
Akron *(G-99)*
Byer Steel Rebar Inc .... E 513 821-6400
Cincinnati *(G-3434)*
C A Joseph Co .... F 330 532-4646
Irondale *(G-11158)*
C-N-D Industries Inc .... E 330 478-8811
Massillon *(G-12965)*
Camelot Manufacturing Inc .... F 419 678-2603
Coldwater *(G-6403)*
CC Ironworks LLC .... G 330 542-0500
New Middletown *(G-14747)*
CCM Welding Inc .... G 330 630-2521
Akron *(G-105)*
Ceco Environmental Corp .... E 513 874-8915
West Chester *(G-19838)*
Central Ohio Fabricators LLC .... E 740 393-3892
Mount Vernon *(G-14474)*
Chagrin Vly Stl Erectors Inc .... F 440 975-1556
Willoughby Hills *(G-20468)*
Champion Bridge Company .... E 937 382-2521
Wilmington *(G-20488)*
Charles Mfg Co .... F 330 395-3490
Warren *(G-19383)*
Charles Ray Evans .... F 740 967-3669
Columbus *(G-6758)*
Chattanooga Laser Cutting LLC .... E 513 779-7200
Cincinnati *(G-3466)*
Chc Manufacturing Inc .... E 513 821-7757
Cincinnati *(G-3467)*
Chc Manufacturing Inc .... G 614 527-1606
Columbus *(G-6759)*
Christman Fabricators Inc .... G 330 477-8077
Canton *(G-2623)*
▲ **Cincinnati Industrial McHy Inc** .... C 513 923-5600
Mason *(G-12843)*
Cincinnati Laser Cutting LLC .... E 513 779-7200
Cincinnati *(G-3498)*
Cincy Glass Inc .... G 513 241-0455
Cincinnati *(G-3514)*
◆ **Clermont Steel Fabricators LLC** .... D 513 732-6033
Batavia *(G-1131)*
Cleveland City Forge Inc .... E 440 647-5400
Wellington *(G-19574)*
▲ **Clifton Steel Company** .... D 216 662-6111
Maple Heights *(G-12569)*
Clipsons Metal Working Inc .... G 513 772-6393
Cincinnati *(G-3528)*
Cohen Brothers Inc .... G 513 422-3696
Middletown *(G-13895)*
Com-Fab Inc .... E 740 857-1107
Plain City *(G-16181)*
Commercial Mtal Fbricators Inc .... E 937 233-4911
Dayton *(G-8100)*

34 FABRICATED METAL PRODUCTS, EXCEPT MACHINERY AND TRANSPORTATION EQUIPMENT

Concord Fabricators Inc ....E 614 875-2500
  Grove City (G-10421)
Contech Engnered Solutions Inc ....F 513 645-7000
  West Chester (G-19680)
Contech Engnered Solutions LLC ....D 513 645-7000
  Middletown (G-13896)
◆ Contech Engnered Solutions LLC ...... C 513 645-7000
  West Chester (G-19681)
▲ Continental GL Sls & Inv Group ....B 614 679-1201
  Powell (G-16318)
County of Lake ....D 440 269-2193
  Willoughby (G-20302)
Coventry Steel Services Inc ....F 216 883-4477
  Cleveland (G-5033)
Cramers Inc ....E 330 477-4571
  Canton (G-2638)
Creative Fab & Welding LLC ....E 937 780-5000
  Leesburg (G-11709)
Curtiss-Wright Flow Control ....D 513 528-7900
  Cincinnati (G-3244)
D T Kothera Inc ....G 440 632-1651
  Middlefield (G-13792)
Dal-Little Fabricating Inc ....G 216 883-3323
  Cleveland (G-5059)
Davis Fabricators Inc ....E 419 898-5297
  Oak Harbor (G-15443)
De-Ko Inc ....G 440 951-2585
  Willoughby (G-20308)
Debra-Kuempel Inc ....E 513 271-6500
  Cincinnati (G-3579)
Debs Welding & Fabrication ....G 330 376-2242
  Akron (G-135)
Defiance Metal Products WI Inc ....C 920 426-9207
  Defiance (G-8621)
Deltec Incorporated ....E 513 732-0800
  Batavia (G-1136)
Diamond Mfg Bluffton Ltd ....D 419 358-0129
  Bluffton (G-1888)
Diamond Wipes Intl Inc ....G 419 562-3575
  Bucyrus (G-2325)
Dietrich Industries Inc ....C 330 372-4014
  Warren (G-19395)
Dietrich Industries Inc ....E 614 438-3210
  Worthington (G-20683)
Dietrich Industries Inc ....D 216 472-1511
  Cleveland (G-5095)
Dietrich Industries Inc ....E 614 438-3210
  Worthington (G-20684)
▲ Diversifd OH Vlly Eqpt & Srvcs ....F 740 458-9881
  Clarington (G-4567)
DMC Welding Incorporated ....G 330 877-1935
  Hartville (G-10689)
Dover Conveyor Inc ....G 740 922-9390
  Midvale (G-13976)
Dover Tank and Plate Company ....E 330 343-4443
  Dover (G-8823)
◆ Dracool-Usa Inc ....E 937 743-5899
  Carlisle (G-2892)
▲ DS Techstar Inc ....G 419 424-0888
  Findlay (G-9681)
Dwayne Bennett Industries ....G 440 466-5724
  Geneva (G-10217)
E B P Inc ....E 216 241-2550
  Cleveland (G-5128)
E W Welding & Fabricating ....G 440 826-9038
  Berea (G-1603)
▼ E-Pak Manufacturing LLC ....D 800 235-1632
  Wooster (G-20588)
▲ Ebner Furnaces Inc ....E 330 335-2311
  Wadsworth (G-19237)
Egypt Structural Steel Proc ....E 419 628-2375
  Minster (G-14213)
Elcoma Metal Fabricating & Sls ....G 330 588-3075
  Canton (G-2666)
◆ Emh Inc ....E 330 220-8600
  Valley City (G-19036)
EPI of Cleveland Inc ....G 330 468-2872
  Twinsburg (G-18769)
Erico International Corp ....B 440 248-0100
  Solon (G-17140)
Evers Welding Co Inc ....E 513 385-7352
  Cincinnati (G-3658)
F M Machine Co ....E 330 773-8237
  Akron (G-163)
Fab Shop Inc ....G 513 860-1332
  Hamilton (G-10556)
▲ Fabco Inc ....E 419 421-4740
  Findlay (G-9682)
▲ Falls Welding & Fabg Inc ....G 330 253-3437
  Akron (G-165)

Farasey Steel Fabricators Inc ....F 216 641-1853
  Cleveland (G-5219)
Fastfeed Corp ....G 330 948-7333
  Lodi (G-12010)
Fenix Fabrication Inc ....E 330 745-8731
  Akron (G-168)
Fiedeldey Stl Fabricators Inc 513 353-3300
  Cincinnati (G-3684)
Flex-Strut Inc ....D 330 372-9999
  Warren (G-19403)
Foster Products Inc ....E 513 735-9770
  Batavia (G-1146)
Franck and Fric Incorporated ....D 216 524-4451
  Cleveland (G-5271)
Frederick Steel Company LLC ....D 513 821-6400
  Cincinnati (G-3712)
Fulton Equipment Co ....E 419 290-5393
  Toledo (G-18299)
Fwt LLC ....G 419 542-1420
  Hicksville (G-10778)
G & R Welding & Machining ....E 937 323-9353
  Springfield (G-17405)
▲ G & W Products LLC ....C 513 860-4050
  Fairfield (G-9499)
▲ Galion-Godwin Truck Bdy Co LLC ..D 330 359-5495
  Millersburg (G-14084)
Gardner Metal Craft Inc ....E 513 539-4538
  Monroe (G-14263)
Garland Welding Co Inc ....F 330 536-6506
  Lowellville (G-12251)
Gb Fabrication Company ....E 419 347-1835
  Shelby (G-16982)
Gen III 614 737-8744
  Columbus (G-6944)
General Steel Corporation ....E 216 883-4200
  Cleveland (G-5314)
George Steel Fabricating Inc ....E 513 932-2887
  Lebanon (G-11655)
Gilson Machine & Tool Co Inc ....E 419 592-2911
  Napoleon (G-14539)
GL Nause Co Inc ....E 513 722-9500
  Loveland (G-12192)
Glenwood Erectors Inc ....G 330 652-9616
  Niles (G-15010)
▲ Gokoh Corporation ....F 937 339-4977
  Troy (G-18662)
▲ Goyal Industries Inc ....E 419 522-7099
  Mansfield (G-12451)
Graber Metal Works Inc ....G 440 237-8422
  North Royalton (G-15274)
Green Point Metals Inc ....E 937 743-4075
  Franklin (G-9887)
◆ Gregory Industries Inc ....D 330 477-4800
  Canton (G-2688)
Grenga Machine & Welding ....F 330 743-1113
  Youngstown (G-20925)
Gunderson Rail Services LLC ....E 330 792-6521
  Youngstown (G-20927)
▲ Gwp Holdings Inc ....D 513 860-4050
  Fairfield (G-9501)
▲ H B Products Inc ....E 937 492-7031
  Sidney (G-17042)
▲ Halvorsen Company ....E 216 341-7500
  Cleveland (G-5367)
Hancock Structural Steel LLC ....F 419 424-1217
  Findlay (G-9699)
Hanson Concrete Products Ohio ......E 614 443-4846
  Columbus (G-6980)
Hays Fabricating & Welding ....E 937 325-0031
  Springfield (G-17412)
Herman Manufacturing LLC ....E 216 251-6400
  Cleveland (G-5398)
High Production Technology LLC ......F 419 591-7000
  Napoleon (G-14541)
Holgate Metal Fab Inc ....E 419 599-2000
  Napoleon (G-14543)
Hoppel Fabrication Specialties ....F 330 823-5700
  Louisville (G-12156)
▲ Horizon Metals Inc ....E 440 235-3338
  Berea (G-1609)
Horning Steel Co ....G 330 633-0028
  Tallmadge (G-17985)
Hr Machine LLC ....G 937 222-7644
  Beavercreek (G-1323)
Hunkar Technologies Inc ....C 513 272-1010
  Cincinnati (G-3829)
▲ Hynes Industries Inc ....G 330 799-3221
  Youngstown (G-20934)
Hyq Technologies LLC ....G 513 225-6911
  Oxford (G-15694)

Indian Creek Fabricators Inc ....E 937 667-7214
  Tipp City (G-18116)
Industrial Hanger Conveyor Co ....G 419 332-2661
  Fremont (G-10028)
Industrial Mill Maintenance ....E 330 746-1155
  Youngstown (G-20939)
Iron Gate Industries LLC ....E 330 264-0626
  Wooster (G-20608)
Ironfab LLC ....F 614 443-3900
  Columbus (G-7049)
Ironhead Fabg & Contg Inc ....D 419 690-0000
  Toledo (G-18354)
J & L Specialty Steel Inc ....G 330 875-6200
  Louisville (G-12158)
J & L Welding Fabricating Inc ....F 330 393-9353
  Warren (G-19412)
J A McMahon Incorporated ....E 330 652-2588
  Niles (G-15017)
J Horst Manufacturing Co ....D 330 828-2216
  Dalton (G-7945)
J P Suggins Mobile Welding ....E 216 566-7131
  Cleveland (G-5486)
J&J Precision Fabricators ....F 330 482-4964
  Columbiana (G-6472)
J&J Precision Machine Ltd ....E 330 923-5783
  Cuyahoga Falls (G-7883)
Jab Sales Inc ....G 440 446-0606
  Cleveland (G-5490)
Jayron Fabrication LLC ....G 740 335-3184
  Leesburg (G-11710)
Jh Industries Inc ....E 330 963-4105
  Twinsburg (G-18797)
Joe Rees Welding ....G 937 652-4067
  Urbana (G-19000)
Johnson-Nash Metal Pdts Inc ....F 513 874-7022
  Fairfield (G-9514)
Jomac Ltd ....G 330 627-7727
  Carrollton (G-2922)
▲ JR Manufacturing Inc ....E 419 375-8021
  Fort Recovery (G-9823)
Js Fabrications Inc ....G 419 333-0323
  Fremont (G-10031)
K & L Die & Manufacturing ....G 419 895-1301
  Greenwich (G-10405)
Kebco Precision Fabricators ....E 330 456-0808
  Canton (G-2722)
Kecoat LLC ....F 330 527-0215
  Garrettsville (G-10195)
Kedar D Army ....G 419 238-6929
  Van Wert (G-19097)
Kellys Welding & Fabricating ....G 440 593-6040
  Conneaut (G-7651)
King Wolf Enterprises LLC ....G 330 853-0450
  East Liverpool (G-9066)
Kings Welding and Fabg Inc ....E 330 738-3592
  Mechanicstown (G-13212)
Kirk Welding & Fabricating ....G 216 961-6403
  Cleveland (G-5538)
Kirwan Industries Inc ....G 513 333-0766
  Cincinnati (G-3913)
▲ Kottler Metal Products Co Inc ......E 440 946-7473
  Willoughby (G-20355)
Kramer Power Equipment Co ....F 937 456-2232
  Eaton (G-9157)
L & W Inc ....D 734 397-6300
  Avon (G-953)
▲ Langdon Inc ....E 513 733-5955
  Cincinnati (G-3930)
Lapham-Hickey Steel Corp ....E 614 443-4881
  Columbus (G-7116)
Laserflex Corporation ....D 614 850-9600
  Hilliard (G-10837)
Lauren Yoakam ....G 440 365-3952
  Elyria (G-9285)
Lazarus Steel LLC ....E 216 391-3245
  Cleveland (G-5569)
▲ Lefeld Welding & Stl Sups Inc ......E 419 678-2397
  Coldwater (G-6416)
Lideco LLC ....G 330 539-9333
  Vienna (G-19200)
Lilly Industries Inc ....E 419 946-7908
  Mount Gilead (G-14427)
Lion Black Products LLC ....F 412 400-6980
  Youngstown (G-20960)
Livingston & Company Ltd ....G 513 553-6430
  New Richmond (G-14811)
Louis Arthur Steel Company ....G 440 997-5545
  Geneva (G-10224)
Louis Arthur Steel Company ....E 440 997-5545
  Geneva (G-10225)

Employee Codes: A=Over 500 employees, B=251-500
C=101-250, D=51-100, E=20-50, F=10-19, G=3-9

Louis Arthur Steel Company ....G.... 440 997-5545
Uniontown *(G-18926)*
Lyco Corporation ....E.... 412 973-9176
Lowellville *(G-12253)*
M & H Fabricating Co Inc ....F.... 937 325-8708
Springfield *(G-17437)*
M & M Fabrication Inc ....F.... 740 779-3071
Chillicothe *(G-3199)*
M & W Welding Inc ....G.... 614 224-0501
Columbus *(G-7139)*
Machine Tool & Fab Corp ....F.... 419 435-7676
Fostoria *(G-9846)*
Mad River Steel Ltd ....G.... 937 845-4046
New Carlisle *(G-14671)*
Magnesium Products Group Inc ....G.... 310 971-5799
Maumee *(G-13128)*
Magnum Piering Inc ....E.... 513 759-3348
West Chester *(G-19874)*
Mahoning Valley Fabricators ....F.... 330 793-8995
Austintown *(G-934)*
Manco Manufacturing Co ....G.... 419 925-4152
Maria Stein *(G-12599)*
▼ Manifold & Phalor Inc ....E.... 614 920-1200
Canal Winchester *(G-2506)*
Manitowoc Company Inc ....G.... 920 746-3332
Cleveland *(G-5612)*
Marc Industries Inc ....G.... 440 944-9305
Willoughby *(G-20369)*
Marsam Metalfab Inc ....E.... 330 405-1520
Twinsburg *(G-18811)*
Martina Metal LLC ....E.... 614 291-9700
Columbus *(G-7155)*
Martins Steel Fabrication ....E.... 330 882-4311
New Franklin *(G-14693)*
Marysville Steel Inc ....E.... 937 642-5971
Marysville *(G-12801)*
Mason Structural Steel Inc ....D.... 440 439-1040
Walton Hills *(G-19312)*
Masonite International Corp ....G.... 937 454-9308
Vandalia *(G-19137)*
Maumee Valley Fabricators Inc ....E.... 419 476-1411
Toledo *(G-18404)*
Maverick Innvtive Slutions LLC ....E.... 419 281-7944
Ashland *(G-723)*
Mc Brown Industries Inc ....F.... 419 963-2800
Findlay *(G-9723)*
Mc Elwain Industries Inc ....F.... 419 532-3126
Ottawa *(G-15658)*
McMillen Steel LLC ....G.... 330 253-9147
Akron *(G-274)*
McNeil Group Inc ....E.... 614 298-0300
Columbus *(G-7169)*
McNeil Holdings LLC ....G.... 614 298-0300
Columbus *(G-7170)*
McWane Inc ....B.... 740 622-6651
Coshocton *(G-7739)*
Mercury Iron and Steel Co ....F.... 440 349-1500
Solon *(G-17190)*
Metal Dynamics Co ....G.... 330 601-0748
Wooster *(G-20622)*
Metal Man Inc ....G.... 614 830-0968
Groveport *(G-10506)*
Metal Sales Manufacturing Corp ....E.... 440 319-3779
Jefferson *(G-11234)*
Metlweb ....E.... 513 563-8822
Cincinnati *(G-4016)*
Miami Steel Fabricators Inc ....G.... 937 299-5550
Dayton *(G-8345)*
Mikes Welding ....G.... 937 675-6587
Jamestown *(G-11220)*
Minova USA Inc ....B.... 740 269-8100
Bowerston *(G-1941)*
Miracle Welding Inc ....G.... 513 746-9977
Franklin *(G-9901)*
Mk Metal Products Inc ....E.... 419 756-3644
Mansfield *(G-12484)*
Mk Trempe Corporation ....E.... 937 492-3548
Sidney *(G-17055)*
Mobile Mini Inc ....F.... 614 449-8655
Columbus *(G-7188)*
Monnig Welding Co ....G.... 513 241-5156
Cincinnati *(G-4042)*
Mound Technologies Inc ....E.... 937 748-2937
Springboro *(G-17338)*
Mr Trailer Sales Inc ....G.... 330 339-7701
New Philadelphia *(G-14789)*
Navpar Inc ....G.... 513 738-2230
Harrison *(G-10660)*
Nct Technologies Group Inc ....E.... 937 882-6800
New Carlisle *(G-14673)*
Neidert Fabricating Inc ....G.... 330 753-3331
Barberton *(G-1088)*
New Wayne Inc ....G.... 740 453-3454
Zanesville *(G-21162)*
Northeast Ohio Contractors LLC ....G.... 216 269-7881
Cleveland *(G-5775)*
Northern Boiler Company ....F.... 216 961-3033
Cleveland *(G-5777)*
▲ Northern Manufacturing Co Inc ....C.... 419 898-2821
Oak Harbor *(G-15446)*
Northwest Installations Inc ....E.... 419 423-5738
Findlay *(G-9732)*
Northwind Industries Inc ....E.... 216 433-0666
Cleveland *(G-5787)*
Nova Structural Steel Inc ....F.... 216 938-7476
Cleveland *(G-5788)*
◆ Ohio Gratings Inc ....B.... 330 477-6707
Canton *(G-2772)*
Ohio Steel Industries Inc ....E.... 740 927-9500
Pataskala *(G-15836)*
Ohio Structures Inc ....E.... 330 547-7705
Berlin Center *(G-1648)*
Ohio Structures Inc ....E.... 330 533-0084
Canfield *(G-2539)*
Olson Sheet Metal Cnstr Co ....G.... 330 745-8225
Barberton *(G-1092)*
Olwin Metal Fabrication LLC ....G.... 937 277-4501
Dayton *(G-8401)*
Outotec Oyj ....E.... 440 783-3336
Strongsville *(G-17775)*
Overhead Door Corporation ....D.... 740 383-6376
Marion *(G-12727)*
Ozone Systems Svcs Group Inc ....G.... 513 899-4131
Morrow *(G-14414)*
▲ P & L Metalcrafts LLC ....F.... 330 793-2178
Youngstown *(G-20987)*
P B Fabrication Mech Contr ....F.... 419 478-4869
Toledo *(G-18454)*
▲ PC Campana Inc ....C.... 440 246-6500
Lorain *(G-12111)*
Pcy Enterprises Inc ....E.... 513 241-5566
Cincinnati *(G-4143)*
Pemjay Inc ....E.... 740 254-4591
Gnadenhutten *(G-10281)*
Perfections Fabricators Inc ....F.... 440 365-5850
Elyria *(G-9310)*
Perry Welding Service Inc ....F.... 330 425-2211
Twinsburg *(G-18836)*
Phillips & Sons Welding & Fabg ....G.... 440 428-1625
Geneva *(G-10228)*
Phoenix Metal Works Inc ....G.... 937 274-5555
Dayton *(G-8424)*
Pioneer Machine Inc ....G.... 330 948-6500
Lodi *(G-12018)*
▲ Pioneer Pipe Inc ....A.... 740 376-2400
Marietta *(G-12653)*
PJs Fabricating Inc ....E.... 330 478-1120
Canton *(G-2786)*
Porters Welding Inc ....F.... 740 452-4181
Zanesville *(G-21169)*
Precision Fabg & Stamping ....G.... 740 453-7310
Zanesville *(G-21172)*
Precision International LLC ....E.... 330 793-0900
Akron *(G-327)*
Precision Steel Services Inc ....D.... 419 476-5702
Toledo *(G-18479)*
Precision Welding & Mfg ....F.... 937 444-6925
Mount Orab *(G-14449)*
Precision Welding Corporation ....E.... 216 524-6110
Cleveland *(G-5912)*
Pro Fab Industries Inc ....G.... 317 297-0461
Dundee *(G-9025)*
Pro-Fab Inc ....E.... 330 644-0044
Akron *(G-332)*
Production Support Inc ....F.... 937 526-3897
Russia *(G-16611)*
Professional Fabricators Inc ....G.... 216 362-1208
Cleveland *(G-5927)*
▲ Promac International Inc ....G.... 440 967-2040
Vermilion *(G-19170)*
Pucel Enterprises Inc ....D.... 216 881-4604
Cleveland *(G-5933)*
Q S I Fabrication ....G.... 419 832-1680
Grand Rapids *(G-10319)*
Qc Industrial Inc ....G.... 740 642-5004
Chillicothe *(G-3218)*
Quality Steel Fabrication ....F.... 937 492-9503
Sidney *(G-17063)*
R L Torbeck Industries Inc ....D.... 513 367-0080
Harrison *(G-10667)*
R S V Wldg Fbrcation Machining ....F.... 419 592-0993
Napoleon *(G-14557)*
Rads LLC ....F.... 330 671-0464
Berea *(G-1623)*
Railing Crafters Ltd ....G.... 440 506-9336
Painesville *(G-15779)*
Rance Industries Inc ....F.... 330 482-1745
Columbiana *(G-6477)*
Rankin Mfg Inc ....E.... 419 929-8338
New London *(G-14735)*
RB Fabricators Inc ....F.... 330 779-0263
Youngstown *(G-21014)*
Rbm Environmental and Cnstr ....E.... 419 693-5840
Oregon *(G-15566)*
Redbuilt LLC ....E.... 740 363-0870
Delaware *(G-8719)*
Retays Welding Company ....E.... 440 327-4100
North Ridgeville *(G-15250)*
Rezmann Karoly ....G.... 216 441-4357
Cleveland *(G-5982)*
Richard Steel Company Inc ....G.... 216 520-6390
Cleveland *(G-5983)*
Ripley Metalworks Ltd ....E.... 937 392-4992
Ripley *(G-16517)*
Rittman Inc ....D.... 330 927-6855
Rittman *(G-16528)*
▼ Riverside Steel Inc ....F.... 330 856-5299
Vienna *(G-19209)*
Riwco Corp ....F.... 937 322-6521
Springfield *(G-17486)*
RLM Fabricating Inc ....E.... 419 729-6130
Toledo *(G-18503)*
Rmi Titanium Company LLC ....G.... 330 544-9470
Niles *(G-15029)*
Robs Welding Technologies Ltd ....G.... 937 890-4963
Dayton *(G-8483)*
▼ Rol- Fab Inc ....E.... 216 662-2500
Cleveland *(G-6001)*
Romar Metal Fabricating Inc ....G.... 740 682-7731
Oak Hill *(G-15460)*
Rose Metal Industries LLC ....F.... 216 881-3355
Cleveland *(G-6002)*
Rose Metal Industries LLC ....E.... 216 426-8615
Cleveland *(G-6003)*
Royal Welding Inc ....G.... 513 829-9353
Fairfield *(G-9560)*
S & G Manufacturing Group LLC ....C.... 614 529-0100
Hilliard *(G-10859)*
▲ Sausser Steel Company Inc ....F.... 419 422-9632
Findlay *(G-9752)*
Sautter Brothers ....G.... 419 468-7443
Galion *(G-10152)*
Schoonover Industries Inc ....E.... 419 289-8332
Ashland *(G-747)*
Seeburger Greenhouse ....G.... 419 832-1834
Grand Rapids *(G-10321)*
Shaffer Metal Fab Inc ....E.... 937 492-1384
Sidney *(G-17076)*
Sintered Metal Industries Inc ....F.... 330 650-4000
Hudson *(G-11073)*
Skinner Sales Group Inc ....E.... 440 572-8455
Medina *(G-13344)*
▲ Smith Truck Cranes & Eqp Co ....F.... 330 929-3303
Cuyahoga Falls *(G-7919)*
Snair Co ....F.... 614 873-7020
Plain City *(G-16212)*
Socar of Ohio Inc ....D.... 419 596-3100
Continental *(G-7668)*
Somerville Manufacturing Inc ....E.... 740 336-7847
Marietta *(G-12674)*
South Central Industrial LLC ....F.... 740 333-5401
Washington Court Hou *(G-19477)*
Specialty Steel Solutions ....G.... 567 674-0011
Kenton *(G-11424)*
Spradlin Bros Welding Co ....F.... 800 219-2182
Springfield *(G-17493)*
St Lawrence Holdings LLC ....E.... 330 562-9000
Maple Heights *(G-12580)*
Stainless Specialties Inc ....E.... 440 942-4242
Eastlake *(G-9130)*
Standard Welding & Steel Pdts ....F.... 330 273-2777
Medina *(G-13346)*
Starr Fabricating Inc ....D.... 330 394-9891
Vienna *(G-19210)*
Stays Lighting Inc ....G.... 440 328-3254
Elyria *(G-9331)*
▼ Steel & Alloy Utility Pdts Inc ....E.... 330 530-2220
Mc Donald *(G-13202)*
▲ Steel Eqp Specialists Inc ....D.... 330 823-8260
Alliance *(G-502)*

Steel It LLC F 513 253-3111
Loveland *(G-12236)*
Steel Quest Inc G 513 772-5030
Cincinnati *(G-4377)*
Steel Services Inc G 513 353-4173
North Bend *(G-15055)*
Steelcon LLC G 330 457-4003
New Waterford *(G-14843)*
Steelial Wldg Met Fbrction Inc E 740 669-5300
Vinton *(G-19216)*
Steve Vore Welding and Steel F 419 375-4087
Fort Recovery *(G-9827)*
Stock Mfg & Design Co Inc D 513 353-3600
Cleves *(G-6377)*
Straightaway Fabrications Ltd E 419 281-9440
Ashland *(G-750)*
Suburban Metal Products Inc F 740 474-4237
Circleville *(G-4559)*
Suburban Stl Sup Co Ltd Partnr G 317 783-6555
Columbus *(G-7498)*
Sulecki Precision Products F 440 255-5454
Mentor *(G-13596)*
Summers Acquisition Corp G 419 423-5800
Findlay *(G-9765)*
Superior Soda Service LLC G 937 657-9700
Beavercreek *(G-1364)*
Superior Welding Co F 614 252-8539
Columbus *(G-7503)*
Surface Recovery Tech LLC F 937 879-5864
Fairborn *(G-9470)*
T & K Welding Co Inc G 216 432-0221
Cleveland *(G-6142)*
Tarrier Steel Company Inc E 614 444-4000
Columbus *(G-7514)*
Tech Dynamics Inc F 419 666-1666
Perrysburg *(G-16010)*
Tech Systems Inc E 419 878-2100
Waterville *(G-19507)*
The Mansfield Strl & Erct Co E 419 522-5911
Mansfield *(G-12528)*
The Mansfield Strl & Erct Co G 419 747-6571
Mansfield *(G-12529)*
Thieman Quality Metal Fab Inc D 419 629-2612
New Bremen *(G-14661)*
Thomas Steel Inc E 419 483-7540
Bellevue *(G-1549)*
Tilton Corporation C 419 227-6421
Lima *(G-11952)*
Transco Railway Products Inc D 330 872-0934
Newton Falls *(G-14994)*
Tri-America Contractors Inc E 740 574-0148
Wheelersburg *(G-20186)*
Tri-Fab Inc E 330 337-3425
Salem *(G-16777)*
Tri-State Fabricators Inc E 513 752-5005
Amelia *(G-550)*
Triangle Precision Industries D 937 299-6776
Dayton *(G-8564)*
Tru-Fab Inc F 937 435-1733
Dayton *(G-8571)*
Tru-Form Steel & Wire Inc E 765 348-5001
Toledo *(G-18583)*
Turn-Key Industrial Svcs LLC D 614 274-1128
Columbus *(G-7551)*
U M D Automated Systems Inc D 740 694-8614
Fredericktown *(G-9981)*
Union Fabricating & Machine Co G 419 626-5963
Sandusky *(G-16858)*
Unique Fabrications Inc F 419 355-1700
Fremont *(G-10060)*
United Metal Fabricators Inc E 216 662-2000
Maple Heights *(G-12582)*
▲ Universal Fabg Cnstr Svcs Inc D 614 274-1128
Columbus *(G-7561)*
Updegraff Inc G 216 621-7600
Cleveland *(G-6241)*
Upright Steel LLC E 216 923-0852
Cleveland *(G-6242)*
V & S Schuler Engineering Inc D 330 452-5200
Canton *(G-2855)*
Valco Industries Inc E 937 399-7400
Springfield *(G-17513)*
Vanscoyk Sheet Metal Corp G 937 845-0581
New Carlisle *(G-14681)*
Verhoff Machine & Welding Inc C 419 596-3202
Continental *(G-7669)*
Vicon Fabricating Company Ltd E 440 205-6700
Mentor *(G-13624)*
Viking Fabricators Inc E 740 374-5246
Marietta *(G-12687)*
Vscorp LLC F 937 305-3562
Tipp City *(G-18144)*
W & W Custom Fabrication Inc G 513 353-4617
Cleves *(G-6382)*
Warmus and Associates Inc F 330 659-4440
Bath *(G-1203)*
◆ Warren Fabricating Corporation D 330 534-5017
Hubbard *(G-11011)*
Warren Fabricating Corporation E 330 544-4101
Niles *(G-15039)*
▲ Waterford Tank Fabrication Ltd D 740 984-4100
Beverly *(G-1663)*
▲ Wauseon Machine & Mfg Inc D 419 337-0940
Wauseon *(G-19537)*
Wecan Fabricators LLC G 740 667-0731
Tuppers Plains *(G-18721)*
Welage Corporation F 513 681-2300
Cincinnati *(G-4495)*
Weldfab Inc G 440 563-3310
Rock Creek *(G-16535)*
Welding Improvement Company G 330 424-9666
Lisbon *(G-11982)*
Weldtec Inc F 419 586-1200
Celina *(G-2992)*
Wernke Wldg & Stl Erection Co F 513 353-4173
North Bend *(G-15058)*
Wernli Realty Inc D 937 258-7878
Beavercreek *(G-1368)*
Westerhaus Metals LLC G 513 240-9441
Cincinnati *(G-4502)*
White Machine & Mfg Co F 740 453-3444
Zanesville *(G-21188)*
◆ Whole Shop Inc F 330 630-5305
Tallmadge *(G-18015)*
Winston Campbell LLC G 614 274-7015
Columbus *(G-7606)*
Wiseman Bros Fabg & Stl Ltd F 740 988-5121
Beaver *(G-1295)*
▼ Witt Industries Inc D 513 871-5700
Mason *(G-12955)*
Wm Lang & Sons Company F 513 541-3304
Cincinnati *(G-4515)*
Woodbury Welding Inc G 937 968-3573
Union City *(G-18906)*
Worthington Industries Inc C 513 539-9291
Monroe *(G-14282)*
Worthngton Stelpac Systems LLC G 937 747-2370
North Lewisburg *(G-15165)*
▲ Ysd Industries Inc D 330 792-6521
Youngstown *(G-21086)*
Ziegler Engineering Inc G 440 582-8515
North Royalton *(G-15312)*
Zimmerman Shtmtl Stl & Wldg G 419 335-3806
Wauseon *(G-19540)*
Zimmerman Steel & Sup Co LLC F 330 828-1010
Dalton *(G-7955)*

3442 Metal Doors, Sash, Frames, Molding & Trim

A B Siemer Inc B 614 888-8855
Columbus *(G-6515)*
A C Shutters Inc G 216 429-2424
Cleveland *(G-4584)*
All Around Garage Door Inc G 440 759-5079
North Ridgeville *(G-15207)*
All Pro Ovrhd Door Systems LLC G 614 444-3667
Columbus *(G-6567)*
Allied Window Inc E 513 559-1212
Cincinnati *(G-3325)*
Aluminum Color Industries Inc D 330 536-6295
Lowellville *(G-12248)*
Amarr Company G 216 573-7100
Independence *(G-11119)*
American Woodwork Specialty Co E 937 263-1053
Dayton *(G-8029)*
Anderson Door Co E 216 475-5700
Cleveland *(G-4712)*
Angel Window Mfg Corp G 440 891-1006
Berea *(G-1590)*
▲ Associated Materials LLC B 330 929-1811
Cuyahoga Falls *(G-7841)*
Associated Materials Group Inc E 330 929-1811
Cuyahoga Falls *(G-7842)*
Associated Mtls Holdings LLC A 330 929-1811
Cuyahoga Falls *(G-7843)*
Bearded Shutter G 440 567-8568
Mantua *(G-12543)*
Bilco Company E 740 455-9020
Zanesville *(G-21107)*
Brainerd Industries Inc E 937 228-0488
Miamisburg *(G-13644)*
Breezeway Screens Inc G 740 599-5222
Danville *(G-7958)*
Burt Manufacturing Company Inc C 330 762-0061
Akron *(G-100)*
Capitol Aluminum & Glass Corp D 800 331-8268
Bellevue *(G-1534)*
▲ Cascade Ohio Inc B 440 593-5800
Conneaut *(G-7642)*
Central Ohio Rtrctable Screens G 614 868-5080
Radnor *(G-16357)*
▲ Champion Opco LLC B 513 327-7338
Cincinnati *(G-3463)*
◆ Champion Win Co Cleveland LLC E 440 899-2562
Macedonia *(G-12283)*
Champion Win Enclosure Dayton E 937 299-6800
Moraine *(G-14337)*
Champion Window Co of Toledo E 419 841-0154
Perrysburg *(G-15933)*
Chase Doors Acquisition Corp G 513 860-5565
West Chester *(G-19840)*
◆ Chase Industries Inc D 513 860-5565
West Chester *(G-19841)*
Cleveland Shutters G 440 234-7600
Berea *(G-1597)*
◆ Clopay Building Pdts Co Inc E 513 770-4800
Mason *(G-12846)*
Clopay Building Pdts Co Inc G 937 526-4301
Russia *(G-16606)*
Clopay Building Pdts Co Inc G 937 440-6403
Troy *(G-18642)*
▲ Clopay Corporation C 800 282-2260
Mason *(G-12847)*
Custom Hitch and Trailer/ Over G 740 289-3925
Piketon *(G-16068)*
Dale Kestler G 513 871-9000
Cincinnati *(G-3574)*
Desco Corporation G 614 888-8855
New Albany *(G-14622)*
◆ Diamond Roll-Up Door Inc D 419 294-3373
Upper Sandusky *(G-18952)*
Division Overhead Door Inc F 513 872-0888
Cincinnati *(G-3597)*
Dj & Woodies Vinyl Frontier G 740 623-2818
Coshocton *(G-7731)*
Duo-Corp E 330 549-2149
North Lima *(G-15170)*
Dynaco Usa Inc G 419 227-3000
Lima *(G-11858)*
Eliason Corporation G 800 828-3655
West Chester *(G-19851)*
Euclid Jalousies Inc G 440 953-1112
Cleveland *(G-5196)*
▲ Fab Tech Inc G 330 926-9556
Brecksville *(G-2036)*
Francis-Schulze Co E 937 295-3941
Russia *(G-16608)*
Friends Ornamental Iron Co G 216 431-6710
Cleveland *(G-5275)*
Haas Door Company C 419 337-9900
Wauseon *(G-19519)*
◆ Hrh Door Corp A 850 208-3400
Mount Hope *(G-14438)*
Hrh Door Corp C 330 828-2291
Dalton *(G-7943)*
Installed Building Pdts LLC E 614 308-9900
Columbus *(G-7029)*
Kawneer Company Inc F 216 252-3203
Cleveland *(G-5520)*
Loxcreen Company Inc F 513 539-2255
Middletown *(G-13921)*
M-D Building Products Inc B 513 539-2255
Middletown *(G-13922)*
Machine Tool & Fab Corp F 419 435-7676
Fostoria *(G-9846)*
Magnode Corporation D 317 243-3553
Trenton *(G-18624)*
Masonite International Corp G 937 454-9308
Vandalia *(G-19137)*
Mestek Inc D 419 288-2703
Holland *(G-10944)*
Mestek Inc D 419 288-2703
Bradner *(G-2015)*
Midwest Curtainwalls Inc D 216 641-7900
Cleveland *(G-5680)*
Modern Builders Supply Inc C 419 241-3961
Toledo *(G-18414)*
National Access Design LLC F 513 351-3400
Cincinnati *(G-4058)*

Employee Codes: A=Over 500 employees, B=251-500
C=101-250, D=51-100, E=20-50, F=10-19, G=3-9
2019 Harris Ohio
Industrial Directory
923

34 FABRICATED METAL PRODUCTS, EXCEPT MACHINERY AND TRANSPORTATION EQUIPMENT — SIC SECTION

▼ Nofziger Door Sales Inc...............C...... 419 337-9900
  Wauseon (G-19530)
Nofziger Door Sales Inc...............F...... 419 445-2961
  Archbold (G-662)
▲ Orrvilon Inc...............C...... 330 684-9400
  Orrville (G-15610)
Otter Group LLC...............F...... 937 315-1199
  Dayton (G-8410)
Overhead Door Corporation ....D...... 740 383-6376
  Marion (G-12727)
Overhead Door Corporation ....F...... 419 294-3874
  Upper Sandusky (G-18970)
Overhead Door ....G...... 419 476-0300
  Toledo (G-18443)
Paul Miracle ....G...... 513 575-3113
  Loveland (G-12220)
Pease Industies Inc...............B...... 513 870-3600
  Fairfield (G-9546)
Phillips Manufacturing Co ....D...... 330 652-4335
  Niles (G-15026)
Provia Holdings Inc ....C...... 330 852-4711
  Sugarcreek (G-17859)
Quality Security Door & Mfg Co ....G...... 440 246-0770
  Lorain (G-12114)
Quanex Screens LLC ....G...... 419 662-5001
  Perrysburg (G-16002)
Renewal By Andersen LLC ....G...... 614 781-9600
  Columbus (G-6506)
S R Door Inc ....C...... 740 927-3558
  Hebron (G-10761)
Senneca Holdings Inc...............D...... 800 543-4455
  Cincinnati (G-4322)
Shade Youngstown & Aluminum Co ......F...... 330 782-2373
  Youngstown (G-21028)
Shurtape Technologies LLC ....B...... 440 937-7000
  Avon (G-966)
Shutter Expressions ....G...... 937 626-0462
  Franklin (G-9920)
Shutterbus Ohio LLC ....G...... 937 726-9634
  Hilliard (G-10861)
▲ Stephen M Trudick ....E...... 440 834-1891
  Burton (G-2371)
◆ Stoett Industries Inc ....E...... 419 542-0247
  Hicksville (G-10783)
Superior Weld and Fabg Co Inc ....G...... 216 249-5122
  Cleveland (G-6128)
Tdm LLC ....G...... 440 969-1442
  Ashtabula (G-806)
Thermal Industries Inc...............G...... 216 464-0674
  Cleveland (G-6166)
Thomas J Weaver Inc ....F...... 740 622-2040
  Coshocton (G-7755)
Traichal Construction Company ....E...... 800 255-3667
  Niles (G-15037)
Tri County Door Service Inc ....F...... 216 531-2245
  Euclid (G-9448)
Vinylume Products Inc ....D...... 330 799-2000
  Youngstown (G-21067)
YKK AP America Inc ....F...... 513 942-7200
  West Chester (G-19823)

3443 Fabricated Plate Work

A A S Amels Sheet Meta L Inc ....E...... 330 793-9326
  Youngstown (G-20830)
A & E Butscha Co ....G...... 513 761-1919
  Cincinnati (G-3275)
▲ A & G Manufacturing Co Inc ....E...... 419 468-7433
  Galion (G-10119)
A C Knox Inc ....G...... 513 921-5028
  Cincinnati (G-3279)
A H Marty Co Ltd ....F...... 216 641-8950
  Cleveland (G-4588)
A Metalcraft Associates Inc ....G...... 937 693-4008
  Botkins (G-1931)
A P O Holdings Inc ....G...... 330 455-8925
  Canton (G-2556)
A-1 Welding & Fabrication ....F...... 440 233-8474
  Lorain (G-12077)
Acme Boiler Co Inc ....E...... 216 961-2471
  Cleveland (G-4605)
Advance Industrial Mfg Inc ....E...... 614 871-3333
  Grove City (G-10411)
Advanced Welding Co ....G...... 937 746-6800
  Franklin (G-9867)
Aetna Plastics Corp ....G...... 330 274-2855
  Mantua (G-12541)
Airtech Mechanical Inc ....F...... 419 292-0074
  Toledo (G-18161)
All American Welding Co ....G...... 614 224-7552
  Columbus (G-6566)

▼ Alloy Engineering Company ....D...... 440 243-6800
  Berea (G-1589)
▼ Allpass Corporation ....F...... 440 998-6300
  Madison (G-12339)
▲ Almo Process Technology Inc ....G...... 513 402-2566
  West Chester (G-19642)
AM Castle & Co ....D...... 330 425-7000
  Bedford (G-1381)
▲ American Tank & Fabricating Co ....C...... 216 252-1500
  Cleveland (G-4698)
AMF Bruns America Lp ....G...... 877 506-3770
  Hudson (G-11031)
▲ Amko Service Company ....E...... 330 364-8857
  Midvale (G-13975)
Apex Welding Incorporated ....F...... 440 232-6770
  Bedford (G-1384)
Ares Inc ....D...... 419 635-2175
  Port Clinton (G-16242)
Armor Consolidated Inc ....G...... 513 923-5260
  Mason (G-12826)
▲ Armor Group Inc ....C...... 513 923-5260
  Mason (G-12827)
▲ Armor Metal Group Mason Inc ....C...... 513 769-0700
  Mason (G-12828)
▲ AT&f Advanced Metals LLC ....E...... 330 684-1122
  Cleveland (G-4756)
Austin Engineering Inc ....G...... 330 848-0815
  Barberton (G-1055)
Ayling and Reichert Co Consent ....E...... 419 898-2471
  Oak Harbor (G-15441)
◆ Babcock & Wilcox Company ....A...... 330 753-4511
  Barberton (G-1059)
Baxter Holdings Inc ....E...... 513 860-3593
  Hamilton (G-10538)
▲ Bico Akron Inc...............D...... 330 794-1716
  Mogadore (G-14231)
BJ Equipment Ltd ....F...... 614 497-1776
  Columbus (G-6673)
Blackwood Sheet Metal Inc ....G...... 614 291-3115
  Columbus (G-6678)
Blevins Metal Fabrication Inc ....E...... 419 522-6082
  Mansfield (G-12412)
Boochers Inc ....G...... 937 667-3414
  Tipp City (G-18101)
Breitinger Company ....C...... 419 526-4255
  Mansfield (G-12414)
Brighton Truedge ....G...... 513 771-2300
  Cincinnati (G-3418)
Brown-Singer Co ....F...... 513 422-9619
  Middletown (G-13888)
▼ Buckeye Fabricating Co ....E...... 937 746-9822
  Springboro (G-17323)
Buckeye Stamping Company ....D...... 614 445-0059
  Columbus (G-6712)
Bwxt Nclear Oprtions Group Inc ....F...... 330 860-1010
  Barberton (G-1068)
C & C Fabrication Inc ....G...... 419 354-3535
  Bowling Green (G-1958)
C & R Inc ....E...... 614 497-1130
  Groveport (G-10486)
C A Joseph Co ....F...... 330 532-4646
  Irondale (G-11158)
C Imperial Inc ....G...... 937 669-5620
  Tipp City (G-18104)
◆ CA Litzler Co Inc ....E...... 216 267-8020
  Cleveland (G-4859)
Capital Tool Company ....E...... 216 661-5750
  Cleveland (G-4871)
▲ Cardinal Pumps Exchangers Inc ....F...... 330 332-8558
  Salem (G-16723)
Cbr Industrial Llc ....G...... 419 645-6447
  Wapakoneta (G-19326)
Cds Technologies Inc ....G...... 800 338-1122
  West Chester (G-19665)
Ceco Environmental Corp ....E...... 513 874-8915
  West Chester (G-19838)
◆ Ceco Group Inc ....G...... 513 458-2600
  Cincinnati (G-3452)
Centerline Machine Inc ....G...... 937 322-4887
  Springfield (G-17372)
Central Fabricators Inc ....E...... 513 621-1240
  Cincinnati (G-3456)
CF Extrusion Technologies LLC ....G...... 844 439-8783
  Uhrichsville (G-18882)
Chart Asia Inc ....D...... 440 753-1490
  Cleveland (G-4913)
Chart Industries Inc ....B...... 440 753-1490
  Cleveland (G-4914)
Chart International Inc ....E...... 440 753-1490
  Cleveland (G-4915)

Cheap Dumpsters LLC ....G...... 614 285-5865
  Columbus (G-6760)
Chempure Products Corporation ....A...... 330 874-4300
  Bolivar (G-1909)
Chute Source LLC ....F...... 330 475-0377
  Akron (G-117)
▲ Cincinnati Heat Exchangers Inc ....E...... 513 874-7232
  Mason (G-12842)
Cincy-Dumpster Inc ....G...... 513 941-3063
  Cleves (G-6357)
Cleveland Steel Specialty Co ....E...... 216 464-9400
  Bedford Heights (G-1466)
Cleveland Track Material Inc ....F...... 216 641-4000
  Cleveland (G-4981)
▲ Clifton Steel Company ....D...... 216 662-6111
  Maple Heights (G-12569)
◆ Columbiana Boiler Company LLC ....E...... 330 482-3373
  Columbiana (G-6460)
▲ Columbiana Holding Co Inc ....D...... 330 482-3373
  Columbiana (G-6461)
Commercial Mtal Fbricators Inc ....E...... 937 233-4911
  Dayton (G-8100)
Compco Industries Inc ....D...... 330 482-6488
  Columbiana (G-6463)
Containment Solutions Inc ....C...... 419 874-8765
  Perrysburg (G-15934)
Contech Bridge Solutions LLC ....F...... 513 645-7000
  West Chester (G-19678)
Contech Cnstr Pdts Hldings Inc ....A...... 513 645-7000
  West Chester (G-19679)
Contech Engnered Solutions Inc ....F...... 513 645-7000
  West Chester (G-19680)
Contech Engnered Solutions LLC ....G...... 614 477-1171
  Columbus (G-6812)
Contech Engnered Solutions LLC ....E...... 513 425-5337
  Middletown (G-13897)
Contech Engnered Solutions LLC ....D...... 513 645-7000
  Middletown (G-13896)
◆ Contech Engnered Solutions LLC ....C...... 513 645-7000
  West Chester (G-19681)
Convault of Ohio Inc ....G...... 614 252-8422
  Columbus (G-6816)
Cooper-Standard Automotive Inc ....B...... 740 342-3523
  New Lexington (G-14714)
Cramers Inc ....E...... 330 477-4571
  Canton (G-2638)
Curtiss-Wright Flow Control ....D...... 513 735-2538
  Batavia (G-1134)
Curtiss-Wright Flow Ctrl Corp ....D...... 513 528-7900
  Cincinnati (G-3245)
Dabar Industries LLC ....F...... 614 873-3949
  Plain City (G-16183)
Debra-Kuempel Inc ....D...... 513 271-6500
  Cincinnati (G-3579)
▲ Defiance Metal Products Co ....B...... 419 784-5332
  Defiance (G-8619)
Deibel Manufacturing LLC ....G...... 330 482-3351
  Leetonia (G-11717)
Diller Metals Inc ....F...... 419 943-3364
  Leipsic (G-11725)
Dj S Weld ....G...... 330 432-2206
  Uhrichsville (G-18885)
Dover Tank and Plate Company ....E...... 330 343-4443
  Dover (G-8823)
Ds Express Carriers Inc ....G...... 419 433-6200
  Norwalk (G-15388)
Dumpsters Inc ....G...... 440 241-6927
  Seven Hills (G-16903)
▲ Dynamic Control North Amer Inc ....F...... 513 860-5094
  Hamilton (G-10552)
▼ E-Pak Manufacturing LLC ....D...... 800 235-1632
  Wooster (G-20588)
Eagle Wldg & Fabrication Inc ....E...... 440 946-0692
  Willoughby (G-20313)
▲ Eaton Fabricating Company Inc ....E...... 440 926-3121
  Grafton (G-10300)
▲ Ebner Furnaces Inc ....D...... 330 335-2311
  Wadsworth (G-19237)
Efco Corp ....E...... 614 876-1226
  Columbus (G-6886)
▲ Eleet Cryogenics Inc ....E...... 330 874-4009
  Bolivar (G-1913)
Elliott Machine Works Inc ....E...... 419 468-4709
  Galion (G-10137)
▲ Ellis & Watts Intl LLC ....G...... 513 752-9000
  Batavia (G-1143)
En-Hanced Products Inc ....G...... 614 882-7400
  Westerville (G-20052)
▲ Enerfab Inc ....B...... 513 641-0500
  Cincinnati (G-3640)

▲ **Enk Tenofour LLC** ....G....... 419 661-1465
Northwood *(G-15336)*
▲ **Exothermics Inc** ....E....... 603 821-5660
Toledo *(G-18286)*
▲ **Fabco Inc** ....E....... 419 421-4740
Findlay *(G-9682)*
Fabrication Shop Inc ....F....... 419 435-7934
Fostoria *(G-9837)*
Fabstar Tanks Inc ....F....... 419 587-3639
Grover Hill *(G-10518)*
▲ **Falls Welding & Fabg Inc** ....G....... 330 253-3437
Akron *(G-165)*
Fiba Technologies Inc ....D....... 330 602-7300
Midvale *(G-13977)*
Fin Tube Products Inc ....F....... 330 334-3736
Wadsworth *(G-19240)*
Fred Winner ....G....... 419 582-2421
New Weston *(G-14845)*
FSRc Tanks Inc ....E....... 234 221-2015
Bolivar *(G-1914)*
Fulton Equipment Co ....E....... 419 290-5393
Toledo *(G-18299)*
Gaspar Inc ....D....... 330 477-2222
Canton *(G-2679)*
◆ **Gayston Corporation** ....C....... 937 743-6050
Miamisburg *(G-13672)*
▲ **General Technologies Inc** ....E....... 419 747-1800
Mansfield *(G-12445)*
▲ **General Tool Company** ....C....... 513 733-5500
Cincinnati *(G-3747)*
Gerald H Smith ....G....... 740 446-3455
Bidwell *(G-1666)*
GL Nause Co Inc ....E....... 513 722-9500
Loveland *(G-12192)*
Gorilla Dumpsters ....G....... 614 344-4677
Dublin *(G-8917)*
Graber Metal Works Inc ....E....... 440 237-8422
North Royalton *(G-15274)*
Grenga Machine & Welding ....F....... 330 743-1113
Youngstown *(G-20925)*
H P E Inc ....F....... 330 833-3161
Massillon *(G-12993)*
▲ **Halvorsen Company** ....E....... 216 341-7500
Cleveland *(G-5367)*
Hamilton Tanks LLC ....F....... 614 445-8446
Columbus *(G-6977)*
▲ **Hammelmann Corporation** ....F....... 937 859-8777
Miamisburg *(G-13673)*
Hard Chrome Plating Consultant ....G....... 216 631-9090
Cleveland *(G-5374)*
Harsco Corporation ....E....... 216 961-1570
Cleveland *(G-5376)*
Hason USA Corp ....E....... 513 248-0287
Milford *(G-14016)*
Heat Exchange Applied Tech ....F....... 330 682-4328
Orrville *(G-15594)*
Heights Dumpster Services LLC ....G....... 937 321-0096
Huber Heights *(G-11019)*
Hershey Machine ....G....... 330 674-2718
Millersburg *(G-14089)*
Hutnik Company ....G....... 330 336-9700
Wadsworth *(G-19246)*
Hydraulic Specialists Inc ....E....... 740 922-3343
Midvale *(G-13978)*
▼ **Hydro-Thrift Corporation** ....E....... 330 837-5141
Massillon *(G-13001)*
Hyq Technologies LLC ....G....... 513 225-6911
Oxford *(G-15694)*
I L R Inc ....G....... 216 587-2212
Cleveland *(G-5433)*
Indian Creek Fabricators Inc ....E....... 937 667-7214
Tipp City *(G-18116)*
Industrial Container Svcs LLC ....E....... 513 921-2056
Cincinnati *(G-3843)*
Industrial Container Svcs LLC ....E....... 513 921-8811
Cincinnati *(G-3844)*
Industrial Container Svcs LLC ....D....... 614 864-1900
Blacklick *(G-1687)*
▲ **Industrial Repair & Mfg Inc** ....D....... 419 822-4232
Delta *(G-8774)*
Industrial Tank & Containment ....F....... 330 448-4876
Brookfield *(G-2107)*
Ironman Metalworks LLC ....G....... 614 907-6629
Groveport *(G-10496)*
J B Kepple Sheet Metal ....G....... 740 393-2971
Mount Vernon *(G-14484)*
Jacp Inc ....G....... 513 353-3660
Miamitown *(G-13747)*
▲ **Jergens Inc** ....C....... 216 486-5540
Cleveland *(G-5495)*
Jh Industries Inc ....E....... 330 963-4105
Twinsburg *(G-18797)*
JMw Welding and Mfg ....E....... 330 484-2428
Canton *(G-2719)*
Kard Welding Inc ....E....... 419 628-2598
Minster *(G-14218)*
▲ **Kendall Holdings Ltd** ....E....... 614 486-4750
Columbus *(G-7086)*
◆ **Kirk & Blum Manufacturing Co** ....C....... 513 458-2600
Cincinnati *(G-3912)*
Laird Technologies Inc ....G....... 234 806-0105
Warren *(G-19416)*
▲ **Langdon Inc** ....E....... 513 733-5955
Cincinnati *(G-3930)*
Lapham-Hickey Steel Corp ....E....... 614 443-4881
Columbus *(G-7116)*
Lion Industries LLC ....E....... 740 699-0369
Saint Clairsville *(G-16636)*
Liquid Luggers LLC ....E....... 330 426-2538
East Palestine *(G-9080)*
▲ **Long-Stanton Mfg Company** ....E....... 513 874-8020
West Chester *(G-19738)*
Louis Arthur Steel Company ....G....... 440 997-5545
Geneva *(G-10224)*
Louis Arthur Steel Company ....G....... 440 997-5545
Uniontown *(G-18926)*
◆ **Loveman Steel Corporation** ....D....... 440 232-6200
Bedford *(G-1423)*
M & H Fabricating Co Inc ....G....... 937 325-8708
Springfield *(G-17438)*
M & M Certified Welding Inc ....F....... 330 467-1729
Macedonia *(G-12311)*
Mack Iron Works Company ....E....... 419 626-3712
Sandusky *(G-16826)*
Macleod Inc ....G....... 513 771-9560
Miamitown *(G-13748)*
Mahle Behr USA Inc ....A....... 937 369-2000
Dayton *(G-8327)*
▼ **Marathon Industrial Cntrs Inc** ....F....... 440 324-2748
Elyria *(G-9291)*
Mark One Manufacturing Ltd ....G....... 419 628-4405
Minster *(G-14220)*
Mercury Iron and Steel Co ....F....... 440 349-1500
Solon *(G-17190)*
Metal Fabricating Corporation ....D....... 216 631-8121
Cleveland *(G-5658)*
▼ **Midwestern Industries Inc** ....C....... 330 837-4203
Massillon *(G-13026)*
Modern Welding Co Ohio Inc ....E....... 740 344-9425
Newark *(G-14898)*
Moore Mr Specialty Company ....G....... 330 332-1229
Salem *(G-16763)*
◆ **Morris Material Handling Inc** ....G....... 937 525-5520
Springfield *(G-17452)*
Munroe Incorporated ....G....... 330 755-7216
Struthers *(G-17821)*
Myers Industries Inc ....E....... 330 253-5592
Akron *(G-293)*
Myers Industries Inc ....C....... 330 336-6621
Wadsworth *(G-19255)*
Nbw Inc ....E....... 216 377-1700
Cleveland *(G-5732)*
▲ **Netshape Technologies Mim Inc** ....F....... 440 248-5456
Solon *(G-17206)*
New Wayne Inc ....G....... 740 453-3454
Zanesville *(G-21162)*
North Coast Dumpster Svcs LLC ....G....... 216 644-5647
Cleveland *(G-5764)*
North High Marathon ....G....... 937 444-1894
Mount Orab *(G-14448)*
Northwest Installations Inc ....E....... 419 423-5738
Findlay *(G-9732)*
Ohio Heat Transfer ....G....... 513 870-5323
Hamilton *(G-10591)*
▲ **Ohio Heat Transfer Ltd** ....F....... 740 695-0635
Saint Clairsville *(G-16643)*
Oil Skimmers Inc ....E....... 440 237-4600
North Royalton *(G-15291)*
P B Fabrication Mech Contr ....F....... 419 478-4869
Toledo *(G-18454)*
◆ **Park Corporation** ....B....... 216 267-4870
Cleveland *(G-5841)*
Parker-Hannifin Corporation ....F....... 330 336-3511
Wadsworth *(G-19262)*
Pcy Enterprises Inc ....E....... 513 241-5566
Cincinnati *(G-4143)*
▲ **Pioneer Pipe Inc** ....A....... 740 376-2400
Marietta *(G-12653)*
Plastran Inc ....G....... 440 237-8404
Cleveland *(G-5888)*
Porter Dumpsters LLC ....G....... 330 659-0043
Richfield *(G-16482)*
Prout Boiler Htg & Wldg Inc ....E....... 330 744-0293
Youngstown *(G-21008)*
Pucel Enterprises Inc ....D....... 216 881-4604
Cleveland *(G-5933)*
Quintus Technologies LLC ....E....... 614 891-2732
Lewis Center *(G-11774)*
◆ **R B Mfg Co** ....F....... 419 626-9464
Wadsworth *(G-19270)*
R4 Holdings LLC ....G....... 614 873-6499
Plain City *(G-16210)*
Rampp Company ....E....... 740 373-7886
Marietta *(G-12662)*
RCE Heat Exchangers LLC ....E....... 330 627-0300
Carrollton *(G-2927)*
Rcr Partnership ....G....... 419 340-1202
Genoa *(G-10235)*
Rebsco Inc ....F....... 937 548-2246
Greenville *(G-10390)*
Retays Welding Company ....E....... 440 327-4100
North Ridgeville *(G-15250)*
Rezmann Karoly ....G....... 216 441-4357
Cleveland *(G-5982)*
Rhodes Manufacturing Co Inc ....E....... 740 743-2614
Somerset *(G-17266)*
▲ **Ridge Corporation** ....D....... 614 421-7434
Etna *(G-9398)*
Rimrock Holdings Corporation ....E....... 614 471-5926
Columbus *(G-7395)*
Rose Metal Industries LLC ....F....... 216 881-3355
Cleveland *(G-6002)*
Ross Hx LLC ....G....... 513 217-1565
Middletown *(G-13949)*
S-P Company Inc ....F....... 330 482-0200
Columbiana *(G-6479)*
▲ **Sausser Steel Company Inc** ....F....... 419 422-9632
Findlay *(G-9752)*
Say Dumpsters ....G....... 937 578-3744
Marysville *(G-12808)*
Schweizer Dipple Inc ....D....... 440 786-8090
Cleveland *(G-6034)*
Sexton Industrial Inc ....C....... 513 530-5555
West Chester *(G-19898)*
▲ **Sgl Technic Inc** ....E....... 440 572-3600
Strongsville *(G-17786)*
Shelburne Corp ....G....... 216 321-9177
Shaker Heights *(G-16936)*
Skinner Sales Group Inc ....E....... 440 572-8455
Medina *(G-13344)*
Snair Co ....F....... 614 873-7020
Plain City *(G-16212)*
Space Dynamics Corp ....E....... 513 792-9800
Blue Ash *(G-1847)*
Spradlin Bros Welding Co ....F....... 800 219-2182
Springfield *(G-17493)*
St Lawrence Holdings LLC ....E....... 330 562-9000
Maple Heights *(G-12580)*
▼ **Steel & Alloy Utility Pdts Inc** ....E....... 330 530-2220
Mc Donald *(G-13202)*
Steel Valley Tank & Welding ....F....... 740 598-4994
Brilliant *(G-2080)*
Steve Vore Welding and Steel ....F....... 419 375-4087
Fort Recovery *(G-9827)*
Sticker Corporation ....F....... 440 946-2100
Willoughby *(G-20438)*
▲ **Strohecker Incorporated** ....E....... 330 426-9496
East Palestine *(G-9085)*
Swagelok Company ....D....... 440 349-5934
Solon *(G-17242)*
Swanton Wldg Machining Co Inc ....D....... 419 826-4816
Swanton *(G-17923)*
Thermogenics Corp ....G....... 513 247-7963
Cincinnati *(G-4418)*
▼ **Toledo Metal Spinning Company** ....E....... 419 535-5931
Toledo *(G-18561)*
Triangle Precision Industries ....D....... 937 299-6776
Dayton *(G-8564)*
Triumph Thermal Systems LLC ....D....... 419 273-2511
Forest *(G-9789)*
TW Tank LLC ....G....... 419 334-2664
Fremont *(G-10057)*
Universal Hydraulik USA Corp ....G....... 419 873-6340
Perrysburg *(G-16020)*
Universal Rack & Equipment Co ....E....... 330 963-6776
Twinsburg *(G-18870)*
▲ **Val-Co Pax Inc** ....D....... 717 354-4586
Coldwater *(G-6423)*
Verhoff Machine & Welding Inc ....C....... 419 596-3202
Continental *(G-7669)*

Employee Codes: A=Over 500 employees, B=251-500
C=101-250, D=51-100, E=20-50, F=10-19, G=3-9
2019 Harris Ohio
Industrial Directory
925

Viking Fabricators Inc ....E 740 374-5246
Marietta *(G-12687)*
Vortec Corporation ....E 513 891-7485
Blue Ash *(G-1866)*
◆ Warren Fabricating Corporation ....D 330 534-5017
Hubbard *(G-11011)*
Washington Products Inc ....F 330 837-5101
Massillon *(G-13057)*
Wastequip Manufacturing Co LLC ....E 330 674-1119
Millersburg *(G-14148)*
▲ Wcr Inc ....E 937 223-0703
Fairborn *(G-9475)*
Wcr Incorporated ....E 740 333-3448
Wshngtn CT Hs *(G-20749)*
Westerman Inc ....D 330 262-6946
Wooster *(G-20665)*
Will-Burt Company ....E 330 682-7015
Orrville *(G-15628)*
▲ Will-Burt Company ....B 330 682-7015
Orrville *(G-15626)*
▲ Worthignton Products Inc ....G 330 452-7400
Canton *(G-2865)*
Worthington Cylinder Corp ....C 740 569-4143
Bremen *(G-2066)*
Worthington Cylinder Corp ....C 330 262-1762
Wooster *(G-20672)*
◆ Worthington Cylinder Corp ....C 614 840-3210
Worthington *(G-20709)*
Worthington Cylinder Corp ....C 440 576-5847
Jefferson *(G-11243)*
Worthington Cylinder Corp ....C 614 438-7900
Columbus *(G-7614)*
Worthington Cylinder Corp ....C 614 840-3800
Westerville *(G-20031)*
Worthington Industries Inc ....C 614 438-3210
Worthington *(G-20710)*

3444 Sheet Metal Work

A A S Amels Sheet Meta L Inc ....E 330 793-9326
Youngstown *(G-20830)*
A & C Welding Inc ....E 330 762-4777
Peninsula *(G-15888)*
A & E Butscha Co ....G 513 761-1919
Cincinnati *(G-3275)*
▲ A & G Manufacturing Co Inc ....E 419 468-7433
Galion *(G-10119)*
A A A Professional Htg & Coolg ....G 513 933-0564
Lebanon *(G-11628)*
A C Shutters Inc ....G 216 429-2424
Cleveland *(G-4584)*
Aba Gutters Inc ....G 440 729-2177
Chesterland *(G-3149)*
Accufab Inc ....G 513 942-1929
West Chester *(G-19636)*
▲ Acro Tool & Die Company ....D 330 773-5173
Akron *(G-29)*
Adjustable Kicker LLC ....G 740 362-9170
Delaware *(G-8650)*
Advance Metal Products Inc ....F 216 741-1800
Cleveland *(G-4623)*
Advanced Welding Co ....E 937 746-6800
Franklin *(G-9867)*
Aerolite Extrusion Company ....D 330 782-1127
Youngstown *(G-20838)*
Ahner Fabricating & Shtmtl Inc ....E 419 626-6641
Sandusky *(G-16793)*
Akron Foundry Co ....E 330 745-3101
Barberton *(G-1050)*
▲ Alan Manufacturing Inc ....E 330 262-1555
Wooster *(G-20560)*
Aleris Rolled Products Inc ....D 740 983-2571
Ashville *(G-814)*
All Metal Fabricators Inc ....F 216 267-0033
Cleveland *(G-4663)*
Allen County Fabrication Inc ....E 419 227-7447
Lima *(G-11834)*
Allfab Inc ....F 614 491-4944
Columbus *(G-6570)*
Allied Fabricating & Wldg Co ....E 614 751-6664
Columbus *(G-6572)*
Allied Mask and Tooling Inc ....G 419 470-2555
Toledo *(G-18164)*
Alro Steel Corporation ....E 419 720-5300
Toledo *(G-18166)*
Alro Steel Corporation ....E 614 878-7271
Columbus *(G-6578)*
Alsco Metals Corporation ....G 740 983-2571
Ashville *(G-815)*
◆ Alsco Metals Corporation ....E 740 983-2571
Dennison *(G-8781)*

Alumetal Manufacturing Company ....E 419 268-2311
Coldwater *(G-6399)*
Aluminum Color Industries Inc ....D 330 536-6295
Lowellville *(G-12248)*
Aluminum Extruded Shapes Inc ....C 513 563-2205
Cincinnati *(G-3328)*
AM Castle & Co ....D 330 425-7000
Bedford *(G-1381)*
AMD Fabricators Inc ....E 440 946-8855
Willoughby *(G-20270)*
American Craft Hardware LLC ....G 440 746-0098
Cleveland *(G-4686)*
American Culvert & Fabg Co ....F 740 432-6334
Cambridge *(G-2422)*
▲ American Frame Corporation ....E 419 893-5595
Maumee *(G-13069)*
American Truck Equipment Inc ....G 216 362-0400
Cleveland *(G-4699)*
Americas Best Siding Co ....G 419 589-5900
Mansfield *(G-12406)*
Amh Holdings LLC ....A 330 929-1811
Cuyahoga Falls *(G-7836)*
▲ Ampp Incorporated ....C 419 666-4747
Perrysburg *(G-15920)*
Anchor Metal Processing Inc ....F 216 362-6463
Cleveland *(G-4707)*
Anchor Metal Processing Inc ....E 216 362-1850
Cleveland *(G-4708)*
Andy Russo Jr Inc ....F 440 585-1456
Wickliffe *(G-20198)*
Anro Logistics Inc ....G 614 428-7490
Westerville *(G-19978)*
Antique Auto Sheet Metal Inc ....E 937 833-4422
Brookville *(G-2161)*
Apex Welding Incorporated ....F 440 232-6770
Bedford *(G-1384)*
Architectural Daylighting LLC ....G 330 460-5000
Medina *(G-13225)*
Architectural Sheet Metals LLC ....G 216 361-9952
Cleveland *(G-4729)*
▲ Armor Group Inc ....C 513 923-5260
Mason *(G-12827)*
▲ Armor Metal Group Mason Inc ....C 513 769-0700
Mason *(G-12828)*
Arsco Custom Metals LLC ....F 513 385-0555
Cincinnati *(G-3356)*
Art Fremont Iron Co ....G 419 332-5554
Fremont *(G-9992)*
Associated Materials LLC ....G 937 236-5679
Dayton *(G-8040)*
▼ Auburn Metal Processing LLC ....E 315 253-2565
Twinsburg *(G-18736)*
Austintown Metal Works Inc ....F 330 259-4673
Youngstown *(G-20848)*
Autoneum North America Inc ....B 419 693-0511
Oregon *(G-15556)*
Avon Lake Sheet Metal Co ....E 440 933-3505
Avon Lake *(G-980)*
Aztec Manufacturing Inc ....E 330 783-9747
Youngstown *(G-20850)*
B Y G Industries Inc ....G 216 961-5436
Cleveland *(G-4785)*
▲ B-R-O-T Incorporated ....E 216 267-5335
Cleveland *(G-4786)*
Bainter Machining Company ....E 740 653-2422
Lancaster *(G-11547)*
Baltimore Fabricators Inc ....G 740 862-6016
Baltimore *(G-1036)*
Bayloff Stmped Pdts Knsman Inc ....D 330 876-4511
Kinsman *(G-11463)*
Beacon Metal Fabricators Inc ....F 216 391-7444
Cleveland *(G-4798)*
Berran Industrial Group Inc ....E 330 253-5800
Akron *(G-85)*
Bickers Metal Products Inc ....E 513 353-4000
Miamitown *(G-13743)*
BJ Equipment Ltd ....F 614 497-1776
Columbus *(G-6673)*
Blesco Services ....G 614 871-4900
Mount Sterling *(G-14460)*
Blevins Metal Fabrication Inc ....E 419 522-6082
Mansfield *(G-12412)*
Bob Lanes Welding Inc ....F 740 373-3567
Marietta *(G-12609)*
Bogie Industries Inc Ltd ....E 330 745-3105
Akron *(G-92)*
Breitinger Company ....C 419 526-4255
Mansfield *(G-12414)*
Bridges Sheet Metal ....G 330 339-3185
New Philadelphia *(G-14760)*

BT Investments II Inc ....G 937 434-4321
Dayton *(G-8066)*
Buckeye Metal Works Inc ....F 614 239-8000
Columbus *(G-6710)*
Bud Corp ....G 740 967-9992
Johnstown *(G-11261)*
Budde Sheet Metal Works Inc ....E 937 224-0868
Dayton *(G-8068)*
Burt Manufacturing Company Inc ....C 330 762-0061
Akron *(G-100)*
Busch & Thiem Inc ....E 419 625-7515
Sandusky *(G-16800)*
C & R Inc ....E 614 497-1130
Groveport *(G-10486)*
C A Joseph Co ....F 330 532-4646
Irondale *(G-11158)*
C G C Systems Inc ....G 330 678-3261
Kent *(G-11302)*
C L W Inc ....G 740 374-8443
Marietta *(G-12611)*
C M L Concrete Construction ....G 330 758-8314
Youngstown *(G-20863)*
C-N-D Industries Inc ....E 330 478-8811
Massillon *(G-12965)*
Cabletek Wiring Products Inc ....E 800 562-9378
Elyria *(G-9230)*
Canton Fabricators Inc ....G 330 830-2900
Massillon *(G-12966)*
Carroll Distrg & Cnstr Sup Inc ....G 513 422-3327
Middletown *(G-13890)*
Carroll Distrg & Cnstr Sup Inc ....G 614 564-9799
Columbus *(G-6747)*
Cbr Industrial Llc ....G 419 645-6447
Wapakoneta *(G-19326)*
◆ Ceco Group Inc ....G 513 458-2600
Cincinnati *(G-3452)*
Centria Inc ....D 740 432-7351
Cambridge *(G-2431)*
Chagrin Metal Fabricating Inc ....G 440 946-6342
Eastlake *(G-9101)*
Champion Window Co of Toledo ....E 419 841-0154
Perrysburg *(G-15933)*
Chute Source LLC ....F 330 475-0377
Akron *(G-117)*
Cincinnati Gutter Supply Inc ....G 513 825-0500
West Chester *(G-19672)*
Cinfab LLC ....C 513 396-6100
Cincinnati *(G-3516)*
Clarkwestern Dietrich Building ....F 330 372-5564
Warren *(G-19384)*
Clarkwestern Dietrich Building ....C 513 870-1100
West Chester *(G-19676)*
▼ Clarkwestern Dietrich Building ....F 513 870-1100
West Chester *(G-19677)*
Cleveland Steel Specialty Co ....E 216 464-9400
Bedford Heights *(G-1466)*
CMA Supply Company Inc ....F 513 942-6663
West Chester *(G-19844)*
Collier Well Eqp & Sup Inc ....F 330 345-3968
Wooster *(G-20580)*
Color Brite Company Inc ....G 216 441-4117
Cleveland *(G-4998)*
Columbus Steelmasters Inc ....F 614 231-2141
Columbus *(G-6803)*
Commercial Mtal Fbricators Inc ....E 937 233-4911
Dayton *(G-8100)*
Compco Industries Inc ....D 330 482-6488
Columbiana *(G-6463)*
Contech Engnered Solutions Inc ....F 513 645-7000
West Chester *(G-19680)*
◆ Contech Engnered Solutions LLC ....C 513 645-7000
West Chester *(G-19681)*
Contech Engnered Solutions LLC ....D 513 645-7000
Middletown *(G-13896)*
Contour Forming Inc ....E 740 345-9777
Newark *(G-14864)*
Controls and Sheet Metal Inc ....E 513 721-3610
Cincinnati *(G-3546)*
COW Industries Inc ....E 614 443-6537
Columbus *(G-6831)*
Cramers Inc ....E 330 477-4571
Canton *(G-2638)*
CRC Metal Products ....G 740 966-0475
Johnstown *(G-11264)*
Creative Concepts ....G 216 513-6463
Medina *(G-13246)*
Crest Awning & Home Imprv Co ....G 440 942-3092
Willoughby *(G-20303)*
Crest Products Inc ....F 440 942-5770
Mentor *(G-13427)*

▲ **Crown Electric Engrg & Mfg LLC** ..... E 513 539-7394
Middletown *(G-13898)*
Custom Crete ..... G 740 726-2433
Waldo *(G-19302)*
Custom Duct & Supply Co Inc ..... G 937 228-2058
Dayton *(G-8118)*
Custom Enclosures Corp ..... G 330 786-9000
Akron *(G-129)*
Custom Metal Products Inc ..... G 614 855-2263
New Albany *(G-14619)*
Custom Metal Products Inc ..... G 614 855-2263
New Albany *(G-14620)*
Custom Metal Shearing Inc ..... F 937 233-6950
Dayton *(G-8120)*
Custom Powdercoating LLC ..... G 937 972-3516
Dayton *(G-8122)*
▲ **D B S Stinless Stl Fabricators** ..... G 513 856-9600
Hamilton *(G-10550)*
Dae Holdings LLC ..... E 502 589-1445
Swanton *(G-17911)*
Datco Mfg Company Inc ..... D 330 781-6100
Youngstown *(G-20887)*
David Cox ..... G 740 254-4858
Gnadenhutten *(G-10277)*
Decor Architectural Products ..... G 419 537-9493
Toledo *(G-18258)*
Defiance Metal Products Co ..... B 419 784-5332
Defiance *(G-8620)*
Delafoil Pennsylvania Inc ..... D 610 327-9565
Perrysburg *(G-15939)*
Delma Corp ..... D 937 253-2142
Dayton *(G-8153)*
Di Lorio Sheet Metal Inc ..... F 216 961-3703
Cleveland *(G-5088)*
Die-Cut Products Co ..... E 216 771-6994
Cleveland *(G-5094)*
Dimensional Metals Inc ..... D 740 927-3633
Reynoldsburg *(G-16435)*
Discount Drainage Supplies LLC ..... G 513 563-8616
Cincinnati *(G-3590)*
Dover Tank and Plate Company ..... E 330 343-4443
Dover *(G-8823)*
Duct Fabricators Inc ..... G 216 391-2400
Cleveland *(G-5116)*
Ducts Inc ..... E 216 391-2400
Cleveland *(G-5117)*
▲ **Duro Dyne Midwest Corp** ..... B 513 870-6000
Hamilton *(G-10551)*
Dynamic Weld Corporation ..... E 419 582-2900
Osgood *(G-15642)*
E & K Products Co Inc ..... G 216 631-2510
Cleveland *(G-5127)*
E B P Inc ..... E 216 241-2550
Cleveland *(G-5128)*
Eagle Wldg & Fabrication Inc ..... E 440 946-0692
Willoughby *(G-20313)*
▲ **Eastern Sheet Metal Inc** ..... D 513 793-3440
Blue Ash *(G-1763)*
▲ **Eaton Fabricating Company Inc** ..... E 440 926-3121
Grafton *(G-10300)*
▲ **Ebner Furnaces Inc** ..... D 330 335-2311
Wadsworth *(G-19237)*
Edwards Sheet Metal Works Inc ..... F 740 694-0010
Fredericktown *(G-9967)*
Efco Corp ..... E 614 876-1226
Columbus *(G-6886)*
Elsass Fabricating Ltd ..... G 937 394-7169
Anna *(G-589)*
Enterprise Welding & Fabg Inc ..... C 440 354-4128
Mentor *(G-13441)*
F M Sheet Metal Fabrication ..... G 937 362-4357
Quincy *(G-16355)*
Fab Steel Co Inc ..... F 419 666-5100
Northwood *(G-15337)*
▲ **Fabco Inc** ..... E 419 421-4740
Findlay *(G-9682)*
Fabcraft Inc ..... G 440 286-6700
Chardon *(G-3111)*
Fabricating Solutions Inc ..... F 330 486-0998
Twinsburg *(G-18773)*
Fabrication Unlimited LLC ..... G 937 492-3166
Sidney *(G-17039)*
Fabtech Ohio ..... G 440 942-0811
Willoughby *(G-20319)*
Falcon Industries Inc ..... E 330 723-0099
Medina *(G-13260)*
Famous Industries Inc ..... E 330 535-1811
Akron *(G-166)*
Famous Industries Inc ..... C 740 397-8842
Mount Vernon *(G-14481)*

Feather Lite Innovations Inc ..... F 513 893-5483
Liberty Twp *(G-11825)*
▲ **Feather Lite Innovations Inc** ..... E 937 743-9008
Springboro *(G-17327)*
Firestone Laser and Mfg LLC ..... E 330 337-9551
Salem *(G-16737)*
First Francis Company Inc ..... E 440 352-8927
Painesville *(G-15739)*
Flood Heliarc Inc ..... F 614 835-3929
Groveport *(G-10489)*
Franck and Fric Incorporated ..... D 216 524-4451
Cleveland *(G-5271)*
Franklin Frames and Cycles ..... G 740 763-3838
Newark *(G-14875)*
Fred Winner ..... G 419 582-2421
New Weston *(G-14845)*
Freeman Enclosure Systems LLC ..... C 877 441-8555
Batavia *(G-1147)*
Fulton Equipment Co ..... E 419 290-5393
Toledo *(G-18299)*
G T Metal Fabricators Inc ..... F 440 237-8745
Cleveland *(G-5284)*
Galion LLC ..... C 419 468-5214
Galion *(G-10138)*
▲ **Galion-Godwin Truck Bdy Co LLC** ... D 330 359-5495
Millersburg *(G-14084)*
Gaspar Inc ..... D 330 477-2222
Canton *(G-2679)*
Geist Co Inc ..... F 216 771-2200
Cleveland *(G-5300)*
Gem City Metal Tech LLC ..... E 937 252-8998
Dayton *(G-8220)*
General Awning Company Inc ..... F 216 749-0110
Cleveland *(G-5305)*
▲ **General Technologies Inc** ..... E 419 747-1800
Mansfield *(G-12445)*
▲ **General Tool Company** ..... C 513 733-5500
Cincinnati *(G-3747)*
▲ **Gentek Building Products Inc** ..... F 800 548-4542
Cuyahoga Falls *(G-7872)*
George Manufacturing Inc ..... E 513 932-1067
Lebanon *(G-11654)*
Gilson Screen Incorporated ..... E 419 256-7711
Malinta *(G-12379)*
GL Nause Co Inc ..... E 513 722-9500
Loveland *(G-12192)*
Global Body & Equipment Co ..... D 330 264-6640
Wooster *(G-20597)*
▲ **Glunt Industries Inc** ..... C 330 399-7585
Warren *(G-19407)*
GNI Erectors ..... G 614 465-7260
Galloway *(G-10179)*
Graber Metal Works Inc ..... E 440 237-8422
North Royalton *(G-15274)*
Great Day Improvements LLC ..... G 330 468-0700
Macedonia *(G-12300)*
Gunderson Rail Services LLC ..... E 330 792-6521
Youngstown *(G-20927)*
Gundlach Sheet Metal Works Inc ..... D 419 626-4525
Sandusky *(G-16814)*
Gutter Topper Ltd ..... G 513 797-5800
Batavia *(G-1150)*
▲ **Gwp Holdings Inc** ..... D 513 860-4050
Fairfield *(G-9501)*
▲ **H B Products Inc** ..... E 937 492-7031
Sidney *(G-17042)*
Hall Company ..... E 937 652-1376
Urbana *(G-18992)*
Halls Sheet Metal Fabrication ..... G 740 965-9264
Galena *(G-10113)*
▲ **Halvorsen Company** ..... E 216 341-7500
Cleveland *(G-5367)*
Harray LLC ..... G 888 568-8371
Cincinnati *(G-3799)*
Harrison Mch & Plastic Corp ..... E 330 527-5641
Garrettsville *(G-10191)*
Hartley Machine Inc ..... G 330 821-0343
Alliance *(G-471)*
Hartzell Mfg Co ..... E 937 859-5955
Miamisburg *(G-13674)*
HCC Holdings Inc ..... G 800 203-1155
Cleveland *(G-5383)*
Heim Sheet Metal Inc ..... G 330 424-7820
Lisbon *(G-11968)*
Hennig Inc ..... G 513 247-0838
Blue Ash *(G-1788)*
▲ **Hidaka Usa Inc** ..... E 614 889-8611
Dublin *(G-8923)*
Higgins Building Mtls No 2 LLC ..... G 740 395-5410
Jackson *(G-11186)*

Highway Safety Corp ..... F 740 387-6991
Marion *(G-12711)*
Hoffman Machining & Repair LLC ..... G 419 547-9204
Clyde *(G-6389)*
Holgate Metal Fab Inc ..... F 419 599-2000
Napoleon *(G-14543)*
Home Sheet Metal & Roofing Co ..... G 419 562-7806
Bucyrus *(G-2334)*
Hvac Inc ..... F 330 343-5511
Dover *(G-8830)*
Indian Creek Fabricators Inc ..... E 937 667-7214
Tipp City *(G-18116)*
Induction Iron Incorporated ..... G 330 501-8852
Youngstown *(G-20938)*
Industrial Fabricators Inc ..... E 614 882-7423
Westerville *(G-20059)*
Industrial Hanger Conveyor Co ..... G 419 332-2661
Fremont *(G-10028)*
Industrial Mill Maintenance ..... E 330 746-1155
Youngstown *(G-20939)*
Interstate Contractors LLC ..... E 513 372-5393
Mason *(G-12897)*
◆ **Isaiah Industries Inc** ..... E 937 773-9840
Piqua *(G-16131)*
Izit Cain Sheet Metal Corp ..... G 937 667-6521
Tipp City *(G-18117)*
J & L Welding Fabricating Inc ..... F 330 393-9353
Warren *(G-19412)*
J B Kepple Sheet Metal ..... G 740 393-2971
Mount Vernon *(G-14484)*
J N Linrose Mfg LLC ..... G 513 867-5500
Hamilton *(G-10574)*
J O Y Aluminum Products Inc ..... F 513 797-1100
Batavia *(G-1155)*
Jacobs Mechanical Co ..... C 513 681-6800
Cincinnati *(G-3866)*
Jeffery A Burns ..... G 419 845-2129
Caledonia *(G-2418)*
Jh Industries Inc ..... E 330 963-4105
Twinsburg *(G-18797)*
Jim Nier Construction Inc ..... F 740 289-3925
Piketon *(G-16072)*
John Baird ..... G 216 440-3595
Spencer *(G-17305)*
Joining Metals Inc ..... F 440 259-1790
Perry *(G-15906)*
Jones Metal Products Company ..... C 740 545-6381
West Lafayette *(G-19931)*
Joyce Manufacturing Co ..... D 440 239-9100
Berea *(G-1615)*
Kalron LLC ..... E 440 647-3039
Wellington *(G-19584)*
Kerber Sheetmetal Works Inc ..... F 937 339-6366
Troy *(G-18681)*
Kettering Roofing & Shtmtl ..... F 513 281-6413
Cincinnati *(G-3906)*
Kilroy Company ..... D 440 951-8700
Eastlake *(G-9117)*
◆ **Kirk & Blum Manufacturing Co** ..... C 513 458-2600
Cincinnati *(G-3912)*
Kirk Williams Company Inc ..... D 614 875-9023
Grove City *(G-10440)*
Kitts Heating & AC ..... G 330 755-9242
Struthers *(G-17818)*
Knight Manufacturing Co Inc ..... G 740 676-5516
Shadyside *(G-16923)*
Korda Manufacturing Inc ..... D 330 262-1555
Wooster *(G-20615)*
Kramer Power Equipment Co ..... F 937 456-2232
Eaton *(G-9157)*
Kuhlman Engineering Co ..... F 419 243-2196
Toledo *(G-18371)*
Kuhn Fabricating Inc ..... G 440 277-4182
Lorain *(G-12098)*
L C Systems Inc ..... G 614 235-9430
Dublin *(G-8940)*
L&M Sheet Metal Ltd ..... G 513 858-6173
Fairfield *(G-9521)*
◆ **Lake Shore Electric Corp** ..... E 440 232-0200
Bedford *(G-1422)*
Lambert Sheet Metal Inc ..... F 614 237-0384
Columbus *(G-7111)*
▲ **Langdon Inc** ..... E 513 733-5955
Cincinnati *(G-3930)*
Lima Sheet Metal Machine & Mfg ..... E 419 229-1161
Lima *(G-11893)*
Locker Konnection Services LLC ..... G 419 334-3956
Fremont *(G-10036)*
▲ **Long-Stanton Mfg Company** ..... E 513 874-8020
West Chester *(G-19738)*

S I C

Employee Codes: A=Over 500 employees, B=251-500
C=101-250, D=51-100, E=20-50, F=10-19, G=3-9
2019 Harris Ohio
Industrial Directory
927

34 FABRICATED METAL PRODUCTS, EXCEPT MACHINERY AND TRANSPORTATION EQUIPMENT

Louis Arthur Steel Company ....G..... 440 997-5545
  Geneva *(G-10224)*
Louis Arthur Steel Company ....G..... 440 997-5545
  Uniontown *(G-18926)*
Lowry Furnace Company Inc ....G..... 330 745-4822
  Akron *(G-260)*
LSI Industries Inc ....E..... 513 793-3200
  Blue Ash *(G-1808)*
▲ Lt Enterprises of Ohio LLC ....E..... 330 526-6908
  North Canton *(G-15099)*
Lukjan Metal Products Inc ....G..... 440 599-8127
  Conneaut *(G-7654)*
Lund Equipment Co Inc ....E..... 330 659-4800
  Bath *(G-1201)*
M H EBY Inc ....E..... 614 879-6901
  West Jefferson *(G-19925)*
M3 Technologies Inc ....F..... 216 898-9936
  Cleveland *(G-5596)*
Mack Iron Works Company ....E..... 419 626-3712
  Sandusky *(G-16826)*
Magnode Corporation ....D..... 317 243-3553
  Trenton *(G-18624)*
Maines Brothers Tin Shop ....G..... 937 393-1633
  Hillsboro *(G-10885)*
Mantych Metalworking Inc ....G..... 937 258-1373
  Dayton *(G-7984)*
Marsam Metalfab Inc ....E..... 330 405-1520
  Twinsburg *(G-18811)*
Martina Metal LLC ....E..... 614 291-9700
  Columbus *(G-7155)*
Matandy Steel & Metal Pdts LLC ....D..... 513 844-2277
  Hamilton *(G-10585)*
Matteo Aluminum Inc ....E..... 440 585-5213
  Wickliffe *(G-20217)*
McGill Airflow LLC ....F..... 614 829-1200
  Columbus *(G-7164)*
▼ McGill Airflow LLC ....G..... 614 829-1200
  Groveport *(G-10503)*
◆ McGill Corporation ....F..... 614 829-1200
  Groveport *(G-10504)*
McWane Inc ....B..... 740 622-6651
  Coshocton *(G-7739)*
Medway Tool Corp ....E..... 937 335-7717
  Troy *(G-18687)*
Meese Inc ....D..... 440 998-1202
  Ashtabula *(G-785)*
Mestek Inc ....D..... 419 288-2703
  Holland *(G-10944)*
Mestek Inc ....D..... 419 288-2703
  Bradner *(G-2015)*
Met-L-Fab Inc ....F..... 513 561-4289
  Cincinnati *(G-4010)*
Metal Fabricating Corporation ....D..... 216 631-8121
  Cleveland *(G-5658)*
Metal Sales Manufacturing Corp ....E..... 440 319-3779
  Jefferson *(G-11234)*
▼ Metal Seal Precision Ltd ....D..... 440 255-8888
  Mentor *(G-13517)*
Metal Seal Precision Ltd ....C..... 440 255-8888
  Willoughby *(G-20380)*
Metal Technology Systems Inc ....E..... 513 563-1882
  Cincinnati *(G-4012)*
Metal-Max Inc ....G..... 330 673-9926
  Kent *(G-11352)*
▲ Metalworking Group Holdings .....E..... 513 521-4119
  Cincinnati *(G-4014)*
Metlweb ....E..... 513 563-8822
  Cincinnati *(G-4016)*
Metrodeck Inc ....F..... 513 541-4370
  Cincinnati *(G-4018)*
Michael Fabricating Inc ....G..... 330 325-8636
  Rootstown *(G-16570)*
▲ Mid-Ohio Products Inc ....D..... 614 771-2795
  Hilliard *(G-10840)*
Midwest Fabrications Inc ....E..... 330 633-0191
  Tallmadge *(G-17993)*
Midwest Metal Fabricators ....F..... 419 739-7077
  Wapakoneta *(G-19344)*
Midwest Metal Fabricators ....F..... 419 739-7077
  Wapakoneta *(G-19345)*
Midwest Spray Booths ....G..... 937 439-6600
  Dayton *(G-8355)*
Mika Metal Fabricating Co ....E..... 440 951-5500
  Willoughby *(G-20382)*
Mike Loppe ....F..... 937 969-8102
  Tremont City *(G-18616)*
Milton West Fabricators Inc ....G..... 937 547-3069
  Greenville *(G-10382)*
Mings Heating & AC ....G..... 216 721-2007
  Cleveland *(G-5693)*

◆ Modern Ice Equipment & Sup Co ...E..... 513 367-2101
  Cincinnati *(G-4038)*
Modern Manufacturing Inc ....F..... 513 251-3600
  Cincinnati *(G-4039)*
Modern Sheet Metal Works Inc ....E..... 513 353-3666
  Miamitown *(G-13749)*
Mor-Lite Co Inc ....G..... 513 661-8587
  Cincinnati *(G-4045)*
▲ MRS Industrial Inc ....E..... 614 308-1070
  Columbus *(G-7199)*
Muehlenkamp Properties Inc ....G..... 513 745-0874
  Cincinnati *(G-4053)*
◆ N Wasserstrom & Sons Inc ....C..... 614 228-5550
  Columbus *(G-7206)*
Nel-Ack Sheet Metal Inc ....G..... 440 357-7844
  Painesville *(G-15765)*
Niles Manufacturing & Finshg ....G..... 330 544-0402
  Niles *(G-15024)*
▲ Nissin Precision N Amer Inc ....D..... 937 836-1910
  Englewood *(G-9372)*
Norstar Aluminum Molds Inc ....G..... 440 632-0853
  Middlefield *(G-13841)*
North Coast Profile Inc ....G..... 330 823-7777
  Alliance *(G-493)*
North Star Metals Mfg Co ....F..... 740 254-4567
  Uhrichsville *(G-18891)*
Northwest Installations Inc ....E..... 419 423-5738
  Findlay *(G-9732)*
Northwind Industries Inc ....E..... 216 433-0666
  Cleveland *(G-5787)*
Nufab Sheet Metal ....G..... 937 235-2030
  Dayton *(G-8391)*
▲ Oatey Supply Chain Svcs Inc ......C..... 216 267-7100
  Cleveland *(G-5795)*
Obr Cooling Towers Inc ....E..... 419 243-3443
  Rossford *(G-16588)*
Ohio Blow Pipe Company ....E..... 216 681-7379
  Cleveland *(G-5801)*
Ohio Fabricators Inc ....E..... 216 391-2400
  Akron *(G-306)*
◆ Ohio Gratings Inc ....B..... 330 477-6707
  Canton *(G-2772)*
Ohio Steel Sheet & Plate Inc ....E..... 800 827-2401
  Hubbard *(G-11007)*
Ohio Trailer Inc ....F..... 330 392-4444
  Warren *(G-19428)*
▼ Options Plus Incorporated ....F..... 740 694-9811
  Fredericktown *(G-9975)*
Owens Corning Sales LLC ....G..... 740 983-1300
  Ashville *(G-819)*
▲ P & L Metalcrafts LLC ....E..... 330 793-2178
  Youngstown *(G-20987)*
P B Fabrication Mech Contr ....F..... 419 478-4869
  Toledo *(G-18454)*
Paint Booth Pros Inc ....G..... 440 653-3982
  Amherst *(G-569)*
Parker-Hannifin Corporation ....F..... 330 336-3511
  Wadsworth *(G-19262)*
Patio Room Factory Inc ....G..... 614 449-7900
  Columbus *(G-7296)*
Patterson & Sons Inc ....F..... 419 281-0897
  Nova *(G-15435)*
Paul Wilke & Son Inc ....F..... 513 921-3163
  Cincinnati *(G-4141)*
Pcy Enterprises Inc ....E..... 513 241-5566
  Cincinnati *(G-4143)*
Pennant Moldings Inc ....C..... 937 584-5411
  Sabina *(G-16617)*
Phillips Awning Co ....F..... 740 653-2433
  Lancaster *(G-11596)*
Phillips Manufacturing Co ....D..... 330 652-4335
  Niles *(G-15026)*
▲ Phillips Shtmtl Fabrications ....G..... 937 223-2722
  Dayton *(G-8423)*
Pioneer Fabrication ....G..... 419 737-9464
  Alvordton *(G-521)*
Plas-Tanks Industries Inc ....E..... 513 942-3800
  Hamilton *(G-10596)*
Precise Metal Form Inc ....F..... 419 636-5221
  Bryan *(G-2305)*
Precision Mtal Fabrication Inc ....D..... 937 235-9261
  Dayton *(G-8434)*
Precision Steel Services Inc ....D..... 419 476-5702
  Toledo *(G-18479)*
Precision Welding Corporation ....E..... 216 524-6910
  Cleveland *(G-5912)*
Premier Stamping and Assembly ......G..... 440 293-8961
  Williamsfield *(G-20259)*
Priest Millwright Service ....G..... 937 780-3405
  Leesburg *(G-11715)*

Prototype Fabricators Company ....F..... 216 252-0080
  Cleveland *(G-5931)*
Quality Craftsman Inc ....F..... 740 474-9685
  Circleville *(G-4555)*
Quality Steel Fabrication ....F..... 937 492-9503
  Sidney *(G-17063)*
Quass Sheet Metal Inc ....G..... 330 477-4841
  Canton *(G-2798)*
R & S Sheet Metal LLC ....G..... 330 857-0225
  Dalton *(G-7952)*
◆ R B Mfg Co ....F..... 419 626-9464
  Wadsworth *(G-19270)*
R L Torbeck Industries Inc ....D..... 513 367-0080
  Harrison *(G-10667)*
Raka Corporation ....D..... 419 476-6572
  Toledo *(G-18498)*
Range One Products & Fabg ....G..... 330 533-1151
  Canfield *(G-2542)*
Rapid Machine Inc ....F..... 419 737-2377
  Pioneer *(G-16094)*
Related Metals Inc ....G..... 330 799-4866
  Canfield *(G-2543)*
Rex Burnett ....G..... 740 927-4669
  Etna *(G-9397)*
Rezmann Karoly ....F..... 216 441-4357
  Cleveland *(G-5982)*
Ridgeview Sheet Metal ....G..... 330 674-3768
  Millersburg *(G-14123)*
▲ Robinson Fin Machines Inc ....E..... 419 674-4152
  Kenton *(G-11421)*
▲ Rockwell Metals Company LLC ...F..... 440 242-2420
  Lorain *(G-12118)*
Roconex Corporation ....F..... 937 339-2616
  Troy *(G-18699)*
Romar Metal Fabricating Inc ....G..... 740 682-7731
  Oak Hill *(G-15460)*
Roofing Annex LLC ....G..... 513 942-0555
  West Chester *(G-19895)*
Royalton Archtctral Fbrication ....F..... 440 582-0400
  North Royalton *(G-15298)*
▼ S & B Metal Products Inc ....E..... 330 487-5790
  Twinsburg *(G-18852)*
S & D Architectural Metals ....G..... 440 582-2560
  North Royalton *(G-15301)*
S & G Manufacturing Group LLC ......C..... 614 529-0100
  Hilliard *(G-10859)*
S & R Sheet Metal ....G..... 937 865-9236
  Dayton *(G-8489)*
S L M Inc ....G..... 216 651-0666
  Cleveland *(G-6022)*
Salsbury Industries Inc ....C..... 614 409-1600
  Columbus *(G-7417)*
Samuel Clark ....F..... 614 855-2263
  New Albany *(G-14636)*
Sarka Shtmtl & Fabrication Inc ....E..... 419 447-4377
  Tiffin *(G-18080)*
▲ Sausser Steel Company Inc ....F..... 419 422-9632
  Findlay *(G-9752)*
Scharenberg Sheet Metal ....G..... 740 664-2431
  New Marshfield *(G-14744)*
Schoonover Industries Inc ....E..... 419 289-8332
  Ashland *(G-747)*
Schweizer Dipple Inc ....D..... 440 786-8090
  Cleveland *(G-6034)*
Scott Fetzer Company ....C..... 216 267-9000
  Cleveland *(G-6035)*
Selmco Metal Fabricators Inc ....F..... 937 498-1331
  Sidney *(G-17075)*
Seneca Sheet Metal Company ....F..... 419 447-8434
  Tiffin *(G-18083)*
Shade Youngstown & Aluminum Co ...G..... 330 782-2373
  Youngstown *(G-21028)*
◆ Shadetree Systems LLC ....F..... 614 844-5990
  Columbus *(G-7443)*
Shaffer Metal Fab Inc ....E..... 937 492-1384
  Sidney *(G-17076)*
Shape Supply Inc ....G..... 513 863-6695
  Hamilton *(G-10604)*
Sheet Metal Products Co Inc ....E..... 440 392-9000
  Mentor *(G-13581)*
▼ Sheffield Metals Cleveland LLC ...F..... 800 283-5262
  Sheffield Village *(G-16975)*
Shriner Sheet Metal Inc ....F..... 330 435-6735
  Creston *(G-7809)*
▲ Siata Ds Inc ....G..... 216 503-7200
  Beachwood *(G-1278)*
▼ Sidney Manufacturing Company ...E..... 937 492-4154
  Sidney *(G-17079)*
Smith Rn Sheet Metal Shop Inc ....E..... 740 653-5011
  Lancaster *(G-11609)*

Snair Co ....F 614 873-7020
Plain City *(G-16212)*
Somerville Manufacturing Inc ....E 740 336-7847
Marietta *(G-12674)*
Spradlin Bros Welding Co ....F 800 219-2182
Springfield *(G-17493)*
Ss Metal Fabricators Inc ....G 937 226-9957
Dayton *(G-8522)*
▲ **Staber Industries Inc** ....E 614 836-5995
Groveport *(G-10513)*
Standard Technologies LLC ....D 419 332-6434
Fremont *(G-10051)*
Starr Fabricating Inc ....D 330 394-9891
Vienna *(G-19210)*
▼ **Steel & Alloy Utility Pdts Inc** ....E 330 530-2220
Mc Donald *(G-13202)*
Steelial Wldg Met Fbrction Inc ....E 740 669-5300
Vinton *(G-19216)*
Steeltec Products LLC ....E 216 681-1114
Cleveland *(G-6103)*
Steve Vore Welding and Steel ....F 419 375-4087
Fort Recovery *(G-9827)*
Suburban Metal Products Inc ....F 740 474-4237
Circleville *(G-4559)*
Sulecki Precision Products ....F 440 255-5454
Mentor *(G-13596)*
Super Sheet Metal ....G 330 482-9045
Leetonia *(G-11722)*
Superior Metal Worx LLC ....F 614 879-9400
Columbus *(G-7501)*
Swanton Wldg Machining Co Inc ....D 419 826-4816
Swanton *(G-17923)*
Systech Handling Inc ....F 419 445-8226
Archbold *(G-670)*
Tangent Air Inc ....E 740 474-1114
Circleville *(G-4560)*
▲ **Technibus Inc** ....D 330 479-4202
Canton *(G-2833)*
▼ **Tectum Inc** ....C 740 345-9691
Newark *(G-14929)*
Tendon Manufacturing Inc ....E 216 663-3200
Cleveland *(G-6159)*
Tex-Tyler Corporation ....E 419 729-4951
Toledo *(G-18548)*
▲ **Thermo Vent Manufacturing Inc** ....F 330 239-0239
Medina *(G-13351)*
Tilton Corporation ....C 419 227-6421
Lima *(G-11952)*
Tkr Metal Fabricating LLC ....G 440 221-2770
Willoughby *(G-20448)*
TL Industries Inc ....C 419 666-8144
Northwood *(G-15346)*
Toledo Window & Awning Inc ....G 419 474-3396
Toledo *(G-18575)*
Tool & Die Systems Inc ....E 440 327-5800
North Ridgeville *(G-15256)*
Torok Supply Company ....G 330 799-6677
Youngstown *(G-21047)*
Tower Tool & Manufacturing Co ....F 330 425-1623
Twinsburg *(G-18864)*
Transtar Holding Company ....G 800 359-3339
Walton Hills *(G-19315)*
Tri-Fab Inc ....E 330 337-3425
Salem *(G-16777)*
Tri-Mac Mfg & Svcs Co ....F 513 896-4445
Hamilton *(G-10613)*
Tri-State Fabricators Inc ....E 513 752-5005
Amelia *(G-550)*
Triangle Precision Industries ....D 937 299-6776
Dayton *(G-8564)*
◆ **Tricor Industrial Inc** ....D 330 264-3299
Wooster *(G-20660)*
Tru Form Metal Products Inc ....G 216 252-3700
Cleveland *(G-6217)*
Unison Industries LLC ....D 937 426-4676
Alpha *(G-518)*
▲ **United McGill Corporation** ....E 614 829-1200
Groveport *(G-10516)*
▲ **Universal Steel Company** ....D 216 883-4972
Cleveland *(G-6240)*
Upside Innovations LLC ....G 513 889-2492
West Chester *(G-19912)*
V & S Schuler Engineering Inc ....D 330 452-5200
Canton *(G-2855)*
V M Systems Inc ....D 419 535-1044
Toledo *(G-18587)*
Valley Metal Works Inc ....E 513 554-1022
Cincinnati *(G-4464)*
Varmland Inc ....F 216 741-1510
Cleveland *(G-6251)*
Verhoff Machine & Welding Inc ....C 419 596-3202
Continental *(G-7669)*
Vicart Prcsion Fabricators Inc ....E 614 771-0080
Hilliard *(G-10874)*
Visual Information Institute ....F 937 376-4361
Xenia *(G-20801)*
W & W Custom Fabrication Inc ....G 513 353-4617
Hamilton *(G-10619)*
▼ **W J Egli Company Inc** ....F 330 823-3666
Alliance *(G-512)*
Waino Sheet Metal Inc ....G 330 945-4226
Stow *(G-17642)*
Warner Fabricating Inc ....F 330 848-3191
Wadsworth *(G-19280)*
◆ **Warren Fabricating Corporation** ....D 330 534-5017
Hubbard *(G-11011)*
Waterville Sheet Metal Company ....G 419 878-5050
Waterville *(G-19508)*
Weber Technologies Inc ....E 440 946-8833
Eastlake *(G-9140)*
Westwood Fvrication Shtmtl Inc ....E 937 837-0494
Dayton *(G-8591)*
Wheeler Sheet Metal Inc ....G 419 668-0481
Norwalk *(G-15417)*
▲ **Will-Burt Company** ....B 330 682-7015
Orrville *(G-15626)*
Wolf Metals Inc ....G 614 461-6361
Columbus *(G-7608)*
Worthington Steel Company ....G 513 702-0130
Middletown *(G-13969)*
▲ **Ysd Industries Inc** ....D 330 792-6521
Youngstown *(G-21086)*
Z Line Kitchen and Bath LLC ....F 614 777-5004
Marysville *(G-12819)*

3446 Architectural & Ornamental Metal Work

A & E Butscha Co ....G 513 761-1919
Cincinnati *(G-3275)*
▲ **A & G Manufacturing Co Inc** ....E 419 468-7433
Galion *(G-10119)*
A & T Ornamental Iron Company ....G 937 859-6006
Miamisburg *(G-13635)*
▲ **Agratronix LLC** ....E 330 562-2222
Streetsboro *(G-17657)*
Akron Products Company ....F 330 576-1750
Wadsworth *(G-19223)*
All Ohio Companies Inc ....F 216 420-9274
Cleveland *(G-4664)*
Annin & Co ....D 740 622-4447
Coshocton *(G-7718)*
Armor Consolidated Inc ....G 513 923-5260
Mason *(G-12826)*
▲ **Armor Group Inc** ....C 513 923-5260
Mason *(G-12827)*
▲ **Armor Metal Group Mason Inc** ....C 513 769-0700
Mason *(G-12828)*
Art Fremont Iron Co ....G 419 332-5554
Fremont *(G-9992)*
▲ **AT&f Advanced Metals LLC** ....E 330 684-1122
Cleveland *(G-4756)*
Autogate Inc ....E 419 588-2796
Berlin Heights *(G-1652)*
Bauer Corporation ....E 800 321-4760
Wooster *(G-20569)*
Beacon Metal Fabricators Inc ....F 216 391-7444
Cleveland *(G-4798)*
Blevins Metal Fabrication Inc ....E 419 522-6082
Mansfield *(G-12412)*
Brown-Campbell Company ....F 216 332-0101
Maple Heights *(G-12567)*
Cappco Tubular Products Inc ....G 216 641-2218
North Olmsted *(G-15183)*
Chc Manufacturing Inc ....E 513 821-7757
Cincinnati *(G-3467)*
Chc Manufacturing Inc ....G 614 527-1606
Columbus *(G-6759)*
City Iron LLC ....G 513 721-5678
Cincinnati *(G-3521)*
Cozmyk Enterprises Inc ....F 614 231-1370
Columbus *(G-6832)*
Cramers Inc ....E 330 477-4571
Canton *(G-2638)*
Debra-Kuempel Inc ....D 513 271-6500
Cincinnati *(G-3579)*
Decor Architectural Products ....G 419 537-9493
Toledo *(G-18258)*
Dover Tank and Plate Company ....E 330 343-4443
Dover *(G-8823)*
E B P Inc ....E 216 241-2550
Cleveland *(G-5128)*
E C S Corp ....F 440 323-1707
Elyria *(G-9247)*
Enginetics Corporation ....F 440 946-8833
Eastlake *(G-9107)*
Federal Iron Works Company ....E 330 482-5910
Columbiana *(G-6465)*
Final Touch Metal Fabricating ....G 216 348-1750
Cleveland *(G-5238)*
Finelli Ornamental Iron Co ....F 440 248-0050
Cleveland *(G-5240)*
Fortin Welding & Mfg Inc ....E 614 291-4342
Columbus *(G-6932)*
Friends Ornamental Iron Co ....G 216 431-6710
Cleveland *(G-5275)*
Geist Co Inc ....F 216 771-2200
Cleveland *(G-5300)*
Gem City Metal Tech LLC ....E 937 252-8998
Dayton *(G-8220)*
Gem Ornamental Iron Co ....G 216 661-6965
Cleveland *(G-5302)*
GL Nause Co Inc ....E 513 722-9500
Loveland *(G-12192)*
Glas Ornamental Metals Inc ....G 330 753-0215
Barberton *(G-1074)*
Graber Metal Works Inc ....E 440 237-8422
North Royalton *(G-15274)*
◆ **Granite Industries Inc** ....D 419 445-4733
Archbold *(G-651)*
Greene Street Wholesale LLC ....G 740 374-5206
Marietta *(G-12628)*
▲ **Gwp Holdings Inc** ....D 513 860-4050
Fairfield *(G-9501)*
Hansen Scaffolding LLC ....F 513 574-9000
West Chester *(G-19863)*
Harsco Corporation ....E 740 387-1150
Marion *(G-12710)*
Hart & Cooley Inc ....C 937 832-7800
Englewood *(G-9361)*
Hayes Bros Ornamental Ir Works ....F 419 531-1491
Toledo *(G-18324)*
Hrh Door Corp ....C 330 828-2291
Dalton *(G-7943)*
Indian Creek Fabricators Inc ....E 937 667-7214
Tipp City *(G-18116)*
J N Linrose Mfg LLC ....G 513 867-5500
Hamilton *(G-10574)*
J S Stairs ....G 440 632-5680
Middlefield *(G-13809)*
James L Wereb ....G 440 942-2405
Willoughby *(G-20347)*
Jason Incorporated ....F 513 860-3400
Hamilton *(G-10576)*
Jerry Harolds Doors Unlimited ....G 740 635-4949
Bridgeport *(G-2076)*
Jim Denigris & Sons Ldscpg ....G 440 449-5548
Cleveland *(G-5499)*
Joyce Manufacturing Co ....D 440 239-9100
Berea *(G-1615)*
L & L Ornamental Iron Co ....F 513 353-1930
Cleves *(G-6369)*
Lakeway Mfg Inc ....E 419 433-3030
Huron *(G-11103)*
▲ **Langdon Inc** ....E 513 733-5955
Cincinnati *(G-3930)*
Lifetime Ironworks LLC ....G 419 443-0567
Tiffin *(G-18065)*
M F Y Inc ....F 330 747-1334
Youngstown *(G-20963)*
M M I Services Inc ....F 440 259-2939
Perry *(G-15908)*
Mack Iron Works Company ....E 419 626-3712
Sandusky *(G-16826)*
▲ **Mataco** ....G 440 546-8355
Broadview Heights *(G-2096)*
Metal Craft Docks Inc ....G 440 286-7135
Painesville *(G-15763)*
Metal Maintenance Inc ....F 513 661-3300
Cleves *(G-6370)*
Michaels Pre-Cast Con Pdts ....F 513 683-1292
Loveland *(G-12215)*
Modern Builders Supply Inc ....C 419 241-3961
Toledo *(G-18414)*
◆ **Momentive Prfmce Mtls Qrtz Inc** ....C 440 878-5700
Strongsville *(G-17765)*
Mound Technologies Inc ....E 937 748-2937
Springboro *(G-17338)*
National Stair Corp ....E 937 325-1347
Springfield *(G-17455)*
Newman Brothers Inc ....E 513 242-0011
Cincinnati *(G-4074)*

S I C

Employee Codes: A=Over 500 employees, B=251-500
C=101-250, D=51-100, E=20-50, F=10-19, G=3-9

34 FABRICATED METAL PRODUCTS, EXCEPT MACHINERY AND TRANSPORTATION EQUIPMENT

Nu Risers Stair Company .... F 937 322-8100
  Springfield *(G-17462)*
◆ Ohio Gratings Inc 330 477-6707
  Canton *(G-2772)*
One Wish LLC .... F 800 505-6883
  Beachwood *(G-1259)*
▲ P & L Metalcrafts LLC .... F 330 793-2178
  Youngstown *(G-20987)*
Phase II Enterprises Inc 330 484-2113
  Canton *(G-2784)*
Quality Architectural and Fabr .... F 937 743-2923
  Franklin *(G-9912)*
Quality Security Door & Mfg Co ..... G 440 246-0770
  Lorain *(G-12114)*
Randy Lewis Inc 330 784-0456
  Akron *(G-342)*
Rezmann Karoly .... G 216 441-4357
  Cleveland *(G-5982)*
Royalton Archtctral Fbrication .... F 440 582-0400
  North Royalton *(G-15298)*
Rural Iron Works LLC 419 647-4617
  Spencerville *(G-17313)*
▲ Sausser Steel Company Inc .... F 419 422-9632
  Findlay *(G-9752)*
Schwab Welding Inc .... G 513 353-4262
  Cincinnati *(G-4308)*
Sewah Studios Inc .... F 740 373-2087
  Marietta *(G-12666)*
Sine Wall LLC .... G 919 453-2011
  West Chester *(G-19796)*
◆ Sky Climber LLC .... E 740 203-3900
  Delaware *(G-8725)*
Southern Ornamental Iron Co .... G 937 278-4319
  Dayton *(G-8512)*
▲ Spallinger Millwright Svc Co ...... D 419 225-5830
  Lima *(G-11942)*
◆ Spillman Company .... E 614 444-2184
  Columbus *(G-7476)*
Stephens Pipe & Steel LLC .... C 740 869-2257
  Mount Sterling *(G-14465)*
Swanton Wldg Machining Co Inc .... D 419 826-4816
  Swanton *(G-17923)*
T E Martindale Enterprises .... E 614 253-6826
  Columbus *(G-7507)*
Tarrier Steel Company Inc .... E 614 444-4000
  Columbus *(G-7514)*
Tim Calvin Access Controls .... G 740 494-4200
  Radnor *(G-16359)*
Triangle Precision Industries .... D 937 299-6776
  Dayton *(G-8564)*
Upright Steel LLC .... E 216 923-0852
  Cleveland *(G-6242)*
Upside Innovations LLC .... G 513 889-2492
  West Chester *(G-19912)*
Van Dyke Custom Iron Inc .... G 614 860-9300
  Columbus *(G-7571)*
Viking Fabricators Inc .... E 740 374-5246
  Marietta *(G-12687)*
Wall Technology Inc .... E 715 532-5548
  Toledo *(G-18594)*
Wanner Metal Worx Inc 740 369-4034
  Delaware *(G-8730)*
▼ Wooster Products Inc .... D 330 264-2844
  Wooster *(G-20669)*
Wooster Products Inc 330 264-2844
  Wooster *(G-20670)*
Wooster Products Inc .... G 330 264-2854
  Wooster *(G-20671)*
Worthington Cnstr Group Inc .... G 216 472-1511
  Cleveland *(G-6326)*
Worthington Mid-Rise Cnstr Inc .... E 216 472-1511
  Cleveland *(G-6327)*
Wright Brothers Inc .... E 513 731-2222
  Cincinnati *(G-4520)*

3448 Prefabricated Metal Buildings & Cmpnts

Affordable Barn Co Ltd .... F 330 674-3001
  Millersburg *(G-14055)*
American Tower Acquisition .... F 419 347-1185
  Shelby *(G-16977)*
Barncraft Storage Buildings 513 738-5654
  Hamilton *(G-10537)*
▲ Benchmark Archtectural Systems .. E 614 444-0110
  Columbus *(G-6662)*
▼ Benko Products Inc .... E 440 934-2180
  Sheffield Village *(G-16966)*
Better Built Barns .... G 606 348-6146
  Winchester *(G-20518)*
Better Living Sunrooms NW Ohio .... G 419 692-4526
  Delphos *(G-8737)*
Cdc Fab Co .... F 419 866-7705
  Maumee *(G-13082)*
Commercial Dock & Door Inc .... E 440 951-1210
  Mentor *(G-13419)*
Consoldted Grnhse Slutions LLC .... G 330 844-8598
  Strongsville *(G-17732)*
Consolidatd Analytical Sys Inc ...... F 513 542-1200
  Cleves *(G-6359)*
Cover Up Building Systems 740 668-8985
  Martinsburg *(G-12765)*
◆ Cropking Incorporated .... F 330 302-4203
  Lodi *(G-12009)*
▲ Enclosure Suppliers LLC .... E 513 782-3900
  Cincinnati *(G-3637)*
Genesis Services LLC .... G 740 896-3734
  Beverly *(G-1661)*
Golden Giant Inc .... E 419 674-4038
  Kenton *(G-11405)*
Great Day Improvements LLC 330 468-0700
  Macedonia *(G-12300)*
Haz-Safe LLC .... F 330 793-0900
  Austintown *(G-933)*
◆ Hoge Lumber Company .... E 419 753-2263
  New Knoxville *(G-14703)*
Homecare Mattress Inc .... F 937 746-2556
  Franklin *(G-9889)*
Jack Walters & Sons Corp 937 653-8986
  Urbana *(G-18999)*
▼ Jet Dock Systems Inc .... E 216 750-2264
  Cleveland *(G-5497)*
Jh Industries Inc 330 963-4105
  Twinsburg *(G-18797)*
Joyce Manufacturing Co .... D 440 239-9100
  Berea *(G-1615)*
Lab-Pro Inc .... G 937 434-9600
  Dayton *(G-8304)*
Ludy Greenhouse Mfg Corp .... D 800 255-5839
  New Madison *(G-14742)*
Metal Craft Docks Inc 440 286-7135
  Painesville *(G-15763)*
Mobile Mini Inc 303 305-9515
  Canton *(G-2756)*
Mobile Mini Inc .... F 614 449-8655
  Columbus *(G-7188)*
Morton Buildings Inc 330 345-6188
  Wooster *(G-20628)*
Morton Buildings Inc .... G 419 399-4549
  Paulding *(G-15866)*
Morton Buildings Inc .... D 419 675-2311
  Kenton *(G-11415)*
Nci Building Systems Inc .... C 937 584-3300
  Middletown *(G-13936)*
ONeals Tarpaulin & Awning Co ..... F 330 788-6504
  Youngstown *(G-20985)*
Otter Group LLC .... F 937 315-1199
  Dayton *(G-8410)*
Overhead Door Corporation .... F 419 294-3874
  Upper Sandusky *(G-18970)*
Patton Aluminum Products Inc ..... F 937 845-9404
  New Carlisle *(G-14676)*
Pioneer Cldding Glzing Systems .... E 216 816-4242
  Cleveland *(G-5879)*
R L Torbeck Industries Inc .... D 513 367-0080
  Harrison *(G-10667)*
Rayhaven Group Inc .... F 330 659-3183
  Richfield *(G-16484)*
Rebsco Inc .... F 937 548-2246
  Greenville *(G-10390)*
Reliable Metal Buildings LLC .... G 419 737-1300
  Fremont *(G-16096)*
◆ Rough Brothers Mfg Inc .... D 513 242-0310
  Cincinnati *(G-4283)*
Rupcol Inc .... G 419 924-5215
  West Unity *(G-19974)*
Shrock Prefab LLC .... F 740 599-9401
  Danville *(G-7965)*
Skyline Corporation .... C 330 852-2483
  Sugarcreek *(G-17864)*
Sorta 4 U LLC .... G 440 365-0091
  Elyria *(G-9330)*
St Marys Iron Works Inc .... F 419 300-6300
  Saint Marys *(G-16702)*
Storage Buildings Unlimited .... G 216 731-0010
  Doylestown *(G-8866)*
Superior Structures Inc .... F 513 942-5954
  Harrison *(G-10674)*
Upside Innovations LLC .... G 513 889-2492
  West Chester *(G-19912)*
Vinyl Tech Storage Barn .... G 330 674-5670
  Millersburg *(G-14143)*
Will-Burt Advnced Cmpsites Inc .... F 330 684-5286
  Orrville *(G-15625)*
Wyse Industrial Carts Inc .... F 419 923-7353
  Wauseon *(G-19539)*
XS Smith Inc .... E 252 940-5060
  Cincinnati *(G-4529)*

3449 Misc Structural Metal Work

Action Group Inc .... D 614 868-8868
  Blacklick *(G-1676)*
Advance Industrial Mfg Inc 614 871-3333
  Grove City *(G-10411)*
▲ Akron Rebar Co 330 745-7100
  Akron *(G-50)*
Alpha Control LLC .... E 740 377-3400
  South Point *(G-17278)*
▼ American Roll Formed Pdts Corp .... C 440 352-0753
  Youngstown *(G-20843)*
Architctral Rfuse Slutions LLC ...... G 330 733-3996
  Akron *(G-69)*
Arrow Tru-Line Inc 419 636-7013
  Bryan *(G-2265)*
Austintown Metal Works Inc .... F 330 259-4673
  Youngstown *(G-20848)*
BMA Metals Group Inc .... G 513 874-5152
  West Chester *(G-19661)*
Bridge Components Incorporated .... G 614 873-0777
  Columbus *(G-6697)*
Buckeye Stamping Company .... D 614 445-0059
  Columbus *(G-6712)*
Burghardt Metal Fabg Inc .... F 330 794-1830
  Akron *(G-99)*
CMF Custom Metal Finishers .... G 513 821-8145
  Cincinnati *(G-3532)*
Custom Control Tech LLC 419 342-5593
  Shelby *(G-16981)*
Ej Usa Inc .... F 330 782-3900
  Youngstown *(G-20898)*
Fabrication Group LLC 216 251-1125
  Cleveland *(G-5213)*
Falcon Fab and Finishes LLC .... G 740 820-4458
  Lucasville *(G-12263)*
Formasters Corporation .... F 440 639-9206
  Mentor *(G-13445)*
Fortin Welding & Mfg Inc .... E 614 291-4342
  Columbus *(G-6932)*
▲ Foundation Systems Anchors Inc .... F 330 454-1700
  Canton *(G-2675)*
Friesingers Inc 740 452-9480
  Zanesville *(G-21139)*
Gateway Concrete Forming Svcs .... D 513 353-2000
  Miamitown *(G-13746)*
Genesis Services LLC .... G 740 896-3734
  Beverly *(G-1661)*
Hartford Steel Sales .... G 513 275-1744
  Hamilton *(G-10570)*
Harvey Brothers Inc .... F 513 541-2622
  Cincinnati *(G-3800)*
Harvey Miller .... G 440 834-9125
  Burton *(G-2359)*
▲ Hynes Industries Inc .... C 330 799-3221
  Youngstown *(G-20934)*
J & L Welding Fabricating Inc .... F 330 393-9353
  Warren *(G-19412)*
Lion Industries LLC .... E 740 699-0369
  Saint Clairsville *(G-16636)*
Lwr Enterprises Inc .... G 740 984-0036
  Waterford *(G-19487)*
▲ Markley Enterprises LLC .... E 513 771-1290
  Cincinnati *(G-3982)*
Matteo Aluminum Inc .... E 440 585-5213
  Wickliffe *(G-20217)*
Metal Sales Manufacturing Corp .... E 440 319-3779
  Jefferson *(G-11234)*
Metrodeck Inc .... F 513 541-4370
  Cincinnati *(G-4018)*
Midwest Curtainwalls Inc .... D 216 641-7900
  Cleveland *(G-5680)*
Mound Steel Corp .... E 937 748-2937
  Springboro *(G-17337)*
Nova Metal Products Inc .... E 440 269-1741
  Eastlake *(G-9127)*
▼ Ohio Bridge Corporation .... C 740 432-6334
  Cambridge *(G-2451)*
Omco Holdings Inc .... E 440 944-2100
  Wickliffe *(G-20220)*
Ontario Mechanical LLC .... E 419 529-2578
  Ontario *(G-15544)*

SIC SECTION 34 FABRICATED METAL PRODUCTS, EXCEPT MACHINERY AND TRANSPORTATION EQUIPMENT

Scs Construction Services Inc.............E....... 513 929-0260
Cincinnati *(G-4311)*
Simcote Inc...E....... 740 382-5000
Marion *(G-12736)*
Skinner Sales Group Inc.......................E....... 440 572-8455
Medina *(G-13344)*
Smith Brothers Erection Inc.................E....... 740 373-3575
Marietta *(G-12671)*
Steel Structures of Ohio LLC...............E....... 330 374-9900
Akron *(G-388)*
Superior Steel Service LLC...................F....... 513 724-0437
Batavia *(G-1188)*
T J F Inc..F....... 419 878-4400
Waterville *(G-19506)*
Tallmadge Spinning & Metal Co...........F....... 330 794-2277
Akron *(G-395)*
Trulite GL Alum Solutions LLC.............D....... 614 876-1057
Columbus *(G-7548)*
Ventari Corporation...............................E....... 937 278-4269
Miamisburg *(G-13731)*
▲ **Ver-Mac Industries Inc**........................E....... 740 397-6511
Mount Vernon *(G-14517)*
Veterans Steel Inc..................................F....... 216 938-7476
Cleveland *(G-6255)*
◆ **Watteredge LLC**...................................D....... 440 933-6110
Avon Lake *(G-1013)*
Will-Burt Company................................E....... 330 682-7015
Orrville *(G-15628)*
▲ **Will-Burt Company**..............................B....... 330 682-7015
Orrville *(G-15626)*
Worthington Industries Inc...................C....... 614 438-3210
Worthington *(G-20710)*
YKK AP America Inc..............................F....... 513 942-7200
West Chester *(G-19823)*

3451 Screw Machine Prdts

Abco Bar & Tube Cutting Svc................E....... 513 697-9487
Maineville *(G-12364)*
Abel Manufacturing Company...............F....... 513 681-5000
Cincinnati *(G-3287)*
Acme Machine Automatics Inc..............D....... 419 453-0010
Ottoville *(G-15679)*
Adams Automatic Inc.............................F....... 440 235-4416
Olmsted Falls *(G-15527)*
Alco Manufacturing................................G....... 440 322-9166
Amherst *(G-553)*
Alco Manufacturing Corp LLC...............D....... 440 458-5165
Elyria *(G-9210)*
Amco Products Inc.................................F....... 937 433-7982
Dayton *(G-7970)*
Amerascrew Inc......................................E....... 419 522-2232
Mansfield *(G-12404)*
American Aero Components LLC.........G....... 937 367-5068
Dayton *(G-8022)*
Amt Machine Systems Limited.............F....... 740 965-2693
Columbus *(G-6594)*
▲ **Ashley F Ward Inc**................................C....... 513 398-1414
Mason *(G-12829)*
Atlas Machine Products Co...................G....... 216 228-3688
Cleveland *(G-4760)*
▲ **Automatic Screw Products Co**..........G....... 216 241-7896
Cleveland *(G-4772)*
Bronco Machine Inc...............................F....... 440 951-5015
Willoughby *(G-20288)*
Bront Machining Inc..............................E....... 937 228-4551
Moraine *(G-14336)*
Chardon Metal Products Co..................E....... 440 285-2147
Chardon *(G-3102)*
Clear Creek Screw Machine Corp..........G....... 740 969-2113
Amanda *(G-525)*
Condo Inc...G....... 330 505-0485
Niles *(G-15004)*
Condo Incorporated...............................D....... 330 609-6021
Warren *(G-19387)*
CT Ferry Screw Products I......................G....... 440 871-1617
Cleveland *(G-5041)*
D L Salkil LLC..G....... 419 841-3341
Toledo *(G-18251)*
▲ **Day-Hio Products Inc**..........................E....... 937 445-0782
Dayton *(G-8127)*
Dove Machine Inc...................................F....... 440 864-2645
Columbia Station *(G-6437)*
Dunham Products Inc.............................F....... 440 232-0885
Walton Hills *(G-19310)*
Eastlake Machine Products Inc..............E....... 440 953-1014
Willoughby *(G-20314)*
Efficient Machine Pdts Corp...................E....... 440 268-0205
Strongsville *(G-17740)*
Elgin Fastener Group LLC......................E....... 216 481-4400
Cleveland *(G-5168)*
Elliott Oren Products Inc........................F....... 419 298-0015
Edgerton *(G-9172)*
Elliott Oren Products Inc........................E....... 419 298-2306
Edgerton *(G-9173)*
▲ **Elyria Manufacturing Corp**................D....... 440 365-4171
Elyria *(G-9252)*
Engels Machining LLC............................G....... 419 485-1500
Montpelier *(G-14308)*
Engstrom Manufacturing Inc.................F....... 513 573-0010
Mason *(G-12866)*
Eureka Screw Machine Pdts Co............G....... 216 883-1715
Cleveland *(G-5198)*
Fairfield Machined Products.................F....... 740 756-4409
Carroll *(G-2905)*
Falmer Screw Pdts & Mfg Inc...............F....... 330 758-0593
Youngstown *(G-20903)*
▲ **Flash Industrial Tech Ltd**....................G....... 440 786-8979
Cleveland *(G-5247)*
Forrest Machine Pdts Co Ltd.................E....... 419 589-3774
Mansfield *(G-12441)*
Fostoria Machine Products....................G....... 419 435-4262
Fostoria *(G-9843)*
Gent Machine Company..........................E....... 216 481-2334
Cleveland *(G-5316)*
Gisco Inc..G....... 937 773-7601
Piqua *(G-16118)*
Global Precision Parts Inc.....................G....... 260 563-9030
Van Wert *(G-19093)*
Great Lakes Defense Svcs LLC..............G....... 216 272-3450
University Heights *(G-18942)*
H & E Machine Company........................F....... 614 443-7635
Columbus *(G-6972)*
H & S Precision Screw Pdts Inc..............E....... 937 437-0316
New Paris *(G-14754)*
H & W Screw Products Inc......................F....... 937 866-2577
Franklin *(G-9888)*
Hamco Manufacturing Inc.......................G....... 440 774-1637
Oberlin *(G-15498)*
Harding Machine Acquisition Co...........D....... 937 666-3031
East Liberty *(G-9048)*
Hebco Products Inc.................................A....... 419 562-7987
Bucyrus *(G-2333)*
Helix Linear Technologies Inc................E....... 216 485-2263
Beachwood *(G-1240)*
Heller Machine Products Inc..................G....... 216 281-2951
Cleveland *(G-5390)*
Hept Machine Inc....................................G....... 937 890-5633
Vandalia *(G-19126)*
Hi-Tech Solutions LLC............................G....... 216 331-3050
Cleveland *(G-5405)*
Houston Machine Products Inc..............E....... 937 322-8022
Springfield *(G-17422)*
▲ **Hy-Production Inc**...............................C....... 330 273-2400
Valley City *(G-19040)*
▲ **Hyland Machine Company**..................E....... 937 233-8600
Dayton *(G-8258)*
Ilsco Corporation....................................E....... 513 367-9100
Harrison *(G-10651)*
Integrity Manufacturing Corp................E....... 937 233-6792
Dayton *(G-8272)*
J & M Cutting Tools Inc..........................G....... 440 622-3900
Mentor *(G-13480)*
JAD Machine Company Inc.....................F....... 419 256-6332
Malinta *(G-12380)*
Karma Metal Products Inc......................F....... 419 524-4371
Mansfield *(G-12466)*
▲ **Kernells Autmtc Machining Inc**..........E....... 419 588-2164
Berlin Heights *(G-1654)*
Kohut Enterprises Inc.............................G....... 440 366-6666
Independence *(G-11138)*
Krausher Machining Inc.........................G....... 440 839-2828
Wakeman *(G-19285)*
Krist Krenz Machine Inc.........................D....... 440 237-1800
North Royalton *(G-15281)*
Kts-Met Bar Products Inc........................G....... 440 288-9308
Lorain *(G-12097)*
▲ **Lake Erie Industries LLC**.....................G....... 216 255-1867
Lakewood *(G-11525)*
Lear Manufacturing Inc..........................G....... 440 327-4545
North Ridgeville *(G-15238)*
Lehner Screw Machine LLC....................E....... 330 688-6616
Akron *(G-250)*
Lenco Industries Inc...............................E....... 937 277-9364
Dayton *(G-8310)*
Machine Tek Systems Inc.......................E....... 330 527-4450
Garrettsville *(G-10197)*
Magnetic Screw Machine Pdts...............G....... 937 348-2807
Marysville *(G-12797)*
Maumee Machine & Tool Corp................E....... 419 385-2501
Toledo *(G-18402)*
McDaniel Products Inc...........................F....... 440 967-5630
Vermilion *(G-19167)*
McDaniel Products Inc...........................E....... 419 524-5841
Mansfield *(G-12478)*
Meistermatic Inc.....................................D....... 216 481-7773
Chesterland *(G-3163)*
Mettlr-Tledo Globl Hldings LLC..............F....... 614 438-4511
Columbus *(G-6502)*
Midwest Precision LLC...........................D....... 440 951-2333
Eastlake *(G-9122)*
▲ **Morgal Machine Tool Co**......................D....... 937 325-5561
Springfield *(G-17451)*
Mosher Machine & Tool Co Inc..............E....... 937 258-8070
Dayton *(G-8369)*
Murray Machine & Tool Inc....................G....... 216 267-1126
Cleveland *(G-5714)*
New Castle Industries Inc......................C....... 724 654-2603
Youngstown *(G-20975)*
▲ **Nook Industries Inc**............................C....... 216 271-7900
Cleveland *(G-5756)*
Obars Machine and Tool Company........E....... 419 535-6307
Toledo *(G-18433)*
▲ **Ohio Metal Products Company**...........E....... 937 228-6101
Dayton *(G-8399)*
Ohio Screw Products Inc........................D....... 440 322-6341
Elyria *(G-9305)*
Paramont Machine Company LLC.........E....... 330 339-3489
New Philadelphia *(G-14792)*
▲ **Pfi Precision Inc**..................................E....... 937 845-3563
New Carlisle *(G-14677)*
Pike Machine Products Co.....................E....... 216 731-1880
Euclid *(G-9433)*
Port Clinton Manufacturing LLC............E....... 419 734-2141
Port Clinton *(G-16255)*
▲ **Precision Fittings LLC**..........................E....... 440 647-4143
Wellington *(G-19589)*
Profile Grinding Inc................................E....... 216 351-0600
Cleveland *(G-5928)*
Qcsm LLC..G....... 216 531-5960
Cleveland *(G-5937)*
R T & T Machining Co Inc.......................F....... 440 974-8479
Mentor *(G-13571)*
R W Screw Products Inc.........................C....... 330 837-9211
Massillon *(G-13044)*
Raka Corporation...................................D....... 419 476-6572
Toledo *(G-18498)*
Richland Screw Machine Pdts................E....... 419 524-1272
Mansfield *(G-12507)*
Roehlers Machine Products...................G....... 937 354-4401
Mount Victory *(G-14522)*
Rtsi LLC..G....... 440 542-3066
Solon *(G-17226)*
Rural Products Inc..................................G....... 419 298-2677
Edgerton *(G-9179)*
S & S Machining Ltd................................F....... 419 524-9525
Mansfield *(G-12510)*
▲ **Semtorq Inc**..F....... 330 487-0600
Twinsburg *(G-18856)*
Shanafelt Manufacturing Co...................E....... 330 455-0315
Canton *(G-2814)*
Stadco Inc...E....... 937 878-0911
Fairborn *(G-9468)*
▲ **Standby Screw Machine Pdts Co**........B....... 440 243-8200
Berea *(G-1625)*
Star Screw Machine Products................G....... 216 361-0307
Cleveland *(G-6096)*
State Machine Co Inc..............................G....... 440 248-1050
Cleveland *(G-6098)*
Superior Bar Products Inc......................G....... 419 784-2590
Defiance *(G-8644)*
◆ **Superior Products Llc**..........................D....... 216 651-9400
Cleveland *(G-6125)*
Supply Technologies LLC.......................D....... 740 363-1971
Delaware *(G-8727)*
Swagelok Hy-Level Company.................C....... 440 238-1260
Strongsville *(G-17798)*
The Delo Screw Products Co...................F....... 740 363-1971
Delaware *(G-8728)*
Toledo Automatic Screw Co....................G....... 419 726-3441
Toledo *(G-18556)*
Toledo Screw Products Inc.....................G....... 419 841-3341
Toledo *(G-18568)*
Tri-K Enterprises Inc...............................G....... 330 832-7380
Canton *(G-2845)*
Triangle Machine Products Co...............E....... 216 524-5872
Cleveland *(G-6208)*
Trojon Gear Inc.......................................F....... 937 254-1737
Dayton *(G-8568)*
Troy Manufacturing Co...........................E....... 440 834-8262
Burton *(G-2373)*

Employee Codes: A=Over 500 employees, B=251-500
C=101-250, D=51-100, E=20-50, F=10-19, G=3-9
2019 Harris Ohio
Industrial Directory
931

34 FABRICATED METAL PRODUCTS, EXCEPT MACHINERY AND TRANSPORTATION EQUIPMENT

Twin Valley Metalcraft Asm LLC ....G...... 937 787-4634
West Alexandria *(G-19622)*
United Auto Worker AFL CIO ....F...... 419 592-0434
Napoleon *(G-14563)*
Usm Precision Products Inc ....D...... 440 975-8600
Wickliffe *(G-20236)*
Valley Tool & Die Inc ....D...... 440 237-0160
North Royalton *(G-15309)*
Vanamatic Company ....D...... 419 692-6085
Delphos *(G-8764)*
Vinco Machine Products Inc 216 475-6708
Cleveland *(G-6263)*
Vulcan Products Co Inc ....F...... 419 468-1039
Galion *(G-10159)*
Warren Screw Machine Inc ....E...... 330 609-6020
Warren *(G-19460)*
Watters Manufacturing Co Inc ....G...... 216 281-8600
Cleveland *(G-6294)*
▲ Whirlaway Corporation ....C...... 440 647-4711
Wellington *(G-19595)*
Whirlaway Corporation ....C...... 440 647-4711
Wellington *(G-19596)*
Whirlaway Corporation ....E...... 440 647-4711
Wellington *(G-19597)*
Whiteford Industries Inc 419 381-1155
Toledo *(G-18599)*
Wood-Sebring Corporation ....G...... 216 267-3191
Cleveland *(G-6321)*
Z and M Screw Machine Products ....G...... 330 467-5822
Garrettsville *(G-10206)*

3452 Bolts, Nuts, Screws, Rivets & Washers

Abco Bar & Tube Cutting Svc ....E...... 513 697-9487
Maineville *(G-12364)*
◆ Agrati - Medina LLC ....C...... 330 725-8853
Medina *(G-13218)*
Agrati - Medina LLC ....G...... 740 467-3199
Millersport *(G-14158)*
Agrati - Tiffin LLC ....D...... 419 447-2221
Tiffin *(G-18041)*
Airfasco Inc ....E...... 330 430-6190
Canton *(G-2561)*
Airfasco Inds Fstner Group LLC ....E...... 330 430-6190
Canton *(G-2562)*
▲ Akko Fastener Inc ....F...... 513 489-8300
Blue Ash *(G-1724)*
▲ Altenloh Brinck & Co Inc ....C...... 419 636-6715
Bryan *(G-2262)*
▲ Altenloh Brinck & Co US Inc ....D...... 419 636-6715
Bryan *(G-2263)*
▲ Amanda Bent Bolt Company ....C...... 740 385-6893
Logan *(G-12021)*
Ampex Metal Products Company ....E...... 216 267-9242
Brookpark *(G-2136)*
Andre Corporation ....E...... 574 293-0207
Mason *(G-12824)*
▲ Atlas Bolt & Screw Company LLC .....C...... 419 289-6171
Ashland *(G-681)*
Auto Bolt Company ....D...... 216 881-3913
Cleveland *(G-4767)*
Bowes Manufacturing Inc ....E...... 216 378-2110
Solon *(G-17117)*
Brainard Rivet Company ....E...... 330 545-4931
Girard *(G-10254)*
Buck Eye Pressure Wash ....G...... 419 385-9274
Toledo *(G-18218)*
Capitol City Mfg Co Inc ....G...... 614 491-1192
Obetz *(G-15506)*
▲ Cold Headed Fas Assemblies Inc .....F...... 330 833-0800
Massillon *(G-12968)*
Cold Heading Co ....D...... 216 581-3000
Cleveland *(G-4996)*
Connell Limited Partnership ....D...... 877 534-8986
Northfield *(G-15316)*
Consolidated Metal Pdts Inc ....C...... 513 251-2624
Cincinnati *(G-3542)*
Core Manufacturing LLC ....G...... 440 946-8002
Mentor *(G-13422)*
▲ Crawford Products Inc ....E...... 614 890-1822
Columbus *(G-6837)*
Curtiss-Wright Flow Ctrl Corp ....D...... 216 373-3200
Cleveland *(G-5045)*
◆ Dayton Superior Corporation ....G...... 937 866-0711
Miamisburg *(G-13655)*
Die-Cut Products Co ....E...... 216 771-6994
Cleveland *(G-5094)*
▲ Dimcogray Corporation ....G...... 937 433-7600
Centerville *(G-3001)*
▲ Dph Discount Pin Inc ....G...... 740 264-2450
Steubenville *(G-17531)*

Edward W Daniel LLC ....E...... 440 647-1960
Wellington *(G-19577)*
Efg Holdings Inc ....G...... 812 689-8990
Brecksville *(G-2030)*
Elgin Fastener Group LLC ....E...... 440 717-7650
Brecksville *(G-2031)*
Elgin Fastener Group LLC ....G...... 216 481-4400
Cleveland *(G-5168)*
Elgin Fastener Group LLC ....F...... 812 689-8990
Brecksville *(G-2032)*
Engstrom Manufacturing Inc 513 573-0010
Mason *(G-12866)*
Express Trading Pins ....G...... 419 394-2550
Saint Marys *(G-16684)*
◆ Facil North America Inc ....C...... 330 487-2500
Twinsburg *(G-18774)*
Fastener Industries Inc ....E...... 440 891-2031
Berea *(G-1607)*
▲ Ferry Cap & Set Screw Company .....C...... 216 649-7400
Lakewood *(G-11517)*
Gauntlet Awards & Engraving ....G...... 937 890-5811
Dayton *(G-8214)*
General Plastex Inc ....E...... 330 745-7775
Barberton *(G-1073)*
Grntwrx LLC ....G...... 440 478-6160
Garrettsville *(G-10190)*
▲ Group Industries Inc ....E...... 216 271-0702
Cleveland *(G-5355)*
▲ Hexagon Industries Inc ....E...... 216 249-0200
Cleveland *(G-5400)*
Hudson Fasteners Inc ....G...... 330 270-9500
Youngstown *(G-20933)*
▲ Industrial Nut Corp ....D...... 419 625-8543
Sandusky *(G-16817)*
Ivan Extruders Co Inc ....G...... 330 644-7400
Akron *(G-220)*
Iwata Bolt USA Inc ....F...... 513 942-5050
Fairfield *(G-9512)*
Jacodar Inc ....G...... 330 832-9557
Massillon *(G-13005)*
Jacodar Fsa LLC ....E...... 330 454-1832
Canton *(G-2715)*
Jenco Manufacturing Inc. ....E...... 216 898-9682
Independence *(G-11137)*
▲ Jergens Inc ....C...... 216 486-5540
Cleveland *(G-5495)*
Jerry Tools Inc ....F...... 513 242-3211
Cincinnati *(G-3871)*
▲ Keystone Bolt & Nut Company ....D...... 216 524-9626
Cleveland *(G-5532)*
Kre Inc ....F...... 216 883-1600
Twinsburg *(G-18802)*
Kyocera Senco Indus Tls Inc ....F...... 800 543-4596
Cincinnati *(G-3256)*
Lapel Pins Unlimited LLC ....G...... 614 562-3218
Lewis Center *(G-11765)*
Lear Mfg Co Inc ....F...... 440 324-1111
Elyria *(G-9286)*
▲ Lerner Enterprises Inc ....E...... 440 323-5529
Elyria *(G-9287)*
Long-Lok Fasteners Corporation ....E...... 513 772-1880
Cincinnati *(G-3950)*
M C Industries Inc ....F...... 440 355-4040
Lagrange *(G-11487)*
Master Products Company ....D...... 216 341-1740
Cleveland *(G-5634)*
▲ Matdan Corporation ....E...... 513 794-0500
Blue Ash *(G-1815)*
Microform Inc ....G...... 440 899-6339
Cleveland *(G-5668)*
Mid-West Fabricating Co ....E...... 740 277-7021
Lancaster *(G-11587)*
Mid-West Fabricating Co ....G...... 740 681-4411
Lancaster *(G-11588)*
◆ Mid-West Fabricating Co ....C...... 740 969-4411
Amanda *(G-526)*
▲ Miller Studio Inc ....D...... 330 339-1100
New Philadelphia *(G-14787)*
Nelson Automotive LLC ....F...... 724 681-0975
Brookpark *(G-2153)*
◆ Nelson Stud Welding Inc ....B...... 440 329-0400
Elyria *(G-9300)*
North Coast Rivet Inc ....F...... 440 366-6829
Elyria *(G-9301)*
▲ Nova Machine Products Inc ....D...... 216 267-3200
Middleburg Heights *(G-13767)*
▲ Ohashi Technica USA Inc ....E...... 740 965-5115
Sunbury *(G-17894)*
Paine Falls Centerpin LLC ....G...... 440 298-3202
Thompson *(G-18026)*

▲ Paulin Industries Inc ....E...... 216 433-7633
Parma *(G-15826)*
Pin High LLC ....G...... 216 577-9999
Avon *(G-958)*
Pin Oak Development LLC ....G...... 440 933-9862
Avon Lake *(G-1000)*
Pin Point Marketing LLC ....G...... 330 336-5863
Wadsworth *(G-19263)*
▲ Precision Fittings LLC ....E...... 440 647-4143
Wellington *(G-19589)*
Pressure Washer Mfrs Assn ....G...... 216 241-7333
Cleveland *(G-5920)*
Pro Roof Washers ....G...... 440 521-2622
Cleveland *(G-5924)*
Quality Concepts Telecom ....E...... 740 385-2003
Logan *(G-12041)*
R S Manufacturing Inc ....G...... 440 946-8002
Mentor *(G-13570)*
▲ Ramco Specialties Inc ....C...... 330 653-5135
Hudson *(G-11069)*
RB&w Manufacturing LLC ....G...... 740 363-1971
Delaware *(G-8718)*
▲ RB&w Manufacturing LLC ....F...... 234 380-8540
Streetsboro *(G-17691)*
Roehlers Machine Products ....G...... 937 354-4401
Mount Victory *(G-14522)*
Ronson Manufacturing Inc. ....G...... 440 256-1463
Willoughby *(G-20423)*
S F S Stadler Inc ....G...... 330 239-7100
Medina *(G-13332)*
Saf-Holland Inc ....E...... 513 874-7888
West Chester *(G-19896)*
Simpson Strong-Tie Company Inc ......C...... 614 876-8060
Columbus *(G-7454)*
▲ Solon Manufacturing Company ....E...... 440 286-7149
Chardon *(G-3137)*
▲ Stafast Products Inc ....E...... 440 357-5546
Painesville *(G-15784)*
▲ Stanley Industrial & Auto LLC ....E...... 614 755-7000
Westerville *(G-20025)*
▲ Steeramerica Inc ....F...... 330 563-4407
Uniontown *(G-18932)*
▲ Stelfast Inc 440 879-0077
Strongsville *(G-17797)*
Supply Technologies LLC ....F...... 614 759-9939
Columbus *(G-7504)*
▲ Supply Technologies LLC ....E...... 440 947-2100
Cleveland *(G-6130)*
Supply Technologies LLC ....G...... 937 898-5795
Dayton *(G-8530)*
T and D Washers LLC ....G...... 419 562-5500
Bucyrus *(G-2344)*
▲ Telefast Industries Inc ....E...... 440 826-0011
Berea *(G-1628)*
Tessec Manufacturing Svcs LLC ....E...... 937 985-3552
Dayton *(G-8553)*
◆ Tinnerman Palnut Engineered PR ....E...... 330 220-5100
Brunswick *(G-2246)*
Troy Screw Products ....G...... 440 946-3381
Mentor *(G-13614)*
Twin Ventures Inc ....F...... 330 405-3838
Twinsburg *(G-18868)*
◆ United Titanium Inc ....C...... 330 264-2111
Wooster *(G-20661)*
Valley Tool & Die Inc ....D...... 440 237-0160
North Royalton *(G-15309)*
W-J Inc ....G...... 440 248-8282
Solon *(G-17259)*
▲ Wallace Forge Company ....D...... 330 488-1203
Canton *(G-2863)*
Wecall Inc ....E...... 440 437-8202
Orwell *(G-15636)*
Wheel Group Holdings LLC ....G...... 614 253-6247
Columbus *(G-7602)*
Wodin Inc ....E...... 440 439-4222
Cleveland *(G-6320)*

3462 Iron & Steel Forgings

Akron Gear & Engineering Inc ....E...... 330 773-6608
Akron *(G-41)*
Alliance Forging Group LLC ....G...... 330 680-4861
Akron *(G-60)*
Alta Mira Corporation ....D...... 330 648-2461
Spencer *(G-17303)*
American Cold Forge LLC ....E...... 419 836-1062
Northwood *(G-15331)*
Anchor Flange Company ....F...... 513 527-4444
Cincinnati *(G-3344)*
▲ Anchor Industries Incorporated ....E...... 440 473-1414
Cleveland *(G-4706)*

Brooker Bros Forging Co Inc ... E ... 419 668-2535
Norwalk *(G-15383)*
Buckeye Gear Co ... F ... 216 292-7998
Chagrin Falls *(G-3038)*
Bula Forge & Machine Inc ... E ... 216 252-7600
Cleveland *(G-4852)*
Cailin Dev Ltd Lblty Co ... F ... 216 408-6261
Cleveland *(G-4862)*
◆ Canton Drop Forge Inc ... B ... 330 477-4511
Canton *(G-2608)*
Carbo Forge Inc ... E ... 419 334-9788
Fremont *(G-10004)*
Cincinnati Gearing Systems Inc ... C ... 513 527-8634
Cincinnati *(G-3494)*
▲ Cleveland Hdwr & Forging Co ... E ... 216 641-5200
Cleveland *(G-4962)*
Cleveland Hollow Boring Inc ... G ... 216 883-1926
Cleveland *(G-4963)*
Cliffs High Performance ... G ... 740 397-2921
Mount Vernon *(G-14476)*
▲ Colfor Manufacturing Inc ... A ... 330 863-7500
Malvern *(G-12387)*
Cordier Group Holdings Inc ... B ... 330 477-4511
Canton *(G-2637)*
Crum Manufacturing Inc ... E ... 419 878-9779
Waterville *(G-19492)*
Dayton Forging Heat Treating ... D ... 937 253-4126
Dayton *(G-8132)*
◆ Dayton Superior Corporation ... C ... 937 866-0711
Miamisburg *(G-13655)*
Dependable Gear Corp ... G ... 440 942-4969
Eastlake *(G-9103)*
Edgerton Forge Inc ... E ... 419 298-2333
Edgerton *(G-9171)*
Edward W Daniel LLC ... E ... 440 647-1960
Wellington *(G-19577)*
▲ Ferrotherm Corporation ... C ... 216 883-9350
Cleveland *(G-5233)*
For Call Inc ... B ... 330 863-0404
Malvern *(G-12390)*
Forge Products Corporation ... D ... 216 231-2600
Cleveland *(G-5262)*
Forging Eqp Solutions Inc ... G ... 330 239-2222
Medina *(G-13263)*
Gear Company of America Inc ... D ... 216 671-5400
Cleveland *(G-5298)*
Geneva Gear & Machine Inc ... F ... 937 866-0318
Dayton *(G-8221)*
GKN PLC ... G ... 740 446-9211
Gallipolis *(G-10165)*
GKN Sinter Metals LLC ... C ... 740 441-3203
Gallipolis *(G-10166)*
▲ J & H Manufacturing LLC ... F ... 330 482-2636
Columbiana *(G-6471)*
Ken Forging Inc ... C ... 440 993-8091
Jefferson *(G-11232)*
King-Indiana Forge Inc ... F ... 330 425-4250
Twinsburg *(G-18800)*
Landerwood Industries Inc ... E ... 440 233-4234
Willoughby *(G-20358)*
Lange Precision Inc ... F ... 513 530-9500
Blue Ash *(G-1802)*
Lextech Industries Ltd ... G ... 216 883-7900
Cleveland *(G-5574)*
Martin Sprocket & Gear Inc ... D ... 419 485-5515
Montpelier *(G-14312)*
Metal Forming & Coining Corp ... D ... 419 897-9530
Maumee *(G-13132)*
Mid-West Forge Corporation ... C ... 216 481-3030
Cleveland *(G-5677)*
Ohio Chain Company LLC ... G ... 419 843-9476
Sylvania *(G-17958)*
▲ Ohio Metal Technologies Inc ... D ... 740 928-8288
Hebron *(G-10756)*
▲ Ohio Star Forge Co ... D ... 330 847-6360
Warren *(G-19427)*
◆ Park-Ohio Holdings Corp ... F ... 440 947-2000
Cleveland *(G-5842)*
Park-Ohio Industries Inc ... C ... 440 947-2000
Cleveland *(G-5843)*
Penn Machine Company ... E ... 814 288-1547
Twinsburg *(G-18829)*
Performance Motorsports ... G ... 513 931-9999
Cincinnati *(G-4149)*
Powers and Sons LLC ... D ... 419 737-2373
Pioneer *(G-16091)*
Presrite Corporation ... B ... 216 441-5990
Cleveland *(G-5918)*
Presrite Corporation ... C ... 440 576-0015
Jefferson *(G-11236)*

▲ Queen City Forging Company ... F ... 513 321-2003
Cincinnati *(G-4237)*
▲ Romark Industries Inc ... G ... 440 333-5480
Westlake *(G-20152)*
Rose Metal Industries LLC ... F ... 216 881-3355
Cleveland *(G-6002)*
▲ Rotek Incorporated ... C ... 330 562-4000
Aurora *(G-904)*
Rudd Equipment Company Inc ... E ... 513 321-7833
Cincinnati *(G-4287)*
▲ Sakamura USA Inc ... F ... 740 223-7777
Marion *(G-12732)*
Satellite Gear Inc ... F ... 216 514-8668
Aurora *(G-907)*
▲ Schaefer Equipment Inc ... D ... 330 372-4006
Warren *(G-19442)*
Shot-Force Pro LLC ... G ... 740 753-3927
Nelsonville *(G-14597)*
◆ Sifco Industries Inc ... B ... 216 881-8600
Cleveland *(G-6063)*
Solmet Technologies Inc ... E ... 330 915-4160
Canton *(G-2819)*
Stahl Gear & Machine Co ... E ... 216 431-2820
Cleveland *(G-6089)*
◆ Summa Holdings Inc ... G ... 440 838-4700
Cleveland *(G-6116)*
T & S Discount Tires Inc ... G ... 440 951-9084
Willoughby *(G-20439)*
Tek Group International Inc ... E ... 330 706-0000
Canal Fulton *(G-2494)*
▲ Tekfor Inc ... B ... 330 202-7420
Wooster *(G-20659)*
▲ Tfo Tech Co Ltd ... C ... 740 426-6381
Jeffersonville *(G-11248)*
TRM Manufacturing Inc ... E ... 330 769-2600
Cuyahoga Falls *(G-7929)*
US Tsubaki Power Transm LLC ... C ... 419 626-4560
Sandusky *(G-16860)*
▲ Wallace Forge Company ... D ... 330 488-1203
Canton *(G-2863)*
Western Reserve Mfg Co ... G ... 216 641-0500
Cleveland *(G-6303)*
Wodin Inc ... E ... 440 439-4222
Cleveland *(G-6320)*
▲ Wright Tool Company ... C ... 330 848-0600
Barberton *(G-1114)*
Wyman-Gordon Company ... E ... 216 341-0085
Cleveland *(G-6330)*

3463 Nonferrous Forgings

American Cold Forge LLC ... E ... 419 836-1062
Northwood *(G-15331)*
Arconic Inc ... A ... 216 641-3600
Newburgh Heights *(G-14934)*
Arconic Inc ... A ... 216 641-3600
Newburgh Heights *(G-14935)*
Arconic Inc ... G ... 330 544-7633
Niles *(G-14998)*
◆ Canton Drop Forge Inc ... B ... 330 477-4511
Canton *(G-2608)*
Clarke Power Services Inc ... E ... 513 771-2200
Cincinnati *(G-3524)*
▲ Cleveland Hdwr & Forging Co ... E ... 216 641-5200
Cleveland *(G-4962)*
▲ Colfor Manufacturing Inc ... A ... 330 863-7500
Malvern *(G-12387)*
Edward W Daniel LLC ... E ... 440 647-1960
Wellington *(G-19577)*
Forge Products Corporation ... D ... 216 231-2600
Cleveland *(G-5262)*
▼ Gateway Industries ... G ... 330 633-3700
Akron *(G-182)*
▲ Guarantee Specialties Inc ... D ... 216 451-9744
Strongsville *(G-17747)*
◆ Mansfield Plumbing Pdts LLC ... A ... 419 938-5211
Perrysville *(G-16030)*
Ohio Conveyor and Supply Inc ... G ... 419 422-3825
Findlay *(G-9733)*
Powers and Sons LLC ... D ... 419 737-2373
Pioneer *(G-16091)*
▲ Rotek Incorporated ... C ... 330 562-4000
Aurora *(G-904)*
Turbine Eng Cmpnents Tech Corp ... E ... 216 692-6173
Cleveland *(G-6222)*
▲ Wallace Forge Company ... D ... 330 488-1203
Canton *(G-2863)*
Wodin Inc ... E ... 440 439-4222
Cleveland *(G-6320)*

3465 Automotive Stampings

◆ A J Rose Mfg Co ... C ... 216 631-4645
Avon *(G-936)*
A J Rose Mfgco ... C ... 216 631-4645
Cleveland *(G-4590)*
Adval Tech US Inc ... G ... 216 362-1850
Cleveland *(G-4620)*
American Quality Molds LLC ... G ... 513 276-7345
Hamilton *(G-10532)*
American Trim LLC ... A ... 419 228-1145
Sidney *(G-17014)*
▲ Anchor Tool & Die Co ... B ... 216 362-1850
Cleveland *(G-4709)*
Antique Auto Sheet Metal Inc ... E ... 937 833-4422
Brookville *(G-2161)*
Arcelormittal Tailored Blanks ... D ... 419 737-3180
Pioneer *(G-16084)*
▲ Artiflex Manufacturing LLC ... B ... 330 262-2015
Wooster *(G-20564)*
Bear Diversified Inc ... G ... 216 883-5494
Cleveland *(G-4799)*
Buyers Products Company ... G ... 440 974-8888
Mentor *(G-13409)*
Cleveland Metal Processing Inc ... C ... 440 243-3404
Cleveland *(G-4968)*
Cole Tool & Die Company ... E ... 419 522-1272
Ontario *(G-15540)*
Custom Floaters LLC ... G ... 216 337-9118
Brookpark *(G-2140)*
Decoma Systems Integration Gro ... D ... 419 324-3387
Toledo *(G-18257)*
▲ Defiance Metal Products Co ... B ... 419 784-5332
Defiance *(G-8619)*
▲ E & W Enterprises Powell Inc ... D ... 937 346-0800
Springfield *(G-17393)*
Elyria Spring & Specialty Inc ... E ... 440 323-5502
Elyria *(G-9256)*
Exact-Tool & Die Inc ... E ... 216 676-9140
Cleveland *(G-5204)*
Falls Stamping & Welding Co ... C ... 330 928-1191
Cuyahoga Falls *(G-7867)*
Falls Stamping & Welding Co ... F ... 216 771-9635
Cleveland *(G-5218)*
▲ Feintool Cincinnati Inc ... C ... 513 247-0110
Blue Ash *(G-1773)*
▲ Feintool US Operations Inc ... C ... 513 247-4061
Blue Ash *(G-1774)*
Fiberglass Link Inc ... G ... 216 531-5515
Cleveland *(G-5236)*
▲ Findlay Products Corporation ... C ... 419 423-3324
Findlay *(G-9687)*
Florida Production Engrg Inc ... D ... 937 996-4361
New Madison *(G-14741)*
▼ FMI Products LLC ... G ... 440 476-8262
Valley City *(G-19037)*
▲ Fuserashi Intl Tech Inc ... E ... 330 273-0140
Valley City *(G-19038)*
Gamco Components Group LLC ... G ... 440 593-1500
Conneaut *(G-7645)*
General Motors LLC ... B ... 330 824-5840
Warren *(G-19406)*
General Motors LLC ... A ... 216 265-5000
Cleveland *(G-5312)*
Gt Technologies Inc ... D ... 419 324-7300
Toledo *(G-18314)*
▲ Guarantee Specialties Inc ... D ... 216 451-9744
Strongsville *(G-17747)*
Hayford Technologies ... D ... 419 524-7627
Mansfield *(G-12455)*
Hercules Acquisition Corp ... E ... 419 287-3223
Pemberville *(G-15884)*
Honda of America Mfg Inc ... C ... 937 644-0724
Marysville *(G-12792)*
Hydro Extrusion North Amer LLC ... C ... 888 935-5759
Sidney *(G-17045)*
Jatdco LLC ... G ... 440 238-6570
Strongsville *(G-17757)*
▲ Kirchhoff Auto Waverly Inc ... D ... 740 947-7763
Waverly *(G-19550)*
Ksi Distribution Inc ... G ... 440 256-2500
Mentor *(G-13491)*
L & W Inc ... D ... 734 397-6300
Avon *(G-953)*
Lakepark Industries Inc ... C ... 419 752-4471
Greenwich *(G-10406)*
Langenau Manufacturing Company ... F ... 216 651-3400
Cleveland *(G-5558)*
Liber Limited LLC ... G ... 440 427-0647
Olmsted Twp *(G-15533)*

Employee Codes: A=Over 500 employees, B=251-500
C=101-250, D=51-100, E=20-50, F=10-19, G=3-9
2019 Harris Ohio
Industrial Directory
933

Ltf Acquisition LLC ....F.... 330 533-0111
Canfield *(G-2533)*
Lwb/ISE LP ....F.... 937 778-3828
Piqua *(G-16139)*
M-Tek Inc ....A.... 419 209-0399
Upper Sandusky *(G-18961)*
▲ **Matsu Ohio Inc** ....C.... 419 298-2394
Edgerton *(G-9176)*
Merrick Manufacturing II LLC ....G.... 937 222-7164
Dayton *(G-8341)*
▲ **Murotech Ohio Corporation** ....C.... 419 394-6529
Saint Marys *(G-16690)*
N N Metal Stampings Inc ....E.... 419 737-2311
Pioneer *(G-16086)*
Nasg Ohio LLC ....F.... 419 634-3125
Ada *(G-7)*
Nebraska Industries Corp ....E.... 419 335-6010
Wauseon *(G-19529)*
Northern Stamping Co ....F.... 216 883-8888
Cleveland *(G-5782)*
▲ **Northern Stamping Co** ....C.... 216 883-8888
Cleveland *(G-5783)*
Northern Stamping Co ....C.... 216 642-8081
Cleveland *(G-5784)*
Oerlikon Friction Systems ....E.... 937 233-9191
Dayton *(G-8395)*
P & A Industries Inc ....C.... 419 422-7070
Findlay *(G-9738)*
Pennant Companies ....B.... 614 451-1782
Columbus *(G-7308)*
◆ **Progressive Stamping Inc** ....C.... 419 453-1111
Ottoville *(G-15683)*
▲ **R K Industries Inc** ....D.... 419 523-5001
Ottawa *(G-15663)*
Select International Corp ....G.... 937 233-9191
Dayton *(G-8503)*
Shiloh Industries Inc ....E.... 330 558-2300
Valley City *(G-19063)*
Shiloh Industries Inc ....A.... 330 558-2000
Valley City *(G-19064)*
Shiloh Industries Inc ....A.... 330 558-2600
Valley City *(G-19065)*
◆ **Shiloh Industries Inc** ....G.... 330 558-2600
Valley City *(G-19066)*
▲ **SSP Industrial Group Inc** ....G.... 330 665-2900
Fairlawn *(G-9619)*
▲ **Stamco Industries Inc** ....E.... 216 731-9333
Cleveland *(G-6091)*
▲ **Stripmatic Products Inc** ....E.... 216 241-7143
Cleveland *(G-6111)*
Sunrise Cooperative Inc ....E.... 419 683-4600
Crestline *(G-7801)*
▲ **T A Bacon Co** ....F.... 216 851-1404
Chesterland *(G-3169)*
▲ **Taylor Metal Products Co** ....C.... 419 522-3471
Mansfield *(G-12526)*
▲ **Tfo Tech Co Ltd** ....C.... 740 426-6381
Jeffersonville *(G-11248)*
Tower Automotive Operations I ....B.... 419 358-8966
Bluffton *(G-1895)*
Tower Automotive Operations I ....C.... 419 483-1500
Bellevue *(G-1550)*
Transitworks LLC ....G.... 855 337-9543
Akron *(G-408)*
Trellborg Sling Prfiles US Inc ....E.... 330 995-9725
Aurora *(G-911)*
▲ **Trucut Incorporated** ....D.... 330 938-9806
Sebring *(G-16896)*
TS Trim Industries Inc ....F.... 614 837-4114
Canal Winchester *(G-2514)*
Valco Industries Inc ....E.... 937 399-7400
Springfield *(G-17513)*
Valley Tool & Die Inc ....D.... 440 237-0160
North Royalton *(G-15309)*
◆ **Vehtek Systems Inc** ....A.... 419 373-8741
Bowling Green *(G-2004)*
Wrena LLC ....E.... 937 667-4403
Tipp City *(G-18146)*
▲ **Yachiyo of America Inc** ....C.... 614 876-3220
Columbus *(G-7620)*
Zip Tool & Die Inc ....F.... 216 267-1117
Cleveland *(G-6343)*

3466 Crowns & Closures

American Flange & Mfg Co Inc ....G.... 740 549-6073
Delaware *(G-8653)*
▲ **Boardman Molded Products Inc** ....D.... 330 788-2400
Youngstown *(G-20854)*
Crown Cork & Seal Usa Inc ....D.... 740 681-3000
Lancaster *(G-11560)*
Eisenhauer Mfg Co LLC ....D.... 419 238-0081
Van Wert *(G-19090)*

3469 Metal Stampings, NEC

◆ **A J Rose Mfg Co** ....C.... 216 631-4645
Avon *(G-936)*
A J Rose Mfgco ....C.... 216 631-4645
Cleveland *(G-4590)*
A-1 Manufacturing Corp ....G.... 216 475-6084
Maple Heights *(G-12563)*
▲ **A-Stamp Industries LLC** ....D.... 419 633-0451
Bryan *(G-2257)*
AAA Stamping Inc ....E.... 216 749-4494
Cleveland *(G-4596)*
Abbott Tool Inc ....E.... 419 476-6742
Toledo *(G-18153)*
Abl Products Inc ....F.... 216 281-2400
Cleveland *(G-4598)*
Accurate Tool Co Inc ....G.... 330 332-9448
Salem *(G-16714)*
▲ **Acro Tool & Die Company** ....D.... 330 773-5173
Akron *(G-29)*
▲ **Advanced Technology Corp** ....C.... 440 293-4064
Andover *(G-577)*
AJD Holding Co ....D.... 330 405-4477
Twinsburg *(G-18728)*
Allied Tool & Die Inc ....F.... 216 941-6196
Cleveland *(G-4673)*
Amaroq Inc ....G.... 419 747-2110
Mansfield *(G-12403)*
Amclo Group Inc ....C.... 216 791-8400
North Royalton *(G-15259)*
▼ **Amcraft Inc** ....G.... 419 729-7900
Toledo *(G-18170)*
American Craft Hardware LLC ....G.... 440 746-0098
Cleveland *(G-4686)*
American Rugged Enclosures ....F.... 513 942-3004
Hamilton *(G-10533)*
American Tool & Mfg Co ....F.... 419 522-2452
Mansfield *(G-12405)*
American Tool and Die Inc ....F.... 419 726-5394
Toledo *(G-18181)*
American Trim LLC ....A.... 419 228-1145
Sidney *(G-17014)*
American Trim LLC ....G.... 419 996-4703
Lima *(G-11837)*
American Trim LLC ....D.... 419 739-4349
Wapakoneta *(G-19318)*
American Trim LLC ....D.... 419 738-9664
Wapakoneta *(G-19319)*
American Trim LLC ....D.... 419 996-4729
Lima *(G-11838)*
American Trim LLC ....D.... 419 996-4703
Lima *(G-11839)*
▲ **American Trim LLC** ....E.... 419 228-1145
Lima *(G-11840)*
American Truck Equipment Inc ....G.... 216 362-0400
Cleveland *(G-4699)*
AMG Industries LLC ....D.... 740 397-4044
Mount Vernon *(G-14467)*
Ampex Metal Products Company ....E.... 216 267-9242
Brookpark *(G-2136)*
Amtekco Industries LLC ....D.... 614 228-6590
Columbus *(G-6596)*
Amtekco Industries Inc ....G.... 614 228-6525
Columbus *(G-6597)*
Anchor Fabricators Inc ....E.... 937 836-5117
Clayton *(G-4571)*
Anchor Tool & Die Co ....D.... 216 362-1850
Cleveland *(G-4710)*
▲ **Anchor Tool & Die Co** ....B.... 216 362-1850
Cleveland *(G-4709)*
Andre Corporation ....E.... 574 293-0207
Mason *(G-12824)*
▲ **Anomatic Corporation** ....B.... 740 522-2203
Johnstown *(G-11255)*
▼ **Armorsource LLC** ....E.... 740 928-0070
Hebron *(G-10738)*
◆ **Arrow Tru-Line Inc** ....C.... 419 446-2785
Archbold *(G-639)*
Arrow Tru-Line Inc ....D.... 419 636-7013
Bryan *(G-2265)*
▲ **Art Metals Group Inc** ....D.... 513 942-8800
Hamilton *(G-10536)*
▲ **Artiflex Manufacturing LLC** ....B.... 330 262-2015
Wooster *(G-20564)*
Artisan Equipment Inc ....F.... 740 756-9135
Carroll *(G-2898)*
▼ **Artisan Tool & Die Corp** ....E.... 216 883-2769
Cleveland *(G-4740)*
Artistic Metal Spinning Inc ....G.... 216 961-3336
Cleveland *(G-4741)*
▲ **Atlantic Durant Technology Inc** ....G.... 440 238-6931
Strongsville *(G-17713)*
▲ **Atlantic Tool & Die Company** ....C.... 440 238-6931
Strongsville *(G-17714)*
Atlantic Tool & Die Company ....C.... 330 769-4500
Seville *(G-16910)*
Automatic Stamp Products Inc ....F.... 216 781-7933
Cleveland *(G-4773)*
Avion Manufacturing Company ....G.... 330 220-1989
Brunswick *(G-2188)*
Ayling and Reichert Co Consent ....E.... 419 898-2471
Oak Harbor *(G-15441)*
Banner Metals Group Inc ....D.... 614 291-3105
Columbus *(G-6646)*
Barnes Group Inc ....G.... 440 526-5900
Brecksville *(G-2021)*
Bates Metal Products Inc ....D.... 740 498-8371
Port Washington *(G-16267)*
Bayloff Stmped Pdts Knsman Inc ....D.... 330 876-4511
Kinsman *(G-11463)*
Bellevue Manufacturing Company ....G.... 419 483-3190
Bellevue *(G-1532)*
Boehm Pressed Steel Company ....E.... 330 220-8000
Valley City *(G-19031)*
Brainerd Industries Inc ....E.... 937 228-0488
Miamisburg *(G-13644)*
Brainin-Advance Industries LLC ....E.... 513 874-9760
West Chester *(G-19663)*
Breitinger Company ....C.... 419 526-4255
Mansfield *(G-12414)*
Brooks Utility Products Group ....F.... 330 455-0301
Canton *(G-2599)*
Brw Tool Inc ....F.... 419 394-3371
Saint Marys *(G-16679)*
Buckeye Metals Industries Inc ....F.... 216 663-4300
Cleveland *(G-4849)*
Buckeye Stamping Company ....D.... 614 445-0059
Columbus *(G-6712)*
Buckley Manufacturing Company ....F.... 513 821-4444
Cincinnati *(G-3429)*
▲ **Bud Industries Inc** ....G.... 440 946-3200
Willoughby *(G-20289)*
C & C Fabrication Inc ....G.... 419 354-3535
Bowling Green *(G-1958)*
▲ **CA Picard Surface Engrg Inc** ....F.... 440 366-5400
Elyria *(G-9229)*
▲ **Calphalon Corporation** ....D.... 770 418-7100
Perrysburg *(G-15927)*
Camelot Manufacturing Inc ....F.... 419 678-2603
Coldwater *(G-6403)*
▲ **Catania Medallic Specialty** ....E.... 440 933-9595
Avon Lake *(G-981)*
Central Ohio Metal Stampi ....E.... 614 861-3332
Columbus *(G-6753)*
Clemens License Agency ....G.... 614 288-8007
Pickerington *(G-16043)*
▲ **Cleveland Die & Mfg Co** ....E.... 440 243-3404
Middleburg Heights *(G-13762)*
Cleveland Hollow Boring Inc ....G.... 216 883-1926
Cleveland *(G-4963)*
Cleveland Metal Stamping Co ....F.... 440 234-0010
Berea *(G-1596)*
Cole Tool & Die Company ....E.... 419 522-1272
Ontario *(G-15540)*
◆ **Com-Corp Industries Inc** ....D.... 216 431-6266
Cleveland *(G-4999)*
Compco Columbiana Company ....G.... 330 482-0200
Columbiana *(G-6462)*
Compco Industries Inc ....D.... 330 482-6488
Columbiana *(G-6463)*
Compressor Technologies Inc ....E.... 937 492-3711
Sidney *(G-17023)*
Connaughton Wldg & Fence LLC ....G.... 513 867-0230
Hamilton *(G-10547)*
Continental Business Entps Inc ....F.... 440 439-4400
Cleveland *(G-5020)*
Contour Forming Inc ....E.... 740 345-9777
Newark *(G-14864)*
▲ **Coreworth Holdings LLC** ....G.... 419 468-7100
Iberia *(G-11112)*
Cqt Kennedy LLC ....D.... 419 238-2442
Van Wert *(G-19086)*
Cubbison Company ....D.... 330 793-2481
Youngstown *(G-20882)*
Customformed Products Inc ....F.... 937 388-0480
Miamisburg *(G-13653)*
D & L Manufacturing Inc ....G.... 440 428-1627
Madison *(G-12346)*

SIC SECTION
34 FABRICATED METAL PRODUCTS, EXCEPT MACHINERY AND TRANSPORTATION EQUIPMENT

D J Klingler Inc G 513 891-2284 — Cincinnati *(G-3570)*

Dayton Tool Co Inc E 937 222-5501 — Dayton *(G-8146)*

Dayton Tractor & Crane G 937 317-5014 — Xenia *(G-20765)*

Deerfield Manufacturing Inc E 513 398-2010 — Mason *(G-12855)*

▲ Defiance Stamping Co D 419 782-5781 — Napoleon *(G-14537)*

Delafoil Pennsylvania Inc D 610 327-9565 — Perrysburg *(G-15939)*

Delta Tool & Die Stl Block Inc F 419 822-5939 — Delta *(G-8767)*

Dependable Stamping Company E 216 486-5522 — Cleveland *(G-5084)*

Deshler Metal Working Co Inc G 419 278-0472 — Deshler *(G-8788)*

▼ Destiny Manufacturing Inc E 330 273-9000 — Brunswick *(G-2199)*

▲ Die Co Inc E 440 942-8856 — Eastlake *(G-9104)*

▲ Die-Matic Corporation D 216 749-4656 — Brooklyn Heights *(G-2119)*

▼ Die-Mension Corporation F 330 273-5872 — Brunswick *(G-2200)*

Doan Machinery & Eqp Co Inc G 216 932-6243 — University Heights *(G-18941)*

Dove Die and Stamping Company E 216 267-3720 — Cleveland *(G-5109)*

Durivage Pattern & Mfg Co E 419 836-8655 — Williston *(G-20262)*

▲ Duro Dyne Midwest Corp B 513 870-6000 — Hamilton *(G-10551)*

Dyco Manufacturing Inc F 419 485-5525 — Montpelier *(G-14307)*

E C Shaw Co E 513 721-6334 — Cincinnati *(G-3616)*

Eagle Precision Products LLC G 440 582-9393 — North Royalton *(G-15270)*

▲ Ecp Corporation E 440 934-0444 — Avon *(G-948)*

Eisenhauer Mfg Co LLC D 419 238-0081 — Van Wert *(G-19090)*

Electrical Control Systems G 937 859-7136 — Dayton *(G-8179)*

Elliott Oren Products Inc E 419 298-2306 — Edgerton *(G-9173)*

Elyria Metal Spinning Fabg Co G 440 323-8068 — Elyria *(G-9253)*

Elyria Spring & Specialty Inc E 440 323-5502 — Elyria *(G-9256)*

▲ Ernie Green Industries Inc G 614 219-1423 — Columbus *(G-6903)*

▲ Ernst Metal Technologies LLC E 937 434-3133 — Moraine *(G-14351)*

Eurocase Architectural Cabinet F 330 674-0681 — Millersburg *(G-14081)*

▲ Even Heat Mfg Ltd F 330 695-9351 — Fredericksburg *(G-9950)*

Exact-Tool & Die Inc E 216 676-9140 — Cleveland *(G-5204)*

F & G Tool and Die Co E 937 746-3658 — Franklin *(G-9880)*

F C Brengman and Assoc LLC E 740 756-4308 — Carroll *(G-2904)*

Fairfield License Center Inc G 513 829-6224 — Hamilton *(G-10557)*

Falls Stamping & Welding Co C 330 928-1191 — Cuyahoga Falls *(G-7867)*

Famous Industries Inc D 740 685-2592 — Byesville *(G-2384)*

Faull & Son LLC F 330 652-4341 — Niles *(G-15008)*

Feinblanking Limited Inc G 513 860-2100 — West Chester *(G-19702)*

▲ Feintool US Operations Inc C 513 247-4061 — Blue Ash *(G-1774)*

▲ Findlay Products Corporation C 419 423-3324 — Findlay *(G-9687)*

Five Handicap Inc F 419 525-2511 — Mansfield *(G-12439)*

Flood Heliarc Inc F 614 835-3929 — Groveport *(G-10489)*

Formasters Corporation F 440 639-9206 — Mentor *(G-13445)*

Formetal Inc F 419 898-2211 — Oak Harbor *(G-15445)*

Frepeg Industries Inc F 440 255-8595 — Mentor *(G-13451)*

Fulton Industries Inc D 419 335-3015 — Wauseon *(G-19516)*

Fulton Manufacturing Inds LLC E 440 546-1435 — Brecksville *(G-2037)*

G & M Metal Products Inc G 513 863-3353 — Hamilton *(G-10561)*

▲ G & W Products LLC C 513 860-4050 — Fairfield *(G-9499)*

Gb Fabrication Company E 419 347-1835 — Shelby *(G-16982)*

Gb Fabrication Company E 419 896-3191 — Shiloh *(G-16993)*

▲ Gb Manufacturing Company D 419 822-5323 — Delta *(G-8772)*

Gem City Metal Tech LLC E 937 252-8998 — Dayton *(G-8220)*

▲ General Technologies Inc E 419 747-1800 — Mansfield *(G-12445)*

Gentzler Tool & Die Corp E 330 896-1941 — Akron *(G-188)*

Global Manufacturing Tech LLC G 440 205-1001 — Mentor *(G-13460)*

Gottschall Tool & Die Inc E 330 332-1544 — Salem *(G-16743)*

Gt Technologies Inc D 419 324-7300 — Toledo *(G-18314)*

▲ Guarantee Specialties Inc D 216 451-9744 — Strongsville *(G-17747)*

Guardian Engineering & Mfg Co G 419 335-1784 — Wauseon *(G-19518)*

▲ Gwp Holdings Inc D 513 860-4050 — Fairfield *(G-9501)*

H&M Mtal Stamping Assembly Inc F 216 898-9030 — Brookpark *(G-2149)*

▲ Hamlin Newco LLC D 330 753-7791 — Akron *(G-196)*

Hamlin Steel Products LLC D 330 753-7791 — Akron *(G-197)*

Hayford Technologies D 419 524-7627 — Mansfield *(G-12455)*

Heatherdowns License Bureau G 419 381-1109 — Toledo *(G-18326)*

Hercules Acquisition Corp E 419 287-3223 — Pemberville *(G-15884)*

Herd Manufacturing Inc E 216 651-4221 — Cleveland *(G-5397)*

▲ Hidaka Usa Inc E 614 889-8611 — Dublin *(G-8923)*

▲ Hill Manufacturing Inc E 419 335-5006 — Wauseon *(G-19520)*

Howland Machine Corp E 330 544-4029 — Niles *(G-15012)*

Hukon Manufacturing Company G 513 721-5562 — Cincinnati *(G-3828)*

Hynes Modern Pattern Co Inc G 937 322-3451 — Springfield *(G-17424)*

Ice Industries Inc G 513 398-2010 — Mason *(G-12889)*

▲ Ice Industries Inc E 419 842-3612 — Sylvania *(G-17943)*

Ice Industries Columbus Inc G 419 842-3600 — Sylvania *(G-17944)*

Impact Industries Inc E 440 327-2360 — North Ridgeville *(G-15230)*

Imperial Die & Mfg Co F 440 268-9080 — Strongsville *(G-17753)*

Imperial Metal Spinning Co G 216 524-5020 — Cleveland *(G-5445)*

Independent Power Consultants G 419 476-8383 — Toledo *(G-18344)*

Independent Stamping Inc E 216 251-3500 — Cleveland *(G-5451)*

Interlake Industries Inc G 440 942-0800 — Willoughby *(G-20345)*

Interlake Stamping Ohio Inc E 440 942-0800 — Willoughby *(G-20346)*

International Trade Group Inc G 614 486-4634 — Columbus *(G-7045)*

J B Stamping Inc E 216 631-0013 — Cleveland *(G-5484)*

▼ J R Machining Inc G 330 528-3406 — Hudson *(G-11058)*

J Schrader Co F 216 961-2890 — Cleveland *(G-5488)*

J Williams & Associates Inc G 330 887-1392 — Westfield Center *(G-20085)*

Jebco Machine Company Inc G 330 452-2909 — Canton *(G-2718)*

▲ Jet Stream International Inc E 330 505-9988 — Niles *(G-15018)*

Jones Metal Products Company C 740 545-6381 — West Lafayette *(G-19931)*

K & B Stamping & Manufacturing G 937 778-8875 — Piqua *(G-16135)*

K & H Industries LLC F 513 921-6770 — Cincinnati *(G-3889)*

K & L Die & Manufacturing G 419 895-1301 — Greenwich *(G-10405)*

Kelch Manufacturing Corp G 440 366-5060 — Elyria *(G-9282)*

◆ Kg63 LLC F 216 941-7766 — Cleveland *(G-5533)*

Knight Manufacturing Co Inc F 740 676-9532 — Shadyside *(G-16922)*

Knight Manufacturing Co Inc G 740 676-5516 — Shadyside *(G-16923)*

Knowlton Manufacturing Co Inc F 513 631-7353 — Cincinnati *(G-3920)*

Kreider Corp D 937 325-8787 — Springfield *(G-17436)*

L & W Inc D 734 397-6300 — Avon *(G-953)*

L C I Inc G 330 948-1922 — Lodi *(G-12013)*

La Ganke & Sons Stamping Co F 216 451-0278 — Columbia Station *(G-6439)*

Lakepark Industries Inc C 419 752-4471 — Greenwich *(G-10406)*

Langenau Manufacturing Company F 216 651-3400 — Cleveland *(G-5558)*

Larosa Die Engineering Inc G 513 284-9195 — Cincinnati *(G-3931)*

Lewark Metal Spinning Inc E 937 275-3303 — Dayton *(G-8312)*

Lextech Industries Ltd G 216 883-7900 — Cleveland *(G-5574)*

▲ Logan Machine Company D 330 633-6163 — Akron *(G-259)*

▲ Long-Stanton Mfg Company E 513 874-8020 — West Chester *(G-19738)*

Lowery Industries G 740 745-5045 — Saint Louisville *(G-16673)*

M S C Industries Inc G 440 474-8788 — Rome *(G-16564)*

Mahoning Valley Manufacturing E 330 537-4492 — Beloit *(G-1571)*

Malin Wire Co E 216 267-9080 — Cleveland *(G-5608)*

▲ Malin Wire Co G 216 267-9080 — Cleveland *(G-5607)*

Mallory Pattern Works Inc G 419 726-8001 — Toledo *(G-18398)*

Mansfield Industries Inc E 419 524-1300 — Mansfield *(G-12477)*

▼ Marc V Concepts Inc F 419 782-6505 — Defiance *(G-8635)*

Mark True Engraving Co G 216 651-7700 — Cleveland *(G-5619)*

Master Products Company D 216 341-1740 — Cleveland *(G-5634)*

▲ Matco Tools Corporation B 330 929-4949 — Stow *(G-17605)*

Maumee Assembly & Stamping LLC D 419 304-2887 — Maumee *(G-13129)*

McAfee Tool & Die Inc E 330 896-9555 — Uniontown *(G-18927)*

McGlennon Metal Products Inc F 614 252-7114 — Columbus *(G-7166)*

Medina Blanking Inc C 330 558-2300 — Valley City *(G-19049)*

Merrick Manufacturing II LLC G 937 222-7164 — Dayton *(G-8341)*

Metal & Wire Products Company D 330 332-9448 — Salem *(G-16760)*

Metal Fabricating Corporation D 216 631-8121 — Cleveland *(G-5658)*

Metal Products Company E 330 652-2558 — Niles *(G-15021)*

Metal Products Company E 330 652-6201 — Niles *(G-15022)*

Metal Stampings Unlimited F 937 328-0206 — Springfield *(G-17445)*

Mic-Ray Metal Products Inc F 216 791-2206 — Cleveland *(G-5665)*

Mid-America Steel Corp E 800 282-3466 — Cleveland *(G-5674)*

Middletown License Agency Inc F 513 422-7225 — Middletown *(G-13928)*

Midway Products Group Inc G 419 422-7070 — Findlay *(G-9725)*

S I C

Employee Codes: A=Over 500 employees, B=251-500 C=101-250, D=51-100, E=20-50, F=10-19, G=3-9
2019 Harris Ohio Industrial Directory
935

Modern Engineering ....G 440 593-5414
Conneaut *(G-7656)*

Modern Pipe Supports Corp ....E 216 361-1666
Cleveland *(G-5700)*

Mohawk Manufacturing Inc ....G 860 632-2345
Mount Vernon *(G-14493)*

Monode Steel Stamp Inc ....E 419 929-3501
New London *(G-14732)*

Monode Steel Stamp Inc ....F 440 975-8802
Mentor *(G-13523)*

▲ **Morgal Machine Tool Co** ....D 937 325-5561
Springfield *(G-17451)*

▼ **Mtd Holdings Inc** ....B 330 225-2600
Valley City *(G-19052)*

N N Metal Stampings Inc ....E 419 737-2311
Pioneer *(G-16086)*

Nebraska Industries Corp ....E 419 335-6010
Wauseon *(G-19529)*

New Bremen Machine & Tool Co ....E 419 629-3295
New Bremen *(G-14657)*

New Can Company Inc ....G 937 547-9050
Greenville *(G-10385)*

New Holland Engineering Inc ....G 740 495-5200
New Holland *(G-14702)*

Neway Stamping & Mfg Inc ....D 440 951-8500
Willoughby *(G-20388)*

Nicholas Press Sales LLC ....G 440 652-6604
Brunswick *(G-2222)*

Niles Manufacturing & Finshg ....C 330 544-0402
Niles *(G-15024)*

Northern Stamping Co ....F 216 883-8888
Cleveland *(G-5782)*

▲ **Northern Stamping Co** ....C 216 883-8888
Cleveland *(G-5783)*

Northwind Industries Inc ....E 216 433-0666
Cleveland *(G-5787)*

Northwood Industries Inc ....F 419 666-2100
Perrysburg *(G-15983)*

Norwood Medical ....G 937 228-4101
Dayton *(G-8385)*

Norwood Medical ....C 937 228-4101
Dayton *(G-8386)*

Norwood Tool Company ....C 937 228-4101
Dayton *(G-8387)*

Ohio Associated Entps LLC ....E 440 354-3148
Painesville *(G-15770)*

▲ **Ohio Gasket and Shim Co Inc** ....E 330 630-0626
Akron *(G-307)*

Ohio Stamping & Machine LLC ....C 937 322-3880
Springfield *(G-17464)*

Ohio Valley Manufacturing Inc ....D 419 522-5818
Mansfield *(G-12497)*

▲ **Omni Manufacturing Inc** ....D 419 394-7424
Saint Marys *(G-16693)*

Omni Manufacturing Inc ....F 419 394-7424
Saint Marys *(G-16694)*

Oneida Group Inc ....C 740 687-2500
Lancaster *(G-11595)*

Orick Stamping ....D 419 331-0600
Elida *(G-9197)*

Ottawa Products Co ....E 419 836-5115
Curtice *(G-7826)*

P & A Industries Inc ....C 419 422-7070
Findlay *(G-9738)*

P M Motor Company ....F 440 327-9999
North Ridgeville *(G-15243)*

▲ **Pacific Manufacturing Ohio Inc** ....B 513 860-3900
Fairfield *(G-9542)*

Pacific Manufacturing Tenn Inc ....E 513 900-7862
Jackson *(G-11194)*

Paramount Stamping & Wldg Co ....D 216 631-1755
Cleveland *(G-5840)*

Parker-Hannifin Corporation ....F 330 336-3511
Wadsworth *(G-19262)*

Parma Heights License Bureau ....G 440 888-0388
Cleveland *(G-5852)*

▼ **Pax Machine Works Inc** ....C 419 586-2337
Celina *(G-2978)*

PDQ Technologies Inc ....F 937 274-4958
Dayton *(G-8419)*

Peerless Metal Products Inc ....E 216 431-6905
Cleveland *(G-5861)*

Pennant Moldings Inc ....C 937 584-5411
Sabina *(G-16617)*

◆ **Pentaflex Inc** ....C 937 325-5551
Springfield *(G-17470)*

Perry Welding Service Inc ....F 330 425-2211
Twinsburg *(G-18836)*

Pettit W T & Sons Co Inc ....G 330 539-6100
Girard *(G-10264)*

Pfahl Gauge & Manufacturing Co ....G 330 633-8402
Akron *(G-319)*

Phillips Mch & Stamping Corp ....G 330 882-6714
New Franklin *(G-14696)*

▲ **Plating Technology Inc** ....D 937 268-6882
Dayton *(G-8428)*

Precision Die & Stamping Inc ....G 513 942-8220
West Chester *(G-19764)*

Precision Metal Products Inc ....F 216 447-1900
Cleveland *(G-5911)*

Precision Pressed Powdered Met ....F 937 433-6802
Dayton *(G-8435)*

Premier Stamping and Assembly ....G 440 293-8961
Williamsfield *(G-20259)*

◆ **Production Products Inc** ....D 734 241-7242
Columbus Grove *(G-7637)*

Progress Tool & Stamping Inc ....E 419 628-2384
Minster *(G-14223)*

Progressive Machine Die Inc ....E 330 405-6600
Macedonia *(G-12321)*

Project Engineering Company ....F 937 743-9114
Miamisburg *(G-13706)*

Public Safety Ohio Department ....G 440 943-5545
Willowick *(G-20481)*

Q Model Inc ....E 330 673-0473
Barberton *(G-1100)*

Quality Fabricated Metals Inc ....E 330 332-7008
Salem *(G-16769)*

Quality Metal Products Inc ....G 440 355-6165
Lagrange *(G-11492)*

Quality Stamping Products Co ....F 216 441-2700
Cleveland *(G-5945)*

Quality Tool Company ....E 419 476-8228
Toledo *(G-18490)*

R K Metals Ltd ....E 513 874-6055
Fairfield *(G-9556)*

R L Rush Tool & Pattern Inc ....G 419 562-9849
Bucyrus *(G-2342)*

Racelite South Coast Inc ....F 216 581-4600
Maple Heights *(G-12578)*

▲ **Range Kleen Mfg Inc** ....B 419 331-8000
Elida *(G-9199)*

Rapid Machine Inc ....F 419 737-2377
Pioneer *(G-16094)*

Ratliff Metal Spinning Co Inc ....E 937 836-3900
Englewood *(G-9374)*

RB&w Manufacturing LLC ....G 740 363-1971
Delaware *(G-8718)*

▲ **RB&w Manufacturing LLC** ....F 234 380-8540
Streetsboro *(G-17691)*

Regal Metal Products Co ....E 330 868-6343
Minerva *(G-14198)*

Regal Metal Products Co ....F 330 868-6343
Minerva *(G-14199)*

Rezmann Karoly ....G 216 441-4357
Cleveland *(G-5982)*

Ridge Tool Manufacturing Co ....A 440 323-5581
Elyria *(G-9322)*

Rittal Corp ....C 440 572-4999
Strongsville *(G-17782)*

Rittal Corp ....F 937 399-0500
Springfield *(G-17484)*

Rittal North America LLC ....C 937 399-0500
Urbana *(G-19010)*

Rjm Stamping Co ....F 614 443-1191
Columbus *(G-7396)*

Robin Industries Inc ....G 216 267-3554
Cleveland *(G-5995)*

Roemer Industries Inc ....D 330 448-2000
Masury *(G-13062)*

Ronfeldt Associates Inc ....D 419 382-5641
Toledo *(G-18506)*

Ronfeldt Manufacturing LLC ....F 419 382-5641
Toledo *(G-18507)*

Ronlen Industries Inc ....E 330 273-6468
Brunswick *(G-2236)*

Roper Lockbox LLC ....G 330 656-5148
Hudson *(G-11071)*

S-P Company Inc ....F 330 482-0200
Columbiana *(G-6479)*

Saco Lowell Parts LLC ....E 330 794-1535
Akron *(G-367)*

Sakas Incorporated ....E 740 862-4114
Baltimore *(G-1042)*

Schoen Industries Inc ....G 330 533-6659
Canfield *(G-2544)*

Schott Metal Products Company ....D 330 773-7873
Akron *(G-373)*

Scott Fetzer Company ....C 216 267-9000
Cleveland *(G-6035)*

Sectional Stamping Inc ....B 440 647-2100
Wellington *(G-19591)*

Seilkop Industries Inc ....E 513 761-1035
Cincinnati *(G-4316)*

◆ **Select Industries Corporation** ....C 937 233-9191
Dayton *(G-8502)*

Service Stampings Inc ....E 440 946-2330
Willoughby *(G-20427)*

Seven Ranges Mfg Corp ....E 330 627-7155
Carrollton *(G-2928)*

Shiloh Automotive Inc ....E 330 558-2600
Valley City *(G-19061)*

Shiloh Corporation ....B 330 558-2600
Valley City *(G-19062)*

Shiloh Industries Inc ....A 440 647-2100
Wellington *(G-19592)*

Shiloh Industries Inc ....A 330 558-2600
Valley City *(G-19065)*

◆ **Shiloh Industries Inc** ....G 330 558-2600
Valley City *(G-19066)*

Smithville Mfg Co ....E 330 345-5818
Wooster *(G-20655)*

Spectrum Machine Inc ....E 330 626-3666
Streetsboro *(G-17699)*

SPR Machine Inc ....G 513 737-8040
Fairfield Township *(G-9586)*

Stamped Steel Products Inc ....F 330 538-3951
North Jackson *(G-15155)*

Stanley Industrial & Auto LLC ....C 614 755-7089
Westerville *(G-20024)*

Stolle Machinery Company LLC ....C 937 497-5400
Sidney *(G-17082)*

Stolle Properties Inc ....A 513 932-8664
Blue Ash *(G-1852)*

▲ **Stripmatic Products Inc** ....E 216 241-7143
Cleveland *(G-6111)*

Stuebing Automatic Machine Co ....E 513 771-8028
Cincinnati *(G-4388)*

Suburban Manufacturing Co ....D 440 953-2024
Eastlake *(G-9133)*

▲ **Sunfield Inc** ....D 740 928-0404
Hebron *(G-10764)*

Superfine Manufacturing Inc ....F 330 897-9024
Fresno *(G-10071)*

◆ **Superior Metal Products Inc** ....E 419 228-1145
Lima *(G-11947)*

Superior Steel Stamp Co ....G 216 431-6460
Cleveland *(G-6127)*

▲ **Supply Technologies LLC** ....C 440 947-2100
Cleveland *(G-6130)*

Supply Technologies LLC ....G 937 898-5795
Dayton *(G-8530)*

Swivel-Tek Industries LLC ....G 419 636-7770
Bryan *(G-2308)*

T & D Fabricating Inc ....E 440 951-5646
Eastlake *(G-9135)*

T and W Stamping Acquisition ....F 330 821-5777
Alliance *(G-505)*

▲ **Takk Industries Inc** ....F 513 353-4306
Cleves *(G-6378)*

▲ **Talan Products Inc** ....D 216 458-0170
Cleveland *(G-6147)*

▲ **Talent Tool & Die Inc** ....E 440 239-8777
Berea *(G-1627)*

▲ **Taylor Metal Products Co** ....C 419 522-3471
Mansfield *(G-12526)*

TEC Design & Manufacturing Inc ....F 937 435-2147
Dayton *(G-8549)*

Tech-Med Inc ....F 216 486-0900
Euclid *(G-9445)*

Tenacity Manufacturing Company ....E 513 821-0201
West Chester *(G-19807)*

The Reliable Spring Wire Frms ....E 440 365-7400
Elyria *(G-9338)*

The W L Jenkins Company ....F 330 477-3407
Canton *(G-2835)*

▲ **Thk Manufacturing America Inc** ....C 740 928-1415
Hebron *(G-10766)*

▼ **Toledo Metal Spinning Company** ....E 419 535-5931
Toledo *(G-18561)*

▲ **Toledo Tool and Die Co Inc** ....E 419 476-4422
Toledo *(G-18574)*

Tool & Die Systems Inc ....E 440 327-5800
North Ridgeville *(G-15256)*

Torr Metal Products Inc ....E 216 671-1616
Cleveland *(G-6189)*

Transportation Ohio Department ....G 740 927-2285
Pataskala *(G-15846)*

▲ **Transue & Williams Stampg Corp** ....F 330 821-5777
Alliance *(G-508)*

Transue & Williams Stampg Corp .... F 330 270-0891
Youngstown *(G-21050)*
Transue Williams Stamping Inc .... G 330 270-0891
Austintown *(G-935)*
▲ **Transue Williams Stamping Inc** .... G 330 829-5007
Alliance *(G-509)*
Treaty City Industries Inc .... F 937 548-9000
Greenville *(G-10398)*
▲ **Triad Metal Products Company** .... D 216 676-6505
Chagrin Falls *(G-3084)*
▲ **Trucut Incorporated** .... D 330 938-9806
Sebring *(G-16896)*
True Turn Industries .... G 440 355-6256
Lagrange *(G-11495)*
▲ **Twist Inc** .... C 937 675-9581
Jamestown *(G-11221)*
Twist Inc .... E 937 675-9581
Jamestown *(G-11222)*
United Die & Mfg Co .... E 330 938-6141
Sebring *(G-16897)*
▲ **Universal Metal Products Inc** .... C 440 943-3040
Wickliffe *(G-20235)*
Universal Metal Products Inc .... E 419 287-3223
Pemberville *(G-15887)*
V K C Inc .... F 440 951-9634
Mentor *(G-13621)*
Valley Tool & Die Inc .... D 440 237-0160
North Royalton *(G-15309)*
▼ **Varbros LLC** .... C 216 267-5200
Cleveland *(G-6250)*
Veeders Mailbox Inc .... G 513 984-8749
Cincinnati *(G-4468)*
Verhoff Machine & Welding Inc .... C 419 596-3202
Continental *(G-7669)*
▲ **Voss Industries LLC** .... C 216 771-7655
Cleveland *(G-6273)*
W M Inc .... E 330 427-6115
Washingtonville *(G-19482)*
Washington Products Inc .... F 330 837-5101
Massillon *(G-13057)*
Weber Technologies Inc .... E 440 946-8833
Eastlake *(G-9140)*
▲ **Wedge Products Inc** .... B 330 405-4477
Twinsburg *(G-18873)*
Weiss Industries Inc .... E 419 526-2480
Mansfield *(G-12539)*
Welage Corporation .... F 513 681-2300
Cincinnati *(G-4495)*
▲ **Whirlaway Corporation** .... C 440 647-4711
Wellington *(G-19595)*
Willow Hill Industries LLC .... D 440 942-3003
Willoughby *(G-20459)*
Winzeler Stamping Co .... D 419 485-3147
Montpelier *(G-14322)*
Wire Products Company Inc .... C 216 267-0777
Cleveland *(G-6316)*
Wisco Products Incorporated .... E 937 228-2101
Dayton *(G-8598)*
▼ **Witt Industries Inc** .... D 513 871-5700
Mason *(G-12955)*
▲ **WLS Fabricating Co** .... E 440 449-0543
Cleveland *(G-6317)*
▲ **WLS Stamping Co** .... D 216 271-5100
Cleveland *(G-6318)*
Wtd Real Estate Inc .... D 440 934-5305
Avon *(G-977)*
▲ **Ysk Corporation** .... B 740 774-7315
Chillicothe *(G-3231)*
ZF North America Inc .... D 419 726-5599
Toledo *(G-18605)*
ZF North America Inc .... E 216 750-2400
Cleveland *(G-6340)*
ZF North America Inc .... B 216 332-7100
Cleveland *(G-6341)*
Zip Tool & Die Inc .... F 216 267-1117
Cleveland *(G-6343)*

3471 Electroplating, Plating, Polishing, Anodizing & Coloring

A & B Deburring Company .... F 513 723-0444
Cincinnati *(G-3274)*
▲ **A J Oster Foils LLC** .... D 330 823-1700
Alliance *(G-447)*
A-Brite LP .... D 216 252-2995
Cleveland *(G-4594)*
Abel Metal Processing Inc .... F 216 881-4156
Cleveland *(G-4597)*
Acme Industrial Group Inc .... F 330 821-3900
Alliance *(G-449)*
ADS Mto .... G 419 424-5231
Findlay *(G-9646)*
Aetna Plating Co .... F 216 341-9111
Cleveland *(G-4637)*
Ak-Isg Steel Coating Company .... D 216 429-6901
Cleveland *(G-4647)*
Akron Plating Co Inc .... F 330 773-6878
Akron *(G-47)*
Allegheny Ludlum LLC .... E 330 875-2244
Louisville *(G-12151)*
Allen Aircraft Products Inc .... E 330 296-1531
Ravenna *(G-16366)*
Allen Aircraft Products Inc .... E 330 296-9621
Ravenna *(G-16365)*
Als Polishing Shop Inc .... G 419 476-8857
Toledo *(G-18167)*
Aluminum Color Industries Inc .... D 330 536-6295
Lowellville *(G-12248)*
Aluminum Extruded Shapes Inc .... C 513 563-2205
Cincinnati *(G-3328)*
Amac Enterprises Inc .... D 216 362-1880
Cleveland *(G-4681)*
▲ **Amac Enterprises Inc** .... C 216 362-1880
Parma *(G-15814)*
American Indus Maintanence .... G 937 254-3400
Dayton *(G-8026)*
American Metal Cleaning Inc .... G 419 255-1828
Toledo *(G-18175)*
American Metal Coatings Inc .... E 216 451-3131
Mentor *(G-13385)*
American Mtal Clg Cncnnati Inc .... G 513 825-1171
Cincinnati *(G-3336)*
American Quality Stripping .... E 419 625-6288
Sandusky *(G-16794)*
Anchor Fabricators Inc .... E 937 836-5117
Clayton *(G-4571)*
Anodizing Specialists Inc .... F 440 951-0257
Mentor *(G-13389)*
▲ **Anomatic Corporation** .... B 740 522-2203
Johnstown *(G-11255)*
Anomatic Corporation .... B 740 522-2203
Newark *(G-14851)*
Applied Metals Tech Ltd .... E 216 741-3236
Brooklyn Heights *(G-2115)*
▲ **Arcelormittal Columbus LLC** .... C 614 492-6800
Columbus *(G-6613)*
Archer Custom Chrome LLC .... G 216 441-2795
Westlake *(G-20099)*
Arem Co .... F 440 974-6740
Mentor *(G-13393)*
Areway Acquisition Inc .... D 216 651-9022
Brooklyn *(G-2111)*
▲ **Atom Blasting & Finishing Inc** .... G 440 235-4765
Columbia Station *(G-6429)*
Auto Core Systems .... G 740 362-5599
Delaware *(G-8657)*
Autocoat .... G 419 636-3830
Bryan *(G-2266)*
◆ **Automated Wheel LLC** .... D 216 651-9022
Cleveland *(G-4771)*
Automation Finishing Inc .... E 216 251-8805
Cleveland *(G-4774)*
B & R Custom Chrome .... G 419 536-7215
Toledo *(G-18197)*
▲ **Badboy Blasters Incorporated** .... F 330 454-2699
Canton *(G-2583)*
Bar Processing Corporation .... D 330 872-0914
Newton Falls *(G-14985)*
▲ **Barker Products Company** .... E 216 249-0900
Cleveland *(G-4792)*
Bedford Anodizing Co .... E 330 650-6052
Hudson *(G-11034)*
Beringer Plating Inc .... G 330 633-8409
Akron *(G-84)*
Best Plating Rack Corp .... F 440 944-3270
Wickliffe *(G-20203)*
Bmd Blasting .... G 614 580-9468
Columbus *(G-6681)*
Boville Indus Coatings Inc .... E 330 669-8558
Smithville *(G-17087)*
Bricker Plating Inc .... G 419 636-1990
Bryan *(G-2271)*
Buffex Metal Finishing Inc .... F 216 631-2202
Cleveland *(G-4851)*
Canton Plating Co Inc .... G 330 452-7808
Canton *(G-2616)*
Carlisle and Finch Company .... E 513 681-6080
Cincinnati *(G-3445)*
Carpe Diem Industries LLC .... E 419 358-0129
Bluffton *(G-1887)*
Carpe Diem Industries LLC .... D 419 659-5639
Columbus Grove *(G-7632)*
Carter Machine Company Inc .... G 419 468-3530
Galion *(G-10125)*
Cascade Plating Inc .... G 440 366-4931
Elyria *(G-9232)*
Case Plating Inc .... G 440 288-8304
Lorain *(G-12083)*
Century Plating Inc .... G 216 531-4131
Cleveland *(G-4902)*
Charles J Meyers .... G 513 922-2866
Cincinnati *(G-3465)*
Chemical Methods Inc .... E 216 476-8400
Strongsville *(G-17725)*
▲ **Chemical Solvents Inc** .... E 216 741-9310
Cleveland *(G-4919)*
Chromatic Inc .... F 216 881-2228
Cleveland *(G-4926)*
Chrome & Speed Cycle LLC .... G 937 429-5656
Beavercreek *(G-1305)*
Chrome Deposit Corporatio .... G 330 773-7800
Akron *(G-116)*
Chrome Deposit Corporation .... E 513 539-8486
Monroe *(G-14257)*
Chrome Deposit Corporation .... E 513 539-8486
Monroe *(G-14258)*
Chrome Industries Inc .... G 216 771-2266
Cleveland *(G-4927)*
Cincinnati Gearing Systems Inc .... D 513 527-8600
Cincinnati *(G-3493)*
City Plating and Polishing LLC .... G 216 267-8158
Cleveland *(G-4933)*
Cleveland Finishing Inc .... G 440 572-5475
Strongsville *(G-17728)*
Cleveland Plating .... G 216 249-0300
Cleveland *(G-4969)*
CMF Custom Metal Finishers .... G 513 821-8145
Cincinnati *(G-3532)*
Columbus Coatings Company .... D 614 492-6800
Columbus *(G-6786)*
Commercial Anodizing Co .... E 440 942-8384
Willoughby *(G-20298)*
▲ **Commercial Honing LLC** .... D 330 343-8896
Dover *(G-8811)*
Commercial Steel Treating Co .... F 216 431-8204
Cleveland *(G-5004)*
Conley Group Inc .... G 330 372-2030
Warren *(G-19388)*
Crystal Koch Finishing Inc .... G 440 366-7526
Elyria *(G-9240)*
Custom Brass Finishing Inc .... G 330 453-0888
Canton *(G-2641)*
Custom Nickel LLC .... G 937 222-1995
Dayton *(G-8121)*
Custom Polishing .... G 937 596-0430
Sidney *(G-17024)*
Custom Powdercoating LLC .... G 937 972-3516
Dayton *(G-8122)*
Customchrome Plating Inc .... F 440 926-3116
Grafton *(G-10296)*
D-G Custom Chrome LLC .... D 513 531-1881
Cincinnati *(G-3571)*
Davro Ltd .... G 216 258-0057
Cleveland *(G-5071)*
Delta Plating Inc .... E 330 452-2300
Canton *(G-2655)*
Derrick Company Inc .... E 513 321-8122
Cincinnati *(G-3583)*
Diamond Hard Chrome Co Inc .... F 216 391-3618
Cleveland *(G-5089)*
▲ **Die Co Inc** .... E 440 942-8856
Eastlake *(G-9104)*
Durable Plating Co .... G 216 391-2132
Cleveland *(G-5121)*
Duray Plating Company Inc .... E 216 941-5540
Cleveland *(G-5122)*
E L Stone Company .... E 330 825-4565
Norton *(G-15365)*
Electro Polish Company Inc .... E 937 222-3611
Dayton *(G-8180)*
Electro Prime Assembly Inc .... F 419 476-0100
Rossford *(G-16583)*
▲ **Electro Prime Group LLC** .... D 419 476-0100
Toledo *(G-18278)*
Electro Prime Group LLC .... D 419 666-5000
Rossford *(G-16584)*
Electro-Metallics Co .... G 513 423-8091
Middletown *(G-13904)*
Electrolizing Corporation Ohio .... E 216 451-3153
Cleveland *(G-5165)*

Employee Codes: A=Over 500 employees, B=251-500
C=101-250, D=51-100, E=20-50, F=10-19, G=3-9
2019 Harris Ohio
Industrial Directory
937

34 FABRICATED METAL PRODUCTS, EXCEPT MACHINERY AND TRANSPORTATION EQUIPMENT SIC SECTION

Electrolizing Corporation Ohio..............F....... 216 451-8653
Cleveland *(G-5166)*
Elyria Plating Corporation......................E....... 440 365-8300
Elyria *(G-9255)*
Engineering Coatings LLC......................G....... 419 485-0077
Montpelier *(G-14309)*
Epd Enterprises Inc..............................D....... 216 961-1200
Cleveland *(G-5184)*
Equinox Enterprises LLC.......................F....... 419 627-0022
Sandusky *(G-16810)*
Erieview Metal Treating Co....................D....... 216 663-1780
Cleveland *(G-5191)*
▲ Ernie Green Industries Inc...............G....... 614 219-1423
Columbus *(G-6903)*
▲ Etched Metal Company......................E....... 440 248-0240
Solon *(G-17142)*
Euclid Refinishing Compnay Inc...........F....... 440 275-3356
Austinburg *(G-920)*
Faithful Mold Polishing Ex....................G....... 330 678-8006
Kent *(G-11321)*
Finishers Inc..G....... 937 773-3177
Piqua *(G-16115)*
Foundry Support Operation...................F....... 440 951-4142
Mentor *(G-13446)*
Future Finishes Inc................................E....... 513 860-0020
Hamilton *(G-10559)*
Gateway Metal Finishing Inc.................E....... 216 267-2580
Cleveland *(G-5296)*
Gei of Columbiana Inc...........................D....... 330 783-0270
Youngstown *(G-20915)*
General Extrusions Inc..........................D....... 330 783-0270
Youngstown *(G-20917)*
GRB Holdings Inc..................................D....... 937 236-3250
Dayton *(G-8235)*
▲ Guaranteed Fnshg Unlimited Inc......E....... 216 252-8200
Cleveland *(G-5358)*
H & R Metal Finishing Inc.....................G....... 440 942-6656
Willoughby *(G-20335)*
Hadronics Inc...D....... 513 321-9350
Cincinnati *(G-3792)*
Hale Performance Coatings Inc............E....... 419 244-6451
Toledo *(G-18319)*
Hall Company...E....... 937 652-1376
Urbana *(G-18992)*
Hartzell Mfg Co......................................E....... 937 859-5955
Miamisburg *(G-13674)*
Hayes Metalfinishing Inc.......................G....... 937 228-7550
Dayton *(G-8245)*
Hearn Plating Co Ltd.............................F....... 419 473-9773
Toledo *(G-18325)*
Hercules Polishing & Plating................F....... 330 455-8871
Canton *(G-2697)*
Highland Precision Plating....................G....... 937 393-9501
Hillsboro *(G-10880)*
Hy-Blast Inc..F....... 513 424-0704
Middletown *(G-13912)*
Indigo 48 LLC...G....... 419 551-6931
Montpelier *(G-14310)*
Industrial Mill Maintenance...................E....... 330 746-1155
Youngstown *(G-20939)*
Industrial Paint & Strip Inc...................E....... 419 568-2222
Waynesfield *(G-19567)*
International Finishing LLC..................G....... 937 293-3340
Dayton *(G-8273)*
Ips Treatments Inc.................................G....... 419 241-5955
Toledo *(G-18352)*
J Horst Manufacturing Co.....................D....... 330 828-2216
Dalton *(G-7945)*
J J Polishing Inc.....................................G....... 614 214-7637
Plain City *(G-16197)*
J M Hamilton Group Inc........................F....... 419 229-4010
Lima *(G-11881)*
J M S Custom Finishing.........................G....... 614 264-9916
Hilliard *(G-10832)*
Jason Incorporated.................................F....... 513 860-3400
Hamilton *(G-10576)*
Jotco Inc...G....... 513 721-4943
Mansfield *(G-12465)*
K-B Plating Inc.......................................F....... 216 341-1115
Cleveland *(G-5514)*
Kel-Mar Inc...E....... 419 806-4600
Bowling Green *(G-1979)*
Kelly Plating Co......................................E....... 216 961-1080
Cleveland *(G-5526)*
Krendl Rack Co Inc.................................G....... 419 667-4800
Venedocia *(G-19154)*
Kyron Plating Corp.................................F....... 216 221-7275
Cleveland *(G-5548)*
L & N Olde Car Co...................................G....... 440 564-7204
Newbury *(G-14959)*

Lake City Plating LLC............................F....... 440 964-3555
Ashtabula *(G-784)*
Lake County Plating Corp.....................F....... 440 255-8835
Mentor *(G-13494)*
Lakeside Custom Plating Inc.................G....... 440 599-2035
Conneaut *(G-7652)*
Leonhardt Plating Company.................E....... 513 242-1410
Cincinnati *(G-3938)*
Lima Sandblasting & Pntg Co...............G....... 419 331-2939
Lima *(G-11892)*
◆ Luke Engineering & Mfg Corp...........E....... 330 335-1501
Wadsworth *(G-19252)*
Luke Engineering & Mfg Corp..............E....... 330 925-3344
Rittman *(G-16525)*
Lustrous Metal Coatings Inc.................E....... 330 478-4653
Canton *(G-2735)*
M I P Inc..F....... 330 744-0215
Youngstown *(G-20964)*
M&L Plating Works LLC.........................G....... 419 255-7701
Toledo *(G-18393)*
Master Chrome Service Inc...................E....... 216 961-2012
Cleveland *(G-5630)*
▲ McCrary Metal Polishing Inc.............F....... 937 492-1979
Port Jefferson *(G-16265)*
McGean-Rohco Inc.................................D....... 216 441-4900
Newburgh Heights *(G-14941)*
Mechanical Finishers Inc LLC................E....... 513 641-5419
Cincinnati *(G-3993)*
Mechanical Finishing Inc.......................E....... 513 641-5419
Cincinnati *(G-3994)*
▲ Mechanical Galv-Plating Corp..........E....... 937 492-3143
Sidney *(G-17051)*
Medina Plating Corp...............................E....... 330 725-4155
Medina *(G-13294)*
Merk Blasting..G....... 513 813-6375
Cincinnati *(G-4008)*
Metal Brite Polishing..............................F....... 937 278-9739
Dayton *(G-8342)*
Metal Finishers Inc.................................F....... 937 492-9175
Sidney *(G-17052)*
Metal Finishing Needs Ltd.....................G....... 216 561-6334
Cleveland *(G-5659)*
Metaltek Industries Inc..........................F....... 937 323-4933
Springfield *(G-17447)*
Metokote Corporation............................D....... 440 934-4686
Sheffield Village *(G-16971)*
Metokote Corporation............................C....... 419 221-2754
Lima *(G-11905)*
Miami Valley Polishing LL......................G....... 937 498-1634
Sidney *(G-17053)*
Miami Valley Polishing LLC...................F....... 937 615-9353
Piqua *(G-16143)*
Micro Lapping & Grinding Co................E....... 216 267-6500
Cleveland *(G-5667)*
Micro Metal Finishing LLC....................D....... 513 541-3095
Cincinnati *(G-4022)*
Micro Products Co Inc...........................D....... 440 943-0258
Willoughby Hills *(G-20471)*
Microfinish Inc..D....... 937 264-1598
Vandalia *(G-19138)*
Microsheen Corporation........................F....... 216 481-5610
Cleveland *(G-5670)*
▲ Microtek Finishing LLC.....................E....... 513 766-5600
West Chester *(G-19879)*
Milestone Services Corp.......................G....... 330 374-9988
Akron *(G-282)*
Mmf Incorporated...................................F....... 614 252-2522
Columbus *(G-7187)*
Moore Chrome Products Co..................E....... 419 843-3510
Sylvania *(G-17952)*
MPC Plastics Inc.....................................D....... 216 881-7220
Cleveland *(G-5708)*
▲ MPC Plating LLC.................................E....... 216 881-7220
Cleveland *(G-5709)*
MPC Plating LLC.....................................E....... 216 881-7220
Cleveland *(G-5710)*
National Plating Corporation................E....... 216 341-6707
Cleveland *(G-5727)*
National Polishing Systems Inc............E....... 330 659-6547
Richfield *(G-16477)*
New Castle Industries Inc.....................C....... 724 654-2603
Youngstown *(G-20975)*
Newsome & Work Metalizing Co..........G....... 330 376-7144
Akron *(G-296)*
Nicks Plating Co Inc...............................F....... 937 773-3175
Piqua *(G-16145)*
Niles Manufacturing & Finshg..............C....... 330 544-0402
Niles *(G-15024)*
▲ Novavision Inc....................................D....... 419 354-1427
Bowling Green *(G-1986)*

Ohio Anodizing Company Inc................F....... 614 252-7855
Columbus *(G-7240)*
◆ Ohio Decorative Products LLC..........C....... 419 647-9033
Spencerville *(G-17311)*
Ohio Electro-Polishing Co Inc...............G....... 419 667-2281
Venedocia *(G-19155)*
▲ Ohio Metal Products Company.........E....... 937 228-6101
Dayton *(G-8399)*
Ohio Metalizing LLC...............................G....... 330 830-1092
Massillon *(G-13030)*
Ohio Roll Grinding Inc............................E....... 330 453-1884
Louisville *(G-12162)*
Oliver Chemical Co Inc...........................G....... 513 541-4540
Cincinnati *(G-4110)*
P & C Metal Polishing Inc.......................E....... 513 771-9143
Cincinnati *(G-4128)*
▼ P & J Industries Inc............................C....... 419 726-2675
Toledo *(G-18452)*
P & J Manufacturing Inc.........................F....... 419 241-7369
Toledo *(G-18453)*
P & L Heat Trting Grinding Inc..............E....... 330 746-1339
Youngstown *(G-20986)*
Parker Rst-Proof Cleveland Inc.............E....... 216 481-6680
Cleveland *(G-5847)*
Parker Trutec Incorporated...................D....... 937 653-8500
Urbana *(G-19007)*
Paxos Plating Inc....................................E....... 330 479-0022
Canton *(G-2782)*
Piedmont Chemical Co Inc.....................G....... 937 428-6640
Dayton *(G-8426)*
Pki Inc...F....... 513 832-8749
Cincinnati *(G-4164)*
Plastic Platers LLC..................................C....... 216 961-1200
Cleveland *(G-5886)*
Plate-All Metal Company Inc.................G....... 330 633-6166
Akron *(G-322)*
Plating Perceptions Inc..........................G....... 330 425-4180
Twinsburg *(G-18837)*
Plating Solutions......................................G....... 513 771-1941
Cincinnati *(G-4167)*
▲ Plating Technology Inc.......................D....... 937 268-6882
Dayton *(G-8428)*
Plating Technology Inc...........................F....... 937 268-6788
Dayton *(G-8429)*
Porter-Guertin Co Inc.............................F....... 513 241-7663
Cincinnati *(G-4174)*
Precious Metal Plating Co......................E....... 440 585-7117
Wickliffe *(G-20228)*
Precision Finishing Systems.................F....... 937 415-5794
Dayton *(G-8431)*
Prince Plating Inc....................................D....... 216 881-7523
Cleveland *(G-5922)*
Pro Line Collision and Pnt LLC..............F....... 937 223-7611
Dayton *(G-8444)*
▲ Quality Plating Co................................G....... 216 361-0151
Cleveland *(G-5942)*
R A Heller Company................................F....... 513 771-6100
Cincinnati *(G-4242)*
Rack Processing Company Inc...............E....... 937 294-1911
Moraine *(G-14388)*
Rack Processing Company Inc...............E....... 937 294-1911
Moraine *(G-14387)*
Raf Acquisition Co...................................F....... 440 572-5999
Valley City *(G-19058)*
Rawac Plating Company.........................E....... 937 322-7491
Springfield *(G-17481)*
REA Polishing Inc.....................................D....... 419 470-0216
Toledo *(G-18499)*
▲ Reifel Industries Inc...........................D....... 419 737-2138
Pioneer *(G-16095)*
Reliable Buffing Co Inc...........................G....... 419 647-4432
Spencerville *(G-17312)*
Rite Way Black & Deburr Inc..................G....... 937 224-7762
Dayton *(G-8478)*
Roberts Demand No 3 Corp....................F....... 216 641-0660
Cleveland *(G-5992)*
Roberts-Demand Corp............................G....... 216 581-1300
Cleveland *(G-5993)*
Russell Products Co Inc..........................G....... 330 535-3391
Akron *(G-360)*
Rykon Plating Inc.....................................G....... 440 933-3273
Avon Lake *(G-1006)*
S & K Metal Polsg & Buffing....................G....... 513 732-6662
Batavia *(G-1182)*
Samuel Steel Pickling Company.............D....... 330 963-3777
Twinsburg *(G-18853)*
▲ Sawyer Technical Materials LLC........E....... 440 951-8770
Willoughby *(G-20424)*
Scot Industries Inc...................................E....... 330 262-7585
Wooster *(G-20651)*

SIC SECTION
34 FABRICATED METAL PRODUCTS, EXCEPT MACHINERY AND TRANSPORTATION EQUIPMENT

Sebring Industrial Plating ......G....... 330 938-6666
Sebring *(G-16895)*
Shalmet Corporation ......G....... 440 236-8840
Elyria *(G-9326)*
Shur Clean Usa LLC ......G....... 513 341-5486
Liberty Township *(G-11820)*
Sifco Applied Srfc Cncepts LLC ......E....... 216 524-0099
Cleveland *(G-6062)*
◆ **Sifco Industries Inc** ......B....... 216 881-8600
Cleveland *(G-6063)*
Smith Electro Chemical Co ......E....... 513 351-7227
Cincinnati *(G-4346)*
Springco Metal Coatings Inc ......C....... 216 941-0020
Cleveland *(G-6087)*
Springfield Metal Finishing ......G....... 937 324-2353
Springfield *(G-17494)*
Stricker Refinishing Inc ......G....... 216 696-2906
Cleveland *(G-6109)*
Sun Polishing Corp ......G....... 440 237-5525
Cleveland *(G-6118)*
Super Fine Shine Inc ......G....... 740 774-1700
Chillicothe *(G-3226)*
Superfinishers Inc ......G....... 330 467-2125
Macedonia *(G-12335)*
▲ **Swagelok** ......G....... 440 349-5657
Solon *(G-17239)*
Tablox Inc ......G....... 440 953-1951
Willoughby *(G-20440)*
Tatham Schulz Incorporated ......E....... 216 861-4431
Cleveland *(G-6149)*
Techniplate Inc ......F....... 216 486-8825
Cleveland *(G-6155)*
Toledo Metal Finishing Inc ......G....... 419 661-1422
Northwood *(G-15347)*
Trans-Acc Inc ......E....... 513 793-6410
Blue Ash *(G-1861)*
Tri-State Fabricators Inc ......E....... 513 752-5005
Amelia *(G-550)*
Tri-State Plating & Polishing ......G....... 304 529-2579
Proctorville *(G-16348)*
Tubetech Inc ......E....... 330 426-9476
East Palestine *(G-9087)*
Tuckers Mold Polishing ......G....... 937 339-3063
Troy *(G-18716)*
▲ **Twist Inc** ......C....... 937 675-9581
Jamestown *(G-11221)*
U S Chrome Corporation Ohio ......F....... 877 872-7716
Dayton *(G-8575)*
United Hard Chrome Corporation ......F....... 330 453-2786
Canton *(G-2849)*
United State Pltg Bumper Svc ......G....... 614 403-4666
Worthington *(G-20706)*
United Surface Finishing Inc ......G....... 330 453-2786
Canton *(G-2851)*
Vacuum Finishing Company ......F....... 440 286-4386
Chardon *(G-3140)*
Vectron Inc ......D....... 440 323-3369
Elyria *(G-9343)*
Wall Polishing LLC ......G....... 937 698-1330
Ludlow Falls *(G-12270)*
Weber Technologies Inc ......E....... 440 946-8833
Eastlake *(G-9140)*
▲ **Whitaker Finishing LLC** ......E....... 419 666-7746
Northwood *(G-15352)*
Witt Enterprises Inc ......E....... 440 992-8333
Ashtabula *(G-812)*
Woodhill Plating Works Company ......E....... 216 883-1344
Cleveland *(G-6322)*
Worthington Industries Inc ......C....... 513 539-9291
Monroe *(G-14282)*
◆ **Worthington Steel Company** ......C....... 614 438-3210
Worthington *(G-20715)*
Yoder Industries Inc ......C....... 937 278-5769
Dayton *(G-8602)*
Youngstown Hard Chrome Plating ......E....... 330 758-9721
Youngstown *(G-21077)*

3479 Coating & Engraving, NEC

A & E Powder Coating Ltd ......G....... 937 525-3750
Springfield *(G-17359)*
A Class Coatings Inc ......F....... 440 960-6869
Lorain *(G-12076)*
A Plus Powder Coaters Inc ......F....... 330 482-4389
Columbiana *(G-6452)*
AAA Galvanizing - Joliet Inc ......E....... 513 871-5700
Cincinnati *(G-3285)*
▲ **Advanced Coatings Intl** ......G....... 330 794-6361
Akron *(G-30)*
Advanced Technical Pdts Sup Co ......F....... 513 851-6858
West Chester *(G-19638)*
Advantage Powder Coating Inc ......D....... 419 782-2363
Defiance *(G-8611)*
Aesthetic Finishers Inc ......E....... 937 778-8777
Piqua *(G-16098)*
Ak-Isg Steel Coating Company ......D....... 216 429-6901
Cleveland *(G-4647)*
Akron Metal Etching Co ......G....... 330 762-7687
Akron *(G-44)*
Akron Steel Treating Co ......E....... 330 773-8211
Akron *(G-53)*
Alpha Coatings Inc ......C....... 419 435-5111
Fostoria *(G-9832)*
◆ **Alsco Metals Corporation** ......E....... 740 983-2571
Dennison *(G-8781)*
American Tchnical Coatings Inc ......G....... 440 401-2270
Westlake *(G-20096)*
American Utility Proc LLC ......E....... 330 535-3000
Akron *(G-65)*
▲ **Anest Iwata Usa Inc** ......G....... 513 755-3100
West Chester *(G-19832)*
Anotex Industries Inc ......G....... 513 860-1165
West Chester *(G-19645)*
▲ **Aps-Materials Inc** ......D....... 937 278-6547
Dayton *(G-8034)*
Aps-Materials Inc ......E....... 937 278-6547
Dayton *(G-8035)*
▲ **Arcelormittal Columbus LLC** ......C....... 614 492-6800
Columbus *(G-6613)*
Architectural and Industrial ......F....... 440 963-0410
Vermilion *(G-19156)*
Armoloy of Ohio Inc ......F....... 937 323-8702
Springfield *(G-17365)*
Art Galvanizing Works Inc ......F....... 216 749-0020
Cleveland *(G-4737)*
Astro-Coatings Inc ......E....... 330 755-1414
Struthers *(G-17816)*
Auld Company ......E....... 614 454-1010
Columbus *(G-6629)*
Austin Finishing Co Inc ......G....... 216 883-0326
Cleveland *(G-4764)*
Azz Incorporated ......E....... 330 445-2170
Canton *(G-2581)*
Balser Inc ......G....... 567 444-4737
Archbold *(G-640)*
Bekaert Corporation ......C....... 330 683-5060
Orrville *(G-15583)*
Benco Industries Inc ......G....... 440 572-3555
Strongsville *(G-17719)*
Bogden Industrial Coatings LLC ......G....... 513 267-5101
Middletown *(G-13887)*
Boville Indus Coatings Inc ......E....... 330 669-8558
Smithville *(G-17087)*
Brilliant Colorworks LLC ......G....... 800 566-4162
Columbus *(G-6701)*
Bta of Motorcars Inc ......G....... 440 716-1000
North Olmsted *(G-15182)*
C L S Finishing Inc ......F....... 330 784-4134
Tallmadge *(G-17974)*
Canfield Coating LLC ......G....... 330 533-3311
Canfield *(G-2524)*
▲ **Cardinal Rubber Company Inc** ......E....... 330 745-2191
Barberton *(G-1069)*
Carpe Diem Industries LLC ......D....... 419 659-5639
Columbus Grove *(G-7632)*
Carpe Diem Industries LLC ......E....... 419 358-0129
Bluffton *(G-1887)*
Carved Stone LLC ......G....... 614 778-9855
Powell *(G-16315)*
Cast Plus Inc ......E....... 937 743-7278
Franklin *(G-9873)*
Central Aluminum Company LLC ......E....... 614 491-5700
Obetz *(G-15508)*
Cincinnati Thermal Spray Inc ......C....... 513 793-1037
Blue Ash *(G-1750)*
Coat All ......G....... 419 659-2757
Columbus Grove *(G-7634)*
Coating Systems Inc ......F....... 513 367-5600
Harrison *(G-10637)*
Columbus Coatings Company ......D....... 614 492-6800
Columbus *(G-6786)*
Corrotec Inc ......E....... 937 325-3585
Springfield *(G-17379)*
Creative Powder Coatings ......G....... 440 322-8197
Elyria *(G-9239)*
Cto Inc ......G....... 330 785-1130
Akron *(G-126)*
Cubbison Company ......D....... 330 793-2481
Youngstown *(G-20882)*
Custom Color Match and Spc ......G....... 419 868-5882
Holland *(G-10921)*
Custom Powdercoating LLC ......G....... 937 972-3516
Dayton *(G-8122)*
Dayton Coating Tech LLC ......G....... 937 278-2060
Dayton *(G-8131)*
▲ **De Nora North America Inc** ......F....... 440 357-4000
Painesville *(G-15730)*
De Vore Engraving Co ......G....... 330 454-6820
Canton *(G-2652)*
Doak Laser ......G....... 740 374-0090
Marietta *(G-12621)*
Duffee Finishing Inc ......G....... 740 965-4848
Sunbury *(G-17885)*
E L Stone Company ......E....... 330 825-4565
Norton *(G-15365)*
Ellison Group Inc ......F....... 513 770-4900
Mason *(G-12861)*
Ellison Srfc Tech - Mexico LLC ......E....... 513 770-4900
Mason *(G-12862)*
Ellison Surface Tech - W LLC ......G....... 513 770-4900
Mason *(G-12863)*
Ellison Surface Tech Inc ......F....... 513 770-4922
Mason *(G-12864)*
Emt Trading Company LLC ......G....... 888 352-8000
Chagrin Falls *(G-3019)*
▲ **Enerfab Inc** ......B....... 513 641-0500
Cincinnati *(G-3640)*
Epco Extrusion Painting Co ......E....... 330 781-6100
Youngstown *(G-20899)*
Erie Ceramic Arts Company LLC ......G....... 419 228-1145
Lima *(G-11860)*
▲ **Etched Metal Company** ......E....... 440 248-0240
Solon *(G-17142)*
F & K Concepts Inc ......G....... 937 426-6843
Springboro *(G-17326)*
Fayette Industrial Coatings ......E....... 419 636-1773
Bryan *(G-2280)*
▲ **Ferro Corporation** ......D....... 216 875-5600
Mayfield Heights *(G-13163)*
Final Finish Corp ......G....... 440 439-3303
Macedonia *(G-12294)*
Gem Coatings Ltd ......E....... 740 589-2998
Athens *(G-832)*
George Manufacturing Inc ......E....... 513 932-1067
Lebanon *(G-11654)*
Georgia Metal Coatings Company ......F....... 770 446-3930
Chardon *(G-3115)*
▲ **Godfrey & Wing Inc** ......E....... 330 562-1440
Aurora *(G-881)*
Great Lakes Etching Finshg Co ......F....... 440 439-3624
Cleveland *(G-5344)*
Greber Machine Tool Inc ......G....... 440 322-3685
Elyria *(G-9264)*
▲ **Greenkote Usa Inc** ......G....... 440 243-2865
Brookpark *(G-2148)*
Gs Wood & Metal Coating LLC ......G....... 419 375-7708
Fort Recovery *(G-9820)*
▲ **Gwp Holdings Inc** ......D....... 513 860-4050
Fairfield *(G-9501)*
Hadronics Inc ......D....... 513 321-9350
Cincinnati *(G-3792)*
Hardcoating Technologies Ltd ......E....... 330 686-2136
Munroe Falls *(G-14523)*
Hardline International Inc ......F....... 419 924-9556
West Unity *(G-19969)*
Hartzell Mfg Co ......E....... 937 859-5955
Miamisburg *(G-13674)*
Harwood Rubber Products Inc ......E....... 330 923-3256
Cuyahoga Falls *(G-7878)*
Hathaway Stamp & Ident Co of C ......F....... 513 621-1052
Cincinnati *(G-3802)*
Herbert E Orr Company ......C....... 419 399-4866
Paulding *(G-15860)*
▲ **Heritage Industrial Finshg Inc** ......D....... 330 798-9840
Akron *(G-205)*
▲ **High Tech Elastomers Inc** ......E....... 937 236-6575
Vandalia *(G-19128)*
Highway Safety Corp ......F....... 740 387-6991
Marion *(G-12711)*
◆ **Howmet Corporation** ......E....... 757 825-7086
Newburgh Heights *(G-14939)*
Hydro Extrusion North Amer LLC ......C....... 888 935-5759
Sidney *(G-17045)*
Imperial Metal Solutions LLC ......F....... 216 781-4094
Cleveland *(G-5444)*
Industrial and Mar Eng Svc Co ......F....... 740 694-0791
Fredericktown *(G-9971)*
Industrial Finishers Inc ......G....... 330 343-7797
Dover *(G-8832)*
Industrial Metal Finishing ......G....... 440 232-2400
Solon *(G-17168)*

S I C

Employee Codes: A=Over 500 employees, B=251-500
C=101-250, D=51-100, E=20-50, F=10-19, G=3-9
2019 Harris Ohio
Industrial Directory
939

34 FABRICATED METAL PRODUCTS, EXCEPT MACHINERY AND TRANSPORTATION EQUIPMENT

Inter-Ion Inc ....E 330 928-9655
 Cuyahoga Falls *(G-7882)*
Interntnal Tchncal Catings Inc ....D 614 449-6669
 Columbus *(G-7046)*
Ionbond LLC ....F 216 831-0880
 Cleveland *(G-5474)*
Ivac Technologies Corp ....F 216 662-4987
 Cleveland *(G-5479)*
J M Hamilton Group Inc ....F 419 229-4010
 Lima *(G-11881)*
Kars Ohio LLC ....G 614 655-1099
 Pataskala *(G-15834)*
Kecamm LLC ....G 330 527-2918
 Garrettsville *(G-10194)*
Laserdealer Inc ....G 440 357-8419
 Mentor *(G-13497)*
Levcoat Powder Coating ....G 614 802-7505
 Columbus *(G-7123)*
Lima Sandblasting & Pntg Co ....G 419 331-2939
 Lima *(G-11892)*
Logan Coatings LLC ....F 740 380-0047
 Logan *(G-12032)*
◆ Loroco Industries Inc ....E 513 891-9544
 Blue Ash *(G-1807)*
M & M Engraving ....G 216 749-7166
 Cleveland *(G-5591)*
Mark True Engraving Company ......G 216 252-7422
 Cleveland *(G-5620)*
Master Marking Company Inc ....F 330 688-6797
 Stow *(G-17604)*
Master Vac Incorporated ....G 419 335-7796
 Wauseon *(G-19527)*
Material Sciences Corporation ....G 330 702-3882
 Canfield *(G-2535)*
Medina Powder Coating Corp ....F 330 952-1977
 Medina *(G-13295)*
Medina Powder Group ....G 330 952-2711
 Medina *(G-13296)*
▲ Mesocoat Inc ....F 216 453-0866
 Euclid *(G-9427)*
Metaltek Industries Inc ....F 937 323-4933
 Springfield *(G-17447)*
Metokote Corporation ....D 440 934-4686
 Sheffield Village *(G-16971)*
Metokote Corporation ....E 270 889-9907
 Lima *(G-11902)*
▲ Metokote Corporation ....B 419 996-7800
 Lima *(G-11903)*
Metokote Corporation ....F 419 227-1100
 Lima *(G-11904)*
Metokote Corporation ....C 419 221-2754
 Lima *(G-11905)*
Metokote Corporation ....D 319 232-6994
 Lima *(G-11906)*
Metokote Corporation ....C 937 235-2811
 Dayton *(G-8343)*
Miamisburg Coating ....F 937 866-1323
 Miamisburg *(G-13693)*
Mmf Inc ....F 614 252-0078
 Columbus *(G-7186)*
Momentive Performance Mtls Inc ...C 740 928-7010
 Hebron *(G-10753)*
Momentive Performance Mtls Inc ...A 440 878-5705
 Richmond Heights *(G-16503)*
◆ Momentive Prfmce Mtls Qrtz Inc ..C 440 878-5700
 Strongsville *(G-17765)*
MSC Walbridge Coatings Inc ....C 419 666-6130
 Walbridge *(G-19297)*
Nation Coating Systems Inc ....G 937 746-7632
 Franklin *(G-9902)*
Niles Manufacturing & Finshg ....C 330 544-0402
 Niles *(G-15024)*
Northeast Coatings Inc ....F 330 784-7773
 Tallmadge *(G-17996)*
Oerlikon Blzers Cating USA Inc ......G 330 343-9892
 Dover *(G-8846)*
Office Magic Inc ....F 510 782-6100
 Medina *(G-13310)*
Ohio Coatings Company ....D 740 859-5500
 Yorkville *(G-20827)*
Ohio Galvanizing Corp ....E 740 387-6474
 Marion *(G-12726)*
▲ Omni Manufacturing Inc ....D 419 394-7424
 Saint Marys *(G-16693)*
Omni Manufacturing Inc ....F 419 394-7424
 Saint Marys *(G-16694)*
Parker Rst-Proof Cleveland Inc ......E 216 481-6680
 Cleveland *(G-5847)*
Parker Trutec Incorporated ....D 937 653-8500
 Urbana *(G-19007)*

▲ Parker Trutec Incorporated ....D 937 323-8833
 Springfield *(G-17469)*
Perfection Finishers Inc ....E 419 337-8015
 Wauseon *(G-19531)*
Pioneer Custom Coating LLC ....G 419 737-3152
 Pioneer *(G-16087)*
Pki Inc ....F 513 832-8749
 Cincinnati *(G-4164)*
Play All LLC ....G 440 992-7529
 Ashtabula *(G-799)*
Poly-Met Inc ....F 330 630-9006
 Akron *(G-323)*
▲ Precision Applied Coatings ....G 614 252-8711
 Columbus *(G-7342)*
Precision Coatings Inc ....F 216 441-0805
 Cleveland *(G-5908)*
Precision Coatings Systems ....E 937 642-4727
 Marysville *(G-12806)*
Pro-TEC Coating Company LLC .....D 419 943-1100
 Leipsic *(G-11734)*
▲ Pro-TEC Coating Company LLC ..C 419 943-1211
 Leipsic *(G-11735)*
Procoat Painting Inc ....G 513 735-2500
 Batavia *(G-1179)*
Production Paint Finishers Inc ....D 937 448-2627
 Bradford *(G-2011)*
Progressive Manufacturing Co ....G 330 784-4717
 Akron *(G-333)*
Progressive Powder Coating Inc ....E 440 974-3478
 Mentor *(G-13559)*
Rack Coating Service Inc ....E 330 854-2869
 Canal Fulton *(G-2491)*
Rack Processing Company Inc ......F 937 294-1911
 Moraine *(G-14388)*
Raf Acquisition Co ....F 440 572-5999
 Valley City *(G-19058)*
▲ Reifel Industries Inc ....D 419 737-2138
 Pioneer *(G-16095)*
Rite Way Black & Deburr Inc ....G 937 224-7762
 Dayton *(G-8478)*
Roban Inc ....G 330 794-1059
 Lakemore *(G-11500)*
Roemer Industries Inc ....D 330 448-2000
 Masury *(G-13062)*
Russell Products Co Inc ....G 330 434-9163
 Akron *(G-361)*
Russell Products Co Inc ....G 216 267-0880
 Akron *(G-362)*
Russell T Bundy Associates Inc ....F 740 965-3008
 Sunbury *(G-17900)*
Russell T Bundy Associates Inc ....E 419 526-4454
 Mansfield *(G-12509)*
Ryder Engraving Inc ....G 740 927-7193
 Pataskala *(G-15842)*
Scholz & Ey Engravers Inc ....F 614 444-8052
 Columbus *(G-7427)*
Seacor Painting Corporation ....G 330 755-6361
 Campbell *(G-2469)*
Semper Quality Industry Inc ....G 440 352-8111
 Mentor *(G-13578)*
SH Bell Company ....E 412 963-9910
 East Liverpool *(G-9068)*
▲ Signature Partners Inc ....D 419 678-1400
 Coldwater *(G-6420)*
Simcote Inc ....E 740 382-5000
 Marion *(G-12736)*
Skinner Powder Coating Inc ....G 937 606-2188
 Piqua *(G-16162)*
▼ Spectrum Metal Finishing Inc ....D 330 758-8358
 Youngstown *(G-21038)*
Springco Metal Coatings Inc ....C 216 941-0020
 Cleveland *(G-6087)*
▲ Star Fab Inc ....C 330 533-9863
 Canfield *(G-2547)*
Sterling Coating ....G 513 942-4900
 West Chester *(G-19799)*
Surftech Inc ....G 440 275-3356
 Austinburg *(G-927)*
T&K Laser Works Inc ....G 937 693-3783
 Botkins *(G-1938)*
▼ Tce International Ltd ....F 800 962-2376
 Perry *(G-15914)*
▲ Techneglas Inc ....G 419 873-2000
 Perrysburg *(G-16011)*
Tendon Manufacturing Inc ....E 216 663-3200
 Cleveland *(G-6159)*
Tennessee Coatings Inc ....F 513 770-4900
 Mason *(G-12949)*
Thornton Powder Coatings Inc ......F 419 522-7183
 Mansfield *(G-12531)*

Tool & Die Systems Inc ....E 440 327-5800
 North Ridgeville *(G-15256)*
Trans-Acc Inc ....E 513 793-6410
 Blue Ash *(G-1861)*
Treemen Industries Inc ....E 330 965-3777
 Boardman *(G-1904)*
Tri-State Fabricators Inc ....E 513 752-5005
 Amelia *(G-550)*
Tsp Inc ....E 513 732-8900
 Batavia *(G-1191)*
Universal Rack & Equipment Co ....E 330 963-6776
 Twinsburg *(G-18870)*
V & S Columbus Galanizing LLC ....D 614 449-8281
 Columbus *(G-7569)*
▲ Vacono America LLC ....E 216 938-7428
 Cleveland *(G-6249)*
Vacuum Finishing Company ....F 440 286-4386
 Chardon *(G-3140)*
▼ Venus Trading LLC ....G 513 374-0066
 Loveland *(G-12243)*
Visimax Technologies Inc ....F 330 405-8330
 Twinsburg *(G-18872)*
Visionmark Nameplate Co LLC ......E 419 977-3131
 New Bremen *(G-14662)*
▲ Voigt & Schweitzer LLC ....F 614 449-8281
 Columbus *(G-7587)*
▲ Water Star Inc ....F 440 996-0800
 Painesville *(G-15797)*
▼ Witt Industries Inc ....D 513 871-5700
 Mason *(G-12955)*
Woodrow Manufacturing Co ....E 937 399-9333
 Springfield *(G-17521)*
X-Treme Finishes Inc ....F 330 474-0614
 Medina *(G-13364)*

3482 Small Arms Ammunition

Ares Inc ....D 419 635-2175
 Port Clinton *(G-16242)*
Big Iron Guns Inc ....G 740 464-0852
 Portsmouth *(G-16279)*
Center Mass Ammo LLC ....G 440 796-6207
 Madison *(G-12342)*
Galion LLC ....C 419 468-5214
 Galion *(G-10138)*
Jmr Enterprises LLC ....G 937 618-1736
 Maineville *(G-12371)*
Johndavid D Jones ....G 740 264-0176
 Wintersville *(G-20539)*
National Bullet Co ....G 800 317-9506
 Eastlake *(G-9125)*
▲ Premier Shot Company Inc ....G 330 405-0583
 Twinsburg *(G-18838)*
R & S Monitions Inc ....G 614 846-0597
 Columbus *(G-7371)*
Toll Compaction Group LLC ....E 740 376-0511
 Belpre *(G-1584)*

3483 Ammunition, Large

Center Mass Ammo LLC ....G 440 796-6207
 Madison *(G-12342)*
L3 Fuzing and Ord Systems Inc ....A 513 943-2000
 Cincinnati *(G-3257)*
▲ Marine Jet Power Inc ....G 614 759-9000
 Blacklick *(G-1689)*
United States Dept of Army ....G 330 358-7311
 Ravenna *(G-16417)*
Vergeline LLC ....G 419 730-0300
 Toledo *(G-18591)*

3484 Small Arms

762mm Firearms LLC ....G 440 655-8572
 Wadsworth *(G-19217)*
Acme Machine Automatics Inc ......D 419 453-0010
 Ottoville *(G-15679)*
▲ American Apex Corporation ....F 614 652-2000
 Plain City *(G-16171)*
Apex Alliance LLC ....G 234 200-5930
 Stow *(G-17569)*
Ares Inc ....D 419 635-2175
 Port Clinton *(G-16242)*
Beech Armament LLC ....G 330 962-4694
 Cuyahoga Falls *(G-7845)*
Faxon Firearms LLC ....G 513 674-2580
 Cincinnati *(G-3677)*
Highpoint Firearms ....E 419 747-9444
 Mansfield *(G-12459)*
Iberia Firearms Inc ....G 419 468-3746
 Galion *(G-10145)*
Inland Manufacturing LLC ....G 937 835-0220
 Dayton *(G-8264)*

Jmr Enterprises LLC....G.... 937 618-1736
Maineville *(G-12371)*
Kaeper Machine Inc....E.... 440 974-1010
Mentor *(G-13488)*
Kelblys Rifle Range Inc....G.... 330 683-0070
North Lawrence *(G-15162)*
Nicana Consulting Inc....G.... 419 615-9703
Kalida *(G-11279)*
▼ **Ohio Ordnance Works Inc**....E.... 440 285-3481
Chardon *(G-3130)*
Parabellum Armament Co LLC....G.... 614 557-5987
Grove City *(G-10456)*
▲ **Quality Replacement Parts Inc**....G.... 216 674-0200
Cleveland *(G-5943)*
Reloading Supplies Corp....G.... 440 228-0367
Ashtabula *(G-802)*
Smokin Guns LLC....G.... 440 324-4003
Elyria *(G-9329)*
TS Sales LLC....F.... 727 804-8060
Mount Gilead *(G-14435)*
X-Treme Shooting Products LLC....G.... 513 313-3464
Batavia *(G-1198)*
▲ **Zshot Inc**....G.... 800 385-8581
Columbus *(G-7628)*

3489 Ordnance & Access, NEC

Advanced Innovation & Mfg Inc....G.... 330 308-6360
New Philadelphia *(G-14756)*
▲ **American Apex Corporation**....F.... 614 652-2000
Plain City *(G-16171)*
Ares Inc....D.... 419 635-2175
Port Clinton *(G-16242)*
Excelitas Technologies Corp....C.... 866 539-5916
Miamisburg *(G-13667)*
General Dynamics-Ots Inc....C.... 937 746-8500
Springboro *(G-17328)*
Hi-Tech Solutions LLC....G.... 216 331-3050
Cleveland *(G-5405)*
Ordnance Cleaning Systems LLC....G.... 440 205-0677
Mentor *(G-13536)*

3491 Industrial Valves

▼ **Akron Steel Fabricators Co**....E.... 330 644-0616
Coventry Township *(G-7764)*
▲ **Alkon Corporation**....D.... 419 355-9111
Fremont *(G-9990)*
Alkon Corporation....E.... 614 799-6650
Dublin *(G-8876)*
Bosch Rexroth Corporation....B.... 330 263-3300
Wooster *(G-20573)*
▲ **Canfield Industries Inc**....G.... 800 554-5071
Youngstown *(G-20864)*
Cfrc Wtr & Enrgy Solutions Inc....G.... 216 479-0290
Cleveland *(G-4906)*
Cincinnati Valve Company....F.... 513 471-8258
Cincinnati *(G-3508)*
▲ **Cincinnati Valve Company**....F.... 513 471-8258
Cincinnati *(G-3509)*
Clark-Reliance Corporation....G.... 440 572-7408
Strongsville *(G-17727)*
▲ **Clark-Reliance Corporation**....C.... 440 572-1500
Strongsville *(G-17726)*
Cleveland Valve & Gauge Co LLC....G.... 216 362-1702
Cleveland *(G-4982)*
Curtiss-Wright Flow Control....D.... 513 735-2538
Batavia *(G-1134)*
Curtiss-Wright Flow Control....D.... 513 528-7900
Cincinnati *(G-3244)*
Curtiss-Wright Flow Ctrl Corp....E.... 440 838-7690
Brecksville *(G-2028)*
Dayton Air Control Pdts LLC....G.... 937 254-4441
Moraine *(G-14343)*
Digital Automation Associates....G.... 419 352-6977
Bowling Green *(G-1969)*
Fisher Controls Intl LLC....G.... 513 285-6000
West Chester *(G-19703)*
Flow Technology Inc....C.... 513 745-6000
Cincinnati *(G-3699)*
▲ **Hearth Products Controls Co**....F.... 937 436-9800
Dayton *(G-7982)*
Honeywell International Inc....A.... 937 484-2000
Urbana *(G-18995)*
Hunt Valve Company Inc....E.... 330 337-9535
Salem *(G-16748)*
Hunt Valve Company Inc....E.... 330 337-9535
Salem *(G-16749)*
Kaplan Industries Inc....F.... 513 386-7762
Harrison *(G-10654)*
◆ **Kaplan Industries Inc**....E.... 856 779-8181
Harrison *(G-10655)*
Keen Manufacturing Inc....G.... 330 427-0045
Washingtonville *(G-19480)*
Maass Midwest Mfg Inc....G.... 419 894-6424
Arcadia *(G-625)*
Machine Component Mfg....F.... 330 454-4566
Canton *(G-2740)*
Manico Inc....G.... 440 946-5333
Willoughby *(G-20367)*
Nupro Company....C.... 440 951-9729
Willoughby *(G-20392)*
Parker-Hannifin Corporation....C.... 419 542-6611
Hicksville *(G-10781)*
Parker-Hannifin Corporation....C.... 937 644-3915
Marysville *(G-12805)*
Phoenix Partners LLC....E.... 734 654-2201
Ottawa Hills *(G-15675)*
Precision Q Systems LLC....G.... 614 286-5142
Westerville *(G-20070)*
▲ **Richards Industries Inc**....C.... 513 533-5600
Cincinnati *(G-4268)*
▲ **Rogers Industrial Products Inc**....E.... 330 535-3331
Akron *(G-353)*
Russments Inc....G.... 513 602-5035
Cincinnati *(G-4290)*
Ruthman Pump and Engineering....E.... 937 783-2411
Blanchester *(G-1706)*
Sdh Flow Controls LLC....G.... 513 624-7001
Cincinnati *(G-4312)*
Seawin Inc....D.... 419 355-9111
Fremont *(G-10050)*
Sherwood Valve LLC....E.... 216 264-5023
Cleveland *(G-6057)*
Sherwood Valve LLC....D.... 216 264-5028
Cleveland *(G-6058)*
▲ **Superb Industries Inc**....D.... 330 852-0500
Sugarcreek *(G-17870)*
Swagelok Company....D.... 440 248-4600
Willoughby Hills *(G-20475)*
◆ **Swagelok Company**....A.... 440 248-4600
Solon *(G-17240)*
Swagelok Company....D.... 440 349-5652
Solon *(G-17241)*
Swagelok Company....E.... 440 349-5836
Solon *(G-17243)*
Transdigm Inc....G.... 216 706-2939
Cleveland *(G-6196)*
▲ **Tylok International Inc**....D.... 216 261-7310
Cleveland *(G-6225)*
▲ **Valvole America LLC**....G.... 330 464-8872
Medina *(G-13360)*
Vickers International Inc....F.... 419 867-2200
Maumee *(G-13159)*
Viking Group Inc....G.... 937 443-0433
Dayton *(G-8580)*
◆ **Waxman Industries Inc**....C.... 440 439-1830
Cleveland *(G-6295)*
▲ **William Powell Company**....D.... 513 852-2000
Cincinnati *(G-4510)*
Xomox Corporation....E.... 513 947-1200
Batavia *(G-1199)*
Xomox Corporation....E.... 936 271-6500
Cincinnati *(G-4527)*
Xomox Corporation....G.... 513 745-6000
Blue Ash *(G-1880)*
Zal Air Products Inc....G.... 440 237-7155
Cleveland *(G-6338)*

3492 Fluid Power Valves & Hose Fittings

▲ **Ace Manufacturing Company**....E.... 513 541-2490
West Chester *(G-19825)*
Aerocontrolex Group Inc....D.... 440 352-6182
Painesville *(G-15706)*
Aeroquip-Vickers Inc....G.... 216 523-5000
Cleveland *(G-4633)*
Air-Way Manufacturing Company....C.... 419 298-2366
Edgerton *(G-9167)*
Aj Fluid Power Sales & Sup Inc....G.... 440 255-7960
Mentor *(G-13380)*
▲ **Alkon Corporation**....D.... 419 355-9111
Fremont *(G-9990)*
▲ **Canfield Industries Inc**....G.... 800 554-5071
Youngstown *(G-20864)*
Cfrc Wtr & Enrgy Solutions Inc....G.... 216 479-0290
Cleveland *(G-4906)*
Commercial Honing Ohio Inc....D.... 330 343-8896
Dover *(G-8812)*
Custom Cltch Jint Hydrlics Inc....F.... 216 431-1630
Cleveland *(G-5046)*
▲ **Dana Limited**....B.... 419 887-3000
Maumee *(G-13099)*
Dixon Valve & Coupling Co LLC....F.... 330 425-3000
Twinsburg *(G-18765)*
DNC Hydraulics LLC....F.... 419 963-2800
Rawson *(G-16421)*
▲ **Dyna-Flex Inc**....F.... 440 946-9424
Mentor *(G-13434)*
◆ **Eaton Aeroquip LLC**....C.... 216 523-5000
Cleveland *(G-5143)*
Eaton Hydraulics LLC....E.... 419 232-7777
Van Wert *(G-19088)*
Eaton-Aeroquip Llc....D.... 419 238-1190
Van Wert *(G-19089)*
Eaton-Aeroquip Llc....D.... 419 891-7775
Maumee *(G-13109)*
Encore Distributing Inc....G.... 513 948-1242
Cincinnati *(G-3638)*
Freudenberg-Nok General Partnr....C.... 419 427-5221
Findlay *(G-9689)*
▲ **Hy-Production Inc**....C.... 330 273-2400
Valley City *(G-19040)*
Hydraulic Parts Store Inc....E.... 330 364-6667
New Philadelphia *(G-14774)*
▼ **Industrial Connections Inc**....G.... 330 274-2155
Mantua *(G-12549)*
Integrated Aircraft Systems....G.... 330 686-2982
Stow *(G-17596)*
Kaman Fluid Power LLC....G.... 330 315-3100
Akron *(G-230)*
◆ **Kirtland Capital Partners LP**....E.... 216 593-0100
Beachwood *(G-1244)*
▲ **Malone Specialty Inc**....F.... 440 255-4200
Mentor *(G-13510)*
Maverick Industries Inc....F.... 440 838-5335
Brecksville *(G-2049)*
Mid-State Sales Inc....G.... 330 744-2158
Youngstown *(G-20971)*
National Aviation Products Inc....F.... 330 688-6494
Stow *(G-17610)*
▲ **National Machine Company**....C.... 330 688-6494
Stow *(G-17611)*
Netherland Rubber Company....F.... 513 733-0883
Cincinnati *(G-4068)*
Ohio Hydraulics Inc....E.... 513 771-2590
Cincinnati *(G-4103)*
Parker-Hannifin Corporation....C.... 419 542-6611
Hicksville *(G-10781)*
Parker-Hannifin Corporation....E.... 440 943-5700
Wickliffe *(G-20225)*
Parker-Hannifin Corporation....C.... 937 962-5566
Lewisburg *(G-11797)*
▲ **Parker-Hannifin Corporation**....B.... 216 896-3000
Cleveland *(G-5848)*
Parker-Hannifin Corporation....B.... 440 943-5700
Wickliffe *(G-20224)*
Parker-Hannifin Corporation....F.... 216 896-3000
Cleveland *(G-5850)*
Parker-Hannifin Corporation....B.... 937 456-5571
Eaton *(G-9163)*
▲ **Ruthman Pump and Engineering**....G.... 513 559-1901
Cincinnati *(G-4291)*
SMC Corporation of America....E.... 330 659-2006
Richfield *(G-16488)*
▲ **SSP Fittings Corp**....C.... 330 425-4250
Twinsburg *(G-18858)*
State Metal Hose Inc....G.... 614 527-4700
Hilliard *(G-10865)*
Summers Acquisition Corp....G.... 740 373-0303
Marietta *(G-12678)*
Superior Holding LLC....G.... 216 651-9400
Cleveland *(G-6121)*
Superior Products LLC....D.... 216 651-9400
Cleveland *(G-6126)*
◆ **Superior Products Llc**....D.... 216 651-9400
Cleveland *(G-6125)*
▲ **Swagelok**....G.... 440 349-5657
Solon *(G-17239)*
Swagelok Company....E.... 440 349-5836
Solon *(G-17243)*
T D Group Holdings LLC....G.... 216 706-2939
Cleveland *(G-6144)*
▲ **Taiyo America Inc**....F.... 419 300-8811
Saint Marys *(G-16703)*
▲ **Thogus Products Company**....D.... 440 933-8850
Avon Lake *(G-1011)*
Transdigm Inc....F.... 216 291-6025
Cleveland *(G-6195)*
Transdigm Inc....G.... 216 706-2939
Cleveland *(G-6196)*
▲ **Tylok International Inc**....D.... 216 261-7310
Cleveland *(G-6225)*

SIC

34 FABRICATED METAL PRODUCTS, EXCEPT MACHINERY AND TRANSPORTATION EQUIPMENT SIC SECTION

Valv-Trol Company ..... F 330 686-2800
  Stow (G-17640)
Valveco Inc ..... D 330 337-9535
  Salem (G-16779)
▲ Valvole America LLC ..... G 330 464-8872
  Medina (G-13360)
Winzeler Stamping Co ..... D 419 485-3147
  Montpelier (G-14322)
Zaytran Corporation ..... E 440 324-2814
  Elyria (G-9348)

3493 Steel Springs, Except Wire

Accurate Tool Co Inc ..... G 330 332-9448
  Salem (G-16714)
Crawford Manufacturing Company ..... F 330 897-1060
  Baltic (G-1026)
▲ Dayton Progress Corporation ..... A 937 859-5111
  Dayton (G-8143)
E & L Spring Shop ..... G 440 632-1439
  Middlefield (G-13796)
Elyria Spring & Specialty Inc ..... E 440 323-5502
  Elyria (G-9256)
Euclid Spring Company Inc ..... E 440 943-3213
  Wickliffe (G-20210)
Golden Spring Co Inc ..... F 937 848-2513
  Bellbrook (G-1495)
Hendrickson International Corp ..... D 740 929-5600
  Hebron (G-10747)
Jamestown Industries Inc ..... D 330 779-0670
  Youngstown (G-20947)
▲ Kern-Liebers Usa Inc ..... D 419 865-2437
  Holland (G-10941)
▲ Liteflex LLC ..... G 937 836-7025
  Englewood (G-9367)
Liteflex LLC ..... G 937 836-7025
  Dayton (G-8314)
Marik Spring Inc ..... F 330 564-0617
  Tallmadge (G-17991)
Matthew Warren Inc ..... E 614 418-0250
  Columbus (G-7160)
◆ Napoleon Spring Works Inc ..... C 419 445-1010
  Archbold (G-660)
Precision Products Group Inc ..... D 330 698-4711
  Apple Creek (G-617)
Rassini Chassis Systems LLC ..... D 419 485-1524
  Montpelier (G-14316)
▼ Service Spring Corp ..... D 419 838-6081
  Maumee (G-13144)
▲ Solon Manufacturing Company ..... E 440 286-7149
  Chardon (G-3137)
Tadd Spring Co Inc ..... E 440 572-1313
  Strongsville (G-17799)
Timac Manufacturing Company ..... F 937 372-3305
  Xenia (G-20796)
Torsion Control Product ..... G 248 597-9997
  Dayton (G-8563)
Tremac Corporation ..... E 937 372-8662
  Xenia (G-20798)
Zsi Manufacturing Inc ..... G 440 266-0701
  Painesville (G-15805)

3494 Valves & Pipe Fittings, NEC

Adaptall America Inc ..... F 330 425-4114
  Twinsburg (G-18727)
Air Tool Service Company ..... F 440 701-1021
  Mentor (G-13379)
◆ Alloy Bllows Prcision Wldg Inc ..... D 440 684-3000
  Cleveland (G-4674)
Amaltech Inc ..... E 440 248-7500
  Solon (G-17105)
Bosch Rexroth Corporation ..... B 330 263-3300
  Wooster (G-20573)
Bowes Manufacturing Inc ..... F 216 378-2110
  Solon (G-17117)
Calvin J Magsig ..... G 419 862-3311
  Elmore (G-9204)
Crane Pumps & Systems Inc ..... B 937 773-2442
  Piqua (G-16187)
Cylinders & Valves Inc ..... G 440 238-7343
  Strongsville (G-17736)
Drainage Pipe & Fitting ..... F 419 538-6337
  Ottawa (G-15651)
Eaton Corporation ..... C 440 826-1115
  Berea (G-1604)
Eaton Corporation ..... C 330 274-0743
  Aurora (G-877)
Edward W Daniel LLC ..... F 440 647-1960
  Wellington (G-19577)
▲ Fcx Performance Inc ..... G 614 324-6050
  Columbus (G-6916)

Fulflo Specialties Company ..... E 937 783-2411
  Blanchester (G-1703)
General Aluminum Mfg Company ..... C 419 739-9300
  Wapakoneta (G-19330)
▲ General Plug and Mfg Co ..... C 440 926-2411
  Grafton (G-10301)
Greater Cleve Pipe Ftting Fund ..... F 216 524-8334
  Cleveland (G-5353)
Grip Force LLC ..... G 440 497-7014
  Eastlake (G-9112)
H P E Inc ..... F 330 833-3161
  Massillon (G-12993)
III Williams LLC ..... G 440 721-8191
  Chardon (G-3118)
Impaction Co ..... G 440 349-5652
  Solon (G-17167)
Insulpro Inc ..... F 614 262-3768
  Columbus (G-7039)
◆ Kirtland Capital Partners LP ..... E 216 593-0100
  Beachwood (G-1244)
▲ Knappco Corporation ..... C 816 741-0786
  West Chester (G-19731)
Lsq Manufacturing Inc ..... F 330 725-4905
  Medina (G-13287)
Machine Component Mfg ..... G 330 454-4566
  Canton (G-2740)
Mack Iron Works Company ..... E 419 626-3712
  Sandusky (G-16826)
Northcoast Valve and Gate Inc ..... G 440 392-9910
  Mentor (G-13530)
Nupro Company ..... C 440 951-9729
  Willoughby (G-20392)
O E M Hydraulics Inc ..... G 740 454-1201
  Zanesville (G-21164)
Oceco Inc ..... F 419 447-0916
  Tiffin (G-18073)
▲ Opw Engineered Systems Inc ..... G 888 771-9438
  Lebanon (G-11680)
Parker-Hannifin Corporation ..... B 937 456-5571
  Eaton (G-9163)
Parker-Hannifin Corporation ..... C 614 279-7070
  Columbus (G-7294)
PHD Manufacturing Inc ..... C 330 482-9256
  Columbiana (G-6476)
Piersante and Associates ..... G 330 533-9904
  Canfield (G-2540)
Pipelines Inc ..... G 330 448-0000
  Masury (G-13061)
▲ Precision Fittings LLC ..... E 440 647-4143
  Wellington (G-19589)
▲ Richards Industries Inc ..... C 513 533-5600
  Cincinnati (G-4268)
Robbins & Myers Inc ..... B 937 327-3111
  Springfield (G-17487)
▲ Robeck Fluid Power Co ..... D 330 562-1140
  Aurora (G-903)
Ruthman Pump and Engineering ..... E 937 783-2411
  Blanchester (G-1706)
Siteone Landscape Supply LLC ..... G 330 220-8691
  Brunswick (G-2239)
▲ SSP Fittings Corp ..... C 330 425-4250
  Twinsburg (G-18858)
Stelter and Brinck Inc ..... E 513 367-9300
  Harrison (G-10672)
Stephens Pipe & Steel LLC ..... C 740 869-2257
  Mount Sterling (G-14465)
Steven L Lones ..... G 740 452-8851
  Zanesville (G-21183)
Superior Holding LLC ..... G 216 651-9400
  Cleveland (G-6121)
Superior Products LLC ..... D 216 651-9400
  Cleveland (G-6126)
◆ Superior Products Llc ..... D 216 651-9400
  Cleveland (G-6125)
▲ Swagelok ..... G 440 349-5657
  Solon (G-17239)
◆ Swagelok Company ..... A 440 248-4600
  Solon (G-17240)
Swagelok Company ..... D 440 349-5652
  Solon (G-17241)
Swagelok Company ..... E 440 944-8988
  Willoughby Hills (G-20476)
Swagelok Company ..... E 440 473-1050
  Cleveland (G-6134)
Swagelok Company ..... E 440 349-5836
  Solon (G-17243)
Swagelok Company ..... F 440 442-6611
  Cleveland (G-6133)
Swagelok Company ..... D 440 349-5934
  Solon (G-17242)

▲ Tech Tool Inc ..... F 330 674-1176
  Millersburg (G-14133)
▲ Thogus Products Company ..... D 440 933-8850
  Avon Lake (G-1011)
▲ Tylok International Inc ..... D 216 261-7310
  Cleveland (G-6225)
US Fittings Inc ..... F 234 212-9420
  Twinsburg (G-18871)
◆ Waxman Industries Inc ..... C 440 439-1830
  Cleveland (G-6295)
Wells Inc ..... F 419 457-2611
  Risingsun (G-16519)
▲ William Powell Company ..... E 513 852-2000
  Cincinnati (G-4510)
Xomox Corporation ..... E 936 271-6500
  Cincinnati (G-4527)
Zeiger Industries ..... E 330 484-4413
  Canton (G-2868)

3495 Wire Springs

A & W Spring Co Inc ..... G 937 222-7284
  Dayton (G-7998)
Aswpengg LLC ..... G 216 292-4620
  Bedford Heights (G-1461)
B & P Spring Production Co ..... F 216 486-4260
  Cleveland (G-4783)
Barnes Group Inc ..... G 440 526-5900
  Brecksville (G-2021)
Barnes Group Inc ..... G 419 891-9292
  Maumee (G-13077)
▲ Bloomingburg Spring & Wire For ..... E 740 437-7614
  Bloomingburg (G-1709)
▲ Dayton Progress Corporation ..... A 937 859-5111
  Dayton (G-8143)
Elyria Spring & Specialty Inc ..... E 440 323-5502
  Elyria (G-9256)
Kern-Liebers Texas Inc ..... E 419 865-2437
  Holland (G-10940)
▲ Kern-Liebers Usa Inc ..... D 419 865-2437
  Holland (G-10941)
Matthew Warren Inc ..... E 614 418-0250
  Columbus (G-7160)
Ohio Wire Form & Spring Co ..... F 614 444-3676
  Columbus (G-7264)
Precision Products Group Inc ..... D 330 698-4711
  Apple Creek (G-617)
Protech Electric LLC ..... F 937 427-0813
  Beavercreek (G-1337)
Regal Spring Co ..... G 614 278-7761
  Columbus (G-7383)
Six C Fabrication Inc ..... C 330 296-5594
  Ravenna (G-16403)
▲ Solon Manufacturing Company ..... E 440 286-7149
  Chardon (G-3137)
▼ Spring Team Inc ..... D 440 275-5981
  Austinburg (G-926)
Spring Works Inc ..... E 614 351-9345
  Columbus (G-7480)
Springtime Manufacturing ..... G 419 697-3720
  Toledo (G-18528)
▲ Stalder Spring Works Inc ..... F 937 322-6120
  Springfield (G-17498)
▲ Supro Spring & Wire Forms Inc ..... E 330 722-5628
  Medina (G-13349)
Tadd Spring Co Inc ..... E 440 572-1313
  Strongsville (G-17799)
The Reliable Spring Wire Frms ..... E 440 365-7400
  Elyria (G-9338)
Trupoint Products ..... F 330 204-3302
  Sugarcreek (G-17872)
▲ Twist Inc ..... G 937 675-9581
  Jamestown (G-11221)
Twist Inc ..... G 937 675-9581
  Jamestown (G-11222)
Wire Products Company Inc ..... C 216 267-0777
  Cleveland (G-6316)
▼ Yost Superior Co ..... E 937 323-7591
  Springfield (G-17522)

3496 Misc Fabricated Wire Prdts

4-Sure Wire Products Inc ..... G 440 563-9263
  Rock Creek (G-16531)
Akron Belting & Supply Company ..... G 330 633-8212
  Akron (G-33)
Alabama Sling Center Inc ..... F 440 239-7000
  Cleveland (G-4649)
◆ Alcan Corporation ..... E 440 460-3307
  Cleveland (G-4650)
All-State Belting LLC ..... G 614 497-4281
  Columbus (G-6569)

▲ **Amanda Bent Bolt Company**............C....... 740 385-6893
Logan *(G-12021)*
American Pennekamp Mfg Inc.............G....... 740 687-0096
Lancaster *(G-11539)*
Assembly Specialty Pdts Inc.................E....... 216 676-5600
Cleveland *(G-4752)*
Blacco Splcing Rgging Loft Inc............G....... 614 444-2888
Columbus *(G-6675)*
▲ **Bloomingburg Spring & Wire For**.....E....... 740 437-7614
Bloomingburg *(G-1709)*
Busch & Thiem Inc................................E....... 419 625-7515
Sandusky *(G-16800)*
C & F Fabrications Inc...........................E....... 937 666-3234
East Liberty *(G-9046)*
Cable and Ctrl Solutions LLC................G....... 937 254-2227
Dayton *(G-7972)*
▲ **Cable Mfg & Assembly Inc**................C....... 330 874-2900
Bolivar *(G-1908)*
Canron Manufacturing Inc.....................F........ 330 497-1131
Greentown *(G-10357)*
Clamps Inc..E....... 419 729-2141
Toledo *(G-18232)*
▲ **Cleveland Wire Cloth & Mfg Co**........E....... 216 341-1832
Cleveland *(G-4985)*
Columbus McKinnon Corporation........D....... 330 424-7248
Lisbon *(G-11965)*
Contitech Usa Inc...................................E....... 937 644-8900
Marysville *(G-12776)*
Darryl Smith...G....... 216 991-5468
Cleveland *(G-5068)*
Dayton Superior Corporation................E....... 815 732-3136
Miamisburg *(G-13656)*
Dayton Wire Products Inc.....................E....... 937 236-8000
Dayton *(G-8149)*
▲ **Die Co Inc**..E....... 440 942-8856
Eastlake *(G-9104)*
Dolin Supply Co......................................E....... 304 529-4171
South Point *(G-17282)*
Eagle Wire Works Inc.............................F....... 216 341-8550
Cleveland *(G-5136)*
Efco Corp...E....... 614 876-1226
Columbus *(G-6886)*
Elyria Spring & Specialty Inc.................E....... 440 323-5502
Elyria *(G-9256)*
Engineered Wire Products Inc..............E....... 330 469-6958
Warren *(G-19400)*
▲ **Engineered Wire Products Inc**.........C....... 419 294-3817
Upper Sandusky *(G-18953)*
▲ **Ever Roll Specialties Co**....................E....... 937 964-1302
Springfield *(G-17399)*
Falcon Fab and Finishes LLC...............G....... 740 820-4458
Lucasville *(G-12263)*
Fastener Industries Inc..........................F....... 216 267-2240
Cleveland *(G-5221)*
Fence One Inc..F....... 216 441-2600
Cleveland *(G-5229)*
Friends Ornamental Iron Co..................G....... 216 431-6710
Cleveland *(G-5275)*
Gateway Concrete Forming Svcs..........D....... 513 353-2000
Miamitown *(G-13746)*
General Chain & Mfg Corp.....................E....... 513 541-6005
Cincinnati *(G-3740)*
Illinois Tool Works Inc............................E....... 216 292-7161
Bedford *(G-1415)*
Industrial Wire Co Inc.............................G....... 216 781-2230
Cleveland *(G-5455)*
Industrial Wire Co Inc.............................G....... 330 723-7471
Medina *(G-13278)*
◆ **Industrial Wire Rope Sup Inc**............G....... 513 941-2443
Cincinnati *(G-3846)*
Interntnal Tchncal Catings Inc..............D....... 614 449-6669
Columbus *(G-7046)*
J B Kepple Sheet Metal..........................G....... 740 393-2971
Mount Vernon *(G-14484)*
K Effs Inc..F....... 614 443-0586
Columbus *(G-7082)*
Kadee Industries Newco Inc..................F....... 440 439-8650
Bedford *(G-1420)*
Kimmatt Corp...G....... 937 228-3811
Dayton *(G-8297)*
▲ **Malin Wire Co**.......................................G....... 216 267-9080
Cleveland *(G-5607)*
▲ **Manufacturers Equipment Co**...........F....... 513 424-3573
Middletown *(G-13924)*
Marik Spring Inc......................................F....... 330 564-0617
Tallmadge *(G-17991)*
Mason Company LLC..............................E....... 937 780-2321
Leesburg *(G-11713)*
▲ **May Conveyor Inc**...............................F....... 440 237-8012
North Royalton *(G-15286)*
▲ **Mazzella Lifting Tech Inc**....................D....... 440 239-7000
Cleveland *(G-5638)*
Mazzella Lifting Tech Inc........................F....... 513 772-4466
Cincinnati *(G-3988)*
◆ **McM Ind Co Inc**....................................F....... 216 292-4506
Cleveland *(G-5644)*
McM Ind Co Inc..E....... 216 641-6300
Cleveland *(G-5645)*
Meese Inc..D....... 440 998-1202
Ashtabula *(G-785)*
Microplex Inc...E....... 330 498-0600
North Canton *(G-15101)*
▼ **Midwestern Industries Inc**..................C....... 330 837-4203
Massillon *(G-13026)*
▲ **Mueller Electric Company Inc**...........E....... 216 771-5225
Akron *(G-290)*
▲ **Ofco Inc**...D....... 740 622-5922
Coshocton *(G-7746)*
Ohio Wire Form & Spring Co..................F....... 614 444-3676
Columbus *(G-7264)*
▼ **Options Plus Incorporated**.................F....... 740 694-9811
Fredericktown *(G-9975)*
▲ **Organized Living Inc**...........................E....... 513 489-9300
Cincinnati *(G-4118)*
Panacea Products Corporation..............D....... 614 429-6320
Columbus *(G-7288)*
◆ **Panacea Products Corporation**.........E....... 614 850-7000
Columbus *(G-7287)*
Parker-Hannifin Corporation..................F....... 330 336-3511
Wadsworth *(G-19262)*
Pittsburgh Wire & Cable..........................G....... 740 886-0202
Proctorville *(G-16344)*
▲ **Polymet Corporation**...........................E....... 513 874-3586
West Chester *(G-19763)*
Precision Wire Products Inc..................G....... 216 265-7580
Cleveland *(G-5913)*
◆ **Premier Manufacturing Corp**.............D....... 216 941-9700
Cleveland *(G-5916)*
Production Plus Corp..............................F....... 740 983-5178
Ashville *(G-820)*
Providence Rees Inc................................E....... 614 833-6231
Columbus *(G-7355)*
▲ **Pwp Inc**...E....... 216 251-2181
Ashland *(G-740)*
▲ **Qualtek Electronics Corp**...................C....... 440 951-3300
Mentor *(G-13567)*
Range One Products & Fabg.................F....... 330 533-1151
Canfield *(G-2542)*
RFS Fabrication.......................................G....... 419 547-0650
Clyde *(G-6395)*
Roy I Kaufman Inc...................................G....... 740 382-0643
Marion *(G-12731)*
▲ **Royal Wire Products Inc**.....................D....... 440 237-8787
North Royalton *(G-15297)*
Rural Iron Works LLC..............................G....... 419 647-4617
Spencerville *(G-17313)*
▲ **Saxon Products Inc**.............................G....... 419 241-6771
Toledo *(G-18513)*
Schweizer Dipple Inc..............................D....... 440 786-8090
Cleveland *(G-6034)*
Seven-Ogun International LLC..............G....... 614 888-8939
Worthington *(G-20703)*
▼ **Spring Team Inc**...................................D....... 440 275-5981
Austinburg *(G-926)*
Starr Fabricating Inc...............................D....... 330 394-9891
Vienna *(G-19210)*
Stephens Pipe & Steel LLC....................C....... 740 869-2257
Mount Sterling *(G-14465)*
▼ **T & R Welding Systems Inc**................F....... 937 228-7517
Dayton *(G-8535)*
▲ **Therm-O-Link Inc**..................................D....... 330 527-2124
Garrettsville *(G-10203)*
Tom Thumb Clip Co Inc...........................F....... 440 953-9606
Willoughby *(G-20450)*
Top Knotch Products Inc.......................G....... 419 543-2266
Cleveland *(G-6186)*
Tri-State Belting Ltd................................G....... 800 330-2358
Cincinnati *(G-4434)*
▲ **Tri-State Wire Rope Supply Inc**.........F....... 513 871-8623
Cincinnati *(G-4437)*
▲ **Tyler Haver Inc**.....................................E....... 440 974-1047
Mentor *(G-13615)*
Unified Screening & Crushing...............G....... 937 836-3201
Englewood *(G-9380)*
▲ **US Screen Co**...G....... 419 736-2400
Sullivan *(G-17882)*
Utility Wire Products Inc........................F....... 216 441-2180
Cleveland *(G-6247)*
▲ **Ver-Mac Industries Inc**........................E....... 740 397-6511
Mount Vernon *(G-14517)*
▼ **W J Egli Company Inc**..........................F....... 330 823-3666
Alliance *(G-512)*
West Equipment Company Inc...............F....... 419 698-1601
Toledo *(G-18597)*
Wire Products Company Inc...................D....... 216 267-0777
Cleveland *(G-6315)*
Wrwp LLC..F....... 330 425-3421
Twinsburg *(G-18875)*
WS Tyler Screening Inc..........................E....... 440 974-1047
Mentor *(G-13630)*
Yankee Wire Cloth Products Inc............E....... 740 545-9129
West Lafayette *(G-19934)*
▼ **Yost Superior Co**....................................E....... 937 323-7591
Springfield *(G-17522)*

3497 Metal Foil & Leaf

▲ **A J Oster Foils LLC**.................................D....... 330 823-1700
Alliance *(G-447)*
CC Investors Management Co LLC.......G....... 740 374-8129
Marietta *(G-12614)*
CCL Label Inc...C....... 216 676-2703
Cleveland *(G-4894)*
CCL Label Inc...E....... 440 878-7000
Brunswick *(G-2194)*

3498 Fabricated Pipe & Pipe Fittings

Addition Mfg Tech LLC............................G....... 513 228-7000
Lebanon *(G-11630)*
◆ **Alloy Bllows Prcision Wldg Inc**............D....... 440 684-3000
Cleveland *(G-4674)*
▼ **American Roll Formed Pdts Corp**.....C....... 440 352-0753
Youngstown *(G-20843)*
▲ **Appian Manufacturing Corp**................E....... 614 445-2230
Columbus *(G-6608)*
Arem Co..F....... 440 974-6740
Mentor *(G-13393)*
Atlas Industrial Contrs LLC....................B....... 614 841-4500
Columbus *(G-6627)*
B S F Inc...F....... 937 890-6121
Dayton *(G-8050)*
B S F Inc...F....... 937 890-6121
Tipp City *(G-18100)*
Beaverson Machine Inc...........................G....... 419 923-8064
Delta *(G-8766)*
Benjamin Steel Company Inc..................E....... 937 233-1212
Springfield *(G-17368)*
Carter Machine Company Inc.................G....... 419 468-3530
Galion *(G-10125)*
Chardon Metal Products Co....................E....... 440 285-2147
Chardon *(G-3102)*
Cleveland Coppersmithing Works..........G....... 330 607-3998
Richfield *(G-16465)*
Cleveland Plastic Fabricat.......................F....... 216 797-7300
Euclid *(G-9409)*
Contractors Steel Company....................E....... 330 425-3050
Twinsburg *(G-18757)*
Crest Bending Inc......................................E....... 419 492-2108
New Washington *(G-14828)*
Defiance Metal Products WI Inc.............C....... 920 426-9207
Defiance *(G-8621)*
Dekay Fabricators Inc..............................G....... 330 793-0826
Youngstown *(G-20888)*
▲ **Duro Dyne Midwest Corp**......................B....... 513 870-6000
Hamilton *(G-10551)*
Eaton Corporation.....................................C....... 440 826-1115
Berea *(G-1604)*
▲ **Ebner Furnaces Inc**................................D....... 330 335-2311
Wadsworth *(G-19237)*
Elliott Tool Technologies Ltd...................D....... 937 253-6133
Dayton *(G-8182)*
◆ **Elster Perfection Corporation**.............D....... 440 428-1171
Geneva *(G-10218)*
Esterle Mold & Machine Co Inc...............E....... 330 686-1685
Stow *(G-17583)*
▲ **Ever Roll Specialties Co**.......................E....... 937 964-1302
Springfield *(G-17399)*
Excel Loading Systems LLC....................G....... 513 265-2936
Blue Ash *(G-1769)*
Fabcraft Inc..G....... 440 286-6700
Chardon *(G-3111)*
Famous Industries Inc..............................D....... 740 685-2592
Byesville *(G-2384)*
Faull & Son LLC..F....... 330 652-4341
Niles *(G-15008)*
Franklin Frames and Cycles....................G....... 740 763-3838
Newark *(G-14875)*
H-P Products Inc.......................................E....... 330 875-7193
Louisville *(G-12155)*
▼ **Hollaender Manufacturing Co**..............D....... 513 772-8800
Cincinnati *(G-3817)*

S I C

Employee Codes: A=Over 500 employees, B=251-500
C=101-250, D=51-100, E=20-50, F=10-19, G=3-9
2019 Harris Ohio
Industrial Directory
943

Hycom Inc....E....330 753-2330
Barberton (G-1076)
Hydra-TEC Inc....G....330 225-8797
Brunswick (G-2213)
▲ Hydro Tube Enterprises Inc....D....440 774-1022
Oberlin (G-15499)
▲ Industrial Quartz Corp....F....440 942-0909
Mentor (G-13469)
Ipsco Tubulars Inc....G....330 448-6772
Brookfield (G-2108)
Jan Squires Inc....G....440 988-7859
Amherst (G-563)
John H Hosking Inc....G....513 821-1080
Middletown (G-13918)
John Maneely Company....E....724 342-6851
Niles (G-15019)
Kenley Enterprises LLC....E....419 630-0921
Bryan (G-2293)
Kings Welding and Fabg Inc....E....330 738-3592
Mechanicstown (G-13212)
◆ Kirtland Capital Partners LP....E....216 593-0100
Beachwood (G-1244)
▲ Kottler Metal Products Co Inc....E....440 946-7473
Willoughby (G-20355)
Lakewood Steel Inc....F....440 965-4226
Wakeman (G-19286)
Lim Services LLC....F....513 217-0801
Middletown (G-13920)
M E P Manufacturing Inc....G....419 855-7723
Genoa (G-10234)
◆ Machine Dynamics & Engrg Inc....D....330 868-5603
Minerva (G-14190)
Mitchell Piping LLC....E....330 245-0258
Hartville (G-10702)
Moss Vale Inc....F....513 939-1970
Fairfield (G-9531)
Normandy Products Company....D....440 632-5050
Middlefield (G-13840)
Parker-Hannifin Corporation....B....937 456-5571
Eaton (G-9163)
Phillips Mfg and Tower Co....D....419 347-1720
Shelby (G-16985)
Phoenix Forge Group LLC....C....800 848-6125
West Jefferson (G-19926)
Pines Manufacturing Inc....E....440 835-5553
Westlake (G-20142)
▲ Pioneer Pipe Inc....A....740 376-2400
Marietta (G-12653)
▲ Pipe Line Development Company....D....440 871-5700
Westlake (G-20144)
Precise Tube Forming Inc....G....440 237-3956
North Royalton (G-15296)
▲ Precision Fittings LLC....E....440 647-4143
Wellington (G-19589)
Propipe Technologies Inc....E....513 424-5311
Middletown (G-13945)
▼ Qual-Fab Inc....E....440 327-5000
Avon (G-960)
Quality Mechanicals Inc....E....513 559-0998
Cincinnati (G-4226)
▲ Rafter Equipment Corporation....E....440 572-3700
Strongsville (G-17781)
Rbm Environmental and Cnstr....E....419 693-5840
Oregon (G-15566)
◆ Rexarc International Inc....E....937 839-4604
West Alexandria (G-19620)
▲ Rhenium Alloys Inc....D....440 365-7388
North Ridgeville (G-15251)
▼ Riker Products Inc....C....419 729-1626
Toledo (G-18501)
Rocks General Maintenance LLC....G....740 323-4711
Thornville (G-18032)
S E Anning Company....G....513 702-4417
Cincinnati (G-4295)
S-P Company Inc....F....330 482-0200
Columbiana (G-6479)
▲ Sanoh America Inc....D....419 425-2600
Findlay (G-9751)
Scot Industries Inc....E....330 262-7585
Wooster (G-20651)
◆ Scott Process Systems Inc....C....330 877-2350
Hartville (G-10705)
Seal Tite LLC....D....937 393-4268
Hillsboro (G-10891)
▲ Sroka Industries Inc....E....440 572-2811
Strongsville (G-17795)
▲ SSP Fittings Corp....C....330 425-4250
Twinsburg (G-18858)
▲ Stam Inc....E....440 974-2500
Mentor (G-13587)
▲ Stripmatic Products Inc....E....216 241-7143
Cleveland (G-6111)
Summers Acquisition Corp....G....419 423-5800
Findlay (G-9765)
Swagelok Company....D....440 349-5934
Solon (G-17242)
Swagelok Company....D....440 349-5652
Solon (G-17241)
T & D Fabricating Inc....E....440 951-5646
Eastlake (G-9135)
▲ Tech Tool Inc....F....330 674-1176
Millersburg (G-14133)
TI Group Auto Systems LLC....C....740 929-2049
Hebron (G-10767)
Tilton Corporation....C....419 227-6421
Lima (G-11952)
Tomco Machining Inc....E....937 264-1943
Dayton (G-8560)
Transit Sittings of NA....G....330 797-2516
Youngstown (G-21049)
Tri-America Contractors Inc....E....740 574-0148
Wheelersburg (G-20186)
Tri-America Contractors Inc....G....740 574-0148
Wheelersburg (G-20187)
Tri-State Fabricators Inc....E....513 752-5005
Amelia (G-550)
Unison Industries LLC....D....937 426-4676
Alpha (G-518)
Unison Industries LLC....B....904 667-9904
Dayton (G-7994)
United Group Services Inc....C....800 633-9690
West Chester (G-19910)
Unity Tube Inc....F....330 426-4282
East Palestine (G-9088)
US Tubular Products Inc....D....330 832-1734
North Lawrence (G-15163)
Vortec Corporation....E....513 891-7485
Blue Ash (G-1866)
▼ W J Egli Company Inc....F....330 823-3666
Alliance (G-512)
Welded Tubes Inc....F....440 437-5144
Orwell (G-15638)
Woodsage Corporation....D....419 476-3553
Holland (G-10967)
Zekelman Industries Inc....C....740 432-2146
Cambridge (G-2463)

3499 Fabricated Metal Prdts, NEC

A&E Machine & Fabrication Inc....F....740 820-4701
Beaver (G-1291)
Accurate Mechanical Inc....E....740 681-1332
Lancaster (G-11538)
Ace Plastics Co....G....330 928-7720
Stow (G-17566)
Alacriant Inc....D....330 562-7191
Streetsboro (G-17658)
Alacriant Inc....E....330 562-7191
Streetsboro (G-17659)
Alchemical Transmutation....C....216 313-8674
Cleveland (G-4651)
▲ Alert Stamping & Mfg Co Inc....E....440 232-5020
Bedford Heights (G-1458)
Alex Products Inc....C....419 399-4500
Paulding (G-15855)
American Scaffolding Inc....G....216 524-7733
Cleveland (G-4697)
Arete Innovative Solutions LLC....G....513 503-2712
Morrow (G-14408)
Avenue Fabricating Inc....E....513 752-1911
Batavia (G-1124)
Axis Corporation....F....937 592-1958
Bellefontaine (G-1505)
B C Composites Corporation....F....330 262-3070
Medina (G-13228)
B K Fabrication & Machine Shop....G....740 695-4164
Saint Clairsville (G-16622)
Bauer Corporation....E....800 321-4760
Wooster (G-20569)
Bc Investment Corporation....G....330 262-3070
Wooster (G-20570)
Ben James Enterprises Inc....G....330 477-9353
Canton (G-2589)
Blue Chip Machine & Tool Ltd....G....419 626-9559
Sandusky (G-16797)
Buckeye Metals....G....740 446-9590
Bidwell (G-1665)
Camaco LLC....A....440 288-4444
Lorain (G-12082)
Candle Cottage....G....937 526-4041
Versailles (G-19176)
Cctm Inc....G....513 934-3533
Lebanon (G-11641)
Cincy Safe Company....E....513 900-9152
Milford (G-14003)
Company Front Awards....G....440 636-5493
Middlefield (G-13786)
COW Industries Inc....E....614 443-6537
Columbus (G-6831)
Cpmg....G....440 263-2780
North Royalton (G-15267)
Crest Craft Company....F....513 271-4858
Blue Ash (G-1754)
Custom Fabrication By Fisher....G....513 738-4600
Okeana (G-15517)
▲ Dern Trophies Corp....F....614 895-3260
Westerville (G-19987)
Detrick Design Fabrication LLC....G....937 620-6736
Troy (G-18651)
Die-Cut Products Co....E....216 771-6994
Cleveland (G-5094)
Diebold Nixdorf Incorporated....A....330 490-4000
North Canton (G-15078)
Donald E Didion II....E....419 483-2226
Bellevue (G-1535)
Drawn Metals Corp....F....937 433-6151
Dayton (G-8168)
▲ Dura Magnetics Inc....F....419 882-0591
Sylvania (G-17939)
▼ Eastern Automated Piping....G....740 535-8184
Mingo Junction (G-14208)
Exair Corporation....E....513 671-3322
Cincinnati (G-3664)
EZ Grout Corporation Inc....E....740 962-2024
Malta (G-12382)
Fabricating Solutions Inc....F....330 486-0998
Twinsburg (G-18773)
Fenix Magnetics Inc....G....440 455-1142
Westlake (G-20113)
Fisher Metal Fabricating....F....419 838-7200
Walbridge (G-19293)
▲ Flexmag Industries Inc....D....740 373-3492
Marietta (G-12624)
Fountain Specialists Inc....G....513 831-5717
Milford (G-14009)
◆ Frame USA....E....513 577-7107
Cincinnati (G-3708)
Frame Warehouse....G....614 861-4582
Reynoldsburg (G-16440)
G & M Metal Products Inc....G....513 863-3353
Hamilton (G-10561)
GCI Metals Inc....G....937 262-7500
Dayton (G-8215)
General Metals Powder Co....D....330 633-1226
Akron (G-186)
Hamilton Fabricators Inc....E....513 735-7773
Batavia (G-1151)
Hamilton Safe Amelia....F....513 753-5694
Amelia (G-540)
▲ Hamilton Safe Co....F....513 874-3733
Cincinnati (G-3794)
▲ Hamilton Security Products Co....G....513 874-3733
Cincinnati (G-3795)
Hit Trophy Inc....G....419 445-5356
Archbold (G-653)
Hoffman Machining & Repair LLC....G....419 547-9204
Clyde (G-6389)
Humble Construction Co....E....614 888-8960
Columbus (G-7010)
Hykon Manufacturing Company....G....330 821-8889
Alliance (G-477)
Ibi Brake Products Inc....G....440 543-7962
Chagrin Falls (G-3052)
J & J Performance Inc....F....330 567-2455
Shreve (G-17004)
J Feldkamp Design Build Ltd....E....513 870-0601
Cincinnati (G-3863)
Jaguar Medical Supplies Inc....G....440 263-2780
North Royalton (G-15279)
▲ Jay Mid-South LLC....C....256 439-6600
Mansfield (G-12462)
Johnson Machining Services LLC....G....937 866-4744
Miamisburg (G-13682)
Kard Welding Inc....E....419 628-2598
Minster (G-14218)
Karyall-Telday Inc....E....216 281-4063
Cleveland (G-5516)
Ksm Metal Fabrication....G....937 339-6366
Troy (G-18683)
Labcraft Inc....E....419 878-4400
Waterville (G-19500)

35 INDUSTRIAL AND COMMERCIAL MACHINERY AND COMPUTER EQUIPMENT

Lam Welding & Met Fabrication ....G 304 839-2404
  Carrollton (G-2924)
Lewark Metal Spinning Inc ....E 937 275-3303
  Dayton (G-8312)
Linsalata Capital Partners Fun ....G 440 684-1400
  Cleveland (G-5579)
M A K Fabricating Inc ....F 330 747-0040
  Youngstown (G-20962)
M E P Manufacturing Inc ....G 419 855-7723
  Genoa (G-10234)
Mab Fabrication Inc 855 622-3221
  Harrison (G-10656)
◆ Magnum Magnetics Corporation ......C 740 373-7770
  Marietta (G-12641)
Mansfield Welding Services LLC ....G 419 594-2738
  Oakwood (G-15471)
Manufacturing Futures Inc ....G 216 903-7993
  Cleveland (G-5613)
Mast Farm Service Ltd ....E 330 893-2972
  Walnut Creek (G-19307)
Mid Ohio Trophy & Awards ....G 419 756-2266
  Mansfield (G-12480)
Mills Aluminum Fab ....G 330 821-4108
  Alliance (G-489)
Miscellnous Mtals Fbrction Inc ....G 740 779-3071
  Chillicothe (G-3200)
MTS Enterprises LLC ....G 937 324-7510
  Springfield (G-17453)
National Security Products ....G 216 566-9962
  Cleveland (G-5729)
▲ New American Reel Company LLC .G 419 258-2900
  Antwerp (G-599)
North American Steel Company ....E 216 475-7300
  Cleveland (G-5759)
▲ North Shore Strapping Inc ....D 216 661-5200
  Brooklyn Heights (G-2128)
▲ Nostalgic Images Inc ....E 419 784-1728
  Defiance (G-8641)
▲ Ohio Gasket and Shim Co Inc ....E 330 630-0626
  Akron (G-307)
Ohio Laser LLC ....E 614 873-7030
  Plain City (G-16204)
▲ Ohio Magnetics Inc ....E 216 662-8484
  Maple Heights (G-12575)
P S Superior Inc ....F 216 587-1000
  Cleveland (G-5833)
Paulg Corporation ....E 914 662-9837
  Columbus (G-7302)
▲ Peter Graham Dunn Inc ....G 330 816-0035
  Dalton (G-7950)
Pfi USA 937 547-0413
  Greenville (G-10386)
Pucel Enterprises Inc ....D 216 881-4604
  Cleveland (G-5933)
Quest Technologies Inc ....G 937 743-1200
  Franklin (G-9913)
R L Torbeck Industries Inc ....E 513 367-0080
  Harrison (G-10667)
Ray Rieser Trophy Co ....G 614 279-1128
  Columbus (G-7379)
Rework Furnishings LLC ....F 614 300-5021
  Columbus (G-7390)
Rise Holdings LLC ....F 440 946-9646
  Willoughby (G-20422)
Rmi Titanium Company LLC ....D 330 455-4010
  Canton (G-2806)
SES Fabracating LLC ....G 440 636-5853
  Windsor (G-20528)
Sharonco Inc ....G 419 882-3443
  Sylvania (G-17960)
Shipping Room Products Inc ....G 216 531-4422
  Cleveland (G-6059)
▲ Smith Security Safes Inc ....G 419 823-1423
  Bowling Green (G-1999)
Spirol International Corp ....D 330 920-3655
  Stow (G-17630)
▲ Sulo Enterprises Inc ....F 440 926-3322
  Grafton (G-10311)
Tosoh SMD Inc ....G 614 875-7912
  Grove City (G-10477)
Tribco Incorporated ....E 216 486-2000
  Cleveland (G-6209)
Universal Dsign Fbrication LLC ....G 419 359-1794
  Sandusky (G-16859)
US Powder Coating Inc ....G 440 255-3090
  Mentor (G-13620)
Vortec Corporation ....E 513 891-7485
  Blue Ash (G-1866)
▲ Voss Industries LLC ....C 216 771-7655
  Cleveland (G-6273)

Voyale Minority Enterprise LLC ....E 216 271-3661
  Cleveland (G-6274)
Walker Magnetics Group Inc ....E 614 492-1614
  Columbus (G-7588)
◆ Walker National Inc ....E 614 492-1614
  Columbus (G-7589)
Warren Steel Specialties Corp ....F 330 399-8360
  Warren (G-19461)
Williamson Safe Inc ....G 937 393-9919
  Hillsboro (G-10895)
▲ Winkle Industries Inc ....D 330 823-9730
  Alliance (G-516)
Yarder Manufacturing Company ....D 419 476-3933
  Toledo (G-18603)
Yarder Manufacturing Company ....G 419 269-3474
  Toledo (G-18604)
Youngstown Specialty Mtls Inc ....G 330 259-1110
  Youngstown (G-21082)

35 INDUSTRIAL AND COMMERCIAL MACHINERY AND COMPUTER EQUIPMENT

3511 Steam, Gas & Hydraulic Turbines & Engines

Aero Propulsion Support Inc ....E 513 367-9452
  Harrison (G-10628)
Alin Machining Company Inc ....D 740 223-0200
  Marion (G-12691)
Arete Innovative Solutions LLC ....G 513 503-2712
  Morrow (G-14408)
▲ Argosy Wind Power Ltd ....G 440 539-1345
  Aurora (G-869)
Babcock & Wilcox Company ....E 330 753-4511
  Barberton (G-1060)
Babcock & Wilcox Company ....G 740 687-6500
  Lancaster (G-11546)
Camfil USA Inc ....G 937 773-0866
  Piqua (G-16106)
Eaton Leasing Corporation ....G 216 382-2292
  Beachwood (G-1235)
Fluid System Service Inc ....G 216 651-2450
  Cleveland (G-5254)
Fluidpower Assembly Inc ....G 419 394-7486
  Saint Marys (G-16685)
▲ Fusion Incorporated ....E 440 946-3300
  Willoughby (G-20327)
GE Aircraft Engines ....G 513 868-9906
  Fairfield Township (G-9581)
General Electric Company ....F 513 243-9317
  West Chester (G-19712)
Kw River Hydroelectric I LLC ....G 513 673-2251
  Cincinnati (G-3927)
▲ Metalex Manufacturing Inc ....C 513 489-0507
  Blue Ash (G-1820)
Muller Engine & Machine Co ....G 937 322-1861
  Springfield (G-17454)
Northel Usa LLC ....G 740 973-0309
  Newark (G-14904)
On-Power Inc ....E 513 228-2100
  Lebanon (G-11679)
Parker Triad Store ....D 937 293-4080
  Moraine (G-14374)
Pfpc Enterprises Inc ....B 513 941-6200
  Cincinnati (G-4155)
R H Industries Inc ....E 216 281-5210
  Cleveland (G-5952)
Siemens Energy Inc ....G 740 504-1947
  Mount Vernon (G-14512)
Siemens Energy Inc ....B 740 393-8897
  Mount Vernon (G-14510)
Steam Engine Works LLC ....G 513 813-3690
  Cincinnati (G-4376)
Steam Turb Alte Reso ....E 740 387-5535
  Marion (G-12737)

3519 Internal Combustion Engines, NEC

▲ American Fine Sinter Co Ltd ....C 419 443-8880
  Tiffin (G-18042)
B A Malcuit Racing Inc ....G 330 878-7111
  Strasburg (G-17645)
Brinkley Technology Group LLC ....F 330 830-2498
  Massillon (G-12963)
Cameron International Corp ....G 740 397-4888
  Mount Vernon (G-14472)
Chemequip Sales Inc ....E 330 724-8300
  Coventry Township (G-7767)

▲ Clarke Fire Prtection Pdts Inc ....D 513 771-2200
  Cincinnati (G-3523)
Country Sales & Service LLC ....F 330 683-2500
  Orrville (G-15588)
Cricket Engines ....G 513 532-2145
  Blanchester (G-1701)
Cummins - Allison Corp ....G 614 529-1940
  Columbus (G-6841)
Cummins - Allison Corp ....G 513 469-2924
  Blue Ash (G-1756)
Cummins - Allison Corp ....G 440 824-5050
  Cleveland (G-5042)
Cummins Bridgeway Columbus LLC ...D 614 771-1000
  Hilliard (G-10822)
Cummins Bridgeway Toledo LLC ....G 419 893-8711
  Maumee (G-13084)
Cummins Inc ....G 614 604-6004
  Grove City (G-10424)
Cummins Inc ....E 614 771-1000
  Hilliard (G-10823)
Debolt Machine Inc ....G 740 454-8082
  Zanesville (G-21127)
Detroit Desl Rmnfacturing Corp ....F 740 439-7701
  Cambridge (G-2434)
◆ Detroit Desl Rmnfctrng-Ast Inc ....B 740 439-7701
  Byesville (G-2382)
◆ Dmax Ltd ....D 937 425-9700
  Moraine (G-14346)
Draime Enterprises Inc ....G 330 837-2254
  Massillon (G-12976)
▲ DW Hercules LLC ....E 330 830-2498
  Massillon (G-12977)
Enginetics Corporation ....C 937 878-3800
  Huber Heights (G-11017)
Ford Motor Company ....A 419 226-7000
  Lima (G-11864)
GE Rolls Royce Fighter ....G 513 243-2787
  Cincinnati (G-3739)
Gellner Engineering Inc ....G 216 398-8500
  Cleveland (G-5301)
▲ General Engine Products LLC ....D 937 704-0160
  Franklin (G-9886)
Graham Ford Power Products ....G 614 801-0049
  Columbus (G-6965)
Great Lakes Diesel ....G 419 433-9898
  Vermilion (G-19160)
▲ Hemco Inc ....G 419 499-4602
  Milan (G-13984)
▲ HK Engine Components LLC ....G 330 830-3500
  Massillon (G-12998)
▲ Hy-Production Inc ....C 330 273-2400
  Valley City (G-19040)
Industrial Parts Depot LLC ....G 440 237-9164
  North Royalton (G-15278)
▼ Jatrodiesel Inc ....F 937 847-8050
  Miamisburg (G-13681)
Jjb Engineer ....G 330 807-0671
  Cuyahoga Falls (G-7885)
Kenworth of Dayton ....F 937 235-2589
  Dayton (G-8294)
Kinstle Truck & Auto Svc Inc ....F 419 738-7493
  Wapakoneta (G-19337)
Maags Automotive & Machine ....G 419 626-1539
  Sandusky (G-16824)
Mantapart ....G 330 549-2389
  New Springfield (G-14820)
Metaldyne Pwrtrain Cmpnnts Inc ....C 330 486-3200
  Twinsburg (G-18818)
Navistar Inc ....E 937 390-5704
  Springfield (G-17459)
Performace Diesel Inc ....F 740 392-3693
  Mount Vernon (G-14500)
Performance Research Inc ....G 614 475-8300
  Columbus (G-7312)
▼ Rozevink Engines LLC ....G 419 789-1159
  Holgate (G-10913)
Western Branch Diesel Inc ....E 330 454-8800
  Canton (G-2864)

3523 Farm Machinery & Eqpt

Afs Technology LLC ....F 937 669-3548
  Ansonia (G-592)
American Baler Co ....D 419 483-5790
  Bellevue (G-1529)
Baker Built Products Inc ....G 419 965-2646
  Ohio City (G-15514)
Beth Otto Independent Case Exa ....G 513 868-0484
  Fairfield (G-9484)
Birds Eye Foods Inc ....E 330 854-0818
  Canal Fulton (G-2477)

Employee Codes: A=Over 500 employees, B=251-500
C=101-250, D=51-100, E=20-50, F=10-19, G=3-9

35 INDUSTRIAL AND COMMERCIAL MACHINERY AND COMPUTER EQUIPMENT

▼ Buckeye Tractor Company Corp .... G 419 659-2162
  Columbus Grove *(G-7631)*
▼ C & S Turf Care Equipment Inc .... F 330 966-4511
  North Canton *(G-15074)*
Cailin Dev Ltd Lblty Co .... F 216 408-6261
  Cleveland *(G-4862)*
CF Extrusion Technologies LLC .... G 844 439-8783
  Uhrichsville *(G-18882)*
◆ Chick Master Incubator Company .... C 330 722-5591
  Medina *(G-13235)*
Consolidated Casework Inc .... G 330 618-6951
  Valley City *(G-19033)*
Country Manufacturing Inc .... F 740 694-9926
  Fredericktown *(G-9964)*
Creamer Metal Products .... E 740 852-1752
  London *(G-12056)*
Empire Plow Company Inc .... E 216 641-2290
  Cleveland *(G-5175)*
END Separation LLC .... G 419 438-0879
  Oakwood *(G-15470)*
Field Gymmy Inc .... G 419 538-6511
  Glandorf *(G-10269)*
Flying Dutchman Inc .... G 740 694-1734
  Smithville *(G-17088)*
◆ Fort Recovery Equipment Inc .... E 419 375-1006
  Fort Recovery *(G-9816)*
Garber Co .... G 937 462-8730
  South Charleston *(G-17272)*
Gerald Grain Center Inc .... F 419 445-2451
  Archbold *(G-650)*
Gilbert Geiser .... G 330 237-7901
  Canton *(G-2684)*
H & S Company Inc .... G 419 394-4444
  Celina *(G-2965)*
H G Violet Inc .... G 419 695-2000
  Delphos *(G-8744)*
▲ Hawkline Nevada LLC .... E 937 444-4295
  Mount Orab *(G-14442)*
▼ Healthpro Brands Inc .... G 513 492-7512
  Loveland *(G-12196)*
Hershy Way Ltd .... G 330 893-2809
  Millersburg *(G-14090)*
Hollmann Inc .... G 513 522-1800
  Cincinnati *(G-3819)*
Hord Elevator LLC .... F 419 562-5934
  Bucyrus *(G-2335)*
◆ Intertec Corporation .... B 419 537-9711
  Toledo *(G-18350)*
◆ J & M Manufacturing Co Inc .... C 419 375-2376
  Fort Recovery *(G-9822)*
Kadant Black Clawson Inc .... D 251 653-8558
  Lebanon *(G-11666)*
Keynes Brothers Inc .... G 740 426-6332
  Jeffersonville *(G-11247)*
Knief Farms A Partnership .... G 937 585-4810
  Lewistown *(G-11801)*
◆ Komar Industries Inc .... E 614 836-2366
  Groveport *(G-10497)*
Koster Crop Tester Inc .... G 330 220-2116
  Brunswick *(G-2217)*
Kriss Kreations .... G 330 405-6102
  Twinsburg *(G-18803)*
Kuhns Mfg Llc .... G 440 693-4630
  North Bloomfield *(G-15065)*
Landscape Group LLC .... G 614 302-4537
  Mount Sterling *(G-14463)*
Ley Industries Inc .... G 419 238-6742
  Van Wert *(G-19100)*
Liebrecht Manufacturing LLC .... F 419 596-3501
  Continental *(G-7667)*
Marion Caldwell .... G 740 446-1042
  Gallipolis *(G-10171)*
Motrin Corporation .... G 740 439-2725
  Cambridge *(G-2450)*
Ntech Industries Inc .... F 707 467-3747
  Dayton *(G-8389)*
Ohio Windmill & Pump Co Inc .... G 330 547-6300
  Berlin Center *(G-1649)*
◆ Pioneer Equipment Company .... F 330 857-6340
  Dalton *(G-7951)*
▲ R L Parsons & Son Equipment Co .... G 614 879-7601
  West Jefferson *(G-19927)*
Randall Richard & Moore LLC .... F 330 455-8873
  Canton *(G-2802)*
▲ Remlinger Manufacturing Co Inc .... E 419 532-3647
  Kalida *(G-11280)*
▲ Rhinestahl Corporation .... D 513 229-5300
  Mason *(G-12933)*
▲ S I Distributing Inc .... F 419 647-4909
  Spencerville *(G-17314)*

Safe-Grain Inc .... G 513 398-2500
  Wapakoneta *(G-19352)*
Shearer Farm Inc .... E 330 345-9023
  Wooster *(G-20653)*
Stein-Way Equipment .... F 330 857-8700
  Apple Creek *(G-619)*
Stephens Pipe & Steel LLC .... C 740 869-2257
  Mount Sterling *(G-14465)*
◆ Sweet Manufacturing Company .... E 937 325-1511
  Springfield *(G-17501)*
TD Landscape Inc .... F 740 694-0244
  Fredericktown *(G-9978)*
Toolco Inc .... G 419 667-3462
  Van Wert *(G-19108)*
Universal Equipment Mfg .... G 614 586-1780
  Columbus *(G-7560)*
◆ Unverferth Mfg Co Inc .... C 419 532-3121
  Kalida *(G-11282)*
Unverferth Mfg Co Inc .... D 419 695-2060
  Delphos *(G-8761)*
▲ Val-Co Pax Inc .... G 717 354-4586
  Coldwater *(G-6423)*
Warren Zachman Contracting .... G 740 389-4503
  Marion *(G-12747)*
Wiley Farms .... G 937 537-0676
  Richwood *(G-16509)*
Woodbury Welding Inc .... G 937 968-3573
  Union City *(G-18906)*
Yoder & Frey Inc .... G 419 445-2070
  Archbold *(G-674)*

3524 Garden, Lawn Tractors & Eqpt

Albright Saw Company Inc .... G 740 887-2107
  Londonderry *(G-12073)*
Bortnick Tractor Sales Inc .... F 330 924-2555
  Cortland *(G-7704)*
California Grounds Care LLC .... G 513 207-0244
  Cincinnati *(G-3437)*
Cannon Salt and Supply Inc .... G 440 232-1700
  Bedford *(G-1392)*
Commercial Turf Products Ltd .... C 330 995-7000
  Streetsboro *(G-17667)*
Cub Cadet LLC .... G 330 273-8669
  Valley City *(G-19034)*
Dinsmore Inc .... G 937 544-3332
  West Union *(G-19961)*
▲ Elan Designs Inc .... G 614 985-5600
  Westerville *(G-20050)*
Extrudex Limited Partnership .... E 440 352-7101
  Painesville *(G-15737)*
Franklin Equipment LLC .... G 614 228-2014
  Groveport *(G-10492)*
Friesen Fab and Equipment .... G 614 873-4354
  Plain City *(G-16192)*
Jani Auto Parts Inc .... G 330 494-2975
  North Canton *(G-15095)*
Johnson Tool Distributors .... G 740 653-6959
  Lancaster *(G-11581)*
Klawhorn Industries Inc .... G 330 335-8191
  Wadsworth *(G-19249)*
Koenig Equipment Inc .... F 937 653-5281
  Urbana *(G-19002)*
◆ Mid-West Fabricating Co .... C 740 969-4411
  Amanda *(G-526)*
Mm Service .... G 330 474-3098
  Streetsboro *(G-17683)*
◆ Mtd Consumer Group Inc .... F 330 225-2600
  Valley City *(G-19051)*
▼ Mtd Holdings Inc .... B 330 225-2600
  Valley City *(G-19052)*
◆ Mtd Products Inc .... B 330 225-2600
  Valley City *(G-19053)*
Mtd Products Inc .... A 419 935-6611
  Willard *(G-20242)*
Mtd Products Inc .... B 330 225-9127
  Valley City *(G-19054)*
Mtd Products Inc .... C 419 342-6455
  Shelby *(G-16984)*
Mtd Products Inc .... D 330 225-1940
  Valley City *(G-19055)*
Norman Knepp .... G 740 978-6339
  Mc Arthur *(G-13183)*
Outback Tree Works .... G 937 332-7300
  Troy *(G-18690)*
◆ Park-Ohio Holdings Corp .... F 440 947-2000
  Cleveland *(G-5842)*
Park-Ohio Industries Inc .... C 440 947-2000
  Cleveland *(G-5843)*
▲ Power Distributors LLC .... D 614 876-3533
  Columbus *(G-7334)*

R J Engineering Company Inc .... G 419 843-8651
  Toledo *(G-18494)*
Rotoline USA LLC .... G 330 677-3223
  Kent *(G-11378)*
Russell Hunt .... F 740 264-1196
  Steubenville *(G-17550)*
Schomaker Natural Resource .... G 513 741-1370
  Cincinnati *(G-4307)*
◆ Scotts Company LLC .... B 937 644-0011
  Marysville *(G-12809)*
Smg Growing Media Inc .... G 937 644-0011
  Marysville *(G-12813)*
◆ Speed North America Inc .... G 330 202-7775
  Wooster *(G-20657)*
Tierra-Derco International LLC .... G 419 929-2240
  New London *(G-14740)*
Tri-Tech Mfg LLC .... G 419 238-0140
  Delphos *(G-8758)*
Village Outdoors .... G 440 256-1172
  Kirtland *(G-11472)*
WH Fetzer & Sons Mfg Inc .... E 419 687-8237
  Plymouth *(G-16235)*

3531 Construction Machinery & Eqpt

A Reed Excavating LLC .... G 740 391-4985
  Beallsville *(G-1288)*
Adairs Pavers .... G 937 454-9302
  Vandalia *(G-19112)*
▼ Aim Attachments .... E 614 539-3030
  Grove City *(G-10412)*
Allied Consolidated Industries .... C 330 744-0808
  Youngstown *(G-20841)*
▲ Allied Construction Pdts LLC .... E 216 431-2600
  Cleveland *(G-4671)*
Allied Construction Pdts LLC .... E 216 431-2600
  Cleveland *(G-4672)*
Altec Industries .... G 419 289-6066
  Ashland *(G-676)*
Altec Industries Inc .... F 205 408-2341
  Cuyahoga Falls *(G-7833)*
American Highway Products LLC .... F 330 874-3270
  Bolivar *(G-1906)*
▲ American Power Pull Corp .... G 419 335-7050
  Wauseon *(G-19509)*
▲ ARM Opco Inc .... E 330 868-7724
  Canton *(G-2575)*
▲ Ballinger Industries Inc .... F 419 422-4533
  Findlay *(G-9655)*
▲ Barbco Inc .... E 330 488-9400
  East Canton *(G-9038)*
Basetek LLC .... F 877 712-2273
  Middlefield *(G-13779)*
▲ Belden Brick Company .... E 330 852-2411
  Sugarcreek *(G-17842)*
Brewpro Inc .... G 513 577-7200
  Cincinnati *(G-3415)*
▲ Buck Equipment Inc .... E 614 539-3039
  Grove City *(G-10419)*
◆ Bucyrus Blades Inc .... C 419 562-6015
  Bucyrus *(G-2318)*
Caterpillar Inc .... D 614 834-2400
  Canal Winchester *(G-2501)*
City of Oxford .... F 513 523-8412
  Oxford *(G-15691)*
Cityscapes International Inc .... C 614 850-2540
  Hilliard *(G-10816)*
Coe Manufacturing Company .... D 440 352-9381
  Painesville *(G-15722)*
Concord Road Equipment Mfg Inc .... E 440 357-5344
  Painesville *(G-15723)*
Concrete Cnstr McHy Co LLC .... G 330 638-1515
  Cortland *(G-7705)*
Concrete Leveling Systems Inc .... G 330 966-8120
  Canton *(G-2634)*
Connor Electric Inc .... E 513 932-5798
  Lebanon *(G-11643)*
▲ Construction Polymers Co .... G 440 591-9018
  Chagrin Falls *(G-3041)*
Crane Pro Services .... G 937 525-5555
  Springfield *(G-17380)*
Custom Machining Solutions LLC .... G 330 221-1523
  Rootstown *(G-16567)*
CW Machine Worx Ltd .... F 740 654-5304
  Carroll *(G-2902)*
D & D Landscaping Inc .... G 330 507-6647
  Brookfield *(G-2104)*
D & L Excavating Ltd .... G 419 271-0635
  Port Clinton *(G-16246)*
Dandy Products Inc .... G 800 591-2284
  Mount Vernon *(G-14477)*

35 INDUSTRIAL AND COMMERCIAL MACHINERY AND COMPUTER EQUIPMENT

▲ David Round Company Inc .... E 330 656-1600
 Streetsboro (G-17668)
Desco Corporation .... G 614 888-8855
 New Albany (G-14622)
Dimensional Metals Inc .... D 740 927-3633
 Reynoldsburg (G-16435)
Donald E Dornon .... G 740 926-9144
 Beallsville (G-1290)
Dover Corporation .... F 513 696-1790
 Mason (G-12857)
Dragon Products LLC .... G 330 345-3968
 Wooster (G-20586)
Duplex Mill & Manufacturing Co .... E 937 325-5555
 Springfield (G-17392)
Dynamic Plastics Inc .... G 937 437-7261
 New Paris (G-14753)
◆ E R Advanced Ceramics Inc .... G 330 426-9433
 East Palestine (G-9077)
▲ E Z Grout Corporation .... E 740 749-3512
 Malta (G-12381)
◆ Eagle Crusher Co Inc .... C 419 468-2288
 Galion (G-10135)
Ers Industries Inc .... E 419 562-6010
 Bucyrus (G-2328)
▲ Fabco Inc .... E 419 421-4740
 Findlay (G-9682)
Field Gymmy Inc .... G 419 538-6511
 Glandorf (G-10269)
▲ Fives St Corp .... E 234 217-9070
 Wadsworth (G-19241)
▲ Forge Industries Inc .... A 330 782-8301
 Youngstown (G-20909)
G & J Asphalt & Material Inc .... F 740 773-6358
 Chillicothe (G-3186)
G & T Manufacturing Co .... F 440 639-7777
 Mentor (G-13453)
Gibson Machinery LLC .... E 440 439-4000
 Cleveland (G-5321)
Gledhill Road Machinery Co .... E 419 468-4400
 Galion (G-10143)
◆ Gradall Industries Inc .... C 330 339-2211
 New Philadelphia (G-14773)
Gradeworks .... G 440 487-4201
 Willoughby (G-20334)
Grand Harbor Yacht Sales & Svc .... G 440 442-2919
 Cleveland (G-5339)
▼ Grasan Equipment Company Inc .... D 419 526-4440
 Mansfield (G-12452)
Great Lakes Machine and Tool .... G 419 836-2346
 Curtice (G-7825)
H Y O Inc .... F 614 488-2861
 Columbus (G-6974)
Harsco Corporation .... E 740 387-1150
 Marion (G-12710)
◆ Haulotte US Inc .... E 419 445-8915
 Archbold (G-652)
Howard & Blake Excavating LLC .... G 740 701-7938
 Richmond Dale (G-16499)
◆ Hudco Manufacturing Inc .... G 440 951-4040
 Willoughby (G-20338)
Hug Manufacturing Corporation .... G 419 668-5086
 Norwalk (G-15400)
▲ Indy Eqp Independence Recycl ...... C 216 524-0999
 Independence (G-11276)
Jbw Systems Inc .... F 614 882-5008
 Westerville (G-20000)
JC Roofing Supply .... G 937 258-9999
 Dayton (G-8281)
Jcl Equipment Co Inc .... G 937 374-1010
 Xenia (G-20779)
▲ Jennmar McSweeney LLC .... C 740 377-3354
 South Point (G-17285)
Jlg Industries Inc .... C 330 684-0132
 Orrville (G-15598)
Jlg Industries Inc .... C 330 684-0200
 Orrville (G-15599)
▲ Jrb Attachments LLC .... G 330 734-3000
 Akron (G-227)
Kaffenbarger Truck Eqp Co .... E 513 772-6800
 Cincinnati (G-3892)
Kenn Feld Group LLC .... F 419 238-1299
 Van Wert (G-19098)
Klumm Bros .... E 419 829-3166
 Holland (G-10942)
◆ Komar Industries Inc .... E 614 836-2366
 Groveport (G-10497)
Koski Construction Co .... G 440 964-8171
 Ashtabula (G-783)
Kubota Tractor Corporation .... F 614 835-3800
 Groveport (G-10499)

Lake Township Trustees .... G 419 836-1143
 Millbury (G-14050)
M S K Partnership .... G 419 394-4444
 Celina (G-2972)
Magna Group LLC .... G 513 388-9463
 Cincinnati (G-3971)
Malta Dynamics LLC .... F 740 749-3512
 Waterford (G-19488)
Mazzella Lifting Tech Inc .... D 440 239-5700
 Cleveland (G-5639)
McNeilus Truck and Mfg Inc .... E 513 874-2022
 Fairfield (G-9528)
McTech Corp .... F 216 391-7700
 Cleveland (G-5649)
Mead Paving .... G 937 322-7414
 Springfield (G-17444)
◆ Mesa Industries Inc .... D 513 321-2950
 Cincinnati (G-4009)
Metro Mech Inc .... G 216 641-6262
 Cleveland (G-5662)
◆ Meyer Products LLC .... D 216 486-1313
 Steubenville (G-17544)
▲ Miller Curber Company LLC .... F 330 782-8081
 Youngstown (G-20972)
▲ Minnich Manufacturing Co Inc .... E 419 903-0010
 Mansfield (G-12482)
Msk Trencher Mfg Inc .... F 419 394-4444
 Celina (G-2977)
Murphy Tractor & Eqp Co Inc .... G 614 876-1141
 Columbus (G-7201)
Murphy Tractor & Eqp Co Inc .... G 937 898-4198
 Vandalia (G-19140)
Murphy Tractor & Eqp Co Inc .... G 419 221-3666
 Lima (G-11909)
Murphy Tractor & Eqp Co Inc .... G 330 477-9304
 Canton (G-2759)
Murphy Tractor & Eqp Co Inc .... G 330 220-4999
 Brunswick (G-2221)
National Oilwell Varco Inc .... E 978 687-0101
 Dayton (G-8376)
New River Equipment Corp .... G 330 669-0040
 North Canton (G-15107)
◆ Npk Construction Equipment Inc ... D 440 232-7900
 Bedford (G-1432)
Ohio Restoration Group LLC .... G 330 568-5815
 Youngstown (G-19083)
Ohio Valley Trackwork Inc .... F 740 446-0181
 Bidwell (G-1667)
◆ Pace Consolidated Inc .... D 440 942-1234
 Willoughby (G-20396)
Pace Engineering Inc .... C 440 942-1234
 Willoughby (G-20397)
Power-Pack Conveyor Company .... E 440 975-9955
 Willoughby (G-20408)
Precision Engineered Tech LLC .... G 330 335-3300
 Wadsworth (G-19266)
◆ Pubco Corporation .... D 216 881-5300
 Cleveland (G-5932)
Quikstir Inc .... F 419 732-2601
 Port Clinton (G-16256)
Rayco Manufacturing LLC .... G 330 264-8699
 Wooster (G-20642)
Richland Twp Garage .... G 419 358-4897
 Bluffton (G-1892)
Rls Parts & Equipment LLC .... G 440 498-1843
 Solon (G-17223)
▲ Rnm Holdings Inc .... E 937 704-9900
 Franklin (G-9916)
Roadsafe Traffic Systems Inc .... G 614 274-9782
 Columbus (G-7398)
◆ Robbins Company .... C 440 248-3303
 Solon (G-17224)
Rogue Manufacturing Inc .... G 937 839-4026
 West Alexandria (G-19621)
Ryman Grinders Inc .... F 330 652-5080
 Niles (G-15035)
Schwieterman Cy Inc .... G 937 548-3965
 Arcanum (G-633)
▲ Scott Port-A-Fold Inc .... E 419 748-8880
 Napoleon (G-14561)
Screen Machine Industries LLC .... G 740 927-3464
 Pataskala (G-15844)
▼ Shaffer Manufacturing Corp .... E 937 652-2151
 Urbana (G-19012)
Shatzels Backhoe Service LLC .... G 937 289-9630
 Clarksville (G-4568)
▲ Sk Machinery Corporation .... G 330 733-7325
 Akron (G-377)
Splendid LLC .... F 614 396-6481
 Columbus (G-7478)

Stillwell Equipment Co Inc .... G 330 650-1029
 Peninsula (G-15898)
Stony Point Metals LLC .... G 330 852-7100
 Sugarcreek (G-17866)
Terex Utilities Inc .... D 513 539-9770
 Monroe (G-14278)
◆ Thorworks Industries Inc .... E 419 626-4375
 Sandusky (G-16855)
▲ Toku America Inc .... F 440 954-9923
 Willoughby (G-20449)
Tri-Way Rebar Inc .... G 330 296-9662
 Ravenna (G-16415)
Turn-Key Tunneling Inc .... E 614 275-4832
 Columbus (G-7552)
▲ Werk-Brau Company .... D 419 422-2912
 Findlay (G-9775)
Wilkett Enterprises LLC .... G 740 384-2890
 Wellston (G-19611)
▲ Wyeth-Scott Company .... G 740 345-4528
 Newark (G-14933)
Youngstown Bending Rolling .... F 330 799-2227
 Youngstown (G-21071)

3532 Mining Machinery & Eqpt

80 Acres Urban Agriculture LLC .... G 513 218-3087
 Cincinnati (G-3273)
▲ Belden Brick Company .... E 330 852-2411
 Sugarcreek (G-17842)
▲ Belle Center Air Tool Co Inc .... G 937 464-7474
 Belle Center (G-1497)
Bowdil Company .... F 800 356-8663
 Canton (G-2596)
Breaker Technology Inc .... E 440 248-7168
 Solon (G-17120)
▼ Brydet Development Corporation ... E 740 623-0455
 Coshocton (G-7723)
Buzz N Shuttle Service .... G 740 223-0567
 Marion (G-12698)
Cailin Dev Ltd Lblty Co .... F 216 408-6261
 Cleveland (G-4862)
Carr Tool Company .... E 513 825-2900
 Fairfield (G-9488)
CF Extrusion Technologies LLC .... G 844 439-8783
 Uhrichsville (G-18882)
Cool Machines Inc .... F 419 232-4871
 Van Wert (G-19083)
▲ Davey Kent Inc .... E 330 673-5400
 Kent (G-11310)
▲ Deep Springs Technology LLC ...... E 419 536-5741
 Toledo (G-18260)
Dover Conveyor Inc .... E 740 922-9390
 Midvale (G-13976)
Eagle Crusher Co Inc .... E 419 562-1183
 Bucyrus (G-2326)
◆ Eagle Crusher Co Inc .... C 419 468-2288
 Galion (G-10135)
Engines Inc of Ohio .... D 740 377-9874
 South Point (G-17283)
Esco Group LLC .... E 419 562-6015
 Bucyrus (G-2329)
▼ Grasan Equipment Company Inc ... D 419 526-4440
 Mansfield (G-12452)
Horizontal Eqp Manufacturing .... G 330 264-2229
 Wooster (G-20604)
◆ Irock Crushers LLC .... G 866 240-0201
 Cleveland (G-5475)
▲ Jennmar McSweeney LLC .... C 740 377-3354
 South Point (G-17285)
▲ Joy Mining Machinery .... C 440 248-7970
 Solon (G-17177)
Kaffenbarger Truck Eqp Co .... E 513 772-6800
 Cincinnati (G-3892)
Kennametal Inc .... C 440 349-5151
 Solon (G-17183)
Komatsu Mining Corp .... F 216 503-5029
 Independence (G-11139)
Maag Automatik Inc .... E 330 677-2225
 Kent (G-11347)
Mike Suponcic .... G 740 635-0654
 Bridgeport (G-2077)
Nolan Company .... G 330 453-7922
 Canton (G-2762)
Nolan Company .... G 740 269-1512
 Bowerston (G-1942)
◆ Npk Construction Equipment Inc ... D 440 232-7900
 Bedford (G-1432)
Penn Machine Company .... E 814 288-1547
 Twinsburg (G-18829)
Pneumatic Parts Co .... F 330 923-6063
 Stow (G-17618)

35 INDUSTRIAL AND COMMERCIAL MACHINERY AND COMPUTER EQUIPMENT SIC SECTION

Riverrock Recycl Crushing LLC............G....... 937 325-2052
Springfield *(G-17485)*
◆ **SMI Holdings Inc**..............................D....... 740 927-3464
Pataskala *(G-15845)*
◆ **Tema Systems Inc**..............................E....... 513 489-7811
Cincinnati *(G-4413)*
Terrasource Global Corporation............D....... 330 923-5254
Cuyahoga Falls *(G-7927)*
◆ **Warren Fabricating Corporation**.......D....... 330 534-5017
Hubbard *(G-11011)*
Zen Industries Inc..................................E....... 216 432-3240
Cleveland *(G-6339)*

3533 Oil Field Machinery & Eqpt

Allied Machine Works Inc.....................G....... 740 454-2534
Zanesville *(G-21097)*
Appalachian Equipment Co LLC...........G....... 330 345-2251
Wooster *(G-20562)*
Arete Innovative Solutions LLC.............G....... 513 503-2712
Morrow *(G-14408)*
Baker Hughes A GE Company LLC........G....... 304 884-6442
Hubbard *(G-11000)*
Buckeye Companies...............................E....... 740 452-3641
Zanesville *(G-21112)*
Cameron International Corp..................G....... 740 654-4260
Lancaster *(G-11552)*
Condition Monitoring Supplies..............G....... 216 941-6868
Strongsville *(G-17731)*
Cyclone Supply Company Inc..............G....... 330 204-0313
Dover *(G-8814)*
Dynamic Leasing Ltd.............................G....... 330 892-0164
New Waterford *(G-14839)*
Edi Holding Company LLC....................G....... 740 401-4000
Belpre *(G-1574)*
Electrnic Dsign For Indust Inc...............E....... 740 401-4000
Belpre *(G-1575)*
◆ **Furukawa Rock Drill Usa Inc**............F....... 330 673-5826
Kent *(G-11324)*
General Electric Company.....................G....... 330 455-2140
Canton *(G-2680)*
H & S Company Inc...............................F....... 419 394-4444
Celina *(G-2965)*
H P E Inc...F....... 330 833-3161
Massillon *(G-12993)*
Jet Rubber Company.............................E....... 330 325-1821
Rootstown *(G-16569)*
Midflow Services LLC...........................F....... 330 674-2399
Millersburg *(G-14111)*
Midflow Services LLC...........................F....... 330 567-3108
Shreve *(G-17006)*
Monroe Drilling Operations....................G....... 740 472-0866
Woodsfield *(G-20548)*
▲ **Multi Products Company**...................E....... 330 674-5981
Millersburg *(G-14117)*
N & N Oil...G....... 740 743-2848
Somerset *(G-17265)*
National Oilwell Varco Inc.....................E....... 440 577-1225
Pierpont *(G-16066)*
Oil Skimmers Inc....................................E....... 440 237-4600
North Royalton *(G-15291)*
Rampp Company...................................E....... 740 373-7886
Marietta *(G-12662)*
▲ **Reberland Equipment Inc**..................F....... 330 698-5883
Apple Creek *(G-618)*
◆ **Rmi Titanium Company LLC**.............E....... 330 652-9952
Niles *(G-15028)*
Robbins & Myers Inc.............................F....... 937 454-3200
Dayton *(G-8482)*
◆ **Saint-Gobain Norpro**..........................C....... 330 673-5860
Stow *(G-17625)*
TEC Design and Mfg LLC.......................G....... 216 362-8962
Cleveland *(G-6152)*
▲ **Tech Tool Inc**.......................................F....... 330 674-1176
Millersburg *(G-14133)*
◆ **Terra Sonic International LLC**...........E....... 740 374-6608
Marietta *(G-12679)*
Tiger General LLC.................................D....... 330 239-4949
Medina *(G-13353)*
Timco Inc...F....... 740 685-2594
Byesville *(G-2393)*
Ultra Premium Oilfld Svcs Ltd...............F....... 330 448-3683
Brookfield *(G-2110)*
Under Hill Water Well.............................G....... 740 852-0858
London *(G-12071)*
Westerman Inc.......................................D....... 330 262-6946
Wooster *(G-20665)*

3534 Elevators & Moving Stairways

Aimco Mfg Inc...G....... 419 476-6572
Toledo *(G-18160)*
▼ **Benko Products Inc**............................E....... 440 934-2180
Sheffield Village *(G-16966)*
◆ **Canton Elevator Inc**............................D....... 330 833-3600
North Canton *(G-15076)*
Dasher Lawless Automation LLC...........E....... 855 755-7275
Warren *(G-19394)*
Edmonds Elevator Company..................F....... 216 781-9135
Thompson *(G-18025)*
▲ **Elevator Cncepts By Wurtec LLC**.......F....... 734 246-4700
Toledo *(G-18280)*
▲ **Federal Equipment Company**............D....... 513 621-5260
Cincinnati *(G-3680)*
▲ **Fujitec America Inc**............................C....... 513 755-6100
Mason *(G-12873)*
Gray-Eering Ltd......................................G....... 740 498-8816
Tippecanoe *(G-18149)*
Heartland Stairways Inc.........................F....... 330 279-2554
Holmesville *(G-10977)*
Heartland Stairways Inc.........................G....... 330 279-2554
Holmesville *(G-10978)*
Holmes Stair Parts Ltd...........................E....... 330 279-2797
Holmesville *(G-10979)*
Otis Elevator Company...........................D....... 216 573-2333
Cleveland *(G-5825)*
Schindler Elevator Corporation.............E....... 419 861-5900
Holland *(G-10956)*
▲ **Sematic Usa Inc**.................................E....... 216 524-0100
Twinsburg *(G-18855)*
◆ **Sweet Manufacturing Company**........E....... 937 325-1511
Springfield *(G-17501)*
Versalift East Inc...................................G....... 610 866-1400
Canton *(G-2859)*

3535 Conveyors & Eqpt

Advanced Equipment Systems LLC.......G....... 216 289-6505
Euclid *(G-9400)*
◆ **Air Technical Industries Inc**................E....... 440 951-5191
Mentor *(G-13378)*
Alba Manufacturing Inc..........................D....... 513 874-0551
Fairfield *(G-9480)*
Allied Consolidated Industries..............C....... 330 744-0808
Youngstown *(G-20841)*
Allied Fabricating & Wldg Co.................E....... 614 751-6664
Columbus *(G-6572)*
▲ **Almo Process Technology Inc**...........G....... 513 402-2566
West Chester *(G-19642)*
◆ **Ambaflex Inc**.......................................E....... 330 478-1858
Canton *(G-2571)*
▲ **American Solving Inc**..........................G....... 440 234-7373
Brookpark *(G-2135)*
Ashtech Corporation..............................G....... 440 646-9911
Gates Mills *(G-10207)*
Automation Systems Designs Inc..........E....... 937 387-0351
Dayton *(G-8044)*
▲ **Barth Industries Co LP**.......................D....... 216 267-0531
Cleveland *(G-4793)*
▲ **Belden Brick Company**.......................E....... 330 852-2411
Sugarcreek *(G-17842)*
◆ **Blair Rubber Company**.......................D....... 330 769-5583
Seville *(G-16912)*
Bobco Enterprises Inc............................F....... 419 867-3560
Toledo *(G-18208)*
▲ **Bry-Air Inc**..E....... 740 965-2974
Sunbury *(G-17883)*
Building & Conveyer Maint LLC..............G....... 303 882-0912
Ravenna *(G-16371)*
Bulk Handling Equipment Co..................G....... 330 468-5703
Northfield *(G-15314)*
▼ **C S Bell Co**...F....... 419 448-0791
Tiffin *(G-18054)*
◆ **CA Litzler Co Inc**.................................E....... 216 267-8020
Cleveland *(G-4859)*
▲ **Cincinnati Mine Machinery Co**............D....... 513 522-7777
Cincinnati *(G-3501)*
Coating Systems Group Inc....................F....... 440 816-9306
Middleburg Heights *(G-13763)*
Con-Belt Inc...F....... 330 273-2003
Valley City *(G-19032)*
Conveyor Metal Works Inc......................E....... 740 477-8700
Frankfort *(G-9861)*
Conveyor Solutions LLC.........................G....... 513 367-4845
Cleves *(G-6360)*
Conveyor Technologies Ltd....................G....... 513 248-0663
Milford *(G-14005)*
◆ **Daifuku America Corporation**............C....... 614 863-1888
Reynoldsburg *(G-16434)*
Decision Systems Inc..............................E....... 330 456-7600
Canton *(G-2653)*
Dillin Engineered Systems Corp.............E....... 419 666-6789
Perrysburg *(G-15940)*
Dover Conveyor Inc................................E....... 740 922-9390
Midvale *(G-13976)*
Duplex Mill & Manufacturing Co............E....... 937 325-5555
Springfield *(G-17392)*
E S Industries Inc...................................G....... 419 643-2625
Lima *(G-11859)*
◆ **Eagle Crusher Co Inc**..........................C....... 419 468-2288
Galion *(G-10135)*
Esco Turbine Tech Cleveland..................F....... 440 953-0053
Eastlake *(G-9110)*
Ethos Corp..G....... 513 242-6336
Cincinnati *(G-3655)*
Fabacraft Inc...E....... 513 677-0500
Maineville *(G-12369)*
▲ **Fabco Inc**...E....... 419 421-4740
Findlay *(G-9682)*
Falcon Industries Inc...............................E....... 330 723-0099
Medina *(G-13260)*
▲ **Federal Equipment Company**..............D....... 513 621-5260
Cincinnati *(G-3680)*
Feedall Inc...F....... 440 942-8100
Willoughby *(G-20321)*
▲ **Fenner Dunlop Port Clinton Inc**.........C....... 419 635-2191
Port Clinton *(G-16247)*
Formtek Inc..D....... 216 292-6300
Cleveland *(G-5263)*
▲ **Formtek Inc**...D....... 216 292-4460
Cleveland *(G-5264)*
Fred D Pfening Company..........................E....... 614 294-5361
Columbus *(G-6938)*
◆ **Glassline Corporation**...........................C....... 419 666-9712
Perrysburg *(G-15958)*
▼ **Grasan Equipment Company Inc**........D....... 419 526-4440
Mansfield *(G-12452)*
Gray-Eering Ltd...G....... 740 498-8816
Tippecanoe *(G-18149)*
◆ **Grob Systems Inc**..................................C....... 419 358-9015
Bluffton *(G-1889)*
Hamilton Air Products Inc.........................G....... 513 874-4030
Fairfield *(G-9503)*
Harsco Corporation...................................E....... 740 387-1150
Marion *(G-12710)*
Hawthorne-Seving Inc...............................E....... 419 643-5531
Cridersville *(G-7810)*
Hoist Equipment Co Inc............................E....... 440 232-0300
Bedford Heights *(G-1472)*
Hostar International Inc............................F....... 440 564-5362
Newbury *(G-14957)*
Ibiza Holdings Inc......................................E....... 513 701-7300
Mason *(G-12888)*
Imperial Technologies Inc.........................F....... 330 491-3200
Canton *(G-2706)*
Innovative Controls Corp...........................D....... 419 691-6684
Toledo *(G-18348)*
Innovative Hdlg & Metalfab LLC................E....... 419 882-7480
Sylvania *(G-17945)*
Ins Robotics Inc..G....... 888 293-5325
Hilliard *(G-10830)*
▲ **Intelligrated Inc**.....................................E....... 866 936-7300
Mason *(G-12891)*
Intelligrated Inc..E....... 513 874-0788
West Chester *(G-19868)*
Intelligrated Headquarters LLC..................G....... 866 936-7300
Mason *(G-12892)*
▲ **Intelligrated Products LLC**....................E....... 740 490-0300
London *(G-12062)*
Intelligrated Sub Holdings Inc....................E....... 513 701-7300
Mason *(G-12893)*
▲ **Intelligrated Systems Inc**......................A....... 866 936-7300
Mason *(G-12894)*
Intelligrated Systems LLC..........................A....... 513 701-7300
Mason *(G-12895)*
◆ **Intelligrated Systems Ohio LLC**............A....... 513 701-7300
Mason *(G-12896)*
Intelligrated Systems Ohio LLC..................G....... 513 682-6600
West Chester *(G-19869)*
Joy Global Underground Min LLC..............F....... 440 248-7970
Cleveland *(G-5507)*
K F T Inc...D....... 513 241-5910
Cincinnati *(G-3890)*
Ka Wanner Inc...E....... 740 251-4636
Marion *(G-12714)*
Kleenline LLC..G....... 800 259-5973
Loveland *(G-12205)*
Kolinahr Systems Inc..................................F....... 513 745-9401
Blue Ash *(G-1801)*
Laser Automation Inc...................................F....... 440 543-9291
Chagrin Falls *(G-3055)*
Ledow Company Inc....................................G....... 330 657-2837
Peninsula *(G-15895)*

◆ **Lewco Inc** .... C 419 625-4014
Sandusky *(G-16822)*
▲ **Logitech Inc** .... E 614 871-2822
Grove City *(G-10441)*
▲ **Manufacturers Equipment Co** .... F 513 424-3573
Middletown *(G-13924)*
Martin Rubber Company .... F 330 336-6604
Seville *(G-16920)*
Martin Sprocket & Gear Inc .... D 419 485-5515
Montpelier *(G-14312)*
▲ **Mayfran International Inc** .... C 440 461-4100
Cleveland *(G-5637)*
Met Fab Fabrication and Mch .... G 513 724-3715
Batavia *(G-1164)*
Metal Equipment Co .... E 440 835-3100
Westlake *(G-20130)*
Mfh Partners Inc .... F 440 461-4100
Cleveland *(G-5664)*
Midwest Conveyor Products Inc .... E 419 281-1235
Ashland *(G-725)*
Midwest Industrial Rubber Inc .... F 614 876-3110
Hilliard *(G-10841)*
Miller Products Inc .... E 330 308-5934
New Philadelphia *(G-14786)*
Mine Equipment Services LLC .... E 740 936-5427
Sunbury *(G-17891)*
Mountaineer Mining Corp .... G 740 418-1817
Jackson *(G-11192)*
Mulhern Belting Inc .... E 201 337-5700
Fairfield *(G-9533)*
◆ **Nesco Inc** .... E 440 461-6000
Cleveland *(G-5741)*
◆ **New Transcon LLC** .... E 440 255-7600
Mentor *(G-13526)*
Nkc of America Inc .... G 937 642-4033
Marysville *(G-12804)*
▲ **Ocs Intellitrak Inc** .... F 513 742-5600
Fairfield *(G-9539)*
▲ **Ohio Magnetics Inc** .... E 216 662-8484
Maple Heights *(G-12575)*
▲ **Opw Engineered Systems Inc** .... G 888 771-9438
Lebanon *(G-11680)*
P B Fabrication Mech Contr .... F 419 478-4869
Toledo *(G-18454)*
Parker-Hannifin Corporation .... F 330 336-3511
Wadsworth *(G-19262)*
Pfpc Enterprises Inc .... B 513 941-6200
Cincinnati *(G-4155)*
▲ **Pneumatic Scale Corporation** .... C 330 923-0491
Cuyahoga Falls *(G-7905)*
Pomacon Inc .... F 330 273-1576
Brunswick *(G-2226)*
Power-Pack Conveyor Company .... E 440 975-9955
Willoughby *(G-20408)*
Precision Conveyor Technology .... F 440 352-3601
Perry *(G-15911)*
Quickdraft Inc .... E 330 477-4574
Canton *(G-2799)*
Rhino Robotics Ltd .... G 513 353-9772
Miamitown *(G-13750)*
Richmond Machine Co .... E 419 485-5740
Montpelier *(G-14318)*
◆ **Robbins Company** .... C 440 248-3303
Solon *(G-17224)*
Rolcon Inc .... F 513 821-7259
Cincinnati *(G-4281)*
Sandusky Fabricating & Sls Inc .... E 419 626-4465
Sandusky *(G-16842)*
Schenck Process LLC .... F 513 576-9200
Chagrin Falls *(G-3074)*
Scott-Randall Systems Inc .... F 937 446-2293
Sardinia *(G-16873)*
Siemens Industry Inc .... E 440 526-2770
Brecksville *(G-2058)*
Sparks Belting Company Inc .... G 216 398-7774
Cleveland *(G-6083)*
▲ **Sst Conveyor Components Inc** .... E 513 583-5500
Loveland *(G-12234)*
Stacy Equipment Co .... G 419 447-6903
Tiffin *(G-18085)*
Stock Fairfield Corporation .... C 440 543-6000
Chagrin Falls *(G-3078)*
◆ **Sweet Manufacturing Company** .... E 937 325-1511
Springfield *(G-17501)*
T J Davies Company Inc .... G 440 248-5510
Solon *(G-17245)*
Tkf Conveyor Systems LLC .... C 513 621-5260
Cincinnati *(G-4423)*
▲ **Webb-Stiles Company** .... D 330 225-7761
Valley City *(G-19069)*
◆ **Webster Industries Inc** .... B 419 447-8232
Tiffin *(G-18092)*

3536 Hoists, Cranes & Monorails

ACC Automation Co Inc .... E 330 928-3821
Akron *(G-26)*
Acme Lifting Products Inc .... G 440 838-4430
Cleveland *(G-4606)*
◆ **Air Technical Industries Inc** .... E 440 951-5191
Mentor *(G-13378)*
Altec Industries Inc .... F 205 408-2341
Cuyahoga Falls *(G-7833)*
American Climber & Mch Corp .... G 330 420-0019
Lisbon *(G-11964)*
American Power Hoist Inc .... G 740 964-2035
Pataskala *(G-15828)*
▲ **American Power Pull Corp** .... G 419 335-7050
Wauseon *(G-19509)*
ARI Phoenix Inc .... E 513 229-3750
Lebanon *(G-11634)*
▲ **Belden Brick Company** .... E 330 852-2411
Sugarcreek *(G-17842)*
Bobco Enterprises Inc .... F 419 867-3560
Toledo *(G-18208)*
Cattron Holdings Inc .... E 234 806-0018
Warren *(G-19381)*
Cincinnati Crane & Hoist LLC .... F 513 202-1408
Harrison *(G-10634)*
Cincinnati Recreation Comm .... G 513 921-5657
Cincinnati *(G-3505)*
Columbus McKinnon Corporation .... D 330 332-5769
Salem *(G-16729)*
Columbus McKinnon Corporation .... D 330 424-7248
Lisbon *(G-11965)*
Crane Training USA Inc .... G 513 755-2177
West Chester *(G-19688)*
▲ **David Round Company Inc** .... E 330 656-1600
Streetsboro *(G-17668)*
Delta Crane Systems Inc .... F 937 324-7425
Springfield *(G-17387)*
◆ **Demag Cranes & Components Corp** C 440 248-2400
Solon *(G-17132)*
▲ **Deuer Manufacturing Inc** .... G 937 254-3812
Dayton *(G-8159)*
▲ **Eaton Electric Holdings LLC** .... B 440 523-5000
Cleveland *(G-5151)*
◆ **Emh Inc** .... E 330 220-8600
Valley City *(G-19036)*
Expert Crane Inc .... E 216 451-9900
Cleveland *(G-5209)*
▲ **Federal Equipment Company** .... D 513 621-5260
Cincinnati *(G-3680)*
▲ **Galion-Godwin Truck Bdy Co LLC** ... D 330 359-5495
Millersburg *(G-14084)*
Gray-Eering Ltd .... G 740 498-8816
Tippecanoe *(G-18149)*
Harsco Corporation .... E 740 387-1150
Marion *(G-12710)*
◆ **Hiab USA Inc** .... D 419 482-6000
Perrysburg *(G-15961)*
Hoist Equipment Co Inc .... E 440 232-0300
Bedford Heights *(G-1472)*
Ibi Brake Products Inc .... G 440 543-7962
Chagrin Falls *(G-3052)*
Indian Lake Boat Lift .... G 937 539-2868
Russells Point *(G-16599)*
Ingersoll-Rand Company .... E 419 633-6800
Bryan *(G-2291)*
◆ **Kci Holding USA Inc** .... C 937 525-5533
Springfield *(G-17430)*
Konecranes Inc .... E 513 755-2800
West Chester *(G-19732)*
Konecranes Inc .... E 937 328-5100
Springfield *(G-17433)*
◆ **Konecranes Inc** .... B 937 525-5533
Springfield *(G-17434)*
Konecranes Inc .... F 440 461-8400
Brecksville *(G-2046)*
Lisbon Hoist Inc .... F 330 424-7283
Lisbon *(G-11974)*
◆ **Mmh Americas Inc** .... G 414 764-6200
Springfield *(G-17449)*
◆ **Mmh Holdings Inc** .... G 937 525-5533
Springfield *(G-17450)*
Morgan Engineering Systems Inc .... E 330 823-6120
Alliance *(G-490)*
Morgan Engineering Systems Inc .... E 330 821-4721
Alliance *(G-491)*
Ohio Mechanical Handling Co .... F 330 773-5165
Akron *(G-308)*
Radocy Inc .... F 419 666-4400
Rossford *(G-16591)*
Replacment Prts Spcialists Inc .... G 440 248-0731
Solon *(G-17221)*
Rnm Holdings Inc .... E 419 867-8712
Holland *(G-10954)*
Rnm Holdings Inc .... F 614 444-5556
Columbus *(G-7397)*
Stahl Cranesystems Inc .... G 843 767-1951
Springfield *(G-17497)*
Terex Utilities Inc .... D 513 539-9770
Monroe *(G-14278)*
Terex Utilities Inc .... F 440 262-3200
Brecksville *(G-2060)*
▲ **Webb-Stiles Company** .... D 330 225-7761
Valley City *(G-19069)*
Westerman Inc .... D 330 262-6946
Wooster *(G-20665)*

3537 Indl Trucks, Tractors, Trailers & Stackers

◆ **Air Technical Industries Inc** .... E 440 951-5191
Mentor *(G-13378)*
AJD Holding Co .... D 330 405-4477
Twinsburg *(G-18728)*
American Truck Equipment Inc .... G 216 362-0400
Cleveland *(G-4699)*
▲ **Belden Brick Company** .... E 330 852-2411
Sugarcreek *(G-17842)*
Boltech Incorporated .... G 330 746-6881
Youngstown *(G-20855)*
Bpr-Rico Elc Trck Spcalist Inc .... D 330 723-4050
Medina *(G-13231)*
▲ **Bpr-Rico Manufacturing Inc** .... D 330 723-4050
Medina *(G-13232)*
◆ **Canton Elevator Inc** .... D 330 833-3600
North Canton *(G-15076)*
Cascade Corporation .... C 937 327-0300
Springfield *(G-17370)*
Chemtrans Logistics Inc .... G 419 447-8041
Tiffin *(G-18056)*
Cincinnati Barge Rail Trml LLC .... G 513 227-3611
Cincinnati *(G-3482)*
City Machine Technologies Inc .... F 330 747-2639
Youngstown *(G-20870)*
▲ **Crescent Metal Products Inc** .... C 440 350-1100
Mentor *(G-13426)*
Crown Credit Company .... F 419 629-2311
New Bremen *(G-14649)*
Crown Equipment Corporation .... D 937 295-4062
Fort Loramie *(G-9793)*
Crown Equipment Corporation .... A 419 586-1100
Celina *(G-2956)*
Crown Equipment Corporation .... G 419 629-9201
New Bremen *(G-14650)*
Crown Equipment Corporation .... D 937 454-7545
Vandalia *(G-19121)*
Crown Equipment Corporation .... D 419 629-2311
New Bremen *(G-14651)*
Crown Equipment Corporation .... E 440 232-7772
Oakwood Village *(G-15479)*
Crown Equipment Corporation .... D 419 629-2311
New Bremen *(G-14653)*
Crown Equipment Corporation .... D 614 274-7700
Grove City *(G-10423)*
Crown Equipment Corporation .... D 513 874-2600
Cincinnati *(G-3560)*
Crown Equipment Corporation .... D 419 629-2311
New Bremen *(G-14652)*
Dale Lute Logging .... G 740 352-1779
Mc Dermott *(G-13192)*
Dragon Products LLC .... E 330 345-3968
Wooster *(G-20586)*
◆ **Eagle Industrial Truck Mfg LLC** .... E 734 442-1000
Swanton *(G-17912)*
Elliott Machine Works Inc .... E 419 468-4709
Galion *(G-10137)*
Fairway Carts Parts & More LLC .... G 234 209-9008
North Canton *(G-15081)*
▲ **Falls Welding & Fabg Inc** .... G 330 253-3437
Akron *(G-165)*
Fame Tool & Mfg Co Inc .... E 513 271-6387
Cincinnati *(G-3670)*
Foerster Instruments Inc .... F 330 332-9100
Salem *(G-16739)*
Foerster Systems Inc .... F 330 332-9100
Salem *(G-16740)*
Forklifts of Americas LLC .... G 440 821-5143
Highland Heights *(G-10790)*

S I C

35 INDUSTRIAL AND COMMERCIAL MACHINERY AND COMPUTER EQUIPMENT SIC SECTION

Forte Indus Eqp Systems Inc.....E.....513 398-2800
Mason *(G-12871)*

Freedom Forklift Sales LLC.....G.....330 289-0879
Akron *(G-177)*

G & T Manufacturing Co.....F.....440 639-7777
Mentor *(G-13453)*

General Electric Company.....B.....513 977-1500
Cincinnati *(G-3741)*

Global Trucking LLC.....F.....614 598-6264
Columbus *(G-6958)*

◆ Gradall Industries Inc.....C.....330 339-2211
New Philadelphia *(G-14773)*

Grand Aire Inc.....E.....419 861-6700
Swanton *(G-17913)*

Grand Harbor Yacht Sales & Svc.....G.....440 442-2919
Cleveland *(G-5339)*

Harsco Corporation.....E.....740 387-1150
Marion *(G-12710)*

Heartland Engineered Pdts LLC.....F.....513 367-0080
Harrison *(G-10645)*

Heritage Truck Equipment Inc.....D.....330 699-4491
Hartville *(G-10695)*

◆ Hobart Brothers LLC.....A.....937 332-5439
Troy *(G-18669)*

Hoist Equipment Co Inc.....E.....440 232-0300
Bedford Heights *(G-1472)*

Hunter Lift Ltd.....E.....330 549-3347
North Lima *(G-15171)*

Hyster-Yale Materials Hdlg Inc.....C.....440 449-9600
Cleveland *(G-5432)*

Integrity Industrial Eqp Inc.....G.....937 238-9275
Huber Heights *(G-11021)*

◆ Intelligrated Systems Ohio LLC.....A.....513 701-7300
Mason *(G-12896)*

Jh Industries Inc.....E.....330 963-4105
Twinsburg *(G-18797)*

▲ Kay Capital Company.....G.....216 531-1010
Cleveland *(G-5521)*

Kinetic Technologies Inc.....F.....440 943-4111
Wickliffe *(G-20214)*

Lange Precision Inc.....F.....513 530-9500
Blue Ash *(G-1802)*

Leebaw Manufacturing Company.....F.....330 533-3368
Canfield *(G-2531)*

Marlow-2000 Inc.....F.....216 362-8500
Cleveland *(G-5625)*

Martin Sheet Metal Inc.....D.....216 377-8200
Cleveland *(G-5627)*

Martin Sprocket & Gear Inc.....D.....419 485-5515
Montpelier *(G-14312)*

McCullough Industries Inc.....E.....419 673-0767
Kenton *(G-11412)*

Mcl Inc.....E.....216 292-3800
Cleveland *(G-5643)*

Medrano Usa Inc.....C.....614 272-5856
Columbus *(G-7172)*

Miller Products Inc.....E.....330 308-5934
New Philadelphia *(G-14786)*

Miners Tractor Sales Inc.....F.....330 325-9914
Rootstown *(G-16571)*

Mitchs Welding & Hitches.....G.....419 893-3117
Maumee *(G-13136)*

Newsafe Transport Service Inc.....F.....740 387-1679
Marion *(G-12725)*

Parobek Trucking Co.....G.....419 869-7500
West Salem *(G-19957)*

Perfecto Industries Inc.....E.....937 778-1900
Piqua *(G-16149)*

Pollock Research & Design Inc.....E.....330 332-3300
Salem *(G-16767)*

Precision Equipment Llc.....G.....330 220-7600
Brunswick *(G-2228)*

Products Innovators.....E.....216 932-5269
Cleveland *(G-5926)*

Pucel Enterprises Inc.....D.....216 881-4604
Cleveland *(G-5933)*

◆ R B Mfg Co.....F.....419 626-9464
Wadsworth *(G-19270)*

River City Body Company.....F.....513 772-9317
Cincinnati *(G-4271)*

Saf-Holland Inc.....G.....513 874-7888
West Chester *(G-19896)*

Saunders Trucking Lcc.....G.....419 210-0551
Fredericktown *(G-9976)*

Scott-Randall Systems Inc.....F.....937 446-2293
Sardinia *(G-16873)*

Shanafelt Manufacturing Co.....E.....330 455-0315
Canton *(G-2814)*

Skylift Inc.....G.....440 960-2100
Lorain *(G-12122)*

Snair Co.....F.....614 873-7020
Plain City *(G-16212)*

▲ Sroka Inc.....E.....440 572-2811
Strongsville *(G-17794)*

St Marys Iron Works Inc.....F.....419 300-6300
Saint Marys *(G-16702)*

Stock Fairfield Corporation.....C.....440 543-6000
Chagrin Falls *(G-3078)*

Surplus Freight Inc.....F.....614 235-7660
Gahanna *(G-10108)*

Suspension Technology Inc.....F.....330 458-3058
Canton *(G-2831)*

◆ Sweet Manufacturing Company.....E.....937 325-1511
Springfield *(G-17501)*

Tarpco Inc.....F.....330 677-8277
Kent *(G-11392)*

Tilt-Or-Lift Inc.....G.....419 893-6944
Maumee *(G-13154)*

▲ Trailer Component Mfg Inc.....E.....440 255-2888
Mentor *(G-13612)*

Transco Railway Products Inc.....E.....419 726-3383
Toledo *(G-18582)*

Trip Transport LLC.....G.....773 969-1402
Columbus *(G-7545)*

Triumphant Enterprises Inc.....E.....513 617-1668
Goshen *(G-10290)*

Venturo Manufacturing Inc.....E.....513 772-8448
Cincinnati *(G-4474)*

▲ Waltco Lift Corp.....C.....330 633-9191
Tallmadge *(G-18013)*

▲ Webb-Stiles Company.....D.....330 225-7761
Valley City *(G-19069)*

◆ Whiteside Manufacturing Co.....E.....740 363-1179
Delaware *(G-8732)*

Working Professionals LLC.....G.....833 244-6299
Canal Winchester *(G-2515)*

Yemaneh Musie.....G.....614 506-3687
Columbus *(G-7622)*

Youngstown-Kenworth Inc.....E.....330 534-9761
Hubbard *(G-11014)*

3541 Machine Tools: Cutting

3 Brothers Torching Inc.....G.....419 339-9985
Lima *(G-11828)*

5 Axis Grinding Inc.....G.....937 312-9797
Dayton *(G-7996)*

A & P Tool Inc.....E.....419 542-6681
Hicksville *(G-10773)*

Abrasive Technology Lapidary.....C.....740 548-4855
Lewis Center *(G-11741)*

Accurate Machining & Welding.....G.....937 584-4518
Sabina *(G-16615)*

Accurate Metal Sawing Svc Co.....E.....440 205-3205
Mentor *(G-13371)*

Accurate Plasma Cutting Inc.....F.....440 943-1655
Wickliffe *(G-20195)*

▲ Acro Tool & Die Company.....D.....330 773-5173
Akron *(G-29)*

Advanced Innovative Mfg Inc.....F.....330 562-2468
Aurora *(G-867)*

Advetech Inc.....E.....330 533-2227
Canfield *(G-2517)*

▼ Alcon Tool Company.....D.....330 773-9171
Akron *(G-57)*

Ald Group LLC.....G.....440 942-9800
Willoughby *(G-20269)*

Alliance Drilling Inc.....F.....330 584-2781
North Benton *(G-15059)*

▲ AM Industrial Group LLC.....E.....216 433-7171
Brookpark *(G-2134)*

Applied Automation Enterprise.....F.....419 929-2428
New London *(G-14728)*

▲ Areway LLC.....D.....216 651-9022
Brooklyn *(G-2112)*

B V Grinding Machining Inc.....G.....440 918-1884
Willoughby *(G-20283)*

Bar Tech Service Inc.....G.....440 943-5286
Wickliffe *(G-20201)*

▲ Barbco Inc.....E.....330 488-9400
East Canton *(G-9038)*

▲ Bardons & Oliver Inc.....C.....440 498-5800
Solon *(G-17112)*

▲ Barth Industries Co LP.....D.....216 267-0531
Cleveland *(G-4793)*

Blairs Cnc Turning Inc.....G.....937 461-1100
Dayton *(G-8057)*

▼ Bor-It Manufacturing Inc.....E.....419 289-6639
Ashland *(G-687)*

Bortnick Tractor Sales Inc.....F.....330 924-2555
Cortland *(G-7704)*

Bud May Inc.....F.....216 676-8850
Cleveland *(G-4850)*

C M M S - Re LLC.....F.....513 489-5111
Blue Ash *(G-1745)*

▼ C S Bell Co.....F.....419 448-0791
Tiffin *(G-18054)*

◆ Callahan Cutting Tools Inc.....G.....614 294-1649
Columbus *(G-6724)*

▲ Cammann Inc.....F.....440 965-4051
Wakeman *(G-19282)*

Cappco Tubular Products Inc.....G.....216 641-2218
North Olmsted *(G-15183)*

Cardinal Builders Inc.....E.....614 237-1000
Columbus *(G-6739)*

Carlton Natco.....G.....216 451-5588
Cleveland *(G-4878)*

Carter Manufacturing Co Inc.....E.....513 398-7303
Mason *(G-12838)*

Center Line Machining LLC.....G.....216 289-6828
Euclid *(G-9408)*

▲ Channel Products Inc.....D.....440 423-0113
Solon *(G-17126)*

Chart Tech Tool Inc.....E.....937 667-3543
Tipp City *(G-18108)*

▲ Cincinnati Gilbert Mch Tl LLC.....E.....513 541-4815
Cincinnati *(G-3497)*

▲ Cincinnati Mine Machinery Co.....D.....513 522-7777
Cincinnati *(G-3501)*

Cleveland Deburring Machine Co.....G.....216 472-0200
Cleveland *(G-4956)*

▼ Coil Technology Inc.....G.....330 601-1350
Wooster *(G-20579)*

Commercial Grinding Services.....E.....330 273-5040
Medina *(G-13238)*

▲ Competetive Carbide Inc.....E.....440 350-9393
Mentor *(G-13421)*

Criterion Tool & Die Inc.....E.....216 267-1733
Brookpark *(G-2139)*

▲ Cutting Systems Inc.....F.....216 928-0500
Cleveland *(G-5052)*

Dan Wilzynski.....G.....800 531-3343
Columbus *(G-6848)*

Dbcr Inc.....E.....330 920-1900
Cuyahoga Falls *(G-7859)*

Dexport Tool Manufacturing Co.....G.....513 625-1600
Loveland *(G-12185)*

Diversified Honing Inc.....E.....330 874-4663
Bolivar *(G-1912)*

Dixie Machinery Inc.....F.....513 360-0091
Monroe *(G-14261)*

E D M Electrofying Inc.....G.....440 322-8900
Elyria *(G-9248)*

▲ Eagle Machinery & Supply Inc.....E.....330 852-1300
Sugarcreek *(G-17849)*

Elliott Tool Technologies Ltd.....D.....937 253-6133
Dayton *(G-8182)*

Falcon Industries Inc.....E.....330 723-0099
Medina *(G-13260)*

Falcon Tool & Machine Inc.....G.....937 534-9999
Moraine *(G-14353)*

Fischer Special Tooling Corp.....F.....440 951-8411
Mentor *(G-13443)*

Fives Landis Corp.....D.....440 709-0700
Painesville *(G-15740)*

Frazier Machine and Prod Inc.....E.....419 661-1656
Perrysburg *(G-15954)*

▼ Fredon Corporation.....D.....440 951-5200
Mentor *(G-13450)*

▲ Gbi Cincinnati Inc.....G.....513 841-8684
Cincinnati *(G-3729)*

General Electric Company.....B.....513 341-0214
West Chester *(G-19714)*

Genex Tool & Die Inc.....F.....330 788-2466
Youngstown *(G-20919)*

▼ George A Mitchell Company.....E.....330 758-5777
Youngstown *(G-20920)*

◆ Glassline Corporation.....C.....419 666-9712
Perrysburg *(G-15958)*

▲ Global Specialty Machines LLC.....F.....513 701-0452
Mason *(G-12881)*

◆ Glt Inc.....F.....937 237-0055
Dayton *(G-8230)*

Grind-All Corporation.....E.....330 220-1600
Brunswick *(G-2211)*

◆ Grt Utilicorp Inc.....E.....330 264-8444
Wooster *(G-20600)*

Gt Machine & Fab.....G.....740 701-9607
Kingston *(G-11458)*

▲ H & D Steel Service Inc.....E.....440 237-3390
North Royalton *(G-15275)*

Hawk Manufacturing LLC ... D ... 330 784-3151 — Akron *(G-201)*
Hawk Manufacturing LLC ... F ... 330 784-4815 — Akron *(G-202)*
Hesler Machine Tool ... G ... 937 299-3833 — Dayton *(G-8248)*
Houston Machine Products Inc ... E ... 937 322-8022 — Springfield *(G-17422)*
Hyper Tool Company ... F ... 440 543-5151 — Chagrin Falls *(G-3051)*
Interstate Tool Corporation ... E ... 216 671-1077 — Cleveland *(G-5471)*
J and S Tool Incorporated ... E ... 216 676-8330 — Cleveland *(G-5482)*
▲ J-C-R Tech Inc ... E ... 937 783-2296 — Blanchester *(G-1704)*
Jacp Inc ... G ... 513 353-3660 — Miamitown *(G-13747)*
K L M Manufacturing Company ... G ... 740 666-5171 — Ostrander *(G-15644)*
▲ Kay Capital Company ... G ... 216 531-1010 — Cleveland *(G-5521)*
Ken Emerick Machine Products ... G ... 440 834-4501 — Burton *(G-2365)*
Kilroy Company ... D ... 440 951-8700 — Eastlake *(G-9117)*
Klawhorn Industries Inc ... G ... 330 335-8191 — Wadsworth *(G-19249)*
Kmi Processing LLC ... G ... 330 862-2185 — Minerva *(G-14187)*
Kmi Processing LLC ... F ... 330 862-2185 — Minerva *(G-14188)*
L M Equipment & Design Inc ... E ... 330 332-9951 — Salem *(G-16754)*
Lahm-Trosper Inc ... F ... 937 252-8791 — Dayton *(G-8305)*
◆ Lawrence Industries Inc ... C ... 216 518-7000 — Cleveland *(G-5566)*
Lawrence Industries Inc ... D ... 216 518-1400 — Cleveland *(G-5567)*
Lees Machinery Inc ... G ... 440 259-2222 — Perry *(G-15907)*
Leland-Gifford Inc ... G ... 330 785-9730 — Akron *(G-251)*
Levan Enterprises Inc ... E ... 330 923-9797 — Stow *(G-17601)*
Machine Component Mfg ... F ... 330 454-4566 — Canton *(G-2740)*
Machine Tl Sltons Unlmited LLC ... F ... 513 761-0709 — Cincinnati *(G-3967)*
◆ Makino Inc ... B ... 513 573-7200 — Mason *(G-12905)*
Martin & Marianne Tools Inc ... G ... 440 255-5107 — Mentor *(G-13511)*
Martindale Electric Company ... E ... 216 521-8567 — Cleveland *(G-5628)*
Masheen Specialties ... E ... 330 652-7535 — Mineral Ridge *(G-14169)*
Master Grinding Company Inc ... G ... 440 944-3680 — Wickliffe *(G-20216)*
Masters Prcision Machining Inc ... F ... 330 419-1933 — Kent *(G-11350)*
▲ Mataco ... G ... 440 546-8355 — Broadview Heights *(G-2096)*
Melin Tool Company Inc ... D ... 216 362-4200 — Cleveland *(G-5654)*
Metal Cutting Technology LLC ... G ... 419 733-1236 — Celina *(G-2975)*
Micron Manufacturing Inc ... D ... 440 355-4200 — Lagrange *(G-11489)*
Midwest Knife Grinding Inc ... F ... 330 854-1030 — Canal Fulton *(G-2486)*
Midwest Ohio Tool Co ... G ... 419 294-1987 — Upper Sandusky *(G-18963)*
Midwest Specialties Inc ... F ... 419 738-8147 — Wapakoneta *(G-19346)*
◆ Milacron Marketing Company LLC ... E ... 513 536-2000 — Batavia *(G-1167)*
▲ Milan Tool Corp ... E ... 216 661-1078 — Cleveland *(G-5685)*
Mk Global Enterprises LLC ... G ... 440 823-0081 — Beachwood *(G-1251)*
Molding Machine Services Inc ... G ... 330 461-2270 — Medina *(G-13303)*
Monaghan & Associates Inc ... E ... 937 253-7706 — Dayton *(G-8365)*
▲ Monarch Lathes LP ... E ... 937 492-4111 — Sidney *(G-17056)*
More Manufacturing LLC ... F ... 937 233-3898 — Tipp City *(G-18123)*
Morlock Asphalt Ltd ... F ... 419 686-4601 — Portage *(G-16271)*
Mrd Solutions LLC ... G ... 440 942-6969 — Eastlake *(G-9124)*
My Catered Table LLC ... G ... 614 882-7323 — Columbus *(G-7205)*
National Machine Tool Company ... G ... 513 541-6682 — Cincinnati *(G-4061)*
◆ Nesco Inc ... E ... 440 461-6000 — Cleveland *(G-5741)*
New Holland Engineering Inc ... G ... 740 495-5200 — New Holland *(G-14702)*
Nmgg Ctg LLC ... G ... 419 447-5211 — Tiffin *(G-18072)*
North East Technologies Inc ... G ... 440 327-9278 — North Ridgeville *(G-15242)*
Northwood Industries Inc ... F ... 419 666-2100 — Perrysburg *(G-15983)*
Obars Machine and Tool Company ... E ... 419 535-6307 — Toledo *(G-18433)*
Oceco Inc ... F ... 419 447-0916 — Tiffin *(G-18073)*
▼ Ohio Broach & Machine Company ... E ... 440 946-1040 — Willoughby *(G-20393)*
Ohio CAM & Tool Co ... G ... 216 531-7900 — Cleveland *(G-5803)*
Ohio Screw Products Inc ... D ... 440 322-6341 — Elyria *(G-9305)*
OReilly Precision Products ... E ... 937 526-4677 — Russia *(G-16610)*
P M R Inc ... G ... 440 937-6241 — Avon *(G-955)*
P R Racing Engines ... G ... 419 472-2277 — Toledo *(G-18455)*
Page Slotting Saw Co Inc ... F ... 419 476-7475 — Toledo *(G-18456)*
Parkn Manufacturing LLC ... F ... 330 723-8172 — Litchfield *(G-11986)*
▲ Peerless Saw Company ... C ... 614 836-5790 — Groveport *(G-10509)*
Phillips Manufacturing Co ... D ... 330 652-4335 — Niles *(G-15026)*
▲ Pilgrim-Harp Co ... G ... 440 249-4185 — Avon *(G-957)*
Pinnacle Precision Pdts LLC ... G ... 440 786-0248 — Bedford *(G-1436)*
Power Engineering LLC ... G ... 513 793-5800 — Cincinnati *(G-4177)*
Precision Honing Inc ... G ... 440 942-7339 — Willoughby *(G-20410)*
▲ Rafter Equipment Corporation ... E ... 440 572-3700 — Strongsville *(G-17781)*
Rapid Machine Inc ... F ... 419 737-2377 — Pioneer *(G-16094)*
Ravana Industries Inc ... G ... 330 536-4015 — Lowellville *(G-12254)*
▲ Raymath Company ... C ... 937 335-1860 — Troy *(G-18697)*
Reliable Products Co Inc ... G ... 419 394-5854 — Saint Marys *(G-16697)*
Republic EDM Services Inc ... G ... 937 278-7070 — Dayton *(G-8473)*
▲ Rex International USA Inc ... E ... 800 321-7950 — Ashtabula *(G-803)*
Ridge Tool Company ... E ... 440 329-4737 — Elyria *(G-9321)*
Ridge Tool Company ... D ... 740 432-8782 — Cambridge *(G-2455)*
◆ Ridge Tool Company ... A ... 440 323-5581 — Elyria *(G-9320)*
Ridge Tool Manufacturing Co ... A ... 440 323-5581 — Elyria *(G-9322)*
Rimrock Holdings Corporation ... E ... 614 471-5926 — Columbus *(G-7395)*
◆ Robbins Company ... C ... 440 248-3303 — Solon *(G-17224)*
▼ Roll-In Saw Inc ... F ... 216 459-9001 — Brookpark *(G-2155)*
Rossi Machinery Services Inc ... G ... 419 281-4488 — Ashland *(G-744)*
Roto Tech Inc ... E ... 937 859-8503 — Dayton *(G-8485)*
Shumaker Racing Components ... G ... 419 238-0801 — Van Wert *(G-19105)*
▲ Single Source Technologies LLC ... B ... 513 573-7200 — Mason *(G-12939)*
Sinico Mtm US Inc ... G ... 216 264-8344 — Cleveland *(G-6067)*
▲ Specialty Metals Processing ... E ... 330 656-2767 — Hudson *(G-11076)*
Stadco Inc ... E ... 937 878-0911 — Fairborn *(G-9468)*
STC International Co Ltd ... G ... 561 308-6002 — Lebanon *(G-11699)*
Stevenson Mfg Co ... G ... 330 532-1581 — Wellsville *(G-19614)*
Strouse Industries Inc ... G ... 440 257-2520 — Mentor *(G-13595)*
Sumitomo Elc Carbide Mfg Inc ... F ... 440 354-0600 — Grand River *(G-10326)*
▲ Superion Inc ... E ... 937 374-0033 — Xenia *(G-20793)*
Supply Dynamics Inc ... E ... 513 965-2000 — Loveland *(G-12238)*
Swagelok Hy-Level Company ... C ... 440 238-1260 — Strongsville *(G-17798)*
Synergy Grinding Inc ... F ... 216 447-4000 — Westlake *(G-20166)*
Systematic Machine Corp ... G ... 440 877-9884 — North Royalton *(G-15305)*
Tailored Systems Inc ... G ... 937 299-3900 — Moraine *(G-14398)*
Technidrill Systems Inc ... E ... 330 678-9980 — Kent *(G-11393)*
Tool Service Co Inc ... G ... 937 254-4000 — Dayton *(G-7992)*
Tooling Connection Inc ... G ... 419 594-3339 — Oakwood *(G-15475)*
Tri-State Tool Grinding Inc ... E ... 513 347-0100 — Cincinnati *(G-4436)*
TSR Machinery Services Inc ... E ... 513 874-9697 — Fairfield *(G-9570)*
Tykma Inc ... D ... 877 318-9562 — Chillicothe *(G-3230)*
U S Alloy Die Corp ... F ... 216 749-9700 — Cleveland *(G-6227)*
U-Sonico ... F ... 423 348-7117 — Springfield *(G-17511)*
◆ Ultra-Met Company ... D ... 937 653-7133 — Urbana *(G-19017)*
▲ Union Process Inc ... E ... 330 929-3333 — Akron *(G-419)*
▲ United Grinding North Amer Inc ... D ... 937 859-1975 — Miamisburg *(G-13730)*
United Wire Edm Inc ... G ... 440 239-8777 — Berea *(G-1630)*
Updike Supply Company ... E ... 937 482-4000 — Huber Heights *(G-11024)*
Usm Acquisition Corporation ... D ... 440 975-8600 — Willoughby *(G-20457)*
▲ Vulcan Tool Company ... G ... 937 253-6194 — Dayton *(G-8581)*
Walter Grinders Inc ... G ... 937 859-1975 — Miamisburg *(G-13737)*
Warner Vess Inc ... G ... 740 585-2481 — Lower Salem *(G-12259)*
West Ohio Tool & Mfg LLC ... G ... 419 678-4745 — Saint Henry *(G-16671)*
West Ohio Tool Company ... F ... 937 842-6688 — Russells Point *(G-16602)*
Whole Solutions ... G ... 330 652-1725 — Mineral Ridge *(G-14174)*
Willow Tool & Machining Ltd ... F ... 440 572-2288 — Strongsville *(G-17808)*
Wonder Machine Services Inc ... E ... 440 937-7500 — Avon *(G-975)*
◆ Zagar Inc ... E ... 216 731-0500 — Cleveland *(G-6336)*

3542 Machine Tools: Forming

Accurate Manufacturing Company ... E ... 614 878-6510 — Columbus *(G-6534)*
▲ Addisonmckee Inc ... C ... 513 228-7000 — Lebanon *(G-11629)*
Advanced Tech Utilization Co ... F ... 440 238-3770 — Strongsville *(G-17706)*
Airam Press Co Ltd ... E ... 937 473-5672 — Covington *(G-7780)*
▲ Ajax Manufacturing Company ... E ... 440 295-0244 — Wickliffe *(G-20196)*
Akron Specialized Products ... G ... 330 762-9269 — Akron *(G-52)*
Allied Mask and Tooling Inc ... G ... 419 470-2555 — Toledo *(G-18164)*
American Fluid Power Inc ... G ... 877 223-8742 — Elyria *(G-9215)*
American Laser and Machine LLC ... G ... 419 214-0880 — Toledo *(G-18173)*
American Metal Tech LLC ... D ... 937 347-1111 — Xenia *(G-20756)*

SIC

Employee Codes: A=Over 500 employees, B=251-500
C=101-250, D=51-100, E=20-50, F=10-19, G=3-9
2019 Harris Ohio
Industrial Directory
951

Anderson & Vreeland Inc ....D.... 419 636-5002
Bryan *(G-2264)*
Apeks LLC ....E.... 740 809-1160
Johnstown *(G-11256)*
Asb Industries Inc ....E.... 330 753-8458
Barberton *(G-1054)*
Ata Tools Inc ....D.... 330 928-7744
Cuyahoga Falls *(G-7844)*
BAC Technologies Ltd ....G.... 937 465-2228
West Liberty *(G-19935)*
Barclay Machine Inc ....F.... 330 337-9541
Salem *(G-16719)*
▲ Barth Industries Co LP ....D.... 216 267-0531
Cleveland *(G-4793)*
Bendco Machine & Tool Inc ....F.... 419 628-3802
Minster *(G-14210)*
Brilex Industries Inc ....D.... 330 744-1114
Youngstown *(G-20858)*
▲ Brilex Industries Inc ....C.... 330 744-1114
Youngstown *(G-20859)*
Columbia Stamping Inc ....F.... 440 236-6677
Columbia Station *(G-6433)*
▲ Columbus Jack Corporation ....D.... 614 747-1596
Swanton *(G-17909)*
▼ Compass Systems & Sales LLC ....D.... 330 733-2111
Norton *(G-15363)*
Connell Limited Partnership ....D.... 877 534-8986
Northfield *(G-15316)*
Diamond America Corporation ....G.... 330 535-3330
Akron *(G-141)*
Diverse Mfg Solutions LLC ....F.... 740 363-3600
Delaware *(G-8672)*
Dover Corporation ....F.... 513 696-1790
Mason *(G-12857)*
▲ DRG Hydraulics Inc ....E.... 216 663-9747
Cleveland *(G-5114)*
E Systems Design & Automtn Inc ....G.... 419 443-0220
Tiffin *(G-18059)*
Eae Logistics Company LLC ....G.... 440 417-4788
Madison *(G-12348)*
Eaton Corporation ....C.... 216 281-2211
Cleveland *(G-5147)*
Eaton Hydraulics LLC ....E.... 419 232-7777
Van Wert *(G-19088)*
Ebog Legacy Inc ....D.... 330 239-4933
Sharon Center *(G-16949)*
Edwards Machine Service Inc ....F.... 937 295-2929
Fort Loramie *(G-9795)*
Elliott Tool Technologies Ltd ....D.... 937 253-6133
Dayton *(G-8182)*
Exito Manufacturing ....G.... 937 291-9871
Beavercreek *(G-1355)*
F & G Tool and Die Co ....E.... 937 746-3658
Franklin *(G-9880)*
Fabriweld Corporation ....G.... 419 668-3358
Norwalk *(G-15393)*
Falls Metal Fabricators Ind ....F.... 330 253-7181
Akron *(G-164)*
First Tool Corp ....E.... 937 254-6197
Dayton *(G-8195)*
Fluidpower Assembly Inc ....G.... 419 394-7486
Saint Marys *(G-16685)*
▲ French Oil Mill Machinery Co ....D.... 937 773-3420
Piqua *(G-16117)*
Gad-Jets Inc ....G.... 937 274-2111
Franklin *(G-9885)*
Gem City Metal Tech LLC ....E.... 937 252-8998
Dayton *(G-8220)*
▼ George A Mitchell Company ....E.... 330 758-5777
Youngstown *(G-20920)*
▲ Green Corp Magnetic Inc ....E.... 614 801-4000
Grove City *(G-10432)*
Hawk Manufacturing LLC ....D.... 330 784-3151
Akron *(G-201)*
Heimann Manufacturing Co ....G.... 937 652-1865
Urbana *(G-18993)*
Hendricks Vacuum Forming Inc ....G.... 330 833-8913
Massillon *(G-12996)*
Henry & Wright Corporation ....F.... 216 851-3750
Cleveland *(G-5394)*
High Production Technology LLC ....F.... 419 591-7000
Napoleon *(G-14541)*
High Production Technology LLC ....G.... 419 599-1511
Napoleon *(G-14542)*
Hill & Griffith Company ....G.... 513 921-1075
Cincinnati *(G-3812)*
◆ Howmet Corporation ....E.... 757 825-7086
Newburgh Heights *(G-14939)*
Hunter Hydraulics Inc ....G.... 330 455-3983
Canton *(G-2701)*
Industrial Machine Tool Svc ....G.... 216 651-1122
Cleveland *(G-5452)*
J and S Tool Incorporated ....E.... 216 676-8330
Cleveland *(G-5482)*
K & L Tool Inc ....F.... 419 258-2086
Antwerp *(G-598)*
▲ Kay Capital Company ....G.... 216 531-1010
Cleveland *(G-5521)*
Kiraly Tool and Die Inc ....F.... 330 744-5773
Youngstown *(G-20954)*
L B Machine & Mfg Co Inc ....G.... 513 471-6137
Okeana *(G-15519)*
Levan Enterprises Inc ....E.... 330 923-9797
Stow *(G-17601)*
▲ Machine Tool Rebuilders Inc ....G.... 614 228-1070
Columbus *(G-7142)*
▲ McNeil & Nrm Inc ....D.... 330 761-1855
Akron *(G-275)*
Metal & Wire Products Company ....D.... 330 332-9448
Salem *(G-16760)*
Meyer Machine Tool Company ....G.... 614 235-0039
Columbus *(G-7176)*
Monode Marking Products Inc ....D.... 440 975-8802
Mentor *(G-13522)*
Monode Marking Products Inc ....F.... 419 929-0346
New London *(G-14731)*
Monode Steel Stamp Inc ....E.... 419 929-3501
New London *(G-14732)*
Monode Steel Stamp Inc ....F.... 440 975-8802
Mentor *(G-13523)*
Multipress Inc ....G.... 614 228-0185
Columbus *(G-7200)*
◆ National Machinery LLC ....B.... 419 447-5211
Tiffin *(G-18070)*
Nidec Minster Corporation ....G.... 419 394-7504
Saint Marys *(G-16691)*
NM Group Global LLC ....G.... 419 447-5211
Tiffin *(G-18071)*
Omni Technical Products Inc ....F.... 216 433-1970
Cleveland *(G-5814)*
Parker-Hannifin Corporation ....C.... 419 644-4311
Metamora *(G-13634)*
Phoenix Hydraulic Presses Inc ....F.... 614 850-8940
Hilliard *(G-10852)*
▲ Pines Manufacturing Inc ....E.... 440 835-5553
Westlake *(G-20141)*
Qpi Multipress Inc ....G.... 614 228-0185
Columbus *(G-7361)*
Quality Products Inc ....D.... 614 228-0185
Swanton *(G-17920)*
R & B Machining Inc ....E.... 937 382-6710
Wilmington *(G-20507)*
▲ Rafter Equipment Corporation ....E.... 440 572-3700
Strongsville *(G-17781)*
Ram Products Inc ....F.... 614 443-4634
Columbus *(G-7377)*
Ready Technology Inc ....F.... 937 228-8181
Dayton *(G-8465)*
▲ Ready Technology Inc ....F.... 937 866-7200
Dayton *(G-8466)*
▼ Recycling Eqp Solutions Corp ....G.... 330 920-1500
Cuyahoga Falls *(G-7912)*
Ritime Incorporated ....F.... 330 273-3443
Cleveland *(G-5986)*
▲ Rogers Industrial Products Inc ....E.... 330 535-3331
Akron *(G-353)*
Rossi Machinery Services Inc ....G.... 419 281-4488
Ashland *(G-744)*
S & H Automation & Eqp Co ....E.... 419 636-0020
Bryan *(G-2306)*
▲ Scotts Miracle-Gro Company ....B.... 937 644-0011
Marysville *(G-12810)*
▲ Semtorq Inc ....F.... 330 487-0600
Twinsburg *(G-18856)*
Slade Gardner ....G.... 440 355-8015
Lagrange *(G-11493)*
Snair Co ....F.... 614 873-7020
Plain City *(G-16212)*
Spencer Manufacturing Company ....D.... 330 648-2461
Spencer *(G-17306)*
▲ Standard Engineering Group Inc ....G.... 330 494-4300
North Canton *(G-15120)*
Starkey Machinery Inc ....E.... 419 468-2560
Galion *(G-10157)*
Stolle Machinery Company LLC ....C.... 937 497-5400
Sidney *(G-17082)*
Stutzman Manufacturing Ltd ....G.... 330 674-4359
Millersburg *(G-14131)*
▼ Taylor - Winfield Corporation ....D.... 330 259-8500
Hubbard *(G-11010)*
TEC Design & Manufacturing Inc ....F.... 937 435-2147
Dayton *(G-8549)*
Terminal Equipment Industries ....G.... 330 468-0322
Northfield *(G-15328)*
▲ THT Presses Inc ....E.... 937 898-2012
Dayton *(G-8558)*
Tri-K Enterprises Inc ....G.... 330 832-7380
Canton *(G-2845)*
▲ Trucut Incorporated ....D.... 330 938-9806
Sebring *(G-16896)*
Turner Machine Co ....F.... 330 332-5821
Salem *(G-16778)*
▲ Twist Inc ....C.... 937 675-9581
Jamestown *(G-11221)*
Twist Inc ....E.... 937 675-9581
Jamestown *(G-11222)*
Uhrichsville Carbide Inc ....F.... 740 922-9197
Uhrichsville *(G-18899)*
Valley Tool & Die Inc ....D.... 440 237-0160
North Royalton *(G-15309)*
Van Burens Welding & Machine ....G.... 740 787-2636
Glenford *(G-10273)*
Vmaxx Inc ....F.... 419 738-4044
Wapakoneta *(G-19358)*
▲ Vulcan Tool Company ....G.... 937 253-6194
Dayton *(G-8581)*
W G Machine Tool Service Co ....G.... 330 723-3428
Medina *(G-13362)*
▲ Yizumi-HPM Corporation ....E.... 740 382-5600
Iberia *(G-11115)*

3543 Industrial Patterns

7 Rowe Court Properties LLC ....G.... 513 874-7236
Hamilton *(G-10526)*
Accuform Manufacturing Inc ....E.... 330 797-9291
Youngstown *(G-20834)*
Air Power Dynamics LLC ....C.... 440 701-2100
Mentor *(G-13377)*
Anchor Pattern Company ....G.... 614 443-2221
Columbus *(G-6601)*
Anger Pattern Company Inc ....G.... 330 882-6519
Clinton *(G-6383)*
API Pattern Works Inc ....E.... 440 269-1766
Willoughby *(G-20274)*
Boko Patterns Models & Molds ....G.... 937 426-9667
Beavercreek *(G-1352)*
Cascade Pattern Company Inc ....E.... 440 323-4300
Elyria *(G-9231)*
Case Pattern Co Inc ....G.... 216 531-0744
Madison *(G-12341)*
Cincinnati Pattern Company ....F.... 513 241-9872
Cincinnati *(G-3503)*
Clinton Foundry Ltd ....F.... 419 243-6885
Toledo *(G-18234)*
Clinton Pattern Works Inc ....F.... 419 243-0855
Toledo *(G-18235)*
▲ Colonial Patterns Inc ....E.... 330 673-6475
Kent *(G-11306)*
Consolidated Pattern Works Inc ....G.... 330 434-6060
Akron *(G-120)*
Dayton Pattern Inc ....G.... 937 277-0761
Dayton *(G-8140)*
Design Pattern Works Inc ....G.... 937 252-0797
Dayton *(G-8157)*
Design Tech Inc ....G.... 937 254-7000
Dayton *(G-8158)*
Elyria Pattern Co Inc ....G.... 440 323-1526
Elyria *(G-9254)*
Feiner Pattern Works Inc ....F.... 513 851-9800
Cincinnati *(G-3681)*
Foster Pattern Works Inc ....G.... 330 482-3612
Columbiana *(G-6466)*
Founder Service & Mfg Co ....F.... 330 584-7759
Deerfield *(G-8609)*
Freeman Manufacturing & Sup Co ....E.... 440 934-1902
Avon *(G-950)*
Geotech Pattern & Mold Inc ....G.... 513 683-2600
Loveland *(G-12191)*
Glazier Pattern & Coach ....G.... 937 492-7355
Houston *(G-10994)*
H&M Machine & Tool LLC ....E.... 419 776-9220
Toledo *(G-18316)*
Humtown Pattern Company ....D.... 330 482-5555
Columbiana *(G-6470)*
Hynes Modern Pattern Co Inc ....G.... 937 322-3451
Springfield *(G-17424)*
Industrial Pattern & Mfg Co ....F.... 614 252-0934
Columbus *(G-7024)*
▲ J-Lenco Inc ....D.... 740 499-2260
Morral *(G-14404)*

952 2019 Harris Ohio Industrial Directory

SIC SECTION 35 INDUSTRIAL AND COMMERCIAL MACHINERY AND COMPUTER EQUIPMENT

Ketco Inc....E....937 426-9331
Beavercreek (G-1324)
Kohl Patterns....G....513 353-3831
Cleves (G-6368)
Lesleys Patterns Ltd....G....937 554-4674
Vandalia (G-19132)
Liberty Pattern and Mold Inc....G....330 788-9463
Youngstown (G-20959)
Lisbon Pattern Limited....G....330 424-7676
Lisbon (G-11975)
Lorain Modern Pattern Inc....F....440 365-6780
Elyria (G-9288)
Maumee Pattern Company....E....419 693-4968
Toledo (G-18403)
Model Engineering Company....G....330 644-3450
Barberton (G-1087)
Morcast Precision Inc....G....614 258-5071
Columbus (G-7195)
Mount Union Pattern Works Inc....G....330 821-2274
Alliance (G-492)
National Pattern Mfg Co....F....330 682-6871
Orrville (G-15605)
North Coast Pattern Inc....G....440 322-5064
Strongsville (G-17771)
PCC Airfoils LLC....C....216 692-7900
Cleveland (G-5857)
Plas-Mac Corp....D....440 349-3222
Solon (G-17216)
R L Rush Tool & Pattern Inc....G....419 562-9849
Bucyrus (G-2342)
Reliable Pattern Works Inc....G....440 232-8820
Cleveland (G-5972)
▲ Ross Aluminum Castings LLC....C....937 492-4134
Sidney (G-17069)
Seaport Mold & Casting Company....F....419 243-1422
Toledo (G-18515)
Seaway Pattern Mfg Inc....E....419 865-5724
Toledo (G-18516)
Seilkop Industries Inc....F....513 679-5680
Cincinnati (G-4317)
Shells Inc....D....330 808-5558
Copley (G-7694)
Sherwood Rtm Corp....G....330 875-7151
Louisville (G-12166)
Sinel Company Inc....F....937 433-4772
Dayton (G-8509)
Spectracam Ltd....G....937 223-3805
Dayton (G-8516)
Tempcraft Corporation....C....216 391-3885
Cleveland (G-6157)
Th Manufacturing Inc....G....330 893-3572
Millersburg (G-14135)
▲ Transducers Direct Llc....F....513 247-0601
Cincinnati (G-4431)
United States Drill Head Co....E....513 941-0300
Cincinnati (G-4450)
Wright Way Patterns....G....513 574-5776
Cincinnati (G-4522)
Xl Pattern Shop Inc....G....330 682-2981
Orrville (G-15629)

3544 Dies, Tools, Jigs, Fixtures & Indl Molds

5me LLC....E....513 719-1600
Cincinnati (G-3232)
5me Holdings LLC....G....859 534-4872
Cincinnati (G-3233)
A & B Tool & Manufacturing....G....419 382-0215
Toledo (G-18151)
A G Industries Inc....F....330 220-0050
Brunswick (G-2185)
Accu Tool Inc....G....937 667-5878
Tipp City (G-18095)
Accu-Rite Tool & Die Co Corp....G....330 497-9959
Canton (G-2557)
Accu-Tek Tool & Die Inc....G....330 726-1946
Salem (G-16713)
Accuform Manufacturing Inc....E....330 797-9291
Youngstown (G-20834)
Accurate Machining & Welding....G....937 584-4518
Sabina (G-16615)
Accurate Tool Co Inc....G....330 332-9448
Salem (G-16714)
Ace American Wire Die Co....F....330 425-7269
Twinsburg (G-18723)
▲ Acro Tool & Die Company....D....330 773-5173
Akron (G-29)
▲ Addisonmckee Inc....C....513 228-7000
Lebanon (G-11629)
Adept Manufacturing Corp....F....937 222-7110
Dayton (G-8009)
Adval Tech US Inc....G....216 362-1850
Cleveland (G-4620)
Advanced Engrg Solutions Inc....D....937 743-6900
Springboro (G-17319)
▲ Advanced Intr Solutions Inc....E....937 550-0065
Springboro (G-17320)
Aims-CMI Technology LLC....F....937 832-2000
Englewood (G-9349)
AJD Holding Co....D....330 405-4477
Twinsburg (G-18728)
Akron Centl Engrv Mold Mch Inc....E....330 794-8704
Akron (G-34)
Allen Tool Co Inc....G....937 987-2037
New Vienna (G-14823)
Allied Tool & Die Inc....F....216 941-6196
Cleveland (G-4673)
▲ Alpha Tool & Mold Inc....F....440 473-2343
Cleveland (G-4676)
Alternative Flash Inc....E....330 334-6111
Wadsworth (G-19225)
Aluminum Fence & Mfg Co....G....330 755-3323
Aurora (G-868)
Amaroq Inc....G....419 747-2110
Mansfield (G-12403)
▼ Amcraft Inc....G....419 729-7900
Toledo (G-18170)
American Cube Mold Inc....G....330 558-0044
Hinckley (G-10898)
American Extrusion Svcs Inc....G....937 743-1210
Springboro (G-17322)
American Punch Co Inc....E....216 731-4501
Euclid (G-9403)
American Tool and Die Inc....F....419 726-5394
Toledo (G-18181)
Amerimold Inc....G....330 628-2190
Mogadore (G-14229)
Amex Dies Inc....F....330 545-9766
Girard (G-10253)
Ampex Metal Products Company....E....216 267-9242
Brookpark (G-2136)
Amtech Tool and Machine Inc....F....330 758-8215
Youngstown (G-20844)
Anchor Glass Container Corp....C....740 452-2743
Zanesville (G-21099)
▲ Anchor Tool & Die Co....B....216 362-1850
Cleveland (G-4709)
Antwerp Tool & Die Inc....F....419 258-5271
Antwerp (G-596)
Apollo Plastics Inc....F....440 951-7774
Mentor (G-13391)
Apollo Products Inc....F....440 269-8551
Willoughby (G-20275)
Apr Tool Inc....G....440 946-0393
Willoughby (G-20278)
Arete Innovative Solutions LLC....G....513 503-2712
Morrow (G-14408)
Argo Tool Corporation....F....330 425-2407
Twinsburg (G-18735)
Arken Manufacturing Inc....G....216 883-6628
Cleveland (G-4733)
Artisan Equipment Inc....F....740 756-9135
Carroll (G-2898)
▼ Artisan Tool & Die Corp....E....216 883-2769
Cleveland (G-4740)
Aspec Inc....G....513 561-9922
Cincinnati (G-3363)
Athens Mold and Machine Inc....D....740 593-6613
Athens (G-823)
Atlantic Tool & Die Company....C....330 239-3700
Sharon Center (G-16945)
▲ Atlantic Tool & Die Company....C....440 238-6931
Strongsville (G-17714)
Atlantic Tool & Die Company....C....330 769-4500
Seville (G-16910)
Aukerman J F Steel Rule Die....G....937 456-4498
Eaton (G-9142)
Automation Plastics Corp....D....330 562-5148
Aurora (G-871)
Automation Tool & Die Inc....D....330 225-8336
Valley City (G-19030)
Autotec Engineering Company....E....419 885-2529
Toledo (G-18195)
B C Wilson Inc....G....937 439-1866
Dayton (G-8049)
B V Mfg Inc....F....330 549-5331
New Springfield (G-14818)
B-K Tool & Design Inc....D....419 532-3890
Kalida (G-11276)
Balancing Company Inc....E....937 898-9111
Vandalia (G-19117)
Banco Die Inc....F....330 821-8511
Alliance (G-456)
Banner Metals Group Inc....D....614 291-3105
Columbus (G-6646)
Barberton Mold & Machine Co....G....330 745-8559
Barberton (G-1063)
▲ Basilius Inc....E....419 536-5810
Toledo (G-18199)
Bk Tool Company Inc....F....513 870-9622
Fairfield (G-9485)
Blick Tool & Die Inc....G....330 343-1277
Dover (G-8809)
Blitz Tool & Die Inc....G....440 237-1177
Cleveland (G-4821)
Bloom Industries Inc....D....330 898-3878
Warren (G-19377)
Blue Ash Tool & Die Co Inc....F....513 793-4530
Blue Ash (G-1737)
Bollinger Tool & Die Inc....G....419 866-5180
Holland (G-10916)
Borke Mold Specialist Inc....E....513 870-8000
West Chester (G-19662)
Brainin-Advance Industries LLC....E....513 874-9760
West Chester (G-19663)
▲ Brinkman Tool & Die Inc....E....937 222-1161
Dayton (G-8062)
Broadway Companies Inc....E....937 890-1888
Dayton (G-8063)
Brothers Tool and Mfg Ltd....F....513 353-9700
Miamitown (G-13744)
Browder Tool Co Inc....G....937 233-6731
Dayton (G-8065)
Bruck Manufacturing Co Inc....G....440 327-6619
North Ridgeville (G-15215)
Brw Tool Inc....F....419 394-3371
Saint Marys (G-16679)
C & D Tool Inc....G....440 942-8463
Eastlake (G-9099)
C-H Tool & Die....G....740 397-7214
Mount Vernon (G-14471)
Caliber Mold and Machine Inc....E....330 633-8171
Akron (G-102)
California Ceramic Supply Co....G....216 531-9185
Euclid (G-9406)
CAM-Lem Inc....G....216 391-7750
Cleveland (G-4863)
▼ Camden Concrete Products....G....937 456-1229
Eaton (G-9145)
Canton Pattern & Mold Inc....G....330 455-4316
Canton (G-2615)
Capital Precision Machine & Tl....G....937 258-1176
Dayton (G-7973)
Capital Tool Company....E....216 661-5750
Cleveland (G-4871)
Carbide Specialist Inc....F....440 951-4027
Willoughby (G-20292)
Carter Manufacturing Co Inc....E....513 398-7303
Mason (G-12838)
Case Pattern Co Inc....G....216 531-0744
Madison (G-12341)
Catalysis Additive Tooling LLC....G....614 715-3674
Powell (G-16316)
Cctm Inc....G....513 934-3533
Lebanon (G-11641)
Centaur Tool & Die Inc....F....419 352-7704
Bowling Green (G-1959)
Centerline Tool & Machine....G....937 222-3600
Dayton (G-8083)
Central Machinery Company LLC....F....740 387-1289
Marion (G-12699)
Century Die Company LLC....D....419 332-2693
Fremont (G-10005)
Chart Tech Tool Inc....E....937 667-3543
Tipp City (G-18108)
Chipmatic Tool & Machine Inc....D....419 862-2737
Elmore (G-9205)
Chippewa Tool & Mfg Co....F....419 849-2790
Woodville (G-20551)
Cincinnati Mold Incorporated....G....513 922-1888
Cincinnati (G-3502)
Cinn Wire E D M Inc....G....513 741-5402
Cincinnati (G-3517)
Circle Mold Incorporated....E....330 633-7017
Tallmadge (G-17976)
Claridon Tool & Die Inc....G....740 389-1944
Caledonia (G-2414)
Classic Tool Inc....G....330 922-1933
Stow (G-17578)
▲ Cleveland Die & Mfg Co....E....440 243-3404
Middleburg Heights (G-13762)

S I C

Employee Codes: A=Over 500 employees, B=251-500 C=101-250, D=51-100, E=20-50, F=10-19, G=3-9
2019 Harris Ohio Industrial Directory
953

35 INDUSTRIAL AND COMMERCIAL MACHINERY AND COMPUTER EQUIPMENT SIC SECTION

Cleveland Metal Processing Inc ....C....... 440 243-3404
Cleveland *(G-4968)*
Cleveland Roll Forming Co ....G....... 216 281-0202
Cleveland *(G-4975)*
◆ **Cleveland Steel Tool Company** ....E....... 216 681-7400
Cleveland *(G-4978)*
Cliffco Stands Inc ....E....... 937 382-3700
Wilmington *(G-20489)*
Clyde Tool & Die Inc ....F....... 419 547-9574
Clyde *(G-6387)*
Cmt Machining & Fabg LLC ....F....... 937 652-3740
Urbana *(G-18983)*
Coach Tool & Die Inc ....G....... 937 890-4716
Dayton *(G-8095)*
Cobb Industries Inc ....G....... 440 946-4695
Mentor *(G-13418)*
Cole Tool & Die Company ....E....... 419 522-1272
Ontario *(G-15540)*
Colonial Machine Company Inc ....D....... 330 673-5859
Kent *(G-11305)*
▲ **Colonial Patterns Inc** ....E....... 330 673-6475
Kent *(G-11306)*
Columbia Stamping Inc ....F....... 440 236-6677
Columbia Station *(G-6433)*
Companies of North Coast LLC ....G....... 216 398-8550
Cleveland *(G-5008)*
Concord Design Inc ....G....... 330 722-5133
Medina *(G-13239)*
Conforming Matrix Corporation ....E....... 419 729-3777
Toledo *(G-18238)*
Conison Tool and Die Inc ....G....... 330 758-1574
Youngstown *(G-20878)*
Connell Limited Partnership ....D....... 877 534-8986
Northfield *(G-15316)*
Container Graphics Corp ....E....... 937 746-5666
Franklin *(G-9875)*
Conti Tool & Die Inc ....G....... 330 633-1414
Akron *(G-121)*
Continental Business Entps Inc ....F....... 440 439-4400
Cleveland *(G-5020)*
Contour Tool Inc ....E....... 440 365-7333
North Ridgeville *(G-15216)*
Cornerstone Manufacturing Inc ....G....... 937 456-5930
Eaton *(G-9146)*
▲ **CP Technologies Company** ....E....... 614 866-9200
Blacklick *(G-1682)*
Criterion Tool & Die Inc ....E....... 216 267-1733
Brookpark *(G-2139)*
Crowe Manufacturing Services ....D....... 800 831-1893
Troy *(G-18644)*
Crum Manufacturing Inc ....E....... 419 878-9779
Waterville *(G-19492)*
Csw of Ny Inc ....F....... 413 589-1311
Sylvania *(G-17935)*
Cubic Blue Inc ....G....... 330 638-2999
Cortland *(G-7708)*
Custom Design & Tool ....G....... 419 865-9773
Holland *(G-10922)*
Custom Machine Inc ....E....... 419 986-5122
Tiffin *(G-18057)*
Customformed Products Inc ....F....... 937 388-0480
Miamisburg *(G-13653)*
D A Fitzgerald Co Inc ....G....... 937 548-0511
Greenville *(G-10367)*
D A Stirling Inc ....G....... 330 923-3195
Cuyahoga Falls *(G-7857)*
D J Metro Mold & Die Inc ....G....... 440 237-1130
North Royalton *(G-15268)*
Darke Precision Inc ....F....... 937 548-2232
Piqua *(G-16110)*
Data Mold and Tool Inc ....G....... 419 878-9861
Waterville *(G-19493)*
Dayton Lamina Corporation ....G....... 937 859-5111
Dayton *(G-8136)*
▲ **Dayton Progress Corporation** ....A....... 937 859-5111
Dayton *(G-8143)*
Dayton Progress Intl Corp ....G....... 937 859-5111
Dayton *(G-8144)*
Dayton Stencil Works Company ....E....... 937 223-3233
Dayton *(G-8145)*
Dayton Tool Co Inc ....E....... 937 222-5501
Dayton *(G-8146)*
Dcd Technologies Inc ....E....... 216 481-0056
Cleveland *(G-5077)*
De-Lux Mold & Machine Inc ....G....... 330 678-1030
Kent *(G-11311)*
▲ **Defiance Metal Products Co** ....B....... 419 784-5332
Defiance *(G-8619)*
▲ **Delco Corporation** ....E....... 330 896-4220
Akron *(G-137)*
Delta Machine & Tool Co ....F....... 216 524-2477
Cleveland *(G-5083)*
Delta Tool & Die Stl Block Inc ....F....... 419 822-5939
Delta *(G-8767)*
▲ **Deuer Developments Inc** ....F....... 937 299-1213
Moraine *(G-14345)*
Diamond Mold & Die Co ....F....... 330 633-5682
Tallmadge *(G-17979)*
Die Cast Division ....G....... 330 769-2013
Seville *(G-16915)*
Die Craft Machining & Engineer ....G....... 513 771-1290
Cincinnati *(G-3588)*
Die Guys Inc ....E....... 330 239-3437
Medina *(G-13252)*
▲ **Die-Matic Corporation** ....D....... 216 749-4656
Brooklyn Heights *(G-2119)*
▼ **Die-Mension Corporation** ....F....... 330 273-5872
Brunswick *(G-2200)*
Die-Namic Tool & Die Inc ....G....... 330 296-6923
Ravenna *(G-16375)*
Diemaster Tool & Mold Inc ....F....... 330 467-4281
Macedonia *(G-12289)*
Direct Wire Service LLP ....G....... 937 526-4447
Versailles *(G-19178)*
Disciple Tool & Machine ....G....... 330 503-7879
Lake Milton *(G-11498)*
Diversified Mold Castings LLC ....E....... 216 663-1814
Cleveland *(G-5100)*
Diversified Tool Systems ....G....... 419 845-2143
Caledonia *(G-2415)*
Dove Die and Stamping Company ....E....... 216 267-3720
Cleveland *(G-5109)*
Dover Machine Co ....F....... 330 343-4123
Dover *(G-8822)*
Doyle Manufacturing Inc ....D....... 419 865-2548
Holland *(G-10926)*
Dreier Tool & Die Corp ....G....... 513 521-8200
Cincinnati *(G-3610)*
◆ **Drt Mfg Co** ....C....... 937 297-6670
Dayton *(G-8171)*
Duco Tool & Die Inc ....F....... 419 628-2031
Minster *(G-14212)*
▲ **Duncan Tool Inc** ....F....... 937 667-9364
Tipp City *(G-18111)*
Durivage Pattern & Mfg Co ....E....... 419 836-8655
Williston *(G-20262)*
Dyco Manufacturing Inc ....F....... 419 485-5525
Montpelier *(G-14307)*
Dynamic Dies Inc ....E....... 513 705-9524
Middletown *(G-13902)*
Dynamic Dies Inc ....E....... 513 705-9524
Middletown *(G-13903)*
Dynamic Tool & Mold Inc ....G....... 440 237-8665
Cleveland *(G-5125)*
Dynamic Tool Die ....G....... 440 834-0007
Middlefield *(G-13795)*
E & E Mold & Die Inc ....G....... 216 898-5853
Cleveland *(G-5126)*
E D M Electrofying Inc ....G....... 440 322-8900
Elyria *(G-9248)*
E D M Fastar Inc ....G....... 216 676-0100
Cleveland *(G-5129)*
▲ **E D M Services Inc** ....G....... 216 486-2068
Euclid *(G-9411)*
Eagle Precision Products LLC ....G....... 440 582-9393
North Royalton *(G-15270)*
Eagle Tool & Die Inc ....G....... 216 671-5055
Cleveland *(G-5135)*
◆ **Edco Inc** ....E....... 419 726-1595
Toledo *(G-18275)*
Edge-Rite Tools Inc ....F....... 216 642-0966
Cleveland *(G-5157)*
Eger Products Inc ....D....... 513 753-4200
Amelia *(G-539)*
▲ **EMI Corp** ....D....... 937 596-5511
Jackson Center *(G-11209)*
Endura Plastics Inc ....D....... 440 951-4466
Kirtland *(G-11467)*
Engineered Mfg & Eqp Co ....G....... 937 642-7776
Marysville *(G-12781)*
Enterprise Tool & Die Company ....F....... 216 351-1300
Cleveland *(G-5181)*
Erickson-Huff Tool and Die ....G....... 740 596-4036
Mc Arthur *(G-13181)*
Estee Mold & Die Inc ....E....... 937 224-7853
Dayton *(G-8188)*
Esterle Mold & Machine Co Inc ....F....... 330 686-1685
Stow *(G-17584)*
Esterle Mold & Machine Co Inc ....E....... 330 686-1685
Stow *(G-17583)*
Euclid Design & Manufacturing ....F....... 440 942-0066
Willoughby *(G-20316)*
Exact-Tool & Die Inc ....E....... 216 676-9140
Cleveland *(G-5204)*
Exito Manufacturing ....G....... 937 291-9871
Beavercreek *(G-1355)*
Exodus Mold & Machine Inc ....G....... 330 854-0282
Canal Fulton *(G-2479)*
Expert Regrind Service Inc ....G....... 937 526-5662
Versailles *(G-19180)*
F & G Tool and Die Co ....E....... 937 294-1405
Moraine *(G-14352)*
Fabrication Shop Inc ....F....... 419 435-7934
Fostoria *(G-9837)*
Faith Tool & Manufacturing ....G....... 440 951-5934
Willoughby *(G-20320)*
Falls Stamping & Welding Co ....C....... 330 928-1191
Cuyahoga Falls *(G-7867)*
Fame Tool & Mfg Co Inc ....E....... 513 271-6387
Cincinnati *(G-3670)*
Fargo Toolite Incorporated ....F....... 440 997-2442
Ashtabula *(G-775)*
Faull & Son LLC ....F....... 330 652-4341
Niles *(G-15008)*
Feller Tool Co Inc ....F....... 440 324-6277
Lorain *(G-12092)*
Fenton Manufacturing Inc ....G....... 440 969-1128
Ashtabula *(G-776)*
▲ **Ferriot Inc** ....C....... 330 786-3000
Akron *(G-169)*
First Machine & Tool Corp ....F....... 440 269-8644
Willoughby *(G-20323)*
First Tool Corp ....E....... 937 254-6197
Dayton *(G-8195)*
Fischer Special Tooling Corp ....F....... 440 951-8411
Mentor *(G-13443)*
Fostoria Machine Products ....G....... 419 435-4262
Fostoria *(G-9843)*
Founder Service & Mfg Co ....F....... 330 584-7759
Deerfield *(G-8609)*
▼ **Fremar Industries Inc** ....E....... 330 220-3700
Brunswick *(G-2207)*
Fremont Cutting Dies Inc ....G....... 419 334-5153
Fremont *(G-10017)*
G & G Header Die Inc ....G....... 330 468-3458
Macedonia *(G-12297)*
G & S Custom Tooling LLC ....G....... 419 286-2888
Fort Jennings *(G-9792)*
Galaxy Products Inc ....G....... 419 843-7337
Sylvania *(G-17940)*
Garvin Tool & Die Inc ....G....... 419 334-2392
Fremont *(G-10022)*
Gasdorf Tool and Mch Co Inc ....E....... 419 227-0103
Lima *(G-11867)*
Gem City Engineering Co ....C....... 937 223-5544
Dayton *(G-8219)*
▲ **General Die Casters Inc** ....E....... 330 678-2528
Twinsburg *(G-18781)*
▲ **General Tool Company** ....C....... 513 733-5500
Cincinnati *(G-3747)*
Gentzler Tool & Die Corp ....E....... 330 896-1941
Akron *(G-188)*
Gilson Machine & Tool Co Inc ....E....... 419 592-2911
Napoleon *(G-14539)*
Glendale Machine Inc ....G....... 440 248-8646
Solon *(G-17150)*
▲ **Gokoh Corporation** ....F....... 937 339-4977
Troy *(G-18662)*
Gordon Tool Inc ....F....... 419 263-3151
Payne *(G-15872)*
Gottschall Tool & Die Inc ....E....... 330 332-1544
Salem *(G-16743)*
Grandon Mfg Co Inc ....G....... 614 294-2694
Columbus *(G-6966)*
Green Machine Tool Inc ....F....... 937 253-0771
Dayton *(G-7980)*
H & R Tool & Machine Co Inc ....G....... 740 452-0784
Zanesville *(G-21143)*
H G Schneider Company ....G....... 614 882-6944
Westerville *(G-20056)*
H K K Machining Co ....E....... 419 924-5116
West Unity *(G-19968)*
H Machining Inc ....F....... 419 636-6890
Bryan *(G-2283)*
H&M Machine & Tool LLC ....E....... 419 776-9220
Toledo *(G-18316)*
Hale Performance Coatings Inc ....E....... 419 244-6451
Toledo *(G-18319)*
Hamilton Custom Molding Inc ....G....... 513 844-6643
Hamilton *(G-10568)*

Hamilton Mold & Machine Co ....E 216 732-8200
Cleveland *(G-5368)*
Hardin Creek Machine & Tool ....F 419 678-4913
Coldwater *(G-6410)*
Hawthorne Tool LLC ....F 440 516-1891
Wickliffe *(G-20212)*
Hedalloy Die Corp ....F 216 341-3768
Cleveland *(G-5388)*
Hedges Selective Tool & Prod ....F 419 478-8670
Toledo *(G-18329)*
Heimann Manufacturing Co ....G 937 652-1865
Urbana *(G-18993)*
▲ Herbert Usa Inc ....D 330 929-4297
Akron *(G-204)*
Herd Manufacturing Inc ....E 216 651-4221
Cleveland *(G-5397)*
Hess Industries Ltd ....F 419 525-4000
Mansfield *(G-12458)*
Hi-Tech Wire Inc ....D 419 678-8376
Saint Henry *(G-16662)*
▲ Hi-Tek Manufacturing Inc ....C 513 459-1094
Mason *(G-12886)*
High Card Industries LLC ....F 330 547-3381
Berlin Center *(G-1646)*
High Tech Mold & Machine Co ....F 330 896-4466
Uniontown *(G-18921)*
Hofacker Prcsion Machining LLC ....F 937 832-7712
Clayton *(G-4574)*
Holland Engraving Company ....F 419 865-2765
Toledo *(G-18332)*
Homeworth Fabrications & Mchs ....F 330 525-5459
Homeworth *(G-10988)*
▲ Honda Engineering N Amer Inc ....B 937 642-5000
Marysville *(G-12789)*
Honda Engineering NA Inc ....F 937 707-5357
Marysville *(G-12790)*
Horizon Industries Corp ....G 937 323-0801
Springfield *(G-17420)*
Hudak Machine & Tool Inc ....G 440 366-8955
Elyria *(G-9266)*
Hunt Products Inc ....E 440 667-2457
Newburgh Heights *(G-14940)*
Hunter Tool and Die Company ....G 937 256-9798
Dayton *(G-8257)*
I-Dee-X Inc ....G 330 788-2186
Youngstown *(G-20935)*
Ibycorp ....G 330 425-8226
Twinsburg *(G-18794)*
Impact Industries Inc ....E 440 327-2360
North Ridgeville *(G-15230)*
Impakt ....G 513 271-9191
Cincinnati *(G-3840)*
Imperial Die & Mfg Co ....F 440 268-9080
Strongsville *(G-17753)*
Independent Stamping Inc ....E 216 251-3500
Cleveland *(G-5451)*
Industrial Automation Service ....G 740 747-2222
Ashley *(G-758)*
Industrial Mold Inc ....E 330 425-7374
Twinsburg *(G-18796)*
▲ Industry Products Co ....B 937 778-0585
Piqua *(G-16130)*
Innovative Plastic Molders LLC ....E 937 898-3775
Dayton *(G-8265)*
Innovative Tool & Die Inc ....G 419 599-0492
Napoleon *(G-14545)*
International Dies Co Inc ....G 330 744-7951
Diamond *(G-8798)*
▲ Ishmael Precision Tool Corp ....E 937 335-8070
Troy *(G-18677)*
IV M Tool & Die ....G 513 625-6464
Williamsburg *(G-20252)*
J & H Corporation ....G 440 357-5982
Painesville *(G-15751)*
J & J Tool & Die Inc ....G 330 343-4721
Dover *(G-8833)*
J & M Industries Inc ....G 440 951-1985
Mentor *(G-13481)*
J and S Tool Incorporated ....E 216 676-8330
Cleveland *(G-5482)*
J M Mold Inc ....G 937 778-0077
Piqua *(G-16132)*
J P Tool Inc ....G 419 354-8696
Bowling Green *(G-1978)*
J W Harwood Co ....F 216 531-6230
Cleveland *(G-5489)*
▲ J-C-R Tech Inc ....E 937 783-2296
Blanchester *(G-1704)*
Jamen Tool & Die Co ....F 330 788-6521
Youngstown *(G-20945)*
Jamen Tool & Die Co ....E 330 782-6731
Youngstown *(G-20946)*
JB Products Co ....G 330 342-0223
Streetsboro *(G-17679)*
JBI Corporation ....F 419 855-3389
Genoa *(G-10233)*
Jena Tool Inc ....D 937 296-1122
Moraine *(G-14361)*
▲ Jergens Inc ....C 216 486-5540
Cleveland *(G-5495)*
Jet Tool and Prototype Co ....G 419 666-1199
Walbridge *(G-19295)*
John F Kilfoil Co ....G 513 791-6150
Cincinnati *(G-3878)*
Johnston Manufacturing Inc ....G 440 269-1420
Mentor *(G-13487)*
Justin P Straub LLC ....G 513 761-0282
Cincinnati *(G-3888)*
K & L Die & Manufacturing ....G 419 895-1301
Greenwich *(G-10405)*
K & L Tool Inc ....F 419 258-2086
Antwerp *(G-598)*
K B Machine & Tool Inc ....G 937 773-1624
Piqua *(G-16136)*
K K Tool Co ....E 937 325-1373
Springfield *(G-17428)*
K P Precision Tool and Mch Co ....G 419 237-2596
Fayette *(G-9633)*
▲ Kalt Manufacturing Company ....D 440 327-2102
North Ridgeville *(G-15235)*
Kastler & Reichlin Inc ....E 440 322-0970
Elyria *(G-9281)*
Kelch Manufacturing Corp ....G 440 366-5060
Elyria *(G-9282)*
Ken Forging Inc ....C 440 993-8091
Jefferson *(G-11232)*
Kent Mold and Manufacturing Co ....E 330 673-3469
Kent *(G-11343)*
KG Tool Company ....G 440 428-8633
Madison *(G-12352)*
Kilroy Company ....D 440 951-8700
Eastlake *(G-9117)*
▲ King Machine and Tool Co ....F 330 833-7217
Massillon *(G-13011)*
Kiraly Tool and Die Inc ....F 330 744-5773
Youngstown *(G-20954)*
Knous Tool & Machine Inc ....G 419 394-3541
Saint Marys *(G-16687)*
Knowlton Manufacturing Co Inc ....F 513 631-7353
Cincinnati *(G-3920)*
Kramer & Kiefer Inc ....G 330 336-8742
Wadsworth *(G-19251)*
Krdc Inc ....G 937 222-2332
Dayton *(G-8301)*
Kreider Corp ....D 937 325-8787
Springfield *(G-17436)*
Krengel Equipment LLC ....C 440 946-3570
Eastlake *(G-9118)*
Krisdale Industries Inc ....G 330 225-2392
Valley City *(G-19043)*
Kurtz Tool & Die Co Inc ....G 330 755-7723
Struthers *(G-17819)*
L B Machine & Mfg Co Inc ....G 513 471-6137
Okeana *(G-15519)*
▼ L C G Machine & Tool Inc ....G 614 261-1651
Columbus *(G-7107)*
La Ganke & Sons Stamping Co ....F 216 451-0278
Columbia Station *(G-6439)*
Lab Quality Machining Inc ....G 513 625-0219
Goshen *(G-10289)*
Lahm-Trosper Inc ....F 937 252-8791
Dayton *(G-8305)*
Lange Precision Inc ....F 513 530-9500
Blue Ash *(G-1802)*
Langenau Manufacturing Company ....F 216 651-3400
Cleveland *(G-5558)*
Lanko Industries Inc ....G 440 269-1641
Mentor *(G-13496)*
Larosa Die Engineering Inc ....G 513 284-9195
Cincinnati *(G-3931)*
Laspina Tool & Die Inc ....F 330 923-9996
Stow *(G-17599)*
▲ Laszeray Technology LLC ....D 440 582-8430
North Royalton *(G-15283)*
Levan Enterprises Inc ....E 330 923-9797
Stow *(G-17601)*
Liberty Die Cast Molds Inc ....F 740 666-7492
Ostrander *(G-15645)*
Liberty Mold & Machine Company ....G 330 278-7825
Hinckley *(G-10904)*
Lideco LLC ....G 330 539-9333
Vienna *(G-19200)*
Lightning Mold & Machine Inc ....F 440 593-6460
Conneaut *(G-7653)*
Line Tool & Die Inc ....G 419 332-2931
Fremont *(G-10035)*
Liqui-Box Corporation ....C 419 209-9085
Upper Sandusky *(G-18960)*
▲ Logan Machine Company ....D 330 633-6163
Akron *(G-259)*
Lomar Enterprises Inc ....F 614 409-9104
Groveport *(G-10501)*
▲ Long-Stanton Mfg Company ....E 513 874-8020
West Chester *(G-19738)*
Lorain Ruled Die Products Inc ....G 440 281-8607
North Ridgeville *(G-15239)*
◆ Loroco Industries Inc ....E 513 891-9544
Blue Ash *(G-1807)*
Lostcreek Tool & Machine Inc ....F 937 773-6022
Piqua *(G-16138)*
Louis G Freeman Co ....E 419 334-9709
Fremont *(G-10037)*
Lowry Tool & Die Inc ....F 330 332-1722
Salem *(G-16755)*
Lrb Tool & Die Ltd ....F 330 898-5783
Warren *(G-19418)*
Lukens Inc ....D 937 440-2500
Troy *(G-18684)*
Lunar Tool & Mold Inc ....F 440 237-2141
North Royalton *(G-15285)*
M & M Dies Inc ....G 216 883-6628
Cleveland *(G-5590)*
M & R Manufacturing Inc ....G 330 633-5725
Tallmadge *(G-17989)*
M S K Tool & Die Inc ....G 440 930-8100
Avon Lake *(G-994)*
Macek Industries ....G 440 205-8711
Mentor *(G-13506)*
Machine Tek Systems Inc ....E 330 527-4450
Garrettsville *(G-10197)*
Machine Tool Design & Fab LLC ....F 419 435-7676
Fostoria *(G-9847)*
Magna Exteriors America Inc ....A 419 662-3256
Northwood *(G-15340)*
Magnum Molding Inc ....G 937 368-3040
Conover *(G-7665)*
◆ Magnum Tool Corp ....G 937 228-0900
Dayton *(G-8323)*
Majestic Tool and Machine Inc ....E 440 248-5058
Solon *(G-17186)*
Malabar Properties LLC ....F 419 884-0071
Mansfield *(G-12473)*
Mallory Pattern Works Inc ....G 419 726-8001
Toledo *(G-18398)*
Mar-Con Tool Company Inc ....E 937 299-2244
Moraine *(G-14367)*
Mar-Metal Mfg Inc ....E 419 447-1102
Upper Sandusky *(G-18962)*
Mar-Vel Tool Co Inc ....E 937 223-2137
Dayton *(G-8331)*
Marsh Technologies Inc ....F 330 545-0085
Girard *(G-10262)*
Martin Machine & Tool Inc ....F 419 373-1711
Bowling Green *(G-1984)*
▼ Martin Pultrusion Group Inc ....G 440 439-9130
Cleveland *(G-5626)*
Martz Mold & Machine Inc ....G 330 928-2159
Cuyahoga Falls *(G-7897)*
Master Craft Products Inc ....F 216 281-5910
Cleveland *(G-5631)*
Master Marking Company Inc ....F 330 688-6797
Stow *(G-17604)*
Match Mold & Machine Inc ....E 330 830-5503
Massillon *(G-13022)*
Maumee Pattern Company ....E 419 693-4968
Toledo *(G-18403)*
Maxtool Company Limited ....G 937 415-5776
Dayton *(G-8334)*
McAfee Tool & Die Inc ....E 330 896-9555
Uniontown *(G-18927)*
McRon Finance Corp ....A 513 487-5000
Cincinnati *(G-3990)*
MD Tool & Die Inc ....G 440 647-6456
Wellington *(G-19586)*
Mdf Enterprises LLC ....G 937 640-3436
Dayton *(G-8336)*
Mdf Tool Corporation ....F 440 237-2277
North Royalton *(G-15287)*
Medway Tool Corp ....E 937 335-7717
Troy *(G-18687)*

Employee Codes: A=Over 500 employees, B=251-500
C=101-250, D=51-100, E=20-50, F=10-19, G=3-9
2019 Harris Ohio
Industrial Directory
955

35 INDUSTRIAL AND COMMERCIAL MACHINERY AND COMPUTER EQUIPMENT

Company	Code	Phone
Meese Inc — Ashtabula (G-785)	D	440 998-1202
Meggitt (erlanger) LLC — Cincinnati (G-4000)	D	513 851-5550
Mercury Machine Co — Solon (G-17191)	D	440 349-3222
Metal & Wire Products Company — Salem (G-16760)	D	330 332-9448
▲ Metalex Manufacturing Inc — Blue Ash (G-1820)	C	513 489-0507
Metro Mech Inc — Cleveland (G-5662)	G	216 641-6262
Metro Tool & Die Co Inc — Englewood (G-9368)	G	937 836-8242
Meyer Machine Tool Company — Columbus (G-7176)	G	614 235-0039
Miami Valley Punch & Mfg — Dayton (G-8347)	E	937 237-0533
▲ Mid-Ohio Products Inc — Hilliard (G-10840)	D	614 771-2795
Midwest Industrial Specialties — Galena (G-10116)	G	740 815-0541
▲ Midwest Mold & Texture Corp — Batavia (G-1165)	E	513 732-1300
Midwest Tool & Engineering Co — Dayton (G-8356)	G	937 224-0756
Mikan Die and Tool LLC — Cleveland (G-5684)	G	216 265-2811
Milacron Holdings Corp — Blue Ash (G-1821)	D	513 487-5000
▲ Milacron Plas Tech Group LLC — Batavia (G-1168)	C	513 536-2000
Milacron Plas Tech Group LLC — Mount Orab (G-14447)	G	937 444-2532
Misumi Investment USA Corp — Dayton (G-8363)	E	937 859-5111
Modern Manufacturing Inc — Cincinnati (G-4039)	F	513 251-3600
Mold Crafters Inc — Dayton (G-8364)	G	937 426-3179
Mold Shop Inc — Sylvania (G-17951)	F	419 829-2041
Mold Solutions — Oberlin (G-15502)	G	800 948-4947
Mold Surface Textures — Kent (G-11357)	G	330 678-8590
Mold-Rite Plastics LLC — Twinsburg (G-18821)	G	330 405-7739
Moldmakers Inc — Kenton (G-11414)	F	419 673-0902
MOM Tools LLC — Cleveland (G-5702)	G	216 283-4014
Monarch Products Co — Minerva (G-14195)	E	330 868-7717
▲ Morgal Machine Tool Co — Springfield (G-17451)	D	937 325-5561
Mosbro Machine and Tool Inc — Northfield (G-15320)	G	330 467-0913
▼ Mtd Holdings Inc — Valley City (G-19052)	B	330 225-2600
Multi Form Mfg — Stow (G-17608)	G	330 922-1933
Mutual Tool LLC — Tipp City (G-18124)	D	937 667-5818
N N Metal Stampings Inc — Pioneer (G-16086)	E	419 737-2311
National Mold Remediation — Columbus (G-7211)	G	614 231-6653
National Pattern Mfg Co — Orrville (G-15605)	F	330 682-6871
National Roller Die Inc — Willoughby (G-20386)	F	440 951-3850
National Steel Rule Die LLC — Vandalia (G-19141)	G	937 667-0967
NBC Industries Inc — Cleveland (G-5731)	F	216 651-9800
Nelson Tool Corporation — Sunbury (G-17892)	F	740 965-1894
◆ Nesco Inc — Cleveland (G-5741)	E	440 461-6000
New Bremen Machine & Tool Co — New Bremen (G-14657)	E	419 629-3295
New Castings Inc — Akron (G-295)	C	330 645-6653
New Die Inc — Toledo (G-18422)	E	419 726-7581
Neway Stamping & Mfg Inc — Willoughby (G-20388)	F	440 951-8500
Nichols Mold Inc — Ravenna (G-16391)	G	330 297-9719
Noble Tool Corp — Dayton (G-8381)	E	937 461-4040
▲ Nordson Xaloy Incorporated — Youngstown (G-20977)	C	724 656-5600
▲ Northeast Tire Molds Inc — Akron (G-302)	G	330 376-6107
Norwalk Precast Molds Inc — Norwalk (G-15410)	E	419 668-1639
Numerics Unlimited Inc — New Carlisle (G-14675)	E	937 849-0100
▲ Oakley Die & Mold Co — Mason (G-12918)	E	513 754-8500
Ogs Tool & Manufacturing — Mansfield (G-12495)	E	419 524-6200
Ohio Associated Entps LLC — Painesville (G-15770)	E	440 354-3148
Ohio Specialty Dies LLC — North Jackson (G-15151)	G	330 538-3396
Ohio Tool & Jig Grind Inc — Dayton (G-8400)	E	937 415-0692
Omega Tool & Die Inc — Dayton (G-8404)	F	937 890-2350
Omni Manufacturing — Saint Marys (G-16692)	G	419 394-7424
▲ Omni Manufacturing Inc — Saint Marys (G-16693)	D	419 394-7424
Omni Manufacturing Inc — Saint Marys (G-16694)	F	419 394-7424
Orick Stamping — Elida (G-9197)	D	419 331-0600
OSG Usa Inc — Mason (G-12919)	F	513 755-3360
P J Tool Company Inc — Dayton (G-8414)	G	937 254-2817
P O McIntire Company — Wickliffe (G-20221)	E	440 269-1848
PA MA Inc — Strongsville (G-17776)	G	440 846-3799
Pace Mold & Machine LLC — Massillon (G-13037)	G	330 879-1777
Pacific Tool & Die Co — Brunswick (G-2223)	F	330 273-7363
Paradise Mold & Die LLC — Cleveland (G-5837)	G	216 362-1945
Paramount Stamping & Wldg Co — Cleveland (G-5840)	D	216 631-1755
Part Rite Inc — North Royalton (G-15294)	G	216 362-4100
Penco Tool LLC — Ashtabula (G-795)	E	440 998-1116
Pendleton Mold & Machine LLC — Ashtabula (G-796)	G	440 998-0041
Perfection Mold & Machine Co — Twinsburg (G-18835)	F	330 784-5435
Perry Welding Service Inc — Twinsburg (G-18836)	F	330 425-2211
Phillips Mch & Stamping Corp — New Franklin (G-14696)	G	330 882-6714
Pier Tool & Die Inc — Columbia Station (G-6443)	F	440 236-3188
Pines Manufacturing Inc — Westlake (G-20142)	G	440 835-5553
Pioneer Precision Tool Inc — Lebanon (G-11684)	G	513 932-8805
Pitco Products Inc — Dayton (G-8427)	F	513 228-7245
▲ Plastic Enterprises Inc — Elyria (G-9312)	E	440 324-3240
Plastic Mold Technology Inc — Barberton (G-1095)	G	330 848-4921
Porter Precision Products Co — Cincinnati (G-4173)	D	513 385-1569
Positool Technologies Inc — Brunswick (G-2227)	G	330 220-4002
Precise Tool Inc — Piqua (G-16156)	G	937 778-3441
Precision Component Inds LLC — Canton (G-2790)	E	330 477-1052
Precision Details Inc — Jackson Center (G-11214)	F	937 596-0068
Precision Die Masters — Mentor (G-13552)	F	440 255-1204
Preferred Pump & Equipment LP — Springfield (G-17475)	G	937 322-4000
Premere Enterprises Inc — Bolivar (G-1922)	G	330 874-3000
Premiere Mold and Machine Co — Bolivar (G-1923)	G	330 874-3000
Preuss Mold & Die — Toledo (G-18481)	G	419 729-9100
Prime Industries Inc — Lorain (G-12113)	E	440 288-3626
Prime Time Machine Inc — Willoughby (G-20411)	G	440 942-7410
Product Tooling Inc — Sunbury (G-17898)	G	740 524-2061
Production Design Services Inc — Dayton (G-8446)	D	937 866-3377
Producto Dieco Corporation — Solon (G-17219)	F	440 542-0000
Progage Inc — Mentor (G-13558)	F	440 951-4477
Progress Tool & Stamping Inc — Minster (G-14223)	E	419 628-2384
Progressive Machine Die Inc — Macedonia (G-12321)	G	330 405-6600
Progrssive Molding Bolivar Inc — Bolivar (G-1925)	C	330 874-3000
Promac Inc — Enon (G-9385)	F	937 864-1961
Promold Inc — Tallmadge (G-18001)	F	330 633-3532
▲ Prospect Mold & Die Company — Cuyahoga Falls (G-7909)	D	330 929-3311
▲ Proto Plastics Inc — Tipp City (G-18129)	F	937 667-8416
▲ PSK Steel Corp — Hubbard (G-11009)	E	330 759-1251
Puehler Tool Co — Cleveland (G-5934)	G	216 447-0101
Pyramid Mold Inc — Kent (G-11370)	F	330 673-5200
Qualiform Inc — Wadsworth (G-19268)	E	330 336-6777
Quality Tooling Systems Inc — Medina (G-13326)	F	330 722-5025
Queen City Tool Works Inc — Fairfield (G-9555)	G	513 874-0111
R & R Machine & Tool Co — Cleveland (G-5948)	G	216 281-7609
R K S Tool & Die Inc — Fairfield (G-9557)	G	513 870-0225
R M Tool & Die Inc — Strongsville (G-17780)	F	440 238-6459
R T & T Machining Co Inc — Mentor (G-13571)	F	440 974-8479
▲ Rage Corporation — Hilliard (G-10857)	D	614 771-4771
Ram Tool Inc — Dayton (G-8463)	G	937 277-0717
Rapid Machine Inc — Pioneer (G-16094)	F	419 737-2377
Rapid Mold Repair & Machine — Akron (G-343)	G	330 253-1000
▲ Raymath Company — Troy (G-18697)	C	937 335-1860
Raymonds Tool & Gauge LLC — Montpelier (G-14317)	F	419 485-8340
▲ Ready Technology Inc — Dayton (G-8466)	F	937 866-7200
Regal Metal Products Co — Minerva (G-14198)	E	330 868-6343
Regal Metal Products Co — Minerva (G-14199)	F	330 868-6343
Renco Mold Inc — Dayton (G-8472)	G	937 233-3233
Reserve Industries Inc — Bay Village (G-1208)	E	440 871-2796
Reuther Mold & Mfg Co Inc — Cuyahoga Falls (G-7913)	D	330 923-5266
▲ Reymond Products Intl Inc — New Philadelphia (G-14796)	E	330 339-3583
Rhinestahl Corporation — Mason (G-12934)	E	513 229-5300
Richard Paskiet Machinists — Canal Fulton (G-2492)	G	330 854-4160
Rme Machining Co — Cincinnati (G-4275)	G	513 541-3328
Rmt Corporation — Dayton (G-8481)	F	513 942-8308
Rock Iron Corporation — Crestline (G-7800)	G	419 529-9411
Rockstedt Tool & Die Inc — Brunswick (G-2235)	F	330 273-9000
Ron-Al Mold & Machine Inc — Kent (G-11377)	F	330 673-7919
Ronfeldt Associates Inc — Toledo (G-18506)	D	419 382-5641
Ronlen Industries Inc — Brunswick (G-2236)	E	330 273-6468

SIC SECTION
35 INDUSTRIAL AND COMMERCIAL MACHINERY AND COMPUTER EQUIPMENT

Ross Special Products Inc F 937 335-8406
Troy *(G-18700)*

Roto-Die Company Inc G 513 942-3500
West Chester *(G-19787)*

Rotocast Technologies Inc E 330 798-9091
Akron *(G-354)*

▲ Royer Technologies Inc G 937 743-6114
Saint Marys *(G-16698)*

RPM Carbide Die Inc E 419 894-6426
Arcadia *(G-626)*

Rural Products Inc G 419 298-2677
Edgerton *(G-9179)*

S-K Mold & Tool Company E 937 339-0299
Tipp City *(G-18132)*

S-K Mold & Tool Company E 937 339-0299
Troy *(G-18701)*

▲ Saehwa IMC Na Inc D 330 645-6653
Akron *(G-369)*

Saehwa IMC Na Inc D 419 752-4511
Akron *(G-368)*

Saint-Gobain Ceramics Plas Inc A 330 673-5860
Stow *(G-17624)*

Schmitmeyer Inc G 937 295-2091
Fort Loramie *(G-9804)*

Schuster Manufacturing Inc G 419 476-5800
Toledo *(G-18514)*

Seaway Pattern Mfg Inc E 419 865-5724
Toledo *(G-18516)*

Seilkop Industries Inc E 513 761-1035
Cincinnati *(G-4316)*

Seilkop Industries Inc E 513 353-3090
Miamitown *(G-13751)*

▼ Sekely Industries Inc C 248 844-9201
Salem *(G-16774)*

Select Machine Co Inc F 330 678-7676
Kent *(G-11384)*

Selzer Tool & Die Inc G 440 365-4124
Elyria *(G-9325)*

Shalix Inc F 216 941-3546
Cleveland *(G-6047)*

Shelburne Corp G 216 321-9177
Shaker Heights *(G-16936)*

Shiloh Automotive Inc E 330 558-2600
Valley City *(G-19061)*

Shiloh Corporation B 330 558-2600
Valley City *(G-19062)*

Shiloh Industries Inc A 330 558-2600
Valley City *(G-19065)*

◆ Shiloh Industries Inc G 330 558-2600
Valley City *(G-19066)*

Shook Tool Inc G 937 337-6471
Ansonia *(G-594)*

Short Run Machine Products Inc F 440 969-1313
Ashtabula *(G-804)*

Sivon Manufacturing LLC G 440 259-5505
Perry *(G-15912)*

Skribs Tool and Die Inc E 440 951-7774
Mentor *(G-13583)*

Skrl Die Casting Inc D 440 946-7200
Willoughby *(G-20431)*

Slabe Tool Company G 740 439-1647
Cambridge *(G-2456)*

Smithville Mfg Co E 330 345-5818
Wooster *(G-20655)*

Sni Inc G 937 427-9447
Beavercreek *(G-1363)*

Snyders Tool & Die Inc G 614 878-2205
Galloway *(G-10180)*

Space Age Coatings LLC G 937 275-5117
Dayton *(G-8514)*

Spectracam Ltd G 937 223-3805
Dayton *(G-8516)*

Spintech LLC F 937 912-3250
Xenia *(G-20791)*

▲ Sroka Industries Inc E 440 572-2811
Strongsville *(G-17795)*

▲ Stanco Precision Manufacturing G 937 274-1785
Dayton *(G-8524)*

Starkey Machinery Inc E 419 468-2560
Galion *(G-10157)*

Straight 72 Inc D 740 943-5730
Marysville *(G-12815)*

Suburban Metal Products Inc F 740 474-4237
Circleville *(G-4559)*

Sulecki Precision Products F 440 255-5454
Mentor *(G-13596)*

Sumitomo Elc Carbide Mfg Inc F 440 354-0600
Grand River *(G-10326)*

Sup-R-Die Inc E 216 252-3930
Cleveland *(G-6119)*

Sup-R-Die Inc G 330 688-7600
Stow *(G-17634)*

Superior Mold & Die Co E 330 688-8251
Munroe Falls *(G-14528)*

Supply Dynamics Inc E 513 965-2000
Loveland *(G-12238)*

Sure Tool & Manufacturing Co E 937 253-9111
Dayton *(G-8531)*

Sutterlin Machine & Tool Co F 440 357-0817
Mentor *(G-13598)*

Symbol Tool & Die Inc G 440 582-5989
North Royalton *(G-15304)*

T & W Tool & Machine Inc G 937 667-2039
Tipp City *(G-18135)*

Taft Tool & Production Co F 419 385-2576
Toledo *(G-18542)*

▲ Talent Tool & Die Inc E 440 239-8777
Berea *(G-1627)*

Tangible Solutions Inc G 937 912-4603
Fairborn *(G-9471)*

Tater Tool & Die Inc G 330 648-1148
Spencer *(G-17307)*

Taylor Tool & Die Inc G 937 845-1491
New Carlisle *(G-14678)*

▲ Te-Co Manufacturing LLC D 937 836-0961
Englewood *(G-9377)*

Tech Industries Inc E 216 861-7337
Cleveland *(G-6153)*

Tech Mold & Tool Co Inc G 937 667-8851
Tipp City *(G-18137)*

Technology House Ltd E 440 248-3025
Streetsboro *(G-17701)*

Tempcraft Corporation C 216 391-3885
Cleveland *(G-6157)*

Tessec Manufacturing Svcs LLC E 937 985-3552
Dayton *(G-8553)*

Tetra Mold & Tool Inc E 937 845-1651
New Carlisle *(G-14679)*

Tig Wood & Die Inc F 937 849-6741
New Carlisle *(G-14680)*

Tipco Punch Inc E 513 874-9140
Hamilton *(G-10611)*

Tm Machine & Tool Inc G 419 478-0310
Toledo *(G-18554)*

▲ Toledo Molding & Die Inc D 419 470-3950
Toledo *(G-18564)*

Toledo Molding & Die Inc C 419 476-0581
Toledo *(G-18563)*

▲ Toledo Tool and Die Co Inc E 419 476-4422
Toledo *(G-18574)*

▲ Tom Smith Industries Inc C 937 832-1555
Englewood *(G-9378)*

Tomahawk Tool Supply G 419 485-8737
Montpelier *(G-14319)*

Tomco Industries G 330 652-7531
Mineral Ridge *(G-14172)*

Tomco Tool Inc G 937 322-5768
Springfield *(G-17507)*

Tool Technologies Van Dyke F 937 349-4900
Marysville *(G-12817)*

Toolcraft Products Inc D 937 223-8271
Dayton *(G-8561)*

Tooling & Components Corp F 419 478-9122
Toledo *(G-18576)*

Tooling Connection Inc G 419 594-3339
Oakwood *(G-15475)*

Tooling Technology LLC D 937 295-3672
Fort Loramie *(G-9810)*

Tooling Zone Inc E 937 550-4180
Springboro *(G-17356)*

Toolrite Manufacturing Inc F 937 278-1962
Dayton *(G-8562)*

Top Tool & Die Inc F 216 267-5878
Cleveland *(G-6187)*

Torr Metal Products Inc E 216 671-1616
Cleveland *(G-6189)*

Tower Tool & Manufacturing Co F 330 425-1623
Twinsburg *(G-18864)*

Tracker Machine Inc G 330 482-4086
Columbiana *(G-6483)*

Tradye Machine & Tool Inc G 740 625-7550
Centerburg *(G-2994)*

Tree City Mold & Machine Co G 330 673-9807
Kent *(G-11396)*

Trexler Rubber Co Inc E 330 296-9677
Ravenna *(G-16414)*

Tri-Craft Inc E 440 826-1050
Cleveland *(G-6206)*

Tri-R Dies Inc E 330 758-8050
Youngstown *(G-21053)*

Trico Machine Products Corp F 216 662-4194
Cleveland *(G-6214)*

▲ Trim Parts Inc E 513 934-0815
Lebanon *(G-11702)*

Trim Tool & Machine Inc E 216 889-1916
Cleveland *(G-6215)*

Trimline Die Corporation E 440 355-6900
Lagrange *(G-11494)*

Troy Precision Carbide Die F 440 834-4477
Burton *(G-2374)*

◆ Troy West LLC G 937 339-2192
Troy *(G-18715)*

Tru-Tex International Corp E 513 825-8844
Cincinnati *(G-4442)*

▲ Trucut Incorporated D 330 938-9806
Sebring *(G-16896)*

True Industries Inc E 330 296-4342
Ravenna *(G-16416)*

True Kote Inc G 419 334-8813
Fremont *(G-10056)*

Turbo Machine & Tool Inc G 216 651-1940
Cleveland *(G-6223)*

Turbo-Mold Inc G 440 352-2530
Painesville *(G-15792)*

Twin Tool LLC G 937 435-8946
Dayton *(G-8574)*

U S Alloy Die Corp F 216 749-9700
Cleveland *(G-6227)*

United Extrusion Dies Inc F 330 533-2915
Canfield *(G-2552)*

United Finshg & Die Cutng Inc F 216 881-0239
Cleveland *(G-6233)*

▲ Universal Tire Molds Inc E 330 253-5101
Akron *(G-422)*

Universal Tool Technology LLC E 937 222-4608
Dayton *(G-8576)*

Unlimited Machine and Tool LLC F 419 269-1730
Toledo *(G-18586)*

V I P Printing & Design G 513 777-7468
West Chester *(G-19913)*

Valley Tool & Die Inc D 440 237-0160
North Royalton *(G-15309)*

Van Wert Machine Inc F 419 692-6836
Delphos *(G-8763)*

Velocity Concept Dev Group LLC G 740 685-2637
Byesville *(G-2395)*

Village Plastics Co G 330 753-0100
Barberton *(G-1112)*

Vinyl Tool & Die Company Inc F 330 782-0254
Youngstown *(G-21066)*

Vinyltech Inc E 330 538-0369
North Jackson *(G-15158)*

▲ Vmi Americas Inc E 330 929-6800
Stow *(G-17641)*

Voisard Tool LLC E 937 526-5451
Russia *(G-16614)*

▲ Vulcan Tool Company G 937 253-6194
Dayton *(G-8581)*

Walest Incorporated G 216 362-8110
Cleveland *(G-6286)*

Walker Tool & Machine Co F 419 661-8000
Perrysburg *(G-16024)*

Wapak Tool & Die Inc G 419 738-6215
Wapakoneta *(G-19359)*

Ward Mold & Machine G 740 472-5303
Woodsfield *(G-20549)*

Warren Fabricating Corporation E 330 544-4101
Niles *(G-15039)*

▲ Wauseon Machine & Mfg Inc D 419 337-0940
Wauseon *(G-19537)*

Waverly Tool Co Ltd G 740 988-4831
Beaver *(G-1294)*

Wayne Trail Technologies Inc D 937 295-2120
Fort Loramie *(G-9811)*

Weiss Industries Inc E 419 526-2480
Mansfield *(G-12539)*

Welage Corporation F 513 681-2300
Cincinnati *(G-4495)*

▲ Wentworth Mold Inc Electra D 937 898-8460
Vandalia *(G-19151)*

White Machine Inc G 440 237-3282
North Royalton *(G-15311)*

Williams Steel Rule Die Co F 216 431-3232
Cleveland *(G-6311)*

Windsor Tool Inc F 216 671-1900
Cleveland *(G-6313)*

Wire Shop Inc E 440 354-6842
Mentor *(G-13628)*

▲ WLS Stamping Co D 216 271-5100
Cleveland *(G-6318)*

S I C

Employee Codes: A=Over 500 employees, B=251-500
C=101-250, D=51-100, E=20-50, F=10-19, G=3-9
2019 Harris Ohio
Industrial Directory
957

Wrena LLC......E...... 937 667-4403
Tipp City *(G-18146)*
Wt Tool & Die Inc......G...... 330 332-2254
Salem *(G-16782)*
▲ **Wurtec Manufacturing Service**......E...... 419 726-1066
Toledo *(G-18602)*
XCEL Mold and Machine Inc......F...... 330 499-8450
Canton *(G-2867)*
Youngstown Die Development......G...... 330 755-0722
Struthers *(G-17826)*
Youngstown Tool & Die Company......D...... 330 747-4464
Youngstown *(G-21083)*
Yugo Mold Inc......F...... 330 606-0710
Akron *(G-441)*

3545 Machine Tool Access

A & B Machine Inc......E...... 937 492-8662
Sidney *(G-17011)*
Able Tool Corporation......E...... 513 733-8989
Cincinnati *(G-3288)*
Advanced Holding Designs Inc......F...... 330 928-4456
Cuyahoga Falls *(G-7831)*
Advantage Tool Supply Inc......G...... 330 896-8869
Uniontown *(G-18907)*
Aeroll Engineering Corp......G...... 216 481-2266
Cleveland *(G-4632)*
▲ **Ajax Industries Inc**......E...... 614 272-6944
Columbus *(G-6556)*
Akron Gear & Engineering Inc......E...... 330 773-6608
Akron *(G-41)*
◆ **Alliance Knife Inc**......E...... 513 367-9000
Harrison *(G-10631)*
▲ **Allied Machine & Engrg Corp**......C...... 330 343-4283
Dover *(G-8803)*
American Truck Equipment Inc......G...... 216 362-0400
Cleveland *(G-4699)*
Anchor Lamina America Inc......E...... 330 952-1595
Medina *(G-13224)*
Angstrom Corp......G...... 330 405-0524
Twinsburg *(G-18733)*
▲ **Angstrom Precision Metals LLC**......D...... 440 255-6700
Mentor *(G-13388)*
Antwerp Tool & Die Inc......F...... 419 258-5271
Antwerp *(G-596)*
Apollo Manufacturing Co LLC......E...... 440 951-9972
Mentor *(G-13390)*
Apollo Products Inc......F...... 440 269-8551
Willoughby *(G-20275)*
Atlantic Tool & Die Company......C...... 330 769-4500
Seville *(G-16910)*
B & R Machine Co Inc......F...... 216 961-7370
Cleveland *(G-4784)*
BAP Manufacturing Inc......E...... 419 332-5041
Fremont *(G-9995)*
Bee Jax Inc......G...... 330 373-0500
Warren *(G-19375)*
Bender Engineering Company......G...... 330 938-2355
Beloit *(G-1568)*
▲ **Big Chief Manufacturing Ltd**......E...... 513 934-3888
Lebanon *(G-11637)*
Blue Ash Tool & Die Co Inc......F...... 513 793-4530
Blue Ash *(G-1737)*
Bully Tools Inc......E...... 740 282-5834
Steubenville *(G-17529)*
Capital Tool Company......E...... 216 661-5750
Cleveland *(G-4871)*
Carbide Probes Inc......E...... 937 490-2994
Beavercreek *(G-1304)*
Carlton Natco......G...... 216 451-5588
Cleveland *(G-4878)*
Certified Comparator Products......G...... 937 426-9677
Beavercreek *(G-1353)*
▲ **Certified Tool & Grinding Inc**......G...... 937 865-5934
Miamisburg *(G-13648)*
Chardon Tool & Supply Co Inc......E...... 440 286-6440
Chardon *(G-3104)*
Chart Tech Tool Inc......E...... 937 667-3543
Tipp City *(G-18108)*
Chippewa Tool & Mfg Co......F...... 419 849-2790
Woodville *(G-20551)*
Cleveland Carbide Tool Co......G...... 440 974-1155
Mentor *(G-13414)*
Cleveland Specialty Insptn Svc......F...... 440 578-1046
Mentor *(G-13415)*
Cnc Indexing Feeding Tech LLC......G...... 513 770-4200
Mason *(G-12851)*
Coleys Inc......F...... 440 967-5630
Vermilion *(G-19158)*
Commercial Grinding Services......E...... 330 273-5040
Medina *(G-13238)*
Connell Limited Partnership......D...... 877 534-8986
Northfield *(G-15316)*
Container Graphics Corp......D...... 419 531-5133
Toledo *(G-18241)*
Contour Tool Inc......E...... 440 365-7333
North Ridgeville *(G-15216)*
▲ **Covert Manufacturing Inc**......B...... 419 468-1761
Galion *(G-10130)*
Cowles Industrial Tool Co LLC......E...... 330 799-9100
Austintown *(G-932)*
Cr Supply LLC......G...... 440 759-5408
Mentor *(G-13425)*
Custom Carbide Cutter Inc......F...... 513 851-6363
West Chester *(G-19847)*
Dark Diamond Tools Inc......G...... 440 701-6424
Chardon *(G-3107)*
Dayton Precision Punch......G...... 937 275-8700
Dayton *(G-8142)*
▲ **Dayton Progress Corporation**......A...... 937 859-5111
Dayton *(G-8143)*
Delta Machine & Tool Co......F...... 216 524-2477
Cleveland *(G-5083)*
Diamond Products Limited......G...... 440 323-4616
Elyria *(G-9241)*
Diamond Reserve Inc......F...... 440 892-7877
Westlake *(G-20108)*
▲ **Diamonds Products LLC**......G...... 440 323-4616
Elyria *(G-9242)*
Dillon Manufacturing Inc......F...... 937 325-8482
Springfield *(G-17388)*
◆ **Drt Mfg Co**......C...... 937 297-6670
Dayton *(G-8171)*
E & J Demark Inc......E...... 419 337-5866
Wauseon *(G-19513)*
E & J Demark Inc......G...... 419 337-5866
Wauseon *(G-19514)*
Edge-Rite Tools Inc......F...... 216 642-0966
Cleveland *(G-5157)*
Electrofuel Industries Inc......G...... 937 783-2846
Batavia *(G-1141)*
Ellison Technologies Inc......G...... 513 874-2736
Hamilton *(G-10553)*
Evandy Co Inc......G...... 216 518-9713
Cleveland *(G-5199)*
Eversharpe Deburring Tool Co......G...... 513 988-6240
Trenton *(G-18618)*
Expert Regrind Service Inc......G...... 937 526-5662
Versailles *(G-19180)*
Feedall Inc......F...... 440 942-8100
Willoughby *(G-20321)*
Ferguson Tools Inc......E...... 419 298-2327
Edgerton *(G-9174)*
Fischer Special Tooling Corp......F...... 440 951-8411
Mentor *(G-13443)*
Flex-E-On Inc......F...... 330 928-4496
Cuyahoga Falls *(G-7868)*
Fox Tool Co Inc......E...... 330 928-3402
Cuyahoga Falls *(G-7869)*
Frecon Engineering......G...... 513 874-8981
West Chester *(G-19707)*
▲ **Frecon Technologies Inc**......F...... 513 874-8981
West Chester *(G-19708)*
▼ **Furukawa Rock Drill USA Co Ltd**......E...... 330 673-5826
Kent *(G-11325)*
Galaxy Products Inc......G...... 419 843-7337
Sylvania *(G-17940)*
Gem Tool LLC......G...... 216 771-8444
Cleveland *(G-5303)*
George Whalley Company......E...... 216 453-0099
Fairport Harbor *(G-9623)*
◆ **Glassline Corporation**......C...... 419 666-9712
Perrysburg *(G-15958)*
◆ **Gleason Metrology Systems Corp**......E...... 937 384-8901
Dayton *(G-8223)*
Greentec Precision Inc......G...... 937 431-1840
Beavercreek *(G-1319)*
H & S Tool Inc......F...... 330 335-1536
Wadsworth *(G-19244)*
H Duane Leis Acquisitions......E...... 937 835-5621
New Lebanon *(G-14710)*
H E Long Company......F...... 513 899-2610
Morrow *(G-14411)*
H Machining Inc......F...... 419 636-6890
Bryan *(G-2283)*
H3d Tool Corporation......G...... 740 498-5181
Newcomerstown *(G-14974)*
Hammill Manufacturing Co......D...... 419 476-0789
Maumee *(G-13115)*
◆ **Hapco Inc**......F...... 330 678-9353
Kent *(G-11331)*
Herco Inc......E...... 740 498-5181
Newcomerstown *(G-14975)*
HI Carb Corp......F...... 216 486-5000
Cleveland *(G-5401)*
HI Tech Tool Corporation......G...... 513 346-4061
Monroe *(G-14266)*
▲ **High Quality Tools Inc**......F...... 440 975-9684
Eastlake *(G-9113)*
▲ **Hudson Supply Company Inc**......G...... 216 518-3000
Cleveland *(G-5424)*
Hydra Air Equipment Inc......G...... 330 274-2222
Mantua *(G-12548)*
Hykon Manufacturing Company......G...... 330 821-8889
Alliance *(G-477)*
Hyper Tool Company......F...... 440 543-5151
Chagrin Falls *(G-3051)*
Imco Carbide Tool Inc......D...... 419 661-6313
Perrysburg *(G-15965)*
Independent Die & Mfg Co......G...... 216 362-6778
Cleveland *(G-5450)*
Interstate Tool Corporation......E...... 216 671-1077
Cleveland *(G-5471)*
J and L Manufacturing Inc......G...... 937 492-0008
Sidney *(G-17047)*
▲ **Jergens Inc**......C...... 216 486-5540
Cleveland *(G-5495)*
Jerry Tools Inc......F...... 513 242-3211
Cincinnati *(G-3871)*
JM Performance Products Inc......F...... 440 357-1234
Fairport Harbor *(G-9624)*
Johnson Bros Rubber Co Inc......E...... 419 752-4814
Greenwich *(G-10404)*
Jones Industrial Service LLC......G...... 419 287-4553
Pemberville *(G-15886)*
Jump N Sales LLC......G...... 513 509-7661
Fairfield Township *(G-9583)*
Kaeper Machine Inc......E...... 440 974-1010
Mentor *(G-13488)*
▲ **Kalt Manufacturing Company**......D...... 440 327-2102
North Ridgeville *(G-15235)*
Karma Metal Products Inc......F...... 419 524-4371
Mansfield *(G-12466)*
Keb Industries Inc......G...... 440 953-4623
Willoughby *(G-20351)*
Kennametal Inc......C...... 440 437-5131
Orwell *(G-15633)*
Kennametal Inc......D...... 216 898-6120
Cleveland *(G-5527)*
Kennametal Inc......C...... 419 877-5358
Whitehouse *(G-20192)*
Kennametal Inc......C...... 440 349-5151
Solon *(G-17183)*
Kilroy Company......D...... 440 951-8700
Eastlake *(G-9117)*
▲ **Knb Tools of America Inc**......F...... 614 733-0400
Plain City *(G-16199)*
▲ **Kyocera SGS Precision Tools**......E...... 330 688-6667
Munroe Falls *(G-14524)*
Kyocera SGS Precision Tools......E...... 330 688-6667
Cuyahoga Falls *(G-7890)*
Kyocera SGS Precision Tools......C...... 330 686-4151
Cuyahoga Falls *(G-7891)*
Kyocera SGS Precision Tools......C...... 330 922-1953
Cuyahoga Falls *(G-7892)*
L C Smith Co......G...... 440 327-1251
Elyria *(G-9283)*
Lange Precision Inc......F...... 513 530-9500
Blue Ash *(G-1802)*
Lear Manufacturing Inc......G...... 440 327-4545
North Ridgeville *(G-15238)*
Levan Enterprises Inc......E...... 330 923-9797
Stow *(G-17601)*
Lord Corporation......C...... 937 278-9431
Dayton *(G-8315)*
LS Starrett Company......D...... 440 835-0005
Westlake *(G-20129)*
M A Harrison Mfg Co Inc......E...... 440 965-4306
Wakeman *(G-19287)*
M S C Industries Inc......G...... 440 474-8788
Rome *(G-16564)*
▲ **Machining Technologies Inc**......E...... 419 862-3110
Elmore *(G-9206)*
Master Carbide Tools Company......F...... 440 352-1112
Painesville *(G-15760)*
Matrix Tool & Machine Inc......E...... 440 255-0300
Mentor *(G-13512)*
Matvest Inc......E...... 614 487-8720
Columbus *(G-7161)*
Mdf Tool Corporation......F...... 440 237-2277
North Royalton *(G-15287)*

Medina Blanking Inc ....C.... 330 558-2300
Valley City *(G-19049)*

Medway Tool Corp ....E.... 937 335-7717
Troy *(G-18687)*

Melin Tool Company Inc ....D.... 216 362-4200
Cleveland *(G-5654)*

▲ **Metalex Manufacturing Inc** ....C.... 513 489-0507
Blue Ash *(G-1820)*

Midwest Tool & Engineering Co ....E.... 937 224-0756
Dayton *(G-8356)*

Mikan Die and Tool LLC ....G.... 216 265-2811
Cleveland *(G-5684)*

Monaghan & Associates Inc ....E.... 937 253-7706
Dayton *(G-8365)*

Morgan Precision Instrs LLC ....G.... 330 896-0846
Akron *(G-287)*

National Machine Company ....E.... 330 688-2584
Stow *(G-17612)*

National Rolled Thread Die Co ....F.... 440 232-8101
Cleveland *(G-5728)*

▲ **Nook Industries Inc** ....C.... 216 271-7900
Cleveland *(G-5756)*

North-West Tool Co ....G.... 937 278-7995
Dayton *(G-8383)*

Northeast Broach & Tool ....G.... 440 918-0048
Eastlake *(G-9126)*

▲ **Oakley Die & Mold Co** ....E.... 513 754-8500
Mason *(G-12918)*

Obars Machine and Tool Company ....E.... 419 535-6307
Toledo *(G-18433)*

▼ **Ohio Broach & Machine Company** ....E.... 440 946-1040
Willoughby *(G-20393)*

Ohio Drill & Tool Co ....G.... 330 525-7161
Homeworth *(G-10990)*

Ohio Drill & Tool Co ....E.... 330 525-7717
Homeworth *(G-10989)*

▲ **Osg-Sterling Die Inc** ....D.... 216 267-1300
Parma *(G-15825)*

P F S Incorporated ....G.... 440 582-1620
Cleveland *(G-5829)*

P O McIntire Company ....E.... 440 269-1848
Wickliffe *(G-20221)*

Pakk Systems LLC ....G.... 440 839-9999
Wakeman *(G-19288)*

Patriot Mfg Group Inc ....D.... 937 746-2117
Carlisle *(G-2896)*

Pemco Inc ....E.... 216 524-2990
Cleveland *(G-5862)*

Performance Superabrasives LLC ....G.... 440 946-7171
Mentor *(G-13547)*

Pike Tool & Manufacturing Co ....G.... 740 947-7462
Waverly *(G-19558)*

PMC Gage Inc ....E.... 440 953-1672
Willoughby *(G-20404)*

PMC Mercury ....G.... 440 953-3300
Willoughby *(G-20405)*

Polhe Tool Inc ....G.... 419 476-2433
Toledo *(G-18473)*

Positrol Inc ....E.... 513 272-0500
Cincinnati *(G-4175)*

Precise Tool & Mfg Corp ....F.... 216 524-1500
Cleveland *(G-5907)*

Precision Component Inds LLC ....E.... 330 477-1052
Canton *(G-2790)*

Precision Gage & Tool Company ....E.... 937 866-9666
Dayton *(G-8432)*

Preston ....F.... 740 788-8208
Newark *(G-14913)*

Production Design Services Inc ....D.... 937 866-3377
Dayton *(G-8446)*

Productive Carbides Inc ....G.... 513 771-7092
Cincinnati *(G-4215)*

Quality Cutter Grinding Co ....F.... 216 362-6444
Cleveland *(G-5941)*

R & J Tool Inc ....F.... 937 833-3200
Brookville *(G-2183)*

R A Heller Company ....F.... 513 771-6100
Cincinnati *(G-4242)*

R Dunn Mold Inc ....G.... 937 773-3388
Piqua *(G-16158)*

R T & T Machining Co Inc ....F.... 440 974-8479
Mentor *(G-13571)*

Red Head Brass Inc ....G.... 330 567-2903
Shreve *(G-17007)*

Reed Machinery Inc ....G.... 330 220-6668
Brunswick *(G-2234)*

▼ **Regal Diamond Products Corp** ....E.... 440 944-7700
Wickliffe *(G-20229)*

Retention Knob Supply & Mfg Co ....F.... 937 686-6405
Huntsville *(G-11088)*

▲ **Rex International USA Inc** ....E.... 800 321-7950
Ashtabula *(G-803)*

Ridge Tool Manufacturing Co ....A.... 440 323-5581
Elyria *(G-9322)*

Riten Industries Incorporated ....E.... 740 335-5353
Wshngtn CT Hs *(G-20742)*

Roehlers Machine Products ....G.... 937 354-4401
Mount Victory *(G-14522)*

▲ **Rol - Tech Inc** ....C.... 214 905-8050
Fort Loramie *(G-9803)*

Rossi Machinery Services Inc ....G.... 419 281-4488
Ashland *(G-744)*

Rotairtech Inc ....G.... 937 435-8178
Kettering *(G-11441)*

Roto Tech Inc ....E.... 937 859-8503
Dayton *(G-8485)*

Roto-Die Inc ....G.... 216 531-4800
Cleveland *(G-6007)*

▲ **Royer Technologies Inc** ....G.... 937 743-6114
Saint Marys *(G-16698)*

▲ **Schober USA Inc** ....G.... 513 489-7393
Fairfield *(G-9561)*

Schumann Enterprises Inc ....E.... 216 267-6850
Cleveland *(G-6033)*

▲ **Setco Sales Company** ....D.... 513 941-5110
Cincinnati *(G-4328)*

Sharp Tool Service Inc ....E.... 330 273-4144
Cleveland *(G-6048)*

Sharper Tooling ....G.... 330 667-2960
Litchfield *(G-11987)*

▲ **Shook Manufactured Pdts Inc** ....G.... 330 848-9780
Akron *(G-375)*

Shook Manufactured Pdts Inc ....G.... 440 247-9130
Chagrin Falls *(G-3029)*

Silver Tool Inc ....E.... 937 865-0012
Miamisburg *(G-13717)*

▲ **Skidmore-Wilhelm Mfg Company** ....E.... 216 481-4774
Solon *(G-17232)*

Sorbothane Inc ....E.... 330 678-9444
Kent *(G-11388)*

Sp3 Cutting Tools Inc ....G.... 937 667-4476
Tipp City *(G-18134)*

Spectrum Machine Inc ....E.... 330 626-3666
Streetsboro *(G-17699)*

Stanley Bittinger ....G.... 740 942-4302
Cadiz *(G-2401)*

Star Metal Products Co Inc ....D.... 440 899-7000
Westlake *(G-20161)*

▼ **Stark Industrial LLC** ....E.... 330 493-9773
North Canton *(G-15122)*

STC International Co Ltd ....G.... 561 308-6002
Lebanon *(G-11699)*

Sumitomo Elc Carbide Mfg Inc ....F.... 440 354-0600
Grand River *(G-10326)*

▲ **Superion Inc** ....E.... 937 374-0033
Xenia *(G-20793)*

Supplier Inspection Svcs Inc ....E.... 937 263-7097
Dayton *(G-8529)*

T M Industries Inc ....G.... 330 627-4410
Carrollton *(G-2930)*

Taft Tool & Production Co ....F.... 419 385-2576
Toledo *(G-18542)*

▲ **Te-Co Manufacturing LLC** ....D.... 937 836-0961
Englewood *(G-9377)*

Technidrill Systems Inc ....E.... 330 678-9980
Kent *(G-11393)*

Thaler Machine Company ....G.... 937 550-2400
Springboro *(G-17355)*

Tomco Tool Inc ....G.... 937 322-5768
Springfield *(G-17507)*

Tool Systems Inc ....F.... 440 461-6363
Cleveland *(G-6182)*

Tormaxx Co ....G.... 513 721-6299
Cincinnati *(G-4426)*

Troyke Manufacturing Company ....F.... 513 769-4242
Cincinnati *(G-4441)*

Uhrichsville Carbide Inc ....F.... 740 922-9197
Uhrichsville *(G-18899)*

United States Drill Head Co ....E.... 513 941-0300
Cincinnati *(G-4450)*

Voisard Tool LLC ....E.... 937 526-5451
Russia *(G-16614)*

Whip Guide Co ....F.... 440 543-5151
Chagrin Falls *(G-3090)*

Whitworth Knife Company ....G.... 513 321-9177
Cincinnati *(G-4507)*

William Darling Company Inc ....G.... 614 878-0085
Columbus *(G-7604)*

Wolff Tool & Manufacturing Co ....F.... 440 933-7797
Avon Lake *(G-1014)*

◆ **Worldwide Machine Tool LLC** ....G.... 614 496-9414
Lewis Center *(G-11788)*

Wright Buffing Wheel Company ....G.... 330 424-7887
Lisbon *(G-11983)*

X-Press Tool Inc ....E.... 330 225-8748
Brunswick *(G-2254)*

3546 Power Hand Tools

Air Tool Service Company ....F.... 440 701-1021
Mentor *(G-13379)*

▲ **Aircraft Dynamics Corporation** ....F.... 419 331-0371
Elida *(G-9193)*

Airmachinescom Inc ....G.... 330 759-1620
Youngstown *(G-20840)*

Alvords Yard & Garden Eqp ....G.... 440 286-2315
Chardon *(G-3098)*

Apex Tool Group LLC ....C.... 937 222-7871
Dayton *(G-8033)*

Black & Decker (us) Inc ....G.... 614 895-3112
Columbus *(G-6676)*

Black & Decker Corporation ....E.... 440 842-9100
Cleveland *(G-4816)*

◆ **Campbell Hausfeld LLC** ....C.... 513 367-4811
Cincinnati *(G-3439)*

Chicago Pneumatic Tool Co LLC ....G.... 704 883-3500
Broadview Heights *(G-2090)*

Corbett R Caudill Chipping Inc ....F.... 740 596-5984
Hamden *(G-10522)*

▲ **ET&f Fastening Systems Inc** ....F.... 800 248-2376
Solon *(G-17141)*

◆ **Furukawa Rock Drill Usa Inc** ....F.... 330 673-5826
Kent *(G-11324)*

▼ **Furukawa Rock Drill USA Co Ltd** ....E.... 330 673-5826
Kent *(G-11325)*

Galaxy Products Inc ....G.... 419 843-7337
Sylvania *(G-17940)*

Hall-Toledo Inc ....F.... 419 893-4334
Maumee *(G-13114)*

Huron Cement Products Company ....E.... 419 433-4161
Huron *(G-11096)*

Ingersoll-Rand Company ....E.... 419 633-6800
Bryan *(G-2291)*

Michabo Inc ....G.... 419 893-4334
Maumee *(G-13133)*

◆ **Npk Construction Equipment Inc** ....D.... 440 232-7900
Bedford *(G-1432)*

Ohio Drill & Tool Co ....E.... 330 525-7717
Homeworth *(G-10989)*

Rboog Industries LLC ....G.... 330 350-0396
Brunswick *(G-2233)*

▲ **Rex International USA Inc** ....E.... 800 321-7950
Ashtabula *(G-803)*

◆ **Ridge Tool Company** ....A.... 440 323-5581
Elyria *(G-9320)*

Ridge Tool Manufacturing Co ....A.... 440 323-5581
Elyria *(G-9322)*

Selbro Inc ....F.... 419 483-9918
Bellevue *(G-1544)*

Senco Brands Inc ....E.... 513 388-2833
Cincinnati *(G-4320)*

▲ **Senco Brands Inc** ....D.... 513 388-2000
Cincinnati *(G-3262)*

▲ **Sensource Global Sourcing LLC** ....G.... 513 659-8283
Cincinnati *(G-3263)*

Sewer Rodding Equipment Co ....E.... 419 991-2065
Lima *(G-11937)*

Stanley Access Tech LLC ....C.... 440 461-5500
Cleveland *(G-6093)*

Stanley Bittinger ....G.... 740 942-4302
Cadiz *(G-2401)*

▲ **Stanley Industrial & Auto LLC** ....D.... 614 755-7000
Westerville *(G-20025)*

Stevens Auto Parts & Towng ....G.... 740 988-2260
Jackson *(G-11195)*

Suburban Manufacturing Co ....D.... 440 953-2024
Eastlake *(G-9133)*

Sumitomo Elc Carbide Mfg Inc ....F.... 440 354-0600
Grand River *(G-10326)*

Superior Pneumatic & Mfg Inc ....F.... 440 871-8780
Cleveland *(G-6122)*

TC Service Co ....E.... 440 954-7500
Willoughby *(G-20441)*

Technidrill Systems Inc ....E.... 330 678-9980
Kent *(G-11393)*

Triad Capital Aat LLC ....G.... 440 236-4163
Columbia Station *(G-6451)*

Uhrichsville Carbide Inc ....F.... 740 922-9197
Uhrichsville *(G-18899)*

White Industrial Tool Inc ....F.... 330 773-6889
Akron *(G-435)*

Employee Codes: A=Over 500 employees, B=251-500
C=101-250, D=51-100, E=20-50, F=10-19, G=3-9
2019 Harris Ohio
Industrial Directory
959

Wolf Machine Company ....C....... 513 791-5194
Blue Ash *(G-1874)*
▲ **Wyeth-Scott Company** ....G....... 740 345-4528
Newark *(G-14933)*
X-Press Tool Inc ....E....... 330 225-8748
Brunswick *(G-2254)*
◆ **Zagar Inc** ....E....... 216 731-0500
Cleveland *(G-6336)*

3547 Rolling Mill Machinery & Eqpt

▲ **Addisonmckee Inc** ....C....... 513 228-7000
Lebanon *(G-11629)*
ADS Machinery Corp ....D....... 330 399-3601
Warren *(G-19362)*
Atkore Plastic Pipe Corp ....D....... 330 627-8002
Carrollton *(G-2916)*
▲ **Bardons & Oliver Inc** ....C....... 440 498-5800
Solon *(G-17112)*
Bendco Machine & Tool Inc ....F....... 419 628-3802
Minster *(G-14210)*
▲ **Circle Machine Rolls Inc** ....E....... 330 938-9010
Sebring *(G-16885)*
◆ **E R Advanced Ceramics Inc** ....E....... 330 426-9433
East Palestine *(G-9077)*
Element Machinery LLC ....G....... 855 447-7648
Toledo *(G-18279)*
▲ **Enprotech Industrial Tech LLC** ....C....... 216 883-3220
Cleveland *(G-5179)*
◆ **Fives Bronx Inc** ....D....... 330 244-1960
North Canton *(G-15083)*
Formtek Inc ....D....... 216 292-6300
Cleveland *(G-5263)*
▲ **Formtek Inc** ....D....... 216 292-4460
Cleveland *(G-5264)*
▲ **Foseco Inc** ....G....... 440 826-4548
Cleveland *(G-5267)*
▼ **George A Mitchell Company** ....E....... 330 758-5777
Youngstown *(G-20920)*
▲ **Graebener Group Tech Ltd** ....G....... 419 591-7033
Napoleon *(G-14540)*
H P E Inc ....F....... 330 833-3161
Massillon *(G-12993)*
Hydranamics Inc ....D....... 419 468-3530
Galion *(G-10144)*
J Horst Manufacturing Co ....D....... 330 828-2216
Dalton *(G-7945)*
▲ **Kottler Metal Products Co Inc** ....E....... 440 946-7473
Willoughby *(G-20355)*
Kusakabe America Corporation ....G....... 216 524-2485
Cleveland *(G-5547)*
Multi Galvanizing LLC ....G....... 330 453-1441
Canton *(G-2758)*
North Coast Profile Inc ....G....... 330 823-7777
Alliance *(G-493)*
◆ **Park Corporation** ....B....... 216 267-4870
Cleveland *(G-5841)*
Perfecto Industries Inc ....E....... 937 778-1900
Piqua *(G-16149)*
Pines Manufacturing Inc ....E....... 440 835-5553
Westlake *(G-20142)*
▲ **Pines Manufacturing Inc** ....E....... 440 835-5553
Westlake *(G-20141)*
Pipeline Automation Syste Inc ....G....... 419 462-8833
Galion *(G-10150)*
▲ **Rafter Equipment Corporation** ....E....... 440 572-3700
Strongsville *(G-17781)*
◆ **Ridge Tool Company** ....A....... 440 323-5581
Elyria *(G-9320)*
Ridge Tool Manufacturing Co ....A....... 440 323-5581
Elyria *(G-9322)*
Rki Inc ....C....... 888 953-9400
Mentor *(G-13573)*
Sentek Corporation ....G....... 614 586-1123
Columbus *(G-7438)*
Steel Eqp Specialists Inc ....E....... 330 829-2626
Alliance *(G-501)*
▲ **Steel Eqp Specialists Inc** ....D....... 330 823-8260
Alliance *(G-502)*
Sticker Corporation ....F....... 440 946-2100
Willoughby *(G-20438)*
Turner Machine Co ....F....... 330 332-5821
Salem *(G-16778)*
◆ **United Rolls Inc** ....D....... 330 456-2761
Canton *(G-2850)*
◆ **Warren Fabricating Corporation** ....D....... 330 534-5017
Hubbard *(G-11011)*
▲ **Wauseon Machine & Mfg Inc** ....D....... 419 337-0940
Wauseon *(G-19537)*
◆ **Xtek Inc** ....B....... 513 733-7800
Cincinnati *(G-4530)*

3548 Welding Apparatus

Accurate Machining & Welding ....G....... 937 584-4518
Sabina *(G-16615)*
Accurate Manufacturing Company ....E....... 614 878-6510
Columbus *(G-6534)*
Aerowave Inc ....G....... 440 731-8464
Elyria *(G-9209)*
Airgas ....G....... 330 345-1257
Wooster *(G-20555)*
AK Fabrication Inc ....F....... 330 458-1037
Canton *(G-2565)*
American Weldquip Inc ....F....... 330 239-0317
Sharon Center *(G-16943)*
◆ **Campbell Hausfeld LLC** ....C....... 513 367-4811
Cincinnati *(G-3439)*
Dennis Corso Co Inc ....G....... 330 673-2411
Kent *(G-11312)*
Fanuc America Corporation ....E....... 513 754-2400
Mason *(G-12870)*
Firelands Manufacturing LLC ....F....... 419 687-8237
Plymouth *(G-16231)*
Fusion Automation Inc ....G....... 440 602-5595
Willoughby *(G-20326)*
Fusion Incorporated ....E....... 440 946-3300
Willoughby *(G-20328)*
Halls Welding & Supplies Inc ....G....... 330 385-9353
East Liverpool *(G-9058)*
Harris Calorific Inc ....G....... 216 383-4107
Cleveland *(G-5375)*
Hobart Brothers Company ....E....... 937 773-5869
Piqua *(G-16127)*
Hobart Brothers Company ....G....... 937 332-5338
Troy *(G-18667)*
Hobart Brothers Company ....G....... 937 332-5023
Troy *(G-18668)*
◆ **Hobart Brothers LLC** ....A....... 937 332-5439
Troy *(G-18669)*
Imax Industries Inc ....F....... 440 639-0242
Painesville *(G-15747)*
J T E Corp ....G....... 937 454-1112
Dayton *(G-8275)*
▲ **Lima Equipment Co** ....G....... 419 222-4181
Lima *(G-11888)*
◆ **Lincoln Electric Company** ....A....... 216 481-8100
Cleveland *(G-5575)*
Lincoln Electric Holdings Inc ....C....... 216 481-8100
Cleveland *(G-5577)*
Lincoln Electric Holdings Inc ....A....... 440 255-7696
Mentor *(G-13500)*
▲ **Lincoln Electric Intl Holdg Co** ....E....... 216 481-8100
Euclid *(G-9424)*
▲ **Luvata Ohio Inc** ....D....... 740 363-1981
Delaware *(G-8704)*
M B Industries Inc ....G....... 419 738-4769
Wapakoneta *(G-19341)*
Mansfield Welding Services LLC ....G....... 419 594-2738
Oakwood *(G-15471)*
◆ **Miller Weldmaster Corporation** ....D....... 330 833-6739
Navarre *(G-14580)*
◆ **Nelson Stud Welding Inc** ....B....... 440 329-0400
Elyria *(G-9300)*
O E Meyer Co ....G....... 419 332-6931
Fremont *(G-10041)*
Otto Konigslow Mfg Co ....F....... 216 851-7900
Cleveland *(G-5826)*
Owen & Sons ....G....... 513 726-5406
Seven Mile *(G-16908)*
Peco Holdings Corp ....F....... 937 667-4451
Tipp City *(G-18126)*
▲ **Polymet Corporation** ....E....... 513 874-3586
West Chester *(G-19763)*
▲ **Postle Industries Inc** ....E....... 216 265-9000
Cleveland *(G-5897)*
Process Development Corp ....E....... 937 890-3388
Dayton *(G-8445)*
▲ **Process Equipment Co Tipp City** ....D....... 937 667-4451
Tipp City *(G-18128)*
◆ **Production Products Inc** ....D....... 734 241-7242
Columbus Grove *(G-7637)*
Quality Components Inc ....F....... 440 255-0606
Mentor *(G-13563)*
Retek Inc ....G....... 440 937-6282
Avon *(G-963)*
◆ **Rexarc International Inc** ....E....... 937 839-4604
West Alexandria *(G-19620)*
◆ **Select-Arc Inc** ....C....... 937 295-5215
Fort Loramie *(G-9805)*
▲ **Semtorq Inc** ....F....... 330 487-0600
Twinsburg *(G-18856)*
Sherbrooke Metals ....E....... 440 942-3520
Willoughby *(G-20429)*
▲ **Spiegelberg Manufacturing Inc** ....E....... 440 324-3042
Strongsville *(G-17792)*
Stryver Mfg Inc ....E....... 937 854-3048
Trotwood *(G-18630)*
▼ **Taylor - Winfield Corporation** ....D....... 330 259-8500
Hubbard *(G-11010)*
Taylor-Winfield Tech Inc ....E....... 330 259-8500
Youngstown *(G-21043)*
Tech-Sonic Inc ....F....... 614 792-3117
Columbus *(G-7519)*
▲ **Techalloy Inc** ....E....... 216 481-8100
Euclid *(G-9446)*
Tokin America Corporation ....G....... 513 644-9743
West Chester *(G-19810)*
Weld-Action Company Inc ....G....... 330 372-1063
Warren *(G-19463)*
▲ **Weldparts Inc** ....G....... 513 530-0064
Blue Ash *(G-1867)*
Westside Supply Co Inc ....G....... 216 267-9353
Brookpark *(G-2159)*
Wonder Weld Inc ....G....... 614 875-1447
Orient *(G-15579)*

3549 Metalworking Machinery, NEC

Added Edge Assembly Inc ....F....... 216 464-4305
Cleveland *(G-4616)*
▲ **Addisonmckee Inc** ....C....... 513 228-7000
Lebanon *(G-11629)*
ADS Machinery Corp ....D....... 330 399-3601
Warren *(G-19362)*
Advance Manufacturing Corp ....E....... 216 333-1684
Cleveland *(G-4622)*
▲ **Arku Coil-Systems Inc** ....G....... 513 985-0500
Blue Ash *(G-1730)*
Armature Coil Equipment Inc ....F....... 216 267-6366
Cleveland *(G-4734)*
Automated Machinery Solutions ....F....... 419 727-1772
Toledo *(G-18194)*
▲ **Automatic Feed Co** ....D....... 419 592-0050
Napoleon *(G-14532)*
Axatronics LLC ....G....... 513 239-5898
Loveland *(G-12178)*
▲ **Bardons & Oliver Inc** ....C....... 440 498-5800
Solon *(G-17112)*
▲ **Barth Industries Co LP** ....D....... 216 267-0531
Cleveland *(G-4793)*
Berran Industrial Group Inc ....E....... 330 253-5800
Akron *(G-85)*
Binns Machinery Company ....G....... 513 242-3388
Cincinnati *(G-3393)*
Bison USA Corp ....G....... 513 713-0513
Hamilton *(G-10541)*
Brilex Industries Inc ....D....... 330 744-1114
Youngstown *(G-20858)*
▲ **Brilex Industries Inc** ....C....... 330 744-1114
Youngstown *(G-20859)*
◆ **CA Litzler Co Inc** ....E....... 216 267-8020
Cleveland *(G-4859)*
▲ **Cammann Inc** ....F....... 440 965-4051
Wakeman *(G-19282)*
Cauffiel Corporation ....G....... 419 843-7262
Toledo *(G-18223)*
Coating Control Inc ....G....... 330 453-9136
Canton *(G-2631)*
Combined Tech Group Inc ....E....... 937 274-4866
Dayton *(G-8098)*
Ctm Integration Incorporated ....E....... 330 332-1800
Salem *(G-16732)*
Dango & Dienenthal Inc ....G....... 330 829-0277
Alliance *(G-463)*
Econ-O-Machine Products Inc ....G....... 937 882-6307
Donnelsville *(G-8801)*
Elite Mfg Solutions LLC ....G....... 330 612-7434
Macedonia *(G-12291)*
EZ Grout Corporation Inc ....E....... 740 962-2024
Malta *(G-12382)*
F L Enterprises ....G....... 216 898-5551
Cleveland *(G-5212)*
Fabriweld Corporation ....G....... 419 668-3358
Norwalk *(G-15393)*
Filmtec Inc ....E....... 419 435-1819
Fostoria *(G-9838)*
Flexomation LLC ....F....... 513 825-0555
Cincinnati *(G-3693)*
Fmt Repair Service Co ....G....... 330 347-7374
Mentor *(G-13444)*
▲ **Formtek Inc** ....D....... 216 292-4460
Cleveland *(G-5264)*

Forrest Machine Pdts Co Ltd.....E..... 419 589-3774
Mansfield ***(G-12441)***
Ged Holdings Inc.....C..... 330 963-5401
Twinsburg ***(G-18780)***
Gem City Engineering Co.....C..... 937 223-5544
Dayton ***(G-8219)***
Generic Systems Inc.....F..... 419 841-8460
Holland ***(G-10932)***
Gilson Machine & Tool Co Inc.....E..... 419 592-2911
Napoleon ***(G-14539)***
▲ **Glunt Industries Inc**.....C..... 330 399-7585
Warren ***(G-19407)***
▲ **Guild International Inc**.....E..... 440 232-5887
Bedford ***(G-1408)***
Hahn Manufacturing Company.....E..... 216 391-9300
Cleveland ***(G-5366)***
Heisler Tool Company.....F..... 440 951-2424
Willoughby ***(G-20336)***
Helix Linear Technologies Inc.....E..... 216 485-2263
Beachwood ***(G-1240)***
Holdren Brothers Inc.....F..... 937 465-7050
West Liberty ***(G-19936)***
▲ **Hunter Defense Tech Inc**.....E..... 216 438-6111
Solon ***(G-17164)***
J Horst Manufacturing Co.....D..... 330 828-2216
Dalton ***(G-7945)***
▲ **Kalt Manufacturing Company**.....D..... 440 327-2102
North Ridgeville ***(G-15235)***
▲ **Kay Capital Company**.....G..... 216 531-1010
Cleveland ***(G-5521)***
Kenley Enterprises LLC.....E..... 419 630-0921
Bryan ***(G-2293)***
▲ **Kent Corporation**.....E..... 440 582-3400
North Royalton ***(G-15280)***
Kilroy Company.....D..... 440 951-8700
Eastlake ***(G-9117)***
Master Marking Company Inc.....F..... 330 688-6797
Stow ***(G-17604)***
Mathew Odonnell.....G..... 440 969-4054
Andover ***(G-585)***
Midwest Laser Systems Inc.....E..... 419 424-0062
Findlay ***(G-9726)***
◆ **Milacron LLC**.....E..... 513 487-5000
Blue Ash ***(G-1822)***
▲ **Oma USA Inc**.....G..... 330 487-0602
Twinsburg ***(G-18824)***
Omega Automation Inc.....D..... 937 890-2350
Dayton ***(G-8402)***
Omega International Inc.....E..... 937 890-2350
Dayton ***(G-8403)***
Peco Holdings Corp.....F..... 937 667-4451
Tipp City ***(G-18126)***
Perfecto Industries Inc.....E..... 937 778-1900
Piqua ***(G-16149)***
▲ **Pines Manufacturing Inc**.....E..... 440 835-5553
Westlake ***(G-20141)***
▲ **Pipe Coil Technology Inc**.....F..... 330 256-6070
Burbank ***(G-2353)***
▲ **Portage Machine Concepts Inc**.....F..... 330 628-2343
Akron ***(G-324)***
Precision Metal Products Inc.....F..... 216 447-1900
Cleveland ***(G-5911)***
▲ **Process Equipment Co Tipp City**.....D..... 937 667-4451
Tipp City ***(G-18128)***
▲ **Rafter Equipment Corporation**.....E..... 440 572-3700
Strongsville ***(G-17781)***
Richard A Limbacher.....G..... 330 897-4515
Stone Creek ***(G-17564)***
Riverside Mch & Automtn Inc.....G..... 419 855-8308
Walbridge ***(G-19299)***
Riverside Mch & Automtn Inc.....D..... 419 855-8308
Genoa ***(G-10236)***
Scott Systems Intl Inc.....F..... 740 383-8383
Marion ***(G-12733)***
▲ **Semtorq Inc**.....F..... 330 487-0600
Twinsburg ***(G-18856)***
Shadetree Machine.....G..... 513 727-8771
Middletown ***(G-13951)***
Simon De Young Corporation.....G..... 440 834-3000
Middlefield ***(G-13853)***
Sir Steak Machinery Inc.....E..... 419 526-9181
Mansfield ***(G-12513)***
South Shore Controls Inc.....E..... 440 259-2500
Perry ***(G-15913)***
Stainless Automation.....G..... 216 961-4550
Cleveland ***(G-6090)***
Standard Car Truck Company.....D..... 740 775-6450
Chillicothe ***(G-3223)***
Stein Inc.....D..... 216 883-7444
Cleveland ***(G-6105)***
Steinbarger Precision Cnc Inc.....G..... 937 376-0322
Xenia ***(G-20792)***
Sticker Corporation.....F..... 440 946-2100
Willoughby ***(G-20438)***
Tdm LLC.....G..... 440 969-1442
Ashtabula ***(G-806)***
Tri-Mac Mfg & Svcs Co.....F..... 513 896-4445
Hamilton ***(G-10613)***
Universal Precision Products.....E..... 330 633-6128
Akron ***(G-421)***

3552 Textile Machinery

Alley Cat Designs Inc.....G..... 937 291-8803
Dayton ***(G-8017)***
American Precision Spindles.....G..... 267 436-6000
Cleveland ***(G-4694)***
▲ **Barudan America Inc**.....F..... 440 248-8770
Solon ***(G-17113)***
◆ **CA Litzler Co Inc**.....E..... 216 267-8020
Cleveland ***(G-4859)***
Impact Sports Wear Inc.....G..... 513 922-7406
North Bend ***(G-15051)***
Karg Corporation.....F..... 330 633-4916
Tallmadge ***(G-17988)***
Knitting Machinery Corp.....G..... 216 851-9900
Cleveland ***(G-5540)***
Knitting Machinery Corp.....F..... 937 548-2338
Greenville ***(G-10379)***
Leesburg Looms Incorporated.....G..... 419 238-2738
Van Wert ***(G-19099)***
▲ **Oma USA Inc**.....G..... 330 487-0602
Twinsburg ***(G-18824)***
Protofab Manufacturing Inc.....G..... 937 849-4983
Medway ***(G-13366)***
R Sportswear LLC.....G..... 937 748-3507
Springboro ***(G-17350)***
Randy Gray.....G..... 513 533-3200
Cincinnati ***(G-4248)***
Schilling Graphics Inc.....E..... 419 468-1037
Galion ***(G-10154)***
Simon De Young Corporation.....G..... 440 834-3000
Middlefield ***(G-13853)***
Solid Light Company Inc.....E..... 740 548-1219
Lewis Center ***(G-11781)***
Truck Stop Embroidery.....G..... 419 257-2860
North Baltimore ***(G-15048)***
Wayne Sporting Goods.....G..... 937 236-6665
Dayton ***(G-8586)***
Wolf Machine Company.....C..... 513 791-5194
Blue Ash ***(G-1874)***

3553 Woodworking Machinery

Axiom Tool Group Inc.....G..... 844 642-4902
Columbus ***(G-6638)***
Bent Wood Solutions LLC.....G..... 330 674-1454
Millersburg ***(G-14065)***
Boko Patterns Models & Molds.....G..... 937 426-9667
Beavercreek ***(G-1352)***
Closettec of North East Ohio.....G..... 216 464-0042
Bedford ***(G-1396)***
Coe Manufacturing Company.....D..... 440 352-9381
Painesville ***(G-15722)***
▲ **Dayton Hawker Corporation**.....F..... 937 293-8147
Dayton ***(G-8135)***
General Intl Pwr Pdts LLC.....G..... 419 877-5234
Whitehouse ***(G-20191)***
ITR Manufacturing LLC.....F..... 419 763-1493
Saint Henry ***(G-16664)***
Kyocera Senco Indus Tls Inc.....F..... 800 543-4596
Cincinnati ***(G-3256)***
McFeelys Inc.....F..... 800 443-7937
Harrison ***(G-10658)***
Midwest Timber & Land Co Inc.....E..... 740 493-2400
Piketon ***(G-16074)***
▲ **Rlfshop LLC**.....G..... 937 898-6070
Dayton ***(G-8480)***
Seilkop Industries Inc.....E..... 513 761-1035
Cincinnati ***(G-4316)***
Trico Enterprises LLC.....E..... 330 674-1157
Millersburg ***(G-14138)***

3554 Paper Inds Machinery

Aleris Recycling Inc.....G..... 216 910-3400
Beachwood ***(G-1219)***
▲ **Baumfolder Corporation**.....E..... 937 492-1281
Sidney ***(G-17019)***
Elite Mill Service & Cnstr.....G..... 513 422-4234
Trenton ***(G-18617)***
Erd Specialty Graphics Inc.....G..... 419 242-9545
Toledo ***(G-18283)***
◆ **Fluid Quip Inc**.....E..... 937 324-0352
Springfield ***(G-17404)***
▲ **French Oil Mill Machinery Co**.....D..... 937 773-3420
Piqua ***(G-16117)***
G Fordyce Co.....G..... 937 393-3241
Hillsboro ***(G-10878)***
▲ **J E Doyle Company**.....E..... 330 564-0743
Norton ***(G-15371)***
Kadant Black Clawson Inc.....D..... 251 653-8558
Lebanon ***(G-11666)***
▲ **Kadant Black Clawson Inc**.....D..... 513 229-8100
Lebanon ***(G-11667)***
Klockner Pentaplast Amer Inc.....G..... 937 743-8040
Franklin ***(G-9893)***
L B Folding Co Inc.....G..... 216 961-0888
North Royalton ***(G-15282)***
Loroco Industries Inc.....E..... 513 554-0356
Cincinnati ***(G-3951)***
▼ **Magna Machine Co**.....C..... 513 851-6900
Cincinnati ***(G-3972)***
Mc Kinley Machinery Inc.....E..... 440 937-6300
Avon ***(G-954)***
▼ **Mtr Martco LLC**.....D..... 513 424-5307
Middletown ***(G-13932)***
National Oilwell Varco LP.....D..... 937 454-3200
Dayton ***(G-8377)***
◆ **Nilpeter Usa Inc**.....C..... 513 489-4400
Cincinnati ***(G-4080)***
▲ **Press Technology & Mfg Inc**.....G..... 937 327-0755
Springfield ***(G-17476)***
Rebiltco Inc.....G..... 513 424-2024
Middletown ***(G-13948)***
Sso Inc.....F..... 440 235-3500
Olmsted Twp ***(G-15536)***
Tri-Mac Mfg & Svcs Co.....F..... 513 896-4445
Hamilton ***(G-10613)***
Universal Precision Products.....E..... 330 633-6128
Akron ***(G-421)***
Vail Rubber Works Inc.....F..... 513 705-2060
Middletown ***(G-13962)***

3555 Printing Trades Machinery & Eqpt

1st Choice Web Solution Inc.....G..... 330 503-1591
Youngstown ***(G-20828)***
A/C Laser Technologies Inc.....F..... 330 784-3355
Akron ***(G-24)***
Advanced Web Corporation.....G..... 740 662-6323
Stewart ***(G-17558)***
Aleris Ohio Management Inc.....F..... 216 910-3400
Cleveland ***(G-4655)***
Allen Green Enterprises LLC.....G..... 330 339-0200
New Philadelphia ***(G-14757)***
Anderson & Vreeland Inc.....D..... 419 636-5002
Bryan ***(G-2264)***
Beehex Inc.....G..... 512 633-5304
Columbus ***(G-6660)***
▼ **Boggs Graphic Equipment LLC**.....G..... 888 837-8101
Maple Heights ***(G-12566)***
Capital Track Company Inc.....G..... 614 595-5088
Columbus ***(G-6734)***
Commonwealth Aluminum Mtls LLC.....G..... 216 910-3400
Beachwood ***(G-1229)***
▲ **Desco Equipment Corp**.....E..... 330 405-1581
Twinsburg ***(G-18762)***
E C Shaw Co.....E..... 513 721-6334
Cincinnati ***(G-3616)***
Flexoplate Inc.....E..... 513 489-0433
Blue Ash ***(G-1776)***
Flexotech Graphics Inc.....F..... 330 929-4743
Stow ***(G-17588)***
FT Group Inc.....E..... 937 746-6439
Cincinnati ***(G-3716)***
Gedico International Inc.....G..... 937 274-2167
Dayton ***(G-8218)***
▲ **Gew Inc**.....G..... 440 237-4439
Cleveland ***(G-5320)***
Graphic Systems Services Inc.....E..... 937 746-0708
Springboro ***(G-17329)***
Great Lakes Graphics Inc.....E..... 216 391-0077
Cleveland ***(G-5345)***
Hadronics Inc.....D..... 513 321-9350
Cincinnati ***(G-3792)***
Hays Fabricating & Welding.....E..... 937 325-0031
Springfield ***(G-17412)***
Hotend Works Inc.....G..... 440 787-3181
Columbia Station ***(G-6438)***
Incorporated Trustees Gospel W.....D..... 216 749-1428
Cleveland ***(G-5449)***
▲ **Kase Equipment**.....D..... 216 642-9040
Cleveland ***(G-5517)***

S I C

Key Blue Prints Inc ....G 614 899-6180
Columbus *(G-7092)*
Klebaum Machinery Inc ....G 330 455-2046
Canton *(G-2724)*
Lyle Printing & Publishing Co ....F 330 337-7172
Salem *(G-16757)*
Moments To Remember USA LLC ....G 330 830-0839
Massillon *(G-13027)*
◆ Nilpeter Usa Inc ....C 513 489-4400
Cincinnati *(G-4080)*
Ohio Graphic Supply Inc ....G 937 433-7537
Dayton *(G-8397)*
◆ Paxar Corporation ....E 845 398-3229
Mentor *(G-13544)*
▲ R & D Equipment Inc ....F 419 668-8439
Norwalk *(G-15413)*
Resource Graphics ....G 513 205-2686
Cincinnati *(G-4261)*
Roconex Corporation ....F 937 339-2616
Troy *(G-18699)*
Roessner Holdings Inc ....G 419 356-2123
Fort Recovery *(G-9826)*
Rotation Dynamics Corporation ....F 937 746-4069
Franklin *(G-9917)*
Schilling Graphics Inc ....E 419 468-1037
Galion *(G-10154)*
Suspension Feeder Corporation ....F 419 763-1377
Fort Recovery *(G-9828)*
▲ Tinker Omega Manufacturing LLC ....E 937 322-2272
Springfield *(G-17506)*
Tykma Inc ....D 877 318-9562
Chillicothe *(G-3230)*
V I P Printing & Design ....G 513 777-7468
West Chester *(G-19913)*
◆ Wood Graphics Inc ....E 513 771-6300
Cincinnati *(G-4516)*

3556 Food Prdts Machinery

Abj Equipfix ....E 419 684-5236
Castalia *(G-2935)*
Acreo Inc ....G 513 734-3327
Amelia *(G-528)*
◆ American Pan Company ....C 937 652-3232
Urbana *(G-18978)*
◆ Anderson International Corp ....D 216 641-1112
Stow *(G-17568)*
Arbor Foods Inc ....E 419 698-4442
Toledo *(G-18188)*
Ashco ....G 330 385-2400
East Liverpool *(G-9050)*
Avure Technologies Inc ....D 513 433-2500
Middletown *(G-13885)*
Biro Manufacturing Company ....F 419 798-4451
North Canton *(G-15073)*
◆ Biro Manufacturing Company ....D 419 798-4451
Marblehead *(G-12584)*
C M Slicechief Co ....G 419 241-7647
Toledo *(G-18220)*
Christy Machine Company ....F 419 332-6451
Fremont *(G-10007)*
▼ Cleveland Gas Systems LLC ....G 216 391-7780
Streetsboro *(G-17665)*
▲ Cleveland Range LLC ....G 216 481-4900
Cleveland *(G-4971)*
▲ Cleveland Range LLC ....C 216 481-4900
Cleveland *(G-4972)*
Country Freezer Units LLC ....G 740 623-8658
Baltic *(G-1024)*
▲ Crescent Metal Products Inc ....C 440 350-1100
Mentor *(G-13426)*
E S Industries Inc ....G 419 643-2625
Lima *(G-11859)*
Ford Piping and Brewry Svc LLC ....G 614 284-2409
Columbus *(G-6929)*
Fred D Pfening Company ....G 614 294-5361
Columbus *(G-6939)*
Fred D Pfening Company ....E 614 294-5361
Columbus *(G-6938)*
▲ French Oil Mill Machinery Co ....D 937 773-3420
Piqua *(G-16117)*
Frost Engineering Inc ....E 513 541-6330
Cincinnati *(G-3715)*
G F Frank and Sons Inc ....F 513 870-9075
West Chester *(G-19709)*
Grice Equipment Repair Inc ....G 937 440-8343
Troy *(G-18664)*
▲ Harry C Lobalzo & Sons Inc ....E 330 666-6758
Akron *(G-199)*
Hawthorne-Seving Inc ....E 419 643-5531
Cridersville *(G-7810)*
Hobart Corporation ....E 937 332-3000
Troy *(G-18671)*
Hobart Corporation ....C 937 332-2797
Piqua *(G-16128)*
Hobart International Holdings ....C 937 332-3000
Troy *(G-18672)*
▼ Ingredient Masters Inc ....G 513 231-7432
Batavia *(G-1154)*
Innovative Controls Corp ....D 419 691-6684
Toledo *(G-18348)*
ITW Food Equipment Group LLC ....F 937 332-3000
Troy *(G-18678)*
ITW Food Equipment Group LLC ....C 937 393-4271
Hillsboro *(G-10882)*
◆ ITW Food Equipment Group LLC ....A 937 332-2396
Troy *(G-18679)*
◆ JE Grote Company Inc ....D 614 868-8414
Columbus *(G-7065)*
John Bean Technologies Corp ....B 419 627-4349
Sandusky *(G-16819)*
Kasel Engineering LLC ....G 937 854-8875
Trotwood *(G-18629)*
▲ Lem Products Holding LLC ....E 513 202-1188
West Chester *(G-19736)*
Lima Sheet Metal Machine & Mfg ....E 419 229-1161
Lima *(G-11893)*
Listermann Mfg Co Inc ....G 513 731-1130
Cincinnati *(G-3946)*
▼ Magna Machine Co ....C 513 851-6900
Cincinnati *(G-3972)*
Maverick Corp Partners LLC ....G 330 669-2631
Smithville *(G-17090)*
▲ Maverick Innvtive Slutions LLC ....E 419 281-7944
Ashland *(G-722)*
▲ Meyer Company ....C 216 587-3400
Cleveland *(G-5663)*
Mojonnier Usa LLC ....G 844 665-6664
Streetsboro *(G-17684)*
◆ N Wasserstrom & Sons Inc ....C 614 228-5550
Columbus *(G-7206)*
National Oilwell Varco LP ....D 937 454-3200
Dayton *(G-8377)*
◆ Nemco Food Equipment Ltd ....D 419 542-7751
Hicksville *(G-10780)*
Norse Dairy Systems Inc ....C 614 294-4931
Columbus *(G-7224)*
◆ Norse Dairy Systems LP ....B 614 421-5297
Columbus *(G-7225)*
Omar Associates LLC ....G 419 426-0610
Attica *(G-858)*
◆ Peerless Foods Inc ....C 937 492-4158
Sidney *(G-17058)*
Premier Industries Inc ....E 513 271-2550
Cincinnati *(G-4187)*
◆ Prime Equipment Group Inc ....D 614 253-8590
Columbus *(G-7347)*
◆ Probake Inc ....F 330 425-4427
Twinsburg *(G-18840)*
Processall Inc ....F 513 771-2266
Cincinnati *(G-4196)*
R and J Corporation ....E 440 871-6009
Westlake *(G-20147)*
Railroad Brewing Company ....G 440 723-8234
Avon *(G-961)*
Richard B Linneman ....G 513 922-5537
Cincinnati *(G-4266)*
Royalton Food Service Eqp Co ....E 440 237-0806
North Royalton *(G-15299)*
Sarka Bros Machining Inc ....G 419 532-2393
Kalida *(G-11281)*
▼ Shaffer Manufacturing Corp ....E 937 652-2151
Urbana *(G-19012)*
▼ Sidney Manufacturing Company ....E 937 492-4154
Sidney *(G-17079)*
▲ Tomlinson Industries LLC ....C 216 587-3400
Cleveland *(G-6181)*
Tpsc Inc ....F 440 439-9320
Bedford Heights *(G-1481)*
▲ Winston Products LLC ....D 440 478-1418
Cleveland *(G-6314)*
Wolf Machine Company ....C 513 791-5194
Blue Ash *(G-1874)*

3559 Special Ind Machinery, NEC

A & M Kiln Dry Ltd ....G 330 852-0505
Dundee *(G-9016)*
A & M Kiln Dry Ltd ....F 330 852-0505
Dundee *(G-9017)*
Acb Three Inc ....G 614 873-4680
Plain City *(G-16168)*
Affinity Information Managemet ....G 419 517-2055
Sylvania *(G-17932)*
Agmet Metals Inc ....E 440 439-7400
Oakwood Village *(G-15476)*
Alstart Enterprises LLC ....F 330 533-3222
Canfield *(G-2521)*
Amano Cincinnati Incorporated ....D 513 697-9000
Loveland *(G-12176)*
American Manufacturing & Eqp ....G 513 829-2248
Fairfield *(G-9482)*
▲ American Plastic Tech Inc ....C 440 632-5203
Middlefield *(G-13777)*
◆ Anderson International Corp ....D 216 641-1112
Stow *(G-17568)*
Aot Inc ....E 937 323-9669
Springfield *(G-17363)*
Aquila Pharmatech LLC ....G 419 386-2527
Waterville *(G-19490)*
ARS Recycling Systems LLC ....F 330 536-8210
Lowellville *(G-12249)*
Auto-Tap Inc ....G 216 671-1043
Cleveland *(G-4769)*
Automated Mfg Solutions Inc ....F 440 878-3711
Strongsville *(G-17716)*
Autotool Inc ....E 614 733-0222
Plain City *(G-16173)*
Beam Machines Inc ....G 513 745-4510
Blue Ash *(G-1732)*
Besten Inc ....G 216 910-2880
Cleveland *(G-4808)*
Bethel Engineering and Eqp Inc ....E 419 568-1100
New Hampshire *(G-14699)*
Bethel Engineering and Eqp Inc ....E 419 568-7976
New Hampshire *(G-14700)*
Bradford Neal Machinery Inc ....G 440 632-1393
Middlefield *(G-13781)*
Broco Products Inc ....G 216 531-0880
Cleveland *(G-4839)*
▲ Buddy Backyard Inc ....E 330 393-9353
Warren *(G-19380)*
Budget Molders Supply Inc ....E 216 367-7050
Macedonia *(G-12281)*
Burton Metal Finishing Inc ....E 614 252-9523
Columbus *(G-6713)*
CAM-Lem Inc ....G 216 391-7750
Cleveland *(G-4863)*
▲ Cammann Inc ....F 440 965-4051
Wakeman *(G-19282)*
Camton Mechanical Inc ....G 614 864-7620
Columbus *(G-6727)*
Cantrell Rfinery Sls Trnsp Inc ....F 937 695-0318
Winchester *(G-20519)*
Cbg Biotech Ltd Co ....E 440 786-7667
Solon *(G-17125)*
Chardon Plastics Machinery ....G 440 564-5360
Chardon *(G-3103)*
Chart International Inc ....E 440 753-1490
Cleveland *(G-4915)*
City of Cleveland ....G 216 664-2711
Cleveland *(G-4931)*
Cohesant Inc ....E 216 910-1700
Beachwood *(G-1228)*
◆ Cold Jet LLC ....C 513 831-3211
Loveland *(G-12183)*
Component Mfg & Design ....F 330 225-8080
Brunswick *(G-2197)*
Conforming Matrix Corporation ....E 419 729-3777
Toledo *(G-18238)*
Conviber Inc ....F 330 723-6006
Medina *(G-13241)*
Corrotec Inc ....E 937 325-3585
Springfield *(G-17379)*
Crowne Group LLC ....D 216 589-0198
Cleveland *(G-5040)*
Customers Car Care Center ....G 419 841-6646
Toledo *(G-18247)*
Decision Systems Inc ....E 330 456-7600
Canton *(G-2653)*
▲ Dengensha America Corporation ....F 440 439-8081
Bedford *(G-1399)*
Design Fabricators of Mantua ....G 330 274-5353
Mantua *(G-12545)*
Designetics Inc ....D 419 866-0700
Holland *(G-10925)*
Devilbiss Ransburg ....F 419 470-2000
Toledo *(G-18262)*
Diptech Systems Inc ....G 330 673-4400
Kent *(G-11314)*
▲ DRG Hydraulics Inc ....E 216 663-9747
Cleveland *(G-5114)*

35 INDUSTRIAL AND COMMERCIAL MACHINERY AND COMPUTER EQUIPMENT

Dura Temp Corporation .... F 419 866-4348
  Holland (G-10929)
◆ Eaton Corporation .... B 440 523-5000
  Cleveland (G-5146)
▲ Eden Cryogenics LLC .... E 614 873-3949
  Plain City (G-16190)
▲ Emco Usa LLC .... F 740 588-1722
  Zanesville (G-21133)
Emhart Glass Manufacturing Inc .... D 567 336-7733
  Perrysburg (G-15945)
Emhart Glass Manufacturing Inc .... G 567 336-8784
  Perrysburg (G-15946)
Empire Systems Inc .... F 440 653-9300
  Avon Lake (G-984)
◆ Encore Plastics Corporation .... C 419 626-8000
  Sandusky (G-16808)
Enerfab Inc .... G 513 771-2300
  Cincinnati (G-3641)
▲ Equipment Manufacturers Intl .... E 216 651-6700
  Cleveland (G-5186)
Fanuc America Corporation .... E 513 754-2400
  Mason (G-12870)
Fawcett Co Inc .... G 330 659-4187
  Richfield (G-16470)
File 13 Inc .... F 937 642-4855
  Marysville (G-12782)
▲ Findlay Machine & Tool Inc .... E 419 434-3100
  Findlay (G-9684)
▲ Freeman Schwabe Machinery LLC .. E 513 947-2888
  Batavia (G-1148)
Fremont Flask Co .... F 419 332-2231
  Fremont (G-10019)
▲ French Oil Mill Machinery Co .... D 937 773-3420
  Piqua (G-16117)
◆ Ganzcorp Investments Inc .... D 330 963-5400
  Twinsburg (G-18778)
Gary Compton .... G 937 339-6829
  Troy (G-18660)
Ged Holdings Inc .... C 330 963-5401
  Twinsburg (G-18780)
General Fabrications Corp .... E 419 625-6055
  Sandusky (G-16813)
Girard Machine Company Inc .... E 330 545-9731
  Girard (G-10261)
▼ Glenn Hunter & Associates Inc .... D 419 533-0925
  Delta (G-8773)
Gloucester Engineering Co Inc .... G 330 722-5168
  Medina (G-13269)
▲ Gokoh Corporation .... F 937 339-4977
  Troy (G-18662)
▼ Grasan Equipment Company Inc .... D 419 526-4440
  Mansfield (G-12452)
◆ Guild Associates Inc .... D 614 798-8215
  Dublin (G-8919)
Guild Associates Inc .... G 843 573-0095
  Dublin (G-8920)
▲ Haeco Inc .... F 513 722-1030
  Loveland (G-12195)
Halifax Industries Inc .... G 216 990-8951
  Hudson (G-11050)
Handle Light Inc .... G 330 772-8901
  Kinsman (G-11464)
Heartland Group Holdings LLC .... E 614 441-4001
  Columbus (G-6985)
Heil Engneered Process Eqp Inc .... F 440 327-6051
  North Ridgeville (G-15228)
▲ Heintz Manufacturers Inc .... G 724 274-6300
  Medina (G-13271)
Hess Technologies Inc .... G 513 228-0909
  Lebanon (G-11662)
▲ High Temperature Systems Inc .... G 440 543-8271
  Chagrin Falls (G-3049)
House Silva-Strongsville Inc .... G 330 464-6419
  Strongsville (G-17750)
Hydratecs Injection Eqp Co .... G 330 773-0491
  Akron (G-210)
I G Brenner Inc .... F 740 345-8845
  Newark (G-14887)
I T W Automotive Finishing .... G 419 470-2000
  Toledo (G-18338)
◆ Industrial Thermal Systems Inc .... F 513 561-2100
  Cincinnati (G-3845)
▼ Ingredient Masters Inc .... G 513 231-7432
  Batavia (G-1154)
Innovative Plastic Machinery .... G 330 478-1825
  Canton (G-2708)
Innovative Recycling Systems .... G 440 498-9200
  Solon (G-17171)
Inpower LLC .... F 740 548-0965
  Lewis Center (G-11763)

▲ Intelliworks Ht .... G 419 660-9050
  Norwalk (G-15401)
◆ Intertec Corporation .... B 419 537-9711
  Toledo (G-18350)
J & S Industrial Mch Pdts Inc .... D 419 691-1380
  Toledo (G-18356)
J M Hamilton Group Inc .... F 419 229-4010
  Lima (G-11881)
J McCaman Enterprises Inc .... F 330 825-2401
  New Franklin (G-14691)
Jaco Manufacturing Company .... F 440 234-4000
  Berea (G-1613)
Jbw Industries Inc .... F 614 882-5008
  Westerville (G-20000)
▲ JC Carter LLC .... G 440 569-1818
  Richmond Heights (G-16502)
◆ Johndow Industries Inc .... F 330 753-6895
  Barberton (G-1078)
Kiln .... G 440 717-1880
  Brecksville (G-2044)
Kilnit Ltd .... G 330 906-0748
  Stow (G-17598)
▲ Kobelco Stewart Bolling Inc .... D 330 655-3111
  Hudson (G-11060)
◆ Koch Knight LLC .... G 330 488-1651
  East Canton (G-9041)
Lam Research Corporation .... C 937 472-3311
  Eaton (G-9158)
Lange Equipment .... G 440 953-1621
  Eastlake (G-9120)
Lifeformations Inc .... F 419 352-2101
  Bowling Green (G-1981)
Linden Industries Inc .... E 330 928-4064
  Cuyahoga Falls (G-7893)
◆ Liquid Development Company .... G 216 641-9366
  Independence (G-11141)
Lube Depot .... G 330 758-0570
  Youngstown (G-20961)
◆ Luke Engineering & Mfg Corp .... E 330 335-1501
  Wadsworth (G-19252)
▲ M M Industries Inc .... E 330 332-5947
  Salem (G-16758)
M W Solutions LLC .... F 419 782-1611
  Defiance (G-8633)
Mactek Corporation .... F 330 487-5477
  Twinsburg (G-18810)
▼ Manifold & Phalor Inc .... F 614 920-1200
  Canal Winchester (G-2506)
Manufctring Bus Dev Sltons LLC .... D 419 294-1313
  Findlay (G-9717)
Mark Carpenter Industries Inc .... G 419 294-4568
  Fremont (G-10039)
McFlusion Inc .... G 800 341-8616
  Twinsburg (G-18814)
▲ McNeil & Nrm Inc .... D 330 761-1855
  Akron (G-275)
McNeil & Nrm Intl Inc .... D 330 253-2525
  Akron (G-276)
Measurement Specialties Inc .... F 937 885-0800
  Dayton (G-8337)
◆ Micro-Pise Msrment Systems LLC ... C 330 541-9100
  Streetsboro (G-17681)
Microcvd Corporation .... G 937 573-8984
  Dayton (G-8350)
▼ Midwestern Industries Inc .... C 330 837-4203
  Massillon (G-13026)
Military Resources LLC .... E 330 263-1040
  Wooster (G-20626)
▼ Military Resources LLC .... D 330 309-9970
  Wooster (G-20627)
Mirion Technologies Ist Corp .... G 614 367-2050
  Pickerington (G-16054)
Modular Assembly Innovations .... F 614 389-4860
  Dublin (G-8947)
Mosbro Machine and Tool Inc .... D 330 467-0913
  Northfield (G-15320)
Nutro Corporation .... D 440 572-3800
  Strongsville (G-17772)
Nutro Inc .... E 440 572-3800
  Strongsville (G-17773)
▲ Ohio Magnetics Inc .... E 216 662-8484
  Maple Heights (G-12575)
Omar McDowell Co .... G 440 808-2280
  Westlake (G-20137)
Palmer Klein Inc .... F 937 323-6339
  Springfield (G-17467)
◆ Palmer Mfg and Supply Inc .... E 937 323-6339
  Springfield (G-17468)
◆ Peerless-Winsmith Inc .... G 614 526-7000
  Dublin (G-8963)

Plastic Partners LLC .... G 425 765-2416
  Salem (G-16766)
▲ Plastic Process Equipment Inc .... E 216 367-7000
  Macedonia (G-12317)
Poly Products Inc .... G 216 391-7659
  Cleveland (G-5893)
▲ Pro Quip Inc .... D 330 468-1850
  Macedonia (G-12320)
Process Development Corp .... E 937 890-3388
  Dayton (G-8445)
Processall Inc .... F 513 771-2266
  Cincinnati (G-4196)
Prodeva Inc .... F 937 596-6713
  Jackson Center (G-11215)
R A K Machine Inc .... F 216 631-7750
  Cleveland (G-5949)
▲ Ratech .... G 513 742-2111
  Cincinnati (G-4249)
Rda Group LLC .... G 440 724-4347
  Avon (G-962)
Regal Industries Inc .... G 440 352-9600
  Painesville (G-15780)
▲ Rhino Rubber LLC .... F 877 744-6603
  North Canton (G-15115)
▲ RMS Equipment LLC .... E 330 564-1360
  Cuyahoga Falls (G-7914)
◆ RP Gatta Inc .... E 330 562-2288
  Aurora (G-905)
▼ RSI Company .... F 216 360-9800
  Beachwood (G-1277)
▲ Rubber City Machinery Corp .... E 330 434-3500
  Akron (G-356)
SDS National LLC .... G 330 759-8066
  Youngstown (G-21026)
◆ Segna Inc .... F 937 335-6700
  Troy (G-18704)
Service Station Equipment Co .... F 216 431-6100
  Cleveland (G-6045)
Shred Away .... G 740 363-6327
  Delaware (G-8724)
Silver Tool Inc .... E 937 865-0012
  Miamisburg (G-13717)
▼ Singleton Corporation .... F 216 651-7800
  Cleveland (G-6066)
Sizetec Inc .... G 330 492-9682
  Canton (G-2817)
Stainless Automation .... G 216 961-4550
  Cleveland (G-6090)
Starkey Machinery Inc .... E 419 468-2560
  Galion (G-10157)
◆ Steelastic Company LLC .... E 330 633-0505
  Cuyahoga Falls (G-7923)
Steinert Industries Inc .... F 330 678-0028
  Kent (G-11390)
Stevens Auto Glaze and SEC LL .... G 440 953-2900
  Eastlake (G-9131)
Stoneworkd .... F 740 920-4099
  Newark (G-14924)
Storetek Engineering Inc .... E 330 294-0678
  Tallmadge (G-18006)
▲ Technical Glass Products Inc .... F 440 639-6399
  Painesville (G-15786)
Tegratek .... G 513 742-5100
  Cincinnati (G-4411)
Tex-Vent Co .... G 614 299-1902
  Columbus (G-7522)
Tiba LLC .... E 614 328-2040
  Columbus (G-7528)
Time Is Money .... G 419 701-6098
  Fostoria (G-9860)
Tks Industrial Company .... D 614 444-5602
  Columbus (G-7531)
▲ Toledo Engineering Co Inc .... C 419 537-9711
  Toledo (G-18558)
▲ Tom Richards Inc .... C 440 974-1300
  Mentor (G-13607)
Tooltex Inc .... F 614 539-3222
  Grove City (G-10475)
Universal Rack & Equipment Co .... E 330 963-6776
  Twinsburg (G-18870)
Velocys Inc .... D 614 733-3300
  Plain City (G-16215)
Vulcan Machinery Corporation .... E 330 376-6025
  Akron (G-428)
▲ Wauseon Machine & Mfg Inc .... D 419 337-0940
  Wauseon (G-19537)
▲ Wentworth Mold Inc Electra .... D 937 898-8460
  Vandalia (G-19151)
Wesco Machine Inc .... F 330 688-6973
  Akron (G-433)

Employee Codes: A=Over 500 employees, B=251-500
C=101-250, D=51-100, E=20-50, F=10-19, G=3-9

35 INDUSTRIAL AND COMMERCIAL MACHINERY AND COMPUTER EQUIPMENT

Wolfe Oil Company LLC ....G....... 513 732-6220
 Williamsburg (G-20257)
◆ Woodman Agitator Inc ....F....... 440 937-9865
 Avon (G-976)
Yost & Son Inc ....G....... 440 779-8025
 North Olmsted (G-15204)
Youngstown Plastic Tooling ....E....... 330 782-7222
 Youngstown (G-21080)
Zed Industries Inc ....D....... 937 667-8407
 Vandalia (G-19152)
Zeeco Equipment Commodity ......G....... 440 838-1102
 Brecksville (G-2063)
▲ Zook Enterprises LLC ....E....... 440 543-1010
 Chagrin Falls (G-3093)

3561 Pumps & Pumping Eqpt

A & F Machine Products Co ....E....... 440 826-0959
 Berea (G-1588)
A P O Holdings Inc ....G....... 330 455-8925
 Canton (G-2556)
▼ Advanced Fuel Systems Inc ....G....... 614 252-8422
 Columbus (G-6545)
▲ All - Flo Pump Company ....E....... 440 354-1700
 Mentor (G-13382)
Ayling and Reichert Co Consent ....E....... 419 898-2471
 Oak Harbor (G-15441)
▲ Belden Brick Company ....E....... 330 852-2411
 Sugarcreek (G-17842)
Bergstrom Company Ltd Partnr ......G....... 440 232-2282
 Cleveland (G-4805)
Blue Chip Pump Inc ....G....... 513 871-7867
 Cincinnati (G-3396)
Certified Labs & Service Inc ....E....... 419 289-7462
 Ashland (G-691)
Chaos Entertainment 937 520-5260
 Dayton (G-8086)
▲ Cima Inc ....E....... 513 382-8976
 Hamilton (G-10546)
City of Newark ....F....... 740 349-6765
 Newark (G-14861)
Cleveland Plastic Fabricat ....F....... 216 797-7300
 Euclid (G-9409)
Crane Co ....G....... 330 337-7861
 Salem (G-16731)
▲ Crane Pumps & Systems Inc ......B....... 937 773-2442
 Piqua (G-16108)
Custom Cltch Jint Hydrlics Inc ....E....... 216 431-1630
 Cleveland (G-5046)
▲ Dreison International Inc ....C....... 216 362-0755
 Cleveland (G-5113)
◆ E R Advanced Ceramics Inc ....E....... 330 426-9433
 East Palestine (G-9077)
Eaton-Aeroquip Llc ....D....... 419 891-7775
 Maumee (G-13109)
▲ Eco-Flo Products Inc ....F....... 877 326-3561
 Ashland (G-703)
Electro-Mechanical Mfg Co Inc .....G....... 330 864-0717
 Akron (G-149)
Eric Allshouse LLC ....G....... 330 533-4258
 Canfield (G-2527)
Excel Fluid Group LLC ....G....... 800 892-2009
 Cleveland (G-5205)
▲ Fischer Global Enterprises LLC ..E....... 513 583-4900
 Loveland (G-12187)
Flow Control US Holding Corp ....G....... 800 843-5628
 Cincinnati (G-3698)
Flow Control US Holding Corp ....G....... 419 289-1144
 Ashland (G-704)
Flowserve Corporation ....G....... 513 874-6990
 Loveland (G-12188)
Flowserve Corporation ....D....... 937 226-4000
 Dayton (G-8200)
Fluid Automation Inc ....E....... 248 912-1970
 North Canton (G-15084)
Frantz Medical Development Ltd ...D....... 440 205-9026
 Mentor (G-13448)
General Electric Company ....D....... 216 883-1000
 Cleveland (G-5306)
General Electric Intl Inc ....E....... 330 963-2066
 Twinsburg (G-18783)
Gerow Equipment Company Inc ....G....... 216 383-8800
 Cleveland (G-5319)
▲ Giant Industries Inc ....E....... 419 531-4600
 Toledo (G-18305)
Gorman-Rupp Company ....E....... 419 886-3001
 Bellville (G-1557)
Gorman-Rupp Company ....B....... 419 755-1011
 Mansfield (G-12448)
Gorman-Rupp Company ....B....... 419 755-1011
 Mansfield (G-12447)

Gorman-Rupp Company ....G....... 419 755-1245
 Mansfield (G-12449)
▲ Graphite Equipment Mfg Co ....G....... 216 271-9500
 Solon (G-17155)
Hpc Manufacturing Inc ....G....... 440 322-8334
 Lorain (G-12095)
▼ Hr Parts N Stuff ....G....... 330 947-2433
 Atwater (G-861)
▲ Hugo Vglsang Maschinenbau GMBH ....E
 330 296-3820
 Ravenna (G-16382)
▲ Hurst Auto-Truck Electric 216 961-1800
 Cleveland (G-5426)
▼ Hydromatic Pumps Inc ....A....... 419 289-1144
 Ashland (G-712)
Ingersoll-Rand Company ....G....... 419 633-6800
 Bryan (G-2291)
◆ Keen Pump Company Inc ....E....... 419 207-9400
 Ashland (G-716)
Lakecraft Inc ....G....... 419 734-2828
 Port Clinton (G-16249)
M T Systems Inc ....G....... 330 453-4646
 Canton (G-2738)
Magnum Piering Inc ....E....... 513 759-3348
 West Chester (G-19874)
▲ Molten Mtal Eqp Innvations LLC ..E....... 440 632-9119
 Middlefield (G-13833)
Neptune Chemical Pump Company ..G....... 513 870-3239
 West Chester (G-19748)
▲ Pckd Enterprises Inc ....E....... 440 632-9119
 Middlefield (G-13844)
Pentair ....F....... 440 248-0100
 Solon (G-17215)
◆ Pentair Flow Technologies LLC ..C....... 419 289-1144
 Ashland (G-734)
▲ Preferred Global Equipment LLC ..D....... 513 530-5800
 Cincinnati (G-4186)
Pyrotek Incorporated ....C....... 440 349-8800
 Aurora (G-901)
Quikstir Inc 419 732-2601
 Port Clinton (G-16256)
▲ Replica Engineering Inc ....F....... 216 252-2204
 Cleveland (G-5976)
Rolcon Inc 513 821-7259
 Cincinnati (G-4281)
Rumpke Transportation Co LLC ....F....... 513 851-0122
 Cincinnati (G-4288)
▲ Ruthman Pump and Engineering ..E....... 513 559-1901
 Cincinnati (G-4291)
◆ Seepex Inc ....C....... 937 864-7150
 Enon (G-9386)
Stahl Gear & Machine Co ....E....... 216 431-2820
 Cleveland (G-6089)
Suburban Manufacturing Co ....D....... 440 953-2024
 Eastlake (G-9133)
Systecon LLC ....G....... 513 777-7722
 West Chester (G-19805)
T D Group Holdings LLC ....G....... 216 706-2939
 Cleveland (G-6144)
Tark Inc ....E....... 937 434-6766
 Dayton (G-8540)
Tat Pumps Inc ....G....... 740 385-0008
 Nelsonville (G-14600)
Thieman Tailgates Inc ....D....... 419 586-7727
 Celina (G-2988)
▲ Tolco Corporation ....D....... 419 241-1113
 Toledo (G-18555)
Tramec Sloan LLC ....F....... 419 468-9122
 Galion (G-10158)
Transdigm Inc ....F....... 216 291-6025
 Cleveland (G-6195)
Transdigm Inc ....E....... 440 352-6182
 Painesville (G-15791)
▲ Valco Cincinnati Inc ....C....... 513 874-6550
 West Chester (G-19914)
Vertiflo Pump Company ....F....... 513 530-0888
 Cincinnati (G-4478)
Vickers International Inc ....F....... 419 867-2200
 Maumee (G-13159)
▲ Warren Rupp Inc ....C....... 419 524-8388
 Mansfield (G-12537)
Waterpro ....F....... 330 372-3565
 Warren (G-19462)
▲ Wayne/Scott Fetzer Company ....C....... 800 237-0987
 Harrison (G-10679)
Westerman Inc ....D....... 330 262-6946
 Wooster (G-20665)

3562 Ball & Roller Bearings

Bearings Manufacturing Company ..E....... 440 846-5517
 Strongsville (G-17718)
Cleveland Caster LLC ....G....... 440 333-1443
 Cleveland (G-4949)
FAg Bearings Corporation ....C....... 513 398-1139
 Mason (G-12869)
Federal-Mogul Powertrain LLC ....C....... 740 432-2393
 Cambridge (G-2437)
Gt Technologies Inc ....C....... 419 782-8955
 Defiance (G-8625)
▲ HMS Industries LLC ....E....... 440 899-0001
 Westlake (G-20124)
▲ Jay Dee Service Corporation .....G....... 330 425-1546
 Macedonia (G-12307)
Miller Bearing Company Inc ....E....... 330 678-8844
 Kent (G-11356)
Nn Inc 440 647-4711
 Wellington (G-19587)
Randolph Research Co ....G....... 330 666-1667
 Akron (G-341)
▲ Rotek Incorporated ....G....... 330 562-4000
 Aurora (G-904)
Schaeffler Group USA Inc ....B....... 330 273-4383
 Valley City (G-19060)
◆ Timken Company ....A....... 234 262-3000
 North Canton (G-15126)
Timken Company ....A....... 419 563-2200
 Bucyrus (G-2345)
Timken Company ....C....... 330 339-1151
 New Philadelphia (G-14804)
Timken Company ....G....... 330 471-4300
 Canton (G-2837)
Timken Company ....F....... 614 836-3337
 Groveport (G-10514)
Timken Company ....G....... 330 471-5028
 Canton (G-2838)
Timken Company 234 262-3000
 North Canton (G-15127)
Timken Company 330 471-4791
 Alliance (G-507)
Timken Company ....A....... 330 471-5043
 Canton (G-2839)
▲ Tsk America Co Ltd ....F....... 513 942-4002
 West Chester (G-19909)
Western Reserve Mfg Co ....G....... 216 641-0500
 Cleveland (G-6303)

3563 Air & Gas Compressors

Aci Services Inc ....E....... 740 435-0240
 Cambridge (G-2421)
Airtech 419 269-1000
 Walbridge (G-19291)
Airtx International Ltd ....F....... 513 631-0660
 Cincinnati (G-3314)
▲ Anest Iwata Air Engrg Inc ....F....... 513 755-3100
 West Chester (G-19644)
Arete Innovative Solutions LLC .....G....... 513 503-2712
 Morrow (G-14408)
Ariel Corporation ....G....... 740 397-0311
 Mount Vernon (G-14468)
Ariel Corporation ....F....... 740 397-0311
 Mount Vernon (G-14469)
▲ Armour Spray Systems Inc ....F....... 216 398-3838
 Cleveland (G-4735)
Atlas Machine and Supply Inc ....G....... 614 351-1603
 Hilliard (G-10807)
▼ Ats Ohio Inc ....C....... 614 888-2344
 Lewis Center (G-11746)
◆ Campbell Hausfeld LLC ....C....... 513 367-4811
 Cincinnati (G-3439)
Cipar Inc ....G....... 216 910-1700
 Beachwood (G-1226)
Cohesant Inc ....E....... 216 910-1700
 Beachwood (G-1228)
Deco Tools Inc ....E....... 419 476-9321
 Toledo (G-18256)
Dresser-Rand Company ....E....... 513 874-8388
 Fairfield (G-9496)
◆ Eaton Comprsr Fabrication Inc ...E....... 877 283-7614
 Englewood (G-9357)
Ecowise LLC ....G....... 216 692-3700
 Cleveland (G-5156)
Edwards Vacuum LLC ....G....... 440 248-4453
 Solon (G-17135)
Ernest Industries Inc ....F....... 937 325-9851
 Springfield (G-17397)
Field Gymmy Inc ....G....... 419 538-6511
 Glandorf (G-10269)

Finishmaster Inc ....D 614 228-4328
Columbus *(G-6924)*

Gardner Denver Nash LLC ....F 440 871-9505
Cleveland *(G-5291)*

General Fabrications Corp ....E 419 625-6055
Sandusky *(G-16813)*

Giti Tech Group Ltd ....G 866 381-7955
West Carrollton *(G-19632)*

Glascraft Inc ....D 330 966-3000
North Canton *(G-15086)*

Kingsly Compression Inc ....G 740 439-0772
Cambridge *(G-2445)*

Lsq Manufacturing Inc ....F 330 725-4905
Medina *(G-13287)*

Mack Industrial LLC ....G 800 918-9986
Perrysburg *(G-15974)*

Nordson Corporation ....D 440 892-1580
Westlake *(G-20132)*

Nordson Corporation ....B 440 985-4000
Amherst *(G-566)*

Nordson Corporation ....B 440 988-9411
Amherst *(G-567)*

Optimair Ltd ....G 419 661-9568
Perrysburg *(G-15992)*

Optime Air MSP Ltd ....G 419 661-9568
Perrysburg *(G-15993)*

Paratus Supply Inc ....F 330 745-3600
Barberton *(G-1093)*

Potemkin Industries Inc ....E 740 397-4888
Mount Vernon *(G-14501)*

▲ Powerex-Iwata Air Tech Inc ....D 888 769-7979
Harrison *(G-10663)*

Quikstir Inc ....F 419 732-2601
Port Clinton *(G-16256)*

Rimrock Holdings Corporation ....E 614 471-5926
Columbus *(G-7395)*

▲ Rotary Compression Tech Inc ....E 937 498-2555
Sidney *(G-17071)*

Rubberset Company ....G 800 345-4939
Cleveland *(G-6015)*

T D Group Holdings LLC ....G 216 706-2939
Cleveland *(G-6144)*

▲ Tolco Corporation ....D 419 241-1113
Toledo *(G-18555)*

Transdigm Inc ....G 216 706-2939
Cleveland *(G-6196)*

Transdigm Inc ....F 216 291-6025
Cleveland *(G-6195)*

Tri State Equipment Company ....G 513 738-7227
Shandon *(G-16942)*

◆ Wiwa LLC ....F 419 757-0141
Alger *(G-444)*

Wiwa LP ....F 419 757-0141
Alger *(G-445)*

3564 Blowers & Fans

A A S Amels Sheet Meta L Inc ....E 330 793-9326
Youngstown *(G-20830)*

Adwest Technologies Inc ....G 513 458-2600
Cincinnati *(G-3304)*

Air Cleaning Solutions ....G 937 832-3600
Dayton *(G-8012)*

Air Cleaning Systems Inc ....G 440 285-3565
Chardon *(G-3096)*

▼ Air-Rite Inc ....E 216 228-8200
Cleveland *(G-4645)*

▲ Airecon Manufacturing Corp ....E 513 561-5522
Cincinnati *(G-3313)*

Allied Separation Tech Inc ....E 704 736-0420
Twinsburg *(G-18732)*

American Manufacturing & Eqp ....G 513 829-2248
Fairfield *(G-9482)*

Americraft Mfg Co Inc ....F 513 489-1047
Cincinnati *(G-3338)*

ARI Phoenix Inc ....E 513 229-3750
Lebanon *(G-11634)*

▲ Beckett Air Incorporated ....D 440 327-9999
North Ridgeville *(G-15209)*

Bha Altair LLC ....G 717 285-8040
Blue Ash *(G-1734)*

▲ Bry-Air Inc ....E 740 965-2974
Sunbury *(G-17883)*

Buckeye BOP LLC ....G 740 498-9898
Newcomerstown *(G-14971)*

Burt Manufacturing Company Inc ....C 330 762-0061
Akron *(G-100)*

Camfil USA Inc ....G 937 773-0866
Piqua *(G-16106)*

Ceco Environmental Corp ....G 513 458-2606
Blue Ash *(G-1748)*

Ceco Filters Inc ....G 513 458-2600
Cincinnati *(G-3451)*

◆ Ceco Group Inc ....G 513 458-2600
Cincinnati *(G-3452)*

Ceco Group Global Holdings LLC ....G 513 458-2600
Cincinnati *(G-3453)*

Cincinnati A Flter Sls Svc Inc ....E 513 242-3400
Cincinnati *(G-3478)*

Clearflite Inc ....G 440 281-7368
Sheffield Lake *(G-16963)*

Complete Filter Media LLC ....E 740 438-0929
Lancaster *(G-11555)*

Criticalaire LLC ....F 513 475-3800
Columbus *(G-6838)*

Criticalaire LLC ....G 614 499-7744
Cincinnati *(G-3559)*

◆ Diamond Power Intl Inc ....B 740 687-6500
Lancaster *(G-11566)*

▲ Dreison International Inc ....C 216 362-0755
Cleveland *(G-5113)*

▲ Duro Dyne Midwest Corp ....B 513 870-6000
Hamilton *(G-10551)*

Durr Megtec LLC ....C 614 258-9501
Columbus *(G-6876)*

▲ Ellis & Watts Intl LLC ....G 513 752-9000
Batavia *(G-1143)*

Envirofab Inc ....F 216 651-1767
Cleveland *(G-5182)*

Famous Industries Inc ....D 740 685-2592
Byesville *(G-2384)*

First Filter LLC ....G 419 666-5260
Perrysburg *(G-15951)*

Flex Technologies Inc ....D 330 359-5415
Mount Eaton *(G-14420)*

▼ Glasfloss Industries Inc ....C 740 687-1100
Lancaster *(G-11577)*

◆ Guardian Technologies LLC ....E 216 706-2250
Euclid *(G-9415)*

Halifax-Fan USA LLC ....G 262 257-9779
Cuyahoga Falls *(G-7876)*

◆ Hartzell Fan Inc ....C 937 773-7411
Piqua *(G-16122)*

Hdt Expeditionary Systems Inc ....E 440 466-6640
Geneva *(G-10222)*

Herman Manufacturing LLC ....F 216 251-6400
Cleveland *(G-5398)*

▲ Howden American Fan Company ....C 513 874-2400
Fairfield *(G-9506)*

Howden American Fan Company ....E 513 874-2400
Fairfield *(G-9507)*

Howden North America Inc ....D 330 867-8540
Medina *(G-13274)*

Howden North America Inc ....E 330 721-7374
Medina *(G-13275)*

▲ Howden North America Inc ....C 513 874-2400
Fairfield *(G-9508)*

Hunter Environmental Corp ....E 440 248-6111
Solon *(G-17165)*

Illinois Tool Works Inc ....C 262 248-8277
Bryan *(G-2289)*

Indoor Envmtl Specialists Inc ....F 937 433-5202
Dayton *(G-8262)*

Jacp Inc ....G 513 353-3660
Miamitown *(G-13747)*

Kirk Williams Company Inc ....D 614 875-9023
Grove City *(G-10440)*

▲ Langdon Inc ....E 513 733-5955
Cincinnati *(G-3930)*

▼ Lau Industries Inc ....C 937 476-6500
Dayton *(G-7983)*

Link-O-Matic Company Inc ....F 765 962-1538
Brookville *(G-2173)*

◆ McGill Airclean LLC ....D 614 829-1200
Columbus *(G-7163)*

◆ McGill Corporation ....F 614 829-1200
Groveport *(G-10504)*

Mestek Inc ....D 419 288-2703
Bradner *(G-2015)*

Met-Pro Technologies LLC ....C 513 458-2600
Cincinnati *(G-4011)*

▼ Midwestern Industries Inc ....C 330 837-4203
Massillon *(G-13026)*

Minova USA Inc ....D 740 377-9146
South Point *(G-17289)*

▲ Multi-Wing America Inc ....E 440 834-9400
Middlefield *(G-13834)*

Neundorfer Inc ....E 440 942-8990
Willoughby *(G-20387)*

Nupro Company ....C 440 951-9729
Willoughby *(G-20392)*

▼ OEM Corporation ....F 937 859-7492
Miamisburg *(G-13702)*

Ohio Blow Pipe Company ....E 216 681-7379
Cleveland *(G-5801)*

Oil Skimmers Inc ....E 440 237-4600
North Royalton *(G-15291)*

Pcy Enterprises Inc ....E 513 241-5566
Cincinnati *(G-4143)*

Plas-Tanks Industries Inc ....E 513 942-3800
Hamilton *(G-10596)*

Process Automation Specialists ....G 330 247-1384
Canal Fulton *(G-2489)*

▲ Qualtek Electronics Corp ....C 440 951-3300
Mentor *(G-13567)*

Quickdraft Inc ....E 330 477-4574
Canton *(G-2799)*

Radon Be Gone Inc ....G 614 268-4440
Columbus *(G-7375)*

Schenck Process LLC ....F 513 576-9200
Chagrin Falls *(G-3074)*

▲ Selas Heat Technology Co LLC ....E 800 523-6500
Streetsboro *(G-17697)*

▲ Skuttle Mfg Co ....F 740 373-9169
Marietta *(G-12670)*

Sly Inc ....F 440 891-3200
Strongsville *(G-17789)*

Starr Fabricating Inc ....D 330 394-9891
Vienna *(G-19210)*

Std Specialty Filters Inc ....F 216 881-3727
Cleveland *(G-6101)*

Stelter and Brinck Inc ....E 513 367-9300
Harrison *(G-10672)*

▲ Thermo Vent Manufacturing Inc ....F 330 239-0239
Medina *(G-13351)*

▲ Tisch Environmental Inc ....F 513 467-9000
Cleves *(G-6379)*

▲ Tlt-Turbo Inc ....G 330 776-5115
Akron *(G-407)*

▲ Tosoh America Inc ....B 614 539-8622
Grove City *(G-10476)*

Troy Filters Ltd ....E 614 777-8222
Columbus *(G-7546)*

▲ United McGill Corporation ....E 614 829-1200
Groveport *(G-10516)*

Usui International Corporation ....E 513 448-0410
Cincinnati *(G-4459)*

Vector Mechanical LLC ....G 216 337-4042
Brookpark *(G-2158)*

▼ Verantis Corporation ....E 440 243-0700
Middleburg Heights *(G-13771)*

Vortec and Paxton Products ....F 513 891-7474
Blue Ash *(G-1865)*

3565 Packaging Machinery

Able Tool Corporation ....E 513 733-8989
Cincinnati *(G-3288)*

Accu Pak Mfg Inc ....G 330 644-3015
Akron *(G-27)*

Advanced Poly-Packaging Inc ....G 330 785-4000
Akron *(G-32)*

Andy Pac Inc ....G 440 748-8800
Columbia Station *(G-6427)*

Ardagh Metal Packaging USA Inc ....G 419 334-4461
Fremont *(G-9991)*

▲ Atlas Vac Machine LLC ....G 513 407-3513
Cincinnati *(G-3368)*

▲ Audion Automation Ltd ....E 216 267-1911
Berea *(G-1591)*

Audion Automation Ltd ....E 216 267-1911
Berea *(G-1592)*

Automated Packg Systems Inc ....D 330 342-2000
Bedford *(G-1386)*

Automated Packg Systems Inc ....C 330 626-2313
Streetsboro *(G-17663)*

Automation Solutions Inc ....G 614 235-4060
Columbus *(G-6633)*

Beckermills Inc ....G 419 738-3450
Wapakoneta *(G-19324)*

▼ Boggs Graphic Equipment LLC ....G 888 837-8101
Maple Heights *(G-12566)*

◆ Combi Packaging Systems Llc ....D 330 456-9333
Canton *(G-2632)*

▲ Crown Closures Machinery ....E 740 681-6593
Lancaster *(G-11559)*

Ctm Integration Incorporated ....E 330 332-1800
Salem *(G-16732)*

Ctm Labeling Systems ....F 330 332-1800
Salem *(G-16733)*

▲ Darifill Inc ....F 614 890-3274
Westerville *(G-20046)*

35 INDUSTRIAL AND COMMERCIAL MACHINERY AND COMPUTER EQUIPMENT SIC SECTION

Dayton Systems Group Inc..................D....... 937 885-5665
Miamisburg *(G-13657)*
Dover Corporation..................F....... 513 696-1790
Mason *(G-12857)*
Dynamic Bar Code Systems Inc..................G....... 330 220-5451
Brunswick *(G-2201)*
Euclid Products Co Inc..................G....... 440 942-7310
Willoughby *(G-20317)*
Exact Equipment Corporation..................F....... 215 295-2000
Columbus *(G-6491)*
Food Equipment Mfg Corp..................E....... 216 672-5859
Bedford Heights *(G-1470)*
G L Industries Inc..................E....... 513 874-1233
Hamilton *(G-10562)*
General Data Healthcare Inc..................G....... 513 752-7978
Cincinnati *(G-3253)*
◆ **Glassline Corporation**..................C....... 419 666-9712
Perrysburg *(G-15958)*
H & G Equipment Inc..................F....... 513 761-2060
Blue Ash *(G-1784)*
◆ **Heat Seal LLC**..................C....... 216 341-2022
Cleveland *(G-5386)*
Hill & Griffith Company..................G....... 513 921-1075
Cincinnati *(G-3812)*
Huhtamaki Inc..................B....... 937 746-9700
Franklin *(G-9890)*
Huhtamaki Inc..................B....... 513 201-1525
Batavia *(G-1153)*
Hunkar Technologies Inc..................C....... 513 272-1010
Cincinnati *(G-3829)*
Impackt..................G....... 513 559-1488
Cincinnati *(G-3839)*
Kaufman Engineered Systems Inc..................D....... 419 878-9727
Waterville *(G-19499)*
▲ **Kennedy Group Incorporated**..................D....... 440 951-7660
Willoughby *(G-20352)*
Kolinahr Systems Inc..................F....... 513 745-9401
Blue Ash *(G-1801)*
Labeldata..................G....... 614 891-5858
Westerville *(G-20063)*
M PI Label Systems..................G....... 330 938-2134
Sebring *(G-16888)*
Madgar Genis Corp..................G....... 330 848-6950
Barberton *(G-1082)*
◆ **Miconvi Properties Inc**..................E....... 440 954-3500
Willoughby *(G-20381)*
Millwood Inc..................G....... 614 717-9099
Powell *(G-16329)*
Millwood Inc..................F....... 513 860-4567
West Chester *(G-19744)*
Millwood Inc..................G....... 330 729-2120
Vienna *(G-19203)*
Millwood Inc..................F....... 404 629-4811
Vienna *(G-19204)*
Millwood Natural LLC..................C....... 330 393-4400
Vienna *(G-19205)*
▲ **Morgan Adhesives Company LLC**...B........ 330 688-1111
Stow *(G-17606)*
Mpi Labels of Baltimore Inc..................F....... 330 938-2134
Sebring *(G-16890)*
MTS Medication Tech Inc..................G....... 440 238-0840
Strongsville *(G-17767)*
◆ **Nilpeter Usa Inc**..................C....... 513 489-4400
Cincinnati *(G-4080)*
Norse Dairy Systems Inc..................C....... 614 294-4931
Columbus *(G-7224)*
◆ **OKL Can Line Inc**..................E....... 513 825-1655
Cincinnati *(G-4108)*
▲ **Pack Line Corp**..................F....... 212 564-0664
Cleveland *(G-5835)*
Pak Master LLC..................E....... 330 523-5319
Richfield *(G-16479)*
Pneumatic Scale..................F....... 330 923-0491
Cuyahoga Falls *(G-7904)*
▲ **Pneumatic Scale Corporation**..................C....... 330 923-0491
Cuyahoga Falls *(G-7905)*
Precision Replacement LLC..................G....... 330 908-0410
Macedonia *(G-12319)*
◆ **Quadrel Inc**..................E....... 440 602-4700
Mentor *(G-13562)*
▲ **Reactive Resin Products Co**..................E....... 419 666-6119
Perrysburg *(G-16003)*
Recon Systems LLC..................G....... 330 488-0368
East Canton *(G-9043)*
Rpmi Packaging Inc..................F....... 513 398-4040
Lebanon *(G-11692)*
S A Langmack Company..................F....... 216 541-0500
Cleveland *(G-6021)*
Samuel Strapping Systems Inc..................D....... 740 522-2500
Heath *(G-10731)*
▲ **Scanacon Incorporated**..................G....... 330 877-7600
Hartville *(G-10704)*
Superior Label Systems Inc..................B....... 513 336-0825
Mason *(G-12944)*
Switchback Group Inc..................E....... 330 523-5200
Richfield *(G-16490)*
System Packaging of Glassline..................C....... 419 666-9712
Perrysburg *(G-16008)*
Unity Enterprises Inc..................G....... 614 231-1370
Columbus *(G-7559)*
Universal Packg Systems Inc..................B....... 513 674-9400
Cincinnati *(G-4452)*
Universal Packg Systems Inc..................B....... 513 732-2000
Batavia *(G-1193)*
Universal Packg Systems Inc..................E....... 513 735-4777
Batavia *(G-1194)*
Vistech Mfg Solutions LLC..................G....... 513 860-1408
Fairfield *(G-9573)*
Vistech Mfg Solutions LLC..................F....... 513 933-9300
Lebanon *(G-11706)*
▲ **Vmi Americas Inc**..................E....... 330 929-6800
Stow *(G-17641)*
W/S Packaging Group Inc..................C....... 513 459-2400
Mason *(G-12953)*

3566 Speed Changers, Drives & Gears

Accurate Gear Manufacturing Co..................G....... 513 761-3220
Cincinnati *(G-3290)*
Akron Gear & Engineering Inc..................E....... 330 773-6608
Akron *(G-41)*
Ametek Tchnical Indus Pdts Inc..................D....... 330 677-3754
Kent *(G-11294)*
Atc Legacy Inc..................G....... 330 590-8105
Sharon Center *(G-16944)*
Avotronics Powertrain Inc..................G....... 614 537-0261
Columbus *(G-6636)*
B & B Gear & Machine Co Inc..................F....... 937 687-1771
New Lebanon *(G-14707)*
▲ **Boneng Transmissions (usa) LLC**....G....... 330 425-1516
Twinsburg *(G-18743)*
Buckeye Gear Co..................F....... 216 292-7998
Chagrin Falls *(G-3038)*
▲ **Bunting Bearings LLC**..................D....... 419 866-7000
Holland *(G-10917)*
Cage Gear & Machine LLC..................F....... 330 452-1532
Canton *(G-2604)*
Canton Gear Mfg Design Co Inc..................F....... 330 455-2771
Canton *(G-2610)*
▲ **Cleveland Gear Company Inc**..................C....... 216 641-9000
Cleveland *(G-4960)*
Dayton Gear & Tool Co Inc..................E....... 937 866-4327
Dayton *(G-8134)*
Dependable Gear Corp..................G....... 440 942-4969
Eastlake *(G-9103)*
Eaton Leasing Corporation..................G....... 216 382-2292
Beachwood *(G-1235)*
Ebog Legacy Inc..................D....... 330 239-4933
Sharon Center *(G-16949)*
▲ **Force Control Industries Inc**..................D....... 513 868-0900
Fairfield *(G-9498)*
▲ **Forge Industries Inc**..................A....... 330 782-8301
Youngstown *(G-20909)*
Gear Company of America Inc..................D....... 216 671-5400
Cleveland *(G-5298)*
Gearing Solutions Inc..................G....... 440 498-9538
Solon *(G-17147)*
▲ **Geartec Inc**..................E....... 440 953-3900
Willoughby *(G-20330)*
Geneva Gear & Machine Inc..................F....... 937 866-0318
Dayton *(G-8221)*
▲ **Great Lakes Power Products Inc**......D....... 440 951-5111
Mentor *(G-13462)*
▲ **Hefty Hoist Inc**..................E....... 740 467-2515
Millersport *(G-14160)*
▲ **Horsburgh & Scott Co**..................C....... 216 432-5858
Cleveland *(G-5418)*
Horsburgh & Scott Co..................G....... 216 383-2909
Cleveland *(G-5419)*
◆ **Industrial Mfg Co LLC**..................F....... 440 838-4700
Brecksville *(G-2041)*
▲ **Jamtek Enterprises Inc**..................G....... 513 738-4700
Harrison *(G-10652)*
Jonmar Gear and Machine Inc..................G....... 330 854-6500
Canal Fulton *(G-2481)*
▲ **Joseph Industries Inc**..................D....... 330 528-0091
Streetsboro *(G-17680)*
▲ **Julie Maynard Inc**..................F....... 937 443-0408
Dayton *(G-8286)*
Kenmore Gear & Machine Co Inc..................G....... 330 753-6671
Akron *(G-234)*
Lincoln Electric Company..................C....... 216 524-8800
Cleveland *(G-5576)*
▲ **Linde Hydraulics Corporation**..................E....... 330 533-6801
Canfield *(G-2532)*
▲ **Luk Clutch Systems LLC**..................E....... 330 264-4383
Wooster *(G-20617)*
Martin Sprocket & Gear Inc..................D....... 419 485-5515
Montpelier *(G-14312)*
Matlock Electric Co Inc..................E....... 513 731-9600
Cincinnati *(G-3986)*
Nidec Indus Automtn USA LLC..................E....... 216 901-2400
Cleveland *(G-5753)*
◆ **Peerless-Winsmith Inc**..................G....... 614 526-7000
Dublin *(G-8963)*
Pentagear Products LLC..................F....... 937 660-8182
Dayton *(G-8420)*
Petro Gear Corporation..................F....... 216 431-2820
Cleveland *(G-5868)*
Radocy Inc..................F....... 419 666-4400
Rossford *(G-16591)*
Richard A Scott..................G....... 937 898-1592
Dayton *(G-8477)*
Right Track Corp..................G....... 937 663-0366
Saint Paris *(G-16710)*
Robertson Manufacturing Co..................F....... 216 531-8222
Cleveland *(G-5994)*
▲ **Satco Inc**..................G....... 330 630-8866
Tallmadge *(G-18002)*
◆ **Schaeffler Transm Systems LLC**......A....... 330 264-4383
Wooster *(G-20649)*
Sew-Eurodrive Inc..................D....... 937 335-0036
Troy *(G-18705)*
Sika Corporation..................D....... 740 387-9224
Marion *(G-12735)*
▲ **Skidmore-Wilhelm Mfg Company**.....E....... 216 481-4774
Solon *(G-17232)*
Spang & Company..................E....... 440 350-6108
Mentor *(G-13585)*
Speed Selector Inc..................F....... 440 543-8233
Chagrin Falls *(G-3077)*
Stahl Gear & Machine Co..................E....... 216 431-2820
Cleveland *(G-6089)*
Tgm Holdings Company..................E....... 419 885-3769
Sylvania *(G-17965)*
Titanium Metals Corporation..................A....... 740 537-1571
Toronto *(G-18612)*
Trojon Gear Inc..................F....... 937 254-1737
Dayton *(G-8568)*
Tymoca Partners LLC..................F....... 440 946-4327
Eastlake *(G-9137)*
◆ **Wasserstrom Company**..................B....... 614 228-6525
Columbus *(G-7591)*
▼ **Westerman Inc**..................C....... 740 569-4143
Bremen *(G-2065)*
Westerman Inc..................D....... 330 262-6946
Wooster *(G-20665)*

3567 Indl Process Furnaces & Ovens

A E F Inc..................D....... 216 360-9800
Cleveland *(G-4585)*
▲ **A Jacks Manufacturing Co**..................E....... 216 531-1010
Cleveland *(G-4591)*
Abp Induction LLC..................F....... 330 830-6252
Massillon *(G-12958)*
Agridry LLC..................E....... 419 459-4399
Edon *(G-9183)*
◆ **Ajax Tocco Magnethermic Corp**........C....... 330 372-8511
Warren *(G-19364)*
Ajax Tocco Magnethermic Corp..................C....... 440 278-7200
Wickliffe *(G-20197)*
Ajax Tocco Magnethermic Corp..................D....... 330 818-8080
Canton *(G-2564)*
Armature Coil Equipment Inc..................F....... 216 267-6366
Cleveland *(G-4734)*
▼ **Benko Products Inc**..................E....... 440 934-2180
Sheffield Village *(G-16966)*
Briskheat Corporation..................E....... 614 429-3232
Columbus *(G-6703)*
◆ **CA Litzler Co Inc**..................E....... 216 267-8020
Cleveland *(G-4859)*
▲ **CA Litzler Holding Company**..................D....... 216 267-8020
Cleveland *(G-4860)*
▲ **CMI Industry Americas Inc**..................D....... 330 332-4661
Salem *(G-16728)*
▲ **Crescent Metal Products Inc**..................C....... 440 350-1100
Mentor *(G-13426)*
Custom Coils..................G....... 330 426-3797
Negley *(G-14589)*
Delta H Technologies LLC..................G....... 740 756-7676
Carroll *(G-2903)*

SIC SECTION 35 INDUSTRIAL AND COMMERCIAL MACHINERY AND COMPUTER EQUIPMENT

Delta H Technologies LLC....................G....... 614 561-8860
Pickerington *(G-16045)*
▲ **Ebner Furnaces Inc**..........................D....... 330 335-2311
Wadsworth *(G-19237)*
Euclid Products Co Inc..........................G....... 440 942-7310
Willoughby *(G-20317)*
▲ **Facultatieve Tech Americas Inc**........E....... 330 723-6339
Medina *(G-13259)*
Furnace Technologies Inc....................D....... 419 878-2100
Waterville *(G-19496)*
Glo-Quartz Electric Heater Co..............E....... 440 255-9701
Mentor *(G-13459)*
Hannon Company.................................D....... 330 456-4728
Canton *(G-2693)*
Haynn Construction Co Inc..................G....... 419 853-4747
West Salem *(G-19954)*
▲ **Heat and Sensor Tech LLC**..............D....... 513 228-0481
Lebanon *(G-11661)*
▲ **I Cerco Inc**.......................................C....... 330 567-2145
Shreve *(G-17003)*
I Cerco Inc..D....... 740 982-2050
Crooksville *(G-7816)*
Induction Services Inc.........................G....... 330 652-4494
Niles *(G-15013)*
Induction Tooling Inc............................E....... 440 237-0711
North Royalton *(G-15277)*
Inter-Power Corporation.......................G....... 330 652-4494
Niles *(G-15014)*
James Thomas Shiveley........................G....... 330 468-2601
Macedonia *(G-12306)*
Kaufman Engineered Systems Inc........D....... 419 878-9727
Waterville *(G-19499)*
◆ **Komar Industries Inc**........................E....... 614 836-2366
Groveport *(G-10497)*
L Haberny Co Inc..................................F....... 440 543-5999
Chagrin Falls *(G-3054)*
Lakeway Mfg Inc...................................E....... 419 433-3030
Huron *(G-11103)*
Lanly Company....................................E....... 216 731-1115
Cleveland *(G-5560)*
◆ **Lewco Inc**..C....... 419 625-4014
Sandusky *(G-16822)*
Magneforce Inc.....................................F....... 330 856-9300
Warren *(G-19421)*
▲ **Micropyretics Heaters Intl Inc**...........F....... 513 772-0404
Cincinnati *(G-4025)*
Miller Core 2 Inc..................................G....... 330 359-0500
Beach City *(G-1213)*
▲ **P S C Inc**...G....... 216 531-3375
Cleveland *(G-5832)*
◆ **Park-Ohio Holdings Corp**..................F....... 440 947-2000
Cleveland *(G-5842)*
Park-Ohio Industries Inc......................C....... 440 947-2000
Cleveland *(G-5843)*
Pillar Induction.....................................G....... 262 317-5300
Warren *(G-19431)*
R K Combustion & Controls.................G....... 937 444-9700
Mount Orab *(G-14451)*
RAD-Con Inc..E....... 440 871-5720
Lakewood *(G-11534)*
Resilience Fund III LP..........................F....... 216 292-0200
Cleveland *(G-5979)*
Robbins Furnace Works Inc.................F....... 440 949-2292
Sheffield Village *(G-16974)*
▲ **Selas Heat Technology Co LLC**........E....... 800 523-6500
Streetsboro *(G-17697)*
Sivon Manufacturing LLC....................G....... 440 259-5505
Perry *(G-15912)*
Specialties Mds Induction Ltd..............G....... 330 394-3338
Warren *(G-19443)*
STA-Warm Electric Company...............F....... 330 296-6461
Ravenna *(G-16408)*
Star Engineering Inc............................E....... 740 342-3514
New Lexington *(G-14724)*
Stelter and Brinck Inc..........................E....... 513 367-9300
Harrison *(G-10672)*
▲ **Strohecker Incorporated**...................E....... 330 426-9496
East Palestine *(G-9085)*
▲ **Surface Combustion Inc**....................C....... 419 891-7150
Maumee *(G-13151)*
T J F Inc...F....... 419 878-4400
Waterville *(G-19506)*
▼ **Taylor - Winfield Corporation**...........D....... 330 259-8500
Hubbard *(G-11010)*
Tegratek..G....... 513 742-5100
Cincinnati *(G-4411)*
Thermo Systems Technology................E....... 216 292-8250
Cleveland *(G-6170)*
▲ **United McGill Corporation**...............E....... 614 829-1200
Groveport *(G-10516)*
Williams Industrial Svc Inc...................E....... 419 353-2120
Bowling Green *(G-2005)*

3568 Mechanical Power Transmission Eqpt, NEC

◆ **A J Rose Mfg Co**................................C....... 216 631-4645
Avon *(G-936)*
A J Rose Mfgco......................................C....... 216 631-4645
Cleveland *(G-4590)*
Abl Products Inc....................................F....... 216 281-2400
Cleveland *(G-4598)*
▲ **Advance Bronze Inc**...........................D....... 330 948-1231
Lodi *(G-12003)*
Advanced Pneumatics Inc.....................G....... 440 953-0700
Mentor *(G-13375)*
Akron Gear & Engineering Inc..............E....... 330 773-6608
Akron *(G-41)*
B S F Inc..F....... 937 890-6121
Dayton *(G-8050)*
B S F Inc..F....... 937 890-6121
Tipp City *(G-18100)*
Ban-Fam Industries Inc..........................G....... 216 265-9588
Cleveland *(G-4788)*
Bdi Inc..F....... 330 498-4980
Canton *(G-2586)*
Bearings Manufacturing Company........E....... 440 846-5517
Strongsville *(G-17718)*
Bowes Manufacturing Inc......................F....... 216 378-2110
Solon *(G-17117)*
▲ **Bucyrus Precision Tech Inc**...............C....... 419 563-9950
Bucyrus *(G-2320)*
Bunting Bearings LLC...........................E....... 419 522-3323
Mansfield *(G-12417)*
City Machine Technologies Inc..............E....... 330 740-8186
Youngstown *(G-20871)*
Cleveland Rebabbitting Service.............G....... 216 433-0123
Cleveland *(G-4974)*
▲ **Climax Metal Products Company**.......D....... 440 943-8898
Mentor *(G-13416)*
Columbus McKinnon Corporation.........D....... 330 424-7248
Lisbon *(G-11965)*
Connell Limited Partnership..................D....... 877 534-8986
Northfield *(G-15316)*
Cook Bonding & Mfg Co Inc..................G....... 216 661-1698
Cleveland *(G-5027)*
Custom Cltch Jint Hydrlics Inc..............F....... 216 431-1630
Cleveland *(G-5046)*
Dependable Gear Corp...........................G....... 440 942-4969
Eastlake *(G-9103)*
▲ **Drive Components**...............................G....... 440 234-6200
Brookpark *(G-2144)*
Dupont Specialty Pdts USA LLC...........C....... 216 901-3600
Cleveland *(G-5120)*
Eaton Corporation...................................C....... 440 826-1115
Berea *(G-1604)*
Eaton Corporation...................................C....... 216 281-2211
Cleveland *(G-5147)*
Eaton Hydraulics LLC.............................E....... 419 232-7777
Van Wert *(G-19088)*
Ebog Legacy Inc......................................D....... 330 239-4933
Sharon Center *(G-16949)*
Eicom Corporation...................................E....... 937 294-5692
Moraine *(G-14349)*
Erie Shore Industrial Svc Co..................G....... 440 933-4301
Avon Lake *(G-985)*
▲ **Euclid Universal Corporation**.............G....... 440 542-0960
Akron *(G-160)*
▲ **Force Control Industries Inc**..............D....... 513 868-0900
Fairfield *(G-9498)*
General Electric Company.......................D....... 216 883-1000
Cleveland *(G-5306)*
General Metals Powder Co......................D....... 330 633-1226
Akron *(G-186)*
Geneva Gear & Machine Inc...................F....... 937 866-0318
Dayton *(G-8221)*
GKN Sinter Metals LLC..........................C....... 740 441-3203
Gallipolis *(G-10166)*
Hite Parts Exchange Inc..........................E....... 614 272-5115
Columbus *(G-7003)*
J L R Products Inc...................................F....... 330 832-9557
Massillon *(G-13004)*
Lextech Industries Ltd.............................G....... 216 883-7900
Cleveland *(G-5574)*
▲ **Logan Clutch Corporation**...................E....... 440 808-4258
Cleveland *(G-5582)*
▲ **Luk Clutch Systems LLC**....................E....... 330 264-4383
Wooster *(G-20617)*
Martin Sprocket & Gear Inc....................D....... 419 485-5515
Montpelier *(G-14312)*
Master Products Company......................D....... 216 341-1740
Cleveland *(G-5634)*
Mechanical Dynamics Analis Ltd............E....... 440 946-0082
Euclid *(G-9426)*
Metro Mech Inc...G....... 216 641-6262
Cleveland *(G-5662)*
Mfh Partners Inc......................................F....... 440 461-4100
Cleveland *(G-5664)*
▲ **Morgal Machine Tool Co**.....................D....... 937 325-5561
Springfield *(G-17451)*
Nidec Minster Corporation......................G....... 419 628-1652
Minster *(G-14221)*
▲ **Nook Industries Inc**.............................C....... 216 271-7900
Cleveland *(G-5756)*
▲ **Opw Engineered Systems Inc**.............G....... 888 771-9438
Lebanon *(G-11680)*
Penn Machine Company..........................E....... 814 288-1547
Twinsburg *(G-18829)*
Poklar Power and Motion Inc..................G....... 513 791-5009
Blue Ash *(G-1832)*
Poly Products Inc.....................................G....... 216 391-7659
Cleveland *(G-5893)*
Rail Bearing Service LLC.........................B....... 234 262-3000
North Canton *(G-15113)*
Rampe Manufacturing Company..............F....... 440 352-8995
Fairport Harbor *(G-9629)*
▲ **Randall Bearings Inc**............................D....... 419 223-1075
Lima *(G-11927)*
Randall Bearings Inc................................F....... 419 678-2486
Coldwater *(G-6419)*
Regal Industries Inc..................................G....... 440 352-9600
Painesville *(G-15780)*
Robertson Manufacturing Co...................F....... 216 531-8222
Cleveland *(G-5994)*
Saf-Holland Inc...G....... 513 874-7888
West Chester *(G-19896)*
Sintered Metal Industries Inc...................F....... 330 650-4000
Hudson *(G-11073)*
Southeastern Shafting Mfg.......................F....... 740 342-4629
New Lexington *(G-14723)*
Stevenson Machine Inc.............................F....... 513 761-4121
Cincinnati *(G-4382)*
▲ **Stripmatic Products Inc**.......................E....... 216 241-7143
Cleveland *(G-6111)*
▲ **Taiho Corporation of America**.............C....... 419 443-1645
Tiffin *(G-18086)*
▲ **Tsk America Co Ltd**...............................F....... 513 942-4002
West Chester *(G-19909)*
US Tsubaki Power Transm LLC...............C....... 419 626-4560
Sandusky *(G-16860)*
▲ **Webb-Stiles Company**..........................D....... 330 225-7761
Valley City *(G-19069)*
Western Branch Diesel Inc.......................E....... 330 454-8800
Canton *(G-2864)*
◆ **Xtek Inc**..B....... 513 733-7800
Cincinnati *(G-4530)*

3569 Indl Machinery & Eqpt, NEC

A S Manufacturing Inc..............................G....... 216 476-0656
Cleveland *(G-4592)*
A-1 Sprinkler Company Inc......................D....... 937 859-6198
Miamisburg *(G-13636)*
▲ **Abanaki Corporation**..............................F....... 440 543-7400
Chagrin Falls *(G-3034)*
▲ **Action Coupling & Eqp Inc**...................D....... 330 279-4242
Holmesville *(G-10972)*
▲ **Advanced Design Industries Inc**...........E....... 440 277-4141
Sheffield Village *(G-16965)*
◆ **Air Technical Industries Inc**..................E....... 440 951-5191
Mentor *(G-13378)*
▲ **Akron Brass Company**...........................E....... 309 444-4440
Wooster *(G-20556)*
Akron Brass Company...............................B....... 330 264-5678
Wooster *(G-20557)*
All-American Fire Eqp Inc........................F....... 800 972-6035
Wshngtn CT Hs *(G-20718)*
▲ **Allied Separation Tech Inc**....................E....... 704 732-8034
Twinsburg *(G-18731)*
American Baler Co.....................................D....... 419 483-5790
Bellevue *(G-1529)*
▲ **American Rescue Technology**...............F....... 937 293-6240
Dayton *(G-8027)*
▲ **Applied Marketing Services**.................E....... 440 716-9962
Westlake *(G-20098)*
Aronit Machine LLC..................................F....... 419 782-4740
Defiance *(G-8613)*
▲ **Ats Systems Oregon Inc**........................B....... 541 738-0932
Lewis Center *(G-11747)*
◆ **Automation Tooling Systems**...............C....... 614 781-8063
Lewis Center *(G-11749)*

Employee Codes: A=Over 500 employees, B=251-500
C=101-250, D=51-100, E=20-50, F=10-19, G=3-9
2019 Harris Ohio
Industrial Directory
967

35 INDUSTRIAL AND COMMERCIAL MACHINERY AND COMPUTER EQUIPMENT

◆ Barney Corporation Inc ....G...... 614 274-9069
  Hilliard *(G-10810)*
Cae Ransohoff Inc ....G...... 513 870-0100
  West Chester *(G-19837)*
Chart International Inc ....E...... 440 753-1490
  Cleveland *(G-4915)*
City of Mansfield ....F...... 419 884-3310
  Mansfield *(G-12425)*
Cleaning Tech Group LLC..............E...... 513 870-0100
  West Chester *(G-19843)*
▲ Cleveland Gear Company Inc .....C...... 216 641-9000
  Cleveland *(G-4960)*
◆ Columbus Industries Inc ....A...... 740 983-2552
  Ashville *(G-816)*
Computer Allied Technology Co......G...... 614 457-2292
  Columbus *(G-6808)*
D C Filter & Chemical Inc ....G...... 419 626-3967
  Sandusky *(G-16802)*
Diamondback Filters..........................G...... 419 494-1156
  Bowling Green *(G-1968)*
Digilube Systems Inc ....F...... 937 748-2209
  Springboro *(G-17325)*
▲ Dosmatic USA Inc ....G...... 972 245-9765
  Cincinnati *(G-3604)*
◆ E R Advanced Ceramics Inc ....E...... 330 426-9433
  East Palestine *(G-9077)*
E S H Inc ....G...... 330 345-1010
  Wooster *(G-20587)*
Eco Mechanical LLC.........................G...... 440 610-9253
  Wellington *(G-19576)*
Edjean Technical Services Inc........G...... 440 647-3300
  Sullivan *(G-17881)*
Elite Fire Services LLC...................F...... 614 586-4255
  Columbus *(G-6891)*
Evoqua Water Technologies LLC....E...... 614 861-5440
  Pickerington *(G-16047)*
Falls Filtration Tech Inc ....E...... 330 928-4100
  Stow *(G-17586)*
Fanuc America Corporation ....G...... 513 754-2400
  Mason *(G-12870)*
Filter Factory-Ttn Inc ....G...... 440 963-2034
  Vermilion *(G-19159)*
Fire Fab Corporation ....G...... 330 759-9834
  Girard *(G-10257)*
Fire Foe Corp.....................................E...... 330 759-9834
  Girard *(G-10258)*
Fluid Automation Inc ....E...... 248 912-1970
  North Canton *(G-15084)*
▲ Foseco Inc ....C...... 440 826-4548
  Cleveland *(G-5267)*
Gem City Engineering Co.................C...... 937 223-5544
  Dayton *(G-8219)*
▲ Globe Pipe Hanger Products Inc..E... 216 362-6300
  Cleveland *(G-5326)*
Gould Fire Protection Inc ....G...... 419 957-2416
  Findlay *(G-9694)*
▲ Groeneveld Atlantic South ....F...... 330 225-4949
  Brunswick *(G-2212)*
▲ Gvs Filtration Inc............................B...... 419 423-9040
  Findlay *(G-9697)*
H P E Inc ....F...... 330 833-3161
  Massillon *(G-12993)*
Hdt Expeditionary Systems Inc ....G...... 216 438-6111
  Solon *(G-17160)*
▲ Hellan Strainer Company ....G...... 216 206-4200
  Cleveland *(G-5389)*
▲ Hunter Defense Tech Inc ....E...... 216 438-6111
  Solon *(G-17164)*
Innovative Assembly Svcs LLC........F...... 419 399-3886
  Paulding *(G-15861)*
Joseph B Stinson Co........................G...... 419 334-4151
  Fremont *(G-10030)*
▲ Joyce/Dayton Corp ....E...... 937 294-6261
  Dayton *(G-8285)*
◆ Kc Robotics Inc ....E...... 513 860-4442
  West Chester *(G-19729)*
▲ Keltec Inc..D...... 330 425-3100
  Twinsburg *(G-18798)*
▲ Koehler Rubber & Supply Co.........F...... 216 749-5100
  Cleveland *(G-5541)*
Koester Corporation ....D...... 419 599-0291
  Napoleon *(G-14548)*
La Mfg Inc ....G...... 513 577-7200
  Cincinnati *(G-3928)*
▲ Laureate Machine & Automtn LLC..G... 419 615-4601
  Leipsic *(G-11728)*
▲ Lawrence Technologies Inc ....G...... 937 274-7771
  Dayton *(G-8308)*
Mac Ltt Inc ....C...... 330 474-3795
  Kent *(G-11348)*

Marmac Co...G...... 937 372-8093
  Xenia *(G-20784)*
Meak Solutions Llc ....G...... 440 796-8209
  Mentor *(G-13513)*
▲ Membrane Specialists LLC ....G...... 513 860-9490
  Hamilton *(G-10586)*
◆ Midwest Filtration LLC ....E...... 513 874-6510
  West Chester *(G-19880)*
Motionsource International LLC ....F...... 440 287-7037
  Solon *(G-17198)*
Motor Systems Incorporated ....E...... 513 576-1725
  Milford *(G-14029)*
National Oilwell Varco Inc ....E...... 978 687-0101
  Dayton *(G-8376)*
Nmgg Ctg LLC...................................G...... 419 447-5211
  Tiffin *(G-18072)*
Nupro Company ....C...... 440 951-9729
  Willoughby *(G-20392)*
Nutro Corporation ....D...... 440 572-3800
  Strongsville *(G-17772)*
Ogden Hydraulics LLC......................G...... 419 686-1108
  Portage *(G-16272)*
Ohlheiser Corp...................................G...... 860 953-7632
  Columbus *(G-7266)*
Oil Skimmers Inc................................E...... 440 237-4600
  North Royalton *(G-15291)*
Omega Automation Inc ....D...... 937 890-2350
  Dayton *(G-8402)*
Omega International Inc ....E...... 937 890-2350
  Dayton *(G-8403)*
Osair Inc...G...... 440 255-8238
  Mentor *(G-13538)*
Parker-Hannifin Corporation ....F...... 330 335-6740
  Wadsworth *(G-19261)*
▲ Parker-Hannifin Corporation ....B...... 216 896-3000
  Cleveland *(G-5848)*
Parker-Hannifin Corporation ....F...... 216 896-3000
  Cleveland *(G-5850)*
Pax Products Inc ....F...... 419 586-2337
  Celina *(G-2979)*
Petro Ware Inc ....D...... 740 982-1302
  Crooksville *(G-7819)*
Phoenix Safety Outfitters LLC..........G...... 614 361-0544
  Springfield *(G-17471)*
▲ Pneumatic Scale Corporation ....C...... 330 923-0491
  Cuyahoga Falls *(G-7905)*
Process Innovations Inc...................G...... 330 856-5192
  Vienna *(G-19207)*
Process Machinery Inc ....E...... 614 278-1055
  Columbus *(G-7352)*
Production Design Services Inc ......D...... 937 866-3377
  Dayton *(G-8446)*
Programmable Control Service ....F...... 740 927-0744
  Pataskala *(G-15838)*
Pyrotek Incorporated.........................C...... 440 349-8800
  Aurora *(G-901)*
Quality Products Inc ....D...... 614 228-0185
  Swanton *(G-17920)*
Radco Fire Protection Inc ....G...... 419 476-0102
  Toledo *(G-18495)*
Raymond W Reisiger ....G...... 740 400-4090
  Baltimore *(G-1041)*
Recognition Robotics Inc.................F...... 440 590-0499
  Elyria *(G-9319)*
Red Head Brass Inc ....G...... 330 567-2903
  Shreve *(G-17007)*
Remtec Corp......................................G...... 513 860-4299
  Mason *(G-12931)*
Remtec Engineering ....E...... 513 860-4299
  Mason *(G-12932)*
Renite Company ....F...... 800 883-7876
  Columbus *(G-7385)*
Rennco Automation Systems Inc ....E...... 419 861-2340
  Holland *(G-10953)*
◆ Rexarc International Inc................F...... 937 839-4604
  West Alexandria *(G-19620)*
▲ Rhba Acquisitions LLC...................D...... 330 567-2903
  Shreve *(G-17008)*
Rimrock Holdings Corporation ....E...... 614 471-5926
  Columbus *(G-7395)*
Rixan Associates Inc ....E...... 937 438-3005
  Dayton *(G-8479)*
◆ Rotex Global LLC ....C...... 513 541-1236
  Cincinnati *(G-4282)*
S A Langmack Company ....F...... 216 541-0500
  Cleveland *(G-6021)*
Sas Automation LLC........................F...... 937 372-5255
  Xenia *(G-20789)*
Selecteon Corporation ....E...... 614 710-1632
  Columbus *(G-7437)*

Stateline Power Corp........................F...... 937 547-1006
  Greenville *(G-10397)*
▼ Steel & Alloy Utility Pdts Inc ....E...... 330 530-2220
  Mc Donald *(G-13202)*
Steven Douglas Corp.......................E...... 440 564-5200
  Newbury *(G-14967)*
◆ Summa Holdings Inc.....................E...... 440 838-4700
  Cleveland *(G-6116)*
Swift Filters Inc ....E...... 440 735-0995
  Oakwood Village *(G-15484)*
TEC Design and Mfg LLC................E...... 216 362-8962
  Cleveland *(G-6152)*
▲ Total Lubrication MGT Co ....E...... 888 478-6996
  Canton *(G-2843)*
Tungsten Capital Partners LLC ....E...... 216 481-4774
  Cleveland *(G-6221)*
Two M Precision Co Inc ....E...... 440 946-2120
  Willoughby *(G-20454)*
Tyler Haver Inc ....D...... 800 255-1259
  Mentor *(G-13616)*
United Fire Apparatus Corp ....E...... 419 645-4083
  Cridersville *(G-7813)*
▲ Versatile Automation Tech Ltd.......E...... 330 220-2600
  Brunswick *(G-2248)*
Viking Group Inc ....G...... 937 443-0433
  Dayton *(G-8580)*
Warren Fire Equipment Inc ....G...... 937 866-8918
  Miamisburg *(G-13738)*
Winston Oil Co Inc ....G...... 740 373-9664
  Marietta *(G-12689)*
Yaskawa America Inc ....G...... 937 847-6200
  Miamisburg *(G-13742)*
Zephyr Industries Inc ....E...... 419 281-4485
  Ashland *(G-756)*
Zhao Hui Filters (us) Inc ....G...... 440 519-9301
  Beachwood *(G-1287)*

3571 Electronic Computers

3d Systems Inc ....C...... 215 757-9611
  Columbus *(G-6512)*
Accurate Insulation LLC...................G...... 302 241-0940
  Columbus *(G-6533)*
Advance Products ....F...... 419 882-8117
  Sylvania *(G-17931)*
Analog Bridge Inc ....G...... 937 901-4832
  Beavercreek *(G-1299)*
Apple Seed LLC ....G...... 330 606-1776
  Akron *(G-67)*
Ascendtech Inc ....E...... 216 458-1101
  Willoughby *(G-20282)*
AT&T Corp..G...... 513 792-9300
  Cincinnati *(G-3365)*
Cardinal Health Tech LLC ....G...... 614 757-5000
  Dublin *(G-8896)*
Chaos Matrix Ltd................................G...... 614 638-4748
  Oberlin *(G-15492)*
◆ Codonics Inc ....C...... 216 226-1066
  Cleveland *(G-4995)*
Computer Zoo Inc ....G...... 937 310-1474
  Bellbrook *(G-1490)*
Dapsco..F...... 937 294-5331
  Moraine *(G-14342)*
Davis Laser Products ....G...... 614 252-7711
  Columbus *(G-6853)*
Dell Inc ....G...... 513 644-1700
  West Chester *(G-19693)*
Delohio Tech......................................F...... 740 816-5628
  Delaware *(G-8671)*
Dupont Electronic Polymers LP ....D...... 937 268-3411
  Dayton *(G-8172)*
Eaj Services LLC...............................F...... 513 792-3400
  Blue Ash *(G-1762)*
◆ Eaton Corporation ....B...... 440 523-5000
  Cleveland *(G-5146)*
First Product Technologies LLC.......Kc.... 440 364-0664
  Independence *(G-11128)*
Fleet Graphics Inc ....G...... 937 252-2552
  Dayton *(G-8198)*
Freedom Usa Inc ....E...... 216 503-6374
  Twinsburg *(G-18776)*
G2 Digital Solutions ....F...... 937 951-1530
  Xenia *(G-20774)*
▲ Golubitsky Corporation ....G...... 800 552-4204
  Cleveland *(G-5329)*
Hardware Exchange Inc ....G...... 440 449-8006
  Solon *(G-17159)*
International Products ....G...... 614 334-1500
  Columbus *(G-7044)*
▲ International Products ....E...... 614 850-3000
  Hilliard *(G-10831)*

SIC SECTION 35 INDUSTRIAL AND COMMERCIAL MACHINERY AND COMPUTER EQUIPMENT

Jordan Reed LLC ....G.... 678 956-1222
Columbus *(G-7076)*
Journey Systems LLC ....F.... 513 831-6200
Milford *(G-14022)*
Kenneth Hickman Co ....F.... 513 348-0016
Batavia *(G-1158)*
Lab Electronics Inc ....G.... 330 674-9818
Millersburg *(G-14104)*
Magnum Computers Inc ....F.... 216 781-1757
Cleveland *(G-5605)*
Mbenztech ....G.... 937 291-1527
Centerville *(G-3003)*
North American Research Corp ....G.... 937 445-5000
Kettering *(G-11438)*
Parker-Hannifin Corporation ....D.... 513 831-2340
Milford *(G-14031)*
PC Systems ....G.... 330 825-7966
Akron *(G-315)*
Potential Labs LLC ....G.... 740 590-0009
Athens *(G-845)*
Powersonic Industries LLC ....E.... 513 429-2329
West Chester *(G-19887)*
Site Tech ....G.... 740 522-0019
Heath *(G-10733)*
Smartronix Inc ....F.... 216 378-3300
Northfield *(G-15325)*
▲ Systemax Manufacturing Inc ....C.... 937 368-2300
Dayton *(G-8533)*
Teradata Operations Inc ....G.... 937 866-0032
Miamisburg *(G-13726)*
Teradata Operations Inc ....D.... 937 242-4030
Miamisburg *(G-13727)*
Terra Comp Technology ....G.... 330 745-8912
Barberton *(G-1111)*
Thomas Ross Associates Inc ....G.... 330 723-1110
Medina *(G-13352)*
Town Cntry Technical Svcs Inc ....F.... 614 866-7700
Reynoldsburg *(G-16457)*
Tracewell Systems Inc ....D.... 614 846-6175
Lewis Center *(G-11787)*
Walter North ....F.... 937 204-6050
Dayton *(G-8582)*

3572 Computer Storage Devices

Capsa Solutions LLC ....D.... 800 437-6633
Canal Winchester *(G-2500)*
CHI Corporation ....F.... 440 498-2300
Cleveland *(G-4920)*
EMC Corporation ....E.... 216 606-2000
Independence *(G-11125)*
Expansion Programs Intl ....G.... 216 631-8544
Cleveland *(G-5208)*
Magnext Ltd ....F.... 614 433-0011
Columbus *(G-7145)*
Quantem Fbo Services ....G.... 603 647-6763
Cincinnati *(G-4230)*
Quantum ....G.... 740 328-2548
Newark *(G-14915)*
Quantum Commerce LLC ....G.... 513 777-0737
West Chester *(G-19774)*
Quantum Integration Llc ....G.... 330 609-0355
Cortland *(G-7715)*
Quantum Sails ....G.... 567 283-5335
Sandusky *(G-16840)*
Quantum World Technologies ....G.... 937 747-3018
Zanesfield *(G-21089)*
Solsys Inc ....G.... 419 886-4683
Mansfield *(G-12518)*
Town Cntry Technical Svcs Inc ....F.... 614 866-7700
Reynoldsburg *(G-16457)*
Tracewell Systems Inc ....D.... 614 846-6175
Lewis Center *(G-11787)*
Western Digital Corporation ....G.... 440 684-1331
Cleveland *(G-6302)*

3575 Computer Terminals

▲ Bluelevel Technologies Inc ....G.... 330 523-5215
Richfield *(G-16463)*
Copier Resources Inc ....G.... 614 268-1100
Columbus *(G-6818)*
Fivepoint LLC ....F.... 937 374-3193
Xenia *(G-20773)*
NCR International Inc ....G.... 937 445-5000
Kettering *(G-11437)*
Parker-Hannifin Corporation ....D.... 513 831-2340
Milford *(G-14031)*
▲ Yutec LLC ....G.... 440 725-5353
Chagrin Falls *(G-3033)*

3577 Computer Peripheral Eqpt, NEC

Abstract Displays Inc ....G.... 513 985-9700
Blue Ash *(G-1719)*
Adaptive Data Inc ....F.... 937 436-2343
Dayton *(G-8007)*
Advanced Microbeam Inc ....G.... 330 394-1255
Vienna *(G-19195)*
AGE Graphics LLC ....F.... 740 989-0006
Little Hocking *(G-11989)*
Airwave Communications Cons ....G.... 419 331-1526
Lima *(G-11832)*
Applied Vision Corporation ....D.... 330 926-2222
Cuyahoga Falls *(G-7839)*
AT&T Corp ....G.... 513 792-9300
Cincinnati *(G-3365)*
Black Box Corporation ....G.... 800 837-7777
Dublin *(G-8890)*
Black Box Corporation ....F.... 800 676-8850
Brecksville *(G-2023)*
Black Box Corporation ....G.... 800 837-7777
Westlake *(G-20101)*
Black Box Corporation ....F.... 614 825-7400
Lewis Center *(G-11751)*
Cisco Systems Inc ....A.... 419 977-2404
New Bremen *(G-14648)*
Cisco Systems Inc ....A.... 937 427-4264
Beavercreek *(G-1306)*
Computer Zoo Inc ....G.... 937 310-1474
Bellbrook *(G-1490)*
Dataq Instruments ....F.... 330 668-1444
Akron *(G-133)*
Eastman Kodak Company ....E.... 937 259-3000
Dayton *(G-8175)*
Electrodynamics Inc ....C.... 847 259-0740
Cincinnati *(G-3247)*
Embedded Planet Inc ....F.... 216 245-4180
Warrensville Heights *(G-19467)*
Enterasys Networks Inc ....B.... 330 245-0240
Akron *(G-157)*
Epic Technologies LLC ....D.... 513 683-5455
Mason *(G-12867)*
Eprintworksplus ....G.... 513 731-3797
Cincinnati *(G-3648)*
Esterline Georgia US LLC ....E.... 937 372-7579
Xenia *(G-20770)*
Gameday Vision ....F.... 330 830-4550
Massillon *(G-12985)*
◆ Gleason Metrology Systems Corp ....E.... 937 384-8901
Dayton *(G-8223)*
Government Acquisitions Inc ....E.... 513 721-8700
Cincinnati *(G-3773)*
Harris Mackessy & Brennan ....C.... 614 221-6831
Westerville *(G-19996)*
Hunkar Technologies Inc ....C.... 513 272-1010
Cincinnati *(G-3829)*
ID Images Inc ....G.... 330 220-7300
Brunswick *(G-2214)*
Intec LLC ....G.... 614 633-7430
Heath *(G-10721)*
Intermec Inc ....G.... 513 874-5882
West Chester *(G-19724)*
Intermec Technologies Corp ....G.... 513 874-5882
West Chester *(G-19725)*
Intermec Technologies Corp ....F.... 513 874-5882
West Chester *(G-19726)*
▲ Kern Inc ....E.... 614 317-2600
Grove City *(G-10439)*
Kern Inc ....G.... 440 930-7315
Cleveland *(G-5531)*
Lazer Action Inc ....G.... 330 630-9200
Akron *(G-249)*
M C Systems Inc ....G.... 513 336-6007
Mason *(G-12904)*
▲ Microcom Corporation ....E.... 740 548-6262
Lewis Center *(G-11767)*
Parker-Hannifin Corporation ....D.... 513 831-2340
Milford *(G-14031)*
◆ Paxar Corporation ....E.... 845 398-3229
Mentor *(G-13544)*
Penca Design Group Ltd ....G.... 440 210-4422
Painesville *(G-15774)*
Perfection Packaging Inc ....G.... 614 866-8558
Gahanna *(G-10098)*
Phase Array Company LLC ....G.... 513 785-0801
West Chester *(G-19759)*
Prentke Romich Company ....C.... 330 262-1984
Wooster *(G-20641)*
▲ Qualtek Electronics Corp ....C.... 440 951-3300
Mentor *(G-13567)*

Royal Specialty Products Inc ....G.... 513 841-1267
Cincinnati *(G-4284)*
▲ Scriptel Corporation ....F.... 614 276-8402
Columbus *(G-7434)*
Signature Technologies Inc ....E.... 937 859-6323
Miamisburg *(G-13716)*
Small Business Products ....G.... 800 553-6485
Cincinnati *(G-4344)*
Star City Art Co ....F.... 937 865-9792
Miamisburg *(G-13720)*
Stellar Systems Inc ....G.... 513 921-8748
Cincinnati *(G-4379)*
Superior Label Systems Inc ....B.... 513 336-0825
Mason *(G-12944)*
▲ Systemax Manufacturing Inc ....C.... 937 368-2300
Dayton *(G-8533)*
T E Hubler Inc ....G.... 419 476-2552
Toledo *(G-18541)*
▲ Tech Pro Inc ....E.... 330 923-3546
Akron *(G-397)*
Timekeeping Systems Inc ....F.... 216 595-0890
Solon *(G-17253)*
▲ University Accessories Inc ....G.... 440 327-4151
North Ridgeville *(G-15257)*
Video Products Inc ....D.... 330 562-2622
Aurora *(G-915)*
▲ Vmetro Inc ....G.... 281 584-0728
Fairborn *(G-9473)*
Xerox Corporation ....D.... 513 539-4858
Monroe *(G-14283)*
Xerox Corporation ....G.... 513 539-4808
Monroe *(G-14284)*
Xponet Inc ....E.... 440 354-6617
Painesville *(G-15801)*
Yonezawa USA Inc ....G.... 614 799-2210
Plain City *(G-16222)*

3578 Calculating & Accounting Eqpt

A & M Creative Group Inc ....E.... 330 452-8940
Canton *(G-2555)*
Allied Retail Solutions ....G.... 330 332-8141
Salem *(G-16716)*
American Merchant Servic ....G.... 216 598-3100
Westlake *(G-20093)*
Bartek Systems ....G.... 614 759-6014
Columbus *(G-6652)*
Cambridge Ohio Production & As ....F.... 740 432-6383
Cambridge *(G-2429)*
Diebold Nixdorf Incorporated ....A.... 330 490-4000
North Canton *(G-15078)*
Diebold Nixdorf Incorporated ....D.... 330 490-4000
North Canton *(G-15079)*
Diebold Nixdorf Incorporated ....B.... 330 490-4000
Canton *(G-2659)*
Ganymede Technologies Corp ....G.... 419 562-5522
Bucyrus *(G-2330)*
Garda CL Technical Svcs Inc ....E.... 937 294-4099
Moraine *(G-14355)*
Ginko Voting Systems LLC ....G.... 937 291-4060
Dayton *(G-8222)*
Glenn Michael Brick ....F.... 740 391-5735
Flushing *(G-9783)*
NCR International Inc ....G.... 937 445-5000
Kettering *(G-11437)*
North American Research Corp ....G.... 937 445-5000
Kettering *(G-11438)*
Outta Box Dispensers LLC ....G.... 937 221-7106
Dayton *(G-8412)*
Peoples Bancorp Inc ....C.... 740 685-1500
Byesville *(G-2391)*
Testlink USA ....F.... 513 272-1081
Cincinnati *(G-4414)*

3579 Office Machines, NEC

Advanced Time Systems ....G.... 440 466-2689
Geneva *(G-10212)*
▲ Baumfolder Corporation ....E.... 937 492-1281
Sidney *(G-17019)*
Cap Data Supply Inc ....G.... 216 252-2280
Cleveland *(G-4869)*
Central Business Products Inc ....G.... 513 385-5899
Cincinnati *(G-3455)*
Collated Products Corp ....F.... 440 946-1950
Chardon *(G-3106)*
Industrial Electronic Service ....F.... 937 746-9750
Carlisle *(G-2893)*
▲ Kern Inc ....E.... 614 317-2600
Grove City *(G-10439)*
Kern Inc ....G.... 440 930-7315
Cleveland *(G-5531)*

S I C

Employee Codes: A=Over 500 employees, B=251-500
C=101-250, D=51-100, E=20-50, F=10-19, G=3-9
2019 Harris Ohio
Industrial Directory
969

Parallel Solutions....G....440 498-9920
Cleveland *(G-5838)*
Pitney Bowes Inc....D....203 426-7025
Brecksville *(G-2054)*
Pitney Bowes Inc....G....216 351-2598
Cleveland *(G-5880)*
Pitney Bowes Inc....D....740 374-5535
Marietta *(G-12655)*
R T Industries Inc....C....937 335-5784
Troy *(G-18695)*
Symatic Inc....E....330 225-1510
Brunswick *(G-2243)*

3581 Automatic Vending Machines

▲ Giant Industries Inc....E....419 531-4600
Toledo *(G-18305)*
Innovative Vend Solutions LLC....E....866 931-9413
Dayton *(G-8267)*
Michele Mellen....G....740 369-1422
Powell *(G-16328)*
Reeces Las Vegas Supplies....G....937 274-5000
Dayton *(G-8467)*
Tranzonic Companies....B....216 535-4300
Richmond Heights *(G-16507)*
▲ Ve Global Vending Inc....F....216 785-2611
Cleveland *(G-6252)*

3582 Commercial Laundry, Dry Clean & Pressing Mchs

Ellis Laundry & Linen Supply....G....330 339-4941
New Philadelphia *(G-14767)*
Ha-International LLC....E....419 537-0096
Toledo *(G-18317)*
▲ Husqvarna US Holding Inc....D....216 898-1800
Cleveland *(G-5427)*
Linen Care Plus Inc....F....614 224-1791
Columbus *(G-7131)*
Process Development Corp....E....937 890-3388
Dayton *(G-8445)*
Swisher Hygiene Inc....G....513 870-4830
West Chester *(G-19905)*
Thompson Distributing Co Inc....G....513 422-9011
Middletown *(G-13957)*
Whirlpool Corporation....B....419 547-7711
Clyde *(G-6397)*

3585 Air Conditioning & Heating Eqpt

A A S Amels Sheet Meta L Inc....E....330 793-9326
Youngstown *(G-20830)*
▲ Adams Manufacturing Company....E....216 662-1600
Cleveland *(G-4613)*
Aeroquip-Vickers Inc....G....216 523-5000
Cleveland *(G-4633)*
Albin Sales Inc....G....740 927-7210
Pataskala *(G-15827)*
All About House....G....614 725-3595
Columbus *(G-6564)*
Anatrace Products LLC....E....419 740-6600
Maumee *(G-13071)*
Aquapro Systems LLC....F....877 278-2797
West Chester *(G-19650)*
Arthurs Refrigeration....G....740 532-0206
Ironton *(G-11161)*
▼ Bard Manufacturing Company Inc....D....419 636-1194
Bryan *(G-2267)*
▲ Beckett Air Incorporated....D....440 327-9999
North Ridgeville *(G-15209)*
Bennett Mechanical Systems LLC....G....513 292-3506
Franklin *(G-9871)*
Bessamaire Sales Inc....E....440 439-1200
Twinsburg *(G-18740)*
BMC Holdings Inc....G....419 636-1194
Bryan *(G-2269)*
Bodor Vents LLC....G....513 348-3853
Blue Ash *(G-1739)*
▲ Boston Beer Company....F....267 240-4429
Cincinnati *(G-3405)*
▲ Briskheat Corporation....C....614 294-3376
Columbus *(G-6702)*
Brookpark Laboratories Inc....G....216 267-7140
Cleveland *(G-4841)*
▲ Bry-Air Inc....E....740 965-2974
Sunbury *(G-17883)*
▼ C Nelson Manufacturing Co....E....419 898-3305
Oak Harbor *(G-15442)*
Carrier Corporation....E....937 275-0645
Dayton *(G-8077)*
Cartwright Construction Inc....G....330 929-3020
Cuyahoga Falls *(G-7846)*

Central Heating & Cooling Inc....G....330 782-7100
Youngstown *(G-20868)*
Certified Service Inc....G....937 643-0393
Dayton *(G-8085)*
CFC Startec LLC....G....330 688-8316
Stow *(G-17575)*
Chilltex LLC....F....937 710-3308
Anna *(G-588)*
Cleveland Smacna....G....440 877-3500
Cleveland *(G-4976)*
Climateright LLC....G....800 725-4628
Columbus *(G-6775)*
Cold Control LLC....G....614 564-7011
Westerville *(G-19986)*
Columbus Heating & Vent Co....C....614 274-1177
Columbus *(G-6790)*
▲ Cryogenic Equipment & Svcs Inc....F....513 761-4200
Cincinnati *(G-3561)*
▲ Csafe LLC....G....937 312-0114
Moraine *(G-14340)*
Daikin Applied Americas Inc....G....614 351-9862
Westerville *(G-20045)*
▲ Dj Beverage Innovations Inc....G....614 769-1569
Plain City *(G-16188)*
Dmtco LLC....G....937 324-0061
Springfield *(G-17389)*
DTE Cool Co....G....513 579-0160
Cincinnati *(G-3611)*
▲ Duro Dyne Midwest Corp....B....513 870-6000
Hamilton *(G-10551)*
▲ Dyoung Enterprise Inc....D....440 918-0505
Willoughby *(G-20312)*
◆ Eaton Aeroquip LLC....C....216 523-5000
Cleveland *(G-5143)*
◆ Ecu Corporation....E....513 898-9294
Cincinnati *(G-3630)*
Edison Solar Inc....F....419 499-0000
Milan *(G-13982)*
◆ Electrolux Professional Inc....E....216 898-1800
Cleveland *(G-5167)*
Ellis & Watts Global Inds Inc....E....513 752-9000
Batavia *(G-1142)*
▲ Ellis & Watts Intl LLC....G....513 752-9000
Batavia *(G-1143)*
◆ Emerson Climate Tech Inc....A....937 498-3011
Sidney *(G-17036)*
Emerson Climate Tech Inc....C....937 498-3011
Sidney *(G-17037)*
Emerson Climate Tech Inc....E....937 498-3587
Sidney *(G-17038)*
Emerson Network Power....G....614 841-8054
Ironton *(G-11164)*
Famous Industries Inc....D....740 685-2592
Byesville *(G-2384)*
Famous Industries Inc....C....740 397-8842
Mount Vernon *(G-14481)*
Famous Realty Cleveland Inc....F....740 685-2533
Byesville *(G-2385)*
▲ Fire From Ice Ventures LLC....F....419 944-6705
Solon *(G-17144)*
Florline Display Products Corp....G....440 975-9449
Willoughby *(G-20324)*
Forzza Corporation....G....440 998-6300
Madison *(G-12350)*
Fred D Pfening Company....E....614 294-5361
Columbus *(G-6938)*
Goodman Distribution Inc....G....440 324-4071
Avon Lake *(G-987)*
Gould Group LLC....G....740 807-4294
Hilliard *(G-10825)*
◆ Guardian Technologies LLC....E....216 706-2250
Euclid *(G-9415)*
Hanon Systems Usa LLC....C....313 920-0583
Carey *(G-2882)*
Hatfield Industries LLC....G....513 225-0456
West Chester *(G-19719)*
Hbb Pro Sales....G....216 901-7900
Cleveland *(G-5381)*
Hdt Expeditionary Systems Inc....E....440 466-6640
Geneva *(G-10222)*
◆ Hickok Ae LLC....D....330 794-9770
Akron *(G-207)*
Hobart Corporation....E....937 332-3000
Troy *(G-18671)*
Hobart Corporation....C....937 332-2797
Piqua *(G-16128)*
▲ Hydro-Dyne Inc....E....330 832-5076
Massillon *(G-13000)*
▼ Hydro-Thrift Corporation....E....330 837-5141
Massillon *(G-13001)*

Insource Tech Inc....F....419 399-3600
Paulding *(G-15862)*
International Beverage Works....G....614 798-5398
Columbus *(G-7043)*
IV J Telecommunications LLC....G....606 694-1762
South Point *(G-17284)*
J D Indoor Comfort Inc....F....440 949-8758
Sheffield Village *(G-16968)*
J&I Duct Fab LLC....F....937 473-2121
Covington *(G-7788)*
Lfg Specialties LLC....E....419 424-4999
Findlay *(G-9715)*
Liebert North America Inc....E....614 888-0246
Columbus *(G-7125)*
◆ Lintern Corporation....E....440 255-9333
Mentor *(G-13501)*
Lockes Heating & Cooling Llc....F....513 793-1900
Blue Ash *(G-1806)*
Mahle Behr USA Inc....A....937 369-2000
Dayton *(G-8327)*
▲ Maverick Innvtive Slutions LLC....E....419 281-7944
Ashland *(G-722)*
Midwest Compressor Co Inc....G....216 941-9200
Cleveland *(G-5679)*
▲ Molecular Dimensions Inc....G....419 740-6600
Maumee *(G-13137)*
Mv Group Inc....G....419 776-1133
Toledo *(G-18419)*
Northeastern Rfrgn Corp....E....440 942-7676
Willoughby *(G-20390)*
NRC Inc....E....440 975-9449
Willoughby *(G-20391)*
Prime Manufacturing Corp....G....937 496-3900
Dayton *(G-8441)*
Professional Supply Inc....F....419 332-7373
Fremont *(G-10046)*
R & R Comfort Experts LLC....G....216 475-3995
Cleveland *(G-5947)*
Rack Draft Service Inc....F....513 353-5520
North Bend *(G-15054)*
Refrigeration Industries Corp....F....740 377-9166
South Point *(G-17293)*
Rs Pro Sales LLC....G....513 699-5329
Cincinnati *(G-4286)*
▼ RSI Company....F....216 360-9800
Beachwood *(G-1277)*
Snap Rite Manufacturing Inc....E....910 897-4080
Cleveland *(G-6075)*
So-Low Environmental Eqp Co....E....513 772-9410
Cincinnati *(G-4350)*
Space Dynamics Corp....E....513 792-9800
Blue Ash *(G-1847)*
Sticker Corporation....F....440 946-2100
Willoughby *(G-20438)*
T J F Inc....F....419 878-4400
Waterville *(G-19506)*
Tactical Envmtl Systems Inc....G....513 831-2663
Milford *(G-14042)*
▲ Taiho Corporation of America....C....419 443-1645
Tiffin *(G-18086)*
Taylor & Moore Co....F....513 733-5530
Cincinnati *(G-4407)*
◆ Tempest Inc....E....216 883-6500
Cleveland *(G-6158)*
Ten Dogs Global Industries LLC....D....513 752-9000
Batavia *(G-1189)*
Thermo King Corporation....F....478 625-7241
Chagrin Falls *(G-3031)*
Trane Company....F....419 491-2278
Holland *(G-10963)*
Trane US Inc....E....513 771-8884
Cincinnati *(G-4429)*
Trane US Inc....C....614 473-3131
Columbus *(G-7536)*
Trane US Inc....C....614 497-6300
Groveport *(G-10515)*
Trane US Inc....D....614 473-8701
Columbus *(G-7537)*
Variflow Equipment Inc....G....513 245-0420
Cincinnati *(G-4467)*
◆ Vertiv Corporation....A....614 888-0246
Columbus *(G-7575)*
Vertiv Group Corporation....A....614 888-0246
Columbus *(G-7576)*
Vertiv Holdings LLC....G....614 888-0246
Columbus *(G-7577)*
Virginia Air Distributors Inc....G....614 262-1129
Columbus *(G-7584)*
Vortec Corporation....E....513 891-7485
Blue Ash *(G-1866)*

Whirlpool Corporation.....C.....614 409-4340
Lockbourne *(G-12000)*

3586 Measuring & Dispensing Pumps

Bandit Machine Inc.....G.....419 281-6595
Ashland *(G-683)*
Bergstrom Company Ltd Partnr.....E.....440 232-2282
Cleveland *(G-4805)*
Cohesant Inc.....E.....216 910-1700
Beachwood *(G-1228)*
Energy Manufacturing Ltd.....G.....419 355-9304
Fremont *(G-10012)*
▲ **Field Stone Inc**.....D.....937 898-3236
Tipp City *(G-18112)*
◆ **Gojo Industries Inc**.....C.....330 255-6000
Akron *(G-189)*
Gojo Industries Inc.....C.....330 255-6525
Stow *(G-17593)*
Gojo Industries Inc.....C.....330 922-4522
Cuyahoga Falls *(G-7874)*
▲ **Graco Ohio Inc**.....D.....330 494-1313
North Canton *(G-15088)*
Hydro Systems Company.....G.....513 271-8800
Milford *(G-14017)*
◆ **Hydro Systems Company**.....E.....513 271-8800
Cincinnati *(G-3832)*
Neptune Chemical Pump Company.....G.....513 870-3239
West Chester *(G-19748)*
Porto Pump Inc.....G.....740 454-2576
Zanesville *(G-21170)*
Precision Conveyor Technology.....F.....440 352-3601
Perry *(G-15911)*
◆ **Seepex Inc**.....C.....937 864-7150
Enon *(G-9386)*
▲ **Tolco Corporation**.....D.....419 241-1113
Toledo *(G-18555)*
Tranzonic Companies.....B.....216 535-4300
Richmond Heights *(G-16507)*
▲ **Valco Cincinnati Inc**.....C.....513 874-6550
West Chester *(G-19914)*
Valco Cincinnati Inc.....G.....513 874-6550
West Chester *(G-19915)*

3589 Service Ind Machines, NEC

Accushred LLC.....F.....419 244-7473
Toledo *(G-18154)*
American Craft Hardware LLC.....G.....440 746-0098
Cleveland *(G-4686)*
American Plastics LLC.....C.....419 423-1213
Findlay *(G-9650)*
▲ **Ameriwater LLC**.....E.....937 461-8833
Dayton *(G-8030)*
Amsoil Inc.....G.....614 274-9851
Columbus *(G-6593)*
Aqua Pennsylvania Inc.....G.....440 257-6190
Mentor On The Lake *(G-13631)*
Askia Inc.....G.....513 828-7443
Cincinnati *(G-3362)*
Aurand Manufacturing & Eqp Co.....G.....513 541-7200
Cincinnati *(G-3371)*
B L Anderson Co Inc.....G.....765 463-1518
West Chester *(G-19654)*
▲ **Baleco International Inc**.....E.....513 353-3000
North Bend *(G-15050)*
Beckman Environmental Svcs Inc.....F.....513 752-3570
Batavia *(G-1127)*
Best Equipment Co Inc.....G.....440 237-3515
North Royalton *(G-15263)*
Buckeye Field Supply Ltd.....G.....513 312-2343
Cincinnati *(G-3428)*
C J Smith Machinery Service.....G.....614 348-1376
Columbus *(G-6719)*
Car-Nation Inc.....G.....330 862-9001
Paris *(G-15808)*
Chiefs Manufacturing & Eqp Co.....G.....216 291-3200
Cleveland *(G-4921)*
Cintas Corporation No 2.....G.....937 236-1506
Dayton *(G-8090)*
City of Ashland.....G.....419 289-8728
Ashland *(G-694)*
City of Athens.....E.....740 592-3344
Athens *(G-825)*
City of Chardon.....F.....440 286-2657
Chardon *(G-3105)*
City of Marietta.....E.....740 374-6864
Marietta *(G-12615)*
City of Middletown.....F.....513 425-7781
Middletown *(G-13894)*
City of Ravenna.....G.....330 296-5214
Ravenna *(G-16372)*
City of Troy.....F.....937 339-4826
Troy *(G-18641)*
City of Xenia.....F.....937 376-7269
Xenia *(G-20762)*
Clark Auto Machine Shop.....G.....216 939-0768
Cleveland *(G-4937)*
Clean Water Conditioning.....G.....614 475-4532
Columbus *(G-6771)*
▲ **Cleveland Range LLC**.....C.....216 481-4900
Cleveland *(G-4972)*
Comp-U-Chem Inc.....G.....740 345-3332
Newark *(G-14863)*
Complete Dry Flood.....G.....513 200-9274
Cincinnati *(G-3539)*
County of Lake.....F.....440 428-1794
Madison *(G-12345)*
County of Lawrence.....F.....740 867-8700
Chesapeake *(G-3144)*
CST Zero Discharged Car Wash S.....G.....740 947-5480
Waverly *(G-19543)*
De Nora Holdings Us Inc.....B.....440 710-5300
Painesville *(G-15729)*
◆ **De Nora Tech LLC**.....D.....440 710-5300
Painesville *(G-15731)*
◆ **Detrex Corporation**.....F.....216 749-2605
Cleveland *(G-5087)*
Dinkmar Inc.....G.....419 468-8516
Galion *(G-10132)*
▲ **E - I Corp**.....F.....614 899-2282
Westerville *(G-19988)*
◆ **Eagle Crusher Co Inc**.....C.....419 468-2288
Galion *(G-10135)*
Eastern Ohio Investments Inc.....G.....740 266-2228
Steubenville *(G-17532)*
▲ **Electric Eel Mfg Co Inc**.....E.....937 323-4644
Springfield *(G-17395)*
▲ **Enting Water Conditioning Inc**.....E.....937 294-5100
Moraine *(G-14350)*
Environmental Closure Systems.....F.....614 759-9186
Reynoldsburg *(G-16437)*
Erichar Inc.....G.....216 402-2628
Cleveland *(G-5188)*
Evers Enterprises Inc.....G.....513 541-7200
Cincinnati *(G-3657)*
Flexcart LLC.....G.....614 348-2517
New Albany *(G-14624)*
▲ **Flow-Liner Systems Ltd**.....E.....800 348-0020
Zanesville *(G-21136)*
Friess Equipment Inc.....G.....330 945-9440
Akron *(G-178)*
▼ **Frontline International Inc**.....F.....330 861-1100
Cuyahoga Falls *(G-7870)*
▲ **Giant Industries Inc**.....E.....419 531-4600
Toledo *(G-18305)*
Greene County.....G.....937 429-0127
Dayton *(G-7981)*
◆ **Henny Penny Corporation**.....A.....937 456-8400
Eaton *(G-9152)*
Hi-Vac Corporation.....G.....740 374-2306
Marietta *(G-12632)*
High-TEC Industrial Services.....C.....937 667-1772
Tipp City *(G-18115)*
Hilo Tech Inc.....G.....440 979-1155
North Olmsted *(G-15192)*
Hirons Memorial Works Inc.....G.....937 444-2917
Mount Orab *(G-14444)*
Hobart Corporation.....E.....937 332-3000
Troy *(G-18671)*
Hobart Corporation.....C.....937 332-2797
Piqua *(G-16128)*
Holdren Brothers Inc.....F.....937 465-7050
West Liberty *(G-19936)*
Illinois Tool Works Inc.....E.....937 335-7171
Troy *(G-18673)*
Image By J & K LLC.....B.....888 667-6929
Maumee *(G-13118)*
Imet Corporation.....G.....440 799-3135
Cleveland *(G-5441)*
J & K Wade Ltd.....G.....419 352-6163
Bowling Green *(G-1977)*
◆ **JE Grote Company Inc**.....D.....614 868-8414
Columbus *(G-7065)*
K S W C Inc.....G.....440 577-1114
Pierpont *(G-16065)*
K2 Pure Solutions LP.....G.....925 526-8112
Uniontown *(G-18922)*
◆ **Kaivac Inc**.....E.....513 887-4600
Hamilton *(G-10577)*
Knight Manufacturing Co Inc.....G.....740 676-5516
Shadyside *(G-16923)*
◆ **Komar Industries Inc**.....E.....614 836-2366
Groveport *(G-10497)*
L A Express.....G.....513 752-6999
Batavia *(G-1162)*
L N Brut Manufacturing Co.....G.....330 833-9045
Navarre *(G-14578)*
Larrys Water Conditioning.....G.....419 887-0290
Maumee *(G-13126)*
Layne Heavy Civil Inc.....E.....513 424-7287
Middletown *(G-13919)*
Lima Sheet Metal Machine & Mfg.....E.....419 229-1161
Lima *(G-11893)*
Link-O-Matic Company Inc.....F.....765 962-1538
Brookville *(G-2173)*
Mack Industries PA Inc.....F.....330 638-7680
Vienna *(G-19202)*
Majic Touch.....G.....330 923-8259
Cuyahoga Falls *(G-7896)*
Master Disposers Inc.....F.....513 553-2289
New Richmond *(G-14812)*
McNish Corporation.....G.....614 899-2282
Westerville *(G-20010)*
Metal Equipment Co.....E.....440 835-3100
Westlake *(G-20130)*
Monarch Water Systems Inc.....F.....937 426-5773
Beavercreek *(G-1333)*
▲ **Mork Process Inc**.....E.....330 928-3700
Worthington *(G-20698)*
Mountain Filtration Systems.....G.....419 395-2526
Defiance *(G-8640)*
MPW Industrial Svcs Group Inc.....D.....740 927-8790
Hebron *(G-10754)*
Mt Vernon Cy Wastewater Trtmnt.....F.....740 393-9502
Mount Vernon *(G-14495)*
N-Viro International Corp.....F.....419 535-6374
Toledo *(G-18421)*
National Pride Equipment Inc.....G.....419 289-2886
Ashland *(G-727)*
Neil Barton.....G.....614 889-9933
Dublin *(G-8953)*
New Aqua LLC.....G.....614 265-9000
Columbus *(G-7215)*
◆ **Norwalk Wastewater Eqp Co**.....E.....419 668-4471
Norwalk *(G-15411)*
◆ **Nss Enterprises Inc**.....C.....419 531-2121
Toledo *(G-18430)*
Oceco Inc.....F.....419 447-0916
Tiffin *(G-18073)*
Oh-LI Commercial Cleaning LLC.....G.....614 390-3628
Grove City *(G-10453)*
▲ **Or-Tec Inc**.....G.....216 475-5225
Maple Heights *(G-12576)*
Peerless Stove & Mfg Co Inc.....F.....419 625-4514
Sandusky *(G-16836)*
Pelton Environmental Products.....G.....440 838-1221
Lewis Center *(G-11770)*
◆ **Pentair Flow Technologies LLC**.....C.....419 289-1144
Ashland *(G-734)*
Pentair Flow Technologies LLC.....G.....419 281-9918
Ashland *(G-735)*
Powerbuff Inc.....F.....419 241-2156
Toledo *(G-18475)*
Powerwash of Ohio.....G.....614 260-2756
Lewis Center *(G-11773)*
R D Baker Enterprises Inc.....G.....937 461-5225
Dayton *(G-8458)*
Reid Asset Management Company.....G.....216 642-3223
Cleveland *(G-5970)*
Reynolds & Co Inc.....G.....937 592-8300
Bellefontaine *(G-1524)*
Samco Technologies Inc.....G.....216 641-5288
Newburgh Heights *(G-14944)*
Sammy S Auto Detail.....F.....614 263-2728
Columbus *(G-7418)*
Samsco Corp.....F.....216 400-8207
Cleveland *(G-6028)*
Smart Sonic Corporation.....G.....818 610-7900
Cleveland *(G-6072)*
St John Ltd Inc.....G.....614 851-8153
Galloway *(G-10181)*
Staley & Sons Powerwashing LLC.....G.....937 843-2713
Russells Point *(G-16601)*
Tangent Company LLC.....G.....440 543-2775
Chagrin Falls *(G-3079)*
◆ **Tema Systems Inc**.....E.....513 489-7811
Cincinnati *(G-4413)*
Tipton Environmental Intl Inc.....F.....513 735-2777
Batavia *(G-1190)*
Tri County Quality Wtr Systems.....G.....740 751-4764
Marion *(G-12745)*

S I C

Employee Codes: A=Over 500 employees, B=251-500
C=101-250, D=51-100, E=20-50, F=10-19, G=3-9
2019 Harris Ohio
Industrial Directory
971

35 INDUSTRIAL AND COMMERCIAL MACHINERY AND COMPUTER EQUIPMENT

Trionetics Inc .... F 216 812-3570
  Brooklyn Heights (G-2133)
Under Pressure Systems Inc .... G 330 602-4466
  New Philadelphia (G-14807)
United McGill .... G 614 829-1226
  Columbus (G-7557)
▲ Veolia Water Technologies Inc ...... D 937 890-4075
  Vandalia (G-19150)
Village of Somerset .... G 740 743-1986
  Somerset (G-17268)
Village of West Alexandria .... G 937 839-4168
  West Alexandria (G-19623)
W3 Ultrasonics LLC .... G 330 284-3667
  North Canton (G-15136)
Waste Water Pollution Control .... F 330 263-5290
  Wooster (G-20663)
Water & Waste Water Eqp Co .... G 440 542-0972
  Solon (G-17260)
Water Systems Services .... G 513 523-6766
  Oxford (G-15702)
Willow Water Treatment Inc .... G 440 254-6313
  Painesville (G-15800)
X-3-5 LLC .... G 513 489-5477
  Cincinnati (G-4526)

3592 Carburetors, Pistons, Rings & Valves

Ad Piston Ring Company LLC .... F 216 781-5200
  Cleveland (G-4612)
Air Conversion Technology Inc .... G 419 841-1720
  Sylvania (G-17933)
Aswpengg LLC .... G 216 292-4620
  Bedford Heights (G-1461)
Auto-Valve Inc .... E 937 854-3037
  Dayton (G-8043)
Brooks Manufacturing .... G 419 244-1777
  Toledo (G-18216)
Buckeye BOP LLC .... G 740 498-9898
  Newcomerstown (G-14971)
▲ Celina Alum Precision Tech Inc .... B 419 586-2278
  Celina (G-2953)
Dover Corporation .... G 440 951-6600
  Mentor (G-13431)
Eaton Usev Holding Company .... G 216 523-5000
  Cleveland (G-5153)
Federal-Mogul Powertrain LLC .... C 740 432-2393
  Cambridge (G-2437)
Federal-Mogul Valve Train Inte .... F 330 460-5828
  Brunswick (G-2203)
▲ Group Industries Inc .... E 216 271-0702
  Cleveland (G-5355)
Hite Parts Exchange Inc .... E 614 272-5115
  Columbus (G-7003)
Manufacturing Division Inc .... G 330 533-6835
  Canfield (G-2534)
Michael N Wheeler .... F 740 377-9777
  South Point (G-17288)
Northcoast Process Controls .... G 440 498-0542
  Cleveland (G-5771)
Oylair Specialty .... G 614 873-3968
  Plain City (G-16205)
Race Winning Brands Inc .... B 440 951-6600
  Mentor (G-13572)
▲ Seabiscuit Motorsports Inc .... B 440 951-6600
  Mentor (G-13577)
Tiffin Foundry & Machine Inc .... E 419 447-3991
  Tiffin (G-18087)

3593 Fluid Power Cylinders & Actuators

B & H Machine Inc .... E 330 868-6425
  Minerva (G-14176)
Carter Machine Company Inc .... G 419 468-3530
  Galion (G-10125)
Cascade Corporation .... C 937 327-0300
  Springfield (G-17370)
Commercial Honing Ohio Inc .... G 330 343-8896
  Dover (G-8813)
▲ Control Line Equipment Inc .... F 216 433-7766
  Cleveland (G-5025)
▲ Custom Hoists Inc .... C 419 368-4721
  Ashland (G-699)
Cylinders & Valves Inc .... G 440 238-7343
  Strongsville (G-17736)
▲ Dana Limited .... B 419 887-3000
  Maumee (G-13099)
Eaton Leasing Corporation .... G 216 382-2292
  Beachwood (G-1235)
Eaton-Aeroquip Llc .... D 419 891-7775
  Maumee (G-13109)
Emerson Process Management .... E 419 529-4311
  Ontario (G-15541)

Emmco Inc .... G 216 429-2020
  Cleveland (G-5172)
▲ Hunger Hydraulics CC Ltd .... F 419 666-4510
  Rossford (G-16586)
Hydranamics Inc .... D 419 468-3530
  Galion (G-10144)
Hydraulic Parts Store Inc .... E 330 364-6667
  New Philadelphia (G-14774)
▲ Hydraulic Products Inc .... G 440 946-4575
  Willoughby (G-20339)
Hydraulic Specialists Inc .... E 740 922-3343
  Midvale (G-13978)
J D Hydraulic Inc .... F 419 686-5234
  Portage (G-16269)
Kyntrol Holdings Inc .... G 440 220-5990
  Eastlake (G-9119)
Kyntronics Inc .... G 440 220-5990
  Solon (G-17184)
Malcolm Hydraulics .... G 330 819-2033
  Atwater (G-862)
▲ Nook Industries Inc .... C 216 271-7900
  Cleveland (G-5756)
North Coast Instruments Inc .... E 216 251-2353
  Cleveland (G-5766)
Northcoast Process Controls .... G 440 498-0542
  Cleveland (G-5771)
▲ Parker-Hannifin Corporation .... B 216 896-3000
  Cleveland (G-5848)
Parker-Hannifin Corporation .... F 216 896-3000
  Cleveland (G-5850)
Parker-Hannifin Corporation .... G 330 336-3511
  Wadsworth (G-19260)
Qcsm LLC .... G 216 531-5960
  Cleveland (G-5937)
R & J Cylinder & Machine Inc .... D 330 364-8263
  New Philadelphia (G-14794)
R & M Fluid Power Inc .... E 330 758-2766
  Youngstown (G-21010)
▲ Robeck Fluid Power Co .... D 330 562-1140
  Aurora (G-903)
Rosenboom Machine & Tool Inc ..... E 419 352-9484
  Bowling Green (G-1998)
Sebring Fluid Power Corp .... G 330 938-9984
  Sebring (G-16894)
▲ Skidmore-Wilhelm Mfg Company .. E 216 481-4774
  Solon (G-17232)
Steel Eqp Specialists Inc .... E 330 829-2626
  Alliance (G-501)
▲ Steel Eqp Specialists Inc .... D 330 823-8260
  Alliance (G-502)
Suburban Manufacturing Co .... D 440 953-2024
  Eastlake (G-9133)
Swagelok Company .... G 440 349-5934
  Solon (G-17242)
United Hydraulics .... F 440 585-0906
  Wickliffe (G-20234)
▲ Waltco Lift Corp .... C 330 633-9191
  Tallmadge (G-18013)
Xomox Corporation .... E 936 271-6500
  Cincinnati (G-4527)
Zaytran Corporation .... E 440 324-2814
  Elyria (G-9348)

3594 Fluid Power Pumps & Motors

Aerocontrolex Group Inc .... D 440 352-6182
  Painesville (G-15706)
Alkid Corporation .... G 216 896-3000
  Cleveland (G-4662)
▲ All - Flo Pump Company .... E 440 354-1700
  Mentor (G-13382)
Ban-Fam Industries Inc .... G 216 265-9588
  Cleveland (G-4788)
Bergstrom Company Ltd Partnr .... E 440 232-2282
  Cleveland (G-4805)
Bosch Rexroth Corporation .... B 330 263-3300
  Wooster (G-20573)
Custom Cltch Jint Hydrlics Inc .... F 216 431-1630
  Cleveland (G-5046)
Cylinders & Valves Inc .... G 440 238-7343
  Strongsville (G-17736)
◆ Eaton Corporation .... B 440 523-5000
  Cleveland (G-5146)
Eaton Hydraulics LLC .... E 419 232-7777
  Van Wert (G-19088)
Eaton Leasing Corporation .... G 216 382-2292
  Beachwood (G-1235)
Eaton-Aeroquip Llc .... D 419 891-7775
  Maumee (G-13109)
Emerson Process Management .... E 419 529-4311
  Ontario (G-15541)

▲ Force Control Industries Inc .... D 513 868-0900
  Fairfield (G-9498)
▼ Furukawa Rock Drill USA Co Ltd .. E 330 673-5826
  Kent (G-11325)
▲ Giant Industries Inc .... E 419 531-4600
  Toledo (G-18305)
Gorman-Rupp Company .... B 419 755-1011
  Mansfield (G-12447)
Gorman-Rupp Company .... G 419 755-1011
  Mansfield (G-12450)
H Y O Inc .... F 614 488-2861
  Columbus (G-6974)
Hite Parts Exchange Inc .... E 614 272-5115
  Columbus (G-7003)
▲ Hy-Production Inc .... C 330 273-2400
  Valley City (G-19040)
Hydraulic Parts Store Inc .... E 330 364-6667
  New Philadelphia (G-14774)
▲ Hydraulic Products Inc .... G 440 946-4575
  Willoughby (G-20339)
Ingersoll-Rand Company .... E 419 633-6800
  Bryan (G-2291)
▲ Linde Hydraulics Corporation ...... E 330 533-6801
  Canfield (G-2532)
Midwest Tool & Engineering Co ...... E 937 224-0756
  Dayton (G-8356)
▲ Opw Inc .... A 800 422-2525
  West Chester (G-19755)
Parker Hannifin Partner B LLC .... G 216 896-3000
  Cleveland (G-5845)
Parker Royalty Partnership .... D 216 896-3000
  Cleveland (G-5846)
Parker-Hannifin Corporation .... C 330 963-0601
  Macedonia (G-12313)
Parker-Hannifin Corporation .... C 937 962-5301
  Lewisburg (G-11796)
Parker-Hannifin Corporation .... C 330 740-8366
  Youngstown (G-20994)
Parker-Hannifin Corporation .... C 513 847-1758
  West Chester (G-19757)
Parker-Hannifin Corporation .... B 440 366-5100
  Elyria (G-9308)
Parker-Hannifin Corporation .... C 330 261-1618
  Berlin Center (G-1650)
Parker-Hannifin Corporation .... F 216 896-3000
  Macedonia (G-12314)
Parker-Hannifin Corporation .... E 440 266-2300
  Mentor (G-13542)
Parker-Hannifin Corporation .... C 440 205-8230
  Mentor (G-13543)
Parker-Hannifin Corporation .... C 937 644-3915
  Marysville (G-12805)
Parker-Hannifin Corporation .... G 216 896-3000
  Cleveland (G-5850)
Parker-Hannifin Corporation .... F 330 743-6893
  Youngstown (G-20995)
▲ Parker-Hannifin Corporation .... B 216 896-3000
  Cleveland (G-5848)
Pfpc Enterprises Inc .... B 513 941-6200
  Cincinnati (G-4155)
Quad Fluid Dynamics Inc .... F 330 220-3005
  Brunswick (G-2231)
R & L Hydraulics Inc .... G 937 399-3407
  Springfield (G-17478)
Radocy Inc .... F 419 666-4400
  Rossford (G-16591)
▲ Robeck Fluid Power Co .... D 330 562-1140
  Aurora (G-903)
▲ Semtorq Inc .... F 330 487-0600
  Twinsburg (G-18856)
Stanley Proctor & Company Inc ...... F 330 425-7814
  Twinsburg (G-18859)
Starkey Machinery Inc .... E 419 468-2560
  Galion (G-10157)
Suburban Manufacturing Co .... D 440 953-2024
  Eastlake (G-9133)
Sunset Industries Inc .... E 216 731-8131
  Euclid (G-9444)
Swagelok Company .... E 440 349-5836
  Solon (G-17243)
Toth Industries Inc .... D 419 729-4669
  Toledo (G-18578)
Vertiflo Pump Company .... F 513 530-0888
  Cincinnati (G-4478)
Vickers International Inc .... F 419 867-2200
  Maumee (G-13159)

3596 Scales & Balances, Exc Laboratory

Advance Weight System Inc .... F 440 926-3691
  Grafton (G-10291)

35 INDUSTRIAL AND COMMERCIAL MACHINERY AND COMPUTER EQUIPMENT

▲ Etched Metal Company ....E 440 248-0240
Solon *(G-17142)*
Exact Equipment Corporation ....F 215 295-2000
Columbus *(G-6491)*
Hobart Corporation ....E 937 332-3000
Troy *(G-18671)*
Hobart Corporation ....C 937 332-2797
Piqua *(G-16128)*
▲ Holtgrven Scale Elctronic Corp ....F 419 422-4779
Findlay *(G-9704)*
Interface Logic Systems Inc ....G 614 236-8388
Columbus *(G-7041)*
K Davis Inc ....G 419 637-2859
Gibsonburg *(G-10249)*
Kanawha Scales & Systems Inc ....F 513 576-0700
Milford *(G-14023)*
Mettler-Toledo LLC ....D 614 438-4511
Worthington *(G-20695)*
Mettler-Toledo LLC ....C 614 438-4390
Worthington *(G-20696)*
Mettler-Toledo LLC ....C 614 841-7300
Columbus *(G-7174)*
Mettler-Toledo Intl Fin Inc ....G 614 438-4511
Columbus *(G-6500)*
◆ Mettler-Toledo Intl Inc ....B 614 438-4511
Columbus *(G-6501)*
Roth Transit Inc ....G 937 773-5051
Piqua *(G-16160)*
T & S Enterprises ....E 419 424-1122
Findlay *(G-9766)*

3599 Machinery & Eqpt, Indl & Commercial, NEC

2-M Manufacturing Company ....E 440 269-1270
Eastlake *(G-9096)*
3d Sales & Consulting Inc ....E 513 422-1198
Middletown *(G-13874)*
3way Machine and Tool Company ....F 419 925-7222
Maria Stein *(G-12597)*
5s Inc ....G 440 968-0212
Montville *(G-14323)*
8888 Butler Investments Inc ....G 440 748-0810
North Ridgeville *(G-15205)*
▲ A & G Manufacturing Co Inc ....F 419 468-7433
Galion *(G-10119)*
A & G Manufacturing Co Inc ....D 419 468-7433
Galion *(G-10120)*
A & L Industries ....E 419 698-3733
Oregon *(G-15551)*
A & L Machine Tool ....G 513 863-2662
Hamilton *(G-10527)*
A & R Machine Co Inc ....G 330 832-4631
Massillon *(G-12957)*
A and V Grinding Inc ....G 937 444-4141
Cincinnati *(G-3276)*
A B & J Machining & Fabg ....E 513 769-5900
Cincinnati *(G-3277)*
A E Ruston Electric LLC ....G 740 286-3022
Jackson *(G-11178)*
A S T Machine Co ....G 740 494-2013
Prospect *(G-16349)*
A&S Machine ....G 440 946-3976
Willoughby *(G-20265)*
A+ Engineering Fabrication Inc ....F 419 832-0748
Grand Rapids *(G-10314)*
A-A1 Machine and Supply Co ....G 440 346-0698
Tallmadge *(G-17970)*
Abbey Machine Products Co ....G 216 481-0080
Medina *(G-13216)*
Abco Bar & Tube Cutting Svc ....G 513 697-9487
Maineville *(G-12364)*
Able Grinding Co Inc ....G 216 961-6555
Cleveland *(G-4600)*
Able Tool Corporation ....E 513 733-8989
Cincinnati *(G-3288)*
Absolute Cnc Machining LLC ....G 937 855-0406
Germantown *(G-10240)*
Absolute Grinding Co Inc ....F 440 974-4030
Mentor *(G-13369)*
Accu Tool Inc ....G 937 667-5878
Tipp City *(G-18095)*
Accu-Grind & Mfg Co Inc ....G 937 224-3303
Dayton *(G-8002)*
Accu-Tech Mfg & Support ....F 440 205-8882
Mentor *(G-13370)*
Accuform Manufacturing Inc ....E 330 797-9291
Youngstown *(G-20834)*
Accurate Automatic Mfg Ltd ....G 330 435-4575
Creston *(G-7802)*

Accurate Machining & Welding ....G 937 584-4518
Sabina *(G-16615)*
Accurate Manufacturing Company ...E 614 878-6510
Columbus *(G-6534)*
Accurate Metal Machining Inc ....C 440 350-8225
Painesville *(G-15704)*
Accurate Tech Inc ....G 440 951-9153
Mentor *(G-13372)*
Ace Boiler & Welding Co Inc ....G 330 745-4443
Barberton *(G-1048)*
▲ Ace Manufacturing Company .....E 513 541-2490
West Chester *(G-19825)*
▲ Ace Precision Industries Inc ....E 330 633-8523
Akron *(G-28)*
Acme Machine Technology LLC ......G 419 594-3349
Oakwood *(G-15468)*
Acrodyne Mfg Co ....G 614 443-5517
Columbus *(G-6538)*
Action Machine & Manufacturing ....G 513 899-3889
Morrow *(G-14407)*
Action Mechanical Repair Inc ....E 513 353-1046
Cincinnati *(G-3294)*
Action Precision Products Inc ....E 419 737-2348
Pioneer *(G-16083)*
▲ Addisonmckee Inc ....C 513 228-7000
Lebanon *(G-11629)*
ADI Machining Inc ....F 440 277-4141
Sheffield Village *(G-16964)*
▲ Advance Apex Inc ....E 614 539-3000
Grove City *(G-10410)*
Advance Manufacturing Corp ....E 216 333-1684
Cleveland *(G-4622)*
Advanced Cylinder Repair Inc ....G 419 289-0538
Ashland *(G-675)*
▲ Advanced Design Industries Inc ..E 440 277-4141
Sheffield Village *(G-16965)*
Advanced Engrg & Mfg Co Inc ....F 330 686-9911
Stow *(G-17567)*
Advanced Indus Machining Inc ....E 614 596-4183
Powell *(G-16307)*
Advanced Machine Solutions LLC ....F 419 733-2537
Wapakoneta *(G-19317)*
Advanced Sleeve Corp ....G 440 205-1055
Mentor *(G-13376)*
Advanced Welding Co ....F 937 746-6800
Franklin *(G-9867)*
Advantage Machine Shop ....G 330 337-8377
Salem *(G-16715)*
Advetech Inc ....E 330 533-2227
Canfield *(G-2517)*
Aero Prep LLC ....G 513 469-8300
Cincinnati *(G-3305)*
Aero-Med Industries Inc ....G 216 459-0004
Cleveland *(G-4631)*
Aeroserv Inc ....F 513 932-9227
Mason *(G-12821)*
Aerotech Enterprise ....F 440 729-2616
Chesterland *(G-3151)*
Aims-CMI Technology LLC ....F 937 832-2000
Englewood *(G-9349)*
Aircraft and Auto Fittings Co ....G 216 486-0047
Cleveland *(G-4646)*
▲ Aja Industries LLC ....G 614 216-9566
Gahanna *(G-10074)*
Akro Tool Co Inc ....G 513 858-1555
Fairfield *(G-9479)*
▼ Akron Equipment Company ....G 330 645-3780
Coventry Township *(G-7763)*
Akron Gear & Engineering Inc ....E 330 773-6608
Akron *(G-41)*
▼ Akron Special Machinery Inc ......E 330 753-1077
Akron *(G-51)*
Albright Machine ....G 419 483-1088
Monroeville *(G-14286)*
Aleco Machine LLC ....G 513 894-6400
Hamilton *(G-10531)*
▲ Alex Products Inc ....B 419 267-5240
Ridgeville Corners *(G-16510)*
▲ Alfons Haar Inc ....F 937 560-2031
Springboro *(G-17321)*
Alfred Machine Co ....D 440 248-4600
Cleveland *(G-4661)*
All Craft Manufacturing Co ....F 513 661-3383
Cincinnati *(G-3321)*
All Purpose Machine ....G 419 238-2794
Van Wert *(G-19075)*
All-Tech Manufacturing Ltd ....E 330 633-1095
Akron *(G-58)*
All-Type Welding & Fabrication ......E 440 439-3990
Cleveland *(G-4669)*

Allen Randall Enterprises Inc ....F 330 374-9850
Akron *(G-59)*
▲ Alliance Automation LLC ....F 419 238-2520
Van Wert *(G-19076)*
Allied Machine Works Inc ....G 740 454-2534
Zanesville *(G-21097)*
Allied Mask and Tooling Inc ....G 419 470-2555
Toledo *(G-18164)*
Allied Pedestal Boom Sys LLC ....G 419 663-0279
Norwalk *(G-15379)*
◆ Alloy Bllows Prcision Wldg Inc ...D 440 684-3000
Cleveland *(G-4674)*
Alloy Machining and Fabg ....E 330 482-5543
Columbiana *(G-6453)*
Alpha Machining LLC ....G 330 889-2207
West Farmington *(G-19919)*
Alpha Omega Dev & Mch Co ....G 440 352-9915
Painesville *(G-15708)*
Alternative Surface Grinding ....E 330 273-3443
Brunswick *(G-2187)*
Alton Products Inc ....F 419 893-0201
Maumee *(G-13068)*
Aluminum Fence & Mfg Co ....G 330 755-3323
Aurora *(G-868)*
Amcan Productions Ltd ....G 330 332-9129
Salem *(G-16717)*
American Aero Components LLC ....G 937 367-5068
Dayton *(G-8022)*
American Punch Co Inc ....E 216 731-4501
Euclid *(G-9403)*
American Tool Works Inc ....G 513 844-6363
Hamilton *(G-10534)*
American Tool Works Inc ....G 513 844-6363
Hamilton *(G-10535)*
Amerimold Inc ....G 330 628-2190
Mogadore *(G-14229)*
Amon Inc ....F 513 734-1700
Amelia *(G-531)*
Ampsco Division ....F 614 444-2181
Columbus *(G-6592)*
▲ Amt Machine Systems Ltd ....F 614 635-8050
Columbus *(G-6595)*
Amtech Tool and Machine Inc ....F 330 758-8215
Youngstown *(G-20844)*
Anchor Fabricators Inc ....E 937 836-5117
Clayton *(G-4571)*
Anchor Metal Processing Inc ....F 216 362-6463
Cleveland *(G-4707)*
Anchor Metal Processing Inc ....E 216 362-1850
Cleveland *(G-4708)*
Andersons Inc ....E 419 891-2930
Maumee *(G-13073)*
Andrew & Sons Inc ....G 419 693-0292
Toledo *(G-18185)*
Andrew Tool Co Inc ....G 440 237-4340
North Royalton *(G-15260)*
▲ Ansco Machine Company ....E 330 929-8181
Peninsula *(G-15889)*
Anstine Machining Corp ....F 330 821-4365
Alliance *(G-455)*
Anvil Products Co ....G 216 883-3740
Cleveland *(G-4719)*
Apex Bolt & Machine Company ....E 419 729-3741
Toledo *(G-18186)*
Applied Experience LLC ....G 614 943-2970
Columbus *(G-6610)*
Apr Tool Inc ....F 440 946-0393
Willoughby *(G-20278)*
Arabian Tools Inc ....G 440 286-3600
Chardon *(G-3099)*
ARC Drilling Inc ....F 216 525-0920
Cleveland *(G-4723)*
Ardar Co Inc ....G 440 582-3371
Cleveland *(G-4731)*
◆ ARM (usa) Inc ....F 740 264-6599
Steubenville *(G-17527)*
Arnold Machine Inc ....F 419 443-1818
Tiffin *(G-18045)*
Arnolds Repair Shop ....G 740 373-5313
Marietta *(G-12604)*
Arsco Custom Metals LLC ....D 513 563-8822
Cincinnati *(G-3357)*
Artisan Equipment Inc ....F 740 756-9135
Carroll *(G-2898)*
Artisan Grinding Service Inc ....F 937 667-7383
Dayton *(G-8038)*
Asb Industries Inc ....E 330 753-8458
Barberton *(G-1054)*
Ashcraft Machine & Supply Inc ......F 740 349-8110
Newark *(G-14853)*

Employee Codes: A=Over 500 employees, B=251-500
C=101-250, D=51-100, E=20-50, F=10-19, G=3-9

2019 Harris Ohio
Industrial Directory

35 INDUSTRIAL AND COMMERCIAL MACHINERY AND COMPUTER EQUIPMENT SIC SECTION

Ashland Precision Tooling LLC............D....... 419 289-1736
Ashland *(G-679)*
Ashta Forge & Machine Inc....................E....... 216 252-7000
Cleveland *(G-4750)*
Aspen Machine and Plastics..................G....... 937 526-4644
Versailles *(G-19173)*
Assembly Machining Wire Pdts............G....... 614 443-1110
Columbus *(G-6622)*
Associated Press Repair Inc..................G....... 216 881-2288
Cleveland *(G-4753)*
Athens Mold and Machine Inc..............D....... 740 593-6613
Athens *(G-823)*
Atlas Gear and Machine Co....................G....... 614 272-6944
Columbus *(G-6626)*
◆ **Atlas Industries Inc**............................C....... 419 355-1000
Fremont *(G-9993)*
Atlas Industries Inc................................B....... 419 637-2117
Tiffin *(G-18046)*
Atlas Industries Inc................................D....... 419 447-4730
Tiffin *(G-18047)*
Atlas Machine and Supply Inc..............G....... 614 351-1603
Hilliard *(G-10807)*
Atlas Machine and Supply Inc..............E....... 502 584-7262
West Chester *(G-19834)*
Atlas Precision Machining Inc..............G....... 937 615-9585
Piqua *(G-16102)*
Ats Machine & Tool Co Inc....................F....... 440 255-1120
Mentor *(G-13394)*
Auglaize Erie Machine Company..........E....... 419 629-2068
New Bremen *(G-14647)*
Austinburg Machine Inc........................G....... 440 275-2001
Austinburg *(G-918)*
Austins Machine Shop............................E....... 614 855-2525
Blacklick *(G-1678)*
Automatic Parts......................................E....... 419 524-5841
Mansfield *(G-12409)*
Autotec Engineering Company..............E....... 419 885-2529
Toledo *(G-18195)*
Axis Tool & Grinding LLC......................G....... 330 535-4713
Akron *(G-75)*
B & B Gear & Machine Co Inc................F....... 937 687-1771
New Lebanon *(G-14707)*
▲ **B & C Research Inc**..............................B....... 330 848-4000
Barberton *(G-1056)*
B & D Machinists Inc..............................F....... 513 831-8588
Milford *(G-13995)*
B & F Manufacturing Co..........................F....... 216 518-0333
Warrensville Heights *(G-19464)*
B & G Machine Company Inc..................G....... 440 946-8787
Mentor *(G-13400)*
B & G Tool Company................................G....... 614 451-2538
Columbus *(G-6640)*
B & H Machine Inc....................................E....... 330 868-6425
Minerva *(G-14176)*
B & R Machine Co Inc..............................F....... 216 961-7370
Cleveland *(G-4784)*
B & T Welding and Machine Co..............G....... 740 687-1908
Lancaster *(G-11545)*
B B & H Tool Company............................G....... 614 868-8634
Reynoldsburg *(G-16429)*
B C Machining Inc....................................G....... 440 593-4763
Conneaut *(G-7641)*
B C Metals Inc..G....... 513 732-9644
Batavia *(G-1125)*
B N Machine Inc..G....... 440 255-5200
Mentor *(G-13401)*
B S F Inc..F....... 937 890-6121
Tipp City *(G-18100)*
B Y G Industries Inc..................................G....... 216 961-5436
Cleveland *(G-4785)*
B&C Machine Co LLC................................B....... 330 745-4013
Barberton *(G-1058)*
Baco Manufacturing Corp........................G....... 440 585-5858
Wickliffe *(G-20199)*
Bainter Machining Company....................F....... 740 756-4598
Carroll *(G-2899)*
Bainter Machining Company....................E....... 740 653-2422
Lancaster *(G-11547)*
Balancing Company Inc............................E....... 937 898-9111
Vandalia *(G-19117)*
Ban-Fam Industries Inc............................G....... 216 265-9588
Cleveland *(G-4788)*
Bar Processing Corp..................................G....... 440 943-0094
Wickliffe *(G-20200)*
▲ **Bardons & Oliver Inc**............................C....... 440 498-5800
Solon *(G-17112)*
Barile Precision Grinding Inc..................E....... 216 267-6500
Cleveland *(G-4791)*
Bartley Offie..G....... 614 235-9050
Columbus *(G-6653)*
Bay West Products....................................G....... 440 835-1991
Bay Village *(G-1205)*
Beacon Metal Fabricators Inc..................F....... 216 391-7444
Cleveland *(G-4798)*
Beckman Machine LLC..............................E....... 513 242-2700
Cincinnati *(G-3386)*
Beemer Machine Company Inc................G....... 330 678-3822
Kent *(G-11300)*
Bender Cycle & Machine Corp................G....... 440 946-0681
Willoughby *(G-20284)*
▲ **Berea Manufacturing Inc**......................F....... 440 260-0590
Berea *(G-1593)*
Bergman Tool & Machine Co....................G....... 419 925-4963
Maria Stein *(G-12598)*
Berran Industrial Group Inc....................E....... 330 253-5800
Akron *(G-85)*
Best Inc..G....... 419 394-2745
Saint Marys *(G-16677)*
Best Mold & Manufacturing Inc..............E....... 330 896-9988
Akron *(G-86)*
Best Performance Inc................................G....... 419 394-2299
Saint Marys *(G-16678)*
Beta Industries Inc....................................E....... 937 299-7385
Dayton *(G-8056)*
Beta Machine Company Inc......................F....... 216 383-0000
Cleveland *(G-4809)*
Beverage Machine & Fabricators............F....... 216 252-5100
Cleveland *(G-4811)*
▲ **Bexley Pen Company Inc**......................G....... 614 351-9988
Columbus *(G-6667)*
Bic Manufacturing Inc..............................E....... 216 531-9393
Euclid *(G-9405)*
Blc Precision Machine Co Inc..................F....... 937 783-1406
Blanchester *(G-1699)*
Bickett Machine and Supply Inc..............G....... 740 353-5710
Portsmouth *(G-16278)*
Bishop Machine Tool & Die......................F....... 740 453-8818
Zanesville *(G-21110)*
Bits & Chips Machining Company..........G....... 513 539-0800
Monroe *(G-14255)*
Black McCuskey Souers............................G....... 330 456-8341
Canton *(G-2593)*
Black Machining & Technology................F....... 513 752-8625
Batavia *(G-1128)*
Blacklick Machine Co Inc..........................G....... 614 866-9300
Blacklick *(G-1680)*
Bleil Chan..G....... 440 352-6012
Mentor *(G-13404)*
Blue Chip Machine & Tool Ltd................G....... 419 626-9559
Sandusky *(G-16797)*
Blue Chip Tool Inc....................................F....... 513 489-3561
Cincinnati *(G-3397)*
Bmi Machine Inc..G....... 614 785-7020
Columbus *(G-6682)*
Bobs Grinding Inc......................................G....... 440 946-6179
Mentor *(G-13405)*
Boggs & Associates Inc..............................G....... 614 237-0600
Columbus *(G-6684)*
Bollari/Davis Inc..F....... 330 296-4445
Ravenna *(G-16370)*
Bomen Marking Products Inc....................G....... 440 582-0053
Cleveland *(G-4829)*
Bond Machine Company Inc......................F....... 937 746-4941
Franklin *(G-9872)*
▼ **Bonnot Company**......................................E....... 330 896-6544
Akron *(G-93)*
Borman Enterprises Inc............................F....... 216 459-9292
Cleveland *(G-4833)*
Bowdil Company..F....... 800 356-8663
Canton *(G-2596)*
Boyce Machine Inc......................................G....... 330 678-3210
Kent *(G-11301)*
Boyds Machine and Met Finshg................F....... 937 698-5623
West Milton *(G-19947)*
Brandts Custom Machining LLC..............G....... 419 566-3192
Mansfield *(G-12413)*
Brinkley Technology Group LLC..............F....... 330 830-2498
Massillon *(G-12963)*
Brocker Machine Inc....................................F....... 330 744-5858
Youngstown *(G-20860)*
Brockman Jig Grinding Service................G....... 937 220-9780
Dayton *(G-8064)*
Brogan Machine Shop..................................G....... 513 683-9054
Loveland *(G-12182)*
Bront Machining Inc....................................E....... 937 228-4551
Moraine *(G-14336)*
Brooklyn Machine & Mfg Co Inc................G....... 216 341-1846
Cleveland *(G-4840)*
Brown Cnc Machinery Inc............................E....... 937 865-9191
Miamisburg *(G-13645)*
Brown Machine Co..G....... 216 631-1255
Cleveland *(G-4845)*
Brown Precision Machine............................G....... 937 675-6585
Jamestown *(G-11218)*
Bruck Manufacturing Co Inc......................G....... 440 327-6619
North Ridgeville *(G-15215)*
Bsm Columbus Llp..G....... 740 755-2380
New Albany *(G-14611)*
Buckeye Field Machining Inc......................G....... 330 336-7036
Norton *(G-15362)*
Buckeye Mch Fabricators Inc......................E....... 419 273-2521
Forest *(G-9785)*
Buckeye State Wldg & Fabg Inc..................F....... 440 322-0319
Elyria *(G-9228)*
Buckys Machine and Fab Ltd......................G....... 419 981-5050
Mc Cutchenville *(G-13191)*
▲ **Bullen Ultrasonics Inc**............................D....... 937 456-7133
Eaton *(G-9144)*
Bullseye Machines LLC................................G....... 419 485-5951
Montpelier *(G-14303)*
Burdens Machine & Welding........................E....... 740 345-9246
Newark *(G-14857)*
▲ **Burke Products Inc**..................................E....... 937 372-3516
Xenia *(G-20759)*
Burn-Rite Mold & Machine Inc....................G....... 330 956-4143
Canton *(G-2602)*
Burton Industries Inc....................................E....... 440 974-1700
Mentor *(G-13407)*
C & D Manufacturing Inc..............................G....... 330 828-8357
Dalton *(G-7937)*
C & K Machine Co Inc....................................G....... 419 237-3203
Fayette *(G-9632)*
C A Joseph Co..F....... 330 532-4646
Irondale *(G-11158)*
▲ **C A Joseph Co**..G....... 330 385-6869
East Liverpool *(G-9051)*
C and J Machine Inc..G....... 330 935-2170
Hartville *(G-10685)*
C G Egli Inc..G....... 937 254-8898
Dayton *(G-8070)*
C M M S - Re Inc..F....... 513 489-5111
Blue Ash *(G-1744)*
C N C Precision Machine Inc..........................D....... 440 548-3880
Parkman *(G-15810)*
C RC Automotive..G....... 513 422-4775
Middletown *(G-13889)*
C-N-D Industries Inc..E....... 330 478-8811
Massillon *(G-12965)*
Cage Gear & Machine LLC................................F....... 330 452-1532
Canton *(G-2604)*
Calvin J Magsig..G....... 419 862-3311
Elmore *(G-9204)*
CAM Machine Inc..E....... 937 663-5000
Saint Paris *(G-16706)*
CAM Machine Inc..G....... 937 663-0680
Saint Paris *(G-16707)*
Capital Machine & Fabrication........................G....... 740 773-4976
Chillicothe *(G-3179)*
Cardinal Machine Company................................F....... 440 238-7050
Strongsville *(G-17722)*
Carnation Machine & Tool Inc..........................G....... 330 823-5352
Alliance *(G-461)*
Carousel Magic LLC..G....... 419 522-6456
Mansfield *(G-12420)*
Carousel Works Inc..E....... 419 522-7558
Mansfield *(G-12421)*
Cascade Unlimited LLC..G....... 440 352-7995
Painesville *(G-15721)*
▲ **Case-Maul Manufacturing Co**..........................F....... 419 524-1061
Mansfield *(G-12422)*
Caskeys Inc..G....... 330 683-0249
Orrville *(G-15586)*
Cave Tool & Manufacturing Inc..........................F....... 937 324-0662
Springfield *(G-17371)*
CBs Boring and Mch Co Inc..................................E....... 419 784-9500
Defiance *(G-8618)*
Cctm Inc..G....... 513 934-3533
Lebanon *(G-11641)*
Ceco Machine & Tool..G....... 937 264-3047
Englewood *(G-9351)*
Cen-Trol Machine Co..G....... 216 524-1932
Cleveland *(G-4899)*
Center Automotive Parts Co................................G....... 330 434-2174
Akron *(G-109)*
Center Line Drilling Inc..G....... 440 951-5920
Willoughby *(G-20294)*
Centerless Grinding Service................................G....... 216 251-4100
Cleveland *(G-4900)*
Centerless Grinding Solutions............................G....... 216 520-4612
Twinsburg *(G-18748)*

SIC SECTION
35 INDUSTRIAL AND COMMERCIAL MACHINERY AND COMPUTER EQUIPMENT

Centerline Tool & Machine .... G 937 222-3600
Dayton *(G-8083)*
Central State Enterprises Inc .... E 419 468-8191
Galion *(G-10127)*
Century Tool & Stamping Inc .... F 216 241-2032
Cleveland *(G-4903)*
Certified Welding Co .... F 216 961-5410
Cleveland *(G-4904)*
Chandler Machine Co Inc .... G 330 688-7615
Stow *(G-17576)*
Chandler Machine Prod Gear .... G 330 688-5585
Stow *(G-17577)*
Chardon Metal Products Co .... E 440 285-2147
Chardon *(G-3102)*
Charles Costa Inc .... F 330 376-3636
Akron *(G-112)*
▼ **Chickasaw Machine & Tl Co Inc** .... F 419 925-4325
Celina *(G-2955)*
Chipman Machining Co Inc .... G 513 681-8515
Cincinnati *(G-3471)*
Chipmatic Tool & Machine Inc .... D 419 862-2737
Elmore *(G-9205)*
Chippewa Industries Inc .... G 248 880-9193
Toledo *(G-18231)*
Chips Manufacturing Inc .... G 440 946-3666
Willoughby *(G-20296)*
Christopher Tool & Mfg Co .... C 440 248-8080
Cleveland *(G-4924)*
▲ **Cincinnati Babbitt Inc** .... F 513 942-5088
Fairfield *(G-9490)*
Cincinnati Precision McHy Inc .... G 513 860-4133
West Chester *(G-19673)*
Cinex Inc .... D 513 921-2825
Cincinnati *(G-3515)*
▲ **Circle Machine Rolls Inc** .... E 330 938-9010
Sebring *(G-16885)*
City Machine Technologies Inc .... E 330 740-8186
Youngstown *(G-20871)*
City Machine Technologies Inc .... E 330 747-2639
Youngstown *(G-20872)*
City Machine Technologies Inc .... G 330 747-2639
Youngstown *(G-20873)*
City Machine Technologies Inc .... F 330 747-2639
Youngstown *(G-20870)*
Clark Machine Service .... G 740 887-2396
Londonderry *(G-12074)*
Cleaning Tech Group LLC .... E 513 870-0100
West Chester *(G-19843)*
Clear Creek Screw Machine Corp .... G 740 969-2113
Amanda *(G-525)*
Cleary Machine Company Inc .... E 937 839-4278
West Alexandria *(G-19617)*
Cleveland Jsm Inc .... D 440 876-3050
Strongsville *(G-17729)*
Cleveland Plastic Fabricat .... F 216 797-7300
Euclid *(G-9409)*
Cleveland Special Tool Inc .... F 440 944-1600
Wickliffe *(G-20207)*
◆ **Cleveland Tool and Machine Inc** .... F 216 267-6010
Cleveland *(G-4979)*
Clipsons Metal Working Inc .... G 513 772-6393
Cincinnati *(G-3528)*
Cmt Machining & Fabg LLC .... F 937 652-3740
Urbana *(G-18983)*
Cnc Custom Machining Inc .... G 330 456-5868
Canton *(G-2630)*
Coit Tool Company Inc .... F 440 946-3377
Willoughby *(G-20297)*
▲ **Cold Headed Fas Assemblies Inc** .... F 330 833-0800
Massillon *(G-12968)*
Coleman Machine Inc .... G 740 695-3006
Saint Clairsville *(G-16628)*
Coleys Inc .... E 440 967-5630
Vermilion *(G-19157)*
▲ **Colfor Manufacturing Inc** .... A 330 863-7500
Malvern *(G-12387)*
Columbia Machine Company .... G 740 452-1736
Zanesville *(G-21121)*
Columbus Advnced Mfg Sftwr Inc .... G 614 410-2300
Delaware *(G-8668)*
Columbus Machine Works Inc .... F 614 409-0244
Columbus *(G-6796)*
Combine Grinding Co Inc .... G 440 439-6148
Bedford *(G-1397)*
Combined Industrial Solutions .... G 513 659-3091
Milford *(G-14004)*
▲ **Commercial Honing LLC** .... D 330 343-8896
Dover *(G-8811)*
Compton Metal Products Inc .... D 937 382-2403
Wilmington *(G-20490)*
Comptons Precision Machine .... F 937 325-9139
Springfield *(G-17378)*
Comturn Manufacturing LLC .... G 219 267-6911
Cleveland *(G-5013)*
Concentric Corporation .... F 440 899-9090
Bay Village *(G-1206)*
Conquest Industries Inc .... E 234 678-5555
Stow *(G-17579)*
Copen Machine Inc .... F 330 678-4598
Kent *(G-11307)*
Core-Tech Inc .... G 440 946-8324
Mentor *(G-13423)*
Coshocton Industries Inc .... G 740 622-4734
Coshocton *(G-7728)*
Craig Bros Machine Co Inc .... G 740 756-9280
Carroll *(G-2901)*
Creative Mold and Machine Inc .... E 440 338-5146
Newbury *(G-14950)*
Creative Processing Inc .... F 440 834-4070
Mantua *(G-12544)*
Creative Tool & Die .... G 614 836-0080
Groveport *(G-10488)*
Crissman Tool & Machine Inc .... G 330 872-1412
Newton Falls *(G-14986)*
Crists Machining Inc .... G 740 653-0041
Lancaster *(G-11558)*
Criterion Tool & Die Inc .... E 216 267-1733
Brookpark *(G-2139)*
Croft & Son Mfg Inc .... G 740 859-2200
Tiltonsville *(G-18093)*
Crowe Manufacturing Services .... D 800 831-1893
Troy *(G-18644)*
Crum Manufacturing Inc .... E 419 878-9779
Waterville *(G-19492)*
Ctek Tool & Machine Company .... G 513 742-0423
Cincinnati *(G-3562)*
Curtiss-Wright Flow Control .... D 513 735-2538
Batavia *(G-1134)*
Custom Crankshaft Inc .... E 330 382-1200
East Liverpool *(G-9054)*
Custom Machine Inc .... E 419 986-5122
Tiffin *(G-18057)*
Custom Manufacturing Solutions .... C 937 372-0777
Dayton *(G-8119)*
Custom Metal Works Inc .... F 419 668-7831
Norwalk *(G-15385)*
Custom Tooling Company Inc .... F 513 733-5790
Cincinnati *(G-3566)*
▲ **Cutting Dynamics Inc** .... C 440 249-4150
Avon *(G-947)*
Cutting Edge Manufacturing LLC .... G 419 547-9204
Clyde *(G-6388)*
Cuyahoga Machine Company LLC .... F 216 267-3560
Brookpark *(G-2142)*
D & B Industries Inc .... G 937 253-8658
Dayton *(G-7975)*
D & B Machine Welding Inc .... G 740 922-4930
Uhrichsville *(G-18884)*
D & D Quality Machining Co Inc .... F 440 942-2772
Willoughby *(G-20304)*
D & E Machine Co .... G 513 932-2184
Lebanon *(G-11646)*
D & J Machine Shop .... G 937 256-2730
Dayton *(G-8123)*
D & L Machine Co Inc .... E 330 785-0781
Akron *(G-132)*
D & L Machining LLC .... G 419 253-1351
Marengo *(G-12590)*
D 4 Industries Inc .... G 419 523-9555
Ottawa *(G-15650)*
D M Tool & Plastics Inc .... F 937 962-4140
Brookville *(G-2166)*
D M Tool & Plastics Inc .... F 937 962-4140
Lewisburg *(G-11790)*
D O Technologies Inc .... F 330 725-4561
Medina *(G-13248)*
D S H Machine Co .... G 440 946-4311
Willoughby *(G-20305)*
▼ **Dale Adams Enterprises Inc** .... G 330 524-2800
Twinsburg *(G-18760)*
Dallas Design & Technology Inc .... G 419 884-9750
Mansfield *(G-12431)*
Dalton Stryker McHining Fcilty .... D 419 682-6328
Stryker *(G-17828)*
Dana Off Highway Products LLC .... E 614 864-1116
Blacklick *(G-1683)*
Dana White Machining Wldg Inc .... G 419 652-3444
Nova *(G-15432)*
David Bixel .... F 440 474-4410
Rock Creek *(G-16532)*
▲ **David Price Metal Services Inc** .... C 419 668-3358
Norwalk *(G-15387)*
Davis Machine Products Inc .... G 440 474-0247
Streetsboro *(G-17670)*
Davis Machining Service .... G 513 528-4917
Cincinnati *(G-3577)*
Day Industries Inc .... G 216 577-6674
Grafton *(G-10297)*
Day-TEC Tool & Mfg Inc .... F 937 847-0022
Miamisburg *(G-13654)*
Deangelo Instrument Inc .... G 330 654-9264
Diamond *(G-8797)*
Dearborn Inc .... E 440 234-1353
Berea *(G-1600)*
Dee Lee Machine Inc .... G 440 259-2245
Madison *(G-12347)*
▲ **Deimling/Jeliho Plastics Inc** .... D 513 752-6653
Amelia *(G-536)*
Del-Ter Precision Machine Inc .... G 330 724-9167
Akron *(G-136)*
Delco LLC .... E 330 896-4220
Akron *(G-138)*
Delta Machine & Tool Co .... F 216 524-2477
Cleveland *(G-5083)*
Delta Manufacturing Inc .... F 330 386-1270
East Liverpool *(G-9056)*
Des Machine Services Inc .... G 330 633-6897
Tallmadge *(G-17978)*
Design & Fabrication Inc .... G 419 294-2414
Upper Sandusky *(G-18951)*
Design Tech Inc .... G 937 254-7000
Dayton *(G-8158)*
Design Technologies & Mfg Co .... F 937 335-0757
Troy *(G-18649)*
Detailed Machining Inc .... E 937 492-1264
Sidney *(G-17029)*
▲ **Detroit Diesl Specialty Tl Inc** .... E 740 435-4452
Byesville *(G-2383)*
Deuce Machining LLC .... G 513 875-2291
Fayetteville *(G-9638)*
Devault Machine & Mould Co LLC .... G 740 654-5925
Lancaster *(G-11563)*
Dg Custom Machine .... G 419 636-8059
Bryan *(G-2279)*
Die-Tech Machine Inc .... G 740 264-2426
Bloomingdale *(G-1710)*
Dilco Industries Inc .... E 330 337-6732
Salem *(G-16734)*
◆ **Dilworth Machine** .... F 330 427-1706
East Palestine *(G-9073)*
Dimension Industries Inc .... F 440 236-3265
Columbia Station *(G-6435)*
Dimension Machine Company Inc .... G 513 242-9996
Cincinnati *(G-3589)*
Diversified Mch Components LLC .... E 440 942-5701
Eastlake *(G-9105)*
DMG Tool & Die LLC .... G 937 407-0810
Bellefontaine *(G-1514)*
Dollman Technical Services .... G 419 877-9404
Toledo *(G-18267)*
Donaldson Company Inc .... D 330 928-4100
Stow *(G-17580)*
Dover Machine Co .... F 330 343-4123
Dover *(G-8822)*
Drabik Manufacturing Inc .... F 216 267-1616
Cleveland *(G-5112)*
Drake Mfg Acquisition LLC .... D 330 847-7291
Warren *(G-19397)*
Drt Holdings Inc .... D 937 298-7391
Dayton *(G-8169)*
Drt Precision Mfg LLC .... E 937 507-4308
Sidney *(G-17032)*
▲ **Dunaway Inc** .... E 330 533-7753
Canfield *(G-2525)*
▲ **Duncan Tool Inc** .... F 937 667-9364
Tipp City *(G-18111)*
Dunham Machine Inc .... G 216 398-4500
Independence *(G-11124)*
Duray Machine Co Inc .... F 440 277-4119
Amherst *(G-561)*
Dynamic Industries Inc .... E 513 861-6767
Cincinnati *(G-3613)*
Dynamic Machine Concepts Inc .... G 216 470-0270
Lagrange *(G-11479)*
Dynapoint Technologies Inc .... E 937 859-5193
Dayton *(G-8173)*
E & J Demark Inc .... E 419 337-5866
Wauseon *(G-19513)*
E & K Products Co Inc .... G 216 631-2510
Cleveland *(G-5127)*

S I C

Employee Codes: A=Over 500 employees, B=251-500
C=101-250, D=51-100, E=20-50, F=10-19, G=3-9
2019 Harris Ohio
Industrial Directory
975

35 INDUSTRIAL AND COMMERCIAL MACHINERY AND COMPUTER EQUIPMENT

▲ E D M Services Inc ....G........ 216 486-2068
  Euclid (G-9411)
E D M Star-One Inc ....F........ 440 647-0600
  Wellington (G-19575)
Eagle Machine and Welding Inc ....G........ 740 345-5210
  Newark (G-14869)
Eagle Manufacturing Inc ....G........ 419 738-3491
  Uniopolis (G-18939)
Eagle Mfg Solutions LLC ....F........ 937 865-0366
  Miamisburg (G-13662)
▲ East End Welding Company ....C........ 330 677-6000
  Kent (G-11317)
East Fork Precision Machine LL........ 513 753-4157
  Amelia (G-538)
Eastlake Machine Products Inc ....E........ 440 953-1014
  Willoughby (G-20314)
▲ Eaton Fabricating Company Inc ....E........ 440 926-3121
  Grafton (G-10300)
Econ-O-Machine Products Inc ....G........ 937 882-6307
  Donnelsville (G-8801)
Edinburg Fixture & Machine ....F........ 330 947-1700
  Rootstown (G-16568)
Eitle Machine Tool Inc ....G........ 419 935-8753
  Attica (G-856)
Ellwood Group Inc ....G........ 216 862-6341
  Cleveland (G-5169)
Eltool Corporation ....G........ 513 723-1772
  Mansfield (G-12436)
Elyria Metal Spinning Fabg Co ....G........ 440 323-8068
  Elyria (G-9253)
EMC Precision Machining II LLC ....F........ 440 365-4171
  Elyria (G-9257)
Emrick Machine & Tool ....G........ 937 692-5901
  Arcanum (G-628)
▲ Energy Machine Inc ....E........ 740 397-1155
  Mount Vernon (G-14480)
Engine Machine Service Inc ....G........ 330 505-1804
  Niles (G-15007)
▲ Enprotech Industrial Tech LLC ....G........ 216 883-3220
  Cleveland (G-5179)
Enterprise C N C Inc ....G........ 440 354-3868
  Mentor (G-13440)
Eos Technology Inc ....E........ 216 281-2999
  Cleveland (G-5183)
Erie Shore Machine Co Inc ....G........ 216 692-1484
  Cleveland (G-5190)
Esterle Mold & Machine Co Inc ....E........ 330 686-1685
  Stow (G-17583)
▲ Esterline & Sons Mfg Co LLC ....F........ 937 265-5278
  Springfield (G-17398)
Eti Tech LLC ....F........ 937 832-4200
  Englewood (G-9358)
Etko Machine Inc ....G........ 330 745-4033
  Norton (G-15367)
Euclid Precision Grinding Co ....G........ 440 946-8888
  Eastlake (G-9111)
▲ Ewart-Ohlson Machine Company ....E........ 330 928-2171
  Cuyahoga Falls (G-7864)
▲ Exact Cutting Service Inc ....E........ 440 546-1319
  Brecksville (G-2035)
Excel Machine & Tool Inc ....F........ 419 678-3318
  Coldwater (G-6408)
Excellent Tool & Die Inc ....G........ 216 671-9222
  Cleveland (G-5206)
EZ Machine Inc ....G........ 330 784-3363
  Akron (G-162)
F & G Tool and Die Co ....E........ 937 294-1405
  Moraine (G-14352)
F & J Grinding Inc ....G........ 440 942-4430
  Willoughby (G-20318)
F & W Auto Supply ....G........ 419 445-3350
  Archbold (G-644)
F A Tech Corp ....E........ 513 942-1920
  West Chester (G-19701)
F M Machine Co ....E........ 330 773-8237
  Akron (G-163)
F3 Defense Systems LLC ....G........ 419 982-2020
  Lima (G-11862)
Fab-Tech Machine Inc ....G........ 937 473-5572
  Covington (G-7785)
Falcon Innovations Inc ....G........ 216 252-0676
  Cleveland (G-5217)
Falcon Tool & Machine Inc ....G........ 937 534-9999
  Moraine (G-14353)
Falmer Screw Pdts & Mfg Inc ....F........ 330 758-0593
  Youngstown (G-20903)
Fargo Toolite Incorporated ....F........ 440 997-2442
  Ashtabula (G-775)
▲ Farmerstown Axle Co ....G........ 330 897-2711
  Baltic (G-1028)

▼ FAS Machinery LLC ....G........ 216 472-3800
  Cleveland (G-5220)
Fasco Machine Products Inc ....G........ 440 437-6242
  Orwell (G-15630)
Fast Fab and Laser LLC ....F........ 937 224-3048
  Dayton (G-8191)
Fate Industries Inc ....G........ 440 327-1770
  North Ridgeville (G-15223)
▲ Faxon Machining Inc ....C........ 513 851-4644
  Cincinnati (G-3678)
Fdc Machine Repair Inc ....E........ 216 362-1082
  Parma (G-15818)
Feilhauers Machine Shop Inc ....E........ 513 202-0545
  Harrison (G-10641)
Feller Tool Co Inc ....F........ 440 324-6277
  Lorain (G-12092)
▲ Ferralloy Inc ....G........ 440 250-1900
  Cleveland (G-5230)
▲ Ferry Industries Inc ....D........ 330 920-9200
  Stow (G-17587)
Fetzer Machining Co Inc ....G........ 937 962-4019
  Lewisburg (G-11791)
Final Machine ....G........ 330 966-1744
  Canton (G-2672)
Finishing Machine Inc ....G........ 419 491-0197
  Holland (G-10931)
First Francis Company Inc ....E........ 440 352-8927
  Painesville (G-15739)
Firstar Precision Corporation ....E........ 216 362-7888
  Brunswick (G-2204)
Five Star Machine & Tool ....G........ 937 420-2170
  Fort Loramie (G-9797)
Fleetline Tool & Die Co ....G........ 216 441-4949
  Cleveland (G-5248)
Flohr Machine Company Inc ....G........ 330 745-3030
  Barberton (G-1070)
◆ Floturn Inc ....C........ 513 860-8040
  West Chester (G-19704)
Floturn Inc ....G........ 513 671-0210
  Cincinnati (G-3697)
Fluid Conservation Systems ....F........ 513 831-9335
  Milford (G-14008)
Focus Manufacturing Inc ....F........ 440 946-8766
  Willoughby (G-20325)
Foltz Machine LLC ....E........ 330 453-9235
  Canton (G-2673)
▲ Forge Industries Inc ....A........ 330 782-8301
  Youngstown (G-20909)
Forrest Machine Shop ....G........ 419 822-5847
  Delta (G-8770)
Forsvara Engineering LLC ....G........ 937 254-9711
  Dayton (G-8202)
Forward Technologies Inc ....F........ 513 489-5111
  Blue Ash (G-1779)
Frazier Machine and Prod Inc ....E........ 419 661-1656
  Perrysburg (G-15954)
Fred W Hanks Company ....G........ 216 731-1774
  Cleveland (G-5274)
▼ Fredon Corporation ....D........ 440 951-5200
  Mentor (G-13450)
Fredrick Welding & Machining ....F........ 614 866-9650
  Reynoldsburg (G-16441)
Friend Engrg & Mch Co Inc ....G........ 419 589-5066
  Mansfield (G-12442)
Fries Machine & Tool Inc ....F........ 937 898-6432
  Dayton (G-8209)
Friess Equipment Inc ....G........ 330 945-9440
  Akron (G-178)
Frisbie Engine & Machine Co ....F........ 513 542-1770
  Cincinnati (G-3714)
◆ Furukawa Rock Drill Usa Inc ....F........ 330 673-5826
  Kent (G-11324)
G & L Machining Inc ....G........ 513 724-2600
  Williamsburg (G-20251)
G & M Precision Machining Inc ....G........ 937 667-1443
  Tipp City (G-18113)
G F Frank and Sons Inc ....F........ 513 870-9075
  West Chester (G-19709)
G Grafton Machine & Rubber ....G........ 330 297-1062
  Ravenna (G-16380)
G H Cutter Services Inc ....G........ 419 476-0476
  Toledo (G-18300)
G L Heller Co Inc ....G........ 419 877-5122
  Whitehouse (G-20190)
G T M Associates Inc ....G........ 440 951-0006
  Mentor (G-13454)
Galactic Precision Mfg LLC ....G........ 937 540-1800
  Englewood (G-9360)
Garber Machine Co ....G........ 330 399-4181
  Warren (G-19404)

Garvey Corporation ....E........ 330 779-0700
  Youngstown (G-20911)
Gasdorf Tool and Mch Co Inc ....E........ 419 227-0103
  Lima (G-11867)
Gaydash Enterprises Inc ....F........ 330 896-4811
  Uniontown (G-18920)
Gb Image Machine Incorporated ....E........ 419 628-4150
  Minster (G-14215)
Gearhart Machine Company ....G........ 330 253-1880
  Akron (G-184)
Gedico International Inc ....G........ 937 274-2167
  Dayton (G-8218)
Gemco Machine & Tool Inc ....F........ 740 344-3111
  Newark (G-14879)
General Machine & Saw Company ....E........ 740 375-5730
  Marion (G-12705)
General Machine & Supply Co ....G........ 740 453-4804
  Zanesville (G-21142)
General Parts Inc ....G........ 614 891-6014
  Westerville (G-20055)
▲ General Plug and Mfg Co ....E........ 440 926-2411
  Grafton (G-10301)
General Sheave Company Inc ....E........ 216 781-8120
  Cleveland (G-5313)
▲ General Tool Company ....E........ 513 733-5500
  Cincinnati (G-3747)
George Steel Fabricating Inc ....E........ 513 932-2887
  Lebanon (G-11655)
Gillam Machine Company ....G........ 330 457-2557
  New Waterford (G-14840)
Gilson Machine & Tool Co Inc ....E........ 419 592-2911
  Napoleon (G-14539)
Girard Machine Company Inc ....E........ 330 545-9731
  Girard (G-10261)
Givens Lifting Systems Inc ....E........ 419 724-9001
  Perrysburg (G-15957)
Glendale Machine Inc ....G........ 440 248-8646
  Solon (G-17150)
▲ Glenridge Machine Co ....E........ 440 975-1055
  Willoughby (G-20332)
▲ Global Srcing Support Svcs LLC .....G........ 800 645-2986
  Cincinnati (G-3765)
▲ Globe Products Inc ....E........ 937 233-0233
  Dayton (G-8229)
▲ Glunt Industries Inc ....C........ 330 399-7585
  Warren (G-19407)
▼ Gmd Industries LLC ....D........ 937 252-3643
  Dayton (G-8231)
Gold Metal Machining Inc ....E........ 614 873-5031
  Plain City (G-16195)
Goodwin Farms ....G........ 513 877-2636
  Pleasant Plain (G-16226)
▲ Goyal Industries Inc ....E........ 419 522-7099
  Mansfield (G-12451)
Graber Metal Works Inc ....E........ 440 237-8422
  North Royalton (G-15274)
Grand Harbor Yacht Sales & Svc ....E........ 440 442-2919
  Cleveland (G-5339)
Grandview Grind ....G........ 614 485-9005
  Columbus (G-6967)
Graphel Corporation ....C........ 513 779-6166
  West Chester (G-19718)
Green Machine Tool Inc ....F........ 937 253-0771
  Dayton (G-7980)
Grenga Machine & Welding ....F........ 330 743-1113
  Youngstown (G-20925)
Grinding Equipment & McHy LLC ....F........ 330 747-2313
  Youngstown (G-20926)
Gt Technologies ....C........ 419 782-8955
  Defiance (G-8625)
Guardian Engineering & Mfg Co ....F........ 419 335-1784
  Wauseon (G-19518)
Guyer Precision Inc ....F........ 440 354-8024
  Painesville (G-15744)
H & B Machine & Tool Inc ....F........ 216 431-3254
  Cleveland (G-5361)
H & H Machine Shop Akron Inc ....E........ 330 773-3327
  Akron (G-193)
H & H Quick Machine Inc ....F........ 330 935-0944
  Louisville (G-12154)
H & M Machine Shop Inc ....F........ 419 453-3414
  Ottoville (G-15680)
H & R Tool & Machine Co Inc ....E........ 740 452-0784
  Zanesville (G-21143)
H & W Tool Co ....G........ 216 795-5520
  Euclid (G-9416)
H R Machine ....G........ 937 838-6289
  Beavercreek (G-1321)
H-W Machine Inc ....G........ 330 477-7231
  Canton (G-2690)

2019 Harris Ohio
Industrial Directory

SIC SECTION
35 INDUSTRIAL AND COMMERCIAL MACHINERY AND COMPUTER EQUIPMENT

▼ **H2o Mechanics LLC**....G....440 554-9515
Newbury *(G-14955)*
Habco Tool and Dev Co Inc....E....440 946-5546
Mentor *(G-13463)*
Hafco-Case Inc....G....216 267-4644
Cleveland *(G-5365)*
Hahn Manufacturing Company....E....216 391-9300
Cleveland *(G-5366)*
Haiss Fabripart LLC....E....330 821-2028
Alliance *(G-470)*
Hale Manufacturing LLC....F....937 382-2127
Wilmington *(G-20497)*
Hannon Company....F....330 343-7758
Dover *(G-8829)*
Happy Time Adventures....G....419 407-6409
Toledo *(G-18323)*
Hardin Creek Machine & Tool....F....419 678-4913
Coldwater *(G-6410)*
Harris Welding and Machine Co....G....419 281-9623
Ashland *(G-708)*
Harris Welding and Machine Co....F....419 281-8351
Ashland *(G-707)*
Hartley Machine Inc....G....330 821-0343
Alliance *(G-471)*
Hashier & Hashier Mfg....G....440 933-4883
Avon Lake *(G-988)*
Haulette Manufacturing Inc....D....419 586-1717
Celina *(G-2966)*
Hawk Engine & Machine....G....440 582-0900
North Royalton *(G-15276)*
Hawk Manufacturing LLC....F....330 784-6234
Akron *(G-200)*
Hawk Manufacturing LLC....F....330 784-4815
Akron *(G-202)*
Hawk Manufacturing LLC....D....330 784-3151
Akron *(G-201)*
▲ **Hazenstab Machine Inc**....F....330 337-1865
Salem *(G-16747)*
Hbe Machine Inc....G....419 668-9426
Monroeville *(G-14288)*
Hearn Plating Co Ltd....F....419 473-9773
Toledo *(G-18325)*
Heisler Tool Company....F....440 951-2424
Willoughby *(G-20336)*
Henderson Fabricating Co Inc....F....216 432-0404
Cleveland *(G-5391)*
Hennacy Machine Company Inc....G....330 785-2940
Akron *(G-203)*
Hephaestus Technologies LLC....E....216 252-0430
Cleveland *(G-5396)*
Herd Manufacturing Inc....E....216 651-4221
Cleveland *(G-5397)*
Hergatt Machine Inc....G....419 589-2931
Mansfield *(G-12457)*
Heritage Tool....F....513 753-7300
Loveland *(G-12197)*
Herman Machine Inc....F....330 633-3261
Tallmadge *(G-17984)*
Hesler Machine Tool....G....937 299-3833
Dayton *(G-8248)*
Heule Tool Corporation....G....513 860-9900
Loveland *(G-12198)*
▲ **Hi-Tek Manufacturing Inc**....C....513 459-1094
Mason *(G-12886)*
High Tech Metal Products LLC....G....419 227-9414
Lima *(G-11874)*
High Tech Mold & Machine Co....F....330 896-4466
Uniontown *(G-18921)*
Highland Products Corp....F....440 352-4777
Mentor *(G-13466)*
Hillman Precision Inc....F....419 289-1557
Ashland *(G-711)*
Hocker Tool and Die Inc....F....937 274-3443
Dayton *(G-8251)*
Hofacker Prcsion Machining LLC....F....937 832-7712
Clayton *(G-4574)*
Hoffman Machining & Repair LLC....G....419 547-9204
Clyde *(G-6389)*
Holdren Brothers Inc....F....937 465-7050
West Liberty *(G-19936)*
Hollow Boring Inc....G....440 951-2929
Mentor *(G-13467)*
Houston Machine Products Inc....E....937 322-8022
Springfield *(G-17422)*
▼ **Hr Parts N Stuff**....G....330 947-2433
Atwater *(G-861)*
Htec Systems Inc....F....937 438-3010
Dayton *(G-8255)*
Hubbell Machine Tooling Inc....F....216 524-1797
Cleveland *(G-5423)*

Hudak Machine & Tool Inc....G....440 366-8955
Elyria *(G-9266)*
Hutnik Company....G....330 336-9700
Wadsworth *(G-19246)*
Hutter Racing Engines Ltd....F....440 285-2175
Chardon *(G-3117)*
▲ **Hy-Production Inc**....C....330 273-2400
Valley City *(G-19040)*
Hydro Supply Co....F....740 454-3842
Zanesville *(G-21147)*
Hylun Machine Co Inc....G....440 256-8755
Willoughby *(G-20340)*
Hyneks Machine and Welding....G....419 281-7966
Ashland *(G-713)*
Hyprolap Finishing Co....G....440 352-0270
Mentor *(G-13468)*
I R B F Company....G....330 633-5100
Tallmadge *(G-17986)*
Iberia Machine Shop Inc....G....419 468-7100
Iberia *(G-11114)*
Imds Corporation....F....330 747-4637
Youngstown *(G-20937)*
Impac Hi-Performance Machining....G....419 726-7100
Toledo *(G-18341)*
Independent Machine & Wldg Inc....G....937 339-7330
Troy *(G-18676)*
Industrial Hanger Conveyor Co....G....419 332-2661
Fremont *(G-10028)*
Industrial Machining Services....E....937 295-2022
Fort Loramie *(G-9799)*
Industrial Shaft and Mfg Inc....G....440 942-9104
Eastlake *(G-9114)*
Innovative Tool & Die Inc....G....419 599-0492
Napoleon *(G-14545)*
Inovent Engineering Inc....G....330 468-0005
Macedonia *(G-12303)*
Integrity Manufacturing Corp....E....937 233-6792
Dayton *(G-8272)*
International Machining Inc....E....330 225-1963
Brunswick *(G-2216)*
◆ **Interscope Manufacturing Inc**....E....513 423-8866
Middletown *(G-13917)*
Intertek Machining & Wldg Inc....F....440 323-3325
Elyria *(G-9269)*
Invotec Engineering Inc....D....937 886-3232
Miamisburg *(G-13680)*
Isco Inc....F....614 792-2206
Columbus *(G-7050)*
IV M Tool & Die....G....513 625-6464
Williamsburg *(G-20252)*
Ivan Extruders Co Inc....G....330 644-7400
Akron *(G-220)*
Izit Cain Sheet Metal Corp....G....937 667-6521
Tipp City *(G-18117)*
J & A Auto Service....G....614 837-6820
Pickerington *(G-16049)*
J & C Industries Inc....F....216 362-8867
Cleveland *(G-5480)*
J & M Maynard Enterprises Inc....F....740 532-3032
Ironton *(G-11167)*
J & M Precision Die Cast Inc....F....440 365-7388
Elyria *(G-9279)*
J & P Products Inc....E....440 974-2830
Mentor *(G-13482)*
J B M Machine Co Inc....G....440 446-0819
Cleveland *(G-5483)*
J B Manufacturing Inc....E....330 676-9744
Kent *(G-11335)*
J Horst Manufacturing Co....D....330 828-2216
Dalton *(G-7945)*
J P Dennis Machine Inc....G....440 474-0247
Rome *(G-16563)*
J S Company....G....440 632-0052
Middlefield *(G-13808)*
J T E Corp....G....937 454-1112
Dayton *(G-8275)*
J Tek Tool & Mold Inc....F....419 547-9476
Clyde *(G-6390)*
J-T Tool Inc....G....937 623-9959
Arcanum *(G-629)*
Jackson Machine & Fabrication....G....740 682-3994
Oak Hill *(G-15452)*
Jade Products Inc....F....440 352-1700
Mentor *(G-13484)*
Jade Tool Co Inc....G....937 376-4740
Xenia *(G-20778)*
Jamar Precision Grinding Co....E....330 220-0099
Hinckley *(G-10903)*
James Eastwood....G....614 444-1340
Columbus *(G-7060)*

James L Wereb....G....440 942-2405
Willoughby *(G-20347)*
Jay-Em Aerospace Corporation....E....330 923-0333
Cuyahoga Falls *(G-7884)*
Jayna Inc....E....937 335-8922
Troy *(G-18680)*
JB Industries Ltd....F....330 856-4587
Warren *(G-19414)*
Jbj Technologies Inc....F....216 469-7297
Euclid *(G-9422)*
▲ **Jbk Manufacturing LLC**....E....937 233-8300
Dayton *(G-8280)*
Jeb Modern Machines Ltd....G....419 639-3937
Republic *(G-16427)*
Jed Industries Inc....E....440 639-9973
Grand River *(G-10323)*
Jed Tool Company....G....937 857-9222
Casstown *(G-2933)*
Jenkins Motor Parts....G....330 525-4011
Beloit *(G-1570)*
Jerl Machine Inc....D....419 873-0270
Perrysburg *(G-15969)*
Jerpbak-Bayless Co....E....440 248-5387
Solon *(G-17176)*
Jesco Products Inc....G....440 233-5828
Grafton *(G-10304)*
Jett Industries Inc....G....740 344-4140
Newark *(G-14889)*
JF Martt and Associates Inc....F....330 938-4000
Sebring *(G-16887)*
Jh Industries Inc....E....330 963-4105
Twinsburg *(G-18797)*
Jilco Precision Mold & Mch Co....G....330 633-9645
Akron *(G-223)*
Jit Company Inc....F....614 529-8010
Hilliard *(G-10834)*
Jj Sleeves Inc....G....440 205-1055
Mentor *(G-13485)*
Johnson Engine & Machine....G....614 876-0724
Hilliard *(G-10835)*
Johnson Machining Services LLC....G....937 866-4744
Miamisburg *(G-13682)*
Johnson Precision Machining....G....513 353-4252
Cleves *(G-6366)*
Jonashtons....G....419 488-2363
Cloverdale *(G-6386)*
Jotco Inc....G....513 721-4943
Mansfield *(G-12465)*
Jrg Performance Technologies....G....216 408-5974
Cleveland *(G-5508)*
Jrs Hydraulic & Welding....G....614 497-1100
Columbus *(G-7079)*
K & G Machine Co....E....216 732-7115
Cleveland *(G-5512)*
K & J Machine Inc....F....740 425-3282
Barnesville *(G-1117)*
K & K Precision Inc....E....513 336-0032
Mason *(G-12898)*
K & M Tool & Machine Co Inc....G....440 572-5130
Strongsville *(G-17758)*
K P Precision Tool and Mch Co....G....419 237-2596
Fayette *(G-9633)*
K S Machine Inc....F....216 687-0459
Cleveland *(G-5513)*
K-M-S Industries Inc....E....440 243-6680
Brookpark *(G-2150)*
▲ **Kalt Manufacturing Company**....D....440 327-2102
North Ridgeville *(G-15235)*
Kaskell Manufacturing Inc....F....937 704-9700
Springboro *(G-17332)*
Kastler & Reichlin Inc....E....440 322-0970
Elyria *(G-9281)*
Kaws Inc....E....513 521-8292
Cincinnati *(G-3898)*
Keban Industries Inc....G....216 446-0159
Cleveland *(G-5522)*
Keck Engineering Inc....G....440 355-9855
Lagrange *(G-11485)*
Kelly Machine Ltd....G....419 825-2006
Swanton *(G-17915)*
▲ **Ken-Dal Corporation**....F....330 644-7118
Coventry Township *(G-7772)*
Kenmore Development & Mch Co....F....330 753-2274
Akron *(G-233)*
Kent Automation Inc....F....330 678-6343
Kent *(G-11339)*
Kent Swigart....G....937 836-5292
Englewood *(G-9365)*
Kerek Industries Ltd Lblty Co....F....440 461-1450
Cleveland *(G-5530)*

S I C

Employee Codes: A=Over 500 employees, B=251-500
C=101-250, D=51-100, E=20-50, F=10-19, G=3-9
2019 Harris Ohio
Industrial Directory
977

35 INDUSTRIAL AND COMMERCIAL MACHINERY AND COMPUTER EQUIPMENT

Kern Machine Tool Inc ....G...... 419 470-1206
 Toledo *(G-18365)*
Kiefer Tool & Mold Inc ....F...... 216 251-0076
 Cleveland *(G-5534)*
Kiley Machine Company Inc ....G...... 513 875-3223
 Fayetteville *(G-9640)*
Kimble Machines Inc ....F...... 419 485-8449
 Montpelier *(G-14311)*
Kings Welding and Fabg Inc ....E...... 330 738-3592
 Mechanicstown *(G-13212)*
Kinninger Prod Wldg Co Inc ....D...... 419 629-3491
 New Bremen *(G-14655)*
Kj Machining Systems Inc ....G...... 440 975-8624
 Willoughby *(G-20353)*
Knape Industries Inc ....E...... 614 885-3016
 Worthington *(G-20693)*
Knight Manufacturing Co Inc ....F...... 740 676-9532
 Shadyside *(G-16922)*
Knous Tool & Machine Inc ....G...... 419 394-3541
 Saint Marys *(G-16687)*
Knowlton Machine Inc ....G...... 419 281-6802
 Ashland *(G-719)*
Knox Machine & Tool ....G...... 740 392-3133
 Mount Vernon *(G-14487)*
Koester Machined Products Co ....F...... 419 782-0291
 Defiance *(G-8632)*
Kole Specialties Inc ....G...... 513 829-1111
 Fairfield *(G-9520)*
Komatec Tool & Die Inc ....G...... 937 252-1133
 Dayton *(G-8300)*
Kopachka Machining Inc ....G...... 440 953-3988
 Willoughby *(G-20354)*
Korff Machine LLC ....G...... 330 332-1566
 Salem *(G-16753)*
Krafft and Associates Inc ....G...... 937 325-4671
 Springfield *(G-17435)*
▲ Kram Precision Machining Inc.........G...... 937 849-1301
 New Carlisle *(G-14670)*
Kramer Power Equipment Co ....F...... 937 456-2232
 Eaton *(G-9157)*
Krdc Inc ....G...... 937 222-2332
 Dayton *(G-8301)*
▼ Krendl Machine Company ....D...... 419 692-3060
 Delphos *(G-8747)*
Kyron Tool and Machine Co Inc ....F...... 614 231-6000
 Columbus *(G-7105)*
L & L Machine Inc ....F...... 419 272-5000
 Edon *(G-9185)*
L & P Machine Company ....G...... 330 527-2753
 Garrettsville *(G-10196)*
L A Machine ....G...... 216 651-1712
 Cleveland *(G-5549)*
L C I Inc ....G...... 330 948-1922
 Lodi *(G-12013)*
L J Manufacturing Inc ....G...... 440 352-1979
 Mentor *(G-13493)*
Lake Erie Machine ....G...... 440 353-9191
 North Ridgeville *(G-15237)*
Lakecraft Inc ....G...... 419 734-2828
 Port Clinton *(G-16249)*
▲ Lako Tool & Mfg ....F...... 419 662-5256
 Perrysburg *(G-15973)*
Lambert Bros Inc ....G...... 513 541-1042
 Cincinnati *(G-3929)*
Langa Tool & Machine Inc ....E...... 440 953-1138
 Willoughby *(G-20359)*
Lange Precision Inc ....G...... 513 530-9500
 Blue Ash *(G-1802)*
Larcom & Mitchell LLC ....F...... 740 595-3750
 Delaware *(G-8701)*
Lariat Machine Inc ....G...... 330 297-5765
 Ravenna *(G-16388)*
Las Motor Sports ....G...... 937 456-2441
 Eaton *(G-9159)*
Laserflex Corporation ....D...... 614 850-9600
 Hilliard *(G-10837)*
Laspina Tool & Die Inc ....F...... 330 923-9996
 Stow *(G-17599)*
Latanick Equipment Inc ....E...... 419 433-2200
 Huron *(G-11104)*
◆ Lawrence Industries Inc ....C...... 216 518-7000
 Cleveland *(G-5566)*
Lawrence Industries Inc ....D...... 216 518-1400
 Cleveland *(G-5567)*
Lawson Precision Machining Inc ....G...... 419 562-1543
 Bucyrus *(G-2337)*
▲ Leadar Roll Inc ....E...... 419 227-2200
 Lima *(G-11885)*
Leader Engnrng-Fabrication Inc ....E...... 419 592-0008
 Napoleon *(G-14549)*

Leader Engnrng-Fabrication Inc ....G...... 419 636-1731
 Bryan *(G-2296)*
Lees Grinding Inc ....E...... 440 572-4610
 Strongsville *(G-17762)*
Lees Machinery Inc ....G...... 440 259-2222
 Perry *(G-15907)*
Lehner Screw Machine LLC ....E...... 330 688-6616
 Akron *(G-250)*
Lem Incorporated ....G...... 330 535-6422
 Munroe Falls *(G-14525)*
Lennox Machine Inc ....F...... 419 525-1020
 Mansfield *(G-12468)*
Leon Newswanger ....G...... 419 896-3336
 Shiloh *(G-16996)*
Lesage Machine Inc ....G...... 419 687-0131
 Plymouth *(G-16232)*
Lightning Mold & Machine Inc ....F...... 440 593-6460
 Conneaut *(G-7653)*
Lima Sheet Metal Machine & Mfg ......E...... 419 229-1161
 Lima *(G-11893)*
Line Tool & Die Inc ....G...... 419 332-2931
 Fremont *(G-10035)*
Lion Mold & Machine Inc ....G...... 330 688-4248
 Stow *(G-17603)*
Lmp Machine LLC ....G...... 740 596-4559
 Zaleski *(G-21088)*
Loecy Precision Manufacturing ....F...... 440 358-0551
 Mentor *(G-13502)*
▲ Logan Machine Company ....D...... 330 633-6163
 Akron *(G-259)*
Lostcreek Tool & Machine Inc ....F...... 937 773-6022
 Piqua *(G-16138)*
Lous Machine Company Inc ....F...... 513 856-9199
 Hamilton *(G-10582)*
Lowell Marcum ....G...... 330 948-2353
 Lodi *(G-12015)*
Lukens Blacksmith Shop ....G...... 513 821-2308
 Cincinnati *(G-3955)*
M & B Machine Inc ....F...... 419 476-8836
 Toledo *(G-18391)*
M & J Machine Shop Inc ....F...... 330 645-0042
 Akron *(G-263)*
M & L Machine ....G...... 937 386-2604
 Seaman *(G-16883)*
M A C Machine ....G...... 410 944-6171
 Canton *(G-2736)*
M L C Technologies Inc ....G...... 513 874-7792
 Hamilton *(G-10583)*
M L Grinding Co ....G...... 440 975-9111
 Willoughby *(G-20364)*
M P Machine Inc ....G...... 440 255-8355
 Mentor *(G-13504)*
M S B Machine Inc ....G...... 330 686-7740
 Munroe Falls *(G-14526)*
Machine Component Mfg ....F...... 330 454-4566
 Canton *(G-2740)*
▲ Machine Concepts Inc ....E...... 419 628-3498
 Minster *(G-14219)*
Machine Development Corp ....G...... 513 825-5885
 Cincinnati *(G-3965)*
Machine Industries Inc ....G...... 216 881-8555
 Cleveland *(G-5599)*
Machine Parts International ....G...... 216 251-4334
 Cleveland *(G-5600)*
Machine Products Company ....E...... 937 890-6600
 Dayton *(G-8320)*
Machine Shop ....G...... 330 494-1251
 Canton *(G-2741)*
Machine Tek Systems Inc ....E...... 330 527-4450
 Garrettsville *(G-10197)*
Machine Tool & Fab Corp ....F...... 419 435-7676
 Fostoria *(G-9846)*
Machine Works Inc ....G...... 513 771-4600
 Cincinnati *(G-3968)*
▲ Machine-Pro Technologies Inc ......D...... 419 584-0086
 Celina *(G-2973)*
Machinex of Dayton Inc ....G...... 937 252-7021
 Dayton *(G-8321)*
▲ Machintek Co ....D...... 513 551-1000
 Fairfield *(G-9522)*
Macpro Inc ....F...... 513 575-3000
 Loveland *(G-12211)*
Mader Automotive Center Inc ....F...... 937 339-2681
 Troy *(G-18685)*
Madison Tool & Die Inc ....G...... 440 354-8642
 Painesville *(G-15759)*
Mag Machine Inc ....G...... 440 946-3381
 Mentor *(G-13507)*
Magic City Machine Inc ....G...... 330 825-0048
 Barberton *(G-1084)*

▼ Magna Machine Co ....C...... 513 851-6900
 Cincinnati *(G-3972)*
Magnolia Machine & Repair Inc ....G...... 330 866-4200
 Magnolia *(G-12360)*
Mahoning Valley Fabricators ....F...... 330 793-8995
 Austintown *(G-934)*
Mainstream Waterjet LLC ....G...... 513 683-5426
 Loveland *(G-12212)*
Majestic Engineering & TI LLC ....G...... 937 845-1079
 New Carlisle *(G-14672)*
▲ Majestic Manufacturing Inc ....E...... 330 457-2447
 New Waterford *(G-14841)*
Majestic Tool and Machine Inc ....G...... 440 248-5058
 Solon *(G-17186)*
▼ Manifold & Phalor Inc ....E...... 614 920-1200
 Canal Winchester *(G-2506)*
Manitowoc Company Inc ....G...... 920 746-3332
 Cleveland *(G-5612)*
Mantych Metalworking Inc ....E...... 937 258-1373
 Dayton *(G-7984)*
Mar-Con Tool Company Inc ....E...... 937 299-2244
 Moraine *(G-14367)*
Margo Tool Technology Inc ....F...... 740 653-8115
 Lancaster *(G-11585)*
Marich Machine & Tool Co Inc ....G...... 216 391-5502
 Cleveland *(G-5617)*
Mark J Myers ....G...... 513 753-7300
 Amelia *(G-543)*
Markham Machine Company Inc ......F...... 330 762-7676
 Akron *(G-270)*
▲ Markley Enterprises LLC ....F...... 513 771-1290
 Cincinnati *(G-3982)*
Markwith Tool Company Inc ....F...... 937 548-6808
 Greenville *(G-10380)*
Marmax Machine Co ....G...... 937 698-9900
 Ludlow Falls *(G-12269)*
Martin Machine & Tool Inc ....F...... 419 373-1711
 Bowling Green *(G-1984)*
Martin Machine Co Inc ....G...... 440 946-5174
 Willoughby *(G-20372)*
Massillon Machine & Die Inc ....G...... 330 833-8913
 Massillon *(G-13020)*
Master Swaging Inc ....G...... 937 596-6171
 Jackson Center *(G-11211)*
▲ Materials Science Intl Inc ....E...... 614 870-0400
 Columbus *(G-7157)*
Matrix Tool & Machine Inc ....G...... 440 255-0300
 Mentor *(G-13512)*
Max Daetwyler Corp ....G...... 937 428-1781
 Miamisburg *(G-13687)*
May Thread Grinding Co ....G...... 440 953-0678
 Willoughby *(G-20373)*
Mc Brown Industries Inc ....G...... 419 963-2800
 Findlay *(G-9723)*
McAttack Machine LLC ....G...... 440 946-3855
 Willoughby *(G-20374)*
McCann Tool & Die Inc ....F...... 330 264-8820
 Wooster *(G-20620)*
▲ McCrary Metal Polishing Inc ....F...... 937 492-1979
 Port Jefferson *(G-16265)*
McDannald Welding & Machining .....G...... 937 644-0300
 Marysville *(G-12802)*
McGuire Machine LLC ....G...... 330 868-3072
 Minerva *(G-14192)*
McIntosh Machine ....G...... 937 687-3936
 New Lebanon *(G-14712)*
▲ McNeil & Nrm Inc ....D...... 330 761-1855
 Akron *(G-275)*
McNeil & Nrm Intl Inc ....D...... 330 253-2525
 Akron *(G-276)*
McPherson Wire Cut Inc ....G...... 330 896-0267
 Canton *(G-2751)*
◆ McSwain Manufacturing LLC ....C...... 513 619-1222
 Cincinnati *(G-3991)*
McTt Machine Tool Inc ....G...... 440 946-9559
 Willoughby *(G-20375)*
Medway Tool Corp ....E...... 937 335-7717
 Troy *(G-18687)*
Meibuhr Co Inc ....G...... 440 942-9375
 Willoughby *(G-20376)*
Meldrum Mechanical Services ....F...... 419 535-3500
 Toledo *(G-18407)*
Melinz Industries Inc ....F...... 440 946-3512
 Willoughby *(G-20378)*
Mellott Bronze Inc ....F...... 330 435-6304
 Creston *(G-7807)*
Memac Industries Inc ....G...... 740 653-4815
 Lancaster *(G-11586)*
Mentor Tool Inc ....G...... 440 942-5273
 Willoughby *(G-20379)*

Meridian Machine Inc .... G 330 308-0296
New Philadelphia *(G-14785)*

Meridian Manufacturing Company .... G 330 793-9632
Youngstown *(G-20970)*

Merit Mold & Tool Products .... G 937 435-0932
Dayton *(G-8340)*

Mes Material Hdlg Systems LLC .... G 740 477-8920
Circleville *(G-4548)*

Messerman Corp .... G 419 782-1136
Defiance *(G-8638)*

Met Fab Fabrication and Mch .... G 513 724-3715
Batavia *(G-1164)*

Meta Manufacturing Corporation .... E 513 793-6382
Blue Ash *(G-1818)*

Metal Equipment Co .... E 440 835-3100
Westlake *(G-20130)*

▲ **Metalex Manufacturing Inc** .... C 513 489-0507
Blue Ash *(G-1820)*

Metals Crankshaft Grinding .... G 216 431-5778
Cleveland *(G-5661)*

Metcut Research Associates Inc .... D 513 271-5100
Cincinnati *(G-4015)*

Metro Design Inc .... F 440 458-4200
Elyria *(G-9295)*

Metzger Machine Co .... F 513 241-3360
Cincinnati *(G-4019)*

◆ **Meyer Tool Inc** .... A 513 681-7362
Cincinnati *(G-4020)*

Mh & Son Machining & Wldg Co .... G 419 621-0690
Sandusky *(G-16829)*

Miami Specialties Inc .... G 937 778-1850
Piqua *(G-16142)*

Miami Valley Precision Inc .... E 937 866-1804
Miamisburg *(G-13691)*

Miami Vly Mfg & Assembly Inc .... F 937 254-6665
Dayton *(G-7986)*

Michaels Tool Service Co Inc .... G 330 772-1119
Burghill *(G-2355)*

Mickes Quality Machining .... G 614 746-6639
Columbus *(G-7177)*

Micro Lapping & Grinding Co .... E 216 267-6500
Cleveland *(G-5667)*

Micro Machine Ltd .... G 330 438-7078
Brewster *(G-2070)*

Micro Machine Works Inc .... F 740 678-8471
Vincent *(G-19214)*

Midway Machining Inc .... F 740 373-8976
Marietta *(G-12647)*

Midway Swiss Turn Inc .... G 330 264-4300
Wooster *(G-20625)*

Midwest Laser Systems Inc .... E 419 424-0062
Findlay *(G-9726)*

Midwest Machine Service Inc .... G 216 631-8151
Cleveland *(G-5682)*

Midwest Production Machining .... G 419 924-5616
West Unity *(G-19972)*

Midwest Specialties Inc .... F 419 738-8147
Wapakoneta *(G-19346)*

Mike Loppe .... F 937 969-8102
Tremont City *(G-18616)*

▲ **Mil-Mar Century Corporation** .... F 937 275-4860
Miamisburg *(G-13694)*

▲ **Milja Inc** .... G 937 223-1988
Dayton *(G-8359)*

Mill & Motion Inc .... F 216 524-4000
Cleveland *(G-5688)*

▲ **Millat Industries Corp** .... D 937 434-6666
Dayton *(G-8360)*

Millennium Mch Techlonlogy LLC .... F 440 269-8080
Willoughby *(G-20383)*

Miller Machine & Mfg LLC .... G 740 439-2283
Cambridge *(G-2448)*

Minerva Welding and Fabg Inc .... E 330 868-7731
Minerva *(G-14194)*

Miracle Welding Inc .... G 513 746-9977
Franklin *(G-9901)*

Mirmat Cnc Machining Inc .... G 440 951-2410
Willoughby *(G-20385)*

▼ **Mission Industrial Group LLC** .... F 740 387-2287
Marion *(G-12721)*

Modern Design Stamping Div .... G 216 382-6318
Cleveland *(G-5698)*

Modern Engineering .... G 440 593-5414
Conneaut *(G-7656)*

Modern Industries Inc .... G 216 432-2855
Cleveland *(G-5699)*

Monovision Machine .... G 330 833-2146
Massillon *(G-13028)*

Monroe Tool and Mfg Co .... F 216 883-7360
Cleveland *(G-5704)*

Montgomery Mch & Fabrication .... E 740 286-2863
Jackson *(G-11191)*

▲ **Monti Incorporated** .... C 513 761-7775
Cincinnati *(G-4043)*

Moran Tool Inc .... G 937 526-5210
Versailles *(G-19188)*

Morning Glory Technologies .... F 440 796-5076
Chesterland *(G-3165)*

Morris Technologies Inc .... C 513 733-1611
Cincinnati *(G-4047)*

Mosher Machine & Tool Co Inc .... E 937 258-8070
Dayton *(G-8369)*

Mossing Machine and Tool .... G 419 476-5657
Toledo *(G-18417)*

Mound Manufacturing Center Inc .... F 937 236-8387
Dayton *(G-8370)*

Msd Products Inc .... G 440 946-0040
Mentor *(G-13524)*

Muller Engine & Machine Co .... G 937 322-1861
Springfield *(G-17454)*

Munson Machine Company Inc .... G 740 967-6867
Johnstown *(G-11270)*

Munson Sales & Engineering .... G 216 496-5436
Chardon *(G-3126)*

Murray Machine & Tool Inc .... G 216 267-1126
Cleveland *(G-5714)*

Muskingum Grinding & Mch Co .... F 740 622-4741
Coshocton *(G-7741)*

Mutual Tool LLC .... D 937 667-5818
Tipp City *(G-18124)*

Myers Machining Inc .... F 330 874-3005
Bolivar *(G-1918)*

Mysta Equipment Co .... G 330 879-5353
Navarre *(G-14581)*

N & W Machining & Fabricating .... G 937 695-5582
Winchester *(G-20523)*

Napoleon Machine LLC .... E 419 591-7010
Napoleon *(G-14553)*

Narrow Way Custom Technology .... E 937 743-1611
Carlisle *(G-2895)*

National Aviation Products Inc .... F 330 688-6494
Stow *(G-17610)*

▲ **National Machine Company** .... C 330 688-6494
Stow *(G-17611)*

National Machine Company .... E 330 688-2584
Stow *(G-17612)*

Nauvod Machine Co .... G 440 632-1990
Middlefield *(G-13837)*

Neff Machinery and Supplies .... E 740 454-0128
Zanesville *(G-21159)*

Neidert Fabricating Inc .... G 330 753-3331
Barberton *(G-1088)*

Neil R Scholl Inc .... F 740 653-6593
Lancaster *(G-11590)*

Nevels Precision Machining LLC .... G 937 387-6037
Dayton *(G-8380)*

New Cut Tool and Mfg Corp .... F 740 676-1666
Shadyside *(G-16924)*

New Pme Inc .... E 513 671-1717
Cincinnati *(G-4071)*

Nexgen Machine Company LLC .... G 440 268-2222
Strongsville *(G-17770)*

▲ **Nfm/Welding Engineers Inc** .... C 330 837-3868
Massillon *(G-13029)*

Nichols Mold Inc .... G 330 297-9719
Ravenna *(G-16391)*

Nippon Stl Smkin Crnkshaft LLC .... F 419 435-0411
Fostoria *(G-9852)*

Nk Machine Inc .... G 513 737-8035
Hamilton *(G-10590)*

NM Group Global LLC .... G 419 447-5211
Tiffin *(G-18071)*

Nn Autocam Precision Component .... G 440 647-4711
Wellington *(G-19588)*

Nobal Enterprises Inc .... G 440 748-0522
Columbia Station *(G-6441)*

Norman Noble Inc .... D 216 761-5387
Cleveland *(G-5757)*

Norman Noble Inc .... C 216 761-2133
Cleveland *(G-5758)*

Norman Noble Inc .... B 216 761-5387
Highland Heights *(G-10795)*

North Canton Tool Co .... G 330 452-0545
Canton *(G-2766)*

Northcoast Prfmce & Mch Co .... G 330 753-7333
Barberton *(G-1089)*

Northend Gear & Machine Inc .... F 513 860-4334
Fairfield *(G-9536)*

Northern Machine Tool Co .... G 216 961-0444
Cleveland *(G-5780)*

Northern Precision Inc .... F 513 860-4701
Fairfield *(G-9537)*

Northmont Tool and Gage Inc .... G 937 836-9879
Clayton *(G-4577)*

Northshore Mold Inc .... G 440 838-8212
Cleveland *(G-5786)*

Northwind Industries Inc .... E 216 433-0666
Cleveland *(G-5787)*

Norwood Medical .... G 937 228-4101
Dayton *(G-8385)*

Norwood Tool Company .... C 937 228-4101
Dayton *(G-8387)*

◆ **Npk Construction Equipment Inc** .... D 440 232-7900
Bedford *(G-1432)*

Nt Machine Inc .... G 440 968-3506
Montville *(G-14324)*

Nu-Tool Industries Inc .... F 440 237-9240
North Royalton *(G-15289)*

Oak Industrial Inc .... G 440 263-2780
North Royalton *(G-15290)*

▲ **Oakley Die & Mold Co** .... E 513 754-8500
Mason *(G-12918)*

Oaks Welding Inc .... G 330 482-4216
Columbiana *(G-6475)*

Oceco Inc .... F 419 447-0916
Tiffin *(G-18073)*

▲ **Odawara Automation Inc** .... E 937 667-8433
Tipp City *(G-18125)*

Odyssey Machine Company Ltd .... G 419 455-6621
Perrysburg *(G-15984)*

of Machining LLC .... G 419 396-7870
Carey *(G-2885)*

▼ **Ohio Broach & Machine Company** .... E 440 946-1040
Willoughby *(G-20393)*

Ohio Engineering and Mfg Sls .... G 937 855-6971
Germantown *(G-10244)*

▲ **Ohio Gasket and Shim Co Inc** .... E 330 630-0626
Akron *(G-307)*

Ohio Hydraulics Inc .... E 513 771-2590
Cincinnati *(G-4103)*

Ohio Metal Fabricating Inc .... F 937 233-2400
Dayton *(G-8398)*

Ohio Metalizing LLC .... G 330 830-1092
Massillon *(G-13030)*

Ohio Precision Inc .... G 330 453-9710
Canton *(G-2775)*

Ohio Roll Grinding Inc .... E 330 453-1884
Louisville *(G-12162)*

Ohio Tool Works LLC .... D 419 281-3700
Ashland *(G-732)*

Ohio Transitional Machine & Tl .... G 419 476-0820
Toledo *(G-18438)*

Ojim Inc .... F 330 832-9557
Massillon *(G-13032)*

Omega International Inc .... E 937 890-2350
Dayton *(G-8403)*

Omega Machine & Tool Inc .... F 440 946-6846
Mentor *(G-13534)*

Omega Tool & Die Inc .... E 937 890-2350
Dayton *(G-8404)*

OReilly Precision Products .... E 937 526-4677
Russia *(G-16610)*

Outlook Tool Inc .... G 937 235-6330
Dayton *(G-8411)*

Ovase Manufacturing LLC .... E 937 275-0617
Dayton *(G-8413)*

Owen S Precision Grinding .... G 513 745-9335
Cincinnati *(G-4126)*

P & G Precision LLC .... G 513 738-3500
Fairfield *(G-9540)*

P & L Heat Trting Grinding Inc .... E 330 746-1339
Youngstown *(G-20986)*

P & P Machine Tool Inc .... G 440 232-7404
Cleveland *(G-5828)*

P & P Mold & Die Inc .... F 330 784-8333
Tallmadge *(G-18000)*

P F S Incorporated .... G 440 582-1620
Cleveland *(G-5829)*

P J Tool Company Inc .... G 937 254-2817
Dayton *(G-8414)*

▲ **P R Machine Works Inc** .... D 419 529-5748
Ontario *(G-15546)*

P R W Tool Inc .... G 440 585-3373
Wickliffe *(G-20222)*

Palmer Industries Inc .... G 330 630-9397
Akron *(G-314)*

Paramont Machine Company LLC .... E 330 339-3489
New Philadelphia *(G-14792)*

Parker-Hannifin Corporation .... F 330 336-3511
Wadsworth *(G-19262)*

Employee Codes: A=Over 500 employees, B=251-500
C=101-250, D=51-100, E=20-50, F=10-19, G=3-9

2019 Harris Ohio
Industrial Directory

979

35 INDUSTRIAL AND COMMERCIAL MACHINERY AND COMPUTER EQUIPMENT SIC SECTION

Part Rite Inc....G.... 216 362-4100
North Royalton *(G-15294)*
Parts Unlimited....G.... 937 558-1527
Dayton *(G-8416)*
Path Technologies Inc....G.... 440 358-1500
Painesville *(G-15772)*
Patriot Precision Products....D.... 330 966-7177
Canton *(G-2779)*
Patton Industries Inc....G.... 419 331-5658
Elida *(G-9198)*
Pattons Truck & Heavy Eqp Svc....F.... 740 385-4067
Logan *(G-12039)*
Paul Popov....G.... 440 582-6677
North Royalton *(G-15295)*
Paul Wilke & Son Inc....F.... 513 921-3163
Cincinnati *(G-4141)*
Peco Holdings Corp....F.... 937 667-4451
Tipp City *(G-18126)*
Pemco Inc....E.... 216 524-2990
Cleveland *(G-5862)*
Penco Tool LLC....E.... 440 998-1116
Ashtabula *(G-795)*
Perfect Prcision Machining Ltd....G.... 330 475-0324
Akron *(G-317)*
Perfection Metal Co....G.... 216 641-0949
Chagrin Falls *(G-3028)*
Perfecto Industries Inc....E.... 937 778-1900
Piqua *(G-16149)*
Perform Metals Inc....G.... 440 286-1951
Chardon *(G-3132)*
Performance Point Grinding....G.... 330 220-0871
Hinckley *(G-10905)*
Performance Services....G.... 419 385-1236
Toledo *(G-18466)*
Perry Welding Service Inc....F.... 330 425-2211
Twinsburg *(G-18836)*
PHI Werkes LLC....G.... 419 586-9222
Celina *(G-2980)*
Phil Matic Screw Products Inc....F.... 440 942-7290
Willoughby *(G-20400)*
Phillips Mfg & Mch Corp....G.... 330 823-9178
Alliance *(G-496)*
Phoenix Tool & Thread Grindng....G.... 216 433-7008
Cleveland *(G-5874)*
Phoenix Tool Co Inc....G.... 330 372-4627
Warren *(G-19430)*
Pierce-Wright Precision Inc....G.... 216 362-2870
Cleveland *(G-5875)*
Pike Machine Products Co....E.... 216 731-1880
Euclid *(G-9433)*
▲ **Pioneer Industrial Systems LLC**....F.... 419 737-9506
Alvordton *(G-522)*
Pioneer Machine Inc....G.... 330 948-6500
Lodi *(G-12018)*
Plas-Mac Corp....D.... 440 349-3222
Solon *(G-17216)*
PME of Ohio Inc....E.... 513 671-1717
Cincinnati *(G-4171)*
Pohl Machining Inc....E.... 513 353-2929
Cleves *(G-6372)*
Polytech Component Corp....E.... 330 726-3235
Youngstown *(G-21001)*
▲ **Positech Corp**....F.... 513 942-7411
Blue Ash *(G-1833)*
Post Products Inc....G.... 330 678-0048
Kent *(G-11366)*
▲ **Precise Tool & Die Company**....E.... 440 951-9173
Willoughby *(G-20409)*
Precision Cnc LLC....E.... 740 689-9009
Lancaster *(G-11598)*
Precision Component Inds LLC....E.... 330 477-1052
Canton *(G-2790)*
Precision Dynamics Inc....G.... 330 697-0611
Akron *(G-326)*
Precision Grinding Corporation....G.... 216 391-7294
Cleveland *(G-5909)*
Precision Hydraulic Connectors....F.... 440 953-3778
Euclid *(G-9437)*
Precision Inc....G.... 330 897-8860
Fresno *(G-10070)*
Precision Machine & Tool Co....F.... 419 334-8405
Fremont *(G-10045)*
Precision Machining Corp....G.... 419 433-3520
Huron *(G-11110)*
Precision McHning Srfacing Inc....G.... 440 439-9850
Cleveland *(G-5910)*
▲ **Precision Production Inc**....E.... 216 252-0372
Strongsville *(G-17778)*
Precision Reflex Inc....F.... 419 629-2603
New Bremen *(G-14659)*
Premier Prod Svc Inds Inc....G.... 330 527-0333
Garrettsville *(G-10201)*
Premier Tool Inc....G.... 937 332-0996
Troy *(G-18694)*
▲ **Pride Cast Metals Inc**....D.... 513 541-1295
Cincinnati *(G-4189)*
Pride Tool Co Inc....F.... 513 563-0070
Cincinnati *(G-4190)*
Pro Gram Engineering Corp....G.... 330 745-1004
Barberton *(G-1099)*
Pro-Tech Manufacturing Inc....F.... 937 444-6484
Mount Orab *(G-14450)*
Process Development Corp....E.... 937 890-3388
Dayton *(G-8445)*
▲ **Process Equipment Co Tipp City**....D.... 937 667-4451
Tipp City *(G-18128)*
Prodeva Inc....F.... 937 596-6713
Jackson Center *(G-11215)*
Product Tooling Inc....G.... 740 524-2061
Sunbury *(G-17898)*
Proficient Machining Co....E.... 440 942-4942
Mentor *(G-13556)*
Profile Grinding Inc....E.... 216 351-0600
Cleveland *(G-5928)*
Progressive Manufacturing Co....G.... 330 784-4717
Akron *(G-333)*
Prohos Inc....G.... 419 877-0153
Whitehouse *(G-20193)*
Prohos Manufacturing Co Inc....G.... 419 877-0153
Whitehouse *(G-20194)*
▼ **Projects Designed & Built**....E.... 419 726-7400
Toledo *(G-18486)*
Promac Inc....E.... 937 864-1961
Enon *(G-9385)*
Prostar Machine & Tool Co....G.... 937 223-1997
Dayton *(G-8451)*
Proto Machine & Mfg Inc....F.... 330 677-1700
Kent *(G-11369)*
Pumphrey Machine Corp....G.... 440 417-0481
Madison *(G-12355)*
Puritas Metal Products Inc....F.... 440 353-1917
North Ridgeville *(G-15247)*
Pvm Incorporated....G.... 614 871-0302
Grove City *(G-10461)*
Q M C Pleasants Inc....G.... 937 278-7302
Dayton *(G-8454)*
Qcsm LLC....G.... 216 531-5960
Cleveland *(G-5937)*
Qpmr Inc....F.... 330 723-1739
Medina *(G-13325)*
Quad Industries Inc....G.... 440 951-4849
Willoughby Hills *(G-20474)*
Qualiturn Inc....E.... 513 868-3333
West Chester *(G-19773)*
Quality CNC Machining Inc....F.... 440 942-0542
Willoughby *(G-20413)*
Quality Craft Machine Inc....F.... 330 928-4064
Cuyahoga Falls *(G-7910)*
Quality Design Machining Inc....G.... 440 352-7290
Mentor *(G-13564)*
Quality Machine Systems LLC....G.... 440 223-2217
Mentor *(G-13565)*
▲ **Quality Machining and Mfg Inc**....F.... 419 899-2543
Sherwood *(G-16992)*
Quality Metal Products Inc....G.... 440 355-6165
Lagrange *(G-11492)*
Quality Mfg Company Inc....G.... 513 921-4500
Cincinnati *(G-4228)*
Quality Screw Products Inc....G.... 440 975-1828
Willoughby *(G-20415)*
Queen City Tool Company Inc....G.... 513 752-4200
Amelia *(G-546)*
Queen City Tool Works Inc....G.... 513 874-0111
Fairfield *(G-9555)*
Quest Technologies Inc....F.... 937 743-1200
Franklin *(G-9913)*
Quick Service Welding & Mch Co....F.... 330 673-3818
Kent *(G-11372)*
R & B Machining Inc....G.... 937 698-3528
Wilmington *(G-20506)*
R & B Machining Inc....E.... 937 382-6710
Wilmington *(G-20507)*
R & D Custom Machine & Tool....E.... 419 727-1700
Toledo *(G-18493)*
R & J Cylinder & Machine Inc....D.... 330 364-8263
New Philadelphia *(G-14794)*
R & M Grinding Inc....G.... 513 732-3330
Owensville *(G-15690)*
R A Heller Company....F.... 513 771-6100
Cincinnati *(G-4242)*
R and S Technologies Inc....F.... 419 483-3691
Bellevue *(G-1542)*
R H Industries Inc....E.... 216 281-5210
Cleveland *(G-5952)*
R J K Enterprises Inc....F.... 440 257-6018
Mentor *(G-13569)*
R L Craig Inc....F.... 330 424-1525
Lisbon *(G-11980)*
▲ **R R R Development Co**....D.... 330 966-8855
North Canton *(G-15112)*
R T & T Machining Co Inc....F.... 440 974-8479
Mentor *(G-13571)*
R T R Slotting & Machine Inc....G.... 330 929-2608
Cuyahoga Falls *(G-7911)*
R Vandewalle Inc....G.... 513 921-2657
Cincinnati *(G-4245)*
▲ **R W Machine & Tool Inc**....E.... 330 296-5211
Ravenna *(G-16398)*
▲ **Radco Industries Inc**....F.... 419 531-4731
Toledo *(G-18496)*
Ram Machining Inc....G.... 740 333-5522
Wshngtn CT Hs *(G-20740)*
▲ **Ram Precision Industries Inc**....D.... 937 885-7700
Dayton *(G-8462)*
Randolph Tool Company Inc....F.... 330 877-4923
Hartville *(G-10703)*
Range One Products & Fabg....F.... 330 533-1151
Canfield *(G-2542)*
Rankin Mfg Inc....E.... 419 929-8338
New London *(G-14735)*
Rapid Mold Repair & Machine....G.... 330 253-1000
Akron *(G-343)*
Ray Townsend....G.... 440 968-3617
Montville *(G-14325)*
Reeces Las Vegas Supplies....G.... 937 274-5000
Dayton *(G-8467)*
Reese Machine Company Inc....F.... 440 992-3942
Ashtabula *(G-801)*
Reesers Machine Inc....G.... 937 548-5847
Greenville *(G-10391)*
Reichard Industries LLC....G.... 330 482-5511
Columbiana *(G-6478)*
Reliance Design Inc....F.... 216 267-5450
Rocky River *(G-16554)*
Rely-On Manufacturing Inc....G.... 937 254-0118
Dayton *(G-8470)*
Remington Engrg Machining Inc....G.... 513 965-8999
Milford *(G-14037)*
Repko Machine Inc....G.... 216 267-1144
Cleveland *(G-5975)*
Reuther Mold & Mfg Co Inc....D.... 330 923-5266
Cuyahoga Falls *(G-7913)*
Revolution Machine Works Inc....G.... 706 505-6525
Burton *(G-2368)*
▲ **Reymond Products Intl Inc**....E.... 330 339-3583
New Philadelphia *(G-14796)*
Rezmann Karoly....G.... 216 441-4357
Cleveland *(G-5982)*
Rl Alto Mfg Inc....F.... 740 914-4230
Marion *(G-12730)*
Richard Paskiet Machinists....G.... 330 854-4160
Canal Fulton *(G-2492)*
Richard Pauley....G.... 740 965-6897
Sunbury *(G-17899)*
Richards Grinding Co Inc....F.... 216 631-7675
Cleveland *(G-5984)*
Richmond Machine Co....E.... 419 485-5740
Montpelier *(G-14318)*
Ridge Machine & Welding Co....G.... 740 537-2821
Toronto *(G-18611)*
Riffle Machine Works Inc....F.... 740 775-2838
Chillicothe *(G-3220)*
Rimeco Products Inc....G.... 440 918-1220
Willoughby *(G-20420)*
Rinaldi and Packard Industries....G.... 330 395-4942
Warren *(G-19440)*
Risher & Co....F.... 216 732-8351
Euclid *(G-9440)*
Rite Machine Inc....G.... 216 267-6911
Cleveland *(G-5985)*
Ritime Incorporated....F.... 330 273-3443
Cleveland *(G-5986)*
Riverside Mch & Automtn Inc....D.... 419 855-8308
Genoa *(G-10236)*
Rjm Tool....G.... 419 355-0900
Fremont *(G-10047)*
◆ **RL Best Company**....E.... 330 758-8601
Boardman *(G-1902)*
Rme Machining Co....G.... 513 541-3328
Cincinnati *(G-4275)*

SIC SECTION
35 INDUSTRIAL AND COMMERCIAL MACHINERY AND COMPUTER EQUIPMENT

Robert Alten Inc ....G....740 653-2640
Lancaster *(G-11603)*
Robert J & Cindy K Hartz ....G....513 521-6215
Cincinnati *(G-4278)*
Robert Long Manufacturing Inc ....G....330 678-0911
Kent *(G-11376)*
Robert Smart Inc ....F....330 454-8881
Canton *(G-2809)*
▲ Roberts Manufacturing Co Inc ....E....419 594-2712
Oakwood *(G-15473)*
Robertson EDM LLC ....G....419 658-2219
Edgerton *(G-9178)*
Robey Tool & Machine ....G....614 251-0412
Columbus *(G-7399)*
Rochester Manufacturing Inc ....F....440 647-2463
Wellington *(G-19590)*
Roerig Machine ....G....440 647-4718
New London *(G-14736)*
Rogar International Inc ....F....419 476-5500
Toledo *(G-18505)*
Rolling Enterprises Inc ....E....937 866-4917
Moraine *(G-14390)*
Roof Die Tool & Machine Inc ....G....614 444-6253
Columbus *(G-7401)*
Rosenboom Machine & Tool Inc ....E....419 352-9484
Bowling Green *(G-1998)*
Rotary Tech Inc ....G....440 862-8568
Burton *(G-2369)*
Rowtac Inc ....G....419 994-4777
Loudonville *(G-12148)*
Royal Tool and Machine LLC ....G....419 836-7781
Northwood *(G-15345)*
Royalton Industries Inc ....F....440 748-9900
Columbia Station *(G-6446)*
Royalton Manufacturing Inc ....F....440 237-2233
Akron *(G-355)*
Royce Co ....G....513 933-0344
Lebanon *(G-11691)*
Rpg Industries Inc ....G....937 698-9801
Tipp City *(G-18131)*
RTZ Manufacturing Co ....G....614 848-8366
Columbus *(G-7405)*
S & N Engineering Svcs Corp ....G....216 433-1700
Cleveland *(G-6020)*
S A E Manufacturing ....G....440 322-9026
Elyria *(G-9324)*
S and S Tool Inc ....G....440 593-4000
Conneaut *(G-7658)*
S C Machine ....G....419 752-6961
Greenwich *(G-10408)*
S J Cox Tool Inc ....G....740 756-1100
Carroll *(G-2909)*
S J K Metalworking Inc ....G....440 564-7877
Newbury *(G-14964)*
S K S Manufacturing Corp ....G....330 669-9133
Smithville *(G-17093)*
S P Z Machine Co ....G....330 848-3286
Barberton *(G-1104)*
S R P M Inc ....E....440 248-8440
Cleveland *(G-6023)*
S T Tool & Design Inc ....F....440 357-1250
Mentor *(G-13576)*
S-K Mold & Tool Company ....E....937 339-0299
Tipp City *(G-18132)*
S-K Mold & Tool Company ....E....937 339-0299
Troy *(G-18701)*
S-P Company Inc ....F....330 482-0200
Columbiana *(G-6479)*
Saehwa IMC Na Inc ....D....419 752-4511
Akron *(G-368)*
Safar Machine Company ....F....330 644-0155
Akron *(G-370)*
Saint Paris Tool and Grinding ....F....937 526-9800
Russia *(G-16613)*
Salco Machine Inc ....F....330 456-8281
Louisville *(G-12165)*
Salem Manufacturing and Sales ....G....614 572-4242
Columbus *(G-7415)*
Salley Tool & Die Co ....F....937 258-3333
Dayton *(G-7989)*
Sample Machining Inc ....E....937 258-3338
Dayton *(G-8492)*
Sandusky Machine & Tool Inc ....F....419 626-8359
Sandusky *(G-16844)*
Santos Industrial Ltd ....G....937 299-7333
Moraine *(G-14393)*
▲ Sattler Companies Inc ....E....330 239-2552
Wadsworth *(G-19276)*
Sauder Machine Ltd ....G....419 896-3722
Plymouth *(G-16234)*
Savanna Tool and Manufacturing ....G....440 327-8330
North Ridgeville *(G-15253)*
Schaffer Grinding Co Inc ....F....323 724-4476
Twinsburg *(G-18854)*
Schmidt Machine Company ....E....419 294-3814
Upper Sandusky *(G-18972)*
Schmitmeyer Inc ....G....937 295-2091
Fort Loramie *(G-9804)*
Schuster Manufacturing Inc ....G....419 476-5800
Toledo *(G-18514)*
Schwab Machine Co Inc ....G....419 626-0245
Sandusky *(G-16847)*
Scott A Zurbrugg ....G....330 821-9814
Alliance *(G-499)*
Sebring Fluid Power Corp ....G....330 938-9984
Sebring *(G-16894)*
Seco Machine Inc ....E....330 499-2150
North Canton *(G-15116)*
Secondary Machining Services ....G....440 593-1272
Conneaut *(G-7659)*
Seeb Industrial Inc ....G....216 896-9016
Bedford *(G-1445)*
Seebach Inc ....F....937 275-3565
Dayton *(G-8501)*
Select Machine Co Inc ....F....330 678-7676
Kent *(G-11384)*
Selzer Tool & Die Inc ....G....440 365-4124
Elyria *(G-9325)*
▲ Semco ....D....800 848-5764
Marion *(G-12734)*
Seme & Son Automotive Inc ....G....216 261-0066
Euclid *(G-9443)*
Shannon Tool Inc ....G....513 563-2300
Cincinnati *(G-4329)*
Shoreline Machine Products Co ....F....216 481-8033
Cleveland *(G-6060)*
Short Run Machine Products Inc ....F....440 969-1313
Ashtabula *(G-804)*
Sietins Plastics Inc ....G....440 232-8515
Cleveland *(G-6061)*
Silver Tool Inc ....E....937 865-0012
Miamisburg *(G-13717)*
Simpson Brothers Machine Works ....G....740 353-6870
Portsmouth *(G-16299)*
Sivon Manufacturing LLC ....G....440 259-5505
Perry *(G-15912)*
Skinner Machining Co ....G....216 486-6636
Cleveland *(G-6069)*
▲ Slabe Machine Products Co ....D....440 946-6555
Willoughby *(G-20432)*
Slimline Surgical Devices LLC ....G....937 335-0496
Troy *(G-18707)*
Sluterbeck Tool & Die Inc ....F....937 836-5736
Clayton *(G-4578)*
Smith Machine Inc ....G....330 821-9898
Alliance *(G-500)*
Smolic Machine Co ....G....440 946-1747
Willoughby *(G-20434)*
Sni Inc ....G....937 427-9447
Beavercreek *(G-1363)*
Snyder Fabrication LLC ....G....419 946-6616
Mount Gilead *(G-14434)*
Snyder Machine Co Inc ....G....419 526-1527
Mansfield *(G-12517)*
Sonoma Grinding Machining Inc ....G....440 918-7990
Willoughby *(G-20435)*
Southeastern Shafting Mfg ....F....740 342-4629
New Lexington *(G-14723)*
Southern Ohio Mfg Inc ....E....513 943-2555
Batavia *(G-1185)*
Southstern Machining Field Svc ....E....740 689-1147
Lancaster *(G-11610)*
Spark LLC ....G....513 924-1559
Cincinnati *(G-4356)*
Spartan Fabrication ....G....330 758-3512
Youngstown *(G-21036)*
Specialty Hose Aerospace Corp ....F....330 497-9650
Canton *(G-2820)*
Spectre EDM ....G....513 469-7700
Blue Ash *(G-1848)*
Spectrum Dynamics Inc ....G....614 486-3223
Columbus *(G-7472)*
Spectrum Machine Inc ....E....330 626-3666
Streetsboro *(G-17699)*
Spectrum Mfg & Sls Inc ....G....614 486-3223
Columbus *(G-7474)*
Spence Technologies Inc ....F....440 946-3035
Willoughby *(G-20436)*
Sponseller Group Inc ....E....419 861-3000
Holland *(G-10959)*
Sponseller Group Inc ....G....937 492-9949
Sidney *(G-17081)*
▲ Sroka Industries Inc ....E....440 572-2811
Strongsville *(G-17795)*
SRS Manufacturing Corp ....F....937 746-3086
Franklin *(G-9921)*
Sst Precision Manufacturing ....F....513 583-5500
Loveland *(G-12235)*
Stafford Gage & Tool Inc ....G....937 277-9944
Dayton *(G-8523)*
Stainless Machine Engineering ....G....330 501-1992
Leetonia *(G-11721)*
▲ Stanco Precision Manufacturing ....G....937 274-1785
Dayton *(G-8524)*
▲ Standard Jig Boring Svc LLC ....E....330 896-9530
Akron *(G-384)*
Standard Jig Boring Svc LLC ....G....330 644-5405
Akron *(G-385)*
Standard Machine Inc ....E....216 631-4440
Cleveland *(G-6092)*
▼ Stanley Industries Inc ....E....216 475-4000
Cleveland *(G-6094)*
Star Precision Tech LLC ....D....440 266-7700
Mentor *(G-13588)*
Starr Machine Inc ....E....740 753-0009
Nelsonville *(G-14598)*
Starwin Industries LLC ....E....937 293-8568
Dayton *(G-8525)*
▲ Steck Manufacturing Co Inc ....F....937 222-0062
Dayton *(G-8527)*
Steel Eqp Specialists Inc ....E....330 829-2626
Alliance *(G-501)*
▲ Steel Eqp Specialists Inc ....D....330 823-8260
Alliance *(G-502)*
Steel Products Corp Akron ....E....330 688-6633
Stow *(G-17631)*
Stefra Inc ....G....440 846-8240
Strongsville *(G-17796)*
Stegemeyer Machine ....G....513 321-5651
Cincinnati *(G-4378)*
Steinbarger Precision Cnc Inc ....G....937 252-0322
Dayton *(G-7990)*
Steinert Industries Inc ....F....330 678-0028
Kent *(G-11390)*
Sterling Grinding Company Inc ....F....614 836-3412
Carroll *(G-2911)*
Stevenson Machine Inc ....F....513 761-4121
Cincinnati *(G-4382)*
Stevenson Mfg Co ....G....330 532-1581
Wellsville *(G-19614)*
Stewarts Machining Inc ....G....513 422-5000
Monroe *(G-14277)*
Stillwater Technologies LLC ....D....937 440-2505
Troy *(G-18713)*
Strassells Machine Inc ....F....419 747-1088
Mansfield *(G-12521)*
Stryver Mfg Inc ....E....937 854-3048
Trotwood *(G-18630)*
Suburban Manufacturing Co ....D....440 953-2024
Eastlake *(G-9133)*
Suburban Metal Products Inc ....F....740 474-4237
Circleville *(G-4559)*
Sulecki Precision Products ....F....440 255-5454
Mentor *(G-13596)*
Summer Global Systems LLC ....G....330 397-1653
Campbell *(G-2470)*
▲ Summit Machine Ltd ....E....330 628-2663
Mogadore *(G-14250)*
Sunset Industries Inc ....E....216 731-8131
Euclid *(G-9444)*
▲ Superalloy Mfg Solutions Corp ....C....513 489-9800
Blue Ash *(G-1854)*
Superfinishers Inc ....G....330 467-2125
Macedonia *(G-12335)*
Superior Machine and Tool ....G....937 308-5771
De Graff *(G-8606)*
Superior Machine Tool Inc ....F....419 675-2363
Kenton *(G-11425)*
Superior Mold & Die Co ....E....330 688-8251
Munroe Falls *(G-14528)*
Superior Precision Products ....G....216 881-3696
Cleveland *(G-6123)*
▲ Superior Quality Machine Co ....E....330 527-7146
Garrettsville *(G-10202)*
Swagelok Company ....C....440 461-7714
Cleveland *(G-6135)*
Swagelok Company ....D....440 248-4600
Willoughby Hills *(G-20475)*
◆ Swagelok Company ....A....440 248-4600
Solon *(G-17240)*

S I C

Employee Codes: A=Over 500 employees, B=251-500
C=101-250, D=51-100, E=20-50, F=10-19, G=3-9
2019 Harris Ohio
Industrial Directory
981

35 INDUSTRIAL AND COMMERCIAL MACHINERY AND COMPUTER EQUIPMENT SIC SECTION

Swagelok Company...D... 440 349-5652
Solon *(G-17241)*
Swagelok Company...E... 440 349-5836
Solon *(G-17243)*
▲ **Swagelok Manufacturing Co LLC**...E... 440 248-4600
Solon *(G-17244)*
Swanton Wldg Machining Co Inc...D... 419 826-4816
Swanton *(G-17923)*
Swartz Manufacturing Inc...G... 440 284-0297
Elyria *(G-9333)*
Swift Tool Inc...G... 330 945-6973
Cuyahoga Falls *(G-7925)*
Swivel-Tek Industries LLC...G... 419 636-7770
Bryan *(G-2308)*
Systech Handling Inc...F... 419 445-8226
Archbold *(G-670)*
Szpak Manufacturing Co Inc...G... 440 236-5233
Columbia Station *(G-6450)*
T & K Welding Co Inc...G... 216 432-0221
Cleveland *(G-6142)*
T & M Machine Products Inc...G... 740 753-2960
Nelsonville *(G-14599)*
T & S Machine Inc...F... 419 453-2101
Wapakoneta *(G-19356)*
T & T Machine Inc...F... 440 354-0605
Painesville *(G-15785)*
T & W Tool & Machine Inc...G... 937 667-2039
Tipp City *(G-18135)*
T E Martindale Enterprises...G... 614 253-6826
Columbus *(G-7507)*
T N T Technologies Inc...G... 330 448-4744
Masury *(G-13063)*
Tailored Systems Inc...G... 937 299-3900
Moraine *(G-14398)*
Tarman Machine Company Inc...F... 614 834-4010
Canal Winchester *(G-2512)*
Tat Machine and Tool Ltd...G... 419 836-7706
Curtice *(G-7827)*
Tc Precision Machine Inc...G... 937 278-3334
Dayton *(G-8547)*
Tdl Tool Inc...F... 937 374-0055
Xenia *(G-20794)*
▲ **Te-Co Manufacturing LLC**...D... 937 836-0961
Englewood *(G-9377)*
Technical Tool & Gauge Inc...F... 330 273-1778
Brunswick *(G-2244)*
Techniform Industries Inc...E... 419 332-8484
Fremont *(G-10054)*
Tegratek...G... 513 742-5100
Cincinnati *(G-4411)*
Tek Gear & Machine Inc...G... 330 455-3331
Canton *(G-2834)*
Tekraft Industries Inc...G... 440 352-8321
Painesville *(G-15787)*
Telcon LLC...D... 330 562-5566
Streetsboro *(G-17702)*
◆ **Tema Systems Inc**...E... 513 489-7811
Cincinnati *(G-4413)*
Tenan Machine & Fabricating...G... 440 997-5100
Ashtabula *(G-807)*
Tendon Manufacturing Inc...E... 216 663-3200
Cleveland *(G-6159)*
Tenney Tool & Supply Co...F... 330 666-2807
Barberton *(G-1110)*
Terydon Inc...F... 330 879-2448
Navarre *(G-14588)*
Tessa Precision Product Inc...E... 440 392-3470
Painesville *(G-15788)*
The Q-P Manufacturing Co Inc...F... 440 946-2120
Chardon *(G-3139)*
Thees Machine & Tool Co...G... 419 586-4766
Celina *(G-2987)*
Thieman Machine...G... 419 628-2474
Minster *(G-14226)*
Thomas Entps of Georgetown...G... 937 378-6300
Georgetown *(G-10238)*
Thread-Rite Tool & Mfg Inc...G... 937 222-2836
Dayton *(G-8555)*
Tiffin Foundry & Machine Inc...E... 419 447-3991
Tiffin *(G-18087)*
Tig Welding Specialties Inc...G... 216 621-1763
Cleveland *(G-6174)*
Timekap Inc...G... 330 747-2122
Youngstown *(G-21045)*
Timon J Reinhart...G... 419 476-1990
Toledo *(G-18552)*
Titan Manufacturing LLC...G... 440 942-2258
Willoughby *(G-20447)*
Tj Bell Inc...G... 330 633-3644
Akron *(G-406)*
Tm Machine & Tool Inc...G... 419 478-0310
Toledo *(G-18554)*
Tmac Machine Inc...G... 330 673-0621
Kent *(G-11394)*
Tom Barbour Auto Parts Inc...F... 740 354-4654
Portsmouth *(G-16303)*
Tool & Die Systems Inc...E... 440 327-5800
North Ridgeville *(G-15256)*
Toolbold Corporation...G... 216 676-9840
Cleveland *(G-6183)*
Toolco Inc...G... 419 667-3462
Van Wert *(G-19108)*
Tooling & Components Corp...F... 419 478-9122
Toledo *(G-18576)*
Total Manufacturing Co Inc...E... 440 205-9700
Mentor *(G-13610)*
Total Quality Machining Inc...F... 937 746-7765
Franklin *(G-9926)*
Total Repair Express Mich LLC...G... 248 690-9410
Stow *(G-17635)*
Toth Industries Inc...D... 419 729-4669
Toledo *(G-18578)*
Tower Tool & Manufacturing Co...F... 330 425-1623
Twinsburg *(G-18864)*
Tq Manufacturing Company Inc...F... 440 255-9000
Mentor *(G-13611)*
Tracer Specialties Inc...G... 216 696-2363
Cleveland *(G-6194)*
Tradye Machine & Tool Inc...G... 740 625-7550
Centerburg *(G-2994)*
▲ **Trailer Component Mfg Inc**...E... 440 255-2888
Mentor *(G-13612)*
Trec Industries Inc...E... 216 741-4114
Cleveland *(G-6201)*
Tri R Tooling Inc...F... 419 522-8665
Mansfield *(G-12533)*
Tri-State Machining LLC...G... 513 257-9442
Cleves *(G-6380)*
▲ **Tri-State Tool & Die Inc**...G... 330 655-2536
Stow *(G-17638)*
Tri-Weld Inc...F... 216 281-6009
Cleveland *(G-6207)*
Triangle Precision Industries...D... 937 299-6776
Dayton *(G-8564)*
Triaxis Machine & Tool LLC...G... 440 230-0303
North Royalton *(G-15308)*
Trinel Inc...F... 216 265-9190
Cleveland *(G-6216)*
Triumph Tool LLC...G... 937 222-6885
Dayton *(G-8567)*
Trojon Gear Inc...F... 937 254-1737
Dayton *(G-8568)*
Trotwood Corporation...E... 937 854-3047
Trotwood *(G-18631)*
Tru-Edge Grinding Inc...E... 419 678-4991
Saint Henry *(G-16668)*
Tru-Fab Technology Inc...F... 440 954-9760
Willoughby *(G-20451)*
Trucast Inc...D... 440 942-4923
Willoughby *(G-20452)*
True Grinding...G... 440 786-7608
Bedford *(G-1452)*
Trv Incorporated...E... 440 951-7722
Willoughby *(G-20453)*
TSS Acquisition Company...G... 513 772-7000
Cincinnati *(G-4444)*
▲ **Tsw Industries Inc**...E... 440 572-7200
Strongsville *(G-17802)*
Tubular Techniques Inc...G... 614 529-4130
Hilliard *(G-10872)*
Turbo Machine & Tool Inc...G... 216 651-1940
Cleveland *(G-6223)*
Turn-All Machine & Gear Co...F... 937 342-8710
Springfield *(G-17510)*
Turner Machine Co...F... 330 332-5821
Salem *(G-16778)*
Twin Valley Metalcraft Asm LLC...G... 937 787-4634
West Alexandria *(G-19622)*
Two M Precision Co Inc...E... 440 946-2120
Willoughby *(G-20454)*
U S Alloy Die Corp...F... 216 749-9700
Cleveland *(G-6227)*
Ultra Machine Inc...G... 440 323-7632
Elyria *(G-9340)*
▲ **Ultra Tech Machinery Inc**...E... 330 929-5544
Cuyahoga Falls *(G-7931)*
▲ **United Grinding and Machine Co**...D... 330 453-7402
Canton *(G-2848)*
United Machine and Tool Inc...G... 440 946-7677
Eastlake *(G-9138)*
▲ **United Precision Services Inc**...G... 513 851-6900
Cincinnati *(G-4449)*
United Tool and Machine Inc...F... 937 843-5603
Lakeview *(G-11505)*
▲ **Universal Fabg Cnstr Svcs Inc**...D... 614 274-1128
Columbus *(G-7561)*
Universal J&Z Machine LLC...E... 216 486-2220
Willoughby *(G-20455)*
Universal Machine Products...G... 513 860-4530
West Chester *(G-19815)*
Universal Prototype Product Co...G... 440 953-3550
Eastlake *(G-9139)*
▲ **Universal Tire Molds Inc**...E... 330 253-5101
Akron *(G-422)*
Universal Tool Technology LLC...E... 937 222-4608
Dayton *(G-8576)*
Updegraff Inc...G... 216 621-7600
Cleveland *(G-6241)*
Upm Inc...G... 419 595-2600
Alvada *(G-520)*
US Machine Prcsion Grnding LLC...G... 440 284-0711
Elyria *(G-9342)*
Usm Acquisition Corporation...D... 440 975-8600
Willoughby *(G-20457)*
V M Machine Co Inc...G... 216 281-4569
Cleveland *(G-6248)*
V-Ash Machine Company...G... 216 267-3400
Cuyahoga Falls *(G-7933)*
Valley Machine Tool Co Inc...E... 513 899-2737
Morrow *(G-14417)*
Vandalia Machining Inc...G... 937 264-9155
Vandalia *(G-19148)*
Vanguard Die & Machine Inc...E... 330 394-4170
Warren *(G-19455)*
Vectron Inc...D... 440 323-3369
Elyria *(G-9343)*
▲ **Ver-Mac Industries Inc**...E... 740 397-6511
Mount Vernon *(G-14517)*
Verhoff Machine & Welding Inc...C... 419 596-3202
Continental *(G-7669)*
Versatile Machine...G... 330 618-9895
Tallmadge *(G-18012)*
Vic Mar Manufacturing Inc...G... 740 687-5434
Lancaster *(G-11617)*
Vicas Manufacturing Co Inc...E... 513 791-7741
Cincinnati *(G-4480)*
Vics Turning Co Inc...G... 216 531-5016
Cleveland *(G-6258)*
Vintage Machine Supply Inc...G... 330 723-0800
Medina *(G-13361)*
Vision Projects Inc...G... 937 667-8648
Tipp City *(G-18142)*
Vorlage Special Tool...G... 419 697-1201
Oregon *(G-15572)*
Vrc Inc...D... 440 243-6666
Berea *(G-1631)*
Vtd Systems Inc...E... 440 323-4122
Elyria *(G-9344)*
Wade Dynamics Inc...G... 216 431-8484
Cleveland *(G-6282)*
▲ **Wagner Machine Inc**...E... 330 706-0700
Norton *(G-15377)*
Walest Incorporated...G... 216 362-8110
Cleveland *(G-6286)*
Walt Myers...G... 937 325-0313
Springfield *(G-17515)*
◆ **Warren Fabricating Corporation**...D... 330 534-5017
Hubbard *(G-11011)*
Warrior Technologies Inc...G... 937 438-0279
Dayton *(G-8584)*
Wauseon Machine & Mfg Inc...G... 419 337-0940
Miamisburg *(G-13739)*
▲ **Wauseon Machine & Mfg Inc**...D... 419 337-0940
Wauseon *(G-19537)*
Wayne Trail Technologies Inc...D... 937 295-2120
Fort Loramie *(G-9811)*
Waynes Precision Machine Inc...G... 330 426-4626
East Palestine *(G-9089)*
Wc Sales Inc...G... 419 836-2300
Northwood *(G-15350)*
We Grind Muzik...G... 614 670-4142
Columbus *(G-7595)*
Webb Machine & Fab Inc...G... 330 717-5745
Berlin Center *(G-1651)*
Weber Tool & Mfg Inc...G... 440 786-0221
Oakwood Village *(G-15488)*
Wedgeworks Mch Tl & Boring Co...G... 216 441-1200
Cleveland *(G-6296)*
Welker Machine & Grinding Co...G... 216 481-1360
Cleveland *(G-6300)*

Wendell Machine Shop ....G.... 330 627-3480
Carrollton *(G-2932)*
Wenrick Machine and Tool Corp ....F.... 937 667-7307
Tipp City *(G-18145)*
Wesco Machine Inc ....F.... 330 688-6973
Akron *(G-433)*
Westerman Acquisition Co LLC ....E.... 330 264-2447
Wooster *(G-20666)*
Westgate Machine Co Inc ....G.... 216 889-9745
North Royalton *(G-15310)*
White Machine & Mfg Co ....F.... 740 453-3444
Zanesville *(G-21188)*
White Machine Inc ....G.... 440 237-3282
North Royalton *(G-15311)*
Whitt Machine Inc ....F.... 513 423-7624
Middletown *(G-13967)*
Wilguss Automotive Machine ....G.... 937 465-0043
West Liberty *(G-19939)*
▲ Will-Burt Company ....B.... 330 682-7015
Orrville *(G-15626)*
Will-Burt Company ....G.... 330 683-9991
Orrville *(G-15627)*
Will-Burt Company ....E.... 330 682-7015
Orrville *(G-15628)*
Williams Machine Co Inc ....G.... 330 534-3058
Hubbard *(G-11012)*
Williams Precision Tool Inc ....F.... 937 384-0608
Miamisburg *(G-13741)*
Willis Cnc ....G.... 440 926-0434
Grafton *(G-10313)*
Willmac Enterprises Inc ....G.... 740 967-1979
Johnstown *(G-11274)*
Willow Tool & Machining Ltd ....F.... 440 572-2288
Strongsville *(G-17808)*
Wipe Out Enterprises ....G.... 937 497-9473
Sidney *(G-17086)*
Wire Shop Inc ....E.... 440 354-6842
Mentor *(G-13628)*
Wise Enterprises Inc ....G.... 330 568-7095
Hubbard *(G-11013)*
Wm Plotz Machine and Forge Co ....F.... 216 861-0441
Cleveland *(G-6319)*
Wodin Inc ....E.... 440 439-4222
Cleveland *(G-6320)*
Wolfe Grinding Inc ....G.... 330 929-6677
Stow *(G-17643)*
Wonder Machine Services Inc ....E.... 440 937-7500
Avon *(G-975)*
Workshop Wire Cut and Mch Inc ....G.... 330 995-6404
Aurora *(G-917)*
Worleys Machine & Fab Inc ....G.... 740 532-3337
Hanging Rock *(G-10624)*
Wray Precision Products Inc ....G.... 513 228-5000
Lebanon *(G-11707)*
Wt Tool & Die Inc ....G.... 330 332-2254
Salem *(G-16782)*
Wulco Inc ....D.... 513 679-2600
Cincinnati *(G-4524)*
▲ Wulco Inc ....D.... 513 679-2600
Cincinnati *(G-4525)*
X-Mil Inc ....E.... 937 444-1323
Mount Orab *(G-14453)*
Xact Spec Industries LLC ....G.... 440 543-8157
Chagrin Falls *(G-3091)*
Xact Spec Industries LLC ....E.... 440 543-8157
Chagrin Falls *(G-3092)*
Xorb Corporation ....G.... 419 354-6021
Bowling Green *(G-2008)*
Yaugher Enterprizes Inc ....G.... 440 968-0151
Montville *(G-14326)*
York Fabrication & Machine ....G.... 419 483-6275
Bellevue *(G-1554)*
Youngstown Hard Chrome Plating ....E.... 330 758-9721
Youngstown *(G-21077)*
Z & Z Manufacturing Inc ....F.... 440 953-2800
Willoughby *(G-20462)*
Zanesville Tool Grinding ....G.... 740 453-9356
Zanesville *(G-21194)*
Zaromet Inc ....G.... 513 891-0773
Blue Ash *(G-1881)*
Zephyr Industries Inc ....G.... 419 281-4485
Ashland *(G-756)*
Ziegler Bros Tool & Mch Inc ....G.... 419 738-6048
Wapakoneta *(G-19361)*
Zitnik Enterprises Inc ....G.... 440 951-0089
Willoughby *(G-20464)*

36 ELECTRONIC AND OTHER ELECTRICAL EQUIPMENT AND COMPONENTS, EXCEPT COMPUTER

3612 Power, Distribution & Specialty Transformers

Acuity Brands Lighting Inc ....B.... 740 349-4343
Newark *(G-14848)*
◆ Ajax Tocco Magnethermic Corp ....C.... 330 372-8511
Warren *(G-19364)*
Alfred J Buescher Jr ....G.... 216 752-3676
Cleveland *(G-4660)*
Arisdyne Systems Inc ....F.... 216 458-1991
Cleveland *(G-4732)*
Clark Substations LLC ....E.... 330 452-5200
Canton *(G-2628)*
Contact Industries Inc ....E.... 419 884-9788
Lexington *(G-11804)*
▲ Control Transformer Inc ....E.... 330 637-6015
Cortland *(G-7706)*
Custom Coil & Transformer Co ....E.... 740 452-5211
Zanesville *(G-21126)*
Darrah Electric Company ....E.... 216 631-0912
Cleveland *(G-5067)*
Delta Transformer Inc ....G.... 513 242-9400
Cincinnati *(G-3581)*
▲ Eaton Electric Holdings LLC ....B.... 440 523-5000
Cleveland *(G-5151)*
Eaton Leasing Corporation ....G.... 216 382-2292
Beachwood *(G-1235)*
Energy Developments Inc ....G.... 440 774-6816
Oberlin *(G-15494)*
Fishel Company ....D.... 614 850-4400
Columbus *(G-6926)*
▲ Fostoria Bshngs Inslators Corp ....G.... 419 435-7514
Fostoria *(G-9839)*
▲ Fostoria Bushings Inc ....G.... 419 435-7514
Fostoria *(G-9840)*
General Electric Company ....D.... 216 883-1000
Cleveland *(G-5306)*
Hannon Company ....D.... 330 456-4728
Canton *(G-2693)*
▲ Japlar Group Inc ....F.... 513 791-7192
Cincinnati *(G-3870)*
Karrier Company Inc ....G.... 330 823-9597
Alliance *(G-480)*
◆ Lake Shore Electric Corp ....E.... 440 232-0200
Bedford *(G-1422)*
◆ LTI Power Systems ....E.... 440 327-5050
Elyria *(G-9290)*
Matlock Electric Co Inc ....E.... 513 731-9600
Cincinnati *(G-3986)*
▼ Morlan & Associates Inc ....E.... 614 889-6152
Hilliard *(G-10842)*
Nautilus Hyosung America Inc ....G.... 937 203-4900
Miamisburg *(G-13697)*
▼ Norlake Manufacturing Company ....D.... 440 353-3200
North Ridgeville *(G-15241)*
▲ Ohio Semitronics Inc ....D.... 614 777-1005
Hilliard *(G-10847)*
▲ Otc Services Inc ....D.... 330 871-2444
Louisville *(G-12163)*
Peak Electric Inc ....G.... 419 726-4848
Toledo *(G-18460)*
▲ Pioneer Transformer Company ....G.... 419 737-2304
Pioneer *(G-16090)*
Precision Switching Inc ....G.... 800 800-8143
Mansfield *(G-12502)*
▲ Qualtek Electronics Corp ....C.... 440 951-3300
Mentor *(G-13567)*
Schneider Electric Usa Inc ....D.... 513 755-5000
West Chester *(G-19792)*
Schneider Electric Usa Inc ....B.... 513 523-4171
Oxford *(G-15700)*
▲ SGB Usa Inc ....E.... 330 472-1187
Tallmadge *(G-18003)*
Siemens Industry Inc ....D.... 937 593-6010
Bellefontaine *(G-1525)*
▲ Specialty Magnetics LLC ....G.... 330 468-8834
Macedonia *(G-12327)*
Spectre Sensors Inc ....G.... 440 250-0372
Westlake *(G-20160)*
◆ Staco Energy Products Co ....G.... 937 253-1191
Miamisburg *(G-13719)*
Tesa Inc ....G.... 614 847-8200
Lewis Center *(G-11784)*
Transcontinental Electric LLC ....G.... 614 496-4379
Columbus *(G-7538)*
Transformer Associates Limited ....G.... 330 430-0750
Canton *(G-2844)*
Unity Cable Technologies Inc ....G.... 419 322-4118
Toledo *(G-18584)*
Vida Ve Corp ....G.... 614 203-2607
Dublin *(G-9008)*
▼ Voltage Regulator Sales & Svcs ....G.... 937 878-0673
Fairborn *(G-9474)*

3613 Switchgear & Switchboard Apparatus

Acorn Technology Corporation ....E.... 216 663-1244
Cleveland *(G-4610)*
Adgo Incorporated ....E.... 513 752-6880
Cincinnati *(G-3239)*
Advanced Controls Inc ....E.... 440 354-5413
Eastlake *(G-9097)*
Agent Technologies Inc ....G.... 513 942-9444
West Chester *(G-19639)*
All Pack Services LLC ....F.... 614 935-0964
Grove City *(G-10413)*
▲ Altronic LLC ....C.... 330 545-9768
Girard *(G-10252)*
Apex Circuits Inc ....G.... 513 942-4400
West Chester *(G-19647)*
Asco Power Technologies LP ....C.... 216 573-7600
Cleveland *(G-4744)*
Asco Power Technologies LP ....E.... 216 573-7600
Cleveland *(G-4745)*
Assembly Works Inc ....G.... 419 433-5010
Huron *(G-11090)*
Auto-Tronic Control Co ....F.... 419 666-5100
Northwood *(G-15333)*
Bentronix Corp ....G.... 440 632-0606
Middlefield *(G-13780)*
▲ Bud Industries Inc ....G.... 440 946-3200
Willoughby *(G-20289)*
CDI Industries Inc ....E.... 440 243-1100
Cleveland *(G-4895)*
City Machine Technologies Inc ....E.... 330 747-2639
Youngstown *(G-20872)*
City Machine Technologies Inc ....G.... 330 747-2639
Youngstown *(G-20873)*
Control Craft LLC ....F.... 513 674-0056
Cincinnati *(G-3544)*
▲ Control Interface Inc ....G.... 513 874-2062
West Chester *(G-19683)*
Custom Craft Controls Inc ....F.... 330 630-9599
Akron *(G-128)*
Cutler Richard DBA Ohio Contro ....G.... 440 892-1858
Cleveland *(G-5050)*
▲ Delta Systems Inc ....C.... 330 626-2811
Streetsboro *(G-17671)*
DRDC Realty Inc ....G.... 419 478-7091
Toledo *(G-18269)*
Dynamics Research & Dev ....G.... 419 478-7091
Toledo *(G-18271)*
Eaton Corporation ....E.... 513 387-2000
West Chester *(G-19696)*
▲ Eaton Electric Holdings LLC ....B.... 440 523-5000
Cleveland *(G-5151)*
Electrical Control Systems ....G.... 937 859-7136
Dayton *(G-8179)*
Electro Controls Inc ....E.... 866 497-1717
Sidney *(G-17035)*
Emerson Network Power ....G.... 614 841-8054
Ironton *(G-11164)*
Empire Power Systems Co ....G.... 440 796-4401
Madison *(G-12349)*
Emt Inc ....G.... 330 399-6939
Warren *(G-19399)*
Epanel Plus Ltd ....F.... 513 772-0888
Cincinnati *(G-3647)*
▲ Etched Metal Company ....E.... 440 248-0240
Solon *(G-17142)*
Fabriweld Corporation ....G.... 419 668-3358
Norwalk *(G-15393)*
Filnor Inc ....F.... 330 821-7667
Alliance *(G-467)*
Flood Heliarc Inc ....F.... 614 835-3929
Groveport *(G-10489)*
General Electric Company ....D.... 216 883-1000
Cleveland *(G-5306)*
Hosler Maps Inc ....G.... 937 855-4173
Germantown *(G-10242)*
Ida Controls ....G.... 440 785-8457
Willoughby *(G-20341)*
◆ Ideal Electric Power Co ....F.... 419 522-3611
Mansfield *(G-12460)*

S I C

Employee Codes: A=Over 500 employees, B=251-500 C=101-250, D=51-100, E=20-50, F=10-19, G=3-9
2019 Harris Ohio Industrial Directory
983

36 ELECTRONIC AND OTHER ELECTRICAL EQUIPMENT AND COMPONENTS, EXCEPT COMPUTER SIC SECTION

Industrial and Mar Eng Svc Co ....F 740 694-0791
Fredericktown *(G-9971)*
Industrial Ctrl Dsign Mint Inc ....F 330 785-9840
Tallmadge *(G-17987)*
Industrial Solutions Inc ....E 614 431-8118
Lewis Center *(G-11762)*
◆ Industrial Thermal Systems Inc ....F 513 561-2100
Cincinnati *(G-3845)*
Innovative Control Systems..................G....... 513 894-3712
Fairfield Township *(G-9582)*
Innovative Controls Corp ....D....... 419 691-6684
Toledo *(G-18348)*
▲ Instrmntation Ctrl Systems Inc.........E 513 662-2600
Cincinnati *(G-3851)*
International Bus Mchs Corp ....B 513 826-1001
Cincinnati *(G-3857)*
Jeff Bonham Electric Inc ....E 937 233-7662
Dayton *(G-8282)*
Koester Corporation ....D....... 419 599-0291
Napoleon *(G-14548)*
◆ Lake Shore Electric Corp....................E 440 232-0200
Bedford *(G-1422)*
Layerzero Power Systems Inc ....E 440 399-9000
Aurora *(G-890)*
Matrix Cable and Mould..........................G....... 513 832-2577
Cincinnati *(G-3987)*
Mercury Iron and Steel Co ....F 440 349-1500
Solon *(G-17190)*
▲ Myers Controlled Power LLC...........C 330 834-3200
North Canton *(G-15105)*
Nolan Manufacturing LLC ....G....... 614 859-2302
Westerville *(G-20012)*
▲ Osborne Coinage Company..............D....... 513 681-5424
Cincinnati *(G-4120)*
Otr Controls LLC....................................G....... 513 621-2197
Cincinnati *(G-4123)*
Pacs Switchgear LLC ....E 740 397-5021
Mount Vernon *(G-14498)*
Panel Control Inc ....G....... 937 394-2201
Anna *(G-591)*
Panel Master LLC...................................E 440 355-4442
Lagrange *(G-11491)*
Panel-Fab Inc..D....... 513 771-1462
Cincinnati *(G-4132)*
Panelmatic Inc...G....... 513 829-3666
Fairfield *(G-9544)*
Panelmatic Inc...E 330 782-8007
Youngstown *(G-20991)*
Panelmatic Cincinnati Inc ....E 513 829-1960
Fairfield *(G-9545)*
▼ Panelmatic Youngstown Inc.............E 330 782-8007
Youngstown *(G-20992)*
Precision Switching Inc..........................G....... 800 800-8143
Mansfield *(G-12502)*
Primex ....E 513 831-9959
Milford *(G-14035)*
Regal Beloit America Inc......................C 419 352-8441
Bowling Green *(G-1996)*
Roemer Industries Inc ....D....... 330 448-2000
Masury *(G-13062)*
Schneider Electric Usa Inc...................C 513 755-5503
Liberty Township *(G-11819)*
Schneider Electric Usa Inc...................D....... 513 755-5000
West Chester *(G-19792)*
Schneider Electric Usa Inc...................C 513 755-5501
Sharonville *(G-16959)*
Scott Fetzer Company ....C 216 267-9000
Cleveland *(G-6035)*
Siemens Industry Inc ....E 419 499-4616
Milan *(G-13989)*
Siemens Industry Inc ....D....... 937 593-6010
Bellefontaine *(G-1525)*
Spb Global LLC.......................................G....... 419 931-6559
Perrysburg *(G-16007)*
▲ Spectra-Tech Manufacturing Inc.......E 513 735-9300
Batavia *(G-1186)*
System Controls Inc................................G....... 216 351-9121
Cleveland *(G-6139)*
Systems Specialty Ctrl Co Inc ....E 419 478-4156
Toledo *(G-18540)*
Tcb Automation LLC ....E 330 556-6444
Dover *(G-8860)*
Te Connectivity Corporation.................C 419 521-9500
Mansfield *(G-12527)*
Technology Products Inc ....G....... 937 652-3412
Urbana *(G-19015)*
Toledo Transducers Inc.........................E 419 724-4170
Holland *(G-10962)*
▲ Trucut Incorporated ....D....... 330 938-9806
Sebring *(G-16896)*
◆ United Rolls Inc ....D....... 330 456-2761
Canton *(G-2850)*
Vacuum Electric Switch Co Inc.............G....... 330 374-5156
Akron *(G-423)*
◆ Vertiv Corporation ....A....... 614 888-0246
Columbus *(G-7575)*

3621 Motors & Generators

Aadco Instruments Inc ....G....... 513 467-1477
Cleves *(G-6354)*
▲ ABM Drives Inc.....................................G....... 513 576-1300
Loveland *(G-12174)*
Accurate Electronics Inc ....C 330 682-7015
Orrville *(G-15581)*
AEP Resources Inc ....F 614 716-1000
Columbus *(G-6548)*
Alliance Torque Converters Inc.............G....... 937 222-3394
Dayton *(G-8019)*
American Mitsuba Corporation ....G....... 989 779-4962
Dublin *(G-8877)*
American Mitsuba Corporation ....G....... 989 779-4962
Dublin *(G-8878)*
Ametek Inc..G....... 302 636-5401
Worthington *(G-20678)*
Ametek Florcare Specialty Mtrs ....F 330 677-3786
Kent *(G-11293)*
Ametek Tchnical Indus Pdts Inc............D....... 330 677-3754
Kent *(G-11294)*
Ares Inc...D....... 419 635-2175
Port Clinton *(G-16242)*
Babcock & Wilcox Entps Inc..................A 330 753-4511
Barberton *(G-1061)*
Brinkley Technology Group LLC ....F 330 830-2498
Massillon *(G-12963)*
Bwx Technologies Inc ....G....... 740 687-4180
Lancaster *(G-11550)*
Charger Connection ....G....... 888 427-5829
Cincinnati *(G-3464)*
Charles Auto Electric Co Inc..................G....... 330 535-6269
Akron *(G-111)*
Chemequip Sales Inc..............................E 330 724-8300
Coventry Township *(G-7767)*
City Machine Technologies Inc..............F 330 747-2639
Youngstown *(G-20870)*
City Machine Technologies Inc..............E 330 740-8186
Youngstown *(G-20871)*
Cummins Inc ....G....... 614 604-6004
Grove City *(G-10424)*
Custom Coil & Transformer Co ....E 740 452-5211
Zanesville *(G-21126)*
◆ Dayton-Phoenix Group Inc ....C 937 496-3900
Dayton *(G-8151)*
◆ Dcm Manufacturing Inc......................E 216 265-8006
Cleveland *(G-5078)*
Design Flux Technologies LLC..............G....... 216 543-6066
Akron *(G-139)*
▲ Dreison International Inc....................C 216 362-0755
Cleveland *(G-5113)*
Econ-O-Machine Products Inc...............G....... 937 882-6307
Donnelsville *(G-8801)*
Electric Service Co Inc ....E 513 271-6387
Cincinnati *(G-3632)*
▲ Electrocraft Arkansas Inc..................D....... 501 268-4203
Gallipolis *(G-10163)*
Energy Technologies Inc........................D....... 419 522-4444
Mansfield *(G-12437)*
Franklin Electric Co Inc..........................A 614 794-2266
Dublin *(G-8915)*
GE Aviation Systems LLC ....B 937 898-5881
Vandalia *(G-19125)*
General Electric Company ....D....... 216 883-1000
Cleveland *(G-5306)*
◆ Gleason Metrology Systems Corp....E 937 384-8901
Dayton *(G-8223)*
▲ Global Innovative Products LLC ......G....... 513 701-0441
Mason *(G-12879)*
▲ Globe Motors Inc..................................C 334 983-3542
Dayton *(G-8226)*
Globe Motors Inc......................................C 937 228-3171
Dayton *(G-8227)*
Globe Motors Inc......................................D....... 937 228-3171
Dayton *(G-8228)*
▲ Grand-Rock Company Inc.................E 440 639-2000
Painesville *(G-15742)*
H W Fairway International Inc...............E 330 678-2540
Kent *(G-11330)*
Hannon Company....................................D....... 330 456-4728
Canton *(G-2693)*
High Performance Servo LLC ....G....... 440 541-3529
Westlake *(G-20123)*
Home Resolver...G....... 440 886-6758
Cleveland *(G-5413)*
▲ Hurst Auto-Truck Electric...................G....... 216 961-1800
Cleveland *(G-5426)*
◆ Ideal Electric Power Co.......................F 419 522-3611
Mansfield *(G-12460)*
Industrial and Mar Eng Svc Co ....F 740 694-0791
Fredericktown *(G-9971)*
JD Power Systems LLC ....F 614 317-9394
Hilliard *(G-10833)*
Kirkwood Holding Inc..............................C 216 267-6200
Cleveland *(G-5539)*
◆ Lake Shore Electric Corp....................E 440 232-0200
Bedford *(G-1422)*
Lesch Btry & Pwr Solution LLC.............G....... 419 884-0219
Mansfield *(G-12469)*
▲ Linde Hydraulics Corporation ....E 330 533-6801
Canfield *(G-2532)*
Martin Diesel Inc ....E 419 782-9911
Defiance *(G-8636)*
Micropower LLC.......................................F 513 382-0100
Cincinnati *(G-4023)*
Mv Designlabs LLC.................................G....... 724 355-7986
Cleveland *(G-5715)*
Nidec Motor Corporation........................C 575 434-0633
Akron *(G-297)*
▲ Ohio Magnetics Inc ....E 216 662-8484
Maple Heights *(G-12575)*
▲ Ohio Semitronics Inc..........................D....... 614 777-1005
Hilliard *(G-10847)*
Ohio Synchro Swim Club........................G....... 614 319-4667
Hilliard *(G-10848)*
Pace Converting Eqp Co Inc..................F 216 631-4555
Cleveland *(G-5834)*
Palesh & Associates Inc.........................G....... 440 942-9168
Willoughby *(G-20398)*
Parker-Hannifin Corporation..................C 330 336-3511
Wadsworth *(G-19260)*
Peerless-Winsmith Inc............................B 330 399-3651
Dublin *(G-8962)*
◆ Peerless-Winsmith Inc ....G....... 614 526-7000
Dublin *(G-8963)*
Precision Design Inc................................G....... 419 289-1553
Ashland *(G-737)*
R E Smith Inc...F 513 771-0645
Cincinnati *(G-4243)*
R Gordon Jones Inc..................................G....... 740 986-8381
Williamsport *(G-20260)*
Ramco Electric Motors Inc......................D....... 937 548-2525
Greenville *(G-10389)*
Regal Beloit America Inc........................C 608 364-8800
Lima *(G-11928)*
Regal Beloit America Inc........................C 937 667-2431
Tipp City *(G-18130)*
Reuland Electric Co.................................G....... 513 825-7314
Cincinnati *(G-4262)*
Safran USA Incorporated ....G....... 513 247-7000
Sharonville *(G-16958)*
Siemens Industry Inc...............................C 513 841-3100
Cincinnati *(G-4334)*
Single Phase Pwr Solutions LLC...........G....... 513 722-5098
Norwood *(G-15429)*
Stateline Power Corp...............................F 937 547-1006
Greenville *(G-10397)*
▲ Surenergy LLC ....F 419 626-8000
Sandusky *(G-16851)*
▲ Swiger Coil Systems Ltd ....C 216 362-7500
Cleveland *(G-6137)*
▲ Tigerpoly Manufacturing Inc ....B 614 871-0045
Grove City *(G-10473)*
Tremont Electric Incorporated...............G....... 888 214-3137
Cleveland *(G-6203)*
▲ Turk+hillinger Usa Inc........................G....... 440 781-1900
Brecksville *(G-2062)*
Turtlecreek Township ....F 513 932-4080
Lebanon *(G-11703)*
◆ Vanner Holdings Inc............................D....... 614 771-2718
Hilliard *(G-10873)*
Visiontech Automation LLC ....G....... 614 554-2013
Dublin *(G-9010)*
Wabtec Corporation.................................G....... 216 362-7500
Cleveland *(G-6280)*
Waibel Electric Co Inc ....F 740 964-2956
Etna *(G-9390)*
▲ Yamada North America Inc...............B 937 462-7111
South Charleston *(G-17275)*

3624 Carbon & Graphite Prdts

Albemarle Corporation............................G....... 330 425-2354
Twinsburg *(G-18729)*

SIC SECTION 36 ELECTRONIC AND OTHER ELECTRICAL EQUIPMENT AND COMPONENTS, EXCEPT COMPUTER

▲ American Spring Wire Corp ....C 216 292-4620
Bedford Heights *(G-1460)*
▲ Angstron Materials Inc ....G 937 331-9884
Dayton *(G-8032)*
Applied Sciences Inc ....E 937 766-2020
Cedarville *(G-2943)*
Buckeye Molded Products Ltd ....F 440 323-2244
Elyria *(G-9226)*
▲ Cammann Inc ....F 440 965-4051
Wakeman *(G-19282)*
◆ De Nora Tech LLC ....D 440 710-5300
Painesville *(G-15731)*
Durr Megtec LLC ....C 614 258-9501
Columbus *(G-6876)*
GE Aviation Systems LLC ....B 937 898-5881
Vandalia *(G-19125)*
Graftech Holdings Inc ....B 216 676-2000
Independence *(G-11134)*
Graftech International Ltd ....D 216 676-2000
Brooklyn Heights *(G-2123)*
Graftech Intl Holdings Inc ....C 216 529-3777
Cleveland *(G-5337)*
Graftech Intl Holdings Inc ....C 330 239-3023
Parma *(G-15821)*
Graftech Intl Holdings Inc ....G 216 676-2000
Brooklyn Heights *(G-2124)*
▲ Graftech Intl Holdings Inc ....C 216 676-2000
Brooklyn Heights *(G-2125)*
Graphel Corporation ....C 513 779-6166
West Chester *(G-19718)*
◆ Graphite Sales Inc ....F 419 652-3388
Nova *(G-15433)*
Graphite Sales Inc ....E 419 652-3388
Nova *(G-15434)*
▲ Mill-Rose Company ....C 440 255-9171
Mentor *(G-13520)*
▼ Morgan Advanced Materials ....C 419 435-8182
Fostoria *(G-9849)*
National Elec Carbn Pdts Inc ....D 419 435-8182
Fostoria *(G-9850)*
Neograf Solutions LLC ....C 216 529-3777
Lakewood *(G-11530)*
Ohio Carbon Blank Inc ....E 440 953-9302
Willoughby *(G-20394)*
Ohio Carbon Industries Inc ....E 419 496-2530
Ashland *(G-730)*
Ohio Power Tool Brush Co ....G 419 736-3010
Ashland *(G-731)*
Pyrograf Products Inc ....F 937 766-2020
Cedarville *(G-2946)*
Pyrotek Incorporated ....C 440 349-8800
Aurora *(G-901)*
▼ R&S Carbon Trading LLC ....G 614 264-3083
Gahanna *(G-10099)*
▲ Randall Bearings Inc ....D 419 223-1075
Lima *(G-11927)*
Randall Bearings Inc ....F 419 678-2486
Coldwater *(G-6419)*
▲ Sangraf International Inc ....F 216 543-3288
Westlake *(G-20154)*
Sentinel Management Inc ....E 440 821-7372
Lorain *(G-12119)*
Sherbrooke Metals ....E 440 942-3520
Willoughby *(G-20429)*
▲ Spectramed Inc ....F 740 263-3059
Gahanna *(G-10106)*
▼ Wolfden Products Inc ....G 614 219-6990
Columbus *(G-7609)*
Xperion E&E USA LLC ....E 740 788-9560
Heath *(G-10735)*
Zyvex Performance Mtls Inc ....E 614 481-2222
Columbus *(G-7629)*

3625 Relays & Indl Controls

Acon Inc ....G 513 276-2111
Tipp City *(G-18096)*
▲ Altronic LLC ....C 330 545-9768
Girard *(G-10252)*
Amano Cincinnati Incorporated ....D 513 697-9000
Loveland *(G-12176)*
Apex Circuits Inc ....G 513 942-4400
West Chester *(G-19647)*
Asco Power Technologies LP ....C 216 573-7600
Cleveland *(G-4744)*
Asco Power Technologies LP ....E 216 573-7600
Cleveland *(G-4745)*
Asco Valve Inc ....F 216 360-0366
Cleveland *(G-4746)*
Automatic Timing & Controls ....G 614 888-8855
New Albany *(G-14606)*
Automation Technology Inc ....E 937 233-6084
Dayton *(G-8045)*
Autoneum North America Inc ....B 419 693-0511
Oregon *(G-15556)*
Avtron Holdings LLC ....B 216 642-1230
Cleveland *(G-4779)*
▼ Axel Austin LLC ....G 440 237-1610
North Royalton *(G-15261)*
Barry Brothers Electric ....G 614 299-8187
Columbus *(G-6651)*
▼ Bay Controls LLC ....E 419 891-4390
Maumee *(G-13079)*
Beckworth Industries Inc ....G 216 268-5557
Cleveland *(G-4801)*
Bost & Filtrex Inc ....F 301 206-9466
Columbus *(G-6689)*
BV Thermal Systems LLC ....F 209 522-3701
Willoughby *(G-20291)*
Cattron Holdings Inc ....E 234 806-0018
Warren *(G-19381)*
◆ Cattron North America Inc ....D 234 806-0018
Warren *(G-19382)*
Central Systems & Control ....G 440 835-0015
Cleveland *(G-4901)*
▲ Chandler Systems Incorporated ....D 888 363-9434
Ashland *(G-693)*
▲ Channel Products Inc ....D 440 423-0113
Solon *(G-17126)*
Cincinnati Ctrl Dynamics Inc ....G 513 242-7300
Cincinnati *(G-3489)*
Clark Substations LLC ....E 330 452-5200
Canton *(G-2628)*
▲ Cleveland Hdwr & Forging Co ....E 216 641-5200
Cleveland *(G-4962)*
Command Alkon Incorporated ....D 614 799-0600
Dublin *(G-8901)*
Comtec Incorporated ....F 330 425-8102
Twinsburg *(G-18756)*
Contact Industries Inc ....E 419 884-9788
Lexington *(G-11804)*
Control Associates Inc ....G 440 708-1770
Chagrin Falls *(G-3042)*
Control Electric Co ....E 216 671-8010
Columbia Station *(G-6434)*
Controllix Corporation ....F 440 232-8757
Walton Hills *(G-19309)*
Controls Inc ....E 330 239-4345
Medina *(G-13240)*
Corrotec Inc ....E 937 325-3585
Springfield *(G-17379)*
Creative Electronic Design ....G 937 256-5106
Beavercreek *(G-1308)*
Curtiss-Wright Controls ....E 937 252-5601
Fairborn *(G-9456)*
Dalton Corporation ....D 419 682-6328
Stryker *(G-17827)*
Das Consulting Services Inc ....F 330 896-4064
Canton *(G-2650)*
Davis Technologies Inc ....F 330 823-2544
Alliance *(G-464)*
Delta Control Inc ....G 937 277-3444
Dayton *(G-8154)*
▲ Delta Systems Inc ....C 330 626-2811
Streetsboro *(G-17671)*
▲ Dimcogray Corporation ....D 937 433-7600
Centerville *(G-3001)*
Divelbiss Corporation ....E 800 245-2327
Fredericktown *(G-9966)*
◆ Eaton Corporation ....B 440 523-5000
Cleveland *(G-5146)*
Eaton Corporation ....C 888 328-6677
Cleveland *(G-5148)*
Eaton Corporation ....C 440 826-1115
Cleveland *(G-5150)*
Eaton Corporation ....G 440 748-2236
Grafton *(G-10299)*
Eaton Corporation ....C 216 281-2211
Cleveland *(G-5147)*
Electrical Control Design Inc ....G 419 443-9290
Perrysburg *(G-15943)*
▲ Electrocraft Ohio Inc ....C 740 441-6200
Gallipolis *(G-10164)*
Electrodynamics Inc ....C 847 259-0740
Cincinnati *(G-3247)*
▲ Ellis & Watts Intl LLC ....G 513 752-9000
Batavia *(G-1143)*
Energy Technologies Inc ....D 419 522-4444
Mansfield *(G-12437)*
Fabriweld Corporation ....G 419 668-3358
Norwalk *(G-15393)*
◆ Filnor Inc ....E 330 821-8731
Alliance *(G-465)*
Filnor Inc ....G 330 829-3180
Alliance *(G-466)*
Filnor Inc ....F 330 821-7667
Alliance *(G-467)*
▼ Fuse Chicken Llc ....G 330 338-7108
Cuyahoga Falls *(G-7871)*
Future Controls Corporation ....E 440 275-3191
Austinburg *(G-922)*
Gc Controls Inc ....G 440 779-4777
North Olmsted *(G-15191)*
GE Aviation Systems LLC ....B 937 898-5881
Vandalia *(G-19125)*
GE Intelligent Platforms Inc ....G 937 459-5404
Greenville *(G-10372)*
Grill ....G 937 673-6768
Eaton *(G-9150)*
Harris Instrument Corporation ....G 740 369-3580
Delaware *(G-8692)*
Helm Instrument Company Inc ....E 419 893-4356
Maumee *(G-13116)*
Hite Parts Exchange Inc ....E 614 272-5115
Columbus *(G-7003)*
Hueston Industries Inc ....G 937 264-8163
Dayton *(G-8256)*
▲ Hurst Auto-Truck Electric ....G 216 961-1800
Cleveland *(G-5426)*
◆ Ideal Electric Power Co ....F 419 522-3611
Mansfield *(G-12460)*
Ignio Systems LLC ....F 419 708-0503
Toledo *(G-18340)*
Independent Digital Consulting ....G 330 753-0777
Norton *(G-15370)*
Industrial and Mar Eng Svc Co ....F 740 694-0791
Fredericktown *(G-9971)*
Innovative Controls Corp ....D 419 691-6684
Toledo *(G-18348)*
Innovative Integrations Inc ....G 216 533-5353
Mesopotamia *(G-13633)*
James R Eaton ....G 937 435-7767
Dayton *(G-8278)*
Job One Control Services ....G 216 347-0133
Cleveland *(G-5500)*
Kahle Technologies Inc ....G 419 523-3951
Ottawa *(G-15657)*
Konecranes Inc ....F 937 328-5123
Columbus *(G-7099)*
Kz Solutions Inc ....G 513 942-9378
West Chester *(G-19733)*
◆ Lake Shore Electric Corp ....E 440 232-0200
Bedford *(G-1422)*
Lincoln Electric Company ....C 216 524-8800
Cleveland *(G-5576)*
M Technologies Inc ....F 330 477-9009
Canton *(G-2739)*
MA Flynn Associates LLC ....G 513 893-7873
Hamilton *(G-10584)*
Maags Automotive & Machine ....G 419 626-1539
Sandusky *(G-16824)*
Miami Control Systems Inc ....G 937 698-5725
West Milton *(G-19949)*
Midwest Minicranes Inc ....G 330 332-3700
Salem *(G-16761)*
Moog Inc ....D 330 682-0010
Orrville *(G-15603)*
◆ Morris Material Handling Inc ....G 937 525-5520
Springfield *(G-17452)*
New ERA Controls Inc ....G 216 641-8683
Cleveland *(G-5747)*
Noise Suppression Technologies ....F 614 275-1818
Columbus *(G-7221)*
Norgren Inc ....C 937 833-4033
Brookville *(G-2179)*
Northcoast Process Controls ....G 440 498-0542
Cleveland *(G-5771)*
▲ Ohio Magnetics Inc ....E 216 662-8484
Maple Heights *(G-12575)*
▲ Ohio Semitronics Inc ....D 614 777-1005
Hilliard *(G-10847)*
Omega Tek Inc ....G 419 756-9580
Mansfield *(G-12499)*
▲ Opw Engineered Systems Inc ....G 888 771-9438
Lebanon *(G-11680)*
Orion Control Panels Inc ....G 513 615-6534
Cincinnati *(G-4119)*
Panel Master LLC ....E 440 355-4442
Lagrange *(G-11491)*
Parkside & Eaton Estate ....G 330 467-2995
Northfield *(G-15321)*

SIC

Employee Codes: A=Over 500 employees, B=251-500
C=101-250, D=51-100, E=20-50, F=10-19, G=3-9
2019 Harris Ohio
Industrial Directory
985

36 ELECTRONIC AND OTHER ELECTRICAL EQUIPMENT AND COMPONENTS, EXCEPT COMPUTER SIC SECTION

Peco II Inc D 614 431-0694
Columbus *(G-7305)*
▲ **Peloton Manufacturing Corp** F 440 205-1600
Mentor *(G-13546)*
▲ **Pepperl + Fuchs Inc** C 330 425-3555
Twinsburg *(G-18830)*
Pepperl + Fuchs Entps Inc G 330 425-3555
Twinsburg *(G-18831)*
PMC Systems Limited E 330 538-2268
North Jackson *(G-15153)*
Positive Safety Mfr Co F 440 951-2130
Willoughby *(G-20407)*
Precision Switching Inc G 800 800-8143
Mansfield *(G-12502)*
Prime Controls Inc G 937 435-8659
Dayton *(G-8440)*
Primex E 513 831-9959
Milford *(G-14035)*
Quality Controls Inc F 513 272-3900
Cincinnati *(G-4225)*
▲ **R-K Electronics Inc** F 513 204-6060
Mason *(G-12929)*
Ramco Electric Motors Inc D 937 548-2525
Greenville *(G-10389)*
Rbb Systems Inc D 330 263-4502
Wooster *(G-20643)*
Regal Beloit America Inc C 608 364-8800
Lima *(G-11928)*
Resinoid Engineering Corp E 740 928-2220
Heath *(G-10730)*
Retek Inc G 440 937-6282
Avon *(G-963)*
Rex Automation Inc G 614 766-4672
Columbus *(G-7391)*
Rockwell Automation Inc D 513 942-9828
West Chester *(G-19785)*
Rockwell Automation Inc B 330 425-3211
Twinsburg *(G-18848)*
Rockwell Automation Inc E 440 604-8410
Cleveland *(G-5998)*
Rockwell Automation Inc E 513 943-1145
Batavia *(G-1180)*
Rockwell Automation Inc D 614 776-3021
Westerville *(G-20022)*
Rockwell Automation Inc D 440 646-5000
Cleveland *(G-5999)*
Rockwell Automation Inc F 440 646-7900
Cleveland *(G-6000)*
▲ **Rogers Industrial Products Inc** E 330 535-3331
Akron *(G-353)*
▲ **Satco Inc** G 330 630-8866
Tallmadge *(G-18002)*
SCC Instruments G 513 856-8444
Hamilton *(G-10602)*
Schneider Electric Usa Inc D 513 755-5000
West Chester *(G-19792)*
Sieb & Meyer America Inc F 513 563-0860
Fairfield *(G-9563)*
SMC Corporation of America E 330 659-2006
Richfield *(G-16488)*
Spang & Company E 440 350-6108
Mentor *(G-13585)*
Stock Fairfield Corporation C 440 543-6000
Chagrin Falls *(G-3078)*
▲ **Superb Industries Inc** D 330 852-0500
Sugarcreek *(G-17870)*
T D Group Holdings LLC G 216 706-2939
Cleveland *(G-6144)*
Te Connectivity Corporation C 419 521-9500
Mansfield *(G-12527)*
Tech Products Corporation E 937 438-1100
Miamisburg *(G-13723)*
Technology Products Inc G 937 652-3412
Urbana *(G-19015)*
Tekworx LLC F 513 533-4777
Blue Ash *(G-1858)*
Temple Israel G 330 762-8617
Akron *(G-399)*
Thermotion Corp F 440 639-8325
Mentor *(G-13605)*
Toledo Electromotive Inc G 419 874-7751
Perrysburg *(G-16019)*
Toledo Transducers Inc E 419 724-4170
Holland *(G-10962)*
Tramec Sloan LLC F 419 468-9122
Galion *(G-10158)*
Transdigm Inc G 216 706-2939
Cleveland *(G-6196)*
Transdigm Inc F 216 291-6025
Cleveland *(G-6195)*
Tri-Tech Research LLC F 440 946-6122
Eastlake *(G-9136)*
Turvey Engineering G 330 427-0125
Washingtonville *(G-19481)*
Tvh Parts Co F 877 755-7311
West Chester *(G-19813)*
Twinsource LLC F 440 248-6800
Solon *(G-17256)*
Utility Relay Co Ltd E 440 708-1000
Chagrin Falls *(G-3087)*
▲ **Valve Related Controls Inc** F 513 677-8724
Loveland *(G-12242)*
Wes-Garde Components Group Inc G 614 885-0319
Westerville *(G-20081)*
Z3 Controls LLC G 419 261-2654
Walbridge *(G-19301)*

3629 Electrical Indl Apparatus, NEC

10155 Broadview Business G 440 546-1901
Broadview Heights *(G-2085)*
Amplified Solar Inc G 216 236-4225
Lakewood *(G-11511)*
Asg Division Jergens Inc G 888 486-6163
Cleveland *(G-4749)*
Avtron Inc E 216 642-1230
Independence *(G-11120)*
▲ **Brookwood Group Inc** F 513 791-3030
Cincinnati *(G-3425)*
Cable and Ctrl Solutions LLC G 937 254-2227
Dayton *(G-7972)*
▲ **Core Technology Inc** F 440 934-9935
Avon *(G-946)*
Cvc Limited 1 LLC G 740 605-3853
Lebanon *(G-11645)*
D C Systems Inc F 330 273-3030
Brunswick *(G-2198)*
Dan-Mar Company Inc E 419 660-8830
Norwalk *(G-15386)*
▲ **Ecotec Ltd LLC** G 937 606-2793
Troy *(G-18652)*
Energy Technologies Inc D 419 522-4444
Mansfield *(G-12437)*
Eti Tech LLC F 937 832-4200
Englewood *(G-9358)*
Exide Technologies G 614 863-3866
Gahanna *(G-10081)*
Graftech Global Entps Inc G 216 676-2000
Cleveland *(G-5336)*
Industrial Application Svs G 419 875-5093
Grand Rapids *(G-10315)*
▲ **Japlar Group Inc** F 513 791-7192
Cincinnati *(G-3870)*
Liebert Field Services Inc D 614 841-5763
Westerville *(G-20007)*
◆ **Lubrizol Global Management** F 216 447-5000
Brecksville *(G-2048)*
Myers Controlled Power LLC G 909 923-1800
Canton *(G-2760)*
Power Source Service LLC G 513 607-4555
Batavia *(G-1177)*
Proteus Electronics Inc G 419 886-2296
Bellville *(G-1563)*
Sarica Manufacturing Company E 937 484-4030
Urbana *(G-19011)*
Spirit Avionics Ltd F 614 237-4271
Columbus *(G-7477)*
Superior Packaging F 419 380-3335
Toledo *(G-18536)*
▲ **Takk Industries Inc** F 513 353-4306
Cleves *(G-6378)*
Tasi Holdings Inc E 513 202-5182
Harrison *(G-10676)*
▲ **Tecmark Corporation** D 440 205-7600
Mentor *(G-13601)*
TL Industries Inc C 419 666-8144
Northwood *(G-15346)*
◆ **Vanner Holdings Inc** D 614 771-2718
Hilliard *(G-10873)*
Waterloo Manufacturing Co Inc G 330 947-2917
Atwater *(G-865)*
Wired Inc G 440 567-8379
Willoughby *(G-20460)*
▲ **Xenotronix/Tli Inc** G 407 331-4793
Northwood *(G-15353)*

3631 Household Cooking Eqpt

Gosun Inc F 888 868-6154
Cincinnati *(G-3772)*
Lapa Lowe Enterprises LLC G 440 944-9410
Willoughby *(G-20360)*
Nacco Industries Inc E 440 229-5151
Cleveland *(G-5719)*
Royalton Food Service Eqp Co E 440 237-0806
North Royalton *(G-15299)*

3632 Household Refrigerators & Freezers

Cold Storage Services LLC G 740 837-0858
London *(G-12054)*
Dover Corporation F 513 870-3206
West Chester *(G-19694)*
◆ **Norcold Inc** B 937 497-3080
Sidney *(G-17057)*
Norcold Inc C 937 447-2241
Gettysburg *(G-10247)*
Whirlpool Corporation B 419 547-7711
Clyde *(G-6397)*
Whirlpool Corporation D 419 423-8123
Findlay *(G-9776)*
Whirlpool Corporation C 614 409-4340
Lockbourne *(G-12000)*
Whirlpool Corporation C 419 523-5100
Ottawa *(G-15672)*
Whirlpool Corporation C 740 383-7122
Marion *(G-12748)*

3633 Household Laundry Eqpt

Carly Co LLC G 937 477-6411
Centerville *(G-3000)*
CSC Serviceworks Holdings G 800 362-3182
Macedonia *(G-12286)*
Junebugs Wash N Dry G 513 988-5863
Trenton *(G-18621)*
▲ **Staber Industries Inc** E 614 836-5995
Groveport *(G-10513)*
Whirlpool Corporation C 740 383-7122
Marion *(G-12748)*
Whirlpool Corporation C 937 547-0773
Greenville *(G-10401)*
Whirlpool Corporation C 419 523-5100
Ottawa *(G-15672)*
Whirlpool Corporation C 614 409-4340
Lockbourne *(G-12000)*
Whirlpool Corporation B 419 547-7711
Clyde *(G-6397)*

3634 Electric Household Appliances

Acorn Technology Corporation E 216 663-1244
Cleveland *(G-4610)*
Aitken Products Inc G 440 466-5711
Geneva *(G-10213)*
Anson Co G 216 524-8838
Bedford *(G-1383)*
Broan-Nutone LLC G 888 336-3948
Blue Ash *(G-1741)*
Ces Nationwide G 937 322-0771
Springfield *(G-17373)*
▲ **Cleveland Range LLC** C 216 481-4900
Cleveland *(G-4972)*
Didonato Products Inc G 330 535-1119
Akron *(G-142)*
Driven Innovations LLC G 330 818-7681
Englewood *(G-9356)*
▲ **Dyoung Enterprise Inc** D 440 918-0505
Willoughby *(G-20312)*
Glo-Quartz Electric Heater Co E 440 255-9701
Mentor *(G-13459)*
◆ **Hmi Industries Inc** E 440 846-7800
Brooklyn *(G-2113)*
Johnson Bros Rubber Co Inc E 419 752-4814
Greenwich *(G-10404)*
▲ **Kitchen Collection LLC** D 740 773-9150
Chillicothe *(G-3198)*
Klawhorn Industries Inc G 330 335-8191
Wadsworth *(G-19249)*
Nacco Industries Inc E 740 773-9150
Chillicothe *(G-3201)*
Nacco Industries Inc E 440 229-5151
Cleveland *(G-5719)*
▲ **Qualtek Electronics Corp** C 440 951-3300
Mentor *(G-13567)*
▲ **Skuttle Mfg Co** F 740 373-9169
Marietta *(G-12670)*
Whirlpool Corporation B 937 548-4126
Greenville *(G-10400)*

3635 Household Vacuum Cleaners

▲ **GMI Holdings Inc** B 330 821-5360
Mount Hope *(G-14437)*

H-P Products Inc ....E 330 875-7193
Louisville *(G-12155)*
Powerclean Equipment Company ....F 513 202-0001
Cleves *(G-6374)*
Rent A Mom Inc ....F 216 901-9599
Seven Hills *(G-16905)*
Scott Fetzer Company ....B 216 228-2403
Cleveland *(G-6036)*
Scott Fetzer Company ....E 216 252-1190
Cleveland *(G-6037)*
Scott Fetzer Company ....B 440 871-2160
Cleveland *(G-6038)*
Scott Fetzer Company ....C 440 439-1616
Harrison *(G-10669)*
Scott Fetzer Company ....D 216 281-1100
Cleveland *(G-6039)*
Scott Fetzer Company ....D 216 433-7797
Cleveland *(G-6040)*
Scott Fetzer Company ....C 440 871-2160
Avon Lake *(G-1007)*
Scott Fetzer Company ....E 216 228-2400
Chagrin Falls *(G-3075)*
▲ **Stanley Steemer Intl Inc** ....C 614 764-2007
Dublin *(G-8994)*
Western/Scott Fetzer Company ....C 440 871-2160
Westlake *(G-20170)*
◆ **Western/Scott Fetzer Company** ....E 440 892-3000
Westlake *(G-20171)*

3639 Household Appliances, NEC

ABC Appliance Inc ....E 419 693-4414
Oregon *(G-15552)*
▲ **Anaheim Manufacturing Company** ...E 800 767-6293
North Olmsted *(G-15181)*
JC and Associates Sylvania LLC ....G 419 824-0011
Sylvania *(G-17947)*
▲ **New Path International LLC** ....E 614 410-3974
Powell *(G-16331)*
▲ **RAD Technologies Incorporated** ....F 513 641-0523
Cincinnati *(G-4246)*
U S Thermal Inc ....G 513 777-7763
West Chester *(G-19814)*
Whirlpool Corporation ....D 419 423-8123
Findlay *(G-9776)*
Whirlpool Corporation ....B 419 547-7711
Clyde *(G-6397)*
Whirlpool Corporation ....C 419 523-5100
Ottawa *(G-15672)*

3641 Electric Lamps

Acuity Brands Lighting Inc ....C 740 349-4409
Newark *(G-14849)*
▲ **Advanced Lighting Tech LLC** ....E 888 440-2358
Solon *(G-17099)*
▲ **Alert Stamping & Mfg Co Inc** ....E 440 232-5020
Bedford Heights *(G-1458)*
Carlisle and Finch Company ....E 513 681-6080
Cincinnati *(G-3445)*
◆ **Clare Sky Inc** ....B 866 558-5706
Cleveland *(G-4936)*
Emitted Energy Inc ....G 513 752-9999
Cincinnati *(G-3249)*
Energy Focus Inc ....C 440 715-1300
Solon *(G-17137)*
▲ **Eye Lighting Intl N Amer Inc** ....C 440 350-7000
Mentor *(G-13442)*
General Electric Company ....C 440 593-1156
Mc Donald *(G-13197)*
General Electric Company ....B 419 563-1200
Bucyrus *(G-2331)*
General Electric Company ....C 330 793-3911
Youngstown *(G-20916)*
General Electric Company ....A 330 297-0861
Mc Donald *(G-13198)*
General Electric Company ....A 330 373-1400
Mc Donald *(G-13199)*
General Electric Company ....B 216 391-8741
Cleveland *(G-5309)*
Johnsons Lamp Shop & Antq Co ....G 937 568-4551
South Vienna *(G-17297)*
Lumitex Inc ....G 949 250-8557
Strongsville *(G-17764)*
▲ **Lumitex Inc** ....D 440 243-8401
Strongsville *(G-17763)*
Magenta Incorporated ....E 216 571-4094
Cleveland *(G-5603)*
◆ **Medallion Lighting Corporation** ....E 440 255-8383
Mentor *(G-13514)*
Resource Exchange Company Inc ....G 440 773-8915
Akron *(G-347)*

3643 Current-Carrying Wiring Devices

Accurate Electronics Inc ....C 330 682-7015
Orrville *(G-15581)*
Alcon Inc ....E 513 722-1037
Loveland *(G-12175)*
Alert Safety Lite Products Co ....F 440 232-5020
Cleveland *(G-4658)*
Amidac Wind Corporation ....G 213 973-4000
Elyria *(G-9216)*
Aviation Technologies Inc ....G 216 706-2960
Cleveland *(G-4776)*
▲ **Bardes Corporation** ....B 513 533-6200
Cincinnati *(G-3379)*
Brooks Utility Products Group ....F 330 455-0301
Canton *(G-2599)*
▲ **Brumall Mfg Coroporation** ....E 440 974-2622
Mentor *(G-13406)*
▲ **Bud Industries Inc** ....G 440 946-3200
Willoughby *(G-20289)*
Burkett Industries Inc ....G 419 332-4391
Fremont *(G-10002)*
Cambridge Ohio Production & As ....F 740 432-6383
Cambridge *(G-2429)*
◆ **Chalfant Manufacturing Company** ....G 330 273-3510
Brunswick *(G-2195)*
Chalfant Manufacturing Company ....F 440 323-9870
Elyria *(G-9236)*
▲ **Channel Products Inc** ....D 440 423-0113
Solon *(G-17126)*
▲ **Connector Manufacturing Co** ....C 513 860-4455
Hamilton *(G-10548)*
Connectronics Corp ....D 419 537-0020
Toledo *(G-18239)*
Cooper Interconnect Inc ....G 800 386-1911
Cleveland *(G-5028)*
▲ **Crown Electric Engrg & Mfg LLC** ....E 513 539-7394
Middletown *(G-13898)*
D & E Electric Inc ....F 513 738-1172
Okeana *(G-15518)*
Desco Corporation ....G 614 888-8855
New Albany *(G-14622)*
▲ **Dreison International Inc** ....C 216 362-0755
Cleveland *(G-5113)*
▲ **Electric Cord Sets Inc** ....G 216 261-1000
Cleveland *(G-5161)*
Empire Power Systems Co ....G 440 796-4401
Madison *(G-12349)*
◆ **Ericson Manufacturing Co** ....D 440 951-8000
Willoughby *(G-20315)*
Erie Copper Works Inc ....G 330 725-5590
Medina *(G-13257)*
Filnor Inc ....F 330 821-7667
Alliance *(G-467)*
GE Aviation Systems LLC ....B 937 898-5881
Vandalia *(G-19125)*
▲ **General Plug and Mfg Co** ....C 440 926-2411
Grafton *(G-10301)*
Hermetic Seal Technology Inc ....F 513 851-4899
Cincinnati *(G-3810)*
Hubbell Incorporated ....E 330 335-2361
Wadsworth *(G-19245)*
▲ **I Sq R Power Cable Co** ....F 330 588-3000
Canton *(G-2704)*
▲ **International Hydraulics Inc** ....E 440 951-7186
Mentor *(G-13474)*
J & S Products Inc ....G 330 686-5840
Stow *(G-17597)*
Kathom Manufacturing Co Inc ....E 513 868-8890
Hamilton *(G-10579)*
▲ **Knappco Corporation** ....C 816 741-0786
West Chester *(G-19731)*
◆ **Lake Shore Electric Corp** ....E 440 232-0200
Bedford *(G-1422)*
Legrand AV Inc ....E 574 267-8101
Blue Ash *(G-1805)*
Legrand North America LLC ....B 937 224-0639
Dayton *(G-8309)*
Mdfritz Technologies Inc ....G 937 314-1234
Centerville *(G-3004)*
▲ **MJM Industries Inc** ....D 440 350-1230
Fairport Harbor *(G-9626)*
▲ **Mueller Electric Company Inc** ....E 216 771-5225
Akron *(G-290)*
Newact Inc ....F 513 321-5177
Batavia *(G-1173)*
Ohio Associated Entps LLC ....C 440 354-3148
Painesville *(G-15769)*
Ohio Vly Lightning Protection ....G 937 987-0245
New Vienna *(G-14825)*

Omnithruster Inc ....F 330 963-6310
Twinsburg *(G-18825)*
P C Power Inc ....G 440 779-4080
North Olmsted *(G-15195)*
Parker-Hannifin Corporation ....C 330 336-3511
Wadsworth *(G-19260)*
Pave Technology Co ....E 937 890-1100
Dayton *(G-8417)*
▲ **Power Grounding Solutions LLC** ....G 440 926-3219
Grafton *(G-10309)*
▲ **Qualtek Electronics Corp** ....C 440 951-3300
Mentor *(G-13567)*
▲ **Rogers Industrial Products Inc** ....E 330 535-3331
Akron *(G-353)*
▲ **Royal Plastics Inc** ....C 440 352-1357
Mentor *(G-13575)*
Ruegg Mfg LLC ....G 330 418-5617
Navarre *(G-14587)*
▲ **Saia-Burgess Lcc** ....D 937 898-3621
Vandalia *(G-19144)*
Schneider Electric Usa Inc ....B 513 523-4171
Oxford *(G-15700)*
Schneider Electric Usa Inc ....D 513 755-5000
West Chester *(G-19792)*
Siemens Industry Inc ....D 937 593-6010
Bellefontaine *(G-1525)*
Simpson Strong-Tie Company Inc ....C 614 876-8060
Columbus *(G-7454)*
SMH Manufacturing Inc ....F 419 884-0071
Lexington *(G-11806)*
▲ **Solon Manufacturing Company** ....E 440 286-7149
Chardon *(G-3137)*
T & S Enterprises ....E 419 424-1122
Findlay *(G-9766)*
▲ **Tecmark Corporation** ....D 440 205-7600
Mentor *(G-13601)*
Tip Products Inc ....E 216 252-2535
Cleveland *(G-6176)*
▲ **Torq Corporation** ....E 440 232-4100
Bedford *(G-1451)*
Turner Lightning Protection Co ....G 614 738-6225
Dublin *(G-9007)*
Vital Connections Incorporated ....E 937 667-3880
Tipp City *(G-18143)*
▲ **Vulcan Tool Company** ....G 937 253-6194
Dayton *(G-8581)*
◆ **Watteredge LLC** ....D 440 933-6110
Avon Lake *(G-1013)*
Weastec Incorporated ....C 937 393-6800
Hillsboro *(G-10893)*
▲ **Wedge Products Inc** ....B 330 405-4477
Twinsburg *(G-18873)*
Wiremax Ltd ....G 419 531-9500
Toledo *(G-18601)*
Xponet Inc ....E 440 354-6617
Painesville *(G-15801)*

3644 Noncurrent-Carrying Wiring Devices

Akron Foundry Co ....E 330 745-3101
Barberton *(G-1050)*
Allied Tube & Conduit Corp ....F 740 928-1018
Hebron *(G-10737)*
▲ **Arnco Corporation** ....C 800 847-7661
Elyria *(G-9219)*
Barracuda Technologies Inc ....F 216 469-1566
Aurora *(G-872)*
Buckeye Raceway LLC ....G 614 272-7888
Columbus *(G-6711)*
▲ **Bud Industries Inc** ....G 440 946-3200
Willoughby *(G-20289)*
Cornerstone Indus Holdings ....G 440 893-9144
Chagrin Falls *(G-3014)*
▲ **Eaton Electric Holdings LLC** ....B 440 523-5000
Cleveland *(G-5151)*
Eger Products Inc ....D 513 753-4200
Amelia *(G-539)*
▲ **Emco Electric International** ....G 440 878-1199
Strongsville *(G-17742)*
◆ **Erico Inc** ....E 440 248-0100
Solon *(G-17138)*
Glt Fabricators Inc ....G 713 670-9700
Solon *(G-17151)*
▼ **Helical Line Products Co** ....E 440 933-9263
Avon Lake *(G-989)*
Highline Raceway LLC ....G 419 883-2042
Butler *(G-2375)*
◆ **Madison Electric Products Inc** ....E 216 391-7776
Bedford Heights *(G-1473)*
Merrico Inc ....G 419 525-2711
Mansfield *(G-12479)*

S I C

36 ELECTRONIC AND OTHER ELECTRICAL EQUIPMENT AND COMPONENTS, EXCEPT COMPUTER SIC SECTION

▲ Monti Incorporated ....C 513 761-7775
Cincinnati *(G-4043)*
▲ Mueller Electric Company Inc ....E 216 771-5225
Akron *(G-290)*
▲ Osborne Coinage Company ....D 513 681-5424
Cincinnati *(G-4120)*
Power Shelf LLC ....G 419 775-6125
Plymouth *(G-16233)*
Preformed Line Products Co ....B 440 461-5200
Mayfield Village *(G-13174)*
Raceway Beverage LLC ....G 513 932-2214
Lebanon *(G-11688)*
Raceway Petroleum Inc ....G 440 989-2660
Lorain *(G-12115)*
▲ Red Seal Electric Co ....E 216 941-3900
Cleveland *(G-5967)*
Regal Beloit America Inc ....C 419 352-8441
Bowling Green *(G-1996)*
Resource Mechanical Insul LLC ....E 248 577-0200
Walbridge *(G-19298)*
◆ Rochling Glastic Composites LP ....C 216 486-0100
Cleveland *(G-5996)*
Saylor Products Corporation ....F 419 832-2125
Grand Rapids *(G-10320)*
State of Ohio Dayton Raceway ....G 937 237-7802
Dayton *(G-8526)*
Treadstone Company ....G 216 410-3435
Twinsburg *(G-18865)*
Tri-Fab Inc ....E 330 337-3425
Salem *(G-16777)*
United Fiberglass America Inc ....F 937 325-7305
Springfield *(G-17512)*
◆ Vertiv Energy Systems Inc ....A 440 288-1122
Lorain *(G-12134)*
Vertiv Group Corporation ....G 440 288-1122
Lorain *(G-12135)*
Von Roll Usa Inc ....E 216 433-7474
Cleveland *(G-6271)*
Weidmann Electrical Tech Inc ....D 937 652-1220
Urbana *(G-19019)*
Zekelman Industries Inc ....C 740 432-2146
Cambridge *(G-2463)*

3645 Residential Lighting Fixtures

Acuity Brands Lighting Inc ....C 740 349-4409
Newark *(G-14849)*
Acuity Brands Lighting Inc ....B 740 349-4343
Newark *(G-14848)*
▲ Advanced Lighting Tech LLC ....E 888 440-2358
Solon *(G-17099)*
▲ Alert Stamping & Mfg Co Inc ....E 440 232-5020
Bedford Heights *(G-1458)*
American Superior Lighting ....G 740 266-2959
Steubenville *(G-17526)*
▲ Besa Lighting Co Inc ....E 614 475-7046
Blacklick *(G-1679)*
◆ Clare Sky Inc ....B 866 558-5706
Cleveland *(G-4936)*
Contract Lighting Inc ....G 614 746-7022
Columbus *(G-6813)*
Country Tin ....G 937 746-7229
Franklin *(G-9877)*
Degaetano Sales ....G 440 729-8877
Chesterland *(G-3156)*
E L Ostendorf Inc ....G 440 247-7631
Chagrin Falls *(G-3016)*
J Schrader Co ....F 216 961-2890
Cleveland *(G-5488)*
JB Machining Concepts LLC ....G 419 523-0096
Ottawa *(G-15655)*
▲ Led Lighting Center Inc ....F 714 271-2633
Toledo *(G-18376)*
Led Lighting Center LLC ....F 888 988-6533
Toledo *(G-18377)*
Lighting Concepts & Control ....G 513 761-6360
West Chester *(G-19737)*
LSI Industries Inc ....E 513 793-3200
Blue Ash *(G-1808)*
Manairco Inc ....G 419 524-2121
Mansfield *(G-12474)*
◆ Medallion Lighting Corporation ....E 440 255-8383
Mentor *(G-13514)*
Mega Bright LLC ....F 330 577-8859
Cuyahoga Falls *(G-7898)*
▲ Microsun Lamps LLC ....G 888 328-8701
Dayton *(G-8351)*
Morel Landscaping LLC ....F 216 551-4395
Richfield *(G-16476)*
Night Lightscapes ....G 419 304-2486
Sylvania *(G-17956)*

Palette Studios Inc ....G 513 961-1316
Cincinnati *(G-4131)*
Pike Machine Products Co ....E 216 731-1880
Euclid *(G-9433)*
Rexel Inc ....G 330 468-1122
Northfield *(G-15323)*
Shannon Ward ....G 330 592-8177
Stow *(G-17627)*
▲ Tresco International Ltd Co ....G 330 757-8131
Youngstown *(G-21051)*

3646 Commercial, Indl & Institutional Lighting Fixtures

Acuity Brands Lighting Inc ....B 740 349-4343
Newark *(G-14848)*
Acuity Brands Lighting Inc ....C 740 349-4409
Newark *(G-14849)*
▲ Advanced Lighting Tech LLC ....E 888 440-2358
Solon *(G-17099)*
▲ Besa Lighting Co Inc ....E 614 475-7046
Blacklick *(G-1679)*
▲ Best Lighting Products Inc ....D 740 964-0063
Etna *(G-9392)*
▲ Bock Company LLC ....G 216 912-7050
Twinsburg *(G-18742)*
▲ Eaton Electric Holdings LLC ....B 440 523-5000
Cleveland *(G-5151)*
Etherium Lighting LLC ....G 310 800-8837
Columbus *(G-6907)*
Evp International LLC ....G 513 761-7614
Cincinnati *(G-3662)*
General Electric Company ....A 216 266-2121
Cleveland *(G-5307)*
General Electric Company ....E 330 458-3200
Canton *(G-2681)*
▲ Genesis Lamp Corp ....F 440 354-0095
Painesville *(G-15741)*
Holophane Corporation ....F 740 349-4194
Newark *(G-14883)*
◆ Holophane Corporation ....C 866 759-1577
Granville *(G-10331)*
Holophane Lighting ....G 330 823-5535
Alliance *(G-475)*
Importers Direct LLC ....E 330 436-3260
Akron *(G-214)*
J Schrader Co ....F 216 961-2890
Cleveland *(G-5488)*
JB Machining Concepts LLC ....G 419 523-0096
Ottawa *(G-15655)*
▲ King Luminaire Company Inc ....E 440 576-9073
Jefferson *(G-11233)*
▲ Led Lighting Center Inc ....F 714 271-2633
Toledo *(G-18376)*
Led Lighting Center LLC ....F 888 988-6533
Toledo *(G-18377)*
Less Cost Lighting Inc ....F 866 633-6883
Etna *(G-9396)*
▲ Light Craft Manufacturing Inc ....F 419 332-0536
Fremont *(G-10034)*
LSI Industries Inc ....C 913 281-1100
Blue Ash *(G-1810)*
LSI Industries Inc ....E 513 793-3200
Blue Ash *(G-1808)*
▲ Lumitex Inc ....D 440 243-8401
Strongsville *(G-17763)*
M-Boss Inc ....E 216 441-6080
Cleveland *(G-5594)*
Magnum Asset Acquisition LLC ....E 330 915-2382
Hudson *(G-11062)*
Mega Bright LLC ....G 216 712-4689
Cleveland *(G-5653)*
Mega Bright LLC ....F 330 577-8859
Cuyahoga Falls *(G-7898)*
Mills Led LLC ....G 800 690-6403
Columbus *(G-7183)*
Mills Led LLC ....G 800 690-6403
Springfield *(G-17448)*
◆ Nordic Light America Inc ....F 614 981-9497
Columbus *(G-7223)*
Norton Industries Inc ....E 888 357-2345
Lakewood *(G-11532)*
Patriot Consulting LLC ....G 614 554-6455
Columbus *(G-7297)*
Pearlwind LLC ....G 216 591-9463
Beachwood *(G-1264)*
Power Source Service LLC ....G 513 607-4555
Batavia *(G-1177)*
Premiere Building Mtls Inc ....G 574 293-5800
Plain City *(G-16207)*

SMS Technologies Inc ....F 419 465-4175
Monroeville *(G-14291)*
Stress-Crete Company ....F 440 576-9073
Jefferson *(G-11239)*
▲ Techbrite LLC ....E 800 246-9977
Cincinnati *(G-4410)*
▲ Teron Lighting Inc ....E 513 858-6004
Fairfield *(G-9568)*
Treemen Industries Inc ....E 330 965-3777
Boardman *(G-1904)*

3647 Vehicular Lighting Eqpt

▲ Advanced Technology Corp ....C 440 293-4064
Andover *(G-577)*
Akron Brass Company ....E 614 529-7230
Columbus *(G-6557)*
Akron Brass Company ....B 330 264-5678
Wooster *(G-20557)*
▲ Akron Brass Company ....B 330 264-5678
Wooster *(G-20558)*
Akron Brass Holding Corp ....G 330 264-5678
Wooster *(G-20559)*
▲ Atc Group Inc ....D 440 293-4064
Andover *(G-579)*
▲ Atc Lighting & Plastics Inc ....C 440 466-7670
Andover *(G-580)*
Federal-Mogul Powertrain LLC ....C 740 432-2393
Cambridge *(G-2437)*
Flasher Light Barricade ....G 513 554-1111
Fairfield *(G-9497)*
Grimes Aerospace Company ....B 937 484-2001
Urbana *(G-18990)*
Intellitronix Corporation ....E 440 359-7200
Eastlake *(G-9115)*
▲ K D Lamp Company ....E 440 293-4064
Andover *(G-583)*
Lighting Products Inc ....D 440 293-4064
Andover *(G-584)*
▲ Stanley Electric US Co Inc ....B 740 852-5200
London *(G-12069)*
Treemen Industries Inc ....E 330 965-3777
Boardman *(G-1904)*
Washington Products Inc ....F 330 837-5101
Massillon *(G-13057)*

3648 Lighting Eqpt, NEC

Acuity Brands Lighting Inc ....B 740 349-4343
Newark *(G-14848)*
◆ ADB Safegate Americas LLC ....B 614 861-1304
Columbus *(G-6542)*
▲ Advanced Lighting Tech LLC ....E 888 440-2358
Solon *(G-17099)*
Akron Brass Company ....E 614 529-7230
Columbus *(G-6557)*
▲ Atc Lighting & Plastics Inc ....C 440 466-7670
Andover *(G-580)*
ATI Irrigation LLC ....G 937 750-2976
Troy *(G-18639)*
Aviation Technologies Inc ....G 216 706-2960
Cleveland *(G-4776)*
Brightguy Inc ....G 440 942-8318
Willoughby *(G-20287)*
Broadview Heights Spotlights ....G 440 526-4404
Broadview Heights *(G-2089)*
Carlisle and Finch Company ....E 513 681-6080
Cincinnati *(G-3445)*
Chromacove LLC ....G 216 264-1104
Cleveland *(G-4925)*
◆ Clare Sky Inc ....B 866 558-5706
Cleveland *(G-4936)*
◆ Current Lighting Solutions LLC ....E 800 435-4448
Cleveland *(G-5043)*
Energy Focus Inc ....C 440 715-1300
Solon *(G-17137)*
◆ Ericson Manufacturing Co ....D 440 951-8000
Willoughby *(G-20315)*
Fidelux Lighting LLC ....G 614 839-0250
Columbus *(G-6919)*
Fulton Industries Inc ....D 419 335-3015
Wauseon *(G-19516)*
General Electric Company ....A 330 373-1400
Mc Donald *(G-13199)*
▲ Genesis Lamp Corp ....F 440 354-0095
Painesville *(G-15741)*
Global E-Lumenation Tech ....G 513 821-8687
Cincinnati *(G-3763)*
▲ Global Lighting Tech Inc ....E 440 922-4584
Brecksville *(G-2039)*
◆ Holophane Corporation ....C 866 759-1577
Granville *(G-10331)*

SIC SECTION 36 ELECTRONIC AND OTHER ELECTRICAL EQUIPMENT AND COMPONENTS, EXCEPT COMPUTER

Hot Spot ... G ... 740 947-8888 Waverly *(G-19548)*
Hughey & Phillips LLC ... E ... 937 652-3500 Urbana *(G-18996)*
Iacono Production Services Inc ... F ... 513 469-5095 Blue Ash *(G-1790)*
Importers Direct LLC ... E ... 330 436-3260 Akron *(G-214)*
Jeff Katz ... G ... 614 834-0404 Pickerington *(G-16051)*
Led Lighting Center LLC ... G ... 888 988-6533 Toledo *(G-18378)*
▲ Lighting Solutions Group LLC ... F ... 614 868-5337 Columbus *(G-7127)*
◆ Lintern Corporation ... E ... 440 255-9333 Mentor *(G-13501)*
LSI Industries Inc ... G ... 513 372-3200 Blue Ash *(G-1809)*
LSI Industries Inc ... B ... 513 793-3200 Blue Ash *(G-1811)*
LSI Industries Inc ... E ... 513 793-3200 Blue Ash *(G-1808)*
▲ Lumitex Inc ... D ... 440 243-8401 Strongsville *(G-17763)*
Manairco Inc ... G ... 419 524-2121 Mansfield *(G-12474)*
Miami Valley Lighting LLC ... G ... 937 224-6000 Dayton *(G-7985)*
◆ Midmark Corporation ... A ... 937 526-3662 Kettering *(G-11434)*
Midmark Corporation ... G ... 937 526-8387 Versailles *(G-19187)*
Moonlighting ... G ... 330 533-3324 Canfield *(G-2538)*
▲ National Biological Corp ... E ... 216 831-0600 Beachwood *(G-1252)*
Photon Labs LLC ... G ... 214 455-0727 Westerville *(G-20017)*
◆ Powertech Inc ... F ... 901 850-9393 Beachwood *(G-1266)*
Pro Lighting LLC ... G ... 614 561-0089 Hilliard *(G-10855)*
Shelly Company ... G ... 330 666-1125 Copley *(G-7695)*
Specialty Systems Electric LLC ... G ... 304 529-3861 Proctorville *(G-16345)*
▼ Sunless Inc ... C ... 440 836-0199 Macedonia *(G-12334)*
◆ Vanner Holdings Inc ... D ... 614 771-2718 Hilliard *(G-10873)*
▲ Will-Burt Company ... B ... 330 682-7015 Orrville *(G-15626)*

3651 Household Audio & Video Eqpt

Advanced Custom Sound ... G ... 330 372-9900 Warren *(G-19363)*
Andersound PA Service ... G ... 216 561-2636 Cleveland *(G-4713)*
▲ Avtek International Inc ... G ... 330 633-7500 Tallmadge *(G-17973)*
Beacon Audio Video Systems Inc ... G ... 937 723-9587 Centerville *(G-2999)*
Bose Corporation ... G ... 614 475-8565 Columbus *(G-6688)*
C T I Audio Inc ... D ... 440 593-1111 Brooklyn Heights *(G-2117)*
▲ Cad Audio LLC ... F ... 440 349-4900 Solon *(G-17121)*
China Enterprises Inc ... G ... 419 885-1485 Toledo *(G-18230)*
Custom Automation Technologies ... G ... 614 939-4228 New Albany *(G-14618)*
▲ Daca Vending Wholesale LLC ... G ... 513 753-1600 Amelia *(G-535)*
Dare Electronics Inc ... E ... 937 335-0031 Troy *(G-18645)*
Digital Media Integration LLC ... G ... 937 305-5582 Dayton *(G-8160)*
Dlng Products ... G ... 440 442-7777 Cleveland *(G-5096)*
Dr Z Amps Inc ... F ... 216 475-1444 Maple Heights *(G-12571)*
E3 Diagnostics Inc ... G ... 937 435-2250 Dayton *(G-8174)*
Electrimotion Inc ... G ... 740 362-0251 Delaware *(G-8675)*
Eprad Inc ... G ... 419 666-3266 Perrysburg *(G-15948)*
Eq Technologies LLC ... G ... 216 548-3684 Cleveland *(G-5185)*

Gadgets Manufacturing Co ... G ... 937 686-5371 Huntsville *(G-11087)*
Greyfield Industries Inc ... F ... 513 860-1785 Trenton *(G-18620)*
House of Hindenach ... G ... 419 422-0392 Findlay *(G-9707)*
Hudson Access Group II ... G ... 330 283-6214 Hudson *(G-11052)*
Janszen Loudspeaker Ltd ... G ... 614 448-1811 Columbus *(G-7063)*
▲ Knukonceptzcom Ltd ... G ... 216 310-6555 Windham *(G-20525)*
Markeys Audio/Visual Inc ... G ... 419 244-8844 Toledo *(G-18399)*
◆ Mitsubishi Elc Auto Amer Inc ... B ... 513 573-6614 Mason *(G-12911)*
Musicmax Inc ... F ... 614 732-0777 Columbus *(G-7202)*
◆ Phantom Sound ... F ... 513 759-4477 Mason *(G-12920)*
▲ Pioneer Automotive Tech Inc ... C ... 937 746-2293 Springboro *(G-17344)*
Pro Audio ... G ... 513 752-7500 Cincinnati *(G-3261)*
Q Music USA LLC ... G ... 239 995-5888 North Olmsted *(G-15196)*
R L Drake Company ... D ... 937 746-4556 Franklin *(G-9914)*
Rs Pro Sales LLC ... G ... 513 699-5329 Cincinnati *(G-4286)*
◆ Snyder Electronics ... G ... 513 738-7200 Harrison *(G-10671)*
Sound Concepts LLC ... G ... 513 703-0147 Mason *(G-12940)*
Soundproof ... G ... 440 864-8864 Grafton *(G-10310)*
South Side Audio LLC ... G ... 614 453-0757 Columbus *(G-7464)*
Tech Products Corporation ... E ... 937 438-1100 Miamisburg *(G-13723)*
Technical Artistry Inc ... G ... 614 299-7777 Columbus *(G-7520)*
Technicolor Usa Inc ... A ... 614 474-8821 Circleville *(G-4561)*
▲ Tls Corp ... E ... 216 574-4759 Cleveland *(G-6177)*
Tune Town Car Audio ... G ... 419 627-1100 Sandusky *(G-16857)*
Undiscovered Radio Network ... G ... 740 533-1032 Ironton *(G-11174)*
Universal Electronics Inc ... D ... 330 487-1110 Twinsburg *(G-18869)*

3652 Phonograph Records & Magnetic Tape

Belkin Production ... E ... 440 247-2722 Chagrin Falls *(G-3009)*
Beverly Snider ... G ... 614 837-5817 Columbus *(G-6665)*
Jk Digital Publishing LLC ... E ... 937 299-0185 Springboro *(G-17331)*
▼ Magstor Inc ... G ... 614 433-0011 Columbus *(G-7146)*
Musicol Inc ... G ... 614 267-3133 Columbus *(G-7203)*
News Reel Inc ... G ... 614 469-0700 Columbus *(G-7218)*
Q C A Inc ... F ... 513 681-8400 Cincinnati *(G-4223)*

3661 Telephone & Telegraph Apparatus

7signal Solutions Inc ... E ... 216 777-2900 Independence *(G-11116)*
▲ Arnco Corporation ... C ... 800 847-7661 Elyria *(G-9219)*
AT&T Corp ... G ... 513 792-9300 Cincinnati *(G-3365)*
Black Box Corporation ... F ... 614 825-7400 Lewis Center *(G-11751)*
C Dcap Modem Line ... G ... 419 748-7409 Mc Clure *(G-13185)*
C Dcap Modem Line ... G ... 440 685-4302 North Bloomfield *(G-15063)*
Commercial Electric Pdts Corp ... E ... 216 241-2886 Cleveland *(G-5002)*
Commtech Solutions Inc ... G ... 440 458-4870 Grafton *(G-10294)*
Cotsworks LLC ... E ... 440 446-8800 Highland Heights *(G-10787)*
Crase Communications Inc ... F ... 419 468-1173 Galion *(G-10131)*

Cutting Edge Technologies Inc ... E ... 216 574-4759 Cleveland *(G-5051)*
DTE Inc ... E ... 419 522-3428 Mansfield *(G-12434)*
Electrodata Inc ... F ... 216 663-3333 Bedford Heights *(G-1469)*
Greyfield Industries Inc ... F ... 513 860-1785 Trenton *(G-18620)*
Headset Wholesalers Ltd ... G ... 419 798-5200 Lakeside Marblehead *(G-11503)*
▲ Kentrox Inc ... D ... 614 798-2000 Dublin *(G-8938)*
Lisa Modem ... G ... 216 551-3365 Cleveland *(G-5581)*
Minor Corporation ... G ... 216 291-8723 Cleveland *(G-5695)*
Mitel (delaware) Inc ... E ... 513 733-8000 West Chester *(G-19745)*
Ocs Telecom LLC ... F ... 740 503-5939 Hilliard *(G-10844)*
Peco II Inc ... D ... 614 431-0694 Columbus *(G-7305)*
Pharmazell Inc ... G ... 440 526-6417 Brecksville *(G-2053)*
Preformed Line Products Co ... B ... 440 461-5200 Mayfield Village *(G-13174)*
Prentke Romich Company ... C ... 330 262-1984 Wooster *(G-20641)*
Pro Oncall Technologies LLC ... F ... 614 761-1400 Dublin *(G-8967)*
Procomsol Ltd ... G ... 216 221-1550 Lakewood *(G-11533)*
Siemens Energy Inc ... G ... 740 393-8464 Mount Vernon *(G-14511)*
▲ Tls Corp ... E ... 216 574-4759 Cleveland *(G-6177)*
◆ Vertiv Energy Systems Inc ... A ... 440 288-1122 Lorain *(G-12134)*
Vertiv Group Corporation ... G ... 440 288-1122 Lorain *(G-12135)*
Vertiv Group Corporation ... F ... 440 460-3600 Cleveland *(G-6253)*
Viasat Inc ... D ... 216 706-7800 Independence *(G-11155)*

3663 Radio & T V Communications, Systs & Eqpt, Broadcast/Studio

Accurate Electronics Inc ... C ... 330 682-7015 Orrville *(G-15581)*
Advanced Telemetrics Intl ... F ... 937 862-6948 Spring Valley *(G-17315)*
AG Antenna Group LLC ... F ... 513 289-6521 Cincinnati *(G-3309)*
◆ Analynk Wireless LLC ... G ... 614 755-5091 Columbus *(G-6599)*
Armada Power LLC ... G ... 614 204-9341 Columbus *(G-6615)*
CDI Industries Inc ... E ... 440 243-1100 Cleveland *(G-4895)*
Central USA Wireless LLC ... E ... 513 469-1500 Cincinnati *(G-3459)*
Circle Prime Manufacturing ... E ... 330 923-0019 Cuyahoga Falls *(G-7850)*
Commscope Technologies LLC ... C ... 216 272-0055 Cleveland *(G-5006)*
Comrod Inc ... G ... 440 455-9186 Westlake *(G-20107)*
Control Industries Inc ... G ... 937 653-7694 Findlay *(G-9671)*
Diamond Electronics Inc ... C ... 740 652-9222 Lancaster *(G-11564)*
Eei Acquisition Corp ... E ... 440 564-5484 Middlefield *(G-13797)*
Electro-Magwave Inc ... G ... 216 453-1160 Cleveland *(G-5164)*
Envision Radio MII ... F ... 216 831-3761 Beachwood *(G-1236)*
Essential Pathways Ohio LLC ... G ... 330 518-3091 Youngstown *(G-20900)*
▲ Gatesair Inc ... D ... 513 459-3400 Mason *(G-12875)*
Globecom Technologies Inc ... G ... 330 408-7008 Canal Fulton *(G-2480)*
Grace Automation Services Inc ... G ... 330 567-3108 Big Prairie *(G-1674)*
Great Lakes Telcom Ltd ... E ... 330 629-8848 Youngstown *(G-20924)*
Greyfield Industries Inc ... F ... 513 860-1785 Trenton *(G-18620)*

S I C

36 ELECTRONIC AND OTHER ELECTRICAL EQUIPMENT AND COMPONENTS, EXCEPT COMPUTER

Hyq Technologies LLC .... G 513 225-6911
  Oxford (G-15694)
Imagine Communications Corp .... D 513 459-3400
  Mason (G-12890)
J Com Data Inc .... G 614 304-1455
  Pataskala (G-15833)
Jason Wilson .... E 937 604-8209
  Tipp City (G-18120)
L-3 Cmmncations Nova Engrg Inc ... C 877 282-1168
  Mason (G-12901)
Liquid Image Corp of America .... G 216 458-9800
  Cleveland (G-5580)
LSI Industries Inc .... B 513 793-3200
  Blue Ash (G-1811)
Manchik Engineering & Co .... G 740 927-4454
  Dublin (G-8945)
▲ Maranatha Industries Inc .... G 419 263-2013
  Payne (G-15873)
McClaflin Mobile Media LLC .... G 419 575-9367
  Bradner (G-2014)
Mentor Radio LLC .... G 216 265-2315
  Elyria (G-9293)
▲ Nissin Precision N Amer Inc .... D 937 836-1910
  Englewood (G-9372)
▲ Ohio Semitronics Inc .... G 614 777-1005
  Hilliard (G-10847)
Peterson Radio Inc .... G 937 549-3731
  Manchester (G-12396)
Pole/Zero Acquisition Inc .... C 513 870-9060
  West Chester (G-19762)
Prentke Romich Company .... G 330 262-1984
  Wooster (G-20641)
Quasonix Inc .... G 513 942-1287
  West Chester (G-19775)
R L Drake Company .... D 937 746-4556
  Franklin (G-9914)
▲ R L Drake Holdings LLC .... F 937 746-4556
  Springboro (G-17349)
Radio Hospital .... G 419 679-1103
  Kenton (G-11419)
Rev38 LLC .... E 937 572-4000
  West Chester (G-19781)
▲ Rf Linx Inc .... G 513 777-2774
  Lebanon (G-11690)
Shenet LLC .... E 614 563-9600
  Columbus (G-7445)
Solar Con Inc .... E 419 865-5877
  Holland (G-10958)
T V Specialties Inc .... F 330 364-6678
  Dover (G-8859)
▲ Tls Corp .... E 216 574-4759
  Cleveland (G-6177)
Track-It Systems .... G 513 522-0083
  Cincinnati (G-4428)
Transel Corporation .... G 513 897-3442
  Harveysburg (G-10706)
▲ Valco Melton Inc .... E 513 874-6550
  West Chester (G-19916)
Watts Antenna Company .... G 740 797-9380
  The Plains (G-18024)
Wireless Retail LLC .... G 614 657-5182
  Blacklick (G-1695)

3669 Communications Eqpt, NEC

A & A Safety Inc .... F 937 567-9781
  Beavercreek (G-1348)
Ademco Inc .... F 513 772-1851
  Blue Ash (G-1721)
Ademco Inc .... G 440 439-7002
  Bedford (G-1379)
Alert Safety Products Inc .... G 513 791-4790
  Blue Ash (G-1725)
Area Wide Protective Inc .... E 330 644-0655
  Kent (G-11296)
Area Wide Protective Inc .... G 419 221-2997
  Lima (G-11842)
Area Wide Protective Inc .... E 513 321-9889
  Fairfield (G-9483)
▲ Athens Technical Specialists .... F 740 592-2874
  Athens (G-824)
Bird Technologies Group Inc .... G 440 248-1200
  Solon (G-17116)
▲ Ceia Usa Ltd .... E 330 405-3190
  Twinsburg (G-18747)
Cincinnati Bell Any Dstnce Inc .... A 513 397-9900
  Cincinnati (G-3483)
City Elyria Communication .... G 440 322-3329
  Elyria (G-9237)
City of Canton .... E 330 489-3370
  Canton (G-2625)

David Boswell .... E 614 441-2497
  Columbus (G-6852)
Ds Express Carriers Inc .... E 419 433-6200
  Norwalk (G-15388)
Faircosa LLC .... G 216 577-9909
  Cleveland (G-5215)
▲ Findaway World LLC .... D 440 893-0808
  Solon (G-17143)
General Dynmics Mssion Systems .... E 513 253-4770
  Beavercreek (G-1317)
Honeywell International Inc .... A 937 484-2000
  Urbana (G-18995)
Honeywell International Inc .... D 937 754-4134
  Fairborn (G-9461)
Hyq Technologies LLC .... G 513 225-6911
  Oxford (G-15694)
Intelligent Signal Tech .... G 614 530-4784
  Loveland (G-12200)
Johnson Controls .... E 419 861-0662
  Maumee (G-13123)
K-Hill Signal Co Inc .... G 740 922-0421
  Uhrichsville (G-18890)
Lightle Enterprises Ohio LLC .... G 740 998-5363
  Frankfort (G-9863)
▲ MD Solutions Inc .... G 866 637-6588
  Plain City (G-16201)
Milicom LLC .... E 216 765-8875
  Beachwood (G-1249)
Offendaway LLC .... G 937 232-3933
  Centerville (G-3005)
Ohio Department Transportation ...... E 614 351-2898
  Columbus (G-7244)
▲ Ohio Magnetics Inc .... E 216 662-8484
  Maple Heights (G-12575)
Paul Peterson Company .... E 614 486-4375
  Columbus (G-7299)
Public Safety Concepts LLC .... G 614 733-0200
  Plain City (G-16208)
Quasonix Inc .... E 513 942-1287
  West Chester (G-19775)
Robert F Sams .... G 330 990-0477
  Akron (G-351)
Safe Systems Inc .... G 216 661-1166
  Cleveland (G-6024)
▲ Saltillo Corporation .... E 330 674-6722
  Millersburg (G-14126)
Security Fence Group Inc .... E 513 681-3700
  Cincinnati (G-4314)
Signature Technologies Inc .... E 937 859-6323
  Miamisburg (G-13716)
▲ Slap N Tickle LLC .... G 419 349-3226
  Toledo (G-18524)
Sound Communications Inc .... F 614 875-8500
  Grove City (G-10470)
Special Way 2 .... G 740 282-8281
  Steubenville (G-17552)
Union Metal Industries Corp .... G 330 456-7653
  Canton (G-2846)
UTC Fire SEC Americas Corp Inc .... G 513 821-7945
  Cincinnati (G-4460)
Viking Group Inc .... G 937 443-0433
  Dayton (G-8580)
Voice Products Inc .... F 216 360-0433
  Cleveland (G-6269)

3671 Radio & T V Receiving Electron Tubes

Fripro Energy LLC .... G 419 865-0002
  Maumee (G-13111)

3672 Printed Circuit Boards

Accurate Electronics Inc .... C 330 682-7015
  Orrville (G-15581)
Adonai Technologies LLC .... E 513 560-9020
  Middletown (G-13875)
Alektronics Inc .... F 937 429-2118
  Beavercreek (G-1349)
Avcom Smt Inc .... F 614 882-8176
  Westerville (G-20035)
▲ Bud Industries Inc .... G 440 946-3200
  Willoughby (G-20289)
C E Electronics Inc .... D 419 636-6705
  Bryan (G-2275)
▼ Cartessa Corporation .... F 513 738-4477
  Shandon (G-16940)
Central Systems & Control .... G 440 835-0015
  Cleveland (G-4901)
Circle Prime Manufacturing .... E 330 923-0019
  Cuyahoga Falls (G-7850)
Circuit Center .... G 513 435-2131
  Dayton (G-8091)

Circuit Services LLC .... G 513 604-7405
  Harrison (G-10636)
Cleveland Coretec Inc .... G 314 727-2087
  North Jackson (G-15144)
Co- Ax Technology Inc .... C 440 914-9200
  Solon (G-17128)
▼ Commercial Mfg Svcs Inc .... G 440 953-2701
  Mentor (G-13420)
Community RE Group-Comvet .... G 440 319-6714
  Ashtabula (G-767)
Ddi North Jackson Corp .... G 330 538-3900
  North Jackson (G-15145)
Debra Harbour .... G 937 440-9618
  Troy (G-18647)
Flextronics International Usa .... A 513 755-2500
  Liberty Township (G-11814)
Interactive Engineering Corp .... G 330 239-6888
  Medina (G-13280)
International Trade Group Inc .... G 614 486-4634
  Columbus (G-7045)
Journey Electronics Corp .... E 513 539-9836
  Monroe (G-14269)
L3 Technologies Inc .... E 513 943-2000
  Cincinnati (G-3258)
Lad Technology Inc .... G 440 461-8002
  Painesville (G-15756)
Levison Enterprises LLC .... E 419 838-7365
  Millbury (G-14051)
Libra Industries Inc .... E 440 974-7770
  Mentor (G-13499)
Malabar Properties LLC .... E 419 884-0071
  Mansfield (G-12473)
Metzenbaum Sheltered Inds Inc ...... G 440 729-1919
  Chesterland (G-3164)
Neo Technology Solutions .... G 513 234-5725
  Mason (G-12914)
▲ Parlex USA LLC .... D 937 898-3621
  Vandalia (G-19142)
Precision Switching Inc .... G 800 800-8143
  Mansfield (G-12502)
▲ Qualtech Technologies Inc .... E 440 946-8081
  Willoughby (G-20416)
▲ R-K Electronics Inc .... F 513 204-6060
  Mason (G-12929)
S Wj LIcred .... G 330 938-6173
  Sebring (G-16892)
Tabtronics Inc .... F 937 222-9969
  Dayton (G-8537)
▲ Techtron Systems Inc .... G 440 505-2990
  Solon (G-17249)
Tetrad Electronics Inc .... D 440 946-6443
  Willoughby (G-20446)
Ttm Technologies Inc .... C 330 538-3900
  North Jackson (G-15156)
United Circuits Inc .... F 440 926-1000
  Grafton (G-10312)
Versitec Manufacturing Inc .... F 440 354-4283
  Painesville (G-15795)
Vexos Electronic Mfg Svcs .... G 855 711-3227
  Lagrange (G-11496)
Visual Information Institute .... F 937 376-4361
  Xenia (G-20801)
▲ Vmetro Inc .... G 281 584-0728
  Fairborn (G-9473)
Wurth Electronics Ics Inc .... E 937 415-7700
  Dayton (G-8601)

3674 Semiconductors

A M D .... G 440 918-8930
  Willoughby (G-20264)
Advanced Dstrbted Gnration LLC .... G 419 530-3792
  Maumee (G-13066)
Advanced Technology Products ...... G 937 349-5221
  Mechanicsburg (G-13210)
Altera Corporation .... E 513 444-2021
  Cincinnati (G-3326)
Altera Corporation .... G 330 650-5200
  Hudson (G-11029)
AT&T Corp .... E 513 792-9300
  Cincinnati (G-3365)
Bestlight Led Corporation .... G 440 205-1552
  Mentor (G-13402)
Biometric Information MGT LLC ...... G 614 456-1296
  Dublin (G-8888)
Bright Focus Sales Inc .... F 216 751-8384
  Cleveland (G-4838)
▲ Burke Products Inc .... E 937 372-3516
  Xenia (G-20759)
Ceso Inc .... D 937 435-8584
  Miamisburg (G-13649)

SIC SECTION 36 ELECTRONIC AND OTHER ELECTRICAL EQUIPMENT AND COMPONENTS, EXCEPT COMPUTER

Cirrus LLC ....G.... 740 272-2012
Delaware *(G-8667)*
Communication Concepts Inc ....G.... 937 426-8600
Beavercreek *(G-1307)*
CPC Logistics Inc ....D.... 513 874-5787
Fairfield *(G-9492)*
Crishtronics Llc ....G.... 440 572-8318
Strongsville *(G-17733)*
D F Electronics Inc ....D.... 513 772-7792
Cincinnati *(G-3569)*
Dan-Mar Company Inc ....E.... 419 660-8830
Norwalk *(G-15386)*
Darrah Electric Company ....E.... 216 631-0912
Cleveland *(G-5067)*
Durr Megtec LLC ....C.... 614 258-9501
Columbus *(G-6876)*
Em4 Inc ....G.... 216 486-6100
Highland Heights *(G-10788)*
Energy Focus Inc ....C.... 440 715-1300
Solon *(G-17137)*
Fidelux Lighting LLC ....G.... 404 941-4182
Columbus *(G-6493)*
Fidelux Lighting LLC ....G.... 614 839-0250
Columbus *(G-6919)*
First Solar Inc ....B.... 419 661-1478
Perrysburg *(G-15952)*
Firstfuelcellscom LLC ....G.... 440 884-2503
Cleveland *(G-5243)*
Gopowerx Inc ....E.... 440 707-6029
Oberlin *(G-15497)*
Heraeus Electro-Nite Co LLC ....G.... 330 725-1419
Medina *(G-13272)*
Hunters Hightech Energy Systm ....G.... 614 275-4777
Columbus *(G-7012)*
Hydrogen 411 Technology LLC ....G.... 440 941-6760
Cleveland *(G-5430)*
Hyper Tech Research Inc ....F.... 614 481-8050
Columbus *(G-7013)*
Integrated Sensors LLC ....G.... 419 536-3212
Ottawa Hills *(G-15673)*
Intel Corporation ....G.... 513 860-9686
West Chester *(G-19723)*
Intel Industries LLC ....G.... 614 551-5702
Cincinnati *(G-3852)*
▲ **Isofoton North America Inc** ....F.... 419 591-4330
Napoleon *(G-14546)*
John B Allen ....G.... 614 488-7122
Columbus *(G-7072)*
Laird Connectivity Inc ....B.... 330 434-7929
Akron *(G-246)*
Leidos Inc ....D.... 937 431-2270
Beavercreek *(G-1326)*
Linear Asics Inc ....G.... 330 474-3920
Twinsburg *(G-18809)*
Lucintech Inc ....G.... 419 265-2641
Toledo *(G-18390)*
Madison Electric (mepco) Inc ....G.... 440 279-0521
Chardon *(G-3124)*
▲ **Materion Brush Inc** ....D.... 216 486-4200
Mayfield Heights *(G-13167)*
◆ **Materion Corporation** ....C.... 216 486-4200
Mayfield Heights *(G-13168)*
Measurement Specialties Inc ....F.... 937 427-1231
Beavercreek *(G-1358)*
Micro Industries Corporation ....D.... 740 548-7878
Westerville *(G-20065)*
Mok Industries LLC ....G.... 614 934-1734
Columbus *(G-7191)*
▲ **Ohio Semitronics Inc** ....D.... 614 777-1005
Hilliard *(G-10847)*
▲ **Pepperl + Fuchs Inc** ....C.... 330 425-3555
Twinsburg *(G-18830)*
Pepperl + Fuchs Entps Inc ....G.... 330 425-3555
Twinsburg *(G-18831)*
Philips Medical Systems Mr ....C.... 440 483-2499
Highland Heights *(G-10798)*
Redhawk Energy Systems LLC ....G.... 740 927-8244
Pataskala *(G-15839)*
Rexon Components Inc ....F.... 440 585-7086
Cleveland *(G-5981)*
Salient Systems Inc ....E.... 614 792-5800
Dublin *(G-8979)*
SCI Engineered Materials Inc ....E.... 614 486-0261
Columbus *(G-7429)*
Selectronics Incorporated ....G.... 440 546-5595
Brecksville *(G-2057)*
Signature Technologies Inc ....E.... 937 859-6323
Miamisburg *(G-13716)*
▲ **Silfex Inc** ....C.... 937 472-3311
Eaton *(G-9166)*
Smart Commercialization Center ....G.... 440 366-4048
Elyria *(G-9327)*
Smart Microsystems Ltd ....F.... 440 366-4257
Elyria *(G-9328)*
Spang & Company ....E.... 440 350-6108
Mentor *(G-13585)*
Spb Global LLC ....G.... 419 931-6559
Perrysburg *(G-16007)*
Special Mtls RES & Tech Inc ....G.... 440 777-4024
North Olmsted *(G-15200)*
▲ **Techneglas Inc** ....G.... 419 873-2000
Perrysburg *(G-16011)*
▲ **Tosoh SMD Inc** ....C.... 614 875-7912
Grove City *(G-10478)*
Transducers Direct Llc ....G.... 513 583-7597
Loveland *(G-12240)*
Tri-Tech Led Systems ....G.... 614 593-2868
Baltimore *(G-1045)*
▲ **Tytek Industries Inc** ....G.... 513 874-7326
Blue Ash *(G-1862)*
▲ **Ustek Incorporated** ....F.... 614 538-8000
Columbus *(G-7567)*
Vega Technology Group LLC ....G.... 216 772-1434
North Canton *(G-15135)*

3675 Electronic Capacitors

CPI Group Limited ....G.... 216 525-0046
Cleveland *(G-5035)*
Elliott Oren Products Inc ....E.... 419 298-2306
Edgerton *(G-9173)*

3676 Electronic Resistors

Filnor Inc ....F.... 330 821-7667
Alliance *(G-467)*
Measurement Specialties Inc ....F.... 937 427-1231
Beavercreek *(G-1358)*

3677 Electronic Coils & Transformers

Adkel Corp ....G.... 740 452-6973
Zanesville *(G-21094)*
Barnes International Inc ....D.... 419 352-7501
Bowling Green *(G-1953)*
▲ **Canfield Industries Inc** ....G.... 800 554-5071
Youngstown *(G-20864)*
Chicopee Engineering Assoc Inc ....E.... 413 592-2273
Twinsburg *(G-18751)*
▼ **Cletronics Inc** ....F.... 330 239-2002
Medina *(G-13237)*
Contech Strmwter Solutions LLC ....G.... 513 645-7000
West Chester *(G-19682)*
Crawford Resources Inc ....G.... 419 624-8400
Lorain *(G-12086)*
Custom Coil & Transformer Co ....E.... 740 452-5211
Zanesville *(G-21126)*
Electric Service Co Inc ....E.... 513 271-6387
Cincinnati *(G-3632)*
Electromotive Inc ....F.... 330 688-6494
Stow *(G-17581)*
Illinois Tool Works Inc ....C.... 262 248-8277
Bryan *(G-2289)*
▲ **Industrial Quartz Corp** ....F.... 440 942-0909
Mentor *(G-13469)*
▲ **Kurz-Kasch Inc** ....D.... 740 498-8343
Newcomerstown *(G-14977)*
M2m Imaging Corporation ....F.... 440 684-9690
Cleveland *(G-5595)*
▲ **Micropure Filtration Inc** ....F.... 952 472-2323
Cleveland *(G-5669)*
Nexjen Technologies Ltd ....G.... 781 572-5737
Avon Lake *(G-998)*
▼ **Norlake Manufacturing Company** ....D.... 440 353-3200
North Ridgeville *(G-15241)*
Nu Stream Filtration Inc ....G.... 937 949-3174
Dayton *(G-8390)*
PCC Airfoils LLC ....C.... 216 692-7900
Cleveland *(G-5857)*
Precision Switching Inc ....G.... 800 800-8143
Mansfield *(G-12502)*
Rapid Mr International LLC ....G.... 614 486-6300
Columbus *(G-7378)*
Schneider Electric Usa Inc ....B.... 513 523-4171
Oxford *(G-15700)*
◆ **Staco Energy Products Co** ....G.... 937 253-1191
Miamisburg *(G-13719)*
Standard Car Truck Company ....D.... 740 775-6450
Chillicothe *(G-3223)*
▲ **Swiger Coil Systems Ltd** ....C.... 216 362-7500
Cleveland *(G-6137)*
▲ **USA Instruments Inc** ....C.... 330 562-1000
Aurora *(G-913)*
Wabtec Corporation ....G.... 216 362-7500
Cleveland *(G-6280)*
Wonder Weld Inc ....G.... 614 875-1447
Orient *(G-15579)*

3678 Electronic Connectors

Ankim Enterprises Incorporated ....E.... 937 599-1121
Sidney *(G-17016)*
Associated Enterprises ....G.... 440 354-2106
Painesville *(G-15712)*
Astro Industries Inc ....E.... 937 429-5900
Beavercreek *(G-1301)*
Aviation Technologies Inc ....G.... 216 706-2960
Cleveland *(G-4776)*
Canadus Power Systems LLC ....F.... 216 831-6600
Twinsburg *(G-18746)*
▲ **Canfield Industries Inc** ....G.... 800 554-5071
Youngstown *(G-20864)*
Connective Design Incorporated ....F.... 937 746-8252
Miamisburg *(G-13651)*
▲ **Connectors Unlimited Inc** ....E.... 440 357-1161
Painesville *(G-15724)*
Connectronics Corp ....D.... 419 537-0020
Toledo *(G-18239)*
Cooper Interconnect Inc ....G.... 800 386-1911
Cleveland *(G-5028)*
D C M Industries Inc ....F.... 937 254-8500
Dayton *(G-8124)*
HCC Industries ....G.... 513 334-5585
Cincinnati *(G-3804)*
HCC/Sealtron ....E.... 513 733-8400
Cincinnati *(G-3805)*
Mueller Electric Company Inc ....E.... 614 888-8855
New Albany *(G-14631)*
▲ **Ohio Associated Entps LLC** ....E.... 440 354-2106
Painesville *(G-15768)*
Ohio Associated Entps LLC ....E.... 440 354-3148
Painesville *(G-15770)*
Ortronics Inc ....G.... 937 224-0639
Dayton *(G-8408)*
◆ **Plcc2 LLC** ....G.... 614 279-1796
Columbus *(G-7328)*
Powell Electrical Systems Inc ....D.... 330 966-1750
Canton *(G-2787)*
Servo Systems Inc ....G.... 440 779-2780
North Olmsted *(G-15198)*
▲ **Spi Inc** ....G.... 937 374-2700
Xenia *(G-20790)*
U S Terminals Inc ....G.... 513 561-8145
Cincinnati *(G-4445)*
Xponet Inc ....E.... 440 354-6617
Painesville *(G-15801)*

3679 Electronic Components, NEC

Accurate Electronics Inc ....C.... 330 682-7015
Orrville *(G-15581)*
Acoh Inc ....G.... 419 741-3195
Ottawa *(G-15647)*
Adcura Mfg ....G.... 937 222-3800
Dayton *(G-8008)*
Advanced Cryogenic Entps LLC ....F.... 330 922-0750
Akron *(G-31)*
▲ **Advanced Quartz Fabrication** ....F.... 440 350-4567
Chardon *(G-3095)*
Advantage Circuits Ltd ....G.... 330 256-7768
Rootstown *(G-16566)*
▲ **Aeroseal LLC** ....E.... 937 428-9300
Centerville *(G-2996)*
Alphabet Inc ....D.... 330 856-3366
Warren *(G-19366)*
American Advnced Assmblies LLC ....E.... 937 339-6267
Troy *(G-18634)*
Ankim Enterprises Incorporated ....E.... 937 599-1121
Sidney *(G-17016)*
Astro Industries Inc ....E.... 937 429-5900
Beavercreek *(G-1301)*
Autosyte ....G.... 440 858-3226
Painesville *(G-15713)*
Aviation Technologies Inc ....G.... 216 706-2960
Cleveland *(G-4776)*
B5 Systems Inc ....G.... 937 372-4768
Xenia *(G-20757)*
Bennett & Bennett Inc ....F.... 937 324-1100
Dayton *(G-8055)*
Berry Investments Inc ....G.... 937 293-0398
Moraine *(G-14334)*
Bionetics Corporation ....E.... 740 788-3800
Heath *(G-10718)*
Black Box Corporation ....F.... 614 825-7400
Lewis Center *(G-11751)*

S I C

36 ELECTRONIC AND OTHER ELECTRICAL EQUIPMENT AND COMPONENTS, EXCEPT COMPUTER SIC SECTION

C E Electronics Inc ....D.... 419 636-6705
Bryan *(G-2275)*
Captor Corporation ....D.... 937 667-8484
Tipp City *(G-18106)*
CEC Electronics Corp ....G.... 330 916-8100
Akron *(G-107)*
▲ Channel Products Inc ....D.... 440 423-0113
Solon *(G-17126)*
▲ Cks Solution Incorporated ....E.... 513 947-1277
Fairfield *(G-9491)*
▲ Cleanlife Energy LLC ....F.... 800 316-2532
Cleveland *(G-4941)*
Cleveland Circuits Corp ....E.... 216 267-9020
Cleveland *(G-4950)*
CMC Electronics Cincinn ....G.... 513 573-6316
Mason *(G-12850)*
Co- Ax Technology Inc ....C.... 440 914-9200
Solon *(G-17128)*
▼ Commercial Mfg Svcs Inc ....G.... 440 953-2701
Mentor *(G-13420)*
Connective Design Incorporated ....F.... 937 746-8252
Miamisburg *(G-13651)*
Cutting Edge Technologies Inc ....E.... 216 574-4759
Cleveland *(G-5051)*
D C M Industries Inc ....F.... 937 254-8500
Dayton *(G-8124)*
Dare Electronics Inc ....E.... 937 335-0031
Troy *(G-18645)*
Darrah Electric Company ....E.... 216 631-0912
Cleveland *(G-5067)*
Don-Ell Corporation ....E.... 419 841-7114
Sylvania *(G-17936)*
Drivetrain USA Inc ....F.... 614 733-0940
Plain City *(G-16189)*
▲ Dynalab Ems Inc ....C.... 614 866-9999
Reynoldsburg *(G-16436)*
Ebulent Technologies Corp ....G.... 925 922-1448
Cuyahoga Falls *(G-7861)*
Educational Electronics Inc ....G.... 234 301-9077
Millersburg *(G-14080)*
Electro-Line Inc ....F.... 937 461-5683
Dayton *(G-8181)*
Electromotive Inc ....F.... 330 688-6494
Stow *(G-17581)*
Electronic Solutions Inc ....F.... 419 666-4700
Perrysburg *(G-15944)*
Empire Power Systems Co ....G.... 440 796-4401
Madison *(G-12349)*
Epic Technologies LLC ....D.... 513 683-5455
Mason *(G-12867)*
Eti Tech LLC ....F.... 937 832-4200
Englewood *(G-9358)*
Ewh Spectrum LLC ....D.... 937 593-8010
Bellefontaine *(G-1515)*
Gmelectric Inc ....G.... 330 477-3392
Canton *(G-2685)*
▲ Great Lakes Glasswerks Inc ....G.... 440 358-0460
Painesville *(G-15743)*
▲ Guitammer Company ....G.... 614 898-9370
Westerville *(G-19995)*
Hall Company ....E.... 937 652-1376
Urbana *(G-18992)*
Idcomm LLC ....G.... 661 250-4081
Willoughby Hills *(G-20469)*
Inductive Components Mfg ....E.... 513 752-4731
Amelia *(G-541)*
▲ Ingram Products Inc ....F.... 904 778-1010
Ashland *(G-714)*
Innocomp ....G.... 440 248-5104
Solon *(G-17170)*
▲ Inservco Inc ....D.... 847 855-9600
Lagrange *(G-11483)*
▲ Inventus Power (ohio) Inc ....F.... 614 351-2191
Dublin *(G-8931)*
▲ J & C Group Inc of Ohio ....E.... 440 205-9658
Mentor *(G-13478)*
John B Allen ....G.... 614 488-7122
Columbus *(G-7072)*
▲ Kent Displays Inc ....C.... 330 673-8784
Kent *(G-11340)*
▲ L & J Cable Inc ....E.... 937 526-9445
Russia *(G-16609)*
La Grange Elec Assemblies Co ....E.... 440 355-5388
Lagrange *(G-11486)*
Laird Technologies Inc ....F.... 330 434-7929
Akron *(G-247)*
Lake Shore Cryotronics Inc ....C.... 614 891-2243
Westerville *(G-20003)*
Leidos Inc ....D.... 937 431-2270
Beavercreek *(G-1326)*
Lintech Electronics LLC ....F.... 513 528-6190
Cincinnati *(G-3259)*
Malabar Properties LLC ....F.... 419 884-0071
Mansfield *(G-12473)*
▲ Mc Gregor & Associates Inc ....C.... 937 833-6768
Brookville *(G-2178)*
Microplex Inc ....E.... 330 498-0600
North Canton *(G-15101)*
Mitchell Electronics Inc ....G.... 740 594-8532
Athens *(G-842)*
Mk Enterprises Inc ....E.... 440 632-0121
Middlefield *(G-13832)*
Mueller Electric Company Inc ....E.... 614 888-8855
New Albany *(G-14631)*
Networked Cmmnctons Sltons LLC ....G.... 440 374-4990
Bedford Heights *(G-1477)*
▼ Niktec LLC ....G.... 513 282-3747
Franklin *(G-9904)*
Ogc Industries Inc ....F.... 330 456-1500
Canton *(G-2770)*
▲ Ohio Semitronics Inc ....D.... 614 777-1005
Hilliard *(G-10847)*
Ohio Wire Harness LLC ....F.... 937 292-7355
Bellefontaine *(G-1523)*
Omega Engineering Inc ....E.... 740 965-9340
Sunbury *(G-17896)*
Ops Wireless ....G.... 419 396-4041
Carey *(G-2886)*
Otr Controls LLC ....G.... 513 621-2197
Cincinnati *(G-4123)*
Parker-Hannifin Corporation ....C.... 937 644-3915
Marysville *(G-12805)*
Per-Tech Inc ....E.... 330 833-8824
Massillon *(G-13038)*
Performance Electronics Ltd ....G.... 513 777-5233
Cincinnati *(G-4148)*
Philips Medical Systems Mr ....C.... 440 483-2499
Highland Heights *(G-10798)*
Power Metrics Inc ....G.... 440 461-9352
Cleveland *(G-5899)*
Precision Manufacturing Co Inc ....D.... 937 236-2170
Dayton *(G-8433)*
Qlog Corp ....G.... 513 874-1211
Hamilton *(G-10599)*
◆ Quality Quartz Engineering Inc ....D.... 937 236-3250
Dayton *(G-8455)*
Quality Quartz of America Inc ....G.... 440 352-2851
Mentor *(G-13566)*
Quality Switch Inc ....E.... 330 872-5707
Newton Falls *(G-14991)*
Quartz Scientific Inc ....E.... 360 574-6254
Fairport Harbor *(G-9628)*
Ra Consultants LLC ....E.... 513 469-6600
Blue Ash *(G-1840)*
Rct Industries Inc ....F.... 937 602-1100
Springboro *(G-17351)*
Rpa Electronic Distributors ....F.... 937 223-7001
Dayton *(G-8486)*
RTD Electronics Inc ....F.... 330 487-0716
Twinsburg *(G-18851)*
▲ S-Tek Inc ....G.... 440 439-8232
Bedford *(G-1443)*
Saint-Gobain Ceramics Plas Inc ....A.... 330 673-5860
Stow *(G-17624)*
Sawyer Research Product ....G.... 440 951-8770
Eastlake *(G-9129)*
▲ Sawyer Technical Materials LLC ....E.... 440 951-8770
Willoughby *(G-20424)*
Schupp Advanced Materials LLC ....G.... 440 488-6416
Willoughby *(G-20426)*
Shiloh Industries Inc ....F.... 937 236-5100
Dayton *(G-8504)*
Showplace Inc ....G.... 419 468-7368
Galion *(G-10155)*
Siglent Technologies Amer Inc ....G.... 440 398-5800
Solon *(G-17231)*
Sinbon Usa LLC ....G.... 937 667-8999
Tipp City *(G-18133)*
SMH Manufacturing Inc ....F.... 419 884-0071
Lexington *(G-11806)*
Sol-Fly Technologies LLC ....G.... 330 465-8883
Wooster *(G-20656)*
Solar Con Inc ....E.... 419 865-5877
Holland *(G-10958)*
Sovereign Circuits Inc ....G.... 330 538-3900
North Jackson *(G-15154)*
▲ Specialty Switch Co ....F.... 330 427-3000
Youngstown *(G-21037)*
Spectron Inc ....G.... 937 461-5590
Dayton *(G-8517)*
▲ Spi Inc ....G.... 937 374-2700
Xenia *(G-20790)*
Suburban Electronics Assembly ....G.... 330 483-4077
Valley City *(G-19067)*
The W L Jenkins Company ....F.... 330 477-3407
Canton *(G-2835)*
◆ Thermtrol Corporation ....E.... 330 497-4148
North Canton *(G-15125)*
Tinycircuits ....G.... 330 329-5753
Akron *(G-405)*
Tk Machining Specialties LLC ....G.... 513 368-3963
Hamilton *(G-10612)*
TL Industries Inc ....C.... 419 666-8144
Northwood *(G-15346)*
▲ Tls Corp ....E.... 216 574-4759
Cleveland *(G-6177)*
▲ Total Cable Solutions Inc ....G.... 513 457-7013
Springboro *(G-17357)*
Tracewell Power Inc ....E.... 614 846-6175
Westerville *(G-20080)*
▲ Twin Point Inc ....F.... 419 923-7525
Delta *(G-8778)*
U S Terminals Inc ....G.... 513 561-8145
Cincinnati *(G-4445)*
Valley Electric Company ....G.... 419 332-6405
Fremont *(G-10061)*
Valtronic Technology Inc ....D.... 440 349-1239
Solon *(G-17257)*
Vertiv Group Corporation ....A.... 614 888-0246
Columbus *(G-7576)*
Vertiv Holdings LLC ....G.... 614 888-0246
Columbus *(G-7577)*
Weldon ....G.... 330 263-9533
Columbus *(G-7599)*
Wetsu Group Inc ....F.... 937 324-9353
Springfield *(G-17517)*
Wifi-Plus Inc ....G.... 877 838-4195
Brunswick *(G-2251)*
▲ Workman Electronic Pdts Inc ....F.... 419 923-7525
Delta *(G-8779)*
Zeus Electronics LLC ....G.... 330 220-1571
Brunswick *(G-2256)*

3691 Storage Batteries

All Power Battery Inc ....G.... 330 453-5236
Canton *(G-2567)*
B W T Inc ....G.... 330 928-9107
Akron *(G-77)*
◆ Crown Battery Manufacturing Co ....B.... 419 334-7181
Fremont *(G-10009)*
Crown Battery Manufacturing Co ....G.... 330 425-3308
Twinsburg *(G-18758)*
Dynalite Corp ....G.... 419 873-1706
Perrysburg *(G-15942)*
Edgewell Per Care Brands LLC ....D.... 330 527-2191
Garrettsville *(G-10188)*
Energizer Manufacturing Inc ....D.... 440 835-7866
Westlake *(G-20112)*
Enersys ....D.... 513 737-2268
West Chester *(G-19698)*
Graywacke Inc ....F.... 419 884-7014
Mansfield *(G-12453)*
Innovative Weld Solutions Ltd ....G.... 937 545-7695
Beavercreek *(G-1356)*
Interstate Batteries Inc ....G.... 740 968-2211
Saint Clairsville *(G-16634)*
Johnson Contrls Btry Group Inc ....A.... 419 865-0542
Holland *(G-10938)*
Lithchem Intl Toxco Inc ....G.... 740 653-6290
Lancaster *(G-11584)*
Ovonic Energy Products Inc ....C.... 937 743-1001
Springboro *(G-17341)*
Retriev Technologies Inc ....D.... 740 653-6290
Lancaster *(G-11602)*
Robert Bosch Btry Systems LLC ....D.... 937 743-1001
Springboro *(G-17352)*
Rus Power Storage LLC ....G.... 937 999-8121
Middletown *(G-13950)*
Toxco Inc ....D.... 740 653-6290
Lancaster *(G-11614)*
Transdigm Inc ....F.... 216 291-6025
Cleveland *(G-6195)*
Transdigm Inc ....G.... 216 706-2939
Cleveland *(G-6196)*
Xerion Advanced Battery Corp ....F.... 720 229-0697
Kettering *(G-11444)*

3692 Primary Batteries: Dry & Wet

D C Systems Inc ....F.... 330 273-3030
Brunswick *(G-2198)*

N S T Battery .... G 937 433-9222
Bellbrook *(G-1496)*
Rus Power Storage LLC .... G 937 999-8121
Middletown *(G-13950)*

3694 Electrical Eqpt For Internal Combustion Engines

▲ Altronic LLC .... C 330 545-9768
Girard *(G-10252)*
Aptiv Services Us LLC .... C 330 505-3150
Warren *(G-19373)*
Brinkley Technology Group LLC .... F 330 830-2498
Massillon *(G-12963)*
Charles Auto Electric Co Inc .... G 330 535-6269
Akron *(G-111)*
Cummins Inc .... G 614 604-6004
Grove City *(G-10424)*
Cuyahoga Rebuilders Inc .... G 440 846-0532
Cleveland *(G-5054)*
Cycle Electric Inc .... F 937 884-7300
Brookville *(G-2165)*
Design Flux Technologies LLC .... G 216 543-6066
Akron *(G-139)*
Egr Products Company Inc .... F 330 833-6554
Dalton *(G-7941)*
Elcor Inc .... E 440 365-5941
Elyria *(G-9249)*
Electra Sound Inc .... D 216 433-9600
Parma *(G-15817)*
◆ Electripack Inc .... E 937 433-2602
Miamisburg *(G-13663)*
Empire Power Systems Co .... G 440 796-4401
Madison *(G-12349)*
Ewh Spectrum LLC .... D 937 593-8010
Bellefontaine *(G-1515)*
Exact-Tool & Die Inc .... E 216 676-9140
Cleveland *(G-5204)*
▲ Ferrotherm Corporation .... C 216 883-9350
Cleveland *(G-5233)*
Flex Technologies Inc .... D 330 359-5415
Mount Eaton *(G-14420)*
Fram Group Operations LLC .... D 419 661-6700
Perrysburg *(G-15953)*
Gmelectric Inc .... G 330 477-3392
Canton *(G-2685)*
▲ GSW Manufacturing Inc .... B 419 423-7111
Findlay *(G-9696)*
▲ Hurst Auto-Truck Electric .... G 216 961-1800
Cleveland *(G-5426)*
Industrial Systems & Solutions .... G 440 205-1658
Mentor *(G-13470)*
Legacy Supplies Inc .... F 330 405-4565
Twinsburg *(G-18805)*
M W Solutions LLC .... F 419 782-1611
Defiance *(G-8633)*
Machine Products Company .... E 937 890-6600
Dayton *(G-8320)*
◆ Mitsubishi Elc Auto Amer Inc .... B 513 573-6614
Mason *(G-12911)*
▲ Mueller Electric Company Inc .... E 216 771-5225
Akron *(G-290)*
◆ Noco Company .... B 216 464-8131
Solon *(G-17208)*
Per-Tech Inc .... E 330 833-8824
Massillon *(G-13038)*
Power Acquisition LLC .... G 614 228-5000
Dublin *(G-8966)*
▲ Satco Inc .... G 330 630-8866
Tallmadge *(G-18002)*
▲ Sk Tech Inc .... C 937 836-3535
Englewood *(G-9375)*
▲ Stanley Electric US Co Inc .... B 740 852-5200
London *(G-12069)*
Stellar Industrial Tech Co .... G 740 654-7052
Lancaster *(G-11612)*
Sumitomo Elc Wirg Systems Inc .... E 937 642-7579
Marysville *(G-12816)*
Thirion Brothers Eqp Co LLC .... G 440 357-8004
Painesville *(G-15790)*
United Controls Group Inc .... G 740 936-0005
Columbus *(G-6507)*
▲ United Ignition Wire Corp .... G 216 898-1112
Cleveland *(G-6234)*
Unity Cable Technologies Inc .... G 419 322-4118
Toledo *(G-18584)*
Weldon Pump Acquition LLC .... E 440 232-2282
Oakwood Village *(G-15489)*

3695 Recording Media

CD Solutions Inc .... G 937 676-2376
Pleasant Hill *(G-16224)*
Characteristic Solutions LLC .... G 614 360-2424
Columbus *(G-6757)*
Folio Photonics LLC .... G 440 420-4500
Solon *(G-17145)*
Future Pos Ohio Inc .... F 330 645-6623
Akron *(G-179)*
Ginko Voting Systems LLC .... G 937 291-4060
Dayton *(G-8222)*
Magnetnotes Ltd .... G 419 593-0060
Toledo *(G-18397)*
Medical Soft Inc .... G 937 293-2575
Oakwood *(G-15464)*
Paragon Robotics LLC .... G 216 313-9299
Bedford Heights *(G-1478)*
Procomsol Ltd .... G 216 221-1550
Lakewood *(G-11533)*
Signalysis Inc .... F 513 528-6164
Cincinnati *(G-4337)*
US Video .... G 440 734-6463
North Olmsted *(G-15202)*
Wm Software Inc .... F 330 558-0501
Brunswick *(G-2253)*

3699 Electrical Machinery, Eqpt & Splys, NEC

A L Callahan Door Sales .... G 419 884-3667
Mansfield *(G-12399)*
Aaron Smith .... G 330 285-1360
Akron *(G-25)*
Access 2 Communications Inc .... G 800 561-1110
Steubenville *(G-17525)*
▲ Action Industries Ltd .... F 216 252-7800
Strongsville *(G-17705)*
▲ Agratronix LLC .... E 330 562-2222
Streetsboro *(G-17657)*
Akron Brass Company .... E 614 529-7230
Columbus *(G-6557)*
▲ Akron Brass Company .... B 330 264-5678
Wooster *(G-20558)*
Akron Brass Holding Corp .... G 330 264-5678
Wooster *(G-20559)*
Akron Foundry Co .... E 330 745-3101
Barberton *(G-1050)*
Alert Safety Lite Products Co .... F 440 232-5020
Cleveland *(G-4658)*
▲ Alert Stamping & Mfg Co Inc .... E 440 232-5020
Bedford Heights *(G-1458)*
Allen Fields Assoc Inc .... G 513 228-1010
Lebanon *(G-11632)*
◆ Allied Moulded Products Inc .... C 419 636-4217
Bryan *(G-2259)*
Ametek Inc .... F 937 440-0800
Troy *(G-18637)*
▼ Automation Metrology Intl LLC .... G 440 354-6436
Mentor *(G-13395)*
Aysco Security Consultants Inc .... E 330 733-8183
Kent *(G-11297)*
Azz Inc .... E 330 456-3241
Canton *(G-2580)*
▲ Barth Industries Co LP .... D 216 267-0531
Cleveland *(G-4793)*
Bert Radebaugh .... G 740 382-8134
Marion *(G-12695)*
Beta Industries Inc .... E 937 299-7385
Dayton *(G-8056)*
Bonham Enterprsises .... G 740 333-0501
Wshngtn CT Hs *(G-20719)*
Bos Electric Supply LLC .... G 937 426-0578
Moraine *(G-14335)*
Buckeye Electrical Products .... E 937 693-7519
Botkins *(G-1935)*
C L S Inc .... G 216 251-5011
Cleveland *(G-4857)*
▲ Cecil C Peck Co .... F 330 785-0781
Akron *(G-108)*
Ces Nationwide .... G 937 322-0771
Springfield *(G-17373)*
Chandler Systems Incorporated .... G 419 281-6829
Ashland *(G-692)*
Checkpoint Systems Inc .... C 937 281-1304
Dayton *(G-8087)*
Christmas Ranch LLC .... E 513 505-3865
Morrow *(G-14409)*
Ci Disposition Co .... E 216 587-5200
Brooklyn Heights *(G-2118)*
Circle Prime Manufacturing .... E 330 923-0019
Cuyahoga Falls *(G-7850)*
Clark Substations LLC .... E 330 452-5200
Canton *(G-2628)*
▲ Cleaning Tech Group LLC .... C 877 933-8278
West Chester *(G-19842)*
Commercial Electric Pdts Corp .... E 216 241-2886
Cleveland *(G-5002)*
Control System Manufacturing .... E 330 542-0000
New Middletown *(G-14749)*
▼ Corrpro Companies Inc .... E 330 723-5082
Medina *(G-13242)*
Corrpro Companies Inc .... F 330 725-6681
Medina *(G-13243)*
Corrpro Companies Intl Inc .... G 330 723-5082
Medina *(G-13244)*
D&M Fencing LLC .... G 419 604-0698
Spencerville *(G-17308)*
Daskal Enterprise LLC .... G 614 848-5700
Columbus *(G-6850)*
Debra Harbour .... G 937 440-9618
Troy *(G-18647)*
Diebold Nixdorf Incorporated .... A 330 490-4000
North Canton *(G-15078)*
E-Beam Services Inc .... E 513 933-0031
Lebanon *(G-11648)*
Eagle Wldg & Fabrication Inc .... E 440 946-0692
Willoughby *(G-20313)*
Elcor Inc .... E 440 365-5941
Elyria *(G-9249)*
▲ Electra - Cord Inc .... D 330 832-8124
Massillon *(G-12979)*
▲ Electrowarmth Products LLC .... G 740 599-7222
Danville *(G-7963)*
Emega Technologies LLC .... G 740 407-3712
Zanesville *(G-21134)*
▲ Emx Industries Inc .... E 216 518-9888
Cleveland *(G-5176)*
Engineered Mfg & Eqp Co .... G 937 642-7776
Marysville *(G-12781)*
Erico Global Company .... G 440 248-0100
Solon *(G-17139)*
Everykey Inc .... G 855 666-5006
Cleveland *(G-5202)*
Executive Security Systems Inc .... G 513 895-2783
Cincinnati *(G-3665)*
▲ Federal Equipment Company .... D 513 621-5260
Cincinnati *(G-3680)*
▲ Fernandes Enterprises LLC .... E 937 890-6444
Dayton *(G-8193)*
Fire-End & Croker Corp .... G 513 870-0517
West Chester *(G-19852)*
FM Manufacturing Inc .... G 419 445-0700
Archbold *(G-646)*
Fortec Medical Lithotripsy LLC .... E 330 656-4301
Streetsboro *(G-17674)*
General Electric Company .... C 216 266-2357
Cleveland *(G-5311)*
Global Laser Tek .... E 513 701-0452
Mason *(G-12880)*
▲ GMI Holdings Inc .... B 330 821-5360
Mount Hope *(G-14437)*
Graham Electric .... G 614 231-8500
Columbus *(G-6964)*
Great Lakes Power Service Co .... G 440 259-0025
Perry *(G-15905)*
H W Fairway International Inc .... E 330 678-2540
Kent *(G-11330)*
Habitec SEC Diversfd Alarm .... G 419 636-1155
Bryan *(G-2284)*
▲ Halex/Scott Fetzer Company .... D 440 439-1616
Bedford Heights *(G-1471)*
Halls Welding & Supplies Inc .... G 330 385-9353
East Liverpool *(G-9058)*
Hannon Company .... D 330 456-4728
Canton *(G-2693)*
Hanon Systems Usa LLC .... C 313 920-0583
Carey *(G-2882)*
Heat Exchange Institute Inc .... G 216 241-7333
Cleveland *(G-5385)*
Henderson Partners LLC .... G 614 883-1310
Columbus *(G-6987)*
Hess Advanced Solutions Llc .... G 937 829-4794
Dayton *(G-8249)*
Highcom Global Security Inc .... F 727 592-9400
Columbus *(G-6997)*
Holland Assocts LLC DBA Archou .... F 513 891-0006
Cincinnati *(G-3818)*
Honeywell International Inc .... A 937 484-2000
Urbana *(G-18995)*
▲ I T Verdin Co .... E 513 241-4010
Cincinnati *(G-3833)*

Employee Codes: A=Over 500 employees, B=251-500
C=101-250, D=51-100, E=20-50, F=10-19, G=3-9
2019 Harris Ohio
Industrial Directory
993

36 ELECTRONIC AND OTHER ELECTRICAL EQUIPMENT AND COMPONENTS, EXCEPT COMPUTER SIC SECTION

I T Verdin Co ....E.... 513 559-3947
Cincinnati *(G-3834)*
Innovar Systems Limited ....F.... 330 538-3942
North Jackson *(G-15147)*
▲ **Insource Technologies Inc** ....C.... 419 399-3600
Paulding *(G-15863)*
▼ **Invue Security Products Inc** ....C.... 330 456-7776
Canton *(G-2711)*
Izit Cain Sheet Metal Corp ....G.... 937 667-6521
Tipp City *(G-18117)*
J II Fire Systems Inc ....G.... 513 574-0609
Cincinnati *(G-3864)*
JC Electric ....E.... 330 760-2915
Garrettsville *(G-10193)*
Jech Technologies Inc ....G.... 740 927-3495
Pickerington *(G-16050)*
▲ **Jobap Assembly Inc** ....F.... 440 632-5393
Middlefield *(G-13810)*
Juggerbot 3d LLC ....G.... 330 406-6900
Youngstown *(G-20950)*
Kiemle-Hankins Company ....E.... 419 661-2430
Perrysburg *(G-15972)*
Kraft Electrical Contg Inc ....E.... 614 836-9300
Groveport *(G-10498)*
Laser Automation Inc ....F.... 440 543-9291
Chagrin Falls *(G-3055)*
Levans Electric & Hvac ....G.... 937 468-2269
Rushsylvania *(G-16596)*
Libra Industries Inc ....C.... 440 974-7770
Mentor *(G-13498)*
Liebert North America Inc ....E.... 614 888-0246
Columbus *(G-7125)*
▼ **Lindsay Precast Inc** ....E.... 800 837-7788
Canal Fulton *(G-2483)*
▲ **Lockheed Martin Integ** ....D.... 330 796-2800
Akron *(G-257)*
Lucky Thirteen Inc ....G.... 216 631-0013
Cleveland *(G-5587)*
◆ **Mace Security Intl Inc** ....D.... 440 424-5321
Cleveland *(G-5598)*
Magnus Engineered Eqp LLC ....E.... 440 942-8488
Willoughby *(G-20366)*
MAI Media Group Llc ....G.... 513 779-0604
West Chester *(G-19875)*
Matlock Electric Co Inc ....E.... 513 731-9600
Cincinnati *(G-3986)*
Midwest Security Services ....G.... 937 853-9000
Dayton *(G-8354)*
Mitsubishi Elc Automtn Inc ....G.... 937 492-3058
Sidney *(G-17054)*
Mixed Logic LLC ....G.... 440 826-1676
Valley City *(G-19050)*
▼ **Modular Security Systems Inc** ....G.... 740 532-7822
Ironton *(G-11169)*
Mr Electric ....G.... 419 289-7474
Mansfield *(G-12488)*
▲ **Mueller Electric Company Inc** ....E.... 216 771-5225
Akron *(G-290)*
Mv Innovative Technologies LLC ....G.... 301 661-0951
Dayton *(G-8373)*
Nabco Entrances Inc ....G.... 419 842-0484
Sylvania *(G-17954)*
Niftech Inc ....F.... 440 257-6018
Mentor *(G-13528)*
▲ **Nook Industries Inc** ....C.... 216 271-7900
Cleveland *(G-5756)*
Northeast Laser Inc ....G.... 330 633-2897
Tallmadge *(G-17997)*
Oakes Door Serv ....G.... 937 323-6188
Springfield *(G-17463)*
Ohio Electric Motor Svc LLC ....G.... 419 525-2225
Mansfield *(G-12496)*
Oldaker Manufacturing Corp ....G.... 419 759-3551
Dunkirk *(G-9036)*
Overhead Door of Salem Inc ....G.... 330 332-9530
Salem *(G-16765)*
▲ **Overly Hautz Motor Base Co** ....E.... 513 932-0025
Lebanon *(G-11681)*
P & B Electric ....G.... 937 754-4695
Fairborn *(G-9465)*
P3labs LLC ....G.... 800 259-8059
North Canton *(G-15108)*
Peerless Laser Processors Inc ....E.... 614 836-5790
Groveport *(G-10508)*
Pentagon Protection Usa LLC ....F.... 614 734-7240
Dublin *(G-8964)*
Pepperl + Fuchs Mfg Inc ....C.... 330 425-3555
Twinsburg *(G-18832)*
◆ **Philips Medical Systems Clevel** ....B.... 440 247-2652
Cleveland *(G-5871)*
Powell Electrical Systems Inc ....D.... 330 966-1750
Canton *(G-2787)*
Primex ....E.... 513 831-9959
Milford *(G-14035)*
▲ **Qualtech Technologies Inc** ....E.... 440 946-8081
Willoughby *(G-20416)*
Rae Systems Inc ....G.... 440 232-0555
Walton Hills *(G-19314)*
Residential Electronic Svcs ....G.... 740 681-9150
Lancaster *(G-11601)*
Resonetics LLC ....D.... 937 865-4070
Kettering *(G-11440)*
Revolaze LLC ....G.... 440 617-0502
Westlake *(G-20150)*
Rexel Inc ....G.... 330 468-1122
Northfield *(G-15323)*
▼ **Riverside Drives Inc** ....E.... 216 362-1211
Cleveland *(G-5988)*
Romanoff Elc Residential LLC ....D.... 614 755-4500
Gahanna *(G-10101)*
RPS America Inc ....G.... 937 231-9339
West Chester *(G-19788)*
▲ **S R Technologies LLC** ....G.... 330 523-7184
Akron *(G-366)*
Say Security Group USA LLC ....F.... 419 634-0004
Ada *(G-8)*
Schneider Electric Usa Inc ....E.... 513 398-9800
West Chester *(G-19793)*
Schneider Electric Usa Inc ....F.... 937 258-8426
Dayton *(G-8495)*
Schneider Electric Usa Inc ....B.... 513 523-4171
Oxford *(G-15700)*
Securcom Inc ....E.... 419 628-1049
Minster *(G-14224)*
Securtex International Inc ....E.... 937 312-1414
Dayton *(G-8500)*
Sew-Eurodrive Inc ....D.... 937 335-0036
Troy *(G-18705)*
Smart Sonic Corporation ....G.... 818 610-7900
Cleveland *(G-6072)*
Spang & Company ....E.... 440 350-6108
Mentor *(G-13585)*
Stephen Radecky ....G.... 440 232-2132
Bedford *(G-1447)*
Stuntronics LLC ....G.... 216 780-1413
Bedford Heights *(G-1480)*
Tech-Sonic Inc ....F.... 614 792-3117
Columbus *(G-7519)*
Technical Sales & Solution ....G.... 614 793-9612
Dublin *(G-9003)*
Technlogy Install Partners LLC ....E.... 888 586-7040
Cleveland *(G-6156)*
Technology Products Inc ....G.... 937 652-3412
Urbana *(G-19015)*
The W L Jenkins Company ....F.... 330 477-3407
Canton *(G-2835)*
Tip Products Inc ....E.... 216 252-2535
Cleveland *(G-6176)*
▲ **Transdermal Inc** ....F.... 440 241-1846
Gates Mills *(G-10209)*
Trinity Door Systems ....G.... 877 603-2018
New Springfield *(G-14822)*
◆ **Vanner Holdings Inc** ....D.... 614 771-2718
Hilliard *(G-10873)*
Vero Security Group Ltd ....G.... 513 731-8376
Cincinnati *(G-4476)*
Villers Enterprises Limited ....G.... 330 818-9838
New Franklin *(G-14688)*
Viotec LLC ....G.... 614 596-2054
Dublin *(G-9009)*
Vortec Corporation ....E.... 513 891-7485
Blue Ash *(G-1866)*
Vti Instruments Corporation ....G.... 216 447-8950
Cleveland *(G-6275)*
Wesco Distribution Inc ....E.... 419 666-1670
Northwood *(G-15351)*
Yaskawa America Inc ....F.... 614 733-3200
Plain City *(G-16220)*

37 TRANSPORTATION EQUIPMENT

3711 Motor Vehicles & Car Bodies

▼ **Accubuilt Inc** ....C.... 419 224-3910
Lima *(G-11829)*
Accubuilt Inc ....C.... 419 224-3910
Lima *(G-11830)*
Aftermarket Parts Company LLC ....B.... 740 369-1056
Delaware *(G-8651)*
◆ **Airstream Inc** ....B.... 937 596-6111
Jackson Center *(G-11205)*
Allen Morgan Trucking & Repair ....G.... 330 336-5192
Norton *(G-15361)*
AM General LLC ....G.... 937 704-0160
Franklin *(G-9868)*
American Honda Motor Co Inc ....G.... 937 339-0157
Troy *(G-18635)*
American Honda Motor Co Inc ....C.... 937 332-6100
Troy *(G-18636)*
American Race Cars ....G.... 419 836-5070
Sandusky *(G-16795)*
AMP Electric Vehicles Inc ....F.... 513 360-4704
Loveland *(G-12177)*
Antique Auto Sheet Metal Inc ....E.... 937 833-4422
Brookville *(G-2161)*
Antram Fire Equipment ....G.... 330 525-7171
North Georgetown *(G-15139)*
Auto Expo USA of Cleveland ....G.... 216 889-3000
Cleveland *(G-4768)*
Autowax Inc ....G.... 440 334-4417
Strongsville *(G-17717)*
Bartley Lawn Service LLC ....G.... 937 435-8884
West Carrollton *(G-19630)*
Biggys Auto Buffet ....G.... 740 455-4663
Zanesville *(G-21106)*
Bobbart Industries Inc ....E.... 419 350-5477
Sylvania *(G-17934)*
Braun Industries Inc ....B.... 419 232-7020
Van Wert *(G-19080)*
Brookville Roadster Inc ....E.... 937 833-4605
Brookville *(G-2162)*
Buses International ....F.... 440 233-4091
Lorain *(G-12081)*
Columbus Fire Fighters Union ....G.... 614 481-8900
Columbus *(G-6788)*
Comprehensive Logistics Co Inc ....E.... 330 793-0504
Youngstown *(G-20877)*
Copley Fire & Rescue Assn ....E.... 330 666-6464
Copley *(G-7681)*
▲ **Custom Chassis Inc** ....G.... 440 839-5574
Wakeman *(G-19283)*
D & D Classic Auto Restoration ....E.... 937 473-2229
Covington *(G-7784)*
Dakkota Integrated Systems LLC ....E.... 517 694-6500
Toledo *(G-18252)*
Eagle Coach Inc ....D.... 513 797-4100
Amelia *(G-537)*
Eldorado National Kansas Inc ....G.... 937 596-6849
Jackson Center *(G-11208)*
Falls Stamping & Welding Co ....C.... 330 928-1191
Cuyahoga Falls *(G-7867)*
▼ **Farber Specialty Vehicles Inc** ....C.... 614 863-6470
Reynoldsburg *(G-16438)*
Ford Motor Company ....A.... 440 933-1215
Avon Lake *(G-986)*
▲ **Galion-Godwin Truck Bdy Co LLC** ....D.... 330 359-5495
Millersburg *(G-14084)*
General Motors LLC ....A.... 330 824-5000
Warren *(G-19405)*
General Motors LLC ....A.... 216 265-5000
Cleveland *(G-5312)*
◆ **Gerling and Associates Inc** ....D.... 740 965-6200
Sunbury *(G-17886)*
Great Lakes Assemblies LLC ....D.... 937 645-3900
East Liberty *(G-9047)*
▼ **Halcore Group Inc** ....C.... 614 539-8181
Grove City *(G-10433)*
◆ **Honda of America Mfg Inc** ....A.... 937 642-5000
Marysville *(G-12791)*
Honda of America Mfg Inc ....B.... 937 642-5000
Marysville *(G-12793)*
Honda of America Mfg Inc ....C.... 937 644-0724
Marysville *(G-12792)*
Horton Enterprises Inc ....G.... 614 539-8181
Grove City *(G-10434)*
Hyq Technologies LLC ....G.... 513 225-6911
Oxford *(G-15694)*
▲ **Jefferson Industries Corp** ....C.... 614 879-5300
West Jefferson *(G-19923)*
JLW - TW Corp ....G.... 216 361-5940
Avon *(G-952)*
Johns Body Shop ....G.... 419 358-1200
Bluffton *(G-1890)*
K K Racing Chassis ....G.... 330 628-2930
Akron *(G-229)*
Kps NAPA ....F.... 740 522-9445
Heath *(G-10725)*
La Boit Specialty Vehicles ....E.... 614 231-7640
Gahanna *(G-10088)*
Lawsons Towing & Auto Wrckg ....F.... 216 883-9050
Cleveland *(G-5568)*

Magic Dragon Machine Inc G 614 539-8004
Grove City *(G-10443)*
Marc Industries Inc G 440 944-9305
Willoughby *(G-20369)*
Mbm Industries Ltd G 937 522-0719
Beavercreek Township *(G-1369)*
Mobile Solutions LLC F 614 286-3944
Columbus *(G-7189)*
Mobis North America LLC E 419 729-6700
Toledo *(G-18413)*
▲ Myers Motors LLC G 330 630-7000
Tallmadge *(G-17994)*
Navistar Inc C 937 390-5848
Springfield *(G-17456)*
Navistar Inc D 937 390-5653
Springfield *(G-17457)*
Navistar Inc D 937 561-3315
Springfield *(G-17458)*
Navistar Inc E 937 390-5704
Springfield *(G-17459)*
Navistar Inc G 513 733-8500
Cincinnati *(G-4064)*
▲ Obs Inc F 330 453-3725
Canton *(G-2769)*
▲ Ogara Hess Eisenhardt G 513 346-1300
West Chester *(G-19751)*
Oshkosh Corporation G 513 745-9436
Cincinnati *(G-4121)*
P C Workshop Inc D 419 399-4805
Paulding *(G-15869)*
Paccar Inc A 740 774-5111
Chillicothe *(G-3205)*
Pittsburgh Glass Works LLC C 419 569-7521
Crestline *(G-7798)*
Progressive Automotive Inc G 740 862-4696
Baltimore *(G-1040)*
Protection Devices Inc G 210 399-2273
West Chester *(G-19770)*
▲ Reberland Equipment Inc F 330 698-5883
Apple Creek *(G-618)*
▲ Rikenkaki America Corporation G 614 336-2744
Dublin *(G-8974)*
Scottrods LLC G 419 499-2705
Monroeville *(G-14290)*
Star Fab Inc E 330 482-1601
Columbiana *(G-6482)*
Subaru of A G 614 793-2358
Dublin *(G-8998)*
◆ Sutphen Corporation C 800 726-7030
Dublin *(G-8999)*
Sutphen Corporation D 937 969-8851
Springfield *(G-17500)*
Svm America Ltd E 937 218-7591
Maineville *(G-12377)*
Tesla Inc G 614 532-5060
Columbus *(G-7521)*
Tesla Inc G 513 745-9111
Blue Ash *(G-1859)*
Thor Industries Inc E 937 596-6111
Jackson Center *(G-11217)*
Titan Bus LLC G 419 523-3593
Ottawa *(G-15669)*
Toledo Pro Fiberglass Inc G 419 241-9390
Toledo *(G-18567)*
United Fire Apparatus Corp G 419 645-4083
Cridersville *(G-7813)*
Universal Composite LLC E 614 507-1646
Sunbury *(G-17901)*
W&W Automotive & Towing Inc F 937 429-1699
Beavercreek Township *(G-1375)*
Warfighter Fcsed Logistics Inc G 740 513-4692
Galena *(G-10117)*
Weastec Incorporated E 614 734-9645
Dublin *(G-9011)*
Weiss Motors G 330 678-5585
Kent *(G-11399)*
Wyatt Specialties Inc G 614 989-5362
Circleville *(G-4565)*

3713 Truck & Bus Bodies

Able Industries Inc G 614 252-1050
Columbus *(G-6528)*
Ace Truck Equipment Co E 740 453-0551
Zanesville *(G-21091)*
◆ Airstream Inc B 937 596-6111
Jackson Center *(G-11205)*
Altec Industries Inc F 205 408-2341
Cuyahoga Falls *(G-7833)*
Alterntive Spport Appratus LLC G 740 922-2727
Midvale *(G-13973)*
Arts Rolloffs & Refuse Inc G 419 991-3730
Lima *(G-11843)*
▲ Atc Lighting & Plastics Inc C 440 466-7670
Andover *(G-580)*
Bores Manufacturing Co Inc F 419 465-2606
Monroeville *(G-14287)*
▼ Bosserman Automotive Engrg LLC G 419 722-2879
Findlay *(G-9660)*
▲ Brothers Body and Eqp LLC F 419 462-1975
Galion *(G-10124)*
Brown Industrial Inc E 937 693-3838
Botkins *(G-1934)*
Bush Specialty Vehicles Inc F 937 382-5502
Wilmington *(G-20487)*
Cascade Corporation C 937 327-0300
Springfield *(G-17370)*
▲ Cleveland Hdwr & Forging Co E 216 641-5200
Cleveland *(G-4962)*
Columbus McKinnon Corporation D 330 424-7248
Lisbon *(G-11965)*
Columbus Mobility Specialist G 614 825-8996
Worthington *(G-20681)*
▲ Cota International Inc F 937 526-5520
Versailles *(G-19177)*
Crosco G 330 477-1999
Canton *(G-2639)*
Dan Patrick Enterprises Inc G 740 477-1006
Circleville *(G-4542)*
Daniel Wagner G 740 942-2928
Cadiz *(G-2397)*
Elliott Machine Works Inc E 419 468-4709
Galion *(G-10137)*
▲ Ellis & Watts Intl LLC G 513 752-9000
Batavia *(G-1143)*
Field Gymmy Inc G 419 538-6511
Glandorf *(G-10269)*
Ford Motor Company A 440 933-1215
Avon Lake *(G-986)*
Friesen Transfer Ltd G 614 873-5672
Plain City *(G-16193)*
▲ Galion-Godwin Truck Bdy Co LLC D 330 359-5495
Millersburg *(G-14084)*
Gerich Fiberglass Inc E 419 362-4591
Mount Gilead *(G-14424)*
H & H Truck Parts LLC G 216 642-4540
Cleveland *(G-5362)*
Hendrickson International Corp D 740 929-5600
Hebron *(G-10747)*
▲ International Brake Inds Inc C 419 227-4421
Lima *(G-11879)*
Johns Body Shop G 419 358-1200
Bluffton *(G-1890)*
▲ Joseph Industries Inc D 330 528-0091
Streetsboro *(G-17680)*
◆ Kaffenbarger Truck Eqp Co C 937 845-3804
New Carlisle *(G-14669)*
Kaffenbarger Truck Eqp Co E 513 772-6800
Cincinnati *(G-3892)*
Kilar Manufacturing Inc E 330 534-8961
Hubbard *(G-11004)*
▲ Kimble Custom Chassis Company D 877 546-2537
New Philadelphia *(G-14778)*
▲ Kimble Mixer Company D 330 308-6700
New Philadelphia *(G-14779)*
▲ King Kutter II Inc E 740 446-0351
Gallipolis *(G-10169)*
Kruz Inc E 330 878-5595
Dover *(G-8835)*
Kuka Toledo Production C 419 727-5500
Toledo *(G-18372)*
La Boit Specialty Vehicles E 614 231-7640
Gahanna *(G-10088)*
▲ Leyman Manufacturing Corp D 513 891-6210
Cincinnati *(G-3939)*
Life Star Rescue Inc E 419 238-2507
Van Wert *(G-19101)*
Mancor Ohio Inc E 937 228-6141
Dayton *(G-8329)*
Mancor Ohio Inc D 937 228-6141
Dayton *(G-8330)*
Marengo Fabricated Steel Ltd F 800 919-2652
Marengo *(G-12593)*
Martin Sheet Metal Inc D 216 377-8200
Cleveland *(G-5627)*
McNeilus Truck and Mfg Inc G 614 868-0760
Gahanna *(G-10089)*
McNeilus Truck and Mfg Inc E 513 874-2022
Fairfield *(G-9528)*
Meritor Inc C 740 348-3498
Granville *(G-10333)*
Miller Industries Inc G 937 293-2223
Dayton *(G-8362)*
Neiss Body & Equipment Corp G 330 828-2409
Dalton *(G-7948)*
Paccar Inc A 740 774-5111
Chillicothe *(G-3205)*
Proform Group Inc E 614 332-9654
Columbus *(G-7354)*
Q T Columbus LLC G 800 758-2410
Columbus *(G-7359)*
▼ QT Equipment Company E 330 724-3055
Akron *(G-334)*
Radar Love Co F 419 951-4750
Findlay *(G-9744)*
▲ Reberland Equipment Inc F 330 698-5883
Apple Creek *(G-618)*
Rke Trucking Co F 614 891-1786
Westerville *(G-20021)*
Schodorf Truck Body & Eqp Co E 614 228-6793
Columbus *(G-7426)*
Silverado Trucks & Accessories G 937 492-8862
Sidney *(G-17080)*
▲ Tarpstop LLC E 419 873-7867
Perrysburg *(G-16009)*
▲ Tremcar USA Inc D 330 878-7708
Strasburg *(G-17654)*
Trim Systems Operating Corp C 614 289-5360
New Albany *(G-14639)*
Valco Industries Inc E 937 399-7400
Springfield *(G-17513)*
▲ Venco Venturo Industries LLC E 513 772-8448
Cincinnati *(G-4473)*
▲ Wallace Forge Company D 330 488-1203
Canton *(G-2863)*
Willard Machine & Welding Inc F 330 467-0642
Macedonia *(G-12338)*
Wilson Seat Company Inc E 513 732-2460
Batavia *(G-1197)*
Youngstown-Kenworth Inc E 330 534-9761
Hubbard *(G-11014)*
Zie Bart Rhino Linings Toledo G 419 841-2886
Toledo *(G-18606)*

3714 Motor Vehicle Parts & Access

1 A Lifesafer Hawaii Inc F 513 651-9560
Blue Ash *(G-1717)*
◆ 31 Inc D 740 498-8324
Newcomerstown *(G-14968)*
A & H Automotive Industries G 614 235-1759
Columbus *(G-6514)*
A G Parts Inc F 937 596-6448
Jackson Center *(G-11204)*
▲ Accel Performance Group LLC C 216 658-6413
Independence *(G-11117)*
Access 2 Communications Inc G 800 561-1110
Steubenville *(G-17525)*
▲ Ach LLC G 419 621-5748
Sandusky *(G-16791)*
▲ Ada Technologies Inc B 419 634-7000
Ada *(G-3)*
◆ Adelmans Truck Parts Corp E 330 456-0206
Canton *(G-2558)*
Adelmans Truck Parts Corp F 216 362-0500
Canton *(G-2559)*
Adient US LLC C 937 383-5200
Greenfield *(G-10345)*
Adient US LLC C 419 662-4950
Northwood *(G-15330)*
▲ Advics Manufacturing Ohio Inc A 513 932-7878
Lebanon *(G-11631)*
Aerotech Styling Inc G 419 923-6970
Lyons *(G-12272)*
◆ Airstream Inc B 937 596-6111
Jackson Center *(G-11205)*
Airtex Industries LLC G 330 899-0340
North Canton *(G-15068)*
Albright Radiator Inc G 330 264-8886
Wooster *(G-20561)*
Alegre Inc F 937 885-6786
Miamisburg *(G-13639)*
Alex Products Inc C 419 399-4500
Paulding *(G-15855)*
All Pro Alum Cylinder Heads G 740 967-7761
Johnstown *(G-11253)*
All Wright Enterprises LLC G 440 259-5656
Perry *(G-15903)*
Allied Separation Tech Inc E 704 736-0420
Twinsburg *(G-18732)*
Alta Mira Corporation D 330 648-2461
Spencer *(G-17303)*

AM General LLC......G...... 937 704-0160
Franklin *(G-9868)*
American Manufacturing & Eqp......G...... 513 829-2248
Fairfield *(G-9482)*
American Showa Inc......A...... 937 783-4961
Blanchester *(G-1698)*
AMP Electric Vehicles Inc......F...... 513 360-4704
Loveland *(G-12177)*
Amsoil Inc......G...... 614 274-9851
Columbus *(G-6593)*
Amsted Industries Incorporated......C...... 614 836-2323
Groveport *(G-10481)*
Angstrom Automotive Group LLC......G...... 440 255-6700
Mentor *(G-13387)*
Aptiv Services Us LLC......B...... 330 306-1000
Warren *(G-19372)*
Aptiv Services Us LLC......C...... 330 367-6000
Vienna *(G-19196)*
▲ **Areway LLC**......D...... 216 651-9022
Brooklyn *(G-2112)*
Arlington Rack & Packaging Co......G...... 419 476-7700
Toledo *(G-18191)*
▲ **ASC Holdco Inc**......G...... 330 899-0340
North Canton *(G-15069)*
◆ **ASC Industries Inc**......C...... 330 899-0340
North Canton *(G-15070)*
▲ **Atc Lighting & Plastics Inc**......C...... 440 466-7670
Andover *(G-580)*
Atlas Industries Inc......D...... 419 447-4730
Tiffin *(G-18047)*
Atlas Industries Inc......B...... 419 637-2117
Tiffin *(G-18046)*
Atwood Mobile Products LLC......E...... 419 258-5531
Antwerp *(G-597)*
Auria Fremont LLC......B...... 419 332-1587
Fremont *(G-9994)*
Auria Holmesville LLC......B...... 330 279-4505
Holmesville *(G-10973)*
Auria Sidney LLC......B...... 937 492-1225
Sidney *(G-17017)*
Auria Sidney LLC......E...... 937 492-1225
Sidney *(G-17018)*
Autoneum North America Inc......G...... 419 690-8924
Oregon *(G-15555)*
Autoneum North America Inc......B...... 419 693-0511
Oregon *(G-15556)*
Axle Surgeons of NW Ohio......G...... 419 822-5775
Delta *(G-8765)*
B A Malcuit Racing Inc......G...... 330 878-7111
Strasburg *(G-17645)*
B&C Machine Co LLC......B...... 330 745-4013
Barberton *(G-1058)*
Beach Manufacturing Co......C...... 937 882-6372
Donnelsville *(G-8800)*
Beasley Fiberglass Inc......G...... 440 357-6644
Painesville *(G-15719)*
Beast Carbon Corporation......G...... 800 909-9051
Cincinnati *(G-3384)*
Bellevue Manufacturing Company......D...... 419 483-3190
Bellevue *(G-1531)*
Bellevue Manufacturing Company......G...... 419 483-3190
Bellevue *(G-1532)*
▲ **Bendix Spcer Fndtion Brake LLC**......D...... 440 329-9709
Elyria *(G-9224)*
Bergstrom Company Ltd Partnr......E...... 440 232-2282
Cleveland *(G-4805)*
Bobbart Industries Inc......E...... 419 350-5477
Sylvania *(G-17934)*
Bores Manufacturing Co Inc......F...... 419 465-2606
Monroeville *(G-14287)*
Buckeye Brake Manufacturing......F...... 740 782-1379
Morristown *(G-14406)*
Buckley Manufacturing Company......F...... 513 821-4444
Cincinnati *(G-3429)*
▲ **Bucyrus Precision Tech Inc**......C...... 419 563-9950
Bucyrus *(G-2320)*
▲ **Buyers Products Company**......C...... 440 974-8888
Mentor *(G-13408)*
Buyers Products Company......G...... 440 974-8888
Mentor *(G-13410)*
Bwi Chassis Dynamics NA Inc......F...... 937 455-5100
Kettering *(G-11427)*
Bwi North America Inc......C...... 937 455-5190
Kettering *(G-11428)*
▲ **Bwi North America Inc**......E...... 937 253-1130
Kettering *(G-11429)*
Cadillac Products Inc......E...... 248 813-8255
Lebanon *(G-11639)*
▲ **Cardington Yutaka Tech Inc**......A...... 419 864-8777
Cardington *(G-2871)*
Carlisle Brake & Friction Inc......F...... 440 528-4000
Solon *(G-17123)*
Certified Power Inc......D...... 419 355-1200
Fremont *(G-10006)*
Chantilly Development Corp......F...... 419 243-8109
Toledo *(G-18227)*
▲ **Chestnut Holdings Inc**......G...... 330 849-6503
Akron *(G-114)*
Cincinnati Drveline Hydraulics......G...... 513 651-2406
Cincinnati *(G-3490)*
Cincinnati Gearing Systems Inc......C...... 513 527-8600
Cincinnati *(G-3496)*
Classic Exhaust......G...... 440 466-5460
Geneva *(G-10216)*
Classic Reproductions......G...... 937 548-9839
Greenville *(G-10364)*
▲ **Cleveland Ignition Co Inc**......G...... 440 439-3688
Cleveland *(G-4964)*
Commercial Vehicle Group Inc......A...... 614 289-5360
New Albany *(G-14615)*
Comprehensive Logistics Co Inc......E...... 440 934-3517
Avon *(G-945)*
Comprehensive Logistics Co Inc......E...... 330 793-0504
Youngstown *(G-20877)*
Connective Design Incorporated......F...... 937 746-8252
Miamisburg *(G-13651)*
Continental Strl Plas Inc......B...... 419 396-1980
Carey *(G-2880)*
Continental Strl Plas Inc......C...... 419 257-2231
North Baltimore *(G-15043)*
Continental Strl Plas Inc......B...... 419 238-4628
Van Wert *(G-19082)*
Cooper-Standard Automotive Inc......B...... 740 342-3523
New Lexington *(G-14714)*
Core Automotive Tech LLC......G...... 614 870-5000
Columbus *(G-6819)*
Cosma International Amer Inc......G...... 419 409-7350
Bowling Green *(G-1966)*
CR Laurence Co Inc......G...... 440 248-0003
Cleveland *(G-5036)*
Cummins Inc......G...... 614 604-6004
Grove City *(G-10424)*
▲ **Custer Products Limited**......F...... 330 490-3158
Massillon *(G-12972)*
Custom Cltch Jint Hydrlics Inc......F...... 216 431-1630
Cleveland *(G-5046)*
Custom Cltch Jint Hydrlics Inc......G...... 330 455-1202
Canton *(G-2642)*
Custom Fab......G...... 330 825-3586
Norton *(G-15364)*
Custom Speed Parts Inc......F...... 440 238-3260
Strongsville *(G-17735)*
▲ **D-Terra Solutions LLC**......G...... 614 450-1040
Powell *(G-16320)*
▼ **Dale Adams Enterprises Inc**......G...... 330 524-2800
Twinsburg *(G-18760)*
◆ **Dana Auto Systems Group LLC**......D...... 419 887-3000
Maumee *(G-13086)*
Dana Automotive Aftermarket......G...... 419 887-3000
Maumee *(G-13087)*
Dana Brazil Holdings I LLC......G...... 419 887-3000
Maumee *(G-13088)*
◆ **Dana Commercial Vhcl Mfg LLC**......G...... 419 887-3000
Maumee *(G-13089)*
◆ **Dana Commercial Vhcl Pdts LLC**......D...... 419 887-3000
Maumee *(G-13090)*
Dana Drive Shaft Pdts Group......G...... 419 227-2001
Lima *(G-11852)*
Dana Driveshaft Mfg LLC......C...... 419 222-9708
Lima *(G-11853)*
▲ **Dana Driveshaft Mfg LLC**......D...... 419 887-3000
Maumee *(G-13091)*
▲ **Dana Driveshaft Products LLC**......D...... 419 887-3000
Maumee *(G-13092)*
◆ **Dana Global Products Inc**......G...... 419 887-3000
Maumee *(G-13093)*
◆ **Dana Heavy Vehicle Systems**......G...... 419 887-3000
Maumee *(G-13094)*
Dana Incorporated......B...... 419 887-3000
Maumee *(G-13095)*
Dana Light Axle Mfg LLC......B...... 419 887-3000
Toledo *(G-18253)*
▲ **Dana Light Axle Mfg LLC**......F...... 419 887-3000
Maumee *(G-13096)*
Dana Limited......G...... 419 887-3000
Maumee *(G-13097)*
Dana Limited......D...... 419 482-2000
Maumee *(G-13098)*
▲ **Dana Limited**......B...... 419 887-3000
Maumee *(G-13099)*
Dana Off Highway Products LLC......E...... 614 864-1116
Blacklick *(G-1683)*
◆ **Dana Off Highway Products LLC**......E...... 419 887-3000
Maumee *(G-13100)*
▲ **Dana Sealing Manufacturing LLC**......D...... 419 887-3000
Maumee *(G-13101)*
▲ **Dana Sealing Products LLC**......E...... 419 887-3000
Maumee *(G-13102)*
Dana Structural Products LLC......G...... 419 887-3000
Maumee *(G-13103)*
▲ **Dana Thermal Products LLC**......E...... 419 887-3000
Maumee *(G-13104)*
Dana World Trade Corporation......G...... 419 887-3000
Maumee *(G-13105)*
David Boswell......E...... 614 441-2497
Columbus *(G-6852)*
Dayton Clutch & Joint Inc......F...... 937 236-9770
Dayton *(G-8130)*
Dayton Superior Pdts Co Inc......G...... 937 332-1930
Troy *(G-18646)*
▲ **Dayton Wheel Concepts Inc**......E...... 937 438-0100
Dayton *(G-8148)*
◆ **Dcm Manufacturing Inc**......E...... 216 265-8006
Cleveland *(G-5078)*
▲ **Denso Automotive Ohio**......G...... 614 336-1261
Dublin *(G-8906)*
Designed Harness Systems Inc......F...... 937 599-2485
Bellefontaine *(G-1512)*
Detroit Toledo Fiber LLC......F...... 248 647-0400
Toledo *(G-18261)*
▼ **Dexol Industries Inc**......G...... 330 633-4477
Akron *(G-140)*
Done Right Engine & Machine......G...... 440 582-1366
Cleveland *(G-5107)*
Doran Mfg LLC......F...... 513 681-5424
Cincinnati *(G-3601)*
Doug Marine Motors Inc......E...... 740 335-3700
Wshngtn CT Hs *(G-20724)*
Dove Machine Inc......F...... 440 864-2645
Columbia Station *(G-6437)*
Dove Manufacturing LLC......G...... 440 506-7935
Grafton *(G-10298)*
▲ **Dreison International Inc**......C...... 216 362-0755
Cleveland *(G-5113)*
Driveline 1 Inc......G...... 614 279-7734
Columbus *(G-6875)*
Dti Molded Products Inc......F...... 937 492-5008
Sidney *(G-17033)*
Eaton Corporation......B...... 440 523-5000
Beachwood *(G-1233)*
Eaton Corporation......C...... 216 281-2211
Cleveland *(G-5147)*
Eaton Corporation......B...... 216 523-5000
Beachwood *(G-1234)*
Eaton Corporation......B...... 216 920-2000
Cleveland *(G-5149)*
◆ **Eaton Corporation**......B...... 440 523-5000
Cleveland *(G-5146)*
Ebog Legacy Inc......D...... 330 239-4933
Sharon Center *(G-16949)*
Edgerton Forge Inc......E...... 419 298-2333
Edgerton *(G-9171)*
Egr Products Company Inc......F...... 330 833-6554
Dalton *(G-7941)*
Enhanced Mfg Solutions LLC......D...... 440 476-1244
Brecksville *(G-2034)*
Entratech Systems LLC......F...... 419 433-7683
Sandusky *(G-16809)*
▲ **Ernie Green Industries Inc**......G...... 614 219-1423
Columbus *(G-6903)*
Exito Manufacturing......G...... 937 291-9871
Beavercreek *(G-1355)*
▲ **F&P America Mfg Inc**......B...... 937 339-0212
Troy *(G-18655)*
Fabberge LLC......G...... 614 365-0056
Plain City *(G-16191)*
Falls Stamping & Welding Co......C...... 330 928-1191
Cuyahoga Falls *(G-7867)*
Farin Industries Inc......F...... 440 275-2755
Austinburg *(G-921)*
▲ **Faurecia Automotive Holdings**......A...... 419 727-5000
Toledo *(G-18288)*
▲ **Faurecia Emissions Control Sys**......C...... 812 341-2000
Toledo *(G-18289)*
Faurecia Exhaust Systems Inc......B...... 937 339-0551
Troy *(G-18656)*
Faurecia Exhaust Systems LLC......C...... 330 824-2807
Warren *(G-19402)*
Faurecia Exhaust Systems Inc......B...... 937 743-0551
Franklin *(G-9882)*

FCA US LLC....A....419 661-3500
Perrysburg (G-15949)
Federal-Mogul Powertrain LLC....C....740 432-2393
Cambridge (G-2437)
▲ Flaming River Industries Inc....F....440 826-4488
Berea (G-1608)
Flex N Gate....G....330 332-6363
Salem (G-16738)
Flex Technologies Inc....D....330 359-5415
Mount Eaton (G-14420)
Florence Alloys Inc....G....330 745-9141
Barberton (G-1071)
Florida Production Engrg Inc....D....937 996-4361
New Madison (G-14741)
▲ Force Control Industries Inc....D....513 868-0900
Fairfield (G-9498)
Ford Motor Company....A....419 226-7000
Lima (G-11864)
Ford Motor Company....A....216 676-7918
Brookpark (G-2147)
Forgeline Inc....F....937 299-0298
Moraine (G-14354)
Fram Group Operations LLC....G....937 316-3000
Greenville (G-10369)
Fram Group Operations LLC....A....419 436-5827
Fostoria (G-9845)
Fram Group Operations LLC....D....419 661-6700
Perrysburg (G-15953)
◆ Friction Products Co....B....330 725-4941
Medina (G-13265)
Frontier Tank Center Inc....E....330 659-3888
Richfield (G-16471)
▲ FT Precision Inc....A....740 694-1500
Fredericktown (G-9970)
Ftd Investments LLC....C....937 833-2161
Brookville (G-2169)
Ftech R&D North America Inc....D....937 339-2777
Troy (G-18659)
▲ G S Wiring Systems Inc....B....419 423-7111
Findlay (G-9691)
Gear Company of America Inc....D....216 671-5400
Cleveland (G-5298)
◆ Gear Star American Performance....G....330 434-5216
Akron (G-183)
Gellner Engineering Inc....G....216 398-8500
Cleveland (G-5301)
General Aluminum Mfg Company....C....419 739-9300
Wapakoneta (G-19330)
General Metals Powder Co....D....330 633-1226
Akron (G-186)
General Motors LLC....B....330 824-5840
Warren (G-19406)
General Motors LLC....A....216 265-5000
Cleveland (G-5312)
Gerich Fiberglass Inc....E....419 362-4591
Mount Gilead (G-14424)
GKN Driveline North Amer Inc....D....419 354-3955
Bowling Green (G-1974)
Goodale Auto-Truck Parts Inc....E....614 294-4777
Columbus (G-6962)
Goodrich Corporation....A....937 339-3811
Troy (G-18663)
▲ Grand-Rock Company Inc....E....440 639-2000
Painesville (G-15742)
Green Acquisition LLC....E....440 930-7600
Avon (G-951)
Green Rdced Emssons Netwrk LLC....G....330 340-0941
Strasburg (G-17648)
Green Tokai Co Ltd....G....937 237-1630
Dayton (G-8237)
◆ Green Tokai Co Ltd....A....937 833-5444
Brookville (G-2170)
Gregory Auto Service....G....513 248-0423
Loveland (G-12194)
▲ GSW Manufacturing Inc....B....419 423-7111
Findlay (G-9696)
Gt Motorsports....G....937 763-7272
Lynchburg (G-12271)
Gt Technologies Inc....C....419 782-8955
Defiance (G-8625)
Gt Technologies Inc....D....419 324-7300
Toledo (G-18314)
H O Fibertrends....G....740 983-3864
Ashville (G-818)
Hall-Toledo Inc....F....419 893-4334
Maumee (G-13114)
◆ Haltec Corporation....C....330 222-1501
Salem (G-16746)
Hanon Systems Usa LLC....C....313 920-0583
Carey (G-2882)

▲ Harco Manufacturing Group LLC....B....937 528-5000
Moraine (G-14359)
Harco Manufacturing Group LLC....C....937 528-5000
Moraine (G-14360)
Hdt Expeditionary Systems Inc....G....216 438-6111
Solon (G-17160)
Hebco Products Inc....A....419 562-7987
Bucyrus (G-2333)
Hendrickson International Corp....D....740 929-5600
Hebron (G-10747)
Hendrickson Usa LLC....C....330 456-7288
Canton (G-2696)
▲ Hfi LLC....B....614 491-0700
Columbus (G-6995)
▲ Hi-Tek Manufacturing Inc....C....513 459-1094
Mason (G-12886)
◆ Hirschvogel Incorporated....C....614 340-5657
Columbus (G-7002)
Hit & Miss Enterprises....G....440 272-5335
Orwell (G-15632)
Hite Parts Exchange Inc....E....614 272-5115
Columbus (G-7003)
Honda of America Mfg Inc....C....937 644-0724
Marysville (G-12792)
▲ Honda Transm Mfg Amer Inc....A....937 843-5555
Russells Point (G-16598)
Horizon Global Americas Inc....D....440 498-0001
Solon (G-17163)
Hot Shot Motor Works M LLC....G....419 294-1997
Upper Sandusky (G-18956)
Hp2g LLC....E....419 906-1525
Napoleon (G-14544)
▲ Hurst Auto-Truck Electric....G....216 961-1800
Cleveland (G-5426)
◆ Hytec Automotive Ind LLC....F....614 527-9370
Columbus (G-7014)
▲ Hytec-Debartolo LLC....F....614 527-9370
Columbus (G-7015)
▲ Ig Watteeuw Usa LLC....F....740 588-1722
Zanesville (G-21148)
Igw USA....G....740 588-1722
Zanesville (G-21149)
Illinois Tool Works Inc....C....513 489-7600
Blue Ash (G-1791)
Illinois Tool Works Inc....C....262 248-8277
Bryan (G-2289)
◆ Imasen Bucyrus Technology Inc....C....419 563-9590
Bucyrus (G-2336)
Industrial Steering Pdts Inc....G....419 636-3300
Bryan (G-2290)
▲ Industry Products Co....B....937 778-0585
Piqua (G-16130)
International Automotive Compo....A....419 335-1000
Wauseon (G-19522)
International Automotive Compo....A....419 433-5653
Huron (G-11099)
▲ International Brake Inds Inc....C....419 227-4421
Lima (G-11879)
◆ Interstate Diesel Service Inc....B....216 881-0015
Cleveland (G-5470)
Inteva Products LLC....F....937 280-8500
Vandalia (G-19129)
Ishikawa Gasket America Inc....C....419 353-7300
Bowling Green (G-1976)
Jae Tech Inc....D....330 698-2000
Apple Creek (G-608)
Johnson Power Ltd....G....419 866-6692
Holland (G-10939)
▼ Johnson Welded Products Inc....C....937 652-1242
Urbana (G-19001)
▲ Joseph Industries Inc....D....330 528-0091
Streetsboro (G-17680)
Josh L Derksen....G....937 548-0080
Greenville (G-10376)
◆ Jr Engineering Inc....C....330 848-0960
Barberton (G-1079)
▲ Julie Maynard Inc....F....937 443-0408
Dayton (G-8286)
K Wm Beach Mfg Co Inc....C....937 399-3838
Springfield (G-17429)
▲ Kalida Manufacturing Inc....C....419 532-2026
Kalida (G-11278)
Karg Fiberglass Inc....G....330 494-2611
Middlebranch (G-13758)
Kasai North America Inc....E....419 209-0470
Upper Sandusky (G-18958)
Kasai North America Inc....F....614 356-1494
Dublin (G-8936)
◆ Keihin Thermal Tech Amer Inc....B....740 869-3000
Mount Sterling (G-14462)

Kenley Enterprises LLC....E....419 630-0921
Bryan (G-2293)
Kerr Friction Products Inc....E....330 455-3983
Canton (G-2723)
Kilar Manufacturing Inc....E....330 534-8961
Hubbard (G-11004)
▲ Knippen Chrysler Dodge Jeep....E....419 695-4976
Delphos (G-8746)
Kongsberg Actuation Systems....F....440 639-8778
Grand River (G-10324)
▲ Kosei St Marys Corporation....A....419 394-7840
Saint Marys (G-16688)
▲ Kth Parts Industries Inc....A....937 663-5941
Saint Paris (G-16709)
Ktri Holdings Inc....G....216 371-1700
Cleveland (G-5546)
Ktsdi LLC....G....330 783-2000
North Lima (G-15173)
Kurts Auto Parts LLC....G....330 723-0166
Medina (G-13286)
▲ Lacal Equipment Inc....E....800 543-6161
Jackson Center (G-11210)
Lakota Racing....G....330 627-7255
Carrollton (G-2923)
▲ Lawrence Technologies Inc....G....937 274-7771
Dayton (G-8308)
▲ Leadec Corp....E....513 731-3590
Blue Ash (G-1804)
▼ Lear Corp....G....614 850-8630
Columbus (G-7118)
Lear Corporation....E....740 928-4358
Hebron (G-10750)
Lear Corporation....C....419 335-6010
Wauseon (G-19526)
Lear Corporation....F....614 850-8630
Columbus (G-7119)
Leggett & Platt Incorporated....G....330 262-6010
Apple Creek (G-611)
Liberty Outdoors LLC....F....330 791-3149
Uniontown (G-18925)
▲ Linde Hydraulics Corporation....E....330 533-6801
Canfield (G-2532)
◆ Lintern Corporation....E....440 255-9333
Mentor (G-13501)
Lorain County Auto Systems Inc....D....248 442-6800
Lorain (G-12101)
▲ Lorain County Auto Systems Inc....E....440 960-7470
Lorain (G-12102)
▲ Luk Clutch Systems LLC....E....330 264-4383
Wooster (G-20617)
Lynn Truck Parts & Service....G....330 966-1470
North Canton (G-15100)
M-Tek Inc....A....419 209-0399
Upper Sandusky (G-18961)
Maags Automotive & Machine....G....419 626-1539
Sandusky (G-16824)
▲ Magna Modular Systems LLC....D....419 324-3387
Toledo (G-18395)
Magna Seating America Inc....C....330 824-3101
Warren (G-19420)
Magnaco Industries Inc....E....216 961-3636
Lodi (G-12016)
Mahle Behr Dayton LLC....B....937 356-2001
Vandalia (G-19134)
Mahle Behr Dayton LLC....B....937 369-2900
Dayton (G-8324)
◆ Mahle Behr Dayton LLC....D....937 369-2900
Dayton (G-8325)
Mahle Behr Service America LLC....G....937 369-2610
Xenia (G-20783)
Mahle Behr USA Inc....G....937 369-2900
Dayton (G-8326)
Mahle Behr USA Inc....C....937 356-2001
Vandalia (G-19135)
Mahle Industries Incorporated....E....937 890-2739
Dayton (G-8328)
Mahle Industries Incorporated....C....740 962-2040
McConnelsville (G-13207)
Majestic Trailers Inc....F....330 798-1698
Akron (G-265)
Marion Industries Inc....A....740 223-0075
Marion (G-12718)
Marmon Highway Tech LLC....E....330 878-5595
Dover (G-8839)
▲ Martin Wheel Co Inc....D....330 633-3278
Tallmadge (G-17992)
Matrix Cable and Mould....G....513 832-2577
Cincinnati (G-3987)
▲ Maval Industries LLC....C....330 405-1600
Twinsburg (G-18813)

SIC

Employee Codes: A=Over 500 employees, B=251-500
C=101-250, D=51-100, E=20-50, F=10-19, G=3-9
2019 Harris Ohio
Industrial Directory
997

▲ **Maxion Wheels Akron LLC** ...E ... 330 794-2310
Akron *(G-272)*
Maxion Wheels Sedalia LLC ...G ... 330 794-2300
Akron *(G-273)*
Meritor Inc ...C ... 740 348-3498
Granville *(G-10333)*
Metro Mech Inc ...G ... 216 641-6262
Cleveland *(G-5662)*
◆ **Mid-West Fabricating Co** ...C ... 740 969-4411
Amanda *(G-526)*
Mid-West Fabricating Co ...G ... 740 681-4411
Lancaster *(G-11588)*
Millat Industries Corp ...E ... 937 535-1500
Dayton *(G-8361)*
▲ **Millat Industries Corp** ...D ... 937 434-6666
Dayton *(G-8360)*
▲ **Mitec Powertrain Inc** ...E ... 567 525-5606
Findlay *(G-9727)*
◆ **Mitsubishi Elc Auto Amer Inc** ...B ... 513 573-6614
Mason *(G-12911)*
Mrs Electronic Inc ...F ... 937 660-6767
Dayton *(G-8371)*
Mueller Gas Products ...D ... 513 424-5311
Middletown *(G-13933)*
Multi-Design Inc ...G ... 440 275-2255
Austinburg *(G-923)*
Navistar Inc ...D ... 937 390-5653
Springfield *(G-17457)*
Navistar Inc ...E ... 937 390-5704
Springfield *(G-17459)*
▲ **Neaton Auto Products Mfg Inc** ...B ... 937 456-7103
Eaton *(G-9162)*
Nebraska Industries Corp ...E ... 419 335-6010
Wauseon *(G-19529)*
▲ **New Sabina Industries Inc** ...C ... 937 584-2433
Sabina *(G-16616)*
▲ **Newman Technology Inc** ...C ... 419 525-1856
Mansfield *(G-12490)*
Nippon Stl Smkin Crnkshaft LLC ...F ... 419 435-0411
Fostoria *(G-9852)*
▲ **Nissin Brake Ohio Inc** ...A ... 419 420-3800
Findlay *(G-9731)*
Nissin Brake Ohio Inc ...E ... 937 642-7556
East Liberty *(G-9049)*
◆ **Noco Company** ...B ... 216 464-8131
Solon *(G-17208)*
▼ **Norlake Manufacturing Company** ...D ... 440 353-3200
North Ridgeville *(G-15241)*
▲ **Norplas Industries Inc** ...B ... 419 662-3317
Northwood *(G-15341)*
North Coast Camshaft Inc ...G ... 216 671-3700
Cleveland *(G-5761)*
North Coast Exotics Inc ...G ... 216 651-5512
Cleveland *(G-5765)*
Northern Stamping Co ...C ... 216 642-8081
Cleveland *(G-5784)*
Norton Manufacturing Co Inc ...F ... 419 435-0411
Fostoria *(G-9853)*
Oakley Industries Sub Assembly ...E ... 419 661-8888
Northwood *(G-15342)*
Oe Exchange LLC ...G ... 440 266-1639
Mentor *(G-13532)*
◆ **Oerlikon Friction Systems** ...C ... 937 449-4000
Dayton *(G-8394)*
Ohio Auto Supply Company ...E ... 330 454-5105
Canton *(G-2771)*
▲ **Ohio Classic Street Rods Inc** ...G ... 440 543-6593
Streetsboro *(G-17686)*
▲ **Ohta Press US Inc** ...F ... 937 374-3382
Xenia *(G-20785)*
▲ **Omsi Transmissions Inc** ...G ... 330 405-7350
Twinsburg *(G-18826)*
Onix Corporation ...E ... 800 844-0076
Perrysburg *(G-15991)*
OReilly Equipment LLC ...G ... 440 564-1234
Newbury *(G-14961)*
◆ **Pacific Industries USA Inc** ...E ... 513 860-3900
Fairfield *(G-9541)*
▲ **Pacific Manufacturing Ohio Inc** ...B ... 513 860-3900
Fairfield *(G-9542)*
▲ **Pako Inc** ...C ... 440 946-8030
Mentor *(G-13540)*
Park-Ohio Industries Inc ...C ... 216 341-2300
Newburgh Heights *(G-14942)*
Parker-Hannifin Corporation ...B ... 440 943-5700
Wickliffe *(G-20224)*
Parker-Hannifin Corporation ...A ... 216 531-3000
Cleveland *(G-5849)*
▲ **Pdi Ground Support Systems Inc** ...D ... 216 271-7344
Solon *(G-17214)*

▲ **Pioneer Automotive Tech Inc** ...C ... 937 746-2293
Springboro *(G-17344)*
Piston Automotive LLC ...D ... 419 464-0250
Toledo *(G-18471)*
▲ **Powers and Sons LLC** ...C ... 419 485-3151
Montpelier *(G-14314)*
Powers and Sons LLC ...D ... 419 737-2373
Pioneer *(G-16091)*
Production Turning LLC ...G ... 937 424-0034
Moraine *(G-14386)*
Ptt Legacy Inc ...D ... 330 239-4933
Sharon Center *(G-16952)*
Pullman Company ...C ... 419 592-2055
Napoleon *(G-14556)*
Pullman Company ...E ... 419 499-2541
Milan *(G-13987)*
▲ **Qualitor Inc** ...G ... 248 204-8600
Lima *(G-11924)*
Quality Reproductions Inc ...G ... 330 335-5000
Wadsworth *(G-19269)*
Race Winning Brands Inc ...B ... 440 951-6600
Mentor *(G-13572)*
Radar Love Co ...F ... 419 951-4750
Findlay *(G-9744)*
▲ **Ramco Specialties Inc** ...C ... 330 653-5135
Hudson *(G-11069)*
▲ **Reactive Resin Products Co** ...E ... 419 666-6119
Perrysburg *(G-16003)*
Reineke Company LLC ...F ... 419 281-5800
Ashland *(G-743)*
Resinoid Engineering Corp ...E ... 740 928-2220
Heath *(G-10730)*
Reynolds Engineered Pdts LLC ...G ... 513 751-4400
Cincinnati *(G-4263)*
▼ **Riker Products Inc** ...C ... 419 729-1626
Toledo *(G-18501)*
Riverside Engines Inc ...G ... 419 927-6838
Tiffin *(G-18077)*
Rochling Automotive USA LLP ...D ... 330 400-5785
Akron *(G-352)*
▲ **Roki America Co Ltd** ...B ... 419 424-9713
Findlay *(G-9747)*
Rubberduck 4x4 ...G ... 513 889-1735
Hamilton *(G-10601)*
▼ **S & A Precision Bearing Inc** ...G ... 440 930-7600
Avon *(G-965)*
Saf-Holland Inc ...G ... 513 874-7888
West Chester *(G-19896)*
Safe Auto Systems LLC ...G ... 216 661-1166
Carroll *(G-2910)*
▲ **Saia-Burgess Lcc** ...D ... 937 898-3621
Vandalia *(G-19144)*
Sanoh America Inc ...C ... 740 392-9200
Mount Vernon *(G-14505)*
▲ **Satco Inc** ...G ... 330 630-8866
Tallmadge *(G-18002)*
◆ **Schaeffler Transm Systems LLC** ...A ... 330 264-4383
Wooster *(G-20649)*
◆ **Schaeffler Transmission LLC** ...C ... 330 264-4383
Wooster *(G-20650)*
Schafer Driveline LLC ...G ... 614 864-1116
Blacklick *(G-1694)*
◆ **Schafer Driveline LLC** ...D ... 740 694-2055
Fredericktown *(G-9977)*
Schott Metal Products Company ...D ... 330 773-7873
Akron *(G-373)*
Scs Gearbox Inc ...F ... 419 483-7278
Bellevue *(G-1543)*
▲ **Seabiscuit Motorsports Inc** ...B ... 440 951-6600
Mentor *(G-13577)*
Senneco Glass Inc ...G ... 330 825-7717
Cuyahoga Falls *(G-7915)*
Sew-Eurodrive Inc ...D ... 937 335-0036
Troy *(G-18705)*
Sfs Group Usa Inc ...C ... 330 239-7100
Medina *(G-13339)*
◆ **Showa Aluminum Corp America** ...G ... 740 895-6422
Wshngtn CT Hs *(G-20744)*
SMH Manufacturing Inc ...F ... 419 884-0071
Lexington *(G-11806)*
Soundwich Inc ...D ... 216 486-2666
Cleveland *(G-6080)*
Spectrum Brands Inc ...F ... 440 357-2600
Painesville *(G-15783)*
Spencer Manufacturing Company ...D ... 330 648-2461
Spencer *(G-17306)*
SPS International Inc ...G ... 216 671-9911
Strongsville *(G-17793)*
Std Specialty Filters Inc ...F ... 216 881-3727
Cleveland *(G-6101)*

▲ **Steck Manufacturing Co Inc** ...F ... 937 222-0062
Dayton *(G-8527)*
Steer & Gear Inc ...E ... 614 231-4064
Columbus *(G-7489)*
Stemco Air Springs ...E ... 234 466-7200
Fairlawn *(G-9620)*
Stoneridge Inc ...A ... 419 884-1219
Lexington *(G-11807)*
▲ **Sumiriko Ohio Inc** ...C ... 419 358-2121
Bluffton *(G-1893)*
Sumitomo Elc Wirg Systems Inc ...E ... 937 642-7579
Marysville *(G-12816)*
Supercharger Systems Inc ...G ... 216 676-5800
Brookpark *(G-2156)*
▼ **Superior Energy Systems LLC** ...F ... 440 236-6009
Columbia Station *(G-6449)*
▲ **Supertrapp Industries Inc** ...D ... 216 265-8400
Cleveland *(G-6129)*
Sutphen Corporation ...D ... 937 969-8851
Springfield *(G-17500)*
▲ **Switzer Performance Engrg** ...F ... 440 774-4219
Oberlin *(G-15505)*
Systems Jay LLC Nanogate ...C ... 419 522-7745
Mansfield *(G-12525)*
▲ **Taiho Corporation of America** ...C ... 419 443-1645
Tiffin *(G-18086)*
Tenneco Automotive Oper Co Inc ...D ... 937 781-4940
Kettering *(G-11442)*
Tetra Mold & Tool Inc ...E ... 937 845-1651
New Carlisle *(G-14679)*
▲ **Tfo Tech Co Ltd** ...C ... 740 426-6381
Jeffersonville *(G-11248)*
◆ **Thyssenkrupp Bilstein Amer Inc** ...C ... 513 881-7600
Hamilton *(G-10610)*
Thyssenkrupp Bilstein Amer Inc ...E ... 513 881-7600
West Chester *(G-19809)*
TI Group Auto Systems LLC ...C ... 740 929-2049
Hebron *(G-10767)*
▲ **Tigerpoly Manufacturing Inc** ...B ... 614 871-0045
Grove City *(G-10473)*
Tko Mfg Services Inc ...E ... 937 299-1637
Moraine *(G-14399)*
Toledo Molding & Die Inc ...C ... 419 692-6022
Delphos *(G-8756)*
Toledo Molding & Die Inc ...D ... 419 692-6022
Delphos *(G-8757)*
Toledo Pro Fiberglass Inc ...G ... 419 241-9390
Toledo *(G-18567)*
▲ **Tom Smith Industries Inc** ...C ... 937 832-1555
Englewood *(G-9378)*
▲ **Trailer Component Mfg Inc** ...E ... 440 255-2888
Mentor *(G-13612)*
Tramec Sloan LLC ...F ... 419 468-9122
Galion *(G-10158)*
Tri-Mac Mfg & Svcs Co ...F ... 513 896-4445
Hamilton *(G-10613)*
▲ **Trim Parts Inc** ...E ... 513 934-0815
Lebanon *(G-11702)*
▲ **Trim Systems Operating Corp** ...D ... 614 289-5360
New Albany *(G-14638)*
Trojon Gear Inc ...F ... 937 254-1737
Dayton *(G-8568)*
TRW Automotive Inc ...C ... 419 237-2511
Fayette *(G-9637)*
TRW Automotive Inc ...E ... 216 750-2400
Cleveland *(G-6220)*
▲ **TS Tech USA Corporation** ...C ... 614 577-1088
Reynoldsburg *(G-16458)*
TS Trim Industries Inc ...B ... 740 593-5958
Athens *(G-852)*
Ugn Inc ...C ... 513 360-3500
Lebanon *(G-11704)*
▲ **Undercar Express LLC** ...E ... 216 531-7004
Cleveland *(G-6229)*
Unique-Chardan Inc ...E ... 419 636-6900
Bryan *(G-2311)*
Unison Industries LLC ...B ... 904 667-9904
Dayton *(G-7994)*
◆ **United Components LLC** ...E ... 812 867-4516
North Canton *(G-15133)*
US Tsubaki Power Transm LLC ...C ... 419 626-4560
Sandusky *(G-16860)*
Usui International Corporation ...C ... 513 448-0410
Sharonville *(G-16960)*
Usui International Corporation ...D ... 734 354-3626
West Chester *(G-19817)*
Utv Hitchworks LLC ...G ... 513 615-8568
Maineville *(G-12378)*
Vanderpool Motor Sports ...G ... 513 424-2166
Middletown *(G-13963)*

▼ Varbros LLC C 216 267-5200
Cleveland *(G-6250)*

▲ Vari-Wall Tube Specialists Inc D 330 482-0000
Columbiana *(G-6485)*

Vehicle Systems Inc G 330 854-0535
Massillon *(G-13056)*

▲ Venco Manufacturing Inc D 513 772-8448
Cincinnati *(G-4472)*

▲ Venco Venturo Industries LLC E 513 772-8448
Cincinnati *(G-4473)*

▲ Ventra Sandusky LLC C 419 627-3600
Sandusky *(G-16861)*

Veoneer Nissin Brake B 419 425-6725
Findlay *(G-9773)*

Visible Solutions Inc G 440 925-2810
Westlake *(G-20168)*

Vivid Wraps LLC G 513 515-8386
Cincinnati *(G-4482)*

W W Williams Company LLC F 330 659-3084
Richfield *(G-16494)*

Walther Engrg & Mfg Co Inc E 937 743-8125
Franklin *(G-9931)*

Warfighter Fcsed Logistics Inc G 740 513-4692
Galena *(G-10117)*

Weastec Incorporated C 937 393-6800
Hillsboro *(G-10893)*

▲ Weastec Incorporated C 937 393-6800
Hillsboro *(G-10894)*

West & Barker Inc E 330 652-9923
Niles *(G-15040)*

Western Branch Diesel Inc E 330 454-8800
Canton *(G-2864)*

Westfield Steel Inc D 937 322-2414
Springfield *(G-17516)*

Wheel Group Holdings LLC G 614 253-6247
Columbus *(G-7602)*

▲ Whirlaway Corporation C 440 647-4711
Wellington *(G-19595)*

Whirlaway Corporation C 440 647-4711
Wellington *(G-19596)*

Whirlaway Corporation E 440 647-4711
Wellington *(G-19597)*

White Mule Company E 740 382-9008
Ontario *(G-15550)*

Woodbridge Group C 419 334-3666
Fremont *(G-10064)*

Workhorse Group Inc D 513 297-3640
Loveland *(G-12245)*

▲ Yachiyo of America Inc C 614 876-3220
Columbus *(G-7620)*

▲ Yamada North America Inc B 937 462-7111
South Charleston *(G-17275)*

3715 Truck Trailers

4w Services F 614 554-5427
Hebron *(G-10736)*

▼ All A Cart Manufacturing Inc F 614 443-5544
Worthington *(G-20675)*

American Mnfcturing Operations G 419 269-1560
Toledo *(G-18176)*

Bair Bodies & Trailers Inc G 330 343-4853
Dover *(G-8806)*

Bell Logistics Co E 740 702-9830
Chillicothe *(G-3177)*

Brothers Equipment Inc G 216 458-0180
Cleveland *(G-4843)*

Bruce High Performance Tran E 440 357-8964
Painesville *(G-15720)*

David Ogilbee G 740 929-2638
Hebron *(G-10741)*

Diamond Trailers Inc E 513 738-4500
Shandon *(G-16941)*

Ds Express Carriers Inc G 419 433-6200
Norwalk *(G-15388)*

▼ East Manufacturing Corporation B 330 325-9921
Randolph *(G-16360)*

East Manufacturing Corporation F 330 325-9921
Randolph *(G-16361)*

Engineered MBL Solutions Inc F 513 724-0247
Batavia *(G-1144)*

Extreme Trailers LLC G 330 440-0026
Dover *(G-8825)*

Gerich Fiberglass Inc E 419 362-4591
Mount Gilead *(G-14424)*

Great Dane LLC E 614 876-0666
Hilliard *(G-10826)*

H & H Equipment Inc G 330 264-5400
Wooster *(G-20601)*

Haulette Manufacturing Inc D 419 586-1717
Celina *(G-2966)*

Heritage Manufacturing Inc G 217 854-2513
Akron *(G-206)*

High Tech Prfmce Trlrs Inc D 440 357-8964
Painesville *(G-15746)*

J & L Body Inc F 216 661-2323
Brooklyn Heights *(G-2126)*

J W Devers & Son Inc F 937 854-3040
Trotwood *(G-18628)*

Jerry Tadlock G 937 544-2851
West Union *(G-19963)*

Jsm Express Inc G 216 331-2008
Euclid *(G-9423)*

Kenan Advantage Group Inc E 614 878-4050
Columbus *(G-7085)*

L C Smith Co G 440 327-1251
Elyria *(G-9283)*

Larry Moore G 740 697-7085
Roseville *(G-16578)*

Longriders Trucking Company G 740 975-7863
Mount Vernon *(G-14489)*

Lyons G 440 224-0676
Kingsville *(G-11460)*

M & W Trailers Inc F 419 453-3331
Ottoville *(G-15682)*

▲ Mac Manufacturing Inc A 330 823-9900
Alliance *(G-483)*

Mac Manufacturing Inc C 330 829-1680
Salem *(G-16759)*

Mac Steel Trailer Ltd E 330 823-9900
Alliance *(G-484)*

▲ Mac Trailer Manufacturing Inc C 330 823-9900
Alliance *(G-485)*

Mac Trailer Service Inc E 330 823-9190
Alliance *(G-486)*

Majestic Trailers Inc F 330 798-1698
Akron *(G-265)*

Martin Allen Trailer LLC G 330 942-0217
Brunswick *(G-2220)*

Moritz International Inc E 419 526-5222
Mansfield *(G-12487)*

Mr Trailer Sales Inc G 330 339-7701
New Philadelphia *(G-14789)*

Navarre Trailer Sales Inc G 330 879-2406
Navarre *(G-14583)*

▼ Nelson Manufacturing Company D 419 523-5321
Ottawa *(G-15660)*

Paccar Inc A 740 774-5111
Chillicothe *(G-3205)*

▲ Pdi Ground Support Systems Inc D 216 271-7344
Solon *(G-17214)*

Pegasus Vans & Trailers Inc E 419 625-8953
Sandusky *(G-16837)*

▲ Quick Loadz Delivery Sys LLC E 888 304-3946
Nelsonville *(G-14594)*

R J Cox Co G 937 548-4699
Arcanum *(G-631)*

Rock Line Products Inc G 419 738-4400
Wapakoneta *(G-19349)*

Saf-Holland Inc G 513 874-7888
West Chester *(G-19896)*

Shilling Transport G 330 948-1105
Lodi *(G-12019)*

Stahl/Scott Fetzer Company C 419 864-8045
Cardington *(G-2876)*

Stahl/Scott Fetzer Company C 800 277-8245
Wooster *(G-20658)*

▼ Trailer One Inc F 330 723-7474
Medina *(G-13354)*

▼ Trailex Inc F 330 533-6814
Canfield *(G-2551)*

Tri County Wheel and Rim Ltd G 419 666-1760
Northwood *(G-15348)*

Wabash National Corporation D 419 434-9409
Findlay *(G-9774)*

3716 Motor Homes

Advanced Rv LLC G 440 283-0405
Willoughby *(G-20267)*

◆ Airstream Inc B 937 596-6111
Jackson Center *(G-11205)*

3721 Aircraft

Aero Composites Inc G 937 849-0244
Medway *(G-13365)*

Air One Jet Center G 513 867-9500
Hamilton *(G-10530)*

Boeing Company F 937 427-1767
Fairborn *(G-9453)*

Boeing Company A 740 788-5805
Newark *(G-14855)*

Boeing Company B 937 431-3503
Wright Patterson Afb *(G-20717)*

Carlson Aircraft Inc G 330 426-3934
East Palestine *(G-9070)*

E Star Aerospace Corporation G 614 396-6868
Westerville *(G-19989)*

Edward S Eveland G 937 233-6568
Dayton *(G-8178)*

Executive Wings Inc G 440 254-1812
Painesville *(G-15736)*

Flightlogix LLC G 513 321-1200
Cincinnati *(G-3694)*

Goodrich Corporation A 937 339-3811
Troy *(G-18663)*

Hexacrafter Ltd G 330 929-0989
Cuyahoga Falls *(G-7879)*

Hyfast Aerospace LLC G 216 712-4158
Parma *(G-15823)*

Lockheed Martin Corporation B 330 796-2800
Akron *(G-256)*

Nextant Aerospace Holdings LLC D 216 261-9000
Cleveland *(G-5752)*

Ruhe Sales Inc F 419 943-3357
Leipsic *(G-11736)*

Sea Air Spc McG and Mld LLC F 440 248-3025
Streetsboro *(G-17695)*

Sky Riders Inc G 440 310-6819
Lorain *(G-12121)*

Snow Aviation Intl Inc C 614 588-2452
Gahanna *(G-10105)*

Star Jet LLC F 614 338-4379
Columbus *(G-7485)*

Stark Airways G 330 526-6416
North Canton *(G-15121)*

Steel Aviation Aircraft Sales G 937 332-7587
Casstown *(G-2934)*

Summit Aerospace Products G 330 612-7341
Northfield *(G-15327)*

Tdc Systems Inc G 440 953-5918
Willoughby *(G-20442)*

Tessec LLC E 937 985-3552
Dayton *(G-8552)*

Tessec Manufacturing Svcs LLC E 937 985-3552
Dayton *(G-8553)*

Textron Inc F 330 626-7800
Streetsboro *(G-17703)*

Theiss Uav Solutions LLC G 330 584-2070
North Benton *(G-15062)*

Toledo Jet Center LLC F 419 866-9050
Swanton *(G-17924)*

Tri-State Model Flyers Inc D 740 886-8429
Proctorville *(G-16347)*

Unmanned Solutions Tech LLC G 937 771-7023
Beavercreek *(G-1366)*

Wanashab Inc G 330 606-6675
Cleveland *(G-6288)*

3724 Aircraft Engines & Engine Parts

Advanced Ground Systems F 513 402-7226
Cincinnati *(G-3300)*

Aero Jet Wash Llc F 866 381-7955
West Carrollton *(G-19628)*

Aerospace Co Inc D 413 998-1637
Cleveland *(G-4635)*

American Aero Components LLC G 937 367-5068
Dayton *(G-8022)*

At Holdings Corporation A 216 692-6000
Cleveland *(G-4755)*

Avion Tool Corporation F 937 278-0779
Dayton *(G-8046)*

Barnes Group Inc A 513 759-3528
West Chester *(G-19655)*

Barnes Group Inc A 513 779-6888
West Chester *(G-19656)*

Certech Inc G 330 405-1033
Twinsburg *(G-18750)*

CFM International Inc D 513 552-2787
West Chester *(G-19667)*

CFM International Inc E 513 563-4180
Cincinnati *(G-3460)*

Challenger Aviation Products G 937 387-6500
Vandalia *(G-19119)*

Eaton Industrial Corporation B 216 523-4205
Cleveland *(G-5152)*

Enginetics Corporation C 937 878-3800
Huber Heights *(G-11017)*

▲ Ferrotherm Corporation C 216 883-9350
Cleveland *(G-5233)*

GE Aircraft Engines E 513 243-2000
Cincinnati *(G-3731)*

SIC

Employee Codes: A=Over 500 employees, B=251-500
C=101-250, D=51-100, E=20-50, F=10-19, G=3-9

2019 Harris Ohio
Industrial Directory

999

37 TRANSPORTATION EQUIPMENT

GE Aviation Systems LLC .... B 937 898-5881
  Vandalia *(G-19124)*
GE Aviation Systems LLC .... C 513 977-1500
  Cincinnati *(G-3733)*
GE Military Systems .... A 513 243-2000
  Cincinnati *(G-3738)*
General Electric Company 513 948-4170
  Cincinnati *(G-3742)*
General Electric Company .... G 513 552-5364
  West Chester *(G-19713)*
General Electric Company .... A 513 552-2000
  Cincinnati *(G-3743)*
▲ Henry Tools Inc 216 291-1011
  Cleveland *(G-5395)*
▲ Hi-Tek Manufacturing Inc 513 459-1094
  Mason *(G-12886)*
Honeywell .... G 614 850-8228
  Columbus *(G-7005)*
Honeywell Automation Control .... F 937 264-2662
  Urbana *(G-18994)*
Honeywell International Inc .... A 216 459-6048
  Independence *(G-11135)*
Honeywell International Inc 440 349-7330
  Solon *(G-17162)*
Lsp Technologies Inc .... E 614 718-3000
  Dublin *(G-8944)*
Magellan Arospc Middletown Inc ..... D 513 422-2751
  Middletown *(G-13923)*
Meak Solutions Llc .... G 440 796-8209
  Mentor *(G-13513)*
Metro Mech Inc .... G 216 641-6262
  Cleveland *(G-5662)*
◆ Meyer Tool Inc .... A 513 681-7362
  Cincinnati *(G-4020)*
Otto Konigslow Mfg Co .... F 216 851-7900
  Cleveland *(G-5826)*
Parker Aircraft Sales .... G 937 833-4820
  Brookville *(G-2180)*
Parker-Hannifin Corporation .... C 440 284-6277
  Elyria *(G-9309)*
Pas Technologies Inc .... D 937 840-1000
  Hillsboro *(G-10889)*
PCC Airfoils LLC .... C 440 255-9770
  Mentor *(G-13545)*
Polycraft Products Inc .... G 513 353-3334
  Cleves *(G-6373)*
Scis Aerospace LLC .... G 216 533-8533
  Medina *(G-13336)*
◆ Sifco Industries Inc .... B 216 881-8600
  Cleveland *(G-6063)*
Snow Aviation Intl Inc .... C 614 588-2452
  Gahanna *(G-10105)*
Spirit Avionics Ltd .... F 614 237-4271
  Columbus *(G-7477)*
Stofiel Aerospace LLC .... G 216 389-0084
  Cleveland *(G-6106)*
Trojon Gear Inc .... F 937 254-1737
  Dayton *(G-8568)*
Turbine Eng Cmpnents Tech Corp .... E 216 692-6173
  Cleveland *(G-6222)*
▲ Turbine Standard Ltd .... F 419 865-0355
  Holland *(G-10964)*
US Aeroteam Inc .... E 937 458-0344
  Dayton *(G-8577)*
Warfighter Fcsed Logistics Inc .... G 740 513-4692
  Galena *(G-10117)*
▲ Welded Ring Products Co .... D 216 961-3800
  Cleveland *(G-6298)*

3728 Aircraft Parts & Eqpt, NEC

8888 Butler Investments Inc .... G 440 748-0810
  North Ridgeville *(G-15205)*
Ace Products Co of Toledo Inc .... G 419 472-1247
  Toledo *(G-18155)*
Achilles Aerospace Pdts Inc .... E 330 425-8444
  Twinsburg *(G-18725)*
▼ Advanced Fuel Systems Inc .... G 614 252-8422
  Columbus *(G-6545)*
Aero Tube & Connector Company .... G 614 885-2514
  Worthington *(G-20673)*
Aerocontrolex Group Inc .... D 440 352-6182
  Painesville *(G-15707)*
Aeroquip-Vickers Inc .... G 216 523-5000
  Cleveland *(G-4633)*
▲ Aerospace Maint Solutions LLC ... E 440 729-7703
  Chesterland *(G-3150)*
Air Force US Dept of .... G 937 245-1962
  Wright Patterson Afb *(G-20716)*
▲ Airtug LLC .... G 440 829-2167
  Avon *(G-940)*
Airwolf Aerospace LLC .... G 440 632-1687
  Middlefield *(G-13774)*
Allen Aircraft Products Inc .... E 330 296-9621
  Ravenna *(G-16365)*
American Aero Components LLC ..... G 937 367-5068
  Dayton *(G-8022)*
At Holdings Corporation .... A 216 692-6000
  Cleveland *(G-4755)*
Aviation Cmpnent Solutions Inc .... F 440 295-6590
  Richmond Heights *(G-16501)*
Aviation Technologies Inc .... G 216 706-2960
  Cleveland *(G-4776)*
Avtron Aerospace Inc .... C 216 750-5152
  Cleveland *(G-4778)*
Aws Industries Inc .... E 513 932-7941
  Lebanon *(G-11635)*
Cleveland Instrument Corp .... G 440 826-1800
  Brookpark *(G-2138)*
▲ Columbus Jack Corporation .... D 614 747-1596
  Swanton *(G-17909)*
Ctl-Aerospace Inc .... C 513 874-7900
  West Chester *(G-19845)*
Ctl-Aerospace Inc .... D 513 874-7900
  West Chester *(G-19846)*
Cuda Composites LLC .... G 937 499-0360
  Dayton *(G-8117)*
Dircksen and Associates Inc .... G 614 238-0413
  Columbus *(G-6865)*
Drt Aerospace LLC .... E 937 298-7391
  West Chester *(G-19695)*
Drt Holdings Inc .... D 937 298-7391
  Dayton *(G-8169)*
Dukes Aerospace Inc .... D 818 998-9811
  Painesville *(G-15732)*
◆ Eaton Aeroquip LLC .... G 216 523-5000
  Cleveland *(G-5143)*
Eaton Hydraulics LLC .... E 419 232-7777
  Van Wert *(G-19088)*
Eaton Industrial Corporation .... B 216 523-4205
  Cleveland *(G-5152)*
Electronic Concepts Engrg Inc .... F 419 861-9000
  Holland *(G-10930)*
Enginetics Corporation .... G 937 878-3800
  Huber Heights *(G-11017)*
Eti Tech LLC .... F 937 832-4200
  Englewood *(G-9358)*
Exito Manufacturing .... G 937 291-9871
  Beavercreek *(G-1355)*
▲ Federal Equipment Company .... D 513 621-5260
  Cincinnati *(G-3680)*
Ferco Tech LLC .... C 937 746-6696
  Franklin *(G-9883)*
Field Aviation Inc .... G 513 792-2282
  Cincinnati *(G-3686)*
◆ Friction Products Co .... B 330 725-4941
  Medina *(G-13265)*
Garsite/Progress LLC .... F 419 424-1100
  Findlay *(G-9692)*
General Electric Company .... B 513 977-1500
  Cincinnati *(G-3741)*
Goodrich Corporation .... A 937 339-3811
  Troy *(G-18663)*
Goodrich Corporation .... B 216 429-4018
  Independence *(G-11133)*
Goodrich Corporation .... G 216 706-2530
  Cleveland *(G-5331)*
Grimes Aerospace Company .... C 937 484-2000
  Urbana *(G-18991)*
▲ GSE Production and Support LLC .. G 972 329-2646
  Swanton *(G-17914)*
Hartzell Propeller Inc .... F 937 778-4200
  Piqua *(G-16125)*
◆ Hartzell Propeller Inc .... C 937 778-4200
  Piqua *(G-16126)*
Hdi Landing Gear Usa Inc .... G 937 325-1586
  Springfield *(G-17413)*
Hdi Landing Gear Usa Inc .... E 440 783-5255
  Strongsville *(G-17748)*
Heico Aerospace Parts Corp .... B 954 987-6101
  Highland Heights *(G-10793)*
Heller Machine Products Inc .... G 216 281-2951
  Cleveland *(G-5390)*
Heroux-Devtek Inc .... F 937 325-1586
  Springfield *(G-17417)*
Hydro-Aire Inc .... C 937 323-3211
  Elyria *(G-9267)*
◆ Industrial Mfg Co LLC .... F 440 838-4700
  Brecksville *(G-2041)*
Jay-Em Aerospace Corporation .... E 330 923-0333
  Cuyahoga Falls *(G-7884)*
JCB Arrowhead Products Inc .... G 440 546-4288
  Brecksville *(G-2043)*
Jeff Cales Customer AVI LLC .... G 330 298-9479
  Ravenna *(G-16384)*
Jonathan Bishop .... G 330 836-6947
  Akron *(G-225)*
L&E Engineering LLC .... E 937 746-6696
  Franklin *(G-9894)*
▲ Lawrence Technologies Inc .... G 937 274-7771
  Dayton *(G-8308)*
▲ Lockheed Martin Integ .... D 330 796-2800
  Akron *(G-257)*
▲ Logan Machine Company .... D 330 633-6163
  Akron *(G-259)*
M & L Machine .... E 937 386-2604
  Seaman *(G-16883)*
Magellan Arospc Middletown Inc ..... D 513 422-2751
  Middletown *(G-13923)*
Mar-Con Tool Company Inc .... E 937 299-2244
  Moraine *(G-14367)*
Master Swaging Inc .... G 937 596-6171
  Jackson Center *(G-11211)*
▲ Maverick Molding Co .... F 513 387-6100
  Blue Ash *(G-1817)*
Meak Solutions Llc .... G 440 796-8209
  Mentor *(G-13513)*
▲ Meggitt Aircraft Braking .... A 330 796-4400
  Akron *(G-278)*
Meggitt Polymers & Composites .... C 513 851-5550
  Cincinnati *(G-4001)*
Microweld Engineering Inc .... F 614 847-9410
  Worthington *(G-20697)*
▼ Midwest Aircraft Products Co .... F 419 884-2164
  Mansfield *(G-12481)*
▲ Milan Tool Corp .... E 216 661-1078
  Cleveland *(G-5685)*
Nextant Aerospace LLC .... E 216 898-4800
  Cleveland *(G-5751)*
Nona Composites LLC .... G 937 490-4814
  Miamisburg *(G-13700)*
▲ Pako Inc .... C 440 946-8030
  Mentor *(G-13540)*
Parker-Hannifin Corporation .... C 440 937-6211
  Avon *(G-956)*
Parker-Hannifin Corporation .... C 440 284-6277
  Elyria *(G-9309)*
PCC Airfoils LLC .... B 740 982-6025
  Crooksville *(G-7818)*
Pitco Products Inc .... F 513 228-7245
  Dayton *(G-8427)*
Proflo Industries LLC .... E 419 436-6008
  Alvada *(G-519)*
Salley Tool & Die Co .... F 937 258-3333
  Dayton *(G-7989)*
Schneller LLC .... D 330 673-1299
  Kent *(G-11381)*
Scis Aerospace LLC .... G 216 533-8533
  Medina *(G-13336)*
Sirio Panel Inc .... G 937 238-3607
  Troy *(G-18706)*
▲ Skidmore-Wilhelm Mfg Company .. E 216 481-4774
  Solon *(G-17232)*
Snow Aviation Intl Inc .... C 614 588-2452
  Gahanna *(G-10105)*
◆ Summa Holdings Inc .... G 440 838-4700
  Cleveland *(G-6116)*
Summit Avionics Inc .... F 330 425-1440
  Twinsburg *(G-18861)*
Taylor Manufacturing Company .... E 937 322-8622
  Springfield *(G-17503)*
Test-Fuchs Corporation .... G 440 708-3505
  Brecksville *(G-2061)*
Tracewell Systems Inc .... D 614 846-6175
  Lewis Center *(G-11787)*
Transdigm Group Incorporated .... C 216 706-2960
  Cleveland *(G-6197)*
Triaxis Machine & Tool LLC .... G 440 230-0303
  North Royalton *(G-15308)*
Triumph Thermal Systems LLC .... D 419 273-2511
  Forest *(G-9789)*
◆ Tronair Inc .... D 419 866-6301
  Swanton *(G-17926)*
Tronair Parent Inc .... G 419 866-6301
  Swanton *(G-17927)*
Truline Industries Inc .... D 440 729-0140
  Chesterland *(G-3171)*
Turbine Eng Cmpnents Tech Corp .... E 216 692-6173
  Cleveland *(G-6222)*
Unison Industries LLC .... B 904 667-9904
  Dayton *(G-7994)*

Unison Industries LLC....B.... 937 427-0550
Beavercreek (G-1345)
Unison Industries LLC....C.... 937 426-0621
Beavercreek (G-1346)
Unison Industries LLC....D.... 937 426-4676
Alpha (G-518)
US Aeroteam Inc....E.... 937 458-0344
Dayton (G-8577)
◆ US Technology Corporation....E.... 330 455-1181
Canton (G-2853)
Wayne Trail Technologies Inc....D.... 937 295-2120
Fort Loramie (G-9811)
Weldon Pump Acquition LLC....E.... 440 232-2282
Oakwood Village (G-15489)
White Machine Inc....G.... 440 237-3282
North Royalton (G-15311)

3731 Shipbuilding & Repairing

Great Lakes Group....C.... 216 621-4854
Cleveland (G-5346)
Lighthouse Youth Services Inc....F.... 513 961-4080
Cincinnati (G-3943)
Manitowoc Company Inc....G.... 920 746-3332
Cleveland (G-5612)
McGinnis Inc....C.... 740 377-4391
South Point (G-17286)
McNational Inc....E.... 740 377-4391
South Point (G-17287)
O-Kan Marine Repair Inc....E.... 740 446-4686
Gallipolis (G-10172)
▲ Oneseal Inc....G.... 973 599-1155
Perrysburg (G-15989)
◆ Pinney Dock & Transport LLC....E.... 440 964-7186
Ashtabula (G-798)
Services Acquisition Co LLC....G.... 330 479-9267
Dennison (G-8786)
Superior Marine Ways Inc....G.... 740 894-6224
South Point (G-17295)
Superior Marine Ways Inc....C.... 740 894-6224
Proctorville (G-16346)
Tack-Anew Inc....E.... 419 734-4212
Port Clinton (G-16262)
V&P Group International LLC....F.... 703 349-6432
Cincinnati (G-4461)
Wadsworth Excavating Inc....G.... 419 898-0771
Oak Harbor (G-15448)
WH Fetzer & Sons Mfg Inc....E.... 419 687-8237
Plymouth (G-16235)

3732 Boat Building & Repairing

Brewster Sugarcreek Twp Histo....F.... 330 767-0045
Brewster (G-2068)
Checkmate Marine Inc....F.... 419 562-3881
Bucyrus (G-2321)
Don Wartko Construction Co....D.... 330 673-5252
Kent (G-11315)
Doyle Sailmaker....G.... 216 486-5732
Cleveland (G-5111)
Duck Water Boats Inc....G.... 330 602-9008
Dover (G-8824)
Dynamic Plastics Inc....G.... 937 437-7261
New Paris (G-14753)
Extreme Marine....G.... 330 963-7800
Twinsburg (G-18772)
Gallagher Wood & Crafts....G.... 513 523-2748
Oxford (G-15693)
Great Midwest Yacht Co....G.... 740 965-4511
Sunbury (G-17887)
Healthcare Benefits Inc....G.... 419 433-4499
Huron (G-11095)
Jacks Marine Inc....G.... 440 997-5060
Ashtabula (G-781)
Marinemax Inc....C.... 918 782-3277
Port Clinton (G-16252)
Mariners Landing Inc....F.... 513 941-3625
Cincinnati (G-3981)
▲ Mentor Inc....G.... 440 255-1250
Mentor On The Lake (G-13632)
▲ Nauticus Inc....G.... 440 746-1290
Brecksville (G-2051)
O-Kan Marine Repair Inc....E.... 740 446-4686
Gallipolis (G-10172)
Racelite South Coast Inc....F.... 216 581-4600
Maple Heights (G-12578)
W of Ohio Inc....G.... 614 873-4664
Plain City (G-16216)
William Thompson....G.... 440 232-4363
Aurora (G-916)
Www Boat Services Inc....G.... 419 626-0883
Sandusky (G-16863)

3743 Railroad Eqpt

A Stucki Company....G.... 412 424-0560
North Canton (G-15067)
Amsted Industries Incorporated....C.... 614 836-2323
Groveport (G-10481)
Amsted Rail Company Inc....F.... 614 836-2323
Groveport (G-10482)
B&C Machine Co LLC....B.... 330 745-4013
Barberton (G-1058)
▲ Buck Equipment Inc....E.... 614 539-3039
Grove City (G-10419)
◆ Dayton-Phoenix Group Inc....C.... 937 496-3900
Dayton (G-8151)
Dennis Lavender....G.... 740 344-3336
Newark (G-14867)
Engines Inc of Ohio....D.... 740 377-9874
South Point (G-17283)
George R Silcott Railway Equip....G.... 614 885-7224
Worthington (G-20687)
Good Day Tools LLC....G.... 513 578-2050
Cincinnati (G-3770)
Gunderson Rail Services LLC....E.... 330 792-6521
Youngstown (G-20927)
▼ Jk-Co LLC....E.... 419 422-5240
Findlay (G-9710)
Johnson Bros Rubber Co Inc....E.... 419 752-4814
Greenwich (G-10404)
K & G Machine Co....E.... 216 732-7115
Cleveland (G-5512)
L B Foster Company....E.... 330 652-1461
Mineral Ridge (G-14168)
Nolan Company....G.... 330 453-7922
Canton (G-2762)
Nolan Company....G.... 740 269-1512
Bowerston (G-1942)
Norfolk Southern Corporation....E.... 419 697-5070
Oregon (G-15563)
Plymouth Locomotive Svc LLC....G.... 419 896-2854
Shiloh (G-16998)
Prime Manufacturing Corp....G.... 937 496-3900
Dayton (G-8441)
R H Little Co....G.... 330 477-3455
Canton (G-2800)
Rail Road Corporation....G.... 614 771-2102
Columbus (G-7376)
Rescar Companies Inc....F.... 630 963-1114
Minerva (G-14200)
Sperling Railway Services Inc....F.... 330 479-2004
Canton (G-2821)
Standard Car Truck Company....D.... 740 775-6450
Chillicothe (G-3223)
Transco Railway Products Inc....D.... 330 872-0934
Newton Falls (G-14994)
Trinity Highway Products Llc....F.... 419 227-1296
Lima (G-11953)
Wabtec Corporation....G.... 440 238-5350
Strongsville (G-17803)
Westinghouse A Brake Tech Corp....D.... 419 526-5323
Mansfield (G-12540)

3751 Motorcycles, Bicycles & Parts

B&D Truck Parts Sls & Svcs LLC....G.... 419 701-7041
Fostoria (G-9835)
Bandit Choppers LLC....G.... 614 556-4416
Pickerington (G-16041)
Beasley Fiberglass Inc....G.... 440 357-6644
Painesville (G-15719)
Behlke Dalene....G.... 330 399-6780
Warren (G-19376)
Carlisle Brake & Friction Inc....E.... 330 725-4941
Medina (G-13234)
◆ Carlisle Brake & Friction Inc....C.... 440 528-4000
Solon (G-17124)
Cherhire Choppers....G.... 740 362-0695
Delaware (G-8665)
▲ Cobra Motorcycles Mfg....E.... 330 207-3844
North Lima (G-15167)
Custom Assembly Inc....E.... 419 622-3040
Haviland (G-10708)
◆ Dco LLC....B.... 419 931-9086
Perrysburg (G-15938)
Edge Cycling Technologies LLC....G.... 937 532-3891
Xenia (G-20768)
Franklin Frames and Cycles....G.... 740 763-3838
Newark (G-14875)
Heritage Tool....F.... 513 753-7300
Loveland (G-12197)
J Tyler Enterprise LLC....G.... 330 774-4490
Youngstown (G-20944)

▲ Ktm North America Inc....D.... 855 215-6360
Amherst (G-564)
Multi-Design Inc....G.... 440 275-2255
Austinburg (G-923)
▲ Newman Technology Inc....C.... 419 525-1856
Mansfield (G-12490)
Old Mill Power Equipment....G.... 740 982-3246
Crooksville (G-7817)
Outback Cycle Shack LLC....G.... 513 554-1048
Cincinnati (G-4125)
Shumaker Racing Components....G.... 419 238-0801
Van Wert (G-19105)
Sinners N Saints LLC....G.... 614 231-7467
Columbus (G-7455)
▲ Spiegler Brake Systems USA LLC....G.... 937 291-1735
Dayton (G-8519)
Sunstar Engrg Americas Inc....F.... 937 743-9049
Franklin (G-9923)
▲ Sunstar Engrg Americas Inc....C.... 937 746-8575
Springboro (G-17354)
◆ Tarantula Performance Racg LLC....G.... 330 273-3456
Hinckley (G-10906)
Thomas D Epperson....G.... 937 855-3300
Germantown (G-10246)
▲ Vari-Wall Tube Specialists Inc....D.... 330 482-0000
Columbiana (G-6485)
Wersells Bike Shop Co....G.... 419 474-7412
Toledo (G-18596)

3761 Guided Missiles & Space Vehicles

Daniel Malek....G.... 330 701-5760
Cuyahoga Falls (G-7858)
Lockheed Martin Corporation....B.... 330 796-2800
Akron (G-256)
Tessec Manufacturing Svcs LLC....E.... 937 985-3552
Dayton (G-8553)

3769 Guided Missile/Space Vehicle Parts & Eqpt, NEC

Curtiss-Wright Controls....E.... 937 252-5601
Fairborn (G-9456)
Defense Co Inc....D.... 413 998-1637
Cleveland (G-5081)
General Electric Company....B.... 513 977-1500
Cincinnati (G-3741)
◆ Gleason Metrology Systems Corp....E.... 937 384-8901
Dayton (G-8223)
Grimes Aerospace Company....B.... 937 484-2001
Urbana (G-18990)
▲ Industrial Quartz Corp....F.... 440 942-0909
Mentor (G-13469)
L3 Cincinnati Electronics Corp....A.... 513 573-6100
Mason (G-12902)
▲ Lockheed Martin Integ....D.... 330 796-2800
Akron (G-257)
Lord Corporation....C.... 937 278-9431
Dayton (G-8315)
▲ Metalex Manufacturing Inc....C.... 513 489-0507
Blue Ash (G-1820)
▲ Millat Industries Corp....D.... 937 434-6666
Dayton (G-8360)
Morris Bean & Company....C.... 937 767-7301
Yellow Springs (G-20812)
Shelburne Corp....G.... 216 321-9177
Shaker Heights (G-16936)
Sunpower Inc....D.... 740 594-2221
Athens (G-851)
Tdm Fuelcell LLC Tdm LLC....G.... 440 969-1442
Chesterland (G-3170)
Te Connectivity Corporation....C.... 419 521-9500
Mansfield (G-12527)
US Aeroteam Inc....E.... 937 458-0344
Dayton (G-8577)

3792 Travel Trailers & Campers

◆ Airstream Inc....B.... 937 596-6111
Jackson Center (G-11205)
American Truck Equipment Inc....G.... 216 362-0400
Cleveland (G-4699)
Berlin Truck Caps Ltd....F.... 330 893-2811
Millersburg (G-14067)
Capitol City Trailers Inc....D.... 614 491-2616
Obetz (G-15507)
Cecil Caudill Trailer Sls Inc....F.... 740 574-0704
Franklin Furnace (G-9933)
D W Truax Enterprise Inc....G.... 740 695-2596
Saint Clairsville (G-16631)
Gerich Fiberglass Inc....E.... 419 362-4591
Mount Gilead (G-14424)

S I C

Hybrid Trailer Co LLC....G....419 433-3022
Huron *(G-11098)*
Isaacs Jr Floyd Thomas....G....513 899-2342
Morrow *(G-14412)*

3795 Tanks & Tank Components

▲ **American Apex Corporation**....F....614 652-2000
Plain City *(G-16171)*
General Dynamics Land....B....419 221-7000
Lima *(G-11869)*
▲ **Joint Systems Mfg Ctr**....G....419 221-9580
Lima *(G-11882)*
Sugartree Square Mercantile....G....740 345-3882
Newark *(G-14926)*
Tencate Advanced Armor USA Inc....D....740 928-0326
Hebron *(G-10765)*
Tessec Manufacturing Svcs LLC....E....937 985-3552
Dayton *(G-8553)*
United States Dept of Army....D....419 221-9500
Lima *(G-11955)*
◆ **US Yachiyo Inc**....C....740 375-4687
Marion *(G-12746)*
Weldon Pump Acquition LLC....E....440 232-2282
Oakwood Village *(G-15489)*

3799 Transportation Eqpt, NEC

Aerodynamic Systems....G....440 463-8820
Chagrin Falls *(G-3035)*
All Power Equipment LLC....F....740 593-3279
Athens *(G-822)*
B & B Industries Inc....G....614 871-3883
Orient *(G-15574)*
Besl Specialized Carrier....G....740 599-6305
Danville *(G-7957)*
Blue Ribbon Trailers Ltd....F....330 538-4114
North Jackson *(G-15142)*
Burkholder Buggy Shop....G....330 674-5891
Millersburg *(G-14074)*
▲ **Cleveland Hdwr & Forging Co**....E....216 641-5200
Cleveland *(G-4962)*
Cleveland Wheels....D....440 937-6211
Avon *(G-944)*
D & A Custom Trailer Inc....G....740 922-2205
Uhrichsville *(G-18883)*
▲ **Farmerstown Axle Co**....G....330 897-2711
Baltic *(G-1028)*
Fitchville East Corp....E....419 929-1510
New London *(G-14729)*
Geyer Transport & Mfg....F....740 382-9008
Marion *(G-12706)*
▲ **GSE Production and Support LLC**....G....972 329-2646
Swanton *(G-17914)*
▲ **Hawkline Nevada LLC**....E....937 444-4295
Mount Orab *(G-14442)*
Hitch-Hiker Mfg Inc....F....330 542-3052
New Middletown *(G-14750)*
Interstate Truckway Inc....E....614 771-1220
Columbus *(G-7047)*
Kedar D Army....G....419 238-6929
Van Wert *(G-19097)*
Kmj Leasing Ltd....E....614 871-3883
Orient *(G-15575)*
▲ **Kolpin Outdoors Corporation**....G....330 328-0772
Cuyahoga Falls *(G-7889)*
▲ **L & R Racing Inc**....E....330 220-3102
Brunswick *(G-2218)*
Loadmaster Trailer Company....F....419 732-3434
Port Clinton *(G-16250)*
London Coach Shop....G....419 347-4803
Shelby *(G-16983)*
▲ **Lux Corporation**....G....419 562-7978
Bucyrus *(G-2338)*
Mx Spring Inc....G....330 426-4600
East Palestine *(G-9081)*
Polaris Industries Inc....E....937 283-1200
Wilmington *(G-20502)*
Premier Uv Products LLC....G....330 715-2452
Cuyahoga Falls *(G-7907)*
R V Spa LLC....G....440 284-4800
Elyria *(G-9316)*
Rankin Mfg Inc....E....419 929-8338
New London *(G-14735)*
Rv Xpress Inc....G....937 418-0127
Piqua *(G-16161)*
Shiloh Carriage Shop LLC....G....419 896-3869
Shiloh *(G-17000)*
Swartz Audie....G....740 820-2341
Minford *(G-14207)*
Thor Industries Inc....E....937 596-6111
Jackson Center *(G-11217)*
Transglobal Inc....G....419 396-9079
Carey *(G-2890)*
Victorian Farms....G....330 628-9188
Atwater *(G-864)*
Walnut Creek Cart Shop....G....330 893-1097
Millersburg *(G-14145)*
◆ **Wholecycle Inc**....E....330 929-8123
Peninsula *(G-15902)*

38 MEASURING, ANALYZING AND CONTROLLING INSTRUMENTS; PHOTOGRAPHIC, MEDICAL AN

3812 Search, Detection, Navigation & Guidance Systs & Instrs

232 Defense LLC....G....419 348-4343
Custar *(G-7828)*
3gc LLC....G....740 703-0580
Cardington *(G-2869)*
Accurate Electronics Inc....C....330 682-7015
Orrville *(G-15581)*
Action Defense LLC....G....440 503-7886
Cleveland *(G-4611)*
◆ **ADB Safegate Americas LLC**....B....614 861-1304
Columbus *(G-6542)*
Advanced Defense Products LLC....G....440 571-2277
Painesville *(G-15705)*
Alternate Defense LLC....G....216 225-5889
Maple Heights *(G-12564)*
American Icon Defense Ltd....G....216 233-5184
Lakewood *(G-11510)*
Atlantic Inertial Systems Inc....E....740 788-3800
Heath *(G-10717)*
Aviation Technologies Inc....G....216 706-2960
Cleveland *(G-4776)*
Ball Aerospace & Tech Corp....C....303 939-4000
Beavercreek *(G-1303)*
Boeing Company....E....740 788-4000
Newark *(G-14854)*
Brookpark Laboratories Inc....G....216 267-7140
Cleveland *(G-4841)*
Btc Inc....E....740 549-2722
Lewis Center *(G-11753)*
Btc Technology Services Inc....G....740 549-2722
Lewis Center *(G-11754)*
Cedar Elec Holdings Corp....D....773 804-6288
West Chester *(G-19666)*
▲ **Ceia Usa Ltd**....E....330 405-3190
Twinsburg *(G-18747)*
Center Mass Defense....G....513 314-8401
Hamilton *(G-10544)*
Central Ohio Defense LLC....G....614 668-6527
Columbus *(G-6752)*
Circle Prime Manufacturing....E....330 923-0019
Cuyahoga Falls *(G-7850)*
Citizens Defense LLC....G....740 645-1101
Thurman *(G-18037)*
Damsel In Defense....G....561 307-4177
North Olmsted *(G-15184)*
Damsel In Defense Diva....G....330 874-2068
Bolivar *(G-1911)*
David Boswell....E....614 441-2497
Columbus *(G-6852)*
Decibel Research Inc....E....256 705-3341
Beavercreek *(G-1310)*
Defense Surplus LLC....G....419 460-9906
Maumee *(G-13106)*
Dragoon Technologies Inc....G....937 439-9223
Dayton *(G-8167)*
Drs Advanced Isr LLC....C....937 429-7408
Beavercreek *(G-1311)*
Drs Mobile Environmntl Svc....G....513 943-1111
Cincinnati *(G-3246)*
Easy Defense Products....G....513 258-2897
Cincinnati *(G-3626)*
▲ **Eaton Aerospace LLC**....F....216 523-5000
Cleveland *(G-5144)*
Eaton Aerospace LLC....E....216 523-5000
Cleveland *(G-5145)*
Electrodynamics Inc....C....847 259-0740
Cincinnati *(G-3247)*
En Garde Deer Defense LLC....G....440 334-7271
Brecksville *(G-2033)*
Enginetics Corporation....C....937 878-3800
Huber Heights *(G-11017)*
▲ **Escort Inc**....D....513 870-8500
West Chester *(G-19699)*
Eti Tech LLC....F....937 832-4200
Englewood *(G-9358)*
Fame Tool & Mfg Co Inc....E....513 271-6387
Cincinnati *(G-3670)*
▲ **Ferrotherm Corporation**....C....216 883-9350
Cleveland *(G-5233)*
Fluid Conservation Systems....F....513 831-9335
Milford *(G-14008)*
Freedom Road Defense....G....740 541-7467
Cambridge *(G-2438)*
Front Line Defense....G....419 516-7992
Ada *(G-6)*
GE Aviation Systems LLC....E....937 898-9600
Dayton *(G-8217)*
GE Aviation Systems LLC....F....513 470-2889
Cincinnati *(G-3732)*
GE Aviation Systems LLC....G....513 552-4278
West Chester *(G-19711)*
▲ **GE Aviation Systems LLC**....G....937 898-9600
Cincinnati *(G-3736)*
General Dynmics Mssion Systems....E....513 253-4770
Beavercreek *(G-1317)*
General Plastics North Corp....E....800 542-2466
Cincinnati *(G-3746)*
Grimes Aerospace Company....B....937 484-2001
Urbana *(G-18990)*
Guardian Strategic Defense LLC....G....937 707-8985
Marysville *(G-12786)*
Harris Corporation....C....973 284-2866
Beavercreek *(G-1322)*
Heller Machine Products Inc....G....216 281-2951
Cleveland *(G-5390)*
Hept Machine Inc....G....937 890-5633
Vandalia *(G-19126)*
HI Tech Aero Spares....G....513 942-4150
West Chester *(G-19721)*
HM Defense....G....513 260-6200
Mount Orab *(G-14445)*
Honeywell International Inc....A....937 484-2000
Urbana *(G-18995)*
Hot Brass Personal Defense....G....419 733-7400
Celina *(G-2969)*
Hunter Defense Tech Inc....C....513 943-7880
Cincinnati *(G-3255)*
IMT Defense Corp....G....614 891-8812
Westerville *(G-19998)*
John Wolf & Co Inc....G....440 942-0083
Willoughby *(G-20348)*
JP Self Defense LLC....G....330 356-1541
Massillon *(G-13007)*
K & M Home Defense LLC....G....313 258-6142
Fairborn *(G-9462)*
Kaman Corporation....E....614 871-1893
Grove City *(G-10438)*
Koroshi School of Defense....G....740 323-3582
Heath *(G-10724)*
L3 Aviation Products Inc....D....614 825-2001
Columbus *(G-7108)*
L3 Cincinnati Electronics Corp....A....513 573-6100
Mason *(G-12902)*
Lake Shore Cryotronics Inc....C....614 891-2243
Westerville *(G-20003)*
Landis Defense Solutions....G....937 938-0688
Moraine *(G-14366)*
Linx Defense LLC....G....805 233-2472
Canton *(G-2734)*
Lockheed Martin Corporation....G....937 429-0100
Beavercreek *(G-1327)*
Lockheed Martin Corporation....B....330 796-7000
Akron *(G-255)*
Lockheed Martin Corporation....E....866 562-2363
Columbus *(G-7134)*
Lockheed Martin Corporation....C....937 429-0100
Beavercreek *(G-1328)*
▲ **Lockheed Martin Integ**....D....330 796-2800
Akron *(G-257)*
Lockheed Martin Integrtd Systm....A....330 796-2800
Akron *(G-258)*
Lunken Charts LLC....G....513 253-7615
Cincinnati *(G-3957)*
MCO Solutions Inc....G....937 205-9512
Dayton *(G-8335)*
Means of Defense....G....740 513-6210
Mount Gilead *(G-14429)*
Midwest Precision Holdings Inc....D....440 497-4086
Eastlake *(G-9121)*
Modern Defense....G....614 505-9338
Columbus *(G-7190)*
Nhvs International Inc....B....440 527-8610
Mentor *(G-13527)*

SIC SECTION 38 MEASURING, ANALYZING AND CONTROLLING INSTRUMENTS; PHOTOGRAPHIC, MEDICAL AN

Northrop Grumman Innovation ....C....... 937 429-9261
Beavercreek *(G-1360)*
Northrop Grumman Systems Corp ....B....... 513 881-3296
West Chester *(G-19881)*
Ohio Defense Services Inc..............G....... 937 608-2371
Dayton *(G-8396)*
Ohio First Defense..........................G....... 513 571-9461
Maineville *(G-12376)*
On Guard Defense LLC ....G....... 740 596-1984
New Plymouth *(G-14809)*
Outlier Solutions LLC......................G....... 330 947-2678
Alliance *(G-494)*
PCC Airfoils LLC..............................C....... 216 692-7900
Cleveland *(G-5857)*
◆ **Peerless-Winsmith Inc**.................G....... 614 526-7000
Dublin *(G-8963)*
Phase Line Defense LLC..................G....... 440 219-0046
Medina *(G-13317)*
Primary Defense LLC.......................G....... 937 673-5703
Toledo *(G-18483)*
Quasonix Inc....................................E....... 513 942-1287
West Chester *(G-19775)*
Rae Systems Inc...............................G....... 440 232-0555
Walton Hills *(G-19314)*
Raytheon Company..........................F....... 937 429-5429
Beavercreek *(G-1339)*
Redco Instrument.............................G....... 440 232-2132
Cleveland *(G-5969)*
◆ **Reuter-Stokes LLC**........................B....... 330 425-3755
Twinsburg *(G-18845)*
Saircorp Ltd......................................G....... 330 669-9099
Smithville *(G-17094)*
Ss Defense LLC................................G....... 937 407-0659
Cridersville *(G-7812)*
▲ **Star Dynamics Corporation** ....D....... 614 334-4510
Hilliard *(G-10864)*
Sunset Industries Inc.........................E....... 216 731-8131
Euclid *(G-9444)*
Talon Defense...................................G....... 419 236-7695
Columbus Grove *(G-7638)*
Te Connectivity Corporation.............C....... 419 521-9500
Mansfield *(G-12527)*
Tmw Systems Inc..............................F....... 615 986-1900
Cleveland *(G-6179)*
Total Self Defense Toledo LLC ....G....... 419 466-5882
Sylvania *(G-17966)*
Tri-State Jet Mfg LLC.......................G....... 513 896-4538
Hamilton *(G-10614)*
Trimble Inc..F....... 937 233-8921
Dayton *(G-8566)*
True Defense Solutions LLC..............G....... 330 325-1695
Rootstown *(G-16573)*
TS Defense LLC.................................G....... 740 446-7716
Bidwell *(G-1671)*
U S Army Corps of Engineers.............F....... 740 537-2571
Toronto *(G-18613)*
UTC Aerospace Systems ....G....... 330 374-3040
Uniontown *(G-18937)*
Valentine Research Inc......................E....... 513 984-8900
Blue Ash *(G-1864)*
Vector Electromagnetics LLC............G....... 937 478-5904
Beavercreek *(G-1367)*
Vici Defense Ltd................................G....... 330 669-3735
Smithville *(G-17096)*
Wall Colmonoy Corporation ....D....... 513 842-4200
Cincinnati *(G-4488)*
Watts Antenna Company...................G....... 740 797-9380
The Plains *(G-18024)*
Yost Labs Inc....................................F....... 740 876-4936
Portsmouth *(G-16305)*

3821 Laboratory Apparatus & Furniture

4r Enterprises Incorporated...............G....... 330 923-9799
Cuyahoga Falls *(G-7829)*
Accuscan Instruments Inc ....F....... 614 878-6644
Columbus *(G-6535)*
◆ **American Isostatic Presses Inc**.........F....... 614 497-3148
Columbus *(G-6583)*
Amteco Inc..G....... 513 217-4430
Middletown *(G-13884)*
Asbeka Custom Products LLC ....F....... 440 352-0839
Painesville *(G-15711)*
Ashton Pumpmatic Inc.......................G....... 937 424-1380
Dayton *(G-8039)*
▲ **Caron Products and Svcs Inc**..........E....... 740 373-6809
Marietta *(G-12612)*
Cellular Technology Limited ....E....... 216 791-5084
Shaker Heights *(G-16929)*
Center For Excptonal Practices...........G....... 330 523-5240
Richfield *(G-16464)*
▲ **Cheminstruments Inc** ....F....... 513 860-1598
West Chester *(G-19668)*
Cheminstruments Inc.........................G....... 513 860-1598
West Chester *(G-19669)*
Chemsultants International Inc ....G....... 513 860-1598
West Chester *(G-19670)*
Chemsultants International Inc ....E....... 440 974-3080
Mentor *(G-13412)*
Continental Hydrodyne Systems..........F....... 330 494-2740
Canton *(G-2635)*
Cortest Inc...F....... 440 942-1235
Willoughby *(G-20301)*
Denton Atd Inc ....E....... 567 265-5200
Huron *(G-11093)*
Dentronix Inc.....................................E....... 330 916-7300
Cuyahoga Falls *(G-7860)*
◆ **E R Advanced Ceramics Inc**............E....... 330 426-9433
East Palestine *(G-9077)*
Eanytime Corporation ....G....... 714 969-7000
Columbus *(G-6882)*
Gdj Inc..G....... 440 975-0258
Mentor *(G-13455)*
◆ **Global Cooling Inc**..........................E....... 740 274-7900
Athens *(G-833)*
H & N Instruments Inc ....G....... 740 344-4351
Newark *(G-14882)*
Ies Systems Inc..................................E....... 330 533-6683
Canfield *(G-2530)*
Ignio Systems LLC.............................F....... 419 708-0503
Toledo *(G-18340)*
Leverett A Anderson Co Inc...............G....... 330 670-1363
Akron *(G-253)*
Malta Dynamics LLC..........................F....... 740 749-3512
Waterford *(G-19488)*
Mettler-Toledo Intl Fin Inc ....G....... 614 438-4511
Columbus *(G-6500)*
◆ **Mettler-Toledo Intl Inc** ....B....... 614 438-4511
Columbus *(G-6501)*
▼ **Nanotech Innovations LLC** ....G....... 440 926-4888
Oberlin *(G-15503)*
Northfield..G....... 440 949-1815
Sheffield Village *(G-16972)*
◆ **Philips Medical Systems Clevel**........B....... 440 247-2652
Cleveland *(G-5871)*
Poi Holdings Inc.................................F....... 937 253-7377
Dayton *(G-7988)*
Powdermet Powder Production...........F....... 216 404-0053
Euclid *(G-9435)*
Qualitech Associates Inc ....G....... 216 265-8702
Cleveland *(G-5939)*
Regal Industries Inc...........................G....... 440 352-9600
Painesville *(G-15780)*
So-Low Environmental Eqp Co ....E....... 513 772-9410
Cincinnati *(G-4350)*
Strategic Technology Entp..................E....... 440 354-2600
Mentor *(G-13594)*
▲ **Tech Pro Inc**...................................E....... 330 923-3546
Akron *(G-397)*
Teledyne Instruments Inc...................E....... 513 229-7000
Mason *(G-12946)*
Teledyne Tekmar Company.................E....... 513 229-7000
Mason *(G-12948)*
Tri-Tech Machining LLC ....G....... 513 575-3959
Milford *(G-14045)*
Universal Scientific Inc.......................G....... 440 428-1777
Madison *(G-12358)*
Waller Brothers Stone Company..........E....... 740 858-1948
Mc Dermott *(G-13195)*

3822 Automatic Temperature Controls

A & P Tool Inc....................................E....... 419 542-6681
Hicksville *(G-10773)*
Action Air & Hydraulics Inc.................G....... 937 372-8614
Xenia *(G-20753)*
Acutemp Thermal Systems..................F....... 937 312-0114
Moraine *(G-14329)*
Ademco Inc.......................................F....... 513 772-1851
Blue Ash *(G-1721)*
Ademco Inc.......................................G....... 440 439-7002
Bedford *(G-1379)*
▲ **Alan Manufacturing Inc** ....E....... 330 262-1555
Wooster *(G-20560)*
◆ **Babcock & Wilcox Company**............A....... 330 753-4511
Barberton *(G-1059)*
Balta Technology Inc..........................G....... 513 724-0247
Batavia *(G-1126)*
▲ **Bry-Air Inc**......................................E....... 740 965-2974
Sunbury *(G-17883)*
Building Ctrl Integrators LLC...............E....... 614 334-3300
Powell *(G-16310)*
Building Ctrl Integrators LLC...............G....... 513 247-6154
Cincinnati *(G-3430)*
Building Ctrl Integrators LLC...............G....... 440 526-6660
Brecksville *(G-2025)*
Building Ctrl Integrators LLC...............G....... 513 860-9600
West Chester *(G-19836)*
Certified Labs & Service Inc ....G....... 419 289-7462
Ashland *(G-691)*
Cfrc Wtr & Enrgy Solutions Inc ....G....... 216 479-0290
Cleveland *(G-4906)*
▲ **Channel Products Inc**.......................D....... 440 423-0113
Solon *(G-17126)*
Cincinnati Air Conditioning Co.............D....... 513 721-5622
Cincinnati *(G-3480)*
▲ **Conery Manufacturing Inc**................F....... 419 289-1444
Ashland *(G-696)*
Cool Times...G....... 513 608-5201
Cincinnati *(G-3547)*
Data Analysis Technologies.................G....... 614 873-0710
Plain City *(G-16186)*
Doan/Pyramid Solutions LLC ....F....... 216 587-9510
Cleveland *(G-5102)*
▲ **Dyoung Enterprise Inc**.....................D....... 440 918-0505
Willoughby *(G-20312)*
▼ **Estabrook Assembly Svcs Inc**..........F....... 440 243-3350
Berea *(G-1606)*
Etc Enterprises LLC...........................G....... 417 262-6382
Delphos *(G-8743)*
Evokes LLC..E....... 513 947-8433
Mason *(G-12868)*
Fes-Ohio Inc......................................G....... 513 772-8566
Cincinnati *(G-3683)*
Follow River Designs LLC...................G....... 614 325-9954
McConnelsville *(G-13204)*
Future Controls Corporation ....E....... 440 275-3191
Austinburg *(G-922)*
Great Lakes Management Inc ....E....... 216 883-6500
Cleveland *(G-5349)*
Grid Sentry LLC ....F....... 937 490-2101
Beavercreek *(G-1320)*
Helm Instrument Company Inc............E....... 419 893-4356
Maumee *(G-13116)*
Honeywell International Inc ....D....... 937 754-4134
Fairborn *(G-9461)*
Honeywell International Inc ....A....... 937 484-2000
Urbana *(G-18995)*
Howden North America Inc ....D....... 330 867-8540
Medina *(G-13274)*
▲ **Hunter Defense Tech Inc**..................E....... 216 438-6111
Solon *(G-17164)*
Ignio Systems LLC..............................F....... 419 708-0503
Toledo *(G-18340)*
Integrated Development & Mfg...........F....... 440 247-5100
Chagrin Falls *(G-3021)*
Integrated Development & Mfg...........E....... 440 543-2423
Chagrin Falls *(G-3053)*
K Davis Inc...G....... 419 637-2859
Gibsonburg *(G-10249)*
Kanawha Scales & Systems Inc ....F....... 513 576-0700
Milford *(G-14023)*
Karman Rubber Company...................E....... 330 864-2161
Akron *(G-232)*
Mader Machine Co Inc.......................E....... 440 355-4505
Lagrange *(G-11488)*
Melink Corporation............................F....... 513 685-0958
Milford *(G-14026)*
Mestek Inc...D....... 419 288-2703
Bradner *(G-2015)*
Mestek Inc...D....... 419 288-2703
Holland *(G-10944)*
Midwest Energy Emissions Corp ....F....... 614 505-6115
Lewis Center *(G-11768)*
Norcold Inc..C....... 937 447-2241
Gettysburg *(G-10247)*
Ohio Coatings Company.....................D....... 740 859-5500
Yorkville *(G-20827)*
Peco II Inc...D....... 614 431-0694
Columbus *(G-7305)*
▲ **Pepperl + Fuchs Inc**.........................C....... 330 425-3555
Twinsburg *(G-18830)*
Pepperl + Fuchs Entps Inc..................G....... 330 425-3555
Twinsburg *(G-18831)*
▲ **Portage Electric Products Inc**...........C....... 330 499-2727
North Canton *(G-15111)*
Prentke Romich Company ....C....... 330 262-1984
Wooster *(G-20641)*
▲ **Qleanair Scandinavia Inc** ....G....... 614 323-1756
Columbus *(G-7360)*
▲ **Sasha Electronics Inc**.......................F....... 419 662-8100
Rossford *(G-16593)*

S I C

38 MEASURING, ANALYZING AND CONTROLLING INSTRUMENTS; PHOTOGRAPHIC, MEDICAL AN SIC SECTION

Schneder Elc Bldngs Amrcas Inc.........D....... 513 398-9800
Lebanon *(G-11694)*
Siemens Industry Inc............................D....... 513 336-2267
Lebanon *(G-11695)*
Siemens Industry Inc............................D....... 614 573-8212
Columbus *(G-7448)*
▲ Skuttle Mfg Co..................................F....... 740 373-9169
Marietta *(G-12670)*
Tetra Tech Inc..F....... 330 286-3683
Canfield *(G-2549)*
▲ Therm-O-Disc Incorporated............A....... 419 525-8500
Mansfield *(G-12530)*
◆ Thermtrol Corporation......................E....... 330 497-4148
North Canton *(G-15125)*
Turner Pressure....................................G....... 614 871-7775
Grove City *(G-10479)*
▲ Ventra Sandusky LLC........................C....... 419 627-3600
Sandusky *(G-16861)*
Vortec Corporation................................E....... 513 891-7485
Blue Ash *(G-1866)*
Young Regulator Company Inc.............E....... 440 232-9452
Bedford *(G-1456)*

3823 Indl Instruments For Meas, Display & Control

ABB Inc..G....... 440 585-8500
Beachwood *(G-1217)*
Air Logic Power Systems LLC..............G....... 513 202-5130
Harrison *(G-10629)*
▲ Airmate Company..............................D....... 419 636-3184
Bryan *(G-2258)*
◆ Alpha Technologies Svcs LLC..........D....... 330 745-1641
Hudson *(G-11027)*
▲ Altronic LLC..C....... 330 545-9768
Girard *(G-10252)*
American Water Services Inc.................G....... 440 243-9840
Strongsville *(G-17709)*
Appleton Grp LLC..................................C....... 330 689-1904
Cuyahoga Falls *(G-7838)*
Aqua Technology Group LLC...............G....... 513 298-1183
West Chester *(G-19648)*
Aquacalc LLC...G....... 916 372-0534
Columbus *(G-6612)*
▼ Arzel Technology Inc.........................E....... 216 831-6068
Cleveland *(G-4743)*
Ascon Tecnologic N Amer LLC..............G....... 216 485-8350
Cleveland *(G-4747)*
Ats Atmtion Globl Svcs USA Inc...........G....... 519 653-4483
Lewis Center *(G-11745)*
Automatic Timing & Controls................G....... 614 888-8855
New Albany *(G-14606)*
Automation and Ctrl Tech Inc...............E....... 614 495-1120
Dublin *(G-8886)*
▼ Automation Metrology Intl LLC.........G....... 440 354-6436
Mentor *(G-13395)*
Automation Technology Inc..................E....... 937 233-6084
Dayton *(G-8045)*
◆ Avure Autoclave Systems Inc...........E....... 614 891-2732
Columbus *(G-6637)*
Avure Technologies Inc..........................F....... 614 891-2732
Lewis Center *(G-11750)*
Beaumont Machine LLC........................F....... 513 701-0421
Mason *(G-12833)*
Brighton Technologies LLC...................E....... 513 469-1800
Saint Bernard *(G-16620)*
Brighton Technologies Group...............G....... 513 469-1800
Cincinnati *(G-3417)*
▲ Bry-Air Inc...E....... 740 965-2974
Sunbury *(G-17883)*
BSK Industries Inc.................................F....... 440 230-9299
North Royalton *(G-15264)*
Burner Tech Unlimited Inc.....................G....... 440 232-3200
Twinsburg *(G-18744)*
C H Washington Water Plan...................G....... 740 636-2382
Wshngtn CT Hs *(G-20721)*
▲ Cammann Inc......................................F....... 440 965-4051
Wakeman *(G-19282)*
▲ Caron Products and Svcs Inc.............E....... 740 373-6809
Marietta *(G-12612)*
▲ Chandler Systems Incorporated.......D....... 888 363-9434
Ashland *(G-693)*
Cincinnati Test Systems Inc..................C....... 513 202-5100
Harrison *(G-10635)*
▲ Clark-Reliance Corporation..............C....... 440 572-1500
Strongsville *(G-17726)*
Cleveland Controls Inc..........................D....... 216 398-0330
Cleveland *(G-4952)*
Cleveland Electric Labs Co...................E....... 800 447-2207
Twinsburg *(G-18754)*
Cleveland Instrument Corp....................G....... 440 826-1800
Brookpark *(G-2138)*
Combustion Process System................G....... 330 922-4161
Cuyahoga Falls *(G-7852)*
Command Alkon Incorporated..............D....... 614 799-0600
Dublin *(G-8901)*
Computer Aided Solutions LLC.............E....... 440 729-2570
Chesterland *(G-3155)*
Comtec Incorporated.............................F....... 330 425-8102
Twinsburg *(G-18756)*
Consolidatd Analytical Sys Inc..............F....... 513 542-1200
Cleves *(G-6359)*
Control Associates Inc...........................G....... 440 708-1770
Chagrin Falls *(G-3042)*
Corro-Tech Equipment Corp.................G....... 216 941-1552
Cleveland *(G-5031)*
Danaher Corporation.............................C....... 440 995-3003
Cleveland *(G-5061)*
Danaher Corporation.............................C....... 440 995-3025
Mentor *(G-13428)*
Data Control Systems Inc......................G....... 330 877-4497
Hartville *(G-10688)*
Deban Enterprises Inc...........................G....... 937 426-4235
Dayton *(G-8152)*
Diamond Power Intl Inc..........................F....... 740 687-4001
Lancaster *(G-11565)*
▲ Doubleday Acquisitions LLC............C....... 937 242-6768
Moraine *(G-14347)*
▲ Dynamic Temperature Sups LLC.......G....... 216 767-5799
Parma *(G-15816)*
Dynetech LLC...E....... 419 690-4281
Toledo *(G-18272)*
▲ Dyoung Enterprise Inc......................D....... 440 918-0505
Willoughby *(G-20312)*
E E Controls Inc......................................G....... 440 585-5554
Willowick *(G-20477)*
Electrodynamics Inc...............................C....... 847 259-0740
Cincinnati *(G-3247)*
Elpro Services Inc..................................G....... 740 568-9900
Marietta *(G-12623)*
Emerson Electric Co..............................C....... 513 731-2020
Cincinnati *(G-3635)*
Emerson Electric Co..............................E....... 440 288-1122
Lorain *(G-12089)*
Emerson Electric Co..............................E....... 440 248-9400
Solon *(G-17136)*
Emerson Process MGT Lllp..................E....... 877 468-6384
Columbus *(G-6490)*
Encompass Automation &......................F....... 419 873-0000
Perrysburg *(G-15947)*
Ernst Flow Industries LLC....................F....... 732 938-5641
Strongsville *(G-17743)*
Facts Inc..E....... 330 928-2332
Cuyahoga Falls *(G-7866)*
Fluid Equipment Corp............................G....... 419 636-0777
Bryan *(G-2281)*
▲ Furnace Parts LLC.............................E....... 216 916-9601
Cleveland *(G-5278)*
Furnace Parts LLC..................................G....... 800 321-0796
Cleveland *(G-5279)*
Future Controls Corporation..................E....... 440 275-3191
Austinburg *(G-922)*
GE Infrastructure Sensing Inc...............B....... 740 928-7010
Hebron *(G-10744)*
Gem Instrument Co................................F....... 330 273-6117
Brunswick *(G-2209)*
Geocorp Inc..E....... 419 433-1101
Huron *(G-11094)*
◆ Gleason Metrology Systems Corp....E....... 937 384-8901
Dayton *(G-8223)*
Glo-Quartz Electric Heater Co..............E....... 440 255-9701
Mentor *(G-13459)*
Godfrey & Wing Inc................................F....... 419 980-4616
Defiance *(G-8624)*
Gooch & Housego (ohio) LLC...............D....... 216 486-6100
Highland Heights *(G-10792)*
H W Fairway International Inc...............E....... 330 678-2540
Kent *(G-11330)*
Harris Corporation..................................C....... 973 284-2866
Beavercreek *(G-1322)*
Harris Instrument Corporation...............G....... 740 369-3580
Delaware *(G-8692)*
Helm Instrument Company Inc..............E....... 419 893-4356
Maumee *(G-13116)*
Henry & Wright Corporation..................F....... 216 851-3750
Cleveland *(G-5394)*
Hickok Incorporated...............................D....... 216 541-8060
Cleveland *(G-5407)*
Homeworth Fabrications & Mchs..........F....... 330 525-5459
Homeworth *(G-10988)*
Honeywell Inc...C....... 513 272-1111
Cincinnati *(G-3825)*
Honeywell International Inc..................A....... 937 484-2000
Urbana *(G-18995)*
Hunkar Technologies Inc.......................C....... 513 272-1010
Cincinnati *(G-3829)*
Huntington Instruments Inc...................G....... 937 767-7001
Yellow Springs *(G-20808)*
▲ Indev Gauging Systems Inc..............E....... 815 282-4463
Dublin *(G-8929)*
Indy Resolutions Ltd..............................G....... 513 475-6625
Cincinnati *(G-3847)*
Infrared Imaging Systems Inc...............G....... 614 989-1148
Marysville *(G-12795)*
Ingersoll-Rand Company........................E....... 419 633-6800
Bryan *(G-2291)*
Innovative Controls Corp.......................D....... 419 691-6684
Toledo *(G-18348)*
Instrument & Valve Services Co...........G....... 513 942-1118
West Chester *(G-19722)*
▼ Intek Inc...E....... 614 895-0301
Westerville *(G-19999)*
John McHael Priester Assoc Inc...........G....... 513 761-8605
Wyoming *(G-20752)*
Journey Electronics Corp......................G....... 513 539-9836
Monroe *(G-14269)*
▲ Keithley Instruments LLC.................C....... 440 248-0400
Solon *(G-17182)*
Koester Corporation...............................D....... 419 599-0291
Napoleon *(G-14548)*
Kuhlman Instrument Company..............G....... 419 668-9533
Norwalk *(G-15402)*
▲ L J Star Incorporated........................E....... 330 405-3040
Twinsburg *(G-18804)*
L3 Cincinnati Electronics Corp..............A....... 513 573-6100
Mason *(G-12902)*
Lake Shore Cryotronics Inc...................C....... 614 891-2243
Westerville *(G-20003)*
Lincoln Electric Company......................C....... 216 524-8800
Cleveland *(G-5576)*
Logan Enterprises Inc............................G....... 937 465-8170
Conover *(G-7664)*
LS Starrett Company...............................D....... 440 835-0005
Westlake *(G-20129)*
M T Systems Inc......................................G....... 330 453-4646
Canton *(G-2738)*
Machine Applications Corp....................G....... 419 621-2322
Sandusky *(G-16825)*
Manico Inc...G....... 440 946-5333
Willoughby *(G-20367)*
▲ Marlin Manufacturing Corp...............D....... 216 676-1340
Cleveland *(G-5623)*
Maxon Corporation.................................G....... 216 459-6056
Independence *(G-11142)*
Measurement Computing Corp..............E....... 440 439-4091
Cleveland *(G-5650)*
▲ Meech Sttic Elminators USA Inc.......F....... 330 564-2000
Copley *(G-7688)*
Mercury Iron and Steel Co.....................F....... 440 349-1500
Solon *(G-17190)*
Mettler-Toledo Intl Fin Inc.....................G....... 614 438-4511
Columbus *(G-6500)*
◆ Mettler-Toledo Intl Inc........................B....... 614 438-4511
Columbus *(G-6501)*
Monitortech Corp....................................G....... 614 231-0500
Columbus *(G-7194)*
▲ MR&e Ltd..G....... 419 872-8180
Toledo *(G-18418)*
Nanostatics Corporation........................F....... 740 477-5900
Circleville *(G-4550)*
Newtech Materials & Analytical.............G....... 330 329-1080
Copley *(G-7690)*
Nidec Indus Automtn USA LLC.............E....... 216 901-2400
Cleveland *(G-5753)*
Nidec Motor Corporation.......................C....... 216 642-1230
Independence *(G-11144)*
Noramar Company Inc...........................G....... 440 338-5740
Novelty *(G-15439)*
Northern Instruments Corp LLC............G....... 216 450-5073
Cleveland *(G-5779)*
▲ Noshok Inc..E....... 440 243-0888
Berea *(G-1620)*
Onevision Corporation...........................G....... 614 794-1144
Westerville *(G-20013)*
Overhoff Technology Corp.....................F....... 513 248-2400
Milford *(G-14030)*
Parker-Hannifin Corporation.................A....... 216 531-3000
Cleveland *(G-5849)*
Poi Holdings Inc.....................................F....... 937 253-7377
Dayton *(G-7988)*

Pride Gage Associates LLC ....G.... 419 318-3793
Toledo (G-18482)
▲ Prime Instruments Inc ....D.... 216 651-0400
Cleveland (G-5921)
Primex ....E.... 513 831-9959
Milford (G-14035)
▼ Production Control Units Inc ....D.... 937 299-5594
Moraine (G-14385)
Production Design Services Inc ....D.... 937 866-3377
Dayton (G-8446)
Prosys Sampling Systems Ltd ....G.... 937 717-4600
Springfield (G-17477)
▲ Q-Lab Corporation ....D.... 440 835-8700
Westlake (G-20146)
Quad/Graphics Inc ....A.... 513 932-1064
Lebanon (G-11687)
Quality Metrology Sys & Sol LL ....G.... 937 431-1800
Beavercreek (G-1338)
R K Combustion & Controls ....G.... 937 444-9700
Mount Orab (G-14451)
Rainin Instrument LLC ....G.... 510 564-1600
Columbus (G-6505)
Ralph Felice Inc ....G.... 330 468-0482
Macedonia (G-12322)
Ram Sensors Inc ....F.... 440 835-3540
Cleveland (G-5959)
▲ Refractory Specialties Inc ....E.... 330 938-2101
Sebring (G-16891)
◆ Reuter-Stokes LLC ....B.... 330 425-3755
Twinsburg (G-18845)
▲ Rhi US Ltd ....F.... 513 753-1254
Cincinnati (G-4264)
▲ Richards Industries Inc ....C.... 513 533-5600
Cincinnati (G-4268)
Rickly Hydrological Co ....E.... 614 297-9877
Columbus (G-7393)
Rosemount Inc ....F.... 513 851-5555
West Chester (G-19786)
Roto Tech Inc ....E.... 937 859-8503
Dayton (G-8485)
Rsa Controls Inc ....G.... 513 476-6277
West Chester (G-19790)
▲ Rsw Technologies LLC ....F.... 419 662-8100
Rossford (G-16592)
Sansei Showa Co Ltd ....E.... 440 248-4440
Cleveland (G-6030)
Scadatech LLC ....G.... 614 552-7726
Reynoldsburg (G-16452)
Schneider Electric Usa Inc ....D.... 513 755-5000
West Chester (G-19792)
Seekirk Inc ....F.... 614 278-9200
Columbus (G-7436)
Seelaus Instrument Co ....G.... 513 733-8222
Miamisburg (G-13714)
▲ Selas Heat Technology Co LLC ....E.... 800 523-6500
Streetsboro (G-17697)
Selective Med Components Inc ....E.... 740 397-7838
Mount Vernon (G-14507)
Shelburne Corp ....G.... 216 321-9177
Shaker Heights (G-16936)
Sherbrooke Metals ....E.... 440 942-3520
Willoughby (G-20429)
Snappskin Inc ....G.... 440 318-4879
Chagrin Falls (G-3030)
▲ Solon Manufacturing Company ....E.... 440 286-7149
Chardon (G-3137)
Stancorp Inc ....G.... 330 545-6615
Girard (G-10267)
Star Combustion Systems LLC ....G.... 513 282-0810
Mason (G-12942)
Stewart Manufacturing Corp ....E.... 937 390-3333
Springfield (G-17499)
Stock Fairfield Corporation ....C.... 440 543-6000
Chagrin Falls (G-3078)
T P F Inc ....G.... 513 761-9968
Cincinnati (G-4403)
Tasi Holdings Inc ....E.... 513 202-5182
Harrison (G-10676)
TE Brown LLC ....G.... 937 223-2241
Dayton (G-8548)
Technology Resources Inc ....G.... 419 241-9248
Toledo (G-18544)
Tecmark Corporation ....E.... 440 205-9188
Mentor (G-13602)
▲ Tecmark Corporation ....D.... 440 205-7600
Mentor (G-13601)
Tecsis LP ....E.... 614 430-0683
Worthington (G-20705)
Telemecanique Sensors ....G.... 800 435-2121
Dayton (G-8551)
▲ Therm-O-Disc Incorporated ....A.... 419 525-8500
Mansfield (G-12530)
Thermacal Inc ....G.... 440 498-1005
Solon (G-17252)
▲ Thk Manufacturing America Inc ....C.... 740 928-1415
Hebron (G-10766)
▲ Tls Corp ....E.... 216 574-4759
Cleveland (G-6177)
Toledo Transducers Inc ....E.... 419 724-4170
Holland (G-10962)
▲ Unicontrol Inc ....D.... 216 398-0330
Cleveland (G-6230)
United Tool Supply Inc ....G.... 513 752-6000
Cincinnati (G-3266)
◆ Vanner Holdings Inc ....D.... 614 771-2718
Hilliard (G-10873)
◆ Vega Americas Inc ....C.... 513 272-0131
Cincinnati (G-4470)
Vertiv Corporation ....B.... 740 547-5100
Ironton (G-11175)
Vertiv North America Inc ....A.... 614 888-0246
Columbus (G-7578)
Vertiv Solutions Inc ....E.... 614 888-0246
Columbus (G-7579)
Visi-Trak Worldwide LLC ....F.... 216 524-2363
Cleveland (G-6264)
Vitec Inc ....F.... 216 464-4670
Bedford (G-1453)
Wabash River Conservancy ....G.... 419 375-2577
Fort Recovery (G-9830)
Weed Instrument Company Inc ....E.... 800 321-0796
Independence (G-11156)
Westerman Inc ....D.... 330 262-6946
Wooster (G-20665)
Wild Fire Systems ....G.... 440 442-8999
Cleveland (G-6308)
Xylem Inc ....D.... 937 767-7241
Yellow Springs (G-20819)
Ysi Environmental Inc ....C.... 937 767-7241
Yellow Springs (G-20824)
◆ Ysi Incorporated ....D.... 937 767-7241
Yellow Springs (G-20825)

3824 Fluid Meters & Counters

Aclara Technologies LLC ....C.... 440 528-7200
Solon (G-17098)
APS Accurate Products & Svcs ....G.... 440 353-9353
North Ridgeville (G-15208)
Aqua Technology Group LLC ....G.... 513 298-1183
West Chester (G-19648)
Automatic Timing & Controls ....G.... 614 888-8855
New Albany (G-14606)
Bif Co LLC ....F.... 330 564-0941
Akron (G-88)
Brooks Manufacturing ....G.... 419 244-1777
Toledo (G-18216)
CNG Fueling LLC ....G.... 330 772-2403
Brookfield (G-2103)
Commercial Electric Pdts Corp ....E.... 216 241-2886
Cleveland (G-5002)
Eaton Corporation ....B.... 440 523-5000
Beachwood (G-1233)
Electrodynamics Inc ....C.... 847 259-0740
Cincinnati (G-3247)
Ernst Flow Industries LLC ....F.... 732 938-5641
Strongsville (G-17743)
Exact Equipment Corporation ....F.... 215 295-2000
Columbus (G-6491)
Flow Line Options Corp ....G.... 330 331-7331
Wadsworth (G-19242)
Fred W Hanks Company ....G.... 216 731-1774
Cleveland (G-5274)
▲ Graco Ohio Inc ....D.... 330 494-1313
North Canton (G-15088)
K-Hill Signal Co Inc ....G.... 740 922-0421
Uhrichsville (G-18890)
Lake Shore Cryotronics Inc ....C.... 614 891-2243
Westerville (G-20003)
Parking & Traffic Control SEC ....F.... 440 243-7565
Cleveland (G-5851)
▲ Triplett Bluffton Corporation ....G.... 419 358-8750
Bluffton (G-1896)
Westmont Inc ....G.... 330 862-3080
Minerva (G-14205)

3825 Instrs For Measuring & Testing Electricity

Accu-Feed Engineering ....G.... 419 668-7990
Norwalk (G-15378)
Aclara Technologies LLC ....C.... 440 528-7200
Solon (G-17098)
Advanced Kiffer Systems Inc ....F.... 216 267-8181
Cleveland (G-4627)
Alpine Gage Inc ....G.... 937 669-8665
Tipp City (G-18099)
Analytica Usa Inc ....G.... 513 348-2333
Dayton (G-8031)
Andeen-Hagerling Inc ....F.... 440 349-0370
Cleveland (G-4711)
Andromeda Research ....G.... 513 831-9708
Cincinnati (G-3346)
Aqua Technology Group LLC ....G.... 513 298-1183
West Chester (G-19648)
Automation Technology Inc ....E.... 937 233-6084
Dayton (G-8045)
Automtiq Msurement Systems LLC ....G.... 614 431-2667
Columbus (G-6634)
Avtron Holdings LLC ....B.... 216 642-1230
Cleveland (G-4779)
Battery Unlimited ....G.... 740 452-5030
Zanesville (G-21104)
Bionix Safety Technologies Ltd ....E.... 419 727-0552
Toledo (G-18202)
▲ Bird Electronic Corporation ....C.... 440 248-1200
Solon (G-17115)
Bird Technologies Group Inc ....G.... 440 248-1200
Solon (G-17116)
CDI Industries Inc ....E.... 440 243-1100
Cleveland (G-4895)
Community Care Network Inc ....E.... 216 671-0977
Cleveland (G-5007)
Contact Industries Inc ....E.... 419 884-9788
Lexington (G-11804)
County of Medina ....F.... 330 723-3641
Medina (G-13245)
Data Power Solutions ....G.... 614 471-1911
Columbus (G-6851)
Desco Corporation ....G.... 614 888-8855
New Albany (G-14622)
Drs Signal Technologies Inc ....E.... 937 429-7470
Beavercreek (G-1312)
▲ Dynamp LLC ....E.... 614 871-6900
Grove City (G-10427)
F Squared Inc ....G.... 419 752-7273
Greenwich (G-10403)
Field Apparatus Service & Tstg ....G.... 513 353-9399
Cincinnati (G-3685)
Fisher Testers LLC ....G.... 937 416-6554
Huber Heights (G-11018)
FT Group Inc ....E.... 937 746-6439
Cincinnati (G-3716)
▲ Hana Microdisplay Tech Inc ....D.... 330 405-4600
Twinsburg (G-18791)
Hannon Company ....D.... 330 456-4728
Canton (G-2693)
Helm Instrument Company Inc ....E.... 419 893-4356
Maumee (G-13116)
Hughes Corporation ....E.... 440 238-2550
Strongsville (G-17751)
▲ Japlar Group Inc ....F.... 513 791-7192
Cincinnati (G-3870)
▲ Keithley Instruments LLC ....C.... 440 248-0400
Solon (G-17182)
Keithley Instruments Intl Corp ....B.... 440 248-0400
Cleveland (G-5525)
Lake Shore Cryotronics Inc ....C.... 614 891-2243
Westerville (G-20003)
Lawhorn Machine & Tool Inc ....G.... 937 884-5674
Phillipsburg (G-16037)
Lomar Enterprises Inc ....F.... 614 409-9104
Groveport (G-10501)
Machine Products Company ....E.... 937 890-6600
Dayton (G-8320)
Midwest Metrology LLC ....G.... 937 832-0965
Englewood (G-9369)
Midwest Telemetry Inc ....G.... 440 725-5718
Kirtland (G-11469)
Mueller Electric Company Inc ....E.... 614 888-8855
New Albany (G-14631)
Nebulatronics Inc ....E.... 440 243-2370
Olmsted Twp (G-15534)
Neptune Equipment Company ....F.... 513 851-8008
Cincinnati (G-4067)
Nu-Di Products Co Inc ....D.... 216 251-9070
Cleveland (G-5793)
O H Technologies Inc ....G.... 440 354-8780
Mentor (G-13531)
Omega Engineering Inc ....E.... 740 965-9340
Sunbury (G-17896)

S I C

38 MEASURING, ANALYZING AND CONTROLLING INSTRUMENTS; PHOTOGRAPHIC, MEDICAL AN

▲ Opw Engineered Systems Inc .... G 888 771-9438
  Lebanon (G-11680)
▼ Orton Edward Jr Crmic Fndation .... E 614 895-2663
  Westerville (G-20014)
P G M Diversified Industries .... G 440 885-3500
  Cleveland (G-5830)
P P M Inc .... F 216 701-0419
  Chagrin Falls (G-3026)
Palstar Inc .... F 937 773-6255
  Piqua (G-16148)
Paneltech LLC .... G 440 516-1300
  Wickliffe (G-20223)
▲ Pile Dynamics Inc .... E 216 831-6131
  Cleveland (G-5877)
▲ Pressco Technology Inc .... D 440 498-2600
  Cleveland (G-5919)
Simplex-It LLC .... G 234 380-1277
  Stow (G-17628)
▲ Skidmore-Wilhelm Mfg Company ..... E 216 481-4774
  Solon (G-17232)
Sontek Corporation .... G 937 767-7241
  Yellow Springs (G-20817)
Speelman Electric Inc .... G 330 633-1410
  Tallmadge (G-18004)
Strong M Llc .... F 614 329-8025
  Columbus (G-7494)
Structural Radar Imaging Inc .... G 425 970-3890
  Toledo (G-18532)
▲ Tech Pro Inc .... E 330 923-3546
  Akron (G-397)
Tektronix Inc .... E 513 870-4729
  West Chester (G-19906)
Tektronix Inc .... E 440 248-0400
  Solon (G-17250)
◆ Tmsi LLC .... G 888 867-4872
  North Canton (G-15130)
▲ Triplett Bluffton Corporation .... G 419 358-8750
  Bluffton (G-1896)
▲ TTI Floor Care North Amer Inc .... B 440 996-2000
  Solon (G-17255)
Val-Con Inc .... G 440 357-1898
  Painesville (G-15794)
Visual Information Institute .... F 937 376-4361
  Xenia (G-20801)
▲ Vmetro Inc .... G 281 584-0728
  Fairborn (G-9473)
▲ Zts Inc .... F 513 271-2557
  Cincinnati (G-4534)

3826 Analytical Instruments

4r Enterprises Incorporated .... G 330 923-9799
  Cuyahoga Falls (G-7829)
Acense LLC .... G 330 242-0046
  Twinsburg (G-18724)
Affymetrix Inc .... C 216 765-5000
  Cleveland (G-4640)
Affymetrix Inc .... F 419 887-1233
  Maumee (G-13067)
Akron Council of Engineering .... G 330 535-8835
  Akron (G-37)
Alliance Healthcare Svcs Inc .... G 330 493-6747
  Canton (G-2568)
▲ Astro Instrumentation LLC .... D 440 238-2005
  Strongsville (G-17712)
Auto Technology Company .... F 440 572-7800
  Strongsville (G-17715)
Bionix Safety Technologies Ltd .... E 419 727-0552
  Toledo (G-18202)
Blue Water Satellite Inc .... G 419 372-0160
  Toledo (G-18207)
Bridge Analyzers Incorporated .... G 216 332-0592
  Bedford Heights (G-1463)
▲ Bry-Air Inc .... E 740 965-2974
  Sunbury (G-17883)
C D C At Cityview .... G 216 426-2020
  Cleveland (G-4856)
◆ Columbus Instruments Intl Corp ...... E 614 276-0593
  Columbus (G-6793)
Compliant Healthcare Tech LLC .... F 216 255-9607
  Cleveland (G-5010)
Compliant Healthcare Tech LLC .... E 216 255-9607
  Cleveland (G-5011)
Consolidatd Analytical Sys Inc .... F 513 542-1200
  Cleves (G-6359)
CST Zero Discharged Car Wash S .... G 740 947-5480
  Waverly (G-19543)
Dentronix Inc .... E 330 916-7300
  Cuyahoga Falls (G-7860)
Diascopic LLC .... G 312 282-1800
  Cleveland (G-5091)

Elkins Earthworks LLC .... G 330 725-7766
  Medina (G-13254)
Envirnmntal Cmpliance Tech LLC ...... G 216 634-0400
  North Royalton (G-15271)
Fertility Solutions Inc .... G 216 491-0030
  Cleveland (G-5234)
Filament LLC .... G 614 732-0754
  Columbus (G-6921)
Health Bridge Imaging LLC .... G 740 423-3300
  Belpre (G-1576)
▲ HEF USA Corporation .... F 937 323-2556
  Springfield (G-17416)
IEC Infrared Systems Inc .... E 440 234-8000
  Middleburg Heights (G-13765)
IEC Infrared Systems LLC .... E 440 234-8000
  Middleburg Heights (G-13766)
Innovative Lab Services LLC .... G 614 554-6446
  Pataskala (G-15832)
Isotopx Inc .... G 508 337-8467
  Hudson (G-11057)
▲ Laserlinc Inc .... E 937 318-2440
  Fairborn (G-9463)
Mansfield Imaging Center LLC .... F 419 756-8899
  Mansfield (G-12476)
Measurenet Technology Ltd .... F 513 396-6765
  Cincinnati (G-3992)
Medical Imaging Dist LLC .... G 800 898-3392
  Mantua (G-12553)
Metron Instruments Inc .... G 216 332-0592
  Bedford Heights (G-1474)
Mettler-Toledo Intl Fin Inc .... E 614 438-4511
  Columbus (G-6500)
◆ Mettler-Toledo Intl Inc .... B 614 438-4511
  Columbus (G-6501)
Mettlr-Tledo Globl Hldings LLC .... F 614 438-4511
  Columbus (G-6502)
Nanotronics Imaging Inc .... G 330 926-9809
  Cuyahoga Falls (G-7900)
NDC Technologies Inc .... C 937 233-9935
  Dayton (G-8379)
Nordson Uv Inc .... F 440 985-4573
  Amherst (G-568)
Northcoast Environmental Labs .... G 330 342-3377
  Streetsboro (G-17685)
Nvision Technology Inc .... F 412 254-4668
  Norton (G-15374)
Ohio Lumex Co Inc .... G 440 264-2500
  Solon (G-17211)
Omnitech Electronics Inc .... F 800 822-1344
  Columbus (G-7271)
▼ Orton Edward Jr Crmic Fndation ... E 614 895-2663
  Westerville (G-20014)
PMC Gage Inc .... E 440 953-1672
  Willoughby (G-20404)
Precision Anlytical Instrs Inc .... G 513 984-1600
  Blue Ash (G-1834)
Pts Prfssnal Technical Svc Inc .... D 513 642-0111
  West Chester (G-19771)
▲ Q-Lab Corporation .... D 440 835-8700
  Westlake (G-20146)
Reid Asset Management Company ... E 216 642-3223
  Cleveland (G-5971)
◆ Reuter-Stokes LLC .... B 330 425-3755
  Twinsburg (G-18845)
◆ Rotex Global LLC .... C 513 541-1236
  Cincinnati (G-4282)
▲ S-Tek Inc .... G 440 439-8232
  Bedford (G-1443)
Summit Diagnostic Imaging LLC ...... E 513 233-3320
  Cincinnati (G-4389)
Targeted Cmpund Monitoring LLC ... G 513 461-3535
  Beavercreek (G-1365)
Teledyne Instruments Inc .... D 603 886-8400
  Mason (G-12947)
Teledyne Instruments Inc .... E 513 229-7000
  Mason (G-12946)
Teledyne Tekmar Company .... E 513 229-7000
  Mason (G-12948)
Test-Fuchs Corporation .... G 440 708-3505
  Brecksville (G-2061)
Thermo Fisher Scientific .... A 740 373-4763
  Marietta (G-12680)
Thermo Fisher Scientific Inc .... F 513 489-2926
  Montgomery (G-14299)
Thermo Fisher Scientific Inc .... G 440 703-1400
  Bedford (G-1449)
◆ Ysi Incorporated .... D 937 767-7241
  Yellow Springs (G-20825)

3827 Optical Instruments

Bsa Industries Inc .... D 614 846-5515
  Columbus (G-6706)
▲ Cleveland Hoya Corp .... D 440 234-5703
  Berea (G-1595)
Di Walt Optical Inc .... F 330 453-8427
  Canton (G-2657)
FT Group Inc .... E 937 746-6439
  Cincinnati (G-3716)
Genvac Aerospace Corp .... F 440 646-9986
  Cleveland (G-5317)
Gooch & Housego (florida) LLC ..... G 321 242-7818
  Cleveland (G-5330)
Gooch & Housego (ohio) LLC .... D 216 486-6100
  Highland Heights (G-10792)
Greenlight Optics LLC .... E 513 247-9777
  Loveland (G-12193)
Holte Eyeware .... E 513 321-4000
  Cincinnati (G-3820)
Hoya Optical Labs .... G 440 239-1924
  Berea (G-1610)
▼ Krendl Machine Company .... D 419 692-3060
  Delphos (G-8747)
Lear Engineering Corp .... F 937 429-0534
  Beavercreek (G-1325)
Mbm Industries Ltd .... G 937 522-0719
  Beavercreek Township (G-1369)
Mercury Iron and Steel Co .... F 440 349-1500
  Solon (G-17190)
Ncrx Optical Solutions Inc .... F 330 239-5353
  Hudson (G-11063)
Point Source Inc .... F 937 855-6020
  Germantown (G-10245)
▲ Trevi Technology Inc .... G 614 754-7175
  Columbus (G-7542)
Uvisir Inc .... G 216 374-9376
  Beachwood (G-1284)
▲ Vampire Optical Coatings Inc ..... G 740 919-4596
  Pataskala (G-15848)
Vance Adams .... G 330 424-9670
  Lisbon (G-11981)
▲ Volk Optical Inc .... D 440 942-6161
  Mentor (G-13625)
Vsp Lab Columbus .... E 614 409-8900
  Lockbourne (G-11999)
Welded Tube Pros LLC .... G 330 854-2966
  Canal Fulton (G-2496)
West Point Optical Group LLC ...... G 614 395-9775
  Mason (G-12954)
Wilson Optical Laboratory Inc .... E 440 357-7000
  Mentor (G-13626)

3829 Measuring & Controlling Devices, NEC

1 A Lifesafer Inc .... G 513 651-9560
  Blue Ash (G-1716)
1 A Lifesafer Hawaii Inc .... F 513 651-9560
  Blue Ash (G-1717)
Aclara Technologies LLC .... C 440 528-7200
  Solon (G-17098)
▲ Advanced Industrial Measuremnt E 937 320-4930
  Miamisburg (G-13637)
Advanced OEM Solutions LLC ..... G 513 846-5755
  Cincinnati (G-3301)
Amano Cincinnati Incorporated ..... D 513 697-9000
  Loveland (G-12176)
American Cube Mold Inc .... G 330 558-0044
  Hinckley (G-10898)
Amron LLC .... G 330 457-8570
  New Waterford (G-14836)
ARC Drilling Inc .... F 216 525-0920
  Cleveland (G-4723)
▲ Arnco Corporation .... C 800 847-7661
  Elyria (G-9219)
AT&T Government Solutions Inc ... D 937 306-3030
  Beavercreek (G-1302)
Automation and Ctrl Tech Inc .... E 614 495-1120
  Dublin (G-8886)
Automation Technology Inc .... E 937 233-6084
  Dayton (G-8045)
Babcock & Wilcox Entps Inc .... A 330 753-4511
  Barberton (G-1061)
Balmac Inc .... F 614 873-8222
  Plain City (G-16175)
▲ Bilz Vibration Technology Inc .... F 330 468-2459
  Macedonia (G-12279)
Bionetics Corporation .... E 740 788-3800
  Heath (G-10718)
▲ Bionix Development Corporation E 419 727-8421
  Toledo (G-18201)

Bionix Safety Technologies Ltd............E....... 419 727-0552
Toledo *(G-18202)*
Blaze Technical Services Inc ....E....... 330 923-0409
Stow *(G-17574)*
▲ Ceia Usa Ltd ....E....... 330 405-3190
Twinsburg *(G-18747)*
Cincinnati Ctrl Dynamics Inc ....G....... 513 242-7300
Cincinnati *(G-3489)*
Continental Testing Inc ....F....... 937 832-3322
Union *(G-18900)*
Control Measurement Inc.......................G....... 440 639-0020
Painesville *(G-15725)*
▲ Controlled Access Inc ....F....... 330 273-6185
Hinckley *(G-10899)*
Cooper-Atkins Corporation....................G....... 513 793-5366
Cincinnati *(G-3549)*
Corcadence Inc ....G....... 216 702-6371
Beachwood *(G-1231)*
David Boswell..E....... 614 441-2497
Columbus *(G-6852)*
Daytronic Corporation...........................F....... 937 866-3300
Miamisburg *(G-13658)*
Denton Atd Inc ....E....... 567 265-5200
Huron *(G-11093)*
Electric Speed Indicator Co ....F....... 216 251-2540
Cleveland *(G-5163)*
▲ Ets Solutions Usa LLC ....G....... 330 666-8696
Bath *(G-1200)*
Euclid Products Co Inc..........................G....... 440 942-7310
Willoughby *(G-20317)*
Excelitas Technologies Corp ....C....... 866 539-5916
Miamisburg *(G-13667)*
▲ Ferry Industries Inc...........................D....... 330 920-9200
Stow *(G-17587)*
Fiomet LLC ....G....... 513 519-7622
Cincinnati *(G-3691)*
Fischer Engineering Company ....G....... 937 754-1750
Dayton *(G-8196)*
▲ Fluke Biomedical LLC ....C....... 440 248-9300
Cleveland *(G-5255)*
▲ Fowler Products Inc...........................F....... 419 683-4057
Crestline *(G-7794)*
Gem Instrument Co................................F....... 330 273-6117
Brunswick *(G-2209)*
General Pump & Eqp Compnay.............G....... 330 455-2100
Canton *(G-2682)*
Gilson Screen Incorporated...................E....... 419 256-7711
Malinta *(G-12379)*
GLC Biotechnology Inc ....G....... 440 349-2193
Hudson *(G-11046)*
◆ Gleason Metrology Systems Corp....E....... 937 384-8901
Dayton *(G-8223)*
Global Gauge Corporation.....................F....... 937 254-3500
Moraine *(G-14356)*
Grale Technologies Inc..........................G....... 724 683-8141
Youngstown *(G-20923)*
Halliday Technologies Inc ....G....... 614 504-4150
Delaware *(G-8691)*
Harris Instrument Corporation ....G....... 740 369-3580
Delaware *(G-8692)*
Helm Instrument Company Inc..............E....... 419 893-4356
Maumee *(G-13116)*
Henry & Wright Corporation ....F....... 216 851-3750
Cleveland *(G-5394)*
Heraeus Electro-Nite Co LLC................G....... 330 725-1419
Medina *(G-13272)*
Hickok Incorporated ....D....... 216 541-8060
Cleveland *(G-5407)*
▲ Honeywell Lebow Products ....C....... 614 850-5000
Columbus *(G-7006)*
Indicator Shop..G....... 513 897-0055
Waynesville *(G-19568)*
Industrial Masurement Ctrl Inc ....G....... 440 877-1140
Cleveland *(G-5453)*
Instrumentors Inc...................................G....... 440 238-3430
Strongsville *(G-17755)*
J C Equipment Sales & Leasing ....G....... 513 772-7612
Cincinnati *(G-3862)*
Jz Technologies LLC ....G....... 937 252-5800
Blue Ash *(G-1799)*
Karman Rubber Company......................E....... 330 864-2161
Akron *(G-232)*
Kicher and Company..............................G....... 440 266-1663
Mentor *(G-13489)*
Krumor Inc ....F....... 216 328-9802
Cleveland *(G-5545)*
Lake Shore Cryotronics Inc ....C....... 614 891-2243
Westerville *(G-20003)*
Lawhorn Machine & Tool Inc ....G....... 937 884-5674
Phillipsburg *(G-16037)*
LH Marshall Company ....F....... 614 294-6433
Columbus *(G-7124)*
Low Stress Grind Inc..............................F....... 513 771-7977
Cincinnati *(G-3952)*
LS Starrett Company ....D....... 440 835-0005
Westlake *(G-20129)*
Magnetic Analysis Corporation ....F....... 330 758-1367
Youngstown *(G-20965)*
Matrix Research Inc...............................D....... 937 427-8433
Beavercreek *(G-1357)*
▼ MB Dynamics Inc ....E....... 216 292-5850
Cleveland *(G-5641)*
Measurement Specialties Inc................D....... 330 659-3312
Akron *(G-277)*
Micro Laboratories Inc ....G....... 440 918-0001
Mentor *(G-13518)*
Micro Systems Development Inc...........G....... 937 438-3567
Dayton *(G-8349)*
Multi Lapping Service Inc......................F....... 440 944-7592
Wickliffe *(G-20218)*
▲ Multilink Inc ....C....... 440 366-6966
Elyria *(G-9298)*
Nanologix Inc ....G....... 330 534-0800
Hubbard *(G-11006)*
National Patent Analytical Sys ....E....... 419 526-6727
Mansfield *(G-12489)*
Nebulatronics Inc...................................E....... 440 243-2370
Olmsted Twp *(G-15534)*
▲ Newall Electronics Inc ....F....... 614 771-0213
Columbus *(G-7216)*
Nidec Motor Corporation.......................C....... 216 642-1230
Independence *(G-11144)*
Novitran LLC ....G....... 513 792-2727
Cincinnati *(G-4091)*
▲ Nucon International Inc ....F....... 614 846-5710
Columbus *(G-7232)*
Omega Automation Inc..........................D....... 937 890-2350
Dayton *(G-8402)*
Omega Engineering Inc.........................E....... 740 965-9340
Sunbury *(G-17896)*
Omega International Inc........................E....... 937 890-2350
Dayton *(G-8403)*
Overhoff Technology Corp.....................F....... 513 248-2400
Milford *(G-14030)*
P H Glatfelter Company.........................G....... 740 289-5100
Piketon *(G-16077)*
▲ Parker-Hannifin Corporation.............B....... 216 896-3000
Cleveland *(G-5848)*
Parker-Hannifin Corporation..................F....... 216 896-3000
Cleveland *(G-5850)*
▲ Perfect Measuring Tape Company ...G....... 419 243-6811
Toledo *(G-18464)*
Plating Test Cell Supply Co ....G....... 216 486-8400
Cleveland *(G-5890)*
PMC Gage Inc..E....... 440 953-1672
Willoughby *(G-20404)*
▲ Portage Electric Products Inc...........C....... 330 499-2727
North Canton *(G-15111)*
Precision Environments Inc..................E....... 513 847-1510
West Chester *(G-19765)*
Prentke Romich Company.....................C....... 330 262-1984
Wooster *(G-20641)*
▲ Pressco Technology Inc....................D....... 440 498-2600
Cleveland *(G-5919)*
▼ Production Control Units Inc ....D....... 937 299-5594
Moraine *(G-14385)*
▲ Q-Lab Corporation ....D....... 440 835-8700
Westlake *(G-20146)*
Quality Controls Inc...............................F....... 513 272-3900
Cincinnati *(G-4225)*
Quidel Dhi..E....... 740 589-3300
Athens *(G-848)*
R J Engineering Company Inc...............G....... 419 843-8651
Toledo *(G-18494)*
Rae Systems Inc ....G....... 440 232-0555
Walton Hills *(G-19314)*
Ralston Instruments LLC ....E....... 440 564-1430
Newbury *(G-14963)*
◆ Reuter-Stokes LLC ....B....... 330 425-3755
Twinsburg *(G-18845)*
Rickly Hydrological Company ....G....... 614 297-9877
Columbus *(G-7394)*
Roto Tech Inc ....E....... 937 859-8503
Dayton *(G-8485)*
Safe-Grain Inc..G....... 513 398-2500
Loveland *(G-12229)*
▲ Saginomiya America Inc...................G....... 614 766-7390
Dublin *(G-8977)*
Science/Electronics Inc..........................F....... 937 224-4444
Dayton *(G-8497)*
Sensotec LLC ....G....... 614 481-8616
Hilliard *(G-10860)*
▲ Skidmore-Wilhelm Mfg Company.....E....... 216 481-4774
Solon *(G-17232)*
▲ Standards Testing Labs Inc ....D....... 330 833-8548
Massillon *(G-13050)*
◆ Struers Inc..D....... 440 871-0071
Westlake *(G-20163)*
▲ Sumiriko Ohio Inc ....C....... 419 358-2121
Bluffton *(G-1893)*
Super Systems Inc.................................E....... 513 772-0060
Cincinnati *(G-4397)*
▲ Te-Co Manufacturing LLC ....D....... 937 836-0961
Englewood *(G-9377)*
▲ Tech Pro Inc.......................................E....... 330 923-3546
Akron *(G-397)*
Tech Products Corporation....................E....... 937 438-1100
Miamisburg *(G-13723)*
Tegam Inc ....E....... 440 466-6100
Geneva *(G-10229)*
Teledyne Instruments Inc......................E....... 513 229-7000
Mason *(G-12946)*
Teledyne Tekmar Company...................E....... 513 229-7000
Mason *(G-12948)*
Teradyne Inc...F....... 937 427-1280
Beavercreek *(G-1343)*
▼ Test Mark Industries Inc ....F....... 330 426-2200
East Palestine *(G-9086)*
Test-Fuchs Corporation ....G....... 440 708-3505
Brecksville *(G-2061)*
Thermo Eberline LLC.............................C....... 440 703-1400
Oakwood Village *(G-15485)*
Tmw Systems Inc...................................F....... 615 986-1900
Cleveland *(G-6179)*
Toledo Transducers Inc.........................E....... 419 724-4170
Holland *(G-10962)*
Tool Technologies Van Dyke..................F....... 937 349-4900
Marysville *(G-12817)*
Tripoint Instruments Inc.........................G....... 513 702-9217
Cincinnati *(G-4440)*
Tuppas Software Corporation................C....... 419 897-7902
Maumee *(G-13156)*
◆ UPA Technology Inc ....F....... 513 755-1380
West Chester *(G-19816)*
Vibration Test Systems Inc ....G....... 330 562-5729
Aurora *(G-914)*
Welding Consultants Inc........................G....... 614 258-7018
Columbus *(G-7598)*
Xcite Systems Corporation....................G....... 513 965-0300
Cincinnati *(G-3267)*

3841 Surgical & Medical Instrs & Apparatus

21stcentury Medical Tech LLC ....G....... 732 310-9367
Akron *(G-13)*
3d Systems Inc.......................................D....... 216 229-2040
Cleveland *(G-4580)*
3M Company...B....... 513 248-1749
Milford *(G-13991)*
Acoflow Therapeutics LLC....................G....... 513 558-0073
Cincinnati *(G-3293)*
Actis Ltd...G....... 614 436-0600
Powell *(G-16306)*
Advanced Medical Solutions Inc...........G....... 937 291-0069
Centerville *(G-2995)*
Aeiou Scientific LLC...............................G....... 614 325-2103
Columbus *(G-6547)*
Altitude Medical Inc ....G....... 440 799-7701
Chardon *(G-3097)*
Applied Medical Technology Inc ....E....... 440 717-4000
Brecksville *(G-2020)*
Apto Orthopaedics Corporation ....E....... 330 572-7544
Akron *(G-68)*
▲ Atc Group Inc ....D....... 440 293-4064
Andover *(G-579)*
Atricure Inc..C....... 513 755-4100
Mason *(G-12830)*
Attention Dsase Diagnstc Group...........G....... 216 577-3075
Cleveland *(G-4763)*
Avalign Technologies Inc.......................F....... 419 542-7743
Hicksville *(G-10776)*
Aws Industries Inc ....E....... 513 932-7941
Lebanon *(G-11635)*
Axon Medical LLC..................................E....... 216 276-0262
Medina *(G-13226)*
Baby Love Prenatal Imaging LLC..........G....... 419 905-7935
Delphos *(G-8736)*
Beam Technologies Inc ....G....... 800 648-1179
Columbus *(G-6655)*
Becton Dickinson and Company............G....... 858 617-4272
Groveport *(G-10484)*

38 MEASURING, ANALYZING AND CONTROLLING INSTRUMENTS; PHOTOGRAPHIC, MEDICAL AN SIC SECTION

▲ **Bionix Development Corporation**.....E....... 419 727-8421
Toledo *(G-18201)*
Blue Bell Bio-Medical Inc.....G....... 419 238-4442
Van Wert *(G-19079)*
Boston Scntfic Nrmdlation Corp.....G....... 513 377-6160
Mason *(G-12836)*
Boston Scntfic Nrmdlation Corp.....G....... 419 720-9510
Toledo *(G-18211)*
Boston Scntfic Nrmdlation Corp.....C....... 330 372-2652
Warren *(G-19378)*
Buckeye Medical Tech LLC.....G....... 330 719-9868
Warren *(G-19379)*
Bulk Molding Compounds Inc.....D....... 419 874-7941
Perrysburg *(G-15926)*
C&W Swiss Inc.....F....... 937 832-2889
Englewood *(G-9350)*
▲ **Casco Mfg Solutions Inc**.....D....... 513 681-0003
Cincinnati *(G-3447)*
Clevex Inc.....G....... 614 675-3757
Columbus *(G-6774)*
Cmd Medtech LLC.....G....... 614 364-4243
Columbus *(G-6777)*
Collaborative For Adaptive Lif.....G....... 216 513-0572
Fairlawn *(G-9601)*
Columbus Vsclar Intrvntion LLC.....E....... 614 917-0696
Westerville *(G-20041)*
◆ **Cordis Corporation**.....A....... 614 757-5000
Dublin *(G-8903)*
Covidien Holding Inc.....F....... 513 948-7219
Cincinnati *(G-3554)*
Cqt Kennedy LLC.....D....... 419 238-2442
Van Wert *(G-19086)*
▼ **Daavlin Distributing Co**.....E....... 419 636-6304
Bryan *(G-2278)*
▲ **Dayton Hawker Corporation**.....F....... 937 293-8147
Dayton *(G-8135)*
Dentronix Inc.....E....... 330 916-7300
Cuyahoga Falls *(G-7860)*
Devicor Med Pdts Holdings Inc.....A....... 513 864-9000
Cincinnati *(G-3586)*
Devicor Medical Products Inc.....G....... 513 864-9000
Cincinnati *(G-3587)*
Diagnostic Hybrids Inc.....C....... 740 593-1784
Athens *(G-828)*
Drt Aerospace LLC.....D....... 937 492-6121
Sidney *(G-17031)*
Drt Medical LLC.....C....... 937 387-0880
Dayton *(G-8170)*
Ebisyn Medical Inc.....G....... 609 759-1101
Dublin *(G-8910)*
Elite Biomedical Solutions LLC.....F....... 513 207-0602
Cincinnati *(G-3248)*
Ellen L Ellsworth.....G....... 440 352-8031
Mentor *(G-13438)*
▲ **Em Innovations Inc**.....G....... 614 853-1504
Galloway *(G-10178)*
◆ **Encore Plastics Corporation**.....C....... 419 626-8000
Sandusky *(G-16808)*
Ennovea Medical LLC.....G....... 855 997-2273
Columbus *(G-6899)*
▼ **Eoi Inc**.....F....... 740 201-3300
Lewis Center *(G-11760)*
Estech Inc.....G....... 805 895-1263
West Chester *(G-19700)*
▲ **Ethicon Endo-Surgery Inc**.....A....... 513 337-7000
Blue Ash *(G-1765)*
Ethicon US LLC.....E....... 513 337-7000
Blue Ash *(G-1767)*
Eye Surgery Center Ohio Inc.....E....... 614 228-3937
Columbus *(G-6912)*
▲ **Falls Welding & Fabg Inc**.....G....... 330 253-3437
Akron *(G-165)*
Filament LLC.....G....... 614 732-0754
Columbus *(G-6921)*
Findlay American Prosthetic &.....G....... 419 424-1622
Findlay *(G-9683)*
Flotbi Inc.....G....... 216 619-5928
Cleveland *(G-5252)*
Frantz Medical Development Ltd.....C....... 440 255-1155
Mentor *(G-13447)*
Frantz Medical Development Ltd.....D....... 440 205-9026
Mentor *(G-13448)*
Frantz Medical Group.....E....... 440 974-8522
Mentor *(G-13449)*
▲ **General Data Company Inc**.....C....... 513 752-7978
Cincinnati *(G-3252)*
Goal Medical LLC.....E....... 541 654-5951
Mentor *(G-13461)*
Gqi Inc.....G....... 330 830-9805
Massillon *(G-12989)*
Grimm Scientific Industries.....F....... 740 374-3412
Marietta *(G-12629)*
Gyrus Acmi LP.....C....... 419 668-8201
Norwalk *(G-15396)*
Haag-Streit Holding Us Inc.....E....... 513 336-7255
Mason *(G-12883)*
Hammill Manufacturing Co.....E....... 419 724-5702
Toledo *(G-18320)*
Heartbeat Company LLC.....G....... 614 423-5646
Westerville *(G-20057)*
Hickok Waekon LLC.....D....... 216 541-8060
Cleveland *(G-5408)*
Howmedica Osteonics Corp.....F....... 937 291-3900
Dayton *(G-8254)*
Immersus Health Company LLC.....G....... 855 994-4325
Cincinnati *(G-3838)*
Immersus Health Company LLC.....G....... 855 994-4325
Blue Ash *(G-1792)*
Integrated Med Solutions Inc.....D....... 440 269-6984
Mentor *(G-13473)*
Intellirod Spine Inc.....G....... 234 678-8965
Akron *(G-217)*
▲ **Invacare Holdings Corporation**.....G....... 440 329-6000
Elyria *(G-9276)*
Invacare International Corp.....G....... 440 329-6000
Elyria *(G-9277)*
Klarity Medical Products LLC.....F....... 740 788-8107
Newark *(G-14891)*
Lababidi Enterprises Inc.....E....... 330 733-2907
Akron *(G-245)*
Liquid Logic LLC.....G....... 937 865-3068
Miamisburg *(G-13685)*
Lumoptik Inc.....G....... 216 577-3905
Shaker Heights *(G-16934)*
Mac Dhui Probe of America Inc.....G....... 440 942-5597
Mentor *(G-13505)*
Markethatch Co Inc.....F....... 330 376-6363
Akron *(G-269)*
▲ **Medinvent LLC**.....G....... 330 247-0921
Medina *(G-13299)*
Medtronic Inc.....F....... 216 642-1977
Cleveland *(G-5652)*
Meridian LLC.....F....... 330 995-0371
Aurora *(G-892)*
◆ **Midmark Corporation**.....A....... 937 526-3662
Kettering *(G-11434)*
▲ **Mill-Rose Company**.....C....... 440 255-9171
Mentor *(G-13520)*
Minimally Invasive Devices Inc.....E....... 614 484-5036
Columbus *(G-7184)*
Morris Technologies Inc.....C....... 513 733-1611
Cincinnati *(G-4047)*
Morrison Medical.....E....... 614 461-4400
Columbus *(G-7197)*
▲ **National Biological Corp**.....E....... 216 831-0600
Beachwood *(G-1252)*
Neptune Aquatic Systems Inc.....G....... 513 575-2989
Loveland *(G-12216)*
Nervive Inc.....F....... 847 274-1790
Cleveland *(G-5740)*
Neurorescue LLC.....G....... 614 354-6453
Lewis Center *(G-11769)*
New Leaf Medical Inc.....G....... 216 391-7749
Cleveland *(G-5748)*
▲ **Norman Noble Inc**.....B....... 216 761-5387
Highland Heights *(G-10794)*
Norman Noble Inc.....E....... 216 851-4007
Euclid *(G-9429)*
North Coast Medi-Tek Inc.....F....... 440 974-0750
Mentor *(G-13529)*
Nuevue Solutions Inc.....G....... 440 836-4772
Rootstown *(G-16572)*
Office Bsed Anesthesia Svcs LLC.....G....... 513 582-5170
Montgomery *(G-14297)*
Olentangy Eye and Laser A.....G....... 614 267-4122
Columbus *(G-7270)*
Optoquest Corporation.....G....... 216 445-3637
Cleveland *(G-5816)*
Patriot Products Inc.....F....... 419 865-9712
Holland *(G-10948)*
Pediavascular Inc.....F....... 216 236-5533
Chagrin Falls *(G-3065)*
Pemco Inc.....E....... 216 524-2990
Cleveland *(G-5862)*
Percuvision LLC.....F....... 614 891-4800
Columbus *(G-7311)*
Perfusion Solutions Inc.....G....... 216 848-1610
Cleveland *(G-5864)*
PMC Smart Solutions LLC.....F....... 513 921-5040
Blue Ash *(G-1831)*
Premiere Farnell Corp.....G....... 937 424-1204
Dayton *(G-8437)*
Prentke Romich Company.....C....... 330 262-1984
Wooster *(G-20641)*
Pulse Worldwide Ltd.....G....... 513 234-7829
Mason *(G-12928)*
Quality Electrodynamics LLC.....C....... 440 638-5106
Mayfield Village *(G-13176)*
▲ **R-Med Inc**.....G....... 419 693-7481
Oregon *(G-15565)*
◆ **Reliance Medical Products Inc**.....D....... 513 398-3937
Mason *(G-12930)*
Resonetics LLC.....D....... 937 865-4070
Kettering *(G-11440)*
Rhinosystems Inc.....F....... 216 351-6262
Brooklyn *(G-2114)*
RJR Surgical Inc.....G....... 216 241-2804
Cleveland *(G-5990)*
Rockdale Systems LLC.....G....... 513 379-3577
Cincinnati *(G-4280)*
Rsb Spine LLC.....F....... 216 241-2804
Cleveland *(G-6014)*
Rultract Inc.....G....... 216 524-2990
Cleveland *(G-6017)*
Sagitta Inc.....G....... 440 570-5393
Cleveland *(G-6025)*
Scottcare Corporation.....E....... 216 362-0550
Cleveland *(G-6041)*
Secqure Surgical Corp.....G....... 513 769-1916
Blue Ash *(G-1845)*
Sense Diagnostics Inc.....G....... 513 515-3853
Cincinnati *(G-4323)*
Smiths Medical Asd Inc.....E....... 800 796-8701
Dublin *(G-8987)*
Smiths Medical Asd Inc.....C....... 614 889-2220
Dublin *(G-8988)*
Smiths Medical Asd Inc.....F....... 614 210-6431
Dublin *(G-8989)*
Smiths Medical North America.....G....... 614 210-7300
Dublin *(G-8990)*
◆ **Smiths Medical Pm Inc**.....F....... 614 210-7300
Dublin *(G-8991)*
Sonogage Inc.....F....... 216 464-1119
Cleveland *(G-6079)*
Sparton Medical Systems Inc.....D....... 440 878-4630
Strongsville *(G-17791)*
Standard Bariatrics Inc.....G....... 513 620-7751
Blue Ash *(G-1850)*
◆ **Steris Corporation**.....A....... 440 354-2600
Mentor *(G-13590)*
Steris Instrument MGT Svcs Inc.....E....... 800 783-9251
Stow *(G-17632)*
Stryker Orthopedic.....G....... 614 766-2990
Dublin *(G-8996)*
Suarez Corporation Industries.....D....... 330 494-4282
Canton *(G-2827)*
Summit Online Products LLC.....G....... 800 326-1972
Powell *(G-16338)*
Surgical Theater LLC.....G....... 216 452-2177
Mayfield Village *(G-13177)*
Surgical Theater LLC.....G....... 216 496-7884
Cleveland *(G-6132)*
Surgrx Inc.....F....... 650 482-2400
Blue Ash *(G-1856)*
Synergy Health North Amer Inc.....D....... 513 398-6406
Mason *(G-12945)*
Theken Companies LLC.....E....... 330 733-7600
Akron *(G-402)*
Thermo Fisher Scientific Inc.....C....... 800 871-8909
Oakwood Village *(G-15486)*
Thompson Partners Inc.....G....... 866 475-2500
Gahanna *(G-10109)*
Torbot Group Inc.....E....... 419 724-1475
Toledo *(G-18577)*
▲ **Transdermal Inc**.....F....... 440 241-1846
Gates Mills *(G-10209)*
◆ **Tri-Tech Medical Inc**.....E....... 800 253-8692
Avon *(G-972)*
Troy Innovative Instrs Inc.....E....... 440 834-9567
Middlefield *(G-13859)*
United Medical Supply Company.....G....... 866 678-8633
Valley City *(G-19068)*
United States Endoscopy.....G....... 440 639-4494
Mentor *(G-13619)*
Valensil Technologies LLC.....G....... 440 937-8181
Avon *(G-973)*
Venturemedgroup Ltd.....G....... 567 661-0768
Toledo *(G-18590)*
Vertebration Inc.....G....... 614 395-3346
Powell *(G-16340)*

Vesco Medical LLC ....F 614 914-5991
   Columbus (G-7580)
World Wide Medical Physics Inc ....G 419 266-7530
   Perrysburg (G-16029)
◆ Ysi Incorporated ....D 937 767-7241
   Yellow Springs (G-20825)

3842 Orthopedic, Prosthetic & Surgical Appliances/Splys

ABI Orthtc/Prosthetic Labs Ltd ....E 330 758-1143
   Youngstown (G-20833)
Ace Prosthetics Inc ....G 614 291-8325
   Columbus (G-6536)
▲ Acor Orthopaedic Inc ....D 216 662-4500
   Cleveland (G-4608)
Acor Orthopaedic Inc ....G 440 532-0117
   Cleveland (G-4609)
Action Prosthetics LLC ....G 937 548-9100
   Greenville (G-10359)
Akron Ent Hearing Services Inc ....G 330 762-8959
   Akron (G-38)
Akron Orthotic Solutions Inc ....G 330 253-3002
   Akron (G-45)
American Orthopedics Inc ....E 614 291-6454
   Columbus (G-6585)
American Ride Wheelchair Coach ......G 216 276-1700
   Cleveland (G-4696)
Anatomical Concepts Inc ....F 330 757-3569
   Youngstown (G-20846)
Anderson Cosmetic & Vein Inst ....G 513 624-7900
   Cincinnati (G-3345)
Ansell Healthcare Products LLC ....D 740 622-4311
   Coshocton (G-7719)
Ansell Healthcare Products LLC ....C 740 295-5414
   Coshocton (G-7720)
Arthur W Guilford III Inc ....G 216 362-1350
   Cleveland (G-4739)
Avalign Technologies Inc ....F 419 542-7743
   Hicksville (G-10776)
Axon Medical LLC ....E 216 276-0262
   Medina (G-13226)
Bahler Medical Inc ....E 614 873-7600
   Plain City (G-16174)
Barton-Carey Medical Products ....F 419 887-1285
   Maumee (G-13078)
◆ Beaufort Rfd Inc ....F 330 239-4331
   Sharon Center (G-16946)
Beeline Purchasing LLC ....G 513 703-3733
   Mason (G-12834)
Beiersdorf Inc ....C 513 682-7300
   West Chester (G-19835)
Bills Sports Center ....G 419 335-2405
   Wauseon (G-19510)
Biocare Orthopedic Prosthetics ....G 614 754-7514
   Columbus (G-6671)
Brace Shop Prosthetic Ortho ....F 513 421-5653
   Cincinnati (G-3407)
Bracemart LLC ....G 440 353-2830
   North Ridgeville (G-15213)
Bulk Molding Compounds Inc ....D 419 874-7941
   Perrysburg (G-15926)
Canton Orthotic Laboratory ....G 330 833-0955
   Canton (G-2614)
Capital Prosthetic & ....F 614 451-0446
   Columbus (G-6732)
Capital Prosthetic & ....E 567 560-2051
   Mansfield (G-12419)
Capital Prosthetic & ....G 740 453-9545
   Zanesville (G-21115)
Capital Prosthetic & ....G 740 522-3331
   Newark (G-14859)
Cardinal Health Inc ....G 614 553-3830
   Dublin (G-8893)
◆ Cardinal Health Inc ....A 614 757-5000
   Dublin (G-8894)
Caro Medical LLC ....G 937 604-8600
   Springboro (G-17324)
Central Ohio Orthtic Prsthetic ....G 614 659-1580
   Dublin (G-8898)
Columbus Prescr Rehabilitation ....G 614 294-1600
   Westerville (G-20040)
Communications Aid Inc ....F 513 475-8453
   Cincinnati (G-3537)
Comprhnsive Brace Limb Ctr LLC ......G 330 337-8333
   Salem (G-16730)
◆ Cordis Corporation ....A 614 757-5000
   Dublin (G-8903)
Cranial Technologies Inc ....G 844 447-5894
   Cincinnati (G-3557)

▲ Daishin Industrial Co ....G 614 766-9535
   Dublin (G-8905)
Dayton Artificial Limb Clinic ....G 937 836-1464
   Englewood (G-9354)
Deco Tools Inc ....E 419 476-9321
   Toledo (G-18256)
Dentronix Inc ....E 330 916-7300
   Cuyahoga Falls (G-7860)
Dj International Inc ....G 440 260-7593
   Berea (G-1602)
Doling & Associates Dental Lab ....E 937 254-0075
   Dayton (G-8164)
DPM Orthodontics Inc ....G 330 673-0334
   Kent (G-11316)
Ear Medical Center Inc ....F 812 537-0031
   Cincinnati (G-3623)
Earthwalk Orthotic ....F 330 837-6569
   Massillon (G-12978)
Ethicon Inc ....C 513 786-7000
   Blue Ash (G-1766)
Evanko Wm/Barringer Richd DDS ......G 330 336-6693
   Wadsworth (G-19238)
▲ Faretec Inc ....F 440 350-9510
   Painesville (G-15738)
Fidelity Orthopedic Inc ....G 937 228-0682
   Dayton (G-8194)
Findlay American Prosthetic & ....G 419 424-1622
   Findlay (G-9683)
Florida Invacare Holdings LLC ....G 800 333-6900
   Elyria (G-9261)
Foot Logic Inc ....G 330 699-0123
   Uniontown (G-18919)
Forbes Rehab Services Inc ....G 419 589-7688
   Mansfield (G-12440)
Forceone LLC ....E 513 939-1018
   Hebron (G-10743)
Francisco Jaume ....G 740 622-1200
   Coshocton (G-7734)
▲ Frohock-Stewart Inc ....E 440 329-6000
   North Ridgeville (G-15226)
Gaitwell Orthotics Pedorthics ....G 513 829-2217
   Cincinnati (G-3721)
Geauga Rhabilitation Engrg Inc ....F 216 536-0826
   Chardon (G-3114)
▲ Gelok International Corp ....F 419 352-1482
   Dunbridge (G-9015)
Gendron Wheel LLC ....G 419 445-6060
   Archbold (G-649)
Gottfried Medical Inc ....E 419 474-2973
   Toledo (G-18309)
▲ Greendale Home Fashions LLC ....D 859 916-5475
   Cincinnati (G-3782)
▲ Guardian Manufacturing Co LLC ...E 419 933-2711
   Willard (G-20240)
Hall Safety Apparel Inc ....F 740 922-3671
   Uhrichsville (G-18887)
Hammill Manufacturing Co ....D 419 476-0789
   Maumee (G-13115)
Hanger Prsthetcs & Ortho Inc ....G 216 475-4211
   Maple Heights (G-12573)
Hanger Prsthetcs & Ortho Inc ....G 440 605-0232
   Mayfield Heights (G-13165)
Hanger Prsthetcs & Ortho Inc ....F 419 841-9852
   Toledo (G-18321)
Hanger Prsthetcs & Ortho Inc ....G 513 421-5653
   Cincinnati (G-3797)
Hanger Prsthetcs & Ortho Inc ....G 330 758-1143
   Youngstown (G-20928)
Hanger Prsthetcs & Ortho Inc ....G 440 892-6665
   Westlake (G-20121)
Hanger Prsthetcs & Ortho Inc ....G 330 374-9544
   Akron (G-198)
Hanger Prsthetcs & Ortho Inc ....G 937 773-2441
   Piqua (G-16120)
Hanger Prsthetcs & Ortho Inc ....F 937 228-5462
   Dayton (G-8243)
Hanger Prsthetcs & Ortho Inc ....F 740 383-2163
   Marion (G-12709)
Hanger Prsthetcs & Ortho Inc ....G 740 266-6400
   Steubenville (G-17536)
Hanger Prsthetcs & Ortho Inc ....G 937 325-5404
   Springfield (G-17411)
Hanger Prsthetcs & Ortho Inc ....F 937 643-1557
   Moraine (G-14358)
Hanger Prsthetcs & Ortho Inc ....G 330 821-4918
   Canton (G-2692)
Hanger Prsthetcs & Ortho Inc ....F 614 481-8338
   Columbus (G-6979)
Hanger Prsthetcs & Ortho Inc ....G 740 354-4775
   Portsmouth (G-16285)

Hanger Prsthetcs & Ortho Inc ....G 419 522-0055
   Marion (G-12708)
Hanger Prsthetcs & Ortho Inc ....G 740 654-1884
   Lancaster (G-11578)
Hanger Prsthetcs & Ortho Inc ....G 740 454-6215
   Zanesville (G-21145)
Healthtech Products ....G 419 271-1761
   Elyria (G-9265)
Healthwares Manufacturing ....F 513 353-3691
   Cleves (G-6364)
Hearing Aid Center of NW Ohio ....G 419 636-8959
   Bryan (G-2286)
Hillman Group Inc ....G 440 248-7000
   Cleveland (G-5409)
Integrated Med Solutions Inc ....D 440 269-6984
   Mentor (G-13473)
Interplex Medical LLC ....E 513 248-5120
   Milford (G-14019)
Invacare Canadian Holdings Inc ....G 440 329-6000
   Elyria (G-9270)
Invacare Canadian Holdings LLC ....G 440 329-6000
   Elyria (G-9271)
Invacare Corporation ....F 440 329-6000
   Elyria (G-9274)
Invacare Corporation ....F 440 329-6000
   North Ridgeville (G-15231)
◆ Invacare Corporation ....A 440 329-6000
   Elyria (G-9272)
Invacare Corporation ....D 800 333-6900
   Elyria (G-9273)
◆ Invacare Corporation (tw) ....E 440 329-6000
   North Ridgeville (G-15232)
Invacare Holdings LLC ....G 440 329-6000
   Elyria (G-9275)
▲ Invacare Holdings Corporation ......G 440 329-6000
   Elyria (G-9276)
Invacare International Corp ....G 440 329-6000
   Elyria (G-9277)
◆ Invacare Respiratory Corp ....E 440 329-6000
   Elyria (G-9278)
▲ Isomedix Inc ....E 440 354-2600
   Mentor (G-13476)
Jobskin Div of Torbot Group ....E 419 724-1475
   Toledo (G-18359)
Jones Metal Products Company ....C 740 545-6381
   West Lafayette (G-19931)
Jones Metal Products Company ....E 740 545-6341
   West Lafayette (G-19932)
▲ Julius Zorn Inc ....D 330 923-4999
   Cuyahoga Falls (G-7886)
Kempf Surgical Appliances Inc ....E 513 984-5758
   Montgomery (G-14295)
Kufbag Inc ....G 614 589-8687
   Westerville (G-20062)
Kuhlmanns Fabrication ....G 513 967-4617
   Hamilton (G-10581)
Leimkuehler Inc ....E 440 899-7842
   Cleveland (G-5573)
Lower Limb Centers LLC ....G 440 365-2502
   Elyria (G-9289)
Luminaud Inc ....G 440 255-9082
   Mentor (G-13503)
M-Co Welling ....G 330 897-1374
   Stone Creek (G-17561)
▲ Marlen Manufacturing & Dev Co ...G 216 292-7060
   Bedford (G-1424)
Marlen Manufacturing & Dev Co ....E 216 292-7546
   Bedford (G-1425)
Materials Engineering & Dev ....G 937 884-5118
   Brookville (G-2177)
▲ Matplus Ltd ....G 440 352-7201
   Painesville (G-15761)
Medco Labs Inc ....F 216 292-7546
   Cleveland (G-5651)
Medical Device Bus Svcs Inc ....E 937 274-5850
   Dayton (G-8338)
Meridian Industries Inc ....D 330 673-1011
   Kent (G-11351)
◆ Midmark Corporation ....A 937 526-3662
   Kettering (G-11434)
Miller Prsthtics Orthotics LLC ....G 740 421-4211
   Belpre (G-1580)
▲ Morning Pride Mfg LLC ....A 937 264-2662
   Dayton (G-8367)
Morning Pride Mfg LLC ....G 937 264-1726
   Dayton (G-8368)
Morris Maico Hearing Aid Svc ....G 419 232-6200
   Van Wert (G-19103)
Mosher Medical Inc ....G 330 668-2252
   Akron (G-289)

Employee Codes: A=Over 500 employees, B=251-500
C=101-250, D=51-100, E=20-50, F=10-19, G=3-9

38 MEASURING, ANALYZING AND CONTROLLING INSTRUMENTS; PHOTOGRAPHIC, MEDICAL AN

Motion Mobility & Design Inc ....F 330 244-9723
 North Canton (G-15103)
MST Inc ....G 419 542-6645
 Hicksville (G-10779)
Mt Pleasant Pharmacy LLC ....G 216 672-4377
 Bedford (G-1429)
Neu Prosthetics & Orthotics ....G 740 363-3522
 Delaware (G-8710)
New Wave Prosthetics Inc ....G 614 782-2361
 Grove City (G-10451)
North Cast Orthtics Prsthetics ....F 440 233-4314
 Lorain (G-12108)
Northestrn OH Foot & Ankl Asoc ....G 330 633-3445
 Akron (G-303)
Novacare Inc ....G 216 704-4817
 Beachwood (G-1254)
O & P Options LLC ....G 513 791-7767
 Montgomery (G-14296)
O P Services Inc ....G 330 723-6679
 Medina (G-13308)
Ohio Safety Products LLC ....G 216 255-3067
 Highland Heights (G-10796)
Ohio State University ....G 614 293-3600
 Columbus (G-7261)
▲ Ohio Willow Wood Company ....G 740 869-3377
 Mount Sterling (G-14464)
Opc Inc ....G 419 531-2222
 Toledo (G-18440)
Optimus LLC ....G 614 263-5462
 Columbus (G-7274)
Optimus LLC ....E 513 918-2320
 Cincinnati (G-4116)
Optimus LLC ....G 937 454-1900
 Dayton (G-8405)
Ortho Prosthetic Center ....G 419 352-8161
 Bowling Green (G-1988)
Orthohlix Surgical Designs Inc ....G 330 869-9562
 Akron (G-312)
Orthotic and Prostetic Spc ....F 216 531-2773
 Euclid (G-9431)
Orthotic and Prosthetic I ....G 330 723-6679
 Medina (G-13313)
Orthotic Prosthetic Center ....G 419 531-2222
 Toledo (G-18441)
Orthotics & Prosthetics Rehab ....F 330 856-2553
 Warren (G-19429)
Osteo Solution ....G 614 485-9790
 Westerville (G-20015)
Osteonovus Inc ....G 617 717-8867
 Toledo (G-18442)
Osteosymbionics LLC ....F 216 881-8500
 Cleveland (G-5824)
Out On A Limb ....G 513 432-5091
 Cincinnati (G-4124)
Pcp Champion ....G 937 392-4301
 Ripley (G-16516)
◆ Philips Medical Systems Clevel ....B 440 247-2652
 Cleveland (G-5871)
Phonak LLC ....G 513 420-4568
 Middletown (G-13940)
Presque Isle Orthotics ....G 216 371-0660
 Beachwood (G-1268)
Prosthetic & Orthotic Services ....G 330 723-6679
 Medina (G-13324)
▲ Prosthetic Design Inc ....G 937 836-1464
 Englewood (G-9373)
Reliable Wheelchair Trans ....G 216 390-3999
 Beachwood (G-1276)
S K M L Inc ....G 330 220-7565
 Valley City (G-19059)
▲ Schaerer Medical Usa Inc ....E 513 561-2241
 Cincinnati (G-4305)
Sentinel Consumer Products Inc ....D 801 825-5671
 Mentor (G-13579)
Smith & Nephew Inc ....E 513 821-5888
 Cincinnati (G-4345)
Smith & Nephew Inc ....G 614 793-0581
 Dublin (G-8986)
Sonus-Usa Inc ....E 419 474-9324
 Toledo (G-18526)
▼ Southpaw Enterprises Inc ....E 937 252-7676
 Moraine (G-14395)
Spinal Balance Inc ....G 419 530-5935
 Swanton (G-17922)
▲ Sroufe Healthcare Products LLC .....E 260 894-4171
 Wadsworth (G-19278)
Stable Step LLC ....E 513 825-1888
 West Chester (G-19798)
Steris Corporation ....G 440 354-2600
 Mentor (G-13589)

◆ Steris Corporation ....A 440 354-2600
 Mentor (G-13590)
Steris Corporation ....C 440 354-2600
 Mentor (G-13591)
Steris Corporation ....D 440 354-2600
 Mentor (G-13592)
Steris Corporation ....F 440 354-2600
 Mentor (G-13593)
▲ Surgical Appliance Inds Inc ....C 513 271-4594
 Cincinnati (G-4401)
Surgical Appliance Inds Inc ....E 937 392-4301
 Ripley (G-16518)
Swanson Orthotic & Prosthetic ....G 419 690-0026
 Oregon (G-15570)
Swanson Prosthetic Center Inc ....G 419 472-8910
 Toledo (G-18538)
Synthetic Body Parts Inc ....G 440 838-0985
 Brecksville (G-2059)
Targeting Customer Safety Inc ....G 330 865-9593
 Akron (G-396)
Thomas Products Co Inc ....E 513 756-9009
 Cincinnati (G-4420)
▲ Tilt 15 Inc ....D 330 239-4192
 Sharon Center (G-16955)
Touch Life Centers LLC ....G 614 388-8075
 Hilliard (G-10871)
Tranzonic Companies ....B 216 535-4300
 Richmond Heights (G-16507)
Visualy Imp Exp Wm Isues Fr Gr ....G 216 561-6864
 Cleveland (G-6265)
▲ Wcm Holdings Inc ....G 513 705-2100
 Cincinnati (G-4493)
Weber Orthopedic Inc ....G 440 934-1812
 Avon (G-974)
▲ West Chester Holdings LLC ....C 800 647-1900
 Cincinnati (G-4499)
Whiteford Industries Inc ....F 419 381-1155
 Toledo (G-18599)
Wilson Mobility LLC ....G 216 921-9457
 Cleveland (G-6312)
▲ World Prep Inc ....G 419 843-3869
 Sylvania (G-17969)
Wright Solutions LLC ....G 937 938-8745
 Dayton (G-8600)
Yanke Bionics Inc ....E 330 762-6411
 Akron (G-438)
Yanke Bionics Inc ....G 330 833-0955
 Massillon (G-13058)
Yanke Bionics Inc ....G 330 668-4070
 Akron (G-439)
Zimmer Inc ....C 614 508-6000
 Columbus (G-7627)
▲ Zimmer Surgical Inc ....B 800 321-5533
 Dover (G-8863)

3843 Dental Eqpt & Splys

Absolute Smile LLC ....G 937 293-9866
 Dayton (G-8000)
Asch-Klaassen Sonics LLC ....G 513 671-3226
 Cincinnati (G-3360)
Branam Oral Health Tech Inc ....G 248 670-0040
 Oregon (G-15557)
▲ Chicago Dental Supply Inc ....G 800 571-5211
 Harrison (G-10633)
◆ Coltene/Whaledent Inc ....C 330 916-8800
 Cuyahoga Falls (G-7851)
Dental Ceramics Inc ....E 330 523-5240
 Richfield (G-16467)
Dental Pure Water Inc ....F 440 234-0890
 Berea (G-1601)
Dentronix Inc ....E 330 916-7300
 Cuyahoga Falls (G-7860)
Dentsply Sirona Inc ....E 419 893-5672
 Maumee (G-13107)
Dentsply Sirona Inc ....D 419 865-9497
 Maumee (G-13108)
Dresch Tolson Dental Labs ....D 419 842-6730
 Sylvania (G-17938)
Duncan Dental Lab LLC ....G 614 793-0330
 Dublin (G-8909)
Mark Dental Laboratory ....G 216 464-6424
 Cleveland (G-5618)
Metz Dental Laboratory Inc ....G 614 252-4444
 Columbus (G-7175)
◆ Midmark Corporation ....A 937 526-3662
 Kettering (G-11434)
Obsidian Biodent ....G 937 938-9244
 Oakwood (G-15465)
Precision Swiss LLC ....G 513 716-7000
 Cincinnati (G-4185)

Smile Brands Inc ....G 440 471-6133
 North Olmsted (G-15199)
Sportsguard Laboratories Inc ....G 330 673-3932
 Kent (G-11389)
Thomas J Raffa DDS Inc ....G 440 997-5208
 Ashtabula (G-808)
United Dental Laboratories ....E 330 253-1810
 Tallmadge (G-18010)
▲ Vacalon Company Inc ....G 614 577-1945
 Pickerington (G-16062)
▲ Wbc Group LLC ....D 866 528-2144
 Hudson (G-11082)

3844 X-ray Apparatus & Tubes

Comet Technologies USA Inc ....F 234 284-7849
 Hudson (G-11038)
Control-X Inc ....G 614 777-9729
 Columbus (G-6815)
Dentsply Sirona Inc ....D 419 865-9497
 Maumee (G-13108)
General Electric Company ....D 216 663-2110
 Cleveland (G-5308)
Metro Design Inc ....F 440 458-4200
 Elyria (G-9295)
North Coast Medical Eqp Inc ....F 440 243-2722
 Berea (G-1619)
◆ Philips Medical Systems Clevel ....B 440 247-2652
 Cleveland (G-5871)
Trionix Research Laboratory ....G 330 425-9055
 Twinsburg (G-18867)
Yxlon ....G 234 284-7862
 Hudson (G-11084)

3845 Electromedical & Electrotherapeutic Apparatus

▼ Alltech Med Systems Amer Inc ....E 440 424-2240
 Solon (G-17104)
Biosense Webster Inc ....G 513 337-3351
 Blue Ash (G-1735)
Brainmaster Technologies Inc ....G 440 232-6000
 Bedford (G-1391)
Cardiac Analytics LLC ....F 614 314-1332
 Powell (G-16314)
Cardiac Arrhythmia Associates ....G 330 759-8169
 Youngstown (G-20865)
Cardioinsight Technologies Inc ....G 216 274-2221
 Independence (G-11121)
Century Biotech Partners Inc ....G 614 746-6998
 Dublin (G-8899)
Checkpoint Surgical Inc ....G 216 378-9107
 Cleveland (G-4917)
▲ Clear Image Technology LLC ....G 440 366-4330
 Westlake (G-20105)
▲ Critical Patient Care Inc ....G 937 434-5455
 Dayton (G-8114)
Ctl Analyzers LLC ....F 216 791-5084
 Shaker Heights (G-16930)
Deerfield Medical Imaging LLC ....G 513 271-5717
 Mason (G-12856)
E3 Diagnostics Inc ....G 937 435-2250
 Dayton (G-8174)
Elastance Imaging LLC ....G 614 579-9520
 Columbus (G-6887)
▼ Eoi Inc ....F 740 201-3300
 Lewis Center (G-11760)
Ep Technologies LLC ....F 234 208-8967
 Akron (G-159)
Flocel Inc ....G 216 619-5903
 Cleveland (G-5251)
Furniss Corporation Ltd ....F 614 871-1470
 Mount Sterling (G-14461)
GE Medical Systems Information ....G 216 663-2110
 Warrensville Heights (G-19468)
Genii Inc ....G 651 501-4810
 Mentor (G-13458)
Great Lkes Nrotechnologies Inc ....E 855 456-3876
 Cleveland (G-5351)
Gvi Medical Devices Corp ....F 330 963-4083
 Twinsburg (G-18789)
Gyrus Acmi LP ....C 419 668-8201
 Norwalk (G-15396)
Hair Science Systems LLC ....G 513 231-8284
 Cincinnati (G-3793)
Health Care Solutions Inc ....G 419 636-4189
 Bryan (G-2285)
Imageiq Inc ....F 855 462-4347
 Cleveland (G-5438)
Imaging Center East Main ....G 614 566-8120
 Columbus (G-7022)

Imalux Corporation F 216 502-0755
Cleveland *(G-5440)*
Infinity Trichology Center G 937 281-0555
Kettering *(G-11433)*
▲ Lumitex Inc D 440 243-8401
Strongsville *(G-17763)*
Magnetic Resonance Tech G 440 942-2922
Willoughby *(G-20365)*
Medforall LLC G 614 947-0791
Columbus *(G-7171)*
Medical Equipment Provider G 937 778-2190
Piqua *(G-16141)*
Medical Quant USA Inc F 440 542-0761
Solon *(G-17189)*
▲ Medinvent LLC G 330 247-0921
Medina *(G-13299)*
Mercury Biomed LLC G 216 777-1492
Cleveland *(G-5655)*
Monitored Therapeutics Inc G 614 761-3555
Dublin *(G-8948)*
Mrpicker G 440 354-6497
Cleveland *(G-5712)*
Nano Mark LLC G 216 409-3104
Cleveland *(G-5720)*
Nasoneb Inc G 330 247-0921
Medina *(G-13306)*
◆ Ndi Medical LLC E 216 378-9106
Cleveland *(G-5733)*
Neuros Medical Inc G 440 951-2565
Willoughby Hills *(G-20472)*
Neurowave Systems Inc G 216 361-1591
Cleveland *(G-5745)*
Nuvasive Manufacturing LLC E 937 343-0400
Fairborn *(G-9464)*
Nxstage Medical Inc G 513 712-1300
Cincinnati *(G-4094)*
Open Sided Mri Cleveland LLC G 804 217-7114
Westlake *(G-20138)*
Osteodynamics G 405 921-9271
Cincinnati *(G-4122)*
Pemco Inc E 216 524-2990
Cleveland *(G-5862)*
◆ Philips Healthcare Cleveland E 440 483-3235
Highland Heights *(G-10797)*
Philips Medical Systems Mr C 440 483-2499
Highland Heights *(G-10798)*
Rapiscan Systems High Energy I G 937 879-4200
Fairborn *(G-9466)*
Relevium Labs Inc G 614 568-7000
Oxford *(G-15699)*
Scallywag Tag G 513 922-4999
Cincinnati *(G-4303)*
Sensetronics LLC G 614 292-2833
Dublin *(G-8983)*
◆ Steris Corporation A 440 354-2600
Mentor *(G-13590)*
Synsei Medical G 609 759-1101
Dublin *(G-9001)*
Valued Relationships Inc C 800 860-4230
Franklin *(G-9928)*
Veressa Medical Inc F 614 591-4201
Columbus *(G-7573)*
▲ Viewray Technologies Inc D 440 703-3210
Oakwood Village *(G-15487)*
Westerville Endoscopy Ctr LLC F 614 568-1666
Westerville *(G-20030)*

3851 Ophthalmic Goods

Albright Albright & Schn G 614 825-4829
Worthington *(G-20674)*
Barnett & Ramel Optical Co Neb E 402 453-4900
Columbus *(G-6648)*
Brunswick Eye & Contact Lens C G 419 439-3381
Defiance *(G-8617)*
Bsa Industries Inc D 614 846-5515
Columbus *(G-6706)*
Bulk Molding Compounds Inc D 419 874-7941
Perrysburg *(G-15926)*
▲ Central Optical Inc E 330 783-9660
Youngstown *(G-20869)*
▲ Classic Optical Labs Inc C 330 759-8245
Youngstown *(G-20875)*
▲ Cleveland Hoya Corp D 440 234-5703
Berea *(G-1595)*
Diversified Ophthalmics Inc F 803 783-3454
Cincinnati *(G-3594)*
Diversified Ophthalmics Inc F 509 324-6364
Cincinnati *(G-3595)*
DMV Corporation G 740 452-4787
Zanesville *(G-21128)*
Essilor Laboratories Amer Inc G 330 425-3003
Twinsburg *(G-18771)*
Essilor Laboratories Amer Inc E 614 274-0840
Columbus *(G-6906)*
Hollywood Family Eye Care G 740 264-1220
Steubenville *(G-17537)*
Jerold Optical Inc G 216 781-4279
Cleveland *(G-5496)*
Lake Cable Optical Lab G 330 497-3022
Canton *(G-2730)*
Libbey Inc F 419 244-5697
Toledo *(G-18384)*
Luxottica of America Inc C 614 409-9381
Lockbourne *(G-11997)*
Malta Dynamics LLC F 740 749-3512
Waterford *(G-19488)*
Mileti Optical Inc G 440 884-6333
Cleveland *(G-5686)*
▲ Nexus Vision Group LLC E 866 492-6499
Grove City *(G-10452)*
Oakley Inc D 949 672-6560
Dayton *(G-8392)*
Opti Vision Inc G 330 650-0919
Hudson *(G-11065)*
▲ Optical Distribution Corp F 937 405-7280
Columbus *(G-7273)*
Rooney Optical Inc E 216 267-5600
Twinsburg *(G-18849)*
Rx Frames N Lenses Ltd G 513 557-2970
Cincinnati *(G-4292)*
Safeway Contact Lens Inc G 330 536-6469
Lowellville *(G-12256)*
Steiner Eoptics Inc D 937 426-2341
Miamisburg *(G-13721)*
Sunforest Vision Center Inc G 419 475-4646
Toledo *(G-18534)*
Terminal Optical Lab G 216 289-7722
Euclid *(G-9447)*
Toledo Optical Laboratory Inc D 419 248-3384
Toledo *(G-18565)*
▲ Volk Optical Inc D 440 942-6161
Mentor *(G-13625)*
Wilson Optical Laboratory Inc E 440 357-7000
Mentor *(G-13626)*

3861 Photographic Eqpt & Splys

Advanced Litho Systems G 419 865-2652
Monclova *(G-14253)*
AGFA Corporation C 513 829-6292
Fairfield *(G-9478)*
Dupont Specialty Pdts USA LLC E 740 474-0220
Circleville *(G-4543)*
E-Waste Systems (ohio) Inc G 614 824-3057
Columbus *(G-6881)*
Eastman Kodak Company E 937 259-3000
Kettering *(G-11431)*
Eprad Inc G 419 666-3266
Perrysburg *(G-15948)*
Gvs Industries Inc G 513 851-3606
Hamilton *(G-10565)*
Horizons Inc Camcode Division E 216 714-0020
Cleveland *(G-5416)*
◆ Horizons Incorporated C 216 475-0555
Cleveland *(G-5417)*
Ink Again G 419 232-4465
Van Wert *(G-19095)*
Jay Tackett G 740 779-1715
Frankfort *(G-9862)*
Kay Zee Inc G 330 339-1268
New Philadelphia *(G-14777)*
◆ Kg63 LLC F 216 941-7766
Cleveland *(G-5533)*
Legrand AV Inc E 574 267-8101
Blue Ash *(G-1805)*
Plastigraphics Inc F 513 771-8848
Cincinnati *(G-4166)*
Precision Remotes LLC E 510 215-6474
Middleburg Heights *(G-13768)*
Rightway Fab & Machine Inc G 937 295-2200
Russia *(G-16612)*
Sensopart USA Inc G 419 931-7696
Perrysburg *(G-16006)*
Smartcopy Inc G 740 392-6162
Mount Vernon *(G-14514)*
Stewart Filmscreen Corp E 513 753-0800
Amelia *(G-548)*
▲ Stretchtape Inc E 216 486-9400
Cleveland *(G-6107)*
Tbh International G 440 323-4651
Elyria *(G-9335)*
Transimage Inc G 937 293-0261
Oakwood *(G-15466)*
Xerox Corporation B 513 554-3200
Blue Ash *(G-1879)*
▲ Xerox Corporation C/O Genco G 503 582-6059
Groveport *(G-10517)*

3873 Watch & Clock Devices & Parts

Amano Cincinnati Incorporated D 513 697-9000
Loveland *(G-12176)*
Amano McGann Inc F 513 683-2906
West Chester *(G-19831)*
▲ Dimcogray Corporation D 937 433-7600
Centerville *(G-3001)*
▲ I T Verdin Co E 513 241-4010
Cincinnati *(G-3833)*
I T Verdin Co E 513 559-3947
Cincinnati *(G-3834)*
Sgi Matrix LLC D 937 438-9033
Miamisburg *(G-13715)*

39 MISCELLANEOUS MANUFACTURING INDUSTRIES

3911 Jewelry: Precious Metal

AR Jester Co G 513 241-1465
Cincinnati *(G-3353)*
Auld Crafters Inc G 614 221-6825
Columbus *(G-6630)*
Baldwin B AA Design G 740 374-5844
Marietta *(G-12608)*
Barany Jewelry Inc G 330 220-4367
Brunswick *(G-2191)*
Benchworks Jewelers Inc G 937 439-4243
Dayton *(G-8054)*
Bensan Jewelers Inc G 216 221-1434
Lakewood *(G-11512)*
Boos Make & Take G 440 647-0000
Wellington *(G-19573)*
C M Stephanoff Jewelers Inc G 440 526-5890
Brecksville *(G-2026)*
Cambridge Mfg Jewelers G 330 528-0207
Hudson *(G-11035)*
Crest Craft Company F 513 271-4858
Blue Ash *(G-1754)*
Davidson Jewelers Inc G 513 932-3936
Lebanon *(G-11647)*
Dimensional Works of Art G 330 657-2681
Peninsula *(G-15891)*
Don Basch Jewelers Inc F 330 467-2116
Macedonia *(G-12290)*
Em Es Be Company LLC G 216 761-9500
Cleveland *(G-5170)*
Farah Jewelers Inc F 614 438-6140
Columbus *(G-6492)*
▲ Ginos Awards Inc E 216 831-6565
Warrensville Heights *(G-19469)*
Gold Mine Inc G 614 378-8308
Dublin *(G-8916)*
Gold Pro Inc G 216 241-5143
Cleveland *(G-5327)*
Goyal Enterprises Inc F 513 874-9303
West Chester *(G-19860)*
Gustave Julian Jewelers Inc G 440 888-1100
Cleveland *(G-5360)*
H P Nielsen Inc G 440 244-4255
Lorain *(G-12094)*
Heather B Moore Inc G 216 932-5430
Cleveland *(G-5387)*
J and L Jewelry Manufacturing G 440 546-9988
Cleveland *(G-5481)*
Jaffe & Gross Jewelry Company G 937 461-9450
Dayton *(G-8276)*
▲ James C Free Inc E 937 298-0171
Dayton *(G-8277)*
James C Free Inc G 513 793-0133
Cincinnati *(G-3868)*
Jensen & Sons Inc F 419 471-1000
Toledo *(G-18358)*
Jewels By Img Inc F 440 461-4464
Cleveland *(G-5498)*
Jostens Inc E 419 874-5835
Perrysburg *(G-15971)*
Jostens Inc G 513 731-5900
Cincinnati *(G-3885)*
Koop Diamond Cutters Inc F 513 621-2838
Cincinnati *(G-3923)*
Levit Jewelers Inc G 440 985-1685
Lorain *(G-12100)*

S I C

Employee Codes: A=Over 500 employees, B=251-500 C=101-250, D=51-100, E=20-50, F=10-19, G=3-9
2019 Harris Ohio Industrial Directory
1011

39 MISCELLANEOUS MANUFACTURING INDUSTRIES

M & M Tobacco ....G....... 330 573-8543
  Carrollton (G-2925)
M B Saxon Co Inc ....F 440 229-5006
  Cleveland (G-5592)
Marcus Jewelers ....G....... 513 474-4950
  Cincinnati (G-3979)
Marfo Company ....D....... 614 276-3352
  Columbus (G-7150)
Michael W Hyes Desgr Goldsmith ....G....... 440 519-0889
  Solon (G-17194)
Mr 14k Inc ....G....... 440 234-6661
  Berea (G-1618)
O C Tanner Company ....G....... 513 583-1100
  Mason (G-12917)
Ohio Silver Co ....G....... 937 767-8261
  Yellow Springs (G-20813)
Old Village ....F 614 791-8467
  Delaware (G-8714)
Phantasm Vapors LLC ....G....... 513 248-2431
  Milford (G-14032)
Puppy Paws Inc ....G....... 440 461-9667
  Cleveland (G-5935)
Rita Caz Jwly Studio & Gallery ....G....... 937 767-7713
  Yellow Springs (G-20814)
Robert W Johnson Inc ....D....... 614 336-4545
  Dublin (G-8975)
Rosenfeld Jewelry Inc ....G....... 440 446-0099
  Cleveland (G-6004)
Roulet Company ....G....... 419 241-2988
  Toledo (G-18508)
Sheiban Jewelry Inc ....F 440 238-0616
  Strongsville (G-17787)
Signet Group Inc ....E 330 668-5901
  Fairlawn (G-9617)
Smokeheal Inc ....G....... 216 255-5119
  Cleveland (G-6074)
Stephen R White ....G....... 740 522-1512
  Newark (G-14923)
Timothy Allen Jewelers Inc ....G....... 440 974-8885
  Mentor (G-13606)
Val Casting Inc ....E 419 562-2499
  Bucyrus (G-2346)
Vapen8r LLC ....G....... 440 934-8273
  Sheffield Village (G-16976)
Weber Jewelers Incorporated ....G....... 937 643-9200
  Dayton (G-8587)
White Jewelers ....G....... 330 264-3324
  Wooster (G-20667)
▲ Whitehouse Bros Inc ....G....... 513 621-2259
  Blue Ash (G-1870)

3914 Silverware, Plated & Stainless Steel Ware

Ahner Fabricating & Shtmtl Inc ....E 419 626-6641
  Sandusky (G-16793)
All American Trophy ....G....... 614 231-8824
  Columbus (G-6565)
B & B Trophies & Awards ....G....... 330 225-6193
  Brunswick (G-2190)
Behrco Inc ....G....... 419 394-1612
  Saint Marys (G-16676)
▲ Ginos Awards Inc ....E 216 831-6565
  Warrensville Heights (G-19469)
Hr Machine LLC ....G....... 937 222-7644
  Beavercreek (G-1323)
Lawnview Industries Inc ....G....... 937 653-5217
  Urbana (G-19003)
▼ Online Engineering Corporation ....G....... 513 561-8878
  Amelia (G-545)
Professional Award Service ....G....... 513 389-3600
  Cincinnati (G-4216)
Quantum Jewelry Dist ....E 330 678-2222
  Kent (G-11371)
Regal Trophy & Awards Company .....…. 877 492-7531
  Sidney (G-17064)
Tempo Manufacturing Company ....G....... 937 773-6613
  Piqua (G-16165)

3915 Jewelers Findings & Lapidary Work

Alex and Ani LLC ....G....... 513 791-1480
  Cincinnati (G-3319)
Alex and Ani LLC ....G....... 216 378-2139
  Beachwood (G-1222)
▲ Dayton Hawker Corporation ....F 937 293-8147
  Dayton (G-8135)
Dentsply Sirona Inc ....D....... 419 865-9497
  Maumee (G-13108)
Koop Diamond Cutters Inc ....F 513 621-2838
  Cincinnati (G-3923)

Lapcraft Inc ....G....... 614 764-8993
  Powell (G-16327)
The-Fischer-Group ....E 513 285-1281
  Fairfield (G-9569)
Zero-D Products Inc ....G....... 440 417-1843
  Willoughby (G-20463)

3931 Musical Instruments

▲ A R Schopps Sons Inc ....E 330 821-8406
  Alliance (G-448)
Bbb Music LLC ....G....... 740 772-2262
  Chillicothe (G-3176)
Belco Works Inc ....B 740 695-0500
  Saint Clairsville (G-16624)
Bell Industries ....F 513 353-2355
  Harrison (G-10632)
Belmont County of Ohio ....G....... 740 699-2140
  Saint Clairsville (G-16625)
Brooks Manufacturing ....G....... 419 244-1777
  Toledo (G-18216)
C E Kegg Inc ....G....... 330 877-8800
  Hartville (G-10686)
▼ Commercial Music Service Co .....G....... 740 746-8500
  Sugar Grove (G-17837)
Conn-Selmer Inc ....B 440 946-6100
  Willoughby (G-20300)
Conn-Selmer Inc ....E 216 391-7723
  Cleveland (G-5014)
D C Ramey Piano Co ....G....... 708 602-3961
  Marysville (G-12779)
D Picking & Co ....G....... 419 562-5016
  Bucyrus (G-2324)
▲ Earthquaker Devices LLC ....F 330 252-9220
  Akron (G-148)
Engels Machining LLC ....G....... 419 485-1500
  Montpelier (G-14308)
Fifth Avenue Fret Shop LLC ....G....... 614 481-8300
  Columbus (G-6920)
Garys Classic Guitars ....G....... 513 891-0555
  Loveland (G-12190)
▲ Grover Musical Products Inc .....E 216 391-1188
  Cleveland (G-5356)
◆ Hanser Music Group Inc ....D....... 859 817-7100
  West Chester (G-19864)
Hisey Bells ....G....... 740 333-7669
  Greenfield (G-10352)
▲ I T Verdin Co ....E 513 241-4010
  Cincinnati (G-3833)
I T Verdin Co ....E 513 559-3947
  Cincinnati (G-3834)
J Zamberlan & Co ....G....... 740 765-9028
  Steubenville (G-17538)
Lima Pipe Organ Co Inc ....E 419 331-5461
  Elida (G-9196)
Loft Violin Shop ....F 614 267-7221
  Columbus (G-7135)
McHael D Goronok String Instrs ....G....... 216 421-4227
  Cleveland (G-5642)
Muller Pipe Organ Co ....F 740 893-1700
  Croton (G-7821)
▲ New Cleveland Group Inc ....G....... 216 932-9310
  Cleveland (G-5746)
▲ Paul Bartel ....G....... 513 541-2000
  Cincinnati (G-4139)
Peebles - Herzog Inc ....G....... 614 279-2211
  Columbus (G-7306)
S I T Strings Co Inc ....G....... 330 434-8010
  Akron (G-365)
Schantz Organ Company ....E 330 682-6065
  Orrville (G-15618)
Sperzel Inc ....E 216 281-6868
  Cleveland (G-6085)
▲ Stewart-Macdonald Mfg Co ....E 740 592-3021
  Athens (G-849)
The Holtkamp Organ Co ....E 216 741-5180
  Cleveland (G-6165)
The W L Jenkins Company ....F 330 477-3407
  Canton (G-2835)
▲ Universal Percussion Inc ....F 330 482-5750
  Columbiana (G-6484)
Victor Organ Company ....G....... 330 792-1321
  Youngstown (G-21062)
Waits Instruments LLC ....G....... 513 600-5996
  Cincinnati (G-4486)
Watson Meeks and Company ....F 937 378-2355
  Georgetown (G-10239)

3942 Dolls & Stuffed Toys

Alice Beougher ....G....... 740 927-2470
  Etna (G-9388)

▲ Classic Toy Company Inc ....G....... 216 851-2000
  Cleveland (G-4940)
Datatex Media Dolls ....G....... 216 598-1000
  Cleveland (G-5070)
Eboni Corner ....G....... 724 518-3065
  Cleveland (G-5154)
Gail J Shumaker Originals ....G....... 330 659-0680
  Richfield (G-16472)
Huston Gifts Dolls and Flowers ....G....... 740 775-9141
  Chillicothe (G-3193)
Middleton Llyd Dolls Inc ....G....... 740 989-2082
  Coolville (G-7674)
▲ Middleton Lee Original Dolls ....F ....
  Columbus (G-7180)

3944 Games, Toys & Children's Vehicles

Advance Novelty Incorporated ....G....... 419 424-0363
  Findlay (G-9647)
▲ Ajj Enterprises LLC ....F 513 755-9562
  West Chester (G-19830)
▲ American Traditions Basket Co ..E 330 854-0900
  Canal Fulton (G-2474)
Applied Concepts Inc ....F 440 229-5033
  Willoughby (G-20277)
◆ Arrow International Inc ....B 216 961-3500
  Cleveland (G-4736)
▲ AW Faber-Castell Usa Inc ....D....... 216 643-4660
  Cleveland (G-4780)
Berlin Wood Products Inc ....E 330 893-3281
  Berlin (G-1639)
Brown Dave Products Inc ....F 513 738-1576
  Hamilton (G-10543)
Brp Inc ....G....... 440 988-4398
  Amherst (G-556)
Container Graphics Corp ....D....... 419 531-5133
  Toledo (G-18241)
Cornpentry ....G....... 513 741-0594
  Cincinnati (G-3551)
Cowells - Arrow Bingo Company ......G....... 216 961-3500
  Cleveland (G-5034)
D L H Locomotive Works ....G....... 937 629-0321
  Springfield (G-17383)
▲ Dunecraft Inc ....E 800 306-4168
  Cleveland (G-5119)
Erockets LLC ....G....... 616 460-2678
  Dayton (G-8187)
Evenflo Company Inc ....D....... 937 773-3971
  Troy (G-18654)
◆ Evenflo Company Inc ....C 937 415-3300
  Miamisburg (G-13666)
First Merit ....G....... 330 849-8750
  Akron (G-172)
◆ Foundations Worldwide Inc ....E 330 722-5033
  Medina (G-13264)
Gingerbread N Bows ....G....... 740 945-1027
  Scio (G-16877)
Hershberger Lawn Structures ....F 330 674-3900
  Millersburg (G-14088)
Ink Factory Inc ....G....... 330 799-0888
  Youngstown (G-20940)
Iron Wind Metals Co LLC ....G....... 513 870-0606
  Cincinnati (G-3859)
Jackpot Festival & Gaming ....G....... 216 531-3500
  Cleveland (G-5491)
Larose Industries LLC ....E 419 237-1600
  Fayette (G-9634)
▲ Late For Sky Production Co ....E 513 531-4400
  Cincinnati (G-3932)
Lawbre Co ....G....... 330 637-3363
  Cortland (G-7712)
Little Cottage Company ....G....... 330 893-4212
  Dundee (G-9021)
M G 3d ....F 614 262-0956
  Columbus (G-7140)
▲ Mag-Nif Inc ....D....... 440 255-9366
  Mentor (G-13508)
Mahoning Valley Manufacturing ....E 330 537-4492
  Beloit (G-1571)
Michaels Stores Inc ....G....... 330 505-1168
  Niles (G-15023)
▲ Molecular Dimensions Inc ....G....... 419 740-6600
  Maumee (G-13137)
Moonstruck Games Inc ....G....... 513 721-3900
  Cincinnati (G-4044)
▲ Parma International Inc ....E 440 237-8650
  North Royalton (G-15293)
▲ Pioneer National Latex Inc ....D....... 419 289-3300
  Ashland (G-736)
Premier Kites & Designs Inc ....G....... 888 416-0174
  Portsmouth (G-16296)

Ramon Robinson....G.... 330 883-3244
Vienna *(G-19208)*
▲ **Ready Made Rc LLC**....G.... 740 936-4500
Lewis Center *(G-11775)*
▲ **Recaro Child Safety LLC**....E.... 248 904-1570
Cincinnati *(G-4253)*
Rockys Hinge Co....G.... 330 539-6296
Girard *(G-10265)*
RPM Consumer Holding Company....G.... 330 273-5090
Medina *(G-13330)*
◆ **S Toys Holdings LLC**....A.... 330 656-0440
Streetsboro *(G-17693)*
Scrambl-Gram Inc....F.... 419 635-2321
Port Clinton *(G-16259)*
◆ **Step2 Company LLC**....B.... 866 429-5200
Streetsboro *(G-17700)*
Step2 Company LLC....B.... 419 938-6343
Perrysville *(G-16032)*
The Guardtower Inc....F.... 614 488-4311
Columbus *(G-7524)*
Unique-Chardan Inc....E.... 419 636-6900
Bryan *(G-2311)*
Vacuum Finishing Company....F.... 440 286-4386
Chardon *(G-3140)*
▲ **Watch-Us Inc**....E.... 513 829-8870
Fairfield *(G-9575)*
Weenk Labs LLC....G.... 614 448-0160
Columbus *(G-7596)*
Wells Manufacturing Co Llc....F.... 937 987-2481
New Vienna *(G-14826)*

3949 Sporting & Athletic Goods, NEC

▲ **1 Iron Golf Inc**....G.... 419 662-9336
Celina *(G-2948)*
AC Shiners Inc....G.... 513 738-1573
Okeana *(G-15515)*
Advanced Fitness Inc....G.... 513 563-1000
Cincinnati *(G-3299)*
Adventurous Child Inc....G.... 513 531-7700
Cincinnati *(G-3303)*
Al-Co Products Inc....F.... 419 399-3867
Latty *(G-11624)*
All Sport Services Corporation....G.... 216 361-1965
Cleveland *(G-4667)*
◆ **American Heritage Billd LLC**....D.... 330 626-3710
Streetsboro *(G-17660)*
American Sports Design Company....D.... 937 865-5431
Centerville *(G-2997)*
▲ **American Whistle Corporation**....F.... 614 846-2918
Columbus *(G-6587)*
Americas Best Bowstrings LLC....G.... 330 893-7155
Millersburg *(G-14058)*
Apex Target Systems LLC....G.... 877 224-6692
Tiffin *(G-18044)*
Aquapro Systems LLC....E.... 513 315-3647
West Chester *(G-19649)*
Arem Co....F.... 440 974-6740
Mentor *(G-13393)*
Backyard Scoreboards LLC....G.... 513 702-6561
Middletown *(G-13886)*
Balbo Industries Inc....G.... 440 333-0630
Rocky River *(G-16543)*
Barnett Spouting Inc....G.... 330 644-0853
Akron *(G-80)*
Baseball Card Corner....G.... 513 677-0464
Loveland *(G-12179)*
Battle Horse Knives LLC....G.... 740 995-9009
Cambridge *(G-2426)*
Bay Area Products Inc....G.... 419 732-2147
Port Clinton *(G-16243)*
Bay Island Company Inc....G.... 513 248-0356
Loveland *(G-12180)*
Black Wing Shooting Center LLC....G.... 740 363-7555
Delaware *(G-8658)*
Board of Park Commissioners....G.... 216 635-3200
Cleveland *(G-4826)*
Boatfun Sports Inc....G.... 513 379-0506
Liberty Township *(G-11811)*
Bracemart LLC....G.... 440 353-2830
North Ridgeville *(G-15213)*
Bradley Enterprises Inc....G.... 330 875-1444
Louisville *(G-12153)*
Brass Tacks Corporation Ltd....G.... 614 599-7954
Dublin *(G-8891)*
Brg Sports Inc....G.... 217 891-1429
North Ridgeville *(G-15214)*
▲ **Bullseye Dart Shoppe Inc**....G.... 440 951-9277
Willoughby *(G-20290)*
Camx Outdoors Inc....G.... 330 474-3969
Kent *(G-11303)*

Careless Heart Enterprises....G.... 740 654-9999
Lancaster *(G-11553)*
Challenge Targets....G.... 859 462-5851
Cincinnati *(G-3462)*
Charles V Snider & Assoc Inc....F.... 440 877-9151
North Royalton *(G-15266)*
Clark & Son Pool Table Company....G.... 330 454-9153
Canton *(G-2626)*
Columbus Canvas Products Inc....F.... 614 375-1397
Columbus *(G-6785)*
▼ **Coulter Ventures Llc**....E.... 614 358-6190
Columbus *(G-6828)*
Country CLB Rtrment Ctr IV LLC....G.... 740 676-2300
Bellaire *(G-1485)*
Creighton Sports Center Inc....G.... 740 865-2521
New Matamoras *(G-14745)*
Daisys Pillows LLC....G.... 937 776-6968
Dayton *(G-8125)*
Darting Around LLC....G.... 330 639-3990
Canton *(G-2649)*
Dayton Stencil Works Company....E.... 937 223-3233
Dayton *(G-8145)*
▲ **Done-Rite Bowling Service Co**....E.... 440 232-3280
Bedford *(G-1402)*
Drop Zone Ltd....G.... 234 806-4604
Warren *(G-19398)*
Drowned Lure....G.... 330 548-5873
Tallmadge *(G-17982)*
Duff Farm....G.... 740 742-2182
Langsville *(G-11621)*
Ebsco Industries Inc....F.... 513 398-2149
Mason *(G-12859)*
▲ **Elite Ftscom Inc**....G.... 740 845-0987
London *(G-12059)*
Equipment Guys Inc....F.... 614 871-9220
Newark *(G-14872)*
Fishermans Central LLC....G.... 330 644-5346
New Franklin *(G-14689)*
▲ **Forrest Enterprises Inc**....G.... 937 773-1714
Piqua *(G-16116)*
Foster Manufacturing....G.... 513 735-9770
Batavia *(G-1145)*
Funtown Playgrounds Inc....E.... 513 871-8585
Cincinnati *(G-3250)*
▲ **Galaxy Balloons Incorporated**....C.... 216 476-3360
Cleveland *(G-5287)*
▲ **Ghostblind Industries Inc**....G.... 740 374-6766
Marietta *(G-12626)*
▲ **GL International LLC**....C.... 330 744-8812
Youngstown *(G-20922)*
Golf Ball Manufacturers LLC....G.... 419 994-5563
Loudonville *(G-12142)*
Golf Car Company Inc....F.... 614 873-1055
Plain City *(G-16196)*
▲ **Golf Galaxy Golfworks Inc**....C.... 740 328-4193
Newark *(G-14880)*
Grey Hawk Golf LLC....G.... 440 355-4844
Lagrange *(G-11481)*
Grey Hawk Golf Club....E.... 440 355-4844
Lagrange *(G-11482)*
Gym Pro LLC....G.... 740 984-4143
Waterford *(G-19485)*
▲ **H & H of Milford Ohio LLC**....G.... 513 576-9004
Milford *(G-14015)*
Hillman Group Inc....G.... 440 248-7000
Cleveland *(G-5409)*
Hofmanns Lures Inc....G.... 937 684-0338
Ansonia *(G-593)*
Hoistech LLC....G.... 440 327-5379
North Ridgeville *(G-15229)*
Hole Hunter Golf Inc....G.... 937 339-5833
Piqua *(G-16129)*
House of Awards and Sports....G.... 419 422-7877
Findlay *(G-9706)*
▲ **Hunters Manufacturing Co Inc**....E.... 330 628-9245
Mogadore *(G-14240)*
Imperial On-Pece Fibrgls Pools....F.... 740 747-2971
Ashley *(G-757)*
Imperial Pools Inc....D.... 513 771-1506
Cincinnati *(G-3842)*
Jason Stuller Pro Shop LLC....G.... 419 882-3197
Sylvania *(G-17946)*
Just Basic Sports Inc....G.... 330 264-7771
Wooster *(G-20611)*
Kabler Farms....G.... 513 732-0501
Batavia *(G-1156)*
▲ **Kent Sporting Goods Co Inc**....D.... 419 929-7021
New London *(G-14730)*
Konkrete City Skateboards....G.... 513 231-0399
Cincinnati *(G-3922)*

L A Productions Co LLC....G.... 330 666-4230
Akron *(G-243)*
Lakota Industries Inc....G.... 937 532-6394
Xenia *(G-20781)*
Lasermark LLC....G.... 513 312-9889
Dayton *(G-8306)*
▲ **Lem Products Holding LLC**....E.... 513 202-1188
West Chester *(G-19736)*
Licensed Spcialty Pdts of Ohio....G.... 419 800-8104
Bradner *(G-2012)*
Line Drive Sportz-Lcrc LLC....G.... 419 794-7150
Maumee *(G-13127)*
Lure Inc....E.... 440 951-8862
Willoughby *(G-20363)*
▼ **M&M Great Adventures LLC**....G.... 937 344-1415
Westerville *(G-20008)*
Mc Alarney Pool Spas and Billd....E.... 740 373-6698
Marietta *(G-12646)*
McSports....G.... 419 586-5555
Celina *(G-2974)*
Meridian Industries Inc....D.... 330 359-5447
Winesburg *(G-20533)*
Meyer Design Inc....E.... 330 434-9176
Akron *(G-280)*
Mudbrook Golf Center....G.... 419 433-2945
Huron *(G-11105)*
N Bass Bait Co....G.... 419 647-4501
Spencerville *(G-17310)*
Neo Tactical Gear....G.... 216 235-2625
Chardon *(G-3127)*
▲ **Ohio Table Pad Company**....D.... 419 872-6400
Perrysburg *(G-15986)*
Ouchless Lures Inc....G.... 330 653-3867
Hudson *(G-11066)*
Peregrine Outdoor Products LLC....G.... 800 595-3850
Lebanon *(G-11683)*
▲ **Phoenix Bat Company**....G.... 614 873-7776
Plain City *(G-16206)*
Playground Equipment Service....G.... 513 481-3776
Cincinnati *(G-4168)*
Practice Center Inc....G.... 513 489-5229
Cincinnati *(G-4183)*
Puck Hogs Pro Shop Inc....G.... 419 540-1388
Toledo *(G-18488)*
R L Y Inc....G.... 513 385-1950
Cincinnati *(G-4244)*
◆ **Rain Drop Products Llc**....E.... 419 207-1229
Ashland *(G-742)*
Raven Concealment Systems LLC....F.... 440 508-9000
North Ridgeville *(G-15249)*
Red Barakuda LLC....G.... 614 596-5432
Columbus *(G-7380)*
Reef Runner Tackle Co Inc....G.... 419 798-9125
Marblehead *(G-12587)*
Reelflyrodcom....G.... 937 434-8472
Dayton *(G-8469)*
Rockbridge Outfitters....G.... 740 654-1956
Lancaster *(G-11604)*
Royal Spa Columbus....G.... 614 529-8569
Lewis Center *(G-11777)*
Shoot A Way Inc....F.... 419 294-4654
Upper Sandusky *(G-18973)*
◆ **Shoot-A-Way Inc**....F.... 419 294-4654
Upper Sandusky *(G-18974)*
Shooting Range Supply LLC....G.... 440 576-7711
Jefferson *(G-11237)*
Smart 3d Solutions LLC....G.... 330 972-7840
Akron *(G-379)*
Snakebite Snaps....G.... 520 227-5442
Cuyahoga Falls *(G-7920)*
Soccer Centre Owners Ltd....E.... 419 893-5425
Maumee *(G-13146)*
Soccer First Inc....G.... 614 889-1115
Dublin *(G-8992)*
Sports Monster Corp....F.... 614 443-0190
Columbus *(G-7479)*
▲ **Sunset Golf LLC**....E.... 419 994-5563
Tallmadge *(G-18007)*
Target Thompson Technology....G.... 330 699-8000
Uniontown *(G-18934)*
Total Tennis Inc....G.... 614 488-5004
Columbus *(G-7535)*
Toy & Sport Trends Inc....E.... 419 748-8880
Napoleon *(G-14562)*
Trendco Inc....G.... 216 661-6903
North Royalton *(G-15307)*
Tuffy Pad Company Inc....F.... 330 688-0043
Stow *(G-17639)*
U S Development Corp....E.... 570 966-5990
Kent *(G-11397)*

Employee Codes: A=Over 500 employees, B=251-500
C=101-250, D=51-100, E=20-50, F=10-19, G=3-9
2019 Harris Ohio
Industrial Directory
1013

39 MISCELLANEOUS MANUFACTURING INDUSTRIES

Ultrabuilt Play Systems Inc .... F 419 652-2294
  Nova *(G-15436)*
Unique-Chardan Inc .... E 419 636-6900
  Bryan *(G-2311)*
Uniwall Manufacturing Co .... F 330 875-1444
  Louisville *(G-12169)*
Vantage Athletic .... G 419 680-5274
  Fremont *(G-10062)*
Vf Outdoor LLC .... G 614 337-1147
  Columbus *(G-7582)*
Victory Athletics Inc .... G 330 274-2854
  Mantua *(G-12561)*
Voll Hockey Inc .... G 216 521-4625
  Lakewood *(G-11536)*
▲ Wake Nation .... F 513 887-9253
  Fairfield *(G-9574)*
Wholesale Bait Co Inc .... G 513 863-2380
  Fairfield *(G-9576)*
Wooden Horse Corporation .... G 419 663-1472
  Norwalk *(G-15419)*
▲ Zebec of North America Inc .... E 513 829-5533
  Fairfield *(G-9579)*
Zwf Golf LLC .... F 937 767-5621
  Fairborn *(G-9476)*

3951 Pens & Mechanical Pencils

▲ Berea Hardwood Co Inc .... G 216 898-8956
  Cleveland *(G-4804)*
▲ Bexley Pen Company Inc .... G 614 351-9988
  Columbus *(G-6667)*

3952 Lead Pencils, Crayons & Artist's Mtrls

Crawford County Arts Council .... G 419 834-4133
  Bucyrus *(G-2323)*
Modern Ink Technology LLC .... F 419 738-9664
  Lima *(G-11908)*
▲ North Shore Strapping Inc .... D 216 661-5200
  Brooklyn Heights *(G-2128)*
Pen Pal LLC .... G 614 348-2517
  New Albany *(G-14633)*
Puracera 3 LLC .... F 513 231-7555
  Cincinnati *(G-4222)*
Ramon Robinson .... G 330 883-3244
  Vienna *(G-19208)*
RPM Consumer Holding Company ..... G 330 273-5090
  Medina *(G-13330)*
Whitten Studios .... G 419 368-8366
  Ashland *(G-755)*

3953 Marking Devices

Ace Rubber Stamp & Off Sup Co .... E 216 771-8483
  Cleveland *(G-4604)*
◆ Akron Paint & Varnish Inc .... D 330 773-8911
  Akron *(G-46)*
Bishop Machine Tool & Die .... F 740 453-8818
  Zanesville *(G-21110)*
Ccsi Inc .... G 800 742-8535
  Akron *(G-106)*
Dayton Stencil Works Company .... E 937 223-3233
  Dayton *(G-8145)*
Desmond Engraving Co Inc .... E 216 265-8338
  Cleveland *(G-5086)*
▼ Dischem International Inc .... G 330 494-5210
  Canton *(G-2660)*
E C Shaw Co .... E 513 721-6334
  Cincinnati *(G-3616)*
East Cleveland Rubber Stamp .... G 216 851-5050
  Cleveland *(G-5137)*
Global Partners USA Co Inc .... G 513 276-4981
  West Chester *(G-19717)*
Greg G Wright & Sons LLC .... E 513 721-3310
  Cincinnati *(G-3784)*
Hathaway Stamp & Ident Co of C ...... F 513 621-1052
  Cincinnati *(G-3802)*
Hathaway Stamp Co .... F 513 621-1052
  Cincinnati *(G-3803)*
Identity Holding Company LLC .... D 216 514-1277
  Cleveland *(G-5435)*
▲ Infosight Corporation .... D 740 642-3600
  Chillicothe *(G-3194)*
▲ Inner Products Sales Inc .... G 216 581-4141
  Bedford *(G-1416)*
Innovative Ceramic Corp .... G 330 385-6515
  East Liverpool *(G-9059)*
Jerry Pulfer .... G 937 778-1861
  Piqua *(G-16134)*
◆ Lectroetch Co .... F 440 934-1249
  Sheffield Village *(G-16970)*
Marathon Mfg & Sup Co .... D 330 343-2656
  New Philadelphia *(G-14783)*

Mark Rite Co .... G 330 757-7229
  Youngstown *(G-20966)*
▲ Mark-All Enterprises LLC .... E 800 433-3615
  Akron *(G-268)*
Marking Devices Inc .... E 216 861-4498
  Cleveland *(G-5622)*
Master Marking Company Inc .... F 330 688-6797
  Stow *(G-17604)*
▲ Microcom Corporation .... E 740 548-6262
  Lewis Center *(G-11767)*
Monode Marking Products Inc .... F 419 929-0346
  New London *(G-14731)*
Monode Steel Stamp Inc .... F 419 929-3501
  New London *(G-14732)*
Quality Rubber Stamp Inc .... G 614 235-2700
  Columbus *(G-7365)*
Quick As A Wink Printing Co .... F 419 224-9786
  Lima *(G-11926)*
Raschke Engraving Inc .... G 330 677-5544
  Kent *(G-11373)*
▲ REA Elektronik Inc .... F 440 232-0555
  Bedford *(G-1440)*
Rise Holdings LLC .... F 440 946-9646
  Willoughby *(G-20422)*
▲ Royal Acme Corporation .... E 216 241-1477
  Cleveland *(G-6009)*
Sprinter Marking Inc .... F 740 453-1000
  Zanesville *(G-21182)*
Stencilsmith LLC .... G 614 876-4350
  Hilliard *(G-10866)*
Superior Steel Stamp Co .... E 216 431-6460
  Cleveland *(G-6127)*
▲ System Seals Inc .... D 440 735-0200
  Cleveland *(G-6140)*
▼ Technology and Services Inc .... F 740 626-2020
  Chillicothe *(G-3227)*
▲ Telesis Technologies Inc .... C 740 477-5000
  Circleville *(G-4562)*
The Metal Marker Mfg Co .... F 440 327-2300
  North Ridgeville *(G-15255)*
Ulrich Rubber Stamp Company .... G 419 339-9939
  Elida *(G-9202)*
Volk Corporation .... G 513 621-1052
  Cincinnati *(G-4483)*
Williams Steel Rule Die Co .... F 216 431-3232
  Cleveland *(G-6311)*
Zitello Fine Art LLC .... G 330 792-8894
  Youngstown *(G-21087)*

3955 Carbon Paper & Inked Ribbons

Adaptive Data Inc .... F 937 436-2343
  Dayton *(G-8007)*
▲ All Write Ribbon Inc .... E 513 753-8300
  Amelia *(G-529)*
Eco-Print Solutions LLC .... G 513 731-3106
  Cincinnati *(G-3629)*
Jay Tackett .... G 740 779-1715
  Frankfort *(G-9862)*
Kehler Enterprises Inc .... G 614 889-8488
  Dublin *(G-8937)*
▲ Kroy LLC .... C 216 426-5600
  Cleveland *(G-5544)*
Nanotechlabs Inc .... G 937 297-9518
  Kettering *(G-11436)*
Newwave Technologies Inc .... G 513 683-1211
  Loveland *(G-12218)*
Progressive Ribbon Inc .... E 513 705-9319
  Middletown *(G-13944)*
◆ Pubco Corporation .... D 216 881-5300
  Cleveland *(G-5932)*
Wood County Ohio .... G 419 353-1227
  Bowling Green *(G-2007)*

3961 Costume Jewelry & Novelties

Cult Couture LLC .... G 330 801-9475
  Cuyahoga Falls *(G-7855)*
Gardella Jewelry LLC .... G 440 877-9261
  North Royalton *(G-15273)*
Johnstons Banks Inc .... G 614 499-4374
  Westerville *(G-20001)*
Prosperity On Payne Inc .... G 216 431-7677
  Cleveland *(G-5930)*
Pughs Designer Jewelers Inc .... G 740 344-9259
  Newark *(G-14914)*
Swarovski North America Ltd .... E 216 292-9737
  Cleveland *(G-6136)*

3965 Fasteners, Buttons, Needles & Pins

A Raymond Tinnerman Indus Inc .... D 330 220-5100
  Brunswick *(G-2186)*

Cailin Dev Ltd Lblty Co .... F 216 408-6261
  Cleveland *(G-4862)*
▲ Cardinal Fstener Specialty Inc ...... E 216 831-3800
  Bedford Heights *(G-1464)*
▲ Catania Medallic Specialty .... E 440 933-9595
  Avon Lake *(G-981)*
▲ Dimcogray Corporation .... D 937 433-7600
  Centerville *(G-3001)*
Dubose Energy Fasteners & Mach ..... F 216 362-1700
  Middleburg Heights *(G-13764)*
Eaglehead Manufacturing Co .... E 216 692-1240
  Euclid *(G-9412)*
Elgin Fastener Group .... G 440 325-4337
  Berea *(G-1605)*
Erico International Corp .... B 440 248-0100
  Solon *(G-17017)*
▲ ET&f Fastening Systems Inc .... F 800 248-2376
  Solon *(G-17141)*
Global Specialties Inc .... G 800 338-0814
  Brunswick *(G-2210)*
Interfast Inc .... E 216 581-3000
  Cleveland *(G-5465)*
▲ Midwest Motor Supply Co .... C 800 233-1294
  Columbus *(G-7181)*
▲ Ohashi Technica USA Mfg Inc ...... E 740 965-9002
  Sunbury *(G-17895)*
Phillips Contractors Sup LLC .... F 216 861-5730
  Cleveland *(G-5872)*
R L Technologies Inc .... G 937 321-5544
  Dayton *(G-8459)*
▲ Ramco Specialties Inc .... G 330 653-5135
  Hudson *(G-11069)*
▲ Silicon USA Inc .... G 330 928-6217
  Cuyahoga Falls *(G-7916)*
Solution Industries LLC .... G 440 816-9500
  Middleburg Heights *(G-13770)*
▲ Stelfast Inc .... E 440 879-0077
  Strongsville *(G-17797)*
Tri-State Fasteners LLC .... G 937 442-1904
  Sardinia *(G-16874)*
W W Cross Industries Inc .... F 330 588-8400
  Canton *(G-2861)*
Wodin Inc .... E 440 439-4222
  Cleveland *(G-6320)*
Youngstown Bolt & Supply Co .... G 330 799-3201
  Youngstown *(G-21072)*
Zipper Manufacturing LLC .... G 937 444-0904
  Williamsburg *(G-20258)*

3991 Brooms & Brushes

Brushes Inc .... E 216 267-8084
  Cleveland *(G-4847)*
D A L E S Corporation .... F 419 255-5335
  Toledo *(G-18250)*
Deco Tools Inc .... E 419 476-9321
  Toledo *(G-18256)*
▲ Demel Enterprises Inc .... F 740 331-1400
  Athens *(G-827)*
Designetics Inc .... D 419 866-0700
  Holland *(G-10925)*
◆ Fimm USA Inc .... F 253 243-1522
  Columbus *(G-6922)*
Hoge Lumber Company .... F 419 753-2351
  New Knoxville *(G-14704)*
◆ Malish Corporation .... C 440 951-5356
  Mentor *(G-13509)*
▲ Mill Rose Laboratories Inc .... E 440 974-6730
  Mentor *(G-13519)*
▲ Mill-Rose Company .... C 440 255-9171
  Mentor *(G-13520)*
Ohio Brush Company .... F 216 791-3265
  Cleveland *(G-5802)*
Ohio Carbon Company .... G 216 251-7274
  Ashland *(G-729)*
Precision Brush Co .... F 440 542-9600
  Solon *(G-17218)*
Public Works Dept Street Div .... E 740 283-6013
  Steubenville *(G-17549)*
▲ Spiral Brushes Inc .... E 330 686-2861
  Stow *(G-17629)*
▲ Stephen M Trudick .... E 440 834-1891
  Burton *(G-2371)*
Taupe Holdings Co .... G 614 330-4600
  Dublin *(G-9002)*
Tod Thin Brushes Inc .... F 440 576-6859
  Jefferson *(G-11242)*
Trent Manufacturing Company .... F 216 391-1551
  Cleveland *(G-6204)*
Unique Packaging & Printing .... F 440 785-6730
  Mentor *(G-13618)*

United Rotary Brush Inc....D....937 644-3515
Plain City *(G-16214)*
Wooster Brush Company....G....440 322-8081
Elyria *(G-9347)*

3993 Signs & Advertising Displays

1 Day Sign....G....419 475-6060
Toledo *(G-18150)*
A & A Safety Inc....E....513 943-6100
Amelia *(G-527)*
A & A Safety Inc....F....937 567-9781
Beavercreek *(G-1348)*
A B C Sign Inc....F....513 241-8884
Cincinnati *(G-3278)*
A Plus Signs & Graphix....G....330 848-4800
Akron *(G-19)*
A Sign For The Times Inc....G....216 297-2977
Cleveland *(G-4593)*
Abbot Image Solutions LLC....G....937 382-6677
Wilmington *(G-20483)*
Abbott Signs....G....937 393-6600
Hillsboro *(G-10876)*
Accu-Sign....G....216 544-2059
Broadview Heights *(G-2086)*
▲ Accutech Sign Shop....G....513 385-3595
Cincinnati *(G-3291)*
Action Enterprise....G....740 522-1678
Newark *(G-14847)*
Action Sign Inc....G....330 966-0390
Greentown *(G-10356)*
Ad-Pro Signs I LLC....G....513 922-5046
Cincinnati *(G-3296)*
Adcraft Decals Inc....E....216 524-2934
Cleveland *(G-4615)*
Advance Sign Group LLC....E....614 429-2111
Columbus *(G-6544)*
Advertising Ideas of Ohio Inc....G....330 745-6555
Barberton *(G-1049)*
▲ Affinity Disp Expositions Inc....C....513 771-2339
Cincinnati *(G-3306)*
Affinity Disp Expositions Inc....D....513 771-2339
Cincinnati *(G-3307)*
AG Designs LLC....G....614 506-2849
Delaware *(G-8652)*
Agile Sign & Ltg Maint Inc....E....440 918-1311
Eastlake *(G-9098)*
Akers Identity LLC....G....330 493-0055
Canton *(G-2566)*
▲ Alberts Screen Print Inc....C....330 753-7559
Norton *(G-15360)*
All Signs and Designs LLC....G....216 267-8588
Cleveland *(G-4666)*
All Signs Express Inc....F....513 489-7744
Blue Ash *(G-1727)*
All Signs of Chillicothe Inc....G....740 773-5016
Chillicothe *(G-3174)*
All Star Group Inc....G....440 323-6060
Elyria *(G-9212)*
All Star Sign Company....E....614 461-9052
Columbus *(G-6568)*
Allied Sign Company Inc....F....614 443-9656
Columbus *(G-6574)*
Alvin L Roepke....F....419 862-3891
Elmore *(G-9203)*
Am Graphics....G....330 799-7319
Youngstown *(G-20842)*
American Awards Inc....F....614 875-1850
Grove City *(G-10414)*
American Executive Gifts Inc....F....330 645-4396
Akron *(G-61)*
▲ American Led-Gible Inc....F....614 851-1100
Columbus *(G-6584)*
American Metal Sign....G....267 521-2670
Ada *(G-4)*
Applied Graphics Ltd....G....419 756-6882
Mansfield *(G-12407)*
Aq Productions Inc....G....614 486-7700
Dublin *(G-8882)*
Archer Corporation....E....330 455-9995
Canton *(G-2574)*
Architctral Identification Inc....E....614 868-8400
Gahanna *(G-10076)*
Art & Sign Corporation....G....419 865-3336
Toledo *(G-18192)*
Art Tees Inc....G....614 338-8337
Columbus *(G-6617)*
Atchley Signs & Graphics....G....614 421-7446
Columbus *(G-6624)*
Atlantic Sign Company Inc....E....513 383-1504
Cincinnati *(G-3367)*
Auld Company....E....614 454-1010
Columbus *(G-6629)*
Auld Lang Signs Inc....G....513 792-5555
Blue Ash *(G-1731)*
Auld Technologies LLC....F....614 755-2853
Columbus *(G-6631)*
Auto Dealer Designs Inc....E....330 374-7666
Akron *(G-74)*
Auto Pro & Design....G....330 833-9237
Massillon *(G-12961)*
B & D Graphics Inc....G....513 641-0855
Cincinnati *(G-3373)*
Baker Plastics Inc....G....330 743-3142
Youngstown *(G-20851)*
Bambeck Inc....G....614 766-1000
Dublin *(G-8887)*
Barnes Advertising Corp....F....740 453-6836
Zanesville *(G-21103)*
Bates Metal Products Inc....D....740 498-8371
Port Washington *(G-16267)*
BDS Packaging Inc....D....937 643-0530
Moraine *(G-14333)*
Becker Signs Inc....G....330 659-4504
Hudson *(G-11033)*
Becker Signs Inc....G....330 659-4504
Richfield *(G-16462)*
Beebe Worldwide Graphics Sign....G....513 241-2726
Blue Ash *(G-1733)*
Behrco Inc....G....419 394-1612
Saint Marys *(G-16676)*
Belco Works Inc....B....740 695-0500
Saint Clairsville *(G-16624)*
Bench Billboard Company Inc....G....513 271-2222
Cincinnati *(G-3388)*
Benchmark Craftsman Inc....E....330 975-4214
Seville *(G-16911)*
Benchmark Signs and Gifts....G....216 973-3718
Northfield *(G-15313)*
Bernard R Doyles Inc....G....216 523-2288
Cleveland *(G-4806)*
Bird Corporation....G....419 424-3095
Findlay *(G-9656)*
Blang Acquisition LLC....F....937 223-2155
Dayton *(G-8058)*
Blink Marketing Inc....G....216 503-2568
Cleveland *(G-4820)*
Bob King Sign Company Inc....G....330 753-2679
Akron *(G-90)*
Boyer Signs & Graphics Inc....E....216 383-7242
Columbus *(G-6691)*
Brainerd Industries Inc....E....937 228-0488
Miamisburg *(G-13644)*
Brandon Screen Printing....F....419 229-9837
Lima *(G-11845)*
Breibach Association....G....614 876-6480
Hilliard *(G-10815)*
Brent Bleh Company....G....513 721-1100
Cincinnati *(G-3410)*
Brilliant Electric Sign Co Ltd....D....216 741-3800
Brooklyn Heights *(G-2116)*
Brockmans Signs Inc....G....513 574-6163
Cincinnati *(G-3422)*
Brown Cnty Bd Mntal Rtardation....E....937 378-4891
Georgetown *(G-10237)*
▲ Buckeye Boxes Inc....C....614 274-8484
Columbus *(G-6707)*
Buds Sign Shop Inc....F....330 744-5555
Youngstown *(G-20861)*
Busch & Thiem Inc....E....419 625-7515
Sandusky *(G-16800)*
Business Idntification Systems....G....614 841-1255
Columbus *(G-6716)*
Byers Sign Co....G....614 561-1224
Columbus *(G-6717)*
C A Kustoms....G....419 332-4395
Fremont *(G-10003)*
C JS Signs....G....330 821-7446
Alliance *(G-459)*
Campbell Signs & Apparel LLC....F....330 386-4768
East Liverpool *(G-9052)*
Canton Sign Co....G....330 456-7151
Canton *(G-2617)*
▲ Casad Company Inc....F....419 586-9457
Coldwater *(G-6404)*
Cdds Inc....G....614 626-8747
Gahanna *(G-10078)*
Cds Signs....G....513 563-7446
Cincinnati *(G-3450)*
Central Graphics Inc....G....330 928-7080
Cuyahoga Falls *(G-7847)*
Century Signs....G....419 352-2666
Bowling Green *(G-1962)*
▲ Cgs Signs LLC....F....419 897-3000
Holland *(G-10919)*
Chatelain Plastics Inc....G....419 422-4323
Findlay *(G-9667)*
Cicogna Electric and Sign Co....D....440 998-2637
Ashtabula *(G-766)*
Classic Sign Company Inc....G....419 420-0058
Findlay *(G-9670)*
Cline Signs LLC....G....513 396-7446
Cincinnati *(G-3527)*
▲ Co Pac Services Inc....F....216 688-1780
Cleveland *(G-4994)*
Columbus Graphics Inc....F....614 577-9360
Reynoldsburg *(G-16432)*
Columbus Sign Company....E....614 252-3133
Columbus *(G-6802)*
Corporate ID Inc....G....614 841-1255
Columbus *(G-6823)*
Creative Blast Co....G....513 251-4177
Cincinnati *(G-3558)*
CTS Signs & Sales....G....419 407-5534
Oregon *(G-15559)*
Cubbison Company....D....330 793-2481
Youngstown *(G-20882)*
Custom Engraving & Screen Prtg....G....440 933-2902
Avon Lake *(G-983)*
Custom Retail Group LLC....G....614 409-9720
Columbus *(G-6843)*
Custom Sign Center Inc....E....614 279-6700
Columbus *(G-6844)*
D & D Next Day Signs Inc....G....419 537-9595
Toledo *(G-18249)*
Dana Signs LLC....G....937 653-3917
Urbana *(G-18987)*
Danite Holdings Ltd....E....614 444-3333
Columbus *(G-6849)*
David Esrati....G....937 228-4433
Dayton *(G-8126)*
Dayton Wire Products Inc....E....937 236-8000
Dayton *(G-8149)*
◆ Dee Sign Co....E....513 779-3333
West Chester *(G-19691)*
Dee Sign Usa LLC....G....513 779-3333
West Chester *(G-19692)*
▲ Dern Trophies Corp....F....614 895-3260
Westerville *(G-19987)*
Design Masters Inc....G....513 772-7175
Cincinnati *(G-3584)*
Design Sign Inc....G....216 398-9900
Cleveland *(G-5085)*
Devries & Associates Inc....F....614 890-3821
Westerville *(G-20047)*
Devries & Associates Inc....G....614 860-0103
Westerville *(G-20048)*
Digimatics Inc....G....419 478-0804
Toledo *(G-18263)*
Digimax Signs....G....513 576-0747
Milford *(G-14007)*
Direct Image Signs Inc....G....440 327-5575
North Ridgeville *(G-15220)*
DJ Signs MD LLC....G....330 344-6643
Akron *(G-144)*
Donald Marlo....G....937 836-4880
Dayton *(G-8165)*
▲ Downing Enterprises Inc....D....330 666-3888
Copley *(G-7683)*
Dyverse Entertainment LLC....G....513 225-3301
Blue Ash *(G-1761)*
E S Sign & Design LLC....G....330 405-4799
Twinsburg *(G-18766)*
▲ Eighth Floor Promotions LLC....C....419 586-6433
Celina *(G-2959)*
Ellet Neon Sales & Service Inc....E....330 628-9907
Akron *(G-150)*
Engravers Gallery & Sign Co....G....330 830-1271
Massillon *(G-12980)*
Enlarging Arts Inc....G....330 434-3433
Akron *(G-156)*
▲ Etched Metal Company....E....440 248-0240
Solon *(G-17142)*
Ew Publishing Company....G....440 979-0025
North Olmsted *(G-15188)*
Exchange Signs....G....330 644-4552
Coventry Township *(G-7769)*
F J Designs Inc....E....330 264-1377
Wooster *(G-20590)*
Fair Publishing House Inc....E....419 668-3746
Norwalk *(G-15394)*

Employee Codes: A=Over 500 employees, B=251-500
C=101-250, D=51-100, E=20-50, F=10-19, G=3-9
2019 Harris Ohio
Industrial Directory
1015

Fastsigns G 513 489-8989
Cincinnati *(G-3674)*
Fastsigns G 330 952-2626
Medina *(G-13261)*
Fastsigns Westerville E 614 890-3821
Westerville *(G-20053)*
Fdi Cabinetry LLC G 513 353-4500
Cleves *(G-6362)*
Federal Heath Sign Company LLC D 740 369-0999
Delaware *(G-8678)*
Fineline Imprints Inc E 740 453-1083
Zanesville *(G-21135)*
Finn Graphics Inc E 513 941-6161
Cincinnati *(G-3690)*
Firehouse Sign Co Inc G 216 267-5300
Brookpark *(G-2146)*
First Stop Signs and Decals G 330 343-1859
New Philadelphia *(G-14769)*
Folks Creative Printers Inc E 740 383-6326
Marion *(G-12702)*
Forsvara Engineering LLC G 937 254-9711
Dayton *(G-8202)*
Forty Nine Degrees LLC F 419 678-0100
Coldwater *(G-6409)*
Fought Signs G 330 262-5901
Wooster *(G-20592)*
Fourteen Ventures Group LLC G 937 866-2341
West Carrollton *(G-19631)*
Fried Daddy G 937 854-4542
Dayton *(G-8207)*
Frontier Signs & Displays Inc G 513 367-0813
Harrison *(G-10642)*
Fulton Sign & Decal Inc G 440 951-1515
Mentor *(G-13452)*
Fultz Sign Co Inc G 419 225-6000
Lima *(G-11866)*
Gail Berner G 937 322-0314
Springfield *(G-17406)*
▲ Galaxy Balloons Incorporated C 216 476-3360
Cleveland *(G-5287)*
◆ Gallo Displays Inc E 216 431-9500
Cleveland *(G-5288)*
Gardner Signs Inc E 419 385-6669
Toledo *(G-18301)*
Gary Lawrence Enterprises Inc G 330 833-7181
Massillon *(G-12986)*
Gauntlet Awards & Engraving G 937 890-5811
Dayton *(G-8214)*
Gedco Inc G 330 828-2044
Dalton *(G-7942)*
Genesis Display Systems Inc G 513 561-1440
Cincinnati *(G-3748)*
Geograph Industries Inc E 513 202-9200
Harrison *(G-10643)*
Gerber Wood Products Inc G 330 857-3901
Kidron *(G-11447)*
▲ Ginos Awards Inc E 216 831-6565
Warrensville Heights *(G-19469)*
Glavin Industries Inc E 440 349-0049
Solon *(G-17149)*
▲ Global Lighting Tech Inc E 440 922-4584
Brecksville *(G-2039)*
Golden Signs and Lighting LLC G 513 248-0895
Milford *(G-14011)*
▲ Golf Marketing Group Inc G 330 963-5155
Twinsburg *(G-18788)*
Grady McCauley Inc D 330 494-9444
North Canton *(G-15089)*
◆ Granite Industries Inc D 419 445-4733
Archbold *(G-651)*
Graphic Detail Inc G 330 678-1724
Kent *(G-11326)*
Great Impressions Signs Design G 614 428-8250
Columbus *(G-6968)*
Greg G Wright & Sons LLC E 513 721-3310
Cincinnati *(G-3784)*
Gus Holthaus Signs Inc E 513 861-0060
Cincinnati *(G-3790)*
Hall Company E 937 652-1376
Urbana *(G-18992)*
Ham Signs LLC G 937 454-9111
Dayton *(G-8242)*
Hart Advertising Inc F 419 668-1194
Norwalk *(G-15397)*
Hendricks Vacuum Forming Inc E 330 837-2040
Massillon *(G-12995)*
Heres Your Sign G 740 574-1248
Franklin Furnace *(G-9935)*
Hillman Group Inc G 440 248-7000
Cleveland *(G-5409)*
HP Manufacturing Company Inc D 216 361-6500
Cleveland *(G-5421)*
HPM Business Systems Inc G 216 520-1330
Cleveland *(G-5422)*
Hulsman Signs G 513 738-3389
Harrison *(G-10649)*
Identitek Systems Inc D 330 832-9844
Massillon *(G-13002)*
Impressions To Go LLC G 614 760-0600
Dublin *(G-8928)*
Industrial and Mar Eng Svc Co F 740 694-0791
Fredericktown *(G-9971)*
Industrial Electronic Service F 937 746-9750
Carlisle *(G-2893)*
Industrial Image G 419 547-1417
Bellevue *(G-1537)*
▲ Inner Products Sales Inc G 216 581-4141
Bedford *(G-1416)*
Innovation Exhibits Inc G 330 726-1324
Youngstown *(G-20941)*
Insignia Signs Inc G 937 866-2341
Dayton *(G-8268)*
Insta Plak Inc F 419 537-1555
Toledo *(G-18349)*
Integral Design Inc F 216 524-0555
Cleveland *(G-5462)*
Interior Graphic Systems LLC G 330 244-0100
Canton *(G-2709)*
International Installations G 330 848-4800
Barberton *(G-1077)*
Interstate Sign Products Inc G 419 683-1962
Crestline *(G-7795)*
Itecgraphix Inc G 440 951-5020
Mentor *(G-13477)*
J & D Berdine Signs Inc G 330 468-0556
Macedonia *(G-12305)*
Jacqueline L Vandyke G 740 593-6779
Athens *(G-837)*
Jalo Inc G 216 661-2222
Cleveland *(G-5492)*
Janeway Signs Inc G 937 237-8433
Dayton *(G-8279)*
JCP Signs & Graphix Inc G 740 965-3058
Galena *(G-10114)*
Jeffrey A Clark G 419 866-8775
Holland *(G-10936)*
Jeffrey L Becht Inc G 937 264-2070
Dayton *(G-8283)*
Jerry Pulfer G 937 778-1861
Piqua *(G-16134)*
Joe Paxton G 614 424-9000
Columbus *(G-7071)*
Jones & Assoc Advg & Design G 330 799-6876
Youngstown *(G-20949)*
Jones Old Rustic Sign E 937 643-1695
Moraine *(G-14362)*
Joseph A Panico & Sons Inc G 614 235-3188
Columbus *(G-7077)*
Judith C Zell G 740 385-0386
Logan *(G-12029)*
Kane Sign Co G 330 253-5263
Akron *(G-231)*
Kasper Enterprises Inc G 419 841-6656
Toledo *(G-18362)*
▲ Kdm Signs Inc C 513 769-1932
Cincinnati *(G-3900)*
Kenneth J Moore G 330 923-8313
Cuyahoga Falls *(G-7887)*
Kessler Sign Company E 740 453-0668
Zanesville *(G-21153)*
Kessler Sign Company G 937 898-0633
Dayton *(G-8295)*
Kief Signs G 513 941-8800
Addyston *(G-12)*
Kim Phillips Sign Co LLC G 330 364-4280
Dover *(G-8834)*
King Retail Solutions Inc F 513 729-5858
Hamilton *(G-10580)*
Kingsway Art & Sign G 330 877-6241
Hartville *(G-10698)*
Kmgrafx Inc G 513 248-4100
Loveland *(G-12206)*
Koebbeco Signs LLC G 513 923-2974
Cincinnati *(G-3921)*
Laad Sign & Lighting Inc F 330 379-2297
Akron *(G-244)*
Lapat Signs G 440 277-6291
Sheffield Village *(G-16969)*
Ledge Hill Signs Limited G 440 461-4445
Cleveland *(G-5570)*
Letter Graphics Sign Co Inc G 330 683-3903
Orrville *(G-15602)*
Limelght Graphic Solutions Inc G 614 793-1996
Dublin *(G-8942)*
Long Sign Co G 614 294-1057
Columbus *(G-7136)*
LSI Industries Inc E 513 793-3200
Blue Ash *(G-1808)*
LSI Industries Inc B 513 793-3200
Blue Ash *(G-1811)*
LSI Retail Graphics LLC D 401 766-7446
North Canton *(G-15098)*
Macray Co LLC G 937 325-1726
Springfield *(G-17440)*
Magnetic Mktg Solutions LLC G 513 721-3801
Cincinnati *(G-3973)*
Maines Inc G 937 322-2084
Springfield *(G-17443)*
Marion Signs & Lighting LLC G 352 236-0936
Columbus *(G-7151)*
Masterpiece Signs & Graphics G 419 358-0077
Bluffton *(G-1891)*
Mayfair Granite Co Inc G 216 382-8150
Cleveland *(G-5636)*
McQueen Advertising Inc G 440 967-1137
Vermilion *(G-19168)*
ME Signs Inc G 419 222-7446
Lima *(G-11898)*
Media Sign Company G 513 564-9500
Cincinnati *(G-3997)*
Medina Signs Post Inc G 330 723-2484
Medina *(G-13297)*
Meka Signs Enterprises Inc G 513 942-5494
West Chester *(G-19878)*
Mel Wacker Sign Inc G 330 832-1726
Massillon *(G-13024)*
Mentor Signs & Graphics Inc G 440 951-7446
Mentor *(G-13516)*
Metalphoto of Cincinnati Inc E 513 772-8281
Cincinnati *(G-4013)*
Metromedia Technologies Inc D 330 264-2501
Wooster *(G-20624)*
Middlefield Sign Co G 440 632-0708
Middlefield *(G-13827)*
Midwest Sign Ctr F 330 493-7330
Canton *(G-2754)*
Mike B Crawford G 330 673-7944
Kent *(G-11355)*
Mitchell Plastics Inc E 330 825-2461
Barberton *(G-1086)*
Moments To Remember USA LLC G 330 830-0839
Massillon *(G-13027)*
Moonlight Specialties G 216 464-6444
Cleveland *(G-5705)*
Moonshine Screen Printing Inc F 513 523-7775
Oxford *(G-15697)*
Morrison Sign Company Inc E 614 276-1181
Columbus *(G-7198)*
Municipal Signs and Sales Inc G 330 457-2421
Columbiana *(G-6474)*
Myers and Lasch Inc G 440 235-2050
Cleveland *(G-5716)*
Names Unlimited Corp G 419 845-2005
Caledonia *(G-2419)*
National Illmination Sign Corp G 419 866-1666
Holland *(G-10945)*
Neon Light Manufacturing Co G 216 851-1000
Cleveland *(G-5739)*
Next Day Sign G 419 537-9595
Toledo *(G-18425)*
Next Day Signs LLC G 614 764-7446
Columbus *(G-7219)*
Norcal Signs Inc G 513 779-6982
West Chester *(G-19749)*
North Coast Theatrical Inc G 330 762-1768
Akron *(G-300)*
North Hill Marble & Granite Co F 330 253-2179
Akron *(G-301)*
Northmont Sign Co Inc G 937 890-0372
Dayton *(G-8384)*
Norton Outdoor Advertising E 513 631-4864
Cincinnati *(G-4089)*
▲ Ohio Awning & Manufacturing Co E 216 861-2400
Cleveland *(G-5799)*
Ohio Displays Inc F 216 961-5600
Elyria *(G-9303)*
Ohio Plastics & Safety Pdts G 330 882-6764
New Franklin *(G-14694)*
Ohio Shelterall Inc F 614 882-1110
Westerville *(G-20068)*

Oliver Signs & Graphics .... G 330 460-2996
Valley City (G-19057)
Omni Media .... G 216 687-0077
Cleveland (G-5813)
Orange Barrel Media LLC .... E 614 294-4898
Columbus (G-7275)
Painted Hill Inv Group Inc .... F 937 339-1756
Troy (G-18691)
Patriot Signage Inc .... G 859 655-9009
Cincinnati (G-4138)
Paul Peterson Safety Div Inc .... E 614 486-4375
Columbus (G-7300)
Penca Design Group Ltd .... G 440 210-4422
Painesville (G-15774)
Pfi Displays Inc .... E 330 925-9015
Rittman (G-16527)
Plastigraphics Inc .... F 513 771-8848
Cincinnati (G-4166)
Power Corp Sign Products Inc .... G 740 344-0468
Newark (G-14912)
Power Media Inc .... G 330 475-0500
Akron (G-325)
PR Signs & Service .... G 614 252-7090
Columbus (G-7340)
Pro Companies Inc .... G 614 738-1222
Pickerington (G-16057)
Pro-Decal Inc .... G 330 484-0089
Canton (G-2793)
Pure Sports Design .... G 937 935-5595
Middletown (G-13946)
Quality Channel Letters .... G 859 866-6500
Miamisburg (G-13707)
▲ Quikey Manufacturing Co Inc .... C 330 633-8106
Akron (G-337)
R & H Signs Unlimited Inc .... G 937 293-3834
Dayton (G-8457)
R M Davis Inc .... G 419 756-6719
Mansfield (G-12503)
R Weir Inc .... G 937 438-5730
Dayton (G-8461)
Ram Z Neon .... G 330 788-5121
Youngstown (G-21013)
Rapid Signs & More Inc .... G 513 553-4040
New Richmond (G-14814)
Ray Meyer Sign Company Inc .... E 513 984-5446
Loveland (G-12226)
Red Hot Studios .... G 330 609-7446
Warren (G-19437)
Redi-Quik Signs Inc .... G 614 228-6641
Columbus (G-7382)
Renoir Visions LLC .... F 419 586-5679
Celina (G-2982)
Ricks Graphic Accents Inc .... G 330 644-4455
Akron (G-349)
Rise N Shine Yard Signs .... G 330 745-5868
Barberton (G-1103)
▲ Rocal Inc .... D 740 998-2122
Frankfort (G-9864)
Roderer Enterprises Inc .... G 513 942-3000
Fairfield (G-9559)
Roemer Industries Inc .... D 330 448-2000
Masury (G-13062)
Rossi Concept Arts .... G 330 453-6366
Canton (G-2811)
▲ Royal Acme Corporation .... E 216 241-1477
Cleveland (G-6009)
Ruff Neon & Lighting Maint Inc .... F 440 350-6267
Painesville (G-15782)
▲ Ruthie Ann Inc .... F 800 231-3567
New Paris (G-14755)
S & S Sign Co .... G 614 837-1511
Canal Winchester (G-2511)
S T Custom Signs .... G 513 733-4227
Cincinnati (G-4298)
S&S Sign Service .... G 614 279-9722
Columbus (G-7411)
Sa-Mor Signs .... G 937 441-4950
Wapakoneta (G-19351)
▲ Sabco Industries Inc .... E 419 531-5347
Toledo (G-18510)
Safety Sign Company .... E 440 238-7722
Strongsville (G-17784)
Scioto Sign Co Inc .... E 419 673-1261
Kenton (G-11422)
Screen Images Inc .... G 440 779-7356
North Olmsted (G-15197)
Screen Works Inc .... E 937 264-9111
Dayton (G-8499)
▲ Sensical Inc .... D 216 641-1141
Solon (G-17229)

Sign A Rama .... G 330 499-4653
North Canton (G-15118)
Sign A Rama .... G 614 337-6000
Gahanna (G-10103)
Sign A Rama Inc .... G 614 932-7005
Powell (G-16335)
Sign A Rama Inc .... G 440 442-5002
Cleveland (G-6064)
Sign A Rama Inc .... G 513 671-2213
Cincinnati (G-4336)
Sign America Incorporated .... E 740 765-5555
Richmond (G-16498)
Sign City Inc .... G 614 486-6700
Mount Gilead (G-14433)
Sign Connection Inc .... G 937 435-4070
Dayton (G-8506)
Sign Design Wooster Inc .... G 330 262-8838
Wooster (G-20654)
Sign Graphics & Design .... G 513 576-1639
Milford (G-14040)
Sign Makers LLC .... G 330 455-0909
Canton (G-2816)
Sign Pro of Lima .... G 419 222-7767
Lima (G-11939)
Sign Shop .... G 740 474-1499
Circleville (G-4558)
Sign Smith LLC .... G 614 519-9144
Marengo (G-12595)
Sign Source USA Inc .... D 419 224-1130
Lima (G-11940)
Sign Technologies LLC .... G 937 439-3970
Dayton (G-8507)
Sign Write .... G 937 559-4388
Beavercreek (G-1341)
Signage Consultants Inc .... G 614 297-7446
Columbus (G-7449)
Signcom Incorporated .... E 614 228-9999
Columbus (G-7451)
Signed By Josette LLC .... G 419 796-9632
Findlay (G-9754)
Signery .... G 513 932-1938
Lebanon (G-11696)
Signery2 LLC .... G 513 738-3048
Hamilton (G-10605)
Significant Impressions Inc .... G 513 874-5223
Fairfield (G-9564)
Signline Graphics & Lettering .... G 740 397-5806
Mount Vernon (G-14513)
Signmaster Inc .... G 614 777-0670
Lewis Center (G-11780)
Signpost Games LLC .... G 614 467-9025
Dublin (G-8985)
Signs 2 Graphics .... G 740 493-2049
Piketon (G-16080)
Signs By George .... G 216 394-2095
Brookfield (G-2109)
Signs Limited LLC .... G 740 282-7715
Steubenville (G-17551)
Signs N Stuff Inc .... G 440 974-3151
Mentor (G-13582)
Signs PDQ Inc .... G 440 951-6651
Willoughby (G-20430)
Signs Unlimited The Graphic .... G 614 836-7446
Logan (G-12043)
Skyline Exhibits Grtr Cncnt .... G 513 671-4460
Cincinnati (G-4343)
Spotted Horse Studio Inc .... G 330 533-2391
Greenford (G-10355)
Standard Signs Incorporated .... F 330 467-2030
Macedonia (G-12332)
Steel Valley Sign .... G 330 755-7446
Struthers (G-17825)
Sterling Associates Inc .... G 330 630-3500
Akron (G-389)
Steven Mercer Inc .... G 740 623-0033
Coshocton (G-7753)
Stine Consulting Inc .... G 513 723-4800
Cincinnati (G-4383)
Summco Inc .... G 330 965-7446
Youngstown (G-21041)
Super Sign Guys LLC .... G 330 477-3887
Canton (G-2830)
Super Signs Inc .... E 480 968-2200
North Bend (G-15056)
Superior Label Systems Inc .... B 513 336-0825
Mason (G-12944)
T-Top Shoppe .... G 330 343-3481
New Philadelphia (G-14803)
▼ Tce International Ltd .... F 800 962-2376
Perry (G-15914)

TE Signs and Ship LLC .... G 440 281-9340
Elyria (G-9336)
◆ Ternion Inc .... E 216 642-6180
Cleveland (G-6161)
Terry & Jack Neon Sign Co .... E 419 229-0674
Lima (G-11950)
Thatcher Enterprises Co Ltd .... G 614 228-2013
Columbus (G-7523)
The Hartman Corp .... G 614 475-5035
Columbus (G-7525)
Think Signs LLC .... G 614 384-0333
Lewis Center (G-11785)
Tim Boutwell .... G 419 358-4653
Bluffton (G-1894)
Toledo Mobile Media LLC .... G 419 389-0687
Toledo (G-18562)
Tract Inc .... G 937 427-3431
Dayton (G-7993)
Traffic Cntrl Sgnls Signs & MA .... G 740 670-7763
Newark (G-14930)
Traffic Detectors & Signs Inc .... G 330 707-9060
Youngstown (G-21048)
Triangle Sign Co .... G 513 863-2578
Hamilton (G-10615)
Tridico Silk Screen & Sign Co .... G 419 526-1695
Mansfield (G-12534)
Triumph Signs & Consulting Inc .... E 513 576-8090
Milford (G-14046)
Ultimate Signs and Graphics .... G 740 633-8928
Martins Ferry (G-12762)
Unionville Center Sign Co .... G 614 873-5834
Unionville Center (G-18938)
Unique Led Products LLC .... G 440 520-4959
Northfield (G-15329)
Unique Straight Line & Sfety S .... G 740 452-2724
Zanesville (G-21185)
United-Maier Signs Inc .... D 513 681-6600
Cincinnati (G-4451)
▲ Vgu Industries Inc .... E 216 676-9093
Cleveland (G-6257)
Vision Graphix Inc .... G 440 835-6540
Westlake (G-20169)
Visionary Signs LLC .... G 614 504-5899
Columbus (G-7585)
Visual Advantage LLC .... G 714 671-0988
Perrysburg (G-16022)
Visual Expressions Sign Co .... G 440 245-6660
Lorain (G-12136)
Vital Signs & Advertising LLC .... G 937 292-7967
Bellefontaine (G-1526)
Warren Enterprises .... G 330 836-6119
Akron (G-431)
Waterford Signs Inc .... G 740 362-7446
Delaware (G-8731)
Westrock Cp LLC .... B 513 745-2400
Blue Ash (G-1868)
Wettle Corporation .... G 419 865-6923
Holland (G-10966)
WH Fetzer & Sons Mfg Inc .... E 419 687-8237
Plymouth (G-16235)
Wholesale Channel Letters .... G 440 256-3200
Kirtland (G-11473)
Wide Area Media LLC .... G 440 356-3133
Westlake (G-20172)
Williams Steel Rule Die Co .... F 216 431-3232
Cleveland (G-6311)
Wilson Seat Company Inc .... E 513 732-2460
Batavia (G-1197)
Wilson Sign Co Inc .... F 937 253-2246
Dayton (G-8595)
Wright John .... G 937 653-4570
Urbana (G-19020)
▲ Wurtec Manufacturing Service .... E 419 726-1066
Toledo (G-18602)
Yes Management Inc .... G 330 747-8593
Columbiana (G-6486)

3995 Burial Caskets

Case Ohio Burial Co .... F 440 779-1992
Cleveland (G-4885)
Clark Grave Vault Company .... C 614 294-3761
Columbus (G-6769)
McCord Products Inc .... F 419 352-3691
Bowling Green (G-1985)
Youngstown Casket Co Inc .... G 330 758-2008
Youngstown (G-21074)
Zane Casket Company Inc .... E 740 452-4680
Zanesville (G-21191)

39 MISCELLANEOUS MANUFACTURING INDUSTRIES

3996 Linoleum & Hard Surface Floor Coverings, NEC

Armstrong World Industries Inc .... D 614 771-9307
  Hilliard (G-10806)
▲ Flowcrete North America Inc .... E 936 539-6700
  Cleveland (G-5253)
Prints & Paints Flr Cvg Co Inc .... E 419 462-5663
  Galion (G-10151)
Schlabach Woodworks Ltd .... E 330 674-7488
  Millersburg (G-14128)

3999 Manufacturing Industries, NEC

11am Industries LLC .... F 330 730-3177
  Barberton (G-1047)
3-D Technical Services Company .... E 937 746-2901
  Franklin (G-9866)
4S Company .... F 330 792-5518
  Youngstown (G-20829)
A-Buck Manufacturing Inc .... G 937 687-3738
  New Lebanon (G-14706)
Abby Industries LLC .... G 513 502-9865
  Eaton (G-9141)
Access Manufacturing Svcs LLC .... G 330 659-9893
  Richfield (G-16461)
Access To Independence Inc .... G 330 296-8111
  Ravenna (G-16363)
Accu Pak Mfg Inc .... G 330 644-3015
  Akron (G-27)
Ace Assembly Packaging Inc .... E 330 866-9117
  Waynesburg (G-19561)
Ace Grinding Co .... G 440 951-6760
  Willoughby (G-20266)
Actual Industries LLC .... G 614 379-2739
  Columbus (G-6541)
Advance Products .... F 419 882-8117
  Sylvania (G-17931)
Advanced Livescan Technologies .... G 440 759-7028
  Cleveland (G-4628)
Aerovent Inc .... G 937 473-3789
  Covington (G-7779)
▲ Al Root Company .... C 330 723-4359
  Medina (G-13219)
Al Root Company .... C 330 725-6677
  Medina (G-13220)
AK Mansfield .... B 419 755-3011
  Mansfield (G-12401)
Alk Industries LLC .... G 513 429-3047
  Cincinnati (G-3320)
All Points Industries Inc .... G 513 826-0681
  Cincinnati (G-3322)
Alliance Mfg Svcs Inc .... G 937 222-3394
  Trotwood (G-18627)
Alt Fuel LLC .... G 419 865-4196
  Toledo (G-18169)
▲ Aluminum Line Products Company .D 440 835-8880
  Westlake (G-20091)
Ambrosia Inc .... G 419 825-1151
  Swanton (G-17904)
American Pioneer Manufacturing .... G 330 457-1400
  New Waterford (G-14835)
Anderson Co Mfg LLC .... G 419 230-7332
  Carey (G-2877)
▲ Anza Inc .... G 513 542-7337
  Cincinnati (G-3349)
API Machining Fabrication Inc .... G 740 369-0455
  Delaware (G-8654)
Aquasurtech OEM Corp .... G 614 577-1203
  Gahanna (G-10075)
◆ Aquatic Technology .... F 440 236-8330
  Columbia Station (G-6428)
Arrowhead Industries .... G 440 349-2846
  Solon (G-17108)
Aster Industries Inc .... F 330 762-7965
  Akron (G-72)
AT&f Nuclear Inc .... G 216 252-1500
  Cleveland (G-4757)
Axalta Coating Systems USA LLC .... D 614 777-7230
  Hilliard (G-10809)
Back Rd Candles & HM Decor LLC .... G 330 461-6075
  Lodi (G-12007)
Bankhurst Industries LLC .... G 216 272-5775
  Solon (G-17111)
Bead Shoppe At Home .... G 330 479-9598
  Canton (G-2587)
Beauty Systems Group LLC .... G 740 456-5434
  New Boston (G-14646)
Beck Studios Inc .... E 513 831-6650
  Milford (G-13997)
Bird Loft .... G 440 988-2473
  Amherst (G-555)

Birge Heavy Industries Ltd .... E 440 821-3249
  Elyria (G-9225)
Bison USA Corp .... G 513 713-0513
  Hamilton (G-10541)
Blue Creek Renewables LLC .... G 419 576-7855
  Paulding (G-15857)
BMC of Barfield Inc .... G 513 860-4455
  Hamilton (G-10542)
Bomb Mfg LLC .... G 419 559-9689
  Fremont (G-10001)
▲ Boss Pet Products Inc .... F 216 332-0832
  Oakwood Village (G-15478)
C&H Industries .... G 330 899-0001
  Canton (G-2603)
Candle Cottage .... G 937 526-4041
  Versailles (G-19176)
Candle-Lite Company LLC .... G 937 780-2711
  Leesburg (G-11708)
Candle-Lite Company LLC .... D 513 563-1113
  Blue Ash (G-1747)
Candles By Joyce .... G 740 886-6355
  Proctorville (G-16343)
Canine Creations .... G 937 667-8576
  Tipp City (G-18105)
Carroll Hills Industries Inc .... D 330 627-5524
  Carrollton (G-2917)
▲ Centaur Inc .... G 419 469-8000
  Toledo (G-18225)
Centerless Grinding Service .... G 216 251-4100
  Cleveland (G-4900)
City Dog .... G 614 228-3647
  Columbus (G-6767)
Cleveland Plant and Flower Co .... E 614 478-9900
  Columbus (G-6773)
◆ CM Paula Company .... E 513 759-7473
  Mason (G-12849)
CNB Machining and Mfg LLC .... G 330 877-7920
  Hartville (G-10687)
Colby Properties LLC .... G 937 390-0816
  Springfield (G-17377)
Columbus Industries Inc .... F 937 544-6896
  West Union (G-19960)
Condos and Trees LLC .... G 419 691-2287
  Northwood (G-15335)
Connelly Industries LLC .... G 330 468-0675
  Macedonia (G-12285)
Connies Candles .... G 740 574-1224
  Wheelersburg (G-20179)
Consolidated Pattern Works Inc .... G 330 434-6060
  Akron (G-120)
Continental Fan Mfg .... G 937 233-5524
  Huber Heights (G-11015)
Country Clippins .... G 740 472-5228
  Woodsfield (G-20543)
Country Lane Custom Buildings .... G 740 485-8481
  Danville (G-7961)
▼ Cr Brands Inc .... D 513 860-5039
  West Chester (G-19686)
Creation Industries LLC .... G 440 554-6286
  Middlefield (G-13787)
◆ Cropking Incorporated .... F 330 302-4203
  Lodi (G-12009)
Custom Made Palm Trees LLC .... G 330 633-0063
  Akron (G-130)
▲ Daca Vending Wholesale LLC .... G 513 753-1600
  Amelia (G-535)
Dano Jr LLC .... G 440 781-5774
  Cleveland (G-5063)
Datco Mfg Company Inc .... E 330 787-1127
  Youngstown (G-20886)
Dcc Corp .... G 330 494-0494
  Canton (G-2651)
Debolt Machine Inc .... G 740 454-8082
  Zanesville (G-21127)
▲ Dem Manufacturing LLC .... F 440 564-7160
  Newbury (G-14951)
Denton Atd Inc .... E 567 265-5200
  Huron (G-11093)
Devault Industries LLC .... G 330 456-6070
  Canton (G-2656)
DSI Parts LLC .... G 937 746-4678
  Miamisburg (G-13661)
Duraflow Industries Inc .... G 440 965-5047
  Wakeman (G-19284)
Duramax Marine Industries .... G 419 668-3728
  Norwalk (G-15390)
Eaglehead Manufacturing Co .... G 440 951-0400
  Eastlake (G-9106)
Elaire Corporation .... G 419 843-2192
  Toledo (G-18276)

Elevated Industries LLC .... G 937 608-3325
  Xenia (G-20760)
Energizer Battery Mfg Inc .... G 330 527-2191
  Garrettsville (G-10189)
Epik Ltd .... G 419 768-2498
  Fredericktown (G-9968)
Erichar Inc .... G 216 402-2628
  Cleveland (G-5188)
Exikon Industries LLC .... F 216 485-2947
  Cleveland (G-5207)
▲ Faith Guiding Cafe LLC .... F 614 245-8451
  New Albany (G-14623)
Fallen Oak Candles Inc .... G 419 204-8162
  Celina (G-2962)
Faw Industries .... G 216 651-9595
  Cleveland (G-5222)
Fbr Industries Inc .... G 330 701-7425
  Mineral Ridge (G-14165)
Fcbdd .... G 614 475-6440
  Columbus (G-6915)
Ferguson Fire Fabrication Inc .... F 614 299-2070
  Columbus (G-6918)
Fin Feather Fur .... G 330 493-8300
  Canton (G-2671)
Fire Safety Services Inc .... G 937 686-2000
  Huntsville (G-11086)
Firelands Manufacturing LLC .... F 419 687-8237
  Plymouth (G-16231)
Fleig Enterprises Inc .... G 216 361-8020
  Cleveland (G-5249)
Fortress Industries LLC .... G 614 402-3045
  Johnstown (G-11266)
Francis Industries LLC .... G 330 333-3352
  Youngstown (G-20910)
Frugal Systems .... G 419 957-7863
  Carey (G-2881)
◆ Gayston Corporation .... C 937 743-6050
  Miamisburg (G-13672)
Gdc Industries LLC .... G 937 640-1212
  Dayton (G-8216)
Gerber Wood Products Inc .... G 330 857-3901
  Kidron (G-11447)
Gibraltar Industries Inc .... G 440 617-9230
  Westlake (G-20118)
▲ GKN Driveline Bowl Green Inc .... E 419 373-7700
  Bowling Green (G-1973)
Glass Mirror Awards Inc .... G 419 638-2221
  Helena (G-10772)
Glasslight Candles LLC .... G 443 509-5505
  Mason (G-12878)
Global Manufacturing Inds .... G 513 271-2180
  Cincinnati (G-3764)
▼ Gojo Industries Inc .... F 800 321-9647
  Cuyahoga Falls (G-7875)
Goodwill Inds NW Ohio Inc .... E 419 255-0070
  Toledo (G-18308)
Gorant Chocolatier LLC .... C 330 726-8821
  Boardman (G-1899)
Grant Solutions .... G 937 344-5558
  Tipp City (G-18114)
Green Door Industries LLC .... G 614 558-1663
  Blacklick (G-1684)
Groff Industries .... F 216 634-9100
  Cleveland (G-5354)
Gsr Industries LLC .... G 440 934-0201
  Cleveland (G-5357)
Gumbys LLC .... G 740 671-0818
  Bellaire (G-1486)
H Rosen Usa LLC .... C 614 354-6707
  Columbus (G-6973)
Hafner Hardwood Connection LLC .... G 419 726-4828
  Toledo (G-18318)
Hartz Mountain Corporation .... D 513 877-2131
  Pleasant Plain (G-16227)
Heart Warming Candles .... G 937 456-2720
  Eaton (G-9151)
Heartland Engineered Pdts LLC .... F 513 367-0080
  Harrison (G-10645)
▲ Henry-Griffitts Limited .... G 419 482-9095
  Maumee (G-13117)
Highland Technologies LLC .... G 513 739-3510
  Mount Orab (G-14443)
HK Technologies .... G 330 337-9710
  Cleveland (G-5411)
Horse Hill Wreath Company .... G 937 272-0701
  Sugarcrk Twp (G-17879)
Housing & Emrgncy Lgstcs Plnnr .... E 209 201-7511
  Lisbon (G-11969)
Hung Pham .... G 614 850-9695
  Columbus (G-7011)

▲ Hunters Manufacturing Co Inc....E.... 330 628-9245
Mogadore (G-14240)
ID Card Systems Inc....G.... 330 963-7446
Twinsburg (G-18795)
Idx Corporation....C.... 937 401-3225
Dayton (G-8259)
J S Manufacturing LLC....G.... 330 815-2136
Kent (G-11336)
J-Fab....G.... 740 384-2649
Wellston (G-19602)
James J Fairbanks Company Inc....G.... 330 534-1374
Hubbard (G-11003)
Janson Industries....D.... 330 455-7029
Canton (G-2716)
Jrb Industries LLC....E.... 567 825-7022
Greenville (G-10377)
Jrf Industries Ltd....G.... 330 665-3130
Copley (G-7687)
JW Manufacturing....G.... 419 375-5536
Fort Recovery (G-9824)
K-Column LLC....G.... 937 269-3696
Eaton (G-9155)
Kendee Candles LLC....G.... 330 899-9898
Uniontown (G-18923)
Key Mobility Services Ltd....G.... 937 374-3226
Xenia (G-20780)
Kf Technologies and Custom Mfg....G.... 419 426-0172
Attica (G-857)
King Model Company....E.... 330 633-0491
Akron (G-238)
Kiser Industries llc....G.... 937 332-6723
Troy (G-18682)
Kitto Katsu Inc....G.... 818 256-6997
Clayton (G-4576)
Kole Industries....G.... 330 353-1751
Canton (G-2728)
L & L Fabricating LLC....G.... 440 647-6649
Wellington (G-19585)
L E P D Industries Ltd....G.... 614 985-1470
Powell (G-16326)
Lance Industries Inc....G.... 740 243-6657
Lancaster (G-11583)
Lawnview Industries Inc....C.... 937 653-5217
Urbana (G-19003)
Lincoln Candle Company Inc....G.... 419 749-4224
Convoy (G-7670)
Linebacker Inc....G.... 614 340-1446
Columbus (G-7130)
▲ Lumi-Lite Candle Company....D.... 740 872-3248
Norwich (G-15421)
Mab Fabrication Inc....G.... 855 622-3221
Harrison (G-10656)
Maca Mold & Machine Co Inc....G.... 330 854-0292
Canal Fulton (G-2485)
◆ Mace Personal Def & SEC Inc....E.... 440 424-5321
Cleveland (G-5597)
◆ Mace Security Intl Inc....D.... 440 424-5321
Cleveland (G-5598)
▲ Makergear LLC....E.... 216 765-0030
Beachwood (G-1246)
Manufacturing Company LLC....G.... 414 708-7583
Cincinnati (G-3977)
▲ Mark-All Enterprises LLC....E.... 800 433-3615
Akron (G-268)
MCS Mfg LLC....G.... 419 923-0169
Lyons (G-12274)
▲ MD Solutions Inc....G.... 866 637-6588
Plain City (G-16201)
Medline Industries Inc....G.... 330 484-1450
Canton (G-2752)
Mels Life Like Hair....G.... 937 278-9486
Dayton (G-8339)
Melvin Grain Co....G.... 937 382-1249
Wilmington (G-20499)
Mibtach Enterprises Inc....G.... 513 941-0387
Cincinnati (G-4021)
Midwest Stamping & Mfg Co....G.... 419 298-2394
Edgerton (G-9177)
◆ Miraclecorp Products....D.... 937 293-9994
Moraine (G-14372)
Model Engineering Company....G.... 330 644-3450
Barberton (G-1087)
Morris Technologies....G.... 330 384-3084
Akron (G-288)
Morris Technologies Inc....C.... 513 733-1611
Cincinnati (G-4047)
N2y LLC....E.... 419 433-9800
Huron (G-11106)
Nail Art....G.... 614 899-7155
Westerville (G-20066)
Nail Secret....G.... 513 459-3373
Maineville (G-12375)
Natural Beauty Hc Express....G.... 440 459-1776
Mayfield Heights (G-13169)
New Republic Industries LLC....F.... 614 580-9927
Marysville (G-12803)
Nexstep Commercial Pdts LLC....G.... 937 322-5163
Springfield (G-17461)
Nichols Industries....G.... 614 866-8451
Columbus (G-7220)
Njf Manufacturing LLC....G.... 419 294-0400
Upper Sandusky (G-18968)
▲ Nl Mfg & Distribution Sys In....G.... 513 422-5216
Middletown (G-13972)
Norkaam Industries LLC....G.... 330 873-9793
Akron (G-298)
Norris North Manufacturing....G.... 330 691-0449
Canton (G-2764)
▲ Norstar International LLC....G.... 513 404-3543
Cincinnati (G-4085)
OBrien Industries LLC....G.... 513 476-0040
Cincinnati (G-4096)
Octsys Security Corp....G.... 614 470-4510
Columbus (G-7239)
Ohio Candle Co Inc....G.... 740 289-8000
Waverly (G-19555)
▲ Ohio Feather Company Inc....G.... 513 921-3373
Cincinnati (G-4101)
Ohio Manufacturing EXT Partnr....G.... 614 644-8788
Columbus (G-7250)
On Display Ltd....E.... 513 841-1600
Batavia (G-1174)
▲ Osborne Coinage Company....D.... 513 681-5424
Cincinnati (G-4120)
▲ Ourpets Company....E.... 440 354-6500
Fairport Harbor (G-9627)
Oveco Industries Electrica....G.... 740 381-3326
Richmond (G-16497)
◆ Partners In Recognition Inc....E.... 937 420-2150
Fort Loramie (G-9801)
Pdi Constellation LLC....G.... 216 271-7344
Solon (G-17213)
Pegasus Industries....G.... 740 772-1049
Chillicothe (G-3207)
Phe Manufacturing....G.... 937 790-1582
Franklin (G-9910)
Pinnacle Sales Inc....G.... 440 734-9195
Westlake (G-20143)
Power Media Inc....G.... 330 475-0500
Akron (G-325)
Priority Vending Inc....G.... 216 361-4100
Cleveland (G-5923)
Prochaska Industries LLC....G.... 440 423-0464
Gates Mills (G-10208)
Production Tl Co Cleveland Inc....F.... 330 425-4466
Twinsburg (G-18841)
Proto Prcsion Mfg Slutions LLC....F.... 614 771-0080
Hilliard (G-10856)
Pyramid Industries LLC....F.... 614 783-1543
Columbus (G-7358)
Quality Compound Mfg....G.... 440 353-0150
North Ridgeville (G-15248)
Quick Tech Business Forms Inc....E.... 937 743-5952
Springboro (G-17347)
R M Industries Inc....G.... 419 529-8970
Mansfield (G-12504)
Rbs Manufacturing Inc....E.... 330 426-9486
East Palestine (G-9082)
Reiser Manufacturing....G.... 330 846-8003
New Waterford (G-14842)
Resource Recycling Inc....F.... 419 222-2702
Lima (G-11929)
Restless Noggins Mfg LLC....G.... 330 526-6908
North Canton (G-15114)
▲ Rhc Inc....G.... 330 874-3750
Bolivar (G-1927)
Rmw Industries Inc....G.... 440 439-1971
Bedford Heights (G-1479)
Rose of Sharon Enterprises....G.... 937 862-4543
Waynesville (G-19572)
Rowend Industries Inc....G.... 419 333-8300
Fremont (G-10049)
Royal Mfg....G.... 419 902-8222
Findlay (G-9750)
RPM Industries....G.... 440 268-8077
Elyria (G-9323)
▲ S & H Industries Inc....G.... 216 831-0550
Cleveland (G-6019)
Safe 4 People Inc....G.... 419 797-4087
Port Clinton (G-16257)
▲ Salon Styling Concepts Ltd....E.... 216 539-0437
Maple Heights (G-12579)
Saltcreek Industries....G.... 330 674-2816
Millersburg (G-14125)
Sarver Industries LLC....G.... 419 455-5509
Tiffin (G-18081)
Scentsible Scents Ltd....G.... 937 572-6690
Dayton (G-8494)
Schell Scenic Studio Inc....G.... 614 444-9550
Columbus (G-7425)
Schreiner Manufacturing....G.... 419 937-0300
New Riegel (G-14817)
Scott Models Inc....F.... 513 771-8005
Cincinnati (G-4309)
Sdi Industries....G.... 513 561-4032
Cincinnati (G-4313)
Season of Wreath....G.... 330 936-7498
Canton (G-2812)
Seavival LLC....G.... 330 252-1151
Akron (G-374)
Serving Veterans Mobility Inc....G.... 937 746-4788
Franklin (G-9918)
Setco Industries Inc....G.... 513 941-5110
Cincinnati (G-4327)
Shafts Mfg....G.... 440 942-6012
Willoughby (G-20428)
Sharc Industries....G.... 216 272-0668
Columbia Station (G-6448)
Shaw Industries Inc....G.... 513 942-3692
West Chester (G-19795)
Skr Enterprises LLC....G.... 419 891-1112
Maumee (G-13145)
Slogans LLC....G.... 330 942-9464
Barberton (G-1105)
Softpoint Industries....G.... 330 668-2645
Copley (G-7696)
Soldier Tech & Armor RES LLC....G.... 330 896-5217
Akron (G-381)
Solomon Industries LLC....G.... 937 558-5334
Troy (G-18708)
◆ Staco Energy Products Co....G.... 937 253-1191
Miamisburg (G-13719)
Sterling Collectables Inc....G.... 419 892-5708
Mansfield (G-12520)
Steves Vans & Accessories LLC....G.... 740 374-3154
Marietta (G-12676)
▲ Sunbright Usa Inc....G.... 440 205-0600
Mentor (G-13597)
Sunsong North America Inc....G.... 919 365-3825
Moraine (G-14397)
Sword Furs....G.... 440 249-5001
Westlake (G-20165)
T and D Industries LLC....G.... 937 321-3424
Dayton (G-8536)
Tangent Company LLC....G.... 440 543-2775
Chagrin Falls (G-3079)
Tango Echo Bravo Mfg Inc....G.... 440 937-3800
North Ridgeville (G-15254)
Texstone Industries....G.... 419 722-4664
Findlay (G-9767)
▲ Thoroughbred Gt Mfg LLC....F.... 330 533-0048
Canfield (G-2550)
Tiffin Scenic Studios Inc....D.... 800 445-1546
Tiffin (G-18089)
Tiger Cat Furniture....G.... 330 220-7232
Brunswick (G-2245)
Tmb Enterprises LLC....F.... 419 243-2189
Holland (G-10961)
Tmh Industries LLC....G.... 954 232-7938
Dublin (G-9005)
Tmt Inc....C.... 419 592-1041
Perrysburg (G-16018)
Toledo Mobile Media LLC....G.... 419 389-0687
Toledo (G-18562)
Trademark Designs Inc....E.... 419 628-3897
Minster (G-14227)
Tri Dlta Metal Fabrication LLC....G.... 937 499-4315
Miamisburg (G-13728)
Triboro Quilt Mfg Corp....F.... 937 222-2132
Vandalia (G-19146)
◆ Truck Fax Inc....G.... 216 921-8866
Cleveland (G-6218)
Ttr Manufacturing....G.... 440 366-5005
Elyria (G-9339)
Tuffy Manufacturing....G.... 330 940-2356
Cuyahoga Falls (G-7930)
Tunnel Vision Hoops LLC....G.... 440 487-0939
Shaker Heights (G-16939)
Twin Oaks Barn....F.... 330 893-3126
Dundee (G-9030)

U S Hair Inc....G....614 235-5190
Columbus *(G-7554)*
V Mast Manufacturing Inc....G....330 409-8116
Canton *(G-2856)*
Vacca Inc....G....513 697-0270
Loveland *(G-12241)*
Valentino Industries LLC....G....330 523-7216
Richfield *(G-16493)*
Vandalia Massage Therapy....G....937 890-8660
Vandalia *(G-19149)*
Velocity Concept Dev Group LLC....G....513 204-2100
Mason *(G-12952)*
Vermilion Dock Masters....G....440 244-5370
Vermilion *(G-19171)*
Vic Maroscher....F....330 332-4958
Salem *(G-16780)*
Virco Virlon Industries Corp....G....216 410-4872
Bedford Heights *(G-1482)*
▲ **Voodoo Industries**....G....440 653-5333
Avon Lake *(G-1012)*
Waterloo Industries Inc....G....800 833-8851
Cleveland *(G-6292)*
Wellington Manufacturing....G....440 647-1162
Wellington *(G-19594)*
Western Reserve Industries LLC....G....330 238-1800
Beloit *(G-1572)*
Wheeler Embroidery....G....740 550-9751
Ironton *(G-11177)*
Wilks Industries....G....330 868-5105
Minerva *(G-14206)*
Willoughby Manufacturing Inc....G....330 402-8217
New Waterford *(G-14844)*
Woodsage Industries LLC....G....419 866-8000
Holland *(G-10968)*
Worldwide Machining & Mfg LLC....G....937 902-5629
Moraine *(G-14400)*
Wreaths & Masn Jars By Krissi....G....419 250-6606
Holland *(G-10970)*
Yoder Manufacturing....G....740 504-5028
Howard *(G-10998)*
Zorich Industries Inc....F....330 482-9803
Columbiana *(G-6488)*

73 BUSINESS SERVICES

7372 Prepackaged Software

252 Tattoo....G....440 235-6699
Columbia Station *(G-6426)*
360water Inc....G....614 294-3600
Columbus *(G-6511)*
4me Group LLC....G....513 898-1083
Terrace Park *(G-18017)*
About Time Software Inc....F....614 759-6295
Pickerington *(G-16038)*
Acclaimd Inc....G....614 219-9519
Columbus *(G-6532)*
Accumulus Software....G....937 435-0861
Dayton *(G-8003)*
Actipro Software LLC....G....888 922-8477
Broadview Heights *(G-2087)*
Acu-Serve Corp....G....330 923-5258
Cuyahoga Falls *(G-7830)*
Advanced Prgrm Resources Inc....E....614 761-9994
Dublin *(G-8874)*
Advant-E Corporation....F....937 429-4288
Beavercreek *(G-1298)*
Agile Global Solutions Inc....E....916 655-7745
Independence *(G-11118)*
Air Force US Dept of....B....937 656-2354
Dayton *(G-7969)*
Alanax Technologies Inc....G....216 469-1545
Belmont *(G-1564)*
Allmax Software Inc....F....419 673-8863
Kenton *(G-11401)*
American Dreams Inc....G....740 385-4444
Thornville *(G-18029)*
American Grphcal Sftwr Systems....G....440 729-0018
Chesterland *(G-3153)*
Ames Development Group Ltd....G....419 704-7812
Toledo *(G-18182)*
Ampersand International Inc....G....216 831-3500
Beachwood *(G-1223)*
Apex Solutions Inc....G....419 843-3434
Toledo *(G-18187)*
Apostrophe Apps LLC....G....513 608-4399
Liberty Twp *(G-11821)*
Application Link Inc....F....614 934-1735
Columbus *(G-6609)*
Applied Systems Inc....E....513 943-0000
Milford *(G-13994)*
Apportis LLC....G....614 832-8362
Dublin *(G-8881)*
Arges....G....440 574-1305
Oberlin *(G-15490)*
Assisted Patrol LLC....G....937 369-0080
Beavercreek *(G-1300)*
Associated Software Cons Inc....F....440 826-1010
Middleburg Heights *(G-13761)*
Asterena Corporation....G....937 605-6470
Dayton *(G-8041)*
Atr Distributing Company....F....513 353-1800
Cincinnati *(G-3369)*
Auto Des Sys Inc....E....614 488-7984
Upper Arlington *(G-18943)*
Automation Software & Engrg....F....330 405-2990
Twinsburg *(G-18737)*
Autorentalsystemscom LLC....G....513 334-1040
Norwood *(G-15423)*
Avasax Ltd....G....937 694-0807
Beavercreek *(G-1350)*
Aver Inc....G....877 841-2775
Columbus *(G-6635)*
Avesta Systems Inc....G....330 650-1800
Hudson *(G-11032)*
Baptist Heritage Revival Soc....G....915 526-2832
Goshen *(G-10285)*
Bass International Sftwr LLC....G....877 227-0155
Westerville *(G-19980)*
Besttransportcom Inc....E....614 888-2378
Columbus *(G-6663)*
Bjond Inc....G....614 537-7246
Columbus *(G-6674)*
Building Block Performance LLC....G....614 918-7476
Plain City *(G-16179)*
Bullseye LLC....G....216 272-7050
Shaker Heights *(G-16926)*
Butler Tech Career Dev Schools....F....513 867-1028
Fairfield Township *(G-9580)*
Cake LLC....G....614 592-7681
Dublin *(G-8892)*
Callcopy Inc....G....614 340-3346
Columbus *(G-6725)*
Capitol Citicom Inc....E....614 472-2679
Columbus *(G-6735)*
Carenection LLC....G....614 468-6045
Columbus *(G-6743)*
Caring Things Inc....G....614 749-9084
Columbus *(G-6744)*
Casentric LLC....G....216 233-6300
Shaker Heights *(G-16928)*
Check Yourself LLC....G....513 685-0868
Blue Ash *(G-1749)*
Cimx LLC....E....513 248-7700
Cincinnati *(G-3476)*
Cincom Systems Inc....C....513 459-1470
Mason *(G-12845)*
Citynet Ohio LLC....E....614 364-7881
Columbus *(G-6768)*
Cleveland Business Supply LLC....G....888 831-0088
Broadview Heights *(G-2091)*
Clientrax Technology Solutions....F....614 875-2245
Grove City *(G-10420)*
Clinicl Otcms Mngmnt Syst LLC....D....330 650-9900
Broadview Heights *(G-2092)*
Cluster Software Inc....F....614 760-9380
Columbus *(G-6776)*
Coffing Corporation....F....513 919-2813
Liberty Twp *(G-11822)*
Columbus Incontact....G....801 245-8369
Columbus *(G-6792)*
Columbus International Corp....F....614 323-1086
Columbus *(G-6794)*
Commercial Transportation Svcs....G....216 267-2000
Cleveland *(G-5005)*
Computer Enterprise Inc....F....216 228-7156
Lakewood *(G-11515)*
Computer System Enhancement....G....513 251-6791
Cincinnati *(G-3541)*
Computer Zoo Inc....G....937 310-1474
Bellbrook *(G-1490)*
Concept Xxi Inc....F....216 831-2121
Beachwood *(G-1230)*
Contractor Tools Online LLC....G....614 264-9392
New Albany *(G-14617)*
Corporate Elevator LLC....F....614 288-1847
Columbus *(G-6822)*
Crabware Ltd....G....330 699-2305
Uniontown *(G-18917)*
Creative Microsystems Inc....D....937 836-4499
Englewood *(G-9353)*
Crimson Gate Consulting Co....G....614 805-0897
Dublin *(G-8904)*
Dakota Software Corporation....D....216 765-7100
Cleveland *(G-5058)*
Dante Solutions Inc....G....440 234-8477
Cleveland *(G-5064)*
Data Genomix Inc....F....216 860-4770
Cleveland *(G-5069)*
Datatrak International Inc....E....440 443-0082
Mayfield Heights *(G-13162)*
Deadbolt Software....G....614 679-2093
Columbus *(G-6855)*
Delphia Consulting LLC....G....614 421-2000
Columbus *(G-6860)*
Delta Media Group Inc....E....330 493-0350
Canton *(G-2654)*
Deneb....G....937 223-4849
Dayton *(G-8156)*
Design & Software Intl....F....513 939-1800
Fairfield *(G-9493)*
Digionyx LLC....G....614 594-9897
London *(G-12058)*
Digisoft Systems Corporation....G....937 833-5016
Brookville *(G-2167)*
Digital Controls Corporation....D....513 746-8118
Miamisburg *(G-13659)*
Drb Systems LLC....C....330 645-3299
Akron *(G-147)*
Eadhere Solutions LLC....G....216 372-6009
Cleveland *(G-5133)*
Echo Mobile Solutions LLC....G....614 282-3756
Pickerington *(G-16046)*
Eci Macola/Max LLC....C....978 539-6186
Dublin *(G-8911)*
Eclipse....G....419 564-7482
Galion *(G-10136)*
Edict Systems Inc....E....937 429-4288
Beavercreek *(G-1313)*
Eighty Six Inc....G....800 760-0722
Huber Heights *(G-11016)*
Einstruction Corp....F....940 565-0004
Youngstown *(G-20896)*
▼ **Einstruction Corporation**....D....330 746-3015
Youngstown *(G-20897)*
Ela Holding Corporation....G....513 200-1374
Cincinnati *(G-3631)*
Elynx Holdings LLC....G....513 612-5969
Cincinnati *(G-3633)*
Elytus Ltd....F....614 824-4985
Columbus *(G-6893)*
EMC Corporation....E....216 606-2000
Independence *(G-11125)*
Empyracom Inc....E....330 744-5570
Canfield *(G-2526)*
Equipsync LLC....G....216 367-6640
Cleveland *(G-5187)*
▲ **Esko-Graphics Inc**....D....937 454-1721
Miamisburg *(G-13665)*
Estreamz Inc....E....513 278-7836
Cincinnati *(G-3654)*
Explorys Inc....D....216 767-4700
Cleveland *(G-5210)*
Exponentia US Inc....E....614 944-5103
Columbus *(G-6911)*
Ezshred LLC....G....440 256-7640
Kirtland *(G-11468)*
Facilities Management Ex LLC....F....844 664-4400
Columbus *(G-6913)*
Field Dailies LLC....G....859 379-2120
Cincinnati *(G-3687)*
Finastra USA Corporation....E....937 435-2335
Miamisburg *(G-13668)*
Flexnova Inc....E....216 288-6961
Cleveland *(G-5250)*
Flypaper Studio Inc....E....602 801-2208
Cincinnati *(G-3700)*
Forcam Inc....F....513 878-2780
Cincinnati *(G-3702)*
Foundation Software Inc....D....330 220-8383
Strongsville *(G-17744)*
Fusionstorm....G....614 431-8000
Columbus *(G-6494)*
Gain LLC....G....440 396-6613
Westerville *(G-19992)*
Gis Dynamics LLC....G....513 847-4931
Blue Ash *(G-1782)*
▼ **Gracie Plum Investments Inc**....E....740 355-9029
Portsmouth *(G-16284)*
Great Migrations LLC....G....614 638-4632
Dublin *(G-8918)*

Guide Technologies LLC ....G....... 513 631-8800
Cincinnati *(G-3789)*
Hab Inc ....E....... 608 785-7650
Solon *(G-17158)*
Hardmagic ....F....... 415 390-6232
Marietta *(G-12631)*
Health Nuts Media LLC ....G....... 818 802-5222
Cleveland *(G-5384)*
Healthedge Software Inc ....G....... 614 431-3711
Powell *(G-16323)*
Hero Pay LLC ....G....... 419 771-0515
Columbus *(G-6991)*
Hommati Franchise Network Inc ....G....... 833 466-6284
Westerville *(G-20058)*
Honeywell International Inc ....D....... 513 745-7200
Cincinnati *(G-3826)*
Hyland Software Inc ....A....... 440 788-5000
Westlake *(G-20125)*
ICC Systems Inc ....G....... 614 524-0299
Sunbury *(G-17889)*
Idialogs LLC ....G....... 937 372-2890
Xenia *(G-20777)*
Igel Technology America LLC ....F....... 954 739-9990
Cincinnati *(G-3837)*
Image Integrations Systems ....F....... 419 872-0003
Perrysburg *(G-15964)*
Incessant Software Inc ....G....... 614 206-2211
Lancaster *(G-11580)*
Infoaccessnet LLC ....E....... 216 328-0100
Cleveland *(G-5456)*
Innago LLC ....G....... 330 554-3101
Hudson *(G-11055)*
Innerapps LLC ....G....... 419 467-3110
Perrysburg *(G-15967)*
Innovative Apps Ltd ....G....... 330 687-2888
New Albany *(G-14626)*
Innovative Bus Cmpt Solutions ....G....... 937 832-3969
Englewood *(G-9363)*
Instaride Cle LLC ....G....... 216 801-4542
Lakewood *(G-11522)*
Integrity Group Consulting Inc ....F....... 614 759-9148
Reynoldsburg *(G-16444)*
Intelligent Mobile Support Inc ....F....... 440 600-7343
Solon *(G-17172)*
Intellinetics Inc ....F....... 614 388-8909
Columbus *(G-7040)*
Interactive Fincl Solutions ....F....... 419 335-1280
Wauseon *(G-19521)*
Intermec Technologies Corp ....F....... 513 874-5882
West Chester *(G-19726)*
Intersoft Group Inc ....F....... 216 765-7351
Cleveland *(G-5469)*
Investment Systems Company ....G....... 440 247-2865
Chagrin Falls *(G-3022)*
Jack A Byte Mltmdia Gaming LLC ....G....... 937 321-1716
Englewood *(G-9364)*
Janova LLC ....F....... 614 638-6785
New Albany *(G-14628)*
Jasstek Inc ....F....... 614 808-3600
Dublin *(G-8932)*
Jda Software Group Inc ....G....... 480 308-3000
Akron *(G-222)*
Jehm Technologies Inc ....G....... 440 355-5558
Lagrange *(G-11484)*
Jst LLC ....G....... 614 423-7815
Westerville *(G-20002)*
Juniper Networks Inc ....D....... 614 932-1432
Dublin *(G-8934)*
Kapios LLC ....G....... 567 661-0772
Toledo *(G-18361)*
Kick Salsa LLC ....G....... 614 330-2499
Columbus *(G-7094)*
King Software Systems ....G....... 330 562-1135
Aurora *(G-889)*
Kronos Incorporated ....G....... 216 867-5609
Independence *(G-11140)*
Lantek Systems Inc ....G....... 513 988-8708
Mason *(G-12903)*
Launchvector Identity LLC ....F....... 216 333-1815
Cleveland *(G-5565)*
Learning Egg LLC ....G....... 330 207-8663
North Jackson *(G-15148)*
Lift Ai LLC ....G....... 419 345-7831
Ottawa Hills *(G-15674)*
Linestream Technologies ....G....... 216 862-7874
Cleveland *(G-5578)*
List Media Inc ....G....... 330 995-0864
Chagrin Falls *(G-3023)*
Lockheed Martin Corporation ....G....... 614 418-1930
Columbus *(G-7133)*
Lost Technology LLP ....G....... 513 685-0054
West Chester *(G-19739)*
Lync Corp ....E....... 513 655-7286
Cincinnati *(G-3959)*
Mae Consulting ....G....... 513 531-8100
Cincinnati *(G-3970)*
Magic Interface Ltd ....G....... 440 498-3700
Solon *(G-17185)*
Mamsys Consulting Services ....G....... 440 287-6824
Solon *(G-17187)*
Mapsys Inc ....E....... 614 255-7258
Columbus *(G-7148)*
Marxware Computing Services ....F....... 216 661-5263
Cleveland *(G-5629)*
Massmatrix Inc ....G....... 614 321-9730
Yellow Springs *(G-20810)*
Mathematical Business Systems ....G....... 440 237-2345
Broadview Heights *(G-2097)*
Matrix Management Solutions ....C....... 330 470-3700
Canton *(G-2747)*
McGaw Technology Inc ....G....... 216 521-3490
Lakewood *(G-11529)*
Merkur Group Inc ....G....... 937 429-4288
Beavercreek *(G-1331)*
Miami Valley Eductl Cmpt Assn ....F....... 937 767-1468
Yellow Springs *(G-20811)*
Microsoft Corporation ....E....... 614 719-5900
Columbus *(G-6503)*
Microsoft Corporation ....E....... 216 986-1440
Cleveland *(G-5671)*
Microsoft Corporation ....G....... 513 826-9630
Cincinnati *(G-4026)*
Microsoft Corporation ....D....... 513 339-2800
Mason *(G-12909)*
Microstrategy Incorporated ....G....... 513 792-2253
Cincinnati *(G-4027)*
Mim Software Inc ....E....... 216 896-9798
Beachwood *(G-1250)*
Mindcrafted Systems Inc ....G....... 440 821-2245
Cleveland *(G-5692)*
Mirus Adapted Tech LLC ....E....... 614 402-4585
Dublin *(G-8946)*
Monitored Therapeutics Inc ....G....... 614 761-3555
Dublin *(G-8948)*
Navistone Inc ....G....... 844 677-3667
Cincinnati *(G-4065)*
Netpark LLC ....F....... 614 866-2495
Gahanna *(G-10094)*
Netsmart Technologies Inc ....E....... 440 942-4040
Solon *(G-17207)*
Neural Holdings LLC ....G....... 734 512-8865
Cincinnati *(G-4069)*
New Life Chapel ....F....... 513 298-2980
Cincinnati *(G-4070)*
Nextmed Systems Inc ....E....... 216 674-0511
Cincinnati *(G-4076)*
Noggin LLC ....G....... 440 305-6188
Cleveland *(G-5755)*
North Coast Security Group LLC ....G....... 614 887-7255
Columbus *(G-7226)*
Now Software Inc ....G....... 614 783-4517
New Albany *(G-14632)*
Nsa Technologies LLC ....C....... 330 576-4600
Akron *(G-304)*
Ohio Cllbrtive Lrng Sltons Inc ....E....... 216 595-5289
Beachwood *(G-1255)*
Ohio Distinctive Enterprises ....E....... 614 459-0453
Columbus *(G-7246)*
Omniboom LLC ....G....... 833 675-3987
Hamilton *(G-10594)*
One Cloud Services LLC ....G....... 513 231-9500
Cincinnati *(G-4112)*
Onx Holdings LLC ....F....... 866 587-2287
Cincinnati *(G-4114)*
Onx USA LLC ....D....... 440 569-2300
Cleveland *(G-5815)*
Open Text Inc ....E....... 614 658-3588
Hilliard *(G-10849)*
Optimal Office Solutions LLC ....G....... 201 257-8516
Cincinnati *(G-4115)*
Optimzed Prdctvity Sltions LLC ....G....... 513 444-2156
Cincinnati *(G-4117)*
Oracle America Inc ....G....... 650 506-7000
Dublin *(G-8957)*
Oracle America Inc ....F....... 513 381-0125
Beachwood *(G-1260)*
Oracle Corporation ....G....... 513 826-6000
Beachwood *(G-1261)*
Oracle Corporation ....C....... 513 826-5632
Beavercreek *(G-1335)*
Oracle Corporation ....G....... 440 264-1620
Cleveland *(G-5817)*
Oracle Systems Corporation ....E....... 513 826-6000
Beachwood *(G-1262)*
Oracle Systems Corporation ....G....... 937 427-5495
Beavercreek *(G-1336)*
Osisoft LLC ....G....... 440 442-2000
Cleveland *(G-5823)*
Osu Labanlens ....G....... 614 688-2356
Columbus *(G-7278)*
Our Voice Initiative Inc ....F....... 740 974-4303
Springboro *(G-17340)*
Pakra LLC ....F....... 614 477-6965
Columbus *(G-7286)*
Parallel Technologies Inc ....D....... 614 798-9700
Dublin *(G-8958)*
Parthenon Global LLC ....G....... 888 332-5303
Cleveland *(G-5853)*
Pathfinder Computer Systems ....G....... 330 928-1961
Barberton *(G-1094)*
Pathos LLC ....G....... 440 497-7278
Chesterland *(G-3168)*
Patrick J Burke & Co ....E....... 513 455-8200
Cincinnati *(G-4137)*
Patriot Software LLC ....D....... 877 968-7147
Canton *(G-2780)*
Patterson Colburne ....G....... 419 866-5544
Holland *(G-10949)*
Paul/Jay Associates ....G....... 740 676-8776
Bellaire *(G-1488)*
PCC Airfolils LLC ....G....... 330 868-7376
Minerva *(G-14197)*
Pdmb Inc ....G....... 513 522-7362
Cincinnati *(G-4144)*
Pearl Tech Corporation ....G....... 614 284-8357
Dublin *(G-8960)*
Peco II Inc ....D....... 614 431-0694
Columbus *(G-7305)*
Perdatum Inc ....G....... 614 761-1578
Hilliard *(G-10850)*
Perennial Software Inc ....F....... 440 247-5602
Chagrin Falls *(G-3027)*
Perfect Probate ....G....... 513 791-4100
Cincinnati *(G-4146)*
Phantom Technology LLC ....G....... 614 710-0074
Hilliard *(G-10851)*
Pkg Technologies Inc ....G....... 513 967-2783
Lebanon *(G-11685)*
Pmj Partners LLC ....G....... 201 360-1914
Columbus *(G-7330)*
Polygon Spaceship ....G....... 440 506-0403
Amherst *(G-571)*
Posm Software LLC ....G....... 859 274-0041
Columbus *(G-7333)*
Preemptive Solutions LLC ....E....... 440 443-7200
Cleveland *(G-5915)*
Preferred Soft Solutions LLC ....G....... 614 975-2750
Columbus *(G-7343)*
Proepo Software Ltd ....G....... 937 243-3825
Wshngtn CT Hs *(G-20736)*
Proficient Information Tech ....G....... 937 470-1300
Dayton *(G-8447)*
Profile Imaging Columbus LLC ....G....... 614 222-2888
Columbus *(G-7353)*
Profound Logic Software Inc ....G....... 937 439-7925
Dayton *(G-8449)*
Protel Systems and Svcs LLC ....G....... 419 913-0825
Maumee *(G-13140)*
Ptc Inc ....F....... 513 791-0330
Cincinnati *(G-4221)*
Pwi Inc ....F....... 732 212-8110
New Albany *(G-14635)*
Qc Software LLC ....G....... 513 469-1424
Cincinnati *(G-4224)*
Quayle Consulting Inc ....G....... 614 868-1363
Pickerington *(G-16058)*
Queen City Technologies ....F....... 513 253-1312
West Chester *(G-19892)*
Quest Software Inc ....D....... 614 336-9223
Dublin *(G-8970)*
R & H Enterprises Llc ....G....... 216 702-4449
Richmond Heights *(G-16504)*
Racedirector LLC ....G....... 440 940-6675
Willoughby *(G-20417)*
Rascal House Inc ....G....... 216 781-0904
Cleveland *(G-5961)*
Rawhide Software Inc ....G....... 419 878-0857
Bowling Green *(G-1993)*
Rebiz LLC ....E....... 844 467-3249
Cleveland *(G-5965)*

Employee Codes: A=Over 500 employees, B=251-500
C=101-250, D=51-100, E=20-50, F=10-19, G=3-9
2019 Harris Ohio
Industrial Directory
1021

Receet Inc....G....513 769-1900
Cincinnati (G-4254)
Reichard Software Corp....G....614 537-8598
Dublin (G-8972)
Research Metrics LLC....G....419 464-3333
Sylvania (G-17959)
Retail Management Products....F....740 548-1725
Lewis Center (G-11776)
Retalix Inc....C....937 384-2277
Miamisburg (G-13712)
Revolution Group Inc....D....614 212-1111
Westerville (G-20020)
Reynolds and Reynolds Company....F....937 485-2805
Beavercreek (G-1362)
Rhino Tech Software LLC....G....614 456-9321
Pickerington (G-16059)
Rhombus Technologies Ltd....G....937 335-1840
Troy (G-18698)
Rina Systems LLC....G....513 469-7462
Cincinnati (G-4270)
Rivals Sports Grille LLC....E....216 267-0005
Middleburg Heights (G-13769)
S L C Software Services....G....513 922-4303
Cincinnati (G-4297)
Sanctuary Software Studio Inc....E....330 666-9690
Fairlawn (G-9616)
Sark Technologies LLC....G....216 932-3171
Cleveland (G-6032)
Satelytics Inc....G....419 419-5380
Toledo (G-18512)
Seapine Software Inc....E....513 754-1655
Mason (G-12938)
Secure Medical Mail LLC....G....216 269-1971
Cleveland (G-6043)
Sest Inc....F....440 777-9777
Westlake (G-20157)
Sherwin Software Solutions....G....440 498-8010
Solon (G-17230)
Showroom Tracker LLC....G....888 407-0094
Canton (G-2815)
Sigmatek Systems LLC....D....513 674-0005
Cincinnati (G-4335)
Simple Vms LLC....G....888 255-8918
Cincinnati (G-4338)
Simplex-It LLC....G....234 380-1277
Stow (G-17628)
Skillsoft Corporation....D....216 524-5200
Independence (G-11150)
Soda Pig LLC....G....646 241-7126
Columbus (G-7458)
Softchoice Corporation....G....614 224-4123
Columbus (G-7459)
Softura Legal Solutions LLC....G....614 220-5611
Columbus (G-7460)
Software Authority Inc....G....216 236-0200
Cleveland (G-6077)
Software Management Group....E....513 618-2165
Cincinnati (G-4351)
Software Solutions Inc....E....513 932-6667
Lebanon (G-11698)
Software To Systems Inc....G....513 893-4367
Fairfield (G-9566)
Southwestern Ohio Instruction....F....937 746-6333
Dayton (G-8513)
Spearfysh Inc....F....330 487-0300
Hudson (G-11075)
Specialized Business Sftwr Inc....E....440 542-9145
Solon (G-17235)
Spitfire Technologies LLC....G....937 463-7729
Dayton (G-8520)
Splicenet Inc....G....513 563-3533
West Chester (G-19901)
Starwin Industries LLC....E....937 293-8568
Dayton (G-8525)
Step It Up LLC....G....720 289-1520
Columbus (G-7490)
Steve Schaefer....G....513 792-9911
Cincinnati (G-4380)
Stewardship Technology Inc....G....866 604-8880
Mount Vernon (G-14515)
Streamsavvy LLC....G....614 256-7955
Columbus (G-7493)
Strongbasics LLC....G....716 903-6151
Columbus (G-7495)
Studium LLC....G....614 402-0359
Dublin (G-8997)
Sunday School Software....G....614 527-8776
Hilliard (G-10867)
Sylvania Moose Lodge No....F....419 885-4953
Sylvania (G-17964)
Symantec Corporation....G....614 793-3060
Dublin (G-9000)
Symantec Corporation....D....216 643-6700
Independence (G-11151)
Syntec LLC....G....440 229-6262
Rocky River (G-16558)
Tahoe Interactive Systems Inc....F....614 891-2323
Westerville (G-20076)
Tarigma Corporation....F....614 436-3734
Columbus (G-7512)
Tata America Intl Corp....B....513 677-6500
Milford (G-14043)
Tech Solutions LLC....G....419 852-7190
Celina (G-2986)
Tech-E-Z LLC....G....419 692-1700
Delphos (G-8755)
Technosoft Inc....F....513 985-9877
Blue Ash (G-1857)
Tekdog Inc....G....614 737-3743
Granville (G-10338)
Terrene Labs LLC....G....513 445-3539
Mason (G-12950)
Thinkware Incorporated....E....513 598-3300
Cincinnati (G-4419)
Timekeeping Systems Inc....F....216 595-0890
Solon (G-17253)
Tmw Systems Inc....C....216 831-6606
Mayfield Heights (G-13171)
Toccata Technologies Inc....G....614 430-9888
Powell (G-16339)
Trapeze Software Group Inc....G....905 629-8727
Beachwood (G-1281)
Triad Governmental Systems....E....937 376-5446
Xenia (G-20799)
True Dinero Records & Tech LLC....G....513 428-4610
Cincinnati (G-4443)
◆ Turning Technologies LLC....C....330 746-3015
Youngstown (G-21055)
Uninterrupted LLC....F....216 771-2323
Akron (G-418)
United Computer Group Inc....G....216 520-1333
Independence (G-11153)
Value Stream Systems Inc....G....330 907-0064
Medina (G-13359)
Veeam Software Corporation....F....614 339-8200
Columbus (G-6508)
Vertex Computer Systems Inc....F....513 662-6888
Cincinnati (G-4477)
Vertical Data LLC....F....330 289-0313
Akron (G-425)
Virtual Boss Inc....G....419 872-7686
Perrysburg (G-16021)
Virtual Hold Technology LLC....D....330 670-2200
Akron (G-427)
Vitalrock LLC....G....888 596-8892
Rocky River (G-16559)
W L Arehart Computing Systems....G....937 383-4710
Wilmington (G-20510)
Web3box Software LLC....G....330 794-7397
Tallmadge (G-18014)
Wellington Wllams Wrldwide LLC....G....423 805-6198
Troy (G-18718)
Wentworth Solutions....F....440 212-7696
Brunswick (G-2249)
Wentworth Technologies LLC....F....440 212-7696
Brunswick (G-2250)
Westmount Technology Inc....G....216 328-2011
Independence (G-11157)
Whatifsportscom Inc....F....513 333-0313
Blue Ash (G-1869)
Wififace LLC....G....419 754-4816
Toledo (G-18600)
Wild Oak LLC....G....513 769-0526
Cincinnati (G-4509)
Willow Frog LLC....G....513 861-4834
Cincinnati (G-4512)
Workflex Solutions LLC....G....513 257-0215
Cincinnati (G-4517)
Works International Inc....G....513 631-6111
Cincinnati (G-4518)
Workspeed Management LLC....E....917 369-9025
Solon (G-17262)
Zipscene LLC....D....513 201-5174
Cincinnati (G-4533)
Znode Inc....F....888 755-5541
Columbus (G-6509)

76 MISCELLANEOUS REPAIR SERVICES

7692 Welding Repair

A & C Welding Inc....E....330 762-4777
Peninsula (G-15888)
▲ A & G Manufacturing Co Inc....E....419 468-7433
Galion (G-10119)
A Metalcraft Associates Inc....G....937 693-4008
Botkins (G-1931)
Abbott Tool Inc....E....419 476-6742
Toledo (G-18153)
Advanced Onsight Welding Svcs....G....513 924-1400
Cincinnati (G-3302)
Advanced Welding Co....E....937 746-6800
Franklin (G-9867)
Advanced Wldg Fabrication Inc....G....440 724-9165
Avon Lake (G-978)
Aetna Welding Co Inc....G....216 883-1801
Cleveland (G-4638)
Aircraft Welding Inc....G....440 951-3863
Willoughby (G-20268)
Airgas Usa LLC....G....614 308-3730
Columbus (G-6554)
Albright Radiator Inc....G....330 264-8886
Wooster (G-20561)
All American Indus Svcs LLC....G....440 255-7525
Mentor (G-13383)
All American Welding Co....G....614 224-7752
Columbus (G-6566)
All Do Weld & Fab LLC....G....740 477-2133
Circleville (G-4536)
All-Type Welding & Fabrication....E....440 439-3990
Cleveland (G-4669)
Allied Fabricating & Wldg Co....E....614 751-6664
Columbus (G-6572)
Alloy Unlimited Weld....G....330 506-8375
Canfield (G-2520)
AMP-Tech Inc....G....419 652-3444
Nova (G-15430)
Amptech Machining & Welding....G....419 652-3444
Nova (G-15431)
Apollo Welding & Fabg Inc....E....440 942-0227
Willoughby (G-20276)
ARC Gas & Supply LLC....E....216 341-5882
Cleveland (G-4724)
ARC Solutions Inc....F....419 542-9272
Hicksville (G-10775)
Arctech Fabricating Inc....E....937 525-9353
Springfield (G-17364)
Arnolds Repair Shop....G....740 373-5313
Marietta (G-12604)
Athens Mold and Machine Inc....D....740 593-6613
Athens (G-823)
Auglaize Welding Company Inc....G....419 738-4422
Wapakoneta (G-19323)
Automation Welding System....G....330 263-1176
Wooster (G-20567)
B & B Welding....G....419 968-2743
Middle Point (G-13756)
B & R Fabricators & Maint Inc....F....513 641-2222
Cincinnati (G-3375)
Baker Built Products Inc....G....419 965-2646
Ohio City (G-15514)
Baker Crane Service Ltd....G....740 453-5868
Zanesville (G-21101)
Baker Welding Llc....G....614 252-6100
Columbus (G-6644)
Baughmans Machine & Weld Shop....G....330 866-9243
Waynesburg (G-19562)
Bayloff Stmped Pdts Knsman Inc....D....330 876-4511
Kinsman (G-11463)
Bear Welding Services LLC....F....740 630-7538
Caldwell (G-2403)
Bens Welding Service Inc....G....937 878-4052
Fairborn (G-9452)
Blackwood Sheet Metal Inc....G....614 291-3115
Columbus (G-6678)
Blevins Metal Fabrication Inc....E....419 522-6082
Mansfield (G-12412)
Bob Lanes Welding Inc....F....740 373-3567
Marietta (G-12609)
Braze Solutions LLC....F....440 349-5100
Solon (G-17119)
Breitinger Company....C....419 526-4255
Mansfield (G-12414)
Bridgetown Welders LLC....G....513 574-4851
Cincinnati (G-3416)

SIC SECTION
76 MISCELLANEOUS REPAIR SERVICES

Broadway Welding & Fabrication ....G...... 513 821-0004
  Cincinnati (G-3420)
Brock RAD & Wldg Fabrication ....G...... 740 773-2540
  Chillicothe (G-3178)
Brocks Welding & Repair Svc ....G...... 740 453-3943
  Zanesville (G-21111)
Brown Industrial Inc ....E...... 937 693-3838
  Botkins (G-1934)
Bse Welding & Fabricating LLC ....F...... 419 547-1043
  Vickery (G-19194)
Buckeye State Welding & Fabg ....E...... 440 322-0344
  Elyria (G-9227)
Buckeye Welding ....G...... 330 674-0944
  Millersburg (G-14072)
▲ Byron Products Inc ....D...... 513 870-9111
  Fairfield (G-9486)
C & M Welding Services LLC ....G...... 419 584-0008
  Celina (G-2951)
C & R Inc ....E...... 614 497-1130
  Groveport (G-10486)
C O Welding & Fabrication Inc ....G...... 419 394-3293
  Saint Marys (G-16680)
C Stoneman Corporation ....G...... 440 942-3325
  Eastlake (G-9100)
C-N-D Industries Inc ....E...... 330 478-8811
  Massillon (G-12965)
Camelot Manufacturing Inc ....F...... 419 678-2603
  Coldwater (G-6403)
Cardinal Welding Inc ....G...... 330 426-2404
  East Palestine (G-9069)
Carol J Guiler ....G...... 614 252-6920
  Columbus (G-6745)
Carter Manufacturing Co Inc ....E...... 513 398-7303
  Mason (G-12838)
▲ Case-Maul Manufacturing Co ....F...... 419 524-1061
  Mansfield (G-12422)
Central Ohio Fabrication LLC ....G...... 740 969-2976
  Amanda (G-524)
Certified Welding Co ....F...... 216 961-5410
  Cleveland (G-4904)
Chipmatic Tool & Machine Inc ....D...... 419 862-2737
  Elmore (G-9205)
Chore Anden ....G...... 330 695-2300
  Fredericksburg (G-9945)
City Machine Technologies Inc ....F...... 330 747-2639
  Youngstown (G-20870)
Cleveland Jsm Inc ....D...... 440 876-3050
  Strongsville (G-17729)
Cleveland Welding & Fabg LLC ....G...... 440 364-5137
  Cleveland (G-4983)
Clipsons Metal Working Inc ....G...... 513 772-6393
  Cincinnati (G-3528)
Cmt Machining & Fabg LLC ....F...... 937 652-3740
  Urbana (G-18983)
Columbus Pipe and Equipment Co ....F...... 614 444-7871
  Columbus (G-6798)
Compton Metal Products Inc ....D...... 937 382-2403
  Wilmington (G-20490)
Comptons Precision Machine ....F...... 937 325-9139
  Springfield (G-17378)
Connaughton Wldg & Fence LLC ....G...... 513 867-0230
  Hamilton (G-10547)
County Wide Welding LLC ....G...... 440 564-1333
  Newbury (G-14949)
Creative Fab & Welding LLC ....E...... 937 780-5000
  Leesburg (G-11709)
Creative Fabrication Ltd ....G...... 740 262-5789
  Richwood (G-16508)
Creative Mold and Machine Inc ....E...... 440 338-5146
  Newbury (G-14950)
Crest Bending Inc ....F...... 419 492-2108
  New Washington (G-14828)
Custom Machine Inc ....E...... 419 986-5122
  Tiffin (G-18057)
Custom Way Welding Inc ....F...... 937 845-9469
  New Carlisle (G-14665)
Custom Weld & Machine Corp ....F...... 330 452-3935
  Canton (G-2643)
D & G Welding Inc ....G...... 419 445-5751
  Archbold (G-643)
D & M Welding & Radiator ....G...... 740 947-9032
  Waverly (G-19544)
Dalin Auto Service ....G...... 440 997-3301
  Ashtabula (G-770)
Davenport Service Group Inc ....G...... 440 487-9353
  Mentor (G-13429)
David Cox ....G...... 740 254-4858
  Gnadenhutten (G-10277)
Dayton Brick Company Inc ....F...... 937 293-4189
  Moraine (G-14344)

Dbcr Inc ....E...... 330 920-1900
  Cuyahoga Falls (G-7859)
Delta Machine & Tool Co ....F...... 216 524-2477
  Cleveland (G-5083)
Des Eck Welding ....G...... 330 698-7271
  Apple Creek (G-603)
Diamond Welding Co Inc ....G...... 216 251-1679
  Cleveland (G-5090)
Diversified Welding Services ....G...... 419 382-1433
  Toledo (G-18265)
Dover Fabrication and Burn Inc ....G...... 330 339-1057
  Dover (G-8820)
Dover Machine Co ....F...... 330 343-4123
  Dover (G-8822)
Drabik Manufacturing Inc ....F...... 216 267-1616
  Cleveland (G-5112)
Ds Welding LLC ....G...... 330 893-4049
  Millersburg (G-14079)
Duco Tool & Die Inc ....F...... 419 628-2031
  Minster (G-14212)
Duray Machine Co Inc ....G...... 440 277-4119
  Amherst (G-561)
Durisek Enterprises Inc ....G...... 216 281-3898
  Cleveland (G-5123)
Dynamic Specialties Inc ....E...... 440 946-2838
  Mentor (G-13435)
Dynamic Weld Corporation ....E...... 419 582-2900
  Osgood (G-15642)
E & M Liberty Welding Inc ....G...... 330 866-2338
  Waynesburg (G-19563)
E & R Welding Inc ....F...... 440 329-9387
  Berlin Heights (G-1653)
E L Davis Inc ....G...... 419 268-2004
  Celina (G-2958)
E W Welding & Fabricating ....G...... 440 826-9038
  Berea (G-1603)
Eagle Machine and Welding Inc ....G...... 740 345-5210
  Newark (G-14869)
Eagle Wldg & Fabrication Inc ....E...... 440 946-0692
  Willoughby (G-20313)
▲ East End Welding Company ....C...... 330 677-6000
  Kent (G-11317)
Euclid Welding Co Inc ....G...... 216 289-0714
  Maple Heights (G-12572)
Fab-Tech Machine Inc ....G...... 937 473-5572
  Covington (G-7785)
Fabrication Shop Inc ....F...... 419 435-7934
  Fostoria (G-9837)
Fabrication Unlimited LLC ....G...... 937 492-3166
  Sidney (G-17039)
Falls Stamping & Welding Co ....C...... 330 928-1191
  Cuyahoga Falls (G-7867)
◆ Fosbel Inc ....E...... 216 362-3900
  Cleveland (G-5265)
Fosbel Holding Inc ....E...... 216 362-3900
  Cleveland (G-5266)
Fred Winner ....G...... 419 582-2421
  New Weston (G-14845)
Fredrick Welding & Machining ....F...... 614 866-9650
  Reynoldsburg (G-16441)
Friess Welding Inc ....F...... 330 644-8160
  Coventry Township (G-7770)
G B Welding & Metal Fabg Co ....G...... 937 444-2091
  Fayetteville (G-9639)
Garland Welding Co Inc ....F...... 330 536-6506
  Lowellville (G-12251)
Gaspar Inc ....D...... 330 477-2222
  Canton (G-2679)
▲ General Technologies Inc ....E...... 419 747-1800
  Mansfield (G-12445)
▲ General Tool Company ....C...... 513 733-5500
  Cincinnati (G-3747)
George Steel Fabricating Inc ....E...... 513 932-2887
  Lebanon (G-11655)
Gilson Machine & Tool Co Inc ....E...... 419 592-2911
  Napoleon (G-14539)
▲ Glenridge Machine Co ....E...... 440 975-1055
  Willoughby (G-20332)
Gmp Welding & Fabrication Inc ....F...... 513 825-7861
  Cincinnati (G-3766)
Greber Machine Tool Inc ....G...... 440 322-3685
  Elyria (G-9264)
Greggs Specialty Services ....F...... 419 478-0803
  Toledo (G-18313)
Gurina Company ....G...... 614 279-3891
  Columbus (G-6971)
H & H Machine Shop Akron Inc ....G...... 330 773-3327
  Akron (G-193)
Habco Tool and Dev Co Inc ....G...... 440 946-5546
  Mentor (G-13463)

Hardline Welding LLC ....G...... 330 858-6289
  Kent (G-11332)
Harris Welding and Machine Co ....F...... 419 281-8351
  Ashland (G-707)
Harris Welding and Machine Co ....G...... 419 281-9623
  Ashland (G-708)
Hartley Machine Inc ....G...... 330 821-0343
  Alliance (G-471)
HI Tecmetal Group Inc ....E...... 216 881-8100
  Cleveland (G-5402)
HI Tecmetal Group Inc ....E...... 440 946-2280
  Willoughby (G-20337)
HI Tecmetal Group Inc ....G...... 440 373-5101
  Wickliffe (G-20213)
▲ Hi-Tek Manufacturing Inc ....C...... 513 459-1094
  Mason (G-12886)
Highs Welding Inc ....G...... 937 464-3029
  Belle Center (G-1499)
Hobart Bros Stick Electrode ....C...... 937 332-5375
  Troy (G-18666)
Hoffman Machining & Repair LLC ....G...... 419 547-9204
  Clyde (G-6389)
Holdren Brothers Inc ....F...... 937 465-7050
  West Liberty (G-19936)
Holdsworth Industrial Fabg ....G...... 330 874-3945
  Bolivar (G-1916)
Hyneks Machine and Welding ....G...... 419 281-7966
  Ashland (G-713)
Independent Machine & Wldg Inc ....G...... 937 339-7330
  Troy (G-18676)
▲ Industry Products Co ....B...... 937 778-0585
  Piqua (G-16130)
Innovative Wldg & Design LLC ....G...... 330 581-1316
  Alliance (G-478)
J & A Machine ....G...... 330 424-5235
  Lisbon (G-11970)
J & L Welding Fabricating Inc ....F...... 330 393-9353
  Warren (G-19412)
J & S Industrial Mch Pdts Inc ....D...... 419 691-1380
  Toledo (G-18356)
J A B Welding Service Inc ....F...... 740 453-5868
  Zanesville (G-21150)
J P Suggins Mobile Welding ....E...... 216 566-7131
  Cleveland (G-5486)
James G Morehouse ....G...... 513 752-2236
  Milford (G-14020)
Jatdco LLC ....G...... 440 238-6570
  Strongsville (G-17757)
Jerl Machine Inc ....D...... 419 873-0270
  Perrysburg (G-15969)
Jerrys Welding Supply Inc ....G...... 937 364-1500
  Hillsboro (G-10883)
JMw Welding and Mfg ....E...... 330 484-2428
  Canton (G-2719)
Johns Welding & Towing Inc ....F...... 419 447-8937
  Tiffin (G-18063)
Jrs Hydraulic & Welding ....G...... 614 497-1100
  Columbus (G-7079)
K & J Machine Inc ....F...... 740 425-3282
  Barnesville (G-1117)
K-M-S Industries Inc ....E...... 440 243-6680
  Brookpark (G-2150)
Kedar D Army ....G...... 419 238-6929
  Van Wert (G-19097)
Kellys Welding & Fabricating ....G...... 440 593-6040
  Conneaut (G-7651)
Kendel Welding & Fabrication ....G...... 330 834-2429
  Massillon (G-13008)
Kings Welding and Fabg Inc ....E...... 330 738-3592
  Mechanicstown (G-13212)
Kirbys Auto & Truck Repair ....G...... 513 934-3999
  Lebanon (G-11669)
Kirk Welding & Fabricating ....G...... 216 961-6403
  Cleveland (G-5538)
▲ Kottler Metal Products Co Inc ....E...... 440 946-7473
  Willoughby (G-20355)
Kramer Power Equipment Co ....F...... 937 456-2232
  Eaton (G-9157)
Kys Welding & Fabrication ....G...... 513 702-9081
  Loveland (G-12207)
L B Industries Inc ....E...... 330 750-1002
  Struthers (G-17820)
Lakecraft Inc ....G...... 419 734-2828
  Port Clinton (G-16249)
Lanes Welding & Repair ....G...... 740 397-2525
  Mount Vernon (G-14488)
Laserflex Corporation ....D...... 614 850-9600
  Hilliard (G-10837)
Liberty Casting Company LLC ....E...... 740 363-1941
  Delaware (G-8703)

Employee Codes: A=Over 500 employees, B=251-500
C=101-250, D=51-100, E=20-50, F=10-19, G=3-9

76 MISCELLANEOUS REPAIR SERVICES

Lima Sheet Metal Machine & Mfg .... E 419 229-1161
  Lima *(G-11893)*
Logan Welding Inc .... G 740 385-9651
  Logan *(G-12034)*
▲ Long-Stanton Mfg Company .... E 513 874-8020
  West Chester *(G-19738)*
Lostcreek Tool & Machine Inc .... F 937 773-6022
  Piqua *(G-16138)*
Lukens Blacksmith Shop .... G 513 821-2308
  Cincinnati *(G-3955)*
Lunar Tool & Mold Inc .... F 440 237-2141
  North Royalton *(G-15285)*
M & M Concepts Inc .... G 937 355-1115
  West Mansfield *(G-19943)*
M & W Welding Inc .... G 614 224-0501
  Columbus *(G-7139)*
Mad Metal Wldg Fabrication LLC .... G 614 256-4163
  Columbus *(G-7144)*
Maintenance and Repair Fabg Co .... G 330 478-1149
  Massillon *(G-13017)*
Majestic Tool and Machine Inc .... E 440 248-5058
  Solon *(G-17186)*
Manufacturing Concepts .... F 330 784-9054
  Tallmadge *(G-17990)*
Marsam Metalfab Inc .... G 330 405-1520
  Twinsburg *(G-18811)*
Martin Welding LLC .... F 937 687-3602
  New Lebanon *(G-14711)*
Mc Elwain Industries Inc .... F 419 532-3126
  Ottawa *(G-15658)*
McDannald Welding & Machining .... G 937 644-0300
  Marysville *(G-12802)*
McIntosh Machine .... G 937 687-3936
  New Lebanon *(G-14712)*
MCO Welding .... G 330 401-6130
  Stone Creek *(G-17562)*
Mecca Rebuilding & Welding Co .... G 419 476-8133
  Toledo *(G-18405)*
Mercers Welding Inc .... G 330 533-3373
  Canfield *(G-2536)*
Meta Manufacturing Corporation .... E 513 793-6382
  Blue Ash *(G-1818)*
Microweld Engineering Inc .... F 614 847-9410
  Worthington *(G-20697)*
Mike Loppe .... F 937 969-8102
  Tremont City *(G-18616)*
Mikes Automotive LLC .... G 937 233-1433
  Dayton *(G-8358)*
Mikes Welding .... G 937 675-6587
  Jamestown *(G-11220)*
Miller Welding Inc .... G 330 364-6173
  Dover *(G-8842)*
Millwrght Wldg Fbrication Svcs .... F 740 533-1510
  Kitts Hill *(G-11475)*
Mitchell Welding LLC .... G 740 259-2211
  Lucasville *(G-12266)*
Monnig Welding Co .... G 513 241-5156
  Cincinnati *(G-4042)*
Montgomery & Montgomery LLC .... G 330 858-9533
  Akron *(G-285)*
National Welding & Tanker Repr .... G 614 875-3399
  Grove City *(G-10449)*
National Welding & Tanker Repr .... G 614 875-3399
  Grove City *(G-10450)*
New Tech Welding Inc .... G 937 426-4801
  Beavercreek *(G-1334)*
Norman Noble Inc .... C 216 761-2133
  Cleveland *(G-5758)*
Northwind Industries Inc .... E 216 433-0666
  Cleveland *(G-5787)*
Oaks Welding Inc .... G 330 482-4216
  Columbiana *(G-6475)*
Oceco Inc .... F 419 447-0916
  Tiffin *(G-18073)*
Ohio Hydraulics Inc .... E 513 771-2590
  Cincinnati *(G-4103)*
Ohio State University .... E 614 292-4139
  Columbus *(G-7260)*
Ohio Trailer Inc .... G 330 392-4444
  Warren *(G-19428)*
Ohio Trailer Supply Inc .... G 614 471-9121
  Columbus *(G-7263)*
Paul Wilke & Son Inc .... F 513 921-3163
  Cincinnati *(G-4141)*
Paulo Products Company .... E 440 942-0153
  Willoughby *(G-20399)*
Penco Tool LLC .... F 440 998-1116
  Ashtabula *(G-795)*
◆ Pentaflex Inc .... G 937 325-5551
  Springfield *(G-17470)*

Perkins Motor Service Ltd .... E 440 277-1256
  Lorain *(G-12112)*
Perry Welding Service Inc .... F 330 425-2211
  Twinsburg *(G-18836)*
Phillips & Sons Welding & Fabg .... G 440 428-1625
  Geneva *(G-10228)*
Phillips Mfg and Tower Co .... G 419 347-1720
  Shelby *(G-16985)*
Phoenix Industries & Apparatus .... F 513 722-1085
  Loveland *(G-12221)*
Phoenix Welding Solutions LLC .... G 330 569-7223
  Garrettsville *(G-10200)*
Precision Mtal Fabrication Inc .... D 937 235-9261
  Dayton *(G-8434)*
Precision Reflex Inc .... F 419 629-2603
  New Bremen *(G-14659)*
Precision Welding Corporation .... E 216 524-6110
  Cleveland *(G-5912)*
Prestons Repair & Welding .... G 937 947-1883
  Laura *(G-11625)*
Pro Fab Welding Service LLC .... G 937 272-2142
  Moraine *(G-14384)*
Product Tooling Inc .... G 740 524-2061
  Sunbury *(G-17898)*
Prout Boiler Htg & Wldg Inc .... G 330 744-0293
  Youngstown *(G-21008)*
Quality Welding Inc .... E 419 483-6067
  Bellevue *(G-1541)*
Quality Wldg & Fabrication LLC .... D 419 225-6208
  Lima *(G-11925)*
Quick Service Welding & Mch Co .... F 330 673-3818
  Kent *(G-11372)*
▲ R K Industries Inc .... D 419 523-5001
  Ottawa *(G-15663)*
R S V Wldg Fbrcation Machining .... F 419 592-0993
  Napoleon *(G-14557)*
Ray Townsend .... G 440 968-3617
  Montville *(G-14325)*
Rbm Environmental and Cnstr .... E 419 693-5840
  Oregon *(G-15566)*
RI Alto Mfg Inc .... F 740 914-4230
  Marion *(G-8564)*
Ridge Machine & Welding Co .... G 740 537-2821
  Toronto *(G-18611)*
RJR & Associates Inc .... G 419 237-2220
  Fayette *(G-9636)*
Robert Alten Inc .... G 740 653-2640
  Lancaster *(G-11603)*
Robert E Moore .... G 513 367-0006
  Harrison *(G-10668)*
Rodney Wells .... G 740 425-2266
  Barnesville *(G-1118)*
Romar Metal Fabricating Inc .... G 740 682-7731
  Oak Hill *(G-15460)*
▲ Rose City Manufacturing Inc .... D 937 325-5561
  Springfield *(G-17489)*
Rose Metal Industries LLC .... F 216 881-3355
  Cleveland *(G-6002)*
Rush Welding & Machine Inc .... G 740 354-7874
  Portsmouth *(G-16297)*
S & S Spring Shop .... G 800 619-4652
  Mount Perry *(G-14458)*
Salem Welding & Supply Company .... G 330 332-4517
  Salem *(G-16772)*
Sammartino Welding & Auto Sls .... G 330 782-6086
  Youngstown *(G-21024)*
Sat Welding LLC .... G 614 747-2641
  Columbus *(G-7421)*
Sauerwein Welding .... G 513 563-2979
  Cincinnati *(G-4301)*
Schmidt Machine Company .... E 419 294-3814
  Upper Sandusky *(G-18972)*
Schwab Welding Inc .... G 513 353-4262
  Cincinnati *(G-4308)*
Selinick Co .... G 440 632-1788
  Middlefield *(G-13851)*
Selzer Tool & Die Inc .... G 440 365-4124
  Elyria *(G-9325)*
▲ Semtorq Inc .... F 330 487-0600
  Twinsburg *(G-18856)*
Simpson & Sons Inc .... F 513 367-0152
  Harrison *(G-10670)*
Slabe Tool Company .... G 740 439-1647
  Cambridge *(G-2456)*
Slade Gardner .... G 440 355-8015
  Lagrange *(G-11493)*
Smith Springs Inc .... G 800 619-4652
  Mount Perry *(G-14459)*
Smp Welding LLC .... F 440 205-9353
  Mentor *(G-13584)*

Somerville Manufacturing Inc .... E 740 336-7847
  Marietta *(G-12674)*
Spradlin Bros Welding Co .... F 800 219-2182
  Springfield *(G-17493)*
Steubenville Truck Center Inc .... E 740 282-2711
  Steubenville *(G-17554)*
Steve Vore Welding and Steel .... F 419 375-4087
  Fort Recovery *(G-9827)*
Stryker Welding .... G 419 682-2301
  Stryker *(G-17835)*
Suburban Metal Products Inc .... F 740 474-4237
  Circleville *(G-4559)*
Superior Weld and Fabg Co Inc .... E 216 249-5122
  Cleveland *(G-6128)*
Systech Handling Inc .... F 419 445-8226
  Archbold *(G-670)*
T & L Welding LLC .... G 937 498-9170
  Sidney *(G-17083)*
▼ T & R Welding Systems Inc .... F 937 228-7517
  Dayton *(G-8535)*
T&T Welding .... G 513 615-1156
  Loveland *(G-12239)*
Tbone Sales LLC .... E 330 897-6131
  Baltic *(G-1033)*
Temperature Controls Company .... F 330 773-6633
  Akron *(G-398)*
Tendon Manufacturing Inc .... E 216 663-3200
  Cleveland *(G-6159)*
Thomas Entps of Georgetown .... G 937 378-6300
  Georgetown *(G-10238)*
Tig Welding Specialties Inc .... G 216 621-1763
  Cleveland *(G-6174)*
Timothy Sasser .... G 740 260-9499
  Byesville *(G-2394)*
Tonys Wldg & Fabrication LLC .... G 740 333-4000
  Wshngtn CT Hs *(G-20746)*
Top Notch Fleet Services LLC .... G 419 260-4057
  Maumee *(G-13155)*
Tri-State Plating & Polishing .... G 304 529-2579
  Proctorville *(G-16348)*
Triangle Precision Industries .... D 937 299-6776
  Dayton *(G-8564)*
Tru-Fab Technology Inc .... F 440 954-9760
  Willoughby *(G-20451)*
Turn-Key Industrial Svcs LLC .... D 614 274-1128
  Columbus *(G-7551)*
TW Tank LLC .... G 419 334-2664
  Fremont *(G-10058)*
Two M Precision Co Inc .... E 440 946-2120
  Willoughby *(G-20454)*
Valley Machine Tool Co Inc .... E 513 899-2737
  Morrow *(G-14417)*
Van Burens Welding & Machine .... G 740 787-2636
  Glenford *(G-10273)*
Viking Fabricators Inc .... E 740 374-5246
  Marietta *(G-12687)*
Waldock Eqp Sls & Svc Inc .... G 419 426-7771
  Attica *(G-860)*
Warlock Inc .... G 614 471-4055
  Columbus *(G-7590)*
Wayne Trail Technologies Inc .... D 937 295-2120
  Fort Loramie *(G-9811)*
Webers Body & Frame .... G 937 839-5946
  West Alexandria *(G-19624)*
Weldfab Inc .... G 440 563-3310
  Rock Creek *(G-16535)*
Welding Consultants Inc .... G 614 258-7018
  Columbus *(G-7598)*
Welding Equipment Repair Co .... G 330 536-2125
  Lowellville *(G-12257)*
Weldments Inc .... F 937 235-9261
  Dayton *(G-8588)*
Wenrick Machine and Tool Corp .... F 937 667-7307
  Tipp City *(G-18145)*
Westerman Acquisition Co LLC .... E 330 264-2447
  Wooster *(G-20666)*
Wg Mobile Welding LLC .... G 440 720-1940
  Highland Heights *(G-10800)*
Whitt Machine Inc .... F 513 423-7624
  Middletown *(G-13967)*
Wiederhold Wldg & Fabrication .... G 513 875-3755
  Fayetteville *(G-9642)*
Wonder Weld Inc .... G 614 875-1447
  Orient *(G-15579)*
Worleys Machine & Fab Inc .... G 740 532-3337
  Hanging Rock *(G-10624)*

7694 Armature Rewinding Shops

▲ 3-D Service Ltd .... C 330 830-3500
  Massillon *(G-12956)*

76 MISCELLANEOUS REPAIR SERVICES

A E Ruston Electric LLC ....G...... 740 286-3022
  Jackson *(G-11178)*
Akron Indus Mtr Sls & Svc Inc.............G...... 330 753-7624
  Norton *(G-15359)*
Al Bradshaw Jr ....G...... 513 422-8870
  Middletown *(G-13882)*
Allan A Irish ....G...... 419 394-3284
  Saint Marys *(G-16675)*
Als High Tech Inc ....F...... 440 232-7090
  Bedford *(G-1380)*
B W Electrical & Maint Svc ....G...... 330 534-7870
  Hubbard *(G-10999)*
Bar1 Motorsports ....F...... 614 284-3732
  Marysville *(G-12771)*
Barry Brothers Electric ....G...... 614 299-8187
  Columbus *(G-6651)*
Bay Electric Co ....G...... 419 625-1046
  Sandusky *(G-16796)*
Bennett Electric Inc ....F...... 800 874-5405
  Norwalk *(G-15382)*
Big River Electric Inc ....G...... 740 446-4360
  Gallipolis *(G-10161)*
Bornhorst Motor Service Inc..............G...... 937 773-0426
  Piqua *(G-16104)*
Brian Franks Electric Inc ....G...... 330 821-5457
  Alliance *(G-458)*
C and O Electric Motor Service ....G...... 614 491-6387
  Columbus *(G-6718)*
C P Electric Motor Repair Inc............G...... 330 425-9593
  Twinsburg *(G-18745)*
Campton Electric Sales & Svc ....G...... 740 826-4429
  New Concord *(G-14682)*
Cardinal Electric LLC ....G...... 740 366-6850
  Newark *(G-14860)*
Carnation Elc Mtr Repr Sls Inc ....G...... 330 823-7116
  Alliance *(G-460)*
City Machine Technologies Inc..........F...... 330 747-2639
  Youngstown *(G-20870)*
City Machine Technologies Inc..........E...... 330 740-8186
  Youngstown *(G-20871)*
Clark-Fowler Enterprises Inc ....E...... 330 262-0906
  Wooster *(G-20578)*
Columbus Electrical Works Co..........F...... 614 294-4651
  Columbus *(G-6787)*
D & J Electric Motor Repair Co ....F...... 330 336-4343
  Wadsworth *(G-19232)*
Diversified Air Systems Inc ....E...... 216 741-1700
  Brooklyn Heights *(G-2121)*
Dolin Supply Co ....E...... 304 529-4171
  South Point *(G-17282)*
E-Z Electric Motor Svc Corp ....F...... 216 581-8820
  Cleveland *(G-5132)*
Econ-O-Machine Products Inc..........G...... 937 882-6507
  Donnelsville *(G-8801)*

Electric Ctrl & Mtr Repr Svc ....G...... 216 881-3143
  Cleveland *(G-5162)*
Electric Motor Svc of Athens ....F...... 740 592-1682
  The Plains *(G-18022)*
Electro Torque ....G...... 614 297-1600
  Columbus *(G-6890)*
Fenton Bros Electric Co ....E...... 330 343-0093
  New Philadelphia *(G-14768)*
Fmh Electric Inc ....F...... 419 782-0671
  Lima *(G-11863)*
Franks Electric Inc ....G...... 513 313-5883
  Cincinnati *(G-3711)*
General Electric Intl Inc ....G...... 410 737-7228
  Cincinnati *(G-3744)*
Hackworth Electric Motors Inc ....G...... 330 345-6049
  Wooster *(G-20602)*
Hannon Company ....E...... 740 453-0527
  Zanesville *(G-21146)*
Hannon Company ....F...... 330 343-7758
  Dover *(G-8829)*
Hennings Quality Service Inc ....F...... 216 941-9120
  Cleveland *(G-5393)*
Home Service Station Inc.................G...... 419 678-2612
  Coldwater *(G-6414)*
Horner Industrial Services Inc ....F...... 513 874-8722
  West Chester *(G-19865)*
Horner Industrial Services Inc ....E...... 937 390-6667
  Springfield *(G-17421)*
Hunnell Electric Co Inc ....G...... 330 773-8278
  Akron *(G-209)*
Integrated Power Services LLC ....E...... 216 433-7808
  Cleveland *(G-5463)*
Integrated Power Services LLC ....E...... 513 863-8816
  Hamilton *(G-10572)*
James W Cunningham ....F...... 419 639-2111
  Green Springs *(G-10344)*
▲ Joe Baker Equipment Sales ....G...... 513 451-1327
  Cincinnati *(G-3875)*
K B Electric Motor Service ....G...... 740 537-1346
  Toronto *(G-18610)*
K C N Technologies LLC ....G...... 440 439-4219
  Bedford *(G-1419)*
Kent Swigart ....G...... 937 836-5292
  Englewood *(G-9365)*
Kiemle-Hankins Company.................E...... 419 661-2430
  Perrysburg *(G-15972)*
Kw Services LLC ....G...... 419 636-3438
  Bryan *(G-2294)*
Kw Services LLC ....G...... 419 228-1325
  Lima *(G-11884)*
Lebanon Electric Motor Svc LLC........G...... 513 932-2889
  Lebanon *(G-11670)*
Lemsco Inc ....G...... 419 242-4005
  Toledo *(G-18381)*

Lima Armature Works Inc.................G...... 419 222-4010
  Lima *(G-11887)*
Lorain Armature & Mtr Repr Inc ....G...... 440 967-2620
  Vermilion *(G-19166)*
M & R Electric Motor Svc Inc ....E...... 937 222-6282
  Dayton *(G-8317)*
Mac Electric Inc................................G...... 419 782-0671
  Lima *(G-11896)*
Machine Doctors Inc.........................G...... 513 422-3060
  Cincinnati *(G-3966)*
Mader Electr Motor & Power Tra........G...... 937 325-5576
  Springfield *(G-17442)*
Magnetech Industrial Svcs Inc ....C...... 330 830-3500
  Massillon *(G-13016)*
Matlock Electric Co Inc....................E...... 513 731-9600
  Cincinnati *(G-3986)*
Mid-Ohio Electric Co........................E...... 614 274-8000
  Columbus *(G-7178)*
Moto-Electric Inc..............................G...... 419 668-7894
  Norwalk *(G-15406)*
◆ National Electric Coil Inc ....B...... 614 488-1151
  Columbus *(G-7209)*
Ohio Electric Motor Svc LLC ....F...... 614 444-1451
  Columbus *(G-7247)*
Ohio Electric Motor Svc LLC ....G...... 419 525-2225
  Mansfield *(G-12496)*
Oliver Pool and Spa Inc ....G...... 740 264-5368
  Steubenville *(G-17548)*
Phillips Electric Co ....F...... 216 361-0014
  Cleveland *(G-5873)*
▲ Setco Sales Company ....D...... 513 941-5110
  Cincinnati *(G-4328)*
Sheldon On Site Inc ....G...... 419 339-1381
  Elida *(G-9200)*
▲ Shoemaker Electric Company ......E...... 614 294-5626
  Columbus *(G-7447)*
Southwest Electric Co ....F...... 330 875-7000
  Louisville *(G-12168)*
Total Maintenance Management........G...... 513 228-2345
  Lebanon *(G-11701)*
Tyler Electric Motor Repair ....G...... 330 836-5537
  Akron *(G-417)*
Watson Electric Motor Svc Inc ....F...... 614 836-9904
  Columbus *(G-7594)*
Wheatley Electric Service Co............G...... 513 531-4951
  Cincinnati *(G-4505)*
Whelco Industrial Ltd ....F...... 419 385-4627
  Perrysburg *(G-16026)*
Whelco Industrial Ltd ....E...... 419 873-6134
  Perrysburg *(G-16027)*
Wyse Electric Motor Repair ....G...... 419 445-5921
  Archbold *(G-673)*

ALPHABETIC SECTION

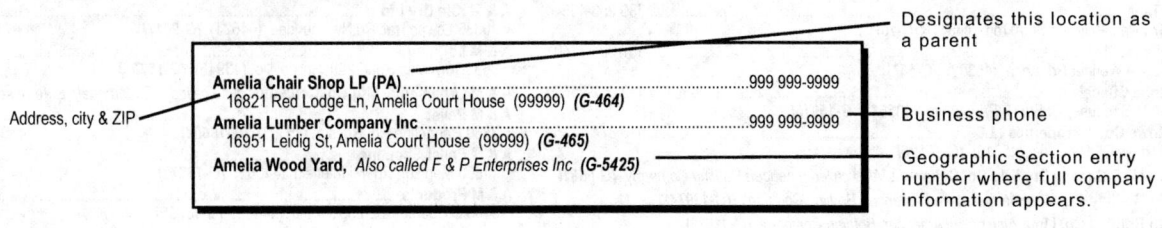

- Designates this location as a parent

Address, city & ZIP

Amelia Chair Shop LP (PA)..999 999-9999
  16821 Red Lodge Ln, Amelia Court House (99999) *(G-464)*
Amelia Lumber Company Inc..999 999-9999
  16951 Leidig St, Amelia Court House (99999) *(G-465)*
Amelia Wood Yard, Also called *F & P Enterprises Inc* *(G-5425)*

- Business phone
- Geographic Section entry number where full company information appears.

See footnotes for symbols and codes identification.

* Companies listed alphabetically.
* Complete physical or mailing address.

---

1 888 U Pitch It...440 796-9028
  7176 Fillmore Ct Mentor (44060) *(G-13368)*
1 A Lifesafer Inc (PA)..513 651-9560
  4290 Glendale Milford Rd Blue Ash (45242) *(G-1716)*
1 A Lifesafer Hawaii Inc..513 651-9560
  4290 Glendale Milford Rd Blue Ash (45242) *(G-1717)*
1 Day Sign...419 475-6060
  4236 Secor Rd Toledo (43623) *(G-18150)*
1 Iron Golf Inc..419 662-9336
  504 Maplewood Ln Colina (45822) *(G-2948)*
1 Stop Graphics, Barberton Also called *Advertising Ideas of Ohio Inc* *(G-1049)*
1-2-3 Gluten Free Inc..216 378-9233
  125 Orange Tree Dr Chagrin Falls (44022) *(G-3007)*
10155 Broadview Business..440 546-1901
  10155 Broadview Rd Broadview Heights (44147) *(G-2085)*
11 92 Holdings LLC..216 920-7790
  8 E Washington St Ste 200 Chagrin Falls (44022) *(G-3008)*
119c Landis Display Co...937 307-9499
  346 Beam Dr Franklin (45005) *(G-9865)*
11am Industries LLC..330 730-3177
  1297 Noble Ave Barberton (44203) *(G-1047)*
1455 Group LLC..330 494-9074
  6116 Market Ave N Canton (44721) *(G-2554)*
1803 Bacon Ltd...740 398-7644
  1081 Norris Dr Columbus (43224) *(G-6510)*
1923 W 25th St Inc...216 696-7529
  1923 W 25th St Cleveland (44113) *(G-4579)*
1967...216 882-4228
  594 Corkhill Rd Apt 402 Bedford (44146) *(G-1377)*
1984 Printing..510 435-8338
  7817 Silver Lake Ct Westerville (43082) *(G-19976)*
1st Choice Contractor, Elyria Also called *Elite Property Group LLC* *(G-9250)*
1st Choice Web Solution Inc..330 503-1591
  3000 Belmont Ave Youngstown (44505) *(G-20828)*
2-M Manufacturing Company.......................................440 269-1270
  34560 Lakeland Blvd Eastlake (44095) *(G-9096)*
20/20 Custom Molded Plast (PA)................................419 485-2020
  14620 Selwyn Dr Montpelier (43543) *(G-14300)*
21st Century Printers Inc...513 771-4150
  326 Northland Blvd Cincinnati (45246) *(G-3268)*
21stcentury Medical Tech LLC.....................................732 310-9367
  526 S Main St Akron (44311) *(G-13)*
232 Defense LLC...419 348-4343
  5371 Otsego Pike Custar (43511) *(G-7828)*
252 Tattoo (PA)...440 235-6699
  24525 Sprague Rd Columbia Station (44028) *(G-6426)*
2cravealloys, Dalton Also called *J Horst Manufacturing Co* *(G-7945)*
2nd Roe LLC...419 499-3031
  12014 Thomas Rd Monroeville (44847) *(G-14285)*
3 Brothers Torching Inc...419 339-9985
  4915 Dutch Hollow Rd Lima (45807) *(G-11828)*
3 Sigma LLC..937 440-3400
  1985 W Stanfield Rd Troy (45373) *(G-18632)*
3-D Service Ltd (PA)...330 830-3500
  800 Nave Rd Se Massillon (44646) *(G-12956)*
3-D Technical Services Company................................937 746-2901
  255 Industrial Dr Franklin (45005) *(G-9866)*
3-Dmed, Franklin Also called *3-D Technical Services Company* *(G-9866)*
3-G Incorporated (PA)..513 921-4515
  4122 Spring Grove Ave Cincinnati (45223) *(G-3269)*
31 Inc..740 498-8324
  100 Enterprise Dr Newcomerstown (43832) *(G-14968)*
360 Communications LLC..330 329-2013
  826 Minota Ave Akron (44306) *(G-14)*
360water Inc..614 294-3600
  965 W 3rd Ave Columbus (43212) *(G-6511)*
3d Corrugated LLC...513 241-8126
  5524 Goldcrest Dr Cincinnati (45238) *(G-3270)*

3d Sales & Consulting Inc..513 422-1198
  408 Vanderveer St Middletown (45044) *(G-13874)*
3d Systems, Barberton Also called *Village Plastics Co* *(G-1112)*
3d Systems Inc..215 757-9611
  950 Taylor Station Rd K Columbus (43230) *(G-6512)*
3d Systems Inc..216 229-2040
  7100 Euclid Ave Cleveland (44103) *(G-4580)*
3dlt LLC...513 452-3358
  8 Peasenhall Ln Cincinnati (45208) *(G-3271)*
3dnsew LLC..740 618-8005
  11813 Wilkins Run Rd Ne Newark (43055) *(G-14846)*
3gc LLC...740 703-0580
  5600 Sw Us 42 Cardington (43315) *(G-2869)*
3i Solutions, Wooster Also called *Ingredient Innovations Intl Co* *(G-20606)*
3jd Inc..513 324-9655
  2823 Northlawn Ave Moraine (45439) *(G-14327)*
3M Company..513 248-1749
  910 Lila Ave Milford (45150) *(G-13991)*
3M Company..330 725-1444
  1030 Lake Rd Medina (44256) *(G-13214)*
3n1 Mens Fashion...513 851-3610
  481 E Kemper Rd Cincinnati (45246) *(G-3272)*
3way Machine and Tool Company...............................419 925-7222
  2411 Cssella Montezuma Rd Maria Stein (45860) *(G-12597)*
4 Him Sales, Morrow Also called *Isaacs Jr Floyd Thomas* *(G-14412)*
4 Over LLC..937 610-0629
  7801 Technology Blvd Dayton (45424) *(G-7995)*
4 Walls Com LLC..216 432-1400
  4700 Lakeside Ave E 173a Cleveland (44114) *(G-4581)*
4-B Wood Custom Cabinets, Seville Also called *4-B Wood Specialties Inc* *(G-16909)*
4-B Wood Specialties Inc..330 769-2188
  255 W Greenwich Rd Seville (44273) *(G-16909)*
4-Sure Wire Products Inc...440 563-9263
  2589 Forman Rd Rock Creek (44084) *(G-16531)*
48 Hr Books Inc...330 374-6917
  2249 14th St Sw Akron (44314) *(G-15)*
48hourprint.com, Cleveland Also called *Advanced Media Corporation* *(G-4629)*
48hr Books, Akron Also called *Printing System Inc* *(G-331)*
4d Screenprinting Ltd..513 353-1070
  5833 Hamilton Cleves Rd Cleves (45002) *(G-6353)*
4everready, Dayton Also called *P3 Secure LLC* *(G-8415)*
4me Group LLC..513 898-1083
  715 Lexington Ave Terrace Park (45174) *(G-18017)*
4r Enterprises Incorporated..330 923-9799
  700 Portage Trl Cuyahoga Falls (44221) *(G-7829)*
4S Company...330 792-5518
  3730 Mahoning Ave Youngstown (44515) *(G-20829)*
4w Services..614 554-5427
  7901 Minecaster Rd Hebron (43025) *(G-10736)*
5 Axis Grinding Inc..937 312-9797
  86 Westpark Rd Dayton (45459) *(G-7996)*
5 BS Inc (PA)...740 454-8453
  1000 5 Bs Dr Zanesville (43701) *(G-21090)*
5-Acre Mill, Hicksville Also called *Adroit Thinking Inc* *(G-10774)*
5874 Sawmill LLC..614 795-1818
  5874 Sawmill Rd Dublin (43017) *(G-8870)*
5me LLC..513 719-1600
  4270 Ivy Pointe Blvd # 100 Cincinnati (45245) *(G-3232)*
5me Holdings LLC (PA)...859 534-4872
  4270 Ivy Pointe Blvd # 100 Cincinnati (45245) *(G-3233)*
5s Inc...440 968-0212
  9755 Plank Rd Montville (44064) *(G-14323)*
6062 Holdings LLC...216 359-9005
  23366 Commerce Park 100b Beachwood (44122) *(G-1216)*
614 Cupcakes LLC...614 245-8800
  4045 Chelsea Grn W New Albany (43054) *(G-14602)*
614 Magazine, Columbus Also called *614 Media Group LLC* *(G-6513)*

(PA)=Parent Co (HQ)=Headquarters (DH)=Div Headquarters

614 Media Group LLC 614 488-4400
458 E Main St Columbus (43215) *(G-6513)*
69 Taps 330 253-4554
374 Paul Williams St Akron (44311) *(G-16)*
6s Products LLC 937 394-7440
12800 Wenger Rd Anna (45302) *(G-587)*
7 Little Cupcakes 419 252-0858
1021 Sandusky St Ste C Perrysburg (43551) *(G-15915)*
7 Rowe Court Properties LLC 513 874-7236
7 Rowe Ct Hamilton (45015) *(G-10526)*
7 Up / R C/Canada Dry Btlg Co, Columbus Also called *American Bottling Company* *(G-6581)*
7 Up Bottling Co, Midvale Also called *American Bottling Company* *(G-13974)*
7 Up Bottling Co, Lima Also called *American Bottling Company* *(G-11836)*
7 Up of Marietta Inc 740 423-9230
871 State Route 618 Little Hocking (45742) *(G-11988)*
7 Up/ Royal Crown, Cincinnati Also called *American Bottling Company* *(G-3330)*
7&7 Woodworking 330 347-6574
11080 Ashland Rd Wooster (44691) *(G-20552)*
717 Inc 440 925-0402
13000 Athens Ave Ste 110 Lakewood (44107) *(G-11507)*
717 Ink, Lakewood Also called *717 Inc* *(G-11507)*
762mm Firearms LLC 440 655-8572
224 High St Wadsworth (44281) *(G-19217)*
77 Coach Supply Ltd 330 674-1454
7426 County Road 77 Millersburg (44654) *(G-14053)*
7d Marketing Inc 330 721-8822
345 N State Rd Medina (44256) *(G-13215)*
7signal Solutions Inc (PA) 216 777-2900
6155 Rockside Rd Ste 110 Independence (44131) *(G-11116)*
80 Acres Urban Agriculture LLC (PA) 513 218-4387
4535 Este Ave Cincinnati (45232) *(G-3273)*
8888 Butler Investments Inc 440 748-0810
8888 Riverwood Dr North Ridgeville (44039) *(G-15205)*
9/10 Castings Inc 216 406-8907
313 Greenway Dr Chardon (44024) *(G-3094)*
9444 Ohio Holding Co 330 359-6291
1658 Us Route 62 E Winesburg (44690) *(G-20529)*
A A S Amels Sheet Meta L Inc 330 793-9326
222 Steel St Youngstown (44509) *(G-20830)*
A & A Discount Tire 330 863-1936
5125 Canton Rd Nw Carrollton (44615) *(G-2914)*
A & A Safety Inc 937 567-9781
4080 Industrial Ln Beavercreek (45430) *(G-1348)*
A & A Safety Inc (PA) 513 943-6100
1126 Ferris Rd Bldg B Amelia (45102) *(G-527)*
A & B Deburring Company 513 723-0444
525 Carr St Cincinnati (45203) *(G-3274)*
A & B Iron & Metal Company 937 228-1561
329 Washington St Dayton (45402) *(G-7997)*
A & B Machine Inc 937 492-8662
2040 Commerce Dr Sidney (45365) *(G-17011)*
A & B Printing, Fort Loramie Also called *Sharp Enterprises Inc* *(G-9806)*
A & B Tool & Manufacturing 419 382-0215
2921 South Ave Toledo (43609) *(G-18151)*
A & B Wood Design Assoc Inc 330 721-2789
3193 Greenwich Rd Wadsworth (44281) *(G-19218)*
A & C Welding Inc 330 762-4777
80 Cuyhoga Fls Indus Pkwy Peninsula (44264) *(G-15888)*
A & D Printing Co 440 975-8001
38287 Airport Pkwy Ste A Willoughby (44094) *(G-20263)*
A & D Wood Products Inc (PA) 419 331-8859
4220 Sherrick Rd Elida (45807) *(G-9192)*
A & E Butscha Co 513 761-1919
110 E Seymour Ave Cincinnati (45216) *(G-3275)*
A & E Powder Coating Ltd 937 525-3750
1511 Sheridan Ave Springfield (45505) *(G-17359)*
A & F Machine Products Co 440 826-0959
454 Geiger St Berea (44017) *(G-1588)*
A & G Manufacturing Co Inc (PA) 419 468-7433
280 Gelsanliter Rd Galion (44833) *(G-10119)*
A & G Manufacturing Co Inc 419 468-7433
165 Gelsanliter Rd Galion (44833) *(G-10120)*
A & H Automotive Industries 614 235-1759
701 Hadley Dr Columbus (43228) *(G-6514)*
A & H Truck Parts, Columbus Also called *A & H Automotive Industries* *(G-6514)*
A & I Metal Finishing, Vermilion Also called *Architectural and Industrial* *(G-19156)*
A & J Woodworking Inc 419 695-5655
808 Ohio St Delphos (45833) *(G-8734)*
A & L Inds Machining & Repr, Oregon Also called *A & L Industries* *(G-15551)*
A & L Industries 419 698-3733
2054 Grange St Oregon (43616) *(G-15551)*
A & L Machine Tool 513 863-2662
3080 Darrtown Rd Hamilton (45013) *(G-10527)*
A & L Metal Processing, Sandusky Also called *Equinox Enterprises LLC* *(G-16810)*
A & M Cheese Co 419 476-8369
253 Waggoner Blvd Toledo (43612) *(G-18152)*
A & M Creative Group Inc 330 452-8940
1704 Ira Turpin Way Ne Canton (44705) *(G-2555)*

A & M Kiln Dry Ltd 330 852-0505
1711 County Road 200 Dundee (44624) *(G-9016)*
A & M Kiln Dry Ltd 330 852-0505
10836 Lower Trail Rd Nw Dundee (44624) *(G-9017)*
A & M Logging 740 543-3171
8633 Township Road 289 Salineville (43945) *(G-16785)*
A & M Ornamental Mfg Co, Columbus Also called *T E Martindale Enterprises* *(G-7507)*
A & M Pallet 937 295-3093
3860 Rangeline Rd Russia (45363) *(G-16604)*
A & M Pallet Shop Inc 440 632-1941
14550 Madison Rd Middlefield (44062) *(G-13772)*
A & M Products 419 595-2092
3060 S County Road 591 Tiffin (44883) *(G-18039)*
A & M Refractories Inc 740 456-8020
202 West Ave New Boston (45662) *(G-14645)*
A & M Woodworking 330 893-1331
6440 State Route 515 Millersburg (44654) *(G-14054)*
A & P Tech Services Inc 330 535-1700
856 Home Ave Akron (44310) *(G-17)*
A & P Technology Inc 513 688-3200
4599 E Tech Dr Cincinnati (45245) *(G-3234)*
A & P Technology Inc 513 688-3200
4622 E Tech Dr Cincinnati (45245) *(G-3235)*
A & P Technology Inc 513 688-3200
4578 E Tech Dr Cincinnati (45245) *(G-3236)*
A & P Technology Inc 513 688-3200
4624 E Tech Dr Cincinnati (45245) *(G-3237)*
A & P Technology Inc (PA) 513 688-3200
4595 E Tech Dr Cincinnati (45245) *(G-3238)*
A & P Tool Inc 419 542-6681
801 Industrial Dr Hicksville (43526) *(G-10773)*
A & P Wood Products Inc 419 673-1196
15790 State Route 31 Kenton (43326) *(G-11400)*
A & R Machine Co Inc 330 832-4631
13212 Vega St Sw Massillon (44647) *(G-12957)*
A & S Inc 866 209-1574
6 N Main St Arcanum (45304) *(G-627)*
A & T Ornamental Iron Company 937 859-6006
415 E Sycamore St Miamisburg (45342) *(G-13635)*
A & W Spring Co Inc 937 222-7284
1000 E 2nd St Ste 8 Dayton (45402) *(G-7998)*
A & W Table Pad Co 800 541-0271
6520 Carnegie Ave Cleveland (44103) *(G-4582)*
A A A Professional Htg & Coolg 513 933-0564
535 N Broadway St Lebanon (45036) *(G-11628)*
A A E, Canton Also called *American Aluminum Extrusions* *(G-2572)*
A Aabaco Plastics Inc 216 663-9494
9520 Midwest Ave Cleveland (44125) *(G-4583)*
A and V Grinding Inc 937 444-4141
1115 Straight St 17 Cincinnati (45214) *(G-3276)*
A B & J Machining & Fabg 513 769-5900
10330 Wayne Ave Cincinnati (45215) *(G-3277)*
A B C Sign Inc 513 241-8884
38 W Mcmicken Ave Cincinnati (45202) *(G-3278)*
A B Siemer Inc 614 888-8855
150 E Campus View Blvd # 250 Columbus (43235) *(G-6515)*
A Best Trmt & Pest Ctrl Sups 330 434-5555
891 Gorge Blvd Akron (44310) *(G-18)*
A Bun In Oven 419 559-3056
1011 Hayes Ave Fremont (43420) *(G-9987)*
A C F, Lima Also called *Allen County Fabrication Inc* *(G-11834)*
A C Hadley - Printing Inc 937 426-0952
1530 Marsetta Dr Beavercreek (45432) *(G-1296)*
A C Knox Inc 513 921-5028
525 Purcell Ave Cincinnati (45205) *(G-3279)*
A C Products Co 330 698-1105
4299 S Apple Creek Rd Apple Creek (44606) *(G-601)*
A C Shutters Inc 216 429-2424
8119 Mansfield Ave Cleveland (44105) *(G-4584)*
A C Williams Co Inc (PA) 330 296-6110
700 N Walnut St Ravenna (44266) *(G-16362)*
A Class Coatings Inc 440 960-6869
4481 Oakhill Blvd Lorain (44053) *(G-12076)*
A Cupcake A Day LLC 330 389-1247
115 W Liberty St Stow (44224) *(G-17565)*
A Designers Workroom 513 251-7396
3066 Madison Rd 3 Cincinnati (45209) *(G-3280)*
A E F Inc 216 360-9800
24050 Commerce Park Fl 2 Cleveland (44122) *(G-4585)*
A E Ruston Electric LLC 740 286-3022
121 N David Ave Jackson (45640) *(G-11178)*
A E T, Maumee Also called *Applied Energy Tech Inc* *(G-13075)*
A E Wilson Holdings Inc 330 405-0316
2307 E Aurora Rd Twinsburg (44087) *(G-18722)*
A F Krainz Co 216 431-4341
1364 E 47th St Cleveland (44103) *(G-4586)*
A F P Ohio, Columbus Also called *Austin Foam Plastics Inc* *(G-6632)*
A G Industries Inc 330 220-0050
2963 Interstate Pkwy Brunswick (44212) *(G-2185)*
A G Mercury, Galion Also called *A & G Manufacturing Co Inc* *(G-10119)*

ALPHABETIC SECTION
A-Gas US Holdings Inc (HQ)

A G Parts Inc 937 596-6448
500 N Linden St Jackson Center (45334) ***(G-11204)***

A G Ruff Paper Specialties Co 513 891-7990
4320 Indeco Ct Blue Ash (45241) ***(G-1718)***

A G S Ohio, Macedonia *Also called AGS Custom Graphics Inc* ***(G-12275)***

A Grade Notes Inc (PA) 614 766-9999
6385 Shier Rings Rd Ste 1 Dublin (43016) ***(G-8871)***

A Graphic Solution 216 228-7223
14900 Detroit Ave Ste 205 Cleveland (44107) ***(G-4587)***

A H Marty Co Ltd 216 641-8950
6900 Union Ave Cleveland (44105) ***(G-4588)***

A H Pelz Co 216 861-1882
2498 Superior Ave E Cleveland (44114) ***(G-4589)***

A I M Specialists, Toledo *Also called Print All Inc* ***(G-18484)***

A I P, Columbus *Also called American Isostatic Presses Inc* ***(G-6583)***

A J Construction Co 330 539-9544
870 Shannon Rd Girard (44420) ***(G-10251)***

A J Oster Foils LLC 330 823-1700
2081 Mccrea St Alliance (44601) ***(G-447)***

A J Rose Mfg Co (PA) 216 631-4645
38000 Chester Rd Avon (44011) ***(G-936)***

A J Rose Mfgco 216 631-4645
3115 W 38th St Cleveland (44109) ***(G-4590)***

A Jack' S Industries, Columbus *Also called Atlas Gear and Machine Co* ***(G-6626)***

A Jacks Manufacturing Co 216 531-1010
1441 Chardon Rd Cleveland (44117) ***(G-4591)***

A K Athletic Equipment Inc 614 920-3069
8015 Howe Industrial Pkwy Canal Winchester (43110) ***(G-2497)***

A K Ready Mix LLC 740 286-8900
441 Dixon Run Rd Jackson (45640) ***(G-11179)***

A L Callahan Door Sales 419 884-3667
35 Industrial Dr Mansfield (44904) ***(G-12399)***

A M C P, Greenfield *Also called American Made Corrugated Packg* ***(G-10346)***

A M D 440 918-8930
4580 Beidler Rd Willoughby (44094) ***(G-20264)***

A M W, Columbus *Also called Assembly Machining Wire Pdts* ***(G-6622)***

A Metalcraft Associates Inc 937 693-4008
18965 State Route 219 Botkins (45306) ***(G-1931)***

A N H 513 576-6240
4065 Clough Woods Dr Batavia (45103) ***(G-1121)***

A P O Holdings Inc 330 455-8925
1405 Timken Pl Sw Canton (44706) ***(G-2556)***

A P Production & Service 740 745-5317
12546 Pleasant Valley Rd Utica (43080) ***(G-19023)***

A P S, Dayton *Also called Aps-Materials Inc* ***(G-8034)***

A P T, Middlefield *Also called American Plastic Tech Inc* ***(G-13777)***

A Park Ohio Company, Wickliffe *Also called PMC Industries Corp* ***(G-20227)***

A Plus Powder Coaters Inc 330 482-4389
1384 Kauffman Ave Columbiana (44408) ***(G-6452)***

A Plus Propane LLC 419 399-4445
8622 Us Route 127 Paulding (45879) ***(G-15854)***

A Plus Signs & Graphics, Barberton *Also called International Installations* ***(G-1077)***

A Plus Signs & Graphix 330 848-4800
833 E Waterloo Rd Akron (44306) ***(G-19)***

A Printed Impression, Newark *Also called Crain-Tharp Printing Inc* ***(G-14866)***

A Quick Copy Center, Cleveland *Also called T H E B Inc* ***(G-6145)***

A R C, Troy *Also called ARC Abrasives Inc* ***(G-18638)***

A R C of Dayton, Dayton *Also called Hayes Reconditioning Group* ***(G-8246)***

A R Harding Publishing Co 614 231-5735
2878 E Main St Columbus (43209) ***(G-6516)***

A R J, Wickliffe *Also called Andy Russo Jr Inc* ***(G-20198)***

A R Schopps Sons Inc 330 821-8406
14536 Oyster Rd Alliance (44601) ***(G-448)***

A Raymond Tinnerman Indus Inc (HQ) 330 220-5100
1060 W 130th St Brunswick (44212) ***(G-2186)***

A Reed Excavating LLC 740 391-4985
52912 State Route 145 Beallsville (43716) ***(G-1288)***

A S C, Middleburg Heights *Also called Associated Software Cons Inc* ***(G-13761)***

A S D, Dayton *Also called Automation Systems Designs Inc* ***(G-8044)***

A S Manufacturing Inc 216 476-0656
4412 W 130th St Cleveland (44135) ***(G-4592)***

A S Nf Producing Inc 330 933-0622
10539 Schlabach Ave Ne Hartville (44632) ***(G-10682)***

A S T Machine Co 740 494-2013
1 N 4th St Prospect (43342) ***(G-16349)***

A S W, Bedford Heights *Also called American Spring Wire Corp* ***(G-1460)***

A Schulman Inc (HQ) 330 666-3751
3637 Ridgewood Rd Fairlawn (44333) ***(G-9589)***

A Schulman Inc 330 498-4840
8562 Port Jackson Ave Nw North Canton (44720) ***(G-15066)***

A Schulman Inc 440 224-7544
110 N Eagle St Geneva (44041) ***(G-10210)***

A Schulman Inc 330 773-2700
1353 Exeter Rd Akron (44306) ***(G-20)***

A Schulman Inc 419 872-1408
12600 Eckel Rd Perrysburg (43551) ***(G-15916)***

A Schulman Inc 909 356-8091
3637 Ridgewood Rd Fairlawn (44333) ***(G-9590)***

A Schulman Inc 330 630-0308
790 E Tallmadge Ave Akron (44310) ***(G-21)***

A Schulman Inc 330 630-3315
1183 Home Ave Akron (44310) ***(G-22)***

A Schulman Compression, Geneva *Also called A Schulman Inc* ***(G-10210)***

A Schulman International Inc (HQ) 330 666-3751
3637 Ridgewood Rd Fairlawn (44333) ***(G-9591)***

A Screen Printed Products 419 352-1535
17715 N Dixie Hwy Bowling Green (43402) ***(G-1943)***

A Service Glass Inc 937 426-4920
1363 N Fairfield Rd Beavercreek (45432) ***(G-1297)***

A Sign For The Times Inc 216 297-2977
4100 Mayfield Rd Cleveland (44121) ***(G-4593)***

A Simona Group Company, Newcomerstown *Also called Boltaron Inc* ***(G-14970)***

A Special Touch Embroidery LLC 740 858-2241
22326 State Route 73 Portsmouth (45663) ***(G-16276)***

A Stucki Company 412 424-0560
7376 Whipple Ave Nw North Canton (44720) ***(G-15067)***

A T & F Co, Cleveland *Also called American Tank & Fabricating Co* ***(G-4698)***

A T C, Westlake *Also called American Tchnical Coatings Inc* ***(G-20096)***

A T E C Diversified, Wilmington *Also called Atec Diversfd Wldg Fabrication* ***(G-20486)***

A T I, Spring Valley *Also called Advanced Telemetrics Intl* ***(G-17315)***

A T Tube Company Inc 330 336-8706
188 S Lyman St Wadsworth (44281) ***(G-19219)***

A To Z Paper Box Co 330 325-8722
4477 Tallmadge Rd Rootstown (44272) ***(G-16565)***

A To Z Portion Ctrl Meats Inc 419 358-2926
201 N Main St Bluffton (45817) ***(G-1883)***

A To Z Wear Ltd 513 923-4662
5647 Cheviot Rd Cincinnati (45247) ***(G-3281)***

A Twist On Olives LLC 614 823-8800
44 N State St Westerville (43081) ***(G-20032)***

A United 330 782-6005
5234 Southern Blvd Ste D Youngstown (44512) ***(G-20831)***

A V C, Canton *Also called Assocted Vsual Cmmncations Inc* ***(G-2577)***

A W S C O, Dayton *Also called American Woodwork Specialty Co* ***(G-8029)***

A W S Incorporated 419 352-5397
520 Hankey Ave Bowling Green (43402) ***(G-1944)***

A W Taylor Lumber Incorporated 440 577-1889
1114 State Route 7 S Pierpont (44082) ***(G-16063)***

A W Tipka Oil & Gas Inc 330 364-4333
2421 Johnstown Rd Ne Dover (44622) ***(G-8802)***

A Z Printing Inc (PA) 513 733-3900
10122 Reading Rd Cincinnati (45241) ***(G-3282)***

A Z Printing Inc 513 745-0700
4077 E Galbraith Rd Cincinnati (45236) ***(G-3283)***

A&E Machine & Fabrication Inc (PA) 740 820-4701
384 State Route 335 Beaver (45613) ***(G-1291)***

A&M Country Woodworking LLC 330 674-1011
7920 Township Road 574 Holmesville (44633) ***(G-10971)***

A&M Woodworking 513 722-5415
1924 W Loveland Ave Loveland (45140) ***(G-12173)***

A&S Machine 440 946-3976
38363 Western Pkwy Unit 1 Willoughby (44094) ***(G-20265)***

A+ Engineering Fabrication Inc 419 832-0748
17562 Beech St Grand Rapids (43522) ***(G-10314)***

A-1 Fabricators Finishers LLC 513 724-0383
4220 Curliss Ln Batavia (45103) ***(G-1122)***

A-1 Manufacturing Corp 216 475-6084
5446 Dunham Rd Maple Heights (44137) ***(G-12563)***

A-1 Printing Inc 419 294-5247
129 W Wyandot Ave Upper Sandusky (43351) ***(G-18945)***

A-1 Printing Inc (PA) 419 562-3111
825 S Sandusky Ave Bucyrus (44820) ***(G-2316)***

A-1 Printing Inc 419 468-5422
139 Harding Way W Galion (44833) ***(G-10121)***

A-1 Sprinkler Company Inc 937 859-6198
2383 Northpointe Dr Miamisburg (45342) ***(G-13636)***

A-1 Welding & Fabrication 440 233-8474
1005 E 32nd St Lorain (44055) ***(G-12077)***

A-1 Welding & Sandblasting, Columbus *Also called Carol J Guiler* ***(G-6745)***

A-A Blueprint Co Inc 330 794-8803
2757 Gilchrist Rd Akron (44305) ***(G-23)***

A-A1 Machine and Supply Co 440 346-0698
3130 Klages Blvd Tallmadge (44278) ***(G-17970)***

A-Best Termite and Pest Ctrl, Akron *Also called A Best Trmt & Pest Ctrl Sups* ***(G-18)***

A-Brite LP 216 252-2995
3000 W 121st St Cleveland (44111) ***(G-4594)***

A-Buck Manufacturing Inc 937 687-3738
12251 Eagle Rd New Lebanon (45345) ***(G-14706)***

A-D Machine, Euclid *Also called Bic Manufacturing Inc* ***(G-9405)***

A-Display Service Corp 614 469-1230
541 Dana Ave Columbus (43223) ***(G-6517)***

A-Gas Americas, Bowling Green *Also called A-Gas US Holdings Inc* ***(G-1945)***

A-Gas US Holdings Inc (HQ) 419 867-8990
1100 Haskins Rd Bowling Green (43402) ***(G-1945)***

ALPHABETIC

A-Gas US Inc (HQ) — ALPHABETIC SECTION

A-Gas US Inc (HQ) 800 372-1301
  1100 Haskins Rd Bowling Green (43402) *(G-1946)*

A-Kobak Container Company 330 225-7791
  1701 W 130th St Hinckley (44233) *(G-10896)*

A-Stamp Industries LLC 419 633-0451
  633 Commerce Dr Bryan (43506) *(G-2257)*

A-Wall, Cleveland Also called Component Systems Inc *(G-5012)*

A-Z Discount Printing, Cincinnati Also called A Z Printing Inc *(G-3282)*

A-Z Packaging Company 614 444-8441
  1221 Harmon Ave Columbus (43223) *(G-6518)*

A.I.M., Aurora Also called Advanced Innovative Mfg Inc *(G-867)*

A.V.E.C., Heath Also called American Vneer Edgebanding Inc *(G-10716)*

A/C Laser Technologies Inc 330 784-3355
  867 Moe Dr Ste F Akron (44310) *(G-24)*

A1 Industrial Painting Inc 330 750-9441
  635 Dumont Ave Struthers Struthers (44471) *(G-17811)*

A2z Pallets LLC 513 652-9026
  1292 Glendale Milford Rd Cincinnati (45215) *(G-3284)*

AA Pallets LLC 216 856-2614
  4326 W 48th St Cleveland (44144) *(G-4595)*

AA1 Tool and Tech Supply, Tallmadge Also called A-A1 Machine and Supply Co *(G-17970)*

AAA, Perrysburg Also called Industrial Hardwood Inc *(G-15966)*

AAA Galvanizing - Joliet Inc 513 871-5700
  4454 Steel Pl Cincinnati (45209) *(G-3285)*

AAA Laminating & Bindery, Fairfield Also called AAA Laminating and Bindery Inc *(G-9477)*

AAA Laminating and Bindery Inc 513 860-2680
  7209 Dixie Hwy Fairfield (45014) *(G-9477)*

AAA Plastics and Pallets Ltd 330 844-2556
  3505 York Rd Orrville (44667) *(G-15580)*

AAA Stamping Inc 216 749-4494
  4001 Pearl Rd Uppr Cleveland (44109) *(G-4596)*

Aabel Plumbing Inc 937 434-4343
  440 Congress Park Dr Dayton (45459) *(G-7999)*

Aadco Instruments Inc 513 467-1477
  145 S Miami Ave Cleves (45002) *(G-6354)*

Aap St. Marys Corp., Saint Marys Also called Kosei St Marys Corporation *(G-16688)*

Aardvark Graphic Enterprises L 419 352-3197
  123 S Main St Bowling Green (43402) *(G-1947)*

Aardvark Screen Prtg & EMB LLC 419 354-6686
  123 S Main St Bowling Green (43402) *(G-1948)*

Aardvark Sportswear Inc 330 793-9428
  5329 Mahoning Ave Youngstown (44515) *(G-20832)*

Aaron Smith 330 285-1360
  385 Rutland Ave Akron (44305) *(G-25)*

Aaronyx Design, Mansfield Also called Aaronyx Publishing *(G-12400)*

Aaronyx Publishing 419 747-2400
  1924 Springmill Rd Mansfield (44903) *(G-12400)*

AB Bonded Locksmiths Inc 513 531-7334
  4344 Montgomery Rd Cincinnati (45212) *(G-3286)*

AB Plastics Inc 513 576-6333
  1287 Us Route 50 Milford (45150) *(G-13992)*

AB Resources LLC 440 922-1098
  6802 W Snowville Rd Ste E Brecksville (44141) *(G-2017)*

AB&j Machng Fabrictn, Cincinnati Also called A B & J Machining & Fabg *(G-3277)*

Aba Gutters Inc 440 729-2177
  13046 Cherry Ln Chesterland (44026) *(G-3149)*

Abacus Biodiesel Complex, Columbus Also called Citi 2 Citi Logistics *(G-6766)*

Abanaki Corporation (PA) 440 543-7400
  17387 Munn Rd Chagrin Falls (44023) *(G-3034)*

ABB Autoclave Systems, Columbus Also called Avure Autoclave Systems Inc *(G-6637)*

ABB Inc 440 585-8500
  23000 Harvard Rd Beachwood (44122) *(G-1217)*

Abbey Carpet, Canton Also called Shaheen Oriental Rug Co Inc *(G-2813)*

Abbey Machine Products Co 216 481-0080
  1011 Lake Rd Medina (44256) *(G-13216)*

Abbot Bindery, Cleveland Also called Irvin Oslin Inc *(G-5476)*

Abbot Image Solutions LLC 937 382-6677
  185 Park Dr Wilmington (45177) *(G-20483)*

Abbott Laboratories 614 624-3191
  585 Cleveland Ave Columbus (43215) *(G-6519)*

Abbott Laboratories 614 624-3192
  350 N 5th St Columbus (43215) *(G-6520)*

Abbott Laboratories 614 624-7677
  3300 Stelzer Rd Columbus (43219) *(G-6521)*

Abbott Laboratories 614 624-6627
  1033 Kingsmill Pkwy Columbus (43229) *(G-6522)*

Abbott Laboratories 614 624-6627
  6550 Singletree Dr Columbus (43229) *(G-6523)*

Abbott Laboratories 800 551-5838
  625 Cleveland Ave Columbus (43215) *(G-6524)*

Abbott Laboratories 614 624-6088
  6 Cleveland Ave Columbus (43215) *(G-6525)*

Abbott Mechanical Services LLC 419 460-4315
  804 W Wayne St Maumee (43537) *(G-13065)*

Abbott Nutrition, Columbus Also called Abbott Laboratories *(G-6519)*

Abbott Nutrition Mfg Inc 614 624-7485
  625 Cleveland Ave Columbus (43215) *(G-6526)*

Abbott Signs (PA) 937 393-6600
  251 John St Hillsboro (45133) *(G-10876)*

Abbott Tool Inc 419 476-6742
  405 Dura Ave Toledo (43612) *(G-18153)*

Abby Industries LLC 513 502-9865
  346 Frizzell Ave Eaton (45320) *(G-9141)*

ABC Appliance Inc 419 693-4414
  3012 Navarre Ave Oregon (43616) *(G-15552)*

ABC Countertops, Toledo Also called Brad Snoderly *(G-18214)*

ABC Inoac Exterior Systems LLC 419 334-8951
  1410 Motor Ave Fremont (43420) *(G-9988)*

ABC Lettering & Embroidery 216 321-8338
  13727 Madison Ave Lakewood (44107) *(G-11508)*

ABC Plastics Inc 330 948-3322
  140 West Dr Lodi (44254) *(G-12002)*

Abco Bar & Tube Cutting Svc 513 697-9487
  7685 S State Route 48 # 1 Maineville (45039) *(G-12364)*

Abecs Community News 419 330-9658
  13900 Frankfort Rd Swanton (43558) *(G-17903)*

Abel Manufacturing Company 513 681-5000
  3474 Beekman St Cincinnati (45223) *(G-3287)*

Abel Metal Processing Inc 216 881-4156
  2105 E 77th St Cleveland (44103) *(G-4597)*

Abeon Medical Corporation 440 262-6000
  8006 Katherine Blvd Brecksville (44141) *(G-2018)*

Abhushan LLC 614 789-0632
  2815 Festival Ln Dublin (43017) *(G-8872)*

ABI Inc 216 378-1336
  26000 Richmond Rd Ste 4 Bedford (44146) *(G-1378)*

ABI Orthtc/Prosthetic Labs Ltd (HQ) 330 758-1143
  930 Trailwood Dr Youngstown (44512) *(G-20833)*

Abitec Corporation (HQ) 614 429-6464
  501 W 1st Ave Columbus (43215) *(G-6527)*

Abj Equipfix 419 684-5236
  202 Lucas St W Castalia (44824) *(G-2935)*

Abl Enterprises, North Olmsted Also called Hometown Threads *(G-15193)*

Abl Lighting Service, Akron Also called Bob King Sign Company Inc *(G-90)*

Abl Products Inc 216 281-2400
  3726 Ridge Rd Cleveland (44144) *(G-4598)*

Abl Screen Printing 440 914-0093
  30300 Solon Indus Pkwy Solon (44139) *(G-17097)*

Able Alloy Inc 216 251-6110
  3500 W 140th St Cleveland (44111) *(G-4599)*

Able Grinding Co Inc 216 961-6555
  10015 Walford Ave Cleveland (44102) *(G-4600)*

Able Industries Inc 614 252-1050
  870 N 20th St Columbus (43219) *(G-6528)*

Able Manufacturing, Columbus Also called Able Industries Inc *(G-6528)*

Able One's Moving Company, Cleveland Also called C P S Enterprises Inc *(G-4858)*

Able Pallet Mfg & Repr 614 444-2115
  1271 Harmon Ave Columbus (43223) *(G-6529)*

Able Printing Company 614 294-4547
  1325 Holly Ave Columbus (43212) *(G-6530)*

Able Tool Corporation 513 733-8989
  617 N Wayne Ave Cincinnati (45215) *(G-3288)*

ABM Drives Inc 513 576-1300
  394 Wards Corner Rd # 110 Loveland (45140) *(G-12174)*

About Cats & Dogs LLC 440 263-8989
  7600 Olde Eight Rd Hudson (44236) *(G-11025)*

About Golf, Maumee Also called Henry-Griffitts Limited *(G-13117)*

About Time Software Inc 614 759-6295
  12790 Pickering Rd Pickerington (43147) *(G-16038)*

Abp Induction LLC 330 830-6252
  607 1st St Sw Massillon (44646) *(G-12958)*

ABRA Auto Body & Glass LP 513 367-9200
  10106 Harrison Ave Harrison (45030) *(G-10627)*

ABRA Auto Body & Glass LP 513 247-3400
  6947 E Kemper Rd Cincinnati (45249) *(G-3289)*

ABRA Auto Body & Glass LP 513 755-7709
  8445 Cncnnati Columbus Rd West Chester (45069) *(G-19635)*

ABRA Autobody & Glass, Harrison Also called ABRA Auto Body & Glass LP *(G-10627)*

ABRA Autobody & Glass, Cincinnati Also called ABRA Auto Body & Glass LP *(G-3289)*

Abrasive Leaders & Innovators, Fairborn Also called Ali Industries Inc *(G-9450)*

Abrasive Source Inc 937 526-9753
  211 W Main St Russia (45363) *(G-16605)*

Abrasive Supply Company Inc 330 894-2818
  25240 State Route 172 Minerva (44657) *(G-14175)*

Abrasive Technology Inc (PA) 740 548-4100
  8400 Green Meadows Dr N Lewis Center (43035) *(G-11740)*

Abrasive Technology Lapidary 740 548-4855
  8400 Green Meadows Dr N Lewis Center (43035) *(G-11741)*

Abraxus Salt Inc 440 743-7669
  5595 Ridge Rd Cleveland (44129) *(G-4601)*

ABS Materials Inc 330 234-7999
  1909 Old Mansfield Rd Wooster (44691) *(G-20553)*

Absolute Cnc Machining LLC 937 855-0406
  2643 Dyton Grmantown Pike Germantown (45327) *(G-10240)*

Absolute Grinding Co Inc 440 974-4030
  7007 Spinach Dr Mentor (44060) *(G-13369)*

Absolute Impressions Inc (PA).....614 840-0599
281 Enterprise Dr Lewis Center (43035) ***(G-11742)***
Absolute Smile LLC.....937 293-9866
4469 Far Hills Ave Dayton (45429) ***(G-8000)***
Absolutely Paper Established.....216 932-4822
14000 Mont Ave Cleveland (44118) ***(G-4602)***
Absorbcore LLC.....440 614-0457
30275 Lorain Rd North Olmsted (44070) ***(G-15180)***
Absorbent Products Company Inc.....419 352-5353
2121 S Woodland Cir Bowling Green (43402) ***(G-1949)***
Abstract Displays Inc.....513 985-9700
6465 Creek Rd Blue Ash (45242) ***(G-1719)***
AC Shiners Inc.....513 738-1573
5747 Jenkins Rd Okeana (45053) ***(G-15515)***
Academy Graphic Comm Inc.....216 661-2550
1000 Brookpark Rd Cleveland (44109) ***(G-4603)***
Acb Three Inc.....614 873-4680
9341 Industrial Pkwy Plain City (43064) ***(G-16168)***
ACC Automation Co Inc.....330 928-3821
475 Wolf Ledges Pkwy Akron (44311) ***(G-26)***
Accel Color, Avon *Also called Accel Corporation* ***(G-937)***
Accel Color, Avon *Also called Accel Corporation* ***(G-938)***
Accel Corporation.....440 327-7418
38620 Chester Rd Avon (44011) ***(G-937)***
Accel Corporation (HQ).....440 934-7711
38620 Chester Rd Avon (44011) ***(G-938)***
Accel Group Inc (PA).....330 336-0317
325 Quadral Dr Wadsworth (44281) ***(G-19220)***
Accel Performance Group LLC (HQ).....216 658-6413
6100 Oak Tree Blvd # 200 Independence (44131) ***(G-11117)***
Accent Drapery Co Inc.....614 488-0741
1180 Goodale Blvd Columbus (43212) ***(G-6531)***
Accent Drapery Supply Co, Columbus *Also called Accent Drapery Co Inc* ***(G-6531)***
Accent Manufacturing Inc (PA).....330 724-7704
1026 Gardner Blvd Norton (44203) ***(G-15355)***
Accent Showroom & Design Ctr, Norton *Also called Accent Manufacturing Inc* ***(G-15355)***
Accent Signs and Graphics, Blue Ash *Also called All Signs Express Inc* ***(G-1727)***
Accents By Renoir, Celina *Also called Renoir Visions LLC* ***(G-2982)***
Accesories Tools, Painesville *Also called Alpha Omega Dev & Mch Co* ***(G-15708)***
Access 2 Communications Inc.....800 561-1110
225 Technology Way Steubenville (43952) ***(G-17525)***
Access Envelope Inc.....513 889-0888
2348 Pleasant Ave Hamilton (45015) ***(G-10528)***
Access Manufacturing Svcs LLC.....330 659-9893
4807 Hawkins Rd Richfield (44286) ***(G-16461)***
Access To Independence Inc.....330 296-8111
4960 S Prospect St Ravenna (44266) ***(G-16363)***
Acclaimd Inc.....614 219-9519
1275 Kinnear Rd Columbus (43212) ***(G-6532)***
Acco Brands USA LLC.....937 495-6323
4751 Hempstead Station Dr Kettering (45429) ***(G-11426)***
Accounting Software Solutions, Solon *Also called Sherwin Software Solutions* ***(G-17230)***
Accro-Cast Corporation.....937 228-0497
4147 Gardendale Ave Dayton (45417) ***(G-8001)***
Accu Pak Mfg Inc.....330 644-3015
2422 Pickle Rd Akron (44312) ***(G-27)***
Accu Tool Inc.....937 667-5878
9765 Julie Ct Tipp City (45371) ***(G-18095)***
Accu-Feed Engineering.....419 668-7990
50 Newton St Norwalk (44857) ***(G-15378)***
Accu-Grind & Mfg Co Inc.....937 224-3303
272 Leo St Dayton (45404) ***(G-8002)***
Accu-Rite Tool & Die Co Corp.....330 497-9959
7295 Sunset Strip Ave Nw Canton (44720) ***(G-2557)***
Accu-Sign.....216 544-2059
3652 Elm Brook Dr Broadview Heights (44147) ***(G-2086)***
Accu-Tech Manufacturing Co.....330 848-8100
195 Olivet Ave Coventry Township (44319) ***(G-7760)***
Accu-Tech Mfg & Support.....440 205-8882
8875 East Ave Mentor (44060) ***(G-13370)***
Accu-Tek Tool & Die Inc.....330 726-1946
1390 Allen Rd Bldg 1 Salem (44460) ***(G-16713)***
Accubuilt Inc (PA).....419 224-3910
2550 Cent Point Pkwy Lima (45804) ***(G-11829)***
Accubuilt Inc.....419 224-3910
2550 Central Point Pkwy Lima (45804) ***(G-11830)***
Accufab Inc.....513 942-1929
9059 Sutton Pl West Chester (45011) ***(G-19636)***
Accufilm, Hebron *Also called Virgail Industries Inc* ***(G-10770)***
Accuform Manufacturing Inc.....330 797-9291
2750 Intertech Dr Youngstown (44509) ***(G-20834)***
Accumulus Software.....937 435-0861
6708 Innsbruck Dr Dayton (45459) ***(G-8003)***
Accuphase Metal Treating LLC.....937 610-5934
2490 Arbor Blvd Moraine (45439) ***(G-14328)***
Accurate Automatic Mfg Ltd.....330 435-4575
141 Factory St Creston (44217) ***(G-7802)***
Accurate Electronics Inc.....330 682-7015
169 S Main St Orrville (44667) ***(G-15581)***
Accurate Fab LLC.....330 562-0566
1400 Miller Pkwy Streetsboro (44241) ***(G-17656)***
Accurate Gear Manufacturing Co.....513 761-3220
16 E 73rd St Cincinnati (45216) ***(G-3290)***
Accurate Insullation LLC.....302 241-0940
495 S High St Ste 50 Columbus (43215) ***(G-6533)***
Accurate Machining & Welding.....937 584-4518
764 N State Route 729 Sabina (45169) ***(G-16615)***
Accurate Manufacturing Company.....614 878-6510
1940 Lone Eagle St Columbus (43228) ***(G-6534)***
Accurate Mechanical Inc.....740 681-1332
566 Mill Park Dr Lancaster (43130) ***(G-11538)***
Accurate Metal Machining Inc.....440 350-8225
882 Callendar Blvd Painesville (44077) ***(G-15704)***
Accurate Metal Sawing Svc Co (PA).....440 205-3205
8989 Tyler Blvd Mentor (44060) ***(G-13371)***
Accurate Plasma Cutting Inc.....440 943-1655
1271 E 289th St Wickliffe (44092) ***(G-20195)***
Accurate Plastics LLC.....330 346-0048
4430 Crystal Pkwy Kent (44240) ***(G-11288)***
Accurate Products Company.....740 498-7202
98 Elizabeth St Newcomerstown (43832) ***(G-14969)***
Accurate Tech Inc.....440 951-9153
7230 Industrial Park Blvd Mentor (44060) ***(G-13372)***
Accurate Tool Co Inc.....330 332-9448
1065 Salem Pkwy Salem (44460) ***(G-16714)***
Accuscan Instruments Inc.....614 878-6644
5098 Trabue Rd Columbus (43228) ***(G-6535)***
Accushred LLC.....419 244-7473
1114 W Central Ave Toledo (43610) ***(G-18154)***
Accutech Films Inc (HQ).....419 678-8700
620 Hardin St Coldwater (45828) ***(G-6398)***
Accutech Plastic Molding Inc.....937 233-0017
5015 Kitridge Rd Dayton (45424) ***(G-8004)***
Accutech Sign Shop.....513 385-3595
9316 Colerain Ave Cincinnati (45251) ***(G-3291)***
Ace, Cleveland *Also called Brothers Equipment Inc* ***(G-4843)***
Ace American Wire Die Co.....330 425-7269
9041 Dutton Dr Twinsburg (44087) ***(G-18723)***
Ace Assembly Packaging Inc.....330 866-9117
133 N Mill St Waynesburg (44688) ***(G-19561)***
Ace Boiler & Welding Co Inc.....330 745-4443
2891 Newpark Dr Barberton (44203) ***(G-1048)***
Ace Equipment Company, Cleveland *Also called Armature Coil Equipment Inc* ***(G-4734)***
Ace Gasket Manufacturing Co.....513 271-6321
7873 Main St Cincinnati (45244) ***(G-3292)***
Ace Grinding Co.....440 951-6760
37518 N Industrial Pkwy Willoughby (44094) ***(G-20266)***
Ace Hydraulics, Bedford *Also called K C N Technologies LLC* ***(G-1419)***
Ace Lumber Company.....330 744-3167
1039 Poland Ave Youngstown (44502) ***(G-20835)***
Ace Manufacturing Company.....513 541-2490
5452 Spellmire Dr West Chester (45246) ***(G-19825)***
Ace Metal Stamping Company, Cleveland *Also called Continental Business Entps Inc* ***(G-5020)***
Ace Plastics Co.....330 928-7720
122 E Tuscarawas Ave Stow (44224) ***(G-17566)***
Ace Precision Industries Inc.....330 633-8523
925 Moe Dr Akron (44310) ***(G-28)***
Ace Printing LLC.....614 855-7227
7788 Central College Rd B New Albany (43054) ***(G-14603)***
Ace Products Co of Toledo Inc.....419 472-1247
4902 Douglas Rd Toledo (43613) ***(G-18155)***
Ace Prosthetics Inc.....614 291-8325
4971 Arlngton Centre Blvd Columbus (43220) ***(G-6536)***
ACE Ready Mix LLC.....330 745-8125
3826 Summit Rd Norton (44203) ***(G-15356)***
Ace Ready Mix Concrete Co Inc.....330 745-8125
3826 Summit Rd Norton (44203) ***(G-15357)***
Ace Rubber Products Division, Akron *Also called Garro Tread Corporation* ***(G-181)***
Ace Rubber Stamp & Off Sup Co.....216 771-8483
3110 Payne Ave Cleveland (44114) ***(G-4604)***
Ace Sanitary, West Chester *Also called Ace Manufacturing Company* ***(G-19825)***
Ace Transfer Company.....937 398-1103
1017 Hometown St Springfield (45504) ***(G-17360)***
Ace Truck Equipment Co.....740 453-0551
1130 Newark Rd Zanesville (43701) ***(G-21091)***
Acense LLC.....330 242-0046
8941 Dutton Dr Twinsburg (44087) ***(G-18724)***
Acer Contracting LLC.....702 236-5917
3840 N High St Ste B Columbus (43214) ***(G-6537)***
Ach LLC.....419 621-5748
3020 Tiffin Ave Sandusky (44870) ***(G-16791)***
Ach Sandusky Plastics, Sandusky *Also called Ach LLC* ***(G-16791)***
Achill Island Composites LLC.....440 838-1746
6981 Chapel Hill Dr Brecksville (44141) ***(G-2019)***
Achilles Aerospace Pdts Inc.....330 425-8444
2100 Enterprise Pkwy Twinsburg (44087) ***(G-18725)***

ALPHABETIC

Aci Industries Ltd (PA) 740 368-4160
970 Pittsburgh Dr Delaware (43015) ***(G-8648)***
Aci Industries Converting Ltd (HQ) 740 368-4160
970 Pittsburgh Dr Delaware (43015) ***(G-8649)***
Aci Services Inc (PA) 740 435-0240
125 Steubenville Ave Cambridge (43725) ***(G-2421)***
Aclara Technologies LLC 440 528-7200
30400 Solon Rd Solon (44139) ***(G-17098)***
Acm, Hinckley *Also called American Cube Mold Inc* ***(G-10898)***
Acm Ohio, Waverly *Also called News Watchman & Paper* ***(G-19553)***
Acme Boiler Co Inc 216 961-2471
3718 Ridge Rd Cleveland (44144) ***(G-4605)***
Acme Company 330 758-2313
9495 Harvard Blvd Poland (44514) ***(G-16236)***
Acme Duplicating Co 216 241-1241
1565 Greenleaf Cir Westlake (44145) ***(G-20086)***
Acme Fence & Lumber, Akron *Also called Randy Lewis Inc* ***(G-342)***
Acme Industrial Group Inc 330 821-3900
540 N Freedom Ave Alliance (44601) ***(G-449)***
Acme Lead Burning Company, Cleveland *Also called Acme Boiler Co Inc* ***(G-4605)***
Acme Lifting Products Inc 440 838-4430
6892 W Snowville Rd Ste 2 Cleveland (44141) ***(G-4606)***
Acme Machine Automatics Inc 419 453-0010
111 Progressive Dr Ottoville (45876) ***(G-15679)***
Acme Machine Technology LLC 419 594-3349
115 Main St Oakwood (45873) ***(G-15468)***
Acme Paper Tube, Cleveland *Also called Acme Spirally Wound Paper Pdts* ***(G-4607)***
Acme Printing, Westlake *Also called Acme Duplicating Co* ***(G-20086)***
Acme Printing Co Inc 419 626-4426
2143 Sherman St Sandusky (44870) ***(G-16792)***
Acme Spirally Wound Paper Pdts 216 267-2950
4810 W 139th St Cleveland (44135) ***(G-4607)***
Acme Steak & Seafood Inc 330 270-8000
31 Bissell Ave Youngstown (44505) ***(G-20836)***
Acme Surface Dynamics Inc 330 821-3900
555 N Freedom Ave Alliance (44601) ***(G-450)***
Aco Polymer Products Inc (HQ) 440 285-7000
9470 Pinecone Dr Mentor (44060) ***(G-13373)***
Acoh Inc 419 741-3195
210 Selhorst Dr Apt 213 Ottawa (45875) ***(G-15647)***
Acon Inc 513 276-2111
11408 Dogleg Rd Tipp City (45371) ***(G-18096)***
Acor Orthopaedic Inc 216 662-4500
18530 S Miles Rd Cleveland (44128) ***(G-4608)***
Acor Orthopaedic Inc 440 532-0117
18700 S Miles Rd Cleveland (44128) ***(G-4609)***
Acorn Technology Corporation 216 663-1244
23103 Miles Rd Cleveland (44128) ***(G-4610)***
Acouflow Therapeutics LLC 513 558-0073
6914 Copperglow Ct Cincinnati (45244) ***(G-3293)***
Acoustical Publications Inc 440 835-0101
27101 E Oviatt Rd Bay Village (44140) ***(G-1204)***
Acreo Inc 513 734-3327
3209 Marshall Dr Amelia (45102) ***(G-528)***
Acro Tool & Die Company 330 773-5173
325 Morgan Ave Akron (44311) ***(G-29)***
Acrodyne Mfg Co 614 443-5517
41 Kingston Ave Columbus (43207) ***(G-6538)***
Acromet Metal Fabricators, Cleveland *Also called G T Metal Fabricators Inc* ***(G-5284)***
Acrylic Arts 440 537-0300
3698 G P Easterly Rd West Farmington (44491) ***(G-19918)***
Acrylicon Inc 614 263-2086
1976 Britains Ln Columbus (43224) ***(G-6539)***
Act, Dublin *Also called Automation and Ctrl Tech Inc* ***(G-8886)***
Act For Sneca Cnty Oprtnty Ctr 419 447-4362
58 Braden Ct Tiffin (44883) ***(G-18040)***
Actega North America Inc 800 426-4657
11264 Grooms Rd Blue Ash (45242) ***(G-1720)***
Action Air & Hydraulics Inc 937 372-8614
1087 Bellbrook Ave Xenia (45385) ***(G-20753)***
Action Blacktop Sealcoating & 937 667-4769
7830 Kessler Frederick Rd Tipp City (45371) ***(G-18097)***
Action Coupling & Eqp Inc 330 279-4242
8248 County Road 245 Holmesville (44633) ***(G-10972)***
Action Defense LLC 440 503-7886
6518 Denison Blvd Cleveland (44130) ***(G-4611)***
Action Door, Mentor On The Lake *Also called Mentor Inc* ***(G-13632)***
Action Enterprise 740 522-1678
416 W Main St Newark (43055) ***(G-14847)***
Action Group Inc 614 868-8868
411 Reynoldsburg New Blacklick (43004) ***(G-1676)***
Action Industries Ltd (PA) 216 252-7800
13325 Darice Pkwy Strongsville (44149) ***(G-17705)***
Action Machine & Manufacturing 513 899-3889
6788 E Us Highway 22 & 3 Morrow (45152) ***(G-14407)***
Action Mechanical Repair Inc 513 353-1046
7760 Harrison Ave Cincinnati (45247) ***(G-3294)***
Action Precision Products Inc 419 737-2348
100 E North Ave Pioneer (43554) ***(G-16083)***
Action Printing & Photography 419 332-9615
626 Grant St Fremont (43420) ***(G-9989)***
Action Printing Inc 330 963-7772
2307 E Aurora Rd Ste 8 Twinsburg (44087) ***(G-18726)***
Action Prosthetics LLC 937 548-9100
1498 N Broadway St Ste 3 Greenville (45331) ***(G-10359)***
Action Rubber Co Inc 937 866-5975
601 Fame Rd Dayton (45449) ***(G-8005)***
Action Sign Inc 330 966-0390
3140 Stage St Greentown (44630) ***(G-10356)***
Action Signs, Newark *Also called Action Enterprise* ***(G-14847)***
Action Sports Apparel Inc 330 848-9300
3070 Wadsworth Rd Norton (44203) ***(G-15358)***
Action Super Abrasive Pdts Inc 330 673-7333
945 Greenbriar Pkwy Kent (44240) ***(G-11289)***
Actipro Software LLC 888 922-8477
8576 Somerset Dr Broadview Heights (44147) ***(G-2087)***
Actis Ltd 614 436-0600
3841b Attucks Dr Powell (43065) ***(G-16306)***
Active Daily Living LLC 513 607-6769
3308 Bishop St Cincinnati (45220) ***(G-3295)***
Activities Press Inc 440 953-1200
7181 Industrial Park Blvd Mentor (44060) ***(G-13374)***
Actual Brewing Company LLC 614 636-3825
655 N James Rd Columbus (43219) ***(G-6540)***
Actual Industries LLC 614 379-2739
655 N James Rd Columbus (43219) ***(G-6541)***
Acu-Serve Corp 330 923-5258
2020 Front St Ste 205 Cuyahoga Falls (44221) ***(G-7830)***
Acuity Brands Lighting Inc 740 349-4343
214 Oakwood Ave Newark (43055) ***(G-14848)***
Acuity Brands Lighting Inc 740 349-4409
465 Mckinley Ave Newark (43055) ***(G-14849)***
ACUITY BRANDS LIGHTING, INC., Newark *Also called Acuity Brands Lighting Inc* ***(G-14848)***
Acuren Inspection Inc 937 228-9729
705 Albany St Dayton (45417) ***(G-8006)***
Acutemp, Moraine *Also called Doubleday Acquisitions LLC* ***(G-14347)***
Acutemp Thermal Systems 937 312-0114
2900 Dryden Rd Moraine (45439) ***(G-14329)***
Ad Piston Ring Company LLC 216 781-5200
3145 Superior Ave E Cleveland (44114) ***(G-4612)***
Ad-Pro Signs I LLC 513 922-5046
11336 Dallas Blvd Cincinnati (45231) ***(G-3296)***
Ada Herald 419 634-6055
229 N Main St Ada (45810) ***(G-2)***
Ada Solutions Inc 440 576-0423
901 Ftville Richmond Rd E Jefferson (44047) ***(G-11223)***
Ada Technologies Inc 419 634-7000
805 E North Ave Ada (45810) ***(G-3)***
Adairs Pavers 937 454-9302
50 Lakin Ct Vandalia (45377) ***(G-19112)***
Adam Printing, West Chester *Also called Cornerstone Industries Lcc* ***(G-19685)***
Adams Automatic Inc 440 235-4416
26070 N Depot St Olmsted Falls (44138) ***(G-15527)***
Adams Bros Concrete Pdts Ltd 740 452-7566
3401 East Pike Zanesville (43701) ***(G-21092)***
Adams Brothers Inc 740 819-0323
1501 Woodlawn Ave Zanesville (43701) ***(G-21093)***
Adams County Lumber, Manchester *Also called Vances Department Store* ***(G-12398)***
Adams Custom Woodworking 513 761-1395
324 W Wyoming Ave Cincinnati (45215) ***(G-3297)***
Adams Fabricating Inc 330 866-2986
10125 Sandyville Ave East Sparta (44626) ***(G-9093)***
Adams Manufacturing Company (PA) 216 662-1600
9790 Midwest Ave Cleveland (44125) ***(G-4613)***
Adams Publishing Group LLC (HQ) 740 592-6612
9300 Johnson Hollow Rd Athens (45701) ***(G-821)***
Adams Signs, Massillon *Also called Identitek Systems Inc* ***(G-13002)***
Adams Street Publishing Co 419 244-9859
1120 Adams St Toledo (43604) ***(G-18156)***
Adapt-A-Pak Inc 937 845-0386
9215 State Route 201 Tipp City (45371) ***(G-18098)***
Adaptall America Inc 330 425-4114
9047 Dutton Dr Twinsburg (44087) ***(G-18727)***
Adaptive Data Inc 937 436-2343
8170 Washington Vlg Dr Dayton (45458) ***(G-8007)***
Adare Pharmaceuticals Inc (HQ) 937 898-9669
845 Center Dr Vandalia (45377) ***(G-19113)***
ADB Safegate Americas LLC 614 861-1304
977 Gahanna Pkwy Columbus (43230) ***(G-6542)***
Adchem Adhesives Inc 440 526-1976
4111 E Royalton Rd Cleveland (44147) ***(G-4614)***
Adcraft Decals Inc 216 524-2934
7708 Commerce Park Oval Cleveland (44131) ***(G-4615)***
Adcura Mfg, Springboro *Also called Rct Industries Inc* ***(G-17351)***
Adcura Mfg 937 222-3800
1314 Farr Dr Dayton (45404) ***(G-8008)***
Add-A-Trap LLC 330 750-0417
488 Como St Struthers (44471) ***(G-17812)***

Added Edge Assembly Inc 216 464-4305
26800 Fargo Ave Ste A Cleveland (44146) *(G-4616)*
Added Touch Decorating Gallery 419 747-3146
1162 Cobblefield Dr Ontario (44903) *(G-15537)*
Addis Glass Fabricating Inc 513 860-3340
9418 Sutton Pl West Chester (45011) *(G-19637)*
Addisonmckee Inc (PA) 513 228-7000
1637 Kingsview Dr Lebanon (45036) *(G-11629)*
Addition Mfg Tech LLC (PA) 513 228-7000
1637 Kingsview Dr Lebanon (45036) *(G-11630)*
Additive Metal Alloys Ltd 800 687-6110
1421 Holloway Rd Ste B Holland (43528) *(G-10914)*
Additive Technology Inc 419 968-2777
404 W Railroad St Middle Point (45863) *(G-13754)*
Adelman's Truck Sales, Canton *Also called Adelmans Truck Parts Corp (G-2558)*
Adelmans Truck Parts Corp (PA) 330 456-0206
2000 Waynesburg Dr Se Canton (44707) *(G-2558)*
Adelmans Truck Parts Corp 216 362-0500
2000 Waynesburg Dr Se Canton (44707) *(G-2559)*
Adelphi Enterprises 937 372-3791
1340 Gultice Rd Xenia (45385) *(G-20754)*
Adelphia, Wellington *Also called Forest City Technologies Inc (G-19581)*
Ademco Inc 513 772-1851
5601 Creek Rd Ste Ab Blue Ash (45242) *(G-1721)*
Ademco Inc 440 439-7002
7710 First Pl Ste A Bedford (44146) *(G-1379)*
Adept Manufacturing Corp 937 222-7110
511 N Findlay St Dayton (45404) *(G-8009)*
Adex International, Cincinnati *Also called Affinity Disp Expositions Inc (G-3306)*
Adex International, Cincinnati *Also called Affinity Disp Expositions Inc (G-3307)*
Adexis, Columbus *Also called Fusionstorm (G-6494)*
Adgo Incorporated 513 752-6880
3988 Mcmann Rd Cincinnati (45245) *(G-3239)*
Adhesves Sealants Coatings Div, Blue Ash *Also called HB Fuller Company (G-1786)*
ADI, Sheffield Village *Also called Advanced Design Industries Inc (G-16965)*
ADI Global Distribution, Blue Ash *Also called Ademco Inc (G-1721)*
ADI Global Distribution, Bedford *Also called Ademco Inc (G-1379)*
ADI Machining Inc 440 277-4141
4686 French Creek Rd Sheffield Village (44054) *(G-16964)*
Adidas North America Inc 330 562-4689
549 S Chillicothe Rd Aurora (44202) *(G-866)*
Adidas Outlet Store Aurora, Aurora *Also called Adidas North America Inc (G-866)*
Adient US LLC 937 383-5200
1147 N Washington St Greenfield (45123) *(G-10345)*
Adient US LLC 419 662-4950
7560 Arbor Dr Northwood (43619) *(G-15330)*
Adjustable Kicker LLC 740 362-9170
45 River St Delaware (43015) *(G-8650)*
Adkel Corp (PA) 740 452-6973
2920 Newark Rd Zanesville (43701) *(G-21094)*
Adkins Marlena 216 704-2751
4729 W 157th St Cleveland (44135) *(G-4617)*
Adkins & Co Inc 216 521-6323
14541 Madison Ave Cleveland (44107) *(G-4618)*
Adkins & Sons, Oak Hill *Also called Denver Adkins (G-15450)*
Adkins Printing, Cleveland *Also called Adkins & Co Inc (G-4618)*
Adler & Company Inc 513 248-1500
6801 Shawnee Run Rd Cincinnati (45243) *(G-3298)*
Adler Team Sports, Euclid *Also called R & A Sports Inc (G-9438)*
ADM, Toledo *Also called Archer-Daniels-Midland Company (G-18189)*
ADM, Fostoria *Also called Archer-Daniels-Midland Company (G-9833)*
ADM, Chillicothe *Also called Archer-Daniels-Midland Company (G-3175)*
ADM, Sugarcreek *Also called Archer-Daniels-Midland Company (G-17841)*
Adma Products, Hudson *Also called Advanced Materials Products (G-11026)*
Admail.net, Chagrin Falls *Also called List Media Inc (G-3023)*
Admark Printing Inc 937 833-5111
310 Sycamore St Brookville (45309) *(G-2160)*
Admaster Supply, New Paris *Also called Ruthie Ann Inc (G-14755)*
Admiral Products Company Inc 216 671-0600
4101 W 150th St Cleveland (44135) *(G-4619)*
Admiral Therapeutics LLC 410 908-8906
3101 Warrington Rd Shaker Heights (44120) *(G-16925)*
Adna Inc 614 397-4974
6866 Mcdougal Ct Dublin (43017) *(G-8873)*
Adohio, Columbus *Also called Ohio Newspaper Services Inc (G-7252)*
Adonai Technologies LLC 513 560-9020
1223 Hook Dr Middletown (45042) *(G-13875)*
Adr Fuel Inc 419 872-2178
353 Elm St Perrysburg (43551) *(G-15917)*
Adria Scientific GL Works Co 440 474-6691
2683 State Route 534 S Geneva (44041) *(G-10211)*
Adroit Thinking Inc 419 542-9363
10860 State Route 2 Hicksville (43526) *(G-10774)*
ADS, Hilliard *Also called Advanced Drainage Systems Inc (G-10803)*
ADS, London *Also called Advanced Drainage Systems Inc (G-12048)*
ADS 419 422-6521
401 Olive St Findlay (45840) *(G-9645)*
ADS Machinery Corp 330 399-3601
1201 Vine Ave Ne Ste 1 Warren (44483) *(G-19362)*
ADS Mto 419 424-5231
12280 County Road 172 Findlay (45840) *(G-9646)*
ADS Ventures Inc (HQ) 614 658-0050
4640 Trueman Blvd Hilliard (43026) *(G-10801)*
Adsetting Service, Cleveland *Also called Royal Acme Corporation (G-6009)*
Adtec, Middle Point *Also called Additive Technology Inc (G-13754)*
Adult Daily Living LLC 330 612-7941
3603 Highspire Dr Coventry Township (44203) *(G-7761)*
Adval Tech US Inc 216 362-1850
12200 Brookpark Rd Cleveland (44130) *(G-4620)*
Advanatage Print Solut 614 519-2392
79 Acton Rd Columbus (43214) *(G-6543)*
Advance Apex Inc (PA) 614 539-3000
2375 Harrisburg Pike Grove City (43123) *(G-10410)*
Advance Bronze Inc (PA) 330 948-1231
139 Ohio St Lodi (44254) *(G-12003)*
Advance Bronzehubco Div (HQ) 304 232-4414
139 Ohio St Lodi (44254) *(G-12004)*
Advance Cnc Machining, Grove City *Also called Advance Apex Inc (G-10410)*
Advance Graphics, Columbus *Also called Hoster Graphics Company Inc (G-7009)*
Advance Industrial Mfg Inc 614 871-3333
1996 Longwood Ave Grove City (43123) *(G-10411)*
Advance Industries Group LLC 216 741-1800
3636 W 58th St Cleveland (44102) *(G-4621)*
Advance Lens Labs, Berea *Also called Cleveland Hoya Corp (G-1595)*
Advance Manufacturing Corp 216 333-1684
6800 Madison Ave Cleveland (44102) *(G-4622)*
Advance Metal Products Inc 216 741-1800
3636 W 58th St Cleveland (44102) *(G-4623)*
Advance Novelty Incorporated 419 424-0363
101 Stanford Pkwy Findlay (45840) *(G-9647)*
Advance Pierre Foods, West Chester *Also called Advancepierre Foods Inc (G-19826)*
Advance Printing Company, Cincinnati *Also called J & P Investments Inc (G-3861)*
Advance Products 419 882-8117
6041 Angleview Dr Sylvania (43560) *(G-17931)*
Advance Reporter (PA) 419 485-4851
115 Broad St Montpelier (43543) *(G-14301)*
Advance Sign Group LLC 614 429-2111
5150 Walcutt Ct Columbus (43228) *(G-6544)*
Advance Weight System Inc 440 926-3691
409 Main St Grafton (44044) *(G-10291)*
Advance Wire Forming Inc 216 432-3250
3636 W 58th St Cleveland (44102) *(G-4624)*
Advanced Bar Technology, Canton *Also called Gerdau Macsteel Atmosphere Ann (G-2683)*
Advanced Biological Mktg Inc 419 232-2461
375 Bonnewitz Ave Van Wert (45891) *(G-19073)*
Advanced Chem Solutions Inc 216 692-3005
150 Allen Ave Orrville (44667) *(G-15582)*
Advanced Chemical Solutions (PA) 330 283-5157
1114 N Court St 196 Medina (44256) *(G-13217)*
Advanced Cleaning Tech LLC 614 504-2014
7533 Merchant Rd Plain City (43064) *(G-16169)*
Advanced Coatings Intl 330 794-6361
2990 Gilchrist Rd # 1100 Akron (44305) *(G-30)*
Advanced Composites Inc 937 575-9814
2810 Howard St Sidney (45365) *(G-17012)*
Advanced Composites Inc (HQ) 937 575-9800
1062 S 4th Ave Sidney (45365) *(G-17013)*
Advanced Controls Inc 440 354-5413
34300 Lakeland Blvd Frnt Eastlake (44095) *(G-9097)*
Advanced Cryogenic Entps LLC 330 922-0750
1034 Home Ave Akron (44310) *(G-31)*
Advanced Custom Sound 330 372-9900
1894 Elm Rd Ne Warren (44483) *(G-19363)*
Advanced Cylinder Repair Inc 419 289-0538
942 State Route 302 Ashland (44805) *(G-675)*
Advanced Defense Products LLC 440 571-2277
11162 Spear Rd Painesville (44077) *(G-15705)*
Advanced Design Industries, Sheffield Village *Also called ADI Machining Inc (G-16964)*
Advanced Design Industries Inc 440 277-4141
4686 French Creek Rd Sheffield Village (44054) *(G-16965)*
Advanced Display Systems, Kent *Also called Mike B Crawford (G-11355)*
Advanced Drainage of Ohio Inc 614 658-0050
4640 Trueman Blvd Hilliard (43026) *(G-10802)*
Advanced Drainage Systems Inc 740 852-9554
288 Lafayette St London (43140) *(G-12047)*
Advanced Drainage Systems Inc 513 863-1384
2650 Hamilton Eaton Rd Hamilton (45011) *(G-10529)*
Advanced Drainage Systems Inc 419 384-3140
501 Basinger Rd Pandora (45877) *(G-15806)*
Advanced Drainage Systems Inc 330 264-4949
3113 W Old Lincoln Way Wooster (44691) *(G-20554)*
Advanced Drainage Systems Inc (PA) 614 658-0050
4640 Trueman Blvd Hilliard (43026) *(G-10803)*

ALPHABETIC

Advanced Drainage Systems Inc.....419 599-9565
1075 Independence Dr Napoleon (43545) ***(G-14530)***
Advanced Drainage Systems Inc.....740 852-2980
400 E High St London (43140) ***(G-12048)***
Advanced Drainage Systems Inc.....419 424-8324
401 Olive St Findlay (45840) ***(G-9648)***
Advanced Dstrbted Gnration LLC.....419 530-3792
1331 Conant St Ste 107 Maumee (43537) ***(G-13066)***
Advanced Elastomer Systems LP.....330 336-7641
1000 Seville Rd Wadsworth (44281) ***(G-19221)***
Advanced Engrg & Mfg Co Inc.....330 686-9911
5026 Hudson Dr Ste D Stow (44224) ***(G-17567)***
Advanced Engrg Solutions Inc.....937 743-6900
250 Advanced Dr Springboro (45066) ***(G-17319)***
Advanced Equipment Systems LLC.....216 289-6505
22800 Lakeland Blvd Euclid (44132) ***(G-9400)***
Advanced F.M.e Products, Mentor *Also called Advanced Pneumatics Inc* ***(G-13375)***
Advanced Fiber LLC.....419 562-1337
100 Crossroads Blvd Bucyrus (44820) ***(G-2317)***
Advanced Fitness Inc.....513 563-1000
11875 Reading Rd Cincinnati (45241) ***(G-3299)***
Advanced Flame Hardening Inc.....216 431-0370
1209 Marquette St Cleveland (44114) ***(G-4625)***
Advanced Fluids Inc.....216 692-3050
18127 Roseland Rd Cleveland (44112) ***(G-4626)***
Advanced Fuel Systems Inc.....614 252-8422
841 Alton Ave Columbus (43219) ***(G-6545)***
Advanced Graphic Solutions, Cleveland *Also called A Graphic Solution* ***(G-4587)***
Advanced Ground Systems.....513 402-7226
1650 Magnolia Dr Cincinnati (45215) ***(G-3300)***
Advanced Holding Designs Inc.....330 928-4456
3332 Cavalier Trl Cuyahoga Falls (44224) ***(G-7831)***
Advanced Incentives Inc.....419 471-9088
1732 W Alexis Rd Toledo (43613) ***(G-18157)***
Advanced Indus Machining Inc (PA).....614 596-4183
3982 Powell Rd Ste 218 Powell (43065) ***(G-16307)***
Advanced Industrial Measuremnt.....937 320-4930
2580 Kohnle Dr Miamisburg (45342) ***(G-13637)***
Advanced Innovation & Mfg Inc.....330 308-6360
326 Pearl Ave Ne New Philadelphia (44663) ***(G-14756)***
Advanced Innovative Mfg Inc.....330 562-2468
116 Lena Dr Operator Aurora (44202) ***(G-867)***
Advanced Intr Solutions Inc.....937 550-0065
250 Advanced Dr Springboro (45066) ***(G-17320)***
Advanced Kiffer Systems Inc.....216 267-8181
4905 Rocky River Dr Cleveland (44135) ***(G-4627)***
Advanced Lighting Tech LLC (PA).....888 440-2358
7905 Cochran Rd Ste 300 Solon (44139) ***(G-17099)***
Advanced Litho Systems.....419 865-2652
4429 Weckerly Rd Monclova (43542) ***(G-14253)***
Advanced Livescan Technologies.....440 759-7028
3575 W 132nd St Cleveland (44111) ***(G-4628)***
Advanced Machine Solutions LLC.....419 733-2537
08764 County Road 33a Wapakoneta (45895) ***(G-19317)***
Advanced Marking Systems Inc (PA).....330 792-8239
6000 Mahoning Ave Ste 50 Youngstown (44515) ***(G-20837)***
Advanced Materials Products.....330 650-4000
1890 Georgetown Rd Hudson (44236) ***(G-11026)***
Advanced Media Corporation.....440 260-9910
6410 Eastland Rd Ste F Cleveland (44142) ***(G-4629)***
Advanced Medical Solutions Inc.....937 291-0069
7026 Corp Way Ste 116 Centerville (45459) ***(G-2995)***
Advanced Microbeam Inc.....330 394-1255
4217 King Graves Rd Ste C Vienna (44473) ***(G-19195)***
Advanced OEM Solutions LLC.....513 846-5755
8044 Montgomery Rd # 700 Cincinnati (45236) ***(G-3301)***
Advanced Onsight Welding Svcs.....513 924-1400
5220 Globe Ave Cincinnati (45212) ***(G-3302)***
Advanced Paper Tube Inc.....216 281-5691
1951 W 90th St Cleveland (44102) ***(G-4630)***
Advanced Plastic Systems Inc.....614 759-6550
990 Gahanna Pkwy Gahanna (43230) ***(G-10073)***
Advanced Plastics Inc.....330 336-6681
307 Water St Wadsworth (44281) ***(G-19222)***
Advanced Pneumatics Inc.....440 953-0700
9413 Hamilton Dr Mentor (44060) ***(G-13375)***
Advanced Poly-Packaging Inc.....330 785-4000
1360 Exeter Rd Akron (44306) ***(G-32)***
Advanced Polymer Coatings Ltd.....440 937-6218
951 Jaycox Rd Avon (44011) ***(G-939)***
Advanced Prgrm Resources Inc (PA).....614 761-9994
2715 Tuller Pkwy Dublin (43017) ***(G-8874)***
Advanced Printing, Youngstown *Also called Advanced Marking Systems Inc* ***(G-20837)***
Advanced Propeller Systems.....937 409-1038
1297 Windsor Dr Dayton (45434) ***(G-7968)***
Advanced Quartz Fabrication.....440 350-4567
11920 Quail Woods Dr Chardon (44024) ***(G-3095)***
Advanced Recycling Systems,, Lowellville *Also called ARS Recycling Systems LLC* ***(G-12249)***
Advanced Rv LLC.....440 283-0405
4590 Hamann Pkwy Willoughby (44094) ***(G-20267)***
Advanced Sleeve Corp.....440 205-1055
8767 East Ave Mentor (44060) ***(G-13376)***
Advanced Specialty Products.....419 882-6528
428 Clough St Bowling Green (43402) ***(G-1950)***
Advanced Tech Utilization Co.....440 238-3770
12005 Prospect Rd Unit 1 Strongsville (44149) ***(G-17706)***
Advanced Technical Pdts Sup Co.....513 851-6858
6186 Centre Park Dr West Chester (45069) ***(G-19638)***
Advanced Technology Corp.....440 293-4064
101 Parker Dr Andover (44003) ***(G-577)***
Advanced Technology Products.....937 349-5221
282 E Sandusky St Mechanicsburg (43044) ***(G-13210)***
Advanced Telemetrics Intl.....937 862-6948
2361 Darnell Dr Spring Valley (45370) ***(G-17315)***
Advanced Time Systems.....440 466-2689
4591 Cork Cold Springs Rd Geneva (44041) ***(G-10212)***
Advanced Translation/Cnsltng.....440 716-0820
3751 Willow Run Westlake (44145) ***(G-20087)***
Advanced Vehicles, Cleveland *Also called Kay Capital Company* ***(G-5521)***
Advanced Web Corporation.....740 662-6323
10999 E Copeland Rd Stewart (45778) ***(G-17558)***
Advanced Welding Co.....937 746-6800
901 N Main St Franklin (45005) ***(G-9867)***
Advanced Wire and Cable, Spring Valley *Also called Max Mighty Inc* ***(G-17317)***
Advanced Wldg Fabrication Inc (PA).....440 724-9165
648 Moore Rd Avon Lake (44012) ***(G-978)***
Advancepierre Foods Inc (HQ).....513 874-8741
9990 Prnceton Glendale Rd West Chester (45246) ***(G-19826)***
Advancepierre Foods Inc.....513 874-8741
9990 Prnceton Glendale Rd West Chester (45246) ***(G-19827)***
Advancepierre Foods Inc.....580 616-4403
1833 Cooper Foster Pk Rd Amherst (44001) ***(G-552)***
Advancing Eco-Agriculture LLC.....800 495-6603
4551 Parks West Rd Middlefield (44062) ***(G-13773)***
Advancperre Foods Holdings Inc (HQ).....800 969-2747
9990 Prnceton Glendale Rd West Chester (45246) ***(G-19828)***
Advant-E Corporation (PA).....937 429-4288
2434 Esquire Dr Beavercreek (45431) ***(G-1298)***
Advantage Circuits Ltd.....330 256-7768
3512 Industry Rd Rootstown (44272) ***(G-16566)***
Advantage Machine Shop.....330 337-8377
777 S Ellsworth Ave Salem (44460) ***(G-16715)***
Advantage Mold Inc.....419 691-5676
525 N Wheeling St Toledo (43605) ***(G-18158)***
Advantage Powder Coating Inc (PA).....419 782-2363
2090 E 2nd St Ste 102 Defiance (43512) ***(G-8611)***
Advantage Printing Inc.....614 272-8259
1369 Royston Dr Columbus (43204) ***(G-6546)***
Advantage Products Corporation (PA).....513 489-2283
11559 Grooms Rd Blue Ash (45242) ***(G-1722)***
Advantage Tent Fittings Inc.....740 773-3015
11661 Pleasant Valley Rd Chillicothe (45601) ***(G-3173)***
Advantage Tool Supply Inc.....330 896-8869
3666 Avanti Ln Uniontown (44685) ***(G-18907)***
Advantage Truck Trailers, Columbus *Also called Kenan Advantage Group Inc* ***(G-7085)***
Advantic LLC.....937 490-4712
4250 Display Ln Dayton (45429) ***(G-8010)***
Advent Designs, Logan *Also called Signs Unlimited The Graphic* ***(G-12043)***
Adventurous Child Inc.....513 531-7700
4781 Duck Creek Rd Cincinnati (45227) ***(G-3303)***
Advertiser-Tribune, The, Tiffin *Also called Augdon Newspapers of Ohio Inc* ***(G-18048)***
Advertising Ideas of Ohio Inc.....330 745-6555
833 Wooster Rd N Barberton (44203) ***(G-1049)***
Advertising Tribune, Tiffin *Also called Ogden Newspapers of Ohio Inc* ***(G-18074)***
Advetech Inc (PA).....330 533-2227
445 W Main St Canfield (44406) ***(G-2517)***
Advetech Inc.....330 533-2227
451 W Main St Canfield (44406) ***(G-2518)***
Advics Manufacturing Ohio Inc.....513 932-7878
1650 Kingsview Dr Lebanon (45036) ***(G-11631)***
Adwest Technologies Inc.....513 458-2600
4625 Red Bank Rd Ste 200 Cincinnati (45227) ***(G-3304)***
Adyl Inc.....330 797-8700
6000 Mahoning Ave Ste 230 Austintown (44515) ***(G-928)***
AEC Brews LLC DBA Old Frhuse B.....513 536-9071
237 W Main St Williamsburg (45176) ***(G-20250)***
Aecom Energy & Cnstr Inc.....419 698-6277
4001 Cedar Point Rd Oregon (43616) ***(G-15553)***
Aeiou Diagnostics, Columbus *Also called Aeiou Scientific LLC* ***(G-6547)***
Aeiou Scientific LLC.....614 325-2103
311 Kendall Pl Columbus (43205) ***(G-6547)***
AEP Resources Inc.....614 716-1000
1 Riverside Plz Columbus (43215) ***(G-6548)***
Aero Composites Inc.....937 849-0244
3400 Spangler Rd Medway (45341) ***(G-13365)***
Aero Fluid Products, Painesville *Also called Dukes Aerospace Inc* ***(G-15732)***
Aero Fluid Products, Painesville *Also called Aerocontrolex Group Inc* ***(G-15707)***

Aero Fulfillment Services Corp (PA)....800 225-7145
3900 Aero Dr Mason (45040) ***(G-12820)***
Aero Jet Wash Llc....866 381-7955
440 Fame Rd West Carrollton (45449) ***(G-19628)***
Aero Prep LLC....513 469-8300
11584 Goldcoast Dr Cincinnati (45249) ***(G-3305)***
Aero Printing Inc....419 695-2931
710 Elida Ave Delphos (45833) ***(G-8735)***
Aero Propulsion Support Inc....513 367-9452
108 May Dr Ste A Harrison (45030) ***(G-10628)***
Aero Propulsion Support Group, Harrison *Also called Aero Propulsion Support Inc* ***(G-10628)***
Aero Refining, Painesville *Also called Panama Jewelers LLC* ***(G-15771)***
Aero Tube & Connector Company....614 885-2514
7100 N High St Worthington (43085) ***(G-20673)***
Aero-Med Industries Inc....216 459-0004
1205 Brookpark Rd Cleveland (44109) ***(G-4631)***
Aerocase Incorporated....440 617-9294
1061 Bradley Rd Westlake (44145) ***(G-20088)***
Aerocontrolex, Cleveland *Also called Transdigm Inc* ***(G-6195)***
Aerocontrolex, Cleveland *Also called Transdigm Inc* ***(G-6196)***
Aerocontrolex Group Inc (HQ)....440 352-6182
313 Gillett St Painesville (44077) ***(G-15706)***
Aerocontrolex Group Inc....440 352-6182
313 Gillett St Painesville (44077) ***(G-15707)***
Aerodynamic Systems....440 463-8820
19020 Brookfield Rd Chagrin Falls (44023) ***(G-3035)***
Aerodyne, Chagrin Falls *Also called Abanaki Corporation* ***(G-3034)***
Aeroflex Powell, Hilliard *Also called Star Dynamics Corporation* ***(G-10864)***
Aerolite Extrusion Company....330 782-1127
4605 Lake Park Rd Youngstown (44512) ***(G-20838)***
Aeroll Engineering Corp....216 481-2266
18511 Euclid Ave Rear Cleveland (44112) ***(G-4632)***
Aeroquip Corp....419 238-1190
1225 W Main St Van Wert (45891) ***(G-19074)***
Aeroquip-Vickers Inc (HQ)....216 523-5000
1111 Superior Ave E Cleveland (44114) ***(G-4633)***
Aeroscena LLC....800 671-1890
10000 Cedar Ave Cleveland (44106) ***(G-4634)***
Aeroseal LLC (PA)....937 428-9300
7989 S Suburban Rd Centerville (45458) ***(G-2996)***
Aeroserv Inc....513 932-9227
201 Industrial Row Dr Mason (45040) ***(G-12821)***
Aerospace Co Inc....413 998-1637
600 Superior Ave E Cleveland (44114) ***(G-4635)***
Aerospace Lubricants Inc....614 878-3600
1600 Georgesville Rd Columbus (43228) ***(G-6549)***
Aerospace Maint Solutions LLC....440 729-7703
8759 Mayfield Rd Chesterland (44026) ***(G-3150)***
Aerospace Mfg Group-Ohio, Blue Ash *Also called Superalloy Mfg Solutions Corp* ***(G-1854)***
Aerospace Simulations, Akron *Also called Lockheed Martin Integrtd Systm* ***(G-258)***
Aerotech Enterprise....440 729-2616
8511 Mulberry Rd Chesterland (44026) ***(G-3151)***
Aerotech Industries Inc....216 881-6660
1435 E 49th St Cleveland (44103) ***(G-4636)***
Aerotech Styling Inc....419 923-6970
14181 County Road 10 2 Lyons (43533) ***(G-12272)***
Aerotorque Corporation, Sharon Center *Also called Atc Legacy Inc* ***(G-16944)***
Aerovent Inc....937 473-3789
800 S High St Covington (45318) ***(G-7779)***
Aerowave Inc....440 731-8464
361 Windward Dr Elyria (44035) ***(G-9209)***
Aerpio Pharmaceuticals Inc....513 985-1920
9987 Carver Rd Ste 420 Blue Ash (45242) ***(G-1723)***
AES, Cincinnati *Also called Aluminum Extruded Shapes Inc* ***(G-3328)***
Aesi, Springboro *Also called Advanced Engrg Solutions Inc* ***(G-17319)***
Aesthetic Finishers Inc....937 778-8777
1502 S Main St Piqua (45356) ***(G-16098)***
Aetna Plastics Corp....330 274-2855
4466 Orchard St Mantua (44255) ***(G-12541)***
Aetna Plating Co....216 341-9111
6511 Morgan Ave Cleveland (44127) ***(G-4637)***
Aetna Welding Co Inc....216 883-1801
4613 Broadway Ave Cleveland (44127) ***(G-4638)***
Afc Company....330 533-5581
5183 W Western Reserve Rd Canfield (44406) ***(G-2519)***
Affinity Disp Expositions Inc (PA)....513 771-2339
1301 Glendale Milford Rd Cincinnati (45215) ***(G-3306)***
Affinity Disp Expositions Inc....513 771-2339
1375 Spring Park Walk Cincinnati (45215) ***(G-3307)***
Affinity Information Managemet....419 517-2055
3359 Silica Rd Sylvania (43560) ***(G-17932)***
Affinity Therapeutics LLC....216 224-9364
11000 Cedar Ave Cleveland (44106) ***(G-4639)***
Affordable Barn Co Ltd....330 674-3001
4260 Township Road 617 Millersburg (44654) ***(G-14055)***
Affordable Bus Support LLC....440 543-5547
17800 Chillicothe Rd Chagrin Falls (44023) ***(G-3036)***
Affordable Cabinet Doors....513 734-9663
205 S Main St Bethel (45106) ***(G-1655)***
Affordable Stump Removal LLC....419 841-8331
2624 Heysler Rd Toledo (43617) ***(G-18159)***
Affymetrix Inc....216 765-5000
26309 Miles Rd Cleveland (44128) ***(G-4640)***
Affymetrix Inc....419 887-1233
434 W Dussel Dr Maumee (43537) ***(G-13067)***
Afi Brands LLC....614 999-6426
5575 Hayden Run Blvd Dublin (43016) ***(G-8875)***
Afs Technology LLC....937 669-3548
400 E Elroy Ansonia Rd Ansonia (45303) ***(G-592)***
After Werk....513 661-9375
3095 Glenmore Ave Cincinnati (45238) ***(G-3308)***
Aftermarket Parts Company LLC....740 369-1056
2338 Us Highway 42 S Delaware (43015) ***(G-8651)***
Afv, Macedonia *Also called Insightfuel LLC* ***(G-12304)***
AG Antenna Group LLC....513 289-6521
11931 Montgomery Rd Cincinnati (45249) ***(G-3309)***
AG Designs LLC....614 506-2849
1165 Dunham Rd Delaware (43015) ***(G-8652)***
AGC Automotive Americas....937 599-3131
1465 W Sandusky Ave Bellefontaine (43311) ***(G-1501)***
AGC Flat Glass North Amer Inc....937 292-7784
31 Hunter Pl Bellefontaine (43311) ***(G-1502)***
AGC Flat Glass North Amer Inc....330 965-1000
365 Mcclurg Rd Ste E Youngstown (44512) ***(G-20839)***
AGC Flat Glass North Amer Inc....330 965-1000
365 Mcclurg Rd Ste E Boardman (44512) ***(G-1897)***
AGC Flat Glass North Amer Inc....937 599-3131
1465 W Sandusky Ave Bellefontaine (43311) ***(G-1503)***
AGE Graphics LLC....740 989-0006
678 Collins Rd Little Hocking (45742) ***(G-11989)***
Agean Marble Manufacturing....513 874-1475
9756 Prnceton Glendale Rd West Chester (45246) ***(G-19829)***
Agent Technologies Inc (PA)....513 942-9444
8216 Princeton Glendale West Chester (45069) ***(G-19639)***
AGFA Corporation....513 829-6292
6104 Monastery Dr Fairfield (45014) ***(G-9478)***
Aggregate Tersornance LLC....330 418-4751
455 Navarre Rd Sw Unit H Canton (44707) ***(G-2560)***
Agile Global Solutions Inc....916 655-7745
5755 Granger Rd Ste 610 Independence (44131) ***(G-11118)***
Agile Sign & Ltg Maint Inc....440 918-1311
35280 Lakeland Blvd Eastlake (44095) ***(G-9098)***
Agile Socks LLC....614 440-2812
168 E Frankfort St Columbus (43206) ***(G-6550)***
Agmet LLC....216 663-8200
5533 Dunham Rd Cleveland (44137) ***(G-4641)***
Agmet Metals Inc....440 439-7400
7800 Medusa Rd Oakwood Village (44146) ***(G-15476)***
Agnone-Kelly Enterprises Inc....800 634-6503
11658 Baen Rd Cincinnati (45242) ***(G-3310)***
Agrana Fruit Us Inc....937 693-3821
16197 County Road 25a Botkins (45306) ***(G-1932)***
Agrati - Medina LLC (HQ)....330 725-8853
941-955 Lake Rd Medina (44256) ***(G-13218)***
Agrati - Medina LLC....740 467-3199
2140 Refugee Rd Ne Millersport (43046) ***(G-14158)***
Agrati - Tiffin LLC....419 447-2221
1988 S County Road 593 Tiffin (44883) ***(G-18041)***
Agratronix LLC....330 562-2222
10375 State Route 43 Streetsboro (44241) ***(G-17657)***
Agri Communicators Inc....614 273-0465
1625 Bethel Rd Ste 203 Columbus (43220) ***(G-6551)***
Agri-Products Inc....216 831-5890
29326 Bolingbrook Rd Cleveland (44124) ***(G-4642)***
Agridry LLC....419 459-4399
3460 Us Highway 20 Edon (43518) ***(G-9183)***
Agrium Advanced Tech US Inc....614 276-5103
701 Kaderly Dr Columbus (43228) ***(G-6552)***
AGS Custom Graphics, Macedonia *Also called Custom Graphics Inc* ***(G-12287)***
AGS Custom Graphics Inc....330 963-7770
8107 Bavaria Rd Macedonia (44056) ***(G-12275)***
Agse Tooling, Cincinnati *Also called Advanced Ground Systems* ***(G-3300)***
Ahalogy....314 974-5599
1140 Main St 3 Cincinnati (45202) ***(G-3311)***
Ahd, Cuyahoga Falls *Also called Advanced Holding Designs Inc* ***(G-7831)***
Ahlstrom West Carrollton LLC....937 859-3621
1 S Elm St Dayton (45449) ***(G-8011)***
Ahmf Inc (PA)....614 921-1223
2245 Wilson Rd Columbus (43228) ***(G-6553)***
Ahner Fabricating & Shtmtl Inc....419 626-6641
2001 E Perkins Ave Sandusky (44870) ***(G-16793)***
Ahresty Wilmington Corporation....937 382-6112
2627 S South St Wilmington (45177) ***(G-20484)***
Al Root Company (PA)....330 723-4359
623 W Liberty St Medina (44256) ***(G-13219)***
Al Root Company....330 725-6677
234 S State Rd Medina (44256) ***(G-13220)***

A L P H A B E T I C

Ailes Millwork Inc 330 678-4300
1520 Enterprise Way Kent (44240) ***(G-11290)***
Aim Attachments 614 539-3030
1720 Feddern Ave Grove City (43123) ***(G-10412)***
Aim Media Midwest Oper LLC 937 335-5634
224 S Market St Troy (45373) ***(G-18633)***
Aimco Mfg Inc 419 476-6572
203 Matzinger Rd Toledo (43612) ***(G-18160)***
Aims-CMI Technology LLC 937 832-2000
65 Haas Dr Englewood (45322) ***(G-9349)***
AIN Industries Inc 440 781-0950
13901 Aspinwall Ave Cleveland (44110) ***(G-4643)***
Air Cleaning Solutions 937 832-3600
8613 N Main St Dayton (45415) ***(G-8012)***
Air Cleaning Systems Inc 440 285-3565
12965 Mayfield Rd Chardon (44024) ***(G-3096)***
Air Compressor Exchange, Perrysburg *Also called Optimair Ltd* ***(G-15992)***
Air Conversion Technology Inc 419 841-1720
3485 Silica Rd Unit A Sylvania (43560) ***(G-17933)***
Air Craft Wheels LLC 440 937-7903
700 N Walnut St Ravenna (44266) ***(G-16364)***
Air Enterprises, LLC, Akron *Also called Hickok Ae LLC* ***(G-207)***
Air Force US Dept of 937 656-2354
4225 Logistics Ave Dayton (45433) ***(G-7969)***
Air Force US Dept of 937 245-1962
5465 Arnold Rd Wright Patterson Afb (45433) ***(G-20716)***
Air Heater Seal Company Inc 740 984-2146
15710 Waterford Rd Waterford (45786) ***(G-19483)***
Air Locke Dock Seal Division, Youngstown *Also called ONeals Tarpaulin & Awning Co* ***(G-20985)***
Air Logic Power Systems LLC 513 202-5130
10100 Progress Way Harrison (45030) ***(G-10629)***
Air One Jet Center 513 867-9500
2808 Bobmeyer Rd Hamilton (45015) ***(G-10530)***
Air Power Dynamics LLC 440 701-2100
7350 Corporate Blvd Mentor (44060) ***(G-13377)***
Air Power of Ohio, Canton *Also called A P O Holdings Inc* ***(G-2556)***
Air Products and Chemicals Inc 513 420-3663
2500 Yankee Rd Middletown (45044) ***(G-13876)***
Air Products and Chemicals Inc 216 781-2801
2820 Quigley Rd Cleveland (44113) ***(G-4644)***
Air Products and Chemicals Inc 513 242-9215
4900 Este Ave Cincinnati (45232) ***(G-3312)***
AIR RITE SERVICE SUPPLY, Cleveland *Also called Air-Rite Inc* ***(G-4645)***
Air Shop, The, Loveland *Also called Paul Miracle* ***(G-12220)***
Air Supply Co, Twinsburg *Also called Allied Separation Tech Inc* ***(G-18731)***
Air Technical Industries Inc 440 951-5191
7501 Clover Ave Mentor (44060) ***(G-13378)***
Air Tool Service Company (PA) 440 701-1021
7722 Metric Dr Mentor (44060) ***(G-13379)***
Air Waves LLC 740 548-1200
7750 Green Meadows Dr A Lewis Center (43035) ***(G-11743)***
Air-Rite Inc 216 228-8200
1290 W 117th St Cleveland (44107) ***(G-4645)***
Air-Way Manufacturing Company 419 298-2366
303 W River St Edgerton (43517) ***(G-9167)***
Airam Press Co Ltd 937 473-5672
2065 Industrial Ct Covington (45318) ***(G-7780)***
Airborne, Centerville *Also called American Sports Design Company* ***(G-2997)***
Aircraft and Auto Fittings Co 216 486-0047
17120 Saint Clair Ave Cleveland (44110) ***(G-4646)***
Aircraft Dynamics Corporation 419 331-0371
418 E Kiracofe Ave Elida (45807) ***(G-9193)***
Aircraft Welding Inc 440 951-3863
38335 Apollo Pkwy Unit 1 Willoughby (44094) ***(G-20268)***
Aircraft Wheels and Breaks, Avon *Also called Cleveland Wheels* ***(G-944)***
Aircraft-Refuelers.com, Findlay *Also called Bosserman Automotive Engrg LLC* ***(G-9660)***
Airecon Manufacturing Corp 513 561-5522
5271 Brotherton Rd Cincinnati (45227) ***(G-3313)***
Airfasco Inc 330 430-6190
2655 Harrison Ave Sw Canton (44706) ***(G-2561)***
Airfasco Inds Fstner Group LLC 330 430-6190
2655 Harrison Ave Sw Canton (44706) ***(G-2562)***
Airgas 330 345-1257
115 N Smyser Rd Wooster (44691) ***(G-20555)***
Airgas Usa LLC 937 228-8594
1223 Mccook Ave Dayton (45404) ***(G-8013)***
Airgas Usa LLC 419 228-2828
1590 Mcclain Rd Lima (45804) ***(G-11831)***
Airgas Usa LLC 614 308-3730
858 Distribution Dr Columbus (43228) ***(G-6554)***
Airgas Usa LLC 440 232-6397
21610 Alexander Rd Oakwood Village (44146) ***(G-15477)***
Airgas Usa LLC 937 237-0621
3800 Dayton Park Dr Dayton (45414) ***(G-8014)***
Airgas Usa LLC 330 454-1330
2505 Shepler Ave Sw Canton (44706) ***(G-2563)***
Airmachinescom Inc 330 759-1620
4705 Belmont Ave Youngstown (44505) ***(G-20840)***
Airmate Company 419 636-3184
16280 County Road D Bryan (43506) ***(G-2258)***
Airplaco Equipment Company, Cincinnati *Also called Mesa Industries Inc* ***(G-4009)***
Airplane Plastics, Tipp City *Also called J & B Rogers Inc* ***(G-18118)***
Airstream Inc (HQ) 937 596-6111
419 W Pike St Jackson Center (45334) ***(G-11205)***
Airtech 419 269-1000
6898 Commodore Dr Walbridge (43465) ***(G-19291)***
Airtech Mechanical Inc 419 292-0074
4444 Monroe St Toledo (43613) ***(G-18161)***
Airtex Industries LLC 330 899-0340
2100 International Pkwy North Canton (44720) ***(G-15068)***
Airtite Mine Products LLC 740 894-8778
1279 County Road 411 Proctorville (45669) ***(G-16342)***
Airtug LLC 440 829-2167
1350 Chester Indus Pkwy Avon (44011) ***(G-940)***
Airtx International Ltd 513 631-0660
6320 Wiehe Rd Cincinnati (45237) ***(G-3314)***
Airwave Communications Cons 419 331-1526
1209 Allentown Rd Lima (45805) ***(G-11832)***
Airwaves, Lewis Center *Also called Solid Light Company Inc* ***(G-11781)***
Airwolf Aerospace LLC 440 632-1687
15369 Madison Rd Middlefield (44062) ***(G-13774)***
Aitken Products Inc 440 466-5711
566 N Eagle St Geneva (44041) ***(G-10213)***
Aj Fluid Power Sales & Sup Inc 440 255-7960
8766 Tyler Blvd Mentor (44060) ***(G-13380)***
Aj Stineburg Wdwkg Studio LLC 614 526-9480
4651 Tatersall Ct Columbus (43230) ***(G-6555)***
Aja Industries LLC 614 216-9566
3857 Wintergreen Blvd Gahanna (43230) ***(G-10074)***
Ajami Holdings Group LLC 216 396-6089
5247 Wilson Mills Rd # 311 Richmond Heights (44143) ***(G-16500)***
Ajax - Ceco, Wickliffe *Also called Ajax Manufacturing Company* ***(G-20196)***
Ajax Industries Inc 614 272-6944
575 N Hague Ave Columbus (43204) ***(G-6556)***
Ajax Jaws, Columbus *Also called Ajax Industries Inc* ***(G-6556)***
Ajax Manufacturing Company 440 295-0244
29100 Lakeland Blvd Wickliffe (44092) ***(G-20196)***
Ajax Tocco Magnethermic Corp (HQ) 330 372-8511
1745 Overland Ave Ne Warren (44483) ***(G-19364)***
Ajax Tocco Magnethermic Corp 440 278-7200
29100 Lakeland Blvd Wickliffe (44092) ***(G-20197)***
Ajax Tocco Magnethermic Corp 330 818-8080
8984 Meridian Cir Nw Canton (44720) ***(G-2564)***
AJD Holding Co (PA) 330 405-4477
2181 Enterprise Pkwy Twinsburg (44087) ***(G-18728)***
Ajj Enterprises LLC 513 755-9562
10073 Commerce Park Dr West Chester (45246) ***(G-19830)***
AK Fabrication Inc 330 458-1037
1500 Allen Ave Se Canton (44707) ***(G-2565)***
AK Mansfield 419 755-3011
913 Bowman St Mansfield (44903) ***(G-12401)***
AK Steel Corporation 419 755-3011
913 Bowman St Mansfield (44903) ***(G-12402)***
AK Steel Corporation 740 450-5600
1724 Linden Ave Zanesville (43701) ***(G-21095)***
AK Steel Corporation 740 829-2206
17400 State Route 16 Coshocton (43812) ***(G-7717)***
AK Steel Corporation 513 425-3694
801 Crawford St Middletown (45044) ***(G-13877)***
AK Steel Corporation 513 425-3593
622 Box Middletown (45042) ***(G-13878)***
AK Steel Corporation 513 231-2552
1080 Nimitzview Dr Cincinnati (45230) ***(G-3315)***
AK Steel Corporation (HQ) 513 425-4200
9227 Centre Pointe Dr West Chester (45069) ***(G-19640)***
AK Steel Door 360, Middletown *Also called Matheson Tri-Gas Inc* ***(G-13925)***
AK Steel Holding Corporation (PA) 513 425-5000
9227 Centre Pointe Dr West Chester (45069) ***(G-19641)***
AK Tube LLC (HQ) 419 661-4150
30400 E Broadway St Walbridge (43465) ***(G-19292)***
Ak-Isg Steel Coating Company 216 429-6901
3531 Campbell Rd Cleveland (44105) ***(G-4647)***
Akers America Inc 330 757-4100
58 S Main St Poland (44514) ***(G-16237)***
Akers Identity LLC 330 493-0055
4150 Belden Village St Nw # 503 Canton (44718) ***(G-2566)***
Akers Packaging Service Inc (PA) 513 422-6312
2820 Lefferson Rd Middletown (45044) ***(G-13879)***
Akers Packaging Service Group, Middletown *Also called Akers Packaging Service Inc* ***(G-13879)***
Akers Packaging Service Group, Middletown *Also called Akers Packaging Solutions Inc* ***(G-13880)***
Akers Packaging Solutions Inc (PA) 513 422-6312
2820 Lefferson Rd Middletown (45044) ***(G-13880)***
Akers Packaging Solutions Inc 304 525-0342
2820 Lefferson Rd Middletown (45044) ***(G-13881)***
Akers Sign, Canton *Also called Akers Identity LLC* ***(G-2566)***

ALPHABETIC SECTION Alchem Corporation

Akko Fastener Inc (PA) 513 489-8300
6855 Cornell Rd Blue Ash (45242) ***(G-1724)***
Akland Printing, Macedonia *Also called Gaspar Services LLC* ***(G-12299)***
Akos Promotions Inc 513 398-6324
668 Reading Rd Ste C Mason (45040) ***(G-12822)***
Akro Polychem Inc 330 864-0360
150 N Miller Rd Ste 300b Fairlawn (44333) ***(G-9592)***
Akro Tool Co Inc 513 858-1555
240 Donald Dr Fairfield (45014) ***(G-9479)***
Akro-Mils, Wadsworth *Also called R B Mfg Co* ***(G-19270)***
Akro-Plastics, Kent *Also called U S Development Corp* ***(G-11398)***
Akron Anodizing & Coating Div, Akron *Also called Russell Products Co Inc* ***(G-360)***
Akron Beacon Journal, Akron *Also called The Beacon Journal Pubg Co* ***(G-400)***
Akron Belting & Supply Company 330 633-8212
1244 Home Ave Akron (44310) ***(G-33)***
Akron Brass Company 309 444-4440
343 Venture Blvd Wooster (44691) ***(G-20556)***
Akron Brass Company 614 529-7230
3656 Paragon Dr Columbus (43228) ***(G-6557)***
Akron Brass Company 330 264-5678
1615 Old Mansfield Rd Wooster (44691) ***(G-20557)***
Akron Brass Company (HQ) 330 264-5678
343 Venture Blvd Wooster (44691) ***(G-20558)***
Akron Brass Holding Corp (HQ) 330 264-5678
343 Venture Blvd Wooster (44691) ***(G-20559)***
Akron Centl Engrv Mold Mch Inc 330 794-8704
1625 Massillon Rd Akron (44312) ***(G-34)***
Akron Coating & Adhesives Inc 330 724-4716
365 Stanton Ave Akron (44301) ***(G-35)***
Akron Cotton Products Inc 330 434-7171
437 W Cedar St Akron (44307) ***(G-36)***
Akron Council of Engineering (PA) 330 535-8835
411 Wolf Ledges Pkwy # 105 Akron (44311) ***(G-37)***
Akron Crate and Pallet LLC 330 524-8955
1545 Mogadore Rd Kent (44240) ***(G-11291)***
Akron Crematory, Akron *Also called Akron Vault Company Inc* ***(G-55)***
Akron Cultured Marble Pdts LLC 330 628-6757
3992 Mogadore Rd Mogadore (44260) ***(G-14228)***
Akron Design & Costume Co 330 644-4849
3425 Manchester Rd Coventry Township (44319) ***(G-7762)***
Akron Dispersions Inc 330 666-0045
3291 Sawmill Rd Copley (44321) ***(G-7676)***
Akron E N T Associates, Akron *Also called Akron Ent Hearing Services Inc* ***(G-38)***
Akron Electric, Barberton *Also called Akron Foundry Co* ***(G-1050)***
Akron Ent Hearing Services Inc 330 762-8959
395 E Market St Akron (44304) ***(G-38)***
Akron Equipment Company (PA) 330 645-3780
3522 Manchester Rd Ste B Coventry Township (44319) ***(G-7763)***
Akron Felt & Chenille Mfg Co 330 733-7778
1205 George Wash Blvd Akron (44312) ***(G-39)***
Akron Foundry Co (PA) 330 745-3101
2728 Wingate Ave Akron (44314) ***(G-40)***
Akron Foundry Co 330 745-3101
1025 Eagon St Barberton (44203) ***(G-1050)***
Akron Gasket & Packg Entps Inc 330 633-3742
445 Northeast Ave Tallmadge (44278) ***(G-17971)***
Akron Gear & Engineering Inc 330 773-6608
501 Morgan Ave Akron (44311) ***(G-41)***
Akron Indus Mtr Sls & Svc Inc 330 753-7624
3041 Barber Rd Norton (44203) ***(G-15359)***
Akron Jewelry Rubber, Willoughby *Also called Zero-D Products Inc* ***(G-20463)***
Akron Legal News Inc 330 296-7578
60 S Summit St Akron (44308) ***(G-42)***
Akron Life, Akron *Also called Baker Media Group LLC* ***(G-78)***
Akron Litho-Print Company Inc 330 434-3145
1026 S Main St Akron (44311) ***(G-43)***
Akron Metal Etching Co 330 762-7687
463 Locust St Akron (44307) ***(G-44)***
Akron Orthotic Solutions Inc 330 253-3002
582 W Market St Akron (44303) ***(G-45)***
Akron Paint & Varnish Inc 330 773-8911
1390 Firestone Pkwy Akron (44301) ***(G-46)***
Akron Plating Co Inc 330 773-6878
1774 Hackberry St Akron (44301) ***(G-47)***
Akron Polymer Products Inc (PA) 330 628-5551
571 Kennedy Rd Akron (44305) ***(G-48)***
Akron Porcelain & Plastic Co, Akron *Also called Akron Porcelain & Plastics Co* ***(G-49)***
Akron Porcelain & Plastics Co (PA) 330 745-2159
2739 Cory Ave Akron (44314) ***(G-49)***
Akron Products Company 330 576-1750
6600 Ridge Rd Wadsworth (44281) ***(G-19223)***
Akron Rebar Co (PA) 330 745-7100
809 W Waterloo Rd Akron (44314) ***(G-50)***
Akron Rebar Co 216 433-0000
16216 Brookpark Rd Cleveland (44135) ***(G-4648)***
Akron Special Machinery Inc (PA) 330 753-1077
2740 Cory Ave Akron (44314) ***(G-51)***
Akron Specialized Products (PA) 330 762-9269
96 E Miller Ave Akron (44301) ***(G-52)***
Akron Steel Fabricators Co 330 644-0616
3291 Manchester Rd Coventry Township (44319) ***(G-7764)***
Akron Steel Treating Co 330 773-8211
336 Morgan Ave Akron (44311) ***(G-53)***
Akron Thermography Inc 330 896-9712
3406 Fortuna Dr Akron (44312) ***(G-54)***
Akron Vault Company Inc 330 784-5475
2399 Gilchrist Rd Akron (44305) ***(G-55)***
Akzo Nobel Chemicals LLC 419 229-0088
1747 Fort Amanda Rd Lima (45804) ***(G-11833)***
Akzo Nobel Coatings Inc 614 294-3361
1313 Windsor Ave Ste 1313 # 1313 Columbus (43211) ***(G-6558)***
Akzo Nobel Coatings Inc 937 322-2671
1550 Progress Rd Springfield (45505) ***(G-17361)***
Akzo Nobel Coatings Inc 614 294-3361
1313 Windsor Ave Columbus (43211) ***(G-6559)***
Akzo Nobel Inc 614 294-3361
1313 Windsor Ave Columbus (43211) ***(G-6560)***
Akzo Nobel Paints LLC 513 242-0530
1754 Tennessee Ave Cincinnati (45229) ***(G-3316)***
Al Bradshaw Jr 513 422-8870
5009 Oxford Middleton Rd Middletown (45042) ***(G-13882)***
Al Fe Heat Treating-Ohio Inc 330 336-0211
979 Seville Rd Wadsworth (44281) ***(G-19224)***
Al Meda Chocolates Inc 419 446-2676
23050 Fulton County Rd E Archbold (43502) ***(G-634)***
Al Yoder Construction Company 330 359-5726
3375 County Road 160 Millersburg (44654) ***(G-14056)***
Al's Electric Motor Service, Bedford *Also called Als High Tech Inc* ***(G-1380)***
Al's Polsg Pltg Powdr Coating, Toledo *Also called Als Polishing Shop Inc* ***(G-18167)***
Al-Co Products Inc 419 399-3867
485 2nd St Latty (45855) ***(G-11624)***
Al-Fe Heat Treating Defiance, Defiance *Also called Al-Fe Heat Treating Inc* ***(G-8612)***
Al-Fe Heat Treating Inc 419 782-7200
2066 E 2nd St Defiance (43512) ***(G-8612)***
Alabama Sling Center Inc 440 239-7000
21000 Aerospace Pkwy Cleveland (44142) ***(G-4649)***
Alacriant Inc (PA) 330 562-7191
1760 Miller Pkwy Streetsboro (44241) ***(G-17658)***
Alacriant Inc 330 562-7191
1760 Miller Pkwy Streetsboro (44241) ***(G-17659)***
Alacwin Nutrition Corporation 614 961-6479
3706 Kimberly Pkwy N Columbus (43232) ***(G-6561)***
Alamarra Inc 800 336-3007
8788 Tyler Blvd Mentor (44060) ***(G-13381)***
Alan BJ Company 330 372-1201
3566 Larchmont Ave Ne Warren (44483) ***(G-19365)***
Alan L Grant Polymer Inc 757 627-4000
1507 Boettler Rd Ste E Uniontown (44685) ***(G-18908)***
Alan Manufacturing Inc 330 262-1555
3927 E Lincoln Way Wooster (44691) ***(G-20560)***
Alanax Technologies Inc 216 469-1545
40714 Cherrywood Dr Belmont (43718) ***(G-1564)***
Alanod Westlake Metal Ind Inc 440 327-8184
36696 Sugar Ridge Rd North Ridgeville (44039) ***(G-15206)***
Alba Manufacturing Inc 513 874-0551
8950 Seward Rd Fairfield (45011) ***(G-9480)***
Albanese Concessions LLC 614 402-4937
6983 Greensview Vlg Dr Canal Winchester (43110) ***(G-2498)***
Albeco, Cleveland *Also called Aluminum Bearing Co of America* ***(G-4679)***
Albemarle Corporation 330 425-2354
1664 Highland Rd Twinsburg (44087) ***(G-18729)***
Albemarle Sorbent Technologies, Twinsburg *Also called Albemarle Corporation* ***(G-18729)***
Albert Bickel 513 530-5700
7116 Leibel Rd Cincinnati (45248) ***(G-3317)***
Albert Bramkamp Printing Co 513 641-1069
4501 Greenlee Ave Cincinnati (45217) ***(G-3318)***
Albert Freytag Inc 419 628-2018
306 Executive Dr Minster (45865) ***(G-14209)***
Albert Screenprint, Norton *Also called Alberts Screen Print Inc* ***(G-15360)***
Alberts Screen Print Inc 330 753-7559
3704 Summit Rd Norton (44203) ***(G-15360)***
Albin Sales Inc 740 927-7210
81 Brandon Dr Pataskala (43062) ***(G-15827)***
Albion Industries Inc 440 238-1955
20246 Progress Dr Strongsville (44149) ***(G-17707)***
Albright Albright & Schn 614 825-4829
89 E Wilson Bridge Rd D Worthington (43085) ***(G-20674)***
Albright Machine 419 483-1088
4296 Us Highway 20 W Monroeville (44847) ***(G-14286)***
Albright Radiator Inc 330 264-8886
331 N Hillcrest Dr Wooster (44691) ***(G-20561)***
Albright Saw Company Inc 740 887-2107
33535 Us Highway 50 Londonderry (45647) ***(G-12073)***
Albright Supply Company, Londonderry *Also called Albright Saw Company Inc* ***(G-12073)***
Alcan Corporation (HQ) 440 460-3307
6060 Parkland Blvd Cleveland (44124) ***(G-4650)***
Alchem Corporation 330 725-2436
525 W Liberty St Medina (44256) ***(G-13221)***

ALPHABETIC

Alchemical Transmutation....216 313-8674
314 E 195th St Cleveland (44119) **(G-4651)**
Alcm, Cleveland *Also called Aluminum Coating Manufacturers* **(G-4680)**
Alco Manufacturing....440 322-9166
105 Middle Ave Amherst (44001) **(G-553)**
Alco Manufacturing Corp LLC (PA)....440 458-5165
10584 Middle Ave Elyria (44035) **(G-9210)**
Alco-Chem Inc (PA)....330 253-3535
45 N Summit St Akron (44308) **(G-56)**
Alcoa, Mogadore *Also called Arconic Inc* **(G-14230)**
Alcoa, Newburgh Heights *Also called Arconic Inc* **(G-14934)**
Alcoa, Barberton *Also called Arconic Inc* **(G-1053)**
Alcoa Power & Propulsion, Newburgh Heights *Also called Howmet Corporation* **(G-14939)**
Alcohol & Drug Addiction Svcs....216 348-4830
2012 W 25th St Ste 600 Cleveland (44113) **(G-4652)**
ALCOHOLICS ANONYMOUS, Cuyahoga Falls *Also called Paradise Inc* **(G-7902)**
Alcon Inc (PA)....513 722-1037
6522 Snider Rd Loveland (45140) **(G-12175)**
Alcon Industries Inc....216 961-1100
7990 Baker Ave Cleveland (44102) **(G-4653)**
Alcon Tool Company....330 773-9171
565 Lafollette St Akron (44311) **(G-57)**
Ald Group LLC....440 942-9800
34201 Melinz Pkwy Unit A Willoughby (44095) **(G-20269)**
Ald Precast Corp (PA)....614 449-3366
400 Frank Rd Columbus (43207) **(G-6562)**
Alden Excavating, Cuyahoga Falls *Also called Alden Sand & Gravel Co Inc* **(G-7832)**
Alden Sand & Gravel Co Inc....330 928-3249
2486 Northampton Rd Cuyahoga Falls (44223) **(G-7832)**
Aldrich Chemical....937 859-1808
3858 Benner Rd Miamisburg (45342) **(G-13638)**
Aldridge Folders, Wadsworth *Also called Keeler Enterprises Inc* **(G-19247)**
Aldridge Folders, Wadsworth *Also called Deshea Printing Company* **(G-19234)**
Aleco Machine LLC....513 894-6400
233 N Martin L King Blvd Hamilton (45011) **(G-10531)**
Alegre Inc....937 885-6786
3101 W Tech Blvd Miamisburg (45342) **(G-13639)**
Alegre Global Supply Solutions, Miamisburg *Also called Alegre Inc* **(G-13639)**
Alektronics Inc....937 429-2118
4095 Executive Dr Beavercreek (45430) **(G-1349)**
Aleris Corporation (PA)....216 910-3400
25825 Science Park Dr # 400 Cleveland (44122) **(G-4654)**
Aleris International Inc (HQ)....216 910-3400
25825 Science Park Dr # 400 Beachwood (44122) **(G-1218)**
Aleris Ohio Management Inc (HQ)....216 910-3400
25825 Science Park Dr # 400 Cleveland (44122) **(G-4655)**
Aleris Recycling Inc....216 910-3400
25825 Science Park Dr # 400 Beachwood (44122) **(G-1219)**
Aleris Rm Inc....216 910-3400
25825 Science Park Dr # 400 Beachwood (44122) **(G-1220)**
Aleris Rolled Pdts Sls Corp....216 910-3400
25825 Science Park Dr Cleveland (44122) **(G-4656)**
Aleris Rolled Products Inc (HQ)....216 910-3400
25825 Science Park Dr # 400 Beachwood (44122) **(G-1221)**
Aleris Rolled Products Inc....740 983-2571
1 Reynolds Rd Ashville (43103) **(G-814)**
Aleris Rolled Products Inc....740 922-2540
7319 Newport Rd Se Uhrichsville (44683) **(G-18879)**
Aleris Rolled Products LLC (HQ)....216 910-3400
25825 Science Park Dr # 400 Cleveland (44122) **(G-4657)**
Alert Safety Lite Products Co....440 232-5020
24500 Solon Rd Cleveland (44146) **(G-4658)**
Alert Safety Products Inc....513 791-4790
11435 Williamson Rd Ste C Blue Ash (45241) **(G-1725)**
Alert Stamping & Mfg Co Inc....440 232-5020
24500 Solon Rd Bedford Heights (44146) **(G-1458)**
Alex and Ani LLC....513 791-1480
7875 Montgomery Rd # 2135 Cincinnati (45236) **(G-3319)**
Alex and Ani LLC....216 378-2139
26300 Cedar Rd Ste 1120 Beachwood (44122) **(G-1222)**
Alex Products Inc....419 399-4500
810 W Gasser Rd Paulding (45879) **(G-15855)**
Alex Products Inc (PA)....419 267-5240
19911 County Rd T Ridgeville Corners (43555) **(G-16510)**
Alexander Wilbert Vault Co (PA)....419 468-3477
1263 State Hwy 598 Galion (44833) **(G-10122)**
Alexis Concrete Enterprise Inc....440 366-0031
672 Sugar Ln Elyria (44035) **(G-9211)**
Alfa Green Supreme, Ottawa *Also called Verhoff Alfalfa Mills Inc* **(G-15670)**
Alfacomp Inc....216 459-1790
4485 Broadview Rd Cleveland (44109) **(G-4659)**
Alfagreen Supreme, Toledo *Also called Ohio Blenders Inc* **(G-18435)**
Alfman Logging LLC....740 982-6227
4499 Township Road 448 Ne Crooksville (43731) **(G-7814)**
Alfons Haar Inc....937 560-2031
150 Advanced Dr Springboro (45066) **(G-17321)**
Alfred J Buescher Jr....216 752-3676
17001 Shaker Blvd Cleveland (44120) **(G-4660)**
Alfred Machine Co (HQ)....440 248-4600
29500 Solon Rd Cleveland (44139) **(G-4661)**
Alfred Nickles Bakery Inc (PA)....330 879-5635
26 Main St N Navarre (44662) **(G-14571)**
Alfred Nickles Bakery Inc....740 453-6522
1147 Newark Rd Zanesville (43701) **(G-21096)**
Alfred Nickles Bakery Inc....937 256-3762
201 Pritz Ave Dayton (45403) **(G-8015)**
Ali Industries Inc....937 878-3946
747 E Xenia Dr Fairborn (45324) **(G-9450)**
Alice Beougher....740 927-2470
13255 National Rd Sw Etna (43068) **(G-9388)**
Alifet USA Inc....513 793-8033
3714 Fallentree Ln Blue Ash (45236) **(G-1726)**
Align Assess Achieve LLC....614 505-6820
900 Michigan Ave Columbus (43215) **(G-6563)**
Alin Machining Company Inc....740 223-0200
875 E Mark St Marion (43302) **(G-12691)**
Alk Industries LLC....513 429-3047
7178 Lamplite Ct Cincinnati (45244) **(G-3320)**
Alkermes Inc....937 382-5642
265 Olinger Cir Wilmington (45177) **(G-20485)**
Alkid Corporation....216 896-3000
6035 Parkland Blvd Cleveland (44124) **(G-4662)**
Alkon Corporation (PA)....419 355-9111
728 Graham Dr Fremont (43420) **(G-9990)**
Alkon Corporation....614 799-6650
6750 Crosby Ct Dublin (43016) **(G-8876)**
All - Flo Pump Company....440 354-1700
8989 Tyler Blvd Mentor (44060) **(G-13382)**
All A Cart Manufacturing Inc....614 443-5544
870 High St Ste 15 Worthington (43085) **(G-20675)**
All About House....614 725-3595
1071 Afton Rd Columbus (43221) **(G-6564)**
All American Energy Coop Assn....440 772-4340
28901 Clemens Rd Ste 119 Westlake (44145) **(G-20089)**
All American Fire Equiptment, Wshngtn CT Hs *Also called All-American Fire Eqp Inc* **(G-20718)**
All American Indus Svcs LLC....440 255-7525
8171 Tyler Blvd Mentor (44060) **(G-13383)**
All American Screen Printing....419 475-0696
2607 W Central Ave Toledo (43606) **(G-18162)**
All American Trophy....614 231-8824
3055 Templeton Rd Ste M Columbus (43209) **(G-6565)**
All American Welding Co....614 224-7752
185 Mcdowell St Columbus (43215) **(G-6566)**
All Around Garage Door Inc....440 759-5079
33434 Liberty Pkwy North Ridgeville (44039) **(G-15207)**
All Coatings Co Inc....330 821-3806
510 W Ely St Alliance (44601) **(G-451)**
All County Phone Directories....419 865-2464
7056 Wexford Hill Ln Holland (43528) **(G-10915)**
All County Phone Directory, Holland *Also called All County Phone Directories* **(G-10915)**
All Craft Manufacturing Co....513 661-3383
6500 Glenway Ave Side 2 Cincinnati (45211) **(G-3321)**
All Cstom Fabricators Erectors, Cleveland *Also called Varmland Inc* **(G-6251)**
All Do Weld & Fab LLC....740 477-2133
28155 River Dr Circleville (43113) **(G-4536)**
All Fired Up Pnt Your Own Pot....330 865-5858
30 Rothrock Loop Copley (44321) **(G-7677)**
All Foam Pdts Safety Foam Proc, Middlefield *Also called All Foam Products Co* **(G-13776)**
All Foam Products Co....330 849-3636
15005 Enterprise Way Middlefield (44062) **(G-13775)**
All Foam Products Co (PA)....330 849-3636
15005 Enterprise Way Middlefield (44062) **(G-13776)**
All For Show Inc....440 729-7186
9321 Winchester Vly Chesterland (44026) **(G-3152)**
All Metal Fabricators Inc....216 267-0033
15400 Commerce Park Dr Cleveland (44142) **(G-4663)**
All Ohio Companies Inc....216 420-9274
2735 Scranton Rd Cleveland (44113) **(G-4664)**
All Ohio Ready Mix Concrete....419 841-3838
622 Eckel Rd Perrysburg (43551) **(G-15918)**
All Ohio Threaded Rod Co Inc....216 426-1800
5349 Saint Clair Ave Cleveland (44103) **(G-4665)**
All Pack Services LLC....614 935-0964
3442 Grant Ave Grove City (43123) **(G-10413)**
All Points Industries Inc....513 826-0681
10590 Hamilton Ave Cincinnati (45231) **(G-3322)**
All Power Battery Inc....330 453-5236
1387 Clarendon Ave Sw # 6 Canton (44710) **(G-2567)**
All Power Equipment LLC (PA)....740 593-3279
8880 United Ln Athens (45701) **(G-822)**
All Prem Cleaners Inc....440 349-3649
33640 Aurora Rd Solon (44139) **(G-17100)**
All Premium Cleaners, Solon *Also called All Prem Cleaners Inc* **(G-17100)**
All Print Ltd....440 349-6868
38415 Flanders Dr Solon (44139) **(G-17101)**
All Pro Alum Cylinder Heads....740 967-7761
5370 Jhnstown Alxndria Rd Johnstown (43031) **(G-11253)**

All Pro Ovrhd Door Systems LLC 614 444-3667
1985 Oakland Park Ave Columbus (43224) **(G-6567)**
All Purpose Machine 419 238-2794
1240 E Main St Van Wert (45891) **(G-19075)**
All Signs and Designs LLC 216 267-8588
5101 W 161st St Cleveland (44142) **(G-4666)**
All Signs Express Inc (PA) 513 489-7744
6610 Corporate Dr Blue Ash (45242) **(G-1727)**
All Signs of Chillicothe Inc 740 773-5016
12035 Pleasant Valley Rd Chillicothe (45601) **(G-3174)**
All Sport Services Corporation 216 361-1965
3635 Perkins Ave Ste 1e Cleveland (44114) **(G-4667)**
All Srvice Plastic Molding Inc 937 415-3674
611 Yellw Spng Fairfld Rd Fairborn (45324) **(G-9451)**
All Srvice Plastic Molding Inc 937 890-0322
900 Falls Creek Dr Vandalia (45377) **(G-19114)**
All Srvice Plastic Molding Inc (PA) 937 890-0322
900 Fall Creek Dr Vandalia (45377) **(G-19115)**
All Star Group Inc 440 323-6060
810 Taylor St Elyria (44035) **(G-9212)**
All Star Sign Company 614 461-9052
112 S Glenwood Ave Columbus (43222) **(G-6568)**
All State GL Block Fctry Inc 440 205-8410
8781 East Ave Mentor (44060) **(G-13384)**
All Steel Structures Inc 330 312-3131
755 N Lisbon St Carrollton (44615) **(G-2915)**
All Systems Colour Inc 937 859-9701
2032 S Alex Rd Ste A Dayton (45449) **(G-8016)**
All Ways Green Lawn & Turf LLC 937 763-4766
1856 Greenbrier Rd Seaman (45679) **(G-16882)**
All Wright Enterprises LLC 440 259-5656
4285 Main St Perry (44081) **(G-15903)**
All Write Ribbon Inc 513 753-8300
3916 Bach Buxton Rd Amelia (45102) **(G-529)**
All-American Fire Eqp Inc 800 972-6035
5101 Us Highway 22 Sw Wshngtn CT Hs (43160) **(G-20718)**
All-Bilt Uniform Corp 513 793-5400
4545 Malsbary Rd Blue Ash (45242) **(G-1728)**
All-Craft Wellman Products, Willoughby *Also called Rise Holdings LLC* **(G-20422)**
All-Line Truck Sales, Hubbard *Also called Youngstown-Kenworth Inc* **(G-11014)**
All-Plant Liquid Plant Food, Ashland *Also called R & J AG Manufacturing Inc* **(G-741)**
All-Rite Rdymx Miami Vly LLC 513 738-1933
7466 New Haven Rd Harrison (45030) **(G-10630)**
All-Seasons Paper Company 440 826-1700
6346 Eastland Rd Cleveland (44142) **(G-4668)**
All-State Belting LLC 614 497-4281
6951 Alan Schwrzwalder St Columbus (43217) **(G-6569)**
All-Tech Manufacturing Ltd 330 633-1095
1477 Industrial Pkwy Akron (44310) **(G-58)**
All-Tra Rubber Processing 330 630-1945
154 Potomac Ave Ste B Tallmadge (44278) **(G-17972)**
All-Type Welding & Fabrication 440 439-3990
7690 Bond St Cleveland (44139) **(G-4669)**
Allan A Irish 419 394-3284
1600 Celina Rd Saint Marys (45885) **(G-16675)**
Allega Concrete Corp 216 447-0814
5585 Canal Rd Cleveland (44125) **(G-4670)**
Allegheny Ludlum LLC 330 875-2244
1500 W Main St Louisville (44641) **(G-12151)**
Allegra Marketing & Printing, Cambridge *Also called H & An LLC* **(G-2442)**
Allegra Marketing Print Mail, Blue Ash *Also called Dsk Imaging LLC* **(G-1759)**
Allegra Print & Imaging, Columbus *Also called Rutobo Inc* **(G-7408)**
Allegra Print & Imaging, Westlake *Also called Allegra Printing & Imaging LLC* **(G-20090)**
Allegra Print & Imaging 419 427-8095
701 W Sandusky St Findlay (45840) **(G-9649)**
Allegra Printing & Imaging LLC 440 449-6989
1486 Barclay Blvd Westlake (44145) **(G-20090)**
Allen Aircraft Products Inc 330 296-9621
312 E Lake St Ravenna (44266) **(G-16365)**
Allen Aircraft Products Inc 330 296-1531
4879 Newton Falls Rd Ravenna (44266) **(G-16366)**
Allen County Fabrication Inc 419 227-7447
999 Industry Ave Lima (45804) **(G-11834)**
Allen County Pallet, Lima *Also called Three AS Inc* **(G-11951)**
Allen Enterprises Inc 740 532-5913
2900 S 9th St Ironton (45638) **(G-11159)**
Allen Fields Assoc Inc 513 228-1010
3525 Grant Ave Ste D Lebanon (45036) **(G-11632)**
Allen Graphics Inc 440 349-4100
27100 Richmond Rd Ste 6 Solon (44139) **(G-17102)**
Allen Green Enterprises LLC 330 339-0200
513 Mill Ave Se New Philadelphia (44663) **(G-14757)**
Allen Harper 740 543-3919
1654 Township Road 266 Amsterdam (43903) **(G-576)**
Allen Kenard Printing Inc 440 323-7405
501 Clark St Elyria (44035) **(G-9213)**
Allen Milk Division, Columbus *Also called Tmarzetti Company* **(G-7532)**
Allen Morgan Trucking & Repair 330 336-5192
4162 Greenwich Rd Norton (44203) **(G-15361)**
Allen Press 614 891-4413
6132 Batavia Rd Westerville (43081) **(G-20033)**
Allen Randall Enterprises Inc 330 374-9850
70 E Miller Ave Akron (44301) **(G-59)**
Allen Tool Co Inc 937 987-2037
300 S 2nd St New Vienna (45159) **(G-14823)**
Allen Zahradnik Inc (PA) 419 729-1201
5902 Edgewater Dr Toledo (43611) **(G-18163)**
Allenbaugh Foods LLC 216 952-3984
14305 Bayes Ave Lakewood (44107) **(G-11509)**
Allergan Inc 614 623-8140
4321 Scioto Pkwy Powell (43065) **(G-16308)**
Allergan Sales LLC 513 271-6800
5000 Brotherton Rd Cincinnati (45209) **(G-3323)**
Allermuir, Maumee *Also called Senator International Inc* **(G-13143)**
Alley Cat Designs Inc 937 291-8803
919 Senate Dr Dayton (45459) **(G-8017)**
Allfab Inc 614 491-4944
2273 Williams Rd Columbus (43207) **(G-6570)**
Allfasteners Usa LLC (HQ) 440 232-6060
959 Lake Rd Medina (44256) **(G-13222)**
Allgeier & Son Inc (PA) 513 574-3735
6386 Bridgetown Rd Cincinnati (45248) **(G-3324)**
Alliance Automation LLC 419 238-2520
560 Bonnewitz Ave Van Wert (45891) **(G-19076)**
Alliance Carpet Cushion Co 740 966-5001
143 Commerce Blvd Johnstown (43031) **(G-11254)**
Alliance Castings Company LLC 330 829-5600
1001 E Broadway St Alliance (44601) **(G-452)**
Alliance Drilling Inc 330 584-2781
20388 N Benton West Rd North Benton (44449) **(G-15059)**
Alliance Equipment Company Inc 330 821-2291
1000 N Union Ave Alliance (44601) **(G-453)**
Alliance Forging Group LLC 330 680-4861
847 Pier Dr 1000 Akron (44307) **(G-60)**
Alliance Healthcare Svcs Inc 330 493-6747
5005 Whipple Ave Nw Canton (44718) **(G-2568)**
Alliance Indus Masking Inc 937 681-5569
204 S Ludlow St Ste 201 Dayton (45402) **(G-8018)**
Alliance Knife Inc 513 367-9000
124 May Dr Harrison (45030) **(G-10631)**
Alliance Manufacturing, Dayton *Also called Alliance Torque Converters Inc* **(G-8019)**
Alliance Mfg Svcs Inc 937 222-3394
5915 Wolf Creek Pike Trotwood (45426) **(G-18627)**
Alliance Petroleum Corporation (HQ) 330 493-0440
4150 Belden Village Mall Canton (44718) **(G-2569)**
Alliance Printing & Publishing 513 422-7611
2520 Atco Ave Middletown (45042) **(G-13883)**
Alliance Publishing Co Inc (HQ) 330 453-1304
40 S Linden Ave Alliance (44601) **(G-454)**
Alliance Torque Converters Inc 937 222-3394
5915 Wolf Creek Pike Dayton (45426) **(G-8019)**
Allied Consolidated Industries (PA) 330 744-0808
2100 Poland Ave Youngstown (44502) **(G-20841)**
Allied Construction Pdts LLC (HQ) 216 431-2600
3900 Kelley Ave Cleveland (44114) **(G-4671)**
Allied Construction Pdts LLC 216 431-2600
1840 E 40th St Cleveland (44103) **(G-4672)**
Allied Corporation Inc (HQ) 330 425-7861
8920 Canyon Falls Blvd # 120 Twinsburg (44087) **(G-18730)**
Allied Custom Molded Products 614 291-0629
1240 Essex Ave Columbus (43201) **(G-6571)**
Allied Fabricating & Wldg Co 614 751-6664
5699 Chantry Dr Columbus (43232) **(G-6572)**
Allied Machine & Engrg Corp (PA) 330 343-4283
120 Deeds Dr Dover (44622) **(G-8803)**
Allied Machine Works Inc 740 454-2534
120 Graham St Zanesville (43701) **(G-21097)**
Allied Mask and Tooling Inc 419 470-2555
6051 Telegraph Rd Ste 6 Toledo (43612) **(G-18164)**
Allied Mineral Products Inc (PA) 614 876-0244
2700 Scioto Pkwy Columbus (43221) **(G-6573)**
Allied Moulded Products Inc (PA) 419 636-4217
222 N Union St Bryan (43506) **(G-2259)**
Allied Moulded Products Inc 419 636-4217
1117 E High St Bryan (43506) **(G-2260)**
Allied Moulded Products Inc 419 636-4217
2103 Industrial Dr Bryan (43506) **(G-2261)**
Allied Pedestal Boom Sys LLC 419 663-0279
75 Norwalk Commons Dr Norwalk (44857) **(G-15379)**
Allied Plastic Co Inc 419 389-1688
3203 South Ave Toledo (43609) **(G-18165)**
Allied Retail Solutions 330 332-8141
1960 S Lincoln Ave Unit 4 Salem (44460) **(G-16716)**
Allied Separation Tech Inc (PA) 704 732-8034
2300 E Enterprise Pkwy Twinsburg (44087) **(G-18731)**
Allied Separation Tech Inc 704 736-0420
2300 E Enterprise Pkwy Twinsburg (44087) **(G-18732)**
Allied Sign Company Inc 614 443-9656
818 Marion Rd Columbus (43207) **(G-6574)**

ALPHABETIC

Allied Silk Screen Inc....937 223-4921
2740 Thunderhawk Ct Dayton (45414) *(G-8020)*
Allied Supplied Company, Twinsburg *Also called Allied Separation Tech Inc (G-18732)*
Allied Tool & Die Inc....216 941-6196
16146 Puritas Ave Cleveland (44135) *(G-4673)*
Allied Tube & Conduit Corp....740 928-1018
250 Capital Dr Hebron (43025) *(G-10737)*
Allied Window Inc....513 559-1212
11111 Canal Rd Cincinnati (45241) *(G-3325)*
Allmax Software Inc....419 673-8863
911 S Main St Kenton (43326) *(G-11401)*
Alloy Bllows Prcision Wldg Inc (PA)....440 684-3000
653 Miner Rd Cleveland (44143) *(G-4674)*
Alloy Engineering Company (PA)....440 243-6800
844 Thacker St Berea (44017) *(G-1589)*
Alloy Fabricators Inc....330 948-3535
700 Wooster St Lodi (44254) *(G-12005)*
Alloy Machining and Fabg....330 482-5543
1028 Lower Elkton Rd Columbiana (44408) *(G-6453)*
Alloy Metal Exchange LLC....216 478-0200
26000 Corbin Dr Bedford Heights (44128) *(G-1459)*
Alloy Polymers, Gahanna *Also called Pahuja Inc (G-10097)*
Alloy Unlimited Weld....330 506-8375
4200 W Middletown Rd Canfield (44406) *(G-2520)*
Alloy Welding & Fabricating....440 914-0650
30340 Solon Indtl Pky B Solon (44139) *(G-17103)*
Allpass Corporation....440 998-6300
222 N Lake St Madison (44057) *(G-12339)*
Allstates Refr Contrs LLC....419 878-4691
218 Mechanic St B Waterville (43566) *(G-19489)*
Alltech Med Systems Amer Inc....440 424-2240
28900 Fountain Pkwy Solon (44139) *(G-17104)*
Allyn Corp (PA)....614 442-3900
1491 Clairmonte Rd Columbus (43221) *(G-6575)*
Alma Mater Sportswear LLC....614 260-8222
3029 Silver Dr Columbus (43224) *(G-6576)*
Alma Mater Wear, Columbus *Also called Alma Mater Sportswear LLC (G-6576)*
Almo Process Technology Inc....513 402-2566
8849 Brookside Ave # 101 West Chester (45069) *(G-19642)*
Almondina Brand Biscuits, Maumee *Also called Y Z Enterprises Inc (G-13161)*
Alonovus Corp....330 674-2300
7368 County Road 623 Millersburg (44654) *(G-14057)*
Aloterra Packaging LLC....281 547-0568
198 Parker Dr Andover (44003) *(G-578)*
Alpco, Westlake *Also called Aluminum Line Products Company (G-20091)*
Alpha Bus Forms & Prtg LLC....419 999-5138
4330 East Rd Lima (45807) *(G-11835)*
Alpha Coatings Inc....419 435-5111
622 S Corporate Dr W Fostoria (44830) *(G-9832)*
Alpha Container Co Inc....937 644-5511
16789 Square Dr Marysville (43040) *(G-12769)*
Alpha Control LLC....740 377-3400
1042 County Road 60 South Point (45680) *(G-17278)*
Alpha Control Fabg & Mfg, South Point *Also called Alpha Control LLC (G-17278)*
Alpha Machining LLC....330 889-2207
394 E Main St West Farmington (44491) *(G-19919)*
Alpha Omega Bioremediation LLC....614 287-2600
2824 Fisher Rd Ste E Columbus (43204) *(G-6577)*
Alpha Omega Dev & Mch Co....440 352-9915
10395 Squires Ct Painesville (44077) *(G-15708)*
Alpha Omega Import Export LLC....740 885-9155
1135 Browns Rd Marietta (45750) *(G-12602)*
Alpha Packaging Holdings Inc....216 252-5595
14801 Emery Ave Cleveland (44135) *(G-4675)*
Alpha Strike, Kent *Also called Primal Screen Inc (G-11368)*
Alpha Technologies Svcs LLC (HQ)....330 745-1641
6279 Hudson Crossing Pkwy Hudson (44236) *(G-11027)*
Alpha Tool & Mold Inc....440 473-2343
83 Alpha Park Cleveland (44143) *(G-4676)*
Alpha Water Conditioning Co, Dayton *Also called R D Baker Enterprises Inc (G-8458)*
Alpha Zeta Holdings Inc (PA)....216 271-1601
2981 Independence Rd Cleveland (44115) *(G-4677)*
Alphabet Inc (HQ)....330 856-3366
8640 E Market St Warren (44484) *(G-19366)*
Alphabet Embroidery Studios....937 372-6557
1291 Bellbrook Ave Xenia (45385) *(G-20755)*
Alphabet Soup Inc....330 467-4418
981 Cessna Dr Macedonia (44056) *(G-12276)*
AlphaGraphics, Strongsville *Also called Blue Crescent Enterprises Inc (G-17720)*
AlphaGraphics, Columbus *Also called DC Reprographics Co (G-6854)*
AlphaGraphics, Columbus *Also called Headlee Enterprises Ltd (G-6496)*
AlphaGraphics, Cleveland *Also called Swimmer Printing Inc (G-6138)*
AlphaGraphics 507 Inc....440 878-9700
14765 Pearl Rd Strongsville (44136) *(G-17708)*
AlphaGraphics Cincinnati, Mason *Also called Morse Enterprises Inc (G-12912)*
AlphaGraphics Valley View, Cleveland *Also called Image Concepts Inc (G-5437)*
AlphaGraphics Westlake, Westlake *Also called Vision Graphix Inc (G-20169)*
Alpine Cabinets Inc....330 273-2131
1515 W 130th St Ste E Hinckley (44233) *(G-10897)*
Alpine Gage Inc....937 669-8665
4325 Lisa Dr Tipp City (45371) *(G-18099)*
Alpla Inc....419 991-9484
3320 Fort Shwnee Indus Dr Lima (45806) *(G-11960)*
Alro Steel Corporation....419 720-5300
3003 Airport Hwy Toledo (43609) *(G-18166)*
Alro Steel Corporation....614 878-7271
555 Hilliard Rome Rd Columbus (43228) *(G-6578)*
Alro Steel Corporation....937 253-6121
821 Springfield St Dayton (45403) *(G-8021)*
Alron....330 477-3405
805 Margo Dr Sw Strasburg (44680) *(G-17644)*
Alron Inc....330 477-3405
5307 Southway St Sw Canton (44706) *(G-2570)*
Als High Tech Inc (PA)....440 232-7090
135 Northfield Rd Bedford (44146) *(G-1380)*
Als Polishing Shop Inc....419 476-8857
1615 W Laskey Rd Toledo (43612) *(G-18167)*
Alsco Metals Corporation....740 983-2571
1 Reynolds Rd Ashville (43103) *(G-815)*
Alsco Metals Corporation (HQ)....740 983-2571
1309 Deer Hill Rd Dennison (44621) *(G-8781)*
Alsico Usa Inc (PA)....330 673-7413
333 Martinel Dr Kent (44240) *(G-11292)*
Alside Supply Center, Dayton *Also called Associated Materials LLC (G-8040)*
Alstart Enterprises LLC....330 533-3222
451 W Main St Canfield (44406) *(G-2521)*
Alt Control Print....419 841-2467
6906 Milrose Ln Toledo (43617) *(G-18168)*
Alt Fuel LLC....419 865-4196
1100 King Rd Toledo (43617) *(G-18169)*
Alta Mira Corporation....330 648-2461
225 N Main St Spencer (44275) *(G-17303)*
Altana....440 954-7600
830 E Erie St Painesville (44077) *(G-15709)*
Altec Industries....419 289-6066
1236 Township Road 1175 Ashland (44805) *(G-676)*
Altec Industries Inc....205 408-2341
307 Munroe Falls Ave Cuyahoga Falls (44221) *(G-7833)*
Alteirs Oil Inc....740 347-4335
140 W Main St Corning (43730) *(G-7699)*
Altenloh Brinck & Co Inc....419 636-6715
2105 County Road 12c Bryan (43506) *(G-2262)*
Altenloh Brinck & Co US Inc (HQ)....419 636-6715
2105 Williams Co Rd 12 C Bryan (43506) *(G-2263)*
Alteo Na LLC....440 460-4600
46 Ravenna St Ste B3 Hudson (44236) *(G-11028)*
Altera Corporation....513 444-2021
9435 Waterstone Blvd # 140 Cincinnati (45249) *(G-3326)*
Altera Corporation....330 650-5200
591 Boston Mills Rd # 600 Hudson (44236) *(G-11029)*
Altera Polymers LLC....864 973-7000
222 S Sycamore St Jefferson (44047) *(G-11224)*
Alternate Defense LLC....216 225-5889
19101 Watercrest Ave Maple Heights (44137) *(G-12564)*
Alternative Flash Inc....330 334-6111
1734 Wall Rd Ste B Wadsworth (44281) *(G-19225)*
Alternative Press Magazine Inc....216 631-1510
1305 W 80th St Ste 21 Cleveland (44102) *(G-4678)*
Alternative Surface Grinding....330 273-3443
1093 Industrial Pkwy N Brunswick (44212) *(G-2187)*
Alterntive Spport Appratus LLC....740 922-2727
5609 Gundy Dr Midvale (44653) *(G-13973)*
Altheirs Oil Inc....740 347-4335
140 E Main St Corning (43730) *(G-7700)*
Altier Brothers Inc....740 347-4329
155 Walnut St Corning (43730) *(G-7701)*
Altitude Medical Inc....440 799-7701
Po Box 770 Chardon (44024) *(G-3097)*
Altivia Petrochemicals LLC....740 532-3420
1019 Haverhill Ohio Haverhill (45636) *(G-10707)*
Altivity Packaging, Middletown *Also called Graphic Packaging Intl Inc (G-13911)*
Altivity Packaging, Solon *Also called Graphic Packaging Intl Inc (G-17153)*
Altivity Packaging, Cincinnati *Also called Multi-Color Corporation (G-4054)*
Alton Products Inc....419 893-0201
425 W Sophia St Maumee (43537) *(G-13068)*
Altraserv LLC....614 889-2500
8350 Industrial Pkwy # 16 Plain City (43064) *(G-16170)*
Altronic LLC (HQ)....330 545-9768
712 Trumbull Ave Girard (44420) *(G-10252)*
Aluchem Inc (PA)....513 733-8519
1 Landy Ln Ste 1 # 1 Cincinnati (45215) *(G-3327)*
Aluchem of Jackson Inc....740 286-2455
14782 Beaver Pike Jackson (45640) *(G-11180)*
Alufab Inc....513 528-7281
1018 Seabrook Way Cincinnati (45245) *(G-3240)*
Alumacast LLC....419 584-1473
300 N Brandon Ave Celina (45822) *(G-2949)*

ALPHABETIC SECTION — American Commodore Tuxedos

Alumetal Manufacturing Company 419 268-2311
4555 Sr 127 Coldwater (45828) *(G-6399)*

Aluminum Bearing Co of America 216 267-8560
4775 W 139th St Cleveland (44135) *(G-4679)*

Aluminum Coating Manufacturers 216 341-2000
7301 Bessemer Ave Cleveland (44127) *(G-4680)*

Aluminum Color Industries Inc (PA) 330 536-6295
369 W Wood St Lowellville (44436) *(G-12248)*

Aluminum Extruded Shapes Inc 513 563-2205
10549 Reading Rd Cincinnati (45241) *(G-3328)*

Aluminum Extrusion Tech LLC 330 533-3994
6155 State Route 446 Canfield (44406) *(G-2522)*

Aluminum Fence & Mfg Co 330 755-3323
189 New Castle Dr Aurora (44202) *(G-868)*

Aluminum Line Products Company (PA) 440 835-8880
24460 Sperry Cir Westlake (44145) *(G-20091)*

Alvin L Roepke 419 862-3891
329 Rice St Elmore (43416) *(G-9203)*

Alvio, Cleveland *Also called Golubitsky Corporation* *(G-5329)*

Alvito Custom Imprints 614 846-8986
7469 Wrthington Galena Rd Worthington (43085) *(G-20676)*

Alvords Yard & Garden Eqp 440 286-2315
12089 Ravenna Rd Chardon (44024) *(G-3098)*

Always Promoting Co., Maumee *Also called Skr Enterprises LLC* *(G-13145)*

AM & PM United, Youngstown *Also called A United* *(G-20831)*

AM Castle & Co 330 425-7000
26800 Miles Rd Bedford (44146) *(G-1381)*

AM General LLC 937 704-0160
2000 Watkins Glen Dr Franklin (45005) *(G-9868)*

Am Graphics 330 799-7319
20 S Maryland Ave Youngstown (44509) *(G-20842)*

AM Industrial Group LLC (PA) 216 433-7171
16000 Commerce Park Dr Brookpark (44142) *(G-2134)*

AM Retail Group Inc 513 539-7837
628 Premium Outlets Dr Monroe (45050) *(G-14254)*

AM Warren LLC 330 841-2800
2234 Main Ave Sw Warren (44481) *(G-19367)*

AMA Fuel Services LLC 513 836-3800
3053 Hart Rd Lebanon (45036) *(G-11633)*

Amac Enterprises Inc (PA) 216 362-1880
5909 W 130th St Parma (44130) *(G-15814)*

Amac Enterprises Inc 216 362-1880
5925 W 130th St Cleveland (44130) *(G-4681)*

Amaltech Inc 440 248-7500
30670 Bainbridge Rd Solon (44139) *(G-17105)*

Aman & Co Inc 330 854-1122
231 Locust St S Canal Fulton (44614) *(G-2473)*

Amanda Bent Bolt Company 740 385-6893
1120 C I C Dr Logan (43138) *(G-12021)*

Amanda Manufacturing, Logan *Also called Amanda Bent Bolt Company* *(G-12021)*

Amano Cincinnati Incorporated 513 697-9000
130 Commerce Dr Loveland (45140) *(G-12176)*

Amano McGann Inc 513 683-2906
10162 International Blvd West Chester (45246) *(G-19831)*

Amaroq Inc 419 747-2110
648 N Trimble Rd Mansfield (44906) *(G-12403)*

Amarr Company 216 573-7100
800 Resource Dr Ste 3 Independence (44131) *(G-11119)*

Amarr Garage Doors, Independence *Also called Amarr Company* *(G-11119)*

Amatech Inc 614 252-2506
1633 Woodland Ave Columbus (43219) *(G-6579)*

Amatech Polycell, Columbus *Also called Polycel Incorporated* *(G-7331)*

Ambaflex Inc 330 478-1858
1530 Raff Rd Sw Canton (44710) *(G-2571)*

Ambassador Heat Transfer, Blue Ash *Also called Space Dynamics Corp* *(G-1847)*

Ambassador Steel Corporation 740 382-9969
850 Barks Rd W Marion (43302) *(G-12692)*

Ambrosia Inc (PA) 419 825-1151
395 W Airport Hwy Swanton (43558) *(G-17904)*

AMC, Wooster *Also called ABS Materials Inc* *(G-20553)*

Amcan Productions Ltd 330 332-9129
3735 Mccracken Rd Salem (44460) *(G-16717)*

Amcan Stair & Rail LLC 937 781-3084
20 Zischler St Springfield (45504) *(G-17362)*

Amclo Group Inc 216 791-8400
9721 York Alpha Dr North Royalton (44133) *(G-15259)*

Amco Products Inc 937 433-7982
500 N Smithville Rd Dayton (45431) *(G-7970)*

Amcor Marine, Lorain *Also called American Metal Chemical Corp* *(G-12078)*

Amcor Rigid Plastics Usa LLC 419 483-4343
975 W Main St Bellevue (44811) *(G-1527)*

Amcor Rigid Plastics Usa LLC 419 592-1998
12993 State Route 110 Napoleon (43545) *(G-14531)*

Amcor Rigid Plastics Usa LLC 419 483-4343
975 W Main St Bellevue (44811) *(G-1528)*

Amcraft Inc 419 729-7900
5144 Enterprise Blvd Toledo (43612) *(G-18170)*

Amcraft Manufacturing, Toledo *Also called Amcraft Inc* *(G-18170)*

AMD Fabricators Inc 440 946-8855
4580 Beidler Rd Willoughby (44094) *(G-20270)*

AMD Plastics LLC (PA) 216 289-4862
27600 Lakeland Blvd Euclid (44132) *(G-9401)*

Ameco USA Metal Fabrication 440 899-9400
4600 W 160th St Cleveland (44135) *(G-4682)*

Amelia Plastics 513 386-4926
3202 Marshall Dr Bldg 8 Amelia (45102) *(G-530)*

Amerascrew Inc 419 522-2232
653 Lida St Mansfield (44903) *(G-12404)*

Ameri-Cal Corporation 330 725-7735
1001 Lake Rd Medina (44256) *(G-13223)*

American Academic Press 216 906-2518
550 Turney Rd Apt C Bedford (44146) *(G-1382)*

American Advnced Assmblies LLC 937 339-6267
37 Harolds Way Troy (45373) *(G-18634)*

American Aero Components LLC 937 367-5068
2601 W Stroop Rd Ste 62 Dayton (45439) *(G-8022)*

American Agritech LLC 480 777-2000
14111 Scottslawn Rd Marysville (43040) *(G-12770)*

American Airless Inc 614 552-0146
7095 Americana Pkwy Reynoldsburg (43068) *(G-16428)*

American Aluminum Extrusions 330 458-0300
4416 Louisville St Ne Canton (44705) *(G-2572)*

American Apex Corporation 614 652-2000
8515 Rausch Dr Plain City (43064) *(G-16171)*

American Assembly Tools, Columbia Station *Also called Triad Capital Aat LLC* *(G-6451)*

American Awards Inc 614 875-1850
2380 Harrisburg Pike Grove City (43123) *(G-10414)*

American Baler Co 419 483-5790
800 E Center St Bellevue (44811) *(G-1529)*

American Band Saw Co 740 452-8168
4049 Newark Rd Zanesville (43701) *(G-21098)*

American Barricade, Dalton *Also called Gedco Inc* *(G-7942)*

American Belleville, Painesville *Also called Zsi Manufacturing Inc* *(G-15805)*

American Book Screening, Cleveland *Also called Betley Printing Co* *(G-4810)*

American Bottling Company 614 237-4201
960 Stelzer Rd Columbus (43219) *(G-6580)*

American Bottling Company 937 236-0333
3131 Transportation Rd Dayton (45404) *(G-8023)*

American Bottling Company 740 922-5253
Old Rte 250 Midvale (44653) *(G-13974)*

American Bottling Company 740 377-4371
2531 County Road 1 South Point (45680) *(G-17279)*

American Bottling Company 740 423-9230
871 State Route 618 Little Hocking (45742) *(G-11990)*

American Bottling Company 614 237-4201
950 Stelzer Rd Columbus (43219) *(G-6581)*

American Bottling Company 419 229-7777
2350 Central Point Pkwy Lima (45804) *(G-11836)*

American Bottling Company 419 535-0777
224 N Byrne Rd Toledo (43607) *(G-18171)*

American Bottling Company 513 381-4891
125 E Court St Ste 820 Cincinnati (45202) *(G-3329)*

American Bottling Company 513 242-5151
5151 Fischer Ave Cincinnati (45217) *(G-3330)*

American Brass, Cleveland *Also called Empire Brass Co* *(G-5173)*

American Brass Manufacturing 216 431-6565
5000 Superior Ave Cleveland (44103) *(G-4683)*

American Brick & Block, Dayton *Also called American Concrete Products* *(G-8025)*

American Bronze Corporation 216 341-7800
2941 Broadway Ave Cleveland (44115) *(G-4684)*

American Brzing Div Paulo Pdts, Willoughby *Also called Paulo Products Company* *(G-20399)*

American Buffing, Carlisle *Also called Qibco Buffing Pads Inc* *(G-2897)*

American Built Custom Pallets 330 532-4780
42120 Glasgow Rd Lisbon (44432) *(G-11963)*

American Canvas Products Inc 419 382-8450
2925 South Ave Toledo (43609) *(G-18172)*

American Carbide Tool Company, Canton *Also called Ohio Metal Working Products* *(G-2773)*

American Carved Crystal, Cleveland *Also called R M Yates Co Inc* *(G-5953)*

American Ceramic Society (PA) 614 890-4700
550 Polaris Pkwy Ste 510 Westerville (43082) *(G-19977)*

American Chemical Products 216 267-7722
5041 W 161st St Cleveland (44142) *(G-4685)*

American City Bus Journals Inc 513 337-9450
120 E 4th St Ste 230 Cincinnati (45202) *(G-3331)*

American City Bus Journals Inc 937 528-4400
40 N Main St Ste 800 Dayton (45423) *(G-8024)*

American Climber & Mch Corp 330 420-0019
38294 Industrial Park Rd Lisbon (44432) *(G-11964)*

American Cold Forge LLC 419 836-1062
5650 Woodville Rd Northwood (43619) *(G-15331)*

American Colloid Company 419 445-9085
809 Myers St Archbold (43502) *(G-635)*

American Colorscans, Columbus *Also called West-Camp Press Inc* *(G-7600)*

American Commodore Tuxedos 440 324-2889
3574 Midway Mall Elyria (44035) *(G-9214)*

(PA)=Parent Co (HQ)=Headquarters (DH)=Div Headquarters

2019 Harris Ohio Industrial Directory

American Community Newspapers 614 888-4567
5255 Sinclair Rd Columbus (43229) *(G-6582)*
American Concrete Products 937 224-1433
1433 S Euclid Ave Dayton (45417) *(G-8025)*
American Confections Co LLC 614 888-8838
90 Logan Pkwy Coventry Township (44319) *(G-7765)*
American Countertops Inc 330 877-0343
7291 Swamp St Ne Hartville (44632) *(G-10683)*
American Craft Hardware LLC 440 746-0098
4025 Riveredge Rd Cleveland (44111) *(G-4686)*
American Cube Mold Inc 330 558-0044
1515 W 130th St Ste C Hinckley (44233) *(G-10898)*
American Culvert & Fabg Co 740 432-6334
201 Wheeling Ave Cambridge (43725) *(G-2422)*
American Custom Industries, Sylvania Also called Bobbart Industries Inc *(G-17934)*
American Custom Polishing, Cincinnati Also called Charles J Meyers *(G-3465)*
American Diesel, Inc., Cleveland Also called Interstate Diesel Service Inc *(G-5470)*
American Doll Accessories 740 590-8458
24924 Brimstone Rd Coolville (45723) *(G-7672)*
American Dreams Inc 740 385-4444
1 Shoreline Dr Thornville (43076) *(G-18029)*
American Electric Furnace Co, Cleveland Also called A E F Inc *(G-4585)*
American Electric Motor Svc, Columbus Also called Electro Torque *(G-6890)*
American Electric Power, Columbus Also called AEP Resources Inc *(G-6548)*
American Energy Corporation 740 926-9152
43521 Mayhugh Hill Rd Beallsville (43716) *(G-1289)*
American Energy Pdts Inc Ind, Mount Vernon Also called Capital City Oil Inc *(G-14473)*
American Executive Gifts Inc 330 645-4396
2098 Sypher Rd Unit C Akron (44306) *(G-61)*
American Extrusion Svcs Inc (HQ) 937 743-1210
235 Advanced Dr Springboro (45066) *(G-17322)*
American Fine Sinter Co Ltd 419 443-8880
957 N County Road 11 Tiffin (44883) *(G-18042)*
American Flange & Mfg Co Inc 740 549-6073
425 Winter Rd Delaware (43015) *(G-8653)*
American Fluid Power Inc 877 223-8742
144 Reaser Ct Elyria (44035) *(G-9215)*
American Foam Products Inc 440 352-3434
753 Liberty St Painesville (44077) *(G-15710)*
American Foods Group LLC 513 733-8898
3480 E Kemper Rd Cincinnati (45241) *(G-3332)*
American Frame Corporation (PA) 419 893-5595
400 Tomahawk Dr Maumee (43537) *(G-13069)*
American Friction Tech LLC 216 823-0861
9300 Midwest Ave Cleveland (44125) *(G-4687)*
American Greetings Corporation (HQ) 216 252-7300
1 American Way Cleveland (44145) *(G-4688)*
American Grphcal Sftwr Systems, Chesterland Also called American Grphcal Sftwr Systems *(G-3153)*
American Grphcal Sftwr Systems 440 729-0018
8000 Wedgewood Dr Chesterland (44026) *(G-3153)*
American Guild of English Hand 937 438-0085
201 E 5th St 19001025 Cincinnati (45202) *(G-3333)*
American Health Packaging, Columbus Also called Amerisource Health Svcs LLC *(G-6590)*
American Heart Association Inc 419 740-6180
4331 Keystone Dr Ste D Maumee (43537) *(G-13070)*
American Heat Treating, Dayton Also called Pride Investments LLC *(G-8439)*
American Heritage Blld LLC 330 626-3710
630 Mondial Pkwy Streetsboro (44241) *(G-17660)*
American Highway Products LLC 330 874-3270
11723 Strasburg Blvd Bolivar (44612) *(G-1906)*
American Honda Motor Co Inc 937 339-0157
151 Commerce Center Blvd Troy (45373) *(G-18635)*
American Honda Motor Co Inc 937 332-6100
101 S Stanfield Rd Troy (45373) *(G-18636)*
American Hvy Plate Sltions LLC 740 331-4620
42722 State Route 7 Ste 1 Clarington (43915) *(G-4566)*
American Icon Defense Ltd 216 233-5184
1510 W Clifton Blvd Lakewood (44107) *(G-11510)*
American Imprssions Sportswear, Worthington Also called American Imprssions Sportswear *(G-20677)*
American Imprssions Sportswear 614 848-6677
6969 Wrthington Galena Rd Worthington (43085) *(G-20677)*
American Indus Maintenance 937 254-3400
605 Springfield St Dayton (45403) *(G-8026)*
American Inks and Coatings Co 513 552-7200
575 Quality Blvd Fairfield (45014) *(G-9481)*
American Insulation Tech LLC 513 733-4248
6071 Branch Hill Guinea P Milford (45150) *(G-13993)*
American Interior Design Inc 216 663-0606
19561 Miles Rd Cleveland (44128) *(G-4689)*
American Ir Met Cleveland LLC 216 266-0509
1240 Marquette St Cleveland (44114) *(G-4690)*
American Isostatic Presses Inc 614 497-3148
1205 S Columbus Arprt Rd Columbus (43207) *(G-6583)*
American Israelite Co 513 621-3145
18 W 9th St Ste 2 Cincinnati (45202) *(G-3334)*
American Israelite Newspaper, Cincinnati Also called American Israelite Co *(G-3334)*

American Jrnl of Drmtpathology 440 542-0041
6554 Dorset Ln Solon (44139) *(G-17106)*
American Laser and Machine LLC 419 214-0880
501 Weston St Toledo (43609) *(G-18173)*
American Lawyers Co Inc (PA) 440 333-5190
853 Westpoint Pkwy # 710 Westlake (44145) *(G-20092)*
American Lawyers Quarterly, Westlake Also called American Lawyers Co Inc *(G-20092)*
American Led-Gible Inc 614 851-1100
1776 Lone Eagle St Columbus (43228) *(G-6584)*
American Legal Publishing Corp 513 421-4248
1 W 4th St Ste 300 Cincinnati (45202) *(G-3335)*
American Light Metals LLC 330 908-3065
635 Highland Rd E Macedonia (44056) *(G-12277)*
American Lithuanian Press 216 531-8150
19807 Cherokee Ave Cleveland (44119) *(G-4691)*
American Made Bags LLC 330 475-1385
999 Sweitzer Ave Akron (44311) *(G-62)*
American Made Corrugated Packg 937 981-2111
1100 N 5th St Greenfield (45123) *(G-10346)*
American Manufacturing Inc (PA) 419 531-9471
2375 Dorr St Ste F Toledo (43607) *(G-18174)*
American Manufacturing & Eqp 513 829-2248
4990 Factory Dr Fairfield (45014) *(G-9482)*
American Merchant Servic 216 598-3100
3076 Waterfall Way Westlake (44145) *(G-20093)*
American Metal Chemical Corp 440 244-1800
200 E 9th St Lorain (44052) *(G-12078)*
American Metal Cleaning Inc 419 255-1828
2512 Albion St Toledo (43610) *(G-18175)*
American Metal Coatings Inc (PA) 216 451-3131
7700 Tyler Blvd Mentor (44060) *(G-13385)*
American Metal Sign 267 521-2670
4750 State Route 309 Ada (45810) *(G-4)*
American Metal Stamping Co LLC 216 531-3100
20900 Saint Clair Ave Euclid (44117) *(G-9402)*
American Metal Tech LLC 937 347-1111
851 Bellbrook Ave Xenia (45385) *(G-20756)*
American Metal Treating Co 216 431-4492
1043 E 62nd St Cleveland (44103) *(G-4692)*
American Mfg & Engrg Co 440 899-9400
910 Cahoon Rd Westlake (44145) *(G-20094)*
American Mfg & Engrg Co 440 899-9400
7500 Grand Division Ave Cleveland (44125) *(G-4693)*
American Mine Door, Cleveland Also called Zen Industries Inc *(G-6339)*
American Mitsuba Corporation 989 779-4962
4140 Tuller Rd Ste 106 Dublin (43017) *(G-8877)*
American Mitsuba Corporation 989 779-4962
4140 Tuller Rd Ste 106 Dublin (43017) *(G-8878)*
American Mnfcturing Operations 419 269-1560
1931 E Manhattan Blvd Toledo (43608) *(G-18176)*
American Mobile Fitness LLC 419 351-1381
2727 N Holland Sylvnia Rd Toledo (43615) *(G-18177)*
American Molded Plastics Inc 330 872-3838
3876 Newton Fls Bailey Rd Newton Falls (44444) *(G-14984)*
American Molding Company Inc 330 620-6799
711 Wooster Rd W Barberton (44203) *(G-1051)*
American Mtal Clg Cncnnati Inc 513 825-1171
475 Northland Blvd Cincinnati (45240) *(G-3336)*
American Office Services Inc 440 899-6888
30257 Clemens Rd Ste C Westlake (44145) *(G-20095)*
American Ohio Locomotive Crane, Bucyrus Also called Ers Industries Inc *(G-2328)*
American Orginal Bldg Pdts LLC 330 786-3000
1000 Arlington Cir Akron (44306) *(G-63)*
American Orthopedics Inc (PA) 614 291-6454
1151 W 5th Ave Columbus (43212) *(G-6585)*
American Paint Recyclers, Lima Also called Brinkman LLC *(G-11846)*
American Paint Recyclers LLC 888 978-6558
4664 Mddle Pint Wetzel Rd Middle Point (45863) *(G-13755)*
American Pan Company, Sunbury Also called Russell T Bundy Associates Inc *(G-17900)*
American Pan Company (PA) 937 652-3232
417 E Water St Ste 2 Urbana (43078) *(G-18978)*
American Paper Converting LLC 419 729-4782
6142 American Rd Toledo (43612) *(G-18178)*
American Pennekamp Mfg Inc 740 687-0096
1495 Longwood Dr Ne Lancaster (43130) *(G-11539)*
American Pioneer Manufacturing 330 457-1400
3672 Silliman St New Waterford (44445) *(G-14835)*
American Plastech LLC 330 538-0576
11635 Mahoning Ave North Jackson (44451) *(G-15140)*
American Plastic Tech Inc 440 632-5203
15229 S State Ave Middlefield (44062) *(G-13777)*
American Plastics LLC 419 423-1213
814 W Lima St Findlay (45840) *(G-9650)*
American Polymer Standards 440 255-2211
8680 Tyler Blvd Mentor (44060) *(G-13386)*
American Posts LLC 419 720-0652
810 Chicago St Toledo (43611) *(G-18179)*
American Power Hoist Inc 740 964-2035
63 E Mill St Pataskala (43062) *(G-15828)*

American Power Pull Corp 419 335-7050
115 E Linfoot St Wauseon (43567) ***(G-19509)***
American Precision Spindles 267 436-6000
670 Alpha Dr Cleveland (44143) ***(G-4694)***
American Printing Inc 330 630-1121
1121 Tower Dr Akron (44305) ***(G-64)***
American Pro-Mold Inc 330 336-4111
350 State St 7 Wadsworth (44281) ***(G-19226)***
American Processing LLC 216 486-4600
17001 Saranac Rd Cleveland (44110) ***(G-4695)***
American Products, Waterville *Also called Duvall Woodworking Inc* ***(G-19494)***
American Punch Co Inc 216 731-4501
1655 Century Corners Pkwy Euclid (44132) ***(G-9403)***
American Quality Door, Marion *Also called Bert Radebaugh* ***(G-12695)***
American Quality Molds LLC 513 276-7345
2275 Millville Ave Ste E Hamilton (45013) ***(G-10532)***
American Quality Stripping 419 625-6288
1750 5th St Sandusky (44870) ***(G-16794)***
American Quicksilver Co 513 871-4517
646 Rushton Rd Cincinnati (45226) ***(G-3337)***
American Qulty Fabrication Inc 937 742-7001
849 Scholz Dr Vandalia (45377) ***(G-19116)***
American Race Cars 419 836-5070
407 E Bogart Rd Sandusky (44870) ***(G-16795)***
American Regent Inc 614 436-2222
6610 New Albany Rd E New Albany (43054) ***(G-14604)***
American Regent Inc 614 436-2222
960 Crupper Ave Columbus (43229) ***(G-6586)***
American Regent Inc 614 436-2222
4150 Lyman Dr Hilliard (43026) ***(G-10804)***
American Rescue Technology 937 293-6240
2780 Culver Ave Dayton (45429) ***(G-8027)***
American Ride Wheelchair Coach 216 276-1700
1368 W 65th St Cleveland (44102) ***(G-4696)***
American Road Machinery, Canton *Also called ARM Opco Inc* ***(G-2575)***
American Rodpump Ltd 440 987-9457
5201 Indian Hill Rd Dublin (43017) ***(G-8879)***
American Roll Formed Pdts Corp (HQ) 440 352-0753
3805 Hendricks Rd Ste A Youngstown (44515) ***(G-20843)***
American Rugged Enclosures (PA) 513 942-3004
4 Standen Dr Hamilton (45015) ***(G-10533)***
American Sand & Gravel Div, Massillon *Also called Kenmore Construction Co Inc* ***(G-13009)***
American Scaffolding Inc 216 524-7733
7600 Wall St Ste 200 Cleveland (44125) ***(G-4697)***
American Showa Inc 937 783-4961
960 Cherry St Blanchester (45107) ***(G-1698)***
American Solving Inc 440 234-7373
6519 Eastland Rd Ste 5 Brookpark (44142) ***(G-2135)***
American Speedy Printing, Zanesville *Also called T & K Heins Corporation* ***(G-21184)***
American Speedy Printing, North Olmsted *Also called E T & K Inc* ***(G-15186)***
American Speedy Printing, Cleveland *Also called E T & K Inc* ***(G-5131)***
American Sports Center, Dayton *Also called Fried Daddy* ***(G-8207)***
American Sports Design Company 937 865-5431
6551 Centervl Bus Pkwy Centerville (45459) ***(G-2997)***
American Spring Wire Corp (PA) 216 292-4620
26300 Miles Rd Bedford Heights (44146) ***(G-1460)***
American Standard Brands, Groveport *Also called As America Inc* ***(G-10483)***
American Standard Brands, Mansfield *Also called As America Inc* ***(G-12408)***
American Steel & Alloys LLC 330 847-0487
4000 Mahoning Ave Nw Warren (44483) ***(G-19368)***
American Steel Assod Pdts Inc 419 531-9471
2375 Dorr St Ste F Toledo (43607) ***(G-18180)***
American Steel Treating Inc (PA) 419 874-2044
525 W 6th St Perrysburg (43551) ***(G-15919)***
American Stirrup, Holmesville *Also called Holmes Wheel Shop Inc* ***(G-10981)***
American Superior Lighting 740 266-2959
1506 Fernwood Rd Steubenville (43953) ***(G-17526)***
American Sweet Bean Co LLC 888 995-0007
8133 N Township Road 72a Tiffin (44883) ***(G-18043)***
American Tank & Fabricating Co (PA) 216 252-1500
12314 Elmwood Ave Cleveland (44111) ***(G-4698)***
American Tchnical Coatings Inc 440 401-2270
28045 Ranney Pkwy Ste H Westlake (44145) ***(G-20096)***
American Tool & Manufacturing, Mansfield *Also called American Tool & Mfg Co* ***(G-12405)***
American Tool & Mfg Co 419 522-2452
211 Newman St Mansfield (44902) ***(G-12405)***
American Tool and Die Inc 419 726-5394
2024 Champlain St Toledo (43611) ***(G-18181)***
American Tool Works Inc 513 844-6363
160 Hancock Ave Hamilton (45011) ***(G-10534)***
American Tool Works Inc (PA) 513 844-6363
160 Hancock Ave Hamilton (45011) ***(G-10535)***
American Tower Acquisition 419 347-1185
5085 State Route 39 W Shelby (44875) ***(G-16977)***
American Traditions Basket Co 330 854-0900
722 Tell Dr Canal Fulton (44614) ***(G-2474)***
American Trim, Lima *Also called Superior Metal Products Inc* ***(G-11947)***
American Trim LLC 419 228-1145
1501 Michigan St Ste 1 Sidney (45365) ***(G-17014)***
American Trim LLC 419 996-4703
999 W Grand Ave Lima (45801) ***(G-11837)***
American Trim LLC 419 739-4349
217 Krein Ave Wapakoneta (45895) ***(G-19318)***
American Trim LLC 419 738-9664
713 Maple St Wapakoneta (45895) ***(G-19319)***
American Trim LLC 419 996-4729
651 N Baxter St Lima (45801) ***(G-11838)***
American Trim LLC 419 996-4703
625 Victory Ave Lima (45801) ***(G-11839)***
American Trim LLC (HQ) 419 228-1145
1005 W Grand Ave Lima (45801) ***(G-11840)***
American Truck Equipment Inc 216 362-0400
5021 W 161st St Cleveland (44142) ***(G-4699)***
American Ultra Specialties Inc 330 656-5000
6855 Industrial Pkwy Hudson (44236) ***(G-11030)***
American Utility Proc LLC 330 535-3000
1246 Princeton St Akron (44301) ***(G-65)***
American Vneer Edgebanding Inc 740 928-2700
1700 James Pkwy Heath (43056) ***(G-10716)***
American Water Services Inc 440 243-9840
17449 W Sprague Rd Strongsville (44136) ***(G-17709)***
American Way Exteriors LLC 855 766-3293
3564 Intercity Dr Dayton (45424) ***(G-8028)***
American Way Manufacturing Inc 330 824-2353
1871 Henn Pkwy Sw Warren (44481) ***(G-19369)***
American Weldquip Inc 330 239-0317
1375 Wolf Creek Trl Sharon Center (44274) ***(G-16943)***
American Whistle Corporation 614 846-2918
6540 Huntley Rd Ste B Columbus (43229) ***(G-6587)***
American Wire & Cable Company (PA) 440 235-1140
7951 Bronson Rd Olmsted Twp (44138) ***(G-15532)***
American Wood Fibers Inc 740 420-3233
2500 Owens Rd Circleville (43113) ***(G-4537)***
American Woodwork Specialty Co 937 263-1053
4301 N James H Mcgee Blvd Dayton (45417) ***(G-8029)***
Americanhort Services Inc 614 884-1203
2130 Stella Ct Ste 200 Columbus (43215) ***(G-6588)***
Americas Best Bowstrings LLC (PA) 330 893-7155
3149 Ohio 39 Millersburg (44654) ***(G-14058)***
Americas Best Cstm Digitizing, Xenia *Also called Alphabet Embroidery Studios* ***(G-20755)***
Americas Best Siding Co 419 589-5900
1395 W Longview Ave Mansfield (44906) ***(G-12406)***
Americas Components, Springfield *Also called Konecranes Inc* ***(G-17433)***
Americhem Inc 330 926-3185
155 E Steels Corners Rd Cuyahoga Falls (44224) ***(G-7834)***
Americhem Inc (PA) 330 929-4213
2000 Americhem Way Cuyahoga Falls (44221) ***(G-7835)***
Americraft Bronze Co, Waterville *Also called Maumee Valley Memorials Inc* ***(G-19501)***
Americraft Carton Inc 419 668-1006
209 Republic St Norwalk (44857) ***(G-15380)***
Americraft Mfg Co Inc 513 489-1047
7937 School Rd Cincinnati (45249) ***(G-3338)***
Americraft Stor Buildings Ltd 330 877-6900
1147 W Maple St Hartville (44632) ***(G-10684)***
Ameridian Specialty Services 513 769-0150
11520 Rockfield Ct Cincinnati (45241) ***(G-3339)***
Amerigraph Llc 614 278-8000
2727 Harrison Rd Columbus (43204) ***(G-6589)***
Amerihua Intl Entps Inc 740 549-0300
707 Radio Dr Lewis Center (43035) ***(G-11744)***
Amerilam Laminating 440 235-4687
4651 W 130th St Cleveland (44135) ***(G-4700)***
Amerimold Inc 330 628-2190
595a Waterloo Rd Ste A Mogadore (44260) ***(G-14229)***
Amerimulch, Twinsburg *Also called Chromascape Inc* ***(G-18752)***
Ameriprint 440 235-6094
8119 Columbia Rd Olmsted Falls (44138) ***(G-15528)***
Amerisource Health Svcs LLC 614 492-8177
2550 John Glenn Ave Ste A Columbus (43217) ***(G-6590)***
Amerisourcebergen Corporation 614 497-3665
6301 Lasalle Dr Lockbourne (43137) ***(G-11992)***
Ameritech Publishing Inc 614 895-6123
2550 Corp Exchange Dr # 310 Columbus (43231) ***(G-6591)***
Ameritech Publishing Inc 330 896-6037
1530 Corp Woods Pkwy # 100 Uniontown (44685) ***(G-18909)***
Ameritux, Elyria *Also called American Commodore Tuxedos* ***(G-9214)***
Ameriwater LLC 937 461-8833
3345 Stop 8 Rd Dayton (45414) ***(G-8030)***
Ameriwood, Steubenville *Also called Express Care* ***(G-17533)***
Amerix Nutra-Pharma 567 204-7756
904 N Cable Rd Lima (45805) ***(G-11841)***
Ames Companies Inc 740 783-2535
21460 Ames Ln Dexter City (45727) ***(G-8791)***
Ames Development Group Ltd 419 704-7812
2339 Drummond Rd Toledo (43606) ***(G-18182)***
Ames Lock Specialties Inc 419 474-2995
2121 W Sylvania Ave Toledo (43613) ***(G-18183)***

ALPHABETIC

(PA)=Parent Co (HQ)=Headquarters (DH)=Div Headquarters
2019 Harris Ohio
Industrial Directory
1043

Ames Locksmith, Toledo Also called Ames Lock Specialties Inc *(G-18183)*

Ametco Manufacturing Corp 440 951-4300
4326 Hamann Pkwy Willoughby (44094) *(G-20271)*

Ametek Inc 419 739-3202
14097 Cemetery Rd Wapakoneta (45895) *(G-19320)*

Ametek Inc 419 739-3200
14101 Cemetery Rd Wapakoneta (45895) *(G-19321)*

Ametek Inc 302 636-5401
530 Lakeview Plaza Blvd C Worthington (43085) *(G-20678)*

Ametek Inc 937 440-0800
66 Industry Ct Ste F Troy (45373) *(G-18637)*

Ametek Electromechanical Group, Kent Also called Ametek Tchnical Indus Pdts Inc *(G-11294)*

Ametek Florcare Specialty Mtrs 330 677-3786
100 E Erie St Ste 200 Kent (44240) *(G-11293)*

Ametek Presto Light Power, Troy Also called Ametek Inc *(G-18637)*

Ametek Tchnical Indus Pdts Inc (HQ) 330 677-3754
100 E Erie St Ste 130 Kent (44240) *(G-11294)*

Ametek Westchester Plastics, Wapakoneta Also called Ametek Inc *(G-19321)*

Amex Dies Inc 330 545-9766
932 N State St Girard (44420) *(G-10253)*

AMF Bruns America Lp 877 506-3770
1797 Georgetown Rd Hudson (44236) *(G-11031)*

AMF Bruns of America, Hudson Also called AMF Bruns America Lp *(G-11031)*

Amfm Inc 440 953-4545
38373 Pelton Rd Willoughby (44094) *(G-20272)*

AMG Industries LLC 740 397-4044
200 Commerce Dr Mount Vernon (43050) *(G-14467)*

AMG Trailer and Equipment, Brunswick Also called Martin Allen Trailer LLC *(G-2220)*

AMG Vanadium LLC 740 435-4600
60790 Southgate Rd Cambridge (43725) *(G-2423)*

Amh Holdings LLC 330 929-1811
3773 State Rd Cuyahoga Falls (44223) *(G-7836)*

Amh Holdings II Inc 330 929-1811
3773 State Rd Cuyahoga Falls (44223) *(G-7837)*

Amherst Party Shop, Amherst Also called Currier Richard & James *(G-559)*

Amidac Wind Corporation 213 973-4000
151 Innovation Dr Elyria (44035) *(G-9216)*

Amir International Foods Inc 614 332-1742
3504 Broadway Grove City (43123) *(G-10415)*

Amish Country Essentials LLC 330 674-3088
4663 Us Rt 62 Millersburg Millersburg (44654) *(G-14059)*

Amish Door Inc (PA) 330 359-5464
1210 Winesburg St Wilmot (44689) *(G-20513)*

Amish Door Restaurant, Wilmot Also called Amish Door Inc *(G-20513)*

Amish Heritg WD Floors & Furn, Middlefield Also called Cherokee Hardwoods Inc *(G-13784)*

Amish Wedding Foods Inc 330 674-9199
316 S Mad Anthony St Millersburg (44654) *(G-14060)*

Amko Service Company, Midvale Also called Fiba Technologies Inc *(G-13977)*

Amko Service Company (HQ) 330 364-8857
3211 Brightwood Rd Midvale (44653) *(G-13975)*

Aml Industries Inc 330 399-5000
520 Pine Ave Se Ste 1 Warren (44483) *(G-19370)*

Amon Inc 513 734-1700
3214 Marshall Dr Amelia (45102) *(G-531)*

Amoney Train Music, Cuyahoga Falls Also called Thickemz Entertainment LLC *(G-7928)*

Amos Media Company (PA) 937 498-2111
911 S Vandemark Rd Sidney (45365) *(G-17015)*

AMP Electric Vehicles Inc 513 360-4704
100 Commerce Dr Loveland (45140) *(G-12177)*

AMP-Tech Inc 419 652-3444
910 County Road 40 Nova (44859) *(G-15430)*

Ampac Holdings LLC (HQ) 513 671-1777
12025 Tricon Rd Cincinnati (45246) *(G-3340)*

Ampac Packaging LLC (HQ) 513 671-1777
12025 Tricon Rd Cincinnati (45246) *(G-3341)*

Ampac Plastics LLC 513 671-1777
12025 Tricon Rd Cincinnati (45246) *(G-3342)*

Ampacet Corp 513 247-5403
4705 Duke Dr Ste 400 Mason (45040) *(G-12823)*

Ampacet Corporation 740 929-5521
1855 James Pkwy Newark (43056) *(G-14850)*

Ampacet Corporation 513 247-5400
4705 Duke Dr 400 Cincinnati (45249) *(G-3343)*

Ampak, Cleveland Also called Heat Seal LLC *(G-5386)*

Ampersand International Inc 216 831-3500
23775 Commerce Park Beachwood (44122) *(G-1223)*

Ampex Metal Products Company (PA) 216 267-9242
5581 W 164th St Brookpark (44142) *(G-2136)*

Ample Industries Inc 937 746-9700
4000 Commerce Center Dr Franklin (45005) *(G-9869)*

Amplified Solar Inc 216 236-4225
1453 Wayne Ave Lakewood (44107) *(G-11511)*

Ampp Incorporated 419 666-4747
28271 Cedar Park Blvd # 5 Perrysburg (43551) *(G-15920)*

Ampsco Division 614 444-2181
2301 Fairwood Ave Columbus (43207) *(G-6592)*

Amptech Machining & Welding 419 652-3444
910 County Road 40 Nova (44859) *(G-15431)*

Amresco LLC 440 349-2805
28600 Fountain Pkwy Solon (44139) *(G-17107)*

Amresco LLC 440 349-2805
29999 Solon Indus Pkwy Cleveland (44139) *(G-4701)*

Amrex Inc 330 678-7050
431 W Elm St Kent (44240) *(G-11295)*

Amrican Spring Wire, Bedford Heights Also called Aswpengg LLC *(G-1461)*

Amrod Bridge & Iron LLC 330 530-8230
105 Ohio Ave Mc Donald (44437) *(G-13196)*

Amron LLC 330 457-8570
47287 State Route 558 New Waterford (44445) *(G-14836)*

Amron Testing, New Waterford Also called Amron LLC *(G-14836)*

Amros Industries Inc 216 433-0010
14701 Industrial Pkwy Cleveland (44135) *(G-4702)*

AMS, Strongsville Also called Automated Mfg Solutions Inc *(G-17716)*

AMS Global Ltd 937 620-1036
119 E Dayton St West Alexandria (45381) *(G-19616)*

Amsoil Inc 614 274-9851
707 Hadley Dr Columbus (43228) *(G-6593)*

Amsted Industries Incorporated 614 836-2323
3900 Bixby Rd Groveport (43125) *(G-10481)*

Amsted Rail Company Inc 614 836-2323
3900 Bixby Rd Groveport (43125) *(G-10482)*

Amt, Brecksville Also called Applied Medical Technology Inc *(G-2020)*

Amt Machine Systems Limited 740 965-2693
1760 Zollinger Rd Ste 2 Columbus (43221) *(G-6594)*

Amt Machine Systems Ltd 614 635-8050
50 W Broad St Ste 1200 Columbus (43215) *(G-6595)*

Amtank Armor 440 268-7735
22555 Ascoa Ct Strongsville (44149) *(G-17710)*

Amtank Armor LLC 216 252-1500
12314 Elmwood Ave Cleveland (44111) *(G-4703)*

Amtech Inc 440 238-2141
11925 Pearl Rd Ste 207 Strongsville (44136) *(G-17711)*

Amtech Laminating Equipment, Strongsville Also called Amtech Inc *(G-17711)*

Amtech Tool and Machine Inc 330 758-8215
100 Mcclurg Rd Youngstown (44512) *(G-20844)*

Amteco Inc 513 217-4430
5773 Elk Creek Rd Middletown (45042) *(G-13884)*

Amtekco Industries LLC (HQ) 614 228-6590
2300 Lockbourne Rd Columbus (43207) *(G-6596)*

Amtekco Industries Inc 614 228-6525
33 W Hinman Ave Columbus (43207) *(G-6597)*

Amthor Steel Inc 330 759-0200
5019 Belmont Ave Youngstown (44505) *(G-20845)*

Amylin Ohio 512 592-8710
8814 Trade Port Dr West Chester (45011) *(G-19643)*

Amys Beauty Jams LLC 330 869-8317
2149 Briar Club Trl Akron (44313) *(G-66)*

An Baiceir Bakery 740 739-0501
116 Reader Ct Etna (43062) *(G-9391)*

Anadem Inc 614 262-2539
3620 N High St Ste 201 Columbus (43214) *(G-6598)*

Anaheim Manufacturing Company 800 767-6293
25300 Al Moen Dr North Olmsted (44070) *(G-15181)*

Analiza Inc (PA) 216 432-9050
3615 Superior Ave E 4407b Cleveland (44114) *(G-4704)*

Analog Bridge Inc 937 901-4832
2897 Kant Pl Beavercreek (45431) *(G-1299)*

Analynk Wireless LLC 614 755-5091
790 Cross Pointe Rd Columbus (43230) *(G-6599)*

Analytic Stress Relieving Inc 804 271-7198
6944 Mcnerney Dr Northwood (43619) *(G-15332)*

Analytica Usa Inc (PA) 513 348-2333
711 E Monu Ave Ste 309 Dayton (45402) *(G-8031)*

Anatomical Concepts Inc 330 757-3569
1399 E Western Reserve Rd Youngstown (44514) *(G-20846)*

Anatrace Products LLC (HQ) 419 740-6600
434 W Dussel Dr Maumee (43537) *(G-13071)*

Anchi Inc 740 653-2527
1115 W 5th Ave Lancaster (43130) *(G-11540)*

Anchor Bronze and Metals Inc 440 549-5653
11470 Euclid Ave Ste 509 Cleveland (44106) *(G-4705)*

Anchor Chemical Co Inc (PA) 440 871-1660
777 Canterbury Rd Westlake (44145) *(G-20097)*

Anchor Corporation 614 836-9590
2160 Cloverleaf St E Columbus (43232) *(G-6600)*

Anchor Fabricators Inc 937 836-5117
386 Talmadge Rd Clayton (45315) *(G-4571)*

Anchor Flange Company 513 527-4444
3959 Virginia Ave Cincinnati (45227) *(G-3344)*

Anchor Fluid Power, Cincinnati Also called Anchor Flange Company *(G-3344)*

Anchor Glass Container Corp 740 452-2743
1206 Brandywine Blvd C Zanesville (43701) *(G-21099)*

Anchor Hocking, Lancaster Also called Anchi Inc *(G-11540)*

Anchor Hocking LLC (HQ) 740 681-6478
519 N Pierce Ave Lancaster (43130) *(G-11541)*

Anchor Hocking LLC 740 687-2500
1115 W 5th Ave Lancaster (43130) *(G-11542)*
Anchor Hocking Company, Lancaster *Also called Anchor Hocking LLC (G-11542)*
Anchor Hocking Company, The, Lancaster *Also called Anchor Hocking LLC (G-11541)*
Anchor Hocking Consmr GL Corp 740 653-2527
1115 W 5th Ave Lancaster (43130) *(G-11543)*
Anchor Hocking Glass Company 740 681-6025
Plant 1 1115 W Fifth Ave Nt St Pla Lancaster (43130) *(G-11544)*
Anchor Hocking Indus GL Div, Lancaster *Also called Ghp II LLC (G-11575)*
Anchor Industries Incorporated 440 473-1414
30775 Solon Indus Pkwy Cleveland (44139) *(G-4706)*
Anchor Lamina America, Dayton *Also called Dayton Lamina Corporation (G-8136)*
Anchor Lamina America Inc 330 952-1595
445 W Liberty St Medina (44256) *(G-13224)*
Anchor Manufacturing Group, Cleveland *Also called Anchor Tool & Die Co (G-4710)*
Anchor Manufacturing Group Inc, Cleveland *Also called Anchor Tool & Die Co (G-4709)*
Anchor Metal Processing Inc 216 362-6463
12200 Brookpark Rd Cleveland (44130) *(G-4707)*
Anchor Metal Processing Inc (PA) 216 362-1850
11830 Brookpark Rd Cleveland (44130) *(G-4708)*
Anchor Pattern Company 614 443-2221
748 Frebis Ave Columbus (43206) *(G-6601)*
Anchor Template Die Div, Cleveland *Also called Paramount Stamping & Wldg Co (G-5840)*
Anchor Tool & Die Co (PA) 216 362-1850
12200 Brookpark Rd Cleveland (44130) *(G-4709)*
Anchor Tool & Die Co 216 362-1850
12200 Brookpark Rd Cleveland (44130) *(G-4710)*
Ancient Infusions LLC 419 659-5110
10246 Road P Columbus Grove (45830) *(G-7630)*
Ancom Business Products, Brunswick *Also called Symatic Inc (G-2243)*
Andal Woodworking 330 897-8059
1411 Township Road 151 Baltic (43804) *(G-1022)*
Andeen-Hagerling Inc 440 349-0370
31200 Bainbridge Rd Ste 2 Cleveland (44139) *(G-4711)*
Anderson & Vreeland Inc 419 636-5002
15348 State Rte 127 E Bryan (43506) *(G-2264)*
Anderson Brothers Entps Inc 440 269-3920
38180 Airport Pkwy Willoughby (44094) *(G-20273)*
Anderson Co Mfg LLC 419 230-7332
415 W North St Carey (43316) *(G-2877)*
Anderson Company, Carey *Also called Anderson Co Mfg LLC (G-2877)*
Anderson Concrete Corp (PA) 614 443-0123
400 Frank Rd Columbus (43207) *(G-6602)*
Anderson Cosmetic & Vein Inst 513 624-7900
7794 5 Mile Rd Ste 270 Cincinnati (45230) *(G-3345)*
Anderson Door Co 216 475-5700
18090 Miles Rd Cleveland (44128) *(G-4712)*
Anderson Energy Inc 740 678-8608
12959 State Route 550 Fleming (45729) *(G-9777)*
Anderson Glass Co Inc 614 476-4877
2816 Morse Rd Columbus (43231) *(G-6603)*
Anderson Graphics Inc 330 745-2165
711 Wooster Rd W Barberton (44203) *(G-1052)*
Anderson International Corp 216 641-1112
4545 Boyce Pkwy Stow (44224) *(G-17568)*
Anderson Pallet & Packg Inc 937 962-2614
210 Western Ave Lewisburg (45338) *(G-11789)*
Anderson Pallet Service, Lewisburg *Also called Anderson Pallet & Packg Inc (G-11789)*
Anderson Printing & Supply LLC 614 891-1100
237 E Broadway Ave Westerville (43081) *(G-20034)*
Anderson Publishing Co (PA) 513 474-9305
9443 Springboro Pike Miamisburg (45342) *(G-13640)*
Anderson Vreeland Midwest, Bryan *Also called Anderson & Vreeland Inc (G-2264)*
Andersons Inc (PA) 419 893-5050
1947 Briarfield Blvd Maumee (43537) *(G-13072)*
Andersons Inc 419 536-0460
801 S Reynolds Rd Toledo (43615) *(G-18184)*
Andersons Inc 419 891-2930
415 Illinois Ave Maumee (43537) *(G-13073)*
Andersons Clymers Ethanol LLC (HQ) 574 722-2627
1947 Briarfield Blvd Maumee (43537) *(G-13074)*
Andersons Plant Nutrient LLC 419 396-3501
1855 County Highway 99 Carey (43316) *(G-2878)*
Andersound PA Service 216 561-2636
15911 Harvard Ave Cleveland (44128) *(G-4713)*
Andras Corp 440 323-2528
840 Infirmary Rd Elyria (44035) *(G-9217)*
Andre Corporation 574 293-0207
4600 N Masn Montgomery Rd Mason (45040) *(G-12824)*
Andre Kitchens, Brice *Also called Carl C Andre Inc (G-2071)*
Andrew & Sons Inc 419 693-0292
2401 Consaul St Toledo (43605) *(G-18185)*
Andrew M Farnham 419 298-4300
2112 County Road C60 Edgerton (43517) *(G-9168)*
Andrew Tool Co Inc 440 237-4340
12146 York Rd Unit 2 North Royalton (44133) *(G-15260)*
Andromeda Research 513 831-9708
648 Quail Run Cincinnati (45244) *(G-3346)*
Andy Pac Inc 440 748-8800
11600 Hawke Rd Columbia Station (44028) *(G-6427)*
Andy Raber 740 622-1386
32441 County Rd Ste 12 Fresno (43824) *(G-10066)*
Andy Russo Jr Inc 440 585-1456
29200 Anderson Rd Wickliffe (44092) *(G-20198)*
Andy's Award, Akron *Also called Miracle Custom Awards & Gifts (G-283)*
Andys Mdterranean Fd Pdts LLC 513 281-9791
906 Nassau St Cincinnati (45206) *(G-3347)*
Anest Iwata Air Engrg Inc 513 755-3100
9525 Glades Dr West Chester (45011) *(G-19644)*
Anest Iwata Usa Inc 513 755-3100
10148 Commerce Park Dr West Chester (45246) *(G-19832)*
Angel Glass Lost 419 353-2831
122 Meeker St Bowling Green (43402) *(G-1951)*
Angel Prtg & Reproduction Co 216 631-5225
1400 W 57th St Cleveland (44102) *(G-4714)*
Angel Window Mfg Corp 440 891-1006
237 Depot St Berea (44017) *(G-1590)*
Angelics A Quilters Haven 330 484-5480
3033 Cleveland Ave S Canton (44707) *(G-2573)*
Angelina Stone & Marble Ltd 740 633-3360
55341 W Center St Bridgeport (43912) *(G-2072)*
Angels Landing Inc 513 687-3681
3430 S Dixie Dr Ste 301 Moraine (45439) *(G-14330)*
Anger Pattern Company Inc 330 882-6519
2999 S 1st St Clinton (44216) *(G-6383)*
Angleboard, Loveland *Also called Signode Industrial Group LLC (G-12232)*
Angry Cupcakes Productions LLC 216 229-2394
2300 E 95th St Cleveland (44106) *(G-4715)*
Angstrom Automotive Group LLC 440 255-6700
8229 Tyler Blvd Mentor (44060) *(G-13387)*
Angstrom Corp 330 405-0524
9221 Ravenna Rd Ste 1 Twinsburg (44087) *(G-18733)*
Angstrom Graphics Inc (PA) 216 271-5300
4437 E 49th St Cleveland (44125) *(G-4716)*
Angstrom Graphics Inc Midwest (HQ) 216 271-5300
4437 E 49th St Cleveland (44125) *(G-4717)*
Angstrom Graphics Southeast (HQ) 216 271-5300
4437 E 49th St Cleveland (44125) *(G-4718)*
Angstrom Precision Metals LLC 440 255-6700
8229 Tyler Blvd Mentor (44060) *(G-13388)*
Angstron Materials Inc 937 331-9884
1240 Mccook Ave Dayton (45404) *(G-8032)*
Anheuser-Busch LLC 614 847-6213
700 Schrock Rd Columbus (43229) *(G-6604)*
Ankim Enterprises Incorporated 937 599-1121
2005 Campbell Rd Sidney (45365) *(G-17016)*
Ann Printing & Promotions 330 399-6564
269 E Market St Warren (44481) *(G-19371)*
Annes Auntie Pretzels 614 418-7021
125 Easton Town Ctr Columbus (43219) *(G-6605)*
Annies Mud Pie Shop LLC 513 871-2529
3130 Wasson Rd Unit 4 Cincinnati (45209) *(G-3348)*
Annin & Co 740 622-4447
700 S 3rd St Coshocton (43812) *(G-7718)*
Anodizing Specialists Inc 440 951-0257
7547 Tyler Blvd Mentor (44060) *(G-13389)*
Anointed Design & Technologies 330 826-1493
1766 Huron Rd Se Massillon (44646) *(G-12959)*
Anomatic Corporation (HQ) 740 522-2203
8880 Innvation Campus Way Johnstown (43031) *(G-11255)*
Anomatic Corporation 740 522-2203
1650 Tamarack Rd Newark (43055) *(G-14851)*
Anotex Industries Inc 513 860-1165
4914 Rialto Rd West Chester (45069) *(G-19645)*
Anro Logistics Inc 614 428-7490
7473 Bentley Pl Westerville (43082) *(G-19978)*
Ansco Machine Company 330 929-8181
60 Cuyhoga Fls Indus Pkwy Peninsula (44264) *(G-15889)*
Ansell Healthcare Products LLC 740 622-4311
925 Chestnut St Coshocton (43812) *(G-7719)*
Ansell Healthcare Products LLC 740 295-5414
925 Chestnut St Coshocton (43812) *(G-7720)*
Anson Co 216 524-8838
18679 Orchard Hill Dr Bedford (44146) *(G-1383)*
Anstine Machining Corp 330 821-4365
15835 Armour St Ne Alliance (44601) *(G-455)*
Antero Resources Corporation 740 760-1000
2335 State Route 821 Marietta (45750) *(G-12603)*
Anthony Business Forms Inc 937 253-0072
3160 Plainfield Rd Dayton (45432) *(G-7971)*
Anthony Decorative Fabrics and 937 299-4637
2701 Lance Dr Moraine (45409) *(G-14331)*
Anthony Mining Co Inc 740 266-8100
72 Airport Rd Wintersville (43953) *(G-20537)*
Anthony Thomas Candy Shoppes, Columbus *Also called Anthony-Thomas Candy Company (G-6607)*
Anthony's Fabric, Moraine *Also called Anthony Decorative Fabrics and (G-14331)*

ALPHABETIC

Anthony-Lee Screen Prtg Inc 419 683-1861
401 S Thoman St Crestline (44827) *(G-7793)*
Anthony-Thomas Candy Company (PA) 614 274-8405
1777 Arlingate Ln Columbus (43228) *(G-6606)*
Anthony-Thomas Candy Company 614 870-8899
4636 W Broad St Columbus (43228) *(G-6607)*
Anthony-Thomas Candy Shoppes, Columbus *Also called Anthony-Thomas Candy Company (G-6606)*
Antique Auto Sheet Metal Inc 937 833-4422
718 Albert Rd Brookville (45309) *(G-2161)*
Antram Fire Equipment 330 525-7171
27970 Winona Rd North Georgetown (44665) *(G-15139)*
Antwerp Bee-Argus 419 258-8161
113 N Main St Antwerp (45813) *(G-595)*
Antwerp Tool & Die Inc 419 258-5271
3167 County Road 424 Antwerp (45813) *(G-596)*
Anvil Products Co 216 883-3740
4535 E 71st St Cleveland (44105) *(G-4719)*
Anything Personalized 330 655-0723
9261 Ravenna Rd Ste 10 Twinsburg (44087) *(G-18734)*
Anza Inc 513 542-7337
3265 Colerain Ave Ste 2 Cincinnati (45225) *(G-3349)*
Aot Inc 937 323-9669
4800 Gateway Blvd Springfield (45502) *(G-17363)*
AP Direct, Mentor *Also called Activities Press Inc (G-13374)*
AP Tech Group Inc 513 761-8111
5130 Rialto Rd West Chester (45069) *(G-19646)*
Ap-Alternatives LLC 419 267-5280
20 345 County Road X Ridgeville Corners (43555) *(G-16511)*
Apartment Finder Magazine, Gahanna *Also called Network Communications Inc (G-10095)*
Apeks LLC 740 809-1160
150 Commerce Blvd Johnstown (43031) *(G-11256)*
Apeks Supercritical, Johnstown *Also called Apeks LLC (G-11256)*
Apex Advanced Technologies LLC 216 898-1595
4857a W 130th St Cleveland (44135) *(G-4720)*
Apex Alliance LLC 234 200-5930
2177 Graham Rd Stow (44224) *(G-17569)*
Apex Aluminum Die Cast Co Inc 937 773-0432
8877 Sherry Dr Piqua (45356) *(G-16099)*
Apex Bolt & Machine Company 419 729-3741
5324 Enterprise Blvd Toledo (43612) *(G-18186)*
Apex Bulk Handlers, Bedford *Also called Apex Welding Incorporated (G-1384)*
Apex Cabinetry 859 581-5300
4536 W Mitchell Ave Cincinnati (45232) *(G-3350)*
Apex Circuits Inc 513 942-4400
5100 Excello Ct West Chester (45069) *(G-19647)*
Apex Crcits Elctrnic Dsign Man, West Chester *Also called Apex Circuits Inc (G-19647)*
Apex Metal Fabricating & Mch, Toledo *Also called Apex Bolt & Machine Company (G-18186)*
Apex Metals, Cleveland *Also called Erieview Metal Treating Co (G-5191)*
Apex Property Management, Richmond Heights *Also called Ajami Holdings Group LLC (G-16500)*
Apex Services, Akron *Also called Aaron Smith (G-25)*
Apex Solutions Inc 419 843-3434
2620 Centennial Rd Ste P Toledo (43617) *(G-18187)*
Apex Target Systems LLC 877 224-6692
37 Heilman St Tiffin (44883) *(G-18044)*
Apex Tool Group LLC 937 222-7871
762 W Stewart St Dayton (45417) *(G-8033)*
Apex Welding Incorporated 440 232-6770
1 Industry Dr Bedford (44146) *(G-1384)*
Apf Legacy Subs LLC (HQ) 513 682-7173
9990 Prnceton Glendale Rd West Chester (45246) *(G-19833)*
Apg Media of Ohio, Athens *Also called Adams Publishing Group LLC (G-821)*
API Machining Fabrication Inc 740 369-0455
377 London Rd Delaware (43015) *(G-8654)*
API Pattern Works Inc 440 269-1766
4456 Hamann Pkwy Willoughby (44094) *(G-20274)*
Apollo GL Mirror Win Screen Co, Cincinnati *Also called Dale Kestler (G-3574)*
Apollo Manufacturing Co LLC 440 951-9972
7911 Enterprise Dr Mentor (44060) *(G-13390)*
Apollo Medical Devices LLC 440 935-5027
11000 Cedar Ave Ste 146 Cleveland (44106) *(G-4721)*
Apollo Plastic, Mentor *Also called Skribs Tool and Die Inc (G-13583)*
Apollo Plastics Inc 440 951-7774
7555 Tyler Blvd Ste 11 Mentor (44060) *(G-13391)*
Apollo Products Inc 440 269-8551
4456 Hamann Pkwy Willoughby (44094) *(G-20275)*
Apollo Welding & Fabg Inc (PA) 440 942-0227
35600 Curtis Blvd Willoughby (44095) *(G-20276)*
Apostrophe Apps LLC 513 608-4399
4452 Millikin Rd Liberty Twp (45011) *(G-11821)*
Appal Energy 740 448-4605
15383 E Kasler Creek Rd Amesville (45711) *(G-551)*
Appalachia Wood Inc (PA) 740 596-2551
31310 State Route 93 Mc Arthur (45651) *(G-13178)*
Appalachian Equipment Co LLC 330 345-2251
2054 Great Trails Dr Wooster (44691) *(G-20562)*
Appalachian Fuels LLC (PA) 606 928-0460
6375 Riverside Dr Ste 200 Dublin (43017) *(G-8880)*
Appalachian Oilfield Svcs LLC 337 216-0066
34602 State Route 7 Sardis (43946) *(G-16875)*
Appalachian Solvents LLC 740 680-3649
5041 Skyline Dr Cambridge (43725) *(G-2424)*
Appalachian Well Surveys Inc 740 255-7652
10291 Ohio Ave Cambridge (43725) *(G-2425)*
Appalachian Wood Floors Inc 740 354-4572
838 Campbell Ave Portsmouth (45662) *(G-16277)*
Apparel Impressions Inc 513 247-0555
11410 Gideon Ln Cincinnati (45249) *(G-3351)*
Apparel Screen Printing Inc 513 733-9495
11255 Reading Rd Ste 1 Cincinnati (45241) *(G-3352)*
Appian Manufacturing Corp 614 445-2230
2025 Camaro Ave Columbus (43207) *(G-6608)*
Apple Seed LLC 330 606-1776
305 High Grove Blvd Akron (44312) *(G-67)*
Appleheart 937 384-0430
2240 E Central Ave Miamisburg (45342) *(G-13641)*
Appleton Grp LLC 330 689-1904
4441 Hickory Trl Cuyahoga Falls (44224) *(G-7838)*
Application Link Inc 614 934-1735
4449 Easton Way Fl 2 Columbus (43219) *(G-6609)*
Applied Automation Enterprise 419 929-2428
24 Cedar St New London (44851) *(G-14728)*
Applied Bingo Mate, Willoughby *Also called Applied Concepts Inc (G-20277)*
Applied Concepts Inc 440 229-5033
36445 Biltmore Pl Ste E Willoughby (44094) *(G-20277)*
Applied Energy Tech Inc 419 537-9052
1720 Indian Wood Cir E Maumee (43537) *(G-13075)*
Applied Engineered Surface, Elyria *Also called Lauren Yoakam (G-9285)*
Applied Engneered Surfaces Inc 440 366-0440
535 Ternes Ln Elyria (44035) *(G-9218)*
Applied Experience LLC 614 943-2970
1003 Kinnear Rd Columbus (43212) *(G-6610)*
Applied Graphics Ltd 419 756-6882
1717 Mccarrick Pkwy Mansfield (44903) *(G-12407)*
Applied Innovations 330 837-5694
1245 Cleveland St Sw Massillon (44647) *(G-12960)*
Applied Marketing Services (HQ) 440 716-9962
28825 Ranney Pkwy Westlake (44145) *(G-20098)*
Applied Materials Finishing 330 336-5645
901 Seville Rd Wadsworth (44281) *(G-19227)*
Applied Medical Technology Inc 440 717-4000
8006 Katherine Blvd Brecksville (44141) *(G-2020)*
Applied Metals Tech Ltd 216 741-3236
1040 Valley Belt Rd Brooklyn Heights (44131) *(G-2115)*
Applied Sciences Inc (PA) 937 766-2020
141 W Xenia Ave Cedarville (45314) *(G-2943)*
Applied Systems Inc 513 943-0000
5300 Dupont Cir Ste B Milford (45150) *(G-13994)*
Applied Vision Corporation (PA) 330 926-2222
2020 Vision Ln Cuyahoga Falls (44223) *(G-7839)*
Apportis LLC 614 832-8362
90 S High St Ste C Dublin (43017) *(G-8881)*
Approved Plbg & Sewer Clg Co, Cleveland *Also called Approved Plumbing Co (G-4722)*
Approved Plumbing Co 216 663-5063
770 Ken Mar Indus Pkwy Cleveland (44147) *(G-4722)*
Appvion Operations Inc 937 859-8261
1030 W Alex Bell Rd West Carrollton (45449) *(G-19629)*
Apr Tool Inc 440 946-0393
4712 Beidler Rd Ste A Willoughby (44094) *(G-20278)*
Aprecia Pharmaceuticals LLC (HQ) 513 864-4107
10901 Kenwood Rd Blue Ash (45242) *(G-1729)*
APS Accurate Products & Svcs 440 353-9353
39050 Center Ridge Rd North Ridgeville (44039) *(G-15208)*
Aps-Materials Inc (PA) 937 278-6547
4011 Riverside Dr Dayton (45405) *(G-8034)*
Aps-Materials Inc 937 278-6547
153 Walbrook Ave Dayton (45405) *(G-8035)*
APT Manufacturing Solutions, Hicksville *Also called A & P Tool Inc (G-10773)*
Aptiv Services Us LLC 330 306-1000
4551 Research Prwy Warren (44483) *(G-19372)*
Aptiv Services Us LLC 330 505-3150
Larchmont North River Rd Warren (44483) *(G-19373)*
Aptiv Services Us LLC 330 367-6000
3400 Aero Park Dr Vienna (44473) *(G-19196)*
Apto Orthopaedics Corporation 330 572-7544
47 N Main St Akron (44308) *(G-68)*
APV Engineered Coatings, Akron *Also called Akron Paint & Varnish Inc (G-46)*
Aq Productions Inc 614 486-7700
5945 Wilcox Pl Ste B Dublin (43016) *(G-8882)*
Aqua Lily Products LLC (PA) 951 246-9610
4485 Glenbrook Rd Willoughby (44094) *(G-20279)*
Aqua Marine Supply, Millersport *Also called Hefty Hoist Inc (G-14160)*
Aqua Ohio, Mentor On The Lake *Also called Aqua Pennsylvania Inc (G-13631)*
Aqua Pennsylvania Inc 440 257-6190
7748 Twilight Dr Mentor On The Lake (44060) *(G-13631)*

ALPHABETIC SECTION Argrov Box Co

Aqua Pro Systems, West Chester *Also called Aquapro Systems LLC* **(G-19649)**
Aqua Science Inc 614 252-5000
1877 E 17th Ave Columbus (43219) **(G-6611)**
Aqua Technology Group LLC 513 298-1183
8104 Beckett Center Dr West Chester (45069) **(G-19648)**
Aquablok Ltd 419 402-4170
230 W Airport Hwy Swanton (43558) **(G-17905)**
Aquablok Ltd (PA) 419 825-1325
175 Woodland Ave Swanton (43558) **(G-17906)**
Aquablue Inc 330 343-0220
1776 Tech Park Dr Ne New Philadelphia (44663) **(G-14758)**
Aquacalc LLC 916 372-0534
1700 Joyce Ave Columbus (43219) **(G-6612)**
Aquanaut Lounge, Hammondsville *Also called Sam Abdallah* **(G-10623)**
Aquapro Systems LLC 513 315-3647
4438 Muhlhauser Rd # 600 West Chester (45011) **(G-19649)**
Aquapro Systems LLC 877 278-2797
4438 Muhlhauser Rd # 500 West Chester (45011) **(G-19650)**
Aquasurtech OEM Corp 614 577-1203
845 Claycraft Rd Gahanna (43230) **(G-10075)**
Aquatic Lighting Systems, Pickerington *Also called Jeff Katz* **(G-16051)**
Aquatic Technology 440 236-8330
26966 Royalton Rd Columbia Station (44028) **(G-6428)**
Aquent Studios 216 266-7551
33433 Curtis Blvd Willoughby (44095) **(G-20280)**
Aquila Pharmatech LLC 419 386-2527
8225 Farnsworth Rd Ste A7 Waterville (43566) **(G-19490)**
AR Jester Co 513 241-1465
6781 Harrison Ave Cincinnati (45247) **(G-3353)**
Arabian Tools Inc 440 286-3600
9632 Brakeman Rd Chardon (44024) **(G-3099)**
Aracor, Fairborn *Also called Rapiscan Systems High Energy I* **(G-9466)**
Aratinabox Companies Inc 330 699-3421
12910 Cleveland Ave Nw Uniontown (44685) **(G-18910)**
Arbor Foods Inc 419 698-4442
3332 Saint Lawrence Dr C Toledo (43605) **(G-18188)**
Arboris LLC 740 522-9350
1780 Tamarack Rd Newark (43055) **(G-14852)**
Arbortech, Wooster *Also called Stahl/Scott Fetzer Company* **(G-20658)**
ARC Abrasives Inc 800 888-4885
2131 Corporate Dr Troy (45373) **(G-18638)**
ARC Blinds Inc 513 889-4864
3850 Bethany Rd Mason (45040) **(G-12825)**
ARC Drilling Inc (PA) 216 525-0920
9551 Corporate Cir Cleveland (44125) **(G-4723)**
ARC Gas & Supply LLC 216 341-5882
4560 Nicky Blvd Ste D Cleveland (44125) **(G-4724)**
ARC Rubber Inc 440 466-4555
100 Water St Geneva (44041) **(G-10214)**
ARC Solutions Inc 419 542-9272
605 Industrial Dr Hicksville (43526) **(G-10775)**
Arcadian Ohio, Lima *Also called Pcs Nitrogen Inc* **(G-11914)**
Arcelormittal Cleveland LLC (HQ) 216 429-6000
3060 Eggers Ave Cleveland (44105) **(G-4725)**
Arcelormittal Cleveland LLC 216 429-6000
3060 Eggers Ave Cleveland (44105) **(G-4726)**
Arcelormittal Columbus LLC 614 492-6800
1800 Watkins Rd Columbus (43207) **(G-6613)**
Arcelormittal Obetz LLC 614 492-8287
4300 Alum Creek Dr Columbus (43207) **(G-6614)**
Arcelormittal Tailored Blanks 419 737-3180
2 Kexon Dr Pioneer (43554) **(G-16084)**
Arcelormittal Tubular 740 382-3979
686 W Fairground St Marion (43302) **(G-12693)**
Arcelormittal Tubular Products 419 347-2424
132 W Main St Shelby (44875) **(G-16978)**
Arcelormittal USA LLC 740 375-2299
686 W Fairground St Marion (43302) **(G-12694)**
Arcelormittal USA LLC 419 347-2424
132 W Main St Shelby (44875) **(G-16979)**
Arcelormittal Warren, Warren *Also called AM Warren LLC* **(G-19367)**
Arch Parent Inc 440 701-7420
9215 Mentor Ave Mentor (44060) **(G-13392)**
Arch Polymers, Marysville *Also called Triple Arrow Industries Inc* **(G-12818)**
Archbold Buckeye Inc 419 445-4466
207 N Defiance St Archbold (43502) **(G-636)**
Archbold Container Corp 800 446-2520
800 W Barre Rd Archbold (43502) **(G-637)**
Archbold Furniture Co 567 444-4666
733 W Barre Rd Archbold (43502) **(G-638)**
Archday, Medina *Also called Architectural Daylighting LLC* **(G-13225)**
Archer Corporation 330 455-9995
1917 Henry Ave Sw Canton (44706) **(G-2574)**
Archer Counter Design Inc 513 396-7526
4433 Verne Ave Cincinnati (45209) **(G-3354)**
Archer Custom Chrome LLC 216 441-2795
25703 Rustic Ln Westlake (44145) **(G-20099)**
Archer Sign, Canton *Also called Archer Corporation* **(G-2574)**
Archer-Daniels-Midland Company 419 705-3292
1308 Miami St Toledo (43605) **(G-18189)**
Archer-Daniels-Midland Company 419 435-6633
608 Findlay St Fostoria (44830) **(G-9833)**
Archer-Daniels-Midland Company 740 702-6179
331 S Watt St Chillicothe (45601) **(G-3175)**
Archer-Daniels-Midland Company 330 852-3025
554 Pleasant Valley Rd Nw Sugarcreek (44681) **(G-17841)**
Archies Too 419 427-2663
2145 S Lake Ct Findlay (45840) **(G-9651)**
Architctral Identification Inc (PA) 614 868-8400
1170 Claycraft Rd Gahanna (43230) **(G-10076)**
Architctral Rfuse Slutions LLC 330 733-3996
525 Kennedy Rd Akron (44305) **(G-69)**
Architechual Etc, Cortland *Also called Lawbre Co* **(G-7712)**
Architectural and Industrial 440 963-0410
1091 Sunnyside Rd Vermilion (44089) **(G-19156)**
Architectural Art Glass Studio 513 731-7336
6106 Ridge Ave Cincinnati (45213) **(G-3355)**
Architectural Arts, Toledo *Also called Digimatics Inc* **(G-18263)**
Architectural Daylighting LLC 330 460-5000
879 S Progress Dr Ste C Medina (44256) **(G-13225)**
Architectural Door Systems LLC 513 808-9900
2810 Highland Ave Norwood (45212) **(G-15422)**
Architectural Fiberglass Inc 216 641-8300
8300 Bessemer Ave Cleveland (44127) **(G-4727)**
Architectural Metal Maint, Cleves *Also called Metal Maintenance Inc* **(G-6370)**
Architectural Products Dev 216 631-6260
6605 Clark Ave Rear 1 Cleveland (44102) **(G-4728)**
Architectural Sheet Metals LLC 216 361-9952
1457 E 39th St Cleveland (44114) **(G-4729)**
Arclin USA LLC 419 726-5013
6175 American Rd Toledo (43612) **(G-18190)**
Arconic Inc 330 835-6000
3340 Gilchrist Rd Mogadore (44260) **(G-14230)**
Arconic Inc 216 391-3885
3960 S Marginal Rd Cleveland (44114) **(G-4730)**
Arconic Inc 330 544-7633
1000 Warren Ave Niles (44446) **(G-14998)**
Arconic Inc 216 641-3600
1600 Harvard Ave Newburgh Heights (44105) **(G-14934)**
Arconic Inc 216 641-3600
1616 Harvard Ave Newburgh Heights (44105) **(G-14935)**
Arconic Inc 330 848-4000
842 Norton Ave Barberton (44203) **(G-1053)**
Arconic Titanium 330 544-7633
1000 Warren Ave Niles (44446) **(G-14999)**
Arctech Fabricating Inc (PA) 937 525-9353
1317 Lagonda Ave Springfield (45503) **(G-17364)**
Ardagh Metal Packaging USA Inc 419 334-4461
2145 Cedar St Fremont (43420) **(G-9991)**
Ardar Co Inc 440 582-3371
12955 York Delta Dr Ste A Cleveland (44133) **(G-4731)**
Arden J Neer Sr 937 585-6733
4859 Township Road 45 Bellefontaine (43311) **(G-1504)**
Area Wide Protective Inc (HQ) 330 644-0655
826 Overholt Rd Kent (44240) **(G-11296)**
Area Wide Protective Inc 419 221-2997
413 Flanders Ave Lima (45801) **(G-11842)**
Area Wide Protective Inc 513 321-9889
9500 Le Saint Dr Fairfield (45014) **(G-9483)**
Arem Co 440 974-6740
7234 Justin Way Mentor (44060) **(G-13393)**
Arena Eye Surgeons, Columbus *Also called Eye Surgery Center Ohio Inc* **(G-6912)**
Arens Corporation (PA) 937 473-2028
395 S High St Covington (45318) **(G-7781)**
Arens Corporation 937 473-2028
22 N High St Covington (45318) **(G-7782)**
Arens Publications & Printing, Covington *Also called Arens Corporation* **(G-7782)**
Ares Inc 419 635-2175
818 Front St Port Clinton (43452) **(G-16242)**
Ares Sportswear Ltd 614 767-1950
3704 Lacon Rd Hilliard (43026) **(G-10805)**
Arete Innovative Solutions LLC 513 503-2712
3050 Shawhan Rd Morrow (45152) **(G-14408)**
Areway Acquisition Inc 216 651-9022
8525 Clinton Rd Brooklyn (44144) **(G-2111)**
Areway LLC 216 651-9022
8525 Clinton Rd Brooklyn (44144) **(G-2112)**
Arf, Youngstown *Also called American Roll Formed Pdts Corp* **(G-20843)**
Argentifex LLC 440 990-1108
4608 Main Ave Ashtabula (44004) **(G-761)**
Arges 440 574-1305
275 N Pleasant St Oberlin (44074) **(G-15490)**
Argo Tool Corporation 330 425-2407
1962 Case Pkwy Twinsburg (44087) **(G-18735)**
Argosy Wind Power Ltd 440 539-1345
70 Aurora Industrial Pkwy Aurora (44202) **(G-869)**
Argrov Box Co 937 898-1700
6030 Webster St Dayton (45414) **(G-8036)**

ALPHABETIC

ARI Phoenix Inc (PA) ALPHABETIC SECTION

ARI Phoenix Inc (PA) 513 229-3750
4119 Binion Way Lebanon (45036) ***(G-11634)***
Ariel Corporation 740 397-0311
35 Blackjack Road Ext Mount Vernon (43050) ***(G-14468)***
Ariel Corporation 740 397-0311
8405 Blackjack Rd Mount Vernon (43050) ***(G-14469)***
Ariel's Oak, Sherrodsville *Also called Ariels Oak Inc* ***(G-16990)***
Ariels Oak Inc 330 343-7453
9486 Cutler Rd Ne Sherrodsville (44675) ***(G-16990)***
Arisdyne Systems Inc 216 458-1991
17909 Cleveland Pkwy Dr # 100 Cleveland (44135) ***(G-4732)***
Arizona Beverages, Cincinnati *Also called Hornell Brewing Co Inc* ***(G-3827)***
Arizona Chemical Company LLC 330 343-7701
875 Harger St Dover (44622) ***(G-8804)***
Arkansas Face Veneer Co Inc (HQ) 937 773-6295
1025 S Roosevelt Ave Piqua (45356) ***(G-16100)***
Arken Manufacturing Inc 216 883-6628
3502 Beyerle Rd Cleveland (44105) ***(G-4733)***
Arku Coil-Systems Inc 513 985-0500
11405 Grooms Rd Blue Ash (45242) ***(G-1730)***
Arlington Rack & Packaging Co 419 476-7700
6120 N Detroit Ave Toledo (43612) ***(G-18191)***
Arlington-Blaine Lumber Co, Delaware *Also called Khempco Bldg Sup Co Ltd Partnr* ***(G-8700)***
Arlo Aluminum & Steel, Dayton *Also called Alro Steel Corporation* ***(G-8021)***
Arm & Hammer, London *Also called Church & Dwight Co Inc* ***(G-12053)***
ARM (usa) Inc 740 264-6599
1506 Fernwood Rd Steubenville (43953) ***(G-17527)***
ARM Opco Inc 330 868-7724
3026 Saratoga Ave Sw Canton (44706) ***(G-2575)***
Armada Fortress LLC 330 953-2185
8061 Market St Youngstown (44512) ***(G-20847)***
Armada Power LLC 614 204-9341
230 West St Ste 150 Columbus (43215) ***(G-6615)***
Armaly Brands, London *Also called Armaly LLC* ***(G-12049)***
Armaly LLC 740 852-3621
110 W 1st St London (43140) ***(G-12049)***
Armature Coil Equipment Inc 216 267-6366
4725 Manufacturing Ave Cleveland (44135) ***(G-4734)***
Armbrust Concrete, Wshngtn CT Hs *Also called Philip Armbrust* ***(G-20735)***
Armeton US Co 419 660-9296
205 Republic St Norwalk (44857) ***(G-15381)***
Armin R Jewett 419 647-6644
607 N Water St Wapakoneta (45895) ***(G-19322)***
Armoloy of Ohio Inc 937 323-8702
1950 E Leffel Ln Springfield (45505) ***(G-17365)***
Armor Consolidated Inc (PA) 513 923-5260
4600 N Mson Montgomery Rd Mason (45040) ***(G-12826)***
Armor Group Inc (HQ) 513 923-5260
4600 N Masn Montgomery Rd Mason (45040) ***(G-12827)***
Armor Metal Group Mason Inc (HQ) 513 769-0700
4600 N Masn Montgomery Rd Mason (45040) ***(G-12828)***
Armormetal, Mason *Also called Armor Metal Group Mason Inc* ***(G-12828)***
Armorsource LLC 740 928-0070
3600 Hebron Rd Hebron (43025) ***(G-10738)***
Armour Spray Systems Inc 216 398-3838
210 Hayes Dr Ste I Cleveland (44131) ***(G-4735)***
Armstrong Custom Moulding Inc 740 922-5931
6408 State Route 800 Se Uhrichsville (44683) ***(G-18880)***
Armstrong Printing, Springfield *Also called Graphic Paper Products Corp* ***(G-17408)***
Armstrong S Printing Ex LLC 937 276-7794
8810 Grovecreek Ct Dayton (45458) ***(G-8037)***
Armstrong World Industries Inc 740 967-1063
451 E Coshocton St Johnstown (43031) ***(G-11257)***
Armstrong World Industries Inc 614 771-9307
4241 Leap Rd Bldg A Hilliard (43026) ***(G-10806)***
Arnco Corporation 800 847-7661
860 Garden St Elyria (44035) ***(G-9219)***
Arnold Machine Inc 419 443-1818
19 Heritage Dr Tiffin (44883) ***(G-18045)***
Arnold Magnetic Technologies, Marietta *Also called Flexmag Industries Inc* ***(G-12624)***
Arnold Printing Inc 330 494-1191
5772 West Blvd Nw Canton (44718) ***(G-2576)***
Arnolds Candies Inc 330 733-4022
931 High Grove Blvd Akron (44312) ***(G-70)***
Arnolds Repair Shop 740 373-5313
101 Simpson St Marietta (45750) ***(G-12604)***
Aromair Fine Fragrance Company 614 984-2896
8860 Smiths Mill Rd # 500 New Albany (43054) ***(G-14605)***
Aronit Machine LLC 419 782-4740
2018 Baltimore St Defiance (43512) ***(G-8613)***
Arrow Coal Grove Inc 740 532-6143
300 Marion Pike Ironton (45638) ***(G-11160)***
Arrow Fabricating Co 216 641-0490
7355 Calley Ln Novelty (44072) ***(G-15437)***
Arrow International Inc (PA) 216 961-3500
9900 Clinton Rd Cleveland (44144) ***(G-4736)***
Arrow Print & Copy, Sylvania *Also called Kevin K Tidd* ***(G-17948)***
Arrow Tru-Line Inc 419 636-7013
720 E Perry St Bryan (43506) ***(G-2265)***
Arrow Tru-Line Inc (PA) 419 446-2785
2211 S Defiance St Archbold (43502) ***(G-639)***
Arrowhead Industries 440 349-2846
33891 Canterbury Rd Solon (44139) ***(G-17108)***
Arrowhead Pallets LLC 440 693-4241
7851 Parkman Mespo Rd Middlefield (44062) ***(G-13778)***
Arrowstrip Inc 740 633-2609
1st & Locust St S Martins Ferry (43935) ***(G-12756)***
ARS Recycling Systems LLC 330 536-8210
4000 Mccartney Rd Lowellville (44436) ***(G-12249)***
Arsco Custom Metals LLC (PA) 513 385-0555
3330 E Kemper Rd Cincinnati (45241) ***(G-3356)***
Arsco Custom Metals LLC 513 563-8822
3330 E Kemper Rd Cincinnati (45241) ***(G-3357)***
Arsco Manufacturing Company, Cincinnati *Also called Arsco Custom Metals LLC* ***(G-3356)***
Art & Sign Corporation 419 865-3336
5458 Angola Rd Toledo (43615) ***(G-18192)***
Art Brands LLC 614 755-4278
225 Business Center Dr Blacklick (43004) ***(G-1677)***
Art Columbus Memorial Inc 614 221-9333
606 W Broad St Columbus (43215) ***(G-6616)***
Art Fremont Iron Co 419 332-5554
307 E State St Fremont (43420) ***(G-9992)***
Art Galvanizing Works Inc 216 749-0020
3935 Valley Rd Cleveland (44109) ***(G-4737)***
Art Guild Binders Inc 513 242-3000
1068 Meta Dr Cincinnati (45237) ***(G-3358)***
Art Metals Group Inc 513 942-8800
3795 Symmes Rd Hamilton (45015) ***(G-10536)***
Art of Beauty Company Inc (PA) 216 438-6363
200 Egbert Rd Bedford (44146) ***(G-1385)***
Art Printing Co Inc 419 281-4371
147 E 2nd St Ashland (44805) ***(G-677)***
Art Pro Graphics 216 236-6465
7279 Summitview Dr Seven Hills (44131) ***(G-16901)***
Art Saylor Logging 740 682-6188
343 Slab Hill Rd Oak Hill (45656) ***(G-15449)***
Art Tees Inc 614 338-8337
39 S Yearling Rd Columbus (43213) ***(G-6617)***
Art Woodworking & Mfg Co 513 681-2986
4238 Dane Ave Cincinnati (45223) ***(G-3359)***
Art Works 740 425-5765
119 E Pike St Barnesville (43713) ***(G-1115)***
Art-American Printing Plates 216 241-4420
1138 W 9th St Fl 4 Cleveland (44113) ***(G-4738)***
Arte Limited, Cleveland *Also called Lawrence Industries Inc* ***(G-5567)***
Artesian Tan, Toledo *Also called Kahuna Bay Spray Tan LLC* ***(G-18360)***
Artex Oil Company, Marietta *Also called James Engineering Inc* ***(G-12636)***
Artex Oil Company 740 373-3313
2337 State Route 821 Marietta (45750) ***(G-12605)***
Artfind Tile, Wooster *Also called Artfinders* ***(G-20563)***
Artfinders 330 264-7706
143 S Market St Wooster (44691) ***(G-20563)***
Arth LLC 513 293-1646
6680 Burlington Dr West Chester (45069) ***(G-19651)***
Arthur Corporation 419 433-7202
1305 Huron Avery Rd Huron (44839) ***(G-11089)***
Arthur Louis Steel Co, Geneva *Also called Louis Arthur Steel Company* ***(G-10225)***
Arthur W Guilford III Inc 216 362-1350
13515 Brookpark Rd Cleveland (44142) ***(G-4739)***
Arthurs Refrigeration 740 532-0206
2156 State Route 93 Ironton (45638) ***(G-11161)***
Artic Diamond, Cincinnati *Also called Brady A Lantz Enterprises Inc* ***(G-3409)***
Artic Diamond, Cincinnati *Also called Brady A Lantz Enterprises* ***(G-3408)***
Artiflex Manufacturing LLC (PA) 330 262-2015
1425 E Bowman St Wooster (44691) ***(G-20564)***
Artisan Equipment Inc 740 756-9135
5770 Winchester Rd Carroll (43112) ***(G-2898)***
Artisan Grinding Service Inc 937 667-7383
1300 Stanley Ave Dayton (45404) ***(G-8038)***
Artisan Mold Co Inc 440 926-4511
1021 Commerce Dr 219 Grafton (44044) ***(G-10292)***
Artisan Tool & Die Corp 216 883-2769
4911 Grant Ave Cleveland (44125) ***(G-4740)***
Artistic Composite & Mold Co 330 352-6632
9225 Stone Rd Litchfield (44253) ***(G-11984)***
Artistic Elements Salon LLC 330 626-2114
8929 State Route 14 Ste C Streetsboro (44241) ***(G-17661)***
Artistic Finishes Inc 440 951-7850
38357 Apollo Pkwy Willoughby (44094) ***(G-20281)***
Artistic Foods Incorporated 330 401-1313
355 Elyria St Lodi (44254) ***(G-12006)***
Artistic Memorials Ltd 419 873-0433
12551 Jefferson St Perrysburg (43551) ***(G-15921)***
Artistic Metal Spinning Inc 216 961-3336
4700 Lorain Ave Cleveland (44102) ***(G-4741)***

Artistic Rock LLC 216 291-8856
3786 Fairoaks Rd Cleveland (44121) **(G-4742)**
Arts Rolloffs & Refuse Inc 419 991-3730
108 Cheshire Cir Lima (45804) **(G-11843)**
Artsinheaven.com, Millersburg *Also called Educational Electronics Inc* **(G-14080)**
Arvinmrtor Commerical Vhcl Sys, Granville *Also called Meritor Inc* **(G-10333)**
Arzel Technology Inc 216 831-6068
4801 Commerce Pkwy Cleveland (44128) **(G-4743)**
Arzel Zoning Technology, Cleveland *Also called Arzel Technology Inc* **(G-4743)**
As America Inc 614 497-9384
6600 Port Rd Ste 200 Groveport (43125) **(G-10483)**
As America Inc 330 337-2219
605 S Ellsworth Ave Salem (44460) **(G-16718)**
As America Inc 419 522-4211
41 Cairns Rd Mansfield (44903) **(G-12408)**
ASAP Ready Mix Inc 513 797-1774
250 Mount Holly Rd Amelia (45102) **(G-532)**
Asb Industries Inc 330 753-8458
1031 Lambert St Barberton (44203) **(G-1054)**
Asbeka Custom Products LLC 440 352-0839
11288 Saint Andrews Way Painesville (44077) **(G-15711)**
ASC Holdco Inc (PA) 330 899-0340
2100 International Pkwy North Canton (44720) **(G-15069)**
ASC Industries Inc (HQ) 330 899-0340
2100 International Pkwy North Canton (44720) **(G-15070)**
Ascendtech Inc 216 458-1101
4772 E 355th St Willoughby (44094) **(G-20282)**
Ascents, Cleveland *Also called Aeroscena LLC* **(G-4634)**
Asch-Klaassen Sonics LLC 513 671-3226
11711 Princeton Pike # 943 Cincinnati (45246) **(G-3360)**
Asco Power Technologies LP 216 573-7600
6255 Halle Dr Cleveland (44125) **(G-4744)**
Asco Power Technologies LP 216 573-7600
8400 E Pleasant Valley Rd Cleveland (44131) **(G-4745)**
Asco Valve Inc 216 360-0366
26401 Emery Rd Ste 105 Cleveland (44128) **(G-4746)**
Ascon Tecnologic N Amer LLC 216 485-8350
1111 Brookpark Rd Cleveland (44109) **(G-4747)**
Ascot Valley Foods LLC (PA) 330 376-9411
205 Ascot Pkwy Cuyahoga Falls (44223) **(G-7840)**
ASG 216 486-6163
15700 S Waterloo Rd Cleveland (44110) **(G-4748)**
Asg Division Jergens Inc 888 486-6163
15700 S Waterloo Rd Cleveland (44110) **(G-4749)**
Ash Sewer & Drain Service 330 376-9714
451 E North St Akron (44304) **(G-71)**
Ashco 330 385-2400
1250 Saint George St # 3 East Liverpool (43920) **(G-9050)**
Ashco Manufacturing Inc 419 838-7157
5234 Tulane Ave Toledo (43611) **(G-18193)**
Ashcraft Machine & Supply Inc 740 349-8110
185 Wilson St Newark (43055) **(G-14853)**
Ashland Conveyor Products, Ashland *Also called Midwest Conveyor Products Inc* **(G-725)**
Ashland Distribution, Dublin *Also called Ashland LLC* **(G-8883)**
Ashland LLC 614 790-3333
5200 Blazer Pkwy Dublin (43017) **(G-8883)**
Ashland LLC 513 682-2405
9451 Meridian Way West Chester (45069) **(G-19652)**
Ashland LLC 419 998-8728
1220 S Metcalf St Lima (45804) **(G-11844)**
Ashland LLC 614 529-3318
1979 Atlas St Columbus (43228) **(G-6618)**
Ashland LLC 513 557-3100
3901 River Rd Cincinnati (45204) **(G-3361)**
Ashland Monument Company Inc 419 281-2688
34 E 2nd St Ashland (44805) **(G-678)**
Ashland Precision Tooling LLC 419 289-1736
1750 S Baney Rd Ashland (44805) **(G-679)**
Ashland Publishing Co 419 281-0581
40 E 2nd St Ashland (44805) **(G-680)**
Ashland R Crawford Knox, Ontario *Also called Child Evngelism Fellowship Inc* **(G-15538)**
Ashland Spcalty Ingredients GP, Dublin *Also called Ashland Specialty Ingredients* **(G-8884)**
Ashland Specialty Ingredients (PA) 302 594-5000
5200 Laser Pkwy Dublin (43017) **(G-8884)**
Ashland Specialty Ingredients 614 529-3311
1979 Atlas St Columbus (43228) **(G-6619)**
Ashland Times Gazette, Ashland *Also called Ashland Publishing Co* **(G-680)**
Ashley F Ward Inc (PA) 513 398-1414
7490 Easy St Mason (45040) **(G-12829)**
Ashta Chemicals Inc 440 997-5221
3509 Middle Rd Ashtabula (44004) **(G-762)**
Ashta Forge & Machine Inc 216 252-7000
3001 W 121st St Cleveland (44111) **(G-4750)**
Ashtabula Rubber Co 440 992-2195
2751 West Ave Ashtabula (44004) **(G-763)**
Ashtabula Star Beacon, Ashtabula *Also called Newspaper Holding Inc* **(G-792)**
Ashtech Corporation 440 646-9911
7155 Settlers Ridge Rd Gates Mills (44040) **(G-10207)**
Ashton LLC 614 833-4165
77 E Columbus St Pickerington (43147) **(G-16039)**
Ashton Pumpmatic Inc 937 424-1380
7670 Mcewen Rd Dayton (45459) **(G-8039)**
Asi Investment Holding Co 330 666-3751
3550 W Market St Fairlawn (44333) **(G-9593)**
Asi Investments Holding Co, Fairlawn *Also called Sunprene Company* **(G-9621)**
Asi Sign Systems, Loveland *Also called Kmgrafx Inc* **(G-12206)**
Asia For Kids, Blue Ash *Also called Master Communications Inc* **(G-1813)**
Asist Translation Services 614 451-6744
4891 Sawmill Rd Ste 200 Columbus (43235) **(G-6620)**
Ask Chemicals 216 961-4690
2191 W 110th St Cleveland (44102) **(G-4751)**
Ask Chemicals LLC 800 848-7485
495 Metro Pl S Ste 250 Dublin (43017) **(G-8885)**
Ask Chemicals LP, Dublin *Also called Ask Chemicals LLC* **(G-8885)**
Askia Inc 513 828-7443
4303 Williamsburg Rd N Cincinnati (45215) **(G-3362)**
Aslan Worldwide 513 671-0671
8583 Rupp Farm Dr West Chester (45069) **(G-19653)**
Asm International 440 338-5151
9639 Kinsman Rd Novelty (44073) **(G-15438)**
Aspec Inc 513 561-9922
5810 Carothers St Cincinnati (45227) **(G-3363)**
Aspen Machine and Plastics 937 526-4644
257 Baker Rd Versailles (45380) **(G-19173)**
Aspery Farms, Streetsboro *Also called Microbiological Labs Inc* **(G-17682)**
Asphalt Fabrics & Specialties 440 786-1077
7710 Bond St Solon (44139) **(G-17109)**
Asphalt Materials Inc 740 373-3040
505 River Ln Marietta (45750) **(G-12606)**
Asphalt Materials Inc 419 693-0626
940 N Wynn Rd Oregon (43616) **(G-15554)**
Asphalt Materials Inc 740 374-5100
13925 State Route 7 Marietta (45750) **(G-12607)**
Asphalt Services Ohio Inc 614 864-4600
4579 Poth Rd Columbus (43213) **(G-6621)**
Assembly Division, Walbridge *Also called Riverside Mch & Automtn Inc* **(G-19299)**
Assembly Machining Wire Pdts 614 443-1110
2375 Refugee Park Columbus (43207) **(G-6622)**
Assembly Specialty Pdts Inc 216 676-5600
14700 Brookpark Rd Cleveland (44135) **(G-4752)**
Assembly Tool Specialists, Twinsburg *Also called Production Tl Co Cleveland Inc* **(G-18841)**
Assembly Works Inc 419 433-5010
1705 Sawmill Pkwy Huron (44839) **(G-11090)**
Assembly Works Matrix Automtn, Huron *Also called Assembly Works Inc* **(G-11090)**
Assisted Patrol LLC 937 369-0080
2130 Hedge Gate Blvd Beavercreek (45431) **(G-1300)**
Assistive Technology of Ohio, Columbus *Also called Ohio State University* **(G-7261)**
Assoc Talents Inc 440 716-1265
3700 Greenbriar Cir Westlake (44145) **(G-20100)**
Associated Associates Inc 330 626-3300
9551 Elliman Rd Mantua (44255) **(G-12542)**
Associated Enterprises 440 354-2106
1382 W Jackson St Painesville (44077) **(G-15712)**
Associated Graphics Inc 614 873-1273
9021 Heritage Dr Ste I Plain City (43064) **(G-16172)**
Associated Hygienic Pdts LLC 770 497-9800
2332 Us Highway 42 S Delaware (43015) **(G-8655)**
Associated Materials LLC (HQ) 330 929-1811
3773 State Rd Cuyahoga Falls (44223) **(G-7841)**
Associated Materials LLC 937 236-5679
3361 Needmore Rd Dayton (45414) **(G-8040)**
Associated Materials Group Inc (PA) 330 929-1811
3773 State Rd Cuyahoga Falls (44223) **(G-7842)**
Associated Mtls Holdings LLC 330 929-1811
3773 State Rd Cuyahoga Falls (44223) **(G-7843)**
Associated Plastics Corp 419 634-3910
502 Eric Wolber Dr Ada (45810) **(G-5)**
Associated Press Repair Inc 216 881-2288
5321 Saint Clair Ave Cleveland (44103) **(G-4753)**
Associated Ready Mix Concrete, Mantua *Also called Associated Associates Inc* **(G-12542)**
Associated Software Cons Inc 440 826-1010
7251 Engle Rd Ste 400 Middleburg Heights (44130) **(G-13761)**
Associated Technical Sales, Franklin *Also called Gad-Jets Inc* **(G-9885)**
Assocted Vsual Cmmncations Inc 330 452-4449
7000 Firestone Ave Ne Canton (44721) **(G-2577)**
Aster Elements Inc 440 942-2799
7100 Euclid Ave Cleveland (44103) **(G-4754)**
Aster Industries Inc 330 762-7965
275 N Arlington St Ste B Akron (44305) **(G-72)**
Asterena Corporation 937 605-6470
1413 Verna Ct Dayton (45458) **(G-8041)**
Astra Products of Ohio Ltd (PA) 330 296-0112
7154 State Route 88 Ravenna (44266) **(G-16367)**
Astro Aluminum Enterprises Inc 330 755-1414
65 Main St Struthers (44471) **(G-17813)**
Astro Industries Inc 937 429-5900
4403 Dayton Xenia Rd Beavercreek (45432) **(G-1301)**

ALPHABETIC

Astro Instrumentation LLC ALPHABETIC SECTION

Astro Instrumentation LLC 440 238-2005
22740 Lunn Rd Strongsville (44149) ***(G-17712)***
Astro Met Inc (PA) 513 772-1242
9974 Springfield Pike Cincinnati (45215) ***(G-3364)***
Astro Shapes LLC (PA) 330 755-1414
65 Main St Struthers (44471) ***(G-17814)***
Astro Shapes LLC 330 755-1414
65 Main St Struthers (44471) ***(G-17815)***
Astro-Coatings Inc 330 755-1414
65 Main St Struthers (44471) ***(G-17816)***
Astro-TEC Mfg Inc 330 854-2209
550 Elm Ridge Ave Canal Fulton (44614) ***(G-2475)***
Aswpengg LLC 216 292-4620
26300 Miles Rd Bedford Heights (44146) ***(G-1461)***
At Holdings Corporation 216 692-6000
23555 Euclid Ave Cleveland (44117) ***(G-4755)***
At Pallet 330 264-3903
4224 E Messner Rd Wooster (44691) ***(G-20565)***
At The Ready Publications LLC 762 822-8549
308 Pleasant St Van Wert (45891) ***(G-19077)***
AT&f Advanced Metals LLC (PA) 330 684-1122
12314 Elmwood Ave Cleveland (44111) ***(G-4756)***
AT&f Nuclear Inc (HQ) 216 252-1500
12314 Elmwood Ave Cleveland (44111) ***(G-4757)***
AT&T Corp 614 223-8236
150 E Gay St Ste 4a Columbus (43215) ***(G-6623)***
AT&T Corp 513 792-9300
7875 Montgomery Rd Ofc Cincinnati (45236) ***(G-3365)***
AT&T Government Solutions Inc 937 306-3030
2940 Presidential Dr # 390 Beavercreek (45324) ***(G-1302)***
Ata Tools Inc 330 928-7744
7 Ascot Pkwy Cuyahoga Falls (44223) ***(G-7844)***
Atc Group Inc (PA) 440 293-4064
101 Parker Dr Andover (44003) ***(G-579)***
Atc Legacy Inc 330 590-8105
1441 Wolf Creek Trl Sharon Center (44274) ***(G-16944)***
Atc Lighting & Plastics, Andover *Also called Atc Group Inc* ***(G-579)***
Atc Lighting & Plastics Inc (HQ) 440 466-7670
101 Parker Dr Andover (44003) ***(G-580)***
Atc Nymold Corporation 440 293-4064
101 Parker Dr Andover (44003) ***(G-581)***
Atc Nymold Corporation (HQ) 440 293-4064
101 Parker Dr Andover (44003) ***(G-582)***
Atchley Signs & Graphics 614 421-7446
1616 Transamerica Ct Columbus (43228) ***(G-6624)***
Atd, Strongsville *Also called Atlantic Durant Technology Inc* ***(G-17713)***
Atec Diversfd Wldg Fabrication 937 546-4399
466 Dehan Rd Wilmington (45177) ***(G-20486)***
Athens Foods Inc 216 676-8500
13600 Snow Rd Cleveland (44142) ***(G-4758)***
Athens Messenger, The, Athens *Also called Messenger Publishing Company* ***(G-839)***
Athens Mold and Machine Inc 740 593-6613
180 Mill St Athens (45701) ***(G-823)***
Athens Technical Specialists 740 592-2874
8157 Us Highway 50 Athens (45701) ***(G-824)***
Athersys Inc (PA) 216 431-9900
3201 Carnegie Ave Cleveland (44115) ***(G-4759)***
ATI, Toledo *Also called Abbott Tool Inc* ***(G-18153)***
ATI, Batavia *Also called Auto Temp Inc* ***(G-1123)***
ATI Allegheny Ludlum, Louisville *Also called Allegheny Ludlum LLC* ***(G-12151)***
ATI Irrigation LLC 937 750-2976
4746 W State Route 55 Troy (45373) ***(G-18639)***
Atk2 Inc 513 661-5869
3111 Harrison Ave Cincinnati (45211) ***(G-3366)***
Atkinson Printing Inc 330 669-3515
2876 N Applecreek Rd Wooster (44691) ***(G-20566)***
Atkore Plastic Pipe Corp 330 627-8002
861 N Lisbon St Carrollton (44615) ***(G-2916)***
Atlantic and Prfmce Rigging, Tiffin *Also called Tiffin Scenic Studios Inc* ***(G-18089)***
Atlantic Co 440 944-8988
26651 Curtiss Wright Pkwy Willoughby Hills (44092) ***(G-20466)***
Atlantic Durant Technology Inc (HQ) 440 238-6931
19963 Progress Dr Strongsville (44149) ***(G-17713)***
Atlantic Inertial Systems Inc 740 788-3800
781 Irving Wick Dr W Heath (43056) ***(G-10717)***
Atlantic Investment 440 567-5054
6117 Antler Xing Lorain (44053) ***(G-12079)***
Atlantic Sign Company Inc 513 383-1504
2328 Florence Ave Cincinnati (45206) ***(G-3367)***
Atlantic Tool & Die Company (PA) 440 238-6931
19963 Progress Dr Strongsville (44149) ***(G-17714)***
Atlantic Tool & Die Company 330 769-4500
4995 Atlantic Dr Seville (44273) ***(G-16910)***
Atlantic Tool & Die Company 330 239-3700
6965 Ridge Rd Sharon Center (44274) ***(G-16945)***
Atlantic Veal & Lamb LLC 330 435-6400
2416 E West Salem Rd Creston (44217) ***(G-7803)***
Atlantic Water Gardens, Mantua *Also called Meridienne International Inc* ***(G-12554)***
Atlantis Sportswear Inc 937 773-0680
344 Fox Dr Piqua (45356) ***(G-16101)***
Atlapac Corp 614 252-2121
2901 E 4th Ave Ste 5 Columbus (43219) ***(G-6625)***
Atlas America Inc 330 339-3155
1026a Cookson Ave Se New Philadelphia (44663) ***(G-14759)***
Atlas Bolt & Screw Company LLC (HQ) 419 289-6171
1628 Troy Rd Ashland (44805) ***(G-681)***
Atlas Dowel & Wood Products Co, Harrison *Also called Puttmann Industries Inc* ***(G-10665)***
Atlas Fasteners For Cnstr, Ashland *Also called Atlas Bolt & Screw Company LLC* ***(G-681)***
Atlas Gear and Machine Co 614 272-6944
575 N Hague Ave Columbus (43204) ***(G-6626)***
Atlas Growth Eagle Ford LLC 330 896-8510
3500 Massillon Rd Uniontown (44685) ***(G-18911)***
Atlas Industrial Contrs LLC (HQ) 614 841-4500
5275 Sinclair Rd Columbus (43229) ***(G-6627)***
Atlas Industries Inc (PA) 419 355-1000
1750 E State St Fremont (43420) ***(G-9993)***
Atlas Industries Inc 419 637-2117
401 Wall St Tiffin (44883) ***(G-18046)***
Atlas Industries Inc 419 447-4730
401 Wall St Tiffin (44883) ***(G-18047)***
Atlas Machine and Supply Inc 502 584-7262
4985 Provident Dr West Chester (45246) ***(G-19834)***
Atlas Machine and Supply Inc 614 351-1603
5040 Nike Dr Hilliard (43026) ***(G-10807)***
Atlas Machine Products Co 216 228-3688
12507 Plover St Cleveland (44107) ***(G-4760)***
Atlas Portable Space Solutions, Cleveland *Also called Atlas Machine Products Co* ***(G-4760)***
Atlas Precision Machining Inc 937 615-9585
8899 Sherry Dr Piqua (45356) ***(G-16102)***
Atlas Printing and Embroidery 440 882-3537
7632 Pleasant View Dr Cleveland (44134) ***(G-4761)***
Atlas Produce LLC 937 223-1446
104 Salem Ave Dayton (45406) ***(G-8042)***
Atlas Roofing Corporation 937 746-9941
675 Oxford Rd Franklin (45005) ***(G-9870)***
Atlas Vac Machine LLC 513 407-3513
9150 Reading Rd Cincinnati (45215) ***(G-3368)***
Atlasbooks, Ashland *Also called Bookmasters Inc* ***(G-686)***
Atmosphere Annealing LLC 330 478-0314
1501 Raff Rd Sw Kenton (43326) ***(G-11402)***
Atom Blasting & Finishing Inc 440 235-4765
24933 Sprague Rd Columbia Station (44028) ***(G-6429)***
Atotech USA Inc 216 398-0550
1000 Harvard Ave Cleveland (44109) ***(G-4762)***
Atr Distributing Company 513 353-1800
11857 Tamper Springs Dr Cincinnati (45240) ***(G-3369)***
Atricure Inc (PA) 513 755-4100
7555 Innovation Way Mason (45040) ***(G-12830)***
Atrium At Anna Maria Inc 330 562-7777
849 N Aurora Rd Aurora (44202) ***(G-870)***
Ats Atmtion Globl Svcs USA Inc 519 653-4483
425 Enterprise Dr Lewis Center (43035) ***(G-11745)***
Ats Machine & Tool Co Inc 440 255-1120
7750 Division Dr Mentor (44060) ***(G-13394)***
Ats Ohio, Lewis Center *Also called Automation Tooling Systems* ***(G-11749)***
Ats Ohio Inc 614 888-2344
425 Enterprise Dr Lewis Center (43035) ***(G-11746)***
Ats Systems Oregon Inc 541 738-0932
425 Enterprise Dr Lewis Center (43035) ***(G-11747)***
Atsi, Athens *Also called Athens Technical Specialists* ***(G-824)***
Attention Dsase Diagnstc Group 216 577-3075
2944 E Derbyshire Rd Cleveland (44118) ***(G-4763)***
Attia Applied Sciences Inc 740 369-1891
548 W Central Ave Delaware (43015) ***(G-8656)***
Attica Hub Office, Attica *Also called Bloomville Gazette Inc* ***(G-855)***
Attractive Kitchens & Flrg LLC 440 406-9299
536 Cleveland St Elyria (44035) ***(G-9220)***
ATW, Hamilton *Also called American Tool Works Inc* ***(G-10535)***
Atwood Mobile Products LLC 419 258-5531
5406 Us 24 Antwerp (45813) ***(G-597)***
Aubrey Rose Apparel LLC 513 728-2681
3862 Race Rd Cincinnati (45211) ***(G-3370)***
Auburn Dairy Products Inc 614 488-2536
2200 Cardigan Ave Columbus (43215) ***(G-6628)***
Auburn Metal Processing LLC (PA) 315 253-2565
1831 Highland Rd Twinsburg (44087) ***(G-18736)***
Audimute Soundproofing & Medic, Beachwood *Also called One Wish LLC* ***(G-1259)***
Audion Automation Ltd (PA) 216 267-1911
775 Berea Industrial Pkwy Berea (44017) ***(G-1591)***
Audion Automation Ltd 216 267-1911
775 Berea Industrial Pkwy Berea (44017) ***(G-1592)***
Audit Forms, Cleveland *Also called Foote Printing Company Inc* ***(G-5260)***
Aufbackgroundscreeningcom 216 831-4113
26101 Village Ln Beachwood (44122) ***(G-1224)***
Augdon Newspapers of Ohio Inc 419 448-3200
320 Nelson St Tiffin (44883) ***(G-18048)***
Auglaize Embroidery Co, Wapakoneta *Also called Judy Dubois* ***(G-19336)***

Auglaize Erie Machine Company 419 629-2068
07148 Quellhorst Rd New Bremen (45869) ***(G-14647)***
Auglaize Welding Company Inc 419 738-4422
106 N Water St Wapakoneta (45895) ***(G-19323)***
August Nine Enterprises, Troy *Also called Debra Harbour* ***(G-18647)***
Aukerman J F Steel Rule Die 937 456-4498
5582 Ozias Rd Eaton (45320) ***(G-9142)***
Auld Company 614 454-1010
1003 Kinnear Rd Columbus (43212) ***(G-6629)***
Auld Crafters Inc 614 221-6825
175 Cleveland Ave Rear Columbus (43215) ***(G-6630)***
Auld Lang Signs Inc 513 792-5555
11109 Kenwood Rd Blue Ash (45242) ***(G-1731)***
Auld Technologies LLC 614 755-2853
2030 Dividend Dr Columbus (43228) ***(G-6631)***
Aultwrks Occupational Medicine 330 491-9675
4650 Hills And Dales Rd N Canton (44708) ***(G-2578)***
Auntie Annes 330 652-1939
5555 Youngstown Warren Rd # 637 Niles (44446) ***(G-15000)***
Aunties Attic 740 548-5059
1550 Lewis Center Rd G Lewis Center (43035) ***(G-11748)***
Aurand Manufacturing & Eqp Co 513 541-7200
1210 Ellis St Cincinnati (45223) ***(G-3371)***
Auria Fremont LLC 419 332-1587
400 S Stone St Fremont (43420) ***(G-9994)***
Auria Holmesville LLC 330 279-4505
8281 County Road 245 Holmesville (44633) ***(G-10973)***
Auria Sidney LLC 937 492-1225
2000 Schlater Dr Sidney (45365) ***(G-17017)***
Auria Sidney LLC (HQ) 937 492-1225
2000 Schlater Dr Sidney (45365) ***(G-17018)***
Auria Solutions, Fremont *Also called Auria Fremont LLC* ***(G-9994)***
Auris Noble LLC (PA) 330 321-6649
3045 Smith Rd Ste 700 Fairlawn (44333) ***(G-9594)***
Auris Noble LLC 330 685-3748
130 E Voris St Ste C Akron (44311) ***(G-73)***
Aurora Plastics LLC (PA) 330 422-0700
9280 Jefferson St Streetsboro (44241) ***(G-17662)***
Austin Engineering Group, Barberton *Also called Austin Engineering Inc* ***(G-1055)***
Austin Engineering Inc 330 848-0815
834 Promenade Cir Barberton (44203) ***(G-1055)***
Austin Finishing Co Inc 216 883-0326
3805 E 91st St Cleveland (44105) ***(G-4764)***
Austin Foam Plastics Inc 614 921-0824
2200 International St Columbus (43228) ***(G-6632)***
Austin Powder Company (HQ) 216 464-2400
25800 Science Park Dr # 300 Cleveland (44122) ***(G-4765)***
Austin Powder Company 740 596-5286
430 Powder Plant Rd Mc Arthur (45651) ***(G-13179)***
Austin Powder Company 419 299-3347
3518 Township Road 142 Findlay (45840) ***(G-9652)***
Austin Powder Company 740 968-1555
74200 Edwards Rd Saint Clairsville (43950) ***(G-16621)***
Austin Powder Holdings Company (HQ) 216 464-2400
25800 Science Park Dr # 300 Cleveland (44122) ***(G-4766)***
Austin Tape and Label Inc 330 928-7999
3350 Cavalier Trl Stow (44224) ***(G-17570)***
Austinburg Machine Inc 440 275-2001
2899 Industrial Park Dr Austinburg (44010) ***(G-918)***
Austins Machine Shop 614 855-2525
4295 N Waggoner Rd Blacklick (43004) ***(G-1678)***
Austintown Metal Works Inc 330 259-4673
45 Victoria Rd Youngstown (44515) ***(G-20848)***
Austintown Printing Inc 330 797-0099
5015 Mahoning Ave Ste 3 Youngstown (44515) ***(G-20849)***
Auto Bolt and Nut Company, The, Cleveland *Also called Auto Bolt Company* ***(G-4767)***
Auto Bolt Company 216 881-3913
4740 Manufacturing Ave Cleveland (44135) ***(G-4767)***
Auto Core Systems 740 362-5599
2097 London Rd Unit A Delaware (43015) ***(G-8657)***
Auto Dealer Designs Inc 330 374-7666
303 W Bartges St Akron (44307) ***(G-74)***
Auto Des Sys Inc 614 488-7984
3518 Riverside Dr Upper Arlington (43221) ***(G-18943)***
Auto Expo USA of Cleveland 216 889-3000
3250 W 117th St Cleveland (44111) ***(G-4768)***
Auto Magic Systems, Steubenville *Also called Eastern Ohio Investments Inc* ***(G-17532)***
Auto Pro & Design 330 833-9237
356 27th St Se Massillon (44646) ***(G-12961)***
Auto Technology Company 440 572-7800
20026 Progress Dr Strongsville (44149) ***(G-17715)***
Auto Temp Inc 513 732-6969
950 Kent Rd Batavia (45103) ***(G-1123)***
Auto-Tap Inc 216 671-1043
3317 W 140th St Cleveland (44111) ***(G-4769)***
Auto-Tronic Control Co 419 666-5100
240 W Andrus Rd Northwood (43619) ***(G-15333)***
Auto-Valve Inc 937 854-3037
1707 Guenther Rd Dayton (45417) ***(G-8043)***
Autobody Supply Company, Columbus *Also called Finishmaster Inc* ***(G-6924)***

Autocoat 419 636-3830
1900 Progress Dr Bryan (43506) ***(G-2266)***
Autogate Inc 419 588-2796
7306 Driver Rd Berlin Heights (44814) ***(G-1652)***
Automated Bldg Components Inc (PA) 419 257-2152
2359 Grant Rd North Baltimore (45872) ***(G-15042)***
Automated Machinery Solutions 419 727-1772
6010 N Summit St Toledo (43611) ***(G-18194)***
Automated Mfg Solutions Inc 440 878-3711
19706 Progress Dr Strongsville (44149) ***(G-17716)***
Automated Packg Systems Inc 330 342-2000
25900 Solon Rd Bedford (44146) ***(G-1386)***
Automated Packg Systems Inc 330 626-2313
600 Mondial Pkwy Streetsboro (44241) ***(G-17663)***
Automated Packg Systems Inc 216 663-2000
13555 Mccracken Rd Cleveland (44125) ***(G-4770)***
Automated Systems Div, Painesville *Also called Coe Manufacturing Company* ***(G-15722)***
Automated Wheel LLC 216 651-9022
8525 Clinton Rd Cleveland (44144) ***(G-4771)***
Automatic Feed Co (PA) 419 592-0050
476 E Riverview Ave Napoleon (43545) ***(G-14532)***
Automatic Feed Company, Napoleon *Also called Automatic Feed Co* ***(G-14532)***
Automatic Parts, Vermilion *Also called McDaniel Products Inc* ***(G-19167)***
Automatic Parts, Mansfield *Also called McDaniel Products Inc* ***(G-12478)***
Automatic Parts 419 524-5841
433 Springmill St Mansfield (44903) ***(G-12409)***
Automatic Screw Products Co 216 241-7896
2070 W 7th St Cleveland (44113) ***(G-4772)***
Automatic Stamp Products Inc 216 781-7933
1822 Columbus Rd Cleveland (44113) ***(G-4773)***
Automatic Timing & Contrls Div, New Albany *Also called Automatic Timing & Controls* ***(G-14606)***
Automatic Timing & Controls (PA) 614 888-8855
7795 Walton Pkwy Ste 175 New Albany (43054) ***(G-14606)***
Automation and Ctrl Tech Inc 614 495-1120
6141 Avery Rd Dublin (43016) ***(G-8886)***
Automation Etc, Cincinnati *Also called Justin P Straub LLC* ***(G-3888)***
Automation Finishing Inc 216 251-8805
3206 W 121st St Cleveland (44111) ***(G-4774)***
Automation Metrology Intl LLC (PA) 440 354-6436
8808 Tyler Blvd Mentor (44060) ***(G-13395)***
Automation Plastics Corp 330 562-5148
150 Lena Dr Aurora (44202) ***(G-871)***
Automation Software & Engrg (PA) 330 405-2990
9321 Ravenna Rd Ste A Twinsburg (44087) ***(G-18737)***
Automation Solutions Inc 614 235-4060
505 S Parkview Ave # 206 Columbus (43209) ***(G-6633)***
Automation Systems Designs Inc 937 387-0351
6222 Webster St Dayton (45414) ***(G-8044)***
Automation Technology Inc 937 233-6084
1900 Troy St Dayton (45404) ***(G-8045)***
Automation Tool & Die Inc 330 225-8336
5576 Innovation Dr Valley City (44280) ***(G-19030)***
Automation Tooling Systems, Lewis Center *Also called Ats Ohio Inc* ***(G-11746)***
Automation Tooling Systems (HQ) 614 781-8063
425 Enterprise Dr Lewis Center (43035) ***(G-11749)***
Automation Welding System 330 263-1176
3132 E Lincoln Way Wooster (44691) ***(G-20567)***
Automotive Industries Division, Huron *Also called International Automotive Compo* ***(G-11099)***
Automtion Rbtic Intgration Div, Miamisburg *Also called Wauseon Machine & Mfg Inc* ***(G-13739)***
Automtiq Msurement Systems LLC 614 431-2667
797 Gatehouse Ln Columbus (43235) ***(G-6634)***
Autoneum North America Inc 419 690-8924
4131 Spartan Dr Oregon (43616) ***(G-15555)***
Autoneum North America Inc 419 693-0511
645 N Lallendorf Rd Oregon (43616) ***(G-15556)***
Autoplas Division, Bellevue *Also called Windsor Mold USA Inc* ***(G-1553)***
Autorentalsystemscom LLC 513 334-1040
1776 Mentor Ave Ste 427 Norwood (45212) ***(G-15423)***
Autosyte 440 858-3226
829 Callendar Blvd Painesville (44077) ***(G-15713)***
Autotec Engineering Company 419 885-2529
6155 Brent Dr Toledo (43611) ***(G-18195)***
Autotool Inc 614 733-0222
7875 Corporate Blvd Plain City (43064) ***(G-16173)***
Autowax Inc 440 334-4417
15015 Foltz Pkwy Strongsville (44149) ***(G-17717)***
Autumn Rush Vineyard LLC 614 312-5748
5686 Dutch Ln Johnstown (43031) ***(G-11258)***
Avadirect.com, Twinsburg *Also called Freedom Usa Inc* ***(G-18776)***
Avalign Technologies Inc (HQ) 419 542-7743
801 Industrial Dr Hicksville (43526) ***(G-10776)***
Avalon, Cleveland *Also called Xapc Co* ***(G-6331)***
Avasax Data Recovery, Beavercreek *Also called Avasax Ltd* ***(G-1350)***
Avasax Ltd 937 694-0807
3895 Oakview Dr Beavercreek (45430) ***(G-1350)***

ALPHABETIC

ALPHABETIC SECTION

Avcom Smt Inc..614 882-8176
213 E Broadway Ave Westerville (43081) *(G-20035)*

Avenue Fabricating Inc....................................513 752-1911
1281 Clough Pike Batavia (45103) *(G-1124)*

Aver Inc...877 841-2775
41 S High St Ste 1400 Columbus (43215) *(G-6635)*

Avery Dennison, Mentor *Also called Paxar Corporation (G-13544)*

Avery Dennison..937 865-2439
200 Monarch Ln Miamisburg (45342) *(G-13642)*

Avery Dennison Corporation...........................440 358-3466
670 Hardy Rd Painesville (44077) *(G-15714)*

Avery Dennison Corporation...........................440 358-4691
7600 Auburn Rd Bldg 18 Painesville (44077) *(G-15715)*

Avery Dennison Corporation...........................440 358-3700
250 Chester St Painesville (44077) *(G-15716)*

Avery Dennison Corporation...........................216 267-8700
15939 Industrial Pkwy Cleveland (44135) *(G-4775)*

Avery Dennison Corporation...........................440 534-6527
8100 Tyler Blvd Mentor (44060) *(G-13396)*

Avery Dennison Corporation...........................440 358-3408
250 Chester St Bldg 11 Painesville (44077) *(G-15717)*

Avery Dennison Corporation...........................513 682-7500
11101 Mosteller Rd Ste 2 Cincinnati (45241) *(G-3372)*

Avery Dennison Corporation...........................614 418-7740
7795 Walton Pkwy Ste 370 New Albany (43054) *(G-14607)*

Avery Dennison Corporation...........................440 358-2828
7100 Lindsay Dr Mentor (44060) *(G-13397)*

Avery Dennison Corporation...........................440 266-2500
7236 Justin Way Mentor (44060) *(G-13398)*

Avery Dennison Corporation...........................440 358-2930
7070 Spinach Dr Bldg 19 Mentor (44060) *(G-13399)*

Avesta Systems Inc (PA)..................................330 650-1800
5601 Hudson Dr Ste 200 Hudson (44236) *(G-11032)*

Avetec Products Group, North Ridgeville *Also called University Accessories Inc (G-15257)*

AVI Staging Technology, Blue Ash *Also called Iacono Production Services Inc (G-1790)*

Aviation Cmpnent Solutions Inc.....................440 295-6590
26451 Curtiss Wright Pkwy # 106 Richmond Heights (44143) *(G-16501)*

Aviation Technologies Inc (HQ).....................216 706-2960
1301 E 9th St Ste 3000 Cleveland (44114) *(G-4776)*

Aviles Construction Company.......................216 939-1084
7011 Clark Ave Cleveland (44102) *(G-4777)*

Avina Specialties Inc.......................................419 592-5646
116 W Washington St Napoleon (43545) *(G-14533)*

Avion Manufacturing Company......................330 220-1989
2950 Westway Dr Ste 106 Brunswick (44212) *(G-2188)*

Avion Tool Corporation...................................937 278-0779
3620 Lenox Dr Dayton (45429) *(G-8046)*

Aviva Metals, Lorain *Also called National Bronze Mtls Ohio Inc (G-12106)*

Avon, Cleveland *Also called Wallseye Concrete Corp (G-6287)*

Avon Concrete, Elyria *Also called Westview Concrete Corp (G-9346)*

Avon Concrete Corporation............................440 937-6264
930 Miller Rd Avon (44011) *(G-941)*

Avon Lake Printing..440 933-2078
227 Miller Rd Avon Lake (44012) *(G-979)*

Avon Lake Sheet Metal Co..............................440 933-3505
33574 Pin Oak Pkwy Avon Lake (44012) *(G-980)*

Avondale Printing Inc......................................330 477-1180
2820 Whipple Ave Nw Canton (44708) *(G-2579)*

Avotronics Powertrain Inc..............................614 537-0261
4200 Regent St Columbus (43219) *(G-6636)*

Avtek International Inc....................................330 633-7500
382 Commerce St Tallmadge (44278) *(G-17973)*

Avtron Inc...216 642-1230
7900 E Pleasant Valley Rd Independence (44131) *(G-11120)*

Avtron Aerospace Inc (PA).............................216 750-5152
7900 E Pleasant Valley Rd Cleveland (44131) *(G-4778)*

Avtron Holdings LLC......................................216 642-1230
7900 E Pleasant Valley Rd Cleveland (44131) *(G-4779)*

Avtron Loadbank, Cleveland *Also called Asco Power Technologies LP (G-4744)*

Avure Autoclave Systems Inc (HQ)................614 891-2732
3721 Corp Dr Columbus (43231) *(G-6637)*

Avure Technologies Inc..................................614 891-2732
8270 Green Meadows Dr N Lewis Center (43035) *(G-11750)*

Avure Technologies Inc..................................513 433-2500
2601 S Verity Pkwy # 13 Middletown (45044) *(G-13885)*

AW Faber-Castell Usa Inc...............................216 643-4660
9450 Allen Dr Ste B Cleveland (44125) *(G-4780)*

Award One, Troy *Also called Designer Awards Inc (G-18650)*

Awardcraft, Celina *Also called Eighth Floor Promotions LLC (G-2959)*

Awb Metals Division, Trenton *Also called Magnode Corporation (G-18624)*

Awesome Yogurt LLC......................................937 643-0879
3337 Lenox Dr Dayton (45429) *(G-8047)*

Awning Fabri Caters Inc..................................216 476-4888
10237 Lorain Ave Cleveland (44111) *(G-4781)*

Awp, Kent *Also called Area Wide Protective Inc (G-11296)*

Aws Industries Inc..513 932-7941
2600 Henkle Dr Lebanon (45036) *(G-11635)*

Axalt Powde Coati Syste Usa I.......................614 600-4104
4130 Lyman Dr Hilliard (43026) *(G-10808)*

Axalta Coating Systems USA LLC..................614 777-7230
4130 Lyman Dr Hilliard (43026) *(G-10809)*

Axatronics LLC..513 239-5898
422 Wards Corner Rd E Loveland (45140) *(G-12178)*

Axel Austin LLC..440 237-1610
10147 Royalton Rd Ste I North Royalton (44133) *(G-15261)*

Axent Graphics LLC.......................................216 362-7560
6270 Engle Rd Brookpark (44142) *(G-2137)*

Axess International LLC.................................330 460-4840
4641 Stag Thicket Ln Brunswick (44212) *(G-2189)*

Axiom Tool Group Inc.....................................844 642-4902
1181 Claycraft Rd Columbus (43230) *(G-6638)*

Axion Strl Innovations LLC (PA)....................740 452-2500
1100 Brandywine Blvd H Zanesville (43701) *(G-21100)*

Axis Corporation...937 592-1958
314 Water Ave Bellefontaine (43311) *(G-1505)*

Axis Tool & Grinding LLC...............................330 535-4713
895 Home Ave Akron (44310) *(G-75)*

Axle Surgeons of NW Ohio............................419 822-5775
811 Helvetia St Delta (43515) *(G-8765)*

Axon Medical LLC..216 276-0262
1484 Medina Rd Ste 117 Medina (44256) *(G-13226)*

Ayers Limestone Quarry Inc..........................740 633-2958
2002 Colerain Pike Martins Ferry (43935) *(G-12757)*

Ayling and Reichert Co Consent....................419 898-2471
411 S Railroad St Oak Harbor (43449) *(G-15441)*

Aysco Security Consultants Inc....................330 733-8183
4075 Karg Industrial Pkwy B Kent (44240) *(G-11297)*

Aza Enterprises LLC......................................740 678-8482
1149 Fisher Ridge Rd Fleming (45729) *(G-9778)*

Aztec Manufacturing Inc................................330 783-9747
4325 Simon Rd Youngstown (44512) *(G-20850)*

Azz Galvanizing - Cincinnati, Cincinnati *Also called AAA Galvanizing - Joliet Inc (G-3285)*

Azz Inc...330 456-3241
1723 Cleveland Ave Sw Canton (44707) *(G-2580)*

Azz Incorporated..330 445-2170
1723 Cleveland Ave Sw Canton (44707) *(G-2581)*

B & A Holistic Fd & Herbs LLC.......................614 747-2200
4550 Heaton Rd Ste B7 Columbus (43229) *(G-6639)*

B & B Beverage Ctr..419 243-0752
1901 Broadway St Toledo (43609) *(G-18196)*

B & B Bindery Inc..330 722-5430
4381 Pine Lake Dr Medina (44256) *(G-13227)*

B & B Box Company Inc..................................419 872-5600
26490 Southpoint Rd Perrysburg (43551) *(G-15922)*

B & B Cast Stone Co Inc.................................740 697-0008
7790 Ransbottom Rd Roseville (43777) *(G-16574)*

B & B Gear & Machine Co Inc.........................937 687-1771
440 W Main St New Lebanon (45345) *(G-14707)*

B & B Industries, Orient *Also called Kmj Leasing Ltd (G-15575)*

B & B Industries Inc..614 871-3883
7001 Harrisburg Pike Orient (43146) *(G-15574)*

B & B Molded Products Inc............................419 592-8700
1250 Ottawa Ave Defiance (43512) *(G-8614)*

B & B Pallet Co..419 435-4530
885 S State Route 587 Fostoria (44830) *(G-9834)*

B & B Paper Converters Inc...........................216 941-8100
12500 Elmwood Ave Frnt Cleveland (44111) *(G-4782)*

B & B Printing Graphics Inc...........................419 893-7068
1689 Lance Pointe Rd Maumee (43537) *(G-13076)*

B & B Trophies & Awards...............................330 225-6193
1317 Pearl Rd Brunswick (44212) *(G-2190)*

B & B Welding...419 968-2743
6647 Middle Pt Wetzel Rd Middle Point (45863) *(G-13756)*

B & C Research Inc...330 848-4000
842 Norton Ave Barberton (44203) *(G-1056)*

B & D Commissary LLC..................................740 743-3890
5705 State Route 204 Ne Mount Perry (43760) *(G-14454)*

B & D Graphics Inc...513 641-0855
300 Township Ave Cincinnati (45216) *(G-3373)*

B & D Machinists Inc......................................513 831-8588
1350 Us Route 50 Milford (45150) *(G-13995)*

B & F Manufacturing Co.................................216 518-0333
19050 Cranwood Pkwy Warrensville Heights (44128) *(G-19464)*

B & G Machine Company Inc..........................440 946-8787
7205 Commerce Dr Mentor (44060) *(G-13400)*

B & G Tool Company......................................614 451-2538
4832 Kenny Rd Columbus (43220) *(G-6640)*

B & H Machine Inc..330 868-6425
15001 Lincoln St Se Minerva (44657) *(G-14176)*

B & J Baking Company Inc.............................513 541-2386
4056 Colerain Ave Cincinnati (45223) *(G-3374)*

B & J Drilling Company Inc............................740 599-6700
13911 Millersburg Rd Danville (43014) *(G-7956)*

B & L Labels and Packg Co Inc......................937 773-9080
421 Fox Dr Piqua (45356) *(G-16103)*

B & P Company Inc..937 298-0265
97 Compark Rd Dayton (45459) *(G-8048)*

B & P Polishing Inc..330 753-4202
123 9th St Nw Barberton (44203) *(G-1057)*

B & P Spring Production Co 216 486-4260
19520 Nottingham Rd Cleveland (44110) *(G-4783)*
B & R Custom Chrome 419 536-7215
469 Dearborn Ave Toledo (43605) *(G-18197)*
B & R Fabricators & Maint Inc 513 641-2222
4524 W Mitchell Ave Cincinnati (45232) *(G-3375)*
B & R Machine Co Inc 216 961-7370
2216 W 65th St Cleveland (44102) *(G-4784)*
B & S Blacktop Co 513 797-5759
1704 Lndale Nchlsville Rd New Richmond (45157) *(G-14810)*
B & S Transport Inc (PA) 330 767-4319
11325 Lawndell Rd Sw Navarre (44662) *(G-14572)*
B & T Welding and Machine Co 740 687-1908
423 S Mount Pleasant Ave Lancaster (43130) *(G-11545)*
B A Malcuit Racing Inc 330 878-7111
707 S Wooster Ave Strasburg (44680) *(G-17645)*
B and L Sales Inc (PA) 330 279-2007
3149 State Rte Ste 39 Millersburg (44654) *(G-14061)*
B B & H Tool Company 614 868-8634
7719 Taylor Rd Sw Reynoldsburg (43068) *(G-16429)*
B B Bradley Company Inc (PA) 440 354-2005
7755 Crile Rd Painesville (44077) *(G-15718)*
B B Bradley Company Inc 614 777-5600
2699 Scioto Pkwy Columbus (43221) *(G-6641)*
B C Composites Corporation 330 262-3070
777 W Smith Rd Medina (44256) *(G-13228)*
B C I, Fairlawn *Also called Buckeye Corrugated Inc* *(G-9599)*
B C I, Powell *Also called Building Ctrl Integrators LLC* *(G-16310)*
B C Machining Inc 440 593-4763
502 E Main Rd Conneaut (44030) *(G-7641)*
B C Metals Inc 513 732-9644
4484 Hartman Ln Batavia (45103) *(G-1125)*
B C Wilson Inc 937 439-1866
85 Compark Rd Dayton (45459) *(G-8049)*
B D G Wrap-Tite Inc 440 349-5400
6200 Cochran Rd Solon (44139) *(G-17110)*
B D P Services Inc 740 828-9685
8255 Blackrun Rd Nashport (43830) *(G-14564)*
B F, Cleveland *Also called Bula Forge & Machine Inc* *(G-4852)*
B G News 419 372-2601
214 W Hall Bgsu Bowling Green (43403) *(G-1952)*
B Hogenkamp & R Harlamert 419 925-0526
3145 Hartke Rd Celina (45822) *(G-2950)*
B J Pallett 419 447-9665
324 4th Ave Tiffin (44883) *(G-18049)*
B K Fabrication & Machine Shop 740 695-4164
70300 Kagg Hill Rd Saint Clairsville (43950) *(G-16622)*
B K Plastics Inc 937 473-2087
1400 Mote Dr Covington (45318) *(G-7783)*
B L Anderson Co Inc 765 463-1518
8887 Eagle Ridge Ct West Chester (45069) *(G-19654)*
B L F Enterprises Inc 937 642-6425
445 S State St Westerville (43081) *(G-20036)*
B M DS Fish N More LLC 419 238-2722
121 South Ave Van Wert (45891) *(G-19078)*
B N Machine Inc 440 255-5200
8853 East Ave Mentor (44060) *(G-13401)*
B O K Inc 937 322-9588
508 W Main St Springfield (45504) *(G-17366)*
B P Exploration, Dayton *Also called BP Products North America Inc* *(G-8060)*
B P Exploration, Bryan *Also called BP Products North America Inc* *(G-2270)*
B P Oil Company 513 671-4107
1201 Omniplex Dr Cincinnati (45240) *(G-3376)*
B P T, Bucyrus *Also called Bucyrus Precision Tech Inc* *(G-2320)*
B Richardson Inc 330 724-2122
25 Elinor Ave Akron (44305) *(G-76)*
B S F Inc (PA) 937 890-6121
8895 N Dixie Dr Dayton (45414) *(G-8050)*
B S F Inc 937 890-6121
320b S 5th St Tipp City (45371) *(G-18100)*
B T C, Dayton *Also called Browder Tool Co Inc* *(G-8065)*
B V Grinding Machining Inc 440 918-1884
1438 E 363rd St Willoughby (44095) *(G-20283)*
B V Mfg Inc 330 549-5331
13426 Woodworth Rd New Springfield (44443) *(G-14818)*
B W Electrical & Maint Svc 330 534-7870
6204 Yungstown Hubbard Rd Hubbard (44425) *(G-10999)*
B W Grinding Co 419 923-1376
15048 County Road 10 3 Lyons (43533) *(G-12273)*
B W T Inc 330 928-9107
353 E Cuyahoga Falls Ave Akron (44310) *(G-77)*
B Y G Industries Inc 216 961-5436
8003 Clinton Rd Cleveland (44144) *(G-4785)*
B&B Distributors LLC 440 324-1293
150 Keep Ct Ste A Elyria (44035) *(G-9221)*
B&C Machine Co LLC 330 745-4013
401 Newell St Barberton (44203) *(G-1058)*
B&D Truck Parts Sls & Svcs LLC 419 701-7041
1498 Perrysburg Rd Fostoria (44830) *(G-9835)*
B&N Coal Inc 740 783-3575
38455 Marietta Rte Dexter City (45727) *(G-8792)*
B-K Tool & Design Inc 419 532-3890
480 W Main St Kalida (45853) *(G-11276)*
B-R-O-T Incorporated 216 267-5335
4730 Briar Rd Cleveland (44135) *(G-4786)*
B-Squared Prtg Mktg Solutions, North Canton *Also called B2 Incorporated* *(G-15071)*
B-Tek Scales LLC 330 471-8900
1510 Metric Ave Sw Canton (44706) *(G-2582)*
B-Wear Sportswear, Zanesville *Also called 5 BS Inc* *(G-21090)*
B2 Incorporated (PA) 330 244-9510
8324c Cleveland Ave Nw North Canton (44720) *(G-15071)*
B5 Systems Inc 937 372-4768
1463 Bellbrook Ave Xenia (45385) *(G-20757)*
Baaron Abrasives Inc 330 263-7737
2015 Great Trails Dr Wooster (44691) *(G-20568)*
Babbert Real Estate Inv Co Ltd (PA) 614 837-8444
7415 Diley Rd Canal Winchester (43110) *(G-2499)*
Babcock & Wilcox Company (HQ) 330 753-4511
20 S Van Buren Ave Barberton (44203) *(G-1059)*
Babcock & Wilcox Company 330 753-4511
91 Stirling Ave Barberton (44203) *(G-1060)*
Babcock & Wilcox Company 740 687-6500
2600 E Main St Lancaster (43130) *(G-11546)*
Babcock & Wilcox Entps Inc (PA) 330 753-4511
20 S Van Buren Ave Barberton (44203) *(G-1061)*
Baby Love Prenatal Imaging LLC 419 905-7935
727 W 2nd St Delphos (45833) *(G-8736)*
BAC Technologies Ltd 937 465-2228
8115 Calland Rd West Liberty (43357) *(G-19935)*
Bacconis Lickety Split 330 924-0418
4194 Greenville Rd Cortland (44410) *(G-7703)*
Back Development LLC 937 671-7896
3700 Northfield Rd Ste 11 Cleveland (44122) *(G-4787)*
Back Rd Candles & HM Decor LLC 330 461-6075
9970 Sanford Rd Lodi (44254) *(G-12007)*
Backyard Scoreboards LLC 513 702-6561
431 Kenridge Dr Middletown (45042) *(G-13886)*
Baco Manufacturing Corp 440 585-5858
29175 Anderson Rd Wickliffe (44092) *(G-20199)*
Bad Brush Design, Holland *Also called Jeffrey A Clark* *(G-10936)*
Badboy Blasters Incorporated 330 454-2699
1720 Wallace Ave Ne Canton (44705) *(G-2583)*
Badizo LLC 844 344-3833
4466 Darrow Rd Ste 3 Stow (44224) *(G-17571)*
Baerlocher Production Usa LLC 513 482-6300
5890 Highland Ridge Dr Cincinnati (45232) *(G-3377)*
Baerlocher Usa LLC (HQ) 330 364-6000
3676 Davis Rd Nw Dover (44622) *(G-8805)*
Baggallini Inc 800 628-0321
13405 Yarmouth Dr Pickerington (43147) *(G-16040)*
Bahler Medical Inc 614 873-7600
8910 Warner Rd Plain City (43064) *(G-16174)*
Bailey & Jensen Inc 937 272-1784
442 Yankee Trace Dr Centerville (45458) *(G-2998)*
Baileys Asphalt Sealing 740 453-9409
2092 Newark Rd South Zanesville (43701) *(G-17301)*
Baillie Lumber Co LP 419 462-2000
3953 County Road 51 Galion (44833) *(G-10123)*
Bainter Machining Company (PA) 740 653-2422
1230 Rainbow Dr Ne Lancaster (43130) *(G-11547)*
Bainter Machining Company 740 756-4598
2945 Carroll Eastern Rd Carroll (43112) *(G-2899)*
Bair Bodies & Trailers Inc 330 343-4853
4562 Bair Rd Nw Dover (44622) *(G-8806)*
Baird Brothers Sawmill Inc 330 533-3122
7060 Crory Rd Canfield (44406) *(G-2523)*
Baird Concrete Products Inc 740 623-8600
15 Locust St Coshocton (43812) *(G-7721)*
Baise Enterprises Inc 614 444-3171
695 Koebel Ave Frnt Columbus (43207) *(G-6642)*
Baise Quality Printing, Columbus *Also called Baise Enterprises Inc* *(G-6642)*
Bake ME Happy LLC 614 477-3642
116 E Moler St Columbus (43207) *(G-6643)*
Bakelite N Sumitomo Amer Inc 419 675-1282
13717 Us Highway 68 Kenton (43326) *(G-11403)*
Baker Built Products Inc 419 965-2646
11877 Walnut Grove Ch Rd Ohio City (45874) *(G-15514)*
Baker Crane Service Ltd 740 453-5868
2820 S River Rd Zanesville (43701) *(G-21101)*
Baker Hughes A GE Company LLC 304 884-6442
8008 Truck World Blvd Hubbard (44425) *(G-11000)*
Baker Logging 740 686-2817
62683 Ok Rd Belmont (43718) *(G-1565)*
Baker McMillen Co (PA) 330 923-8300
3688 Wyoga Lake Rd Stow (44224) *(G-17572)*
Baker McMillen Co 330 923-3303
3688 Wyoga Lake Rd Stow (44224) *(G-17573)*
Baker Media Group LLC 330 253-0056
1653 Merriman Rd Ste 116 Akron (44313) *(G-78)*

ALPHABETIC

Baker Plastics Inc....330 743-3142
900 Mahoning Ave Youngstown (44502) *(G-20851)*
Baker Welding Llc....614 252-6100
2901 Eastport Ave Bldg 95 Columbus (43219) *(G-6644)*
Baker-Shindler Builders Sup Co, Defiance *Also called Baker-Shindler Contracting Co (G-8615)*
Baker-Shindler Contracting Co (PA)....419 782-5080
525 Cleveland Ave Defiance (43512) *(G-8615)*
Baker-Shindler Contracting Co....419 399-4841
121 German St Cecil (45821) *(G-2942)*
Baker-Shindler Ready Mix, Cecil *Also called Baker-Shindler Contracting Co (G-2942)*
Bakers Welding, Zanesville *Also called J A B Welding Service Inc (G-21150)*
Bakerwell Inc (PA)....330 276-2161
10420 County Road 620 Killbuck (44637) *(G-11448)*
Bakerwell Inc....614 898-7590
6295 Maxtown Rd Ste 300 Westerville (43082) *(G-19979)*
Bakerwell Service Rigs Inc (HQ)....330 276-2161
10420 County Road 620 Killbuck (44637) *(G-11449)*
Balance Disorder Institute, Cincinnati *Also called Ear Medical Center Inc (G-3623)*
Balancing Company Inc (PA)....937 898-9111
898 Center Dr Vandalia (45377) *(G-19117)*
Balbo Industries Inc (PA)....440 333-0630
20630 Center Ridge Rd Rocky River (44116) *(G-16543)*
Baldie Corporation....513 503-0953
4520 Lucerne Ave Cincinnati (45227) *(G-3378)*
Baldwin, Hilliard *Also called Merry X-Ray Chemical Corp (G-10839)*
Baldwin B AA Design....740 374-5844
256 Front St Marietta (45750) *(G-12608)*
Baleco International Inc....513 353-3000
3200 State Line Rd North Bend (45052) *(G-15050)*
Ball Bounce and Sport Inc (PA)....419 289-9310
1 Hedstrom Dr Ashland (44805) *(G-682)*
Ball Aerospace & Tech Corp....303 939-4000
2875 Presidential Dr # 180 Beavercreek (45324) *(G-1303)*
Ball Corp....419 483-4343
975 W Main St Bellevue (44811) *(G-1530)*
Ball Corporation....419 423-3071
1800 Production Dr Findlay (45840) *(G-9653)*
Ball Corporation....330 244-2313
3075 Brookline Rd North Canton (44720) *(G-15072)*
Ball Corporation....614 771-9112
2690 Charter St Columbus (43228) *(G-6645)*
Ball Corporation....330 244-2800
2121 Warner Rd Se Canton (44707) *(G-2584)*
Ball Metal Beverage Cont Corp....419 423-3071
12340 Township Rd 99 E Findlay (45840) *(G-9654)*
Ball Metal Beverage Cont Div, Findlay *Also called Ball Metal Beverage Cont Corp (G-9654)*
Ball Plastic Container Div, Bellevue *Also called Amcor Rigid Plastics Usa LLC (G-1528)*
Ballas Egg Products, Zanesville *Also called BE Products Inc (G-21105)*
Ballas Egg Products Corp....614 453-0386
40 N 2nd St Zanesville (43701) *(G-21102)*
Ballinger Industries Inc (PA)....419 422-4533
2500 Fostoria Ave Findlay (45840) *(G-9655)*
Ballreich Bros Inc....419 447-1814
186 Ohio Ave Tiffin (44883) *(G-18050)*
Ballreichs Potato Chips Snacks, Tiffin *Also called Ballreich Bros Inc (G-18050)*
Balmac Inc....614 873-8222
8205 Estates Pkwy Ste N Plain City (43064) *(G-16175)*
Balser Inc....567 444-4737
502 Jackson St Archbold (43502) *(G-640)*
Balta Technology Inc....513 724-0247
4350 Batavia Rd Batavia (45103) *(G-1126)*
Baltic Country Meats....330 897-7025
3320 State Route 557 Baltic (43804) *(G-1023)*
Baltic Meats, Baltic *Also called Baltic Country Meats (G-1023)*
Baltimore Fabricators Inc....740 862-6016
9420 Lancaster Krkersvlle Baltimore (43105) *(G-1036)*
Bam Fuel Inc....740 397-6674
21191 Floralwood Dr Howard (43028) *(G-10995)*
Bambeck Inc....614 766-1000
4362 Tuller Rd Dublin (43017) *(G-8887)*
Ban-Fam Industries Inc....216 265-9588
4740 Briar Rd Cleveland (44135) *(G-4788)*
Bancequity Petroleum Corp....330 468-5935
8821 Freeway Dr Macedonia (44056) *(G-12278)*
Banco Die Inc....330 821-8511
11322 Union Ave Ne Alliance (44601) *(G-456)*
Bandit Choppers LLC....614 556-4416
237 Lillian Dr Pickerington (43147) *(G-16041)*
Bandit Machine Inc....419 281-6595
261 E 8th St Ashland (44805) *(G-683)*
Bands Company Inc....330 674-0446
164 E Jackson St Millersburg (44654) *(G-14062)*
Bang Printing of Ohio Inc....800 678-1222
3765 Sunnybrook Rd Kent (44240) *(G-11298)*
Bankhurst Industries LLC....216 272-5775
6075 Cochran Rd Solon (44139) *(G-17111)*
Banks Manufacturing Company....440 458-8661
40259 Banks Rd Grafton (44044) *(G-10293)*
Banner Mattress & Furniture Co, Toledo *Also called Banner Mattress Co Inc (G-18198)*
Banner Mattress Co Inc (PA)....419 324-7181
2544 N Reynolds Rd Toledo (43615) *(G-18198)*
Banner Metals Group Inc....614 291-3105
1308 Holly Ave Columbus (43212) *(G-6646)*
Bansal Enterprises Inc....330 633-9355
1538 Home Ave Akron (44310) *(G-79)*
BAP Manufacturing Inc....419 332-5041
601 N Stone St Ste 1 Fremont (43420) *(G-9995)*
Baptist Heritage Revival Soc....915 526-2832
10632 Eltzroth Rd Goshen (45122) *(G-10285)*
Bar 25 LLC....216 621-4000
1939 W 25th St Cleveland (44113) *(G-4789)*
Bar Codes Unlimited Inc....937 434-2633
683 Miamisburg Ctrvl 21 Ste Dayton (45459) *(G-8051)*
Bar Processing Corp....440 943-0094
1271 E 289th St Wickliffe (44092) *(G-20200)*
Bar Processing Corporation....330 872-0914
1000 Windham Rd Newton Falls (44444) *(G-14985)*
Bar Tech Service Inc....440 943-5286
30012 Lakeland Blvd Wickliffe (44092) *(G-20201)*
Bar1 Motorsports....614 284-3732
1757 Creekview Dr Marysville (43040) *(G-12771)*
Barany Jewelry Inc....330 220-4367
3702 Center Rd Brunswick (44212) *(G-2191)*
Barbara A Eisenhardt....614 436-9690
7726 Cloister Dr Columbus (43235) *(G-6647)*
Barbasol LLC....419 903-0738
2011 Ford Dr Ashland (44805) *(G-684)*
Barbco Inc....330 488-9400
315 Pekin Dr Se East Canton (44730) *(G-9038)*
Barber Spring Ohio, Chillicothe *Also called Standard Car Truck Company (G-3223)*
Barberton Facility, Barberton *Also called Babcock & Wilcox Company (G-1060)*
Barberton Herald, Barberton *Also called Richardson Publishing Company (G-1102)*
Barberton Magic Press Printing....330 753-9578
699 Wooster Rd N Barberton (44203) *(G-1062)*
Barberton Mold & Machine Co....330 745-8559
465 5th St Ne Barberton (44203) *(G-1063)*
Barberton Printcraft....330 848-3000
520 Wooster Rd W Barberton (44203) *(G-1064)*
Barberton Steel Industries Inc....330 745-6837
240 E Huston St Barberton (44203) *(G-1065)*
Barbs Custom Embroidery....419 393-2226
14845 State Route 111 Defiance (43512) *(G-8616)*
Barbs Embroidery....614 875-9933
2700 Brunswick Dr Grove City (43123) *(G-10416)*
Barbs Graffiti Inc (PA)....216 881-5550
3111 Carnegie Ave Cleveland (44115) *(G-4790)*
Barclay Machine Inc....330 337-9541
650 S Broadway Ave Salem (44460) *(G-16719)*
Barclay Rolls, Salem *Also called Barclay Machine Inc (G-16719)*
Bard Manufacturing Company Inc (PA)....419 636-1194
1914 Randolph Dr Bryan (43506) *(G-2267)*
Bardes Corporation (PA)....513 533-6200
4730 Madison Rd Cincinnati (45227) *(G-3379)*
Bardons & Oliver Inc (PA)....440 498-5800
5800 Harper Rd Solon (44139) *(G-17112)*
Bardwell Winery, Mount Orab *Also called Wedco LLC (G-14452)*
Bargain Hunter, Millersburg *Also called Graphic Publications Inc (G-14085)*
Barile Precision Grinding Inc....216 267-6500
12320 Plaza Dr Cleveland (44130) *(G-4791)*
Baring Distributors, Cleveland *Also called Bdi Inc (G-4796)*
Barker Products Company....216 249-0900
1028 E 134th St Cleveland (44110) *(G-4792)*
Barkett Fruit Co Inc (PA)....330 364-6645
1213 E 3rd St Dover (44622) *(G-8807)*
Barkman Products LLC....330 893-2520
2550 Township Road 121 Millersburg (44654) *(G-14063)*
Barlamy Supply, Wapakoneta *Also called Jewett Supply (G-19335)*
Barley's Brewing Company, Columbus *Also called Brewpub Restaurant Corp (G-6696)*
Barncraft Storage Buildings....513 738-5654
2527 Millville Shandon Rd Hamilton (45013) *(G-10537)*
Barnes Advertising Corp....740 453-6836
1580 Fairview Rd Zanesville (43701) *(G-21103)*
Barnes Group Inc....513 759-3528
9826 Crescent Park Dr West Chester (45069) *(G-19655)*
Barnes Group Inc....513 779-6888
9826 Crescent Park Dr West Chester (45069) *(G-19656)*
Barnes Group Inc....440 526-5900
10367 Brecksville Rd Brecksville (44141) *(G-2021)*
Barnes Group Inc....419 891-9292
370 W Dussel Dr Ste A Maumee (43537) *(G-13077)*
Barnes International Inc....419 352-7501
555 Van Camp Rd Bowling Green (43402) *(G-1953)*
Barnes Services LLC....440 319-2088
20677 Centuryway Rd Maple Heights (44137) *(G-12565)*
Barnett & Ramel Optical Co Neb....402 453-4900
6510 Huntley Rd Columbus (43229) *(G-6648)*

Barnett Spouting Inc 330 644-0853
204 E Ralston Ave Akron (44301) *(G-80)*
Barney Corporation Inc (PA) 614 274-9069
4089 Leap Rd Hilliard (43026) *(G-10810)*
Barney Schoolers, Akron Also called Barnett Spouting Inc *(G-80)*
Barnhart Printing Corp 330 456-2279
1107 Melchoir Pl Sw Canton (44707) *(G-2585)*
Barnhart Publishing, Canton Also called Barnhart Printing Corp *(G-2585)*
Barnstorm Brewing Company LLC 419 852-9366
706 N 2nd St Coldwater (45828) *(G-6400)*
Baroque Violin Shop, Cincinnati Also called Paul Bartel *(G-4139)*
Barr Engineering Incorporated 614 892-0162
5710 Westbourne Ave Columbus (43213) *(G-6649)*
Barr Engineering Incorporated (PA) 614 714-0299
2800 Corp Exchange Dr # 240 Columbus (43231) *(G-6650)*
Barr Laboratories Inc 513 731-9900
5040 Duramed Rd Cincinnati (45213) *(G-3380)*
Barracuda Technologies Inc 216 469-1566
2900 State Route 82 Aurora (44202) *(G-872)*
Barrett & Sons Pallet & Lbr Co, East Liverpool Also called Joe Barrett *(G-9060)*
Barrett Paving Materials Inc 513 271-6200
3751 Commerce Dr Middletown (45005) *(G-13970)*
Barry Brothers Electric 614 299-8187
1100 Leona Ave Columbus (43201) *(G-6651)*
Barta Viorel 440 735-1699
26245 Broadway Ave Bedford (44146) *(G-1387)*
Bartan Design Inc 216 267-6474
10316 Edgerton Rd North Royalton (44133) *(G-15262)*
Bartek Systems 614 759-6014
6155 Chinaberry Dr Columbus (43213) *(G-6652)*
Bartells Cupcakery 330 957-1793
4555 Norquest Blvd Austintown (44515) *(G-929)*
Barth Industries Co LP (PA) 216 267-0531
12650 Brookpark Rd Cleveland (44130) *(G-4793)*
Bartley Lawn Service LLC 937 435-8884
69 W Alex Bell Rd West Carrollton (45449) *(G-19630)*
Bartley Offie 614 235-9050
3760 E 5th Ave Columbus (43219) *(G-6653)*
Bartleys Lawn Services, West Carrollton Also called Bartley Lawn Service LLC *(G-19630)*
Barton-Carey Medical Products (PA) 419 887-1285
1331 Conant St Ste 102 Maumee (43537) *(G-13078)*
Bartter & Sons 419 651-0374
1761 Township Road 85 Jeromesville (44840) *(G-11249)*
Barudan America Inc (HQ) 440 248-8770
30901 Carter St Frnt A Solon (44139) *(G-17113)*
Basco Manufacturing Company (PA) 513 573-1900
7201 Snider Rd Mason (45040) *(G-12831)*
Basco Shower Enclosures, Mason Also called Basco Manufacturing Company *(G-12831)*
Baseball Card Corner 513 677-0464
1812 Arrowhead Trl Loveland (45140) *(G-12179)*
Baseline Printing Inc 330 369-3204
1262 Youngstown Rd Se Warren (44484) *(G-19374)*
Basetek LLC (PA) 877 712-2273
14975 White Rd Middlefield (44062) *(G-13779)*
BASF Catalysts LLC 440 322-3741
120 Pine St Elyria (44035) *(G-9222)*
BASF Catalysts LLC 216 360-5005
23800 Mercantile Rd Cleveland (44122) *(G-4794)*
BASF Corporation 937 547-6700
1175 Martin St Greenville (45331) *(G-10360)*
BASF Corporation 419 877-5308
6125 Industrial Pkwy Whitehouse (43571) *(G-20188)*
BASF Corporation 440 329-2525
120 Pine St Elyria (44035) *(G-9223)*
BASF Corporation 513 482-3000
4900 Este Ave Cincinnati (45232) *(G-3381)*
Basic Cases Inc 216 662-3900
19561 Miles Rd Cleveland (44128) *(G-4795)*
Basic Coatings LLC 419 241-2156
400 Van Camp Rd Bowling Green (43402) *(G-1954)*
Basic Grain Products Inc 614 408-3091
300 E Vine St Coldwater (45828) *(G-6401)*
Basic Grain Products Inc 419 678-2304
300-310 E Vine St Coldwater (45828) *(G-6402)*
Basic Packaging Ltd 330 634-9665
2986 Indian Hill Dr Lima (45806) *(G-11961)*
Basilius Inc 419 536-5810
4338 South Ave Toledo (43615) *(G-18199)*
Basinger Inc 614 771-8300
2222 Wilson Rd Columbus (43228) *(G-6654)*
Bass International Sftwr LLC (PA) 877 227-0155
752 N State St Westerville (43082) *(G-19980)*
Bassett Nut Company, Holland Also called Jml Holdings Inc *(G-10937)*
Baswa Acoustics North Amer LLC 216 475-7197
21863 Aurora Rd Bedford (44146) *(G-1388)*
Bates Metal Products Inc 740 498-8371
403 E Mn St Port Washington (43837) *(G-16267)*
Bates Printing Inc 330 833-5830
150 23rd St Se Massillon (44646) *(G-12962)*

Bath & Body Works LLC (HQ) 614 856-6000
7 Limited Pkwy E Reynoldsburg (43068) *(G-16430)*
Bath & Brass Emporium The, Columbus Also called Savko Plastic Pipe & Fittings *(G-7422)*
Battershell Cabinets 419 542-6448
312 Defiance Ave Hicksville (43526) *(G-10777)*
Battery Unlimited 740 452-5030
1080 Linden Ave Zanesville (43701) *(G-21104)*
Battle Horse Knives LLC 740 995-9009
700 S 9th St Cambridge (43725) *(G-2426)*
Bauer Corporation (PA) 800 321-4760
2540 Progress Dr Wooster (44691) *(G-20569)*
Bauer Ladder, Wooster Also called Bauer Corporation *(G-20569)*
Baughman Tile Company 800 837-3160
8516 Road 137 Paulding (45879) *(G-15856)*
Baughmans Machine & Weld Shop 330 866-9243
6498 June Rd Nw Waynesburg (44688) *(G-19562)*
Bauman Custom Woodworking LLC 330 482-4330
13650 Green Beaver Rd Salem (44460) *(G-16720)*
Baumfolder Corporation 937 492-1281
1660 Campbell Rd Sidney (45365) *(G-17019)*
Bautec N Technoform Amer Inc 330 487-6600
1755 Entp Pkwy Ste 300 Twinsburg (44087) *(G-18738)*
Bawls Acquisition LLC 888 731-9708
8840 Commons Blvd Ste 101 Twinsburg (44087) *(G-18739)*
Baxter Burial Vault Service 513 641-1010
909 E Ross Ave Cincinnati (45217) *(G-3382)*
Baxter Holdings Inc 513 860-3593
3370 Port Union Rd Hamilton (45014) *(G-10538)*
Baxter-Wilbert Burial Vault, Cincinnati Also called Baxter Burial Vault Service *(G-3382)*
Baxters LLC 234 678-5484
1259 Ashford Ln Akron (44313) *(G-81)*
Bay Area Products Inc 419 732-2147
4942 W Fremont Rd Port Clinton (43452) *(G-16243)*
Bay Business Forms Inc 937 322-3000
1803 W Columbia St Springfield (45504) *(G-17367)*
Bay Controls LLC 419 891-4390
6528 Weatherfield Ct Maumee (43537) *(G-13079)*
Bay Electric Co 419 625-1046
2612 Columbus Ave Sandusky (44870) *(G-16796)*
Bay Island Company Inc 513 248-0356
585 Ibold Rd Loveland (45140) *(G-12180)*
Bay Manufacturing, Milan Also called Hemco Inc *(G-13984)*
Bay Packing, Lancaster Also called C J Kraft Enterprises Inc *(G-11551)*
Bay West Products 440 835-1991
31008 Walker Rd Bay Village (44140) *(G-1205)*
Bay World International Inc 419 525-2222
395 Reed St Mansfield (44903) *(G-12410)*
Bayard Inc 937 293-1415
2621 Dryden Rd Ste 300 Moraine (45439) *(G-14332)*
Bayberry Co, Canal Fulton Also called American Traditions Basket Co *(G-2474)*
Bayes, Roy Products, Columbus Also called Roy L Bayes *(G-7404)*
Bayley Envelope Inc 330 821-2150
119 E State St Alliance (44601) *(G-457)*
Bayloff Stmped Pdts Knsman Inc 330 876-4511
8091 State Route 5 Kinsman (44428) *(G-11463)*
Bayswater Beverages LLC 312 224-8012
705 Wakefield Dr Cincinnati (45226) *(G-3383)*
Bbb Music LLC 740 772-2262
20 E Water St Chillicothe (45601) *(G-3176)*
Bbi Well Service, Dellroy Also called Beucler Brothers Inc *(G-8733)*
Bc Investment Corporation (PA) 330 262-3070
1505 E Bowman St Wooster (44691) *(G-20570)*
Bcast Stainless Products LLC 614 873-3945
9000 Heritage Dr Plain City (43064) *(G-16176)*
Bcfab Inc (PA) 419 532-2899
15751 Road 19 Fort Jennings (45844) *(G-9791)*
BCI, Toledo Also called Block Communications Inc *(G-18206)*
BCi and V Investments Inc 330 538-0660
11675 Mahoning Ave North Jackson (44451) *(G-15141)*
BCI International, Dublin Also called Smiths Medical Pm Inc *(G-8991)*
Bcmr Publications LLC 740 441-7778
430 2nd Ave Gallipolis (45631) *(G-10160)*
Bcs Metal Prep LLC 440 663-1100
31000 Solon Rd Solon (44139) *(G-17114)*
BCT, Akron Also called Akron Thermography Inc *(G-54)*
BCT Alarm Services Inc 440 669-8153
103 Milan Ave Ste 4 Amherst (44001) *(G-554)*
Bdi Inc (PA) 216 642-9100
8000 Hub Pkwy Cleveland (44125) *(G-4796)*
Bdi Inc 330 498-4980
417 Applegrove St Nw Canton (44720) *(G-2586)*
Bdl Supply, South Charleston Also called Buckeye Diamond Logistics Inc *(G-17271)*
BDS Packaging Inc 937 643-0530
3155 Elbee Rd Ste 201 Moraine (45439) *(G-14333)*
BE Products Inc 740 453-0386
40 N 2nd St Zanesville (43701) *(G-21105)*
Bea-Ecc Apparels Inc 216 650-6336
1287 W 76th St Cleveland (44102) *(G-4797)*

Beach City Lumber LLC..........330 878-4097
5177 Austin Ln Nw Strasburg (44680) ***(G-17646)***
Beach Company..........740 622-0905
240 Browns Ln Coshocton (43812) ***(G-7722)***
Beach Manufacturing Co..........937 882-6372
118 N Hampton Rd Donnelsville (45319) ***(G-8800)***
Beach Mfg Plastic Molding Div..........937 882-6400
7816 W National Rd New Carlisle (45344) ***(G-14663)***
Beachs Trees Selective Harvest..........513 289-5976
915 Wilma Cir Cincinnati (45245) ***(G-3241)***
Beachy Barns Ltd..........614 873-4193
8720 Amish Pike Plain City (43064) ***(G-16177)***
Beacon Audio Video Systems Inc..........937 723-9587
155 N Main St Centerville (45459) ***(G-2999)***
Beacon Metal Fabricators Inc..........216 391-7444
5425 Hamilton Ave Ste D Cleveland (44114) ***(G-4798)***
Beacon, The, Port Clinton *Also called Schaffner Publication Inc* ***(G-16258)***
Bead Shoppe At Home..........330 479-9598
2872 Whipple Ave Nw Canton (44708) ***(G-2587)***
Beam Machines Inc..........513 745-4510
5101 Creek Rd Blue Ash (45242) ***(G-1732)***
Beam Technologies Inc..........800 648-1179
266 N 4th St Ste 200 Columbus (43215) ***(G-6655)***
Bean Bag City, Spring Valley *Also called Sailors Tailor Inc* ***(G-17318)***
Bean Counter LLC..........419 636-0705
1210 W High St Ste C Bryan (43506) ***(G-2268)***
Bear Cabinetry LLC..........216 481-9282
23560 Lakeland Blvd Euclid (44132) ***(G-9404)***
Bear Diversified Inc (PA)..........216 883-5494
4580 E 71st St Cleveland (44125) ***(G-4799)***
Bear Welding Services LLC..........740 630-7538
18210 Myrtle Ake Rd Caldwell (43724) ***(G-2403)***
Bearcat Construction Inc..........513 314-0867
4457 Bethany Rd Mason (45040) ***(G-12832)***
Bearded Shutter..........440 567-8568
10821 John Edward Dr Mantua (44255) ***(G-12543)***
Bearing & Transm Sup Co Div, Macedonia *Also called Jay Dee Service Corporation* ***(G-12307)***
Bearing Precious Seed (PA)..........513 575-1706
1369 Woodville Pike B Milford (45150) ***(G-13996)***
Bearings Manufacturing Company (PA)..........440 846-5517
15157 Foltz Pkwy Strongsville (44149) ***(G-17718)***
Beasley Fiberglass Inc..........440 357-6644
799 Lakeshore Blvd Painesville (44077) ***(G-15719)***
Beast Carbon Corporation..........800 909-9051
607 Shepherd Dr Unit 9 Cincinnati (45215) ***(G-3384)***
Beatty Foods LLC..........330 327-2442
1117 Brant Ave Nw Canton (44708) ***(G-2588)***
Beaufort Rfd Inc..........330 239-4331
1420 Wolfcreek Trl Sharon Center (44274) ***(G-16946)***
Beaumont Brothers Pottery, Crooksville *Also called Beaumont Brothers Stoneware* ***(G-7815)***
Beaumont Brothers Stoneware (PA)..........740 982-0055
410 Keystone St Crooksville (43731) ***(G-7815)***
Beaumont Machine LLC..........513 701-0421
7697 Innovation Way Mason (45040) ***(G-12833)***
Beauty Cft Met Fabricators Inc..........440 439-0710
5439 Perkins Rd Bedford (44146) ***(G-1389)***
Beauty Systems Group LLC..........740 456-5434
3606 Rhodes Ave New Boston (45662) ***(G-14646)***
Beaver Productions..........330 352-4603
2251 Cooledge Ave Akron (44305) ***(G-82)***
Beaver Wood Products..........740 226-6211
190 Buck Hollow Rd Beaver (45613) ***(G-1292)***
Beaverson Machine Inc..........419 923-8064
11600 County Road 10 2 Delta (43515) ***(G-8766)***
Bechem Lubrication Tech LLC..........440 543-9845
8401 Chagrin Rd Ste 5a Chagrin Falls (44023) ***(G-3037)***
Beck & Orr Inc..........614 276-8809
3097 W Broad St Columbus (43204) ***(G-6656)***
Beck Energy Corp..........330 297-6891
160 N Chestnut St Ravenna (44266) ***(G-16368)***
Beck Sand & Gravel Inc..........330 626-3863
2820 Webb Rd Ravenna (44266) ***(G-16369)***
Beck Studios Inc..........513 831-6650
1001 Tech Dr Milford (45150) ***(G-13997)***
Beckenhorst Press Inc..........614 451-6461
960 Old Henderson Rd Columbus (43220) ***(G-6657)***
Becker Gallagher Legal Pubg..........513 677-5044
8790 Governors Hill Dr # 102 Cincinnati (45249) ***(G-3385)***
Becker Signs Inc..........330 659-4504
6381 Chittenden Rd Ste E9 Hudson (44236) ***(G-11033)***
Becker Signs Inc..........330 659-4504
4762 Black Rd Richfield (44286) ***(G-16462)***
Beckermills Inc..........419 738-3450
15286 State Route 67 Wapakoneta (45895) ***(G-19324)***
Beckers Bakeshop Inc..........216 752-4161
13510 Miles Ave Cleveland (44105) ***(G-4800)***
Beckett Air Incorporated (PA)..........440 327-9999
37850 Taylor Pkwy North Ridgeville (44039) ***(G-15209)***
Beckett Gas Inc (PA)..........440 327-3141
38000 Beckett Pkwy North Ridgeville (44039) ***(G-15210)***
Beckman & Gast Company (PA)..........419 678-4195
282 W Kremer Hoying Rd Saint Henry (45883) ***(G-16659)***
Beckman Environmental Svcs Inc..........513 752-3570
4259 Armstrong Blvd Batavia (45103) ***(G-1127)***
Beckman Machine LLC..........513 242-2700
4684 Paddock Rd Cincinnati (45229) ***(G-3386)***
Beckman Xmo, Columbus *Also called S Beckman Print & G* ***(G-7410)***
Beckman Xmo..........614 864-2232
376 Morrison Rd Ste D Columbus (43213) ***(G-6658)***
Beckwith Orchards Inc..........330 673-6433
1617 Lake Rockwell Rd Kent (44240) ***(G-11299)***
Beckworth Industries Inc..........216 268-5557
14511 Saranac Rd Cleveland (44110) ***(G-4801)***
Becky Brisker..........614 266-6575
2260 E Main St Columbus (43209) ***(G-6659)***
Becky Knapp..........330 854-4400
136 N Canal St Canal Fulton (44614) ***(G-2476)***
Becton Dickinson and Company..........858 617-4272
2727 London Groveport Rd Groveport (43125) ***(G-10484)***
Bedford Anodizing Co (PA)..........330 650-6052
82 Aurora St Hudson (44236) ***(G-11034)***
Bedford Cabinet Inc..........440 439-4830
21891 Forbes Rd Ste 102 Cleveland (44146) ***(G-4802)***
Bedford Gear, Solon *Also called Joy Mining Machinery* ***(G-17177)***
Bee Jax Inc..........330 373-0500
156 Vermont Ave Sw Warren (44485) ***(G-19375)***
Bee Valve, Elyria *Also called Plastic Enterprises Inc* ***(G-9313)***
Beebe Worldwide Graphics Sign..........513 241-2726
9933 Alliance Rd Ste 2 Blue Ash (45242) ***(G-1733)***
Beech Armament LLC..........330 962-4694
105 Marc Dr Cuyahoga Falls (44223) ***(G-7845)***
Beech Engineering & Mfg, New Philadelphia *Also called Miller Products Inc* ***(G-14786)***
Beechvale Laminating..........330 674-2804
7241 Township Road 572 Millersburg (44654) ***(G-14064)***
Beehex Inc..........512 633-5304
1130 Gahanna Pkwy Columbus (43230) ***(G-6660)***
Beekman Logging..........740 493-2763
204 Wyckoff Rd Piketon (45661) ***(G-16067)***
Beeline Purchasing LLC..........513 703-3733
4454 N Mallard Cv Mason (45040) ***(G-12834)***
Beemer Machine Company Inc..........330 678-3822
1530 Enterprise Way Kent (44240) ***(G-11300)***
Beertubes.com, Plain City *Also called Dj Beverage Innovations Inc* ***(G-16188)***
Beevinwood Inc..........937 678-9910
5748 Clark Rd West Manchester (45382) ***(G-19940)***
Behlke Dalene..........330 399-6780
958 Tod Ave Nw Warren (44485) ***(G-19376)***
Behr Dayton Thermal Products, Dayton *Also called Mahle Behr USA Inc* ***(G-8327)***
Behrco Inc..........419 394-1612
1865 Celina Rd Saint Marys (45885) ***(G-16676)***
Beiersdorf Inc..........513 682-7300
5232 E Provident Dr West Chester (45246) ***(G-19835)***
Bekaert Corporation..........330 683-5060
322 E Pine St Orrville (44667) ***(G-15583)***
Bekaert Corporation..........330 683-5060
510 Collins Blvd Orrville (44667) ***(G-15584)***
Bekaert Corporation..........330 835-5124
3200 W Market St Ste 303 Fairlawn (44333) ***(G-9595)***
Bekaert Corporation..........330 867-3325
3200 W Market St Ste 303 Fairlawn (44333) ***(G-9596)***
Bekaert North America MGT Corp (HQ)..........330 867-3325
3200 W Market St Ste 303 Fairlawn (44333) ***(G-9597)***
Belco Works..........740 695-0500
68425 Hammond Rd Saint Clairsville (43950) ***(G-16623)***
Belco Works Inc..........740 695-0500
340 Fox Shannon Pl Saint Clairsville (43950) ***(G-16624)***
Belden & Blake Corporation..........330 602-5551
1748 Saltwell Rd Nw Dover (44622) ***(G-8808)***
Belden Brick Company..........330 852-2411
750 Edelweiss Dr Ne Sugarcreek (44681) ***(G-17842)***
Belden Brick Company LLC..........330 456-0031
700 Edelweiss Dr Ne Sugarcreek (44681) ***(G-17843)***
Belden Brick Company LLC..........330 265-2030
690 Dover Rd Ne Sugarcreek (44681) ***(G-17844)***
Belden Brick Plant 3, Sugarcreek *Also called Belden Brick Company LLC* ***(G-17844)***
Beldex Land Company LLC (PA)..........740 783-3575
38455 State Rte 821 S Dexter City (45727) ***(G-8793)***
Belkin Production..........440 247-2722
44 N Main St Chagrin Falls (44022) ***(G-3009)***
Bell Binders LLC..........419 242-3201
320 21st St Toledo (43604) ***(G-18200)***
Bell Burial Vault Co..........513 896-9044
804 Belle Ave Hamilton (45015) ***(G-10539)***
Bell Industries..........513 353-2355
9843 New Haven Rd Harrison (45030) ***(G-10632)***
Bell Logistics Co..........740 702-9830
27311 Old Route 35 Chillicothe (45601) ***(G-3177)***

ALPHABETIC SECTION — Berry Film Products Co Inc (HQ)

Bell Ohio Inc 605 332-6721
  6300 Commerce Center Dr Groveport (43125) *(G-10485)*
Bell Optical, Twinsburg Also called Essilor Laboratories Amer Inc *(G-18771)*
Bell Vault & Monument Works 937 866-2444
  1019 S Main St Miamisburg (45342) *(G-13643)*
Bella Stone Cincinnati 513 772-3552
  239 Northland Blvd Cincinnati (45246) *(G-3387)*
Bellbrook Transport Inc (HQ) 937 233-5555
  3361 Successful Way Dayton (45414) *(G-8052)*
Belle Center Air Tool Co Inc 937 464-7474
  202 N Elizabeth St Belle Center (43310) *(G-1497)*
Belle Printing 937 592-5161
  118 S Main St Bellefontaine (43311) *(G-1506)*
Bellefontaine Examiner 937 592-3060
  127 E Chillicothe Ave Bellefontaine (43311) *(G-1507)*
Bellevue Gazette, Oberlin Also called Gazette Publishing Company *(G-15495)*
Bellevue Manufacturing Company (PA) 419 483-3190
  520 Goodrich Rd Bellevue (44811) *(G-1531)*
Bellevue Manufacturing Company 419 483-3190
  300 Ashford Ave Bellevue (44811) *(G-1532)*
Bellisio 740 286-5505
  100 E Broadway St Jackson (45640) *(G-11181)*
Bellisio Foods Inc 740 286-5505
  100 E Broadway St Jackson (45640) *(G-11182)*
Bellissimo Distribution LLC 216 431-3344
  3820 Lakeside Ave E Cleveland (44114) *(G-4803)*
Bello Verde LLC 614 365-3000
  464 E Main St Ste 100 Columbus (43215) *(G-6661)*
Bellville Flowers and Gifts, Bellville Also called Colleen D Turner *(G-1555)*
Bellwyck Clinical Services, West Chester Also called Bellwyck Packg Solutions Inc *(G-19657)*
Bellwyck Packg Solutions Inc 513 874-1200
  8946 Global Way West Chester (45069) *(G-19657)*
Belmon Coutn Recoder's Office, Saint Clairsville Also called Belmont County of Ohio *(G-16625)*
Belmont Community Health Ctr, Bellaire Also called Belmont Community Hospital *(G-1483)*
Belmont Community Hospital 740 671-1216
  4697 Harrison St Bellaire (43906) *(G-1483)*
Belmont County of Ohio 740 699-2140
  101 W Main St Ste 205 Saint Clairsville (43950) *(G-16625)*
Belmont Stamping, Shadyside Also called Knight Manufacturing Co Inc *(G-16923)*
Beloit Fuel LLC 330 584-1915
  9379 First East St North Benton (44449) *(G-15060)*
Belot Concrete Block, Tiltonsville Also called Walden Industries Inc *(G-18094)*
Belpre Sand and Gravel Company, Dexter City Also called Beldex Land Company LLC *(G-8793)*
Belton Foods 937 890-7768
  2701 Thunderhawk Ct Dayton (45414) *(G-8053)*
Belvino LLC 440 715-0076
  526 Manor Brook Dr Chagrin Falls (44022) *(G-3010)*
Bemis Company Inc 330 923-5281
  1972 Akron Peninsula Rd Akron (44313) *(G-83)*
Bemis Company Inc 419 334-9465
  730 Industrial Dr Fremont (43420) *(G-9996)*
Bemis North America, Akron Also called Bemis Company Inc *(G-83)*
Ben James Enterprises Inc 330 477-9353
  4110 Southway St Sw Canton (44706) *(G-2589)*
Ben Logging, Sarahsville Also called Ned A Shreve *(G-16866)*
Ben Venue Laboratories, Bedford Also called Boehringer Ingelheim USA Corp *(G-1390)*
Bena Inc 419 299-3313
  1390 Township Road 229 Van Buren (45889) *(G-19071)*
Bench Billboard Company Inc 513 271-2222
  6805 Cambridge Ave Cincinnati (45227) *(G-3388)*
Benchmark Archtectural Systems 614 444-0110
  720 Marion Rd Columbus (43207) *(G-6662)*
Benchmark Cabinets 740 397-4615
  17239 Sycamore Rd Mount Vernon (43050) *(G-14470)*
Benchmark Cabinets 740 694-1144
  97 Mount Vernon Ave Fredericktown (43019) *(G-9963)*
Benchmark Craftsman Inc 330 975-4214
  4700 Greenwich Rd Seville (44273) *(G-16911)*
Benchmark Craftsmen, Seville Also called Benchmark Craftsman Inc *(G-16911)*
Benchmark Land Management LLC 513 310-7850
  9431 Butler Warren Rd West Chester (45069) *(G-19658)*
Benchmark Prints 419 332-7640
  2252 W State St Fremont (43420) *(G-9997)*
Benchmark Signs and Gifts 216 973-3718
  80 Hazel Dr Northfield (44067) *(G-15313)*
Benchworks Jewelers Inc 937 439-4243
  133 E Franklin St Dayton (45459) *(G-8054)*
Benco Industries Inc 440 572-3555
  19231 Royalton Rd Strongsville (44149) *(G-17719)*
Bendco Machine & Tool Inc 419 628-3802
  283 W 1st St Minster (45865) *(G-14210)*
Bender Cycle & Machine Corp 440 946-0681
  1476 E 359th St Willoughby (44095) *(G-20284)*
Bender Engineering Company 330 938-2355
  17934 Mill St Beloit (44609) *(G-1568)*

Bendix Spcer Fndtion Brake LLC (HQ) 440 329-9709
  901 Cleveland St Elyria (44035) *(G-9224)*
Bendon Inc (PA) 419 207-3600
  1840 S Baney Rd Ashland (44805) *(G-685)*
Benjamin Media Inc 330 467-7588
  10050 Brecksville Rd Brecksville (44141) *(G-2022)*
Benjamin P Forbes Company 440 838-4400
  800 Ken Mar Indus Pkwy Broadview Heights (44147) *(G-2088)*
Benjamin Steel Company Inc 937 233-1212
  777 Benjamin Dr Springfield (45502) *(G-17368)*
Benko Products Inc 440 934-2180
  5350 Evergreen Pkwy Sheffield Village (44054) *(G-16966)*
Benmit Division, North Lawrence Also called US Tubular Products Inc *(G-15163)*
Benners Custom Woodworking (PA) 513 932-9159
  1004 W Main St Lebanon (45036) *(G-11636)*
Bennett & Bennett Inc (PA) 937 324-1100
  1744 Thomas Paine Pkwy Dayton (45459) *(G-8055)*
Bennett Displays, Geneva Also called Dwayne Bennett Industries *(G-10217)*
Bennett Electric Inc 800 874-5405
  211 Republic St Norwalk (44857) *(G-15382)*
Bennett Mechanical Systems LLC 513 292-3506
  5157 Union Rd Franklin (45005) *(G-9871)*
Bennett Plastics Inc 740 432-2209
  197 N 2nd St Cambridge (43725) *(G-2427)*
Bens Welding Service Inc 937 878-4052
  605 Middle St Fairborn (45324) *(G-9452)*
Bensan Jewelers Inc 216 221-1434
  14410 Madison Ave Lakewood (44107) *(G-11512)*
Bent Nail Millwork, Lodi Also called Oak Front Inc *(G-12017)*
Bent Wood Solutions LLC 330 674-1454
  7426 County Road 77 Millersburg (44654) *(G-14065)*
Bentronix Corp 440 632-0606
  14999 Madison Rd Middlefield (44062) *(G-13780)*
Berea Hardwood Co Inc 216 898-8956
  18745 Sheldon Rd Cleveland (44130) *(G-4804)*
Berea Manufacturing Inc 440 260-0590
  480 Geiger St Berea (44017) *(G-1593)*
Berea Printing Company 440 243-1080
  1060 W Bagley Rd Ste 102 Berea (44017) *(G-1594)*
Bergen, W J & Co, Solon Also called William J Bergen & Co *(G-17261)*
Berghausen Corporation 513 541-5631
  4524 Este Ave Cincinnati (45232) *(G-3389)*
Bergholz 7, Bergholz Also called Rosebud Mining Company *(G-1635)*
Bergman Safety Spanner Co Inc 419 691-1462
  3002 Woodville Rd Ste B Northwood (43619) *(G-15334)*
Bergman Tool & Machine Co 419 925-4963
  8066 Industrial Dr Maria Stein (45860) *(G-12598)*
Bergstein Oil & Gas Partnr 513 771-6220
  11464 Lippelman Rd # 200 Cincinnati (45246) *(G-3390)*
Bergstrom Company Ltd Partnr 440 232-2282
  640 Golden Oak Pkwy Cleveland (44146) *(G-4805)*
Beringer Plating Inc 330 633-8409
  1211 Devalera St Akron (44310) *(G-84)*
Berlekamp Plastics Inc 419 334-4481
  2587 County Road 99 Fremont (43420) *(G-9998)*
Berlin Boat Covers 330 547-7600
  17740 W Akron Canfield Rd Berlin Center (44401) *(G-1645)*
Berlin Boat Covers Ulphostery, Berlin Center Also called Berlin Boat Covers *(G-1645)*
Berlin Custom Leather Ltd 330 674-3768
  5085 Township Road 353 Millersburg (44654) *(G-14066)*
Berlin Gardens Gazebos Ltd 330 893-3411
  5045 State Rte 39 Berlin (44610) *(G-1637)*
Berlin Inds Protector Pdts, Youngstown Also called Berlin Industries Inc *(G-20852)*
Berlin Industries Inc 330 549-2100
  1275 Boardman Poland Rd # 1 Youngstown (44514) *(G-20852)*
Berlin Natural Bakery Inc 330 893-2734
  5126 County Rd 120 Berlin (44610) *(G-1638)*
Berlin Parts, Millersburg Also called Berlin Truck Caps Ltd *(G-14067)*
Berlin Truck Caps Ltd 330 893-2811
  4560 State Route 39 Millersburg (44654) *(G-14067)*
Berlin Wood Products Inc 330 893-3281
  5039 County Rd 120 Berlin (44610) *(G-1639)*
Berlin Woodworking 330 893-3234
  4575 Township Road 366 Millersburg (44654) *(G-14068)*
Bermex, Columbus Also called Matvest Inc *(G-7161)*
Bernard Laboratories Inc 513 681-7373
  1738 Townsend St Cincinnati (45223) *(G-3391)*
Bernard R Doyles Inc 216 523-2288
  2102 Saint Clair Ave Ne Cleveland (44114) *(G-4806)*
Bernard Specialty Co 216 881-2200
  2800 E 55th St Frnt Cleveland (44104) *(G-4807)*
Berner Screen Print, Springfield Also called Gail Berner *(G-17406)*
Berran Industrial Group Inc 330 253-5800
  570 Wolf Ledges Pkwy Akron (44311) *(G-85)*
Berry Company 513 768-7800
  312 Plum St Ste 600 Cincinnati (45202) *(G-3392)*
Berry Film Products Co Inc (HQ) 800 225-6729
  8585 Duke Blvd Mason (45040) *(G-12835)*

(PA)=Parent Co (HQ)=Headquarters (DH)=Div Headquarters

Berry Global Inc — ALPHABETIC SECTION

Berry Global Inc 419 887-1602
  1695 Indian Wood Cir Maumee (43537) *(G-13080)*

Berry Global Inc 330 896-6700
  1275 Ethan Ave Streetsboro (44241) *(G-17664)*

Berry Investments Inc 937 293-0398
  3055 Kettering Blvd # 418 Moraine (45439) *(G-14334)*

Berry Plastics Filmco Inc 330 562-6111
  1450 S Chillicothe Rd Aurora (44202) *(G-873)*

Berry Woodworking 513 734-6133
  2244 Berry Rd Amelia (45102) *(G-533)*

Bert Radebaugh 740 382-8134
  1544 Marion Marysville Rd Marion (43302) *(G-12695)*

Bertin Steel Processing Inc 440 943-0094
  1271 E 289th St Ste 1 Wickliffe (44092) *(G-20202)*

Besa Lighting Co Inc 614 475-7046
  6695 Taylor Rd Blacklick (43004) *(G-1679)*

Bescast Inc 440 946-5300
  4600 E 355th St Willoughby (44094) *(G-20285)*

Besco, Batavia Also called Beckman Environmental Svcs Inc *(G-1127)*

Besi Manufacturing Inc (PA) 513 874-0232
  9087 Sutton Pl West Chester (45011) *(G-19659)*

Besl Specialized Carrier 740 599-6305
  16559 Skyline Dr Danville (43014) *(G-7957)*

Bessamaire Sales Inc 440 439-1200
  1869 E Aurora Rd Ste 700 Twinsburg (44087) *(G-18740)*

Best Bite Grill LLC 419 344-7462
  22 N Center St Versailles (45380) *(G-19174)*

Best Controls Company, Ashland Also called Chandler Systems Incorporated *(G-693)*

Best Equipment Co Inc 440 237-3515
  12620 York Delta Dr North Royalton (44133) *(G-15263)*

Best Fab Co., Elyria Also called Stays Lighting Inc *(G-9331)*

Best Glass, Dayton Also called Kimmatt Corp *(G-8297)*

Best Inc 419 394-2745
  Hc 116 Saint Marys (45885) *(G-16677)*

Best Lighting Products Inc (HQ) 740 964-0063
  1213 Etna Pkwy Etna (43062) *(G-9392)*

Best Logging, Stockport Also called Roger L Best *(G-17560)*

Best Mold & Manufacturing Inc 330 896-9988
  1546 E Turkeyfoot Lake Rd Akron (44312) *(G-86)*

Best Performance Inc 419 394-2299
  14381 State Route 116 Saint Marys (45885) *(G-16678)*

Best Plating Rack Corp 440 944-3270
  1321 E 289th St Wickliffe (44092) *(G-20203)*

Best Process Solutions Inc 330 220-1440
  1071 Industrial Pkwy N Brunswick (44212) *(G-2192)*

Best Snow Plow, Willoughby Also called Marc Industries Inc *(G-20369)*

Besten Equipment Inc 216 581-1166
  388 S Main St Ste 700 Akron (44311) *(G-87)*

Besten Inc 216 910-2880
  4416 Lee Rd Cleveland (44128) *(G-4808)*

Bestlight Led Corporation 440 205-1552
  8909 East Ave Mentor (44060) *(G-13402)*

Besttransportcom Inc 614 888-2378
  1103 Schrock Rd Ste 100 Columbus (43229) *(G-6663)*

Bestway Cabinets LLC 614 306-3518
  3525 Ridgewood Dr Hilliard (43026) *(G-10811)*

Beta Industries Inc (PA) 937 299-7385
  2860 Culver Ave Dayton (45429) *(G-8056)*

Beta Machine Company Inc 216 383-0000
  17702 S Waterloo Rd Cleveland (44119) *(G-4809)*

Betco Corporation Ltd (HQ) 419 241-2156
  400 Van Camp Rd Bowling Green (43402) *(G-1955)*

Beth Otto Independent Case Exa 513 868-0484
  544 Walter Ave Fairfield (45014) *(G-9484)*

Bethart Enterprises Inc (PA) 513 863-6161
  531 Main St Hamilton (45013) *(G-10540)*

Bethart Enterprises Inc 513 777-8707
  8548 Lakota Dr W Ste B West Chester (45069) *(G-19660)*

Bethart Printing Services, Hamilton Also called Bethart Enterprises Inc *(G-10540)*

Bethart Printing Services, West Chester Also called Bethart Enterprises Inc *(G-19660)*

Bethel Engineering and Eqp Inc (PA) 419 568-1100
  13830 Mcbeth Rd New Hampshire (45870) *(G-14699)*

Bethel Engineering and Eqp Inc 419 568-7976
  13830 Mcbeth Rd New Hampshire (45870) *(G-14700)*

Betley Printing Co 216 206-5600
  3816 Cullen Dr Cleveland (44105) *(G-4810)*

Better Built Barns (PA) 606 348-6146
  10628 Russellville Winchs Winchester (45697) *(G-20518)*

Better Foam Insulation, South Point Also called Pyro-Chem Corporation *(G-17292)*

Better Living Concepts Inc 330 494-2213
  7233 Freedom Ave Nw Canton (44720) *(G-2590)*

Better Living Sunrooms NW Ohio 419 692-4526
  205 S Pierce St Delphos (45833) *(G-8737)*

Better Than Sex Ice Cream LLC 614 444-5505
  1352 Parsons Ave Columbus (43206) *(G-6664)*

Betula USA, Cincinnati Also called NTS Enterprises Ltd *(G-4092)*

Beucler Brothers Inc 330 735-2267
  7237 Flint Rd Sw Dellroy (44620) *(G-8733)*

Bevcorp Properties, Willoughby Also called Miconvi Properties Inc *(G-20381)*

Beverage Dock, Dayton Also called Csv Inc *(G-8115)*

Beverage Machine & Fabricators 216 252-5100
  13301 Lakewood Hts Blvd Cleveland (44107) *(G-4811)*

Beverly Snider 614 837-5817
  3900 Noe Bixby Rd Columbus (43232) *(G-6665)*

Bexley Fabrics Inc 614 231-7272
  2476 E Main St Columbus (43209) *(G-6666)*

Bexley Pen Company Inc 614 351-9988
  2840 Fisher Rd Ste B Columbus (43204) *(G-6667)*

Bfs Supply, Cincinnati Also called Frederick Steel Company LLC *(G-3712)*

Bg News, Bowling Green Also called B G News *(G-1952)*

Bha Altair LLC 717 285-8040
  4440 Creek Rd Blue Ash (45242) *(G-1734)*

Bharat Trading, West Chester Also called Goyal Enterprises Inc *(G-19860)*

Biaginis Draperies 614 876-1706
  3082 Alton Darby Creek Rd Hilliard (43026) *(G-10812)*

Bic Manufacturing Inc 216 531-9393
  26420 Cntury Corners Pkwy Euclid (44132) *(G-9405)*

Blc Precision Machine Co Inc 937 783-1406
  3004 Cherry St Blanchester (45107) *(G-1699)*

Bickers Metal Products Inc 513 353-4000
  5825 State Rte128 Miamitown (45041) *(G-13743)*

Bickett Machine and Supply Inc 740 353-5710
  1411 Robinson Ave Portsmouth (45662) *(G-16278)*

Bickford Flavors, Wickliffe Also called Bickford Laboratories Inc *(G-20204)*

Bickford Laboratories Inc 440 354-7747
  1197 E 305th St Wickliffe (44092) *(G-20204)*

Bico Akron Inc 330 794-1716
  3100 Gilchrist Rd Mogadore (44260) *(G-14231)*

Bico Steel Service Centers, Mogadore Also called Bico Akron Inc *(G-14231)*

Biedenbach Logging 740 732-6477
  48443 Seneca Lake Rd Sarahsville (43779) *(G-16865)*

Biery Cheese Co (PA) 330 875-3381
  6544 Paris Ave Louisville (44641) *(G-12152)*

Bif Co LLC 330 564-0941
  1405 Home Ave Akron (44310) *(G-88)*

Bif, LLC, Akron Also called Bif Co LLC *(G-88)*

Big Bills Trucking LLC 614 850-0626
  6023 Homestead Ct Hilliard (43026) *(G-10813)*

Big Chief Manufacturing Ltd 513 934-3888
  250 Harmon Ave Lebanon (45036) *(G-11637)*

Big Gus Onion Rings Inc 216 883-9045
  4500 Turney Rd Cleveland (44105) *(G-4812)*

Big Iron Guns Inc 740 464-0852
  1712 11th St Portsmouth (45662) *(G-16279)*

Big Kahuna Graphics LLC 330 455-2625
  1255 Prospect Ave Sw Canton (44706) *(G-2591)*

Big Noodle LLC 614 558-7170
  687 Kenwick Rd Columbus (43209) *(G-6668)*

Big Productions Inc 440 775-0015
  45300b Us Highway 20 Oberlin (44074) *(G-15491)*

Big River Electric Inc 740 446-4360
  299 Upper River Rd Gallipolis (45631) *(G-10161)*

Big Sky Petroleum, New Concord Also called Robert Barr *(G-14686)*

Biggys Auto Buffet 740 455-4663
  806 W Main St Zanesville (43701) *(G-21106)*

Bigmar Inc 740 966-5800
  9711 Sportsman Club Rd Johnstown (43031) *(G-11259)*

Bigmouth Donut Company LLC 216 264-0250
  1361 E 55th St Cleveland (44103) *(G-4813)*

Bil-Jac Foods Inc (PA) 330 722-7888
  3337 Medina Rd Medina (44256) *(G-13229)*

Bil-Jax, Archbold Also called Haulotte US Inc *(G-652)*

Bilco Company 740 455-9020
  3400 Jim Granger Dr Zanesville (43701) *(G-21107)*

Bill Hall Well Service 330 695-4671
  10180 James Rd Fredericksburg (44627) *(G-9943)*

Bill Wyatt Inc 330 535-1113
  8857 Lake Shore Blvd Mentor (44060) *(G-13403)*

Bill's Counter Tops, Saint Clairsville Also called D Lewis Inc *(G-16630)*

Billock, John N Cpo, Warren Also called Orthotics & Prosthetics Rehab *(G-19429)*

Bills Sports Center 419 335-2405
  1495 N Shoop Ave Wauseon (43567) *(G-19510)*

Bilz Vibration Technology Inc 330 468-2459
  895 Highland Rd E Ste F Macedonia (44056) *(G-12279)*

Bimac, Moraine Also called Santos Industrial Ltd *(G-14392)*

Bimac Machine, Moraine Also called Santos Industrial Ltd *(G-14393)*

Bimbo Bakeries Usa Inc 740 797-4449
  33 N Plains Rd The Plains (45780) *(G-18019)*

Bimbo Bakeries Usa Inc 740 797-4449
  33 Plains Rd The Plains (45780) *(G-18020)*

Bimbo Bakeries USA Cleveland 216 641-5700
  4570 E 71st St Cleveland (44105) *(G-4814)*

Bimbo Qsr Ohio LLC (HQ) 740 454-6876
  3005 E Pointe Dr Zanesville (43701) *(G-21108)*

Bimbo Qsr Ohio LLC 740 454-6876
  3005 E Pointe Dr Zanesville (43701) *(G-21109)*

Bindery & Spc Pressworks Inc.....614 873-4623
351 W Bigelow Ave Plain City (43064) ***(G-16178)***
Bindery Tech Inc.....440 934-3247
35205 Center Ridge Rd North Ridgeville (44039) ***(G-15211)***
Bindtech LLC.....615 834-0404
5344 Bragg Rd Cleveland (44127) ***(G-4815)***
Binns Machinery Company.....513 242-3388
330 Railroad Ave Cincinnati (45217) ***(G-3393)***
Bio-Blood Components Inc.....614 294-3183
1393 N High St Columbus (43201) ***(G-6669)***
Bio-Systems Corporation.....608 365-9550
400 Van Camp Rd Bowling Green (43402) ***(G-1956)***
Biobent Holdings LLC.....513 658-5560
1275 Kinnear Rd Ste 239 Columbus (43212) ***(G-6670)***
Biobent Polymers, Columbus *Also called Biobent Holdings LLC* ***(G-6670)***
Biocare Orthopedic Prosthetics.....614 754-7514
2976 E Broad St Columbus (43209) ***(G-6671)***
Biocurv Medical Instruments (PA).....330 454-6621
3054 Tuscarawas St W Canton (44708) ***(G-2592)***
Biofocus Inc, Dayton *Also called Galapagos Inc* ***(G-8213)***
Biometric Information MGT LLC.....614 456-1296
6059 Frantz Rd Ste 102 Dublin (43017) ***(G-8888)***
Bionetics Corporation.....740 788-3800
781 Irving Wick Dr W # 1 Heath (43056) ***(G-10718)***
Bionetics-Desg-, Heath *Also called Bionetics Corporation* ***(G-10718)***
Bionix Development Corporation (PA).....419 727-8421
315 Matzinger Rd Toledo (43612) ***(G-18201)***
Bionix Radiation Therapy, Toledo *Also called Bionix Development Corporation* ***(G-18201)***
Bionix Safety Technologies Ltd (HQ).....419 727-0552
5154 Enterprise Blvd Toledo (43612) ***(G-18202)***
Biorx LLC (HQ).....866 442-4679
7167 E Kemper Rd Cincinnati (45249) ***(G-3394)***
Biosense Webster Inc.....513 337-3351
4545 Creek Rd Blue Ash (45242) ***(G-1735)***
Biothane Coated Webbing Corp.....440 327-0485
34655 Mills Rd North Ridgeville (44039) ***(G-15212)***
Biowish Technologies Inc.....312 572-6700
2724 Erie Ave Ste B Cincinnati (45208) ***(G-3395)***
Bip Printing Solutions LLC.....216 832-5673
24755 Highpoint Rd Ste 1 Beachwood (44122) ***(G-1225)***
Bird Control International.....330 425-2377
1393 Highland Rd Twinsburg (44087) ***(G-18741)***
Bird Corporation.....419 424-3095
100 Stanford Pkwy Findlay (45840) ***(G-9656)***
Bird Electronic Corporation.....440 248-1200
30303 Aurora Rd Solon (44139) ***(G-17115)***
Bird Equipment LLC.....330 549-1004
11950 South Ave North Lima (44452) ***(G-15166)***
Bird Loft.....440 988-2473
141 N Leavitt Rd Amherst (44001) ***(G-555)***
Bird Technologies Group Inc (PA).....440 248-1200
30303 Aurora Rd Solon (44139) ***(G-17116)***
Bird Watcher's Digest, Marietta *Also called Pardson Inc* ***(G-12651)***
Birdfish Brewing Company LLC.....330 397-4010
16 S Main St Columbiana (44408) ***(G-6454)***
Birds Eye Foods Inc.....330 854-0818
611 Elm Ridge Ave Canal Fulton (44614) ***(G-2477)***
Birge Heavy Industries Ltd.....440 821-3249
322 Furnace St Elyria (44035) ***(G-9225)***
Birmurco, Seville *Also called Island Delights Inc* ***(G-16917)***
Biro Manufacturing Company.....419 798-4451
6658 Promway Ave Nw North Canton (44720) ***(G-15073)***
Biro Manufacturing Company (PA).....419 798-4451
1114 W Main St Marblehead (43440) ***(G-12584)***
Bishop International, Akron *Also called Jonathan Bishop* ***(G-225)***
Bishop Machine Shop, Zanesville *Also called Bishop Machine Tool & Die* ***(G-21110)***
Bishop Machine Tool & Die.....740 453-8818
2304 Hoge Ave Zanesville (43701) ***(G-21110)***
Bishop Well Service Corp.....330 264-2023
416 N Bauer Rd Wooster (44691) ***(G-20571)***
Bison Leather Co.....419 517-1737
7409 W Central Ave Toledo (43617) ***(G-18203)***
Bison USA Corp.....513 713-0513
5325 Muhlhauser Rd Hamilton (45011) ***(G-10541)***
Bison Wldg & Fabrication Inc.....440 944-4770
29301 Clayton Ave Wickliffe (44092) ***(G-20205)***
Bisson Custom Plastic.....937 653-4966
238 Logan St Urbana (43078) ***(G-18979)***
Bitec, Dayton *Also called Sample Machining Inc* ***(G-8492)***
Bites Baking Company LLC.....614 457-6092
8090 Summerhouse Dr W Dublin (43016) ***(G-8889)***
Bits & Chips Machining Company.....513 539-0800
730 Lebanon St Monroe (45050) ***(G-14255)***
BITTERSWEET FARMS, Whitehouse *Also called Bittersweet Inc* ***(G-20189)***
Bittersweet Inc (PA).....419 875-6986
12660 Archbold Whthuse Rd Whitehouse (43571) ***(G-20189)***
Bittinger Carbide, Cadiz *Also called Stanley Bittinger* ***(G-2401)***
Bituminous Products Company.....419 693-3933
352 George Hardy Dr Toledo (43605) ***(G-18204)***

Bizzy Bee, Columbus *Also called K B Printing* ***(G-7081)***
Bizzy Bee Printing Inc.....614 771-1222
1500 W 3rd Ave Ste 106 Columbus (43212) ***(G-6672)***
BJ Equipment Ltd.....614 497-1776
4522 Lockbourne Rd Columbus (43207) ***(G-6673)***
BJ Oilfield Services Ltd.....419 768-2408
2944 County Road 186 Cardington (43315) ***(G-2870)***
Bjond Inc.....614 537-7246
1463 Briarmeadow Dr Columbus (43235) ***(G-6674)***
Bk Tool Company Inc.....513 870-9622
300 Security Dr Fairfield (45014) ***(G-9485)***
Bkhn Inc.....513 831-4402
55 W Techne Center Dr Milford (45150) ***(G-13998)***
Bkt USA Inc.....330 836-1090
2660 W Market St Ste 100 Fairlawn (44333) ***(G-9598)***
Blacco Splcing Rgging Loft Inc (PA).....614 444-2888
1976 Alum Creek Dr Columbus (43207) ***(G-6675)***
Black McCuskey Souers (PA).....330 456-8341
220 Market Ave S Ste 612 Canton (44702) ***(G-2593)***
Black & Decker (us) Inc.....614 895-3112
1948 Schrock Rd Columbus (43229) ***(G-6676)***
Black & Decker Corporation.....440 842-9100
12100 Snow Rd Ste 1 Cleveland (44130) ***(G-4816)***
Black Box Corporation.....800 837-7777
5400 Frantz Rd Ste 240 Dublin (43016) ***(G-8890)***
Black Box Corporation.....800 676-8850
6650 W Snowville Rd Ste R Brecksville (44141) ***(G-2023)***
Black Box Corporation.....800 837-7777
26100 1st St Westlake (44145) ***(G-20101)***
Black Box Corporation.....614 825-7400
255 Enterprise Dr Lewis Center (43035) ***(G-11751)***
Black Box Network Services, Lewis Center *Also called Black Box Corporation* ***(G-11751)***
Black Cloister Brewing Co LLC.....419 481-3891
619 Monroe St Toledo (43604) ***(G-18205)***
Black Machining & Technology.....513 752-8625
4020 Bach Buxton Rd Batavia (45103) ***(G-1128)***
Black Radish Creamery Ltd.....614 323-6016
7064 Cunningham Dr New Albany (43054) ***(G-14608)***
Black River Display Group, Mansfield *Also called Black River Group Inc* ***(G-12411)***
Black River Group Inc (PA).....419 524-6699
140 Park Ave E Mansfield (44902) ***(G-12411)***
Black Swamp Distillery.....419 344-4347
118 N Arch St Fremont (43420) ***(G-9999)***
Black Wing Shooting Center LLC.....740 363-7555
3722 Marysville Rd Delaware (43015) ***(G-8658)***
Blackburns Fabrication Inc.....614 875-0784
2467 Jackson Pike Columbus (43223) ***(G-6677)***
Blacklick Machine Co Inc.....614 866-9300
265 North St Blacklick (43004) ***(G-1680)***
Blackstone Mining, Dennison *Also called Kenneth Mc Beth* ***(G-8784)***
Blackthorn LLC.....937 836-9296
6113 Brookville Salem Rd Clayton (45315) ***(G-4572)***
Blackwood Sheet Metal Inc.....614 291-3115
844 Kerr St Columbus (43215) ***(G-6678)***
Blade Manufacturing Co Inc.....614 294-1649
915 Distribution Dr Ste A Columbus (43228) ***(G-6679)***
Blade Manufacturing Co, The, Columbus *Also called Callahan Cutting Tools Inc* ***(G-6724)***
Blains Folding Service Inc.....216 631-4700
4103 Detroit Ave Cleveland (44113) ***(G-4817)***
Blair Logging.....740 934-2730
30530 Lebanon Rd Lower Salem (45745) ***(G-12258)***
Blair Rubber Company.....330 769-5583
5020 Enterprise Pkwy Seville (44273) ***(G-16912)***
Blairs Cnc Turning Inc.....937 461-1100
245 Leo St Dayton (45404) ***(G-8057)***
Blako Industries Inc.....419 246-6172
10850 Middleton Pike Dunbridge (43414) ***(G-9014)***
Blanchard Refining Company LLC.....419 422-2121
539 S Main St Findlay (45840) ***(G-9657)***
Blanchard Terminal Company LLC.....419 422-2121
539 S Main St Findlay (45840) ***(G-9658)***
Blanchester Foundry Co Inc.....937 783-2091
214 Cherry St Blanchester (45107) ***(G-1700)***
Blaney Hardwoods Ohio Inc (PA).....740 678-8288
425 Timberline Dr Vincent (45784) ***(G-19212)***
Blang Acquisition LLC.....937 223-2155
1608 Kuntz Rd Dayton (45404) ***(G-8058)***
Blankenship Logging LLC.....740 372-3833
433 Curtis Smith Rd Otway (45657) ***(G-15684)***
Blankenship Lumber Inc.....740 372-0191
5356 State Route 348 Otway (45657) ***(G-15685)***
Blaster Chemical Co Inc.....216 901-5800
8500 Sweet Valley Dr Cleveland (44125) ***(G-4818)***
BLaster Corporation.....216 901-5800
8500 Sweet Valley Dr Cleveland (44125) ***(G-4819)***
BLASTWRAP, Columbus *Also called Highcom Global Security Inc* ***(G-6997)***
Blaze Oil & Gas Inc.....330 345-6700
1699 Nupp Dr Wooster (44691) ***(G-20572)***
Blaze Technical Services Inc.....330 923-0409
1445 Commerce Dr Stow (44224) ***(G-17574)***

ALPHABETIC

Bleachtech LLC 216 921-1980
320 Ryan Rd Seville (44273) *(G-16913)*
Bleil Chan 440 352-6012
9451 Jackson St Mentor (44060) *(G-13404)*
Bleil Manufacturing Company, Mentor *Also called Bleil Chan* *(G-13404)*
Blend of Seven Winery, Delaware *Also called Sandra Weddington* *(G-8722)*
Blendzall Inc 740 633-1333
310 S 1st St Martins Ferry (43935) *(G-12758)*
Blesco Services 614 871-4900
8905 Mckendree Rd Mount Sterling (43143) *(G-14460)*
Blevins Fabrication, Mansfield *Also called Blevins Metal Fabrication Inc* *(G-12412)*
Blevins Metal Fabrication Inc 419 522-6082
288 Illinois Ave S Mansfield (44905) *(G-12412)*
Blick Tool & Die Inc 330 343-1277
117 E Front St Dover (44622) *(G-8809)*
Blind Factory Showroom 614 771-6549
3670 Parkway Ln Ste M Hilliard (43026) *(G-10814)*
Blind Outlet (PA) 614 895-2002
574 W Schrock Rd Westerville (43081) *(G-20037)*
Blinds Plus and More, Mason *Also called Cincinnati Window Shade Inc* *(G-12844)*
Blink Marketing Inc 216 503-2568
1925 Saint Clair Ave Ne Cleveland (44114) *(G-4820)*
Blink Marketing & Signs, Cleveland *Also called Blink Marketing Inc* *(G-4820)*
Blink Print & Mail, Toledo *Also called Northcoast Pmm LLC* *(G-18428)*
Blitz Tool & Die Inc 440 237-1177
11941 Abbey Rd Ste I Cleveland (44133) *(G-4821)*
Bloch Printing Company 330 576-6760
3569 Copley Rd Copley (44321) *(G-7678)*
Block Communications Inc (PA) 419 724-6212
405 Madison Ave Ste 2100 Toledo (43604) *(G-18206)*
Blockamerica Corporation 614 274-0700
750 Kaderly Dr Columbus (43228) *(G-6680)*
Blonde Swan 419 307-8591
307 W State St Fremont (43420) *(G-10000)*
Bloom Center Biodiesel LLC 937 585-6412
4974 Township Road 79 Lewistown (43333) *(G-11800)*
Bloom Industries Inc 330 898-3878
1052 Mahoney Ave Nw Warren (44483) *(G-19377)*
Bloom Lake Iron Ore Mine Ltd 216 694-5700
200 Public Sq Cleveland (44114) *(G-4822)*
Blooming Services, Dennison *Also called Blooms Printing Inc* *(G-8782)*
Bloomingburg Spring & Wire For 740 437-7614
83 Main St Bloomingburg (43106) *(G-1709)*
Blooms Printing Inc 740 922-1765
4792 N 4th Street Ext Se Dennison (44621) *(G-8782)*
Bloomville Gazette Inc 419 426-3491
26 N Main St Attica (44807) *(G-855)*
Blt Inc 513 631-5050
2834 Highland Ave Norwood (45212) *(G-15424)*
Blue Ash Paper Sales LLC 513 891-9544
5000 Creek Rd Blue Ash (45242) *(G-1736)*
Blue Ash Tool & Die Co Inc 513 793-4530
4245 Creek Rd Blue Ash (45241) *(G-1737)*
Blue Bell Bio-Medical Inc 419 238-4442
1260 Industrial Dr Van Wert (45891) *(G-19079)*
Blue Chip Machine & Tool Ltd 419 626-9559
4211 Venice Rd Sandusky (44870) *(G-16797)*
Blue Chip Pump Inc 513 871-7867
1045 Meta Dr Cincinnati (45237) *(G-3396)*
Blue Chip Tool Inc 513 489-3561
11511 Goldcoast Dr Cincinnati (45249) *(G-3397)*
Blue Cottage Bakery LLC 216 221-9733
15612 Lake Ave Lakewood (44107) *(G-11513)*
Blue Creek Renewables LLC 419 576-7855
7909 Broughton Pike Paulding (45879) *(G-15857)*
Blue Crescent Enterprises Inc 440 878-9700
19645 Progress Dr Strongsville (44149) *(G-17720)*
Blue Cube Operations LLC 440 248-1223
9456 Freeway Dr Macedonia (44056) *(G-12280)*
Blue Fox Group, The, Mount Vernon *Also called Smartcopy Inc* *(G-14514)*
Blue Grass Cooperage - Jackson, Wellston *Also called Brown-Forman Corporation* *(G-19598)*
Blue Jay Entps of Tscrwas Cnty 330 874-2048
9852 Hess Mill Rd Ne Bolivar (44612) *(G-1907)*
Blue Line Painting LLC 440 951-2583
19520 Nottingham Rd Cleveland (44110) *(G-4823)*
Blue Machine, Cincinnati *Also called Power Engineering LLC* *(G-4177)*
Blue Pawn, Cuyahoga Falls *Also called Simon & Simon Blue Pond Inc* *(G-7918)*
Blue Point Capitl Partners LLC (PA) 216 535-4700
127 Public Sq Ste 5100 Cleveland (44114) *(G-4824)*
Blue Racer Midstream LLC 740 630-7556
11388 E Pike Rd Unit B Cambridge (43725) *(G-2428)*
Blue Ribbon Screen Graphics 216 226-6200
1473 Hollow Wood Ln Avon (44011) *(G-942)*
Blue Ribbon Trailers Ltd 330 538-4114
12800 Leonard Pkwy North Jackson (44451) *(G-15142)*
Blue Ridge Paper Products Inc 440 235-7200
7920 Mapleway Dr Olmsted Falls (44138) *(G-15529)*

Blue Streak Services Inc 216 223-3282
25001 Emery Rd Ste 410 Cleveland (44128) *(G-4825)*
Blue Water Satellite Inc 419 372-0160
1510 N Westwood Ave Toledo (43606) *(G-18207)*
Bluefoot Energy Services, Steubenville *Also called Bluefoot Industrial LLC* *(G-17528)*
Bluefoot Industrial LLC 740 314-5299
224 N 3rd St Steubenville (43952) *(G-17528)*
Bluelevel Technologies Inc 330 523-5215
3778 Timberlake Dr Richfield (44286) *(G-16463)*
Bluelogos Inc 614 898-9971
130 Graphic Way Westerville (43081) *(G-20038)*
Blueserv Reprograhics LLC 937 426-6410
3313 Seajay Dr Beavercreek (45430) *(G-1351)*
Bluffton News Pubg & Prtg Co (PA) 419 358-8010
101 S Main St Bluffton (45817) *(G-1884)*
Bluffton News, The, Bluffton *Also called Bluffton News Pubg & Prtg Co* *(G-1884)*
Bluffton Precast Concrete Co 419 358-6946
8950 Dixie Hwy Bluffton (45817) *(G-1885)*
Bluffton Stone Co 419 358-6941
310 Quarry Dr Bluffton (45817) *(G-1886)*
BMA Metals Group Inc 513 874-5152
7770 W Chester Rd Ste 120 West Chester (45069) *(G-19661)*
BMC, Perrysburg *Also called Bulk Molding Compounds Inc* *(G-15926)*
BMC, Strongsville *Also called Bearings Manufacturing Company* *(G-17718)*
BMC Holdings Inc (PA) 419 636-1194
1914 Randolph Dr Bryan (43506) *(G-2269)*
BMC of Barfield Inc 513 860-4455
3501 Symmes Rd Hamilton (45015) *(G-10542)*
Bmd Blasting 614 580-9468
1840 Federal Pkwy Columbus (43207) *(G-6681)*
Bmi Machine Inc 614 785-7020
8354 Fairway Dr Columbus (43235) *(G-6682)*
Bnoat Oncology 330 285-2537
411 Wolf Ledges Pkwy Akron (44311) *(G-89)*
Board of Park Commissioners 216 635-3200
4101 Fulton Pkwy Cleveland (44144) *(G-4826)*
Boardman Molded Intl LLC 330 788-2400
1110 Thalia Ave Youngstown (44512) *(G-20853)*
Boardman Molded Products Inc (PA) 330 788-2400
1110 Thalia Ave Youngstown (44512) *(G-20854)*
Boardman News 330 758-6397
8302 Southern Blvd Ste 2 Boardman (44512) *(G-1898)*
Boardman Printing, Youngstown *Also called Nomis Publications Inc* *(G-20976)*
Boardman Steel Inc 330 758-0951
156 Nulf Dr Columbiana (44408) *(G-64455)*
Boatfun Sports Inc 513 379-0506
6548 Westminster Ct Liberty Township (45044) *(G-11811)*
Bob Evans Farms Inc 937 372-4493
640 Birch Rd Xenia (45385) *(G-20758)*
Bob Evans Farms Inc (HQ) 614 491-2225
8111 Smiths Mill Rd New Albany (43054) *(G-14609)*
Bob Evans Farms Inc 740 245-5305
791 Farmview Rd Bidwell (45614) *(G-1664)*
Bob King Sign Company Inc 330 753-2679
1631 East Ave Akron (44314) *(G-90)*
Bob Lanes Welding Inc 740 373-3567
545 Rummer Rd Marietta (45750) *(G-12609)*
Bob Ready, North Canton *Also called LSI Retail Graphics LLC* *(G-15098)*
Bob Smith 513 242-7700
9933 Alliance Rd Blue Ash (45242) *(G-1738)*
Bobbart Industries Inc 419 350-5477
5035 Alexis Rd Ste 1 Sylvania (43560) *(G-17934)*
Bobco Enterprises Inc 419 867-3560
2910 Glanzman Rd Toledo (43614) *(G-18208)*
Bobit Business Media Inc 330 899-2200
3515 Massillon Rd Ste 350 Uniontown (44685) *(G-18912)*
Bobs Custom Str Interiors LLC 567 316-7490
5333 Secor Rd Ste 19 Toledo (43623) *(G-18209)*
Bobs Grinding Inc 440 946-6179
7564 Tyler Blvd Ste D Mentor (44060) *(G-13405)*
Bocchi Laboratories Ohio LLC 614 741-7458
9200 Smiths Mill Rd N New Albany (43054) *(G-14610)*
Bock & Pierce Enterprises 513 474-9500
8550 Beechmont Ave # 800 Cincinnati (45255) *(G-3398)*
Bock Company LLC 216 912-7050
2476 Edison Blvd Twinsburg (44087) *(G-18742)*
Bock Lighting, Twinsburg *Also called Bock Company LLC* *(G-18742)*
Bocor Holdings LLC 330 494-1221
7793 Pittsburg Ave Nw Canton (44720) *(G-2594)*
Bocor Producing, Canton *Also called Bocor Holdings LLC* *(G-2594)*
Bodnar Printing Co Inc 440 277-8295
3480 Colorado Ave Lorain (44052) *(G-12080)*
Bodor Vents LLC 513 348-3853
11013 Kenwood Rd Blue Ash (45242) *(G-1739)*
Bodycote Imt Inc 740 852-5000
443 E High St London (43140) *(G-12050)*
Bodycote Kolsterising, London *Also called Bodycote Thermal Proc Inc* *(G-12051)*
Bodycote Thermal Proc Inc 614 444-1181
1515 Universal Rd Columbus (43207) *(G-6683)*

Bodycote Thermal Proc Inc 513 921-2300
710 Burns St Cincinnati (45204) **(G-3399)**
Bodycote Thermal Proc Inc 440 473-2020
5475 Avion Park Dr Cleveland (44143) **(G-4827)**
Bodycote Thermal Proc Inc 216 475-0400
14701 Industrial Ave Cleveland (44137) **(G-4828)**
Bodycote Thermal Proc Inc 740 852-4955
443 E High St London (43140) **(G-12051)**
Bodyvega Nutrition LLC 708 712-5743
3493 Torrey Pines Dr Akron (44333) **(G-91)**
Boehm Inc (PA) 614 875-9010
2050 Hardy Parkway St Grove City (43123) **(G-10417)**
Boehm Pressed Steel Company 330 220-8000
5440 Wegman Dr Valley City (44280) **(G-19031)**
Boehr Print 419 358-1350
2703 N Main St Ste 1 Findlay (45840) **(G-9659)**
Boehringer Ingelheim USA Corp 440 232-3320
300 Northfield Rd Bedford (44146) **(G-1390)**
Boehrnger Inglheim Phrmcctcals 440 286-5667
11540 Autumn Ridge Dr Chardon (44024) **(G-3100)**
Boeing Company 740 788-4000
801 Irving Wick Dr W Newark (43056) **(G-14854)**
Boeing Company 937 427-1767
2600 Paramount Pl Ste 400 Fairborn (45324) **(G-9453)**
Boeing Company 740 788-5805
801 Irving Wick Dr W Newark (43056) **(G-14855)**
Boeing Company 937 431-3503
5200 Vincent Ave Wright Patterson Afb (45433) **(G-20717)**
Boes, Wilbert J, New Riegel *Also called New Riegel Cafe Inc* **(G-14816)**
Bogden Industrial Coatings LLC 513 267-5101
5020 Eck Rd Middletown (45042) **(G-13887)**
Boggs & Associates Inc 614 237-0600
3555 E Fulton St Columbus (43227) **(G-6684)**
Boggs Graphic Equipment LLC 888 837-8101
14901 Broadway Ave Maple Heights (44137) **(G-12566)**
Boggs Recycling Inc 800 837-8101
12355 Kinsman Rd Unit J Newbury (44065) **(G-14946)**
Bogie Industries Inc Ltd 330 745-3105
1100 Home Ave Akron (44310) **(G-92)**
Bohlender Engravg, Cincinnati *Also called Bohlender Engraving Company* **(G-3400)**
Bohlender Engraving Company 513 621-4095
1599 Central Pkwy Cincinnati (45214) **(G-3400)**
Boich Companies LLC 614 221-0101
41 S High St Ste 3750s Columbus (43215) **(G-6685)**
Bojos Cream 330 270-3332
1412 S Raccoon Rd Austintown (44515) **(G-930)**
Boko Patterns Models & Molds 937 426-9667
4130 Industrial Ln Beavercreek (45430) **(G-1352)**
Boldman Printing LLC 937 653-3431
1333 N Main St Urbana (43078) **(G-18980)**
Bollari/Davis Inc 330 296-4445
5292 S Prospect St Ravenna (44266) **(G-16370)**
Bollin & Sons Inc 419 693-6573
6001 Brent Dr Toledo (43611) **(G-18210)**
Bollin Label Systems, Toledo *Also called Bollin & Sons Inc* **(G-18210)**
Bollinger Tool & Die Inc 419 866-5180
959 Hamilton Dr Holland (43528) **(G-10916)**
Bolon Timber LLC 740 567-4102
45436 Smithberger Rd Lewisville (43754) **(G-11802)**
Bolons Custom Kitchens Inc 330 499-0092
6287 Promler St Nw Canton (44720) **(G-2595)**
Boltaron Inc 740 498-5900
1 General St Newcomerstown (43832) **(G-14970)**
Boltech Incorporated 330 746-6881
1201 Crescent St Youngstown (44502) **(G-20855)**
Bomb Mfg LLC 419 559-9689
530 S Taft Ave Fremont (43420) **(G-10001)**
Bomba S Custom Woodworking 330 699-9075
3748 Dogwood St Nw Uniontown (44685) **(G-18913)**
Bomen Marking Products Inc 440 582-0053
12905 York Delta Dr Ste A Cleveland (44133) **(G-4829)**
Bonbonneri Bakery, Cincinnati *Also called Bonbonneri Inc* **(G-3401)**
Bonbonneri Inc 513 321-3399
2030 Madison Rd Ste 1 Cincinnati (45208) **(G-3401)**
Bond Chemicals Inc 330 725-5935
1154 W Smith Rd Medina (44256) **(G-13230)**
Bond Distributing LLC 440 461-7920
701 Beta Dr Ste 8 Cleveland (44143) **(G-4830)**
Bond Machine Company Inc 937 746-4941
921 N Main St Franklin (45005) **(G-9872)**
Bond Quarters Horses 614 354-4028
23574 Cadiz Rd Freeport (43973) **(G-9984)**
Bonded Pallets 513 541-1855
1801 John St Cincinnati (45214) **(G-3402)**
Boneng Transmissions (usa) LLC 330 425-1516
1670 Entp Pkwy Unit E Twinsburg (44087) **(G-18743)**
Bonfoey Co 216 621-0178
1710 Euclid Ave Cleveland (44115) **(G-4831)**
Bonham Doors & Openers, Wshngtn CT Hs *Also called Bonham Enterprsises* **(G-20719)**
Bonham Enterprsises 740 333-0501
2555 Us Highway 62 Ne Wshngtn CT Hs (43160) **(G-20719)**
Bonne Bell LLC (PA) 440 835-2440
1006 Crocker Rd Westlake (44145) **(G-20102)**
Bonnot Company 330 896-6544
1301 Home Ave Akron (44310) **(G-93)**
Bonsal American Inc 513 398-7300
5155 Fischer Ave Cincinnati (45217) **(G-3403)**
Boochers Inc 937 667-3414
320 S 5th St Tipp City (45371) **(G-18101)**
Boogie Wipes, Cincinnati *Also called Little Busy Bodies LLC* **(G-3948)**
Book Store, Columbus *Also called US Government Publishing Off* **(G-7566)**
Bookbinders Incorporated 330 848-4980
90 16th St Sw Ste C Barberton (44203) **(G-1066)**
Bookcolor Bindery Services 614 252-2941
1685 Woodland Ave Columbus (43219) **(G-6686)**
Bookfactory LLC 937 226-7100
2302 S Edwin C Moses Blvd Dayton (45417) **(G-8059)**
Bookman & Son Fine Jewelry, Cleveland *Also called J and L Jewelry Manufacturing* **(G-5481)**
Bookmasters Inc (PA) 419 281-1802
30 Amberwood Pkwy Ashland (44805) **(G-686)**
Bookmyer LLP 419 447-3883
144 S Washington St Ste B Tiffin (44883) **(G-18051)**
Boomerang Rubber Inc 937 693-4611
105 Dinsmore St Botkins (45306) **(G-1933)**
Boos Make & Take 440 647-0000
676 N Main St Wellington (44090) **(G-19573)**
Bor-It Manufacturing Inc 419 289-6639
1687 Cleveland Rd Ashland (44805) **(G-687)**
Borchers Americas Inc (HQ) 440 899-2950
811 Sharon Dr Westlake (44145) **(G-20103)**
Borden Bakers Inc 614 457-9800
4723 Reed Rd Columbus (43220) **(G-6687)**
Borden Dairy Co Cincinnati LLC 513 948-8811
415 John St Cincinnati (45215) **(G-3404)**
Borden Dairy Company Ohio LLC 216 671-2300
3068 W 106th St Cleveland (44111) **(G-4832)**
Bores Manufacturing Co Inc 419 465-2606
300 Sandusky St Monroeville (44847) **(G-14287)**
Bores, J F Mfg, Monroeville *Also called Bores Manufacturing Co Inc* **(G-14287)**
Borke Mold Specialist Inc 513 870-8000
9541 Glades Dr West Chester (45011) **(G-19662)**
Borman Enterprises Inc 216 459-9292
1311 Brookpark Rd Cleveland (44109) **(G-4833)**
Bornhorst Motor Service Inc 937 773-0426
8270 N Dixie Dr Piqua (45356) **(G-16104)**
Bornhorst Printing Company Inc 419 738-5901
10139 County Road 25a Wapakoneta (45895) **(G-19325)**
Bortnick Tractor Sales Inc 330 924-2555
6192 Warren Rd Cortland (44410) **(G-7704)**
Bos Electric Supply LLC 937 426-0578
2388 Arbor Blvd Moraine (45439) **(G-14335)**
Bosca Accesories, Springfield *Also called Hugo Bosca Company Inc* **(G-17423)**
Bosch Rexroth Corporation 330 263-3300
1683 Enterprise Pkwy Wooster (44691) **(G-20573)**
Bosco Pup Co LLC 614 833-0349
290 Parkwood Ave Pickerington (43147) **(G-16042)**
Boscott Metals Inc 937 448-2018
138 S Miami Ave Bradford (45308) **(G-2009)**
Bose Corporation 614 475-8565
155 Easton Town Ctr Fl 1 Columbus (43219) **(G-6688)**
Bose Showcase Store, Columbus *Also called Bose Corporation* **(G-6688)**
Boss Pet Products Inc (HQ) 216 332-0832
7730 First Pl Ste E Oakwood Village (44146) **(G-15478)**
Bosserman Automotive Engrg LLC 419 722-2879
18919 Olympic Dr Findlay (45840) **(G-9660)**
Bost & Filtrex Inc (HQ) 301 206-9466
1783 Kenny Rd Columbus (43212) **(G-6689)**
Boston Beer Company 267 240-4429
1625 Central Pkwy Cincinnati (45214) **(G-3405)**
Boston Scntfic Nrmdlation Corp 513 377-6160
4267 S Haven Dr Mason (45040) **(G-12836)**
Boston Scntfic Nrmdlation Corp 419 720-9510
3130 Executive Pkwy Toledo (43606) **(G-18211)**
Boston Scntfic Nrmdlation Corp 330 372-2652
2174 Sarkies Dr Ne Warren (44483) **(G-19378)**
Boston Stoker Inc (PA) 937 890-6401
10855 Engle Rd Vandalia (45377) **(G-19118)**
Botanicare, Marysville *Also called American Agritech LLC* **(G-12770)**
Bottomline Ink Corporation 419 897-8000
7829 Ponderosa Rd Perrysburg (43551) **(G-15923)**
Boulder Daily Camera, Cincinnati *Also called Brv Inc* **(G-3427)**
Boville Indus Coatings Inc 330 669-8558
7459 Leichty Rd Smithville (44677) **(G-17087)**
Bowdil Company 800 356-8663
2030 Industrial Pl Se Canton (44707) **(G-2596)**
Bowerston Shale Company 740 763-3921
1329 Seven Hills Rd Newark (43055) **(G-14856)**

ALPHABETIC

Bowerston Shale Company (PA) 740 269-2921
515 Main St Bowerston (44695) *(G-1939)*
Bowes Manufacturing Inc 216 378-2110
30340 Solon Industrial Solon (44139) *(G-17117)*
Bowes Mill and Cabinet LLC 440 236-3255
33549 E Royalton Rd # 7 Columbia Station (44028) *(G-6430)*
Bowman Cabinet Shop 419 331-8209
4880 N Cable Rd Elida (45807) *(G-9194)*
Bows Barrettes & Baubles 440 247-2697
4180 Chagrin River Rd Moreland Hills (44022) *(G-14401)*
Box Seat Publishing LLC 513 519-2812
8635 Willowview Ct Cincinnati (45251) *(G-3406)*
Boxdrop Mansfield Mattress, Mansfield Also called Mlp Interent Enterprises LLC *(G-12483)*
Boxes & Such 440 237-7122
1118 Mindy Ln Wooster (44691) *(G-20574)*
Boxit Corporation (HQ) 216 631-6900
5555 Walworth Ave Cleveland (44102) *(G-4834)*
Boxit Corporation 216 416-9475
3000 Quigley Rd B Cleveland (44113) *(G-4835)*
Boyce Ltd 614 236-8901
2173 S James Rd Columbus (43232) *(G-6690)*
Boyce Machine Inc 330 678-3210
3609 Mogadore Rd Kent (44240) *(G-11301)*
Boyd Sanitation 740 697-7940
5525 4th St Roseville (43777) *(G-16575)*
Boyds Machine and Met Finshg 937 698-5623
7650 S Kssler Frderick Rd West Milton (45383) *(G-19947)*
Boyer Signs & Graphics Inc 216 383-7242
3200 Valleyview Dr Columbus (43204) *(G-6691)*
BP, Cincinnati Also called B P Oil Company *(G-3376)*
BP, Cincinnati Also called N M R Inc *(G-4056)*
BP, Cincinnati Also called North Bend Express *(G-4086)*
BP Products North America Inc 937 461-3621
621 Brandt St Dayton (45404) *(G-8060)*
BP Products North America Inc 419 537-9540
2450 Hill Ave Toledo (43607) *(G-18212)*
BP Products North America Inc 419 636-2249
710 E Wilson St Bryan (43506) *(G-2270)*
Bpm Realty Inc 614 221-6811
195 N Grant Ave Fl 2a Columbus (43215) *(G-6692)*
Bpr-Rico Elc Trck Spcalist Inc 330 723-4050
691 W Liberty St Medina (44256) *(G-13231)*
Bpr-Rico Manufacturing Inc 330 723-4050
691 W Liberty St Medina (44256) *(G-13232)*
Bpr/Rico, Medina Also called Bpr-Rico Manufacturing Inc *(G-13232)*
Bprex Halthcare Brookville LLC (HQ) 847 541-9700
1899 N Wilkinson Way Perrysburg (43551) *(G-15924)*
Bprex Plastic Packaging Inc (HQ) 419 247-5000
1 Seagate Toledo (43604) *(G-18213)*
BR Mulch Inc 937 667-8288
620 Ginghamsburg Rd Tipp City (45371) *(G-18102)*
Brace Shop Prosthetic Ortho (HQ) 513 421-5653
111 Wellington Pl Ste 8 Cincinnati (45219) *(G-3407)*
Bracemart LLC 440 353-2830
36097 Westminister Ave North Ridgeville (44039) *(G-15213)*
Brad Snoderly 419 476-0184
444 W Laskey Rd Ste K Toledo (43612) *(G-18214)*
Braden-Sutphin Ink, Cleveland Also called Wikoff Color Corporation *(G-6307)*
Braden-Sutphin Ink Company, Cleveland Also called Red Tie Group Inc *(G-5968)*
Bradford Neal Machinery Inc 440 632-1393
14503 Old State Rd Middlefield (44062) *(G-13781)*
Bradley Enterprises Inc (PA) 330 875-1444
3750 Beck Ave Louisville (44641) *(G-12153)*
Bradley Stone Industries LLC 440 519-3277
30801 Carter St Solon (44139) *(G-17118)*
Bradleys Beacons Ltd 419 447-7560
296 Hedges St Tiffin (44883) *(G-18052)*
Bradner Oil Company Inc 419 288-2945
Wayne Rd Wayne (43466) *(G-19560)*
Bradshaw Manufacturing, Cleveland Also called Hutchinson-Stevens Inc *(G-5428)*
Brady A Lantz Enterprises 513 742-4921
11242 Sebring Dr Cincinnati (45240) *(G-3408)*
Brady A Lantz Enterprises Inc 513 742-4921
11242 Sebring Dr Cincinnati (45240) *(G-3409)*
Brahler Inc 330 966-7730
4041 Batton St Nw Ste 104 Canton (44720) *(G-2597)*
Brain Child Products LLC 419 698-4020
146 Main St Toledo (43605) *(G-18215)*
Brainard Rivet Company 330 545-4931
222 Harry St Girard (44420) *(G-10254)*
Brainerd Industries Inc (PA) 937 228-0488
680 Precision Ct Miamisburg (45342) *(G-13644)*
Brainin-Advance Industries LLC 513 874-9760
4348 Le Saint Ct West Chester (45014) *(G-19663)*
Brainmaster Technologies Inc 440 232-6000
195 Willis St 3 Bedford (44146) *(G-1391)*
Brakers Publishing & Prtg Svc 440 576-0136
166 W Cedar St Jefferson (44047) *(G-11225)*

Bramkamp Printing Company Inc 513 241-1865
9933 Alliance Rd Ste 2 Blue Ash (45242) *(G-1740)*
Branam Oral Health Tech Inc (PA) 248 670-0040
3140 Dustin Rd Oregon (43616) *(G-15557)*
Branch 300, Groveport Also called Kurtz Bros Inc *(G-10500)*
Branch 49, Columbus Also called Laird Plastics Inc *(G-7110)*
Brand Castle LLC (PA) 216 292-7700
5111 Richmond Rd Frnt Bedford Heights (44146) *(G-1462)*
Brandon Screen Printing 419 229-9837
326 S West St Lima (45801) *(G-11845)*
Brands' Marina, Port Clinton Also called Tack-Anew Inc *(G-16262)*
Brandts Candies 440 942-1016
1238 Lost Nation Rd Willoughby (44094) *(G-20286)*
Brandts Custom Machining LLC 419 566-3192
1183 Stewart Rd N Mansfield (44905) *(G-12413)*
Brass & Bronze Ingot Division, Cincinnati Also called G A Avril Company *(G-3719)*
Brass Accents Inc 330 332-9500
1693 Salem Pkwy W Salem (44460) *(G-16721)*
Brass Bull 1 LLC 740 335-8030
1020 Leesburg Ave Wshngtn CT Hs (43160) *(G-20720)*
Brass Lantern Antiques, Waynesville Also called John Purdum *(G-19569)*
Brass Tacks Corporation Ltd (PA) 614 599-7954
4177 Wyandotte Woods Blvd Dublin (43016) *(G-8891)*
Brasspack Packing Supply, Mansfield Also called Skybox Investments Inc *(G-12514)*
Brat Printing, Cincinnati Also called Randy Gray *(G-4248)*
Braun Industries Inc 419 232-7020
1170 Production Dr Van Wert (45891) *(G-19080)*
Braun Machine Technologies LLC 330 777-5433
4175 Warren Sharon Rd Vienna (44473) *(G-19197)*
Braze Solutions LLC 440 349-5100
6850 Cochran Rd Solon (44139) *(G-17119)*
Brazing Service Inc 440 871-1120
24480 Sperry Cir Westlake (44145) *(G-20104)*
Bread Kneads Inc 419 422-3863
510 S Blanchard St Findlay (45840) *(G-9661)*
Breaker Technology Inc 440 248-7168
30625 Solon Ind Pkwy Solon (44139) *(G-17120)*
Breaking Bread Pizza Company 614 754-4777
9042 Cotter St Lewis Center (43035) *(G-11752)*
Breakthrough Media Ministries, Canal Winchester Also called World Harvest Church Inc *(G-2516)*
Breckenridge Paper & Packaging, Huron Also called Central Ohio Paper & Packg Inc *(G-11092)*
Brecksville Broadview Gazette 440 526-7977
7014 Mill Rd Brecksville (44141) *(G-2024)*
Breezeway Screens Inc 740 599-5222
513 Market St Danville (43014) *(G-7958)*
Breibach & Associates, Hilliard Also called Breibach Association *(G-10815)*
Breibach Association 614 876-6480
5117 Grandon Dr Hilliard (43026) *(G-10815)*
Breining Mechanical Sytems, Massillon Also called Canton Fabricators Inc *(G-12966)*
Breitenbach Bed & Breakfast, Dover Also called Breitenbach Wine Cellar Inc *(G-8810)*
Breitenbach Wine Cellar Inc 330 343-3603
5934 Old Route 39 Nw Dover (44622) *(G-8810)*
Breitinger Company 419 526-4255
595 Oakenwaldt St Mansfield (44905) *(G-12414)*
Breits Inc 216 651-5800
5218 Detroit Ave Cleveland (44102) *(G-4836)*
Bren-Ko Patterns, Hamilton Also called 7 Rowe Court Properties LLC *(G-10526)*
Brendel Producing Company 330 854-4151
8215 Arlington Ave Nw Canton (44720) *(G-2598)*
Brendons Fiber Works 614 353-6599
306 E Jeffrey Pl Columbus (43214) *(G-6693)*
Brenmar Construction Inc 740 286-2151
900 Morton St Jackson (45640) *(G-11183)*
Brenner International, Newark Also called I G Brenner Inc *(G-14887)*
Brent Bleh Company 513 721-1100
917 Vine St Cincinnati (45202) *(G-3410)*
Brent Carter Enterprises Inc 513 731-1440
4404 Forest Ave Cincinnati (45212) *(G-3411)*
Brentmoor Hams LLC 513 677-0813
10367 Brentmoor Dr Loveland (45140) *(G-12181)*
Brentwood Originals Inc 330 793-2255
1309 N Meridian Rd Youngstown (44509) *(G-20856)*
Brentwood Printing & Sty 513 522-2679
8630 Winton Rd Cincinnati (45231) *(G-3412)*
Brett Purdum 740 626-2890
10989 Cropp St South Salem (45681) *(G-17296)*
Brew Kettle Inc 440 234-8788
8377 Pearl Rd Strongsville (44136) *(G-17721)*
Brew Kettle Strongsville LLC 440 915-7074
3520 Longwood Dr Medina (44256) *(G-13233)*
Brew Monkeys LLC 513 330-8806
36 E 7th St Ste 1510 Cincinnati (45202) *(G-3413)*
Brewer Company (PA) 800 394-0017
1354 Us Route 50 Milford (45150) *(G-13999)*
Brewer Company 440 944-3800
30060 Lakeland Blvd Wickliffe (44092) *(G-20206)*

Brewer Company 614 279-8688
  472 Brehl Ave Columbus (43223) *(G-6694)*
Brewer Company 513 576-6300
  7300 Main St Cincinnati (45244) *(G-3414)*
Brewer Industries LLC 216 469-0808
  318 Bentleyville Rd Chagrin Falls (44022) *(G-3011)*
Brewer Products, Cincinnati Also called La Mfg Inc *(G-3928)*
Brewer Products Co, Cincinnati Also called Brewpro Inc *(G-3415)*
Brewercote, Milford Also called Brewer Company *(G-13999)*
Brewery Real Estate Partnr 614 224-9023
  467 N High St Columbus (43215) *(G-6695)*
Brewpro Inc 513 577-7200
  9483 Reading Rd Cincinnati (45215) *(G-3415)*
Brewpub Restaurant Corp 614 228-2537
  467 N High St Columbus (43215) *(G-6696)*
Brewster Cheese Company (PA) 330 767-3492
  800 Wabash Ave S Brewster (44613) *(G-2067)*
BREWSTER HISTORICAL SOCIETY, Brewster Also called Brewster Sugarcreek Twp Histo *(G-2068)*
Brewster Sugarcreek Twp Histo 330 767-0045
  45 Wabash Ave S Brewster (44613) *(G-2068)*
Brg Sports Inc 217 891-1429
  7501 Performance Ln North Ridgeville (44039) *(G-15214)*
Brian Franks Electric Inc 330 821-5457
  11424 Beech St Ne Alliance (44601) *(G-458)*
Brian Rengh, Cleveland Also called Atlas Printing and Embroidery *(G-4761)*
Briar Hill Furniture 330 223-2109
  7061 Bane Rd Ne Kensington (44427) *(G-11284)*
Briar Hill Stone Company 330 377-5100
  12470 State Route 520 Glenmont (44628) *(G-10274)*
Briarwood Manufacturing, Van Wert Also called Kedar D Army *(G-19097)*
Briarwood Valley Farms 419 736-2298
  502 Us Highway 224 Sullivan (44880) *(G-17880)*
Brick and Barrel 503 927-0629
  1844 Columbus Rd Cleveland (44113) *(G-4837)*
Bricker Plating Inc 419 636-1990
  612 E Edgerton St Bryan (43506) *(G-2271)*
Bricolage Inc 614 853-6789
  2989 Lewis Centre Way Grove City (43123) *(G-10418)*
Bridge Analyzers Incorporated 216 332-0592
  5198 Richmond Rd Bedford Heights (44146) *(G-1463)*
Bridge Components Incorporated 614 873-0777
  3476 Millikin Ct Columbus (43228) *(G-6697)*
Bridge Components Inds Inc 614 873-0777
  3476 Millikin Ct Columbus (43228) *(G-6698)*
Bridges Sheet Metal 330 339-3185
  1184 Tuscarawas Ave Nw New Philadelphia (44663) *(G-14760)*
Bridgestone Americas Center Fo 330 379-7575
  1659 S Main St Akron (44301) *(G-94)*
Bridgestone APM Company 419 294-6989
  235 Commerce Way Upper Sandusky (43351) *(G-18946)*
Bridgestone APM Company 419 294-6304
  245 Commerce Way Upper Sandusky (43351) *(G-18947)*
Bridgestone Procurement Holdin (HQ) 337 882-1200
  381 W Wilbeth Rd Akron (44301) *(G-95)*
Bridgetek, Dayton Also called Contech Bridge Solutions LLC *(G-8103)*
Bridgetek, West Chester Also called Contech Bridge Solutions LLC *(G-19678)*
Bridgetown Welders LLC 513 574-4851
  4489 Bridgetown Rd Cincinnati (45211) *(G-3416)*
Bridgits Bath LLC 937 259-1960
  1226 Pursell Ave Dayton (45420) *(G-8061)*
Brier Hill Slag Company (PA) 330 743-8170
  18 Hogue St Youngstown (44502) *(G-20857)*
Bright Focus Sales Inc 216 751-8384
  2310 Superior Ave E # 225 Cleveland (44114) *(G-4838)*
Bright Now Dental, North Olmsted Also called Smile Brands Inc *(G-15199)*
Brighteye Innovations LLC 800 573-0052
  1760 Wadsworth Rd Akron (44320) *(G-96)*
Brightguy Inc 440 942-8318
  38205b Stevens Blvd Willoughby (44094) *(G-20287)*
Brighton Collectibles LLC 614 418-7561
  217 Easton Town Ctr Columbus (43219) *(G-6699)*
Brighton Mills, Cincinnati Also called H Nagel & Son Co *(G-3791)*
Brighton Technologies LLC 513 469-1800
  5129 Kieley Pl Saint Bernard (45217) *(G-16620)*
Brighton Technologies Group 513 469-1800
  5129 Kieley Pl Ste A Cincinnati (45217) *(G-3417)*
Brighton Truedge 513 771-2300
  4955 Spring Grove Ave Cincinnati (45232) *(G-3418)*
Brightstar Propane & Fuels 614 891-8395
  6190 Frost Rd Westerville (43082) *(G-19981)*
Brilex Industries Inc 330 744-1114
  101 Andrews Ave Youngstown (44503) *(G-20858)*
Brilex Industries Inc (PA) 330 744-1114
  1201 Crescent St Youngstown (44502) *(G-20859)*
Brilex Tech Services, Youngstown Also called Brilex Industries Inc *(G-20859)*
Brilista Foods Company Inc (PA) 614 299-4132
  1000 Goodale Blvd Columbus (43212) *(G-6700)*

Brilliant Colorworks LLC 800 566-4162
  2940 E 14th Ave Columbus (43219) *(G-6701)*
Brilliant Electric Sign Co Ltd 216 741-3800
  4811 Van Epps Rd Brooklyn Heights (44131) *(G-2116)*
Brinkley Technology Group LLC 330 830-2498
  2770 Erie St S Massillon (44646) *(G-12963)*
Brinkman LLC 419 204-5934
  1524 Adak Ave Lima (45805) *(G-11846)*
Brinkman Tool & Die Inc 937 222-1161
  325 Kiser St Dayton (45404) *(G-8062)*
Brinkman Turkey Farms Inc (PA) 419 365-5127
  16314 State Route 68 Findlay (45840) *(G-9662)*
Brinkman's Country Corner, Findlay Also called Brinkman Turkey Farms Inc *(G-9662)*
Brio Coffee Co, Plain City Also called Altraserv LLC *(G-16170)*
Briskheat Corporation (PA) 614 294-3376
  4800 Hilton Corporate Dr Columbus (43232) *(G-6702)*
Briskheat Corporation 614 429-3232
  460 E Starr Ave Columbus (43201) *(G-6703)*
Bristol-Myers Squibb Company 800 321-1335
  999 Polaris Pkwy Ste 100 Columbus (43240) *(G-6489)*
Brite Brazing, Wickliffe Also called HI Tecmetal Group Inc *(G-20213)*
Broad Street Financial Company (PA) 614 228-0326
  1515 Lake Shore Dr # 225 Columbus (43204) *(G-6704)*
Broadband Hospitality, Youngstown Also called Great Lakes Telcom Ltd *(G-20924)*
Broadstreet Energy Company, Columbus Also called Broad Street Financial Company *(G-6704)*
Broadview Heights Spotlights 440 526-4404
  9543 Broadview Rd Broadview Heights (44147) *(G-2089)*
Broadview Journal, The, Richfield Also called Scriptype Publishing Inc *(G-16485)*
Broadway Companies Inc (PA) 937 890-1888
  6161 Ventnor Ave Dayton (45414) *(G-8063)*
Broadway Printing LLC 513 621-3429
  530 Reading Rd Cincinnati (45202) *(G-3419)*
Broadway Welding & Fabrication 513 821-0004
  25 E 76th St Cincinnati (45216) *(G-3420)*
Broan-Nutone LLC 888 336-3948
  9825 Kenwood Rd Ste 301 Blue Ash (45242) *(G-1741)*
Brocar Products Inc 513 922-2888
  4335 River Rd Cincinnati (45204) *(G-3421)*
Brock Burial Vault Inc 740 894-5246
  1043 County Road 120 South Point (45680) *(G-17280)*
Brock RAD & Wldg Fabrication 740 773-2540
  370 Douglas Ave Chillicothe (45601) *(G-3178)*
Brocker Machine Inc 330 744-5858
  1530 Poland Ave Youngstown (44502) *(G-20860)*
Brockman Jig Grinding Service 937 220-9780
  1535 Stanley Ave Dayton (45404) *(G-8064)*
Brockmans Signs Inc 513 574-6163
  6041 Harrison Ave Ste 5 Cincinnati (45248) *(G-3422)*
Brocks Chimney 740 819-2489
  4620 Gorsuch Rd Nashport (43830) *(G-14565)*
Brocks RAD Wldg Fabrication I, Chillicothe Also called Brock RAD & Wldg Fabrication *(G-3178)*
Brocks Welding & Repair Svc 740 453-3943
  3985 East Pike Zanesville (43701) *(G-21111)*
Broco Products Inc 216 531-0880
  18624 Syracuse Ave Cleveland (44110) *(G-4839)*
Brodwill LLC 513 258-2716
  3900 Rose Hill Ave Ste C Cincinnati (45229) *(G-3423)*
Broestl & Wallis Fine Jewelers, Lakewood Also called Bensan Jewelers Inc *(G-11512)*
Brogan Machine Shop 513 683-9054
  501 Lovelnd Madera Rd # 2 Loveland (45140) *(G-12182)*
Broken Spinning Wheel 419 825-1609
  14230 Monclova Rd Swanton (43558) *(G-17907)*
Bronco Machine Inc 440 951-5015
  38411 Apollo Pkwy Willoughby (44094) *(G-20288)*
Bront Machining Inc 937 228-4551
  2601 W Dorothy Ln Moraine (45439) *(G-14336)*
Bronx Taylor Wilson, North Canton Also called Fives Bronx Inc *(G-15083)*
Bronze and Beautiful, Waverly Also called Hot Spot *(G-19548)*
Broodle Brands LLC 855 276-6353
  8361 Broadwell Rd Ste 100 Cincinnati (45244) *(G-3424)*
Brooke Printers Inc 614 235-6800
  358 Lincoln Ave Ste C Lancaster (43130) *(G-11548)*
Brooker Bros Forging Co Inc 419 668-2535
  102 Jefferson St Norwalk (44857) *(G-15383)*
Brookhill Center Industries 419 876-3932
  7989 State Route 108 Ottawa (45875) *(G-15648)*
Brooklyn Machine & Mfg Co Inc 216 341-1846
  5180 Grant Ave Cleveland (44125) *(G-4840)*
Brookpark Laboratories Inc 216 267-7140
  4595 Manufacturing Ave Cleveland (44135) *(G-4841)*
Brooks Manufacturing 419 244-1777
  1102 N Summit St Toledo (43604) *(G-18216)*
Brooks Meter Devices, Canton Also called Brooks Utility Products Group *(G-2599)*
Brooks Utility Products Group 330 455-0301
  3359 Bruening Ave Sw Canton (44706) *(G-2599)*

Brookville Roadster Inc 937 833-4605
718 Albert Rd Brookville (45309) ***(G-2162)***
Brookville Star 937 833-2545
14 Mulberry St Brookville (45309) ***(G-2163)***
Brookwood Group Inc 513 791-3030
3210 Wasson Rd Cincinnati (45209) ***(G-3425)***
Broshco Fabricated Products, Mansfield *Also called Jay Industries Inc* ***(G-12461)***
Brost Foundry Company (PA) 216 641-1131
2934 E 55th St Cleveland (44127) ***(G-4842)***
Brost Foundry Company 419 522-1133
198 Wayne St Mansfield (44902) ***(G-12415)***
Brothers Body and Eqp LLC 419 462-1975
352 South St Bldg 24 Galion (44833) ***(G-10124)***
Brothers Equipment Inc 216 458-0180
1335 E 171st St Cleveland (44110) ***(G-4843)***
Brothers Printing Co Inc 216 621-6050
2000 Euclid Ave Cleveland (44115) ***(G-4844)***
Brothers Publishing Co LLC 937 548-3330
100 Washington Ave Greenville (45331) ***(G-10361)***
Brothers Tool and Mfg Ltd 513 353-9700
8300 Harrison Ave Miamitown (45041) ***(G-13744)***
Broty Enterprises Inc (PA) 330 674-6900
88 W Jackson St Millersburg (44654) ***(G-14069)***
Broughton Foods Company (HQ) 740 373-4121
1701 Greene St Marietta (45750) ***(G-12610)***
Broughton Foods Company 800 598-7545
8099 County Road 1 South Point (45680) ***(G-17281)***
Browder Tool Co Inc 937 233-6731
5924 Executive Blvd Dayton (45424) ***(G-8065)***
Brower Products Inc (HQ) 937 563-1111
401 Northland Blvd Cincinnati (45240) ***(G-3426)***
Brown Box Company, Findlay *Also called Square One Solutions LLC* ***(G-9761)***
Brown Cnc Machinery Inc 937 865-9191
433 E Maple Ave Miamisburg (45342) ***(G-13645)***
Brown Cnty Bd Mntal Rtardation 937 378-4891
325 W State St Ste A2 Georgetown (45121) ***(G-10237)***
Brown Company of Findlay Ltd 419 425-3002
225 Stanford Pkwy Findlay (45840) ***(G-9663)***
Brown County Press, Mount Orab *Also called Clermont Sun Publishing Co* ***(G-14441)***
Brown Dave Products Inc 513 738-1576
4560 Layhigh Rd Hamilton (45013) ***(G-10543)***
Brown Fired Heater Div, Elyria *Also called Es Thermal Inc* ***(G-9260)***
Brown Forest Products 937 544-1515
652 State Route 348 Otway (45657) ***(G-15686)***
Brown Industrial Inc 937 693-3838
311 W South St Botkins (45306) ***(G-1934)***
Brown Machine Co 216 631-1255
16151 Puritas Ave Cleveland (44135) ***(G-4845)***
Brown Precision Machine 937 675-6585
13 S Buckles Ave Jamestown (45335) ***(G-11218)***
Brown Publishing Co 937 544-2391
229 N Cross St West Union (45693) ***(G-19959)***
Brown Publishing Co Inc (PA) 740 286-2187
1 Acy Ave Ste D Jackson (45640) ***(G-11184)***
Brown Publishing Inc LLC 513 794-5040
4229 Saint Andrews Pl Blue Ash (45236) ***(G-1742)***
Brown Wood Products Company 330 339-8000
7783 Crooked Run Rd Sw New Philadelphia (44663) ***(G-14761)***
Brown-Campbell Company 216 332-0101
14400 Industrial Ave S Maple Heights (44137) ***(G-12567)***
Brown-Campbell Steel, Maple Heights *Also called Brown-Campbell Company* ***(G-12567)***
Brown-Forman Corporation 740 384-3027
468 Salem Church Rd Wellston (45692) ***(G-19598)***
Brown-Singer Co 513 422-9619
108 Dorset Dr Middletown (45044) ***(G-13888)***
Brownie Points Inc 614 860-8470
5712 Westbourne Ave Columbus (43213) ***(G-6705)***
Brownlee Engineering & Mfg, Canton *Also called Machine Component Mfg* ***(G-2740)***
Brp Inc 440 988-4398
114 Hidden Tree Ln Amherst (44001) ***(G-556)***
Brp Manufacturing Company 800 858-0482
637 N Jackson St Lima (45801) ***(G-11847)***
BRT Extrusions Inc 330 544-0177
1818 N Main St Unit 1 Niles (44446) ***(G-15001)***
Brubaker Metalcrafts Inc 937 456-5834
209 N Franklin St Eaton (45320) ***(G-9143)***
Bruce Box Co Inc 740 533-0670
161 Big Doney Rd Unit A Ironton (45638) ***(G-11162)***
Bruce High Performance Tran 440 357-8964
1 High Tech Ave Painesville (44077) ***(G-15720)***
Bruck Manufacturing Co Inc 440 327-6619
33471 Liberty Pkwy North Ridgeville (44039) ***(G-15215)***
Bruening Glass Works Inc 440 333-4768
20157 Lake Rd Cleveland (44116) ***(G-4846)***
Bruewer Woodwork Mfg Co 513 353-3505
10000 Cilley Rd Cleves (45002) ***(G-6355)***
Brufist LLC 330 221-4472
122 1/2 S Maple St Bowling Green (43402) ***(G-1957)***
Brumall Mfg Coroporation 440 974-2622
7850 Division Dr Mentor (44060) ***(G-13406)***
Brune Printing Co 419 399-2756
310 W Perry St Paulding (45879) ***(G-15858)***
Brunswick Eye & Contact Lens C 419 439-3381
2011 S Clinton St Defiance (43512) ***(G-8617)***
Brushes Inc 216 267-8084
5400 Smith Rd Cleveland (44142) ***(G-4847)***
Brushes Inc 216 267-8084
5400 Smith Rd Cleveland (44142) ***(G-4848)***
Brv Inc 513 977-3000
312 Walnut St Ste 2800 Cincinnati (45202) ***(G-3427)***
Brw Tool Inc 419 394-3371
502 Scott St Saint Marys (45885) ***(G-16679)***
Bry-Air Inc 740 965-2974
10793 E State Route 37 Sunbury (43074) ***(G-17883)***
Bryan Metals LLC (HQ) 419 636-4571
1103 S Main St Bryan (43506) ***(G-2272)***
Bryan Packaging Inc 419 636-2600
620 E Perry St Bryan (43506) ***(G-2273)***
Bryan Publishing Company (PA) 419 636-1111
127 S Walnut St Bryan (43506) ***(G-2274)***
Bryan Publishing Company 419 485-3113
319 W Main St Montpelier (43543) ***(G-14302)***
Bryce Hill Inc 937 663-4152
8801 State Route 36 Saint Paris (43072) ***(G-16705)***
Bryce Hill Inc (PA) 937 325-0651
2301 Sheridan Ave Springfield (45505) ***(G-17369)***
Brydet Development Corporation 740 623-0455
16867 State Route 83 Coshocton (43812) ***(G-7723)***
Bsa Industries Inc 614 846-5515
6510 Huntley Rd Columbus (43229) ***(G-6706)***
BSC Environmental, Bowling Green *Also called Bio-Systems Corporation* ***(G-1956)***
Bse Welding & Fabricating LLC 419 547-1043
1787 N State Route 510 Vickery (43464) ***(G-19194)***
BSK Industries Inc (PA) 440 230-9299
10143 Royalton Rd Ste C North Royalton (44133) ***(G-15264)***
Bsm Columbus Llp 740 755-2380
2677 Harrison Rd New Albany (43054) ***(G-14611)***
BT Energy Corporation (PA) 740 373-6134
1635 Warren Chapel Rd Fleming (45729) ***(G-9779)***
BT Investments II Inc 937 434-4321
601 Congress Park Dr Dayton (45459) ***(G-8066)***
Bta Enterprises Inc 937 277-0881
4090 Little Richmond Rd Dayton (45417) ***(G-8067)***
Bta of Motorcars Inc 440 716-1000
27500 Lorain Rd North Olmsted (44070) ***(G-15182)***
Btc Inc 740 549-2722
8842 Whitney Dr Lewis Center (43035) ***(G-11753)***
Btc Technology Services Inc 740 549-2722
617 Carle Ave Lewis Center (43035) ***(G-11754)***
Btg Labs, Saint Bernard *Also called Brighton Technologies LLC* ***(G-16620)***
Btg Labs, Cincinnati *Also called Brighton Technologies Group* ***(G-3417)***
BTS Ice Cream, Columbus *Also called Better Than Sex Ice Cream LLC* ***(G-6664)***
Btw LLC 419 382-4443
2226 Greenlawn Dr Toledo (43614) ***(G-18217)***
Bu E Comp Inc 419 284-3381
7092 S State Route 19 Bloomville (44818) ***(G-1712)***
Bucher Printing, Dayton *Also called Keithley Enterprises Inc* ***(G-8290)***
Buck Creek Pallet 937 653-3098
713 Muzzy Rd Urbana (43078) ***(G-18981)***
Buck Equipment Inc 614 539-3039
1720 Feddern Ave Grove City (43123) ***(G-10419)***
Buck Eye Pressure Wash 419 385-9274
5242 Angola Rd Ste 130 Toledo (43615) ***(G-18218)***
Buckeye Abrasive Inc 330 753-1041
1020 Eagon St Barberton (44203) ***(G-1067)***
Buckeye Aluminum Foundry Inc (PA) 440 428-7180
457 N Lake St Madison (44057) ***(G-12340)***
Buckeye Asphalt Paving Co, Toledo *Also called Lucas County Asphalt Inc* ***(G-18389)***
Buckeye Blow Out Preventer, Newcomerstown *Also called Buckeye BOP LLC* ***(G-14971)***
Buckeye BOP LLC 740 498-9898
401 Enterprise Dr Newcomerstown (43832) ***(G-14971)***
Buckeye Boxes Inc (PA) 614 274-8484
601 N Hague Ave Columbus (43204) ***(G-6707)***
Buckeye Boxes Inc 937 599-2551
1133 W Columbus Ave Bellefontaine (43311) ***(G-1508)***
Buckeye Boxes Inc 614 274-8484
601 N Hague Ave Columbus (43204) ***(G-6708)***
Buckeye Brake Manufacturing 740 782-1379
40168 National Rd W Morristown (43759) ***(G-14406)***
Buckeye Brine LLC 740 575-4482
23986 Airport Rd Coshocton (43812) ***(G-7724)***
Buckeye Building Products, Reynoldsburg *Also called Buckeye Ready-Mix LLC* ***(G-16431)***
Buckeye Business Forms Inc 614 882-1890
7307 Red Bank Rd Westerville (43082) ***(G-19982)***
Buckeye Business Products, Cleveland *Also called Kroy LLC* ***(G-5544)***
Buckeye Companies (PA) 740 452-3641
999 Zane St Zanesville (43701) ***(G-21112)***
Buckeye Components LLC 330 482-5163
1340 State Route 14 Columbiana (44408) ***(G-6456)***

Buckeye Composites, Kettering *Also called Nanotechlabs Inc* ***(G-11436)***
Buckeye Container Division, Wooster *Also called Buckeye Corrugated Inc* ***(G-20575)***
Buckeye Corrugated Inc (PA)...330 576-0590
822 Kumho Dr Ste 400 Fairlawn (44333) ***(G-9599)***
Buckeye Corrugated Inc...330 264-6336
3350 Long Rd Wooster (44691) ***(G-20575)***
Buckeye Counters...330 682-0902
10207 Ely Rd Orrville (44667) ***(G-15585)***
Buckeye Cstm Screen Print EMB...614 237-0196
3822 Elbern Ave Columbus (43213) ***(G-6709)***
Buckeye Custom Fab, Fort Jennings *Also called Bcfab Inc* ***(G-9791)***
Buckeye Delivery, Mansfield *Also called Buckeye Vault Service Inc* ***(G-12416)***
Buckeye Design & Engr Svc LLC...419 375-4241
2600 Wabash Rd Fort Recovery (45846) ***(G-9812)***
Buckeye Diamond Logistics Inc (PA)...937 462-8361
15 Sprague Rd South Charleston (45368) ***(G-17271)***
Buckeye Diamond Logistics Inc...937 644-2194
21963 Northwest Pkwy Marysville (43040) ***(G-12772)***
Buckeye Dimensions LLC...330 857-0223
1543 Zuercher Rd Dalton (44618) ***(G-7936)***
Buckeye Distillery...937 877-1901
130 W Plum St Tipp City (45371) ***(G-18103)***
Buckeye Electrical Products...937 693-7519
100 Commerce Dr Botkins (45306) ***(G-1935)***
Buckeye Energy Resources Inc...740 452-9506
999 Zane St Zanesville (43701) ***(G-21113)***
Buckeye Engraving, Kent *Also called Raschke Engraving Inc* ***(G-11373)***
Buckeye Fabricating Co...937 746-9822
245 S Pioneer Blvd Springboro (45066) ***(G-17323)***
BUCKEYE FASTENERS COMPANY, Girard *Also called Brainard Rivet Company* ***(G-10254)***
BUCKEYE FASTENERS COMPANY, Streetsboro *Also called Joseph Industries Inc* ***(G-17680)***
Buckeye Fbricators of Leetonia...330 427-0330
38009 Butcher Rd Leetonia (44431) ***(G-11716)***
Buckeye Field Machining Inc...330 336-7036
2131 Wadsworth Rd Ste 500 Norton (44203) ***(G-15362)***
Buckeye Field Supply Ltd...513 312-2343
8190 Beechmont Ave 262a Cincinnati (45255) ***(G-3428)***
Buckeye Franklin Co...330 859-2465
3471 New Zoarville Rd Ne Zoarville (44656) ***(G-21195)***
Buckeye Gear Co...216 292-7998
16354 Stone Ridge Rd Chagrin Falls (44023) ***(G-3038)***
Buckeye Lake Beacon, Buckeye Lake *Also called Impact Publications* ***(G-2315)***
Buckeye Lake Shopper Reporter...740 246-4741
14886 State Route 13 Thornville (43076) ***(G-18030)***
Buckeye Mch Fabricators Inc...419 273-2521
610 E Lima St Forest (45843) ***(G-9785)***
Buckeye Medical Tech LLC...330 719-9868
405 Niles Cortland Rd Se # 202 Warren (44484) ***(G-19379)***
Buckeye Metal Works Inc...614 239-8000
3240 Petzinger Rd Columbus (43232) ***(G-6710)***
Buckeye Metals, Cleveland *Also called W R G Inc* ***(G-6279)***
Buckeye Metals...740 446-9590
185 Curr Rd Bidwell (45614) ***(G-1665)***
Buckeye Metals Industries Inc...216 663-4300
3238 E 82nd St Cleveland (44104) ***(G-4849)***
Buckeye Molded Products Ltd...440 323-2244
443 Oberlin Elyria Rd Elyria (44035) ***(G-9226)***
Buckeye Oil Producing Co...330 264-8847
544 E Liberty St Wooster (44691) ***(G-20576)***
Buckeye Pallett...330 359-5919
3463 County Road 160 Millersburg (44654) ***(G-14070)***
Buckeye Paper Co Inc...330 477-5925
5233 Southway St Sw # 523 Canton (44706) ***(G-2600)***
Buckeye Polymers Inc (PA)...330 948-3007
104 Lee St Lodi (44254) ***(G-12008)***
Buckeye Post...330 724-2800
1266 Grant St Akron (44301) ***(G-97)***
Buckeye Prep Magazine, New Albany *Also called Buckeye Prep Report Magazine* ***(G-14612)***
Buckeye Prep Report Magazine...614 855-6977
8599 Swisher Creek Xing New Albany (43054) ***(G-14612)***
Buckeye Products...740 969-4718
6745 Chillicothe Lancster Amanda (43102) ***(G-523)***
Buckeye Raceway LLC...614 272-7888
4050 W Broad St Columbus (43228) ***(G-6711)***
Buckeye Ready Mix, Columbus *Also called Anderson Concrete Corp* ***(G-6602)***
Buckeye Ready-Mix...419 294-2389
6326 County Highway 61 Upper Sandusky (43351) ***(G-18948)***
Buckeye Ready-Mix LLC...740 967-4801
7720 Jhnstown Alxndria Rd Johnstown (43031) ***(G-11260)***
Buckeye Ready-Mix LLC...614 879-6316
6600 State Route 29 West Jefferson (43162) ***(G-19921)***
Buckeye Ready-Mix LLC...740 387-8846
627 Likens Rd Marion (43302) ***(G-12696)***
Buckeye Ready-Mix LLC (PA)...614 575-2132
7657 Taylor Rd Sw Reynoldsburg (43068) ***(G-16431)***
Buckeye Ready-Mix LLC...937 642-2951
838 N Main St Marysville (43040) ***(G-12773)***
Buckeye Ready-Mix LLC...740 654-4423
1750 Logan Langster Rd Lancaster (43130) ***(G-11549)***
Buckeye Rocker, Millersburg *Also called M H Woodworking LLC* ***(G-14108)***
Buckeye Rubber Products, Lima *Also called Brp Manufacturing Company* ***(G-11847)***
Buckeye Sanitary Service, Springfield *Also called Reed Elvin Burl II* ***(G-17482)***
Buckeye Seating LLC...330 473-2379
6960 County Road 672 Millersburg (44654) ***(G-14071)***
Buckeye Shapeform, Columbus *Also called Buckeye Stamping Company* ***(G-6712)***
Buckeye Sports Bulletin, Columbus *Also called Columbus-Sports Publications* ***(G-6804)***
Buckeye Stamping Company...614 445-0059
555 Marion Rd Columbus (43207) ***(G-6712)***
Buckeye State Welding & Fabg...440 322-0344
175 Woodford Ave Elyria (44035) ***(G-9227)***
Buckeye State Wldg & Fabg Inc (PA)...440 322-0319
131 Buckeye St Elyria (44035) ***(G-9228)***
Buckeye Steel Inc...740 425-2306
607 Watt Ave Barnesville (43713) ***(G-1116)***
Buckeye Tractor Company Corp...419 659-2162
11313 Slabtown Rd Columbus Grove (45830) ***(G-7631)***
Buckeye Vault Service Inc...419 747-1976
2253 Stiving Rd Mansfield (44903) ***(G-12416)***
Buckeye Volleyball Center LLC...614 764-1075
7824 Maplecreek Ct Powell (43065) ***(G-16309)***
Buckeye Welding...330 674-0944
2507 Township Road 110 Millersburg (44654) ***(G-14072)***
Buckhorn, Milford *Also called Bkhn Inc* ***(G-13998)***
Buckhorn Inc (HQ)...513 831-4402
55 W Techne Center Dr A Milford (45150) ***(G-14000)***
Buckhorn Material Hdlg Group...513 831-4402
55 W Techne Center Dr A Milford (45150) ***(G-14001)***
Buckley Manufacturing Company...513 821-4444
10333 Wayne Ave Ste 1 Cincinnati (45215) ***(G-3429)***
Buckman Machine Works Inc...330 525-7665
24841 Georgetown Rd Homeworth (44634) ***(G-10987)***
Bucktask, Columbus *Also called Pmj Partners LLC* ***(G-7330)***
Buckys Machine and Fab Ltd...419 981-5050
8376 S County Road 47 Mc Cutchenville (44844) ***(G-13191)***
Bucyrus Blades Inc (HQ)...419 562-6015
260 E Beal Ave Bucyrus (44820) ***(G-2318)***
Bucyrus Extruded Composites, Bloomville *Also called Buecomp Inc* ***(G-1713)***
Bucyrus Graphics Inc...419 562-2906
214 W Liberty St Bucyrus (44820) ***(G-2319)***
Bucyrus Ice Company, Bucyrus *Also called Velvet Ice Cream Company* ***(G-2348)***
Bucyrus Precision Tech Inc...419 563-9950
200 Crossroads Blvd Bucyrus (44820) ***(G-2320)***
Bud Corp...740 967-9992
158 Commerce Blvd Johnstown (43031) ***(G-11261)***
Bud Industries Inc (PA)...440 946-3200
4605 E 355th St Willoughby (44094) ***(G-20289)***
Bud May Inc...216 676-8850
16850 Hummel Rd Cleveland (44142) ***(G-4850)***
Budd Co Plastics Div...419 238-4332
1276 Industrial Dr Van Wert (45891) ***(G-19081)***
Budde Sheet Metal Works Inc (PA)...937 224-0868
305 Leo St Dayton (45404) ***(G-8068)***
Buddy Backyard Inc...330 393-9353
140 Dana St Ne Warren (44483) ***(G-19380)***
Buderer Drug Co (PA)...419 626-3429
633 Hancock St Sandusky (44870) ***(G-16798)***
Buderer Drug Company Inc (PA)...419 627-2800
633 Hancock St Sandusky (44870) ***(G-16799)***
Buderer Drug Company Inc...419 873-2800
26611 Dixie Hwy Ste 119 Perrysburg (43551) ***(G-15925)***
Buderer Drug Company Inc...440 934-3100
38530 Chester Rd Ste 400 Avon (44011) ***(G-943)***
Budget Blinds, Strongsville *Also called Cascade Group of Ohio Limited* ***(G-17723)***
Budget Molders Supply Inc...216 367-7050
8303 Corporate Park Dr Macedonia (44056) ***(G-12281)***
Budget Newspaper, The, Sugarcreek *Also called Sugarcreek Budget Publishers* ***(G-17867)***
Buds Sign Shop Inc...330 744-5555
892 Mahoning Ave Youngstown (44502) ***(G-20861)***
Buecomp Inc...419 284-3840
7016 S State Route 19 Bloomville (44818) ***(G-1713)***
Buffalo Abrasives Inc...614 891-6450
1093 Smoke Burr Dr Westerville (43081) ***(G-20039)***
Buffalo Peanuts, Columbus *Also called Nuts Are Good Inc* ***(G-7233)***
Buffex Metal Finishing Inc...216 631-2202
1935 W 96th St Ste L Cleveland (44102) ***(G-4851)***
Bugh Vinyl Products Inc...330 305-0978
8933 Cleveland Ave Nw Canton (44720) ***(G-2601)***
Buhi Imports...440 224-0013
3210 E Center St North Kingsville (44068) ***(G-15159)***
Buildcret Concrete, Glenford *Also called James Ryan Soloman* ***(G-10270)***
Builder Tech Wholesale LLC...419 535-7606
2931 South Ave Toledo (43609) ***(G-18219)***
Builder Tech Windows, Toledo *Also called Builder Tech Wholesale LLC* ***(G-18219)***
Builders Straight Edge, Elyria *Also called B&B Distributors LLC* ***(G-9221)***

ALPHABETIC

Building & Conveyer Maint LLC...303 882-0912
8756 Peck Rd Ravenna (44266) ***(G-16371)***
Building Block Performance LLC...614 918-7476
7920 Corporate Blvd Ste C Plain City (43064) ***(G-16179)***
Building Concepts Inc (PA)...419 298-2371
444 N Michigan Ave Edgerton (43517) ***(G-9169)***
Building Ctrl Integrators LLC (PA)...614 334-3300
383 N Liberty St Powell (43065) ***(G-16310)***
Building Ctrl Integrators LLC...513 247-6154
300 E Bus Way Ste 200 Cincinnati (45241) ***(G-3430)***
Building Ctrl Integrators LLC...440 526-6660
6900 W Snowville Rd Brecksville (44141) ***(G-2025)***
Building Ctrl Integrators LLC...513 860-9600
10174 International Blvd West Chester (45246) ***(G-19836)***
Building Rlationships Together, Niles *Also called BRT Extrusions Inc* ***(G-15001)***
Built-Rite Box & Crate Inc...330 263-0936
608 Freedlander Rd Wooster (44691) ***(G-20577)***
Bula Forge & Machine Inc...216 252-7600
3001 W 121st St Cleveland (44111) ***(G-4852)***
Bulk Apothecary, Aurora *Also called Natural Essentials Inc* ***(G-895)***
Bulk Carrier Trnsp Eqp Co...330 339-3333
2743 Brightwood Rd Se New Philadelphia (44663) ***(G-14762)***
Bulk Handling Equipment Co...330 468-5703
28 W Aurora Rd Northfield (44067) ***(G-15314)***
Bulk Molding Compounds Inc...419 874-7941
12600 Eckel Rd Perrysburg (43551) ***(G-15926)***
Bull Moose Tube Company...330 448-4878
1433 Standard Ave Masury (44438) ***(G-13059)***
Bulldogsecurity, Steubenville *Also called Access 2 Communications Inc* ***(G-17525)***
Bullen Ultrasonics Inc...937 456-7133
1301 Miller Williams Rd Eaton (45320) ***(G-9144)***
Bullseye LLC...216 272-7050
2830 Attleboro Rd Shaker Heights (44120) ***(G-16926)***
Bullseye Activewear Inc...330 220-1720
2947 Nationwide Pkwy Brunswick (44212) ***(G-2193)***
Bullseye Dart Shoppe Inc...440 951-9277
950c Erie Rd Willoughby (44095) ***(G-20290)***
Bullseye Machines LLC...419 485-5951
1224 Charlies Way Montpelier (43543) ***(G-14303)***
Bully Tools Inc...740 282-5834
14 Technology Way Steubenville (43952) ***(G-17529)***
Bunge North America Foundation...740 383-1181
751 E Farming St Marion (43302) ***(G-12697)***
Bunge North America Foundation...419 483-5340
605 Goodrich Rd Bellevue (44811) ***(G-1533)***
Bunge North America Foundation...740 426-6332
12574 State Route 41 Jeffersonville (43128) ***(G-11245)***
Bunker Hill Cheese Co Inc...330 893-2131
6005 County Road 77 Millersburg (44654) ***(G-14073)***
Bunny B, Cuyahoga Falls *Also called Ascot Valley Foods LLC* ***(G-7840)***
Buns of Delaware Inc...740 363-2867
14 W Winter St Delaware (43015) ***(G-8659)***
Buns Restaurant & Bakery, Delaware *Also called Buns of Delaware Inc* ***(G-8659)***
Bunting Bearings LLC...419 522-3323
153 E 5th St Mansfield (44902) ***(G-12417)***
Bunting Bearings LLC (PA)...419 866-7000
1001 Holland Park Blvd Holland (43528) ***(G-10917)***
Burdens Machine & Welding...740 345-9246
94 S 5th St Newark (43055) ***(G-14857)***
Burghardt Manufacturing Inc...330 253-7590
1524 Massillon Rd Akron (44306) ***(G-98)***
Burghardt Metal Fabg Inc...330 794-1830
1638 Mcchesney Rd Akron (44306) ***(G-99)***
Burgie Brauerei Inc...740 344-1620
860 Village Pkwy Newark (43055) ***(G-14858)***
Burial Vaults By Neher, Springfield *Also called Neher Burial Vault Company* ***(G-17460)***
Burke & Company, Cincinnati *Also called Patrick J Burke & Co* ***(G-4137)***
Burke Products Inc...937 372-3516
1355 Enterprise Ln Xenia (45385) ***(G-20759)***
Burkett Advnced Composite Tech, West Liberty *Also called BAC Technologies Ltd* ***(G-19935)***
Burkett Industries Inc...419 332-4391
507 Vine St Fremont (43420) ***(G-10002)***
Burkettsville Stockyard, Burkettsville *Also called Werling and Sons Inc* ***(G-2356)***
Burkholder Buggy Shop...330 674-5891
7400 County Road 77 Millersburg (44654) ***(G-14074)***
Burn-Rite Mold & Machine Inc...330 956-4143
2401 Shepler Ch Ave Sw Canton (44706) ***(G-2602)***
Burner Tech Unlimited Inc...440 232-3200
1499 Enterprise Pkwy Twinsburg (44087) ***(G-18744)***
Burns & Rink Enterprises LLC...513 421-7799
2016 Elm St Cincinnati (45202) ***(G-3431)***
Burrrows Paper Corroc Div, Franklin *Also called Novolex Holdings Inc* ***(G-9905)***
Burt Manufacturing Company Inc...330 762-0061
44 E South St Akron (44311) ***(G-100)***
Burton Industries Inc...440 974-1700
7875 Division Dr Mentor (44060) ***(G-13407)***
Burton Metal Finishing Inc...614 252-9523
1711 Woodland Ave Columbus (43219) ***(G-6713)***
Burton Metal Finishing, Inc. &, Columbus *Also called Burton Metal Finishing Inc* ***(G-6713)***
Burton Rubber Processing, Burton *Also called Hexpol Compounding LLC* ***(G-2360)***
Busch & Thiem Inc...419 625-7515
1316 Cleveland Rd Sandusky (44870) ***(G-16800)***
Busch Properties Inc...614 888-0946
1103 Schrock Rd Ste 200 Columbus (43229) ***(G-6714)***
Buschman Corporation...216 431-6633
4100 Payne Ave Ste 1 Cleveland (44103) ***(G-4853)***
Buses International...440 233-4091
702 N Ridge Rd E Lorain (44055) ***(G-12081)***
Bush Inc...216 362-6700
15901 Industrial Pkwy Cleveland (44135) ***(G-4854)***
Bush Integrated, Cleveland *Also called PJ Bush Associates Inc* ***(G-5881)***
Bush Specialty Vehicles Inc...937 382-5502
80 Park Dr Wilmington (45177) ***(G-20487)***
Bushong Auto Service, Troy *Also called Mader Automotive Center Inc* ***(G-18685)***
Bushworks Incorporated...937 767-1713
144 Cliff St Ste A Yellow Springs (45387) ***(G-20805)***
Business Courier, Cincinnati *Also called American City Bus Journals Inc* ***(G-3331)***
Business First Columbus Inc (HQ)...614 461-4040
300 Marconi Blvd Ste 105 Columbus (43215) ***(G-6715)***
Business Fnctnality Forms Svcs...614 557-9420
4367 Grays Market Dr Gahanna (43230) ***(G-10077)***
Business Idntification Systems...614 841-1255
6185 Huntley Rd Ste M Columbus (43229) ***(G-6716)***
Business Journal...330 744-5023
25 E Boardman St Ste 306 Youngstown (44503) ***(G-20862)***
Business Journal, The, Youngstown *Also called Business Journal* ***(G-20862)***
Business Stationery, Cleveland *Also called Identity Holding Company LLC* ***(G-5435)***
Busse Combat Knives, Wauseon *Also called Busse Knife Co* ***(G-19511)***
Busse Knife Co...419 923-6471
11651 County Road 12 Wauseon (43567) ***(G-19511)***
Busson Digital Printing Inc...330 753-8373
1061 Eastern Rd Wadsworth (44281) ***(G-19228)***
Busy Bee Lumber...330 674-1305
5965 Township Road 355 Millersburg (44654) ***(G-14075)***
Butera Manufacturing Inc...440 516-3698
2935 Lynn Dr Willoughby Hills (44092) ***(G-20467)***
Butera Manufacturing Inds...216 761-8800
1068 E 134th St Cleveland (44110) ***(G-4855)***
Butler Machine, Columbus *Also called Bmi Machine Inc* ***(G-6682)***
Butler Tech Career Dev Schools...513 867-1028
3611 Hmlton Middletown Rd Fairfield Township (45011) ***(G-9580)***
Butt Hut, Findlay *Also called Smoke Rings Inc* ***(G-9757)***
Butt Hut of America Inc...419 443-1997
1972 W Market St Tiffin (44883) ***(G-18053)***
Buttkicker, Westerville *Also called Guitammer Company* ***(G-19995)***
Buy Truck Wheels, Galena *Also called Ws Trading LLC* ***(G-10118)***
Buyers Products Company (PA)...440 974-8888
9049 Tyler Blvd Mentor (44060) ***(G-13408)***
Buyers Products Company...440 974-8888
8120 Tyler Blvd Mentor (44060) ***(G-13409)***
Buyers Products Company...440 974-8888
7700 Tyler Blvd Mentor (44060) ***(G-13410)***
Buzz N Shuttle Service...740 223-0567
333 Executive Dr Apt I Marion (43302) ***(G-12698)***
Buzz Seating Inc (PA)...877 263-5737
623 N Wayne Ave Cincinnati (45215) ***(G-3432)***
BV Thermal Systems LLC...209 522-3701
38241 Willoughby Pkwy Willoughby (44094) ***(G-20291)***
Bw Supply Co., Lyons *Also called B W Grinding Co* ***(G-12273)***
BWAY Corporation...513 388-2200
8200 Broadwell Rd Cincinnati (45244) ***(G-3433)***
Bwaypackaging, Cincinnati *Also called BWAY Corporation* ***(G-3433)***
Bwi Chassis Dynamics NA Inc...937 455-5100
3100 Research Blvd Kettering (45420) ***(G-11427)***
Bwi Group, Kettering *Also called Bwi North America Inc* ***(G-11429)***
Bwi North America Inc...937 455-5190
3100 Res Blvd Ste 210 Kettering (45420) ***(G-11428)***
Bwi North America Inc (HQ)...937 253-1130
3100 Res Blvd Ste 240 Kettering (45420) ***(G-11429)***
Bwx Technologies Inc...740 687-4180
2600 E Main St Lancaster (43130) ***(G-11550)***
Bwxt Nclear Oprtions Group Inc...330 860-1010
91 Stirling Ave Barberton (44203) ***(G-1068)***
Byedak Construction Ltd...937 414-6153
7406 New Pris Gttysbrg Rd New Paris (45347) ***(G-14752)***
Byer Steel Rebar Inc...513 821-6400
200 W North Bend Rd Cincinnati (45216) ***(G-3434)***
Byers Sign Co...614 561-1224
2940 E 14th Ave Columbus (43219) ***(G-6717)***
Byler Truss...330 465-5412
1271 State Route 96 Ashland (44805) ***(G-688)***
Byrd Prcurement Specialist Inc...419 936-0019
12150 Monclova Rd Swanton (43558) ***(G-17908)***
Byron Products Inc...513 870-9111
3781 Port Union Rd Fairfield (45014) ***(G-9486)***

C & B Logging Inc 740 347-4844
9821 State Route 13 Se Glouster (45732) ***(G-10275)***
C & C Fabrication Inc 419 354-3535
18237 N Dixie Hwy Bowling Green (43402) ***(G-1958)***
C & C Metal Products, Wooster *Also called Global Body & Equipment Co* ***(G-20597)***
C & C Mobile Homes LLC 740 663-5535
1580 Valley Rd Waverly (45690) ***(G-19541)***
C & D Counters 740 259-5529
359b Back St Lucasville (45648) ***(G-12260)***
C & D Manufacturing Inc 330 828-8357
374 Eckard Rd Dalton (44618) ***(G-7937)***
C & D Tool Inc 440 942-8463
35595 Curtis Blvd Unit F Eastlake (44095) ***(G-9099)***
C & F Fabrications Inc 937 666-3234
3100 State St East Liberty (43319) ***(G-9046)***
C & G Associates Inc 419 756-6583
3130 Hastings Newville Rd Mansfield (44903) ***(G-12418)***
C & K Machine Co Inc 419 237-3203
604 N Park St Fayette (43521) ***(G-9632)***
C & L Erectors & Riggers Inc 740 332-7185
16412 Thompson Ridge Rd Laurelville (43135) ***(G-11626)***
C & L Supply, Logan *Also called Kilbarger Construction Inc* ***(G-12030)***
C & M Rubber Co Inc 937 299-2782
414 Littell Ave Dayton (45419) ***(G-8069)***
C & M Welding Services LLC 419 584-0008
1405 James Dr Celina (45822) ***(G-2951)***
C & R Inc (PA) 614 497-1130
5600 Clyde Moore Dr Groveport (43125) ***(G-10486)***
C & S Associates Inc 440 461-9661
729 Miner Rd Highland Heights (44143) ***(G-10786)***
C & S Turf Care Equipment Inc 330 966-4511
6207 Dressler Rd Nw North Canton (44720) ***(G-15074)***
C & W Custom Wdwkg Co Inc 513 891-6340
11949 Tramway Dr Cincinnati (45241) ***(G-3435)***
C A I R Ohio 513 281-8200
10999 Reed Hartman Hwy # 207 Blue Ash (45242) ***(G-1743)***
C A Joseph Co (PA) 330 385-6869
13712 Old Frdericktown Rd East Liverpool (43920) ***(G-9051)***
C A Joseph Co 330 532-4646
170 Broadway St Irondale (43932) ***(G-11158)***
C A Kustoms 419 332-4395
524 N Stone St Fremont (43420) ***(G-10003)***
C A P Industries Inc 937 773-1824
543 Staunton St Piqua (45356) ***(G-16105)***
C and J Machine Inc 330 935-2170
403 State Route 44 Hartville (44632) ***(G-10685)***
C and O Electric Motor Service 614 491-6387
3105 Hillgate Rd Columbus (43207) ***(G-6718)***
C B & S Spouting Inc 937 866-1600
4609 Slders Hm Mmsburg Rd Miamisburg (45342) ***(G-13646)***
C B C, Marysville *Also called Contract Building Components* ***(G-12777)***
C B Mfg & Sls Co Inc (PA) 937 866-5986
4455 Infirmary Rd Miamisburg (45342) ***(G-13647)***
C D C At Cityview 216 426-2020
6606 Carnegie Ave Cleveland (44103) ***(G-4856)***
C D I, Miamisburg *Also called Connective Design Incorporated* ***(G-13651)***
C D R Pigments Dispersions Div, Cincinnati *Also called Flint Group US LLC* ***(G-3695)***
C Dcap Modem Line 419 748-7409
232 S East St Mc Clure (43534) ***(G-13185)***
C Dcap Modem Line 440 685-4302
8829 State Route 45 North Bloomfield (44450) ***(G-15063)***
C E D Process Minerals Inc (PA) 330 666-5500
863 N Clvland Mssillon Rd Akron (44333) ***(G-101)***
C E Electronics Inc 419 636-6705
2107 Industrial Dr Bryan (43506) ***(G-2275)***
C E Kegg Inc (PA) 330 877-8800
1184 Woodland St Sw Hartville (44632) ***(G-10686)***
C E White Co (HQ) 419 492-2157
417 N Kibler St New Washington (44854) ***(G-14827)***
C F Doors, Cleveland *Also called Clear Fold Door Inc* ***(G-4942)***
C F Poeppelman Inc (PA) 937 448-2191
4755 N State Route 721 Bradford (45308) ***(G-2010)***
C F Poeppelman Inc 937 526-5137
10175 Old State Route 121 Versailles (45380) ***(G-19175)***
C G C Systems Inc 330 678-3261
4763 Sherman Rd Kent (44240) ***(G-11302)***
C G Egli Inc 937 254-8898
515 Springfield St Dayton (45403) ***(G-8070)***
C G S, Cleveland *Also called Centerless Grinding Service* ***(G-4900)***
C H R Industries Inc 440 361-0744
185 Water St Ste 6 Geneva (44041) ***(G-10215)***
C H T, Cleveland *Also called Compliant Healthcare Tech LLC* ***(G-5011)***
C H Washington Water Plan 740 636-2382
220 Park Ave Wshngtn CT Hs (43160) ***(G-20721)***
C Imperial Inc 937 669-5620
1322 Commerce Park Dr Tipp City (45371) ***(G-18104)***
C J Kraft Enterprises Inc 740 653-9606
301 S Maple St Lancaster (43130) ***(G-11551)***
C J Krehbiel Company 513 271-6035
3962 Virginia Ave Cincinnati (45227) ***(G-3436)***
C J Smith Machinery Service 614 348-1376
3000 E Main St Ste B Columbus (43209) ***(G-6719)***
C JS Signs 330 821-7446
1670 Charl Ann Dr Alliance (44601) ***(G-459)***
C L D, Franklin *Also called 119c Landis Display Co* ***(G-9865)***
C L S Finishing Inc 330 784-4134
409 Munroe Falls Rd Tallmadge (44278) ***(G-17974)***
C L S Inc 216 251-5011
3812 W 150th St Cleveland (44111) ***(G-4857)***
C L W Inc 740 374-8443
1201 Gilman Ave Marietta (45750) ***(G-12611)***
C M A Supply Company, West Chester *Also called CMA Supply Company Inc* ***(G-19844)***
C M C, Hamilton *Also called Connector Manufacturing Co* ***(G-10548)***
C M L Concrete Construction 330 758-8314
482 Garden Valley Ct Youngstown (44512) ***(G-20863)***
C M M S - Re Inc 513 489-5111
6130 Interstate Cir Blue Ash (45242) ***(G-1744)***
C M M S - Re LLC (PA) 513 489-5111
6130 Interstate Cir Blue Ash (45242) ***(G-1745)***
C M Slicechief Co 419 241-7647
3333 Maple St Toledo (43608) ***(G-18220)***
C M Stephanoff Jewelers Inc 440 526-5890
8718 Bradford Ln Brecksville (44141) ***(G-2026)***
C M Tech, Delaware *Also called Cast Metals Technology Inc* ***(G-8661)***
C Massouh Printing, Canal Fulton *Also called C Massouh Printing Co Inc* ***(G-2478)***
C Massouh Printing Co Inc 330 408-7330
590 Elm Ridge Ave Canal Fulton (44614) ***(G-2478)***
C Massouh Printing Co Inc 330 832-6334
9589 Portage St Nw Massillon (44646) ***(G-12964)***
C Massouh Printing Services, Massillon *Also called C Massouh Printing Co Inc* ***(G-12964)***
C N C Precision Machine Inc 440 548-3880
18360 Industrial Cir Parkman (44080) ***(G-15810)***
C Nelson Manufacturing Co 419 898-3305
265 N Lake Winds Pkwy Oak Harbor (43449) ***(G-15442)***
C O Welding & Fabrication Inc 419 394-3293
850 S Main St Saint Marys (45885) ***(G-16680)***
C P Electric Motor Repair Inc 330 425-9593
2212 E Aurora Rd Twinsburg (44087) ***(G-18745)***
C P S Enterprises Inc 216 441-7969
9815 Reno Ave Cleveland (44105) ***(G-4858)***
C RC Automotive 513 422-4775
460 N Verity Pkwy Middletown (45042) ***(G-13889)***
C S A Enterprises 740 342-9367
932 S Main St New Lexington (43764) ***(G-14713)***
C S Bell Co 419 448-0791
170 W Davis St Tiffin (44883) ***(G-18054)***
C S I, Toledo *Also called Chem-Sales Inc* ***(G-18228)***
C S I, Harrison *Also called Coating Systems Inc* ***(G-10637)***
C S Johns Company, Berea *Also called Mr 14k Inc* ***(G-1618)***
C S T Geometric Forms, Lorain *Also called Custom Sink Top Mfg* ***(G-12087)***
C Soltesz Co 614 529-5494
4374 Dublin Rd Columbus (43221) ***(G-6720)***
C Square Lumber Products 740 557-3129
1541 S Elliott Rd Stockport (43787) ***(G-17559)***
C Stoneman Corporation 440 942-3325
100 E Shore Blvd Eastlake (44095) ***(G-9100)***
C T Chemicals Inc 513 459-9744
4110 Columbia Rd Lebanon (45036) ***(G-11638)***
C T I Audio Inc 440 593-1111
220 Eastview Dr Ste 1 Brooklyn Heights (44131) ***(G-2117)***
C W Ohio, Conneaut *Also called Cascade Ohio Inc* ***(G-7642)***
C&H Industries 330 899-0001
2054 Jaquelyn Dr Canton (44720) ***(G-2603)***
C&W Swiss Inc 937 832-2889
100 Lau Pkwy Englewood (45315) ***(G-9350)***
C-H Tool & Die 740 397-7214
711 N Sandusky St Mount Vernon (43050) ***(G-14471)***
C-Hawk Trailers, Bucyrus *Also called Lux Corporation* ***(G-2338)***
C-Link Enterprises LLC 937 222-2829
1825 Webster St Dayton (45404) ***(G-8071)***
C-N-D Industries Inc 330 478-8811
359 State Ave Nw Massillon (44647) ***(G-12965)***
C-Tech Industries, West Chester *Also called Tvh Parts Co* ***(G-19813)***
C.T.L. Steel Division, Columbus *Also called Clark Grave Vault Company* ***(G-6769)***
C2g, Dayton *Also called Legrand North America LLC* ***(G-8309)***
CA Litzler Co Inc 216 267-8020
4800 W 160th St Cleveland (44135) ***(G-4859)***
CA Litzler Holding Company (PA) 216 267-8020
4800 W 160th St Cleveland (44135) ***(G-4860)***
CA Picard Surface Engrg Inc 440 366-5400
1206 E Broad St Elyria (44035) ***(G-9229)***
Cabell Huntington 740 867-2665
29 Candy Ln Chesapeake (45619) ***(G-3143)***
Cabinet 2 Countertops, North Canton *Also called Navigator Construction LLC* ***(G-15106)***
Cabinet Restylers, Ashland *Also called Thiels Replacement Systems Inc* ***(G-751)***

ALPHABETIC

Cabinet Solutions By Design, Cincinnati *Also called Brower Products Inc* ***(G-3426)***
Cabinet Source 330 336-5600
8100 Wadsworth Rd Wadsworth (44281) ***(G-19229)***
Cabinet Specialties Inc 330 695-3463
10738 Criswell Rd Fredericksburg (44627) ***(G-9944)***
Cabinet Studio, Bedford *Also called Barta Viorel* ***(G-1387)***
Cabinet Systems Inc 440 237-1924
9830 York Theta Dr Cleveland (44133) ***(G-4861)***
Cabinet Works, Columbus *Also called Cabintpak Kitchens of Columbus* ***(G-6721)***
Cabinetry By Ebbing 419 678-2191
5765 State Route 219 Celina (45822) ***(G-2952)***
Cabinetworks Unlimited LLC 234 320-4107
1725 Salem Pkwy W Salem (44460) ***(G-16722)***
Cabintpak Kitchens of Columbus 614 294-4646
899 King Ave Columbus (43212) ***(G-6721)***
Cable and Ctrl Solutions LLC 937 254-2227
4726 Springfield St Dayton (45431) ***(G-7972)***
Cable Mfg & Assembly Inc (PA) 330 874-2900
10896 Industrial Pkwy Nw Bolivar (44612) ***(G-1908)***
Cable Quest, Twinsburg *Also called Print Management Partners Inc* ***(G-18839)***
Cabletek Wiring Products Inc 800 562-9378
1150 Taylor St Elyria (44035) ***(G-9230)***
Cabot Lumber Inc 740 545-7109
304 E Union Ave West Lafayette (43845) ***(G-19929)***
Cac Energy Ltd 937 867-5593
1025 N Main St Dayton (45405) ***(G-8072)***
Cad Audio LLC 440 349-4900
6573 Cochran Rd Ste I Solon (44139) ***(G-17121)***
Cadbury Schweppes Bottling 614 238-0469
950 Stelzer Rd Columbus (43219) ***(G-6722)***
Cadenza Enterprises LLC 937 428-6058
6533 Halberd Ct Dayton (45459) ***(G-8073)***
Cadillac Papers, Hamilton *Also called Gvs Industries Inc* ***(G-10565)***
Cadillac Products Inc 248 813-8255
265 S West St Lebanon (45036) ***(G-11639)***
Cado Door & Design Inc 330 343-4288
5964 Main St Se New Philadelphia (44663) ***(G-14763)***
Cado Woodworking, New Philadelphia *Also called Cado Door & Design Inc* ***(G-14763)***
Cae Ransohoff Inc 513 870-0100
4933 Provident Dr West Chester (45246) ***(G-19837)***
Caesarcreek Pallets Ltd 937 416-4447
4392 Shawnee Trl Jamestown (45335) ***(G-11219)***
Cafco Filter, Cincinnati *Also called Cincinnati A Flter Sls Svc Inc* ***(G-3478)***
Cage Gear & Machine LLC 330 452-1532
1776 Gateway Blvd Se Canton (44707) ***(G-2604)***
Cages By Jim, Cleveland *Also called Precision Wire Products Inc* ***(G-5913)***
Cahill Services Inc 216 410-5595
13000 Athens Ave Ste 104e Lakewood (44107) ***(G-11514)***
Cailin Dev Ltd Lblty Co 216 408-6261
8960 70th St Cleveland (44102) ***(G-4862)***
Cake Arts Supplies 419 472-4959
2858 W Sylvania Ave Toledo (43613) ***(G-18221)***
Cake Arts Supplies & Bakery, Toledo *Also called Cake Arts Supplies* ***(G-18221)***
Cake Decor 614 836-5533
607 Main St Groveport (43125) ***(G-10487)***
Cake LLC 614 592-7681
6724 Perimeter Loop Rd # 254 Dublin (43017) ***(G-8892)***
Cal Sales Embroidery 440 236-3820
13975 Station Rd Columbia Station (44028) ***(G-6431)***
Cal-Maine Foods Inc 937 337-9576
3078 Washington Rd Rossburg (45362) ***(G-16581)***
Cal-Maine Foods Inc 937 968-4874
1039 Zumbrum Rd Union City (45390) ***(G-18901)***
Calcol Inc 216 245-6301
23425 Bryden Rd Shaker Heights (44122) ***(G-16927)***
Caldwell Lumber & Supply Co 740 732-2306
17990 Woodsfield Rd Caldwell (43724) ***(G-2404)***
Caldwell Redi Mix Company (PA) 740 732-2906
45997 Marietta Rd Caldwell (43724) ***(G-2405)***
Caldwell Redi Mix Company 740 685-6554
209 Pioneer Rd Byesville (43723) ***(G-2379)***
Caldwell Redi-Mix Concrete, Caldwell *Also called Caldwell Redi Mix Company* ***(G-2405)***
Calgon Carbon Corporation 614 258-9501
835 N Cassady Ave Columbus (43219) ***(G-6723)***
Caliber Mold and Machine Inc 330 633-8171
1461 Industrial Pkwy Akron (44310) ***(G-102)***
California Ceramic Supply Co 216 531-9185
19451 Roseland Ave Ste A Euclid (44117) ***(G-9406)***
California Creamery Operators 440 264-5351
30003 Bainbridge Rd Solon (44139) ***(G-17122)***
California Grounds Care LLC 513 207-0244
5827 Berte St Cincinnati (45230) ***(G-3437)***
Call & Post, Cleveland *Also called King Media Enterprises Inc* ***(G-5535)***
Callahan Cutting Tools Inc 614 294-1649
915 Distribution Dr Ste A Columbus (43228) ***(G-6724)***
Callcopy Inc (HQ) 614 340-3346
555 S Front St Columbus (43215) ***(G-6725)***
Callender Group, The, Mentor *Also called Lake Publishing Inc* ***(G-13495)***
Calm, Fairlawn *Also called Collaborative For Adaptive Lif* ***(G-9601)***
Calmego Specialized Pdts LLC 937 669-5620
1569 Martindale Rd Greenville (45331) ***(G-10362)***
Calphalon Corporation (HQ) 770 418-7100
310 3rd St Perrysburg (43551) ***(G-15927)***
Calphalon Corporation 419 666-8700
310 3rd St Perrysburg (43551) ***(G-15928)***
Calvary Christian Ch of Ohio 740 828-9000
338 W 3rd St Frazeysburg (43822) ***(G-9937)***
Calvary Industries Inc (PA) 513 874-1113
9233 Seward Rd Fairfield (45014) ***(G-9487)***
Calvert Wire & Cable Corp 330 494-3248
4276 Strausser St Nw North Canton (44720) ***(G-15075)***
Calvin J Magsig 419 862-3311
343 Clinton St Elmore (43416) ***(G-9204)***
Calvin Lanier 937 952-4221
4003 Foxboro Dr Dayton (45416) ***(G-8074)***
Calzurocom 800 257-9472
8055 Corp Blvd Unit B Plain City (43064) ***(G-16180)***
CAM Co Inc (PA) 740 922-4533
6270 Wolf Run Rd Se Dennison (44621) ***(G-8783)***
CAM Machine Inc 937 663-5000
513 S Springfield St Saint Paris (43072) ***(G-16706)***
CAM Machine Inc 937 663-0680
3833 State Route 235 N Saint Paris (43072) ***(G-16707)***
CAM-Lem Inc 216 391-7750
1768 E 25th St Cleveland (44114) ***(G-4863)***
Camaco LLC 440 288-4444
3400 River Indus Pk Rd Lorain (44052) ***(G-12082)***
Camaco Lorain, Lorain *Also called Camaco LLC* ***(G-12082)***
Camargo Construction, Cincinnati *Also called Adler & Company Inc* ***(G-3298)***
Camargo Phrm Svcs LLC (PA) 513 561-3329
9825 Kenwood Rd Ste 203 Blue Ash (45242) ***(G-1746)***
Camargo Publications Inc 513 779-7177
7270 N Mingo Ln Cincinnati (45243) ***(G-3438)***
Cambridge Box & Gift Shop, Cambridge *Also called Cambridge Packaging Inc* ***(G-2430)***
Cambridge Cable Service Co 740 685-5775
58945 Country Club Rd Byesville (43723) ***(G-2380)***
Cambridge Jewelers, Hudson *Also called Cambridge Mfg Jewelers* ***(G-11035)***
Cambridge Mfg Jewelers 330 528-0207
76 Maple Dr Ste 1 Hudson (44236) ***(G-11035)***
Cambridge Mill Products Inc 330 863-1121
6005 Alliance Rd Nw Malvern (44644) ***(G-12385)***
Cambridge Ohio Production & As 740 432-6383
1521 Morton Ave Cambridge (43725) ***(G-2429)***
Cambridge Packaging Inc 740 432-3351
60794 Southgate Rd Cambridge (43725) ***(G-2430)***
Camden Concrete Products 937 456-1229
4952 State Route 732 W Eaton (45320) ***(G-9145)***
Camden Ready Mix, West Alexandria *Also called Wysong Gravel Co Inc* ***(G-19626)***
Camden Ready Mix Co (PA) 937 456-4539
478 Cmden Cllege Cornr Rd Camden (45311) ***(G-2464)***
Cameco Communications 937 840-9490
128 S High St Hillsboro (45133) ***(G-10877)***
Camela Nitschke Ribbonry 419 872-0073
119 Louisiana Ave Perrysburg (43551) ***(G-15929)***
Camelot Cellars Winery 614 441-8860
901 Oak St Columbus (43205) ***(G-6726)***
Camelot Digital, Cleveland *Also called Camelot Typesetting Company* ***(G-4864)***
Camelot Manufacturing Inc 419 678-2603
210 Butler St Coldwater (45828) ***(G-6403)***
Camelot Printing, Lodi *Also called Stephen Andrews Inc* ***(G-12020)***
Camelot Typesetting Company 216 574-8973
2570 Superior Ave E # 201 Cleveland (44114) ***(G-4864)***
Cameo Countertops Inc (PA) 419 865-6371
1610 Kieswetter Rd Holland (43528) ***(G-10918)***
Cameo Inc 419 661-9611
995 3rd St Perrysburg (43551) ***(G-15930)***
Cameron Drilling Co Inc 740 453-3300
3636 Adamsville Rd Zanesville (43701) ***(G-21114)***
Cameron International Corp 740 397-4888
8043 Columbus Rd Mount Vernon (43050) ***(G-14472)***
Cameron International Corp 740 654-4260
471 Quarry Rd Se Lancaster (43130) ***(G-11552)***
Cameron Packaging Inc 419 222-9404
250 E Hanthorn Rd Lima (45804) ***(G-11848)***
Camfil Farr, Piqua *Also called Camfil USA Inc* ***(G-16106)***
Camfil USA Inc 937 773-0866
405 Fox Dr Piqua (45356) ***(G-16106)***
Cammann Inc 440 965-4051
7105 State Route 60 Wakeman (44889) ***(G-19282)***
Cammel Saw Company Inc 330 477-3764
4898 Hills & Dales Rd Nw Canton (44708) ***(G-2605)***
Campbell Group, Cincinnati *Also called Campbell Hausfeld LLC* ***(G-3439)***
Campbell Hausfeld LLC (HQ) 513 367-4811
225 Pictoria Dr Ste 210 Cincinnati (45246) ***(G-3439)***
Campbell Signs & Apparel LLC 330 386-4768
47366 Y And O Rd East Liverpool (43920) ***(G-9052)***

Campbell Soup Company 419 592-1010
110 E Maumee Ave Napoleon (43545) *(G-14534)*
Campbells Candies 330 493-1805
3074 Chaucer Dr Ne Canton (44721) *(G-2606)*
Camphire Drilling Inc 740 599-6928
8 Ross St Danville (43014) *(G-7959)*
Campton Electric Sales & Svc 740 826-4429
11615 Norfield Rd New Concord (43762) *(G-14682)*
Cams, Delaware Also called Columbus Advnced Mfg Sftwr Inc *(G-8668)*
Camslide South, Ridgeville Corners Also called Magna International Amer Inc *(G-16512)*
Camton Mechanical Inc 614 864-7620
4531 Ellery Dr Columbus (43227) *(G-6727)*
Camx Outdoors Inc 330 474-3969
1500 Enterprise Way Kent (44240) *(G-11303)*
Canaan Country Meats 330 435-4778
11970 Canaan Center Rd Creston (44217) *(G-7804)*
Canadus Power Systems LLC 216 831-6600
9347 Ravenna Rd Ste A Twinsburg (44087) *(G-18746)*
Canal Dover Furniture LLC 330 359-5375
8211 Township Road 652 Millersburg (44654) *(G-14076)*
Canal Winchester Facility, Canal Winchester Also called Nifco America Corporation *(G-2508)*
Canberra Corporation 419 724-4300
3610 N Hlland Sylvania Rd Toledo (43615) *(G-18222)*
Candle Cottage 937 526-4041
732 E Main St Versailles (45380) *(G-19176)*
Candle-Lite Company LLC 937 780-2711
250 Eastern Ave Leesburg (45135) *(G-11708)*
Candle-Lite Company LLC (HQ) 513 563-1113
10521 Millington Ct Ste B Blue Ash (45242) *(G-1747)*
Candles By Joyce 740 886-6355
343 Township Road 1233 Proctorville (45669) *(G-16343)*
Candy Bar, Put In Bay Also called Gift Cove Inc *(G-16352)*
Canfield Coating LLC 330 533-3311
460 W Main St Canfield (44406) *(G-2524)*
Canfield Industrial Park, Canfield Also called Afc Company *(G-2519)*
Canfield Industries Inc (PA) 800 554-5071
8510 Foxwood Ct Youngstown (44514) *(G-20864)*
Canfield Manufacturing Co Inc 330 533-3333
489 Rosemont Rd North Jackson (44451) *(G-15143)*
Canine Creations 937 667-8576
120b W Broadway St Tipp City (45371) *(G-18105)*
Cannon Salt and Supply Inc 440 232-1700
26041 Cannon Rd Bedford (44146) *(G-1392)*
Canron Manufacturing Inc 330 497-1131
3979 State St Nw Greentown (44630) *(G-10357)*
Cansto Coatings Ltd 216 231-6115
9320 Woodland Ave Cleveland (44104) *(G-4865)*
Cansto Paint and Varnish Co 216 231-6115
9320 Woodland Ave Cleveland (44104) *(G-4866)*
Cantelli Block and Brick Inc (PA) 419 433-0102
1001 Sawmill Pkwy Huron (44839) *(G-11091)*
Cantex Inc 330 995-3665
11444 Chamberlain Rd 1 Aurora (44202) *(G-874)*
Canton Cabinet Co 330 455-2585
1415 7th St Nw Canton (44703) *(G-2607)*
Canton Cut Stone, North Canton Also called Sims-Lohman Inc *(G-15119)*
Canton Drop Forge Inc 330 477-4511
4575 Southway St Sw Canton (44706) *(G-2608)*
Canton Elevator Inc 330 833-3600
2575 Greensburg Rd North Canton (44720) *(G-15076)*
Canton Fabricators Inc (PA) 330 830-2900
1115 Industrial Ave Sw Massillon (44647) *(G-12966)*
Canton Fuel 330 455-3400
1600 30th St Ne Canton (44714) *(G-2609)*
Canton Gear Mfg Design Co Inc 330 455-2771
1600 Tuscarawas St E Canton (44707) *(G-2610)*
Canton Graphic Arts Service 330 456-9868
800 Cleveland Ave Sw Canton (44702) *(G-2611)*
Canton Hot Rolled Plant, Canton Also called Republic Steel Inc *(G-2805)*
Canton OH Rubber Speclty Prods 330 454-3847
1387 Clarendon Ave Sw Canton (44710) *(G-2612)*
Canton Oil Well Service Inc 330 494-1221
7793 Pittsburg Ave Nw Canton (44720) *(G-2613)*
Canton Orthotic Laboratory 330 833-0955
811 12th St Nw Canton (44703) *(G-2614)*
Canton Pattern & Mold Inc 330 455-4316
914 Sylvan Ct Ne Canton (44705) *(G-2615)*
Canton Pattern and Mold, Canton Also called Canton Pattern & Mold Inc *(G-2615)*
Canton Plating Co Inc 330 452-7808
903 9th St Ne Canton (44704) *(G-2616)*
Canton Sign Co 330 456-7151
222 5th St Ne Canton (44702) *(G-2617)*
Canton Sterilized Wiping Cloth 330 455-5179
1401 Waynesburg Dr Se Canton (44707) *(G-2618)*
Cantrell Rfinery Sls Trnsp Inc 937 695-0318
18856 State Route 136 Winchester (45697) *(G-20519)*
Canvas 123 Inc 312 805-0563
277 Oak Grove Dr Coventry Township (44319) *(G-7766)*

Canvas Exchange Inc 216 749-2233
5777 Grant Ave Cleveland (44105) *(G-4867)*
Canvas Salon and Skin Bar 614 336-3942
3893 Powell Rd Powell (43065) *(G-16311)*
Canvas Specialty Mfg Co 216 881-0647
4045 Saint Clair Ave Cleveland (44103) *(G-4868)*
Canyon Run Engineering, Troy Also called Slimline Surgical Devices LLC *(G-18707)*
Cap & Associates Incorporated 614 863-3363
445 Mccormick Blvd Columbus (43213) *(G-6728)*
Cap City Direct LLC 614 252-6245
3203 E 11th Ave Columbus (43219) *(G-6729)*
Cap Data Supply Inc 216 252-2280
15227 Triskett Rd Cleveland (44111) *(G-4869)*
Capehart Enterprises LLC 614 769-7746
1724 Northwest Blvd B1 Columbus (43212) *(G-6730)*
Capital Chemical Co 330 494-9535
5340 Mayfair Rd Canton (44720) *(G-2619)*
Capital City Awning Company 614 221-5404
577 N 4th St Columbus (43215) *(G-6731)*
Capital City Energy Group Inc 614 485-3110
3789 Attucks Dr Powell (43065) *(G-16312)*
Capital City Millwork Inc 614 939-0670
150 E Dublin Granville Rd New Albany (43054) *(G-14613)*
Capital City Oil Inc 740 397-4483
375 Columbus Rd Mount Vernon (43050) *(G-14473)*
Capital Engraving Company 440 237-7760
11963 Abbey Rd Cleveland (44133) *(G-4870)*
Capital Machine & Fabrication 740 773-4976
162 Commercial Cir Chillicothe (45601) *(G-3179)*
Capital Office Supply, Columbus Also called Dewitt Group Inc *(G-6862)*
Capital Oil & Gas Inc 330 533-1828
6075 Silica Rd Austintown (44515) *(G-931)*
Capital Precision Machine & TI 937 258-1176
1865 Radio Rd Dayton (45431) *(G-7973)*
Capital Prosthetic & (PA) 614 451-0446
4678 Larwell Dr Columbus (43220) *(G-6732)*
Capital Prosthetic & 567 560-2051
625 Cline Ave Mansfield (44907) *(G-12419)*
Capital Prosthetic & 740 453-9545
4035 Northpointe Dr A Zanesville (43701) *(G-21115)*
Capital Prosthetic & 740 522-3331
55 S Terrace Ave Newark (43055) *(G-14859)*
Capital Prsthetic Orthotic Ctr, Newark Also called Capital Prosthetic & *(G-14859)*
Capital Resin Corporation 614 445-7177
324 Dering Ave Columbus (43207) *(G-6733)*
Capital Spring, Columbus Also called Matthew Warren Inc *(G-7160)*
Capital Toe Grinding, Columbus Also called HI Lite Plastic Products *(G-6996)*
Capital Tool Company 216 661-5750
1110 Brookpark Rd Cleveland (44109) *(G-4871)*
Capital Tool Grinding Co, Columbus Also called Bartley Offie *(G-6653)*
Capital Track Company Inc 614 595-5088
1364 Cardwell Sq S Columbus (43229) *(G-6734)*
Capitol Aluminum & Glass Corp 800 331-8268
1276 W Main St Bellevue (44811) *(G-1534)*
Capitol Citicom Inc 614 472-2679
2225 Citygate Dr Ste A Columbus (43219) *(G-6735)*
Capitol City Mfg Co Inc 614 491-1192
3881 Groveport Rd Obetz (43207) *(G-15506)*
Capitol City Trailers Inc 614 491-2616
3960 Groveport Rd Obetz (43207) *(G-15507)*
Capitol Square Printing Inc 614 221-2850
59 E Gay St Columbus (43215) *(G-6736)*
Capozzolo Printers Inc 513 542-7874
4000 Hamilton Ave Cincinnati (45223) *(G-3440)*
Cappco Tubular Products Inc 216 641-2218
26777 Lorain Rd Ste 216 North Olmsted (44070) *(G-15183)*
Caps 216 524-0418
8300 Sweet Valley Dr # 301 Cleveland (44125) *(G-4872)*
Capsa Solutions LLC 800 437-6633
8170 Dove Pkwy Canal Winchester (43110) *(G-2500)*
Capt, Celina Also called Celina Alum Precision Tech Inc *(G-2953)*
Captor Corporation 937 667-8484
5040 S County Road 25a Tipp City (45371) *(G-18106)*
Car Bros Inc 440 232-1840
7177 Northfield Rd Bedford (44146) *(G-1393)*
Car-Nation Inc 330 862-9001
1216 Fox Ave Se Paris (44669) *(G-15808)*
Carat Patch, The, Newark Also called Stephen R White *(G-14923)*
Caraustar Industrial and Con 330 868-4111
460 Knox Ct Minerva (44657) *(G-14177)*
Caraustar Industries Inc 216 961-5060
3400 Vega Ave Cleveland (44113) *(G-4873)*
Caraustar Industries Inc 614 529-5535
3024 Charter St Columbus (43228) *(G-6737)*
Caraustar Industries Inc 513 871-7112
5500 Wooster Pike Cincinnati (45226) *(G-3441)*
Caraustar Industries Inc 216 939-3001
7960 Lorain Ave Cleveland (44102) *(G-4874)*

(PA)=Parent Co (HQ)=Headquarters (DH)=Div Headquarters

Caraustar Industries Inc ...330 665-7700
202 Montrose West Ave # 315 Copley (44321) ***(G-7679)***

Caraustar Industries Inc ...740 862-4167
310 W Water St Baltimore (43105) ***(G-1037)***

Caravan Packaging Inc (PA) ...440 243-4100
6427 Eastland Rd Cleveland (44142) ***(G-4875)***

Carbide Probes Inc ...937 490-2994
1328 Research Park Dr Beavercreek (45432) ***(G-1304)***

Carbide Specialist Inc ...440 951-4027
36430 Reading Ave Ste 10 Willoughby (44094) ***(G-20292)***

Carbo Forge Inc ...419 334-9788
150 State Route 523 Fremont (43420) ***(G-10004)***

Carbogene USA LLC ...215 378-4306
2252 Sedgwick Dr Columbus (43220) ***(G-6738)***

Carboline Company ...800 848-4645
2379 Miramar Blvd University Heights (44118) ***(G-18940)***

Carbon Group, The, Solon *Also called Carlisle Brake & Friction Inc* ***(G-17123)***

Carbon Products, West Chester *Also called Graphel Corporation* ***(G-19718)***

Carbonklean Llc ...614 980-9515
24 Village Pointe Dr Powell (43065) ***(G-16313)***

Carbonless & Cut Sheet Forms ...740 826-1700
1948 John Glenn Hwy New Concord (43762) ***(G-14683)***

Carbonless On Demandcom ...330 837-8611
332 Erie St S Massillon (44646) ***(G-12967)***

Carden Door Company LLC ...513 459-2233
1224 Castle Dr Mason (45040) ***(G-12837)***

Cardiac Analytics LLC ...614 314-1332
5683 Liberty Rd N Powell (43065) ***(G-16314)***

Cardiac Arrhythmia Associates ...330 759-8169
3622 Belmont Ave Ste 1112 Youngstown (44505) ***(G-20865)***

Cardinal Aggregate ...419 872-4380
8026 Fremont Pike Perrysburg (43551) ***(G-15931)***

Cardinal Builders Inc ...614 237-1000
4409 E Main St Columbus (43213) ***(G-6739)***

Cardinal Building Supply LLC ...614 706-4499
1000 Edgehill Rd Ste B Columbus (43212) ***(G-6740)***

Cardinal Container Corporation ...614 497-3033
3700 Lockbourne Rd Columbus (43207) ***(G-6741)***

Cardinal CT Company ...740 892-2324
140 Carey St Utica (43080) ***(G-19024)***

Cardinal Custom Cabinets Ltd ...216 281-1570
8201 Almira Ave Ste 10 Cleveland (44102) ***(G-4876)***

Cardinal Electric LLC ...740 366-6850
1725 Mount Vernon Rd Newark (43055) ***(G-14860)***

Cardinal Fstener Specialty Inc ...216 831-3800
5185 Richmond Rd Bedford Heights (44146) ***(G-1464)***

Cardinal Glass Industries Inc ...740 892-2324
140 Carey St Utica (43080) ***(G-19025)***

Cardinal Health Inc ...614 553-3830
7200 Cardinal Pl W Dublin (43017) ***(G-8893)***

Cardinal Health Inc (PA) ...614 757-5000
7000 Cardinal Pl Dublin (43017) ***(G-8894)***

Cardinal Health 414 LLC (HQ) ...614 757-5000
7000 Cardinal Pl Dublin (43017) ***(G-8895)***

Cardinal Health 414 LLC ...614 473-0786
2215 Citygate Dr Ste D Columbus (43219) ***(G-6742)***

Cardinal Health 414 LLC ...513 759-1900
9866 Windisch Rd Bldg 3 West Chester (45069) ***(G-19664)***

Cardinal Health Tech LLC (HQ) ...614 757-5000
7000 Cardinal Pl Dublin (43017) ***(G-8896)***

Cardinal Machine Company ...440 238-7050
14459 Foltz Pkwy Strongsville (44149) ***(G-17722)***

Cardinal Printing Inc ...330 773-7300
112 W Wilbeth Rd Akron (44301) ***(G-103)***

Cardinal Products Inc ...440 237-8280
11929 Abbey Rd Ste D North Royalton (44133) ***(G-15265)***

Cardinal Pumps Exchangers Inc (HQ) ...330 332-8558
1425 Quaker Ct Salem (44460) ***(G-16723)***

Cardinal Rubber Company Inc ...330 745-2191
939 Wooster Rd N Barberton (44203) ***(G-1069)***

Cardinal Truss & Components, Edgerton *Also called Building Concepts Inc* ***(G-9169)***

Cardinal Welding Inc ...330 426-2404
895 E Taggart St East Palestine (44413) ***(G-9069)***

Cardington Yutaka Tech Inc (HQ) ...419 864-8777
575 W Main St Cardington (43315) ***(G-2871)***

Cardioinsight Technologies Inc ...216 274-2221
3 Summit Park Dr Ste 400 Independence (44131) ***(G-11121)***

Cardpak, Solon *Also called Rohrer Corporation* ***(G-17225)***

Care Cabinetry Inc ...216 481-7445
1410 Chardon Rd Frnt Euclid (44117) ***(G-9407)***

Carefusion, Groveport *Also called Becton Dickinson and Company* ***(G-10484)***

Careless Heart Enterprises (PA) ...740 654-9999
600 N Columbus St Lancaster (43130) ***(G-11553)***

Carenection LLC ...614 468-6045
1103 Schrock Rd Ste 205 Columbus (43229) ***(G-6743)***

Carepoint Partners, Canfield *Also called Molorokalin Inc* ***(G-2537)***

Carey Color Inc ...330 239-1835
6835 Ridge Rd Sharon Center (44274) ***(G-16947)***

Carey Color Llc/Cincinnati ...513 241-5210
1361 Tennessee Ave Cincinnati (45229) ***(G-3442)***

Carey Digital Solutions, Cincinnati *Also called Carey Color Llc/Cincinnati* ***(G-3442)***

Carey Precast Concrete Company ...419 396-7142
3420 Township Highway 98 Carey (43316) ***(G-2879)***

Cargill Incorporated ...330 745-0031
2065 Manchester Rd Akron (44314) ***(G-104)***

Cargill Incorporated ...937 236-1971
3201 Needmore Rd Dayton (45414) ***(G-8075)***

Cargill Incorporated ...513 941-7400
5204 River Rd Cincinnati (45233) ***(G-3443)***

Cargill Incorporated ...937 498-4555
2400 Industrial Dr Sidney (45365) ***(G-17020)***

Cargill Incorporated ...216 651-7200
2400 Ships Channel Cleveland (44113) ***(G-4877)***

Cargill Incorporated ...419 394-3374
1400 Mckinley Rd Saint Marys (45885) ***(G-16681)***

Cargill Premix and Nutrition, Brookville *Also called Provimi North America Inc* ***(G-2182)***

Carhartt Inc ...513 657-7130
2685 Edmondson Rd Cincinnati (45209) ***(G-3444)***

Carhoff, Cleveland *Also called L-Mor Inc* ***(G-5551)***

Caring Things Inc ...614 749-9084
435 W State St Columbus (43215) ***(G-6744)***

Carl C Andre Inc ...614 864-0123
2894 Brice Rd Brice (43109) ***(G-2071)***

Carl E Oeder Sons Sand & Grav ...513 494-1555
1000 Mason Morrow Rd Lebanon (45036) ***(G-11640)***

Carl Rittberger Sr Inc ...740 452-2767
1900 Lutz Ln Zanesville (43701) ***(G-21116)***

Carlisle and Finch Company ...513 681-6080
4562 W Mitchell Ave Cincinnati (45232) ***(G-3445)***

Carlisle Brake & Friction Inc ...440 528-4000
29001 Solon Rd Solon (44139) ***(G-17123)***

Carlisle Brake & Friction Inc ...330 725-4941
920 Lake Rd Medina (44256) ***(G-13234)***

Carlisle Brake & Friction Inc (HQ) ...440 528-4000
6180 Cochran Rd Solon (44139) ***(G-17124)***

Carlisle Oak ...330 852-8734
3872 Township Road 162 Sugarcreek (44681) ***(G-17845)***

Carlisle Plastics Company Inc ...937 845-9411
320 Ohio St New Carlisle (45344) ***(G-14664)***

Carlisle Prtg Walnut Creek Ltd ...330 852-9922
2673 Township Road 421 Sugarcreek (44681) ***(G-17846)***

Carlson Aircraft Inc ...330 426-3934
51028 State Route 14 East Palestine (44413) ***(G-9070)***

Carlson Quality Brake, Lima *Also called International Brake Inds Inc* ***(G-11879)***

Carlton Natco ...216 451-5588
13020 Saint Clair Ave Cleveland (44108) ***(G-4878)***

Carlton Oil Corp ...740 473-2629
961 Greene St Newport (45768) ***(G-14983)***

Carly Co LLC ...937 477-6411
235 N Main St Centerville (45459) ***(G-3000)***

Carmel Trader Publishing Inc ...330 478-9200
4501 Hills & Dales Rd Nw Canton (44708) ***(G-2620)***

Carmens Installation Co ...216 321-4040
2865 Mayfield Rd Cleveland (44118) ***(G-4879)***

Carmeuse Lime Inc ...419 638-2511
3964 County Road 41 Millersville (43435) ***(G-14163)***

Carmeuse Lime Inc ...419 986-2000
1967 W County Rd 42 Tiffin (44883) ***(G-18055)***

Carmeuse Lime Inc ...419 986-5200
1967 W County Rd 42 Bettsville (44815) ***(G-1660)***

Carmeuse Lime & Stone, Millersville *Also called Carmeuse Lime Inc* ***(G-14163)***

Carmeuse Natural Chemicals, Bettsville *Also called Carmeuse Lime Inc* ***(G-1660)***

Carnation Elc Mtr Repr Sls Inc ...330 823-7116
232 N Lincoln Ave Alliance (44601) ***(G-460)***

Carnation Machine & Tool Inc ...330 823-5352
14632 Oyster Rd Alliance (44601) ***(G-461)***

Carnegie Plas Cabinetry Inc ...216 451-3300
1755 Coit Ave Cleveland (44112) ***(G-4880)***

Carnegie Promotions Inc ...440 442-2099
697 Davidson Dr Cleveland (44143) ***(G-4881)***

Carney Plastics Inc ...330 746-8273
1010 W Rayen Ave Youngstown (44502) ***(G-20866)***

Caro Medical LLC ...937 604-8600
6791 Bunnell Hill Rd Springboro (45066) ***(G-17324)***

Carol J Guiler ...614 252-6920
1359 E 5th Ave Columbus (43219) ***(G-6745)***

Carol Mickley (PA) ...740 599-7870
2 Richard St Danville (43014) ***(G-7960)***

Carolina Color Corp Ohio ...740 363-6622
100 Colomet Dr Delaware (43015) ***(G-8660)***

Carolina Stair Supply Inc (PA) ...740 922-3333
316 Herrick St Uhrichsville (44683) ***(G-18881)***

Carols Ultra Stitch & Variety ...419 935-8991
122 S Myrtle Ave Willard (44890) ***(G-20238)***

Carolyn Chemical Company ...614 252-5000
1601 Woodland Ave Columbus (43219) ***(G-6746)***

Caron Products and Svcs Inc ...740 373-6809
27640 State Route 7 Marietta (45750) ***(G-12612)***

Carousel Carvings, Marion *Also called Todd W Goings* ***(G-12743)***

ALPHABETIC SECTION — Cathie D Hubbard

Carousel Magic LLC 419 522-6456
44 W 4th St Mansfield (44902) *(G-12420)*

Carousel Works Inc 419 522-7558
1285 Pollock Pkwy Mansfield (44905) *(G-12421)*

Carpe Diem Industries LLC (PA) 419 659-5639
4599 Campbell Rd Columbus Grove (45830) *(G-7632)*

Carpe Diem Industries LLC 419 358-0129
505 E Jefferson St Bluffton (45817) *(G-1887)*

Carper Well Service Inc 740 374-2567
30745 State Route 7 Marietta (45750) *(G-12613)*

Carquest Auto Parts, Beloit Also called Jenkins Motor Parts *(G-1570)*

Carquest Auto Parts, Westerville Also called General Parts Inc *(G-20055)*

Carr Bros Inc 440 232-3700
7177 Northfield Rd Bedford (44146) *(G-1394)*

Carr Bros Bldrs Sup & Coal Co 440 232-3700
7177 Northfield Rd Cleveland (44146) *(G-4882)*

Carr Supply Co 937 316-6300
900 Sater St Greenville (45331) *(G-10363)*

Carr Supply Co 937 276-2555
4800 Webster St Dayton (45414) *(G-8076)*

Carr Tool Company 513 825-2900
575 Security Dr Fairfield (45014) *(G-9488)*

Carrera Holdings Inc 216 687-1311
101 W Prospect Ave Cleveland (44115) *(G-4883)*

Carriage House Printery LLC 740 243-7493
5458 Carroll Northern Rd Carroll (43112) *(G-2900)*

Carrier Corporation 937 275-0645
6050 Milo Rd Dayton (45414) *(G-8077)*

Carrillo Pallets LLC 513 942-2210
1292 Glendale Milford Rd Cincinnati (45215) *(G-3446)*

Carroll Distrg & Cnstr Sup Inc 513 422-3327
6688 Georgetown Ln Middletown (45042) *(G-13890)*

Carroll Distrg & Cnstr Sup Inc 614 564-9799
2929 E 14th Ave Columbus (43219) *(G-6747)*

Carroll Exhibit and Print Svcs 216 361-2325
5150 Prospect Ave Cleveland (44103) *(G-4884)*

Carroll Graphic, Cleveland Also called Carroll Exhibit and Print Svcs *(G-4884)*

Carroll Hills Industries Inc 330 627-5524
540 High St Nw Carrollton (44615) *(G-2917)*

Carrollton Publishing Company 330 627-5591
43 E Main St Carrollton (44615) *(G-2918)*

Carruth Studio Inc (PA) 419 878-3060
1178 Farnsworth Rd Waterville (43566) *(G-19491)*

Carry Grandview Out 614 487-0305
710 Neil Ave Columbus (43215) *(G-6748)*

Cars and Parts Magazine 937 498-0803
911 S Vandemark Rd Sidney (45365) *(G-17021)*

Carson Industries LLC 419 592-2309
1675 Industrial Dr Napoleon (43545) *(G-14535)*

Carson-Saeks Inc (PA) 937 278-5311
2601 Timber Ln Dayton (45414) *(G-8078)*

Carter Drapery Service Inc 419 289-2530
1301 County Road 1356 Ashland (44805) *(G-689)*

Carter Evans Enterprises Inc 614 920-2276
3354 Battee Rd Granville (43023) *(G-10327)*

Carter Machine Company Inc (PA) 419 468-3530
820 Edward St Galion (44833) *(G-10125)*

Carter Manufacturing Co Inc 513 398-7303
4220 State Route 42 Mason (45040) *(G-12838)*

Carter Scott-Browne 513 398-3970
4220 State Route 42 Mason (45040) *(G-12839)*

Carter-Jones Lumber Company 330 674-9060
6139 State Route 39 Millersburg (44654) *(G-14077)*

Carter-Jones Lumber Company 440 834-8164
14601 Kinsman Rd Middlefield (44062) *(G-13782)*

Cartessa Corporation 513 738-4477
4825 Cncnnati Brkville Rd Shandon (45063) *(G-16940)*

Carton Service Incorporated (PA) 419 342-5010
First Quality Dr Shelby (44875) *(G-16980)*

Cartwright Cnstr H B A C, Cuyahoga Falls Also called Cartwright Construction Inc *(G-7846)*

Cartwright Construction Inc 330 929-3020
4898 Wild Lake Rd Cuyahoga Falls (44224) *(G-7846)*

Caruso's Coffee, Brecksville Also called Pmd Enterprises Inc *(G-2055)*

Carved N Stone, Powell Also called Carved Stone LLC *(G-16315)*

Carved Stone LLC 614 778-9855
505 Village Park Dr Powell (43065) *(G-16315)*

Caryns Cuisine 614 237-4143
155 N Remington Rd Columbus (43209) *(G-6749)*

Cas, Cleves Also called Consolidatd Analytical Sys Inc *(G-6359)*

Cas Data Loggers, Chesterland Also called Computer Aided Solutions LLC *(G-3155)*

Casad Company Inc 419 586-9457
450 S 2nd St Coldwater (45828) *(G-6404)*

Cascade Corporation 937 327-0300
2501 Sheridan Ave Springfield (45505) *(G-17370)*

Cascade Cut Stone 419 422-4341
41 Township Highway 87 Findlay (45839) *(G-9664)*

Cascade Group of Ohio Limited 440 572-2480
14761 Pearl Rd Strongsville (44136) *(G-17723)*

Cascade Ohio Inc 440 593-5800
1209 Maple Ave Conneaut (44030) *(G-7642)*

Cascade Pattern Company Inc 440 323-4300
519 Ternes Ln Elyria (44035) *(G-9231)*

Cascade Plating Inc 440 366-4931
210 Abbe Rd S Elyria (44035) *(G-9232)*

Cascade Unlimited LLC 440 352-7995
2510 Hale Rd Painesville (44077) *(G-15721)*

Casco Mfg Solutions Inc 513 681-0003
3107 Spring Grove Ave Cincinnati (45225) *(G-3447)*

Case Crafters Inc 937 667-9473
211 S 1st St Tipp City (45371) *(G-18107)*

Case Farms Chicken, Winesburg Also called Case Farms of Ohio Inc *(G-20530)*

Case Farms of Ohio Inc (HQ) 330 359-7141
1818 County Rd 160 Winesburg (44690) *(G-20530)*

Case Farms of Ohio Inc 330 878-7118
1225 Hensel Ave Ne Strasburg (44680) *(G-17647)*

Case Ohio Burial Co (PA) 440 779-1992
1720 Columbus Rd Cleveland (44113) *(G-4885)*

Case Pattern Co Inc 216 531-0744
2380 Forest Glen Rd Madison (44057) *(G-12341)*

Case Plating Inc 440 288-8304
736 Idaho Ave Lorain (44052) *(G-12083)*

Case-Maul Clamps Inc 419 668-6563
69 N West St Norwalk (44857) *(G-15384)*

Case-Maul Manufacturing Co 419 524-1061
30 Harker St Mansfield (44903) *(G-12422)*

Casentric LLC 216 233-6300
23700 Fairmount Blvd Shaker Heights (44122) *(G-16928)*

Cashmere & Twig LLC 740 404-8468
181 Lowery Ln New Concord (43762) *(G-14684)*

Caskey's Recreation, Orrville Also called Caskeys Inc *(G-15586)*

Caskeys Inc 330 683-0249
14847 Fosnight Rd Orrville (44667) *(G-15586)*

Caspa Home Page Inc 216 781-0748
1501 N Marginal Rd # 166 Cleveland (44114) *(G-4886)*

Cass Frames Inc 419 468-2863
6052 State Route 19 Galion (44833) *(G-10126)*

Cassady Woodworks Inc 937 256-7948
446 N Smithville Rd Dayton (45431) *(G-7974)*

Casselberry Clinic Inc 440 995-0555
5555 Mayfield Rd Cleveland (44124) *(G-4887)*

Cast Metals Incorporated 419 278-2010
104 W North St Deshler (43516) *(G-8787)*

Cast Metals Technology Inc 937 968-5460
305 Se Deerfield Rd Union City (45390) *(G-18902)*

Cast Metals Technology Inc (PA) 740 363-1690
550 Liberty Rd Delaware (43015) *(G-8661)*

Cast Plus Inc 937 743-7278
415 Oxford Rd Franklin (45005) *(G-9873)*

Cast Specialties Inc 216 292-7393
26711 Miles Rd Cleveland (44128) *(G-4888)*

Castalia Trenching & Ready Mix 419 684-5502
4814 State Route 269 S Castalia (44824) *(G-2936)*

Castalloy Inc 216 961-7990
7990 Baker Ave Cleveland (44102) *(G-4889)*

Castco Inc 440 365-2333
527 Ternes Ln Elyria (44035) *(G-9233)*

Castek Aluminum Inc 440 365-2333
527 Ternes Ln Elyria (44035) *(G-9234)*

Castelli Marble Inc (PA) 216 361-2410
1521 E 47th St Cleveland (44103) *(G-4890)*

Casting Solutions LLC 740 452-9371
2345 Licking Rd Zanesville (43701) *(G-21117)*

Castings Usa Inc 330 339-3611
2061 Brightwood Rd Se New Philadelphia (44663) *(G-14764)*

Castlebar Corporation 330 451-6511
406 15th St Sw Canton (44707) *(G-2621)*

Castmor Products Inc 440 953-1103
4708 Beidler Rd Willoughby (44094) *(G-20293)*

Castruction Company Inc 330 332-9622
1588 Salem Pkwy Salem (44460) *(G-16724)*

Cat's Meow Village, The, Wooster Also called F J Designs Inc *(G-20590)*

Cat-Wood Metalworks, Moraine Also called Rolling Enterprises Inc *(G-14390)*

Catalent Pharma Solutions LLC 614 757-4757
7000 Cardinal Pl Dublin (43017) *(G-8897)*

Catalysis Additive Tooling LLC 614 715-3674
35 Clairedan Dr Powell (43065) *(G-16316)*

Catania Medallic Specialities, Avon Lake Also called Catania Medallic Specialty *(G-981)*

Catania Medallic Specialty 440 933-9595
668 Moore Rd Avon Lake (44012) *(G-981)*

Catawba Island Brewing Co 419 960-7764
2330 East Harbor Rd Port Clinton (43452) *(G-16244)*

Cateringstone 513 410-1064
6119 Kenwood Rd Cincinnati (45243) *(G-3448)*

Caterpillar Inc 614 834-2400
8170 Dove Pkwy Canal Winchester (43110) *(G-2501)*

Cathie D Hubbard 937 593-0316
305 E Williams Ave Bellefontaine (43311) *(G-1509)*

Catholic Charity Hispanic Off ... 216 696-2197
2012 W 25th St Ste 507 Cleveland (44113) *(G-4891)*

Catholic Diocese of Columbus ... 614 224-5195
197 E Gay St Ste 4 Columbus (43215) *(G-6750)*

Catholic Exponent, Youngstown Also called Roman Cthlic Dioces Youngstown *(G-21021)*

Catholic Times, Columbus Also called Catholic Diocese of Columbus *(G-6750)*

Catress LLC ... 740 695-0918
50482 National Rd Saint Clairsville (43950) *(G-16626)*

Cats Printing Inc ... 216 381-8181
3980 Mayfield Rd Cleveland (44121) *(G-4892)*

Cattron Holdings Inc (HQ) ... 234 806-0018
655 N River Rd Nw Ste A Warren (44483) *(G-19381)*

Cattron North America Inc (HQ) ... 234 806-0018
655 N River Rd Nw Ste A Warren (44483) *(G-19382)*

Cauffiel Corporation (PA) ... 419 843-7262
3171 N Repub Blvd Ste 102 Toledo (43615) *(G-18223)*

Cave Tool & Manufacturing Inc ... 937 324-0662
20 Walnut St Springfield (45505) *(G-17371)*

Caven and Sons Meat Packing Co ... 937 368-3841
7850 E Us Rte 36 Conover (45317) *(G-7662)*

CB Manufacturing & Sls Co Inc ... 937 866-5986
4475 Infirmary Rd Dayton (45449) *(G-8079)*

Cbd Media Holdings LLC (HQ) ... 513 217-9483
312 Plum St Ste 900 Cincinnati (45202) *(G-3449)*

Cbf, Solon Also called Carlisle Brake & Friction Inc *(G-17124)*

Cbg Biotech Ltd Co ... 440 786-7667
30175 Solon Indus Pkwy Solon (44139) *(G-17125)*

Cbl Products ... 216 321-2599
1661 Cumberland Rd Cleveland (44118) *(G-4893)*

Cbr Industrial Llc ... 419 645-6447
20086 Wapakoneta Cridersv Wapakoneta (45895) *(G-19326)*

CBs Boring and Mch Co Inc ... 419 784-9500
2064 E 2nd St Defiance (43512) *(G-8618)*

CC Investors Management Co LLC ... 740 374-8129
30765 State Route 7 Marietta (45750) *(G-12614)*

CC Ironworks LLC ... 330 542-0500
10613 Main St New Middletown (44442) *(G-14747)*

CC Pallets LLC ... 513 442-8766
212 Cambridge Ave Terrace Park (45174) *(G-18018)*

CCI, Cincinnati Also called Albert Bickel *(G-3317)*

CCL Design, Brunswick Also called CCL Label Inc *(G-2194)*

CCL Design Electronics, Strongsville Also called CCL Label Inc *(G-17724)*

CCL Label Inc ... 216 676-2703
15939 Industrial Pkwy Cleveland (44135) *(G-4894)*

CCL Label Inc ... 440 878-7000
2845 Center Rd Brunswick (44212) *(G-2194)*

CCL Label Inc ... 440 878-7277
17700 Foltz Pkwy Strongsville (44149) *(G-17724)*

CCM Welding Inc ... 330 630-2521
895 Moe Dr Ste D11 Akron (44310) *(G-105)*

Ccp Industries, Richmond Heights Also called Tranzonic Companies *(G-16506)*

Ccsi Inc ... 800 742-8535
221 Beaver St Akron (44304) *(G-106)*

CCT, Shelby Also called Custom Control Tech LLC *(G-16981)*

Cctm Inc ... 513 934-3533
838 Carson Dr Lebanon (45036) *(G-11641)*

CD / Dvd Distribution, Dayton Also called Chaos Entertainment *(G-8086)*

CD Solutions Inc ... 937 676-2376
100 W Monument St Pleasant Hill (45359) *(G-16224)*

Cdc Corporation ... 715 532-5548
1445 Holland Rd Maumee (43537) *(G-13081)*

Cdc Fab Co ... 419 866-7705
1445 Holland Rd Maumee (43537) *(G-13082)*

Cdds Inc ... 614 626-8747
950 Taylor Station Rd U Gahanna (43230) *(G-10078)*

CDI, Avon Also called Cutting Dynamics Inc *(G-947)*

CDI Industries Inc ... 440 243-1100
6800 Lake Abrams Dr Cleveland (44130) *(G-4895)*

Cdmc, Cleveland Also called Cleveland Deburring Machine Co *(G-4956)*

Cdracks.com, Xenia Also called The Wood Shed *(G-20795)*

Cds Signs ... 513 563-7446
11024 Reading Rd Cincinnati (45241) *(G-3450)*

Cds Technologies Inc ... 800 338-1122
9025 Centre Pointe Dr West Chester (45069) *(G-19665)*

CEC Electronics Corp ... 330 916-8100
1739 Akron Peninsula Rd Akron (44313) *(G-107)*

Cecil C Peck Co ... 330 785-0781
1029 Arlington Cir Akron (44306) *(G-108)*

Cecil Caudill Trailer Sls Inc ... 740 574-0704
6679 Gallia Pike Franklin Furnace (45629) *(G-9933)*

Ceco Environmental Corp ... 513 458-2606
6245 Creek Rd Blue Ash (45242) *(G-1748)*

Ceco Environmental Corp ... 513 874-8915
9759 Inter Ocean Dr West Chester (45246) *(G-19838)*

Ceco Equipment Company, Akron Also called Custom Enclosures Corp *(G-129)*

Ceco Filters Inc ... 513 458-2600
4625 Red Bank Rd Ste 200 Cincinnati (45227) *(G-3451)*

Ceco Group Inc (HQ) ... 513 458-2600
4625 Red Bank Rd Ste 200 Cincinnati (45227) *(G-3452)*

Ceco Group Global Holdings LLC (HQ) ... 513 458-2600
4625 Red Bank Rd Ste 200 Cincinnati (45227) *(G-3453)*

Ceco Machine & Tool ... 937 264-3047
111 Quinter Farm Rd Englewood (45322) *(G-9351)*

Cedar America, Columbus Also called Woodcor America Inc *(G-7611)*

Cedar Chest ... 937 878-9097
405 W Main St Fairborn (45324) *(G-9454)*

Cedar Craft Products Inc ... 614 759-1600
776 Reynldsbrg New Albany Blacklick (43004) *(G-1681)*

Cedar Elec Holdings Corp ... 773 804-6288
5440 W Chester Rd West Chester (45069) *(G-19666)*

Cedar Outdoor Furniture Inc ... 330 863-2580
8229 Old Canal Ln Nw Malvern (44644) *(G-12386)*

Cedar Point Laundry ... 419 627-2274
1 Cedar Point Dr Sandusky (44870) *(G-16801)*

Cedar Products LLC ... 937 892-0070
380 Duffey Rd Peebles (45660) *(G-15877)*

Cedar Woodworking, Delaware Also called Cedee Cedar Inc *(G-8662)*

Cedarville Quarry, Cedarville Also called Martin Marietta Materials Inc *(G-2945)*

Cedee Cedar Inc (PA) ... 740 363-3148
3903 Us Highway 42 S Delaware (43015) *(G-8662)*

Ceen, Toledo Also called Ames Development Group Ltd *(G-18182)*

Ceia Usa Ltd ... 330 405-3190
9155 Dutton Dr Twinsburg (44087) *(G-18747)*

Ceja Publishing ... 216 319-0268
3654 Atherstone Rd Cleveland (44121) *(G-4896)*

Celcore Inc (PA) ... 440 234-7888
7850 Freeway Cir Ste 100 Cleveland (44130) *(G-4897)*

Celebrations ... 419 381-8088
2910 Glanzman Rd Unit 1 Toledo (43614) *(G-18224)*

Celebrations Monogramming, Cleveland Also called Kathy Simecek *(G-5518)*

Celina Alum Precision Tech Inc ... 419 586-2278
7059 Staeger Rd Celina (45822) *(G-2953)*

Celina Industries, Celina Also called Celina Tent Inc *(G-2954)*

Celina Tent Inc ... 419 586-3610
5373 State Route 29 Celina (45822) *(G-2954)*

Cell 4less, Lima Also called Airwave Communications Cons *(G-11832)*

Cell-O-Core Co ... 330 239-4370
6935 Ridge Rd Sharon Center (44274) *(G-16948)*

Cellera LLC ... 513 539-1500
1045 Reed Dr Ste C Monroe (45050) *(G-14256)*

Cellular Technology Limited ... 216 791-5084
20521 Chagrin Blvd # 200 Shaker Heights (44122) *(G-16929)*

Cellular Technology Ltd, Shaker Heights Also called Ctl Analyzers LLC *(G-16930)*

Celstar Group Inc (PA) ... 937 224-1730
40 N Main St Ste 1730 Dayton (45423) *(G-8080)*

Celsus, Cincinnati Also called Smithfield Bioscience Inc *(G-4347)*

Celtic Forms, Cincinnati Also called National Adhesives Inc *(G-4059)*

Cem - Fairborn Plant, Xenia Also called Cemex Cnstr Mtls ATL LLC *(G-20760)*

Cemedine North America LLC ... 513 618-4652
2142 Western Ave Cincinnati (45214) *(G-3454)*

Cement Products Inc ... 419 524-4342
389 Park Ave E Mansfield (44905) *(G-12423)*

Cemex Cnstr Mtls ATL LLC ... 937 878-8651
3250 Linebaugh Rd Xenia (45385) *(G-20760)*

Cemex Construction Corporation ... 440 449-0872
10176 Page Dr Mentor (44060) *(G-13411)*

Cemex Construction Mtls Inc ... 440 449-0872
6525 Highland Rd Cleveland (44143) *(G-4898)*

Cemex Materials LLC ... 937 268-6706
1504 N Gettysburg Ave Dayton (45417) *(G-8081)*

Cemex Materials LLC ... 937 268-6706
4385 N James H Mcgee Blvd Dayton (45417) *(G-8082)*

Cemex USA Inc ... 937 879-8350
2600 Paramount Pl Fairborn (45324) *(G-9455)*

Cen-Trol Machine Co ... 216 524-1932
7601 Commerce Park Oval Cleveland (44131) *(G-4899)*

Cengage Learning Inc ... 513 234-5967
770 Broadway Mason (45040) *(G-12840)*

Censtar Coatings Inc ... 330 723-8000
11829 Jeffrey Rd West Salem (44287) *(G-19953)*

Centaur Inc (PA) ... 419 469-8000
2401 Front St Toledo (43605) *(G-18225)*

Centaur Tool & Die Inc ... 419 352-7704
2019 Wood Bridge Blvd Bowling Green (43402) *(G-1959)*

Centennial Screen Printing ... 419 422-5548
1785 S Romick Pkwy Findlay (45840) *(G-9665)*

Center Automotive Parts Co ... 330 434-2174
274 E South St Akron (44311) *(G-109)*

Center Concrete Inc (PA) ... 800 453-4224
8790 Us Rt 6 Edgerton (43517) *(G-9170)*

Center For Excptonal Practices ... 330 523-5240
3404 Brecksville Rd Richfield (44286) *(G-16464)*

Center For Inquiry Inc ... 330 671-7192
6413 Riverview Rd Peninsula (44264) *(G-15890)*

Center Line Drilling Inc ... 440 951-5920
33000 Lakeland Blvd Willoughby (44095) *(G-20294)*

Center Line Machining LLC 216 289-6828
25700 Lakeland Blvd Euclid (44132) ***(G-9408)***
Center Mass Ammo LLC 440 796-6207
6642 Middle Ridge Rd Madison (44057) ***(G-12342)***
Center Mass Defense 513 314-8401
4421 Hamilton Cleves Rd Hamilton (45013) ***(G-10544)***
Centerless Grinding Service 216 251-4100
19500 S Miles Rd Cleveland (44128) ***(G-4900)***
Centerless Grinding Solutions 216 520-4612
8440 Tower Dr Twinsburg (44087) ***(G-18748)***
Centerline Machine Inc 937 322-4887
4949 Urbana Rd Springfield (45502) ***(G-17372)***
Centerline Tool & Machine 937 222-3600
1330 E 2nd St Dayton (45403) ***(G-8083)***
Centerra Co-Op (PA) 419 281-2153
813 Clark Ave Ashland (44805) ***(G-690)***
Centerra Co-Op 800 362-9598
161 E Jefferson St Jefferson (44047) ***(G-11226)***
Centor Inc (HQ) 567 336-8094
1899 N Wilkinson Way Perrysburg (43551) ***(G-15932)***
Centor Inc 800 321-3391
5091 County Rd 120 Berlin (44610) ***(G-1640)***
Central Allied Enterprises Inc 330 879-2132
6331 Blough Ave Sw Navarre (44662) ***(G-14573)***
Central Aluminum Company LLC 614 491-5700
2045 Broehm Rd Obetz (43207) ***(G-15508)***
Central Business Products Inc 513 385-5899
3722 Vernier Dr Cincinnati (45251) ***(G-3455)***
Central Coated Products Inc 330 821-9830
2025 Mccrea St Alliance (44601) ***(G-462)***
Central Coca-Cola Btlg Co Inc 740 474-2180
387 Walnut St Circleville (43113) ***(G-4538)***
Central Coca-Cola Btlg Co Inc 330 875-1487
1560 Triplett Blvd Akron (44306) ***(G-110)***
Central Coca-Cola Btlg Co Inc 419 476-6622
3970 Catawba St Toledo (43612) ***(G-18226)***
Central Coca-Cola Btlg Co Inc 330 783-1982
531 E Indianola Ave Youngstown (44502) ***(G-20867)***
Central Coca-Cola Btlg Co Inc 330 487-0212
8295 Bavaria Dr E Macedonia (44056) ***(G-12282)***
Central Coca-Cola Btlg Co Inc 614 863-7200
4500 Groves Rd Columbus (43232) ***(G-6751)***
Central Coca-Cola Btlg Co Inc 419 522-2653
100 Industrial Pkwy Mansfield (44903) ***(G-12424)***
Central Coca-Cola Btlg Co Inc 440 324-3335
1410 Lake Ave Elyria (44035) ***(G-9235)***
Central Coca-Cola Btlg Co Inc 740 452-3608
154 S 7th St Zanesville (43701) ***(G-21118)***
Central Coca-Cola Btlg Co Inc 330 425-4401
1882 Highland Rd Twinsburg (44087) ***(G-18749)***
Central Coca-Cola Btlg Co Inc 440 269-1433
4800 E 355th St Willoughby (44094) ***(G-20295)***
Central Design Services 513 829-7027
5417 Dixie Hwy Fairfield (45014) ***(G-9489)***
Central Fabricators Inc 513 621-1240
408 Poplar St Cincinnati (45214) ***(G-3456)***
Central Graphics Inc 330 928-7080
1658 State Rd Cuyahoga Falls (44223) ***(G-7847)***
Central Heating & Cooling Inc 330 782-7100
5626 South Ave Ste 1 Youngstown (44512) ***(G-20868)***
Central Machinery Company LLC 740 387-1289
1339 E Fairground Rd Marion (43302) ***(G-12699)***
Central Market Specialty Meats, Columbus *Also called Karn Meats Inc* ***(G-7083)***
Central Ohio Bldg Components, Newark *Also called Columbus Roof Trusses Inc* ***(G-14862)***
Central Ohio Defense LLC 614 668-6527
292 E Weisheimer Rd Columbus (43214) ***(G-6752)***
Central Ohio Fabrication LLC 740 969-2976
8143 Bowers Rd Sw Amanda (43102) ***(G-524)***
Central Ohio Fabricators LLC 740 393-3892
105 Progress Dr Mount Vernon (43050) ***(G-14474)***
Central Ohio Metal Stampi 614 861-3332
1055 Claycraft Rd Columbus (43230) ***(G-6753)***
Central Ohio Orthtic Prsthetic 614 659-1580
248 Bradenton Ave Dublin (43017) ***(G-8898)***
Central Ohio Paper & Packg Inc (PA) 419 621-9239
2350 University Dr E Huron (44839) ***(G-11092)***
Central Ohio Printing Corp 740 852-1616
55 W High St London (43140) ***(G-12052)***
Central Ohio Rtrctable Screens 614 868-5080
6737 Thomas Rd Radnor (43066) ***(G-16357)***
Central Ohio Welding, Columbus *Also called COW Industries Inc* ***(G-6831)***
Central Oil Asphalt Corp (PA) 614 224-8111
8 E Long St Ste 400 Columbus (43215) ***(G-6754)***
Central Optical Inc 330 783-9660
6981 Southern Blvd Ste B Youngstown (44512) ***(G-20869)***
Central Power Systems, Columbus *Also called Power Distributors LLC* ***(G-7334)***
Central Ready Mix LLC (PA) 513 402-5001
6310 E Kemper Rd Ste 125 Cincinnati (45241) ***(G-3457)***
Central Ready Mix LLC 513 367-1939
7340 Dry Fork Rd Cleves (45002) ***(G-6356)***
Central Ready-Mix of Ohio LLC 614 252-3452
6310 E Kemper Rd Ste 125 Cincinnati (45241) ***(G-3458)***
Central State Enterprises Inc 419 468-8191
1331 Freese Works Pl Galion (44833) ***(G-10127)***
Central Systems & Control 440 835-0015
26933 Westwood Rd Ste 400 Cleveland (44145) ***(G-4901)***
Central USA Wireless LLC 513 469-1500
11210 Montgomery Rd Cincinnati (45249) ***(G-3459)***
Centrex Plastics, Findlay *Also called American Plastics LLC* ***(G-9650)***
Centrex Plastics LLC 419 423-1213
814 W Lima St Findlay (45840) ***(G-9666)***
Centria Inc 740 432-7351
530 N 2nd St Cambridge (43725) ***(G-2431)***
Centria Coil Coating Services, Cambridge *Also called Centria Inc* ***(G-2431)***
Century Biotech Partners Inc 614 746-6998
7765 Dublin Rd Dublin (43017) ***(G-8899)***
Century Container LLC (HQ) 330 457-2367
5331 State Route 7 New Waterford (44445) ***(G-14837)***
Century Container LLC 330 457-2367
32 W Railroad St Columbiana (44408) ***(G-6457)***
Century Die Company LLC 419 332-2693
215 N Stone St Fremont (43420) ***(G-10005)***
Century Graphics Inc 614 895-7698
9101 Hawthorne Pt Westerville (43082) ***(G-19983)***
Century Industries Corporation 330 457-2367
5331 State Route 7 New Waterford (44445) ***(G-14838)***
Century Marketing Corporation 419 354-2591
1145 Fairview Ave Bowling Green (43402) ***(G-1960)***
Century Marketing Corporation (HQ) 419 354-2591
12836 S Dixie Hwy Bowling Green (43402) ***(G-1961)***
Century Mold Company Inc 513 539-9283
55 Wright Dr Middletown (45044) ***(G-13891)***
Century Plating Inc 216 531-4131
18006 S Waterloo Rd Cleveland (44119) ***(G-4902)***
Century Signs 419 352-2666
169 S Main St Bowling Green (43402) ***(G-1962)***
Century Tool & Stamping Inc 216 241-2032
1510 University Rd Cleveland (44113) ***(G-4903)***
Centurylabel, Bowling Green *Also called Century Marketing Corporation* ***(G-1961)***
Cep Holdings LLC 330 665-2900
3560 W Market St Ste 340 Fairlawn (44333) ***(G-9600)***
Cephas Enterprises LLC 513 317-5685
4740 Dues Dr Unit F West Chester (45246) ***(G-19839)***
Ceramitec, Columbus *Also called Wk Brick Company* ***(G-7607)***
Ceranode Division, Dayton *Also called Aps-Materials Inc* ***(G-8035)***
Cermet Technologies, Cleveland *Also called Postle Industries Inc* ***(G-5897)***
Certainteed Corporation 419 499-2581
11519 Us Highway 250 N Milan (44846) ***(G-13981)***
Certech Inc 330 405-1033
2181 Pinnacle Pkwy Twinsburg (44087) ***(G-18750)***
Certified Comparator Products 937 426-9677
1174 Grange Hall Rd Beavercreek (45430) ***(G-1353)***
Certified Heat Treating Inc (PA) 937 866-0245
4475 Infirmary Rd Dayton (45449) ***(G-8084)***
Certified Labs & Service Inc 419 289-7462
535 E 7th St Ashland (44805) ***(G-691)***
Certified Oil Company Inc 614 421-7500
949 King Ave Columbus (43212) ***(G-6755)***
Certified Power Inc 419 355-1200
1110 Napoleon St Fremont (43420) ***(G-10006)***
Certified Service Inc 937 643-0393
2876 Culver Ave Dayton (45429) ***(G-8085)***
Certified Tool & Grinding Inc 937 865-5934
4455 Infirmary Rd Miamisburg (45342) ***(G-13648)***
Certified Walk In Tubs 614 436-4848
926 Freeway Dr N Columbus (43229) ***(G-6756)***
Certified Welding Co 216 961-5410
9603 Clinton Rd Cleveland (44144) ***(G-4904)***
Certon Technologies Inc (PA) 440 786-7185
60 S Park St Bedford (44146) ***(G-1395)***
Ces Nationwide 937 322-0771
567 E Leffel Ln Springfield (45505) ***(G-17373)***
Ceso Inc (PA) 937 435-8584
3601 Rigby Rd Ste 310 Miamisburg (45342) ***(G-13649)***
Cetek, Cleveland *Also called Fosbel Inc* ***(G-5265)***
Cetek Ltd 216 362-3900
6779 Engle Rd Ste A Cleveland (44130) ***(G-4905)***
CF Extrusion Technologies LLC 844 439-8783
101 E 3rd St Uhrichsville (44683) ***(G-18882)***
CFC Startec LLC 330 688-8316
2213 Arndale Rd Stow (44224) ***(G-17575)***
CFM International Inc (PA) 513 552-2787
6440 Aviation Way West Chester (45069) ***(G-19667)***
CFM International Inc 513 563-4180
1 Neumann Way Cincinnati (45215) ***(G-3460)***
CFM Religion Pubg Group LLC (PA) 513 931-4050
8805 Governors Hill Dr # 400 Cincinnati (45249) ***(G-3461)***
Cfrc Wtr & Enrgy Solutions Inc 216 479-0290
850 Euclid Ave Ste 1314 Cleveland (44114) ***(G-4906)***

ALPHABETIC

Cft Systems, Fairport Harbor *Also called George Whalley Company* ***(G-9623)***
Cgas Exploration Inc (HQ)...614 436-4631
110 E Wilson Bridge Rd # 250 Worthington (43085) ***(G-20679)***
Cgas Inc (PA)...614 975-4697
110 E Wilson Bridge Rd # 250 Worthington (43085) ***(G-20680)***
Cgh Global, Cincinnati *Also called Cgh-Global Emerg Mngmt Strateg* ***(G-3242)***
Cgh-Global Emerg Mngmt Strateg...800 376-0655
851 Ohio Pike Ste 203 Cincinnati (45245) ***(G-3242)***
Cgs, Medina *Also called Commercial Grinding Services* ***(G-13238)***
Cgs Imaging, Holland *Also called Cgs Signs LLC* ***(G-10919)***
Cgs Signs LLC...419 897-3000
6950 Hall St Holland (43528) ***(G-10919)***
Ch Enterprises, Toledo *Also called Greggs Specialty Services* ***(G-18313)***
Ch Tool & Die, Mount Vernon *Also called C-H Tool & Die* ***(G-14471)***
Chagrin Metal Fabricating Inc...440 946-6342
34201 Melinz Pkwy Unit B Eastlake (44095) ***(G-9101)***
Chagrin Valley Publishing Co...440 247-5335
525 Washington St Chagrin Falls (44022) ***(G-3012)***
Chagrin Valley Times, Chagrin Falls *Also called Chagrin Valley Publishing Co* ***(G-3012)***
Chagrin Vly Stl Erectors Inc...440 975-1556
2278 River Rd Willoughby Hills (44094) ***(G-20468)***
Chalet Debonne Vineyards Inc...440 466-3485
7840 Doty Rd Madison (44057) ***(G-12343)***
Chalet In The Valley, Millersburg *Also called Guggisberg Cheese Inc* ***(G-14086)***
Chalfant Loading Dock Eqp, Cleveland *Also called Chalfant Sew Fabricators Inc* ***(G-4907)***
Chalfant Manufacturing Company (HQ)...330 273-3510
50 Pearl Rd Ste 212 Brunswick (44212) ***(G-2195)***
Chalfant Manufacturing Company...440 323-9870
7005 W River Rd S Elyria (44035) ***(G-9236)***
Chalfant Sew Fabricators Inc...216 521-7922
11525 Madison Ave Cleveland (44102) ***(G-4907)***
Chalk Outline Pictures...216 291-3944
4773 Hillary Ln Cleveland (44143) ***(G-4908)***
Challenge Targets...859 462-5851
2524 Spring Grove Ave Cincinnati (45214) ***(G-3462)***
Challenger Aviation Products...937 387-6500
4433 Old Springfield Rd Vandalia (45377) ***(G-19119)***
Challenger Hardware Company...216 591-1141
800 Resource Dr Ste 8 Independence (44131) ***(G-11122)***
Cham Cor Industries Inc...740 967-9015
117 W Coshocton St Johnstown (43031) ***(G-11262)***
Champa Ventures LLC...614 726-1801
6314 Belvedere Green Blvd Dublin (43016) ***(G-8900)***
Champion, Cincinnati *Also called Enclosure Suppliers LLC* ***(G-3637)***
Champion Bridge Company...937 382-2521
261 E Sugartree St Wilmington (45177) ***(G-20488)***
Champion Company (PA)...937 324-5681
400 Harrison St Springfield (45505) ***(G-17374)***
Champion Company...937 324-5681
1100 Kenton St Springfield (45505) ***(G-17375)***
CHAMPION INDUSTRIES DIV, Troy *Also called R T Industries Inc* ***(G-18695)***
Champion Manufacturing Inc...419 253-7930
4025 Bennington Way Marengo (43334) ***(G-12588)***
Champion Opco LLC (PA)...513 327-7338
12121 Champion Way Cincinnati (45241) ***(G-3463)***
Champion Rivet Company, Twinsburg *Also called Kre Inc* ***(G-18802)***
Champion Webbing Company Inc...330 920-1007
2748 2nd St Cuyahoga Falls (44221) ***(G-7848)***
Champion Win Co Cleveland LLC...440 899-2562
9011 Freeway Dr Ste 1 Macedonia (44056) ***(G-12283)***
Champion Win Enclosure Dayton...937 299-6800
2012 Springboro W Bldg 4 Moraine (45439) ***(G-14337)***
Champion Window Co of Toledo...419 841-0154
7546 Ponderosa Rd Ste A Perrysburg (43551) ***(G-15933)***
Champion Windows Manufacturing, Cincinnati *Also called Champion Opco LLC* ***(G-3463)***
Chandler Machine Co Inc...330 688-7615
4960 Hudson Dr Stow (44224) ***(G-17576)***
Chandler Machine Prod Gear...330 688-5585
4960 Hudson Dr Stow (44224) ***(G-17577)***
Chandler Mch & Prod Gear & Bro, Stow *Also called Chandler Machine Co Inc* ***(G-17576)***
Chandler Systems Incorporated...419 281-6829
710 Orange St Ashland (44805) ***(G-692)***
Chandler Systems Incorporated...888 363-9434
710 Orange St Ashland (44805) ***(G-693)***
Chang Audio, Toledo *Also called China Enterprises Inc* ***(G-18230)***
Channel Products Inc (PA)...440 423-0113
30700 Solon Indus Pkwy Solon (44139) ***(G-17126)***
Chantilly Development Corp...419 243-8109
3101 Monroe St Toledo (43606) ***(G-18227)***
Chaos Entertainment...937 520-5260
7570 Mount Whitney St Dayton (45424) ***(G-8086)***
Chaos Matrix Ltd...614 638-4748
44451 Kipton Nickle Plate Oberlin (44074) ***(G-15492)***
Chaplet & Chill Division, Canton *Also called The W L Jenkins Company* ***(G-2835)***
Chappell Door Company, Washington Court Hou *Also called Courthouse Manufacturing LLC* ***(G-19476)***
Chappell-Zimmerman Inc...330 337-8711
641 Olive St Salem (44460) ***(G-16725)***
Characteristic Solutions LLC...614 360-2424
829 Bethel Rd Ste 105 Columbus (43214) ***(G-6757)***
Characters Inc...937 335-1976
190 Peters Ave Ste A Troy (45373) ***(G-18640)***
Chardon Custom Polymers LLC...440 285-2161
373 Washington St Chardon (44024) ***(G-3101)***
Chardon Metal Products Co...440 285-2147
206 5th Ave Chardon (44024) ***(G-3102)***
Chardon Plastics Machinery...440 564-5360
11680 Butternut Rd Chardon (44024) ***(G-3103)***
Chardon Tool & Supply Co Inc...440 286-6440
115 Parker Ct Chardon (44024) ***(G-3104)***
Charger Connection...888 427-5829
7779 Meadowcreek Dr Cincinnati (45244) ***(G-3464)***
Charger Press Inc...513 542-3113
6088 Rte128 Miamitown (45041) ***(G-13745)***
Charisma Products Inc...614 846-8888
6342 Worthington Rd Westerville (43082) ***(G-19984)***
Charizma Corp...216 621-2220
1400 E 30th St Ste 201 Cleveland (44114) ***(G-4909)***
Charles Auto Electric Co Inc...330 535-6269
600 Grant St Akron (44311) ***(G-111)***
Charles C Lewis Company...440 439-3150
1 W Interstate St Ste 200 Cleveland (44146) ***(G-4910)***
Charles Costa Inc...330 376-3636
924 Home Ave Akron (44310) ***(G-112)***
Charles Daniel Young...937 968-3423
1324 Wasson Rd Union City (45390) ***(G-18903)***
Charles Huffman & Associates...216 295-0850
19214 Gladstone Rd Warrensville Heights (44122) ***(G-19465)***
Charles J Meyers...513 922-2866
866 Suncreek Ct Cincinnati (45238) ***(G-3465)***
Charles Messina...216 663-3344
16645 Granite Rd Cleveland (44137) ***(G-4911)***
Charles Mfg Co...330 395-3490
3021 Sferra Ave Nw Warren (44483) ***(G-19383)***
Charles Ray Evans...740 967-3669
1055 Gibbard Ave Columbus (43201) ***(G-6758)***
Charles Rewinding Div, Canton *Also called Hannon Company* ***(G-2693)***
Charles Svec Inc (PA)...216 662-5200
5470 Dunham Rd Maple Heights (44137) ***(G-12568)***
Charles V Snider & Assoc Inc...440 877-9151
10139 Royalton Rd Ste K North Royalton (44133) ***(G-15266)***
Charles Wisvari...740 671-9960
3266 Guernsey St Bellaire (43906) ***(G-1484)***
Charlotte M Peters...216 798-8997
3452 W 126th St Cleveland (44111) ***(G-4912)***
Charm Harness and Boot Ltd...330 893-0402
4432 County Road 70 Charm (44617) ***(G-3141)***
Chart Asia Inc...440 753-1490
1 Infinity Corp Ctr Dr Cleveland (44125) ***(G-4913)***
Chart Industries Inc...440 753-1490
5885 Landerbrook Dr # 150 Cleveland (44124) ***(G-4914)***
Chart International Inc (HQ)...440 753-1490
1 Infinity Corp Ctr Dr Cleveland (44125) ***(G-4915)***
Chart Tech Tool Inc...937 667-3543
4060 Lisa Dr Tipp City (45371) ***(G-18108)***
Charter Manufacturing Co Inc...216 883-3800
4300 E 49th St Cleveland (44125) ***(G-4916)***
Charter Nex Films - Del OH Inc...740 369-2770
1188 S Houk Rd Delaware (43015) ***(G-8663)***
Charter Nex Holding Company...740 369-2770
1188 S Houk Rd Delaware (43015) ***(G-8664)***
Chase Brass and Copper Co LLC (HQ)...419 485-3193
14212 Selwyn Dr Montpelier (43543) ***(G-14304)***
Chase Doors, West Chester *Also called Chase Industries Inc* ***(G-19841)***
Chase Doors Acquisition Corp...513 860-5565
10021 Commerce Park Dr West Chester (45246) ***(G-19840)***
Chase Industries Inc (HQ)...513 860-5565
10021 Commerce Park Dr West Chester (45246) ***(G-19841)***
Chassis Division, Springfield *Also called Sutphen Corporation* ***(G-17500)***
Chatelain Plastics Inc...419 422-4323
413 N Main St Findlay (45840) ***(G-9667)***
Chattanooga Laser Cutting LLC...513 779-7200
891 Redna Ter Cincinnati (45215) ***(G-3466)***
Chautauqua Fiberglass & Plasti...513 423-8840
2601 S Verity Pkwy Middletown (45044) ***(G-13892)***
Chc Manufacturing Inc (PA)...513 821-7757
10270 Wayne Ave Cincinnati (45215) ***(G-3467)***
Chc Manufacturing Inc...614 527-1606
2343 Westbrooke Dr Columbus (43228) ***(G-6759)***
Cheap Dumpsters LLC...614 285-5865
5042 Astoria Ave Columbus (43207) ***(G-6760)***
Check Yourself LLC...513 685-0868
4422 Carver Woods Dr # 110 Blue Ash (45242) ***(G-1749)***
Checkered Express Inc...330 530-8169
2501 W Liberty St Girard (44420) ***(G-10255)***

ALPHABETIC SECTION

Checkmate Marine Inc...419 562-3881
  3691 State Route 4 Bucyrus (44820) *(G-2321)*
Checkpoint Surgical Inc...216 378-9107
  22901 Millcreek Blvd # 110 Cleveland (44122) *(G-4917)*
Checkpoint Systems Inc...937 281-1304
  7620 Mcewen Rd Dayton (45459) *(G-8087)*
Checkpoint Systems Inc...330 456-7776
  1510 4th St Se Canton (44707) *(G-2622)*
Chef 2 Chef Foods...216 696-0080
  1893 E 55th St Cleveland (44103) *(G-4918)*
Chefs Pantry Inc (HQ)..440 288-0146
  1833 Cooper Foster Pk Rd Amherst (44001) *(G-557)*
Chelsea House Fabrics, Columbus Also called Style-Line Incorporated *(G-7497)*
Chem 1 Inc...216 475-7443
  19220 Miles Rd Warrensville Heights (44128) *(G-19466)*
Chem Instruments, West Chester Also called Chemsultants International Inc *(G-19670)*
Chem Technologies Ltd..440 632-9311
  14875 Bonner Dr Middlefield (44062) *(G-13783)*
Chem-Sales Inc..419 531-4292
  3860 Dorr St Toledo (43607) *(G-18228)*
Chemcore Inc (PA)..937 228-6118
  20 Madison St Dayton (45402) *(G-8088)*
Chemequip Sales Inc..330 724-8300
  1004 Swartz Rd Coventry Township (44319) *(G-7767)*
Chemical Instruments, West Chester Also called Cheminstruments Inc *(G-19669)*
Chemical Methods Inc...216 476-8400
  20338 Progress Dr Strongsville (44149) *(G-17725)*
Chemical Solvents Inc (PA)....................................216 741-9310
  3751 Jennings Rd Cleveland (44109) *(G-4919)*
Chemical Systems, Cleveland Also called Sports Care Products Inc *(G-6086)*
Chemigon LLC..330 592-1875
  520 S Main St Ste 2519 Akron (44311) *(G-113)*
Chemineer, Dayton Also called National Oilwell Varco Inc *(G-8376)*
Chemineer, Dayton Also called National Oilwell Varco LP *(G-8377)*
Cheminstruments Inc (PA).....................................513 860-1598
  510 Commercial Dr West Chester (45014) *(G-19668)*
Cheminstruments Inc..513 860-1598
  510 Commercial Dr West Chester (45014) *(G-19669)*
Chemionics Corporation..330 733-8834
  390 Munroe Falls Rd Tallmadge (44278) *(G-17975)*
Chemmasters Inc..440 428-2105
  300 Edwards St Madison (44057) *(G-12344)*
Chempace Corporation..419 535-0101
  339 Arco Dr Toledo (43607) *(G-18229)*
Chempak International LLC (PA)..........................440 543-8511
  10175 Queens Way Ste 8 Chagrin Falls (44023) *(G-3039)*
Chempure Products Corporation...........................330 874-4300
  148 Central Ave Bolivar (44612) *(G-1909)*
Chemspec...330 896-0355
  1559 Corporate Woods Pkwy # 150 Uniontown (44685) *(G-18914)*
Chemspec Ltd..330 896-0355
  1559 Corporate Woods Pkwy Uniontown (44685) *(G-18915)*
Chemspec Polymer Additives, Uniontown Also called Chemspec Ltd *(G-18915)*
Chemspec Usa LLC..330 669-8512
  9287 Smucker Rd Orrville (44667) *(G-15587)*
Chemsultants International Inc..............................513 860-1598
  510 Commercial Dr West Chester (45014) *(G-19670)*
Chemsultants International Inc (PA).......................440 974-3080
  9079 Tyler Blvd Mentor (44060) *(G-13412)*
Chemtrade Chemicals US LLC..............................513 422-6319
  305 Richmond St Middletown (45044) *(G-13893)*
Chemtrade Refinery Svcs Inc.................................419 641-4151
  7680 Ottawa Rd Cairo (45820) *(G-2402)*
Chemtrans Logistics Inc..419 447-8041
  281 Hancock St Tiffin (44883) *(G-18056)*
Chemwise...419 425-3604
  1752 W Romick Pkwy Findlay (45840) *(G-9668)*
Cheney Pulp and Paper Company..........................937 746-9991
  1000 Anderson St Franklin (45005) *(G-9874)*
Chep (usa) Inc...614 497-9448
  2130 New World Dr Columbus (43207) *(G-6761)*
Cherhire Choppers..740 362-0695
  4059 State Route 37 E A Delaware (43015) *(G-8665)*
Cherokee Hardwoods Inc (PA)..............................440 632-0322
  16741 Newcomb Rd Middlefield (44062) *(G-13784)*
Cheryl & Co (HQ)..614 776-1500
  646 Mccorkle Blvd Westerville (43082) *(G-19985)*
Cheryl & Co...614 776-1500
  4465 Industrial Center Dr Obetz (43207) *(G-15509)*
Cheryl A Lucas..614 755-2100
  388 Morrison Rd Columbus (43213) *(G-6762)*
Cheryl Heintz...937 492-3310
  231 Sandpiper Pl Sidney (45365) *(G-17022)*
Chester F Hale..740 379-2437
  60 Dry Ridge Rd Patriot (45658) *(G-15849)*
Chester Hoist, Salem Also called Columbus McKinnon Corporation *(G-16729)*
Chester Labs Inc...513 458-3871
  900 Section Rd Ste A Cincinnati (45237) *(G-3468)*
Chester Packaging LLC..513 458-3840
  1900 Section Rd Ste A Cincinnati (45237) *(G-3469)*
Chesterhill Stone Co..740 849-2338
  6305 Saltillo Rd East Fultonham (43735) *(G-9045)*
Chesterland Cabinet Company..............................440 564-1157
  10389 Kinsman Rd Newbury (44065) *(G-14947)*
Chesterland News Inc...440 729-7667
  8389 Mayfield Rd Ste B-4 Chesterland (44026) *(G-3154)*
Chestnut Holdings Inc (PA)....................................330 849-6503
  670 W Market St Akron (44303) *(G-114)*
Chevron Ae Resources LLC..................................330 896-8510
  3500 Massillon Rd Ste 100 Uniontown (44685) *(G-18916)*
Chevron Ae Resources LLC..................................330 654-4343
  1823 State Route 14 Deerfield (44411) *(G-8607)*
Chez Rama Restaurant...614 237-9315
  3669 E Livingston Ave Columbus (43227) *(G-6763)*
CHI Corporation (PA)..440 498-2300
  5265 Naiman Pkwy Ste H Cleveland (44139) *(G-4920)*
Chica Bands LLC..513 871-4300
  6216 Madison Rd Cincinnati (45227) *(G-3470)*
Chicago Dental Supply Inc.....................................800 571-5211
  10051 Simonson Rd Unit 9 Harrison (45030) *(G-10633)*
Chicago Pneumatic Tool Co LLC...........................704 883-3500
  9100 Market Pl Rear Broadview Heights (44147) *(G-2090)*
Chick Master Incubator Company (PA)..................330 722-5591
  945 Lafayette Rd Medina (44256) *(G-13235)*
Chickasaw Machine & TI Co Inc............................419 925-4325
  3050 Chickasaw Rd Celina (45822) *(G-2955)*
Chicopee Engineering Assoc Inc............................413 592-2273
  2300 E Enterprise Pkwy Twinsburg (44087) *(G-18751)*
Chieffos Frozen Foods Inc.....................................330 652-1222
  406 S Main St Niles (44446) *(G-15002)*
Chiefs Manufacturing & Eqp Co.............................216 291-3200
  4325 Monticello Blvd Cleveland (44121) *(G-4921)*
Chilcote Company...216 781-6000
  2160 Superior Ave E Cleveland (44114) *(G-4922)*
Child Evngelism Fellowship Inc..............................440 218-4982
  641 Acorn Pl Cuyahoga Falls (44221) *(G-7849)*
Child Evngelism Fellowship Inc..............................419 756-7799
  535 Beer Rd Ontario (44906) *(G-15538)*
Chili Logging Ltd..740 545-9502
  30240 County Road 10 Fresno (43824) *(G-10067)*
Chillicothe Facility, Chillicothe Also called P H Glatfelter Company *(G-3204)*
Chillicothe Gazette, Chillicothe Also called Gannett Co Inc *(G-3188)*
Chillicothe Packaging Corp....................................740 773-5800
  4168 State Route 159 Chillicothe (45601) *(G-3180)*
Chillicothe Packing, Chillicothe Also called Churmac Industries Inc *(G-3182)*
Chilltex LLC..937 710-3308
  7440 Hoying Rd Anna (45302) *(G-588)*
Chime Master Systems, Sugar Grove Also called Commercial Music Service Co *(G-17837)*
China Enterprises Inc..419 885-1485
  5151 Monroe St Toledo (43623) *(G-18230)*
Chipman Machining Co Inc....................................513 681-8515
  2900 Spring Grove Ave Cincinnati (45225) *(G-3471)*
Chipmatic Tool & Machine Inc..............................419 862-2737
  212 Ottawa St Elmore (43416) *(G-9205)*
Chipmunk Logging & Lumber LLC........................440 537-5124
  15810 Chipmunk Ln Middlefield (44062) *(G-13785)*
Chippewa Industries Inc..248 880-9193
  1309 W Bancroft St Toledo (43606) *(G-18231)*
Chippewa Tool & Mfg Co.......................................419 849-2790
  1101 Oak St Woodville (43469) *(G-20551)*
Chips Manufacturing Inc..440 946-3666
  35720 Lakeland Blvd Willoughby (44095) *(G-20296)*
Chocolate Pig Inc (PA)..440 461-4511
  5338 Mayfield Rd Cleveland (44124) *(G-4923)*
Choice Brands Adhesives Ltd...............................800 330-5566
  666 Redna Ter Ste 500 Cincinnati (45215) *(G-3472)*
Chore Anden..330 695-2300
  11461 Salt Creek Rd Fredericksburg (44627) *(G-9945)*
Chris Erhart Foundry & Mch Co.............................513 421-6550
  1240 Mehring Way Cincinnati (45203) *(G-3473)*
Chris Haughey..937 652-3338
  1463 S Us Highway 68 Urbana (43078) *(G-18982)*
Chris Nckel Cstm Ltherwork LLC..........................614 262-2672
  80 E Kelso Rd Columbus (43202) *(G-6764)*
Chris Stepp..513 248-0822
  927 State Route 28 Unit B Milford (45150) *(G-14002)*
Chrisnik Inc...513 738-2920
  7461 Cncnnati Brkville Rd Okeana (45053) *(G-15516)*
Christian Blue Pages (PA).....................................937 847-2583
  521 Byers Rd Ste 102 Miamisburg (45342) *(G-13650)*
Christian Citizen USA, Vandalia Also called Cross Communications Inc *(G-19120)*
Christian Happenings Magazine, Columbus Also called Wordcross Enterprises Inc *(G-7612)*
Christina A Kraft PHD...330 375-7474
  75 Arch St Ste 410 Akron (44304) *(G-115)*
Christman Fabricators Inc....................................330 477-8077
  4668 Navarre Rd Sw Canton (44706) *(G-2623)*
Christman Quarry, Lewisville Also called Gerald Christman *(G-11803)*

Christman Supply Co Inc ALPHABETIC SECTION

Christman Supply Co Inc......740 472-0046
239 Oaklawn Ave Woodsfield (43793) ***(G-20542)***
Christmas Ranch LLC......513 505-3865
3205 S Waynesville Rd Morrow (45152) ***(G-14409)***
Christopher Tool & Mfg Co......440 248-8080
30500 Carter St Frnt Cleveland (44139) ***(G-4924)***
Christy Machine Company......419 332-6451
118 Birchard Ave Fremont (43420) ***(G-10007)***
Chroma Color, Delaware *Also called Carolina Color Corp Ohio* ***(G-8660)***
Chroma Color Corporation......740 363-6622
100 Colomet Dr Delaware (43015) ***(G-8666)***
Chromacove LLC......216 264-1104
9000 Bank St Cleveland (44125) ***(G-4925)***
Chromaflo Technologies Corp (PA)......440 997-0081
2600 Michigan Ave Ashtabula (44004) ***(G-764)***
Chromaflo Technologies Corp......513 733-5111
620 Shepherd Dr Cincinnati (45215) ***(G-3474)***
Chromaflo Technologies Corp......440 997-5137
1603 W 29th St Ashtabula (44004) ***(G-765)***
Chromascape Inc (PA)......330 998-7574
2055 Enterprise Pkwy Twinsburg (44087) ***(G-18752)***
Chromatic Inc......216 881-2228
839 E 63rd St Cleveland (44103) ***(G-4926)***
Chrome & Speed Cycle LLC......937 429-5656
3490 Dayton Xenia Rd C Beavercreek (45432) ***(G-1305)***
Chrome Deposit Corporatio......330 773-7800
1566 Firestone Pkwy Akron (44301) ***(G-116)***
Chrome Deposit Corporation......513 539-8486
341 Lawton Ave Monroe (45050) ***(G-14257)***
Chrome Deposit Corporation......513 539-8486
341 Lawton Ave Monroe (45050) ***(G-14258)***
Chrome Industries Inc......216 771-2266
3041 Perkins Ave Cleveland (44114) ***(G-4927)***
Chronicle Telegram......330 725-4166
885 W Liberty St Medina (44256) ***(G-13236)***
Chronicle Your Life Story......614 456-7576
123 S Virginialee Rd Columbus (43209) ***(G-6765)***
Chub Gibsons Logging......740 884-4079
391 Fyffe Hollow Rd Chillicothe (45601) ***(G-3181)***
Chuck Meadors Plastics Co......440 813-4466
150 S Cucumber St Jefferson (44047) ***(G-11227)***
Church & Dwight Co Inc......740 852-3621
110 W 1st St London (43140) ***(G-12053)***
Church & Dwight Co Inc......419 992-4244
2501 E County Rd 34 Old Fort (44861) ***(G-15524)***
Church Budget Monthly Inc......330 337-1122
157 W Pershing St Salem (44460) ***(G-16726)***
Church-Budget Envelope Company......800 446-9780
271 S Ellsworth Ave Salem (44460) ***(G-16727)***
Churchill Steel Plate Ltd......330 425-9000
7851 Bavaria Rd Twinsburg (44087) ***(G-18753)***
Churmac Industries, Chillicothe *Also called Chillicothe Packaging Corp* ***(G-3180)***
Churmac Industries Inc......740 773-5800
4168 State Route 159 Chillicothe (45601) ***(G-3182)***
Chute Source LLC......330 475-0377
525 Kennedy Rd Akron (44305) ***(G-117)***
Ci Disposition Co......216 587-5200
1000 Valley Belt Rd Brooklyn Heights (44131) ***(G-2118)***
Cicogna Electric and Sign Co (PA)......440 998-2637
4330 N Bend Rd Ashtabula (44004) ***(G-766)***
Cigars of Cincy......513 931-5926
1467 Larann Ln Cincinnati (45231) ***(G-3475)***
Cil Isotope Separations LLC......937 376-5413
1689 Burnett Dr Xenia (45385) ***(G-20761)***
Cima Inc......513 382-8976
1010b Eaton Ave Hamilton (45013) ***(G-10545)***
Cima Inc......513 382-8976
1010 Eaton Ave Hamilton (45013) ***(G-10546)***
Cima Plastics Group, Twinsburg *Also called Stewart Acquisition LLC* ***(G-18860)***
Cimbar Performance Mnrl WV LLC......330 532-2034
2400 Clark Ave Wellsville (43968) ***(G-19612)***
Cimino Box & Pallet Company, Cleveland *Also called Cimino Box Inc* ***(G-4928)***
Cimino Box Inc......216 961-7377
8500 Clinton Rd Ste 6 Cleveland (44144) ***(G-4928)***
Cimx LLC......513 248-7700
4625 Red Bank Rd Ste 200 Cincinnati (45227) ***(G-3476)***
Cimx Software, Cincinnati *Also called Cimx LLC* ***(G-3476)***
Cinchempro Inc......513 724-6111
458 W Main St Batavia (45103) ***(G-1129)***
Cincinati Book Publicsher, Cincinnati *Also called Psa Consulting Inc* ***(G-4220)***
Cincinnati - Vulcan Company......513 242-5300
5353 Spring Grove Ave Cincinnati (45217) ***(G-3477)***
Cincinnati A Flter Sls Svc Inc......513 242-3400
4815 Para Dr Cincinnati (45237) ***(G-3478)***
Cincinnati Advg Pdts LLC (HQ)......513 346-7310
12150 Northwest Blvd Cincinnati (45246) ***(G-3479)***
Cincinnati Air Conditioning Co......513 721-5622
2080 Northwest Dr Cincinnati (45231) ***(G-3480)***
Cincinnati Assn For The Blind......513 221-8558
2045 Gilbert Ave Cincinnati (45202) ***(G-3481)***
Cincinnati Babbitt Inc......513 942-5088
9217 Seward Rd Fairfield (45014) ***(G-9490)***
Cincinnati Barge Rail Trml LLC......513 227-3611
1707 Riverside Dr Cincinnati (45202) ***(G-3482)***
Cincinnati Bell Any Dstnce Inc......513 397-9900
221 E 4th St Ste 700 Cincinnati (45202) ***(G-3483)***
Cincinnati Bindery & Packg Inc......859 816-0282
2838 Spring Grove Ave Cincinnati (45225) ***(G-3484)***
Cincinnati Biorefining Corp (HQ)......513 482-8800
470 Este Ave Cincinnati (45232) ***(G-3485)***
Cincinnati Blacktop Company......513 681-0952
4992 Gray Rd Cincinnati (45232) ***(G-3486)***
Cincinnati Chemical Processing, Batavia *Also called Cinchempro Inc* ***(G-1129)***
Cincinnati City Boat Ramp, Cincinnati *Also called Cincinnati Recreation Comm* ***(G-3505)***
Cincinnati Cold Drawn Inc......513 874-3296
9108 Sutton Pl West Chester (45011) ***(G-19671)***
Cincinnati Convertors Inc......513 731-6600
1730 Cleneay Ave Cincinnati (45212) ***(G-3487)***
Cincinnati Crane & Hoist LLC......513 202-1408
10860 Paddys Run Rd Harrison (45030) ***(G-10634)***
Cincinnati Crt Index Press Inc......513 241-1450
119 W Central Pkwy Cincinnati (45202) ***(G-3488)***
Cincinnati Ctrl Dynamics Inc......513 242-7300
4924 Para Dr Cincinnati (45237) ***(G-3489)***
Cincinnati Division, Monroe *Also called Terex Utilities Inc* ***(G-14278)***
Cincinnati Dowel & WD Pdts Co......937 444-2502
135 Oak St Mount Orab (45154) ***(G-14439)***
Cincinnati Drveline Hydraulics......513 651-2406
1220 W 8th St Cincinnati (45203) ***(G-3490)***
Cincinnati Enquirer......513 721-2700
312 Elm St Fl 18 Cincinnati (45202) ***(G-3491)***
Cincinnati Enquirer, The, Cincinnati *Also called Gannett Co Inc* ***(G-3723)***
Cincinnati Flame Hardening Co, Fairfield *Also called Detroit Flame Hardening Co* ***(G-9494)***
Cincinnati Ftn Sq News Inc......513 421-4049
8739 S Shore Pl Mason (45040) ***(G-12841)***
Cincinnati Gasket & Indus GL, Cincinnati *Also called Cincinnati Gasket Pkg Mfg Inc* ***(G-3492)***
Cincinnati Gasket Pkg Mfg Inc......513 761-3458
40 Illinois Ave Cincinnati (45215) ***(G-3492)***
Cincinnati Gearing Systems Inc (PA)......513 527-8600
5757 Mariemont Ave Cincinnati (45227) ***(G-3493)***
Cincinnati Gearing Systems Inc......513 527-8634
301 Milford Pkwy Cincinnati (45227) ***(G-3494)***
Cincinnati Gearing Systems Inc......513 527-8600
5757 Mariemont Ave Cincinnati (45227) ***(G-3495)***
Cincinnati Gearing Systems Inc......513 527-8600
5757 Mariemont Ave Cincinnati (45227) ***(G-3496)***
Cincinnati Gilbert Mch Tl LLC......513 541-4815
3366 Beekman St Cincinnati (45223) ***(G-3497)***
Cincinnati Glass Block Day GL, Cincinnati *Also called Pierce GL Inc* ***(G-4158)***
Cincinnati Gutter Supply Inc......513 825-0500
9345 Prnceton Glendale Rd West Chester (45011) ***(G-19672)***
Cincinnati Heat Exchangers Inc......513 874-7232
6404 Thornberry Ct # 440 Mason (45040) ***(G-12842)***
Cincinnati Industrial McHy Inc......513 923-5600
4600 N Masn Montgomery Rd Mason (45040) ***(G-12843)***
Cincinnati Laser Cutting LLC......513 779-7200
891 Redna Ter Cincinnati (45215) ***(G-3498)***
Cincinnati Machines Inc......513 536-2432
4165 Half Acre Rd Batavia (45103) ***(G-1130)***
Cincinnati Magazine......513 421-4300
441 Vine St Ste 200 Cincinnati (45202) ***(G-3499)***
Cincinnati Marlins Inc......513 761-3320
616 W North Bend Rd Cincinnati (45224) ***(G-3500)***
Cincinnati Metal Fabricating, Cincinnati *Also called Cincinnati Laser Cutting LLC* ***(G-3498)***
Cincinnati Mine Machinery Co......513 522-7777
2950 Jonrose Ave Cincinnati (45239) ***(G-3501)***
Cincinnati Mold Incorporated......513 922-1888
225 Stille Dr Cincinnati (45233) ***(G-3502)***
Cincinnati Paperboard, Cincinnati *Also called Caraustar Industries Inc* ***(G-3441)***
Cincinnati Pattern Company......513 241-9872
2405 Spring Grove Ave Cincinnati (45214) ***(G-3503)***
Cincinnati Precision McHy Inc......513 860-4133
9083 Sutton Pl West Chester (45011) ***(G-19673)***
Cincinnati Preserving Company (HQ)......513 771-2000
3015 E Kemper Rd Cincinnati (45241) ***(G-3504)***
Cincinnati Print Solutions LLC......513 943-9500
4007 Bach Buxton Rd Amelia (45102) ***(G-534)***
Cincinnati Printers Co Inc......513 860-9053
9053 Le Saint Dr West Chester (45014) ***(G-19674)***
Cincinnati Prof Door Sls Div, Cincinnati *Also called Division Overhead Door Inc* ***(G-3597)***
Cincinnati Recreation Comm......513 921-5657
3540 Southside Ave Cincinnati (45204) ***(G-3505)***
Cincinnati Renewable Fuels LLC......513 482-8800
4700 Este Ave Cincinnati (45232) ***(G-3506)***
Cincinnati Retread Systems, Fairfield *Also called American Manufacturing & Eqp* ***(G-9482)***
Cincinnati Specialties LLC......513 242-3300
501 Murray Rd Cincinnati (45217) ***(G-3507)***

ALPHABETIC SECTION
Clampco Products Inc (PA)

Cincinnati Stair, Loveland *Also called Jaco Inc* ***(G-12202)***
Cincinnati Test Systems Inc (PA)...513 202-5100
10100 Progress Way Harrison (45030) ***(G-10635)***
Cincinnati Thermal Spray Inc...513 793-1037
5901 Creek Rd Blue Ash (45242) ***(G-1750)***
Cincinnati Valve Company...513 471-8258
1245 Hill Smith Dr Cincinnati (45215) ***(G-3508)***
Cincinnati Valve Company...513 471-8258
1245 Hill Smith Dr Cincinnati (45215) ***(G-3509)***
Cincinnati Valve Lunkenheimer, Cincinnati *Also called Cincinnati Valve Company* ***(G-3508)***
Cincinnati Window Decor, Cincinnati *Also called Cincinnati Window Shade Inc* ***(G-3510)***
Cincinnati Window Shade Inc...513 398-8510
5633 Tylersville Rd Ste 1 Mason (45040) ***(G-12844)***
Cincinnati Window Shade Inc (PA)...513 631-7200
3004 Harris Ave Cincinnati (45212) ***(G-3510)***
Cincinnati Wood Products Co...513 542-0569
2644 Colerain Ave Cincinnati (45214) ***(G-3511)***
Cincinnati Woodworks Inc...513 241-6412
2161 Elysian Pl Cincinnati (45219) ***(G-3512)***
Cincinnatti Premier Candy LLC...513 253-0079
5141 Fischer Ave Cincinnati (45217) ***(G-3513)***
Cincom Systems Inc...513 459-1470
4605 Duke Dr Mason (45040) ***(G-12845)***
Cincy Deli & Carryout, Cincinnati *Also called Zygo Inc* ***(G-4535)***
Cincy Glass Inc...513 241-0455
3249 Fredonia Ave Cincinnati (45229) ***(G-3514)***
Cincy Safe Company...513 900-9152
1607 State Route 131 Milford (45150) ***(G-14003)***
Cincy-Dumpster Inc...513 941-3063
50 Timea Ave Cleves (45002) ***(G-6357)***
Cinderella...937 312-9969
2700 Mmsburg Cntrville Rd Dayton (45459) ***(G-8089)***
Cindoco Wood Products Co...937 444-2504
410 Mount Clifton Dr Mount Orab (45154) ***(G-14440)***
Cinex Inc...513 921-2825
2641 Cummins St Cincinnati (45225) ***(G-3515)***
Cinfab LLC...513 396-6100
5240 Lester Rd Cincinnati (45213) ***(G-3516)***
Cinn Wire E D M Inc...513 741-5402
6850 Colerain Ave Cincinnati (45239) ***(G-3517)***
Cinncinati Bindery, Cincinnati *Also called Spring Grove Manufacturing* ***(G-4362)***
Cintas Corporation (PA)...513 459-1200
6800 Cintas Blvd Cincinnati (45262) ***(G-3518)***
Cintas Corporation...513 631-5750
5570 Ridge Ave Cincinnati (45213) ***(G-3519)***
Cintas Corporation No 2...937 236-1506
903 Brandt St Bldg A Dayton (45404) ***(G-8090)***
Cintas Corporation No 2...330 966-7800
3865 Highland Park Nw Canton (44720) ***(G-2624)***
Cintas Sales Corporation (HQ)...513 459-1200
6800 Cintas Blvd Cincinnati (45262) ***(G-3520)***
Cintas Uniforms AP Fcilty Svcs, Cincinnati *Also called Cintas Corporation* ***(G-3519)***
CIP International Inc...513 874-9925
9575 Le Saint Dr West Chester (45014) ***(G-19675)***
Cipar Inc (HQ)...216 910-1700
3601 Green Rd Ste 308 Beachwood (44122) ***(G-1226)***
Circle Machine Rolls Inc...330 938-9010
245 W Kentucky Ave Sebring (44672) ***(G-16885)***
Circle Mold & Machine Co, Tallmadge *Also called Circle Mold Incorporated* ***(G-17976)***
Circle Mold Incorporated...330 633-7017
85 S Thomas Rd Tallmadge (44278) ***(G-17976)***
Circle Prime Manufacturing...330 923-0019
2114 Front St Cuyahoga Falls (44221) ***(G-7850)***
Circleville Glass Operations, Circleville *Also called Technicolor Usa Inc* ***(G-4561)***
Circleville Oil Co...740 477-3341
224 Lancaster Pike Circleville (43113) ***(G-4539)***
Circuit Center...513 435-2131
4738 Gateway Cir Dayton (45440) ***(G-8091)***
Circuit Services LLC...513 604-7405
351 Deerfield Dr Harrison (45030) ***(G-10636)***
Cirrus LLC...740 272-2012
120 Homestead Ln Delaware (43015) ***(G-8667)***
Cisco Systems Inc...419 977-2404
130 S Washington St New Bremen (45869) ***(G-14648)***
Cisco Systems Inc...937 427-4264
2661 Commons Blvd Ste 133 Beavercreek (45431) ***(G-1306)***
Citco Diamond & Cbn Products, Painesville *Also called Fives Landis Corp* ***(G-15740)***
Citgo Petroleum Corporation...419 698-8055
1840 Otter Creek Rd Oregon (43616) ***(G-15558)***
Citi 2 Citi Logistics...614 306-4109
6031 E Main St Columbus (43213) ***(G-6766)***
Citizens Defense LLC...740 645-1101
7388 Cora Mill Rd Thurman (45685) ***(G-18037)***
Citizens USA...937 280-2001
3651 Wright Way Rd Dayton (45424) ***(G-8092)***
City Dog...614 228-3647
510 E Main St Columbus (43215) ***(G-6767)***
City Elyria Communication...440 322-3329
851 Garden St Elyria (44035) ***(G-9237)***
City Girl Magazine LLC...216 481-4110
801 E 212th St Cleveland (44119) ***(G-4929)***
City Iron LLC...513 721-5678
4136 Colerain Ave Cincinnati (45223) ***(G-3521)***
City Machine Technologies Inc (PA)...330 747-2639
773 W Rayen Ave Youngstown (44502) ***(G-20870)***
City Machine Technologies Inc...330 740-8186
825 Martin Luther King Jr Youngstown (44502) ***(G-20871)***
City Machine Technologies Inc...330 747-2639
773 W Rayen Ave Youngstown (44502) ***(G-20872)***
City Machine Technologies Inc...330 747-2639
448 Andrews Ave Youngstown (44505) ***(G-20873)***
City of Ashland...419 289-8728
310 W 12th St Ashland (44805) ***(G-694)***
City of Athens...740 592-3344
395 W State St Athens (45701) ***(G-825)***
City of Canton...330 489-3370
2436 30th St Ne Canton (44705) ***(G-2625)***
City of Chardon...440 286-2657
201 N Hambden St Chardon (44024) ***(G-3105)***
City of Cleveland...216 664-3013
1735 Lakeside Ave E Cleveland (44114) ***(G-4930)***
City of Cleveland...216 664-2711
500 Lakeside Ave E Cleveland (44114) ***(G-4931)***
City of Columbus...614 645-3152
7000 State Route 104 Lockbourne (43137) ***(G-11993)***
City of Conneaut...440 599-7071
480 Lake Rd Conneaut (44030) ***(G-7643)***
City of Kent...330 673-8897
497 Middlebury Rd Kent (44240) ***(G-11304)***
City of Lancaster...740 687-6670
1424 Campground Rd Lancaster (43130) ***(G-11554)***
City of Mansfield...419 884-3310
2010 S Lexngtn Sprngml Rd Mansfield (44904) ***(G-12425)***
City of Marietta...740 374-6864
2000 4th St Marietta (45750) ***(G-12615)***
City of Middletown...513 425-7781
805 Columbia Ave Middletown (45042) ***(G-13894)***
City of Mount Vernon...740 393-9508
1550 Old Delaware Rd Mount Vernon (43050) ***(G-14475)***
City of Newark, Newark *Also called Traffic Cntrl Sgnls Signs & MA* ***(G-14930)***
City of Newark...740 349-6765
164 Waterworks Rd Newark (43055) ***(G-14861)***
City of Oxford...513 523-8412
945 Collins Run Rd Oxford (45056) ***(G-15691)***
City of Parma...440 885-8816
6611 Ridge Rd Fl 2 Cleveland (44129) ***(G-4932)***
City of Ravenna...330 296-5214
3722 Hommon Rd Ravenna (44266) ***(G-16372)***
City of Troy...937 339-4826
300 E Staunton Rd Troy (45373) ***(G-18641)***
City of Xenia...937 376-7269
1831 Us Route 68 N Xenia (45385) ***(G-20762)***
City Plating and Polishing LLC...216 267-8158
4821 W 130th St Cleveland (44135) ***(G-4933)***
City Printing Co Inc...330 747-5691
122 Oak Hill Ave Youngstown (44502) ***(G-20874)***
City Scrap & Salvage Co...330 753-5051
760 Flora Ave Akron (44314) ***(G-118)***
City Visitor Inc...216 661-6666
5755 Granger Rd Ste 600 Cleveland (44131) ***(G-4934)***
City Visitor Publications, Cleveland *Also called City Visitor Inc* ***(G-4934)***
Citynet Ohio LLC...614 364-7881
343 N Front St Ste 400 Columbus (43215) ***(G-6768)***
Cityscapes International Inc...614 850-2540
4200 Lyman Ct Hilliard (43026) ***(G-10816)***
Citywide Materials Inc...513 533-1111
5263 Wooster Pike Cincinnati (45226) ***(G-3522)***
Citywide Ready Mix, Cincinnati *Also called Citywide Materials Inc* ***(G-3522)***
Civacon, West Chester *Also called Knappco Corporation* ***(G-19731)***
Civica CMI, Englewood *Also called Creative Microsystems Inc* ***(G-9353)***
Civitas Media, Miamisburg *Also called Heartland Publications LLC* ***(G-13675)***
Cjk USA Print Possibilities, Cincinnati *Also called C J Krehbiel Company* ***(G-3436)***
Cjr Desserts...513 549-6403
7272 Northgate Dr Maineville (45039) ***(G-12365)***
Cjt's, Ironton *Also called Wheeler Embroidery* ***(G-11177)***
CK Technologies LLC (HQ)...419 485-1110
1701 Magda Dr Montpelier (43543) ***(G-14305)***
Ckm Ventures LLC (PA)...216 623-0370
2635 Payne Ave Cleveland (44114) ***(G-4935)***
Cks Solution Incorporated (PA)...513 947-1277
4293 Muhlhauser Rd Fairfield (45014) ***(G-9491)***
Claflin Company Inc...330 650-0582
5270 Hudson Dr Hudson (44236) ***(G-11036)***
Clair Zeits...419 643-8980
7896 N Cool Rd Columbus Grove (45830) ***(G-7633)***
Clampco Products Inc (PA)...330 336-8857
1743 Wall Rd Wadsworth (44281) ***(G-19230)***

ALPHABETIC

Clamps Inc 419 729-2141
  5960 American Rd E Toledo (43612) *(G-18232)*
Clancys Cabinet Shop 419 445-4455
  3751 County Road 26 Archbold (43502) *(G-641)*
Clarcor Industrial Air, Blue Ash *Also called Bha Altair LLC (G-1734)*
Clare Sky Inc (HQ) 866 558-5706
  7711 E Pleasant Valley Rd Cleveland (44131) *(G-4936)*
Clarence Tussel Jr 440 576-3415
  141 E Jefferson St Jefferson (44047) *(G-11228)*
Clariant Corporation 513 791-2964
  10999 Reed Hartman Hwy # 201 Blue Ash (45242) *(G-1751)*
Claridon Tool & Die Inc 740 389-1944
  4985 Marion Mt Gilead Rd Caledonia (43314) *(G-2414)*
Clark & Son Billiard Supply, Canton *Also called Clark & Son Pool Table Company (G-2626)*
Clark & Son Pool Table Company 330 454-9153
  2737 Cleveland Ave Nw Canton (44709) *(G-2626)*
Clark Associates Inc 419 334-3838
  702 W State St Ste A Fremont (43420) *(G-10008)*
Clark Auto Machine Shop 216 939-0768
  4607 Clark Ave Cleveland (44102) *(G-4937)*
Clark Dietrich Building, Warren *Also called Clarkwestern Dietrich Building (G-19384)*
Clark Grave Vault Company (PA) 614 294-3761
  375 E 5th Ave Columbus (43201) *(G-6769)*
Clark Machine Service 740 887-2396
  33926 Us Highway 50 Londonderry (45647) *(G-12074)*
Clark Optimization LLC 330 417-2164
  1222 Easton St Ne Canton (44721) *(G-2627)*
Clark Prfmce Fabrication LLC 701 721-1378
  5647 Rowena Dr Dayton (45415) *(G-8093)*
Clark Rbr Plastic Intl Sls Inc (PA) 440 255-9793
  8888 East Ave Mentor (44060) *(G-13413)*
Clark Rm Inc 419 425-9889
  400 Crystal Ave Findlay (45840) *(G-9669)*
Clark Son Actn Liquidation Inc 330 866-9330
  10233 Sandyville Ave Se East Sparta (44626) *(G-9094)*
Clark Substations LLC 330 452-5200
  2240 Allen Ave Se Canton (44707) *(G-2628)*
Clark Wood Specialties Inc 330 499-8711
  9235 Shadybrook St Nw Clinton (44216) *(G-6384)*
Clark-Fowler Elc Mtr & Sups, Wooster *Also called Clark-Fowler Enterprises Inc (G-20578)*
Clark-Fowler Enterprises Inc. 330 262-0906
  510 W Henry St Wooster (44691) *(G-20578)*
Clark-Reliance Corporation (PA) 440 572-1500
  16633 Foltz Pkwy Strongsville (44149) *(G-17726)*
Clark-Reliance Corporation 440 572-7408
  16633 Foltz Pkwy Strongsville (44149) *(G-17727)*
Clarke Fire Protection Product, Cincinnati *Also called Clarke Power Services Inc (G-3524)*
Clarke Fire Prtection Pdts Inc (HQ) 513 771-2200
  3133 E Kemper Rd Cincinnati (45241) *(G-3523)*
Clarke Power Services Inc 513 771-2200
  3133 E Kemper Rd Cincinnati (45241) *(G-3524)*
Clarke-Boxit Corporation 716 487-1950
  5601 Walworth Ave Cleveland (44102) *(G-4938)*
Clarksville Stave & Lumber Co 937 376-4618
  2808 Jasper Rd Xenia (45385) *(G-20763)*
Clarkwestern Dietrich Building 330 372-5564
  1985 N River Rd Ne Warren (44483) *(G-19384)*
Clarkwestern Dietrich Building 513 870-1100
  9050 Centre Pointe Dr West Chester (45069) *(G-19676)*
Clarkwestern Dietrich Building (HQ) 513 870-1100
  9050 Centre Pointe Dr West Chester (45069) *(G-19677)*
Classic Countertops LLC 330 882-4220
  1519 Kenmore Blvd Akron (44314) *(G-119)*
Classic Delight Inc 419 394-7955
  310 S Park Dr Saint Marys (45885) *(G-16682)*
Classic Exhaust 440 466-5460
  805 Pro Gram Pkwy Geneva (44041) *(G-10216)*
Classic Laminations Inc 440 735-1333
  7703 First Pl Ste B Cleveland (44146) *(G-4939)*
Classic Metal Roofing Systems, Piqua *Also called Isaiah Industries Inc (G-16131)*
Classic Metals Ltd 330 763-1162
  7051 State Route 83 Holmesville (44633) *(G-10974)*
Classic Monuments, Piqua *Also called Piqua Granite & Marble Co Inc (G-16153)*
Classic Optical Labs Inc 330 759-8245
  3710 Belmont Ave Youngstown (44505) *(G-20875)*
Classic Recipe Chili Inc 513 771-1441
  10592 Taconic Ter Cincinnati (45215) *(G-3525)*
Classic Reproductions 937 548-9839
  5315 Meeker Rd Greenville (45331) *(G-10364)*
Classic Sign Company Inc 419 420-0058
  112 Lagrange St Findlay (45840) *(G-9670)*
Classic Stone Company Inc 614 833-3946
  4090 Janitrol Rd Columbus (43228) *(G-6770)*
Classic Tool Inc 330 922-1933
  4278 Hudson Dr Stow (44224) *(G-17578)*
Classic Toy Company Inc 216 851-2000
  12825 Taft Ave Cleveland (44108) *(G-4940)*
Clay Burley Products Co (PA) 740 452-3633
  455 Gordon St Roseville (43777) *(G-16576)*
Clay Burley Products Co 740 697-0221
  451 Gordon St Roseville (43777) *(G-16577)*
Clay LBC Co 740 492-5055
  59260 County Road 9 Newcomerstown (43832) *(G-14972)*
Clay Logan Products Company 740 385-2184
  201 S Walnut St Logan (43138) *(G-12022)*
Clayton Manufacturing Company 513 563-1300
  3051 Exon Ave Cincinnati (45241) *(G-3526)*
Clayton Mfg Co, Cincinnati *Also called Clayton Manufacturing Company (G-3526)*
Clean Water Conditioning 614 475-4532
  305 Sumption Dr Columbus (43230) *(G-6771)*
Cleancut, West Chester *Also called Safeway Safety Step LLC (G-19791)*
Cleaning By Sndra Msters Touch 216 524-6827
  6516 Gale Dr Seven Hills (44131) *(G-16902)*
Cleaning Lady Inc 419 589-5566
  190 Stewart Rd N Mansfield (44905) *(G-12426)*
Cleaning Tech Group LLC (HQ) 877 933-8278
  4933 Provident Dr West Chester (45246) *(G-19842)*
Cleaning Tech Group LLC 513 870-0100
  4933 Provident Dr West Chester (45246) *(G-19843)*
Cleaning Technologies Grp, Tiffin *Also called Nmgg Ctg LLC (G-18072)*
Cleanlife Energy LLC 800 316-2532
  2400 Superior Ave E # 205 Cleveland (44114) *(G-4941)*
Cleanlife Products, Springboro *Also called No Rinse Laboratories LLC (G-17339)*
Clear Channel, Lima *Also called Iheartcommunications Inc (G-11876)*
Clear Creek Screw Machine Corp 740 969-2113
  4900 Julian Rd Sw Amanda (43102) *(G-525)*
Clear Fold Door Inc 440 735-1351
  7703 First Pl Ste A Cleveland (44146) *(G-4942)*
Clear Image Technology LLC 440 366-4330
  26202 Detroit Rd Ste 340 Westlake (44145) *(G-20105)*
Clear Images LLC 419 241-9347
  121 11th St Toledo (43604) *(G-18233)*
Clear One LLC 800 279-3724
  99 S Remington Rd Columbus (43209) *(G-6772)*
Clear Run Lumber Co 740 747-2665
  2830 State Route 229 Marengo (43334) *(G-12589)*
Clearfield Ohio Holdings Inc 740 947-5121
  300 E 2nd St Waverly (45690) *(G-19542)*
Clearflite Inc 440 281-7368
  5445 E Lake Rd Sheffield Lake (44054) *(G-16963)*
Clearly Visible Mobile Wash 440 543-9299
  7302 Jackson Rd Chagrin Falls (44023) *(G-3040)*
Clearpath Utility Solutions LLC 740 661-4240
  8155 Ridge Rd Zanesville (43701) *(G-21119)*
Clearsonic Manufacturing Inc 828 772-9809
  1223 Norton Rd Hudson (44236) *(G-11037)*
Clearwater One LLC 216 554-4747
  21400 Lorain Rd Cleveland (44126) *(G-4943)*
Clearwater Wood Group LLC 567 644-9951
  4401 Hunts Landing Rd Hebron (43025) *(G-10739)*
Cleary Machine Company Inc 937 839-4278
  4858 Us Route 35 E West Alexandria (45381) *(G-19617)*
Clecorr Inc 216 961-5500
  10610 Berea Rd Rear Cleveland (44102) *(G-4944)*
Clecorr Packaging, Cleveland *Also called Clecorr Inc (G-4944)*
Clemens License Agency 614 288-8007
  12825 Wheaton Ave Pickerington (43147) *(G-16043)*
Clermont Steel Fabricators LLC 513 732-6033
  2565 Old State Route 32 Batavia (45103) *(G-1131)*
Clermont Sun Publishing Co 937 444-3441
  219 S High St Mount Orab (45154) *(G-14441)*
Cletronics Inc 330 239-2002
  2262 Port Centre Dr Medina (44256) *(G-13237)*
Cleveland AEC West LLC 216 362-6000
  14000 Keystone Pkwy Cleveland (44135) *(G-4945)*
Cleveland Bagel Company LLC 216 385-7723
  4309 Larrain Ave Cleveland (44113) *(G-4946)*
Cleveland Bagel Company, The, Cleveland *Also called Cleveland Bagel Company LLC (G-4946)*
Cleveland Bean Sprout Inc 216 881-2112
  2675 E 40th St Cleveland (44115) *(G-4947)*
Cleveland Black Oxide, Cleveland *Also called Tatham Schulz Incorporated (G-6149)*
Cleveland Black Pages, Cleveland *Also called Lanier & Associates Inc (G-5559)*
Cleveland Business Supply LLC 888 831-0088
  8193 Avery Rd Ste 200 Broadview Heights (44147) *(G-2091)*
Cleveland Canvas Goods Mfg Co 216 361-4567
  1960 E 57th St Cleveland (44103) *(G-4948)*
Cleveland Carbide Tool Co 440 974-1155
  7755 Division Dr Mentor (44060) *(G-13414)*
Cleveland Caster LLC 440 333-1443
  19885 Detroit Rd 243 Cleveland (44116) *(G-4949)*
Cleveland Church Supply, Cleveland *Also called Novak J F Manufacturing Co LLC (G-5790)*
Cleveland Circuits Corp 216 267-9020
  15516 Industrial Pkwy Cleveland (44135) *(G-4950)*
Cleveland Citizen Pubg Co 216 861-4283
  2012 W 25th St Ste 900 Cleveland (44113) *(G-4951)*
Cleveland City Forge Inc 440 647-5400
  46950 State Route 18 Wellington (44090) *(G-19574)*

Cleveland Coca-Cola Btlg Inc....216 690-2653
25000 Miles Rd Bedford Heights (44146) *(G-1465)*
Cleveland Controls Inc....216 398-0330
1111 Brookpark Rd Cleveland (44109) *(G-4952)*
Cleveland Coppersmithing Works....330 607-3998
4830 Hawkins Rd Richfield (44286) *(G-16465)*
Cleveland Copy & Prtg Svc LLC (PA)....216 861-0324
1835 E 30th St Fl 3 Cleveland (44114) *(G-4953)*
Cleveland Coretec Inc....314 727-2087
12080 Debartolo Dr North Jackson (44451) *(G-15144)*
Cleveland Cstm Pllet Crate Inc....216 881-1414
4201 Lakeside Ave E Cleveland (44114) *(G-4954)*
Cleveland Custom Cabinets LLC....213 663-0606
19561 Miles Rd Cleveland (44128) *(G-4955)*
Cleveland Deburring Machine Co....216 472-0200
3370 W 140th St Cleveland (44111) *(G-4956)*
Cleveland Die & Mfg, Middleburg Heights *Also called Cleveland Die & Mfg Co (G-13762)*
Cleveland Die & Mfg Co (PA)....440 243-3404
20303 1st Ave Middleburg Heights (44130) *(G-13762)*
Cleveland Digital Imaging Svcs, Cleveland *Also called Caraustar Industries Inc (G-4874)*
Cleveland Division, Brecksville *Also called Terex Utilities Inc (G-2060)*
Cleveland Drapery Stitch Inc....216 252-3857
12890 Berea Rd Cleveland (44111) *(G-4957)*
Cleveland East Ed Wns Jurnl....216 228-1379
1663 Saint Charles Ave Cleveland (44107) *(G-4958)*
Cleveland Electric Labs, Twinsburg *Also called Cleveland Electric Labs Co (G-18754)*
Cleveland Electric Labs Co (PA)....800 447-2207
1776 Enterprise Pkwy Twinsburg (44087) *(G-18754)*
Cleveland Finishing Inc....440 572-5475
16979 Falmouth Dr Strongsville (44136) *(G-17728)*
Cleveland Flame Hardening, Euclid *Also called Detroit Flame Hardening Co (G-9410)*
Cleveland FP Inc (PA)....216 249-4900
12819 Coit Rd Cleveland (44108) *(G-4959)*
Cleveland Gas Systems LLC....216 391-7780
10325 State Route 43 N Streetsboro (44241) *(G-17665)*
Cleveland Gear Company Inc (HQ)....216 641-9000
3249 E 80th St Cleveland (44104) *(G-4960)*
Cleveland Granite & Marble LLC....216 291-7637
4121 Carnegie Ave Cleveland (44103) *(G-4961)*
Cleveland Hdwr & Forging Co (PA)....216 641-5200
3270 E 79th St Cleveland (44104) *(G-4962)*
Cleveland Hollow Boring Inc....216 883-1926
4501 Lakeside Ave E Cleveland (44114) *(G-4963)*
Cleveland Hoya Corp....440 234-5703
94 Pelret Industrial Pkwy Berea (44017) *(G-1595)*
Cleveland Ignition Co Inc....440 439-3688
600 Golden Oak Pkwy Cleveland (44146) *(G-4964)*
Cleveland Indus Training Ctr, Cleveland *Also called Borman Enterprises Inc (G-4833)*
Cleveland Instrument Corp....440 826-1800
6430 Eastland Rd Ste 2 Brookpark (44142) *(G-2138)*
Cleveland Iron Workers Members....216 687-2290
2121 Euclid Ave Mm304 Cleveland (44115) *(G-4965)*
Cleveland Jewish News, Cleveland *Also called Cleveland Jewish Publ Co (G-4966)*
Cleveland Jewish Publ Co....216 454-8300
23880 Commerce Park Ste 1 Cleveland (44122) *(G-4966)*
Cleveland Jewish Publ Co Fdn....216 454-8300
23800 Commerce Park Beachwood (44122) *(G-1227)*
Cleveland Jsm Inc....440 876-3050
11792 Alameda Dr Strongsville (44149) *(G-17729)*
Cleveland Letter Service Inc....216 781-8300
8351 Clover Ln Chagrin Falls (44022) *(G-3013)*
Cleveland Magazine, Cleveland *Also called Great Lakes Publishing Company (G-5350)*
Cleveland Menu Printing Inc....216 241-5256
1441 E 17th St Cleveland (44114) *(G-4967)*
Cleveland Metal Processing Inc (PA)....440 243-3404
20303 1st Ave Cleveland (44130) *(G-4968)*
Cleveland Metal Stamping Co....440 234-0010
1231 W Bagley Rd Ste 1 Berea (44017) *(G-1596)*
Cleveland Plant and Flower Co....614 478-9900
2370 Marilyn Ln Columbus (43219) *(G-6773)*
Cleveland Plastic Fabricat....216 797-7300
25861 Tungsten Rd Euclid (44132) *(G-9409)*
Cleveland Plating....216 249-0300
1028 E 134th St Cleveland (44110) *(G-4969)*
Cleveland Printwear Inc....216 521-5500
13300 Madison Ave Cleveland (44107) *(G-4970)*
Cleveland Prosthetic Center, Cleveland *Also called Acor Orthopaedic Inc (G-4609)*
Cleveland Punch and Die Co, Ravenna *Also called True Industries Inc (G-16416)*
Cleveland Quarries, Vermilion *Also called Irg Operating LLC (G-19163)*
Cleveland Range LLC....216 481-4900
18901 Euclid Ave Cleveland (44117) *(G-4971)*
Cleveland Range LLC (HQ)....216 481-4900
18301 Saint Clair Ave Cleveland (44110) *(G-4972)*
Cleveland Ready Mix....216 399-6688
4860 Orchard Rd Cleveland (44128) *(G-4973)*
Cleveland Rebabbitting Service....216 433-0123
15593 Brookpark Rd Cleveland (44142) *(G-4974)*
Cleveland Rebar, Akron *Also called Akron Rebar Co (G-50)*
Cleveland Recycling Plant, Cleveland *Also called Caraustar Industries Inc (G-4873)*
Cleveland Roll Forming Co....216 281-0202
3170 W 32nd St Cleveland (44109) *(G-4975)*
Cleveland Safe Co, Cleveland *Also called National Security Products (G-5729)*
Cleveland Scene, Cleveland *Also called Voice Media Group Inc (G-6268)*
Cleveland Shiprepair Company, Cleveland *Also called Manitowoc Company Inc (G-5612)*
Cleveland Shutters....440 234-7600
204 Depot St Berea (44017) *(G-1597)*
Cleveland Smacna....440 877-3500
6060 Royalton Rd Cleveland (44133) *(G-4976)*
Cleveland Special Tool Inc....440 944-1600
1351 E 286th St Wickliffe (44092) *(G-20207)*
Cleveland Specialty Insptn Svc....440 578-1046
8562 East Ave Mentor (44060) *(G-13415)*
Cleveland Specialty Pdts Inc....216 281-8300
2130 W 110th St Cleveland (44102) *(G-4977)*
Cleveland Steel Container Corp....330 656-5600
10048 Aurora Hudson Rd Streetsboro (44241) *(G-17666)*
Cleveland Steel Container Corp....330 544-2271
412 Mason St Niles (44446) *(G-15003)*
Cleveland Steel Specialty Co....216 464-9400
26001 Richmond Rd Bedford Heights (44146) *(G-1466)*
Cleveland Steel Tool Company....216 681-7400
474 E 105th St Cleveland (44108) *(G-4978)*
Cleveland Syrup Corp (PA)....330 963-1900
2200 Highland Rd Twinsburg (44087) *(G-18755)*
Cleveland Tool and Machine Inc (PA)....216 267-6010
5240 Smith Rd Ste 3 Cleveland (44142) *(G-4979)*
Cleveland Track Material Inc (HQ)....216 641-4000
6600 Bessemer Ave Cleveland (44127) *(G-4980)*
Cleveland Track Material Inc....216 641-4000
6600 Bessemer Ave Cleveland (44127) *(G-4981)*
Cleveland Valve & Gauge Co LLC....216 362-1702
4755 W 150th St Ste H Cleveland (44135) *(G-4982)*
Cleveland Welding & Fabg LLC....440 364-5137
4410 Perkins Ave Cleveland (44103) *(G-4983)*
Cleveland Wheels....440 937-6211
1160 Center Rd Avon (44011) *(G-944)*
Cleveland Whiskey LLC....216 881-8481
1768 E 25th St Cleveland (44114) *(G-4984)*
Cleveland Wire Cloth & Mfg Co....216 341-1832
3573 E 78th St Cleveland (44105) *(G-4985)*
Cleveland-Cliffs Inc (PA)....216 694-5700
200 Public Sq Ste 3300 Cleveland (44114) *(G-4986)*
Clevelandcom....216 862-7159
1801 Superior Ave E Cleveland (44114) *(G-4987)*
Clevelandcrystals, Highland Heights *Also called Gooch & Housego (ohio) LLC (G-10792)*
Clevex Inc (PA)....614 675-3757
1275 Kinnear Rd Ste 223 Columbus (43212) *(G-6774)*
Clevland Valve & Gauge Co, Ottawa Hills *Also called Phoenix Partners LLC (G-15675)*
Clicks Document Management, Cleveland *Also called Marcus Uppe Inc (G-5616)*
Clientrax Software, Grove City *Also called Clientrax Technology Solutions (G-10420)*
Clientrax Technology Solutions....614 875-2245
3347 Mcdowell Rd Grove City (43123) *(G-10420)*
Cliffco Stands Inc....937 382-3700
397 Starbuck Rd Wilmington (45177) *(G-20489)*
Cliffs, Cleveland *Also called Northshore Mining Company (G-5785)*
Cliffs & Associates Ltd....216 694-5700
1100 Superior Ave E # 1500 Cleveland (44114) *(G-4988)*
Cliffs High Performance....740 397-2921
20579 Berry Rd Mount Vernon (43050) *(G-14476)*
Cliffs Logan County Coal LLC....216 694-5700
200 Public Sq Ste 3300 Cleveland (44114) *(G-4989)*
Cliffs Michigan Operation....216 694-5303
District 1072 Ste 1500 Cleveland (44114) *(G-4990)*
Cliffs Mining Company....216 694-5700
200 Public Sq Ste 3300 Cleveland (44114) *(G-4991)*
Cliffs Minnesota Minerals Co....216 694-5700
1100 Superior Ave E Cleveland (44114) *(G-4992)*
Clifton Steel Company (PA)....216 662-6111
16500 Rockside Rd Maple Heights (44137) *(G-12569)*
Climateright Air, Columbus *Also called Climateright LLC (G-6775)*
Climateright LLC....800 725-4628
777 Manor Park Dr Columbus (43228) *(G-6775)*
Climax Metal Products Company....440 943-8898
8141 Tyler Blvd Mentor (44060) *(G-13416)*
Climax Packaging Machinery, Hamilton *Also called G L Industries Inc (G-10562)*
Cline Signs LLC....513 396-7446
3272 Highland Ave Cincinnati (45213) *(G-3527)*
Clinical Specialties Inc (PA)....888 873-7888
6955 Treeline Dr Ste A Brecksville (44141) *(G-2027)*
Clinicl Otcms Mngmnt Syst LLC....330 650-9900
9200 S Hills Blvd Ste 200 Broadview Heights (44147) *(G-2092)*
Clint's Prntng, Beavercreek *Also called Clints Printing Inc (G-1354)*
Clinton Foundry Ltd....419 243-6885
1202 W Bancroft St Toledo (43606) *(G-18234)*
Clinton Pattern Works Inc....419 243-0855
1215 W Bancroft St Toledo (43606) *(G-18235)*

ALPHABETIC

Clinton Supply, Ravenna Also called Tri-Way Rebar Inc (G-16415)
Clints Printing Inc 937 426-2771
　3963 Rockfield Dr Beavercreek (45430) (G-1354)
Clipper Magazine LLC 937 534-0470
　2360 W Dorothy Ln Ste 101 Moraine (45439) (G-14338)
Clipper Products Inc 513 688-7300
　675 Cncnnati Batavia Pike Cincinnati (45245) (G-3243)
Clipson S Metalworking, Cincinnati Also called Clipsons Metal Working Inc (G-3528)
Clipsons Metal Working Inc 513 772-6393
　127 Novner Dr Cincinnati (45215) (G-3528)
Clopay Building Pdts Co Inc (HQ) 513 770-4800
　8585 Duke Blvd Mason (45040) (G-12846)
Clopay Building Pdts Co Inc 937 526-4301
　101 N Liberty St Russia (45363) (G-16606)
Clopay Building Pdts Co Inc 937 440-6403
　1400 W Market St Troy (45373) (G-18642)
Clopay Corporation (HQ) 800 282-2260
　8585 Duke Blvd Mason (45040) (G-12847)
Clopay Corporation 440 542-9215
　7905 Cochran Rd Ste 500 Solon (44139) (G-17127)
Clopay Corporation 513 742-1984
　1260 W Sharon Rd Cincinnati (45240) (G-3529)
Clopay Plastic Products Co Inc, Mason Also called Berry Film Products Co Inc (G-12835)
Clorox Company 513 445-1840
　4680 Parkway Dr 130 Mason (45040) (G-12848)
Clorox Sales Company 440 892-1700
　24500 Center Ridge Rd # 240 Westlake (44145) (G-20106)
Closet Factory, The, Cleveland Also called Home Stor & Off Solutions Inc (G-5414)
Closets By Mike 740 607-2212
　517 Winton Ave Zanesville (43701) (G-21120)
Closettec of North East Ohio 216 464-0042
　5222 Richmond Rd Bedford (44146) (G-1396)
Cloud 9 Naturally Inc 403 348-9704
　53840 National Rd Bridgeport (43912) (G-2073)
Clouth Sprenger LLC 937 642-8390
　14681 Industrial Pkwy Marysville (43040) (G-12774)
Clover Pallet LLC 330 454-5592
　5219 Violet Knoll Ave Ne Canton (44705) (G-2629)
Cloverdale Food Processing, Amherst Also called Chefs Pantry Inc (G-557)
Cloverleaf Office Slutions LLC 614 219-9050
　5394 Old Creek Ln Hilliard (43026) (G-10817)
Clovernook Center For The Bli (PA) 513 522-3860
　7000 Hamilton Ave Cincinnati (45231) (G-3530)
Clovervale Farms Inc (HQ) 440 960-0146
　8133 Cooper Foster Pk Rd Amherst (44001) (G-558)
Clovervale Foods, Amherst Also called Clovervale Farms Inc (G-558)
CLS, Canton Also called Concrete Leveling Systems Inc (G-2634)
Club 513 LLC 800 530-2574
　201 E 5th St Fl 19 Cincinnati (45202) (G-3531)
Cluster Software Inc 614 760-9380
　2674 Billingsley Rd Columbus (43235) (G-6776)
Clyde Foam, Clyde Also called Clyde Tool & Die Inc (G-6387)
Clyde Tool & Die Inc (PA) 419 547-9574
　524 S Church St Clyde (43410) (G-6387)
CM Paula Company (PA) 513 759-7473
　6049 Hi Tek Ct Mason (45040) (G-12849)
CM Printing, Columbus Also called Dispatch Printing Company (G-6868)
CMA, Bolivar Also called Cable Mfg & Assembly Inc (G-1908)
CMA Supply Company Inc 513 942-6663
　9984 Commerce Park Dr West Chester (45246) (G-19844)
CMC Consulting, Cleveland Also called CMC Pharmaceuticals Inc (G-4993)
CMC Daymark Corporation 419 354-2591
　12830 S Dixie Hwy Bowling Green (43402) (G-1963)
CMC Electronics Cincinn 513 573-6316
　7500 Innovation Way Mason (45040) (G-12850)
CMC Group Inc (PA) 419 354-2591
　12836 S Dixie Hwy Bowling Green (43402) (G-1964)
CMC Pharmaceuticals Inc (PA) 216 600-9430
　7100 Euclid Ave Ste 152 Cleveland (44103) (G-4993)
Cmd Medtech LLC 614 364-4243
　3585 Interchange Rd Columbus (43204) (G-6777)
CMF Custom Metal Finishers 513 821-8145
　7616 Anthony Wayne Ave Cincinnati (45216) (G-3532)
Cmg Company Plant 2, West Mansfield Also called M & M Concepts Inc (G-19943)
CMI, Lancaster Also called Crists Machining Inc (G-11558)
CMI Holding Company Crawford 419 468-9122
　1310 Freese Works Pl Galion (44833) (G-10128)
CMI Industry Americas Inc (HQ) 330 332-4661
　435 W Wilson St Salem (44460) (G-16728)
CMS, Strongsville Also called Condition Monitoring Supplies (G-17731)
Cmsi, Mentor Also called Commercial Mfg Svcs Inc (G-13420)
Cmt Machining & Fabg LLC 937 652-3740
　1411 Knnard Kingscreek Rd Urbana (43078) (G-18983)
Cnb LLC 419 528-3109
　84 Briggs Dr Ontario (44906) (G-15539)
CNB Machining and Mfg LLC 330 877-7920
　1052 Manning Rd Nw Hartville (44632) (G-10687)

Cnc Custom Machining Inc 330 456-5868
　1314 Henry Ave Sw Canton (44706) (G-2630)
Cnc Indexing Feeding Tech LLC (PA) 513 770-4200
　7944 Innovation Way Ste B Mason (45040) (G-12851)
Cnc Machine Shop, Brunswick Also called Firstar Precision Corporation (G-2204)
Cnd Machine, Massillon Also called C-N-D Industries Inc (G-12965)
CNG Business Group 614 771-0877
　4974 Scoto Darby Rd Ste A Hilliard (43026) (G-10818)
CNG Fueling LLC 330 772-2403
　1266 State Route 7 Ne F Brookfield (44403) (G-2103)
Cnr Marketing Ltd 937 293-1030
　7925 Paragon Rd 100 Dayton (45459) (G-8094)
Cns Inc (PA) 513 631-7073
　3716 Montgomery Rd Cincinnati (45207) (G-3533)
Co Pac Services Inc 216 688-1780
　3113 W 110th St Cleveland (44111) (G-4994)
Co- Ax Technology Inc 440 914-9200
　30301 Emerald Valley Pkwy Solon (44139) (G-17128)
Co-Op Tool, Toledo Also called Hammill Manufacturing Co (G-18320)
Coach Tool & Die Inc 937 890-4716
　5728 Webster St Dayton (45414) (G-8095)
Coal Resources Inc 740 338-3100
　46226 National Rd Saint Clairsville (43950) (G-16627)
Coal Services Inc 740 795-5220
　155 Highway 7 S Powhatan Point (43942) (G-16341)
Coal Services Group, Powhatan Point Also called Coal Services Inc (G-16341)
Coalescence LLC 614 861-3639
　3455 Millennium Ct Columbus (43219) (G-6778)
Coastal Diamond, Mentor Also called Performance Superabrasives LLC (G-13547)
Coastal Diamond Incorporated 440 946-7171
　7255 Industrial Park Blvd A Mentor (44060) (G-13417)
Coat All 419 659-2757
　4599 Campbell Rd Columbus Grove (45830) (G-7634)
Coate Concrete Products Inc (PA) 937 698-4181
　7330 W State Route 571 West Milton (45383) (G-19948)
Coating Applications Intl LLC 513 956-5222
　2860 Cooper Rd Ste 200 Cincinnati (45241) (G-3534)
Coating Control Inc 330 453-9136
　825 Navarre Rd Sw Canton (44707) (G-2631)
Coating Systems Inc 513 367-5600
　150 Sales Ave Harrison (45030) (G-10637)
Coating Systems Group Inc 440 816-9306
　6909 Engle Rd Bldg C Middleburg Heights (44130) (G-13763)
Coatings & Colorants, Cincinnati Also called Evonik Corporation (G-3661)
Coaxial Dynamics, Cleveland Also called CDI Industries Inc (G-4895)
Cobb Industries Inc 440 946-4695
　7605 Saint Clair Ave Mentor (44060) (G-13418)
Cobblers Corner LLC 330 482-4005
　1115 Village Plz Columbiana (44408) (G-6458)
Coblentz Brothers Inc 330 857-7211
　7101 S Kohler Rd Apple Creek (44606) (G-602)
Coblentz Chocolate Co, Walnut Creek Also called Walnut Creek Chocolate Company (G-19308)
Cobra Motorcycles Mfg 330 207-3844
　11511 Springfield Rd North Lima (44452) (G-15167)
Cobra Plastics Inc 330 425-3669
　1244 Highland Rd E Macedonia (44056) (G-12284)
Coburn Inc (PA) 419 368-4051
　636 Ashland Cnty Rd 30 A Hayesville (44838) (G-10714)
Coca-Cola 937 446-4644
　136 Fairview Ave Sardinia (45171) (G-16867)
Coca-Cola Bottling Co Cnsld 419 422-3743
　201 N Shore Dr Lima (45801) (G-11849)
Coca-Cola Bottling Co Cnsld 740 353-3133
　5050 Old Scioto Trl Portsmouth (45662) (G-16280)
Coca-Cola Bottling Co Cnsld 937 878-5000
　1000 Coca Cola Blvd Dayton (45424) (G-8096)
Coca-Cola Bottling Co Cnsld 513 527-6600
　5100 Duck Creek Rd Cincinnati (45227) (G-3535)
Coca-Cola Company 614 491-6305
　2455 Watkins Rd Columbus (43207) (G-6779)
Coca-Cola Company 937 446-4644
　7906 Yochum Rd Sardinia (45171) (G-16868)
Codonics Inc (PA) 216 226-1066
　17991 Englewood Dr Ste D Cleveland (44130) (G-4995)
Coe Manufacturing Company (HQ) 440 352-9381
　70 W Erie St Ste 150 Painesville (44077) (G-15722)
Coffelt Candy Inc (PA) 937 399-8772
　6050 Urbana Rd Springfield (45502) (G-17376)
Coffey and Associates, West Chester Also called D C Controls LLC (G-19848)
Coffing Corporation (PA) 513 919-2813
　5336 Lesourdsville Rd Liberty Twp (45011) (G-11822)
Cohen Brothers Inc (PA) 513 422-3696
　1520 14th Ave Middletown (45044) (G-13895)
Cohesant Inc (PA) 216 910-1700
　3601 Green Rd Ste 308 Beachwood (44122) (G-1228)
Coil Specialty Chemicals LLC 740 236-2407
　2375 Glendale Rd Marietta (45750) (G-12616)

ALPHABETIC SECTION — Columbus Messenger Company

Coil Technology Inc 330 601-1350
2109 Great Trails Dr Wooster (44691) *(G-20579)*
Coil Tek, Wooster Also called Coil Technology Inc *(G-20579)*
Coin World, Sidney Also called Amos Media Company *(G-17015)*
Coit Tool Company Inc 440 946-3377
38134 Western Pkwy Unit 3 Willoughby (44094) *(G-20297)*
Col-Pump Company Inc 330 482-1029
131 E Railroad St Columbiana (44408) *(G-6459)*
Colburn Dairy, Waverly Also called C & C Mobile Homes LLC *(G-19541)*
Colby Properties LLC 937 390-0816
2071 N Bechtle Ave Springfield (45504) *(G-17377)*
Colby Woodworking Inc 937 224-7676
1912 Lucille Dr Dayton (45404) *(G-8097)*
Cold Control LLC 614 564-7011
470 Olde Worthington Rd # 200 Westerville (43082) *(G-19986)*
Cold Duck Screen Prtg & EMB Co 330 426-1900
540 Sugar Camp Dr East Palestine (44413) *(G-9071)*
Cold Headed Fas Assemblies Inc 330 833-0800
1875 Harsh Ave Se Ste 3 Massillon (44646) *(G-12968)*
Cold Heading Co 216 581-3000
4444 Lee Rd Cleveland (44128) *(G-4996)*
Cold Jet LLC (PA) 513 831-3211
455 Wards Corner Rd # 100 Loveland (45140) *(G-12183)*
Cold Stone Creamery, Columbus Also called R D Lucky LLC *(G-7373)*
Cold Storage Services LLC 740 837-0858
54 S Main St London (43140) *(G-12054)*
Coldstone Creamery, Powell Also called Stella Lou LLC *(G-16336)*
Coldwell Family Tree Farm 330 506-9012
33320 Hull Rd Salineville (43945) *(G-16786)*
Cole Pak Inc 937 652-3910
1030 S Edgewood Ave Urbana (43078) *(G-18984)*
Cole Tool & Die Company 419 522-1272
466 State Route 314 N Ontario (44903) *(G-15540)*
Coleman Machine Inc 740 695-3006
49381 Firpoint Maynard Rd Saint Clairsville (43950) *(G-16628)*
Coleman Machine Company, Saint Clairsville Also called Coleman Machine Inc *(G-16628)*
Coleys Inc 440 967-5630
1775 Liberty Ave Vermilion (44089) *(G-19157)*
Coleys Inc 440 967-5630
1775 Liberty Ave Vermilion (44089) *(G-19158)*
Colfor Manufacturing Inc 330 863-7500
3255 Alliance Rd Nw Malvern (44644) *(G-12387)*
Colgate-Palmolive Company 212 310-2000
8800 Guernsey Indus Blvd Cambridge (43725) *(G-2432)*
Collaborative For Adaptive Lif 216 513-0572
3250 W Market St Ste 205 Fairlawn (44333) *(G-9601)*
Collated Products Corp 440 946-1950
8480 Brakeman Rd Chardon (44024) *(G-3106)*
Colleen D Turner 419 886-4810
72 Main St Bellville (44813) *(G-1555)*
College Issue, Piqua Also called Atlantis Sportswear Inc *(G-16101)*
Collier Well Eqp & Sup Inc (PA) 330 345-3968
3310 Columbus Rd Wooster (44691) *(G-20580)*
Colliers Cstmizing Fabrication 937 523-0420
1675 W County Line Rd Urbana (43078) *(G-18985)*
Collins & Venco Venturo, Cincinnati Also called Venco Manufacturing Inc *(G-4472)*
Collotype Labels Usa Inc 513 381-1480
4053 Clough Woods Dr Batavia (45103) *(G-1132)*
Colonels Quarters 740 385-3374
131 Park Pl Circleville (43113) *(G-4540)*
Colonial Cabinets Inc 440 355-9663
337 S Center St Lagrange (44050) *(G-11478)*
Colonial Heights Mhp LLC 740 314-5182
917 Two Ridge Rd Wintersville (43953) *(G-20538)*
Colonial Machine Company Inc 330 673-5859
1041 Mogadore Rd Kent (44240) *(G-11305)*
Colonial Patterns Inc 330 673-6475
920 Overholt Rd Kent (44240) *(G-11306)*
Colonial Rubber Company (PA) 330 296-2831
706 Oakwood St Ravenna (44266) *(G-16373)*
Colonial Surface Solutions, Columbus Grove Also called Carpe Diem Industries LLC *(G-7632)*
Colonial Woodcraft Inc 513 779-8088
1004 W Main St Lebanon (45036) *(G-11642)*
Colony Hardware, Cleveland Also called Phillips Contractors Sup LLC *(G-5872)*
Color 3 Embroidery Inc 330 652-9495
387 Chestnut Ave Ne Warren (44483) *(G-19385)*
Color Bar Printing Centers Inc 216 595-3939
4576 Renaissance Pkwy Cleveland (44128) *(G-4997)*
Color Brite Company Inc 216 441-4117
5209 Grant Ave Cleveland (44125) *(G-4998)*
Color Process Inc 440 268-7100
13900 Prospect Rd Strongsville (44149) *(G-17730)*
Coloramic Process Inc 440 275-1199
2883 Industrial Park Dr Austinburg (44010) *(G-919)*
Coloramics LLC 614 876-1171
4077 Weaver Ct S Hilliard (43026) *(G-10819)*
Coloring Book Solutions LLC 419 281-9641
426 E 8th St Ashland (44805) *(G-695)*

Colormatrix 440 930-1000
33587 Walker Rd Avon Lake (44012) *(G-982)*
Colormatrix Group Inc (HQ) 216 622-0100
680 N Rocky River Dr Berea (44017) *(G-1598)*
Colormatrix Holdings Inc (HQ) 440 930-3162
680 N Rocky River Dr Berea (44017) *(G-1599)*
Colors, North Canton Also called Jane Valentine *(G-15094)*
Colortech Graphics & Printing (PA) 614 766-2400
4000 Business Park Dr Columbus (43204) *(G-6780)*
Coltene/Whaledent Inc (HQ) 330 916-8800
235 Ascot Pkwy Cuyahoga Falls (44223) *(G-7851)*
Columbia, Vandalia Also called Datwyler Sling Sltions USA Inc *(G-19122)*
Columbia Cabinets Inc 440 748-1010
33549 E Royalton Rd 4-5 Columbia Station (44028) *(G-6432)*
Columbia Chemical Corporation 330 225-3200
1000 Western Dr Brunswick (44212) *(G-2196)*
Columbia Energy Group 614 460-4683
200 Civic Center Dr Columbus (43215) *(G-6781)*
Columbia Gas Meter Shop 614 460-5519
5315 Fisher Rd Columbus (43228) *(G-6782)*
Columbia Industries, Solon Also called Skidmore-Wilhelm Mfg Company *(G-17232)*
Columbia Industries, Cleveland Also called Qcsm LLC *(G-5937)*
Columbia Machine Company 740 452-1736
961 Hughes St Zanesville (43701) *(G-21121)*
Columbia Midstream Group LLC 330 542-1095
10846 Stateline Rd New Middletown (44442) *(G-14748)*
Columbia Stamping Inc 440 236-6677
13676 Station Rd Columbia Station (44028) *(G-6433)*
Columbia Steel and Wire Inc 330 468-2709
30 W Aurora Rd Northfield (44067) *(G-15315)*
Columbiana Boiler Company LLC 330 482-3373
200 W Railroad St Columbiana (44408) *(G-6460)*
Columbiana Holding Co Inc (PA) 330 482-3373
200 W Railroad St Columbiana (44408) *(G-6461)*
Columbus Advnced Mfg Sftwr Inc 614 410-2300
105 Innovation Ct Ste J Delaware (43015) *(G-8668)*
Columbus Alive Inc 614 221-2449
34 S 3rd St Columbus (43215) *(G-6783)*
Columbus Brewing Co, Columbus Also called District Brewing Co Inc *(G-6870)*
Columbus Bride 614 888-4567
34 S 3rd St Columbus (43215) *(G-6784)*
Columbus Canvas Products Inc 614 375-1397
577 N 4th St Columbus (43215) *(G-6785)*
Columbus Coatings Company 614 492-6800
1800 Watkins Rd Columbus (43207) *(G-6786)*
Columbus Dispatch, Lewis Center Also called Dispatch Printing Company *(G-11757)*
Columbus Electrical Works Co 614 294-4651
777 N 4th St Columbus (43215) *(G-6787)*
Columbus Equipment Company 740 455-4036
818 Lee St Zanesville (43701) *(G-21122)*
Columbus Fire Fighters Union 614 481-8900
379 W Broad St Columbus (43215) *(G-6788)*
Columbus Gasket & Supply, Columbus Also called Columbus Gasket Co Inc *(G-6789)*
Columbus Gasket Co Inc 614 878-6041
1875 Lone Eagle St Columbus (43228) *(G-6789)*
Columbus Graphics Inc 614 577-9360
7295 Rickly St Reynoldsburg (43068) *(G-16432)*
Columbus Heating & Vent Co 614 274-1177
182 N Yale Ave Columbus (43222) *(G-6790)*
Columbus Humungous Apparel LLC 614 824-2657
2913 Manola Dr Ste 100 Columbus (43209) *(G-6791)*
Columbus Incontact 801 245-8369
555 S Front St Columbus (43215) *(G-6792)*
Columbus Industries Inc (PA) 740 983-2552
2938 State Route 752 Ashville (43103) *(G-816)*
Columbus Industries Inc 937 544-6896
11545 State Route 41 West Union (45693) *(G-19960)*
Columbus Instruments Intl Corp 614 276-0593
950 N Hague Ave Columbus (43204) *(G-6793)*
Columbus International Corp 614 323-1086
200 E Campus View Blvd # 200 Columbus (43235) *(G-6794)*
Columbus Jack Corporation 614 747-1596
1 Air Cargo Pkwy E Swanton (43558) *(G-17909)*
Columbus Jack Regent, Swanton Also called Columbus Jack Corporation *(G-17909)*
Columbus Kdc 614 656-1130
8825 Smiths Mill Rd New Albany (43054) *(G-14614)*
Columbus Kombucha Company LLC 614 262-0000
930 Freeway Dr N Columbus (43229) *(G-6795)*
Columbus Machine Works Inc 614 409-0244
2491 Fairwood Ave Columbus (43207) *(G-6796)*
Columbus McKinnon Corporation 330 332-5769
240 Pennsylvania Ave Salem (44460) *(G-16729)*
Columbus McKinnon Corporation 330 424-7248
7573 State Route 45 Lisbon (44432) *(G-11965)*
Columbus Messenger Company (PA) 614 272-5422
3500 Sullivant Ave Columbus (43204) *(G-6797)*
Columbus Messenger Company 740 852-0809
78 S Main St London (43140) *(G-12055)*

(PA)=Parent Co (HQ)=Headquarters (DH)=Div Headquarters

Columbus Mobility Specialist....614 825-8996
6330 Proprietors Rd Ste F Worthington (43085) ***(G-20681)***
Columbus Oil Field Exploration, Powell *Also called Columbus Oilfield Exploration* ***(G-16317)***
Columbus Oilfield Exploration....614 895-9520
80 Grace Dr Ste G Powell (43065) ***(G-16317)***
Columbus Pipe and Equipment Co....614 444-7871
763 E Markison Ave Columbus (43207) ***(G-6798)***
Columbus Prescr Rehabilitation....614 294-1600
975 Eastwind Dr Ste 155 Westerville (43081) ***(G-20040)***
Columbus Processing Co LLC....614 492-8287
4300 Alum Creek Dr Columbus (43207) ***(G-6799)***
Columbus Roof Trusses Inc (PA)....614 272-6464
2525 Fisher Rd Columbus (43204) ***(G-6800)***
Columbus Roof Trusses Inc....740 763-3000
400 Marne Dr Newark (43055) ***(G-14862)***
Columbus Serum Co....614 793-0615
7570 Donora Ln Columbus (43235) ***(G-6801)***
Columbus Sign Company (PA)....614 252-3133
1515 E 5th Ave Columbus (43219) ***(G-6802)***
Columbus Steelmasters Inc....614 231-2141
660 Concrea Rd Columbus (43219) ***(G-6803)***
Columbus Underground, Columbus *Also called Evans Creative Group LLC* ***(G-6909)***
Columbus Vsclar Intrvntion LLC....614 917-0696
895 S State St Westerville (43081) ***(G-20041)***
Columbus Washboard Company Ltd....740 380-3828
14 Gallagher Ave Logan (43138) ***(G-12023)***
Columbus-Sports Publications....614 486-2202
1350 W 5th Ave Ste 30 Columbus (43212) ***(G-6804)***
Com-Corp Industries Inc....216 431-6266
7601 Bittern Ave Cleveland (44103) ***(G-4999)***
Com-Fab Inc....740 857-1107
4657 Price Hilliards Rd Plain City (43064) ***(G-16181)***
Com-Net Software Specialists, Miamisburg *Also called Signature Technologies Inc* ***(G-13716)***
Combi Packaging Systems Llc....330 456-9333
6299 Dressler Rd Nw Canton (44720) ***(G-2632)***
Combine Grinding Co Inc....440 439-6148
7005 Krick Rd Ste C Bedford (44146) ***(G-1397)***
Combined Container Board....513 530-5700
7741 School Rd Cincinnati (45249) ***(G-3536)***
Combined Industrial Solutions....513 659-3091
944 Klondyke Rd Milford (45150) ***(G-14004)***
Combined Tech Group Inc....937 274-4866
6061 Milo Rd Dayton (45414) ***(G-8098)***
Combustion Process System....330 922-4161
2104 Front St Cuyahoga Falls (44221) ***(G-7852)***
Comcorp Inc....718 981-1234
1801 Superior Ave E Cleveland (44114) ***(G-5000)***
Comdess Company Inc....330 769-2094
8733 Wooster Pike Rd Seville (44273) ***(G-16914)***
Comdoc Inc....330 899-8000
330 W Spring St Ste 100 Columbus (43215) ***(G-6805)***
Comet Technologies USA Inc....234 284-7849
5675 Hudson Indus Pkwy Hudson (44236) ***(G-11038)***
Comex Group, Cleveland *Also called Comex North America Inc* ***(G-5001)***
Comex North America Inc (HQ)....303 307-2100
101 W Prospect Ave # 1020 Cleveland (44115) ***(G-5001)***
Comfort Line Ltd....419 729-8520
5500 Enterprise Blvd Toledo (43612) ***(G-18236)***
Command Alkon Incorporated....614 799-0600
6750 Crosby Ct Dublin (43016) ***(G-8901)***
Command Plastic Corporation....800 321-8001
124 West Ave Tallmadge (44278) ***(G-17977)***
Commconnect....937 414-0505
5747 Executive Blvd Dayton (45424) ***(G-8099)***
Commercial Anodizing Co....440 942-8384
38387 Apollo Pkwy Willoughby (44094) ***(G-20298)***
Commercial Bar & Cabinetry....330 743-1420
12 S Worthington St Youngstown (44502) ***(G-20876)***
Commercial Cabinets, Youngstown *Also called Commercial Bar & Cabinetry* ***(G-20876)***
Commercial Cutng Graphics LLC....419 526-4800
208 Central Ave Mansfield (44905) ***(G-12427)***
Commercial Decal of Ohio Inc....330 385-7178
46686 Y And O Rd East Liverpool (43920) ***(G-9053)***
Commercial Dock & Door Inc....440 951-1210
7653 Saint Clair Ave Mentor (44060) ***(G-13419)***
Commercial Electric Pdts Corp (PA)....216 241-2886
1821 E 40th St Cleveland (44103) ***(G-5002)***
Commercial Fluid Power, Dover *Also called Commercial Honing LLC* ***(G-8811)***
Commercial Grinding Services....330 273-5040
1155 Industrial Pkwy # 1 Medina (44256) ***(G-13238)***
Commercial Honing LLC (PA)....330 343-8896
2997 Progress St Dover (44622) ***(G-8811)***
Commercial Honing Ohio Inc (PA)....330 343-8896
2997 Progress St Dover (44622) ***(G-8812)***
Commercial Honing Ohio Inc....330 343-8896
2997 Progress St Dover (44622) ***(G-8813)***
Commercial Innovations Inc....216 641-7500
3812 E 91st St Cleveland (44105) ***(G-5003)***
Commercial Interior Products, West Chester *Also called CIP International Inc* ***(G-19675)***
Commercial Lubricants Inc....614 475-5952
2854 Johnstown Rd Columbus (43219) ***(G-6806)***
Commercial Metal Forming, Youngstown *Also called Star Forming Manufacturing LL* ***(G-21039)***
Commercial Mfg Svcs Inc....440 953-2701
7123 Industrial Park Blvd Mentor (44060) ***(G-13420)***
Commercial Minerals Inc....330 549-2165
10900 South Ave North Lima (44452) ***(G-15168)***
Commercial Mtal Fbricators Inc....937 233-4911
150 Commerce Park Dr Dayton (45404) ***(G-8100)***
Commercial Music Service Co....740 746-8500
6312 Goss Rd Sugar Grove (43155) ***(G-17837)***
Commercial Prtg of Greenvill....937 548-3835
314 S Broadway St Greenville (45331) ***(G-10365)***
Commercial Steel Treating Co....216 431-8204
1394 E 39th St Cleveland (44114) ***(G-5004)***
Commercial Transportation Svcs....216 267-2000
12487 Plaza Dr Cleveland (44130) ***(G-5005)***
Commercial Turf Products Ltd....330 995-7000
1777 Miller Pkwy Streetsboro (44241) ***(G-17667)***
Commercial Vehicle Group Inc (PA)....614 289-5360
7800 Walton Pkwy New Albany (43054) ***(G-14615)***
Commissary Brewing....614 636-3164
1400 Dublin Rd Columbus (43215) ***(G-6807)***
Commonwealth Aluminum Mtls LLC....216 910-3400
25825 Science Park Dr # 400 Beachwood (44122) ***(G-1229)***
Commscope Technologies LLC....216 272-0055
1668 Sunview Rd Cleveland (44124) ***(G-5006)***
Commtech Solutions Inc....440 458-4870
38900 Arbor Ct Grafton (44044) ***(G-10294)***
Communication Concepts Inc....937 426-8600
508 Mill Stone Dr Beavercreek (45434) ***(G-1307)***
Communication Resources Inc....800 992-2144
4786 Dressler Rd Nw Ste 3 Canton (44718) ***(G-2633)***
Communications Aid Inc....513 475-8453
222 Piedmont Ave Ste 5200 Cincinnati (45219) ***(G-3537)***
Community Action Program Corp....740 374-8501
696 Wayne St Marietta (45750) ***(G-12617)***
Community Action Wic Hlth Svc, Marietta *Also called Community Action Program Corp* ***(G-12617)***
Community Care Network Inc (PA)....216 671-0977
4614 Prospect Ave Ste 240 Cleveland (44103) ***(G-5007)***
Community Care On Wheels....330 882-5506
2 Kauffmans Crk Clinton (44216) ***(G-6385)***
Community Mirror, The, Maumee *Also called Mirror* ***(G-13134)***
Community Post, Minster *Also called Horizon Publications Inc* ***(G-14217)***
Community RE Group-Comvet....440 319-6714
3220 Station Ave Ashtabula (44004) ***(G-767)***
Comp-U-Chem Inc....740 345-3332
195 Dayton Rd Ne Newark (43055) ***(G-14863)***
Companies of North Coast LLC (HQ)....216 398-8550
4605 Spring Rd Cleveland (44131) ***(G-5008)***
Company Front Awards....440 636-5493
12653 Madison Rd Middlefield (44062) ***(G-13786)***
Compass, Moraine *Also called Angels Landing Inc* ***(G-14330)***
Compass Energy LLC....866 665-2225
17877 Saint Clair Ave # 1 Cleveland (44110) ***(G-5009)***
Compass Systems & Sales LLC....330 733-2111
5185 New Haven Cir Norton (44203) ***(G-15363)***
Compco Columbiana Company (PA)....330 482-0200
400 W Railroad St Ste 1 Columbiana (44408) ***(G-6462)***
Compco Industries, Columbiana *Also called Compco Columbiana Company* ***(G-6462)***
Compco Industries Inc (HQ)....330 482-6488
400 W Railroad St Ste 1 Columbiana (44408) ***(G-6463)***
Competetive Carbide Inc....440 350-9393
9332 Pinecone Dr Mentor (44060) ***(G-13421)***
Competitive Carbide, Mentor *Also called Competetive Carbide Inc* ***(G-13421)***
Competitive Press Inc....330 289-1968
144 Scenic View Dr Copley (44321) ***(G-7680)***
Complements Lighting, Mentor *Also called Medallion Lighting Corporation* ***(G-13514)***
Complete Business Machines, Cleveland *Also called D and D Business Equipment Inc* ***(G-5056)***
Complete Cylinder Service Inc....513 772-1500
1240 Glendale Milford Rd Cincinnati (45215) ***(G-3538)***
Complete Dry Flood....513 200-9274
6006 Madison Rd Cincinnati (45227) ***(G-3539)***
Complete Energy Services Inc....440 577-1070
7338 Us Route 6 Pierpont (44082) ***(G-16064)***
Complete Expressions WD Works....614 245-4152
6718 Albany Station Dr New Albany (43054) ***(G-14616)***
Complete Filter Media LLC....740 438-0929
1000 Mcgrery Rd Se Lancaster (43130) ***(G-11555)***
Compliant Access Products LLC....513 518-4525
5885 Hamilton Cleves Rd Cleves (45002) ***(G-6358)***
Compliant Healthcare Tech LLC....216 255-9607
7123 Pearl Rd Ste 305 Cleveland (44130) ***(G-5010)***

ALPHABETIC SECTION — Consolidated Graphics Inc

Compliant Healthcare Tech LLC (PA) 216 255-9607
7123 Pearl Rd Ste 305 Cleveland (44130) *(G-5011)*

Component Mfg & Design 330 225-8080
3121 Interstate Pkwy Brunswick (44212) *(G-2197)*

Component Systems Inc 216 252-9292
2245 W 114th St Cleveland (44102) *(G-5012)*

Composite Advantage, Dayton Also called Cpca Manufacturing LLC *(G-8109)*

Composite Concepts Inc 440 247-3844
615 Bunker Ln Mason (45040) *(G-12852)*

Composite Group, The, Fairlawn Also called Hpc Holdings LLC *(G-9608)*

Composite Technical Svcs LLC 937 660-3783
2000 Composite Dr Kettering (45420) *(G-11430)*

Composite Technologies Co LLC 937 228-2880
401 N Keowee St Dayton (45404) *(G-8101)*

Compost Cincy 513 278-8178
5800 Este Ave Cincinnati (45232) *(G-3540)*

Compost Facility, Lockbourne Also called City of Columbus *(G-11993)*

Comprehensive Logistics Co Inc 440 934-3517
1200 A Chester Indus Pkwy Avon (44011) *(G-945)*

Comprehensive Logistics Co Inc 330 793-0504
365 Victoria Rd Youngstown (44515) *(G-20877)*

Compressor Technologies Inc 937 492-3711
211 E Russell Rd Sidney (45365) *(G-17023)*

Comprhnsive Brace Limb Ctr LLC (PA) 330 337-8333
2235 E Pershing St Salem (44460) *(G-16730)*

Compton Metal Products Inc 937 382-2403
416 Steele Rd Wilmington (45177) *(G-20490)*

Comptons Precision Machine 937 325-9139
224 Dayton Ave Springfield (45506) *(G-17378)*

Comptroll, Solon Also called Kyntronics Inc *(G-17184)*

Compu-Print, Canton Also called Better Living Concepts Inc *(G-2590)*

Computational Engineering Svcs 513 745-0313
10979 Reed Hartman Hwy # 210 Blue Ash (45242) *(G-1752)*

Computer Aided Solutions LLC 440 729-2570
8437 Mayfield Rd Ste 104a Chesterland (44026) *(G-3155)*

Computer Allied Technology Co 614 457-2292
3385 Somerford Rd Columbus (43221) *(G-6808)*

Computer Enterprise Inc 216 228-7156
1530 Saint Charles Ave Lakewood (44107) *(G-11515)*

Computer Forms Printing, Westerville Also called Jeffrey Reedy *(G-20060)*

Computer Stitch Designs Inc 330 856-7826
1414 Henn Hyde Rd Ne Warren (44484) *(G-19386)*

Computer System Enhancement 513 251-6791
1053 Kreis Ln Cincinnati (45205) *(G-3541)*

Computer Workshop Inc (PA) 614 798-9505
5131 Post Rd Ste 102 Dublin (43017) *(G-8902)*

Computer Zoo Inc 937 310-1474
1930 N Lakeman Dr Ste 106 Bellbrook (45305) *(G-1490)*

Computercrafts 614 231-7559
2936 Brownlee Ave Columbus (43209) *(G-6809)*

Comrod Inc 440 455-9186
909 Canterbury Rd Ste A Westlake (44145) *(G-20107)*

Coms Interactive, Broadview Heights Also called Clinicl Otcms Mngmnt Syst LLC *(G-2092)*

Comtec Incorporated 330 425-8102
1800 Enterprise Pkwy Twinsburg (44087) *(G-18756)*

Comturn Manufacturing LLC 219 267-6911
13704 Enterprise Ave Cleveland (44135) *(G-5013)*

Con-AG, Saint Marys Also called Conag Inc *(G-16683)*

Con-Belt Inc 330 273-2003
5656 Innovation Dr Valley City (44280) *(G-19032)*

Con-Cure, Pioneer Also called Premiere Con Solutions LLC *(G-16092)*

Conag Inc 419 394-8870
16672 County Road 66a Saint Marys (45885) *(G-16683)*

Conagra Brands Inc 513 229-0305
7300 Central Parke Blvd Mason (45040) *(G-12853)*

Conagra Brands Inc 419 445-8015
901 Stryker St Archbold (43502) *(G-642)*

Conagra Brands Inc 740 465-3912
2970 County Highway 74 Morral (43337) *(G-14403)*

Conagra Fods Pckaged Foods LLC 937 440-2800
801 Dye Mill Rd Troy (45373) *(G-18643)*

Concentric Corporation 440 899-9090
27101 E Oviatt Rd Ste 8 Bay Village (44140) *(G-1206)*

Concept Manufacturing LLC 812 677-2043
101 Butternut Cove Pl Johnstown (43031) *(G-11263)*

Concept Printing of Wauseon 419 335-6627
775 N Shoop Ave Wauseon (43567) *(G-19512)*

Concept Wear, Columbus Also called Srm Graphics Inc *(G-7482)*

Concept Xxi Inc 216 831-2121
23600 Merc Rd Ste 101 Beachwood (44122) *(G-1230)*

Concord Design Inc 330 722-5133
3382 S Weymouth Rd Medina (44256) *(G-13239)*

Concord Fabricators Inc 614 875-2500
6511 Seeds Rd Grove City (43123) *(G-10421)*

Concord Road Equipment Mfg Inc 440 357-5344
348 Chester St Painesville (44077) *(G-15723)*

Concord Steel of Ohio, Warren Also called Conley Group Inc *(G-19388)*

Concorde Castings Inc 440 953-0053
34000 Lakeland Blvd Willoughby (44095) *(G-20299)*

Concrete Cnstr McHy Co LLC 330 638-1515
5210 State Route 46 Cortland (44410) *(G-7705)*

Concrete Leveling Systems Inc (PA) 330 966-8120
5046 East Blvd Nw Canton (44718) *(G-2634)*

Concrete Material Supply LLC 419 261-6404
1 Maritime Plz Fl 4 Toledo (43604) *(G-18237)*

Concrete Sealants Inc 937 845-8776
9325 State Route 201 Tipp City (45371) *(G-18109)*

Condition Monitoring Supplies 216 941-6868
20338 Progress Dr Strongsville (44149) *(G-17731)*

Condo Inc 330 505-0485
49 W Federal St Niles (44446) *(G-15004)*

Condo Incorporated 330 609-6021
3869 Niles Rd Se Warren (44484) *(G-19387)*

Condos and Trees LLC 419 691-2287
2674 Woodville Rd Northwood (43619) *(G-15335)*

Conduit Pipe Products Company 614 879-9114
1501 W Main St West Jefferson (43162) *(G-19922)*

Conery Manufacturing Inc 419 289-1444
1380 Township Road 743 Ashland (44805) *(G-696)*

Conform Automotive, Sidney Also called Dti Molded Products Inc *(G-17033)*

Conforming Matrix Corporation 419 729-3777
6255 Suder Ave Toledo (43611) *(G-18238)*

Conison Tool and Die Inc 330 758-1574
8100 Southern Blvd Youngstown (44512) *(G-20878)*

Conley Group Inc 330 372-2030
197 W Market St Ste 202 Warren (44481) *(G-19388)*

Conn-Selmer Inc 440 946-6100
34199 Curtis Blvd Willoughby (44095) *(G-20300)*

Conn-Selmer Inc 216 391-7723
1440 E 36th St Ste 501 Cleveland (44114) *(G-5014)*

Connaughton Wldg & Fence LLC 513 867-0230
440 Hensel Pl Hamilton (45011) *(G-10547)*

Conneaut Township Park, Conneaut Also called City of Conneaut *(G-7643)*

Connect Television 614 876-4402
4811 Northwest Pkwy Hilliard (43026) *(G-10820)*

Connective Design Incorporated 937 746-8252
3010 S Tech Blvd Miamisburg (45342) *(G-13651)*

Connector Manufacturing Co (HQ) 513 860-4455
3501 Symmes Rd Hamilton (45015) *(G-10548)*

Connectors Unlimited Inc (PA) 440 357-1161
1359 W Jackson St Painesville (44077) *(G-15724)*

Connectronics Corp (HQ) 419 537-0020
2745 Avondale Ave Toledo (43607) *(G-18239)*

Connell Limited Partnership 877 534-8986
154 E Aurora Rd Pmb 186 Northfield (44067) *(G-15316)*

Connelly Industries LLC 330 468-0675
9651 N Bedford Rd Macedonia (44056) *(G-12285)*

Connies Candles 740 574-1224
9103 Ohio River Rd Wheelersburg (45694) *(G-20179)*

Connolly Construction Co Inc 937 644-8831
179 Emmaus Rd Marysville (43040) *(G-12775)*

Connor Electric Inc 513 932-5798
605 N Liberty Keuter Rd Lebanon (45036) *(G-11643)*

Conns Potato Chip Co Inc (PA) 740 452-4615
1805 Kemper Ct Zanesville (43701) *(G-21123)*

Conover Lumber Company Inc 937 368-3010
7960 N Alcony Conover Rd Conover (45317) *(G-7663)*

Conquest Industries Inc 234 678-5555
4488 Allen Rd Stow (44224) *(G-17579)*

Conquest Maps 614 654-1627
5696 Westbourne Ave Columbus (43213) *(G-6810)*

Conseal, Tipp City Also called Concrete Sealants Inc *(G-18109)*

Consol Energy 740 232-2140
47355 National Rd Saint Clairsville (43950) *(G-16629)*

Consoldated Graphics Group Inc 216 881-9191
1614 E 40th St Cleveland (44103) *(G-5015)*

Consoldted Grnhse Slutions LLC 330 844-8598
14800 Foltz Pkwy Strongsville (44149) *(G-17732)*

Consoldted Precision Pdts Corp (HQ) 216 453-4800
1621 Euclid Ave Ste 1850 Cleveland (44115) *(G-5016)*

Consoldted Precision Pdts Corp 440 953-0053
34000 Lakeland Blvd Eastlake (44095) *(G-9102)*

Consolidatd Analytical Sys Inc 513 542-1200
201 S Miami Ave Cleves (45002) *(G-6359)*

Consolidated Biscuit Company, Mc Comb Also called Hearthside Food Solutions LLC *(G-13189)*

Consolidated Biscuit Company 419 293-2911
312 Rader Rd Mc Comb (45858) *(G-13187)*

Consolidated Casework Inc 330 618-6951
708 Marks Rd Ste 201 Valley City (44280) *(G-19033)*

Consolidated Coatings Corp 216 514-7596
3735 Green Rd Cleveland (44122) *(G-5017)*

Consolidated Container Co 330 394-0905
2880 Sferra Ave Nw Warren (44483) *(G-19389)*

Consolidated Gas Coop Inc 419 946-6600
5255 State Route 95 Mount Gilead (43338) *(G-14422)*

Consolidated Graphics Inc 740 654-2112
3950 Lancaster New Lxngtn Lancaster (43130) *(G-11556)*

Consolidated Metal Pdts Inc....513 251-2624
1028 Depot St Cincinnati (45204) **(G-3542)**
Consolidated Pattern Works Inc....330 434-6060
754 E Glenwood Ave Akron (44310) **(G-120)**
Consolidated Solutions, Cleveland *Also called Consolidated Web* **(G-5018)**
Consolidated Solutions, Cleveland *Also called Consoldated Graphics Group Inc* **(G-5015)**
Consolidated Vehicle Converter, Dayton *Also called Julie Maynard Inc* **(G-8286)**
Consolidated Web....216 881-7816
3831 Kelley Ave Cleveland (44114) **(G-5018)**
Constar International, Hebron *Also called Plastipak Packaging Inc* **(G-10757)**
Construction Bulletin Inc....330 782-3733
4178 Market St Lowr Youngstown (44512) **(G-20879)**
Construction Polymers Co....440 591-9018
8160 Devon Ct Chagrin Falls (44023) **(G-3041)**
Construction Techniques Inc (HQ)....216 267-7310
15887 Snow Rd Ste 100 Cleveland (44142) **(G-5019)**
Consuetudo Abscisum Inc....419 281-8002
921 Jacobson Ave Ashland (44805) **(G-697)**
Consumer Guild Foods Inc....419 726-3406
5035 Enterprise Blvd Toledo (43612) **(G-18240)**
Consumer Source Inc....513 621-7300
431 Elliott Ave Cincinnati (45215) **(G-3543)**
Consumeracq Inc (PA)....440 277-9305
2509 N Ridge Rd E Lorain (44055) **(G-12084)**
Consumers Builders Supply Co (PA)....440 277-9306
2509 N Ridge Rd E Lorain (44055) **(G-12085)**
Consumers News Services Inc (HQ)....740 888-6000
5300 Crosswind Dr Columbus (43228) **(G-6811)**
Consumers News Services Inc....614 875-2307
4048 Broadway Grove City (43123) **(G-10422)**
Consun Food Industries Inc....440 322-6301
123 Gateway Blvd N Elyria (44035) **(G-9238)**
Contact Industries Inc....419 884-9788
25 Industrial Dr Lexington (44904) **(G-11804)**
Container Graphics Corp....937 746-5666
1 Miller St Franklin (45005) **(G-9875)**
Container Graphics Corp....419 531-5133
305 Ryder Rd Toledo (43607) **(G-18241)**
Container King Inc....937 652-3087
955 Lippincott Rd Urbana (43078) **(G-18986)**
Container Manufacturing Ltd....937 264-2370
6450 Poe Ave Ste 511 Dayton (45414) **(G-8102)**
Containment Solutions Inc....419 874-8765
103 Secor Woods Ln Perrysburg (43551) **(G-15934)**
Contech Bridge Solutions LLC....937 878-2170
7941 New Carlisle Pike Dayton (45424) **(G-8103)**
Contech Bridge Solutions LLC (HQ)....513 645-7000
9025 Cntrpinte Dr Ste 400 West Chester (45069) **(G-19678)**
Contech Cnstr Pdts Hldings Inc....513 645-7000
9025 Centre Pointe Dr # 400 West Chester (45069) **(G-19679)**
Contech Engnered Solutions Inc (PA)....513 645-7000
9025 Ctr Pinte Dr Ste 400 West Chester (45069) **(G-19680)**
Contech Engnered Solutions LLC....513 645-7000
1001 Grove St Middletown (45044) **(G-13896)**
Contech Engnered Solutions LLC....614 477-1171
1103 Schrock Rd Ste 105 Columbus (43229) **(G-6812)**
Contech Engnered Solutions LLC....513 425-5337
1001 Grove St Middletown (45044) **(G-13897)**
Contech Engnered Solutions LLC (HQ)....513 645-7000
9025 Centre Pointe Dr # 400 West Chester (45069) **(G-19681)**
Contech Strmwter Solutions LLC....513 645-7000
9025 Centre Pointe Dr # 400 West Chester (45069) **(G-19682)**
Contemprary Image Labeling Inc....513 583-5699
2034 Mckinley Blvd Lebanon (45036) **(G-11644)**
Conti Tool & Die Inc....330 633-1414
1333 Devalera St Akron (44310) **(G-121)**
Continental Business Entps Inc (PA)....440 439-4400
7311 Northfield Rd Cleveland (44146) **(G-5020)**
Continental Contitech, Marysville *Also called Contitech Usa Inc* **(G-12776)**
Continental Contitech, Fairlawn *Also called Contitech Usa Inc* **(G-9603)**
Continental Fan Mfg....937 233-5524
6274 Executive Blvd Huber Heights (45424) **(G-11015)**
Continental GL Sls & Inv Group....614 679-1201
315 Ashmoore Ct Powell (43065) **(G-16318)**
Continental Group, Powell *Also called Continental GL Sls & Inv Group* **(G-16318)**
Continental Hydrodyne Systems....330 494-2740
2216 Glenmont Dr Nw Canton (44708) **(G-2635)**
Continental Metal Proc Co (PA)....216 268-0000
18711 Cleveland Ave Cleveland (44110) **(G-5021)**
Continental Metal Proc Co....216 268-0000
14919 Saranac Rd Cleveland (44110) **(G-5022)**
Continental Products Company (PA)....216 383-3932
2926 Chester Ave Cleveland (44114) **(G-5023)**
Continental Products Company....216 531-0710
2926 Chester Ave Cleveland (44114) **(G-5024)**
Continental Strl Plas Inc....440 945-4800
333 Gore Rd Conneaut (44030) **(G-7644)**
Continental Strl Plas Inc....419 396-1980
2915 County Rd 96 Carey (43316) **(G-2880)**
Continental Strl Plas Inc....419 257-2231
100 S Poe Rd North Baltimore (45872) **(G-15043)**
Continental Strl Plas Inc....419 238-4628
1276 Industrial Dr Van Wert (45891) **(G-19082)**
Continental Testing Inc....937 832-3322
104 S Main St Union (45322) **(G-18900)**
Continental Tire Americas LLC....419 633-4221
927 S Union Bryan Bryan (43506) **(G-2276)**
Contingncy Prcrement Group LLC....513 204-9590
2800 Millbank Row Maineville (45039) **(G-12366)**
Contitech North America Inc (HQ)....330 664-7180
703 S Clvlnd Massillon Rd Fairlawn (44333) **(G-9602)**
Contitech Usa Inc....937 644-8900
13601 Industrial Pkwy Marysville (43040) **(G-12776)**
Contitech Usa Inc (HQ)....330 664-7000
703 S Clvland Mssillon Rd Fairlawn (44333) **(G-9603)**
Contour Forming Inc....740 345-9777
215 Oakwood Ave Newark (43055) **(G-14864)**
Contour Tool Inc....440 365-7333
38830 Taylor Pkwy North Ridgeville (44035) **(G-15216)**
Contours, Orrville *Also called Bekaert Corporation* **(G-15583)**
Contract Building Components....937 644-0739
14540 Industrial Pkwy Marysville (43040) **(G-12777)**
Contract Lighting Inc....614 746-7022
1207 Grandview Ave Columbus (43212) **(G-6813)**
Contract Lumber Inc....614 751-1109
200 Schofield Dr Columbus (43213) **(G-6814)**
Contractor Tools Online LLC....614 264-9392
Uknown New Albany (43054) **(G-14617)**
Contractors Steel Company....330 425-3050
8383 Boyle Pkwy Twinsburg (44087) **(G-18757)**
Control Associates Inc....440 708-1770
10205 Queens Way Unit 2 Chagrin Falls (44023) **(G-3042)**
Control Craft LLC....513 674-0056
2130 Schappelle Ln Cincinnati (45240) **(G-3544)**
Control Electric Co....216 671-8010
12130 Eaton Commerce Pkwy Columbia Station (44028) **(G-6434)**
Control Industries Inc....937 653-7694
1700 Fostoria Ave Ste 300 Findlay (45840) **(G-9671)**
Control Interface Inc....513 874-2062
517 Commercial Dr West Chester (45014) **(G-19683)**
Control Line Equipment Inc....216 433-7766
14750 Industrial Pkwy Cleveland (44135) **(G-5025)**
Control Measurement Inc....440 639-0020
1400 Mentor Ave Ste 5 Painesville (44077) **(G-15725)**
Control System Manufacturing....330 542-0000
10725 Struthers Rd New Middletown (44442) **(G-14749)**
Control System Upgrades, Cincinnati *Also called Magna Group LLC* **(G-3971)**
Control Transformer Inc....330 637-6015
3701 Warren Meadville Rd Cortland (44410) **(G-7706)**
Control-X Inc....614 777-9729
2289 Westbrooke Dr Columbus (43228) **(G-6815)**
Controlled Access Inc....330 273-6185
1515 W 130th St Ste A Hinckley (44233) **(G-10899)**
Controlled Release Society Inc....513 948-8000
110 E 69th St Cincinnati (45216) **(G-3545)**
Controllix Corporation....440 232-8757
21415 Alexander Rd Walton Hills (44146) **(G-19309)**
Controls and Sheet Metal Inc (PA)....513 721-3610
1051 Sargent St Cincinnati (45203) **(G-3546)**
Controls Inc....330 239-4345
5204 Portside Dr Medina (44256) **(G-13240)**
Convault of Ohio Inc....614 252-8422
841 Alton Ave Columbus (43219) **(G-6816)**
Converge Group Inc....419 281-0000
1850 S Baney Rd Ashland (44805) **(G-698)**
Conversion Tech Intl Inc....419 924-5566
700 Oak St West Unity (43570) **(G-19967)**
Convertapax, Midvale *Also called Maintenance Repair Supply Inc* **(G-13980)**
Converters/Prepress Inc....937 743-0935
301 Industry Dr Carlisle (45005) **(G-2891)**
Conveyor Metal Works Inc....740 477-8700
2717 Bush Mill Rd Frankfort (45628) **(G-9861)**
Conveyor Solutions LLC....513 367-4845
6705 Dry Fork Rd Cleves (45002) **(G-6360)**
Conveyor Technologies Ltd....513 248-0663
501 Techne Center Dr B Milford (45150) **(G-14005)**
Conviber, Medina *Also called Heintz Manufacturers Inc* **(G-13271)**
Conviber Inc....330 723-6006
1066 Industrial Pkwy Medina (44256) **(G-13241)**
Conway Greene Co Inc....216 619-8091
1400 E 30th St Ste 402 Cleveland (44114) **(G-5026)**
Conwed Designscape....715 532-5548
1445 Holland Rd Maumee (43537) **(G-13083)**
Cook Bonding & Mfg Co Inc....216 661-1698
701 W Schaaf Rd Cleveland (44109) **(G-5027)**
Cook, R D Company, Columbus *Also called R D Cook Company LLC* **(G-7372)**
Cooked Foods, Fairfield *Also called Koch Meat Co Inc* **(G-9519)**
Cookie Bouquets Inc....614 888-2171
6665 Huntley Rd Ste F Columbus (43229) **(G-6817)**

ALPHABETIC SECTION Coshocton Ethanol LLC

Cookie Cupboard, Cleveland *Also called Mid American Ventures Inc* ***(G-5673)***
Cool Machines Inc ... 419 232-4871
740 Fox Rd Van Wert (45891) ***(G-19083)***
Cool Seal Usa LLC ... 419 666-1111
232 J St Perrysburg (43551) ***(G-15935)***
Cool Times ... 513 608-5201
6127 Fairway Dr Cincinnati (45212) ***(G-3547)***
Coolant Control Inc (PA) ... 513 471-8770
5353 Spring Grove Ave Cincinnati (45217) ***(G-3548)***
Coomercial Forg Heat Treatment, Cleveland *Also called Cleveland Hollow Boring Inc* ***(G-4963)***
Coons Homemade Candies ... 740 496-4141
16451 County Highway 113 Harpster (43323) ***(G-10626)***
Cooper - Eaton Center, Cleveland *Also called Cooper Interconnect Inc* ***(G-5028)***
Cooper Energy Services, Mount Vernon *Also called Cameron International Corp* ***(G-14472)***
Cooper Farms, Oakwood *Also called Cooper Hatchery Inc* ***(G-15469)***
Cooper Farms, Saint Henry *Also called V H Cooper & Co Inc* ***(G-16670)***
Cooper Farms Inc (PA) ... 419 375-4116
2321 State Route 49 Fort Recovery (45846) ***(G-9813)***
Cooper Farms Inc ... 419 375-4119
2351 Wabash Rd Fort Recovery (45846) ***(G-9814)***
Cooper Farms Inc ... 419 375-4619
3310 State Route 49 Fort Recovery (45846) ***(G-9815)***
Cooper Farms Cooked Meat, Van Wert *Also called Cooper Foods* ***(G-19084)***
Cooper Farms Cooked Meats, Van Wert *Also called Cooper Hatchery Inc* ***(G-19085)***
Cooper Farms East Mill, Fort Recovery *Also called Cooper Farms Inc* ***(G-9814)***
Cooper Foods, Fort Recovery *Also called V H Cooper & Co Inc* ***(G-9829)***
Cooper Foods ... 419 232-2440
6893 Us Route 127 Van Wert (45891) ***(G-19084)***
Cooper Hatchery Inc (PA) ... 419 594-3325
22348 Road 140 Oakwood (45873) ***(G-15469)***
Cooper Hatchery Inc ... 419 238-4869
6793 Us Route 127 Van Wert (45891) ***(G-19085)***
Cooper Interconnect Inc ... 800 386-1911
1000 Eaton Blvd Cleveland (44122) ***(G-5028)***
Cooper Tire & Rubber Company (PA) ... 419 423-1321
701 Lima Ave Findlay (45840) ***(G-9672)***
Cooper Tire & Rubber Company ... 419 424-4202
900 Lima Ave Findlay (45840) ***(G-9673)***
Cooper Tire & Rubber Company ... 419 424-4384
1625 Lake Casscade Pkwy Findlay (45840) ***(G-9674)***
Cooper Tire Vhcl Test Ctr Inc (HQ) ... 419 423-1321
701 Lima Ave Findlay (45840) ***(G-9675)***
Cooper-Atkins Corporation ... 513 793-5366
11353 R Hartman Hwy 110 Cincinnati (45241) ***(G-3549)***
Cooper-Standard Automotive Inc ... 740 342-3523
2378 State Route 345 Ne New Lexington (43764) ***(G-14714)***
Cooper-Standard Automotive Inc ... 419 352-3533
1175 N Main St Bowling Green (43402) ***(G-1965)***
Coopers Mill Inc ... 419 562-4215
1414 N Sandusky Ave Bucyrus (44820) ***(G-2322)***
Copac, Cambridge *Also called Cambridge Ohio Production & As* ***(G-2429)***
Copen Machine Inc ... 330 678-4598
501 Dodge St Kent (44240) ***(G-11307)***
Copernicus Therapeutics Inc ... 216 707-1776
11000 Cedar Ave Ste 145 Cleveland (44106) ***(G-5029)***
Copier Resources Inc ... 614 268-1100
4800 Evanswood Dr Columbus (43229) ***(G-6818)***
Copley Fire & Rescue Assn ... 330 666-6464
1540 S Clvland Msslon Rd Copley (44321) ***(G-7681)***
Copley Ohio Newspapers Inc (HQ) ... 585 598-0030
500 Market Ave S Canton (44702) ***(G-2636)***
Copley Ohio Newspapers Inc ... 330 364-5577
629 Wabash Ave Nw New Philadelphia (44663) ***(G-14765)***
Copley Ohio Newspapers Inc ... 330 833-2631
729 Lincoln Way E Massillon (44646) ***(G-12969)***
COPLEY TOWNSHIP FIRE DEPT, Copley *Also called Copley Fire & Rescue Assn* ***(G-7681)***
Copperloy, Twinsburg *Also called Jh Industries Inc* ***(G-18797)***
Copy Cat Printing, Portsmouth *Also called Keystone Printing & Copy Cat* ***(G-16286)***
Copy Cats Printing LLC ... 440 345-5966
6659 Pearl Rd Ste 101 Cleveland (44130) ***(G-5030)***
Copy Print, Kent *Also called Rhoads Printing Center Inc* ***(G-11375)***
Copy Right of Ohio LLC ... 614 431-1303
7445 Montgomery Rd B Plain City (43064) ***(G-16182)***
Copy Right Printing, Plain City *Also called Copy Right of Ohio LLC* ***(G-16182)***
Copy Source Inc ... 937 642-7140
108 N Main St Marysville (43040) ***(G-12778)***
Copyrite Printing, Wheelersburg *Also called Greg Blume* ***(G-20182)***
Cora Cupcakes ... 440 227-7145
95 Park Rd Painesville (44077) ***(G-15726)***
Corbett R Caudill Chipping Inc ... 740 596-5984
35887 State Route 324 Hamden (45634) ***(G-10522)***
Corcadence Inc ... 216 702-6371
26701 Bernwood Rd Beachwood (44122) ***(G-1231)***
Cordier Group Holdings Inc ... 330 477-4511
4575 Southway St Sw Canton (44706) ***(G-2637)***
Cordis Corporation (HQ) ... 614 757-5000
7000 Cardinal Pl Dublin (43017) ***(G-8903)***
Core Automotive Tech LLC (HQ) ... 614 870-5000
800 Manor Park Dr Columbus (43228) ***(G-6819)***
Core Composites Cincinnati LLC ... 513 724-6111
4174 Half Acre Rd Batavia (45103) ***(G-1133)***
Core Manufacturing LLC ... 440 946-8002
8878 East Ave Mentor (44060) ***(G-13422)***
Core Molding Technologies Inc (PA) ... 614 870-5000
800 Manor Park Dr Columbus (43228) ***(G-6820)***
Core Quantum Technologies Inc ... 614 214-7210
1275 Kinnear Rd Columbus (43212) ***(G-6821)***
Core Technology Inc ... 440 934-9935
1260 Moore Rd Ste E Avon (44011) ***(G-946)***
Core-Tech Inc ... 440 946-8324
7850 Enterprise Dr Mentor (44060) ***(G-13423)***
Corell's Potato Chips, Beach City *Also called Daniel Meenan* ***(G-1211)***
Coreworth Holdings LLC ... 419 468-7100
8402 County Rd Iberia (43325) ***(G-11112)***
Corner Copy Shop, The, Beavercreek *Also called Flowers Print Inc* ***(G-1315)***
Cornerstone Brands Inc ... 866 668-5962
5568 W Chester Rd West Chester (45069) ***(G-19684)***
Cornerstone Indus Holdings (PA) ... 440 893-9144
100 Park Pl Chagrin Falls (44022) ***(G-3014)***
Cornerstone Industries Lcc ... 513 871-4546
10132 Mosteller Ln West Chester (45069) ***(G-19685)***
Cornerstone Manufacturing Inc ... 937 456-5930
861 Us Route 35 Eaton (45320) ***(G-9146)***
Cornerstone Printing Inc ... 614 861-2138
443 Knob Ave Reynoldsburg (43068) ***(G-16433)***
Cornerstone Spclty WD Pdts LLC ... 513 772-5560
12020 Tramway Dr Cincinnati (45241) ***(G-3550)***
Cornpentry ... 513 741-0594
2122 Schappelle Ln Cincinnati (45240) ***(G-3551)***
Corns Quality Woodworking LLC ... 419 589-4899
1525 Chew Rd Mansfield (44903) ***(G-12428)***
CORNWELL QUALITY TOOLS, Van Wert *Also called Cqt Kennedy LLC* ***(G-19086)***
Cornwell Quality Tools Company ... 330 628-2627
200 N Cleveland Ave Mogadore (44260) ***(G-14232)***
Corp, Dana, Lima *Also called Dana Drive Shaft Pdts Group* ***(G-11852)***
Corpad Company Inc ... 419 522-7818
555 Park Ave E Mansfield (44905) ***(G-12429)***
Corporate Dcment Solutions Inc ... 513 595-8200
11120 Ashburn Rd Cincinnati (45240) ***(G-3552)***
Corporate Elevator LLC ... 614 288-1847
35 E Gay St Ste 218 Columbus (43215) ***(G-6822)***
Corporate ID Inc ... 614 841-1255
6185 Huntley Rd Ste M Columbus (43229) ***(G-6823)***
Corporate Printing, Cincinnati *Also called Newhouse & Faulkner Inc* ***(G-4073)***
Corporate Printing, Liberty Twp *Also called Kuwatch Printing LLC* ***(G-11827)***
Corporate Supply LLC ... 614 876-8400
3608 Sugar Loaf Ct Columbus (43221) ***(G-6824)***
Corrchoice Inc (HQ) ... 330 833-5705
777 3rd St Nw Massillon (44647) ***(G-12970)***
Corro-Tech Equipment Corp ... 216 941-1552
4034 W 163rd St Cleveland (44135) ***(G-5031)***
Corrosion Resistant Technology ... 800 245-3769
560 Club Dr Aurora (44202) ***(G-875)***
Corrotec Inc ... 937 325-3585
1125 W North St Springfield (45504) ***(G-17379)***
Corrpro Companies Inc (HQ) ... 330 723-5082
1055 W Smith Rd Medina (44256) ***(G-13242)***
Corrpro Companies Inc ... 330 725-6681
1055 W Smith Rd Medina (44256) ***(G-13243)***
Corrpro Companies Intl Inc ... 330 723-5082
1055 W Smith Rd Medina (44256) ***(G-13244)***
Corrpro Waterworks, Medina *Also called Corrpro Companies Inc* ***(G-13243)***
Corrugated Chemicals Inc ... 513 561-7773
3865 Virginia Ave Cincinnati (45227) ***(G-3553)***
Cors Products, Canton *Also called Canton OH Rubber Speclty Prods* ***(G-2612)***
Cortape Inc ... 330 929-6700
60 Marc Dr Cuyahoga Falls (44223) ***(G-7853)***
Cortest Inc ... 440 942-1235
38322 Apollo Pkwy Willoughby (44094) ***(G-20301)***
Cortland Hardwood Products LLC ... 330 638-3232
124 Pearl St Cortland (44410) ***(G-7707)***
Corvac Composites LLC ... 248 807-0969
1025 N Washington St Greenfield (45123) ***(G-10347)***
Cory Electronics ... 440 951-9424
7665 Mentor Ave 335 Mentor (44060) ***(G-13424)***
COS Blueprint Inc (PA) ... 330 376-0022
590 N Main St Akron (44310) ***(G-122)***
Coshocton Community Choir ... 740 623-0554
142 N 4th St Coshocton (43812) ***(G-7725)***
Coshocton Community Choir Inc ... 740 622-8571
530 Cambridge Rd Coshocton (43812) ***(G-7726)***
Coshocton Ethanol LLC ... 740 623-3046
18137 County Road 271 Coshocton (43812) ***(G-7727)***

ALPHABETIC

Coshocton Industries Inc (PA) ...740 622-4734
605 N 15th St Coshocton (43812) ***(G-7728)***
Coshocton Orthopedic Center, Coshocton *Also called Francisco Jaume* ***(G-7734)***
Coshocton Pallet & Door Bldg ...740 622-9766
23222 County Road 621 Coshocton (43812) ***(G-7729)***
Coshocton Pallet & Door Co, Coshocton *Also called Thomas J Weaver Inc* ***(G-7755)***
Coshocton Stainless, Coshocton *Also called AK Steel Corporation* ***(G-7717)***
Cosma International Amer Inc ...419 409-7350
2125 Wood Bridge Blvd Bowling Green (43402) ***(G-1966)***
Cosmo Corporation ...330 359-5429
211 Winesburg St Wilmot (44689) ***(G-20514)***
Cosmo Plastics Co, Wilmot *Also called Cosmo Corporation* ***(G-20514)***
Coso Media LLC ...330 904-5889
5603 Darrow Rd Ste 500 Hudson (44236) ***(G-11039)***
Costa Machine, Akron *Also called Charles Costa Inc* ***(G-112)***
Costume Specialists Inc (PA) ...614 464-2115
211 N 5th St Ste 100 Columbus (43215) ***(G-6825)***
Costume Specialists Inc ...614 464-2115
211 N 5th St Ste 100 Columbus (43215) ***(G-6826)***
Cota International Inc ...937 526-5520
67 Industrial Pkwy Versailles (45380) ***(G-19177)***
Cotsworks LLC (PA) ...440 446-8800
749 Miner Rd Highland Heights (44143) ***(G-10787)***
Cott Systems Inc ...614 847-4405
2800 Corp Exchange Dr # 300 Columbus (43231) ***(G-6827)***
Cotton Pickin Tees & Caps ...419 636-3595
215 W Bryan St Bryan (43506) ***(G-2277)***
Cotton Wood Pallet Co, Galion *Also called Cottonwood Pallet Inc* ***(G-10129)***
Cottonwood Pallet Inc ...419 468-9703
9541 Mrral Krkptrick Rd E Galion (44833) ***(G-10129)***
Couch Business Development Inc ...937 253-1099
32 Bates St Dayton (45402) ***(G-8104)***
Coulter Ventures Llc (PA) ...614 358-6190
545 E 5th Ave Columbus (43201) ***(G-6828)***
Counter Concepts Inc ...330 848-4848
15535 Portage St Doylestown (44230) ***(G-8864)***
Counter Creation Plus L L C ...419 826-7449
106 Church St Swanton (43558) ***(G-17910)***
Counter Method Inc ...614 206-3192
13767 E State Route 37 Sunbury (43074) ***(G-17884)***
Counter Rhythm Group ...513 379-6587
441 E Redbud Aly Columbus (43206) ***(G-6829)***
Counter- Advice Inc ...937 291-1600
7002 State Route 123 Franklin (45005) ***(G-9876)***
Countertop Sales ...614 626-4476
5767 Westbourne Ave Columbus (43213) ***(G-6830)***
Countertop Xpress ...440 358-0500
381 Fountain Ave Painesville (44077) ***(G-15727)***
Countertops Helmart, Cincinnati *Also called Helmart Company Inc* ***(G-3806)***
Country Caterers Inc (PA) ...740 389-1013
409 Mrion Cardington Rd W Marion (43302) ***(G-12700)***
Country CLB Rtrment Ctr IV LLC ...740 676-2300
55801 Conno Mara Dr Bellaire (43906) ***(G-1485)***
Country Clippins ...740 472-5228
237 S Main St Woodsfield (43793) ***(G-20543)***
Country Comfort Woodworking ...330 695-4408
2 Mi Sw Of Mt Eaton Fredericksburg (44627) ***(G-9946)***
Country Crust Bakery ...888 860-2940
4918 State Route 41 S Bainbridge (45612) ***(G-1015)***
Country Freezer Units LLC ...740 623-8658
50938 Township Road 220 Baltic (43804) ***(G-1024)***
Country Ice Cream Freezer, Baltic *Also called Country Freezer Units LLC* ***(G-1024)***
Country Lane Custom Buildings ...740 485-8481
21318 Pealer Mill Rd Danville (43014) ***(G-7961)***
Country Maid Ice Cream Inc ...330 659-6830
3252 W Streetsboro Rd Richfield (44286) ***(G-16466)***
Country Manufacturing Inc ...740 694-9926
333 Salem Ave Ext Fredericktown (43019) ***(G-9964)***
Country Molding ...440 564-5235
12375 Kinsman Rd Newbury (44065) ***(G-14948)***
Country Parlour Ice Cream Co ...440 237-4040
12905 York Delta Dr Ste C Cleveland (44133) ***(G-5032)***
Country Pure Foods Inc (HQ) ...330 848-6875
222 W Main St Ste 401 Akron (44308) ***(G-123)***
Country Sales & Service LLC ...330 683-2500
255 Tracy Bridge Rd Orrville (44667) ***(G-15588)***
Country Savings Magazine, Burton *Also called Fontanelle Group Inc* ***(G-2358)***
Country Tin ...937 746-7229
228 S Main St Franklin (45005) ***(G-9877)***
Countryside Construction, Danville *Also called Country Lane Custom Buildings* ***(G-7961)***
Countryside Pumping Inc ...330 628-0058
1496 Martin Rd Mogadore (44260) ***(G-14233)***
County Classifieds ...937 592-8847
117 E Patterson Ave Bellefontaine (43311) ***(G-1510)***
County Line, Bryan *Also called Bryan Publishing Company* ***(G-2274)***
County Line Wood Working LLC ...330 316-3057
1482 County Road 600 Baltic (43804) ***(G-1025)***
County of Lake ...440 428-1794
7815 Cashen Rd Madison (44057) ***(G-12345)***
County of Lake ...440 269-2193
2100 Joseph Lloyd Pkwy Willoughby (44094) ***(G-20302)***
County of Lawrence ...740 867-8700
11100 Private Dr Chesapeake (45619) ***(G-3144)***
County of Medina ...330 723-3641
144 N Broadway St Ste 117 Medina (44256) ***(G-13245)***
County of Summit ...330 865-8065
1828 Smith Rd Akron (44313) ***(G-124)***
County Wide Welding LLC ...440 564-1333
14999 Cross Creek Pkwy Newbury (44065) ***(G-14949)***
Countyline Co-Op Inc (PA) ...419 287-3241
425 E Front St Pemberville (43450) ***(G-15883)***
Courthouse Manufacturing LLC ...740 335-2727
1730 Wash Ave Solar Ln Washington Court Hou (43160) ***(G-19476)***
Covap Inc ...513 793-1855
10829 Millington Ct Ste 1 Blue Ash (45242) ***(G-1753)***
Coventry Steel Services Inc ...216 883-4477
4200 E 71st St Ste 1 Cleveland (44105) ***(G-5033)***
Cover Up Building Systems ...740 668-8985
101 N Market St Martinsburg (43037) ***(G-12765)***
Covered Bridge Press, Cleveland *Also called Curt Harler Inc* ***(G-5044)***
Covert Manufacturing Inc (PA) ...419 468-1761
328 S East St Galion (44833) ***(G-10130)***
Covestro LLC ...740 929-2015
Newark Industrial Park Hebron (43025) ***(G-10740)***
Covia Holdings Corporation (HQ) ...440 214-3284
3 Summit Park Dr Ste 700 Independence (44131) ***(G-11123)***
Covidien Holding Inc ...513 948-7219
2111 E Galbraith Rd Cincinnati (45237) ***(G-3554)***
COW Industries Inc (PA) ...614 443-6537
1875 Progress Ave Columbus (43207) ***(G-6831)***
Cowells - Arrow Bingo Company ...216 961-3500
9900 Clinton Rd Cleveland (44144) ***(G-5034)***
Cowgill Printing Co ...216 741-2076
4427 Brookpark Rd Parma (44134) ***(G-15815)***
Cowles Industrial Tool Co LLC ...330 799-9100
185 N Four Mile Run Rd Austintown (44515) ***(G-932)***
Cox Inc ...740 858-4400
11201 State Route 104 Lucasville (45648) ***(G-12261)***
Cox Interior Inc ...270 789-3129
4080 Webster Ave Norwood (45212) ***(G-15425)***
Cox Machine & Fabrication, Carroll *Also called S J Cox Tool Inc* ***(G-2909)***
Cox Media Group Ohio Inc (HQ) ...937 225-2000
1611 S Main St Dayton (45409) ***(G-8105)***
Cox Media Group Ohio Inc ...937 743-6700
1611 S Main St Dayton (45409) ***(G-8106)***
Cox Newspapers LLC ...513 696-4500
200 Harmon Ave Liberty Township (45044) ***(G-11812)***
Cox Newspapers LLC ...937 866-3331
230 S 2nd St Miamisburg (45342) ***(G-13652)***
Cox Newspapers LLC ...937 225-2000
1611 S Main St Dayton (45409) ***(G-8107)***
Cox Newspapers LLC ...513 863-8200
7320 Yankee Rd Liberty Township (45044) ***(G-11813)***
Cox Newspapers LLC ...513 523-4139
30 W Park Pl Uppr Uppr Oxford (45056) ***(G-15692)***
Cox Painting, Wilmington *Also called Cox Printing Co* ***(G-20491)***
Cox Precast, Lucasville *Also called Cox Inc* ***(G-12261)***
Cox Printing Co ...937 382-2312
1087 Wayne Rd Wilmington (45177) ***(G-20491)***
Cox Publishing Hq ...937 225-2000
1611 S Main St Dayton (45409) ***(G-8108)***
Cox Trailer, Arcanum *Also called R J Cox Co* ***(G-631)***
Cox Wood Product Inc ...740 372-4735
5715 State Route 348 Otway (45657) ***(G-15687)***
Cozmyk Enterprises, Columbus *Also called Unity Enterprises Inc* ***(G-7559)***
Cozmyk Enterprises Inc ...614 231-1370
3757 Courtright Ct Columbus (43227) ***(G-6832)***
CP Chemicals Group LP ...440 833-3000
28960 Lakeland Blvd Wickliffe (44092) ***(G-20208)***
CP Industries Inc ...740 763-2886
11047 Lambs Ln Newark (43055) ***(G-14865)***
CP Metals Inc ...724 510-4293
2880 Sferra Ave Nw Warren (44483) ***(G-19390)***
CP Technologies Company ...614 866-9200
6615 Taylor Rd Blacklick (43004) ***(G-1682)***
CP Trading Group, Wickliffe *Also called CP Chemicals Group LP* ***(G-20208)***
CPC Logistics Inc ...513 874-5787
8695 Seward Rd Fairfield (45011) ***(G-9492)***
Cpca Manufacturing LLC ...937 723-9031
750 Rosedale Dr Dayton (45402) ***(G-8109)***
Cpg - Ohio LLC (PA) ...513 825-4800
470 Northland Blvd Cincinnati (45240) ***(G-3555)***
Cpg Armor Company, Maineville *Also called Contingncy Prcrement Group LLC* ***(G-12366)***
Cpg International LLC ...937 655-8766
894 Prairie Rd Wilmington (45177) ***(G-20492)***
Cpg Printing & Graphics, Toledo *Also called Culaine Inc* ***(G-18244)***
CPI, Holland *Also called Creative Products Inc* ***(G-10920)***

CPI Group Limited 216 525-0046
13858 Tinkers Creek Rd Cleveland (44125) *(G-5035)*

CPI Industrial Co 614 445-0800
2300 Parsons Ave Columbus (43207) *(G-6833)*

Cpic Automotive Inc 740 587-3262
1226 Weaver Dr Granville (43023) *(G-10328)*

Cpmg 440 263-2780
12955 York Delta Dr Ste G North Royalton (44133) *(G-15267)*

Cpmm Services Group Inc 614 447-0165
3785 Indianola Ave Columbus (43214) *(G-6834)*

Cpp, Coshocton Also called Ansell Healthcare Products LLC *(G-7720)*

Cpp Cleveland, Eastlake Also called Consoldted Precision Pdts Corp *(G-9102)*

Cpp Pomona, Cleveland Also called Consoldted Precision Pdts Corp *(G-5016)*

Cq Printing, Strongsville Also called J & J Bechke Inc *(G-17756)*

Cqt Kennedy LLC 419 238-2442
1260 Industrial Dr Van Wert (45891) *(G-19086)*

Cr Brands Inc (HQ) 513 860-5039
8790 Beckett Rd West Chester (45069) *(G-19686)*

Cr Holding Inc (HQ) 513 860-5039
9100 Centre Pointe Dr West Chester (45069) *(G-19687)*

CR Laurence Co Inc 440 248-0003
31600 Carter St Cleveland (44139) *(G-5036)*

Cr Supply LLC 440 759-5408
7661 Ohio St Mentor (44060) *(G-13425)*

CRA-Z-Art, Palmer Paint, Fayette Also called Larose Industries LLC *(G-9634)*

Crabar Business Systems, Leipsic Also called Crabar/Gbf Inc *(G-11724)*

Crabar/Gbf Inc 419 269-1720
4444 N Detroit Ave Toledo (43612) *(G-18242)*

Crabar/Gbf Inc (HQ) 419 943-2141
68 Vine St Leipsic (45856) *(G-11723)*

Crabar/Gbf Inc 740 622-0222
24170 Hangar Ct Coshocton (43812) *(G-7730)*

Crabar/Gbf Inc 419 943-2141
68 Vine St Leipsic (45856) *(G-11724)*

Crabro Printing Inc 740 533-3404
314 Chestnut St Ironton (45638) *(G-11163)*

Crabware Ltd 330 699-2305
3842 Park Ridge Dr Uniontown (44685) *(G-18917)*

Craco Embroidery Inc 513 563-6999
37 Techview Dr Cincinnati (45215) *(G-3556)*

Crafco Inc 330 270-3034
912 Salt Springs Rd Youngstown (44509) *(G-20880)*

Crafted Surface and Stone LLC 440 658-3799
26050 Richmond Rd Ste D Bedford Heights (44146) *(G-1467)*

Crafts For Kids, Solon Also called Katherine A Stull Inc *(G-17181)*

Craftwood, Mount Orab Also called Cindoco Wood Products Co *(G-14440)*

Craig Bros Machine Co Inc 740 756-9280
5846 Winchester Rd Carroll (43112) *(G-2901)*

Craig Saylor 740 352-8363
53020 State Route 124 Portland (45770) *(G-16275)*

Crain Communications Inc 216 522-1383
700 W Saint Clair Ave # 310 Cleveland (44113) *(G-5037)*

Crain Communications Inc 330 836-9180
1725 Merriman Rd Ste 300 Akron (44313) *(G-125)*

Crain's Cleveland Business, Cleveland Also called Crain Communications Inc *(G-5037)*

Crain-Tharp Printing Inc 740 345-9823
11 W Main St Newark (43055) *(G-14866)*

Cramers Inc 330 477-4571
4944 Southway St Sw Canton (44706) *(G-2638)*

Crane Blending Center 614 542-1199
2141 Fairwood Ave Columbus (43207) *(G-6835)*

Crane Chempharma & Energy, Cincinnati Also called Xomox Corporation *(G-4527)*

Crane Co 330 337-7861
1453 Allen Rd Salem (44460) *(G-16731)*

Crane Plastics, Columbus Also called Engineered Profiles LLC *(G-6896)*

Crane Plastics Mfg Ltd 614 754-3700
2141 Fairwood Ave Columbus (43207) *(G-6836)*

Crane Pro Services, West Chester Also called Konecranes Inc *(G-19732)*

Crane Pro Services, Brecksville Also called Konecranes Inc *(G-2046)*

Crane Pro Services 937 525-5555
4401 Gateway Blvd Springfield (45502) *(G-17380)*

Crane Pumps & Systems Inc 937 773-2442
420 3rd St Piqua (45356) *(G-16107)*

Crane Pumps & Systems Inc (HQ) 937 773-2442
420 3rd St Piqua (45356) *(G-16108)*

Crane Training USA Inc 513 755-2177
7908 Cincinnati Dayton Rd H West Chester (45069) *(G-19688)*

Crane Xomox, Blue Ash Also called Xomox Corporation *(G-1880)*

Cranial Technologies Inc 844 447-5894
4030 Smith Rd Ste 105 Cincinnati (45209) *(G-3557)*

Crase Communications Inc 419 468-1173
120 Harding Way E Ste 104 Galion (44833) *(G-10131)*

Crawford Acquisition Corp 216 486-0702
16130 Saint Clair Ave Cleveland (44110) *(G-5038)*

Crawford Computer Center, Solon Also called Swagelok Company *(G-17243)*

Crawford County Arts Council 419 834-4133
1810 E Mansfield St Bucyrus (44820) *(G-2323)*

Crawford Manufacturing Company 330 897-1060
52496 State Route 651 Baltic (43804) *(G-1026)*

Crawford Products Inc 614 890-1822
3637 Corporate Dr Columbus (43231) *(G-6837)*

Crawford Resources Inc 419 624-8400
1326 Coper Foster Pk Rd W Lorain (44053) *(G-12086)*

Crazy Richards, Plain City Also called Krema Group Inc *(G-16200)*

CRC Metal Products 740 966-0475
29 Greenscapes Ct Johnstown (43031) *(G-11264)*

Creamer Metal Products (PA) 740 852-1752
77 S Madison Rd London (43140) *(G-12056)*

Creatia Inc 937 368-3100
7990 Sodom Ballou Rd Fletcher (45326) *(G-9782)*

Creation Industries LLC 440 554-6286
15236 Shedd Rd Middlefield (44062) *(G-13787)*

Creative Blast Co 513 251-4177
3627 Spring Grove Ave Cincinnati (45223) *(G-3558)*

Creative Cabinets Ltd 740 689-0603
1807 Snoke Rd Sw Lancaster (43130) *(G-11557)*

Creative Commercial Finishing 513 722-9393
1298 State Route 28 Ste B Loveland (45140) *(G-12184)*

Creative Concepts 216 513-6463
620 E Smith Rd Ste W1 Medina (44256) *(G-13246)*

Creative Countertops Ohio LLC 937 540-9450
477 E Wenger Rd Englewood (45322) *(G-9352)*

Creative Curbing America LLC 419 738-7668
1634 Springfield Ave Wapakoneta (45895) *(G-19327)*

Creative Design Marble Inc 937 434-8892
7901 S Suburban Rd Dayton (45458) *(G-8110)*

Creative Documents Solutions 740 389-4252
1629 Marion Waldo Rd Marion (43302) *(G-12701)*

Creative Electronic Design 937 256-5106
2565 Celia Dr Beavercreek (45434) *(G-1308)*

Creative Fab & Welding LLC 937 780-5000
9691 Stafford Rd Leesburg (45135) *(G-11709)*

Creative Fabrication Ltd 740 262-5789
20110 Predmore Rd Richwood (43344) *(G-16508)*

Creative Foam Dayton Mold 937 279-9987
3337 N Dixie Dr Dayton (45414) *(G-8111)*

Creative Fuels LLC 330 923-2222
1093 Foxglove Cir Cuyahoga Falls (44223) *(G-7854)*

Creative Impressions Inc 937 435-5296
4611 Gateway Cir Dayton (45440) *(G-8112)*

Creative Microsystems Inc 937 836-4499
52 Hillside Ct Englewood (45322) *(G-9353)*

Creative Millwork Ohio Inc 440 992-3566
1801 W 47th St Ashtabula (44004) *(G-768)*

Creative Mold and Machine Inc 440 338-5146
10385 Kinsman Rd Newbury (44065) *(G-14950)*

Creative Packaging LLC 740 452-8497
1781 Kemper Ct Zanesville (43701) *(G-21124)*

Creative Packaging Concepts, Elyria Also called Wayne Pak Ltd *(G-9345)*

Creative Plastic Concepts LLC (HQ) 419 927-9588
206 S Griffith St Sycamore (44882) *(G-17930)*

Creative Plastics Intl 937 596-6769
18163 Snider Rd Jackson Center (45334) *(G-11206)*

Creative Powder Coatings 440 322-8197
6412 Gateway Blvd S Elyria (44035) *(G-9239)*

Creative Print Solutions LLC 614 989-1471
71 Granby Pl W Westerville (43081) *(G-20042)*

Creative Processing Inc 440 834-4070
17540 Rapids Rd Mantua (44255) *(G-12544)*

Creative Products Inc 419 866-5501
1430 Kieswetter Rd Holland (43528) *(G-10920)*

Creative Stitches Monogramming 740 667-3592
87 Cornes Rd Little Hocking (45742) *(G-11991)*

Creative Tool & Die 614 836-0080
244 Main St Groveport (43125) *(G-10488)*

Creative Woodworks 330 897-1432
5209 Evans Creek Rd Sw Sugarcreek (44681) *(G-17847)*

Creative Woodworks 440 355-8155
16940 Indian Hollow Rd Grafton (44044) *(G-10295)*

Creativity For Kids, Cleveland Also called AW Faber-Castell Usa Inc *(G-4780)*

Creek Smoothies LLC 937 429-1519
3195 Dayton Xenia Rd Beavercreek (45434) *(G-1309)*

Creekside Cottage Winery LLC 330 694-1013
8818 Cleveland Ave Se Magnolia (44643) *(G-12359)*

Creekside Springs LLC 330 679-1010
32 Washington St Salineville (43945) *(G-16787)*

Creighton Sports Center Inc (PA) 740 865-2521
205 Broadway Ave New Matamoras (45767) *(G-14745)*

Cremeans Concrete and Sup Co 740 446-1142
161 Georges Creek Rd Gallipolis (45631) *(G-10162)*

Cres Cor, Mentor Also called Crescent Metal Products Inc *(G-13426)*

Crescent Metal Products Inc (PA) 440 350-1100
5925 Heisley Rd Mentor (44060) *(G-13426)*

Crescent Services LLC 405 603-1200
11137 E Pike Rd Cambridge (43725) *(G-2433)*

Cresset Chemical Co Inc (PA) 419 669-2041
13255 Main St Weston (43569) *(G-20175)*

Cresset Chemical Co Inc 419 669-2041
13490 Silver St Weston (43569) ***(G-20176)***
Crest Aluminum Products, Mentor *Also called Crest Products Inc* ***(G-13427)***
Crest Awning & Home Imprv Co 440 942-3092
1571 E 361st St Bldg 1 Willoughby (44095) ***(G-20303)***
Crest Bending Inc 419 492-2108
108 John St New Washington (44854) ***(G-14828)***
Crest Craft Company 513 271-4858
4460 Lake Forest Dr # 232 Blue Ash (45242) ***(G-1754)***
Crest Graphics Inc 513 271-2200
9933 Alliance Rd Ste 1 Blue Ash (45242) ***(G-1755)***
Crest Products Inc 440 942-5770
8287 Tyler Blvd Mentor (44060) ***(G-13427)***
Crestar Crusts Inc 740 335-4813
1104 Clinton Ave Wshngtn CT Hs (43160) ***(G-20722)***
Crestar Foods, Wshngtn CT Hs *Also called Crestar Crusts Inc* ***(G-20722)***
Crg Plastics Inc 937 298-2025
2661 Culver Ave Dayton (45429) ***(G-8113)***
Crg Worldwide, Columbus *Also called Custom Retail Group LLC* ***(G-6843)***
Cri Digital, Columbus *Also called Copier Resources Inc* ***(G-6818)***
Cricket, Blacklick *Also called Wireless Retail LLC* ***(G-1695)***
Cricket Engines 513 532-2145
10810 Cincinnati Chillico Blanchester (45107) ***(G-1701)***
Crime and Trauma Scene Clean, Dayton *Also called Sara Hudson* ***(G-8493)***
Crimson Gate Consulting Co (PA) 614 805-0897
3274 Heatherstone Ct Dublin (43017) ***(G-8904)***
Crisenbery Logging LLC 740 256-1439
7818 Lincoln Pike Patriot (45658) ***(G-15850)***
Crishtronics Llc 440 572-8318
15249 Sassafras Dr Strongsville (44136) ***(G-17733)***
Crispie Creme of Chillicothe 740 774-3770
47 N Bridge St Chillicothe (45601) ***(G-3183)***
Criss Cross Directories, North Canton *Also called Haines & Company Inc* ***(G-15090)***
Crissman Tool & Machine Inc 330 872-1412
3877 Hallock Sook Rd Newton Falls (44444) ***(G-14986)***
Cristal USA Inc 440 994-1400
2900 Middle Rd Ashtabula (44004) ***(G-769)***
Crists Machining Inc 740 653-0041
1910 Hamburg Rd Sw Lancaster (43130) ***(G-11558)***
Criswell Furniture LLC 330 695-2082
8139 Criswell Rd Fredericksburg (44627) ***(G-9947)***
Criterion Instrument, Brookpark *Also called Criterion Tool & Die Inc* ***(G-2139)***
Criterion Tool & Die Inc 216 267-1733
5349 W 161st St Brookpark (44142) ***(G-2139)***
Critical Patient Care Inc 937 434-5455
4738 Gateway Cir Ste B Dayton (45440) ***(G-8114)***
Criticalaire LLC 513 475-3800
6155 Huntley Rd Ste A Columbus (43229) ***(G-6838)***
Criticalaire LLC (PA) 614 499-7744
11325 R Hartman Hwy 100 Cincinnati (45241) ***(G-3559)***
Croft & Son Mfg Inc 740 859-2200
509 Highland Ave Tiltonsville (43963) ***(G-18093)***
Cromwell Aleene 937 547-2281
101 W Main St Greenville (45331) ***(G-10366)***
Crook Miller Company, Stow *Also called Baker McMillen Co* ***(G-17572)***
Crooked River Coffee Co 440 442-8330
761 Beta Dr Ste E Cleveland (44143) ***(G-5039)***
Cropking Incorporated 330 302-4203
134 West Dr Lodi (44254) ***(G-12009)***
Crosco 330 477-1999
5246 18th St Sw Canton (44706) ***(G-2639)***
Crosco Wood Products, Fredericksburg *Also called Miller Crist* ***(G-9953)***
Crosco Wood Products 330 857-0228
1543 Zuercher Rd Dalton (44618) ***(G-7938)***
Cross Communications Inc 937 304-0010
250 N Cassel Rd Vandalia (45377) ***(G-19120)***
Crosscreek Pallet Co 440 632-1940
14530 Madison Rd Middlefield (44062) ***(G-13788)***
Crosstown Bindery, Cincinnati *Also called Patricia Lee Burd* ***(G-4136)***
Crow Works LLC 888 811-2769
179 Straits Ln Killbuck (44637) ***(G-11450)***
Crowe Manufacturing Services 800 831-1893
2731 Walnut Ridge Dr Troy (45373) ***(G-18644)***
Crowes Cabinets Inc 330 729-9911
590 E West Reserve Bldg 8 Youngstown (44514) ***(G-20881)***
Crown Auto Top Mfg Co, Columbus *Also called Crown Dielectric Inds Inc* ***(G-6839)***
Crown Battery Manufacturing Co (PA) 419 334-7181
1445 Majestic Dr Fremont (43420) ***(G-10009)***
Crown Battery Manufacturing Co 330 425-3308
1750 Highland Rd Ste 3 Twinsburg (44087) ***(G-18758)***
Crown Closures Machinery 740 681-6593
1765 W Fair Ave Lancaster (43130) ***(G-11559)***
Crown Cork & Seal Usa Inc 419 727-8201
5201 Enterprise Blvd Toledo (43612) ***(G-18243)***
Crown Cork & Seal Usa Inc 330 833-1011
700 16th St Se Massillon (44646) ***(G-12971)***
Crown Cork & Seal Usa Inc 937 299-2027
5005 Springboro Pike Moraine (45439) ***(G-14339)***
Crown Cork & Seal Usa Inc 740 681-3000
940 Mill Park Dr Lancaster (43130) ***(G-11560)***
Crown Cork & Seal Usa Inc 740 681-6593
1765 W Fair Ave Lancaster (43130) ***(G-11561)***
Crown Credit Company 419 629-2311
44 S Washington St New Bremen (45869) ***(G-14649)***
Crown Dielectric Inds Inc 614 224-5161
830 W Broad St Columbus (43222) ***(G-6839)***
Crown Electric Engrg & Mfg LLC 513 539-7394
175 Edison Dr Middletown (45044) ***(G-13898)***
Crown Equipment Corporation 937 295-4062
300 S Tower St Fort Loramie (45845) ***(G-9793)***
Crown Equipment Corporation 419 586-1100
410 Grand Lake Rd Celina (45822) ***(G-2956)***
Crown Equipment Corporation 419 629-9201
120 W Monroe St New Bremen (45869) ***(G-14650)***
Crown Equipment Corporation 937 454-7545
750 Center Dr Vandalia (45377) ***(G-19121)***
Crown Equipment Corporation 419 629-2311
624 W Monroe St New Bremen (45869) ***(G-14651)***
Crown Equipment Corporation 440 232-7772
26400 Broadway Ave Ste B Oakwood Village (44146) ***(G-15479)***
Crown Equipment Corporation 419 629-2311
40 S Washington St New Bremen (45869) ***(G-14652)***
Crown Equipment Corporation 419 629-2311
510 W Monroe St New Bremen (45869) ***(G-14653)***
Crown Equipment Corporation 614 274-7700
2100 Southwest Blvd Grove City (43123) ***(G-10423)***
Crown Equipment Corporation 513 874-2600
10685 Medallion Dr Cincinnati (45241) ***(G-3560)***
Crown Lift Trucks, Fort Loramie *Also called Crown Equipment Corporation* ***(G-9793)***
Crown Lift Trucks, Celina *Also called Crown Equipment Corporation* ***(G-2956)***
Crown Lift Trucks, New Bremen *Also called Crown Equipment Corporation* ***(G-14650)***
Crown Lift Trucks, Vandalia *Also called Crown Equipment Corporation* ***(G-19121)***
Crown Lift Trucks, New Bremen *Also called Crown Equipment Corporation* ***(G-14651)***
Crown Lift Trucks, Oakwood Village *Also called Crown Equipment Corporation* ***(G-15479)***
Crown Lift Trucks, New Bremen *Also called Crown Equipment Corporation* ***(G-14653)***
Crown Lift Trucks, Grove City *Also called Crown Equipment Corporation* ***(G-10423)***
Crown Lift Trucks, Cincinnati *Also called Crown Equipment Corporation* ***(G-3560)***
Crown Mats & Mating, Fremont *Also called Ludlow Composites Corporation* ***(G-10038)***
Crown North America, Apple Creek *Also called Leggett & Platt Incorporated* ***(G-611)***
Crown Plastics Co 513 367-0238
116 May Dr Harrison (45030) ***(G-10638)***
Crown Printing Inc 740 477-2511
118 S Scioto St Circleville (43113) ***(G-4541)***
Crowne Group LLC (PA) 216 589-0198
127 Public Sq Ste 5110 Cleveland (44114) ***(G-5040)***
Crowning Food Company 937 323-4699
1966 Commerce Cir Springfield (45504) ***(G-17381)***
Crownover Lumber Co Inc (PA) 740 596-5229
501 Fairview Ave Mc Arthur (45651) ***(G-13180)***
Crude Oil Buyer, Gnadenhutten *Also called Echo Drilling Inc* ***(G-10278)***
Crude Oil Company 740 452-3335
1819 Newark Rd Zanesville (43701) ***(G-21125)***
Cruise Quarters 614 777-6022
4013 Main St Hilliard (43026) ***(G-10821)***
Cruise Quarters and Tours 614 891-6089
730 Mohican Way Westerville (43081) ***(G-20043)***
Cruisin Times Magazine 440 331-4615
20545 Center Ridge Rd Ll40 Rocky River (44116) ***(G-16544)***
Crum Manufacturing Inc 419 878-9779
1265 Wtrville Monclova Rd Waterville (43566) ***(G-19492)***
Crumbs Bakery, Athens *Also called Crumbs Inc* ***(G-826)***
Crumbs Inc 740 592-3803
94 Columbus Rd Athens (45701) ***(G-826)***
Crummitt & Son Vault Corp (PA) 304 281-2420
329 N 2nd St Martins Ferry (43935) ***(G-12759)***
Crushproof Tubing Co 419 293-2111
100 North St Mc Comb (45858) ***(G-13188)***
Cryogenic Equipment & Svcs Inc 513 761-4200
11959 Tramway Dr Ste 1 Cincinnati (45241) ***(G-3561)***
Cryogenic Technical Services, Plain City *Also called Drivetrain USA Inc* ***(G-16189)***
Cryoplus Inc 330 683-3375
2429 N Millborne Rd Wooster (44691) ***(G-20581)***
Cryovac Inc 513 771-7770
7410 Union Centre Blvd West Chester (45014) ***(G-19689)***
Crystal Art Imports Inc (PA) 614 430-8180
6185 Huntley Rd Ste K Columbus (43229) ***(G-6840)***
Crystal Carvers Inc 800 365-9782
4040 Essex Ct Powell (43065) ***(G-16319)***
Crystal Classics, Columbus *Also called Crystal Art Imports Inc* ***(G-6840)***
Crystal Koch Finishing Inc 440 366-7526
630 Sugar Ln Elyria (44035) ***(G-9240)***
Crystalite, Lewis Center *Also called Abrasive Technology Lapidary* ***(G-11741)***
Cs Products 330 452-8566
1307 Gross Ave Ne Canton (44705) ***(G-2640)***
Csa Nutrition Services Inc 800 257-3788
10 Nutrition Way Brookville (45309) ***(G-2164)***

ALPHABETIC SECTION — Custom Coils

Csafe LLC 937 312-0114
2900 Dryden Rd Moraine (45439) *(G-14340)*
Csc Ltd 330 841-6011
4000 Mahoning Ave Nw Warren (44483) *(G-19391)*
CSC Serviceworks Holdings 800 362-3182
8515 Freeway Dr Ste D Macedonia (44056) *(G-12286)*
Cse-Industrial Products Group, Cincinnati Also called Computer System Enhancement *(G-3541)*
Csi Infusion Services, Brecksville Also called Clinical Specialties Inc *(G-2027)*
Csl Plasma Inc 937 325-4200
435 E Columbia St Springfield (45503) *(G-17382)*
CSM Horvath Ledgebrook 419 522-1133
198 Wayne St Mansfield (44902) *(G-12430)*
CSP Carey, Carey Also called Continental Strl Plas Inc *(G-2880)*
CSP North Baltimore, North Baltimore Also called Continental Strl Plas Inc *(G-15043)*
CSP Van Wert, Van Wert Also called Continental Strl Plas Inc *(G-19082)*
Csqp Quick Printing, Berea Also called Whiskey Fox Corporation *(G-1632)*
CSS Publishing Co Inc 419 227-1818
5450 N Dixie Hwy Lima (45807) *(G-11850)*
Cssi & Quality Printing, Kent Also called Customer Service Systems Inc *(G-11308)*
CST Zero Discharged Car Wash S 740 947-5480
223 Virginia Ln Waverly (45690) *(G-19543)*
Csv Inc 937 438-1142
2080 E Rahn Rd Dayton (45440) *(G-8115)*
Csw of Ny Inc 413 589-1311
3545 Silica Rd Unit E Sylvania (43560) *(G-17935)*
CT Ferry Screw Products I 440 871-1617
1660 Queen Annes Gate Cleveland (44145) *(G-5041)*
CTB Consulting LLC 216 712-7764
19056 Old Detroit Rd Rocky River (44116) *(G-16545)*
Ctc Plastics (HQ) 937 228-9184
401 N Keowee St Dayton (45404) *(G-8116)*
Ctek Tool & Machine Company 513 742-0423
11310 Southland Rd Cincinnati (45240) *(G-3562)*
Ctg, Miamisburg Also called Certified Tool & Grinding Inc *(G-13648)*
Ctl Analyzers, Shaker Heights Also called Cellular Technology Limited *(G-16929)*
Ctl Analyzers LLC (PA) 216 791-5084
20521 Chagrin Blvd # 200 Shaker Heights (44122) *(G-16930)*
Ctl-Aerospace Inc (PA) 513 874-7900
5616 Spellmire Dr West Chester (45246) *(G-19845)*
Ctl-Aerospace Inc 513 874-7900
9970 International Blvd West Chester (45246) *(G-19846)*
Ctm Integration Incorporated 330 332-1800
1318 Quaker Cir Salem (44460) *(G-16732)*
Ctm Labeling Systems 330 332-1800
1318 Quaker Cir Salem (44460) *(G-16733)*
Ctna Tire Plant, Bryan Also called Continental Tire Americas LLC *(G-2276)*
Cto Inc 330 785-1130
2035 S Main St Akron (44301) *(G-126)*
CTS, Kettering Also called Composite Technical Svcs LLC *(G-11430)*
CTS Signs & Sales 419 407-5534
1030 Crescuus Rd Oregon (43616) *(G-15559)*
Cub Cadet LLC 330 273-8669
5903 Grafton Rd Valley City (44280) *(G-19034)*
Cubbison Company (PA) 330 793-2481
380 Victoria Rd Youngstown (44515) *(G-20882)*
Cubic Blue Inc 330 638-2999
2934 Warren Meadville Rd Cortland (44410) *(G-7708)*
Cuda Composites LLC 937 499-0360
1788 S Metro Pkwy Dayton (45459) *(G-8117)*
Culaine Inc 419 345-4984
1036 W Laskey Rd Toledo (43612) *(G-18244)*
Culinary Standards, Blue Ash Also called Rsw Distributors LLC *(G-1841)*
Culligan, Zanesville Also called US Water Company LLC *(G-21186)*
Cult Couture LLC 330 801-9475
1110 Munroe Falls Ave Cuyahoga Falls (44221) *(G-7855)*
Cultured Marble Inc 330 549-2282
11331 South Ave North Lima (44452) *(G-15169)*
Cumberland Limestone LLC 740 638-3942
53681 Spencer Rd Cumberland (43732) *(G-7823)*
Cummins - Allison Corp 614 529-1940
2222 Wilson Rd Columbus (43228) *(G-6841)*
Cummins - Allison Corp 440 824-5050
6777 Engle Rd Ste H Cleveland (44130) *(G-5042)*
Cummins - Allison Corp 513 469-2924
11256 Cornell Park Dr Blue Ash (45242) *(G-1756)*
Cummins Bridgeway Columbus LLC 614 771-1000
4000 Lyman Dr Hilliard (43026) *(G-10822)*
Cummins Bridgeway Toledo LLC 419 893-8711
801 Illinois Ave Maumee (43537) *(G-13084)*
Cummins Inc 614 604-6004
2297 Southwest Blvd Ste K Grove City (43123) *(G-10424)*
Cummins Inc 614 771-1000
4000 Lyman Dr Hilliard (43026) *(G-10823)*
Cummins-Allison, Columbus Also called Cummins - Allison Corp *(G-6841)*
Cupboard Distributing, Urbana Also called Chris Haughey *(G-18982)*
Cupcake Divaz 216 509-3850
5480 Autumn Ln North Ridgeville (44039) *(G-15217)*
Cupcake Wishes 440 315-3856
34340 Bainbridge Rd North Ridgeville (44039) *(G-15218)*
Cupcakes For A Cure 419 764-1719
26595 Woodmont Dr Perrysburg (43551) *(G-15936)*
Curation Foods Inc 419 931-1029
12700 S Dixie Hwy Bowling Green (43402) *(G-1967)*
Curless Printing Company 937 783-2403
202 E Main St Unit 1 Blanchester (45107) *(G-1702)*
Current Inc 330 392-5151
455 N River Rd Nw Warren (44483) *(G-19392)*
Current Lighting Solutions LLC (HQ) 800 435-4448
1975 Noble Rd Ste 338e Cleveland (44112) *(G-5043)*
Current Technology, Columbus Also called Data Power Solutions *(G-6851)*
Currier Richard & James 440 988-4132
540 Mcintosh Ln Amherst (44001) *(G-559)*
Curt Harler Inc 440 238-4556
12936 Falling Water Rd Cleveland (44136) *(G-5044)*
Curtis Chemical Inc 330 656-2514
6020 Ogilby Dr Hudson (44236) *(G-11040)*
Curtiss-Wright Controls 937 252-5601
2600 Paramount Pl Ste 200 Fairborn (45324) *(G-9456)*
Curtiss-Wright Flow Control 513 735-2538
750 Kent Rd Batavia (45103) *(G-1134)*
Curtiss-Wright Flow Control 513 528-7900
4600 E Tech Dr Cincinnati (45245) *(G-3244)*
Curtiss-Wright Flow Ctrl Corp 440 838-7690
10195 Brecksville Rd Brecksville (44141) *(G-2028)*
Curtiss-Wright Flow Ctrl Corp 216 267-3200
18001 Sheldon Rd Cleveland (44130) *(G-5045)*
Curtiss-Wright Flow Ctrl Corp 513 528-7900
4600 E Tech Dr Cincinnati (45245) *(G-3245)*
Curv Imaging LLC 614 890-2878
841 Green Crest Dr Westerville (43081) *(G-20044)*
Curves and More Woodworking 614 239-7837
2002 Zettler Rd Columbus (43232) *(G-6842)*
Cusc International Ltd 513 881-2000
3 Standen Dr Hamilton (45015) *(G-10549)*
Cushman Foundry LLC 513 984-5570
5300 Creek Rd Blue Ash (45242) *(G-1757)*
Cushman Foundry Div, Cincinnati Also called Sawbrook Steel Castings Co *(G-4302)*
Custar Stone Co 419 669-4327
9072 County Road 424 Napoleon (43545) *(G-14536)*
Custer Products Limited 330 490-3158
1320 Sanders Ave Sw Massillon (44647) *(G-12972)*
Custom Aerosol Packaging, Piqua Also called C A P Industries Inc *(G-16105)*
Custom Aluminum Boxes 440 864-2664
210 Cooper Foster Park Rd Amherst (44001) *(G-560)*
Custom Apparel LLC 330 633-2626
1180 Brittain Rd Akron (44305) *(G-127)*
Custom Assembly Inc 419 622-3040
2952 Road 107 Haviland (45851) *(G-10708)*
Custom Automation Technologies 614 939-4228
1267 Bayboro Dr New Albany (43054) *(G-14618)*
Custom Blast & Coat Inc 419 225-6024
1511 S Dixie Hwy Lima (45804) *(G-11851)*
Custom Boat Covers, Aurora Also called William Thompson *(G-916)*
Custom Bobbin Winding, Zanesville Also called Adkel Corp *(G-21094)*
Custom Brackets, Cleveland Also called J B M Machine Co Inc *(G-5483)*
Custom Brass Finishing Inc 330 453-0888
1541 Raff Rd Sw Canton (44710) *(G-2641)*
Custom Built Crates Inc 513 248-4422
1700 Victory Park Dr Milford (45150) *(G-14006)*
Custom Canvas & Boat Repair 419 732-3314
29 S Bridge Rd Lakeside (43440) *(G-11501)*
Custom Canvas & Upholstery, Lakeside Also called Custom Canvas & Boat Repair *(G-11501)*
Custom Carbide Cutter Inc 513 851-6363
133 Circle Freeway Dr West Chester (45246) *(G-19847)*
Custom Carving Source LLC 513 407-1008
3182 Beekman St Cincinnati (45223) *(G-3563)*
Custom Cases For Collectibles, Hamilton Also called Specialty Plas Fabrications *(G-10607)*
Custom Cast Marbleworks Inc 513 769-6505
3154 Exon Ave Cincinnati (45241) *(G-3564)*
Custom Chassis Inc 440 839-5574
52826 State Route 303 Wakeman (44889) *(G-19283)*
Custom Chemical Packaging LLC 330 331-7416
4086 Watercourse Dr Medina (44256) *(G-13247)*
Custom Chrome Plating, Grafton Also called Customchrome Plating Inc *(G-10296)*
Custom Cltch Jint Hydrlcs Inc (PA) 216 431-1630
3417 Saint Clair Ave Ne Cleveland (44114) *(G-5046)*
Custom Cltch Jint Hydrlcs Inc 330 455-1202
1313 15th St Sw Canton (44706) *(G-2642)*
Custom Cntrwght Plate Proc Inc 330 448-2347
7799 Locust St Masury (44438) *(G-13060)*
Custom Coil & Transformer Co 740 452-5211
2900 Newark Rd Zanesville (43701) *(G-21126)*
Custom Coils 330 426-3797
51305 Carmel Achor Rd Negley (44441) *(G-14589)*

Custom Color Match and Spc
ALPHABETIC SECTION

Custom Color Match and Spc 419 868-5882
8930 Airport Hwy Holland (43528) **(G-10921)**
Custom Control Tech LLC 419 342-5593
4469 Funk Rd Shelby (44875) **(G-16981)**
Custom Counter Tops & Spc Co 330 637-4856
161 W Main St Cortland (44410) **(G-7709)**
Custom Craft Controls Inc 330 630-9599
1620 Triplett Blvd Akron (44306) **(G-128)**
Custom Craft Drap Inc 330 929-5728
1924 Portage Trl Cuyahoga Falls (44223) **(G-7856)**
Custom Crankshaft Inc 330 382-1200
1730 Annesley Rd East Liverpool (43920) **(G-9054)**
Custom Crete 740 726-2433
6928 Gillette Rd Waldo (43356) **(G-19302)**
Custom Cutting Company, Ashland *Also called Consuetudo Abscisum Inc* **(G-697)**
Custom Deco LLC 419 698-2900
1345 Miami St Toledo (43605) **(G-18245)**
Custom Deco South Inc 419 698-2900
1343 Miami St Toledo (43605) **(G-18246)**
Custom Design & Tool 419 865-9773
8900 Geiser Rd Holland (43528) **(G-10922)**
Custom Design Cabinets & Tops 440 639-9900
379 Fountain Ave Painesville (44077) **(G-15728)**
Custom Design Kitchen & Bath, Painesville *Also called Custom Design Cabinets & Tops* **(G-15728)**
Custom Displays LLC 330 454-8850
9838 Bimeler St Ne Bolivar (44612) **(G-1910)**
Custom Duct & Supply Co Inc 937 228-2058
912 Cincinnati St Dayton (45417) **(G-8118)**
Custom Enclosures Corp 330 786-9000
1951 S Main St Akron (44301) **(G-129)**
Custom Engraving & Screen Prtg 440 933-2902
690 Avon Belden Rd Ste 1b Avon Lake (44012) **(G-983)**
Custom Fab 330 825-3586
5281 S Hametown Rd Norton (44203) **(G-15364)**
Custom Fabrication By Fisher 513 738-4600
100 Weaver Rd Okeana (45053) **(G-15517)**
Custom Floaters LLC 216 337-9118
5161 W 161st St Brookpark (44142) **(G-2140)**
Custom Floaters LLC 216 536-8979
6519 Eastland Rd Ste 101 Brookpark (44142) **(G-2141)**
Custom Foam Products Inc (PA) 937 295-2700
900 Tower Dr Fort Loramie (45845) **(G-9794)**
Custom Formed Products, Miamisburg *Also called Customformed Products Inc* **(G-13653)**
Custom Fresheners 888 241-9109
423 Knapp St Fremont (43420) **(G-10010)**
Custom GL Sltions Millbury LLC 419 855-7706
24145 W Moline Martin Rd Millbury (43447) **(G-14048)**
Custom Glass Solutions LLC (PA) 248 340-1800
600 Lkview Plz Blvd Ste A Worthington (43085) **(G-20682)**
Custom Glass Solutions Upper S 419 294-4921
12688 State Highway 67 Upper Sandusky (43351) **(G-18949)**
Custom Graphics Inc 330 963-7770
8107 Bavaria Dr E Macedonia (44056) **(G-12287)**
Custom Hitch & Trailer, Piketon *Also called Custom Hitch and Trailer/ Over* **(G-16068)**
Custom Hitch and Trailer/ Over 740 289-3925
4237 Us Highway 23 Piketon (45661) **(G-16068)**
Custom Hoists Inc (HQ) 419 368-4721
771 County Road 30a Ashland (44805) **(G-699)**
Custom Imprint 440 238-4488
19573 Progress Dr Strongsville (44149) **(G-17734)**
Custom Industries Inc 216 251-2804
10701 Briggs Rd Cleveland (44111) **(G-5047)**
Custom Machine Inc 419 986-5122
3315 W Township Road 158 Tiffin (44883) **(G-18057)**
Custom Machining Solutions LLC 330 221-1523
5605 Tallmadge Rd Rootstown (44272) **(G-16567)**
Custom Made Palm Trees & Tiki, Akron *Also called Custom Made Palm Trees LLC* **(G-130)**
Custom Made Palm Trees LLC 330 633-0063
1201 Devalera St Akron (44310) **(G-130)**
Custom Manufacturing Solutions (PA) 937 372-0777
1129 Miamisburg Centervil Dayton (45449) **(G-8119)**
Custom Marine Canvas Training 419 732-8362
250 Se Catawba Rd Ste C Port Clinton (43452) **(G-16245)**
Custom Material Hdlg Eqp LLC 513 235-5336
7868 Gapstow Brg Cincinnati (45231) **(G-3565)**
Custom Metal Products Inc 614 855-2263
5037 Babbitt Rd New Albany (43054) **(G-14619)**
Custom Metal Products Inc (PA) 614 855-2263
5037 Babbitt Rd New Albany (43054) **(G-14620)**
Custom Metal Shearing Inc 937 233-6950
80 Commerce Park Dr Dayton (45404) **(G-8120)**
Custom Metal Works Inc (PA) 419 668-7831
193 Akron Rd Norwalk (44857) **(G-15385)**
Custom Millcraft Corp 513 874-7080
9092 Le Saint Dr West Chester (45014) **(G-19690)**
Custom Molded Products LLC 937 382-1070
92 Grant St Wilmington (45177) **(G-20493)**
Custom Nickel LLC 937 222-1995
45 N Clinton St Dayton (45402) **(G-8121)**
Custom Palet Manufacturing 440 693-4603
9291 N Girdle Rd Middlefield (44062) **(G-13789)**
Custom Polishing 937 596-0430
559 Plum Ridge Trl Sidney (45365) **(G-17024)**
Custom Powdercoating LLC 937 972-3516
2211 Bellefontaine Ave Dayton (45404) **(G-8122)**
Custom Powdr Coating By Greber, Elyria *Also called Greber Machine Tool Inc* **(G-9264)**
Custom Products Corporation (PA) 440 528-7100
7100 Cochran Rd Solon (44139) **(G-17129)**
Custom Pultrusions Inc (HQ) 330 562-5201
1331 S Chillicothe Rd Aurora (44202) **(G-876)**
Custom Retail Group LLC 614 409-9720
6311 Busch Blvd Columbus (43229) **(G-6843)**
Custom Rubber Corporation 216 391-2928
1274 E 55th St Cleveland (44103) **(G-5048)**
Custom Screen Printing (PA) 330 963-3131
1869 E Aurora Rd Ste 100 Twinsburg (44087) **(G-18759)**
Custom Sign Center Inc 614 279-6700
3200 Valleyview Dr Columbus (43204) **(G-6844)**
Custom Sink Top Mfg 440 245-6220
302 W 12th St Lorain (44052) **(G-12087)**
Custom Speed Parts Inc 440 238-3260
19769 Progress Dr Strongsville (44149) **(G-17735)**
Custom Sporstwear Imprints LLC 330 335-8326
238 High St Wadsworth (44281) **(G-19231)**
Custom Stamp Makers Inc 216 351-1470
4901 Brookpark Rd Cleveland (44134) **(G-5049)**
Custom Surroundings Inc 330 483-9020
6450 Grafton Rd Valley City (44280) **(G-19035)**
Custom Tarpaulin Products Inc 330 758-1801
8095 Southern Blvd Youngstown (44512) **(G-20883)**
Custom Tooling Company Inc 513 733-5790
603 Wayne Park Dr Cincinnati (45215) **(G-3566)**
Custom Way Welding Inc 937 845-9469
2217 N Dayton Lakeview Rd New Carlisle (45344) **(G-14665)**
Custom Weld & Machine Corp 330 452-3935
1500 Henry Ave Sw Canton (44706) **(G-2643)**
Custom Welding, Columbus *Also called Warlock Inc* **(G-7590)**
Custom Woodworking Inc 419 456-3330
214 S Main St Ottawa (45875) **(G-15649)**
Customchrome Plating Inc 440 926-3116
963 Mechanic St Grafton (44044) **(G-10296)**
Customer Printing Inc 330 629-8676
592 Industrial Rd Youngstown (44509) **(G-20884)**
Customer Service Systems Inc 330 677-2877
1250 W Main St Ste A Kent (44240) **(G-11308)**
Customers Car Care Center 419 841-6646
5299 Monroe St Toledo (43623) **(G-18247)**
Customformed Products Inc 937 388-0480
645 Precision Ct Miamisburg (45342) **(G-13653)**
Customized Girl, Columbus *Also called E Retailing Associates LLC* **(G-6880)**
Customized Vinyl Sales 330 518-3238
50814 Hadley Rd East Palestine (44413) **(G-9072)**
Cut Off Blades Inc 440 543-2947
426 Chipping Ln Chagrin Falls (44023) **(G-3043)**
Cutler Richard DBA Ohio Contro 440 892-1858
21506 Ellen Dr Cleveland (44126) **(G-5050)**
Cutter Equipment Company, Canton *Also called Randall Richard & Moore LLC* **(G-2802)**
Cutting Dynamics Inc (PA) 440 249-4150
980 Jaycox Rd Avon (44011) **(G-947)**
Cutting Edge , The, Perry *Also called Tce International Ltd* **(G-15914)**
Cutting Edge Countertops Inc 419 873-9500
1300 Flagship Dr Perrysburg (43551) **(G-15937)**
Cutting Edge Manufacturing LLC 419 547-9204
1744 W Mcpherson Hwy B Clyde (43410) **(G-6388)**
Cutting Edge Roofing Products, Tallmadge *Also called Trans Foam Inc* **(G-18009)**
Cutting Edge Technologies Inc 216 574-4759
1241 Superior Ave E Cleveland (44114) **(G-5051)**
Cutting Systems Inc 216 928-0500
15593 Brookpark Rd Cleveland (44142) **(G-5052)**
Cuyahoga Co Med Examiner S Off 216 721-5610
11001 Cedar Ave Cleveland (44106) **(G-5053)**
Cuyahoga Concrete Products, Cleveland *Also called Osborne Inc* **(G-5821)**
Cuyahoga Falls Plant, Cuyahoga Falls *Also called Terrasource Global Corporation* **(G-7927)**
Cuyahoga Group, The, North Ridgeville *Also called Cuyahoga Vending Co Inc* **(G-15219)**
Cuyahoga Machine Company LLC 216 267-3560
5250 W 137th St Brookpark (44142) **(G-2142)**
Cuyahoga Rebuilders Inc 440 846-0532
5111 Brookpark Rd Cleveland (44134) **(G-5054)**
Cuyahoga Vending Co Inc 440 353-9595
39405 Taylor Pkwy North Ridgeville (44035) **(G-15219)**
Cvc Limited 1 LLC 740 605-3853
568 S Liberty Keuter Rd Lebanon (45036) **(G-11645)**
Cvg National Seating Co LLC 219 872-7295
7800 Walton Pkwy New Albany (43054) **(G-14621)**
Cvg Trim Systems, New Albany *Also called Trim Systems Operating Corp* **(G-14638)**
CW Machine Worx Ltd 740 654-5304
4805 Scooby Ln Carroll (43112) **(G-2902)**

ALPHABETIC SECTION

CWC Partners LLC 567 208-1573
228 Stadium Dr Findlay (45840) *(G-9676)*
Cwh Graphics LLC 866 241-8515
23196 Miles Rd Ste A Bedford Heights (44128) *(G-1468)*
Cwm Smoothie LLC 419 283-6387
2859 N Hlland Sylvania Rd Toledo (43615) *(G-18248)*
Cyberutility LLC 216 298-8723
1599 Maywood Rd Cleveland (44121) *(G-5055)*
Cycle Electric Inc 937 884-7300
8734 Dyton Grenville Pike Brookville (45309) *(G-2165)*
Cyclone Supply Company Inc (PA) 330 204-0313
524 River St Dover (44622) *(G-8814)*
Cylinders & Valves Inc 440 238-7343
20811 Westwood Dr Strongsville (44149) *(G-17736)*
Cylindrical Fabrications, Cleveland Also called Cleveland Track Material Inc *(G-4980)*
Cypress Valley Log Homes, Marietta Also called Gillard Construction Inc *(G-12627)*
Cyril-Scott Company, The, Lancaster Also called Consolidated Graphics Inc *(G-11556)*
D & A Custom Trailer Inc 740 922-2205
6700 Moores Ridge Rd Se Uhrichsville (44683) *(G-18883)*
D & A Rofael Enterprises Inc 513 751-4929
3026 Burnet Ave Cincinnati (45219) *(G-3567)*
D & B Industries Inc 937 253-8658
5031 Linden Ave Ste B Dayton (45432) *(G-7975)*
D & B Machine Welding Inc 740 922-4930
1128 N Main St Uhrichsville (44683) *(G-18884)*
D & D Classic Auto Restoration 937 473-2229
2300 Mote Dr Covington (45318) *(G-7784)*
D & D Energy Co 330 495-1631
6033 Marelis Ave Ne Canton (44721) *(G-2644)*
D & D Landscaping Inc 330 507-6647
7012 Warren Sharon Rd Brookfield (44403) *(G-2104)*
D & D Mining Co Inc 330 549-3127
3379 E Garfield Rd New Springfield (44443) *(G-14819)*
D & D Next Day Signs Inc 419 537-9595
2112 N Reynolds Rd Toledo (43615) *(G-18249)*
D & D Plastics Inc 330 376-0668
581 E Tallmadge Ave Akron (44310) *(G-131)*
D & D Quality Machining Co Inc 440 942-2772
36495 Reading Ave Ste 1 Willoughby (44094) *(G-20304)*
D & E Cut Stock, Middlefield Also called David J Fisher *(G-13793)*
D & E Electric Inc 513 738-1172
7055 Okana Drewersburg Rd Okeana (45053) *(G-15518)*
D & E Machine Co 513 932-2184
962 S Us Route 42 Lebanon (45036) *(G-11646)*
D & G Welding Inc 419 445-5751
302 W Barre Rd Archbold (43502) *(G-643)*
D & H Meats Inc 419 387-7767
400 S Blanchard Vanlue (45890) *(G-19153)*
D & J Distributing & Mfg 419 865-2552
1302 Holloway Rd Holland (43528) *(G-10923)*
D & J Electric Motor Repair Co 330 336-4343
1734 Wall Rd Unit Office Wadsworth (44281) *(G-19232)*
D & J Machine Shop 937 256-2730
442 Todd St Dayton (45403) *(G-8123)*
D & J Printing Inc 330 678-5868
3765 Sunnybrook Rd Kent (44240) *(G-11309)*
D & K Designs, Millersburg Also called Lamar D Steiner *(G-14105)*
D & L Energy Inc 330 270-1201
3930 Fulton Dr Nw Ste 200 Canton (44718) *(G-2645)*
D & L Excavating Ltd 419 271-0635
969 N Rymers Rd Port Clinton (43452) *(G-16246)*
D & L Machine Co Inc 330 785-0781
1029 Arlington Cir Akron (44306) *(G-132)*
D & L Machining LLC 419 253-1651
4621 Township Road 21 Marengo (43334) *(G-12590)*
D & L Manufacturing Inc 440 428-1627
2715 Bennett Rd Madison (44057) *(G-12346)*
D & M Printing, Massillon Also called David A and Mary A Mathis *(G-12973)*
D & M Saw & Tool Inc 513 871-5433
2974 P G Graves Ln Cincinnati (45241) *(G-3568)*
D & M Welding, Moraine Also called Dayton Brick Company Inc *(G-14344)*
D & M Welding & Radiator 740 947-9032
9093 State Route 220 Waverly (45690) *(G-19544)*
D & R Supply Inc 330 855-3781
18228 Fulton Rd Marshallville (44645) *(G-12752)*
D 4 Industries Inc 419 523-9555
685 Woodland Dr Ottawa (45875) *(G-15650)*
D A Fitzgerald Co Inc 937 548-0511
1045 Sater St Greenville (45331) *(G-10367)*
D A L E S Corporation 419 255-5335
1402 Jackson St Toledo (43604) *(G-18250)*
D A Stirling Inc 330 923-3195
2740 Hudson Dr Cuyahoga Falls (44221) *(G-7857)*
D and D Asp Sealcoating LLC 614 288-3597
13199 E Crosset Hill Dr Pickerington (43147) *(G-16044)*
D and D Business Equipment Inc 440 777-5441
3298 Columbia Rd Cleveland (44145) *(G-5056)*
D Anderson Corp 330 433-0606
6872 Glengarry Ave Nw Canton (44718) *(G-2646)*

D B S Stinless Stl Fabricators 513 856-9600
21 Standen Dr Hamilton (45015) *(G-10550)*
D C, Cleveland Also called Die-Cut Products Co *(G-5094)*
D C Controls LLC 513 225-0813
4836 Duff Dr Ste E West Chester (45246) *(G-19848)*
D C Filter & Chemical Inc 419 626-3967
1517 5th St Sandusky (44870) *(G-16802)*
D C G, Cleveland Also called Directconnectgroup Ltd *(G-5097)*
D C I, Akron Also called Digital Color Intl LLC *(G-143)*
D C M Industries Inc 937 254-8500
1901 E 5th St Dayton (45403) *(G-8124)*
D C Ramey Piano Co 708 602-3961
17768 Woodview Dr Marysville (43040) *(G-12779)*
D C Systems Inc 330 273-3030
1251 Industrial Pkwy N Brunswick (44212) *(G-2198)*
D D D Hams Inc 440 487-9572
34234 Aurora Rd Solon (44139) *(G-17130)*
D F Electronics Inc 513 772-7792
200 Novner Dr Cincinnati (45215) *(G-3569)*
D I, Canfield Also called Dunaway Inc *(G-2525)*
D J Decorative Stone Inc 937 848-6462
3180 Ferry Rd Bellbrook (45305) *(G-1491)*
D J Klingler Inc 513 891-2284
9999 Montgomery Rd Cincinnati (45242) *(G-3570)*
D J Metro Mold & Die Inc 440 237-1130
9841 York Alpha Dr Ste J North Royalton (44133) *(G-15268)*
D K Manufacturing 740 654-5566
2118 Commerce St Lancaster (43130) *(G-11562)*
D L H Locomotive Works 937 629-0321
1528 Mitchell Blvd Springfield (45503) *(G-17383)*
D L Salkil LLC 419 841-3341
8261 W Bancroft St Toledo (43617) *(G-18251)*
D L T, Cincinnati Also called Dominion Liquid Tech LLC *(G-3600)*
D Lewis Inc 740 695-2615
52235 National Rd Saint Clairsville (43950) *(G-16630)*
D M C, Lagrange Also called Dynamic Machine Concepts Inc *(G-11479)*
D M I, Reynoldsburg Also called Dimensional Metals Inc *(G-16435)*
D M J F Inc 440 845-1155
6571 Pearl Rd Cleveland (44130) *(G-5057)*
D M L Steel Tech 513 737-9911
6974 Zenith Ct Liberty Twp (45011) *(G-11823)*
D M Pallet Service Inc 614 491-0881
2019 Rathmell Rd Columbus (43207) *(G-6845)*
D M Tool & Plastics Inc 937 962-4140
11150 Baltimore Brookville (45309) *(G-2166)*
D M Tool & Plastics Inc (PA) 937 962-4140
4140 Us Route 40 E Lewisburg (45338) *(G-11790)*
D M U, Dayton Also called Dayton Molded Urethanes LLC *(G-8139)*
D M V Supply Corporation 330 847-0450
3047 Anderson Anthony Warren (44481) *(G-19393)*
D M Z Machine Co, Willoughby Also called Zitnik Enterprises Inc *(G-20464)*
D Martone Industries Inc 440 632-5800
15060 Madison Rd Middlefield (44062) *(G-13790)*
D N A, Plain City Also called Daily Needs Assistance *(G-16184)*
D O Technologies Inc 330 725-4561
667 Lafayette Rd Medina (44256) *(G-13248)*
D P I, Toledo Also called Decorative Panels Intl Inc *(G-18259)*
D P Products Inc 440 834-9663
14790 Brkshire Ind Pkwy Middlefield (44062) *(G-13791)*
D Picking & Co 419 562-5016
119 S Walnut St Bucyrus (44820) *(G-2324)*
D S H Machine Co 440 946-4311
36255 Reading Ave Ste A Willoughby (44094) *(G-20305)*
D T Kothera Inc 440 632-1651
15422 Georgia Rd Middlefield (44062) *(G-13792)*
D W Dickey, Lisbon Also called D W Dickey and Son Inc *(G-11966)*
D W Dickey and Son Inc (PA) 330 424-1441
7896 Dickey Dr Lisbon (44432) *(G-11966)*
D W Truax Enterprise Inc 740 695-2596
52499 National Rd Saint Clairsville (43950) *(G-16631)*
D&D Classic Restoration, Covington Also called D & D Classic Auto Restoration *(G-7784)*
D&D Design Concepts Inc 513 752-2191
4360 Winding Creek Blvd Batavia (45103) *(G-1135)*
D&D Logging 740 679-2573
52759 State Route 379 Woodsfield (43793) *(G-20544)*
D&M Fencing LLC 419 604-0698
08656 Deep Cut Rd Spencerville (45887) *(G-17308)*
D'Ing Meeting Room Products, Cleveland Also called DIng Products *(G-5096)*
D-G Custom Chrome LLC 513 531-1881
5200 Lester Rd Cincinnati (45213) *(G-3571)*
D-Terra Solutions LLC 614 450-1040
35 Clairedan Dr Powell (43065) *(G-16320)*
D.B.G. Cleaners, Mansfield Also called Our Detergent Inc *(G-12500)*
D.O.V.E.S., Clarington Also called Diversifd OH Vlly Eqpt & Srvcs *(G-4567)*
Daavlin Distributing Co 419 636-6304
205 W Bement St Bryan (43506) *(G-2278)*
Dabar Industries LLC 614 873-3949
8475 Rausch Dr Plain City (43064) *(G-16183)*

Dac, Dover *Also called Direct Action Co Inc* ***(G-8816)***
Daca Vending Wholesale LLC....513 753-1600
1105b W Ohio Pike Amelia (45102) ***(G-535)***
Dacon Industries Co....330 298-9491
4839 Washington Ave Ravenna (44266) ***(G-16374)***
Dacraft, Miamisburg *Also called Waxco International Inc* ***(G-13740)***
Dadco Inc (PA)....513 489-2244
7365 E Kemper Rd Ste C Cincinnati (45249) ***(G-3572)***
Dadco Inc....513 489-2244
12151 Best Pl Cincinnati (45241) ***(G-3573)***
Daddy Katz LLC....937 296-0347
3250 Kettering Blvd Moraine (45439) ***(G-14341)***
Dae Holdings LLC....502 589-1445
1 Air Cargo Pkwy E Swanton (43558) ***(G-17911)***
Dae Industries, Swanton *Also called Dae Holdings LLC* ***(G-17911)***
Daffin Candies, Girard *Also called Daffins Candies* ***(G-10256)***
Daffins Candies (PA)....330 545-0325
700 N State St Girard (44420) ***(G-10256)***
Dai Ceramics Inc....440 946-6964
38240 Airport Pkwy Willoughby (44094) ***(G-20306)***
Daido Metal Bellefontaine LLC....937 592-5010
1215 S Greenwood St Bellefontaine (43311) ***(G-1511)***
Daifuku America Corporation (HQ)....614 863-1888
6700 Tussing Rd Reynoldsburg (43068) ***(G-16434)***
Daifuku Co, Reynoldsburg *Also called Daifuku America Corporation* ***(G-16434)***
Daikin Applied Americas Inc....614 351-9862
192 Heatherdown Dr Westerville (43081) ***(G-20045)***
Daily Agency Inc....937 456-9808
309 N Barron St Eaton (45320) ***(G-9147)***
Daily Chief Union....419 294-2331
111 W Wyandot Ave Upper Sandusky (43351) ***(G-18950)***
Daily Dog....419 708-4923
8325 Hill Ave Holland (43528) ***(G-10924)***
Daily Fostoria Review Co....419 435-6641
113 E Center St Fostoria (44830) ***(G-9836)***
Daily Gazette....937 372-4444
1836 W Park Sq Xenia (45385) ***(G-20764)***
Daily Globe, Shelby *Also called Shelby Daily Globe Inc* ***(G-16988)***
Daily Growler Inc....614 656-2337
2812 Fishinger Rd Upper Arlington (43221) ***(G-18944)***
Daily Kent Stater, Kent *Also called Kent State University* ***(G-11345)***
Daily Legal News, Cleveland *Also called Legal News Publishing Co* ***(G-5572)***
Daily Legal News Inc....330 747-7777
100 E Federal St Ste 126 Youngstown (44503) ***(G-20885)***
Daily Needs Assistance....614 824-8340
340 W Main St Plain City (43064) ***(G-16184)***
Daily Needs Personal Care LLC....614 598-8383
11560 State Route 104 Ashville (43103) ***(G-817)***
Daily Record, The, Millersburg *Also called Holmes County Hub Inc* ***(G-14097)***
Daily Reporter....614 224-4835
580 S High St Ste 316 Columbus (43215) ***(G-6846)***
Daily Squawk LLC....937 426-6247
3214 Bob White Pl Dayton (45431) ***(G-7976)***
Daily Standard The, Celina *Also called Standard Printing Co Inc* ***(G-2985)***
Dairy Clean, Delaware *Also called Frischco Inc* ***(G-8680)***
Dairy Farmers America Inc....330 670-7800
1035 Medina Rd Ste 300 Medina (44256) ***(G-13249)***
Dairy Pak Div, Olmsted Falls *Also called Blue Ridge Paper Products Inc* ***(G-15529)***
Dairy Shed....937 848-3504
55 Bellbrook Plz Bellbrook (45305) ***(G-1492)***
Dairymens, Cleveland *Also called Borden Dairy Company Ohio LLC* ***(G-4832)***
Daishin Industrial Co....614 766-9535
6490 Shier Rings Rd Ste E Dublin (43016) ***(G-8905)***
Daisy Brand LLC....330 202-4376
3600 N Geyers Chapel Rd Wooster (44691) ***(G-20582)***
Daisys Pillows LLC....937 776-6968
4694 Free Pike Dayton (45416) ***(G-8125)***
Dak Enterprises Inc (PA)....740 828-3291
18062 Timber Trails Rd Marysville (43040) ***(G-12780)***
Dakkota Integrated Systems LLC....517 694-6500
315 Matzinger Rd Unit G Toledo (43612) ***(G-18252)***
Dakota Software Corporation (PA)....216 765-7100
1375 Euclid Ave Ste 500 Cleveland (44115) ***(G-5058)***
Dal-Little Fabricating Inc....216 883-3323
11707 Putnam Ave Cleveland (44105) ***(G-5059)***
Dalaco Materials LLC....513 893-5483
4805 Hamilton Middltwn Liberty Twp (45011) ***(G-11824)***
Dale Adams Enterprises Inc....330 524-2800
1658 Highland Rd Ste 1 Twinsburg (44087) ***(G-18760)***
Dale Kestler....513 871-9000
3475 Cardiff Ave Cincinnati (45209) ***(G-3574)***
Dale Lute Logging....740 352-1779
2696 Henley Deemer Rd Mc Dermott (45652) ***(G-13192)***
Dalin Auto Service....440 997-3301
3041 S Ridge Rd W Ashtabula (44004) ***(G-770)***
Dallas Design & Technology Inc....419 884-9750
184 Industrial Dr Mansfield (44904) ***(G-12431)***
Dallas Instantwhip Inc....614 488-2536
2200 Cardigan Ave Columbus (43215) ***(G-6847)***
Dalmatian Press LLC....419 207-3600
605 Westlake Dr Ashland (44805) ***(G-700)***
Dalton Combustion Systems Inc....216 447-0647
9701 Stone Rd Cleveland (44125) ***(G-5060)***
Dalton Corporation....419 682-6328
310 Ellis St Stryker (43557) ***(G-17827)***
Dalton Stryker McHining Fcilty....419 682-6328
310 Ellis St Stryker (43557) ***(G-17828)***
Dalton Veal....330 828-8337
14978 Arnold Rd Dalton (44618) ***(G-7939)***
Dalton Wood Products Inc....330 682-0727
101 N Swinehart Rd Orrville (44667) ***(G-15589)***
Damar Products Inc (PA)....937 492-9023
17222 State Route 47 E Sidney (45365) ***(G-17025)***
Damar Products Inc....937 492-9023
516 Park St Sidney (45365) ***(G-17026)***
Damsel In Defense....561 307-4177
7484 Willow Woods Dr North Olmsted (44070) ***(G-15184)***
Damsel In Defense Diva....330 874-2068
11331 Whitetail Run St Nw Bolivar (44612) ***(G-1911)***
Dan K Williams Inc....419 893-3251
1350 Ford St Maumee (43537) ***(G-13085)***
Dan Patrick Enterprises Inc....740 477-1006
8564 Zane Trail Rd Circleville (43113) ***(G-4542)***
Dan S Miller & David S Miller....937 464-9061
9535 County Road 97 Belle Center (43310) ***(G-1498)***
Dan Shrock Cement....440 548-2498
9344 Pritchard Rd Parkman (44080) ***(G-15811)***
Dan Wilzynski....800 531-3343
2000 Fairwood Ave Columbus (43207) ***(G-6848)***
Dan-Loc Express, Piqua *Also called Dan-Loc Group LLC* ***(G-16109)***
Dan-Loc Group LLC....937 778-0485
294 Fox Dr Piqua (45356) ***(G-16109)***
Dan-Mar Company Inc....419 660-8830
200 Bluegrass Dr E Norwalk (44857) ***(G-15386)***
Dana Auto Systems Group LLC (HQ)....419 887-3000
3939 Technology Dr Maumee (43537) ***(G-13086)***
Dana Automotive Aftermarket (HQ)....419 887-3000
3939 Technology Dr Maumee (43537) ***(G-13087)***
Dana Brazil Holdings I LLC (HQ)....419 887-3000
3939 Technology Dr Maumee (43537) ***(G-13088)***
Dana Commercial Vehicle Pdts, Maumee *Also called Dana Commercial Vhcl Mfg LLC* ***(G-13089)***
Dana Commercial Vhcl Mfg LLC (HQ)....419 887-3000
3939 Technology Dr Maumee (43537) ***(G-13089)***
Dana Commercial Vhcl Pdts LLC (HQ)....419 887-3000
3939 Technology Dr Maumee (43537) ***(G-13090)***
Dana Drive Shaft Pdts Group....419 227-2001
777 Bible Rd Lima (45801) ***(G-11852)***
Dana Driveshaft Mfg LLC....419 222-9708
777 Bible Rd Lima (45801) ***(G-11853)***
Dana Driveshaft Mfg LLC (HQ)....419 887-3000
3939 Technology Dr Maumee (43537) ***(G-13091)***
Dana Driveshaft Products, Lima *Also called Dana Driveshaft Mfg LLC* ***(G-11853)***
Dana Driveshaft Products, Maumee *Also called Dana Driveshaft Mfg LLC* ***(G-13091)***
Dana Driveshaft Products LLC (HQ)....419 887-3000
3939 Technology Dr Maumee (43537) ***(G-13092)***
Dana Global Products Inc (HQ)....419 887-3000
3939 Technology Dr Maumee (43537) ***(G-13093)***
Dana Graphics Inc....513 351-4400
2200 Dana Ave Fl 2 Cincinnati (45208) ***(G-3575)***
Dana Heavy Vehicle Systems (HQ)....419 887-3000
3939 Technology Dr Maumee (43537) ***(G-13094)***
Dana Heavy Vhcl Systems Group, Maumee *Also called Dana Heavy Vehicle Systems* ***(G-13094)***
Dana Incorporated (PA)....419 887-3000
3939 Technology Dr Maumee (43537) ***(G-13095)***
Dana Information Technology, Maumee *Also called Dana Limited* ***(G-13098)***
Dana Light Axle Mfg LLC....419 887-3000
3044 Jeep Pkwy Toledo (43610) ***(G-18253)***
Dana Light Axle Mfg LLC (HQ)....419 887-3000
3939 Technology Dr Maumee (43537) ***(G-13096)***
Dana Light Axle Products, Maumee *Also called Dana Light Axle Mfg LLC* ***(G-13096)***
Dana Limited....419 887-3000
6515 Maumee Western Rd Maumee (43537) ***(G-13097)***
Dana Limited....419 482-2000
580 Longbow Dr Maumee (43537) ***(G-13098)***
Dana Limited (HQ)....419 887-3000
3939 Technology Dr Maumee (43537) ***(G-13099)***
Dana Off Highway Products LLC....614 864-1116
6635 Taylor Rd Blacklick (43004) ***(G-1683)***
Dana Off Highway Products LLC (HQ)....419 887-3000
3939 Technology Dr Maumee (43537) ***(G-13100)***
Dana Sealing Manufacturing LLC (HQ)....419 887-3000
3939 Technology Dr Maumee (43537) ***(G-13101)***
Dana Sealing Products, Maumee *Also called Dana Sealing Manufacturing LLC* ***(G-13101)***

Dana Sealing Products LLC (HQ) 419 887-3000
3939 Technology Dr Maumee (43537) *(G-13102)*
Dana Signs LLC 937 653-3917
1052 S Main St Frnt Frnt Urbana (43078) *(G-18987)*
Dana Structural Products LLC (HQ) 419 887-3000
3939 Technology Dr Maumee (43537) *(G-13103)*
Dana Thermal Products LLC (HQ) 419 887-3000
3939 Technology Dr Maumee (43537) *(G-13104)*
Dana White Machining Wldg Inc 419 652-3444
910 County Road 40 Nova (44859) *(G-15432)*
Dana World Trade Corporation (HQ) 419 887-3000
3939 Technology Dr Maumee (43537) *(G-13105)*
Danaher Corporation 440 995-3003
6095 Parkland Blvd # 310 Cleveland (44124) *(G-5061)*
Danaher Corporation 440 995-3025
7171 Industrial Park Blvd Mentor (44060) *(G-13428)*
Dandi Enterprises Inc 419 516-9070
6353 Som Center Rd Solon (44139) *(G-17131)*
Dandy Products Inc 800 591-2284
1095 Harcourt Rd Ste C Mount Vernon (43050) *(G-14477)*
Dandy Products Inc 513 625-3000
3314 State Route 131 Goshen (45122) *(G-10286)*
Dango & Dienenthal Inc 330 829-0277
21 E Chestnut St Alliance (44601) *(G-463)*
Daniel Malek 330 701-5760
2315 21st St Cuyahoga Falls (44223) *(G-7858)*
Daniel Meenan 330 756-2818
614 Pine St Nw Beach City (44608) *(G-1211)*
Daniel Wagner 740 942-2928
39170 Welsh Rd Cadiz (43907) *(G-2397)*
Daniels Amish Collection LLC 330 276-0110
100 Straits Ln Killbuck (44637) *(G-11451)*
Danis Sweet Cupcakes 614 581-8978
283 N Clayton St Centerburg (43011) *(G-2993)*
Danite Holdings Ltd 614 444-3333
1640 Harmon Ave Columbus (43223) *(G-6849)*
Danite Sign Co, Columbus Also called Danite Holdings Ltd *(G-6849)*
Danmarco, Norwalk Also called Dan-Mar Company Inc *(G-15386)*
Danner Press Corp 330 454-5692
1411 Navarre Rd Sw Canton (44706) *(G-2647)*
Danny Cabinet Co 440 667-6635
11983 Abbey Rd Unit 1 Cleveland (44133) *(G-5062)*
Dano Jr LLC 440 781-5774
6185 Ridgebury Blvd Cleveland (44124) *(G-5063)*
Danone Us LLC 513 229-0092
7577 Central Parke Blvd Mason (45040) *(G-12854)*
Danone Us LLC 419 628-3861
216 Southgate Minster (45865) *(G-14211)*
Dansco Mfg & Pmpg Unit Svc LP 330 452-3677
2149 Moore Ave Se Canton (44707) *(G-2648)*
Dansizen Printing Co Inc 330 966-4962
4525 Aultman Ave Nw North Canton (44720) *(G-15077)*
Dante Solutions Inc 440 234-8477
7261 Engle Rd Ste 105 Cleveland (44130) *(G-5064)*
Dap Products Inc 937 667-4461
875 N 3rd St Tipp City (45371) *(G-18110)*
Dapsco 937 294-5331
3110 Kettering Blvd Moraine (45439) *(G-14342)*
Darby Creek Millwork Co 614 873-3267
10001 Plain Cy Grgesville Plain City (43064) *(G-16185)*
Dare Electronics Inc 937 335-0031
3245 S County Road 25a Troy (45373) *(G-18645)*
Darifill Inc 614 890-3274
750 Green Crest Dr Westerville (43081) *(G-20046)*
Darin Jordan 740 819-3525
3460 Gorsuch Rd Nashport (43830) *(G-14566)*
Dark Diamond Tools Inc 440 701-6424
10319 Sawmill Dr Chardon (44024) *(G-3107)*
Darke Precision Inc 937 548-2232
291 Fox Dr Piqua (45356) *(G-16110)*
Darko Inc 330 425-9805
26401 Richmond Rd Bedford (44146) *(G-1398)*
Darling Ingredients Inc 972 717-0300
3105 Spring Grove Ave Cincinnati (45225) *(G-3576)*
Darling Ingredients Inc 216 351-3440
1002 Belt Line Ave Cleveland (44109) *(G-5065)*
Darling International, Cincinnati Also called Darling Ingredients Inc *(G-3576)*
Darling International Inc 216 651-9300
1002 Peltnine Ave Cleveland (44109) *(G-5066)*
Darrah Electric Company (PA) 216 631-0912
5914 Merrill Ave Cleveland (44102) *(G-5067)*
Darryl Smith 216 991-5468
3571 E 147th St Cleveland (44120) *(G-5068)*
Darting Around LLC 330 639-3990
3032 Martindale Rd Ne Canton (44714) *(G-2649)*
Darusta Woodlife Division, Tipp City Also called Dap Products Inc *(G-18110)*
Das Consulting Services Inc (PA) 330 896-4064
5178 Mayfair Rd Canton (44720) *(G-2650)*
Das Deutsch Cheese, Middlefield Also called Middlfeld Original Cheese Coop *(G-13828)*
Dasher Lawless Automation LLC 855 755-7275
310 Dana St Ne Warren (44483) *(G-19394)*
Daskal Enterprise LLC (PA) 614 848-5700
6522 Singletree Dr Columbus (43229) *(G-6850)*
Data Analysis Technologies 614 873-0710
7715 Corporate Blvd Plain City (43064) *(G-16186)*
Data Control Systems Inc 330 877-4497
13611 Kaufman Ave Nw Hartville (44632) *(G-10688)*
Data Cooling Technologies LLC 330 954-3800
3092 Euclid Heights Blvd Cleveland Heights (44118) *(G-6347)*
Data Genomix Inc 216 860-4770
1215 W 10th St Ste B Cleveland (44113) *(G-5069)*
Data Mold and Tool Inc 419 878-9861
160 Concord St Waterville (43566) *(G-19493)*
Data Power Solutions 614 471-1911
804 Hedley Pl Columbus (43230) *(G-6851)*
Dataq Instruments 330 668-1444
241 Springside Dr Akron (44333) *(G-133)*
Datatex Media Dolls 216 598-1000
7027 Columbia Rd Cleveland (44138) *(G-5070)*
Datatrak International Inc 440 443-0082
5900 Landerbrook Dr # 170 Mayfield Heights (44124) *(G-13162)*
Datco Mfg Company Inc 330 787-1127
4605 Lake Park Rd Youngstown (44512) *(G-20886)*
Datco Mfg Company Inc (PA) 330 781-6100
4605 Lake Park Rd Youngstown (44512) *(G-20887)*
Datono Products, Dayton Also called Dayton Stencil Works Company *(G-8145)*
Datwyler Sling Sltions USA Inc 937 387-2800
875 Center Dr Vandalia (45377) *(G-19122)*
Daubenmires Printing 513 425-7223
1527 Central Ave Middletown (45044) *(G-13899)*
Dave's Welding & Excavation, Gnadenhutten Also called David Cox *(G-10277)*
Davenport Service Group Inc 440 487-9353
7561 Tyler Blvd Ste 9 Mentor (44060) *(G-13429)*
Daves Pallets 740 525-4938
710 Thomas St Belpre (45714) *(G-1573)*
Davey Drill, Kent Also called Davey Kent Inc *(G-11310)*
Davey Kent Inc 330 673-5400
200 W Williams St Kent (44240) *(G-11310)*
David A and Mary A Mathis 330 837-8611
332 Erie St S Massillon (44646) *(G-12973)*
David A Waldron & Associates (PA) 330 264-7275
2285 Eagle Pass Ste A Wooster (44691) *(G-20583)*
David Adkins Logging 740 533-0297
1260 Township Road 256 Kitts Hill (45645) *(G-11474)*
David Bixel 440 474-4410
2683 State Route 534 Rock Creek (44084) *(G-16532)*
David Boswell 614 441-2497
1777 Franklin Park S Columbus (43205) *(G-6852)*
David Brandeberry 937 653-4680
703 Miami St Urbana (43078) *(G-18988)*
David Butler Tax Service 419 626-8086
415 Tiffin Ave Sandusky (44870) *(G-16803)*
David Cox 740 254-4858
9664 Gilmore Rd Se Gnadenhutten (44629) *(G-10277)*
David E Easterday and Co Inc 330 359-0700
1225 Us Route 62 Unit C Wilmot (44689) *(G-20515)*
David Esrati 937 228-4433
100 Bonner St Dayton (45410) *(G-8126)*
David Evans Foods, Cincinnati Also called Cincinnati Preserving Company *(G-3504)*
David J Fisher (PA) 440 636-2256
9794 State Route 534 Middlefield (44062) *(G-13793)*
David Ogilbee 740 929-2638
1881 Beaver Run Rd Se Hebron (43025) *(G-10741)*
David Price Metal Services Inc 419 668-3358
360 Eastpark Dr Norwalk (44857) *(G-15387)*
David R Hill Inc 740 685-5168
132 S 2nd St Byesville (43723) *(G-2381)*
David Round Company Inc 330 656-1600
10200 Wellman Rd Streetsboro (44241) *(G-17668)*
David Wolfe Design Inc 330 633-6124
829 Moe Dr Akron (44310) *(G-134)*
Davids Stone Company LLC 740 373-1996
514 4th St Marietta (45750) *(G-12618)*
Davidson Converting Inc 330 626-2118
1611 Frost Rd Streetsboro (44241) *(G-17669)*
Davidson Jewelers Inc 513 932-3936
726 E Main St Lebanon (45036) *(G-11647)*
Davidson Meat Processing Plant, Waynesville Also called Patrick M Davidson *(G-19571)*
Davies Interiors, Mansfield Also called Davies Since 1900 *(G-12432)*
Davies Since 1900 .... 419 756-4212
913 S Main St Mansfield (44907) *(G-12432)*
Davis Caulking & Sealant LLC 740 286-3825
199 Garfield Rd Wellston (45692) *(G-19599)*
Davis Design Group, Medina Also called Ddg Incorporated *(G-13250)*
Davis Fabricators Inc 419 898-5297
15765 W State Route 2 Oak Harbor (43449) *(G-15443)*
Davis Laser Products 614 252-7711
2700 E 6th Ave Columbus (43219) *(G-6853)*

Davis Machine Products Inc — 440 474-0247
74 Sapphire Ln Streetsboro (44241) *(G-17670)*

Davis Machining Service — 513 528-4917
602 Comet Dr Cincinnati (45244) *(G-3577)*

Davis Technologies Inc — 330 823-2544
837 W Main St Alliance (44601) *(G-464)*

Davis Welding Company, Celina Also called E L Davis Inc *(G-2958)*

Davro Ltd — 216 258-0057
1200 E 152nd St Cleveland (44110) *(G-5071)*

Dawn Enterprises Inc (PA) — 216 642-5506
9155 Sweet Valley Dr Cleveland (44125) *(G-5072)*

Day Industries Inc — 216 577-6674
690 Island Rd Grafton (44044) *(G-10297)*

Day Pre-Cast Products Co — 419 536-2909
801 N Westwood Ave Toledo (43607) *(G-18254)*

Day-Glo Color Corp (HQ) — 216 391-7070
4515 Saint Clair Ave Cleveland (44103) *(G-5073)*

Day-Glo Color Corp — 216 391-7070
4518 Hamilton Ave Cleveland (44114) *(G-5074)*

Day-Glo Color Corp — 216 391-7070
1570 Highland Rd Twinsburg (44087) *(G-18761)*

Day-Hio Products Inc — 937 445-0782
709 Webster St Dayton (45404) *(G-8127)*

Day-TEC Tool & Mfg Inc — 937 847-0022
4900 Lyons Rd Unit A Miamisburg (45342) *(G-13654)*

Daymark Security Systems, Bowling Green Also called CMC Daymark Corporation *(G-1963)*

Dayson Polymers LLC (PA) — 330 335-5237
9774 Trease Rd Wadsworth (44281) *(G-19233)*

Dayton Air Control Pdts LLC — 937 254-4441
2785 Lance Dr Moraine (45409) *(G-14343)*

Dayton Artificial Limb Clinic — 937 836-1464
700 Harco Dr Englewood (45315) *(G-9354)*

Dayton Bag & Burlap Co — 937 253-1722
448 Huffman Ave Dayton (45403) *(G-8128)*

Dayton Brick Company Inc — 937 293-4189
2300 Arbor Blvd Moraine (45439) *(G-14344)*

Dayton Business Journal, Dayton Also called American City Bus Journals Inc *(G-8024)*

Dayton City Paper New LLC — 937 222-8855
126 N Main St Ste 240 Dayton (45402) *(G-8129)*

Dayton Clutch & Joint Inc (PA) — 937 236-9770
2005 Troy St 1 Dayton (45404) *(G-8130)*

Dayton Coating Tech LLC — 937 278-2060
1926 E Siebenthaler Ave Dayton (45414) *(G-8131)*

Dayton Dailey News — 937 743-2387
5000 Commerce Center Dr Franklin (45005) *(G-9878)*

Dayton Daily News, Dayton Also called Cox Newspapers LLC *(G-8107)*

Dayton Forging Heat Treating — 937 253-4126
215 N Findlay St Dayton (45403) *(G-8132)*

Dayton Fruit Tree Label Co — 937 223-4650
1225 Ray St Dayton (45404) *(G-8133)*

Dayton Garden Labels, Dayton Also called Dayton Fruit Tree Label Co *(G-8133)*

Dayton Gear & Tool Co Inc — 937 866-4327
500 Fame Rd Dayton (45449) *(G-8134)*

Dayton Hawker Corporation — 937 293-8147
2844 Culver Ave Dayton (45429) *(G-8135)*

Dayton Heidelberg Distrg Co — 440 989-1027
5901 Baumhart Rd Lorain (44053) *(G-12088)*

Dayton Industrial Drum Inc — 937 253-8933
1880 Radio Rd Dayton (45431) *(G-7977)*

Dayton Lamina Corporation (HQ) — 937 859-5111
500 Progress Rd Dayton (45449) *(G-8136)*

Dayton Laser & Aesthetic Medic — 937 208-8282
6611 Clyo Rd Ste E Dayton (45459) *(G-8137)*

Dayton Mailing Services Inc — 937 222-5056
100 S Keowee St Dayton (45402) *(G-8138)*

Dayton Manufacturing Company, Dayton Also called Delma Corp *(G-8153)*

Dayton Molded Urethanes LLC — 937 279-9987
3337 N Dixie Dr Dayton (45414) *(G-8139)*

Dayton Pattern Inc — 937 277-0761
5591 Wadsworth Rd Dayton (45414) *(G-8140)*

Dayton Polymeric Products Inc — 937 279-9987
3337 N Dixie Dr Dayton (45414) *(G-8141)*

Dayton Precision Punch — 937 275-8700
4900 Webster St Dayton (45414) *(G-8142)*

Dayton Progress Corporation (HQ) — 937 859-5111
500 Progress Rd Dayton (45449) *(G-8143)*

Dayton Progress Intl Corp — 937 859-5111
500 Progress Rd Dayton (45449) *(G-8144)*

Dayton Richmond, Miamisburg Also called Dayton Superior Corporation *(G-13656)*

Dayton Stencil Works Company — 937 223-3233
113 E 2nd St Dayton (45402) *(G-8145)*

Dayton Superior Corporation (HQ) — 937 866-0711
1125 Byers Rd Miamisburg (45342) *(G-13655)*

Dayton Superior Corporation — 815 732-3136
1125 Byers Rd Miamisburg (45342) *(G-13656)*

Dayton Superior Corporation — 937 682-4015
270 Rush St Rushsylvania (43347) *(G-16595)*

Dayton Superior Pdts Co Inc — 937 332-1930
1370 Lytle Rd Troy (45373) *(G-18646)*

Dayton Systems Group Inc — 937 885-5665
3003 S Tech Blvd Miamisburg (45342) *(G-13657)*

Dayton Technologies — 513 539-5474
351 N Garver Rd Monroe (45050) *(G-14259)*

Dayton Tool Co Inc — 937 222-5501
1825 E 1st St Dayton (45403) *(G-8146)*

Dayton Tractor & Crane — 937 317-5014
1861 Us Route 42 S Xenia (45385) *(G-20765)*

Dayton Weekly News — 937 223-8060
118 Salem Ave Dayton (45406) *(G-8147)*

Dayton Wheel Concepts Inc — 937 438-0100
115 Compark Rd Dayton (45459) *(G-8148)*

Dayton Wire Products Inc — 937 236-8000
7 Dayton Wire Pkwy Dayton (45404) *(G-8149)*

Dayton Wire Wheel, Dayton Also called Dayton Wheel Concepts Inc *(G-8148)*

Dayton Wright Composite — 937 469-3962
3251 Mccall St Dayton (45417) *(G-8150)*

Dayton-Phoenix Group Inc (PA) — 937 496-3900
1619 Kuntz Rd Dayton (45404) *(G-8151)*

Daytronic Corporation (HQ) — 937 866-3300
2566 Kohnle Dr Miamisburg (45342) *(G-13658)*

Db Parent Inc — 513 475-3265
3630 E Kemper Rd Cincinnati (45241) *(G-3578)*

Db Rediheat Inc — 216 361-0530
4516 Saint Clair Ave Cleveland (44103) *(G-5075)*

Dbcr Inc — 330 920-1900
3400 Cavalier Trl Cuyahoga Falls (44224) *(G-7859)*

Dbd, Akron Also called 360 Communications LLC *(G-14)*

Dbhi Inc (HQ) — 216 267-7100
4700 W 160th St Cleveland (44135) *(G-5076)*

DC Reprographics Co — 614 297-1200
1254 Courtland Ave Columbus (43201) *(G-6854)*

Dc- Digital, Carlisle Also called Industrial Electronic Service *(G-2893)*

Dcc Corp (PA) — 330 494-0494
5757 Mayfair Rd Canton (44720) *(G-2651)*

Dcd Technologies Inc — 216 481-0056
17920 S Waterloo Rd Cleveland (44119) *(G-5077)*

Dcm Manufacturing Inc (HQ) — 216 265-8006
4540 W 160th St Cleveland (44135) *(G-5078)*

Dco LLC (HQ) — 419 931-9086
900 E Boundary St Ste 8a Perrysburg (43551) *(G-15938)*

DCS Technologies Corporation — 937 743-4060
6501 State Route 123 Franklin (45005) *(G-9879)*

DCW Acquisition Inc — 216 451-0666
10646 Leuer Ave Cleveland (44108) *(G-5079)*

Dd Foundry Inc (PA) — 216 362-4100
15583 Brookpark Rd Brookpark (44142) *(G-2143)*

Ddg Incorporated — 440 343-5060
3593 Medina Rd Medina (44256) *(G-13250)*

Ddi North Jackson Corp — 330 538-3900
12080 Debartolo Dr North Jackson (44451) *(G-15145)*

Ddnews — 440 331-6600
19035 Old Detroit Rd Rocky River (44116) *(G-16546)*

De Bra - Kuempel, Cincinnati Also called Debra-Kuempel Inc *(G-3579)*

De Milta Sand and Gravel Inc — 440 942-2015
921 Erie Rd Willoughby (44095) *(G-20307)*

De Nora Holdings Us Inc — 440 710-5300
7590 Discovery Ln Painesville (44077) *(G-15729)*

De Nora North America Inc — 440 357-4000
7590 Discovery Ln Painesville (44077) *(G-15730)*

De Nora Tech LLC (HQ) — 440 710-5300
7590 Discovery Ln Painesville (44077) *(G-15731)*

De Vore Engraving Co — 330 454-6820
1017 Tuscarawas St E Canton (44707) *(G-2652)*

De-Ko Inc — 440 951-2585
38334 Willoughby Pkwy Willoughby (44094) *(G-20308)*

De-Lux Mold & Machine Inc — 330 678-1030
6523 Pleasant Ave Kent (44240) *(G-11311)*

Deadbolt Software — 614 679-2093
43 Amazon Pl Columbus (43214) *(G-6855)*

Deaks Form Tools Inc — 440 286-2353
9954a Cutts Rd Chardon (44024) *(G-3108)*

Dealer Communications, Twinsburg Also called Horizon Communications Inc *(G-18792)*

Dean Foods Co — 419 473-9621
4117 Fitch Rd Toledo (43613) *(G-18255)*

Deangelo Instrument Inc — 330 654-9264
3200 Mcclintocksburg Rd Diamond (44412) *(G-8797)*

Dearborn Inc — 440 234-1353
678 Front St Berea (44017) *(G-1600)*

Dearth Resources Inc (PA) — 937 325-0651
2301 Sheridan Ave Springfield (45505) *(G-17384)*

Dearth Resources Inc — 937 663-4171
8801 State Route 36 Springfield (45501) *(G-17385)*

Deban Enterprises Inc — 937 426-4235
611 Congress Park Dr Dayton (45459) *(G-8152)*

Debandale Printing Inc — 330 725-5122
2785 Sharon Copley Rd Medina (44256) *(G-13251)*

Debolt Machine Inc — 740 454-8082
4208 West Pike Zanesville (43701) *(G-21127)*

Debra Harbour..937 440-9618
  251 S Mulberry St # 220 Troy (45373) *(G-18647)*
Debra-Kuempel Inc (HQ)..513 271-6500
  3976 Southern Ave Cincinnati (45227) *(G-3579)*
Debs Welding & Fabrication..330 376-2242
  950 Rhodes Ave Akron (44307) *(G-135)*
Deca Manufacturing, Lexington Also called SMH Manufacturing Inc *(G-11806)*
Deca Manufacturing, Mansfield Also called Malabar Properties LLC *(G-12473)*
Decal Impressions, Cincinnati Also called Magnetic Mktg Solutions LLC *(G-3973)*
Decaplus, Middletown Also called Natural Beauty Products Inc *(G-13935)*
Decaria Brothers Inc..330 385-0825
  104 E 5th St East Liverpool (43920) *(G-9055)*
Decent Hill Press, Hilliard Also called Decent Hill Publishers LLC *(G-10824)*
Decent Hill Publishers LLC..216 548-1255
  2825 Wynneleaf St Hilliard (43026) *(G-10824)*
Deceuninck North America LLC (PA).............................513 539-4444
  351 N Garver Rd Monroe (45050) *(G-14260)*
Decibel Research Inc..256 705-3341
  2661 Commons Blvd Ste 136 Beavercreek (45431) *(G-1310)*
Decision Systems Inc..330 456-7600
  2935 Woodcliff Dr Nw Canton (44718) *(G-2653)*
Decker Custom Wood Llc..419 332-3464
  505 W Mcgormley Rd Fremont (43420) *(G-10011)*
Decker Custom Wood Working, Fremont Also called Decker Custom Wood Llc *(G-10011)*
Decker Drilling Inc..740 749-3939
  11565 State Route 676 Vincent (45784) *(G-19213)*
Decko Products Inc..419 626-5757
  2105 Superior St Sandusky (44870) *(G-16804)*
Deco Plas Properties LLC..419 485-0632
  700 Randolph St Montpelier (43543) *(G-14306)*
Deco Tools Inc..419 476-9321
  1541 Coining Dr Toledo (43612) *(G-18256)*
Decoma Systems Integration Gro.................................419 324-3387
  1800 Nathan Dr Toledo (43611) *(G-18257)*
Decor Architectural Products..419 537-9493
  2375 Dorr St Ste E Toledo (43607) *(G-18258)*
Decorative Panels Intl Inc (HQ)......................................419 535-5921
  2900 Hill Ave Toledo (43607) *(G-18259)*
Decorative Veneer Inc (PA)..216 741-5511
  2121 Saint Clair Ave Ne Cleveland (44114) *(G-5080)*
Dedtru, Stow Also called Total Repair Express Mich LLC *(G-17635)*
Dee Lee Machine Inc...440 259-2245
  3921 Townline Rd Madison (44057) *(G-12347)*
Dee Printing Inc...614 777-8700
  4999 Transamerica Dr Columbus (43228) *(G-6856)*
Dee Sign Co (PA)...513 779-3333
  6163 Allen Rd West Chester (45069) *(G-19691)*
Dee Sign Usa LLC..513 779-3333
  6163 Allen Rd West Chester (45069) *(G-19692)*
Dee-Jays Custom Butchering..740 694-7492
  17460 Ankneytown Rd Fredericktown (43019) *(G-9965)*
Deemsys Inc (PA)..614 322-9928
  800 Cross Pointe Rd Afg Gahanna (43230) *(G-10079)*
Deep Springs Technology LLC.......................................419 536-5741
  4750 W Bancroft St Ste 1 Toledo (43615) *(G-18260)*
Deer Creek Custom Canvas LLC....................................740 495-9239
  23799 State Route 207 New Holland (43145) *(G-14701)*
Deer Creek Honey Farms Ltd...740 852-0899
  551 E High St London (43140) *(G-12057)*
Deer Valley Woodworking, Fresno Also called Andy Raber *(G-10066)*
Deerfield Digital, Cincinnati Also called Laurenee Ltd LLC *(G-3934)*
Deerfield Farms Service Inc..800 589-8606
  9041 U S Route 224 Deerfield (44411) *(G-8608)*
Deerfield Manufacturing Inc..513 398-2010
  320 N Mason Montgomery Rd Mason (45040) *(G-12855)*
Deerfield Medical Imaging LLC......................................513 271-5717
  9311 S Masn Montgomery Rd Mason (45040) *(G-12856)*
Deerfield Ventures Inc...614 875-0688
  2224 Stringtown Rd Grove City (43123) *(G-10425)*
Defense Co Inc..413 998-1637
  600 Superior Ave E Cleveland (44114) *(G-5081)*
Defense Surplus LLC..419 460-9906
  706 Waite Ave Maumee (43537) *(G-13106)*
Defiance Crescent News, The, Defiance Also called The Defiance Publishing Co *(G-8645)*
Defiance Metal Products Co (HQ)..................................419 784-5332
  21 Seneca St Defiance (43512) *(G-8619)*
Defiance Metal Products Co...419 784-5332
  6728 N State Route 66 Defiance (43512) *(G-8620)*
Defiance Metal Products WI Inc.....................................920 426-9207
  21 Seneca St Defiance (43512) *(G-8621)*
Defiance Operations, Defiance Also called Gt Technologies Inc *(G-8625)*
Defiance Stamping Co..419 782-5781
  800 Independence Dr Napoleon (43545) *(G-14537)*
Deflecto LLC..330 602-0840
  303 Oxford St Ste A Dover (44622) *(G-8815)*
Degaetano Sales..440 729-8877
  8408 Mayfield Rd Chesterland (44026) *(G-3156)*
Degussa Construction, Beachwood Also called Master Builders LLC *(G-1247)*

Degussa Incorporated..513 733-5111
  620 Shepherd Dr Cincinnati (45215) *(G-3580)*
Dei Fratelli, Northwood Also called Hirzel Canning Company *(G-15338)*
Deibel Manufacturing LLC...330 482-3351
  41659 Esterly Dr Leetonia (44431) *(G-11717)*
Deimling/Jeliho Plastics Inc..513 752-6653
  4010 Bach Buxton Rd Amelia (45102) *(G-536)*
Dejak Machine Tool Company, Euclid Also called Eaglehead Manufacturing Co *(G-9412)*
Dekay Fabricators Inc..330 793-0826
  295 S Meridian Rd Youngstown (44509) *(G-20888)*
Del Holdash..440 427-0611
  29891 Westminster Dr North Olmsted (44070) *(G-15185)*
Del-Ter Precision Machine Inc.......................................330 724-9167
  1038 Triplett Blvd Akron (44306) *(G-136)*
Dela-Glassware Ltd LLC..740 369-6737
  130 N Liberty St Delaware (43015) *(G-8669)*
Delafoil Pennsylvania Inc..610 327-9565
  1775 Progress Dr Perrysburg (43551) *(G-15939)*
Delano Foods, Canton Also called Hiland Group Incorporated *(G-2699)*
Delaware Company, Cleveland Also called Tremont Electric Incorporated *(G-6203)*
Delaware Gazette Company..740 363-1161
  40 N Sandusky St Ste 202 Delaware (43015) *(G-8670)*
Delco Corporation...330 896-4220
  3300 Massillon Rd Akron (44312) *(G-137)*
Delco LLC..330 896-4220
  3300 Massillon Rd Akron (44312) *(G-138)*
Deliciously Different Candies, Canal Fulton Also called Becky Knapp *(G-2476)*
Delille Oxygen Company (PA)...614 444-1177
  772 Marion Rd Columbus (43207) *(G-6857)*
Delille Oxygen Company..937 325-9595
  1101 W Columbia St Springfield (45504) *(G-17386)*
Delite Fruit Juices..614 470-4333
  185 N Yale Ave Columbus (43222) *(G-6858)*
Dell Fixtures Inc...614 449-1750
  321 Dering Ave Columbus (43207) *(G-6859)*
Dell Inc...513 644-1700
  9701 Windisch Rd West Chester (45069) *(G-19693)*
Delma Corp...937 253-2142
  3327 Elkton Ave Dayton (45403) *(G-8153)*
Delmar E Hicks (PA)...740 354-4333
  2310 A St Portsmouth (45662) *(G-16281)*
Delo Screw Products, Delaware Also called Supply Technologies LLC *(G-8727)*
Delo Screw Products, Delaware Also called RB&w Manufacturing LLC *(G-8718)*
Delohio Tech..740 816-5628
  2061 State Route 521 Delaware (43015) *(G-8671)*
Delores E OBeirn..440 582-3610
  13022 Kingston Way Cleveland (44133) *(G-5082)*
Delphi, Warren Also called Aptiv Services Us LLC *(G-19372)*
Delphi, Warren Also called Aptiv Services Us LLC *(G-19373)*
Delphi, Vienna Also called Aptiv Services Us LLC *(G-19196)*
Delphi, Vandalia Also called Mahle Behr USA Inc *(G-19135)*
Delphi-T - Vandalia Ptc, Dayton Also called Mahle Industries Incorporated *(G-8328)*
Delphia Consulting LLC...614 421-2000
  250 E Broad St Ste 1150 Columbus (43215) *(G-6860)*
Delphos Herald Inc (PA)..419 695-0015
  405 N Main St Delphos (45833) *(G-8738)*
Delphos Herald Inc...419 399-4015
  113 S Williams St Paulding (45879) *(G-15859)*
Delphos Herald Inc...419 695-0015
  405 N Main St Delphos (45833) *(G-8739)*
Delphos Plant 2, Delphos Also called Toledo Molding & Die Inc *(G-8757)*
Delphos Tent and Awning Inc..419 692-5776
  1454 N Main St Delphos (45833) *(G-8740)*
Delta Control Inc (PA)...937 277-3444
  2532 Nordic Rd Dayton (45414) *(G-8154)*
Delta Crane Systems Inc..937 324-7425
  624 Aberfelda Dr Springfield (45504) *(G-17387)*
Delta H Technologies LLC..740 756-7676
  62 High St Carroll (43112) *(G-2903)*
Delta H Technologies LLC..614 561-8860
  8847 Easton Dr Pickerington (43147) *(G-16045)*
Delta Machine & Tool Co..216 524-2477
  7575 Wall St Cleveland (44125) *(G-5083)*
Delta Manufacturing Inc...330 386-1270
  49207 Clctta Smthferry Rd East Liverpool (43920) *(G-9056)*
Delta Media Group Inc..330 493-0350
  4726 Hills And Dales Rd N Canton (44708) *(G-2654)*
Delta Plating Inc..330 452-2300
  2125 Harrison Ave Sw Canton (44706) *(G-2655)*
Delta Systems Inc..330 626-2811
  1734 Frost Rd Streetsboro (44241) *(G-17671)*
Delta Tool & Die Stl Block Inc..419 822-5939
  5226 County Road 6 Delta (43515) *(G-8767)*
Delta Transformer Inc...513 242-9400
  406 Blade Ave Cincinnati (45216) *(G-3581)*
Deltacraft, Cleveland Also called Millcraft Group LLC *(G-5689)*
Deltec Incorporated..513 732-0800
  4230 Grissom Dr Batavia (45103) *(G-1136)*

Deltech Polymers Corporation 937 339-3150
1250 S Union St Troy (45373) *(G-18648)*

Deluca Vineyards 440 685-4242
8954 State Route 45 North Bloomfield (44450) *(G-15064)*

Deluxe Corporation 330 342-1500
10030 Phillipp Pkwy Hudson (44236) *(G-11041)*

Dem Manufacturing LLC 440 564-7160
10357 Kinsman Rd Newbury (44065) *(G-14951)*

Dem Technology LLC 937 223-1317
755 Albany St Dayton (45417) *(G-8155)*

Demag Cranes & Components Corp (HQ) 440 248-2400
6675 Parkland Blvd # 200 Solon (44139) *(G-17132)*

Demel Enterprises Inc 740 331-1400
10980 Northpoint Dr Athens (45701) *(G-827)*

Dendratec Ltd 330 473-4878
1417 Zuercher Rd Dalton (44618) *(G-7940)*

Deneb (PA) 937 223-4849
270 Regency Ridge Dr # 200 Dayton (45459) *(G-8156)*

Deneb Software, Dayton Also called Deneb *(G-8156)*

Dengensha America Corporation 440 439-8081
7647 First Pl Bedford (44146) *(G-1399)*

Denizen Inc 937 615-9561
130 Fox Dr Piqua (45356) *(G-16111)*

Denmac Metalworks, Marion Also called Central Machinery Company LLC *(G-12699)*

Denney Plastics Machining LLC 330 308-5300
149 Stonecreek Rd Nw New Philadelphia (44663) *(G-14766)*

Dennis Corso Co Inc 330 673-2411
266 Martinel Dr Bldg A Kent (44240) *(G-11312)*

Dennis Lavender 740 344-3336
200 Maholm St Newark (43055) *(G-14867)*

Denoon Lumber Company LLC 740 768-2220
571 County Highway 52 Bergholz (43908) *(G-1634)*

Denso Automotive Ohio 614 336-1261
260 Cramer Creek Ct Dublin (43017) *(G-8906)*

Dental Ceramics Inc 330 523-5240
3404 Brecksville Rd Richfield (44286) *(G-16467)*

Dental Pure Water Inc 440 234-0890
336 Daisy Ave Ste 102b Berea (44017) *(G-1601)*

Dental Sealants 440 582-3466
7029 Royalton Rd North Royalton (44133) *(G-15269)*

Denton & Anderson Mktg Div, Hubbard Also called Taylor - Winfield Corporation *(G-11010)*

Denton Atd Inc (PA) 567 265-5200
900 Denton Dr Huron (44839) *(G-11093)*

Dentronix Inc 330 916-7300
235 Ascot Pkwy Cuyahoga Falls (44223) *(G-7860)*

Dentsply Sirona Inc 419 893-5672
520 Illinois Ave Maumee (43537) *(G-13107)*

Dentsply Sirona Inc 419 865-9497
3535 Briarfield Blvd Maumee (43537) *(G-13108)*

Denver Adkins 740 682-3123
642 Phillip Kuhn Rd Oak Hill (45656) *(G-15450)*

Deodora Vineyards & Winery LLC 513 238-1167
1071 Celestial St # 2402 Cincinnati (45202) *(G-3582)*

Dependable Gear Corp 440 942-4969
1422 E 363rd St Eastlake (44095) *(G-9103)*

Dependable Stamping Company 216 486-5522
1160 E 222nd St Cleveland (44117) *(G-5084)*

Derby Fabg Solutions LLC 937 498-4054
570 Lester Ave Sidney (45365) *(G-17027)*

Dermamed Coatin 330 474-3786
271 Progress Blvd Kent (44240) *(G-11313)*

Dern Trophies Corp 614 895-3260
6225 Frost Rd Westerville (43082) *(G-19987)*

Dern Trophy Mfg, Westerville Also called Dern Trophies Corp *(G-19987)*

Derrick Company Inc 513 321-8122
4560 Kellogg Ave Cincinnati (45226) *(G-3583)*

Derrick Petroleum Inc 740 668-5711
Market St Bladensburg (43005) *(G-1696)*

Deruijter Intl USA Inc 419 678-3909
120 Harvest Dr Coldwater (45828) *(G-6405)*

Des Eck Welding 330 698-7271
10777 E Moreland Rd Apple Creek (44606) *(G-603)*

Des Machine Services Inc 330 633-6897
351 Tacoma Ave Tallmadge (44278) *(G-17978)*

Des Tech, Troy Also called Design Technologies & Mfg Co *(G-18649)*

Desco Corporation (PA) 614 888-8855
7795 Walton Pkwy Ste 175 New Albany (43054) *(G-14622)*

Desco Equipment Corp 330 405-1581
1903 Case Pkwy Twinsburg (44087) *(G-18762)*

Deshea Printing Company 330 336-7601
924 Seville Rd Wadsworth (44281) *(G-19234)*

Deshler Flag, Liberty Center Also called Mickens Inc *(G-11809)*

Deshler Metal Working Co Inc 419 278-0472
140 S East Ave Deshler (43516) *(G-8788)*

Design & Fabrication Inc 419 294-2414
400 Malabar Dr Upper Sandusky (43351) *(G-18951)*

Design & Software Intl (PA) 513 939-1800
526 Nilles Rd Ste 2 Fairfield (45014) *(G-9493)*

Design Avenue Inc 330 487-5280
1710 Enterprise Pkwy Twinsburg (44087) *(G-18763)*

Design Concrete Surfaces, Kent Also called Don Wartko Construction Co *(G-11315)*

Design Fabricators of Mantua 330 274-5353
10612 Main St Mantua (44255) *(G-12545)*

Design Farm, Millersburg Also called Simple Products LLC *(G-14129)*

Design Flux Technologies LLC 216 543-6066
526 S Main St Ste 108 Akron (44311) *(G-139)*

Design Magnetics Ltd 234 380-5500
7941 Valley View Rd Hudson (44236) *(G-11042)*

Design Masters Inc 513 772-7175
800 Redna Ter Cincinnati (45215) *(G-3584)*

Design Molded Plastics Inc 330 963-4400
8220 Bavaria Rd Macedonia (44056) *(G-12288)*

Design Original Inc 937 596-5121
402 Jackson St Jackson Center (45334) *(G-11207)*

Design Pattern Works Inc 937 252-0797
2312 E 3rd St Dayton (45403) *(G-8157)*

Design Sign Inc 216 398-9900
6380 Nelwood Rd Cleveland (44130) *(G-5085)*

Design Tech Inc 937 254-7000
1531 Keystone Ave Dayton (45403) *(G-8158)*

Design Technologies & Mfg Co 937 335-0757
2000 Corporate Dr Troy (45373) *(G-18649)*

Design Trac Inc 330 759-3131
4136 Logan Way Youngstown (44505) *(G-20889)*

Design Wheel and Hub, Akron Also called Schott Metal Products Company *(G-373)*

Design-N-Wood LLC 937 419-0479
3700 Michigan St Sidney (45365) *(G-17028)*

Designed Harness Systems Inc 937 599-2485
227 Water Ave Bellefontaine (43311) *(G-1512)*

Designer Awards Inc 937 339-4444
101 S Market St Troy (45373) *(G-18650)*

Designer Cntemporary Laminates 440 946-8207
37105 Code Ave Willoughby (44094) *(G-20309)*

Designer Doors Inc 330 772-6391
4810 State Route 7 Burghill (44404) *(G-2354)*

Designer Stone Co 740 492-1300
303 E Main St Port Washington (43837) *(G-16268)*

Designetics Inc (PA) 419 866-0700
1624 Eber Rd Holland (43528) *(G-10925)*

Desinger Window Treatment Inc 419 822-4967
302 Superior St Delta (43515) *(G-8768)*

Desmond Engraving Co Inc 216 265-8338
13410 Enterprise Ave D Cleveland (44135) *(G-5086)*

Desmond-Stephan Mfgcompany 937 653-7181
121 W Water St Urbana (43078) *(G-18989)*

Desserts By Sandy LLC 513 385-8755
8071 Redhaven Ct Cincinnati (45247) *(G-3585)*

Dester Corporation 419 362-8020
1200 E Kibby St Bldg 32 Lima (45804) *(G-11854)*

Dester Corporation 419 362-8020
1200 E Kibby St Bldg 6 Lima (45804) *(G-11855)*

Destin Die Casting LLC 937 347-1111
851 Bellbrook Ave Xenia (45385) *(G-20766)*

Destin Die Casting, LLC, Xenia Also called American Metal Tech LLC *(G-20756)*

Destination Donuts LLC 614 370-0754
59 Spruce St Columbus (43215) *(G-6861)*

Destiny Manufacturing Inc 330 273-9000
2974 Interstate Pkwy Brunswick (44212) *(G-2199)*

Detailed Machining Inc 937 492-1264
2490 Ross St Sidney (45365) *(G-17029)*

Detrex Corporation (HQ) 216 749-2605
1000 Belt Line Ave Cleveland (44109) *(G-5087)*

Detrick Design Fabrication LLC 937 620-6736
425 Wisteria Dr Troy (45373) *(G-18651)*

Detroit Desl Rmnfacturing Corp 740 439-7701
8475 Reitler Rd Cambridge (43725) *(G-2434)*

Detroit Desl Rmnfctrng-Ast Inc 740 439-7701
60703 Country Club Rd Byesville (43723) *(G-2382)*

Detroit Diesl Specialty TI Inc 740 435-4452
60703 Country Club Rd Byesville (43723) *(G-2383)*

Detroit Flame Hardening Co 216 531-4273
24951 Tungsten Rd Euclid (44117) *(G-9410)*

Detroit Flame Hardening Co 513 942-1400
375 Security Dr Fairfield (45014) *(G-9494)*

Detroit Technologies Inc 937 492-2708
1630 Ferguson Ct Sidney (45365) *(G-17030)*

Detroit Toledo Fiber LLC 248 647-0400
1245 E Manhattan Blvd Toledo (43608) *(G-18261)*

Deuce Machining LLC 513 875-2291
3088 Us Highway 50 Fayetteville (45118) *(G-9638)*

Deuer Developments Inc 937 299-1213
3434 Encrete Ln Moraine (45439) *(G-14345)*

Deuer Manufacturing Inc 937 254-3812
1100 S Smithville Rd Dayton (45403) *(G-8159)*

Deufol Worldwide Packaging LLC 440 232-1100
19800 Alexander Rd Bedford (44146) *(G-1400)*

Devault Industries LLC 330 456-6070
3500 12th St Nw Canton (44708) *(G-2656)*

Devault Machine & Mould Co LLC 740 654-5925
2294 Commerce St Lancaster (43130) *(G-11563)*

Devicor Med Pdts Holdings Inc 513 864-9000
300 E Business Way Fl 5 Cincinnati (45241) *(G-3586)*

Devicor Medical Products Inc (HQ) 513 864-9000
300 E Business Way Fl 5 Cincinnati (45241) *(G-3587)*

Devilbiss Ransburg 419 470-2000
320 Phillips Ave Toledo (43612) *(G-18262)*

Devries & Associates Inc 614 890-3821
654 Brooksedge Blvd Ste A Westerville (43081) *(G-20047)*

Devries & Associates Inc (PA) 614 860-0103
5117 E Main St Westerville (43081) *(G-20048)*

Deward Publishing Co Ltd 800 300-9778
278 Scott Rd Chillicothe (45601) *(G-3184)*

Dewey Smith Quarter Horses 682 597-2424
2679 Township Road 55 Bellefontaine (43311) *(G-1513)*

Dewitt Group Inc 614 847-5919
777 Dearborn Park Ln E Columbus (43085) *(G-6862)*

Dewitt Inc 216 662-0800
14450 Industrial Ave N Maple Heights (44137) *(G-12570)*

Dexol Industries Inc 330 633-4477
844 E Tallmadge Ave Akron (44310) *(G-140)*

Dexport Tool Manufacturing Co 513 625-1600
855 Carpenter Rd Loveland (45140) *(G-12185)*

Dexter Hardwoods Inc 740 783-4141
145 Jefferson St Dexter City (45727) *(G-8794)*

Dg Custom Machine 419 636-8059
840 E Edgerton St Bryan (43506) *(G-2279)*

Dhpp, Dover *Also called Dover High Prfmce Plas Inc (G-8821)*

Dhs Innovations, Bellefontaine *Also called Designed Harness Systems Inc (G-1512)*

Di Lorio Sheet Metal Inc 216 961-3703
5002 Clark Ave Cleveland (44102) *(G-5088)*

Di Walt Optical Inc 330 453-8427
1112 12th St Ne Canton (44705) *(G-2657)*

DIA Enterprises Inc 740 802-7075
731 Decliff Rd N New Bloomington (43341) *(G-14644)*

Diagnostic Hybrids Inc 740 593-1784
2005 E State St Ste 100 Athens (45701) *(G-828)*

Dialogue House Associates Inc 216 342-5170
23400 Mercantile Rd Ste 2 Beachwood (44122) *(G-1232)*

Diamant Coating Systems Ltd 513 515-3078
3495 Mustafa Dr Sharonville (45241) *(G-16956)*

Diamond Aluminum Co, Middletown *Also called John H Hosking Inc (G-13918)*

Diamond America Corporation 330 535-3330
520 S Main St Ste 2456 Akron (44311) *(G-141)*

Diamond Cellar, The, Dublin *Also called Robert W Johnson Inc (G-8975)*

Diamond Electronics, Lancaster *Also called Diamond Power Intl Inc (G-11565)*

Diamond Electronics Inc 740 652-9222
1858 Cedar Hill Rd Lancaster (43130) *(G-11564)*

Diamond Hard Chrome Co Inc 216 391-3618
6110 Grand Ave Cleveland (44104) *(G-5089)*

Diamond Heavy Haul, Shandon *Also called Diamond Trailers Inc (G-16941)*

Diamond Innovations Inc (PA) 614 438-2000
6325 Huntley Rd Columbus (43229) *(G-6863)*

Diamond Machine and Mfg, Bluffton *Also called Carpe Diem Industries LLC (G-1887)*

Diamond Mfg Bluffton Ltd 419 358-0129
505 E Jefferson St Bluffton (45817) *(G-1888)*

Diamond Mold & Die Co 330 633-5682
109 E Garwood Dr Tallmadge (44278) *(G-17979)*

Diamond Oilfield Tech LLC 234 806-4185
4494 Warren Sharon Rd Vienna (44473) *(G-19198)*

Diamond Pallets LLC 419 281-2908
1505 Center Lane Dr Ashland (44805) *(G-701)*

Diamond Plastics Inc 419 759-3838
211 W Geneva St Dunkirk (45836) *(G-9034)*

Diamond Power Intl Inc 740 687-4001
2530 E Main St Lancaster (43130) *(G-11565)*

Diamond Power Intl Inc (HQ) 740 687-6500
2600 E Main St Lancaster (43130) *(G-11566)*

Diamond Power Specialty, Lancaster *Also called Diamond Power Intl Inc (G-11566)*

Diamond Products Limited 440 323-4616
1111 Taylor St Elyria (44035) *(G-9241)*

Diamond Reserve Inc 440 892-7877
801 Sharon Dr Westlake (44145) *(G-20108)*

Diamond Roll-Up Door Inc 419 294-3373
295 Commerce Way Upper Sandusky (43351) *(G-18952)*

Diamond Sparkler Mfg Co (PA) 330 746-1064
555 Martin Luther King Jr Youngstown (44502) *(G-20890)*

Diamond Trailers Inc 513 738-4500
5045 Cncnnt Brookville Rd Shandon (45063) *(G-16941)*

Diamond Welding Co Inc 216 251-1679
11030 Briggs Rd Cleveland (44111) *(G-5090)*

Diamond Wipes Intl Inc 419 562-3575
1375 Isaac Beal Rd Bucyrus (44820) *(G-2325)*

Diamondback Filters 419 494-1156
11602 Sugar Ridge Rd Bowling Green (43402) *(G-1968)*

Diamonds Products LLC 440 323-4616
1250 E Broad St Elyria (44035) *(G-9242)*

Diamonite Plant, Shreve *Also called I Cerco Inc (G-17003)*

Diano Construction and Sup Co 330 456-7229
1000 Warner Rd Se Canton (44707) *(G-2658)*

Diano Supply Co, Canton *Also called Diano Construction and Sup Co (G-2658)*

Diascopic LLC 312 282-1800
16173 Cleviden Rd Cleveland (44112) *(G-5091)*

Diasome Pharmaceuticals Inc 216 444-7110
10000 Cedar Ave Ste 6 Cleveland (44106) *(G-5092)*

Dickens Foundry, Arcadia *Also called Maass Midwest Mfg Inc (G-625)*

Dickman Directories Inc 740 548-6130
6145 Columbus Pike Lewis Center (43035) *(G-11755)*

Dicks Counter D M 440 322-3312
275 Warden Ave Elyria (44035) *(G-9243)*

Didion's Mechanical, Bellevue *Also called Donald E Didion II (G-1535)*

Didonato Products Inc 330 535-1119
1145 Highbrook St Ste 507 Akron (44301) *(G-142)*

Die Cast Division 330 769-2013
271 W Greenwich Rd Seville (44273) *(G-16915)*

Die Co Inc 440 942-8856
1889 E 337th St Eastlake (44095) *(G-9104)*

Die Craft Division, Cincinnati *Also called Markley Enterprises LLC (G-3982)*

Die Craft Machining & Engineer 513 771-1290
1705 Magnolia Dr Cincinnati (45215) *(G-3588)*

Die Guys Inc 330 239-3437
5238 Portside Dr Medina (44256) *(G-13252)*

Die Services Ltd 216 883-5800
9200 Inman Ave Cleveland (44105) *(G-5093)*

Die-Cut Products Co 216 771-6994
1801 E 30th St Cleveland (44114) *(G-5094)*

Die-Matic Corporation 216 749-4656
201 Eastview Dr Brooklyn Heights (44131) *(G-2119)*

Die-Mension Corporation 330 273-5872
3020 Nationwide Pkwy Brunswick (44212) *(G-2200)*

Die-Namic Tool & Die Inc 330 296-6923
100 Romito St Ste D Ravenna (44266) *(G-16375)*

Die-Tech Machine Inc 740 264-2426
1650 County Road 22a Bloomingdale (43910) *(G-1710)*

Diebold Nixdorf Incorporated (PA) 330 490-4000
5995 Mayfair Rd North Canton (44720) *(G-15078)*

Diebold Nixdorf Incorporated 330 490-4000
5995 Mayfair Rd North Canton (44720) *(G-15079)*

Diebold Nixdorf Incorporated 330 490-4000
5571 Global Gtwy Canton (44720) *(G-2659)*

Diemaster Tool & Mold Inc 330 467-4281
895 Highland Rd E 5 Macedonia (44056) *(G-12289)*

Diesel Fltrtion Spcialists LLC 740 698-0255
5475 Ste Rte 681 New Marshfield (45766) *(G-14743)*

Diesel Recon Service Inc 513 625-1887
2641 State Route 28 Pleasant Plain (45162) *(G-16225)*

Dietrich Industries Inc 330 372-4014
1300 Phoenix Rd Ne Warren (44483) *(G-19395)*

Dietrich Industries Inc 614 438-3210
200 W Old Wlson Bridge Rd Worthington (43085) *(G-20683)*

Dietrich Industries Inc 330 372-2868
1985 N River Rd Ne Warren (44483) *(G-19396)*

Dietrich Industries Inc 216 472-1511
818 E 73rd St Cleveland (44103) *(G-5095)*

Dietrich Industries Inc 614 438-3210
200 W Old Wlson Bridge Rd Worthington (43085) *(G-20684)*

Dietrich Metal Framing, Warren *Also called Dietrich Industries Inc (G-19395)*

Dietrich Von Hildebrand Legacy 703 496-7821
1235 University Blvd Steubenville (43952) *(G-17530)*

Dietsch Brothers Incorporated (PA) 419 422-4474
400 W Main Cross St Findlay (45840) *(G-9677)*

Digicom Inc 216 642-3838
5405 Valley Belt Rd Ste A Brooklyn Heights (44131) *(G-2120)*

Digilube Systems Inc 937 748-2209
216 E Mill St Springboro (45066) *(G-17325)*

Digimatics Inc 419 478-0804
4011 Vermaas Ave Toledo (43612) *(G-18263)*

Digimax Signs 513 576-0747
759 Us Route 50 Milford (45150) *(G-14007)*

Digionyx LLC 614 594-9897
8420 Opossum Run Rd London (43140) *(G-12058)*

Digisoft Systems Corporation 937 833-5016
4520 Clayton Rd Brookville (45309) *(G-2167)*

Digital & Analog Design, Dublin *Also called Pro Oncall Technologies LLC (G-8967)*

Digital Automation Associates 419 352-6977
310 W Gypsy Lane Rd Bowling Green (43402) *(G-1969)*

Digital Color Intl LLC 330 762-6959
1653 Merriman Rd Ste 211 Akron (44313) *(G-143)*

Digital Controls Corporation (PA) 513 746-8118
444 Alexandersville Rd Miamisburg (45342) *(G-13659)*

Digital Graphics, Cleveland *Also called Alfacomp Inc (G-4659)*

Digital Graphics 330 707-1720
4589 Dobbins Rd Youngstown (44514) *(G-20891)*

Digital Media Integration LLC 937 305-5582
9090 State Route 48 B Dayton (45458) *(G-8160)*

Digital Shorts Inc 937 228-1700
136 N Saint Clair St # 100 Dayton (45402) *(G-8161)*

Digital Solutions, Bellaire *Also called Paul/Jay Associates (G-1488)*

Digital Technologies, Rossford *Also called Sasha Electronics Inc (G-16593)*

Digital Visuals Inc   ALPHABETIC SECTION

Digital Visuals Inc 513 420-9466
   15 N Clinton St Middletown (45042) *(G-13900)*
Digitek Corp 513 794-3190
   5665 Creek Rd Blue Ash (45242) *(G-1758)*
Dik Jaxon Products Co 937 890-7350
   6195 Webster St Dayton (45414) *(G-8162)*
Dilco Industries Inc 330 337-6732
   300 Benton Rd Salem (44460) *(G-16734)*
Dillen Products, Middlefield Also called Myers Industries Inc *(G-13836)*
Diller Metals Inc 419 943-3364
   507 S Eastom St Leipsic (45856) *(G-11725)*
Dillin Engineered Systems Corp 419 666-6789
   8030 Broadstone Rd Perrysburg (43551) *(G-15940)*
Dillon Manufacturing Inc 937 325-8482
   2115 Progress Rd Springfield (45505) *(G-17388)*
Dilworth Machine 330 427-1706
   51552 Chain School Rd East Palestine (44413) *(G-9073)*
Dimco-Gray Company, Centerville Also called Dimcogray Corporation *(G-3001)*
Dimcogray Corporation (PA) 937 433-7600
   900 Dimco Way Centerville (45458) *(G-3001)*
Dimension Hardwood Veneers Inc 419 272-2245
   509 Woodville St Edon (43518) *(G-9184)*
Dimension Industries Inc 440 236-3265
   27335 Royalton Rd Columbia Station (44028) *(G-6435)*
Dimension Machine Company Inc 513 242-9996
   6614 Lebanon St Cincinnati (45216) *(G-3589)*
Dimensional Equipment Div, Elida Also called Patton Industries Inc *(G-9198)*
Dimensional Metals Inc (PA) 740 927-3633
   58 Klema Dr N Reynoldsburg (43068) *(G-16435)*
Dimensional Works of Art 330 657-2681
   2355 Main St Peninsula (44264) *(G-15891)*
Dimensions Three Inc 614 539-5180
   6157 Enterprise Pkwy Grove City (43123) *(G-10426)*
Dimex LLC 740 374-3100
   28305 State Route 7 Marietta (45750) *(G-12619)*
Dinesol Plastics Inc 330 544-7171
   195 E Park Ave Niles (44446) *(G-15005)*
DIng Products 440 442-7777
   5695 Cherokee Dr Cleveland (44124) *(G-5096)*
Dinkmar Inc 419 468-8516
   9357 Township Road 48 Galion (44833) *(G-10132)*
Dinol US Inc 740 548-1656
   8520 Cotter St Lewis Center (43035) *(G-11756)*
Dinos Drive Thru LLC 330 263-1111
   1541 Jones Ave Wooster (44691) *(G-20584)*
Dinsmore Inc 937 544-3332
   11780 State Route 41 West Union (45693) *(G-19961)*
Diocesan Publications Inc Ohio (PA) 614 718-9500
   6161 Wilcox Rd Dublin (43016) *(G-8907)*
Diptech Systems Inc (PA) 330 673-4400
   4485 Crystal Pkwy Ste 100 Kent (44240) *(G-11314)*
Diramed LLC 614 487-3660
   5000 Arlington Centre 2 Columbus (43220) *(G-6864)*
Dircksen and Associates Inc 614 238-0413
   743 S Front St Columbus (43206) *(G-6865)*
Direct Action Co Inc 330 364-3219
   6668 Old Route 39 Nw Dover (44622) *(G-8816)*
Direct Digital Graphics Inc 330 405-3770
   1716 Enterprise Pkwy Twinsburg (44087) *(G-18764)*
Direct Disposables LLC 440 717-3335
   10605 Snowville Rd Brecksville (44141) *(G-2029)*
Direct Image Signs Inc 440 327-5575
   7820 Maddock Rd North Ridgeville (44039) *(G-15220)*
Direct Wire Service LLP 937 526-4447
   100 Subler Dr Versailles (45380) *(G-19178)*
Directconnectgroup Ltd 216 281-2866
   5501 Cass Ave Cleveland (44102) *(G-5097)*
Directional One Svcs Inc USA 740 371-5031
   2163a-1 Gwb Complex Marietta (45750) *(G-12620)*
Dirt Works Excavating, Wellston Also called Wilkett Enterprises LLC *(G-19611)*
Dirussos Sausage Inc 330 744-1208
   1035 W Rayen Ave Youngstown (44502) *(G-20892)*
DIRVA LITHUANIAN NEWSPAPER, Cleveland Also called American Lithuanian Press *(G-4691)*
Disalvo Deli & Italian Store, Dayton Also called Disalvos Deli & Italian Store *(G-8163)*
Disalvos Deli & Italian Store 937 298-5053
   1383 E Stroop Rd Dayton (45429) *(G-8163)*
Disante Socks 614 481-3243
   1540 Westwood Ave Columbus (43212) *(G-6866)*
Dischem International Inc 330 494-5210
   4252 Strausser St Nw Canton (44720) *(G-2660)*
Disciple Tool & Machine 330 503-7879
   189 Se River Rd Lake Milton (44429) *(G-11498)*
Discount Drainage Supplies LLC 513 563-8616
   200 Cavett Ave Cincinnati (45215) *(G-3590)*
Discount Dring Sups Cincinnati, Cincinnati Also called Discount Drainage Supplies LLC *(G-3590)*
Discover Publications 614 785-1111
   6425 Busch Blvd Columbus (43229) *(G-6867)*

Discus Sofware, Columbus Also called Characteristic Solutions LLC *(G-6757)*
Diskin Enterprises LLC 330 527-4308
   10421 Industrial Dr Garrettsville (44231) *(G-10187)*
Dismat Corporation 419 531-8963
   336 N Westwood Ave Toledo (43607) *(G-18264)*
DISPATCH PRINTING, Columbus Also called Wolfe Associates Inc *(G-7610)*
Dispatch Printing Company 740 548-5331
   7801 N Central Dr Lewis Center (43035) *(G-11757)*
Dispatch Printing Company 614 885-6020
   5253 Sinclair Rd Columbus (43229) *(G-6868)*
Display Dynamics Inc 937 832-2830
   1 Display Point Dr Englewood (45315) *(G-9355)*
Distillata Company (PA) 216 771-2900
   1608 E 24th St Cleveland (44114) *(G-5098)*
Distinct Advantage Cabinetry, Toledo Also called Online Mega Sellers Corp *(G-18439)*
Distinct Cbntry Innvations LLC 937 661-1051
   31 S Church St New Lebanon (45345) *(G-14708)*
Distinctive Building Elem 419 420-5528
   15476 E State Route 12 Findlay (45840) *(G-9678)*
Distinctive Marble & Gran Inc 614 760-0003
   7635 Commerce Pl Plain City (43064) *(G-16187)*
Distinctive Surfaces LLC 614 431-0898
   5158 Sinclair Rd Columbus (43229) *(G-6869)*
Distribution Center, West Chester Also called Martin-Brower Company LLC *(G-19741)*
Distributor Graphics Inc 440 260-0024
   6909 Engle Rd Ste 13 Cleveland (44130) *(G-5099)*
District Brewing Co Inc 614 224-3626
   2555 Harrison Rd Columbus (43204) *(G-6870)*
Ditsch Usa LLC 513 782-8888
   311 Northland Blvd Cincinnati (45246) *(G-3591)*
Dittmar Sales and Service 740 653-7933
   132 W 6th Ave Lancaster (43130) *(G-11567)*
Ditz Designs, Norwalk Also called Hen House Inc *(G-15398)*
Divelbiss Corporation 800 245-2327
   9778 Mount Gilead Rd Fredericktown (43019) *(G-9966)*
Diverse Mfg Solutions LLC 740 363-3600
   970 Pittsburgh Dr Ste 22 Delaware (43015) *(G-8672)*
Diversey Inc 513 326-8300
   200 Crowne Point Pl Cincinnati (45241) *(G-3592)*
Diverseylever Inc 513 554-4200
   3630 E Kemper Rd Cincinnati (45241) *(G-3593)*
Diversfied Mch Pdts Gnsvlle GA, Columbus Also called Prime Equipment Group Inc *(G-7347)*
Diversifd OH Vlly Eqpt & Srvcs 740 458-9881
   50817 State Route 556 Clarington (43915) *(G-4567)*
Diversified Air Systems Inc (PA) 216 741-1700
   4760 Van Epps Rd Brooklyn Heights (44131) *(G-2121)*
Diversified Brands 216 595-8777
   26300 Fargo Ave Bedford (44146) *(G-1401)*
Diversified Honing Inc 330 874-4663
   11064 Industrial Pkwy Nw Bolivar (44612) *(G-1912)*
Diversified Mch Components LLC 440 942-5701
   34099 Melinz Pkwy Unit D Eastlake (44095) *(G-9105)*
Diversified Mold & Castings Co, Cleveland Also called Diversified Mold Castings LLC *(G-5100)*
Diversified Mold and Castings, Cleveland Also called Plaster Process Castings Co *(G-5885)*
Diversified Mold Castings LLC 216 663-1814
   19800 Miles Rd Cleveland (44128) *(G-5100)*
Diversified Ophthalmics Inc 803 783-3454
   250 Mccullough St Cincinnati (45226) *(G-3594)*
Diversified Ophthalmics Inc 509 324-6364
   250 Mccullough St Cincinnati (45226) *(G-3595)*
Diversified Products & Svcs 740 393-6202
   1250 Vernonview Dr Mount Vernon (43050) *(G-14478)*
Diversified Ready Mix Ltd 330 628-3355
   1680 Southeast Ave Tallmadge (44278) *(G-17980)*
Diversified SE Division, Cincinnati Also called Diversified Ophthalmics Inc *(G-3594)*
Diversified Sign, West Chester Also called Dee Sign Co *(G-19691)*
Diversified Technology Inc 330 722-4995
   650 W Smith Rd Ste 10 Medina (44256) *(G-13253)*
Diversified Tool Systems 419 845-2143
   5357 Mrion Wllmsport Rd E Caledonia (43314) *(G-2415)*
Diversified Welding Services 419 382-1433
   3541 Marine Rd Toledo (43609) *(G-18265)*
Diversified Woodworking, Findlay Also called Old Mill Custom Cabinetry Co *(G-9734)*
Diversipak Inc (PA) 513 321-7884
   838 Reedy St Cincinnati (45202) *(G-3596)*
Diversity-Vuteq LLC 614 490-5034
   1015 Taylor Rd Gahanna (43230) *(G-10080)*
Divine Prtg T-Shirts & More 419 241-8208
   3433 Monroe St Toledo (43606) *(G-18266)*
Division 20, Canal Winchester Also called Nurdcon LLC *(G-2509)*
Division Gorman-Rupp Company, Bellville Also called Gorman-Rupp Company *(G-1557)*
Division of Selling Materials, Dover Also called Smith Concrete Co *(G-8854)*
Division Overhead Door Inc (PA) 513 872-0888
   861 Dellway St Cincinnati (45229) *(G-3597)*
Dixie Flyer & Printing Co 937 687-0088
   424 Rosetta St New Lebanon (45345) *(G-14709)*

Dixie Machinery Inc ...513 360-0091
845 Todhunter Rd Monroe (45050) ***(G-14261)***
Dixitech Cnc, Monroe *Also called Dixie Machinery Inc* ***(G-14261)***
Dixon Valve & Coupling Co LLC ...330 425-3000
1900 Enterprise Pkwy Twinsburg (44087) ***(G-18765)***
Diy Holster LLC ...419 921-2168
7836 Oberlin Rd Elyria (44035) ***(G-9244)***
Dj & Woodies Vinyl Frontier ...740 623-2818
2339 County Road 16 Coshocton (43812) ***(G-7731)***
Dj Beverage Innovations Inc ...614 769-1569
8400 Indl Pkwy Bldg 2 Plain City (43064) ***(G-16188)***
Dj International Inc ...440 260-7593
35 2nd Ave Berea (44017) ***(G-1602)***
Dj Pallets ...216 701-9183
23845 Royalton Rd Columbia Station (44028) ***(G-6436)***
Dj S Weld ...330 432-2206
424 N Main St Uhrichsville (44683) ***(G-18885)***
DJ Signs MD LLC ...330 344-6643
224 W Exchange St Ste 290 Akron (44302) ***(G-144)***
Djc Holdings, Huron *Also called N2y LLC* ***(G-11106)***
DJM Plastics Ltd ...419 424-5250
1530 Harvard Ave Findlay (45840) ***(G-9679)***
DK Manfcturing Frazeysburg Inc (HQ) ...740 828-3291
119 W 2nd St Frazeysburg (43822) ***(G-9938)***
DK Manufacturing Lancaster Inc ...740 654-5566
2118 Commerce St Lancaster (43130) ***(G-11568)***
Dla Document Services ...216 522-3535
1240 E 9th St Rm B31 Cleveland (44199) ***(G-5101)***
Dla Document Services ...937 257-6014
4165 Communications Blvd Dayton (45433) ***(G-7978)***
Dlhbowles Inc (PA) ...330 478-2503
2422 Leo Ave Sw Canton (44706) ***(G-2661)***
Dlhbowles Inc ...330 478-2503
2422 Leo Ave Sw Canton (44706) ***(G-2662)***
Dlhbowles Inc ...330 479-7595
2310 Leo Ave Sw Canton (44706) ***(G-2663)***
Dlhbowles Inc ...330 488-0716
336 Wood St S East Canton (44730) ***(G-9039)***
DLM Plastics, Findlay *Also called DJM Plastics Ltd* ***(G-9679)***
Dlwoodworking ...740 927-2693
9330 Hollow Rd Sw Pataskala (43062) ***(G-15829)***
Dlz Ohio Inc (HQ) ...614 888-0040
6121 Huntley Rd Columbus (43229) ***(G-6871)***
Dm Pallet Service, Columbus *Also called Ohio Wood Recycling Inc* ***(G-7265)***
Dmax Ltd (HQ) ...937 425-9700
3100 Dryden Rd Moraine (45439) ***(G-14346)***
DMC Welding Incorporated ...330 877-1935
9975 Market Ave N Hartville (44632) ***(G-10689)***
DMG Tool & Die LLC ...937 407-0810
1215 S Greenwood St Bellefontaine (43311) ***(G-1514)***
Dmk Industries Inc ...513 727-4549
1801 Made Dr Middletown (45044) ***(G-13901)***
Dmtco LLC ...937 324-0061
302 S Center St Springfield (45506) ***(G-17389)***
DMV Corporation ...740 452-4787
1024 Military Rd Zanesville (43701) ***(G-21128)***
DNC Hydraulics LLC ...419 963-2800
5219 County Road 313 Rawson (45881) ***(G-16421)***
Dnd Emulsions Inc ...419 525-4988
270 Park Ave E Mansfield (44902) ***(G-12433)***
Dnd Products Inc ...440 286-7275
13262 Chardon Windsor Rd Chardon (44024) ***(G-3109)***
Dnl Oil Corp ...740 342-4970
7913 State Route 37 E New Lexington (43764) ***(G-14715)***
Dno Inc ...614 231-3601
3650 E 5th Ave Columbus (43219) ***(G-6872)***
Do All Sheet Metal, New Albany *Also called Samuel Clark* ***(G-14636)***
Do All Sheet Metal, New Albany *Also called Custom Metal Products Inc* ***(G-14620)***
Do All Sheetmetal, New Albany *Also called Custom Metal Products Inc* ***(G-14619)***
Do It Best, Cincinnati *Also called Hyde Park Lumber Company* ***(G-3830)***
Do It Best, Caldwell *Also called Caldwell Lumber & Supply Co* ***(G-2404)***
Doak Laser ...740 374-0090
2801 Waterford Rd Marietta (45750) ***(G-12621)***
Doan Machinery & Eqp Co Inc ...216 932-6243
2636 S Belvoir Blvd University Heights (44118) ***(G-18941)***
Doan/Pyramid Solutions LLC ...216 587-9510
5069 Corbin Dr Cleveland (44128) ***(G-5102)***
Doc Howards Distillery ...440 488-9463
7737 Lucretia Ct Mentor (44060) ***(G-13430)***
Docmann Printing & Assoc Inc ...440 975-1775
5275 Naiman Pkwy Ste E Solon (44139) ***(G-17133)***
Docupros Digital Printing, Blue Ash *Also called Bob Smith* ***(G-1738)***
Docustar, Cincinnati *Also called Vya Inc* ***(G-4485)***
Dodds Monument Inc (PA) ...937 372-2736
123 W Main St Xenia (45385) ***(G-20767)***
Dodge Company, Dayton *Also called Ronald T Dodge Co* ***(G-8484)***
Dodge Data & Analytics LLC ...513 763-3660
7265 Kenwood Rd Ste 200 Cincinnati (45236) ***(G-3598)***
Dog Daily ...216 624-0735
1180 Blanchester Rd Cleveland (44124) ***(G-5103)***
Dog Depot ...513 771-9274
950 S Troy Ave Cincinnati (45246) ***(G-3599)***
Doglok Inc ...440 223-1836
3512 River Rd Perry (44081) ***(G-15904)***
Dole Fresh Vegetables Inc ...937 525-4300
600 Benjamin Dr Springfield (45502) ***(G-17390)***
Dolgencorp LLC ...740 289-4790
7095 Us Highway 23 Piketon (45661) ***(G-16069)***
Dolin Supply Co ...304 529-4171
702 Solida Rd South Point (45680) ***(G-17282)***
Doling & Associates Dental Lab ...937 254-0075
3318 Successful Way Dayton (45414) ***(G-8164)***
Doll Inc ...419 586-7880
1901 Havemann Rd Celina (45822) ***(G-2957)***
Doll Printing, Celina *Also called Doll Inc* ***(G-2957)***
Dollar General, Piketon *Also called Dolgencorp LLC* ***(G-16069)***
Dollman Technical Services ...419 877-9404
2910 Glanzman Rd Toledo (43614) ***(G-18267)***
Dome Drilling Co (PA) ...440 892-9434
2001 Crocker Rd Ste 420 Westlake (44145) ***(G-20109)***
Dome Drilling Co ...330 262-5113
4489 E Lincoln Way Wooster (44691) ***(G-20585)***
Dome Energicorp ...440 892-4900
2001 Crocker Rd Ste 420 Westlake (44145) ***(G-20110)***
Dome Resources, Westlake *Also called Dome Drilling Co* ***(G-20109)***
Domestic Casting Company LLC ...717 532-6615
620 Liberty Rd Delaware (43015) ***(G-8673)***
Domestic Oil & Gas Co Inc ...440 232-3150
19600 Rockside Rd Cleveland (44146) ***(G-5104)***
Dometic Sanitation Corporation ...330 439-5550
13128 State Route 226 Big Prairie (44611) ***(G-1673)***
Domicone Printing Inc ...937 878-3080
854 Kauffman Ave Fairborn (45324) ***(G-9457)***
Dominion Enterprises ...216 472-1870
26301 Curtiss Wright Pkwy Cleveland (44143) ***(G-5105)***
Dominion Labels & Forms ...419 784-1041
232 Adams St Defiance (43512) ***(G-8622)***
Dominion Liquid Tech LLC ...513 272-2824
3965 Virginia Ave Cincinnati (45227) ***(G-3600)***
Domino Foods Inc ...216 432-3222
2075 E 65th St Cleveland (44103) ***(G-5106)***
Domino Sugar, Cleveland *Also called Domino Foods Inc* ***(G-5106)***
Domtar Paper Company LLC ...740 333-0003
1803 Lowes Blvd Wshngtn CT Hs (43160) ***(G-20723)***
Don Basch Jewelers Inc ...330 467-2116
8210 Mcidonia Comm Blvd36 Macedonia (44056) ***(G-12290)***
Don Gamertsfelder ...740 797-4495
10416 State Route 682 The Plains (45780) ***(G-18021)***
Don Puckett Lumber Inc ...740 887-4191
31263 Beech Grove Rd Londonderry (45647) ***(G-12075)***
Don Walter Kitchen Distrs Inc ...330 793-9338
260 Victoria Rd Youngstown (44515) ***(G-20893)***
Don Wartko Construction Co (PA) ...330 673-5252
975 Tallmadge Rd Kent (44240) ***(G-11315)***
Don-Ell Corporation (PA) ...419 841-7114
8450 Central Ave Sylvania (43560) ***(G-17936)***
Don-Ell Corporation ...419 841-7114
8456 Central Ave Sylvania (43560) ***(G-17937)***
Donahue's Hilltop Supply, Cambridge *Also called Donahues Hilltop Ice Company* ***(G-2435)***
Donahues Hilltop Ice Company ...740 432-3348
1112 Highland Ave Cambridge (43725) ***(G-2435)***
Donald E Didion II ...419 483-2226
1027b County Road 308 Bellevue (44811) ***(G-1535)***
Donald E Dornon ...740 926-9144
44592 Game Ridge Rd Beallsville (43716) ***(G-1290)***
Donald Marlo ...937 836-4880
5003 Brock Ln Dayton (45415) ***(G-8165)***
Donald Schloemer ...419 933-2002
2441 Niver Rd Willard (44890) ***(G-20239)***
Donaldson Company Inc ...330 928-4100
115 E Steels Corners Rd Stow (44224) ***(G-17580)***
Done Right Engine & Machine ...440 582-1366
12955 York Delta Dr Ste J Cleveland (44133) ***(G-5107)***
Done-Rite Bowling Service Co (PA) ...440 232-3280
20434 Krick Rd Bedford (44146) ***(G-1402)***
Dongan Electric Mfg Co, Pioneer *Also called Pioneer Transformer Company* ***(G-16090)***
Donisi Mirror Company, Loveland *Also called R G C Inc* ***(G-12225)***
Donnelley Financial LLC ...216 621-8384
1300 E 9th St Ste 1200 Cleveland (44114) ***(G-5108)***
Donze Enterprises, Grafton *Also called Great Works Publishing Inc* ***(G-10303)***
Door Fabrication Services Inc ...937 454-9207
3250 Old Springfield Rd # 1 Vandalia (45377) ***(G-19123)***
Doran Manufacturing Co., Cincinnati *Also called Osborne Coinage Company* ***(G-4120)***
Doran Mfg LLC ...513 681-5424
2851 Massachusetts Ave Cincinnati (45225) ***(G-3601)***
Dorel Home Furnishings Inc ...419 447-7448
458 2nd Ave Tiffin (44883) ***(G-18058)***

A L P H A B E T I C

Doris Kimble 330 343-1226
  3596 State Route 39 Nw Dover (44622) *(G-8817)*
Dornback Furnace Division, Cleveland Also called Adams Manufacturing Company *(G-4613)*
Dorothy Crooker 513 385-0888
  5984 Cheviot Rd Cincinnati (45247) *(G-3602)*
Dorum Color Co Inc 330 773-1900
  2229 Stahl Rd Coventry Township (44319) *(G-7768)*
Doscher's Candy Company, Cincinnati Also called Doschers Candies LLC *(G-3603)*
Doschers Candies LLC 513 381-8656
  6926 Main St Cincinnati (45244) *(G-3603)*
Dosmatic USA Inc (PA) 972 245-9765
  3798 Round Bottom Rd Cincinnati (45244) *(G-3604)*
Dotcentral LLC 330 809-0112
  1650 Deerford Ave Sw Massillon (44647) *(G-12974)*
Double b Printing LLC 740 593-7393
  17 W Washington St Athens (45701) *(G-829)*
Double Dippin Inc 937 847-2572
  949 Blanche Dr Miamisburg (45342) *(G-13660)*
Double Eagle, Lima Also called Lima Armature Works Inc *(G-11887)*
Doubleday Acquisitions LLC 937 242-6768
  2900 Dryden Rd Moraine (45439) *(G-14347)*
Doug Marine Motors Inc 740 335-3700
  1120 Clinton Ave Wshngtn CT Hs (43160) *(G-20724)*
Doug Smith 740 345-1398
  55 W Church St Newark (43055) *(G-14868)*
Douglas Industries LLC 740 775-2400
  379 Douglas Ave Chillicothe (45601) *(G-3185)*
Douglas S Kutz 440 238-8426
  19395 Knowlton Pkwy # 103 Strongsville (44149) *(G-17737)*
Douglas W & B C Richardson 440 247-5262
  62 Wychwood Dr Chagrin Falls (44022) *(G-3015)*
Douthit Communications Inc (PA) 419 625-5825
  520 Warren St Sandusky (44870) *(G-16805)*
DOV Graphics Inc 513 241-5150
  2230 Gilbert Ave Cincinnati (45206) *(G-3605)*
Dove Cds Inc 330 928-9160
  290 West Ave Ste J Tallmadge (44278) *(G-17981)*
Dove Die and Stamping Company 216 267-3720
  15665 Brookpark Rd Cleveland (44142) *(G-5109)*
Dove Graphics Inc 440 238-1800
  13500 Pearl Rd Cleveland (44136) *(G-5110)*
Dove Machine Inc 440 864-2645
  27100 Royalton Rd Columbia Station (44028) *(G-6437)*
Dove Manufacturing LLC 440 506-7935
  12900 Reed Rd Grafton (44044) *(G-10298)*
Dover Atwood Corp 330 809-0630
  1875 Harsh Ave Se Ste 1 Massillon (44646) *(G-12975)*
Dover Cabinet Inc 330 343-9074
  1568 State Route 39 Nw Dover (44622) *(G-8818)*
Dover Chemical Corporation (HQ) 330 343-7711
  3676 Davis Rd Nw Dover (44622) *(G-8819)*
Dover Conveyor Inc 740 922-9390
  3323 Brightwood Rd Midvale (44653) *(G-13976)*
Dover Corporation 440 951-6600
  7201 Industrial Park Blvd Mentor (44060) *(G-13431)*
Dover Corporation 513 870-3206
  9393 Prnceton Glendale Rd West Chester (45011) *(G-19694)*
Dover Corporation 513 696-1790
  4680 Parkway Dr Ste 203 Mason (45040) *(G-12857)*
Dover Cryogenics, Midvale Also called Amko Service Company *(G-13975)*
Dover Fabrication and Burn Inc (HQ) 330 339-1057
  2996 Progress St Dover (44622) *(G-8820)*
Dover High Prfmce Plas Inc 330 343-3477
  140 Williams Dr Nw Dover (44622) *(G-8821)*
Dover Machine Co 330 343-4123
  2208 State Route 516 Nw Dover (44622) *(G-8822)*
Dover Phila Heating & Cooling, Dover Also called Hvac Inc *(G-8830)*
Dover Tank and Plate Company 330 343-4443
  5725 Crown Rd Nw Dover (44622) *(G-8823)*
Dover Tower Company, The, Dover Also called T V Specialties Inc *(G-8859)*
Dover Wipes Company 513 983-1100
  1 Procter And Gamble Plz Cincinnati (45202) *(G-3606)*
Dovetail Dimensions 330 674-9533
  6534 Township Road 603 Millersburg (44654) *(G-14078)*
Dow Cameron Oil & Gas LLC 740 452-1568
  5555 Eden Park Dr Zanesville (43701) *(G-21129)*
Dow Chemical, Hebron Also called Transcendia Inc *(G-10768)*
Dow Chemical Company 419 423-6500
  3441 N Main St Findlay (45840) *(G-9680)*
Dow Chemical Company 937 839-4612
  10 Electric St West Alexandria (45381) *(G-19618)*
Dow Chemical Company 740 929-5100
  3700 Hebron Rd Hebron (43025) *(G-10742)*
Dow Chemical Company 937 254-1550
  555 Gaddis Blvd Dayton (45403) *(G-8166)*
Dow Jones & Company Inc 419 352-4696
  1201 Brim Rd Bowling Green (43402) *(G-1970)*
Dow Silicones Corporation 330 319-1127
  3835 Copley Rd Copley (44321) *(G-7682)*

Dowa Tht America Inc 419 354-4144
  2130 S Woodland Cir Bowling Green (43402) *(G-1971)*
Dowco LLC 330 773-6654
  1374 Markle St Akron (44306) *(G-145)*
Down Decor, Cincinnati Also called Downhome Inc *(G-3607)*
Down Home 740 393-1186
  9 N Main St Mount Vernon (43050) *(G-14479)*
Down Home Leather, Mount Vernon Also called Down Home *(G-14479)*
Down-Lite International Inc (PA) 513 229-3696
  8153 Duke Blvd Mason (45040) *(G-12858)*
Downey Enterprises Inc 740 587-4258
  2087 Jones Rd Granville (43023) *(G-10329)*
Downhome Inc 513 921-3373
  1 Kovach Dr Cincinnati (45215) *(G-3607)*
Downing Enterprises Inc 330 666-3888
  1287 Centerview Cir Copley (44321) *(G-7683)*
Downing Exhibits, Copley Also called Downing Enterprises Inc *(G-7683)*
Downlite, Mason Also called Down-Lite International Inc *(G-12858)*
Downtown Print Shop 419 242-9164
  500 Madison Ave Fl 1 Toledo (43604) *(G-18268)*
Doyle Manufacturing Inc 419 865-2548
  1440 Holloway Rd Holland (43528) *(G-10926)*
Doyle Sailmaker 216 486-5732
  805 E 185th St Cleveland (44119) *(G-5111)*
Doyle Systems, Norton Also called J E Doyle Company *(G-15371)*
Dp Operating Company Inc 330 938-2172
  19220 State Route 62 Beloit (44609) *(G-1569)*
Dp Products LLC 440 834-9663
  14395 Aquilla Rd Burton (44021) *(G-2357)*
Dp2 Energy LLC 330 376-5068
  697 W Market St Akron (44303) *(G-146)*
Dpa Investments Inc 440 992-3377
  3050 Lake Rd E Ashtabula (44004) *(G-771)*
Dpa Investments Inc 513 737-7100
  3700 Dixie Hwy Fairfield (45014) *(G-9495)*
Dpa Investments Inc 440 992-7039
  1741 W 47th St Ashtabula (44004) *(G-772)*
Dph Discount Pin Inc 740 264-2450
  30 Snug Hbr Steubenville (43953) *(G-17531)*
Dpi Inc 419 273-1400
  110 N Davis St Forest (45843) *(G-9786)*
DPM Orthodontics Inc 330 673-0334
  1519 Enterprise Way Ste H Kent (44240) *(G-11316)*
Dr Hess Products LLC 800 718-8022
  1000 Hedstrom Dr Ste B Ashland (44805) *(G-702)*
Dr Pepper, Cincinnati Also called Dr Pepper Snapple Group *(G-3608)*
Dr Pepper Bottlers Associates 330 746-7651
  500 Pepsi Pl Youngstown (44502) *(G-20894)*
Dr Pepper Bottling Company 740 452-2721
  335 N 6th St Zanesville (43701) *(G-21130)*
Dr Pepper Snapple Group 419 223-0072
  2480 Saint Johns Rd Lima (45804) *(G-11856)*
Dr Pepper Snapple Group 513 242-5151
  1115 Regina Graeter Way Cincinnati (45216) *(G-3608)*
Dr Pepper/Seven Up Inc 419 229-7777
  2350 Central Point Pkwy Lima (45804) *(G-11857)*
Dr Z Amplification, Maple Heights Also called Dr Z Amps Inc *(G-12571)*
Dr Z Amps Inc 216 475-1444
  17011 Broadway Ave Maple Heights (44137) *(G-12571)*
Dr. Pepper 7 Up Columbus, Columbus Also called American Bottling Company *(G-6580)*
Drabik Manufacturing Inc 216 267-1616
  15601 Commerce Park Dr Cleveland (44142) *(G-5112)*
Dracool-Usa Inc (PA) 937 743-5899
  30 Eagle Ct Carlisle (45005) *(G-2892)*
Dragon Beverage Inc 614 506-5592
  1945 Judwick Dr Columbus (43229) *(G-6873)*
Dragon Products LLC 330 345-3968
  3310 Columbus Rd Wooster (44691) *(G-20586)*
Dragon Racing Service, Loveland Also called Gregory Auto Service *(G-12194)*
Dragonflies and Angels Press 740 964-9149
  103 Venetian Way Sw Pataskala (43062) *(G-15830)*
Dragoon Technologies Inc (PA) 937 439-9223
  900 Senate Dr Dayton (45459) *(G-8167)*
Dragoonitcn, Dayton Also called Dragoon Technologies Inc *(G-8167)*
Draime Enterprises Inc 330 837-2254
  1300 Erie St S Unit C Massillon (44646) *(G-12976)*
Drain Products LLC (PA) 419 230-4549
  13051 County Road 301 Lakeview (43331) *(G-11504)*
Drainage Pipe & Fitting 419 538-6337
  450 Tile Company St Ottawa (45875) *(G-15651)*
Drainage Products Inc 419 622-6951
  100 W Main St Haviland (45851) *(G-10709)*
Drake Brothers Ltd 415 819-4941
  1215 Forsythe Ave Columbus (43201) *(G-6874)*
Drake Mfg Acquisition LLC 330 847-7291
  4371 N Leavitt Rd Nw Warren (44485) *(G-19397)*
Drake Monument Company 937 399-7941
  524 W Mccreight Ave Springfield (45504) *(G-17391)*

ALPHABETIC SECTION — Duplex Mill & Manufacturing Co

Drapery Stitch Cincinnati Inc 513 561-2443
5601 Wooster Pike Cincinnati (45227) *(G-3609)*

Drapery Stitch of Delphos 419 692-3921
50 Summers Ln Delphos (45833) *(G-8741)*

Drawn Metals Corp 937 433-6151
331 Congress Park Dr Dayton (45459) *(G-8168)*

Drb Systems LLC (HQ) 330 645-3299
3245 Pickle Rd Akron (44312) *(G-147)*

DRDC Realty Inc (PA) 419 478-7091
4401 Jackman Rd Toledo (43612) *(G-18269)*

Dreamscape Media LLC (PA) 877 983-7326
1417 Timber Wolf Dr Holland (43528) *(G-10927)*

Dreco Inc 440 327-6021
7887 Root Rd North Ridgeville (44039) *(G-15221)*

Dreier Tool & Die Corp 513 521-8200
2865 Compton Rd Cincinnati (45251) *(G-3610)*

Dreison International Inc (PA) 216 362-0755
4540 W 160th St Cleveland (44135) *(G-5113)*

Dresch Tolson Dental Labs 419 842-6730
8730 Resource Park Dr Sylvania (43560) *(G-17938)*

Dresden Specialties Inc (PA) 740 754-2451
305 Main St Dresden (43821) *(G-8868)*

Dresden Specialties Inc 740 452-7100
710 Main St Zanesville (43701) *(G-21131)*

Dresser-Rand Company 513 874-8388
8655 Seward Rd Fairfield (45011) *(G-9496)*

DRG Hydraulics Inc 216 663-9747
18200 S Miles Rd Cleveland (44128) *(G-5114)*

Drifter Marine Inc 419 666-8144
28271 Cedar Park Blvd # 6 Perrysburg (43551) *(G-15941)*

Drive Components 440 234-6200
6519 Eastland Rd Ste 106 Brookpark (44142) *(G-2144)*

Driveline 1 Inc 614 279-7734
1369 Frank Rd Columbus (43223) *(G-6875)*

Driven Innovations LLC 330 818-7681
140 Harrisburg Dr Englewood (45322) *(G-9356)*

Drivetrain USA Inc 614 733-0940
8445 Rausch Dr Plain City (43064) *(G-16189)*

Drop Zone Ltd 234 806-4604
3680 N River Rd Ne Warren (44484) *(G-19398)*

Drowned Lure 330 548-5873
3295 Klages Blvd Tallmadge (44278) *(G-17982)*

Drr, Brunswick Also called L & R Racing Inc *(G-2218)*

Drs Advanced Isr LLC (HQ) 937 429-7408
2601 Mission Point Blvd Beavercreek (45431) *(G-1311)*

Drs Industries Inc 419 861-0334
1067 Hamilton Dr Holland (43528) *(G-10928)*

Drs Mobile Environmntl Svc 513 943-1111
4043 Mcmann Rd Cincinnati (45245) *(G-3246)*

Drs Signal Technologies Inc 937 429-7470
4393 Dayton Xenia Rd Beavercreek (45432) *(G-1312)*

Drt Aerospace LLC 937 492-6121
1950 Campbell Rd Sidney (45365) *(G-17031)*

Drt Aerospace LLC (HQ) 937 298-7391
8694 Rite Track Way West Chester (45069) *(G-19695)*

Drt Holdings Inc (PA) 937 298-7391
618 Greenmount Blvd Dayton (45419) *(G-8169)*

Drt Medical LLC (HQ) 937 387-0880
4201 Little York Rd Dayton (45414) *(G-8170)*

Drt Mfg Co (HQ) 937 297-6670
618 Greenmount Blvd Dayton (45419) *(G-8171)*

Drt Precision Mfg LLC (HQ) 937 507-4308
1985 Campbell Rd Sidney (45365) *(G-17032)*

Drum Parts, Cleveland Also called Group Industries Inc *(G-5355)*

Drum Runner, Marion Also called Mission Industrial Group LLC *(G-12721)*

Drummond Corp 440 834-9660
14990 Brkshire Indus Pkwy Middlefield (44062) *(G-13794)*

Drummond Dolomite Inc 440 942-7000
7954 Reynolds Rd Mentor (44060) *(G-13432)*

Drummond Dolomite Quarry, Mentor Also called Drummond Dolomite Inc *(G-13432)*

Drycal Inc 440 974-1999
7355 Production Dr Mentor (44060) *(G-13433)*

Ds Express Carriers Inc (PA) 419 433-6200
203 Republic St Norwalk (44857) *(G-15388)*

Ds Technologies Group Ltd 419 841-5388
2537 Wimbledon Park Blvd Toledo (43617) *(G-18270)*

DS Techstar Inc 419 424-0888
1219 W Main Cross St Findlay (45840) *(G-9681)*

Ds Welding LLC 330 893-4049
3982 State Route 39 Millersburg (44654) *(G-14079)*

DSC Supply Company LLC 614 891-1100
237 E Broadway Ave Ste A Westerville (43081) *(G-20049)*

Dsg-Canusa, Loveland Also called Shawcor Inc *(G-12231)*

DSI Parts LLC 937 746-4678
2133 Lyons Rd Miamisburg (45342) *(G-13661)*

Dsk Imaging LLC 513 554-1797
6839 Ashfield Dr Blue Ash (45242) *(G-1759)*

DSM Industries Inc 440 585-1100
1340 E 289th St Wickliffe (44092) *(G-20209)*

DTE Cool Co 513 579-0160
105 E 4th St Ste G100 Cincinnati (45202) *(G-3611)*

DTE Inc 419 522-3428
110 Baird Pkwy Mansfield (44903) *(G-12434)*

Dti, Alliance Also called Davis Technologies Inc *(G-464)*

Dti Molded Products Inc 937 492-5008
250 Stolle Ave Sidney (45365) *(G-17033)*

DTR Equipment Inc 419 692-3000
1430 N Main St Delphos (45833) *(G-8742)*

Dts, Parma Also called Dynamic Temperature Sups LLC *(G-15816)*

Dublin Millwork Co Inc 614 889-7776
7575 Fishel Dr S Dublin (43016) *(G-8908)*

Dublin Plastics Inc 216 641-5904
9202 Reno Ave Cleveland (44105) *(G-5115)*

Dubose Energy Fasteners & Mach 216 362-1700
18737 Sheldon Rd Middleburg Heights (44130) *(G-13764)*

Duck Tape, Avon Also called Shurtech Brands LLC *(G-967)*

Duck Water Boats Inc 330 602-9008
3817 Blacksnake Hl Rd Ne Dover (44622) *(G-8824)*

Duco Tool & Die Inc 419 628-2031
19 S Main St Minster (45865) *(G-14212)*

Duct Fabricators Inc 216 391-2400
883 Addison Rd Cleveland (44103) *(G-5116)*

Ducts Inc 216 391-2400
883 Addison Rd Cleveland (44103) *(G-5117)*

Dudick Inc 330 562-1970
1818 Miller Pkwy Streetsboro (44241) *(G-17672)*

Dues Jersey Farm 419 678-2102
4131 Philothea Rd Coldwater (45828) *(G-6406)*

Dues Lumbermill, Coldwater Also called Dues Jersey Farm *(G-6406)*

Duff Farm 740 742-2182
30762 Old Dexter Rd Langsville (45741) *(G-11621)*

Duff Quarry Inc (PA) 937 686-2811
9042 State Route 117 Huntsville (43324) *(G-11085)*

Duff Quarry Inc 419 273-2518
3798 State Route 53 Forest (45843) *(G-9787)*

Duffee Finishing Inc 740 965-4848
4860 N County Line Rd Sunbury (43074) *(G-17885)*

Duffy Family Partner 330 650-6716
356 Kendall Park Rd Peninsula (44264) *(G-15892)*

Dugan Drilling Incorporated 740 668-3811
27238 New Guilford Rd Walhonding (43843) *(G-19305)*

Duke Graphics Inc 440 946-0606
33212 Lakeland Blvd Willoughby (44095) *(G-20310)*

Duke Printing, Willoughby Also called Duke Graphics Inc *(G-20310)*

Dukes Aerospace Inc 818 998-9811
313 Gillett St Painesville (44077) *(G-15732)*

Dulcelicious Cupcakes and More 440 385-7706
22368 Lorain Rd Cleveland (44126) *(G-5118)*

Dulle Associates 513 723-9600
848 Woodshire Dr Cincinnati (45233) *(G-3612)*

Dulle Printing, Cincinnati Also called Dulle Associates *(G-3612)*

Duma Deer Processing LLC 330 805-3429
831 Waterloo Rd Mogadore (44260) *(G-14234)*

Dumas Meats Inc 330 628-3438
857 Randolph Rd Mogadore (44260) *(G-14235)*

Dumpsters Inc 440 241-6927
772 Hillside Rd Seven Hills (44131) *(G-16903)*

Dunagan Logging 740 599-9368
16844 Pritchard Rd Danville (43014) *(G-7962)*

Dunaway Inc 330 533-7753
5959 Leffingwell Rd Canfield (44406) *(G-2525)*

Duncan Brothers Drilling Inc (PA) 330 426-9507
1264 Howell Ave East Palestine (44413) *(G-9074)*

Duncan Brothers Drilling Inc 330 426-9507
1264 Howell Ave East Palestine (44413) *(G-9075)*

Duncan Dental Lab LLC 614 793-0330
6175 Shamrock Ct Ste A Dublin (43016) *(G-8909)*

Duncan Press Corporation 330 477-4529
5049 Yukon St Nw Canton (44708) *(G-2664)*

Duncan Tool Inc 937 667-9364
9790 Julie Ct Tipp City (45371) *(G-18111)*

Dunecraft Inc 800 306-4168
19201 Cranwood Pkwy Cleveland (44128) *(G-5119)*

Dunham Machine Inc 216 398-4500
1311 E Schaaf Rd Bldg A Independence (44131) *(G-11124)*

Dunham Products Inc 440 232-0885
7400 Northfield Rd Walton Hills (44146) *(G-19310)*

Dunhams Sports 330 334-3257
180 Great Oaks Trl Ste C Wadsworth (44281) *(G-19235)*

Dunkin Donuts 330 336-2500
809 High St Wadsworth (44281) *(G-19236)*

Dunkin' Donuts, Solon Also called Dandi Enterprises Inc *(G-17131)*

Dunn S Tank Service Inc 330 863-2200
6036 Alliance Rd Nw Malvern (44644) *(G-12388)*

Duo-Corp 330 549-2149
280 Miley Rd North Lima (44452) *(G-15170)*

Duplex Mill & Manufacturing Co 937 325-5555
415 Sigler St Springfield (45506) *(G-17392)*

Dupli-Systems Inc 440 234-9415
8260 Dow Cir Strongsville (44136) **(G-17738)**
Dupont Electronic Polymers LP 937 268-3411
1515 Nicholas Rd Dayton (45417) **(G-8172)**
Dupont Specialty Pdts USA LLC 740 474-0220
S Dupont Rd Rr 23 Circleville (43113) **(G-4543)**
Dupont Specialty Pdts USA LLC 216 901-3600
6200 Hillcrest Dr Cleveland (44125) **(G-5120)**
Dupont Specialty Pdts USA LLC 740 474-0635
800 Dupont Rd Circleville (43113) **(G-4544)**
Dupont Vespel Parts and Shapes, Cleveland *Also called Dupont Specialty Pdts USA LLC* **(G-5120)**
Dupont Vespel Parts and Shapes, Circleville *Also called Dupont Specialty Pdts USA LLC* **(G-4544)**
Dupps Printing and Supply Co, Port Clinton *Also called William J Dupps* **(G-16264)**
Dura Bilt Drapery & Upholstery 440 269-8438
4041 Erie St Willoughby (44094) **(G-20311)**
Dura Magnetics Inc 419 882-0591
5500 Schultz Dr Sylvania (43560) **(G-17939)**
Dura Temp Corporation 419 866-4348
949 S Mccord Rd Holland (43528) **(G-10929)**
Dura-Line Corporation 440 322-1000
860 Garden St Elyria (44035) **(G-9245)**
Durable Corporation 800 537-1603
75 N Pleasant St Norwalk (44857) **(G-15389)**
Durable Plating Co 216 391-2132
4404 Saint Clair Ave Cleveland (44103) **(G-5121)**
Duracorp LLC 740 549-3336
7787 Graphics Way Lewis Center (43035) **(G-11758)**
Duracote Corporation 330 296-9600
350 N Diamond St Ravenna (44266) **(G-16376)**
Duraflow Industries Inc 440 965-5047
15706 Garfield Rd Wakeman (44889) **(G-19284)**
Duramax Global Corp 440 834-5400
17990 Great Lakes Pkwy Hiram (44234) **(G-10909)**
Duramax Marine, Hiram *Also called Duramax Global Corp* **(G-10909)**
Duramax Marine Industries 419 668-3728
53 Saint Marys St Norwalk (44857) **(G-15390)**
Durango Boot, Nelsonville *Also called Georgia-Boot Inc* **(G-14593)**
Durashield, Urbana *Also called American Pan Company* **(G-18978)**
Duray Machine Co Inc 440 277-4119
400 Ravenglass Blvd Amherst (44001) **(G-561)**
Duray Plating Company Inc 216 941-5540
13701 Triskett Rd Cleveland (44111) **(G-5122)**
Durbin Minuteman Press 513 791-9171
11130 Kenwood Rd Blue Ash (45242) **(G-1760)**
Durez Corporation 567 295-6400
13717 State Route 68 Kenton (43326) **(G-11404)**
Durisek Enterprises Inc 216 281-3898
5200 Train Ave Cleveland (44102) **(G-5123)**
Durivage Pattern & Mfg Co 419 836-8655
20522 State Route 579 W Williston (43468) **(G-20262)**
Duro Dyne Midwest Corp 513 870-6000
3825 Symmes Rd Hamilton (45015) **(G-10551)**
Durox Company 440 238-5350
12312 Alameda Dr Strongsville (44149) **(G-17739)**
Durr Megtec LLC 614 258-9501
835 N Cassady Ave Columbus (43219) **(G-6876)**
Durr Megtec LLC 614 340-4154
2120 Citygate Dr Columbus (43219) **(G-6877)**
DUrso Bakery Inc 330 652-4741
212 S Cedar Ave Niles (44446) **(G-15006)**
Dusty's Salvage & Supply, New Lexington *Also called Dnl Oil Corp* **(G-14715)**
Dutch Barn Builders, Old Washington *Also called Hershbergers Dutch Market LLP* **(G-15526)**
Dutch Design Products LLC 330 674-1167
8216 State Route 241 Fredericksburg (44627) **(G-9948)**
Dutch Heritage Woodcraft 330 893-2211
4363 State Route 39 Berlin (44610) **(G-1641)**
Dutch Legacy LLC 330 359-0270
2425 Us Route 62 Dundee (44624) **(G-9018)**
Dutch Quality Stone Inc 877 359-7866
18012 Dover Rd Mount Eaton (44659) **(G-14419)**
Dutch Valley Woodcraft Ltd 330 695-2364
5833 Township Road 610 Fredericksburg (44627) **(G-9949)**
Dutch Valley Woodworking Inc 330 852-4319
State Rte 39 Sugarcreek (44681) **(G-17848)**
Dutchcraft Truss Component Inc 330 862-2220
2212 Fox Ave Se Minerva (44657) **(G-14178)**
Duvall Woodworking Inc 419 878-9581
7551 Dutch Rd Waterville (43566) **(G-19494)**
Dvi Retal, Middletown *Also called Digital Visuals Inc* **(G-13900)**
Dvuv LLC 216 741-5511
4641 Hinckley Indus Pkwy Cleveland (44109) **(G-5124)**
DW Hercules LLC 330 830-2498
2770 Erie St S Massillon (44646) **(G-12977)**
Dwayne Bennett Industries 440 466-5724
6708 N Ridge Rd W Geneva (44041) **(G-10217)**
Dwayne Hall 740 685-5270
57501 Cherry Hill Rd Senecaville (43780) **(G-16899)**
Dyco Manufacturing Inc 419 485-5525
12708 State Route 576 Montpelier (43543) **(G-14307)**
Dyenamo Distributing 419 462-9474
6124 State Route 19 Galion (44833) **(G-10133)**
Dyna Floor, Solon *Also called Dynafloor Systems Inc* **(G-17134)**
Dyna Tech Molding & Beta 330 296-2315
367 N Freedom St Ravenna (44266) **(G-16377)**
Dyna Vac Plastics Inc 937 773-0092
921 S Downing St Piqua (45356) **(G-16112)**
Dyna-Flex Inc 440 946-9424
7300 Industrial Park Blvd Mentor (44060) **(G-13434)**
Dynaco Usa Inc 419 227-3000
1075 Prosperity Rd Lima (45801) **(G-11858)**
Dynafloor Systems Inc 330 467-6005
35079 Quartermane Cir Solon (44139) **(G-17134)**
Dynalab Ems Inc 614 866-9999
555 Lancaster Ave Reynoldsburg (43068) **(G-16436)**
Dynalite Corp 419 873-1706
26040a Glenwood Rd Ste A Perrysburg (43551) **(G-15942)**
Dynamic Bar Code Systems Inc 330 220-5451
3139 Ipswich Ct Brunswick (44212) **(G-2201)**
Dynamic Control North Amer Inc (PA) 513 860-5094
3042 Symmes Rd Hamilton (45015) **(G-10552)**
Dynamic Design & Systems Inc 440 708-1010
7639 Washington St Chagrin Falls (44023) **(G-3044)**
Dynamic Dies Inc 513 705-9524
1310 Hook Dr Middletown (45042) **(G-13902)**
Dynamic Dies Inc 513 705-9524
1310 Hook Dr Middletown (45042) **(G-13903)**
Dynamic Industries Inc 513 861-6767
3611 Woodburn Ave Cincinnati (45207) **(G-3613)**
Dynamic Leasing Ltd 330 892-0164
3790 State Route 7 New Waterford (44445) **(G-14839)**
Dynamic Machine Concepts Inc 216 470-0270
233 Commerce Dr Unit A Lagrange (44050) **(G-11479)**
Dynamic Metal Services, Bedford Heights *Also called Alloy Metal Exchange LLC* **(G-1459)**
Dynamic Plastics Inc 937 437-7261
8207 H W Rd New Paris (45347) **(G-14753)**
Dynamic Specialties Inc 440 946-2838
7471 Tyler Blvd Ste E Mentor (44060) **(G-13435)**
Dynamic Temperature Sups LLC 216 767-5799
12448 Plaza Dr Parma (44130) **(G-15816)**
Dynamic Tool & Mold Inc 440 237-8665
12126 York Rd Unit N Cleveland (44133) **(G-5125)**
Dynamic Tool Die 440 834-0007
14925 White Rd Middlefield (44062) **(G-13795)**
Dynamic Weld Corporation 419 582-2900
242 N St Osgood (45351) **(G-15642)**
Dynamics Manufacturing, Toledo *Also called Dynamics Research & Dev* **(G-18271)**
Dynamics Research & Dev 419 478-7091
4401 Jackman Rd Toledo (43612) **(G-18271)**
Dynamp LLC 614 871-6900
3735 Gantz Rd Ste D Grove City (43123) **(G-10427)**
Dynapoint Technologies Inc 937 859-5193
475 Progress Rd Dayton (45449) **(G-8173)**
Dynatech Systems Inc 440 365-1774
161 Reaser Ct Elyria (44035) **(G-9246)**
Dyneon LLC 859 334-4500
2165 Cablecar Ct Cincinnati (45244) **(G-3614)**
Dynetech LLC 419 690-4281
916 N Summit St Toledo (43604) **(G-18272)**
Dyoung Enterprise Inc 440 918-0505
38241 Willoughby Pkwy Willoughby (44094) **(G-20312)**
Dyverse Entertainment LLC 513 225-3301
10979 Reed Hartman Hwy Blue Ash (45242) **(G-1761)**
Dyverse Marketing Solutions, Blue Ash *Also called Dyverse Entertainment LLC* **(G-1761)**
E & E Mold & Die Inc 216 898-5853
4605 Manufacturing Ave Cleveland (44135) **(G-5126)**
E & E Nameplates Inc 419 468-3617
760 E Walnut St Galion (44833) **(G-10134)**
E & E Parts Machining, Strongsville *Also called Stefra Inc* **(G-17796)**
E & E Ready Rooms, Saint Clairsville *Also called D W Truax Enterprise Inc* **(G-16631)**
E & E Screen Prtg & Cstm EMB 614 235-2177
901 Robinwood Ave Ste G Columbus (43213) **(G-6878)**
E & I, Westerville *Also called McNish Corporation* **(G-20010)**
E & J Demark Inc (PA) 419 337-5866
1115 N Ottokee St Wauseon (43567) **(G-19513)**
E & J Demark Inc 419 337-5866
1115 N Ottokee St Wauseon (43567) **(G-19514)**
E & J Gallo Winery 513 381-4050
125 E Court St Cincinnati (45202) **(G-3615)**
E & K Products Co Inc 216 631-2510
3520 Cesko Ave Cleveland (44109) **(G-5127)**
E & L Spring Shop 440 632-1439
16035 Nauvoo Rd Middlefield (44062) **(G-13796)**
E & M Liberty Welding Inc 330 866-2338
141 James St Waynesburg (44688) **(G-19563)**
E & R Welding Inc 440 329-9387
32 South St Berlin Heights (44814) **(G-1653)**

ALPHABETIC SECTION Early Bird, The, Greenville

E & W Enterprises Powell Inc (HQ) 937 346-0800
2020 Progress Rd Springfield (45505) ***(G-17393)***
E - I Corp 614 899-2282
214 Hoff Rd Unit M Westerville (43082) ***(G-19988)***
E A Cox Inc 740 858-4400
11201 State Route 104 Lucasville (45648) ***(G-12262)***
E B P Inc 216 241-2550
2041 W 17th St Cleveland (44113) ***(G-5128)***
E Bee Printing Inc 614 224-0416
70 S 4th St Columbus (43215) ***(G-6879)***
E C Babbert Inc 614 837-8444
7415 Diley Rd Canal Winchester (43110) ***(G-2502)***
E C E, Holland *Also called Electronic Concepts Engrg Inc* ***(G-10930)***
E C S, Dayton *Also called Electrical Control Systems* ***(G-8179)***
E C S, Reynoldsburg *Also called Environmental Closure Systems* ***(G-16437)***
E C S Corp 440 323-1707
8015 Murray Ridge Rd Elyria (44035) ***(G-9247)***
E C Shaw Co 513 721-6334
1242 Mehring Way Cincinnati (45203) ***(G-3616)***
E D I, Belpre *Also called Electrnic Dsign For Indust Inc* ***(G-1575)***
E D M Electrofying Inc 440 322-8900
34 Artemas Ct Elyria (44035) ***(G-9248)***
E D M Fastar Inc 216 676-0100
13410 Enterprise Ave Cleveland (44135) ***(G-5129)***
E D M Services Inc 216 486-2068
21724 Saint Clair Ave Euclid (44117) ***(G-9411)***
E D M Star-One Inc 440 647-0600
745 Shiloh Ave Wellington (44090) ***(G-19575)***
E E Controls Inc 440 585-5554
30301 Fairway Blvd Willowick (44095) ***(G-20477)***
E E M C O, Cleveland *Also called Eaton Aerospace LLC* ***(G-5144)***
E H T Company, Euclid *Also called Euclid Heat Treating Co* ***(G-9413)***
E I Ceramics LLC 513 772-7001
2600 Commerce Blvd Cincinnati (45241) ***(G-3617)***
E J Bognar Inc 330 426-9292
51887 E Taggart St East Palestine (44413) ***(G-9076)***
E J Skok Industries (PA) 216 292-7533
26901 Richmond Rd Bedford (44146) ***(G-1403)***
E L Davis Inc 419 268-2004
6032 State Route 219 Celina (45822) ***(G-2958)***
E L Mustee & Sons Inc (PA) 216 267-3100
5431 W 164th St Brookpark (44142) ***(G-2145)***
E L Ostendorf Inc 440 247-7631
3425 Roundwood Rd Chagrin Falls (44022) ***(G-3016)***
E L Stone Company 330 825-4565
2998 Eastern Rd Norton (44203) ***(G-15365)***
E M E C, Marysville *Also called Engineered Mfg & Eqp Co* ***(G-12781)***
E M I, Cleveland *Also called Equipment Manufacturers Intl* ***(G-5186)***
E M I Plastic Equipment, Jackson Center *Also called EMI Corp* ***(G-11209)***
E M S, Delaware *Also called Engineered Mtls Systems Inc* ***(G-8677)***
E M S, Batavia *Also called Engineered MBL Solutions Inc* ***(G-1144)***
E M Wave, Cleveland *Also called Electro-Magwave Inc* ***(G-5164)***
E P S Specialists Ltd Inc 513 489-3676
7875 School Rd Cincinnati (45249) ***(G-3618)***
E Pompili & Sons Inc 216 581-8080
12307 Broadway Ave Cleveland (44125) ***(G-5130)***
E R Advanced Ceramics Inc 330 426-9433
600 E Clark St East Palestine (44413) ***(G-9077)***
E R B Enterprises Inc 740 948-9174
8205 Factory Shops Blvd Jeffersonville (43128) ***(G-11246)***
E Retailing Associates LLC 614 300-5785
2282 Westbrooke Dr Columbus (43228) ***(G-6880)***
E S C, Akron *Also called Ellet Neon Sales & Service Inc* ***(G-150)***
E S H Inc 330 345-1010
390 W South St Wooster (44691) ***(G-20587)***
E S Industries Inc (PA) 419 643-2625
110 Brookview Ct Lima (45801) ***(G-11859)***
E S S, North Canton *Also called Environmental Sampling Sup Inc* ***(G-15080)***
E S Sign & Design LLC 330 405-4799
9478 Ravenna Rd Twinsburg (44087) ***(G-18766)***
E Star Aerospace Corporation 614 396-6868
470 Olde Worthington Rd # 200 Westerville (43082) ***(G-19989)***
E Systems Design & Automtn Inc 419 443-0220
226 Heritage Dr Tiffin (44883) ***(G-18059)***
E T & K Inc 440 777-7375
23545 Lorain Rd North Olmsted (44070) ***(G-15186)***
E T & K Inc 440 888-4780
9809 Running Brook Dr Cleveland (44130) ***(G-5131)***
E T I, Mansfield *Also called Energy Technologies Inc* ***(G-12437)***
E W Perry Service Co Inc 419 473-1231
4216 W Alexis Rd Toledo (43623) ***(G-18273)***
E W Welding & Fabricating 440 826-9038
336 Wyleswood Dr Berea (44017) ***(G-1603)***
E Z Binderys 513 733-0005
10122 Reading Rd Cincinnati (45241) ***(G-3619)***
E Z Grout Corporation 740 749-3512
1833 N Riverview Rd Malta (43758) ***(G-12381)***
E Z Rout Inc 330 467-4814
102 E Aurora Rd Northfield (44067) ***(G-15317)***
E-Beam Services Inc 513 933-0031
2775 Henkle Dr Unit B Lebanon (45036) ***(G-11648)***
E-Pak Manufacturing LLC 800 235-1632
1109 Pittsburg Ave Wooster (44691) ***(G-20588)***
E-Waste Systems (ohio) Inc 614 824-3057
1033 Brentnell Ave # 300 Columbus (43219) ***(G-6881)***
E-Z Electric Motor Svc Corp 216 581-8820
8510 Bessemer Ave Cleveland (44127) ***(G-5132)***
E-Z Grader Company 440 247-7511
300 Industrial Pkwy Ste A Chagrin Falls (44022) ***(G-3017)***
E-Z Label Co, Brookfield *Also called E-Z Stop Service Center* ***(G-2105)***
E-Z Pack, Cincinnati *Also called Wayne Signer Enterprises Inc* ***(G-4492)***
E-Z Stop Service Center 330 448-2236
354 Bedford Rd Se Brookfield (44403) ***(G-2105)***
E.C. Kitzel & Sons, Cleveland *Also called Schumann Enterprises Inc* ***(G-6033)***
E2 Merchandising Inc 513 860-5444
9706 Inter Ocean Dr West Chester (45246) ***(G-19849)***
E3 Diagnostics Inc 937 435-2250
74 Marco Ln Dayton (45458) ***(G-8174)***
E3 Gordon Stowe, Dayton *Also called E3 Diagnostics Inc* ***(G-8174)***
Eadhere Solutions LLC (PA) 216 372-6009
6815 Euclid Ave Cleveland (44103) ***(G-5133)***
Eae Logistics Company LLC 440 417-4788
5907 S Ridge Rd Madison (44057) ***(G-12348)***
Eagle Advertising 216 881-0800
4101 Commerce Ave Cleveland (44103) ***(G-5134)***
Eagle Coach Inc 513 797-4100
3344 State Route 132 Amelia (45102) ***(G-537)***
Eagle Coach Company, Amelia *Also called Eagle Coach Inc* ***(G-537)***
Eagle Creek Inc 513 385-4442
9799 Prechtel Rd Cincinnati (45252) ***(G-3620)***
Eagle Crusher Co Inc (PA) 419 468-2288
525 S Market St Galion (44833) ***(G-10135)***
Eagle Crusher Co Inc 419 562-1183
521 E Southern Ave Bucyrus (44820) ***(G-2326)***
Eagle Elastomer Inc 330 923-7070
70 Cuyhoga Fls Indus Pkwy Peninsula (44264) ***(G-15893)***
Eagle Family Foods Group LLC (PA) 330 382-3725
4020 Kinross Lakes Pkwy # 3 Richfield (44286) ***(G-16468)***
Eagle Fireworks Co (PA) 740 373-3357
26400 State Route 7 Marietta (45750) ***(G-12622)***
Eagle Hardwoods, Windsor *Also called Hershberger Manufacturing* ***(G-20526)***
Eagle Image Inc 513 662-3000
4742 Blue Rock Rd Cincinnati (45247) ***(G-3621)***
Eagle Industrial Truck Mfg LLC 734 442-1000
1 Air Cargo Pkwy E Swanton (43558) ***(G-17912)***
Eagle Laboratory Glass Co LLC 440 354-8350
440 W Prospect St Painesville (44077) ***(G-15733)***
Eagle Machine and Welding Inc 740 345-5210
18 W Walnut St Newark (43055) ***(G-14869)***
Eagle Machinery & Supply Inc 330 852-1300
422 Dutch Valley Dr Ne Sugarcreek (44681) ***(G-17849)***
Eagle Manufacturing Inc 419 738-3491
88 High St Uniopolis (45888) ***(G-18939)***
Eagle Mfg Solutions LLC 937 865-0366
2585 Belvo Rd Miamisburg (45342) ***(G-13662)***
Eagle Precision Products LLC 440 582-9393
13800 Progress Pkwy Ste J North Royalton (44133) ***(G-15270)***
Eagle Print, Delphos *Also called Delphos Herald Inc* ***(G-8738)***
Eagle Printing & Graphics LLC 937 773-7900
318 N Wayne St Piqua (45356) ***(G-16113)***
Eagle Tool & Die Inc 216 671-5055
10805 Briggs Rd Cleveland (44111) ***(G-5135)***
Eagle Tugs, Swanton *Also called Eagle Industrial Truck Mfg LLC* ***(G-17912)***
Eagle Wire Works Inc 216 341-8550
3173 E 66th St Fl 3 Cleveland (44127) ***(G-5136)***
Eagle Wldg & Fabrication Inc 440 946-0692
1766 Joseph Lloyd Pkwy Willoughby (44094) ***(G-20313)***
Eagle Wright Innovations Inc 937 640-8093
2591 Lance Dr Moraine (45409) ***(G-14348)***
Eagleburgmann Industries LP 513 563-7325
3478 Hauck Rd Ste A Cincinnati (45241) ***(G-3622)***
Eaglehead Manufacturing Co 216 692-1240
23555 Euclid Ave Euclid (44117) ***(G-9412)***
Eaglehead Manufacturing Co 440 951-0400
35280 Lakeland Blvd Eastlake (44095) ***(G-9106)***
Eagles Club 740 962-6490
407 W Riverside Dr McConnelsville (43756) ***(G-13203)***
Eaj Services LLC 513 792-3400
4350 Glendale Milford Rd # 170 Blue Ash (45242) ***(G-1762)***
Eanytime Corporation 714 969-7000
833 Grandview Ave Ste B Columbus (43215) ***(G-6882)***
Ear Medical Center Inc (PA) 812 537-0031
2121 Alpine Pl Apt 1101 Cincinnati (45206) ***(G-3623)***
Earl D Arnold Printing Company 513 533-6900
630 Lunken Park Dr Cincinnati (45226) ***(G-3624)***
Early Bird, The, Greenville *Also called Brothers Publishing Co LLC* ***(G-10361)***

ALPHABETIC

(PA)=Parent Co (HQ)=Headquarters (DH)=Div Headquarters
2019 Harris Ohio Industrial Directory
1103

Earnest Brew Works...419 340-2589
4342 S Detroit Ave Toledo (43614) *(G-18274)*
Earth Anatomy Fabrication LLC...740 244-5316
4092 Greenwich Rd Norton (44203) *(G-15366)*
Earth and Atmospheric Sciences, Dayton *Also called Science/Electronics Inc (G-8497)*
Earth Dreams Jewelry, North Royalton *Also called Gardella Jewelry LLC (G-15273)*
Earthganic Elements LLC...513 430-0503
1150 Nature Run Rd Batavia (45103) *(G-1137)*
Earthquaker Devices LLC...330 252-9220
350 W Bowery St Akron (44307) *(G-148)*
Earthwalk Orthotic...330 837-6569
500 Vista Ave Se Massillon (44646) *(G-12978)*
Easi, Berea *Also called Estabrook Assembly Svcs Inc (G-1606)*
East Chemical Plant, Marysville *Also called Scotts Miracle-Gro Company (G-12811)*
East Cleveland Rubber Stamp...216 851-5050
16501 Euclid Ave Cleveland (44112) *(G-5137)*
East End Welding Company...330 677-6000
357 Tallmadge Rd Kent (44240) *(G-11317)*
East Fairfield Coal Co...330 542-1010
13699 Youngstown Pittsbur Petersburg (44454) *(G-16033)*
East Fork Precision Machine LL...513 753-4157
3874 Gordon Dr Amelia (45102) *(G-538)*
East Manufacturing Corporation (PA)...330 325-9921
1871 State Rte 44 Randolph (44265) *(G-16360)*
East Manufacturing Corporation...330 325-9921
3865 Waterloo Rd Randolph (44265) *(G-16361)*
East Oberlin Cabinets...440 775-1166
13184 Hale Rd Oberlin (44074) *(G-15493)*
East Palestine Decorating LLC...330 426-9600
870 W Main St East Palestine (44413) *(G-9078)*
East Side Fuel Plus Operations...419 563-0777
1505 N Sandusky Ave Bucyrus (44820) *(G-2327)*
East West Copolymer & Rbr LLC...225 267-3713
28026 Gates Mills Blvd Cleveland (44124) *(G-5138)*
East West Copolymer LLC...225 267-3400
28026 Gates Mills Blvd Cleveland (44124) *(G-5139)*
East Woodworking Company...216 791-5950
2044 Random Rd Cleveland (44106) *(G-5140)*
Easterday & Co, Wilmot *Also called David E Easterday and Co Inc (G-20515)*
Easterdays Printing Center...330 726-1182
86 Boardman Poland Rd Youngstown (44512) *(G-20895)*
Eastern Automated Piping...740 535-8184
424 State St Mingo Junction (43938) *(G-14208)*
Eastern Enterprise, Springfield *Also called Comptons Precision Machine (G-17378)*
Eastern Graphic Arts...419 994-5815
214 N Jefferson St Loudonville (44842) *(G-12141)*
Eastern Lawrnce Cty Watr Reclm, Chesapeake *Also called County of Lawrence (G-3144)*
Eastern Ohio Investments Inc...740 266-2228
213 Braybarton Blvd Steubenville (43952) *(G-17532)*
Eastern Ohio Newspapers Inc...740 633-1131
200 S 4th St Martins Ferry (43935) *(G-12760)*
Eastern Reserve Development...614 319-3179
3888 Stonewater Dr Columbus (43221) *(G-6883)*
Eastern Sheet Metal Inc (HQ)...513 793-3440
8959 Blue Ash Rd Blue Ash (45242) *(G-1763)*
Eastern Slipcover Company Inc...440 951-2310
6399 Cumberland Dr Mentor (44060) *(G-13436)*
Eastgate Custom Graphics Ltd...513 528-7922
4459 Mt Carmel Tobasco Rd Cincinnati (45244) *(G-3625)*
Eastlake Machine Products Inc...440 953-1014
1956 Joseph Lloyd Pkwy Willoughby (44094) *(G-20314)*
Eastlake Mfg Facility, Willoughby *Also called Conn-Selmer Inc (G-20300)*
Eastman Kodak Company...937 259-3000
3100 Research Blvd # 250 Kettering (45420) *(G-11431)*
Eastman Kodak Company...937 259-3000
3000 Research Blvd Dayton (45420) *(G-8175)*
Easton-Mccarthy Division, Wooster *Also called Baaron Abrasives Inc (G-20568)*
Eastside Daily News, Cleveland *Also called Easy Side Publishing Co Inc (G-5142)*
Eastword Publications Dev...216 781-9594
812 Huron Rd E Ste 401 Cleveland (44115) *(G-5141)*
Easy Board Inc...440 205-8836
8621 Station St Mentor (44060) *(G-13437)*
Easy Care Products Inc...330 405-1380
8870 Darrow Rd Ste F106 Twinsburg (44087) *(G-18767)*
Easy Defense Products...513 258-2897
2660 Hummingbird Ct Cincinnati (45239) *(G-3626)*
Easy Side Publishing Co Inc...216 721-1674
11400 Woodland Ave Cleveland (44104) *(G-5142)*
Easy Way Leisure Corporation (PA)...513 731-5640
8950 Rossash Rd Cincinnati (45236) *(G-3627)*
Easy Way Products, Cincinnati *Also called Easy Way Leisure Corporation (G-3627)*
Easyfit Products Inc...740 362-9900
320 London Rd Ste 302 Delaware (43015) *(G-8674)*
Eat Moore Cupcakes...513 713-8139
1212 Forest Run Dr Batavia (45103) *(G-1138)*
Eaton Aeroquip LLC (HQ)...216 523-5000
1000 Eaton Blvd Cleveland (44122) *(G-5143)*
Eaton Aerospace LLC (HQ)...216 523-5000
1000 Eaton Blvd Cleveland (44122) *(G-5144)*
Eaton Aerospace LLC...216 523-5000
2000 Apollo Dr Cleveland (44142) *(G-5145)*
Eaton Comprsr Fabrication Inc...877 283-7614
1000 Cass Dr Englewood (45315) *(G-9357)*
Eaton Corporation (HQ)...440 523-5000
1000 Eaton Blvd Cleveland (44122) *(G-5146)*
Eaton Corporation...440 523-5000
1000 Eaton Blvd Beachwood (44122) *(G-1233)*
Eaton Corporation...419 238-1190
1225 W Main St Van Wert (45891) *(G-19087)*
Eaton Corporation...330 274-0743
115 Lena Dr Aurora (44202) *(G-877)*
Eaton Corporation...216 281-2211
9919 Clinton Rd Cleveland (44144) *(G-5147)*
Eaton Corporation...513 387-2000
9902 Windisch Rd West Chester (45069) *(G-19696)*
Eaton Corporation...440 826-1115
1000 W Bagley Rd Berea (44017) *(G-1604)*
Eaton Corporation...888 328-6677
6055 Rckside Woods Blvd N Cleveland (44131) *(G-5148)*
Eaton Corporation...216 523-5000
1000 Eaton Blvd Beachwood (44122) *(G-1234)*
Eaton Corporation...216 920-2000
333 Babbitt Rd Ste 100 Cleveland (44123) *(G-5149)*
Eaton Corporation...440 826-1115
6055 Rckside Woods Blvd N Cleveland (44131) *(G-5150)*
Eaton Corporation...440 748-2236
12043 Avon Belden Rd Grafton (44044) *(G-10299)*
Eaton Electric Holdings LLC (HQ)...440 523-5000
1000 Eaton Blvd Cleveland (44122) *(G-5151)*
Eaton Fabricating Company Inc...440 926-3121
1009 Mcalpin Ct Grafton (44044) *(G-10300)*
Eaton Global Hose, Cleveland *Also called Eaton Aeroquip LLC (G-5143)*
Eaton Global Hose, Van Wert *Also called Eaton-Aeroquip Llc (G-19089)*
Eaton Hydraulics LLC...419 232-7777
1225 W Main St Van Wert (45891) *(G-19088)*
Eaton Industrial Corporation (HQ)...216 523-4205
23555 Euclid Ave Cleveland (44117) *(G-5152)*
Eaton Leasing Corporation (HQ)...216 382-2292
1000 Eaton Blvd Beachwood (44122) *(G-1235)*
Eaton Township, Grafton *Also called Eaton Corporation (G-10299)*
Eaton Usev Holding Company (HQ)...216 523-5000
1111 Suprr Eatn Ctr 173 Cleveland (44114) *(G-5153)*
Eaton-Aeroquip Llc...419 891-7775
1660 Indian Wood Cir Maumee (43537) *(G-13109)*
Eaton-Aeroquip Llc...419 238-1190
1225 W Main St Van Wert (45891) *(G-19089)*
Ebel Tape & Label, Cincinnati *Also called Ebel-Binder Printing Co (G-3628)*
Ebel-Binder Printing Co...513 471-1067
1630 Dalton Ave 1 Cincinnati (45214) *(G-3628)*
Ebisyn Medical Inc...609 759-1101
6474 Weston Cir W Dublin (43016) *(G-8910)*
Ebner Furnaces Inc...330 335-2311
224 Quadral Dr Wadsworth (44281) *(G-19237)*
Ebnerfab, Wadsworth *Also called Ebner Furnaces Inc (G-19237)*
Ebo Group, Inc., Sharon Center *Also called Ebog Legacy Inc (G-16949)*
Ebog Legacy Inc (HQ)...330 239-4933
1441 Wolf Creek Trl Sharon Center (44274) *(G-16949)*
Eboni Corner...724 518-3065
1780 S Belvoir Blvd Cleveland (44121) *(G-5154)*
Ebsco Industries Inc...513 398-2149
1111 Western Row Rd Mason (45040) *(G-12859)*
Ebsco Industries Inc...513 398-3695
4680 Parkway Dr Ste 200 Mason (45040) *(G-12860)*
Ebulent Technologies Corp...925 922-1448
Falls Town Ctr Cuyahoga Falls (44221) *(G-7861)*
Ecc Company, Groveport *Also called Lomar Enterprises Inc (G-10501)*
Eccles Saw & Tool, Cincinnati *Also called D & M Saw & Tool Inc (G-3568)*
Echo Drilling Inc (PA)...740 498-8560
11 Crestview Mnr Newcomerstown (43832) *(G-14973)*
Echo Drilling Inc...740 254-4127
367 Echo Rd Se Gnadenhutten (44629) *(G-10278)*
Echo EMR Inc...937 322-4972
2755 Columbus Rd Springfield (45503) *(G-17394)*
Echo Environmental Waverly LLC...740 286-2810
479 Indl Pk Dr Waverly (45690) *(G-19545)*
Echo Mobile Solutions LLC...614 282-3756
108 Leasure Dr Pickerington (43147) *(G-16046)*
Echographics Inc...440 846-2330
9454 Grist Mill Dr North Ridgeville (44039) *(G-15222)*
Eci...419 483-2738
8802 Portland Rd Castalia (44824) *(G-2937)*
Eci Macola/Max LLC (HQ)...978 539-6186
5455 Rings Rd Ste 100 Dublin (43017) *(G-8911)*
Ecil Met TEC, Avon Lake *Also called Reliacheck Manufacturing Inc (G-1005)*
Eckart Aluminum, Painesville *Also called Eckart America Corporation (G-15734)*
Eckart America, Painesville *Also called Obron Atlantic Corporation (G-15767)*
Eckart America Corporation (HQ)...440 954-7600
830 E Erie St Painesville (44077) *(G-15734)*

Eckel Industries Inc 978 772-0480
10021 Commerce Park Dr West Chester (45246) *(G-19850)*
Eclipse 419 564-7482
126 N Union St Galion (44833) *(G-10136)*
Eclipse Blind Systems Inc 330 296-0112
7154 State Route 88 Ravenna (44266) *(G-16378)*
Eclipse Resources - Ohio LLC 740 452-4503
4900 Boggs Rd Zanesville (43701) *(G-21132)*
Ecm Biofilms Inc 440 350-1400
Victoria Pl Ste 225 Painesville (44077) *(G-15735)*
Eco Chem Alternative Fuels LLC 614 764-3835
565 Metro Pl S Ste 300 Dublin (43017) *(G-8912)*
Eco Fuel Solution LLC 440 282-8592
779 Sunrise Dr Amherst (44001) *(G-562)*
Eco Mechanical LLC 440 610-9253
47559 Hughes Rd Wellington (44090) *(G-19576)*
Eco-Flo Products Inc (PA) 877 326-3561
1899 Cottage St Ashland (44805) *(G-703)*
Eco-Groupe Inc (PA) 937 898-2603
6161 Ventnor Ave Dayton (45414) *(G-8176)*
Eco-Print Solutions LLC 513 731-3106
6893 High Meadows Dr Cincinnati (45230) *(G-3629)*
Ecolab Inc 513 932-0830
726 E Main St Ste F Lebanon (45036) *(G-11649)*
Econ-O-Machine Products Inc 937 882-6307
160 E Main St Donnelsville (45319) *(G-8801)*
Econo Products Inc 330 923-4101
101 Ascot Pkwy Cuyahoga Falls (44223) *(G-7862)*
Economy Forms, Columbus *Also called Efco Corp (G-6886)*
Economy Straightening Service 216 432-4410
896 E 70th St Cleveland (44103) *(G-5155)*
Ecotec Ltd LLC 937 606-2793
150 Marybill Dr S Troy (45373) *(G-18652)*
Ecowise LLC 216 692-3700
17000 Saint Clair Ave Cleveland (44110) *(G-5156)*
Ecp, Akron *Also called Enzyme Catalyzed Polymers LLC (G-158)*
Ecp Corporation 440 934-0444
1305 Chester Indus Pkwy Avon (44011) *(G-948)*
Ect, North Royalton *Also called Envirnmntal Cmpliance Tech LLC (G-15271)*
Ecu Corporation (PA) 513 898-9294
7209 E Kemper Rd Cincinnati (45249) *(G-3630)*
Edac Composites, Cincinnati *Also called Meggitt (erlanger) LLC (G-4000)*
Edco Inc (HQ) 419 726-1595
5244 Enterprise Blvd # 5 Toledo (43612) *(G-18275)*
Edco Producing 419 947-2515
869 Meadow Dr Mount Gilead (43338) *(G-14423)*
Edco Tool & Die, Toledo *Also called Edco Inc (G-18275)*
Edelmann Provision Company 513 881-5800
10000 Martins Way Harrison (45030) *(G-10639)*
Eden Cryogenics LLC 614 873-3949
8475 Rausch Dr Plain City (43064) *(G-16190)*
Edge Adhesives-Oh, Grove City *Also called Rubex Inc (G-10463)*
Edge Cycling Technologies LLC 937 532-3891
1549 Woodside Way Xenia (45385) *(G-20768)*
Edge Makers, Columbus *Also called Dan Wilzynski (G-6848)*
Edge Plastics Inc (PA) 419 522-6696
449 Newman St Mansfield (44902) *(G-12435)*
Edge-Rite Tools Inc 216 642-0966
7700 Exchange St Cleveland (44125) *(G-5157)*
Edgerton Forge Inc (HQ) 419 298-2333
257 E Morrison St Edgerton (43517) *(G-9171)*
Edgewater Canvas Co, Toledo *Also called Allen Zahradnik Inc (G-18163)*
Edgewell Per Care Brands LLC 937 228-0105
973 S Perry St Dayton (45402) *(G-8177)*
Edgewell Per Care Brands LLC 440 835-7500
25225 Detroit Rd Westlake (44145) *(G-20111)*
Edgewell Per Care Brands LLC 330 527-2191
10545 Freedom St Garrettsville (44231) *(G-10188)*
Edgewell Personal Care LLC 937 492-1057
1810 Progress Way Sidney (45365) *(G-17034)*
Edi Holding Company LLC (PA) 740 401-4000
100 Ayers Blvd Belpre (45714) *(G-1574)*
Edible Arrangement, Twinsburg *Also called Kriss Kreations (G-18803)*
Edict Systems Inc 937 429-4288
2434 Esquire Dr Beavercreek (45431) *(G-1313)*
Edinburg Fixture & Machine 330 947-1700
3101 State Route 14 Rootstown (44272) *(G-16568)*
Edison Solar Inc 419 499-0000
3809 State Route 113 E Milan (44846) *(G-13982)*
Edjean Technical Services Inc 440 647-3300
246 Us Highway 224 Ste A Sullivan (44880) *(G-17881)*
Edjetech Services, Sullivan *Also called Edjean Technical Services Inc (G-17881)*
Edmar Chemical Company 440 247-9560
539 Washington St Chagrin Falls (44022) *(G-3018)*
Edmonds Elevator Company 216 781-9135
6777 Sidley Rd Thompson (44086) *(G-18025)*
Edsal Sandusky Corporation 419 626-5465
117 E Washington Row Sandusky (44870) *(G-16806)*
Educational Electronics Inc 234 301-9077
101 Lakeview Dr Apt 28 Millersburg (44654) *(G-14080)*
Educational Equipment, Kent *Also called Michael Kaufman Companies Inc (G-11353)*
Educational Equipment, Kent *Also called Michael Kaufman Companies Inc (G-11354)*
Educational Publisher Inc 614 485-0721
1091 W 1st Ave Columbus (43212) *(G-6884)*
Edw C Levy Co 330 484-6328
3715 Whipple Ave Sw Canton (44706) *(G-2665)*
Edw C Levy Co 419 822-8286
6565 County Road 9 Delta (43515) *(G-8769)*
Edward Keiter & Sons 937 382-3249
1235 Stone Rd Wilmington (45177) *(G-20494)*
Edward S Eveland 937 233-6568
6175 Falkland Dr Dayton (45424) *(G-8178)*
Edward W Daniel LLC 440 647-1960
46950 State Route 18 S Wellington (44090) *(G-19577)*
Edwards Culvert Co, Fredericktown *Also called Edwards Sheet Metal Works Inc (G-9967)*
Edwards Electrical & Mech 614 485-2003
685 Grandview Ave Columbus (43215) *(G-6885)*
Edwards Machine Service Inc 937 295-2929
8800 State Route 66 Fort Loramie (45845) *(G-9795)*
Edwards Sheet Metal Works Inc 740 694-0010
10439 Sparta Rd Fredericktown (43019) *(G-9967)*
Edwards Vacuum LLC 440 248-4453
7905 Cochran Rd Ste 100 Solon (44139) *(G-17135)*
Eei Acquisition Corp 440 564-5484
15175 Kinsman Rd Middlefield (44062) *(G-13797)*
Efco Corp 614 876-1226
3900 Zane Trace Dr Columbus (43228) *(G-6886)*
Effective Air, Bedford *Also called Anson Co (G-1383)*
Efficient Machine Pdts Corp 440 268-0205
12133 Alameda Dr Strongsville (44149) *(G-17740)*
Efg Holdings Inc (PA) 812 689-8990
10217 Brecksville Rd # 101 Brecksville (44141) *(G-2030)*
Eg Enterprise Services Inc 216 431-3300
5000 Euclid Ave Ste 100 Cleveland (44103) *(G-5158)*
Eg Industries, Columbus *Also called Ernie Green Industries Inc (G-6903)*
Eg Industries, Circleville *Also called Florida Production Engrg Inc (G-4545)*
Egc Enterprises Inc 440 285-5835
140 Parker Ct Chardon (44024) *(G-3110)*
Eger Products Inc (PA) 513 753-4200
1132 Ferris Rd Amelia (45102) *(G-539)*
Eger Products Inc 513 735-1400
4226 Grissom Dr Batavia (45103) *(G-1139)*
Egr Products Company Inc (PA) 330 833-6554
55 Eckard Rd Dalton (44618) *(G-7941)*
Egypt Structural Steel Proc 419 628-2375
480 Osterloh Rd Minster (45865) *(G-14213)*
Eia, Cleveland *Also called Everything In America (G-5203)*
Eicom Corporation 937 294-5692
3249 Dryden Rd Moraine (45439) *(G-14349)*
Eighth Floor Promotions LLC 419 586-6433
1 Visions Pkwy Celina (45822) *(G-2959)*
Eighty Six Inc 800 760-0722
8823 Salon Cir Huber Heights (45424) *(G-11016)*
Eileen Musser Shiela 937 295-4212
80 S Main St Fort Loramie (45845) *(G-9796)*
Einstruction Corp 940 565-0004
255 W Federal St Youngstown (44503) *(G-20896)*
Einstruction Corporation (HQ) 330 746-3015
255 W Federal St Youngstown (44503) *(G-20897)*
Eisenhauer Mfg Co LLC 419 238-0081
409 Center St Van Wert (45891) *(G-19090)*
Eitle Machine Tool Inc 419 935-8753
6036 Coder Rd Attica (44807) *(G-856)*
Ej Usa Inc 216 692-3001
4160 Glenridge Rd Cleveland (44121) *(G-5159)*
Ej Usa Inc 330 782-3900
4150 Simon Rd Youngstown (44512) *(G-20898)*
Ej Usa Inc 614 871-2436
1855 Feddern Ave Grove City (43123) *(G-10428)*
El Nuevo Naranjo 614 863-4212
6142 Glenworth Ct Galloway (43119) *(G-10177)*
Ela Holding Corporation 513 200-1374
5403 Haft Rd Cincinnati (45247) *(G-3631)*
Elaire Corporation 419 843-2192
7944 W Central Ave Ste 10 Toledo (43617) *(G-18276)*
Elan Designs Inc 614 985-5600
10 E Schrock Rd 110 Westerville (43081) *(G-20050)*
Elanco Animal Health, Germantown *Also called Eli Lilly and Company (G-10241)*
Elano Div, Beavercreek *Also called Unison Industries LLC (G-1345)*
Elano Machine Operations, Alpha *Also called Unison Industries LLC (G-518)*
Elastance Imaging LLC 614 579-9520
226 E Beechwold Blvd Columbus (43214) *(G-6887)*
Elaston Company 330 863-2865
448 E Mohawk Dr Malvern (44644) *(G-12389)*
Elastostar Rubber Corp 614 841-4400
7030 Huntley Rd Ste B Columbus (43229) *(G-6888)*

ALPHABETIC

Elbern Publications ALPHABETIC SECTION

Elbern Publications...614 235-2643
3120 Elbern Ave Columbus (43209) ***(G-6889)***
Elbex Corporation...330 673-3233
300 Martinel Dr Kent (44240) ***(G-11318)***
Elco Corporation...440 997-6131
1100 State Rd Ashtabula (44004) ***(G-773)***
Elco Corporation (HQ)...800 321-0467
1000 Belt Line Ave Cleveland (44109) ***(G-5160)***
Elcoma Metal Fabricating & Sls...330 588-3075
521 Lawrence Rd Ne Canton (44704) ***(G-2666)***
Elcor Inc...440 365-5941
640 Sugar Ln Elyria (44035) ***(G-9249)***
Elden Draperies of Toledo Inc...419 535-1909
1845 N Reynolds Rd Toledo (43615) ***(G-18277)***
Eldorado National Kansas Inc...937 596-6849
419 W Pike St Jackson Center (45334) ***(G-11208)***
Electr-Gnral Plas Corp Clumbus...614 871-2915
6200 Enterprise Pkwy Grove City (43123) ***(G-10429)***
Electra - Cord Inc...330 832-8124
1320 Sanders Ave Sw Massillon (44647) ***(G-12979)***
Electra Sound Inc (PA)...216 433-9600
5260 Commerce Pkwy W Parma (44130) ***(G-15817)***
Electra Tarp Inc...330 477-7168
2900 Perry Dr Sw Canton (44706) ***(G-2667)***
Electraform Industries Div, Vandalia *Also called Wentworth Mold Inc Electra* ***(G-19151)***
Electrasound TV & Appl Svc, Parma *Also called Electra Sound Inc* ***(G-15817)***
Electric Cord Sets Inc (PA)...216 261-1000
4700 Manufacturing Ave Cleveland (44135) ***(G-5161)***
Electric Ctrl & Mtr Repr Svc...216 881-3143
6717 Saint Clair Ave Cleveland (44103) ***(G-5162)***
Electric Eel Mfg Co Inc...937 323-4644
501 W Leffel Ln Springfield (45506) ***(G-17395)***
Electric Motor Service, Piqua *Also called Bornhorst Motor Service Inc* ***(G-16104)***
Electric Motor Svc of Athens...740 592-1682
6 E 4th St The Plains (45780) ***(G-18022)***
Electric Service Co Inc...513 271-6387
5331 Hetzell St Cincinnati (45227) ***(G-3632)***
Electric Speed Indicator Co...216 251-2540
12234 Triskett Rd Cleveland (44111) ***(G-5163)***
Electrical Control Design Inc...419 443-9290
25571 Fort Meigs Rd Ste D Perrysburg (43551) ***(G-15943)***
Electrical Control Systems...937 859-7136
3731 W Alex Bell Rd Dayton (45449) ***(G-8179)***
Electrical Insulation Company, Delta *Also called Workman Electronic Pdts Inc* ***(G-8779)***
Electrical Machinery & Repair, Green Springs *Also called James W Cunningham* ***(G-10344)***
Electrimotion Inc...740 362-0251
1484 Dale Ford Rd Delaware (43015) ***(G-8675)***
Electripack Inc...937 433-2602
2064 Byers Rd Miamisburg (45342) ***(G-13663)***
Electrnic Dsign For Indust Inc...740 401-4000
100 Ayers Blvd Belpre (45714) ***(G-1575)***
Electro Controls Inc...866 497-1717
1625 Ferguson Ct Sidney (45365) ***(G-17035)***
Electro Polish Company Inc...937 222-3611
332 Vermont Ave Dayton (45404) ***(G-8180)***
Electro Prime Assembly Inc...419 476-0100
63 Dixie Hwy Ste 7 Rossford (43460) ***(G-16583)***
Electro Prime Group LLC (PA)...419 476-0100
4510 Lint Ave Ste B Toledo (43612) ***(G-18278)***
Electro Prime Group LLC...419 666-5000
63 Dixie Hwy Ste 7 Rossford (43460) ***(G-16584)***
Electro Torque...614 297-1600
900 Gray St Columbus (43201) ***(G-6890)***
Electro-Cap International Inc...937 456-6099
1011 W Lexington Rd Eaton (45320) ***(G-9148)***
Electro-Line Inc...937 461-5683
118 S Terry St Dayton (45403) ***(G-8181)***
Electro-Magwave Inc...216 453-1160
6111 Carey Dr Ste 1 Cleveland (44125) ***(G-5164)***
Electro-Mechanical Mfg Co Inc...330 864-0717
1351 S Clvlnd Mhlln Rd Akron (44321) ***(G-149)***
Electro-Metallics Co...513 423-8091
3004 Lefferson Rd Middletown (45044) ***(G-13904)***
Electro-Plating & Fabricating, Cleveland *Also called Roberts Demand No 3 Corp* ***(G-5992)***
ELECTROBURR, Wellington *Also called Rochester Manufacturing Inc* ***(G-19590)***
Electrocoat, Medina *Also called Office Magic Inc* ***(G-13310)***
Electrocraft Arkansas Inc...501 268-4203
250 Mccormick Rd Gallipolis (45631) ***(G-10163)***
Electrocraft Ohio Inc...740 441-6200
250 Mccormick Rd Gallipolis (45631) ***(G-10164)***
Electrodata Inc...216 663-3333
23400 Aurora Rd Ste 5 Bedford Heights (44146) ***(G-1469)***
Electroduct LLC...330 220-9300
1126 Industrial Pkwy N Brunswick (44212) ***(G-2202)***
Electrodynamics Inc...847 259-0740
3975 Mcmann Rd Cincinnati (45245) ***(G-3247)***
Electrodyne Company Inc...513 732-2822
4188 Taylor Rd Batavia (45103) ***(G-1140)***
Electrofuel Industries Inc...937 783-2846
77 N Depot Rd Batavia (45103) ***(G-1141)***
Electrolizing Corporation Ohio (PA)...216 451-3153
1325 E 152nd St Cleveland (44112) ***(G-5165)***
Electrolizing Corporation Ohio...216 451-8653
1655 Collamer Ave Cleveland (44110) ***(G-5166)***
Electrolux Professional Inc (HQ)...216 898-1800
20445 Emerald Pkwy Cleveland (44135) ***(G-5167)***
Electromechanical North Amer, Milford *Also called Parker-Hannifin Corporation* ***(G-14031)***
Electromechanical North Amer, Wadsworth *Also called Parker-Hannifin Corporation* ***(G-19262)***
Electromotive Inc (PA)...330 688-6494
4880 Hudson Dr Stow (44224) ***(G-17581)***
Electronic Concepts Engrg Inc...419 861-9000
1465 Timber Wolf Dr Holland (43528) ***(G-10930)***
Electronic Imaging Svcs Inc...740 549-2487
8273 Green Meadows Dr N # 400 Lewis Center (43035) ***(G-11759)***
Electronic Services, Fairborn *Also called Voltage Regulator Sales & Svcs* ***(G-9474)***
Electronic Solutions Inc...419 666-4700
28271 Cedar Park Blvd Perrysburg (43551) ***(G-15944)***
Electrovations Inc...330 274-3558
350 Harris Dr Aurora (44202) ***(G-878)***
Electrowarmth Products LLC...740 599-7222
513 Market St Danville (43014) ***(G-7963)***
Eleet Cryogenics Inc (PA)...330 874-4009
11132 Industrial Pkwy Nw Bolivar (44612) ***(G-1913)***
Elegant Embroidery Llc...440 878-0904
11053 Prospect Rd Strongsville (44149) ***(G-17741)***
Elektro Kopy, Columbus *Also called Instant Impressions Inc* ***(G-7030)***
Element Machinery LLC...855 447-7648
4801 Bennett Rd Toledo (43612) ***(G-18279)***
Element One Home Staging...740 972-4714
2502 Starford Dr Dublin (43016) ***(G-8913)***
Element14 US Holdings Inc (HQ)...330 523-4280
4180 Highlander Pkwy Richfield (44286) ***(G-16469)***
Elements LLC...937 663-5837
556 N Heck Hill Rd Saint Paris (43072) ***(G-16708)***
Elevated Industries LLC...937 608-3325
1835 Wlberforce Switch Rd Xenia (45385) ***(G-20769)***
Elevator Cncepts By Wurtec LLC...734 246-4700
6200 Brent Dr Toledo (43611) ***(G-18280)***
Elgin Fastener Group...440 325-4337
777 W Bagley Rd Berea (44017) ***(G-1605)***
Elgin Fastener Group LLC...440 717-7650
10147 Brecksville Rd Brecksville (44141) ***(G-2031)***
Elgin Fastener Group LLC (HQ)...812 689-8990
10217 Brecksville Rd # 101 Brecksville (44141) ***(G-2032)***
Elgin Fastener Group LLC...216 481-4400
1491 Chardon Rd Cleveland (44117) ***(G-5168)***
Eli Lilly and Company...937 855-3300
7440 Weaver Rd Germantown (45327) ***(G-10241)***
Eliason Corporation...800 828-3655
10021 Commerce Park Dr West Chester (45246) ***(G-19851)***
Eliokem Inc...330 734-1100
175 Ghent Rd Fairlawn (44333) ***(G-9604)***
Eliokem Materials and Concepts, Fairlawn *Also called Eliokem Inc* ***(G-9604)***
Elite Biomedical Solutions LLC...513 207-0602
756 Old State Route 74 C Cincinnati (45245) ***(G-3248)***
Elite Enclosure Company, Sidney *Also called Mk Trempe Corporation* ***(G-17055)***
Elite Fire Services LLC...614 586-4255
1520 Harmon Ave Ste 667 Columbus (43223) ***(G-6891)***
Elite Ftscom Inc...740 845-0987
1402 State Route 665 London (43140) ***(G-12059)***
Elite Mfg Solutions LLC...330 612-7434
7792 Capital Blvd Ste 6 Macedonia (44056) ***(G-12291)***
Elite Mill Service & Cnstr...513 422-4234
5757 Cottonrun Rd Trenton (45067) ***(G-18617)***
Elite Property Group LLC...216 356-7469
1036 N Pasadena Ave Elyria (44035) ***(G-9250)***
Elite Tactical Supply, Wadsworth *Also called 762mm Firearms LLC* ***(G-19217)***
Elitefts, London *Also called Elite Ftscom Inc* ***(G-12059)***
Elizabeths Closet...513 646-5025
8847 Dover Dr Maineville (45039) ***(G-12367)***
Elkay Plumbing Products Co...419 841-1820
7634 New West Rd Toledo (43617) ***(G-18281)***
Elken Co...513 459-7207
2905 Afton Valley Ct Maineville (45039) ***(G-12368)***
Elkhead Gas & Oil Co...740 763-3966
12163 Marne Rd Newark (43055) ***(G-14870)***
Elkins Earthworks LLC...330 725-7766
865 W Liberty St Ste 220 Medina (44256) ***(G-13254)***
Ellen L Ellsworth...440 352-8031
9930 Johnnycake Ridge Rd 4b Mentor (44060) ***(G-13438)***
Ellet Neon Sales & Service Inc...330 628-9907
3041 E Waterloo Rd Akron (44312) ***(G-150)***
Ellinger Monument Inc...740 385-3687
27841 Fairview Cmtry Rd Rockbridge (43149) ***(G-16536)***
Elliott Machine Works Inc...419 468-4709
1351 Freese Works Pl Galion (44833) ***(G-10137)***

Elliott Oren Products Inc 419 298-0015
113 Industrial Dr Edgerton (43517) ***(G-9172)***
Elliott Oren Products Inc (PA) 419 298-2306
128 W Vine St Edgerton (43517) ***(G-9173)***
Elliott Tool Technologies Ltd (PA) 937 253-6133
1760 Tuttle Ave Dayton (45403) ***(G-8182)***
Ellis & Watts Global Inds Inc 513 752-9000
4400 Glen Willow Lake Ln Batavia (45103) ***(G-1142)***
Ellis & Watts Intl LLC 513 752-9000
4400 Glen Willow Lake Ln Batavia (45103) ***(G-1143)***
Ellis Laundry & Linen Supply 330 339-4941
213 8th Street Ext Sw New Philadelphia (44663) ***(G-14767)***
Ellison Group Inc (PA) 513 770-4900
8118 Corp Way Ste 201 Mason (45040) ***(G-12861)***
Ellison Srfc Tech - Mexico LLC 513 770-4900
8093 Columbia Rd Ste 201 Mason (45040) ***(G-12862)***
Ellison Surface Tech - W LLC (HQ) 513 770-4900
8093 Columbia Rd Ste 201 Mason (45040) ***(G-12863)***
Ellison Surface Tech Inc (HQ) 513 770-4922
8118 Corp Way Ste 201 Mason (45040) ***(G-12864)***
Ellison Surfc Technologies-Tn, Mason *Also called Tennessee Coatings Inc* ***(G-12949)***
Ellison Technologies Inc 513 874-2736
5333 Muhlhauser Rd Hamilton (45011) ***(G-10553)***
Elloras Cave Publishing Inc 330 253-3521
1056 Home Ave Akron (44310) ***(G-151)***
Ellwood Engineered Castings Co 330 568-3000
7158 Hubbard Masury Rd Hubbard (44425) ***(G-11001)***
Ellwood Group Inc 216 862-6341
777 E 79th St Cleveland (44103) ***(G-5169)***
Elmer S Inc 614 225-4000
180 E Broad St Fl 4 Columbus (43215) ***(G-6892)***
Elmore Mfg Co, Elmore *Also called Calvin J Magsig* ***(G-9204)***
Elpro Services Inc 740 568-9900
210 Mill Creek Rd Marietta (45750) ***(G-12623)***
Elra Industries Inc 513 868-6228
550 S Erie Hwy Hamilton (45011) ***(G-10554)***
Elsaan Energy LLC 740 294-9399
26100 Township Road 52 Walhonding (43843) ***(G-19306)***
Elsass Fabricating Ltd 937 394-7169
11385 Amsterdam Rd Anna (45302) ***(G-589)***
Elsons International, Cleveland *Also called International Cont Systems LLC* ***(G-5468)***
Elster Perfection Corporation (HQ) 440 428-1171
436 N Eagle St Geneva (44041) ***(G-10218)***
Eltool Corporation 513 723-1772
1400 Park Ave E Mansfield (44905) ***(G-12436)***
Elwood Crankshaft Group, Cleveland *Also called Ellwood Group Inc* ***(G-5169)***
Ely Road Reel Company Ltd 330 683-1818
9081 Ely Rd Apple Creek (44606) ***(G-604)***
Elynx Holdings LLC (HQ) 513 612-5969
11500 Northlake Dr # 200 Cincinnati (45249) ***(G-3633)***
Elyria Concrete Step Company, Elyria *Also called E C S Corp* ***(G-9247)***
Elyria Copy Center Inc 440 323-4145
325 Lake Ave Elyria (44035) ***(G-9251)***
Elyria Manufacturing Corp (PA) 440 365-4171
145 Northrup St Elyria (44035) ***(G-9252)***
Elyria Metal Spinning Fabg Co 440 323-8068
7511 W River Rd S Elyria (44035) ***(G-9253)***
Elyria Pattern Co Inc 440 323-1526
6785 W River Rd S Elyria (44035) ***(G-9254)***
Elyria Plastic Products, Elyria *Also called P P E Inc* ***(G-9306)***
Elyria Plating Corporation 440 365-8300
118 Olive St Elyria (44035) ***(G-9255)***
Elyria Spring & Specialty Inc 440 323-5502
123 Elbe St Elyria (44035) ***(G-9256)***
Elytus Ltd 614 824-4985
601 S High St Columbus (43215) ***(G-6893)***
Em Es Be Company LLC 216 761-9500
246 E 131st St Ste 2 Cleveland (44108) ***(G-5170)***
Em Innovations Inc 614 853-1504
6106 Bausch Rd Galloway (43119) ***(G-10178)***
Em4 Inc 216 486-6100
676 Alpha Dr Highland Heights (44143) ***(G-10788)***
EMB Designs, Coldwater *Also called K Ventures Inc* ***(G-6415)***
Embedded Planet Inc 216 245-4180
4760 Richmond Rd Ste 400 Warrensville Heights (44128) ***(G-19467)***
Embedee LLC 419 678-7007
625 Cron St Coldwater (45828) ***(G-6407)***
Embroid ME 216 459-9250
4311 Ridge Rd Cleveland (44144) ***(G-5171)***
Embroidered ID Inc 440 974-8113
7845 Hidden Hollow Dr Mentor (44060) ***(G-13439)***
Embroidered Identity, Mentor *Also called Embroidered ID Inc* ***(G-13439)***
Embroidery Design Group LLC 614 798-8152
2564 Billingsley Rd Columbus (43235) ***(G-6894)***
Embroidme, Gahanna *Also called Cdds Inc* ***(G-10078)***
Embroidme 330 484-8484
3611 Cleveland Ave S Canton (44707) ***(G-2668)***
EMC Corporation 216 606-2000
6480 Rcksde Wds Blvd S # 330 Independence (44131) ***(G-11125)***
EMC Precision Machining, Elyria *Also called Elyria Manufacturing Corp* ***(G-9252)***
EMC Precision Machining II LLC (PA) 440 365-4171
145 Northrup St Elyria (44035) ***(G-9257)***
Emco Electric International 440 878-1199
19449 Progress Dr Strongsville (44149) ***(G-17742)***
Emco Usa LLC 740 588-1722
1000 Linden Ave Zanesville (43701) ***(G-21133)***
EMD Millipore Corporation 513 631-0445
2909 Highland Ave Norwood (45212) ***(G-15426)***
Emega Technologies LLC 740 407-3712
205 N 5th St Zanesville (43701) ***(G-21134)***
Emerald Hilton Davis, Cincinnati *Also called Emerald Performance Mtls LLC* ***(G-3634)***
Emerald Performance Mtls LLC 513 841-4000
2235 Langdon Farm Rd Cincinnati (45237) ***(G-3634)***
Emerald Performance Mtls LLC 330 374-2418
240 W Emerling Ave Akron (44301) ***(G-152)***
Emerald Polymer Additives LLC (HQ) 330 374-2424
240 W Emerling Ave Akron (44301) ***(G-153)***
Emerald Specialty Polymers LLC 330 374-2424
240 W Emerling Ave Akron (44301) ***(G-154)***
Emerald Transformer Ppm LLC 800 908-8800
1672 Highland Rd Twinsburg (44087) ***(G-18768)***
Emergency Products & RES Inc 330 673-5003
890 W Main St Kent (44240) ***(G-11319)***
Emerine Estates Inc 440 293-8199
5689 Loveland Rd Jefferson (44047) ***(G-11229)***
Emerson Climate Tech Inc (HQ) 937 498-3011
1675 Campbell Rd Sidney (45365) ***(G-17036)***
Emerson Climate Tech Inc 937 498-3011
756 Brooklyn Ave Sidney (45365) ***(G-17037)***
Emerson Climate Tech Inc 937 498-3587
1351 N Vandemark Rd Sidney (45365) ***(G-17038)***
Emerson Electric Co 513 731-2020
6000 Fernview Ave Cincinnati (45212) ***(G-3635)***
Emerson Electric Co 440 288-1122
1509 Iowa Ave Lorain (44052) ***(G-12089)***
Emerson Electric Co 440 248-9400
31100 Bainbridge Rd Solon (44139) ***(G-17136)***
Emerson Network Power 614 841-8054
3040 S 9th St Ironton (45638) ***(G-11164)***
Emerson Network Power System, Westerville *Also called Liebert Field Services Inc* ***(G-20007)***
Emerson Process Management 419 529-4311
2500 Park Ave W Ontario (44906) ***(G-15541)***
Emerson Process MGT Lllp 877 468-6384
8460 Orion Pl Ste 110 Columbus (43240) ***(G-6490)***
Emery Oleochemicals LLC (HQ) 513 762-2500
4900 Este Ave Cincinnati (45232) ***(G-3636)***
Emes Supply LLC 216 400-8025
35622 Vine St Willowick (44095) ***(G-20478)***
Emh Inc (PA) 330 220-8600
550 Crane Dr Valley City (44280) ***(G-19036)***
Emhart Glass Manufacturing Inc 567 336-7733
1899 N Wilkinson Way Perrysburg (43551) ***(G-15945)***
Emhart Glass Manufacturing Inc 567 336-8784
7401 Fremont Pike 6 Perrysburg (43551) ***(G-15946)***
EMI Corp (PA) 937 596-5511
801 W Pike St Jackson Center (45334) ***(G-11209)***
Emitted Energy Inc 513 752-9999
754 Cincinnati Batavia Pi Cincinnati (45245) ***(G-3249)***
Emmco, Akron *Also called Electro-Mechanical Mfg Co Inc* ***(G-149)***
Emmco Inc 216 429-2020
4540 E 71st St Cleveland (44105) ***(G-5172)***
Empire Bakery Commissary LLC (PA) 513 793-6241
11243 Cornell Park Dr Blue Ash (45242) ***(G-1764)***
Empire Brass Co 216 431-6565
5000 Superior Ave Cleveland (44103) ***(G-5173)***
Empire Die Casting Company, Macedonia *Also called American Light Metals LLC* ***(G-12277)***
Empire Diecasting, Macedonia *Also called SRS Die Casting Holdings LLC* ***(G-12330)***
Empire Iron Mining Partnership (PA) 216 694-5700
1100 Superior Ave E Fl 15 Cleveland (44114) ***(G-5174)***
Empire Packing Company LP 901 948-4788
4780 Alliance Dr Mason (45040) ***(G-12865)***
Empire Plow Company Inc (HQ) 216 641-2290
3140 E 65th St Cleveland (44127) ***(G-5175)***
Empire Power Systems Co 440 796-4401
6211 Shore Dr Madison (44057) ***(G-12349)***
Empire Systems Inc 440 653-9300
33683 Walker Rd Avon Lake (44012) ***(G-984)***
Empress Chili, Cincinnati *Also called Classic Recipe Chili Inc* ***(G-3525)***
Empyracom Inc 330 744-5570
6550 Seville Dr Ste A Canfield (44406) ***(G-2526)***
Emrick Machine & Tool 937 692-5901
211 S Sycamore St Arcanum (45304) ***(G-628)***
Emroid ME 614 789-1898
6065 Shreven Dr Westerville (43081) ***(G-20051)***
Ems/Hooptech (PA) 513 829-7768
9185 Le Saint Dr West Chester (45014) ***(G-19697)***

ALPHABETIC

Emt Inc...330 399-6939
1201 Vine Ave Ne Ste 2 Warren (44483) *(G-19399)*
Emt Trading Company LLC...888 352-8000
147 Bell St Chagrin Falls (44022) *(G-3019)*
Emta Inc...440 734-6464
28875 Lorain Rd North Olmsted (44070) *(G-15187)*
Emx Industries Inc...216 518-9888
4564 Johnston Pkwy Cleveland (44128) *(G-5176)*
En Garde Deer Defense LLC...440 334-7271
10292 Fitzwater Rd Brecksville (44141) *(G-2033)*
En-Hanced Products Inc...614 882-7400
229 E Broadway Ave Westerville (43081) *(G-20052)*
Enclosure Suppliers LLC...513 782-3900
12119 Champion Way Cincinnati (45241) *(G-3637)*
Encompass Automation &...419 873-0000
622 Eckel Rd Perrysburg (43551) *(G-15947)*
Encore Distributing Inc...513 948-1242
8060 Reading Rd Ste 6 Cincinnati (45237) *(G-3638)*
Encore Industries Inc (PA)...419 626-8000
319 Howard Dr Sandusky (44870) *(G-16807)*
Encore Plastics, Sandusky *Also called Encore Industries Inc (G-16807)*
Encore Plastics Corporation...740 432-1652
725 Water St Cambridge (43725) *(G-2436)*
Encore Plastics Corporation (HQ)...419 626-8000
319 Howard Dr Sandusky (44870) *(G-16808)*
Encore Precast LLC...513 726-5678
416 W Ritter Seven Mile (45062) *(G-16907)*
END Separation LLC...419 438-0879
12742 Road 191 Oakwood (45873) *(G-15470)*
Endoglobe, Oregon *Also called R-Med Inc (G-15565)*
Endura Plastics, Kirtland *Also called Stewart Acquisition LLC (G-11471)*
Endura Plastics Inc...440 951-4466
7955 Euclid Chardon Rd Kirtland (44094) *(G-11467)*
Endurance Manufacturing Inc...330 628-2600
213 Randolph Rd Mogadore (44260) *(G-14236)*
Enduro Rubber Company...330 296-9603
685 S Chestnut St Ravenna (44266) *(G-16379)*
Enerchem Incorporated...513 745-0580
8373 Squirrelridge Dr Cincinnati (45243) *(G-3639)*
Enerco Group Inc (PA)...216 916-3000
4560 W 160th St Cleveland (44135) *(G-5177)*
Enerco Technical Products Inc...216 916-3000
4560 W 160th St Cleveland (44135) *(G-5178)*
Enerfab Inc (PA)...513 641-0500
4955 Spring Grove Ave Cincinnati (45232) *(G-3640)*
Enerfab Inc...513 771-2300
11861 Mosteller Rd Cincinnati (45241) *(G-3641)*
Energizer Battery Mfg Inc...330 527-2191
10545 Freedom St Garrettsville (44231) *(G-10189)*
Energizer Manufacturing Inc...440 835-7866
25225 Detroit Rd Westlake (44145) *(G-20112)*
Energy Corportive, Coshocton *Also called Ngo Development Corporation (G-7743)*
Energy Developments Inc...440 774-6816
43550 Oberlin Elyria Rd Oberlin (44074) *(G-15494)*
Energy Focus Inc (PA)...440 715-1300
32000 Aurora Rd Ste B Solon (44139) *(G-17137)*
Energy Machine Inc...740 397-1155
100 Commerce Dr Mount Vernon (43050) *(G-14480)*
Energy Manufacturing Ltd...419 355-9304
1830 Old Oak Harbour Rd Fremont (43420) *(G-10012)*
Energy Storage Technologies...937 312-0114
7610 Mcewen Rd Dayton (45459) *(G-8183)*
Energy Technologies Inc...419 522-4444
219 Park Ave E Mansfield (44902) *(G-12437)*
Energy Transfer, Minerva *Also called Machine Dynamics & Engrg Inc (G-14190)*
Enersys...513 737-2268
9436 Meridian Way West Chester (45069) *(G-19698)*
Enervest Ltd...330 877-6747
125 State Route 43 Hartville (44632) *(G-10690)*
Engelhard Corp...440 322-3741
120 Pine St Elyria (44035) *(G-9258)*
Engels Machining LLC...419 485-1500
13299 State Route 107 Montpelier (43543) *(G-14308)*
Engine Machine Service Inc...330 505-1804
865 Summit Ave Unit 2 Niles (44446) *(G-15007)*
Engineered Conductive Mtl LLC...740 362-4444
132 Johnson Dr Delaware (43015) *(G-8676)*
Engineered Endeavors, Middlefield *Also called Eei Acquisition Corp (G-13797)*
Engineered Marble Inc...614 308-0041
4064 Fisher Rd Columbus (43228) *(G-6895)*
Engineered Material Handling, Valley City *Also called Emh Inc (G-19036)*
Engineered MBL Solutions Inc...513 724-0247
4350 Batavia Rd Batavia (45103) *(G-1144)*
Engineered Mfg & Eqp Co...937 642-7776
11611 Industrial Pkwy Marysville (43040) *(G-12781)*
Engineered Mtls Systems Inc...740 362-4444
100 Innovation Ct Delaware (43015) *(G-8677)*
Engineered Plastics Corp...330 376-7700
420 Kenmore Blvd Akron (44301) *(G-155)*
Engineered Polymer Systems LLC...216 255-2116
2600 Medina Rd Medina (44256) *(G-13255)*
Engineered Products, Twinsburg *Also called EPI of Cleveland Inc (G-18769)*
Engineered Profiles LLC...614 754-3700
2141 Fairwood Ave Columbus (43207) *(G-6896)*
Engineered Wire Products Inc...330 469-6958
3121 W Market St Warren (44485) *(G-19400)*
Engineered Wire Products Inc (HQ)...419 294-3817
1200 N Warpole St Upper Sandusky (43351) *(G-18953)*
Engineering Chain Div, Sandusky *Also called US Tsubaki Power Transm LLC (G-16860)*
Engineering Coatings LLC...419 485-0077
1826 Magda Dr Montpelier (43543) *(G-14309)*
Engineering Dept, Troy *Also called Hobart Corporation (G-18671)*
Engines Inc of Ohio...740 377-9874
101 Commerce Dr South Point (45680) *(G-17283)*
Enginetics, Huber Heights *Also called Mpe Aeroengines Inc (G-11022)*
Enginetics Aero Space, Huber Heights *Also called Enginetics Corporation (G-11017)*
Enginetics Aerospace, Eastlake *Also called Enginetics Corporation (G-9107)*
Enginetics Corporation...440 946-8833
34000 Melinz Pkwy Eastlake (44095) *(G-9107)*
Enginetics Corporation (HQ)...937 878-3800
7700 New Carlisle Pike Huber Heights (45424) *(G-11017)*
Enginred Plstic Components Inc...513 228-0298
315 S West St Lebanon (45036) *(G-11650)*
Engler Printing Co...419 332-2181
808 W State St Fremont (43420) *(G-10013)*
Engravers Gallery & Sign Co...330 830-1271
10 Lincoln Way E Massillon (44646) *(G-12980)*
Engstrom Manufacturing Inc...513 573-0010
4503b State Route 42 Mason (45040) *(G-12866)*
Enhanced Mfg Solutions LLC...440 476-1244
2890 Boston Mills Rd Brecksville (44141) *(G-2034)*
ENI USA R & M CO. INC., Medina *Also called Eni USA R & M Co Inc (G-13256)*
Eni USA R & M Co Inc...330 723-6457
740 S Progress Dr Medina (44256) *(G-13256)*
Enk Tenofour LLC...419 661-1465
2533 Tracy Rd Northwood (43619) *(G-15336)*
Enlarging Arts Inc...330 434-3433
2280 Tinkham Rd Akron (44313) *(G-156)*
Enlyton Ltd...614 888-9220
1216 Kinnear Rd Columbus (43212) *(G-6897)*
Ennis Inc...800 537-8648
4444 N Detroit Ave Toledo (43612) *(G-18282)*
Ennis Business Forms of Ohio, Coshocton *Also called Crabar/Gbf Inc (G-7730)*
Ennis-Leispic, Leipsic *Also called Crabar/Gbf Inc (G-11723)*
Ennovea LLC...814 838-6664
2030 Dividend Dr Columbus (43228) *(G-6898)*
Ennovea Medical LLC...855 997-2273
2030 Dividend Dr Columbus (43228) *(G-6899)*
Enpac LLC...440 975-0070
34355 Melinz Pkwy Eastlake (44095) *(G-9108)*
Enpress LLC...440 510-0108
34899 Curtis Blvd Eastlake (44095) *(G-9109)*
Enprotech Industrial Tech LLC (HQ)...216 883-3220
4259 E 49th St Cleveland (44125) *(G-5179)*
Enquirer Printing Co Inc...513 241-1956
7188 Main St Cincinnati (45244) *(G-3642)*
Enquirer Printing Company...513 241-1956
7188 Main St Cincinnati (45244) *(G-3643)*
Enrevo Pyro LLC...203 517-5002
6874 Strimbu Dr Brookfield (44403) *(G-2106)*
Ensign Product Company Inc...216 341-5911
3528 E 76th St Cleveland (44105) *(G-5180)*
Entec International Systems, Lakewood *Also called RAD-Con Inc (G-11534)*
Enterasys Networks Inc...330 245-0240
1093 Corsham Cir Akron (44312) *(G-157)*
Enterprise / Ameriseal Inc...937 284-3003
33 Walnut St Springfield (45505) *(G-17396)*
Enterprise C N C Inc...440 354-3868
9280 Pineneedle Dr Mentor (44060) *(G-13440)*
Enterprise Electric, Lakewood *Also called Computer Enterprise Inc (G-11515)*
Enterprise Plastics Inc...330 346-0496
1500 Enterprise Way Kent (44240) *(G-11320)*
Enterprise Tool & Die Company...216 351-1300
4940 Schaaf Ln Cleveland (44131) *(G-5181)*
Enterprise Welding & Fabg Inc...440 354-4128
6257 Heisley Rd Mentor (44060) *(G-13441)*
Entertrainment Junction...513 326-1100
2721 E Sharon Rd Cincinnati (45241) *(G-3644)*
Enting Water Conditioning Inc (PA)...937 294-5100
3211 Dryden Rd Frnt Frnt Moraine (45439) *(G-14350)*
Entratech Systems LLC (PA)...419 433-7683
202 Fox Rd Sandusky (44870) *(G-16809)*
Entrochem Inc...614 946-7602
1245 Kinnear Rd Columbus (43212) *(G-6900)*
Entrotech Inc...614 946-7602
1245 Kinnear Rd Columbus (43212) *(G-6901)*
Envelope 1 Inc (PA)...330 482-3900
41969 State Route 344 Columbiana (44408) *(G-6464)*

ALPHABETIC SECTION Ernst Enterprises Inc

Envelope Mart of Ohio Inc 440 365-8177
1540 Lowell St Elyria (44035) ***(G-9259)***
Envirnmntal Archtctral Signage, Findlay *Also called Bird Corporation* ***(G-9656)***
Envirnmntal Cmpliance Tech LLC 216 634-0400
13953 Progress Pkwy North Royalton (44133) ***(G-15271)***
Envirnmntal Prtctive Ctngs LLC 740 363-6180
5999 Houseman Rd Ostrander (43061) ***(G-15643)***
Enviro Polymers & Chemicals 937 427-1315
3045 Rodenbeck Dr Ste D Beavercreek (45432) ***(G-1314)***
Envirofab Inc 216 651-1767
7914 Lake Ave Cleveland (44102) ***(G-5182)***
Environment Chemical Corp 330 453-5200
2167 Crestwick Dr Uniontown (44685) ***(G-18918)***
Environmental Closure Systems 614 759-9186
536 Killin Ct Reynoldsburg (43068) ***(G-16437)***
Environmental Doctor, Dayton *Also called Indoor Envmtl Specialists Inc* ***(G-8262)***
Environmental Growth Chambers, Chagrin Falls *Also called Integrated Development & Mfg* ***(G-3021)***
Environmental Products Div, Sheffield Village *Also called Benko Products Inc* ***(G-16966)***
Environmental Sampling Sup Inc (HQ) 330 497-9396
4101 Shuffel St Nw North Canton (44720) ***(G-15080)***
Environmental Wall Systems 440 542-6600
77 Milford Dr Ste 283 Hudson (44236) ***(G-11043)***
Environmental Water Engrg, Bowling Green *Also called J & K Wade Ltd* ***(G-1977)***
Envirozyme LLC 800 232-2847
400 Van Camp Rd Bowling Green (43402) ***(G-1972)***
Envision Radio Mll 216 831-3761
3733 Park East Dr Ste 222 Beachwood (44122) ***(G-1236)***
Envoi Design Inc 513 651-4229
1332 Main St Frnt Cincinnati (45202) ***(G-3645)***
Enzyme Catalyzed Polymers LLC 330 310-1072
2295 W Market St Ste D Akron (44313) ***(G-158)***
Enzyme Industries of The U S A 740 929-4975
2090 James Pkwy Newark (43056) ***(G-14871)***
Eoi Inc 740 201-3300
8377 Green Meadows Dr N C Lewis Center (43035) ***(G-11760)***
Eos Technology Inc 216 281-2999
8525 Clinton Rd Cleveland (44144) ***(G-5183)***
Ep Bollinger LLC 513 941-1101
2664 Saint Georges Ct Cincinnati (45233) ***(G-3646)***
EP Ferris & Associates Inc 614 299-2999
880 King Ave Columbus (43212) ***(G-6902)***
Ep Technologies LLC 234 208-8967
520 S Main St Ste 2455 Akron (44311) ***(G-159)***
Epanel Plus Ltd 513 772-0888
271 Northland Blvd Cincinnati (45246) ***(G-3647)***
Epco, Germantown *Also called Thomas D Epperson* ***(G-10246)***
Epco Extrusion Painting Co 330 781-6100
4605 Lake Park Rd Youngstown (44512) ***(G-20899)***
Epcor Foundries, Cincinnati *Also called Seilkop Industries Inc* ***(G-4316)***
Epd Enterprises Inc 216 961-1200
9921 Clinton Rd Cleveland (44144) ***(G-5184)***
Epg Inc 330 995-5125
500 Lena Dr Aurora (44202) ***(G-879)***
Epg Inc (HQ) 330 995-9725
1780 Miller Pkwy Streetsboro (44241) ***(G-17673)***
Epi Global, Millbury *Also called Levison Enterprises LLC* ***(G-14051)***
EPI of Cleveland Inc 330 468-2872
2224 E Enterprise Pkwy Twinsburg (44087) ***(G-18769)***
Epic Steel, Cleveland *Also called E B P Inc* ***(G-5128)***
Epic Technologies LLC 513 683-5455
4240 Irwin Simpson Rd Mason (45040) ***(G-12867)***
Epik Ltd 419 768-2498
7196 Mount Gilead Rd Fredericktown (43019) ***(G-9968)***
Epix Tube Co Inc (PA) 937 529-4858
5800 Wolf Creek Pike Dayton (45426) ***(G-8184)***
Epluno LLC 800 249-5275
4501 Lyons Rd Miamisburg (45342) ***(G-13664)***
Epoxy Chemicals, Cleveland *Also called Euclid Chemical Company* ***(G-5193)***
Epoxy Systems Blstg Cating Inc 513 924-1800
5640 Morgan Rd Cleves (45002) ***(G-6361)***
Epr, Kent *Also called Emergency Products & RES Inc* ***(G-11319)***
Eprad Inc 419 666-3266
28271 Cedar Park Blvd # 1 Perrysburg (43551) ***(G-15948)***
Eprintworksplus 513 731-3797
5846 Hamilton Ave Cincinnati (45224) ***(G-3648)***
Epro Inc 419 426-5053
10890 E County Road 6 Bloomville (44818) ***(G-1714)***
Eps Specialties Ltd Inc 513 489-3676
7875 School Rd 77 Cincinnati (45249) ***(G-3649)***
Eq Technologies LLC 216 548-3684
11601 Wade Park Ave Cleveland (44106) ***(G-5185)***
Eqm Technologies & Energy Inc (PA) 513 825-7500
1800 Carillion Blvd Cincinnati (45240) ***(G-3650)***
Equinox Enterprises LLC 419 627-0022
1920 George St Sandusky (44870) ***(G-16810)***
Equipment Guys Inc 614 871-9220
185 Westgate Dr Newark (43055) ***(G-14872)***
Equipment Manufacturers Intl 216 651-6700
16151 Puritas Ave Cleveland (44135) ***(G-5186)***
Equipment Spcalists Dayton LLC 937 415-2151
5595 Webster St Dayton (45414) ***(G-8185)***
Equipsync LLC 216 367-6640
4755 W 150th St Cleveland (44135) ***(G-5187)***
Equistar, Fairport Harbor *Also called Lyondell Chemical Company* ***(G-9625)***
Equistar Chemicals LP 513 530-4000
11530 Northlake Dr Cincinnati (45249) ***(G-3651)***
Equity Oil & Gas Funds Inc (PA) 234 231-1004
4704 Barrow Ste 1 Stow (44224) ***(G-17582)***
Erath Veneer Corp Virginia 540 483-5223
2825 Hallie Ln B Granville (43023) ***(G-10330)***
Erd Specialty Graphics Inc 419 242-9545
3250 Monroe St Toledo (43606) ***(G-18283)***
Erdie Industries Inc 440 288-0166
1205 Colorado Ave Lorain (44052) ***(G-12090)***
Ergo Desktop LLC 567 890-3746
457 Grand Lake Rd Celina (45822) ***(G-2960)***
Ergocan, Toledo *Also called Mon-Say Corp* ***(G-18415)***
Eric Allshouse LLC 330 533-4258
9666 Lisbon Rd Canfield (44406) ***(G-2527)***
Eric Mondene 740 965-2842
4278 Harlem Rd Galena (43021) ***(G-10111)***
Eric Nickel 614 818-2488
5563 Covington Meadows Ct Westerville (43082) ***(G-19990)***
Erichar Inc 216 402-2628
2051 W Ridgewood Dr Cleveland (44134) ***(G-5188)***
Erickson-Huff Tool and Die 740 596-4036
61698 Locker Plant Rd Mc Arthur (45651) ***(G-13181)***
Erico Inc 440 248-0100
34600 Solon Rd Solon (44139) ***(G-17138)***
Erico Global Company 440 248-0100
31700 Solon Rd Solon (44139) ***(G-17139)***
Erico International Corp 440 248-0100
34600 Solon Rd Solon (44139) ***(G-17140)***
Ericson Manufacturing Co 440 951-8000
4323 Hamann Pkwy Willoughby (44094) ***(G-20315)***
Erie Black Top, Castalia *Also called Erie Materials Inc* ***(G-2938)***
Erie Ceramic Arts Company LLC 419 228-1145
1005 W Grand Ave Lima (45801) ***(G-11860)***
Erie Chinese Journal 216 324-2959
9810 Ravenna Rd Ste 1 Twinsburg (44087) ***(G-18770)***
Erie Copper Works Inc 330 725-5590
230 N State Rd Medina (44256) ***(G-13257)***
Erie Lake Plastic Inc 440 333-4880
19940 Ingersoll Dr Cleveland (44116) ***(G-5189)***
Erie Laser Ink LLC 419 346-0600
911 Jefferson Ave Toledo (43604) ***(G-18284)***
Erie Materials Inc 419 483-4648
9200 Portland Rd Castalia (44824) ***(G-2938)***
Erie Shore Industrial Svc Co 440 933-4301
683 Moore Rd Ste A Avon Lake (44012) ***(G-985)***
Erie Shore Machine Co Inc 216 692-1484
18602 Syracuse Ave Cleveland (44110) ***(G-5190)***
Erie Shores Mattress, Perrysburg *Also called J C Logan Barie LLC* ***(G-15968)***
Erie Steel Ltd 419 478-3743
5540 Jackman Rd Toledo (43613) ***(G-18285)***
Erieview Metal Treating Co 216 663-1780
4465 Johnston Pkwy Cleveland (44128) ***(G-5191)***
Erik V Lamb 330 962-1540
1638 S Clvland Mssllon Rd Copley (44321) ***(G-7684)***
Ernest Industries Inc 937 325-9851
1221 Groop Rd Springfield (45504) ***(G-17397)***
Ernest Trucking, Dayton *Also called Bellbrook Transport Inc* ***(G-8052)***
Ernie Green Industries Inc (PA) 614 219-1423
2030 Dividend Dr Columbus (43228) ***(G-6903)***
Ernst Concrete, Dayton *Also called Ernst Enterprises Inc* ***(G-8186)***
Ernst Custom Cabinets LLC 513 376-9554
4686 Paddock Rd Ste 99 Cincinnati (45229) ***(G-3652)***
Ernst Enterprises Inc 937 878-9378
5325 Medway Rd Fairborn (45324) ***(G-9458)***
Ernst Enterprises Inc (PA) 937 233-5555
3361 Successful Way Dayton (45414) ***(G-8186)***
Ernst Enterprises Inc 513 874-8300
4250 Columbia Rd Lebanon (45036) ***(G-11651)***
Ernst Enterprises Inc 937 848-6811
2181 Ferry Rd Bellbrook (45305) ***(G-1493)***
Ernst Enterprises Inc 614 443-9456
711 Stimmel Rd Columbus (43223) ***(G-6904)***
Ernst Enterprises Inc 937 866-9441
4710 Soldiers Home Rd Carrollton (44615) ***(G-2919)***
Ernst Enterprises Inc 614 308-0063
569 N Wilson Rd Columbus (43204) ***(G-6905)***
Ernst Enterprises Inc 419 222-2015
377 S Central Ave Lima (45804) ***(G-11861)***
Ernst Enterprises Inc 937 339-6249
805 S Union St Troy (45373) ***(G-18653)***
Ernst Enterprises Inc 513 422-3651
2504 S Main St Middletown (45044) ***(G-13905)***

ALPHABETIC

Ernst Flow Industries LLC ... 732 938-5641
16633 Foltz Pkwy Strongsville (44149) ***(G-17743)***
Ernst Metal Technologies LLC (HQ) ... 937 434-3133
2920 Kreitzer Rd Moraine (45439) ***(G-14351)***
Ernst Ready Mix Division, Lima *Also called Ernst Enterprises Inc* ***(G-11861)***
Ernst Sporting Gds Minster LLC ... 937 526-9822
32 E Main St Versailles (45380) ***(G-19179)***
Erockets LLC ... 616 460-2678
2790 Thunderhawk Ct Dayton (45414) ***(G-8187)***
Erodetech Inc ... 330 725-9181
4986 Gateway Dr Medina (44256) ***(G-13258)***
Ers Industries Inc ... 419 562-6010
811 Hopley Ave Bucyrus (44820) ***(G-2328)***
Ervan Guttman Co ... 513 791-0767
8208 Blue Ash Rd Rear Cincinnati (45236) ***(G-3653)***
Ervin Lee Logging ... 330 771-0039
8555 Stump Rd Minerva (44657) ***(G-14179)***
Ervin Yoder ... 330 359-5862
7700 County Rd 77 Mount Hope (44660) ***(G-14436)***
Es Manufacturing Inc ... 888 331-3443
55 Builders Dr Newark (43055) ***(G-14873)***
Es Sign and Design, Twinsburg *Also called E S Sign & Design LLC* ***(G-18766)***
Es Steiner Dairy, Baltic *Also called Tri State Dairy LLC* ***(G-1034)***
Es Steiner Dairy LLC ... 330 897-5555
115 S Mill St Baltic (43804) ***(G-1027)***
Es Thermal Inc ... 440 323-3291
300 Ceran Elyria (44035) ***(G-9260)***
ES&w, Lakewood *Also called Euclid Steel & Wire Inc* ***(G-11516)***
ESAB Group Incorporated ... 440 813-2506
3325 Middle Rd Ashtabula (44004) ***(G-774)***
Escher Division, Toledo *Also called Maumee Valley Fabricators Inc* ***(G-18404)***
Esco Group LLC ... 419 562-6015
260 E Beal Ave Bucyrus (44820) ***(G-2329)***
Esco Turbine Tech Cleveland ... 440 953-0053
34000 Lakeland Blvd Eastlake (44095) ***(G-9110)***
Escort Inc ... 513 870-8500
5440 W Chester Rd West Chester (45069) ***(G-19699)***
Esko-Graphics Inc (HQ) ... 937 454-1721
8535 Gander Creek Dr Miamisburg (45342) ***(G-13665)***
Eskoartwork, Miamisburg *Also called Esko-Graphics Inc* ***(G-13665)***
Esm Products Inc ... 937 492-4644
5445 Behm Rd Lot 5 Celina (45822) ***(G-2961)***
Esperia Holdings LLC (PA) ... 714 249-7888
8035 W Lake Winds Dr Oak Harbor (43449) ***(G-15444)***
Essco Aircraft, Barberton *Also called Stadvec Inc* ***(G-1107)***
Essence Maker ... 440 729-3894
12819 Opalocka Dr Chesterland (44026) ***(G-3157)***
Essential Earth Elements LLC ... 740 632-0682
808 Market St Toronto (43964) ***(G-18607)***
Essential Learning Products, Hilliard *Also called Teachers Publishing Group* ***(G-10868)***
Essential Pathways Ohio LLC ... 330 518-3091
726 E Boston Ave Youngstown (44502) ***(G-20900)***
Essential Sealing Products Inc (PA) ... 440 543-8108
10145 Queens Way Chagrin Falls (44023) ***(G-3045)***
Essential Wonders Inc ... 888 525-5282
2926 State Rd Ste 202 Cuyahoga Falls (44223) ***(G-7863)***
Essi Acoustical Products ... 216 251-7888
11750 Berea Rd Ste 1 Cleveland (44111) ***(G-5192)***
Essilor Laboratories Amer Inc ... 330 425-3003
9221 Ravenna Rd # 3 Twinsburg (44087) ***(G-18771)***
Essilor Laboratories Amer Inc ... 614 274-0840
3671 Interchange Rd Columbus (43204) ***(G-6906)***
Essity Prof Hygiene N Amer LLC ... 513 217-3644
700 Columbia Ave Middletown (45042) ***(G-13906)***
ESSITY PROFESSIONAL HYGIENE NORTH AMERICA LLC, Middletown *Also called Essity Prof Hygiene N Amer LLC* ***(G-13906)***
Est, Walton Hills *Also called Intigral Inc* ***(G-19311)***
Est Analytical, West Chester *Also called Pts Prfssnal Technical Svc Inc* ***(G-19771)***
Estabrook Assembly Svcs Inc ... 440 243-3350
700 W Bagley Rd Berea (44017) ***(G-1606)***
Estech Inc ... 805 895-1263
6217 Centre Park Dr West Chester (45069) ***(G-19700)***
Estee Lauder Companies Inc ... 310 994-9651
6279 Tri Ridge Blvd # 250 Loveland (45140) ***(G-12186)***
Estee Mold & Die Inc ... 937 224-7853
612 Linden Ave Dayton (45403) ***(G-8188)***
Esterle Mold & Machine Co Inc (PA) ... 330 686-1685
1539 Commerce Dr Stow (44224) ***(G-17583)***
Esterle Mold & Machine Co Inc ... 330 686-1685
1567 Commerce Dr Stow (44224) ***(G-17584)***
Esterline & Sons Mfg Co LLC ... 937 265-5278
6508 Old Clifton Rd Springfield (45502) ***(G-17398)***
Esterline Georgia US LLC (HQ) ... 937 372-7579
600 Bellbrook Ave Xenia (45385) ***(G-20770)***
Esterman Printing Services, Cincinnati *Also called Robert Esterman* ***(G-4277)***
Estreamz Inc ... 513 278-7836
1118 Groesbeck Rd Cincinnati (45224) ***(G-3654)***

ET&f Fastening Systems Inc ... 800 248-2376
29019 Solon Rd Solon (44139) ***(G-17141)***
Etc Enterprises LLC ... 417 262-6382
330 Sunderland Rd S Delphos (45833) ***(G-8743)***
Etc Lighthing and Plastic, Andover *Also called K D Lamp Company* ***(G-583)***
Etched In Stone ... 614 302-8924
5680 Horns Mill Rd Sugar Grove (43155) ***(G-17838)***
Etched Metal Company ... 440 248-0240
30200 Solon Indus Pkwy Solon (44139) ***(G-17142)***
Etching Concepts ... 419 691-9086
621 Bruns Dr Rossford (43460) ***(G-16585)***
Etherium Lighting LLC ... 310 800-8837
6969 Alum Creek Dr Columbus (43217) ***(G-6907)***
Ethicon Endo - Surgery, Blue Ash *Also called Ethicon Inc* ***(G-1766)***
Ethicon Endo-Surgery Inc (HQ) ... 513 337-7000
4545 Creek Rd Blue Ash (45242) ***(G-1765)***
Ethicon Inc ... 513 786-7000
10123 Alliance Rd Blue Ash (45242) ***(G-1766)***
Ethicon US LLC (HQ) ... 513 337-7000
4545 Creek Rd 3 Blue Ash (45242) ***(G-1767)***
Ethos Corp ... 513 242-6336
1045 Meta Dr Cincinnati (45237) ***(G-3655)***
Eti Tech LLC ... 937 832-4200
75 Holiday Dr Englewood (45322) ***(G-9358)***
Etko Machine Inc ... 330 745-4033
2796 Barber Rd Norton (44203) ***(G-15367)***
Etl Performance Products Inc ... 234 575-7226
1717 Pennsylvania Ave Salem (44460) ***(G-16735)***
Etna Products Incorporated (PA) ... 440 543-9845
16824 Park Circle Dr Chagrin Falls (44023) ***(G-3046)***
Ets Schaefer LLC ... 330 468-6600
8050 Highland Pointe Pkwy Macedonia (44056) ***(G-12292)***
Ets Schaefer LLC (HQ) ... 330 468-6600
3700 Park East Dr Ste 300 Beachwood (44122) ***(G-1237)***
Ets Solutions Usa LLC ... 330 666-8696
3900 Ira Rd Bath (44210) ***(G-1200)***
Euclid Chemical Company (HQ) ... 800 321-7628
19218 Redwood Rd Cleveland (44110) ***(G-5193)***
Euclid Chemical Company ... 216 292-5000
3735 Green Rd Beachwood (44122) ***(G-1238)***
Euclid Chemical Company ... 216 531-9222
19218 Redwood Rd Cleveland (44110) ***(G-5194)***
Euclid Coffee Co Inc ... 216 481-3330
17230 S Waterloo Rd Cleveland (44110) ***(G-5195)***
Euclid Design & Manufacturing ... 440 942-0066
38333 Willoughby Pkwy Willoughby (44094) ***(G-20316)***
Euclid Heat Treating Co ... 216 481-8444
1408 E 222nd St Euclid (44117) ***(G-9413)***
Euclid Jalousies Inc ... 440 953-1112
490 E 200th St Cleveland (44119) ***(G-5196)***
Euclid Media Group LLC (PA) ... 216 241-7550
737 Bolivar Rd Cleveland (44115) ***(G-5197)***
Euclid Precision Grinding Co ... 440 946-8888
35400 Lakeland Blvd Eastlake (44095) ***(G-9111)***
Euclid Products Co Inc ... 440 942-7310
38341 Western Pkwy Unit A Willoughby (44094) ***(G-20317)***
Euclid Refinishing Compnay Inc (PA) ... 440 275-3356
2937 Industrial Park Dr Austinburg (44010) ***(G-920)***
Euclid Spring Company Inc ... 440 943-3213
30006 Lakeland Blvd Wickliffe (44092) ***(G-20210)***
Euclid Steel & Wire Inc ... 216 731-6744
13000 Athens Ave Ste 101 Lakewood (44107) ***(G-11516)***
Euclid Universal Corporation ... 440 542-0960
1503 Exeter Rd Akron (44306) ***(G-160)***
Euclid Vidaro Mfg. Co., Kent *Also called Alsico Usa Inc* ***(G-11292)***
Euclid Welding Co Inc ... 216 289-0714
16500 Rockside Rd Maple Heights (44137) ***(G-12572)***
Eugene Stewart ... 937 898-1117
5671 Webster St Dayton (45414) ***(G-8189)***
Eureeka, Lima *Also called Accubuilt Inc* ***(G-11830)***
Eureka Screw Machine Co, Cleveland *Also called Eureka Screw Machine Pdts Co* ***(G-5198)***
Eureka Screw Machine Pdts Co ... 216 883-1715
3960 E 91st St Cleveland (44105) ***(G-5198)***
Eurocase Architectural Cabinet ... 330 674-0681
7488 State Route 241 Millersburg (44654) ***(G-14081)***
European Wax Center, Cincinnati *Also called Puracera 3 LLC* ***(G-4222)***
Eurostampa North America Inc (HQ) ... 513 821-2275
1440 Seymour Ave Cincinnati (45237) ***(G-3656)***
Eurotherm, North Olmsted *Also called Gc Controls Inc* ***(G-15191)***
Evan Ragouzis Co ... 513 242-5900
4 Standen Dr Hamilton (45015) ***(G-10555)***
Evandy Co Inc ... 216 518-9713
5450 Dunham Rd Cleveland (44137) ***(G-5199)***
Evanko Wm/Barringer Richd DDS ... 330 336-6693
185 Wadsworth Rd Ste K Wadsworth (44281) ***(G-19238)***
Evans Adhesive Corporation (HQ) ... 614 451-2665
925 Old Henderson Rd Columbus (43220) ***(G-6908)***
Evans Bakery Inc ... 937 228-4151
700 Troy St Dayton (45404) ***(G-8190)***

Evans Creative Group LLC...614 657-9439
11 E Gay St Columbus (43215) *(G-6909)*
Evans Industries Inc...330 453-1122
606 Walnut Ave Ne Canton (44702) *(G-2669)*
Even Heat Mfg Ltd...330 695-9351
8241 Tr 601 Fredericksburg (44627) *(G-9950)*
Evenflo Company Inc...937 773-3971
1801 W Main St Troy (45373) *(G-18654)*
Evenflo Company Inc (HQ)...937 415-3300
225 Byers Rd Miamisburg (45342) *(G-13666)*
Evening Leader, The, Saint Marys *Also called Horizon Ohio Publications Inc (G-16686)*
Ever Roll Specialties Co...937 964-1302
3988 Lawrenceville Dr Springfield (45504) *(G-17399)*
Eveready Printing Inc...216 587-2389
20700 Miles Pkwy Cleveland (44128) *(G-5200)*
Eveready Products Corporation...216 661-2755
1101 Belt Line Ave Cleveland (44109) *(G-5201)*
Everett Industries LLC...330 372-3700
3601 Larchmont Ave Ne Warren (44483) *(G-19401)*
Everflow Eastern Partners LP...330 537-3863
29093 Salem Alliance Rd Salem (44460) *(G-16736)*
Everflow Eastern Partners LP (PA)...330 533-2692
585 W Main St Canfield (44406) *(G-2528)*
Evergreen Packaging Inc...440 235-7200
7920 Mapleway Dr Olmsted Falls (44138) *(G-15530)*
Evergreen Plastics, Clyde *Also called Polychem Corporation (G-6392)*
Everhard Products Inc (PA)...330 453-7786
1016 9th St Sw Canton (44707) *(G-2670)*
Everly Concrete Products...740 635-1415
53620 Farmington Rd Bridgeport (43912) *(G-2074)*
Everris NA Inc (HQ)...614 726-7100
4950 Blazer Pkwy Dublin (43017) *(G-8914)*
Evers Enterprises Inc...513 541-7200
1210 Ellis St Cincinnati (45223) *(G-3657)*
Evers Welding Co Inc...513 385-7352
4849 Blue Rock Rd Cincinnati (45247) *(G-3658)*
Eversharpe Deburring Tool Co...513 988-6240
10 Baltimore Ave Trenton (45067) *(G-18618)*
Evertz Technology Service Usa...513 422-8400
2601 S Verity Pkwy # 102 Middletown (45044) *(G-13907)*
Everykey Inc...855 666-5006
12018 Mayfield Rd Cleveland (44106) *(G-5202)*
Everything In America...347 871-6872
4141 Stilmore Rd Cleveland (44121) *(G-5203)*
Everythings Image Inc...513 469-6727
9933 Alliance Rd Ste 2 Blue Ash (45242) *(G-1768)*
Evokes LLC...513 947-8433
8118 Corp Way Ste 212 Mason (45040) *(G-12868)*
Evolution Crtive Solutions Inc...513 681-4450
7107 Shona Dr Cincinnati (45237) *(G-3659)*
Evolution Crtive Solutions LLC...513 681-4450
7107 Shona Dr Ste 110 Cincinnati (45237) *(G-3660)*
Evolution Resources LLC...937 438-2390
480 Congress Park Dr Centerville (45459) *(G-3002)*
Evonik Corporation...513 554-8969
620 Shepherd Dr Cincinnati (45215) *(G-3661)*
Evoqua Water Technologies LLC...614 861-5440
1154 Hill Rd N Pickerington (43147) *(G-16047)*
Evp International LLC...513 761-7614
10179 Wayne Ave Cincinnati (45215) *(G-3662)*
Ew Publishing Company...440 979-0025
24181 Lorain Rd North Olmsted (44070) *(G-15188)*
EW Scripps Company (PA)...513 977-3000
312 Walnut St Ste 2800 Cincinnati (45202) *(G-3663)*
Ewart-Ohlson Machine Company...330 928-2171
1435 Main St Cuyahoga Falls (44221) *(G-7864)*
Ewh Spectrum LLC...937 593-8010
221 W Chillicothe Ave Bellefontaine (43311) *(G-1515)*
Exact Cutting Service Inc...440 546-1319
6892 W Snwvlle Rd Ste 108 Brecksville (44141) *(G-2035)*
Exact Equipment Corporation (HQ)...215 295-2000
1900 Polaris Pkwy Columbus (43240) *(G-6491)*
Exact Pipe Tools...330 922-8150
141 Broad Blvd Ste 201 Cuyahoga Falls (44221) *(G-7865)*
Exact-Tool & Die Inc...216 676-9140
5425 W 140th St Cleveland (44142) *(G-5204)*
Exair Corporation (PA)...513 671-3322
11510 Goldcoast Dr Cincinnati (45249) *(G-3664)*
Exal Corporation (PA)...330 744-9505
1 Performance Pl Youngstown (44502) *(G-20901)*
Excalibur Exploration Inc...330 966-7003
9720 Cleveland Ave Nw Greentown (44630) *(G-10358)*
Excel Fluid Group LLC...800 892-2009
15939 Industrial Pkwy Cleveland (44135) *(G-5205)*
Excel Loading Systems LLC...513 265-2936
675 N Deis Dr Ste 276 Blue Ash (45242) *(G-1769)*
Excel Machine & Tool Inc...419 678-3318
212 Butler St Coldwater (45828) *(G-6408)*
Excelitas Technologies Corp...866 539-5916
1100 Vanguard Blvd Miamisburg (45342) *(G-13667)*
Excellent Tool & Die Inc...216 671-9222
10921 Briggs Rd Cleveland (44111) *(G-5206)*
Excello Fabric Finishers Inc...740 622-7444
802 S 2nd St Coshocton (43812) *(G-7732)*
Excelsior Marking, Akron *Also called Mark-All Enterprises LLC (G-268)*
Excelsior Printing Co...740 927-2934
1014 Putnam Rd Sw Pataskala (43062) *(G-15831)*
Excelsior Solutions...937 848-2569
1742 River Ridge Dr Spring Valley (45370) *(G-17316)*
Exchange Printing Company...330 773-7842
969 Grant St Akron (44311) *(G-161)*
Exchange Signs...330 644-4552
3152 Manchester Rd Coventry Township (44319) *(G-7769)*
Exco Resources LLC...740 254-4061
3618 Fallen Timber Rd Se Tippecanoe (44699) *(G-18147)*
Executive Security Systems Inc...513 895-2783
332 Cherry St Cincinnati (45246) *(G-3665)*
Executive Wings Inc...440 254-1812
13550 Carter Rd Painesville (44077) *(G-15736)*
Exelon Energy Company...614 797-4377
470 Olde Worthington Rd # 375 Westerville (43082) *(G-19991)*
Exide Technologies...614 863-3866
861 Taylor Rd Unit G Gahanna (43230) *(G-10081)*
Exikon Industries LLC...216 485-2947
15215 Chatfield Ave Cleveland (44111) *(G-5207)*
Exito Manufacturing...937 291-9871
4120 Industrial Ln Ste B Beavercreek (45430) *(G-1355)*
Exochem Corporation (PA)...800 807-7464
2421 E 28th St Lorain (44055) *(G-12091)*
Exochem Corporation...330 426-9898
90 Kemple Dr East Palestine (44413) *(G-9079)*
Exodus Mold & Machine Inc...330 854-0282
960 Milan St N Canal Fulton (44614) *(G-2479)*
Exonanorna LLC...614 928-3512
1507 Chambers Rd Ste 301 Columbus (43212) *(G-6910)*
Exothermics Inc...603 821-5660
5040 Enterprise Blvd Toledo (43612) *(G-18286)*
Exotica Fresheners Co, Holland *Also called D & J Distributing & Mfg (G-10923)*
Exp Fuels Inc...419 382-7713
3070 Airport Hwy Toledo (43609) *(G-18287)*
Expansion Programs Intl...216 631-8544
11115 Edgewater Dr Cleveland (44102) *(G-5208)*
Experimental Machine, Brecksville *Also called Exact Cutting Service Inc (G-2035)*
Expert Crane Inc...216 451-9900
5755 Grant Ave Cleveland (44105) *(G-5209)*
Expert Gasket & Seal LLC...330 468-0066
9011 Freeway Dr Ste 5 Macedonia (44056) *(G-12293)*
Expert Regrind Service Inc...937 526-5662
20 S Pearl St Versailles (45380) *(G-19180)*
Expert TS...330 263-4588
221 Beall Ave Wooster (44691) *(G-20589)*
Expertise, Wooster *Also called Expert TS (G-20589)*
Explorys Inc...216 767-4700
1111 Superior Ave E # 2600 Cleveland (44114) *(G-5210)*
Exponentia US Inc...614 944-5103
424 Beecher Rd Ste A Columbus (43230) *(G-6911)*
Express Care...740 266-2501
197 Main St Steubenville (43953) *(G-17533)*
Express Energy Svcs Oper LP...740 337-4530
1515 Franklin St Toronto (43964) *(G-18608)*
Express Graphic Prtg & Design...513 728-3344
9695 Hamilton Ave Cincinnati (45231) *(G-3666)*
Express Lube, Massillon *Also called Melanda Inc (G-13025)*
Express Trading Pins...419 394-2550
105 Marbello Ct Saint Marys (45885) *(G-16684)*
Extendit Company...330 743-4343
601 Jones St Youngstown (44502) *(G-20902)*
Extol of Ohio Inc (PA)...419 668-2072
208 Republic St Norwalk (44857) *(G-15391)*
Extol of Ohio Inc...419 668-2072
208 Republic St Norwalk (44857) *(G-15392)*
Extra Seal, Newcomerstown *Also called 31 Inc (G-14968)*
Extreme Marine...330 963-7800
2057 E Aurora Rd Ste Lm Twinsburg (44087) *(G-18772)*
Extreme Trailers LLC...330 440-0026
317 E Broadway St Dover (44622) *(G-8825)*
Extruded Silicon Products Inc...330 733-0101
3300 Gilchrist Rd Mogadore (44260) *(G-14237)*
Extrudex Aluminum Inc...330 538-4444
12051 Mahoning Ave North Jackson (44451) *(G-15146)*
Extrudex Limited Partnership (PA)...440 352-7101
310 Figgie Dr Painesville (44077) *(G-15737)*
Exxcite Marketing Inc...513 271-4550
7949 Graves Rd Cincinnati (45243) *(G-3667)*
Exxcite Marketing Products, Cincinnati *Also called Exxcite Marketing Inc (G-3667)*
Exxon, Wadsworth *Also called Advanced Elastomer Systems LP (G-19221)*
Eye Lighting Intl N Amer Inc...440 350-7000
9150 Hendricks Rd Mentor (44060) *(G-13442)*

ALPHABETIC

(PA)=Parent Co (HQ)=Headquarters (DH)=Div Headquarters

Eye Surgery Center Ohio Inc (PA)....614 228-3937
262 Neil Ave Ste 320 Columbus (43215) ***(G-6912)***
Eye3data, West Chester *Also called MAI Media Group Llc* ***(G-19875)***
Eyescience Labs LLC....614 885-7100
493 Village Park Dr Powell (43065) ***(G-16321)***
EZ Brite Brands Inc....440 871-7817
806 Sharon Dr Ste C Cleveland (44145) ***(G-5211)***
EZ Grout Corporation Inc....740 962-2024
1833 N Riverview Rd Malta (43758) ***(G-12382)***
EZ Machine Inc....330 784-3363
2359 Triplett Blvd Akron (44312) ***(G-162)***
Ezg Manufacturing, Malta *Also called EZ Grout Corporation Inc* ***(G-12382)***
Ezg Manufacturing, Malta *Also called E Z Grout Corporation* ***(G-12381)***
Ezshred LLC (PA)....440 256-7640
7621 Euclid Chardon Rd Kirtland (44094) ***(G-11468)***
F & B Engraving Tls & Sup LLC....937 332-7994
308 W Statler Rd Piqua (45356) ***(G-16114)***
F & G Tool and Die Co (PA)....937 294-1405
3024 Dryden Rd Moraine (45439) ***(G-14352)***
F & G Tool and Die Co....937 746-3658
130 Industrial Dr Franklin (45005) ***(G-9880)***
F & J Grinding Inc....440 942-4430
36495 Reading Ave Ste 2 Willoughby (44094) ***(G-20318)***
F & J Manufacturing, Dayton *Also called Weber Jewelers Incorporated* ***(G-8587)***
F & K Concepts Inc....937 426-6843
264 Hiawatha Trl Springboro (45066) ***(G-17326)***
F & M Coal Company....740 544-5203
3925 County Road 56 Toronto (43964) ***(G-18609)***
F & W Auto Supply....419 445-3350
111 Depot St Archbold (43502) ***(G-644)***
F A S T, Cincinnati *Also called Field Apparatus Service & Tstg* ***(G-3685)***
F A Tech Corp....513 942-1920
9065 Sutton Pl West Chester (45011) ***(G-19701)***
F and W Publications Inc....513 531-2690
4700 E Galbraith Rd Cincinnati (45236) ***(G-3668)***
F C Brengman and Assoc LLC....740 756-4308
86 High St Carroll (43112) ***(G-2904)***
F H Bonn Co Inc....937 323-7024
4300 Gateway Blvd Springfield (45502) ***(G-17400)***
F I C, Akron *Also called Foundation Industries Inc* ***(G-176)***
F I T, Valley City *Also called Fuserashi Intl Tech Inc* ***(G-19038)***
F J Designs Inc....330 264-1377
2163 Great Trails Dr Wooster (44691) ***(G-20590)***
F L Distributors, Cleveland *Also called F L Enterprises* ***(G-5212)***
F L Enterprises....216 898-5551
4740 Briar Rd Cleveland (44135) ***(G-5212)***
F M Machine Co....330 773-8237
1114 Triplett Blvd Akron (44306) ***(G-163)***
F M Sheet Metal Fabrication....937 362-4357
13019 Shanley Rd Quincy (43343) ***(G-16355)***
F P C Printing Inc....937 743-8136
119 Art Ave Franklin (45005) ***(G-9881)***
F P M, Lancaster *Also called Fabricated Packaging Mtls Inc* ***(G-11570)***
F S, Batavia *Also called Freeman Schwabe Machinery LLC* ***(G-1148)***
F S A, Canton *Also called Foundation Systems Anchors Inc* ***(G-2675)***
F Squared Inc....419 752-7273
9 Sunset Dr Greenwich (44837) ***(G-10403)***
F W Dodge, Cincinnati *Also called Dodge Data & Analytics LLC* ***(G-3598)***
F&P America Mfg Inc (HQ)....937 339-0212
2101 Corporate Dr Troy (45373) ***(G-18655)***
F+w Media Inc (HQ)....513 531-2690
10151 Carver Rd Ste 200 Blue Ash (45242) ***(G-1770)***
F+w Media Inc....603 253-8148
10151 Carver Rd Ste 200 Blue Ash (45242) ***(G-1771)***
F3 Defense Systems LLC....419 982-2020
1601 S Dixie Hwy Lima (45804) ***(G-11862)***
FA Siberling Naturelm Mtro Prk, Akron *Also called County of Summit* ***(G-124)***
Fab Form, Mentor *Also called V K C Inc* ***(G-13621)***
Fab Shop Inc....513 860-1332
1520 Bender Ave Hamilton (45011) ***(G-10556)***
Fab Steel Co Inc....419 666-5100
240 W Andrus Rd Northwood (43619) ***(G-15337)***
Fab Tech Inc....330 926-9556
6500 W Snowville Rd Brecksville (44141) ***(G-2036)***
Fab-Tech Machine Inc....937 473-5572
2 W Spring St Covington (45318) ***(G-7785)***
Fab3 Group, Cleveland *Also called Duct Fabricators Inc* ***(G-5116)***
Fabacraft Inc....513 677-0500
201 Grandin Rd Maineville (45039) ***(G-12369)***
Fabacraft Co, Maineville *Also called Fabacraft Inc* ***(G-12369)***
Fabberge LLC....614 365-0056
8034 Corporate Blvd Ste B Plain City (43064) ***(G-16191)***
Fabco Inc (HQ)....419 421-4740
616 N Blanchard St Findlay (45840) ***(G-9682)***
Fabcon Companies LLC....614 875-8601
3400 Jackson Pike Grove City (43123) ***(G-10430)***
Fabcraft Inc....440 286-6700
344 Center St Chardon (44024) ***(G-3111)***
Fabohio Inc....740 922-4233
521 E 7th St Uhrichsville (44683) ***(G-18886)***
Fabric Square Shop....330 752-3044
2091 Liberty Rd Stow (44224) ***(G-17585)***
Fabricated Packaging Mtls Inc....740 681-1750
296 Quarry Rd Se Lancaster (43130) ***(G-11569)***
Fabricated Packaging Mtls Inc (PA)....740 654-3492
2109 Commerce St Lancaster (43130) ***(G-11570)***
Fabricating Solutions Inc....330 486-0998
7920 Bavaria Rd Twinsburg (44087) ***(G-18773)***
Fabrication Division, Maumee *Also called Andersons Inc* ***(G-13073)***
Fabrication Group LLC....216 251-1125
3453 W 140th St Cleveland (44111) ***(G-5213)***
Fabrication Shop Inc....419 435-7934
1395 Buckley St Fostoria (44830) ***(G-9837)***
Fabrication Unlimited LLC....937 492-3166
4343 State Route 29 E Sidney (45365) ***(G-17039)***
Fabriweld Corporation....419 668-3358
360 Eastpark Dr Norwalk (44857) ***(G-15393)***
Fabstar Tanks Inc....419 587-3639
20302 Road 48 Grover Hill (45849) ***(G-10518)***
Fabtech Machine, Covington *Also called Fab-Tech Machine Inc* ***(G-7785)***
Fabtech Ohio....440 942-0811
38311 Apollo Pkwy Ste 3 Willoughby (44094) ***(G-20319)***
Facemyer Forest Products Inc....740 992-7425
State Rte 7 Middleport (45760) ***(G-13872)***
Facemyer Lumber Co Inc (PA)....740 992-5965
31940 Bailey Run Rd Pomeroy (45769) ***(G-16240)***
Facial Sensation Products....937 293-2280
12 Beverly Pl Oakwood (45419) ***(G-15461)***
Facil North America Inc (HQ)....330 487-2500
2242 Pinnacle Pkwy # 100 Twinsburg (44087) ***(G-18774)***
Facilities Management Ex LLC....844 664-4400
800 Yard St Ste 115 Columbus (43212) ***(G-6913)***
Facts Inc....330 928-2332
2737 Front St Cuyahoga Falls (44221) ***(G-7866)***
Facultatieve Tech Americas Inc....330 723-6339
940 Lake Rd Medina (44256) ***(G-13259)***
FAg Bearings Corporation....513 398-1139
4035 N Ascot Pl Mason (45040) ***(G-12869)***
Fair Publishing, Norwalk *Also called Rotary Printing Company* ***(G-15414)***
Fair Publishing House Inc....419 668-3746
15 Schauss Ave Norwalk (44857) ***(G-15394)***
Fairborn Cement Company LLC....937 879-8393
3250 Linebaugh Rd Xenia (45385) ***(G-20771)***
Fairchild Printing Co....216 641-4192
5807 Fleet Ave Cleveland (44105) ***(G-5214)***
Faircosa LLC....216 577-9909
4296 E 167th St Cleveland (44128) ***(G-5215)***
Fairfield License Center Inc....513 829-6224
530 Wessel Dr Ste L Hamilton (45014) ***(G-10557)***
Fairfield Machined Products....740 756-4409
5594 Winchester Rd Carroll (43112) ***(G-2905)***
Fairfield Woodworks Ltd....740 689-1953
1612 E Main St Lancaster (43130) ***(G-11571)***
Fairmont Creamery LLC....216 357-2560
1720 Willey Ave Cleveland (44113) ***(G-5216)***
Fairmount Minerals, Independence *Also called Fairmount Santrol Inc* ***(G-11127)***
Fairmount Minerals LLC....269 926-9450
3 Summit Park Dr Ste 700 Independence (44131) ***(G-11126)***
Fairmount Santrol, Independence *Also called Fairmount Minerals LLC* ***(G-11126)***
Fairmount Santrol Inc (HQ)....440 214-3200
3 Summit Park Dr Ste 700 Independence (44131) ***(G-11127)***
Fairview Log Homes, Millersburg *Also called Al Yoder Construction Company* ***(G-14056)***
Fairway Carts Parts & More LLC....234 209-9008
6944 Wales Ave Nw North Canton (44720) ***(G-15081)***
Fairy Dust Ltd Inc....513 251-0065
3528 Warsaw Ave Cincinnati (45205) ***(G-3669)***
Faith Guiding Cafe LLC....614 245-8451
5195 Hampsted Vlg Ctr Way New Albany (43054) ***(G-14623)***
Faith Tool & Manufacturing....440 951-5934
36575 Reading Ave Willoughby (44094) ***(G-20320)***
Faithful Mold Polishing Ex....330 678-8006
4485 Crystal Pkwy Kent (44240) ***(G-11321)***
Falcon Fab and Finishes LLC....740 820-4458
3368 Piketon Rd Lucasville (45648) ***(G-12263)***
Falcon Fabrication, Lucasville *Also called Falcon Fab and Finishes LLC* ***(G-12263)***
Falcon Foundry Company....330 536-6221
96 6th St Lowellville (44436) ***(G-12250)***
Falcon Industries Inc (PA)....330 723-0099
180 Commerce Dr Medina (44256) ***(G-13260)***
Falcon Innovations Inc....216 252-0676
3316 W 118th St Cleveland (44111) ***(G-5217)***
Falcon Tool & Machine Inc....937 534-9999
2795 Lance Dr Moraine (45409) ***(G-14353)***
Fallen Oak Candles Inc....419 204-8162
917 Lilac St Celina (45822) ***(G-2962)***
Falls Filtration Tech Inc....330 928-4100
115 E Steels Corners Rd Stow (44224) ***(G-17586)***

Falls Metal Fabricators Ind 330 253-7181
  760 Home Ave Akron (44310) *(G-164)*
Falls Stamping & Welding Co (PA) 330 928-1191
  2900 Vincent St Cuyahoga Falls (44221) *(G-7867)*
Falls Stamping & Welding Co 216 771-9635
  1720 Fall St Cleveland (44113) *(G-5218)*
Falls Welding & Fabg Inc 330 253-3437
  608 Grant St Akron (44311) *(G-165)*
Falmer Screw Pdts & Mfg Inc 330 758-0593
  690 Mcclurg Rd Youngstown (44512) *(G-20903)*
Fame Tool & Mfg Co Inc 513 271-6387
  5340 Hetzell St Cincinnati (45227) *(G-3670)*
Family Fun, Louisville *Also called Bradley Enterprises Inc* *(G-12153)*
Family Medical Clinic & Laser 740 345-2767
  44 S 29th St Newark (43055) *(G-14874)*
Family Motor Coach Assn Inc (PA) 513 474-3622
  8291 Clough Pike Cincinnati (45244) *(G-3671)*
Family Motor Coaching Inc 513 474-3622
  8291 Clough Pike Cincinnati (45244) *(G-3672)*
Family Packaging Inc (PA) 937 325-4106
  504 W Euclid Ave Springfield (45506) *(G-17401)*
Family Values Magazine 419 566-1102
  3027 Fox Rd Mansfield (44904) *(G-12438)*
Family Woodworks LLC 740 289-4071
  286 Taylor Hollow Rd Piketon (45661) *(G-16070)*
Famous Industries Inc (HQ) 330 535-1811
  2620 Ridgewood Rd Ste 200 Akron (44313) *(G-166)*
Famous Industries Inc 740 685-2592
  356 W Main St Byesville (43723) *(G-2384)*
Famous Industries Inc 740 397-8842
  325 Commerce Dr Mount Vernon (43050) *(G-14481)*
Famous Kiss-N-Korn Shop, Cleveland *Also called Crawford Acquisition Corp* *(G-5038)*
Famous Realty Cleveland Inc 740 685-2533
  354 W Main St Byesville (43723) *(G-2385)*
Famous Supply, Byesville *Also called Famous Realty Cleveland Inc* *(G-2385)*
Fanci Forms, Upper Sandusky *Also called Mar-Metal Mfg Inc* *(G-18962)*
Fannie May Confections Inc 330 494-0833
  5353 Lauby Rd North Canton (44720) *(G-15082)*
Fantastic Sams Hair Care Salon 740 456-4296
  4490 Gallia St Portsmouth (45662) *(G-16282)*
Fantasy Candies, Cleveland *Also called Chocolate Pig Inc* *(G-4923)*
Fanuc America Corporation 513 754-2400
  7700 Innovation Way Mason (45040) *(G-12870)*
Fanz Stop 937 310-1436
  63 Bellbrook Plz Bellbrook (45305) *(G-1494)*
Far Associates, Macedonia *Also called Ralph Felice Inc* *(G-12322)*
Farah Jewelers Inc 614 438-6140
  1500 Polaris Pkwy # 2156 Columbus (43240) *(G-6492)*
Farasey Steel Fabricators Inc 216 641-1853
  4000 Iron Ct Cleveland (44115) *(G-5219)*
Farber Specialty Vehicles Inc 614 863-6470
  7052 Americana Pkwy Reynoldsburg (43068) *(G-16438)*
Faretec Inc 440 350-9510
  1610 W Jackson St Unit 6 Painesville (44077) *(G-15738)*
Fargo Toolite Incorporated 440 997-2442
  998 Stevenson Rd Ashtabula (44004) *(G-775)*
Farin Industries Inc 440 275-2755
  2844 Industrial Park Dr Austinburg (44010) *(G-921)*
Farm & Dairy, Salem *Also called Lyle Printing & Publishing Co* *(G-16756)*
Farm Products Division, Dayton *Also called Putnam Plastics Inc* *(G-8452)*
Farmed Materials Inc 513 680-4046
  300 E Business Way # 200 Cincinnati (45241) *(G-3673)*
Farmer Smiths Market, Dover *Also called Barkett Fruit Co Inc* *(G-8807)*
Farmers Commission Company (HQ) 419 294-2371
  520 W Wyandot Ave Upper Sandusky (43351) *(G-18954)*
Farmerstown Axle Co 330 897-2711
  2816 State Route 557 Baltic (43804) *(G-1028)*
Farmland News LLC 419 445-9456
  104 Depot St Archbold (43502) *(G-645)*
Farmside Wood 330 695-5100
  11833 Harrison Rd Apple Creek (44606) *(G-605)*
Farmstead Acres Woodworking 330 695-6492
  9106 County Road 201 Fredericksburg (44627) *(G-9951)*
Farquhar Heating and Air, Dayton *Also called BT Investments II Inc* *(G-8066)*
Farsight Management Inc 330 602-8338
  6790 Middle Run Rd Nw Dover (44622) *(G-8826)*
FAS Machinery LLC 216 472-3800
  9916 Broadway Ave Cleveland (44125) *(G-5220)*
Fasco Machine Products Inc 440 437-6242
  554 E Main St Orwell (44076) *(G-15630)*
Fast Fab and Laser LLC 937 224-3048
  401 Kiser St Dayton (45404) *(G-8191)*
Fastenal Company 419 629-3024
  575 W Monroe St New Bremen (45869) *(G-14654)*
Fastener Industries Inc 440 891-2031
  33 Lou Groza Blvd Berea (44017) *(G-1607)*
Fastener Industries Inc 216 267-2240
  5250 W 164th St Cleveland (44142) *(G-5221)*

Fastfeed Corp 330 948-7333
  124 S Academy St Lodi (44254) *(G-12010)*
Fastformingcom LLC 330 927-3277
  300 Morning Star Dr Rittman (44270) *(G-16520)*
Fastpatch Ltd 513 367-1838
  10774 Carolina Trace Rd Harrison (45030) *(G-10640)*
Fastsigns, Cleveland *Also called Ledge Hill Signs Limited* *(G-5570)*
Fastsigns, Lima *Also called ME Signs Inc* *(G-11898)*
Fastsigns, Youngstown *Also called Summco Inc* *(G-21041)*
Fastsigns, Akron *Also called Sterling Associates Inc* *(G-389)*
Fastsigns, Dayton *Also called Janeway Signs Inc* *(G-8279)*
Fastsigns, Cincinnati *Also called Stine Consulting Inc* *(G-4383)*
Fastsigns, Cleveland *Also called Bernard R Doyles Inc* *(G-4806)*
Fastsigns, Cincinnati *Also called Cline Signs LLC* *(G-3527)*
Fastsigns, Bedford *Also called Inner Products Sales Inc* *(G-1416)*
Fastsigns, Westerville *Also called Devries & Associates Inc* *(G-20048)*
Fastsigns, Dublin *Also called Limelght Graphic Solutions Inc* *(G-8942)*
Fastsigns, Westerville *Also called Devries & Associates Inc* *(G-20047)*
Fastsigns, Dayton *Also called R Weir Inc* *(G-8461)*
Fastsigns, Columbus *Also called Thatcher Enterprises Co Ltd* *(G-7523)*
Fastsigns, Fairfield *Also called Roderer Enterprises Inc* *(G-9559)*
Fastsigns, Blue Ash *Also called Auld Lang Signs Inc* *(G-1731)*
Fastsigns, North Olmsted *Also called Ew Publishing Company* *(G-15188)*
Fastsigns 513 489-8989
  12125 Montgomery Rd Cincinnati (45249) *(G-3674)*
Fastsigns 330 952-2626
  2736 Medina Rd Medina (44256) *(G-13261)*
Fastsigns Westerville 614 890-3821
  654 Brooksedge Blvd Ste A Westerville (43081) *(G-20053)*
Fate Industries Inc 440 327-1770
  36682 Sugar Ridge Rd North Ridgeville (44039) *(G-15223)*
Faull & Son LLC 330 652-4341
  515 Holford Ave Niles (44446) *(G-15008)*
Faurecia Automotive Holdings 419 727-5000
  543 Matzinger Rd Toledo (43612) *(G-18288)*
Faurecia Emissions Control Sys (HQ) 812 341-2000
  543 Matzinger Rd Toledo (43612) *(G-18289)*
Faurecia Exhaust Systems Inc 937 339-0551
  1255 Archer Dr Troy (45373) *(G-18656)*
Faurecia Exhaust Systems LLC 330 824-2807
  1849 Ellsworth Bailey Rd Warren (44481) *(G-19402)*
Faurecia Exhaust Systems Inc 937 743-0551
  2301 Commerce Center Dr Franklin (45005) *(G-9882)*
Faw Industries 216 651-9595
  14837 Detroit Ave 207 Cleveland (44107) *(G-5222)*
Fawcett Co Inc 330 659-4187
  3863 Congress Pkwy Richfield (44286) *(G-16470)*
Fawn Confectionery (PA) 513 574-9612
  4271 Harrison Ave Cincinnati (45211) *(G-3675)*
Fax Medley Group Inc 513 272-1932
  7754 Camargo Rd Ste 18 Cincinnati (45243) *(G-3676)*
Faxon Firearms LLC 513 674-2580
  11101 Adwood Dr Cincinnati (45240) *(G-3677)*
Faxon Machining Inc 513 851-4644
  11101 Adwood Dr Cincinnati (45240) *(G-3678)*
Fayette Industrial Coatings 419 636-1773
  533 Commerce Dr Ste A Bryan (43506) *(G-2280)*
FB Ins, Fostoria *Also called Fostoria Bushings Inc* *(G-9840)*
FBC Chemical Corporation 216 341-2000
  7301 Bessemer Ave Cleveland (44127) *(G-5223)*
Fbf Limited 513 541-6300
  2980 Spring Grove Ave Cincinnati (45225) *(G-3679)*
Fbg Bottling Group LLC 614 554-4646
  1523 Alum Creek Dr Columbus (43209) *(G-6914)*
Fbr Industries Inc 330 701-7425
  1336 Seaborn St Ste 7 Mineral Ridge (44440) *(G-14165)*
Fca LLC 309 644-2424
  6611 Hoke Rd Clayton (45315) *(G-4573)*
FCA US LLC 419 661-3500
  8000 Chrysler Dr Perrysburg (43551) *(G-15949)*
Fcbdd 614 475-6440
  2879 Johnstown Rd Columbus (43219) *(G-6915)*
Fci Inc 216 251-5200
  4661 Giles Rd Cleveland (44135) *(G-5224)*
Fcr Suspension, East Palestine *Also called Mx Spring Inc* *(G-9081)*
Fcs, Milford *Also called Fluid Conservation Systems* *(G-14008)*
Fcs Graphics Inc 216 771-5177
  2169 Saint Clair Ave Ne Cleveland (44114) *(G-5225)*
Fcx Performance Inc (HQ) 614 324-6050
  3000 E 14th Ave Columbus (43219) *(G-6916)*
Fd Machinery, Highland Heights *Also called Fd Rolls Corp* *(G-10789)*
Fd Rolls Corp 216 536-1433
  5405 Avion Park Dr Highland Heights (44143) *(G-10789)*
Fdc Machine Repair Inc 216 362-1082
  5585 Venture Dr Parma (44130) *(G-15818)*
Fdi Cabinetry LLC 513 353-4500
  5555 Dry Fork Rd Cleves (45002) *(G-6362)*

Fdi Enterprises 440 269-8282
  17700 Saint Clair Ave Cleveland (44110) *(G-5226)*
Feather Lite Innovations Inc 513 893-5483
  4805 Hmlton Middletown Rd Liberty Twp (45011) *(G-11825)*
Feather Lite Innovations Inc (PA) 937 743-9008
  650 Pleasant Valley Dr Springboro (45066) *(G-17327)*
Fechheimer Brothers Company (HQ) 513 793-5400
  4545 Malsbary Rd Blue Ash (45242) *(G-1772)*
Federal Barcode Label Systems 440 748-8060
  33438 Liberty Pkwy North Ridgeville (44039) *(G-15224)*
Federal Equipment Company (PA) 513 621-5260
  5298 River Rd Cincinnati (45233) *(G-3680)*
Federal Gear, Eastlake Also called *Tymoca Partners LLC* *(G-9137)*
Federal Heath Sign Company LLC 740 369-0999
  1020 Pittsburgh Dr Ste B Delaware (43015) *(G-8678)*
Federal Hose Manufacturing, Painesville Also called *First Francis Company Inc* *(G-15739)*
Federal Iron Works Company 330 482-5910
  42082 State Route 344 Columbiana (44408) *(G-6465)*
Federal Metal Co, Bedford Also called *Oakwood Industries Inc* *(G-1433)*
Federal Metal Company 440 232-8700
  7250 Division St Bedford (44146) *(G-1404)*
Federal Process Corporation (PA) 216 464-6440
  4520 Richmond Rd Cleveland (44128) *(G-5227)*
Federal-Mogul Powertrain LLC 740 432-2393
  6420 Glenn Hwy Cambridge (43725) *(G-2437)*
Federal-Mogul Powertrain LLC 419 238-1053
  150 Fisher Ave Van Wert (45891) *(G-19091)*
Federal-Mogul Valve Train Inte 330 460-5828
  1035 Western Dr Brunswick (44212) *(G-2203)*
Fedex Corporation 740 687-0334
  1612 N Memorial Dr Lancaster (43130) *(G-11572)*
Fedex Office & Print Svcs Inc 937 335-3816
  1886 W Main St Troy (45373) *(G-18657)*
Fedex Office & Print Svcs Inc 937 436-0677
  1189 Mmsburg Cntrville Rd Dayton (45459) *(G-8192)*
Fedex Office & Print Svcs Inc 330 376-6002
  322 E Exchange St Akron (44304) *(G-167)*
Fedex Office & Print Svcs Inc 614 621-1100
  180 N High St Columbus (43215) *(G-6917)*
Fedex Office & Print Svcs Inc 419 866-5464
  2306 S Reynolds Rd Toledo (43614) *(G-18290)*
Fedex Office & Print Svcs Inc 614 898-0000
  604 W Schrock Rd Westerville (43081) *(G-20054)*
Fedex Office & Print Svcs Inc 614 575-0800
  2668 Brice Rd Reynoldsburg (43068) *(G-16439)*
Fedex Office & Print Svcs Inc 216 573-1511
  6901 Rockside Rd Cleveland (44131) *(G-5228)*
Feedall Inc 440 942-8100
  38379 Pelton Rd Willoughby (44094) *(G-20321)*
Feikert Concrete, Millersburg Also called *Feikert Sand & Gravel Co Inc* *(G-14082)*
Feikert Sand & Gravel Co Inc 330 674-0038
  6971 County Road 189 Millersburg (44654) *(G-14082)*
Feilhauers Machine Shop Inc (PA) 513 202-0545
  421 Industrial Dr Harrison (45030) *(G-10641)*
Feinblanking Limited Inc 513 860-2100
  9461 Le Saint Dr West Chester (45014) *(G-19702)*
Feiner Pattern Works Inc 513 851-9800
  11335 Sebring Dr Cincinnati (45240) *(G-3681)*
Feinkost Ingredient Co U S A 330 948-3006
  103 Billman St Lodi (44254) *(G-12011)*
Feinkost Ingredients, Lodi Also called *Feinkost Ingredient Co U S A* *(G-12011)*
Feintool Cincinnati Inc (HQ) 513 247-0110
  11280 Cornell Park Dr Blue Ash (45242) *(G-1773)*
Feintool US Operations Inc (HQ) 513 247-4061
  11280 Cornell Park Dr Blue Ash (45242) *(G-1774)*
Feld Printing Co 513 271-6806
  6806 Main St Cincinnati (45244) *(G-3682)*
Felicity Plastics Machinery 513 876-7003
  892 Neville Penn Schoolho Felicity (45120) *(G-9643)*
Feller Tool Co Inc 440 324-6277
  7405 Industrial Pkwy Dr Lorain (44053) *(G-12092)*
Fellow's, Willoughby Also called *Fionas Fineries* *(G-20322)*
Femc, Bedford Heights Also called *Food Equipment Mfg Corp* *(G-1470)*
Fence One Inc 216 441-2600
  11111 Broadway Ave Cleveland (44125) *(G-5229)*
Fenix LLC (HQ) 419 739-3400
  820 Willipie St Wapakoneta (45895) *(G-19328)*
Fenix Fabrication Inc 330 745-8731
  2689 Wingate Ave Akron (44314) *(G-168)*
Fenix Magnetics Inc 440 455-1142
  909 Canterbury Rd Ste K Westlake (44145) *(G-20113)*
Fenner Dunlop (toledo) LLC 419 531-5300
  146 S Westwood Ave Toledo (43607) *(G-18291)*
Fenner Dunlop Port Clinton Inc 419 635-2191
  5225 W Lakeshore Dr Port Clinton (43452) *(G-16247)*
Fenton Bros Electric Co 330 343-0093
  235 Ray Ave Ne New Philadelphia (44663) *(G-14768)*
Fenton Manufacturing Inc 440 969-1128
  6600 Depot Rd Ashtabula (44004) *(G-776)*

Fenton's Festival of Lights, New Philadelphia Also called *Fenton Bros Electric Co* *(G-14768)*
Fenwick Frame Shppe Art Gllery, Toledo Also called *Fenwick Gallery of Fine Arts* *(G-18292)*
Fenwick Gallery of Fine Arts (PA) 419 475-1651
  3433 W Alexis Rd Frnt Toledo (43623) *(G-18292)*
Ferco Tech LLC 937 746-6696
  291 Conover Dr Franklin (45005) *(G-9883)*
Ferguson Fire Fabrication Inc 614 299-2070
  1640 Clara St Columbus (43211) *(G-6918)*
Ferguson Tools Inc 419 298-2327
  103 Industrial Dr Edgerton (43517) *(G-9174)*
Fergusons Cut Glass Works 419 734-0808
  5890 East Harbor Rd Marblehead (43440) *(G-12585)*
Fergusons Finishing Inc 419 241-9123
  126 N Ontario St Toledo (43604) *(G-18293)*
Fernandes Enterprises LLC (PA) 937 890-6444
  2801 Ontario Ave Dayton (45414) *(G-8193)*
Ferralloy Inc 440 250-1900
  28001 Ranney Pkwy Cleveland (44145) *(G-5230)*
Ferrante Wine Farm Inc 440 466-8466
  558 Rte 307 Geneva (44041) *(G-10219)*
Ferriot Inc 330 786-3000
  1000 Arlington Cir Akron (44306) *(G-169)*
Ferro Corporation 216 577-7144
  7050 Krick Rd Bedford (44146) *(G-1405)*
Ferro Corporation (PA) 216 875-5600
  6060 Parkland Blvd # 250 Mayfield Heights (44124) *(G-13163)*
Ferro Corporation 216 875-6178
  4150 E 56th St Ste 1 Cleveland (44105) *(G-5231)*
Ferro Corporation 216 875-5600
  6060 Parkland Blvd # 250 Cleveland (44124) *(G-5232)*
Ferro Corporation 330 682-8015
  1560 N Main St Orrville (44667) *(G-15590)*
Ferro International Svcs Inc 216 875-5600
  6060 Parkland Blvd # 250 Mayfield Heights (44124) *(G-13164)*
Ferrotherm Corporation 216 883-9350
  4758 Warner Rd Cleveland (44125) *(G-5233)*
Ferrous Processing and Trading, Cleveland Also called *Fpt Cleveland LLC* *(G-5270)*
Ferrum Industries Inc (HQ) 440 519-1768
  1831 Highland Rd Twinsburg (44087) *(G-18775)*
Ferry & Quintax, Stow Also called *Ferry Industries Inc* *(G-17587)*
Ferry Cap & Set Screw Company (HQ) 216 649-7400
  13300 Bramley Ave Lakewood (44107) *(G-11517)*
Ferry Industries Inc (PA) 330 920-9200
  4445 Allen Rd Ste A Stow (44224) *(G-17587)*
Fertility Solutions Inc 216 491-0030
  11811 Shaker Blvd Ste 330 Cleveland (44120) *(G-5234)*
Fes Incorporated, Cincinnati Also called *Fes-Ohio Inc* *(G-3683)*
Fes-Ohio Inc 513 772-8566
  4030 Mt Carml Tbsc Rd # 227 Cincinnati (45255) *(G-3683)*
Feslers Refinishing 740 622-4849
  315 Main St Coshocton (43812) *(G-7733)*
Fetzer Machining Co Inc 937 962-4019
  5192 Pyrmont Rd Lewisburg (45338) *(G-11791)*
Few Atmtive GL Applcations Inc 234 249-1880
  1660 Enterprise Pkwy Wooster (44691) *(G-20591)*
Fft Sidney LLC 937 492-2709
  1630 Ferguson Ct Sidney (45365) *(G-17040)*
Fgb International LLC (PA) 440 359-0000
  7670 First Pl Cleveland (44146) *(G-5235)*
Fgm Media Inc 440 376-0487
  13981 Stoney Creek Dr North Royalton (44133) *(G-15272)*
Fiba Technologies Inc 330 602-7300
  3211 Brightwood Rd Midvale (44653) *(G-13977)*
Fiber -Tech Industries Inc 740 335-9400
  2000 Kenskill Ave Wshngtn CT Hs (43160) *(G-20725)*
Fiber Sales & Development, Urbana Also called *J Rettenmaier USA LP* *(G-18998)*
Fiber Systems, Dayton Also called *Industrial Fiberglass Spc Inc* *(G-8263)*
Fibercorr Mills LLC 330 837-5151
  670 17th St Nw Massillon (44647) *(G-12981)*
Fiberglass Engineering Co, Cleveland Also called *Hanlon Industries Inc* *(G-5371)*
Fiberglass Link Inc 216 531-5515
  18607 Saint Clair Ave Cleveland (44110) *(G-5236)*
Fiberglass Technology Inds Inc 740 335-9400
  2000 Kenskill Ave Wshngtn CT Hs (43160) *(G-20726)*
Fibertech Networks 614 436-3565
  720 Lakeview Plaza Blvd Worthington (43085) *(G-20685)*
Fibreboard Corporation (HQ) 419 248-8000
  1 Owens Corning Pkwy Toledo (43659) *(G-18294)*
Fibretuff Med Biopolymers LLC 419 346-8728
  238 W 7th St Perrysburg (43551) *(G-15950)*
Fidelity Orthopedic Inc 937 228-0682
  8514 N Main St Dayton (45415) *(G-8194)*
Fidelux Lighting LLC 404 941-4182
  8415 Pulsar Pl Ste 300 Columbus (43240) *(G-6493)*
Fidelux Lighting LLC 614 839-0250
  3000 Corp Exchange Dr # 600 Columbus (43231) *(G-6919)*
Fiedeldey Stl Fabricators Inc 513 353-3300
  8487 E Miami River Rd Cincinnati (45247) *(G-3684)*

Field Apparatus Service & Tstg 513 353-9399
4040 Rev Dr Cincinnati (45232) ***(G-3685)***
Field Aviation Inc (PA) 513 792-2282
8044 Montgomery Rd # 400 Cincinnati (45236) ***(G-3686)***
Field Dailies LLC 859 379-2120
323 W 5th St Apt 3 Cincinnati (45202) ***(G-3687)***
Field Gymmy Inc 419 538-6511
138-143 S Main St Glandorf (45848) ***(G-10269)***
Field Stone Inc 937 898-3236
2750 Us Route 40 Tipp City (45371) ***(G-18112)***
Fields Associates Inc 513 426-8652
2134 Hatmaker St Ste 3 Cincinnati (45204) ***(G-3688)***
Fifth Avenue Fret Shop LLC 614 481-8300
1597 W 5th Ave Columbus (43212) ***(G-6920)***
Fifth Avenue Lumber Co 614 833-6655
5200 Winchester Pike Canal Winchester (43110) ***(G-2503)***
Fifty West Brewing Company 513 834-8789
7668 Wooster Pike Cincinnati (45227) ***(G-3689)***
Fifty West Brewing,, Cincinnati *Also called Fifty West Brewing Company* ***(G-3689)***
Fig- Games, Mason *Also called Fun-In-Games Inc* ***(G-12874)***
Figleaf Brewing Company, Middletown *Also called Unbridled Brewing Company LLC* ***(G-13961)***
Figley Stamping Company, Defiance *Also called Marc V Concepts Inc* ***(G-8635)***
Filament LLC 614 732-0754
1507 Chambers Rd Fl 1 Columbus (43212) ***(G-6921)***
File 13 Inc 937 642-4855
232 N Main St Ste K Marysville (43040) ***(G-12782)***
File Sharpening Company Inc 937 376-8268
360 W Church St Xenia (45385) ***(G-20772)***
Filia 330 322-1200
560 Rockglen Dr Wadsworth (44281) ***(G-19239)***
Fillous & Ruppel Inc 216 431-0470
7411 Cedar Ave Cleveland (44103) ***(G-5237)***
Filmco, Aurora *Also called Kapstone Container Corporation* ***(G-886)***
Filmtec Inc 419 435-1819
1120 Sandusky St Fostoria (44830) ***(G-9838)***
Filnor Inc (PA) 330 821-8731
227 N Freedom Ave Alliance (44601) ***(G-465)***
Filnor Inc 330 829-3180
181 N Arch Ave Alliance (44601) ***(G-466)***
Filnor Inc 330 821-7667
227 N Freedom Ave Alliance (44601) ***(G-467)***
Filter Factory-Ttn Inc 440 963-2034
3409 Liberty Ave Ste 100 Vermilion (44089) ***(G-19159)***
Filters.com, Hilliard *Also called Barney Corporation Inc* ***(G-10810)***
Fimm USA Inc 253 243-1522
5454 Alkire Rd Columbus (43228) ***(G-6922)***
Fin Feather Fur 330 493-8300
4080 Belden Village St Nw Canton (44718) ***(G-2671)***
Fin Pan Inc (PA) 513 870-9200
3255 Symmes Rd Hamilton (45015) ***(G-10558)***
Fin Tube Products Inc 330 334-3736
188 S Lyman St Ste 100 Wadsworth (44281) ***(G-19240)***
Final Finish Corp 440 439-3303
596 Highland Rd E Macedonia (44056) ***(G-12294)***
Final Machine 330 966-1744
8397 Cleveland Ave Nw Canton (44720) ***(G-2672)***
Final Touch Metal Fabricating 216 348-1750
2290 Scranton Rd Cleveland (44113) ***(G-5238)***
Finastra USA Corporation 937 435-2335
8555 Gander Creek Dr Miamisburg (45342) ***(G-13668)***
Findaway World LLC 440 893-0808
31999 Aurora Rd Solon (44139) ***(G-17143)***
Findlay American Prosthetic & 419 424-1622
12474 County Road 99 Findlay (45840) ***(G-9683)***
Findlay Division, Findlay *Also called Shelly Company* ***(G-9753)***
Findlay Machine & Tool Inc 419 434-3100
2000 Industrial Dr Findlay (45840) ***(G-9684)***
Findlay Pallet Inc 419 423-0511
300 Bell Ave Findlay (45840) ***(G-9685)***
Findlay Pallett Inc 419 423-0511
102 Crystal Ave Findlay (45840) ***(G-9686)***
Findlay Party Mart, Findlay *Also called Ottawa Oil Co Inc* ***(G-9737)***
Findlay Products Corporation 419 423-3324
2045 Industrial Dr Findlay (45840) ***(G-9687)***
Findlay Terminal, Findlay *Also called Michigan Sugar Company* ***(G-9724)***
Fine Line Embroidery Company 330 788-9070
4660 Lake Park Rd Youngstown (44512) ***(G-20904)***
Fine Line Embroidery Company (PA) 440 331-7030
20525 Detroit Rd Ste 9 Rocky River (44116) ***(G-16547)***
Fine Line Graphics Inc 330 920-6096
1972 Akron Peninsula Rd Akron (44313) ***(G-170)***
Fine Line Graphics Corp (PA) 614 486-0276
1481 Goodale Blvd Columbus (43212) ***(G-6923)***
Fine Lines, Wadsworth *Also called Quality Reproductions Inc* ***(G-19269)***
Fine Lines Laser Engraving 419 337-6313
12825 County Road 14 Wauseon (43567) ***(G-19515)***
Fine Points Inc 216 229-6644
12620 Larchmere Blvd Cleveland (44120) ***(G-5239)***
Fine Print LLC 419 702-7087
508 Oak Ave Lakeside Marblehead (43440) ***(G-11502)***
Fine Wood Design Inc 440 327-0751
35535 Center Ridge Rd North Ridgeville (44039) ***(G-15225)***
Fineline Imprints Inc 740 453-1083
516 State St Zanesville (43701) ***(G-21135)***
Finelli Architectural Iron Co, Cleveland *Also called Finelli Ornamental Iron Co* ***(G-5240)***
Finelli Ornamental Iron Co 440 248-0050
30815 Solon Rd Cleveland (44139) ***(G-5240)***
Finish Line Binderies, Cleveland *Also called Bindtech LLC* ***(G-4815)***
Finishers Inc 937 773-3177
1718 Commerce Dr Piqua (45356) ***(G-16115)***
Finishing Machine Inc 419 491-0197
707 Lost Lakes Dr Holland (43528) ***(G-10931)***
Finishing Touch 440 263-9264
22084 Lorain Rd Cleveland (44126) ***(G-5241)***
Finishmaster Inc 614 228-4328
212 N Grant Ave Columbus (43215) ***(G-6924)***
Finite Fibers, Akron *Also called Dowco LLC* ***(G-145)***
Fink Meat Company Inc 937 390-2750
2475 Troy Rd Springfield (45504) ***(G-17402)***
Finn Graphics Inc 513 941-6161
220 Stille Dr Cincinnati (45233) ***(G-3690)***
Fiomet LLC 513 519-7622
2717 Erie Ave Cincinnati (45208) ***(G-3691)***
Fionas Fineries 440 796-7426
9077 Billings Rd Willoughby (44094) ***(G-20322)***
Fire Ball Press 614 280-0100
27 E 5th Ave Columbus (43201) ***(G-6925)***
Fire Fab Corporation 330 759-9834
999 Trumbull Ave Girard (44420) ***(G-10257)***
Fire Foe Corp 330 759-9834
999 Trumbull Ave Girard (44420) ***(G-10258)***
Fire From Ice Ventures LLC 419 944-6705
30333 Emerald Valley Pkwy Solon (44139) ***(G-17144)***
Fire Pit Gallery, The, Bristolville *Also called Strutt Products LLC* ***(G-2084)***
Fire Safety Services Inc 937 686-2000
6228 Township Road 95 Huntsville (43324) ***(G-11086)***
Fire Tetrahedron Journal 567 220-6477
3110 E County Road 50 C Tiffin (44883) ***(G-18060)***
Fire-Dex LLC 330 723-0000
780 S Progress Dr Medina (44256) ***(G-13262)***
Fire-End & Croker Corp 513 870-0517
4690 Interstate Dr Ste P West Chester (45246) ***(G-19852)***
Firehouse Sign Co Inc 216 267-5300
5241 W 161st St Brookpark (44142) ***(G-2146)***
Firehouse Sub, Findlay *Also called Trixies Pickles Inc* ***(G-9771)***
Firelands Farmer, The, New London *Also called Sdg News Group Inc* ***(G-14737)***
Firelands Fas-Print LLC 419 668-3045
59 Benedict Ave Norwalk (44857) ***(G-15395)***
Firelands Manufacturing LLC 419 687-8237
500 Industrial Park Dr Plymouth (44865) ***(G-16231)***
Firelands Winery 419 625-5474
917 Bardshar Rd Sandusky (44870) ***(G-16811)***
Fireline Inc 330 259-0647
8560 Foxwood Ct Youngstown (44514) ***(G-20905)***
Fireline Inc (PA) 330 743-1164
300 Andrews Ave Youngstown (44505) ***(G-20906)***
Fireline Tcon, Youngstown *Also called Fireline Inc* ***(G-20906)***
Firestone Laser and Mfg LLC 330 337-9551
949 S Broadway Ave Salem (44460) ***(G-16737)***
Firestone Polymers LLC (HQ) 330 379-7000
381 W Wilbeth Rd Akron (44301) ***(G-171)***
Firovac, Apple Creek *Also called Reberland Equipment Inc* ***(G-618)***
First Catholc Slovak Union U S (PA) 216 642-9406
6611 Rockside Rd Cleveland (44131) ***(G-5242)***
First Choice Packaging Inc (PA) 419 333-4100
1501 W State St Fremont (43420) ***(G-10014)***
First Choice Packg Solutions, Fremont *Also called First Choice Packaging Inc* ***(G-10014)***
First Filter LLC 419 666-5260
620 1st St Ampoint Perrysburg (43551) ***(G-15951)***
First Francis Company Inc (HQ) 440 352-8927
25 Florence Ave Painesville (44077) ***(G-15739)***
First Impression Wear 937 456-3900
120 E Main St Eaton (45320) ***(G-9149)***
First Impressions Printing, Lancaster *Also called Brooke Printers Inc* ***(G-11548)***
First Machine & Tool Corp 440 269-8644
38181 Airport Pkwy Willoughby (44094) ***(G-20323)***
First Merit 330 849-8750
106 S Main St Fl 6 Akron (44308) ***(G-172)***
First Product Technologies LLC 440 364-0664
6100 Oak Tree Blvd Independence (44131) ***(G-11128)***
First Solar Inc 419 661-1478
28101 Cedar Park Blvd Perrysburg (43551) ***(G-15952)***
First Solar Electric, Perrysburg *Also called First Solar Inc* ***(G-15952)***
First Stop Signs and Decals 330 343-1859
1347 4th St Nw New Philadelphia (44663) ***(G-14769)***
First Tool Corp (PA) 937 254-6197
612 Linden Ave Dayton (45403) ***(G-8195)***

A L P H A B E T I C

Firstar Precision Corporation — ALPHABETIC SECTION

Firstar Precision Corporation 216 362-7888
2867 Nationwide Pkwy Brunswick (44212) *(G-2204)*

Firstfuelcellscom LLC 440 884-2503
11163 Blossom Ave Cleveland (44130) *(G-5243)*

Fischer Engineering Company 937 754-1750
8220 Expansion Way Dayton (45424) *(G-8196)*

Fischer Global Enterprises LLC 513 583-4900
155 Commerce Dr Loveland (45140) *(G-12187)*

Fischer Special Tooling Corp 440 951-8411
7219 Commerce Dr Mentor (44060) *(G-13443)*

Fish Express 513 661-3000
2463 Harrison Ave Cincinnati (45211) *(G-3692)*

Fishburn Tank Truck Service 419 253-6031
5012 State Route 229 Marengo (43334) *(G-12591)*

Fishel Company 614 850-4400
1600 Walcutt Rd Columbus (43228) *(G-6926)*

Fisher Controls Intl LLC 513 285-6000
5453 W Chester Rd West Chester (45069) *(G-19703)*

Fisher Drug, Sandusky Also called Buderer Drug Co *(G-16798)*

Fisher Metal Fabricating 419 838-7200
27953 E Broadway St Walbridge (43465) *(G-19293)*

Fisher Pallet 440 632-0863
8496 Bundysburg Rd Middlefield (44062) *(G-13798)*

Fisher Sand & Gravel Inc 330 745-9239
3322 Clark Mill Rd Norton (44203) *(G-15368)*

Fisher Testers LLC 937 416-6554
5079 Kerridge Rd Huber Heights (45424) *(G-11018)*

Fishermans Central LLC 330 644-5346
5461 Manchester Rd New Franklin (44319) *(G-14689)*

Fiske Brothers Refining Co 419 691-2491
1500 Oakdale Ave Toledo (43605) *(G-18295)*

Fitchville East Corp 419 929-1510
1732 Us Highway 250 S New London (44851) *(G-14729)*

Fitchville East Storage, New London Also called Fitchville East Corp *(G-14729)*

Fithian-Wilbert Burial Vlt Co 330 758-2327
6234 Market St Youngstown (44512) *(G-20907)*

Fitness Fuel Training 330 807-7353
1021 Southeast Ave Tallmadge (44278) *(G-17983)*

Fitness Serve, Rocky River Also called Balbo Industries Inc *(G-16543)*

Five Handicap Inc (PA) 419 525-2511
127 N Walnut St Mansfield (44902) *(G-12439)*

Five Points Distillery LLC 937 776-4634
122 Van Buren St Dayton (45402) *(G-8197)*

Five Star Graphics Inc 330 545-5077
201 W Liberty St Girard (44420) *(G-10259)*

Five Star Machine & Tool 937 420-2170
403 S Main St Fort Loramie (45845) *(G-9797)*

Fivecoat Lumber Inc 740 254-4681
2400 Larson Rd Se Gnadenhutten (44629) *(G-10279)*

Fivepoint LLC 937 374-3193
825 Bellbrook Ave Unit B Xenia (45385) *(G-20773)*

Fives Bronx Inc 330 244-1960
8817 Pleasantwood Ave Nw North Canton (44720) *(G-15083)*

Fives Landis Corp 440 709-0700
7605 Discovery Ln Painesville (44077) *(G-15740)*

Fives N Amercn Combustn Inc (HQ) 216 271-6000
4455 E 71st St Cleveland (44105) *(G-5244)*

Fives N Amercn Combustn Inc 734 207-7008
4455 E 71st St Cleveland (44105) *(G-5245)*

Fives N Amercn Combustn Inc 412 655-0101
4455 E 71st St Cleveland (44105) *(G-5246)*

Fives St Corp 234 217-9070
1 Park Centre Dr Ste 210 Wadsworth (44281) *(G-19241)*

Fixture Dimensions Inc 513 360-7512
4355 Salzman Rd Middletown (45044) *(G-13908)*

Fkci, Springboro Also called F & K Concepts Inc *(G-17326)*

Fki Logistex, West Chester Also called Intelligrated Systems Ohio LLC *(G-19869)*

Flag Lady Inc 614 263-1776
4567 N High St Columbus (43214) *(G-6927)*

Flag Lady's Flag Store, The, Columbus Also called Flag Lady Inc *(G-6927)*

Flambeau 440 632-6131
15981 Valplast St Middlefield (44062) *(G-13799)*

Flambeau 330 239-0202
1468 Wolfe Creek Trl Sharon Center (44274) *(G-16950)*

Flaming River Industries Inc 440 826-4488
800 Poertner Dr Berea (44017) *(G-1608)*

Flash Industrial Tech Ltd 440 786-8979
30 Industry Dr Cleveland (44146) *(G-5247)*

Flasher Light Barricade 513 554-1111
4896 Factory Dr Fairfield (45014) *(G-9497)*

Flashions Sportswear Ltd 937 323-5885
1002 N Bechtle Ave Springfield (45504) *(G-17403)*

Flat Rocks Brewing Company 419 270-3582
127 W Washington St Napoleon (43545) *(G-14538)*

Flavor Systems International 513 870-0420
9930 Commerce Park Dr West Chester (45246) *(G-19853)*

Flavor Systems Intl Inc (HQ) 513 870-4900
5404 Duff Dr West Chester (45246) *(G-19854)*

Flavorseal LLC 440 937-3900
35179 Avon Commerce Pkwy Avon (44011) *(G-949)*

Fleet Graphics Inc 937 252-2552
1701 Thomas Paine Pkwy Dayton (45459) *(G-8198)*

Fleetchem LLC 513 539-1111
651 N Garver Rd Monroe (45050) *(G-14262)*

Fleetline Tool & Die Co 216 441-4949
7803 Harvard Ave Cleveland (44105) *(G-5248)*

Fleetmaster Express Inc 419 425-0666
5250 Distribution Dr Findlay (45840) *(G-9688)*

Fleetwood Craftsman, Johnstown Also called Fleetwood Custom Countertops *(G-11265)*

Fleetwood Custom Countertops (PA) 740 965-9833
15710 Center Village Rd Johnstown (43031) *(G-11265)*

Flegal Brothers Inc 419 298-3539
104 Industrial Dr Edgerton (43517) *(G-9175)*

Fleig Enterprises Inc 216 361-8020
940 E 67th St Cleveland (44103) *(G-5249)*

Fleming Construction Co 740 494-2177
5298 Marion Marysville Rd Prospect (43342) *(G-16350)*

Flesher Sand & Gravel, Norton Also called Fisher Sand & Gravel Inc *(G-15368)*

Flex N Gate 330 332-6363
800 Pennsylvania Ave Salem (44460) *(G-16738)*

Flex Pro Label Inc 513 489-4417
11465 Deerfield Rd Blue Ash (45242) *(G-1775)*

Flex Technologies Inc 330 359-5415
16183 E Main St Mount Eaton (44659) *(G-14420)*

Flex Technologies Inc 330 897-6311
3430 State Route 93 Baltic (43804) *(G-1029)*

Flex-Core Division, Hilliard Also called Morlan & Associates Inc *(G-10842)*

Flex-E-On Inc 330 928-4496
3332 Cavalier Trl Cuyahoga Falls (44224) *(G-7868)*

Flex-Strut Inc 330 372-9999
2900 Commonwealth Ave Ne Warren (44483) *(G-19403)*

Flexarm, Wapakoneta Also called Midwest Specialties Inc *(G-19346)*

Flexcart LLC 614 348-2517
5868 Kitzmiller Rd New Albany (43054) *(G-14624)*

Flexmag Industries Inc (HQ) 740 373-3492
107 Industry Rd Marietta (45750) *(G-12624)*

Flexnova Inc 216 288-6961
6100 Oak Tree Blvd Cleveland (44131) *(G-5250)*

Flexomation LLC 513 825-0555
11701 Chesterdale Rd Cincinnati (45246) *(G-3693)*

Flexoplate Inc 513 489-0433
6504 Corporate Dr Blue Ash (45242) *(G-1776)*

Flexotech Graphics Inc (PA) 330 929-4743
4830 Hudson Dr Stow (44224) *(G-17588)*

Flexsys America LP (HQ) 330 666-4111
260 Springside Dr Akron (44333) *(G-173)*

Flextronics International Usa 513 755-2500
6224 Windham Ct Liberty Township (45044) *(G-11814)*

Flight Operations, Cleveland Also called Swagelok Company *(G-6133)*

Flight Specialties Components, Highland Heights Also called Heico Aerospace Parts Corp *(G-10793)*

Flightlogix LLC 513 321-1200
4510 Airport Rd Cincinnati (45226) *(G-3694)*

Flint Group Global Packaging, Lebanon Also called Flint Group US LLC *(G-11652)*

Flint Group US LLC 513 771-1900
410 Glendale Milford Rd Cincinnati (45215) *(G-3695)*

Flint Group US LLC 513 934-6500
2675 Henkle Dr Lebanon (45036) *(G-11652)*

Flint Ridge Vineyard LLC 740 787-2116
3970 Pert Hill Rd Hopewell (43746) *(G-10992)*

Flipside Inc (PA) 440 600-7274
44 N Main St Chagrin Falls (44022) *(G-3020)*

Flocel Inc 216 619-5903
4415 Euclid Ave Ste 421 Cleveland (44103) *(G-5251)*

Flohr Machine Company Inc 330 745-3030
1028 Coventry Rd Barberton (44203) *(G-1070)*

Flohrmachine.com, Barberton Also called Flohr Machine Company Inc *(G-1070)*

Flood Heliarc Inc 614 835-3929
4181 Venture Pl Groveport (43125) *(G-10489)*

Floorcraft Designs, Toledo Also called Property Assist Inc *(G-18487)*

Florence Alloys Inc 330 745-9141
121 Snyder Ave Barberton (44203) *(G-1071)*

Florida Invacare Holdings LLC 800 333-6900
1 Invacare Way Elyria (44035) *(G-9261)*

Florida Production Engrg Inc 937 996-4361
1855 State Route 121 N New Madison (45346) *(G-14741)*

Florida Production Engrg Inc 740 420-5252
30627 Orr Rd Circleville (43113) *(G-4545)*

Florida Tile Inc 513 891-1122
10840 Millington Ct Blue Ash (45242) *(G-1777)*

Florida Tile Inc 614 436-2511
7029 Huntley Rd Ste B Columbus (43229) *(G-6928)*

Florida Tile Inc 937 293-5151
2105 Lyons Rd Miamisburg (45342) *(G-13669)*

Florline Display Products Corp 440 975-9449
38160 Western Pkwy Willoughby (44094) *(G-20324)*

Flory Cabinetry, Covington Also called Harold Flory *(G-7787)*

Flotbi Inc 216 619-5928
4415 Euclid Ave Ste 421 Cleveland (44103) *(G-5252)*

Fowler Products Inc 419 683-4057
810 Colby Rd Crestline (44827) ***(G-7794)***
Fowlers Milling Co Inc 440 286-2024
12500 Fowlers Mill Rd Chardon (44024) ***(G-3112)***
Fox Hollow Pallet, Winchester *Also called Leroy Yutzy* ***(G-20522)***
Fox Hollow Pallet 937 386-2872
3519 Graces Run Rd Winchester (45697) ***(G-20520)***
Fox Lite Inc 937 864-1966
8300 Dayton Rd Fairborn (45324) ***(G-9459)***
Fox Supply LLC 419 628-3051
40 Columbia Dr Minster (45865) ***(G-14214)***
Fox Tool Co Inc 330 928-3402
1471 Main St Cuyahoga Falls (44221) ***(G-7869)***
Fox Valley Forge, Cleveland *Also called Cleveland Hdwr & Forging Co* ***(G-4962)***
Foxtail Foods, Fairfield *Also called Perkins & Marie Callenders LLC* ***(G-9548)***
Foxtronix Inc 937 866-2112
2240 E Central Ave Ste 4 Miamisburg (45342) ***(G-13670)***
Fpt Cleveland LLC (HQ) 216 441-3800
8550 Aetna Rd Cleveland (44105) ***(G-5270)***
Fragapane Bakeries Inc (PA) 440 779-6050
28625 Lorain Rd North Olmsted (44070) ***(G-15190)***
Fragapane Bakery & Deli, North Olmsted *Also called Fragapane Bakeries Inc* ***(G-15190)***
Fram Group Operations LLC 937 316-3000
851 Jackson St Greenville (45331) ***(G-10369)***
Fram Group Operations LLC 419 436-5827
1600 N Union St Fostoria (44830) ***(G-9845)***
Fram Group Operations LLC 419 661-6700
28399 Cedar Park Blvd Perrysburg (43551) ***(G-15953)***
Frame Depot Inc 330 652-7865
1043 Youngstown Warren Rd Niles (44446) ***(G-15009)***
Frame USA 513 577-7107
225 Northland Blvd Cincinnati (45246) ***(G-3708)***
Frame Warehouse 614 861-4582
7502 E Main St Reynoldsburg (43068) ***(G-16440)***
Francis Industries LLC 330 333-3352
1424 Albert St Youngstown (44505) ***(G-20910)***
Francis Manufacturing Company 937 526-4551
500 E Mn St Russia (45363) ***(G-16607)***
Francis-Schulze Co 937 295-3941
3880 Rangeline Rd Russia (45363) ***(G-16608)***
Francisco Jaume 740 622-1200
311 S 15th St Ste 206 Coshocton (43812) ***(G-7734)***
Franck and Fric Incorporated 216 524-4451
7919 Old Rockside Rd Cleveland (44131) ***(G-5271)***
Franjinhas Inc 440 463-1523
17656 Fairfax Ln Strongsville (44136) ***(G-17745)***
Frank Brunckhorst Company LLC 614 662-5300
2225 Spiegel Dr Groveport (43125) ***(G-10491)***
Frank Csapo 330 435-4458
157 Myers St Creston (44217) ***(G-7805)***
Frank Csapo Oil & Gas Producer, Creston *Also called Frank Csapo* ***(G-7805)***
Frank J Prucha & Associates 216 642-3838
6916 Daisy Ave Cleveland (44131) ***(G-5272)***
Frank L Harter & Son Inc 513 574-1330
3778 Frondorf Ave Cincinnati (45211) ***(G-3709)***
Frank W Schaefer, Perrysburg *Also called Schaefer Group Inc* ***(G-16004)***
Frankes Wood Products LLC 937 642-0706
825 Collins Ave Marysville (43040) ***(G-12783)***
Frankie Tatum 614 216-1556
56 Winner Ave Columbus (43203) ***(G-6934)***
Frankies Graphics Inc 440 979-0824
3770 Windsong Ct Westlake (44145) ***(G-20114)***
Franklin 419 699-5757
747 Michigan Ave Waterville (43566) ***(G-19495)***
Franklin Art Glass Studios 614 221-2972
222 E Sycamore St Columbus (43206) ***(G-6935)***
Franklin Brazing Met Treating, Lebanon *Also called Kando of Cincinnati Inc* ***(G-11668)***
Franklin Cabinet Company Inc 937 743-9606
2500 Commerce Center Dr Franklin (45005) ***(G-9884)***
Franklin Communications Inc 614 459-9769
4401 Carriage Hill Ln Columbus (43220) ***(G-6936)***
Franklin Covey Co 513 792-0099
7875 Montgomery Rd # 1202 Cincinnati (45236) ***(G-3710)***
Franklin Electric Co Inc 614 794-2266
555 Metro Pl N Dublin (43017) ***(G-8915)***
Franklin Equipment LLC (PA) 614 228-2014
4141 Hamilton Square Blvd Groveport (43125) ***(G-10492)***
Franklin Field Service 614 885-1779
7065 Huntley Rd Columbus (43229) ***(G-6937)***
Franklin Frames and Cycles 740 763-3838
7179 Reform Rd Newark (43055) ***(G-14875)***
Franklin Gas & Oil Company LLC 330 264-8739
1615 W Old Lincoln Way Wooster (44691) ***(G-20593)***
Franklin Graphics, North Canton *Also called Paul Stipkovich* ***(G-15110)***
Franklin Iron & Metal Corp 937 253-8184
1939 E 1st St Dayton (45403) ***(G-8206)***
Franklin Mfg Div, Franklin *Also called Faurecia Exhaust Systems Inc* ***(G-9882)***
Franklin's Printing, Franklin *Also called F P C Printing Inc* ***(G-9881)***
Franklins Printing Company 740 452-6375
984 Beverly Ave Zanesville (43701) ***(G-21138)***
Franks Casing 330 236-4264
607 1st St Sw Massillon (44646) ***(G-12982)***
Franks Electric Inc 513 313-5883
2640 Colerain Ave Cincinnati (45214) ***(G-3711)***
Franks Electric Motor Repair, Cincinnati *Also called Franks Electric Inc* ***(G-3711)***
Franks Sawmill Inc 419 682-3831
Rr 195 Stryker (43557) ***(G-17829)***
Frantz Medical Development Ltd (PA) 440 255-1155
7740 Metric Dr Mentor (44060) ***(G-13447)***
Frantz Medical Development Ltd 440 205-9026
7740 Metric Dr Mentor (44060) ***(G-13448)***
Frantz Medical Group 440 974-8522
7740 Metric Dr Mentor (44060) ***(G-13449)***
Frasernet Inc 216 691-6686
2940 Noble Rd Ste 1 Cleveland (44121) ***(G-5273)***
Frazeysburg Restaurant & Bky, Frazeysburg *Also called Calvary Christian Ch of Ohio* ***(G-9937)***
Frazier Machine and Prod Inc 419 661-1656
26489 Southpoint Rd Perrysburg (43551) ***(G-15954)***
Frd, Kent *Also called Furukawa Rock Drill USA Co Ltd* ***(G-11325)***
Freak-N-Fries Inc 440 453-1877
204 Taylor Blvd Lagrange (44050) ***(G-11480)***
Frecon Engineering 513 874-8981
9319 Prnceton Glendale Rd West Chester (45011) ***(G-19707)***
Frecon Technologies, West Chester *Also called Frecon Engineering* ***(G-19707)***
Frecon Technologies Inc 513 874-8981
9319 Prnceton Glendale Rd West Chester (45011) ***(G-19708)***
Fred D Pfening Company (PA) 614 294-5361
1075 W 5th Ave Columbus (43212) ***(G-6938)***
Fred D Pfening Company 614 294-5361
1075 W 5th Ave Columbus (43212) ***(G-6939)***
Fred Marvin and Associates Inc 330 784-9211
4484 Allen Rd Stow (44224) ***(G-17590)***
Fred Marvin Associates, Stow *Also called Fred Marvin and Associates Inc* ***(G-17590)***
Fred W Hanks Company 216 731-1774
25018 Lakeland Blvd Cleveland (44132) ***(G-5274)***
Fred Winner 419 582-2421
7860 Cohn Rd New Weston (45348) ***(G-14845)***
Frederick Steel Company LLC 513 821-6400
630 Glendale Milford Rd Cincinnati (45215) ***(G-3712)***
Fredericksburg Facility, Fredericksburg *Also called Robin Industries Inc* ***(G-9958)***
Fredon Corporation 440 951-5200
8990 Tyler Blvd Mentor (44060) ***(G-13450)***
Fredrick Welding & Machining 614 866-9650
6840 Americana Pkwy Reynoldsburg (43068) ***(G-16441)***
Free Bird Publications Ltd 216 673-0229
1410 S Carptr Rd Apt 238 Brunswick (44212) ***(G-2206)***
Free Press Standard, Carrollton *Also called Carrollton Publishing Company* ***(G-2918)***
Freedom Asphalt Sealant & Line 937 416-1053
1241 Stephens St Miamisburg (45342) ***(G-13671)***
Freedom Forklift Sales LLC 330 289-0879
1114 Garman Rd Akron (44313) ***(G-177)***
Freedom Health LLC 330 562-0888
65 Aurora Industrial Pkwy Aurora (44202) ***(G-880)***
Freedom Road Defense 740 541-7467
1 Orchard Ln Cambridge (43725) ***(G-2438)***
Freedom Usa Inc 216 503-6374
2045 Midway Dr Twinsburg (44087) ***(G-18776)***
Freeman Enclosure Systems LLC 877 441-8555
4160 Half Acre Rd Batavia (45103) ***(G-1147)***
Freeman Manufacturing & Sup Co (PA) 440 934-1902
1101 Moore Rd Avon (44011) ***(G-950)***
Freeman Schwabe Machinery LLC 513 947-2888
4064 Clough Woods Dr Batavia (45103) ***(G-1148)***
Freeport Press Inc (PA) 330 308-3300
2127 Reiser Ave Se New Philadelphia (44663) ***(G-14770)***
Freeport Press Inc 740 658-4000
2127 Reiser Ave Se New Philadelphia (44663) ***(G-14771)***
Fremar Industries Inc 330 220-3700
2808 Westway Dr Brunswick (44212) ***(G-2207)***
Fremont Company (PA) 419 334-8995
802 N Front St Fremont (43420) ***(G-10015)***
Fremont Company 419 334-8995
802 N Front St Fremont (43420) ***(G-10016)***
Fremont Company 419 363-2924
150 Hickory St Rockford (45882) ***(G-16539)***
Fremont Cutting Dies Inc 419 334-5153
3179 Us 20 E Fremont (43420) ***(G-10017)***
Fremont Discover Ltd 419 332-8696
315 Garrison St Fremont (43420) ***(G-10018)***
Fremont Flask Co 419 332-2231
1000 Wolfe Ave Fremont (43420) ***(G-10019)***
Fremont Quick Print 419 334-8808
2870 W Us Highway 6 Helena (43435) ***(G-10771)***
French Oil Mill Machinery Co (PA) 937 773-3420
1035 W Greene St Piqua (45356) ***(G-16117)***
French USA, Piqua *Also called French Oil Mill Machinery Co* ***(G-16117)***

ALPHABETIC

(PA)=Parent Co (HQ)=Headquarters (DH)=Div Headquarters
2019 Harris Ohio Industrial Directory
1119

Frepeg Industries Inc 440 255-8595
8624 East Ave Mentor (44060) **(G-13451)**
Fresh Aire Farms, Union City *Also called Charles Daniel Young* **(G-18903)**
Fresh and Limited, Sidney *Also called Freshway Foods Inc* **(G-17041)**
Fresh Mark Inc (PA) 330 834-3669
1888 Southway St Se Massillon (44646) **(G-12983)**
Fresh Mark Inc 330 832-7491
1888 Southway St Sw Massillon (44646) **(G-12984)**
Fresh Mark Inc 330 332-8508
1735 S Lincoln Ave Salem (44460) **(G-16741)**
Fresh Mark Sugardale, Massillon *Also called Fresh Mark Inc* **(G-12984)**
Fresh Press LLC 513 378-1402
6567 Estate Ln Loveland (45140) **(G-12189)**
Fresh Prints, Youngstown *Also called Zitello Fine Art LLC* **(G-21087)**
Fresh Products LLC 419 531-9741
30600 Oregon Rd Perrysburg (43551) **(G-15955)**
Fresh Sausage Specialists, Harrison *Also called Edelmann Provision Company* **(G-10639)**
Fresh Table LLC 513 381-3774
1801 Race St Ste 45 Cincinnati (45202) **(G-3713)**
Fresh Vegetable Technology, Columbus *Also called National Fruit Vegetable Tech* **(G-7210)**
Freshway Foods Inc (PA) 937 498-4664
601 Stolle Ave Sidney (45365) **(G-17041)**
Freudenberg-Nok General Partnr 937 335-3306
1275 Archer Dr Troy (45373) **(G-18658)**
Freudenberg-Nok General Partnr 419 427-5221
555 Marathon Blvd Findlay (45840) **(G-9689)**
Freudenberg-Nok Sealing Tech, Troy *Also called Freudenberg-Nok General Partnr* **(G-18658)**
Freudenberg-Nok Sealing Tech 877 331-8427
11617 State Route 13 Milan (44846) **(G-13983)**
Frickco Inc 740 887-2017
54660 Pretty Run Rd South Bloomingville (43152) **(G-17270)**
Friction Products Co 330 725-4941
920 Lake Rd Medina (44256) **(G-13265)**
Friday's Creations, Hilliard *Also called CNG Business Group* **(G-10818)**
Fried Daddy 937 854-4542
448 N Union Rd Dayton (45417) **(G-8207)**
Friend Engrg & Mch Co Inc 419 589-5066
67 Illinois Ave S Mansfield (44905) **(G-12442)**
Friends Business Source, Findlay *Also called Friends Service Co Inc* **(G-9690)**
Friends of Bears Mill Inc 937 548-5112
6450 Arcanum Bearsmill Rd Greenville (45331) **(G-10370)**
Friends Ornamental Iron Co 216 431-6710
1593 E 41st St Cleveland (44103) **(G-5275)**
Friends Service Co Inc 800 427-1704
4604 Salem Ave Dayton (45416) **(G-8208)**
Friends Service Co Inc 800 427-1704
948 Cherry St Kent (44240) **(G-11322)**
Friends Service Co Inc (PA) 419 427-1704
2300 Bright Rd Findlay (45840) **(G-9690)**
Fries Machine & Tool Inc 937 898-6432
5729 Webster St Dayton (45414) **(G-8209)**
Friesen Fab & Equipment, Plain City *Also called Friesen Fab and Equipment* **(G-16192)**
Friesen Fab and Equipment 614 873-4354
10030 Smith Calhoun Rd Plain City (43064) **(G-16192)**
Friesen Transfer Ltd 614 873-5672
9280 Iams Rd Plain City (43064) **(G-16193)**
Friesingers Inc 740 452-9480
120 Graham St Zanesville (43701) **(G-21139)**
Friess Equipment Inc 330 945-9440
2222 Akron Peninsula Rd Akron (44313) **(G-178)**
Friess Welding Inc 330 644-8160
3342 S Main St Coventry Township (44319) **(G-7770)**
Frigid Units Inc 419 478-4000
5072 Lewis Ave Toledo (43612) **(G-18297)**
Fripro Energy LLC 419 865-0002
7008 Garden Rd Maumee (43537) **(G-13111)**
Frisbie Engine & Machine Co (PA) 513 542-1770
2635 Spring Grove Ave Cincinnati (45214) **(G-3714)**
Frisby Printing Company 330 665-4565
3571 Brookwall Dr Unit C Fairlawn (44333) **(G-9605)**
Frischco Inc 740 363-7537
715 Sunbury Rd Delaware (43015) **(G-8680)**
Frito-Lay North America Inc 972 334-7000
1626 Old Mansfield Rd Wooster (44691) **(G-20594)**
Frito-Lay North America Inc 330 477-7009
4030 16th St Sw Canton (44710) **(G-2676)**
Frito-Lay North America Inc 614 508-3004
6611 Broughton Ave Columbus (43213) **(G-6940)**
Frito-Lay North America Inc 513 229-3000
5181 Natorp Blvd Ste 400 Mason (45040) **(G-12872)**
Fritzie Freeze Inc 419 727-0818
5137 N Summit St Unit 1 Toledo (43611) **(G-18298)**
Frog Ranch Foods Ltd 740 767-3705
5 S High St Glouster (45732) **(G-10276)**
Frogs In Bloom 330 678-9508
1112 Delores Ave Kent (44240) **(G-11323)**
Frohock-Stewart Inc 440 329-6000
39400 Taylor Pkwy North Ridgeville (44035) **(G-15226)**
Front Line Defense 419 516-7992
2783 Heritage Pl Ada (45810) **(G-6)**
Frontier Signs & Displays Inc 513 367-0813
525 New Biddinger Rd Harrison (45030) **(G-10642)**
Frontier Tank Center Inc 330 659-3888
3800 Congress Pkwy Richfield (44286) **(G-16471)**
Frontiers Unlimited, Lisbon *Also called Vance Adams* **(G-11981)**
Frontline International Inc 330 861-1100
187 Ascot Pkwy Cuyahoga Falls (44223) **(G-7870)**
Frost Engineering Inc 513 541-6330
3408 Beekman St Cincinnati (45223) **(G-3715)**
Frostop, Columbus *Also called Fbg Bottling Group LLC* **(G-6914)**
Frozen Specialties Inc 419 445-9015
720 W Barre Rd Archbold (43502) **(G-647)**
Frozen Specialties Inc (HQ) 419 445-9015
8600 S Wilkinson Way G Perrysburg (43551) **(G-15956)**
Frsteam By Sun Cleaners, Carroll *Also called Sun Cleaners & Laundry Inc* **(G-2912)**
Frugal Systems 419 957-7863
21250 County Road 26 Carey (43316) **(G-2881)**
Frutarom USA Holding Inc (HQ) 201 861-9500
5404 Duff Dr West Chester (45246) **(G-19855)**
Frutarom USA Inc (HQ) 513 870-4900
5404 Duff Dr West Chester (45246) **(G-19856)**
Frutarom USA Inc 513 870-4900
9950 Commerce Park Dr West Chester (45246) **(G-19857)**
Frutarom USA Inc 513 870-4900
9930 Commerce Park Dr West Chester (45246) **(G-19858)**
Frutarom USA Inc 513 870-4900
10139 Commerce Park Dr West Chester (45246) **(G-19859)**
Fry Foods Inc 419 448-0831
99 Maule Rd Tiffin (44883) **(G-18061)**
Fryes Soccer Shoppe 937 832-2230
709 Taywood Rd Englewood (45322) **(G-9359)**
FSI, Perrysburg *Also called Frozen Specialties Inc* **(G-15956)**
FSI/Mfp Inc 419 445-9015
720 W Barre Rd Archbold (43502) **(G-648)**
FSRc Tanks Inc 234 221-2015
11029 Industrial Pkwy Nw Bolivar (44612) **(G-1914)**
FT Group Inc 937 746-6439
4710 Madison Rd Cincinnati (45227) **(G-3716)**
FT Precision Inc 740 694-1500
9731 Mount Gilead Rd Fredericktown (43019) **(G-9970)**
Ftd Investments LLC 937 833-2161
379 Albert Rd Brookville (45309) **(G-2169)**
Ftech R&D North America Inc (HQ) 937 339-2777
1191 Horizon West Ct Troy (45373) **(G-18659)**
Ftp, Fredericktown *Also called FT Precision Inc* **(G-9970)**
Fts International Inc 330 754-2375
1520 Wood Ave Se East Canton (44730) **(G-9040)**
Fuchs Franklin Div, Twinsburg *Also called Fuchs Lubricants Co* **(G-18777)**
Fuchs Lubricants Co 330 963-0400
8036 Bavaria Rd Twinsburg (44087) **(G-18777)**
Fuel America 419 586-5609
204 E Market St Celina (45822) **(G-2963)**
Fuel G USA LLC 440 617-0950
1457 Mendelssohn Dr Westlake (44145) **(G-20115)**
Fuhrmann Orchards LLC 740 776-6406
510 Hansgen Morgan Rd Wheelersburg (45694) **(G-20181)**
Fujitec America Inc (HQ) 513 755-6100
7258 Innovation Way Mason (45040) **(G-12873)**
Fukuvi Usa Inc 937 236-7288
7631 Progress Ct Dayton (45424) **(G-8210)**
Fulflo Specialties Company, Cincinnati *Also called Ruthman Pump and Engineering* **(G-4291)**
Fulflo Specialties Company 937 783-2411
459 E Fancy St Blanchester (45107) **(G-1703)**
Full Circle Oil Field Svcs Inc 740 371-5422
2327 State Route 821 B Marietta (45750) **(G-12625)**
Full Circle Technologies LLC 216 650-0007
1175 Piermont Rd Cleveland (44121) **(G-5276)**
Full Gospel Baptist Times 614 279-3307
3415 El Paso Dr Columbus (43204) **(G-6941)**
Fullgospel Publishing 216 339-1973
16781 Chagrin Blvd # 134 Shaker Heights (44120) **(G-16931)**
Fullton Mill Services, Delta *Also called Edw C Levy Co* **(G-8769)**
Fulton County Expositor, Wauseon *Also called Gazette Publishing Company* **(G-19517)**
Fulton County Processing Ltd 419 822-9266
7800 State Route 109 Delta (43515) **(G-8771)**
Fulton Equipment Co (PA) 419 290-5393
823 Hamilton St Toledo (43607) **(G-18299)**
Fulton Industries Inc (PA) 419 335-3015
135 E Linfoot St Wauseon (43567) **(G-19516)**
Fulton Manufacturing Inds LLC 440 546-1435
6600 W Snowville Rd # 6500 Brecksville (44141) **(G-2037)**
Fulton Sign & Decal Inc 440 951-1515
7144 Industrial Park Blvd Mentor (44060) **(G-13452)**
Fultz Sign Co Inc 419 225-6000
3350 Slabtown Rd Lima (45801) **(G-11866)**

Fun-In-Games Inc......866 587-1004
9378 Mason Montgomery Rd Mason (45040) *(G-12874)*
Functional Formularies, West Chester *Also called Nutritional Medicinals LLC (G-19750)*
Functional Imaging Ltd......740 689-2466
2368 Pine Crest Dr Lancaster (43130) *(G-11573)*
Functional Products Inc......330 963-3060
8282 Bavaria Dr E Macedonia (44056) *(G-12296)*
Funke Signature Holdings, Cincinnati *Also called Annies Mud Pie Shop LLC (G-3348)*
Funny Times Inc......216 371-8600
2176 Lee Rd Cleveland (44118) *(G-5277)*
Funsports Brands, Liberty Township *Also called Boatfun Sports Inc (G-11811)*
Funtown Playgrounds Inc......513 871-8585
839 Cypresspoint Ct Cincinnati (45245) *(G-3250)*
Fur-Fish-Game, Columbus *Also called A R Harding Publishing Co (G-6516)*
Furn Tech, Waterville *Also called Labcraft Inc (G-19500)*
Furn Tech, Waterville *Also called Furnace Technologies Inc (G-19496)*
Furnace Parts, Independence *Also called Weed Instrument Company Inc (G-11156)*
Furnace Parts LLC......216 916-9601
4755 W 150th St Ste C Cleveland (44135) *(G-5278)*
Furnace Parts LLC......800 321-0796
6133 Rockside Rd Ste 300 Cleveland (44131) *(G-5279)*
Furnace Technologies Inc......419 878-2100
1070 Disher Dr Waterville (43566) *(G-19496)*
Furniss Corporation Ltd......614 871-1470
15812 State Route 56 W Mount Sterling (43143) *(G-14461)*
Furniture By Otmar Inc (PA)......937 435-2039
301 Mmsburg Cnterville Rd Dayton (45459) *(G-8211)*
Furniture By Otmar Inc......513 891-5141
9500 Montgomery Rd Cincinnati (45242) *(G-3717)*
Furniture Concepts Inc......216 292-9100
4925 Galaxy Pkwy Ste G Cleveland (44128) *(G-5280)*
Furukawa Rock Drill Usa Inc (HQ)......330 673-5826
705 Lake St Kent (44240) *(G-11324)*
Furukawa Rock Drill USA Co Ltd (PA)......330 673-5826
711 Lake St Kent (44240) *(G-11325)*
Fuse Chicken Llc......330 338-7108
2251 Front St Ste 200 Cuyahoga Falls (44221) *(G-7871)*
Fuserashi Intl Tech Inc......330 273-0140
5401 Innovation Dr Valley City (44280) *(G-19038)*
Fusion Automation Inc (HQ)......440 602-5595
4658 E 355th St Willoughby (44094) *(G-20326)*
Fusion Ceramics Inc (PA)......330 627-5821
160 Scio Rd Se Carrollton (44615) *(G-2920)*
Fusion Incorporated......440 946-3300
4658 E 355th St Willoughby (44094) *(G-20327)*
Fusion Incorporated......440 946-3300
4711 Topps Indus Pkwy Willoughby (44094) *(G-20328)*
Fusion Noodle Co......740 589-5511
30 E Union St Athens (45701) *(G-830)*
Fusionstorm......614 431-8000
1900 Polaris Pkwy Ste 385 Columbus (43240) *(G-6494)*
Future Controls Corporation......440 275-3191
1419 State Route 45 Austinburg (44010) *(G-922)*
Future Finishes Inc......513 860-0020
40 Standen Dr Hamilton (45015) *(G-10559)*
Future Poly Tech Inc......614 942-1209
393 N Eastern Ave Saint Henry (45883) *(G-16660)*
Future Polytech Inc......419 763-1352
393 N Eastern Ave Saint Henry (45883) *(G-16661)*
Future Pos Ohio Inc......330 645-6623
2561 S Arlington Rd Akron (44319) *(G-179)*
Future Productions Inc......330 478-0477
4601 11th St Nw Canton (44708) *(G-2677)*
Future Screen Inc......440 838-5055
9009 Broadview Rd Unit B Cleveland (44147) *(G-5281)*
Fuyao Glass America Inc (HQ)......937 496-5777
2801 W Stroop Rd Dayton (45439) *(G-8212)*
Fwt LLC......419 542-1420
761 W High St Hicksville (43526) *(G-10778)*
Fww, Canton *Also called Super Sign Guys LLC (G-2830)*
Fx Digital Media Inc (PA)......216 241-4040
1600 E 23rs St Rs Cleveland (44114) *(G-5282)*
Fx Digital Media Inc......216 241-4040
2400 Superior Ave E # 100 Cleveland (44114) *(G-5283)*
Fypon Ltd......800 446-3040
1750 Indian Wood Cir Maumee (43537) *(G-13112)*
G & C Raw LLC......937 827-0010
225 N West St Versailles (45380) *(G-19181)*
G & C Raw Dog Food, Versailles *Also called G & C Raw LLC (G-19181)*
G & D Twinsburg, Twinsburg *Also called Giesecke & Devrient Amer Inc (G-18785)*
G & G Header Die Inc......330 468-3458
1200 Saybrook Dr Macedonia (44056) *(G-12297)*
G & G Originals, Cleveland *Also called Glauners Wholesale Inc (G-5323)*
G & H Drilling Inc......330 674-4868
5550 County Road 314 Millersburg (44654) *(G-14083)*
G & J, Toledo *Also called Mecca Rebuilding & Welding Co (G-18405)*
G & J Asphalt & Material Inc......740 773-6358
379 Seney Rd Chillicothe (45601) *(G-3186)*
G & J Extrusions Inc......330 753-0162
1580 Turkeyfoot Lake Rd New Franklin (44203) *(G-14690)*
G & J Pepsi-Cola Bottlers Inc......740 354-9191
4587 Gallia Pike Franklin Furnace (45629) *(G-9934)*
G & J Pepsi-Cola Bottlers Inc......740 774-2148
400 E 7th St Chillicothe (45601) *(G-3187)*
G & J Pepsi-Cola Bottlers Inc (PA)......513 785-6060
9435 Waterstone Blvd # 390 Cincinnati (45249) *(G-3718)*
G & J Pepsi-Cola Bottlers Inc......937 392-4937
1111 S 2nd St Ripley (45167) *(G-16513)*
G & J Pepsi-Cola Bottlers Inc......513 896-3700
2580 Bobmeyer Rd Hamilton (45015) *(G-10560)*
G & J Pepsi-Cola Bottlers Inc......740 593-3366
2001 E State St Athens (45701) *(G-831)*
G & J Pepsi-Cola Bottlers Inc......614 253-8771
1241 Gibbard Ave Columbus (43219) *(G-6942)*
G & J Pepsi-Cola Bottlers Inc......740 452-2721
335 N 6th St Zanesville (43701) *(G-21140)*
G & L Machining Inc......513 724-2600
299 N 3rd St Williamsburg (45176) *(G-20251)*
G & M Metal Products Inc......513 863-3353
1001 Fairview Ave Hamilton (45015) *(G-10561)*
G & M Precision Machining Inc......937 667-1443
9785 Wildcat Rd Tipp City (45371) *(G-18113)*
G & R Welding & Machining......937 323-9353
4690 E National Rd Springfield (45505) *(G-17405)*
G & S Bar and Wire LLC......260 747-4154
4000 E Lincoln Way Wooster (44691) *(G-20595)*
G & S Custom Tooling LLC......419 286-2888
18406 Road 20 Fort Jennings (45844) *(G-9792)*
G & T Manufacturing Co......440 639-7777
6085 Pinecone Dr Mentor (44060) *(G-13453)*
G & W Products LLC......513 860-4050
8675 Seward Rd Fairfield (45011) *(G-9499)*
G A Avril Company (PA)......513 641-0566
4445 Kings Run Dr Cincinnati (45232) *(G-3719)*
G A Avril Company......513 731-5133
2108 Eagle Ct Cincinnati (45237) *(G-3720)*
G A Guilford & Sons, Cleveland *Also called Arthur W Guilford III Inc (G-4739)*
G A Spring Advertising......330 343-9030
2101 N Wooster Ave Dover (44622) *(G-8827)*
G A Wintzer and Son Company......419 739-4913
12279 S Dixey Hwy Wapakoneta (45895) *(G-19329)*
G B Welding & Metal Fabg Co......937 444-2091
3288 Mcmullen Rd Fayetteville (45118) *(G-9639)*
G Big Inc (PA)......740 867-5758
441 Rockwood Ave Chesapeake (45619) *(G-3145)*
G Big Inc......740 532-9123
300 Marion Pike Ironton (45638) *(G-11165)*
G F Frank and Sons Inc......513 870-9075
9075 Le Saint Dr West Chester (45014) *(G-19709)*
G Fordyce Co......937 393-3241
210 Hobart Dr Hillsboro (45133) *(G-10878)*
G Grafton Machine & Rubber......330 297-1062
640 Cleveland Rd Ravenna (44266) *(G-16380)*
G H Cutter Services Inc......419 476-0476
6203 N Detroit Ave Toledo (43612) *(G-18300)*
G I Plastek Inc......440 230-1942
24700 Center Ridge Rd # 8 Westlake (44145) *(G-20116)*
G Keener & Co......937 846-1210
2936 Liberty Rd New Carlisle (45344) *(G-14666)*
G L Heller Co Inc......419 877-5122
6246 Industrial Pkwy Whitehouse (43571) *(G-20190)*
G L Industries Inc......513 874-1233
25 Standen Dr Hamilton (45015) *(G-10562)*
G M R Technology Inc......440 992-6003
2131 Aetna Rd Ashtabula (44004) *(G-777)*
G Metal, Stow *Also called Glebus Alloys LLC (G-17592)*
G Q Business Products......513 792-4750
11380 Grooms Rd Blue Ash (45242) *(G-1780)*
G R K Manufacturing Co Inc......513 863-3131
1200 Dayton St Hamilton (45011) *(G-10563)*
G S K Inc......937 547-1611
915 Front St Greenville (45331) *(G-10371)*
G S Link & Associates......513 722-2457
1881 Main St Goshen (45122) *(G-10287)*
G S S, Barberton *Also called Glass Surface Systems Inc (G-1075)*
G S S, Springboro *Also called Graphic Systems Services Inc (G-17329)*
G S Wiring Systems Inc (HQ)......419 423-7111
1801 Production Dr Findlay (45840) *(G-9691)*
G T M Associates Inc......440 951-0006
7112 Industrial Park Blvd Mentor (44060) *(G-13454)*
G T Metal Fabricators Inc......440 237-8745
12126 York Rd Unit E Cleveland (44133) *(G-5284)*
G W Cobb Co......216 341-0100
3914 Broadway Ave 16 Cleveland (44115) *(G-5285)*
G W Smith and Sons Inc......937 253-5114
1700 Spaulding Rd Dayton (45432) *(G-7979)*
G W Steffen Bookbinders Inc......330 963-0300
8212 Bavaria Dr E Macedonia (44056) *(G-12298)*

ALPHABETIC

G W Tool & Die Co, Fort Loramie *Also called Schmitmeyer Inc* ***(G-9804)***
G&M Media Packaging Inc.....419 636-5461
1 Toy St Bryan (43506) ***(G-2282)***
G-M-I Inc.....440 953-8811
4822 E 355th St Willoughby (44094) ***(G-20329)***
G.S. Steel Company, Cuyahoga Falls *Also called Dbcr Inc* ***(G-7859)***
G2 Digital Solutions.....937 951-1530
1841 Trebein Rd Xenia (45385) ***(G-20774)***
G2 Print Plus.....614 276-0500
3787 Interchange Rd Columbus (43204) ***(G-6943)***
Gabriel Logan LLC (PA).....740 380-6809
1689 E Front St Logan (43138) ***(G-12024)***
Gabriel Performance Pdts LLC (HQ).....866 800-2436
388 S Main St Ste 340 Akron (44311) ***(G-180)***
Gabriel Performance Pdts LLC.....440 992-3200
725 State Rd Ashtabula (44004) ***(G-778)***
Gad-Jets Inc.....937 274-2111
323 Industrial Dr Franklin (45005) ***(G-9885)***
Gadd Logging.....513 312-3941
823 E Jameson Ct Trenton (45067) ***(G-18619)***
Gadgets Manufacturing Co.....937 686-5371
9366 State Route 117 Huntsville (43324) ***(G-11087)***
Gail Berner.....937 322-0314
514 W Columbia St Springfield (45504) ***(G-17406)***
Gail J Shumaker Originals.....330 659-0680
3999 Brush Rd Richfield (44286) ***(G-16472)***
Gail Zeilmann.....440 888-4858
3560 W 105th St Cleveland (44111) ***(G-5286)***
Gain LLC.....440 396-6613
8475 Fallgold Ln Westerville (43082) ***(G-19992)***
Gaitwell Orthotics Pedorthics.....513 829-2217
1 N Commerce Park Dr # 306 Cincinnati (45215) ***(G-3721)***
Galactic Precision Mfg LLC.....937 540-1800
345 Huls Dr Englewood (45315) ***(G-9360)***
Galapagos Inc (PA).....937 890-3068
3345 Old Salem Rd Dayton (45415) ***(G-8213)***
Galaxy Balloons Incorporated.....216 476-3360
11750 Berea Rd Ste 3 Cleveland (44111) ***(G-5287)***
Galaxy Products Inc.....419 843-7337
3403 Silica Rd Sylvania (43560) ***(G-17940)***
Galena Vault Ltd.....740 965-2200
4909 Harlem Rd Galena (43021) ***(G-10112)***
Galion LLC.....419 468-5214
515 N East St Galion (44833) ***(G-10138)***
Galion Canvas Products (PA).....419 468-5333
385 S Market St Galion (44833) ***(G-10139)***
Galion Dump Bodies, Millersburg *Also called Galion-Godwin Truck Bdy Co LLC* ***(G-14084)***
Galion Packaging Co Inc.....419 468-2548
340 S East St Galion (44833) ***(G-10140)***
Galion-Godwin Truck Bdy Co LLC.....330 359-5495
7415 Peabody Kent Rd Millersburg (44654) ***(G-14084)***
Gallagher Lumber Co.....330 274-2333
10272 Vaughn Rd Mantua (44255) ***(G-12546)***
Gallagher Wood & Crafts.....513 523-2748
2715 Scott Rd Oxford (45056) ***(G-15693)***
Galleria Co (HQ).....513 983-1490
1 Procter And Gamble Plz Cincinnati (45202) ***(G-3722)***
Galley Printing Inc.....330 220-5577
2892 Westway Dr Brunswick (44212) ***(G-2208)***
Galley Printing Company, Brunswick *Also called Galley Printing Inc* ***(G-2208)***
Gallo Displays Inc (PA).....216 431-9500
4922 E 49th St Cleveland (44125) ***(G-5288)***
Galt Alloys, Canton *Also called Rmi Titanium Company LLC* ***(G-2807)***
Galt Alloys Inc Main Ofc.....330 453-4678
122 Central Plz N Canton (44702) ***(G-2678)***
Gamco, Cleveland *Also called General Aluminum Mfg Company* ***(G-5304)***
Gamco Componets Group LLC.....440 593-1500
1370 Chamberlain Blvd Conneaut (44030) ***(G-7645)***
Gameday Vision.....330 830-4550
1147 Oberlin Ave Sw Massillon (44647) ***(G-12985)***
Gametime Apparel & Dezigns LLC.....740 255-5254
2327 E Wheeling Ave Cambridge (43725) ***(G-2439)***
Ganger Enterprises Inc.....614 776-3985
214 Hoff Rd Unit D Westerville (43082) ***(G-19993)***
Gannett Co Inc.....740 345-4053
22 N 1st St Newark (43055) ***(G-14876)***
Gannett Co Inc.....513 721-2700
312 Elm St Ste 1400 Cincinnati (45202) ***(G-3723)***
Gannett Co Inc.....740 654-1321
123 S Broad St Ste 233 Lancaster (43130) ***(G-11574)***
Gannett Co Inc.....740 773-2111
50 W Main St Chillicothe (45601) ***(G-3188)***
Gannett Co Inc.....419 521-7341
163 E Center St Marion (43302) ***(G-12703)***
Gannett Co Inc.....740 452-4561
3871 Gorsky Dr Zanesville (43701) ***(G-21141)***
Gannett Co Inc.....419 332-5511
1700 Cedar St Fremont (43420) ***(G-10020)***
Gannett Co Inc.....419 522-3311
70 W 4th St Mansfield (44903) ***(G-12443)***
Gannett Co Inc.....740 349-1100
2 N 1st St Newark (43055) ***(G-14877)***
Gannett Publishing Svcs LLC.....419 522-3311
70 W 4th St Mansfield (44903) ***(G-12444)***
Gannett Stllite Info Ntwrk Inc.....513 721-2700
312 Elm St Ste 1400 Cincinnati (45202) ***(G-3724)***
Gannett Stllite Info Ntwrk LLC.....419 334-1012
1800 E State St Ste B Fremont (43420) ***(G-10021)***
Gannons Discount Blinds.....216 398-2761
2725 Ralph Ave Cleveland (44109) ***(G-5289)***
Ganymede Technologies Corp.....419 562-5522
1685 Marion Rd Bucyrus (44820) ***(G-2330)***
Ganzcorp Investments Inc.....330 963-5400
2300 Pinnacle Pkwy Twinsburg (44087) ***(G-18778)***
Garber Co.....937 462-8730
5818 Old State Route 42 South Charleston (45368) ***(G-17272)***
Garber Farms, Greenville *Also called Russell L Garber* ***(G-10394)***
Garber Machine Co.....330 399-4181
1788 Drexel Ave Nw Warren (44485) ***(G-19404)***
Garda CL Technical Svcs Inc.....937 294-4099
2690 Lance Dr Moraine (45409) ***(G-14355)***
Gardella Jewelry LLC.....440 877-9261
7432 Julia Dr North Royalton (44133) ***(G-15273)***
Garden Art Innovations LLC.....330 697-0007
30 2nd St Sw Barberton (44203) ***(G-1072)***
Garden of Delight LLC.....513 300-7205
5540 Chandler St Cincinnati (45227) ***(G-3725)***
Garden of Flavor LLC.....216 702-7991
7501 Carnegie Ave Cleveland (44103) ***(G-5290)***
Garden Street Iron & Metal (PA).....513 853-3700
2885 Spring Grove Ave Cincinnati (45225) ***(G-3726)***
Gardener, Cleveland *Also called Gardner Denver Nash LLC* ***(G-5291)***
Gardenscape, Archbold *Also called Tri-State Garden Supply Inc* ***(G-672)***
Gardner Business Media Inc.....513 527-8800
6925 Valley Ave Cincinnati (45244) ***(G-3727)***
Gardner Denver Nash LLC.....440 871-9505
7420 Pine River Ct Cleveland (44130) ***(G-5291)***
Gardner Lumber Co Inc.....740 254-4664
5805 Laurel Creek Rd Se Tippecanoe (44699) ***(G-18148)***
Gardner Metal Craft Inc.....513 539-4538
490 S Main St Monroe (45050) ***(G-14263)***
Gardner Signs Inc (PA).....419 385-6669
3800 Airport Hwy Toledo (43615) ***(G-18301)***
Gareth Stevens Publishing LP.....800 542-2595
23221 Morgan Ct Strongsville (44149) ***(G-17746)***
Garfield Alloys Inc (PA).....216 587-4843
4878 Chaincraft Rd Cleveland (44125) ***(G-5292)***
Garick LLC (PA).....216 581-0100
13600 Broadway Ave Ste 1 Cleveland (44125) ***(G-5293)***
Garland Industries Inc (PA).....216 641-7500
3800 E 91st St Cleveland (44105) ***(G-5294)***
Garland Welding Co Inc.....330 536-6506
804 E Liberty St Lowellville (44436) ***(G-12251)***
Garland/Dbs Inc.....216 641-7500
3800 E 91st St Cleveland (44105) ***(G-5295)***
Garment Specialties Inc.....330 425-2928
1885 E Aurora Rd Twinsburg (44087) ***(G-18779)***
Garner Industries Inc.....740 349-0238
767 Country Club Dr Newark (43055) ***(G-14878)***
Garro Tread Corporation (PA).....330 376-3125
100 Beech St Akron (44308) ***(G-181)***
Garsite/Progress LLC.....419 424-1100
1005 Lima Ave Findlay (45840) ***(G-9692)***
Garvey Corporation.....330 779-0700
1019 Ohio Works Dr Youngstown (44510) ***(G-20911)***
Garvin Industries Div, Strongsville *Also called Guarantee Specialties Inc* ***(G-17747)***
Garvin Tool & Die Inc.....419 334-2392
3000 State Route 412 Fremont (43420) ***(G-10022)***
Gary Brown Farm & Sawmill.....740 372-5022
3575 State Route 348 Otway (45657) ***(G-15688)***
Gary Compton.....937 339-6829
3245 Piqua Troy Rd Troy (45373) ***(G-18660)***
Gary I Teach Jr.....614 582-7483
4855 Rsdale Mlford Ctr Rd London (43140) ***(G-12060)***
Gary L Gast.....419 626-5915
2024 Campbell St Sandusky (44870) ***(G-16812)***
Gary Lawrence Enterprises Inc.....330 833-7181
21 Charles Ave Sw Massillon (44646) ***(G-12986)***
Garys Chesecakes Fine Desserts.....513 574-1700
5285 Crookshank Rd Side Cincinnati (45238) ***(G-3728)***
Garys Classic Guitars.....513 891-0555
6692 Sandy Shores Dr Loveland (45140) ***(G-12190)***
Gas & Grills, Willoughby *Also called Lapa Lowe Enterprises LLC* ***(G-20360)***
Gas Analytical Services Inc.....330 539-4267
1688 Shannon Rd Girard (44420) ***(G-10260)***
Gas Enterprise Company, Wingett Run *Also called James L Williams* ***(G-20536)***
Gas Products, Cambridge *Also called Aci Services Inc* ***(G-2421)***
Gas Tran Systems, Streetsboro *Also called Cleveland Gas Systems LLC* ***(G-17665)***
Gas Turbine Fuel Systems, Mentor *Also called Parker-Hannifin Corporation* ***(G-13542)***

Gasdorf Tool and Mch Co Inc 419 227-0103
445 N Mcdonel St Lima (45801) *(G-11867)*
Gasflux Company 440 365-1941
32 Hawthorne St Elyria (44035) *(G-9262)*
Gasko Fabricated Products LLC (HQ) 330 239-1781
4049 Ridge Rd Medina (44256) *(G-13266)*
Gaslamp Popcorn Company 951 684-6767
6575 Bellefontaine Rd Lima (45804) *(G-11868)*
Gasoila Thred-Taper, Cleveland *Also called Federal Process Corporation (G-5227)*
Gaspar Inc 330 477-2222
1545 Whipple Ave Sw Canton (44710) *(G-2679)*
Gaspar Services LLC 330 467-8292
7791 Capital Blvd Ste 2 Macedonia (44056) *(G-12299)*
Gasser Chair Co Inc (PA) 330 534-2234
4136 Logan Way Youngstown (44505) *(G-20912)*
Gasser Chair Co Inc 330 534-2234
4136 Logan Way Youngstown (44505) *(G-20913)*
Gasser Chair Co Inc 330 759-2234
2457 Logan Ave Youngstown (44505) *(G-20914)*
Gate West Coast Ventures LLC 513 891-1000
4412 Carver Woods Dr # 105 Blue Ash (45242) *(G-1781)*
Gatesair Inc (HQ) 513 459-3400
5300 Kings Island Dr Mason (45040) *(G-12875)*
Gateway Concrete Forming Svcs 513 353-2000
5938 Hamilton Cleves Rd Miamitown (45041) *(G-13746)*
Gateway Industrial Pdts Inc 440 324-4112
160 Freedom Ct Elyria (44035) *(G-9263)*
Gateway Industries 330 633-3700
1236 Brittain Rd Akron (44310) *(G-182)*
Gateway Metal Finishing Inc 216 267-2580
5310 W 161st St Ste J Cleveland (44142) *(G-5296)*
Gateway Printing, Wadsworth *Also called Rohrer Corporation (G-19275)*
Gathering Place, Galion *Also called Ginnys Custom Framing Gallery (G-10142)*
Gatton Packaging Inc 419 886-2577
99 East St Bellville (44813) *(G-1556)*
Gauntlet Awards & Engraving 937 890-5811
9153 N Dixie Dr Dayton (45414) *(G-8214)*
Gaydash Enterprises Inc 330 896-4811
3640 Tabs Dr Uniontown (44685) *(G-18920)*
Gaydash Industries, Uniontown *Also called Gaydash Enterprises Inc (G-18920)*
Gayston Corporation 937 743-6050
721 Richard St Miamisburg (45342) *(G-13672)*
Gazette Publishing, Conneaut *Also called The Gazette Printing Co Inc (G-7660)*
Gazette Publishing Company (PA) 419 483-4190
42 S Main St Oberlin (44074) *(G-15495)*
Gazette Publishing Company 419 335-2010
1270 N Shoop Ave Ste A Wauseon (43567) *(G-19517)*
Gazzette, The, Medina *Also called Medina County Publications Inc (G-13293)*
Gb Fabrication Company 419 347-1835
2510 Taylortown Rd Shelby (44875) *(G-16982)*
Gb Fabrication Company (HQ) 419 896-3191
60 Scott St Shiloh (44878) *(G-16993)*
Gb Image Machine Incorporated (PA) 419 628-4150
351 Industrial Dr Minster (45865) *(G-14215)*
Gb Liquidating Company Inc 513 248-7600
22 Whitney Dr Milford (45150) *(G-14010)*
Gb Manufacturing Company (PA) 419 822-5323
1120 E Main St Delta (43515) *(G-8772)*
Gbc International LLC 513 943-7283
1091 Ohio Pike Cincinnati (45245) *(G-3251)*
Gbc Metals LLC 330 823-1700
2081 Mccrea St Alliance (44601) *(G-469)*
Gbi Cincinnati Inc 513 841-8684
7700 Shawnee Run Rd Cincinnati (45243) *(G-3729)*
Gbm Golf, Loudonville *Also called Golf Ball Manufacturers LLC (G-12142)*
GBS Corp (PA) 330 494-5330
7233 Freedom Ave Nw North Canton (44720) *(G-15085)*
GBS Corp 330 929-8050
3658 Wyoga Lake Rd Stow (44224) *(G-17591)*
GBS Corp 330 863-1828
224 Morges Rd Malvern (44644) *(G-12391)*
GBS Filing Solutions, Malvern *Also called GBS Corp (G-12391)*
GBS Printech Solutions, North Canton *Also called GBS Corp (G-15085)*
Gc Controls Inc 440 779-4777
3926 Pine Cir North Olmsted (44070) *(G-15191)*
GCI Digital Imaging Inc 513 521-7446
5031 Winton Rd Cincinnati (45232) *(G-3730)*
GCI Metals Inc 937 262-7500
7660 W 3rd St Dayton (45417) *(G-8215)*
Gdc Inc 574 533-3128
1700 Old Mansfield Rd Wooster (44691) *(G-20596)*
Gdc Industries LLC 937 367-7229
1423 Research Park Dr Beavercreek (45432) *(G-1316)*
Gdc Industries LLC 937 640-1212
49 Front St Dayton (45402) *(G-8216)*
Gdic Group LLC (PA) 330 468-0700
1300 E 9th St Fl 20 Cleveland (44114) *(G-5297)*
Gdj Inc 440 975-0258
7585 Tyler Blvd Mentor (44060) *(G-13455)*
Gdw Woodworking LLC 513 494-3041
120 Vista Ridge Dr South Lebanon (45065) *(G-17276)*
Gdy Installations Inc 419 467-0036
302 Arco Dr Toledo (43607) *(G-18302)*
GE, Aurora *Also called USA Instruments Inc (G-913)*
GE, Beavercreek *Also called Unison Industries LLC (G-1346)*
GE Additive, West Chester *Also called General Electric Company (G-19714)*
GE Aircraft Engines 513 868-9906
5871 Greenlawn Rd Fairfield Township (45011) *(G-9581)*
GE Aircraft Engines 513 243-2000
1 Neumann Way Cincinnati (45215) *(G-3731)*
GE Aviation Services, Cincinnati *Also called GE Aviation Systems LLC (G-3733)*
GE Aviation Systems LLC 937 898-5881
740 E National Rd Vandalia (45377) *(G-19124)*
GE Aviation Systems LLC 937 898-9600
6800 Poe Ave Dayton (45414) *(G-8217)*
GE Aviation Systems LLC 513 470-2889
10270 Saint Rita Ln Cincinnati (45215) *(G-3732)*
GE Aviation Systems LLC 513 977-1500
201 W Crescentville Rd Cincinnati (45246) *(G-3733)*
GE Aviation Systems LLC 513 733-1611
11988 Tramway Dr Cincinnati (45241) *(G-3734)*
GE Aviation Systems LLC 513 889-5150
5223 Muhlhauser Rd West Chester (45011) *(G-19710)*
GE Aviation Systems LLC 513 552-5663
123 Merchant St Cincinnati (45246) *(G-3735)*
GE Aviation Systems LLC 513 552-4278
9100 Centre Pointe Dr West Chester (45069) *(G-19711)*
GE Aviation Systems LLC (HQ) 937 898-9600
1 Neumann Way Cincinnati (45215) *(G-3736)*
GE Aviation Systems LLC 937 898-5881
740 E National Rd Vandalia (45377) *(G-19125)*
GE Healthcare Inc 513 241-5955
346 Gest St Cincinnati (45203) *(G-3737)*
GE Healthcare Inc 502 452-4311
34825 Lakeview Dr Solon (44139) *(G-17146)*
GE Infrastructure Sensing Inc 740 928-7010
611 O Neill Dr Hebron (43025) *(G-10744)*
GE Intelligent Platforms Inc 937 459-5404
5438 S State Route 49 Greenville (45331) *(G-10372)*
GE Medical Systems Information 216 663-2110
18683 S Miles Rd Warrensville Heights (44128) *(G-19468)*
GE Military Systems 513 243-2000
1 Neumann Way Cincinnati (45215) *(G-3738)*
GE Rolls Royce Fighter 513 243-2787
1 Neumann Way 318a Cincinnati (45215) *(G-3739)*
GE Water & Process Tech, New Philadelphia *Also called Suez Wts Usa Inc (G-14802)*
Gear Company of America Inc 216 671-5400
14300 Lorain Ave Cleveland (44111) *(G-5298)*
Gear Products Co, Willoughby *Also called T & S Discount Tires Inc (G-20439)*
Gear Star American Performance 330 434-5216
132 N Howard St Akron (44308) *(G-183)*
Gearhart Machine Company 330 253-1880
1145 Highbrook St Ste 508 Akron (44301) *(G-184)*
Gearing Solutions Inc 440 498-9538
5905 Harper Rd Ste A Solon (44139) *(G-17147)*
Geartec Inc 440 953-3900
4245 Hamann Pkwy Willoughby (44094) *(G-20330)*
Geauga Coatings LLC 440 286-5571
15120 Sisson Rd Chardon (44024) *(G-3113)*
Geauga Concrete Inc 440 338-4915
10509 Kinsman Rd Newbury (44065) *(G-14952)*
Geauga Feed and Grain Supply 440 564-5000
11030 Kinsman Rd Newbury (44065) *(G-14953)*
Geauga Group LLC 440 543-8797
11024 Wingate Dr Chagrin Falls (44023) *(G-3047)*
Geauga Rehab Engineering, Chardon *Also called Geauga Rhabilitation Engrg Inc (G-3114)*
Geauga Rhabilitation Engrg Inc (PA) 216 536-0826
13376 Ravenna Rd Chardon (44024) *(G-3114)*
Gebauer Company 216 581-3030
4444 E 153rd St Cleveland (44128) *(G-5299)*
Ged Holdings Inc 330 963-5401
9280 Dutton Dr Twinsburg (44087) *(G-18780)*
Gedco Inc 330 828-2044
130 Briarwood Dr Dalton (44618) *(G-7942)*
Gedico International Inc 937 274-2167
4050 Grafix Blvd Dayton (45417) *(G-8218)*
Gehm & Sons Limited (PA) 330 724-8423
825 S Arlington St Akron (44306) *(G-185)*
Gei, Youngstown *Also called General Extrusions Inc (G-20917)*
Gei of Columbiana Inc 330 783-0270
4040 Lake Park Rd Youngstown (44512) *(G-20915)*
Geist Co Inc 216 771-2200
1814 W 30th St Cleveland (44113) *(G-5300)*
Gellner Engineering Inc 216 398-8500
2827 Brookpark Rd Cleveland (44134) *(G-5301)*
Gelok International Corp 419 352-1482
20189 Pine Lake Rd Dunbridge (43414) *(G-9015)*

A L P H A B E T I C

Gem Beverages Inc 740 384-2411
106 E 11th St Wellston (45692) *(G-19600)*
Gem City Engineering & Mfg, Dayton *Also called Gem City Engineering Co (G-8219)*
Gem City Engineering Co (PA) 937 223-5544
401 Leo St Dayton (45404) *(G-8219)*
Gem City Golf Club, Fairborn *Also called Zwf Golf LLC (G-9476)*
Gem City Metal Tech LLC 937 252-8998
1825 E 1st St Dayton (45403) *(G-8220)*
Gem Coatings Ltd 740 589-2998
5840 Industrial Park Rd Athens (45701) *(G-832)*
Gem Instrument Co 330 273-6117
2832 Nationwide Pkwy Brunswick (44212) *(G-2209)*
Gem Ornamental Iron Co 216 661-6965
4681 Broadview Rd Cleveland (44109) *(G-5302)*
Gem Tool LLC 216 771-8444
127 Public Sq Cleveland (44114) *(G-5303)*
Gemco Machine & Tool Inc 740 344-3111
88 Decrow Ave Newark (43055) *(G-14879)*
Gemini Fiber Corporation 330 874-4131
11145 Industrial Pkwy Nw Bolivar (44612) *(G-1915)*
Gemini Products, Brecksville *Also called Knight Ergonomics Inc (G-2045)*
Gempco, Akron *Also called General Metals Powder Co (G-186)*
Gen III 614 737-8744
2300 Lockbourne Rd Columbus (43207) *(G-6944)*
Gendron Wheel LLC 419 445-6060
400 E Lugbill Rd Archbold (43502) *(G-649)*
General Aluminum Mfg Company (HQ) 330 297-1225
6065 Parkland Blvd Cleveland (44124) *(G-5304)*
General Aluminum Mfg Company 330 297-1020
5159 S Prospect St Ravenna (44266) *(G-16381)*
General Aluminum Mfg Company 419 739-9300
13663 Short Rd Wapakoneta (45895) *(G-19330)*
General Aluminum Mfg Company 440 593-6225
1370 Chamberlain Blvd Conneaut (44030) *(G-7646)*
General Aquatics, Cincinnati *Also called Flow Control US Holding Corp (G-3698)*
General Awning Company Inc 216 749-0110
1350 E Granger Rd Cleveland (44131) *(G-5305)*
General Bar Inc 440 835-2000
25000 Center Ridge Rd # 3 Westlake (44145) *(G-20117)*
General Book Binding, Chesterland *Also called Hf Group LLC (G-3161)*
General Chain & Mfg Corp 513 541-6005
3274 Beekman St Cincinnati (45223) *(G-3740)*
General Color Investments Inc 330 868-4161
250 Bridge St Minerva (44657) *(G-14180)*
General Cutlery Inc (PA) 419 332-2316
1918 N County Road 232 Fremont (43420) *(G-10023)*
General Data Company Inc (PA) 513 752-7978
4354 Ferguson Dr Cincinnati (45245) *(G-3252)*
General Data Healthcare Inc 513 752-7978
4043 Mcmann Rd Cincinnati (45245) *(G-3253)*
General Die Casters Inc 330 467-6700
6212 Akron Peninsula Rd Northfield (44067) *(G-15318)*
General Die Casters Inc (PA) 330 678-2528
2150 Highland Rd Twinsburg (44087) *(G-18781)*
General Dyn Lima Army T P, Lima *Also called General Dynamics Land (G-11869)*
General Dynamics Land 419 221-7000
1161 Buckeye Rd Lima (45804) *(G-11869)*
General Dynamics-Ots Inc 937 746-8500
200 S Pioneer Blvd Springboro (45066) *(G-17328)*
General Dynmics Mssion Systems 513 253-4770
2673 Commons Blvd Ste 200 Beavercreek (45431) *(G-1317)*
General Electric Company 440 593-1156
3159 Wildwood Dr Mc Donald (44437) *(G-13197)*
General Electric Company 419 563-1200
1250 S Walnut St Bucyrus (44820) *(G-2331)*
General Electric Company 740 623-5379
1350 S 2nd St Coshocton (43812) *(G-7735)*
General Electric Company 216 883-1000
4477 E 49th St Cleveland (44125) *(G-5306)*
General Electric Company 216 266-2121
1975 Noble Rd Cleveland (44112) *(G-5307)*
General Electric Company 513 977-1500
201 W Crescentville Rd Cincinnati (45246) *(G-3741)*
General Electric Company 513 243-9317
9050 Centre Pointe Dr West Chester (45069) *(G-19712)*
General Electric Company 740 385-2114
Hc 93 Box N Logan (43138) *(G-12025)*
General Electric Company 330 425-3755
8499 Darrow Rd Twinsburg (44087) *(G-18782)*
General Electric Company 330 455-2140
1807 Allen Ave Se Canton (44707) *(G-2680)*
General Electric Company 216 663-2110
18683 S Miles Rd Cleveland (44128) *(G-5308)*
General Electric Company 330 793-3911
280 N Meridian Rd Youngstown (44509) *(G-20916)*
General Electric Company 513 948-4170
445 S Cooper Ave Cincinnati (45215) *(G-3742)*
General Electric Company 740 928-7010
611 O Neill Dr Hebron (43025) *(G-10745)*
General Electric Company 330 297-0861
3159 Wildwood Dr Mc Donald (44437) *(G-13198)*
General Electric Company 330 373-1400
3159 Wildwood Dr Mc Donald (44437) *(G-13199)*
General Electric Company 216 391-8741
1814 E 45th St Cleveland (44103) *(G-5309)*
General Electric Company 513 552-5364
9100 Centre Pointe Dr # 4 West Chester (45069) *(G-19713)*
General Electric Company 216 268-3846
1099 Ivanhoe Rd Cleveland (44110) *(G-5310)*
General Electric Company 216 266-2357
21800 Tungsten Rd Cleveland (44117) *(G-5311)*
General Electric Company 513 341-0214
6380 Aviation Way West Chester (45069) *(G-19714)*
General Electric Company 330 458-3200
5555 Massillon Rd Bldg D Canton (44720) *(G-2681)*
General Electric Company 513 552-2000
1 Neumann Way Cincinnati (45215) *(G-3743)*
General Electric Intl Inc 410 737-7228
191 Rosa Parks St Cincinnati (45202) *(G-3744)*
General Electric Intl Inc 330 963-2066
8941 Dutton Dr Twinsburg (44087) *(G-18783)*
General Engine Products LLC 937 704-0160
2000 Watkins Glen Dr Franklin (45005) *(G-9886)*
General Environmental Science 216 464-0680
3659 Green Rd Ste 306 Beachwood (44122) *(G-1239)*
General Equipped Products, Columbus *Also called U S Fuel Development Co (G-7553)*
General Extrusions Inc 330 783-0270
4040 Lake Park Rd Youngstown (44512) *(G-20917)*
General Fabrications Corp 419 625-6055
7777 Milan Rd Sandusky (44870) *(G-16813)*
General Films Inc 888 436-3456
645 S High St Covington (45318) *(G-7786)*
General Glass & Screen Inc 440 350-9033
6095 Pinecone Dr Mentor (44060) *(G-13456)*
General Industrial Supply, Piqua *Also called Gisco Inc (G-16118)*
General Intl Pwr Pdts LLC 419 877-5234
6243 Industrial Pkwy Whitehouse (43571) *(G-20191)*
General Machine & Saw Company (PA) 740 382-1104
740 W Center St Marion (43302) *(G-12704)*
General Machine & Saw Company 740 375-5730
305 Davis St Marion (43302) *(G-12705)*
General Machine & Supply Co 740 453-4804
3135 Lookout Dr Zanesville (43701) *(G-21142)*
General Machine and Mould Co, Lancaster *Also called Devault Machine & Mould Co LLC (G-11563)*
General Metals Powder Co (PA) 330 633-1226
1195 Home Ave Akron (44310) *(G-186)*
General Mills Inc 513 771-8200
11301 Mosteller Rd Cincinnati (45241) *(G-3745)*
General Mills Inc 513 770-0558
5181 Natorp Blvd Ste 540 Mason (45040) *(G-12876)*
General Mills Inc 419 269-3100
1250 W Laskey Rd Toledo (43612) *(G-18303)*
General Mills Inc 740 286-2170
2403 S Pennsylvania Ave Wellston (45692) *(G-19601)*
General Motors LLC 419 782-7010
26427 State Route 281 Defiance (43512) *(G-8623)*
General Motors LLC 330 824-5000
2300 Hallock Young Rd Sw Warren (44481) *(G-19405)*
General Motors LLC 330 824-5840
2369 Ellsworth Bailey Rd Warren (44481) *(G-19406)*
General Motors LLC 216 265-5000
5400 Chevrolet Blvd Cleveland (44130) *(G-5312)*
General Nano, Cincinnati *Also called Veelo Technologies LLC (G-4469)*
General Parts Inc 614 891-6014
24 E Schrock Rd Westerville (43081) *(G-20055)*
General Plastex Inc 330 745-7775
35 Stuver Pl Barberton (44203) *(G-1073)*
General Plastics North Corp 800 542-2466
5220 Vine St Cincinnati (45217) *(G-3746)*
General Plug and Mfg Co (PA) 440 926-2411
455 Main St Grafton (44044) *(G-10301)*
General Precision Corporation 440 951-9380
4553 Beidler Rd Willoughby (44094) *(G-20331)*
General Pump & Eqp Compnay 330 455-2100
3276 Bruening Ave Sw Canton (44706) *(G-2682)*
General Sheave Company Inc 216 781-8120
1335 Main Ave Cleveland (44113) *(G-5313)*
General Steel Corporation 216 883-4200
3344 E 80th St Cleveland (44127) *(G-5314)*
General Technologies Inc 419 747-1800
855 W Longview Ave Mansfield (44906) *(G-12445)*
General Theming Contrs LLC 614 252-6342
3750 Courtright Ct Columbus (43227) *(G-6945)*
General Tool Company (PA) 513 733-5500
101 Landy Ln Cincinnati (45215) *(G-3747)*
Generals Books 614 870-1861
522 Norton Rd Columbus (43228) *(G-6946)*

Generations Coffee Company LLC (HQ)....440 546-0901
60100 W Snowell Brecksville (44141) ***(G-2038)***
Generic Systems Inc....419 841-8460
10560 Geiser Rd Holland (43528) ***(G-10932)***
Genesco Inc....330 633-8179
2000 Brittain Rd Ste 681 Akron (44310) ***(G-187)***
Genesis Display Systems Inc....513 561-1440
4004 Erie Ct Cincinnati (45227) ***(G-3748)***
Genesis Graphics....937 335-5332
14 N Walnut St Ste 2 Troy (45373) ***(G-18661)***
Genesis Lamp Corp....440 354-0095
375 N Saint Clair St Painesville (44077) ***(G-15741)***
Genesis Plastic Tech LLC....440 542-0722
27200 Tinkers Ct Solon (44139) ***(G-17148)***
Genesis Quality Printing Inc....440 975-5700
7250 Commerce Dr Ste G Mentor (44060) ***(G-13457)***
Genesis Services LLC....740 896-3734
565 Straight Run Rd Beverly (45715) ***(G-1661)***
Genesis Steel Corp....740 282-2300
6th & Adams St Steubenville (43952) ***(G-17535)***
Geneva Gear & Machine Inc....937 866-0318
339 Progress Rd Dayton (45449) ***(G-8221)***
Geneva Liberty Steel Ltd (PA)....330 740-0103
947 Martin Luther King Jr Youngstown (44502) ***(G-20918)***
Geneva Rubber Company, Cortland *Also called Control Transformer Inc* ***(G-7706)***
Genex Mold, Canton *Also called Dlhbowles Inc* ***(G-2662)***
Genex Tool & Die Inc....330 788-2466
4000 Lake Park Rd Youngstown (44512) ***(G-20919)***
Genie Company, The, Mount Hope *Also called GMI Holdings Inc* ***(G-14437)***
Genie Repros Inc....216 965-0213
2211 Hamilton Ave Cleveland (44114) ***(G-5315)***
Genii Inc....651 501-4810
5976 Heisley Rd Mentor (44060) ***(G-13458)***
GENMAK GENEVA LIBERTY, Youngstown *Also called Geneva Liberty Steel Ltd* ***(G-20918)***
Gennaro Pavers....330 536-6825
6065 Arrel Smith Rd Lowellville (44436) ***(G-12252)***
Genoa Healthcare....740 370-0759
901 Washington St Portsmouth (45662) ***(G-16283)***
Genoa Healthcare LLC....513 727-0471
1036 S Verity Pkwy Middletown (45044) ***(G-13909)***
Genoa Healthcare LLC....567 202-8326
1832 Adams St Toledo (43604) ***(G-18304)***
Genoa Healthcare LLC....513 541-0164
5837 Hamilton Ave Cincinnati (45224) ***(G-3749)***
Genpak LLC....614 276-5156
845 Kaderly Dr Columbus (43228) ***(G-6947)***
Gent Machine Company....216 481-2334
12315 Kirby Ave Cleveland (44108) ***(G-5316)***
Gentek Building Products Inc (HQ)....800 548-4542
3773 State Rd Cuyahoga Falls (44223) ***(G-7872)***
Gentzler Tool & Die Corp (PA)....330 896-1941
3903 Massillon Rd Akron (44312) ***(G-188)***
Genvac Aerospace Corp (PA)....440 646-9986
110 Alpha Park Cleveland (44143) ***(G-5317)***
Geo Specialty Chemical....330 650-0237
2685 Blue Heron Dr Hudson (44236) ***(G-11045)***
Geo-Tech Polymers LLC....614 797-2300
423 Hopewell Rd Ste 2 Waverly (45690) ***(G-19546)***
Geocentral, Mason *Also called CM Paula Company* ***(G-12849)***
Geocore Drilling Inc....419 864-4011
2918 Us Highway 42 Cardington (43315) ***(G-2872)***
Geocorp Inc....419 433-1101
9010 River Rd Huron (44839) ***(G-11094)***
Geodyne One, Columbus *Also called Mori Shuji* ***(G-7196)***
Geograph Industries Inc....513 202-9200
475 Industrial Dr Harrison (45030) ***(G-10643)***
Geopetro LLC....614 885-9350
7100 N High St Ste 303 Worthington (43085) ***(G-20686)***
George & Underwood LLP....513 409-5631
530 N Broadway St Lebanon (45036) ***(G-11653)***
George A Mitchell Company....330 758-5777
557 Mcclurg Rd Youngstown (44512) ***(G-20920)***
George Manufacturing Inc....513 932-1067
160 Harmon Ave Lebanon (45036) ***(G-11654)***
George R Klein News, Cleveland *Also called Ckm Ventures LLC* ***(G-4935)***
George R Silcott Railway Equip....614 885-7224
564 E Dublin Granville Rd Worthington (43085) ***(G-20687)***
George Steel Fabricating Inc....513 932-2887
1207 S Us Route 42 Lebanon (45036) ***(G-11655)***
George Weston Co....614 868-7565
1020 Claycraft Rd Ste D Columbus (43230) ***(G-6948)***
George Whalley Company....216 453-0099
1180 High St Ste 1 Fairport Harbor (44077) ***(G-9623)***
Georges Donuts Inc....330 963-9902
7995 Darrow Rd Twinsburg (44087) ***(G-18784)***
Georgetown Vineyards Inc....740 435-3222
62920 Georgetown Rd Cambridge (43725) ***(G-2440)***
Georgia Metal Coatings Company....770 446-3930
275 Industrial Pkwy Chardon (44024) ***(G-3115)***
Georgia-Boot Inc....740 753-1951
39 E Canal St Nelsonville (45764) ***(G-14593)***
Georgia-Pacific LLC....740 477-3347
2850 Owens Rd Circleville (43113) ***(G-4546)***
Georgia-Pacific LLC....513 336-4200
5181 Natorp Blvd Ste 520 Mason (45040) ***(G-12877)***
Georgia-Pacific LLC....614 491-9100
1975 Watkins Rd Columbus (43207) ***(G-6949)***
Georgia-Pacific LLC....513 536-3020
4225 Curliss Ln Batavia (45103) ***(G-1149)***
Georgia-Pacific LLC....330 794-4444
3265 Gilchrist Rd Mogadore (44260) ***(G-14238)***
Georgia-Pacific LLC....513 942-4800
9048 Port Union Rialto Rd West Chester (45069) ***(G-19715)***
Geotech Pattern & Mold Inc....513 683-2600
272 E Kemper Rd Loveland (45140) ***(G-12191)***
Gerald Christman....740 838-2475
47278 Swazey Rd Lewisville (43754) ***(G-11803)***
Gerald D Damron....740 894-3680
197 Township Road 1156 Chesapeake (45619) ***(G-3146)***
Gerald Grain Center Inc....419 445-2451
3265 County Road 24 Archbold (43502) ***(G-650)***
Gerald H Smith....740 446-3455
670 Buck Ridge Rd Bidwell (45614) ***(G-1666)***
Gerald L Hermann Co Inc....513 661-1818
3325 Harrison Ave Cincinnati (45211) ***(G-3750)***
Gerber & Sons Inc (PA)....330 897-6201
201 E Main St Baltic (43804) ***(G-1030)***
Gerber Farm Division Inc....800 362-7381
5889 Kidron Rd Kidron (44636) ***(G-11446)***
Gerber Wood Products Inc....330 857-3901
6075 Kidron Rd Kidron (44636) ***(G-11447)***
Gerdau Macsteel Atmosphere Ann....330 478-0314
1501 Raff Rd Sw Canton (44710) ***(G-2683)***
Gergel-Kellem Company Inc....216 398-2000
4544 Hinckley Indus Pkwy Cleveland (44109) ***(G-5318)***
Gerich Fiberglass Inc....419 362-4591
7004 Us Highway 42 Mount Gilead (43338) ***(G-14424)***
Gerling and Associates Inc....740 965-6200
138 Stelzer Ct Sunbury (43074) ***(G-17886)***
GERM GUARDIAN, Euclid *Also called Guardian Technologies LLC* ***(G-9415)***
Gerow Equipment Company Inc....216 383-8800
706 E 163rd St Cleveland (44110) ***(G-5319)***
Gerstco Division, Wooster *Also called Artiflex Manufacturing LLC* ***(G-20564)***
Gerstenslager Construction....330 832-3604
343 16th St Se Massillon (44646) ***(G-12987)***
Gerstenslager Hardwood Pdts, Massillon *Also called Gerstenslager Construction* ***(G-12987)***
Gerstner International, Dayton *Also called H Gerstner & Sons Inc* ***(G-8241)***
Gervasi Vineyard, Canton *Also called Vervasi Vineyard & Itln Bistro* ***(G-2860)***
Gew Inc....440 237-4439
11941 Abbey Rd Ste X Cleveland (44133) ***(G-5320)***
Geyer Transport & Mfg....740 382-9008
1443 N Main St Marion (43302) ***(G-12706)***
Geyers Markets Inc....419 468-9477
230 Portland Way N Galion (44833) ***(G-10141)***
Geygan Enterprises Inc....513 932-4222
101 Dave Ave Ste E Lebanon (45036) ***(G-11656)***
GFS Chemicals Inc (PA)....740 881-5501
3041 Home Rd Powell (43065) ***(G-16322)***
GFS Chemicals Inc....614 224-5345
851 Mckinley Ave Columbus (43222) ***(G-6950)***
GFS Chemicals Inc....614 351-5347
800 Kaderly Dr Columbus (43228) ***(G-6951)***
Ghent Manufacturing, Lebanon *Also called GMI Companies Inc* ***(G-11657)***
Ghostblind Industries Inc....740 374-6766
2347a State Route 821 Marietta (45750) ***(G-12626)***
Ghp II LLC (HQ)....740 687-2500
1115 W 5th Ave Lancaster (43130) ***(G-11575)***
Ghp II LLC....740 681-6825
2893 W Fair Ave Lancaster (43130) ***(G-11576)***
Gia Russa (PA)....330 743-6050
574 Mcclurg Rd Youngstown (44512) ***(G-20921)***
Giannios Candy Co Inc (PA)....330 755-7000
430 Youngstown Poland Rd Struthers (44471) ***(G-17817)***
Giant Eagle, Tallmadge *Also called Tamarkin Company* ***(G-18008)***
Giant Industries Inc....419 531-4600
900 N Westwood Ave Toledo (43607) ***(G-18305)***
Gibbco, Cincinnati *Also called Trans Ash Inc* ***(G-4430)***
Gibbs E & Associates LLC....614 939-1672
7386 Hampsted Sq S New Albany (43054) ***(G-14625)***
Gibraltar Industries Inc....440 617-9230
26314 Center Ridge Rd Westlake (44145) ***(G-20118)***
Gibson Bakery, Oberlin *Also called Gibson Bros Inc* ***(G-15496)***
Gibson Bros Inc....440 774-2401
23 W College St Oberlin (44074) ***(G-15496)***
Gibson Machinery LLC....440 439-4000
181 Oak Leaf Oval Cleveland (44146) ***(G-5321)***
Gibson, Jo K, Marietta *Also called Rockbottom Oil & Gas* ***(G-12664)***

ALPHABETIC

Gie Media Inc (PA) — ALPHABETIC SECTION

Gie Media Inc (PA) 800 456-0707
  5811 Canal Rd Cleveland (44125) *(G-5322)*
Giesecke & Devrient Amer Inc 330 425-1515
  2020 Enterprise Pkwy Twinsburg (44087) *(G-18785)*
Giesecke & Devrient Can 330 425-1515
  2020 Enterprise Pkwy Twinsburg (44087) *(G-18786)*
Giesecke+devrient 330 405-8442
  1960 Enterprise Pkwy Twinsburg (44087) *(G-18787)*
Gift Cove Inc 419 285-2920
  170 Delaware St Put In Bay (43456) *(G-16352)*
Gifted Nutrition, Stow Also called Badizo LLC *(G-17571)*
Gilbert Geiser 330 237-7901
  3301 Longview Pl Nw Canton (44720) *(G-2684)*
Giles Logging LLC 406 855-5284
  7340 Richman Rd Spencer (44275) *(G-17304)*
Gilkey Window Company Inc 513 769-9663
  3528 Hauck Rd Cincinnati (45241) *(G-3751)*
Gilkey Window Company Inc (PA) 513 769-4527
  3625 Hauck Rd Cincinnati (45241) *(G-3752)*
Gillam Machine Company 330 457-2557
  1888 Macklin Rd New Waterford (44445) *(G-14840)*
Gillard Construction Inc 740 376-9744
  1308 Greene St Marietta (45750) *(G-12627)*
Gillig Custom Winery Inc 419 202-6057
  1720 Northridge Rd Findlay (45840) *(G-9693)*
Gills Petroleum LLC 740 702-2600
  213 S Paint St Chillicothe (45601) *(G-3189)*
Gillz LLC (PA) 904 330-1094
  28915 Clemens Rd Ste 20 Westlake (44145) *(G-20119)*
Gilson Machine & Tool Co Inc 419 592-2911
  529 Freedom Dr Napoleon (43545) *(G-14539)*
Gilson Screen Incorporated 419 256-7711
  8-810 K 2 Rd Malinta (43535) *(G-12379)*
Giminetti Baking Company 513 751-7655
  2900 Gilbert Ave Cincinnati (45206) *(G-3753)*
Gingerbread N Bows 740 945-1027
  202 W Main St Scio (43988) *(G-16877)*
Ginko Systems, Dayton Also called Ginko Voting Systems LLC *(G-8222)*
Ginko Voting Systems LLC 937 291-4060
  600 Progress Rd Dayton (45449) *(G-8222)*
Ginnys Custom Framing Gallery 419 468-7240
  1135 Cherington Dr Galion (44833) *(G-10142)*
Gino's Jewelers & Trophy Mfrs, Warrensville Heights Also called Ginos Awards Inc *(G-19469)*
Ginos Awards Inc 216 831-6565
  4701 Richmond Rd Ste 200 Warrensville Heights (44128) *(G-19469)*
Girard Machine Company Inc 330 545-9731
  700 Dot St Girard (44420) *(G-10261)*
Gis Dynamics LLC 513 847-4931
  11315 Williamson Rd Blue Ash (45241) *(G-1782)*
Gisco Inc 937 773-7601
  308 W Statler Rd Piqua (45356) *(G-16118)*
Giti Tech Group Ltd 866 381-7955
  440 Fame Rd West Carrollton (45449) *(G-19632)*
Givaudan 513 482-2536
  110 E 69th St Cincinnati (45216) *(G-3754)*
Givaudan Flavors Corporation 513 948-4933
  100 E 69th St Cincinnati (45216) *(G-3755)*
Givaudan Flavors Corporation 513 948-8000
  110 E 70th St Cincinnati (45216) *(G-3756)*
Givaudan Flvors Fragrances Inc (HQ) 513 948-8000
  1199 Edison Dr Cincinnati (45216) *(G-3757)*
Givaudan Fragrances Corp (HQ) 513 948-3428
  1199 Edison Dr Ste 1-2 Cincinnati (45216) *(G-3758)*
Givaudan Fragrances Corp 513 948-3428
  100 E 69th St Cincinnati (45216) *(G-3759)*
Givaudan Roure US Inc (HQ) 513 948-8000
  1199 Edison Dr Cincinnati (45216) *(G-3760)*
Givaudan US, Cincinnati Also called Givaudan Roure US Inc *(G-3760)*
Givens Lifting Systems Inc 419 724-9001
  26437 Southpoint Rd Perrysburg (43551) *(G-15957)*
Gizmo, Chagrin Falls Also called Whip Guide Co *(G-3090)*
GK Packaging Inc (PA) 614 873-3900
  7680 Commerce Pl Plain City (43064) *(G-16194)*
GKN Driveline Bowl Green Inc (HQ) 419 373-7700
  2223 Wood Bridge Blvd Bowling Green (43402) *(G-1973)*
GKN Driveline Bowling Green, Bowling Green Also called GKN Driveline North Amer Inc *(G-1974)*
GKN Driveline North Amer Inc 419 354-3955
  2223 Wood Bridge Blvd Bowling Green (43402) *(G-1974)*
GKN PLC 740 446-9211
  2160 Eastern Ave Gallipolis (45631) *(G-10165)*
GKN Sinter Metals, Gallipolis Also called GKN PLC *(G-10165)*
GKN Sinter Metals LLC 740 441-3203
  2160 Eastern Ave Gallipolis (45631) *(G-10166)*
GKN Sinter Metals 419 238-8200
  1180 Kear Rd Rear Bldg250 Van Wert (45891) *(G-19092)*
GKN Sinter Metals Mfg Svcs, Van Wert Also called GKN Sinter Metals LLC *(G-19092)*

GL International LLC 330 744-8812
  215 Sinter Ct Youngstown (44510) *(G-20922)*
GL Nause Co Inc 513 722-9500
  1971 Phoenix Dr Loveland (45140) *(G-12192)*
Glas Ornamental Metals Inc 330 753-0215
  1559 Waterloo Rd Barberton (44203) *(G-1074)*
Glascraft Inc 330 966-3000
  8400 Port Jackson Ave Nw North Canton (44720) *(G-15086)*
Glasfloss Industries Inc (PA) 740 687-1100
  2168 Commerce St Lancaster (43130) *(G-11577)*
Glass Axis 614 291-4250
  610 W Town St Columbus (43215) *(G-6952)*
Glass Block Warehouse, The, Columbus Also called Blockamerica Corporation *(G-6680)*
Glass Coatings & Concepts LLC 513 539-5300
  300 Lawton Ave Monroe (45050) *(G-14264)*
Glass Fabricators Inc 216 529-1919
  2160 Halstead Ave Lakewood (44107) *(G-11518)*
Glass Medic America, Westerville Also called Glass Medic Inc *(G-19994)*
Glass Medic Inc 800 356-4009
  6996 Four Seasons Dr Westerville (43082) *(G-19994)*
Glass Mirror Awards Inc 419 638-2221
  703 County Road 26 Helena (43435) *(G-10772)*
Glass Seale Ltd 513 733-1464
  1700 Hunt Rd Cincinnati (45215) *(G-3761)*
Glass Specialties, Fredericksburg Also called Yoder Window & Siding Ltd *(G-9961)*
Glass Surface Systems Inc 330 745-8500
  24 Brown St Barberton (44203) *(G-1075)*
Glasslight Candles LLC 443 509-5505
  8706 Charleston Ridge Dr Mason (45040) *(G-12878)*
Glassline Corporation (PA) 419 666-9712
  28905 Glenwood Rd Perrysburg (43551) *(G-15958)*
Glassrock Plant, Glenford Also called Pioneer Sands LLC *(G-10271)*
Glasstech Inc (PA) 419 661-9500
  995 4th St Perrysburg (43551) *(G-15959)*
Glauners Wholesale Inc 216 398-7088
  5011 Brookpark Rd Cleveland (44134) *(G-5323)*
Glavin Industries Inc 440 349-0049
  6835 Cochran Rd Ste A Solon (44139) *(G-17149)*
Glavin Specialty Co, Solon Also called Glavin Industries Inc *(G-17149)*
Glawe Awnings, Fairborn Also called Glawe Manufacturing Co Inc *(G-9460)*
Glawe Manufacturing Co Inc 937 754-0064
  851 Zapata Dr Fairborn (45324) *(G-9460)*
Glaxosmithkline LLC 937 623-2680
  741 Chaffin Rdg Columbus (43214) *(G-6953)*
Glaxosmithkline LLC 440 552-2895
  37381 Stone Creek Dr North Ridgeville (44039) *(G-15227)*
Glaxosmithkline LLC 330 608-2365
  4273 Ridge Crest Dr Copley (44321) *(G-7685)*
Glaxosmithkline LLC 614 570-5970
  359 Garden Rd Columbus (43214) *(G-6954)*
Glaxosmithkline LLC 330 241-4447
  6250 Highland Meadows Dr Medina (44256) *(G-13267)*
Glazier Pattern & Coach 937 492-7355
  3720 Loramie Wash Rd Houston (45333) *(G-10994)*
GLC Biotechnology Inc 440 349-2193
  7925 Megan Meadow Dr Hudson (44236) *(G-11046)*
Gleason M & M Precision, Dayton Also called Gleason Metrology Systems Corp *(G-8223)*
Gleason Metrology Systems Corp (HQ) 937 384-8901
  300 Progress Rd Dayton (45449) *(G-8223)*
Glebus Alloys LLC 330 867-9999
  883 Hampshire Rd Ste E Stow (44224) *(G-17592)*
Gledhill Road Machinery Co 419 468-4400
  765 Portland Way S Galion (44833) *(G-10143)*
Glen D Lala 937 274-7770
  2610 Willowburn Ave Dayton (45417) *(G-8224)*
Glen-Gery Caledonia Plant, Caledonia Also called Glen-Gery Corporation *(G-2416)*
Glen-Gery Corporation 419 845-3321
  5692 Rinker Rd Caledonia (43314) *(G-2416)*
Glen-Gery Corporation 419 468-5002
  County Rd 9 Iberia (43325) *(G-11113)*
Glendale Machine Inc 440 248-8646
  30625 Solon Industrial # 1 Solon (44139) *(G-17150)*
Glenn Hunter & Associates Inc 419 533-0925
  1222 County Road 6 Delta (43515) *(G-8773)*
Glenn Michael Brick 740 391-5735
  108 Wood St Flushing (43977) *(G-9783)*
Glenn O Hawbaker Inc 330 308-0533
  2565 Mthias Raceway Rd Sw New Philadelphia (44663) *(G-14772)*
Glenn Ravens Winery 740 545-1000
  56183 County Road 143 West Lafayette (43845) *(G-19930)*
Glenridge Machine Co 440 975-1055
  4610 Beidler Rd Willoughby (44094) *(G-20332)*
Glens Bedford Garden Center 330 305-1971
  9486 Cleveland Ave Nw North Canton (44720) *(G-15087)*
Glenwood Erectors Inc 330 652-9616
  905 Summit Ave Niles (44446) *(G-15010)*
Glf International Inc (PA) 216 621-6901
  3690 Orange Pl Ste 495 Cleveland (44122) *(G-5324)*
Gli, Cleveland Also called Great Lakes Integrated Inc *(G-5347)*

2019 Harris Ohio Industrial Directory

(G-0000) Company's Geographic Section entry number

Gli Pool Products, Youngstown *Also called GL International LLC* ***(G-20922)***
Glidden Professional Paint Ctr, Cincinnati *Also called Akzo Nobel Paints LLC* ***(G-3316)***
Glidden Professional Paint Ctr, Canton *Also called PPG Architectural Finishes Inc* ***(G-2788)***
Glister Inc 614 252-6400
3065 Switzer Ave Columbus (43219) ***(G-6955)***
Glo-Quartz Electric Heater Co 440 255-9701
7084 Maple St Mentor (44060) ***(G-13459)***
Global Biochem 513 792-2218
8044 Montgomery Rd Cincinnati (45236) ***(G-3762)***
Global Bioprotect LLC 336 861-0162
8720 Orion Pl Ste 110 Columbus (43240) ***(G-6495)***
Global Body & Equipment Co 330 264-6640
2061 Sylvan Rd Wooster (44691) ***(G-20597)***
Global Chemical Inc 419 242-1004
1925 Nebraska Ave Toledo (43607) ***(G-18306)***
Global Coal Sales Group LLC (HQ) 614 221-0101
41 S High St Ste 3750s Columbus (43215) ***(G-6956)***
Global Cooling Inc 740 274-7900
6000 Poston Rd Athens (45701) ***(G-833)***
Global Design Factory LLC 330 322-8775
1227 Norton Rd 3b Hudson (44236) ***(G-11047)***
Global E-Lumenation Tech 513 821-8687
3289 Spring Grove Ave Cincinnati (45225) ***(G-3763)***
Global Furnishings Inc 216 595-0901
1621 E 41st St Cleveland (44103) ***(G-5325)***
Global Gauge Corporation 937 254-3500
3200 Kettering Blvd Moraine (45439) ***(G-14356)***
Global Gear LLC 941 830-0531
8336 W Craig Dr Chagrin Falls (44023) ***(G-3048)***
Global Glass Block Inc 216 731-2333
23570 Lakeland Blvd Euclid (44132) ***(G-9414)***
Global Graphite Group LLC 216 538-0362
4807 Rockside Rd Independence (44131) ***(G-11132)***
Global Health Services Inc 513 777-8111
901 Boyle Rd Hamilton (45013) ***(G-10564)***
Global Innovative Products LLC 513 701-0441
7697 Innovation Way # 200 Mason (45040) ***(G-12879)***
Global Laser Tek 513 701-0452
7697 Innovation Way # 700 Mason (45040) ***(G-12880)***
Global Lighting Tech Inc 440 922-4584
55 Andrews Cir Ste 1 Brecksville (44141) ***(G-2039)***
Global Manufacturing Inds (PA) 513 271-2180
7710 Shawnee Run Rd Cincinnati (45243) ***(G-3764)***
Global Manufacturing Solutions 937 236-8315
2001 Kuntz Rd Dayton (45404) ***(G-8225)***
Global Manufacturing Tech LLC 440 205-1001
8671 Tyler Blvd Unit F Mentor (44060) ***(G-13460)***
Global Mining Holding Co LLC (PA) 614 221-0101
41 S High St Columbus (43215) ***(G-6957)***
Global Oil & Gas Services LLC 330 807-1490
2337 Watson Marshall Rd Mc Donald (44437) ***(G-13200)***
Global Oilfield Services LLC 419 756-8027
3401 State Route 13 Mansfield (44904) ***(G-12446)***
Global Packaging & Exports Inc (PA) 513 454-2020
9166 Sutton Pl West Chester (45011) ***(G-19716)***
Global Partners USA Co Inc 513 276-4981
7544 Bermuda Trce West Chester (45069) ***(G-19717)***
Global Plastic Tech Inc 440 879-6045
1657 Broadway Lorain (44052) ***(G-12093)***
Global Precision Parts, East Liberty *Also called Harding Machine Acquisition Co* ***(G-9048)***
Global Precision Parts, Ottoville *Also called Acme Machine Automatics Inc* ***(G-15679)***
Global Precision Parts Inc 260 563-9030
7600 Us Route 127 Van Wert (45891) ***(G-19093)***
Global Specialties Inc 800 338-0814
2950 Westway Dr Ste 110 Brunswick (44212) ***(G-2210)***
Global Specialty Machines LLC (PA) 513 701-0452
7697 Innovation Way # 700 Mason (45040) ***(G-12881)***
Global Srcing Support Svcs LLC 800 645-2986
260 E University Ave Cincinnati (45219) ***(G-3765)***
Global Technology Center, Holland *Also called Tekni-Plex Inc* ***(G-10960)***
Global Tool, Dayton *Also called Ovase Manufacturing LLC* ***(G-8413)***
Global Trucking LLC 614 598-6264
3723 Ellerdale Dr Columbus (43230) ***(G-6958)***
Global Wood Products LLC 440 442-5859
734 Alpha Dr Ste J Highland Heights (44143) ***(G-10791)***
Globe Metallurgical Inc (HQ) 740 984-2361
Co Rd 32 Waterford (45786) ***(G-19484)***
Globe Motors Inc (HQ) 334 983-3542
2275 Stanley Ave Dayton (45404) ***(G-8226)***
Globe Motors Inc 937 228-3171
1944 Troy St Dayton (45404) ***(G-8227)***
Globe Motors Inc 937 228-3171
2275 Stanley Ave Dayton (45404) ***(G-8228)***
Globe Pipe Hanger Products Inc 216 362-6300
14601 Industrial Pkwy Cleveland (44135) ***(G-5326)***
Globe Products Inc (PA) 937 233-0233
5051 Kitridge Rd Dayton (45424) ***(G-8229)***
Globe Specialty Metals, Waterford *Also called Globe Metallurgical Inc* ***(G-19484)***
Globecom Technologies Inc 330 408-7008
8542 Kepler Ave Nw Canal Fulton (44614) ***(G-2480)***
Globus Printing & Packg Co Inc (PA) 419 628-2381
1 Executive Pkwy Minster (45865) ***(G-14216)***
Glorias 330 264-8963
2023 Portage Rd Wooster (44691) ***(G-20598)***
Glorious Cupcakes 216 544-2325
3132 Sterling Lake Dr Medina (44256) ***(G-13268)***
Gloucester Engineering Co Inc 330 722-5168
220 Lafayette Rd Medina (44256) ***(G-13269)***
Glt Inc (PA) 937 237-0055
3341 Successful Way Dayton (45414) ***(G-8230)***
Glt Fabricators Inc (PA) 713 670-9700
6810 Cochran Rd Solon (44139) ***(G-17151)***
Glt Products, Solon *Also called Great Lakes Textiles Inc* ***(G-17156)***
Glunt Industries Inc 330 399-7585
319 N River Rd Nw Warren (44483) ***(G-19407)***
Gluten-Free Expressions 740 928-0338
520 E Main St Hebron (43025) ***(G-10746)***
GM Logging 740 501-0819
204 Cole Dr Johnstown (43031) ***(G-11267)***
GM Management, Zanesville *Also called General Machine & Supply Co* ***(G-21142)***
Gmd Industries LLC 937 252-3643
1414 E 2nd St Dayton (45403) ***(G-8231)***
Gmelectric Inc 330 477-3392
4606 Southway St Sw Canton (44706) ***(G-2685)***
Gmerecords, Reynoldsburg *Also called Swagg Productions2015llc* ***(G-16455)***
GMI Companies Inc (PA) 513 932-3445
2999 Henkle Dr Lebanon (45036) ***(G-11657)***
GMI Companies Inc 937 981-0244
512 S Washington St Greenfield (45123) ***(G-10348)***
GMI Companies Inc 937 981-7724
512 S Washington St Greenfield (45123) ***(G-10349)***
GMI Holdings Inc (HQ) 330 821-5360
1 Door Dr Mount Hope (44660) ***(G-14437)***
Gmp Welding & Fabrication Inc 513 825-7861
11175 Adwood Dr Cincinnati (45240) ***(G-3766)***
GMR Furniture Services Ltd 216 244-5072
7403 Dorothy Ave Parma (44129) ***(G-15820)***
GNI Erectors 614 465-7260
8907 Stillwater Dr Galloway (43119) ***(G-10179)***
Gnrl Chemical L 419 255-0193
1661 Campbell St Toledo (43607) ***(G-18307)***
Gns, Danville *Also called Besl Specialized Carrier* ***(G-7957)***
Go Cupcake 937 299-4985
5017 Rolling Woods Trl Dayton (45429) ***(G-8232)***
Go For Broke Amusement, Flushing *Also called Glenn Michael Brick* ***(G-9783)***
Goal Medical LLC 541 654-5951
7555 Tyler Blvd Mentor (44060) ***(G-13461)***
Godfrey & Wing Inc (PA) 330 562-1440
220 Campus Dr Aurora (44202) ***(G-881)***
Godfrey & Wing Inc 419 980-4616
2066 E 2nd St Defiance (43512) ***(G-8624)***
Gofast LLC 419 562-8027
963 Hopley Ave Bucyrus (44820) ***(G-2332)***
Gofs, Mansfield *Also called Global Oilfield Services LLC* ***(G-12446)***
Goin' Postal, Defiance *Also called M-Fischer Enterprises LLC* ***(G-8634)***
Gojo Industries Inc (PA) 330 255-6000
1 Gojo Plz Ste 500 Akron (44311) ***(G-189)***
Gojo Industries Inc 330 255-6000
3783 State Rd Cuyahoga Falls (44223) ***(G-7873)***
Gojo Industries Inc 330 255-6525
1366 Commerce Dr Stow (44224) ***(G-17593)***
Gojo Industries Inc 330 922-4522
3783 State Rd Cuyahoga Falls (44223) ***(G-7874)***
Gojo Industries Inc 800 321-9647
200 W Steels Corners Rd Cuyahoga Falls (44223) ***(G-7875)***
Gokoh Corporation (HQ) 937 339-4977
1280 Archer Dr Troy (45373) ***(G-18662)***
Gold 2 Green Ltd 304 551-1172
319 Main St Bridgeport (43912) ***(G-2075)***
Gold Key Processing Inc 440 632-0901
14910 Madison Rd Middlefield (44062) ***(G-13800)***
Gold Metal Machining Inc 614 873-5031
216 W Bigelow Ave Plain City (43064) ***(G-16195)***
Gold Mine Inc 614 378-8308
4951 Gillingham Way Dublin (43017) ***(G-8916)***
Gold N Krisp Chips & Pretzels 330 832-8395
1900 Erie Ave Nw Massillon (44646) ***(G-12988)***
Gold Pro Inc 216 241-5143
850 Euclid Ave Ste 518 Cleveland (44114) ***(G-5327)***
Gold Rush Jerky, Litchfield *Also called Medina Foods Inc* ***(G-11985)***
Gold Star Chili Inc (PA) 513 231-4541
650 Lunken Park Dr Cincinnati (45226) ***(G-3767)***
Gold Star Chili Inc 513 631-1990
5420 Ridge Ave Cincinnati (45213) ***(G-3768)***
Gold Star Chili-Burnet, Cincinnati *Also called D & A Rofael Enterprises Inc* ***(G-3567)***
Golda Inc (PA) 216 464-5490
24050 Commerce Park Cleveland (44122) ***(G-5328)***

ALPHABETIC

Golden Dynamic Inc.....614 575-1222
950 Taylor Station Rd M Columbus (43230) ***(G-6959)***
Golden Eagle, Upper Sandusky *Also called New Eezy-Gro Inc* ***(G-18967)***
Golden Giant Inc.....419 674-4038
13300 S Vision Dr Kenton (43326) ***(G-11405)***
Golden Giants Building System, Kenton *Also called Golden Giant Inc* ***(G-11405)***
Golden Graphics Ltd.....419 673-6260
314 W Franklin St Kenton (43326) ***(G-11406)***
Golden Jersey Inn, Yellow Springs *Also called Youngs Jersey Dairy Inc* ***(G-20823)***
Golden Signs and Lighting LLC.....513 248-0895
120-150 Olympic Rd Milford (45150) ***(G-14011)***
Golden Spring Co Inc.....937 848-2513
2143 Ferry Rd Bellbrook (45305) ***(G-1495)***
Golden Turtle Chocolate Fctry.....513 932-1990
120 S Broadway St Ste 1 Lebanon (45036) ***(G-11658)***
Goldsmith & Eggleton LLC.....203 855-6000
300 1st St Wadsworth (44281) ***(G-19243)***
Golf Ball Manufacturers LLC.....419 994-5563
326 N Water St Loudonville (44842) ***(G-12142)***
Golf Car Company Inc.....614 873-1055
8899 Memorial Dr Plain City (43064) ***(G-16196)***
Golf Dsign Screcards Unlimited, Columbus *Also called Scorecards Unlimited LLC* ***(G-7432)***
Golf Galaxy Golfworks Inc.....740 328-4193
4820 Jacksontown Rd Newark (43056) ***(G-14880)***
Golf Graphics, Bluffton *Also called Tim Boutwell* ***(G-1894)***
Golf Marketing Group Inc.....330 963-5155
9221 Ravenna Rd Ste 7 Twinsburg (44087) ***(G-18788)***
Golfpremiums.com, Columbus *Also called Corporate Supply LLC* ***(G-6824)***
Golfworks, The, Newark *Also called Golf Galaxy Golfworks Inc* ***(G-14880)***
Golubitsky Corporation.....800 552-4204
4364 Cranwood Pkwy Cleveland (44128) ***(G-5329)***
Gomez Salsa LLC.....513 314-1978
8575 Coolwood Ct Cincinnati (45236) ***(G-3769)***
Gonda Wood Products, Grafton *Also called Joe Gonda Company Inc* ***(G-10305)***
Gongwer News Service Inc (PA).....614 221-1992
17 S High St Ste 630 Columbus (43215) ***(G-6960)***
Gongwer News Service Inc (HQ).....614 221-1992
17 S High St Ste 630 Columbus (43215) ***(G-6961)***
Gonzoil Inc.....330 497-5888
5260 Fulton Dr Nw Canton (44718) ***(G-2686)***
Gooch & Housego (florida) LLC (HQ).....321 242-7818
676 Alpha Dr Cleveland (44143) ***(G-5330)***
Gooch & Housego (ohio) LLC.....216 486-6100
676 Alpha Dr Highland Heights (44143) ***(G-10792)***
Good Beans Coffee Roasters LLC.....513 310-9516
1381 Cottonwood Dr Milford (45150) ***(G-14012)***
Good Day Tools LLC.....513 578-2050
4603 Carter Ave Cincinnati (45212) ***(G-3770)***
Good Earth Good Eating LLC.....513 256-5935
6317 Starridge Ct Cincinnati (45248) ***(G-3771)***
Good Fortunes Inc.....440 942-2888
1486 E 361st St Willoughby (44095) ***(G-20333)***
Good Greens, Oakwood Village *Also called Good Nutrition LLC* ***(G-15480)***
Good Impressions LLC.....740 392-4327
205 S Mulberry St Mount Vernon (43050) ***(G-14482)***
Good JP.....419 207-8484
854 Willow Ln Ashland (44805) ***(G-706)***
Good News, Middlefield *Also called Suburban Communications Inc* ***(G-13855)***
Good Nutrition LLC.....216 534-6617
7710 First Pl Oakwood Village (44146) ***(G-15480)***
Good Wood Inc (PA).....740 484-1500
42591 Bina Rd Belmont (43718) ***(G-1566)***
Goodale Auto-Truck Parts Inc.....614 294-4777
1100 E 5th Ave Columbus (43201) ***(G-6962)***
Goodell Farms.....330 274-2161
5212 Goodell Rd Mantua (44255) ***(G-12547)***
Goodman Distribution Inc.....440 324-4071
760 Moore Rd Avon Lake (44012) ***(G-987)***
Goodrich Avionics, Columbus *Also called L3 Aviation Products Inc* ***(G-7108)***
Goodrich Corporation.....937 339-3811
101 Waco St Troy (45373) ***(G-18663)***
Goodrich Corporation.....216 429-4018
6225 Oak Tree Blvd Independence (44131) ***(G-11133)***
Goodrich Corporation.....216 706-2530
8000 Marble Ave Cleveland (44105) ***(G-5331)***
Goodrich Corporation.....216 429-4655
925 Keynote Cir Ste 300 Brooklyn Heights (44131) ***(G-2122)***
Goodrich Landing Gear Division, Independence *Also called Goodrich Corporation* ***(G-11133)***
Goodwill Inds NW Ohio Inc.....419 255-0070
525 Cherry St Toledo (43604) ***(G-18308)***
Goodwin Farms.....513 877-2636
10092 State Route 132 Pleasant Plain (45162) ***(G-16226)***
Goodyear International Corp (HQ).....330 796-2121
200 E Innovation Way Akron (44316) ***(G-190)***
Goodyear Tire & Rubber Company (PA).....330 796-2121
200 E Innovation Way Akron (44316) ***(G-191)***
Goodyear Tire & Rubber Company.....216 265-1800
18901 Snow Rd Cleveland (44142) ***(G-5332)***
Goosefoot Acres Inc (PA).....330 225-7184
5879 Center Rd Valley City (44280) ***(G-19039)***
Goosefoot Acres Cntr For, Valley City *Also called Goosefoot Acres Inc* ***(G-19039)***
Gopowerx Inc.....440 707-6029
283 Eastern Ave Oberlin (44074) ***(G-15497)***
Gorant Chocolatier LLC (PA).....330 726-8821
8301 Market St Boardman (44512) ***(G-1899)***
Gorant's Yum Yum Tree, Boardman *Also called Gorant Chocolatier LLC* ***(G-1899)***
Gordon Bernard Company LLC.....513 248-7600
22 Whitney Dr Milford (45150) ***(G-14013)***
Gordon Brothers Btlg Group Inc.....330 337-8754
776 N Ellsworth Ave Salem (44460) ***(G-16742)***
Gordon Tool Inc.....419 263-3151
1301 State Route 49 Payne (45880) ***(G-15872)***
Gordons Graphics Inc.....330 863-2322
123 S Reed Ave Malvern (44644) ***(G-12392)***
Gorell Enterprises Inc (PA).....724 465-1800
10250 Philipp Pkwy Streetsboro (44241) ***(G-17675)***
Gorell Windows & Doors, Streetsboro *Also called Gorell Enterprises Inc* ***(G-17675)***
Gorey Construction, Medina *Also called Robert Gorey* ***(G-13328)***
Gorilla Dumpsters.....614 344-4677
7686 Fishel Dr N B Dublin (43016) ***(G-8917)***
Gorman-Rupp Company.....419 886-3001
180 Hines Ave Bellville (44813) ***(G-1557)***
Gorman-Rupp Company (PA).....419 755-1011
600 S Airport Rd Mansfield (44903) ***(G-12447)***
Gorman-Rupp Company.....419 755-1011
305 Bowman St Mansfield (44903) ***(G-12448)***
Gorman-Rupp Company.....419 755-1245
100 Rump Rd Mansfield (44903) ***(G-12449)***
Gorman-Rupp Company.....419 755-1011
100 Rupp Rd Mansfield (44903) ***(G-12450)***
Gortons Inc.....216 362-1050
13525 Hummel Rd Cleveland (44142) ***(G-5333)***
Gospel Trumpet Publishing.....937 548-9876
5065 S State Route 49 Greenville (45331) ***(G-10373)***
Gosun Inc.....888 868-6154
1217 Ellis St Cincinnati (45223) ***(G-3772)***
Got Graphix Llc.....330 703-9047
3265 W Market St Fairlawn (44333) ***(G-9606)***
Gotcha Covered.....513 829-7555
4854 Factory Dr Fairfield (45014) ***(G-9500)***
Gotta Groove Records Inc.....216 431-7373
3615 Superior Ave E 4201a Cleveland (44114) ***(G-5334)***
Gottfried Medical Inc.....419 474-2973
2920 Centennial Rd Toledo (43617) ***(G-18309)***
Gottschall Tool & Die Inc.....330 332-1544
14028 W Middletown Rd Salem (44460) ***(G-16743)***
Gougler Industries Inc, Kent *Also called Furukawa Rock Drill Usa Inc* ***(G-11324)***
Gould Fire Protection Inc.....419 957-2416
633 Bristol Dr Findlay (45840) ***(G-9694)***
Gould Group LLC.....740 807-4294
4653 Trueman Blvd Ste 120 Hilliard (43026) ***(G-10825)***
Government Acquisitions Inc.....513 721-8700
720 E Pete Rose Way # 330 Cincinnati (45202) ***(G-3773)***
Government Specialty Pdts LLC (PA).....937 672-9473
9588 Quailwood Trl Dayton (45458) ***(G-8233)***
Goyal Enterprises Inc.....513 874-9303
4836 Business Center Way West Chester (45246) ***(G-19860)***
Goyal Industries Inc.....419 522-7099
382 Park Ave E Mansfield (44905) ***(G-12451)***
Gpi, Xenia *Also called Graphic Packaging Intl Inc* ***(G-20775)***
GPM, Franklin *Also called Green Point Metals Inc* ***(G-9887)***
Gqi Inc.....330 830-9805
2650 Richville Dr Sw # 105 Massillon (44646) ***(G-12989)***
Gr Golf, New Washington *Also called Wurms Woodworking Company* ***(G-14834)***
Gra-Mag Truck Intr Systems LLC (HQ).....740 490-1000
470 E High St London (43140) ***(G-12061)***
Graber Metal Works Inc.....440 237-8422
9664 Akins Rd Ste 1 North Royalton (44133) ***(G-15274)***
Grabo Interiors Inc.....216 391-6677
3605 Perkins Ave Cleveland (44114) ***(G-5335)***
Grace Automation Services Inc.....330 567-3108
8140 State Route 514 Big Prairie (44611) ***(G-1674)***
Grace Imaging LLC.....419 874-2127
28400 Cedar Park Blvd C Perrysburg (43551) ***(G-15960)***
Grace Metals Ltd.....234 380-1433
685 Ashbrooke Way Hudson (44236) ***(G-11048)***
Gracie Plum Investments Inc.....740 355-9029
609 2nd St Unit 2 Portsmouth (45662) ***(G-16284)***
Graco Ohio Inc (HQ).....330 494-1313
8400 Port Jackson Ave Nw North Canton (44720) ***(G-15088)***
Gradall Industries Inc (HQ).....330 339-2211
406 Mill Ave Sw New Philadelphia (44663) ***(G-14773)***
Gradeworks.....440 487-4201
10655 Hickory Hill Ct Willoughby (44094) ***(G-20334)***
Grady McCauley Inc.....330 494-9444
9260 Pleasantwood Ave Nw North Canton (44720) ***(G-15089)***

Graebener Group Tech Ltd ... 419 591-7033
476 E Riverview Ave Napoleon (43545) *(G-14540)*
Graeter's Ice Cream, Columbus *Also called Superior Tasting Products Inc (G-7502)*
Graeter's Ice Cream, Cincinnati *Also called International Brand Services (G-3856)*
Graeters Manufacturing Co (PA) ... 513 721-3323
1175 Regina Graeter Way Cincinnati (45216) *(G-3774)*
Graf Custom Hardwood, Portsmouth *Also called Appalachian Wood Floors Inc (G-16277)*
Graffiti Co, Cleveland *Also called Barbs Graffiti Inc (G-4790)*
Graffiti Foods Limited ... 614 759-1921
333 Outerbelt St Columbus (43213) *(G-6963)*
Grafisk Msknfabrik-America LLC ... 630 432-4370
603 Norgal Dr Ste F Lebanon (45036) *(G-11659)*
Grafix, Cleveland *Also called Graphic Art Systems Inc (G-5341)*
Graftech Global Entps Inc ... 216 676-2000
12900 Snow Rd Cleveland (44130) *(G-5336)*
Graftech Holdings Inc ... 216 676-2000
6100 Oak Tree Blvd # 300 Independence (44131) *(G-11134)*
Graftech International Ltd (HQ) ... 216 676-2000
982 Keynote Cir Ste 6 Brooklyn Heights (44131) *(G-2123)*
Graftech Intl Holdings Inc ... 216 529-3777
11709 Madison Ave Cleveland (44107) *(G-5337)*
Graftech Intl Holdings Inc ... 330 239-3023
12300 Snow Rd Parma (44130) *(G-15821)*
Graftech Intl Holdings Inc ... 216 676-2000
982 Keynote Cir Brooklyn Heights (44131) *(G-2124)*
Graftech Intl Holdings Inc (HQ) ... 216 676-2000
982 Keynote Cir Brooklyn Heights (44131) *(G-2125)*
Grafton Ready Mix Concret Inc ... 440 926-2911
1155 Elm St Grafton (44044) *(G-10302)*
Graham Electric ... 614 231-8500
2855 Banwick Rd Columbus (43232) *(G-6964)*
Graham Ford Power Products ... 614 801-0049
850 Harmon Ave Columbus (43223) *(G-6965)*
Graham Packaging Co Europe LLC ... 513 398-5000
1225 Castle Dr Mason (45040) *(G-12882)*
Graham Packaging Company LP ... 740 439-4242
8800 Guernsey Industrial Cambridge (43725) *(G-2441)*
Graham Packaging Company LP ... 513 874-1770
290 Circle Freeway Dr West Chester (45246) *(G-19861)*
Graham Packaging Company LP ... 419 334-4197
725 Industrial Dr Fremont (43420) *(G-10024)*
Graham Packaging Pet Tech Inc ... 419 334-4197
725 Industrial Dr Fremont (43420) *(G-10025)*
Graham Packg Plastic Pdts Inc (HQ) ... 717 849-8500
1 Seagate Ste 10 Toledo (43604) *(G-18310)*
Graham Packg Plastic Pdts Inc ... 419 421-8037
170 Stanford Pkwy 7 Findlay (45840) *(G-9695)*
Grain Craft Inc ... 216 621-3206
1635 Merwin Ave Cleveland (44113) *(G-5338)*
Grale Technologies Inc ... 724 683-8141
1019 Ohio Works Dr Youngstown (44510) *(G-20923)*
Gramag LLC ... 614 875-8435
2999 Lewis Centre Way Grove City (43123) *(G-10431)*
Graminex LLC ... 419 278-1023
2 300 County Rd C Deshler (43516) *(G-8789)*
Grand Aire Inc (PA) ... 419 861-6700
11777 W Airport Svc Rd Swanton (43558) *(G-17913)*
Grand Harbor Yacht Sales & Svc ... 440 442-2919
706 Alpha Dr Cleveland (44143) *(G-5339)*
Grand Rapids Printing Ink Co ... 859 261-4530
95 Glendale Milford Rd Cincinnati (45215) *(G-3775)*
Grand River Asphalt ... 440 352-2254
6 Coast Guard Rd Grand River (44045) *(G-10322)*
Grand Slam Acres, Celina *Also called B Hogenkamp & R Harlamert (G-2950)*
Grand Unification Press Inc ... 330 683-1187
2380 Wayne St Orrville (44667) *(G-15592)*
Grand-Rock Company Inc ... 440 639-2000
395 Fountain Ave Painesville (44077) *(G-15742)*
Grandinroad Catalog, West Chester *Also called Cornerstone Brands Inc (G-19684)*
Grandon Mfg Co Inc ... 614 294-2694
530 Dow Ave Columbus (43211) *(G-6966)*
Grandpa Jack's, Chillicothe *Also called Crispie Creme of Chillicothe (G-3183)*
Grandpas Pottery ... 937 382-6442
3558 W State Route 73 Wilmington (45177) *(G-20495)*
Grandview Grind ... 614 485-9005
1423 Grandview Ave Columbus (43212) *(G-6967)*
Grandview Materials Inc ... 614 488-6998
8598 Cotter St Lewis Center (43035) *(G-11761)*
Granex Industries Inc (PA) ... 440 248-4915
32400 Aurora Rd Ste 4 Solon (44139) *(G-17152)*
Granger Pipeline Corporation ... 330 454-8095
111 2nd St Nw Ste 202 Canton (44702) *(G-2687)*
Granger Plastic Company ... 513 424-1955
1600 M A D E Indus Dr Middletown (45044) *(G-13910)*
Granite Fabricators Inc ... 216 228-3669
1250 Marquette St Cleveland (44114) *(G-5340)*
Granite Industries Inc ... 419 445-4733
595 E Lugbill Rd Archbold (43502) *(G-651)*
Grant John ... 937 298-0633
2715 Culver Ave Dayton (45429) *(G-8234)*
Grant Solutions ... 937 344-5558
7745 Winding Way N Tipp City (45371) *(G-18114)*
Grant Street Pallet Inc ... 330 424-0355
39196 Grant St Lisbon (44432) *(G-11967)*
Granville Milling Co ... 740 345-1305
145 N Cedar St Newark (43055) *(G-14881)*
Granville Milling Drive-Thru, Newark *Also called Granville Milling Co (G-14881)*
Graphel Corporation ... 513 779-6166
6115 Centre Park Dr West Chester (45069) *(G-19718)*
Graphic Art Systems Inc ... 216 581-9050
5800 Pennsylvania Ave Cleveland (44137) *(G-5341)*
Graphic Arts Rubber, Cuyahoga Falls *Also called Econo Products Inc (G-7862)*
Graphic Awards, Columbus *Also called Joe Paxton (G-7071)*
Graphic Detail Inc ... 330 678-1724
936 Greenbriar Pkwy Kent (44240) *(G-11326)*
Graphic Expressions Signs ... 330 422-7446
8540 State Route 14 Ste D Streetsboro (44241) *(G-17676)*
Graphic Image ... 937 320-0302
2210 Shumway Ct Beavercreek (45431) *(G-1318)*
Graphic Info Systems Inc ... 513 948-1300
7665 Production Dr Cincinnati (45237) *(G-3776)*
Graphic Packaging Intl Inc ... 513 424-4200
407 Charles St Middletown (45042) *(G-13911)*
Graphic Packaging Intl Inc ... 440 248-4370
6385 Cochran Rd Solon (44139) *(G-17153)*
Graphic Packaging Intl Inc ... 937 372-8001
1439 Lavelle Dr Xenia (45385) *(G-20775)*
Graphic Packaging Intl LLC ... 740 387-6543
1171 W Center St Marion (43302) *(G-12707)*
Graphic Packaging Intl LLC ... 419 673-0711
1300 S Main St Kenton (43326) *(G-11407)*
Graphic Paper Products Corp (HQ) ... 937 325-5503
581 W Leffel Ln Springfield (45506) *(G-17407)*
Graphic Paper Products Corp ... 937 325-3912
222 E Main St Springfield (45503) *(G-17408)*
Graphic Plus ... 740 701-1860
712 Overlook Heights Ln Chillicothe (45601) *(G-3190)*
Graphic Print Solutions Inc ... 513 948-3344
7633 Production Dr Cincinnati (45237) *(G-3777)*
Graphic Publications Inc ... 330 674-2300
7368 County Road 623 Millersburg (44654) *(G-14085)*
Graphic Publications Inc ... 330 343-4377
123 W 3rd St Dover (44622) *(G-8828)*
Graphic Solutions Company ... 513 484-3067
3438 Middleton Ave Cincinnati (45220) *(G-3778)*
Graphic Stitch Inc ... 937 642-6707
169 Grove St Rm A Marysville (43040) *(G-12784)*
Graphic Systems Services Inc ... 937 746-0708
400 S Pioneer Blvd Springboro (45066) *(G-17329)*
Graphic Touch Inc ... 330 337-3341
451 E Pershing St Salem (44460) *(G-16744)*
Graphicom Press Inc ... 937 767-1916
302 Orton Rd Yellow Springs (45387) *(G-20806)*
Graphics By Design Avenue, Twinsburg *Also called Design Avenue Inc (G-18763)*
Graphics To Go LLC ... 937 382-4100
761 S Nelson Ave Wilmington (45177) *(G-20496)*
Graphicsource Inc ... 440 248-9200
30405 Solon Rd Ste 12 Solon (44139) *(G-17154)*
Graphite Equipment Mfg Co ... 216 271-9500
5577 Valley Ln Solon (44139) *(G-17155)*
Graphite Sales Inc (PA) ... 419 652-3388
220 Township Road 791 Nova (44859) *(G-15433)*
Graphite Sales Inc ... 419 652-3388
220 Township Road 791 Nova (44859) *(G-15434)*
Graphix Junction ... 234 284-8392
5170 Hudson Dr Ste B Hudson (44236) *(G-11049)*
Graphix Network ... 740 941-3771
122 N High St Waverly (45690) *(G-19547)*
Graphtech Communications Inc ... 216 676-1020
4724 W 150th St Cleveland (44135) *(G-5342)*
Grasan Equipment Company Inc ... 419 526-4440
440 S Illinois Ave Mansfield (44907) *(G-12452)*
Gravel Doctor of Ohio LLC ... 844 472-8353
2985 Canal Dr Millersport (43046) *(G-14159)*
Gravel Doctor of Ohio, The, Millersport *Also called Gravel Doctor of Ohio LLC (G-14159)*
Gravel-Tech ... 513 703-3672
4005 E Fster Mineville Rd Morrow (45152) *(G-14410)*
Gray & Company Publishers ... 216 431-2665
1588 E 40th St Ste 1b Cleveland (44103) *(G-5343)*
Gray Tech International, Cleveland *Also called Hephaestus Technologies LLC (G-5396)*
Gray-Eering Ltd ... 740 498-8816
3158 Sandy Ridge Rd Se Tippecanoe (44699) *(G-18149)*
Graymont Dolime (oh) Inc ... 419 855-8682
21880 W State Route 163 Genoa (43430) *(G-10232)*
Graywacke Inc ... 419 884-7014
300 S Mill St Mansfield (44904) *(G-12453)*
GRB Holdings Inc ... 937 236-3250
131 Janney Rd Dayton (45404) *(G-8235)*

ALPHABETIC

(PA)=Parent Co (HQ)=Headquarters (DH)=Div Headquarters
2019 Harris Ohio Industrial Directory 1129

Gre'n Disc, Strasburg Also called Green Rdced Emssons Netwrk LLC *(G-17648)*
Grean Technologies LLC 513 510-7116
 902 N Garver Rd Monroe (45050) *(G-14265)*
Great American Cookie Company 419 474-9417
 5001 Monroe St Ste Fc13 Toledo (43623) *(G-18311)*
Great Dane LLC 614 876-0666
 4080 Lyman Dr Hilliard (43026) *(G-10826)*
Great Dane Trailers, Hilliard Also called Great Dane LLC *(G-10826)*
Great Day Improvements LLC (HQ) 330 468-0700
 700 Highland Rd E Macedonia (44056) *(G-12300)*
Great Harvest Bread, Westerville Also called B L F Enterprises Inc *(G-20036)*
Great Impressions Signs Design 614 428-8250
 3800 Agler Rd Columbus (43219) *(G-6968)*
Great Lake Fence, Cleveland Also called Fence One Inc *(G-5229)*
Great Lakes Assemblies LLC 937 645-3900
 11590 Tr 298 East Liberty (43319) *(G-9047)*
Great Lakes Cheese Co Inc (PA) 440 834-2500
 17825 Great Lakes Pkwy Hiram (44234) *(G-10910)*
Great Lakes Crushing Ltd 440 944-5500
 30831 Euclid Ave Wickliffe (44092) *(G-20211)*
Great Lakes Defense Svcs LLC 216 272-3450
 2319 Miramar Blvd University Heights (44118) *(G-18942)*
Great Lakes Diesel 419 433-9898
 5148 Concord Dr Vermilion (44089) *(G-19160)*
Great Lakes Embroidery, Chardon Also called Screen Craft Plastics *(G-3135)*
Great Lakes Engraving Corp 419 867-1607
 1736 Henthorne Dr Maumee (43537) *(G-13113)*
Great Lakes Etching Finshg Co 440 439-3624
 7010 Krick Rd Ste 3 Cleveland (44146) *(G-5344)*
Great Lakes Glasswerks Inc 440 358-0460
 360 W Prospect St Painesville (44077) *(G-15743)*
Great Lakes Graphics Inc 216 391-0077
 3354 Superior Ave E Cleveland (44114) *(G-5345)*
Great Lakes Group 216 621-4854
 4500 Division Ave Cleveland (44102) *(G-5346)*
Great Lakes Integrated Inc (PA) 216 651-1500
 4005 Clark Ave Cleveland (44109) *(G-5347)*
Great Lakes Lithograph 216 651-1500
 4005 Clark Ave Cleveland (44109) *(G-5348)*
Great Lakes Machine and Tool 419 836-2346
 10705 Jerusalem Rd Curtice (43412) *(G-7825)*
Great Lakes Management Inc (PA) 216 883-6500
 2700 E 40th St Ste 1 Cleveland (44115) *(G-5349)*
Great Lakes McHy & Automtn LLC 419 208-2004
 1839 Port Clinton Rd Fremont (43420) *(G-10026)*
Great Lakes Mfg Group Ltd 440 391-8266
 19035 Old Detroit Rd Rocky River (44116) *(G-16548)*
Great Lakes Popcorn Company 419 732-3080
 60 Madison St Port Clinton (43452) *(G-16248)*
Great Lakes Power Products Inc (PA) 440 951-5111
 7455 Tyler Blvd Mentor (44060) *(G-13462)*
Great Lakes Power Service Co 440 259-0025
 3691 Shepard Rd Perry (44081) *(G-15905)*
Great Lakes Printing Inc 440 993-8781
 2926 Lake Ave Ashtabula (44004) *(G-779)*
Great Lakes Publishing Company (PA) 216 771-2833
 1422 Euclid Ave Ste 730 Cleveland (44115) *(G-5350)*
Great Lakes Reprographic, Maumee Also called Great Lakes Engraving Corp *(G-13113)*
Great Lakes Stair & Mllwk Co 330 225-2005
 1545 W 130th St Ste A1 Hinckley (44233) *(G-10900)*
Great Lakes Telcom Ltd 330 629-8848
 590 E Western Reserve Rd Youngstown (44514) *(G-20924)*
Great Lakes Textiles Inc (PA) 440 914-1122
 6810 Cochran Rd Solon (44139) *(G-17156)*
Great Lakes Textiles Inc 440 201-1300
 11 Industry Dr Bedford (44146) *(G-1406)*
Great Lakes Towing, Cleveland Also called Great Lakes Group *(G-5346)*
Great Lakes Window Inc 419 666-5555
 30499 Tracy Rd Walbridge (43465) *(G-19294)*
Great Lkes Nrotechnologies Inc 855 456-3876
 6100 Rockside Woods # 415 Cleveland (44131) *(G-5351)*
Great Midwest Tobacco Inc 513 745-0450
 10825 Medallion Dr Cincinnati (45241) *(G-3779)*
Great Midwest Yacht Co 740 965-4511
 140 E Granville St Sunbury (43074) *(G-17887)*
Great Migrations LLC 614 638-4632
 7453 Katesbridge Ct Dublin (43017) *(G-8918)*
Great Oppurtunities Inc 614 868-1899
 1750 Idlewild Dr Columbus (43232) *(G-6969)*
Great Western Juice Company 216 475-5770
 16153 Libby Rd Cleveland (44137) *(G-5352)*
Great Works Publishing Inc 440 926-1100
 1080 Cleveland St Grafton (44044) *(G-10303)*
Greater Cincinnati Bowl Assn 513 761-7387
 611 Mercury Dr Cincinnati (45244) *(G-3780)*
Greater Cleve Pipe Ftting Fund 216 524-8334
 6305 Halle Dr Cleveland (44125) *(G-5353)*
Greater Ohio Ethanol LLC (PA) 567 940-9500
 7227 Harding Hwy Lima (45801) *(G-11870)*

Greber Machine Tool Inc 440 322-3685
 313 Clark St Elyria (44035) *(G-9264)*
Green Acquisition LLC 440 930-7600
 1141 Jaycox Rd Avon (44011) *(G-951)*
Green Acres Furniture Ltd 330 359-6251
 7412 Massillon Rd Sw Navarre (44662) *(G-14574)*
Green Bay Packaging Inc 419 332-5593
 2323 Commerce Dr Fremont (43420) *(G-10027)*
Green Bay Packaging Inc 513 228-5560
 760 Kingsview Dr Lebanon (45036) *(G-11660)*
Green Bearing Co, Avon Also called Green Acquisition LLC *(G-951)*
Green Brothers Enterprises 937 444-3323
 516 Sicily Rd Sardinia (45171) *(G-16869)*
Green Corp Magnetic Inc 614 801-4000
 4342 Mcdowell Rd Grove City (43123) *(G-10432)*
Green County Wtr Sup & Trtmnt, Dayton Also called Greene County *(G-7981)*
Green Door Industries LLC 614 558-1663
 7844 Waggoner Trace Dr Blacklick (43004) *(G-1684)*
Green Energy Inc 330 262-5112
 4489 E Lincoln Way Wooster (44691) *(G-20599)*
Green Gourmet Foods LLC 740 400-4212
 515 N Main St Baltimore (43105) *(G-1038)*
Green Harvest Energy LLC 330 716-3068
 1340 State Route 14 Columbiana (44408) *(G-6467)*
Green Leaf Printing and Design 937 222-3634
 1001 E 2nd St Ste 2485 Dayton (45402) *(G-8236)*
Green Machine Tool Inc 937 253-0771
 1865 Radio Rd Dayton (45431) *(G-7980)*
Green Point Metals Inc (PA) 937 743-4075
 301 Shotwell Dr Franklin (45005) *(G-9887)*
Green Rdced Emssons Netwrk LLC 330 340-0941
 5029 Hilltop Dr Nw Strasburg (44680) *(G-17648)*
Green Recycling Works LLC 513 278-7111
 1530 Tremont St Cincinnati (45214) *(G-3781)*
Green Room Brewing LLC 614 596-3655
 1101 N 4th St Columbus (43201) *(G-6970)*
Green Tokai Co Ltd 937 237-1630
 3700 Inpark Dr Dayton (45414) *(G-8237)*
Green Tokai Co Ltd (HQ) 937 833-5444
 55 Robert Wright Dr Brookville (45309) *(G-2170)*
Green Vision Materials Inc 440 564-5500
 11220 Kinsman Rd Newbury (44065) *(G-14954)*
Green Willow Inc 937 436-5290
 90 Compark Rd Ste A Dayton (45459) *(G-8238)*
Greenbrier Rail Services, Youngstown Also called Gunderson Rail Services LLC *(G-20927)*
Greendale Home Fashions LLC 859 916-5475
 5500 Muddy Creek Rd Cincinnati (45238) *(G-3782)*
Greene County 937 429-0127
 1122 Beaver Valley Rd Dayton (45434) *(G-7981)*
Greene Fuel Plaza Inc 937 532-4826
 3151 E Dorothy Ln Kettering (45420) *(G-11432)*
Greene Street Wholesale LLC 740 374-5206
 1310 Greene St Marietta (45750) *(G-12628)*
Greenes Fence, Solon Also called Mi-Lar Fence Co Inc *(G-17193)*
Greenes Fence Co Inc 216 464-3160
 5250 Naiman Pkwy Ste B Solon (44139) *(G-17157)*
Greenfield Research Inc (PA) 937 981-7763
 347 Edgewood Ave Greenfield (45123) *(G-10350)*
Greenfield Research Inc 937 876-9224
 324 S Washington St Greenfield (45123) *(G-10351)*
Greenkote Usa Inc 440 243-2865
 6435 Eastland Rd Brookpark (44142) *(G-2148)*
Greenlight Optics LLC 513 247-9777
 8940 Glendale Milford Rd Loveland (45140) *(G-12193)*
Greeno Company, Cincinnati Also called Tri-State Belting Ltd *(G-4434)*
Greenrock Ltd 646 388-4281
 341 W Benson St Cincinnati (45215) *(G-3783)*
Greentec Precision Inc 937 431-1840
 2372 Lakeview Dr Ste F Beavercreek (45431) *(G-1319)*
Greenville Technology Inc 937 642-6744
 15000 Industrial Pkwy Marysville (43040) *(G-12785)*
Greenville Technology Inc (HQ) 937 548-3217
 5755 State Route 571 Greenville (45331) *(G-10374)*
Greenwood Printing & Graphics 419 727-3275
 3615 Stickney Ave Toledo (43608) *(G-18312)*
Greenworld Enterprises Inc 800 525-6999
 61 Circle Freeway Dr West Chester (45246) *(G-19862)*
Greer & Whitehead Cnstr Inc 513 202-1757
 510 S State St Ste D Harrison (45030) *(G-10644)*
Greg Blume 740 574-2308
 7459 Ohio River Rd Wheelersburg (45694) *(G-20182)*
Greg G Wright & Sons LLC 513 721-3310
 10200 Springfield Pike Cincinnati (45215) *(G-3784)*
Gregg Macmillan 513 248-2121
 2002 Ford Cir Ste A Milford (45150) *(G-14014)*
Greggs Specialty Services 419 478-0803
 306 Dura Ave Toledo (43612) *(G-18313)*
Gregoire Moulin 614 861-4582
 7502 E Main St Reynoldsburg (43068) *(G-16442)*

ALPHABETIC SECTION — Guide Technologies LLC (PA)

Gregory Auto Service...513 248-0423
  224 Beech Rd Loveland (45140) *(G-12194)*
Gregory Industries Inc (PA).......................................330 477-4800
  4100 13th St Sw Canton (44710) *(G-2688)*
Gregory Roll Form Inc..330 477-4800
  4100 13th St Sw Canton (44710) *(G-2689)*
Gregory Stone Co Inc...937 275-7455
  1860 N Gettysburg Ave Dayton (45417) *(G-8239)*
Gregs Eagle Tire Co Inc...330 837-1983
  3425 Lincoln Way E Massillon (44646) *(G-12990)*
Greif Inc (PA)..740 549-6000
  425 Winter Rd Delaware (43015) *(G-8681)*
Greif Inc..740 657-6500
  366 Greif Pkwy Delaware (43015) *(G-8682)*
Greif Inc..740 657-6500
  366 Greif Pkwy Delaware (43015) *(G-8683)*
Greif Inc..419 238-0565
  975 Glenn St Van Wert (45891) *(G-19094)*
Greif Inc..740 549-6000
  425 Winter Rd Delaware (43015) *(G-8684)*
Greif Inc..740 549-6000
  425 Winter Rd Delaware (43015) *(G-8685)*
Greif Inc..330 879-2101
  9420 Warmington St Sw Navarre (44662) *(G-14575)*
Greif Inc..937 548-4111
  366 Greif Pkwy Delaware (43015) *(G-8686)*
Greif Inc..330 879-2936
  787 Warmington Rd Se Massillon (44646) *(G-12991)*
Greif Bros Corp Ohio Inc...740 549-6000
  425 Winter Rd Delaware (43015) *(G-8687)*
Greif Packaging LLC..330 879-2101
  787 Warmington Rd Sw Massillon (44646) *(G-12992)*
Greif Packaging LLC (HQ)...740 549-6000
  366 Greif Pkwy Delaware (43015) *(G-8688)*
Greif Paper Packg & Svcs LLC.................................740 549-6000
  425 Winter Rd Delaware (43015) *(G-8689)*
Greif USA LLC (HQ)...740 549-6000
  366 Greif Pkwy Delaware (43015) *(G-8690)*
Grenga Machine & Welding.......................................330 743-1113
  56 Wayne Ave Youngstown (44502) *(G-20925)*
Grey Hawk Golf LLC..440 355-4844
  665 U S Grant St Lagrange (44050) *(G-11481)*
Grey Hawk Golf Club..440 355-4844
  665 U S Grant St Lagrange (44050) *(G-11482)*
Greyden Press, Springboro *Also called Jk Digital Publishing LLC (G-17331)*
Greyfield Industries Inc...513 860-1785
  3104 Wayne Madison Rd Trenton (45067) *(G-18620)*
Grice Equipment Repair Inc......................................937 440-8343
  518 Garfield Ave Troy (45373) *(G-18664)*
Grid Industrial Heating Inc..330 332-9931
  1108 Salem Pkwy Salem (44460) *(G-16745)*
Grid Sentry LLC...937 490-2101
  3915 Germany Ln Beavercreek (45431) *(G-1320)*
Grief Brothers, Delaware *Also called Greif Inc (G-8682)*
Griffin Cider Works LLC..440 785-7418
  2165 Elmwood Dr Westlake (44145) *(G-20120)*
Griffin Fisher Co Inc..513 961-2110
  1126 Wlliam Hward Taft Rd Cincinnati (45206) *(G-3785)*
Griffin Wheel, Groveport *Also called Amsted Industries Incorporated (G-10481)*
Grill..937 673-6768
  100 Morton Rd Eaton (45320) *(G-9150)*
Grimes Aerospace Company....................................937 484-2001
  550 State Route 55 Urbana (43078) *(G-18990)*
Grimes Aerospace Company....................................937 484-2000
  515 N Russell St Urbana (43078) *(G-18991)*
Grimes Sand & Gravel..740 865-3990
  165 Holdren Ln New Matamoras (45767) *(G-14746)*
Grimm Scientific Industries......................................740 374-3412
  1403 Pike St Marietta (45750) *(G-12629)*
Grind-All Corporation..330 220-1600
  1113 Industrial Pkwy N Brunswick (44212) *(G-2211)*
Grinding Equipment & McHy LLC..............................330 747-2313
  15 S Worthington St Youngstown (44502) *(G-20926)*
Grip Force LLC..440 497-7014
  990 Quentin Rd Eastlake (44095) *(G-9112)*
Grippo Potato Chip Co Inc..513 923-1900
  6750 Colerain Ave Cincinnati (45239) *(G-3786)*
Grit Guard Inc..937 592-9003
  3690 County Road 10 Bellefontaine (43311) *(G-1516)*
Grntwrx LLC...440 478-6160
  8205 Clover Ln Garrettsville (44231) *(G-10190)*
Gro2 Bags & Accessories LLC.................................740 622-0928
  1760 Buena Vista Dr Coshocton (43812) *(G-7736)*
Grob Systems Inc..419 358-9015
  1070 Navajo Dr Bluffton (45817) *(G-1889)*
Groeneveld Atlantic South..330 225-4949
  1130 Industrial Pkwy N # 7 Brunswick (44212) *(G-2212)*
Groff Industries..216 634-9100
  2201 W 110th St Cleveland (44102) *(G-5354)*
Groovemaster Music, Perrysburg *Also called Tiny Lion Music Groups (G-16017)*

Gross & Sons Custom Millwork................................419 227-0214
  1219 Grant St Lima (45801) *(G-11871)*
Gross Lumber Inc..330 683-2055
  8848 Ely Rd Apple Creek (44606) *(G-606)*
Groundhogs 2000 LLC...440 653-1647
  33 Industry Dr Bedford (44146) *(G-1407)*
Group Industries Inc (PA)...216 271-0702
  7580 Garfield Blvd Cleveland (44125) *(G-5355)*
Grove City Record, Grove City *Also called Consumers News Services Inc (G-10422)*
Grove Engineered Products Inc...............................419 659-5939
  201 E Cross St Columbus Grove (45830) *(G-7635)*
Grover Musical Products Inc (PA)............................216 391-1188
  9287 Midwest Ave Cleveland (44125) *(G-5356)*
Grover Trophy Musical Products, Cleveland *Also called Grover Musical Products Inc (G-5356)*
Grow With ME Bibs, Hartville *Also called Grow With Me- Creations (G-10691)*
Grow With Me- Creations..800 850-1889
  14236 Wade Ave Ne Hartville (44632) *(G-10691)*
Growco Inc...419 886-4628
  844 Kochheiser Rd Mansfield (44904) *(G-12454)*
Growers Choice Ltd...330 262-8754
  5505 S Elyria Rd Shreve (44676) *(G-17001)*
Growmark Fs LLC..330 386-7626
  100 River Rd East Liverpool (43920) *(G-9057)*
Grt Utilicorp Inc..330 264-8444
  9268 Ashland Rd Wooster (44691) *(G-20600)*
Gruppo Mossi & Ghisolfi, Sharon Center *Also called M & G Polymers Usa LLC (G-16951)*
Grypmat Inc..419 953-7607
  6886 Nancy Ave Celina (45822) *(G-2964)*
Gs Wood & Metal Coating LLC..................................419 375-7708
  2096 Saint Joe Rd Fort Recovery (45846) *(G-9820)*
GSC Neon...216 310-6243
  6301 Aldenham Dr Mayfield Hts (44143) *(G-13173)*
GSE Production and Support LLC (PA)....................972 329-2646
  1 Air Cargo Pkwy E Swanton (43558) *(G-17914)*
GSE Spares, Swanton *Also called GSE Production and Support LLC (G-17914)*
Gsf Energy LLC...513 825-0504
  10795 Hughes Rd Cincinnati (45251) *(G-3787)*
Gsr Industries LLC..440 934-0201
  21648 N Park Dr Cleveland (44126) *(G-5357)*
GSW Manufacturing Inc..419 423-7111
  1801 Production Dr Findlay (45840) *(G-9696)*
Gt Industrial Supply Inc...513 771-7000
  4350 Indeco Ct Ste B Blue Ash (45241) *(G-1783)*
Gt Machine & Fab..740 701-9607
  16655 Charleston Pike Kingston (45644) *(G-11458)*
Gt Motorsports..937 763-7272
  7323 Oh 135 Lynchburg (45142) *(G-12271)*
Gt Technlgies Tledo Operations, Toledo *Also called Gt Technologies Inc (G-18314)*
Gt Technologies Inc..419 782-8955
  1125 Precision Way Defiance (43512) *(G-8625)*
Gt Technologies Inc..419 324-7300
  99 N Fearing Blvd Toledo (43607) *(G-18314)*
GTC, Brookville *Also called Green Tokai Co Ltd (G-2170)*
GTC Artist With Machines, Columbus *Also called General Theming Contrs LLC (G-6945)*
Gtlp Holdings LLC (PA)...513 489-6700
  7911 School Rd Cincinnati (45249) *(G-3788)*
Guadalupe Publishing Inc...614 450-2474
  60 Dellenbaugh Loop Etna (43062) *(G-9393)*
Guarantee Specialties Inc..216 451-9744
  21693 Drake Rd Strongsville (44149) *(G-17747)*
Guaranteed Fnshg Unlimited Inc..............................216 252-8200
  3200 W 121st St Cleveland (44111) *(G-5358)*
Guardian Co Inc..216 721-2262
  2754 Woodhill Rd Cleveland (44104) *(G-5359)*
Guardian Engineering & Mfg Co...............................419 335-1784
  965 Fairway Ln Wauseon (43567) *(G-19518)*
Guardian Gloves, Willard *Also called Guardian Manufacturing Co LLC (G-20240)*
Guardian Industries LLC..614 431-6309
  600 Lkview Plz Blvd Ste A Worthington (43085) *(G-20688)*
Guardian Lima LLC..567 940-9500
  2485 Houx Pkwy Lima (45804) *(G-11872)*
Guardian Manufacturing Co LLC..............................419 933-2711
  302 S Conwell Ave Willard (44890) *(G-20240)*
Guardian Millbury, Millbury *Also called Custom GL Sltions Millbury LLC (G-14048)*
Guardian Strategic Defense LLC..............................937 707-8985
  1540 Horizon Dr Marysville (43040) *(G-12786)*
Guardian Technologies LLC......................................216 706-2250
  26251 Bluestone Blvd # 7 Euclid (44132) *(G-9415)*
Guari Inc (PA)..330 733-4005
  2215 E Waterloo Rd # 101 Akron (44312) *(G-192)*
Guerin-Zimmerman Co, Cleveland *Also called B Y G Industries Inc (G-4785)*
GUERNSEY INDUSTRIES, Byesville *Also called Ken Harper (G-2388)*
Guetle Die & Stamping, Mansfield *Also called Amaroq Inc (G-12403)*
Guggisberg Cheese Inc (PA).....................................330 893-2550
  5060 State Route 557 Millersburg (44654) *(G-14086)*
Guide Technologies LLC (PA)...................................513 631-8800
  7363 E Kemper Rd Ste Ab Cincinnati (45249) *(G-3789)*

Guild Associates Inc (PA)....614 798-8215
5750 Shier Rings Rd Dublin (43016) ***(G-8919)***
Guild Associates Inc....843 573-0095
4412 Tuller Rd Dublin (43017) ***(G-8920)***
Guild Biosciences, Dublin *Also called Guild Associates Inc* ***(G-8919)***
Guild Biosciences, Dublin *Also called Guild Associates Inc* ***(G-8920)***
Guild International Inc....440 232-5887
7273 Division St Bedford (44146) ***(G-1408)***
Guitammer Company....614 898-9370
6117 Maxtown Rd Westerville (43082) ***(G-19995)***
Guitar Digest Inc....740 592-4614
23 Curtis St Athens (45701) ***(G-834)***
Gulfport Energy Corporation....740 251-0407
67185 Executive Dr Saint Clairsville (43950) ***(G-16632)***
Gumbys LLC....740 671-0818
2300 Belmont St Bellaire (43906) ***(G-1486)***
Gunderson Rail Services LLC....330 792-6521
3710 Hendricks Rd Bldg 2a Youngstown (44515) ***(G-20927)***
Gundlach, Cincinnati *Also called Rotex Global LLC* ***(G-4282)***
Gundlach Sheet Metal Works Inc (PA)....419 626-4525
910 Columbus Ave Sandusky (44870) ***(G-16814)***
Gurina Company....614 279-3891
1379 River St Columbus (43222) ***(G-6971)***
Gus Holthaus Signs Inc....513 861-0060
817 Ridgeway Ave Cincinnati (45229) ***(G-3790)***
Gustave Julian Jewelers Inc....440 888-1100
7432 State Rd Cleveland (44134) ***(G-5360)***
Gutter Topper Ltd....513 797-5800
4111 Founders Blvd Batavia (45103) ***(G-1150)***
Guttman Oil, Westerville *Also called Brightstar Propane & Fuels* ***(G-19981)***
Guy's Award Winning Barbeque, Newton Falls *Also called Guys Barbeque Inc* ***(G-14987)***
Guyer Precision Inc....440 354-8024
280 W Prospect St Painesville (44077) ***(G-15744)***
Guys Barbeque Inc....330 872-7256
4498 W Oakland St Sw Newton Falls (44444) ***(G-14987)***
Guys Brewing Gear....330 554-9362
1325 Chelton Dr Kent (44240) ***(G-11327)***
Gvc Plastics & Metals LLC....440 232-9360
7051 Krick Rd Bedford (44146) ***(G-1409)***
Gvi Medical Devices Corp....330 963-4083
1470 Enterprise Pkwy Twinsburg (44087) ***(G-18789)***
Gvimd, Twinsburg *Also called Gvi Medical Devices Corp* ***(G-18789)***
Gvs Filtration Inc (HQ)....419 423-9040
2150 Industrial Dr Findlay (45840) ***(G-9697)***
Gvs Industries Inc....513 851-3606
1030 Beissinger Rd Hamilton (45013) ***(G-10565)***
Gwen Rosenberg Enterprises LLC....330 678-1893
175 E Erie St Ste 201 Kent (44240) ***(G-11328)***
Gwp Holdings Inc....513 860-4050
8675 Seward Rd Fairfield (45011) ***(G-9501)***
Gym Pro LLC....740 984-4143
50 Washington St Waterford (45786) ***(G-19485)***
Gyrus Acmi LP....419 668-8201
93 N Pleasant St Norwalk (44857) ***(G-15396)***
H & An LLC....740 435-0200
1224 Southgate Pkwy Cambridge (43725) ***(G-2442)***
H & B Machine & Tool Inc....216 431-3254
1390 E 40th St Cleveland (44103) ***(G-5361)***
H & C Building Supplies, Huron *Also called Huron Cement Products Company* ***(G-11096)***
H & C Building Supplies, Sandusky *Also called Huron Cement Products Company* ***(G-16816)***
H & D Drilling Co Inc....740 745-2236
11183 Pleasant Valley Rd Frazeysburg (43822) ***(G-9939)***
H & D Steel Service Inc....440 237-3390
9960 York Alpha Dr North Royalton (44133) ***(G-15275)***
H & D Steel Service Center, North Royalton *Also called H & D Steel Service Inc* ***(G-15275)***
H & E Machine Company....614 443-7635
1646 Fairwood Ave Columbus (43206) ***(G-6972)***
H & G Equipment Inc (PA)....513 761-2060
10837 Millington Ct Blue Ash (45242) ***(G-1784)***
H & H Engineered Molded Pdts....440 415-1814
436 N Eagle St Geneva (44041) ***(G-10220)***
H & H Equipment Inc....330 264-5400
6247 Ashland Rd Wooster (44691) ***(G-20601)***
H & H Industries Inc....740 682-7721
5400 State Route 93 Oak Hill (45656) ***(G-15451)***
H & H Machine Shop Akron Inc....330 773-3327
955 Grant St Akron (44311) ***(G-193)***
H & H of Milford Ohio LLC....513 576-9004
1194 Wintercrest Cir Milford (45150) ***(G-14015)***
H & H Quick Machine Inc....330 935-0944
7816 Edison St Louisville (44641) ***(G-12154)***
H & H Sailcraft, New Paris *Also called Dynamic Plastics Inc* ***(G-14753)***
H & H Screen Process Inc....937 253-7520
1220 Wyoming St Dayton (45410) ***(G-8240)***
H & H Tooling, Westlake *Also called Pines Manufacturing Inc* ***(G-20142)***
H & H Tree Service LLC....440 632-0551
15530 Old State Rd Middlefield (44062) ***(G-13801)***
H & H Truck Parts LLC....216 642-4540
5500s Cloverleaf Pkwy Cleveland (44125) ***(G-5362)***
H & K Pallet Services....937 608-1140
1039 Jasper Ave Xenia (45385) ***(G-20776)***
H & M Fabricating, Burton *Also called Harvey Miller* ***(G-2359)***
H & M Machine Shop Inc....419 453-3414
290 State Route 189 Ottoville (45876) ***(G-15680)***
H & M Metal Processing Co....330 745-3075
1414 Kenmore Blvd Akron (44314) ***(G-194)***
H & N Instruments Inc....740 344-4351
219 N Westmoor Ave Newark (43055) ***(G-14882)***
H & R Metal Finishing Inc....440 942-6656
1650 E 361st St Unit L Willoughby (44095) ***(G-20335)***
H & R Tool & Machine Co Inc....740 452-0784
18 Jefferson St Zanesville (43701) ***(G-21143)***
H & S Company Inc....419 394-4444
7219 Harris Rd Celina (45822) ***(G-2965)***
H & S Drilling Co Inc....740 828-2411
101 E 3rd St Frazeysburg (43822) ***(G-9940)***
H & S Operating Company Inc....330 830-8178
2581 County Rd 160 Winesburg (44690) ***(G-20531)***
H & S Precision Screw Pdts Inc....937 437-0316
8205 H W Rd New Paris (45347) ***(G-14754)***
H & S Steel Treating Inc....330 678-5245
4142 Mogadore Rd Kent (44240) ***(G-11329)***
H & S Tool Inc....330 335-1536
715 Weber Dr Wadsworth (44281) ***(G-19244)***
H & W Screw Products Inc....937 866-2577
335 Industrial Dr Franklin (45005) ***(G-9888)***
H & W Tool Co....216 795-5520
1363 Chardon Rd Ste 3 Euclid (44117) ***(G-9416)***
H B Products Inc....937 492-7031
1661 Saint Marys Rd Sidney (45365) ***(G-17042)***
H C Starck Inc....216 692-6990
1250 E 222nd St Euclid (44117) ***(G-9417)***
H C Starck Inc....216 692-3990
21801 Tungsten Rd Euclid (44117) ***(G-9418)***
H D C, Miamisburg *Also called Hooven - Dayton Corp* ***(G-13677)***
H Duane Leis Acquisitions....937 835-5621
443 S Diamond Mill Rd New Lebanon (45345) ***(G-14710)***
H E Long Company....513 899-2610
3910 Anderson Rd Morrow (45152) ***(G-14411)***
H G Schneider Company....614 882-6944
291 Broad St Westerville (43081) ***(G-20056)***
H G Violet Inc....419 695-2000
2103 N Main St Delphos (45833) ***(G-8744)***
H Gerstner & Sons Inc....937 228-1662
20 Gerstner Way Dayton (45402) ***(G-8241)***
H Goodman Inc....216 341-0200
3201 Harvard Ave Newburgh Heights (44105) ***(G-14936)***
H I Smith Oil & Gas Inc....330 279-2361
8255 County Road 192 Holmesville (44633) ***(G-10975)***
H I T, Painesville *Also called Hardy Industrial Tech LLC* ***(G-15745)***
H K K Machining Co....419 924-5116
1201 Oak St West Unity (43570) ***(G-19968)***
H K M, Cleveland *Also called Hkm Drect Mkt Cmmnications Inc* ***(G-5412)***
H K M Drect Mktg Cmmunications, Sheffield Village *Also called Hkm Drect Mkt Cmmnications Inc* ***(G-16967)***
H Machining Inc....419 636-6890
720 Commerce Dr Bryan (43506) ***(G-2283)***
H Nagel & Son Co....513 665-4550
2641 Spring Grove Ave Cincinnati (45214) ***(G-3791)***
H O Fibertrends....740 983-3864
235 State Route 674 S Ashville (43103) ***(G-818)***
H P E Inc....330 833-3161
2025 Harsh Ave Se Massillon (44646) ***(G-12993)***
H P Manufacturing Co....216 361-6500
3740 Prospect Ave E Cleveland (44115) ***(G-5363)***
H P Nielsen Inc....440 244-4255
753 Broadway Lorain (44052) ***(G-12094)***
H P Streicher Inc (PA)....419 841-4715
2955 Gradwohl Rd Toledo (43617) ***(G-18315)***
H R Machine....937 838-6289
2972 Homeway Dr Beavercreek (45434) ***(G-1321)***
H Rosen Usa LLC....614 354-6707
1195 Technology Dr Columbus (43230) ***(G-6973)***
H S Morgan Limited Partnership (PA)....513 870-4400
3158 Production Dr Fairfield (45014) ***(G-9502)***
H S Processing LP....216 641-6995
4600 Heidtman Pkwy Cleveland (44105) ***(G-5364)***
H W Chair Co, Millersburg *Also called Hochstetler Wood* ***(G-14093)***
H W Fairway International Inc....330 678-2540
716 N Mantua St Kent (44240) ***(G-11330)***
H Y O Inc....614 488-2861
2550 W 5th Ave Columbus (43204) ***(G-6974)***
H&H Custom Homes, Loudonville *Also called Mohican Log Homes Inc* ***(G-12144)***
H&M Machine & Tool LLC....419 776-9220
3823 Seiss Ave Toledo (43612) ***(G-18316)***
H&M Mtal Stamping Assembly Inc....216 898-9030
5325 W 140th St Brookpark (44142) ***(G-2149)***

H-P Products Inc...330 875-7193
2000 W Main St Louisville (44641) ***(G-12155)***
H-W Machine Inc...330 477-7231
4028 Southway St Sw Canton (44706) ***(G-2690)***
H. Meyer Dairy, Cincinnati *Also called Borden Dairy Co Cincinnati LLC* ***(G-3404)***
H2o Mechanics LLC...440 554-9515
15708 Park View Dr Newbury (44065) ***(G-14955)***
H3d Tool Corporation (PA)...740 498-5181
295 Enterprise Dr Newcomerstown (43832) ***(G-14974)***
Ha-International LLC...419 537-0096
4243 South Ave Toledo (43615) ***(G-18317)***
Ha-Ste Manufacturing Co Inc...937 968-4858
119 E Elm St Union City (45390) ***(G-18904)***
Haag-Streit Holding Us Inc (HQ)...513 336-7255
3535 Kings Mills Rd Mason (45040) ***(G-12883)***
Haas Door Company...419 337-9900
320 Sycamore St Wauseon (43567) ***(G-19519)***
Haas Doors, Wauseon *Also called Nofziger Door Sales Inc* ***(G-19530)***
Haas Jordan Company, Holland *Also called Tmb Enterprises LLC* ***(G-10961)***
Hab Computer Services, Solon *Also called Hab Inc* ***(G-17158)***
Hab Inc...608 785-7650
28925 Fountain Pkwy Solon (44139) ***(G-17158)***
Habco Tool and Dev Co Inc...440 946-5546
7725 Metric Dr Mentor (44060) ***(G-13463)***
Habitec SEC Diversfd Alarm...419 636-1155
115 N Lynn St Bryan (43506) ***(G-2284)***
Hacienda Publications LLC...216 202-5440
20970 Wilmore Ave Euclid (44123) ***(G-9419)***
Hacker Wood Products Inc...513 737-4462
2144 Jackson Rd Hamilton (45011) ***(G-10566)***
Hackman Frames LLC...614 841-0007
502 Schrock Rd Columbus (43229) ***(G-6975)***
Hackworth Electric Motors Inc...330 345-6049
4952 Cleveland Rd Wooster (44691) ***(G-20602)***
Hackworth Electrical Contrs In, Wooster *Also called Hackworth Oil Field Electric* ***(G-20603)***
Hackworth Oil Field Electric...330 345-6504
4931 Cleveland Rd Wooster (44691) ***(G-20603)***
Hadley Printing, Beavercreek *Also called A C Hadley - Printing Inc* ***(G-1296)***
Hadlock Plastics LLC...440 466-4876
110 N Eagle St Geneva (44041) ***(G-10221)***
Hadronics Inc...513 321-9350
4570 Steel Pl Cincinnati (45209) ***(G-3792)***
Haeco Inc (PA)...513 722-1030
6504 Snider Rd Loveland (45140) ***(G-12195)***
Haessly Lumber Sales Co (PA)...740 373-6681
25 Sheets Run Rd Marietta (45750) ***(G-12630)***
Hafco-Case Inc...216 267-4644
12212 Sprecher Ave Cleveland (44135) ***(G-5365)***
Hafner Hardwood Connection LLC...419 726-4828
2845 111th St Toledo (43611) ***(G-18318)***
Hahn Manufacturing Company...216 391-9300
5332 Hamilton Ave Cleveland (44114) ***(G-5366)***
Hahs Factory Outlet...330 405-4227
1993 Case Pkwy Twinsburg (44087) ***(G-18790)***
Haines & Company Inc (PA)...330 494-9111
8050 Freedom Ave Nw A North Canton (44720) ***(G-15090)***
Haines Criss Cross (PA)...330 494-9111
8050 Freedom Ave Nw North Canton (44720) ***(G-15091)***
Haines Publishing Inc...330 494-9111
8050 Freedom Ave Nw Canton (44720) ***(G-2691)***
Hair & Nail Impressions...937 399-0221
2330 Northmoor Dr Springfield (45503) ***(G-17409)***
Hair Science Systems LLC...513 231-8284
445 Bishopsbridge Dr Cincinnati (45255) ***(G-3793)***
Haiss Fabripart LLC...330 821-2028
22421 Lake Park Blvd Alliance (44601) ***(G-470)***
Hake Head LLC...614 291-2244
1855 E 17th Ave Columbus (43219) ***(G-6976)***
Hal Mar Printing, Warren *Also called Mackland Co Inc* ***(G-19419)***
Halcore Group Inc (HQ)...614 539-8181
3800 Mcdowell Rd Grove City (43123) ***(G-10433)***
Hale Logging, Patriot *Also called Chester F Hale* ***(G-15849)***
Hale Manufacturing LLC...937 382-2127
1065 Wayne Rd Wilmington (45177) ***(G-20497)***
Hale Performance Coatings Inc...419 244-6451
2282 Albion St Toledo (43606) ***(G-18319)***
Halex, Harrison *Also called Scott Fetzer Company* ***(G-10669)***
Halex, A Scott Fetzer Company, Bedford Heights *Also called Halex/Scott Fetzer Company* ***(G-1471)***
Halex/Scott Fetzer Company (HQ)...440 439-1616
23901 Aurora Rd Bedford Heights (44146) ***(G-1471)***
Halifax Industries Inc...216 990-8951
2060 Garden Ln Hudson (44236) ***(G-11050)***
Halifax-Fan USA LLC...262 257-9779
1474 Main St Cuyahoga Falls (44221) ***(G-7876)***
Hall Company...937 652-1376
420 E Water St Urbana (43078) ***(G-18992)***
Hall Safety Apparel Inc...740 922-3671
1020 W 1st St Uhrichsville (44683) ***(G-18887)***
Hall Trencher Service, South Webster *Also called Roger Hall* ***(G-17299)***
Hall's Sheet Metal Fabricating, Galena *Also called Halls Sheet Metal Fabrication* ***(G-10113)***
Hall-Toledo Inc...419 893-4334
525 W Sophia St Maumee (43537) ***(G-13114)***
Haller Enterprises Inc...330 733-9693
1621 E Market St Akron (44305) ***(G-195)***
Halliburton Energy Svcs Inc...740 617-2917
4999 E Pointe Dr Zanesville (43701) ***(G-21144)***
Halliday Holdings Inc...740 335-1430
1544 Old Us 35 Se Wshngtn CT Hs (43160) ***(G-20727)***
Halliday Technologies Inc...614 504-4150
105 Innovation Ct Ste F Delaware (43015) ***(G-8691)***
Hallmark Industries Inc (PA)...937 864-7378
2233 N Limestone St Springfield (45503) ***(G-17410)***
Halls Sheet Metal Fabrication...740 965-9264
10001 Center Village Rd Galena (43021) ***(G-10113)***
Halls Welding & Supplies Inc...330 385-9353
49037 Clctta Smthferry Rd East Liverpool (43920) ***(G-9058)***
Haltec Corporation...330 222-1501
32585 N Price Rd Salem (44460) ***(G-16746)***
Halvey Quarter Horses...614 648-0483
6230 Havens Corners Rd Blacklick (43004) ***(G-1685)***
Halvorsen Company...216 341-7500
7500 Grand Division Ave # 1 Cleveland (44125) ***(G-5367)***
Ham Signs LLC...937 454-9111
6020 N Dixie Dr Dayton (45414) ***(G-8242)***
Haman Enterprises Inc...614 888-7574
7525 Pingue Dr Worthington (43085) ***(G-20689)***
Haman Midwest, Worthington *Also called Haman Enterprises Inc* ***(G-20689)***
Hamco Manufacturing Inc...440 774-1637
48882 State Route 511 Oberlin (44074) ***(G-15498)***
Hamilton Air Products Inc...513 874-4030
3143 Production Dr Fairfield (45014) ***(G-9503)***
Hamilton Animal Products LLC...937 293-9994
2425 W Dorothy Ln Moraine (45439) ***(G-14357)***
Hamilton Arts Inc...937 767-1834
750 Union St Yellow Springs (45387) ***(G-20807)***
Hamilton Brass & Alum Castings...513 867-0400
706 S 8th St Hamilton (45011) ***(G-10567)***
Hamilton Custom Molding Inc...513 844-6643
1365 Shuler Ave Hamilton (45011) ***(G-10568)***
Hamilton Fabricators Inc...513 735-7773
4008 Borman Dr Batavia (45103) ***(G-1151)***
Hamilton Journal News Inc...513 863-8200
7320 Yankee Rd Liberty Township (45044) ***(G-11815)***
Hamilton Journalnews, Liberty Township *Also called Cox Newspapers LLC* ***(G-11813)***
Hamilton Manufacturing Corp...419 867-4858
1026 Hamilton Dr Holland (43528) ***(G-10933)***
Hamilton Mold & Machine Co...216 732-8200
25016 Lakeland Blvd Cleveland (44132) ***(G-5368)***
Hamilton Rti Inc...330 652-9951
1000 Warren Ave Niles (44446) ***(G-15011)***
Hamilton Safe, Cincinnati *Also called Hamilton Security Products Co* ***(G-3795)***
Hamilton Safe Amelia...513 753-5694
3997 Bach Buxton Rd Amelia (45102) ***(G-540)***
Hamilton Safe Co (PA)...513 874-3733
7775 Cooper Rd Cincinnati (45242) ***(G-3794)***
Hamilton Security Products Co (PA)...513 874-3733
7775 Cooper Rd Cincinnati (45242) ***(G-3795)***
Hamilton Tanks LLC...614 445-8446
2200 Refugee Rd Columbus (43207) ***(G-6977)***
Hamlet Protein Inc...567 525-5627
5289 Hamlet Dr Findlay (45840) ***(G-9698)***
Hamlin Newco LLC...330 753-7791
2741 Wingate Ave Akron (44314) ***(G-196)***
Hamlin Steel Products LLC...330 753-7791
2741 Wingate Ave Akron (44314) ***(G-197)***
Hammelmann Corporation (HQ)...937 859-8777
436 Southpointe Dr Miamisburg (45342) ***(G-13673)***
Hammill Manufacturing Co (PA)...419 476-0789
360 Tomahawk Dr Maumee (43537) ***(G-13115)***
Hammill Manufacturing Co...419 724-5702
1517 Coining Dr Toledo (43612) ***(G-18320)***
Hampshire Co...937 773-3493
9225 State Route 66 Piqua (45356) ***(G-16119)***
Hampton Publishing Company...513 777-9543
7739 Derbyshire Ct Liberty Township (45044) ***(G-11816)***
Hana Microdisplay Tech Inc...330 405-4600
2061 Case Pkwy S Twinsburg (44087) ***(G-18791)***
Hanby Farms Inc...740 763-3554
10790 Newark Rd Nashport (43830) ***(G-14567)***
Hanchett Paper Company...513 782-4440
12121 Best Pl Cincinnati (45241) ***(G-3796)***
Hancock Structural Steel LLC...419 424-1217
813 E Bigelow Ave Findlay (45840) ***(G-9699)***
Hancor Holding Corporation (HQ)...419 422-6521
401 Olive St Findlay (45840) ***(G-9700)***
Hancor Inc (HQ)...614 658-0050
4640 Trueman Blvd Hilliard (43026) ***(G-10827)***

ALPHABETIC

Hancor Inc...419 424-8225
433 Olive St Findlay (45840) ***(G-9701)***
Hancor Inc...419 424-8222
12370 Jackson Township Rd Findlay (45839) ***(G-9702)***
Handcrafted Jewelry Inc...330 650-9011
116 N Main St Hudson (44236) ***(G-11051)***
Handicraft LLC...216 295-1950
26225 Broadway Ave Bedford (44146) ***(G-1410)***
Handkerchief House, The, Hudson *Also called Thompson Assoc Hudson Ohio* ***(G-11079)***
Handle Light Inc...330 772-8901
5533 State Route 7 Kinsman (44428) ***(G-11464)***
Hands On International LLC...513 502-9000
8541 Charleston Ridge Dr Mason (45040) ***(G-12884)***
Handy Twine Knife Co...419 294-3424
5676 County Highway 330 Upper Sandusky (43351) ***(G-18955)***
Hang Time Group Inc...216 771-5885
5340 Hamilton Ave Ste 107 Cleveland (44114) ***(G-5369)***
Hang-UPS Instllation Group Inc...614 239-7004
3751 April Ln Columbus (43227) ***(G-6978)***
Hanger Clinic, Cincinnati *Also called Hanger Prsthetcs & Ortho Inc* ***(G-3797)***
Hanger Clinic, Youngstown *Also called Hanger Prsthetcs & Ortho Inc* ***(G-20928)***
Hanger Clinic, Portsmouth *Also called Hanger Prsthetcs & Ortho Inc* ***(G-16285)***
Hanger Prsthetcs & Ortho Inc...216 475-4211
16480 Broadway Ave Maple Heights (44137) ***(G-12573)***
Hanger Prsthetcs & Ortho Inc...440 605-0232
6001 Landerhaven Dr Ste A Mayfield Heights (44124) ***(G-13165)***
Hanger Prsthetcs & Ortho Inc...419 841-9852
3435 N Hlland Sylvania Rd Toledo (43615) ***(G-18321)***
Hanger Prsthetcs & Ortho Inc...513 421-5653
2135 Dana Ave Ste 100 Cincinnati (45207) ***(G-3797)***
Hanger Prsthetcs & Ortho Inc...740 454-6215
930 Orchard Hill Rd Zanesville (43701) ***(G-21145)***
Hanger Prsthetcs & Ortho Inc...330 758-1143
930 Trailwood Dr Youngstown (44512) ***(G-20928)***
Hanger Prsthetcs & Ortho Inc...440 892-6665
29101 Health Campus Dr # 104 Westlake (44145) ***(G-20121)***
Hanger Prsthetcs & Ortho Inc...330 374-9544
388 S Main St Ste 205 Akron (44311) ***(G-198)***
Hanger Prsthetcs & Ortho Inc...937 773-2441
9179 N County Road 25a 2b Piqua (45356) ***(G-16120)***
Hanger Prsthetcs & Ortho Inc...937 228-5462
1 Elizabeth Pl Ste 300 Dayton (45417) ***(G-8243)***
Hanger Prsthetcs & Ortho Inc...740 354-4775
1611 27th St Ste 303 Portsmouth (45662) ***(G-16285)***
Hanger Prsthetcs & Ortho Inc...419 522-0055
1136 Independence Ave Marion (43302) ***(G-12708)***
Hanger Prsthetcs & Ortho Inc...740 383-2163
1136 Independence Ave Marion (43302) ***(G-12709)***
Hanger Prsthetcs & Ortho Inc...740 266-6400
2605 Sunset Blvd Unit C Steubenville (43952) ***(G-17536)***
Hanger Prsthetcs & Ortho Inc...937 325-5404
30 Warder St Ste 125 Springfield (45504) ***(G-17411)***
Hanger Prsthetcs & Ortho Inc...937 643-1557
2000 Springboro W Moraine (45439) ***(G-14358)***
Hanger Prsthetcs & Ortho Inc...330 821-4918
4663 Whipple Ave Nw Canton (44718) ***(G-2692)***
Hanger Prsthetcs & Ortho Inc...614 481-8338
1357 Dublin Rd Columbus (43215) ***(G-6979)***
Hanger Prsthetcs & Ortho Inc...740 654-1884
111 N Ewing St Lancaster (43130) ***(G-11578)***
Hanini Seven Oil...216 857-0172
6501 Denison Ave Cleveland (44102) ***(G-5370)***
Hanlon Industries Inc...216 261-7056
1280 E 286th St Cleveland (44132) ***(G-5371)***
Hann Box Works...740 962-3752
4678 N State Route 60 Nw McConnelsville (43756) ***(G-13205)***
Hann Construction, McConnelsville *Also called Hann Box Works* ***(G-13205)***
Hann Manufacturing Inc...740 962-3752
4678 N State Route 60 Nw McConnelsville (43756) ***(G-13206)***
Hannibal Co Inc...614 846-5060
6536 Proprietors Rd Worthington (43085) ***(G-20690)***
Hannon Company (PA)...330 456-4728
1605 Waynesburg Dr Se Canton (44707) ***(G-2693)***
Hannon Company...330 343-7758
801 Commercial Pkwy Dover (44622) ***(G-8829)***
Hannon Company...740 453-0527
218 Adams St Zanesville (43701) ***(G-21146)***
Hanon Systems Usa LLC...313 920-0583
581 Arrowhead Dr Carey (43316) ***(G-2882)***
Hanover Publishing Co...440 838-0911
7569 Sanctuary Cir Brecksville (44141) ***(G-2040)***
Hanover Winery Inc...513 304-9702
2121 Morman Rd Hamilton (45013) ***(G-10569)***
Hans Rothenbuhler & Son Inc...440 632-6000
15815 Nauvoo Rd Middlefield (44062) ***(G-13802)***
Hansa Bewery LLC...216 631-6585
2717 Lorain Ave Cleveland (44113) ***(G-5372)***
Hansen Coupling Division, Berea *Also called Eaton Corporation* ***(G-1604)***
Hansen Scaffolding LLC (PA)...513 574-9000
193 Circle Freeway Dr West Chester (45246) ***(G-19863)***
Hansen-Mueller Co...419 729-5535
1800 N Water St Toledo (43611) ***(G-18322)***
Hanser Music Group Inc (PA)...859 817-7100
9615 Inter Ocean Dr West Chester (45246) ***(G-19864)***
Hanson Aggregates, Sandusky *Also called Wagner Quarries Company* ***(G-16862)***
Hanson Aggregates East...513 353-1100
7000 Dry Fork Rd Cleves (45002) ***(G-6363)***
Hanson Aggregates East LLC...740 773-2172
33 Renick Ave Chillicothe (45601) ***(G-3191)***
Hanson Aggregates East LLC...937 587-2671
848 Plum Run Rd Peebles (45660) ***(G-15878)***
Hanson Aggregates East LLC...330 467-7890
7925 Empire Pkwy Macedonia (44056) ***(G-12301)***
Hanson Aggregates East LLC...419 483-4390
9220 Portland Rd Castalia (44824) ***(G-2939)***
Hanson Aggregates East LLC...937 442-6009
13526 Overstake Rd Winchester (45697) ***(G-20521)***
Hanson Aggregates LLC...419 841-3413
4100 Centennial Rd Sylvania (43560) ***(G-17941)***
Hanson Aggregates Mid West, Bloomville *Also called Hanson Aggregates Midwest LLC* ***(G-1715)***
Hanson Aggregates Midwest LLC...419 882-0123
8130 Brint Rd Sylvania (43560) ***(G-17942)***
Hanson Aggregates Midwest LLC...419 983-2211
4575 S County Road 49 Bloomville (44818) ***(G-1715)***
Hanson Aggregates Midwest LLC...419 878-2006
600 S River Rd Waterville (43566) ***(G-19497)***
Hanson Concrete Products Ohio...614 443-4846
1500 Haul Rd Columbus (43207) ***(G-6980)***
Hanson Pipe & Precast Hamburg, Dayton *Also called Forterra Pipe & Precast LLC* ***(G-8203)***
Hanson Pipe & Products, Columbus *Also called Hanson Concrete Products Ohio* ***(G-6980)***
Hanson Ready Mix Inc...614 221-5345
816 Mckinley Ave Columbus (43222) ***(G-6981)***
Hantech, Findlay *Also called Hancor Inc* ***(G-9701)***
Hapco Inc...330 678-9353
390 Portage Blvd Kent (44240) ***(G-11331)***
Happy Booker, Cincinnati *Also called Art Guild Binders Inc* ***(G-3358)***
Happy Time Adventures...419 407-6409
3434 Secor Rd Toledo (43606) ***(G-18323)***
Happy Trails Rv, Cleveland *Also called Electric Cord Sets Inc* ***(G-5161)***
Har Adhesive Technologies, Bedford *Also called Certon Technologies Inc* ***(G-1395)***
Har Equipment Sales Inc...440 786-7189
60 S Park St Bedford (44146) ***(G-1411)***
Harbisonwalker Intl Inc...330 326-2010
9686 E Center St Windham (44288) ***(G-20524)***
Harbisonwalker Intl Inc...440 234-8002
6950 Engle Rd Cleveland (44130) ***(G-5373)***
Harbisonwalker Intl Inc...513 576-6240
4065a Clough Woods Dr Batavia (45103) ***(G-1152)***
Harbisonwalker Intl Inc...330 868-4141
1316 Alliance Rd Nw Minerva (44657) ***(G-14181)***
Harbor Castings Inc (PA)...330 499-7178
2508 Bailey Rd Cuyahoga Falls (44221) ***(G-7877)***
Harbor Freight Tools Usa Inc...937 415-0770
1941 Needmore Rd Dayton (45414) ***(G-8244)***
Harbor Industrial Corp...440 599-8366
859 W Jackson St Conneaut (44030) ***(G-7647)***
Harco Manufacturing Group LLC (PA)...937 528-5000
3535 Kettering Blvd Moraine (45439) ***(G-14359)***
Harco Manufacturing Group LLC...937 528-5000
3535 Kettering Blvd 200 Moraine (45439) ***(G-14360)***
Hard Chrome Plating Consultant...216 631-9090
2196 W 59th St Cleveland (44102) ***(G-5374)***
Hard Drive Co, Barberton *Also called Florence Alloys Inc* ***(G-1071)***
Hardcoating Technologies Ltd...330 686-2136
103 S Main St Munroe Falls (44262) ***(G-14523)***
Hardin County Publishing Co (HQ)...419 674-4066
201 E Columbus St Kenton (43326) ***(G-11408)***
Hardin Creek Machine & Tool...419 678-4913
200 Hardin St Coldwater (45828) ***(G-6410)***
Harding Machine Acquisition Co...937 666-3031
13060 State Route 287 East Liberty (43319) ***(G-9048)***
Hardline International Inc...419 924-9556
1107 Oak St West Unity (43570) ***(G-19969)***
Hardline Welding LLC...330 858-6289
2161 Mogadore Rd Kent (44240) ***(G-11332)***
Hardmagic...415 390-6232
125 Frederick St Marietta (45750) ***(G-12631)***
Hardware Exchange Inc...440 449-8006
6573 Cochran Rd Ste F Solon (44139) ***(G-17159)***
Hardwood Connection, The, Toledo *Also called Hafner Hardwood Connection LLC* ***(G-18318)***
Hardwood Flrg & Paneling Inc...440 834-1710
15320 Burton Windsor Rd Middlefield (44062) ***(G-13803)***
Hardwood Lumber Co, Burton *Also called Stephen M Trudick* ***(G-2371)***
Hardwood Solutions...330 359-5755
112 E Main St Wilmot (44689) ***(G-20516)***
Hardwood Store Inc...937 864-2899
340 Enon Rd Enon (45323) ***(G-9384)***

Hardy Industrial Tech LLC 440 350-6300
679 Hardy Rd Painesville (44077) ***(G-15745)***
Harlan Graphic Arts Svcs Inc 513 251-5700
4752 River Rd Cincinnati (45233) ***(G-3798)***
Harland Sharp, Strongsville *Also called Custom Speed Parts Inc* ***(G-17735)***
Harmon John 740 934-2032
36300 Greenbrier Rd Graysville (45734) ***(G-10341)***
Harmon Sign Company, Toledo *Also called Kasper Enterprises Inc* ***(G-18362)***
Harmon, John K, Graysville *Also called Harmon John* ***(G-10341)***
Harmony Systems and Svc Inc 937 778-1082
1711 Commerce Dr Piqua (45356) ***(G-16121)***
Harn Vault Service Inc (PA) 330 832-1995
422 East St Minerva (44657) ***(G-14182)***
Harness Shop, Charm *Also called Charm Harness and Boot Ltd* ***(G-3141)***
Harold Flory 937 473-3030
5225 W Myers Rd Covington (45318) ***(G-7787)***
Harper Engraving & Printing Co (PA) 614 276-0700
2626 Fisher Rd Columbus (43204) ***(G-6982)***
Harray LLC 888 568-8371
266 W Mitchell Ave Cincinnati (45232) ***(G-3799)***
Harris Mackessy & Brennan 614 221-6831
570 Polaris Pkwy Ste 125 Westerville (43082) ***(G-19996)***
Harris Broadcast, Mason *Also called Imagine Communications Corp* ***(G-12890)***
Harris Calorific Inc 216 383-4107
22801 Saint Clair Ave Cleveland (44117) ***(G-5375)***
Harris Corporation 973 284-2866
3500 Pentagon Blvd # 300 Beavercreek (45431) ***(G-1322)***
Harris Hawk 800 459-4295
306 W Main St Mason (45040) ***(G-12885)***
Harris Instrument Corporation 740 369-3580
155 Johnson Dr Delaware (43015) ***(G-8692)***
Harris Paper Crafts Inc 614 299-2141
266 E 5th Ave Columbus (43201) ***(G-6983)***
Harris Products Group, The, Euclid *Also called J W Harris Co Inc* ***(G-9421)***
Harris Welding and Machine Co (PA) 419 281-8351
2219 Cottage St Ashland (44805) ***(G-707)***
Harris Welding and Machine Co 419 281-9623
2219 Cottage St Ashland (44805) ***(G-708)***
Harrison 20 Mtd Borefinery LLC 740 796-4797
9665 Young America Rd Adamsville (43802) ***(G-9)***
Harrison County Coal Company (PA) 740 338-3100
46226 National Rd Saint Clairsville (43950) ***(G-16633)***
Harrison Ethanol, Adamsville *Also called Harrison 20 Mtd Borefinery LLC* ***(G-9)***
Harrison Hub, Scio *Also called M3 Midstream LLC* ***(G-16878)***
Harrison Mch & Plastic Corp (PA) 330 527-5641
11614 State Route 88 Garrettsville (44231) ***(G-10191)***
Harrison News Herald Inc 740 942-2118
144 S Main St Lowr Cadiz (43907) ***(G-2398)***
Harrison Paint Company (PA) 330 455-5120
1329 Harrison Ave Sw Canton (44706) ***(G-2694)***
Harry C Lobalzo & Sons Inc (PA) 330 666-6758
61 N Cleveland Akron (44333) ***(G-199)***
Harry London Candies Inc (HQ) 330 494-0833
5353 Lauby Rd North Canton (44720) ***(G-15092)***
Harry London Chocolates, North Canton *Also called Harry London Candies Inc* ***(G-15092)***
Harrys Pallets LLC 330 704-1056
7029 Flenner St Sw Navarre (44662) ***(G-14576)***
Harsco Corporation 740 387-1150
3477 Harding Hwy E Marion (43302) ***(G-12710)***
Harsco Corporation 740 367-7322
5486 State Route 7 N Cheshire (45620) ***(G-3148)***
Harsco Corporation 216 961-1570
7900 Hub Pkwy Cleveland (44125) ***(G-5376)***
Harsco Corporation 330 372-1781
101 Tidewater St Ne Warren (44483) ***(G-19408)***
Hart & Cooley Inc 937 832-7800
1 Lau Pkwy Englewood (45315) ***(G-9361)***
Hart Advertising Inc 419 668-1194
6975 E Seminary St Norwalk (44857) ***(G-15397)***
Hartco Printing Company (PA) 614 761-1292
4106 Delancy Park Dr Dublin (43016) ***(G-8921)***
Hartco Products, The, Dublin *Also called Hartco Printing Company* ***(G-8921)***
Hartford Steel Sales 513 275-1744
6 S 2nd St Ste 214 Hamilton (45011) ***(G-10570)***
Hartley Machine Inc 330 821-0343
22640 Hartley Rd Alliance (44601) ***(G-471)***
Hartline Products Coinc (PA) 216 291-2303
4568 Mayfield Rd Ste 202 Cleveland (44121) ***(G-5377)***
Hartline Products Coinc 216 851-7189
15035 Woodworth Rd Ste 3 Cleveland (44110) ***(G-5378)***
Hartman Baseball Cards, Columbus *Also called The Hartman Corp* ***(G-7525)***
Hartman Distributing LLC 740 616-7764
1262 Bluejack Ln Heath (43056) ***(G-10719)***
Hartman Printing Co 419 946-2854
425 W Marion St Mount Gilead (43338) ***(G-14425)***
Hartmann Incorporated 513 276-7318
4615 Carlynn Dr Blue Ash (45241) ***(G-1785)***
Hartsgrove Machine, Rock Creek *Also called David Bixel* ***(G-16532)***
Hartville Chocolate Factory, Hartville *Also called Hartville Chocolates Inc* ***(G-10692)***
Hartville Chocolates Inc 330 877-1999
114 S Prospect Ave Hartville (44632) ***(G-10692)***
Hartville Locker Service Inc 330 877-9547
119 Sunnyside St Sw Hartville (44632) ***(G-10693)***
Hartville News, Hartville *Also called Knowles Press Inc* ***(G-10699)***
Hartville Plastics Inc 330 877-9090
322 Lake Ave Ne Hartville (44632) ***(G-10694)***
Hartz Mountain Corporation 513 877-2131
5374 Long Spurling Rd Pleasant Plain (45162) ***(G-16227)***
Hartzell Fan Inc (PA) 937 773-7411
910 S Downing St Piqua (45356) ***(G-16122)***
Hartzell Hardwoods Inc (PA) 937 773-7054
1025 S Roosevelt Ave Piqua (45356) ***(G-16123)***
Hartzell Industries Inc (PA) 937 773-6295
1025 S Roosevelt Ave Piqua (45356) ***(G-16124)***
Hartzell Mfg Co 937 859-5955
2533 Technical Dr Miamisburg (45342) ***(G-13674)***
Hartzell Propeller Inc 937 778-4200
1 Propeller Pl Piqua (45356) ***(G-16125)***
Hartzell Propeller Inc (HQ) 937 778-4200
1 Propeller Pl Piqua (45356) ***(G-16126)***
Hartzell Service Center, Piqua *Also called Hartzell Propeller Inc* ***(G-16125)***
Harvard Coil Processing Inc 216 883-6366
5400 Harvard Ave Cleveland (44105) ***(G-5379)***
Harvest Land Co-Op Inc 937 884-5526
141 S Commerce St Verona (45378) ***(G-19172)***
Harvey Brothers Inc (PA) 513 541-2622
3492 Spring Grove Ave Cincinnati (45223) ***(G-3800)***
Harvey Miller 440 834-9125
16828 Jug Rd Burton (44021) ***(G-2359)***
Harvey Whitney Books Company 513 793-3555
4906 Cooper Rd Cincinnati (45242) ***(G-3801)***
Harwood Rubber Products Inc 330 923-3256
1365 Orlen Ave Cuyahoga Falls (44221) ***(G-7878)***
Hashier & Hashier Mfg 440 933-4883
644 Moore Rd Avon Lake (44012) ***(G-988)***
Hason USA Corp 513 248-0287
1262 Us Highway 50 Milford (45150) ***(G-14016)***
Hatchery, Strasburg *Also called Case Farms of Ohio Inc* ***(G-17647)***
Hatfield Industries LLC 513 225-0456
9717 Flagstone Way West Chester (45069) ***(G-19719)***
Hathaway, Cincinnati *Also called Volk Corporation* ***(G-4483)***
Hathaway Stamp & Ident Co of C 513 621-1052
635 Main St Cincinnati (45202) ***(G-3802)***
Hathaway Stamp Co 513 621-1052
635 Main St Ste 1 Cincinnati (45202) ***(G-3803)***
Hathaway Stamp Identification, Cincinnati *Also called Hathaway Stamp & Ident Co of C* ***(G-3802)***
Hattenbach Company (PA) 216 881-5200
5309 Hamilton Ave Cleveland (44114) ***(G-5380)***
Hattenbach Company 330 744-2732
52 E Myrtle Ave Youngstown (44507) ***(G-20929)***
Haueter Construction Co 440 834-8220
15349 Ravenna Rd Newbury (44065) ***(G-14956)***
Haul, Mark Sales/Service/Parts, Navarre *Also called Navarre Trailer Sales Inc* ***(G-14583)***
Haul-Away Containers Inc 440 546-1879
3554 Brecksville Rd # 500 Richfield (44286) ***(G-16473)***
Haulette Manufacturing Inc 419 586-1717
8271 Us Route 127 Celina (45822) ***(G-2966)***
Haulotte US Inc (HQ) 419 445-8915
125 Taylor Pkwy Archbold (43502) ***(G-652)***
Haus Cider Mill & Fruit Farm, Canfield *Also called Haus Mathias* ***(G-2529)***
Haus Mathias 330 533-5305
6742 W Calla Rd Canfield (44406) ***(G-2529)***
Hauser Landscaping, Middlefield *Also called Hauser Services Llc* ***(G-13804)***
Hauser Services Llc 440 632-5126
15668 Old State Rd Middlefield (44062) ***(G-13804)***
Haute Chocolate Inc 513 793-9999
9424 Shelly Ln Montgomery (45242) ***(G-14294)***
Haviland Culvert Company 419 622-6951
100 W Main Haviland (45851) ***(G-10710)***
Haviland Drainage Products Co (PA) 419 622-4611
100 W Main St Haviland (45851) ***(G-10711)***
Haviland Plastic Products Co 419 622-3110
119 W Main St Haviland (45851) ***(G-10712)***
Hawaii Revealed, Lancaster *Also called Wizard Publications Inc* ***(G-11619)***
Hawk Engine & Machine 440 582-0900
12166 York Rd Unit 1 North Royalton (44133) ***(G-15276)***
Hawk Manufacturing LLC 330 784-6234
2642 Gilchrist Rd Akron (44305) ***(G-200)***
Hawk Manufacturing LLC (HQ) 330 784-3151
380 Kennedy Rd Akron (44305) ***(G-201)***
Hawk Manufacturing LLC 330 784-4815
382 Kennedy Rd Akron (44305) ***(G-202)***
Hawk Performance, Medina *Also called Friction Products Co* ***(G-13265)***
Hawkline Nevada LLC 937 444-4295
200 Front St Mount Orab (45154) ***(G-14442)***

ALPHABETIC

(PA)=Parent Co (HQ)=Headquarters (DH)=Div Headquarters
2019 Harris Ohio Industrial Directory
1135

Hawks & Associates Inc...513 752-4311
1029 Seabrook Way Cincinnati (45245) ***(G-3254)***
Hawks Tag, Cincinnati *Also called Hawks & Associates Inc* ***(G-3254)***
Hawthorne Bolt Works Corp...330 723-0555
1020 Industrial Pkwy Medina (44256) ***(G-13270)***
Hawthorne Hydrophonics/Botanic, Marysville *Also called Hawthorne Hydroponics LLC* ***(G-12787)***
Hawthorne Hydroponics LLC...480 777-2000
14111 Scottslawn Rd Marysville (43040) ***(G-12787)***
Hawthorne Hydroponics LLC (HQ)...800 221-1760
14111 Scottslawn Rd Marysville (43040) ***(G-12788)***
Hawthorne Tool LLC...440 516-1891
1340 Lloyd Rd Ste C Wickliffe (44092) ***(G-20212)***
Hawthorne Wire Ltd...216 712-4747
13000 Athens Ave Ste 101 Lakewood (44107) ***(G-11519)***
Hawthorne Wire Services Ltd...216 712-4747
13000 Athens Ave Ste 101 Lakewood (44107) ***(G-11520)***
Hawthorne-Seving Inc...419 643-5531
320 W Main St Cridersville (45806) ***(G-7810)***
Hayden Valley Foods Inc...614 539-7233
3150 Urbancrest Indus Urbancrest (43123) ***(G-19021)***
Hayes Bros Ornamental Ir Works...419 531-1491
1830 N Reynolds Rd Toledo (43615) ***(G-18324)***
Hayes Lemmerz Intl-Commrcl Hwy, Akron *Also called Maxion Wheels Akron LLC* ***(G-272)***
Hayes Metalfinishing Inc...937 228-7550
2617 Stanley Ave Dayton (45404) ***(G-8245)***
Hayes Reconditioning Group...937 299-8013
1301 Robert Dickey Pkwy Dayton (45409) ***(G-8246)***
Hayes, Michael Designer, Solon *Also called Michael W Hyes Desgr Goldsmith* ***(G-17194)***
Hayford Technologies...419 524-7627
500 S Airport Rd Mansfield (44903) ***(G-12455)***
Haynes Manufacturing Company, Westlake *Also called R and J Corporation* ***(G-20147)***
Haynn Construction Co Inc...419 853-4747
14866 N Elyria Rd West Salem (44287) ***(G-19954)***
Hays Cleveland, Cleveland *Also called Unicontrol Inc* ***(G-6230)***
Hays Fabricating & Welding...937 325-0031
633 E Leffel Ln Springfield (45505) ***(G-17412)***
Hays Orchard & Cider Mill LLC...330 482-2924
3622 Middleton Rd Columbiana (44408) ***(G-6468)***
Haz-Safe LLC...330 793-0900
3850 Hendricks Rd Austintown (44515) ***(G-933)***
Hazel and Rye Artisan Bkg Co...330 454-6658
220 Market Ave S Ste 110 Canton (44702) ***(G-2695)***
Hazelbaker Industries Ltd...614 276-2631
1661 Old Henderson Rd Columbus (43220) ***(G-6984)***
Hazenstab Machine Inc...330 337-1865
1575 Salem Pkwy Salem (44460) ***(G-16747)***
HB, Sidney *Also called H B Products Inc* ***(G-17042)***
HB Fuller Company...513 719-3600
4450 Malsbary Rd Blue Ash (45242) ***(G-1786)***
HB Fuller Company...513 719-3600
4440 Malsbary Rd Blue Ash (45242) ***(G-1787)***
Hbb Pro Sales (PA)...216 901-7900
9700 Rockside Rd Ste 120 Cleveland (44125) ***(G-5381)***
Hbd/Thermoid Inc...937 593-5010
1301 W Sandusky Ave Bellefontaine (43311) ***(G-1517)***
Hbd/Thermoid Inc (HQ)...614 526-7000
5200 Upper Metro Pl Dublin (43017) ***(G-8922)***
Hbe Machine Inc...419 668-9426
1100 State Route 61 N Monroeville (44847) ***(G-14288)***
HBK Stoneworks...740 817-2244
9292 Jhnstown Alxndria Rd Johnstown (43031) ***(G-11268)***
Hc Apparel, Columbus *Also called Columbus Humungous Apparel LLC* ***(G-6791)***
HC Starck Inc...216 692-3990
21801 Tungsten Rd Cleveland (44117) ***(G-5382)***
Hc Transport, Cincinnati *Also called Home City Ice Company* ***(G-3822)***
HCC Holdings Inc...800 203-1155
4700 W 160th St Cleveland (44135) ***(G-5383)***
HCC Industries...513 334-5585
9705 Reading Rd Cincinnati (45215) ***(G-3804)***
HCC/Sealtron (HQ)...513 733-8400
9705 Reading Rd Cincinnati (45215) ***(G-3805)***
Hdi Landing Gear Usa Inc (HQ)...937 325-1586
663 Montgomery Ave Springfield (45506) ***(G-17413)***
Hdi Landing Gear Usa Inc...440 783-5255
15900 Foltz Pkwy Strongsville (44149) ***(G-17748)***
Hdt Engineered Technologies, Solon *Also called Hunter Defense Tech Inc* ***(G-17164)***
Hdt Expeditionary Systems Inc...216 438-6111
30500 Aurora Rd Ste 100 Solon (44139) ***(G-17160)***
Hdt Expeditionary Systems Inc...440 466-6640
5455 Route 307 W Geneva (44041) ***(G-10222)***
Hdt Expeditionary Systems Inc (HQ)...216 438-6111
30500 Aurora Rd Ste 100 Solon (44139) ***(G-17161)***
Headlee Enterprises Ltd...614 785-0011
9015 Antares Ave Columbus (43240) ***(G-6496)***
Headset Wholesalers Ltd...419 798-5200
2411 S Commodore Ct Lakeside Marblehead (43440) ***(G-11503)***
Headwaters Incorporated...989 671-1500
745 Us Route 52 Manchester (45144) ***(G-12394)***
Health Bridge Imaging LLC...740 423-3300
809 Farson St Unit 107 Belpre (45714) ***(G-1576)***
Health Care Products Inc...419 678-9620
410 Nisco St Coldwater (45828) ***(G-6411)***
Health Care Solutions Inc...419 636-4189
5673 State Route 15 Bryan (43506) ***(G-2285)***
Health Mor At Home Cbp, Brooklyn *Also called Hmi Industries Inc* ***(G-2113)***
Health Nuts Media LLC...818 802-5222
4225 W 229th St Cleveland (44126) ***(G-5384)***
Healthcare Benefits Inc...419 433-4499
1212 Cleveland Rd W Huron (44839) ***(G-11095)***
Healthedge Software Inc...614 431-3711
50 S Liberty St Ste 200 Powell (43065) ***(G-16323)***
Healthpro Brands Inc...513 492-7512
12044 Millstone Ct Loveland (45140) ***(G-12196)***
Healthtech Products...419 271-1761
1 Invacare Way Elyria (44035) ***(G-9265)***
Healthwares Manufacturing...513 353-3691
5838b Hamilton Cleves Rd Cleves (45002) ***(G-6364)***
Healthy Living...937 962-4705
4248 New Market Banta Rd Lewisburg (45338) ***(G-11792)***
Hearing Aid Center of NW Ohio...419 636-8959
1318 E High St Ste B Bryan (43506) ***(G-2286)***
Hearing Aid Ctr of NW Ohio The, Bryan *Also called Hearing Aid Center of NW Ohio* ***(G-2286)***
Hearn Plating Co Ltd...419 473-9773
3184 Bellevue Rd Toledo (43606) ***(G-18325)***
Heart Warming Candles...937 456-2720
6806 Cumbersville St Eaton (45320) ***(G-9151)***
Heartbeat Company LLC...614 423-5646
895 S State St Westerville (43081) ***(G-20057)***
Hearth Products Controls Co...937 436-9800
3050 Plainfield Rd Dayton (45432) ***(G-7982)***
Hearthside Food Solutions LLC...419 293-2911
312 Rader Rd Mc Comb (45858) ***(G-13189)***
Heartland Bread & Roll, Worthington *Also called Hannibal Co Inc* ***(G-20690)***
Heartland Communications, Utica *Also called Utica Herald* ***(G-19028)***
Heartland Communications Div, Pataskala *Also called Pataskala Post* ***(G-15837)***
Heartland Design Concepts...419 774-0199
29 Illinois Ave S Mansfield (44905) ***(G-12456)***
Heartland Education Community...330 684-3034
200 N Main St Orrville (44667) ***(G-15593)***
Heartland Engineered Pdts LLC...513 367-0080
355 Industrial Dr Harrison (45030) ***(G-10645)***
Heartland Group Holdings LLC (HQ)...614 441-4001
4001 E 5th Ave Columbus (43219) ***(G-6985)***
Heartland Home Cabinetry Ltd...740 936-5100
35 S Galena Rd Unit C Sunbury (43074) ***(G-17888)***
Heartland Publications LLC (HQ)...860 664-1075
4500 Lyons Rd Miamisburg (45342) ***(G-13675)***
Heartland Publications LLC...740 446-2342
825 3rd Ave Gallipolis (45631) ***(G-10167)***
Heartland Stairway Ltd...330 279-2554
7080 Township Road 601 Millersburg (44654) ***(G-14087)***
Heartland Stairways Inc...330 279-2554
7964 Township Road 565 Holmesville (44633) ***(G-10976)***
Heartland Stairways Inc (PA)...330 279-2554
8230 County Road 245 Holmesville (44633) ***(G-10977)***
Heartland Stairways Inc...330 279-2554
Township Road 245 Holmesville (44633) ***(G-10978)***
Heartland Steel, Inc., Washington Court Hou *Also called South Central Industrial LLC* ***(G-19477)***
Heartland Thermography, West Chester *Also called Lasting First Impressions Inc* ***(G-19872)***
Heat & Sensor, Lebanon *Also called Heat and Sensor Tech LLC* ***(G-11661)***
Heat and Sensor Tech LLC...513 228-0481
627 Norgal Dr Lebanon (45036) ***(G-11661)***
Heat Exchange Applied Tech...330 682-4328
150b Allen Ave Orrville (44667) ***(G-15594)***
Heat Exchange Institute Inc...216 241-7333
1300 Sumner Ave Cleveland (44115) ***(G-5385)***
Heat Seal LLC...216 341-2022
4922 E 49th St Cleveland (44125) ***(G-5386)***
Heat Treating Inc (PA)...937 325-3121
1762 W Pleasant St Springfield (45506) ***(G-17414)***
Heat Treating Inc...937 325-3121
1807 W Pleasant St Springfield (45506) ***(G-17415)***
Heat Treating Inc...614 759-9963
675 Cross Pointe Rd Gahanna (43230) ***(G-10082)***
Heat Treating Technologies...419 224-8324
1799 E 4th St Lima (45804) ***(G-11873)***
Heatermeals, Cincinnati *Also called Luxfer Magtech Inc* ***(G-3958)***
Heather B Moore Inc...216 932-5430
4502 Prospect Ave Cleveland (44103) ***(G-5387)***
Heatherdowns License Bureau...419 381-1109
4460 Heatherdowns Blvd Toledo (43614) ***(G-18326)***
Heating & Cooling Products, Mount Vernon *Also called Famous Industries Inc* ***(G-14481)***
Heatstar, Cleveland *Also called Mr Heater Inc* ***(G-5711)***
Hebco Products Inc...419 562-7987
1232 Whetstone St Bucyrus (44820) ***(G-2333)***

ALPHABETIC SECTION — Herff Jones LLC

Hebraic Way Press Company 330 614-4872
2615 S Seneca Ave Alliance (44601) *(G-472)*

Hec Investments Inc 937 278-9123
4800 Wadsworth Rd Dayton (45414) *(G-8247)*

Heck's Diamond Printing, Toledo Also called Hecks Direct Mail & Prtg Svc *(G-18328)*

Heckmann Wtr Resources Cvr Inc 740 844-0045
9350 East Pike Norwich (43767) *(G-15420)*

Hecks Direct Mail & Prtg Svc (PA) 419 697-3505
417 Main St Toledo (43605) *(G-18327)*

Hecks Direct Mail & Prtg Svc 419 661-6028
202 W Florence Ave Toledo (43605) *(G-18328)*

Hedalloy Die Corp 216 341-3768
3266 E 49th St Cleveland (44127) *(G-5388)*

Hedges Printing Co 740 422-8500
6490 Revenge Rd Sw Lancaster (43130) *(G-11579)*

Hedges Selective Tool & Prod 419 478-8670
702 W Laskey Rd Toledo (43612) *(G-18329)*

Hedstrom Fitness, Ashland Also called Ball Bounce and Sport Inc *(G-682)*

HEF USA Corporation (PA) 937 323-2556
2015 Progress Rd Springfield (45505) *(G-17416)*

Heffelfingers Meats Inc 419 368-7131
469 County Road 30a Jeromesville (44840) *(G-11250)*

Hefty Hoist Inc 740 467-2515
2397a Refugee St Millersport (43046) *(G-14160)*

Heico Aerospace Parts Corp (HQ) 954 987-6101
375 Alpha Park Highland Heights (44143) *(G-10793)*

Heidtman Steel Products, Toledo Also called Centaur Inc *(G-18225)*

Heidtman Steel Products Inc (HQ) 419 691-4646
2401 Front St Toledo (43605) *(G-18330)*

Heights Dumpster Services LLC 937 321-0096
5742 Mallard Dr Huber Heights (45424) *(G-11019)*

Heil Engneered Process Eqp Inc 440 327-6051
37000 Center Ridge Rd North Ridgeville (44039) *(G-15228)*

Heim Sheet Metal Inc 330 424-7820
525 E Chestnut St Lisbon (44432) *(G-11968)*

Heimann Manufacturing Co 937 652-1865
1140 N Main St Urbana (43078) *(G-18993)*

Heinen's 8, Aurora Also called Heinens Inc *(G-882)*

Heinens Inc 330 562-5297
115 N Chillicothe Rd Aurora (44202) *(G-882)*

Heinis Cheese Chalet, Millersburg Also called Bunker Hill Cheese Co Inc *(G-14073)*

Heintz Conveying Belt Service, Medina Also called Conviber Inc *(G-13241)*

Heintz Manufacturers Inc 724 274-6300
1066 Industrial Pkwy Medina (44256) *(G-13271)*

Heinz Foreign Investment Co (HQ) 330 837-8331
1301 Oberlin Ave Sw Massillon (44647) *(G-12994)*

Heinz Frozen Foods, Massillon Also called HJ Heinz Company LP *(G-12997)*

Heisler Tool Company 440 951-2424
38228 Western Pkwy Willoughby (44094) *(G-20336)*

Heitkamp & Kremer Printing 419 925-4121
6184 State Route 274 Celina (45822) *(G-2967)*

Helena Agri-Enterprises LLC 614 275-4200
800 Distribution Dr Columbus (43228) *(G-6986)*

Helena Agri-Enterprises LLC 419 596-3806
200 N Main St Continental (45831) *(G-7666)*

Helex Division, Cincinnati Also called A C Knox Inc *(G-3279)*

Helical Line Products Co 440 933-9263
659 Miller Rd Avon Lake (44012) *(G-989)*

Helix Linear Technologies Inc 216 485-2263
23200 Commerce Park Beachwood (44122) *(G-1240)*

Hellan Strainer Company 216 206-4200
3249 E 80th St Cleveland (44104) *(G-5389)*

Heller Acquisitions Inc 937 833-2676
227 Market St Brookville (45309) *(G-2171)*

Heller Machine Products Inc 216 281-2951
1971 W 90th St Cleveland (44102) *(G-5390)*

Heller Sports Center, Montpelier Also called W C Heller & Co Inc *(G-14321)*

Helm Instrument Company Inc 419 893-4356
361 W Dussel Dr Maumee (43537) *(G-13116)*

Helmart Company Inc 513 941-3095
4960 Hillside Ave Cincinnati (45233) *(G-3806)*

Hely & Weber Orthopedic, Avon Also called Weber Orthopedic Inc *(G-974)*

Hematite Inc 937 540-9889
300 Lau Pkwy Englewood (45315) *(G-9362)*

Hemco Inc 419 499-4602
1413 State Route 113 E Milan (44846) *(G-13984)*

Hemmelgarn & Sons Inc 419 678-2351
3763 Philothea Rd Coldwater (45828) *(G-6412)*

Hen House Inc 419 663-3377
100 Northwest St Norwalk (44857) *(G-15398)*

Hen of Woods LLC 513 833-7357
1432 Main St Cincinnati (45202) *(G-3807)*

Henderson Builders Inc 419 665-2684
1610 County Road 90 Gibsonburg (43431) *(G-10248)*

Henderson Fabricating Co Inc 216 432-0404
6217 Central Ave Cleveland (44104) *(G-5391)*

Henderson Partners LLC 614 883-1310
4424 N High St Columbus (43214) *(G-6987)*

Henderson Trucking, Delaware Also called Rjw Trucking Company Ltd *(G-8720)*

Hendricks Vacuum Forming Inc (PA) 330 837-2040
3500 17th St Sw Massillon (44647) *(G-12995)*

Hendricks Vacuum Forming Inc 330 833-8913
3536 17th St Sw Massillon (44647) *(G-12996)*

Hendrickson Auxiliary Axles, Hebron Also called Hendrickson International Corp *(G-10747)*

Hendrickson International Corp 740 929-5600
277 N High St Hebron (43025) *(G-10747)*

Hendrickson Trailer, Canton Also called Hendrickson Usa LLC *(G-2696)*

Hendrickson Usa LLC 330 456-7288
2070 Industrial Pl Se Canton (44707) *(G-2696)*

Henkel Adhesive Corporation 513 677-5800
1356 Tecumseh Dr Maineville (45039) *(G-12370)*

Henkel Corporation 740 363-1351
421 London Rd Delaware (43015) *(G-8693)*

Henkel Corporation 216 475-3600
18731 Cranwood Pkwy Cleveland (44128) *(G-5392)*

Henkel Surface Technologies, Delaware Also called Henkel Corporation *(G-8693)*

Henkel US Operations Corp 440 255-8900
7405 Production Dr Mentor (44060) *(G-13464)*

Henkel US Operations Corp 440 250-7700
26235 1st St Westlake (44145) *(G-20122)*

Henkel US Operations Corp 513 830-0260
9435 Waterstone Blvd Cincinnati (45249) *(G-3808)*

Henly Corporation 419 476-0851
520 W Laskey Rd Toledo (43612) *(G-18331)*

Hennacy Machine Company Inc 330 785-2940
1209 Triplett Blvd Akron (44306) *(G-203)*

Hennig Inc 513 247-0838
11431 Williamson Rd Ste A Blue Ash (45241) *(G-1788)*

Hennings Quality Service Inc 216 941-9120
3115 Berea Rd Cleveland (44111) *(G-5393)*

Henny Penny Corporation (PA) 937 456-8400
1219 Us Route 35 Eaton (45320) *(G-9152)*

Henry & Wright Corporation 216 851-3750
739 E 140th St Ste 1 Cleveland (44110) *(G-5394)*

Henry Bussman 614 224-0417
70 S 4th St Columbus (43215) *(G-6988)*

Henry Tools Inc 216 291-1011
498 S Belvoir Blvd Cleveland (44121) *(G-5395)*

Henry-Griffitts Limited (HQ) 419 482-9095
352 Tomahawk Dr Maumee (43537) *(G-13117)*

Hensel Ready Mix 419 253-9200
4050 Bennington Way Marengo (43334) *(G-12592)*

Hensel Ready Mix Inc (PA) 419 675-1808
9925 County Road 265 Kenton (43326) *(G-11409)*

Hensel Ready Mix Inc 614 755-6365
477 Claycraft Rd Columbus (43230) *(G-6989)*

Henty USA 513 984-5590
7260 Edington Dr Cincinnati (45249) *(G-3809)*

Hephaestus Technologies LLC 216 252-0430
3811 W 150th St Cleveland (44111) *(G-5396)*

Hept Machine Inc 937 890-5633
19 E Alkaline Springs Rd Vandalia (45377) *(G-19126)*

Heraeus Electro-Nite Co LLC 330 725-1419
6469 Fenn Rd Medina (44256) *(G-13272)*

Heraeus Precious Metals North 937 264-1000
970 Industrial Park Dr Vandalia (45377) *(G-19127)*

Herald Inc 419 492-2133
625 S Kibler St New Washington (44854) *(G-14829)*

Herald Looms 330 948-1080
118 Lee St Lodi (44254) *(G-12012)*

Herald Reflector Inc (PA) 419 668-3771
61 E Monroe St Norwalk (44857) *(G-15399)*

Herald Star Newspaper, Steubenville Also called Weirton Daily Times *(G-17557)*

Herbert E Orr Company 419 399-4866
335 W Wall St Paulding (45879) *(G-15860)*

Herbert Usa Inc 330 929-4297
1480 Industrial Pkwy Akron (44310) *(G-204)*

Herbert Wood Products Inc 440 834-1410
15089 White Rd Middlefield (44062) *(G-13805)*

Herco Inc 740 498-5181
295 Enterprise Dr Newcomerstown (43832) *(G-14975)*

Hercules, Wickliffe Also called Universal Metal Products Inc *(G-20235)*

Hercules Acquisition Corp 419 287-3223
850 W Front St Pemberville (43450) *(G-15884)*

Hercules Engine Components, Massillon Also called Brinkley Technology Group LLC *(G-12963)*

Hercules Engine Components, Massillon Also called DW Hercules LLC *(G-12977)*

Hercules Industries Inc 740 494-2620
7194 Prospect Delaware Rd Prospect (43342) *(G-16351)*

Hercules Polishing & Plating 330 455-8871
4883 Southway St Sw Canton (44706) *(G-2697)*

Hercules Stamping Co, Pemberville Also called Hercules Acquisition Corp *(G-15884)*

Herd Manufacturing Inc 216 651-4221
9227 Clinton Rd Cleveland (44144) *(G-5397)*

Heres Your Sign 740 574-1248
304 Lafayette Ln Franklin Furnace (45629) *(G-9935)*

Herff Jones LLC 740 357-2160
37 Lucasville Mdfrd Rd Lucasville (45648) *(G-12264)*

Herff Jones LLC 330 678-8138
4468 Berry Hl Stow (44224) *(G-17594)*

Hergatt Machine Inc 419 589-2931
2530 Pavonia Rd Mansfield (44903) *(G-12457)*

Heritage Bag Company 513 874-3311
4255 Thunderbird Ln West Chester (45014) *(G-19720)*

Heritage Inc 614 860-1185
2087 State Route 256 T Reynoldsburg (43068) *(G-16443)*

Heritage Industrial Finshg Inc 330 798-9840
1874 Englewood Ave Akron (44312) *(G-205)*

Heritage Lounge, Reynoldsburg *Also called Heritage Inc (G-16443)*

Heritage Manufacturing Inc 217 854-2513
1600 E Waterloo Rd Akron (44306) *(G-206)*

Heritage Marble of Ohio Inc 614 436-1464
7086 Huntley Rd Columbus (43229) *(G-6990)*

Heritage Marbles, Columbus *Also called Heritage Marble of Ohio Inc (G-6990)*

Heritage Plas An Atkore Intl, Carrollton *Also called Atkore Plastic Pipe Corp (G-2916)*

Heritage Press Inc 419 289-9209
651 Sandusky St Ashland (44805) *(G-709)*

Heritage Sleep Products LLC 440 437-4425
243 Staley Rd Orwell (44076) *(G-15631)*

Heritage Tool 513 753-7300
6225 N Shadow Hill Way Loveland (45140) *(G-12197)*

Heritage Tool & Manufacturing, Amelia *Also called Mark J Myers (G-543)*

Heritage Truck Equipment Inc 330 699-4491
661 Powell Ave Hartville (44632) *(G-10695)*

Herman Machine Inc 330 633-3261
252 Northeast Ave Tallmadge (44278) *(G-17984)*

Herman Manufacturing LLC 216 251-6400
13825 Triskett Rd Cleveland (44111) *(G-5398)*

Hermann Pickle Company (PA) 330 527-2696
11964 State Route 88 Garrettsville (44231) *(G-10192)*

Hermetic Seal Technology Inc 513 851-4899
2150 Schappelle Ln Cincinnati (45240) *(G-3810)*

Hero Pay LLC 419 771-0515
341 S 3rd St Ste 107 Columbus (43215) *(G-6991)*

Herold Salads Inc 216 991-7500
17512 Miles Ave Cleveland (44128) *(G-5399)*

Heroux Devtek Landing Gear Div, Strongsville *Also called Hdi Landing Gear Usa Inc (G-17748)*

Heroux-Devtek Inc 937 325-1586
663 Montgomery Ave Springfield (45506) *(G-17417)*

Heroux-Devtek Springfield, Springfield *Also called Heroux-Devtek Inc (G-17417)*

Herr Foods Incorporated 740 773-8282
476 E 7th St Chillicothe (45601) *(G-3192)*

Hershberger Lawn Structures 330 674-3900
8990 State Route 39 Millersburg (44654) *(G-14088)*

Hershberger Manufacturing 440 272-5555
7584 Rockwood Rd Windsor (44099) *(G-20526)*

Hershbergers Dutch Market LLP 740 489-5322
228 Old National Rd Old Washington (43768) *(G-15526)*

Hershey Machine 330 674-2718
5502 State Route 557 Millersburg (44654) *(G-14089)*

Hershy Way Ltd 330 893-2809
5918 County Road 201 Millersburg (44654) *(G-14090)*

Heskamp Printing Co Inc 513 871-6770
5514 Fair Ln Cincinnati (45227) *(G-3811)*

Hesler Machine Tool 937 299-3833
607 Brookfield Rd Dayton (45429) *(G-8248)*

Hess & Gault Lumber Co 419 281-3105
707 County Road 1302 Ashland (44805) *(G-710)*

Hess Advanced Solutions Llc 937 829-4794
7415 Chambersburg Rd Dayton (45424) *(G-8249)*

Hess Advanced Technology Inc 937 268-4377
7415 Chambersburg Rd Huber Heights (45424) *(G-11020)*

Hess Industries Ltd 419 525-4000
108 Sawyer Pkwy Mansfield (44903) *(G-12458)*

Hess Print Solutions, Kent *Also called Press of Ohio Inc (G-11367)*

Hess Print Solutions, Kent *Also called D & J Printing Inc (G-11309)*

Hess Technologies Inc 513 228-0909
200 Harmon Ave Lebanon (45036) *(G-11662)*

Heule Tool Corporation 513 860-9900
131 Commerce Dr Loveland (45140) *(G-12198)*

Hexa Americas Inc 937 497-7900
1150 S Vandemark Rd Sidney (45365) *(G-17043)*

Hexacrafter Ltd 330 929-0989
2750 Northampton Rd Cuyahoga Falls (44223) *(G-7879)*

Hexagon Industries Inc 216 249-0200
1135 Ivanhoe Rd Cleveland (44110) *(G-5400)*

Hexion Inc (HQ) 614 225-4000
180 E Broad St Fl 26 Columbus (43215) *(G-6992)*

Hexion LLC (HQ) 614 225-4000
180 E Broad St Fl 26 Columbus (43215) *(G-6993)*

Hexion US Finance Corp 614 225-4000
180 E Broad St Columbus (43215) *(G-6994)*

Hexpol Compounding LLC 440 834-4644
14330 Kinsman Rd Burton (44021) *(G-2360)*

Hexpol Compounding LLC 440 682-4038
3939a Mogadore Indus Pkwy Mogadore (44260) *(G-14239)*

Hexpol Compounding LLC (HQ) 440 834-4644
14330 Kinsman Rd Burton (44021) *(G-2361)*

Hexpol Holding Inc (HQ) 440 834-4644
14330 Kinsman Rd Burton (44021) *(G-2362)*

Hexpol Polymers, Burton *Also called Hexpol Compounding LLC (G-2361)*

Hexpol Silicone, Mogadore *Also called Hexpol Compounding LLC (G-14239)*

Hf Group 440 729-9411
8844 Mayfield Rd Chesterland (44026) *(G-3158)*

Hf Group LLC (PA) 440 729-2445
8844 Mayfield Rd Chesterland (44026) *(G-3159)*

Hf Group LLC 440 729-9411
8844 Mayfield Rd Chesterland (44026) *(G-3160)*

Hf Group LLC 440 729-9411
8844 Mayfield Rd Chesterland (44026) *(G-3161)*

Hfi LLC (PA) 614 491-0700
59 Gender Rd Columbus (43215) *(G-6995)*

Hggc Citadel Plas Holdings Inc (HQ) 330 666-3751
3637 Ridgewood Rd Fairlawn (44333) *(G-9607)*

Hhi, Canton *Also called Hunter Hydraulics Inc (G-2701)*

Hhi Company Inc (PA) 330 455-3983
2512 Columbus Rd Ne Canton (44705) *(G-2698)*

Hi Carb Corp 216 486-5000
23610 Saint Clair Ave Cleveland (44117) *(G-5401)*

Hi Lite Plastic Products 614 235-9050
3760 E 5th Ave Columbus (43219) *(G-6996)*

Hi Tech Aero Spares 513 942-4150
9436 Meridian Way West Chester (45069) *(G-19721)*

Hi Tech Graphics, Cincinnati *Also called Nickum Enterprises Inc (G-4077)*

Hi Tech Printing, Fairfield *Also called ID Images LLC (G-9509)*

Hi Tech Tool Corporation 513 346-4061
415 Breaden Dr Ste 1 Monroe (45050) *(G-14266)*

Hi Tecmetal Group Inc (PA) 216 881-8100
1101 E 55th St Cleveland (44103) *(G-5402)*

Hi Tecmetal Group Inc 440 373-5101
28910 Lakeland Blvd Wickliffe (44092) *(G-20213)*

Hi Tecmetal Group Inc 440 946-2280
34800 Lakeland Blvd Willoughby (44095) *(G-20337)*

Hi Tecmetal Group Inc 216 941-0440
10601 Briggs Rd Cleveland (44111) *(G-5403)*

Hi Tecmetal Group Inc 216 881-8100
1432 E 47th St Cleveland (44103) *(G-5404)*

Hi Tek Mold 440 942-4090
7777 Saint Clair Ave Mentor (44060) *(G-13465)*

Hi-Point Firearms, Mansfield *Also called Highpoint Firearms (G-12459)*

Hi-Stat A Stoneridge Co, Lexington *Also called Stoneridge Inc (G-11807)*

Hi-Tech Extrusions Ltd 440 286-4000
12621 Chardon Windsor Rd Chardon (44024) *(G-3116)*

Hi-Tech Solutions LLC 216 331-3050
510 Karl Dr Cleveland (44143) *(G-5405)*

Hi-Tech Wire Inc 419 678-8376
631 E Washington St Saint Henry (45883) *(G-16662)*

Hi-Tek Manufacturing Inc 513 459-1094
6050 Hi Tek Ct Mason (45040) *(G-12886)*

Hi-Vac Corporation 740 374-2306
27895 State Route 7 Marietta (45750) *(G-12632)*

Hiab USA Inc (HQ) 419 482-6000
12233 Williams Rd Perrysburg (43551) *(G-15961)*

Hibbing Taconite A Joint Ventr (HQ) 216 694-5700
200 Public Sq Ste 3300 Cleveland (44114) *(G-5406)*

Hickok Ae LLC 330 794-9770
735 Glaser Pkwy Akron (44306) *(G-207)*

Hickok Incorporated (PA) 216 541-8060
10514 Dupont Ave Cleveland (44108) *(G-5407)*

Hickok Waekon LLC 216 541-8060
10514 Dupont Ave Cleveland (44108) *(G-5408)*

Hickory Harvest Foods, Coventry Township *Also called Ohio Hickory Harvest Brand Pro (G-7775)*

Hickory Lane Welding, Fredericksburg *Also called Chore Anden (G-9945)*

Hidaka Usa Inc 614 889-8611
5761 Shier Rings Rd Dublin (43016) *(G-8923)*

Higgins Building Mtls No 2 LLC 740 395-5410
2000 Acy Ave Jackson (45640) *(G-11186)*

High Card Industries LLC 330 547-3381
15439 W Akron Canfield Rd Berlin Center (44401) *(G-1646)*

High Concrete Group LLC 937 748-2412
95 Mound Park Dr Springboro (45066) *(G-17330)*

High Definition Tooling, Newcomerstown *Also called H3d Tool Corporation (G-14974)*

High Kinky Plastic, Maple Heights *Also called Jr Larry Knight (G-12574)*

High Low Winery 844 466-4456
588 Medina Rd Medina (44256) *(G-13273)*

High Performance Servo LLC 440 541-3529
1477 E Crossings Pl Westlake (44145) *(G-20123)*

High Production Technology LLC (HQ) 419 591-7000
476 E Riverview Ave Napoleon (43545) *(G-14541)*

High Production Technology LLC 419 599-1511
13068 County Road R Napoleon (43545) *(G-14542)*

High Quality Plastics 419 422-8290
2000 Fostoria Ave Findlay (45840) *(G-9703)*

ALPHABETIC SECTION HM Defense

High Quality Tools Inc (PA)..........440 975-9684
34940 Lakeland Blvd Eastlake (44095) ***(G-9113)***
High Tech Elastomers Inc (PA)..........937 236-6575
885 Scholz Dr Vandalia (45377) ***(G-19128)***
High Tech Metal Products LLC..........419 227-9414
2300 Central Point Pkwy Lima (45804) ***(G-11874)***
High Tech Mold & Machine Co..........330 896-4466
3771 Tabs Dr Uniontown (44685) ***(G-18921)***
High Tech Molding & Design Inc..........330 726-1676
27 W Indianola Ave Youngstown (44507) ***(G-20930)***
High Tech Prfmce Trlrs Inc..........440 357-8964
1 High Tech Ave Painesville (44077) ***(G-15746)***
High Temperature Systems Inc..........440 543-8271
16755 Park Circle Dr Chagrin Falls (44023) ***(G-3049)***
High-TEC Industrial Services..........937 667-1772
15 Industry Park Ct Tipp City (45371) ***(G-18115)***
Highcom Global Security Inc (HQ)..........727 592-9400
2901 E 4th Ave Unit J Columbus (43219) ***(G-6997)***
Highland Computer Forms Inc (PA)..........937 393-4215
1025 W Main St Hillsboro (45133) ***(G-10879)***
Highland County Press, Hillsboro *Also called Cameco Communications* ***(G-10877)***
Highland Precision Plating..........937 393-9501
6940 State Route 124 Hillsboro (45133) ***(G-10880)***
Highland Products Corp..........440 352-4777
9331 Mercantile Dr Mentor (44060) ***(G-13466)***
Highland Technologies LLC..........513 739-3510
630 Harwood Rd Mount Orab (45154) ***(G-14443)***
Highlights For Children Inc..........614 486-0631
4555 Lyman Dr Hilliard (43026) ***(G-10828)***
Highlights Press Inc..........614 487-2767
1800 Watermark Dr Columbus (43215) ***(G-6998)***
Highline Raceway LLC..........419 883-2042
1766 Cassell Rd Butler (44822) ***(G-2375)***
Highpoint Firearms..........419 747-9444
1015 Springmill St Mansfield (44906) ***(G-12459)***
Highs Welding Inc..........937 464-3029
3065 County Road 150 Belle Center (43310) ***(G-1499)***
Highschoolball Inc..........330 321-8536
82 Wakefield Run Blvd Hinckley (44233) ***(G-10901)***
Hightech Signs, Fairfield *Also called Significant Impressions Inc* ***(G-9564)***
Highway Safety Corp..........740 387-6991
473 W Fairground St Marion (43302) ***(G-12711)***
Hikma Labs Inc..........614 276-4000
1809 Wilson Rd Columbus (43228) ***(G-6999)***
Hikma Pharmaceuticals USA Inc..........732 542-1191
2130 Rohr Rd Lockbourne (43137) ***(G-11994)***
Hikma Pharmaceuticals USA Inc..........732 542-1191
300 Northfield Rd Bedford (44146) ***(G-1412)***
Hikma Pharmaceuticals USA Inc..........614 276-4000
1809 Wilson Rd Columbus (43228) ***(G-7000)***
Hiland Group Incorporated (PA)..........330 499-8404
7600 Supreme St Nw Canton (44720) ***(G-2699)***
Hildreth Mfg LLC..........740 375-5832
1657 Cascade Dr Marion (43302) ***(G-12712)***
Hill James R & Hill Earley W..........740 591-4203
41085 Townsend Rd Albany (45710) ***(G-442)***
Hill & Associates Inc..........740 685-5168
132 S 6th St Byesville (43723) ***(G-2386)***
Hill & Griffith Company (PA)..........513 921-1075
1085 Summer St Cincinnati (45204) ***(G-3812)***
Hill Bryce Concrete, Springfield *Also called Dearth Resources Inc* ***(G-17384)***
Hill Finishing..........740 623-0650
32795 Township Road 219 Millersburg (44654) ***(G-14091)***
Hill Manufacturing Inc..........419 335-5006
318 W Chestnut St Wauseon (43567) ***(G-19520)***
Hillcrest..........740 824-4849
31580 Township Rd Brinkhaven (43006) ***(G-2081)***
Hillcrest Lumber Ltd..........330 359-5721
8669 Zuercher Rd Apple Creek (44606) ***(G-607)***
Hilleary-Whitaker Inc..........614 766-4694
2646 Billingsley Rd Columbus (43235) ***(G-7001)***
Hilles Burial Vaults Inc..........330 823-2251
2145 S Union Ave Alliance (44601) ***(G-473)***
Hilliard Cat Shack LLC..........614 527-9711
5484 Pearson Ct Hilliard (43026) ***(G-10829)***
Hillman Group Inc..........440 248-7000
31100 Solon Rd Cleveland (44139) ***(G-5409)***
Hillman Group Inc..........800 800-4900
12400 Plaza Dr Parma (44130) ***(G-15822)***
Hillman Precision Inc..........419 289-1557
462 E 9th St Ste 1 Ashland (44805) ***(G-711)***
Hillshire Brands Company..........330 758-8885
95 Karago Ave Youngstown (44512) ***(G-20931)***
Hillside Pallet..........440 272-5425
8552 Cox Rd Windsor (44099) ***(G-20527)***
Hillside Winery..........419 456-3108
221 Main St Gilboa (45875) ***(G-10250)***
Hillside Wood Ltd..........330 359-5991
8413 Township Road 652 Millersburg (44654) ***(G-14092)***
Hilltop Basic Resources Inc (PA)..........513 651-5000
1 W 4th St Ste 1100 Cincinnati (45202) ***(G-3813)***
Hilltop Basic Resources Inc..........937 882-6357
1665 Enon Rd Springfield (45502) ***(G-17418)***
Hilltop Basic Resources Inc..........937 859-3616
4710 Soldiers Home W Miamisburg (45342) ***(G-13676)***
Hilltop Basic Resources Inc..........937 795-2020
8030 Rte 52 Us Aberdeen (45101) ***(G-1)***
Hilltop Basic Resources Inc..........513 621-1500
511 W Water St Cincinnati (45202) ***(G-3814)***
Hilltop Big Bend Quarry LLC..........513 651-5000
1 W 4th St Ste 1100 Cincinnati (45202) ***(G-3815)***
Hilltop Concrete, Cincinnati *Also called Hilltop Basic Resources Inc* ***(G-3813)***
Hilltop Concrete, Cincinnati *Also called Hilltop Basic Resources Inc* ***(G-3814)***
Hilltop Energy Inc..........330 859-2108
6978 Lindentree Rd Ne Mineral City (44656) ***(G-14164)***
Hilltop Printing..........419 782-9898
1815 Baltimore St Defiance (43512) ***(G-8626)***
Hilltop Stone Llc..........513 651-5000
1 W 4th St Ste 1100 Cincinnati (45202) ***(G-3816)***
Hilo Tech Inc..........440 979-1155
31532 Lorain Rd North Olmsted (44070) ***(G-15192)***
Hinchcliff Lumber Company..........440 238-5200
13550 Falling Water Rd # 105 Strongsville (44136) ***(G-17749)***
Hinchcliff Products Co, Strongsville *Also called Hinchcliff Lumber Company* ***(G-17749)***
Hinckley Wood Products..........330 220-9999
1545 W 130th St Hinckley (44233) ***(G-10902)***
Hines Builders Inc..........937 335-4586
1587 Lytle Rd Troy (45373) ***(G-18665)***
Hines Specialty Vehicle Group, New Philadelphia *Also called Kimble Mixer Company* ***(G-14779)***
Hinkle Fine Foods Inc..........937 836-3665
4800 Wadsworth Rd Dayton (45414) ***(G-8250)***
Hinkle Manufacturing, Perrysburg *Also called Orbis Corporation* ***(G-15994)***
Hinkle Manufacturing LLC (PA)..........313 584-0400
348 5th St Perrysburg (43551) ***(G-15962)***
Hipsy LLC..........513 403-5333
4951 Dixie Hwy Fairfield (45014) ***(G-9504)***
Hirons Memorial Works Inc..........937 444-2917
14950 Us Highway 68 Mount Orab (45154) ***(G-14444)***
Hirschvogel Incorporated..........614 340-5657
2230 S 3rd St Columbus (43207) ***(G-7002)***
Hirt Publishing Co Inc..........419 946-3010
245 Neal Ave Ste A Mount Gilead (43338) ***(G-14426)***
Hirt Publishing Co Inc (PA)..........419 523-5709
224 E Main St Ottawa (45875) ***(G-15652)***
Hirt Publishing Co Inc..........419 523-5709
224 E Main St Ottawa (45875) ***(G-15653)***
Hirzel Canning Company..........419 287-3288
115 Columbus St Pemberville (43450) ***(G-15885)***
Hirzel Canning Company (PA)..........419 693-0531
411 Lemoyne Rd Northwood (43619) ***(G-15338)***
Hirzel Canning Company..........419 523-3225
325 E Williamstown Rd Ottawa (45875) ***(G-15654)***
Hisey Bells..........740 333-7669
581 Capps Rd Greenfield (45123) ***(G-10352)***
Hit & Miss Ent Antiq Engs Prts, Orwell *Also called Hit & Miss Enterprises* ***(G-15632)***
Hit & Miss Enterprises..........440 272-5335
4461 Montgomery Rd Orwell (44076) ***(G-15632)***
Hit Trophy Inc..........419 445-5356
4989 State Route 66 Archbold (43502) ***(G-653)***
Hitch-Hiker Mfg Inc..........330 542-3052
10065 Rapp Rd New Middletown (44442) ***(G-14750)***
Hite Parts Exchange Inc..........614 272-5115
2235 Mckinley Ave Columbus (43204) ***(G-7003)***
Hitech Shapes & Designs, Cincinnati *Also called Seilkop Industries Inc* ***(G-4317)***
Hitti Enterprises Inc..........440 243-4100
6427 Eastland Rd Cleveland (44142) ***(G-5410)***
HJ Heinz Company LP (HQ)..........330 837-8331
1301 Oberlin Ave Sw Massillon (44647) ***(G-12997)***
Hj Systems Inc..........614 351-9777
230 N Central Ave Columbus (43222) ***(G-7004)***
HK Engine Components LLC (HQ)..........330 830-3500
800 Nave Rd Se Massillon (44646) ***(G-12998)***
HK Logging & Lumber Ltd..........440 632-1997
16465 Farley Rd Middlefield (44062) ***(G-13806)***
HK Technologies..........330 337-9710
2828 Clinton Ave Cleveland (44113) ***(G-5411)***
Hkb Enterprises Inc..........330 733-3200
2215 E Waterloo Rd # 303 Akron (44312) ***(G-208)***
Hkm Drect Mkt Cmmnications Inc (PA)..........216 651-9500
5501 Cass Ave Cleveland (44102) ***(G-5412)***
Hkm Drect Mkt Cmmnications Inc..........440 934-3060
2931 Abbe Rd Sheffield Village (44054) ***(G-16967)***
Hl Oilfield Services LLC..........740 783-1156
19797 Harl Weiller Rd Caldwell (43724) ***(G-2406)***
HM Defense..........513 260-6200
222 Homan Way Mount Orab (45154) ***(G-14445)***

ALPHABETIC

HM Wire International Inc | ALPHABETIC SECTION

HM Wire International Inc 330 244-8501
2125 46th St Nw Canton (44709) *(G-2700)*
Hmb Information Sys Developers, Westerville *Also called Harris Mackessy & Brennan (G-19996)*
Hmi Industries Inc (PA) 440 846-7800
1 American Rd Ste 1250 Brooklyn (44144) *(G-2113)*
HMS Industries LLC 440 899-0001
27995 Ranney Pkwy Westlake (44145) *(G-20124)*
Hmt Inc (PA) 440 599-7005
360 Commerce St Conneaut (44030) *(G-7648)*
Hobart, Hillsboro *Also called ITW Food Equipment Group LLC (G-10882)*
Hobart, Troy *Also called ITW Food Equipment Group LLC (G-18679)*
Hobart Bros Stick Electrode 937 332-5375
101 Trade Sq E Troy (45373) *(G-18666)*
Hobart Brothers Company 937 773-5869
8585 Industry Park Dr Piqua (45356) *(G-16127)*
Hobart Brothers Company 937 332-5338
400 Trade Sq E Troy (45373) *(G-18667)*
Hobart Brothers Company 937 332-5023
1260 Bruckner Dr Troy (45373) *(G-18668)*
Hobart Brothers LLC (HQ) 937 332-5439
101 Trade Sq E Troy (45373) *(G-18669)*
Hobart Cabinet Company 937 335-4666
301 E Water St Troy (45373) *(G-18670)*
Hobart Corporation 937 332-3000
401 S Market St Troy (45373) *(G-18671)*
Hobart Corporation 937 332-2797
8515 Industry Park Dr Piqua (45356) *(G-16128)*
Hobart International Holdings 937 332-3000
701 S Ridge Ave Troy (45373) *(G-18672)*
Hobart Sales & Service, Akron *Also called Harry C Lobalzo & Sons Inc (G-199)*
Hobby Printing, Dayton *Also called Oscar Hicks (G-8409)*
Hochstetler Milling LLC 419 368-0004
552 State Route 95 Loudonville (44842) *(G-12143)*
Hochstetler Wood 330 893-2384
6791 County Road 77 Millersburg (44654) *(G-14093)*
Hochstetler Wood Ltd 330 893-1601
6791 County Road 77 Millersburg (44654) *(G-14094)*
Hocker Tool and Die Inc 937 274-3443
5161 Webster St Dayton (45414) *(G-8251)*
Hocking Hills Energy & Well SE 740 385-6690
32919 Logan Horns Mill Rd Logan (43138) *(G-12026)*
Hocking Hills Hardwoods, Laurelville *Also called T & D Thompson Inc (G-11627)*
Hocking Valley Concrete Inc (PA) 740 385-2165
35255 Hocking Dr Logan (43138) *(G-12027)*
Hocking Valley Concrete Inc 740 342-1948
1500 Commerce Dr New Lexington (43764) *(G-14716)*
Hocking Valley Concrete Inc 740 385-2165
35255 Hocking Dr Logan (43138) *(G-12028)*
Hoehnes Custom Woodworking 937 693-8008
9600 Amsterdam Rd Anna (45302) *(G-590)*
Hofacker Prcsion Machining LLC 937 832-7712
7560 Jacks Ln Clayton (45315) *(G-4574)*
Hoffee John 330 868-3553
207 N Market St Minerva (44657) *(G-14183)*
Hoffman Hinge and Hardware LLC 330 935-2240
11750 Marlboro Ave Ne Alliance (44601) *(G-474)*
Hoffman Machining & Repair LLC 419 547-9204
1744 W Mcpherson Hwy Clyde (43410) *(G-6389)*
Hoffman Meat Processing 419 864-3994
157 S 4th St Cardington (43315) *(G-2873)*
Hofmanns Lures Inc 937 684-0338
5350 State Route 47 Ansonia (45303) *(G-593)*
Hoge Brush, New Knoxville *Also called Hoge Lumber Company (G-14703)*
Hoge Lumber Company (PA) 419 753-2263
701 S Main St State New Knoxville (45871) *(G-14703)*
Hoge Lumber Company 419 753-2351
202 E South St New Knoxville (45871) *(G-14704)*
Hoist Equipment Co Inc (PA) 440 232-0300
26161 Cannon Rd Bedford Heights (44146) *(G-1472)*
Hoistech LLC 440 327-5379
5131 Mills Indus Pkwy North Ridgeville (44039) *(G-15229)*
Holdren Brothers Inc 937 465-7050
301 Runkle St West Liberty (43357) *(G-19936)*
Holdsworth Industrial Fabg 330 874-3945
10407 Welton Rd Ne Bolivar (44612) *(G-1916)*
Hole Hunter Golf Driving Range, Piqua *Also called Hole Hunter Golf Inc (G-16129)*
Hole Hunter Golf Inc 937 339-5833
438 S Downing St Piqua (45356) *(G-16129)*
Holes Custom Woodworking 419 586-8171
6875 Nancy Ave Celina (45822) *(G-2968)*
Holgate Metal Fab Inc 419 599-2000
555 Independence Dr Napoleon (43545) *(G-14543)*
Holiday Hmes Rvrview Crossings, Harrison *Also called Holiday Homes Inc (G-10646)*
Holiday Homes Inc 513 353-9777
10620 Sand Run Rd Harrison (45030) *(G-10646)*
Holistic Botanicals, Bellville *Also called Natural Options Aromatherapy (G-1560)*
Holistic Foods Herbs and Books, Columbus *Also called B & A Holistic Fd & Herbs LLC (G-6639)*
Holistic Measures 216 261-0329
26241 Lake Shore Blvd Euclid (44132) *(G-9420)*
Hollaender Manufacturing Co 513 772-8800
10285 Wayne Ave Cincinnati (45215) *(G-3817)*
Holland Assocts LLC DBA Archou 513 891-0006
316 W 4th St Ste 201 Cincinnati (45202) *(G-3818)*
Holland Engineering Co, Toledo *Also called Holland Engraving Company (G-18332)*
Holland Engraving Company 419 865-2765
7340 Dorr St Toledo (43615) *(G-18332)*
Holland Grills Distributing, Spencerville *Also called S I Distributing Inc (G-17314)*
Holland Springfield Journal 419 874-2528
117 E 2nd St Perrysburg (43551) *(G-15963)*
Hollmann Inc 513 522-1800
1617 W Belmar Pl Cincinnati (45224) *(G-3819)*
Hollow Boring Inc 440 951-2929
7832 Enterprise Dr Mentor (44060) *(G-13467)*
Hollphane, Newark *Also called Acuity Brands Lighting Inc (G-14849)*
Hollys Custom Print Inc 740 928-2697
1001 O Neill Dr Hebron (43025) *(G-10748)*
Hollywood Family Eye Care 740 264-1220
276 S Hollywood Blvd Steubenville (43952) *(G-17537)*
Hollywood Imprints LLC 614 501-6040
1000 Morrison Rd Ste D Gahanna (43230) *(G-10083)*
Holm Industries Inc (PA) 330 562-2900
1300 Danner Dr Aurora (44202) *(G-883)*
Holmco Division, Winesburg *Also called Robin Industries Inc (G-20534)*
Holmes By Products Co 330 893-2322
3175 Township Road 411 Millersburg (44654) *(G-14095)*
Holmes Cheese Co 330 674-6451
9444 State Route 39 Millersburg (44654) *(G-14096)*
Holmes County Hub Inc 330 674-1811
6 W Jackson St Ste C Millersburg (44654) *(G-14097)*
Holmes Limestone Co (PA) 330 893-2721
4255 State Rte 39 Berlin (44610) *(G-1642)*
Holmes Lumber & Bldg Ctr Inc 330 674-9060
6139 Hc 39 Millersburg (44654) *(G-14098)*
Holmes Lumber & Supply, Millersburg *Also called Holmes Lumber & Bldg Ctr Inc (G-14098)*
Holmes Panel 330 897-5040
3052 State Route 557 Baltic (43804) *(G-1031)*
Holmes Prcut/Troyer Imprinting 330 359-0000
7540 Peabody Kent Rd Dundee (44624) *(G-9019)*
Holmes Printing, Springfield *Also called Holmes W & Sons Printing (G-17419)*
Holmes Printing Solutions LLC 330 234-9699
8757 County Road 77 Fredericksburg (44627) *(G-9952)*
Holmes Redimix Inc 330 674-0865
5420 County Road 349 Millersburg (44654) *(G-14099)*
Holmes Stair Parts Ltd 330 279-2797
8614 Township Road 561 Holmesville (44633) *(G-10979)*
Holmes Supply Corp 330 279-2634
7571 State Route 83 Holmesville (44633) *(G-10980)*
Holmes W & Sons Printing 937 325-1509
401 E Columbia St Springfield (45503) *(G-17419)*
Holmes Wheel Shop Inc 330 279-2891
7969 County Road 189 Holmesville (44633) *(G-10981)*
Holophane Corporation 740 349-4194
515 Mckinley Ave Newark (43055) *(G-14883)*
Holophane Corporation (HQ) 866 759-1577
3825 Columbus Rd Bldg A Granville (43023) *(G-10331)*
Holophane Lighting 330 823-5535
12720 Beech St Ne Alliance (44601) *(G-475)*
Holte Eyeware 513 321-4000
2651 Observatory Ave # 1 Cincinnati (45208) *(G-3820)*
Holtgrven Scale Elctronic Corp 419 422-4779
420 E Lincoln St Findlay (45840) *(G-9704)*
Holthaus Lackner Signs, Cincinnati *Also called Gus Holthaus Signs Inc (G-3790)*
Homan Metals LLC 513 721-5010
1253 Knowlton St Cincinnati (45223) *(G-3821)*
Home Bakery 419 678-3018
109 W Main St Coldwater (45828) *(G-6413)*
Home Care Products LLC (HQ) 919 693-1002
7160 Chagrin Rd Ste 220 Chagrin Falls (44023) *(G-3050)*
Home City Ice Company 513 353-9346
5709 State Rte 128 Harrison (45030) *(G-10647)*
Home City Ice Company 513 941-0340
6045 Bridgetown Rd Ste 1 Cincinnati (45248) *(G-3822)*
Home City Ice Company 614 836-2877
4505 S Hamilton Rd Groveport (43125) *(G-10493)*
Home City Ice Company 513 851-4040
11920 Kemper Springs Dr Cincinnati (45240) *(G-3823)*
Home City Ice Company 937 461-6028
1020 Gateway Dr Dayton (45404) *(G-8252)*
Home City Ice Company 419 562-4953
150 Johnson Dr Delaware (43015) *(G-8694)*
Home City Ice Company 440 439-5001
20282 Hannan Pkwy Bedford (44146) *(G-1413)*
Home Idea Center Inc 419 375-4951
1100 Commerce St Fort Recovery (45846) *(G-9821)*

Home Pro, Columbus *Also called Certified Walk In Tubs* ***(G-6756)***
Home Quarters North Canto....330 806-5336
1428 Edison St Nw Hartville (44632) ***(G-10696)***
Home Resolver....440 886-6758
11121 Magdala Dr Cleveland (44130) ***(G-5413)***
Home Service Station Inc....419 678-2612
116 S 1st St Coldwater (45828) ***(G-6414)***
Home Sheet Metal & Roofing Co....419 562-7806
211 W Galen St Bucyrus (44820) ***(G-2334)***
Home Stor & Off Solutions Inc....216 362-4660
5305 Commerce Pkwy W Cleveland (44130) ***(G-5414)***
Homecare Mattress Inc....937 746-2556
303 Conover Dr Franklin (45005) ***(G-9889)***
Homeland AG Fuels LLC....216 763-1004
25700 Science Park Dr # 210 Cleveland (44122) ***(G-5415)***
Homestat Farm Ltd (PA)....614 718-3060
6065 Frantz Rd Ste 206 Dublin (43017) ***(G-8924)***
Homestead Beer Company....740 522-8018
811 Irving Wick Dr W Heath (43056) ***(G-10720)***
Homestead Collections....419 422-8286
11300 Township Rd 99 Findlay (45840) ***(G-9705)***
Homestead Landscapers....740 435-8480
67137 Old 21 Rd 21st Cambridge (43725) ***(G-2443)***
Homestretch Inc....419 738-6604
203 E Auglaize St Wapakoneta (45895) ***(G-19331)***
Homestretch Sportswear Inc....419 678-4282
491 S Eastern Ave Saint Henry (45883) ***(G-16663)***
Hometown Food Company....419 470-7914
1250 W Laskey Rd Toledo (43612) ***(G-18333)***
Hometown Threads....440 779-6053
4636 Great Northern Blvd North Olmsted (44070) ***(G-15193)***
Homewood Press Inc....419 478-0695
400 E State Line Rd Toledo (43612) ***(G-18334)***
Homeworth Fabrications & Mchs....330 525-5459
23094 Georgetown Rd Homeworth (44634) ***(G-10988)***
Homeworth Sales & Services, Homeworth *Also called Ohio Drill & Tool Co* ***(G-10990)***
Homeworth Sales Service Div, Homeworth *Also called Ohio Drill & Tool Co* ***(G-10989)***
Hommati Franchise Network Inc....833 466-6284
6264 S Sunbury Rd Ste 100 Westerville (43081) ***(G-20058)***
Honda Engineering N Amer Inc....937 642-5000
24000 Honda Pkwy Marysville (43040) ***(G-12789)***
Honda Engineering NA Inc....937 707-5357
24000 Honda Pkwy Marysville (43040) ***(G-12790)***
Honda Mdwest Consolidation Ctr, Troy *Also called American Honda Motor Co Inc* ***(G-18635)***
Honda of America Mfg Inc (HQ)....937 642-5000
24000 Honda Pkwy Marysville (43040) ***(G-12791)***
Honda of America Mfg Inc....937 644-0724
19900 State Route 739 Marysville (43040) ***(G-12792)***
Honda of America Mfg Inc....937 642-5000
25000 Honda Pkwy Marysville (43040) ***(G-12793)***
Honda Support Office, Marysville *Also called Honda of America Mfg Inc* ***(G-12792)***
Honda Transm Mfg Amer Inc....937 843-5555
6964 State Route 235 N Russells Point (43348) ***(G-16598)***
Honey Cell Inc Mid West....513 360-0280
6480 Hamilton Lebanon Rd Monroe (45044) ***(G-14267)***
Honey Sweetie Acres LLC....513 456-6090
2710 Spring Hill Rd Goshen (45122) ***(G-10288)***
Honeybaked Ham Company (PA)....513 583-9700
11935 Mason Montgomery Rd # 110 Cincinnati (45249) ***(G-3824)***
Honeycomb Midwest....513 360-0280
6480 Hamilton Lebanon Rd Monroe (45044) ***(G-14268)***
Honeymoon Paper Products Inc (PA)....513 755-7200
7100 Dixie Hwy Fairfield (45014) ***(G-9505)***
Honeywell, Lancaster *Also called Diamond Electronics Inc* ***(G-11564)***
Honeywell, Urbana *Also called Grimes Aerospace Company* ***(G-18990)***
Honeywell, Perrysburg *Also called Fram Group Operations LLC* ***(G-15953)***
Honeywell....614 850-8228
2199 Dividend Dr Columbus (43228) ***(G-7005)***
Honeywell Authorized Dealer, Sandusky *Also called Gundlach Sheet Metal Works Inc* ***(G-16814)***
Honeywell Authorized Dealer, Cincinnati *Also called Cincinnati Air Conditioning Co* ***(G-3480)***
Honeywell Authorized Dealer, Anna *Also called Chilltex LLC* ***(G-588)***
Honeywell Authorized Dealer, Cincinnati *Also called Wine Cellar Innovations LLC* ***(G-4513)***
Honeywell Automation Control....937 264-2662
550 State Route 55 Urbana (43078) ***(G-18994)***
Honeywell First Responder Pdts, Dayton *Also called Morning Pride Mfg LLC* ***(G-8367)***
Honeywell Inc....513 272-1111
3940 Virginia Ave Cincinnati (45227) ***(G-3825)***
Honeywell International Inc....216 459-6048
950 Keynote Cir Ste 90 Independence (44131) ***(G-11135)***
Honeywell International Inc....440 349-7330
5935 Stephanie Ln Solon (44139) ***(G-17162)***
Honeywell International Inc....937 484-2000
550 State Route 55 Urbana (43078) ***(G-18995)***
Honeywell International Inc....513 745-7200
1280 Kemper Meadow Dr Cincinnati (45240) ***(G-3826)***
Honeywell International Inc....937 754-4134
1232 Dytn Yllow Sprng Rd Fairborn (45324) ***(G-9461)***
Honeywell Lebow Products....614 850-5000
2080 Arlingate Ln Columbus (43228) ***(G-7006)***
Honeywell Lightning & Elec, Urbana *Also called Grimes Aerospace Company* ***(G-18991)***
Honeywell Senfopec, Columbus *Also called Honeywell Lebow Products* ***(G-7006)***
Hood Packaging Corporation....937 382-6681
1961 Rombach Ave Wilmington (45177) ***(G-20498)***
Hookah Rush....614 267-6463
2422 N High St Columbus (43202) ***(G-7007)***
Hoopes Fertilizer Works Inc (PA)....330 894-2121
24104 Us Route 30 East Rochester (44625) ***(G-9090)***
Hoopes Fertilizer Works Inc....330 821-3550
9866 Freshley Ave Ne # 166 Alliance (44601) ***(G-476)***
Hoot and Holler,, Cincinnati *Also called Owl Be Sweatin* ***(G-4127)***
Hooven - Dayton Corp (PA)....937 233-4473
511 Byers Rd Miamisburg (45342) ***(G-13677)***
Hoover & Wells Inc....419 691-9220
2011 Seaman St Toledo (43605) ***(G-18335)***
Hoover Group....419 525-3159
411 Eby Rd Shiloh (44878) ***(G-16994)***
Hopco Resources Inc....614 882-8533
2829 E Dblin Granville Rd Columbus (43231) ***(G-7008)***
Hope Timber & Marketing Group (PA)....740 344-1788
141 Union St Newark (43055) ***(G-14884)***
Hope Timber Mulch Inc....740 344-1788
141 Union St Newark (43055) ***(G-14885)***
Hope Timber Pallet Recycl Inc....740 344-1788
141 Union St Newark (43055) ***(G-14886)***
Hopedale Mining LLC....740 937-2225
86900 Sinfield Rd Hopedale (43976) ***(G-10991)***
Hopewell Industries Inc (PA)....740 622-3563
637 Chestnut St Coshocton (43812) ***(G-7737)***
Hopewood Inc....330 359-5656
8087 Township Road 652 Millersburg (44654) ***(G-14100)***
Hoppel Fabrication Specialties....330 823-5700
9481 Columbus Rd Ste 1 Louisville (44641) ***(G-12156)***
Hord Elevator LLC....419 562-5934
1016 State Route 98 Bucyrus (44820) ***(G-2335)***
Horizon Communications Inc....330 968-6959
8870 Darrow Rd Ste F106 Twinsburg (44087) ***(G-18792)***
Horizon Global Americas Inc....440 498-0001
29000 Aurora Rd Ste 2 Solon (44139) ***(G-17163)***
Horizon Industries Corp....937 323-0801
1801 W Columbia St Springfield (45504) ***(G-17420)***
Horizon Metals Inc....440 235-3338
8059 Lewis Rd Ste 102 Berea (44017) ***(G-1609)***
Horizon Ohio Publications Inc (HQ)....419 394-7414
102 E Spring St Saint Marys (45885) ***(G-16686)***
Horizon Ohio Publications Inc....419 738-2128
520 Industrial Dr Wapakoneta (45895) ***(G-19332)***
Horizon Publications Inc....419 628-2369
326 N Main St Ste 200 Minster (45865) ***(G-14217)***
Horizon Publications Inc....419 738-2128
520 Industrial Dr Wapakoneta (45895) ***(G-19333)***
Horizons Inc Camcode Division....216 714-0020
18531 S Miles Rd Cleveland (44128) ***(G-5416)***
Horizons Incorporated (PA)....216 475-0555
18531 S Miles Rd Cleveland (44128) ***(G-5417)***
Horizontal Eqp Manufactoring....330 264-2229
3310 Columbus Rd Wooster (44691) ***(G-20604)***
Hornell Brewing Co Inc....516 812-0384
644 Linn St Ste 318 Cincinnati (45203) ***(G-3827)***
Horner Industrial Services Inc....937 390-6667
5330 Prosperity Dr Springfield (45502) ***(G-17421)***
Horner Industrial Services Inc....513 874-8722
4721 Interstate Dr West Chester (45246) ***(G-19865)***
Horning Steel Co....330 633-0028
167 Southwest Ave Tallmadge (44278) ***(G-17985)***
Horsburgh & Scott Co (PA)....216 432-5858
5114 Hamilton Ave Cleveland (44114) ***(G-5418)***
Horsburgh & Scott Co....216 383-2909
1441 Chardon Rd Cleveland (44117) ***(G-5419)***
Horse Hill Wreath Company....937 272-0701
1205 S Alpha Bellbrook Rd Sugarcrk Twp (45305) ***(G-17879)***
Horsemens Pride Inc....800 232-7950
10008 State Route 43 Streetsboro (44241) ***(G-17677)***
Horst Packing Inc....330 482-2997
3535 Renkenberger Rd Columbiana (44408) ***(G-6469)***
Horton Emergency Vehicles, Grove City *Also called Halcore Group Inc* ***(G-10433)***
Horton Enterprises Inc....614 539-8181
3800 Mcdowell Rd Grove City (43123) ***(G-10434)***
Horwitz & Pintis Co....419 666-2220
1604 Tracy St Toledo (43605) ***(G-18336)***
Hosler Maps Inc....937 855-4173
115 N Plum St Germantown (45327) ***(G-10242)***
Hospeco, Richmond Heights *Also called Tranzonic Companies* ***(G-16507)***
Hostar International Inc (PA)....440 564-5362
15000 Cross Creek Pkwy Newbury (44065) ***(G-14957)***
Hoster Graphics Company Inc....614 299-9770
1349 Delashmut Ave Columbus (43212) ***(G-7009)***

(PA)=Parent Co (HQ)=Headquarters (DH)=Div Headquarters

Hot Brass Personal Defense 419 733-7400
101 S Sugar St Celina (45822) **(G-2969)**
Hot Cards.com, Cleveland *Also called Fx Digital Media Inc* **(G-5283)**
HOT Graphic Services Inc 419 242-7000
2595 Tracy Rd Northwood (43619) **(G-15339)**
Hot Mama Foods Inc 419 474-3402
5839 Secor Rd Toledo (43623) **(G-18337)**
Hot Shot Motor Works M LLC 419 294-1997
555 S Warpole St Rear Upper Sandusky (43351) **(G-18956)**
Hot Spot 740 947-8888
800 W 2nd St Waverly (45690) **(G-19548)**
Hotend Works Inc 440 787-3181
11470 Hawke Rd Unit 9 Columbia Station (44028) **(G-6438)**
House of 10000 Picture Frames 937 254-5541
2210 Wilmington Pike Dayton (45420) **(G-8253)**
House of Awards and Sports 419 422-7877
419 N Main St Findlay (45840) **(G-9706)**
House of Delara Fragrances 216 651-5803
1810 W 47th St Cleveland (44102) **(G-5420)**
House of Hindenach 419 422-0392
408 N Main St Findlay (45840) **(G-9707)**
House of Plastics, Cleveland *Also called HP Manufacturing Company Inc* **(G-5421)**
House Silva-Strongsville Inc 330 464-6419
Al156 Southpark Mall Al Strongsville (44136) **(G-17750)**
Housetrends 513 794-4103
4601 Malsbary Rd 104 Blue Ash (45242) **(G-1789)**
Housing & Emrgncy Lgstcs Plnnr 209 201-7511
36905 State Route 30 Lisbon (44432) **(G-11969)**
Houston Machine Products Inc 937 322-8022
1065 W Leffel Ln Springfield (45506) **(G-17422)**
Howard & Blake Excavating LLC 740 701-7938
1030 Main St Richmond Dale (45673) **(G-16499)**
Howard B Claflin Co 330 928-1704
2475 2nd St Cuyahoga Falls (44221) **(G-7880)**
Howard Grant Corp 330 743-3151
316 Alexander St Youngstown (44502) **(G-20932)**
Howden American Fan Company (HQ) 513 874-2400
2933 Symmes Rd Fairfield (45014) **(G-9506)**
Howden American Fan Company 513 874-2400
3235 Homeward Way Fairfield (45014) **(G-9507)**
Howden North America Inc 330 867-8540
411 Independence Dr Medina (44256) **(G-13274)**
Howden North America Inc 330 721-7374
935 Heritage Dr Medina (44256) **(G-13275)**
Howden North America Inc 513 874-2400
2933 Symmes Rd Fairfield (45014) **(G-9508)**
Howland Machine Corp 330 544-4029
947 Summit Ave Niles (44446) **(G-15012)**
Howland Printing Inc 330 637-8255
3117 Niles Cortland Rd Ne Cortland (44410) **(G-7710)**
Howmedica Osteonics Corp 937 291-3900
474 Windsor Park Dr Dayton (45459) **(G-8254)**
Howmet Aluminum Casting Inc (HQ) 216 641-4340
1600 Harvard Ave Newburgh Heights (44105) **(G-14937)**
Howmet Castings & Services Inc (HQ) 216 641-4400
1616 Harvard Ave Newburgh Heights (44105) **(G-14938)**
Howmet Corporation (HQ) 757 825-7086
1616 Harvard Ave Newburgh Heights (44105) **(G-14939)**
Hoxworth Blood Center, Cincinnati *Also called University of Cincinnati* **(G-4453)**
Hoya Optical Labs 440 239-1924
869 W Bagley Rd Berea (44017) **(G-1610)**
HP Manufacturing Company Inc (PA) 216 361-6500
3705 Carnegie Ave Cleveland (44115) **(G-5421)**
Hp2g LLC 419 906-1525
2611 Scott St Napoleon Napoleon (43545) **(G-14544)**
Hpc Holdings LLC (HQ) 330 666-3751
3637 Ridgewood Rd Fairlawn (44333) **(G-9608)**
Hpc Manufacturing Inc 440 322-8334
7405 Industrial Pkwy Dr Lorain (44053) **(G-12095)**
HPM Business Systems Inc 216 520-1330
21887 Lorain Rd 300 Cleveland (44126) **(G-5422)**
HPM North America Corp, Iberia *Also called Yizumi-HPM Corporation* **(G-11115)**
Hr Machine LLC 937 222-7644
2972 Homeway Dr Beavercreek (45434) **(G-1323)**
Hr Parts N Stuff 330 947-2433
2002 Industry Rd Atwater (44201) **(G-861)**
Hrh Door Corp (PA) 850 208-3400
1 Door Dr Mount Hope (44660) **(G-14438)**
Hrh Door Corp 330 828-2291
14512 Lincoln Way E Dalton (44618) **(G-7943)**
Hrh Door Corp 440 593-5226
1001 Chamberlain Blvd Conneaut (44030) **(G-7649)**
Hsm Wire International Inc 330 244-8501
820 S Valley Blvd Nw North Canton (44720) **(G-15093)**
Hst, Cincinnati *Also called Hermetic Seal Technology Inc* **(G-3810)**
Htci Co 937 845-1204
12170 Milton Carlisle Rd New Carlisle (45344) **(G-14667)**
Htec Systems Inc 937 438-3010
561 Congress Park Dr Dayton (45459) **(G-8255)**
Hub Plastics Inc 614 861-1791
725 Reynoldsburg New Blacklick (43004) **(G-1686)**
Hubbard Company 419 784-4455
612 Clinton St Defiance (43512) **(G-8627)**
Hubbard Feeds, Botkins *Also called Ridley USA Inc* **(G-1936)**
Hubbard Feeds, Botkins *Also called Ridley USA Inc* **(G-1937)**
Hubbard Publishing Co 937 592-3060
127 E Chillicothe Ave Bellefontaine (43311) **(G-1518)**
Hubbell Incorporated 330 335-2361
8711 Wadsworth Rd Wadsworth (44281) **(G-19245)**
Hubbell Machine Tooling Inc 216 524-1797
7507 Exchange St Cleveland (44125) **(G-5423)**
Hubert Enterprises Inc 513 367-8600
9555 Dry Fork Rd Harrison (45030) **(G-10648)**
Hudak Machine & Tool Inc 440 366-8955
144 Eady Ct Elyria (44035) **(G-9266)**
Hudco Manufacturing Inc 440 951-4040
38250 Western Pkwy Willoughby (44094) **(G-20338)**
Hudson Access Group II 330 283-6214
2460 Bramfield Way Hudson (44236) **(G-11052)**
Hudson Extrusions Inc 330 653-6015
1255 Norton Rd Hudson (44236) **(G-11053)**
Hudson Fasteners Inc 330 270-9500
241 W Federal St 512 Youngstown (44503) **(G-20933)**
Hudson Feeds, Okolona *Also called Republic Mills Inc* **(G-15523)**
Hudson Leather Ltd 419 485-8531
14700 State Route 15 Pioneer (43554) **(G-16085)**
Hudson Leather Co, Pioneer *Also called Hudson Leather Ltd* **(G-16085)**
Hudson Printing of Medina LLC 330 591-4800
2425 Medina Rd Ste 206 Medina (44256) **(G-13276)**
Hudson Supply Company Inc 216 518-3000
4500 Lee Rd Ste 120 Cleveland (44128) **(G-5424)**
Hudson Village Pizza Inc 330 968-4563
3825 Kay Dr Stow (44224) **(G-17595)**
Hueston Industries Inc 937 264-8163
3020 Production Ct Dayton (45414) **(G-8256)**
Hug Manufacturing Corporation 419 668-5086
2858 Arcade Rd Norwalk (44857) **(G-15400)**
Hughes Corporation (PA) 440 238-2550
16900 Foltz Pkwy Strongsville (44149) **(G-17751)**
Hughey & Phillips LLC 937 652-3500
240 W Twain Ave Urbana (43078) **(G-18996)**
Hugo Bosca Company Inc (PA) 937 323-5523
1905 W Jefferson St Springfield (45506) **(G-17423)**
Hugo Boss Usa Inc 216 671-8100
4600 Piderman Rd Cleveland (44144) **(G-5425)**
Hugo Sand Company 216 570-1212
7055 State Route 43 Kent (44240) **(G-11333)**
Hugo Vglsang Maschinenbau GMBH 330 296-3820
7966 State Route 44 Ravenna (44266) **(G-16382)**
Huhtamaki Inc 937 746-9700
4000 Commerce Center Dr Franklin (45005) **(G-9890)**
Huhtamaki Inc 513 201-1525
1985 James E Sauls Sr Dr Batavia (45103) **(G-1153)**
Huhtamaki Inc 937 987-3078
5566 New Vienna Rd New Vienna (45159) **(G-14824)**
Huhtamaki Plastics, New Vienna *Also called Huhtamaki Inc* **(G-14824)**
Hukon Manufacturing Company 513 721-5562
2111 Freeman Ave Cincinnati (45214) **(G-3828)**
Hull Builders Supply, Sandusky *Also called Hull Ready Mix Concrete Inc* **(G-16815)**
Hull Builders Supply Inc 440 967-3159
685 Main St Vermilion (44089) **(G-19161)**
Hull Ready Mix Concrete Inc 419 625-8070
4419 Tiffin Ave Sandusky (44870) **(G-16815)**
Hulsman Signs 513 738-3389
10001 State Route 128 Harrison (45030) **(G-10649)**
Humbert Screen Graphix, Canton *Also called Tim L Humbert* **(G-2836)**
Humble Construction Co 614 888-8960
3441 Morse Rd Columbus (43231) **(G-7010)**
Hummingbird Graphics LLC 216 595-8835
4425 Renaissance Pkwy Warrensville Heights (44128) **(G-19470)**
Humphrey Popcorn Company (PA) 216 662-6629
11606 Pearl Rd Strongsville (44136) **(G-17752)**
Humtown Pattern Company 330 482-5555
44708 Clmbana Wterford Rd Columbiana (44408) **(G-6470)**
Humtown Products, Columbiana *Also called Humtown Pattern Company* **(G-6470)**
Hundley Cellars LLC 843 368-5016
6451 N River Rd W Geneva (44041) **(G-10223)**
Hung Pham 614 850-9695
5291 Westpointe Plaza Dr Columbus (43228) **(G-7011)**
Hunger Hydraulics CC Ltd 419 666-4510
63 Dixie Hwy Ste 1 Rossford (43460) **(G-16586)**
Hunger Industrial Complex, Rossford *Also called Hunger Hydraulics CC Ltd* **(G-16586)**
Hunkar Technologies Inc (PA) 513 272-1010
2368 Victory Pkwy Ste 210 Cincinnati (45206) **(G-3829)**
Hunnell Electric Co Inc 330 773-8278
950 Grant St Akron (44311) **(G-209)**
Hunnell Electric Motor Repair, Akron *Also called Hunnell Electric Co Inc* **(G-209)**

Hunt Imaging LLC (PA) 440 826-0433
210 Sheldon Rd Berea (44017) ***(G-1611)***
Hunt Products Inc 440 667-2457
3982 E 42nd St Newburgh Heights (44105) ***(G-14940)***
Hunt Valve Company Inc 330 337-9535
1913 E State St Salem (44460) ***(G-16748)***
Hunt Valve Company Inc 330 337-9535
1913 E State St Salem (44460) ***(G-16749)***
Hunter Defense Tech Inc 513 943-7880
1032 Seabrook Way Cincinnati (45245) ***(G-3255)***
Hunter Defense Tech Inc (PA) 216 438-6111
30500 Aurora Rd Ste 100 Solon (44139) ***(G-17164)***
Hunter Environmental Corp 440 248-6111
30525 Aurora Rd Solon (44139) ***(G-17165)***
Hunter Eureka Pipeline LLC 740 374-2940
125 Putnam St Marietta (45750) ***(G-12633)***
Hunter Hydraulics Inc 330 455-3983
2512 Columbus Rd Ne Canton (44705) ***(G-2701)***
Hunter Lift Ltd 330 549-3347
11233 South Ave North Lima (44452) ***(G-15171)***
Hunter Manufacturing Company, Solon *Also called Hunter Environmental Corp* ***(G-17165)***
Hunter Tool and Die Company 937 256-9798
2104 E 1st St Dayton (45403) ***(G-8257)***
Hunters Hightech Energy Systm 614 275-4777
2059 Big Tree Dr Columbus (43223) ***(G-7012)***
Hunters Manufacturing Co Inc (PA) 330 628-9245
1325 Waterloo Rd Mogadore (44260) ***(G-14240)***
Huntington Hardwood Lbr Co Inc 440 647-2283
28211 Baker Rd Wellington (44090) ***(G-19583)***
Huntington Instruments Inc 937 767-7001
303 N Walnut St Yellow Springs (45387) ***(G-20808)***
Huntsman 614 659-0155
5407 Lanark Ct Dublin (43017) ***(G-8925)***
Huron Cement Products Company (PA) 419 433-4161
617 Main St Huron (44839) ***(G-11096)***
Huron Cement Products Company 419 433-4161
2925 Venice Rd Sandusky (44870) ***(G-16816)***
Huron Hometown News 419 433-1401
304 Williams St Huron (44839) ***(G-11097)***
Huron Products 419 483-5608
601 E Center St Bellevue (44811) ***(G-1536)***
Hurst Auto-Truck Electric 216 961-1800
9004 Madison Ave Cleveland (44102) ***(G-5426)***
Husac Paving 513 200-2818
114 S Walnut St Harrison (45030) ***(G-10650)***
Husky Energy, Dublin *Also called Husky Marketing and Supply Co* ***(G-8927)***
Husky Energy 614 766-5633
5550 Blazer Pkwy Ste 200 Dublin (43017) ***(G-8926)***
Husky Lima Refinery 419 226-2300
1150 S Metcalf St Lima (45804) ***(G-11875)***
Husky Marketing and Supply Co, Dublin *Also called Husky Energy* ***(G-8926)***
Husky Marketing and Supply Co 614 210-2300
5550 Blazer Pkwy Ste 200 Dublin (43017) ***(G-8927)***
Husqvarna Construction Pdts, Cleveland *Also called Husqvarna US Holding Inc* ***(G-5427)***
Husqvarna US Holding Inc (HQ) 216 898-1800
20445 Emerald Pkwy Cleveland (44135) ***(G-5427)***
Huston Gift Shop, Chillicothe *Also called Huston Gifts Dolls and Flowers* ***(G-3193)***
Huston Gifts Dolls and Flowers 740 775-9141
306 Fairway Ave Chillicothe (45601) ***(G-3193)***
Hutchinson-Stevens Inc 216 281-8585
9627 Clinton Rd Cleveland (44144) ***(G-5428)***
Huth Ready Mix & Supply Co 330 833-4191
501 5th St Nw Massillon (44647) ***(G-12999)***
Huth Ready-Mix & Supply Co, Massillon *Also called Huth Ready Mix & Supply Co* ***(G-12999)***
Hutnik Company 330 336-9700
350 State St Ste 5 Wadsworth (44281) ***(G-19246)***
Hutter Racing Engines Ltd 440 285-2175
12550 Gar Hwy Chardon (44024) ***(G-3117)***
Hvac, Akron *Also called Lowry Furnace Company Inc* ***(G-260)***
Hvac Inc 330 343-5511
133 W 3rd St Dover (44622) ***(G-8830)***
Hw Chair, Brinkhaven *Also called Hillcrest* ***(G-2081)***
Hy-Blast Inc 513 424-0704
70 Enterprise Dr Middletown (45044) ***(G-13912)***
Hy-Grade Corporation (PA) 216 341-7711
3993 E 93rd St Cleveland (44105) ***(G-5429)***
Hy-Production Inc 330 273-2400
6000 Grafton Rd Valley City (44280) ***(G-19040)***
Hybrid Trailer Co LLC 419 433-3022
912 University Dr S Huron (44839) ***(G-11098)***
Hycom Inc 330 753-2330
374 5th St Nw Barberton (44203) ***(G-1076)***
Hyde Brothers Prtg & Mktg LLC (PA) 740 373-2054
2343 State Route 821 E Marietta (45750) ***(G-12634)***
Hyde Park Lumber Company 513 271-1500
3360 Red Bank Rd Cincinnati (45227) ***(G-3830)***
Hydra Air Equipment Inc 330 274-2222
9222 State Route 44 Mantua (44255) ***(G-12548)***
Hydra-TEC Inc 330 225-8797
3027 Nationwide Pkwy Brunswick (44212) ***(G-2213)***
Hydranamics, Galion *Also called Carter Machine Company Inc* ***(G-10125)***
Hydranamics Div Carter Mch Co, Galion *Also called Hydranamics Inc* ***(G-10144)***
Hydranamics Inc 419 468-3530
820 Edward St Galion (44833) ***(G-10144)***
Hydrant Hat LLC 440 224-1007
5759 S Wright St Kingsville (44048) ***(G-11459)***
Hydratech Engineered Pdts LLC 513 827-9169
10448 Chester Rd Cincinnati (45215) ***(G-3831)***
Hydratecs Injection Eqp Co 330 773-0491
430 Morgan Ave Akron (44311) ***(G-210)***
Hydraulic Parts Store Inc 330 364-6667
145 1st Dr Ne New Philadelphia (44663) ***(G-14774)***
Hydraulic Products Inc 440 946-4575
4540 Beidler Rd Willoughby (44094) ***(G-20339)***
Hydraulic Specialists Inc 740 922-3343
5655 Gundy Dr Midvale (44653) ***(G-13978)***
Hydro Aluminum Fayetteville 937 492-9194
401 N Stolle Ave Sidney (45365) ***(G-17044)***
Hydro Extrusion North Amer LLC 888 935-5759
401 N Stolle Ave Sidney (45365) ***(G-17045)***
Hydro Supply Co 740 454-3842
3112 East Pike Zanesville (43701) ***(G-21147)***
Hydro Systems Company 513 271-8800
401 Milford Pkwy Milford (45150) ***(G-14017)***
Hydro Systems Company (HQ) 513 271-8800
3798 Round Bottom Rd Cincinnati (45244) ***(G-3832)***
Hydro Tube Enterprises Inc (PA) 440 774-1022
137 Artino St Oberlin (44074) ***(G-15499)***
Hydro-Aire Inc 440 323-3211
241 Abbe Rd S Elyria (44035) ***(G-9267)***
Hydro-Dyne Inc 330 832-5076
225 Wetmore Ave Se Massillon (44646) ***(G-13000)***
Hydro-Thrift Corporation 330 837-5141
1301 Sanders Ave Sw Massillon (44647) ***(G-13001)***
Hydro-Vac, Cleveland *Also called HI Tecmetal Group Inc* ***(G-5402)***
Hydrodec Inc (HQ) 330 454-8202
2021 Steinway Blvd Se Canton (44707) ***(G-2702)***
Hydrodec of North America LLC 330 454-8202
2021 Steinway Blvd Se Canton (44707) ***(G-2703)***
Hydrofresh Ltd 419 785-3221
1571 Gressel Dr Delphos (45833) ***(G-8745)***
Hydrogen 411 Technology LLC 440 941-6760
7777 W 130th St Cleveland (44130) ***(G-5430)***
Hydrogen Energy Systems LLC 330 236-0358
12 E Exchange St Fl 8 Akron (44308) ***(G-211)***
Hydromatic Pumps Inc 419 289-1144
1101 Myers Pkwy Ashland (44805) ***(G-712)***
Hydromotive Engineering Co 330 425-4266
9261 Ravenna Rd Bldg B1b2 Twinsburg (44087) ***(G-18793)***
Hydrothrift, Massillon *Also called Hydro-Thrift Corporation* ***(G-13001)***
Hyfast Aerospace LLC 216 712-4158
12313 Plaza Dr Parma (44130) ***(G-15823)***
Hygenic Acquisition Co 330 633-8460
1245 Home Ave Akron (44310) ***(G-212)***
Hygenic Corporation (HQ) 330 633-8460
1245 Home Ave Akron (44310) ***(G-213)***
Hygient Corporation 440 796-7964
5815 Landerbrook Dr # 24702 Cleveland (44124) ***(G-5431)***
Hykon Manufacturing Company 330 821-8889
163 E State St Alliance (44601) ***(G-477)***
Hyland Machine Company 937 233-8600
1900 Kuntz Rd Dayton (45404) ***(G-8258)***
Hyland Screw Machine Products, Dayton *Also called Hyland Machine Company* ***(G-8258)***
Hyland Software Inc (HQ) 440 788-5000
28500 Clemens Rd Westlake (44145) ***(G-20125)***
Hyload Inc (HQ) 330 336-6604
5020 Enterprise Pkwy Seville (44273) ***(G-16916)***
Hylun Machine Co Inc 440 256-8755
9220 Woods Way Dr Willoughby (44094) ***(G-20340)***
Hyneks Machine & Weld Shop, Ashland *Also called Hyneks Machine and Welding* ***(G-713)***
Hyneks Machine and Welding 419 281-7966
1372 State Route 603 Ashland (44805) ***(G-713)***
Hynes Industries Inc (PA) 330 799-3221
3805 Hendricks Rd Ste A Youngstown (44515) ***(G-20934)***
Hynes Modern Pattern Co Inc 937 322-3451
2141 Erie Ave Springfield (45505) ***(G-17424)***
Hype Socks LLC 855 497-3769
8836 Commerce Loop Dr Columbus (43240) ***(G-6497)***
Hyper Tech Research Inc 614 481-8050
539 Industrial Mile Rd Columbus (43228) ***(G-7013)***
Hyper Tool Company 440 543-5151
16829 Park Circle Dr Chagrin Falls (44023) ***(G-3051)***
Hyperion, Columbus *Also called Diamond Innovations Inc* ***(G-6863)***
Hyponex Corporation (HQ) 937 644-0011
14111 Scottslawn Rd Marysville (43040) ***(G-12794)***
Hyponex Corporation 330 262-1300
3875 S Elyria Rd Shreve (44676) ***(G-17002)***

ALPHABETIC

Hyprolap Finishing Co 440 352-0270
9300 Pinecone Dr Mentor (44060) ***(G-13468)***
Hyq Technologies LLC 513 225-6911
2897 Miamiview Ct Apt A Oxford (45056) ***(G-15694)***
Hyq Teq, Oxford *Also called Hyq Technologies LLC* ***(G-15694)***
Hyson Products, Brecksville *Also called Barnes Group Inc* ***(G-2021)***
Hyster-Yale Materials Hdlg Inc (PA) 440 449-9600
5875 Landerbrook Dr # 300 Cleveland (44124) ***(G-5432)***
Hytec Automotive, Columbus *Also called Hytec-Debartolo LLC* ***(G-7015)***
Hytec Automotive Ind LLC 614 527-9370
4419 Equity Dr Columbus (43228) ***(G-7014)***
Hytec-Debartolo LLC 614 527-9370
4419 Equity Dr Columbus (43228) ***(G-7015)***
Hytech Silicone Products Inc 330 297-1888
6112 Knapp Rd Ravenna (44266) ***(G-16383)***
Hytek Coatings Inc 513 424-0131
1700 S University Blvd Middletown (45044) ***(G-13913)***
I B C S, Englewood *Also called Innovative Bus Cmpt Solutions* ***(G-9363)***
I B-Tech, Bucyrus *Also called Imasen Bucyrus Technology Inc* ***(G-2336)***
I C M I, Amelia *Also called Inductive Components Mfg* ***(G-541)***
I C S, Groveport *Also called Innovtive Crtive Solutions LLC* ***(G-10494)***
I Cerco Inc 740 982-2050
416 Maple Ave Crooksville (43731) ***(G-7816)***
I Cerco Inc (PA) 330 567-2145
453 W Mcconkey St Shreve (44676) ***(G-17003)***
I D I, Wapakoneta *Also called Ingredia Inc* ***(G-19334)***
I Dream of Cakes 937 533-6024
995 Camden Rd Eaton (45320) ***(G-9153)***
I E C, Bolivar *Also called Inventive Extrusions Corp* ***(G-1917)***
I E R Industries, Macedonia *Also called Ier Fujikura Inc* ***(G-12302)***
I F C O Systems, Cincinnati *Also called Ifco Systems Us LLC* ***(G-3836)***
I G Brenner Inc 740 345-8845
32 E North St Newark (43055) ***(G-14887)***
I H Schlezinger Inc 614 252-1188
1041 Joyce Ave Columbus (43219) ***(G-7016)***
I Heart Cupcakes 614 787-3896
372 Hanton Way Columbus (43213) ***(G-7017)***
I L R Inc 216 587-2212
5240 Greenhurst Ext Cleveland (44137) ***(G-5433)***
I L S, Cleveland *Also called Supply Technologies LLC* ***(G-6130)***
I P D, North Royalton *Also called Industrial Parts Depot LLC* ***(G-15278)***
I P Specrete Inc 216 721-2050
10703 Quebec Ave Cleveland (44106) ***(G-5434)***
I R B F Company 330 633-5100
195 Potomac Ave Ste A Tallmadge (44278) ***(G-17986)***
I S I, Lewis Center *Also called Industrial Solutions Inc* ***(G-11762)***
I Schumann & Co, Bedford *Also called I Schumann & Co LLC* ***(G-1414)***
I Schumann & Co LLC 440 439-2300
22500 Alexander Rd Bedford (44146) ***(G-1414)***
I Sq R Power Cable Co 330 588-3000
4300 Chamber Ave Sw Canton (44706) ***(G-2704)***
I T Verdin Co (PA) 513 241-4010
444 Reading Rd Cincinnati (45202) ***(G-3833)***
I T Verdin Co 513 559-3947
3900 Kellogg Ave Cincinnati (45226) ***(G-3834)***
I T W Automotive Finishing 419 470-2000
320 Phillips Ave Toledo (43612) ***(G-18338)***
I-Convert, Caldwell *Also called Interntnal Cnvrter Cldwell Inc* ***(G-2407)***
I-Dee-X Inc 330 788-2186
4302 Lake Park Rd Youngstown (44512) ***(G-20935)***
I-Group Technologies LLC 877 622-3377
3509 Brightwood Rd Se New Philadelphia (44663) ***(G-14775)***
I.T. Plastics, Mentor *Also called Industrial Thermoset Plas Inc* ***(G-13471)***
I2, Hubbard *Also called Independence 2 LLC* ***(G-11002)***
I3, Mesopotamia *Also called Innovative Integrations Inc* ***(G-13633)***
Iabf Inc 614 279-4498
1890 Mckinley Ave Columbus (43222) ***(G-7018)***
Iacono Production Services Inc 513 469-5095
11420 Deerfield Rd Blue Ash (45242) ***(G-1790)***
IAMS Company (HQ) 800 675-3849
8700 S Masn Montgomery Rd Mason (45040) ***(G-12887)***
IAMS Company 419 943-4267
3700 State Route 65 Leipsic (45856) ***(G-11726)***
IAMS Company 937 962-7782
6571 State Route 503 N Lewisburg (45338) ***(G-11793)***
Iberia Firearms Inc 419 468-3746
3929 State Route 309 Galion (44833) ***(G-10145)***
Iberia Machine Shop Inc 419 468-7100
8402 County Rd 30 Iberia (43325) ***(G-11114)***
Ibex Rapid Cooks, Troy *Also called ITW Food Equipment Group LLC* ***(G-18678)***
Ibi, Chillicothe *Also called Ingle-Barr Inc* ***(G-3195)***
Ibi Brake Products Inc 440 543-7962
16751 Hilltop Park Pl Chagrin Falls (44023) ***(G-3052)***
Ibidltd-Blue Green Energy 909 547-5160
1456 N Summit St Toledo (43604) ***(G-18339)***
Ibiza Holdings Inc 513 701-7300
7901 Innovation Way Mason (45040) ***(G-12888)***
IBM, Cincinnati *Also called International Bus Mchs Corp* ***(G-3857)***
Ibycorp 330 425-8226
8968 Dutton Dr Twinsburg (44087) ***(G-18794)***
Ibycorp Tool & Die, Twinsburg *Also called Ibycorp* ***(G-18794)***
Ic Roofing, Mason *Also called Interstate Contractors LLC* ***(G-12897)***
Ic3d Inc 614 344-0414
1697 Westbelt Dr Columbus (43228) ***(G-7019)***
Ic3d Printers, Columbus *Also called Ic3d Inc* ***(G-7019)***
Icandi Graphics LLC 330 723-8337
650 W Smith Rd Ste 3 Medina (44256) ***(G-13277)***
Icaot, Painesville *Also called International Cntr Artfcial or* ***(G-15749)***
ICC, Brecksville *Also called Integrated Chem Concepts Inc* ***(G-2042)***
ICC Safety Service Inc 614 261-4557
1070 Leona Ave Columbus (43201) ***(G-7020)***
ICC Systems Inc 614 524-0299
5665 Blue Church Rd # 202 Sunbury (43074) ***(G-17889)***
Ice Industries Inc 513 398-2010
320 N Mason Montgomery Rd Mason (45040) ***(G-12889)***
Ice Industries Inc (PA) 419 842-3612
3810 Herr Rd Sylvania (43560) ***(G-17943)***
Ice Industries Columbus Inc 419 842-3600
3810 Herr Rd Sylvania (43560) ***(G-17944)***
Ice Industries Deerfield, Mason *Also called Deerfield Manufacturing Inc* ***(G-12855)***
Ice Industries Ronfeldt, Toledo *Also called Ronfeldt Manufacturing LLC* ***(G-18507)***
Ice Water Airboats, Dover *Also called Duck Water Boats Inc* ***(G-8824)***
ICEE USA 513 771-0630
44 Carnegie Way West Chester (45246) ***(G-19866)***
ICI Paints Store, Columbus *Also called Akzo Nobel Inc* ***(G-6560)***
Icibinding Corporation (PA) 440 729-2445
8834 Mayfield Rd Ste A Chesterland (44026) ***(G-3162)***
ICO Holdings LLC 330 666-3751
3550 W Market St Fairlawn (44333) ***(G-9609)***
ICO Mold LLC 419 867-3900
6415 Angola Rd Holland (43528) ***(G-10934)***
ICO Technology Inc 330 666-3751
3550 W Market St Fairlawn (44333) ***(G-9610)***
ICP Adhesives and Sealants Inc (HQ) 330 753-4585
2775 Barber Rd Norton (44203) ***(G-15369)***
Ics Electrical Services, Cincinnati *Also called Instrmntation Ctrl Systems Inc* ***(G-3851)***
Ics-Cargo Clean, Cincinnati *Also called Industrial Container Svcs LLC* ***(G-3843)***
Ics-Cargo Clean, Cincinnati *Also called Industrial Container Svcs LLC* ***(G-3844)***
Ictm Inc 330 629-6060
7204 Glenwood Ave Youngstown (44512) ***(G-20936)***
ID Card Systems Inc 330 963-7446
2248 E Enterprise Pkwy Twinsburg (44087) ***(G-18795)***
ID Images Inc 330 220-7300
2991 Interstate Pkwy Brunswick (44212) ***(G-2214)***
ID Images LLC 513 874-5325
3741 Port Union Rd Fairfield (45014) ***(G-9509)***
ID Images LLC (PA) 330 220-7300
2991 Interstate Pkwy Brunswick (44212) ***(G-2215)***
ID Plastech Engraving, Cincinnati *Also called Professional Award Service* ***(G-4216)***
Ida Controls 440 785-8457
38593 Bell Rd Willoughby (44094) ***(G-20341)***
Idcomm LLC 661 250-4081
32315 White Rd Willoughby Hills (44092) ***(G-20469)***
Idea Works, Sugarcreek *Also called Middaugh Enterprises Inc* ***(G-17852)***
Ideal Baking Co, Lakemore *Also called Four Generations Inc* ***(G-11499)***
Ideal Door, Mason *Also called Clopay Building Pdts Co Inc* ***(G-12846)***
Ideal Electric Power Co 419 522-3611
330 E 1st St Mansfield (44902) ***(G-12460)***
Ideas & Ad Ventures Inc 513 542-7154
2614 Spring Grove Ave Cincinnati (45214) ***(G-3835)***
Identitek Systems Inc 330 832-9844
1100 Industrial Ave Sw Massillon (44647) ***(G-13002)***
Identity Holding Company LLC 216 514-1277
4944 Commerce Pkwy Cleveland (44128) ***(G-5435)***
Identity Syncronizer, Perrysburg *Also called Innerapps LLC* ***(G-15967)***
Idialogs LLC 937 372-2890
121 Pawleys Plantation Ct Xenia (45385) ***(G-20777)***
Idx Corporation 937 401-3225
2875 Needmore Rd Dayton (45414) ***(G-8259)***
Idx Dayton LLC 937 401-3460
2875 Needmore Rd Dayton (45414) ***(G-8260)***
Idx Supply Division, Youngstown *Also called I-Dee-X Inc* ***(G-20935)***
IEC Infrared Systems Inc 440 234-8000
7803 Freeway Cir Middleburg Heights (44130) ***(G-13765)***
IEC Infrared Systems LLC 440 234-8000
7803 Freeway Cir Middleburg Heights (44130) ***(G-13766)***
Ieg Plastics LLC 937 565-4211
223 Lock And Load Rd Bellefontaine (43311) ***(G-1519)***
Ier Fujikura Inc (PA) 330 425-7121
8271 Bavaria Dr E Macedonia (44056) ***(G-12302)***
Ies Systems Inc 330 533-6683
464 Lisbon St Canfield (44406) ***(G-2530)***
Ifco Systems North America Inc 330 669-2726
179 S Gilbert Dr Smithville (44677) ***(G-17089)***

ALPHABETIC SECTION

Ifco Systems Us LLC..513 769-0377
  10725 Evendale Dr Cincinnati (45241) *(G-3836)*
Ig Watteeuw Usa LLC...740 588-1722
  1000 Linden Ave Zanesville (43701) *(G-21148)*
Igc Software, Reynoldsburg Also called Integrity Group Consulting Inc *(G-16444)*
Igel Technology America LLC..................................954 739-9990
  2106 Florence Ave Cincinnati (45206) *(G-3837)*
Ignio Systems LLC..419 708-0503
  444 W Laskey Rd Ste V Toledo (43612) *(G-18340)*
Ignition Interlock, Blue Ash Also called 1 A Lifesafer Inc *(G-1716)*
Igo Home Products, Cleveland Also called Toolovation LLC *(G-6185)*
Igw USA..740 588-1722
  1000 Linden Ave Zanesville (43701) *(G-21149)*
Iheartcommunications Inc.......................................740 335-0941
  1535 N North St Wshngtn CT Hs (43160) *(G-20728)*
Iheartcommunications Inc.......................................419 223-2060
  667 W Market St Lima (45801) *(G-11876)*
Ihi Connectors R, Mentor Also called International Hydraulics Inc *(G-13474)*
Ihod USA LLC...216 459-7179
  127 Public Sq Ste 4120 Cleveland (44114) *(G-5436)*
III Olive LLC Spicy..937 247-5969
  3650 Rigby Rd Miamisburg (45342) *(G-13678)*
III Williams LLC..440 721-8191
  11993 Ravenna Rd Ste 12 Chardon (44024) *(G-3118)*
Iko Production Inc...937 746-4561
  1200 S Main St Franklin (45005) *(G-9891)*
Illinois Tool Works Inc..440 914-3100
  6875 Parkland Blvd Solon (44139) *(G-17166)*
Illinois Tool Works Inc..216 292-7161
  26101 Fargo Ave Bedford (44146) *(G-1415)*
Illinois Tool Works Inc..937 335-7171
  701 S Ridge Ave Troy (45374) *(G-18673)*
Illinois Tool Works Inc..937 332-2839
  750 Lincoln Ave Troy (45373) *(G-18674)*
Illinois Tool Works Inc..513 489-7600
  6600 Cornell Rd Blue Ash (45242) *(G-1791)*
Illinois Tool Works Inc..419 633-3236
  730 E South St Bryan (43506) *(G-2287)*
Illinois Tool Works Inc..419 636-3161
  730 E South St Bryan (43506) *(G-2288)*
Illinois Tool Works Inc..262 248-8277
  730 E South St Bryan (43506) *(G-2289)*
Illinois Tool Works Inc..519 376-8886
  401 W Market St Troy (45373) *(G-18675)*
Illusions Screenprinting..330 263-7770
  214 N Bever St Wooster (44691) *(G-20605)*
Ilpea Industries Inc..330 562-2916
  1300 Danner Dr Aurora (44202) *(G-884)*
Ilsco, Cincinnati Also called Bardes Corporation *(G-3379)*
Ilsco Corporation...513 367-9100
  119 May Dr Harrison (45030) *(G-10651)*
Image Armor LLC..877 673-4377
  3509 Brightwood Rd Se Midvale (44653) *(G-13979)*
Image By J & K LLC..888 667-6929
  1575 Henthorne Dr Maumee (43537) *(G-13118)*
Image Concepts Inc...216 524-9000
  8200 Sweet Valley Dr # 107 Cleveland (44125) *(G-5437)*
Image Graphics, Columbia Station Also called Perrons Printing Company *(G-6442)*
Image Group of Toledo Inc.....................................419 866-3300
  1255 Corporate Dr Holland (43528) *(G-10935)*
Image Industries Inc..937 832-7969
  5700 Swan Dr Clayton (45315) *(G-4575)*
Image Integrations Systems (PA)..........................419 872-0003
  885 Commerce Dr Ste B Perrysburg (43551) *(G-15964)*
Image Pavement Maintenance................................937 833-9200
  425 Carr Dr Brookville (45309) *(G-2172)*
Image Print Inc...614 776-3985
  214 Hoff Rd Unit D Westerville (43082) *(G-19997)*
Image Print Inc...614 430-8470
  6417 Busch Blvd Columbus (43229) *(G-7021)*
Imageiq Inc...855 462-4347
  26801 Miles Rd Ste 103 Cleveland (44128) *(G-5438)*
Imagemart Inc..216 486-4767
  17320 Saint Clair Ave Cleveland (44110) *(G-5439)*
Imagen Brands, Mason Also called Ebsco Industries Inc *(G-12860)*
Imagine Communications Corp.............................513 459-3400
  5300 Kings Island Dr # 101 Mason (45040) *(G-12890)*
Imagine This Renovations......................................330 833-6739
  4220 Alabama Ave Sw Navarre (44662) *(G-14577)*
Imaging Center East Main......................................614 566-8120
  500 E Main St 2nd Columbus (43215) *(G-7022)*
Imaging Sciences LLC..440 975-9640
  38174 Willoughby Pkwy Willoughby (44094) *(G-20342)*
Imalux Corporation...216 502-0755
  11000 Cedar Ave Ste 250 Cleveland (44106) *(G-5440)*
Imasen Bucyrus Technology Inc............................419 563-9590
  260 Crossroads Blvd Bucyrus (44820) *(G-2336)*
Imax Industries Inc..440 639-0242
  117 W Walnut Ave Painesville (44077) *(G-15747)*

Imco Carbide Tool Inc...419 661-6313
  28170 Cedar Park Blvd Perrysburg (43551) *(G-15965)*
Imco Recycling of Ohio LLC..................................740 922-2373
  7335 Newport Rd Se Uhrichsville (44683) *(G-18888)*
Imds Corporation...330 747-4637
  935 Augusta Dr Youngstown (44512) *(G-20937)*
Imesco, Fredericktown Also called Industrial and Mar Eng Svc Co *(G-9971)*
Imet Corporation..440 799-3135
  13400 Glenside Rd Cleveland (44110) *(G-5441)*
IMI Precision, Brookville Also called Norgren Inc *(G-2179)*
IMI-Irving Materials Inc...513 844-8444
  600 Augspurger Rd Hamilton (45011) *(G-10571)*
Iml Containers Ohio Inc...330 754-1066
  5365 E Center Dr Ne Canton (44721) *(G-2705)*
Immersus Health Company LLC (PA)...................855 994-4325
  2 Hill And Hollow Ln Cincinnati (45208) *(G-3838)*
Immersus Health Company LLC............................855 994-4325
  4351 Creek Rd Blue Ash (45241) *(G-1792)*
Immigration Law Systems Inc................................614 252-3078
  1620 E Broad St Ste 107 Columbus (43203) *(G-7023)*
Impac Hi-Performance Machining.........................419 726-7100
  5515 Enterprise Blvd Toledo (43612) *(G-18341)*
Impackt...513 559-1488
  3700 Pocahontas Ave Cincinnati (45227) *(G-3839)*
Impact Armor Technologies LLC...........................216 706-2024
  17000 Saint Clair Ave Cleveland (44110) *(G-5442)*
Impact Cutoff Div, Maumee Also called Hammill Manufacturing Co *(G-13115)*
Impact Industries Inc..440 327-2360
  5120 Mills Indus Pkwy North Ridgeville (44039) *(G-15230)*
Impact Products LLC (HQ).....................................419 841-2891
  2840 Centennial Rd Toledo (43617) *(G-18342)*
Impact Promotions, North Bend Also called Impact Sports Wear Inc *(G-15051)*
Impact Publications...740 928-5541
  4675 Walnut Rd Buckeye Lake (43008) *(G-2315)*
Impact Sports Wear Inc..513 922-7406
  99 St Annes Ave North Bend (45052) *(G-15051)*
Impact Weekly, Dayton Also called Dayton City Paper New LLC *(G-8129)*
Impaction Co..440 349-5652
  6100 Cochran Rd Solon (44139) *(G-17167)*
Impakt...513 271-9191
  5721 Dragon Way Ste 217 Cincinnati (45227) *(G-3840)*
Imperial Adhesives..513 351-1300
  6315 Wiehe Rd Cincinnati (45237) *(G-3841)*
Imperial Alum - Minerva LLC..................................330 868-7765
  217 Roosevelt St Minerva (44657) *(G-14184)*
Imperial Castings, Tipp City Also called C Imperial Inc *(G-18104)*
Imperial Countertops..216 851-0888
  10646 Leuer Ave Cleveland (44108) *(G-5443)*
Imperial Die & Mfg Co..440 268-9080
  22930 Royalton Rd Strongsville (44149) *(G-17753)*
Imperial Metal Solutions LLC................................216 781-4094
  2284 Scranton Rd Cleveland (44113) *(G-5444)*
Imperial Metal Spinning Co....................................216 524-5020
  7600 Exchange St Cleveland (44125) *(G-5445)*
Imperial On-Pece Fibrgls Pools..............................740 747-2971
  255 S Franklin St Ashley (43003) *(G-757)*
Imperial Orthodontics, Urbana Also called Triage Ortho Group *(G-19016)*
Imperial Plastics Inc..330 927-5065
  80 Industrial St Rittman (44270) *(G-16521)*
Imperial Pools Inc...513 771-1506
  12090 Best Pl Cincinnati (45241) *(G-3842)*
Imperial Technologies Inc (HQ).............................330 491-3200
  4155 Martindale Rd Ne Canton (44705) *(G-2706)*
Imperial Tent Company, Coldwater Also called Embedee LLC *(G-6407)*
Importers Direct LLC..330 436-3260
  1559 S Main St Akron (44301) *(G-214)*
Impressions - A Print Shop....................................440 449-6966
  370 Alpha Park Cleveland (44143) *(G-5446)*
Impressions To Go LLC..614 760-0600
  6121 Pirthshire St Dublin (43016) *(G-8928)*
Imprints..330 650-0467
  77 Maple Dr Hudson (44236) *(G-11054)*
Improv Electronics, Kent Also called Kent Displays Inc *(G-11340)*
IMS, Shaker Heights Also called Institute Mthmtical Statistics *(G-16932)*
IMT Defense Corp..614 891-8812
  5386 Club Dr Westerville (43082) *(G-19998)*
In Box Publications LLC...330 592-4288
  977 Hampton Ridge Dr Akron (44313) *(G-215)*
In Good Hlth & Animal Wellness............................330 908-1234
  9425 Olde 8 Rd Ste 4 Northfield (44067) *(G-15319)*
In Stiches Ctr For Ltrgcal Art, Cleveland Also called Strictly Stitchery Inc *(G-6110)*
In-Touch Corp..440 268-0881
  13500 Pearl Rd Ste 139 Cleveland (44136) *(G-5447)*
Inc., K.I.W.I., Twinsburg Also called Kiwi Promotional AP & Prtg Co *(G-18801)*
Inca Presswood-Pallets Ltd (PA)...........................330 343-3361
  3005 Progress St Dover (44622) *(G-8831)*
Inceptor Inc..419 726-8804
  1301 Progress Ave Toledo (43612) *(G-18343)*

Incessant Software Inc....614 206-2211
8577 Ohio Wesleyan Ct Nw Lancaster (43130) ***(G-11580)***
Incinerator Specialists, Medina *Also called Facultatieve Tech Americas Inc* ***(G-13259)***
Incorporated Trst Gspl Wk Scty....216 749-2100
2000 Brookpark Rd Cleveland (44109) ***(G-5448)***
Incorporated Trustees Gospel W....216 749-1428
1980 Brookpark Rd Cleveland (44109) ***(G-5449)***
Incredible Plastics, Warren *Also called Bloom Industries Inc* ***(G-19377)***
Incredible Solutions Inc....330 898-3878
1052 Mahoning Ave Nw Warren (44483) ***(G-19409)***
Independence 2 LLC....800 414-0545
623 W Liberty St Hubbard (44425) ***(G-11002)***
Independent Awning & Canvas Co....937 223-9661
324 Jones St Dayton (45410) ***(G-8261)***
Independent Can Company....440 593-5300
1049 Chamberlain Blvd Conneaut (44030) ***(G-7650)***
Independent Container, Delaware *Also called Greif Inc* ***(G-8683)***
Independent Die & Mfg Co....216 362-6778
5161 W 161st St Cleveland (44142) ***(G-5450)***
Independent Digital Consulting....330 753-0777
2081 Wadsworth Rd Norton (44203) ***(G-15370)***
Independent Machine & Wldg Inc....937 339-7330
35 Marybill Dr S Troy (45373) ***(G-18676)***
Independent Particle Labs....330 477-2016
5353 Swepstone St Nw Canton (44708) ***(G-2707)***
Independent Power Consultants....419 476-8383
6051 Telegraph Rd Ste 19 Toledo (43612) ***(G-18344)***
Independent Protection Systems....330 832-7992
2510 Upland Ave Sw Massillon (44647) ***(G-13003)***
Independent Restaurateur, Newark *Also called Plus Publications Inc* ***(G-14911)***
Independent Stamping Inc....216 251-3500
12025 Zelis Rd Cleveland (44135) ***(G-5451)***
Independent Steel Company LLC....330 225-7741
615 Liverpool Dr Valley City (44280) ***(G-19041)***
Independent The, Massillon *Also called Copley Ohio Newspapers Inc* ***(G-12969)***
Indev Gauging Systems Inc....815 282-4463
6141 Avery Rd Dublin (43016) ***(G-8929)***
Indian Creek Distillery....937 846-1443
7095 Staley Rd New Carlisle (45344) ***(G-14668)***
Indian Creek Fabricators Inc....937 667-7214
1350 Commerce Park Dr Tipp City (45371) ***(G-18116)***
Indian Creek Structures, Rome *Also called J Aaron Weaver* ***(G-16562)***
Indian Lake Boat Lift....937 539-2868
129 Wilgus W Russells Point (43348) ***(G-16599)***
Indian Lake Shoppers Edge....937 843-6600
204 1/2 Lincoln Blvd Russells Point (43348) ***(G-16600)***
Indian River Industries....740 965-4377
31 E Granville St Sunbury (43074) ***(G-17890)***
Indicator Advisory Corporation....419 726-9000
3061 Shoreland Ave Toledo (43611) ***(G-18345)***
Indicator Shop....513 897-0055
8875 Bellbrook Rd Waynesville (45068) ***(G-19568)***
Indie-Peasant Enterprises....740 590-8240
88 Columbus Cir Athens (45701) ***(G-835)***
Indigo 48 LLC....419 551-6931
1607 Magda Dr Montpelier (43543) ***(G-14310)***
Indoor Dog Litter, Barberton *Also called Slogans LLC* ***(G-1105)***
Indoor Envmtl Specialists Inc....937 433-5202
438 Windsor Park Dr Dayton (45459) ***(G-8262)***
Indra Holdings Corp (PA)....513 682-8200
9655 International Blvd West Chester (45246) ***(G-19867)***
Induction Hrdning Spclists Inc....234 678-6820
75 Cuyhoga Fls Indus Pkwy Peninsula (44264) ***(G-15894)***
Induction Iron Incorporated....330 501-8852
3710 Hendricks Rd Bldg 1 Youngstown (44515) ***(G-20938)***
Induction Management Svcs LLC....440 947-2000
1745 Overland Ave Ne Warren (44483) ***(G-19410)***
Induction Services Inc....330 652-4494
1713 N Main St Niles (44446) ***(G-15013)***
Induction Tooling Inc....440 237-0711
12510 York Delta Dr North Royalton (44133) ***(G-15277)***
Inductive Components Mfg....513 752-4731
1200 Ferris Rd Amelia (45102) ***(G-541)***
Industrial Aluminum Foundry, Columbus *Also called Iabf Inc* ***(G-7018)***
Industrial and Mar Eng Svc Co....740 694-0791
13843 Armentrout Rd Fredericktown (43019) ***(G-9971)***
Industrial Application Svs....419 875-5093
13453 Woodbrier Ln Grand Rapids (43522) ***(G-10315)***
Industrial Automation Service....740 747-2222
4590 State Route 229 Ashley (43003) ***(G-758)***
Industrial Connections Inc....330 274-2155
11730 Timber Point Trl Mantua (44255) ***(G-12549)***
Industrial Container Svcs LLC....513 921-2056
1258 Knowlton St Cincinnati (45223) ***(G-3843)***
Industrial Container Svcs LLC....513 921-8811
837 Depot St Cincinnati (45204) ***(G-3844)***
Industrial Container Svcs LLC....614 864-1900
1385 Blatt Blvd Gahanna A Indsutrial Blacklick (43004) ***(G-1687)***
Industrial Crate & Lumber Div, Zanesville *Also called Southeast Ohio Timber Pdts Co* ***(G-21181)***
Industrial Ctrl Design & Maint, Tallmadge *Also called Industrial Ctrl Dsign Mint Inc* ***(G-17987)***
Industrial Ctrl Dsign Mint Inc....330 785-9840
311 Geneva Ave Tallmadge (44278) ***(G-17987)***
Industrial Electronic Service....937 746-9750
325 Industry Dr Carlisle (45005) ***(G-2893)***
Industrial Fabricators Inc....614 882-7423
265 E Broadway Ave Westerville (43081) ***(G-20059)***
Industrial Fiberglass Spc Inc....937 222-9000
521 Kiser St Dayton (45404) ***(G-8263)***
Industrial Finishers Inc....330 343-7797
3690 State Route 800 Ne Dover (44622) ***(G-8832)***
Industrial Hanger Conveyor Co....419 332-2661
886 N County Road 232 Fremont (43420) ***(G-10028)***
Industrial Hardwood Inc....419 666-2503
521 F St Perrysburg (43551) ***(G-15966)***
Industrial Hose Product Div, Wickliffe *Also called Parker-Hannifin Corporation* ***(G-20225)***
Industrial Image....419 547-1417
5630 State Route 113 Bellevue (44811) ***(G-1537)***
Industrial Machine Service, Cardington *Also called Jack Gruber* ***(G-2874)***
Industrial Machine Tool Svc....216 651-1122
3560 Ridge Rd Cleveland (44102) ***(G-5452)***
Industrial Machining Services....937 295-2022
700 Tower Dr Fort Loramie (45845) ***(G-9799)***
Industrial Masurement Ctrl Inc....440 877-1140
9901 Beechwood Dr Cleveland (44133) ***(G-5453)***
Industrial Metal Finishing....440 232-2400
7680 Bond St Solon (44139) ***(G-17168)***
Industrial Mfg Co LLC (HQ)....440 838-4700
8223 Brecksville Rd Ste 1 Brecksville (44141) ***(G-2041)***
Industrial Mill Maintenance....330 746-1155
1609 Wilson Ave Ste 2 Youngstown (44506) ***(G-20939)***
Industrial Mold Inc....330 425-7374
2057 E Aurora Rd Twinsburg (44087) ***(G-18796)***
Industrial Molded Plastics....330 673-1464
425 1/2 W Grant St Kent (44240) ***(G-11334)***
Industrial Nut Corp....419 625-8543
1425 Tiffin Ave Sandusky (44870) ***(G-16817)***
Industrial Packaging Products....440 734-2663
22259 Spencer Ln Cleveland (44126) ***(G-5454)***
Industrial Paint & Strip Inc....419 568-2222
1000 Commerce Ct Waynesfield (45896) ***(G-19567)***
Industrial Parts Depot LLC....440 237-9164
11266 Royalton Rd North Royalton (44133) ***(G-15278)***
Industrial Pattern & Mfg Co....614 252-0934
899 N 20th St Columbus (43219) ***(G-7024)***
Industrial Prfctn Mold & Mch, Twinsburg *Also called Industrial Mold Inc* ***(G-18796)***
Industrial Pulley & Machine Co....937 355-4910
151 E Center St West Mansfield (43358) ***(G-19942)***
Industrial Quartz Corp....440 942-0909
7552 Saint Clair Ave D Mentor (44060) ***(G-13469)***
Industrial Repair & Mfg Inc (PA)....419 822-4232
1140 E Main St Ste A Delta (43515) ***(G-8774)***
Industrial Screen Process (PA)....419 255-4900
17 17th St Toledo (43604) ***(G-18346)***
Industrial Shaft and Mfg Inc....440 942-9104
34201 Melinz Pkwy Unit A Eastlake (44095) ***(G-9114)***
Industrial Solutions Inc....614 431-8118
8333 Green Meadows Dr N A Lewis Center (43035) ***(G-11762)***
Industrial Steering Pdts Inc....419 636-3300
426 N Lewis St Bryan (43506) ***(G-2290)***
Industrial Systems & Solutions....440 205-1658
8812 Tyler Blvd Mentor (44060) ***(G-13470)***
Industrial Tank & Containment....330 448-4876
411 State Route 7 Se # 3 Brookfield (44403) ***(G-2107)***
Industrial Thermal Systems Inc....513 561-2100
3914 Virginia Ave Cincinnati (45227) ***(G-3845)***
Industrial Thermoset Plas Inc....440 975-0411
7675 Jenther Dr Mentor (44060) ***(G-13471)***
Industrial Timber & Land Co....740 596-5294
35748 State Route 93 Hamden (45634) ***(G-10523)***
Industrial Timber & Lumber Co, Cleveland *Also called Itl Corp* ***(G-5478)***
Industrial Timber & Lumber Co....800 829-9663
23925 Commerce Park Beachwood (44122) ***(G-1241)***
Industrial Timber and Lbr LLC, Beachwood *Also called Itl LLC* ***(G-1242)***
Industrial WD Prts Fabrication, Archbold *Also called Liechty Specialties Inc* ***(G-655)***
Industrial Wire Co Inc (PA)....216 781-2230
2805 Superior Ave E Cleveland (44114) ***(G-5455)***
Industrial Wire Co Inc....330 723-7471
6867 Wooster Pike Medina (44256) ***(G-13278)***
Industrial Wire Rope Sup Inc (PA)....513 941-2443
7390 Harrison Ave Cincinnati (45247) ***(G-3846)***
Industry Products Co (PA)....937 778-0585
500 W Statler Rd Piqua (45356) ***(G-16130)***
Indy Eqp Independence Recycl....216 524-0999
6220 E Schaaf Rd Independence (44131) ***(G-11136)***
Indy Resolutions Ltd....513 475-6625
1776 Mentor Ave Ste 130 Cincinnati (45212) ***(G-3847)***

ALPHABETIC SECTION

Ineos LLC (PA) 419 226-1200
1900 Fort Amanda Rd Lima (45804) *(G-11877)*
Ineos ABS (usa) LLC (HQ) 513 467-2400
356 Three Rivers Pkwy Addyston (45001) *(G-11)*
Ineos Nitriles USA LLC 419 226-1200
1900 Fort Amanda Rd Lima (45804) *(G-11878)*
Infant Food Project Inc 614 239-5763
638 S Hampton Rd Columbus (43213) *(G-7025)*
Infinit Nutrition LLC 513 791-3500
11240 Cornell Park Dr # 110 Blue Ash (45242) *(G-1793)*
Infinity Trichology Center 937 281-0555
5250 Far Hills Ave Kettering (45429) *(G-11433)*
Infinium Wall Systems Inc 440 572-5000
22555 Ascoa Ct Strongsville (44149) *(G-17754)*
Inflatable Images, Brunswick Also called Scherba Industries Inc *(G-2238)*
Info-Graphics Inc 440 498-1640
5960 Liberty Rd Solon (44139) *(G-17169)*
Infoaccessnet LLC 216 328-0100
8801 E Pleasant Valley Rd Cleveland (44131) *(G-5456)*
Informa Media Inc 216 696-7000
1300 E 9th St Cleveland (44114) *(G-5457)*
Infosight Corporation 740 642-3600
20700 Us Highway 23 Chillicothe (45601) *(G-3194)*
Infrared Imaging Systems Inc 614 989-1148
22718 Holycross Epps Rd Marysville (43040) *(G-12795)*
Ingersoll Rand, Holland Also called Trane Company *(G-10963)*
Ingersoll-Rand Co 704 655-4000
8799 Peach Orchard Rd Hillsboro (45133) *(G-10881)*
Ingersoll-Rand Company 419 633-6800
209 N Main St Bryan (43506) *(G-2291)*
Ingle-Barr Inc (PA) 740 702-6117
20 Plyleys Ln Chillicothe (45601) *(G-3195)*
Ingles Logging 740 379-2909
19094 State Route 141 Patriot (45658) *(G-15851)*
Ingles Logging 740 379-2760
17748 State Route 141 Patriot (45658) *(G-15852)*
Ingram Products Inc 904 778-1010
1376 Township Road 743 Ashland (44805) *(G-714)*
Ingredia Inc 419 738-4060
625 Commerce Rd Wapakoneta (45895) *(G-19334)*
Ingredient Innovations Intl Co 330 262-4440
146 S Bever St Wooster (44691) *(G-20606)*
Ingredient Masters Inc 513 231-7432
377 E Main St Batavia (45103) *(G-1154)*
Ingredient Technology Division, Elyria Also called Lanxess Solutions US Inc *(G-9284)*
Inhance Technologies LLC 614 846-6400
6575 Huntley Rd Ste D Columbus (43229) *(G-7026)*
Initial Designs Inc 419 475-3900
2453 Tremainsville Rd # 2 Toledo (43613) *(G-18347)*
Initially Yours 216 228-4478
15028 Madison Ave Lakewood (44107) *(G-11521)*
Injection Alloys Incorporated 513 422-8819
1700 Made Industrial Dr Middletown (45044) *(G-13914)*
Injection Molding Specialist 440 639-7896
251 W Prospect St Painesville (44077) *(G-15748)*
Ink Again 419 232-4465
115 N Washington St Van Wert (45891) *(G-19095)*
Ink Factory Inc 330 799-0888
2750 Salt Springs Rd Youngstown (44509) *(G-20940)*
Ink Inc 330 875-4789
200 S Bauman Ct Louisville (44641) *(G-12157)*
Ink It Press 440 967-9062
13500 W Lake Rd Vermilion (44089) *(G-19162)*
Ink Production Services Inc 513 733-9338
9648 Wayne Ave Cincinnati (45215) *(G-3848)*
Ink Technology Corporation (PA) 216 486-6720
18320 Lanken Ave Cleveland (44119) *(G-5458)*
Ink Well, Grove City Also called Deerfield Ventures Inc *(G-10425)*
Ink Well, Akron Also called Bansal Enterprises Inc *(G-79)*
Ink Well, Bedford Heights Also called Cwh Graphics LLC *(G-1468)*
Ink Well 614 861-7113
969 Claycraft Rd Gahanna (43230) *(G-10084)*
Inkwell, The, Westerville Also called Technoprint Inc *(G-20077)*
Inland Hardwood Corporation 740 373-7187
25 Sheets Run Rd Marietta (45750) *(G-12635)*
Inland Manufacturing LLC 937 835-0220
6785 W 3rd St Dayton (45417) *(G-8264)*
Inland Products Inc (PA) 614 443-3425
599 Frank Rd Columbus (43223) *(G-7027)*
Inland Wood Products, Marietta Also called Inland Hardwood Corporation *(G-12635)*
Inline Label Company 513 217-5662
4720 Emerald Way Middletown (45044) *(G-13915)*
Inn Maid Products, Westerville Also called Tmarzetti Company *(G-20029)*
Innago LLC 330 554-3101
77 Milford Dr Hudson (44236) *(G-11055)*
Inner City Abrasives LLC 216 391-4402
7209 Saint Clair Ave 101b Cleveland (44103) *(G-5459)*
Inner Fire Sports LLC 719 244-6622
2558 Madison Rd Apt 18 Cincinnati (45208) *(G-3849)*
Inner Products Sales Inc 216 581-4141
5221 Northfield Rd A Bedford (44146) *(G-1416)*
Innerapps LLC 419 467-3110
28350 Kensington Ln # 200 Perrysburg (43551) *(G-15967)*
Innerwood & Company 513 677-2229
688 Elizabeth Ln Loveland (45140) *(G-12199)*
Inno-Pak Holding Inc 740 363-0090
1932 Pittsburgh Dr Delaware (43015) *(G-8695)*
Innocomp 440 248-5104
33195 Wagon Wheel Dr Solon (44139) *(G-17170)*
Innocor Foam Tech - Acp Inc 419 647-4172
200 E North St Spencerville (45887) *(G-17309)*
Innmark Communications LLC 513 285-1040
375 Northpointe Dr Fairfield (45014) *(G-9510)*
Innmark Communications LLC 937 454-5555
3233 S Tech Blvd Miamisburg (45342) *(G-13679)*
Innovar Systems Limited 330 538-3942
12155 Commissioner Dr North Jackson (44451) *(G-15147)*
Innovated Health LLC 330 858-0651
2241 Front St Fl 1 Cuyahoga Falls (44221) *(G-7881)*
Innovation Exhibits Inc 330 726-1324
85 Karago Ave Ste 1&2 Youngstown (44512) *(G-20941)*
Innovation Sales LLC 330 239-0400
803 E Washington St # 210 Medina (44256) *(G-13279)*
Innovations In Plastic Inc 216 541-6060
1643 Eddy Rd Cleveland (44112) *(G-5460)*
Innovative Apps Ltd 330 687-2888
8000 Walton Pkwy Ste 208 New Albany (43054) *(G-14626)*
Innovative Assembly Svcs LLC 419 399-3886
400 W Wall St Paulding (45879) *(G-15861)*
Innovative Bus Cmpt Solutions 937 832-3969
303 Shady Tree Ct Englewood (45315) *(G-9363)*
Innovative Ceramic Corp 330 385-6515
432 Walnut St East Liverpool (43920) *(G-9059)*
Innovative Computer Forms, Columbus Also called Bizzy Bee Printing Inc *(G-6672)*
Innovative Control Systems 513 894-3712
5870 Fairham Rd Fairfield Township (45011) *(G-9582)*
Innovative Controls Corp 419 691-6684
1354 E Broadway St Toledo (43605) *(G-18348)*
Innovative Creations, Dayton Also called Glen D Lala *(G-8224)*
Innovative Hdlg & Metalfab LLC 419 882-7480
7755 Sylvania Ave Sylvania (43560) *(G-17945)*
Innovative Industries, Macedonia Also called James Thomas Shiveley *(G-12306)*
Innovative Integrations Inc 216 533-5353
7877 Girdle Rd Mesopotamia (44439) *(G-13633)*
Innovative Lab Services LLC 614 554-6446
7123 National Rd Sw Rear Pataskala (43062) *(G-15832)*
Innovative Plastic Machinery 330 478-1825
5252 Southway St Sw Canton (44706) *(G-2708)*
Innovative Plastic Molders LLC 937 898-3775
7438 Webster St Dayton (45414) *(G-8265)*
Innovative Recycling Systems 440 498-9200
31655 Arthur Rd Solon (44139) *(G-17171)*
Innovative Retail Displays Inc 937 237-7708
2127 Troy St Dayton (45404) *(G-8266)*
Innovative Stiching, North Baltimore Also called Truck Stop Embroidery *(G-15049)*
Innovative Tool & Die Inc 419 599-0492
1700 Industrial Dr Napoleon (43545) *(G-14545)*
Innovative Vend Solutions LLC 866 931-9413
2048 S Alex Rd Dayton (45449) *(G-8267)*
Innovative Weld Solutions Ltd 937 545-7695
4030 N Emerald Ct Beavercreek (45430) *(G-1356)*
Innovative Wldg & Design LLC 330 581-1316
24946 Hartley Rd Alliance (44601) *(G-478)*
Innovative Woodworking Inc 513 531-1940
1901 Ross Ave Cincinnati (45212) *(G-3850)*
Innovtive Cnfction Sltions LLC 440 835-8001
28025 Ranney Pkwy Westlake (44145) *(G-20126)*
Innovtive Crtive Solutions LLC 614 491-9638
5835 Green Pointe Dr S B Groveport (43125) *(G-10494)*
Inovent Engineering Inc 330 468-0005
8877 Freeway Dr Macedonia (44056) *(G-12303)*
Inpaco Corporation 614 888-9288
6950 Wrthington Galena Rd Worthington (43085) *(G-20691)*
Inpower LLC 740 548-0965
8311 Green Meadows Dr N Lewis Center (43035) *(G-11763)*
Ins Robotics Inc 888 293-5325
3600 Parkway Ln Hilliard (43026) *(G-10830)*
Inservco Inc (HQ) 847 855-9600
110 Commerce Dr Lagrange (44050) *(G-11483)*
Inside Outfitters, Lewis Center Also called Lumenomics Inc *(G-11766)*
Insightfuel LLC 330 998-7380
1333 Highland Rd E Ste P Macedonia (44056) *(G-12304)*
Insignia Signs Inc 937 866-2341
300 Gargrave Rd Dayton (45449) *(G-8268)*
Inskeep Brothers Inc 614 898-6620
3193 E Dblin Granville Rd Columbus (43231) *(G-7028)*
Inskeep Brothers Printers, Columbus Also called Inskeep Brothers Inc *(G-7028)*
Insley Printing Inc 614 885-5973
666 High St Ste 400 Worthington (43085) *(G-20692)*

ALPHABETIC SECTION

Insource Tech Inc 419 399-3600
  12124 Road 111 Paulding (45879) *(G-15862)*
Insource Technologies Inc 419 399-3600
  12124 Road 111 Paulding (45879) *(G-15863)*
Insta Plak Inc (PA) 419 537-1555
  5025 Dorr St Toledo (43615) *(G-18349)*
Insta-Gro Manufacturing Inc 419 845-3046
  8217 Linn Hipsher Rd Caledonia (43314) *(G-2417)*
Insta-Plak, Toledo Also called Insta Plak Inc *(G-18349)*
Insta-Print Inc 216 741-6500
  3101 Brookpark Rd Cleveland (44134) *(G-5461)*
Instacopy, Salem Also called Sanscan Inc *(G-16773)*
Installed Building Pdts LLC 614 308-9900
  1320 Mckinley Ave Ste A Columbus (43222) *(G-7029)*
Instant Impressions Inc 614 538-9844
  4499 Kenny Rd Columbus (43220) *(G-7030)*
Instant Replay 937 592-0534
  334 E Columbus Ave Bellefontaine (43311) *(G-1520)*
Instant Whip Detroit, Columbus Also called Instantwhip Detroit Inc *(G-7033)*
Instantorder, Celina Also called Tech Solutions LLC *(G-2986)*
Instantwhip Connecticut Inc (PA) 614 488-2536
  2200 Cardigan Ave Columbus (43215) *(G-7031)*
Instantwhip Detroit Inc (PA) 614 488-2536
  2200 Cardigan Ave Columbus (43215) *(G-7032)*
Instantwhip Detroit Inc 800 544-9447
  2200 Cardigan Ave Columbus (43215) *(G-7033)*
Instantwhip Foods Inc (PA) 614 488-2536
  2200 Cardigan Ave Columbus (43215) *(G-7034)*
Instantwhip National Office, Columbus Also called Dallas Instantwhip Inc *(G-6847)*
Instantwhip of Buffalo Inc (HQ) 614 488-2536
  2200 Cardigan Ave Columbus (43215) *(G-7035)*
Instantwhip of Pennsylvania, Columbus Also called Instantwhip Products Co PA *(G-7036)*
Instantwhip Products Co PA (HQ) 614 488-2536
  2200 Cardigan Ave Columbus (43215) *(G-7036)*
Instantwhip-Chicago Inc (PA) 614 488-2536
  2200 Cardigan Ave Columbus (43215) *(G-7037)*
Instantwhip-Columbus Inc (HQ) 614 871-9447
  3855 Marlane Dr Grove City (43123) *(G-10435)*
Instantwhip-Dayton Inc (PA) 937 235-5930
  5820 Executive Blvd Dayton (45424) *(G-8269)*
Instantwhip-Dayton Inc 937 435-4371
  967 Senate Dr Dayton (45459) *(G-8270)*
Instantwhip-Syracuse Inc (PA) 614 488-2536
  2200 Cardigan Ave Columbus (43215) *(G-7038)*
Instaride Cle LLC 216 801-4542
  15026 Madison Ave Lakewood (44107) *(G-11522)*
Institute Mthmtical Statistics 216 295-2340
  3163 Somerset Dr Shaker Heights (44122) *(G-16932)*
Instrmntation Ctrl Systems Inc 513 662-2600
  11355 Sebring Dr Cincinnati (45240) *(G-3851)*
Instruction & Design Concepts 937 439-2698
  441 Maple Springs Dr Dayton (45458) *(G-8271)*
Instrumatics, Cleveland Also called Cleveland Circuits Corp *(G-4950)*
Instrument & Valve Services Co 513 942-1118
  4400 Muhlhauser Rd West Chester (45011) *(G-19722)*
Instrumentors Inc 440 238-3430
  22077 Drake Rd Strongsville (44149) *(G-17755)*
Insulpro Inc 614 262-3768
  4650 Indianola Ave Columbus (43214) *(G-7039)*
Intec LLC 614 633-7430
  351 S 30th St Ste E Heath (43056) *(G-10721)*
Integra Enclosures Inc (PA) 440 269-4966
  7750 Pyler Blvd Willoughby (44094) *(G-20343)*
Integra Enclosures Limited 440 269-4966
  8989 Tyler Blvd Mentor (44060) *(G-13472)*
Integral Design Inc 216 524-0555
  7670 Hub Pkwy Cleveland (44125) *(G-5462)*
Integrated Aircraft Systems 330 686-2982
  1337 Commerce Dr Ste 9 Stow (44224) *(G-17596)*
Integrated Chem Concepts Inc 440 838-5666
  6650 W Snowville Rd Ste F Brecksville (44141) *(G-2042)*
Integrated Development & Mfg (PA) 440 247-5100
  510 Washington St Chagrin Falls (44022) *(G-3021)*
Integrated Development & Mfg 440 543-2423
  8401 Washington St Chagrin Falls (44023) *(G-3053)*
Integrated Med Solutions Inc 440 269-6984
  7124 Industrial Park Blvd Mentor (44060) *(G-13473)*
Integrated Power Services LLC 216 433-7808
  5325 W 130th St Cleveland (44130) *(G-5463)*
Integrated Power Services LLC 513 863-8816
  2175a Schlichter Dr Hamilton (45015) *(G-10572)*
Integrated Sensors LLC 419 536-3212
  2403 Evergreen Rd Ottawa Hills (43606) *(G-15673)*
Integrated Systems Professiona 614 875-0104
  4110 Demorest Rd Grove City (43123) *(G-10436)*
Integrity Group Consulting Inc 614 759-9148
  6432 E Main St Ste 201 Reynoldsburg (43068) *(G-16444)*
Integrity Industrial Eqp Inc 937 238-9275
  7401 Bridgewater Rd Huber Heights (45424) *(G-11021)*
Integrity Manufacturing Corp 937 233-6792
  3723 Inpark Dr Dayton (45414) *(G-8272)*
Integrity Print Solutions Inc 330 818-0161
  567 E Turkeyfoot Lake Rd Akron (44319) *(G-216)*
Intek Inc 614 895-0301
  751 Intek Way Westerville (43082) *(G-19999)*
Intel Corporation 513 860-9686
  5785 Woodbridge Ln West Chester (45069) *(G-19723)*
Intel Industries LLC 614 551-5702
  773 Laverty Ln Cincinnati (45230) *(G-3852)*
Intelitool Manufacturing Svcs 440 953-1071
  36335 Reading Ave Ste 4 Willoughby (44094) *(G-20344)*
Intelligent Mobile Support Inc 440 600-7343
  31320 Solon Rd Ste 17 Solon (44139) *(G-17172)*
Intelligent Signal Tech 614 530-4784
  6318 Dustywind Ln Loveland (45140) *(G-12200)*
Intelligrated Inc (HQ) 866 936-7300
  7901 Innovation Way Mason (45040) *(G-12891)*
Intelligrated Inc 513 874-0788
  10045 International Blvd West Chester (45246) *(G-19868)*
Intelligrated Headquarters LLC 866 936-7300
  7901 Innovation Way Mason (45040) *(G-12892)*
Intelligrated Products LLC 740 490-0300
  475 E High St London (43140) *(G-12062)*
Intelligrated Sub Holdings Inc (PA) 513 701-7300
  7901 Innovation Way Mason (45040) *(G-12893)*
Intelligrated Systems Inc (HQ) 866 936-7300
  7901 Innovation Way Mason (45040) *(G-12894)*
Intelligrated Systems LLC 513 701-7300
  7901 Innovation Way Mason (45040) *(G-12895)*
Intelligrated Systems Ohio LLC (HQ) 513 701-7300
  7901 Innovation Way Mason (45040) *(G-12896)*
Intelligrated Systems Ohio LLC 513 682-6600
  10045 International Blvd West Chester (45246) *(G-19869)*
Intellinetics Inc (PA) 614 388-8909
  2190 Dividend Dr Columbus (43228) *(G-7040)*
Intellirod Spine Inc 234 678-8965
  554 White Pond Dr Ste F Akron (44320) *(G-217)*
Intellitronix Corporation 440 359-7200
  34099 Melinz Pkwy Unit E Eastlake (44095) *(G-9115)*
Intelliworks Ht 419 660-9050
  61 Saint Marys St Norwalk (44857) *(G-15401)*
Inter American Products Inc (HQ) 800 645-2233
  1240 State Ave Cincinnati (45204) *(G-3853)*
Inter Cab Corporation 216 351-0770
  8551 Brookpark Rd Cleveland (44129) *(G-5464)*
Inter Tel, West Chester Also called Mitel (delaware) Inc *(G-19745)*
Inter Valley Communication, Greenfield Also called Hisey Bells *(G-10352)*
Inter-Ion Inc 330 928-9655
  157 Ascot Pkwy Cuyahoga Falls (44223) *(G-7882)*
Inter-Power Corporation 330 652-4494
  1713 N Main St Niles (44446) *(G-15014)*
Interactive Engineering Corp 330 239-6888
  884 Medina Rd Medina (44256) *(G-13280)*
Interactive Fincl Solutions 419 335-1280
  122 S Fulton St Wauseon (43567) *(G-19521)*
Intercontinental Chemical Corp (PA) 513 541-7100
  4660 Spring Grove Ave Cincinnati (45232) *(G-3854)*
Interden Industries Inc 419 368-9011
  2377 County Road 175 Lakeville (44638) *(G-11506)*
Interface Logic Systems Inc 614 236-8388
  3311 E Livingston Ave Columbus (43227) *(G-7041)*
Interfast Inc 216 581-3000
  4444 Lee Rd Cleveland (44128) *(G-5465)*
Intergroup International Ltd 216 965-0257
  1653 Merriman Rd Ste 211 Akron (44313) *(G-218)*
Interior Dnnage Spcialites Inc 614 291-0900
  470 E Starr Ave Columbus (43201) *(G-7042)*
Interior Graphic Systems LLC 330 244-0100
  4550 Aultman Rd Canton (44720) *(G-2709)*
Interior Products Co Inc 216 641-1919
  3615 Superior Ave E 3104f Cleveland (44114) *(G-5466)*
Interlake Industries Inc (PA) 440 942-0800
  4732 E 355th St Willoughby (44094) *(G-20345)*
Interlake Stamping Ohio Inc 440 942-0800
  4732 E 355th St Willoughby (44094) *(G-20346)*
Interlube Corporation 513 531-1777
  4646 Baker St Cincinnati (45212) *(G-3855)*
Intermec Inc 513 874-5882
  9290 Le Saint Dr West Chester (45014) *(G-19724)*
Intermec Media Products, West Chester Also called Intermec Ultra Print Inc *(G-19727)*
Intermec Technologies Corp 513 874-5882
  9290 Le Saint Dr West Chester (45014) *(G-19725)*
Intermec Technologies Corp 513 874-5882
  9290 Le Saint Dr West Chester (45014) *(G-19726)*
Intermec Ultra Print Inc 513 874-5882
  9290 Le Saint Dr West Chester (45014) *(G-19727)*
International Advg Concepts 440 331-4733
  4285 W 217th St Cleveland (44126) *(G-5467)*

International Automotive 330 279-6557
8281 County Road 245 Holmesville (44633) *(G-10982)*
International Automotive Compo 419 335-1000
555 W Linfoot St Wauseon (43567) *(G-19522)*
International Automotive Compo 419 433-5653
1608 Sawmill Pkwy Huron (44839) *(G-11099)*
International Beverage Works 614 798-5398
5636 Moorgate Dr Columbus (43235) *(G-7043)*
International Brake Inds Inc (HQ) 419 227-4421
1840 Mccullough St Lima (45801) *(G-11879)*
International Brand Services 513 376-8209
3397 Erie Ave Apt 215 Cincinnati (45208) *(G-3856)*
International Bus Mchs Corp 513 826-1001
1 Procter And Gamble Plz Cincinnati (45202) *(G-3857)*
International Cntr Artfcial or 440 358-1102
10 W Erie St Ste 200 Painesville (44077) *(G-15749)*
International Cont Systems LLC 216 481-8219
16601 Saint Clair Ave Cleveland (44110) *(G-5468)*
International Dies Co Inc 330 744-7951
3400 Newton Falls Rd Diamond (44412) *(G-8798)*
International Financial Svcs, Cincinnati *Also called International Supply Corp (G-3858)*
International Finishing LLC 937 293-3340
2223 S Dixie Dr Dayton (45409) *(G-8273)*
International Hydraulics Inc 440 951-7186
7700 Saint Clair Ave Mentor (44060) *(G-13474)*
International Installations (PA) 330 848-4800
833 Wooster Rd N Barberton (44203) *(G-1077)*
International Laminating Corp 937 254-8181
1712 Springfield St Ste 2 Dayton (45403) *(G-8274)*
International Machining Inc 330 225-1963
2885 Nationwide Pkwy Brunswick (44212) *(G-2216)*
International Metal Supply LLC 330 764-1004
3995 Medina Rd Ste 200 Medina (44256) *(G-13281)*
International Mill Service, Marion *Also called Tms International Corporation (G-12741)*
International Multifoods Corp (HQ) 330 682-3000
1 Strawberry Ln Orrville (44667) *(G-15595)*
International Multifoods Corp 440 323-5100
6325 Gateway Blvd S Elyria (44035) *(G-9268)*
International Noodle Company 614 888-0665
341 Enterprise Dr Lewis Center (43035) *(G-11764)*
International Paper, Kenton *Also called Graphic Packaging Intl LLC (G-11407)*
International Paper Company 330 264-1322
689 Palmer St Wooster (44691) *(G-20607)*
International Paper Company 937 456-4131
900 State Route 35 W Eaton (45320) *(G-9154)*
International Paper Company 740 397-5215
8800 Granville Rd Mount Vernon (43050) *(G-14483)*
International Paper Company 740 383-4061
1600 Cascade Dr Marion (43302) *(G-12713)*
International Paper Company 937 578-7718
13307 Industrial Pkwy Marysville (43040) *(G-12796)*
International Paper Company 800 473-0830
912 Nelbar St Middletown (45042) *(G-13916)*
International Paper Company 877 447-2737
5806 Jeb Stuart Dr Milford (45150) *(G-14018)*
International Paper Company 440 428-5116
3200 County Line Rd Madison (44057) *(G-12351)*
International Paper Company 740 363-9882
865 Pittsburgh Dr Delaware (43015) *(G-8696)*
International Paper Company 740 439-3527
60700 Hope Ave Byesville (43723) *(G-2387)*
International Paper Company 740 369-7691
875 Pittsburgh Dr Delaware (43015) *(G-8697)*
International Paper Company 740 522-3123
1851 Tamarack Rd Newark (43055) *(G-14888)*
International Paper Company 800 422-4657
808 Fontaine St Kenton (43326) *(G-11410)*
International Paper Company 330 626-7300
700 Mondial Pkwy Streetsboro (44241) *(G-17678)*
International Paper Company 513 248-6000
6283 Tri Ridge Blvd Loveland (45140) *(G-12201)*
International Precision 330 342-0407
1570 Terex Rd Hudson (44236) *(G-11056)*
International Products 614 334-1500
2701 Charter St Ste A Columbus (43228) *(G-7044)*
International Products (HQ) 614 850-3000
4119 Leap Rd Hilliard (43026) *(G-10831)*
International Sources Inc 440 735-9890
380 Golden Oak Pkwy Bedford (44146) *(G-1417)*
International Steel Group 330 841-2800
2234 Main Street Ext Sw Warren (44481) *(G-19411)*
International Supply Corp 513 793-0393
3284 E Sharon Rd Cincinnati (45241) *(G-3858)*
International Technical 330 505-1218
852 Ann Ave Niles (44446) *(G-15015)*
International Trade Group Inc 614 486-4634
2920 North Star Rd Columbus (43221) *(G-7045)*
Interntnal Cnvrter Cldwell Inc 740 732-5665
17153 Industrial Hwy Caldwell (43724) *(G-2407)*
Interntnal Pckg Pallets Crates, Sidney *Also called Wappoo Wood Products Inc (G-17084)*
Interntnal Plstic Cmpnents Inc 330 744-0625
75 Mccartney Rd Campbell (44405) *(G-2468)*
Interntnal Tchncal Catings Inc 614 449-6669
845 E Markison Ave Columbus (43207) *(G-7046)*
Interpak Inc 440 974-8999
7278 Justin Way Mentor (44060) *(G-13475)*
Interplex Medical LLC 513 248-5120
25 Whitney Dr Ste 114 Milford (45150) *(G-14019)*
Interscope Manufacturing Inc 513 423-8866
2901 Carmody Blvd Middletown (45042) *(G-13917)*
Intersoft Group Inc 216 765-7351
26380 Curtiss Wright Pkwy # 303 Cleveland (44143) *(G-5469)*
Interstate Batteries Inc 740 968-2211
44925 Lafferty Rd Saint Clairsville (43950) *(G-16634)*
Interstate Battery System Amer, Saint Clairsville *Also called Interstate Batteries Inc (G-16634)*
Interstate Contractors LLC 513 372-5393
762 Reading Rd G Mason (45040) *(G-12897)*
Interstate Diesel Service Inc (PA) 216 881-0015
5300 Lakeside Ave E Cleveland (44114) *(G-5470)*
Interstate Gas Supply Inc (PA) 614 659-5000
6100 Emerald Pkwy Dublin (43016) *(G-8930)*
Interstate Sign Products Inc 419 683-1962
432 E Main St Crestline (44827) *(G-7795)*
Interstate Tool Corporation 216 671-1077
4538 W 130th St Cleveland (44135) *(G-5471)*
Interstate Truckway Inc 614 771-1220
5440 Renner Rd Columbus (43228) *(G-7047)*
Intertape Polymr Woven USA Inc 704 279-3011
1800 E Pleasant St Springfield (45505) *(G-17425)*
Intertec Corporation 419 537-9711
3400 Executive Pkwy Toledo (43606) *(G-18350)*
Intertek Machining & Wldg Inc 440 323-3325
6805 W River Rd S Elyria (44035) *(G-9269)*
Intertex World Resources Inc 770 214-5551
4518 Fulton Dr Nw Ste 101 Canton (44718) *(G-2710)*
Interweave Press LLC 513 531-2690
10151 Carver Rd Ste 200 Blue Ash (45242) *(G-1794)*
Inteva Products LLC 937 280-8500
707 Crossroads Ct Vandalia (45377) *(G-19129)*
Intier Sting Systems-Lordstown, Warren *Also called Magna Seating America Inc (G-19420)*
Intigral Inc (PA) 440 439-0980
7850 Northfield Rd Walton Hills (44146) *(G-19311)*
Intigral Inc 440 439-0980
45 Karago Ave Youngstown (44512) *(G-20942)*
Into Great Brands Inc 888 771-5656
1010 Taylor Station Rd A Gahanna (43230) *(G-10085)*
Intrusion-Prepakt Inc (PA) 440 238-6950
15910 Pearl Rd Ste 101 Cleveland (44136) *(G-5472)*
Invacare Canadian Holdings Inc 440 329-6000
1 Invacare Way Elyria (44035) *(G-9270)*
Invacare Canadian Holdings LLC 440 329-6000
1 Invacare Way Elyria (44035) *(G-9271)*
Invacare Corporation (PA) 440 329-6000
1 Invacare Way Elyria (44035) *(G-9272)*
Invacare Corporation 800 333-6900
1320 Taylor St Elyria (44035) *(G-9273)*
Invacare Corporation 440 329-6000
1200 Taylor St Elyria (44035) *(G-9274)*
Invacare Corporation 440 329-6000
38683 Taylor Pkwy North Ridgeville (44035) *(G-15231)*
Invacare Corporation (tw) 440 329-6000
39400 Taylor Pkwy North Ridgeville (44035) *(G-15232)*
Invacare Hme, North Ridgeville *Also called Invacare Corporation (G-15231)*
Invacare Holdings LLC 440 329-6000
1 Invacare Way Elyria (44035) *(G-9275)*
Invacare Holdings Corporation 440 329-6000
1 Invacare Way Elyria (44035) *(G-9276)*
Invacare International Corp (HQ) 440 329-6000
1 Invacare Way Elyria (44035) *(G-9277)*
Invacare It & Financial Svcs, Elyria *Also called Invacare Corporation (G-9273)*
Invacare Rentals, Elyria *Also called Healthtech Products (G-9265)*
Invacare Respiratory Corp 440 329-6000
899 Cleveland St Elyria (44035) *(G-9278)*
Inventive Extrusions Corp 330 874-3000
10882 Fort Laurens Rd Nw Bolivar (44612) *(G-1917)*
Inventus Power (ohio) Inc (HQ) 614 351-2191
5115 Prkcnter Ave Ste 275 Dublin (43017) *(G-8931)*
Investment Systems Company 440 247-2865
37840 Jackson Rd Chagrin Falls (44022) *(G-3022)*
Invisible Chef, The, Canton *Also called Jaz Foods Inc (G-2717)*
Invisible Repair Products Inc 330 798-0441
1021 Evans Ave Akron (44305) *(G-219)*
Invotec Engineering Inc (PA) 937 886-3232
10909 Industry Ln Miamisburg (45342) *(G-13680)*
Invue Security Products Inc 330 456-7776
1510 4th St Se Canton (44707) *(G-2711)*
INX International Ink Co 707 693-2990
350 Homan Rd Lebanon (45036) *(G-11663)*

INX International Ink Co 513 282-2920
  350 Homan Rd Lebanon (45036) (G-11664)
INX International Ink Co 440 239-1766
  18001 Englewood Dr Unit P Cleveland (44130) (G-5473)
Ion Vacuum Technologies, Cleveland Also called Ivac Technologies Corp (G-5479)
Ionbond LLC 216 831-0880
  24700 Highpoint Rd Cleveland (44122) (G-5474)
Ioppolo Concrete Corporation 440 439-6606
  10 Industry Dr Bedford (44146) (G-1418)
Iosil Energy Corporation 614 295-8680
  5700 Green Pointe Dr N Groveport (43125) (G-10495)
Iotech, Cleveland Also called Measurement Computing Corp (G-5650)
IPA Ltd 614 523-3974
  199 Mckenna Creek Dr Columbus (43230) (G-7048)
Ipex USA LLC 513 942-9910
  4507 Lesaint Ct Fairfield (45014) (G-9511)
Ipm Inc 419 248-8000
  1 Owens Corning Pkwy Toledo (43659) (G-18351)
Ips, Wadsworth Also called Parker-Hannifin Corporation (G-19261)
Ips Treatments Inc 419 241-5955
  3254 Hill Ave Toledo (43607) (G-18352)
Ipsco Tubulars Inc 330 448-6772
  6880 Parkway Dr Brookfield (44403) (G-2108)
Ipsg, Columbus Also called International Products (G-7044)
Ipsg / Micro Center, Hilliard Also called International Products (G-10831)
Iptc, Troy Also called Ishmael Precision Tool Corp (G-18677)
Irg Operating LLC 440 963-4008
  850 W River Rd Vermilion (44089) (G-19163)
Irish Electric Motor Service, Saint Marys Also called Allan A Irish (G-16675)
Irock Crushers LLC 866 240-0201
  5531 Canal Rd Cleveland (44125) (G-5475)
Iron Bean Inc 518 641-9917
  2269 Ragan Woods Dr Toledo (43614) (G-18353)
Iron City Wood Products Inc 330 755-2772
  900 Albert St Youngstown (44505) (G-20943)
Iron Gate Industries LLC 330 264-0626
  1435 S Honeytown Rd Wooster (44691) (G-20608)
Iron Horse Engineering, Parkman Also called Montville Plastics & Rbr LLC (G-15812)
Iron Vault Distillery LLC 419 747-7560
  3880 Horizon Dr Ontario (44903) (G-15542)
Iron Wind Metals Co LLC 513 870-0606
  10488 Chester Rd Cincinnati (45215) (G-3859)
Ironfab LLC 614 443-3900
  1771 Progress Ave Columbus (43207) (G-7049)
Ironhead Fabg & Contg Inc 419 690-0000
  2245 Front St Toledo (43605) (G-18354)
Ironhouse Pallets 330 635-5218
  5212 Mills Indus Pkwy North Ridgeville (44039) (G-15233)
Ironics Inc 330 652-0583
  750 S Main St Niles (44446) (G-15016)
Ironman Metalworks LLC 614 907-6629
  250 Lowery Ct Ste A Groveport (43125) (G-10496)
Ironrock Capital Incorporated 330 484-4887
  1201 Millerton St Se Canton (44707) (G-2712)
Ironton Publications Inc 740 532-1441
  2903 S 5th St Ironton (45638) (G-11166)
Ironton Tribune The, Ironton Also called Ironton Publications Inc (G-11166)
Iroquois Pallet 513 677-0048
  9417 Bainwoods Dr Cincinnati (45249) (G-3860)
Irvin Oslin Inc 216 361-7555
  2800 E 55th St Frnt Cleveland (44104) (G-5476)
Irvine Wood Recovery Inc 513 831-0060
  110 Glendale Milford Rd Miamiville (45147) (G-13752)
Irving Materials Inc 513 523-7127
  6601 Ringwood Rd Oxford (45056) (G-15695)
Irving Materials Inc 513 844-8444
  600 Augspurger Rd Hamilton (45011) (G-10573)
Irwin Engraving & Printing Co 216 391-7300
  5318 Saint Clair Ave # 1 Cleveland (44103) (G-5477)
Isaacs Jr Floyd Thomas 513 899-2342
  3480 E Us Highway 22 & 3 Morrow (45152) (G-14412)
Isaiah Industries Inc (PA) 937 773-9840
  8510 Industry Park Dr Piqua (45356) (G-16131)
Isco Inc 614 792-2206
  6360 Fiesta Dr Columbus (43235) (G-7050)
Ishikawa Gasket America Inc (HQ) 419 353-7300
  828 Van Camp Rd Bowling Green (43402) (G-1975)
Ishikawa Gasket America Inc 419 353-7300
  828 Van Camp Rd Bowling Green (43402) (G-1976)
Ishmael Precision Tool Corp 937 335-8070
  55 Industry Ct Troy (45373) (G-18677)
Ishos Bros Fuel Ventures Inc 586 634-0187
  1289 Conant St Maumee (43537) (G-13119)
Ishos Bros Fuel Ventures Inc 419 913-5718
  2446 W Alexis Rd Toledo (43613) (G-18355)
ISK Americas Incorporated (HQ) 440 357-4600
  7474 Auburn Rd Painesville (44077) (G-15750)
Isky North America Inc 937 823-9595
  21 Kenbrook Dr Vandalia (45377) (G-19130)

Island Delights Inc 866 887-4100
  240 W Greenwich Rd Seville (44273) (G-16917)
ISO Technologies Inc 740 344-9554
  200 Milliken Dr Hebron (43025) (G-10749)
ISO Technologies Inc 740 928-0084
  1870 James Pkwy Heath (43056) (G-10722)
Isochem Incorporated 614 775-9328
  7721 Sutton Pl New Albany (43054) (G-14627)
Isofoton North America Inc 419 591-4330
  800 Independence Dr Napoleon (43545) (G-14546)
Isomedix Inc 440 354-2600
  5960 Heisley Rd Mentor (44060) (G-13476)
Isostatic Pressing Svcs LLC 614 370-2140
  1205 S Columbus Arprt Rd Columbus (43207) (G-7051)
Isotopx Inc 508 337-8467
  12 Pinewood Ln Hudson (44236) (G-11057)
Isp, Grove City Also called Integrated Systems Professiona (G-10436)
Isp Chemicals LLC 614 876-3637
  1979 Atlas St Columbus (43228) (G-7052)
Isp Lima LLC 419 998-8700
  12220 S Metcalf St Lima (45804) (G-11880)
Isps, Toledo Also called Industrial Screen Process (G-18346)
ISS, Mentor Also called Industrial Systems & Solutions (G-13470)
Ist International, Loveland Also called Intelligent Signal Tech (G-12200)
It XCEL Consulting LLC 513 847-8261
  7112 Office Park Dr West Chester (45069) (G-19728)
It's Sew Much More, Columbus Also called Cheryl A Lucas (G-6762)
Itc Manufacturing, Columbus Also called Interntnal Tchncal Catings Inc (G-7046)
Itecgraphix Inc 440 951-5020
  7417 Mentor Ave Mentor (44060) (G-13477)
Iten Industries Inc (PA) 440 997-6134
  4602 Benefit Ave Ashtabula (44004) (G-780)
Itg Brands LLC 614 431-0044
  6740 Huntley Rd Columbus (43229) (G-7053)
Itl LLC 216 831-3140
  23925 Commerce Park Beachwood (44122) (G-1242)
Itl Corp (HQ) 216 831-3140
  23925 Commerce Park Cleveland (44122) (G-5478)
Itps, Niles Also called International Technical (G-15015)
ITR Manufacturing LLC 419 763-1493
  811 Ash St Saint Henry (45883) (G-16664)
Itran Electronics Recycling 330 659-0801
  4100 Congress Pkwy W Richfield (44286) (G-16474)
ITW Evercoat, Blue Ash Also called Illinois Tool Works Inc (G-1791)
ITW Filtration Products, Bryan Also called Illinois Tool Works Inc (G-2289)
ITW Food Equipment Group LLC 937 332-3000
  401 W Market St Troy (45373) (G-18678)
ITW Food Equipment Group LLC 937 393-4271
  1495 N High St Hillsboro (45133) (G-10882)
ITW Food Equipment Group LLC (HQ) 937 332-2396
  701 S Ridge Ave Troy (45374) (G-18679)
ITW Hobart, Troy Also called Illinois Tool Works Inc (G-18674)
ITW Hobart Brothers, Troy Also called Hobart Brothers LLC (G-18669)
ITW Powertrain Components, Bryan Also called Illinois Tool Works Inc (G-2287)
IV J Telecommunications LLC 606 694-1762
  101 Lea St South Point (45680) (G-17284)
IV M Tool & Die 513 625-6464
  3227 Us Highway 50 Williamsburg (45176) (G-20252)
Ivac Technologies Corp 216 662-4987
  18678 Cranwood Pkwy Cleveland (44128) (G-5479)
Ivan Extruders Co Inc 330 644-7400
  2404 Pickle Rd Akron (44312) (G-220)
Ivans Insurance Solutions, Milford Also called Applied Systems Inc (G-13994)
IVEX Protective Packaging Inc (HQ) 937 498-9298
  2600 Campbell Rd Sidney (45365) (G-17046)
Ivi Mining Group Ltd 740 418-7745
  72116 Grey Rd Vinton (45686) (G-19215)
Iwata Bolt USA Inc 513 942-5050
  102 Iwata Dr Fairfield (45014) (G-9512)
Izit Cain Sheet Metal Corp 937 667-6521
  222 N 6th St Tipp City (45371) (G-18117)
J & A Auto Service 614 837-6820
  101 E Columbus St Pickerington (43147) (G-16049)
J & A Machine 330 424-5235
  8362 Thomas Rd Lisbon (44432) (G-11970)
J & B Feed Co Inc 419 335-5821
  140 S Brunell St Wauseon (43567) (G-19523)
J & B Rogers Inc 937 669-2677
  9785 Julie Ct Tipp City (45371) (G-18118)
J & C Group Inc of Ohio 440 205-9658
  6781 Hopkins Rd Mentor (44060) (G-13478)
J & C Industries Inc 216 362-8867
  4808 W 130th St Cleveland (44135) (G-5480)
J & D Berdine Signs Inc 330 468-0556
  746 E Aurora Rd Ste 3 Macedonia (44056) (G-12305)
J & D Mining Inc 330 339-4935
  3497 University Dr Ne New Philadelphia (44663) (G-14776)
J & D Printing, Dayton Also called Grant John (G-8234)

J & F Furniture Shop ...330 852-2478
3521 Township Road 166 Sugarcreek (44681) ***(G-17850)***
J & H Corporation ...440 357-5982
444 Newell St Painesville (44077) ***(G-15751)***
J & H Manufacturing LLC ...330 482-2636
1652 Columbiana Lisbon Rd Columbiana (44408) ***(G-6471)***
J & J Bechke Inc (PA) ...440 238-1441
12931 Pearl Rd Strongsville (44136) ***(G-17756)***
J & J Logging ...740 896-2827
7100 Highland Ridge Rd Lowell (45744) ***(G-12246)***
J & J Performance Inc ...330 567-2455
410 E Wood St Shreve (44676) ***(G-17004)***
J & J Performance Paintball, Shreve *Also called J & J Performance Inc* ***(G-17004)***
J & J Snack Foods Corp ...440 248-2084
5351 Naiman Pkwy Ste B Solon (44139) ***(G-17173)***
J & J Tool & Die Inc ...330 343-4721
203 W 4th St Dover (44622) ***(G-8833)***
J & J Woodcraft, Berlin *Also called J-J Berlin Woodcraft Inc* ***(G-1643)***
J & K Cabinetry Incorporated ...513 860-3461
9920 Prnceton Glendale Rd West Chester (45246) ***(G-19870)***
J & K Pallet Inc ...937 526-5117
30 Subler Dr Versailles (45380) ***(G-19182)***
J & K Powder Coating ...330 540-6145
1336 Seaborn St Mineral Ridge (44440) ***(G-14166)***
J & K Printing ...330 456-5306
1728 Navarre Rd Sw Canton (44706) ***(G-2713)***
J & K Wade Ltd ...419 352-6163
143 E Wooster St Ste B Bowling Green (43402) ***(G-1977)***
J & L Body Inc ...216 661-2323
4848 Van Epps Rd Brooklyn Heights (44131) ***(G-2126)***
J & L Door ...330 684-1496
13505 Bodine Rd Dalton (44618) ***(G-7944)***
J & L Management Corporation ...440 205-1199
8634 Station St Mentor (44060) ***(G-13479)***
J & L Specialty Steel Inc ...330 875-6200
1500 W Main St Louisville (44641) ***(G-12158)***
J & L Steel Bar LLC ...440 526-0050
3587 Antony Dr Broadview Heights (44147) ***(G-2093)***
J & L Welding Fabricating Inc ...330 393-9353
140 Dana St Ne Warren (44483) ***(G-19412)***
J & L Wood Products Inc (PA) ...937 667-4064
910 Ginghamsburg Rd Tipp City (45371) ***(G-18119)***
J & M Construction LLP ...740 454-8986
8780 Hopewell National Rd Hopewell (43746) ***(G-10993)***
J & M Cutting Tools Inc ...440 622-3900
9401 Hamilton Dr Mentor (44060) ***(G-13480)***
J & M Industries Inc ...440 951-1985
7775 Division Dr Mentor (44060) ***(G-13481)***
J & M Machine, Fairport Harbor *Also called JM Performance Products Inc* ***(G-9624)***
J & M Manufacturing Co Inc ...419 375-2376
284 Railroad St Fort Recovery (45846) ***(G-9822)***
J & M Maynard Enterprises Inc (PA) ...740 532-3032
501 N 2nd St Ironton (45638) ***(G-11167)***
J & M Precision Die Cast Inc ...440 365-7388
1329 Taylor St Elyria (44035) ***(G-9279)***
J & M Steel, Ironton *Also called J & M Maynard Enterprises Inc* ***(G-11167)***
J & M Welding & Fabricating, Rock Creek *Also called Weldfab Inc* ***(G-16535)***
J & O Plastics Inc ...330 927-3169
12475 Sheets Rd Rittman (44270) ***(G-16522)***
J & P Investments Inc ...513 821-2299
8100 Reading Rd Cincinnati (45237) ***(G-3861)***
J & P Products Inc ...440 974-2830
8865 East Ave Mentor (44060) ***(G-13482)***
J & R Woodworking ...330 893-0713
4925 Private Road 386 Millersburg (44654) ***(G-14101)***
J & S Industrial Mch Pdts Inc ...419 691-1380
123 Oakdale Ave Toledo (43605) ***(G-18356)***
J & S Products Inc ...330 686-5840
4534 Berry Hl Stow (44224) ***(G-17597)***
J & W Canvas Company ...330 652-7678
1386 Church St Mineral Ridge (44440) ***(G-14167)***
J A B Welding Service Inc ...740 453-5868
2820 S River Rd Zanesville (43701) ***(G-21150)***
J A H Woodworking LLC ...740 266-6949
39 Belvedere Dr Bloomingdale (43910) ***(G-1711)***
J A McMahon Incorporated ...330 652-2588
6 E Park Ave Niles (44446) ***(G-15017)***
J Aaron Weaver ...440 474-9185
5759 Us Highway 6 Rome (44085) ***(G-16562)***
J America LLC ...614 914-2091
580 N 4th St Ste 620 Columbus (43215) ***(G-7054)***
J and J Sales, Delaware *Also called Aci Industries Converting Ltd* ***(G-8649)***
J and L Jewelry Manufacturing ...440 546-9988
8803 Brecksville Rd # 6 Cleveland (44141) ***(G-5481)***
J and L Manufacturing Inc ...937 492-0008
9401 State Route 29 N Sidney (45365) ***(G-17047)***
J and N Inc ...234 759-3741
80 Eastgate Dr North Lima (44452) ***(G-15172)***
J and S Tool Incorporated ...216 676-8330
15330 Brookpark Rd Cleveland (44135) ***(G-5482)***
J B K Manufacturing & Dev, Dayton *Also called Jbk Manufacturing LLC* ***(G-8280)***
J B Kepple Sheet Metal ...740 393-2971
1010 Vernonview Dr Mount Vernon (43050) ***(G-14484)***
J B M Machine Co Inc ...440 446-0819
32 Alpha Park Cleveland (44143) ***(G-5483)***
J B Manufacturing Inc ...330 676-9744
4465 Crystal Pkwy Kent (44240) ***(G-11335)***
J B Products, Streetsboro *Also called JB Products Co* ***(G-17679)***
J B Stamping Inc ...216 631-0013
7413 Associate Ave Cleveland (44144) ***(G-5484)***
J C Equipment Sales & Leasing ...513 772-7612
2300 E Kemper Rd Unit 11a Cincinnati (45241) ***(G-3862)***
J C L S Enterprises LLC ...740 472-0314
742 Lewisville Rd Woodsfield (43793) ***(G-20545)***
J C Logan Barie LLC ...567 336-6523
194 E South Boundary St Perrysburg (43551) ***(G-15968)***
J C Robinson Products, Cincinnati *Also called James C Robinson* ***(G-3869)***
J Com Data Inc ...614 304-1455
6706 Watkins Rd Sw Pataskala (43062) ***(G-15833)***
J D B Partners Inc ...513 874-3056
6601 Dixie Hwy Ste C Fairfield (45014) ***(G-9513)***
J D Drilling Co ...740 949-2512
107 S 3rd St Racine (45771) ***(G-16356)***
J D Hydraulic Inc ...419 686-5234
Rr 25 Portage (43451) ***(G-16269)***
J D Indoor Comfort Duct Clg, Sheffield Village *Also called J D Indoor Comfort Inc* ***(G-16968)***
J D Indoor Comfort Inc ...440 949-8758
4040 Colorado Ave Sheffield Village (44054) ***(G-16968)***
J D Knisley Logging ...740 634-3207
112 W 3rd St Bainbridge (45612) ***(G-1016)***
J D L Hardwoods ...440 272-5630
9024 N Girdle Rd Middlefield (44062) ***(G-13807)***
J E Doyle Company ...330 564-0743
5186 New Haven Cir Norton (44203) ***(G-15371)***
J E Johnson Pallett Inc ...614 424-9663
1465 E 17th Ave Columbus (43219) ***(G-7055)***
J Feldkamp Design Build Ltd ...513 870-0601
10036 Springfield Pike Cincinnati (45215) ***(G-3863)***
J G Pads, Akron *Also called Markethatch Co Inc* ***(G-269)***
J H Plastics ...419 937-2035
4720 W Us Highway 224 Tiffin (44883) ***(G-18062)***
J Horst Manufacturing Co ...330 828-2216
279 E Main St Dalton (44618) ***(G-7945)***
J I C, West Jefferson *Also called Jefferson Industries Corp* ***(G-19923)***
J I T Pallets Inc ...330 424-0355
39196 Grant St Lisbon (44432) ***(G-11971)***
J Il Fire Systems Inc ...513 574-0609
3628 Harrison Ave Cincinnati (45211) ***(G-3864)***
J J Merlin Systems Inc ...330 666-8609
1245 S Cleveland Massillo Copley (44321) ***(G-7686)***
J J Polishing Inc ...614 214-7637
8520 Rausch Dr Plain City (43064) ***(G-16197)***
J K Logging & Chipwood Company ...330 738-3571
3218 Oasis Rd Ne Salineville (43945) ***(G-16788)***
J K Precast, Wshngtn CT Hs *Also called James Kimmey* ***(G-20730)***
J K Precast LLC ...740 335-2188
1001 Armbrust Ave Wshngtn CT Hs (43160) ***(G-20729)***
J L R Products Inc ...330 832-9557
1212 Oberlin Ave Sw Massillon (44647) ***(G-13004)***
J L Wannemacher Sales & Svc ...419 453-3445
26992 Us 224 W Ottoville (45876) ***(G-15681)***
J M C Rollmasters, Mentor *Also called Johnston Manufacturing Inc* ***(G-13487)***
J M Hamilton Group Inc ...419 229-4010
1700 Elida Rd Lima (45805) ***(G-11881)***
J M Machinery, New Franklin *Also called J McCaman Enterprises Inc* ***(G-14691)***
J M Meat Processing ...740 259-3030
360 S Zuefle Dr Mc Dermott (45652) ***(G-13193)***
J M Mold Inc ...937 778-0077
1707 Commerce Dr Piqua (45356) ***(G-16132)***
J M S Custom Finishing ...614 264-9916
4468 Circle Dr Hilliard (43026) ***(G-10832)***
J M Smucker, Orrville *Also called International Multifoods Corp* ***(G-15595)***
J M Smucker Company (PA) ...330 682-3000
1 Strawberry Ln Orrville (44667) ***(G-15596)***
J M Smucker Company ...330 684-1500
333 Wadsworth Rd Orrville (44667) ***(G-15597)***
J M Smucker Company ...513 482-8000
5204 Spring Grove Ave Cincinnati (45217) ***(G-3865)***
J M Smucker Company ...440 323-5100
6325 Gateway Blvd S Elyria (44035) ***(G-9280)***
J M Smucker Company ...330 497-0073
Akron Canton Reg Aprt 7 Canton (44720) ***(G-2714)***
J McCaman Enterprises Inc ...330 825-2401
3032 Franks Rd New Franklin (44216) ***(G-14691)***
J McCoy Lumber Co Ltd (PA) ...937 587-3423
6 N Main St Peebles (45660) ***(G-15879)***
J McCoy Lumber Co Ltd ...937 544-2968
733 Vaughn Ridge Rd West Union (45693) ***(G-19962)***

ALPHABETIC

J N Linrose Mfg LLC....513 867-5500
999 East Ave Hamilton (45011) ***(G-10574)***
J O Y Aluminum Products Inc....513 797-1100
4111 Founders Blvd Batavia (45103) ***(G-1155)***
J P Dennis Machine Inc....440 474-0247
4380 State Route 534 Rome (44085) ***(G-16563)***
J P Industrial Products Inc (PA)....330 424-1110
11988 State Route 45 Lisbon (44432) ***(G-11972)***
J P Industrial Products Inc....330 424-3388
State Rte 518 Lisbon (44432) ***(G-11973)***
J P Quality Printing Inc....216 791-6303
12614 Larchmere Blvd Cleveland (44120) ***(G-5485)***
J P Sand & Gravel Company....614 497-0083
5911 Lockbourne Rd Lockbourne (43137) ***(G-11995)***
J P Suggins Mobile Welding....216 566-7131
2020 Saint Clair Ave Ne Cleveland (44114) ***(G-5486)***
J P Tool Inc....419 354-8696
2019 Wood Bridge Blvd Bowling Green (43402) ***(G-1978)***
J Pappas, East Liverpool *Also called Joseph G Pappas* ***(G-9061)***
J R Custom Unlimited....513 894-9800
2620 Bobmeyer Rd Hamilton (45015) ***(G-10575)***
J R Engineering, Barberton *Also called Jr Engineering Inc* ***(G-1079)***
J R Goslee Co....330 723-4904
1154 W Smith Rd Medina (44256) ***(G-13282)***
J R M Chemical Inc....216 475-8488
4881 Neo Pkwy Cleveland (44128) ***(G-5487)***
J R Machining Inc....330 528-3406
5170 Hudson Dr Ste G Hudson (44236) ***(G-11058)***
J R S Hydraulic Welding, Columbus *Also called Jrs Hydraulic & Welding* ***(G-7079)***
J R Tool & Die, Wooster *Also called McCann Tool & Die Inc* ***(G-20620)***
J Rettenmaier USA LP....440 385-6701
216 Oberlin Rd Oberlin (44074) ***(G-15500)***
J Rettenmaier USA LP....937 652-2101
1228 Muzzy Rd Urbana (43078) ***(G-18997)***
J Rettenmaier USA LP....937 652-2101
1228 Muzzy Rd Urbana (43078) ***(G-18998)***
J S C Publishing....614 424-6911
958 King Ave Columbus (43212) ***(G-7056)***
J S Company....440 632-0052
16351 Nauvoo Rd Middlefield (44062) ***(G-13808)***
J S Manufacturing LLC....330 815-2136
4631 Mogadore Rd Kent (44240) ***(G-11336)***
J S Stairs....440 632-5680
16118 Old State Rd Middlefield (44062) ***(G-13809)***
J Schrader Co....216 961-2890
4603 Fenwick Ave Cleveland (44102) ***(G-5488)***
J Smokin....330 466-7087
9797 Benner Rd Rittman (44270) ***(G-16523)***
J T E Corp....937 454-1112
5675 Webster St Dayton (45414) ***(G-8275)***
J T M, Solon *Also called Jtm Products Inc* ***(G-17178)***
J Tek Tool & Mold Inc....419 547-9476
304 Elm St Clyde (43410) ***(G-6390)***
J Tyler Enterprise LLC....330 774-4490
66 Parkgate Ave Youngstown (44515) ***(G-20944)***
J Valtier Gas and Oil Co Inc....740 342-2839
10416 State Route 37 Malta (43758) ***(G-12383)***
J W Devers & Son Inc....937 854-3040
5 N Broadway St Trotwood (45426) ***(G-18628)***
J W Goss Co Inc (PA)....330 395-0739
410 South St Sw Warren (44483) ***(G-19413)***
J W Harris Co Inc....216 481-8100
22801 Saint Clair Ave Euclid (44117) ***(G-9421)***
J W Harwood Co (PA)....216 531-6230
18001 Roseland Rd Cleveland (44112) ***(G-5489)***
J W P, Urbana *Also called Johnson Welded Products Inc* ***(G-19001)***
J Williams & Associates Inc....330 887-1392
8761 Virginia Dr Westfield Center (44251) ***(G-20085)***
J Zamberlan & Co....740 765-9028
100 Keagler Dr Bldg 4 Steubenville (43953) ***(G-17538)***
J&B Postal and Print Svcs LLC....740 363-7653
175 S Sandusky St Delaware (43015) ***(G-8698)***
J&I Duct Fab LLC....937 473-2121
7502 W State Route 41 Covington (45318) ***(G-7788)***
J&J Precision Fabricators....330 482-4964
1341 Heck Rd Columbiana (44408) ***(G-6472)***
J&J Precision Machine Ltd....330 923-5783
1474 Main St Cuyahoga Falls (44221) ***(G-7883)***
J&R Pallet Ltd....740 226-1112
1100 Travis Rd Waverly (45690) ***(G-19549)***
J-C-R Tech Inc....937 783-2296
936 Cherry St Blanchester (45107) ***(G-1704)***
J-Fab....740 384-2649
21 N Wisconsin Ave Wellston (45692) ***(G-19602)***
J-J Berlin Woodcraft Inc (PA)....330 893-9171
4805 State Rt 39 Main St Berlin (44610) ***(G-1643)***
J-Lenco Inc....740 499-2260
664 N High St Morral (43337) ***(G-14404)***
J-M Designs LLC....419 794-2114
128 W Wayne St Maumee (43537) ***(G-13120)***
J-Mak Industries, Columbus *Also called Panacea Products Corporation* ***(G-7287)***
J-T Tool Inc....937 623-9959
6995 Hllnsburg Sampson Rd Arcanum (45304) ***(G-629)***
J-Vac Industries Inc....740 384-2155
202 S Pennsylvania Ave Wellston (45692) ***(G-19603)***
J3 Point-Of-Sale, Bucyrus *Also called Ganymede Technologies Corp* ***(G-2330)***
Jab Sales Inc (PA)....440 446-0606
39 Alpha Park Cleveland (44143) ***(G-5490)***
Jabco & Associates Inc....513 752-0600
1188 Ferris Rd Amelia (45102) ***(G-542)***
JAC Construction Ohio Llc....440 564-5005
14985 Cross Creek Pkwy Newbury (44065) ***(G-14958)***
Jack A Byte Mltmdia Gaming LLC....937 321-1716
893 S Main St 375 Englewood (45322) ***(G-9364)***
Jack Gruber....740 408-2718
2606 County Rd Ste 184 Cardington (43315) ***(G-2874)***
Jack Huffman....740 384-5178
1210 Hiram West Rd Wellston (45692) ***(G-19604)***
Jack Walker Printing Co....440 352-4222
9517 Jackson St Mentor (44060) ***(G-13483)***
Jack Walters & Sons Corp....937 653-8986
5045 N Us Highway 68 Urbana (43078) ***(G-18999)***
Jackabyte, Englewood *Also called Jack A Byte Mltmdia Gaming LLC* ***(G-9364)***
Jackie Os Pub Brewery LLC....740 274-0777
25 Campbell St Athens (45701) ***(G-836)***
Jackpot Festival & Gaming....216 531-3500
650a E 185th St Cleveland (44119) ***(G-5491)***
Jacks Marine Inc....440 997-5060
2612 Arlington Ave Ashtabula (44004) ***(G-781)***
Jackson Deluxe Cleaners Ltd (PA)....419 592-2826
522 Hobson St Napoleon (43545) ***(G-14547)***
Jackson Machine & Fabrication....740 682-3994
6679 State Route 93 Oak Hill (45656) ***(G-15452)***
Jackson Monument Inc....740 286-1590
14 Fairmount St Jackson (45640) ***(G-11187)***
Jackson Tube Service Inc (PA)....937 773-8550
8210 Industry Park Dr Piqua (45356) ***(G-16133)***
Jackson Wells Services....419 886-2017
1201 Mill Rd Bellville (44813) ***(G-1558)***
Jacksonlea, Hamilton *Also called Jason Incorporated* ***(G-10576)***
Jaco Inc....513 722-3947
1451 State Route 28 Ste D Loveland (45140) ***(G-12202)***
Jaco Manufacturing Company (PA)....440 234-4000
468 Geiger St Berea (44017) ***(G-1612)***
Jaco Manufacturing Company....440 234-4000
90 Karl St Berea (44017) ***(G-1613)***
Jaco Products, Middlefield *Also called D Martone Industries Inc* ***(G-13790)***
Jacobi Carbons Inc....215 546-3900
432 Mccormick Blvd Columbus (43213) ***(G-7057)***
Jacobs & Sons Logging LLC....419 678-3802
132 N Sycamore St Saint Henry (45883) ***(G-16665)***
Jacobs Mechanical Co....513 681-6800
4500 W Mitchell Ave Cincinnati (45232) ***(G-3866)***
Jacoby Old Smokehouse, West Unity *Also called Jacoby Packing Co* ***(G-19970)***
Jacoby Packing Co....419 924-2684
505 S Main St West Unity (43570) ***(G-19970)***
Jacoby Tarbox Co, Strongsville *Also called Clark-Reliance Corporation* ***(G-17727)***
Jacodar Inc....330 832-9557
1212 Oberlin Ave Sw Massillon (44647) ***(G-13005)***
Jacodar Fsa LLC....330 454-1832
2300 Allen Ave Se Canton (44707) ***(G-2715)***
Jacp Inc (PA)....513 353-3660
5928 Hamilton Cleves Rd Miamitown (45041) ***(G-13747)***
Jacqua's Monogramming & Design, Findlay *Also called Jaquas Monogramming & Design* ***(G-9708)***
Jacqueline L Vandyke....740 593-6779
10414 State Route 550 Athens (45701) ***(G-837)***
JAD Machine Company Inc....419 256-6332
10620 County Road J Malinta (43535) ***(G-12380)***
Jade Products Inc....440 352-1700
9309 Mercantile Dr Mentor (44060) ***(G-13484)***
Jade Tool Co Inc....937 376-4740
1280 Burnett Dr Xenia (45385) ***(G-20778)***
Jadlyn Inc....330 670-9545
1930 N Clvland Msslton Rd Akron (44333) ***(G-221)***
Jae Tech Inc....330 698-2000
32 Hunter St Apple Creek (44606) ***(G-608)***
Jafe Decorating Co Inc....937 547-1888
1250 Martin St Greenville (45331) ***(G-10375)***
Jaffe & Gross Jewelry Company....937 461-9450
3951 Far Hills Ave Dayton (45429) ***(G-8276)***
Jagger Cone Company Inc....419 682-1816
304 Ellis St Stryker (43557) ***(G-17830)***
Jaguar Medical Supplies Inc....440 263-2780
12955 York Delta Dr Ste G North Royalton (44133) ***(G-15279)***
Jain America Foods Inc (HQ)....614 850-9400
1819 Walcutt Rd Ste 1 Columbus (43228) ***(G-7058)***
Jain America Holdings Inc....614 850-9400
1819 Walcutt Rd Ste 1 Columbus (43228) ***(G-7059)***

Jain Americas, Columbus *Also called Jain America Foods Inc* ***(G-7058)***
Jakes Sportswear Ltd 740 746-8356
112 Elm St Sugar Grove (43155) ***(G-17839)***
Jakmar Incorporated 513 631-4303
3280 Hageman Ave Cincinnati (45241) ***(G-3867)***
Jakprints Inc 877 246-3132
34440 Vine St Willowick (44095) ***(G-20479)***
Jalco Industries Inc 740 286-3808
330 Athens St Jackson (45640) ***(G-11188)***
Jalo Inc 216 661-2222
7619 Brookpark Rd Cleveland (44129) ***(G-5492)***
Jamac Inc 419 625-9790
422 Buchanan St Sandusky (44870) ***(G-16818)***
Jamar Precision Grinding Co 330 220-0099
2661 Center Rd Hinckley (44233) ***(G-10903)***
Jamen Tool & Die Co (PA) 330 788-6521
4450 Lake Park Rd Youngstown (44512) ***(G-20945)***
Jamen Tool & Die Co 330 782-6731
914 E Indianola Ave Youngstown (44502) ***(G-20946)***
James Alexander President, Cincinnati *Also called Baldie Corporation* ***(G-3378)***
James Bunnell Inc 513 353-1100
7000 Dry Fork Rd Cleves (45002) ***(G-6365)***
James C Free Inc (PA) 937 298-0171
3100 Far Hills Ave Dayton (45429) ***(G-8277)***
James C Free Inc 513 793-0133
9555 Main St Ste 1 Cincinnati (45242) ***(G-3868)***
James C Robinson 513 969-7482
442 Chestnut St Apt 1 Cincinnati (45203) ***(G-3869)***
James Eastwood 614 444-1340
663 Harmon Plz Columbus (43223) ***(G-7060)***
James Engineering Inc 740 373-9521
2163 State Route 821 Marietta (45750) ***(G-12636)***
James F Seme 440 759-6455
292 Karl St Berea (44017) ***(G-1614)***
James Free Jewelers, Dayton *Also called James C Free Inc* ***(G-8277)***
James Free Jewellers, Cincinnati *Also called James C Free Inc* ***(G-3868)***
James G Morehouse 513 752-2236
4814a Woodlawn Dr Milford (45150) ***(G-14020)***
James J Fairbanks Company Inc 330 534-1374
7342 Hubbard Bedford Rd Hubbard (44425) ***(G-11003)***
James Kimmey 740 335-5746
1000 Armbrust Ave Wshngtn CT Hs (43160) ***(G-20730)***
James L Wereb 440 942-2405
38005 Apollo Pkwy Ste 2 Willoughby (44094) ***(G-20347)***
James L Williams 740 865-3382
52 Tr 12 Wingett Run (45789) ***(G-20536)***
James Logan Logging, Jackson *Also called For Every Home* ***(G-11185)***
James McGuire 614 483-9825
190 Ziegler Ave Columbus (43207) ***(G-7061)***
James O Emert Jr 330 650-6990
7920 Princewood Dr Hudson (44236) ***(G-11059)***
James Oshea 614 262-3188
326 Richards Rd Columbus (43214) ***(G-7062)***
James R Bernhardt Producing 330 345-5306
6717 Cleveland Rd Wooster (44691) ***(G-20609)***
James R Eaton 937 435-7767
535 Clareridge Ln Dayton (45458) ***(G-8278)***
James R Smail Inc 330 264-7500
2285 Eagle Pass Ste B Wooster (44691) ***(G-20610)***
James Ryan Soloman 740 659-2304
5471 High Point Rd Glenford (43739) ***(G-10270)***
James Thomas Shiveley 330 468-2601
585 Highland Rd E Macedonia (44056) ***(G-12306)***
James W Cunningham 419 639-2111
125 Baker St Green Springs (44836) ***(G-10344)***
Jamestown Cont Cleveland Inc 216 831-3700
4500 Renaissance Pkwy Cleveland (44128) ***(G-5493)***
Jamestown Industries Inc 330 779-0670
650 N Meridian Rd Ste 3 Youngstown (44509) ***(G-20947)***
Jamtek Enterprises Inc 513 738-4700
10845 State Route 128 Harrison (45030) ***(G-10652)***
Jan Squires Inc 440 988-7859
7985 Leavitt Rd Amherst (44001) ***(G-563)***
Jane Valentine 330 452-3154
912 Woodside Ave Se North Canton (44720) ***(G-15094)***
Janell Inc 740 532-9111
1014 S 2nd St Ironton (45638) ***(G-11168)***
Janet Sullivan 419 658-2333
3480 State Route 15 Ney (43549) ***(G-14997)***
Janeway Signs Inc 937 237-8433
7825 Waynetowne Blvd Dayton (45424) ***(G-8279)***
Jani Auto Parts Inc 330 494-2975
6434 Wise Ave Nw North Canton (44720) ***(G-15095)***
Janorpot LLC 330 564-0232
3175 Gilchrist Rd Mogadore (44260) ***(G-14241)***
Janova LLC 614 638-6785
7570 N Goodrich Sq New Albany (43054) ***(G-14628)***
Janson Industries 330 455-7029
1200 Garfield Ave Sw Canton (44706) ***(G-2716)***
Janszen Loudspeaker Ltd 614 448-1811
480 Trade Rd Columbus (43204) ***(G-7063)***
Japlar Group Inc 513 791-7192
3210 Wasson Rd Cincinnati (45209) ***(G-3870)***
Japlar Schauer, Cincinnati *Also called Japlar Group Inc* ***(G-3870)***
Jaquas Monogramming & Design 419 422-2244
1016 Tiffin Ave Ste E Findlay (45840) ***(G-9708)***
Jarman Printing Company LLC 330 823-8585
350 S Union Ave Alliance (44601) ***(G-479)***
Jasa Asphalt Russell Standard, Akron *Also called Russell Standard Corporation* ***(G-363)***
Jasmine Distributing Ltd 216 251-9420
12117 Berea Rd Cleveland (44111) ***(G-5494)***
Jason C Gibson 740 663-4520
414 Bethel Rd Chillicothe (45601) ***(G-3196)***
Jason Incorporated 513 860-3400
3440 Symmes Rd Hamilton (45015) ***(G-10576)***
Jason Incorporated 419 668-4474
12406 Us Rte 250 Milan (44846) ***(G-13985)***
Jason Stuller Pro Shop LLC (PA) 419 882-3197
5201 Corey Rd Sylvania (43560) ***(G-17946)***
Jason Wilson 937 604-8209
5575 Ross Rd Tipp City (45371) ***(G-18120)***
Jasstek Inc 614 808-3600
555 Metro Pl N Ste 100 Dublin (43017) ***(G-8932)***
Jatdco, Seville *Also called Atlantic Tool & Die Company* ***(G-16910)***
Jatdco LLC 440 238-6570
19963 Progress Dr Strongsville (44149) ***(G-17757)***
Jatrodiesel Inc 937 847-8050
845 N Main St Miamisburg (45342) ***(G-13681)***
Javanation 419 584-1705
108 S Main St Celina (45822) ***(G-2970)***
Jax Wax Inc 614 476-6769
3145 E 17th Ave Columbus (43219) ***(G-7064)***
Jaxon's, Dayton *Also called Dik Jaxon Products Co* ***(G-8162)***
Jay Dee Service Corporation 330 425-1546
1320 Highland Rd E Macedonia (44056) ***(G-12307)***
Jay Industries Inc 419 747-4161
1595 W Longview Ave Mansfield (44906) ***(G-12461)***
Jay Mid-South LLC 256 439-6600
150 Longview Ave E Mansfield (44903) ***(G-12462)***
Jay Tackett 740 779-1715
387 Musselman Station Rd Frankfort (45628) ***(G-9862)***
Jay-Em Aerospace Corporation 330 923-0333
75 Marc Dr Cuyahoga Falls (44223) ***(G-7884)***
Jaymac Systems Inc 440 498-0810
34300 Sherbrook Park Dr Solon (44139) ***(G-17174)***
Jayna Inc (PA) 937 335-8922
15 Marybill Dr S Troy (45373) ***(G-18680)***
Jayron Fabrication LLC 740 335-3184
13140 New Martinsburg Rd Leesburg (45135) ***(G-11710)***
Jaytee Division, Mentor *Also called Arem Co* ***(G-13393)***
Jaz Foods Inc 800 456-7115
1818 Hopple Ave Sw Canton (44706) ***(G-2717)***
Jazz Textile Impressions 419 242-5940
1425 Holland Rd Maumee (43537) ***(G-13121)***
JB Industries Ltd (PA) 330 856-4587
160 Clifton Dr Ne Ste 4 Warren (44484) ***(G-19414)***
JB Machining Concepts LLC 419 523-0096
995 Sugar Mill Dr Ottawa (45875) ***(G-15655)***
JB Polymers Inc 216 941-7041
55 S Main St Ste 204 Oberlin (44074) ***(G-15501)***
JB Products Co 330 342-0223
10299 Wellman Rd Streetsboro (44241) ***(G-17679)***
Jbc Technologies Inc 440 327-4522
7887 Bliss Pkwy North Ridgeville (44039) ***(G-15234)***
JBI Corporation 419 855-3389
22325 State Route 51 W Genoa (43430) ***(G-10233)***
Jbj Technologies Inc 216 469-7297
185 E 280th St Euclid (44132) ***(G-9422)***
Jbk Manufacturing LLC 937 233-8300
2127 Troy St Dayton (45404) ***(G-8280)***
Jbm Enterprises, Powell *Also called Michele Mellen* ***(G-16328)***
Jbm Technologies Inc 419 368-4362
1926 State Rte 179 Hayesville (44838) ***(G-10715)***
Jbs Industries, Lebanon *Also called Mix-Masters Inc* ***(G-11673)***
Jbs Instruments, Columbus *Also called Aquacalc LLC* ***(G-6612)***
Jbt Foodtech, Sandusky *Also called John Bean Technologies Corp* ***(G-16819)***
Jbw Systems Inc 614 882-5008
5840 Chandler Ct Westerville (43082) ***(G-20000)***
JC and Associates Sylvania LLC 419 824-0011
5129 Main St Sylvania (43560) ***(G-17947)***
JC Carter LLC 440 569-1818
26451 Curtiss Wright Pkwy # 106 Richmond Heights (44143) ***(G-16502)***
JC Carter Nozzles, Richmond Heights *Also called JC Carter LLC* ***(G-16502)***
JC Electric 330 760-2915
9717 State Route 88 Garrettsville (44231) ***(G-10193)***
JC Roofing Supply (PA) 937 258-9999
1535 Keystone Ave Dayton (45403) ***(G-8281)***

A L P H A B E T I C

JCB Arrowhead Products Inc..........440 546-4288
8223 Brecksville Rd # 100 Brecksville (44141) ***(G-2043)***
JCB Payroll Solutions, Cincinnati *Also called Fields Associates Inc* ***(G-3688)***
Jcd, Pataskala *Also called J Com Data Inc* ***(G-15833)***
Jci Jones Chemicals Inc..........330 825-2531
2500 Vanderhoof Rd New Franklin (44203) ***(G-14692)***
Jck Industries..........419 433-6277
730 River Rd Huron (44839) ***(G-11100)***
Jcl Equipment Co Inc..........937 374-1010
915 Trumbull St Xenia (45385) ***(G-20779)***
JCP Signs & Graphix Inc..........740 965-3058
12920 Gorsuch Rd Galena (43021) ***(G-10114)***
JD Power Systems LLC..........614 317-9394
3979 Parkway Ln Hilliard (43026) ***(G-10833)***
Jda Software Group Inc..........480 308-3000
308 N Clvland Mssillon Rd Akron (44333) ***(G-222)***
JE Grote Company Inc (PA)..........614 868-8414
1160 Gahanna Pkwy Columbus (43230) ***(G-7065)***
Jeb Modern Machines Ltd..........419 639-3937
3360 N State Route 19 Republic (44867) ***(G-16427)***
Jebco Machine Company Inc..........330 452-2909
1311 Greenfield Ave Sw Canton (44706) ***(G-2718)***
Jec Forest & Paper Related Co, Oakwood *Also called Johnson Energy Company* ***(G-15462)***
Jech Technologies Inc..........740 927-3495
13962 Olde Post Rd Pickerington (43147) ***(G-16050)***
Jed Industries Inc..........440 639-9973
320 River St Grand River (44045) ***(G-10323)***
Jed Tool Company..........937 857-9222
8058 E Troy Urbana Rd Casstown (45312) ***(G-2933)***
Jeff Bonham Electric Inc..........937 233-7662
3647 Wright Way Rd Dayton (45424) ***(G-8282)***
Jeff Cales Customer AVI LLC..........330 298-9479
8101 State Route 44 A Ravenna (44266) ***(G-16384)***
Jeff Katz (PA)..........614 834-0404
6265 Mamie Dr Pickerington (43147) ***(G-16051)***
Jeff Pendergrass..........513 575-1226
6037 Mill Row Ct Milford (45150) ***(G-14021)***
Jeffco Sheltered Workshop..........740 264-4608
256 John Scott Hwy Steubenville (43952) ***(G-17539)***
Jefferson Industries Corp (HQ)..........614 879-5300
6670 State Route 29 West Jefferson (43162) ***(G-19923)***
Jefferson Smurfit Corporation..........440 248-4370
6385 Cochran Rd Solon (44139) ***(G-17175)***
Jeffery A Burns..........419 845-2129
7430 Linn Hipsher Rd Caledonia (43314) ***(G-2418)***
Jeffrey A Clark..........419 866-8775
148 N King Rd Holland (43528) ***(G-10936)***
Jeffrey Adams Logging Inc..........740 634-2286
3656 Us Highway 50 W Bainbridge (45612) ***(G-1017)***
Jeffrey Brandewie..........937 726-7765
30 E Park St Fort Loramie (45845) ***(G-9800)***
Jeffrey L Becht Inc..........937 264-2070
2781 Thunderhawk Ct Dayton (45414) ***(G-8283)***
Jeffrey Reedy..........614 794-9292
237 E Broadway Ave Ste D Westerville (43081) ***(G-20060)***
Jeffrey Weaver, Sharon Center *Also called Sharon Printing Co Inc* ***(G-16953)***
Jeffs Bakery..........937 890-9703
210 Groveview Ave Dayton (45415) ***(G-8284)***
Jehm Technologies Inc..........440 355-5558
612 N Center St Ste 201 Lagrange (44050) ***(G-11484)***
Jeld-Wen Inc..........740 397-1144
1201 Newark Rd Mount Vernon (43050) ***(G-14485)***
Jeld-Wen Inc..........740 964-1431
91 Heritage Dr Etna (43062) ***(G-9394)***
Jeld-Wen Inc..........740 397-3403
335 Commerce Dr Mount Vernon (43050) ***(G-14486)***
Jeld-Wen Millwork Masters, Etna *Also called Jeld-Wen Inc* ***(G-9394)***
Jeld-Wen Windows, Mount Vernon *Also called Jeld-Wen Inc* ***(G-14485)***
Jena Tool Inc..........937 296-1122
5219 Springboro Pike Moraine (45439) ***(G-14361)***
Jenco Manufacturing Inc..........216 898-9682
7682 Valley Vista Rd Independence (44131) ***(G-11137)***
Jenkins Motor Parts..........330 525-4011
38 Westville Lake Rd Beloit (44609) ***(G-1570)***
Jennmar McSweeney LLC..........740 377-3354
235 Commerce Dr South Point (45680) ***(G-17285)***
Jensar Manufacturing LLC..........419 727-8320
1230 S Expressway Dr Toledo (43608) ***(G-18357)***
Jensen & Sons Inc..........419 471-1000
4481 Monroe St Toledo (43613) ***(G-18358)***
Jergens Inc (PA)..........216 486-5540
15700 S Waterloo Rd Cleveland (44110) ***(G-5495)***
Jerguson, Strongsville *Also called Clark-Reliance Corporation* ***(G-17726)***
Jerico Industries, Minerva *Also called Jerico Plastic Industries Inc* ***(G-14185)***
Jerico Plastic Industries Inc (PA)..........330 868-4600
250 Bridge St Bldg 92 Minerva (44657) ***(G-14185)***
Jerl Machine Inc..........419 873-0270
11140 Avenue Rd Perrysburg (43551) ***(G-15969)***
Jerold Optical Inc..........216 781-4279
800 Huron Rd E Cleveland (44115) ***(G-5496)***
Jerpbak-Bayless Co..........440 248-5387
34150 Solon Rd Solon (44139) ***(G-17176)***
Jerry Harolds Doors Unlimited (PA)..........740 635-4949
415 Hall St Bridgeport (43912) ***(G-2076)***
Jerry Moore Inc (PA)..........330 877-1155
1010 Sunnyside St Sw Hartville (44632) ***(G-10697)***
Jerry Pulfer..........937 778-1861
900 S Main St Piqua (45356) ***(G-16134)***
Jerry Tadlock..........937 544-2851
5645 State Route 125 West Union (45693) ***(G-19963)***
Jerry Tools Inc..........513 242-3211
6200 Vine St Cincinnati (45216) ***(G-3871)***
Jerry's Welding Supply ICN, Hillsboro *Also called Jerrys Welding Supply Inc* ***(G-10883)***
Jerrys Welding Supply Inc..........937 364-1500
5367 Us Highway 50 Hillsboro (45133) ***(G-10883)***
JES Foods/Celina Inc..........419 586-7446
1800 Industrial Dr Celina (45822) ***(G-2971)***
Jesco Products Inc..........440 233-5828
11811 Robson Rd Grafton (44044) ***(G-10304)***
Jester Jewelers, Cincinnati *Also called AR Jester Co* ***(G-3353)***
Jet Container Company..........614 444-2133
1033 Brentnell Ave # 100 Columbus (43219) ***(G-7066)***
Jet Dock Systems Inc..........216 750-2264
9601 Corporate Cir Cleveland (44125) ***(G-5497)***
Jet Electric, Williamsport *Also called R Gordon Jones Inc* ***(G-20260)***
Jet Machine, Cincinnati *Also called Wulco Inc* ***(G-4524)***
Jet Machine & Manufacturing, Cincinnati *Also called Wulco Inc* ***(G-4525)***
Jet Rubber Company..........330 325-1821
4457 Tallmadge Rd Rootstown (44272) ***(G-16569)***
Jet Stream International Inc..........330 505-9988
931 Summit Ave Unit 3 Niles (44446) ***(G-15018)***
Jet Tool and Prototype Co..........419 666-1199
230 W Perry St Walbridge (43465) ***(G-19295)***
Jetcoat LLC..........800 394-0047
472 Brehl Ave Columbus (43223) ***(G-7067)***
Jetfuel Sports Inc..........614 327-3300
8000 Walton Pkwy New Albany (43054) ***(G-14629)***
Jett Industries Inc..........740 344-4140
180 Grant St Newark (43055) ***(G-14889)***
Jett's Professional Embroidery, Greenfield *Also called Jetts Embroideries* ***(G-10353)***
Jetts Embroideries..........937 981-3716
1060 Jefferson St Greenfield (45123) ***(G-10353)***
Jewelry Art, Hudson *Also called Handcrafted Jewelry Inc* ***(G-11051)***
Jewels By Img Inc..........440 461-4464
5470 Mayfield Rd Cleveland (44124) ***(G-5498)***
Jewett Supply..........419 738-9882
607 N Water St Wapakoneta (45895) ***(G-19335)***
Jewish Journal Monthly Mag..........330 746-3251
505 Gypsy Ln Youngstown (44504) ***(G-20948)***
JF Martt and Associates Inc..........330 938-4000
501 N Johnson Rd Sebring (44672) ***(G-16887)***
Jh Industries Inc..........330 963-4105
1981 E Aurora Rd Twinsburg (44087) ***(G-18797)***
Jh Instruments, Columbus *Also called Fcx Performance Inc* ***(G-6916)***
Jh Woodworking LLC..........330 276-7600
11259 Township Road 71 Killbuck (44637) ***(G-11452)***
Jhg Retail Services LLC..........216 447-0831
7951 Merrymaker Ln Cincinnati (45236) ***(G-3872)***
Jilco Precision Mold & Mch Co..........330 633-9645
1245 Devalera St Akron (44310) ***(G-223)***
Jim Bumen Construction Company (PA)..........740 663-2659
3218 S Bridge St Chillicothe (45601) ***(G-3197)***
Jim Denigris & Sons Ldscpg..........440 449-5548
1520 Longwood Dr Cleveland (44124) ***(G-5499)***
Jim H Niemeyer..........419 422-2465
1004 W Sandusky St Findlay (45840) ***(G-9709)***
Jim Nier Construction Inc..........740 289-2629
3877 Us Highway 23 Piketon (45661) ***(G-16071)***
Jim Nier Construction Inc (PA)..........740 289-3925
340 Bailey Chapel Rd Piketon (45661) ***(G-16072)***
Jims Donut Shop..........937 898-4222
122 E National Rd Vandalia (45377) ***(G-19131)***
Jit Company Inc..........614 529-8010
2180 Venus Dr Hilliard (43026) ***(G-10834)***
Jit Milrob, Aurora *Also called JIT Packaging Inc* ***(G-885)***
JIT Packaging Inc (PA)..........330 562-8080
250 Page Rd Aurora (44202) ***(G-885)***
JIT Packaging Inc..........513 934-0905
1550 Kingsview Dr Lebanon (45036) ***(G-11665)***
Jj Seville LLC..........330 769-2071
22 Milton St Seville (44273) ***(G-16918)***
Jj Sleeves Inc..........440 205-1055
6850 Patterson Dr Mentor (44060) ***(G-13485)***
Jjb Engineer..........330 807-0671
2695 N Haven Blvd Ste 10 Cuyahoga Falls (44223) ***(G-7885)***
Jjc Plastics Ltd..........330 334-3637
4021 Deerspring Ct Norton (44203) ***(G-15372)***

Jjc Products Inc......330 666-4582
3670 Forest Oaks Dr Akron (44333) *(G-224)*
Jjkb Enterprises LLC......513 731-4332
6125 Montgomery Rd Unit 1 Cincinnati (45213) *(G-3873)*
Jjs3 Foundation......513 751-3292
11925 Kemper Springs Dr Cincinnati (45240) *(G-3874)*
Jk Digital Publishing LLC......937 299-0185
20 Heatherwoode Cir Springboro (45066) *(G-17331)*
Jk-Co LLC......419 422-5240
16960 E State Route 12 Findlay (45840) *(G-9710)*
Jlg Industries Inc......330 684-0132
2927 Paradise St Orrville (44667) *(G-15598)*
Jlg Industries Inc......330 684-0200
600 E Chestnut St Orrville (44667) *(G-15599)*
Jlm Logging LLC......330 340-4863
3334 County Road 160 Millersburg (44654) *(G-14102)*
Jls Funeral Home......614 625-1220
2322 Randy Ct Columbus (43232) *(G-7068)*
JLW - TW Corp......216 361-5940
35350 Chester Rd Avon (44011) *(G-952)*
JM Gournet Popcorn, Toledo *Also called Celebrations* *(G-18224)*
JM Logging Inc......740 441-0941
1624 Graham School Rd Gallipolis (45631) *(G-10168)*
JM Performance Products Inc......440 357-1234
1234 High St Fairport Harbor (44077) *(G-9624)*
JM Printing......740 412-8666
134 W Main St Circleville (43113) *(G-4547)*
JM Smucker Co......330 684-8274
918 N Main St Orrville (44667) *(G-15600)*
Jmac Inc (PA)......614 436-2418
200 W Nationwide Blvd # 1 Columbus (43215) *(G-7069)*
Jmc Steel Group......216 910-3700
3201 Entp Pkwy Ste 150 Beachwood (44122) *(G-1243)*
JMJ Paper Inc......216 941-8100
681 Moore Rd Ste D Avon Lake (44012) *(G-990)*
JMJ Paper Inc......419 332-6675
1900 Napoleon St Fremont (43420) *(G-10029)*
Jml Holdings Inc......419 866-7500
6210 Merger Dr Holland (43528) *(G-10937)*
Jmr Enterprises LLC......937 618-1736
7808 Hyatts Ln Maineville (45039) *(G-12371)*
JMS Composites, Springfield *Also called JMS Industries Inc* *(G-17426)*
JMS Industries Inc......937 325-3502
3240 E National Rd Springfield (45505) *(G-17426)*
JMw Welding and Mfg......330 484-2428
512 45th St Sw Canton (44706) *(G-2719)*
Jnc,, Piketon *Also called Jim Nier Construction Inc* *(G-16072)*
Jnj Distributors, Cincinnati *Also called Great Midwest Tobacco Inc* *(G-3779)*
Job News (PA)......513 984-5724
10250 Alliance Rd Ste 201 Blue Ash (45242) *(G-1795)*
Job News USA......614 310-1700
150 E Campus View Blvd # 120 Columbus (43235) *(G-7070)*
Job One Control Services......216 347-0133
6893 Lantern Ln Cleveland (44130) *(G-5500)*
Jobap Assembly Inc......440 632-5393
16090 Industrial Pkwy # 9 Middlefield (44062) *(G-13810)*
Jobskin Div of Torbot Group......419 724-1475
5030 Advantage Dr Ste 101 Toledo (43612) *(G-18359)*
Jobskin Division, Toledo *Also called Torbot Group Inc* *(G-18577)*
Joe Baker Equipment Sales......513 451-1327
1000 Devils Backbone Rd Cincinnati (45233) *(G-3875)*
Joe Barrett......216 385-2384
13583 Old Frdericktown Rd East Liverpool (43920) *(G-9060)*
Joe Busby......513 821-1716
439 S Cooper Ave Cincinnati (45215) *(G-3876)*
Joe D'S Printing, North Olmsted *Also called Emta Inc* *(G-15187)*
Joe Gonda Company Inc......440 458-6000
50000 Gondawood Dr Grafton (44044) *(G-10305)*
Joe McClelland Inc (PA)......740 452-3036
98 E La Salle St Zanesville (43701) *(G-21151)*
Joe P Fischer Woodcraft......513 474-4316
8455 Greenleaf Dr Cincinnati (45255) *(G-3877)*
Joe P Fischer Woodcraft......513 530-9600
4627 Carlynn Dr Blue Ash (45241) *(G-1796)*
Joe Paxton......614 424-9000
960 King Ave Columbus (43212) *(G-7071)*
Joe Rees Welding......937 652-4067
326 W Twain Ave Urbana (43078) *(G-19000)*
Joe Sestito......614 871-7778
5553 Spring Hill Rd Grove City (43123) *(G-10437)*
Joe The Printer Guy LLC......216 651-3880
1590 Parkwood Rd Lakewood (44107) *(G-11523)*
Joes Saw Shop......440 834-1196
14530 Butternut Rd Burton (44021) *(G-2363)*
Johannings Inc......330 875-1706
3244 S Nickelplate St Louisville (44641) *(G-12159)*
John B Allen......614 488-7122
2346 Brandon Rd Columbus (43221) *(G-7072)*
John Baird......216 440-3595
12646 Lovers Lane Rd Spencer (44275) *(G-17305)*
John Bean Technologies Corp......419 627-4349
1622 1st St Sandusky (44870) *(G-16819)*
John Byler......330 627-7635
5130 Germano Rd Se Carrollton (44615) *(G-2921)*
John C Meier Grape Juice Co, Cincinnati *Also called Meiers Wine Cellars Inc* *(G-4003)*
John C Starr......740 852-5592
15 S Main St London (43140) *(G-12063)*
John Christ Winery Inc......440 933-9672
32421 Walker Rd Avon Lake (44012) *(G-991)*
John D Oil and Gas Company......440 255-6325
7001 Center St Mentor (44060) *(G-13486)*
John Deere Authorized Dealer, Wooster *Also called Shearer Farm Inc* *(G-20653)*
John Deere Authorized Dealer, Urbana *Also called Koenig Equipment Inc* *(G-19002)*
John Deere Authorized Dealer, Mentor *Also called Great Lakes Power Products Inc* *(G-13462)*
John Deere Authorized Dealer, Hilliard *Also called JD Power Systems LLC* *(G-10833)*
John Deere Authorized Dealer, Canton *Also called Western Branch Diesel Inc* *(G-2864)*
John Deere Authorized Dealer, Perry *Also called Great Lakes Power Service Co* *(G-15905)*
John Deere Authorized Dealer, Columbus *Also called Murphy Tractor & Eqp Co Inc* *(G-7201)*
John Deere Authorized Dealer, Vandalia *Also called Murphy Tractor & Eqp Co Inc* *(G-19140)*
John Deere Authorized Dealer, Lima *Also called Murphy Tractor & Eqp Co Inc* *(G-11909)*
John Deere Authorized Dealer, Canton *Also called Murphy Tractor & Eqp Co Inc* *(G-2759)*
John Deere Authorized Dealer, Brunswick *Also called Murphy Tractor & Eqp Co Inc* *(G-2221)*
John Downey Company, Granville *Also called Downey Enterprises Inc* *(G-10329)*
John F Kilfoil Co......513 791-6150
3799 Madison Rd Cincinnati (45209) *(G-3878)*
John Frieda Prof Hair Care Inc (HQ)......800 521-3189
2535 Spring Grove Ave Cincinnati (45214) *(G-3879)*
John H Hosking Inc......513 821-1080
4665 Emerald Way Middletown (45044) *(G-13918)*
John J Yoder Logging......330 749-6324
6776 Mount Hope Rd Apple Creek (44606) *(G-609)*
John Kolesar and Sons Inc......216 221-7117
13437 Detroit Ave Cleveland (44107) *(G-5501)*
John Krizay Inc......330 332-5607
1777 Pennsylvania Ave Salem (44460) *(G-16750)*
John Krusinski......216 441-0100
6300 Heisley Ave Cleveland (44105) *(G-5502)*
John L Garber Materials Corp......419 884-1567
2745 Gass Rd Mansfield (44904) *(G-12463)*
John M Hand......937 902-1327
6417 Enterprise Rd West Alexandria (45381) *(G-19619)*
John Maneely Company......724 342-6851
1800 Hunter Ave Niles (44446) *(G-15019)*
John McCulloch Distillery......937 725-5588
414 Cemetery Rd Martinsville (45146) *(G-12766)*
John McHael Priester Assoc Inc......513 761-8605
266 Elm Ave Wyoming (45215) *(G-20752)*
John P Ellis Clinic Podiatry......440 460-0444
730 Som Center Rd Ste 350 Cleveland (44143) *(G-5503)*
John Purdum......513 897-9686
100 S Main St Waynesville (45068) *(G-19569)*
John R Jurgensen Co......937 293-3112
1780 Enon Rd Springfield (45502) *(G-17427)*
John S Swift Company Inc......513 721-4147
8044 Montgomery Rd # 700 Cincinnati (45236) *(G-3880)*
John Stehlin & Sons Co Inc......513 385-6164
10134 Colerain Ave Cincinnati (45251) *(G-3881)*
John Stieg & Associates......614 889-7954
8621 Kirkhill Ct Dublin (43017) *(G-8933)*
John Wolf & Co Inc......440 942-0083
36420 Biltmore Pl Ste 1 Willoughby (44094) *(G-20348)*
John Zidian Company, Youngstown *Also called Gia Russa* *(G-20921)*
Johndavid D Jones......740 264-0176
590 Woodvue Ln Wintersville (43953) *(G-20539)*
Johndow Industries Inc......330 753-6895
151 Snyder Ave Barberton (44203) *(G-1078)*
Johnny Chin Insurance Agency......513 777-8695
9676 Cncnnati Columbus Rd West Chester (45241) *(G-19871)*
Johnny Johnson Sports, Ontario *Also called Unisport Inc* *(G-15549)*
Johns Body Shop......419 358-1200
200 Lake Dr Bluffton (45817) *(G-1890)*
Johns Jerky & Snack Meats LLC......937 207-7008
12499 Clmbus Cncinnati Rd South Charleston (45368) *(G-17273)*
Johns Manville Corporation......419 782-0180
1410 Columbus Ave Defiance (43512) *(G-8628)*
Johns Manville Corporation......419 499-1400
49 Lockwood Rd Milan (44846) *(G-13986)*
Johns Manville Corporation......419 878-8111
7500 Dutch Rd Waterville (43566) *(G-19498)*
Johns Manville Corporation......419 784-7000
925 Carpenter Rd Defiance (43512) *(G-8629)*
Johns Manville Corporation......419 784-7000
3rd And Perry Defiance (43512) *(G-8630)*
Johns Manville Corporation......419 467-8189
1020 Ford St Maumee (43537) *(G-13122)*
Johns Manville Corporation......419 878-8111
408 Perry St Plant 02 2 Plant Defiance (43512) *(G-8631)*

ALPHABETIC

Johns Welding & Towing Inc 419 447-8937
850 N County Road 11 Tiffin (44883) *(G-18063)*
Johnson Bros Greenwich, Greenwich *Also called Johnson Bros Rubber Co Inc (G-10404)*
Johnson Bros Rubber Co Inc (PA) 419 853-4122
42 W Buckeye St West Salem (44287) *(G-19955)*
Johnson Bros Rubber Co Inc 419 752-4814
41 Center St Greenwich (44837) *(G-10404)*
Johnson Brothers Holdings LLC 614 868-5273
717 Oak St Columbus (43205) *(G-7073)*
Johnson Contrls Authorized Dlr, Akron *Also called Famous Industries Inc (G-166)*
Johnson Contrls Authorized Dlr, Northwood *Also called Yanfeng US Automotive (G-15354)*
Johnson Contrls Btry Group Inc 419 865-0542
10300 Industrial St Holland (43528) *(G-10938)*
Johnson Controls 419 861-0662
3661 Brrfeld Blvd Ste 101 Maumee (43537) *(G-13123)*
Johnson Controls Inc 419 636-4211
918 S Union St Bryan (43506) *(G-2292)*
Johnson Controls Inc 216 587-0100
9797 Midwest Ave Cleveland (44125) *(G-5504)*
Johnson Controls Inc 513 671-6338
11648 Springfield Pike Cincinnati (45246) *(G-3882)*
Johnson Energy Company 937 435-5401
127 Lookout Dr Oakwood (45409) *(G-15462)*
Johnson Engine & Machine 614 876-0724
2899 Walcutt Rd Hilliard (43026) *(G-10835)*
Johnson Machining Services LLC 937 866-4744
4505 Infirmary Rd Miamisburg (45342) *(G-13682)*
Johnson Mtthey Prcess Tech Inc 330 298-7005
785 N Freedom St Ravenna (44266) *(G-16385)*
Johnson Power Ltd 419 866-6692
1236 Clark St Holland (43528) *(G-10939)*
Johnson Precision Machining 513 353-4252
5919 Hamilton Cleves Rd Cleves (45002) *(G-6366)*
Johnson Printing 740 922-4821
216 E 5th St Uhrichsville (44683) *(G-18889)*
Johnson Tool Distributors 740 653-6959
1059 Rockmill Rd Nw Lancaster (43130) *(G-11581)*
Johnson Welded Products Inc 937 652-1242
625 S Edgewood Ave Urbana (43078) *(G-19001)*
Johnson-Nash Metal Pdts Inc 513 874-7022
9265 Seward Rd Fairfield (45014) *(G-9514)*
Johnsonite, Solon *Also called Tarkett USA Inc (G-17247)*
Johnsonite Inc 440 632-3441
16035 Industrial Pkwy Middlefield (44062) *(G-13811)*
Johnsonite Rubber Flooring, Middlefield *Also called Johnsonite Inc (G-13811)*
Johnsons Lamp Shop & Antq Co 937 568-4551
8518 E National Rd South Vienna (45369) *(G-17297)*
Johnsons Real Ice Cream Co 614 231-0014
2728 E Main St Columbus (43209) *(G-7074)*
Johnston Manufacturing Inc 440 269-1420
7611 Saint Clair Ave Mentor (44060) *(G-13487)*
Johnston-Morehouse-Dickey Co 614 866-0452
4647 Poth Rd Columbus (43213) *(G-7075)*
Johnston-Morehouse-Dickey Co 330 405-6050
1290 Highland Rd E Macedonia (44056) *(G-12308)*
Johnstons Banks Inc 614 499-4374
6927 Sherbrook Dr Westerville (43082) *(G-20001)*
Joining Metals Inc 440 259-1790
3314 Blackmore Rd Perry (44081) *(G-15906)*
Joint Systems Mfg Ctr 419 221-9580
1155 Buckeye Rd Bldg 147 Lima (45804) *(G-11882)*
Jolly Pats, Streetsboro *Also called Horsemens Pride Inc (G-17677)*
Jomac Ltd 330 627-7727
182 Scio Rd Se Carrollton (44615) *(G-2922)*
Jonashtons 419 488-2363
12485 State Route 634 Cloverdale (45827) *(G-6386)*
Jonathan Bishop 330 836-6947
200 Hampshire Rd Akron (44313) *(G-225)*
Jones & Assoc Advg & Design 330 799-6876
5015 Mahoning Ave Ste 1 Youngstown (44515) *(G-20949)*
Jones Industrial Service LLC 419 287-4553
17221 Eisenhour Rd Pemberville (43450) *(G-15886)*
Jones Metal Products Company (PA) 740 545-6381
200 N Center St West Lafayette (43845) *(G-19931)*
Jones Metal Products Company 740 545-6341
305 N Center St West Lafayette (43845) *(G-19932)*
Jones Old Rustic Sign 937 643-1695
2758 Viking Ln Moraine (45439) *(G-14362)*
Jones Potato Chip Co (PA) 419 529-9424
823 Bowman St Mansfield (44903) *(G-12464)*
Jones Printing Services Inc 440 946-7300
1519 E 367th St Ste 1 Eastlake (44095) *(G-9116)*
Jones Processing 330 772-2193
State Rte 7 Hartford (44424) *(G-10681)*
Jones Propane Supply, Carrollton *Also called Jomac Ltd (G-2922)*
Jones Signs, Moraine *Also called Jones Old Rustic Sign (G-14362)*
Jones Zylon Company, West Lafayette *Also called Jones Metal Products Company (G-19931)*
Jones-Hamilton Co (PA) 419 666-9838
30354 Tracy Rd Walbridge (43465) *(G-19296)*
Joneszylon Company LLC 740 545-6341
300 N Center St West Lafayette (43845) *(G-19933)*
Jonmar Gear and Machine Inc 330 854-6500
13786 Warwick Dr Nw Canal Fulton (44614) *(G-2481)*
Jordan E Armour 330 252-0290
1145 Highbrook St Ste 103 Akron (44301) *(G-226)*
Jordan Reed LLC 678 956-1222
5855 Parliament Dr Columbus (43213) *(G-7076)*
Jordan Young International, London *Also called Textiles Inc (G-12070)*
Jordon Auto Service & Tire Inc 216 214-6528
5201 Carnegie Ave Cleveland (44103) *(G-5505)*
Jos-Tech Inc 330 678-3260
852 W Main St Kent (44240) *(G-11337)*
Jose Madrid Salsa, Zanesville *Also called Michael Zakany LLC (G-21156)*
Joseph A Panico & Sons Inc (PA) 614 235-3188
4605 E 5th Ave Columbus (43219) *(G-7077)*
Joseph Adams Corp 330 225-9125
5740 Grafton Rd Valley City (44280) *(G-19042)*
Joseph B Stinson Co 419 334-4151
2300 Napoleon Rd Fremont (43420) *(G-10030)*
Joseph Berning Printing Co 513 721-0781
1850 Dalton Ave Cincinnati (45214) *(G-3883)*
Joseph G Betz & Sons 513 481-0322
4219 Saint Martins Pl Cincinnati (45211) *(G-3884)*
Joseph G Pappas 330 383-2917
3197 Forest Hills Dr East Liverpool (43920) *(G-9061)*
Joseph Industries, Cleveland *Also called Charles Messina (G-4911)*
Joseph Industries Inc 330 528-0091
10039 Aurora Hudson Rd Streetsboro (44241) *(G-17680)*
Joseph Knapp 330 832-3515
151 Lennox Ave Sw Massillon (44646) *(G-13006)*
Joseph Sabatino 330 332-5879
1834 Depot Rd Salem (44460) *(G-16751)*
Joseph T Snyder Industries 216 883-6900
9210 Loren Ave Cleveland (44105) *(G-5506)*
Josh L Derksen 937 548-0080
200 N Broadway St Greenville (45331) *(G-10376)*
Joshua Enterprises Inc 419 872-9699
12900 Eckel Junction Rd Perrysburg (43551) *(G-15970)*
Joshua Label Company, Perrysburg *Also called Joshua Enterprises Inc (G-15970)*
Joshua Leigh Enterprises Inc 330 244-9200
2191 E Maple St Canton (44720) *(G-2720)*
Joslyn Manufacturing Company 330 467-8111
9400 Valley View Rd Macedonia (44056) *(G-12309)*
Jostens Inc 419 874-5835
1833 Eaglecrest Rd Perrysburg (43551) *(G-15971)*
Jostens Inc 513 731-5900
3047 Madison Rd Ste 207 Cincinnati (45209) *(G-3885)*
Jotco Inc 513 721-4943
1400 Park Ave E Mansfield (44905) *(G-12465)*
Joules Angstrom UV Printing (PA) 740 964-9113
104 Heritage Dr Etna (43062) *(G-9395)*
Journal Leader, Caldwell *Also called Southeast Publications Inc (G-2412)*
Journal News 513 829-7900
5120 Dixie Hwy Fairfield (45014) *(G-9515)*
Journal Register Company 440 951-0000
7085 Mentor Ave Willoughby (44094) *(G-20349)*
Journal Register Company 440 245-6901
2500 W Erie Ave Lorain (44053) *(G-12096)*
Journey Electronics Corp 513 539-9836
902 N Garver Rd Monroe (45050) *(G-14269)*
Journey Systems LLC (PA) 513 831-6200
25 Whitney Dr Ste 100 Milford (45150) *(G-14022)*
Joy Global Underground Min LLC 440 248-7970
6160 Cochran Rd Cleveland (44139) *(G-5507)*
Joy Mining Machinery 440 248-7970
6160 Cochran Rd Solon (44139) *(G-17177)*
Joyce Manufacturing Co (PA) 440 239-9100
1125 Berea Indus Pkwy Berea (44017) *(G-1615)*
Joyce Windows, Berea *Also called Joyce Manufacturing Co (G-1615)*
Joyce/Dayton Corp (HQ) 937 294-6261
3300 S Dixie Dr Ste 101 Dayton (45439) *(G-8285)*
JP Good Co, Ashland *Also called Good JP (G-706)*
JP Industrial, Lisbon *Also called J P Industrial Products Inc (G-11972)*
JP Self Defense LLC 330 356-1541
2870 Lincoln Way E Massillon (44646) *(G-13007)*
JPS Print 614 235-8947
1014 Parsons Ave Columbus (43206) *(G-7078)*
JPS Technologies Inc (PA) 513 984-6400
11110 Deerfield Rd Blue Ash (45242) *(G-1797)*
JPS Technologies Inc 513 984-6400
11118 Deerfield Rd Blue Ash (45242) *(G-1798)*
Jr Engineering Inc (PA) 330 848-0960
123 9th St Nw Barberton (44203) *(G-1079)*
Jr Kennel Mfg 937 780-6104
12196 Wilmington Ave Leesburg (45135) *(G-11711)*

Jr Larry Knight...216 762-3141
5260 Cato St Maple Heights (44137) ***(G-12574)***
JR Manufacturing Inc (PA)...419 375-8021
900 Industrial Dr W Fort Recovery (45846) ***(G-9823)***
Jrb Attachments LLC (HQ)...330 734-3000
820 Glaser Pkwy Akron (44306) ***(G-227)***
Jrb Industries LLC...567 825-7022
3425 State Route 571 Greenville (45331) ***(G-10377)***
Jrf Industries Ltd...330 665-3130
3675 Copley Rd Copley (44321) ***(G-7687)***
Jrg Performance Technologies...216 408-5974
340 Balmoral Dr Cleveland (44143) ***(G-5508)***
Jroll LLC...330 661-0600
985 Boardman Aly Medina (44256) ***(G-13283)***
Jrs Hydraulic & Welding...614 497-1100
2774 Groveport Rd Columbus (43207) ***(G-7079)***
Js Fabrications Inc...419 333-0323
1400 E State St Fremont (43420) ***(G-10031)***
Jsc Employee Leasing Corp (PA)...330 773-8971
1560 Firestone Pkwy Akron (44301) ***(G-228)***
Jscs Group Inc...513 563-4900
690 Northland Blvd Cincinnati (45240) ***(G-3886)***
Jsm Express Inc...216 331-2008
27301 Markbarry Ave Euclid (44132) ***(G-9423)***
Jst LLC...614 423-7815
6240 Frost Rd Ste C Westerville (43082) ***(G-20002)***
Jt Premier Printing Corp...216 831-8785
18780 Cranwood Pkwy Cleveland (44128) ***(G-5509)***
Jtm Food Group, Harrison *Also called Jtm Provisions Company Inc* ***(G-10653)***
Jtm Products Inc...440 287-2302
31025 Carter St Solon (44139) ***(G-17178)***
Jtm Provisions Company Inc...513 367-4900
200 Sales Ave Harrison (45030) ***(G-10653)***
Judith C Zell...740 385-0386
21313 State Route 93 S Logan (43138) ***(G-12029)***
Judith Leiber LLC (PA)...614 449-4217
4300 E 5th Ave Columbus (43219) ***(G-7080)***
Judy Dubois...419 738-6979
4 N Wood St Wapakoneta (45895) ***(G-19336)***
Judy Mills Company Inc (PA)...513 271-4241
3360 Red Bank Rd Cincinnati (45227) ***(G-3887)***
Juggerbot 3d LLC...330 406-6900
241 W Federal St Youngstown (44503) ***(G-20950)***
Julie Maynard Inc...937 443-0408
4991 Hempstead Station Dr Dayton (45429) ***(G-8286)***
Julius Zorn Inc...330 923-4999
3690 Zorn Dr Cuyahoga Falls (44223) ***(G-7886)***
Jump N Sales LLC...513 509-7661
6745 Gilmore Rd Ste E Fairfield Township (45011) ***(G-9583)***
Junebugs Wash N Dry...513 988-5863
6435 E State St Trenton (45067) ***(G-18621)***
Juniper Networks Inc...614 932-1432
545 Metro Pl S Ste 164 Dublin (43017) ***(G-8934)***
Just Basic Sports Inc...330 264-7771
1615 N Geyers Chapel Rd Wooster (44691) ***(G-20611)***
Just Business Inc...866 577-3303
1612 Prosser Ave Ste 100 Dayton (45409) ***(G-8287)***
Just Name It Inc...614 626-8662
268 Drexel Pl Pickerington (43147) ***(G-16052)***
Just Natural Provision Company...216 431-7922
4800 Crayton Ave Cleveland (44104) ***(G-5510)***
Just Plastics Inc...419 468-5506
869 Smith St Galion (44833) ***(G-10146)***
Justin P Straub LLC...513 761-0282
14 De Camp Ave Cincinnati (45216) ***(G-3888)***
Juvenile Furniture Specialties, Sugarcreek *Also called J & F Furniture Shop* ***(G-17850)***
Juzo, Cuyahoga Falls *Also called Julius Zorn Inc* ***(G-7886)***
JW Log and Lumber, Carrollton *Also called John Byler* ***(G-2921)***
JW Manufacturing...419 375-5536
317 Watkins Rd Fort Recovery (45846) ***(G-9824)***
Jz Technologies LLC...937 252-5800
3420 Aston Pl Blue Ash (45241) ***(G-1799)***
K & B Acquisitions Inc...937 253-1163
3013 Linden Ave Dayton (45410) ***(G-8288)***
K & B Stamping & Manufacturing...937 778-8875
9676 Looney Rd Piqua (45356) ***(G-16135)***
K & E Chemical Co Inc...216 341-0500
3960 E 93rd St Cleveland (44105) ***(G-5511)***
K & G Machine Co...216 732-7115
26981 Tungsten Rd Cleveland (44132) ***(G-5512)***
K & H Industries LLC...513 921-6770
1041 Evans St Ste 2 Cincinnati (45204) ***(G-3889)***
K & J Holdings Inc...330 726-0828
8060 Southern Blvd Youngstown (44512) ***(G-20951)***
K & J Machine Inc...740 425-3282
326 Fairmont Ave Barnesville (43713) ***(G-1117)***
K & K Auto & Truck Parts, Logan *Also called Pattons Truck & Heavy Eqp Svc* ***(G-12039)***
K & K Precision Inc...513 336-0032
5001 N Masn Montgomery Rd Mason (45040) ***(G-12898)***
K & L Die & Manufacturing...419 895-1301
7541 Olvsburg Ftchvlle Rd Greenwich (44837) ***(G-10405)***
K & L Ready Mix Inc...419 943-2200
300 Putnam Dr Leipsic (45856) ***(G-11727)***
K & L Ready Mix Inc (PA)...419 523-4376
10391 State Route 15 Ottawa (45875) ***(G-15656)***
K & L Ready Mix Inc...419 532-3585
105 S 6th St Kalida (45853) ***(G-11277)***
K & L Ready Mix Inc...419 293-2937
5511 State Route 613 Mc Comb (45858) ***(G-13190)***
K & L Tool Inc...419 258-2086
5141 Us 24 Antwerp (45813) ***(G-598)***
K & M Home Defense LLC...313 258-6142
325 Wallace Dr Fairborn (45324) ***(G-9462)***
K & M Tool & Machine Co Inc...440 572-5130
17383 Foltz Pkwy Strongsville (44149) ***(G-17758)***
K & R Pretzel Co...937 299-2231
1700 Flesher Ave Dayton (45420) ***(G-8289)***
K A P C O, Kent *Also called Kent Adhesive Products Co* ***(G-11338)***
K B Electric Motor Service...740 537-1346
915 Banfield Ave Toronto (43964) ***(G-18610)***
K B Electric Service, Toronto *Also called K B Electric Motor Service* ***(G-18610)***
K B Machine & Tool Inc...937 773-1624
1500 S Main St Piqua (45356) ***(G-16136)***
K B Printing...614 771-1222
1199 Goodale Blvd Columbus (43212) ***(G-7081)***
K C N Technologies LLC...440 439-4219
20637 Krick Rd Bedford (44146) ***(G-1419)***
K C P, Beachwood *Also called Kirtland Capital Partners LP* ***(G-1244)***
K Cupcakes...440 576-3464
222 Elliott Ave Jefferson (44047) ***(G-11230)***
K D Hardwoods Inc...440 834-1772
14195 Kinsman Rd Burton (44021) ***(G-2364)***
K D Lamp Company...440 293-4064
101 Parker Dr Andover (44003) ***(G-583)***
K Davis Inc...419 637-2859
526 N Webster St Gibsonburg (43431) ***(G-10249)***
K Effs Inc...614 443-0586
2117 S High St Columbus (43207) ***(G-7082)***
K F D Inc...330 773-4300
39 Alice Dr Unit B Coventry Township (44319) ***(G-7771)***
K F T Inc...513 241-5910
726 Mehring Way Cincinnati (45203) ***(G-3890)***
K G M, Cincinnati *Also called Knoble Glass & Metal Inc* ***(G-3919)***
K K Racing Chassis...330 628-2930
485 Taylor Ave Akron (44312) ***(G-229)***
K K Tool Co...937 325-1373
115 S Center St Springfield (45502) ***(G-17428)***
K L M Manufacturing Company...740 666-5171
56 Huston St Ostrander (43061) ***(G-15644)***
K M B Inc...330 889-3451
1306 State Route 88 Bristolville (44402) ***(G-2082)***
K M C, Cleveland *Also called Knitting Machinery Corp* ***(G-5540)***
K P Precision Tool and Mch Co...419 237-2596
606 N Park St Fayette (43521) ***(G-9633)***
K Petroleum Inc (PA)...614 532-5420
81 Mill St Ste 205 Gahanna (43230) ***(G-10086)***
K S Machine Inc...216 687-0459
3215 Superior Ave E Cleveland (44114) ***(G-5513)***
K S W C Inc...440 577-1114
697 State Line Rd Pierpont (44082) ***(G-16065)***
K Ventures Inc...419 678-2308
211 E Main St Coldwater (45828) ***(G-6415)***
K Wm Beach Mfg Co Inc...937 399-3838
4655 Urbana Rd Springfield (45502) ***(G-17429)***
K-B Plating Inc...216 341-1115
3685 E 78th St Cleveland (44105) ***(G-5514)***
K-Column LLC...937 269-3696
438 7 Mile Rd Eaton (45320) ***(G-9155)***
K-Hill Signal Co Inc...740 922-0421
326 W 3rd St Uhrichsville (44683) ***(G-18890)***
K-M-S Industries Inc...440 243-6680
6519 Eastland Rd Ste 1 Brookpark (44142) ***(G-2150)***
K.M.I. Printing, Chardon *Also called Key Maneuvers Inc* ***(G-3119)***
K.M.S., Brookpark *Also called K-M-S Industries Inc* ***(G-2150)***
K/H Enterprises, Fairfield *Also called Kaaa/Hamilton Enterprises Inc* ***(G-9516)***
K2 Petroleum & Supply LLC...937 503-2614
11371 Village Brook Dr # 1321 Cincinnati (45249) ***(G-3891)***
K2 Pure Solutions LP (PA)...925 526-8112
3515 Massillon Rd Ste 290 Uniontown (44685) ***(G-18922)***
Ka Wanner Inc...740 251-4636
370 W Fairground St Marion (43302) ***(G-12714)***
Kaaa/Hamilton Enterprises Inc...513 874-5874
3143 Production Dr Fairfield (45014) ***(G-9516)***
Kabler Farms...513 732-0501
4529 Elmwood Rd Batavia (45103) ***(G-1156)***
Kacy Architectural Millwork, Howard *Also called Kacy Stairs* ***(G-10996)***
Kacy Stairs...740 599-5201
19762 Nunda Rd Howard (43028) ***(G-10996)***

Kad Holdings Inc ALPHABETIC SECTION

Kad Holdings Inc 614 792-3399
5887 Karric Square Dr Dublin (43016) ***(G-8935)***
Kadant Black Clawson Inc 251 653-8558
1425 Kingsview Dr Lebanon (45036) ***(G-11666)***
Kadant Black Clawson Inc (HQ) 513 229-8100
1425 Kingsview Dr Lebanon (45036) ***(G-11667)***
Kadee Industries Newco Inc 440 439-8650
7160 Krick Rd Ste A Bedford (44146) ***(G-1420)***
Kaeden Books, Westlake *Also called Kaeden Corporation* ***(G-20127)***
Kaeden Corporation 440 617-1400
806 Sharon Dr Ste F Westlake (44145) ***(G-20127)***
Kaeper Machine Inc 440 974-1010
8680 Twinbrook Rd Mentor (44060) ***(G-13488)***
Kaffenbarger Truck Eqp Co (PA) 937 845-3804
10100 Ballentine Pike New Carlisle (45344) ***(G-14669)***
Kaffenbarger Truck Eqp Co 513 772-6800
3260 E Kemper Rd Cincinnati (45241) ***(G-3892)***
Kahiki Foods Inc 614 322-3180
1100 Morrison Rd Gahanna (43230) ***(G-10087)***
Kahle Technologies Inc 419 523-3951
1204 E 3rd St Ottawa (45875) ***(G-15657)***
Kahny Printing Inc 513 251-2911
4766 River Rd Cincinnati (45233) ***(G-3893)***
Kahuna Bay Spray Tan LLC 419 386-2387
757 Warehouse Rd Ste E-F Toledo (43615) ***(G-18360)***
Kaiser Aluminum Fab Pdts LLC 740 522-1151
600 Kaiser Dr Heath (43056) ***(G-10723)***
Kaiser Aluminum Newark Works, Heath *Also called Kaiser Aluminum Fab Pdts LLC* ***(G-10723)***
Kaiser Foods Inc (PA) 513 621-2053
500 York St Cincinnati (45214) ***(G-3894)***
Kaiser Foods Inc 513 241-6833
2155 Kindel Ave Cincinnati (45214) ***(G-3895)***
Kaiser Pickles, Cincinnati *Also called Kaiser Foods Inc* ***(G-3895)***
Kaiser Pickles LLC 513 621-2053
500 York St Cincinnati (45214) ***(G-3896)***
Kaivac Inc (PA) 513 887-4600
2680 Van Hook Ave Hamilton (45015) ***(G-10577)***
Kalcor Coatings Company 440 946-4700
37721 Stevens Blvd Willoughby (44094) ***(G-20350)***
Kaleidoscope Magazine LLC 216 566-5500
1677 E 40th St Cleveland (44103) ***(G-5515)***
Kalida Manufacturing Inc 419 532-2026
801 Ottawa St Kalida (45853) ***(G-11278)***
Kalinich Fence Company Inc 440 238-6127
12223 Prospect Rd Strongsville (44149) ***(G-17759)***
Kalmbach Feeds Inc (PA) 419 294-3838
7148 State Highway 199 Upper Sandusky (43351) ***(G-18957)***
Kalron LLC 440 647-3039
143 Erie St Wellington (44090) ***(G-19584)***
Kalt Manufacturing Company 440 327-2102
36700 Sugar Ridge Rd North Ridgeville (44039) ***(G-15235)***
Kam Manufacturing Inc 419 238-6037
1197 Grill Rd Van Wert (45891) ***(G-19096)***
Kam Services, Newark *Also called Kathy Edie* ***(G-14890)***
Kaman Corporation 614 871-1893
3735 Gantz Rd Ste C Grove City (43123) ***(G-10438)***
Kaman Fluid Power LLC 330 315-3100
195 S Main St Ste 400 Akron (44308) ***(G-230)***
Kamco Industries Inc (HQ) 419 924-5511
1001 E Jackson St West Unity (43570) ***(G-19971)***
Kamps Inc 937 526-9333
10709 Reed Rd Versailles (45380) ***(G-19183)***
Kanan Enterprises Inc (PA) 440 248-8484
31900 Solon Rd Solon (44139) ***(G-17179)***
Kanan Enterprises Inc 440 349-0719
6401 Davis Indus Pkwy Solon (44139) ***(G-17180)***
Kanawha Scales & Systems Inc 513 576-0700
26 Whitney Dr Milford (45150) ***(G-14023)***
Kando of Cincinnati Inc 513 459-7782
2025 Mckinley Blvd Lebanon (45036) ***(G-11668)***
Kane Sign Co 330 253-5263
486 E Glenwood Ave Akron (44310) ***(G-231)***
Kanel Brothers Church Supplies, Canton *Also called Kanel Brothers Supply* ***(G-2721)***
Kanel Brothers Supply 330 499-4802
8280 Kent Ave Ne Canton (44721) ***(G-2721)***
Kangaroo Brand Mops, Union City *Also called Ha-Ste Manufacturing Co Inc* ***(G-18904)***
KAO USA Inc (HQ) 513 421-1400
2535 Spring Grove Ave Cincinnati (45214) ***(G-3897)***
KAO USA Inc 513 421-1400
8778 Lesaint Dr Hamilton (45011) ***(G-10578)***
Kap Signs, Dayton *Also called Blang Acquisition LLC* ***(G-8058)***
Kapios LLC 567 661-0772
2865 N Reynolds Rd 220d Toledo (43615) ***(G-18361)***
Kapios Health, Toledo *Also called Kapios LLC* ***(G-18361)***
Kaplan Industries Inc 513 386-7762
6255 Kilby Rd Harrison (45030) ***(G-10654)***
Kaplan Industries Inc (PA) 856 779-8181
6255 Kilby Rd Harrison (45030) ***(G-10655)***
Kapstone Container Corporation 330 562-6111
1450 S Chillicothe Rd Aurora (44202) ***(G-886)***
Kar-Del Plastics Inc 419 289-9739
1177 Faultless Dr Ashland (44805) ***(G-715)***
Kard Bridge Products, Minster *Also called Kard Welding Inc* ***(G-14218)***
Kard Welding Inc 419 628-2598
480 Osterloh Rd Minster (45865) ***(G-14218)***
Kardol Quality Products LLC (PA) 513 933-8206
9933 Alliance Rd Ste 2 Blue Ash (45242) ***(G-1800)***
Karen Carson Creations, Dayton *Also called Carson-Saeks Inc* ***(G-8078)***
Karg Corporation 330 633-4916
241 Southwest Ave Tallmadge (44278) ***(G-17988)***
Karg Fiberglass Inc 330 494-2611
2831 Diamond St Middlebranch (44652) ***(G-13758)***
Karl Industries Inc 330 562-4100
11415 Chamberlain Rd Aurora (44202) ***(G-887)***
Karlco Oilfield Services Inc 440 576-3415
141 E Jefferson St Jefferson (44047) ***(G-11231)***
Karma Metal Products Inc 419 524-4371
556 Caldwell Ave Mansfield (44905) ***(G-12466)***
Karman Rubber Company (PA) 330 864-2161
2331 Copley Rd Akron (44320) ***(G-232)***
Karn Meats Inc 614 252-3712
922 Taylor Ave Columbus (43219) ***(G-7083)***
Karrier Company Inc 330 823-9597
1065 S Liberty Ave Alliance (44601) ***(G-480)***
Kars Ohio LLC 614 655-1099
6359 Summit Rd Sw Pataskala (43062) ***(G-15834)***
Karyall-Telday Inc 216 281-4063
8221 Clinton Rd Cleveland (44144) ***(G-5516)***
Kasai North America Inc 419 209-0470
1111 N Warpole St Upper Sandusky (43351) ***(G-18958)***
Kasai North America Inc 614 356-1494
655 Metro Pl S Ste 560 Dublin (43017) ***(G-8936)***
Kase Equipment 216 642-9040
7400 Hub Pkwy Cleveland (44125) ***(G-5517)***
Kasel Engineering LLC 937 854-8875
5911 Wolf Creek Pike Trotwood (45426) ***(G-18629)***
Kaskell Manufacturing Inc 937 704-9700
240 Hiawatha Trl Springboro (45066) ***(G-17332)***
Kasper Enterprises Inc 419 841-6656
7844 W Central Ave Toledo (43617) ***(G-18362)***
Kastler & Reichlin Inc 440 322-0970
710 Taylor St Elyria (44035) ***(G-9281)***
Katherine A Stull Inc 440 349-3977
7079 Navajo Trl Solon (44139) ***(G-17181)***
Kathom Manufacturing Co Inc 513 868-8890
661 Williams Ave Hamilton (45015) ***(G-10579)***
Kathy Edie 740 763-4887
2737 Licking Valley Rd Newark (43055) ***(G-14890)***
Kathy Simecek 440 886-2468
8506 Pin Oak Dr Cleveland (44130) ***(G-5518)***
Kathys Krafts and Kollectibles 423 787-3709
3303 Hamilton Rd Medina (44256) ***(G-13284)***
Katies Light House LLC 419 645-5451
300 Dupler Ave Cridersville (45806) ***(G-7811)***
Katies Snack Foods LLC 614 440-0780
3929 Hill Park Rd Hilliard (43026) ***(G-10836)***
Kaufman Container Company (PA) 216 898-2000
1000 Keystone Pkwy # 100 Cleveland (44135) ***(G-5519)***
Kaufman Engineered Systems Inc 419 878-9727
1260 Wtrville Monclova Rd Waterville (43566) ***(G-19499)***
Kaufman Mulch Inc 330 893-3676
3988 County Road 135 Millersburg (44654) ***(G-14103)***
Kaufman Trucking, Millersburg *Also called Kaufman Mulch Inc* ***(G-14103)***
Kawneer Company Inc 216 252-3203
4536 Industrial Pkwy Cleveland (44135) ***(G-5520)***
Kaws Inc 513 521-8292
2680 Civic Center Dr Cincinnati (45231) ***(G-3898)***
Kay Capital Company (HQ) 216 531-1010
1441 Chardon Rd Cleveland (44117) ***(G-5521)***
Kay Toledo Tag Inc 419 729-5479
6050 Benore Rd Toledo (43612) ***(G-18363)***
Kay Zee Inc 330 339-1268
1279 Crestview Ave Sw New Philadelphia (44663) ***(G-14777)***
Kbc Services 513 693-3743
9993 Union Cemetery Rd Loveland (45140) ***(G-12203)***
Kbi Group Inc 614 873-5825
7370 Merchant Rd Plain City (43064) ***(G-16198)***
Kbr, Cincinnati *Also called Kitchens By Rutenschroer Inc* ***(G-3914)***
Kc Robotics Inc 513 860-4442
9000 Le Saint Dr West Chester (45014) ***(G-19729)***
Kcg Inc 614 238-9450
3939 E 5th Ave Columbus (43219) ***(G-7084)***
Kci Holding USA Inc (HQ) 937 525-5533
4401 Gateway Blvd Springfield (45502) ***(G-17430)***
Kci Works, Canal Winchester *Also called Kellogg Cabinets Inc* ***(G-2504)***
Kcs Cleaning Service 740 418-5479
7550 State Route 93 Oak Hill (45656) ***(G-15453)***
Kdc Innovation, New Albany *Also called Tri-Tech Laboratories Inc* ***(G-14637)***

ALPHABETIC SECTION
Kennedy Mint Inc

Kdc Lynchburg, Johnstown *Also called Kdc US Holdings Inc* ***(G-11269)***
Kdc US Holdings Inc....740 927-2817
8825 Smiths Mill Rd N Johnstown (43031) ***(G-11269)***
Kdlamp Company, Andover *Also called Atc Lighting & Plastics Inc* ***(G-580)***
Kdm Screen Printing, Cincinnati *Also called Kdm Signs Inc* ***(G-3900)***
Kdm Signs Inc....513 769-3900
3000 Exon Ave Cincinnati (45241) ***(G-3899)***
Kdm Signs Inc (PA)....513 769-1932
10450 Medallion Dr Cincinnati (45241) ***(G-3900)***
Keb Industries Inc....440 953-4623
2166 Joseph Lloyd Pkwy Willoughby (44094) ***(G-20351)***
Keban Industries Inc....216 446-0159
7500 Wall St Ste 100 Cleveland (44125) ***(G-5522)***
Kebco Precision Fabricators....330 456-0808
3145 Columbus Rd Ne Canton (44705) ***(G-2722)***
Kecamm LLC....330 527-2918
10404 Industrial Dr Garrettsville (44231) ***(G-10194)***
Keck Engineering Inc....440 355-9855
39610 Whitney Rd Lagrange (44050) ***(G-11485)***
Keco Plating, Cleveland *Also called Roberts-Demand Corp* ***(G-5993)***
Kecoat LLC....330 527-0215
10610 Freedom St Garrettsville (44231) ***(G-10195)***
Kedar D Army....419 238-6929
11373 Van Wert Decatur Rd Van Wert (45891) ***(G-19097)***
Kee Printing Inc....937 456-6851
118 W Monfort St Eaton (45320) ***(G-9156)***
Keebler Company....513 271-3500
1 Trade St Cincinnati (45227) ***(G-3901)***
Keeler Enterprises Inc....330 336-7601
924 Seville Rd Wadsworth (44281) ***(G-19247)***
Keen Manufacturing Inc....330 427-0045
240 High St Washingtonville (44490) ***(G-19480)***
Keen Pump Company Inc....419 207-9400
471 E State Rte 250 E Ashland (44805) ***(G-716)***
Keener Printing Inc....216 531-7595
401 E 200th St Cleveland (44119) ***(G-5523)***
Keener Rubber Company....330 821-1880
14700 Commerce St Ne Alliance (44601) ***(G-481)***
Keeney Sand & Stone Inc....440 254-4582
13320 Girdled Rd Painesville (44077) ***(G-15752)***
Kegg Pipe Organ Builders, Hartville *Also called C E Kegg Inc* ***(G-10686)***
Kehl-Kolor Inc....419 281-3107
824 Us Highway 42 Ashland (44805) ***(G-717)***
Kehler Enterprises Inc....614 889-8488
323 W Bridge St Dublin (43017) ***(G-8937)***
Kehoe Brothers Printing Inc....216 351-4100
910 W Schaaf Rd Cleveland (44109) ***(G-5524)***
Keihin Thermal Tech Amer Inc....740 869-3000
10500 Oday Harrison Rd Mount Sterling (43143) ***(G-14462)***
Keith Grimm....419 899-2725
100 W Pearl St Sherwood (43556) ***(G-16991)***
Keithley Enterprises Inc....937 890-1878
3425 Garianne Dr Dayton (45414) ***(G-8290)***
Keithley Instruments LLC (HQ)....440 248-0400
28775 Aurora Rd Solon (44139) ***(G-17182)***
Keithley Instruments Intl Corp....440 248-0400
28775 Aurora Rd Cleveland (44139) ***(G-5525)***
Kel-Mar Inc....419 806-4600
436 N Enterprise St Bowling Green (43402) ***(G-1979)***
Kelblys Rifle Range Inc....330 683-0070
7222 Dalton Fox Lake Rd North Lawrence (44666) ***(G-15162)***
Kelch Manufacturing Corp....440 366-5060
626 Sugar Ln Elyria (44035) ***(G-9282)***
Kelchner Inc (HQ)....937 704-9890
50 Advanced Dr Springboro (45066) ***(G-17333)***
Kelco Hardwood Floors Inc....440 354-0974
10137 Johnnycake Ridge Rd Painesville (44077) ***(G-15753)***
Kelic, Waterville *Also called Rimer Enterprises Inc* ***(G-19504)***
Kelley Bible Books, Dayton *Also called Kelley Communication Dev* ***(G-8291)***
Kelley Communication Dev....937 298-6132
2312 Candlewood Dr Dayton (45419) ***(G-8291)***
Kelleys Island Wine Co....419 746-2678
418 Woodford Rd Kelleys Island (43438) ***(G-11283)***
Kellogg Cabinets Inc....614 833-9596
7711 Diley Rd Canal Winchester (43110) ***(G-2504)***
Kellogg Company....513 271-3500
1 Trade St Cincinnati (45227) ***(G-3902)***
Kellogg Company....614 879-9659
125 Enterprise Pkwy West Jefferson (43162) ***(G-19924)***
Kellogg Company....513 792-2700
8044 Montgomery Rd # 700 Cincinnati (45236) ***(G-3903)***
Kellogg Company....614 855-3437
124 Hyatts Rd Delaware (43015) ***(G-8699)***
Kellogg Company....740 453-5501
1675 Fairview Rd Zanesville (43701) ***(G-21152)***
Kellogg Yard, Cincinnati *Also called Martin Marietta Materials Inc* ***(G-3983)***
Kellstone....419 621-8140
201 Putnam St Sandusky (44870) ***(G-16820)***
Kelly Cabinet Company LLC....614 563-2971
525 Thrush Rill Ct Powell (43065) ***(G-16324)***
Kelly Duplex, Springfield *Also called Duplex Mill & Manufacturing Co* ***(G-17392)***
Kelly Foods Corporation (PA)....330 722-8855
3337 Medina Rd Medina (44256) ***(G-13285)***
Kelly Machine Ltd....419 825-2006
7245 County Road 1 3 Swanton (43558) ***(G-17915)***
Kelly Plating Co....216 961-1080
10316 Madison Ave Cleveland (44102) ***(G-5526)***
Kelly Printing, Obetz *Also called Michael R Kelly* ***(G-15511)***
Kelly Prints LLC....440 356-6361
24112 Lorain Rd North Olmsted (44070) ***(G-15194)***
Kelly-Creswell Company, Springfield *Also called Ernest Industries Inc* ***(G-17397)***
Kellys Welding & Fabricating....440 593-6040
285 N Amboy Rd Conneaut (44030) ***(G-7651)***
Keltec Inc (PA)....330 425-3100
2300 E Enterprise Pkwy Twinsburg (44087) ***(G-18798)***
Keltec-Technolab, Twinsburg *Also called Keltec Inc* ***(G-18798)***
Kem Advertising and Prtg LLC....330 818-5061
564 W Tuscarawas Ave # 104 Barberton (44203) ***(G-1080)***
Kemex Laboratories, Monroe *Also called Grean Technologies LLC* ***(G-14265)***
Kemper Automotive....800 783-8004
1380 E 2nd St Franklin (45005) ***(G-9892)***
Kempf Surgical Appliances Inc....513 984-5758
10567 Montgomery Rd Montgomery (45242) ***(G-14295)***
Ken AG Inc....419 281-1204
101 E 7th St Ashland (44805) ***(G-718)***
Ken Emerick Machine Products....440 834-4501
14504 Main Market Rd Burton (44021) ***(G-2365)***
Ken Forging Inc....440 993-8091
1049 Griggs Rd Jefferson (44047) ***(G-11232)***
Ken Harper....740 439-4452
60772 Southgate Rd Byesville (43723) ***(G-2388)***
Ken Veney Industries LLC....330 336-5825
690 Weber Dr Wadsworth (44281) ***(G-19248)***
Ken-Dal Corporation....330 644-7118
644 Killian Rd Coventry Township (44319) ***(G-7772)***
Ken-Tools, Akron *Also called Summit Tool Company* ***(G-392)***
Kenamerican Resources Inc (HQ)....740 338-3100
46226 National Rd Saint Clairsville (43950) ***(G-16635)***
Kenan Advantage Group Inc....614 878-4050
500 Manor Park Dr Columbus (43228) ***(G-7085)***
Kencraft Co Inc....419 536-0333
821 N Westwood Ave Toledo (43607) ***(G-18364)***
Kendall & Sons Company....937 222-6996
2800 E 3rd St Dayton (45403) ***(G-8292)***
Kendall Holdings Ltd (PA)....614 486-4750
2111 Builders Pl Columbus (43204) ***(G-7086)***
Kendall Printing, Dayton *Also called Kendall & Sons Company* ***(G-8292)***
Kendall/Hunt Publishing Co....877 275-4725
8805 Governors Hill Dr # 400 Cincinnati (45249) ***(G-3904)***
Kendee Candles LLC....330 899-9898
4761 Buhl Blvd Uniontown (44685) ***(G-18923)***
Kendel Welding & Fabrication....330 834-2429
1700 Navarre Rd Se Massillon (44646) ***(G-13008)***
Kendra Screen Print....440 967-8820
3817 Liberty Ave Vermilion (44089) ***(G-19164)***
Kenlake Foods, Cincinnati *Also called Inter American Products Inc* ***(G-3853)***
Kenley Enterprises LLC....419 630-0921
418 N Lynn St Bryan (43506) ***(G-2293)***
Kenmore Construction Co Inc....330 832-8888
9500 Forty Corners Rd Nw Massillon (44647) ***(G-13009)***
Kenmore Development & Mch Co....330 753-2274
1395 Kenmore Blvd Akron (44314) ***(G-233)***
Kenmore Gear & Machine Co Inc....330 753-6671
2129 Jennifer St Akron (44313) ***(G-234)***
Kenn Feld Group LLC....419 238-1299
10305 Liberty Union Rd Van Wert (45891) ***(G-19098)***
Kennametal Inc....440 437-5131
180 Penniman Rd Orwell (44076) ***(G-15633)***
Kennametal Inc....216 898-6120
18105 Cleveland Pkwy Dr Cleveland (44135) ***(G-5527)***
Kennametal Inc....419 877-5358
6325 Industrial Pkwy Whitehouse (43571) ***(G-20192)***
Kennametal Inc....440 349-5151
6865 Cochran Rd Solon (44139) ***(G-17183)***
Kennedy Catalogs LLC....513 753-1518
4177 Knollview Ct Batavia (45103) ***(G-1157)***
Kennedy Graphics, Cleveland *Also called Kennedy Mint Inc* ***(G-5528)***
Kennedy Graphics Inc (PA)....419 223-9825
1640 N Main St Lima (45801) ***(G-11883)***
Kennedy Group Incorporated (PA)....440 951-7660
38601 Kennedy Pkwy Willoughby (44094) ***(G-20352)***
Kennedy Ink Company Inc (PA)....513 871-2515
5230 Wooster Pike Cincinnati (45226) ***(G-3905)***
Kennedy Ink Company Inc....937 461-5600
110 Vermont Ave Dayton (45404) ***(G-8293)***
Kennedy Mint Inc....440 572-3222
12102 Pearl Rd Rear Cleveland (44136) ***(G-5528)***

ALPHABETIC

Kennedys Bakery Inc 740 432-2301
1025 Wheeling Ave Cambridge (43725) *(G-2444)*

Kenneth Hickman Co 513 348-0016
4266 Tranquility Ct Batavia (45103) *(G-1158)*

Kenneth J Moore 330 923-8313
3775 Wyoga Lake Rd Cuyahoga Falls (44224) *(G-7887)*

Kenneth Mc Beth 740 922-9494
514 Stillwater Ave Denison (44621) *(G-8784)*

Kenneth Schrock 937 544-7566
3735 Wheat Ridge Rd West Union (45693) *(G-19964)*

Kenneth Shannon 513 777-8888
5438 Kyles Station Rd Liberty Twp (45011) *(G-11826)*

Kennewegs Wood Products 330 832-1540
973 Vindell Ave Nw Massillon (44647) *(G-13010)*

Kennick Mold & Die Inc 216 631-3535
3601 Detroit Ave Cleveland (44113) *(G-5529)*

Kenoil Inc 330 262-1144
1537 Blachleyville Rd Wooster (44691) *(G-20612)*

Kenosha Beef International Ltd 614 771-1330
1821 Dividend Dr Columbus (43228) *(G-7087)*

Kens His & Hers Shop Inc 330 872-3190
5 S Milton Blvd Ste C Newton Falls (44444) *(G-14988)*

Kensington Plant, Kensington Also called M3 Midstream LLC *(G-11285)*

Kent Adhesive Products Co 330 678-1626
1000 Cherry St Kent (44240) *(G-11338)*

Kent Automation Inc 330 678-6343
449 Dodge St Kent (44240) *(G-11339)*

Kent Corporation 440 582-3400
9601 York Alpha Dr North Royalton (44133) *(G-15280)*

Kent Displays Inc (PA) 330 673-8784
343 Portage Blvd Kent (44240) *(G-11340)*

Kent Elastomer Products, Winesburg Also called Meridian Industries Inc *(G-20533)*

Kent Elastomer Products, Kent Also called Meridian Industries Inc *(G-11351)*

Kent Elastomer Products Inc 800 331-4762
3890 Mogadore Indus Pkwy Mogadore (44260) *(G-14242)*

Kent Elastomer Products Inc (HQ) 330 673-1011
1500 Saint Clair Ave Kent (44240) *(G-11341)*

Kent Information Services Inc 330 672-2110
6185 2nd Ave Kent (44240) *(G-11342)*

Kent Mold and Manufacturing Co 330 673-3469
1190 W Main St Kent (44240) *(G-11343)*

Kent Parks Recreation, Kent Also called City of Kent *(G-11304)*

Kent Paverbrick LLC 330 995-7000
11437 Chamberlain Rd Aurora (44202) *(G-888)*

Kent Sporting Goods Co Inc (PA) 419 929-7021
433 Park Ave New London (44851) *(G-14730)*

Kent State University 330 672-7913
307 Lwry Hall Terrance Dr Kent (44242) *(G-11344)*

Kent State University 330 672-2586
205 Frlanklin Hall Kent (44242) *(G-11345)*

Kent Stow Screen Printing Inc 330 923-5118
1340 Home Ave Ste F Akron (44310) *(G-235)*

Kent Swigart 937 836-5292
301 W Wenger Rd Englewood (45322) *(G-9365)*

Kentak Products Company 330 386-3700
1230 Railroad St Ste 1 East Liverpool (43920) *(G-9062)*

Kentak Products Company (PA) 330 382-2000
1230 Railroad St Ste 1 East Liverpool (43920) *(G-9063)*

Kentak Products Company 330 532-6211
1230 Railroad St Ste 1 East Liverpool (43920) *(G-9064)*

Kenton Iron Products Inc (PA) 419 674-4178
347 Vine St Kenton (43326) *(G-11411)*

Kenton Times, Kenton Also called Ray Barnes Newspaper Inc *(G-11420)*

Kenton Times, The, Kenton Also called Hardin County Publishing Co *(G-11408)*

Kentrox Inc (HQ) 614 798-2000
5800 Innovation Dr Dublin (43016) *(G-8938)*

Kenway Corp 937 767-1660
504 Xenia Ave Yellow Springs (45387) *(G-20809)*

Kenwel Printers Inc 614 261-1011
4272 Indianola Ave Columbus (43214) *(G-7088)*

Kenworth of Dayton 937 235-2589
7740 Center Point 70 Blvd Dayton (45424) *(G-8294)*

Kenyon Co, Coshocton Also called Novelty Advertising Co Inc *(G-7745)*

Kenyon Review 740 427-5208
104 College Dr Fl 2 Gambier (43022) *(G-10182)*

Kepcor Inc 330 868-6434
215 Bridge St Minerva (44657) *(G-14186)*

Kerber Sheetmetal Works Inc 937 339-6366
104 Foss Way Troy (45373) *(G-18681)*

Kerek Industries Ltd Lblty Co 440 461-1450
750 Beta Dr Ste A Cleveland (44143) *(G-5530)*

Kerf Waterjet, Dayton Also called Forsvara Engineering LLC *(G-8202)*

Kern Inc (HQ) 614 317-2600
3940 Gantz Rd Ste A Grove City (43123) *(G-10439)*

Kern Inc 440 930-7315
755 Alpha Dr Cleveland (44143) *(G-5531)*

Kern Machine Tool Inc 419 470-1206
367 E State Line Rd Toledo (43612) *(G-18365)*

Kern-Liebers Texas Inc 419 865-2437
1510 Albon Rd Holland (43528) *(G-10940)*

Kern-Liebers Usa Inc (HQ) 419 865-2437
1510 Albon Rd Holland (43528) *(G-10941)*

Kernells Autmtc Machining Inc 419 588-2164
10511 State Rte 61 N Berlin Heights (44814) *(G-1654)*

Kerr Friction Products Inc 330 455-3983
2512 Columbus Rd Ne Canton (44705) *(G-2723)*

Kerry Flavor Systems Us LLC 513 539-7373
1055 Reed Dr Monroe (45050) *(G-14270)*

Kerry Inc 760 685-2548
100 Hope Ave Byesville (43723) *(G-2389)*

Kerry Inc 440 229-5200
5800 Landerbrook Dr # 300 Mayfield Heights (44124) *(G-13166)*

Kerry Ingredients, Byesville Also called Kerry Inc *(G-2389)*

Kerry Ingredients & Flavours, Monroe Also called Kerry Flavor Systems Us LLC *(G-14270)*

Kes Industries LLC (PA) 330 405-2813
8040 Bavaria Rd Twinsburg (44087) *(G-18799)*

Kessler Outdoor Advertising, Zanesville Also called Kessler Sign Company *(G-21153)*

Kessler Sign Company (PA) 740 453-0668
2669 National Rd Zanesville (43701) *(G-21153)*

Kessler Sign Company 937 898-0633
5804 Poe Ave Dayton (45414) *(G-8295)*

Kessler Studios Inc 513 683-7500
273 E Broadway St Loveland (45140) *(G-12204)*

Ketco Inc 937 426-9331
1348 Research Park Dr Beavercreek (45432) *(G-1324)*

Keteli Teamwear LLC 740 373-7969
313 Greene St Marietta (45750) *(G-12637)*

Ketman Corporation 330 262-1688
205 W Liberty St Wooster (44691) *(G-20613)*

Kettering Monogramming, Dayton Also called Zimmer Enterprises Inc *(G-8604)*

Kettering Roofing & Shtmtl 513 281-6413
3210 Jefferson Ave Ste 1 Cincinnati (45220) *(G-3906)*

Keuchel & Associates Inc 330 945-9455
175 Muffin Ln Cuyahoga Falls (44223) *(G-7888)*

Keurig Dr Pepper Inc 614 237-4201
950 Stelzer Rd Columbus (43219) *(G-7089)*

Keurig Dr Pepper Inc 419 535-0777
224 N Byrne Rd Toledo (43607) *(G-18366)*

Keurig Dr Pepper Inc 614 237-4201
960 Stelzer Rd Columbus (43219) *(G-7090)*

Kever Incorporated 614 552-9000
4581 Poth Rd Columbus (43213) *(G-7091)*

Kever Printing & Promotions, Columbus Also called Kever Incorporated *(G-7091)*

Kevin G Ryba Inc 419 627-2010
3727 Perkins Ave Huron (44839) *(G-11101)*

Kevin K Tidd 419 885-5603
5505 Roan Rd Sylvania (43560) *(G-17948)*

Key Blue Prints Inc 614 899-6180
1920 Schrock Rd Columbus (43229) *(G-7092)*

Key Finishes LLC 614 351-8393
727 Harrison Dr Columbus (43204) *(G-7093)*

Key Maneuvers Inc (PA) 440 285-0774
10639 Grant St Ste C Chardon (44024) *(G-3119)*

Key Marketing Group 440 748-3479
11185 Arrowhead Dr Grafton (44044) *(G-10306)*

Key Mobility Services Ltd 937 374-3226
1944 Us Route 68 N Xenia (45385) *(G-20780)*

Key Press Inc 513 721-1203
2135 Central Pkwy Cincinnati (45214) *(G-3907)*

Key Resin Company (HQ) 513 943-4225
4050 Clough Woods Dr Batavia (45103) *(G-1159)*

Keyah International Trdg LLC (PA) 937 399-3140
4655 Urbana Rd Springfield (45502) *(G-17431)*

Keynes Brothers Inc 740 426-6332
12574 State Route 41 Jeffersonville (43128) *(G-11247)*

Keysco Tools, Cleveland Also called S & H Industries Inc *(G-6018)*

Keystone Bolt & Nut Company 216 524-9626
7600 Hub Pkwy Cleveland (44125) *(G-5532)*

Keystone Foods Inc 419 257-2341
2208 Grant Rd North Baltimore (45872) *(G-15044)*

Keystone Press Inc 419 243-7326
1801 Broadway St Toledo (43609) *(G-18367)*

Keystone Printing & Copy Cat 740 354-6542
842 4th St Portsmouth (45662) *(G-16286)*

Keystone Printing Co 330 385-9519
648 Saint Clair Ave East Liverpool (43920) *(G-9065)*

Keystone Threaded Products, Cleveland Also called Keystone Bolt & Nut Company *(G-5532)*

Keytel Systems, Reynoldsburg Also called Town Cntry Technical Svcs Inc *(G-16457)*

Kf Technologies and Custom Mfg 419 426-0172
12178 E County Road 6 Attica (44807) *(G-857)*

KG Tool Company 440 428-8633
5640 Middle Ridge Rd Madison (44057) *(G-12352)*

Kg63 LLC 216 941-7766
15501 Chatfield Ave Cleveland (44111) *(G-5533)*

Khempco Bldg Sup Co Ltd Partnr (PA) 740 549-0465
130 Johnson Dr Delaware (43015) *(G-8700)*

ALPHABETIC SECTION
Kirwan Industries Inc

Kicher and Company (PA).....440 266-1663
6942 Spinach Dr Mentor (44060) ***(G-13489)***
Kichler Lighting, Cleveland *Also called Clare Sky Inc* ***(G-4936)***
Kick Salsa LLC.....614 330-2499
5281 Spring Beauty Ct Columbus (43230) ***(G-7094)***
Kid Concoctions Company.....440 572-1800
18511 Whitemarsh Ln Strongsville (44149) ***(G-17760)***
Kiddi Pops, Dalton *Also called Yost Candy Co* ***(G-7954)***
Kief Signs.....513 941-8800
3 E Main St Addyston (45001) ***(G-12)***
Kiefer Tool & Mold Inc.....216 251-0076
3855 W 150th St Cleveland (44111) ***(G-5534)***
Kiemle-Hankins Company (PA).....419 661-2430
94 H St Perrysburg (43551) ***(G-15972)***
Kight Creations, Dayton *Also called Naomi Kight* ***(G-8375)***
Kilar Manufacturing Inc.....330 534-8961
2616 N Main St Hubbard (44425) ***(G-11004)***
Kilbarger Construction Inc.....740 385-6019
450 Gallagher Ave Logan (43138) ***(G-12030)***
Kilbarger Investment Co, Logan *Also called Kilbarger Investments Inc* ***(G-12031)***
Kilbarger Investments Inc.....740 385-6019
450 Gallagher Ave Logan (43138) ***(G-12031)***
Kiley Machine Company Inc.....513 875-3223
4196 Anderson State Rd Fayetteville (45118) ***(G-9640)***
Kiley Mold Company LLC.....513 875-3223
4200 Anderson State Rd Fayetteville (45118) ***(G-9641)***
Killbuck Creek Distillery LLC.....740 502-2880
42879 Us Highway 36 B Warsaw (43844) ***(G-19475)***
Killbuck Creek Oil Co.....330 601-0921
2538 Columbus Rd Wooster (44691) ***(G-20614)***
Killbuck Oilfield Services.....330 276-6706
9277 Township Road 92 Killbuck (44637) ***(G-11453)***
Killer Brownie Ltd.....937 535-5690
6135 Far Hills Ave Dayton (45459) ***(G-8296)***
Killian Latex Inc.....330 644-6746
2064 Killian Rd Akron (44312) ***(G-236)***
Kiln.....440 717-1880
7225 Fitzwater Rd Brecksville (44141) ***(G-2044)***
Kiln of Hyde Park Inc.....513 321-3307
1286 Herschel Ave Cincinnati (45208) ***(G-3908)***
Kilnit Ltd.....330 906-0748
1625 Graham Rd Stow (44224) ***(G-17598)***
Kilroy Company (PA).....440 951-8700
34929 Curtis Blvd Ste 104 Eastlake (44095) ***(G-9117)***
Kiltex Corporation.....330 644-6746
2064 Killian Rd Akron (44312) ***(G-237)***
Kim Brauer & Company LLC.....330 540-9152
7465 Huntington Dr Apt 6 Youngstown (44512) ***(G-20952)***
Kim Phillips Sign Co LLC.....330 364-4280
812 Boulevard St Dover (44622) ***(G-8834)***
Kimball Midwest, Columbus *Also called Midwest Motor Supply Co* ***(G-7181)***
Kimberly-Clark Corporation.....513 864-3780
209 W 7th St Cincinnati (45202) ***(G-3909)***
Kimberly-Clark Corporation.....513 794-1005
9277 Centre Pointe Dr # 200 West Chester (45069) ***(G-19730)***
Kimble Custom Chassis Company.....877 546-2537
1951 Reiser Ave Se New Philadelphia (44663) ***(G-14778)***
Kimble Machines Inc.....419 485-8449
124 S Jonesville St Montpelier (43543) ***(G-14311)***
Kimble Manufacturing Company, New Philadelphia *Also called Kimble Custom Chassis Company* ***(G-14778)***
Kimble Mixer Company.....330 308-6700
1951 Reiser Ave Se New Philadelphia (44663) ***(G-14779)***
Kimmatt Corp.....937 228-3811
326 Troy St Dayton (45404) ***(G-8297)***
Kimpton Printing & Spc Co.....330 467-1640
400 Highland Rd E Macedonia (44056) ***(G-12310)***
Kimpton Prtg & Specialities, Macedonia *Also called Kimpton Printing & Spc Co* ***(G-12310)***
Kind Special Alloys Us LLC.....330 788-2437
1221 Velma Ct Youngstown (44512) ***(G-20953)***
Kinetic Dsign Group - Columbus, Cincinnati *Also called Spark LLC* ***(G-4356)***
Kinetic Technologies Inc.....440 943-4111
1350 Rockefeller Rd Wickliffe (44092) ***(G-20214)***
King Bag and Manufacturing Co (PA).....513 541-5440
1500 Spring Lawn Ave Cincinnati (45223) ***(G-3910)***
King Bros Feed & Supply, Bristolville *Also called K M B Inc* ***(G-2082)***
King Castings, Akron *Also called King Model Company* ***(G-238)***
King Drilling Co.....330 769-3434
24 E Main St Seville (44273) ***(G-16919)***
King Energy Inc.....330 297-5508
6050 State Route 14 Lot 7 Ravenna (44266) ***(G-16386)***
King Kold Inc.....937 836-2731
331 N Main St Englewood (45322) ***(G-9366)***
King Kutter II Inc.....740 446-0351
2150 Eastern Ave Gallipolis (45631) ***(G-10169)***
King Limestone Inc.....740 638-3942
53681 Spencer Rd Cumberland (43732) ***(G-7824)***
King Luminaire, Jefferson *Also called Stress-Crete Company* ***(G-11239)***
King Luminaire Company Inc (HQ).....440 576-9073
1153 State Route 46 N Jefferson (44047) ***(G-11233)***
King Machine and Tool Co.....330 833-7217
1237 Sanders Ave Sw Massillon (44647) ***(G-13011)***
King Media Enterprises Inc.....216 588-6700
11800 Shaker Blvd Cleveland (44120) ***(G-5535)***
King Mill's Woodworking, Plain City *Also called Kbi Group Inc* ***(G-16198)***
King Model Company.....330 633-0491
365 Kenmore Blvd Akron (44301) ***(G-238)***
King Nut Companies, Solon *Also called Kanan Enterprises Inc* ***(G-17179)***
King Nut Companies, Plant 2, Solon *Also called Kanan Enterprises Inc* ***(G-17180)***
King of The Road, Troy *Also called Crowe Manufacturing Services* ***(G-18644)***
King Quarries Inc.....740 732-2923
41820 Parrish Ridge Rd Caldwell (43724) ***(G-2408)***
King Retail Solutions Inc.....513 729-5858
3865 Symmes Rd Hamilton (45015) ***(G-10580)***
King Software Systems.....330 562-1135
680 Briarcliff Dr Aurora (44202) ***(G-889)***
King Vineyards.....440 967-4191
5903 Coen Rd Vermilion (44089) ***(G-19165)***
King Wolf Enterprises LLC.....330 853-0450
1865 Park Way East Liverpool (43920) ***(G-9066)***
King-Indiana Forge Inc.....330 425-4250
8250 Boyle Pkwy Twinsburg (44087) ***(G-18800)***
Kings Command Foods LLC.....937 526-3553
770 N Center St Versailles (45380) ***(G-19184)***
Kings Welding and Fabg Inc.....330 738-3592
5259 Bane Rd Ne Mechanicstown (44651) ***(G-13212)***
Kingscote Chemicals Inc.....330 523-5300
3778 Timberlake Dr Richfield (44286) ***(G-16475)***
Kingscote Chemicals Inc.....937 886-9100
3334 S Tech Blvd Miamisburg (45342) ***(G-13683)***
Kingscote-Formulabs, Miamisburg *Also called Kingscote Chemicals Inc* ***(G-13683)***
Kingsford Ink LLC.....216 507-4032
2663 Noble Rd Apt 4 Cleveland Heights (44121) ***(G-6349)***
Kingsly Compression Inc.....740 439-0772
3956 Glenn Hwy Cambridge (43725) ***(G-2445)***
Kingspan Benchmark, Columbus *Also called Benchmark Archtectural Systems* ***(G-6662)***
Kingsway Art & Sign.....330 877-6241
1555 Andrews St Ne Hartville (44632) ***(G-10698)***
Kingswood Company, The, Columbus *Also called Glister Inc* ***(G-6955)***
Kinnemeyers Cornerstone Cab Co, Cleves *Also called Kinnemyers Cornerstone Cab Inc* ***(G-6367)***
Kinnemyers Cornerstone Cab Inc.....513 353-3030
6000 Hamilton Cleves Rd Cleves (45002) ***(G-6367)***
Kinninger Prod Wldg Co Inc.....419 629-3491
710 Kuenzel Dr New Bremen (45869) ***(G-14655)***
Kinsella Manufacturing Co Inc.....513 561-5285
7880 Camargo Rd Cincinnati (45243) ***(G-3911)***
Kinstle Ster/West Star Truck C, Wapakoneta *Also called Kinstle Truck & Auto Svc Inc* ***(G-19337)***
Kinstle Truck & Auto Svc Inc.....419 738-7493
1770 Wapak Fisher Rd Wapakoneta (45895) ***(G-19337)***
Kinzua Environmental Inc.....216 881-4040
1176 E 38th St Ste 1 Cleveland (44114) ***(G-5536)***
Kip-Craft Incorporated (PA).....216 898-5500
4747 W 160th St Cleveland (44135) ***(G-5537)***
Kipps Gravel Company Inc.....513 732-1024
4987 State Route 222 Batavia (45103) ***(G-1160)***
Kiraly Tool and Die Inc.....330 744-5773
1250 Crescent St Youngstown (44502) ***(G-20954)***
Kirby and Sons Inc.....419 927-2260
4876 County Highway 43 Upper Sandusky (43351) ***(G-18959)***
Kirby Customer Service Center, Cleveland *Also called Scott Fetzer Company* ***(G-6040)***
Kirby Sand & Gravel, Upper Sandusky *Also called Kirby and Sons Inc* ***(G-18959)***
Kirbys Auto & Truck Repair.....513 934-3999
875 Columbus Ave Lebanon (45036) ***(G-11669)***
Kirchhoff Auto Waverly Inc (HQ).....740 947-7763
611 W 2nd St Waverly (45690) ***(G-19550)***
Kirk & Blum Manufacturing Co (HQ).....513 458-2600
4625 Red Bank Rd Ste 200 Cincinnati (45227) ***(G-3912)***
Kirk Excavating & Construction.....614 444-4008
821 Stimmel Rd Columbus (43223) ***(G-7095)***
Kirk Key Interlock Company LLC.....330 833-8223
9048 Meridian Cir Nw North Canton (44720) ***(G-15096)***
Kirk Welding & Fabricating.....216 961-6403
10410 Madison Ave Cleveland (44102) ***(G-5538)***
Kirk Williams Company Inc.....614 875-9023
2734 Home Rd Grove City (43123) ***(G-10440)***
Kirkwood Holding Inc (PA).....216 267-6200
1239 Rockside Rd Cleveland (44134) ***(G-5539)***
Kirtland Capital Partners LP (PA).....216 593-0100
3201 Entp Pkwy Ste 200 Beachwood (44122) ***(G-1244)***
Kirtland Cpitl Partners III LP (PA).....440 585-9010
2550 Som Center Rd # 105 Willoughby Hills (44094) ***(G-20470)***
Kirwan Industries Inc.....513 333-0766
1964 Central Ave Cincinnati (45214) ***(G-3913)***

ALPHABETIC

ALPHABETIC SECTION

Kiser Industries llc..937 332-6723
　507 Michigan Ave Troy (45373) *(G-18682)*

Kissicakes - N-Sweets LLC...................................614 940-2779
　7660 Silver Fox Dr Columbus (43235) *(G-7096)*

Kistler Instrument Corp..937 268-5920
　3061 Dorf Dr Dayton (45439) *(G-8298)*

Kit MB Systems Inc...330 945-4500
　925 Glaser Pkwy Akron (44306) *(G-239)*

Kitchen & Bath Factory Inc..................................440 510-8111
　7170 Hawthorne Dr Mentor (44060) *(G-13490)*

Kitchen Collection LLC (HQ)................................740 773-9150
　71 E Water St Chillicothe (45601) *(G-3198)*

Kitchen Designs Plus Inc......................................419 536-6605
　2725 N Reynolds Rd Toledo (43615) *(G-18368)*

Kitchen Works Inc...440 353-0939
　34425 Lorain Rd Ste 5 North Ridgeville (44039) *(G-15236)*

Kitchens By Rutenschroer Inc (PA).....................513 251-8333
　950 Laidlaw Ave Cincinnati (45237) *(G-3914)*

Kitt's Heating & AC Co, Struthers Also called Kitts Heating & AC *(G-17818)*

Kitto Katsu Inc..818 256-6997
　7445 Lockwood St Clayton (45315) *(G-4576)*

Kitts Heating & AC..330 755-9242
　289 Elm St Ste 1 Struthers (44471) *(G-17818)*

Kittyhawk Molding Company Inc.........................937 746-3663
　10 Eagle Ct Carlisle (45005) *(G-2894)*

Kiwi Promotional AP & Prtg Co............................330 487-5115
　2170 E Aurora Rd Twinsburg (44087) *(G-18801)*

Kj Machining Systems Inc....................................440 975-8624
　38254 Airport Pkwy Unit C Willoughby (44094) *(G-20353)*

Klarity Medical Products LLC...............................740 788-8107
　1987 Coffman Rd Newark (43055) *(G-14891)*

Klawhorn Industries Inc.......................................330 335-8191
　456 South Blvd Wadsworth (44281) *(G-19249)*

Klb Industries Inc...937 592-9010
　Orchard & Elm St Bellefontaine (43311) *(G-1521)*

Klc Brands Inc..201 456-4115
　2692 Madison Rd Cincinnati (45208) *(G-3915)*

Klebaum Machinery Inc.......................................330 455-2046
　1303 13th St Se Canton (44707) *(G-2724)*

Kleen Polymers Inc..330 336-4212
　145 Rainbow St Wadsworth (44281) *(G-19250)*

Kleen Test Products, Beach City Also called Meridian Industries Inc *(G-1212)*

Kleen Test Products Corp....................................330 878-5586
　216 12th St Ne Strasburg (44680) *(G-17649)*

Kleenline LLC..800 259-5973
　6279 Tri Ridge Blvd # 410 Loveland (45140) *(G-12205)*

Klenk Industries Inc...330 453-7857
　1016 9th St Sw Canton (44707) *(G-2725)*

Klingshirn Winery Inc..440 933-6666
　33050 Webber Rd Avon Lake (44012) *(G-992)*

Klingstedt Brothers Company.............................330 456-8319
　425 Schroyer Ave Sw Canton (44702) *(G-2726)*

Klivlend Cask Distilling LLC................................216 926-1682
　149 Hayer Dr Painesville (44077) *(G-15754)*

Klockner Pentaplast Amer Inc.............................937 743-8040
　400 Shotwell Dr Franklin (45005) *(G-9893)*

Klockner Pentaplast Amer Inc.............................937 548-7272
　1671 Martindale Rd Greenville (45331) *(G-10378)*

Klosterman Baking Co (PA).................................513 242-5667
　4760 Paddock Rd Cincinnati (45229) *(G-3916)*

Klosterman Baking Co...937 322-9588
　508 W Main St Springfield (45504) *(G-17432)*

Klosterman Baking Co...937 743-9021
　350 S Pioneer Blvd Springboro (45066) *(G-17334)*

Klosterman Baking Co...513 398-2707
　1130 Reading Rd Mason (45040) *(G-12899)*

Klosterman Baking Co...614 338-8111
　2655 Courtright Rd Columbus (43232) *(G-7097)*

Klosterman Baking Co...513 242-1004
　1000 E Ross Ave Cincinnati (45217) *(G-3917)*

Klumm Bros...419 829-3166
　9241 W Bancroft St Holland (43528) *(G-10942)*

Klw Plastics Inc..678 674-2990
　930 Deneen Ave Monroe (45050) *(G-14271)*

Klw Plastics Inc (HQ)...513 539-2673
　980 Deneen Ave Monroe (45050) *(G-14272)*

Kmak Group LLC..937 308-1023
　480 E High St London (43140) *(G-12064)*

KMC Precision Machine, Canton Also called Klebaum Machinery Inc *(G-2724)*

Kmgrafx Inc...513 248-4100
　394 Wards Corner Rd # 100 Loveland (45140) *(G-12206)*

Kmi Processing LLC (PA).....................................330 862-2185
　15383 Lisbon St Ne Minerva (44657) *(G-14187)*

Kmi Processing LLC...330 862-2185
　15441 Lisbon St Ne Minerva (44657) *(G-14188)*

Kmj Leasing Ltd...614 871-3883
　7001 Harrisburg Pike Orient (43146) *(G-15575)*

KMS 2000 Inc (PA)..330 454-9444
　315 12th St Nw Canton (44703) *(G-2727)*

Kn Rubber LLC (HQ)..419 739-4200
　1400 Lunar Dr Wapakoneta (45895) *(G-19338)*

Kn8designs LLC...859 380-5926
　4016 Allston St Cincinnati (45209) *(G-3918)*

Knape Industries Inc...614 885-3016
　6592 Proprietors Rd Worthington (43085) *(G-20693)*

Knapke Custom Cabinetry Ltd............................937 459-8866
　9306 Kelch Rd Versailles (45380) *(G-19185)*

Knapp Enterprises, Massillon Also called Joseph Knapp *(G-13006)*

Knapp Foundry Co Inc...330 434-0916
　1207 Sweitzer Ave Akron (44301) *(G-240)*

Knappco Corporation..816 741-0786
　9393 Prnceton Glendale Rd West Chester (45011) *(G-19731)*

Knauff Bros Logging & Lumber..........................740 634-2432
　494 Houseman Town Rd Bainbridge (45612) *(G-1018)*

Knauff Logging, Bainbridge Also called Knauff Bros Logging & Lumber *(G-1018)*

Knb Tools of America Inc....................................614 733-0400
　8440 Rausch Dr Plain City (43064) *(G-16199)*

Kne LLC...859 356-1690
　12 Suffolk Ct Fairfield (45014) *(G-9517)*

Kneading Dough LLC...719 310-5774
　7912 S Masn Montgomery Rd Mason (45040) *(G-12900)*

Kneiss Saw & Tool Supply, Dayton Also called Form-A-Chip Inc *(G-8201)*

Knepp's Power Equipment, Mc Arthur Also called Norman Knepp *(G-13183)*

Knief Farms A Partnership..................................937 585-4810
　10532 County Road 13 Lewistown (43333) *(G-11801)*

Knight Ergonomics Inc..440 746-0044
　6650 W Snowville Rd Ste G Brecksville (44141) *(G-2045)*

Knight Industries Corp..419 478-8550
　5949 Telegraph Rd Toledo (43612) *(G-18369)*

Knight Manufacturing Co Inc (PA).....................740 676-9532
　399 E 40th St Shadyside (43947) *(G-16922)*

Knight Manufacturing Co Inc.............................740 676-5516
　E 40th St Shadyside (43947) *(G-16923)*

Knippen Chrysler Dodge Jeep............................419 695-4976
　800 W 5th St Delphos (45833) *(G-8746)*

Knisley Lumber...740 634-2935
　160 Potts Hill Rd Bainbridge (45612) *(G-1019)*

Knitting Machinery Corp (PA).............................216 851-9900
　15625 Saranac Rd Cleveland (44110) *(G-5540)*

Knitting Machinery Corp.....................................937 548-2338
　607 Riffle Ave Greenville (45331) *(G-10379)*

Knoble Glass & Metal Inc (PA)............................513 753-1246
　8650 Green Rd Cincinnati (45255) *(G-3919)*

Knous Tool & Machine Inc...................................419 394-3541
　14184 State Route 116 Saint Marys (45885) *(G-16687)*

Knowles Press Inc..330 877-9345
　316 E Maple St Hartville (44632) *(G-10699)*

Knowlton Machine Inc...419 281-6802
　726 Virginia Ave Ashland (44805) *(G-719)*

Knowlton Manufacturing Co Inc.........................513 631-7353
　2524 Leslie Ave Cincinnati (45212) *(G-3920)*

Knox County Citizen, Galion Also called Knox County Printing Co *(G-10147)*

Knox County Printing Co.....................................740 848-4032
　129 Harding Way E Galion (44833) *(G-10147)*

Knox Energy Inc (PA)...740 927-6731
　11872 Worthington Rd Nw Pataskala (43062) *(G-15835)*

Knox Machine & Tool...740 392-3133
　250 Columbus Rd Mount Vernon (43050) *(G-14487)*

Knukonceptzcom Ltd...216 310-6555
　7227 Anderson Rd Windham (44288) *(G-20525)*

Kobelco Stewart Bolling Inc................................330 655-3111
　1600 Terex Rd Hudson (44236) *(G-11060)*

Koch Crystal Finishing, Elyria Also called Crystal Koch Finishing Inc *(G-9240)*

Koch Foods of Cincinnati LLC.............................513 874-3500
　4100 Port Union Rd Fairfield (45014) *(G-9518)*

Koch Knight LLC (HQ)..330 488-1651
　5385 Orchardview Dr Se East Canton (44730) *(G-9041)*

Koch Meat Co Inc...513 874-3500
　4100 Port Union Rd Fairfield (45014) *(G-9519)*

Kodiak Springs Water Co, Pierpont Also called K S W C Inc *(G-16065)*

Koebbeco Signs LLC...513 923-2974
　5683 Springdale Rd Cincinnati (45251) *(G-3921)*

Koehler Rubber & Supply Co...............................216 749-5100
　800 W Resource Dr Cleveland (44131) *(G-5541)*

Koenig Equipment Inc...937 653-5281
　3130 E Us Highway 36 Urbana (43078) *(G-19002)*

Koester Corporation (PA)....................................419 599-0291
　813 N Perry St Napoleon (43545) *(G-14548)*

Koester Machined Products Co..........................419 782-0291
　136 Fox Run Dr Defiance (43512) *(G-8632)*

Kohl Patterns..513 353-3831
　7983 Morgan Rd Cleves (45002) *(G-6368)*

Kohut Enterprises Inc..440 366-6666
　5281 Butternut Ridge Dr Independence (44131) *(G-11138)*

Koki Laboratories Inc..330 773-7669
　1081 Rosemary Blvd Akron (44306) *(G-241)*

Kokosing Materials Inc..419 522-2715
　215 Oak St Mansfield (44907) *(G-12467)*

Kokosing Materials Inc 740 745-3341
9134 Mount Vernon Rd Saint Louisville (43071) ***(G-16672)***
Kokosing Materials Inc 614 891-5090
6189 Westerville Rd Westerville (43081) ***(G-20061)***
Kokosing Materials Inc 614 491-1199
4755 S High St Columbus (43207) ***(G-7098)***
Kol-Cap Manufacturing Co, Cleveland *Also called Walest Incorporated* ***(G-6286)***
Kole Industries 330 353-1751
121 34th St Ne Canton (44714) ***(G-2728)***
Kole Specialties Inc 513 829-1111
4695 Industry Dr Ste A Fairfield (45014) ***(G-9520)***
Kolhfab Cstm Plstic Fbrication 937 237-2098
2025 Webster St Dayton (45404) ***(G-8299)***
Kolinahr Systems Inc 513 745-9401
6840 Ashfield Dr Blue Ash (45242) ***(G-1801)***
Kolpin Outdoors Corporation 330 328-0772
3479 State Rd Cuyahoga Falls (44223) ***(G-7889)***
Koltcz Concrete Block Co 440 232-3630
7660 Oak Leaf Rd Bedford (44146) ***(G-1421)***
Komar Industries Inc (PA) 614 836-2366
4425 Marketing Pl Groveport (43125) ***(G-10497)***
Komatec Tool & Die Inc 937 252-1133
1415 E 2nd St Dayton (45403) ***(G-8300)***
Komatsu Mining Corp 216 503-5029
981 Keynote Cir Ste 8 Independence (44131) ***(G-11139)***
Konecranes Inc 513 755-2800
9879 Crescent Park Dr West Chester (45069) ***(G-19732)***
Konecranes Inc 937 328-5123
1110 Claycraft Rd Ste C Columbus (43230) ***(G-7099)***
Konecranes Inc 937 328-5100
4505 Gateway Blvd Springfield (45502) ***(G-17433)***
Konecranes Inc (HQ) 937 525-5533
4401 Gateway Blvd Springfield (45502) ***(G-17434)***
Konecranes Inc 440 461-8400
6400 W Snowville Rd Ste 1 Brecksville (44141) ***(G-2046)***
Koneta Inc 419 739-4200
1400 Lunar Dr Wapakoneta (45895) ***(G-19339)***
Koneta Rubber, Wapakoneta *Also called Kn Rubber LLC* ***(G-19338)***
Kongsberg Actuation Systems 440 639-8778
301 Olive St Grand River (44045) ***(G-10324)***
Kongsberg Automotive, Grand River *Also called Kongsberg Actuation Systems* ***(G-10324)***
Konkrete City Skateboards 513 231-0399
2109 Beechmont Ave Cincinnati (45230) ***(G-3922)***
Konoil Inc 330 499-9811
6477 Frank Ave Nw Canton (44720) ***(G-2729)***
Konys, Mark Glass Design, Cleveland *Also called Bruening Glass Works Inc* ***(G-4846)***
Koop Diamond Cutters Inc 513 621-2838
214 E 8th St Fl 4 Cincinnati (45202) ***(G-3923)***
Kopachko Machining Inc 440 953-3988
38341 Western Pkwy Willoughby (44094) ***(G-20354)***
Koppers Ind Inc 740 776-2149
400 Harding Ave Portsmouth (45662) ***(G-16287)***
Koppers Industries Inc 740 776-3238
6501 Pershing Ave Portsmouth (45662) ***(G-16288)***
Korda Manufacturing Inc 330 262-1555
3927 E Lincoln Way Wooster (44691) ***(G-20615)***
Korff Holdings LLC 330 332-1566
310 E Euclid Ave Salem (44460) ***(G-16752)***
Korff Machine LLC 330 332-1566
310 E Euclid Ave Salem (44460) ***(G-16753)***
Koroseal Interior Products LLC (PA) 330 668-7600
3875 Embassy Pkwy Ste 110 Fairlawn (44333) ***(G-9611)***
Koroshi School of Defense 740 323-3582
12955 Fairview Rd Heath (43056) ***(G-10724)***
Kosei St Marys Corporation 419 394-7840
1100 Mckinley Rd Saint Marys (45885) ***(G-16688)***
Koski Construction Co (PA) 440 997-5337
5841 Woodman Ave Ashtabula (44004) ***(G-782)***
Koski Construction Co 440 964-8171
1149 E 5th St Ashtabula (44004) ***(G-783)***
Koster Crop Tester Inc 330 220-2116
3077 Nationwide Pkwy Brunswick (44212) ***(G-2217)***
Koster Moisture Tester, Brunswick *Also called Koster Crop Tester Inc* ***(G-2217)***
Kottler Metal Products Co Inc 440 946-7473
1595 Lost Nation Rd Willoughby (44094) ***(G-20355)***
Kountry Pride Enterprises 330 868-3345
10167 Malibu Rd Ne Minerva (44657) ***(G-14189)***
Kovacevic Printing Inc 440 887-1000
13367 Smith Rd Cleveland (44130) ***(G-5542)***
Kovatch Castings Inc 330 896-9944
3743 Tabs Dr Uniontown (44685) ***(G-18924)***
Kowalski Heat Treating Co 216 631-4411
3611 Detroit Ave Cleveland (44113) ***(G-5543)***
Kps NAPA 740 522-9445
441 Hopewell Dr Heath (43056) ***(G-10725)***
Krafft and Associates Inc 937 325-4671
991 W Leffel Ln Springfield (45506) ***(G-17435)***
Kraft Electrical Contg Inc 614 836-9300
4407 Professional Pkwy Groveport (43125) ***(G-10498)***
Kraft Foods, Toledo *Also called Mondelez Global LLC* ***(G-18416)***
Kraft Heinz Company, Massillon *Also called Kraft Heinz Company* ***(G-13012)***
Kraft Heinz Company 330 837-8331
1301 Oberlin Ave Sw Massillon (44647) ***(G-13012)***
Kraft Heinz Foods Company 419 332-7357
1200n N 5th St Fremont (43420) ***(G-10032)***
Kraft Heinz Foods Company 740 622-0523
1660 S 2nd St Coshocton (43812) ***(G-7738)***
Kraft House No 5 ....614 396-9091
5 S Liberty St Powell (43065) ***(G-16325)***
Kraft of Writing 614 620-2476
46 Webster Park Ave Columbus (43214) ***(G-7100)***
Kraftee Kreations, Cleveland *Also called Our Family Mall* ***(G-5827)***
Kraftmaid Cabinetry, Orwell *Also called Masco Cbinetry Middlefield LLC* ***(G-15634)***
Kraftmaid Trucking Inc (PA) 440 632-2531
16052 Industrial Pkwy Middlefield (44062) ***(G-13812)***
Kram Precision Machining Inc 937 849-1301
1751 Dalton Dr New Carlisle (45344) ***(G-14670)***
Kramer & Kiefer Inc 330 336-8742
2662 Valley Side Ave Wadsworth (44281) ***(G-19251)***
Kramer Graphics Inc 937 296-9600
2408 W Dorothy Ln Moraine (45439) ***(G-14363)***
Kramer Power Equipment Co 937 456-2232
2388 State Route 726 N Eaton (45320) ***(G-9157)***
Kramer Printing, Mentor *Also called J & L Management Corporation* ***(G-13479)***
Kraton Emplyees Recreation CLB 740 423-7571
2419 State Route 618 Belpre (45714) ***(G-1577)***
Kraton Polymers US LLC 740 423-7571
2419 State Rd 618 Belpre (45714) ***(G-1578)***
Krausher Machining Inc 440 839-2828
4267 Butler Rd Wakeman (44889) ***(G-19285)***
Krazy Glue, West Jefferson *Also called Toagosei America Inc* ***(G-19928)***
Krdc Inc 937 222-2332
90 Vermont Ave Dayton (45404) ***(G-8301)***
Kre Inc 216 883-1600
2181 Enterprise Pkwy Twinsburg (44087) ***(G-18802)***
Kreider Corp 937 325-8787
2000 S Yellow Springs St Springfield (45506) ***(G-17436)***
Krema Group Inc 614 889-4824
7920 Corporate Blvd Ste B Plain City (43064) ***(G-16200)***
Krema Nut Co, Columbus *Also called Brilista Foods Company Inc* ***(G-6700)***
Krema Peanut Butter, Dublin *Also called Krema Products Inc* ***(G-8939)***
Krema Products Inc (PA) 614 889-4824
45 N High St Dublin (43017) ***(G-8939)***
Krendl Machine Company 419 692-3060
1201 Spencerville Rd Delphos (45833) ***(G-8747)***
Krendl Rack Co Inc 419 667-4800
18413 Haver Rd Venedocia (45894) ***(G-19154)***
Krengel Equipment LLC 440 946-3570
34580 Lakeland Blvd Eastlake (44095) ***(G-9118)***
Krengel Manufacturing, Eastlake *Also called Krengel Equipment LLC* ***(G-9118)***
Krisdale Industries Inc 330 225-2392
649 Marks Rd Valley City (44280) ***(G-19043)***
Krispy Kreme 322, Columbus *Also called Krispy Kreme Doughnut Corp* ***(G-7101)***
Krispy Kreme Doughnut Corp 614 798-0812
3690 W Dblin Granville Rd Columbus (43235) ***(G-7101)***
Kriss Kreations 330 405-6102
9224 Darrow Rd Twinsburg (44087) ***(G-18803)***
Krist Krenz Machine Inc 440 237-1800
9801 York Alpha Dr North Royalton (44133) ***(G-15281)***
Kristine Marie's Olfactorium, Cleveland *Also called Olfactorium Corp Inc* ***(G-5811)***
Kroehler Furniture Mfg Co Inc 828 459-9865
4300 E 5th Ave Columbus (43219) ***(G-7102)***
Kroger 00510, Findlay *Also called Kroger Co* ***(G-9711)***
Kroger Co 740 671-5164
400 28th St Bellaire (43906) ***(G-1487)***
Kroger Co 740 335-4030
548 Clinton Ave Wshngtn CT Hs (43160) ***(G-20731)***
Kroger Co 740 264-5057
264 S Hollywood Blvd Steubenville (43952) ***(G-17540)***
Kroger Co 513 683-4001
2900 W Us Hwy 22 3 Unit 1 Maineville (45039) ***(G-12372)***
Kroger Co 513 742-9500
1212 W Kemper Rd Ste 1 Cincinnati (45240) ***(G-3924)***
Kroger Co 740 374-2523
40 Acme St Marietta (45750) ***(G-12638)***
Kroger Co 419 423-2065
101 6th St Findlay (45840) ***(G-9711)***
Kroger Co 937 277-0950
1934 Needmore Rd Dayton (45414) ***(G-8302)***
Kroger Co 614 263-1766
3417 N High St Columbus (43214) ***(G-7103)***
Kroger Co 937 743-5900
725 W Central Ave Springboro (45066) ***(G-17335)***
Kroger Co 614 575-3742
7000 E Broad St Columbus (43213) ***(G-7104)***
Kroner Publications Inc (PA) 330 544-5500
1123 W Park Ave Niles (44446) ***(G-15020)***
Kronos Incorporated 216 867-5609
6100 Oak Tree Blvd # 410 Independence (44131) ***(G-11140)***

ALPHABETIC

Kroy LLC (HQ) 216 426-5600
  3830 Kelley Ave Cleveland (44114) *(G-5544)*

Krumor Inc 216 328-9802
  7655 Hub Pkwy Ste 206 Cleveland (44125) *(G-5545)*

Krusinski's Meat Market, Cleveland *Also called John Krusinski (G-5502)*

Kruz Inc 330 878-5595
  6332 Columbia Rd Nw Dover (44622) *(G-8835)*

KS Designs Inc 513 241-5953
  3636 Muddy Creek Rd Apt 1 Cincinnati (45238) *(G-3925)*

KSA Limited Partnership 740 776-3238
  6501 Pershing Ave Portsmouth (45662) *(G-16289)*

Kse Manufacturing 937 409-9831
  175 S Lester Ave Sidney (45365) *(G-17048)*

Ksi Distribution Inc (PA) 440 256-2500
  8724 Tyler Blvd Mentor (44060) *(G-13491)*

Ksm Metal Fabrication 937 339-6366
  104 Foss Way Troy (45373) *(G-18683)*

Ksm Metal Fabrications, Troy *Also called Kerber Sheetmetal Works Inc (G-18681)*

Ksn Clearing LLC 304 269-3306
  736 2nd Ave Gallipolis (45631) *(G-10170)*

Kth Parts Industries Inc (PA) 937 663-5941
  1111 State Route 235 N Saint Paris (43072) *(G-16709)*

Ktm North America Inc (PA) 855 215-6360
  1119 Milan Ave Amherst (44001) *(G-564)*

Ktri Holdings Inc (PA) 216 371-1700
  127 Public Sq Ste 5110 Cleveland (44114) *(G-5546)*

Kts Cstm Lgs/Xclsvely You Inc 440 285-9803
  602 South St Ste C-2 Chardon (44024) *(G-3120)*

Kts Custom Logos 440 285-9803
  602 South St Ste C-2 Chardon (44024) *(G-3121)*

Kts-Met Bar Products Inc 440 288-9308
  967 G St Lorain (44052) *(G-12097)*

Ktsdi LLC 330 783-2000
  801 E Middletown Rd North Lima (44452) *(G-15173)*

Kubota Authorized Dealer, Athens *Also called All Power Equipment LLC (G-822)*

Kubota Tractor Corporation 614 835-3800
  6300 At One Kubota Way Groveport (43125) *(G-10499)*

Kufbag Inc 614 589-8687
  1333 Cobblestone Ave Westerville (43081) *(G-20062)*

Kuhlman Construction Products, Maumee *Also called Kuhlman Corporation (G-13124)*

Kuhlman Corporation (PA) 419 897-6000
  1845 Indian Wood Cir Maumee (43537) *(G-13124)*

Kuhlman Corporation 419 321-1670
  444 Kuhlman Dr Toledo (43609) *(G-18370)*

Kuhlman Engineering Co 419 243-2196
  840 Champlain St Toledo (43604) *(G-18371)*

Kuhlman Instrument Company 419 668-9533
  54 Summit St Norwalk (44857) *(G-15402)*

Kuhlmanns Fabrication 513 967-4617
  1753 Millville Oxford Rd Hamilton (45013) *(G-10581)*

Kuhls Hot Sportspot 513 474-2282
  7860 Beechmont Ave Cincinnati (45255) *(G-3926)*

Kuhn Fabricating Inc 440 277-4182
  1637 E 28th St Lorain (44055) *(G-12098)*

Kuhns Mfg Llc 440 693-4630
  4210 Kinsman Rd Nw North Bloomfield (44450) *(G-15065)*

Kuka Toledo Production 419 727-5500
  3770 Stickney Ave Toledo (43608) *(G-18372)*

Kurts Auto Parts LLC 330 723-0166
  4093 Watercourse Dr Medina (44256) *(G-13286)*

Kurtz Bros Inc 614 491-0868
  2850 Rohr Rd Groveport (43125) *(G-10500)*

Kurtz Bros Compost Services 330 864-2621
  2677 Riverview Rd Akron (44313) *(G-242)*

Kurtz Tool & Die Co Inc 330 755-7723
  164 State St Struthers (44471) *(G-17819)*

Kurz-Kasch Inc 740 498-8343
  199 E State St Newcomerstown (43832) *(G-14976)*

Kurz-Kasch Inc (HQ) 740 498-8343
  199 E State St Newcomerstown (43832) *(G-14977)*

Kurzkasch Inc Wilm Div 740 498-8345
  199 E State St Newcomerstown (43832) *(G-14978)*

Kusakabe America Corporation 216 524-2485
  6116 W Creek Rd Cleveland (44131) *(G-5547)*

Kustom Cases LLC 240 380-6275
  130 Oxford Ave Dayton (45402) *(G-8303)*

Kutol Products Company Inc 513 527-5500
  100 Partnership Way Sharonville (45241) *(G-16957)*

Kutrite Manufacturing, Tremont City *Also called Mike Loppe (G-18616)*

Kuwatch Printing LLC 513 759-5850
  7163 Ashview Ln Liberty Twp (45011) *(G-11827)*

Kw River Hydroelectric I LLC 513 673-2251
  5667 Krystal Ct Ste 100 Cincinnati (45252) *(G-3927)*

Kw Services LLC 419 636-3438
  527 S Union St Bryan (43506) *(G-2294)*

Kw Services LLC 419 228-1325
  1864 Mccullough St Lima (45801) *(G-11884)*

Kwik Kopy Printing, Blue Ash *Also called Larmax Inc (G-1803)*

Kwik Kopy Printing, Columbus *Also called Hilleary-Whitaker Inc (G-7001)*

Kwik Kopy Printing, Youngstown *Also called Austintown Printing Inc (G-20849)*

Kyle Publications Inc 419 754-4234
  2611 Montebello Rd Toledo (43607) *(G-18373)*

Kyntrol Holdings Inc (PA) 440 220-5990
  34700 Lakeland Blvd Eastlake (44095) *(G-9119)*

Kyntronics, Inc (HQ) 440 220-5990
  6565 Davis Indus Pkwy Solon (44139) *(G-17184)*

Kyocera Senco Indus Tls Inc (HQ) 800 543-4596
  4270 Ivy Pointe Blvd Cincinnati (45245) *(G-3256)*

Kyocera SGS Precision Tools (PA) 330 688-6667
  55 S Main St Munroe Falls (44262) *(G-14524)*

Kyocera SGS Precision Tools 330 688-6667
  2824 2nd St Cuyahoga Falls (44221) *(G-7890)*

Kyocera SGS Precision Tools 330 686-4151
  150 Marc Dr Cuyahoga Falls (44223) *(G-7891)*

Kyocera SGS Precision Tools 330 922-1953
  238 Marc Dr Cuyahoga Falls (44223) *(G-7892)*

Kyron Plating Corp 216 221-7275
  1336 W 114th St Cleveland (44102) *(G-5548)*

Kyron Tool and Machine Co Inc 614 231-6000
  2900 Banwick Rd Columbus (43232) *(G-7105)*

Kys Welding & Fabrication 513 702-9081
  154 Shoemaker Dr Loveland (45140) *(G-12207)*

Kz Solutions Inc 513 942-9378
  9440 Sutton Pl West Chester (45011) *(G-19733)*

L & C Plastic Bags Inc 937 473-2968
  500 Dick Minnich Dr Covington (45318) *(G-7789)*

L & F Lauch LLC 513 732-5805
  950 Kent Rd Batavia (45103) *(G-1161)*

L & H Printing 937 855-4512
  34 W Market St Germantown (45327) *(G-10243)*

L & H Printing Co, Germantown *Also called L & H Printing (G-10243)*

L & H Wood Products, Sidney *Also called Langston Pallets (G-17049)*

L & I Natural Resources Inc 513 683-2045
  10369 Cones Rd Loveland (45140) *(G-12208)*

L & J Cable Inc 937 526-9445
  102 Industrial Dr Russia (45363) *(G-16609)*

L & J Drive Thru 330 767-2185
  212 Wabash Ave N Brewster (44613) *(G-2069)*

L & L Fabricating LLC 440 647-6649
  46419 Whitney Rd Wellington (44090) *(G-19585)*

L & L Machine Inc 419 272-5000
  2919 County Road 2l Edon (43518) *(G-9185)*

L & L Ornamental Iron Co 513 353-1930
  6024 Hamilton Cleves Rd Cleves (45002) *(G-6369)*

L & L Plastics, Felicity *Also called L C Liming & Sons Inc (G-9644)*

L & L Railings, Cleves *Also called L & L Ornamental Iron Co (G-6369)*

L & M Mineral Co 330 852-3696
  2010 County Road 144 Sugarcreek (44681) *(G-17851)*

L & N Olde Car Co 440 564-7204
  9992 Kinsman Rd Newbury (44065) *(G-14959)*

L & P Machine Company 330 527-2753
  8488 State Route 305 Garrettsville (44231) *(G-10196)*

L & R Racing Inc 330 220-3102
  900 Theora Dr Brunswick (44212) *(G-2218)*

L & S Liette Express 419 394-7077
  2286 Celina Rd Saint Marys (45885) *(G-16689)*

L & T Collins Inc 740 345-4494
  44 S 4th St Newark (43055) *(G-14892)*

L & W Inc 734 397-6300
  1190 Jaycox Rd Avon (44011) *(G-953)*

L A Express (PA) 513 752-6999
  1148 Marian Dr Batavia (45103) *(G-1162)*

L A Machine 216 651-1712
  3818 Trent Ave Cleveland (44109) *(G-5549)*

L A Productions Co LLC (PA) 330 666-4230
  1333 Collier Rd Akron (44320) *(G-243)*

L A Products Co, Akron *Also called L A Productions Co LLC (G-243)*

L and J Woodworking 330 359-3216
  9035 Senff Rd Dundee (44624) *(G-9020)*

L and S Express Fuel Center 330 549-9566
  10125 Market St North Lima (44452) *(G-15174)*

L B Folding Co Inc 216 961-0888
  12126 York Rd Unit F North Royalton (44133) *(G-15282)*

L B Foster Company 330 652-1461
  1193 Salt Springs Rd Mineral Ridge (44440) *(G-14168)*

L B Industries Inc 330 750-1002
  534 Lowellville Rd Struthers (44471) *(G-17820)*

L B L Lithographers Inc (PA) 440 350-0106
  365 W Prospect St Painesville (44077) *(G-15755)*

L B L Printing, Painesville *Also called L B L Lithographers Inc (G-15755)*

L B Machine & Mfg Co Inc 513 471-6137
  6624 Layhigh Rd Okeana (45053) *(G-15519)*

L B Manufacturing, Byesville *Also called Famous Industries Inc (G-2384)*

L B Weiss Construction Inc 440 205-1774
  8677 Twinbrook Rd Mentor (44060) *(G-13492)*

L Brands Inc 614 479-2000
  3 Limited Pkwy Columbus (43230) *(G-7106)*

ALPHABETIC SECTION — Lake Plating, Elyria

L C F Inc 330 877-3322
 114 S Prospect Ave Hartville (44632) *(G-10700)*
L C G Machine & Tool Inc 614 261-1651
 2923 Grasmere Ave Columbus (43224) *(G-7107)*
L C I Inc 330 948-1922
 101 West Dr Lodi (44254) *(G-12013)*
L C Liming & Sons Inc 513 876-2555
 3200 State Route 756 Felicity (45120) *(G-9644)*
L C Smith Co 440 327-1251
 196 Morgan Ave Elyria (44035) *(G-9283)*
L C Systems Inc 614 235-9430
 6135 Memorial Dr Ste 106f Dublin (43017) *(G-8940)*
L D C, Independence *Also called Liquid Development Company* *(G-11141)*
L E P D Industries Ltd 614 985-1470
 2292 Clairborne Dr Powell (43065) *(G-16326)*
L Garbers Sons Sawmilling LLC 419 335-6362
 6444 County Road 12 Wauseon (43567) *(G-19524)*
L Haberny Co Inc 440 543-5999
 10115 Queens Way Chagrin Falls (44023) *(G-3054)*
L J Manufacturing Inc 440 352-1979
 9436 Mercantile Dr Mentor (44060) *(G-13493)*
L J Minor Corp 216 861-8350
 2621 W 25th St Cleveland (44113) *(G-5550)*
L J Smith Inc (HQ) 740 269-2221
 35280 Scio Bowerston Rd Bowerston (44695) *(G-1940)*
L J Star Incorporated 330 405-3040
 2396 Edison Blvd Twinsburg (44087) *(G-18804)*
L M Animal Farms, Pleasant Plain *Also called Hartz Mountain Corporation* *(G-16227)*
L M Berry and Company (PA) 937 296-2121
 3170 Kettering Blvd Moraine (45439) *(G-14364)*
L M Engineering Inc 330 270-2400
 2720 Intertech Dr Youngstown (44509) *(G-20955)*
L M Equipment & Design Inc 330 332-9951
 11000 Youngstown Salem Rd Salem (44460) *(G-16754)*
L N Brut Manufacturing Co 330 833-9045
 4680 Alabama Ave Sw Navarre (44662) *(G-14578)*
L N S Pallets 330 936-7507
 6144 Smith Rd Sw Navarre (44662) *(G-14579)*
L P S I, Cleveland *Also called Laser Printing Solutions Inc* *(G-5563)*
L S Manufacturing Inc 614 885-7988
 480 E Wilson Bridge Rd C Worthington (43085) *(G-20694)*
L&E Engineering LLC 937 746-6696
 291 Conover Dr Franklin (45005) *(G-9894)*
L&H Threaded Rods Corp 937 294-6666
 3050 Dryden Rd Moraine (45439) *(G-14365)*
L&L Excavating & Land Clearing 740 682-7823
 56 Jim Reese Rd Oak Hill (45656) *(G-15454)*
L&M Sheet Metal Ltd 513 858-6173
 5010 Factory Dr Fairfield (45014) *(G-9521)*
L&W Cleveland, Avon *Also called L & W Inc* *(G-953)*
L-3 Cmmncations Nova Engrg Inc 877 282-1168
 4393 Digital Way Mason (45040) *(G-12901)*
L-3 Cmmnctions Electrodynamics, Cincinnati *Also called Electrodynamics Inc* *(G-3247)*
L-3 Communications Cincinnati, Mason *Also called L3 Cincinnati Electronics Corp* *(G-12902)*
L-3 Fuzing and Ord Systems Inc, Cincinnati *Also called L3 Fuzing and Ord Systems Inc* *(G-3257)*
L-K Industry Inc 937 526-3000
 176 N West St Versailles (45380) *(G-19186)*
L-Mor Inc 216 541-2224
 13404 Saint Clair Ave Cleveland (44110) *(G-5551)*
L.E.M. Products, West Chester *Also called Lem Products Holding LLC* *(G-19736)*
L3 Aviation Products Inc 614 825-2001
 1105 Schrock Rd Ste 800 Columbus (43229) *(G-7108)*
L3 Cincinnati Electronics Corp (HQ) 513 573-6100
 7500 Innovation Way Mason (45040) *(G-12902)*
L3 Fuzing and Ord Systems Inc 513 943-2000
 3975 Mcmann Rd Cincinnati (45245) *(G-3257)*
L3 Technologies Inc 513 943-2000
 3975 Mcmann Rd Cincinnati (45245) *(G-3258)*
La Boit Specialty Vehicles (PA) 614 231-7640
 700 Cross Pointe Rd Gahanna (43230) *(G-10088)*
La Dua Inc 440 243-9600
 17123 Hilliard Rd Lakewood (44107) *(G-11524)*
La Ganke & Sons Stamping Co 216 451-0278
 13676 Station Rd Columbia Station (44028) *(G-6439)*
La Grange Elec Assemblies Co 440 355-5388
 349 S Center St Lagrange (44050) *(G-11486)*
La Mfg Inc 513 577-7200
 9483 Reading Rd Cincinnati (45215) *(G-3928)*
La Perla Inc (PA) 419 534-2074
 2742 Hill Ave Toledo (43607) *(G-18374)*
La Rose Paving Co Inc 440 632-0330
 16590 Nauvoo Rd Middlefield (44062) *(G-13813)*
La Voz Hispania Newspaper 614 274-4505
 3552 Sullivant Ave Columbus (43204) *(G-7109)*
Laad Sign & Lighting Inc 330 379-2297
 830 Moe Dr Ste B Akron (44310) *(G-244)*
Lab Electronics Inc 330 674-9818
 5640 Township Road 353 Millersburg (44654) *(G-14104)*
Lab Quality Machining Inc 513 625-0219
 6311 Roudebush Rd Goshen (45122) *(G-10289)*
Lab-Pro Inc 937 434-9600
 11019 Cold Spring Dr Dayton (45458) *(G-8304)*
Lababidi Enterprises Inc 330 733-2907
 2167 Forest Oak Dr Akron (44312) *(G-245)*
Labcraft Inc 419 878-4400
 1070 Disher Dr Waterville (43566) *(G-19500)*
Label Aid Inc 419 433-2888
 608 Rye Beach Rd Huron (44839) *(G-11102)*
Label Print Technologies LLC 800 475-4030
 3380 Gilchrist Rd Mogadore (44260) *(G-14243)*
Label Technique Southeast LLC 440 951-7660
 38601 Kennedy Pkwy Willoughby (44094) *(G-20356)*
Labeldata 614 891-5858
 275 Old County Line Rd I Westerville (43081) *(G-20063)*
Laborie Enterprises LLC 419 686-6245
 10892 S Dixie Hwy Portage (43451) *(G-16270)*
Lacal Equipment Inc 800 543-6161
 901 W Pike St Jackson Center (45334) *(G-11210)*
Laces For Less, Cincinnati *Also called Joe Busby* *(G-3876)*
Lachina Creative Inc 216 292-7959
 3791 Green Rd Cleveland (44122) *(G-5552)*
Lad Technology Inc 440 461-8002
 7830 Hermitage Rd Painesville (44077) *(G-15756)*
Lafarge North America Inc 419 399-4861
 11435 County Rd 176 Paulding (45879) *(G-15864)*
Lafarge North America Inc 419 798-4486
 831 S Quarry Rd Marblehead (43440) *(G-12586)*
Lafarge North America Inc 216 781-9330
 2500 Elm St Cleveland (44113) *(G-5553)*
Lafarge North America Inc 419 241-5256
 840 Water St Toledo (43604) *(G-18375)*
Lafarge North America Inc 419 897-7656
 1645 Indian Wood Cir Maumee (43537) *(G-13125)*
Lafarge North America Inc 330 393-5656
 6205 Newton Fls Bailey Rd Warren (44481) *(G-19415)*
Lafarge North America Inc 740 423-5900
 1684 State Route 618 Belpre (45714) *(G-1579)*
Lafargeholcim, Paulding *Also called Lafarge North America Inc* *(G-15864)*
Lafargeholcim, Cleveland *Also called Lafarge North America Inc* *(G-5553)*
Lafargeholcim, Toledo *Also called Lafarge North America Inc* *(G-18375)*
Lagc Ltd 419 886-2141
 11729 Leedy Rd Fredericktown (43019) *(G-9972)*
Lahm Tool, Dayton *Also called Lahm-Trosper Inc* *(G-8305)*
Lahm-Trosper Inc 937 252-8791
 1030 Springfield St Dayton (45403) *(G-8305)*
Laipplys Prtg Mktg Sltions Inc 740 387-9282
 270 E Center St Marion (43302) *(G-12715)*
Laird Connectivity Inc (HQ) 330 434-7929
 50 S Main St Ste 1100 Akron (44308) *(G-246)*
Laird Plastics Inc 614 272-0777
 2220 International St Columbus (43228) *(G-7110)*
Laird Technologies Inc 234 806-0105
 655 N River Rd Nw Warren (44483) *(G-19416)*
Laird Technologies Inc 330 434-7929
 50 S Main St Ste 1100 Akron (44308) *(G-247)*
Laird Technologies Inc 216 939-2300
 4707 Detroit Ave Cleveland (44102) *(G-5554)*
Lake Cable Optical Lab 330 497-3022
 4837 Frank Ave Nw Canton (44720) *(G-2730)*
Lake Cable Optical Laboratory, Canton *Also called Lake Cable Optical Lab* *(G-2730)*
Lake City Plating LLC 440 964-3555
 1701 Lake Ave Ashtabula (44004) *(G-784)*
Lake Cnty Deptmntl Retrdtn/Dvl, Willoughby *Also called County of Lake* *(G-20302)*
Lake Community News 440 946-2577
 36081 Lake Shore Blvd # 5 Willoughby (44095) *(G-20357)*
Lake County Auto Recyclers 440 428-2886
 427 Newell St Painesville (44077) *(G-15757)*
Lake County Plating Corp 440 255-8835
 7790 Division Dr Mentor (44060) *(G-13494)*
Lake Erie Asphalt Paving Inc 440 526-5191
 5510 Oakes Rd Brecksville (44141) *(G-2047)*
Lake Erie Frozen Foods Mfg Co 419 289-9204
 1830 Orange Rd Ashland (44805) *(G-720)*
Lake Erie Graphics Inc 216 575-1333
 5372 W 130th St Brookpark (44142) *(G-2151)*
Lake Erie Industries LLC 216 255-1867
 13000 Athens Ave Ste 101 Lakewood (44107) *(G-11525)*
Lake Erie Iron and Metal, Cleveland *Also called Welders Supply Inc* *(G-6299)*
Lake Erie Machine 440 353-9191
 5165 Mills Indus Pkwy North Ridgeville (44039) *(G-15237)*
Lake Erie Rubber Recycling LLC 440 570-6027
 19940 Echo Dr Strongsville (44149) *(G-17761)*
Lake Metals, Ravenna *Also called A C Williams Co Inc* *(G-16362)*
Lake Park Tool & Machine LLC 330 788-2437
 1221 Velma Ct Youngstown (44512) *(G-20956)*
Lake Plating, Elyria *Also called Cascade Plating Inc* *(G-9232)*

Lake Publishing Inc — ALPHABETIC SECTION

Lake Publishing Inc 440 299-8500
  9853 Johnnycake Ridge Rd # 107 Mentor (44060) *(G-13495)*

Lake Region Oil Inc 330 828-8420
  26 N Cochran St Dalton (44618) *(G-7946)*

Lake Screen Printing Inc 440 244-5707
  1924 Broadway Lorain (44052) *(G-12099)*

Lake Shore Cryotronics Inc (PA) 614 891-2243
  575 Mccorkle Blvd Westerville (43082) *(G-20003)*

Lake Shore Electric Corp 440 232-0200
  205 Willis St Bedford (44146) *(G-1422)*

Lake Township Trustees 419 836-1143
  3800 Ayers Rd Millbury (43447) *(G-14050)*

Lake Wood Product Inc (PA) 419 832-0150
  13020 Box Rd Grand Rapids (43522) *(G-10316)*

Lakecraft Inc (PA) 419 734-2828
  1010 W Lakeshore Dr Port Clinton (43452) *(G-16249)*

Lakepark Industries Inc 419 752-4471
  40 Seminary St Greenwich (44837) *(G-10406)*

Lakeshore Feed & Seed Inc 216 961-5729
  5116 Clark Ave Cleveland (44102) *(G-5555)*

Lakeshore Graphic Industries 419 626-8631
  617 Hancock St Sandusky (44870) *(G-16821)*

Lakeside Cabins Ltd 419 896-2299
  7389 State Route 13 N Shiloh (44878) *(G-16995)*

Lakeside Custom Plating Inc 440 599-2035
  373 Commerce St Conneaut (44030) *(G-7652)*

Lakeside Sand & Gravel Inc 330 274-2569
  3498 Frost Rd Mantua (44255) *(G-12550)*

Lakeside Sport Shop Inc 330 637-2862
  2115 Wlson Sharpsville Rd Cortland (44410) *(G-7711)*

Lakeview Farms Inc 419 695-9925
  1700 Gressel Dr Delphos (45833) *(G-8748)*

Lakeview Farms LLC 419 695-9925
  1600 Gressel Dr Delphos (45833) *(G-8749)*

Lakeview Farms LLC 419 695-9925
  1600 Gressel Dr Delphos (45833) *(G-8750)*

Lakeway Mfg Inc (PA) 419 433-3030
  730 River Rd Huron (44839) *(G-11103)*

Lakewood Observer Inc 216 712-7070
  14900 Detroit Ave Ste 205 Lakewood (44107) *(G-11526)*

Lakewood Steel Inc 440 965-4226
  13616 State Route 113 Wakeman (44889) *(G-19286)*

Lako Tool & Mfg 419 662-5256
  7400 Ponderosa Rd Perrysburg (43551) *(G-15973)*

Lakota Archery, Xenia Also called Lakota Industries Inc *(G-20781)*

Lakota Industries Inc 937 532-6394
  1463 Bellbrook Ave Xenia (45385) *(G-20781)*

Lakota Printing Inc 513 755-3666
  7967 Cincinnati Dayton Rd J West Chester (45069) *(G-19734)*

Lakota Racing 330 627-7255
  109 12th St Nw Carrollton (44615) *(G-2923)*

Lally Pipe & Tube, Struthers Also called L B Industries Inc *(G-17820)*

Lam Pro Inc 216 426-0661
  4701 Crayton Ave Ste A Cleveland (44104) *(G-5556)*

Lam Research Corporation 937 472-3311
  960 S Franklin St Eaton (45320) *(G-9158)*

Lam Tech, Tiffin Also called Laminate Technologies Inc *(G-18064)*

Lam Welding & Met Fabrication 304 839-2404
  2269 Waynesburg Rd Nw Carrollton (44615) *(G-2924)*

Lamar D Steiner 330 466-1479
  6815 State Route 39 Millersburg (44654) *(G-14105)*

Lamar Proforma 440 285-2277
  12636 Mayfield Rd Ste 1 Chardon (44024) *(G-3122)*

Lambert Bros Inc 513 541-1042
  1337 Bates Ave Cincinnati (45225) *(G-3929)*

Lambert Bros Nutangs, Cincinnati Also called Lambert Bros Inc *(G-3929)*

Lambert Sheet Metal Inc 614 237-0384
  3776 E 5th Ave Columbus (43219) *(G-7111)*

Laminate Shop 740 749-3536
  1145 Klinger Rd Waterford (45786) *(G-19486)*

Laminate Technologies Inc (PA) 419 448-0812
  161 Maule Rd Tiffin (44883) *(G-18064)*

Lamor Corporation 440 871-8000
  841 Hamlet Ln Apt A2 Westlake (44145) *(G-20128)*

Lamports Filter Media Inc 216 881-2050
  837 E 79th St Cleveland (44103) *(G-5557)*

Lancaster Colony Corporation (PA) 614 224-7141
  380 Polaris Pkwy Ste 400 Westerville (43082) *(G-20004)*

Lancaster Colony Corporation 614 792-9774
  380 Polaris Pkwy Ste 400 Westerville (43082) *(G-20005)*

Lancaster Colony Corporation 614 224-7141
  380 Polaris Pkwy Ste 400 Westerville (43082) *(G-20006)*

Lancaster Colony Design Group, Westerville Also called Lancaster Colony Corporation *(G-20005)*

Lancaster Commercial Pdts LLC 740 286-5081
  2353 Westbrooke Dr Columbus (43228) *(G-7112)*

Lancaster Eagle Gazette, Lancaster Also called Gannett Co Inc *(G-11574)*

Lancaster Municipal Gas, Lancaster Also called City of Lancaster *(G-11554)*

Lancaster West Side Coal Co (PA) 740 862-4713
  700 Van Buren Ave Lancaster (43130) *(G-11582)*

Lance Industries Inc 740 243-6657
  1361 Sugar Grove Rd Se Lancaster (43130) *(G-11583)*

Lancio, Bath Also called Mollard Conducting Batons Inc *(G-1202)*

Land & Shore Drilling, Millersburg Also called G & H Drilling Inc *(G-14083)*

Land OLakes Inc 330 879-2158
  8485 Navarre Rd Sw Massillon (44646) *(G-13013)*

Land OLakes Inc 330 678-1578
  2001 Mogadore Rd Kent (44240) *(G-11346)*

Landec Corporation 419 931-1095
  12700 S Dixie Hwy Bowling Green (43402) *(G-1980)*

Landen Desktop Pubg Ctr Inc 513 683-5181
  8976 Columbia Rd Loveland (45140) *(G-12209)*

Landen Digital Publishing, Loveland Also called Landen Desktop Pubg Ctr Inc *(G-12209)*

Landerwood Industries Inc 440 233-4234
  4245 Hamann Pkwy Willoughby (44094) *(G-20358)*

Landis Defense Solutions 937 938-0688
  5335 Springboro Pike Moraine (45439) *(G-14366)*

Landmark Plastic Corporation (PA) 330 785-2200
  1331 Kelly Ave Akron (44306) *(G-248)*

Landon Vault Company 614 443-5505
  1477 Frebis Ave Columbus (43206) *(G-7113)*

Landsberg Cincinnati Div 1017, Monroe Also called Orora Packaging Solutions *(G-14274)*

Landscape & Christmas Tree, Akron Also called Acro Tool & Die Company *(G-29)*

Landscape Group LLC 614 302-4537
  15740 Scioto Darby Rd Mount Sterling (43143) *(G-14463)*

Lanes Welding & Repair 740 397-2525
  9180 Kinney Rd Mount Vernon (43050) *(G-14488)*

Lang Stone Company Inc (PA) 614 235-4099
  4099 E 5th Ave Columbus (43219) *(G-7114)*

Langa Tool & Machine Inc 440 953-1138
  36430 Reading Ave Ste 1 Willoughby (44094) *(G-20359)*

Langdon Inc 513 733-5955
  9865 Wayne Ave Cincinnati (45215) *(G-3930)*

Lange Equipment 440 953-1621
  1585 E 361st St Unit D Eastlake (44095) *(G-9120)*

Lange Precision Inc 513 530-9500
  6971 Cornell Rd Blue Ash (45242) *(G-1802)*

Langenau Manufacturing Company 216 651-3400
  7306 Madison Ave Cleveland (44102) *(G-5558)*

Langston Pallets 937 492-8769
  1650 Miami Conservancy Rd Sidney (45365) *(G-17049)*

Langstons Ultmate Clg Svcs Inc 330 298-9150
  3764 Summit Rd Ravenna (44266) *(G-16387)*

Lanier & Associates Inc 216 391-7735
  1814 E 40th St Ste 1c Cleveland (44103) *(G-5559)*

Lanko Industries Inc 440 269-1641
  7301 Industrial Park Blvd Mentor (44060) *(G-13496)*

Lanly Company 216 731-1115
  26201 Tungsten Rd Cleveland (44132) *(G-5560)*

Lansing Bros Sawmill 937 588-4291
  897 Chenoweth Fork Rd Piketon (45661) *(G-16073)*

Lantek Systems Inc 513 988-8708
  5155 Financial Way Ste 2 Mason (45040) *(G-12903)*

Lantz Lumber & Saw Shop 740 286-5658
  637 Industry Dr Jackson (45640) *(G-11189)*

Lanxess Corporation 440 279-2367
  145 Parker Ct Chardon (44024) *(G-3123)*

Lanxess Solutions US Inc 440 324-6060
  110 Liberty Ct Elyria (44035) *(G-9284)*

Lanz Printing Co Inc 614 221-1724
  257 Cleveland Ave Columbus (43215) *(G-7115)*

Lapa Lowe Enterprises LLC 440 944-9410
  5900 Som Center Rd Ste 16 Willoughby (44094) *(G-20360)*

Lapat Signs 440 277-6291
  4151 E River Rd Sheffield Village (44054) *(G-16969)*

Lapchi LLC 216 360-0104
  23533 Mercantile Rd # 103 Cleveland (44122) *(G-5561)*

Lapcraft Inc 614 764-8993
  195 W Olentangy St Unit A Powell (43065) *(G-16327)*

Lapel Pins Unlimited LLC 614 562-3218
  5649 Ketch St Lewis Center (43035) *(G-11765)*

Lapham-Hickey Steel Corp 419 399-4803
  815 W Gasser Rd Paulding (45879) *(G-15865)*

Lapham-Hickey Steel Corp 614 443-4881
  753 Marion Rd Columbus (43207) *(G-7116)*

Larcom & Mitchell LLC 740 595-3750
  1800 Pittsburgh Dr Delaware (43015) *(G-8701)*

Largemachining.com, Dayton Also called Gedico International Inc *(G-8218)*

Lariat Machine Inc 330 297-5765
  826 Cleveland Rd Ravenna (44266) *(G-16388)*

Lariccias Italian Foods 330 729-0222
  7438 Southern Blvd Youngstown (44512) *(G-20957)*

Larmax Inc 513 984-0783
  10945 Reed Hartman Hwy # 210 Blue Ash (45242) *(G-1803)*

Larmco Windows Inc (PA) 216 502-2832
  8400 Sweet Valley Dr # 404 Cleveland (44125) *(G-5562)*

Larosa Die Engineering Inc 513 284-9195
  3320 Robinet Dr Cincinnati (45238) *(G-3931)*

ALPHABETIC SECTION

Larose Industries LLC 419 237-1600
40 E Industrial Pkwy Fayette (43521) *(G-9634)*
Larry Moore 740 697-7085
6680 Ransbottom Rd Roseville (43777) *(G-16578)*
Larrys Drive Thru & Mini Mart 330 953-0512
3305 Center Rd Youngstown (44514) *(G-20958)*
Larrys Water Conditioning 419 887-0290
720 Illinois Ave Ste I Maumee (43537) *(G-13126)*
Las Motor Sports 937 456-2441
1694 Eaton Lewisburg Rd Eaton (45320) *(G-9159)*
Laser Automation Inc 440 543-9291
16771 Hilltop Park Pl Chagrin Falls (44023) *(G-3055)*
Laser Cartridge Express, Bowling Green Also called Wood County Ohio *(G-2007)*
Laser Cutting Shapes, Columbus Also called Daskal Enterprise LLC *(G-6850)*
Laser Horizons 330 208-0575
1879 Caroline Ave Norton (44203) *(G-15373)*
Laser Images Inc 419 668-8348
28 W Main St Norwalk (44857) *(G-15403)*
Laser Printing Solutions Inc 216 351-4444
6040 Hillcrest Dr Cleveland (44125) *(G-5563)*
Lasercap, Gates Mills Also called Transdermal Inc *(G-10209)*
Laserdealer Inc 440 357-8419
9323 Hamilton Dr Mentor (44060) *(G-13497)*
Laserflex Corporation (HQ) 614 850-9600
3649 Parkway Ln Hilliard (43026) *(G-10837)*
Laserlinc Inc 937 318-2440
777 Zapata Dr Fairborn (45324) *(G-9463)*
Lasermark LLC 513 312-9889
530 N Union Rd Dayton (45417) *(G-8306)*
Laspina Tool & Die Inc 330 923-9996
4282 Hudson Dr Stow (44224) *(G-17599)*
Last Word, The, Port Clinton Also called Scrambl-Gram Inc *(G-16259)*
Lasting First Impressions Inc 513 870-6900
36 Carnegie Way West Chester (45246) *(G-19872)*
Lasting Impression Direct 216 464-1960
23500 Mercantile Rd Beachwood (44122) *(G-1245)*
Lasting Impression Llc 614 806-1186
4415 Berthstone Dr Columbus (43231) *(G-7117)*
Laszeray Technology LLC 440 582-8430
12315 York Delta Dr North Royalton (44133) *(G-15283)*
Latanick Equipment Inc 419 433-2200
720 River Rd Huron (44839) *(G-11104)*
Late For Sky Production Co 513 531-4400
1292 Glendale Milford Rd Cincinnati (45215) *(G-3932)*
LAtelier Custom Woodworking 234 759-3359
11905 Woodworth Rd North Lima (44452) *(G-15175)*
Latham Limestone LLC 740 493-2677
6424 State Route 124 Latham (45646) *(G-11622)*
Latham Lumber & Pallet Co Inc 740 493-2707
9445 Street Rte 124 Latham (45646) *(G-11623)*
Latin Quarter 513 271-5400
6904 Wooster Pike Cincinnati (45227) *(G-3933)*
Latrobe Spcialty Mtls Dist Inc (HQ) 330 609-5137
1551 Vienna Pkwy Vienna (44473) *(G-19199)*
Latrobe Specialty Mtls Co LLC 419 335-8010
14614 County Road H Wauseon (43567) *(G-19525)*
Lattasburg Lumberworks Co LLC 330 202-7671
9399 Lattasburg Rd West Salem (44287) *(G-19956)*
Latte Living 440 364-2201
11005 Johnson Dr Cleveland (44130) *(G-5564)*
Lau Industries Inc (HQ) 937 476-6500
4509 Springfield St Dayton (45431) *(G-7983)*
Lauber Manufacturing Co 419 446-2450
3751 County Road 26 Archbold (43502) *(G-654)*
Laughing Star Montessory 513 683-5682
8725 Davis Rd Maineville (45039) *(G-12373)*
Launchvector Identity LLC 216 333-1815
3635 Perkins Ave Ste 6a Cleveland (44114) *(G-5565)*
Laura Dawson 513 777-2513
7827 Plantation Dr West Chester (45069) *(G-19735)*
Laureate Machine & Automtn LLC 419 615-4601
100 Laureate Dr Leipsic (45856) *(G-11728)*
Lauren International Ltd (HQ) 330 339-3373
2228 Reiser Ave Se New Philadelphia (44663) *(G-14780)*
Lauren Manufacturing, New Philadelphia Also called Lauren International Ltd *(G-14780)*
Lauren Manufacturing LLC 330 339-3373
2228 Reiser Ave Se New Philadelphia (44663) *(G-14781)*
Lauren Yoakam 440 365-3952
591 Ternes Ln Elyria (44035) *(G-9285)*
Laurenee Ltd LLC 513 662-2225
3509 Harrison Ave Cincinnati (45211) *(G-3934)*
Laurentia Winery 440 296-9170
6869 River Rd Madison (44057) *(G-12353)*
Lavander Bridal Salon 330 602-0333
218 W 3rd St Dover (44622) *(G-8836)*
Lavish Lyfe Magazine 937 938-5816
19 Colgate Ave Dayton (45417) *(G-8307)*
Lavy Inc 937 692-8189
1977 Gttysburg Ptsburg Rd Arcanum (45304) *(G-630)*
Lavy's Marathon, Arcanum Also called Lavy Inc *(G-630)*

Lawbre Co 330 637-3363
3311 Warren Meadville Rd Cortland (44410) *(G-7712)*
Lawft (PA) 419 422-5293
1016 N Blanchard St Findlay (45840) *(G-9712)*
Lawhorn Machine & Tool Inc 937 884-5674
25 E Walnut St Phillipsburg (45354) *(G-16037)*
Lawnview Industries Inc 937 653-5217
1250 E Us Highway 36 Urbana (43078) *(G-19003)*
Lawrence Industries Inc (PA) 216 518-7000
4500 Lee Rd Ste 120 Cleveland (44128) *(G-5566)*
Lawrence Industries Inc 216 518-1400
4500 Lee Rd Ste 120 Cleveland (44128) *(G-5567)*
Lawrence Machine, Massillon Also called Gary Lawrence Enterprises Inc *(G-12986)*
Lawrence Pallets & Solutions 740 259-4283
620 Owensville Rd Lucasville (45648) *(G-12265)*
Lawrence Technologies Inc 937 274-7771
2571 Timber Ln Dayton (45414) *(G-8308)*
Lawson Precision Machining Inc 419 562-1543
3981 Crestline Rd Bucyrus (44820) *(G-2337)*
Lawsons Towing & Auto Wrckg 216 883-9050
14114 Miles Ave Cleveland (44128) *(G-5568)*
Layerzero Power Systems Inc 440 399-9000
1500 Danner Dr Aurora (44202) *(G-890)*
Layne Heavy Civil Inc 513 424-7287
6451 Germantown Rd Middletown (45042) *(G-13919)*
Lazars Art Gllery Crtive Frmng 330 477-8351
2940 Woodlawn Ave Nw Canton (44708) *(G-2731)*
Lazarus Steel LLC 216 391-3245
901 Addison Rd Cleveland (44103) *(G-5569)*
Lazer Action Inc 330 630-9200
1534 Brittain Rd Akron (44310) *(G-249)*
Lazer Systems Inc (PA) 513 641-4002
850 E Ross Ave Cincinnati (45217) *(G-3935)*
LBC Clay Co LLC 330 674-0674
4501 Township Road 307 Millersburg (44654) *(G-14106)*
Lc, Cleveland Also called Logan Clutch Corporation *(G-5582)*
Lcas, Lorain Also called Lorain County Auto Systems Inc *(G-12102)*
Lcp Tech Inc 513 271-1389
8120 Indian Hill Rd Cincinnati (45243) *(G-3936)*
Le Gourmet Chef, Chillicothe Also called Kitchen Collection LLC *(G-3198)*
LE Smith Company (PA) 419 636-4555
1030 E Wilson St Bryan (43506) *(G-2295)*
Le Summer Kidron Inc 330 857-2031
6856 Kidron Rd Apple Creek (44606) *(G-610)*
Leadar Roll Inc (PA) 419 227-2200
893 Shawnee Rd Lima (45805) *(G-11885)*
Leadec Corp (HQ) 513 731-3590
9395 Kenwood Rd Ste 200 Blue Ash (45242) *(G-1804)*
Leader Engnrng-Fabrication Inc (PA) 419 592-0008
695 Independence Dr Napoleon (43545) *(G-14549)*
Leader Engnrng-Fabrication Inc 419 636-1731
County Rd D 50 Bryan (43506) *(G-2296)*
Leader Printing, Newark Also called Ryans Newark Leader Ex Prtg *(G-14916)*
Leader Publications Inc 330 665-9595
3075 Smith Rd Ste 204 Fairlawn (44333) *(G-9612)*
Leaf & Thorn Press 614 396-6055
1080 Pebble Brook Dr Columbus (43240) *(G-6498)*
Leaf Lono Earth Alterntv Fuels 614 829-7159
4204 Town Square Dr Canal Winchester (43110) *(G-2505)*
Leap Publishing Services Inc 234 738-0082
4301 Darrow Rd Ste 1200a Stow (44224) *(G-17600)*
Lear Corp 614 850-8630
2181 International St Columbus (43228) *(G-7118)*
Lear Corporation 740 928-4358
180 N High St Hebron (43025) *(G-10750)*
Lear Corporation 419 335-6010
447 E Walnut St Wauseon (43567) *(G-19526)*
Lear Corporation 614 850-8630
2181 International St Columbus (43228) *(G-7119)*
Lear Engineering Corp 937 429-0534
2942 Stauffer Dr Beavercreek (45434) *(G-1325)*
Lear Manufacturing Inc 440 327-4545
7855 Race Rd North Ridgeville (44039) *(G-15238)*
Lear Mfg Co Inc 440 324-1111
147 Freedom Ct Elyria (44035) *(G-9286)*
Lear Romec, Elyria Also called Hydro-Aire Inc *(G-9267)*
Learning Egg LLC 330 207-8663
9332 Silica Rd North Jackson (44451) *(G-15148)*
Learning Egg, The, North Jackson Also called Learning Egg LLC *(G-15148)*
Lebanon Electric Motor Svc LLC 513 932-2889
602 E Main St Lebanon (45036) *(G-11670)*
Lectroetch Co 440 934-1249
5342 Evergreen Pkwy Sheffield Village (44054) *(G-16970)*
Led Lighting Center Inc (PA) 714 271-2633
6120 N Detroit Ave # 1020 Toledo (43612) *(G-18376)*
Led Lighting Center LLC (HQ) 888 988-6533
6120 N Detroit Ave Toledo (43612) *(G-18377)*
Led Lighting Center LLC. 888 988-6533
6120 N Detroit Ave Toledo (43612) *(G-18378)*

LED-ANDON, Columbus ALPHABETIC SECTION

LED-ANDON, Columbus *Also called American Led-Gible Inc* ***(G-6584)***
Ledex & Dormeyer Products, Vandalia *Also called Saia-Burgess Lcc* ***(G-19144)***
Ledge Hill Signs Limited....440 461-4445
5369 Mayfield Rd Cleveland (44124) ***(G-5570)***
Ledow Company Inc....330 657-2837
3011 Oak Hill Rd Peninsula (44264) ***(G-15895)***
Lee A Williams Jr....419 225-6751
205 W Elm St Lima (45801) ***(G-11886)***
Lee Corporation....513 771-3602
12055 Mosteller Rd Cincinnati (45241) ***(G-3937)***
Lee Oil & Gas Inc....937 223-8891
326 Spirea Dr Oakwood (45419) ***(G-15463)***
Lee Plastic Company LLC....937 456-5720
1100 Us Route 35 Eaton (45320) ***(G-9160)***
Lee Printers, Cincinnati *Also called Lee Corporation* ***(G-3937)***
Lee Saylor Logging LLC....740 682-0479
565 Cress Rd Oak Hill (45656) ***(G-15455)***
Lee Williams Meats Inc (PA)....419 729-3893
3002 131st St Toledo (43611) ***(G-18379)***
Leebaw Manufacturing Company....330 533-3368
3 Industrial Park Dr Canfield (44406) ***(G-2531)***
Leeper Printing Co Inc....419 243-2604
710 S Saint Clair St Toledo (43609) ***(G-18380)***
Lees Grinding Inc....440 572-4610
15620 Foltz Pkwy Strongsville (44149) ***(G-17762)***
Lees Machinery Inc....440 259-2222
4089 N Ridge Rd Perry (44081) ***(G-15907)***
Leesburg Loom & Supply, Van Wert *Also called Leesburg Looms Incorporated* ***(G-19099)***
Leesburg Looms Incorporated....419 238-2738
201 N Cherry St Van Wert (45891) ***(G-19099)***
Leesburg Modern Sales Inc....937 780-2613
12607 Monroe Rd Leesburg (45135) ***(G-11712)***
Leesville Plant, Dennison *Also called M3 Midstream LLC* ***(G-8785)***
Leetonia Tool Company....330 427-6944
142 Main St Leetonia (44431) ***(G-11718)***
Lefco Worthington LLC....216 432-4422
18451 Euclid Ave Cleveland (44112) ***(G-5571)***
Lefeld Supplies Rental, Coldwater *Also called Lefeld Welding & Stl Sups Inc* ***(G-6416)***
Lefeld Welding & Stl Sups Inc (PA)....419 678-2397
600 N 2nd St Coldwater (45828) ***(G-6416)***
Legacy Farmers Cooperative (PA)....419 423-2611
6566 County Road 236 Findlay (45840) ***(G-9713)***
Legacy Finishing Inc....937 743-7278
415 Oxford Rd Franklin (45005) ***(G-9895)***
Legacy Oak and Hardwoods LLC....330 859-2656
7138 Mount Pleasant Rd Ne Zoarville (44656) ***(G-21196)***
Legacy Supplies Inc....330 405-4565
8252 Darrow Rd Ste E Twinsburg (44087) ***(G-18805)***
Legal News Publishing Co....216 696-3322
2935 Prospect Ave E Cleveland (44115) ***(G-5572)***
Legalcraft Inc....330 494-1261
302 Hallum St Sw Canton (44720) ***(G-2732)***
Legendary Ink Inc....614 766-5101
1559 Granville St Columbus (43203) ***(G-7120)***
Leggett & Platt Incorporated....330 262-6010
7315 E Lincoln Way Apple Creek (44606) ***(G-611)***
Legrand AV Inc....574 267-8101
11500 Williamson Rd Blue Ash (45241) ***(G-1805)***
Legrand North America LLC....937 224-0639
6500 Poe Ave Dayton (45414) ***(G-8309)***
Lehigh Cement Company LLC....330 499-9100
8282 Middlebranch Ave Ne Middlebranch (44652) ***(G-13759)***
Lehigh Hanson Ecc Inc....330 499-9100
8282 Middlebranch Ave Ne Middlebranch (44652) ***(G-13760)***
Lehigh Hanson Ecc Inc....614 497-2001
1550 Williams Rd Columbus (43207) ***(G-7121)***
Lehman & Sons....330 857-7404
3328 S Kohler Rd Orrville (44667) ***(G-15601)***
Lehner Screw Machine LLC....330 688-6616
1169 Brittain Rd Akron (44305) ***(G-250)***
Lehner Signs Inc....614 258-0500
2983 Switzer Ave Columbus (43219) ***(G-7122)***
Lehr Awning Co, Mansfield *Also called P C R Restorations Inc* ***(G-12501)***
Leiden Cabinet Company LLC (PA)....330 425-8555
2385 Edison Blvd Twinsburg (44087) ***(G-18806)***
Leidos Inc....937 431-2270
3745 Pentagon Blvd Beavercreek (45431) ***(G-1326)***
Leimkuehler Inc (PA)....440 899-7842
4625 Detroit Ave Cleveland (44102) ***(G-5573)***
Leipsic Messenger Newspaper, Leipsic *Also called Mickens Inc* ***(G-11729)***
Leland-Gifford Inc....330 785-9730
1029 Arlington Cir Akron (44306) ***(G-251)***
Lem Incorporated....330 535-6422
71 S River Rd Munroe Falls (44262) ***(G-14525)***
Lem Products Holding LLC....513 202-1188
4440 Muhlhauser Rd # 300 West Chester (45011) ***(G-19736)***
Lemsco Inc....419 242-4005
2056 Canton Ave Toledo (43620) ***(G-18381)***
Lemsco-Girkins, Toledo *Also called Lemsco Inc* ***(G-18381)***
Lena Fiore Inc....330 659-0020
2188 Majesty Ct Akron (44333) ***(G-252)***
Lenas Amish Granola....330 600-1599
11051 County Road 329 Shreve (44676) ***(G-17005)***
Lenco Industries Inc....937 277-9364
3301 Klepinger Rd Dayton (45406) ***(G-8310)***
Lennox Machine Inc....419 525-1020
1471 Sprang Pkwy Mansfield (44903) ***(G-12468)***
Lennox Machine Shop, Mansfield *Also called Lennox Machine Inc* ***(G-12468)***
Lenz Inc....937 277-9364
3301 Klepinger Rd Dayton (45406) ***(G-8311)***
Lenz Company, Dayton *Also called Lenz Inc* ***(G-8311)***
Leon Newswanger....419 896-3336
7828 Planktown North Rd Shiloh (44878) ***(G-16996)***
Leonhardt Plating Company....513 242-1410
5753 Este Ave Cincinnati (45232) ***(G-3938)***
Leppert Companies Inc....614 889-2818
8779 Tartan Fields Dr Dublin (43017) ***(G-8941)***
Lerner Enterprises Inc....440 323-5529
811 Taylor St Elyria (44035) ***(G-9287)***
Leroi Gas Compressors, Sidney *Also called Rotary Compression Tech Inc* ***(G-17071)***
Leroy Yutzy....937 386-2872
191 Russellville Rd Winchester (45697) ***(G-20522)***
Lesage Machine Inc....419 687-0131
5269 State Route 598 Plymouth (44865) ***(G-16232)***
Lesch Boat Cover Canvas Co LLC....419 668-6374
43 1/2 Saint Marys St Norwalk (44857) ***(G-15404)***
Lesch Btry & Pwr Solution LLC....419 884-0219
2744 Lexington Ave Mansfield (44904) ***(G-12469)***
Lesco Inc....740 633-6366
100 Picoma Rd Martins Ferry (43935) ***(G-12761)***
Lesher Printers Inc....419 332-8253
810 N Wilson Ave Fremont (43420) ***(G-10033)***
Lesleys Patterns Ltd....937 554-4674
405 Halifax Dr Vandalia (45377) ***(G-19132)***
Less Cost Lighting Inc....866 633-6883
1213 Etna Pkwy Etna (43062) ***(G-9396)***
Let's Rage, Cleveland *Also called Rageon Inc* ***(G-5958)***
Lets Golf Daily Inc....330 966-3373
3199 Whitewood St Nw North Canton (44720) ***(G-15097)***
Letter Graphics Sign Co Inc....330 683-3903
400 W Market St Orrville (44667) ***(G-15602)***
Letter Shop....937 981-3117
247 Jefferson St Greenfield (45123) ***(G-10354)***
Letterman Printing Inc....513 523-1111
316 S College Ave Oxford (45056) ***(G-15696)***
Lettermans LLC....330 345-2628
344 Beall Ave Wooster (44691) ***(G-20616)***
Levan Enterprises Inc (PA)....330 923-9797
4585 Allen Rd Stow (44224) ***(G-17601)***
Levans Electric & Hvac....937 468-2269
275 Mill St W Rushsylvania (43347) ***(G-16596)***
Levcoat Powder Coating....614 802-7505
2773 Westbelt Dr Columbus (43228) ***(G-7123)***
Leveck Lighting Products Inc (PA)....937 667-4421
8415 S State Route 202 Tipp City (45371) ***(G-18121)***
Level Packaging LLC....614 392-2412
12517 County Road 99 Findlay (45840) ***(G-9714)***
Leverett A Anderson Co Inc....330 670-1363
1245 S Clvld Masslln Rd Akron (44321) ***(G-253)***
Levi Strauss & Co....513 539-7822
211 Premium Outlets Dr Monroe (45050) ***(G-14273)***
Levison Enterprises LLC....419 838-7365
4470 Moline Martin Rd Millbury (43447) ***(G-14051)***
Levit Jewelers Inc....440 985-1685
4274 Oberlin Ave Lorain (44053) ***(G-12100)***
Lewark Metal Spinning Inc....937 275-3303
2746 Keenan Ave Dayton (45414) ***(G-8312)***
Lewco Inc....419 625-4014
706 Lane St Sandusky (44870) ***(G-16822)***
Lewisburg Container Company (HQ)....937 962-2681
275 W Clay St Lewisburg (45338) ***(G-11794)***
Lexington Abrasives Inc....330 821-1166
16123 Armour St Ne Alliance (44601) ***(G-482)***
Lexington Rubber Group Inc....330 425-8352
3565 Highland Park Nw Canton (44720) ***(G-2733)***
Lexington Rubber Group Inc (HQ)....330 425-8472
1700 Highland Rd Twinsburg (44087) ***(G-18807)***
Lexis Nexis, Miamisburg *Also called Relx Inc* ***(G-13708)***
Lexisnexis, Miamisburg *Also called Relx Inc* ***(G-13710)***
Lexisnexis Group (HQ)....937 865-6800
9443 Springboro Pike Miamisburg (45342) ***(G-13684)***
Lextech Industries Ltd....216 883-7900
6800 Union Ave Cleveland (44105) ***(G-5574)***
Ley Industries Inc....419 238-6742
121 S Walnut St Van Wert (45891) ***(G-19100)***
Leyman Liftgates, Cincinnati *Also called Leyman Manufacturing Corp* ***(G-3939)***
Leyman Manufacturing Corp....513 891-6210
10335 Wayne Ave Cincinnati (45215) ***(G-3939)***

ALPHABETIC SECTION
Linger Photo Engraving Corp

Lfe Instruments, Bluffton *Also called Triplett Bluffton Corporation* ***(G-1896)***
Lfg Specialties LLC 419 424-4999
16406 E Us Route 224 Findlay (45840) ***(G-9715)***
LH Marshall Company 614 294-6433
1601 Woodland Ave Columbus (43219) ***(G-7124)***
Lib Therapeutics LLC 859 240-7764
5375 Medpace Way Cincinnati (45227) ***(G-3940)***
Libart North America, Hicksville *Also called Stoett Industries Inc* ***(G-10783)***
Libbey Glass Factory Outlet, Toledo *Also called Libbey Inc* ***(G-18384)***
Libbey Glass Inc (HQ) 419 325-2100
300 Madison Ave Fl 4 Toledo (43604) ***(G-18382)***
Libbey Glass Inc 419 729-7272
940 Ash St Toledo (43611) ***(G-18383)***
Libbey Inc 419 244-5697
205 S Erie St Toledo (43604) ***(G-18384)***
Libbey Inc (PA) 419 325-2100
300 Madison Ave Toledo (43604) ***(G-18385)***
Liber Limited LLC 440 427-0647
7162 Windwood Way Olmsted Twp (44138) ***(G-15533)***
Liberty Casting Company LLC (PA) 740 363-1941
550 Liberty Rd Delaware (43015) ***(G-8702)***
Liberty Casting Company LLC 740 363-1941
407 Curtis St Delaware (43015) ***(G-8703)***
Liberty Die Cast Molds Inc 740 666-7492
57 2nd St Ostrander (43061) ***(G-15645)***
Liberty Die Casting Company 419 636-3971
872 E Trevitt St Bryan (43506) ***(G-2297)***
Liberty Fabricating & Steel, Middlefield *Also called D T Kothera Inc* ***(G-13792)***
Liberty Mold & Machine Company 330 278-7825
1369 Ridge Rd Ste B Hinckley (44233) ***(G-10904)***
Liberty Ornamental Products, Bryan *Also called Liberty Die Casting Company* ***(G-2297)***
Liberty Outdoors LLC 330 791-3149
1519 Boettler Rd Ste A Uniontown (44685) ***(G-18925)***
Liberty Pattern and Mold Inc 330 788-9463
1131 Meadowbrook Ave Youngstown (44512) ***(G-20959)***
Liberty Steel Pressed Pdts LLC 330 538-2236
11650 Mahoning Ave North Jackson (44451) ***(G-15149)***
Libido Edge Labs LLC 740 344-1401
4331 Rock Haven Rd Newark (43055) ***(G-14893)***
Libra Industries, Willoughby *Also called Focus Manufacturing Inc* ***(G-20325)***
Libra Industries Inc (PA) 440 974-7770
7770 Division Dr Mentor (44060) ***(G-13498)***
Libra Industries Inc 440 974-7770
7715 Metric Dr Mentor (44060) ***(G-13499)***
Licensed Spcialty Pdts of Ohio 419 800-8104
130 Cherry St Bradner (43406) ***(G-2012)***
Lideco LLC 330 539-9333
972 Yngtn Kngs Rd Se Vienna (44473) ***(G-19200)***
Lids, Akron *Also called Genesco Inc* ***(G-187)***
Liebert Field Services Inc 614 841-5763
610 Executive Campus Dr Westerville (43082) ***(G-20007)***
Liebert North America Inc (HQ) 614 888-0246
1050 Dearborn Dr Columbus (43085) ***(G-7125)***
Liebrecht Excavating, Continental *Also called Liebrecht Manufacturing LLC* ***(G-7667)***
Liebrecht Manufacturing LLC 419 596-3501
Rd H 13 Continental (45831) ***(G-7667)***
Liechty Specialties, Archbold *Also called Nef Ltd* ***(G-661)***
Liechty Specialties Inc 419 445-6696
1901 S Defiance St Archbold (43502) ***(G-655)***
Life Star Rescue Inc 419 238-2507
1171 Production Dr Van Wert (45891) ***(G-19101)***
Life Support Development Ltd 614 221-1765
777 Dearborn Park Ln R Columbus (43085) ***(G-7126)***
Life Time Embroidery, Brookville *Also called Heller Acquisitions Inc* ***(G-2171)***
Lifeformations Inc 419 352-2101
2029 Wood Bridge Blvd Bowling Green (43402) ***(G-1981)***
Lifegas, Columbus *Also called Linde Gas North America LLC* ***(G-7129)***
Lifestyle Nutraceuticals Ltd 513 376-7218
5911 Turpin Hills Dr Cincinnati (45244) ***(G-3941)***
Lifetime Fenders, Canfield *Also called Ltf Acquisition LLC* ***(G-2533)***
Lifetime Ironworks LLC 419 443-0567
244 Coe St Tiffin (44883) ***(G-18065)***
Lifo Enterprises Inc 513 225-8801
810 Carrington Pl Apt 206 Loveland (45140) ***(G-12210)***
Lift Ai LLC 419 345-7831
2348 Manchester Blvd Ottawa Hills (43606) ***(G-15674)***
Light Craft Direct, Fremont *Also called Light Craft Manufacturing Inc* ***(G-10034)***
Light Craft Manufacturing Inc 419 332-0536
220 Sullivan Rd Fremont (43420) ***(G-10034)***
Light Vision 513 351-9444
1776 Mentor Ave Cincinnati (45212) ***(G-3942)***
Lighted House Numbers, Circleville *Also called Sign Shop* ***(G-4558)***
Lighthouse Youth Services Inc 513 961-4080
2522 Highland Ave Cincinnati (45219) ***(G-3943)***
Lighting Concepts & Control 513 761-6360
9753 Crescent Park Dr West Chester (45069) ***(G-19737)***
Lighting Products Inc 440 293-4064
101 Parker Dr Andover (44003) ***(G-584)***
Lighting Solutions Group LLC 614 868-5337
153 Outerbelt St Columbus (43213) ***(G-7127)***
Lightle Enterprises Ohio LLC (PA) 740 998-5363
22 E Springfield St Frankfort (45628) ***(G-9863)***
Lightning Bolt Fastners, Mount Gilead *Also called Lilly Industries Inc* ***(G-14427)***
Lightning Mold & Machine Inc 440 593-6460
509 W Main Rd Conneaut (44030) ***(G-7653)***
Lightstab Ltd Co 216 751-5800
3103 Morley Rd Shaker Heights (44122) ***(G-16933)***
Lilienthal Southeastern Inc 740 439-1640
1609 N 11th St Cambridge (43725) ***(G-2446)***
Lilleys Fabrication and Design, Morrow *Also called Stephen R Lilley* ***(G-14415)***
Lilly Industries Inc (PA) 419 946-7908
6437 County Road 20 Mount Gilead (43338) ***(G-14427)***
Lily Tiger Press 513 591-0817
1945 Dunham Way Cincinnati (45238) ***(G-3944)***
Lim Services LLC 513 217-0801
3351 Cincinnati Dayton Rd Middletown (45044) ***(G-13920)***
Lima Armature Works Inc 419 222-4010
142 E Pearl St Lima (45801) ***(G-11887)***
Lima Army Tank Plant, Lima *Also called United States Dept of Army* ***(G-11955)***
Lima Equipment Co 419 222-4181
895 Shawnee Rd Lima (45805) ***(G-11888)***
Lima Millwork Inc 419 331-3303
4251 East Rd Elida (45807) ***(G-9195)***
Lima Pallet Company Inc 419 229-5736
1470 Neubrecht Rd Lima (45801) ***(G-11889)***
Lima Pipe Organ Co Inc 419 331-5461
408 E Kiracofe Ave Elida (45807) ***(G-9196)***
Lima Refining Company (HQ) 419 226-2300
1150 S Metcalf St Lima (45804) ***(G-11890)***
Lima Refining Company 419 226-2300
1150 S Metcalf St Lima (45804) ***(G-11891)***
Lima Sandblasting & Pntg Co 419 331-2939
4310 East Rd Lima (45807) ***(G-11892)***
Lima Sheet Metal Machine & Mfg 419 229-1161
1001 Bowman Rd Lima (45804) ***(G-11893)***
Lima Sporting Goods Inc 419 222-1036
1404 Allentown Rd Lima (45805) ***(G-11894)***
Limelght Graphic Solutions Inc 614 793-1996
2829 Festival Ln Dublin (43017) ***(G-8942)***
Liming Printing Inc 937 374-2646
1450 S Patton St Xenia (45385) ***(G-20782)***
Limited Too 937, Dayton *Also called Tween Brands Inc* ***(G-8572)***
Lincoln Candle Company Inc 419 749-4224
6588 Pollock Rd Convoy (45832) ***(G-7670)***
Lincoln Electric Company (HQ) 216 481-8100
22801 Saint Clair Ave Cleveland (44117) ***(G-5575)***
Lincoln Electric Company 216 524-8800
7550 Hub Pkwy Cleveland (44125) ***(G-5576)***
Lincoln Electric Holdings Inc (PA) 216 481-8100
22801 Saint Clair Ave Cleveland (44117) ***(G-5577)***
Lincoln Electric Holdings Inc 440 255-7696
6500 Heisley Rd Mentor (44060) ***(G-13500)***
Lincoln Electric Intl Holdg Co (HQ) 216 481-8100
22801 Saint Clair Ave Euclid (44117) ***(G-9424)***
Lincoln Library Press, Cleveland *Also called Eastword Publications Dev* ***(G-5141)***
Lind Stoneworks Ltd 614 866-9733
175 Oberlin Ct N Columbus (43230) ***(G-7128)***
Linde Gas North America LLC 614 846-7048
7029 Huntley Rd Columbus (43229) ***(G-7129)***
Linde Gas USA LLC 330 425-3989
2045 E Aurora Rd Twinsburg (44087) ***(G-18808)***
Linde Hydraulics Corporation (HQ) 330 533-6801
5089 W Western Reserve Rd Canfield (44406) ***(G-2532)***
Linden Industries Inc 330 928-4064
137 Ascot Pkwy Cuyahoga Falls (44223) ***(G-7893)***
Linden Monuments 419 468-4130
104 Linden Dr Galion (44833) ***(G-10148)***
Lindsay Package Systems Inc 330 854-4511
6845 Erie Ave Nw Canal Fulton (44614) ***(G-2482)***
Lindsay Precast Inc (PA) 800 837-7788
5820 Erie Ave Nw Canal Fulton (44614) ***(G-2483)***
Lindsey Graphics Inc 330 995-9241
112 Parkview Dr Aurora (44202) ***(G-891)***
Line Drive Sportz-Lcrc LLC 419 794-7150
2901 Key St Ste 1 Maumee (43537) ***(G-13127)***
Line Tool & Die Inc 419 332-2931
933 Napoleon St Fremont (43420) ***(G-10035)***
Line-X of Akron/Medina, Medina *Also called X-Treme Finishes Inc* ***(G-13364)***
Linear Asics Inc 330 474-3920
2061 Case Pkwy S Twinsburg (44087) ***(G-18809)***
Linebacker Inc 614 340-1446
1275 Kinnear Rd Columbus (43212) ***(G-7130)***
Linen Care Plus Inc 614 224-1791
84 N Glenwood Ave Columbus (43222) ***(G-7131)***
Linestream Technologies 216 862-7874
1468 W 9th St Ste 435 Cleveland (44113) ***(G-5578)***
Linger Photo Engraving Corp 513 579-1380
2230 Gilbert Ave Cincinnati (45206) ***(G-3945)***

ALPHABETIC

(PA)=Parent Co (HQ)=Headquarters (DH)=Div Headquarters
2019 Harris Ohio
Industrial Directory
1169

Link's Auto, Cleveland *Also called Fiberglass Link Inc* ***(G-5236)***
Link-O-Matic Company Inc....765 962-1538
13359 Brkville Pyrmont Rd Brookville (45309) ***(G-2173)***
Links Country Meats....419 683-2195
7252 Leesville Rd Crestline (44827) ***(G-7796)***
Linsalata Capital Partners Fun....440 684-1400
5900 Landerbrook Dr # 280 Cleveland (44124) ***(G-5579)***
Lintec USA Holding Inc (HQ)....781 935-7850
4560 Darrow Rd Stow (44224) ***(G-17602)***
Lintech Electronics LLC....513 528-6190
4435 Aicholtz Rd Ste 500 Cincinnati (45245) ***(G-3259)***
Lintern Corporation (PA)....440 255-9333
8685 Station St Mentor (44060) ***(G-13501)***
Linx Defense LLC....805 233-2472
2230 University Ave Nw Canton (44709) ***(G-2734)***
Lion Apparel Inc (HQ)....937 898-1949
7200 Poe Ave Ste 400 Dayton (45414) ***(G-8313)***
Lion Black Products LLC....412 400-6980
3710 Hendricks Rd Youngstown (44515) ***(G-20960)***
Lion Clothing Inc....419 692-9981
206 N Main St Delphos (45833) ***(G-8751)***
Lion Industries LLC....740 699-0369
49068 Reservoir Rd Saint Clairsville (43950) ***(G-16636)***
Lion Mold & Machine Inc....330 688-4248
4510 Darrow Rd Stow (44224) ***(G-17603)***
Lion's Den Sport Shop, Minerva *Also called Hoffee John* ***(G-14183)***
Lippincott & Peto Inc....330 864-2122
1741 Akron Peninsula Rd Akron (44313) ***(G-254)***
Liqui-Box Corporation....419 289-9696
1817 Masters Ave Ashland (44805) ***(G-721)***
Liqui-Box Corporation....419 209-9085
519 Raybestos Dr Upper Sandusky (43351) ***(G-18960)***
Liquid Control, North Canton *Also called Graco Ohio Inc* ***(G-15088)***
Liquid Development Company (PA)....216 641-9366
5708 E Schaaf Rd Independence (44131) ***(G-11141)***
Liquid Image Corp of America....216 458-9800
3700 Prospect Ave E Cleveland (44115) ***(G-5580)***
Liquid Logic LLC....937 865-3068
720 Mound Rd Ste 250 Miamisburg (45342) ***(G-13685)***
Liquid Luggers LLC....330 426-2538
183 Edgeworth Ave East Palestine (44413) ***(G-9080)***
Lisa Arters....330 435-1804
117 Maple Ave Creston (44217) ***(G-7806)***
Lisa Modem....216 551-3365
4195 Zalley Rd Cleveland (44109) ***(G-5581)***
Lisbon Hoist Inc....330 424-7283
321 S Beaver St Lisbon (44432) ***(G-11974)***
Lisbon Pattern Limited....330 424-7676
7629 State Route 45 Lisbon (44432) ***(G-11975)***
List Media Inc....330 995-0864
46 Shopping Plz Ste 122 Chagrin Falls (44022) ***(G-3023)***
Listermann Brewery Supply, Cincinnati *Also called Listermann Mfg Co Inc* ***(G-3946)***
Listermann Mfg Co Inc....513 731-1130
1621 Dana Ave Cincinnati (45207) ***(G-3946)***
Litco International Inc (PA)....330 539-5433
1 Litco Dr Vienna (44473) ***(G-19201)***
Litco Manufacturing LLC....330 539-5433
1512 Phoenix Rd Ne Warren (44483) ***(G-19417)***
Litco Wood Products, Apple Creek *Also called Millwood Inc* ***(G-614)***
Lite Metals Company....330 296-6110
700 N Walnut St Ravenna (44266) ***(G-16389)***
Liteflex LLC (PA)....937 836-7025
100 Holiday Dr Englewood (45322) ***(G-9367)***
Liteflex LLC....937 836-7025
3600 Maywood Ave Dayton (45417) ***(G-8314)***
Lithchem Intl Toxco Inc....740 653-6290
265 Quarry Rd Se Lancaster (43130) ***(G-11584)***
Lithium Innovations Co LLC....419 843-6051
3171 N Repub Blvd Ste 101 Toledo (43615) ***(G-18386)***
Litho-Craft Lithography Inc....513 542-6404
7107 Shona Dr 130 Cincinnati (45237) ***(G-3947)***
Little Busy Bodies LLC....513 351-5700
1130 Findlay St Cincinnati (45214) ***(G-3948)***
Little Cottage Company....330 893-4212
6673 State Route 515 Dundee (44624) ***(G-9021)***
Little Ghost Roasters....614 325-2065
247 1/2 King Ave Columbus (43201) ***(G-7132)***
Little Printing Company....937 773-4595
4317 W Us Route 36 Piqua (45356) ***(G-16137)***
Littlern Corporation....330 848-8847
77 2nd St Sw Barberton (44203) ***(G-1081)***
Litzinger Logging....740 743-2245
314 S Columbus St Somerset (43783) ***(G-17264)***
Liverpool Manufacturing, Valley City *Also called Shiloh Automotive Inc* ***(G-19061)***
Livingston & Company Ltd....513 553-6430
1103 Ten Mile Rd New Richmond (45157) ***(G-14811)***
Lizzie Maes Birdseed & Dg Co....330 927-1795
11315 Steiner Rd Rittman (44270) ***(G-16524)***
LLC Bowman Leather....330 893-1954
6705 Private Road 387 Millersburg (44654) ***(G-14107)***
LLC Kurtz Bros Central Ohio....614 733-3074
6279 Houchard Rd Dublin (43016) ***(G-8943)***
LLC Ring Masters....330 832-1511
240 6th St Nw Massillon (44647) ***(G-13014)***
Lloyd F Helber....740 756-9607
3820 Clmbus Lncster Rd Nw Carroll (43112) ***(G-2906)***
Lloyd Library & Museum....513 721-3707
917 Plum St Cincinnati (45202) ***(G-3949)***
LMC, Akron *Also called Logan Machine Company* ***(G-259)***
LMI Custom Mixing LLC....740 435-0444
804 Byesville Rd Cambridge (43725) ***(G-2447)***
Lmp, Hartville *Also called Louisville Molded Products* ***(G-10701)***
Lmp Machine LLC....740 596-4559
115 E Chestnut St Zaleski (45698) ***(G-21088)***
Loadmaster Scale Mfgr, Findlay *Also called Holtgrven Scale Elctronic Corp* ***(G-9704)***
Loadmaster Trailer Company....419 732-3434
2354 East Harbor Rd Port Clinton (43452) ***(G-16250)***
Loadmaster Trailers Mfg, Port Clinton *Also called Loadmaster Trailer Company* ***(G-16250)***
Lobo Awrds Screen Prtg Graphix....740 972-9087
627 Bellefontaine Ave Marion (43302) ***(G-12716)***
Local Insight Yellow Pages Inc....330 650-7100
100 Executive Pkwy Hudson (44236) ***(G-11061)***
Lock-N-Logs Log Homes, Coolville *Also called M & G Truss Rafters* ***(G-7673)***
Lockbourne AG Center Inc....614 491-0635
10 Commerce St Lockbourne (43137) ***(G-11996)***
Locke Industrial Maint Svcs, Middletown *Also called Lim Services LLC* ***(G-13920)***
Locker Konnection Services LLC....419 334-3956
405 Jackson St Fremont (43420) ***(G-10036)***
Locker Room Inc....419 445-9600
223 N Defiance St Archbold (43502) ***(G-656)***
Locker Room Lettering Ltd....419 359-1761
7316 Magill Rd Castalia (44824) ***(G-2940)***
Lockes Heating & Cooling Llc....513 793-1900
10229 Kenwood Rd Blue Ash (45242) ***(G-1806)***
Lockheed Martin Corporation....614 418-1930
2720 Airport Dr Ste 100 Columbus (43219) ***(G-7133)***
Lockheed Martin Corporation....937 429-0100
2940 Presidential Dr # 290 Beavercreek (45324) ***(G-1327)***
Lockheed Martin Corporation....330 796-7000
1210 Massillon Rd Akron (44315) ***(G-255)***
Lockheed Martin Corporation....866 562-2363
2740 Airport Dr Ste 150 Columbus (43219) ***(G-7134)***
Lockheed Martin Corporation....937 429-0100
2940 Presidential Dr # 290 Beavercreek (45324) ***(G-1328)***
Lockheed Martin Corporation....330 796-2800
1210 Massillon Rd Akron (44315) ***(G-256)***
Lockheed Martin Integ....330 796-2800
1210 Massillon Rd Akron (44315) ***(G-257)***
Lockheed Martin Integrtd Systm....330 796-2800
1210 Massillon Rd Akron (44315) ***(G-258)***
Lockheed Martin Investments....937 429-0100
2940 Presidential Dr # 290 Beavercreek (45324) ***(G-1329)***
Lockrey Manafacturing, Toledo *Also called Aimco Mfg Inc* ***(G-18160)***
Lockrey Manufacturing, Toledo *Also called Raka Corporation* ***(G-18498)***
Loctite, Westlake *Also called Henkel US Operations Corp* ***(G-20122)***
Loctote LLC....614 407-0882
1010 Jackson Hole Dr Blacklick (43004) ***(G-1688)***
Lodi Foundry Co Inc....330 948-1516
106 Billman St Lodi (44254) ***(G-12014)***
Loecy Precision Manufacturing....440 358-0551
9180 Hilo Farm Dr Mentor (44060) ***(G-13502)***
Loft Violin Shop....614 267-7221
4604 N High St Columbus (43214) ***(G-7135)***
Logan Clutch Corporation....440 808-4258
28855 Ranney Pkwy Cleveland (44145) ***(G-5582)***
Logan Coatings LLC....740 380-0047
2255 E Front St Logan (43138) ***(G-12032)***
Logan Enterprises Inc....937 465-8170
12229 W State Route 29 Conover (45317) ***(G-7664)***
LOGAN FOUNDRY & MACHINE, Logan *Also called Clay Logan Products Company* ***(G-12022)***
Logan Machine Company (PA)....330 633-6163
1405 Home Ave Akron (44310) ***(G-259)***
Logan Screen Printing....740 385-3303
119 W Main St Logan (43138) ***(G-12033)***
Logan Screen Printing & EMB, Logan *Also called Logan Screen Printing* ***(G-12033)***
Logan Welding Inc....740 385-9651
37062 Hocking Dr Logan (43138) ***(G-12034)***
Logitech Inc....614 871-2822
6423 Seeds Rd Grove City (43123) ***(G-10441)***
Logo This....419 445-1355
301 Ditto St Ste E Archbold (43502) ***(G-657)***
Logos On Lee....216 862-5226
3105 Mayfield Rd Cleveland (44118) ***(G-5583)***
Logotec, Cleveland *Also called Madison Group Inc* ***(G-5602)***
Loken Oil Field Services LLC....740 749-3495
2190 Olinn Rd Marietta (45750) ***(G-12639)***
Lokring Technology LLC....440 942-0880
38376 Apollo Pkwy Willoughby (44094) ***(G-20361)***

Lollipop Stop..........614 991-5192
4595 Hunting Creek Dr Grove City (43123) ***(G-10442)***
Loma Lux Laboratories, Solon *Also called Plymouth Healthcare Pdts LLC* ***(G-17217)***
Lomar Enterprises Inc..........614 409-9104
5905 Green Pointe Dr S G Groveport (43125) ***(G-10501)***
London Coach Shop..........419 347-4803
2962 London East Rd Shelby (44875) ***(G-16983)***
Long Sign Co..........614 294-1057
979 E 5th Ave Columbus (43201) ***(G-7136)***
Long View Steel Corp..........419 747-1108
1555 W Longview Ave Mansfield (44906) ***(G-12470)***
Long-Lok Fasteners Corporation..........513 772-1880
10630 Chester Rd Cincinnati (45215) ***(G-3950)***
Long-Stanton Mfg Company..........513 874-8020
9388 Sutton Pl West Chester (45011) ***(G-19738)***
Longriders Trucking Company..........740 975-7863
7 Delano St Mount Vernon (43050) ***(G-14489)***
Longs Custom Doors..........419 339-2331
229 S Greenlawn Ave Lima (45807) ***(G-11895)***
Longyear Company..........740 373-2190
1010 Greene St Marietta (45750) ***(G-12640)***
Lopaus Point Inc..........614 302-7242
250 W Dodridge St Columbus (43202) ***(G-7137)***
Lorain Armature & Mtr Repr Inc..........440 967-2620
960 Sunnyside Rd Vermilion (44089) ***(G-19166)***
Lorain County Auto Systems Inc..........248 442-6800
3400 River Indus Pk Rd Lorain (44052) ***(G-12101)***
Lorain County Auto Systems Inc (HQ)..........440 960-7470
7470 Industrial Pkwy Dr Lorain (44053) ***(G-12102)***
Lorain Modern Pattern Inc..........440 365-6780
159 Woodbury St Elyria (44035) ***(G-9288)***
Lorain Printing Company..........440 288-6000
1310 Colorado Ave Lorain (44052) ***(G-12103)***
Lorain Quickprint, Monroeville *Also called Nari Inc* ***(G-14289)***
Lorain Ruled Die Products Inc..........440 281-8607
6287 Lear Nagle Rd Ste 4 North Ridgeville (44039) ***(G-15239)***
Lord Corporation..........937 278-9431
4644 Wadsworth Rd Dayton (45414) ***(G-8315)***
Lordstown Cnstr Recovery, Warren *Also called Lafarge North America Inc* ***(G-19415)***
Lore Inc..........513 969-8481
5526 Garrett Dr Milford (45150) ***(G-14024)***
LOreal Usa Inc..........440 248-3700
30601 Carter St Cleveland (44139) ***(G-5584)***
Lorenz Corporation (PA)..........937 228-6118
501 E 3rd St Dayton (45402) ***(G-8316)***
Lori Holding Co (PA)..........740 342-3230
1400 Commerce Dr New Lexington (43764) ***(G-14717)***
Loris Printing & Party Center, Sandusky *Also called Loris Printing Inc* ***(G-16823)***
Loris Printing Inc..........419 626-6648
2111 Cleveland Rd Sandusky (44870) ***(G-16823)***
Loroco Industries Inc (PA)..........513 891-9544
5000 Creek Rd Blue Ash (45242) ***(G-1807)***
Loroco Industries Inc..........513 554-0356
10600 Evendale Dr Cincinnati (45241) ***(G-3951)***
Lost Nation Fuel..........440 951-9088
3525 Lost Nation Rd Willoughby (44094) ***(G-20362)***
Lost Technology LLP..........513 685-0054
9501 Woodland Hills Dr West Chester (45011) ***(G-19739)***
Lostcreek Tool & Machine Inc..........937 773-6022
1150 S Main St Piqua (45356) ***(G-16138)***
Louis Arthur Steel Company (PA)..........440 997-5545
185 Water St Geneva (44041) ***(G-10224)***
Louis Arthur Steel Company..........440 997-5545
200 North Ave E Geneva (44041) ***(G-10225)***
Louis Arthur Steel Company..........440 997-5545
3700 Massillon Rd Ste 360 Uniontown (44685) ***(G-18926)***
Louis G Freeman Co..........513 263-1720
4064 Clough Woods Dr Batavia (45103) ***(G-1163)***
Louis G Freeman Co..........419 334-9709
911 Graham Dr Fremont (43420) ***(G-10037)***
Louis Instantwhip-St Inc (PA)..........614 488-2536
2200 Cardigan Ave Columbus (43215) ***(G-7138)***
Louis Trauth Dairy LLC (HQ)..........859 431-7553
9991 Commerce Park Dr West Chester (45246) ***(G-19873)***
Louise Sweet LLC..........419 460-5505
3827 Beechway Blvd Toledo (43614) ***(G-18387)***
Louisville Herald Inc..........330 875-5610
308 S Mill St Louisville (44641) ***(G-12160)***
Louisville Molded Products..........330 877-9740
13122 Duquette Ave Ne Hartville (44632) ***(G-10701)***
Lous Machine Company Inc..........513 856-9199
102 Hastings Ave Hamilton (45011) ***(G-10582)***
Lous Sausage Ltd..........216 752-5060
14723 Miles Ave Cleveland (44128) ***(G-5585)***
Love Chocolate Factory, Hartville *Also called L C F Inc* ***(G-10700)***
Loveland Graphics, Cincinnati *Also called Eastgate Custom Graphics Ltd* ***(G-3625)***
Loveman Steel Corporation..........440 232-6200
5455 Perkins Rd Bedford (44146) ***(G-1423)***
Low Stress Grind Inc..........513 771-7977
12077 Mosteller Rd Cincinnati (45241) ***(G-3952)***
Lowell Marcum..........330 948-2353
328 Bank St Lodi (44254) ***(G-12015)***
Lower Limb Centers LLC..........440 365-2502
1100 Abbe Rd N Ste D Elyria (44035) ***(G-9289)***
Lowery Industries..........740 745-5045
10975 Houdeshell Rd Saint Louisville (43071) ***(G-16673)***
Lowry Furnace Company Inc..........330 745-4822
663 Flora Ave Akron (44314) ***(G-260)***
Lowry Tool & Die Inc..........330 332-1722
986 Salem Pkwy Salem (44460) ***(G-16755)***
Loxcreen Company Inc..........513 539-2255
100 Westheimer Dr Middletown (45044) ***(G-13921)***
Lozinak & Sons Inc..........440 877-1819
8695 York Rd North Royalton (44133) ***(G-15284)***
LP Propane Gas, Mc Arthur *Also called Nimco Inc* ***(G-13182)***
LPC Publishing Co..........216 721-1800
2026 Murray Hill Rd # 10 Cleveland (44106) ***(G-5586)***
Lrb Tool & Die Ltd..........330 898-5783
3303 Parkman Rd Nw Warren (44481) ***(G-19418)***
Lrbg Chemicals USA Inc..........419 244-5856
2112 Sylvan Ave Toledo (43606) ***(G-18388)***
LS Bombshelles..........513 254-6898
3940 Vine St Cincinnati (45217) ***(G-3953)***
LS Starrett Company..........440 835-0005
24500 Detroit Rd Westlake (44145) ***(G-20129)***
Ls2 Printing..........937 544-1000
111 E Main St West Union (45693) ***(G-19965)***
Lsc Communications Inc..........419 935-0111
1145 S Conwell Ave Willard (44890) ***(G-20241)***
LSI Graphic Solutions Plus, North Canton *Also called Grady McCauley Inc* ***(G-15089)***
LSI Industries Inc..........513 793-3200
10000 Alliance Rd Blue Ash (45242) ***(G-1808)***
LSI Industries Inc..........513 372-3200
10170 Alliance Rd Blue Ash (45242) ***(G-1809)***
LSI Industries Inc..........913 281-1100
10000 Alliance Rd Blue Ash (45242) ***(G-1810)***
LSI Industries Inc (PA)..........513 793-3200
10000 Alliance Rd Blue Ash (45242) ***(G-1811)***
LSI Retail Graphics LLC..........401 766-7446
9260 Pleasantwood Ave Nw North Canton (44720) ***(G-15098)***
Lsmi, Columbus *Also called Lambert Sheet Metal Inc* ***(G-7111)***
Lsp Technologies Inc..........614 718-3000
6145 Scherers Pl Dublin (43016) ***(G-8944)***
Lsq Manufacturing Inc..........330 725-4905
1140 Industrial Pkwy Medina (44256) ***(G-13287)***
Lt Enterprises of Ohio LLC..........330 526-6908
334 Orchard Ave Ne North Canton (44720) ***(G-15099)***
Lt Wright Handcrafted Knife Co..........740 317-1404
130 Warren Ln Unit B Steubenville (43953) ***(G-17541)***
Ltf Acquisition LLC..........330 533-0111
430 W Main St Canfield (44406) ***(G-2533)***
Ltg Polymers Limited..........330 854-5609
7612 Onyx Ave Nw Massillon (44646) ***(G-13015)***
LTI Power Systems..........440 327-5050
10800 Middle Ave Hngr B Elyria (44035) ***(G-9290)***
Lube & Chem Products, Cincinnati *Also called Interlube Corporation* ***(G-3855)***
Lube Depot..........330 758-0570
6122 Market St Youngstown (44512) ***(G-20961)***
Lube Depot..........330 854-6345
2185 Locust St S Canal Fulton (44614) ***(G-2484)***
Lubricant Additives, Wickliffe *Also called Lubrizol Corporation* ***(G-20215)***
LUBRIZOL ADVANCED MATERIALS, INC., Avon Lake *Also called Lubrizol Advanced Mtls Inc* ***(G-993)***
LUBRIZOL ADVANCED MATERIALS, INC., Bowling Green *Also called Lubrizol Advanced Mtls Inc* ***(G-1982)***
Lubrizol Advanced Mtls Inc, Brecksville *Also called Lubrizol Global Management* ***(G-2048)***
Lubrizol Advanced Mtls Inc..........440 933-0400
550 Moore Rd Avon Lake (44012) ***(G-993)***
Lubrizol Advanced Mtls Inc..........419 352-5565
1142 N Main St Bowling Green (43402) ***(G-1982)***
Lubrizol Corporation (HQ)..........440 943-4200
29400 Lakeland Blvd Wickliffe (44092) ***(G-20215)***
Lubrizol Corporation..........440 357-7064
155 Freedom Rd Painesville (44077) ***(G-15758)***
Lubrizol Corporation..........216 447-6212
1779 Marvo Dr Akron (44306) ***(G-261)***
Lubrizol Global Management (HQ)..........216 447-5000
9911 Brecksville Rd Brecksville (44141) ***(G-2048)***
Lubrizol Production Plant, Painesville *Also called Lubrizol Corporation* ***(G-15758)***
Luc Ice Inc..........419 734-2201
728 S Railroad St Port Clinton (43452) ***(G-16251)***
Lucas County Asphalt Inc..........419 476-0705
7540 Hollow Creek Dr Toledo (43617) ***(G-18389)***
Lucintech Inc..........419 265-2641
1510 N Westwood Ave Toledo (43606) ***(G-18390)***
Lucio Vanni LLC..........440 823-6103
1545 Wooster Rd Rocky River (44116) ***(G-16549)***
Lucius Fence Decking Irrigat..........419 450-9907
8146 Us Highway 224 New Riegel (44853) ***(G-14815)***

ALPHABETIC

Luckey Farmers Inc 419 287-3275
2320 Bowling Green Rd E Bradner (43406) *(G-2013)*
Lucky Paws LLC 859 620-2525
5541 Foley Rd Cincinnati (45238) *(G-3954)*
Lucky Thirteen Inc 216 631-0013
7413 Associate Ave Cleveland (44144) *(G-5587)*
Lucky Thirteen Laser, Cleveland Also called Lucky Thirteen Inc *(G-5587)*
Ludlow Composites Corporation 419 332-5531
2100 Commerce Dr Fremont (43420) *(G-10038)*
Ludowici Roof Tile Inc 740 342-1995
4757 Tile Plant Rd Se New Lexington (43764) *(G-14718)*
Ludwig Music Publishing Co 440 926-1100
1080 Cleveland St Grafton (44044) *(G-10307)*
Ludy Greenhouse Mfg Corp (PA) 800 255-5839
122 Railroad St New Madison (45346) *(G-14742)*
Luk Clutch Systems LLC (HQ) 330 264-4383
3401 Old Airport Rd Wooster (44691) *(G-20617)*
Luk USA LLC, Wooster Also called Schaeffler Transmission LLC *(G-20650)*
Luke Engineering & Mfg Corp (PA) 330 335-1501
456 South Blvd Wadsworth (44281) *(G-19252)*
Luke Engineering & Mfg Corp 330 925-3344
11 Pipestone Rd Rittman (44270) *(G-16525)*
Lukens Inc 937 440-2500
1040 S Dorset Rd Troy (45373) *(G-18684)*
Lukens Blacksmith Shop 513 821-2308
30 Compton Rd Cincinnati (45216) *(G-3955)*
Lukjan Metal Products Inc (PA) 440 599-8127
645 Industry Rd Conneaut (44030) *(G-7654)*
Luma Electric Company 419 843-7842
3419 Silica Rd Sylvania (43560) *(G-17949)*
Lumacurve Airfield Signs, Macedonia Also called Standard Signs Incorporated *(G-12332)*
Lumberjack Pallet Recycl LLC 513 821-7543
81 Caldwell Dr Cincinnati (45216) *(G-3956)*
Lumenomics Inc 614 798-3500
8333 Green Meadows Dr N Lewis Center (43035) *(G-11766)*
Lumi Craft, Norwich Also called Lumi-Lite Candle Company *(G-15421)*
Lumi-Lite Candle Company 740 872-3248
102 Sundale Rd Norwich (43767) *(G-15421)*
Luminaud Inc 440 255-9082
8688 Tyler Blvd Mentor (44060) *(G-13503)*
Luminex HD&f Company, Blue Ash Also called Luminex Home Decor *(G-1812)*
Luminex Home Decor (PA) 513 563-1113
10521 Millington Ct Blue Ash (45242) *(G-1812)*
Lumitex Inc (PA) 440 243-8401
8443 Dow Cir Strongsville (44136) *(G-17763)*
Lumitex Inc 949 250-8557
8443 Dow Cir Strongsville (44136) *(G-17764)*
Lumoptik Inc 216 577-3905
2700 W Park Blvd Shaker Heights (44120) *(G-16934)*
Lunar Tool & Mold Inc 440 237-2141
9860 York Alpha Dr North Royalton (44133) *(G-15285)*
Lund Equipment Co Inc 330 659-4800
2400 N Clvlnd Mssillon Rd Bath (44210) *(G-1201)*
Lund Printing Co 330 628-4047
2962 Trenton Rd Akron (44312) *(G-262)*
Lunken Charts LLC 513 253-7615
262 Wilmer Ave Cincinnati (45226) *(G-3957)*
Lure Inc 440 951-8862
38040 3rd St Willoughby (44094) *(G-20363)*
Lustrous Metal Coatings Inc 330 478-4653
1541 Raff Rd Sw Canton (44710) *(G-2735)*
Luvata Ohio Inc (HQ) 740 363-1981
1376 Pittsburgh Dr Delaware (43015) *(G-8704)*
Lux Corporation 419 562-7978
4613 Stetzer Rd Bucyrus (44820) *(G-2338)*
Luxaire Cushion Co 330 872-0995
2410 S Center St Newton Falls (44444) *(G-14989)*
Luxco Inc 216 671-6300
3116 Berea Rd Cleveland (44111) *(G-5588)*
Luxfer Magtech Inc (HQ) 513 772-3066
2940 Highland Ave Ste 210 Cincinnati (45212) *(G-3958)*
Luxottica of America Inc 614 409-9381
2150 Bixby Rd Lockbourne (43137) *(G-11997)*
Luxottica Optical Mfg, Lockbourne Also called Luxottica of America Inc *(G-11997)*
Luxus Arms, Mount Orab Also called Luxus Products LLC *(G-14446)*
Luxus Products LLC 937 444-6500
222 Homan Way Mount Orab (45154) *(G-14446)*
Luxx Ultra-Tech Inc 330 483-6051
7334 Lonesome Pine Trl Medina (44256) *(G-13288)*
Lwb/ISE LP 937 778-3828
9160 Country Club Rd Piqua (45356) *(G-16139)*
Lwc, Maumee Also called Larrys Water Conditioning *(G-13126)*
Lwr Enterprises Inc 740 984-0036
4310 Sparling Rd Waterford (45786) *(G-19487)*
Lyco Corporation 412 973-9176
1089 N Hubbard Rd Lowellville (44436) *(G-12253)*
Lyle Printing & Publishing Co (PA) 330 337-3419
185 E State St Salem (44460) *(G-16756)*
Lyle Printing & Publishing Co 330 337-7172
193 S Howard Ave Salem (44460) *(G-16757)*
Lync Corp 513 655-7286
2963 Commodore Ln Apt 2 Cincinnati (45251) *(G-3959)*
Lynn James Contracting LLC 419 467-4505
12490 County Road 5 Delta (43515) *(G-8775)*
Lynn Truck Parts & Service 330 966-1470
2690 Missenden St Nw North Canton (44720) *(G-15100)*
Lynns Logos Inc 440 786-1156
386 Broadway Ave Cleveland (44146) *(G-5589)*
Lynx Chemical 513 856-9161
370 Industrial Dr Franklin (45005) *(G-9896)*
Lyondell Chemical Company 440 352-9393
110 3rd St Fairport Harbor (44077) *(G-9625)*
Lyondell Chemical Company 513 530-4000
11530 Northlake Dr Cincinnati (45249) *(G-3960)*
Lyondellbasell 513 530-4000
11530 Northlake Dr Cincinnati (45249) *(G-3961)*
Lyons 440 224-0676
5231 State Route 193 Kingsville (44048) *(G-11460)*
M & B Asphalt Company Inc 419 992-4235
2100 W Senc County Rd 42 Tiffin (44883) *(G-18066)*
M & B Asphalt Company Inc 419 992-4236
1525 W County Road 42 Old Fort (44861) *(G-15525)*
M & B Machine Inc 419 476-8836
4801 Bennett Rd Toledo (43612) *(G-18391)*
M & G Polymers Usa LLC 330 239-7400
6951 Ridge Rd Sharon Center (44274) *(G-16951)*
M & G Truss Rafters 740 667-3166
26077 Congrove St Coolville (45723) *(G-7673)*
M & H Fabricating Co Inc (PA) 937 325-8708
717 Mound St Springfield (45505) *(G-17437)*
M & H Fabricating Co Inc 937 325-8708
823 Mound St Springfield (45505) *(G-17438)*
M & H Screen Printing 740 522-1957
1486 Hebron Rd Newark (43056) *(G-14894)*
M & J Machine Shop Inc 330 645-0042
2420 Pickle Rd Akron (44312) *(G-263)*
M & L Machine 937 386-2604
17400 State Route 247 Seaman (45679) *(G-16883)*
M & M Certified Welding Inc 330 467-1729
556 Highland Rd E Ste 3 Macedonia (44056) *(G-12311)*
M & M Concepts Inc 937 355-1115
2633 State Route 292 West Mansfield (43358) *(G-19943)*
M & M Dies Inc 216 883-6628
3502 Beyerle Rd Cleveland (44105) *(G-5590)*
M & M Engraving 216 749-7166
5411 State Rd Cleveland (44134) *(G-5591)*
M & M Fabrication Inc 740 779-3071
18828 Us Highway 50 Chillicothe (45601) *(G-3199)*
M & M Foods, Cleveland Also called Mama Mias Foods Inc *(G-5610)*
M & M Hardwoods, Sugarcreek Also called Tusco Hardwoods LLC *(G-17873)*
M & M Tobacco 330 573-8543
701 Canton Rd Nw Carrollton (44615) *(G-2925)*
M & R Electric Motor Svc Inc 937 222-6282
1516 E 5th St Dayton (45403) *(G-8317)*
M & R Manufacturing Inc 330 633-5725
41 Industry St Tallmadge (44278) *(G-17989)*
M & R Phillips Enterprises 740 323-0580
6242 Jacksontown Rd Newark (43056) *(G-14895)*
M & R Redi Mix Inc (PA) 419 445-7771
521 Commercial St Pettisville (43553) *(G-16034)*
M & R Redi Mix Inc 419 748-8442
L207 County Road 1c Mc Clure (43534) *(G-13186)*
M & W Trailers Inc 419 453-3331
525 E Main St Ottoville (45876) *(G-15682)*
M & W Welding Inc 614 224-0501
72 N Glenwood Ave Columbus (43222) *(G-7139)*
M & Y Marketing 937 322-3423
2651 Danbury Rd Springfield (45505) *(G-17439)*
M A C Machine 410 944-6171
1111 Faircrest St Se Canton (44707) *(G-2736)*
M A Harrison Mfg Co Inc 440 965-4306
14307 State Route 113 Wakeman (44889) *(G-19287)*
M A K Fabricating Inc 330 747-0040
1609 Wilson Ave Youngstown (44506) *(G-20962)*
M A Miller 440 636-5697
16790 Pioneer Rd Middlefield (44062) *(G-13814)*
M B Industries Inc 419 738-4769
310 Commerce Rd Wapakoneta (45895) *(G-19340)*
M B Industries Inc (PA) 419 738-4769
11158 Infirmary Rd Wapakoneta (45895) *(G-19341)*
M B Saxon Co Inc 440 229-5006
47 Alpha Park Cleveland (44143) *(G-5592)*
M B Trucking, Dover Also called Sugarcreek Lime Service *(G-8858)*
M C D Plastics & Manufacturing, Piqua Also called Miami Specialties Inc *(G-16142)*
M C Industries Inc 440 355-4040
111 Commerce Dr Lagrange (44050) *(G-11487)*
M C L Window Coverings Inc 513 868-6000
6741 Gilmore Rd Ste H Fairfield Township (45011) *(G-9584)*

M C Systems Inc 513 336-6007
4455 Bethany Rd Unit C Mason (45040) *(G-12904)*
M D M Graphics Inc 859 816-7375
10600 Chester Rd Cincinnati (45215) *(G-3962)*
M D Solutions, Plain City *Also called MD Solutions Inc (G-16201)*
M E P Manufacturing Inc (PA) 419 855-7723
214 E 4th St Genoa (43430) *(G-10234)*
M F Y Inc 330 747-1334
1640 Wilson Ave Youngstown (44506) *(G-20963)*
M G 3d 614 262-0956
320 E Weber Rd Columbus (43202) *(G-7140)*
M G Q Inc 419 992-4236
1525 W County Road 42 Tiffin (44883) *(G-18067)*
M Grafix LLC 419 528-8665
384 Gatewood Dr Apt 2 Mansfield (44907) *(G-12471)*
M H EBY Inc 614 879-6901
4435 State Route 29 West Jefferson (43162) *(G-19925)*
M H Logging & Lumber 740 694-1988
14582 Montgomery Rd Fredericktown (43019) *(G-9973)*
M H Woodworking LLC 330 893-3929
2789 County Rd Ste 600 Millersburg (44654) *(G-14108)*
M I P Inc 330 744-0215
701 Jones St Youngstown (44502) *(G-20964)*
M J Coates Construction Co (PA) 937 886-9546
9809 Saddle Creek Trl Dayton (45458) *(G-8318)*
M J S Oil Inc 937 982-3519
23296 Treaty Line Rd West Mansfield (43358) *(G-19944)*
M K Morse Company (PA) 330 453-8187
1101 11th St Se Canton (44707) *(G-2737)*
M L B Molded Urethane Pdts LLC 419 825-9140
1680 Us Highway 20a Swanton (43558) *(G-17916)*
M L C Technologies Inc 513 874-7792
4 Standen Dr Hamilton (45015) *(G-10583)*
M L Grinding Co 440 975-9111
34620 Lakeland Blvd Willoughby (44095) *(G-20364)*
M M I Services Inc 440 259-2939
3235 Elizabeth Dr Unit 34 Perry (44081) *(G-15908)*
M M Industries Inc 330 332-5947
36135 Salem Grange Rd Salem (44460) *(G-16758)*
M Mazzone & Sons Bakery Inc 216 631-6511
3519 Clark Ave Cleveland (44109) *(G-5593)*
M P G, Maumee *Also called Magnesium Products Group Inc (G-13128)*
M P I Labeltek, Wadsworth *Also called Miller Products Inc (G-19254)*
M P I Logistics, Massillon *Also called Martin Pallet Inc (G-13018)*
M P Machine Inc 440 255-8355
8743 East Ave Mentor (44060) *(G-13504)*
M Pharmaceutical USA 859 868-3131
4030 Mount Carmel Tobasco Ste 327 Cincinnati (45255) *(G-3963)*
M Pl Label Systems 330 938-2134
450 Courtney Rd Sebring (44672) *(G-16888)*
M R I Education Foundation 513 281-3400
5400 Kennedy Ave Cincinnati (45213) *(G-3964)*
M R S, Columbus *Also called MRS Industrial Inc (G-7199)*
M R T, Middletown *Also called 3d Sales & Consulting Inc (G-13874)*
M Russell & Associates Inc 419 478-8795
3250 Monroe St Toledo (43606) *(G-18392)*
M S B Machine Inc 330 686-7740
36 Castle Dr Munroe Falls (44262) *(G-14526)*
M S C Industries Inc 440 474-8788
5131 Ireland Rd Rome (44085) *(G-16564)*
M S K Partnership 419 394-4444
7219 Harris Rd Celina (45822) *(G-2972)*
M S K Tool & Die Inc 440 930-8100
685 Moore Rd Ste B Avon Lake (44012) *(G-994)*
M T, Elmore *Also called Machining Technologies Inc (G-9206)*
M T D Service Division, Shelby *Also called Mtd Products Inc (G-16984)*
M T O, Saint Marys *Also called Murotech Ohio Corporation (G-16690)*
M T S, Cincinnati *Also called Metal Technology Systems Inc (G-4012)*
M T Systems Inc 330 453-4646
400 Schroyer Ave Sw Canton (44702) *(G-2738)*
M Technologies Inc 330 477-9009
1818 Hopple Ave Sw Canton (44706) *(G-2739)*
M W Solutions LLC 419 782-1611
1802 Baltimore St Ste B Defiance (43512) *(G-8633)*
M Web Type Inc 614 272-8973
3500 Sullivant Ave Columbus (43204) *(G-7141)*
M&L Plating Works LLC (PA) 419 255-7701
425 Jefferson Ave Ste 520 Toledo (43604) *(G-18393)*
M&M Great Adventures LLC 937 344-1415
586 Deer Trl Westerville (43082) *(G-20008)*
M&S Machine and Manufacturing, Cincinnati *Also called Modern Manufacturing Inc (G-4039)*
M-Boss Inc 216 441-6080
4510 E 71st St Ste 2 Cleveland (44105) *(G-5594)*
M-Co Welling 330 897-1374
10949 Gnther Miller Rd Sw Stone Creek (43840) *(G-17561)*
M-D Building Products Inc 513 539-2255
100 Westheimer Dr Middletown (45044) *(G-13922)*
M-Fischer Enterprises LLC 419 782-5309
925 S Clinton St Ste B Defiance (43512) *(G-8634)*
M-Tek Inc 419 209-0399
1111 N Warpole St Upper Sandusky (43351) *(G-18961)*
M. A. I., Delaware *Also called Midwest Acoust-A-Fiber Inc (G-8705)*
M.S. Barkin Company, Cleveland *Also called Em Es Be Company LLC (G-5170)*
M/W International Inc 440 526-6900
2525 E Royalton Rd Broadview Heights (44147) *(G-2094)*
M21 Industries LLC 937 781-1377
721 Springfield St Dayton (45403) *(G-8319)*
M2m Imaging Corporation 440 684-9690
5427 Wilson Mills Rd Cleveland (44143) *(G-5595)*
M3 Midstream LLC 740 945-1170
37950 Crimm Rd Scio (43988) *(G-16878)*
M3 Midstream LLC 330 679-5580
10 E Main St Salineville (43945) *(G-16789)*
M3 Midstream LLC 330 223-2220
11543 Sr 644 Kensington (44427) *(G-11285)*
M3 Midstream LLC 740 431-4168
8349 Azalea Rd Sw Dennison (44621) *(G-8785)*
M3 Technologies Inc 216 898-9936
13910 Enterprise Ave Cleveland (44135) *(G-5596)*
M7 Technologies, Youngstown *Also called Garvey Corporation (G-20911)*
MA Flynn Associates LLC 513 893-7873
4115 Tonya Trl Hamilton (45011) *(G-10584)*
Maag Automatik Inc 330 677-2225
235 Progress Blvd Kent (44240) *(G-11347)*
Maag Reduction Engineering, Kent *Also called Maag Automatik Inc (G-11347)*
Maags Automotive & Machine 419 626-1539
1640 Columbus Ave Sandusky (44870) *(G-16824)*
Maass Midwest Mfg Inc 419 894-6424
19710 State Route 12 Arcadia (44804) *(G-625)*
Mab Fabrication Inc 855 622-3221
320 N State St Harrison (45030) *(G-10656)*
Mabar Printing Service 419 257-3659
400 N Tarr St North Baltimore (45872) *(G-15045)*
Mabsc, Akron *Also called Meggitt Aircraft Braking (G-278)*
Mac Advertising Co, Dayton *Also called Donald Marlo (G-8165)*
Mac Dhui Probe of America Inc 440 942-5597
7867 Enterprise Dr 9 Mentor (44060) *(G-13505)*
Mac Electric, Lima *Also called Fmh Electric Inc (G-11863)*
Mac Electric Inc 419 782-0671
1240 Fairgreen Ave Lima (45805) *(G-11896)*
Mac Instruments, Sandusky *Also called Machine Applications Corp (G-16825)*
Mac Its LLC (PA) 937 454-0722
1625 Fieldstone Way Vandalia (45377) *(G-19133)*
Mac Liquid Tank Trailer, Kent *Also called Mac Ltt Inc (G-11348)*
Mac Ltt Inc 330 474-3795
1400 Fairchild Ave Kent (44240) *(G-11348)*
Mac Manufacturing Inc (PA) 330 823-9900
14599 Commerce St Ne Alliance (44601) *(G-483)*
Mac Manufacturing Inc 330 829-1680
1453 Allen Rd Salem (44460) *(G-16759)*
Mac Mfg and Test Facilities, Youngstown *Also called Magnetic Analysis Corporation (G-20965)*
Mac Oil Field Service Inc 330 674-7371
7861 Township Road 306 Millersburg (44654) *(G-14109)*
Mac Printing Company 937 393-1101
406 N West St Hillsboro (45133) *(G-10884)*
Mac Ritchie Materials Inc 419 288-2790
6126 S Main St West Millgrove (43467) *(G-19946)*
Mac Steel Trailer Ltd 330 823-9900
14599 Commerce St Ne Alliance (44601) *(G-484)*
Mac Tools, Westerville *Also called Stanley Industrial & Auto LLC (G-20024)*
Mac Trailer Manufacturing Inc (PA) 330 823-9900
14599 Commerce St Ne Alliance (44601) *(G-485)*
Mac Trailer Service Inc 330 823-9190
14504 Commerce St Ne Alliance (44601) *(G-486)*
Maca Mold & Machine Co Inc 330 854-0292
761 Elm Ridge Ave Canal Fulton (44614) *(G-2485)*
Macdivitt Rubber Company LLC 440 259-5937
3291 Center Rd Perry (44081) *(G-15909)*
Mace Personal Def & SEC Inc (HQ) 440 424-5321
4400 Carnegie Ave Cleveland (44103) *(G-5597)*
Mace Security Intl Inc (PA) 440 424-5321
4400 Carnegie Ave Cleveland (44103) *(G-5598)*
Macek Industries 440 205-8711
8830 Tyler Blvd Mentor (44060) *(G-13506)*
Machine & Tool Accessories Co, Broadview Heights *Also called Mataco (G-2096)*
Machine Applications Corp 419 621-2322
3410 Tiffin Ave Sandusky (44870) *(G-16825)*
Machine Component Mfg 330 454-4566
3410 Perry Dr Nw Canton (44708) *(G-2740)*
Machine Concepts Inc 419 628-3498
2167 State Route 66 Minster (45865) *(G-14219)*
Machine Development Corp 513 825-5885
7707 Affinity Dr Cincinnati (45231) *(G-3965)*
Machine Doctors, Middletown *Also called Al Bradshaw Jr (G-13882)*

ALPHABETIC

Machine Doctors Inc   ALPHABETIC SECTION

Machine Doctors Inc 513 422-3060
  3490 Mustafa Dr Cincinnati (45241) *(G-3966)*
Machine Dynamics & Engrg Inc 330 868-5603
  9312 Arrow Rd Nw Minerva (44657) *(G-14190)*
Machine Industries Inc (PA) 216 881-8555
  5200 Perkins Ave Cleveland (44103) *(G-5599)*
Machine Parts International 216 251-4334
  10925 Briggs Rd Cleveland (44111) *(G-5600)*
Machine Products, Loveland *Also called Macpro Inc (G-12211)*
Machine Products Company 937 890-6600
  5660 Webster St Dayton (45414) *(G-8320)*
Machine Shop 330 494-1251
  410 Viking St Nw Canton (44720) *(G-2741)*
Machine Tek Systems Inc 330 527-4450
  10400 Industrial Dr Garrettsville (44231) *(G-10197)*
Machine Tl Sltons Unlmited LLC 513 761-0709
  8711 Reading Rd Cincinnati (45215) *(G-3967)*
Machine Tool & Fab Corp 419 435-7676
  1401 Sandusky St Fostoria (44830) *(G-9846)*
Machine Tool Design & Fab LLC 419 435-7676
  1401 Sandusky St Fostoria (44830) *(G-9847)*
Machine Tool Division, Bluffton *Also called Grob Systems Inc (G-1889)*
Machine Tool Rebuilders Inc 614 228-1070
  2042 Leonard Ave Columbus (43219) *(G-7142)*
Machine Tools Supply, Huber Heights *Also called Updike Supply Company (G-11024)*
Machine Works Inc 513 771-4600
  979 Redna Ter Cincinnati (45215) *(G-3968)*
Machine-Pro Technologies Inc 419 584-0086
  1321 W Market St Celina (45822) *(G-2973)*
Machined Glass Specialist Inc 937 743-6166
  245 Hiawatha Trl Springboro (45066) *(G-17336)*
Machined Seals, Cleveland *Also called SKF Usa Inc (G-6068)*
Machinex of Dayton Inc 937 252-7021
  2121 Old Vienna Dr Dayton (45459) *(G-8321)*
Machining Technologies Inc (PA) 419 862-3110
  468 Maple St Elmore (43416) *(G-9206)*
Machintek Co 513 551-1000
  3721 Port Union Rd Fairfield (45014) *(G-9522)*
Mack Concrete Industries Inc (HQ) 330 483-3111
  201 Columbia Rd Valley City (44280) *(G-19044)*
Mack Concrete Industries Inc 330 784-7008
  124 Darrow Rd Ste 7 Akron (44305) *(G-264)*
Mack Industrial LLC 800 918-9986
  3258 Sterlingwood Ln Perrysburg (43551) *(G-15974)*
Mack Industries 419 353-7081
  507 Derby Ave Bowling Green (43402) *(G-1983)*
Mack Industries Inc (PA) 330 460-7005
  1321 Industrial Pkwy N # 500 Brunswick (44212) *(G-2219)*
Mack Industries PA Inc (HQ) 330 483-3111
  201 Columbia Rd Valley City (44280) *(G-19045)*
Mack Industries PA Inc 330 638-7680
  2207 Slem Hutchings Rd Ne Vienna (44473) *(G-19202)*
Mack Iron Works Company 419 626-3712
  124 Warren St Sandusky (44870) *(G-16826)*
Mack Ready Mix Concrete Inc 330 483-3111
  201 Columbia Rd Valley City (44280) *(G-19046)*
Mack Ready-Mix, Akron *Also called Mack Concrete Industries Inc (G-264)*
Mack Transport, Brunswick *Also called Mack Industries Inc (G-2219)*
Macke Brothers Inc 513 771-7500
  10355 Spartan Dr Cincinnati (45215) *(G-3969)*
Mackland Co Inc 330 399-5034
  155 North St Nw Warren (44483) *(G-19419)*
Macleod Inc 513 771-9560
  5928 Hamilton Cleves Rd Miamitown (45041) *(G-13748)*
Macmillan Graphics, Milford *Also called Gregg Macmillan (G-14014)*
Macpherson & Company, Berea *Also called Macpherson Engineering Inc (G-1616)*
Macpherson Engineering Inc 440 243-6565
  95 Pelret Industrial Pkwy Berea (44017) *(G-1616)*
Macpro Inc 513 575-3000
  1456 Fay Rd Unit B Loveland (45140) *(G-12211)*
Macray Co LLC 937 325-1726
  100 W North St Springfield (45504) *(G-17440)*
Macro Meric, Aurora *Also called Saco Aei Polymers Inc (G-906)*
Mactac, Stow *Also called Morgan Adhesives Company LLC (G-17606)*
Mactek Corporation 330 487-5477
  2112 Case Pkwy Ste 1 Twinsburg (44087) *(G-18810)*
Macwood Inc 614 279-7676
  397 Martha Ave Columbus (43223) *(G-7143)*
Macwood Custom Woodworking, Columbus *Also called Macwood Inc (G-7143)*
Mad Metal Wldg Fabrication LLC 614 256-4163
  3435 Polley Rd Columbus (43221) *(G-7144)*
Mad River Steel Ltd 937 845-4046
  2141 N Dayton Lakeview Rd New Carlisle (45344) *(G-14671)*
Mad River Steel Company, New Carlisle *Also called Mad River Steel Ltd (G-14671)*
Mad River Topsoil Inc 937 882-6115
  5625 Lower Valley Pike Springfield (45506) *(G-17441)*
Madaen Natural Products Inc 800 600-1445
  141 Broad Blvd Lowr Cuyahoga Falls (44221) *(G-7894)*

Mader Automotive Center Inc (PA) 937 339-2681
  225 S Walnut St Troy (45373) *(G-18685)*
Mader Dampers, Lagrange *Also called Mader Machine Co Inc (G-11488)*
Mader Electr Motor & Power Tra 937 325-5576
  205 E Main St Springfield (45503) *(G-17442)*
Mader Machine Co Inc 440 355-4505
  422 Commerce Dr E Lagrange (44050) *(G-11488)*
Maderite LLC 937 570-1042
  6915 Roberta Dr Tipp City (45371) *(G-18122)*
Madgar Genis Corp 330 848-6950
  131 Snyder Ave Barberton (44203) *(G-1082)*
Madison Electric (mepco) Inc 440 279-0521
  11993 Ravenna Rd Ste 12 Chardon (44024) *(G-3124)*
Madison Electric Products Inc (PA) 216 391-7776
  26401 Fargo Ave Bedford Heights (44146) *(G-1473)*
Madison Graphics 216 226-5770
  13130 Detroit Ave Cleveland (44107) *(G-5601)*
Madison Group Inc 216 362-9000
  15919 Industrial Pkwy Cleveland (44135) *(G-5602)*
Madison Messenger, Columbus *Also called Columbus Messenger Company (G-6797)*
Madison Messenger, London *Also called Columbus Messenger Company (G-12055)*
Madison Press, London *Also called Central Ohio Printing Corp (G-12052)*
Madison Press Inc 216 521-3789
  1381 Summit Ave Lakewood (44107) *(G-11527)*
Madison Tool & Die Inc 440 354-8642
  147 Elevator Ave Painesville (44077) *(G-15759)*
Madsen Wire Products Inc 937 829-6561
  101 Madison St Dayton (45402) *(G-8322)*
Mae Consulting 513 531-8100
  700 W Pete Rose Way 531b Cincinnati (45203) *(G-3970)*
Mae Materials LLC 740 778-2242
  8336 Bennett School House South Webster (45682) *(G-17298)*
Mag Acquisitions LLC 513 988-6351
  400 E State St Trenton (45067) *(G-18622)*
Mag Machine Inc 440 946-3381
  7243 Industrial Park Blvd Mentor (44060) *(G-13507)*
Mag Resources LLC 330 294-0494
  711 Wooster Rd W Barberton (44203) *(G-1083)*
Mag-Nif Inc 440 255-9366
  8820 East Ave Mentor (44060) *(G-13508)*
Magellan Arospc Middletown Inc (HQ) 513 422-2751
  2320 Wedekind Dr Middletown (45042) *(G-13923)*
Magenta Incorporated 216 571-4094
  3185a W 33rd St Cleveland (44109) *(G-5603)*
Mageros Candies 330 534-1146
  132 N Main St Hubbard (44425) *(G-11005)*
Magic City Machine Inc 330 825-0048
  21 4th St Nw Barberton (44203) *(G-1084)*
Magic Dragon Machine Inc 614 539-8004
  3451 Grant Ave Grove City (43123) *(G-10443)*
Magic Interface Ltd 440 498-3700
  7295 Popham Pl Solon (44139) *(G-17185)*
Magic Press Printery, Barberton *Also called Barberton Magic Press Printing (G-1062)*
Magic Rack, Ashville *Also called Production Plus Corp (G-820)*
Magic Wok Enterprises, Toledo *Also called Magic Wok Inc (G-18394)*
Magic Wok Inc (PA) 419 531-1818
  3352 W Laskey Rd Toledo (43623) *(G-18394)*
Magna, Northwood *Also called Norplas Industries Inc (G-15341)*
Magna Exteriors America Inc 419 662-3256
  7825 Caple Blvd Northwood (43619) *(G-15340)*
Magna Group LLC 513 388-9463
  2340 Clydes Xing Cincinnati (45244) *(G-3971)*
Magna International Amer Inc 905 853-3604
  19911 County Rd Ridgeville Corners (43555) *(G-16512)*
Magna Machine Co (PA) 513 851-6900
  11180 Southland Rd Cincinnati (45240) *(G-3972)*
Magna Modular Systems LLC (HQ) 419 324-3387
  1800 Nathan Dr Toledo (43611) *(G-18395)*
Magna Modular Systems, Inc., Toledo *Also called Magna Modular Systems LLC (G-18395)*
Magna Products, Grafton *Also called Sulo Enterprises Inc (G-10311)*
Magna Seating America Inc 330 824-3101
  1702 Henn Pkwy Sw Warren (44481) *(G-19420)*
Magnaco Industries Inc (PA) 216 961-3636
  140 West Dr Lodi (44254) *(G-12016)*
Magneco/Metrel Inc 330 426-9468
  51365 State Route 154 Negley (44441) *(G-14590)*
Magneforce Inc 330 856-9300
  155 Shaffer Dr Ne Warren (44484) *(G-19421)*
Magnesium Elektron North Amer 419 424-8878
  115 Stanford Pkwy Findlay (45840) *(G-9716)*
Magnesium Products Group Inc 310 971-5799
  3928 Azalea Cir Maumee (43537) *(G-13128)*
Magnesium Refining Tech Inc (PA) 419 483-9199
  29695 Pettibone Rd Cleveland (44139) *(G-5604)*
Magnesium Refining Tech Inc 419 483-9199
  301 County Road 177 Bellevue (44811) *(G-1538)*
Magnetech, Massillon *Also called 3-D Service Ltd (G-12956)*
Magnetech Industrial Svcs Inc 330 830-3500
  800 Nave Rd Se Massillon (44646) *(G-13016)*

ALPHABETIC SECTION

Magnetic Analysis Corporation 330 758-1367
675 Mcclurg Rd Youngstown (44512) *(G-20965)*
Magnetic Mktg Solutions LLC 513 721-3801
2111 Kindel Ave Cincinnati (45214) *(G-3973)*
Magnetic Packaging LLC 419 720-4366
946 Kane St Ste C Toledo (43612) *(G-18396)*
Magnetic Resonance Tech 440 942-2922
4261 Hamann Pkwy Willoughby (44094) *(G-20365)*
Magnetic Screw Machine Pdts 937 348-2807
23241 State Route 37 Marysville (43040) *(G-12797)*
Magnetic Source, Marietta Also called Master Magnetics Inc *(G-12545)*
Magnetnotes Ltd 419 593-0060
946 Kane St Ste A Toledo (43612) *(G-18397)*
Magnext Ltd 614 433-0011
7100 Huntley Rd Columbus (43229) *(G-7145)*
Magnode, Trenton Also called Mag Acquisitions LLC *(G-18622)*
Magnode Corporation (HQ) 513 988-6351
400 E State St Trenton (45067) *(G-18623)*
Magnode Corporation 317 243-3553
400 E State St Trenton (45067) *(G-18624)*
Magnolia Machine & Repair Inc 330 866-4200
3315 Magnolia Rd Nw Magnolia (44643) *(G-12360)*
Magnum Asset Acquisition LLC 330 915-2382
5675 Hudson Industrial Hudson (44236) *(G-11062)*
Magnum Computers Inc 216 781-1757
868 Montford Rd Cleveland (44121) *(G-5605)*
Magnum Inks & Coatings, Marietta Also called Magnum Magnetics Corporation *(G-12641)*
Magnum Innovations, Hudson Also called Magnum Asset Acquisition LLC *(G-11062)*
Magnum Magnetics Corporation 740 516-6237
17289 Industrial Hwy Caldwell (43724) *(G-2409)*
Magnum Magnetics Corporation (PA) 740 373-7770
801 Masonic Park Rd Marietta (45750) *(G-12641)*
Magnum Molding Inc 937 368-3040
7435 N Bollinger Rd Conover (45317) *(G-7665)*
Magnum Piering Inc 513 759-3348
156 Circle Freeway Dr West Chester (45246) *(G-19874)*
Magnum Press, Columbus Also called Resilient Holdings Inc *(G-7387)*
Magnum Products, Columbus Also called Kcg Inc *(G-7084)*
Magnum Tool Corp 937 228-0900
1407 Stanley Ave Dayton (45404) *(G-8323)*
Magnus Engineered Eqp LLC 440 942-8488
4500 Beidler Rd Willoughby (44094) *(G-20366)*
Magnus Equipment, Cleveland Also called Reid Asset Management Company *(G-5970)*
Magnus Equipment, Willoughby Also called Reid Asset Management Company *(G-20419)*
Magnus International Group Inc (PA) 216 592-8355
16533 Chillicothe Rd A Chagrin Falls (44023) *(G-3056)*
Magretech, Bellevue Also called Magnesium Refining Tech Inc *(G-1538)*
Magstor Inc 614 433-0011
7100 Huntley Rd Columbus (43229) *(G-7146)*
Mahan Packing Co Inc 330 889-2454
6540 State Route 45 Bristolville (44402) *(G-2083)*
Mahar Spar Industries Inc 216 249-7143
341 E 131st St Cleveland (44108) *(G-5606)*
Mahle Behr Dayton LLC 937 356-2001
250 Northwoods Blvd # 47 Vandalia (45377) *(G-19134)*
Mahle Behr Dayton LLC 937 369-2900
1720 Webster St Dayton (45404) *(G-8324)*
Mahle Behr Dayton LLC (HQ) 937 369-2900
1600 Webster St Dayton (45404) *(G-8325)*
Mahle Behr Service America LLC 937 369-2610
1003 Bellbrook Ave Xenia (45385) *(G-20783)*
Mahle Behr USA Inc 937 369-2900
1600 Webster St Dayton (45404) *(G-8326)*
Mahle Behr USA Inc 937 356-2001
250 Northwoods Blvd # 47 Vandalia (45377) *(G-19135)*
Mahle Behr USA Inc 937 369-2000
1600 Webster St Dayton (45404) *(G-8327)*
Mahle Industries Incorporated 937 890-2739
1600 Webster St Dayton (45404) *(G-8328)*
Mahle Industries Incorporated 740 962-2040
5130 N State Route 60 Nw McConnelsville (43756) *(G-13207)*
Mahoning Valley Fabricators 330 793-8995
3697 Oakwood Ave Austintown (44515) *(G-934)*
Mahoning Valley Manufacturing 330 537-4492
17796 Rte 62 Beloit (44609) *(G-1571)*
MAI Manufacturing, Marysville Also called Straight 72 Inc *(G-12815)*
MAI Media Group Llc 513 779-0604
9624 Cincinnati Columbus West Chester (45241) *(G-19875)*
Main Awning & Tent Inc 513 621-6947
415 W Seymour Ave Cincinnati (45216) *(G-3974)*
Main Fare Box Division, Willoughby Also called Euclid Products Co Inc *(G-20317)*
Main Street Cambritt Cookies, Cuyahoga Falls Also called Main Street Gourmet LLC *(G-7895)*
Main Street Gourmet LLC 330 929-0000
170 Muffin Ln Cuyahoga Falls (44223) *(G-7895)*
Main Street Ice Cream Parlor, Van Wert Also called B M DS Fish N More LLC *(G-19078)*
Main Street Lighting Standards, Medina Also called Msls Group LLC *(G-13305)*

Maine Rubber Preforms LLC 216 210-2094
16090 Industrial Pkwy # 1 Middlefield (44062) *(G-13815)*
Maine's Sign's & Designs, Springfield Also called Maines Inc *(G-17443)*
Maines Brothers Tin Shop 937 393-1633
121 S West St Hillsboro (45133) *(G-10885)*
Maines Inc 937 322-2084
1718 E Pleasant St Springfield (45505) *(G-17443)*
Maines, Clyde Sons Tin Shop, Hillsboro Also called Maines Brothers Tin Shop *(G-10885)*
Mainstream Waterjet LLC 513 683-5426
108 Northeast Dr Loveland (45140) *(G-12212)*
Maintenance + Inc 330 264-6262
1051 W Liberty St Wooster (44691) *(G-20618)*
Maintenance and Repair Fabg Co 330 478-1149
427 Harding Ave Nw Massillon (44646) *(G-13017)*
Maintenance Building, Oxford Also called City of Oxford *(G-15691)*
Maintenance Repair Supply Inc 740 922-3006
5539 Gundy Dr Midvale (44653) *(G-13980)*
Maiweave, Springfield Also called Intertape Polymr Woven USA Inc *(G-17425)*
Majestic Engineering & TI LLC 937 845-1079
107 W Washington St New Carlisle (45344) *(G-14672)*
Majestic Manufacturing Inc 330 457-2447
4536 State Route 7 New Waterford (44445) *(G-14841)*
Majestic Plastics Inc 937 593-9500
811 N Main St Bellefontaine (43311) *(G-1522)*
Majestic Sportswear Company 937 773-1144
2545 Landman Mill Rd Piqua (45356) *(G-16140)*
Majestic Tool and Machine Inc 440 248-5058
30700 Carter St Ste C Solon (44139) *(G-17186)*
Majestic Trailer & Hitch, Akron Also called Majestic Trailers Inc *(G-265)*
Majestic Trailers Inc (PA) 330 798-1698
1750 E Waterloo Rd Akron (44306) *(G-265)*
Majic Touch 330 923-8259
4133 State Rd Cuyahoga Falls (44223) *(G-7896)*
Major Metals Company 419 886-4600
844 Kochheiser Rd Mansfield (44904) *(G-12472)*
Makergear LLC 216 765-0030
23632 Merc Rd Unit G Beachwood (44122) *(G-1246)*
Makino, Mason Also called Single Source Technologies LLC *(G-12939)*
Makino Inc (HQ) 513 573-7200
7680 Innovation Way Mason (45040) *(G-12905)*
Malabar Properties LLC 419 884-0071
300 S Mill St Mansfield (44904) *(G-12473)*
Malco Laminated Inc 513 541-8300
4251 Spring Grove Ave Cincinnati (45223) *(G-3975)*
Malco Products Inc 330 753-0361
12155 Fisher Ave Ne Alliance (44601) *(G-487)*
Malco Products Inc 330 753-0361
393 W Wilbeth Rd Akron (44301) *(G-266)*
Malco Products Alliance Packg, Alliance Also called Malco Products Inc *(G-487)*
Malcolm Hydraulics 330 819-2033
6581 Waterloo Rd Atwater (44201) *(G-862)*
Malcuit Racing Engines, Strasburg Also called B A Malcuit Racing Inc *(G-17645)*
Malin Co, Cleveland Also called Malin Wire Co *(G-5608)*
Malin Company, Cleveland Also called Brushes Inc *(G-4848)*
Malin Wire Co (HQ) 216 267-9080
5400 Smith Rd Cleveland (44142) *(G-5607)*
Malin Wire Co 216 267-9080
5400 Smith Rd Cleveland (44142) *(G-5608)*
Malish Corporation (PA) 440 951-5356
7333 Corporate Blvd Mentor (44060) *(G-13509)*
Mall Compan, The, Mansfield Also called R M Davis Inc *(G-12503)*
Malley's Chocolates, Lakewood Also called Malleys Candies *(G-11528)*
Malley's Chocolates, Cleveland Also called Malleys Candies Inc *(G-5609)*
Malleys Candies (PA) 216 362-8700
1685 Victoria Ave Lakewood (44107) *(G-11528)*
Malleys Candies Inc 216 529-6262
13400 Brookpark Rd Cleveland (44135) *(G-5609)*
Mallinckrodt LLC 513 948-5751
2111 E Galbraith Rd Cincinnati (45237) *(G-3976)*
Mallory Pattern Works Inc 419 726-8001
5340 Enterprise Blvd Toledo (43612) *(G-18398)*
Malone Specialty Inc 440 255-4200
8900 East Ave Mentor (44060) *(G-13510)*
Malta Dynamics LLC (PA) 740 749-3512
405 Watertown Rd Waterford (45786) *(G-19488)*
Mama Mias Foods Inc 216 281-2188
3270 W 67th Pl Cleveland (44102) *(G-5610)*
Mameco International Inc 216 752-4400
4475 E 175th St Cleveland (44128) *(G-5611)*
Mammas Mandel 513 827-2457
7952 Hedgewood Cir Mason (45040) *(G-12906)*
Mammotone, Cincinnati Also called Devicor Medical Products Inc *(G-3587)*
Mamsys Consulting Services 440 287-6824
35865 Spatterdock Ln Solon (44139) *(G-17187)*
Manairco Inc 419 524-2121
28 Industrial Pkwy Mansfield (44903) *(G-12474)*
Manchik Engineering & Co 740 927-4454
7070 Avery Rd Dublin (43017) *(G-8945)*

Manco Inc
  6531 State Route 503 N Lewisburg (45338) *(G-11795)* 937 962-2661

Manco Manufacturing Co 419 925-4152
  2411 Rolfes Rd Maria Stein (45860) *(G-12599)*

Mancor Ohio Inc (HQ) 937 228-6141
  1008 Leonhard St Dayton (45404) *(G-8329)*

Mancor Ohio Inc 937 228-6141
  600 Kiser St Dayton (45404) *(G-8330)*

Mandi A Tripp 740 380-1216
  12691 Ovid Rd Rockbridge (43149) *(G-16537)*

Mane Inc (HQ) 513 248-9876
  2501 Henkle Dr Lebanon (45036) *(G-11671)*

Mane Inc 513 248-9876
  1093 Mane Way Lebanon (45036) *(G-11672)*

Mane Calafornia, Lebanon Also called Mane Inc *(G-11671)*

Manfacturing, Dayton Also called Daisys Pillows LLC *(G-8125)*

Manico Inc 440 946-5333
  37105 Code Ave Willoughby (44094) *(G-20367)*

Manifest Productions LLC 614 806-3054
  272 S Front St Apt 601 Columbus (43215) *(G-7147)*

Manifold & Phalor Inc 614 920-1200
  10385 Busey Rd Nw Canal Winchester (43110) *(G-2506)*

Manitowoc Company Inc 920 746-3332
  1847 Columbus Rd Cleveland (44113) *(G-5612)*

Manitwoc Ovens Advnced Cooking, Cleveland Also called Cleveland Range LLC *(G-4972)*

Mannings Packing Co 937 446-3278
  100 College Ave Sardinia (45171) *(G-16870)*

Mannings USA 614 836-0021
  351 Lowery Ct Ste 3 Groveport (43125) *(G-10502)*

Manoranjan Shaffer & Heidkamp, Dayton Also called Watson Haran & Company Inc *(G-8585)*

Mansfield Asphalt Paving Inc 740 453-0721
  3570 S River Rd Zanesville (43701) *(G-21154)*

Mansfield Blanking Div, Valley City Also called Shiloh Corporation *(G-19062)*

Mansfield Brick & Supply Co (PA) 419 526-1191
  320 N Diamond St Mansfield (44902) *(G-12475)*

Mansfield Fabricated Products, Mansfield Also called The Mansfield Strl & Erct Co *(G-12528)*

Mansfield Fabricated Products, Mansfield Also called The Mansfield Strl & Erct Co *(G-12529)*

Mansfield Graphics, Mansfield Also called Five Handicap Inc *(G-12439)*

Mansfield Imaging Center LLC 419 756-8899
  536 S Trimble Rd Ste A Mansfield (44906) *(G-12476)*

Mansfield Industries Inc 419 524-1300
  1776 Harrington Mem Rd Mansfield (44903) *(G-12477)*

Mansfield Journal Co 330 364-8641
  629 Wabash Ave Nw New Philadelphia (44663) *(G-14782)*

Mansfield Operations, Mansfield Also called AK Steel Corporation *(G-12402)*

Mansfield Paint Co Inc 330 725-2436
  525 W Liberty St Medina (44256) *(G-13289)*

Mansfield Plumbing Pdts LLC (HQ) 419 938-5211
  150 E 1st St Perrysville (44864) *(G-16030)*

Mansfield Plumbing Pdts LLC 330 496-2301
  13211 State Route 226 Big Prairie (44611) *(G-1675)*

Mansfield Welding Services LLC 419 594-2738
  20027 State Route 613 Oakwood (45873) *(G-15471)*

MANSION HOMES, Bryan Also called Manufactured Housing Entps Inc *(G-2298)*

Mantaline Corporation 330 274-2264
  4754 E High St Mantua (44255) *(G-12551)*

Mantapart 330 549-2389
  1161 E Garfield Rd Unit 2 New Springfield (44443) *(G-14820)*

Mantey Vineyards, Sandusky Also called Firelands Winery *(G-16811)*

Mantra Haircare LLC 440 526-3304
  305 Ken Mar Indus Pkwy Broadview Heights (44147) *(G-2095)*

Mantua Bed Frames, Solon Also called Mantua Manufacturing Co *(G-17188)*

Mantua Manufacturing Co (PA) 800 333-8333
  31050 Diamond Pkwy Solon (44139) *(G-17188)*

Mantych Metalworking Inc 937 258-1373
  3175 Plainfield Rd Dayton (45432) *(G-7984)*

Manufactured Housing Entps Inc 419 636-4511
  9302 Us Highway 6 Bryan (43506) *(G-2298)*

Manufacturer, Medina Also called Hawthorne Bolt Works Corp *(G-13270)*

Manufacturers Equipment Co 513 424-3573
  35 Enterprise Dr Middletown (45044) *(G-13924)*

Manufacturing Animal Food Phrm, Batavia Also called Ingredient Masters Inc *(G-1154)*

Manufacturing Company LLC 414 708-7583
  3468 Cornell Pl Cincinnati (45220) *(G-3977)*

Manufacturing Concepts 330 784-9054
  409 Munroe Falls Rd Tallmadge (44278) *(G-17990)*

Manufacturing Division, Willard Also called Lsc Communications Inc *(G-20241)*

Manufacturing Division Inc 330 533-6835
  445 W Main St Canfield (44406) *(G-2534)*

Manufacturing Futures Inc (PA) 216 903-7993
  40 Haskell Dr Cleveland (44108) *(G-5613)*

Manufctring Bus Dev Sltons LLC 419 294-1313
  1950 Industrial Dr Findlay (45840) *(G-9717)*

MAP SYSTEMS AND SOLUTIONS, Columbus Also called Mapsys Inc *(G-7148)*

Mapco, Mansfield Also called Midwest Aircraft Products Co *(G-12481)*

Mapes Concrete Construction 513 245-2631
  5691 Cheviot Rd Apt 3 Cincinnati (45247) *(G-3978)*

Maple City Rubber Company 419 668-8261
  55 Newton St Norwalk (44857) *(G-15405)*

Maple Creek Mining Inc (HQ) 740 926-9205
  56854 Pleasant Ridge Rd Alledonia (43902) *(G-446)*

Maple Grove Companies, Tiffin Also called M G Q Inc *(G-18067)*

Maple Grove Materials, Tiffin Also called M & B Asphalt Company Inc *(G-18066)*

Maple Grove Materials Inc 419 992-4235
  1525 W City Rd Ste 42 Tiffin (44883) *(G-18068)*

Maple Grove Stone, Old Fort Also called M & B Asphalt Company Inc *(G-15525)*

Maple Hill Woodworking 330 674-2500
  2726 Trl 128 Millersburg (44654) *(G-14110)*

Maple Valley Cleaners, Akron Also called Norkaam Industries LLC *(G-298)*

Maple Valley Sug Bush & Farms, Chardon Also called Dnd Products Inc *(G-3109)*

Mapledale Farm Inc 440 286-3389
  12613 Woodin Rd Chardon (44024) *(G-3125)*

Mapledale Landscaping, Chardon Also called Mapledale Farm Inc *(G-3125)*

Mapsys Inc (PA) 614 255-7258
  920 Michigan Ave Columbus (43215) *(G-7148)*

Mar Chele Inc 937 429-2300
  2727 Fairfield Cmns Blvd Beavercreek (45431) *(G-1330)*

Mar Chele Inc (PA) 937 833-3400
  18 Market St Brookville (45309) *(G-2174)*

Mar Mor Inc 216 961-6900
  3591 W 56th St Cleveland (44102) *(G-5614)*

Mar Zane, Youngstown Also called Shelly and Sands Inc *(G-21029)*

Mar-Bal Inc (PA) 440 543-7526
  10095 Queens Way Chagrin Falls (44023) *(G-3057)*

Mar-Bal Inc 440 543-7526
  10095 Queens Way Chagrin Falls (44023) *(G-3058)*

Mar-Bal Pultrusion Inc 440 953-0456
  38310 Apollo Pkwy Willoughby (44094) *(G-20368)*

Mar-Con Tool Company Inc 937 299-2244
  2301 Arbor Blvd Moraine (45439) *(G-14367)*

Mar-Metal Mfg Inc 419 447-1102
  420 N Warpole St Upper Sandusky (43351) *(G-18962)*

Mar-Vel Tool Co Inc 937 223-2137
  858 Hall Ave Dayton (45404) *(G-8331)*

Mar-Zane Inc (HQ) 740 453-0721
  3570 S River Rd Zanesville (43701) *(G-21155)*

Mar-Zane Inc 740 782-1240
  38824 National Rd Bethesda (43719) *(G-1657)*

Mar-Zane Inc 740 685-5178
  59903 Vocational Rd Byesville (43723) *(G-2390)*

Mar-Zane Inc 330 626-2079
  9551 Elliman Rd Mantua (44255) *(G-12552)*

Mar-Zane Inc 419 529-2086
  1300 W 4th St Ontario (44906) *(G-15543)*

Mar-Zane Materials, Zanesville Also called Mar-Zane Inc *(G-21155)*

Maramor Chocolates, Columbus Also called Hake Head LLC *(G-6976)*

Maranatha Industries Inc 419 263-2013
  102 S Main St Payne (45880) *(G-15873)*

Marathon At Sawmill 614 734-0836
  7200 Sawmill Rd Columbus (43235) *(G-7149)*

Marathon Canton Refinery, Canton Also called Mplx Terminals LLC *(G-2757)*

Marathon Industrial Cntrs Inc 440 324-2748
  100 Freedom Ct Elyria (44035) *(G-9291)*

Marathon Mfg & Sup Co 330 343-2656
  5165 Main St Ne New Philadelphia (44663) *(G-14783)*

Marathon Oil Company 419 422-2121
  539 S Main St Findlay (45840) *(G-9718)*

Marathon Petroleum Company LP (HQ) 419 422-2121
  539 S Main St Findlay (45840) *(G-9719)*

Marathon Petroleum Coporation 419 422-2121
  539 S Main St Findlay (45840) *(G-9720)*

Marathon Petroleum Corporation (PA) 419 422-2121
  539 S Main St Findlay (45840) *(G-9721)*

Marazita Graphics Inc 330 773-6462
  1100 Triplett Blvd Akron (44306) *(G-267)*

Marbee Inc 419 422-9441
  2703 N Main St Ste 1 Findlay (45840) *(G-9722)*

Marbee Printing & Graphic Art, Findlay Also called Marbee Inc *(G-9722)*

Marble Arch Products Inc 937 746-8388
  263 Industrial Dr Franklin (45005) *(G-9897)*

Marble Cliff Block & Bldrs Sup, Lockbourne Also called J P Sand & Gravel Company *(G-11995)*

Marble Cliff Block & Bldrs Sup, Columbus Also called Oberfields LLC *(G-7236)*

Marble Cliff Limestone Inc 614 488-3030
  2650 Old Dublin Rd Hilliard (43026) *(G-10838)*

Marble Works 216 496-7745
  17827 Roseland Rd Cleveland (44112) *(G-5615)*

Marblelife of Central Ohio 614 837-6146
  8440 Blacklick Eastern Rd Pickerington (43147) *(G-16053)*

Marc Industries Inc 440 944-9305
  35140 Lakeland Blvd Willoughby (44095) *(G-20369)*

ALPHABETIC SECTION

Marc V Concepts Inc 419 782-6505
   401 Agnes St Defiance (43512) *(G-8635)*
Marchione Studio Inc 330 454-7408
   1225 Minerva Ct Nw Canton (44703) *(G-2742)*
Marco Printed Products Co 937 433-7030
   25 W Whipp Rd Dayton (45459) *(G-8332)*
Marco Printed Products Co Inc (PA) 937 433-5680
   14 Marco Ln Dayton (45458) *(G-8333)*
Marco's Paper, Dayton Also called Marco Printed Products Co Inc *(G-8333)*
Marco's Papers, Dayton Also called Marco Printed Products Co *(G-8332)*
Marcum Crew Cut Inc 740 862-3400
   6080 Fisher Rd Nw Baltimore (43105) *(G-1039)*
Marcum Development LLC 330 466-8231
   2245 Flickinger Hill Rd Wooster (44691) *(G-20619)*
Marcum Machine Shop, Lodi Also called Lowell Marcum *(G-12015)*
Marcus Jewelers 513 474-4950
   2022 8 Mile Rd Cincinnati (45244) *(G-3979)*
Marcus Uppe Inc 216 263-4000
   815 Superior Ave E # 714 Cleveland (44114) *(G-5616)*
Marengo Fabricated Steel Ltd (PA) 800 919-2652
   1089 County Road 26 Marengo (43334) *(G-12593)*
Marfo Company (PA) 614 276-3352
   799 N Hague Ave Columbus (43204) *(G-7150)*
Margaret Trentman 513 948-1700
   5123 Montgomery Rd Cincinnati (45212) *(G-3980)*
Margo Tool Technology Inc 740 653-8115
   2616 Setter Ct Nw Lancaster (43130) *(G-11585)*
Maric Drilling Company Inc 330 830-8178
   2581 County Rd 160 Winesburg (44690) *(G-20532)*
Marich Machine & Tool Co Inc 216 391-5502
   3815 Lakeside Ave E Cleveland (44114) *(G-5617)*
Maries Candies LLC 937 465-3061
   311 Zanesfield Rd West Liberty (43357) *(G-19937)*
Marietta Coal Co (PA) 740 695-2197
   67705 Friends Church Rd Saint Clairsville (43950) *(G-16637)*
Marietta Eramet Inc 740 374-1000
   16705 State Route 7 Marietta (45750) *(G-12642)*
Marietta Martin Materials Inc 937 335-8313
   250 Dye Mill Rd Troy (45373) *(G-18686)*
Marietta Martin Materials Inc 919 781-4550
   9843 Dyton Grenville Pike Brookville (45309) *(G-2175)*
Marietta Martin Materials Inc 937 766-2351
   3744 Turnbull Rd Cedarville (45314) *(G-2944)*
Marietta Martin Materials Inc 937 884-5814
   9843 State Route 49 Brookville (45309) *(G-2176)*
Marietta Mobility, Marietta Also called Steves Vans & Accessories LLC *(G-12676)*
Marietta Resources Corporation 740 373-6305
   704 Pike St Marietta (45750) *(G-12643)*
Marik Spring Inc 330 564-0617
   121 Northeast Ave Tallmadge (44278) *(G-17991)*
Marine Development, Cincinnati Also called Machine Development Corp *(G-3965)*
Marine Jet Power Inc 614 759-9000
   6740 Commerce Court Dr Blacklick (43004) *(G-1689)*
Marinemax Inc 918 782-3277
   1991 Ne Catawba Rd Port Clinton (43452) *(G-16252)*
Mariner's Landing Marina, Cincinnati Also called Mariners Landing Inc *(G-3981)*
Mariners Landing Inc 513 941-3625
   7405 Forbes Rd Cincinnati (45233) *(G-3981)*
Marino Maintenance Co, Canton Also called Phase II Enterprises Inc *(G-2784)*
Marion Caldwell 740 446-1042
   1262 Lincoln Pike Rear Gallipolis (45631) *(G-10171)*
Marion Ethanol LLC 740 383-4400
   1660 Hillman Ford Rd Marion (43302) *(G-12717)*
Marion Industries Inc 740 223-0075
   999 Kellogg Pkwy Marion (43302) *(G-12718)*
Marion Signs & Lighting LLC 352 236-0936
   3200 Valleyview Dr Columbus (43204) *(G-7151)*
Marion Star, Marion Also called Gannett Co Inc *(G-12703)*
Marios Drive Thru 330 452-8793
   914 12th St Ne Canton (44704) *(G-2743)*
Mariotti Printing Co LLC 440 245-4120
   513 E 28th St Lorain (44055) *(G-12104)*
Mark Advertising Agency Inc 419 626-9000
   1600 5th St Sandusky (44870) *(G-16827)*
Mark Carpenter Industries Inc 419 294-4568
   2300 Napoleon Rd Fremont (43420) *(G-10039)*
Mark Daily 937 369-5358
   807 N Maple St Eaton (45320) *(G-9161)*
Mark Dental Laboratory 216 464-6424
   24300 Chagrin Blvd # 310 Cleveland (44122) *(G-5618)*
Mark Grzianis St Treats Ex Inc (PA) 330 414-6266
   1294 Windward Ln Kent (44240) *(G-11349)*
Mark J Myers (PA) 513 753-7300
   80 W Main St Amelia (45102) *(G-543)*
Mark Matthews Glass, Archbold Also called Matthews Art Glass *(G-658)*
Mark Nelson 740 282-5334
   980 Lincoln Ave Steubenville (43952) *(G-17542)*
Mark One Manufacturing Ltd 419 628-4405
   351 Industrial Dr Ste 9 Minster (45865) *(G-14220)*

Mark Rasche 614 882-1810
   6962 Harlem Rd Westerville (43082) *(G-20009)*
Mark Rite Co 330 757-7229
   206 Evergreen Dr Youngstown (44514) *(G-20966)*
Mark True Engraving Co 216 651-7700
   1250 W 76th St Cleveland (44102) *(G-5619)*
Mark True Engraving Company 216 252-7422
   3264 W 105th St Cleveland (44111) *(G-5620)*
Mark West Energy, Cadiz Also called Markwest Energy Partners LP *(G-2399)*
Mark-All Enterprises LLC 800 433-3615
   888 W Waterloo Rd Akron (44314) *(G-268)*
Mark-N-Mend Inc 440 951-2003
   38151 Airport Pkwy Ste 54 Willoughby (44094) *(G-20370)*
Markers Inc 440 933-5927
   33490 Pin Oak Pkwy Avon Lake (44012) *(G-995)*
Market Direct, Cincinnati Also called Jscs Group Inc *(G-3886)*
Market Garden Brewery, Cleveland Also called Bar 25 LLC *(G-4789)*
Market Media Creations, Coshocton Also called Sprint Print Inc *(G-7752)*
Market Ready 513 289-9231
   1129 Avalon Dr Maineville (45039) *(G-12374)*
Market-Master, New Richmond Also called Master Disposers Inc *(G-14812)*
Markethatch Co Inc 330 376-6363
   91 E Voris St Akron (44311) *(G-269)*
Marketing Comm Resource Inc 440 484-3010
   4800 E 345th St Willoughby (44094) *(G-20371)*
Marketing Directions Inc 440 835-5550
   28005 Clemens Rd Cleveland (44145) *(G-5621)*
Marketing Essentials LLC 419 629-0080
   14 N Washington St New Bremen (45869) *(G-14656)*
Markeys Audio/Visual Inc 419 244-8844
   24 S Saint Clair St Toledo (43604) *(G-18399)*
Markham Machine Company Inc 330 762-7676
   160 N Union St Akron (44304) *(G-270)*
Marking Devices Inc 216 861-4498
   3110 Payne Ave Cleveland (44114) *(G-5622)*
Markko Vineyard 440 593-3197
   4500 S Ridge Rd W Conneaut (44030) *(G-7655)*
Markley Enterprises LLC 513 771-1290
   1705 Magnolia Dr Cincinnati (45215) *(G-3982)*
Marks Brew Thru 330 699-1755
   2455 Canton Rd Akron (44312) *(G-271)*
Markt 740 397-5900
   1095 Harcourt Rd Ste A Mount Vernon (43050) *(G-14490)*
Markwest Energy Partners LP 740 942-0463
   78405 Cadiz New Athens Rd Cadiz (43907) *(G-2399)*
Markwest Utica Emg LLC 740 942-4810
   46700 Giacobbi Rd Jewett (43986) *(G-11252)*
Markwith Tool Company Inc 937 548-6808
   5261 S State Route 49 Greenville (45331) *(G-10380)*
Marky Welding, North Bend Also called Steel Services Inc *(G-15055)*
Marlboro Manufacturing Inc 330 935-2221
   11750 Marlboro Ave Ne Alliance (44601) *(G-488)*
Marlen Manufacturing & Dev Co (PA) 216 292-7060
   5150 Richmond Rd Bedford (44146) *(G-1424)*
Marlen Manufacturing & Dev Co 216 292-7546
   5156 Richmond Rd Bedford (44146) *(G-1425)*
Marlin Manufacturing Corp (PA) 216 676-1340
   12800 Corporate Dr Cleveland (44130) *(G-5623)*
Marlin Thermocouple Wire Inc 440 835-1950
   12800 Corporate Dr Cleveland (44130) *(G-5624)*
Marlite Inc 330 343-6621
   609 S Tuscarawas Ave Dover (44622) *(G-8837)*
Marlite Inc (HQ) 330 343-6621
   1 Marlite Dr Dover (44622) *(G-8838)*
Marlow-2000 Inc 216 362-8500
   13811 Enterprise Ave Cleveland (44135) *(G-5625)*
Marmac Co 937 372-8093
   1231 Bellbrook Ave Xenia (45385) *(G-20784)*
Marmax Machine Co 937 698-9900
   2425 S State Route 48 Ludlow Falls (45339) *(G-12269)*
Marmon Highway Tech LLC 330 878-5595
   6332 Columbia Rd Nw Dover (44622) *(G-8839)*
Marne Plastics LLC 614 732-4666
   808 Distribution Dr Columbus (43228) *(G-7152)*
Marpro, Cincinnati Also called Cincinnatti Premier Candy LLC *(G-3513)*
Marrow County Sentinel, Mount Gilead Also called Hirt Publishing Co Inc *(G-14426)*
Marrow County Sentinel 419 946-3010
   245 Neal Ave Ste A Mount Gilead (43338) *(G-14428)*
Mars Petcare Us Inc 614 878-7242
   5115 Fisher Rd Columbus (43228) *(G-7153)*
Marsam Metalfab Inc 330 405-1520
   1870 Enterprise Pkwy Twinsburg (44087) *(G-18811)*
Marsh Industries Inc 330 308-8667
   1117 Bowers Ave Nw New Philadelphia (44663) *(G-14784)*
Marsh Technologies Inc 330 545-0085
   30 W Main St Ste A Girard (44420) *(G-10262)*
Marsh Valley Forest Pdts Ltd 440 632-1889
   14141 Old State Rd Middlefield (44062) *(G-13816)*

Marshall Plastics Inc 937 653-4740
590 S Edgewood Ave Urbana (43078) ***(G-19004)***
Marshalltown Packaging Inc 641 753-5272
601 N Hague Ave Columbus (43204) ***(G-7154)***
Marshallville Packing Co Inc 330 855-2871
50 E Market St Marshallville (44645) ***(G-12753)***
Marshas Buckeyes LLC 419 872-7666
25631 Fort Meigs Rd Ste E Perrysburg (43551) ***(G-15975)***
Mart Plus Fuel 216 261-0420
21820 Lake Shore Blvd Euclid (44123) ***(G-9425)***
Martans Foods 330 483-9009
6460 Grafton Rd Valley City (44280) ***(G-19047)***
Martin & Marianne Tools Inc 440 255-5107
9335 Kathleen Dr Mentor (44060) ***(G-13511)***
Martin Allen Trailer LLC 330 942-0217
2888 Nationwide Pkwy Brunswick (44212) ***(G-2220)***
Martin Bauder Woodworking LLC 513 735-0659
1498 Binning Rd Milford (45150) ***(G-14025)***
Martin Block Company 740 286-7507
290 Twin Oaks Dr Jackson (45640) ***(G-11190)***
Martin Cab Div, Cleveland *Also called Martin Sheet Metal Inc* ***(G-5627)***
Martin Diesel Inc 419 782-9911
27809 County Road 424 Defiance (43512) ***(G-8636)***
Martin Industrial Truck, Cleveland *Also called Marlow-2000 Inc* ***(G-5625)***
Martin Industries Inc 419 862-2694
473 Maple St Elmore (43416) ***(G-9207)***
Martin M Hardin 740 282-1234
411 N 7th St Steubenville (43952) ***(G-17543)***
Martin Machine & Tool Inc 419 373-1711
435 W Woodland Cir Bowling Green (43402) ***(G-1984)***
Martin Machine Co Inc 440 946-5174
37151 Ben Hur Ave Ste D Willoughby (44094) ***(G-20372)***
Martin Marietta Aggragate, West Chester *Also called Martin Marietta Materials Inc* ***(G-19740)***
Martin Marietta Aggregates, Harrison *Also called Martin Marietta Materials Inc* ***(G-10657)***
Martin Marietta Aggregates, Cedarville *Also called Marietta Martin Materials Inc* ***(G-2944)***
Martin Marietta Aggregates, Brookville *Also called Marietta Martin Materials Inc* ***(G-2176)***
Martin Marietta Materials Inc 513 701-1120
4900 Parkway Dr Mason (45040) ***(G-12907)***
Martin Marietta Materials Inc 513 701-1140
9277 Centre Pointe Dr # 250 West Chester (45069) ***(G-19740)***
Martin Marietta Materials Inc 513 200-2303
170 Pilot Rd Harrison (45030) ***(G-10657)***
Martin Marietta Materials Inc 513 353-1400
10905 Us 50 North Bend (45052) ***(G-15052)***
Martin Marietta Materials Inc 937 766-2351
3744 Turnbull Rd Cedarville (45314) ***(G-2945)***
Martin Marietta Materials Inc 513 871-7152
4439 Kellogg Ave Cincinnati (45226) ***(G-3983)***
Martin Pallet Inc 330 832-5309
1414 Industrial Ave Sw Massillon (44647) ***(G-13018)***
Martin Paper Products Inc 740 756-9271
5907 Clmbus Lncster Rd Nw Carroll (43112) ***(G-2907)***
Martin Printing Co 419 224-9176
1804 Wendell Ave Lima (45805) ***(G-11897)***
Martin Pultrusion Group Inc 440 439-9130
20801 Miles Rd Ste B Cleveland (44128) ***(G-5626)***
Martin Rubber Company 330 336-6604
5020 Panther Pkwy Seville (44273) ***(G-16920)***
Martin Sheet Metal Inc 216 377-8200
7108 Madison Ave Cleveland (44102) ***(G-5627)***
Martin Sprocket & Gear Inc 419 485-5515
350 S Airport Rd Montpelier (43543) ***(G-14312)***
Martin Welding LLC (PA) 937 687-3602
1472 W Main St New Lebanon (45345) ***(G-14711)***
Martin Wheel Co Inc 330 633-3278
342 West Ave Tallmadge (44278) ***(G-17992)***
Martin-Brower Company LLC 513 773-2301
4260 Port Union Rd West Chester (45011) ***(G-19741)***
Martin-Palmer Tl & Die Co Div, Dayton *Also called Krdc Inc* ***(G-8301)***
Martina Metal LLC 614 291-9700
1575 Shawnee Ave Columbus (43211) ***(G-7155)***
Martindale Electric Company 216 521-8567
1375 Hird Ave Cleveland (44107) ***(G-5628)***
Martinez Food Products LLC 419 720-6973
1220 Belmont Ave Toledo (43607) ***(G-18400)***
Martins Partitions, Lancaster *Also called Thorwald Holdings Inc* ***(G-11613)***
Martins Steel Fabrication 330 882-4311
2115 Center Rd New Franklin (44216) ***(G-14693)***
Martys Print Shop 740 373-3454
307 3rd St Marietta (45750) ***(G-12644)***
Martz Mold & Machine Inc 330 928-2159
1365 Munroe Falls Ave Cuyahoga Falls (44221) ***(G-7897)***
Martz Well Service 330 323-7417
5101 Rocky Rill Ave Ne Canton (44705) ***(G-2744)***
Marula Publishing LLC 513 549-5218
6539 Harrison Ave Ste 154 Cincinnati (45247) ***(G-3984)***
Marvin Mix 614 774-9337
3113 Kentwood Pl Columbus (43227) ***(G-7156)***
Marwil, Fort Loramie *Also called Rol - Tech Inc* ***(G-9803)***
Marwin Ball Valves Div, Cincinnati *Also called Richards Industries Inc* ***(G-4268)***
Marxware Computing Services 216 661-5263
4963 Schaaf Ln Cleveland (44131) ***(G-5629)***
Mary Ann Donut Shoppe Inc (PA) 330 478-1655
5032 Yukon St Nw Canton (44708) ***(G-2745)***
Mary Ann Donuts, Canton *Also called Mary Ann Donut Shoppe Inc* ***(G-2745)***
Mary James Inc 419 599-2941
1025 Clairmont Ave Napoleon (43545) ***(G-14550)***
Marysville Auto Plant, Marysville *Also called Honda of America Mfg Inc* ***(G-12791)***
Marysville Monument Company 937 642-7039
703 E 5th St Marysville (43040) ***(G-12798)***
Marysville Newspaper Inc (PA) 937 644-9111
207 N Main St Marysville (43040) ***(G-12799)***
Marysville Printing Company 937 644-4959
127 S Main St Marysville (43040) ***(G-12800)***
Marysville Steel Inc 937 642-5971
323 E 8th St Marysville (43040) ***(G-12801)***
Marzetti Distribution Center, Grove City *Also called Tmarzetti Company* ***(G-10474)***
Masco Cabinetry LLC 440 632-2547
15535 S State Ave Middlefield (44062) ***(G-13817)***
Masco Cbinetry Middlefield LLC (HQ) 440 632-5333
15535 S State Ave Middlefield (44062) ***(G-13818)***
Masco Cbinetry Middlefield LLC 440 632-5058
16052 Industrial Pkwy Middlefield (44062) ***(G-13819)***
Masco Cbinetry Middlefield LLC 440 437-8537
150 Grand Valley Ave Orwell (44076) ***(G-15634)***
Mascot Shop, The, Akron *Also called Kent Stow Screen Printing Inc* ***(G-235)***
Masheen Specialties 330 652-7535
3519 Union St Mineral Ridge (44440) ***(G-14169)***
Mason Company LLC 937 780-2321
260 Depot Ln Leesburg (45135) ***(G-11713)***
Mason Producing Inc 740 913-0686
10010 Center Village Rd Galena (43021) ***(G-10115)***
Mason Steel, Walton Hills *Also called Mason Structural Steel Inc* ***(G-19312)***
Mason Structural Steel Inc 440 439-1040
7500 Northfield Rd Walton Hills (44146) ***(G-19312)***
Mason's Century Signs, Bowling Green *Also called Century Signs* ***(G-1962)***
Masonite Corporation 937 454-9207
3250 Old Springfield Rd # 1 Vandalia (45377) ***(G-19136)***
Masonite International Corp 937 454-9308
875 Center Dr Vandalia (45377) ***(G-19137)***
Masons Sand and Gravel Co 614 491-3611
2385 Rathmell Rd Obetz (43207) ***(G-15510)***
Mass-Marketing Inc 513 860-6200
7209 Dixie Hwy Fairfield (45014) ***(G-9523)***
Massageblocks.com, Powell *Also called Summit Online Products LLC* ***(G-16338)***
Massillon Asphalt Co 330 833-6330
1833 Riverside Dr Nw Massillon (44647) ***(G-13019)***
Massillon Machine & Die, Massillon *Also called Hendricks Vacuum Forming Inc* ***(G-12996)***
Massillon Machine & Die Inc 330 833-8913
3536 17th St Sw Massillon (44647) ***(G-13020)***
Massillon Materials Inc (PA) 330 837-4767
26 N Cochran St Dalton (44618) ***(G-7947)***
Massillon Metaphysics 330 837-1653
912 Amherst Rd Ne Massillon (44646) ***(G-13021)***
Massillon Washed Gravel Co, Navarre *Also called Central Allied Enterprises Inc* ***(G-14573)***
Massmatrix Inc 614 321-9730
302 Corry St Yellow Springs (45387) ***(G-20810)***
Mast Farm Service Ltd 330 893-2972
3585 State Rte 39 Walnut Creek (44687) ***(G-19307)***
Master Builders LLC (HQ) 216 831-5500
23700 Chagrin Blvd Beachwood (44122) ***(G-1247)***
Master Carbide Tools Company 440 352-1112
55 Florence Ave Painesville (44077) ***(G-15760)***
Master Caster Company, Cleveland *Also called Master Mfg Co Inc* ***(G-5632)***
Master Chemical Corporation (PA) 419 874-7902
501 W Boundary St Perrysburg (43551) ***(G-15976)***
Master Chrome Service Inc 216 961-2012
5709 Herman Ave Cleveland (44102) ***(G-5630)***
Master Communications Inc 208 821-3473
4480 Lake Forest Dr # 302 Blue Ash (45242) ***(G-1813)***
Master Craft Products Inc 216 281-5910
10621 Briggs Rd Cleveland (44111) ***(G-5631)***
Master Disposers Inc 513 553-2289
2128 Idlett Hill Rd New Richmond (45157) ***(G-14812)***
Master Draw Lubricants, Chagrin Falls *Also called Etna Products Incorporated* ***(G-3046)***
Master Fluid Solutions, Perrysburg *Also called Master Chemical Corporation* ***(G-15976)***
Master Grinding Company Inc 440 944-3680
28917 Anderson Rd Wickliffe (44092) ***(G-20216)***
Master Label Company Inc 419 625-8095
1048 Cleveland Rd Sandusky (44870) ***(G-16828)***
Master Magnetics Inc 740 373-0909
108 Industry Rd Marietta (45750) ***(G-12645)***
Master Marking Company Inc 330 688-6797
4830 Hudson Dr Stow (44224) ***(G-17604)***
Master Mfg Co Inc 216 641-0500
9200 Inman Ave Cleveland (44105) ***(G-5632)***
Master Print Center, Cincinnati *Also called Gerald L Hermann Co Inc* ***(G-3750)***

Master Printing Company.....216 351-2246
3112 Broadview Rd Cleveland (44109) ***(G-5633)***
Master Products Company.....216 341-1740
6400 Park Ave Cleveland (44105) ***(G-5634)***
Master Swaging Inc.....937 596-6171
210 Washington St Jackson Center (45334) ***(G-11211)***
Master Tool Div, Grand River *Also called Sumitomo Elc Carbide Mfg Inc* ***(G-10326)***
Master Vac Incorporated.....419 335-7796
741 Parkview St Wauseon (43567) ***(G-19527)***
Master-Halco Inc.....513 869-7600
620 Commerce Center Dr Fairfield (45011) ***(G-9524)***
Mastercraft Mfg Inc.....330 893-3366
4136 Logan Way Youngstown (44505) ***(G-20967)***
Masterfoods USA, Columbus *Also called Mars Petcare Us Inc* ***(G-7153)***
Masterpiece Publisher L P.....513 948-1000
8046 Debonair Ct Cincinnati (45237) ***(G-3985)***
Masterpiece Signs & Graphics.....419 358-0077
902 N Main St Bluffton (45817) ***(G-1891)***
Masters Group Inc.....440 893-1900
7160 Chagrin Rd Ste 160 Chagrin Falls (44023) ***(G-3059)***
Masters Pharmaceutical Inc.....513 290-2969
8695 Seward Rd Fairfield (45011) ***(G-9525)***
Masters Prcision Machining Inc.....330 419-1933
4465 Crystal Pkwy Kent (44240) ***(G-11350)***
Mastertech Diamond Products Co, Painesville *Also called Master Carbide Tools Company* ***(G-15760)***
Mastic Home Exteriors Inc.....937 497-7008
2405 Campbell Rd Sidney (45365) ***(G-17050)***
Mastropietro Winery Inc.....330 547-2151
14558 Ellsworth Rd Berlin Center (44401) ***(G-1647)***
Mat Basics Incorporated.....513 793-0313
4546 Cornell Rd Blue Ash (45241) ***(G-1814)***
Mataco.....440 546-8355
2861 E Royalton Rd Broadview Heights (44147) ***(G-2096)***
Matalco (us) Inc.....330 452-4760
4420 Louisville St Ne Canton (44705) ***(G-2746)***
Matandy Steel & Metal Pdts LLC.....513 844-2277
1200 Central Ave Hamilton (45011) ***(G-10585)***
Matandy Steel Sales, Hamilton *Also called Matandy Steel & Metal Pdts LLC* ***(G-10585)***
Match Mold & Machine Inc.....330 830-5503
1100 Nova Dr Se Massillon (44646) ***(G-13022)***
Matco Tools Corporation (HQ).....330 929-4949
4403 Allen Rd Stow (44224) ***(G-17605)***
Matdan Corporation.....513 794-0500
10855 Millington Ct Blue Ash (45242) ***(G-1815)***
Material Sciences Corporation.....330 702-3882
460 W Main St Canfield (44406) ***(G-2535)***
Materials Engineering & Dev.....937 884-5118
11150 Bltmr Phllpsburg Rd Brookville (45309) ***(G-2177)***
Materials Science Intl Inc.....614 870-0400
1660 Georgesville Rd Columbus (43228) ***(G-7157)***
Materion Brush Inc (HQ).....216 486-4200
6070 Parkland Blvd Ste 1 Mayfield Heights (44124) ***(G-13167)***
Materion Brush Inc.....419 862-2745
14710 W Prtage River S Rd Elmore (43416) ***(G-9208)***
Materion Brush Inc.....440 960-5660
7375 Industrial Pkwy Lorain (44053) ***(G-12105)***
Materion Corporation (PA).....216 486-4200
6070 Parkland Blvd Ste 1 Mayfield Heights (44124) ***(G-13168)***
Materion Technical Mtls Inc.....216 486-4200
6070 Parkland Blvd Cleveland (44124) ***(G-5635)***
Mathematical Business Systems.....440 237-2345
1261 Valley Park Dr Broadview Heights (44147) ***(G-2097)***
Matheson Gas Products, Twinsburg *Also called Matheson Tri-Gas Inc* ***(G-18812)***
Matheson Tri-Gas Inc.....513 727-9638
1801 Crawford St Middletown (45044) ***(G-13925)***
Matheson Tri-Gas Inc.....419 865-8881
1720 Trade Rd Holland (43528) ***(G-10943)***
Matheson Tri-Gas Inc.....330 425-4407
1650 Enterprise Pkwy Twinsburg (44087) ***(G-18812)***
Mathew Odonnell.....440 969-4054
6645 2nd Ave Andover (44003) ***(G-585)***
Mathews Printing Company.....614 444-1010
1250 S Front St Columbus (43206) ***(G-7158)***
Matlock Electric Co Inc (PA).....513 731-9600
2780 Highland Ave Cincinnati (45212) ***(G-3986)***
Matly Digital Solutions LLC.....513 860-3435
6625 Dixie Hwy Ste E Fairfield (45014) ***(G-9526)***
Matplus Ltd.....440 352-7201
76 Burton St Painesville (44077) ***(G-15761)***
Matrix Cable and Mould.....513 832-2577
11785 Highway Dr Ste 900 Cincinnati (45241) ***(G-3987)***
Matrix Management Solutions.....330 470-3700
5200 Stoneham Rd Canton (44720) ***(G-2747)***
Matrix Plastics Co Inc.....330 666-7730
171 Granger Rd Unit 156 Medina (44256) ***(G-13290)***
Matrix Plastics Co Inc.....330 666-2395
171 Granger Rd Unit 156 Medina (44256) ***(G-13291)***
Matrix Research Inc.....937 427-8433
3844 Research Blvd Beavercreek (45430) ***(G-1357)***
Matrix Sys Auto Finishes LLC.....248 668-8135
600 Nova Dr Se Massillon (44646) ***(G-13023)***
Matrix Tool & Machine Inc.....440 255-0300
7870 Division Dr Mentor (44060) ***(G-13512)***
Matsu Ohio Inc.....419 298-2394
228 E Morrison St Edgerton (43517) ***(G-9176)***
Matteo Aluminum Inc.....440 585-5213
1261 E 289th St Wickliffe (44092) ***(G-20217)***
Matterworks.....740 200-0071
2135 James Pkwy Heath (43056) ***(G-10726)***
Matthew Bender & Company Inc.....518 487-3000
9443 Springboro Pike Miamisburg (45342) ***(G-13686)***
Matthew Koster.....440 887-9000
720 Marks Rd Ste C Valley City (44280) ***(G-19048)***
Matthew R Copp (PA).....614 276-8959
2291 Scioto Harper Dr Columbus (43204) ***(G-7159)***
Matthew Warren Inc.....614 418-0250
2000 Jetway Blvd Columbus (43219) ***(G-7160)***
Matthews Art Glass.....419 335-2448
22611 State Route 2 Archbold (43502) ***(G-658)***
Mattress Mart, Plain City *Also called Quilting Inc* ***(G-16209)***
Mature Living News Magazine.....419 241-8880
3601 W Alexis Rd Ste 112 Toledo (43623) ***(G-18401)***
Matvest Inc.....614 487-8720
1380 Dublin Rd Ste 200 Columbus (43215) ***(G-7161)***
Maull Tool & Die Supply Llc.....513 646-4229
112 Pheasantlake Dr Loveland (45140) ***(G-12213)***
Maumee Assembly & Stamping LLC.....419 304-2887
920 Illinois Ave Maumee (43537) ***(G-13129)***
Maumee Bay Kitchen & Bath Cent.....419 882-4390
5758 Main St Ste 1 Sylvania (43560) ***(G-17950)***
Maumee Bay Kitchen & Bath Ctr, Sylvania *Also called Maumee Bay Kitchen & Bath Cent* ***(G-17950)***
Maumee Hose & Belting Co, Maumee *Also called Maumee Hose & Fitting Inc* ***(G-13130)***
Maumee Hose & Fitting Inc.....419 893-7252
720 Illinois Ave Ste H Maumee (43537) ***(G-13130)***
Maumee Machine & Tool Corp.....419 385-2501
2960 South Ave Toledo (43609) ***(G-18402)***
Maumee Pattern Company.....419 693-4968
1019 Hazelwood St Toledo (43605) ***(G-18403)***
Maumee Quick Print Inc.....419 893-4321
406 Illinois Ave Maumee (43537) ***(G-13131)***
Maumee Valley Fabricators Inc.....419 476-1411
4801 Bennett Rd Toledo (43612) ***(G-18404)***
Maumee Valley Memorials Inc (HQ).....419 878-9030
111 Anthony Wayne Trl Waterville (43566) ***(G-19501)***
Mauser Usa LLC.....513 398-1300
1229 Castle Dr Mason (45040) ***(G-12908)***
Mauser Usa LLC.....614 856-5982
219 Commerce Dr Mount Vernon (43050) ***(G-14491)***
Mauser USA LLC.....614 856-5982
219 Commerce Dr Mount Vernon (43050) ***(G-14492)***
Maval Industries LLC.....330 405-1600
1555 Enterprise Pkwy Twinsburg (44087) ***(G-18813)***
Maval Manufacturing, Twinsburg *Also called Maval Industries LLC* ***(G-18813)***
Maverick Corp Partners LLC (PA).....330 669-2631
301 W Prospect St Smithville (44677) ***(G-17090)***
Maverick Corporation.....513 469-9919
11285 Grooms Rd Blue Ash (45242) ***(G-1816)***
Maverick Desk, Fairfield *Also called Workstream Inc* ***(G-9577)***
Maverick Industries Inc.....440 838-5335
5945 W Snowville Rd Brecksville (44141) ***(G-2049)***
Maverick Innvtive Slutions LLC (PA).....419 281-7944
532 County Road 1600 Ashland (44805) ***(G-722)***
Maverick Innvtive Slutions LLC.....419 281-7944
532 County Road 1600 Ashland (44805) ***(G-723)***
Maverick Molding Co.....513 387-6100
11359 Grooms Rd Blue Ash (45242) ***(G-1817)***
Mavericks Stainless, Mansfield *Also called Mk Metal Products Inc* ***(G-12484)***
Max Daetwyler Corp.....937 428-1781
2133 Lyons Rd Miamisburg (45342) ***(G-13687)***
Max Mighty Inc.....937 862-9530
2434 Darnell Dr Spring Valley (45370) ***(G-17317)***
Maximum Graphix Inc.....440 353-3301
33426 Liberty Pkwy North Ridgeville (44039) ***(G-15240)***
Maxion Wheels Akron LLC (HQ).....330 794-2310
428 Seiberling St Akron (44306) ***(G-272)***
Maxion Wheels Sedalia LLC.....330 794-2300
428 Seiberling St Akron (44306) ***(G-273)***
Maxon Corporation.....216 459-6056
950 Keynote Cir Ste 113 Independence (44131) ***(G-11142)***
Maxtool Company Limited.....937 415-5776
2946 Production Ct Dayton (45414) ***(G-8334)***
May Conveyor Inc.....440 237-8012
9981 York Theta Dr North Royalton (44133) ***(G-15286)***
May Lin Silicone Products Inc.....330 825-9019
955 Wooster Rd W Barberton (44203) ***(G-1085)***
May Thread Grinding Co.....440 953-0678
38401 Apollo Pkwy Ste F Willoughby (44094) ***(G-20373)***

ALPHABETIC

(PA)=Parent Co (HQ)=Headquarters (DH)=Div Headquarters
2019 Harris Ohio Industrial Directory
1179

Mayco Colors, Hilliard *Also called Coloramics LLC* ***(G-10819)***
Mayfair Granite Co Inc....216 382-8150
4202 Mayfield Rd Cleveland (44121) ***(G-5636)***
Mayfair Memorial, Cleveland *Also called Mayfair Granite Co Inc* ***(G-5636)***
Mayflower Vehicle Systems LLC....419 668-8132
7800 Walton Pkwy New Albany (43054) ***(G-14630)***
Mayfran International Inc (HQ)....440 461-4100
6650 Beta Dr Cleveland (44143) ***(G-5637)***
Maynard Company, The, Cleveland *Also called Bud May Inc* ***(G-4850)***
Mayo, R A Industries, East Palestine *Also called Robert Mayo Industries* ***(G-9083)***
Maysville Harness Shop Ltd....330 695-9977
8572 Mount Hope Rd Apple Creek (44606) ***(G-612)***
Maysville Materials LLC....740 849-0474
6535 Old Town Rd Mount Perry (43760) ***(G-14455)***
Maysville Ready Mix Con Co, Aberdeen *Also called Hilltop Basic Resources Inc* ***(G-1)***
Mazzella Crane & Hoist Svcs, Cincinnati *Also called Mazzella Lifting Tech Inc* ***(G-3988)***
Mazzella Lifting Tech Inc (HQ)....440 239-7000
21000 Aerospace Pkwy Cleveland (44142) ***(G-5638)***
Mazzella Lifting Tech Inc....513 772-4466
10605 Chester Rd Cincinnati (45215) ***(G-3988)***
Mazzella Lifting Tech Inc....440 239-5700
21000 Aerospace Pkwy Cleveland (44142) ***(G-5639)***
Mazzolini Artcraft Co Inc....216 431-7529
1607 E 41st St Cleveland (44103) ***(G-5640)***
Mazzone Bakery, Cleveland *Also called M Mazzone & Sons Bakery Inc* ***(G-5593)***
MB Dynamics Inc....216 292-5850
25865 Richmond Rd Cleveland (44146) ***(G-5641)***
MB Manufacturing Corp....513 682-1461
2904 Symmes Rd Fairfield (45014) ***(G-9527)***
Mbenztech....937 291-1527
5528 Liberty Bell Cir Centerville (45459) ***(G-3003)***
Mbm Industries Ltd....937 522-0719
801 Space Dr Beavercreek Township (45434) ***(G-1369)***
Mbm Lumber....937 459-7448
1588 Cox Rd Union City (45390) ***(G-18905)***
Mbs Acquisition, Mason *Also called Remtec Engineering* ***(G-12932)***
Mc Alarney Pool Spas and Billd....740 373-6698
908 Pike St Marietta (45750) ***(G-12646)***
Mc Brown Industries Inc....419 963-2800
10534 Township Road 128 Findlay (45840) ***(G-9723)***
Mc Cartney Industries, Mentor *Also called Semper Quality Industry Inc* ***(G-13578)***
Mc Concepts Llc....330 933-6402
2459 55th St Ne Canton (44721) ***(G-2748)***
Mc Connells Market....740 765-4300
2189 State Route 43 Richmond (43944) ***(G-16496)***
Mc Cully Supply & Sales Inc....330 497-2211
5559 Fulton Dr Nw Ste A Canton (44718) ***(G-2749)***
Mc Elwain Industries Inc....419 532-3126
17941 Road L Ottawa (45875) ***(G-15658)***
Mc Graphix Div of Th Newfax, Toledo *Also called Newfax Corporation* ***(G-18424)***
Mc Graw-Hill Educational Pubg, Ashland *Also called McGraw-Hill School Education H* ***(G-724)***
Mc Gregor & Associates Inc....937 833-6768
365 Carr Dr Brookville (45309) ***(G-2178)***
Mc Happy's Bake Shoppe, Belpre *Also called Wal-Bon of Ohio Inc* ***(G-1586)***
Mc Happys Donuts, Athens *Also called McHappys Donuts of Parkersburg* ***(G-838)***
Mc Industries, Fremont *Also called Mark Carpenter Industries Inc* ***(G-10039)***
Mc Kinley Machinery Inc....440 937-6300
1265 Lear Industrial Pkwy Avon (44011) ***(G-954)***
Mc Products, Wooster *Also called E S H Inc* ***(G-20587)***
Mc Vay Ventures Inc....614 890-1516
40 W College Ave Westerville (43081) ***(G-20064)***
McAfee Tool & Die Inc....330 896-9555
1717 Boettler Rd Uniontown (44685) ***(G-18927)***
McAlarney Pols Spas Billd More, Marietta *Also called Mc Alarney Pool Spas and Billd* ***(G-12646)***
McArthur Lumber and Post, Mc Arthur *Also called Appalachia Wood Inc* ***(G-13178)***
McAttack Machine LLC....440 946-3855
38338 Apollo Pkwy Bldg 2 Willoughby (44094) ***(G-20374)***
McCann Plastics Inc....330 499-1515
5600 Mayfair Rd Canton (44720) ***(G-2750)***
McCann Tool & Die Inc....330 264-8820
3230 Columbus Rd Wooster (44691) ***(G-20620)***
McCc Sportswear Inc....513 583-9210
9944 Prnceton Glendale Rd West Chester (45246) ***(G-19876)***
McClaflin Mobile Media LLC....419 575-9367
106 Caldwell St Bradner (43406) ***(G-2014)***
McClellan Rand L....614 462-4782
65 E State St Columbus (43215) ***(G-7162)***
McConnell Ready Mix....440 458-4325
37500 Butternut Ridge Rd Elyria (44039) ***(G-9292)***
McConnell's Farm Market, Richmond *Also called Mc Connells Market* ***(G-16496)***
McCord Monuments, Bowling Green *Also called McCord Products Inc* ***(G-1985)***
McCord Products Inc....419 352-3691
1135 N Main St Bowling Green (43402) ***(G-1985)***
McCrary Metal Polishing Inc....937 492-1979
207 Pasco Montra Rd Port Jefferson (45360) ***(G-16265)***
McCullough Industries Inc....419 673-0767
13047 County Road 175 Kenton (43326) ***(G-11412)***
McDaniel Envelope Co Inc....330 868-5929
1400 Union Ave Se Minerva (44657) ***(G-14191)***
McDaniel Products Inc (PA)....440 967-5630
1775 Liberty Ave Vermilion (44089) ***(G-19167)***
McDaniel Products Inc....419 524-5841
433 Springmill St Mansfield (44903) ***(G-12478)***
McDannald Welding & Machining....937 644-0300
11879 State Route 736 Marysville (43040) ***(G-12802)***
McDonald & Woodward Pubg Co....740 321-1140
431b E College St Granville (43023) ***(G-10332)***
McDonald & Woodward Publishing....740 641-2691
695 Tall Oaks Dr Newark (43055) ***(G-14896)***
McDonald Steel Corporation....330 530-9118
100 Ohio Ave Mc Donald (44437) ***(G-13201)***
McElroy Contract Packaging....330 262-0855
249 S Bauer Rd Wooster (44691) ***(G-20621)***
McFadden Logging....740 599-6902
305 S Mickley St Danville (43014) ***(G-7964)***
McFeelys Inc....800 443-7937
320 N State St Harrison (45030) ***(G-10658)***
McFlusion Inc....800 341-8616
2112 Case Pkwy Ste 8 Twinsburg (44087) ***(G-18814)***
McGaw Technology Inc....216 521-3490
17439 Lake Ave Lakewood (44107) ***(G-11529)***
McGean-Rohco Inc....216 441-4900
2910 Harvard Ave Newburgh Heights (44105) ***(G-14941)***
McGill Airclean LLC....614 829-1200
1777 Refugee Rd Columbus (43207) ***(G-7163)***
McGill Airflow LLC....614 829-1200
2400 Fairwood Ave Columbus (43207) ***(G-7164)***
McGill Airflow LLC (HQ)....614 829-1200
1 Mission Park Groveport (43125) ***(G-10503)***
McGill Corporation (PA)....614 829-1200
1 Mission Park Groveport (43125) ***(G-10504)***
McGill Septic Tank Co....330 876-2171
8913 State St Kinsman (44428) ***(G-11465)***
McGinnis Inc (HQ)....740 377-4391
502 2nd St E South Point (45680) ***(G-17286)***
McGlaughln Oil Compny/Fas Lube (PA)....614 231-2518
3750 E Livingston Ave Columbus (43227) ***(G-7165)***
McGlennon Metal Products Inc....614 252-7114
940 N 20th St Columbus (43219) ***(G-7166)***
McGovney Ready Mix Inc....740 353-4111
55 River Ave Portsmouth (45662) ***(G-16290)***
McGovney River Terminal, Portsmouth *Also called McGovney Ready Mix Inc* ***(G-16290)***
McGraw-Hill Global Educatn LLC....614 755-4151
860 Taylor Station Rd Blacklick (43004) ***(G-1690)***
McGraw-Hill School Education H....419 207-7400
1250 George Rd Ashland (44805) ***(G-724)***
McGraw-Hill School Education H....614 430-4000
8787 Orion Pl Columbus (43240) ***(G-6499)***
McGregor Metalworking, Springfield *Also called Morgal Machine Tool Co* ***(G-17451)***
McGuire Machine LLC....330 868-3072
1400 Union Ave Se Minerva (44657) ***(G-14192)***
McHael D Goronok String Instrs....216 421-4227
10823 Magnolia Dr Cleveland (44106) ***(G-5642)***
McHappys Donuts of Parkersburg....740 593-8744
384 Richland Ave Athens (45701) ***(G-838)***
McHenry Industries Inc....330 799-8930
85 Victoria Rd Youngstown (44515) ***(G-20968)***
McI Inc (HQ)....216 292-3800
22901 Millcreek Blvd Cleveland (44122) ***(G-5643)***
McIntosh Machine....937 687-3936
11 S Church St New Lebanon (45345) ***(G-14712)***
McJak Candy Company LLC....330 722-3531
1087 Branch Rd Medina (44256) ***(G-13292)***
McKay-Gross Div....330 683-2055
8848 Ely Rd Apple Creek (44606) ***(G-613)***
McKinley Leather, Marion *Also called Williams Leather Products Inc* ***(G-12749)***
McKinleys Meadery LLC....740 928-0229
4412 Keller Rd Hebron (43025) ***(G-10751)***
McL Inc....614 861-6259
5240 E Main St Columbus (43213) ***(G-7167)***
McL Whitehall, Columbus *Also called McL Inc* ***(G-7167)***
McLeod Bar Group LLC....614 299-2099
234 King Ave Columbus (43201) ***(G-7168)***
McM Ind Co Inc (PA)....216 292-4506
22901 Millcreek Blvd Cleveland (44122) ***(G-5644)***
McM Ind Co Inc....216 641-6300
7800 Finney Ave Cleveland (44105) ***(G-5645)***
McM Industries, Cleveland *Also called McM Ind Co Inc* ***(G-5644)***
McM Precision Castings Inc....419 669-3226
13133 Beech St Weston (43569) ***(G-20177)***
McMath & Sheets Unlimited Inc....216 381-0010
4427 Mayfield Rd Cleveland (44121) ***(G-5646)***
McMillen Steel LLC....330 253-9147
1372 Kenmore Blvd Akron (44314) ***(G-274)***

McMillion Lock & Key 937 473-5342
8822 N Rangeline Rd Covington (45318) **(G-7790)**
McNamaras Pub Inc 216 671-8820
3498 W 146th St Cleveland (44111) **(G-5647)**
McNational Inc (PA) 740 377-4391
502 2nd St E South Point (45680) **(G-17287)**
McNeil & Nrm Inc (HQ) 330 761-1855
96 E Crosier St Akron (44311) **(G-275)**
McNeil & Nrm Intl Inc (HQ) 330 253-2525
96 E Crosier St Akron (44311) **(G-276)**
McNeil Group Inc 614 298-0300
1701 Woodland Ave Columbus (43219) **(G-7169)**
McNeil Holdings LLC 614 298-0300
1701 Woodland Ave Columbus (43219) **(G-7170)**
McNeil Industries Inc 440 951-7756
835 Richmond Rd Ste 2 Painesville (44077) **(G-15762)**
McNeilus Truck and Mfg Inc 614 868-0760
1130 Morrison Rd Gahanna (43230) **(G-10089)**
McNeilus Truck and Mfg Inc 513 874-2022
8997 Lesaint Dr Fairfield (45014) **(G-9528)**
McNerney & Associates LLC (PA) 513 241-9951
440 Northland Blvd Cincinnati (45240) **(G-3989)**
McNish Corporation 614 899-2282
214 Hoff Rd Unit M Westerville (43082) **(G-20010)**
McO Inc (PA) 216 341-8914
7555 Bessemer Ave Cleveland (44127) **(G-5648)**
MCO Solutions Inc 937 205-9512
8820 Sugarcreek Pt Dayton (45458) **(G-8335)**
MCO Welding 330 401-6130
10949 Gnther Miller Rd Sw Stone Creek (43840) **(G-17562)**
McPherson Wire Cut Inc 330 896-0267
5208 Mayfair Rd Canton (44720) **(G-2751)**
McPp, Bellevue *Also called Mitsubishi Chls Perf Plyrs Inc* **(G-1540)**
McQueen Advertising Inc 440 967-1137
2010 Vermilion Rd Vermilion (44089) **(G-19168)**
McQueen Sign Co, Vermilion *Also called McQueen Advertising Inc* **(G-19168)**
McRon Finance Corp 513 487-5000
3010 Disney St Cincinnati (45209) **(G-3990)**
MCS Mfg LLC 419 923-0169
15210 County Road 10 3 Lyons (43533) **(G-12274)**
MCS Midwest LLC (PA) 513 217-0805
3876 Hendrickson Rd Franklin (45005) **(G-9898)**
McSports 419 586-5555
1945 Havemann Rd Celina (45822) **(G-2974)**
McSwain Manufacturing LLC 513 619-1222
189 Container Pl Cincinnati (45246) **(G-3991)**
McTech Corp 216 391-7700
5000 Crayton Ave Cleveland (44104) **(G-5649)**
McTt Machine Tool Inc 440 946-9559
38131 Arprt Pkwy Unit 207 Willoughby (44094) **(G-20375)**
McWane Inc 740 622-6651
2266 S 6th St Coshocton (43812) **(G-7739)**
MD Solutions Inc 866 637-6588
8225 Estates Pkwy Plain City (43064) **(G-16201)**
MD Tool & Die Inc 440 647-6456
755 Industrial Ave Wellington (44090) **(G-19586)**
Mdf Enterprises LLC 937 640-3436
821 Hall Ave Dayton (45404) **(G-8336)**
Mdf Tool Corporation 440 237-2277
10166 Royalton Rd North Royalton (44133) **(G-15287)**
Mdfritz Technologies Inc 937 314-1234
59 E Franklin St Centerville (45459) **(G-3004)**
Mdi of Ohio Inc 937 866-2345
802 N 4th St Miamisburg (45342) **(G-13688)**
ME Signs Inc 419 222-7446
2155 Elida Rd Lima (45805) **(G-11898)**
Mead Paving 937 322-7414
1023 W Perrin Ave Springfield (45506) **(G-17444)**
Meadow Burke Products, West Chester *Also called Merchants Metals LLC* **(G-19743)**
Meadwestvaco, Kettering *Also called Westrock Mwv LLC* **(G-11443)**
Meak Solutions Llc 440 796-8209
7315 Industrial Park Blvd Mentor (44060) **(G-13513)**
Mealey Industrial Lubricants, Cleveland *Also called Mar Mor Inc* **(G-5614)**
Means of Defense 740 513-6210
7326 State Route 19 Mount Gilead (43338) **(G-14429)**
Measurement Computing Corp (HQ) 440 439-4091
25971 Cannon Rd Cleveland (44146) **(G-5650)**
Measurement Specialties Inc 330 659-3312
2236 N Cleveland Massillo Akron (44333) **(G-277)**
Measurement Specialties Inc 937 427-1231
2670 Indian Ripple Rd Beavercreek (45440) **(G-1358)**
Measurement Specialties Inc 937 885-0800
10522 Success Ln Dayton (45458) **(G-8337)**
Measurenet Technology Ltd 513 396-6765
4242 Airport Rd Ste 101 Cincinnati (45226) **(G-3992)**
Mec 419 483-4852
540 Goodrich Rd Bellevue (44811) **(G-1539)**
Mecc-Usa LLC (PA) 513 891-0301
9468 Meridian Way West Chester (45069) **(G-19742)**
Mecca Rebuilding & Welding Co 419 476-8133
615 Phillips Ave Toledo (43612) **(G-18405)**
Mecco Inc 513 422-3651
2100 S Main St Middletown (45044) **(G-13926)**
Mechanical Dynamics Analis Ltd 440 946-0082
1250 E 222nd St Euclid (44117) **(G-9426)**
Mechanical Elastomerics Inc 330 863-1014
3266 Coral Rd Nw Malvern (44644) **(G-12393)**
Mechanical Finishers Inc LLC 513 641-5419
6350 Este Ave Cincinnati (45232) **(G-3993)**
Mechanical Finishing Inc 513 641-5419
6350 Este Ave Cincinnati (45232) **(G-3994)**
Mechanical Galv-Plating Corp 937 492-3143
933 Oak Ave Sidney (45365) **(G-17051)**
Mechanicsburg Sand & Gravel 937 834-2606
5734 State Route 4 Mechanicsburg (43044) **(G-13211)**
Meco, Middletown *Also called Manufacturers Equipment Co* **(G-13924)**
Med Center Systems LLC 513 942-6066
10179 Commerce Park Dr West Chester (45246) **(G-19877)**
Medalist Laserfab, Defiance *Also called Defiance Metal Products Wl Inc* **(G-8621)**
Medallion Lighting Corporation 440 255-8383
8710 East Ave Mentor (44060) **(G-13514)**
Medco Adhesive Coated Products, Cleveland *Also called Medco Labs Inc* **(G-5651)**
Medco Labs Inc 216 292-7546
5156 Richmond Rd Cleveland (44146) **(G-5651)**
Meders Special Tees 513 921-3800
618 Delhi Ave Cincinnati (45204) **(G-3995)**
Medex, Dublin *Also called Saint-Gobain Prfmce Plas Corp* **(G-8978)**
Medforall LLC 614 947-0791
1500 W 3rd Ave Ste 111 Columbus (43212) **(G-7171)**
Medi Home Health Agency Inc 740 472-3220
117 S Main St Woodsfield (43793) **(G-20546)**
Media Procurement Services Inc 513 977-3000
312 Walnut St Cincinnati (45202) **(G-3996)**
Media Sign Company 513 564-9500
2111 Kindel Ave Cincinnati (45214) **(G-3997)**
Medical & Home Health, Westlake *Also called Applied Marketing Services* **(G-20098)**
Medical Device Bus Svcs Inc 937 274-5850
2747 Armstrong Ln Dayton (45414) **(G-8338)**
Medical Elastomer Dev Inc 330 425-8352
1700 Highland Rd Twinsburg (44087) **(G-18815)**
Medical Equipment Provider 937 778-2190
102 Fox Dr Piqua (45356) **(G-16141)**
Medical Imaging, Cincinnati *Also called Summit Diagnostic Imaging LLC* **(G-4389)**
Medical Imaging Dist LLC 800 898-3392
11823 State Route 44 Mantua (44255) **(G-12553)**
Medical Imaging Equipment, Cleveland *Also called Philips Medical Systems Clevel* **(G-5871)**
Medical Quant USA Inc 440 542-0761
6521 Davis Indus Pkwy Solon (44139) **(G-17189)**
Medical Resources, Lewis Center *Also called Eoi Inc* **(G-11760)**
Medical Soft Inc 937 293-2575
1800 Southwood Ln W Oakwood (45419) **(G-15464)**
Medina Blanking Inc (HQ) 330 558-2300
5580 Wegman Dr Valley City (44280) **(G-19049)**
Medina County Publications Inc 330 721-4040
885 W Liberty St Medina (44256) **(G-13293)**
Medina County Recorders, Medina *Also called County of Medina* **(G-13245)**
Medina Foods Inc 330 725-1390
9706 Crow Rd Litchfield (44253) **(G-11985)**
Medina Fuel, Coshocton *Also called MFC Drilling Inc* **(G-7740)**
Medina Plating Corp 330 725-4155
940 Lafayette Rd Medina (44256) **(G-13294)**
Medina Powder Coating Corp 330 952-1977
930 Lafayette Rd Unit C Medina (44256) **(G-13295)**
Medina Powder Group 330 952-2711
910 Lake Rd Ste B Medina (44256) **(G-13296)**
Medina Signs Post Inc 330 723-2484
411 W Smith Rd Medina (44256) **(G-13297)**
Medina Supply Company (HQ) 330 723-3681
230 E Smith Rd Medina (44256) **(G-13298)**
Medina Supply Company 330 425-0752
1516 Highland Rd Twinsburg (44087) **(G-18816)**
Medina Tool & Die, Wadsworth *Also called Kramer & Kiefer Inc* **(G-19251)**
Medinvent LLC 330 247-0921
1133 Medina Rd Ste 500 Medina (44256) **(G-13299)**
Medkeff-Nye, Barberton *Also called Madgar Genis Corp* **(G-1082)**
Medline Industries Inc 330 484-1450
3800 Commerce St Sw Canton (44706) **(G-2752)**
Medpace Holdings Inc (PA) 513 579-9911
5375 Medpace Way Cincinnati (45227) **(G-3998)**
Medpace Research Inc 513 579-9911
5375 Medpace Way Cincinnati (45227) **(G-3999)**
Medrano Usa Inc 614 272-5856
4311 Janitrol Rd Ste 500 Columbus (43228) **(G-7172)**
Medtrace, Akron *Also called Vertical Data LLC* **(G-425)**
Medtronic Inc 216 642-1977
5005 Rockside Rd Ste 1160 Cleveland (44131) **(G-5652)**

ALPHABETIC

(PA)=Parent Co (HQ)=Headquarters (DH)=Div Headquarters
2019 Harris Ohio Industrial Directory
1181

Medway Tool Corp 937 335-7717
2100 Corporate Dr Troy (45373) *(G-18687)*

Meech Sttic Elminators USA Inc 330 564-2000
1298 Centerview Cir Copley (44321) *(G-7688)*

Meeks Pastry Shop 419 782-4871
315 Clinton St Defiance (43512) *(G-8637)*

Meese Inc 440 998-1202
4920 State Rd Ashtabula (44004) *(G-785)*

Mega Bright LLC 216 712-4689
4979 W 130th St Cleveland (44135) *(G-5653)*

Mega Bright LLC 330 577-8859
2251 Front St Cuyahoga Falls (44221) *(G-7898)*

Mega Plastics Co 330 527-2211
10610 Freedom St Garrettsville (44231) *(G-10198)*

Megaform Computer Products, Vandalia Also called Misato Computer Products Inc *(G-19139)*

Meggitt (erlanger) LLC 513 851-5550
10293 Burlington Rd Cincinnati (45231) *(G-4000)*

Meggitt Aircraft Braking (HQ) 330 796-4400
1204 Massillon Rd Akron (44306) *(G-278)*

Meggitt Polymers & Composites 513 851-5550
10293 Burlington Rd Cincinnati (45231) *(G-4001)*

Megna Plastics, Cleveland Also called Dal-Little Fabricating Inc *(G-5059)*

Mehaffie Pie Company, Dayton Also called K & B Acquisitions Inc *(G-8288)*

MEI, Wapakoneta Also called Midwest Elastomers Inc *(G-19343)*

MEI, Malvern Also called Mechanical Elastomerics Inc *(G-12393)*

Meibuhr Co Inc 440 942-9375
38301 Apollo Pkwy Ste 1 Willoughby (44094) *(G-20376)*

Meierjohan-Wengler Inc 513 771-6074
10340 Julian Dr Cincinnati (45215) *(G-4002)*

Meiers Wine Cellars Inc 513 891-2900
6955 Plainfield Rd Cincinnati (45236) *(G-4003)*

Meiring Precision, Ludlow Falls Also called Marmax Machine Co *(G-12269)*

Meister Media Worldwide Inc (PA) 440 942-2000
37733 Euclid Ave Willoughby (44094) *(G-20377)*

Meistermatic Inc 216 481-7773
12446 Bentbrook Dr Chesterland (44026) *(G-3163)*

Mek Van Wert Inc 419 203-4902
1265 Industrial Dr Van Wert (45891) *(G-19102)*

Meka Signs Enterprises Inc 513 942-5494
10126 Prncton Glendale Rd West Chester (45246) *(G-19878)*

Mel Heitkamp Builders Ltd 419 375-0405
635 Secret Judy Rd Fort Recovery (45846) *(G-9825)*

Mel Stevens U-Cart Concrete 419 478-2600
6151 Telegraph Rd Toledo (43612) *(G-18406)*

Mel Wacker Sign Inc 330 832-1726
13076 Barrs Rd Sw Massillon (44647) *(G-13024)*

Mel's Lifelike Hair, Dayton Also called Mels Life Like Hair *(G-8339)*

Mel-Ba Manufacturing, Independence Also called Kohut Enterprises Inc *(G-11138)*

Melanda Inc 330 833-0517
2646 Lincoln Way Nw Massillon (44647) *(G-13025)*

Meldrum Mechanical Services 419 535-3500
4455 South Ave Toledo (43615) *(G-18407)*

Melin Tool Company Inc 216 362-4200
5565 Venture Dr Ste C Cleveland (44130) *(G-5654)*

Melink Corporation (PA) 513 685-0958
5140 River Valley Rd Milford (45150) *(G-14026)*

Melinz Industries Inc (PA) 440 946-3512
34099 Melinz Pkwy Unit D Willoughby (44095) *(G-20378)*

Mellott Bronze Inc 330 435-6304
4634 E Sterling Rd Creston (44217) *(G-7807)*

Melnor Graphics LLC 419 476-8808
5225 Telegraph Rd Toledo (43612) *(G-18408)*

Mels Life Like Hair 937 278-9486
6140 N Main St Dayton (45415) *(G-8339)*

Melt Inc 330 426-3545
51621 Darlington Rd Negley (44441) *(G-14591)*

Melvin Grain Co 937 382-1249
413 Melvin Rd Wilmington (45177) *(G-20499)*

Melvin Stone Co LLC 513 771-0820
11641 Mosteller Rd Ste 2 Cincinnati (45241) *(G-4004)*

Melvin Stone Company LLC 740 998-5016
3333 Plano Rd Wshngtn CT Hs (43160) *(G-20732)*

Memac Industries Inc 740 653-4815
324 Quarry Rd Se Lancaster (43130) *(G-11586)*

Membrane Specialists LLC (PA) 513 860-9490
2 Rowe Ct Hamilton (45015) *(G-10586)*

Menard Inc 513 250-4566
2789 Cunningham Rd Cincinnati (45241) *(G-4005)*

Menard Inc 513 583-1444
3787 W State Route 22 3 Loveland (45140) *(G-12214)*

Menard Inc 419 998-4321
2614 N Eastown Rd Lima (45807) *(G-11899)*

Menards, Loveland Also called Menard Inc *(G-12214)*

Menasha Packaging Company LLC 740 773-8204
2842 Spiegel Dr Groveport (43125) *(G-10505)*

Mennel Milling Company 740 385-6824
1 W Front St Logan (43138) *(G-12035)*

Mennel Milling Company 419 436-5130
320 Findlay St Fostoria (44830) *(G-9848)*

Mennel Milling Company 740 385-6824
1 W Front St Logan (43138) *(G-12036)*

Mennel Milling Logan, Logan Also called Mennel Milling Company *(G-12035)*

Mennel Milling Logan, Logan Also called Mennel Milling Company *(G-12036)*

Mentor Glass Supplies and Repr 440 255-9444
8985 Osborne Dr Mentor (44060) *(G-13515)*

Mentor Inc 440 255-1250
5983 Andrews Rd Mentor On The Lake (44060) *(G-13632)*

Mentor Radio LLC 216 265-2315
151 Innovation Dr Ste 320 Elyria (44035) *(G-9293)*

Mentor Signs & Graphics Inc 440 951-7446
7522a Tyler Blvd Ste A Mentor (44060) *(G-13516)*

Mentor Tool Inc 440 942-5273
990 Erie Rd Unit D Willoughby (44095) *(G-20379)*

Meranda Nixon Estate Wine LLC 937 515-8013
6517 Laycock Rd Ripley (45167) *(G-16514)*

Mercer Color Corporation 419 678-8273
425 Hardin St Coldwater (45828) *(G-6417)*

Mercer Landmark Inc 419 363-3391
450 Strable Rd Rockford (45882) *(G-16540)*

Mercers Welding Inc 330 533-3373
6336 W Calla Rd Canfield (44406) *(G-2536)*

Merchants Metals LLC 513 942-0268
8760 Global Way Bldg 1 West Chester (45069) *(G-19743)*

Mercury Biomed LLC 216 777-1492
29001 Cedar Rd Ste 326 Cleveland (44124) *(G-5655)*

Mercury Iron and Steel Co 440 349-1500
6275 Cochran Rd Solon (44139) *(G-17190)*

Mercury Machine Co 440 349-3222
30250 Carter St Solon (44139) *(G-17191)*

Mercury Plastics LLC 440 632-5281
15760 Madison Rd Middlefield (44062) *(G-13820)*

Meridian Arts and Graphics 330 759-9099
16 Belgrade St Youngstown (44505) *(G-20969)*

Meridian Bioscience Inc (PA) 513 271-3700
3471 River Hills Dr Cincinnati (45244) *(G-4006)*

Meridian Brick LLC 937 294-1548
250 Industrial Dr Franklin (45005) *(G-9899)*

Meridian Industries Inc 330 359-5447
7369 Peabody Kent Rd Winesburg (44690) *(G-20533)*

Meridian Industries Inc 330 359-5809
9901 Chestnut Ridge Rd Nw Beach City (44608) *(G-1212)*

Meridian Industries Inc 330 673-1011
1500 Saint Clair Ave Kent (44240) *(G-11351)*

Meridian Life Science Inc (HQ) 513 271-3700
3471 River Hills Dr Cincinnati (45244) *(G-4007)*

Meridian LLC 330 995-0371
325 Harris Dr Aurora (44202) *(G-892)*

Meridian Machine Inc 330 308-0296
702 Steele Hill Rd Nw New Philadelphia (44663) *(G-14785)*

Meridian Manufacturing Company 330 793-9632
1191 N Meridian Rd Youngstown (44509) *(G-20970)*

Meridienne International Inc 330 274-8317
4494 Orchard St Mantua (44255) *(G-12554)*

Merit Foundry Co Inc 216 741-4282
2289 N Saint James Pkwy Cleveland (44106) *(G-5656)*

Merit Mold & Tool Products 937 435-0932
4648 Gateway Cir Dayton (45440) *(G-8340)*

Meritech, Painesville Also called Ohio Associated Entps LLC *(G-15770)*

Meritor Inc 740 348-3498
4009 Columbus Rd Ste 111 Granville (43023) *(G-10333)*

Merk Blasting 513 813-6375
3917 Biehl Ave Cincinnati (45248) *(G-4008)*

Merkur Group Inc 937 429-4288
2434 Esquire Dr Beavercreek (45431) *(G-1331)*

Merrick Manufacturing II LLC 937 222-7164
836 Hall Ave Dayton (45404) *(G-8341)*

Merrico Inc 419 525-2711
541 Grant St Mansfield (44903) *(G-12479)*

Merrill Corporation 614 801-4700
3400 Southpark Pl Ste H Grove City (43123) *(G-10444)*

Merritt Woodwork, Mentor Also called Profac Inc *(G-13555)*

Merry X-Ray Chemical Corp 614 219-2011
4770 Northwest Pkwy Hilliard (43026) *(G-10839)*

Mes, Sunbury Also called Mine Equipment Services LLC *(G-17891)*

Mes Material Hdlg Systems LLC 740 477-8920
28196 Scippo Creek Rd Circleville (43113) *(G-4548)*

Mesa Industries Inc (PA) 513 321-2950
4027 Eastern Ave Cincinnati (45226) *(G-4009)*

Mesocoat Inc 216 453-0866
24112 Rockwell Dr Euclid (44117) *(G-9427)*

Mesocoat Advanced Coating Tech, Euclid Also called Mesocoat Inc *(G-9427)*

Mespo Woodworking 440 693-4041
4421 Donley Rd Middlefield (44062) *(G-13821)*

Messenger Press, Celina Also called Heitkamp & Kremer Printing *(G-2967)*

Messenger Publishing Company 740 592-6612
9300 Johnson Hollow Rd Athens (45701) *(G-839)*

ALPHABETIC SECTION

Messer LLC 330 608-3008
4179 Meadow Wood Ln Uniontown (44685) *(G-18928)*

Messer LLC 513 831-4742
State Road 126160 St State Ro Miamiville (45147) *(G-13753)*

Messer LLC 419 227-9585
961 Industry Ave Lima (45804) *(G-11900)*

Messer LLC 216 533-7256
6300 Halle Dr Cleveland (44125) *(G-5657)*

Messer LLC 614 539-2259
1699 Feddern Ave Grove City (43123) *(G-10445)*

Messer LLC 330 394-4541
2000 Pine Ave Se Warren (44483) *(G-19422)*

Messer LLC 419 221-5043
1680 Buckeye Rd Lima (45804) *(G-11901)*

Messer LLC 419 822-3909
6744 County Road 10 Delta (43515) *(G-8776)*

Messerman Corp 419 782-1136
407 Agnes St Defiance (43512) *(G-8638)*

Messerman Machine Co, Defiance Also called Messerman Corp *(G-8638)*

Messinger Press, Celina Also called Society of The Precious Blood *(G-2984)*

Mestek Inc 419 288-2703
120 Plin St Bradner (43406) *(G-2015)*

Mestek Inc 419 288-2703
7301 International Dr Holland (43528) *(G-10944)*

Met Fab Fabrication and Mch 513 724-3715
2974 Waitensburg Pike Batavia (45103) *(G-1164)*

Met-All Industries, Canal Fulton Also called Aman & Co Inc *(G-2473)*

Met-L-Fab Inc 513 561-4289
5313 Robert Ave Cincinnati (45248) *(G-4010)*

Met-Pro Technologies LLC (HQ) 513 458-2600
4625 Red Bank Rd Cincinnati (45227) *(G-4011)*

Meta Manufacturing Corporation 513 793-6382
8901 Blue Ash Rd Ste 1 Blue Ash (45242) *(G-1818)*

Metal & Wire Products Company (PA) 330 332-9448
1065 Salem Pkwy Salem (44460) *(G-16760)*

Metal Brite Polishing 937 278-9739
2445 Neff Rd Unit 4 Dayton (45414) *(G-8342)*

Metal Building Intr Pdts Co 440 322-6500
750 Adams St Elyria (44035) *(G-9294)*

Metal Coating Company, Lima Also called J M Hamilton Group Inc *(G-11881)*

Metal Craft Docks Inc 440 286-7135
156 Burton St Painesville (44077) *(G-15763)*

Metal Cutting Technology LLC 419 733-1236
5410 Golden Pond Rd Celina (45822) *(G-2975)*

Metal Dynamics Co 330 601-0748
4047 Unit A Lincoln Way Wooster (44691) *(G-20622)*

Metal Equipment Co 440 835-3100
1985 Savannah Pkwy Westlake (44145) *(G-20130)*

Metal Fabricating Corporation 216 631-8121
10408 Berea Rd Cleveland (44102) *(G-5658)*

Metal Finishers Inc 937 492-9175
2600 Fair Rd Sidney (45365) *(G-17052)*

Metal Finishing Divison, Ravenna Also called Allen Aircraft Products Inc *(G-16366)*

Metal Finishing Needs Ltd 216 561-6334
16025 Van Aken Blvd Cleveland (44120) *(G-5659)*

Metal Forming & Coining Corp (PA) 419 897-9530
1007 Illinois Ave Maumee (43537) *(G-13132)*

Metal Improvement Company LLC 513 489-6484
11131 Luschek Dr Blue Ash (45241) *(G-1819)*

Metal Improvement Company LLC 330 425-1490
1652 Highland Rd Twinsburg (44087) *(G-18817)*

Metal Maintenance Inc 513 661-3300
322 N Finley St Cleves (45002) *(G-6370)*

Metal Man Inc 614 830-0968
4681 Homer Ohio Ln Ste A Groveport (43125) *(G-10506)*

Metal Manufacturing, Elyria Also called Elyria Metal Spinning Fabg Co *(G-9253)*

Metal Matic 513 422-6007
1701 Made Dr Middletown (45044) *(G-13927)*

Metal Merchants Usa Inc 330 723-3228
445 W Liberty St Medina (44256) *(G-13300)*

Metal Products Company (PA) 330 652-2558
112 Erie St Niles (44446) *(G-15021)*

Metal Products Company 330 652-6201
1818 N Main St Unit 4 Niles (44446) *(G-15022)*

Metal Sales Manufacturing Corp 440 319-3779
352 E Erie St Jefferson (44047) *(G-11234)*

Metal Seal Precision Ltd (PA) 440 255-8888
8687 Tyler Blvd Mentor (44060) *(G-13517)*

Metal Seal Precision Ltd 440 255-8888
4369 Hamann Pkwy Willoughby (44094) *(G-20380)*

Metal Shredders Inc 937 866-0777
5101 Farmersville W Miamisburg (45342) *(G-13689)*

Metal Stampings Unlimited 937 328-0206
552 W Johnny Lytle Ave Springfield (45506) *(G-17445)*

Metal Technology Systems Inc 513 563-1882
675 Redna Ter Cincinnati (45215) *(G-4012)*

Metal-Mation Inc 216 651-1083
2391 W 38th St Cleveland (44113) *(G-5660)*

Metal-Max Inc 330 673-9926
1540 Enterprise Way Kent (44240) *(G-11352)*

Metaldyne Pwrtrain Cmpnnts Inc 330 486-3200
8001 Bavaria Rd Twinsburg (44087) *(G-18818)*

Metaldyne Twinsburg, Twinsburg Also called Metaldyne Pwrtrain Cmpnnts Inc *(G-18818)*

Metalex Manufacturing Inc (PA) 513 489-0507
5750 Cornell Rd Blue Ash (45242) *(G-1820)*

Metalico Akron Inc (HQ) 330 376-1400
943 Hazel St Akron (44305) *(G-279)*

Metalico Annaco, Akron Also called Metalico Akron Inc *(G-279)*

Metallic Resources Inc 330 425-3155
2368 E Enterprise Pkwy Twinsburg (44087) *(G-18819)*

Metallurgical Service Inc 937 294-2681
2221 Arbor Blvd Moraine (45439) *(G-14368)*

Metalmark, Chagrin Falls Also called Emt Trading Company LLC *(G-3019)*

Metalphoto of Cincinnati Inc 513 772-8281
1080 Skillman Dr Cincinnati (45215) *(G-4013)*

Metals and Additives Corp Inc 740 654-6555
4850 Elder Rd Ne Pleasantville (43148) *(G-16228)*

Metals Crankshaft Grinding 216 431-5778
1435 E 45th St Cleveland (44103) *(G-5661)*

Metals Recovery Services LLC 614 870-0364
1400 Norton Rd Columbus (43228) *(G-7173)*

Metals USA Crbn Flat Rlled Inc 937 882-6354
5750 Lower Valley Pike Springfield (45502) *(G-17446)*

Metals USA Crbn Flat Rlled Inc (HQ) 330 264-8416
1070 W Liberty St Wooster (44691) *(G-20623)*

Metalsmiths, Cleveland Also called Metro Mech Inc *(G-5662)*

Metaltek Industries Inc 937 323-4933
829 Pauline St Springfield (45503) *(G-17447)*

Metalworking Group Holdings (PA) 513 521-4119
9070 Pippin Rd Cincinnati (45251) *(G-4014)*

Metalworking Group, The, Cincinnati Also called Metalworking Group Holdings *(G-4014)*

Metcalf Design & Printing Ctr, Gahanna Also called Sjpm Inc *(G-10104)*

Metcut Research Associates Inc (PA) 513 271-5100
3980 Rosslyn Dr Cincinnati (45209) *(G-4015)*

Meteor Automotive, Dover Also called Meteor Sealing Systems LLC *(G-8840)*

Meteor Sealing Systems LLC 330 343-9595
400 S Tuscarawas Ave Dover (44622) *(G-8840)*

Metlweb 513 563-8822
3330 E Kemper Rd Cincinnati (45241) *(G-4016)*

Metokote Corporation 440 934-4686
5477 Evergreen Pkwy Sheffield Village (44054) *(G-16971)*

Metokote Corporation 270 889-9907
1340 Neubrecht Rd Lima (45801) *(G-11902)*

Metokote Corporation (HQ) 419 996-7800
1340 Neubrecht Rd Lima (45801) *(G-11903)*

Metokote Corporation 419 227-1100
1340 Neubrecht Rd Lima (45801) *(G-11904)*

Metokote Corporation 419 221-2754
1340 Neubrecht Rd Lima (45801) *(G-11905)*

Metokote Corporation 319 232-6994
1340 Neubrecht Rd Lima (45801) *(G-11906)*

Metokote Corporation 419 996-7800
1340 Neubrecht Rd Lima (45801) *(G-11907)*

Metokote Corporation 937 235-2811
8040 Center Point 70 Blvd Dayton (45424) *(G-8343)*

Metro Design Inc 440 458-4200
10740 Middle Ave Elyria (44035) *(G-9295)*

Metro Flex Inc 937 299-5360
3304 Encrete Ln Moraine (45439) *(G-14369)*

Metro Mech Inc 216 641-6262
3599 E 49th St Cleveland (44105) *(G-5662)*

Metro Recycling Company 513 251-1800
19 W Vine St Cincinnati (45215) *(G-4017)*

Metro Tool & Die Co Inc 937 836-8242
11974 Putnam Rd Englewood (45322) *(G-9368)*

Metrodeck Inc 513 541-4370
4795 Day Rd Cincinnati (45252) *(G-4018)*

Metromedia Technologies Inc 330 264-2501
1061 Venture Blvd Wooster (44691) *(G-20624)*

Metron Instruments Inc 216 332-0592
5198 Richmond Rd Bedford Heights (44146) *(G-1474)*

Metropolitan Ceramics Div, Canton Also called Ironrock Capital Incorporated *(G-2712)*

Mettler-Toledo LLC 614 438-4511
720 Dearborn Park Ln Worthington (43085) *(G-20695)*

Mettler-Toledo LLC 614 438-4390
1150 Dearborn Dr Worthington (43085) *(G-20696)*

Mettler-Toledo LLC 614 841-7300
6600 Huntley Rd Columbus (43229) *(G-7174)*

Mettler-Toledo Intl Fin Inc (HQ) 614 438-4511
1900 Polaris Pkwy Fl 6 Columbus (43240) *(G-6500)*

Mettler-Toledo Intl Inc (PA) 614 438-4511
1900 Polaris Pkwy Fl 6 Columbus (43240) *(G-6501)*

Mettlr-Tledo Globl Hldings LLC (HQ) 614 438-4511
1900 Polaris Pkwy Columbus (43240) *(G-6502)*

Metz Dental Laboratory Inc 614 252-4444
1271 E Broad St Columbus (43205) *(G-7175)*

Metz Dental Laboratory, The, Columbus Also called Metz Dental Laboratory Inc *(G-7175)*

Metzenbaum Sheltered Inds Inc 440 729-1919
8090 Cedar Rd Chesterland (44026) *(G-3164)*

Metzger Machine Co....513 241-3360
2165 Spring Grove Ave Cincinnati (45214) ***(G-4019)***
Metzgers....419 861-8611
150 Arco Dr Toledo (43607) ***(G-18409)***
Mexichem Specialty Resins Inc (HQ)....440 930-1435
33653 Walker Rd Avon Lake (44012) ***(G-996)***
Meyer Company (PA)....216 587-3400
13700 Broadway Ave Cleveland (44125) ***(G-5663)***
Meyer Design Inc....330 434-9176
100 N High St Akron (44308) ***(G-280)***
Meyer Machine Tool Company....614 235-0039
3434 E 7th Ave Columbus (43219) ***(G-7176)***
Meyer Products LLC....216 486-1313
324 N 7th St Steubenville (43952) ***(G-17544)***
Meyer Tool Inc (PA)....513 681-7362
3055 Colerain Ave Cincinnati (45225) ***(G-4020)***
Meyerpt, Hudson *Also called Wbc Group LLC* ***(G-11082)***
Meyers Printing & Design Inc....937 461-6000
254 Leo St Dayton (45404) ***(G-8344)***
MFC, Maumee *Also called Metal Forming & Coining Corp* ***(G-13132)***
MFC Drilling Inc....740 622-5600
46281 Us Highway 36 Coshocton (43812) ***(G-7740)***
Mfg Composite Systems Company....440 997-5851
2925 Mfg Pl Ashtabula (44004) ***(G-786)***
Mfg CSC, Ashtabula *Also called Mfg Composite Systems Company* ***(G-786)***
Mfh Partners Inc (PA)....440 461-4100
6650 Beta Dr Cleveland (44143) ***(G-5664)***
Mfi, Cincinnati *Also called Mechanical Finishers Inc LLC* ***(G-3993)***
Mfs Supply LLC (PA)....440 248-5300
31100 Solon Rd Ste E Solon (44139) ***(G-17192)***
MGM Construction Inc....440 234-7660
1480 W Bagley Rd Ste 1 Berea (44017) ***(G-1617)***
MGM Roofing, Berea *Also called MGM Construction Inc* ***(G-1617)***
Mh & Son Machining & Wldg Co....419 621-0690
210 W Perkins Ave Ste 10 Sandusky (44870) ***(G-16829)***
Mhi, Cincinnati *Also called Micropyretics Heaters Intl Inc* ***(G-4025)***
Mhp Flooring, Millersburg *Also called Mount Hope Planing* ***(G-14115)***
Mi-Lar Fence Co Inc (PA)....216 464-3160
5250 Naiman Pkwy Ste B Solon (44139) ***(G-17193)***
Mia Express Inc....330 896-8180
3238 Robins Trce Akron (44319) ***(G-281)***
Miami Control Systems Inc....937 698-5725
955 S Main St West Milton (45383) ***(G-19949)***
Miami Graphics Services Inc....937 698-4013
225 N Jay St West Milton (45383) ***(G-19950)***
Miami Machine, Cleves *Also called Pohl Machining Inc* ***(G-6372)***
Miami Specialties Inc....937 778-1850
172 Robert M Davis Pkwy Piqua (45356) ***(G-16142)***
Miami Steel Fabricators Inc....937 299-5550
1525 Manchester Rd Dayton (45449) ***(G-8345)***
Miami Valley Counters & Spc....937 865-0562
8515 Dyton Cncinnati Pike Miamisburg (45342) ***(G-13690)***
Miami Valley Eductl Cmpt Assn....937 767-1468
330 E Enon Rd Yellow Springs (45387) ***(G-20811)***
Miami Valley Gasket Co Inc....937 228-0781
1222 E 3rd St Dayton (45402) ***(G-8346)***
Miami Valley Lighting LLC....937 224-6000
1065 Woodman Dr Dayton (45432) ***(G-7985)***
Miami Valley Paper LLC....937 746-6451
413 Oxford Rd Franklin (45005) ***(G-9900)***
Miami Valley Pizza Hut Inc....419 586-5900
1152 E Market St Celina (45822) ***(G-2976)***
Miami Valley Plastics Inc....937 273-3200
310 S Main St Eldorado (45321) ***(G-9189)***
Miami Valley Polishing LL....937 498-1634
1317 Pinetree Ct Sidney (45365) ***(G-17053)***
Miami Valley Polishing LLC....937 615-9353
170 Fox Dr Piqua (45356) ***(G-16143)***
Miami Valley Precision Inc....937 866-1804
456 Alexandersville Rd Miamisburg (45342) ***(G-13691)***
Miami Valley Press Inc....937 547-0771
6132 Kruckeburg Rd Greenville (45331) ***(G-10381)***
Miami Valley Punch & Mfg....937 237-0533
3425 Successful Way Dayton (45414) ***(G-8347)***
Miami Valley Ready Mix Inc....513 738-2616
9540 Hamilton Cleves Hwy Harrison (45030) ***(G-10659)***
Miami Vly Mfg & Assembly Inc....937 254-6665
1889 Radio Rd Dayton (45431) ***(G-7986)***
Miami Vly Packg Solutions Inc....937 224-1800
1752 Stanley Ave Dayton (45404) ***(G-8348)***
Miami Wabash, Franklin *Also called Miami Valley Paper LLC* ***(G-9900)***
Miami-Cast Inc....937 866-2951
901 N Main St Miamisburg (45342) ***(G-13692)***
Miamisburg Coating....937 866-1323
925 N Main St Miamisburg (45342) ***(G-13693)***
Miamisburg News, Miamisburg *Also called Cox Newspapers LLC* ***(G-13652)***
Miba Sinter USA LLC....740 962-4242
5045 N State Route 60 Nw McConnelsville (43756) ***(G-13208)***
Mibtach Enterprises Inc....513 941-0387
2629 Lytham Ct Cincinnati (45233) ***(G-4021)***
Mic-Ray Metal Products Inc....216 791-2206
9016 Manor Ave Cleveland (44104) ***(G-5665)***
Mica Laminates, Columbus *Also called Somerset Galleries Inc* ***(G-7461)***
Micah Specialty Foods....405 320-3325
18014 Garden Blvd Warrensville Heights (44128) ***(G-19471)***
Miceli Dairy Products Co (PA)....216 791-6222
2721 E 90th St Cleveland (44104) ***(G-5666)***
Michabo Inc (PA)....419 893-4334
525 W Sophia St Maumee (43537) ***(G-13133)***
Michael D Strickland....740 682-6902
2730 Hickory Grove Rd Oak Hill (45656) ***(G-15456)***
Michael Day Enterprises LLC....330 335-5100
9774 Trease Rd Wadsworth (44281) ***(G-19253)***
Michael Fabricating Inc....330 325-8636
4003 State Route 44 Rootstown (44272) ***(G-16570)***
Michael Kaufman Companies Inc (PA)....330 673-4881
845 Overholt Rd Kent (44240) ***(G-11353)***
Michael Kaufman Companies Inc....330 673-4881
845 Overholt Rd Kent (44240) ***(G-11354)***
Michael N Wheeler....740 377-9777
1004 4th St E South Point (45680) ***(G-17288)***
Michael R Kelly....614 491-1745
1657 Victor Ave Obetz (43207) ***(G-15511)***
Michael W Hyes Desgr Goldsmith....440 519-0889
28200 Miles Rd Unit F Solon (44139) ***(G-17194)***
Michael Zakany LLC....740 221-3934
601 Putnam Ave Zanesville (43701) ***(G-21156)***
Michaels 9837, Niles *Also called Michaels Stores Inc* ***(G-15023)***
Michaels Pre-Cast Con Pdts....513 683-1292
1917 Adams Rd Loveland (45140) ***(G-12215)***
Michaels Stores Inc....330 505-1168
5555 Youngstown Warren Rd # 914 Niles (44446) ***(G-15023)***
Michaels Tool Service Co Inc....330 772-1119
8346 Milligan East Rd Burghill (44404) ***(G-2355)***
Michele Mellen....740 369-1422
5680 Liberty Rd N Powell (43065) ***(G-16328)***
Michigan Report, Columbus *Also called Gongwer News Service Inc* ***(G-6960)***
Michigan Sugar Company....419 332-9931
1101 N Front St Fremont (43420) ***(G-10040)***
Michigan Sugar Company....419 423-1666
1343 Greenwood St Findlay (45840) ***(G-9724)***
Mickens Inc (PA)....419 533-2401
107 East St Ste 1 Liberty Center (43532) ***(G-11809)***
Mickens Inc....419 943-2590
117 E Main St Leipsic (45856) ***(G-11729)***
Mickes Quality Machining....614 746-6639
488 Trade Rd Columbus (43204) ***(G-7177)***
Miconvi Properties Inc....440 954-3500
4711 E 355th St Willoughby (44094) ***(G-20381)***
Micro Industries Corporation (PA)....740 548-7878
8399 Green Meadows Dr N Westerville (43081) ***(G-20065)***
Micro Laboratories Inc....440 918-0001
7158 Industrial Park Blvd Mentor (44060) ***(G-13518)***
Micro Lapping & Grinding Co....216 267-6500
12320 Plaza Dr Cleveland (44130) ***(G-5667)***
Micro Machine Ltd....330 438-7078
275 7th St Sw Brewster (44613) ***(G-2070)***
Micro Machine Works Inc....740 678-8471
10499 State Route 339 Vincent (45784) ***(G-19214)***
Micro Metal Finishing LLC....513 541-3095
3448 Spring Grove Ave Cincinnati (45225) ***(G-4022)***
Micro Mower, West Jefferson *Also called R L Parsons & Son Equipment Co* ***(G-19927)***
Micro Products Co Inc....440 943-0258
26653 Curtiss Wright Pkwy Willoughby Hills (44092) ***(G-20471)***
Micro Systems Development Inc....937 438-3567
419 E 6th St Dayton (45402) ***(G-8349)***
Micro Tool Service, New Lebanon *Also called H Duane Leis Acquisitions* ***(G-14710)***
Micro-Pise Msrment Systems LLC....330 541-9100
555 Mondial Pkwy Streetsboro (44241) ***(G-17681)***
Microbiological Labs Inc....330 626-2264
9593 Page Rd Streetsboro (44241) ***(G-17682)***
Microcom Corporation....740 548-6262
8220 Green Meadows Dr N Lewis Center (43035) ***(G-11767)***
Microcvd Corporation....937 573-8984
10150 Meadow Woods Ln Dayton (45458) ***(G-8350)***
Microfinish Inc....937 264-1598
865 Scholz Dr Vandalia (45377) ***(G-19138)***
Microform Inc....440 899-6339
29529 Goulders Grn Cleveland (44140) ***(G-5668)***
Micron Manufacturing Inc....440 355-4200
186 Commerce Dr Lagrange (44050) ***(G-11489)***
Microplex Inc....330 498-0600
7568 Whipple Ave Nw North Canton (44720) ***(G-15101)***
Microplex Printware Corp....440 374-2424
100 Northfield Rd Bedford (44146) ***(G-1426)***
Micropower LLC....513 382-0100
10470 Evendale Dr Cincinnati (45241) ***(G-4023)***

Micropress America LLC 513 746-0689
4240 Minmor Dr Cincinnati (45217) ***(G-4024)***
Micropure Filtration Inc 952 472-2323
837 E 79th St Cleveland (44103) ***(G-5669)***
Micropyretics Heaters Intl Inc 513 772-0404
750 Redna Ter Cincinnati (45215) ***(G-4025)***
Microsheen Corporation 216 481-5610
1100 E 222nd St Ste 1 Cleveland (44117) ***(G-5670)***
Microsoft Corporation 614 719-5900
8800 Lyra Dr Ste 400 Columbus (43240) ***(G-6503)***
Microsoft Corporation 216 986-1440
6050 Oak Tree Blvd # 300 Cleveland (44131) ***(G-5671)***
Microsoft Corporation 513 826-9630
7875 Montgomery Rd # 2205 Cincinnati (45236) ***(G-4026)***
Microsoft Corporation 513 339-2800
4605 Duke Dr Ste 800 Mason (45040) ***(G-12909)***
Microstrategy Incorporated 513 792-2253
8044 Montgomery Rd # 700 Cincinnati (45236) ***(G-4027)***
Microsun Lamps LLC 888 328-8701
7890 Center Point 70 Blvd Dayton (45424) ***(G-8351)***
Microtek Finishing LLC 513 766-5600
5579 Spellmire Dr West Chester (45246) ***(G-19879)***
Microweld Engineering Inc 614 847-9410
7451 Oakmeadows Dr Worthington (43085) ***(G-20697)***
Mid, Mantua *Also called Medical Imaging Dist LLC* ***(G-12553)***
Mid, Columbus *Also called Minimally Invasive Devices Inc* ***(G-7184)***
Mid America Chemical Corp 216 749-0100
4701 Spring Rd Cleveland (44131) ***(G-5672)***
Mid American Ventures Inc 216 524-0974
7600 Wall St Ste 205 Cleveland (44125) ***(G-5673)***
Mid Ohio Net, Delaware *Also called Delaware Gazette Company* ***(G-8670)***
Mid Ohio Packaging LLC 740 383-9200
2135 Innovation Dr Marion (43302) ***(G-12719)***
Mid Ohio Screen Print Inc 614 875-1774
4163 Kelnor Dr Grove City (43123) ***(G-10446)***
Mid Ohio Trophy & Awards 419 756-2266
131 W Cook Rd Mansfield (44907) ***(G-12480)***
Mid Ohio Wood Products Inc 740 323-0427
535 Franklin Ave Newark (43056) ***(G-14897)***
Mid Ohio Wood Recycling Inc 419 673-8470
16289 State Route 31 Kenton (43326) ***(G-11413)***
Mid West Fabricating Co, Amanda *Also called Mid-West Fabricating Co* ***(G-526)***
Mid's Spaghetti Sauce, Navarre *Also called RC Industries Inc* ***(G-14586)***
Mid-America Stainless, Cleveland *Also called Mid-America Steel Corp* ***(G-5674)***
Mid-America Steel Corp 800 282-3466
20900 Saint Clair Ave Cleveland (44117) ***(G-5674)***
Mid-Continent Coal and Coke Co 216 283-5700
761 Stones Levee Cleveland (44113) ***(G-5675)***
Mid-Continent Minerals Corp (PA) 216 283-5700
20600 Chagrin Blvd # 850 Cleveland (44122) ***(G-5676)***
Mid-Continent River Dock, Cleveland *Also called Mid-Continent Coal and Coke Co* ***(G-5675)***
Mid-Ohio Electric Co 614 274-8000
1170 Mckinley Ave Columbus (43222) ***(G-7178)***
Mid-Ohio Products Inc 614 771-2795
4329 Reynolds Dr Hilliard (43026) ***(G-10840)***
Mid-Ohio Regional Plg Comm 614 351-9210
501 Industry Dr Columbus (43204) ***(G-7179)***
Mid-Ohio Tubing LLC (HQ) 419 883-2066
145 W Elm St Butler (44822) ***(G-2376)***
Mid-Ohio Tubing LLC 419 886-0220
500 Main St Bellville (44813) ***(G-1559)***
Mid-State Sales Inc 330 744-2158
854 Mahoning Ave Youngstown (44502) ***(G-20971)***
Mid-West Fabricating Co (PA) 740 969-4411
313 N Johns St Amanda (43102) ***(G-526)***
Mid-West Fabricating Co 740 277-7021
885 Mill Park Dr Lancaster (43130) ***(G-11587)***
Mid-West Fabricating Co 740 681-4411
3115 W Fair Ave Lancaster (43130) ***(G-11588)***
Mid-West Forge Corporation (PA) 216 481-3030
17301 Saint Clair Ave Cleveland (44110) ***(G-5677)***
Mid-West Poly Pak Inc 330 658-2921
89 E Marion St Doylestown (44230) ***(G-8865)***
Mid-Wood Inc 419 257-3331
101 E State St North Baltimore (45872) ***(G-15046)***
Middaugh Enterprises Inc 330 852-2471
211 Yoder Ave Nw Sugarcreek (44681) ***(G-17852)***
Middaugh Printers 330 852-2471
226 W 2nd St Dover (44622) ***(G-8841)***
Middlefield Cheese House Inc 440 632-5228
15815 Nauvoo Rd Middlefield (44062) ***(G-13822)***
Middlefield Glass Incorporated 440 632-5699
17447 Kinsman Rd Middlefield (44062) ***(G-13823)***
Middlefield Mix Inc 440 632-0157
15815 Nauvoo Rd Middlefield (44062) ***(G-13824)***
Middlefield Pallet Inc 440 632-0553
15940 Burton Windsor Rd Middlefield (44062) ***(G-13825)***
Middlefield Plastics Inc 440 834-4638
15235 Burton Windsor Rd Middlefield (44062) ***(G-13826)***
Middlefield Sign Co 440 632-0708
14895 N State Ave Unit G Middlefield (44062) ***(G-13827)***
Middleton Llyd Dolls Inc (PA) 740 989-2082
23689 Mountain Bell Rd Coolville (45723) ***(G-7674)***
Middleton Lee Original Dolls (HQ) ....
2400 Corporate Exch Dr Columbus (43231) ***(G-7180)***
Middleton Printing Co Inc 614 294-7277
81 Mill St Ste 300 Gahanna (43230) ***(G-10090)***
Middletown License Agency Inc 513 422-7225
3232 Roosevelt Blvd Middletown (45044) ***(G-13928)***
Middletown Pharmacy Inc 513 705-6252
4421 Roosevelt Blvd Ste H Middletown (45044) ***(G-13929)***
Middletown Tube Works Inc 513 727-0080
2201 Trine St Middletown (45044) ***(G-13930)***
Middletownusacom 513 594-2831
6730 Roosevelt Ave Middletown (45005) ***(G-13971)***
Middlfeld Original Cheese Coop 440 632-5567
16942 Kinsman Rd Middlefield (44062) ***(G-13828)***
Middlton Lloyd Doll Fctry Outl, Coolville *Also called Middleton Llyd Dolls Inc* ***(G-7674)***
Midflow Services LLC 330 674-2399
812 S Washington St Millersburg (44654) ***(G-14111)***
Midflow Services LLC (PA) 330 567-3108
10774 Township Road 506 Shreve (44676) ***(G-17006)***
Midlake Products & Mfg Co 330 875-4202
819 N Nickelplate St Louisville (44641) ***(G-12161)***
Midland Engineering, Canton *Also called Decision Systems Inc* ***(G-2653)***
Midland Oil Co 740 787-2557
14687 National Rd Se Brownsville (43721) ***(G-2184)***
Midlands Millroom Supply Inc 330 453-9100
1911 36th St Ne Canton (44705) ***(G-2753)***
Midmark Corporation (PA) 937 526-3662
1700 S Patterson Blvd # 400 Kettering (45409) ***(G-11434)***
Midmark Corporation 937 526-8387
160 Industrial Pkwy Versailles (45380) ***(G-19187)***
Midtown Pallet & Recycling 419 241-1311
1987 Hawthorne St Toledo (43606) ***(G-18410)***
Midway Machining Inc 740 373-8976
1060 Gravel Bank Rd Marietta (45750) ***(G-12647)***
Midway Products Group, Greenwich *Also called Lakepark Industries Inc* ***(G-10406)***
Midway Products Group Inc 419 422-7070
2045 Industrial Dr Findlay (45840) ***(G-9725)***
Midway Swiss Turn Inc 330 264-4300
2160 Great Trails Dr Wooster (44691) ***(G-20625)***
Midwest Acoust-A-Fiber Inc (PA) 740 369-3624
759 Pittsburgh Dr Delaware (43015) ***(G-8705)***
Midwest Acoust-A-Fiber Inc 740 363-6247
487 London Rd Delaware (43015) ***(G-8706)***
Midwest Aircraft Products Co 419 884-2164
125 S Mill St Mansfield (44904) ***(G-12481)***
Midwest Box Company 216 281-9021
9801 Walford Ave Ste C Cleveland (44102) ***(G-5678)***
Midwest Centerless Grinding, Cincinnati *Also called A and V Grinding Inc* ***(G-3276)***
Midwest Composites LLC 419 738-2431
302 Krein Ave Wapakoneta (45895) ***(G-19342)***
Midwest Compost Inc 419 547-7979
7250 State Route 101 E Clyde (43410) ***(G-6391)***
Midwest Compressor Co Inc (PA) 216 941-9200
12901 Elmwood Ave Cleveland (44111) ***(G-5679)***
Midwest Container Corporation 513 870-3000
375 Northpointe Dr Fairfield (45014) ***(G-9529)***
Midwest Conveyor Products Inc 419 281-1235
1919 Cellar Dr Ashland (44805) ***(G-725)***
Midwest Curtainwalls Inc 216 641-7900
5171 Grant Ave Cleveland (44125) ***(G-5680)***
Midwest Elastomers Inc 419 738-8844
700 Industrial Dr Wapakoneta (45895) ***(G-19343)***
Midwest Energy Emissions Corp 614 505-6115
670 Enterprise Dr Ste D Lewis Center (43035) ***(G-11768)***
Midwest Exposure Magazine 937 626-6738
1509 S Smithville Rd Dayton (45410) ***(G-8352)***
Midwest Fabrications Inc 330 633-0191
516 Commerce St Tallmadge (44278) ***(G-17993)***
Midwest Filtration LLC 513 874-6510
9775 International Blvd West Chester (45246) ***(G-19880)***
Midwest Fireworks Mfg Co II 330 584-7000
8550 State Route 224 Deerfield (44411) ***(G-8610)***
Midwest Granite & Stone, Holland *Also called Schena Company Ltd* ***(G-10955)***
Midwest Graphics, Columbus *Also called Our Nine LLC* ***(G-7280)***
Midwest Industrial Products 216 771-8555
7424 Bessemer Ave Cleveland (44127) ***(G-5681)***
Midwest Industrial Rubber Inc 614 876-3110
4847 Northwest Pkwy Hilliard (43026) ***(G-10841)***
Midwest Industrial Specialties 740 815-0541
5521 Summer Blvd Galena (43021) ***(G-10116)***
Midwest Iron and Metal Co 937 222-5992
461 Homestead Ave Dayton (45417) ***(G-8353)***
Midwest Knife Grinding Inc 330 854-1030
492 Elm Ridge Ave Ste 4 Canal Fulton (44614) ***(G-2486)***
Midwest Laser Systems Inc 419 424-0062
1101 Commerce Pkwy Findlay (45840) ***(G-9726)***

ALPHABETIC

Midwest Machine, West Unity *Also called Midwest Production Machining* ***(G-19972)***
Midwest Machine Service Inc..............216 631-8151
4700 Train Ave Ste 1 Cleveland (44102) ***(G-5682)***
Midwest Metal Fabricators..............419 739-7077
712 Maple St Wapakoneta (45895) ***(G-19344)***
Midwest Metal Fabricators..............419 739-7077
712 Maple St Wapakoneta (45895) ***(G-19345)***
Midwest Metrology LLC..............937 832-0965
341 Smith Dr Englewood (45315) ***(G-9369)***
Midwest Minicranes Inc..............330 332-3700
1350 Pennsylvania Ave Salem (44460) ***(G-16761)***
Midwest Mold & Texture Corp..............513 732-1300
4270 Armstrong Blvd Batavia (45103) ***(G-1165)***
Midwest Molding Inc..............614 873-1572
8245 Estates Pkwy Plain City (43064) ***(G-16202)***
Midwest Motor Supply Co (PA)..............800 233-1294
4800 Roberts Rd Columbus (43228) ***(G-7181)***
Midwest Ohio Tool Co..............419 294-1987
215 Tarhe Trl Upper Sandusky (43351) ***(G-18963)***
Midwest Plastic Systems Inc..............513 553-4380
100 Front St New Richmond (45157) ***(G-14813)***
Midwest Plastics, Lima *Also called W T Inc* ***(G-11957)***
Midwest Precision Holdings Inc (HQ)..............440 497-4086
34700 Lakeland Blvd Eastlake (44095) ***(G-9121)***
Midwest Precision LLC..............440 951-2333
34700 Lakeland Blvd Eastlake (44095) ***(G-9122)***
Midwest Precision Products..............440 237-9500
9940 York Alpha Dr Cleveland (44133) ***(G-5683)***
Midwest Production Machining..............419 924-5616
10484 State Route 191 West Unity (43570) ***(G-19972)***
Midwest Quality Bedding Inc..............614 504-5971
3860 Morse Rd Columbus (43219) ***(G-7182)***
Midwest Security Services..............937 853-9000
4050 Benfield Dr Dayton (45429) ***(G-8354)***
Midwest Service, Middletown *Also called Vail Rubber Works Inc* ***(G-13962)***
Midwest Sign Center, Canton *Also called Midwest Sign Ctr* ***(G-2754)***
Midwest Sign Ctr..............330 493-7330
4210 Cleveland Ave Nw Canton (44709) ***(G-2754)***
Midwest Specialties Inc..............419 738-8147
851 Industrial Dr Wapakoneta (45895) ***(G-19346)***
Midwest Spray Booths..............937 439-6600
7672 Mcewen Rd Dayton (45459) ***(G-8355)***
Midwest Spray Drying Company..............419 294-4221
422 W Guthrie Dr Upper Sandusky (43351) ***(G-18964)***
Midwest Stamping & Mfg Co..............419 298-2394
228 E Morrison St Edgerton (43517) ***(G-9177)***
Midwest Telemetry Inc..............440 725-5718
7935 Chardon Rd B7 Kirtland (44094) ***(G-11469)***
Midwest Timber & Land Co Inc..............740 493-2400
88 Jasper Rd Piketon (45661) ***(G-16074)***
Midwest Tool & Engineering Co..............937 224-0756
112 Webster St Dayton (45402) ***(G-8356)***
Midwest Welding & Boiler Co, Cleveland *Also called Durisek Enterprises Inc* ***(G-5123)***
Midwest Woodworking Co Inc..............513 631-6684
4019 Montgomery Rd Cincinnati (45212) ***(G-4028)***
Midwestern Bag Co Inc..............419 241-3112
3230 Monroe St Toledo (43606) ***(G-18411)***
Midwestern Industries Inc (PA)..............330 837-4203
915 Oberlin Ave Sw Massillon (44647) ***(G-13026)***
Mielke Furniture Repair Inc..............419 625-4572
3209 Columbus Ave Sandusky (44870) ***(G-16830)***
Migraine Proof LLC..............330 635-7874
6890 Meadowood Dr Medina (44256) ***(G-13301)***
Miiler Brewing Company..............513 896-9200
2525 Wayne Madison Rd Trenton (45067) ***(G-18625)***
Mika Metal Fabricating Co..............440 951-5500
4530 Hamann Pkwy Willoughby (44094) ***(G-20382)***
Mikan Die and Tool LLC..............216 265-2811
13410 Enterprise Ave Cleveland (44135) ***(G-5684)***
Mike B Crawford..............330 673-7944
606 Mogadore Rd Kent (44240) ***(G-11355)***
Mike Loppe..............937 969-8102
2 W Main St Tremont City (45372) ***(G-18616)***
Mike Strickland Logging, Oak Hill *Also called Michael D Strickland* ***(G-15456)***
Mike Suponcic..............740 635-0654
68940 Blaine Chermont Rd Bridgeport (43912) ***(G-2077)***
Mike-Sells Potato Chip Co (HQ)..............937 228-9400
333 Leo St Dayton (45404) ***(G-8357)***
Mikes Automotive LLC..............937 233-1433
7581 Brandt Pike Unit B Dayton (45424) ***(G-8358)***
Mikes Mill Shop Inc..............419 538-6091
14768 Road J Ottawa (45875) ***(G-15659)***
Mikes Welding..............937 675-6587
5589 Us Highway 35 E Jamestown (45335) ***(G-11220)***
Mil-Mar Century Corporation..............937 275-4860
8641 Washington Church Rd Miamisburg (45342) ***(G-13694)***
Milacron Holdings Corp (PA)..............513 487-5000
10200 Alliance Rd Ste 200 Blue Ash (45242) ***(G-1821)***
Milacron LLC..............513 536-2000
4165 Half Acre Rd Batavia (45103) ***(G-1166)***
Milacron LLC (HQ)..............513 487-5000
10200 Alliance Rd Ste 200 Blue Ash (45242) ***(G-1822)***
Milacron Marketing Company LLC (HQ)..............513 536-2000
4165 Half Acre Rd Batavia (45103) ***(G-1167)***
Milacron Plas Tech Group LLC (HQ)..............513 536-2000
4165 Half Acre Rd Batavia (45103) ***(G-1168)***
Milacron Plas Tech Group LLC..............937 444-2532
418 W Main St Mount Orab (45154) ***(G-14447)***
Milan Tool Corp..............216 661-1078
8989 Brookpark Rd Cleveland (44129) ***(G-5685)***
Milark Industries, Mansfield *Also called Hayford Technologies* ***(G-12455)***
Miles Park Window Treatments, Beachwood *Also called Miles Pk Vntian Blind Shds Mfg* ***(G-1248)***
Miles Pk Vntian Blind Shds Mfg..............216 239-0850
23880 Commerce Park # 100 Beachwood (44122) ***(G-1248)***
Miles Rubber & Packing Company (PA)..............330 425-3888
9020 Dutton Dr Twinsburg (44087) ***(G-18820)***
Milestone Services Corp..............330 374-9988
551 Beacon St Akron (44311) ***(G-282)***
Milestone Veneer, Granville *Also called Milestone Ventures LLC* ***(G-10334)***
Milestone Ventures LLC (PA)..............317 908-2093
2924 Hallie Ln Granville (43023) ***(G-10334)***
Mileti Optical & Hearing Ctr, Cleveland *Also called Mileti Optical Inc* ***(G-5686)***
Mileti Optical Inc..............440 884-6333
5957 State Rd Ste 1 Cleveland (44134) ***(G-5686)***
Milford Printers (PA)..............513 831-6630
317 Main St Milford (45150) ***(G-14027)***
Milford Printers..............513 831-6630
18 Locust St Milford (45150) ***(G-14028)***
Milicom LLC..............216 765-8875
23307 Commerce Park Beachwood (44122) ***(G-1249)***
Military Resources LLC..............330 263-1040
1036 Burbank Rd Wooster (44691) ***(G-20626)***
Military Resources LLC (PA)..............330 309-9970
1834 Cleveland Rd Ste 301 Wooster (44691) ***(G-20627)***
Milja Inc..............937 223-1988
1254 Stanley Ave Dayton (45404) ***(G-8359)***
Milk & Honey..............330 492-5884
3400 Cleveland Ave Nw # 1 Canton (44709) ***(G-2755)***
Milkmen Design LLC..............440 590-5788
2332 Prospect Ave E Cleveland (44115) ***(G-5687)***
Mill & Motion Inc..............216 524-4000
5415 E Schaaf Rd Ste 101 Cleveland (44131) ***(G-5688)***
Mill Brook, Euclid *Also called Schwebel Baking Company* ***(G-9442)***
Mill Rose Laboratories Inc..............440 974-6730
7310 Corp Blvd Mentor (44060) ***(G-13519)***
Mill-Rose Company (PA)..............440 255-9171
7995 Tyler Blvd Mentor (44060) ***(G-13520)***
Millat Industries Corp (PA)..............937 434-6666
4901 Croftshire Dr Dayton (45440) ***(G-8360)***
Millat Industries Corp..............937 535-1500
7611 Center Pt I 70 Blvd Dayton (45424) ***(G-8361)***
Millcraft Group LLC (PA)..............216 441-5500
6800 Grant Ave Cleveland (44105) ***(G-5689)***
Millcraft Paper Company..............216 429-9860
4640 Hinckley Indus Pkwy Cleveland (44109) ***(G-5690)***
Millennium, Ashtabula *Also called Cristal USA Inc* ***(G-769)***
Millennium Adhesive Pdts Inc..............440 708-1212
178 E Washington St Ste 1 Chagrin Falls (44022) ***(G-3024)***
Millennium Adhesive Products..............440 708-1212
17340 Munn Rd Chagrin Falls (44023) ***(G-3060)***
Millennium Mch Techlonlogy LLC..............440 269-8080
38323 Apollo Pkwy Ste 7 Willoughby (44094) ***(G-20383)***
Miller & Son Logging..............330 738-2031
8521 Clover Rd Ne Mechanicstown (44651) ***(G-13213)***
Miller and Slay Wdwkg LLC..............513 265-3816
8284 Winters Ln Mason (45040) ***(G-12910)***
Miller Bearing Company Inc..............330 678-8844
420 Portage Blvd Kent (44240) ***(G-11356)***
Miller Bros Paving Inc (HQ)..............419 445-1015
1613 S Defiance St Archbold (43502) ***(G-659)***
Miller Cabinet Ltd..............614 873-4221
6217 Converse Huff Rd Plain City (43064) ***(G-16203)***
Miller Casting Inc..............330 482-2923
1634 Lower Elkton Rd Columbiana (44408) ***(G-6473)***
Miller Consolidated Industries (PA)..............937 294-2681
2221 Arbor Blvd Moraine (45439) ***(G-14370)***
Miller Core 2 Inc..............330 359-0500
9823 Chestnut Ridge Rd Nw Beach City (44608) ***(G-1213)***
Miller Crist..............330 359-7877
10258 S Kansas Rd Fredericksburg (44627) ***(G-9953)***
Miller Curber Company LLC..............330 782-8081
4020 Simon Rd Youngstown (44512) ***(G-20972)***
Miller Engine & Machine Co, Springfield *Also called Muller Engine & Machine Co* ***(G-17454)***
Miller Enterprises Ohio LLC..............330 852-4009
1360 County Road 108 Sugarcreek (44681) ***(G-17853)***
Miller Industries Inc..............937 293-2223
139 Auto Club Dr Dayton (45402) ***(G-8362)***
Miller Leasing, Baltic *Also called Crawford Manufacturing Company* ***(G-1026)***

Miller Logging	440 693-4001
5327 Parks West Rd Middlefield (44062) *(G-13829)*	
Miller Logging Inc	330 279-4721
8373 State Route 83 Holmesville (44633) *(G-10983)*	
Miller Lumber Co Inc	330 674-0273
7101 State Route 39 Millersburg (44654) *(G-14112)*	
Miller Machine & Mfg LLC	740 439-2283
62056 Greendale Rd Cambridge (43725) *(G-2448)*	
Miller Manufacturing Inc	330 852-0689
2705 Shetler Rd Nw Sugarcreek (44681) *(G-17854)*	
Miller Pallet Company	937 464-4483
9216 County Road 97 Belle Center (43310) *(G-1500)*	
Miller Printing Co, Springfield Also called Graphic Paper Products Corp *(G-17407)*	
Miller Products Inc	330 308-5934
642 Wabash Ave Nw New Philadelphia (44663) *(G-14786)*	
Miller Products Inc	330 335-3110
985 Seville Rd Wadsworth (44281) *(G-19254)*	
Miller Prsthtics Orthotics LLC	740 421-4211
2354 Richmiller Ln Belpre (45714) *(G-1580)*	
Miller Publishing Company	937 866-3331
230 S 2nd St Miamisburg (45342) *(G-13695)*	
Miller Studio Inc	330 339-1100
734 Fair Ave Nw New Philadelphia (44663) *(G-14787)*	
Miller Truss LLC	440 321-0126
15345 Georgia Rd Middlefield (44062) *(G-13830)*	
Miller Welding Inc	330 364-6173
2718 Broad Run Dar Rd Nw Dover (44622) *(G-8842)*	
Miller Weldmaster Corporation (PA)	330 833-6739
4220 Alabama Ave Sw Navarre (44662) *(G-14580)*	
Miller Wire & Cable, Cleveland Also called Marlin Thermocouple Wire Inc *(G-5624)*	
Miller Wood Design, Sugarcreek Also called Miller Manufacturing Inc *(G-17854)*	
Miller, Jim Furniture, Springfield Also called Hallmark Industries Inc *(G-17410)*	
Millercoors LLC	513 896-9200
2525 Wayne Madison Rd Trenton (45067) *(G-18626)*	
Millers Liniments LLC	440 548-5800
17150 Bundysburg Rd Middlefield (44062) *(G-13831)*	
Millers Storage Barns LLC	330 893-3293
4230 State Route 39 Millersburg (44654) *(G-14113)*	
Millersburg Ice Co	330 674-3016
25 S Grant St Millersburg (44654) *(G-14114)*	
Millmcrawley, Greenville Also called Markwith Tool Company Inc *(G-10380)*	
Mills Aluminum Fab	330 821-4108
W 23 Rd St Alliance (44601) *(G-489)*	
Mills Company	740 375-0770
3007 Harding Hwy E 4n Marion (43302) *(G-12720)*	
Mills Customs Woodworks	216 407-3600
3950 Prospect Ave E Cleveland (44115) *(G-5691)*	
Mills Led LLC (PA)	800 690-6403
81 S 5th St Ste 201 Columbus (43215) *(G-7183)*	
Mills Led LLC	800 690-6403
845 E High St Springfield (45505) *(G-17448)*	
Mills Metal Finishing, Columbus Also called Mmf Inc *(G-7186)*	
Mills Walls, Broadview Heights Also called M/W International Inc *(G-2094)*	
Millstone Coffee Inc (HQ)	513 983-1100
1 Procter And Gamble Plz Cincinnati (45202) *(G-4029)*	
Milltree Lumber Holdings	740 226-2090
535 Coal Dock Rd Waverly (45690) *(G-19551)*	
Millwood Inc	330 359-5220
18279 Dover Rd Dundee (44624) *(G-9022)*	
Millwood Inc	330 857-3075
8208 S Kohler Rd Apple Creek (44606) *(G-614)*	
Millwood Inc	740 226-2090
535 Coal Dock Rd Waverly (45690) *(G-19552)*	
Millwood Inc	614 717-9099
9743 Fairway Dr Powell (43065) *(G-16329)*	
Millwood Inc	440 914-0540
30311 Emerald Valley Pkwu Solon (44139) *(G-17195)*	
Millwood Inc	513 860-4567
4438 Muhlhauser Rd # 100 West Chester (45011) *(G-19744)*	
Millwood Inc	330 729-2120
3708 International Blvd Vienna (44473) *(G-19203)*	
Millwood Inc	404 629-4811
3708 International Blvd Vienna (44473) *(G-19204)*	
Millwood Logging, Gnadenhutten Also called Millwood Lumber Inc *(G-10280)*	
Millwood Lumber Inc	740 254-4681
2400 Larson Rd Se Gnadenhutten (44629) *(G-10280)*	
Millwood Natural LLC	330 393-4400
3708 International Blvd Vienna (44473) *(G-19205)*	
Millwood Pallet Co, Dundee Also called Millwood Inc *(G-9022)*	
Millwood Plant, Howard Also called Pioneer Sands LLC *(G-10997)*	
Millwood Wholesale Inc	330 359-6109
7969 Township Road 662 Dundee (44624) *(G-9023)*	
Millwork Design Solutions Inc	440 946-8637
4547 Beidler Rd Willoughby (44094) *(G-20384)*	
Millwork Designs Inc	740 335-5203
230 Topaz Ln Wshngtn CT Hs (43160) *(G-20733)*	
Millwork Fabricators Inc	937 299-5452
3176 Kettering Blvd Moraine (45439) *(G-14371)*	
Millwrght Wldg Fbrication Svcs	740 533-1510
1590 County Road 105 Kitts Hill (45645) *(G-11475)*	
Milnot Company	888 656-3245
735 Taylor Rd Ste 200 Gahanna (43230) *(G-10091)*	
Milo Bennett Corp	419 874-1492
12922 Eckel Junction Rd Perrysburg (43551) *(G-15977)*	
Milos Whole World Gourmet LLC	740 589-6456
94 Columbus Rd Athens (45701) *(G-840)*	
Milsek Furniture Polish Inc	330 542-2700
1351 Quaker Cir Salem (44460) *(G-16762)*	
Milton West Fabricators Inc	937 547-3069
4773 Hllnsburg Tampico Rd Greenville (45331) *(G-10382)*	
Mim Software Inc (PA)	216 896-9798
25800 Science Park Dr # 180 Beachwood (44122) *(G-1250)*	
Mindcrafted Systems Inc	440 821-2245
1969 Newbury Dr Cleveland (44145) *(G-5692)*	
Minderman Marine Products Inc	419 732-2626
129 Buckeye Blvd Port Clinton (43452) *(G-16253)*	
Mine Equipment Services LLC (PA)	740 936-5427
3958 State Route 3 Sunbury (43074) *(G-17891)*	
Miner's Bishop Tractor Sales, Rootstown Also called Miners Tractor Sales Inc *(G-16571)*	
Mineral Processing, Carey Also called Andersons Plant Nutrient LLC *(G-2878)*	
Mineral Processing Company	419 396-3501
1855 County Highway 99 Carey (43316) *(G-2883)*	
Mineral Technology Metal Cast, Archbold Also called American Colloid Company *(G-635)*	
Miners Tractor Sales Inc (PA)	330 325-9914
6941 Tallmadge Rd Rootstown (44272) *(G-16571)*	
Minerva Dairy Inc	330 868-4196
430 Radloff Ave Minerva (44657) *(G-14193)*	
Minerva Maid, Minerva Also called Minerva Dairy Inc *(G-14193)*	
Minerva Tube Plant, Minerva Also called Caraustar Industrial and Con *(G-14177)*	
Minerva Welding and Fabg Inc	330 868-7731
22133 Us Route 30 Minerva (44657) *(G-14194)*	
Mings Heating & AC	216 721-2007
11902 Larchmere Blvd Cleveland (44120) *(G-5693)*	
Mini Graphics Inc.	513 563-8600
7306 Euclid Ave Cincinnati (45243) *(G-4030)*	
Mini Mix Inc	513 353-3811
5852 Hamilton Cleves Rd Cleves (45002) *(G-6371)*	
Miniature Plastic Molding Inc	440 564-7210
6750 Arnold Miller Pkwy Solon (44139) *(G-17196)*	
Minimally Invasive Devices Inc	614 484-5036
1275 Kinnear Rd Columbus (43212) *(G-7184)*	
Mining Reclamation Inc	740 327-5555
15953 State Route 60 S Dresden (43821) *(G-8869)*	
Minnich Manufacturing Co Inc	419 903-0010
1444 State Route 42 Mansfield (44903) *(G-12482)*	
Minnicks Drive-Thru	513 868-6126
828 East Ave Hamilton (45011) *(G-10587)*	
Minnie Hanmons Catering Inc	216 815-7744
1738 Coit Ave Cleveland (44112) *(G-5694)*	
Minor Corporation	216 291-8723
1599 Maywood Rd Cleveland (44121) *(G-5695)*	
Minotas Trophies & Awards	440 720-1288
40 Alpha Park Cleveland (44143) *(G-5696)*	
Minova USA Inc	740 377-9146
101 Valley Dr South Point (45680) *(G-17289)*	
Minova USA Inc	740 269-8100
600 Boyce Dr Bowerston (44695) *(G-1941)*	
Minster Farmers, Minster Also called Sunrise Cooperative Inc *(G-14225)*	
Minteq International Inc	330 343-8821
5864 Crown Street Ext Nw Dover (44622) *(G-8843)*	
Minuteman Distribution, Millersport Also called Agrati - Medina LLC *(G-14158)*	
Minuteman of Heath, Newark Also called L & T Collins Inc *(G-14892)*	
Minuteman Press, Cincinnati Also called Bock & Pierce Enterprises *(G-3398)*	
Minuteman Press, Parma Also called Fourjays Inc *(G-15819)*	
Minuteman Press, Ontario Also called Cnb LLC *(G-15539)*	
Minuteman Press, Columbus Also called Henry Bussman *(G-6988)*	
Minuteman Press, Fairlawn Also called Frisby Printing Company *(G-9605)*	
Minuteman Press, Athens Also called Double b Printing LLC *(G-829)*	
Minuteman Press, Cincinnati Also called Mmp Printing Inc *(G-4035)*	
Minuteman Press, Youngstown Also called Seifert Printing Company *(G-21027)*	
Minuteman Press, Lebanon Also called Geygan Enterprises Inc *(G-11656)*
Minuteman Press, Fairfield Also called J D B Partners Inc *(G-9513)*
Minuteman Press, Medina Also called Debandale Printing Inc *(G-13251)*
Minuteman Press, Troy Also called Schiffer Group Inc *(G-18703)*
Minuteman Press, Toledo Also called Stepping Stone Enterprises Inc *(G-18529)*
Minuteman Press, Columbus Also called Capehart Enterprises LLC *(G-6730)*
Minuteman Press, Dayton Also called Green Willow Inc *(G-8238)*
Minuteman Press, Cleveland Also called Williams Executive Entps Inc *(G-6310)*
Minuteman Press, Cleveland Also called Kovacevic Printing Inc *(G-5542)*
Minuteman Press, North Olmsted Also called Kelly Prints LLC *(G-15194)*
Minuteman Press, Lewis Center Also called Shallow Lake Corp *(G-11779)*
Minuteman Press, Dublin Also called Kad Holdings Inc *(G-8935)*
Minuteman Press, Dayton Also called Premier Printing and Packg Inc *(G-8436)*

Minuteman Press, Chagrin Falls *Also called Affordable Bus Support LLC* ***(G-3036)***
Minuteman Press.....440 946-3311
7450 Mentor Ave Mentor (44060) ***(G-13521)***
Minuteman Press.....419 782-8002
214 Clinton St Defiance (43512) ***(G-8639)***
Minuteman Press.....513 772-0500
2312 E Sharon Rd Cincinnati (45241) ***(G-4031)***
Minuteman Press.....614 337-2334
265 Lincoln Cir Ste C Columbus (43230) ***(G-7185)***
Minuteman Press.....937 429-8610
2372 Lakeview Dr Beavercreek (45431) ***(G-1332)***
Minuteman Press.....330 725-4121
455 W Liberty St Medina (44256) ***(G-13302)***
Minuteman Press Inc.....513 741-9056
9904 Colerain Ave Cincinnati (45251) ***(G-4032)***
Minuteman Press of Athens LLC.....740 593-7393
17 W Washington St Athens (45701) ***(G-841)***
Minuteman Press of Elyria.....440 365-9377
631 Abbe Rd S Elyria (44035) ***(G-9296)***
Minutman Press Frfeld Cnty LLC.....740 689-1992
135 N Columbus St Lancaster (43130) ***(G-11589)***
Mio Vino.....513 407-0486
7908 Blue Ash Rd Cincinnati (45236) ***(G-4033)***
Mlp Interent Enterprises LLC.....614 917-8705
720c 5th Ave Mansfield (44905) ***(G-12483)***
Mir, Hilliard *Also called Midwest Industrial Rubber Inc* ***(G-10841)***
Miracle Air, Franklin *Also called Miracle Welding Inc* ***(G-9901)***
Miracle Core Filters, Sandusky *Also called D C Filter & Chemical Inc* ***(G-16802)***
Miracle Custom Awards & Gifts.....330 376-8335
565 Wolf Ledges Pkwy A Akron (44311) ***(G-283)***
Miracle Documents.....513 651-2222
2300 Montana Ave Ste 301 Cincinnati (45211) ***(G-4034)***
Miracle Metal Finishing, Cleveland *Also called Kyron Plating Corp* ***(G-5548)***
Miracle Welding Inc.....513 746-9977
141 Industrial Dr Ste 200 Franklin (45005) ***(G-9901)***
Miraclecorp Products (PA).....937 293-9994
2425 W Dorothy Ln Moraine (45439) ***(G-14372)***
Mirion Technologies Ist Corp.....614 367-2050
12954 Stonecreek Dr Ste C Pickerington (43147) ***(G-16054)***
Mirmat Cnc Machining Inc.....440 951-2410
4550 Hamann Pkwy Willoughby (44094) ***(G-20385)***
Mirror.....419 893-8135
113 W Wayne St Maumee (43537) ***(G-13134)***
Mirror Publishing Co Inc.....419 893-8135
113 W Wayne St Maumee (43537) ***(G-13135)***
Mirror, The, Maumee *Also called Mirror Publishing Co Inc* ***(G-13135)***
Mirror-Coat, Cincinnati *Also called Southern Adhesive Coatings* ***(G-4355)***
Mirus Adapted Tech LLC.....614 402-4585
288 Cramer Creek Ct Dublin (43017) ***(G-8946)***
Mis, Ashland *Also called Maverick Innvtive Slutions LLC* ***(G-722)***
Mis Micro Information Services, Cincinnati *Also called Steve Schaefer* ***(G-4380)***
Misato Computer Products Inc.....937 890-8410
850 Industrial Park Dr Vandalia (45377) ***(G-19139)***
Miscellnous Mtals Fbrction Inc.....740 779-3071
18828 Us Highway 50 Chillicothe (45601) ***(G-3200)***
Misco Refractometer, Solon *Also called Mercury Iron and Steel Co* ***(G-17190)***
Mission Industrial Group LLC.....740 387-2287
3602 Harding Hwy E Marion (43302) ***(G-12721)***
Mission Support, Beavercreek *Also called Leidos Inc* ***(G-1326)***
Misumi Investment USA Corp (HQ).....937 859-5111
500 Progress Rd Dayton (45449) ***(G-8363)***
Mitchell Bros Ice Cream Inc.....216 861-2799
1867 W 25th St Cleveland (44113) ***(G-5697)***
Mitchell Electronics Inc.....740 594-8532
1005 E State St Ste 5 Athens (45701) ***(G-842)***
Mitchell Piping LLC.....330 245-0258
1101 Sunnyside St Sw C Hartville (44632) ***(G-10702)***
Mitchell Plastics Inc.....330 825-2461
130 31st St Nw Barberton (44203) ***(G-1086)***
Mitchell Welding LLC.....740 259-2211
11761 State Route 104 Lucasville (45648) ***(G-12266)***
Mitchellace Inc (PA).....740 354-2813
830 Murray St Portsmouth (45662) ***(G-16291)***
Mitchs Welding & Hitches.....419 893-3117
802 Kingsbury St Maumee (43537) ***(G-13136)***
Mitec Powertrain Inc.....567 525-5606
4000 Fostoria Ave Findlay (45840) ***(G-9727)***
Mitel (delaware) Inc.....513 733-8000
9100 W Chester Towne Ctr West Chester (45069) ***(G-19745)***
Mitsubishi Chls Perf Plyrs Inc.....419 483-2931
350 N Buckeye St Bellevue (44811) ***(G-1540)***
Mitsubishi Elc Auto Amer Inc (HQ).....513 573-6614
4773 Bethany Rd Mason (45040) ***(G-12911)***
Mitsubishi Elc Automtn Inc.....937 492-3058
213 N Ohio Ave Sidney (45365) ***(G-17054)***
Mix-Masters Inc.....513 228-2800
2550 Henkle Dr Lebanon (45036) ***(G-11673)***
Mixed Logic LLC.....440 826-1676
5907 E Law Rd Valley City (44280) ***(G-19050)***
Mixmill, Cincinnati *Also called Processall Inc* ***(G-4196)***
Mizer Printing & Graphics.....740 942-3343
160 Cunningham Ave Ste C Cadiz (43907) ***(G-2400)***
Mj Coates Homes, Dayton *Also called M J Coates Construction Co* ***(G-8318)***
Mjc Enterprises Inc.....330 669-3744
7820 Blough Rd Sterling (44276) ***(G-17523)***
MJM Industries Inc.....440 350-1230
1200 East St Fairport Harbor (44077) ***(G-9626)***
Mjs Plastics Inc.....937 548-1000
1355 Sater St Greenville (45331) ***(G-10383)***
Mk Enterprises Inc.....440 632-0121
11162 Industrial Pkwy Middlefield (44062) ***(G-13832)***
Mk Global Enterprises LLC.....440 823-0081
23980 Chagrin Blvd # 204 Beachwood (44122) ***(G-1251)***
Mk Metal Products Inc (PA).....419 756-3644
90 Sawyer Pkwy Mansfield (44903) ***(G-12484)***
Mk Trempe Corporation.....937 492-3548
2349 Industrial Dr Sidney (45365) ***(G-17055)***
ML Advertising & Design LLC.....419 447-6523
185 Jefferson St Tiffin (44883) ***(G-18069)***
ML Erectors LLC.....440 328-3227
827 Walnut St Elyria (44035) ***(G-9297)***
Mlad Graphic Design Services, Tiffin *Also called ML Advertising & Design LLC* ***(G-18069)***
MLS Systems, Findlay *Also called Midwest Laser Systems Inc* ***(G-9726)***
Mm Outsourcing LLC.....937 661-4300
355 S South St Leesburg (45135) ***(G-11714)***
Mm Service.....330 474-3098
8936 State Route 14 Streetsboro (44241) ***(G-17683)***
Mmei, Middlefield *Also called Molten Mtal Eqp Innvations LLC* ***(G-13833)***
Mmf Inc (PA).....614 252-0078
1977 Mcallister Ave Columbus (43205) ***(G-7186)***
Mmf Incorporated.....614 252-2522
1977 Mcallister Ave Columbus (43205) ***(G-7187)***
Mmh Americas Inc (HQ).....414 764-6200
4401 Gateway Blvd Springfield (45502) ***(G-17449)***
Mmh Holdings Inc (HQ).....937 525-5533
4401 Gateway Blvd Springfield (45502) ***(G-17450)***
Mmi Textiles Inc.....440 899-8050
29260 Clemens Rd Bldg Ii Westlake (44145) ***(G-20131)***
Mmp Printing Inc.....513 381-0990
10570 Chester Rd Cincinnati (45215) ***(G-4035)***
Mmp Toledo.....419 472-0505
5847 Secor Rd Toledo (43623) ***(G-18412)***
Mn8-Foxfire, Cincinnati *Also called Evp International LLC* ***(G-3662)***
Mobile Conversions Inc.....513 797-1991
3354 State Route 132 Amelia (45102) ***(G-544)***
Mobile Mini Inc.....303 305-9515
8045 Dawnwood Ave Ne Canton (44721) ***(G-2756)***
Mobile Mini Inc.....614 449-8655
871 Buckeye Park Rd Columbus (43207) ***(G-7188)***
Mobile Office Solutions, Batavia *Also called Foster Products Inc* ***(G-1146)***
Mobile Operations, Van Wert *Also called Eaton Corporation* ***(G-19087)***
Mobile Solutions LLC.....614 286-3944
149 N Hamilton Rd Columbus (43213) ***(G-7189)***
Mobis North America LLC.....419 729-6700
3900 Stickney Ave Toledo (43608) ***(G-18413)***
Mock Shoppe, Greenville *Also called Cromwell Aleene* ***(G-10366)***
Mock Woodworking Company LLC.....740 452-2701
4400 West Pike Zanesville (43701) ***(G-21157)***
Model and Tool Making, Andover *Also called Mathew Odonnell* ***(G-585)***
Model Engineering Company.....330 644-3450
800 Robinson Ave Barberton (44203) ***(G-1087)***
Model Graphics & Media Inc.....513 541-2355
2614 Crescentville Rd West Chester (45069) ***(G-19746)***
Model Pattern & Foundry Co.....513 542-2322
3242 Spring Grove Ave Cincinnati (45225) ***(G-4036)***
Modern AG Supply Inc.....419 753-3484
302 S Main St New Knoxville (45871) ***(G-14705)***
Modern Builders Supply Inc (PA).....419 241-3961
3500 Phillips Ave Toledo (43608) ***(G-18414)***
Modern Builders Supply Inc.....419 526-0002
85 Smith Ave Mansfield (44905) ***(G-12485)***
Modern China Inc (PA).....330 938-6104
550 E Ohio Ave Sebring (44672) ***(G-16889)***
Modern Defense.....614 505-9338
2394 N High St Columbus (43202) ***(G-7190)***
Modern Design Stamping Div.....216 382-6318
1618 Maple Rd Cleveland (44121) ***(G-5698)***
Modern Designs Inc.....330 644-1771
310 Killian Rd Coventry Township (44319) ***(G-7773)***
Modern Displays Inc.....513 471-1639
4301 Schulte Dr Cincinnati (45205) ***(G-4037)***
Modern Engineering.....440 593-5414
527 W Adams St Conneaut (44030) ***(G-7656)***
Modern Ice Equipment & Sup Co (PA).....513 367-2101
5709 Harrison Ave Cincinnati (45248) ***(G-4038)***
Modern Industries Inc.....216 432-2855
6610 Metta Ave Cleveland (44103) ***(G-5699)***

Modern Ink Technology LLC 419 738-9664
1005 W Grand Ave Lima (45801) ***(G-11908)***
Modern Manufacturing Inc (PA) 513 251-3600
240 Stille Dr Cincinnati (45233) ***(G-4039)***
Modern Mold Corporation 440 236-9600
27684 Royalton Rd Columbia Station (44028) ***(G-6440)***
Modern Pipe Supports Corp 216 361-1666
4734 Commerce Ave Cleveland (44103) ***(G-5700)***
Modern Plastics Recovery Inc 419 622-4611
100 Main St Haviland (45851) ***(G-10713)***
Modern Retail Solutions LLC 330 527-4308
10421 Industrial Dr Garrettsville (44231) ***(G-10199)***
Modern Safety Techniques, Hicksville *Also called MST Inc* ***(G-10779)***
Modern Sheet Metal Works Inc 513 353-3666
6037 State Rte 128 Miamitown (45041) ***(G-13749)***
Modern Time Dealer, Uniontown *Also called Bobit Business Media Inc* ***(G-18912)***
Modern Tour, Cincinnati *Also called Modern Ice Equipment & Sup Co* ***(G-4038)***
Modern Welding Co Ohio Inc 740 344-9425
1 Modern Way Newark (43055) ***(G-14898)***
Modernfold, Youngstown *Also called W B Becherer Inc* ***(G-21068)***
Modroto 800 772-7659
4920 State Rd Ashtabula (44004) ***(G-787)***
Modular Assembly Innovations (PA) 614 389-4860
600 Stonehenge Pkwy # 100 Dublin (43017) ***(G-8947)***
Modular Security Systems Inc 740 532-7822
1804 N 2nd St Ironton (45638) ***(G-11169)***
Module 21 Bldg Company, Dayton *Also called M21 Industries LLC* ***(G-8319)***
Moeller Brew Barn LLC 419 925-3005
8595 Irwin St Maria Stein (45860) ***(G-12600)***
Mohawk Fine Papers Inc 440 969-2000
6800 Center Rd Ashtabula (44004) ***(G-788)***
Mohawk Industries Inc 800 837-3812
3565 Urbancrest Indus Dr Grove City (43123) ***(G-10447)***
Mohawk Manufacturing Inc 860 632-2345
306 E Gambier St Mount Vernon (43050) ***(G-14493)***
Mohican Industries Inc 330 869-0500
1225 W Market St Akron (44313) ***(G-284)***
Mohican Log Homes Inc 419 994-4088
2441 State Route 60 Loudonville (44842) ***(G-12144)***
Mohican Wood Products 740 599-5655
20460 Nunda Rd Butler (44822) ***(G-2377)***
Mohler Lumber Company 330 499-5461
4214 Portage St Nw North Canton (44720) ***(G-15102)***
Mojonnier Usa LLC 844 665-6664
10325 State Route 43 N Streetsboro (44241) ***(G-17684)***
Mok Industries LLC 614 934-1734
4449 Easton Way Columbus (43219) ***(G-7191)***
Mold Crafters Inc 937 426-3179
1531 Keystone Ave Dayton (45403) ***(G-8364)***
Mold Masters Intl Inc 440 953-0220
34000 Melinz Pkwy Eastlake (44095) ***(G-9123)***
Mold Shop Inc 419 829-2041
8520 Central Ave Sylvania (43560) ***(G-17951)***
Mold Solutions 800 948-4947
55 S Main St Ste 131 Oberlin (44074) ***(G-15502)***
Mold Surface Textures 330 678-8590
4485 Crystal Pkwy Ste 300 Kent (44240) ***(G-11357)***
Mold Tech, Painesville *Also called Xponet Inc* ***(G-15801)***
Mold-Rite Plastics LLC 330 405-7739
2300 Highland Rd Twinsburg (44087) ***(G-18821)***
Molded Extruded 216 475-5491
23940 Miles Rd Bedford Heights (44128) ***(G-1475)***
Molded Fiber Glass Companies (PA) 440 997-5851
2925 Mfg Pl Ashtabula (44004) ***(G-789)***
Molded Fiber Glass Companies 440 997-5851
4401 Benefit Ave Ashtabula (44004) ***(G-790)***
Molded Fiber Glass Research 440 994-5100
1315 W 47th St Ashtabula (44004) ***(G-791)***
Molded Parts Division, North Kingsville *Also called Premix Inc* ***(G-15160)***
Molders Choice Inc 440 248-8500
5380 Naiman Pkwy Ste E Solon (44139) ***(G-17197)***
Molders World Inc 513 469-6653
11471 Deerfield Rd Blue Ash (45242) ***(G-1823)***
Molding Dynamics Inc 440 786-8100
7009 Krick Rd Bedford (44146) ***(G-1427)***
Molding Machine Services Inc 330 461-2270
301 Lake Rd Medina (44256) ***(G-13303)***
Molding Technologies, Hebron *Also called MTI Acquisition LLC* ***(G-10755)***
Molding Technologies Ltd 740 929-2065
85 N High St Hebron (43025) ***(G-10752)***
Moldmakers Inc 419 673-0902
13608 Us Highway 68 Kenton (43326) ***(G-11414)***
Molecular Dimensions Inc 419 740-6600
434 W Dussel Dr Maumee (43537) ***(G-13137)***
Molecular Research Center (PA) 513 841-0900
5645 Montgomery Rd Cincinnati (45212) ***(G-4040)***
Molecular Theranostics LLC 216 595-1968
1768 E 25th St Ste 208 Cleveland (44114) ***(G-5701)***
Moleman 513 662-3017
1314 Pennsbury Dr Cincinnati (45238) ***(G-4041)***
Moleman Mole Trapping, Cincinnati *Also called Moleman* ***(G-4041)***
Mollard Conducting Batons Inc 330 659-7081
2236 N Clvland Msslon Rd Bath (44210) ***(G-1202)***
Molorokalin Inc (HQ) 330 629-1332
4137 Boardman Canfield Rd Ll04 Canfield (44406) ***(G-2537)***
Molten Metals, Middlefield *Also called Pckd Enterprises Inc* ***(G-13844)***
Molten Mtal Eqp Innvations LLC 440 632-9119
15510 Old State Rd Middlefield (44062) ***(G-13833)***
Molten North America Corp (HQ) 419 425-2700
1835 Industrial Dr Findlay (45840) ***(G-9728)***
MOM Tools LLC 216 283-4014
3659 Green Rd Ste 304 Cleveland (44122) ***(G-5702)***
Momentive Performance 281 325-3536
180 E Broad St Columbus (43215) ***(G-7192)***
Momentive Performance Mtls, Richmond Heights *Also called Momentive Performance Mtls Inc* ***(G-16503)***
Momentive Performance Mtls Inc 614 986-2495
180 E Broad St Columbus (43215) ***(G-7193)***
Momentive Performance Mtls Inc 740 928-7010
611 O Neill Dr Hebron (43025) ***(G-10753)***
Momentive Performance Mtls Inc 440 878-5705
24400 Highland Rd Richmond Heights (44143) ***(G-16503)***
Momentive Prfmce Mtls Qrtz Inc 440 878-5700
22557 Lunn Rd Strongsville (44149) ***(G-17765)***
Momentive Specialty Chem Inc 740 452-5451
2055 Grief Rd Zanesville (43701) ***(G-21158)***
Moments To Remember USA LLC 330 830-0839
1250 Sanders Ave Sw Massillon (44647) ***(G-13027)***
Momentum Technologies Intl, Uniontown *Also called Alan L Grant Polymer Inc* ***(G-18908)***
Mon-Say Corp 419 720-0163
2735 Dorr St Toledo (43607) ***(G-18415)***
Monaghan & Associates Inc 937 253-7706
30 N Clinton St Dayton (45402) ***(G-8365)***
Monaghan Tooling Group, Dayton *Also called Monaghan & Associates Inc* ***(G-8365)***
Monarch, Cleveland *Also called Integrated Power Services LLC* ***(G-5463)***
Monarch Engraving Inc 440 638-1500
8293 Dow Cir Strongsville (44136) ***(G-17766)***
Monarch Lathes LP 937 492-4111
615 Oak Ave Sidney (45365) ***(G-17056)***
Monarch Products Co 330 868-7717
105 Short St Minerva (44657) ***(G-14195)***
Monarch Steel Company Inc 216 587-8000
4650 Johnston Pkwy Cleveland (44128) ***(G-5703)***
Monarch Water Systems Inc 937 426-5773
689 Greystone Dr Beavercreek (45434) ***(G-1333)***
Monco Enterprises Inc (PA) 937 461-0034
700 Liberty Ln Dayton (45449) ***(G-8366)***
Mondelez Global LLC 419 691-5200
2221 Front St Toledo (43605) ***(G-18416)***
Mondo Polymer Technologies Inc 740 376-9396
27620 State Rte 7 Reno (45773) ***(G-16425)***
Money Jewelry Vaults 937 366-6391
236 E Sugartree St Wilmington (45177) ***(G-20500)***
Monitored Therapeutics Inc 614 761-3555
6543 Commerce Pkwy Ste A Dublin (43017) ***(G-8948)***
Monitortech Corp 614 231-0500
661 N James Rd Columbus (43219) ***(G-7194)***
Monnig Welding Co 513 241-5156
521 Harriet St Cincinnati (45203) ***(G-4042)***
Monode Marking Products Inc (PA) 440 975-8802
9200 Tyler Blvd Mentor (44060) ***(G-13522)***
Monode Marking Products Inc 419 929-0346
149 High St New London (44851) ***(G-14731)***
Monode Steel Stamp Inc (PA) 419 929-3501
149 High St New London (44851) ***(G-14732)***
Monode Steel Stamp Inc 440 975-8802
7620 Tyler Blvd Mentor (44060) ***(G-13523)***
Monovision Machine 330 833-2146
125 Walnut Rd Se Massillon (44646) ***(G-13028)***
Monroe County Beacon Inc 740 472-0734
103 E Court St Woodsfield (43793) ***(G-20547)***
Monroe Drilling Operations 740 472-0866
46886 Moore Ridge Rd Woodsfield (43793) ***(G-20548)***
Monroe Tool and Mfg Co 216 883-7360
3900 E 93rd St Cleveland (44105) ***(G-5704)***
Monroe Water Sys Treatmnt Plnt, Sardis *Also called Monroe Water System* ***(G-16876)***
Monroe Water System 740 472-1030
35100 State Route 7 Sardis (43946) ***(G-16876)***
Monsanto Company 937 548-7858
1051 Landsdowne Ave Greenville (45331) ***(G-10384)***
Montgomery & Montgomery LLC 330 858-9533
80 N Pershing Ave Akron (44313) ***(G-285)***
Montgomery License Bureau, Cincinnati *Also called D J Klingler Inc* ***(G-3570)***
Montgomery Mch & Fabrication 740 286-2863
206 Watts Blevins Rd Jackson (45640) ***(G-11191)***
Montgomerys Pallet Service 330 297-6677
7937 State Route 44 Ravenna (44266) ***(G-16390)***

ALPHABETIC

Monti Incorporated (PA)...513 761-7775
4510 Reading Rd Cincinnati (45229) ***(G-4043)***
Montview Corporation...330 723-3409
404 W Liberty St Medina (44256) ***(G-13304)***
Montville Plastics & Rbr LLC...440 548-3211
15567 Main Market Rd Parkman (44080) ***(G-15812)***
Moo Technologies Inc...513 732-5805
950 Kent Rd Batavia (45103) ***(G-1169)***
Moog Inc...330 682-0010
1701 N Main St Orrville (44667) ***(G-15603)***
Moonlight Specialties...216 464-6444
4555 Renaissance Pkwy # 105 Cleveland (44128) ***(G-5705)***
Moonlighting...330 533-3324
8627 Gibson Rd Canfield (44406) ***(G-2538)***
Moonshine Screen Printing Inc...513 523-7775
23 N College Ave Oxford (45056) ***(G-15697)***
Moonstruck Games Inc...513 721-3900
312 Walnut St Ste 2275 Cincinnati (45202) ***(G-4044)***
Moorchild LLC...513 649-8867
6 S Broad St Middletown (45044) ***(G-13931)***
Moore Mc Millen Holdings...330 745-3075
1850 Front St Cuyahoga Falls (44221) ***(G-7899)***
Moore Chrome Products Co...419 843-3510
3525 Silica Rd Sylvania (43560) ***(G-17952)***
Moore Industries Inc...419 485-5572
1317 Henricks Dr Montpelier (43543) ***(G-14313)***
Moore Metal Finishing, Sylvania *Also called Moore Chrome Products Co* ***(G-17952)***
Moore Mr Specialty Company...330 332-1229
1050 Pennsylvania Ave Salem (44460) ***(G-16763)***
Moore Outdoor Sign Craftsman, Westerville *Also called Ohio Shelterall Inc* ***(G-20068)***
Moore Well Services Inc...330 650-4443
246 N Cleveland Ave Mogadore (44260) ***(G-14244)***
Moosehead Cigar Company Llc...513 266-7207
5180 Potomac Dr Fairfield (45014) ***(G-9530)***
Mopac, Marion *Also called Mid Ohio Packaging LLC* ***(G-12719)***
Mor-Lite Co Inc...513 661-8587
2344 Wyoming Ave Cincinnati (45214) ***(G-4045)***
Mor-X Plastics, Youngstown *Also called Jamen Tool & Die Co* ***(G-20946)***
Moran Tool Inc...937 526-5210
261 Baker Rd Versailles (45380) ***(G-19188)***
Morcast Precision Inc...614 258-5071
1615 Woodland Ave Columbus (43219) ***(G-7195)***
More Manufacturing LLC...937 233-3898
4025 Lisa Dr Ste A Tipp City (45371) ***(G-18123)***
More Than Gourmet Inc...330 762-6652
929 Home Ave Akron (44310) ***(G-286)***
Morehouse Welding, Milford *Also called James G Morehouse* ***(G-14020)***
Morel Landscaping LLC...216 551-4395
3684 Forest Run Dr Richfield (44286) ***(G-16476)***
Morey Woodworking LLC...937 623-5280
377 E Loy Rd Piqua (45356) ***(G-16144)***
Morgal Machine Tool Co...937 325-5561
2100 S Yellow Springs St Springfield (45506) ***(G-17451)***
Morgan Adhesives Company LLC (HQ)...330 688-1111
4560 Darrow Rd Stow (44224) ***(G-17606)***
Morgan Advanced Ceramics Inc...440 232-8604
232 Forbes Rd Bedford (44146) ***(G-1428)***
Morgan Advanced Ceramics Inc...330 405-1033
2181 Pinnacle Pkwy Twinsburg (44087) ***(G-18822)***
Morgan Advanced Materials, Bedford *Also called Morgan Advanced Ceramics Inc* ***(G-1428)***
Morgan Advanced Materials, Twinsburg *Also called Morgan Advanced Ceramics Inc* ***(G-18822)***
Morgan Advanced Materials...419 435-8182
200 N Town St Fostoria (44830) ***(G-9849)***
Morgan County Herald, McConnelsville *Also called Morgan County Publishing Co* ***(G-13209)***
Morgan County Publishing Co...740 962-3377
89 W Main St McConnelsville (43756) ***(G-13209)***
Morgan Engineering Systems Inc...330 823-6120
1049 S Mahoning Ave Alliance (44601) ***(G-490)***
Morgan Engineering Systems Inc...330 821-4721
1182 E Summit St Alliance (44601) ***(G-491)***
Morgan Litho, Cleveland *Also called T D Dynamics Inc* ***(G-6143)***
Morgan Precision Instrs LLC...330 896-0846
3375 Miller Park Rd Akron (44312) ***(G-287)***
Morgan Wood Products Inc...614 336-4000
9761 Fairway Dr Powell (43065) ***(G-16330)***
Mori Shuji...614 459-1296
3755 Mountview Rd Columbus (43220) ***(G-7196)***
Moritz Concrete Inc...419 529-3232
362 N Trimble Rd Mansfield (44906) ***(G-12486)***
Moritz International Inc...419 526-5222
665 N Main St Mansfield (44902) ***(G-12487)***
Moritz Materials Inc (PA)...419 281-0575
859 Faultless Dr Ashland (44805) ***(G-726)***
Mork Process Inc...330 928-3700
400 W Wilson Bridge Rd # 130 Worthington (43085) ***(G-20698)***
Morlan & Associates Inc (PA)...614 889-6152
4970 Scioto Darby Rd D Hilliard (43026) ***(G-10842)***
Morlock Asphalt Ltd...419 686-4601
9362 Mermill Rd Portage (43451) ***(G-16271)***
Morning Glory Technologies...440 796-5076
12826 Morning Glory Trl Chesterland (44026) ***(G-3165)***
Morning Journal, Lisbon *Also called Ogden Newspapers Ohio Inc* ***(G-11976)***
Morning Journal, Lorain *Also called Journal Register Company* ***(G-12096)***
Morning Pride Mfg LLC (HQ)...937 264-2662
1 Innovation Ct Dayton (45414) ***(G-8367)***
Morning Pride Mfg LLC...937 264-1726
4978 Riverton Dr Dayton (45414) ***(G-8368)***
Morning Sun Technologies Inc...513 461-1417
7191 Morning Sun Rd Oxford (45056) ***(G-15698)***
Morris Bean & Company...937 767-7301
777 E Hyde Rd Yellow Springs (45387) ***(G-20812)***
Morris Clean It N Sweep Clean...513 200-8222
327 Crestline Ave Cincinnati (45205) ***(G-4046)***
Morris Maico Hearing Aid Svc...419 232-6200
117 N Washington St Van Wert (45891) ***(G-19103)***
Morris Material Handling, Springfield *Also called Mmh Holdings Inc* ***(G-17450)***
Morris Material Handling Inc (HQ)...937 525-5520
4401 Gateway Blvd Springfield (45502) ***(G-17452)***
Morris Technologies, Cincinnati *Also called GE Aviation Systems LLC* ***(G-3734)***
Morris Technologies...330 384-3084
1741 S Main St Akron (44301) ***(G-288)***
Morris Technologies Inc...513 733-1611
11988 Tramway Dr Cincinnati (45241) ***(G-4047)***
Morrison Custom Welding, Wooster *Also called Iron Gate Industries LLC* ***(G-20608)***
Morrison Media Group-Cmj LLP...216 973-4005
11800 Shaker Blvd Cleveland (44120) ***(G-5706)***
Morrison Medical...614 461-4400
3735 Paragon Dr Columbus (43228) ***(G-7197)***
Morrison Sign Company Inc...614 276-1181
2757 Scioto Pkwy Columbus (43221) ***(G-7198)***
Morrow Gravel, Morrow *Also called Valley Asphalt Corporation* ***(G-14416)***
Morrow Gravel Company Inc...513 899-2000
4850 Stubbs Mills Rd Morrow (45152) ***(G-14413)***
Morrow Gravel Company Inc (PA)...513 771-0820
11641 Mosteller Rd Cincinnati (45241) ***(G-4048)***
Morse Enterprises Inc...513 229-3600
6678 Tri Way Dr Mason (45040) ***(G-12912)***
Morselicious Cupcakes...216 408-7508
17341 Independence Ct Brookpark (44142) ***(G-2152)***
Morton Buildings Inc...330 345-6188
1055 Columbus Avenue Ext Wooster (44691) ***(G-20628)***
Morton Buildings Inc...419 399-4549
1099 N Williams St Paulding (45879) ***(G-15866)***
Morton Buildings Inc...419 675-2311
14483 State Route 31 Kenton (43326) ***(G-11415)***
Morton Buildings Plant, Kenton *Also called Morton Buildings Inc* ***(G-11415)***
Morton International LLC...513 941-1578
5340 River Rd Cincinnati (45233) ***(G-4049)***
Morton Salt, Cincinnati *Also called Morton International LLC* ***(G-4049)***
Morton Salt Inc...440 354-9901
570 Headlands Rd Painesville (44077) ***(G-15764)***
Morton Salt Inc...330 925-3015
151 Industrial Ave Rittman (44270) ***(G-16526)***
Mos International Inc...330 329-0905
3213 Peterboro Dr Stow (44224) ***(G-17607)***
Mosbro Machine and Tool Inc...330 467-0913
8135 Crystal Creek Rd Northfield (44067) ***(G-15320)***
Moser Leather Company, Hamilton *Also called Old West Industries Inc* ***(G-10592)***
Mosher Machine & Tool Co Inc...937 258-8070
1420 Springfield St Dayton (45403) ***(G-8369)***
Mosher Medical Inc...330 668-2252
150 Springside Dr 220b Akron (44333) ***(G-289)***
Moss Vale Inc...513 939-1970
160 Donald Dr B Fairfield (45014) ***(G-9531)***
Mosser Glass Incorporated...740 439-1827
9279 Cadiz Rd Cambridge (43725) ***(G-2449)***
Mossing Machine and Tool...419 476-5657
5225 Telegraph Rd Toledo (43612) ***(G-18417)***
Motion Mobility & Design Inc...330 244-9723
6490 Promler St Nw North Canton (44720) ***(G-15103)***
Motionsource International LLC...440 287-7037
31200 Solon Rd Ste 7 Solon (44139) ***(G-17198)***
Moto Photo, Shaker Heights *Also called SMS Communications Inc* ***(G-16937)***
Moto-Electric Inc...419 668-7894
262 Cleveland Rd Norwalk (44857) ***(G-15406)***
Motor Systems Incorporated...513 576-1725
460 Milford Pkwy Milford (45150) ***(G-14029)***
Motorcarbon Elements LLC...304 617-4047
600 Technology Dr South Point (45680) ***(G-17290)***
Motorkote & Dura Lube, Gahanna *Also called Into Great Brands Inc* ***(G-10085)***
Motors & Drives Division, Cincinnati *Also called Siemens Industry Inc* ***(G-4334)***
Motrin Corporation...740 439-2725
1070 Byesville Rd Cambridge (43725) ***(G-2450)***
Motts Oils & More...330 601-1645
137 W Liberty St Wooster (44691) ***(G-20629)***

Motz Mobile Containers Inc..........513 772-6689
3153 Madison Rd Apt 1 Cincinnati (45209) ***(G-4050)***
Mound Laser Photonics Center, Kettering *Also called Resonetics LLC* ***(G-11440)***
Mound Manufacturing Center Inc..........937 236-8387
33 Commerce Park Dr Dayton (45404) ***(G-8370)***
Mound Printing Company Inc..........937 866-2872
2455 Belvo Rd Miamisburg (45342) ***(G-13696)***
Mound Steel Corp..........937 748-2937
25 Mound Park Dr Springboro (45066) ***(G-17337)***
Mound Technologies Inc..........937 748-2937
25 Mound Park Dr Springboro (45066) ***(G-17338)***
Mount Eaton Division, Mount Eaton *Also called Flex Technologies Inc* ***(G-14420)***
Mount Hope Harness & Shoe, Mount Hope *Also called Ervin Yoder* ***(G-14436)***
Mount Hope Planing..........330 359-0538
7598 Tr652 Millersburg (44654) ***(G-14115)***
Mount Union Pattern Works Inc..........330 821-2274
920 Auld St Alliance (44601) ***(G-492)***
Mount Vernon News, Mount Vernon *Also called Progressive Communications* ***(G-14503)***
Mount Vernon Packaging Inc..........740 397-3221
135 Progress Dr Mount Vernon (43050) ***(G-14494)***
Mountain Filtration Systems..........419 395-2526
26705 Blanchard Rd Defiance (43512) ***(G-8640)***
Mountain Top Frozen Pies Div, Columbus *Also called Quality Bakery Company Inc* ***(G-7364)***
Mountaineer Mining Corp..........740 418-1817
885 Sternberger Rd Jackson (45640) ***(G-11192)***
Mowhawk Lumber Ltd..........330 698-5333
2931 S Carr Rd Apple Creek (44606) ***(G-615)***
Moyer Vineyards Inc..........937 549-2957
3859 Us Highway 52 Manchester (45144) ***(G-12395)***
Moyer Winery & Restaurant, Manchester *Also called Moyer Vineyards Inc* ***(G-12395)***
Moyno, Springfield *Also called Robbins & Myers Inc* ***(G-17487)***
Mp Biomedicals LLC..........440 337-1200
29525 Fountain Pkwy Solon (44139) ***(G-17199)***
Mp Printing & Design Inc..........740 456-2045
4302 Gallia St Portsmouth (45662) ***(G-16292)***
Mpc Inc..........440 835-1405
5350 Tradex Pkwy Cleveland (44102) ***(G-5707)***
MPC Plastics Inc..........216 881-7220
1859 E 63rd St Cleveland (44103) ***(G-5708)***
MPC Plating LLC (PA)..........216 881-7220
1859 E 63rd St Cleveland (44103) ***(G-5709)***
MPC Plating LLC..........216 881-7220
1859 E 63rd St Cleveland (44103) ***(G-5710)***
Mpe Aeroengines Inc (HQ)..........937 878-3800
7700 New Carlisle Pike Huber Heights (45424) ***(G-11022)***
Mpi Label Systems., Sebring *Also called Mpi Labels of Baltimore Inc* ***(G-16890)***
Mpi Labels of Baltimore Inc (HQ)..........330 938-2134
450 Courtney Rd Sebring (44672) ***(G-16890)***
Mplx Terminals LLC..........330 479-5539
2408 Gambrinus Ave Sw Canton (44706) ***(G-2757)***
MPS Manufacturing Company LLC..........330 343-1435
326 Pearl Ave Ne New Philadelphia (44663) ***(G-14788)***
MPW Industrial Svcs Group Inc (PA)..........740 927-8790
9711 Lancaster Rd Hebron (43025) ***(G-10754)***
Mr 14k Inc..........440 234-6661
370 W Bagley Rd Berea (44017) ***(G-1618)***
Mr Box, Mansfield *Also called Skybox Packaging LLC* ***(G-12515)***
Mr Direct, Inc., Toledo *Also called Elkay Plumbing Products Co* ***(G-18281)***
Mr Electric..........419 289-7474
24 Bell St Mansfield (44906) ***(G-12488)***
Mr Emblem Inc..........419 697-1888
3209 Navarre Ave Oregon (43616) ***(G-15561)***
Mr Heater, Cleveland *Also called Enerco Group Inc* ***(G-5177)***
Mr Heater Inc..........216 916-3000
4560 W 160th St Cleveland (44135) ***(G-5711)***
Mr Label Inc..........513 681-2088
5018 Gray Rd Cincinnati (45232) ***(G-4051)***
Mr Neon Sign, Canton *Also called Rossi Concept Arts* ***(G-2811)***
Mr Trailer Sales Inc..........330 339-7701
1565 Steele Hill Rd Nw New Philadelphia (44663) ***(G-14789)***
MR&e Ltd..........419 872-8180
3146 W Lincolnshire Blvd Toledo (43606) ***(G-18418)***
Mr. Heater, Cleveland *Also called Enerco Technical Products Inc* ***(G-5178)***
MRC, Cincinnati *Also called Molecular Research Center* ***(G-4040)***
MRC Global (us) Inc..........614 475-4033
700 Taylor Rd Gahanna (43230) ***(G-10092)***
Mrd Solutions LLC..........440 942-6969
34201 Melinz Pkwy Unit A Eastlake (44095) ***(G-9124)***
Mrdd Solutions, Wauseon *Also called Interactive Fincl Solutions* ***(G-19521)***
Mro Built Inc..........330 526-0555
6410 Promway Ave Nw North Canton (44720) ***(G-15104)***
Mrpicker..........440 354-6497
595 Miner Rd Cleveland (44143) ***(G-5712)***
Mrs Electronic Inc..........937 660-6767
2149 Winners Cir Dayton (45404) ***(G-8371)***
MRS Industrial Inc..........614 308-1070
2583 Harrison Rd Columbus (43204) ***(G-7199)***
Mrs Mllers Hmmade Noodles Ltd..........330 694-5814
9140 County Road 192 Fredericksburg (44627) ***(G-9954)***
Mrs Turbos Cookies, Columbus *Also called Turbos FBC LLC* ***(G-7550)***
MSC Walbridge Coatings Inc..........419 666-6130
30610 E Broadway St Walbridge (43465) ***(G-19297)***
Msd Products Inc..........440 946-0040
7842 Enterprise Dr Mentor (44060) ***(G-13524)***
Msg Premier Molded Fiber, Ashtabula *Also called Molded Fiber Glass Companies* ***(G-790)***
MSI, Chesterland *Also called Metzenbaum Sheltered Inds Inc* ***(G-3164)***
MSI, Milford *Also called Motor Systems Incorporated* ***(G-14029)***
Msk Trencher Mfg Inc..........419 394-4444
7219 Harris Rd Celina (45822) ***(G-2977)***
Msls Group LLC..........330 723-4431
1080 Industrial Pkwy Medina (44256) ***(G-13305)***
Mssi, Ironton *Also called Modular Security Systems Inc* ***(G-11169)***
MST, Kent *Also called Mold Surface Textures* ***(G-11357)***
MST Inc..........419 542-6645
11370 Breininger Rd Hicksville (43526) ***(G-10779)***
Mt Carmel Brewing Company..........513 519-7161
4362 Mt Carmel Tobasco Rd Cincinnati (45244) ***(G-4052)***
Mt Eaton Pallet Ltd..........330 893-2986
4761 County Road 207 Millersburg (44654) ***(G-14116)***
Mt Perry Foods Inc..........740 743-3890
5705 State Route 204 Ne Mount Perry (43760) ***(G-14456)***
Mt Pleasant Blacktopping Inc..........513 874-3777
3199 Production Dr Fairfield (45014) ***(G-9532)***
Mt Pleasant Pharmacy LLC..........216 672-4377
631 Lee Rd Apt 1228 Bedford (44146) ***(G-1429)***
Mt Vernon Cy Wastewater Trtmnt..........740 393-9502
3 Cougar Dr Unit 3 # 3 Mount Vernon (43050) ***(G-14495)***
Mtd Consumer Group Inc (HQ)..........330 225-2600
5965 Grafton Rd Valley City (44280) ***(G-19051)***
Mtd Consumer Products Supply, Valley City *Also called Mtd Products Inc* ***(G-19055)***
Mtd Holdings Inc (PA)..........330 225-2600
5965 Grafton Rd Valley City (44280) ***(G-19052)***
Mtd Products Inc (HQ)..........330 225-2600
5965 Grafton Rd Valley City (44280) ***(G-19053)***
Mtd Products Inc..........419 935-6611
979 S Conwell Ave Willard (44890) ***(G-20242)***
Mtd Products Inc..........330 225-9127
680 Liverpool Dr Valley City (44280) ***(G-19054)***
Mtd Products Inc..........419 342-6455
305 Mansfield Ave Shelby (44875) ***(G-16984)***
Mtd Products Inc..........330 225-1940
5903 Grafton Rd Valley City (44280) ***(G-19055)***
MTI Acquisition LLC..........740 929-2065
85 N High St Hebron (43025) ***(G-10755)***
Mto Suncoke, Middletown *Also called Suncoke Energy Nc* ***(G-13955)***
Mtr Martco LLC..........513 424-5307
3350 Yankee Rd Middletown (45044) ***(G-13932)***
MTS Enterprises LLC..........937 324-7510
1330 Perry St Springfield (45504) ***(G-17453)***
MTS Medication Tech Inc..........440 238-0840
21550 Drake Rd Strongsville (44149) ***(G-17767)***
Mudbrook Golf Center..........419 433-2945
1609 Mudbrook Rd Huron (44839) ***(G-11105)***
Muehlenkamp Properties Inc..........513 745-0874
4317 Kugler Mill Rd Cincinnati (45236) ***(G-4053)***
Mueller Art Cover & Binding Co..........440 238-3303
12005 Alameda Dr Strongsville (44149) ***(G-17768)***
Mueller Color, Blue Ash *Also called Superior Printing Ink Co Inc* ***(G-1855)***
Mueller Electric Company Inc..........614 888-8855
7795 Walton Pkwy Ste 175 New Albany (43054) ***(G-14631)***
Mueller Electric Company Inc..........216 771-5225
2850 Gilchrist Rd Ste 5 Akron (44305) ***(G-290)***
Mueller Gas Products..........513 424-5311
1800 Clayton Ave Middletown (45042) ***(G-13933)***
Muir Graphics Inc..........419 882-7993
5454 Alger Dr Ste A Sylvania (43560) ***(G-17953)***
Muirfield Wine Company LLC..........614 799-9222
7154 Muirfield Dr Dublin (43017) ***(G-8949)***
Mulch Madness LLC..........330 920-9900
8022 S Riverside Dr Aurora (44202) ***(G-893)***
Mulch Man..........937 866-5370
4595 Fairpark Ave Dayton (45431) ***(G-7987)***
Mulch Man Greenline Products, Dayton *Also called Mulch Man* ***(G-7987)***
Mulch Masters of Ohio, Miamisburg *Also called Gayston Corporation* ***(G-13672)***
Mulch World..........419 873-6852
8232 Fremont Pike Perrysburg (43551) ***(G-15978)***
Mulhern Belting Inc..........201 337-5700
310 Osborne Dr Fairfield (45014) ***(G-9533)***
Mull Iron, Rittman *Also called Rittman Inc* ***(G-16528)***
Muller Engine & Machine Co..........937 322-1861
1414 S Yellow Springs St Springfield (45506) ***(G-17454)***
Muller Pipe Organ Co..........740 893-1700
122 N High St Croton (43013) ***(G-7821)***
Muller Pipe Organ Company, Croton *Also called Muller Pipe Organ Co* ***(G-7821)***

ALPHABETIC

Mullet Enterprises Inc (PA)..........330 852-4681
138 2nd St Nw Sugarcreek (44681) ***(G-17855)***
Mullet Enterprises Inc..........330 897-3911
28003 Adams Twp Rd 101 Bakersville (43803) ***(G-1021)***
Mullin Print Solutions..........216 383-2901
84 E 197th St Euclid (44119) ***(G-9428)***
Mullins Rubber Products Inc..........937 233-4211
2949 Valley Pike Dayton (45404) ***(G-8372)***
Multi Cast LLC..........419 335-0010
225 E Linfoot St Wauseon (43567) ***(G-19528)***
Multi Form Mfg..........330 922-1933
4278 Hudson Dr Stow (44224) ***(G-17608)***
Multi Galvanizing LLC..........330 453-1441
825 Navarre Rd Sw Canton (44707) ***(G-2758)***
Multi Lapping Service Inc..........440 944-7592
30032 Lakeland Bvld Wickliffe (44092) ***(G-20218)***
Multi Products Company..........330 674-5981
7188 State Route 39 Millersburg (44654) ***(G-14117)***
Multi Radiance Medical, Solon *Also called Medical Quant USA Inc* ***(G-17189)***
Multi-Color, Batavia *Also called Verstraete In Mold Lab* ***(G-1195)***
Multi-Color, Mason *Also called Spear USA Inc* ***(G-12941)***
Multi-Color Australia LLC..........513 381-1480
4053 Clough Woods Dr Batavia (45103) ***(G-1170)***
Multi-Color Corporation..........513 459-3283
5510 Courseview Dr Mason (45040) ***(G-12913)***
Multi-Color Corporation..........513 396-5600
4500 Beech St Cincinnati (45212) ***(G-4054)***
Multi-Color Corporation (PA)..........513 381-1480
4053 Clough Woods Dr Batavia (45103) ***(G-1171)***
Multi-Color Corporation..........513 943-0080
4053 Clough Woods Dr Batavia (45103) ***(G-1172)***
Multi-Craft Litho Inc..........859 581-2754
4440 Creek Rd Blue Ash (45242) ***(G-1824)***
Multi-Design Inc..........440 275-2255
2844 Industrial Park Dr Austinburg (44010) ***(G-923)***
Multi-Form Plastics, Batavia *Also called Plastikos Corporation* ***(G-1176)***
Multi-Wing America Inc..........440 834-9400
15030 Brkshire Indus Pkwy Middlefield (44062) ***(G-13834)***
Multibase Inc..........330 666-0505
3835 Copley Rd Copley (44321) ***(G-7689)***
Multicorr Corp..........502 935-1000
425 Winter Rd Delaware (43015) ***(G-8707)***
Multifab, Elyria *Also called Multilink Inc* ***(G-9298)***
Multilink Inc..........440 366-6966
580 Ternes Ln Elyria (44035) ***(G-9298)***
Multiplast Systems Inc..........440 349-0800
33355 Station St Solon (44139) ***(G-17200)***
Multiple Products Company, Cleveland *Also called Kg63 LLC* ***(G-5533)***
Multipress Inc..........614 228-0185
1250 Refugee Ln Columbus (43207) ***(G-7200)***
Mum Industries Inc..........440 269-4966
8989 Tyler Blvd Mentor (44060) ***(G-13525)***
Mumfords Potato Chips & Deli..........937 653-3491
325 N Main St Urbana (43078) ***(G-19005)***
Muncy Co, The, Springfield *Also called E & W Enterprises Powell Inc* ***(G-17393)***
Municipal Brew Works LLC..........513 889-8369
306 Ashley Brook Dr Hamilton (45013) ***(G-10588)***
Municipal Signs and Sales Inc..........330 457-2421
1219 Mcclosky Rd Columbiana (44408) ***(G-6474)***
Munroe Incorporated..........330 755-7216
25 Union St Struthers (44471) ***(G-17821)***
Munson Machine Company Inc..........740 967-6867
80 E College Ave Johnstown (43031) ***(G-11270)***
Munson Sales & Engineering..........216 496-5436
13260 Crows Hollow Dr Chardon (44024) ***(G-3126)***
Murdock Inc..........513 471-7700
7180 Anderson Woods Dr Cincinnati (45244) ***(G-4055)***
Murotech Ohio Corporation..........419 394-6529
550 Mckinley Rd Saint Marys (45885) ***(G-16690)***
Murphy Industries Inc..........740 387-7890
1650 Cascade Dr Marion (43302) ***(G-12722)***
Murphy James Construction LLC..........740 667-3626
4146 N Torch Rd Coolville (45723) ***(G-7675)***
Murphy Tractor & Eqp Co Inc..........614 876-1141
2121 Walcutt Rd Columbus (43228) ***(G-7201)***
Murphy Tractor & Eqp Co Inc..........937 898-4198
1015 Industrial Park Dr Vandalia (45377) ***(G-19140)***
Murphy Tractor & Eqp Co Inc..........419 221-3666
3550 Saint Johns Rd Lima (45804) ***(G-11909)***
Murphy Tractor & Eqp Co Inc..........330 477-9304
1509 Raff Rd Sw Canton (44710) ***(G-2759)***
Murphy Tractor & Eqp Co Inc..........330 220-4999
1240 Industrial Rd Pkwy N Brunswick (44212) ***(G-2221)***
Murphy's Landing Casual Dining, Middletown *Also called Moorchild LLC* ***(G-13931)***
Murr Corporation..........330 264-2223
201 N Buckeye St Wooster (44691) ***(G-20630)***
Murr Printing and Graphics, Wooster *Also called Murr Corporation* ***(G-20630)***
Murray American Energy Inc..........740 338-3100
46226 National Rd Saint Clairsville (43950) ***(G-16638)***
Murray Display Fixtures Ltd..........614 875-1594
2300 Southwest Blvd Grove City (43123) ***(G-10448)***
Murray Energy Corporation (PA)..........740 338-3100
46226 National Rd Saint Clairsville (43950) ***(G-16639)***
Murray Fabrics Inc (PA)..........216 881-4041
837 E 79th St Cleveland (44103) ***(G-5713)***
Murray Kentucky Energy Inc (HQ)..........740 338-3100
46226 National Rd Saint Clairsville (43950) ***(G-16640)***
Murray Machine & Tool Inc..........216 267-1126
17801 Sheldon Rd Side Cleveland (44130) ***(G-5714)***
Murrubber Technologies Inc..........330 688-4881
1350 Commerce Dr Stow (44224) ***(G-17609)***
Muscle Feast LLC (PA)..........740 877-8808
1320 Boston Rd Nashport (43830) ***(G-14568)***
Music Systems, North Olmsted *Also called Q Music USA LLC* ***(G-15196)***
Musicmax Inc..........614 732-0777
1517 Hess St Ste 200 Columbus (43212) ***(G-7202)***
Musicol Inc..........614 267-3133
780 Oakland Park Ave Columbus (43224) ***(G-7203)***
Muskingum Grinding & Mch Co..........740 622-4741
2155 Otsego Ave Coshocton (43812) ***(G-7741)***
Mustang Aerial Services Inc..........740 373-9262
27620 State Route 7 Reno (45773) ***(G-16426)***
Mustang Dynamometer, Twinsburg *Also called Ganzcorp Investments Inc* ***(G-18778)***
Mustang Printing, Wauseon *Also called Tomahawk Printing LLC* ***(G-19534)***
Mustang Printing..........419 592-2746
119 W Washington St Napoleon (43545) ***(G-14551)***
Mustard Seed Health Fd Mkt Inc..........440 519-3663
6025 Kruse Dr Ste 100 Solon (44139) ***(G-17201)***
Mutual Tool LLC..........937 667-5818
1350 Commerce Park Dr Tipp City (45371) ***(G-18124)***
Mv Designlabs LLC..........724 355-7986
17138 Lorain Ave Ste 201 Cleveland (44111) ***(G-5715)***
Mv Group Inc..........419 776-1133
303 Morris St Toledo (43604) ***(G-18419)***
Mv Innovative Technologies LLC..........301 661-0951
711 E Monu Ave Ste 102 Dayton (45402) ***(G-8373)***
Mveca, Yellow Springs *Also called Miami Valley Eductl Cmpt Assn* ***(G-20811)***
Mvp Pharmacy..........614 449-8000
1931 Parsons Ave Columbus (43207) ***(G-7204)***
Mvp Plastics Inc (PA)..........440 834-1790
15005 Enterprise Way Middlefield (44062) ***(G-13835)***
MWC Publishing Co, Dayton *Also called Dayton Weekly News* ***(G-8147)***
Mx Spring Inc..........330 426-4600
39 Wilderson Ave East Palestine (44413) ***(G-9081)***
My Catered Table LLC..........614 882-7323
1871 N High St Columbus (43210) ***(G-7205)***
My Floors By Prints and Paints, Galion *Also called Prints & Paints Flr Cvg Co Inc* ***(G-10151)***
My Lady Muffins LLC..........937 854-5317
2475 N Snyder Rd Dayton (45426) ***(G-8374)***
My Second Home Early Lrng Schl, Marysville *Also called New Republic Industries LLC* ***(G-12803)***
My Way Home Finder Magazine..........419 841-6201
5215 Monroe St Ste 14 Toledo (43623) ***(G-18420)***
Myairplane.com, Cardington *Also called 3gc LLC* ***(G-2869)***
Mye Automotive Inc..........330 253-5592
1293 S Main St Akron (44301) ***(G-291)***
Myers and Lasch Inc..........440 235-2050
8026 Columbia Rd Cleveland (44138) ***(G-5716)***
Myers Controlled Power LLC (HQ)..........330 834-3200
219 E Maple St 100-200e North Canton (44720) ***(G-15105)***
Myers Controlled Power LLC..........909 923-1800
133 Taft Ave Ne Canton (44720) ***(G-2760)***
Myers Industries Inc (PA)..........330 253-5592
1293 S Main St Akron (44301) ***(G-292)***
Myers Industries Inc..........440 632-1006
15150 Madison Rd Middlefield (44062) ***(G-13836)***
Myers Industries Inc..........330 336-6621
250 Seville Rd Wadsworth (44281) ***(G-19255)***
Myers Industries Inc..........330 253-5592
1293 S Main St Akron (44301) ***(G-293)***
Myers Machining Inc..........330 874-3005
11789 Strasburg Bolivar Bolivar (44612) ***(G-1918)***
Myers Motors LLC..........330 630-7000
180 South Ave Tallmadge (44278) ***(G-17994)***
Myko Industries..........216 431-0900
896 E 70th St Cleveland (44103) ***(G-5717)***
Myrlen, Cincinnati *Also called Ep Bollinger LLC* ***(G-3646)***
Myron D Budd..........330 682-5866
480 S Crown Hill Rd Orrville (44667) ***(G-15604)***
Mysta Equipment Co..........330 879-5353
6434 Werstler Ave Sw Navarre (44662) ***(G-14581)***
Mystic Chemical Products Co..........216 251-4416
3561 W 105th St Cleveland (44111) ***(G-5718)***
Mytee Products Inc..........440 591-4301
1335 S Chillicothe Rd Aurora (44202) ***(G-894)***
N & N Oil..........740 743-2848
6111 State Route 13 Ne Somerset (43783) ***(G-17265)***

N & W Machining & Fabricating 937 695-5582
8 Mathias Rd Winchester (45697) *(G-20523)*
N A C, Findlay *Also called Nichidai America Corporation (G-9730)*
N A D, Cincinnati *Also called National Access Design LLC (G-4058)*
N Bass Bait Co 419 647-4501
08780 Deep Cut Rd Spencerville (45887) *(G-17310)*
N C W Nicoloff Cab Works LLC 513 821-1400
3200 Profit Dr Fairfield (45014) *(G-9534)*
N E C Columbus, Columbus *Also called National Electric Coil Inc (G-7209)*
N F M, Massillon *Also called Nfm/Welding Engineers Inc (G-13029)*
N G C, North Royalton *Also called Next Gerenation Crimping (G-15288)*
N J E M A Magazine, Cincinnati *Also called Sesh Communications (G-4326)*
N M Hansen Machine and Tool, Toledo *Also called Rogar International Inc (G-18505)*
N M R Inc 513 530-9075
7555 Fields Ertel Rd Cincinnati (45241) *(G-4056)*
N N I, Cleveland *Also called Norman Noble Inc (G-5757)*
N N Metal Stampings Inc (PA) 419 737-2311
510 S Maple St Pioneer (43554) *(G-16086)*
N S T Battery 937 433-9222
4496 W Franklin St Bellbrook (45305) *(G-1496)*
N W P Manufacturing, Waldo *Also called Nwp Manufacturing Inc (G-19303)*
N Wasserstrom & Sons Inc (HQ) 614 228-5550
2300 Lockbourne Rd Columbus (43207) *(G-7206)*
N Wasserstrom & Sons Inc 614 737-5410
862 E Jenkins Ave Columbus (43207) *(G-7207)*
N-Molecular Inc 440 439-5356
7650 Frst Pl Bldg B Ste A Oakwood Village (44146) *(G-15481)*
N-Stock Box Inc 513 423-0319
1500 S University Blvd Middletown (45044) *(G-13934)*
N-Viro International Corp 419 535-6374
2254 Centennial Rd Toledo (43617) *(G-18421)*
N2y LLC 419 433-9800
909 University Dr S Huron (44839) *(G-11106)*
N8 Medical Inc 614 537-7246
6000 Memorial Dr Dublin (43017) *(G-8950)*
NA Financial Service Center, Cleveland *Also called Eaton Corporation (G-5150)*
Nabco Entrances Inc 419 842-0484
3407 Silica Rd Sylvania (43560) *(G-17954)*
Nac Products 330 644-3117
3200 S Main St Coventry Township (44319) *(G-7774)*
Nacco Industries Inc 740 773-9150
71 E Water St Chillicothe (45601) *(G-3201)*
Nacco Industries Inc (PA) 440 229-5151
5875 Landerbrook Dr # 220 Cleveland (44124) *(G-5719)*
Nachurs Alpine Solutions Corp (HQ) 740 382-5701
421 Leader St Marion (43302) *(G-12723)*
Nail Art 614 899-7155
5470 Westerville Rd Westerville (43081) *(G-20066)*
Nail Artist, Westerville *Also called Nail Art (G-20066)*
Nail Secret 513 459-3373
3187 Wstn Row Rd Ste 105 Maineville (45039) *(G-12375)*
Naked Lime 937 485-1932
2405 County Line Rd Beavercreek (45430) *(G-1359)*
Nalcon Ready Mix Inc 419 422-4341
12484 State Route 701 Kenton (43326) *(G-11416)*
Names Unlimited Corp 419 845-2005
3787 Marion Galion Rd Caledonia (43314) *(G-2419)*
Nanak Bakery 614 882-0882
895 S State St Westerville (43081) *(G-20067)*
Nanbrands LLC 513 313-9581
8405 Indian Hill Rd Cincinnati (45243) *(G-4057)*
Nancy Blanket, Mount Sterling *Also called Watershed Mangement LLC (G-14466)*
Nancys Draperies 330 855-7751
57 S Main St Marshallville (44645) *(G-12754)*
Nano Fabrix, Columbus *Also called Nano Innovations LLC (G-7208)*
Nano Innovations LLC 614 203-5706
2121 Riverside Dr Columbus (43221) *(G-7208)*
Nano Mark LLC 216 409-3104
4415 Euclid Ave Cleveland (44103) *(G-5720)*
Nanofiber Solutions Inc 614 453-5877
4389 Weaver Ct N Hilliard (43026) *(G-10843)*
Nanolap Technologies LLC 877 658-4949
85 Harrisburg Dr Englewood (45322) *(G-9370)*
Nanologix Inc 330 534-0800
843 N Main St Hubbard (44425) *(G-11006)*
Nanomeld LLC 740 477-5900
18646 Us Rte 23 N Circleville (43113) *(G-4549)*
Nanosperse LLC 937 296-5030
2000 Composite Dr Kettering (45420) *(G-11435)*
Nanostatics Corporation 740 477-5900
18646 Us Rte 23 Circleville (43113) *(G-4550)*
Nanotech Innovations LLC 440 926-4888
132 Artino St Oberlin (44074) *(G-15503)*
Nanotechlabs Inc (PA) 937 297-9518
2000 Composite Dr Kettering (45420) *(G-11436)*
Nanotronics Imaging Inc (PA) 330 926-9809
2251 Front St Ste 109-111 Cuyahoga Falls (44221) *(G-7900)*

Naomi Kight 937 278-0040
132 Marson Dr Dayton (45405) *(G-8375)*
Nap Asset Holdings Ltd 330 633-0599
411 Geneva Ave Tallmadge (44278) *(G-17995)*
NAPA Auto Parts, North Canton *Also called Jani Auto Parts Inc (G-15095)*
Napoleon Inc 419 592-5055
595 E Riverview Ave Napoleon (43545) *(G-14552)*
Napoleon Machine LLC 419 591-7010
476 E Riverview Ave Napoleon (43545) *(G-14553)*
Napoleon Products Co, Napoleon *Also called United Auto Worker AFL CIO (G-14563)*
Napoleon Spring Works Inc (HQ) 419 445-1010
111 Weires Dr Archbold (43502) *(G-660)*
Napoli's Pizza, Belpre *Also called Wal-Bon of Ohio Inc (G-1585)*
Napolitano Monument, Cincinnati *Also called 3-G Incorporated (G-3269)*
Naptime Productions LLC 419 662-9521
107 Hidden Cove St Rossford (43460) *(G-16587)*
Nari Inc 440 960-2280
5190 State Route 99 N Monroeville (44847) *(G-14289)*
Narrow Way Custom Technology 937 743-1611
100 Industry Dr Carlisle (45005) *(G-2895)*
Nasg Ohio LLC 419 634-3125
605 E Montford Ave Ada (45810) *(G-7)*
Nasoneb Inc 330 247-0921
1133 Medina Rd Ste 500 Medina (44256) *(G-13306)*
Natgascar, Cleveland *Also called Ecowise LLC (G-5156)*
Nation Coating Systems Inc 937 746-7632
501 Shotwell Dr Franklin (45005) *(G-9902)*
National Access Design LLC 513 351-3400
1924 Losantiville Ave Cincinnati (45237) *(G-4058)*
National Adhesives Inc 513 683-8650
9435 Waterstone Blvd # 200 Cincinnati (45249) *(G-4059)*
National Aviation Products Inc (HQ) 330 688-6494
4880 Hudson Dr Stow (44224) *(G-17610)*
National Bank Note Company (PA) 216 281-7792
9800 Detroit Ave Ste 1 Cleveland (44102) *(G-5721)*
National Bedding Company LLC 513 825-4172
1680 Carillion Blvd Cincinnati (45240) *(G-4060)*
National Beverage, Obetz *Also called Shasta Beverages Inc (G-15513)*
National Beverage Corp 614 491-5415
4685 Groveport Rd Obetz (43207) *(G-15512)*
National Bias Fabric Co 216 361-0530
4516 Saint Clair Ave Cleveland (44103) *(G-5722)*
National Biological Corp 216 831-0600
23700 Mercantile Rd Beachwood (44122) *(G-1252)*
National Bios Fabric Company, Cleveland *Also called Db Rediheat Inc (G-5075)*
National Brass Company Inc 216 651-8530
3179 W 33rd St Cleveland (44109) *(G-5723)*
National Bronze Mtls Ohio Inc 440 277-1226
5311 W River Rd Lorain (44055) *(G-12106)*
National Bullet Co 800 317-9506
34971 Glen Dr Eastlake (44095) *(G-9125)*
National Colloid Company 740 282-1171
906 Adams St Steubenville (43952) *(G-17545)*
National Diamond Tl & Coating, Westlake *Also called Diamond Reserve Inc (G-20108)*
National Dirctry of Morts Inc 440 247-3561
285 Park Pl Chagrin Falls (44022) *(G-3025)*
National Elec Carbn Pdts Inc 419 435-8182
200 N Town St Fostoria (44830) *(G-9850)*
National Electric Coil Inc (PA) 614 488-1151
800 King Ave Columbus (43212) *(G-7209)*
National Electro-Coatings Inc 216 898-0080
15655 Brookpark Rd Cleveland (44142) *(G-5724)*
National Engrg Archtctral Svcs, Columbus *Also called Barr Engineering Incorporated (G-6649)*
National Engrg Archtctral Svcs, Columbus *Also called Barr Engineering Incorporated (G-6650)*
National Extrusion & Mfg Co, Bellefontaine *Also called Klb Industries Inc (G-1521)*
National Fasteners Inc 216 771-6473
4581 Spring Rd Brooklyn Heights (44131) *(G-2127)*
National Fleet Svcs Ohio LLC 440 930-5177
607 Miller Rd Avon Lake (44012) *(G-997)*
National Foods Packaging Inc 216 415-7102
8200 Madison Ave Cleveland (44102) *(G-5725)*
National Fruit Vegetable Tech 740 400-4055
250 Civic Center Dr Columbus (43215) *(G-7210)*
National Gas & Oil Company (HQ) 740 344-2102
1500 Granville Rd Newark (43055) *(G-14899)*
National Gas & Oil Corporation (HQ) 740 344-2102
1500 Granville Rd Newark (43055) *(G-14900)*
National Glass Svc Group LLC 614 652-3699
5500 Frantz Rd Ste 100 Dublin (43017) *(G-8951)*
National Hwy Maint Systems LLC 330 922-3649
4361 State Rd Peninsula (44264) *(G-15896)*
National Illmination Sign Corp 419 866-1666
6525 Angola Rd Holland (43528) *(G-10945)*
National Lien Digest, Highland Heights *Also called C & S Associates Inc (G-10786)*
National Lime and Stone Co 419 396-7671
370 N Patterson St Carey (43316) *(G-2884)*

ALPHABETIC

National Lime and Stone Co...419 657-6745
18430 Main Street Rd Wapakoneta (45895) ***(G-19347)***
National Lime and Stone Co...330 262-1317
1455 Timken Rd Wooster (44691) ***(G-20631)***
National Lime and Stone Co...740 548-4206
2406 S Section Line Rd Delaware (43015) ***(G-8708)***
National Lime and Stone Co...419 562-0771
4580 Bethel Rd Bucyrus (44820) ***(G-2339)***
National Lime and Stone Co...740 387-3485
700 Likens Rd Marion (43302) ***(G-12724)***
National Lime and Stone Co...419 228-3434
1314 Findlay Rd Lima (45801) ***(G-11910)***
National Lime and Stone Co...330 339-2144
2942 Brightwood Rd Se New Philadelphia (44663) ***(G-14790)***
National Lime and Stone Co...419 423-3400
9860 County Road 313 Findlay (45840) ***(G-9729)***
National Lime and Stone Co...419 642-6690
18264 State Route 189 Columbus Grove (45830) ***(G-7636)***
National Lime and Stone Co...614 497-0083
5911 Lockbourne Rd Lockbourne (43137) ***(G-11998)***
National Lime and Stone Co...419 294-3049
14407 Township Rd 124 Upper Sandusky (43351) ***(G-18965)***
National Lime and Stone Co...216 883-9840
4200 E 71st St Cleveland (44105) ***(G-5726)***
National Lime Stone, Wooster *Also called National Lime and Stone Co* ***(G-20631)***
National Lime Stone Clmbus Reg, Delaware *Also called National Lime and Stone Co* ***(G-8708)***
National Machine Company (HQ)...330 688-6494
4880 Hudson Dr Stow (44224) ***(G-17611)***
National Machine Company...330 688-2584
1330 Commerce Dr Stow (44224) ***(G-17612)***
National Machine Tool Company...513 541-6682
2013 E Galbraith Rd Cincinnati (45215) ***(G-4061)***
National Machinery LLC (HQ)...419 447-5211
161 Greenfield St Tiffin (44883) ***(G-18070)***
National Metal Shapes Inc...740 363-9559
425 S Sandusky St Ste 1 Delaware (43015) ***(G-8709)***
National Mold Remediation...614 231-6653
3923 E Main St Columbus (43213) ***(G-7211)***
National Molded Products Inc...440 365-3400
147 Kenwood St Elyria (44035) ***(G-9299)***
National Ntwrk EMB Prfssionals...502 212-7500
3100 Surrey Hill Ln Stow (44224) ***(G-17613)***
National Office, Cleveland *Also called National Electro-Coatings Inc* ***(G-5724)***
National Oil Products, Hamilton *Also called Wallover Oil Hamilton Inc* ***(G-10620)***
National Oilwell Varco Inc...978 687-0101
5870 Poe Ave Dayton (45414) ***(G-8376)***
National Oilwell Varco Inc...440 577-1225
7338 N Richmond Rd Pierpont (44082) ***(G-16066)***
National Oilwell Varco LP...937 454-3200
5870 Poe Ave Dayton (45414) ***(G-8377)***
National Pallet & Mulch LLC...937 237-1643
3550 Intercity Dr Dayton (45424) ***(G-8378)***
National Patent Analytical Sys...419 526-6727
2090 Harrington Mem Rd Mansfield (44903) ***(G-12489)***
National Pattern Mfg Co...330 682-6871
1318 N Main St Orrville (44667) ***(G-15605)***
National Peening...216 342-9155
23800 Corbin Dr Unit B Bedford Heights (44128) ***(G-1476)***
National Plating Corporation...216 341-6707
6701 Hubbard Ave Ste 1 Cleveland (44127) ***(G-5727)***
National Polishing Systems Inc...330 659-6547
5145 Brecksville Rd # 101 Richfield (44286) ***(G-16477)***
National Polymer Dev Co Inc...440 708-1245
10200 Gottschalk Pkwy # 4 Chagrin Falls (44023) ***(G-3061)***
National Polymer Inc...440 708-1245
10200 Gottschalk Pkwy Chagrin Falls (44023) ***(G-3062)***
National Pride Equipment Inc...419 289-2886
1266 Middle Rowsburg Rd Ashland (44805) ***(G-727)***
National Production, Newark *Also called Ngo Development Corporation* ***(G-14903)***
National Psychologist, The, Columbus *Also called Ohio Psychlogy Pblications Inc* ***(G-7256)***
National Rolled Thread Die Co...440 232-8101
7051 Krick Rd Cleveland (44146) ***(G-5728)***
National Roller Die Inc...440 951-3850
4750 Beidler Rd Unit 4 Willoughby (44094) ***(G-20386)***
National Screen Production, Cleveland *Also called Charizma Corp* ***(G-4909)***
National Security Products...216 566-9962
1636 Saint Clair Ave Ne Cleveland (44114) ***(G-5729)***
National Smallwares, Columbus *Also called Wasserstrom Company* ***(G-7591)***
National Stair Corp...937 325-1347
20 Zischler St Springfield (45504) ***(G-17455)***
National Starch Chemical...513 830-0260
9435 Waterstone Blvd # 200 Cincinnati (45249) ***(G-4062)***
National Steel Rule Die LLC...937 667-0967
3580 Lightner Rd Vandalia (45377) ***(G-19141)***
National Super Service Co, Toledo *Also called Nss Enterprises Inc* ***(G-18430)***
National Thermoform, Fort Loramie *Also called Jeffrey Brandewie* ***(G-9800)***
National Tool & Equipment Inc...330 629-8665
60 Karago Ave Youngstown (44512) ***(G-20973)***
National Welding & Tanker Repr...614 875-3399
2036 Hendrix Dr Grove City (43123) ***(G-10449)***
National Welding & Tanker Repr...614 875-3399
2036 Hendrix Dr Grove City (43123) ***(G-10450)***
Nationwide Chemical Products...419 714-7075
24851 E Broadway Rd Perrysburg (43551) ***(G-15979)***
Natural Beauty Hc Express...440 459-1776
6809 Mayfield Rd Apt 550 Mayfield Heights (44124) ***(G-13169)***
Natural Beauty Products Inc...513 420-9400
50 S Main St Middletown (45044) ***(G-13935)***
Natural Country Farms Inc (HQ)...330 753-2293
681 W Waterloo Rd Akron (44314) ***(G-294)***
Natural Essentials Inc...330 562-8022
1199 S Chillicothe Rd Aurora (44202) ***(G-895)***
Natural Gas Construction Inc...330 364-9240
1737 Red Hill Rd Nw Dover (44622) ***(G-8844)***
Natural Options Aromatherapy...419 886-3736
610 State Route 97 W Bellville (44813) ***(G-1560)***
Naturally Smart Labs LLC...216 503-9398
7820 E Pleasant Valley Rd Independence (44131) ***(G-11143)***
Nature Friendly Products LLC...216 464-5490
24050 Commerce Park # 101 Cleveland (44122) ***(G-5730)***
Nature Pure LLC...937 358-2364
26560 Storms Rd West Mansfield (43358) ***(G-19945)***
Nature Pure LLC (PA)...937 358-2364
26586 State Route 739 Raymond (43067) ***(G-16424)***
Nature Trek...513 314-3916
5979 Wind St Cincinnati (45227) ***(G-4063)***
Natures Own Source LLC...440 838-5135
7033 Mill Rd Brecksville (44141) ***(G-2050)***
Naturym LLC...614 284-3068
1255 N Hamilton Rd Gahanna (43230) ***(G-10093)***
Nauticus Inc...440 746-1290
8080 Snowville Rd Brecksville (44141) ***(G-2051)***
Nautilus Hyosung America Inc...937 203-4900
2076 Byers Rd Miamisburg (45342) ***(G-13697)***
Nauvod Machine Co...440 632-1990
16254 Nauvoo Rd Middlefield (44062) ***(G-13837)***
Nauvoo Custom Woodworking...440 632-9502
17231 Nauvoo Rd Middlefield (44062) ***(G-13838)***
Navage, Brooklyn *Also called Rhinosystems Inc* ***(G-2114)***
Navarre Industries Inc...330 767-3003
10384 Navarre Rd Sw Navarre (44662) ***(G-14582)***
Navarre Trailer Sales Inc...330 879-2406
4633 Erie Ave Sw Navarre (44662) ***(G-14583)***
Navidea Biopharmaceuticals Inc...614 793-7500
4995 Bradenton Ave # 240 Dublin (43017) ***(G-8952)***
Navigator Construction LLC...330 244-0221
7530 Tim Ave Nw Ste B North Canton (44720) ***(G-15106)***
Navistar Inc...937 390-5848
6125 Urbana Rd Springfield (45502) ***(G-17456)***
Navistar Inc...937 390-5653
349 W County Line Rd Springfield (45502) ***(G-17457)***
Navistar Inc...937 561-3315
811 N Murray St Springfield (45503) ***(G-17458)***
Navistar Inc...937 390-5704
4949 Urbana Rd Frnt Springfield (45502) ***(G-17459)***
Navistar Inc...513 733-8500
11775 Highway Dr Cincinnati (45241) ***(G-4064)***
Navistone Inc...844 677-3667
1308 Race St Ste 103 Cincinnati (45202) ***(G-4065)***
Navpar Inc...513 738-2230
11029 State Route 128 Harrison (45030) ***(G-10660)***
Naw Petroleum Service...740 464-7988
208 Copperfield Dr Chillicothe (45601) ***(G-3202)***
Nbbi...614 888-8320
1055 Crupper Ave Columbus (43229) ***(G-7212)***
NBC Industries Inc...216 651-9800
4700 Train Ave Ste 3 Cleveland (44102) ***(G-5731)***
Nbw Inc...216 377-1700
4556 Industrial Pkwy Cleveland (44135) ***(G-5732)***
NC Works Inc...937 514-7781
3500 Commerce Center Dr Franklin (45005) ***(G-9903)***
Ncc, Cleveland *Also called North Coast Container Corp* ***(G-5763)***
Nccd, Wooster *Also called North Central Concrete Design* ***(G-20632)***
Nci Building Systems Inc...937 584-3300
2400 Yankee Rd Middletown (45044) ***(G-13936)***
NCM, Cleveland *Also called North Coast Media LLC* ***(G-5768)***
NCR International Inc (HQ)...937 445-5000
1700 S Patterson Blvd Kettering (45409) ***(G-11437)***
Ncrx Optical Solutions Inc (PA)...330 239-5353
105 Executive Pkwy # 401 Hudson (44236) ***(G-11063)***
Nct Technologies Group Inc (PA)...937 882-6800
7867 W National Rd New Carlisle (45344) ***(G-14673)***
NDC Technologies Inc...937 233-9935
8001 Technology Blvd Dayton (45424) ***(G-8379)***
Ndi Medical LLC (PA)...216 378-9106
22901 Millcreek Blvd # 110 Cleveland (44122) ***(G-5733)***
Ndw Textiles, Westlake *Also called Mmi Textiles Inc* ***(G-20131)***

Neal Publications Inc ... 419 874-4787
127 W Indiana Ave Perrysburg (43551) ***(G-15980)***
Nease Co LLC (HQ) ... 513 587-2800
9774 Windisch Rd West Chester (45069) ***(G-19747)***
Nease Co LLC ... 513 738-1255
10740 Paddys Run Rd Harrison (45030) ***(G-10661)***
Nease Performance Chemicals, West Chester *Also called Nease Co LLC* ***(G-19747)***
Nease Performance Chemicals, Harrison *Also called Nease Co LLC* ***(G-10661)***
Neaton Auto Products Mfg Inc (HQ) ... 937 456-7103
975 S Franklin St Eaton (45320) ***(G-9162)***
Nebraska Industries Corp ... 419 335-6010
447 E Walnut St Wauseon (43567) ***(G-19529)***
Nebulatronics Inc ... 440 243-2370
24542 Nobottom Rd Olmsted Twp (44138) ***(G-15534)***
Necco American, Columbus *Also called Appian Manufacturing Corp* ***(G-6608)***
Ned A Shreve ... 740 732-6465
48398 Seneca Lake Rd Sarahsville (43779) ***(G-16866)***
Neer's Engineering Labs, Bellefontaine *Also called Arden J Neer Sr* ***(G-1504)***
Nef Ltd ... 419 445-6696
1901 S Defiance St Archbold (43502) ***(G-661)***
Neff Machinery and Supplies ... 740 454-0128
112 S Shawnee Ave Zanesville (43701) ***(G-21159)***
Neff Parts, Zanesville *Also called Neff Machinery and Supplies* ***(G-21159)***
Neff-Perkins Company ... 440 632-1658
16080 Industrial Pkwy Middlefield (44062) ***(G-13839)***
Nehemiah Manufacturing Co LLC ... 513 351-5700
1907 South St Cincinnati (45204) ***(G-4066)***
Neher Burial Vault Company ... 937 399-4494
1903 Saint Paris Pike Springfield (45504) ***(G-17460)***
Neidert Fabricating Inc ... 330 753-3331
712 Wooster Rd W Barberton (44203) ***(G-1088)***
Neighborhood News Pubg Co ... 216 441-2141
8613 Garfield Blvd Cleveland (44125) ***(G-5734)***
Neil Barton ... 614 889-9933
8215 Dublin Rd Dublin (43017) ***(G-8953)***
Neil R Scholl Inc ... 740 653-6593
54 Snoke Hill Rd Ne Lancaster (43130) ***(G-11590)***
Neiss Body & Equipment Corp ... 330 828-2409
17485 Old Lincoln Way Dalton (44618) ***(G-7948)***
Nel-Ack Sheet Metal Inc ... 440 357-7844
546 Hoyt St Ste 18 Painesville (44077) ***(G-15765)***
Nelis Printing Co ... 330 757-4114
5146 Sterling Ave Youngstown (44515) ***(G-20974)***
Nelson Aluminum Foundry Inc ... 440 543-1941
17093 Munn Rd Chagrin Falls (44023) ***(G-3063)***
Nelson Automotive LLC ... 724 681-0975
6430 Eastland Rd Ste 3 Brookpark (44142) ***(G-2153)***
Nelson Constantinelli Ltd ... 800 680-1029
545 Metro Pl S Ste 100 Dublin (43017) ***(G-8954)***
Nelson Manufacturing Company ... 419 523-5321
6448 State Route 224 Ottawa (45875) ***(G-15660)***
Nelson Sand & Gravel Inc ... 440 224-0198
5720 State Route 193 Kingsville (44048) ***(G-11461)***
Nelson Stud Welding Inc (HQ) ... 440 329-0400
7900 W Ridge Rd Elyria (44035) ***(G-9300)***
Nelson Tool Corporation ... 740 965-1894
388 N County Line Rd Sunbury (43074) ***(G-17892)***
Nelson's Woodcrafts, Steubenville *Also called Mark Nelson* ***(G-17542)***
Nemco Food Equipment Ltd (PA) ... 419 542-7751
301 Meuse Argonne St Hicksville (43526) ***(G-10780)***
Neo Tactical Gear ... 216 235-2625
11540 Glenmora Dr Chardon (44024) ***(G-3127)***
Neo Tech ... 937 845-0999
123 S Main St New Carlisle (45344) ***(G-14674)***
Neo Technology Solutions ... 513 234-5725
4240 Irwin Simpson Rd Mason (45040) ***(G-12914)***
Neograf Solutions LLC ... 216 529-3777
11709 Madison Ave Lakewood (44107) ***(G-11530)***
Neola Inc (PA) ... 330 926-0514
3914 Clk Pnte Trl Ste 103 Stow (44224) ***(G-17614)***
Neola Inc ... 740 622-5341
632 Main St Coshocton (43812) ***(G-7742)***
Neon ... 216 761-4782
15201 Euclid Ave Cleveland (44112) ***(G-5735)***
Neon Beach Tan ... 440 933-3051
2259 Kresge Dr Amherst (44001) ***(G-565)***
Neon By Deon LLC ... 440 292-5626
7801 Day Dr Unit 29522 Cleveland (44129) ***(G-5736)***
Neon City ... 440 301-2000
11500 Madison Ave Cleveland (44102) ***(G-5737)***
Neon Goldfish Mktg Solutions ... 419 842-4462
6912 Spring Valley Dr # 208 Holland (43528) ***(G-10946)***
Neon Health Services Inc ... 216 231-7700
4800 Payne Ave Cleveland (44103) ***(G-5738)***
Neon Hussy LLC ... 513 374-7644
237 E 12th Ave Columbus (43201) ***(G-7213)***
Neon Light Manufacturing Co ... 216 851-1000
12655 Coit Rd Cleveland (44108) ***(G-5739)***
Neon Paintbrush ... 419 436-1202
461 W Lytle St Lot 153 Fostoria (44830) ***(G-9851)***
Nephrogenex, Cincinnati *Also called Medpace Research Inc* ***(G-3999)***
Neptune Aquatic Systems Inc ... 513 575-2989
6641 Smith Rd Loveland (45140) ***(G-12216)***
Neptune Chemical Pump Company ... 513 870-3239
9393 Princetone Glendale West Chester (45011) ***(G-19748)***
Neptune Equipment Company ... 513 851-8008
11082 Southland Rd Cincinnati (45240) ***(G-4067)***
Nervive Inc ... 847 274-1790
5900 Landerbrook Dr # 350 Cleveland (44124) ***(G-5740)***
Nesco Inc (PA) ... 440 461-6000
6140 Parkland Blvd # 110 Cleveland (44124) ***(G-5741)***
Nesco Resource, Cleveland *Also called Nesco Inc* ***(G-5741)***
Nestier, Milford *Also called Buckhorn Material Hdlg Group* ***(G-14001)***
Nestle Brands Company ... 440 264-6600
30000 Bainbridge Rd Solon (44139) ***(G-17202)***
Nestle Food Service Factory, Cleveland *Also called Nestle Usa Inc* ***(G-5744)***
Nestle Prepared Foods Company (HQ) ... 440 248-3600
30003 Bainbridge Rd Solon (44139) ***(G-17203)***
Nestle Prepared Foods Company ... 440 349-5757
5750 Harper Rd Solon (44139) ***(G-17204)***
Nestle Purina Petcare Company ... 740 454-8575
5 N 2nd St Zanesville (43701) ***(G-21160)***
Nestle Usa Inc ... 216 524-7738
7645 Granger Rd Cleveland (44125) ***(G-5742)***
Nestle Usa Inc ... 216 524-3397
7605 Granger Rd Cleveland (44125) ***(G-5743)***
Nestle Usa Inc ... 440 349-5757
30003 Bainbridge Rd Solon (44139) ***(G-17205)***
Nestle Usa Inc ... 513 576-4930
6279 Tri Ridge Blvd # 100 Loveland (45140) ***(G-12217)***
Nestle Usa Inc ... 216 861-8350
2621 W 25th St Cleveland (44113) ***(G-5744)***
Netherland Rubber Company (PA) ... 513 733-0883
2931 Exon Ave Cincinnati (45241) ***(G-4068)***
Netpark LLC ... 614 866-2495
1182 Claycraft Rd Gahanna (43230) ***(G-10094)***
Netshape Technologies Mim Inc ... 440 248-5456
31005 Solon Rd Solon (44139) ***(G-17206)***
Netsmart Technologies Inc ... 440 942-4040
30775 Bnbridge Rd Ste 200 Solon (44139) ***(G-17207)***
Nettleton Steel Treating Div, Cleveland *Also called Thermal Treatment Center Inc* ***(G-6167)***
Neturen America Corporation ... 513 863-1900
2995 Moser Ct Hamilton (45011) ***(G-10589)***
Network Communications Inc ... 614 934-1919
467 Waterbury Ct Ste B Gahanna (43230) ***(G-10095)***
Network Printing & Graphics ... 614 230-2084
443 Crestview Rd Columbus (43202) ***(G-7214)***
Networked Cmmnctons Sltons LLC ... 440 374-4990
23400 Aurora Rd Ste 5 Bedford Heights (44146) ***(G-1477)***
Neu Prosthetics & Orthotics ... 740 363-3522
2848 Jericho Pl Delaware (43015) ***(G-8710)***
Neumeisters Candy Shoppe LLC ... 419 294-3647
139 N Sandusky Ave Upper Sandusky (43351) ***(G-18966)***
Neundorfer Inc ... 440 942-8990
4590 Hamann Pkwy Willoughby (44094) ***(G-20387)***
Neundorfer Engineering Service, Willoughby *Also called Neundorfer Inc* ***(G-20387)***
Neural Holdings LLC ... 734 512-8865
9867 Beech Dr Cincinnati (45231) ***(G-4069)***
Neurorescue LLC ... 614 354-6453
2004 Alum Village Dr Lewis Center (43035) ***(G-11769)***
Neuros Medical Inc ... 440 951-2565
35010 Chardon Rd Ste 210 Willoughby Hills (44094) ***(G-20472)***
Neurowave Systems Inc ... 216 361-1591
2490 Lee Blvd Ste 300 Cleveland (44118) ***(G-5745)***
Neusole Glassworks, Cincinnati *Also called Jjs3 Foundation* ***(G-3874)***
Nevels Precision Machining LLC ... 937 387-6037
2770 Thunderhawk Ct Dayton (45414) ***(G-8380)***
New Age Design & Tool Inc ... 440 355-5400
162 Commerce Dr Lagrange (44050) ***(G-11490)***
New American Reel Company LLC ... 419 258-2900
5278 County Road 424 A Antwerp (45813) ***(G-599)***
New Aqua LLC ... 614 265-9000
3707 Interchange Rd Columbus (43204) ***(G-7215)***
New Bakery of Zanesville LLC ... 614 764-3100
1 Dave Thomas Blvd Dublin (43017) ***(G-8955)***
New Bloomer Candy Company LLC ... 740 452-7501
1445 Deercreek Dr Zanesville (43701) ***(G-21161)***
New Bremen Machine & Tool Co ... 419 629-3295
705 Kuenzel Dr New Bremen (45869) ***(G-14657)***
New Can Company Inc ... 937 547-9050
1367 Sater St Greenville (45331) ***(G-10385)***
New Castings Inc ... 330 645-6653
2200 Massillon Rd Akron (44312) ***(G-295)***
New Castle Industries Inc (HQ) ... 724 654-2603
375 Victoria Rd Ste 1 Youngstown (44515) ***(G-20975)***
New Century Sales LLC ... 513 422-3631
2905 Lopane Ave Middletown (45044) ***(G-13937)***
New Cleveland Group Inc ... 216 932-9310
2917 Mayfield Rd Cleveland (44118) ***(G-5746)***

ALPHABETIC

(PA)=Parent Co (HQ)=Headquarters (DH)=Div Headquarters
2019 Harris Ohio Industrial Directory
1195

New Cumberland Lock & Dam, Toronto *Also called U S Army Corps of Engineers* ***(G-18613)***
New Cut Tool and Mfg Corp....740 676-1666
1 New Cut Rd Shadyside (43947) ***(G-16924)***
New Dawn Designs....330 759-3500
1282 Trumbull Ave Ste E Girard (44420) ***(G-10263)***
New Die Inc....419 726-7581
2828 E Manhattan Blvd Toledo (43611) ***(G-18422)***
New Dimension Metals Corp....937 299-2233
3050 Dryden Rd Moraine (45439) ***(G-14373)***
New Eezy-Gro Inc....419 927-6110
9841 County Highway 49 Upper Sandusky (43351) ***(G-18967)***
New ERA Controls Inc....216 641-8683
11002 Edgepark Dr Cleveland (44125) ***(G-5747)***
New Holland Engineering Inc....740 495-5200
43 E Front St New Holland (43145) ***(G-14702)***
New Horizons Baking Company (PA)....419 668-8226
211 Woodlawn Ave Norwalk (44857) ***(G-15407)***
New Image Plastics Mfg Co....330 854-3010
241 Market St W Canal Fulton (44614) ***(G-2487)***
New Leaf Medical Inc....216 391-7749
1768 E 25th St Cleveland (44114) ***(G-5748)***
New Life Chapel....513 298-2980
10195 Giverny Blvd Cincinnati (45241) ***(G-4070)***
New London Foundry Inc....419 929-2073
80 Walnut St New London (44851) ***(G-14733)***
New London Regalia Mfg Co....419 929-1516
1 Harmony Pl New London (44851) ***(G-14734)***
New Mansfield Brass & Alum Co....419 492-2166
636 S Center St New Washington (44854) ***(G-14830)***
New Mulch In A Bottle Limited....724 290-2341
140 Gross St Ste 116 Marietta (45750) ***(G-12648)***
New Path International LLC....614 410-3974
1476 Manning Pkwy Ste A Powell (43065) ***(G-16331)***
New Pme Inc....513 671-1717
518 W Crescentville Rd Cincinnati (45246) ***(G-4071)***
New Republic Industries LLC....614 580-9927
497 Bridle Dr Marysville (43040) ***(G-12803)***
New Riegel Cafe Inc....419 595-2255
14 N Perry St New Riegel (44853) ***(G-14816)***
New River Equipment Corp....330 669-0040
7793 Pittsburg Ave Nw North Canton (44720) ***(G-15107)***
New Sabina Industries Inc (HQ)....937 584-2433
12555 Us Highway 22 And 3 Sabina (45169) ***(G-16616)***
New Tech Welding Inc....937 426-4801
2972 Lantz Rd Beavercreek (45434) ***(G-1334)***
New Track Media LLC....513 421-6500
10151 Carver Rd Ste 200 Blue Ash (45242) ***(G-1825)***
New Transcon LLC....440 255-7600
8824 Twinbrook Rd Mentor (44060) ***(G-13526)***
New Urban Distributors LLC....216 373-2349
13940 Cedar Rd Ste 224 Cleveland (44118) ***(G-5749)***
New Vulco Mfg & Sales Co LLC....513 242-2672
5353 Spring Grove Ave Cincinnati (45217) ***(G-4072)***
New Waste Concepts Inc....877 736-6924
26624 Glenwood Rd Perrysburg (43551) ***(G-15981)***
New Wave Prosthetics Inc....614 782-2361
3454 Grant Ave Grove City (43123) ***(G-10451)***
New Wayne Inc....740 453-3454
1555 Ritchey Pkwy Zanesville (43701) ***(G-21162)***
New World Energy Resources (PA)....740 344-4087
1500 Granville Rd Newark (43055) ***(G-14901)***
New York Frozen Foods, Bedford *Also called Tmarzetti Company* ***(G-1450)***
New York Frozen Foods....614 846-2232
380 Polaris Pkwy Ste 400 Westerville (43082) ***(G-20011)***
New York Frozen Foods Inc (HQ)....216 292-5655
25900 Fargo Ave Bedford (44146) ***(G-1430)***
Newact Inc....513 321-5177
2084 James E Sauls Sr Dr Batavia (45103) ***(G-1173)***
Newall Electronics Inc....614 771-0213
1803 Obrien Rd Columbus (43228) ***(G-7216)***
Newark Downtown Center Inc....740 403-5454
8 Arcade Pl Newark (43055) ***(G-14902)***
Newark Recovery & Recycling, Columbus *Also called Caraustar Industries Inc* ***(G-6737)***
Newark Water Plant, Newark *Also called City of Newark* ***(G-14861)***
Neway Stamping & Mfg Inc....440 951-8500
4820 E 345th St Willoughby (44094) ***(G-20388)***
Newberry Wood Enterprises Inc (PA)....440 238-6127
12223 Prospect Rd Strongsville (44149) ***(G-17769)***
Newbury Sandblasting & Pntg, Newbury *Also called L & N Olde Car Co* ***(G-14959)***
Newbury Woodworks....440 564-5273
10958 Kinsman Rd Unit 2 Newbury (44065) ***(G-14960)***
Newell Brands Inc....330 733-1184
212 Progress Blvd Kent (44240) ***(G-11358)***
Newell Brands Inc....330 733-7771
3200 Gilchrist Rd Mogadore (44260) ***(G-14245)***
Newell Rubbermaid, Mogadore *Also called Newell Brands Inc* ***(G-14245)***
Newfax Corporation (PA)....419 241-5157
333 W Woodruff Ave Toledo (43604) ***(G-18423)***
Newfax Corporation....419 893-4557
3333 W Wooddrift Toledo (43624) ***(G-18424)***
Newhouse & Faulkner Inc....513 721-1660
215 E 9th St Cincinnati (45202) ***(G-4073)***
Newhouse Printing Company, Dover *Also called R & J Printing Enterprises Inc* ***(G-8847)***
Newkor Inc....216 631-7800
10410 Berea Rd Cleveland (44102) ***(G-5750)***
Newman Brothers Inc....513 242-0011
5609 Center Hill Ave Cincinnati (45216) ***(G-4074)***
Newman International Inc....513 932-7379
964 W Main St Lebanon (45036) ***(G-11674)***
Newman Sanitary Gasket, Lebanon *Also called Newman International Inc* ***(G-11674)***
Newman Sanitary Gasket Company....513 932-7379
964 W Main St Lebanon (45036) ***(G-11675)***
Newman Technology Inc (HQ)....419 525-1856
100 Cairns Rd Mansfield (44903) ***(G-12490)***
Newmast Mktg & Communications....614 837-1200
2060 Integrity Dr N Columbus (43209) ***(G-7217)***
Newpage Group Inc....937 242-9500
8540 Gander Creek Dr Miamisburg (45342) ***(G-13698)***
Newpage Holding Corporation....877 855-7243
8540 Gander Creek Dr Miamisburg (45342) ***(G-13699)***
News Gazette Printing Company....419 227-2527
324 W Market St Lima (45801) ***(G-11911)***
News Office, Beauro, Warren *Also called Vindicator Printing Company* ***(G-19456)***
News Reel Inc....614 469-0700
5 E Long St Ste 1001 Columbus (43215) ***(G-7218)***
News Reel Mag By & For Blind, Columbus *Also called News Reel Inc* ***(G-7218)***
News Tribune, Hicksville *Also called Tribune Printing Inc* ***(G-10785)***
News Watchman & Paper....740 947-2149
860 W Emmitt Ave Ste 5 Waverly (45690) ***(G-19553)***
Newsafe Transport Service Inc....740 387-1679
979 Pole Lane Rd Marion (43302) ***(G-12725)***
Newsome & Work Metalizing Co....330 376-7144
258 Kenmore Blvd Akron (44301) ***(G-296)***
Newspaper Holding Inc....440 998-2323
4626 Park Ave Ashtabula (44004) ***(G-792)***
Newspaper Network Central OH....419 524-3545
70 W 4th St Mansfield (44903) ***(G-12491)***
Newspaper Network Central Ohio, Newark *Also called Gannett Co Inc* ***(G-14877)***
Newspaper Solutions LLC....937 694-9370
116 Old Carriage Dr Englewood (45322) ***(G-9371)***
Newswanger Machine, Shiloh *Also called Leon Newswanger* ***(G-16996)***
Newtech Materials & Analytical....330 329-1080
618 Tresham Ct Copley (44321) ***(G-7690)***
Newton Asphalt Paving Inc....330 878-5648
8344 Central Rd Nw Strasburg (44680) ***(G-17650)***
Newton Falls Printing....330 872-3532
27 E Broad St Newton Falls (44444) ***(G-14990)***
Newwave Technologies Inc....513 683-1211
968 Paxton Guinea Rd Loveland (45140) ***(G-12218)***
Nexeo Solutions LLC....800 531-7106
5200 Blazer Pkwy Dublin (43017) ***(G-8956)***
Nexergy, Inc., Dublin *Also called Inventus Power (ohio) Inc* ***(G-8931)***
Nexgen Machine Company LLC....440 268-2222
19768 Progress Dr Strongsville (44149) ***(G-17770)***
Nexicor, Cincinnati *Also called Senco Brands Inc* ***(G-3262)***
Nexjen Technologies Ltd....781 572-5737
362 Bethany Ct Avon Lake (44012) ***(G-998)***
Nexstep Commercial Pdts LLC....937 322-5163
625 Burt St Springfield (45505) ***(G-17461)***
Next, Cincinnati *Also called Nilpeter Usa Inc* ***(G-4080)***
Next Day Access-Central Ohio, Franklin *Also called Homecare Mattress Inc* ***(G-9889)***
Next Day Sign....419 537-9595
2112 N Reynolds Rd Toledo (43615) ***(G-18425)***
Next Day Signs LLC....614 764-7446
6403 Nicholas Dr Columbus (43235) ***(G-7219)***
Next Design & Build LLC....330 907-3042
4735 Massillon Rd # 520 Green (44232) ***(G-10343)***
Next Dimension Components Inc....440 576-0194
223 S Spruce St Jefferson (44047) ***(G-11235)***
Next Generation Bag Inc....419 884-1327
230 Industrial Dr Mansfield (44904) ***(G-12492)***
Next Generation Films Inc....419 884-8150
215 Industrial Dr Mansfield (44904) ***(G-12493)***
Next Generation Films Inc (PA)....419 884-8150
230 Industrial Dr Lexington (44904) ***(G-11805)***
Next Generation Plastics LLC....330 668-1200
3075 Smith Rd Ste 101 Fairlawn (44333) ***(G-9613)***
Next Gerenation Crimping....440 237-6300
9880 York Alpha Dr North Royalton (44133) ***(G-15288)***
Next Resins, Sylvania *Also called Next Specialty Resins Inc* ***(G-17955)***
Next Sales LLC....330 704-4126
3258 Dogwood Ln Nw Dover (44622) ***(G-8845)***
Next Specialty Resins Inc (PA)....419 843-4600
3315 Centennial Rd Ste J Sylvania (43560) ***(G-17955)***
Next Step, Centerville *Also called Advanced Medical Solutions Inc* ***(G-2995)***
Next Step Socks LLC....216 534-8077
2042 Richland Ave Lakewood (44107) ***(G-11531)***
Next Wave Marketing Innovation, Dayton *Also called David Esrati* ***(G-8126)***

Nextant Aerospace LLC 216 898-4800
18601 Cleveland Pkwy Dr Cleveland (44135) *(G-5751)*
Nextant Aerospace Holdings LLC 216 261-9000
355 Richmond Rd Ste 8 Cleveland (44143) *(G-5752)*
Nextgen Fiber Optics LLC (PA) 513 549-4691
720 E Pete Rose Way # 410 Cincinnati (45202) *(G-4075)*
Nextgen Materials LLC 513 858-2365
160a Donald Dr Fairfield (45014) *(G-9535)*
Nextmed Systems Inc (PA) 216 674-0511
16 Triangle Park Dr Cincinnati (45246) *(G-4076)*
Nextstep Networking, Blue Ash *Also called Eaj Services LLC (G-1762)*
Nexus Vision Group LLC 866 492-6499
2156 Southwest Blvd Grove City (43123) *(G-10452)*
Nfm/Welding Engineers Inc (PA) 330 837-3868
577 Oberlin Ave Sw Massillon (44647) *(G-13029)*
Ngc Red Hill, Dover *Also called Natural Gas Construction Inc (G-8844)*
Ngo Development Corporation (HQ) 740 344-3790
1500 Granville Rd Newark (43055) *(G-14903)*
Ngo Development Corporation 740 622-9560
504 N 3rd St Coshocton (43812) *(G-7743)*
Ngp Printing Professional, Lima *Also called News Gazette Printing Company (G-11911)*
Nhvs International Inc 440 527-8610
7600 Tyler Blvd Mentor (44060) *(G-13527)*
Niagara Bottling LLC 614 751-7420
1700 Eastgate Pkwy Gahanna (43230) *(G-10096)*
Niagara Custombilt Mfg, Cleveland *Also called S A Langmack Company (G-6021)*
Niagara Stamping Co, Cleveland *Also called Robin Industries Inc (G-5995)*
Nibco Inc 513 228-1426
2800 Henkle Dr Lebanon (45036) *(G-11676)*
Nicana Consulting Inc 419 615-9703
801 Oak Pkwy Kalida (45853) *(G-11279)*
Nichidai America Corporation 419 423-7511
15630 E State Route 12 # 4 Findlay (45840) *(G-9730)*
Nicholas Press Sales LLC 440 652-6604
3077 Nationwide Pkwy Brunswick (44212) *(G-2222)*
Nicholas Ray Enterprises LLC 330 454-4811
3605 Mahoning Rd Ne Canton (44705) *(G-2761)*
Nichols Aluminum-Alabama LLC 256 353-1550
25825 Science Park Dr # 400 Beachwood (44122) *(G-1253)*
Nichols Industries 614 866-8451
4555 Groves Rd Ste 16 Columbus (43232) *(G-7220)*
Nichols Mold Inc 330 297-9719
222 W Lake St Ravenna (44266) *(G-16391)*
Nickles Bakery 45, Zanesville *Also called Alfred Nickles Bakery Inc (G-21096)*
Nicks Plating Co Inc 937 773-3175
6980 Free Rd Piqua (45356) *(G-16145)*
Nickum Enterprises Inc 513 561-2292
6105 Madison Rd Cincinnati (45227) *(G-4077)*
Nicofibers Inc 740 394-2491
9702 Iron Point Rd Se Shawnee (43782) *(G-16961)*
Nidec Indus Automtn USA LLC 216 901-2400
7800 Hub Pkwy Cleveland (44125) *(G-5753)*
Nidec Industrial Solutions, Independence *Also called Nidec Motor Corporation (G-11144)*
Nidec Minster, Saint Marys *Also called Nidec Minster Corporation (G-16691)*
Nidec Minster Corporation 419 628-1652
115 N Ohio St Minster (45865) *(G-14221)*
Nidec Minster Corporation 419 394-7504
331 S Park Dr Saint Marys (45885) *(G-16691)*
Nidec Motor Corporation 216 642-1230
7555 E Pleasant Vly Independence (44131) *(G-11144)*
Nidec Motor Corporation 575 434-0633
1503 Exeter Rd Akron (44306) *(G-297)*
Nielsen Jewelers, Lorain *Also called H P Nielsen Inc (G-12094)*
Niese Farms 419 347-1204
7506 Cole Rd Crestline (44827) *(G-7797)*
Nifco America Corporation (HQ) 614 920-6800
8015 Dove Pkwy Canal Winchester (43110) *(G-2507)*
Nifco America Corporation 614 836-3808
8015 Dove Pkwy Canal Winchester (43110) *(G-2508)*
Nifco America Corporation 614 836-8691
4485 S Hamilton Rd Groveport (43125) *(G-10507)*
Niftech, Mentor *Also called R J K Enterprises Inc (G-13569)*
Niftech Inc 440 257-6018
5565 Wilson Dr Mentor (44060) *(G-13528)*
Niftech Precision Race Pdts, Mentor *Also called Niftech Inc (G-13528)*
Nifty Promo Products, Middletown *Also called Backyard Scoreboards LLC (G-13886)*
Nigerian Assn Pharmacists & PH 513 861-2329
483 Northland Blvd Cincinnati (45240) *(G-4078)*
Night Lightscapes 419 304-2486
3303 Herr Rd Sylvania (43560) *(G-17956)*
Nihon Company, Urbana *Also called Parker Trutec Incorporated (G-19007)*
Nija Foods LLC 513 377-7495
323 Warren Ave Cincinnati (45220) *(G-4079)*
Nikkicakes 330 606-5745
806 Myrtle Ave Cuyahoga Falls (44221) *(G-7901)*
Niklee Co 440 944-0082
2959 Canterbury Ct Willoughby Hills (44092) *(G-20473)*
Niktec LLC 513 282-3747
127 Industrial Dr Franklin (45005) *(G-9904)*
Niles Manufacturing & Finshg 330 544-0402
465 Walnut St Niles (44446) *(G-15024)*
Niles Roll Service Inc (PA) 330 544-0026
704 Warren Ave Niles (44446) *(G-15025)*
Nilodor Inc 800 443-4321
10966 Industrial Pkwy Nw Bolivar (44612) *(G-1919)*
Nilpeter Usa Inc 513 489-4400
11550 Goldcoast Dr Cincinnati (45249) *(G-4080)*
Nimco Inc 740 596-4477
33711 State Route 93 Mc Arthur (45651) *(G-13182)*
Nine Giant Brewing LLC 510 220-5104
3204 Nash Ave Cincinnati (45226) *(G-4081)*
Nipm, Canal Fulton *Also called New Image Plastics Mfg Co (G-2487)*
Nippon Stl Smkin Crnkshaft LLC 419 435-0411
1815 Sandusky St Fostoria (44830) *(G-9852)*
Nissen Chemitec America Inc 740 852-3200
350 E High St London (43140) *(G-12065)*
Nissen Lumber & Coal Co Inc (PA) 419 836-8035
5700 Navarre Ave Oregon (43616) *(G-15562)*
Nissin Brake Ohio Inc (HQ) 419 420-3800
1901 Industrial Dr Findlay (45840) *(G-9731)*
Nissin Brake Ohio Inc 937 642-7556
25790 State Route 287 East Liberty (43319) *(G-9049)*
Nissin Precision N Amer Inc 937 836-1910
375 Union Rd Englewood (45315) *(G-9372)*
Nitrojection 440 834-8790
8430 Mayfield Rd Chesterland (44026) *(G-3166)*
Nitto Inc 937 773-4820
1620 S Main St Piqua (45356) *(G-16146)*
Nitto Denko Avecia Inc 513 679-3000
8560 Reading Rd Cincinnati (45215) *(G-4082)*
Niya Goods, Powell *Also called Toccata Technologies Inc (G-16339)*
Njf Manufacturing LLC 419 294-0400
7387 Township Highway 104 Upper Sandusky (43351) *(G-18968)*
Njm Furniture Outlet Inc 330 893-3514
6899 County Road 672 Millersburg (44654) *(G-14118)*
Nk Machine Inc 513 737-8035
1550 Pleasant Ave Hamilton (45015) *(G-10590)*
Nkc of America Inc 937 642-4033
24000 Honda Pkwy Gate E Marysville (43040) *(G-12804)*
Nl Mfg & Distribution Sys In 513 422-5216
6107 Market Ave Middletown (45005) *(G-13972)*
NM Group Global LLC (PA) 419 447-5211
161 Greenfield St Tiffin (44883) *(G-18071)*
Nmg Aerospace, Stow *Also called National Machine Company (G-17611)*
Nmgg Ctg LLC (PA) 419 447-5211
161 Greenfield St Tiffin (44883) *(G-18072)*
Nmtc, Inc., Stow *Also called Matco Tools Corporation (G-17605)*
Nn Inc 440 647-4711
125 Bennett St Wellington (44090) *(G-19587)*
Nn Autocam Precision Component 440 647-4711
720 Shiloh Ave Wellington (44090) *(G-19588)*
Nnodum Pharmaceuticals Corp 513 861-2329
483 Northland Blvd Cincinnati (45240) *(G-4083)*
No Burn Inc 330 336-1500
1392 High St Ste 211 Wadsworth (44281) *(G-19256)*
No Burn North America Inc 419 841-6055
2930 Centennial Rd Toledo (43617) *(G-18426)*
No Name Lumber LLC 740 289-3722
165 No Name Rd Piketon (45661) *(G-16075)*
No Rinse Laboratories LLC 937 746-7357
868 Pleasant Valley Dr Springboro (45066) *(G-17339)*
Nobal Enterprises Inc 440 748-0522
11470 Hawke Rd Unit 3 Columbia Station (44028) *(G-6441)*
Noble Denim Workshop 513 560-5640
2929 Spring Grove Ave Cincinnati (45225) *(G-4084)*
Noble Tool Corp 937 461-4040
1535 Stanley Ave Dayton (45404) *(G-8381)*
Nock and Son Company (PA) 440 871-5525
27320 W Oviatt Rd Cleveland (44140) *(G-5754)*
Nock and Son Company 740 682-7741
4138 Monroe Hollow Rd Oak Hill (45656) *(G-15457)*
Noco Company 216 464-8131
30339 Diamond Pkwy # 102 Solon (44139) *(G-17208)*
Nof Metal Coatings N Amer Inc (HQ) 440 285-2231
275 Industrial Pkwy Chardon (44024) *(G-3128)*
Nofziger Door Sales Inc (PA) 419 337-9900
320 Sycamore St Wauseon (43567) *(G-19530)*
Nofziger Door Sales Inc 419 445-2961
111 Taylor Pkwy Archbold (43502) *(G-662)*
Noggin LLC 440 305-6188
3500 Lorain Ave Ste 300 Cleveland (44113) *(G-5755)*
Noise Suppression Technologies 614 275-1818
4182 Fisher Rd Columbus (43228) *(G-7221)*
Nolan Company (PA) 330 453-7922
1016 9th St Sw Canton (44707) *(G-2762)*
Nolan Company 740 269-1512
300 Boyce Dr Bowerston (44695) *(G-1942)*

ALPHABETIC

Nolan Manufacturing LLC · 614 859-2302
493 Blue Heron Ct Westerville (43082) *(G-20012)*

Nolan Mfg Co - Electronics Div, Westerville Also called Nolan Manufacturing LLC *(G-20012)*

Nom Nom Nom · 614 302-4815
2818 Banwick Rd Columbus (43232) *(G-7222)*

Nomac Drilling LLC · 330 476-7040
1258 Panda Rd Se Carrollton (44615) *(G-2926)*

Nomac Drilling LLC · 724 324-2205
67090 Executive Dr Saint Clairsville (43950) *(G-16641)*

Nomis Publications Inc · 330 965-2380
8570 Foxwood Ct Youngstown (44514) *(G-20976)*

Non-Ferrous Casting Co · 937 228-1162
736 Albany St Dayton (45417) *(G-8382)*

Non-Ferrous Heat Treating, Maple Heights Also called Dewitt Inc *(G-12570)*

Non-Injectable Manufacturing, Columbus Also called Hikma Pharmaceuticals USA Inc *(G-7000)*

Nona Composites LLC · 937 490-4814
510 Earl Blvd Miamisburg (45342) *(G-13700)*

None, Curtice Also called Ottawa Products Co *(G-7826)*

Nook Industries Inc (PA) · 216 271-7900
4950 E 49th St Cleveland (44125) *(G-5756)*

NOOTROPICS CITY DBA, Canton Also called Aggregate Tersornance LLC *(G-2560)*

Noramar Company Inc · 440 338-5740
8501 Kinsman Rd Novelty (44072) *(G-15439)*

Noramco, Euclid Also called North American Plas Chem Inc *(G-9430)*

Norbar Torque Tools Inc · 440 953-1175
36400 Biltmore Pl Willoughby (44094) *(G-20389)*

Norcal Signs Inc · 513 779-6982
6163 Allen Rd West Chester (45069) *(G-19749)*

Norcia Bakery · 330 454-1077
624 Belden Ave Ne Canton (44704) *(G-2763)*

Norcold Inc (HQ) · 937 497-3080
600 S Kuther Rd Sidney (45365) *(G-17057)*

Norcold Inc · 937 447-2241
1 Century Dr Gettysburg (45328) *(G-10247)*

Nordec Inc · 330 940-3700
900 Hampshire Rd Stow (44224) *(G-17615)*

Nordic Light America Inc · 614 981-9497
426 Mccormick Blvd Columbus (43213) *(G-7223)*

Nordson Corporation (PA) · 440 892-1580
28601 Clemens Rd Westlake (44145) *(G-20132)*

Nordson Corporation · 440 985-4000
100 Nordson Dr Ms81 Amherst (44001) *(G-566)*

Nordson Corporation · 440 988-9411
555 Jackson St Amherst (44001) *(G-567)*

Nordson Uv Inc · 440 985-4573
555 Jackson St Amherst (44001) *(G-568)*

Nordson Xaloy Incorporated (HQ) · 724 656-5600
375 Victoria Rd Ste 1 Youngstown (44515) *(G-20977)*

Norfolk Southern Corporation · 419 697-5070
3830 Corduroy Rd Oregon (43616) *(G-15563)*

Norgren Inc · 937 833-4033
325 Carr Dr Brookville (45309) *(G-2179)*

Noritake Co Inc · 513 234-0770
4990 Alliance Dr Mason (45040) *(G-12915)*

Norkaam Industries LLC · 330 873-9793
1477 Copley Rd Akron (44320) *(G-298)*

Norlab Dyes, Lorain Also called Norlab Inc *(G-12107)*

Norlab Inc · 440 282-5265
7465 Industrial Pkwy Dr Lorain (44053) *(G-12107)*

Norlake Manufacturing Company · 440 353-3200
39301 Taylor Pkwy North Ridgeville (44035) *(G-15241)*

Norman Knepp · 740 978-6339
62969 Us Highway 50 Mc Arthur (45651) *(G-13183)*

Norman Noble Inc (PA) · 216 761-5387
5507 Avion Park Dr Highland Heights (44143) *(G-10794)*

Norman Noble Inc · 216 851-4007
931 E 228th St Euclid (44123) *(G-9429)*

Norman Noble Inc · 216 761-5387
5507 Avion Park Dr Cleveland (44143) *(G-5757)*

Norman Noble Inc · 216 761-2133
6120 Parkland Blvd # 306 Cleveland (44124) *(G-5758)*

Norman Noble Inc · 216 761-5387
5340 Avion Park Dr Highland Heights (44143) *(G-10795)*

Normandy Products Company · 440 632-5050
16125 Industrial Pkwy Middlefield (44062) *(G-13840)*

Normant Candy Co · 419 886-4214
1821 Mock Rd Mansfield (44904) *(G-12494)*

Normant's Salt Water Taffy, Mansfield Also called Normant Candy Co *(G-12494)*

Norplas Industries, Northwood Also called Magna Exteriors America Inc *(G-15340)*

Norplas Industries Inc (HQ) · 419 662-3317
7825 Caple Blvd Northwood (43619) *(G-15341)*

Norris North Manufacturing · 330 691-0449
1500 Henry Ave Sw Canton (44706) *(G-2764)*

Norse Dairy Systems Inc · 614 294-4931
1700 E 17th Ave Columbus (43219) *(G-7224)*

Norse Dairy Systems LP · 614 421-5297
1740 Joyce Ave Columbus (43219) *(G-7225)*

Norstar Aluminum Molds Inc · 440 632-0853
15986 Valplast St Middlefield (44062) *(G-13841)*

Norstar International LLC · 513 404-3543
9435 Waterstone Blvd # 290 Cincinnati (45249) *(G-4085)*

North American Auger Mining · 740 622-8782
1816 Bayberry Ln Coshocton (43812) *(G-7744)*

North American Cast Stone Inc · 440 286-1999
13271 Bass Lake Rd Chardon (44024) *(G-3129)*

North American Coating Labs, Mentor Also called Wilson Optical Laboratory Inc *(G-13626)*

North American Dist Ctr, Cambridge Also called Ridge Tool Company *(G-2455)*

North American Plas Chem Inc (PA) · 216 531-3400
1400 E 222nd St Euclid (44117) *(G-9430)*

North American Research Corp · 937 445-5000
1700 S Patterson Blvd Kettering (45409) *(G-11438)*

North American Stamping Group, Ada Also called Nasg Ohio LLC *(G-7)*

North American Steel Company · 216 475-7300
18300 Miles Rd Cleveland (44128) *(G-5759)*

North Amrcn Sstnable Enrgy Ltd · 440 539-7133
1360 Grant Dr Parma (44134) *(G-15824)*

North Bend Express · 513 481-4623
3295 North Bend Rd Cincinnati (45239) *(G-4086)*

North Canton Plastics Inc · 330 497-0071
6658 Promway Ave Nw Canton (44720) *(G-2765)*

North Canton Tool Co · 330 452-0545
1156 Marion Ave Sw Canton (44707) *(G-2766)*

North Cape Manufacturing, Streetsboro Also called Technology House Ltd *(G-17701)*

North Cast Orthtics Prsthetics (PA) · 440 233-4314
6100 S Broadway Ste 104 Lorain (44053) *(G-12108)*

North Central Concrete Design · 419 606-1908
3331 E Lincoln Way Wooster (44691) *(G-20632)*

North Central Insulation Inc (PA) · 419 886-2030
7539 State Route 13 Bellville (44813) *(G-1561)*

North Central Processing Inc (PA) · 216 623-1090
761 Stones Levee Cleveland (44113) *(G-5760)*

North Coast Business Journal · 419 734-4838
205 Se Catawba Rd Ste G Port Clinton (43452) *(G-16254)*

North Coast Camshaft Inc · 216 671-3700
10910 Briggs Rd Cleveland (44111) *(G-5761)*

North Coast Composites Inc · 216 398-8550
4605 Spring Rd Cleveland (44131) *(G-5762)*

North Coast Container Corp (PA) · 216 441-6214
8806 Crane Ave Cleveland (44105) *(G-5763)*

North Coast Custom Molding Inc · 419 905-6447
211 W Geneva St Dunkirk (45836) *(G-9035)*

North Coast Dumpster Svcs LLC · 216 644-5647
3740 Carnegie Ave Cleveland (44115) *(G-5764)*

North Coast Exotics Inc · 216 651-5512
3159 W 68th St Cleveland (44102) *(G-5765)*

North Coast Holdings Inc (PA) · 330 535-7177
768 E North St Akron (44305) *(G-299)*

North Coast Instruments Inc · 216 251-2353
14615 Lorain Ave Cleveland (44111) *(G-5766)*

North Coast Litho Inc · 216 881-1952
4701 Manufacturing Ave Cleveland (44135) *(G-5767)*

North Coast Medi-Tek Inc · 440 974-0750
8603 East Ave Mentor (44060) *(G-13529)*

North Coast Media LLC · 216 706-3700
1360 E 9th St Ste 1070 Cleveland (44114) *(G-5768)*

North Coast Medical Eqp Inc · 440 243-2722
96 Lincoln Ave Berea (44017) *(G-1619)*

North Coast Minority Media LLC · 216 407-4327
1360 E 9th St Cleveland (44114) *(G-5769)*

North Coast Pattern Inc · 440 322-5064
10587 Scottsdale Dr Strongsville (44136) *(G-17771)*

North Coast Profile Inc · 330 823-7777
255 E Perry St Alliance (44601) *(G-493)*

North Coast Publications, Cleveland Also called North Coast Minority Media LLC *(G-5769)*

North Coast Rivet Inc · 440 366-6829
700 Sugar Ln Elyria (44035) *(G-9301)*

North Coast Security Group LLC · 614 887-7255
750 E Long St Ste 3000 Columbus (43203) *(G-7226)*

North Coast Theatrical Inc (PA) · 330 762-1768
2181 Killian Rd Unit A Akron (44312) *(G-300)*

North Coast Voice Mag · 440 415-0999
143 S Cedar St Geneva (44041) *(G-10226)*

North East Fuel Inc · 330 264-4454
3927 Cleveland Rd Wooster (44691) *(G-20633)*

North East Technologies Inc · 440 327-9278
5127 Mills Indus Pkwy North Ridgeville (44039) *(G-15242)*

North End Press Incorporated · 740 653-6514
235 S Columbus St Lancaster (43130) *(G-11591)*

North Fork Southern, Columbus Also called Rail Road Corporation *(G-7376)*

North High Brewing LLC · 614 407-5278
1125 Cleveland Ave Columbus (43201) *(G-7227)*

North Hill Marathon · 937 444-1894
570 N High St Mount Orab (45154) *(G-14448)*

North Hill Marble & Granite Co · 330 253-2179
448 N Howard St Akron (44310) *(G-301)*

North Jckson Specialty Stl LLC · 330 538-9621
2058 S Bailey Rd North Jackson (44451) *(G-15150)*

North Shore Safety, Mentor Also called Tecmark Corporation (G-13602)
North Shore Stone Inc 614 870-7531
915 Manor Park Dr Columbus (43228) (G-7228)
North Shore Strapping Inc (PA) 216 661-5200
1400 Valley Belt Rd Brooklyn Heights (44131) (G-2128)
North Shore Strapping Inc 216 661-5200
9401 Maywood Ave Cleveland (44102) (G-5770)
North Star Bluescope Steel LLC 419 822-2200
6767 County Road 9 Delta (43515) (G-8777)
North Star Metals Mfg Co 740 254-4567
6850 Edwards Ridge Rd Se Uhrichsville (44683) (G-18891)
North Toledo Graphics LLC 419 476-8808
5225 Telegraph Rd Toledo (43612) (G-18427)
North View Woodworking 330 359-6286
8422 State Route 93 Nw Dundee (44624) (G-9024)
North-West Tool Co 937 278-7995
2725 Kearns Ave Dayton (45414) (G-8383)
Northcoast Advertising, Ashland Also called Heritage Press Inc (G-709)
Northcoast Environmental Labs 330 342-3377
10100 Wellman Rd Streetsboro (44241) (G-17685)
Northcoast Pmm LLC 419 540-8667
4725 Southbridge Rd Toledo (43623) (G-18428)
Northcoast Prfmce & Mch Co 330 753-7333
1190 Wooster Rd N Barberton (44203) (G-1089)
Northcoast Process Controls 440 498-0542
6283 Sunnywood Dr Cleveland (44139) (G-5771)
Northcoast Tape & Label Inc 440 439-3200
24300 Solon Rd Ste 7 Cleveland (44146) (G-5772)
Northcoast Valve and Gate Inc 440 392-9910
9437 Mercantile Dr Mentor (44060) (G-13530)
Northeast Blueprint & Sup Co 216 261-7500
1230 E 286th St Cleveland (44132) (G-5773)
Northeast Box Company 440 992-5500
1726 Griswold Ave Ashtabula (44004) (G-793)
Northeast Broach & Tool 440 918-0048
990 Erie Rd Unit H Eastlake (44095) (G-9126)
Northeast Cabinet Co LLC 614 759-0800
6063 Taylor Rd Columbus (43230) (G-7229)
Northeast Coatings Inc 330 784-7773
415 Munroe Falls Rd Tallmadge (44278) (G-17996)
Northeast Laser Inc 330 633-2897
461 Commerce St Tallmadge (44278) (G-17997)
Northeast OH Neighborhood Heal 216 751-3100
13301 Miles Ave Cleveland (44105) (G-5774)
Northeast Ohio Contractors LLC 216 269-7881
3555 W 69th St Cleveland (44102) (G-5775)
Northeast Piping Supply, Wooster Also called Northeast Tubular Service Inc (G-20634)
Northeast Scene Inc 216 241-7550
737 Bolivar Rd Cleveland (44115) (G-5776)
Northeast Suburban Life 513 248-8600
312 Elm St Cincinnati (45202) (G-4087)
Northeast Tire Molds Inc (HQ) 330 376-6107
159 Opportunity Pkwy Akron (44307) (G-302)
Northeast Tubular Service Inc 330 262-1881
6740 E Lincoln Way Wooster (44691) (G-20634)
Northeastern Machinery, Warren Also called Rinaldi and Packard Industries (G-19440)
Northeastern Oilfield Svcs LLC (PA) 330 581-3304
1537 Waynesburg Dr Se Canton (44707) (G-2767)
Northeastern Plastics Inc 330 453-5925
112 Navarre Rd Sw Canton (44707) (G-2768)
Northeastern Process Cooling, Willoughby Also called NRC Inc (G-20391)
Northeastern Rfrgn Corp 440 942-7676
38274 Western Pkwy Willoughby (44094) (G-20390)
Northel Usa LLC 740 973-0309
5772 Bear Hollow Rd Se Newark (43056) (G-14904)
Northend Gear & Machine Inc 513 860-4334
475 Security Dr Fairfield (45014) (G-9536)
Northern Boiler Company 216 961-3033
3453 W 86th St Cleveland (44102) (G-5777)
Northern Chem Blnding Corp Inc 216 781-7799
360 Literary Rd Cleveland (44113) (G-5778)
Northern Concrete Pipe Inc 419 841-3361
3756 Centennial Rd Sylvania (43560) (G-17957)
Northern Fabricator, Cleveland Also called Northern Boiler Company (G-5777)
Northern Instruments Corp LLC 216 450-5073
23205 Mercantile Rd Cleveland (44122) (G-5779)
Northern Machine Tool Co 216 961-0444
3453 W 86th St Cleveland (44102) (G-5780)
Northern Manufacturing Co Inc 419 898-2821
150 N Lake Winds Pkwy Oak Harbor (43449) (G-15446)
Northern Mobile Electric, Canton Also called M Technologies Inc (G-2739)
Northern Ohio Printing Inc 216 398-0000
4721 Hinckley Indus Pkwy Cleveland (44109) (G-5781)
Northern Precision Inc 513 860-4701
3245 Production Dr Fairfield (45014) (G-9537)
Northern Stamping Co 216 883-8888
5900 Harvard Ave Cleveland (44105) (G-5782)
Northern Stamping Co (HQ) 216 883-8888
6600 Chapek Pkwy Cleveland (44125) (G-5783)

Northern Stamping Co 216 642-8081
7750 Hub Pkwy Cleveland (44125) (G-5784)
Northern Stamping Plant 2, Cleveland Also called Northern Stamping Co (G-5784)
Northern Stamping, Inc., Cleveland Also called Northern Stamping Co (G-5783)
Northern States Metals Company 860 521-6001
3207 Innovation Pl Youngstown (44509) (G-20978)
Northestrn OH Foot & Ankl Asoc 330 633-3445
1557 Vernon Odom Blvd # 102 Akron (44320) (G-303)
Northfield 440 949-1815
5190 Oster Rd Sheffield Village (44054) (G-16972)
Northlake Steel Corporation 330 220-7717
5455 Wegman Dr Valley City (44280) (G-19056)
Northmont Sign Co Inc 937 890-0372
8400 N Main St Dayton (45415) (G-8384)
Northmont Tool and Gage Inc 937 836-9879
8741 Kimmel Rd Clayton (45315) (G-4577)
Northpointe Cabinetry LLC 740 455-4045
4800 Frazeysburg Rd Zanesville (43701) (G-21163)
Northrop Grumman Innovation 937 429-9261
1365 Technology Ct Beavercreek (45430) (G-1360)
Northrop Grumman Systems Corp 513 881-3296
460 W Crescentville Rd West Chester (45246) (G-19881)
Northshore Mining Company (HQ) 216 694-5700
200 Public Sq Cleveland (44114) (G-5785)
Northshore Mold Inc 440 838-8212
2861 E Royalton Rd Cleveland (44147) (G-5786)
Northside Meat Co Inc 513 681-4111
2910 Sidney Ave Cincinnati (45225) (G-4088)
Northstar Asphalt, Canton Also called Stark Materials Inc (G-2822)
Northstar Publishing 330 721-9126
437 Lafayette Rd Ste 310 Medina (44256) (G-13307)
Northwest Installations Inc 419 423-5738
1903 Blanchard Ave Findlay (45840) (G-9732)
Northwest Molded Plastics 419 459-4414
14372 County Road 4 Edon (43518) (G-9186)
Northwest Print Inc 419 385-3375
12900 Eckel Junction Rd C Perrysburg (43551) (G-15982)
Northwest Printing, Westerville Also called Ganger Enterprises Inc (G-19993)
Northwest Products, Stryker Also called Quadco Rehabilitation Ctr Inc (G-17832)
Northwest Products Div, Archbold Also called Quadco Rehabilitation Center (G-665)
Northwest Realty, Montpelier Also called Bryan Publishing Company (G-14302)
Northwest Signal, Napoleon Also called Napoleon Inc (G-14552)
Northwind Industries Inc 216 433-0666
15500 Commerce Park Dr Cleveland (44142) (G-5787)
Northwood Energy Corporation 614 457-1024
941 Chatham Ln Ste 100 Columbus (43221) (G-7230)
Northwood Industries Inc 419 666-2100
7650 Ponderosa Rd Perrysburg (43551) (G-15983)
Norton Industries Inc 888 357-2345
1366 W 117th St Lakewood (44107) (G-11532)
Norton Manufacturing Co Inc 419 435-0411
455 W 4th St Fostoria (44830) (G-9853)
Norton Outdoor Advertising 513 631-4864
5280 Kennedy Ave Cincinnati (45213) (G-4089)
Norwalk Concrete Inds Inc (PA) 419 668-8167
80 Commerce Dr Norwalk (44857) (G-15408)
Norwalk Concrete Inds Inc 419 668-8167
80 Commerce Dr Norwalk (44857) (G-15409)
Norwalk Precast Molds Inc 419 668-1639
205 Industrial Pkwy Norwalk (44857) (G-15410)
Norwalk Reflector, Norwalk Also called Herald Reflector Inc (G-15399)
Norwalk Wastewater Eqp Co 419 668-4471
220 Republic St Norwalk (44857) (G-15411)
Norweco, Norwalk Also called Norwalk Wastewater Eqp Co (G-15411)
Norwesco Inc 740 335-6236
2424 Kenskill Ave Wshngtn CT Hs (43160) (G-20734)
Norwesco Inc 740 654-6402
3111 Wilson Rd Lancaster (43130) (G-11592)
Norwich Overseas Inc (HQ) 513 983-1100
8700 S Masn Montgomery Rd Mason (45040) (G-12916)
Norwood Medical, Dayton Also called Norwood Tool Company (G-8387)
Norwood Medical 937 228-4101
2055 Winners Cir Dayton (45404) (G-8385)
Norwood Medical 937 228-4101
2101 Winners Cir Dayton (45404) (G-8386)
Norwood Tool Company (PA) 937 228-4101
2122 Winners Cir Dayton (45404) (G-8387)
Noshok Inc (PA) 440 243-0888
1010 W Bagley Rd Berea (44017) (G-1620)
Nostalgic Images Inc 419 784-1728
26012 Nostalgic Rd Defiance (43512) (G-8641)
Noster Rubber Company Inc 419 299-3387
1481 Township Road 229 Van Buren (45889) (G-19072)
Nostrum Laboratories Inc 419 636-1168
705 E Mulberry St Bryan (43506) (G-2299)
Noteworthy Woodworking 330 297-0509
6361 Marchinn Dr Ravenna (44266) (G-16392)
Noun Research and Dev Svcs, Columbus Also called David Boswell (G-6852)

Nov Tuboscope, Lorain *Also called Tuboscope Pipeline Svcs Inc* ***(G-12130)***
Nova Chemicals Inc........440 352-3381
786 Hardy Rd Painesville (44077) ***(G-15766)***
Nova Creative Group Inc........937 291-8653
7812 Mcewen Rd Ste 300 Dayton (45459) ***(G-8388)***
Nova Films and Foils Inc........440 201-1300
11 Industry Dr Bedford (44146) ***(G-1431)***
Nova Machine Products Inc (HQ)........216 267-3200
18001 Sheldon Rd Middleburg Heights (44130) ***(G-13767)***
Nova Metal Products Inc........440 269-1741
1455 E 328th St Eastlake (44095) ***(G-9127)***
Nova Polymers Inc........888 484-6682
15348 Rt 127 E Bryan (43506) ***(G-2300)***
Nova Structural Steel Inc........216 938-7476
900 E 69th St Cleveland (44103) ***(G-5788)***
Novacare Inc........216 704-4817
24400 Highpoint Rd Ste 10 Beachwood (44122) ***(G-1254)***
Novacare Prosthetics Orthotics, Oregon *Also called Swanson Orthotic & Prosthetic* ***(G-15570)***
Novacel Inc........937 335-5611
421 S Union St Troy (45373) ***(G-18688)***
Novacel Inc........413 283-3468
421 Union St Troy (45373) ***(G-18689)***
Novagard Solutions Inc (PA)........216 881-3890
5109 Hamilton Ave Cleveland (44114) ***(G-5789)***
Novak J F Manufacturing Co LLC........216 741-5112
2701 Meyer Ave Cleveland (44109) ***(G-5790)***
Novak Supply LLC........216 741-5112
2701 Meyer Ave Cleveland (44109) ***(G-5791)***
Novartis Corporation........919 577-5000
1880 Waycross Rd Cincinnati (45240) ***(G-4090)***
Novartis Vaccines & Diagnostic, Cincinnati *Also called Novartis Corporation* ***(G-4090)***
Novatex North America Inc........419 282-4264
1070 Faultless Dr Ashland (44805) ***(G-728)***
Novation Solutions LLC........330 620-1189
30 2nd St Sw Barberton (44203) ***(G-1090)***
Novavision Inc (PA)........419 354-1427
524 E Woodland Cir Bowling Green (43402) ***(G-1986)***
Novel Writing Workshop, Blue Ash *Also called F+w Media Inc* ***(G-1770)***
Novelis........440 392-6150
11815 Oakhurst Ave Concord Township (44077) ***(G-7640)***
Novelis Corporation........330 841-3456
390 Griswold St Ne Warren (44483) ***(G-19423)***
Novelty Advertising Co Inc........740 622-3113
1148 Walnut St Coshocton (43812) ***(G-7745)***
Noveon Fcc Inc........440 943-4200
29400 Lakeland Blvd Wickliffe (44092) ***(G-20219)***
Noveon Incorporated........216 447-5000
9921 Brecksville Rd Brecksville (44141) ***(G-2052)***
Novex Inc........330 335-2371
258 Main St Wadsworth (44281) ***(G-19257)***
Novex Products Incorporated........440 244-3330
2707 Toledo Ave Ste A Lorain (44055) ***(G-12109)***
Novitran LLC........513 792-2727
8100 Deer Path Cincinnati (45243) ***(G-4091)***
Novo Foam Products LLC........440 892-3325
1991 Crocker Rd Ste 600 Westlake (44145) ***(G-20133)***
Novolex, Coldwater *Also called Accutech Films Inc* ***(G-6398)***
Novolex Holdings Inc........740 397-2555
101 Commerce Dr Mount Vernon (43050) ***(G-14496)***
Novolex Holdings Inc........937 746-1933
2000 Commerce Center Dr Franklin (45005) ***(G-9905)***
Now Software Inc........614 783-4517
3720 Head Of Pond Rd New Albany (43054) ***(G-14632)***
Noxgear LLC........937 248-1860
2264 Green Island Dr Columbus (43228) ***(G-7231)***
Npa Coatings Inc........216 651-5900
11110 Berea Rd Ste 1 Cleveland (44102) ***(G-5792)***
Npk Construction Equipment Inc (HQ)........440 232-7900
7550 Independence Dr Bedford (44146) ***(G-1432)***
NPS, Richfield *Also called National Polishing Systems Inc* ***(G-16477)***
Nr Lee Restoration Ltd........419 692-2233
7470 Grone Rd Delphos (45833) ***(G-8752)***
NRC Inc........440 975-9449
38160 Western Pkwy Willoughby (44094) ***(G-20391)***
NRG Smoothies LLC........972 800-1002
1887 Youngstown Vienna (44473) ***(G-19206)***
Nsa Technologies LLC........330 576-4600
3867 Medina Rd Ste 256 Akron (44333) ***(G-304)***
Nsg Glass North America Inc........419 247-4800
811 Madison Ave Toledo (43604) ***(G-18429)***
Nsi Crankshaft, Fostoria *Also called Nippon Stl Smkin Crnkshaft LLC* ***(G-9852)***
Nss Enterprises Inc (PA)........419 531-2121
3115 Frenchmens Rd Toledo (43607) ***(G-18430)***
Nsti, Columbus *Also called Noise Suppression Technologies* ***(G-7221)***
Nt, Toledo *Also called North Toledo Graphics LLC* ***(G-18427)***
Nt Machine Inc........440 968-3506
10080 Clay St Montville (44064) ***(G-14324)***
Nt Machine Inorp, Montville *Also called Nt Machine Inc* ***(G-14324)***
Nta Graphics Inc........419 476-8808
5225 Telegraph Rd Toledo (43612) ***(G-18431)***
Ntech Industries Inc........707 467-3747
5475 Kellenburger Rd Dayton (45424) ***(G-8389)***
NTS Enterprises Ltd (PA)........513 531-1166
1550 Magnolia Dr Cincinnati (45215) ***(G-4092)***
Nu Pet Company (HQ)........330 682-3000
1 Strawberry Ln Orrville (44667) ***(G-15606)***
Nu Risers Stair Company........937 322-8100
2748 Columbus Rd Springfield (45503) ***(G-17462)***
Nu Stream Filtration Inc........937 949-3174
1257 Stanley Ave Dayton (45404) ***(G-8390)***
Nu-Di Corporation, Cleveland *Also called Nu-Di Products Co Inc* ***(G-5793)***
Nu-Di Products Co Inc........216 251-9070
12730 Triskett Rd Cleveland (44111) ***(G-5793)***
Nu-Tool Industries Inc........440 237-9240
9920 York Alpha Dr North Royalton (44133) ***(G-15289)***
Nucam, Twinsburg *Also called Semtorq Inc* ***(G-18856)***
Nucon International Inc (PA)........614 846-5710
7000 Huntley Rd Columbus (43229) ***(G-7232)***
Nucor Bright Bar Orville LLC........330 682-5555
555 Collins Blvd Orrville (44667) ***(G-15607)***
Nuevue Solutions Inc........440 836-4772
4209 State Route 44 D-134 Rootstown (44272) ***(G-16572)***
Nufab Sheet Metal........937 235-2030
4750 Hempstead Station Dr Dayton (45429) ***(G-8391)***
Nuflux LLC........330 399-1122
2395 State Route 5 Cortland (44410) ***(G-7713)***
Numerics Unlimited Inc........937 849-0100
1700 Dalton Dr New Carlisle (45344) ***(G-14675)***
Numerics Unlimited North, Sidney *Also called Compressor Technologies Inc* ***(G-17023)***
Nupco Inc........419 629-2259
06561 County Road 66a New Bremen (45869) ***(G-14658)***
Nupro Company........440 951-9729
4800 E 345th St Willoughby (44094) ***(G-20392)***
Nurdcon LLC........614 208-5898
6645 Kodiak Dr Canal Winchester (43110) ***(G-2509)***
Nurture Brands LLC........513 307-2338
177 Wyoming Woods Ln Cincinnati (45215) ***(G-4093)***
Nutech Company LLC........440 867-8900
4496 Mahoning Ave Ste 919 Youngstown (44515) ***(G-20979)***
Nutrien AG Solutions Inc........614 873-4253
9972 State Route 38 Milford Center (43045) ***(G-14047)***
Nutrien AG Solutions Inc........513 941-4100
10743 Brower Rd North Bend (45052) ***(G-15053)***
Nutrifresh Eggs........567 224-7676
342 Plymouth East Rd Willard (44890) ***(G-20243)***
Nutrimir LLC........614 600-2478
408 Tipperary Loop Delaware (43015) ***(G-8711)***
Nutrimir Personalized Wellness, Delaware *Also called Nutrimir LLC* ***(G-8711)***
Nutritional Medicinals LLC........937 433-4673
9277 Centre Pointe Dr # 220 West Chester (45069) ***(G-19750)***
Nutro Corporation........440 572-3800
11515 Alameda Dr Strongsville (44149) ***(G-17772)***
Nutro Inc........440 572-3800
11515 Alameda Dr Strongsville (44149) ***(G-17773)***
Nutro Machinery, Strongsville *Also called Nutro Corporation* ***(G-17772)***
Nuts Are Good Inc (PA)........586 619-2400
Busch Blvd Columbus (43229) ***(G-7233)***
Nuvasive Manufacturing LLC........937 343-0400
1 Herald Sq Fairborn (45324) ***(G-9464)***
Nuvox........614 232-9115
111 N 4th St Columbus (43215) ***(G-7234)***
Nvision Technology Inc........412 254-4668
2769 Pinegate Dr Norton (44203) ***(G-15374)***
Nwc HUD Corp II........419 228-8400
1404 N West St Lima (45801) ***(G-11912)***
Nwp Manufacturing Inc........419 894-6871
2862 County Road 146 Waldo (43356) ***(G-19303)***
Nxstage Medical Inc........513 712-1300
12065 Montgomery Rd Cincinnati (45249) ***(G-4094)***
NY Logging & Lumber........740 679-2085
61285 Shannon Run Rd Quaker City (43773) ***(G-16353)***
Nyeco Gas Inc........419 447-2712
905 Pierce St Sandusky (44870) ***(G-16831)***
Nyp Corp (frmr Ny-Pters Corp)........440 428-0129
2711 Bennett Rd Madison (44057) ***(G-12354)***
O & P Options LLC........513 791-7767
10547 Montgomery Rd # 600 Montgomery (45242) ***(G-14296)***
O A R Vinyl Window Co, Middlefield *Also called O A R Vinyl Windows & Siding* ***(G-13842)***
O A R Vinyl Windows & Siding........440 636-5573
12880 Clay St Middlefield (44062) ***(G-13842)***
O C I, Waverly *Also called Oak Chips Inc* ***(G-19554)***
O C Tanner Company........513 583-1100
8569 S Mason Montgomery R Mason (45040) ***(G-12917)***
O Connor Office Pdts & Prtg........740 852-2209
60 W High St London (43140) ***(G-12066)***
O D M, Mason *Also called Oakley Die & Mold Co* ***(G-12918)***

O E M Hydraulics Inc 740 454-1201
1150 Newark Rd Zanesville (43701) *(G-21164)*
O E M Sales, Germantown *Also called Ohio Engineering and Mfg Sls (G-10244)*
O E Meyer Co 419 332-6931
1005 Everett Rd Fremont (43420) *(G-10041)*
O G Bell, Avon Lake *Also called Wolff Tool & Manufacturing Co (G-1014)*
O Gauge Railroading, Hilliard *Also called Ogr Publishing Inc (G-10845)*
O H Technologies Inc 440 354-8780
9300 Progress Pkwy Mentor (44060) *(G-13531)*
O K Brugmann Jr & Sons Inc 330 274-2106
4083 Mennonite Rd Mantua (44255) *(G-12555)*
O K Coal & Concrete, Zanesville *Also called Joe McClelland Inc (G-21151)*
O P Services Inc 330 723-6679
799 N Court St Medina (44256) *(G-13308)*
O S C, Columbus *Also called Octsys Security Corp (G-7239)*
O'Beirn Printing Co, Cleveland *Also called Delores E OBeirn (G-5082)*
O'Reilly Precision Tool, Russia *Also called OReilly Precision Products (G-16610)*
O-1, Perrysburg *Also called Owens-Illinois General Inc (G-15998)*
O-I, Perrysburg *Also called Owens-Brockway Glass Cont Inc (G-15995)*
O-I, Toledo *Also called Owens-Illinois De Puerto Rico (G-18451)*
O-Kan Marine Repair Inc 740 446-4686
267 Upper River Rd Gallipolis (45631) *(G-10172)*
O.c Tanner Recognition, Mason *Also called O C Tanner Company (G-12917)*
Oak Chips Inc 740 947-4159
9329 State Route 220 A Waverly (45690) *(G-19554)*
Oak Dale Drilling Inc 740 385-5888
149 Ruth Ave Logan (43138) *(G-12037)*
Oak Front Inc 330 948-4500
830 Bank St Lodi (44254) *(G-12017)*
Oak Heritage, Yellow Springs *Also called Kenway Corp (G-20809)*
Oak Hills Carton Co 513 948-4200
6310 Este Ave Cincinnati (45232) *(G-4095)*
Oak Industrial Inc 440 263-2780
12955 York Delta Dr Ste G North Royalton (44133) *(G-15290)*
Oak Pointe Stair Systems Inc 740 498-9820
96 New Pace Rd Newcomerstown (43832) *(G-14979)*
Oak Printing Company 440 238-3316
19540 Progress Dr Strongsville (44149) *(G-17774)*
Oak Tree Intl Holdings Inc 702 462-7295
1209 Lowell St Elyria (44035) *(G-9302)*
Oak View Enterprises Inc 513 860-4446
100 Crossroads Blvd Bucyrus (44820) *(G-2340)*
Oakbridge Timber Framing 419 994-1052
9001 Township Road 461 Loudonville (44842) *(G-12145)*
Oakes Door Serv 937 323-6188
5298 Troy Rd Springfield (45502) *(G-17463)*
Oakes Foundry Inc 330 372-4010
700 Bronze Rd Ne Warren (44483) *(G-19424)*
Oakley Inc 949 672-6560
1421 Springfield St # 2 Dayton (45403) *(G-8392)*
Oakley Die & Mold Co 513 754-8500
7595 Innovation Way Mason (45040) *(G-12918)*
Oakley Full Gospel Baptist Ch, Columbus *Also called Full Gospel Baptist Times (G-6941)*
Oakley Industries Sub Assembly 419 661-8888
6317 Fairfield Dr Northwood (43619) *(G-15342)*
Oakmoor Pallet 216 926-1858
795 Sharon Dr Ste 210 Westlake (44145) *(G-20134)*
Oakmoor Pallet 440 385-7340
795 Sharon Dr Westlake (44145) *(G-20135)*
Oaks Welding Inc 330 482-4216
201 Prospect St Columbiana (44408) *(G-6475)*
Oaktree Wireline LLC 330 352-7250
1825 E High Ave New Philadelphia (44663) *(G-14791)*
Oakvale Farm Cheese Inc 740 857-1230
1283 State Route 29 Ne London (43140) *(G-12067)*
Oakwood Furniture Inc 740 896-3162
10105 State Route 60 Lowell (45744) *(G-12247)*
Oakwood Industries Inc (PA) 440 232-8700
7250 Division St Bedford (44146) *(G-1433)*
Oakwood Laboratories LLC (PA) 440 359-0000
7670 First Pl Ste A Oakwood Village (44146) *(G-15482)*
Oakwood Laboratories LLC 440 505-2011
27070 Miles Rd Solon (44139) *(G-17209)*
Oakwood Register, The, Dayton *Also called Winkler Co Inc (G-8596)*
Oasis Consumer Healthcare LLC 216 394-0544
737 Bolivar Rd Ste 4500 Cleveland (44115) *(G-5794)*
Oasis Embroidery 614 785-7266
6663 Huntley Rd Ste R Columbus (43229) *(G-7235)*
Oasis Mediterranean Cuisine 419 269-1459
1520 W Laskey Rd Toledo (43612) *(G-18432)*
Oatey Company, Cleveland *Also called Oatey Supply Chain Svcs Inc (G-5795)*
Oatey Supply Chain Svcs Inc (HQ) 216 267-7100
20600 Emerald Pkwy Cleveland (44135) *(G-5795)*
Obars Machine and Tool Company (PA) 419 535-6307
115 N Westwood Ave 125 Toledo (43607) *(G-18433)*
Obars Welding & Fabg Div, Toledo *Also called Obars Machine and Tool Company (G-18433)*
Oberfields LLC (HQ) 740 369-7644
528 London Rd Delaware (43015) *(G-8712)*
Oberfields LLC 614 491-7643
4033 Alum Creek Dr Columbus (43207) *(G-7236)*
Oberfields LLC 740 369-7644
471 Kintner Pkwy Sunbury (43074) *(G-17893)*
Oberfields LLC 614 252-0955
1165 Alum Creek Dr Columbus (43209) *(G-7237)*
Oberfields LLC 937 885-3711
10075 Sheehan Rd Dayton (45458) *(G-8393)*
Oberfields Holdings LLC (PA) 740 369-7644
528 London Rd Delaware (43015) *(G-8713)*
Obersons Nurs & Landscapes Inc 513 894-0669
3951 River Rd Fairfield (45014) *(G-9538)*
Obersons Snow and Ice MGT, Fairfield *Also called Obersons Nurs & Landscapes Inc (G-9538)*
Obr Cooling Towers Inc 419 243-3443
9665 S Compass Dr Rossford (43460) *(G-16588)*
OBrien Cut Stone Company (PA) 216 663-7800
19100 Miles Rd Cleveland (44128) *(G-5796)*
OBrien Cut Stone Company 216 663-7800
19100 Miles Rd Cleveland (44128) *(G-5797)*
OBrien Industries LLC 513 476-0040
2131 Oxford Ave Cincinnati (45230) *(G-4096)*
Obron Atlantic Corporation 440 954-7600
830 E Erie St Painesville (44077) *(G-15767)*
Obs Inc 330 453-3725
1324 Tuscarawas St W Canton (44702) *(G-2769)*
Obs Specialty Vehicles, Canton *Also called Obs Inc (G-2769)*
Obsidian Biodent 937 938-9244
260 Ridgewood Ave Oakwood (45409) *(G-15465)*
OCC, Ashland *Also called Ohio Carbon Company (G-729)*
Occassionaly Yours, Beavercreek *Also called Shops By Todd Inc (G-1340)*
Occidental Chemical Corp 513 242-2900
4701 Paddock Rd Cincinnati (45229) *(G-4097)*
Occidental Chemical Corp 330 764-3441
3984 Dogleg Trl Medina (44256) *(G-13309)*
Occidental Chemical Durez 419 675-5300
13717 Us Highway 68 Kenton (43326) *(G-11417)*
Ocean Providence Columbus LLC 614 272-5973
3699 Interchange Rd Columbus (43204) *(G-7238)*
Ocean Spray Cranberries Inc 513 455-5770
6281 Tri Ridge Blvd # 300 Loveland (45140) *(G-12219)*
Oceanside Foods 440 554-7810
32859 Lake Rd Avon Lake (44012) *(G-999)*
Oceco Co, Tiffin *Also called Oceco Inc (G-18073)*
Oceco Inc 419 447-0916
1616 S County Road 1 Tiffin (44883) *(G-18073)*
Ochc, Cleveland *Also called Oasis Consumer Healthcare LLC (G-5794)*
Ocm LLC (HQ) 937 247-2700
4500 Lyons Rd Miamisburg (45342) *(G-13701)*
Ocs Intellitrak Inc 513 742-5600
8660 Seward Rd Fairfield (45011) *(G-9539)*
Ocs Telecom LLC 740 503-5939
4138 Weaver Ct E Hilliard (43026) *(G-10844)*
Octal Extrusion Corp 513 881-6100
5399 E Provident Dr West Chester (45246) *(G-19882)*
Octsys Security Corp (PA) 614 470-4510
341 S 3rd St Ste 100-42 Columbus (43215) *(G-7239)*
Odacs Inc 513 761-0539
8634 Reading Rd Cincinnati (45215) *(G-4098)*
Odawara Automation Inc 937 667-8433
4805 S County Road 25a Tipp City (45371) *(G-18125)*
Odell Electronic Cleaning Stns, Westlake *Also called Aerocase Incorporated (G-20088)*
Odi, Elyria *Also called Ohio Displays Inc (G-9303)*
Odortech Distributing LLC 216 339-0773
35 Ashbourne Dr Westlake (44145) *(G-20136)*
Odyssey Canvas Works Inc 937 392-4422
6689 Us Highway 52 Ripley (45167) *(G-16515)*
Odyssey Cellars Inc 330 782-0177
4033 Hopkins Rd Youngstown (44511) *(G-20980)*
Odyssey Machine Company Ltd 419 455-6621
26675 Eckel Rd 5 Perrysburg (43551) *(G-15984)*
Odyssey Press Inc 614 410-0356
913 Superior Dr Huron (44839) *(G-11107)*
Odyssey Printwear, Aurora *Also called Odyssey Spirits Inc (G-896)*
Odyssey Spirits Inc 330 562-1523
7286 N Aurora Rd Aurora (44202) *(G-896)*
Oe Exchange LLC (PA) 440 266-1639
8200 Tyler Blvd Mentor (44060) *(G-13532)*
Oeder Carl E Sons Sand & Grav 513 494-1238
1000 Mason Mrrow Mlgrv Rd Lebanon (45036) *(G-11677)*
OEM, West Chester *Also called Ctl-Aerospace Inc (G-19845)*
OEM Corporation 937 859-7492
3660 Benner Rd Miamisburg (45342) *(G-13702)*
Oen Custom Cabinets Inc 419 738-8115
8 Willipie St Wapakoneta (45895) *(G-19348)*
Oen Kitchen & Bath Showroom, Wapakoneta *Also called Oen Custom Cabinets Inc (G-19348)*

Oerlikon Blzers Cating USA Inc 330 343-9892
120 Deeds Dr Dover (44622) ***(G-8846)***
Oerlikon Friction Systems (HQ) 937 449-4000
240 Detrick St Dayton (45404) ***(G-8394)***
Oerlikon Friction Systems 937 233-9191
240 Detrick St Dayton (45404) ***(G-8395)***
of Machining LLC 419 396-7870
2140 State Rd 568 Carey (43316) ***(G-2885)***
Ofco Inc 740 622-5922
111 N 14th St Coshocton (43812) ***(G-7746)***
Off Contact Inc 419 255-5546
4756 W Bancroft St Toledo (43615) ***(G-18434)***
Off Contact Productions, Toledo *Also called Off Contact Inc* ***(G-18434)***
Offendaway LLC 937 232-3933
9498 Ash Hollow Ln Centerville (45458) ***(G-3005)***
Office Bsed Ansthesia Svcs LLC 513 582-5170
10296 Gentlewind Dr Montgomery (45242) ***(G-14297)***
Office Magic Inc (PA) 510 782-6100
2290 Wilbur Rd Medina (44256) ***(G-13310)***
Office Print N Copy 740 695-3616
104 N Marietta St Saint Clairsville (43950) ***(G-16642)***
Offset Theory, Cleveland *Also called McMath & Sheets Unlimited Inc* ***(G-5646)***
Ogara Hess Eisenhardt 513 346-1300
9113 Le Saint Dr West Chester (45014) ***(G-19751)***
Ogc Industries Inc 330 456-1500
934 Wells Ave Nw Canton (44703) ***(G-2770)***
Ogden Hydraulics LLC 419 686-1108
396 W Main St Portage (43451) ***(G-16272)***
Ogden Newspapers Inc 304 748-0606
401 Herald Sq Steubenville (43952) ***(G-17546)***
Ogden Newspapers Inc 330 629-6200
240 Franklin St Se Warren (44483) ***(G-19425)***
Ogden Newspapers Inc 330 332-4601
161 N Lincoln Ave Salem (44460) ***(G-16764)***
Ogden Newspapers Inc 740 283-4711
401 Herald Sq Steubenville (43952) ***(G-17547)***
Ogden Newspapers Inc 330 841-1600
240 Franklin St Se Warren (44483) ***(G-19426)***
Ogden Newspapers of Ohio Inc 419 448-3200
320 Nelson St Tiffin (44883) ***(G-18074)***
Ogden Newspapers Ohio Inc (HQ) 330 424-9541
308 Maple St Lisbon (44432) ***(G-11976)***
Ogg Garick, Cleveland *Also called Garick LLC* ***(G-5293)***
Ogr Publishing Inc 330 757-3020
5825 Redsand Rd Hilliard (43026) ***(G-10845)***
Ogs Industries, Akron *Also called Ohio Gasket and Shim Co Inc* ***(G-307)***
Ogs Tool & Manufacturing 419 524-6200
3520 N Main St Mansfield (44903) ***(G-12495)***
Oh-Ll Commercial Cleaning LLC 614 390-3628
1905 Lake Crest Dr Grove City (43123) ***(G-10453)***
Ohashi Technica USA Inc (HQ) 740 965-5115
111 Burrer Dr Sunbury (43074) ***(G-17894)***
Ohashi Technica USA Mfg Inc 740 965-9002
99 Burrer Dr Sunbury (43074) ***(G-17895)***
Ohigro Inc (PA) 740 726-2429
6720 Gillette Rd Waldo (43356) ***(G-19304)***
Ohio Aluminum Chemicals LLC 513 860-3842
4544 Muhlhauser Rd West Chester (45011) ***(G-19752)***
Ohio Aluminum Industries Inc 216 641-8865
4840 Warner Rd Cleveland (44125) ***(G-5798)***
Ohio Anodizing Company Inc 614 252-7855
915 N 20th St Columbus (43219) ***(G-7240)***
Ohio Art Company (PA) 419 636-3141
1 Toy St Bryan (43506) ***(G-2301)***
Ohio Asphaltic Limestone Corp 937 364-2191
8591 Mad River Rd Hillsboro (45133) ***(G-10886)***
Ohio Associated Entps LLC (PA) 440 354-2106
97 Corwin Dr Painesville (44077) ***(G-15768)***
Ohio Associated Entps LLC 440 354-3148
1359 W Jackson St Painesville (44077) ***(G-15769)***
Ohio Associated Entps LLC 440 354-3148
72 Corwin Dr Painesville (44077) ***(G-15770)***
Ohio Association Realtors Inc 614 228-6675
200 E Town St Columbus (43215) ***(G-7241)***
Ohio Auto Supply Company 330 454-5105
1128 Tuscarawas St W Canton (44702) ***(G-2771)***
Ohio Awning & Manufacturing Co (PA) 216 861-2400
5777 Grant Ave Cleveland (44105) ***(G-5799)***
Ohio Beauty Cut Stone, Akron *Also called Ohio Beauty Inc* ***(G-305)***
Ohio Beauty Inc 330 644-2241
40 W Turkeyfoot Lake Rd Akron (44319) ***(G-305)***
Ohio Belt Control Supply Co, Wadsworth *Also called D & J Electric Motor Repair Co* ***(G-19232)***
Ohio Beverage Systems Inc 216 475-3900
9200 Midwest Ave Cleveland (44125) ***(G-5800)***
Ohio Biofuels 614 886-6518
3613 Woodbridge Pl Cincinnati (45226) ***(G-4099)***
Ohio Biosystems Coop Inc 419 980-7663
135 N Market St Loudonville (44842) ***(G-12146)***
Ohio Blenders Inc (PA) 419 726-2655
2404 N Summit St Toledo (43611) ***(G-18435)***
Ohio Blow Pipe Company (PA) 216 681-7379
446 E 131st St Cleveland (44108) ***(G-5801)***
Ohio Box & Crate Inc 440 526-3133
16751 Tavern Rd Burton (44021) ***(G-2366)***
Ohio Box and Crate Co, Burton *Also called Ohio Box & Crate Inc* ***(G-2366)***
Ohio Bridge Corporation 740 432-6334
201 Wheeling Ave Cambridge (43725) ***(G-2451)***
Ohio Broach & Machine Company 440 946-1040
35264 Topps Indus Pkwy Willoughby (44094) ***(G-20393)***
Ohio Brush Company 216 791-3265
2680 Lisbon Rd Cleveland (44104) ***(G-5802)***
Ohio CAM & Tool Co 216 531-7900
23572 Saint Clair Ave Cleveland (44117) ***(G-5803)***
Ohio Candle Co Inc 740 289-8000
7040 Us Rte 23 Waverly (45690) ***(G-19555)***
Ohio Carbon Blank Inc 440 953-9302
38403 Pelton Rd Willoughby (44094) ***(G-20394)***
Ohio Carbon Company 216 251-7274
1201 Jacobson Ave Ashland (44805) ***(G-729)***
Ohio Carbon Industries Inc 419 496-2530
1201 Jacobson Ave Ashland (44805) ***(G-730)***
Ohio Cast Stone Co LLC 614 444-2278
45 W Barthman Ave Columbus (43207) ***(G-7242)***
Ohio Centech 513 477-8779
444 Hidden Valley Ln Cincinnati (45215) ***(G-4100)***
Ohio Chain Company LLC 419 843-9476
7757 Little Rd Sylvania (43560) ***(G-17958)***
Ohio Chemical Two 614 482-8073
8132 Linden Leaf Cir Columbus (43235) ***(G-7243)***
Ohio City Pasta, Cleveland *Also called Food Designs Inc* ***(G-5259)***
Ohio City Power 216 651-6250
4427 Franklin Blvd Cleveland (44113) ***(G-5804)***
Ohio Classic Street Rods Inc 440 543-6593
10145 Philipp Pkwy Streetsboro (44241) ***(G-17686)***
Ohio Cllbrtive Lrng Sltons Inc (PA) 216 595-5289
24700 Chagrin Blvd # 104 Beachwood (44122) ***(G-1255)***
Ohio Coatings Company 740 859-5500
2100 Tin Plate Pl Yorkville (43971) ***(G-20827)***
Ohio Community Media, Miamisburg *Also called Ocm LLC* ***(G-13701)***
Ohio Community Media 740 848-4064
59 W College St Fredericktown (43019) ***(G-9974)***
Ohio Conveyor and Supply Inc 419 422-3825
845 Hurd Ave Findlay (45840) ***(G-9733)***
OHIO CRAFT MUSEUM, Columbus *Also called Ohio Designer Craftsmen Entps* ***(G-7245)***
Ohio Crankshaft Div, Newburgh Heights *Also called Park-Ohio Industries Inc* ***(G-14942)***
Ohio Cut Sheet, Strongsville *Also called Dupli-Systems Inc* ***(G-17738)***
Ohio Decorative Products LLC (PA) 419 647-9033
220 S Elizabeth St Spencerville (45887) ***(G-17311)***
Ohio Defense Services Inc 937 608-2371
143 S Monmouth St Dayton (45403) ***(G-8396)***
Ohio Department Transportation 614 351-2898
1606 W Broad St Columbus (43223) ***(G-7244)***
Ohio Designer Craftsmen Entps (HQ) 614 486-7119
1665 W 5th Ave Columbus (43212) ***(G-7245)***
Ohio Displays Inc 216 961-5600
825 Leona St Elyria (44035) ***(G-9303)***
Ohio Distinctive Enterprises 614 459-0453
6500 Fiesta Dr Columbus (43235) ***(G-7246)***
Ohio Distinctive Software, Columbus *Also called Ohio Distinctive Enterprises* ***(G-7246)***
Ohio Drill & Tool Co (PA) 330 525-7717
23255 Georgetown Rd Homeworth (44634) ***(G-10989)***
Ohio Drill & Tool Co 330 525-7161
23303 South St Homeworth (44634) ***(G-10990)***
Ohio Eagle Distributing LLC 513 539-8483
9300 Allen Rd West Chester (45069) ***(G-19753)***
Ohio Elastomers 440 354-9750
3470 Blackmore Rd Perry (44081) ***(G-15910)***
Ohio Electric Control, Ashland *Also called Precision Design Inc* ***(G-737)***
Ohio Electric Motor Svc LLC 419 525-2225
311 E 3rd St Mansfield (44902) ***(G-12496)***
Ohio Electric Motor Svc LLC (PA) 614 444-1451
1909 E Livingston Ave Columbus (43209) ***(G-7247)***
Ohio Electric Motors, Dublin *Also called Peerless-Winsmith Inc* ***(G-8963)***
Ohio Electro-Polishing Co Inc 419 667-2281
15085 Main St Venedocia (45894) ***(G-19155)***
Ohio Engineering and Mfg Co, Wadsworth *Also called Hutnik Company* ***(G-19246)***
Ohio Engineering and Mfg Sls 937 855-6971
11610 State Route 725 Germantown (45327) ***(G-10244)***
Ohio Envelope Manufacturing Co 216 267-2920
5161 W 164th St Cleveland (44142) ***(G-5805)***
Ohio Fabricators, Coshocton *Also called Ofco Inc* ***(G-7746)***
Ohio Fabricators Inc 216 391-2400
1452 Kenmore Blvd Akron (44314) ***(G-306)***
Ohio Farms Packing Co Ltd 330 435-6400
2416 E West Salem Rd Creston (44217) ***(G-7808)***
Ohio Feather Company Inc 513 921-3373
1 Kovach Dr Cincinnati (45215) ***(G-4101)***

ALPHABETIC SECTION — Ohio State University

Ohio First Defense 513 571-9461
3530 Arbor Hill Ln Maineville (45039) *(G-12376)*

Ohio Flame 330 953-0863
7655 Spring Park Dr Youngstown (44512) *(G-20981)*

Ohio Flame Hardening Company (PA) 513 336-6160
4110 Columbia Rd Lebanon (45036) *(G-11678)*

Ohio Flame Hardening Company 513 733-5162
637 N Wayne Ave Cincinnati (45215) *(G-4102)*

Ohio Flexible Packaging Co 513 494-1800
512 S Main St South Lebanon (45065) *(G-17277)*

Ohio Flock-Cote Company Inc 440 914-1122
6810 Cochran Rd Solon (44139) *(G-17210)*

Ohio Foam Corporation 614 252-4877
1513 Alum Creek Dr Columbus (43209) *(G-7248)*

Ohio Foam Corporation (PA) 419 563-0399
820 Plymouth St Bucyrus (44820) *(G-2341)*

Ohio Foam Corporation 330 799-4553
1201 Ameritech Blvd Youngstown (44509) *(G-20982)*

Ohio Foam Corporation 419 492-2151
529 S Kibler St New Washington (44854) *(G-14831)*

Ohio Fresh Eggs LLC (PA) 740 893-7200
11212 Croton Rd Croton (43013) *(G-7822)*

Ohio Fresh Eggs LLC 937 354-2233
20449 County Road 245 Mount Victory (43340) *(G-14520)*

Ohio Galvanizing Corp 740 387-6474
467 W Fairground St Marion (43302) *(G-12726)*

Ohio Gasket and Shim Co Inc (PA) 330 630-0626
976 Evans Ave Akron (44305) *(G-307)*

Ohio Graphic Supply Inc 937 433-7537
530 W Whipp Rd Dayton (45459) *(G-8397)*

Ohio Gratings Inc (PA) 330 477-6707
5299 Southway St Sw Canton (44706) *(G-2772)*

Ohio Gravure Technologies Inc 937 439-1582
1241 Byers Rd Miamisburg (45342) *(G-13703)*

Ohio Guns, Ashtabula Also called Reloading Supplies Corp *(G-802)*

Ohio Heat Transfer 513 870-5323
3400 Port Union Rd Hamilton (45014) *(G-10591)*

Ohio Heat Transfer Ltd 740 695-0635
66721 Executive Dr Saint Clairsville (43950) *(G-16643)*

Ohio Hickory Harvest Brand Pro 330 644-6266
90 Logan Pkwy Coventry Township (44319) *(G-7775)*

Ohio Hydraulics Inc 513 771-2590
2510 E Sharon Rd Ste 1 Cincinnati (45241) *(G-4103)*

Ohio Industrial Supply, Dayton Also called Tool Service Co Inc *(G-7992)*

Ohio Knitting Mills, Cleveland Also called Okm LLC *(G-5808)*

Ohio Lab Pharma LLC 484 522-2601
4738 Gateway Cir J184 Kettering (45440) *(G-11439)*

Ohio Label Inc 614 777-0180
5005 Transamerica Dr Columbus (43228) *(G-7249)*

Ohio Laminating & Binding Inc 614 771-4868
4364 Reynolds Dr Hilliard (43026) *(G-10846)*

Ohio Laser LLC 614 873-7030
8260 Estates Pkwy Plain City (43064) *(G-16204)*

Ohio Legal Blank Co 216 281-7792
9800 Detroit Ave Ste 1 Cleveland (44102) *(G-5806)*

Ohio Lumex Co Inc 440 264-2500
30350 Bruce Indus Pkwy Solon (44139) *(G-17211)*

Ohio Magnetics Inc 216 662-8484
5400 Dunham Rd Maple Heights (44137) *(G-12575)*

Ohio Manufacturing EXT Partnr 614 644-8788
77 S High St Columbus (43215) *(G-7250)*

Ohio Mattress 740 739-8219
1408 Ety Rd Nw Lancaster (43130) *(G-11593)*

Ohio Mechanical Handling Co 330 773-5165
1856 S Main St Akron (44301) *(G-308)*

Ohio Metal Fabricating Inc 937 233-2400
6057 Milo Rd Dayton (45414) *(G-8398)*

Ohio Metal Products Company 937 228-6101
35 Bates St Dayton (45402) *(G-8399)*

Ohio Metal Technologies Inc 740 928-8288
470 John Alford Pkwy Hebron (43025) *(G-10756)*

Ohio Metal Working Products 330 455-2009
3620 Progress St Ne Canton (44705) *(G-2773)*

Ohio Metalizing LLC 330 830-1092
2519 Erie St S Massillon (44646) *(G-13030)*

Ohio Metallurgical Service Inc 440 365-4104
1033 Clark St Elyria (44035) *(G-9304)*

Ohio Mill Supply, Cleveland Also called Ohio Mills Corporation *(G-5807)*

Ohio Mills Corporation (PA) 216 431-3979
1719 E 39th St Cleveland (44114) *(G-5807)*

Ohio Mirror Technologies Inc (PA) 419 399-5903
114 W Jackson St Paulding (45879) *(G-15867)*

Ohio Mirror Technologies Inc 419 399-5903
384 W Wall St Paulding (45879) *(G-15868)*

Ohio Natural Gas Services Inc 740 796-3305
5600 East Pike Zanesville (43701) *(G-21165)*

Ohio News Network 614 460-3700
770 Twin Rivers Dr Columbus (43215) *(G-7251)*

Ohio News Network, The, Columbus Also called Ohio News Network *(G-7251)*

Ohio Newspaper Services Inc 614 486-6677
1335 Dublin Rd Ste 216b Columbus (43215) *(G-7252)*

Ohio Newspapers Foundation 614 486-6677
1335 Dublin Rd Ste 216b Columbus (43215) *(G-7253)*

Ohio Nut & Bolt Company Div, Berea Also called Fastener Industries Inc *(G-1607)*

Ohio Ordnance Works Inc 440 285-3481
310 Park Dr Chardon (44024) *(G-3130)*

Ohio Oxide Corporation Del 740 654-6555
4850 Elder Rd Ne Pleasantville (43148) *(G-16229)*

Ohio Packaging (HQ) 330 833-2884
777 3rd St Nw Massillon (44647) *(G-13031)*

Ohio Packing Company (PA) 614 445-0627
1306 Harmon Ave Columbus (43223) *(G-7254)*

Ohio Paper Tube Co 330 478-5171
3422 Navarre Rd Sw Canton (44706) *(G-2774)*

Ohio Pet Foods Inc (HQ) 330 424-1431
38251 Indl Pk Rd Lisbon (44432) *(G-11977)*

Ohio Pickling & Processing LLC 419 241-9601
1149 Campbell St Toledo (43607) *(G-18436)*

Ohio Plastics & Safety Pdts 330 882-6764
6140 Manchester Rd New Franklin (44319) *(G-14694)*

Ohio Plastics Belting Co 330 882-6764
6140 Manchester Rd New Franklin (44319) *(G-14695)*

Ohio Plastics Company 740 828-3291
3933 Price Rd Ne Newark (43055) *(G-14905)*

Ohio Plywood Box 513 242-9125
5555 Vine St Cincinnati (45216) *(G-4104)*

Ohio Power Tool Brush Co 419 736-3010
1201 Jacobson Ave Ashland (44805) *(G-731)*

Ohio Precision Inc 330 453-9710
1239 Market Ave S Canton (44707) *(G-2775)*

Ohio Precision Molding Inc 330 745-9393
122 E Tuscarawas Ave Barberton (44203) *(G-1091)*

Ohio Press, Antwerp Also called Antwerp Bee-Argus *(G-595)*

Ohio Print Source, Canton Also called 1455 Group LLC *(G-2554)*

Ohio Printed Products Inc 330 659-0909
3920 Congress Pkwy Richfield (44286) *(G-16478)*

Ohio Processors Inc (HQ) 740 852-9243
2200 Cardigan Ave Columbus (43215) *(G-7255)*

Ohio Psychlogy Pblications Inc 614 861-1999
620 Taylor Station Rd F Columbus (43230) *(G-7256)*

Ohio Pure Foods Inc (HQ) 330 753-2293
681 W Waterloo Rd Akron (44314) *(G-309)*

Ohio Restoration Group LLC 330 568-5815
557 S Meridian Rd Ste 4 Youngstown (44509) *(G-20983)*

Ohio Rights Group 614 300-0529
1021 E Broad St Columbus (43205) *(G-7257)*

Ohio River Valley Cabinet 740 975-8846
4 Waterworks Rd Newark (43055) *(G-14906)*

Ohio Roll Grinding Inc 330 453-1884
5165 Louisville St Louisville (44641) *(G-12162)*

Ohio Safety Products LLC 216 255-3067
675 Alpha Dr Highland Heights (44143) *(G-10796)*

Ohio Safety Supply, Highland Heights Also called Ohio Safety Products LLC *(G-10796)*

Ohio Screw Products Inc 440 322-6341
818 Lowell St Elyria (44035) *(G-9305)*

Ohio Select Imprinted Fabrics, Reynoldsburg Also called Ohio State Institute of Fin *(G-16445)*

Ohio Semitronics Inc (PA) 614 777-1005
4242 Reynolds Dr Hilliard (43026) *(G-10847)*

Ohio Shelterall Inc 614 882-1110
6060 Westerville Rd Westerville (43081) *(G-20068)*

Ohio Silver Co 937 767-8261
245 Xenia Ave Yellow Springs (45387) *(G-20813)*

Ohio Slitting & Storage 937 452-1108
7000 N Main St Camden (45311) *(G-2465)*

Ohio Specialty Dies LLC 330 538-3396
293 Rosemont Rd North Jackson (44451) *(G-15151)*

Ohio Specialty Mfg Co 419 531-5402
2008 N Hlland Sylvania Rd Toledo (43615) *(G-18437)*

Ohio Stamping & Machine LLC 937 322-3880
1305 Innisfallen Ave Springfield (45506) *(G-17464)*

Ohio Standard Bread, Medina Also called Trogdon Publishing Inc *(G-13355)*

Ohio Star Forge Co 330 847-6360
4000 Mahoning Ave Nw Warren (44483) *(G-19427)*

Ohio State Institute of Fin 614 861-8811
7394 E Main St Reynoldsburg (43068) *(G-16445)*

Ohio State Pallet Corp 614 332-3961
2175 Broehm Rd Homer (43027) *(G-10985)*

Ohio State Plastics 614 299-5618
1917 Joyce Ave Columbus (43219) *(G-7258)*

Ohio State University 614 292-7656
1060 Carmack Rd Rm 39 Columbus (43210) *(G-7259)*

Ohio State University 614 292-4139
1248 Arthur E Adams Dr Columbus (43221) *(G-7260)*

Ohio State University 614 293-3600
2050 Kenny Rd Fl 9 Columbus (43221) *(G-7261)*

Ohio State University 614 292-1462
1070 Carmack Rd Rm 180 Columbus (43210) *(G-7262)*

(PA)=Parent Co (HQ)=Headquarters (DH)=Div Headquarters

Ohio State University Press, Columbus *Also called Ohio State University* ***(G-7262)***
Ohio Steel Industries Inc 740 927-9500
13792 Broad St Sw Pataskala (43062) ***(G-15836)***
Ohio Steel Sheet & Plate Inc 800 827-2401
7845 Chestnut Ridge Rd Hubbard (44425) ***(G-11007)***
Ohio Structures Inc 330 547-7705
6120 S Pricetown Rd Berlin Center (44401) ***(G-1648)***
Ohio Structures Inc (HQ) 330 533-0084
535 N Broad St Ste 5 Canfield (44406) ***(G-2539)***
Ohio Synchro Swim Club 614 319-4667
4405 Landmark Ln Hilliard (43026) ***(G-10848)***
Ohio Table Pad Co Georgia Div, Perrysburg *Also called Ohio Table Pad Company* ***(G-15986)***
Ohio Table Pad Company 419 872-6400
350 3 Meadows Dr Perrysburg (43551) ***(G-15985)***
Ohio Table Pad Company (PA) 419 872-6400
350 3 Meadows Dr Perrysburg (43551) ***(G-15986)***
Ohio Table Pad of Indiana 419 872-6400
350 3 Meadows Dr Perrysburg (43551) ***(G-15987)***
Ohio Tile & Marble Co (PA) 513 541-4211
3809 Spring Grove Ave Cincinnati (45223) ***(G-4105)***
Ohio Timberland Products 419 682-6322
102 Railroad Ave Stryker (43557) ***(G-17831)***
Ohio Tool & Jig Grind Inc 937 415-0692
5724 Webster St Dayton (45414) ***(G-8400)***
Ohio Tool Works LLC 419 281-3700
1374 Enterprise Pkwy Ashland (44805) ***(G-732)***
Ohio Trailer Inc 330 392-4444
1899 Tod Ave Sw Warren (44485) ***(G-19428)***
Ohio Trailer Supply Inc 614 471-9121
2966 Westerville Rd Columbus (43224) ***(G-7263)***
Ohio Transitional Machine & Tl 419 476-0820
3940 Castener St Toledo (43612) ***(G-18438)***
Ohio University 740 593-4010
28 Union St Ground Fl Athens (45701) ***(G-843)***
Ohio Valley Adhesives 513 454-1800
6148 Rapid Run Rd Cincinnati (45233) ***(G-4106)***
Ohio Valley Alloy Services Inc 740 373-1900
100 Westview Ave Marietta (45750) ***(G-12649)***
Ohio Valley Coal, Saint Clairsville *Also called Ohio Valley Resources Inc* ***(G-16645)***
Ohio Valley Coal Company (HQ) 740 926-1351
46226 National Rd Saint Clairsville (43950) ***(G-16644)***
Ohio Valley Energy Systems 330 799-2268
200 Victoria Rd Bldg 4 Youngstown (44515) ***(G-20984)***
Ohio Valley Herbal Products 330 382-1229
1250 Saint George St # 5 East Liverpool (43920) ***(G-9067)***
Ohio Valley Ink, Cincinnati *Also called Grand Rapids Printing Ink Co* ***(G-3775)***
Ohio Valley Manufacturing Inc 419 522-5818
1501 Harrington Mem Rd Mansfield (44903) ***(G-12497)***
Ohio Valley Resources Inc 740 795-5220
46226 National Rd Saint Clairsville (43950) ***(G-16645)***
Ohio Valley Specialty Company 740 373-2276
115 Industry Rd Marietta (45750) ***(G-12650)***
Ohio Valley Trackwork Inc 740 446-0181
39 Fairview Rd Bidwell (45614) ***(G-1667)***
Ohio Valley Trading and Exch, Lancaster *Also called Rockbridge Outfitters* ***(G-11604)***
Ohio Valley Transloading Co 740 795-4967
46226 National Rd Saint Clairsville (43950) ***(G-16646)***
Ohio Valley Truss Co (PA) 937 393-3995
6000 Us Highway 50 Hillsboro (45133) ***(G-10887)***
Ohio Valley Truss Co 937 393-3995
887 1/2 W Main St Hillsboro (45133) ***(G-10888)***
Ohio Valley Veneer Inc 740 493-2901
16523 State Route 124 Piketon (45661) ***(G-16076)***
Ohio Valley Veneer Co, Piketon *Also called Ohio Valley Veneer Inc* ***(G-16076)***
Ohio Vly Lightning Protection 937 987-0245
520 Leeka Rd New Vienna (45159) ***(G-14825)***
Ohio Vly Stmpng-Assemblies Inc 419 522-0983
500 Newman St Mansfield (44902) ***(G-12498)***
Ohio Willow Wood Company 740 869-3377
15441 Scioto Darby Rd Mount Sterling (43143) ***(G-14464)***
Ohio Windmill & Pump Co Inc 330 547-6300
8389 S Pricetown Rd Berlin Center (44401) ***(G-1649)***
Ohio Wire Cloth, Englewood *Also called Unified Screening & Crushing* ***(G-9380)***
Ohio Wire Form & Spring Co 614 444-3676
2270 S High St Columbus (43207) ***(G-7264)***
Ohio Wire Harness LLC 937 292-7355
225 Lincoln Ave Bellefontaine (43311) ***(G-1523)***
Ohio Wood Fabrication, Sandusky *Also called Gary L Gast* ***(G-16812)***
Ohio Wood Recycling Inc 614 491-0881
2019 Rathmell Rd Columbus (43207) ***(G-7265)***
Ohio Woodlands, Salineville *Also called Coldwell Family Tree Farm* ***(G-16786)***
Ohio Woodworking Co Inc 513 631-0870
5035 Beech St Cincinnati (45212) ***(G-4107)***
Ohio's Country Journal, Columbus *Also called Agri Communicators Inc* ***(G-6551)***
Ohiomet, Elyria *Also called Ohio Metallurgical Service Inc* ***(G-9304)***
Ohlheiser Corp 860 953-7632
1900 Jetway Blvd Columbus (43219) ***(G-7266)***
Ohlinger Publishing Svcs Inc 614 261-5360
28 W Henderson Rd Columbus (43214) ***(G-7267)***
Ohmart Vega, Cincinnati *Also called Vega Americas Inc* ***(G-4470)***
Ohmep, Columbus *Also called Ohio Manufacturing EXT Partnr* ***(G-7250)***
Ohta Press US Inc 937 374-3382
1125 S Patton St Xenia (45385) ***(G-20785)***
Oil & Go LLC 330 854-6345
2185 Locust St S Canal Fulton (44614) ***(G-2488)***
Oil Bar LLC (PA) 614 501-9815
2740 Eastland Mall Columbus (43232) ***(G-7268)***
Oil Bar LLC 614 880-3950
1500 Polaris Pkwy # 2072 Columbus (43240) ***(G-6504)***
Oil Enterprises, Logan *Also called Ralph Robinson Inc* ***(G-12042)***
Oil Kraft Div, Cincinnati *Also called US Industrial Lubricants Inc* ***(G-4458)***
Oil Skimmers Inc 440 237-4600
12800 York Rd Ste G North Royalton (44133) ***(G-15291)***
Oil Tooling and Stamping, Ontario *Also called Cole Tool & Die Company* ***(G-15540)***
Oiler Processing 740 892-2640
53 S Central Ave Utica (43080) ***(G-19026)***
Oiler's Meat Processing, Utica *Also called Oiler Processing* ***(G-19026)***
Oils By Nature Incorporated 330 468-8897
5712 Abbyshire Dr 1a Hudson (44236) ***(G-11064)***
Ojim Inc (PA) 330 832-9557
1212 Oberlin Ave Sw Massillon (44647) ***(G-13032)***
OK Industries Inc 419 435-2361
2307 W Corporate Dr W Fostoria (44830) ***(G-9854)***
Okamoto Sandusky Mfg LLC 419 626-1633
3130 W Monroe St Sandusky (44870) ***(G-16832)***
Okamoto USA, Sandusky *Also called Okamoto Sandusky Mfg LLC* ***(G-16832)***
OKeefe Casting Co 440 277-5427
2401 E 28th St Lorain (44055) ***(G-12110)***
OKL Can Line Inc 513 825-1655
11235 Sebring Dr Cincinnati (45240) ***(G-4108)***
Okm LLC 216 272-6375
4701 Perkins Ave Ste 1 Cleveland (44103) ***(G-5808)***
Olan Plastics Inc 614 834-6526
6550 Olan Dr Canal Winchester (43110) ***(G-2510)***
Olay LLC 787 535-2191
11530 Reed Hartman Hwy Blue Ash (45241) ***(G-1826)***
Old Country Sausage Kitchen 216 662-5988
15711 Libby Rd Cleveland (44137) ***(G-5809)***
Old Es LLC 330 468-6600
8050 Highland Pointe Pkwy Macedonia (44056) ***(G-12312)***
Old Firehouse Brewery, Williamsburg *Also called AEC Brews LLC DBA Old Frhuse B* ***(G-20250)***
Old Mason Winery Inc 937 698-1122
4199 S Iddings Rd West Milton (45383) ***(G-19951)***
Old Mill Custom Cabinetry Co 419 423-8897
310 E Crawford St Findlay (45840) ***(G-9734)***
Old Mill Power Equipment 740 982-3246
100 China St Crooksville (43731) ***(G-7817)***
Old Mill Winery Inc 440 466-5560
403 S Broadway Geneva (44041) ***(G-10227)***
Old Rar Inc (PA) 216 910-3400
3700 Park East Dr Ste 300 Beachwood (44122) ***(G-1256)***
Old Salt Tees 440 463-0628
9777 Little Mountain Rd Mentor (44060) ***(G-13533)***
Old Trail Printing Company 614 443-4852
100 Fornoff Rd Columbus (43207) ***(G-7269)***
Old Village 614 791-8467
2878 Jericho Pl Delaware (43015) ***(G-8714)***
Old West Industries Inc (PA) 513 889-0500
1421 Boyle Rd Bldg B Hamilton (45013) ***(G-10592)***
Old World Foods Inc 216 341-5665
3545 E 76th St Cleveland (44105) ***(G-5810)***
Oldaker M F G, Dunkirk *Also called Oldaker Manufacturing Corp* ***(G-9036)***
Oldaker Manufacturing Corp 419 759-3551
301 N Main St Dunkirk (45836) ***(G-9036)***
Oldcastle Apg Midwest Inc 440 949-1815
5190 Oster Rd Sheffield Village (44054) ***(G-16973)***
Oldcastle Buildingenvelope Inc 419 661-5079
291 M St Perrysburg (43551) ***(G-15988)***
Oldcastle Companies 800 899-8455
13762 Road 179 Oakwood (45873) ***(G-15472)***
Oldcastle Precast Inc 419 592-2309
1675 Industrial Dr Napoleon (43545) ***(G-14554)***
Olde Home Market LLC 614 738-3975
2517 Old Home Rd Grove City (43123) ***(G-10454)***
Olde Man Granola LLC 419 819-9576
7227 W State Route 12 Findlay (45840) ***(G-9735)***
Olde Schlhuse Vnyrd Winery LLC 937 273-6023
8538 State Route 726 Eldorado (45321) ***(G-9190)***
Olde Wood Ltd 330 866-1441
7557 Willowdale Ave Se Magnolia (44643) ***(G-12361)***
Oldforge Tools Inc (HQ) 330 535-7177
768 E North St Akron (44305) ***(G-310)***
Olen Corporation 419 294-2611
6326 County Highway 61 Upper Sandusky (43351) ***(G-18969)***
Olen Corporation 330 262-6821
3001 Prairie Ln Wooster (44691) ***(G-20635)***

Olen Corporation 740 745-5865
9134 Mount Vernon Rd Saint Louisville (43071) *(G-16674)*
Olentangy Eye and Laser A 614 267-4122
3525 Olentngy Rvr Rd # 5310 Columbus (43214) *(G-7270)*
Olfactorium Corp Inc 216 663-8831
12395 Mccracken Rd Cleveland (44125) *(G-5811)*
Olin Brass, Alliance *Also called Gbc Metals LLC (G-469)*
Olivamed LLC 937 401-0821
401 Shotwell Dr Franklin (45005) *(G-9906)*
Olive Branch 614 563-3139
2337 Finley Guy Rd London (43140) *(G-12068)*
Olive Smuckers Oil 513 646-7103
5204 Spring Grove Ave Cincinnati (45217) *(G-4109)*
Olive Tap (PA) 330 721-6500
30 Public Sq Medina (44256) *(G-13311)*
Oliver Chemical Co Inc 513 541-4540
2908 Spring Grove Ave Cincinnati (45225) *(G-4110)*
Oliver Pool and Spa Inc 740 264-5368
512 Main St Steubenville (43953) *(G-17548)*
Oliver Printing & Packg Co LLC (PA) 330 425-7890
1760 Enterprise Pkwy Twinsburg (44087) *(G-18823)*
Oliver Products Company 513 860-6880
3840 Symmes Rd Hamilton (45015) *(G-10593)*
Oliver Signs & Graphics 330 460-2996
5880 Myrtle Hill Rd Valley City (44280) *(G-19057)*
Oliver Steel Plate, Bedford *Also called AM Castle & Co (G-1381)*
Oliver-Tolas Healthcare Packg, Hamilton *Also called Oliver Products Company (G-10593)*
Olmsted Falls Plant, Olmsted Falls *Also called Evergreen Packaging Inc (G-15530)*
Olmsted Ice Inc 440 235-8411
8134 Bronson Rd Olmsted Twp (44138) *(G-15535)*
Olmsted Printing Inc 440 234-2600
1060 W Bagley Rd Ste 102 Berea (44017) *(G-1621)*
Olson Sheet Metal Cnstr Co 330 745-8225
465 Glenn St Barberton (44203) *(G-1092)*
Olwin Metal Fabrication LLC 937 277-4501
1933 Kuntz Rd Dayton (45404) *(G-8401)*
Olymco, Canton *Also called Delta Plating Inc (G-2655)*
Olympia Candies, Strongsville *Also called Robert E McGrath Inc (G-17783)*
Olympic Enterprises, Canton *Also called Nicholas Ray Enterprises LLC (G-2761)*
Olympic Forest Products Co 216 421-2775
2200 Carnegie Ave Cleveland (44115) *(G-5812)*
Om Group, Westlake *Also called Borchers Americas Inc (G-20103)*
Oma USA Inc 330 487-0602
9329 Ravenna Rd Ste A Twinsburg (44087) *(G-18824)*
Omar Associates LLC 419 426-0610
625 N State Route 4 Attica (44807) *(G-858)*
Omar McDowell Co 440 808-2280
25109 Detroit Rd Ste 320 Westlake (44145) *(G-20137)*
Omative North America, Cincinnati *Also called Optimzed Prdctvity Sltions LLC (G-4117)*
Omco Holdings Inc (PA) 440 944-2100
30396 Lakeland Blvd Wickliffe (44092) *(G-20220)*
Omega Automation Inc 937 890-2350
2850 Needmore Rd Dayton (45414) *(G-8402)*
Omega Cementing Co 330 695-7147
3776 S Millborne Rd Apple Creek (44606) *(G-616)*
Omega Engineering Inc 740 965-9340
149 Stelzer Ct Sunbury (43074) *(G-17896)*
Omega International Inc (HQ) 937 890-2350
6192 Webster St Dayton (45414) *(G-8403)*
Omega Logging Inc (PA) 330 534-0378
2550 State Line Rd Hubbard (44425) *(G-11008)*
Omega Machine & Tool Inc 440 946-6846
7590 Jenther Dr Mentor (44060) *(G-13534)*
Omega One, Willoughby *Also called Amfm Inc (G-20272)*
Omega Polymer Technologies Inc (PA) 330 562-5201
1331 S Chillicothe Rd Aurora (44202) *(G-897)*
Omega Pultrusions Incorporated 330 562-5201
1331 S Chillicothe Rd Aurora (44202) *(G-898)*
Omega Tek Inc 419 756-9580
649 Old Mill Run Rd Mansfield (44906) *(G-12499)*
Omega Tool & Die Inc 937 890-2350
2850 Needmore Rd Dayton (45414) *(G-8404)*
Omega Tool and Die, Dayton *Also called Omega Tool & Die Inc (G-8404)*
Omegadyne, Sunbury *Also called Omega Engineering Inc (G-17896)*
Omer J Smith Inc 513 921-4717
9112 Le Saint Dr West Chester (45014) *(G-19754)*
Ommc, Toledo *Also called Mobis North America LLC (G-18413)*
Omni Business Forms Inc 513 860-0111
4747 Devitt Dr West Chester (45246) *(G-19883)*
Omni Die Casting Inc 330 830-5500
1100 Nova Dr Se Massillon (44646) *(G-13033)*
Omni Manufacturing 419 394-7424
901 Mckinley Rd Saint Marys (45885) *(G-16692)*
Omni Manufacturing Inc (PA) 419 394-7424
901 Mckinley Rd Saint Marys (45885) *(G-16693)*
Omni Manufacturing Inc 419 394-7424
220 Cleveland Ave Saint Marys (45885) *(G-16694)*
Omni Media 216 687-0077
1375 E 9th St Fl 10 Cleveland (44114) *(G-5813)*
Omni Tech Electronics, Columbus *Also called Accuscan Instruments Inc (G-6535)*
Omni Technical Products Inc 216 433-1970
15300 Industrial Pkwy Cleveland (44135) *(G-5814)*
Omni USA Inc 330 830-5500
1100 Nova Dr Se Massillon (44646) *(G-13034)*
Omniboom LLC 833 675-3987
20 High St Hamilton (45011) *(G-10594)*
Omnicare Phrm of Midwest LLC (HQ) 513 719-2600
201 E 4th St Ste 900 Cincinnati (45202) *(G-4111)*
Omnitec, Painesville *Also called Ohio Associated Entps LLC (G-15769)*
Omnitech Electronics Inc 800 822-1344
5090 Trabue Rd Columbus (43228) *(G-7271)*
Omnithruster Inc 330 963-6310
2201 Pinnacle Pkwy Ste A Twinsburg (44087) *(G-18825)*
Omnova Overseas Inc (HQ) 330 869-4200
175 Ghent Rd Fairlawn (44333) *(G-9614)*
Omnova Solutions Inc 330 628-6550
165 S Cleveland Ave Mogadore (44260) *(G-14246)*
Omnova Solutions Inc 330 734-1237
1380 Tech Way Akron (44306) *(G-311)*
Omnova Solutions Inc (PA) 216 682-7000
25435 Harvard Rd Beachwood (44122) *(G-1257)*
Omnova Wallcovering USA Inc (HQ) 216 682-7000
25435 Harvard Rd Beachwood (44122) *(G-1258)*
Omsi Transmissions Inc 330 405-7350
9319 Ravenna Rd Ste A Twinsburg (44087) *(G-18826)*
Omya Distribution LLC (HQ) 513 387-4600
9987 Carver Rd Ste 300 Blue Ash (45242) *(G-1827)*
Omya Industries Inc (HQ) 513 387-4600
9987 Carver Rd Ste 300 Blue Ash (45242) *(G-1828)*
On Display Ltd 513 841-1600
1250 Clough Pike Batavia (45103) *(G-1174)*
On Guard Defense LLC 740 596-1984
66211 Bethel Rd New Plymouth (45654) *(G-14809)*
On-Power Inc 513 228-2100
3525 Grant Ave Ste A Lebanon (45036) *(G-11679)*
One Cloud Services LLC 513 231-9500
1080 Nimitzview Dr # 400 Cincinnati (45230) *(G-4112)*
One Liberty Street 419 352-6298
813 Hamilton Ct Bowling Green (43402) *(G-1987)*
One Styling, Maple Heights *Also called Salon Styling Concepts Ltd (G-12579)*
One Time, Cleveland *Also called Bond Distributing LLC (G-4830)*
One Wish LLC 800 505-6883
23945 Mercantile Rd Ste H Beachwood (44122) *(G-1259)*
One With Nature, Cuyahoga Falls *Also called Madaen Natural Products Inc (G-7894)*
One-Write Company 740 654-2128
3750 Lancaster New Lexing Lancaster (43130) *(G-11594)*
ONeals Tarpaulin & Awning Co 330 788-6504
549 W Indianola Ave Youngstown (44511) *(G-20985)*
Oneida Group Inc (PA) 740 687-2500
519 N Pierce Ave Lancaster (43130) *(G-11595)*
ONeil & Associates Inc (PA) 937 865-0800
495 Byers Rd Miamisburg (45342) *(G-13704)*
Oneseal Inc (HQ) 973 599-1155
1300 3rd St Perrysburg (43551) *(G-15989)*
Onetouchpoint East Corp 513 421-1600
1441 Western Ave Cincinnati (45214) *(G-4113)*
Onevision Corporation (PA) 614 794-1144
5805 Chandler Ct Ste A Westerville (43082) *(G-20013)*
Onevuex, Westerville *Also called Bass International Sftwr LLC (G-19980)*
Onix Corporation (PA) 800 844-0076
27100 Oakmead Dr Perrysburg (43551) *(G-15990)*
Onix Corporation 800 844-0076
27100 Oakmead Dr Perrysburg (43551) *(G-15991)*
Online Engineering Corporation 513 561-8878
3947 Bach Buxton Rd Amelia (45102) *(G-545)*
Online Mega Sellers Corp (PA) 888 384-6468
4236 W Alexis Rd Toledo (43623) *(G-18439)*
Onnyx 419 627-9872
3911 Venice Rd Sandusky (44870) *(G-16833)*
Onstage Publications, Dayton *Also called Just Business Inc (G-8287)*
Ontario Mechanical LLC 419 529-2578
2880 Park Ave W Ontario (44906) *(G-15544)*
Onx Enterprise Solutions, Cincinnati *Also called Onx Holdings LLC (G-4114)*
Onx Holdings LLC (HQ) 866 587-2287
221 E 4th St Cincinnati (45202) *(G-4114)*
Onx USA LLC (HQ) 440 569-2300
5910 Landerbrook Dr # 250 Cleveland (44124) *(G-5815)*
Oogeep 740 587-0410
1718 Columbus Rd Granville (43023) *(G-10335)*
Ooteksofpak, Columbus *Also called Tarigma Corporation (G-7512)*
Opal Diamond LLC 330 653-5876
20033 Detroit Rd Rocky River (44116) *(G-16550)*
Opc Inc 419 531-2222
419 N Reynolds Rd Toledo (43615) *(G-18440)*
OPC Inc, Toledo *Also called Orthotic Prosthetic Center (G-18441)*

ALPHABETIC

ALPHABETIC SECTION

Open House Magazine Inc..................................614 523-7775
   1537 Guilford Rd Columbus (43221) *(G-7272)*
Open Sided Mri Cleveland LLC..............................804 217-7114
   30400 Detroit Rd Ste 30 Westlake (44145) *(G-20138)*
Open Text Inc...614 658-3588
   3671 Ridge Mill Dr Hilliard (43026) *(G-10849)*
Operational Support Svcs LLC..............................419 425-0889
   1850 Industrial Dr Findlay (45840) *(G-9736)*
Opm, Barberton Also called Ohio Precision Molding Inc *(G-1091)*
Opp, Toledo Also called Ohio Pickling & Processing LLC *(G-18436)*
Ops Wireless..419 396-4041
   807 E Findlay St Carey (43316) *(G-2886)*
Opt Brush, Ashland Also called Ohio Power Tool Brush Co *(G-731)*
Opta Minerals (usa) Inc (HQ)..............................330 659-3003
   4807 Rockside Rd Ste 400 Independence (44131) *(G-11145)*
Optem, Medina Also called Ovation Polymer Technology and *(G-13314)*
Optem Inc...330 723-5686
   1030 W Smith Rd Medina (44256) *(G-13312)*
Opti, Aurora Also called Omega Polymer Technologies Inc *(G-897)*
Opti Vision Inc (PA)......................................330 650-0919
   5697 Darrow Rd Hudson (44236) *(G-11065)*
Optical Distribution Corp.................................937 405-7280
   401 N Front St Ste 350 Columbus (43215) *(G-7273)*
Optimair Ltd..419 661-9568
   29102 Glenwood Rd Perrysburg (43551) *(G-15992)*
Optimal Led, Toledo Also called Led Lighting Center Inc *(G-18376)*
Optimal Office Solutions LLC..............................201 257-8516
   25 Merchant St Ste 135 Cincinnati (45246) *(G-4115)*
Optimalled, Toledo Also called Led Lighting Center LLC *(G-18377)*
Optime Air MSP Ltd..419 661-9568
   29102 Glenwood Rd Perrysburg (43551) *(G-15993)*
Optimum Blinds, Brilliant Also called Optimun Blinds Inc *(G-2079)*
Optimum Graphics, Westerville Also called Optimum System Products Inc *(G-20069)*
Optimum System Products Inc (PA).........................614 885-4464
   921 Eastwind Dr Ste 133 Westerville (43081) *(G-20069)*
Optimun Blinds Inc..740 598-5808
   204 Ohio St Brilliant (43913) *(G-2079)*
Optimus LLC...614 263-5462
   975 Bethel Rd Columbus (43214) *(G-7274)*
Optimus LLC...513 918-2320
   4623 Wesley Ave Ste B Cincinnati (45212) *(G-4116)*
Optimus LLC (PA)..937 454-1900
   8517 N Dixie Dr Dayton (45414) *(G-8405)*
Optimus Prosthetics, Columbus Also called Optimus LLC *(G-7274)*
Optimus Prosthetics, Dayton Also called Optimus LLC *(G-8405)*
Optimzed Prdctvity Sltions LLC............................513 444-2156
   9435 Waterstone Blvd Cincinnati (45249) *(G-4117)*
Options Plus Incorporated.................................740 694-9811
   143 Tuttle Ave Fredericktown (43019) *(G-9975)*
Optonicus, Dayton Also called Mv Innovative Technologies LLC *(G-8373)*
Optoquest Corporation.....................................216 445-3637
   10000 Cedar Ave Cleveland (44106) *(G-5816)*
Opw Inc...800 422-2525
   9393 Prnceton Glendale Rd West Chester (45011) *(G-19755)*
Opw Engineered Systems, West Chester Also called Opw Fueling Components Inc *(G-19756)*
Opw Engineered Systems Inc (HQ)...........................888 771-9438
   2726 Henkle Dr Lebanon (45036) *(G-11680)*
Opw Engineering Systems, West Chester Also called Opw Inc *(G-19755)*
Opw Fluid Transfer Group, Mason Also called Dover Corporation *(G-12857)*
Opw Fueling Components Inc (HQ)...........................800 422-2525
   9393 Prnceton Glendale Rd West Chester (45011) *(G-19756)*
Or-Tec Inc..216 475-5225
   14500 Industrial Ave S Maple Heights (44137) *(G-12576)*
Oracle America Inc..650 506-7000
   4378 Tuller Rd Dublin (43017) *(G-8957)*
Oracle America Inc..513 381-0125
   3333 Richmond Rd Ste 420 Beachwood (44122) *(G-1260)*
Oracle Corporation..513 826-6000
   3333 Richmond Rd Ste 420 Beachwood (44122) *(G-1261)*
Oracle Corporation..513 826-5632
   3610 Pentagon Blvd # 205 Beavercreek (45431) *(G-1335)*
Oracle Corporation..440 264-1620
   30500 Bruce Indus Pkwy Cleveland (44139) *(G-5817)*
Oracle Systems Corporation................................513 826-6000
   3333 Richmond Rd Ste 420 Beachwood (44122) *(G-1262)*
Oracle Systems Corporation................................937 427-5495
   2661 Commons Blvd Beavercreek (45431) *(G-1336)*
Orange Barrel Media LLC...................................614 294-4898
   250 N Hartford Ave Columbus (43222) *(G-7275)*
Orange Frazer Press Inc...................................937 382-3196
   37 1/2 W Main St Wilmington (45177) *(G-20501)*
Orbis Corporation...262 560-5000
   348 5th St Perrysburg (43551) *(G-15994)*
Orbis Corporation...937 652-1361
   200 Elm St Urbana (43078) *(G-19006)*
Orbis Corporation...440 974-3857
   7212 Justin Way Mentor (44060) *(G-13535)*
Orbis Corporation...513 737-9489
   1621 Hanover Ct Hamilton (45013) *(G-10595)*
Orbis Rpm LLC...419 307-8511
   592 Claycraft Rd Columbus (43230) *(G-7276)*
Orbis Rpm LLC...740 772-6355
   5938 State Route 159 Chillicothe (45601) *(G-3203)*
Orbis Rpm LLC...419 355-8310
   2100 Cedar St Fremont (43420) *(G-10042)*
Orbit Manufacturing Inc...................................513 732-6097
   4291 Armstrong Blvd Batavia (45103) *(G-1175)*
Orbytel Print and Packg Inc...............................216 267-8734
   4901 Johnston Pkwy Cleveland (44128) *(G-5818)*
Orchem Corporation..513 874-9700
   15 W 4th St Ste 450 Dayton (45402) *(G-8406)*
Ordnance Cleaning Systems LLC.............................440 205-0677
   7895 Division Dr Mentor (44060) *(G-13536)*
Oregon Printing, Dayton Also called Oregon Village Print Shoppe *(G-8407)*
Oregon Village Print Shoppe...............................937 222-9418
   29 N June St Dayton (45403) *(G-8407)*
OReilly Equipment LLC.....................................440 564-1234
   14555 Ravenna Rd Newbury (44065) *(G-14961)*
OReilly Precision Products................................937 526-4677
   560 E Main St Russia (45363) *(G-16610)*
Organic Coating Products, Lima Also called Modern Ink Technology LLC *(G-11908)*
Organic Roots Horticulture LLC............................330 620-1108
   6158 State Route 303 Ravenna (44266) *(G-16393)*
Organic Spa Magazine Ltd (PA).............................440 331-5750
   19537 Lake Rd 203 Rocky River (44116) *(G-16551)*
Organic Technologies, Coshocton Also called Wiley Organics Inc *(G-7758)*
Organized Living Inc (PA).................................513 489-9300
   3100 E Kemper Rd Cincinnati (45241) *(G-4118)*
Organon Inc...440 729-2290
   7407 Cedar Rd Chesterland (44026) *(G-3167)*
Orick Stamping..419 331-0600
   614 E Kiracofe Ave Elida (45807) *(G-9197)*
Original Mattress Factory, Columbus Also called Ahmf Inc *(G-6553)*
Original Mattress Factory Inc (PA)........................216 661-8388
   4930 State Rd Cleveland (44134) *(G-5819)*
Original Mattress Factory Inc.............................513 752-6600
   4450 Eastgate Blvd # 265 Cincinnati (45245) *(G-3260)*
Orion Control Panels Inc..................................513 615-6534
   5012 Calvert St Ste B Cincinnati (45209) *(G-4119)*
Orion Engineered Carbons LLC..............................740 423-9571
   11135 State Route 7 Belpre (45714) *(G-1581)*
Orion Lighting Solutions, Plain City Also called Premiere Building Mtls Inc *(G-16207)*
Orlando Baking Company (PA)...............................216 361-1872
   7777 Grand Ave Cleveland (44104) *(G-5820)*
Orora Packaging Solutions.................................513 539-8274
   930 Deneen Ave Monroe (45050) *(G-14274)*
Orpro Prosthetics & Orthotics, Piqua Also called Hanger Prsthetcs & Ortho Inc *(G-16120)*
Orpro Prosthetics & Orthotics, Dayton Also called Hanger Prsthetcs & Ortho Inc *(G-8243)*
Orpro Prosthetics & Orthotics, Springfield Also called Hanger Prsthetcs & Ortho Inc *(G-17411)*
Orpro Prosthetics & Orthotics, Moraine Also called Hanger Prsthetcs & Ortho Inc *(G-14358)*
Orrcast Aluminum Foundry, Orrville Also called Myron D Budd *(G-15604)*
Orrville Printing Co Inc..................................330 682-5066
   1645 N Main St Orrville (44667) *(G-15608)*
Orrville Trucking & Grading Co (PA).......................330 682-4010
   475 Orr St Orrville (44667) *(G-15609)*
Orrvilon Inc..330 684-9400
   1400 Dairy Ln Orrville (44667) *(G-15610)*
Ortho Prosthetic Center...................................419 352-8161
   1224 W Wooster St Bowling Green (43402) *(G-1988)*
Orthohlix Surgical Designs Inc............................330 869-9562
   3975 Embassy Pkwy Akron (44333) *(G-312)*
Orthotic and Prostetic Spc................................216 531-2773
   20650 Lakeland Blvd Euclid (44119) *(G-9431)*
Orthotic and Prosthetic I.................................330 723-6679
   799 N Court St Ste 1 Medina (44256) *(G-13313)*
Orthotic Prosthetic Center................................419 531-2222
   419 N Reynolds Rd Toledo (43615) *(G-18441)*
Orthotics & Prosthetics Rehab.............................330 856-2553
   700 Howland Wilson Rd Se Warren (44484) *(G-19429)*
Orton Edward Jr Crmic Fndation............................614 895-2663
   6991 S Old 3c Hwy Westerville (43082) *(G-20014)*
Ortronics Inc...937 224-0639
   6500 Poe Ave Dayton (45414) *(G-8408)*
Orwell Printing...440 285-2233
   10639 Grant St Ste C Chardon (44024) *(G-3131)*
OS Kelly Corporation (HQ).................................937 322-4921
   318 E North St Springfield (45503) *(G-17465)*
OS Power Tong Inc...330 866-3815
   7330 Minerva Rd Se Waynesburg (44688) *(G-19564)*
Osair Inc (PA)..440 974-6500
   7001 Center St Mentor (44060) *(G-13537)*
Osair Inc...440 255-8238
   8649 East Ave Mentor (44060) *(G-13538)*
Osborne Inc (PA)..440 942-7000
   7954 Reynolds Rd Mentor (44060) *(G-13539)*

Osborne Inc 216 771-0010
2100 Central Furnace Ct Cleveland (44115) **(G-5821)**
Osborne Inc 440 232-1440
26481 Cannon Rd Cleveland (44146) **(G-5822)**
Osborne Coinage Company (PA) 513 681-5424
2851 Massachusetts Ave Cincinnati (45225) **(G-4120)**
Osborne Materials Company (PA) 440 357-7026
1 Williams St Grand River (44045) **(G-10325)**
Osburn Associates Inc (PA) 740 385-5732
9383 Vanatta Rd Logan (43138) **(G-12038)**
Oscar Brugmann Sand & Gravel 330 274-8224
3828 Dudley Rd Mantua (44255) **(G-12556)**
Oscar Hicks 937 435-4350
9860 Atchison Rd Dayton (45458) **(G-8409)**
Osco Industries Inc (PA) 740 354-3183
734 11th St Portsmouth (45662) **(G-16293)**
Osco Industries Inc 740 286-5004
165 Athens St Jackson (45640) **(G-11193)**
OSG Usa Inc 513 755-3360
3611 Socialvl Fstr Rd # 102 Mason (45040) **(G-12919)**
Osg-Sterling Die Inc 216 267-1300
12502 Plaza Dr Parma (44130) **(G-15825)**
Oshkosh Corporation 513 745-9436
7875 Montgomery Rd Spc 87 Cincinnati (45236) **(G-4121)**
OSI, Hilliard *Also called Ohio Semitronics Inc* **(G-10847)**
OSI Global Sourcing LLC 614 471-4800
2575 Ferris Rd Columbus (43224) **(G-7277)**
OSI Software, Cleveland *Also called Osisoft LLC* **(G-5823)**
Osisoft LLC 440 442-2000
5885 Landerbrook Dr # 310 Cleveland (44124) **(G-5823)**
OSister Jams & Jellies 419 968-2505
12198 Mddlpoint Wetzel Rd Delphos (45833) **(G-8753)**
Osmans Pies Inc 330 607-9083
3678 Elm Rd Stow (44224) **(G-17616)**
Osnaburg Quilt Fibr Art Guild 330 488-2591
6855 Orchardview Dr Se East Canton (44730) **(G-9042)**
Osteo Solution 614 485-9790
117 Commerce Park Dr Westerville (43082) **(G-20015)**
Osteodynamics 405 921-9271
3130 Highland Ave Fl 3 Cincinnati (45219) **(G-4122)**
Osteonovus Inc 617 717-8867
1510 N Westwood Ave # 1080 Toledo (43606) **(G-18442)**
Osteosymbionics LLC 216 881-8500
1768 E 25th St Ste 316 Cleveland (44114) **(G-5824)**
Oster Enterprises, Massillon *Also called Oster Sand and Gravel Inc* **(G-13035)**
Oster Sand and Gravel Inc (PA) 330 494-5472
5947 Whipple Ave Nw Canton (44720) **(G-2776)**
Oster Sand and Gravel Inc 330 874-3322
3467 Dover Zoar Rd Ne Bolivar (44612) **(G-1920)**
Oster Sand and Gravel Inc 330 833-2649
1955 Riverside Dr Nw Massillon (44647) **(G-13035)**
Osu Arabidopsis Resource, Columbus *Also called Ohio State University* **(G-7259)**
Osu Industrial Welding Sy, Columbus *Also called Ohio State University* **(G-7260)**
Osu Labanlens 614 688-2356
1813 N High St Columbus (43210) **(G-7278)**
Otb, Dayton *Also called Outta Box Dispensers LLC* **(G-8412)**
Otc Services Inc 330 871-2444
1776 Constitution Ave Louisville (44641) **(G-12163)**
Otis Elevator Company 216 573-2333
9800 Rockside Rd Ste 1200 Cleveland (44125) **(G-5825)**
Otr Controls LLC 513 621-2197
40 E Mcmicken Ave Cincinnati (45202) **(G-4123)**
Ots, Columbus *Also called Ohio Trailer Supply Inc* **(G-7263)**
Ottawa Oil Co Inc 419 425-3301
1100 Trenton Ave Findlay (45840) **(G-9737)**
Ottawa Products Co 419 836-5115
1602 N Curtice Rd Ste A Curtice (43412) **(G-7826)**
Ottawa Rubber Company (PA) 419 865-1378
1600 Commerce Rd Holland (43528) **(G-10947)**
Otter Group LLC 937 315-1199
2725 Needmore Rd Dayton (45414) **(G-8410)**
Otto Konigslow Mfg Co 216 851-7900
13300 Coit Rd Cleveland (44110) **(G-5826)**
Ottokee Group Inc 419 636-1932
17768 County Road H50 Bryan (43506) **(G-2302)**
Ouchless Lures Inc 330 653-3867
305 Kilbourne Dr Hudson (44236) **(G-11066)**
Our Detergent Inc 419 589-5571
101 Knight Pkwy Mansfield (44903) **(G-12500)**
Our Family Mall 216 761-8669
13400 6th Ave Cleveland (44112) **(G-5827)**
Our Fifth Street LLC 614 866-4065
12920 Stonecreek Dr Ste A Pickerington (43147) **(G-16055)**
Our Heart Health Care Svcs LLC 614 943-5216
1336 E Main St Columbus (43205) **(G-7279)**
Our Nine LLC 614 844-6655
6740 Huntley Rd Ste F Columbus (43229) **(G-7280)**
Our Voice Initiative Inc 740 974-4303
237 Creekside Dr Springboro (45066) **(G-17340)**
Ourpets Company (HQ) 440 354-6500
1300 East St Fairport Harbor (44077) **(G-9627)**
Ourvoiceusa, Springboro *Also called Our Voice Initiative Inc* **(G-17340)**
Out On A Limb 513 432-5091
5311 Springdale Rd Cincinnati (45251) **(G-4124)**
Outback Cycle Shack LLC 513 554-1048
7923 Blue Ash Rd Cincinnati (45236) **(G-4125)**
Outback Tree Works 937 332-7300
808 N Market St Troy (45373) **(G-18690)**
Outdoor Army Navy Stores, Ashtabula *Also called Outdoor Army Store of Ashtbula* **(G-794)**
Outdoor Army Store of Ashtbula 440 992-8791
4420 Main Ave Ashtabula (44004) **(G-794)**
Outdoorwarehouse, Cleveland *Also called Marble Works* **(G-5615)**
Outhouse Paper Etc Inc 937 382-2800
319 Collett Rd Waynesville (45068) **(G-19570)**
Outlier Solutions LLC 330 947-2678
14835 Mccallum Ave Ne Alliance (44601) **(G-494)**
Outlook Tool Inc 937 235-6330
360 Fame Rd Dayton (45449) **(G-8411)**
Outotec North America, Strongsville *Also called Outotec Oyj* **(G-17775)**
Outotec Oyj 440 783-3336
11288 Alameda Dr Strongsville (44149) **(G-17775)**
Outta Box Dispensers LLC 937 221-7106
811 E 4th St Dayton (45402) **(G-8412)**
Ovase Manufacturing LLC 937 275-0617
1990 Berwyck Ave Dayton (45414) **(G-8413)**
Ovation Polymer Technology and 330 723-5686
1030 W Smith Rd Medina (44256) **(G-13314)**
Oveco Industries Electrica 740 381-3326
100 Kragel Rd Ste 4 Richmond (43944) **(G-16497)**
Oven Windows, Saint Henry *Also called West Ohio Tool & Mfg LLC* **(G-16671)**
Overhead Door Company, Toledo *Also called Overhead Inc* **(G-18443)**
Overhead Door Corporation 740 383-6376
1332 E Fairground Rd Marion (43302) **(G-12727)**
Overhead Door Corporation 419 294-3874
781 Rt 30w Upper Sandusky (43351) **(G-18970)**
Overhead Door of Salem Inc 330 332-9530
3864 Mccracken Rd Salem (44460) **(G-16765)**
Overhead Inc 419 476-0300
340 New Towne Square Dr Toledo (43612) **(G-18443)**
Overhoff Technology Corp 513 248-2400
1160 Us Route 50 Milford (45150) **(G-14030)**
Overly Hautz Company, Lebanon *Also called Overly Hautz Motor Base Co* **(G-11681)**
Overly Hautz Motor Base Co 513 932-0025
285 S West St Lebanon (45036) **(G-11681)**
Overseas Packing LLC 440 232-2917
19800 Alexander Rd Bedford (44146) **(G-1434)**
Ovonic Energy Products Inc 937 743-1001
50 Ovonic Way Springboro (45066) **(G-17341)**
Owen & Sons 513 726-5406
206 S Main St Seven Mile (45062) **(G-16908)**
Owen S Precision Grinding 513 745-9335
8383 Blue Ash Rd Cincinnati (45236) **(G-4126)**
Owens Corning 419 248-8000
9318 Erie Ave Sw Navarre (44662) **(G-14584)**
Owens Corning 740 964-1727
1 Corning Pkwy Toledo (43659) **(G-18444)**
Owens Corning 614 754-4098
2050 Integrity Dr S Columbus (43209) **(G-7281)**
Owens Corning 419 248-8000
1 Owens Corning Pkwy Toledo (43659) **(G-18445)**
Owens Corning (PA) 419 248-8000
1 Owens Corning Pkwy Toledo (43659) **(G-18446)**
Owens Corning Ht Inc 419 248-8000
Owens Corning World Toledo (43659) **(G-18447)**
Owens Corning Sales LLC (HQ) 419 248-8000
1 Owens Corning Pkwy Toledo (43659) **(G-18448)**
Owens Corning Sales LLC 740 328-2300
400 Case Ave Newark (43055) **(G-14907)**
Owens Corning Sales LLC 614 399-3915
100 Blackjack Road Ext Mount Vernon (43050) **(G-14497)**
Owens Corning Sales LLC 740 587-3562
2790 Columbus Rd Granville (43023) **(G-10336)**
Owens Corning Sales LLC 740 983-1300
1 Reynolds Rd Ashville (43103) **(G-819)**
Owens Corning Sales LLC 330 634-0460
170 South Ave Tallmadge (44278) **(G-17998)**
Owens Corning Sales LLC 330 764-7800
890 W Smith Rd Medina (44256) **(G-13315)**
Owens Corning Sales LLC 419 248-5751
11451 W Airport Svc Rd Swanton (43558) **(G-17917)**
Owens Corning Sales LLC 330 633-6735
275 Southwest Ave Tallmadge (44278) **(G-17999)**
Owens Corning Sales LLC 614 539-0830
3750 Brookham Dr Ste K Grove City (43123) **(G-10455)**
Owens Crning Cmposite Mtls LLC 419 248-8000
1 Owens Corning Pkwy Toledo (43659) **(G-18449)**
Owens Precisn Grindg, Cincinnati *Also called Owen S Precision Grinding* **(G-4126)**

ALPHABETIC

(PA)=Parent Co (HQ)=Headquarters (DH)=Div Headquarters
2019 Harris Ohio Industrial Directory
1207

Owens-Brockway Glass Cont Inc (HQ) 567 336-8449
1 Michael Owens Way Perrysburg (43551) *(G-15995)*
Owens-Brockway Packaging Inc (HQ) 567 336-5000
1 Michael Owens Way Perrysburg (43551) *(G-15996)*
Owens-Corning Capital LLC 419 248-8000
1 Owens Corning Pkwy Toledo (43659) *(G-18450)*
Owens-Illinois Inc (PA) 567 336-5000
1 Michael Owens Way Perrysburg (43551) *(G-15997)*
Owens-Illinois De Puerto Rico (PA) 419 874-9708
1 Seagate Toledo (43604) *(G-18451)*
Owens-Illinois General Inc (HQ) 567 336-5000
1 Michael Owens Way Perrysburg (43551) *(G-15998)*
Owens-Illinois Group Inc (HQ) 567 336-5000
1 Michael Owens Way Perrysburg (43551) *(G-15999)*
Owl Be Sweatin 513 260-2026
4914 Ridge Ave Cincinnati (45209) *(G-4127)*
Oxford Mining Company Inc 740 342-7666
2500 Township Rd 205 New Lexington (43764) *(G-14719)*
Oxford Mining Company Inc 330 878-5120
7551 Reed Rd Nw Strasburg (44680) *(G-17651)*
Oxford Mining Company Inc (HQ) 740 622-6302
544 Chestnut St Coshocton (43812) *(G-7747)*
Oxford Mining Company Inc 740 588-0190
1855 Kemper Ct Zanesville (43701) *(G-21166)*
Oxford Mining Company LLC (HQ) 740 622-6302
544 Chestnut St Coshocton (43812) *(G-7748)*
Oxford Mining Company - KY LLC 740 622-6302
544 Chestnut St Coshocton (43812) *(G-7749)*
Oxford Mining Inc 330 339-4546
4371 Rice Rd Sw Stone Creek (43840) *(G-17563)*
Oxford Press, Oxford Also called Cox Newspapers LLC *(G-15692)*
Oxyrase Inc 419 589-8800
3000 Park Ave W Ontario (44906) *(G-15545)*
Oylair Specialty 614 873-3968
9029 Heritage Dr Plain City (43064) *(G-16205)*
Ozone Systems Svcs Group Inc 513 899-4131
6687 State Route 132 Morrow (45152) *(G-14414)*
P & A Industries Inc 419 422-7070
600 Crystal Ave Findlay (45840) *(G-9738)*
P & B Electric 937 754-4695
1835 Successful Dr Fairborn (45324) *(G-9465)*
P & C Metal Polishing Inc 513 771-9143
340 Glendale Milford Rd Cincinnati (45215) *(G-4128)*
P & E Sales Ltd 330 829-0100
1595 W Main St Alliance (44601) *(G-495)*
P & G Precision LLC 513 738-3500
3955 Kraus Ln Fairfield (45014) *(G-9540)*
P & J Industries Inc (PA) 419 726-2675
4934 Lewis Ave Toledo (43612) *(G-18452)*
P & J Manufacturing Inc 419 241-7369
1644 Campbell St Toledo (43607) *(G-18453)*
P & L Heat Trting Grinding Inc 330 746-1339
313 E Wood St Youngstown (44503) *(G-20986)*
P & L Metalcrafts LLC 330 793-2178
1050 Ohio Works Dr Youngstown (44510) *(G-20987)*
P & L Precision Grinding LLC 330 746-8081
948 Poland Ave Youngstown (44502) *(G-20988)*
P & M Enterprises Group Inc 330 316-0387
1900 Mahoning Rd Ne Canton (44705) *(G-2777)*
P & P Machine Tool Inc 440 232-7404
26189 Broadway Ave Cleveland (44146) *(G-5828)*
P & P Mold & Die Inc 330 784-8333
1034 S Munroe Rd Tallmadge (44278) *(G-18000)*
P & R Specialty Inc 937 773-0263
1835 W High St Piqua (45356) *(G-16147)*
P & S Energy Inc 330 652-2525
3729 Union St Mineral Ridge (44440) *(G-14170)*
P & S Welding Co 330 274-2850
11611 Mantua Center Rd Mantua (44255) *(G-12557)*
P & T Millwork Inc 440 543-2151
10090 Queens Way Chagrin Falls (44023) *(G-3064)*
P & T Products Inc 419 621-1966
472 Industrial Pkwy Sandusky (44870) *(G-16834)*
P A I, Blue Ash Also called Precision Anlytical Instrs Inc *(G-1834)*
P A X, Lebanon Also called Pax Corrugated Products Inc *(G-11682)*
P B Fabrication Mech Contr 419 478-4869
750 W Laskey Rd Toledo (43612) *(G-18454)*
P C M Co (PA) 330 336-8040
291 W Bergey St Wadsworth (44281) *(G-19258)*
P C Power Inc 440 779-4080
23792 Lorain Rd Ste 300 North Olmsted (44070) *(G-15195)*
P C R Inc 330 945-7721
1135 Portage Trail Ext Akron (44313) *(G-313)*
P C R Restorations Inc 419 747-7957
933 W Longview Ave Mansfield (44906) *(G-12501)*
P C S, Pataskala Also called Programmable Control Service *(G-15838)*
P C T, Burbank Also called Pipe Coil Technology Inc *(G-2353)*
P C Workshop Inc 419 399-4805
900 W Caroline St Paulding (45879) *(G-15869)*

P F S Incorporated 440 582-1620
9861 York Alpha Dr Cleveland (44133) *(G-5829)*
P G I, Cleveland Also called Pinnacle Graphics & Imaging *(G-5878)*
P G M Diversified Industries 440 885-3500
6514 Alexandria Dr Cleveland (44130) *(G-5830)*
P Graham Dunn Inc (PA) 330 828-2105
630 Henry St Dalton (44618) *(G-7949)*
P H Glatfelter Company 419 333-6700
2275 Commerce Dr Fremont (43420) *(G-10043)*
P H Glatfelter Company 740 289-5100
200 Schuster Rd Piketon (45661) *(G-16077)*
P H Glatfelter Company 740 772-3111
232 E 8th St Chillicothe (45601) *(G-3204)*
P H I, Toledo Also called Pilkington Holdings Inc *(G-18469)*
P J McNerney & Associates, Cincinnati Also called McNerney & Associates LLC *(G-3989)*
P J Tool Company Inc 937 254-2817
1115 Springfield St Dayton (45403) *(G-8414)*
P L M Corporation 216 341-8008
7424 Bessemer Ave Cleveland (44127) *(G-5831)*
P M C, Blue Ash Also called Plastic Moldings Company Llc *(G-1830)*
P M I Food Equipment Group, Piqua Also called Hobart Corporation *(G-16128)*
P M Machine Inc 440 942-6537
38205 Western Pkwy Willoughby (44094) *(G-20395)*
P M Motor -Fan Blade Company, North Ridgeville Also called P M Motor Company *(G-15243)*
P M Motor Company 440 327-9999
37850 Taylor Pkwy North Ridgeville (44039) *(G-15243)*
P M R Inc 440 937-6241
4661 Jaycox Rd Avon (44011) *(G-955)*
P O McIntire Company (PA) 440 269-1848
29191 Anderson Rd Wickliffe (44092) *(G-20221)*
P P C Greatstuff Co, Mansfield Also called Shelly Fisher *(G-12512)*
P P E Inc 440 322-8577
710 Taylor St Elyria (44035) *(G-9306)*
P P F, Bradford Also called Production Paint Finishers Inc *(G-2011)*
P P G, Milford Also called PPG Industries Inc *(G-14033)*
P P G Chemicals Group, Barberton Also called PPG Industries Inc *(G-1096)*
P P G Refinishing Group, Delaware Also called PPG Industries Inc *(G-8715)*
P P G Refinishing Group, Columbus Also called PPG Industries Inc *(G-7339)*
P P G Regional Support Center, Chillicothe Also called PPG Industries Inc *(G-3214)*
P P I Graphics, Canton Also called KMS 2000 Inc *(G-2727)*
P P M Inc 216 701-0419
35 High Ct Chagrin Falls (44022) *(G-3026)*
P R Machine Works Inc 419 529-5748
1825 Nussbaum Pkwy Ontario (44906) *(G-15546)*
P R Racing Engines 419 472-2277
1951 W Sylvania Ave Toledo (43613) *(G-18455)*
P R U Industries Inc 937 746-8702
8401 Claude Thomas Rd Franklin (45005) *(G-9907)*
P R W Tool Inc 440 585-3373
30036 Lakeland Blvd Wickliffe (44092) *(G-20222)*
P S Awards, Cleveland Also called P S Superior Inc *(G-5833)*
P S C Inc 216 531-3375
21761 Tungsten Rd Cleveland (44117) *(G-5832)*
P S P Inc 330 283-5635
7337 Westview Rd Kent (44240) *(G-11359)*
P S Plastics Inc 614 262-7070
2020 Britains Ln Columbus (43224) *(G-7282)*
P S Superior Inc 216 587-1000
9257 Midwest Ave Cleveland (44125) *(G-5833)*
P T C, Lima Also called Precision Thrmplstc Componts *(G-11962)*
P T I Inc 419 445-2800
100 Taylor Pkwy Archbold (43502) *(G-663)*
P T X, Cleveland Also called Plastran Inc *(G-5888)*
P W C, Brunswick Also called Prime Wood Craft Inc *(G-2229)*
P&G, Cincinnati Also called Procter & Gamble Company *(G-4198)*
P&M Publishing 740 353-3300
2225 8th St Portsmouth (45662) *(G-16294)*
P&S Bakery Inc 330 707-4141
3279 E Western Reserve Rd Youngstown (44514) *(G-20989)*
P-Americas LLC 740 266-6121
450 Luray Dr Wintersville (43953) *(G-20540)*
P-Americas LLC 513 948-5100
2121 Sunnybrook Dr Cincinnati (45237) *(G-4129)*
P-Americas LLC 419 227-3541
1750 Greely Chapel Rd Lima (45804) *(G-11913)*
P-Americas LLC 614 253-8771
1241 Gibbard Ave Columbus (43219) *(G-7283)*
P-Americas LLC 440 323-5524
925 Lorain Blvd Elyria (44035) *(G-9307)*
P-Americas LLC 330 336-3553
904 Seville Rd Wadsworth (44281) *(G-19259)*
P-Americas LLC 330 837-4224
815 Oberlin Ave Sw Massillon (44647) *(G-13036)*
P-Americas LLC 330 963-0090
2351 Edison Blvd Ste 2 Twinsburg (44087) *(G-18827)*

P-Americas LLC 330 746-7652
500 Pepsi Pl Youngstown (44502) *(G-20990)*
P3 Secure LLC 937 610-5500
3535 Salem Ave Dayton (45406) *(G-8415)*
P3labs LLC 800 259-8059
6545 Market Ave N Ste 100 North Canton (44720) *(G-15108)*
PA MA Inc 440 846-3799
11288 Alameda Dr Strongsville (44149) *(G-17776)*
PA Stratton & Co Inc 419 660-9979
3768 State Route 20 Collins (44826) *(G-6425)*
PAC Drilling O & G LLC 330 874-3781
1037 Lawnridge St Ne Bolivar (44612) *(G-1921)*
Pac Manufacturing, Middletown *Also called Pac Worldwide Corporation* *(G-13938)*
Pac Worldwide Corporation 800 610-9367
3131 Cincinnati Dayton Rd Middletown (45044) *(G-13938)*
Paccar Inc 740 774-5111
65 Kenworth Dr Chillicothe (45601) *(G-3205)*
Pace Consolidated Inc (PA) 440 942-1234
4800 Beidler Rd Willoughby (44094) *(G-20396)*
Pace Converting Eqp Co Inc 216 631-4555
8500 Lake Ave Cleveland (44102) *(G-5834)*
Pace Engineering, Willoughby *Also called Pace Consolidated Inc* *(G-20396)*
Pace Engineering Inc 440 942-1234
4800 Beidler Rd Willoughby (44094) *(G-20397)*
Pace Mold & Machine LLC 330 879-1777
8225 Navarre Rd Sw Massillon (44646) *(G-13037)*
Pacer's Embroidery Barn, Granville *Also called Carter Evans Enterprises Inc* *(G-10327)*
Pacific Industries USA Inc 513 860-3900
8955 Seward Rd Fairfield (45011) *(G-9541)*
Pacific Manufacturing Ohio Inc 513 860-3900
8955 Seward Rd Fairfield (45011) *(G-9542)*
Pacific Manufacturing Tenn Inc 513 900-7862
555 Smith Ln Jackson (45640) *(G-11194)*
Pacific Tool & Die Co 330 273-7363
1035 Western Dr Brunswick (44212) *(G-2223)*
Pacific Valve, Piqua *Also called Crane Pumps & Systems Inc* *(G-16107)*
Pack Line Corp 212 564-0664
22900 Miles Rd Cleveland (44128) *(G-5835)*
Packaging Corporation America 513 424-3542
1824 Baltimore St Middletown (45044) *(G-13939)*
Packaging Corporation America 419 282-5809
929 Faultless Dr Ashland (44805) *(G-733)*
Packaging Corporation America 513 860-1145
3840 Port Union Rd Fairfield (45014) *(G-9543)*
Packaging Corporation America 513 582-0690
791 Saint Thomas Ct Cincinnati (45230) *(G-4130)*
Packaging Corporation America 740 344-1126
205 S 21st St Newark (43055) *(G-14908)*
Packaging Corporation America 330 644-9542
708 Killian Rd Ste 1 Coventry Township (44319) *(G-7776)*
Packaging Div, Mount Vernon *Also called Novolex Holdings Inc* *(G-14496)*
Packaging Material Direct Inc 989 482-8400
30405 Solon Rd Ste 9 Solon (44139) *(G-17212)*
Packaging Materials Inc 740 432-6337
62805 Bennett Ave Cambridge (43725) *(G-2452)*
Packaging Specialties Inc 330 723-6000
300 Lake Rd Medina (44256) *(G-13316)*
Packaging Tech LLC 216 374-7308
17325 Euclid Ave Ste 3045 Cleveland (44112) *(G-5836)*
Pacs Switchgear LLC 740 397-5021
8405 Blackjack Rd Mount Vernon (43050) *(G-14498)*
Pactiv LLC 815 547-1200
2120 Westbelt Dr Columbus (43228) *(G-7284)*
Pactiv LLC 614 771-5400
2120 Westbelt Dr Columbus (43228) *(G-7285)*
Pactiv LLC 330 644-9542
708 Killian Rd Coventry Township (44319) *(G-7777)*
Page One Group 740 397-4240
10 E Vine St Ste C Mount Vernon (43050) *(G-14499)*
Page Slotting Saw Co Inc 419 476-7475
3820 Lagrange St Toledo (43612) *(G-18456)*
Pahl Ready Mix Concrete Inc (PA) 419 636-4238
14586 Us Highway 127 Ew Bryan (43506) *(G-2303)*
Pahl Ready Mix Concrete Inc 419 636-4238
600 S River Rd Waterville (43566) *(G-19502)*
Pahuja Inc 614 864-3989
1125 Gahanna Pkwy Gahanna (43230) *(G-10097)*
Paine Falls Centerpin LLC 440 298-3202
6342 Ledge Rd Thompson (44086) *(G-18026)*
Painesville Pride, Willoughby *Also called Lake Community News* *(G-20357)*
Painesville Publishing Co 440 354-4142
2883 Industrial Park Dr Austinburg (44010) *(G-924)*
Paint Booth Pros Inc 440 653-3982
577 Fieldstone Dr Amherst (44001) *(G-569)*
Painted Hill Inv Group Inc 937 339-1756
402 E Main St Troy (45373) *(G-18691)*
Pak Master LLC 330 523-5319
3778 Timberlake Dr Richfield (44286) *(G-16479)*
Pakk Systems LLC 440 839-9999
39 W Main St Wakeman (44889) *(G-19288)*
Paklab, Batavia *Also called Universal Packg Systems Inc* *(G-1193)*
Paklab, Cincinnati *Also called Universal Packg Systems Inc* *(G-4452)*
Pako Inc 440 946-8030
7615 Jenther Dr Mentor (44060) *(G-13540)*
Pakra LLC 614 477-6965
449 E Mound St Columbus (43215) *(G-7286)*
Paleomd LLC 248 854-0031
26245 Broadway Ave Ste B Bedford (44146) *(G-1435)*
Palesh & Associates Inc 440 942-9168
3659 Lost Nation Rd Willoughby (44094) *(G-20398)*
Palette Studios Inc 513 961-1316
2501 Woodburn Ave Cincinnati (45206) *(G-4131)*
Pallet & Cont Corp of Amer 419 255-1256
901 Buckingham St Toledo (43607) *(G-18457)*
Pallet Distributors Inc 330 852-3531
10343 Copperhead Rd Nw Sugarcreek (44681) *(G-17856)*
Pallet Guys 440 897-3001
12720 N Star Dr North Royalton (44133) *(G-15292)*
Pallet Man The, Lisbon *Also called Paul E Cekovich* *(G-11979)*
Pallet Pros 440 537-9087
12500 Island Rd Grafton (44044) *(G-10308)*
Pallet Specs Plus LLC 513 351-3200
1701 Mills Ave Norwood (45212) *(G-15427)*
Pallet World Inc 419 874-9333
8272 Fremont Pike Perrysburg (43551) *(G-16000)*
Pallets-Fam-In-place-packaging, Versailles *Also called Kamps Inc* *(G-19183)*
Palmer Bros Transit Mix Con 419 332-6363
210 N Stone St Fremont (43420) *(G-10044)*
Palmer Bros Transit Mix Con (PA) 419 352-4681
12205 E Gypsy Lane Rd Bowling Green (43402) *(G-1989)*
Palmer Bros Transit Mix Con 419 447-2018
1900 S County Road 1 Tiffin (44883) *(G-18075)*
Palmer Bros Transit Mix Con 419 686-2366
12580 Greensburg Pike Portage (43451) *(G-16273)*
Palmer Engineered Products Inc 937 322-1481
1310 W Main St Springfield (45504) *(G-17466)*
Palmer Industries Inc 330 630-9397
920 Moe Dr Akron (44310) *(G-314)*
Palmer Klein Inc 937 323-6339
18 N Bechtle Ave Springfield (45504) *(G-17467)*
Palmer Mfg and Supply Inc 937 323-6339
18 N Bechtle Ave Springfield (45504) *(G-17468)*
Palmer Products, Akron *Also called Palmer Industries Inc* *(G-314)*
Palpac Industries Inc 419 523-3230
610 N Agner St Ottawa (45875) *(G-15661)*
Palstar Inc 937 773-6255
9676 Looney Rd Piqua (45356) *(G-16148)*
Pama Tool & Die, Strongsville *Also called PA MA Inc* *(G-17776)*
Pan-Glo, Mansfield *Also called Russell T Bundy Associates Inc* *(G-12509)*
Panacea Products Corporation (PA) 614 850-7000
2711 International St Columbus (43228) *(G-7287)*
Panacea Products Corporation 614 429-6320
1825 Joyce Ave Columbus (43219) *(G-7288)*
Panam Imaging Systems, Cleveland *Also called Horizons Incorporated* *(G-5417)*
Panama Jewelers LLC 440 376-6987
7250 Brakeman Rd Painesville (44077) *(G-15771)*
Pandrol Inc 419 592-5050
25 Interstate Dr Napoleon (43545) *(G-14555)*
Panel Control Inc 937 394-2201
107 Shue Dr Anna (45302) *(G-591)*
Panel Master LLC 440 355-4442
191 Commerce Dr Lagrange (44050) *(G-11491)*
Panel-Fab Inc 513 771-1462
10520 Taconic Ter Cincinnati (45215) *(G-4132)*
Panelbloc Inc 440 974-8877
8665 Tyler Blvd Mentor (44060) *(G-13541)*
Panelmatic Inc (PA) 513 829-3666
258 Donald Dr Fairfield (45014) *(G-9544)*
Panelmatic Inc 330 782-8007
1125 Meadowbrook Ave Youngstown (44512) *(G-20991)*
Panelmatic Cincinnati Inc 513 829-1960
258 Donald Dr Fairfield (45014) *(G-9545)*
Panelmatic Youngstown, Youngstown *Also called Panelmatic Inc* *(G-20991)*
Panelmatic Youngstown Inc 330 782-8007
1125 Meadowbrook Ave Youngstown (44512) *(G-20992)*
Paneltech LLC 440 516-1300
1430 Lloyd Rd Wickliffe (44092) *(G-20223)*
Pang Rubber Company, Johnstown *Also called Truflex Rubber Products Co* *(G-11273)*
Pantac Usa Ltd 614 423-6743
6155 Huntley Rd Ste D Columbus (43229) *(G-7289)*
Papel Couture 614 848-5700
6522 Singletree Dr Columbus (43229) *(G-7290)*
Paper Moon Winery 440 967-2500
2008 State Rd Vermilion (44089) *(G-19169)*
Paper Products Company, West Chester *Also called Omer J Smith Inc* *(G-19754)*
Paper Service Inc 330 227-3546
12022 Leslie Rd Lisbon (44432) *(G-11978)*
Paper Systems Incorporated (PA) 937 746-6841
185 S Pioneer Blvd Springboro (45066) *(G-17342)*

A L P H A B E T I C

Paper Vault   **ALPHABETIC SECTION**

Paper Vault 614 859-5538
869 Montrose Ave Columbus (43209) *(G-7291)*
Papworth Prints 614 428-6137
4355 Boulder Creek Dr Columbus (43230) *(G-7292)*
Parabellum Armament Co LLC 614 557-5987
3142 Broadway Ste 200 Grove City (43123) *(G-10456)*
Paradigm International Inc 740 370-2428
4239 Us Highway 23 Piketon (45661) *(G-16078)*
Paradise Inc 330 928-3789
1710 Front St Cuyahoga Falls (44221) *(G-7902)*
Paradise Mold & Die LLC 216 362-1945
10815 Briggs Rd Cleveland (44111) *(G-5837)*
Paragan Tool and Die, Berlin Center *Also called High Card Industries LLC* *(G-1646)*
Paragon Custom Plastics Inc 419 636-6060
402 N Union St Bryan (43506) *(G-2304)*
Paragon Machine Company, Bedford *Also called Done-Rite Bowling Service Co* *(G-1402)*
Paragon Metal Fabricators, Cincinnati *Also called Muehlenkamp Properties Inc* *(G-4053)*
Paragon Plastics 330 542-9825
5551 E Calla Rd New Middletown (44442) *(G-14751)*
Paragon Press 513 281-9911
2239 Fulton Ave Cincinnati (45206) *(G-4133)*
Paragon Robotics LLC 216 313-9299
5386 Majestic Pkwy Ste 2 Bedford Heights (44146) *(G-1478)*
Paragon Woodworking LLC 614 402-1459
800 Reynolds Ave Columbus (43201) *(G-7293)*
Paragraphics Inc 330 493-1074
2011 29th St Nw Canton (44709) *(G-2778)*
Parallel Solutions 440 498-9920
5380 Naiman Pkwy Ste B Cleveland (44139) *(G-5838)*
Parallel Technologies Inc 614 798-9700
4868 Blazer Pkwy Dublin (43017) *(G-8958)*
Paramelt Argueso Kindt Inc 216 252-4122
12651 Elmwood Ave Cleveland (44111) *(G-5839)*
Paramont Machine Company LLC 330 339-3489
963 Commercial Ave Se New Philadelphia (44663) *(G-14792)*
Paramount Distillers, Cleveland *Also called Luxco Inc* *(G-5588)*
Paramount Products 419 832-0235
10550 Prov Neap Swan Rd Grand Rapids (43522) *(G-10317)*
Paramount Stamping & Wldg Co 216 631-1755
1200 W 58th St Cleveland (44102) *(G-5840)*
Paratus Supply Inc 330 745-3600
635 Wooster Rd W Barberton (44203) *(G-1093)*
Pardson Inc 740 373-5285
149 Acme St Marietta (45750) *(G-12651)*
Park Corporation (PA) 216 267-4870
6200 Riverside Dr Cleveland (44135) *(G-5841)*
Park PLC Prntg Cpyg & Dgtl IMG 330 799-1739
3410 Canfield Rd Ste B Youngstown (44511) *(G-20993)*
Park Press Direct 419 626-4426
2143 Sherman St Sandusky (44870) *(G-16835)*
Park-Hio Frged McHned Pdts LLC 216 692-7200
23000 Euclid Ave Euclid (44117) *(G-9432)*
Park-Ohio Holdings Corp (PA) 440 947-2000
6065 Parkland Blvd Ste 1 Cleveland (44124) *(G-5842)*
Park-Ohio Industries Inc (HQ) 440 947-2000
6065 Parkland Blvd Ste 1 Cleveland (44124) *(G-5843)*
Park-Ohio Industries Inc 216 341-2300
3800 Harvard Ave Newburgh Heights (44105) *(G-14942)*
Park-Ohio Products Inc 216 961-7200
7000 Denison Ave Cleveland (44102) *(G-5844)*
Parker Aircraft Sales 937 833-4820
212 Church St Brookville (45309) *(G-2180)*
Parker Hannifin, Berlin Center *Also called Parker-Hannifin Corporation* *(G-1650)*
Parker Hannifin Partner B LLC 216 896-3000
6035 Parkland Blvd Cleveland (44124) *(G-5845)*
Parker Royalty Partnership 216 896-3000
6035 Parkland Blvd Cleveland (44124) *(G-5846)*
Parker Rst-Proof Cleveland Inc 216 481-6680
1688 Arabella Rd Cleveland (44112) *(G-5847)*
Parker Triad Store 937 293-4080
2402 Springboro Pike Moraine (45439) *(G-14374)*
Parker Trutec Incorporated (HQ) 937 323-8833
4700 Gateway Blvd Springfield (45502) *(G-17469)*
Parker Trutec Incorporated 937 653-8500
4795 Upper Valley Pike Urbana (43078) *(G-19007)*
Parker-Hannifin Corporation (PA) 216 896-3000
6035 Parkland Blvd Cleveland (44124) *(G-5848)*
Parker-Hannifin Corporation 937 456-5571
725 N Beech St Eaton (45320) *(G-9163)*
Parker-Hannifin Corporation 440 943-5700
30240 Lakeland Blvd Wickliffe (44092) *(G-20224)*
Parker-Hannifin Corporation 330 336-3511
135 Quadral Dr Wadsworth (44281) *(G-19260)*
Parker-Hannifin Corporation 330 963-0601
1390 Highland Rd E Macedonia (44056) *(G-12313)*
Parker-Hannifin Corporation 513 831-2340
50 W Techne Center Dr H Milford (45150) *(G-14031)*
Parker-Hannifin Corporation 614 279-7070
3885 Gateway Blvd Columbus (43228) *(G-7294)*
Parker-Hannifin Corporation 937 962-5301
700 W Cumberland St Lewisburg (45338) *(G-11796)*
Parker-Hannifin Corporation 330 673-2700
838 Overholt Rd Kent (44240) *(G-11360)*
Parker-Hannifin Corporation 330 740-8366
1911 Logan Ave Youngstown (44505) *(G-20994)*
Parker-Hannifin Corporation 330 335-6740
135 Quadral Dr Wadsworth (44281) *(G-19261)*
Parker-Hannifin Corporation 513 847-1758
9050 Centre Pointe Dr # 310 West Chester (45069) *(G-19757)*
Parker-Hannifin Corporation 419 542-6611
373 Meuse Argonne St Hicksville (43526) *(G-10781)*
Parker-Hannifin Corporation 440 366-5100
520 Ternes Ln Elyria (44035) *(G-9308)*
Parker-Hannifin Corporation 419 644-4311
16810 Fulton County Rd 2 Metamora (43540) *(G-13634)*
Parker-Hannifin Corporation 330 261-1618
14010 Ellsworth Rd Berlin Center (44401) *(G-1650)*
Parker-Hannifin Corporation 216 896-3000
1390 Highland Rd E Macedonia (44056) *(G-12314)*
Parker-Hannifin Corporation 330 296-2871
1300 N Freedom St Ravenna (44266) *(G-16394)*
Parker-Hannifin Corporation 440 937-6211
1160 Center Rd Avon (44011) *(G-956)*
Parker-Hannifin Corporation 440 284-6277
711 Taylor St Elyria (44035) *(G-9309)*
Parker-Hannifin Corporation 440 266-2300
8940 Tyler Blvd Mentor (44060) *(G-13542)*
Parker-Hannifin Corporation 440 205-8230
8940 Tyler Blvd Mentor (44060) *(G-13543)*
Parker-Hannifin Corporation 440 943-5700
30242 Lakeland Blvd Wickliffe (44092) *(G-20225)*
Parker-Hannifin Corporation 216 531-3000
6035 Parkland Blvd Cleveland (44124) *(G-5849)*
Parker-Hannifin Corporation 937 962-5566
704 W Cumberland St Lewisburg (45338) *(G-11797)*
Parker-Hannifin Corporation 937 644-3915
14249 Industrial Pkwy Marysville (43040) *(G-12805)*
Parker-Hannifin Corporation 330 336-3511
135 Quadral Dr Wadsworth (44281) *(G-19262)*
Parker-Hannifin Corporation 216 896-3000
6035 Parkland Blvd Cleveland (44124) *(G-5850)*
Parker-Hannifin Corporation 330 743-6893
58 Hubbard Rd Youngstown (44505) *(G-20995)*
Parker-Hannifin Corporation 330 296-2871
1300 N Freedom St Ravenna (44266) *(G-16395)*
Parking & Traffic Control SEC 440 243-7565
13651 Newton Rd Cleveland (44130) *(G-5851)*
Parking Facilities, Cleveland *Also called City of Cleveland* *(G-4931)*
Parkins Asphalt Sealing 419 422-2399
1710 Olney Ave Findlay (45840) *(G-9739)*
Parkn Manufacturing LLC 330 723-8172
8035 Norwalk Rd Ste 107 Litchfield (44253) *(G-11986)*
Parks West Pallet Llc 440 693-4651
4566 Parks West Rd Middlefield (44062) *(G-13843)*
Parkside & Eaton Estate 330 467-2995
8689 Parkside Dr Northfield (44067) *(G-15321)*
Parlex USA LLC (HQ) 937 898-3621
801 Scholz Dr Vandalia (45377) *(G-19142)*
Parma Heights License Bureau 440 888-0388
6339 Olde York Rd Cleveland (44130) *(G-5852)*
Parma International Inc 440 237-8650
13927 Progress Pkwy North Royalton (44133) *(G-15293)*
Parma Seven Hills Gazette, Brecksville *Also called Brecksville Broadview Gazette* *(G-2024)*
Paro Services Co (PA) 330 467-1300
1755 Entp Pkwy Ste 100 Twinsburg (44087) *(G-18828)*
Parobek Trucking Co 419 869-7500
192 State Route 42 West Salem (44287) *(G-19957)*
Parrot Energy Company 330 637-0151
180 Portal Dr Cortland (44410) *(G-7714)*
Parry Co 740 884-4893
33630 Old Route 35 Chillicothe (45601) *(G-3206)*
Part Rite Inc 216 362-4100
12855 York Delta Dr North Royalton (44133) *(G-15294)*
Parthenon Global LLC 888 332-5303
3615 Superior Ave E Cleveland (44114) *(G-5853)*
Parthenon Globalsystems, LLC, Cleveland *Also called Parthenon Global LLC* *(G-5853)*
Partitions Plus LLC 419 422-2600
12517 County Road 99 Findlay (45840) *(G-9740)*
Partners In Recognition Inc 937 420-2150
405 S Main St Fort Loramie (45845) *(G-9801)*
Partners Manufacturing Group 419 468-8516
9357 Township Road 48 Galion (44833) *(G-10149)*
Parts Unlimited 937 558-1527
5221 Shiloh Springs Rd Dayton (45426) *(G-8416)*
Party Animal Inc 440 471-1030
909 Crocker Rd Westlake (44145) *(G-20139)*
Party On, Austintown *Also called Adyl Inc* *(G-928)*
Pas Technologies Inc 937 840-1000
214 Hobart Dr Hillsboro (45133) *(G-10889)*

Pat's Cleaners, Cleveland *Also called Pats Nu-Style Cleaners Inc* ***(G-5854)***
Pataskala License Bureau, Pataskala *Also called Transportation Ohio Department* ***(G-15846)***
Pataskala Post 740 964-6226
190 E Broad St Ste 2 Pataskala (43062) ***(G-15837)***
Patches LLC 513 304-4882
1696 Pin Oak Ln Williamsburg (45176) ***(G-20253)***
Patent Construction Systems, Marion *Also called Harsco Corporation* ***(G-12710)***
Patenthealth LLC 330 208-1111
8000 Freedom Ave Nw North Canton (44720) ***(G-15109)***
Path Technologies Inc 440 358-1500
437 W Prospect St Painesville (44077) ***(G-15772)***
Patheon Pharmaceuticals Inc 513 948-9111
2110 E Galbraith Rd Cincinnati (45237) ***(G-4134)***
Pathfinder Computer Systems 330 928-1961
345 5th St Ne Barberton (44203) ***(G-1094)***
Pathos LLC 440 497-7278
7948 Mayfield Rd Chesterland (44026) ***(G-3168)***
Pathos Printing, Chesterland *Also called Pathos LLC* ***(G-3168)***
Patio Enclosures, Macedonia *Also called Great Day Improvements LLC* ***(G-12300)***
Patio Enclosures (PA) 513 733-4646
11949 Tramway Dr Cincinnati (45241) ***(G-4135)***
Patio Print & Promotions, Columbus *Also called Patio Printing Inc* ***(G-7295)***
Patio Printing Inc 614 785-9553
6663 Huntley Rd Ste S Columbus (43229) ***(G-7295)***
Patio Room Factory Inc 614 449-7900
2659 Beulah Rd Columbus (43211) ***(G-7296)***
Patjim Holdings Company 419 727-1298
3444 N Summit St Toledo (43611) ***(G-18458)***
Patriarch Trucking LLC 877 875-5402
68500 Mrrstown Flshing Rd Flushing (43977) ***(G-9784)***
Patricia Lee Burd 513 302-4860
310 Culvert St Cincinnati (45202) ***(G-4136)***
Patrician Furniture Builders 330 746-6354
1097 Wick Ave Youngstown (44505) ***(G-20996)***
Patrick J Burke & Co 513 455-8200
901 Adams Crossing Fl 1 Cincinnati (45202) ***(G-4137)***
Patrick M Davidson 513 897-2971
6490 Corwin Ave Waynesville (45068) ***(G-19571)***
Patrick Products Inc 419 943-4137
150 S Werner St Leipsic (45856) ***(G-11730)***
Patrick's, Leipsic *Also called Pretium Packaging LLC* ***(G-11732)***
Patriot 419 864-8411
217 W Main St Cardington (43315) ***(G-2875)***
Patriot Building Solutions, Wheelersburg *Also called Patriot Holdings Unlimited LLC* ***(G-20183)***
Patriot Consulting LLC 614 554-6455
20 E Frambes Ave Columbus (43201) ***(G-7297)***
Patriot Distributing, Columbus *Also called Patriot Consulting LLC* ***(G-7297)***
Patriot Energy LLC 330 923-4442
1574 Main St Cuyahoga Falls (44221) ***(G-7903)***
Patriot Holdings Unlimited LLC 740 574-2112
956 Patriot Ridge Dr Wheelersburg (45694) ***(G-20183)***
Patriot Mfg Group Inc 937 746-2117
512 Linden Ave Carlisle (45005) ***(G-2896)***
Patriot Mobility, Holland *Also called Patriot Products Inc* ***(G-10948)***
Patriot Precision Products 330 966-7177
8817 Pleasantwood Ave Nw Canton (44720) ***(G-2779)***
Patriot Products Inc 419 865-9712
1133 Corporate Dr Ste B Holland (43528) ***(G-10948)***
Patriot Seating Inc 330 779-0768
1584 Tamarisk Trl Youngstown (44514) ***(G-20997)***
Patriot Signage Inc 859 655-9009
10561 Chester Rd Cincinnati (45215) ***(G-4138)***
Patriot Software LLC 877 968-7147
4883 Dressler Rd Nw # 301 Canton (44718) ***(G-2780)***
Patriot Special Metals Inc 330 538-9621
2058 S Bailey Rd North Jackson (44451) ***(G-15152)***
Patriot Special Metals Inc 330 580-9600
2201 Harrison Ave Sw Canton (44706) ***(G-2781)***
Patriotic Buildings LLC 740 853-3970
1753 Patriot Rd Patriot (45658) ***(G-15853)***
Patron Graphics, Cincinnati *Also called Registered Images Inc* ***(G-4257)***
Pats Delicious LLC 614 441-7047
737 Parkwood Ave Columbus (43219) ***(G-7298)***
Pats Nu-Style Cleaners Inc 216 676-4855
5851 Smith Rd Cleveland (44142) ***(G-5854)***
Patterson Colburne (PA) 419 866-5544
1100 S Hlland Sylvania Rd Holland (43528) ***(G-10949)***
Patterson & Sons Inc 419 281-0897
10 Township Road 1031 Nova (44859) ***(G-15435)***
Patterson-Britton Printing 216 781-7997
2165 Lakeside Ave E Cleveland (44114) ***(G-5855)***
Patton Aluminum Products Inc 937 845-9404
65 Quick Rd New Carlisle (45344) ***(G-14676)***
Patton Industries Inc 419 331-5658
1950 Beery Rd Elida (45807) ***(G-9198)***
Pattons Truck & Heavy Eqp Svc 740 385-4067
35640 Hocking Dr Logan (43138) ***(G-12039)***
Paul A Grim Inc 740 385-9637
15104 State Route 328 Logan (43138) ***(G-12040)***
Paul Bartel (PA) 513 541-2000
1038 W North Bend Rd Cincinnati (45224) ***(G-4139)***
Paul Blausey Farms, Genoa *Also called Rcr Partnership* ***(G-10235)***
Paul E Cekovich 330 424-3213
9403 Black Rd Lisbon (44432) ***(G-11979)***
Paul H Rohe Company Inc 513 326-6789
11641 Mosteller Rd Cincinnati (45241) ***(G-4140)***
Paul J Tatulinski Ltd 330 584-8251
1595 W Main St North Benton (44449) ***(G-15061)***
Paul Miracle 513 575-3113
6749 Oakland Rd Loveland (45140) ***(G-12220)***
Paul Peterson Company (PA) 614 486-4375
950 Dublin Rd Columbus (43215) ***(G-7299)***
Paul Peterson Safety Div Inc 614 486-4375
950 Dublin Rd Columbus (43215) ***(G-7300)***
Paul Popov 440 582-6677
13800 Progress Pkwy Ste A North Royalton (44133) ***(G-15295)***
Paul R Lipp & Son Inc 330 227-9614
47563 Pancake Clarkson Rd Rogers (44455) ***(G-16560)***
Paul S Blanch, Bedford Heights *Also called Alert Stamping & Mfg Co Inc* ***(G-1458)***
Paul Stipkovich 330 499-7391
515 Browning Ave Nw North Canton (44720) ***(G-15110)***
Paul Wilke & Son Inc 513 921-3163
1965 Grand Ave Cincinnati (45214) ***(G-4141)***
Paul Yoder 740 439-5811
13051 Deerfield Rd Senecaville (43780) ***(G-16900)***
Paul/Jay Associates 740 676-8776
3057 Union St Bellaire (43906) ***(G-1488)***
Paula and Julies Cookbooks LLC 614 863-1193
6034 Mcnaughten Grove Ln Columbus (43213) ***(G-7301)***
Pauler Communications Inc (PA) 440 243-1229
3046 Brecksville Rd Ste B Richfield (44286) ***(G-16480)***
Pauley's Machine Shop, Sunbury *Also called Richard Pauley* ***(G-17899)***
Paulg Corporation 914 662-9837
1601 W 5th Ave Columbus (43212) ***(G-7302)***
Paulin Industries Inc 216 433-7633
12400 Plaza Dr U1 Parma (44130) ***(G-15826)***
Paulo Products Company 440 942-0153
4428 Hamann Pkwy Willoughby (44094) ***(G-20399)***
Pave Technology Co 937 890-1100
2751 Thunderhawk Ct Dayton (45414) ***(G-8417)***
Pavestone LLC 513 474-3783
8479 Broadwell Rd Cincinnati (45244) ***(G-4142)***
Pawnee Maintenance Inc 740 373-6861
101 Rathbone Rd Marietta (45750) ***(G-12652)***
Paws & Remember Nwo 419 662-9000
2121 Tracy Rd Northwood (43619) ***(G-15343)***
Pax Corrugated Products Inc 513 932-9855
1899 Kingsview Dr Lebanon (45036) ***(G-11682)***
Pax Machine Works Inc 419 586-2337
5139 Monroe Rd Celina (45822) ***(G-2978)***
Pax Products Inc 419 586-2337
5097 Monroe Rd Celina (45822) ***(G-2979)***
Paxar Corporation (HQ) 845 398-3229
8080 Norton Pkwy 22 Mentor (44060) ***(G-13544)***
Paxar Corporation 937 681-4541
7801 Technology Blvd Dayton (45424) ***(G-8418)***
Paxos Plating Inc 330 479-0022
4631 Navarre Rd Sw Canton (44706) ***(G-2782)***
Paycard USA Inc 702 216-6801
5854 Whitebark Pine Trl Dublin (43016) ***(G-8959)***
Payne Family LLC II 513 861-7600
5871 Creek Rd Blue Ash (45242) ***(G-1829)***
Pbf Energy Partners LP 419 698-6724
3143 Goddard Rd Toledo (43606) ***(G-18459)***
PBM Covington LLC 937 473-2050
400 Hazel St Covington (45318) ***(G-7791)***
PC, Columbus *Also called Papel Couture* ***(G-7290)***
PC Campana Inc (PA) 440 246-6500
6155 Park Square Dr Ste 1 Lorain (44053) ***(G-12111)***
PC Systems 330 825-7966
307 Montrose Ave Akron (44310) ***(G-315)***
PCA, Fairfield *Also called Packaging Corporation America* ***(G-9543)***
PCA, Cincinnati *Also called Packaging Corporation America* ***(G-4130)***
PCA/Akron 312, Coventry Township *Also called Packaging Corporation America* ***(G-7776)***
Pca/Ashland 307, Ashland *Also called Packaging Corporation America* ***(G-733)***
Pca/Middletown 353, Middletown *Also called Packaging Corporation America* ***(G-13939)***
PCA/Newark 365, Newark *Also called Packaging Corporation America* ***(G-14908)***
PCC Airfoils LLC 330 868-6441
3860 Union Ave Se Minerva (44657) ***(G-14196)***
PCC Airfoils LLC 740 982-6025
101 China St Crooksville (43731) ***(G-7818)***
PCC Airfoils LLC 440 350-6150
870 Renaissance Pkwy Painesville (44077) ***(G-15773)***
PCC Airfoils LLC 216 766-6206
25201 Chagrin Blvd # 290 Beachwood (44122) ***(G-1263)***

ALPHABETIC

(PA)=Parent Co (HQ)=Headquarters (DH)=Div Headquarters
2019 Harris Ohio Industrial Directory
1211

PCC Airfoils LLC (HQ)....216 831-3590
3401 Entp Pkwy Ste 200 Cleveland (44122) ***(G-5856)***
PCC Airfoils LLC....216 692-7900
1781 Octavia Rd Cleveland (44112) ***(G-5857)***
PCC Airfoils LLC....440 255-9770
8607 Tyler Blvd Mentor (44060) ***(G-13545)***
PCC Airfolils LLC....330 868-7376
3860 Union Ave Se Minerva (44657) ***(G-14197)***
PCC Ceramic Group 1....440 516-3672
1470 E 289th St Wickliffe (44092) ***(G-20226)***
PCI, West Chester *Also called Professional Case Inc* ***(G-19890)***
Pckd Enterprises Inc....440 632-9119
15510 Old State Rd Middlefield (44062) ***(G-13844)***
Pcna, Cincinnati *Also called Peter Cremer North America LP* ***(G-4153)***
Pcp Champion....937 392-4301
300 Congress St Ripley (45167) ***(G-16516)***
Pcs Nitrogen Inc....419 226-1200
1900 Fort Amanda Rd Lima (45804) ***(G-11914)***
Pcs Nitrogen Ohio LP....419 879-8989
2200 Fort Amanda Rd Lima (45804) ***(G-11915)***
Pcs Phosphate Company Inc....513 738-1261
10818 Paddys Run Rd Harrison (45030) ***(G-10662)***
Pct Industries, Perry *Also called Precision Conveyor Technology* ***(G-15911)***
Pcy Enterprises Inc....513 241-5566
3111 Spring Grove Ave Cincinnati (45225) ***(G-4143)***
PD&b, Toledo *Also called Projects Designed & Built* ***(G-18486)***
Pdi, Cleveland *Also called Pile Dynamics Inc* ***(G-5877)***
Pdi, Englewood *Also called Prosthetic Design Inc* ***(G-9373)***
Pdi Constellation LLC....216 271-7344
6225 Cochran Rd Solon (44139) ***(G-17213)***
Pdi Ground Support Systems Inc....216 271-7344
6225 Cochran Rd Solon (44139) ***(G-17214)***
PDI GROUP, THE, Solon *Also called Pdi Ground Support Systems Inc* ***(G-17214)***
Pdmb Inc....513 522-7362
9600 Colerain Ave Ste 110 Cincinnati (45251) ***(G-4144)***
PDQ Installation Co, Parma *Also called GMR Furniture Services Ltd* ***(G-15820)***
PDQ Printing Service....216 241-5443
1914 Clark Ave Cleveland (44109) ***(G-5858)***
PDQ Technologies Inc....937 274-4958
2608 Nordic Rd Dayton (45414) ***(G-8419)***
Pds, Fairfield *Also called CPC Logistics Inc* ***(G-9492)***
Pdsi Technical Services, Dayton *Also called Production Design Services Inc* ***(G-8446)***
Peabody Coal Company....740 450-2420
2810 East Pike Apt 3 Zanesville (43701) ***(G-21167)***
Peak Electric Inc....419 726-4848
320 N Byrne Rd Toledo (43607) ***(G-18460)***
Peak Foods Llc....937 440-0707
1903 W Main St Ste B Troy (45373) ***(G-18692)***
Peanut Roaster, The, Sandusky *Also called Thorfood LLC* ***(G-16854)***
Pearl Healthwear Inc (PA)....440 446-0265
5900 Maurice Ave Cleveland (44127) ***(G-5859)***
Pearl Lighting, Beachwood *Also called Pearlwind LLC* ***(G-1264)***
Pearl Tech Corporation (PA)....614 284-8357
545 Metro Pl S Ste 100 Dublin (43017) ***(G-8960)***
Pearl Valley Cheese Inc....740 545-6002
54760 Township Road 90 Fresno (43824) ***(G-10068)***
Pearlwind LLC....216 591-9463
24800 Chagrin Blvd # 101 Beachwood (44122) ***(G-1264)***
Pearson Education Inc....614 876-0371
4350 Equity Dr Columbus (43228) ***(G-7303)***
Pearson Education Inc....614 841-3700
445 Hutchinson Ave # 400 Columbus (43235) ***(G-7304)***
Pease Industies Inc....513 870-3600
7100 Dixie Hwy Fairfield (45014) ***(G-9546)***
Peck Engraving Co....216 221-1556
14398 Detroit Ave Cleveland (44107) ***(G-5860)***
Peco Holdings Corp (PA)....937 667-4451
6555 S State Route 202 Tipp City (45371) ***(G-18126)***
Peco II Inc....614 431-0694
7060 Huntley Rd Columbus (43229) ***(G-7305)***
Pedestrian Press....419 244-6488
2233 Robinwood Ave Toledo (43620) ***(G-18461)***
Pediavascular Inc....216 236-5533
7181 Chagrin Rd Ste 250 Chagrin Falls (44023) ***(G-3065)***
Peebles - Herzog Inc....614 279-2211
50 Hayden Ave Columbus (43222) ***(G-7306)***
Peebles Creative Group Inc....614 487-2011
4260 Tuller Rd Ste 200 Dublin (43017) ***(G-8961)***
Peebles Messenger Newspaper....937 587-1451
58 S Main St Peebles (45660) ***(G-15880)***
Peer Pantry LLC....216 236-4087
30901 Lake Shore Blvd Willowick (44095) ***(G-20480)***
Peerless Foods Inc....937 492-4158
500 S Vandemark Rd Sidney (45365) ***(G-17058)***
Peerless Foods Equipment, Sidney *Also called Peerless Foods Inc* ***(G-17058)***
Peerless Laser Processors Inc....614 836-5790
4353 Directors Blvd Groveport (43125) ***(G-10508)***
Peerless Metal Products Inc....216 431-6905
6017 Superior Ave Cleveland (44103) ***(G-5861)***
Peerless Printing Company....513 721-4657
2250 Gilbert Ave Ste 1 Cincinnati (45206) ***(G-4145)***
Peerless Prof Cooking Eqp, Sandusky *Also called Peerless Stove & Mfg Co Inc* ***(G-16836)***
Peerless Pump Clveland Svc Ctr, Cleveland *Also called Wm Plotz Machine and Forge Co* ***(G-6319)***
Peerless Saw Company (PA)....614 836-5790
4353 Directors Blvd Groveport (43125) ***(G-10509)***
Peerless Stove & Mfg Co Inc....419 625-4514
334 Harrison St Sandusky (44870) ***(G-16836)***
Peerless-Winsmith Inc....330 399-3651
5200 Upper Metro Pl # 110 Dublin (43017) ***(G-8962)***
Peerless-Winsmith Inc (HQ)....614 526-7000
5200 Upper Metro Pl # 110 Dublin (43017) ***(G-8963)***
Pegasus Industries....740 772-1049
104 S Mcarthur St Chillicothe (45601) ***(G-3207)***
Pegasus Printing Group, Youngstown *Also called Customer Printing Inc* ***(G-20884)***
Pegasus Products Company Inc....330 677-1123
315 Gougler Ave Kent (44240) ***(G-11361)***
Pegasus Vans & Trailers Inc....419 625-8953
4003 Tiffin Ave Sandusky (44870) ***(G-16837)***
Peggys Pride....614 464-2511
183 E Rich St Columbus (43215) ***(G-7307)***
Pelham Precious Metals LLC....419 708-7975
3105 Pelham Rd Toledo (43606) ***(G-18462)***
Pelletier Brothers Mfg....740 774-4704
4000 Sulphur Lick Rd Chillicothe (45601) ***(G-3208)***
Peloton Manufacturing Corp....440 205-1600
8909 East Ave Mentor (44060) ***(G-13546)***
Pelton Environmental Products....440 838-1221
8638 Cotter St Lewis Center (43035) ***(G-11770)***
Pelz Lettering Inc....419 625-3567
5003 Milan Rd Sandusky (44870) ***(G-16838)***
Pemco Inc....216 524-2990
5663 Brecksville Rd Cleveland (44131) ***(G-5862)***
Pemco North Canton Division, Canton *Also called Powell Electrical Systems Inc* ***(G-2787)***
Pemjay Inc....740 254-4591
318 E Tuscarawas Ave Gnadenhutten (44629) ***(G-10281)***
Pemro Corporation....800 440-5441
125 Alpha Park Cleveland (44143) ***(G-5863)***
Pemro Distribution, Cleveland *Also called Pemro Corporation* ***(G-5863)***
Pen Brands LLC....216 674-1430
220 Eastview Dr Ste 102 Brooklyn Heights (44131) ***(G-2129)***
Pen Pal LLC....614 348-2517
5868 Kitzmiller Rd New Albany (43054) ***(G-14633)***
Penca Design Group Ltd....440 210-4422
1325 Yale Pl Painesville (44077) ***(G-15774)***
Penco Tool LLC....440 998-1116
2621 West Ave Ashtabula (44004) ***(G-795)***
Pendaform Company....740 826-5000
200 S Friendship Dr New Concord (43762) ***(G-14685)***
Pendant Armor, West Chester *Also called Roboworld Molded Products LLC* ***(G-19784)***
Pendleton Mold & Machine LLC....440 998-0041
4624 State Rd Ashtabula (44004) ***(G-796)***
Penguin Enterprises Inc....440 899-5112
869 Canterbury Rd Ste 2 Westlake (44145) ***(G-20140)***
Penguin Serv Ice....614 848-6511
530 Lakeview Plaza Blvd Worthington (43085) ***(G-20699)***
Pengywn, Columbus *Also called H Y O Inc* ***(G-6974)***
Penick Gas & Oil....740 323-3040
1504 Blue Jay Rd Newark (43056) ***(G-14909)***
Peninsula Publishing LLC....330 524-3359
302 N Cleveland Massillon Akron (44333) ***(G-316)***
Penn Machine Company....814 288-1547
2182 E Aurora Rd Twinsburg (44087) ***(G-18829)***
Pennant, Pioneer *Also called N N Metal Stampings Inc* ***(G-16086)***
Pennant Companies (PA)....614 451-1782
2000 Bethel Rd Ste D Columbus (43220) ***(G-7308)***
Pennant Moldings Inc....937 584-5411
12381 Route 22 E Sabina (45169) ***(G-16617)***
Pennex Aluminum....330 427-6704
1 Commerce Ave Leetonia (44431) ***(G-11719)***
Pennslyvania Hill, Youngstown *Also called Armada Fortress LLC* ***(G-20847)***
Penny Fab, Columbus *Also called Charles Ray Evans* ***(G-6758)***
Penny Printing Inc....330 645-2955
2957 S Main St Coventry Township (44319) ***(G-7778)***
Pentaflex Inc....937 325-5551
4981 Gateway Blvd Springfield (45502) ***(G-17470)***
Pentagear Products LLC....937 660-8182
6161 Webster St Dayton (45414) ***(G-8420)***
Pentagon Protection Usa LLC....614 734-7240
5500 Frantz Rd Ste 100 Dublin (43017) ***(G-8964)***
Pentair....440 248-0100
34600 Solon Rd Solon (44139) ***(G-17215)***
Pentair Flow Technologies LLC (HQ)....419 289-1144
1101 Myers Pkwy Ashland (44805) ***(G-734)***
Pentair Flow Technologies LLC....419 281-9918
740 E 9th St Ashland (44805) ***(G-735)***

Pentair Water, Ashland *Also called Pentair Flow Technologies LLC* ***(G-734)***
Pentair Water Ashland Oper, Ashland *Also called Flow Control US Holding Corp* ***(G-704)***
Penwood Mfg 330 359-5600
30505 Tr 212 Fresno (43824) ***(G-10069)***
People's Defender, West Union *Also called Brown Publishing Co* ***(G-19959)***
Peoples Bancorp Inc 740 685-1500
221 S 2nd St Byesville (43723) ***(G-2391)***
Pep Brainin Fairfield Division, West Chester *Also called Brainin-Advance Industries LLC* ***(G-19663)***
Pepcon Concrete, Bradford *Also called C F Poeppelman Inc* ***(G-2010)***
Pepcon Concrete, Versailles *Also called C F Poeppelman Inc* ***(G-19175)***
Pepi, North Canton *Also called Portage Electric Products Inc* ***(G-15111)***
Pepperidge Farm Incorporated 614 457-4800
1174 Kenny Centre Mall Columbus (43220) ***(G-7309)***
Pepperidge Farm Incorporated 419 933-2611
3320 State Route 103 E Willard (44890) ***(G-20244)***
Pepperidge Farm Thrift Store, Columbus *Also called Pepperidge Farm Incorporated* ***(G-7309)***
Pepperl + Fuchs Inc (HQ) 330 425-3555
1600 Enterprise Pkwy Twinsburg (44087) ***(G-18830)***
Pepperl + Fuchs Entps Inc (HQ) 330 425-3555
1600 Enterprise Pkwy Twinsburg (44087) ***(G-18831)***
Pepperl + Fuchs Mfg Inc 330 425-3555
1600 Enterprise Pkwy Twinsburg (44087) ***(G-18832)***
Pepsi-Cola Metro Btlg Co Inc 937 461-4664
526 Milburn Ave Dayton (45404) ***(G-8421)***
Pepsi-Cola Metro Btlg Co Inc 614 261-8193
2553 N High St Columbus (43202) ***(G-7310)***
Pepsi-Cola Metro Btlg Co Inc 330 963-0426
1999 Enterprise Pkwy Twinsburg (44087) ***(G-18833)***
Pepsi-Cola Metro Btlg Co Inc 330 963-5300
1999 Enterprise Pkwy Twinsburg (44087) ***(G-18834)***
Pepsi-Cola Metro Btlg Co Inc 419 534-2186
3245 Hill Ave Toledo (43607) ***(G-18463)***
Pepsico, Franklin Furnace *Also called G & J Pepsi-Cola Bottlers Inc* ***(G-9934)***
Pepsico, Chillicothe *Also called G & J Pepsi-Cola Bottlers Inc* ***(G-3187)***
Pepsico, Cincinnati *Also called P-Americas LLC* ***(G-4129)***
Pepsico, Columbus *Also called Pepsi-Cola Metro Btlg Co Inc* ***(G-7310)***
Pepsico, Columbus *Also called G & J Pepsi-Cola Bottlers Inc* ***(G-6942)***
Pepsico, Twinsburg *Also called Pepsi-Cola Metro Btlg Co Inc* ***(G-18834)***
Pepsico, Toledo *Also called Pepsi-Cola Metro Btlg Co Inc* ***(G-18463)***
Pepsico, Columbus *Also called P-Americas LLC* ***(G-7283)***
Pepsico, Elyria *Also called P-Americas LLC* ***(G-9307)***
Pepsico, Wadsworth *Also called P-Americas LLC* ***(G-19259)***
Pepsico, Massillon *Also called P-Americas LLC* ***(G-13036)***
Pepsico, Zanesville *Also called G & J Pepsi-Cola Bottlers Inc* ***(G-21140)***
Pepsico, Youngstown *Also called P-Americas LLC* ***(G-20990)***
Per-Tech Inc 330 833-8824
113 Erie St S Massillon (44646) ***(G-13038)***
Percuvision LLC 614 891-4800
2030 Dividend Dr Columbus (43228) ***(G-7311)***
Perdatum Inc 614 761-1578
4098 Main St Hilliard (43026) ***(G-10850)***
Peregrine Field Gear, Lebanon *Also called Peregrine Outdoor Products LLC* ***(G-11683)***
Peregrine Outdoor Products LLC (PA) 800 595-3850
4317 N State Route 48 # 3 Lebanon (45036) ***(G-11683)***
Perennial Software Inc 440 247-5602
547 Washington St Ste 11 Chagrin Falls (44022) ***(G-3027)***
Perez Foods LLC 419 264-0303
515 Richholt St Holgate (43527) ***(G-10912)***
Perfect Measuring Tape Company (PA) 419 243-6811
1116 N Summit St Toledo (43604) ***(G-18464)***
Perfect Prcision Machining Ltd 330 475-0324
920 Clay St Akron (44311) ***(G-317)***
Perfect Probate 513 791-4100
2036 8 Mile Rd Cincinnati (45244) ***(G-4146)***
Perfect Score, The, Bedford Heights *Also called Tpsc Inc* ***(G-1481)***
Perfection Bakeries Inc 614 866-8171
6720 Commerce Court Dr Blacklick (43004) ***(G-1691)***
Perfection Bakeries Inc 419 221-2359
1278 W Robb Ave Lima (45801) ***(G-11916)***
Perfection Bakeries Inc 513 942-1442
374 Circle Freeway Dr C West Chester (45246) ***(G-19884)***
Perfection Fine Products, Cleveland *Also called Great Western Juice Company* ***(G-5352)***
Perfection Finishers Inc 419 337-8015
1151 N Ottokee St Wauseon (43567) ***(G-19531)***
Perfection In Carbide, Canfield *Also called Advetech Inc* ***(G-2517)***
Perfection Metal Co 216 641-0949
15085 N Deepwood Ln Chagrin Falls (44022) ***(G-3028)***
Perfection Mold & Machine Co 330 784-5435
2057 E Aurora Rd Ste Hi Twinsburg (44087) ***(G-18835)***
Perfection Packaging Inc 614 866-8558
885 Claycraft Rd Gahanna (43230) ***(G-10098)***
Perfection Printing 513 874-2173
9560 Le Saint Dr Fairfield (45014) ***(G-9547)***
Perfections Fabricators Inc 440 365-5850
680 Sugar Ln Elyria (44035) ***(G-9310)***
Perfecto Industries Inc 937 778-1900
1729 W High St Piqua (45356) ***(G-16149)***
Perfettes Sausage LLC 330 792-0775
1264 S Schenley Ave Youngstown (44511) ***(G-20998)***
Perform Metals Inc 440 286-1951
124 Industrial Pkwy Chardon (44024) ***(G-3132)***
Performa La Mar Printing Inc 440 632-9800
15912 W High St Middlefield (44062) ***(G-13845)***
Performace Diesel Inc 740 392-3693
16901 Mcvay Rd Mount Vernon (43050) ***(G-14500)***
Performance Abrasives Inc 513 733-9283
10330 Wayne Ave Cincinnati (45215) ***(G-4147)***
Performance Additives Amer LLC 330 365-9256
906 Cookson Ave Se New Philadelphia (44663) ***(G-14793)***
Performance Electronics Ltd 513 777-5233
11529 Goldcoast Dr Cincinnati (45249) ***(G-4148)***
Performance Lettering & Signs, Athens *Also called Jacqueline L Vandyke* ***(G-837)***
Performance Motorsports 513 931-9999
2545 W Galbraith Rd Cincinnati (45239) ***(G-4149)***
Performance Packaging Inc 419 478-8805
5219 Telegraph Rd Toledo (43612) ***(G-18465)***
Performance Plastics Ltd 513 321-8404
4435 Brownway Ave Cincinnati (45209) ***(G-4150)***
Performance Point Grinding 330 220-0871
1669 W 130th St Ste 302 Hinckley (44233) ***(G-10905)***
Performance Research Inc 614 475-8300
3328 Westerville Rd Columbus (43224) ***(G-7312)***
Performance Services 419 385-1236
828 Warehouse Rd Ste 8 Toledo (43615) ***(G-18466)***
Performance Superabrasives LLC 440 946-7171
7255 Industrial Park Blvd A Mentor (44060) ***(G-13547)***
Performance Technologies LLC 330 875-1216
3690 Tulane Ave Louisville (44641) ***(G-12164)***
Performanx Specialty Chem LLC (PA) 614 300-7001
300 Westdale Ave Westerville (43082) ***(G-20016)***
Performanx Specialty Chem LLC 614 300-7001
423 Hopewell Rd Waverly (45690) ***(G-19556)***
Performnce Plymr Solutions Inc 937 298-3713
2711 Lance Dr Moraine (45409) ***(G-14375)***
Perfume Counter 513 885-5989
11700 Princeton Pike Cincinnati (45246) ***(G-4151)***
Perfusion Solutions Inc 216 848-1610
4320 Mayfield Rd Ste 108 Cleveland (44121) ***(G-5864)***
Periflo/Px Pumps USA, Loveland *Also called Fischer Global Enterprises LLC* ***(G-12187)***
Perkinelmer Hlth Sciences Inc 330 825-4525
520 S Main St Ste 2423 Akron (44311) ***(G-318)***
Perkins & Marie Callenders LLC 513 881-7900
6880 Fairfield Bus Ctr Dr Fairfield (45014) ***(G-9548)***
Perkins Logging LLC 740 288-7311
361 Perkins Rd Chillicothe (45601) ***(G-3209)***
Perkins Motor Service Ltd (PA) 440 277-1256
1864 E 28th St Lorain (44055) ***(G-12112)***
Perkins Wood Products 740 884-4046
8686 Limerick Rd Chillicothe (45601) ***(G-3210)***
Perma-Fix of Dayton Inc 937 268-6501
300 Cherokee Dr Dayton (45417) ***(G-8422)***
Permaguide 330 456-8519
2427 9th St Sw Canton (44710) ***(G-2783)***
Permanent Impressions 740 892-3045
12182 Bruce Rd Utica (43080) ***(G-19027)***
Permco Inc 330 626-2801
1500 Frost Rd Streetsboro (44241) ***(G-17687)***
Permian Oil & Gas Division, Newark *Also called National Gas & Oil Corporation* ***(G-14900)***
Perrigo 937 473-2050
400 Hazel St Covington (45318) ***(G-7792)***
Perrons Printing Company 440 236-8870
27500 Royalton Rd Ste D Columbia Station (44028) ***(G-6442)***
Perry County Tribune 740 342-4121
399 Lincoln Park Dr Ste A New Lexington (43764) ***(G-14720)***
Perry Service Co., Toledo *Also called E W Perry Service Co Inc* ***(G-18273)***
Perry Welding Service Inc 330 425-2211
2075 Case Pkwy S Twinsburg (44087) ***(G-18836)***
Perrysburg Messenger-Journal, Perrysburg *Also called Welch Publishing Co* ***(G-16025)***
Personal Plumber Service Corp 440 324-4321
42343 N Ridge Rd Elyria (44035) ***(G-9311)***
Personal Stitch Monogramming 440 282-7707
924 Amchester Dr Amherst (44001) ***(G-570)***
Personnel Selection Services 440 835-3255
31517 Walker Rd Cleveland (44140) ***(G-5865)***
Perstorp Polyols Inc 419 729-5448
600 Matzinger Rd Toledo (43612) ***(G-18467)***
PES, Cincinnati *Also called Burns & Rink Enterprises LLC* ***(G-3431)***
Pesce Baking Company Ltd 330 746-6537
45 N Hine St Youngstown (44506) ***(G-20999)***
Peska Inc (PA) 440 998-4664
3600 N Ridge Rd E Ashtabula (44004) ***(G-797)***
Pet Goods Mfg, Columbus *Also called Tarahill Inc* ***(G-7511)***

ALPHABETIC

(PA)=Parent Co (HQ)=Headquarters (DH)=Div Headquarters
2019 Harris Ohio Industrial Directory
1213

Pet Processors LLc..................440 354-4321
1350 Bacon Rd Painesville (44077) *(G-15775)*
Pete Emmert Co..................740 455-3924
5580 Pleasant Valley Rd Nashport (43830) *(G-14569)*
Pete Gaietto & Associates Inc..................513 771-0903
1900 Section Rd Cincinnati (45237) *(G-4152)*
Peter Cremer North America LP (HQ)..................513 471-7200
3117 Southside Ave Cincinnati (45204) *(G-4153)*
Peter Graham Dunn Inc..................330 816-0035
1417 Zuercher Rd Dalton (44618) *(G-7950)*
Peter Ll Education Group, Moraine *Also called Pjl Enterprise Inc (G-14377)*
Peters Cabinetry..................937 884-7514
8766 N County Line Rd Brookville (45309) *(G-2181)*
Peterson Heat Treating, Kent *Also called H & S Steel Treating Inc (G-11329)*
Peterson Radio Inc..................937 549-3731
9711 Us Highway 52 Manchester (45144) *(G-12396)*
Petfiber LLC..................216 767-4482
17000 Saint Clair Ave # 1 Cleveland (44110) *(G-5866)*
Petit Gourmet, Maumee *Also called Twenty Second Cntury Foods LLC (G-13157)*
Petnet Solutions Inc..................865 218-2000
2139 Auburn Ave Cincinnati (45219) *(G-4154)*
Petnet Solutions Inc..................865 218-2000
11100 Euclid Ave Cleveland (44106) *(G-5867)*
Petro Evaluation Services Inc..................330 264-4454
3927 Cleveland Rd Wooster (44691) *(G-20636)*
Petro Gear Corporation (PA)..................216 431-2820
3901 Hamilton Ave Cleveland (44114) *(G-5868)*
Petro Quest Inc (PA)..................740 593-3800
3 W Stimson Ave Athens (45701) *(G-844)*
Petro Ware Inc..................740 982-1302
713 Keystone St Crooksville (43731) *(G-7819)*
Petroliance..................614 475-5952
2854 Johnstown Rd Columbus (43219) *(G-7313)*
Petroliance LLC..................216 441-7200
8500 Clinton Rd Ste 11 Cleveland (44144) *(G-5869)*
Petros Concrete Inc (PA)..................330 868-6130
7105 Lardon Rd Nw Waynesburg (44688) *(G-19565)*
Petrox Inc..................330 653-5526
10005 Ellsworth Rd Streetsboro (44241) *(G-17688)*
Petry Power Systems, Kent *Also called P S P Inc (G-11359)*
Pettigrew Pumping Inc..................330 297-7900
4171 Sandy Lake Rd Ravenna (44266) *(G-16396)*
Pettisville Grain Co (PA)..................419 446-2547
18251 County Road D E Pettisville (43553) *(G-16035)*
Pettisville Meats Inc..................419 445-0921
3082 Main St Pettisville (43553) *(G-16036)*
Pettit W T & Sons Co Inc..................330 539-6100
1670 Keefer Rd Girard (44420) *(G-10264)*
Pettits Pallets Inc..................614 351-4920
11812 London Rd Orient (43146) *(G-15576)*
Pexco Packaging Corp..................419 470-5935
795 Berdan Ave Toledo (43610) *(G-18468)*
Pf Management Inc..................513 874-8741
9990 Prnceton Glendale Rd West Chester (45246) *(G-19885)*
Pfahl Gauge & Manufacturing Co..................330 633-8402
665 Harden Ave Akron (44310) *(G-319)*
Pfi Displays Inc (PA)..................330 925-9015
40 Industrial St Rittman (44270) *(G-16527)*
Pfi Precision Inc..................937 845-3563
2011 N Dayton Lakeview Rd New Carlisle (45344) *(G-14677)*
Pfi Precision Machining, New Carlisle *Also called Pfi Precision Inc (G-14677)*
Pfi USA..................937 547-0413
5963 Jysville St Johns Rd Greenville (45331) *(G-10386)*
Pfizer Inc..................513 342-9056
9878 Windisch Rd West Chester (45069) *(G-19758)*
Pfizer Inc..................614 496-0990
8192 Bibury Ln Dublin (43016) *(G-8965)*
Pfizer Inc..................216 591-0642
2000 Auburn Dr Ste 200 Beachwood (44122) *(G-1265)*
Pfizer Inc..................937 746-3603
160 Industrial Dr Franklin (45005) *(G-9908)*
Pflaum Publishing Group..................937 293-1415
3055 Kettering Blvd # 100 Moraine (45439) *(G-14376)*
Pfmi, West Chester *Also called Pf Management Inc (G-19885)*
Pfpc Enterprises Inc..................513 941-6200
5750 Hillside Ave Cincinnati (45233) *(G-4155)*
Pgc Feeds, Pettisville *Also called Pettisville Grain Co (G-16035)*
PGT Healthcare LLP (HQ)..................513 983-1100
1 Procter And Gamble Plz Cincinnati (45202) *(G-4156)*
Pgw, Crestline *Also called Pittsburgh Glass Works LLC (G-7798)*
Phagevax Inc..................740 502-9010
855 Sharon Valley Rd # 101 Newark (43055) *(G-14910)*
Phantasm Designs..................419 538-6737
112 W Main St Ottawa (45875) *(G-15662)*
Phantasm Vapors LLC (PA)..................513 248-2431
951 Lila Ave Milford (45150) *(G-14032)*
Phantom Fireworks Inc..................419 237-2185
25840 Us Highway 20 Fayette (43521) *(G-9635)*
Phantom Sound..................513 759-4477
104 Reading Rd Mason (45040) *(G-12920)*
Phantom Technology LLC..................614 710-0074
3116 Scioto Darby Exec Ct Hilliard (43026) *(G-10851)*
Pharma Packaging Solutions, Shelby *Also called Carton Service Incorporated (G-16980)*
Pharma Tegix LLC..................740 879-4015
3177 Mccammon Chase Dr Lewis Center (43035) *(G-11771)*
Pharmacia Hepar LLC..................937 746-3603
160 Industrial Dr Franklin (45005) *(G-9909)*
Pharmazell Inc..................440 526-6417
8921 Brecksville Rd Brecksville (44141) *(G-2053)*
Pharmcutical Dev Solutions LLC..................732 766-5222
7116 Vista Creek Ct Powell (43065) *(G-16332)*
Phase Array Company LLC..................513 785-0801
9365 Allen Rd West Chester (45069) *(G-19759)*
Phase II Enterprises Inc..................330 484-2113
2154 Bolivar Rd Sw Canton (44706) *(G-2784)*
Phase Line Defense LLC..................440 219-0046
2610 Lester Rd Medina (44256) *(G-13317)*
Phase One, Dayton *Also called Poi Holdings Inc (G-7988)*
PHC Divison Bic Manufacturing, Euclid *Also called Precision Hydraulic Connectors (G-9437)*
PHD Manufacturing Inc..................330 482-9256
44018 Clmbana Wterford Rd Columbiana (44408) *(G-6476)*
Phe Manufacturing..................937 790-1582
331 Industrial Dr Franklin (45005) *(G-9910)*
Phg Retail Services, Cincinnati *Also called Jhg Retail Services LLC (G-3872)*
PHI Werkes LLC..................419 586-9222
1201 Havemann Rd Celina (45822) *(G-2980)*
Phil D De Mint..................740 474-7777
6345 State Route 56 E Circleville (43113) *(G-4551)*
Phil Matic Screw Products Inc..................440 942-7290
1457 E 357th St Willoughby (44095) *(G-20400)*
Phil Vedda & Sons Inc..................216 671-2222
12000 Berea Rd Cleveland (44111) *(G-5870)*
Phil's Custom Cabinets, Circleville *Also called Phil D De Mint (G-4551)*
Philadelphia Instantwhip Inc..................614 488-2536
2200 Cardigan Ave Columbus (43215) *(G-7314)*
Philip Armbrust..................740 335-7285
4939 Branen Dr Wshngtn CT Hs (43160) *(G-20735)*
Philips Healthcare Cleveland..................440 483-3235
595 Miner Rd Highland Heights (44143) *(G-10797)*
Philips Medical Systems Clevel (HQ)..................440 247-2652
595 Miner Rd Cleveland (44143) *(G-5871)*
Philips Medical Systems Mr..................440 483-2499
603 Alpha Dr Highland Heights (44143) *(G-10798)*
Phillips & Sons Welding & Fabg..................440 428-1625
6720 N Ridge Rd W Geneva (44041) *(G-10228)*
Phillips Awning Co..................740 653-2433
2052 W Fair Ave Lancaster (43130) *(G-11596)*
Phillips Companies (PA)..................937 426-5461
620 Phillips Dr Beavercreek Township (45434) *(G-1370)*
Phillips Companies..................937 431-7987
555 Old Springfield Rd Vandalia (45377) *(G-19143)*
Phillips Companies..................937 426-5461
620 Phillips Dr Beavercreek Township (45434) *(G-1371)*
Phillips Contractors Sup LLC..................216 861-5730
1800 E 30th St Cleveland (44114) *(G-5872)*
Phillips Electric Co..................216 361-0014
4126 Saint Clair Ave Cleveland (44103) *(G-5873)*
Phillips Manufacturing Co..................330 652-4335
504 Walnut St Niles (44446) *(G-15026)*
Phillips Mch & Stamping Corp..................330 882-6714
5290 S Main St New Franklin (44319) *(G-14696)*
Phillips Mfg & Mch Corp..................330 823-9178
118 1/2 E Ely St Alliance (44601) *(G-496)*
Phillips Mfg and Tower Co (PA)..................419 347-1720
5578 State Route 61 N Shelby (44875) *(G-16985)*
Phillips Packaging Inc..................937 484-4702
1050 Phoenix Dr Unit B Urbana (43078) *(G-19008)*
Phillips Ready Mix Co..................937 426-5151
620 Phillips Dr Beavercreek Township (45434) *(G-1372)*
Phillips Sand & Gravel Co, Beavercreek Township *Also called Phillips Companies (G-1371)*
Phillips Shtmtl Fabrications..................937 223-2722
1215 Ray St Dayton (45404) *(G-8423)*
Phillips Syrup, Westlake *Also called Innovtive Cnfction Sltions LLC (G-20126)*
Phillipsburg Quarry, Brookville *Also called Marietta Martin Materials Inc (G-2175)*
Philpott Indus Plas Entps Ltd..................330 225-3344
1010 Industrial Pkwy N Brunswick (44212) *(G-2224)*
Philpott Intl Entps Ltd, Brunswick *Also called Philpott Indus Plas Entps Ltd (G-2224)*
Philpott Rubber and Plastics, Aurora *Also called Philpott Rubber LLC (G-899)*
Philpott Rubber Company, Brunswick *Also called Philpott Rubber LLC (G-2225)*
Philpott Rubber LLC (HQ)..................330 225-3344
1010 Industrial Pkwy N Brunswick (44212) *(G-2225)*
Philpott Rubber LLC..................330 225-3344
375 Gentry Dr Aurora (44202) *(G-899)*
Pho & Rice LLC..................216 563-1122
1780 Coventry Rd Cleveland Heights (44118) *(G-6350)*
Phoenix Asphalt Company Inc..................330 339-4935
18025 Imperial Rd Magnolia (44643) *(G-12362)*

Phoenix Associates....440 543-9701
16760 W Park Circle Dr Chagrin Falls (44023) ***(G-3066)***
Phoenix Bat Company....614 873-7776
7801 Corp Blvd Unit E Plain City (43064) ***(G-16206)***
Phoenix Forge Group LLC....800 848-6125
1501 W Main St West Jefferson (43162) ***(G-19926)***
Phoenix Hydraulic Presses Inc....614 850-8940
4329 Reynolds Dr Hilliard (43026) ***(G-10852)***
Phoenix Hydraulics and Contrls, South Point *Also called Michael N Wheeler* ***(G-17288)***
Phoenix Industries & Apparatus....513 722-1085
6466 Snider Rd Apt C Loveland (45140) ***(G-12221)***
Phoenix Metal Fabricators, Dayton *Also called Phoenix Metal Works Inc* ***(G-8424)***
Phoenix Metal Works Inc....937 274-5555
2528 Ashcraft Rd Dayton (45414) ***(G-8424)***
Phoenix Mold & Die, Elyria *Also called Kastler & Reichlin Inc* ***(G-9281)***
Phoenix Partners LLC....734 654-2201
3464 Brookside Rd Ottawa Hills (43606) ***(G-15675)***
Phoenix Safety Outfitters LLC....614 361-0544
1619 Commerce Rd Springfield (45504) ***(G-17471)***
Phoenix Technologies Intl LLC (PA)....419 353-7738
1098 Fairview Ave Bowling Green (43402) ***(G-1990)***
Phoenix Tool & Thread Grindng....216 433-7008
4760 Briar Rd Cleveland (44135) ***(G-5874)***
Phoenix Tool Co Inc....330 372-4627
1351 Phoenix Rd Ne Warren (44483) ***(G-19430)***
Phoenix Welding Solutions LLC....330 569-7223
7606 Norton Rd Garrettsville (44231) ***(G-10200)***
Phoenix/Electrotek LLC....740 681-1412
890 Mill Park Dr Lancaster (43130) ***(G-11597)***
Phonak LLC....513 420-4568
2951 Cincinnati Dayton Rd Middletown (45044) ***(G-13940)***
Photo Journals, Sandusky *Also called Douthit Communications Inc* ***(G-16805)***
Photo Star....419 495-2696
307 State St Willshire (45898) ***(G-20482)***
Photo-Type Engraving Company....614 308-1900
2500 Harrison Rd Columbus (43204) ***(G-7315)***
Photo-Type Engraving Company....614 308-7914
2500 Harrison Rd Columbus (43204) ***(G-7316)***
Photon Labs LLC....214 455-0727
752 N State St Westerville (43082) ***(G-20017)***
Phpk Technologies, Columbus *Also called Kendall Holdings Ltd* ***(G-7086)***
Phymet Inc....937 743-8061
75 N Pioneer Blvd Springboro (45066) ***(G-17343)***
Pi-Tech, Dayton *Also called Proficient Information Tech* ***(G-8447)***
Pickaway News Journal....740 851-3072
375 Edwards Rd Circleville (43113) ***(G-4552)***
Pickens Window Service Inc....513 931-4432
7824 Hamilton Ave Cincinnati (45231) ***(G-4157)***
Pickett Concrete, Chesapeake *Also called G Big Inc* ***(G-3145)***
Pickett Concrete, Ironton *Also called G Big Inc* ***(G-11165)***
Pickett Enterprises Inc....937 428-6747
4643 Knollcroft Rd Dayton (45426) ***(G-8425)***
Pieco Inc (PA)....419 422-5335
2151 Industrial Dr Findlay (45840) ***(G-9741)***
Pieco Inc....937 399-5100
5225 Prosperity Dr Springfield (45502) ***(G-17472)***
Piedmont Chemical Co Inc....937 428-6640
1516 Silver Lake Dr Dayton (45458) ***(G-8426)***
Pier Tool & Die Inc....440 236-3188
27369 Royalton Rd Columbia Station (44028) ***(G-6443)***
Pierce GL Inc....513 772-7202
12100 Mosteller Rd # 500 Cincinnati (45241) ***(G-4158)***
Pierce Ohio, Willoughby *Also called Plastic Fabrication Svcs Inc* ***(G-20402)***
Pierce-Wright Precision Inc....216 362-2870
13606 Enterprise Ave Cleveland (44135) ***(G-5875)***
Pierre Holding Corp (HQ)....513 874-8741
9990 Prnceton Glendale Rd West Chester (45246) ***(G-19886)***
Pierre's Ice Cream Company, Cleveland *Also called Royal Ice Cream Co* ***(G-6012)***
Pierres French Ice Cream Inc....216 431-2555
6519 Carnegie Ave Cleveland (44103) ***(G-5876)***
Piersante and Associates....330 533-9904
230 Russo Dr Canfield (44406) ***(G-2540)***
Pietra Naturale Inc....937 438-8882
140 Industrial Dr Franklin (45005) ***(G-9911)***
Pigments Division, Cincinnati *Also called Sun Chemical Corporation* ***(G-4391)***
Pike County Paper Inc....740 947-5522
14572 Us Highway 23 Ste C Waverly (45690) ***(G-19557)***
Pike Machine Products Co....216 731-1880
23460 Lakeland Blvd Euclid (44132) ***(G-9433)***
Pike Tool & Manufacturing Co....740 947-7462
754 W 2nd St Waverly (45690) ***(G-19558)***
Piland Parts....330 686-3083
3215 Darrow Rd Stow (44224) ***(G-17617)***
Pile Dynamics Inc....216 831-6131
30725 Aurora Rd Cleveland (44139) ***(G-5877)***
Pilgrim-Harp Co....440 249-4185
35050 Avon Commerce Pkwy Avon (44011) ***(G-957)***
Pilington Libbey-Owens-Ford Co, Rossford *Also called Pilkington North America Inc* ***(G-16589)***
Pilkington Holdings Inc (HQ)....419 247-3731
811 Madison Ave Fl 1 Toledo (43604) ***(G-18469)***
Pilkington North America Inc....800 547-9280
2401 E Broadway St Northwood (43619) ***(G-15344)***
Pilkington North America Inc....419 247-3211
140 Dixie Hwy Rossford (43460) ***(G-16589)***
Pilkington North America Inc....419 247-3731
3440 Centerpoint Dr Ste C Urbancrest (43123) ***(G-19022)***
Pilkington North America Inc (HQ)....419 247-3731
811 Madison Ave Fl 3 Toledo (43604) ***(G-18470)***
Pillar Induction....262 317-5300
1745 Overland Ave Ne Warren (44483) ***(G-19431)***
Pillsbury Company LLC....740 286-2170
2403 S Pennsylvania Ave Wellston (45692) ***(G-19605)***
Pillsbury Company LLC....419 845-3751
4136 Martel Rd Caledonia (43314) ***(G-2420)***
Pilorusso Construction Div, Lowellville *Also called Lyco Corporation* ***(G-12253)***
Pilot Chemical, Newark *Also called CP Industries Inc* ***(G-14865)***
Pilot Chemical Company Ohio (PA)....513 326-0600
2744 E Kemper Rd Cincinnati (45241) ***(G-4159)***
Pilot Chemical Company Ohio....513 733-4880
606 Shepherd Dr Cincinnati (45215) ***(G-4160)***
Pilot Chemical Corp (HQ)....513 326-0600
2744 E Kemper Rd Cincinnati (45241) ***(G-4161)***
Pilot Chemical Corp....513 424-9700
3439 Yankee Rd Middletown (45044) ***(G-13941)***
Pilot Plastics Inc....330 920-1718
200 Cyhoga Fls Indus Pkwy Peninsula (44264) ***(G-15897)***
Pilot Production Solutions LLC....513 602-1467
6253 Crooked Creek Dr Mason (45040) ***(G-12921)***
Pin High LLC....216 577-9999
37040 Detroit Rd Avon (44011) ***(G-958)***
Pin Oak Development LLC....440 933-9862
32329 Orchard Park Dr Avon Lake (44012) ***(G-1000)***
Pin Oak Energy Partners LLC....888 748-0763
209 S Main St Ste 501 Akron (44308) ***(G-320)***
Pin Point Marketing LLC....330 336-5863
302 Eric Ln Wadsworth (44281) ***(G-19263)***
Pine Acres Woodcraft....330 852-0190
123 Pleasant Valley Rd Nw Sugarcreek (44681) ***(G-17857)***
Pine Ridge Meat Processing, Fleming *Also called Pine Ridge Processing* ***(G-9780)***
Pine Ridge Processing....740 749-3166
4559 Anderson Rd Fleming (45729) ***(G-9780)***
Pines Engineering, Wickliffe *Also called Ajax Tocco Magnethermic Corp* ***(G-20197)***
Pines Manufacturing Inc (PA)....440 835-5553
29100 Lakeland Blvd Westlake (44145) ***(G-20141)***
Pines Manufacturing Inc....440 835-5553
30505 Clemens Rd Westlake (44145) ***(G-20142)***
Pines Technology, Westlake *Also called Pines Manufacturing Inc* ***(G-20141)***
Pink Corner Office Inc....614 547-9350
8595 Columbus Pike # 106 Lewis Center (43035) ***(G-11772)***
Pinky & Thumb LLC....614 939-5216
5216 Sugar Run Dr New Albany (43054) ***(G-14634)***
Pinnacle Graphics & Imaging....216 781-1800
1138 W 9th St Ste Ll Cleveland (44113) ***(G-5878)***
Pinnacle Industrial Entps Inc....419 352-8688
513 Napoleon Rd Bowling Green (43402) ***(G-1991)***
Pinnacle Metal Products, Columbus *Also called McNeil Group Inc* ***(G-7169)***
Pinnacle Plastic Products, Bowling Green *Also called Pinnacle Industrial Entps Inc* ***(G-1991)***
Pinnacle Precision Pdts LLC....440 786-0248
624 Golden Oak Pkwy Bedford (44146) ***(G-1436)***
Pinnacle Press Inc....330 453-7060
2960 Harrisburg Rd Ne Canton (44705) ***(G-2785)***
Pinnacle Roller Co....513 369-4830
2147 Spring Grove Ave Cincinnati (45214) ***(G-4162)***
Pinnacle Sales Inc....440 734-9195
159 Crocker Park Blvd # 400 Westlake (44145) ***(G-20143)***
Pinney Dock & Transport LLC....440 964-7186
1149 E 5th St Ashtabula (44004) ***(G-798)***
Pioneer Automotive Tech Inc (HQ)....937 746-2293
100 S Pioneer Blvd Springboro (45066) ***(G-17344)***
Pioneer City Casting Company....740 423-7533
904 Campus Dr Belpre (45714) ***(G-1582)***
Pioneer Cldding Glzing Systems....216 816-4242
2550 Brookpark Rd Cleveland (44134) ***(G-5879)***
Pioneer Custom Coating LLC....419 737-3152
255 Industrial Ave Bldg D Pioneer (43554) ***(G-16087)***
Pioneer Custom Molding Inc....419 737-3252
3 Kexon Dr Pioneer (43554) ***(G-16088)***
Pioneer Equipment Company....330 857-6340
16875 Jericho Rd Dalton (44618) ***(G-7951)***
Pioneer Fabrication....419 737-9464
17455 County Road P Alvordton (43501) ***(G-521)***
Pioneer Forge Div, Pioneer *Also called Powers and Sons LLC* ***(G-16091)***
Pioneer Group, Marietta *Also called Pioneer Pipe Inc* ***(G-12653)***
Pioneer Hi-Bred Intl Inc....419 748-8051
15180 Henry Wood Rd Grand Rapids (43522) ***(G-10318)***

ALPHABETIC

Pioneer Homes Inc 419 737-2371
  1018 Lakeshore Dr Pioneer (43554) *(G-16089)*
Pioneer Industrial Systems LLC (PA) 419 737-9506
  16442 Us Highway 20 Alvordton (43501) *(G-522)*
Pioneer Machine Inc 330 948-6500
  104 S Prospect St Lodi (44254) *(G-12018)*
Pioneer National Latex Inc (HQ) 419 289-3300
  246 E 4th St Ashland (44805) *(G-736)*
Pioneer Pipe Inc 740 376-2400
  2021 Hanna Rd Marietta (45750) *(G-12653)*
Pioneer Plastics Corporation 330 896-2356
  3330 Massillon Rd Akron (44312) *(G-321)*
Pioneer Precision Tool Inc 513 932-8805
  5100 Bunnell Hill Rd Lebanon (45036) *(G-11684)*
Pioneer Sands LLC 740 659-2241
  2446 State Route 204 Glenford (43739) *(G-10271)*
Pioneer Sands LLC 740 599-7773
  26900 Coshocton Rd Howard (43028) *(G-10997)*
Pioneer Table Pad, Cleveland *Also called A & W Table Pad Co (G-4582)*
Pioneer Transformer Company 419 737-2304
  500 Cedar St Pioneer (43554) *(G-16090)*
PIP and Huds LLC 740 208-5519
  334 2nd Ave Gallipolis (45631) *(G-10173)*
PIP Enterprises LLC 740 373-5276
  220 Indian Run Rd Marietta (45750) *(G-12654)*
PIP Printing, Columbus *Also called Preisser Inc (G-7344)*
PIP Printing, Mentor *Also called Ultra Impressions Inc (G-13617)*
PIP Printing 440 951-2606
  35401 Euclid Ave Ste 109 Willoughby (44094) *(G-20401)*
Pipe Coil Technology Inc 330 256-6070
  111 Cardington Ln Burbank (44214) *(G-2353)*
Pipe Line Development Company 440 871-5700
  870 Canterbury Rd Westlake (44145) *(G-20144)*
Pipeline Automation Syste Inc 419 462-8833
  215 Harding Way W Galion (44833) *(G-10150)*
Pipeline Dept, Oregon *Also called Standard Oil Company (G-15569)*
Pipelines Inc 330 448-0000
  7800 Addison Rd Masury (44438) *(G-13061)*
Piqua Champion Foundry Inc 937 773-3375
  918 S Main St Piqua (45356) *(G-16150)*
Piqua Chocolate Company Inc (PA) 937 773-1981
  310 Spring St Piqua (45356) *(G-16151)*
Piqua Emery Cutter & Fndry Co 937 773-4134
  821 S Downing St Piqua (45356) *(G-16152)*
Piqua Emery Foundry, Piqua *Also called Piqua Emery Cutter & Fndry Co (G-16152)*
Piqua Granite & Marble Co Inc (PA) 937 773-2000
  123 N Main St Piqua (45356) *(G-16153)*
Piqua Materials Inc 937 773-4824
  1750 W Statler Rd Piqua (45356) *(G-16154)*
Piqua Materials Inc (PA) 513 771-0820
  11641 Mosteller Rd Ste 1 Cincinnati (45241) *(G-4163)*
Piqua Mineral Division, Piqua *Also called Piqua Materials Inc (G-16154)*
Piqua Paper Box Company 937 773-0313
  616 Covington Ave Piqua (45356) *(G-16155)*
Piqua Plant, Piqua *Also called Srm Concrete LLC (G-16163)*
Piqua Sign, Piqua *Also called Jerry Pulfer (G-16134)*
Pique Stripping Division, Moraine *Also called Rack Processing Company Inc (G-14388)*
Pirtek Reading Road, Cincinnati *Also called Encore Distributing Inc (G-3638)*
Piston Automotive LLC 419 464-0250
  1212 E Alexis Rd Toledo (43612) *(G-18471)*
Piston Group, Toledo *Also called Piston Automotive LLC (G-18471)*
Pita Wrap LLC 330 886-8091
  4721 Market St Boardman (44512) *(G-1900)*
Pitco Products Inc 513 228-7245
  120 N Terry St Dayton (45403) *(G-8427)*
Pitney Bowes Inc 203 426-7025
  6910 Treeline Dr Ste C Brecksville (44141) *(G-2054)*
Pitney Bowes Inc 216 351-2598
  4640 Hnckley Indus Prkway Cleveland (44109) *(G-5880)*
Pitney Bowes Inc 740 374-5535
  111 Marshall Rd Marietta (45750) *(G-12655)*
Pitt Plastics Inc (HQ) 614 868-8660
  3980 Groves Rd Ste A Columbus (43232) *(G-7317)*
Pittsburgh Glass Works LLC 419 569-7521
  5064 Lincoln Hwy Crestline (44827) *(G-7798)*
Pittsburgh Glass Works LLC 740 774-8762
  850 Southern Ave Chillicothe (45601) *(G-3211)*
Pittsburgh Wire & Cable 740 886-0202
  99 Township Road 1248 Proctorville (45669) *(G-16344)*
Pixslap Inc 937 559-2671
  1634 Central Ave Middletown (45044) *(G-13942)*
Pixuru, Coventry Township *Also called Canvas 123 Inc (G-7766)*
Pizzazz, Wooster *Also called Just Basic Sports Inc (G-20611)*
PJ Bush Associates Inc 216 362-6700
  15901 Industrial Pkwy Cleveland (44135) *(G-5881)*
Pj Woodwork LLC 419 886-0008
  16 E Ogle St Bellville (44813) *(G-1562)*
Pj's, Canton *Also called PJs Fabricating Inc (G-2786)*

Pjl Enterprise Inc (HQ) 937 293-1415
  3055 Kettering Blvd # 100 Moraine (45439) *(G-14377)*
Pjl Enterprise Inc 937 293-1415
  2019 Springboro W Moraine (45439) *(G-14378)*
Pjs Corrugated Inc 419 644-3383
  2330 Us Highway 20 Swanton (43558) *(G-17918)*
PJs Fabricating Inc 330 478-1120
  1511 Linwood Ave Sw Canton (44710) *(G-2786)*
Pjs Wholesale Inc 614 402-9363
  2551 Westbelt Dr Columbus (43228) *(G-7318)*
Pkg Technologies Inc 513 967-2783
  212 N Broadway St Ste 7 Lebanon (45036) *(G-11685)*
Pki Inc 513 832-8749
  4500 Reading Rd Cincinnati (45229) *(G-4164)*
Plabell Rubber Products Corp (PA) 419 691-5878
  300 S Saint Clair St # 324 Toledo (43604) *(G-18472)*
Placecrete Inc 937 298-2121
  2475 Arbor Blvd Moraine (45439) *(G-14379)*
Plain City Molding, Plain City *Also called GK Packaging Inc (G-16194)*
Plain Dealer Publishing Co (HQ) 216 999-5000
  4800 Tiedeman Rd Cleveland (44144) *(G-5882)*
Plain Dealer Publishing Co 614 228-8200
  155 E Broad St Fl 23 Columbus (43215) *(G-7319)*
Plain Dealer Publishing Co 216 999-5000
  4800 Tiedeman Rd Cleveland (44144) *(G-5883)*
Plain Dealer, The, Cleveland *Also called Plain Dealer Publishing Co (G-5882)*
Plains Precut Ltd 330 893-3300
  4917 County Road 207 Millersburg (44654) *(G-14119)*
Plan B Toys Ltd 614 751-6605
  4036 London Lancaster Rd Groveport (43125) *(G-10510)*
Planet Display & Packaging Inc 216 251-9641
  12500 Berea Rd Cleveland (44111) *(G-5884)*
Plank and Hide Co 888 462-6852
  2721a E Sharon Rd Cincinnati (45241) *(G-4165)*
Plant 2, Ashtabula *Also called Iten Industries Inc (G-780)*
Plant 2, Wooster *Also called Wooster Products Inc (G-20671)*
Plant 2, Columbus *Also called Fred D Pfening Company (G-6939)*
Plant 25, Lima *Also called Metokote Corporation (G-11904)*
Plant 5, Dayton *Also called Oerlikon Friction Systems (G-8395)*
Plant 8, Sugarcreek *Also called Belden Brick Company LLC (G-17843)*
Plant Maintenance Engineering, Cincinnati *Also called New Pme Inc (G-4071)*
Plant Two, Cleveland *Also called Falls Stamping & Welding Co (G-5218)*
Plas-Mac Corp 440 349-3222
  30250 Carter St Solon (44139) *(G-17216)*
Plas-Tanks Industries Inc (PA) 513 942-3800
  39 Standen Dr Hamilton (45015) *(G-10596)*
Plas-TEC Corp 419 272-2731
  601 W Indiana St Edon (43518) *(G-9187)*
Plaskolite LLC (PA) 614 294-3281
  400 W Nationwide Blvd # 400 Columbus (43215) *(G-7320)*
Plaskolite LLC 740 450-1109
  1175 5 Bs Dr Zanesville (43701) *(G-21168)*
Plaskolite LLC 614 294-3281
  400 W Nationwide Blvd # 400 Columbus (43215) *(G-7321)*
Plaster Process Castings Co 216 663-1814
  19800 Miles Rd Cleveland (44128) *(G-5885)*
Plastex Industries Inc 419 531-0189
  7106 Country Creek Rd Maumee (43537) *(G-13138)*
Plasti-Kemm Inc 330 239-1555
  2805 Stony Hill Rd Medina (44256) *(G-13318)*
Plastic Card Inc (PA) 330 896-5555
  3711 Boettler Oaks Dr Uniontown (44685) *(G-18929)*
Plastic Color Division, Minerva *Also called General Color Investments Inc (G-14180)*
Plastic Compounders Inc 740 432-7371
  1125 Utica Dr Cambridge (43725) *(G-2453)*
Plastic Enterprises Inc (PA) 440 324-3240
  41520 Schadden Rd Elyria (44035) *(G-9312)*
Plastic Enterprises Inc 440 366-0220
  1150 Taylor St Elyria (44035) *(G-9313)*
Plastic Extrusion Tech Ltd 440 632-5611
  15229 S State Ave Middlefield (44062) *(G-13846)*
Plastic Fabrication Svcs Inc 440 953-9990
  38167 Airport Pkwy Unit 1 Willoughby (44094) *(G-20402)*
Plastic Forming Company Inc 330 830-5167
  201 Vista Ave Se Massillon (44646) *(G-13039)*
Plastic Materials Inc (PA) 330 468-5706
  775 Highland Rd E Macedonia (44056) *(G-12315)*
Plastic Materials Inc 330 468-0184
  775 Highland Rd E Macedonia (44056) *(G-12316)*
Plastic Mold Technology Inc 330 848-4921
  40 Stuver Pl Barberton (44203) *(G-1095)*
Plastic Moldings Company Llc (PA) 513 921-5040
  9825 Kenwood Rd Ste 302 Blue Ash (45242) *(G-1830)*
Plastic Pallet & Container Inc 330 650-6700
  2239 Edgeview Dr Hudson (44236) *(G-11067)*
Plastic Partners LLC 425 765-2416
  1801 Newgarden Rd Salem (44460) *(G-16766)*
Plastic Platers LLC 216 961-1200
  9921 Clinton Rd Cleveland (44144) *(G-5886)*

Plastic Process Equipment Inc (PA).....216 367-7000
8303 Corporate Park Dr Macedonia (44056) **(G-12317)**
Plastic Products and Supply.....330 744-5076
1305 Lilac St Youngstown (44502) **(G-21000)**
Plastic Regrinders Inc.....740 659-2346
3161 Cooperriders Rd Nw Glenford (43739) **(G-10272)**
Plastic Selection Group Inc (PA).....614 464-2008
692 N High St Ste 310 Columbus (43215) **(G-7322)**
Plastic Suppliers Inc (PA).....614 471-9100
2400 Marilyn Ln Columbus (43219) **(G-7323)**
Plastic Suppliers Inc.....214 467-3700
2400 Marilyn Ln Columbus (43219) **(G-7324)**
Plastic Suppliers Inc.....614 475-8010
2400 Marilyn Ln Columbus (43219) **(G-7325)**
Plastic Works Inc (PA).....419 433-6576
10502 Mudbrook Rd Huron (44839) **(G-11108)**
Plastic Works Inc.....440 331-5575
19851 Ingersoll Dr Cleveland (44116) **(G-5887)**
Plastic-Kemm, Medina *Also called Plasti-Kemm Inc* **(G-13318)**
Plasticards Inc (PA).....330 896-5555
3711 Boettler Oaks Dr Uniontown (44685) **(G-18930)**
Plastics Converting Solutions.....330 722-2537
5341 River Styx Rd Medina (44256) **(G-13319)**
Plastics Division, Stow *Also called Esterle Mold & Machine Co Inc* **(G-17583)**
Plastics Machinery Magazine, Akron *Also called Peninsula Publishing LLC* **(G-316)**
Plastics R Unique Inc.....330 334-4820
330 Grandview Ave Wadsworth (44281) **(G-19264)**
Plastigraphics Inc.....513 771-8848
722 Redna Ter Cincinnati (45215) **(G-4166)**
Plastikos Corporation.....513 732-0961
700 Kent Rd Batavia (45103) **(G-1176)**
Plastipak Packaging Inc.....740 928-4435
610 O Neill Dr Bldg 22 Hebron (43025) **(G-10757)**
Plastipak Packaging Inc.....937 596-6142
18015 State Route 65 Jackson Center (45334) **(G-11212)**
Plastipak Packaging Inc.....937 596-5166
300 Washington St Jackson Center (45334) **(G-11213)**
Plasto-Tech Corporation.....440 323-6300
708 Lowell St Elyria (44035) **(G-9314)**
Plastran Inc.....440 237-8404
9841 York Alpha Dr Ste N Cleveland (44133) **(G-5888)**
Plastrx Inc.....513 847-4032
7682 Wetherington Dr West Chester (45069) **(G-19760)**
Plate Engraving Corporation.....330 239-2155
2324 Sharon Copley Rd Medina (44256) **(G-13320)**
Plate-All Metal Company Inc.....330 633-6166
1210 Devalera St Akron (44310) **(G-322)**
Platform Beers LLC.....440 539-3245
4125 Lorain Ave Cleveland (44113) **(G-5889)**
Plating Perceptions Inc.....330 425-4180
8815 Herrick Rd Twinsburg (44087) **(G-18837)**
Plating Process Systems Inc.....440 951-9667
7561 Tyler Blvd Ste 5 Mentor (44060) **(G-13548)**
Plating Solutions.....513 771-1941
871 Redna Ter Cincinnati (45215) **(G-4167)**
Plating Technology Inc (PA).....937 268-6882
1525 W River Rd Dayton (45417) **(G-8428)**
Plating Technology Inc.....937 268-6788
1525 W River Rd Dayton (45417) **(G-8429)**
Plating Test Cell Supply Co.....216 486-8400
948 Wayside Rd B Cleveland (44110) **(G-5890)**
Play All LLC.....440 992-7529
4542 Main Ave Ashtabula (44004) **(G-799)**
Play Mor, Millersburg *Also called Hershberger Lawn Structures* **(G-14088)**
Playall Trophies Awards Engrv, Ashtabula *Also called Play All LLC* **(G-799)**
Playground Equipment Service.....513 481-3776
2980 Diehl Rd Cincinnati (45211) **(G-4168)**
Playtex Manufacturing Inc.....937 498-4710
1905 Progress Way Sidney (45365) **(G-17059)**
Plaza At Sawmill Pl.....614 889-6121
6472 Sawmill Rd Columbus (43235) **(G-7326)**
PLC Connections, Columbus *Also called Plcc2 LLC* **(G-7328)**
PLC Connections LLC.....614 279-1796
673 N Wilson Rd Columbus (43204) **(G-7327)**
Plcc2 LLC.....614 279-1796
673 N Wilson Rd Columbus (43204) **(G-7328)**
Pleasant Valley Ready Mix Inc.....330 852-2613
559 Pleasant Valley Rd Nw Sugarcreek (44681) **(G-17858)**
Pleasant Valley Wdwkg LLC.....440 636-5860
13424 Clay St Middlefield (44062) **(G-13847)**
Plextrusions Inc.....330 668-2587
38870 Taylor Pkwy North Ridgeville (44035) **(G-15244)**
Plibrico Company LLC.....740 682-7755
454 County Road 33 Oak Hill (45656) **(G-15458)**
Plidco Ppline Repr Ppline Mint, Westlake *Also called Pipe Line Development Company* **(G-20144)**
Plott Graphic Directions Inc.....614 475-0217
859 Harmony Dr Columbus (43230) **(G-7329)**
Pluggers Inc.....330 383-7692
1617 Warren Ave Niles (44446) **(G-15027)**
Plus Mark LLC.....216 252-6770
1 American Rd Cleveland (44144) **(G-5891)**
Plus Publications Inc.....740 345-5542
57 S 3rd St Newark (43055) **(G-14911)**
Ply Gem Industries Inc.....937 492-1111
2600 Campbell Rd Sidney (45365) **(G-17060)**
Ply Gem Siding Group, Sidney *Also called Mastic Home Exteriors Inc* **(G-17050)**
Plymouth Foam LLC.....740 254-1188
1 Souther Gateway St Gnadenhutten (44629) **(G-10282)**
Plymouth Healthcare Pdts LLC.....440 542-0762
6521 Davis Indus Pkwy Solon (44139) **(G-17217)**
Plymouth Locomotive Svc LLC.....419 896-2854
48 E Main St Shiloh (44878) **(G-16997)**
Plymouth Locomotive Svc LLC.....419 896-2854
8118 Shiloh Norwalk Rd Shiloh (44878) **(G-16998)**
PM Coal Company LLC.....440 256-7624
9717 Chillicothe Rd Willoughby (44094) **(G-20403)**
PM Company, West Chester *Also called Pmco LLC* **(G-19761)**
PM Graphics Inc.....330 650-0861
10170 Philipp Pkwy Streetsboro (44241) **(G-17689)**
PM Motor Fan Blade Company, North Ridgeville *Also called Beckett Air Incorporated* **(G-15209)**
PMC Acquisitions Inc.....419 429-0042
2040 Industrial Dr Findlay (45840) **(G-9742)**
PMC Gage Inc (PA).....440 953-1672
38383 Willoughby Pkwy Willoughby (44094) **(G-20404)**
PMC Industries Corp.....440 943-3300
29100 Lakeland Blvd Wickliffe (44092) **(G-20227)**
PMC Lonestar, Willoughby *Also called PMC Gage Inc* **(G-20404)**
PMC Mercury (PA).....440 953-3300
38383 Willoughby Pkwy Willoughby (44094) **(G-20405)**
PMC Smart Solutions LLC.....513 921-5040
9825 Kenwood Rd Ste 300 Blue Ash (45242) **(G-1831)**
PMC Specialties Group Inc (HQ).....513 242-3300
501 Murray Rd Cincinnati (45217) **(G-4169)**
PMC Specialties Group Inc.....513 242-3300
5220 Vine St Cincinnati (45217) **(G-4170)**
PMC Systems Limited.....330 538-2268
12155 Commissioner Dr North Jackson (44451) **(G-15153)**
Pmco LLC.....513 825-7626
9220 Glades Dr West Chester (45011) **(G-19761)**
Pmd Enterprises Inc.....440 546-0901
6100 W Snowville Rd Brecksville (44141) **(G-2055)**
PME of Ohio Inc (PA).....513 671-1717
518 W Crescentville Rd Cincinnati (45246) **(G-4171)**
PME- Babbit Bearings, Cincinnati *Also called PME of Ohio Inc* **(G-4171)**
PMI, Macedonia *Also called Plastic Materials Inc* **(G-12316)**
Pmj Partners LLC.....201 360-1914
281 Lenappe Dr Columbus (43214) **(G-7330)**
Pneumatic Parts Co.....330 923-6063
888 Hampshire Rd Stow (44224) **(G-17618)**
Pneumatic Scale.....330 923-0491
4485 Allen Rd Cuyahoga Falls (44224) **(G-7904)**
Pneumatic Scale Angelus, Cuyahoga Falls *Also called Pneumatic Scale Corporation* **(G-7905)**
Pneumatic Scale Corporation (HQ).....330 923-0491
10 Ascot Pkwy Cuyahoga Falls (44223) **(G-7905)**
Podnar Plastics Inc.....330 673-2255
343 Portage Blvd Unit 3 Kent (44240) **(G-11362)**
Podnar Plastics Inc (PA).....330 673-2255
1510 Mogadore Rd Kent (44240) **(G-11363)**
Poet Biorefining, Marion *Also called Marion Ethanol LLC* **(G-12717)**
Poet Biorefining-Leipsic, Leipsic *Also called Summit Ethanol LLC* **(G-11737)**
Poet Brfining- Fostoria 23200, Fostoria *Also called Fostoria Ethanol LLC* **(G-9841)**
Pohl Machining Inc (PA).....513 353-2929
4901 Hamilton Cleves Rd Cleves (45002) **(G-6372)**
Poi Holdings Inc (HQ).....937 253-7377
3203 Plainfield Rd Dayton (45432) **(G-7988)**
Point Five Golf Co, Loveland *Also called Bay Island Company Inc* **(G-12180)**
Point Source Inc.....937 855-6020
7996 Butter St Germantown (45327) **(G-10245)**
Poklar Power and Motion Inc.....513 791-5009
10979 Reed Hartman Hwy # 111 Blue Ash (45242) **(G-1832)**
Poklar Power Motion, Blue Ash *Also called Poklar Power and Motion Inc* **(G-1832)**
Poland Concrete Products Inc (PA).....330 757-1241
70 Poland Mnr Poland (44514) **(G-16238)**
Poland Print Shop, North Lima *Also called Print Factory Pll* **(G-15176)**
Polar Inc.....937 297-0911
2297 N Moraine Dr Moraine (45439) **(G-14380)**
Polar Air, Englewood *Also called Eaton Comprsr Fabrication Inc* **(G-9357)**
Polar Products Inc.....330 253-9973
3380 Cavalier Trl Stow (44224) **(G-17619)**
Polaris Industries Inc.....937 283-1200
3435 Airborne Rd Ste A Wilmington (45177) **(G-20502)**
Polaris Technologies, Toledo *Also called Modern Builders Supply Inc* **(G-18414)**

Pole/Zero Acquisition Inc....513 870-9060
5558 Union Centre Dr West Chester (45069) ***(G-19762)***
Polgenix Inc....440 537-9691
11000 Cedar Ave Ste 100 Cleveland (44106) ***(G-5892)***
Polhe Tool Inc....419 476-2433
312 W Laskey Rd Toledo (43612) ***(G-18473)***
Polimeros Usa LLC....216 591-0175
26210 Emery Rd Ste 202 Warrensville Heights (44128) ***(G-19472)***
Poling Group, Coventry Township *Also called Akron Steel Fabricators Co* ***(G-7764)***
Poling Group, The, Akron *Also called Akron Special Machinery Inc* ***(G-51)***
Polished Pearl LLP....513 659-8824
11419 Brattle Ln Montgomery (45249) ***(G-14298)***
Polka DOT Pin Cushion Inc....330 659-0233
3807 Brecksville Rd Ste 8 Richfield (44286) ***(G-16481)***
Pollock Research & Design Inc....330 332-3300
1134 Salem Pkwy Salem (44460) ***(G-16767)***
Poly Concepts LLC....419 678-3300
712 Ash St Saint Henry (45883) ***(G-16666)***
Poly Flex, Baltic *Also called Flex Technologies Inc* ***(G-1029)***
Poly Green Technologies LLC....419 529-9909
1237 W 4th St Ontario (44906) ***(G-15547)***
Poly Products Inc....216 391-7659
837 E 79th St Cleveland (44103) ***(G-5893)***
Poly Works....419 678-3758
4830 State Route 219 Coldwater (45828) ***(G-6418)***
Poly-Carb Inc....440 248-1223
9456 Freeway Dr Macedonia (44056) ***(G-12318)***
Poly-Met Inc....330 630-9006
1997 Nolt Dr Akron (44312) ***(G-323)***
Polycase Division, Avon *Also called Ecp Corporation* ***(G-948)***
Polycel Incorporated....614 252-2400
1633 Woodland Ave Columbus (43219) ***(G-7331)***
Polychem Corporation (HQ)....440 357-1500
6277 Heisley Rd Mentor (44060) ***(G-13549)***
Polychem Corporation....440 357-1500
7214 Justin Way Mentor (44060) ***(G-13550)***
Polychem Corporation....419 547-1400
202 Watertower Dr Clyde (43410) ***(G-6392)***
Polychem Dispersions Inc....800 545-3530
16066 Industrial Pkwy Middlefield (44062) ***(G-13848)***
Polycraft Products Inc....513 353-3334
5511 Hamilton Cleves Rd Cleves (45002) ***(G-6373)***
Polyfill LLC....937 493-0041
960 N Vandemark Rd Sidney (45365) ***(G-17061)***
Polyflex LLC....440 946-0758
4803 E 345th St Willoughby (44094) ***(G-20406)***
Polygon Spaceship....440 506-0403
5536 Linn Dr Amherst (44001) ***(G-571)***
Polygon Spaceship Games, Amherst *Also called Polygon Spaceship* ***(G-571)***
Polygroup Inc....877 476-5972
9341 Hickory Hill Ct Loveland (45140) ***(G-12222)***
Polymer & Steel Tech Inc....440 510-0108
34899 Curtis Blvd Eastlake (44095) ***(G-9128)***
Polymer Additives Inc (HQ)....216 875-7200
7500 E Pleasant Valley Rd Independence (44131) ***(G-11146)***
Polymer Additives Inc....216 262-7016
7050 Krick Rd Walton Hills (44146) ***(G-19313)***
Polymer Additives Inc....216 875-7273
1636 Wayside Rd Cleveland (44112) ***(G-5894)***
Polymer Additives Inc....216 875-5840
1636 Wayside Rd Cleveland (44112) ***(G-5895)***
Polymer Additives Holdings Inc (HQ)....216 875-7200
7500 E Pleasant Valley Rd Independence (44131) ***(G-11147)***
Polymer Concepts Inc....440 953-9605
7555 Tyler Blvd Ste 1 Mentor (44060) ***(G-13551)***
Polymer Packaging Inc (PA)....330 832-2000
8333 Navarre Rd Se Massillon (44646) ***(G-13040)***
Polymer Protective Packaging, Massillon *Also called Polymer Packaging Inc* ***(G-13040)***
Polymer Tech & Svcs Inc (PA)....740 929-5500
1835 James Pkwy Heath (43056) ***(G-10727)***
Polymera Inc....740 527-2069
511 Milliken Dr Hebron (43025) ***(G-10758)***
Polymerics Inc (PA)....330 434-6665
2828 2nd St Cuyahoga Falls (44221) ***(G-7906)***
Polymerics Inc....330 677-1131
1540 Saint Clair Ave Kent (44240) ***(G-11364)***
Polymers By Design LLC....937 361-7398
2150 Monroe Concord Rd Troy (45373) ***(G-18693)***
Polymet Corporation....513 874-3586
7397 Union Centre Blvd West Chester (45014) ***(G-19763)***
Polynew Inc....330 897-3202
3557 State Route 93 Baltic (43804) ***(G-1032)***
Polynt Composites USA Inc....816 391-6000
1321 1st St Sandusky (44870) ***(G-16839)***
Polyone Corporation....419 668-4844
80 N West St Norwalk (44857) ***(G-15412)***
Polyone Corporation....740 423-7571
2419 State Route 618 Belpre (45714) ***(G-1583)***
Polyone Corporation....216 622-0100
680 N Rocky River Dr Berea (44017) ***(G-1622)***
Polyone Corporation....440 930-1000
733 E Water St North Baltimore (45872) ***(G-15047)***
Polyone Corporation....800 727-4338
1050 Landsdowne Ave Greenville (45331) ***(G-10387)***
Polyone Corporation....937 548-2133
1050 Landsdowne Ave Greenville (45331) ***(G-10388)***
Polyone Corporation....330 834-3812
1675 Navarre Rd Se Massillon (44646) ***(G-13041)***
Polyone Corporation (PA)....440 930-1000
33587 Walker Rd Avon Lake (44012) ***(G-1001)***
Polyone Corporation....440 930-3817
33587 Walker Rd Rdb-418 Avon Lake (44012) ***(G-1002)***
Polyone Funding Corporation....440 930-1000
33587 Walker Rd Avon Lake (44012) ***(G-1003)***
Polyone LLC....440 930-1000
33587 Walker Rd Avon Lake (44012) ***(G-1004)***
Polyquest Inc....330 888-9448
762 Valley Brook Cir Sagamore Hills (44067) ***(G-16619)***
Polyshield Corporation....614 755-7674
8643 Chateau Dr Pickerington (43147) ***(G-16056)***
Polytech Component Corp....330 726-3235
8469 Southern Blvd Youngstown (44512) ***(G-21001)***
Poma GL Specialty Windows Inc....330 965-1000
365 Mcclurg Rd Ste E Boardman (44512) ***(G-1901)***
Pomacon Inc....330 273-1576
2996 Interstate Pkwy Brunswick (44212) ***(G-2226)***
Pompili Precast Concrete, Cleveland *Also called E Pompili & Sons Inc* ***(G-5130)***
Ponderosa Consulting Services (PA)....330 264-2298
4060 Millbrook Rd Wooster (44691) ***(G-20637)***
Pool Office Manager, Hilliard *Also called Phantom Technology LLC* ***(G-10851)***
Pooles Printing & Office Svcs....419 475-9000
4036 Monroe St Toledo (43606) ***(G-18474)***
Pop A Top Cruise Thru....419 947-5855
157 S Main St Mount Gilead (43338) ***(G-14430)***
Pop/Pos Advantage....440 543-9452
17911 Snyder Rd Ste A Chagrin Falls (44023) ***(G-3067)***
Popped....330 678-1893
175 E Erie St Ste 201 Kent (44240) ***(G-11365)***
Poppees Popcorn Inc....440 327-0775
38727 Taylor Pkwy North Ridgeville (44035) ***(G-15245)***
Poppos Advantage Group, Chagrin Falls *Also called Pop/Pos Advantage* ***(G-3067)***
Pops Printed Apparel LLC....614 372-5651
1758 N High St Unit 2 Columbus (43201) ***(G-7332)***
Porath Business Services Inc....216 626-0060
21000 Miles Pkwy Cleveland (44128) ***(G-5896)***
Porath Printing, Cleveland *Also called Porath Business Services Inc* ***(G-5896)***
Porcelain Enamels, Cleveland *Also called Ferro Corporation* ***(G-5232)***
Porkbelly Bbq, Bowling Green *Also called Roare-Q LLC* ***(G-1997)***
Porocel Industries LLC (PA)....513 733-8519
1 Landy Ln Cincinnati (45215) ***(G-4172)***
Port Clinton Manufacturing LLC....419 734-2141
328 W Perry St Port Clinton (43452) ***(G-16255)***
Porta-Kleen, Lancaster *Also called Pro-Kleen Industrial Svcs Inc* ***(G-11599)***
Portage Electric Products Inc....330 499-2727
7700 Freedom Ave Nw North Canton (44720) ***(G-15111)***
Portage Knife Company, Akron *Also called Portage Machine Concepts Inc* ***(G-324)***
Portage Machine Concepts Inc....330 628-2343
75 Skelton Rd Akron (44312) ***(G-324)***
Portage Resources Inc....330 856-2622
8650 Kimblewick Ln Ne Warren (44484) ***(G-19432)***
Portage Septic Tank, Warren *Also called Richmond Concrete Products* ***(G-19439)***
Porter Dumpsters LLC....330 659-0043
2868 Southern Rd Richfield (44286) ***(G-16482)***
Porter Hybrids Inc....937 382-2324
1683 N State Route 134 Wilmington (45177) ***(G-20503)***
Porter Precision Products Co (PA)....513 385-1569
2734 Banning Rd Cincinnati (45239) ***(G-4173)***
Porter-Guertin Co Inc....513 241-7663
2150 Colerain Ave Cincinnati (45214) ***(G-4174)***
Porters Welding Inc (PA)....740 452-4181
601 Linden Ave Zanesville (43701) ***(G-21169)***
Portion Pac Inc (HQ)....513 398-0400
7325 Snider Rd Mason (45040) ***(G-12922)***
Porto Pump Inc....740 454-2576
8th And South St Zanesville (43702) ***(G-21170)***
Portsmouth Block & Brick, Portsmouth *Also called Portsmouth Block Inc* ***(G-16295)***
Portsmouth Block Inc....740 353-4113
2700 Gallia St Portsmouth (45662) ***(G-16295)***
Portsmouth Division, Portsmouth *Also called Osco Industries Inc* ***(G-16293)***
Positech Corp....513 942-7411
11310 Williamson Rd Blue Ash (45241) ***(G-1833)***
Positive Images, Newton Falls *Also called Kens His & Hers Shop Inc* ***(G-14988)***
Positive Safety Mfr Co....440 951-2130
34099 Melinz Pkwy Unit A Willoughby (44095) ***(G-20407)***
Positool Technologies Inc....330 220-4002
2985 Nationwide Pkwy Brunswick (44212) ***(G-2227)***
Positrol Inc....513 272-0500
3890 Virginia Ave Cincinnati (45227) ***(G-4175)***

Positrol Workholding, Cincinnati Also called Positrol Inc (G-4175)
Posm Software LLC 859 274-0041
4925 Sharon Hill Dr Columbus (43235) (G-7333)
Possible Plastics Inc 614 277-2100
1620 Feddern Ave Bldg B Grove City (43123) (G-10457)
Post 513 768-8000
312 Elm St Lockland (45215) (G-12001)
Post Newspapers 330 721-7678
5164 Normandy Park Dr # 100 Medina (44256) (G-13321)
Post Printing Co (PA) 859 254-7714
205 W 4th St Minster (45865) (G-14222)
Post Products Inc 330 678-0048
1600 Franklin Ave Kent (44240) (G-11366)
Post, The, Athens Also called Ohio University (G-843)
Posterservice Incorporated (PA) 513 577-7100
225 Northland Blvd Cincinnati (45246) (G-4176)
Postle Industries Inc 216 265-9000
5500 W 164th St Cleveland (44142) (G-5897)
Potemkin Industries Inc (PA) 740 397-4888
8043 Columbus Rd Mount Vernon (43050) (G-14501)
Potential Labs LLC 740 590-0009
101 S May Ave Athens (45701) (G-845)
Potter House 419 584-1705
108 S Main St Celina (45822) (G-2981)
Potters Industries LLC 216 621-0840
2380 W 3rd St Cleveland (44113) (G-5898)
Pottery Making Illustrate, Westerville Also called American Ceramic Society (G-19977)
POv Print Communication Inc 440 591-5443
16715 W Park Circle Dr Chagrin Falls (44023) (G-3068)
Powder Alloy Corporation 513 984-4016
101 Northeast Dr Loveland (45140) (G-12223)
Powder Coatings, Strongsville Also called PPG Industries Inc (G-17777)
Powder Kote Industries, Cincinnati Also called Pki Inc (G-4164)
Powdermet Inc (PA) 216 404-0053
24112 Rockwell Dr Euclid (44117) (G-9434)
Powdermet Powder Production 216 404-0053
24112 Rockwell Dr Ste D Euclid (44117) (G-9435)
Powell Electrical Systems Inc 330 966-1750
8967 Pleasantwood Ave Nw Canton (44720) (G-2787)
Powell Logging 740 372-6131
7593 State Route 348 Otway (45657) (G-15689)
Powell Prints LLC 614 771-4830
3991 Main St Hilliard (43026) (G-10853)
Powell Valve, Cincinnati Also called William Powell Company (G-4510)
Powell Village Winery LLC 614 290-5898
50 S Liberty St Powell (43065) (G-16333)
Power Acquisition LLC (HQ) 614 228-5000
5025 Bradenton Ave # 130 Dublin (43017) (G-8966)
Power Corp Sign Products Inc 740 344-0468
632 Swansea Rd Newark (43055) (G-14912)
Power Distributors LLC (PA) 614 876-3533
3700 Paragon Dr Columbus (43228) (G-7334)
Power Engineering LLC 513 793-5800
507 N Wayne Ave Cincinnati (45215) (G-4177)
Power Engineering Technology, Wyoming Also called John McHael Priester Assoc Inc (G-20752)
Power Grounding Solutions LLC 440 926-3219
1001 Commerce Dr Grafton (44044) (G-10309)
Power Management Inc (PA) 937 222-2909
420 Davis Ave Dayton (45403) (G-8430)
Power Media Inc 330 475-0500
546 Grant St Akron (44311) (G-325)
Power Metrics Inc 440 461-9352
17 Alpha Park Cleveland (44143) (G-5899)
Power Shelf LLC 419 775-6125
500 Industrial Park Dr Plymouth (44865) (G-16233)
Power Source Service LLC 513 607-4555
5400 Belle Meade Dr Batavia (45103) (G-1177)
Power-Pack Conveyor Company 440 975-9955
38363 Airport Pkwy Willoughby (44094) (G-20408)
Powerbuff Inc 419 241-2156
1001 Brown Ave Toledo (43607) (G-18475)
Powerclean Equipment Company 513 202-0001
5945 Dry Fork Rd Cleves (45002) (G-6374)
Powerex-Iwata Air Tech Inc 888 769-7979
150 Production Dr Harrison (45030) (G-10663)
Powerhouse Factories Inc 513 719-6417
1111 Saint Gregory St Cincinnati (45202) (G-4178)
Powerlasers, Pioneer Also called Arcelormittal Tailored Blanks (G-16084)
Powermount Systems Inc 740 499-4330
1602 Larue Marseilles Rd La Rue (43332) (G-11476)
Powers and Sons LLC 419 737-2373
101 Industrial Ave Pioneer (43554) (G-16091)
Powers and Sons LLC (HQ) 419 485-3151
1613 Magda Dr Montpelier (43543) (G-14314)
Powersonic Industries LLC 513 429-2329
5406 Spellmire Dr West Chester (45246) (G-19887)
Powersteps, West Chester Also called Stable Step LLC (G-19798)
Powertech Inc 901 850-9393
25805 Frmunt Blvd Apt 203 Beachwood (44122) (G-1266)
Powerwash of Ohio 614 260-2756
8029 Cranes Crossing Dr Lewis Center (43035) (G-11773)
Powrkleen, Medina Also called Woodbine Products Company (G-13363)
Ppafco Inc 614 488-7259
1096 Ridge St Columbus (43215) (G-7335)
Ppe, Macedonia Also called Plastic Process Equipment Inc (G-12317)
PPG 4331, Cincinnati Also called PPG Industries Inc (G-4179)
PPG 4332, Cincinnati Also called PPG Industries Inc (G-4182)
PPG 4333, Cincinnati Also called PPG Industries Inc (G-4180)
PPG 4335, Middletown Also called PPG Industries Inc (G-13943)
PPG 4338, Fairfield Also called PPG Industries Inc (G-9549)
PPG 4339, Cincinnati Also called PPG Industries Inc (G-4181)
PPG 4341, West Chester Also called PPG Industries Inc (G-19888)
PPG 5404, Columbus Also called PPG Industries Inc (G-7338)
PPG 5412, Circleville Also called PPG Industries Inc (G-4554)
PPG 5414, Wooster Also called PPG Industries Inc (G-20638)
PPG 5537, Columbus Also called PPG Industries Inc (G-7337)
PPG 5538, Reynoldsburg Also called PPG Industries Inc (G-16446)
PPG 5539, Grove City Also called PPG Industries Inc (G-10458)
PPG 9282, Hilliard Also called PPG Industries Inc (G-10854)
PPG Architectural Coatings LLC 419 433-5664
350 Sprowl Rd Huron (44839) (G-11109)
PPG Architectural Finishes Inc 330 477-8165
4575 Tuscarawas St W Canton (44708) (G-2788)
PPG Chillicothe, Chillicothe Also called PPG Industries Inc (G-3212)
PPG Industries Inc 330 825-0831
4829 Fairland Rd Barberton (44203) (G-1096)
PPG Industries Inc 513 737-1893
91 N Brookwood Ave Hamilton (45013) (G-10597)
PPG Industries Inc 440 572-2800
19699 Progress Dr Strongsville (44149) (G-17777)
PPG Industries Inc 740 774-8734
848 Southern Ave Chillicothe (45601) (G-3212)
PPG Industries Inc 440 232-1260
7650 First Pl Ste E Bedford (44146) (G-1437)
PPG Industries Inc 216 671-7793
14800 Emery Ave Cleveland (44135) (G-5900)
PPG Industries Inc 740 363-9610
760 Pittsburgh Dr Delaware (43015) (G-8715)
PPG Industries Inc 513 576-0360
500 Techne Center Dr Milford (45150) (G-14033)
PPG Industries Inc 614 252-6384
1380 E 5th Ave Columbus (43219) (G-7336)
PPG Industries Inc 330 825-6328
900 Columbia Ct At 16th & Barberton (44203) (G-1097)
PPG Industries Inc 740 474-3161
559 Pittsburgh Rd Circleville (43113) (G-4553)
PPG Industries Inc 740 774-7600
848 Southern Ave Chillicothe (45601) (G-3213)
PPG Industries Inc 740 774-7600
848 Southern Ave Chillicothe (45601) (G-3214)
PPG Industries Inc 740 774-7600
848 Southern Ave Chillicothe (45601) (G-3215)
PPG Industries Inc 419 683-2400
5066 Lincoln Hwy Crestline (44827) (G-7799)
PPG Industries Inc 513 231-3200
7198 Beechmont Ave Cincinnati (45230) (G-4179)
PPG Industries Inc 740 474-3945
221 E Main St Circleville (43113) (G-4554)
PPG Industries Inc 513 829-6006
726 Nilles Rd Fairfield (45014) (G-9549)
PPG Industries Inc 513 661-5220
6462 Glenway Ave Cincinnati (45211) (G-4180)
PPG Industries Inc 614 277-0620
2362 Stringtown Rd Grove City (43123) (G-10458)
PPG Industries Inc 614 921-9228
5054 Cemetery Rd Hilliard (43026) (G-10854)
PPG Industries Inc 513 424-1241
4480 Marie Dr Middletown (45044) (G-13943)
PPG Industries Inc 513 984-6761
9865 Montgomery Rd Cincinnati (45242) (G-4181)
PPG Industries Inc 614 939-2365
5548 N Hamilton Rd Columbus (43230) (G-7337)
PPG Industries Inc 614 268-2609
2840 N High St Columbus (43202) (G-7338)
PPG Industries Inc 513 779-2727
9304 Cincinnati Columbus West Chester (45241) (G-19888)
PPG Industries Inc 513 242-3050
4600 Reading Rd Cincinnati (45229) (G-4182)
PPG Industries Inc 614 501-7360
6585 E Main St Reynoldsburg (43068) (G-16446)
PPG Industries Inc 330 262-9741
239 W Liberty St Wooster (44691) (G-20638)
PPG Industries Inc 513 576-3100
500 Techne Center Dr Milford (45150) (G-14034)

PPG Industries Inc — ALPHABETIC SECTION

PPG Industries Inc 330 824-2537
  2823 Ellsworth Bailey Rd Warren (44481) (G-19433)
PPG Industries Inc 614 846-3128
  777 Dearborn Park Ln C Columbus (43085) (G-7339)
PPG Industries Ohio Inc 740 363-9610
  760 Pittsburgh Dr Delaware (43015) (G-8716)
PPG Industries Ohio Inc 216 486-5300
  23000 Saint Clair Ave Euclid (44117) (G-9436)
PPG Industries Ohio Inc (HQ) 216 671-0050
  3800 W 143rd St Cleveland (44111) (G-5901)
PPG Oak Creek, Cleveland Also called PPG Industries Ohio Inc (G-5901)
PPG Regional Support Center, Chillicothe Also called PPG Industries Inc (G-3213)
Ppg-Metokote, Lima Also called Metokote Corporation (G-11903)
Ppi, Cleveland Also called Plastic Platers LLC (G-5886)
Ppl Holding Company 216 514-1840
  25201 Chagrin Blvd # 360 Cleveland (44122) (G-5902)
Pps, Mason Also called Pilot Production Solutions LLC (G-12921)
PQ Corporation 216 341-2578
  5200 Harvard Ave Newburgh Heights (44105) (G-14943)
PR Signs & Service 614 252-7090
  3049 E 14th Ave Columbus (43219) (G-7340)
Practice Center Inc (PA) 513 489-5229
  7621 E Kemper Rd Cincinnati (45249) (G-4183)
Prairie Lane Corporation 330 262-3322
  4489 Prairie Ln Wooster (44691) (G-20639)
Prairie Lane Gravel Co, Wooster Also called Prairie Lane Corporation (G-20639)
Prasco LLC (PA) 513 204-1100
  6125 Commerce Ct Mason (45040) (G-12923)
Prasco Laboratories, Mason Also called Prasco LLC (G-12923)
Pratt (jet Corr) Inc 937 390-7100
  1515 Baker Rd Springfield (45504) (G-17473)
Pratt Displays, Mason Also called Pratt Industries Inc (G-12924)
Pratt Industries Inc 513 770-0851
  4700 Duke Dr Ste 140 Mason (45040) (G-12924)
Pratt Industries USA, Springfield Also called Pratt (jet Corr) Inc (G-17473)
Praxair Inc 440 994-1000
  3102 Lake Rd E Ashtabula (44004) (G-800)
Praxair Inc 216 778-5555
  2500 Metrohealth Dr Cleveland (44109) (G-5903)
Praxair Inc 440 237-8690
  14788 York Rd Cleveland (44133) (G-5904)
Praxair Inc 419 698-8005
  3742 Cedar Point Rd Oregon (43616) (G-15564)
Praxair Inc 419 729-7732
  6055 Brent Dr Toledo (43611) (G-18476)
Praxair Inc 740 453-0346
  130 N 3rd St Zanesville (43701) (G-21171)
Praxair Inc 937 323-6408
  403 W Columbia St Springfield (45504) (G-17474)
Praxair Inc 740 373-6449
  10 Morris Loop Rd Marietta (45750) (G-12656)
Praxair Inc 419 422-1353
  961 Industry Ave Lima (45804) (G-11917)
Praxair Inc 330 264-6633
  4265 E Lincoln Way Unit A Wooster (44691) (G-20640)
Praxair Inc 419 652-3562
  5480 Cloverleaf Pkwy # 6 Cleveland (44125) (G-5905)
Praxair Inc 440 944-8844
  5324 Grant Ave Cleveland (44125) (G-5906)
Praxair Inc 740 374-5525
  2034 Blue Knob Rd Marietta (45750) (G-12657)
Praxair Inc 330 453-9904
  2225 Bolivar Rd Sw Canton (44706) (G-2789)
Praxair Inc 419 666-5206
  Dixie Hwy Rossford (43460) (G-16590)
Praxair Inc 330 747-4126
  2211 Poland Ave Youngstown (44502) (G-21002)
Praxair Inc 330 825-4449
  4805 Fairland Rd Barberton (44203) (G-1098)
Praxair Distribution Inc 614 443-7687
  450 Greenlawn Ave Columbus (43223) (G-7341)
Praxair Distribution Inc 419 422-1353
  961 Industry Ave Lima (45804) (G-11918)
Praxair Distribution Inc 513 821-2192
  8376 Reading Rd Cincinnati (45237) (G-4184)
Praxair Distribution Inc 419 476-0738
  5254 Jackman Rd Ste A Toledo (43613) (G-18477)
Praxair Distribution Inc 937 283-3400
  105 Praxair Way Wilmington (45177) (G-20504)
PRC - Desoto International Inc 800 772-9378
  848 Southern Ave Chillicothe (45601) (G-3216)
PRC Desoto International, Chillicothe Also called PRC - Desoto International Inc (G-3216)
Prcc Holdings Inc 330 798-4790
  175 Montrose West Ave # 200 Copley (44321) (G-7691)
Precast Services Inc 614 428-4541
  6494 Taylor Rd Sw Reynoldsburg (43068) (G-16447)
Precious Metal Plating Co 440 585-7117
  30335 Palisades Pkwy Wickliffe (44092) (G-20228)

Precise Metal Form Inc 419 636-5221
  810 Commerce Dr Bryan (43506) (G-2305)
Precise Pallets LLC 513 560-8236
  4211 Curliss Ln Batavia (45103) (G-1178)
Precise Tool & Die Company 440 951-9173
  38128 Willoughby Pkwy Willoughby (44094) (G-20409)
Precise Tool & Mfg Corp 216 524-1500
  5755 Canal Rd Cleveland (44125) (G-5907)
Precise Tool Inc 937 778-3441
  9676 Looney Rd Piqua (45356) (G-16156)
Precise Tube Forming Inc 440 237-3956
  9591 York Alpha Dr Ste 7 North Royalton (44133) (G-15296)
Precision Aggregates, Portage Also called Palmer Bros Transit Mix Con (G-16273)
Precision Aluminum Inc 330 335-2351
  733 Weber Dr Wadsworth (44281) (G-19265)
Precision Anlytical Instrs Inc 513 984-1600
  10857 Millington Ct Blue Ash (45242) (G-1834)
Precision Applied Coatings 614 252-8711
  3021 E 4th Ave Ste B Columbus (43219) (G-7342)
Precision Automotive Plastics, Bellevue Also called Windsor Mold Inc (G-1552)
Precision Brush Co 440 542-9600
  6700 Parkland Blvd Solon (44139) (G-17218)
Precision Business Solutions 419 661-8700
  447 J St Perrysburg (43551) (G-16001)
Precision Cnc LLC 740 689-9009
  1858 Cedar Hill Rd Lancaster (43130) (G-11598)
Precision Coatings Inc 216 441-0805
  3289 E 80th St Cleveland (44104) (G-5908)
Precision Coatings Systems 937 642-4727
  948 Columbus Ave Marysville (43040) (G-12806)
Precision Component & Mch Inc 740 867-6366
  17 Rosslyn Rd Chesapeake (45619) (G-3147)
Precision Component Inds LLC 330 477-1052
  5325 Southway St Sw Canton (44706) (G-2790)
Precision Conveyor Technology 440 352-3601
  3785 Lane Rd Ext Perry (44081) (G-15911)
Precision Custom Products Inc 937 585-4011
  4590 County Road 35 De Graff (43318) (G-8605)
Precision Cutoff LLC 419 866-8000
  7400 Airport Hwy Holland (43528) (G-10950)
Precision Design Inc 419 289-1553
  2395 Rock Rd Ashland (44805) (G-737)
Precision Details Inc 937 596-0068
  104 Washington St Jackson Center (45334) (G-11214)
Precision Die & Stamping Inc 513 942-8220
  9800 Harwood Ct West Chester (45014) (G-19764)
Precision Die Masters 440 255-1204
  8724 East Ave Mentor (44060) (G-13552)
Precision Dynamics Inc 330 697-0611
  1270 Linden Ave Akron (44310) (G-326)
Precision Engineered Tech LLC 330 335-3300
  1785 Wall Rd Wadsworth (44281) (G-19266)
Precision Environments Inc 513 847-1510
  9830 Windisch Rd West Chester (45069) (G-19765)
Precision Equipment Llc 330 220-7600
  1460 W 130th St Ste C Brunswick (44212) (G-2228)
Precision Fab Products Inc 937 526-5681
  10061 Old State Route 121 Versailles (45380) (G-19189)
Precision Fabg & Stamping 740 453-7310
  1755 Kemper Ct Zanesville (43701) (G-21172)
Precision Fabrications Inc 937 297-8606
  272 High St Sunbury (43074) (G-17897)
Precision Finishing Systems 937 415-5794
  6101 Webster St Dayton (45414) (G-8431)
Precision Fittings LLC 440 647-4143
  709 N Main St Wellington (44090) (G-19589)
Precision Foam Fabrication Inc 330 270-2440
  2716 Intertech Dr Youngstown (44509) (G-21003)
Precision Forged Products, Gallipolis Also called GKN Sinter Metals LLC (G-10166)
Precision Gage & Tool Company 937 866-9666
  375 Gargrave Rd Dayton (45449) (G-8432)
Precision Geophysical Inc (PA) 330 674-2198
  2695 State Route 83 Millersburg (44654) (G-14120)
Precision Geophysical Inc 740 849-3044
  4700 Rucker Rd Mount Perry (43760) (G-14457)
Precision Graphic Services 419 241-5189
  436 Wade St Toledo (43604) (G-18478)
Precision Grinding Corporation 216 391-7294
  6717 Saint Clair Ave Cleveland (44103) (G-5909)
Precision Honing Inc 440 942-7339
  33000 Lakeland Blvd Willoughby (44095) (G-20410)
Precision Hydraulic Connectors 440 953-3778
  26420 Cntury Corners Pkwy Euclid (44132) (G-9437)
Precision Imprint 740 592-5916
  26 E State St Athens (45701) (G-846)
Precision Inc 330 897-8860
  33725 County Road 10 Fresno (43824) (G-10070)
Precision International LLC 330 793-0900
  843 N Cleveland Akron (44322) (G-327)

Precision Laser & Forming 419 943-4350
6500 Road 5 Leipsic (45856) *(G-11731)*
Precision Machine & Tool Co 419 334-8405
1016 N 5th St Fremont (43420) *(G-10045)*
Precision Machining Corp 419 433-3520
9307 Wikel Rd Huron (44839) *(G-11110)*
Precision Manufacturing Co Inc 937 236-2170
2149 Valley Pike Dayton (45404) *(G-8433)*
Precision McHning Srfacing Inc 440 439-9850
5435 Perkins Rd Cleveland (44146) *(G-5910)*
Precision Metal Products Inc 216 447-1900
7641 Commerce Park Oval Cleveland (44131) *(G-5911)*
Precision Metalforming Assn (PA) 216 241-1482
6363 Oak Tree Blvd Independence (44131) *(G-11148)*
Precision Mtal Fabrication Inc (PA) 937 235-9261
191 Heid Ave Dayton (45404) *(G-8434)*
Precision of Ohio Inc 330 793-0900
3850 Hendricks Rd Youngstown (44515) *(G-21004)*
Precision Pallet Inc 419 381-8191
3919 W Bancroft St Ottawa Hills (43606) *(G-15676)*
Precision Polymer Casting LLC 440 343-0461
140 Greentree Rd Moreland Hills (44022) *(G-14402)*
Precision Polymers Inc 614 322-9951
6919 Americana Pkwy Reynoldsburg (43068) *(G-16448)*
Precision Pressed Powdered Met 937 433-6802
1522 Manchester Rd Dayton (45449) *(G-8435)*
Precision Production Inc 216 252-0372
8250 Dow Cir Strongsville (44136) *(G-17778)*
Precision Products Group Inc 330 698-4711
339 Mill St Apple Creek (44606) *(G-617)*
Precision Q Systems LLC 614 286-5142
285 Old County Line Rd B Westerville (43081) *(G-20070)*
Precision Reflex Inc 419 629-2603
710 Streine Dr New Bremen (45869) *(G-14659)*
Precision Remotes LLC 510 215-6474
7803 Freeway Cir Middleburg Heights (44130) *(G-13768)*
Precision Replacement LLC 330 908-0410
9009 Freeway Dr Unit 7 Macedonia (44056) *(G-12319)*
Precision Specialty Metals Inc 800 944-2255
200 W Old Wlson Bridge Rd Worthington (43085) *(G-20700)*
Precision Steel Services Inc (PA) 419 476-5702
31 E Sylvania Ave Toledo (43612) *(G-18479)*
Precision Strip Inc 937 667-6255
315 Park Ave Tipp City (45371) *(G-18127)*
Precision Strip Inc 419 674-4186
190 Bales Rd Kenton (43326) *(G-11418)*
Precision Swiss LLC 513 716-7000
9580 Wayne Ave Cincinnati (45215) *(G-4185)*
Precision Switching Inc 800 800-8143
2090 Harrington Mem Rd Mansfield (44903) *(G-12502)*
Precision Tek Manufacturing, Mason *Also called Ashley F Ward Inc* *(G-12829)*
Precision Temp, Cincinnati *Also called RAD Technologies Incorporated* *(G-4246)*
Precision Thrmplstc Componts 419 227-4500
3765 Saint Johns Rd Lima (45806) *(G-11962)*
Precision Welding & Mfg 937 444-6925
101 Day Rd Mount Orab (45154) *(G-14449)*
Precision Welding Corporation 216 524-6110
7900 Exchange St Cleveland (44125) *(G-5912)*
Precision Wire Products Inc (PA) 216 265-7580
4791 W 139th St Cleveland (44135) *(G-5913)*
Precision Wood & Metal Co 419 221-1512
3960 E Bluelick Rd Lima (45801) *(G-11919)*
Precision Wood Products Inc (PA) 937 787-3523
2456 Aukerman Creek Rd Camden (45311) *(G-2466)*
Precision Woodwork Ltd 440 257-3002
6385 Mentor Park Blvd Mentor (44060) *(G-13553)*
Precisions Paint Systems LLC 740 894-6224
5852 County Road 1 South Point (45680) *(G-17291)*
Precison Clean Rooms, West Chester *Also called Precision Environments Inc* *(G-19765)*
Precison Coating Technology, Cleveland *Also called Precision Coatings Inc* *(G-5908)*
Predict Inc 216 642-3223
9555 Rockside Rd Ste 350 Cleveland (44125) *(G-5914)*
Predict Technologies Div, Cleveland *Also called Reid Asset Management Company* *(G-5971)*
Preemptive Solutions LLC 440 443-7200
767 Beta Dr Cleveland (44143) *(G-5915)*
Preferred Compounding, Copley *Also called Prcc Holdings Inc* *(G-7691)*
Preferred Compounding Corp (PA) 330 798-4790
175 Montrose West Ave # 200 Copley (44321) *(G-7692)*
Preferred Global Equipment LLC 513 530-5800
7800 Redsky Dr Cincinnati (45249) *(G-4186)*
Preferred Printing (PA) 937 492-6961
3700 Michigan St Sidney (45365) *(G-17062)*
Preferred Pump & Equipment LP 937 322-4000
561 E Leffel Ln Springfield (45505) *(G-17475)*
Preferred Soft Solutions LLC 614 975-2750
2906 Kool Air Way Columbus (43231) *(G-7343)*
Preferred Solutions Inc 216 642-1200
7819 Broadview Rd Ste 6 Seven Hills (44131) *(G-16904)*
Preform Sealants, Twinsburg *Also called Kes Industries LLC* *(G-18799)*
Preform Technologies LLC 419 720-0355
11362 S Airfield Rd Swanton (43558) *(G-17919)*
Preformed Line Products Co (PA) 440 461-5200
660 Beta Dr Mayfield Village (44143) *(G-13174)*
Prehistoric Antiquities 937 747-2225
7045 State Route 245 North Lewisburg (43060) *(G-15164)*
Preisser Inc 614 345-0199
3560 Millikin Ct Ste A Columbus (43228) *(G-7344)*
Premar Manufacturing Ltd 440 250-0373
803 Sharon Dr Westlake (44145) *(G-20145)*
Premere Enterprises Inc 330 874-3000
10882 Fort Laurens Rd Nw Bolivar (44612) *(G-1922)*
Premere Precast Products 740 533-3333
317 Hecla St Ironton (45638) *(G-11170)*
Premier Building Solutions Inc (PA) 330 244-2907
480 Nova Dr Se Massillon (44646) *(G-13042)*
Premier Coatings Ltd 513 942-1070
9390 Le Saint Dr West Chester (45014) *(G-19766)*
Premier Construction Company 513 874-2611
9361 Seward Rd Fairfield (45014) *(G-9550)*
Premier Farnell Holding Inc (HQ) 330 523-4273
4180 Highlander Pkwy Richfield (44286) *(G-16483)*
Premier Feeds LLC (HQ) 937 584-2411
292 N Howard St Sabina (45169) *(G-16618)*
Premier Industries Inc 513 271-2550
5721 Dragon Way Ste 113 Cincinnati (45227) *(G-4187)*
Premier Ink Systems Inc (PA) 513 367-2300
10420 N State St Harrison (45030) *(G-10664)*
Premier Inv Cast Group LLC 937 299-7333
3034 Dryden Rd Moraine (45439) *(G-14381)*
Premier Inv Cast Group LLC 413 727-2860
3034 Dryden Rd Moraine (45439) *(G-14382)*
Premier Kites & Designs Inc 888 416-0174
1004 Findlay St Portsmouth (45662) *(G-16296)*
Premier Manufacturing Corp (HQ) 216 941-9700
3003 Priscilla Ave Cleveland (44134) *(G-5916)*
Premier Material Concepts, Findlay *Also called Rowmark LLC* *(G-9749)*
Premier Metal Trading LLC (PA) 440 247-9494
26949 Chagrin Blvd # 306 Beachwood (44122) *(G-1267)*
Premier OEM, Cuyahoga Falls *Also called Kolpin Outdoors Corporation* *(G-7889)*
Premier Pallet & Recycling 330 767-2221
11361 Lawndell Rd Sw Navarre (44662) *(G-14585)*
Premier Printing and Packg Inc 937 436-5290
90 Compark Rd Ste A Dayton (45459) *(G-8436)*
Premier Printing Corporation 216 478-9720
18780 Cranwood Pkwy Cleveland (44128) *(G-5917)*
Premier Printing Solutions 740 374-2836
115 Pineview Cir Marietta (45750) *(G-12658)*
Premier Prod Svc Inds Inc 330 527-0333
10384 Industrial Dr C Garrettsville (44231) *(G-10201)*
Premier Seals Mfg, Akron *Also called Premier Seals Mfg LLC* *(G-328)*
Premier Seals Mfg LLC 330 861-1060
909 W Waterloo Rd Akron (44314) *(G-328)*
Premier Shot Company Inc 330 405-0583
1666 Enterprise Pkwy Twinsburg (44087) *(G-18838)*
Premier Southern Ticket, Cincinnati *Also called Gtlp Holdings LLC* *(G-3788)*
Premier Southern Ticket Co Inc 513 489-6700
7911 School Rd Cincinnati (45249) *(G-4188)*
Premier Stamping and Assembly 440 293-8961
7924 Mill St Williamsfield (44093) *(G-20259)*
Premier Tanning & Nutrition 419 342-6259
35 Mansfield Ave Shelby (44875) *(G-16986)*
Premier Tool Inc 937 332-0996
1333 E Main St Troy (45373) *(G-18694)*
Premier Uv Products LLC 330 715-2452
1738 Front St Cuyahoga Falls (44221) *(G-7907)*
Premiere Building Mtls Inc (PA) 574 293-5800
8200 Memorial Dr Ste A Plain City (43064) *(G-16207)*
Premiere Con Solutions LLC 419 737-9808
508 Cedar St Pioneer (43554) *(G-16092)*
Premiere Farnell Corp 937 424-1204
650 Congress Park Dr Dayton (45459) *(G-8437)*
Premiere Medical Resources Inc 330 923-5899
2750 Front St Cuyahoga Falls (44221) *(G-7908)*
Premiere Mold and Machine Co 330 874-3000
10882 Fort Laurens Rd Nw Bolivar (44612) *(G-1923)*
Premiere Printing & Signs Inc 330 688-6244
778 Mccauley Rd Unit 120 Stow (44224) *(G-17620)*
Premiere Stamping, Williamsfield *Also called Premier Stamping and Assembly* *(G-20259)*
Premium Panel & Tread 330 695-9979
4910 Harrison Rd Fredericksburg (44627) *(G-9955)*
Premix Inc (HQ) 440 224-2181
3365 E Center St North Kingsville (44068) *(G-15160)*
Prentke Romich Company (PA) 330 262-1984
1022 Heyl Rd Wooster (44691) *(G-20641)*
Preserving Your Memories 614 861-4283
1862 Drugan Ct Sw Reynoldsburg (43068) *(G-16449)*
Presque Isle Medical Tech, Beachwood *Also called Presque Isle Orthotics* *(G-1268)*
Presque Isle Orthotics 216 371-0660
2101 Richmond Rd Ste 1000 Beachwood (44122) *(G-1268)*

ALPHABETIC

Presrite Corporation (PA) — 216 441-5990
3665 E 78th St Cleveland (44105) *(G-5918)*

Presrite Corporation — 440 576-0015
322 S Cucumber St Jefferson (44047) *(G-11236)*

Press Chemical & Phrm Lab — 614 863-2802
2700 E Main St Ste 102 Columbus (43209) *(G-7345)*

Press For Less Printing Firm I — 931 912-4606
1836 Stubbs Mill Rd Lebanon (45036) *(G-11686)*

Press of Ohio Inc — 330 678-5868
3765 Sunnybrook Rd Kent (44240) *(G-11367)*

Press Technology & Mfg Inc — 937 327-0755
1401 Fotler St Springfield (45504) *(G-17476)*

Pressco Technology Inc (PA) — 440 498-2600
29200 Aurora Rd Cleveland (44139) *(G-5919)*

Pressed Coffee Bar & Eatery — 330 746-8030
215 Lincoln Ave Youngstown (44503) *(G-21005)*

Presslers Meats Inc — 330 644-5636
2553 Pressler Rd Akron (44312) *(G-329)*

Pressmark Inc — 740 373-6005
641 State Route 821 Ste A Marietta (45750) *(G-12659)*

Pressure Technology Ohio Inc — 215 628-1975
7996 Auburn Rd Painesville (44077) *(G-15776)*

Pressure Washer Mfrs Assn — 216 241-7333
1300 Sumner Ave Cleveland (44115) *(G-5920)*

Prestige Display and Packg LLC — 513 285-1040
420 Distribution Cir Fairfield (45014) *(G-9551)*

Prestige Enterprise Intl Inc — 513 469-6044
11343 Grooms Rd Blue Ash (45242) *(G-1835)*

Prestige Fireworks LLC — 513 492-7726
222 Van Buren Dr Mason (45040) *(G-12925)*

Prestige Printing — 937 236-8468
5888 Executive Blvd Dayton (45424) *(G-8438)*

Prestige Store Interiors Inc — 419 476-2106
4500 N Detroit Ave Toledo (43612) *(G-18480)*

Preston — 740 788-8208
42 Sandalwood Dr Newark (43055) *(G-14913)*

Prestons Repair & Welding — 937 947-1883
11611 State Route 571 Laura (45337) *(G-11625)*

Prestress Services Inds LLC (PA) — 859 299-0461
2250 N Hartford Ave Columbus (43222) *(G-7346)*

Prestress Services Inds LLC — 614 871-2900
3350 Jackson Pike Grove City (43123) *(G-10459)*

Pretium Packaging LLC — 419 943-3733
150 S Werner St Leipsic (45856) *(G-11732)*

Pretreatment & Specialty Pdts, Euclid Also called PPG Industries Ohio Inc *(G-9436)*

Pretzel Fest, Brookville Also called Mar Chele Inc *(G-2174)*

Preuss Mold & Die — 419 729-9100
1010 Matzinger Rd Toledo (43612) *(G-18481)*

PRI Marine, Columbus Also called Performance Research Inc *(G-7312)*

Price Farms Organics Ltd — 740 369-1000
4838 Warrensburg Rd Delaware (43015) *(G-8717)*

Price Management Services Ltd — 419 298-5423
10307 Road 107 Paulding (45879) *(G-15870)*

Pride and True Garage, Cincinnati Also called Outback Cycle Shack LLC *(G-4125)*

Pride Cast Metals Inc — 513 541-1295
2737 Colerain Ave Cincinnati (45225) *(G-4189)*

Pride Gage Associates LLC — 419 318-3793
7862 W Central Ave Ste D Toledo (43617) *(G-18482)*

Pride Investments LLC — 937 461-1121
1346 Morris Ave Dayton (45417) *(G-8439)*

Pride of Geneva — 440 466-5695
18106 Snyder Rd Chagrin Falls (44023) *(G-3069)*

Pride Tool Co Inc — 513 563-0070
10200 Wayne Ave Cincinnati (45215) *(G-4190)*

Pridecraft Enterprises, Cincinnati Also called Standard Textile Co Inc *(G-4372)*

Priesman Printery — 419 898-2526
218 W Water St Oak Harbor (43449) *(G-15447)*

Priest Millwright Service — 937 780-3405
101 Miller St Leesburg (45135) *(G-11715)*

Priest Services Inc (PA) — 440 333-1123
1127 Linda St 5885 Mayfield Heights (44124) *(G-13170)*

Priest Services Inc — 440 333-1123
1127 Linda St Rocky River (44116) *(G-16552)*

Primal Life Organics LLC — 419 356-3843
3637 Torrey Pines Dr Akron (44333) *(G-330)*

Primal Screen Inc — 330 677-1766
1021 Mason Ave Kent (44240) *(G-11368)*

Primary Colors Design Corp — 419 903-0403
1899 Cottage St Ashland (44805) *(G-738)*

Primary Defense LLC — 937 673-5703
3217 Schneider Rd Toledo (43614) *(G-18483)*

Primary Packaging Incorporated — 330 874-3131
10810 Industrial Pkwy Nw Bolivar (44612) *(G-1924)*

Prime Conduit Inc (PA) — 216 464-3400
23240 Chagrin Blvd # 405 Beachwood (44122) *(G-1269)*

Prime Controls Inc — 937 435-8659
4528 Gateway Cir Dayton (45440) *(G-8440)*

Prime Engineered Plastics Corp — 330 452-5110
1505 Howington Cir Se Canton (44707) *(G-2791)*

Prime Equipment Group Inc — 614 253-8590
2000 E Fulton St Columbus (43205) *(G-7347)*

Prime Industries Inc — 440 288-3626
1817 Iowa Ave Lorain (44052) *(G-12113)*

Prime Instruments Inc — 216 651-0400
9805 Walford Ave Cleveland (44102) *(G-5921)*

Prime Manufacturing Corp (HQ) — 937 496-3900
1619 Kuntz Rd Dayton (45404) *(G-8441)*

Prime Printing Inc (PA) — 937 438-3707
8929 Kingsridge Dr Dayton (45458) *(G-8442)*

Prime Time Machine Inc — 440 942-7410
38302 Arprt Pkwy Unit 10 Willoughby (44094) *(G-20411)*

Prime Wood Craft Inc (HQ) — 216 738-2222
1120 W 130th St Brunswick (44212) *(G-2229)*

Primeline Industries, Akron Also called Sml Inc *(G-380)*

Primex — 513 831-9959
400 Techne Center Dr # 104 Milford (45150) *(G-14035)*

Prince Plating Inc — 216 881-7523
1530 E 40th St Cleveland (44103) *(G-5922)*

Principle Business Entps Inc (PA) — 419 352-1551
20189 Pine Lake Rd Bowling Green (43402) *(G-1992)*

Principled Dynamics Inc — 419 351-6303
6920 Hall St Holland (43528) *(G-10951)*

Print All Inc — 419 534-2880
380 S Erie St Toledo (43604) *(G-18484)*

Print Craft Inc — 513 931-6828
8045 Colerain Ave Cincinnati (45239) *(G-4191)*

Print Digital, Stow Also called Print-Digital Incorporated *(G-17621)*

Print Direct For Less 2 Inc — 440 236-8870
27500 Royalton Rd Columbia Station (44028) *(G-6444)*

Print Factory PII — 330 549-9640
11471 South Ave North Lima (44452) *(G-15176)*

Print Management Partners Inc — 330 650-5300
2265 E Enterprise Pkwy A Twinsburg (44087) *(G-18839)*

Print Marketing Inc — 330 625-1500
11820 Black River Schl Rd Homerville (44235) *(G-10986)*

Print Masters Ltd — 740 450-2885
941 W Main St Zanesville (43701) *(G-21173)*

Print Shop Design and Print — 440 232-2391
366 Broadway Ave Bedford (44146) *(G-1438)*

Print Shop of Canton Inc — 330 497-3212
6536 Promler St Nw Canton (44720) *(G-2792)*

Print Shop, The, Newark Also called Spencer-Walker Press Inc *(G-14921)*

Print Shop, The, Wshngtn CT Hs Also called Brass Bull 1 LLC *(G-20720)*

Print Solutions Today LLC — 614 848-4500
657 Collingwood Dr Westerville (43081) *(G-20071)*

Print Syndicate Inc — 614 657-8318
1275 Kinnear Rd Columbus (43212) *(G-7348)*

Print Syndicate LLC — 614 519-0341
901 W 3rd Ave Ste A Columbus (43212) *(G-7349)*

Print Zone — 513 733-0067
9588 Cncnnati Columbus Rd West Chester (45241) *(G-19889)*

Print-Digital Incorporated — 330 686-5945
4688 Darrow Rd Stow (44224) *(G-17621)*

Print-N-Copy, Saint Clairsville Also called Office Print N Copy *(G-16642)*

Printcraft Inc — 440 599-8903
866 W Jackson St Conneaut (44030) *(G-7657)*

Printed Image — 614 221-1412
41 S Grant Ave Columbus (43215) *(G-7350)*

Printed Image, The, Columbus Also called V & C Enterprises Co *(G-7568)*

Printers Bindery, Cincinnati Also called Printers Bindery Services Inc *(G-4192)*

Printers Bindery Services Inc — 513 821-8039
925 Freeman Ave Cincinnati (45203) *(G-4192)*

Printers Devil Inc — 330 650-1218
77 Maple Dr Hudson (44236) *(G-11068)*

Printers Edge Inc — 330 372-2232
4965 Mahoning Ave Nw Warren (44483) *(G-19434)*

Printers Emergency Service LLC — 513 421-7799
2016 Elm St Side A Cincinnati (45202) *(G-4193)*

Printex Incorporated (PA) — 740 773-0088
185 E Main St Chillicothe (45601) *(G-3217)*

Printex Incorporated — 740 947-8800
101 Victory Dr Waverly (45690) *(G-19559)*

Printex-Same Day Printing, Chillicothe Also called Printex Incorporated *(G-3217)*

Printing & Reproduction Div, Cleveland Also called City of Cleveland *(G-4930)*

Printing 3d Parts Inc — 330 759-9099
16 Belgrade St Youngstown (44505) *(G-21006)*

Printing Arts Press — 740 397-6106
8028 Newark Rd Mount Vernon (43050) *(G-14502)*

Printing Center of Xenia — 937 372-1687
402 W Church St Xenia (45385) *(G-20786)*

Printing Center, The, Xenia Also called Sandy Smittcamp *(G-20788)*

Printing Company, The, Columbus Also called Newmast Mktg & Communications *(G-7217)*

Printing Concepts, Stow Also called Traxium LLC *(G-17637)*

Printing Connection Inc — 216 898-4878
5221 W 161st St Brookpark (44142) *(G-2154)*

Printing Depot Inc — 330 783-5341
3828 Southern Blvd Youngstown (44507) *(G-21007)*

Printing Express 937 276-7794
  3350 Kettering Blvd Moraine (45439) *(G-14383)*
Printing Express Inc 740 532-7003
  1229 S 3rd St Ironton (45638) *(G-11171)*
Printing For Less 937 743-8268
  45 Tahlequah Trl Springboro (45066) *(G-17345)*
Printing Partner, Cleveland Also called John Kolesar and Sons Inc *(G-5501)*
Printing Partners, Brunswick Also called Wirick Press Inc *(G-2252)*
Printing Partners, Solon Also called Allen Graphics Inc *(G-17102)*
Printing Plant, Cincinnati Also called Tech/III Inc *(G-4409)*
Printing Service Company 937 425-6100
  3233 S Tech Blvd Miamisburg (45342) *(G-13705)*
Printing Services 440 708-1999
  16750 Park Circle Dr Chagrin Falls (44023) *(G-3070)*
Printing System Inc 330 375-9128
  2249 14th St Sw Akron (44314) *(G-331)*
Printpoint Printing Inc 937 223-9041
  150 S Patterson Blvd Dayton (45402) *(G-8443)*
Printprod Inc 937 228-2181
  6142 American Rd Toledo (43612) *(G-18485)*
Prints & Paints Flr Cvg Co Inc 419 462-5663
  888 Bucyrus Rd Galion (44833) *(G-10151)*
Printxcel, Toledo Also called Crabar/Gbf Inc *(G-18242)*
Printzone 513 733-0067
  11974 Lebanon Rd Cincinnati (45241) *(G-4194)*
Priority Custom Molding Inc 937 431-8770
  840 Distribution Dr Beavercreek Township (45434) *(G-1373)*
Priority Vending Inc 216 361-4100
  3425 Prospect Ave E Cleveland (44115) *(G-5923)*
Prism Powder Coatings Ltd 330 225-5626
  2890 Carquest Dr Brunswick (44212) *(G-2230)*
Pristine Exteriors 330 957-5664
  5925 Renninger Rd New Franklin (44319) *(G-14697)*
Privacyware, New Albany Also called Pwi Inc *(G-14635)*
Pro Audio 513 752-7500
  671 Cncnnati Batavia Pike Cincinnati (45245) *(G-3261)*
Pro Cal, Middlefield Also called The Hc Companies Inc *(G-13857)*
Pro Companies Inc 614 738-1222
  1162 Hill Rd N Pickerington (43147) *(G-16057)*
Pro Fab, Cleveland Also called Professional Fabricators Inc *(G-5927)*
Pro Fab Industries Inc 317 297-0461
  9368 Massillon Rd Dundee (44624) *(G-9025)*
Pro Fab Welding Service LLC 937 272-2142
  2765 Lance Dr Moraine (45409) *(G-14384)*
Pro Forma Supply International, Steubenville Also called Supply International Inc *(G-17555)*
Pro Gram Engineering Corp 330 745-1004
  475 5th St Ne Barberton (44203) *(G-1099)*
Pro Hardware 13074, Sugarcreek Also called Stony Point Hardwoods *(G-17865)*
Pro Lighting LLC 614 561-0089
  5864 Hunting Haven Dr Hilliard (43026) *(G-10855)*
Pro Line Collision and Pnt LLC (PA) 937 223-7611
  1 Armor Pl Dayton (45417) *(G-8444)*
Pro Mold Design Inc 440 352-1212
  9853 Johnnycake Ridge Rd # 308 Mentor (44060) *(G-13554)*
Pro Oncall Technologies LLC 614 761-1400
  4374 Tuller Rd Ste B Dublin (43017) *(G-8967)*
Pro Printing Inc 614 276-8366
  4191 W Broad St Columbus (43228) *(G-7351)*
Pro Quip Inc 330 468-1850
  850 Highland Rd E Macedonia (44056) *(G-12320)*
Pro Roof Washers 440 521-2622
  1403 Ford Rd Cleveland (44124) *(G-5924)*
Pro Sign Design, Middletown Also called Pure Sports Design *(G-13946)*
Pro Street Chassis Shop, Norton Also called Allen Morgan Trucking & Repair *(G-15361)*
Pro-Decal Inc 330 484-0089
  3638 Cleveland Ave S Canton (44707) *(G-2793)*
Pro-Fab Inc 330 644-0044
  2570 Pressler Rd Akron (44312) *(G-332)*
Pro-Kleen Industrial Svcs Inc 740 689-1886
  1030 Mill Park Dr Lancaster (43130) *(G-11599)*
Pro-Pak Industries Inc (PA) 419 729-0751
  1125 Ford St Maumee (43537) *(G-13139)*
Pro-Pet LLC 419 394-3374
  1601 Mckinley Rd Saint Marys (45885) *(G-16695)*
Pro-Print Business Center, Dover Also called G A Spring Advertising *(G-8827)*
Pro-Soy, Upper Sandusky Also called Midwest Spray Drying Company *(G-18964)*
Pro-TEC Coating Company LLC 419 943-1100
  5000 Pro-Tec Pkwy Leipsic (45856) *(G-11733)*
Pro-TEC Coating Company LLC 419 943-1100
  4500 Protec Pkwy Leipsic (45856) *(G-11734)*
Pro-TEC Coating Company LLC (PA) 419 943-1211
  5500 Pro-Tec Pkwy Leipsic (45856) *(G-11735)*
Pro-Tech Manufacturing Inc 937 444-6484
  14994 Hillcrest Rd Mount Orab (45154) *(G-14450)*
Proampac, Cincinnati Also called Ampac Holdings LLC *(G-3340)*
Proampac Pg Borrower LLC (PA) 513 671-1777
  12025 Tricon Rd Cincinnati (45246) *(G-4195)*

Probake Inc 330 425-4427
  2057 E Aurora Rd Ste Pq Twinsburg (44087) *(G-18840)*
Process Automation Specialists 330 247-1384
  7405 Diamondback Ave Nw Canal Fulton (44614) *(G-2489)*
Process Development Corp 937 890-3388
  6060 Milo Rd Dayton (45414) *(G-8445)*
Process Equipment Co Tipp City (HQ) 937 667-4451
  4754 Us Route 40 Tipp City (45371) *(G-18128)*
Process Equipment Company, Tipp City Also called Process Equipment Co Tipp City *(G-18128)*
Process Innovations Inc 330 856-5192
  4219 King Graves Rd Vienna (44473) *(G-19207)*
Process Machinery Inc 614 278-1055
  860 Kaderly Dr Columbus (43228) *(G-7352)*
Process Sltions For Indust Inc 330 702-1685
  480 S Broad St Ste A Canfield (44406) *(G-2541)*
Process Technology, Mentor Also called Tom Richards Inc *(G-13607)*
Processall Inc 513 771-2266
  4600 N Masn Montgomery Rd Cincinnati (45215) *(G-4196)*
Prochaska Industries LLC 440 423-0464
  7959 Gates Mills Est Dr Gates Mills (44040) *(G-10208)*
Procoat Painting Inc 513 735-2500
  601 W Main St Unit B Batavia (45103) *(G-1179)*
Procomsol Ltd 216 221-1550
  13001 Athens Ave Ste 220 Lakewood (44107) *(G-11533)*
Procter & Gamble 513 207-8931
  1611 Northwood Dr Cincinnati (45237) *(G-4197)*
Procter & Gamble Company (PA) 513 983-1100
  1 Procter And Gamble Plz Cincinnati (45202) *(G-4198)*
Procter & Gamble Company 513 983-1100
  6210 Center Hill Ave Cincinnati (45224) *(G-4199)*
Procter & Gamble Company 513 266-4375
  5280 Vine St Cincinnati (45217) *(G-4200)*
Procter & Gamble Company 513 871-7557
  654 Wilmer Ave Hngr 4 Cincinnati (45226) *(G-4201)*
Procter & Gamble Company 513 983-1100
  5299 Spring Grove Ave Cincinnati (45217) *(G-4202)*
Procter & Gamble Company 419 998-5891
  840 N Thayer Rd Lima (45801) *(G-11920)*
Procter & Gamble Company 513 482-6789
  4460 Kings Run Dr Cincinnati (45232) *(G-4203)*
Procter & Gamble Company 513 672-4044
  8868 Beckett Rd West Chester (45069) *(G-19767)*
Procter & Gamble Company 513 634-5069
  6300 Center Hill Ave Fl 2 Cincinnati (45224) *(G-4204)*
Procter & Gamble Company 513 627-7115
  5348 Vine St Cincinnati (45217) *(G-4205)*
Procter & Gamble Company 513 634-9600
  8256 Union Centre Blvd West Chester (45069) *(G-19768)*
Procter & Gamble Company 513 634-9110
  8611 Beckett Rd West Chester (45069) *(G-19769)*
Procter & Gamble Company 513 983-1100
  2 Procter And Gamble Plz Cincinnati (45202) *(G-4206)*
Procter & Gamble Company 513 934-3406
  600 S Waynesville Rd Oregonia (45054) *(G-15573)*
Procter & Gamble Company 513 627-7779
  5201 Spring Grove Ave Cincinnati (45217) *(G-4207)*
Procter & Gamble Company 513 945-0340
  6280 Center Hill Ave Cincinnati (45224) *(G-4208)*
Procter & Gamble Company 513 626-2500
  11530 Reed Hartman Hwy Blue Ash (45241) *(G-1836)*
Procter & Gamble Company 513 622-1000
  8700 Mason Montgomery Rd Mason (45040) *(G-12926)*
Procter & Gamble Company 513 242-5752
  5289 Vine St Cincinnati (45217) *(G-4209)*
Procter & Gamble Company 410 527-5735
  2200 Southwest Blvd Grove City (43123) *(G-10460)*
Procter & Gamble Far East Inc (HQ) 513 983-1100
  1 Procter And Gamble Plz Cincinnati (45202) *(G-4210)*
Procter & Gamble Hair Care LLC 513 983-4502
  1 Procter And Gamble Plz Cincinnati (45202) *(G-4211)*
Procter & Gamble Mfg Co (HQ) 513 983-1100
  1 Procter And Gamble Plz Cincinnati (45202) *(G-4212)*
Procter & Gamble Mfg Co 419 226-5500
  3875 Reservoir Rd Lima (45801) *(G-11921)*
Procter & Gamble Paper Pdts Co (HQ) 513 983-1100
  1 Procter And Gamble Plz Cincinnati (45202) *(G-4213)*
Procter & Gamble Paper Pdts Co 513 983-2222
  301 E 6th St Cincinnati (45202) *(G-4214)*
Procter Gamble Co 513 698-7675
  3550 Symmes Rd Hamilton (45015) *(G-10598)*
Procter Gamble Olay Co - Cayey, Blue Ash Also called Olay LLC *(G-1826)*
Proctoer & Gamble 513 983-1100
  11530 Reed Hartman Hwy Blue Ash (45241) *(G-1837)*
Prodeva Inc 937 596-6713
  100 Jerry Dr Jackson Center (45334) *(G-11215)*
Produce Packaging Inc 216 391-6129
  7501 Carnegie Ave Cleveland (44103) *(G-5925)*
Product Machine Company, North Royalton Also called Paul Popov *(G-15295)*

Product Tooling Inc — ALPHABETIC SECTION

Product Tooling Inc 740 524-2061
  4290 N 3 Bs And K Rd Sunbury (43074) *(G-17898)*
Production, Cuyahoga Falls *Also called Gojo Industries Inc* *(G-7873)*
Production Control Units Inc 937 299-5594
  2280 W Dorothy Ln Moraine (45439) *(G-14385)*
Production Design Services Inc (PA) 937 866-3377
  313 Mound St Dayton (45402) *(G-8446)*
Production Div, Youngstown *Also called Gasser Chair Co Inc* *(G-20914)*
Production Paint Finishers Inc 937 448-2627
  140 Center St Bradford (45308) *(G-2011)*
Production Plant, Dayton *Also called U S Chrome Corporation Ohio* *(G-8575)*
Production Plus Corp 740 983-5178
  101 S Business Pl Ashville (43103) *(G-820)*
Production Products Inc 734 241-7242
  200 Sugar Grove Ln Columbus Grove (45830) *(G-7637)*
Production Screw Machine, Dayton *Also called Gmd Industries LLC* *(G-8231)*
Production Support Inc 937 526-3897
  105 Francis St Russia (45363) *(G-16611)*
Production TI Co Cleveland Inc 330 425-4466
  9002 Dutton Dr Twinsburg (44087) *(G-18841)*
Production Turning LLC 937 424-0034
  2490 Arbor Blvd Unit A Moraine (45439) *(G-14386)*
Productive Carbides Inc 513 771-7092
  10265 Spartan Dr Ste K Cincinnati (45215) *(G-4215)*
Producto Dieco Corporation (HQ) 440 542-0000
  30600 Aurora Rd Ste 160 Solon (44139) *(G-17219)*
Products Chemical, Cleveland *Also called Strib Industries Inc* *(G-6108)*
Products Innovators 216 932-5269
  2567 Lafayette Dr Cleveland (44118) *(G-5926)*
Proepo Software Ltd 937 243-3825
  609 E Paint St Wshngtn CT Hs (43160) *(G-20736)*
Profac Inc 440 942-0205
  7198 Industrial Park Blvd Mentor (44060) *(G-13555)*
Professional Award Service 513 389-3600
  3901 N Bend Rd Cincinnati (45211) *(G-4216)*
Professional Case Inc 513 682-2520
  9790 Inter Ocean Dr West Chester (45246) *(G-19890)*
Professional Detailing Pdts, Canton *Also called Ohio Auto Supply Company* *(G-2771)*
Professional Fabricators Inc 216 362-1208
  15708 Brookpark Rd Cleveland (44135) *(G-5927)*
Professional Oilfield Services 740 685-5168
  221 1/2 S 6th St Byesville (43723) *(G-2392)*
Professional Packaging Company (PA) 440 238-8850
  22360 Royalton Rd Strongsville (44149) *(G-17779)*
Professional Plastics Corp 614 336-2498
  4863 Rays Cir Dublin (43016) *(G-8968)*
Professional Screen Printing 740 687-0760
  731 N Pierce Ave Lancaster (43130) *(G-11600)*
Professional Supply Inc 419 332-7373
  504 Liberty St Fremont (43420) *(G-10046)*
Proficient Information Tech 937 470-1300
  301 W 1st St Dayton (45402) *(G-8447)*
Proficient Machining Co 440 942-4942
  7522 Tyler Blvd Unit B-G Mentor (44060) *(G-13556)*
Proficient Plastics Inc 440 205-9700
  7777 Saint Clair Ave Mentor (44060) *(G-13557)*
Profile Digital Printing LLC 937 866-4241
  5449 Marina Dr Dayton (45449) *(G-8448)*
Profile Discovery, Columbus *Also called Profile Imaging Columbus LLC* *(G-7353)*
Profile Grinding Inc 216 351-0600
  4593 Spring Rd Cleveland (44131) *(G-5928)*
Profile Imaging Columbus LLC 614 222-2888
  46 N High St Ste 200 Columbus (43215) *(G-7353)*
Profile Plastics Inc 330 452-7000
  1226 Prospect Ave Sw Canton (44706) *(G-2794)*
Profile Products LLC 330 452-2630
  1525 Waynesburg Dr Se Canton (44707) *(G-2795)*
Profile Rubber Corporation 330 239-1703
  6784 Ridge Rd Wadsworth (44281) *(G-19267)*
Profiles In Design Inc 513 751-2212
  860 Dellway St Cincinnati (45229) *(G-4217)*
Profiles In Diversity Journal, Westlake *Also called Rector Inc* *(G-20149)*
Profit Energy Company Inc 740 472-1018
  36829 Township Road 2067 Jerusalem (43747) *(G-11251)*
Proflo Industries LLC 419 436-6008
  2679 S Us Highway 23 Alvada (44802) *(G-519)*
Proform Group Inc 614 332-9654
  1715 Georgesville Rd Columbus (43228) *(G-7354)*
Proforma, Cortland *Also called Howland Printing Inc* *(G-7710)*
Proforma Advantage 440 781-5255
  640 Som Center Rd Mayfield Village (44143) *(G-13175)*
Proforma Buckeye, Westerville *Also called Buckeye Business Forms Inc* *(G-19982)*
Proforma Cnr Marketing, Dayton *Also called Cnr Marketing Ltd* *(G-8094)*
Proforma Joe Thomas Group, Cleveland *Also called In-Touch Corp* *(G-5447)*
Proforma Print & Imaging 216 520-8400
  655 Metro Pl S Ste 600 Dublin (43017) *(G-8969)*
Proforma Signature Solutions, Brooklyn Heights *Also called R&D Marketing Group Inc* *(G-2130)*

Proforma Solution Ventures, Avon Lake *Also called Solution Ventures Inc* *(G-1008)*
Proforma Steinbacher & Assoc 330 241-5370
  3745 Medina Rd Ste A Medina (44256) *(G-13322)*
Proforma Systems Advantage 419 224-8747
  1207 Findlay Rd Lima (45801) *(G-11922)*
Profound Logic Software Inc 937 439-7925
  396 Congress Park Dr Dayton (45459) *(G-8449)*
Proft & Gamble 513 945-0340
  6280 Center Hill Ave Cincinnati (45224) *(G-4218)*
Profusion Industries LLC (PA) 800 938-2858
  822 Kumho Dr Ste 202 Fairlawn (44333) *(G-9615)*
Profusion Industries LLC 740 374-6400
  700 Bf Goodrich Rd Marietta (45750) *(G-12660)*
Progage Inc 440 951-4477
  7555 Tyler Blvd Ste 6 Mentor (44060) *(G-13558)*
Programmable Control Service 740 927-0744
  6900 Blacks Rd Sw Pataskala (43062) *(G-15838)*
Prographics Printing Center, Cincinnati *Also called Brent Carter Enterprises Inc* *(G-3411)*
Progress Tool & Stamping Inc 419 628-2384
  207 Southgate Minster (45865) *(G-14223)*
Progress Tool Co, Minster *Also called Progress Tool & Stamping Inc* *(G-14223)*
Progressive Automotive 740 862-4696
  125 W Rome St Baltimore (43105) *(G-1040)*
Progressive Book Binding Co, Northfield *Also called Progressive Folding Binding Co* *(G-15322)*
Progressive Communications 740 397-5333
  18 E Vine St Mount Vernon (43050) *(G-14503)*
Progressive Foam Tech Inc 330 756-3200
  6753 Chestnut Ridge Rd Nw Beach City (44608) *(G-1214)*
Progressive Folding Binding Co 216 621-1893
  8082 Augusta Ln Northfield (44067) *(G-15322)*
Progressive Furniture Inc (HQ) 419 446-4500
  502 Middle St Archbold (43502) *(G-664)*
Progressive International, Archbold *Also called Progressive Furniture Inc* *(G-664)*
Progressive Labels LLC 570 688-9636
  38601 Kennedy Pkwy Willoughby (44094) *(G-20412)*
Progressive Machine Die Inc 330 405-6600
  8406 Bavaria Dr E Macedonia (44056) *(G-12321)*
Progressive Manufacturing Co 330 784-4717
  300 Massillon Rd Akron (44312) *(G-333)*
Progressive Molding Tech 330 220-7030
  5234 Portside Dr Medina (44256) *(G-13323)*
Progressive Pain Relief, Cleveland *Also called Casselberry Clinic Inc* *(G-4887)*
Progressive Plastics, Cleveland *Also called Alpha Packaging Holdings Inc* *(G-4675)*
Progressive Powder Coating Inc 440 974-3478
  7742 Tyler Blvd Mentor (44060) *(G-13559)*
Progressive Printers Inc 937 222-1267
  6700 Homestretch Rd Dayton (45414) *(G-8450)*
Progressive Ribbon Inc (PA) 513 705-9319
  1533 Central Ave Middletown (45044) *(G-13944)*
Progressive Stamping Inc 419 453-1111
  200 Progressive Dr Ottoville (45876) *(G-15683)*
Progressive Tool Division, Delphos *Also called Van Wert Machine Inc* *(G-8763)*
Progressor Times 419 396-7567
  1198 E Findlay St Carey (43316) *(G-2887)*
Progrssive Molding Bolivar Inc 330 874-3000
  10882 Fort Laurens Rd Nw Bolivar (44612) *(G-1925)*
Progrssive Mtllizing Machining, Akron *Also called Progressive Manufacturing Co* *(G-333)*
Prohos Inc 419 877-0153
  10755 Logan St Whitehouse (43571) *(G-20193)*
Prohos Manufacturing Co Inc 419 877-0153
  10755 Logan St Whitehouse (43571) *(G-20194)*
Proimage Printing & Design LLC 937 312-9544
  1803 Roxbury Dr Xenia (45385) *(G-20787)*
Project Aloha, New Albany *Also called Pinky & Thumb LLC* *(G-14634)*
Project Engineering Company 937 743-9114
  3010 S Tech Blvd Miamisburg (45342) *(G-13706)*
Projects Designed & Built 419 726-7400
  5949 American Rd E Toledo (43612) *(G-18486)*
Proline Finishing, Dayton *Also called Pro Line Collision and Pnt LLC* *(G-8444)*
Proline Screenwear 440 205-3700
  8586 East Ave Mentor (44060) *(G-13560)*
Proline Truss 419 895-9980
  29 Free Rd Shiloh (44878) *(G-16999)*
Promac Inc 937 864-1961
  350 Conley Dr Enon (45323) *(G-9385)*
Promac International Inc 440 967-2040
  1121 Sunnyside Rd Vermilion (44089) *(G-19170)*
Promatch Solutions LLC 937 299-0185
  20 Heatherwoode Cir Springboro (45066) *(G-17346)*
Promo Costumes Inc 740 383-5176
  381 W Center St Marion (43302) *(G-12728)*
Promo Sparks 513 844-2211
  1120 Hicks Blvd Ste 1 Fairfield (45014) *(G-9552)*
Promold Inc 330 633-3532
  487 Commerce St Tallmadge (44278) *(G-18001)*
Promold Gauer, Tallmadge *Also called Promold Inc* *(G-18001)*

Promospark Inc....513 844-2211
1120 Hicks Blvd Ste 201 Fairfield (45014) *(G-9553)*
Promotional Fixtures, Rittman *Also called Pfi Displays Inc (G-16527)*
Promotional Spring, Miamisburg *Also called Mound Printing Company Inc (G-13696)*
Promotions Plus Inc....440 582-2855
3402 Magnolia Way Broadview Heights (44147) *(G-2098)*
Proof Research Acd, Moraine *Also called Performnce Plymr Solutions Inc (G-14375)*
Property Assist Inc....419 480-1700
1755 W Sylvania Ave Toledo (43613) *(G-18487)*
Propharma Sales LLC....513 486-3353
5770 Gateway Ste 203 Mason (45040) *(G-12927)*
Propipe Technologies Inc....513 424-5311
1800 Clayton Ave Middletown (45042) *(G-13945)*
Propress Inc....216 631-8200
3135 Berea Rd Ste 1 Cleveland (44111) *(G-5929)*
Prospect Mold & Die Company....330 929-3311
1100 Main St Cuyahoga Falls (44221) *(G-7909)*
Prosperity On Payne Inc....216 431-7677
1814 E 40th St Ste 5e Cleveland (44103) *(G-5930)*
Prostar Machine & Tool Co....937 223-1997
2039 Webster St Dayton (45404) *(G-8451)*
Prosthetic & Orthotic Services....330 723-6679
799 N Court St Ste 1 Medina (44256) *(G-13324)*
Prosthetic Design Inc....937 836-1464
700 Harco Dr Englewood (45315) *(G-9373)*
Prosys Sampling Systems Ltd....937 717-4600
3800 Old Mill Rd Springfield (45502) *(G-17477)*
Protec Industries Incorporated....440 937-4142
1384 Lear Industrial Pkwy Avon (44011) *(G-959)*
Protech Electric LLC....937 427-0813
1632 Beaverbrook Dr Beavercreek (45432) *(G-1337)*
Protech Industries, Avon *Also called Protec Industries Incorporated (G-959)*
Protection Devices Inc....210 399-2273
9113 Le Saint Dr West Chester (45014) *(G-19770)*
Protective Industrial Polymers....440 327-0015
7875 Bliss Pkwy North Ridgeville (44039) *(G-15246)*
Protein Express Inc....513 769-9654
10931 Reed Hartman Hwy B Blue Ash (45242) *(G-1838)*
Protein Express Laboratories....513 769-9654
10931 R Hartman Hwy B Blue Ash (45242) *(G-1839)*
Protel Systems and Svcs LLC (PA)....419 913-0825
1298 Conant St Ste 504 Maumee (43537) *(G-13140)*
Proteus Electronics Inc....419 886-2296
161 Spayde Rd Bellville (44813) *(G-1563)*
Protista Tool, Canton *Also called Gilbert Geiser (G-2684)*
Proto Machine & Mfg Inc....330 677-1700
2190 State Route 59 Kent (44240) *(G-11369)*
Proto Plastics Inc....937 667-8416
316 Park Ave Tipp City (45371) *(G-18129)*
Proto Prcsion Mfg Slutions LLC....614 771-0080
4101 Leap Rd Hilliard (43026) *(G-10856)*
Proto Precision Fabricators, Hilliard *Also called Proto Prcsion Mfg Slutions LLC (G-10856)*
Proto Precision Fabricators, Hilliard *Also called Vicart Prcsion Fabricators Inc (G-10874)*
Proto-Mold Products Co Inc....937 778-1959
1750 Commerce Dr Piqua (45356) *(G-16157)*
Protofab Manufacturing Inc....937 849-4983
8 University Rd Medway (45341) *(G-13366)*
Prototype Fabricators Company....216 252-0080
10911 Briggs Rd Cleveland (44111) *(G-5931)*
Prout Boiler Htg & Wldg Inc....330 744-0293
3124 Temple St Youngstown (44510) *(G-21008)*
Provia - Heritage Stone, Sugarcreek *Also called Provia Holdings Inc (G-17859)*
Provia Holdings Inc (PA)....330 852-4711
2150 State Route 39 Sugarcreek (44681) *(G-17859)*
Provia LLC....330 852-4711
1550 County Road 140 Sugarcreek (44681) *(G-17860)*
Providence Rees Inc....614 833-6231
2111 Builders Pl Columbus (43204) *(G-7355)*
Provimi North America Inc....937 770-2400
6531 State Route 503 N Lewisburg (45338) *(G-11798)*
Provimi North America Inc (HQ)....937 770-2400
10 Collective Way Brookville (45309) *(G-2182)*
Province of St John The Baptis....513 241-5615
28 W Liberty St Cincinnati (45202) *(G-4219)*
Prowrite Inc....614 864-2004
7644 Slate Ridge Blvd Reynoldsburg (43068) *(G-16450)*
PS Copy, Westlake *Also called Penguin Enterprises Inc (G-20140)*
PS Graphics Inc....440 356-9656
20284 Orchard Grove Ave Rocky River (44116) *(G-16553)*
Psa Consulting Inc....513 382-4315
19 Garfield Pl Ste 211 Cincinnati (45202) *(G-4220)*
PSC Holdings Inc (PA)....740 454-6253
109 Graham St Zanesville (43701) *(G-21174)*
Psd Partners LLC (PA)....419 294-3838
5968 State Highway 199 Carey (43316) *(G-2888)*
Psg, Columbus *Also called Plastic Selection Group Inc (G-7322)*
PSI, Springboro *Also called Paper Systems Incorporated (G-17342)*
PSI Products, Canfield *Also called Process Sltions For Indust Inc (G-2541)*
PSK Steel Corp....330 759-1251
2960 Gale Dr Hubbard (44425) *(G-11009)*
Pt Tech Inc., Sharon Center *Also called Ptt Legacy Inc (G-16952)*
Ptc Enterprises Inc....419 272-2524
3047 County Road K Edon (43518) *(G-9188)*
Ptc Inc....513 791-0330
625 Eden Park Dr Ste 860 Cincinnati (45202) *(G-4221)*
Ptc Industries, Cleveland *Also called Parking & Traffic Control SEC (G-5851)*
Pti, Bowling Green *Also called Phoenix Technologies Intl LLC (G-1990)*
Ptmj Enterprises....440 543-8000
32000 Aurora Rd Solon (44139) *(G-17220)*
Ptr Daily LLC....330 673-1990
4501 Eastwicke Blvd Stow (44224) *(G-17622)*
Pts, Heath *Also called Polymer Tech & Svcs Inc (G-10727)*
Pts Prfssnal Technical Svc Inc (PA)....513 642-0111
503 Commercial Dr West Chester (45014) *(G-19771)*
Ptt Legacy Inc....330 239-4933
1441 Wolf Creek Trl Sharon Center (44274) *(G-16952)*
Pubco Corporation (PA)....216 881-5300
3830 Kelley Ave Cleveland (44114) *(G-5932)*
Public Safety Concepts LLC....614 733-0200
8495 Estates Ct Plain City (43064) *(G-16208)*
Public Safety Ohio Department....440 943-5545
31517 Vine St Willowick (44095) *(G-20481)*
Public School Works, Cincinnati *Also called Works International Inc (G-4518)*
Public Works Dept Street Div....740 283-6013
238 S Lake Erie St Steubenville (43952) *(G-17549)*
Publishing Company, Bellefontaine *Also called Cathie D Hubbard (G-1509)*
Publishing Group Ltd....614 572-1240
781 Northwest Blvd # 202 Columbus (43212) *(G-7356)*
Pucel Enterprises Inc....216 881-4604
1440 E 36th St Cleveland (44114) *(G-5933)*
Puck Hogs Pro Shop Inc....419 540-1388
1258 W Alexis Rd Toledo (43612) *(G-18488)*
Puehler Tool Co....216 447-0101
7670 Hub Pkwy Cleveland (44125) *(G-5934)*
Pughs Designer Jewelers Inc....740 344-9259
44 S 2nd St Newark (43055) *(G-14914)*
Puhd....216 244-3336
20806 Aurora Rd Bedford (44146) *(G-1439)*
Pukka Inc (PA)....419 429-7808
337 S Main St Fl 4 Findlay (45840) *(G-9743)*
Pukka Headwear, Findlay *Also called Pukka Inc (G-9743)*
Pullman Company....419 592-2055
11800 County Road 424 Napoleon (43545) *(G-14556)*
Pullman Company....419 499-2541
33 Lockwood Rd Milan (44846) *(G-13987)*
Pulse Journal....513 829-7900
7320 Yankee Rd Liberty Township (45044) *(G-11817)*
Pulse Worldwide Ltd....513 234-7829
7554 Central Parke Blvd Mason (45040) *(G-12928)*
Pumphrey Machine Corp....440 417-0481
7240 N Ridge Rd Madison (44057) *(G-12355)*
Pumps Group, North Canton *Also called Airtex Industries LLC (G-15068)*
Pumps Group, The, North Canton *Also called ASC Holdco Inc (G-15069)*
Pun-U, Cincinnati *Also called Lifestyle Nutraceuticals Ltd (G-3941)*
Puppy Paws Inc....440 461-9667
6763 Stafford Dr Cleveland (44124) *(G-5935)*
Puracera 3 LLC....513 231-7555
7466 Beechmont Ave # 409 Cincinnati (45255) *(G-4222)*
Pure Foods LLC....303 358-8375
675 Alpha Dr Ste E Highland Heights (44143) *(G-10799)*
Pure Sports Design....937 935-5595
3125 Yankee Rd Ste 1 Middletown (45044) *(G-13946)*
Pure Water Global Inc....419 737-2352
50 Industrial Ave Pioneer (43554) *(G-16093)*
Purebred Publishing Inc....614 339-5393
1224 Alton Darby Creek Rd C Columbus (43228) *(G-7357)*
Puremonics, Cleveland *Also called CPI Group Limited (G-5035)*
Purina Animal Nutrition LLC....740 335-0207
767 Old Chillicothe Rd Se Wshngtn CT Hs (43160) *(G-20737)*
Purina Animal Nutrition LLC....419 224-2015
1111 N Cole St Lima (45805) *(G-11923)*
Purina Animal Nutrition LLC....330 682-1951
635 Collins Blvd Orrville (44667) *(G-15611)*
Purina Animal Nutrition LLC....330 879-2158
8485 Navarre Rd Sw Massillon (44646) *(G-13043)*
Purina Mills LLC....330 682-1951
635 Collins Blvd Orrville (44667) *(G-15612)*
Puritas Metal Products Inc....440 353-1917
7720 Race Rd North Ridgeville (44039) *(G-15247)*
Purple Land Management LLC....740 238-4259
51461 Jennifer Ln Ste 110 Saint Clairsville (43950) *(G-16647)*
Purushealth LLC....800 601-0580
3558 Lee Rd Shaker Heights (44120) *(G-16935)*
Purvi Oil Inc....419 207-8234
654 Us Highway 250 E Ashland (44805) *(G-739)*
Purvis Milling Co, West Union *Also called Dinsmore Inc (G-19961)*

ALPHABETIC

Putnam County Sentinel, Ottawa *Also called Hirt Publishing Co Inc* ***(G-15652)***
Putnam County Sentinel, Ottawa *Also called Hirt Publishing Co Inc* ***(G-15653)***
Putnam Plastics Inc..........937 866-6261
255 S Alex Rd Dayton (45449) ***(G-8452)***
Puttco Inc..........937 299-1527
2613 Oakley Ave Dayton (45419) ***(G-8453)***
Puttmann Industries Inc..........513 202-9444
320 N State St Harrison (45030) ***(G-10665)***
Pvh Corp..........330 562-4440
549 S Chilcthe Rd Ste 340 Aurora (44202) ***(G-900)***
Pvm Incorporated..........614 871-0302
3515 Grove City Rd Grove City (43123) ***(G-10461)***
PVS Chemical Solutions Inc..........330 666-0888
3149 Copley Rd Copley (44321) ***(G-7693)***
PVS Plastics Technology Corp..........937 233-4376
6290 Executive Blvd Huber Heights (45424) ***(G-11023)***
Pwi Inc..........732 212-8110
5195 Hampsted Vlg Ctr Way New Albany (43054) ***(G-14635)***
Pwp Inc..........216 251-2181
532 County Road 1600 Ashland (44805) ***(G-740)***
Pymatning Spcialty Pallets LLC..........440 293-3306
4683 Stanhope Klloggvl Rd Andover (44003) ***(G-586)***
Pyramid Industries LLC..........614 783-1543
2825 Booty Dr Columbus (43207) ***(G-7358)***
Pyramid Mold & Machine Company, Kent *Also called Pyramid Mold Inc* ***(G-11370)***
Pyramid Mold Inc..........330 673-5200
222 Martinel Dr Kent (44240) ***(G-11370)***
Pyramid Plastics Inc..........216 641-5904
9202 Reno Ave Cleveland (44105) ***(G-5936)***
Pyramid Treating Inc..........330 325-2811
3031 Sanford Rd Atwater (44201) ***(G-863)***
Pyro-Chem Corporation..........740 377-2244
2491 County Road 1 South Point (45680) ***(G-17292)***
Pyrograf Products Inc..........937 766-2020
154 W Xenia Ave Cedarville (45314) ***(G-2946)***
Pyromatics Corp (PA)..........440 352-3500
9321 Pineneedle Dr Mentor (44060) ***(G-13561)***
Pyrotek Incorporated..........440 349-8800
355 Campus Dr Aurora (44202) ***(G-901)***
Q C A Inc..........513 681-8400
2832 Spring Grove Ave Cincinnati (45225) ***(G-4223)***
Q C Printing..........419 475-4266
3650 Upton Ave Toledo (43613) ***(G-18489)***
Q Holding Company (HQ)..........330 425-8472
1700 Highland Rd Twinsburg (44087) ***(G-18842)***
Q M C Pleasants Inc..........937 278-7302
5648 Wadsworth Rd Dayton (45414) ***(G-8454)***
Q M P, Cleves *Also called Stock Mfg & Design Co Inc* ***(G-6377)***
Q Model Inc..........330 673-0473
711 Wooster Rd W Barberton (44203) ***(G-1100)***
Q Music USA LLC..........239 995-5888
5730 Great Northern Blvd E1 North Olmsted (44070) ***(G-15196)***
Q S I Fabrication..........419 832-1680
10333 S River Rd Grand Rapids (43522) ***(G-10319)***
Q T Columbus LLC..........800 758-2410
1330 Stimmel Rd Columbus (43223) ***(G-7359)***
Q&D Indrustrial Floors, Farmersville *Also called Quality Durable Indus Floors* ***(G-9631)***
Q-Lab Corporation (PA)..........440 835-8700
800 Canterbury Rd Westlake (44145) ***(G-20146)***
Qc Industrial Inc..........740 642-5004
526 Red Bud Rd Chillicothe (45601) ***(G-3218)***
Qc Plastics, Dayton *Also called Queen City Polymers Inc* ***(G-8456)***
Qc Prntng By Quality Craft, Toledo *Also called Q C Printing* ***(G-18489)***
Qc Software LLC..........513 469-1424
11800 Conrey Rd Ste 150 Cincinnati (45249) ***(G-4224)***
Qcforge.com, Cincinnati *Also called Queen City Forging Company* ***(G-4237)***
Qcp, Holland *Also called Quality Care Products LLC* ***(G-10952)***
Qcsm LLC..........216 531-5960
9335 Mccracken Blvd Cleveland (44125) ***(G-5937)***
Qes Pressure Control LLC..........740 489-5721
64201 Wintergreen Rd Lore City (43755) ***(G-12139)***
Qibco Buffing Pads Inc (PA)..........937 743-0805
301 Industry Dr Ste B Carlisle (45005) ***(G-2897)***
Qkardz.com, Columbus *Also called Johnson Brothers Holdings LLC* ***(G-7073)***
Qleanair Scandinavia Inc..........614 323-1756
941 Medinah Ter Columbus (43235) ***(G-7360)***
Qlog Corp..........513 874-1211
33 Standen Dr Hamilton (45015) ***(G-10599)***
Qol Meds, Middletown *Also called Genoa Healthcare LLC* ***(G-13909)***
Qpi Cincinnati LLC..........513 755-2670
6455 Gano Rd West Chester (45069) ***(G-19772)***
Qpi Multipress Inc..........614 228-0185
370 S 5th St Ste 2 Columbus (43215) ***(G-7361)***
Qpmr Inc..........330 723-1739
7599 Hidden Acres Dr Medina (44256) ***(G-13325)***
Qsi, Fairport Harbor *Also called Quartz Scientific Inc* ***(G-9628)***
Qsr, Twinsburg *Also called Lexington Rubber Group Inc* ***(G-18807)***
QT Equipment Company (PA)..........330 724-3055
151 W Dartmore Ave Akron (44301) ***(G-334)***
Quad Fluid Dynamics Inc..........330 220-3005
2826 Westway Dr Brunswick (44212) ***(G-2231)***
Quad Industries Inc..........440 951-4849
37151 Rogers Rd Willoughby Hills (44094) ***(G-20474)***
Quad/Graphics Inc..........513 932-1064
760 Fujitec Dr Lebanon (45036) ***(G-11687)***
Quadcast..........330 854-4511
6845 Erie Ave Nw Canal Fulton (44614) ***(G-2490)***
Quadco Rehabilitation Center..........419 445-1950
600 Oak St Archbold (43502) ***(G-665)***
Quadco Rehabilitation Ctr Inc (PA)..........419 682-1011
427 N Defiance St Stryker (43557) ***(G-17832)***
Quadra - Tech Inc..........614 445-0690
864 E Jenkins Ave Columbus (43207) ***(G-7362)***
Quadrel Inc..........440 602-4700
7670 Jenther Dr Mentor (44060) ***(G-13562)***
Quadrel Labeling Systems, Mentor *Also called Quadrel Inc* ***(G-13562)***
Quadriga Americas LLC (HQ)..........614 890-6090
480 Olde Worthington Rd # 350 Westerville (43082) ***(G-20018)***
Quaker Chemical Corporation (HQ)..........513 422-9600
3431 Yankee Rd Middletown (45044) ***(G-13947)***
Quaker City Casting, Salem *Also called Korff Holdings LLC* ***(G-16752)***
Quaker City Septic Tanks LLC..........330 427-2239
290 E High St Leetonia (44431) ***(G-11720)***
Quaker Express Stamping Inc..........330 332-9266
1134 Salem Pkwy Salem (44460) ***(G-16768)***
Qual-Fab Inc..........440 327-5000
34250 Mills Rd Avon (44011) ***(G-960)***
Qualco LLC..........614 257-7408
2211 S James Rd Columbus (43232) ***(G-7363)***
Quali Tee Design..........740 335-8497
1270 Us Highway 22 Nw # 9 Wshngtn CT Hs (43160) ***(G-20738)***
Quali-Tee Design Sports..........937 382-7997
50 W Sugartree St Wilmington (45177) ***(G-20505)***
Quali-Tee Design Sportswear, Wilmington *Also called Quali-Tee Design Sports* ***(G-20505)***
Qualico Inc..........216 271-2550
3201 E 66th St Cleveland (44127) ***(G-5938)***
Qualiform Inc..........330 336-6777
689 Weber Dr Wadsworth (44281) ***(G-19268)***
Qualitech Associates Inc..........216 265-8702
11324 Brookpark Rd Cleveland (44130) ***(G-5939)***
Qualitee Design Sportswear Co (PA)..........740 333-8337
1270 Us Highway 22 Nw # 9 Wshngtn CT Hs (43160) ***(G-20739)***
Qualitor Inc (HQ)..........248 204-8600
1840 Mccullough St Lima (45801) ***(G-11924)***
Qualiturn Inc..........513 868-3333
9081 Le Saint Dr West Chester (45014) ***(G-19773)***
Quality Architectural and Fabr..........937 743-2923
8 Shotwell Dr Franklin (45005) ***(G-9912)***
Quality Assurance, Fremont *Also called Kraft Heinz Foods Company* ***(G-10032)***
Quality Bakery Company Inc (HQ)..........614 846-2232
380 Polaris Pkwy Ste 400 Westerville (43082) ***(G-20019)***
Quality Bakery Company Inc..........614 224-1424
50 N Glenwood Ave Columbus (43222) ***(G-7364)***
Quality Bar Inc..........330 755-0000
17 Union St Ste 7 Struthers (44471) ***(G-17822)***
Quality Black Oxide, Dayton *Also called Hayes Metalfinishing Inc* ***(G-8245)***
Quality Block & Supply Inc (HQ)..........330 364-4411
Rr 250 Mount Eaton (44659) ***(G-14421)***
Quality Blow Molding Inc..........440 458-6550
635 Oberlin Elyria Rd Elyria (44035) ***(G-9315)***
Quality Borate Co LLC..........216 896-1949
3690 Orange Pl Ste 495 Cleveland (44122) ***(G-5940)***
Quality Care Products LLC..........734 847-2704
6920 Hall St Holland (43528) ***(G-10952)***
Quality Castings Company (PA)..........330 682-6871
1200 N Main St Orrville (44667) ***(G-15613)***
Quality Channel Letters..........859 866-6500
1115 N 11th St Miamisburg (45342) ***(G-13707)***
Quality CNC Machining Inc..........440 942-0542
38195 Airport Pkwy Willoughby (44094) ***(G-20413)***
Quality Components Inc..........440 255-0606
8825 East Ave Mentor (44060) ***(G-13563)***
Quality Compound Mfg..........440 353-0150
5212 Mills Indus Pkwy North Ridgeville (44039) ***(G-15248)***
Quality Concepts Telecom..........740 385-2003
19485 Harble Rd Logan (43138) ***(G-12041)***
Quality Controls Inc..........513 272-3900
3411 Church St Cincinnati (45244) ***(G-4225)***
Quality Craft Machine Inc..........330 928-4064
137 Ascot Pkwy Cuyahoga Falls (44223) ***(G-7910)***
Quality Craftsman Inc..........740 474-9685
28155 River Dr Circleville (43113) ***(G-4555)***
Quality Cutter Grinding Co..........216 362-6444
15501 Commerce Park Dr Cleveland (44142) ***(G-5941)***
Quality Design Machining Inc..........440 352-7290
9349 Hamilton Dr Mentor (44060) ***(G-13564)***

Quality Durable Indus Floors 937 696-2833
5005 Farmersvl German Pik Farmersville (45325) *(G-9631)*
Quality Electrodynamics LLC 440 638-5106
6655 Beta Dr Ste 100 Mayfield Village (44143) *(G-13176)*
Quality Envelope Inc 513 942-7578
9792 Inter Ocean Dr West Chester (45246) *(G-19891)*
Quality Fabricated Metals Inc 330 332-7008
14000 W Middletown Rd Salem (44460) *(G-16769)*
Quality Fabrications LLC 330 695-2478
7108 Township Road 569 Fredericksburg (44627) *(G-9956)*
Quality Forms, Piqua *Also called Little Printing Company (G-16137)*
Quality Frp Fabrications 440 942-9067
1450 E 363rd St Willoughby (44095) *(G-20414)*
Quality Gold Inc (PA) 513 942-7659
500 Quality Blvd Fairfield (45014) *(G-9554)*
Quality Image Embroidery & AP 440 230-1109
2643 Royalwood Rd Broadview Heights (44147) *(G-2099)*
Quality Innovative Pdts LLC 330 990-9888
787 Wye Rd Akron (44333) *(G-335)*
Quality Liquid Feeds Inc 330 532-4635
2402 Clark Ave Wellsville (43968) *(G-19613)*
Quality Machine, Dayton *Also called Q M C Pleasants Inc (G-8454)*
Quality Machine Systems LLC 440 223-2217
7875 Enterprise Dr Mentor (44060) *(G-13565)*
Quality Machining and Mfg Inc 419 899-2543
14168 State Route 18 Sherwood (43556) *(G-16992)*
Quality Match Plate Co 330 889-2462
4211 State Route 534 Southington (44470) *(G-17302)*
Quality Mechanicals Inc 513 559-0998
1225 Streng St Cincinnati (45223) *(G-4226)*
Quality Metal Products Inc 440 355-6165
210 Commerce Dr Lagrange (44050) *(G-11492)*
Quality Metal Treating Company 931 432-7467
2980 Spring Grove Ave Cincinnati (45225) *(G-4227)*
Quality Metal Works, Cleveland *Also called Rezmann Karoly (G-5982)*
Quality Metrology Sys & Sol LL 937 431-1800
425 Mill Stone Dr Beavercreek (45434) *(G-1338)*
Quality Mfg Company Inc 513 921-4500
4323 Spring Grove Ave Cincinnati (45223) *(G-4228)*
Quality Molded, Akron *Also called New Castings Inc (G-295)*
Quality Office Products, Dayton *Also called SPAOS Inc (G-8515)*
Quality Parts, Jackson Center *Also called A G Parts Inc (G-11204)*
Quality Plastic Machine Repair, Medina *Also called Qpmr Inc (G-13325)*
Quality Plating Co 216 361-0151
1443 E 40th St Cleveland (44103) *(G-5942)*
Quality Pllets Recyclables LLC 419 396-3244
410 E Findlay St Carey (43316) *(G-2889)*
Quality Poly Corp 330 453-9559
3000 Atlantic Blvd Ne Rear Canton (44705) *(G-2796)*
Quality Print Shop Inc 740 992-3345
255 Mill St Middleport (45760) *(G-13873)*
Quality Printing & Publishing, Hamilton *Also called Quality Publishing Co (G-10600)*
Quality Printing Co, Bucyrus *Also called Bucyrus Graphics Inc (G-2319)*
Quality Products Inc (PA) 614 228-0185
1 Air Cargo Pkwy E Swanton (43558) *(G-17920)*
Quality Publishing Co 513 863-8210
3200 Symmes Rd Hamilton (45015) *(G-10600)*
Quality Quartz Engineering Inc 937 236-3250
131 Janney Rd Dayton (45404) *(G-8455)*
Quality Quartz of America Inc 440 352-2851
9362 Hamilton Dr Mentor (44060) *(G-13566)*
Quality Quick Print, Troy *Also called Western Ohio Graphics (G-18719)*
Quality Ready Mix Inc (PA) 419 394-8870
16672 County Road 66a Saint Marys (45885) *(G-16696)*
Quality Replacement Parts Inc 216 674-0200
9099 Bank St Ste 2 Cleveland (44125) *(G-5943)*
Quality Reproductions Inc 330 335-5000
127 Hartman Rd Wadsworth (44281) *(G-19269)*
Quality Rubber Stamp Inc 614 235-2700
3314 Refugee Rd Columbus (43232) *(G-7365)*
Quality Screw Products Inc 440 975-1828
38302 Arprt Pkwy Unit 15 Willoughby (44094) *(G-20415)*
Quality Seating Company Inc 330 747-0181
4136 Logan Way Youngstown (44505) *(G-21009)*
Quality Security Door & Mfg Co (PA) 440 246-0770
1925 Broadway Lorain (44052) *(G-12114)*
Quality Sewing Inc 216 475-0411
5656 Dunham Rd Cleveland (44137) *(G-5944)*
Quality Spt & Silk Screen Sp 513 769-8300
9217 Reading Rd Cincinnati (45215) *(G-4229)*
Quality Spt Silk Screen & EMB, Cincinnati *Also called Quality Spt & Silk Screen Sp (G-4229)*
Quality Stamp Co, East Liverpool *Also called Innovative Ceramic Corp (G-9059)*
Quality Stamping, Toledo *Also called Quality Tool Company (G-18490)*
Quality Stamping Products Co (PA) 216 441-2700
5322 Bragg Rd Cleveland (44127) *(G-5945)*
Quality Steel Fabrication 937 492-9503
2500 Fair Rd Sidney (45365) *(G-17063)*
Quality Stitch Embroidery Inc 614 237-0480
4300 E Main St Columbus (43213) *(G-7366)*
Quality Switch Inc 330 872-5707
715 Arlington Blvd Newton Falls (44444) *(G-14991)*
Quality Synthetic Rubber, Twinsburg *Also called Q Holding Company (G-18842)*
Quality Tool Company 419 476-8228
577 Mel Simon Dr Toledo (43612) *(G-18490)*
Quality Tooling Systems Inc 330 722-5025
650 W Smith Rd Ste 4 Medina (44256) *(G-13326)*
Quality Welding Inc 419 483-6067
104 Ronald Ln Bellevue (44811) *(G-1541)*
Quality Wldg & Fabrication LLC 419 225-6208
4330 East Rd Lima (45807) *(G-11925)*
Quality-Service Products Inc 614 447-9522
528 E Hudson St Columbus (43202) *(G-7367)*
Qualtech NP, Batavia *Also called Curtiss-Wright Flow Control (G-1134)*
Qualtech NP, Cincinnati *Also called Curtiss-Wright Flow Ctrl Corp (G-3245)*
Qualtech NP, Cincinnati *Also called Curtiss-Wright Flow Control (G-3244)*
Qualtech Technologies Inc 440 946-8081
1685b Joseph Lloyd Pkwy Willoughby (44094) *(G-20416)*
Qualtek Electronics Corp 440 951-3300
7610 Jenther Dr Mentor (44060) *(G-13567)*
Quanex Building Products, Akron *Also called Quanex Ig Systems Inc (G-336)*
Quanex Ig Systems Inc 740 439-2338
2411 E Wheeling Ave Cambridge (43725) *(G-2454)*
Quanex Ig Systems Inc (HQ) 216 910-1519
388 S Main St Ste 700 Akron (44311) *(G-336)*
Quanex Screens LLC 419 662-5001
7597 Broadmoor Rd Perrysburg (43551) *(G-16002)*
Quantem Fbo Services 603 647-6763
1077 Celestial St Cincinnati (45202) *(G-4230)*
Quantum 740 328-2548
400 Case Ave Newark (43055) *(G-14915)*
Quantum Commerce LLC 513 777-0737
6748 Dimmick Rd West Chester (45069) *(G-19774)*
Quantum Energy LLC (PA) 440 285-7381
10405 Locust Grove Dr Chardon (44024) *(G-3133)*
Quantum Integration Llc 330 609-0355
1980 Niles Cortland Rd Ne Cortland (44410) *(G-7715)*
Quantum Jewelry Dist 330 678-2222
4631 Mogadore Rd Kent (44240) *(G-11371)*
Quantum Sails 567 283-5335
207 W Water St Sandusky (44870) *(G-16840)*
Quantum World Technologies 937 747-3018
6973 Township Road 177 Zanesfield (43360) *(G-21089)*
Quarries LLC 513 306-2924
12157 Brisben Pl Cincinnati (45249) *(G-4231)*
Quarrymasters Inc 330 612-0474
7761 Hill Church St Se Canton (44730) *(G-2797)*
Quarter Bistro 513 271-5400
6904 Wooster Pike Cincinnati (45227) *(G-4232)*
Quarter Mile Fabrication LLC 440 298-1272
7289 Leroy Thompson Rd Thompson (44086) *(G-18027)*
Quartz, Mentor *Also called Aco Polymer Products Inc (G-13373)*
Quartz Scientific Inc (PA) 360 574-6254
819 East St Fairport Harbor (44077) *(G-9628)*
Quasonix Inc (PA) 513 942-1287
6025 Schumacher Park Dr West Chester (45069) *(G-19775)*
Quass Sheet Metal Inc 330 477-4841
5018 Yukon St Nw Canton (44708) *(G-2798)*
Quayle Consulting Inc 614 868-1363
8572 N Spring Ct Pickerington (43147) *(G-16058)*
Qube Corporation 440 543-2393
16744 W Park Circle Dr Chagrin Falls (44023) *(G-3071)*
Quebecor World Johnson Hardin 614 326-0299
3600 Red Bank Rd Cincinnati (45227) *(G-4233)*
Queen City Awning & Tent Co 513 530-9660
7225 E Kemper Rd Cincinnati (45249) *(G-4234)*
Queen City Bearers, Amelia *Also called Queen City Tool Company Inc (G-546)*
Queen City Carpets LLC 513 823-8238
6539 Harrison Ave 304 Cincinnati (45247) *(G-4235)*
Queen City Foam Inc 513 741-7722
1000 Redna Ter Cincinnati (45215) *(G-4236)*
Queen City Forging Company 513 321-2003
235b Tennyson St Cincinnati (45226) *(G-4237)*
Queen City Office Machine 513 251-7200
3984 Trevor Ave Cincinnati (45211) *(G-4238)*
Queen City Pallets Inc 513 821-6700
7744 Reinhold Dr Cincinnati (45237) *(G-4239)*
Queen City Paper, Cincinnati *Also called Vemuri International LLC (G-4471)*
Queen City Polymers, West Chester *Also called Riotech International Ltd (G-19782)*
Queen City Polymers Inc (PA) 513 779-0990
6101 Schumacher Park Dr West Chester (45069) *(G-19776)*
Queen City Polymers Inc 937 236-2710
365 Leo St Dayton (45404) *(G-8456)*
Queen City Reprographics 513 326-2300
2863 E Sharon Rd Cincinnati (45241) *(G-4240)*
Queen City Sausage & Provision 513 541-5581
1136 Straight St Cincinnati (45214) *(G-4241)*

ALPHABETIC

Queen City Steel Treating Co, Cincinnati *Also called Fbf Limited* ***(G-3679)***
Queen City Technologies....513 253-1312
34 W Crescentville Rd West Chester (45246) ***(G-19892)***
Queen City Tool Company Inc....513 752-4200
3939 Bach Buxton Rd Amelia (45102) ***(G-546)***
Queen City Tool Works Inc....513 874-0111
125 Constitution Dr Ste 2 Fairfield (45014) ***(G-9555)***
Ques Industries Inc....216 267-8989
5420 W 140th St Cleveland (44142) ***(G-5946)***
Quest Lasercut, Franklin *Also called Quest Technologies Inc* ***(G-9913)***
Quest Service Labs, Twinsburg *Also called A E Wilson Holdings Inc* ***(G-18722)***
Quest Service Labs Inc....330 405-0316
2307 E Aurora Rd Unit B10 Twinsburg (44087) ***(G-18843)***
Quest Software Inc....614 336-9223
6500 Emerald Pkwy Ste 400 Dublin (43016) ***(G-8970)***
Quest Solutions Group LLC....513 703-4520
8046 Green Lake Dr Liberty Township (45044) ***(G-11818)***
Quest Technologies Inc....937 743-1200
600 Commerce Center Dr Franklin (45005) ***(G-9913)***
Questline Inc....614 255-3166
5500 Frantz Rd Ste 150 Dublin (43017) ***(G-8971)***
Questmark, Cincinnati *Also called Diversipak Inc* ***(G-3596)***
Quez Media Marketing Inc....216 910-0202
6100 Oak Tree Blvd # 200 Independence (44131) ***(G-11149)***
Quick As A Wink Printing Co....419 224-9786
321 W High St Lima (45801) ***(G-11926)***
Quick Loadz Delivery Sys LLC....888 304-3946
185 W Canal St Nelsonville (45764) ***(G-14594)***
Quick Print, Lorain *Also called Slutzkers Quickprint Center* ***(G-12123)***
Quick Print, Canton *Also called USA Quickprint Inc* ***(G-2854)***
Quick Print Center, New Philadelphia *Also called Robert H Shackelford* ***(G-14799)***
Quick Service Welding & Mch Co....330 673-3818
117 E Summit St Kent (44240) ***(G-11372)***
Quick Sign Works, Cincinnati *Also called Brent Bleh Company* ***(G-3410)***
Quick Tab II Inc (PA)....419 448-6622
241 Heritage Dr Tiffin (44883) ***(G-18076)***
Quick Tech Business Forms Inc....937 743-5952
408 Sharts Dr Springboro (45066) ***(G-17347)***
Quick Tech Graphics Inc....937 743-5952
408 Sharts Dr Frnt Springboro (45066) ***(G-17348)***
Quickdraft Inc....330 477-4574
1525 Perry Dr Sw Canton (44710) ***(G-2799)***
Quickstitch Plus LLC....614 476-3186
124 Granville St Columbus (43230) ***(G-7368)***
Quidel Corporation....740 589-3300
1055 E State St Ste 100 Athens (45701) ***(G-847)***
Quidel Dhi....740 589-3300
2005 E State St Athens (45701) ***(G-848)***
Quikey Manufacturing Co Inc (PA)....330 633-8106
1500 Industrial Pkwy Akron (44310) ***(G-337)***
Quikrete Cincinnati, Harrison *Also called Quikrete Companies Inc* ***(G-10666)***
Quikrete Companies Inc....614 885-4406
6225 Huntley Rd Columbus (43229) ***(G-7369)***
Quikrete Companies Inc....513 367-6135
5425 Kilby Rd Harrison (45030) ***(G-10666)***
Quikrete Companies LLC....419 241-1148
873 Western Ave Toledo (43609) ***(G-18491)***
Quikrete Companies LLC....330 296-6080
2693 Lake Rockwell Rd Ravenna (44266) ***(G-16397)***
Quikrete of Cleveland, Ravenna *Also called Quikrete Companies LLC* ***(G-16397)***
Quikspray, Port Clinton *Also called Quikstir Inc* ***(G-16256)***
Quikstir Inc....419 732-2601
2105 W Lakeshore Dr Port Clinton (43452) ***(G-16256)***
Quilting Inc (PA)....614 504-5971
7600 Industrial Pkwy Plain City (43064) ***(G-16209)***
Quilting Creations Intl....330 874-4741
8778 Towpath Rd Ne Bolivar (44612) ***(G-1926)***
Quintus Technologies LLC....614 891-2732
8270 Green Meadows Dr N Lewis Center (43035) ***(G-11774)***
Qumont Chemical Co....419 241-1057
359 Hamilton St Ste 3 Toledo (43604) ***(G-18492)***
Qure Medical, Twinsburg *Also called Medical Elastomer Dev Inc* ***(G-18815)***
R & A Sports Inc....216 289-2254
23780 Lakeland Blvd Euclid (44132) ***(G-9438)***
R & B Enterprises USA Inc....330 674-2227
1868 County Road 150 Millersburg (44654) ***(G-14121)***
R & B Machining Inc (PA)....937 698-3528
2695 Progress Way Wilmington (45177) ***(G-20506)***
R & B Machining Inc....937 382-6710
2695 Progress Way Wilmington (45177) ***(G-20507)***
R & C Pkg & Cstm Butchering, Bidwell *Also called R&C Packing & Custom Butcher* ***(G-1668)***
R & D Custom Machine & Tool....419 727-1700
5961 American Rd E Toledo (43612) ***(G-18493)***
R & D Equipment Inc....419 668-8439
206 Republic St Norwalk (44857) ***(G-15413)***
R & D Group, Columbus *Also called Research and Development Group* ***(G-7386)***
R & D Hilltop Lumber Inc....740 342-3051
2126 State Route 93 Se New Lexington (43764) ***(G-14721)***
R & H Enterprises Llc....216 702-4449
4933 Karen Isle Dr Richmond Heights (44143) ***(G-16504)***
R & H Signs Unlimited Inc....937 293-3834
3048 Wilmington Pike Dayton (45429) ***(G-8457)***
R & J AG Manufacturing Inc....419 962-4707
821 State Route 511 Ashland (44805) ***(G-741)***
R & J Bardon Inc....614 457-5500
4676 Larwell Dr Columbus (43220) ***(G-7370)***
R & J Contracting, Caledonia *Also called Jeffery A Burns* ***(G-2418)***
R & J Cylinder & Machine Inc....330 364-8263
464 Robinson Dr Se New Philadelphia (44663) ***(G-14794)***
R & J Drilling Company Inc....740 763-3991
18586 Pinewood Trl Frazeysburg (43822) ***(G-9941)***
R & J Printing Enterprises Inc....330 343-1242
111 N Walnut St Dover (44622) ***(G-8847)***
R & J Tool Inc....937 833-3200
10550 Upper Lewisburg Brookville (45309) ***(G-2183)***
R & K Industrial Supply, Coshocton *Also called T JS Oil & Gas Inc* ***(G-7754)***
R & L Hydraulics Inc....937 399-3407
109 Tremont City Rd Springfield (45502) ***(G-17478)***
R & L Truss Inc....419 587-3440
17985 Road 60 Grover Hill (45849) ***(G-10519)***
R & L Wood Products....937 444-2496
16137 Eastwood Rd Williamsburg (45176) ***(G-20254)***
R & M Fluid Power Inc....330 758-2766
7953 Southern Blvd Youngstown (44512) ***(G-21010)***
R & M Grinding Inc....513 732-3330
5080 State Rd 132 Owensville (45160) ***(G-15690)***
R & R Comfort Experts LLC....216 475-3995
13370 Hathaway Rd Cleveland (44125) ***(G-5947)***
R & R Engine & Machine, Coventry Township *Also called Chemequip Sales Inc* ***(G-7767)***
R & R Machine & Tool Co....216 281-7609
3148 W 32nd St Ste 3 Cleveland (44109) ***(G-5948)***
R & R Tool Inc....937 783-8665
1449a Middleboro Rd Blanchester (45107) ***(G-1705)***
R & S Label, Oberlin *Also called R R Donnelley & Sons Company* ***(G-15504)***
R & S Monitions Inc....614 846-0597
181 Rosslyn Ave Columbus (43214) ***(G-7371)***
R & S Sheet Metal LLC....330 857-0225
5966 Mount Eaton Rd S Dalton (44618) ***(G-7952)***
R & T Microcenters of Ohio, Toledo *Also called T E Hubler Inc* ***(G-18541)***
R & W Printing Company....513 575-0131
1394 Stella Dr Loveland (45140) ***(G-12224)***
R A Hamed International Inc....330 247-0190
8400 Darrow Rd Twinsburg (44087) ***(G-18844)***
R A Heller Company....513 771-6100
10530 Chester Rd Cincinnati (45215) ***(G-4242)***
R A K Machine Inc....216 631-7750
5900 Walworth Ave Cleveland (44102) ***(G-5949)***
R A M Plastics Co Inc....330 549-3107
11401 South Ave North Lima (44452) ***(G-15177)***
R A M Precision Tool, Dayton *Also called Ram Precision Industries Inc* ***(G-8462)***
R and D Incorporated....216 581-6328
16645 Granite Rd Maple Heights (44137) ***(G-12577)***
R and J Corporation....440 871-6009
24142 Detroit Rd Westlake (44145) ***(G-20147)***
R and S Technologies Inc....419 483-3691
2474 State Route 4 Bellevue (44811) ***(G-1542)***
R Anthony Enterprises LLC....419 341-0961
2626 Whetstone River Rd S Marion (43302) ***(G-12729)***
R B Mfg Co....419 626-9464
250 Seville Rd Wadsworth (44281) ***(G-19270)***
R C A Rubber Company....330 784-1291
1833 E Market St Akron (44305) ***(G-338)***
R C Family Wood Products....937 295-2393
5590 State Route 47 Fort Loramie (45845) ***(G-9802)***
R C M, Akron *Also called Rubber City Machinery Corp* ***(G-356)***
R C Moore Lumber Co....740 732-4950
820 Miller St Caldwell (43724) ***(G-2410)***
R C Musson Rubber Co....330 773-7651
1320 E Archwood Ave Akron (44306) ***(G-339)***
R C Packaging Systems....248 684-6363
6277 Heisley Rd Mentor (44060) ***(G-13568)***
R C Poling Company Inc....740 939-0023
2105 Clay Rd Junction City (43748) ***(G-11275)***
R Carney Thomas....740 342-3388
1600 Commerce Dr New Lexington (43764) ***(G-14722)***
R D Baker Enterprises Inc....937 461-5225
765 Liberty Ln Dayton (45449) ***(G-8458)***
R D Cook Company LLC....614 262-0550
883 E Hudson St Columbus (43211) ***(G-7372)***
R D Holder Oil Co Inc....740 522-3136
1000 Keller Dr Heath (43056) ***(G-10728)***
R D Lucky LLC....614 570-8005
5336 Shiloh Dr Columbus (43220) ***(G-7373)***
R D Thompson Paper Pdts Co Inc....419 994-3614
1 Madison St Loudonville (44842) ***(G-12147)***
R Design & Printing Co....614 299-1420
30 E 4th Ave Columbus (43201) ***(G-7374)***

ALPHABETIC SECTION

Radcliffe Steel, Berea

R Dunn Mold Inc 937 773-3388
  9055 State Route 66 Piqua (45356) *(G-16158)*
R E May Inc 216 771-6332
  1401 E 24th St Cleveland (44114) *(G-5950)*
R E Smith Inc 513 771-0645
  10330 Chester Rd Cincinnati (45215) *(G-4243)*
R F Cook Manufacturing Co, Stow Also called Levan Enterprises Inc *(G-17601)*
R F W Holdings Inc 440 331-8300
  1200 Smith Ct Cleveland (44116) *(G-5951)*
R G C Inc 513 683-3110
  507 Loveland Madeira Rd Loveland (45140) *(G-12225)*
R Gordon Jones Inc 740 986-8381
  20849 Five Points Pike Williamsport (43164) *(G-20260)*
R H Industries Inc 216 281-5210
  3155 W 33rd St Cleveland (44109) *(G-5952)*
R H Little Co 330 477-3455
  4434 Southway St Sw Canton (44706) *(G-2800)*
R J Cox Co 937 548-4699
  8903 State Route 571 Arcanum (45304) *(G-631)*
R J Dobay Enterprises Inc 440 227-1005
  14704 Main Market Rd Burton (44021) *(G-2367)*
R J Engineering Company Inc 419 843-8651
  2860 Heysler Rd Toledo (43617) *(G-18494)*
R J K Enterprises Inc 440 257-6018
  5565 Wilson Dr Mentor (44060) *(G-13569)*
R K Combustion & Controls 937 444-9700
  212 Hughes Blvd Mount Orab (45154) *(G-14451)*
R K Industries Inc 419 523-5001
  725 N Locust St Ottawa (45875) *(G-15663)*
R K Metals Ltd 513 874-6055
  3235 Homeward Way Fairfield (45014) *(G-9556)*
R K S Tool & Die Inc 513 870-0225
  200 Security Dr Fairfield (45014) *(G-9557)*
R L Corbett Co, The, Cleveland Also called Modern Design Stamping Div *(G-5698)*
R L Craig Inc 330 424-1525
  6496 State Route 45 Lisbon (44432) *(G-11980)*
R L Drake Company 937 746-4556
  230 Industrial Dr Franklin (45005) *(G-9914)*
R L Drake Holdings LLC (HQ) 937 746-4556
  710 Pleasant Valley Dr Springboro (45066) *(G-17349)*
R L Industries Inc 513 874-2800
  9355 Le Saint Dr West Chester (45014) *(G-19777)*
R L Parsons & Son Equipment Co 614 879-7601
  7155 State Route 142 Se West Jefferson (43162) *(G-19927)*
R L Rush Tool & Pattern Inc 419 562-9849
  1620 Whetstone St Bucyrus (44820) *(G-2342)*
R L S Corporation 740 773-1440
  990 Eastern Ave Chillicothe (45601) *(G-3219)*
R L S Recycling, Chillicothe Also called R L S Corporation *(G-3219)*
R L Technologies Inc (PA) 937 321-5544
  1711 Mccall St Dayton (45402) *(G-8459)*
R L Torbeck Industries Inc 513 367-0080
  355 Industrial Dr Harrison (45030) *(G-10667)*
R L Y Inc 513 385-1950
  5874 Cheviot Rd Cincinnati (45247) *(G-4244)*
R M Davis Inc 419 756-6719
  517 Walfield Dr Mansfield (44904) *(G-12503)*
R M Industries Inc 419 529-8970
  95 Ohio Brass Rd Mansfield (44902) *(G-12504)*
R M Tool & Die Inc 440 238-6459
  19768 Progress Dr Strongsville (44149) *(G-17780)*
R M Wood Co 419 845-2661
  5795 County Road 30 Mount Gilead (43338) *(G-14431)*
R M Yates Co Inc 216 441-0900
  4452 Warner Rd Cleveland (44105) *(G-5953)*
R Molds, Euclid Also called California Ceramic Supply Co *(G-9406)*
R P A, Dayton Also called Rpa Electronic Distributors *(G-8486)*
R R Donnelley, Hebron Also called RR Donnelley & Sons Company *(G-10760)*
R R Donnelley, Streetsboro Also called R R Donnelley & Sons Company *(G-17690)*
R R Donnelley & Sons Company 740 376-9276
  88 Products Ln Marietta (45750) *(G-12661)*
R R Donnelley & Sons Company 513 552-1512
  8720 Global Way West Chester (45069) *(G-19778)*
R R Donnelley & Sons Company 330 562-5250
  10400 Danner Dr Streetsboro (44241) *(G-17690)*
R R Donnelley & Sons Company 440 774-2101
  450 Sterns Rd Oberlin (44074) *(G-15504)*
R R R Development Co (PA) 330 966-8855
  8817 Pleasantwood Ave Nw North Canton (44720) *(G-15112)*
R S C, Columbus Also called Safecor Health LLC *(G-7412)*
R S C Sales Company 423 581-4916
  1347 E 4th St Dayton (45402) *(G-8460)*
R S Imprints 330 872-5905
  5 S Milton Blvd Newton Falls (44444) *(G-14992)*
R S Manufacturing Inc 440 946-8002
  8878 East Ave Mentor (44060) *(G-13570)*
R S V Wldg Fbrcation Machining 419 592-0993
  M063 County Road 12 Napoleon (43545) *(G-14557)*

R Sportswear LLC 937 748-3507
  8068 Forest Glen Dr Springboro (45066) *(G-17350)*
R T & T Machining Co Inc 440 974-8479
  8195 Tyler Blvd Mentor (44060) *(G-13571)*
R T Communications Inc 330 726-7892
  6031 Applecrest Dr Youngstown (44512) *(G-21011)*
R T H Processing Inc 419 692-3000
  1430 N Main St Delphos (45833) *(G-8754)*
R T Industries Inc (PA) 937 335-5784
  110 Foss Way Troy (45373) *(G-18695)*
R T R Slotting & Machine Inc 330 929-2608
  2742 2nd St Cuyahoga Falls (44221) *(G-7911)*
R V Spa LLC 440 284-4800
  42345 Oberlin Elyria Rd Elyria (44035) *(G-9316)*
R Vandewalle Inc 513 921-2657
  4030 Delhi Ave Cincinnati (45204) *(G-4245)*
R W Machine & Tool Inc 330 296-5211
  7944 State Route 44 Ravenna (44266) *(G-16398)*
R W Michael Printing Co 330 923-9277
  665 E Cuyahoga Falls Ave Akron (44310) *(G-340)*
R W Screw Products Inc 330 837-9211
  999 Oberlin Ave Sw Massillon (44647) *(G-13044)*
R W Sidley Inc 440 224-2664
  3062 E Center St Kingsville (44068) *(G-11462)*
R W Sidley Incorporated (PA) 440 352-9343
  436 Casement Ave Painesville (44077) *(G-15777)*
R W Sidley Incorporated 440 298-3232
  7123 Madison Rd Thompson (44086) *(G-18028)*
R W Sidley Incorporated 440 564-2221
  10688 Kinsman Rd Newbury (44065) *(G-14962)*
R W Sidley Incorporated 330 499-5616
  7545 Pittsburg Ave Nw Canton (44720) *(G-2801)*
R W Sidley Incorporated 330 392-2721
  425 N River Rd Nw Warren (44483) *(G-19435)*
R W Sidley Incorporated 330 750-1661
  395 Lowellville Rd Struthers (44471) *(G-17823)*
R W Sidley Incorporated 440 352-9343
  436 Casement Ave Painesville (44077) *(G-15778)*
R W Sidley Incorporated 330 793-7374
  3424 Oregon Ave Youngstown (44509) *(G-21012)*
R Weir Inc 937 438-5730
  978 Mmsburg Cnterville Rd Dayton (45459) *(G-8461)*
R&C Packing & Custom Butcher 740 245-9440
  3836 State Route 850 Bidwell (45614) *(G-1668)*
R&D Machine Inc 937 339-2545
  1204 S Crawford St Troy (45373) *(G-18696)*
R&D Marketing Group Inc 216 398-9100
  4597 Van Epps Rd Brooklyn Heights (44131) *(G-2130)*
R&S Carbon Trading LLC 614 264-3083
  146 N Hamilton Rd Ste 127 Gahanna (43230) *(G-10099)*
R-K Electronics Inc 513 204-6060
  7405 Industrial Row Dr Mason (45040) *(G-12929)*
R-Med Inc 419 693-7481
  3465 Navarre Ave Oregon (43616) *(G-15565)*
R. Joseph Group, Columbus Also called Musicmax Inc *(G-7202)*
R.W., Willoughby Also called Spence Technologies Inc *(G-20436)*
R4 Holdings LLC 614 873-6499
  7795 Corporate Blvd Plain City (43064) *(G-16210)*
Ra Consultants LLC 513 469-6600
  10856 Kenwood Rd Blue Ash (45242) *(G-1840)*
Ra Recycling, LLC, Beachwood Also called Real Alloy Recycling LLC *(G-1272)*
Raber Lumber Co 330 893-2797
  4112 State Rte 557 Charm (44617) *(G-3142)*
Race Winning Brands Inc (HQ) 440 951-6600
  7201 Industrial Park Blvd Mentor (44060) *(G-13572)*
Racedirector LLC 440 940-6675
  38613 Andrews Ridge Way Willoughby (44094) *(G-20417)*
Racelite South Coast Inc 216 581-4600
  16518 Broadway Ave Maple Heights (44137) *(G-12578)*
Raceway Beverage LLC 513 932-2214
  11 S Broadway St Lebanon (45036) *(G-11688)*
Raceway Petroleum Inc 440 989-2660
  3040 Oberlin Ave Lorain (44052) *(G-12115)*
Rack Coating Service Inc 330 854-2869
  5760 Erie Ave Nw Canal Fulton (44614) *(G-2491)*
Rack Draft Service Inc 513 353-5520
  11109 Guard Ln North Bend (45052) *(G-15054)*
Rack Processing Company Inc (PA) 937 294-1911
  2350 Arbor Blvd Moraine (45439) *(G-14387)*
Rack Processing Company Inc 937 294-1911
  2350 Arbor Blvd Moraine (45439) *(G-14388)*
Raco Cutting Inc (PA) 937 293-1228
  2230 E River Rd Moraine (45439) *(G-14389)*
RAD Technologies Incorporated 513 641-0523
  11 Sunnybrook Dr Cincinnati (45237) *(G-4246)*
RAD-Con Inc (PA) 440 871-5720
  13001 Athens Ave Ste 300 Lakewood (44107) *(G-11534)*
Radar Love Co 419 951-4750
  5500 Fostoria Ave Findlay (45840) *(G-9744)*
Radcliffe Steel, Berea Also called Rads LLC *(G-1623)*

(PA)=Parent Co (HQ)=Headquarters (DH)=Div Headquarters

Radco Fire Protection Inc...419 476-0102
444 W Laskey Rd Ste S Toledo (43612) ***(G-18495)***
Radco Industries Inc...419 531-4731
3226 Frenchmens Rd Toledo (43607) ***(G-18496)***
Raddells Sausage...216 486-1944
478 E 152nd St Cleveland (44110) ***(G-5954)***
Radici Plastics Usa Inc...330 336-7611
960 Seville Rd Wadsworth (44281) ***(G-19271)***
Radio Hospital...419 679-1103
30 N Main St Kenton (43326) ***(G-11419)***
Radioshack, Cuyahoga Falls *Also called 4r Enterprises Incorporated* ***(G-7829)***
Radix Wire & Cable LLC...216 731-9191
26000 Lakeland Blvd Cleveland (44132) ***(G-5955)***
Radix Wire Co (PA)...216 731-9191
26000 Lakeland Blvd Cleveland (44132) ***(G-5956)***
Radix Wire Co...216 731-9191
26260 Lakeland Blvd Cleveland (44132) ***(G-5957)***
Radix Wire Company...330 995-3677
350 Harris Dr Aurora (44202) ***(G-902)***
Radix Wire Company, The, Cleveland *Also called Radix Wire Co* ***(G-5956)***
Radocy Inc...419 666-4400
30652 E River Rd Rossford (43460) ***(G-16591)***
Radon Be Gone Inc...614 268-4440
4319 Indianola Ave Columbus (43214) ***(G-7375)***
Rads LLC...330 671-0464
135 Blaze Industrial Pkwy Berea (44017) ***(G-1623)***
Rae Systems Inc...440 232-0555
7307 Young Dr Ste B Walton Hills (44146) ***(G-19314)***
Raf Acquisition Co...440 572-5999
5478 Grafton Rd Valley City (44280) ***(G-19058)***
Rafter Equipment Corporation...440 572-3700
12430 Alameda Dr Strongsville (44149) ***(G-17781)***
Rage Corporation (PA)...614 771-4771
3949 Lyman Dr Hilliard (43026) ***(G-10857)***
Rage Plastics, Hilliard *Also called Rage Corporation* ***(G-10857)***
Rageon Inc...617 633-0544
1163 E 40th St Ste 2 Cleveland (44114) ***(G-5958)***
Ragman Inc...419 255-8068
1201 N Summit St Toledo (43604) ***(G-18497)***
Ragon House Collection, Bolivar *Also called Rhc Inc* ***(G-1927)***
Rail Bearing Service Inc, North Canton *Also called Rail Bearing Service LLC* ***(G-15113)***
Rail Bearing Service LLC...234 262-3000
4500 Mount Pleasant St Nw North Canton (44720) ***(G-15113)***
Rail Road Corporation...614 771-2102
4881 Trabue Rd Columbus (43228) ***(G-7376)***
Railing Crafters Ltd...440 506-9336
632 Argonne Dr Painesville (44077) ***(G-15779)***
Railroad Brewing Company...440 723-8234
1010 Center Rd Avon (44011) ***(G-961)***
Railtech Boutet, Inc., Napoleon *Also called Pandrol Inc* ***(G-14555)***
Railtech Matweld Inc...419 592-5050
15 Interstate Dr Napoleon (43545) ***(G-14558)***
Railtech Matweld Inc (HQ)...419 591-3770
25 Interstate Dr Napoleon (43545) ***(G-14559)***
Rain Drop Products Llc...419 207-1229
2121 Cottage St Ashland (44805) ***(G-742)***
Rainbow Bedding...330 852-3127
3421 Township Road 166 Sugarcreek (44681) ***(G-17861)***
Rainbow Cultured Marble...330 225-3400
1442 W 130th St Brunswick (44212) ***(G-2232)***
Rainbow Hills Vineyards Inc...740 545-9305
26349 Township Road 251 Newcomerstown (43832) ***(G-14980)***
Rainbow Industries Inc...937 323-6493
5975 E National Rd Springfield (45505) ***(G-17479)***
Rainbow Plastics, Mentor *Also called Rlr Industries Inc* ***(G-13574)***
Rainbow Printing, Uniontown *Also called Plastic Card Inc* ***(G-18929)***
Rainbow Printing, Uniontown *Also called Plasticards Inc* ***(G-18930)***
Rainbow Tarp, Springfield *Also called Rainbow Industries Inc* ***(G-17479)***
Raindow Hills Vineyards, Newcomerstown *Also called Rainbow Hills Vineyards Inc* ***(G-14980)***
Rainin Instrument LLC...510 564-1600
1900 Polaris Pkwy Columbus (43240) ***(G-6505)***
Raka Corporation...419 476-6572
203 Matzinger Rd Toledo (43612) ***(G-18498)***
Ral Robotics Investment Group, Stone Creek *Also called Richard A Limbacher* ***(G-17564)***
Ralph Felice Inc...330 468-0482
1532 Newport Dr Macedonia (44056) ***(G-12322)***
Ralph Robinson Inc...740 385-2747
700 Ohio Ave Logan (43138) ***(G-12042)***
Ralphie Gianni Mfg & Co...216 507-3873
250 E 271st St Euclid (44132) ***(G-9439)***
Ralston Food, Lancaster *Also called Treehouse Private Brands Inc* ***(G-11615)***
Ralston Instruments LLC...440 564-1430
15035 Cross Creek Pkwy Newbury (44065) ***(G-14963)***
Ram Machining Inc...740 333-5522
806 Delaware St Wshngtn CT Hs (43160) ***(G-20740)***
Ram Precision Industries Inc...937 885-7700
11125 Yankee St Ste A Dayton (45458) ***(G-8462)***
Ram Products Inc...614 443-4634
1091 Stimmel Rd Columbus (43223) ***(G-7377)***
Ram Racewares, Warren *Also called Behlke Dalene* ***(G-19376)***
Ram Sensors Inc (PA)...440 835-3540
875 Canterbury Rd Cleveland (44145) ***(G-5959)***
Ram Sensors Inc...440 835-3540
875 Canterbury Rd Ste 875 # 875 Westlake (44145) ***(G-20148)***
Ram Tool Inc...937 277-0717
1944 Neva Dr Dayton (45414) ***(G-8463)***
Ram Z Neon...330 788-5121
1227 E Indianola Ave Youngstown (44502) ***(G-21013)***
Ramco Electric Motors Inc...937 548-2525
5763 Jysville St Johns Rd Greenville (45331) ***(G-10389)***
Ramco Specialties Inc (PA)...330 653-5135
5445 Hudson Indus Pkwy Hudson (44236) ***(G-11069)***
Ramon Robinson...330 883-3244
475 Niles Vienna Rd Vienna (44473) ***(G-19208)***
Ramona Southworth...740 226-8202
2882 Adams Rd Beaver (45613) ***(G-1293)***
Ramp Creek III Ltd...740 522-0660
1100 Thornwood Dr Lot 1 Heath (43056) ***(G-10729)***
Rampe Manufacturing Company...440 352-8995
1246 High St Fairport Harbor (44077) ***(G-9629)***
Rampp Company (PA)...740 373-7886
20445 State Route 550 Ofc Marietta (45750) ***(G-12662)***
Ramzi, Cleveland *Also called Safe Systems Inc* ***(G-6024)***
Rance Industries Inc...330 482-1745
1361 Heck Rd Columbiana (44408) ***(G-6477)***
Randall Richard & Moore LLC...330 455-8873
3710 Progress St Ne Canton (44705) ***(G-2802)***
Randall Bearings Inc (PA)...419 223-1075
1046 S Greenlawn Ave Lima (45804) ***(G-11927)***
Randall Bearings Inc...419 678-2486
821 Weis St Coldwater (45828) ***(G-6419)***
Randall Foods Inc (PA)...513 793-6525
312 Walnut St Ste 1600 Cincinnati (45202) ***(G-4247)***
Randd Assoc Prtg & Promotions...937 294-1874
330 Progress Rd Dayton (45449) ***(G-8464)***
Randolph Research Co...330 666-1667
2449 Kensington Rd Akron (44333) ***(G-341)***
Randolph Tool Company Inc...330 877-4923
750 Wales Dr Hartville (44632) ***(G-10703)***
Randy Carter Logging Inc...740 634-2604
1100 Schmidt Rd Bainbridge (45612) ***(G-1020)***
Randy Gray...513 533-3200
4142 Airport Rd Fl 1 Cincinnati (45226) ***(G-4248)***
Randy Lewis Inc...330 784-0456
1053 Bank St Akron (44305) ***(G-342)***
Randy R Wilson...740 454-4440
5225 W State Route 12 Findlay (45840) ***(G-9745)***
Randys, Toledo *Also called Slap N Tickle LLC* ***(G-18524)***
Randys Countertops Inc...740 881-5831
3208 Home Rd Powell (43065) ***(G-16334)***
Randys Pickles LLC...440 864-6611
2203 Superior Ave E Cleveland (44114) ***(G-5960)***
Range Hood Store, The, Marysville *Also called Z Line Kitchen and Bath LLC* ***(G-12819)***
Range Kleen Mfg Inc...419 331-8000
4240 East Rd Elida (45807) ***(G-9199)***
Range One Products & Fabg...330 533-1151
580 W Main St Canfield (44406) ***(G-2542)***
Range Rsurces - Appalachia LLC...330 866-3301
1748 Saltwell Rd Nw Dover (44622) ***(G-8848)***
Ranir Dcp...616 698-8880
4701 E Paris Bay Village (44140) ***(G-1207)***
Rankin Mfg Inc...419 929-8338
201 N Main St New London (44851) ***(G-14735)***
Ransohoff, West Chester *Also called Cleaning Tech Group LLC* ***(G-19842)***
Ransom & Randolph...419 794-1210
520 Illinois Ave Maumee (43537) ***(G-13141)***
Rantek Products LLC...419 485-2421
1826 Magda Dr Ste A Montpelier (43543) ***(G-14315)***
Rapid Blanket Restorer Corp...330 821-6326
8735 Palomino Trl Willoughby (44094) ***(G-20418)***
Rapid Copy Printing, Cincinnati *Also called Dorothy Crooker* ***(G-3602)***
Rapid Machine Inc...419 737-2377
610 N State St Pioneer (43554) ***(G-16094)***
Rapid Mold Repair & Machine...330 253-1000
813 Home Ave Akron (44310) ***(G-343)***
Rapid Mr International LLC...614 486-6300
1500 Lake Shore Dr # 310 Columbus (43204) ***(G-7378)***
Rapid Quality Manufacturing, West Chester *Also called GE Aviation Systems LLC* ***(G-19710)***
Rapid Signs & More Inc...513 553-4040
1044 Old Us Highway 52 New Richmond (45157) ***(G-14814)***
Rapid Signs & Sportswear, New Richmond *Also called Rapid Signs & More Inc* ***(G-14814)***
Rapiscan Systems High Energy I...937 879-4200
514 E Dytn Yllow Sprng Rd Fairborn (45324) ***(G-9466)***
Rapistan Systems, Brecksville *Also called Siemens Industry Inc* ***(G-2058)***
Raptis Coffee Inc...330 399-7011
341 Main Ave Sw Warren (44481) ***(G-19436)***

ALPHABETIC SECTION
Rector Inc

Rascal House Inc............216 781-0904
1836 Euclid Ave Ste 800 Cleveland (44115) ***(G-5961)***
Rasche Cabinetmakers, Westerville *Also called Mark Rasche* ***(G-20009)***
Raschke Engraving Inc............330 677-5544
4485 Crystal Pkwy Ste 200 Kent (44240) ***(G-11373)***
Rassini Chassis Systems LLC............419 485-1524
1812 Magda Dr Montpelier (43543) ***(G-14316)***
Ratech............513 742-2111
11110 Adwood Dr Cincinnati (45240) ***(G-4249)***
Ratliff Metal Spinning Co Inc............937 836-3900
40 Harrisburg Dr Englewood (45322) ***(G-9374)***
Rauh Polymers Inc............330 376-1120
420 Kenmore Blvd Akron (44301) ***(G-344)***
Ravago Americas LLC............419 924-9090
600 Oak St West Unity (43570) ***(G-19973)***
Ravana Industries Inc............330 536-4015
6170 Center Rd Lowellville (44436) ***(G-12254)***
Raven Concealment Systems LLC............440 508-9000
7889 Root Rd North Ridgeville (44039) ***(G-15249)***
Raven Industries Inc............937 323-4625
2130 Progress Rd Springfield (45505) ***(G-17480)***
Ravens Sales & Service, Dover *Also called Kruz Inc* ***(G-8835)***
Ravenworks Deer Skin............937 354-5151
34477 Shertzer Rd Mount Victory (43340) ***(G-14521)***
Rawac Plating Company............937 322-7491
125 N Bell Ave Springfield (45504) ***(G-17481)***
Rawhide Press, Bowling Green *Also called Rawhide Software Inc* ***(G-1993)***
Rawhide Software Inc (PA)............419 878-0857
17552 W River Rd Bowling Green (43402) ***(G-1993)***
Rawlins Pallet & Lumber, Wheelersburg *Also called Forrest Rawlins* ***(G-20180)***
Ray Barnes Newspaper Inc (PA)............419 674-4066
201 E Columbus St 207 Kenton (43326) ***(G-11420)***
Ray Communications Inc............330 686-0226
1337 Commerce Dr Ste 11 Stow (44224) ***(G-17623)***
Ray Fogg Construction Inc............216 351-7976
981 Keynote Cir Ste 15 Cleveland (44131) ***(G-5962)***
Ray L Lute LL............740 372-7703
494 Coldicott Hill Rd Lucasville (45648) ***(G-12267)***
Ray Lewis & Son Incorporated............937 644-4015
916 Delaware Ave Marysville (43040) ***(G-12807)***
Ray Meyer Sign Company Inc............513 984-5446
8942 Glendale Milford Rd Loveland (45140) ***(G-12226)***
Ray Rieser Trophy Co............614 279-1128
3852 Sullivant Ave Columbus (43228) ***(G-7379)***
Ray Townsend............440 968-3617
9168 Clay St Montville (44064) ***(G-14325)***
Rayco Manufacturing LLC............330 264-8699
4255 E Lincoln Way Wooster (44691) ***(G-20642)***
Raydar Inc of Ohio............330 334-6111
1734 Wall Rd Ste B Wadsworth (44281) ***(G-19272)***
Rayhaven Group Inc............330 659-3183
3842 Congress Pkwy Ste A Richfield (44286) ***(G-16484)***
Rayle Coal Co............740 695-2197
67705 Friends Church Rd Saint Clairsville (43950) ***(G-16648)***
Raymath Company............937 335-1860
2323 W State Route 55 Troy (45373) ***(G-18697)***
Raymond W Reisiger............740 400-4090
11885 Paddock View Ct Nw Baltimore (43105) ***(G-1041)***
Raymonds Tool & Gauge LLC............419 485-8340
6726 County Road N30 Montpelier (43543) ***(G-14317)***
Rays Sausage Inc............216 921-8782
3146 E 123rd St Cleveland (44120) ***(G-5963)***
Raytec Systems, Stow *Also called Ray Communications Inc* ***(G-17623)***
Raytheon Company............937 429-5429
2970 Presidential Dr # 300 Beavercreek (45324) ***(G-1339)***
RB Fabricators Inc............330 779-0263
4021 Mahoning Ave Youngstown (44515) ***(G-21014)***
RB Tool and Manufacturing, Cincinnati *Also called Kaws Inc* ***(G-3898)***
RB&w Manufacturing LLC............740 363-1971
700 London Rd Delaware (43015) ***(G-8718)***
RB&w Manufacturing LLC (HQ)............234 380-8540
10080 Wellman Rd Streetsboro (44241) ***(G-17691)***
Rba Inc............330 336-6700
487 College St Wadsworth (44281) ***(G-19273)***
Rbb Systems Inc............330 263-4502
1909 Old Mansfield Rd Wooster (44691) ***(G-20643)***
Rbi Solar Inc (HQ)............513 242-2051
5513 Vine St Cincinnati (45217) ***(G-4250)***
Rbm Environmental and Cnstr............419 693-5840
4526 Bayshore Rd Oregon (43616) ***(G-15566)***
Rboog Industries LLC............330 350-0396
3132 Ipswich Ct Brunswick (44212) ***(G-2233)***
Rbs Manufacturing Inc............330 426-9486
145 E Martin St East Palestine (44413) ***(G-9082)***
RC Industries Inc............330 879-5486
620 Main St N Navarre (44662) ***(G-14586)***
RC Lonestar Inc............513 467-0430
6381 River Rd Cincinnati (45233) ***(G-4251)***
RC Outsourcing LLC............330 536-8500
102 E Water St Lowellville (44436) ***(G-12255)***
RCE Heat Exchangers LLC............330 627-0300
3165 Folsam Rd Nw Carrollton (44615) ***(G-2927)***
Rcf Kitchens Indiana LLC............765 478-6600
87 Shelford Way Beavercreek (45440) ***(G-1361)***
Rci, Sidney *Also called Ross Casting & Innovation LLC* ***(G-17070)***
Rcl Benziger, Cincinnati *Also called Kendall/Hunt Publishing Co* ***(G-3904)***
Rcl Publishing Group LLC............972 390-6400
8805 Governors Hill Dr # 400 Cincinnati (45249) ***(G-4252)***
RCM Engineering Company............330 666-0575
2089 N Clvland Msslon Rd Akron (44333) ***(G-345)***
Rcr Partnership............419 340-1202
424 N Martin Williston Rd Genoa (43430) ***(G-10235)***
Rcs Brewhouse............440 984-3103
223 Church St Amherst (44001) ***(G-572)***
Rct Industries Inc............937 602-1100
7494 Deep Woods Ct Springboro (45066) ***(G-17351)***
Rda Group LLC............440 724-4347
2131 Clifton Way Avon (44011) ***(G-962)***
RE Connors Construction Ltd............740 644-0261
13352 Forrest Rd Ne Thornville (43076) ***(G-18031)***
REA Elektronik Inc............440 232-0555
7307 Young Dr Ste B Bedford (44146) ***(G-1440)***
REA Polishing Inc............419 470-0216
1606 W Laskey Rd Toledo (43612) ***(G-18499)***
Reactive Resin Products Co............419 666-6119
327 5th St Perrysburg (43551) ***(G-16003)***
Reading Rock Inc (PA)............513 874-2345
4600 Devitt Dr West Chester (45246) ***(G-19893)***
Ready Field Solutions LLC............330 562-0550
1240 Ethan Ave Streetsboro (44241) ***(G-17692)***
Ready Made Rc LLC............740 936-4500
7719 Graphics Way Ste F Lewis Center (43035) ***(G-11775)***
Ready Technology Inc............937 228-8181
630 Kiser St Dayton (45404) ***(G-8465)***
Ready Technology Inc (HQ)............937 866-7200
333 Progress Rd Unit A Dayton (45449) ***(G-8466)***
Ready To Go LLC............216 862-8572
17325 Euclid Ave Cleveland (44112) ***(G-5964)***
Real Alloy Holding LLC (PA)............216 755-8900
3700 Park East Dr Ste 300 Beachwood (44122) ***(G-1270)***
Real Alloy Recycling LLC............346 444-8540
3700 Park East Dr Ste 100 Beachwood (44122) ***(G-1271)***
Real Alloy Recycling LLC (HQ)............216 755-8900
3700 Park East Dr Ste 300 Beachwood (44122) ***(G-1272)***
Real Alloy Specialty Pdts LLC............216 755-8836
3700 Park East Dr Ste 300 Beachwood (44122) ***(G-1273)***
Real Alloy Specialty Pdts LLC............440 322-0072
440 Huron St Elyria (44035) ***(G-9317)***
Real Alloy Specialty Products............440 563-3487
2639 E Water St Rock Creek (44084) ***(G-16533)***
Real Alloy Specialty Products (HQ)............216 755-8836
3700 Park East Dr Ste 300 Beachwood (44122) ***(G-1274)***
Real Alloy Specialty Products............440 322-0072
320 Huron St Elyria (44035) ***(G-9318)***
Real Alloy Specification LLC (HQ)............216 755-8900
3700 Park East Dr Ste 300 Beachwood (44122) ***(G-1275)***
Real Geese, Bradner *Also called Licensed Spcialty Pdts of Ohio* ***(G-2012)***
Real Products Manufacturing, Ney *Also called Janet Sullivan* ***(G-14997)***
Real Solution Communication, Akron *Also called Robert F Sams* ***(G-351)***
Really Cool Foods, Beavercreek *Also called Rcf Kitchens Indiana LLC* ***(G-1361)***
Ream and Haager Laboratory............330 343-3711
179 W Broadway St Dover (44622) ***(G-8849)***
Reberland Equipment Inc............330 698-5883
5963 Fountain Nook Rd Apple Creek (44606) ***(G-618)***
Rebiltco Inc............513 424-2024
8775 Thomas Rd Middletown (45042) ***(G-13948)***
Rebiz LLC............844 467-3249
1925 Saint Clair Ave Ne Cleveland (44114) ***(G-5965)***
Rebsco Inc............937 548-2246
4362 Us Route 36 Greenville (45331) ***(G-10390)***
Recaro Child Safety LLC............248 904-1570
4921 Para Dr Cincinnati (45237) ***(G-4253)***
Receet Inc............513 769-1900
4055 Executive Park Dr # 140 Cincinnati (45241) ***(G-4254)***
Reclamation Technologies Inc (HQ)............800 372-1301
1100 Haskins Rd Bowling Green (43402) ***(G-1994)***
Reclamation Technologies Inc............419 867-8990
1100 Haskins Rd Bowling Green (43402) ***(G-1995)***
Recob Great Lakes Express Inc............216 265-7940
20600 Sheldon Rd Cleveland (44142) ***(G-5966)***
Recognition Robotics Inc (PA)............440 590-0499
151 Innovation Dr Elyria (44035) ***(G-9319)***
Recon Systems LLC (PA)............330 488-0368
330 Wood St S East Canton (44730) ***(G-9043)***
Recov Beverages LLC............513 518-9794
331 W 4th St Apt 2 Cincinnati (45202) ***(G-4255)***
Recto Molded Products Inc............513 871-5544
4425 Appleton St Cincinnati (45209) ***(G-4256)***
Rector Inc............440 892-0444
1991 Crocker Rd Ste 320 Westlake (44145) ***(G-20149)***

ALPHABETIC

Recycled Systems Furniture Inc 614 880-9110
401 E Wilson Bridge Rd Worthington (43085) *(G-20701)*
Recycling Div, Cleveland *Also called Resolute FP US Inc (G-5980)*
Recycling Div, Columbus *Also called Resolute FP US Inc (G-7388)*
Recycling Div, Cincinnati *Also called Resolute FP US Inc (G-4260)*
Recycling Eqp Solutions Corp 330 920-1500
276 Remington Rd Ste C Cuyahoga Falls (44224) *(G-7912)*
Red Barakuda LLC 614 596-5432
4439 Shoupmill Dr Columbus (43230) *(G-7380)*
Red Barn Cabinet Co 937 884-9800
8046 State Route 722 Arcanum (45304) *(G-632)*
Red Barn Screen Printing & EMB 740 474-6657
1144 Northridge Rd Circleville (43113) *(G-4556)*
Red Barn, The, Circleville *Also called Red Barn Screen Printing & EMB (G-4556)*
Red Bone Services LLC 330 364-0022
1213 Stonecreek Rd Sw New Philadelphia (44663) *(G-14795)*
Red Book, Chagrin Falls *Also called National Dirctry of Morts Inc (G-3025)*
Red Diamond Plant, Mc Arthur *Also called Austin Powder Company (G-13179)*
Red Head Brass, Shreve *Also called Rhba Acquisitions LLC (G-17008)*
Red Head Brass Inc 330 567-2903
643 Legion Dr Shreve (44676) *(G-17007)*
Red Hill Development Company, Dover *Also called Doris Kimble (G-8817)*
Red Hot Studios 330 609-7446
728 Shadowood Ln Se Warren (44484) *(G-19437)*
Red Lion Nursery Inc 937 704-9840
3505 N State Route 741 Lebanon (45036) *(G-11689)*
Red Sea Truck Line, Columbus *Also called Yemaneh Musie (G-7622)*
Red Seal Electric Co 216 941-3900
3835 W 150th St Cleveland (44111) *(G-5967)*
Red Tie Group Inc (HQ) 216 271-2300
3650 E 93rd St Cleveland (44105) *(G-5968)*
Red Tie Group Inc 614 443-9100
2272 S High St Columbus (43207) *(G-7381)*
Red Vette Printing Company 740 364-1766
75 Fern Hill Dr Granville (43023) *(G-10337)*
Redbuilt LLC 740 363-0870
200 Colomet Dr Delaware (43015) *(G-8719)*
Redco Instrument 440 232-2132
659 Broadway Ave Cleveland (44146) *(G-5969)*
Redex Industries Inc (PA) 330 332-9800
1176 Salem Pkwy Salem (44460) *(G-16770)*
Redhawk Energy Systems LLC 740 927-8244
10340 Palmer Rd Sw Pataskala (43062) *(G-15839)*
Redi Rock Structures Oki LLC 513 965-9221
1050 Round Bottom Rd Milford (45150) *(G-14036)*
Redi-Quik Signs Inc 614 228-6641
123 E Spring St Columbus (43215) *(G-7382)*
Redmond Waltz Electric, Cleveland *Also called Phillips Electric Co (G-5873)*
Reds Auto Glass Shop, Warren *Also called J W Goss Co Inc (G-19413)*
Reebar Die Casting Inc 419 878-7591
1177 Farnsworth Rd Waterville (43566) *(G-19503)*
Reeces Las Vegas Supplies (PA) 937 274-5000
5425 Fishburg Rd Dayton (45424) *(G-8467)*
Reed Elvin Burl II 937 399-3242
1236 Villa Rd Springfield (45503) *(G-17482)*
Reed Machinery Inc 330 220-6668
629 Marsh Way Brunswick (44212) *(G-2234)*
Reef Runner Tackle Co Inc 419 798-9125
102 Cherry St Marblehead (43440) *(G-12587)*
Reel Image 937 296-9036
2520 Blackhawk Rd Dayton (45420) *(G-8468)*
Reelflyrodcom 937 434-8472
7635 Wilmington Pike D Dayton (45458) *(G-8469)*
Reese Machine Company Inc 440 992-3942
2501 State Rd Ashtabula (44004) *(G-801)*
Reesers Machine Inc 937 548-5847
2624 Fox Rd Greenville (45331) *(G-10391)*
Refcotec, Orrville *Also called Refractory Coating Tech Inc (G-15614)*
Refractory Coating Tech Inc 330 683-2200
542 Collins Blvd Orrville (44667) *(G-15614)*
Refractory Specialties Inc 330 938-2101
230 W California Ave Sebring (44672) *(G-16891)*
Refrigeration Industries Corp 740 377-9166
719 County Road 1 South Point (45680) *(G-17293)*
Regal Beloit America Inc 419 352-8441
427 Van Camp Rd Bowling Green (43402) *(G-1996)*
Regal Beloit America Inc 608 364-8800
200 E Chapman Rd Lima (45801) *(G-11928)*
Regal Beloit America Inc 937 667-2431
531 N 4th St Tipp City (45371) *(G-18130)*
Regal Cabinet Inc 419 865-3932
315 N Holland Sylvania Rd Toledo (43615) *(G-18500)*
Regal Diamond Products Corp 440 944-7700
1405 E 286th St Wickliffe (44092) *(G-20229)*
Regal Industries Inc 440 352-9600
857 Richmond Rd Painesville (44077) *(G-15780)*
Regal Metal Products Co (PA) 330 868-6343
3615 Union Ave Se Minerva (44657) *(G-14198)*
Regal Metal Products Co 330 868-6343
162 Arbor Rd Ne Minerva (44657) *(G-14199)*
Regal Spring Co 614 278-7761
2140 Eakin Rd Ste J Columbus (43223) *(G-7383)*
Regal Trophy & Awards Company 877 492-7531
1269 Wapakoneta Ave Sidney (45365) *(G-17064)*
Regalia Products Inc 614 579-8399
2117 S High St Columbus (43207) *(G-7384)*
Register Herald Office 937 456-5553
200 Eaton Lewisburg Rd # 105 Eaton (45320) *(G-9164)*
Registered Images Inc 859 781-9200
6545 Wiehe Rd Cincinnati (45237) *(G-4257)*
Regol-G Industries, Cleveland *Also called DCW Acquisition Inc (G-5079)*
Rehn Co, Toledo *Also called Whiteford Industries Inc (G-18599)*
Reichard Controls, Dublin *Also called Reichard Software Corp (G-8972)*
Reichard Industries LLC (PA) 330 482-5511
338 S Main St Columbiana (44408) *(G-6478)*
Reichard Software Corp 614 537-8598
655 Metro Pl S Ste 600 Dublin (43017) *(G-8972)*
Reid Asset Management Company (PA) 216 642-3223
9555 Rockside Rd Ste 350 Cleveland (44125) *(G-5970)*
Reid Asset Management Company 216 642-3223
9555 Rockside Rd Ste 350 Cleveland (44125) *(G-5971)*
Reid Asset Management Company 440 942-8488
4500 Beidler Rd Willoughby (44094) *(G-20419)*
Reifel Industries Inc 419 737-2138
201 Ohio St Pioneer (43554) *(G-16095)*
Reighart Steel Products, Willoughby *Also called Sticker Corporation (G-20438)*
Reinecker Party Center & Catrg, Macedonia *Also called Reineckers Bakery Ltd (G-12323)*
Reineckers Bakery Ltd 330 467-2221
8575 Freeway Dr Macedonia (44056) *(G-12323)*
Reineke Company LLC 419 281-5800
1025 Faultless Dr Ashland (44805) *(G-743)*
Reisbeck Fd Mkts St Clirsville, Saint Clairsville *Also called Riesbeck Food Markets Inc (G-16649)*
Reiser Manufacturing 330 846-8003
4571 Millrock Rd New Waterford (44445) *(G-14842)*
Reiter Dairy of Akron Inc (HQ) 937 323-5777
1961 Commerce Cir Springfield (45504) *(G-17483)*
Reiter Dairy of Akron Inc 513 795-6962
9991 Commerce Park Dr West Chester (45246) *(G-19894)*
Reiter Dairy of Akron Inc 419 424-5060
10456 State Route 224 W Findlay (45840) *(G-9746)*
Rek Associates LLC 419 294-3838
11218 County Highway 44 Upper Sandusky (43351) *(G-18971)*
Reladyne Inc (PA) 513 489-6000
8280 Montgomery Rd # 101 Cincinnati (45236) *(G-4258)*
Related Metals Inc 330 799-4866
6011 Deer Spring Run Canfield (44406) *(G-2543)*
Relay Rail Div., Mineral Ridge *Also called L B Foster Company (G-14168)*
Relevium Labs Inc (PA) 614 568-7000
4663 Katie Ln Ste O Oxford (45056) *(G-15699)*
Reliable Buffing & Polishing, Spencerville *Also called Reliable Buffing Co Inc (G-17312)*
Reliable Buffing Co Inc 419 647-4432
222 N College St Spencerville (45887) *(G-17312)*
Reliable Castings Corporation 937 497-5217
1521 W Michigan Ave Sidney (45365) *(G-17065)*
Reliable Metal Buildings LLC 419 737-1300
16570 Us Highway 20ns Pioneer (43554) *(G-16096)*
Reliable Mfg Co LLC 740 756-9373
4411 Carroll Southern Rd Carroll (43112) *(G-2908)*
Reliable Pattern Works Inc 440 232-8820
590 Golden Oak Pkwy Cleveland (44146) *(G-5972)*
Reliable Products Co Inc 419 394-5854
315 S Park Dr Saint Marys (45885) *(G-16697)*
Reliable Wheelchair Trans 216 390-3999
28899 Harvard Rd Beachwood (44122) *(G-1276)*
Reliacheck Manufacturing Inc 440 933-6162
33554 Pin Oak Pkwy Avon Lake (44012) *(G-1005)*
Reliance Design Inc 216 267-5450
3463 Archwood Dr Rocky River (44116) *(G-16554)*
Reliance Medical Products Inc (HQ) 513 398-3937
3535 Kings Mills Rd Mason (45040) *(G-12930)*
Reloading Supplies Corp 440 228-0367
1040 Devon Dr Ashtabula (44004) *(G-802)*
Relx Inc 937 865-6800
9443 Springboro Pike Miamisburg (45342) *(G-13708)*
Relx Inc 937 865-6800
4700 Lyons Rd Miamisburg (45342) *(G-13709)*
Relx Inc 937 865-6800
9333 Springboro Pike Miamisburg (45342) *(G-13710)*
Rely-On Manufacturing Inc 937 254-0118
955 Springfield St Dayton (45403) *(G-8470)*
Remel Products, Oakwood Village *Also called Thermo Fisher Scientific Inc (G-15486)*
Remington Engrg Machining Inc 513 965-8999
5105 River Valley Rd Milford (45150) *(G-14037)*
Remington Products Co 330 335-1571
961 Seville Rd Wadsworth (44281) *(G-19274)*
Remington Steel, Springfield *Also called Westfield Steel Inc (G-17516)*

Remlinger Manufacturing Co Inc 419 532-3647
16394 Us 224 Kalida (45853) ***(G-11280)***
Remnant Room 937 938-7350
1915 S Alex Rd Dayton (45449) ***(G-8471)***
Remram Recovery LLC 740 667-0092
49705 E Park Dr Tuppers Plains (45783) ***(G-18720)***
Remtec Corp 513 860-4299
6049 Hi Tek Ct Mason (45040) ***(G-12931)***
Remtec Engineering 513 860-4299
6049 Hi Tek Ct Mason (45040) ***(G-12932)***
Remtec International, Bowling Green *Also called Reclamation Technologies Inc* ***(G-1994)***
Remtec International, Bowling Green *Also called Reclamation Technologies Inc* ***(G-1995)***
Remtron, Warren *Also called Cattron North America Inc* ***(G-19382)***
Renco Mold Inc 937 233-3233
2801 Ome Ave Dayton (45414) ***(G-8472)***
Renco Printing Inc 216 267-5585
5261 W 161st St Cleveland (44142) ***(G-5973)***
Renee Barrett Winery 513 471-1340
8129 Austin Ridge Dr Cincinnati (45247) ***(G-4259)***
Renegade Brands LLC 216 342-4347
3201 Enterprise Pkwy # 490 Cleveland (44122) ***(G-5974)***
Renegade Candle Company, New Albany *Also called Faith Guiding Cafe LLC* ***(G-14623)***
Renegade Materials Corporation 508 579-7888
3363 S Tech Blvd Miamisburg (45342) ***(G-13711)***
Renegade Well Services LLC 330 488-6055
215 Trump Ave Ne Canton (44730) ***(G-2803)***
Renewable Energy, Parma *Also called North Amrcn Sstnable Enrgy Ltd* ***(G-15824)***
Renewal By Andersen LLC 614 781-9600
400 Lazelle Rd Ste 1 Columbus (43240) ***(G-6506)***
Renewal Parts Maintenance, Euclid *Also called Mechanical Dynamics Analis Ltd* ***(G-9426)***
Renite Company 800 883-7876
2500 E 5th Ave Columbus (43219) ***(G-7385)***
Renite Lubrication Engineers, Columbus *Also called Renite Company* ***(G-7385)***
Rennco Automation Systems Inc 419 861-2340
971 Hamilton Dr Holland (43528) ***(G-10953)***
Renoir Visions LLC 419 586-5679
1 Visions Pkwy Celina (45822) ***(G-2982)***
Renosol Seating, Hebron *Also called Lear Corporation* ***(G-10750)***
Rent A Mom Inc 216 901-9599
4531 Hillside Rd Seven Hills (44131) ***(G-16905)***
Rent-A-John, Columbus *Also called BJ Equipment Ltd* ***(G-6673)***
Repko Machine Inc 216 267-1144
5081 W 164th St Cleveland (44142) ***(G-5975)***
Replacment Prts Spcialists Inc (PA) 440 248-0731
30400 Solon Indus Pkwy Solon (44139) ***(G-17221)***
Replex Mirror Company 740 397-5535
11 Mount Vernon Ave Mount Vernon (43050) ***(G-14504)***
Replex Plastics, Mount Vernon *Also called Replex Mirror Company* ***(G-14504)***
Replica Engineering Inc 216 252-2204
3483 W 140th St Cleveland (44111) ***(G-5976)***
Reporter Newspaper Inc 330 535-7061
1088 S Main St Akron (44301) ***(G-346)***
Repository, Canton *Also called Copley Ohio Newspapers Inc* ***(G-2636)***
Repp, Blue Ash *Also called Check Yourself LLC* ***(G-1749)***
Repro Acquisition Company LLC 216 738-3800
25001 Rockwell Dr Cleveland (44117) ***(G-5977)***
Repro Depot, Medina *Also called Montview Corporation* ***(G-13304)***
Reprocenter, The, Cleveland *Also called Repro Acquisition Company LLC* ***(G-5977)***
Republic Anode Fabricators, Valley City *Also called Raf Acquisition Co* ***(G-19058)***
Republic EDM Services Inc 937 278-7070
5660 Wadsworth Rd Dayton (45414) ***(G-8473)***
Republic Engineered Products 440 277-2000
1807 E 28th St Lorain (44055) ***(G-12116)***
Republic Metals, Cleveland *Also called Vwm-Republic Inc* ***(G-6276)***
Republic Mills Inc 419 758-3511
888 School St Okolona (43545) ***(G-15523)***
Republic Powdered Metals Inc (HQ) 330 225-3192
2628 Pearl Rd Medina (44256) ***(G-13327)***
Republic Steel, Lorain *Also called Republic Engineered Products* ***(G-12116)***
Republic Steel (HQ) 330 438-5435
2633 8th St Ne Canton (44704) ***(G-2804)***
Republic Steel 330 837-7024
401 Rose Ave Se Massillon (44646) ***(G-13045)***
Republic Steel Inc 330 438-5533
2633 8th St Ne Canton (44704) ***(G-2805)***
Republic Steel Inc 440 277-2000
1807 E 28th St Lorain (44055) ***(G-12117)***
Republic Steel Wire Proc LLC 440 996-0740
31000 Solon Rd Solon (44139) ***(G-17222)***
Republic Wire Inc 513 860-1800
5525 Union Centre Dr West Chester (45069) ***(G-19779)***
RES Q Cleaning Solutions Inc 740 964-9494
638 Klema Dr E Reynoldsburg (43068) ***(G-16451)***
Rescar Companies Inc 630 963-1114
177 Curry St Minerva (44657) ***(G-14200)***
Resco Products Inc 330 372-3716
1929 Larchmont Ave Ne Warren (44483) ***(G-19438)***
Resco Products Inc 330 488-1226
6878 Osnaburg St Se East Canton (44730) ***(G-9044)***
Resco Products Inc 740 682-7794
3542 State Route 93 Oak Hill (45656) ***(G-15459)***
Research & Development Div, Bedford *Also called Hikma Pharmaceuticals USA Inc* ***(G-1412)***
Research & Development II, Mentor *Also called Steris Corporation* ***(G-13589)***
Research Abrasive Products Inc 440 944-3200
1400 E 286th St Wickliffe (44092) ***(G-20230)***
Research and Development Group 614 261-0454
1208 E Hudson St Columbus (43211) ***(G-7386)***
Research Metrics LLC 419 464-3333
5121 Whiteford Rd Sylvania (43560) ***(G-17959)***
Research Organics LLC 216 883-8025
4353 E 49th St Cleveland (44125) ***(G-5978)***
Research Technologies Intl, Cleveland *Also called Detrex Corporation* ***(G-5087)***
Reserve Energy Exploration Co 440 543-0770
10155 Gottschalk Pkwy # 1 Chagrin Falls (44023) ***(G-3072)***
Reserve Industries Inc 440 871-2796
386 Lake Park Dr Bay Village (44140) ***(G-1208)***
Reserve Millwork Inc 216 531-6982
26881 Cannon Rd Bedford (44146) ***(G-1441)***
Residential Electronic Svcs 740 681-9150
3155 Lancstr Kirkrsvll Nw Lancaster (43130) ***(G-11601)***
Residents of Sawmill Park 614 659-6678
2765 Sawmill Park Dr Dublin (43017) ***(G-8973)***
Resilience Fund III LP (PA) 216 292-0200
25101 Chagrin Blvd Cleveland (44122) ***(G-5979)***
Resilient Holdings Inc 614 847-5600
6155 Huntley Rd Ste F Columbus (43229) ***(G-7387)***
Resinoid Engineering Corp (PA) 740 928-6115
251 Oneill Dr Hebron (43025) ***(G-10759)***
Resinoid Engineering Corp 740 928-2220
2040 James Pkwy Heath (43056) ***(G-10730)***
Resolute FP US Inc 216 961-3900
3400 Vega Ave Cleveland (44113) ***(G-5980)***
Resolute FP US Inc 614 443-6300
995 Marion Rd Columbus (43207) ***(G-7388)***
Resolute FP US Inc 513 242-3671
5535 Vine St Cincinnati (45217) ***(G-4260)***
Resonetics LLC 937 865-4070
2941 College Dr Kettering (45420) ***(G-11440)***
Resource Exchange Company Inc 440 773-8915
383 Abbyshire Rd Akron (44319) ***(G-347)***
Resource Fuels LLC (PA) 614 221-0101
41 S High St Ste 3750s Columbus (43215) ***(G-7389)***
Resource Graphics 513 205-2686
2230 Gilbert Ave Cincinnati (45206) ***(G-4261)***
Resource Mechanical Insul LLC 248 577-0200
6842 Commodore Dr Walbridge (43465) ***(G-19298)***
Resource Mtl Hdlg & Recycl Inc (PA) 440 834-0727
14970 Brkshire Indus Pkwy Middlefield (44062) ***(G-13849)***
Resource Recycling Inc 419 222-2702
1596 Neubrecht Rd Lima (45801) ***(G-11929)***
Restless Noggins Mfg LLC 330 526-6908
334 Orchard Ave Ne North Canton (44720) ***(G-15114)***
Retail Display Group, Columbus *Also called Plaskolite LLC* ***(G-7321)***
Retail Management Products 740 548-1725
8851 Whitney Dr Lewis Center (43035) ***(G-11776)***
Retalix Inc 937 384-2277
2490 Technical Dr Miamisburg (45342) ***(G-13712)***
Retays Welding Company 440 327-4100
7650 Race Rd North Ridgeville (44039) ***(G-15250)***
Retco Mold & Machine, Tallmadge *Also called M & R Manufacturing Inc* ***(G-17989)***
Retek Inc 440 937-6282
34550 Chester Rd Avon (44011) ***(G-963)***
Retention Knob Supply & Mfg Co 937 686-6405
4905 State Route 274 W Huntsville (43324) ***(G-11088)***
Retriev Technologies Inc 740 653-6290
265 Quarry Rd Se Lancaster (43130) ***(G-11602)***
Retterbush Fiberglass Corp 937 778-1936
719 Long St Piqua (45356) ***(G-16159)***
Retterbush Graphic and Packg 513 779-4466
6187 Schumacher Park Dr West Chester (45069) ***(G-19780)***
Retterer Manufacturing Company, Caledonia *Also called Claridon Tool & Die Inc* ***(G-2414)***
Rettig Family Pallets Inc 419 264-1540
12484 State Route 110 Napoleon (43545) ***(G-14560)***
Reuland Electric Co 513 825-7314
9620 Colerain Ave Ste 22 Cincinnati (45251) ***(G-4262)***
Reuter-Stokes LLC 330 425-3755
8499 Darrow Rd Ste 1 Twinsburg (44087) ***(G-18845)***
Reuter-Stokes, Inc., Twinsburg *Also called Reuter-Stokes LLC* ***(G-18845)***
Reuther Mold & Manufacturing, Cuyahoga Falls *Also called Reuther Mold & Mfg Co Inc* ***(G-7913)***
Reuther Mold & Mfg Co Inc 330 923-5266
1225 Munroe Falls Ave Cuyahoga Falls (44221) ***(G-7913)***
Rev38 LLC 937 572-4000
8888 Beckett Rd West Chester (45069) ***(G-19781)***
Revenue Management Group LLC 419 993-2200
2348 Baton Rouge Lima (45805) ***(G-11930)***

Revere Building Products, Cuyahoga Falls *Also called Gentek Building Products Inc* ***(G-7872)***
Revere Plas Systems Group LLC (HQ)....419 547-6918
401 Elm St Clyde (43410) ***(G-6393)***
Revere Plastics Systems LLC (HQ)....419 547-6918
401 Elm St Clyde (43410) ***(G-6394)***
Review Times, The, Fostoria *Also called Daily Fostoria Review Co* ***(G-9836)***
Review, The, Alliance *Also called Alliance Publishing Co Inc* ***(G-454)***
Revlis Corporation....330 535-2108
2845 Newpark Dr Barberton (44203) ***(G-1101)***
Revlon, Barberton *Also called Revlis Corporation* ***(G-1101)***
Revolaze LLC....440 617-0502
31000 Viking Pkwy Westlake (44145) ***(G-20150)***
Revolution Group Inc....614 212-1111
600 N Cleveland Ave # 110 Westerville (43082) ***(G-20020)***
Revolution Machine Works Inc....706 505-6525
14646 Ravenna Rd Unit B Burton (44021) ***(G-2368)***
Revonoc Inc....440 548-3491
18125 Madison Rd Parkman (44080) ***(G-15813)***
Rework Furnishings LLC....614 300-5021
1271 Edgehill Rd Bldg B Columbus (43212) ***(G-7390)***
Rex American Resources Corp (PA)....937 276-3931
7720 Paragon Rd Dayton (45459) ***(G-8474)***
Rex Auto Seat Covers, Lima *Also called Rex Manufacturing Co* ***(G-11931)***
Rex Automation Inc....614 766-4672
2211 Aspenwood Ln Columbus (43235) ***(G-7391)***
Rex Burnett....740 927-4669
26 1st Ave Sw Etna (43062) ***(G-9397)***
Rex International USA Inc....800 321-7950
3744 Jefferson Rd Ashtabula (44004) ***(G-803)***
Rex Manufacturing Co....419 224-5751
805 S Cable Rd Lima (45805) ***(G-11931)***
Rexam Closure Systems, Perrysburg *Also called Bprex Halthcare Brookville Inc* ***(G-15924)***
Rexam Plastic Packaging, Toledo *Also called Bprex Plastic Packaging Inc* ***(G-18213)***
Rexam PLC....330 893-2451
5091 County Road 120 Millersburg (44654) ***(G-14122)***
Rexarc International Inc....937 839-4604
35 E 3rd St West Alexandria (45381) ***(G-19620)***
Rexel Inc....330 468-1122
805 Millstream Run Northfield (44056) ***(G-15323)***
Rexon Components Inc....440 585-7086
24500 Highpoint Rd Cleveland (44122) ***(G-5981)***
Reymond Products Intl Inc....330 339-3583
2066 Brightwood Rd Se New Philadelphia (44663) ***(G-14796)***
Reynolds & Co Inc....937 592-8300
1515 S Main St Bellefontaine (43311) ***(G-1524)***
Reynolds and Reynolds Company....419 584-7000
824 Murlin Ave Celina (45822) ***(G-2983)***
Reynolds and Reynolds Company....937 485-4771
354 Mound St Dayton (45402) ***(G-8475)***
Reynolds and Reynolds Company....937 449-4039
115 S Ludlow St Dayton (45402) ***(G-8476)***
Reynolds and Reynolds Company....937 485-2805
2405 County Line Rd Beavercreek (45430) ***(G-1362)***
Reynolds Cabinetry & Millwork, Cincinnati *Also called Village Cabinet Shop Inc* ***(G-4481)***
Reynolds Engineered Pdts LLC....513 751-4400
4242 Airport Rd Ste 103 Cincinnati (45226) ***(G-4263)***
Reynolds Industries Group LLC....614 864-6199
7463 Old River Dr Blacklick (43004) ***(G-1692)***
Reynolds Industries Inc....330 889-9466
380 W Main St West Farmington (44491) ***(G-19920)***
Reynoldsburg Trophy, Grove City *Also called American Awards Inc* ***(G-10414)***
REZ STONE, Toledo *Also called Hoover & Wells Inc* ***(G-18335)***
Rez-Tech Corporation....330 673-4009
1510 Mogadore Rd Kent (44240) ***(G-11374)***
Rezas Roast LLC....937 823-1193
611 Yellow Spgs Fairborn (45324) ***(G-9467)***
Rezkem Chemicals LLC....330 653-9104
56 Milford Dr Ste 100 Hudson (44236) ***(G-11070)***
Rezmann Karoly....216 441-4357
7216 Bessemer Ave Cleveland (44127) ***(G-5982)***
Rf Linx Inc....513 777-2774
2142 Greentree Rd Lebanon (45036) ***(G-11690)***
RFS Fabrication....419 547-0650
2515 County Road 213 Clyde (43410) ***(G-6395)***
Rh Enterprises, Richmond Heights *Also called R & H Enterprises Llc* ***(G-16504)***
Rhba Acquisitions LLC....330 567-2903
643 Legion Dr Shreve (44676) ***(G-17008)***
Rhc Inc....330 874-3750
10841 Fisher Rd Nw Bolivar (44612) ***(G-1927)***
Rhe-Tech Colors, Sandusky *Also called Thermocolor LLC* ***(G-16852)***
Rheaco Builders Inc....330 425-3090
1941 E Aurora Rd Twinsburg (44087) ***(G-18846)***
Rhenium Alloys Inc (PA)....440 365-7388
38683 Taylor Pkwy North Ridgeville (44035) ***(G-15251)***
Rhetech Color, Sandusky *Also called Thermocolor LLC* ***(G-16853)***
Rhi US Ltd (HQ)....513 753-1254
3956 Virginia Ave Cincinnati (45227) ***(G-4264)***
Rhinestahl AMG, Mason *Also called Rhinestahl Corporation* ***(G-12933)***
Rhinestahl Corporation (PA)....513 229-5300
1111 Western Row Rd Mason (45040) ***(G-12933)***
Rhinestahl Corporation....513 229-5300
7687 Innovation Way Mason (45040) ***(G-12934)***
Rhino Robotics Ltd....513 353-9772
5928 State Rte 128 Miamitown (45041) ***(G-13750)***
Rhino Rubber LLC (PA)....877 744-6603
7054 Meadowlands Ave Nw North Canton (44720) ***(G-15115)***
Rhino Tech Software LLC....614 456-9321
13938 Nantucket Ave Pickerington (43147) ***(G-16059)***
Rhinosystems Inc....216 351-6262
1 American Rd Ste 1100 Brooklyn (44144) ***(G-2114)***
Rhoads Printing Center Inc (PA)....330 678-2042
302 N Water St Kent (44240) ***(G-11375)***
Rhodes Manufacturing Co Inc....740 743-2614
7045 Buckeye Valley Rd Ne Somerset (43783) ***(G-17266)***
Rhombus Technologies Ltd....937 335-1840
755 Barnhart Rd Troy (45373) ***(G-18698)***
Rl Alto Mfg Inc....740 914-4230
1632 Cascade Dr Marion (43302) ***(G-12730)***
Ribbon Technology Corporation....614 864-5444
825 Taylor Station Rd Gahanna (43230) ***(G-10100)***
Riblet Packaging Co....937 652-3087
955 Lippincott Rd Urbana (43078) ***(G-19009)***
Ribs King Inc....513 791-1942
9406 Main St Cincinnati (45242) ***(G-4265)***
Ribtec, Gahanna *Also called Ribbon Technology Corporation* ***(G-10100)***
Ricci Anthony....330 758-5761
755 Boardman Canfield Rd Youngstown (44512) ***(G-21015)***
Riceland Cabinet Inc....330 601-1071
326 N Hillcrest Dr Ste A Wooster (44691) ***(G-20644)***
Riceland Cabinet Corporation....330 601-1071
326 N Hillcrest Dr Ste A Wooster (44691) ***(G-20645)***
Ricers Residential Svcs LLC....567 203-7414
3526 State Route 314 Shelby (44875) ***(G-16987)***
Rich Industries Inc....330 339-4113
2384 Brightwood Rd Se New Philadelphia (44663) ***(G-14797)***
Rich Print, Youngstown *Also called Ricci Anthony* ***(G-21015)***
Rich Products Corporation....614 771-1117
4600 Northwest Pkwy Hilliard (43026) ***(G-10858)***
Richard A Limbacher....330 897-4515
7148 Rocky Ridge Rd Sw Stone Creek (43840) ***(G-17564)***
Richard A Scott....937 898-1592
8000 Allison Ave Dayton (45415) ***(G-8477)***
Richard B Linneman....513 922-5537
5642 Victory Dr Cincinnati (45233) ***(G-4266)***
Richard Benhase & Associates....513 772-1896
11741 Chesterdale Rd Cincinnati (45246) ***(G-4267)***
Richard Farm Shop, Clyde *Also called RFS Fabrication* ***(G-6395)***
Richard Paskiet Machinists....330 854-4160
468 Etheridge Blvd S Canal Fulton (44614) ***(G-2492)***
Richard Pauley....740 965-6897
3308 N State Route 61 Sunbury (43074) ***(G-17899)***
Richard Steel Company Inc....216 520-6390
11110 Avon Ave Cleveland (44105) ***(G-5983)***
Richard's Fence Company, Akron *Also called Richards Whl Fence Co Inc* ***(G-348)***
Richards and Simmons Inc....614 268-3909
33 W Schreyer Pl Columbus (43214) ***(G-7392)***
Richards Grinding Co Inc....216 631-7675
4914 Walworth Ave Cleveland (44102) ***(G-5984)***
Richards Industries Inc....513 533-5600
3170 Wasson Rd Cincinnati (45209) ***(G-4268)***
Richards Intrors Bldg Cmpnents, Youngstown *Also called Shade Youngstown & Aluminum Co* ***(G-21028)***
Richards Maple Products Inc....440 286-4160
545 Water St Chardon (44024) ***(G-3134)***
Richards Whl Fence Co Inc....330 773-0423
1600 Firestone Pkwy Akron (44301) ***(G-348)***
Richardson Printing Corp (PA)....740 373-5362
201 Acme St Marietta (45750) ***(G-12663)***
Richardson Publishing Company....330 753-1068
70 4th St Nw Ste 1 Barberton (44203) ***(G-1102)***
Richardson Supply Ltd....614 539-3033
2080 Hardy Parkway St Grove City (43123) ***(G-10462)***
Richardson Woodworking....614 893-8850
3834 Mann Rd Blacklick (43004) ***(G-1693)***
Richelieu Foods Inc....740 335-4813
1104 Clinton Ave Wshngtn CT Hs (43160) ***(G-20741)***
Richland Blue Printcom Inc....419 524-2781
1069 Park Ave W Mansfield (44906) ***(G-12505)***
Richland Laminated Columns LLC....419 895-0036
8252 State Route 13 Greenwich (44837) ***(G-10407)***
Richland Newhope Industries (PA)....419 774-4400
150 E 4th St Mansfield (44902) ***(G-12506)***
Richland Screw Machine Pdts....419 524-1272
531 Grant St Mansfield (44903) ***(G-12507)***
Richland Twp Garage....419 358-4897
8435 Dixie Hwy Bluffton (45817) ***(G-1892)***

Richmond Builders Supply, Saint Henry *Also called St Henry Tile Co Inc* ***(G-16667)***
Richmond Concrete Products....330 673-7892
3640 Kibler Toot Rd Sw Warren (44481) ***(G-19439)***
Richmond Machine Co....419 485-5740
1528 Travis Dr Montpelier (43543) ***(G-14318)***
Richmonds Woodworks Inc....330 343-8184
1115 Oak Shadows Dr Ne New Philadelphia (44663) ***(G-14798)***
Richtech Industries Inc....440 937-4401
34000 Lear Indus Pkwy Avon (44011) ***(G-964)***
Richwood Gazette, Marysville *Also called Marysville Newspaper Inc* ***(G-12799)***
Ricking Paper and Specialty Co....513 825-3551
525 Northland Blvd Cincinnati (45240) ***(G-4269)***
Rickly Hydrological Co....614 297-9877
1700 Joyce Ave Columbus (43219) ***(G-7393)***
Rickly Hydrological Company....614 297-9877
1700 Joyce Ave Columbus (43219) ***(G-7394)***
Ricks Graphic Accents Inc....330 644-4455
3554 S Arlington Rd Akron (44312) ***(G-349)***
Ridge Corporation....614 421-7434
1201 Etna Pkwy Etna (43062) ***(G-9398)***
Ridge Machine & Welding Co....740 537-2821
1015 Railroad St Toronto (43964) ***(G-18611)***
Ridge Tool Company (HQ)....440 323-5581
400 Clark St Elyria (44035) ***(G-9320)***
Ridge Tool Company....440 329-4737
321 Sumner St Elyria (44035) ***(G-9321)***
Ridge Tool Company....740 432-8782
9877 Brick Church Rd Cambridge (43725) ***(G-2455)***
Ridge Tool Manufacturing Co....440 323-5581
400 Clark St Elyria (44035) ***(G-9322)***
Ridge Township Stone Quarry....419 968-2222
16905 Middle Point Rd Van Wert (45891) ***(G-19104)***
Ridgeview Sheet Metal....330 674-3768
4772 Township Road 352 Millersburg (44654) ***(G-14123)***
Ridgeway Lumber, West Union *Also called Kenneth Schrock* ***(G-19964)***
Ridgewood Brake Co, Cleveland *Also called Beckworth Industries Inc* ***(G-4801)***
Ridgid, Elyria *Also called Ridge Tool Company* ***(G-9320)***
Ridley USA Inc....800 837-8222
104 Oak St Botkins (45306) ***(G-1936)***
Ridley USA Inc....937 693-6393
104 Oak St Botkins (45306) ***(G-1937)***
Riegle Colors....937 548-8444
3566 N Creek Dr Greenville (45331) ***(G-10392)***
Riesbeck Food Markets Inc....740 695-3401
104 Plaza Dr Saint Clairsville (43950) ***(G-16649)***
Rieter Automotive-Oregon Plant, Oregon *Also called Autoneum North America Inc* ***(G-15556)***
Riffle & Sons, Chillicothe *Also called Riffle Machine Works Inc* ***(G-3220)***
Riffle Machine Works Inc (PA)....740 775-2838
5746 State Route 159 Chillicothe (45601) ***(G-3220)***
Riggenbach Kitchens....330 669-2113
790 E Main St Smithville (44677) ***(G-17091)***
Right Away Division, Blue Ash *Also called Wornick Company* ***(G-1877)***
Right Srce Cmmunications Group, Cincinnati *Also called Jjkb Enterprises LLC* ***(G-3873)***
Right Track Corp....937 663-0366
11124 Helltown Rd Saint Paris (43072) ***(G-16710)***
Righter Plumbing....614 604-7197
1451 Galway Bnd N Pataskala (43062) ***(G-15840)***
Rightway Fab & Machine Inc....937 295-2200
4101 Rangeline Rd Russia (45363) ***(G-16612)***
Rightway Food Service....419 223-4075
3255 Saint Johns Rd Lima (45804) ***(G-11932)***
Rikenkaki America Corporation....614 336-2744
5985 Wilcox Pl Ste D Dublin (43016) ***(G-8974)***
Riker Products Inc....419 729-1626
4901 Stickney Ave Toledo (43612) ***(G-18501)***
Rimeco Products Inc....440 918-1220
2002 Joseph Lloyd Pkwy Willoughby (44094) ***(G-20420)***
Rimer Enterprises Inc....419 878-8156
916 Rimer Dr Waterville (43566) ***(G-19504)***
Rimm Kleen Systems, West Unity *Also called Hardline International Inc* ***(G-19969)***
Rimrock Holdings Corporation (HQ)....614 471-5926
1700 Jetway Blvd Columbus (43219) ***(G-7395)***
Rina Systems LLC....513 469-7462
8180 Corp Pk Dr Ste 140 Cincinnati (45242) ***(G-4270)***
Rinaldi and Packard Industries....330 395-4942
775 And A Half Nles Rd Se Warren (44483) ***(G-19440)***
Ring Container Tech LLC....937 492-0961
603 Oak Ave Sidney (45365) ***(G-17066)***
Ring Masters, Brunswick *Also called Alternative Surface Grinding* ***(G-2187)***
Ringer Screen Print, North Kingsville *Also called Wholesale Imprints Inc* ***(G-15161)***
Ringneck Brewing Company, Strongsville *Also called Brew Kettle Inc* ***(G-17721)***
Rinker Materials....330 654-2511
4200 Universal Dr Diamond (44412) ***(G-8799)***
Rinos Woodworking Shop Inc....440 946-1718
36475 Biltmore Pl Willoughby (44094) ***(G-20421)***
Rinz-N-Reuz, Bowling Green *Also called Diamondback Filters* ***(G-1968)***
Riotech International Ltd (PA)....513 779-0990
6101 Schumacher Park Dr West Chester (45069) ***(G-19782)***
Ripley Metalworks Ltd....937 392-4992
111 Waterworks Rd Ripley (45167) ***(G-16517)***
Ripple Swimwear, Dublin *Also called Afi Brands LLC* ***(G-8875)***
Ris, Bedford *Also called Stephen Radecky* ***(G-1447)***
Rise Holdings LLC....440 946-9646
4839 E 345th St Willoughby (44094) ***(G-20422)***
Rise N Shine Yard Signs....330 745-5868
606 Grandview Ave Barberton (44203) ***(G-1103)***
Risher & Co....216 732-8351
27011 Tungsten Rd Euclid (44132) ***(G-9440)***
Rising Moon Custom Apparel....614 882-1336
19 E College Ave Westerville (43081) ***(G-20072)***
Rita Caz Jwly Studio & Gallery....937 767-7713
220 Xenia Ave Ste 2 Yellow Springs (45387) ***(G-20814)***
Ritchie Foods LLC....440 354-7474
212 High St Fairport Harbor (44077) ***(G-9630)***
Rite Machine Inc....216 267-6911
13704 Enterprise Ave Cleveland (44135) ***(G-5985)***
Rite Way Black & Deburr Inc....937 224-7762
1138 E 2nd St Dayton (45403) ***(G-8478)***
Riten Industries Incorporated....740 335-5353
1100 Lakeview Ave Wshngtn CT Hs (43160) ***(G-20742)***
Ritime Incorporated....330 273-3443
6363 York Rd Ste 104 Cleveland (44130) ***(G-5986)***
Rittal Corp....440 572-4999
19541 Winding Trl Strongsville (44149) ***(G-17782)***
Rittal Corp....937 399-0500
3100 Upper Valley Pike Springfield (45504) ***(G-17484)***
Rittal North America LLC....937 399-0500
1 Rittal Pl Urbana (43078) ***(G-19010)***
Rittman Inc....330 927-6855
10 Mull Dr Rittman (44270) ***(G-16528)***
Rivals Sports Grille LLC....216 267-0005
6710 Smith Rd Middleburg Heights (44130) ***(G-13769)***
River Bend Chair Co, Lebanon *Also called Colonial Woodcraft Inc* ***(G-11642)***
River City Body Company....513 772-9317
2660 Commerce Blvd Cincinnati (45241) ***(G-4271)***
River City Pharma....513 870-1680
8695 Seward Rd Fairfield (45011) ***(G-9558)***
River Corp....513 641-3355
32 W Mitchell Ave Cincinnati (45217) ***(G-4272)***
River East Custom Cabinets....419 244-3226
221 S Saint Clair St Toledo (43604) ***(G-18502)***
River Foundry Supply, Cleveland *Also called River Smelting & Ref Mfg Co* ***(G-5987)***
River Smelting & Ref Mfg Co....216 459-2100
4195 Bradley Rd Cleveland (44109) ***(G-5987)***
Riverbend Sand Rock and Gravel, Miamisburg *Also called Hilltop Basic Resources Inc* ***(G-13676)***
Rivercity Woodworking Inc....513 860-1900
9837 Harwood Ct West Chester (45014) ***(G-19783)***
Rivercor LLC....330 784-1113
1560 Firestone Pkwy Akron (44301) ***(G-350)***
Riverrock Recycl Crushing LLC....937 325-2052
2484 Lindair Dr Springfield (45502) ***(G-17485)***
Riverside Cnstr Svcs Inc....513 723-0900
218 W Mcmicken Ave Cincinnati (45214) ***(G-4273)***
Riverside Drives Inc....216 362-1211
4509 W 160th St Cleveland (44135) ***(G-5988)***
Riverside Drives Disc, Cleveland *Also called Riverside Drives Inc* ***(G-5988)***
Riverside Engines Inc....419 927-6838
7381 S State Route 231 Tiffin (44883) ***(G-18077)***
Riverside Homemade Ice Cream, Marion *Also called Country Caterers Inc* ***(G-12700)***
Riverside Mch & Automtn Inc (PA)....419 855-8308
1240 N Genoa Clay Ctr Rd Genoa (43430) ***(G-10236)***
Riverside Mch & Automtn Inc....419 855-8308
28701 E Broadway St Walbridge (43465) ***(G-19299)***
Riverside Mfg LLC....937 492-3100
2309 Industrial Dr Sidney (45365) ***(G-17067)***
Riverside Mfg Acquisition LLC....585 458-2090
5344 Bragg Rd Cleveland (44127) ***(G-5989)***
Riverside Steel Inc....330 856-5299
3102 Warren Sharon Rd Vienna (44473) ***(G-19209)***
Rivertown Brewing Company LLC....513 827-9280
6550 Hamilton Lebanon Rd Monroe (45044) ***(G-14275)***
Riverview Indus WD Pdts Inc....330 669-8509
646 Industrial Blvd Wooster (44691) ***(G-20646)***
Riverview Indus WD Pdts Inc....330 669-8509
179 S Gilbert Dr Smithville (44677) ***(G-17092)***
Riverview Packaging Inc....937 743-9530
101 Shotwell Dr Franklin (45005) ***(G-9915)***
Riverview Productions Inc....740 441-1150
652 Jackson Pike Gallipolis (45631) ***(G-10174)***
Riverview Raquetball Club, Willoughby *Also called Melinz Industries Inc* ***(G-20378)***
Riwco Corp....937 322-6521
2330 Columbus Rd Springfield (45503) ***(G-17486)***
Rixan Associates Inc....937 438-3005
7560 Paragon Rd Dayton (45459) ***(G-8479)***

ALPHABETIC

(PA)=Parent Co (HQ)=Headquarters (DH)=Div Headquarters
2019 Harris Ohio Industrial Directory
1235

Rj Drilling Company Inc......740 763-3991
5755 Licking Valley Rd Se Nashport (43830) ***(G-14570)***
Rjm Stamping Co......614 443-1191
1641 Universal Rd Columbus (43207) ***(G-7396)***
Rjm Tool......419 355-0900
1718 Sycamore St Fremont (43420) ***(G-10047)***
RJR & Associates Inc......419 237-2220
21550 County Road L Fayette (43521) ***(G-9636)***
RJR Surgical Inc......216 241-2804
2530 Superior Ave E # 703 Cleveland (44114) ***(G-5990)***
Rjw Trucking Company Ltd......740 363-5343
124 Henderson Ct Delaware (43015) ***(G-8720)***
Rke Trucking Co......614 891-1786
6305 Frost Rd Westerville (43082) ***(G-20021)***
Rki Inc (PA)......888 953-9400
8901 Tyler Blvd Mentor (44060) ***(G-13573)***
RL Best Company......330 758-8601
723 Bev Rd Boardman (44512) ***(G-1902)***
Rl Smith Graphics, Youngstown *Also called Rl Smith Graphics LLC* ***(G-21016)***
Rl Smith Graphics LLC......330 629-8616
493 Bev Rd Bldg 7b Youngstown (44512) ***(G-21016)***
Rl Smith Printing Co......330 747-9590
4030 Simon Rd Youngstown (44512) ***(G-21017)***
Rlfshop LLC......937 898-6070
6530 Poe Ave Dayton (45414) ***(G-8480)***
RLM Fabricating Inc......419 729-6130
4801 Bennett Rd Toledo (43612) ***(G-18503)***
Rlr Industries Inc......440 951-9501
8677 Tyler Blvd Unit B Mentor (44060) ***(G-13574)***
Rls Parts & Equipment LLC......440 498-1843
33595 Bnbridge Rd Ste 204 Solon (44139) ***(G-17223)***
Rm Advisory Group Inc......513 242-2100
5300 Vine St Cincinnati (45217) ***(G-4274)***
Rme Machining Co......513 541-3328
2900 Spring Grove Ave Cincinnati (45225) ***(G-4275)***
Rmi Titanium Company LLC (HQ)......330 652-9952
1000 Warren Ave Niles (44446) ***(G-15028)***
Rmi Titanium Company LLC......330 455-4010
1935 Warner Rd Se Canton (44707) ***(G-2806)***
Rmi Titanium Company LLC......330 544-9470
2000 Warren Ave Niles (44446) ***(G-15029)***
Rmi Titanium Company LLC......330 471-1844
208 15th St Sw Canton (44707) ***(G-2807)***
Rmi Titanium Company LLC......330 544-7633
1000 Warren Ave Niles (44446) ***(G-15030)***
Rmi Titanium Company LLC......330 652-9955
1000 Warren Ave Niles (44446) ***(G-15031)***
Rml Tool Inc......216 941-1615
15115 Chatfield Ave B Cleveland (44111) ***(G-5991)***
RMS Equipment LLC......330 564-1360
1 Vision Ln Cuyahoga Falls (44223) ***(G-7914)***
RMS Equipment Company, Cuyahoga Falls *Also called RMS Equipment LLC* ***(G-7914)***
Rmt Corporation......513 942-8308
2552 Titus Ave Dayton (45414) ***(G-8481)***
Rmt Holdings Inc......419 221-1168
1025 Findlay Rd Lima (45801) ***(G-11933)***
Rmw Industries Inc......440 439-1971
24869 Aurora Rd Bedford Heights (44146) ***(G-1479)***
Rn Cabinets & More Ltd......330 275-0203
3916 County Road 200 Fredericksburg (44627) ***(G-9957)***
Rnm Holdings Inc......419 867-8712
1810 Eber Rd Ste C Holland (43528) ***(G-10954)***
Rnm Holdings Inc (PA)......937 704-9900
550 Conover Dr Franklin (45005) ***(G-9916)***
Rnm Holdings Inc......614 444-5556
2350 Refugee Park Columbus (43207) ***(G-7397)***
Rnr Enterprises LLC......330 852-3022
1361 County Road 108 Sugarcreek (44681) ***(G-17862)***
Rnw Holdings Inc......330 792-0600
200 Division Street Ext Youngstown (44510) ***(G-21018)***
Ro-MAI Industries Inc......330 425-9090
1605 Enterprise Pkwy Twinsburg (44087) ***(G-18847)***
Roach Wood Products & Plas Inc......740 532-4855
25 Township Road 328 Ironton (45638) ***(G-11172)***
Road Maintenance Products......740 465-7181
194 Center St Morral (43337) ***(G-14405)***
Roadsafe Traffic Systems Inc......614 274-9782
1350 Stimmel Rd Columbus (43223) ***(G-7398)***
Roare-Q LLC......419 801-4040
10232 Middleton Pike Bowling Green (43402) ***(G-1997)***
Roastery, The, Fairborn *Also called Rezas Roast LLC* ***(G-9467)***
Rob's Specialties, Wintersville *Also called Robs Creative Screen Printing* ***(G-20541)***
Roban Inc......330 794-1059
1319 Main St Lakemore (44250) ***(G-11500)***
Robbins Inc (PA)......513 871-8988
4777 Eastern Ave Cincinnati (45226) ***(G-4276)***
Robbins & Myers Inc......937 327-3111
1895 W Jefferson St Springfield (45506) ***(G-17487)***
Robbins & Myers Inc......937 454-3200
5870 Poe Ave Ste A Dayton (45414) ***(G-8482)***
Robbins Company (HQ)......440 248-3303
29100 Hall St Ste 100 Solon (44139) ***(G-17224)***
Robbins Furnace Works Inc......440 949-2292
3739 Colorado Ave Sheffield Village (44054) ***(G-16974)***
Robbins Sports Surfaces, Cincinnati *Also called Robbins Inc* ***(G-4276)***
Robeck Fluid Power Co......330 562-1140
350 Lena Dr Aurora (44202) ***(G-903)***
Roberds Converting Co Inc......513 683-6667
113 Northeast Dr Loveland (45140) ***(G-12227)***
Robert A Reich Company......440 808-0033
24930 Detroit Rd D Westlake (44145) ***(G-20151)***
Robert Alten Inc......740 653-2640
449 S Ewing St Lancaster (43130) ***(G-11603)***
Robert Ashcraft......740 667-3690
4350 Bethany Ridge Rd Guysville (45735) ***(G-10520)***
Robert Barr......740 826-7325
1245 Friendship Dr New Concord (43762) ***(G-14686)***
Robert Becker Impressions Inc......419 385-5303
4646 Angola Rd Toledo (43615) ***(G-18504)***
Robert Bosch Btry Systems LLC......937 743-1001
50 Ovonic Way Springboro (45066) ***(G-17352)***
Robert C Bost Associates Inc, Columbus *Also called Bost & Filtrex Inc* ***(G-6689)***
Robert E McGrath Inc......440 572-7747
11606 Pearl Rd Strongsville (44136) ***(G-17783)***
Robert E Moore......513 367-0006
10430 New Biddinger Rd Harrison (45030) ***(G-10668)***
Robert Esterman......513 541-3311
2929 Spring Grove Ave # 100 Cincinnati (45225) ***(G-4277)***
Robert F Sams......330 990-0477
1148 Monteray Dr Akron (44305) ***(G-351)***
Robert Gorey......330 725-7272
6811 Stone Rd Medina (44256) ***(G-13328)***
Robert H Shackelford (PA)......330 364-2221
147 Ashwood Ln Ne New Philadelphia (44663) ***(G-14799)***
Robert J & Cindy K Hartz......513 521-6215
8734 Woodview Dr Cincinnati (45231) ***(G-4278)***
Robert Long Manufacturing Inc......330 678-0911
4192 Karg Industrial Pkwy Kent (44240) ***(G-11376)***
Robert Mayo Industries......330 426-2587
157 E Martin St East Palestine (44413) ***(G-9083)***
Robert Nickel......419 448-8256
125 Minerva St Tiffin (44883) ***(G-18078)***
Robert Perez Carpentry......330 497-0043
430 Browning Ave Nw Canton (44720) ***(G-2808)***
Robert Raack......216 932-6127
2943 Berkshire Rd Cleveland Heights (44118) ***(G-6351)***
Robert Rothschild Farm LLC......937 653-7397
3015 E Kemper Rd Cincinnati (45241) ***(G-4279)***
Robert Rothschild Market Cafe, Cincinnati *Also called Robert Rothschild Farm LLC* ***(G-4279)***
Robert Smart Inc......330 454-8881
1100 High Ave Sw Canton (44707) ***(G-2809)***
Robert Tuneberg......440 899-9277
27016 Knickerbocker Rd # 1 Bay Village (44140) ***(G-1209)***
Robert W Johnson Inc (PA)......614 336-4545
6280 Sawmill Rd Dublin (43017) ***(G-8975)***
Robert Winner Sons Inc (PA)......419 582-4321
8544 State Route 705 Yorkshire (45388) ***(G-20826)***
Robert Winner Sons Inc......937 548-7513
2259 State Route 502 Greenville (45331) ***(G-10393)***
Roberts Brothers, Steubenville *Also called Fort Stben Burial Estates Assn* ***(G-17534)***
Roberts Demand No 3 Corp......216 641-0660
4008 E 89th St Cleveland (44105) ***(G-5992)***
Roberts Graphic Center......330 788-4642
5375 Market St Youngstown (44512) ***(G-21019)***
Roberts Manufacturing Co Inc......419 594-2712
24338 Road 148 Oakwood (45873) ***(G-15473)***
Roberts Screw Products, Rushsylvania *Also called Dayton Superior Corporation* ***(G-16595)***
Roberts-Demand Corp......216 581-1300
17401 S Miles Rd Cleveland (44128) ***(G-5993)***
Robertson Cabinets Inc......937 698-3755
1090 S Main St West Milton (45383) ***(G-19952)***
Robertson EDM LLC......419 658-2219
9294 State Route 249 Edgerton (43517) ***(G-9178)***
Robertson Incorporated (PA)......937 323-3747
14 N Lowry Ave Ste 200 Springfield (45504) ***(G-17488)***
Robertson Manufacturing Co......216 531-8222
17917 Roseland Rd Cleveland (44112) ***(G-5994)***
Robey Tool & Machine......614 251-0412
1593 E 5th Ave Columbus (43219) ***(G-7399)***
Robin Enterprises Company......614 891-0250
111 N Otterbein Ave Westerville (43081) ***(G-20073)***
Robin Industries Inc......330 359-5418
7227 State Route 515 Winesburg (44690) ***(G-20534)***
Robin Industries Inc......330 695-9300
300 W Clay St Fredericksburg (44627) ***(G-9958)***
Robin Industries Inc......216 267-3554
4780 W 139th St Cleveland (44135) ***(G-5995)***
Robin Industries Inc......330 893-3501
5200 County Rd 120 Berlin (44610) ***(G-1644)***

ALPHABETIC SECTION

Robinson Fin Machines Inc 419 674-4152
13670 Us Highway 68 Kenton (43326) *(G-11421)*

Robinson Ordnance, Maineville Also called Jmr Enterprises LLC *(G-12371)*

Robinson Wood Products, Vienna Also called Ramon Robinson *(G-19208)*

Robloc Inc 330 723-5853
3593 Medina Rd Medina (44256) *(G-13329)*

Robotworx, Marion Also called Scott Systems Intl Inc *(G-12733)*

Robotworx, Marion Also called Ka Wanner Inc *(G-12714)*

Roboworld Molded Products LLC 513 720-6900
8216 Princeton Glendale West Chester (45069) *(G-19784)*

Robs Creative Screen Printing 740 264-6383
350 Cadiz Rd Wintersville (43953) *(G-20541)*

Robs Welding Technologies Ltd 937 890-4963
2920 Production Ct Dayton (45414) *(G-8483)*

Rocal Inc (PA) 740 998-2122
3186 County Road 550 Frankfort (45628) *(G-9864)*

Rochester Manufacturing Inc 440 647-2463
24765 Quarry Rd Wellington (44090) *(G-19590)*

Rochling Automotive USA LLP 330 400-5785
2275 Picton Pkwy Akron (44312) *(G-352)*

Rochling Glastic Composites LP (HQ) 216 486-0100
4321 Glenridge Rd Cleveland (44121) *(G-5996)*

Rock Decor Company 330 857-7625
2877 Kidron Rd Orrville (44667) *(G-15615)*

Rock Iron Corporation 419 529-9411
1221 Warehouse Dr Crestline (44827) *(G-7800)*

Rock Line Products Inc 419 738-4400
401 Industrial Dr Wapakoneta (45895) *(G-19349)*

Rock Lite, Maple Heights Also called Charles Svec Inc *(G-12568)*

Rock Mill Division, Lancaster Also called Mid-West Fabricating Co *(G-11588)*

Rock Tenn, Ravenna Also called Westrock Rkt Company *(G-16420)*

Rockbottom Oil & Gas 740 374-2478
1 Court House Ln Ste 3 Marietta (45750) *(G-12664)*

Rockbridge Outfitters 740 654-1956
2805 Clmbus Lncster Rd Nw Lancaster (43130) *(G-11604)*

Rockdale Systems LLC 513 379-3577
6 Rowley Ct Cincinnati (45246) *(G-4280)*

Rocknstarr Holdings LLC 330 509-9086
112 S Meridian Rd Youngstown (44509) *(G-21020)*

Rockport Cnstr & Mtls Inc 216 432-9465
3092 Rockefeller Ave Cleveland (44115) *(G-5997)*

Rockport Ready Mix, Cleveland Also called Rockport Cnstr & Mtls Inc *(G-5997)*

Rocks General Maintenance LLC 740 323-4711
10019 Jacksontown Rd Thornville (43076) *(G-18032)*

Rockside Winery & Vineyards LL 740 687-4414
2363 Lncster Newark Rd Ne Lancaster (43130) *(G-11605)*

Rockstedt Tool & Die Inc 330 273-9000
2974 Interstate Pkwy Brunswick (44212) *(G-2235)*

Rocktenn Merchandising Display, West Chester Also called Westrock Rkt LLC *(G-19821)*

Rockwell Automation Inc 513 942-9828
9355 Allen Rd West Chester (45069) *(G-19785)*

Rockwell Automation Inc 330 425-3211
8440 Darrow Rd Twinsburg (44087) *(G-18848)*

Rockwell Automation Inc 440 604-8410
760 Beta Dr Ste A Cleveland (44143) *(G-5998)*

Rockwell Automation Inc 513 943-1145
1195 Clough Pike Batavia (45103) *(G-1180)*

Rockwell Automation Inc 614 776-3021
350 Worthington Rd Ste A Westerville (43082) *(G-20022)*

Rockwell Automation Inc 440 646-5000
1 Allen Bradley Dr Cleveland (44124) *(G-5999)*

Rockwell Automation Inc 440 646-7900
6680 Beta Dr Cleveland (44143) *(G-6000)*

Rockwell Metals Company LLC 440 242-2420
3709 W Erie Ave Lorain (44053) *(G-12118)*

Rockwood Door & Millwork, Millersburg Also called Rockwood Products Ltd *(G-14124)*

Rockwood Products Ltd 330 893-2392
5264 Township Road 401 Millersburg (44654) *(G-14124)*

Rocky Brands Inc (PA) 740 753-1951
39 E Canal St Nelsonville (45764) *(G-14595)*

Rocky Brands Inc 740 753-1951
39 E Canal St Nelsonville (45764) *(G-14596)*

Rocky Mountain Chocolate, Jeffersonville Also called E R B Enterprises Inc *(G-11246)*

Rocky River Brewing Co 440 895-2739
21290 Center Ridge Rd Rocky River (44116) *(G-16555)*

Rockys Hinge Co 330 539-6296
1660 Harding Ave Girard (44420) *(G-10265)*

Roco Industries, Painesville Also called Ropama Inc *(G-15781)*

Roconex Corporation 937 339-2616
20 Marybill Dr S Troy (45373) *(G-18699)*

Rodco Petroleum Inc 330 477-9823
4600 Castlebar St Nw Canton (44708) *(G-2810)*

Roderer Enterprises Inc 513 942-3000
6560 Dixie Hwy Ste E Fairfield (45014) *(G-9559)*

Rodney Wells 740 425-2266
34225 Holland Rd Barnesville (43713) *(G-1118)*

Rods Welding and Rebuilding, Barnesville Also called Rodney Wells *(G-1118)*

Roe Transportation Entps Inc 937 497-7161
3680 W Michigan St Sidney (45365) *(G-17068)*

Roehlers Machine Products 937 354-4401
117 Taylor St E Mount Victory (43340) *(G-14522)*

Roemer Industries Inc 330 448-2000
1555 Masury Rd Masury (44438) *(G-13062)*

Roerig Machine 440 647-4718
27348 State Route 511 New London (44851) *(G-14736)*

Roessner Holdings Inc 419 356-2123
482 State Route 119 Fort Recovery (45846) *(G-9826)*

Roettger Hardwood Inc 937 693-6811
17066 Kettlersville Rd Kettlersville (45336) *(G-11445)*

Rogar International Inc 419 476-5500
4015 Dewey St Toledo (43612) *(G-18505)*

Roger Hall 740 778-2861
429 Railroad Hollow Rd South Webster (45682) *(G-17299)*

Roger Hoover 330 857-1815
571 Kidron Rd Orrville (44667) *(G-15616)*

Roger L Best 740 590-9133
3080 Blind Rd Stockport (43787) *(G-17560)*

Roger's Quick Print, Newark Also called Doug Smith *(G-14868)*

Rogers Industrial Products Inc 330 535-3331
532 S Main St Akron (44311) *(G-353)*

Rogers Mill Inc (PA) 330 227-3214
7431 Depot St Rogers (44455) *(G-16561)*

Rogue Fitness, Columbus Also called Coulter Ventures Llc *(G-6828)*

Rogue Manufacturing Inc 937 839-4026
304 Stotler Rd West Alexandria (45381) *(G-19621)*

Rohrer Corporation (PA) 330 335-1541
717 Seville Rd Wadsworth (44281) *(G-19275)*

Rohrer Corporation 440 542-3100
29601 Solon Rd Solon (44139) *(G-17225)*

Roki America Co Ltd 419 424-9713
2001 Production Dr Findlay (45840) *(G-9747)*

Rol - Tech Inc 214 905-8050
4814 Calvert Dr Fort Loramie (45845) *(G-9803)*

Rol- Fab Inc 216 662-2500
4949 Johnston Pkwy Cleveland (44128) *(G-6001)*

Rolcon Inc 513 821-7259
510 Station Ave Cincinnati (45215) *(G-4281)*

Roll Formed Products Co Div, Youngstown Also called Hynes Industries Inc *(G-20934)*

Roll-In Saw Inc 216 459-9001
15851 Commerce Park Dr Brookpark (44142) *(G-2155)*

Roll-Kraft, Mentor Also called Rki Inc *(G-13573)*

Roller Plant, Canton Also called Timken Company *(G-2839)*

Roller Source Inc 440 748-4033
34100 E Royalton Rd Columbia Station (44028) *(G-6445)*

Rolling Enterprises Inc 937 866-4917
2701 Lance Dr Moraine (45409) *(G-14390)*

Roman Cthlic Docese Youngstown 330 744-8451
144 W Wood St Fl 1 Youngstown (44503) *(G-21021)*

Romanoff Elc Residential LLC 614 755-4500
1288 Research Rd Gahanna (43230) *(G-10101)*

Romar Metal Fabricating Inc 740 682-7731
201 Zane Oak Rd Oak Hill (45656) *(G-15460)*

Romark Industries Inc 440 333-5480
24500 Center Ridge Rd # 250 Westlake (44145) *(G-20152)*

Ron-Al Mold & Machine Inc 330 673-7919
1057 Mason Ave Kent (44240) *(G-11377)*

Rona Enterprises Inc 740 927-9971
30 W Broad St Pataskala (43062) *(G-15841)*

Ronald J Dobay Enterprises, Burton Also called R J Dobay Enterprises Inc *(G-2367)*

Ronald T Dodge Co 937 439-4497
55 Westpark Rd Dayton (45459) *(G-8484)*

Rondy & Co., Barberton Also called Tahoma Rubber & Plastics Inc *(G-1109)*

Ronfeldt Associates Inc 419 382-5641
2345 S Byrne Rd Toledo (43614) *(G-18506)*

Ronfeldt Manufacturing LLC (HQ) 419 382-5641
2345 S Byrne Rd Toledo (43614) *(G-18507)*

Ronlen Industries Inc 330 273-6468
2809 Nationwide Pkwy Brunswick (44212) *(G-2236)*

Rons Texstyles LLC 513 936-9975
457 Thorburn Pl Columbus (43230) *(G-7400)*

Ronson Manufacturing Inc 440 256-1463
9933 Chillicothe Rd Willoughby (44094) *(G-20423)*

Ronyak Brothers Paving, Burton Also called Shalersville Asphalt Co *(G-2370)*

Roof Die Tool & Machine Inc 614 444-6253
2000 S High St Columbus (43207) *(G-7401)*

Roof To Road LLC 740 986-6923
27910 Chillicothe Pike Williamsport (43164) *(G-20261)*

Roofing Annex LLC 513 942-0555
4866 Duff Dr Ste D West Chester (45246) *(G-19895)*

Rooney Optical Inc (PA) 216 267-5600
9221 Ravenna Rd Ste 3 Twinsburg (44087) *(G-18849)*

Root Candles, Medina Also called Al Root Company *(G-13220)*

Roots Poultry Inc 419 332-0041
3721 W State St Fremont (43420) *(G-10048)*

Ropama Inc 440 358-1304
380 W Prospect St Painesville (44077) *(G-15781)*

Roper Lockbox LLC ALPHABETIC SECTION

Roper Lockbox LLC 330 656-5148
7600 Olde Eight Rd Hudson (44236) ***(G-11071)***
Roppe Corporation....419 435-8546
1602 N Union St Fostoria (44830) ***(G-9855)***
Roppe Holding Company....419 435-6601
106 N Main St Fostoria (44830) ***(G-9856)***
Rose City Manufacturing Inc....937 325-5561
900 W Leffel Ln Springfield (45506) ***(G-17489)***
Rose Metal Industries LLC (PA)....216 881-3355
1536 E 43rd St Cleveland (44103) ***(G-6002)***
Rose Metal Industries LLC....216 426-8615
1155 Marquette St Cleveland (44114) ***(G-6003)***
Rose of Sharon Enterprises....937 862-4543
9243 Old Stage Rd Waynesville (45068) ***(G-19572)***
Rose Products and Services Inc....614 443-7647
545 Stimmel Rd Columbus (43223) ***(G-7402)***
Rosebud Mining Company....740 658-4217
28490 Birmingham Rd Freeport (43973) ***(G-9985)***
Rosebud Mining Company....740 768-2097
9076 County Road 53 Bergholz (43908) ***(G-1635)***
Rosebud Mining Company....740 922-9122
5600 Pleasant Vly Rd Se Uhrichsville (44683) ***(G-18892)***
Rosemount Inc....513 851-5555
4400 Muhlhauser Rd West Chester (45011) ***(G-19786)***
Rosenboom Machine & Tool Inc....419 352-9484
1032 S Maple St Bowling Green (43402) ***(G-1998)***
Rosenfeld Jewelry Inc....440 446-0099
5668 Mayfield Rd Cleveland (44124) ***(G-6004)***
Roseville Hardwood....740 221-8712
103 Church St Roseville (43777) ***(G-16579)***
Ross Aluminum Castings LLC....937 492-4134
815 Oak Ave Sidney (45365) ***(G-17069)***
Ross Casting & Innovation LLC....937 497-4500
402 S Kuther Rd Sidney (45365) ***(G-17070)***
Ross Co Redi Mix Co Inc....740 333-6833
1865 Old Us 35 Se Wshngtn CT Hs (43160) ***(G-20743)***
Ross County License Bureau, Willowick *Also called Public Safety Ohio Department* ***(G-20481)***
Ross Hx LLC....513 217-1565
2908 Cincinnati Dayton Rd Middletown (45044) ***(G-13949)***
Ross Printing Co., Cleveland *Also called Yuckon International Corp* ***(G-6334)***
Ross Products Division, Columbus *Also called Abbott Laboratories* ***(G-6522)***
Ross Products Division, Columbus *Also called Abbott Laboratories* ***(G-6525)***
Ross Special Products Inc....937 335-8406
2500 W State Route 55 Troy (45373) ***(G-18700)***
Ross Tmber Harvstg For MGT Inc....513 383-6933
5300 Rapp Ln Batavia (45103) ***(G-1181)***
Ross-Co Redi-Mix Co Inc (PA)....740 775-4466
689 Marietta Rd Chillicothe (45601) ***(G-3221)***
Rossborough, Independence *Also called Opta Minerals (usa) Inc* ***(G-11145)***
Rossborough Supply Co....216 941-6115
3425 Service Rd Cleveland (44111) ***(G-6005)***
Rossi Concept Arts....330 453-6366
1019 Mckinley Ave Nw Canton (44703) ***(G-2811)***
Rossi Machinery Services Inc (PA)....419 281-4488
1529 Cottage St Ashland (44805) ***(G-744)***
Rossi Pasta Factory Inc....740 376-2065
106 Front St Marietta (45750) ***(G-12665)***
Rost Boundry, Mansfield *Also called CSM Horvath Ledgebrook* ***(G-12430)***
Roswell Inc....419 433-4709
9808 Barrows Rd Huron (44839) ***(G-11111)***
Rotadyne, Franklin *Also called Rotation Dynamics Corporation* ***(G-9917)***
Rotairtech Inc....937 435-8178
4668 Gateway Cir Kettering (45440) ***(G-11441)***
Rotary Compression Tech Inc....937 498-2555
211 E Russell Rd Sidney (45365) ***(G-17071)***
Rotary Forms Press Inc (PA)....937 393-3426
835 S High St Hillsboro (45133) ***(G-10890)***
Rotary Printing Company (PA)....419 668-4821
15 Schauss Ave Norwalk (44857) ***(G-15414)***
Rotary Products Inc (PA)....740 747-2623
117 E High St Ashley (43003) ***(G-759)***
Rotary Products Inc....740 747-2623
202 W High St Ashley (43003) ***(G-760)***
Rotary Tech Inc....440 862-8568
12710 Kinsman Rd Burton (44021) ***(G-2369)***
Rotation Dynamics Corporation....937 746-4069
315 Industrial Dr Franklin (45005) ***(G-9917)***
Rotech Products Incorporated....216 476-3722
16901 Albers Ave Cleveland (44111) ***(G-6006)***
Rotek Incorporated (HQ)....330 562-4000
1400 S Chillicothe Rd Aurora (44202) ***(G-904)***
Rotex Global LLC....513 541-1236
1230 Knowlton St Cincinnati (45223) ***(G-4282)***
Rotex Silver Recovery Co, Lebanon *Also called Hess Technologies Inc* ***(G-11662)***
Roth Ready Mix Concrete Co, Cincinnati *Also called S J Roth Enterprises Inc* ***(G-4296)***
Roth Transit Inc....937 773-5051
8590 Industry Park Dr Piqua (45356) ***(G-16160)***
Roto Met Rice, West Chester *Also called Roto-Die Company Inc* ***(G-19787)***
Roto Mold, Mentor *Also called Interpak Inc* ***(G-13475)***
Roto Solutions Inc....330 279-2424
8300 County Rd 189 Holmesville (44633) ***(G-10984)***
Roto Systems, Warrensville Heights *Also called Polimeros Usa LLC* ***(G-19472)***
Roto Tech Inc....937 859-8503
351 Fame Rd Ste A Dayton (45449) ***(G-8485)***
Roto-Die Inc....216 531-4800
21751 Tungsten Rd Cleveland (44117) ***(G-6007)***
Roto-Die Company Inc....513 942-3500
4430 Muhlhauser Rd West Chester (45011) ***(G-19787)***
Roto-Rooter, Cleveland *Also called Gsr Industries LLC* ***(G-5357)***
Rotocast Technologies Inc....330 798-9091
1900 Englewood Ave Akron (44312) ***(G-354)***
Rotoline USA LLC....330 677-3223
4429 Crystal Pkwy Ste B Kent (44240) ***(G-11378)***
Rotopolymers....216 645-0333
26210 Emery Rd Ste 202 Cleveland (44128) ***(G-6008)***
Rotosolutions Inc....419 903-0800
1401 Jacobson Ave Ashland (44805) ***(G-745)***
Rough Brothers Mfg Inc....513 242-0310
5513 Vine St Ste 1 Cincinnati (45217) ***(G-4283)***
Roulet Company....419 241-2988
4221 Lewis Ave Toledo (43612) ***(G-18508)***
Rouse Marketing, Blue Ash *Also called Alifet USA Inc* ***(G-1726)***
Route 14 Promos, Ravenna *Also called Route 14 Storage Inc* ***(G-16399)***
Route 14 Storage Inc....330 296-0084
7830 State Route 14 Ravenna (44266) ***(G-16399)***
Rowe Premix Inc....937 678-9015
10107 Us Rr 127 Box N West Manchester (45382) ***(G-19941)***
Rowend Industries Inc....419 333-8300
1035 Napoleon St Ste 101 Fremont (43420) ***(G-10049)***
Rowmark LLC (PA)....419 425-8974
5409 Hamlet Dr Findlay (45840) ***(G-9748)***
Rowmark LLC....419 429-0042
2040 Industrial Dr Findlay (45840) ***(G-9749)***
Rowtac Inc....419 994-4777
16125 Township Road 458 Loudonville (44842) ***(G-12148)***
Roxane Laboratories....614 276-4000
1900 Arlingate Ln Columbus (43228) ***(G-7403)***
Roxane Laboratories, Inc., Columbus *Also called Hikma Labs Inc* ***(G-6999)***
Roy Holtzapple John Johns....419 657-2460
18526 Williams Rd Wapakoneta (45895) ***(G-19350)***
Roy I Kaufman Inc....740 382-0643
1672 Marion Uppr Sndsk Rd Marion (43302) ***(G-12731)***
Roy L Bayes....614 274-6729
1593 Harrisburg Pike Columbus (43223) ***(G-7404)***
Royal Acme, Cleveland *Also called Ace Rubber Stamp & Off Sup Co* ***(G-4604)***
Royal Acme Corporation (PA)....216 241-1477
3110 Payne Ave Cleveland (44114) ***(G-6009)***
Royal Adhesives & Sealants LLC....440 708-1212
17340 Munn Rd Chagrin Falls (44023) ***(G-3073)***
Royal Appliance Manufacturing, Solon *Also called TTI Floor Care North Amer Inc* ***(G-17255)***
Royal Cabinet Design Co Inc....216 267-5330
15800 Commerce Park Dr Cleveland (44142) ***(G-6010)***
Royal Chemical Company Ltd....330 467-1300
1755 Entp Pkwy Ste 100 Twinsburg (44087) ***(G-18850)***
Royal Gateau....216 351-3553
4276 Pearl Rd Cleveland (44109) ***(G-6011)***
Royal Ice Cream Co....216 432-1144
6200 Euclid Ave Cleveland (44103) ***(G-6012)***
Royal Mfg....419 902-8222
2447 Tiffin Ave Findlay (45840) ***(G-9750)***
Royal Pad Products, Blue Ash *Also called Loroco Industries Inc* ***(G-1807)***
Royal Plastics Inc....440 352-1357
9410 Pineneedle Dr Mentor (44060) ***(G-13575)***
Royal Powder Corporation....216 898-0074
4800 Briar Rd Cleveland (44135) ***(G-6013)***
Royal Spa Columbus....614 529-8569
9022 Cotter St Lewis Center (43035) ***(G-11777)***
Royal Specialty Products Inc....513 841-1267
4114 Montgomery Rd Cincinnati (45212) ***(G-4284)***
Royal Tool and Machine LLC....419 836-7781
5740 Woodville Rd Northwood (43619) ***(G-15345)***
Royal Welding Inc....513 829-9353
5000 Factory Dr Fairfield (45014) ***(G-9560)***
Royal Wire Products Inc (PA)....440 237-8787
13450 York Delta Dr North Royalton (44133) ***(G-15297)***
Royalton Archtctral Fbrication....440 582-0400
13155 York Delta Dr North Royalton (44133) ***(G-15298)***
Royalton Food Service Eqp Co....440 237-0806
9981 York Theta Dr North Royalton (44133) ***(G-15299)***
Royalton Industries Inc....440 748-9900
12450 Eaton Commerce Pkwy Columbia Station (44028) ***(G-6446)***
Royalton Manufacturing Inc....440 237-2233
1169 Brittain Rd Akron (44305) ***(G-355)***
Royalton Recorder....440 237-2235
13737 State Rd North Royalton (44133) ***(G-15300)***
Royce Co....513 933-0344
2340 Lebanon Rd Lebanon (45036) ***(G-11691)***

Royer Technologies Inc 937 743-6114
00907 Willies Way Saint Marys (45885) ***(G-16698)***
Rozevink Engines LLC 419 789-1159
14316 State Route 281 Holgate (43527) ***(G-10913)***
Rozzi Company Inc (PA) 513 683-0620
118 Karl Brown Way Loveland (45140) ***(G-12228)***
Rozzi Company Inc 513 683-0620
6047 State Route 350 Martinsville (45146) ***(G-12767)***
RP Gatta Inc 330 562-2288
435 Gentry Dr Aurora (44202) ***(G-905)***
Rpa Electronic Distributors 937 223-7001
122 S Terry St Dayton (45403) ***(G-8486)***
Rpg Industries Inc 937 698-9801
3571 Ginghmsbg Frdrck Rd Tipp City (45371) ***(G-18131)***
RPI Color Service Inc 513 471-4040
1950 Radcliff Dr Cincinnati (45204) ***(G-4285)***
RPI Graphic Data Solutions, Cincinnati *Also called RPI Color Service Inc* ***(G-4285)***
RPM Carbide Die Inc 419 894-6426
202 E South St Arcadia (44804) ***(G-626)***
RPM Consumer Holding Company (HQ) 330 273-5090
2628 Pearl Rd Medina (44256) ***(G-13330)***
RPM Industries 440 268-8077
1444 Lowell St Elyria (44035) ***(G-9323)***
RPM International Inc (PA) 330 273-5090
2628 Pearl Rd Medina (44256) ***(G-13331)***
Rpmi Packaging Inc 513 398-4040
3899 S Us Route 42 Lebanon (45036) ***(G-11692)***
Rpp Containers, Cincinnati *Also called Dadco Inc* ***(G-3572)***
Rpp Containers, Cincinnati *Also called Dadco Inc* ***(G-3573)***
RPS, Solon *Also called Replacment Prts Spcialists Inc* ***(G-17221)***
RPS America Inc (PA) 937 231-9339
8808 Beckett Center Dr West Chester (45069) ***(G-19788)***
RR Donnelley, West Chester *Also called R R Donnelley & Sons Company* ***(G-19778)***
RR Donnelley & Sons Company 513 870-4040
8740 Global Way West Chester (45069) ***(G-19789)***
RR Donnelley & Sons Company 740 928-6110
190 Milliken Dr Hebron (43025) ***(G-10760)***
Rrysburg Sunoco, Waterville *Also called Franklin* ***(G-19495)***
Rs Pro Sales LLC 513 699-5329
1512 Eastern Ave Cincinnati (45202) ***(G-4286)***
Rsa Controls Inc 513 476-6277
6422 Fountains Blvd West Chester (45069) ***(G-19790)***
Rsb Spine LLC 216 241-2804
2530 Superior Ave E # 703 Cleveland (44114) ***(G-6014)***
Rsfi Office Furniture, Worthington *Also called Recycled Systems Furniture Inc* ***(G-20701)***
RSI Company (PA) 216 360-9800
24050 Commerce Park # 200 Beachwood (44122) ***(G-1277)***
Rsw Distributors LLC 502 587-8877
4700 Ashwood Dr Ste 200 Blue Ash (45241) ***(G-1841)***
Rsw Technologies LLC 419 662-8100
135 Dixie Hwy Rossford (43460) ***(G-16592)***
RTD Electronics Inc 330 487-0716
1632 Entp Pkwy Ste D Twinsburg (44087) ***(G-18851)***
Rti, Niles *Also called Rmi Titanium Company LLC* ***(G-15029)***
Rti, Niles *Also called Arconic Inc* ***(G-14998)***
Rti Alloys 330 652-9952
1000 Warren Ave Niles (44446) ***(G-15032)***
Rti Alloys Tpd, Canton *Also called Rmi Titanium Company LLC* ***(G-2806)***
Rti Finance Corp 330 652-9952
1000 Warren Ave Niles (44446) ***(G-15033)***
Rti Niles, Niles *Also called Rmi Titanium Company LLC* ***(G-15028)***
Rti Niles, Niles *Also called Rmi Titanium Company LLC* ***(G-15030)***
Rti Niles, Niles *Also called Rti Finance Corp* ***(G-15033)***
Rti Niles 330 455-4010
1000 Warren Ave Niles (44446) ***(G-15034)***
Rtprocess LLC 937 366-6215
311 Davids Dr Wilmington (45177) ***(G-20508)***
RTS Companies (us) Inc 440 275-3077
2900 Industrial Park Dr Austinburg (44010) ***(G-925)***
Rtsi LLC 440 542-3066
6161 Cochran Rd Ste G Solon (44139) ***(G-17226)***
RTZ Manufacturing Co 614 848-8366
6530 Huntley Rd Columbus (43229) ***(G-7405)***
Rub-R-Road Inc 330 678-7050
431 W Elm St Kent (44240) ***(G-11379)***
Rubber & Plastics News, Akron *Also called Crain Communications Inc* ***(G-125)***
Rubber Associates Inc 330 745-2186
1522 Turkeyfoot Lake Rd New Franklin (44203) ***(G-14698)***
Rubber City Machinery Corp 330 434-3500
1 Thousand Sweitzer Ave Akron (44311) ***(G-356)***
Rubber Seal Products, Dayton *Also called Teknol Inc* ***(G-8550)***
Rubber Triangle, Twinsburg *Also called Treadstone Company* ***(G-18865)***
Rubber World Magazine, Akron *Also called Lippincott & Peto Inc* ***(G-254)***
Rubber World Magazine Inc 330 864-2122
1741 Akron Peninsula Rd Akron (44313) ***(G-357)***
Rubber-Tech Inc 937 274-1114
5208 Wadsworth Rd Dayton (45414) ***(G-8487)***

Rubberduck 4x4 ....513 889-1735
1622 Smith Rd Hamilton (45013) ***(G-10601)***
Rubberite Corp 832 457-0654
1575 Frebis Ln Columbus (43206) ***(G-7406)***
Rubberite Cypress Sponge, Columbus *Also called Rubberite Corp* ***(G-7406)***
Rubbermaid, Kent *Also called Newell Brands Inc* ***(G-11358)***
Rubbermaid Incorporated 330 733-7771
3200 Gilchrist Rd Mogadore (44260) ***(G-14247)***
Rubberset Company 800 345-4939
101 W Prospect Ave Cleveland (44115) ***(G-6015)***
Rubbertec Industrial Pdts Co 740 657-3345
7580 Commerce Ct Lewis Center (43035) ***(G-11778)***
Ruber Polymer, Akron *Also called P C R Inc* ***(G-313)***
Rubex Inc 614 875-6343
3709 Grove City Rd Grove City (43123) ***(G-10463)***
Rubys Country Store 330 359-0406
2467 Us Route 62 Dundee (44624) ***(G-9026)***
Ruda Print & Graphics 419 331-7832
4129 Elida Rd Lima (45807) ***(G-11934)***
Rudd Equipment Company Inc 513 321-7833
11807 Enterprise Dr Cincinnati (45241) ***(G-4287)***
Rudolph Foods Company Inc (PA) 909 383-7463
6575 Bellefontaine Rd Lima (45804) ***(G-11935)***
Rudy's Strudel & Bakery, Cleveland *Also called Rudys Strudel Shop* ***(G-6016)***
Rudys Strudel Shop 440 886-4430
5580 Ridge Rd Cleveland (44129) ***(G-6016)***
Ruegg Mfg LLC 330 418-5617
13955 Elton St Sw Navarre (44662) ***(G-14587)***
Ruff Neon & Lighting Maint Inc 440 350-6267
295 W Prospect St Painesville (44077) ***(G-15782)***
Ruhe Sales Inc (PA) 419 943-3357
5450 State Route 109 Leipsic (45856) ***(G-11736)***
Rultract Inc 216 524-2990
5663 Brecksville Rd Cleveland (44131) ***(G-6017)***
Rumford Paper Company 937 242-9230
8540 Gander Creek Dr Miamisburg (45342) ***(G-13713)***
Rumpke Container Service, Cincinnati *Also called Rumpke Transportation Co LLC* ***(G-4289)***
Rumpke Transportation Co LLC (HQ) 513 851-0122
10795 Hughes Rd Cincinnati (45251) ***(G-4288)***
Rumpke Transportation Co LLC 513 242-4600
553 Vine St Cincinnati (45202) ***(G-4289)***
Runkles Sawmill LLC 937 663-0115
2534 Dialton Rd Saint Paris (43072) ***(G-16711)***
Rupcol Inc 419 924-5215
509 Parkway St West Unity (43570) ***(G-19974)***
Ruple Trucking, Willoughby Hills *Also called Chagrin Vly Stl Erectors Inc* ***(G-20468)***
Rupp Construction Inc 330 855-2781
18228 Fulton Rd Marshallville (44645) ***(G-12755)***
Rural Farm Distributors Co 419 747-6807
2690 Bowman Street Rd Mansfield (44903) ***(G-12508)***
Rural Iron Works LLC 419 647-4617
510 N Saint Marys Rd Spencerville (45887) ***(G-17313)***
Rural Products Inc 419 298-2677
6266 Us Highway 6 Edgerton (43517) ***(G-9179)***
Rural Urban Record Inc 440 236-8982
24487 Squire Rd Columbia Station (44028) ***(G-6447)***
Rus Power Storage LLC 937 999-8121
3210 S Main St Middletown (45044) ***(G-13950)***
Ruscilli Real Estate Services 614 923-6400
5100 Prkcnter Ave Ste 100 Dublin (43017) ***(G-8976)***
Ruscoe Company (PA) 330 253-8148
485 Kenmore Blvd Akron (44301) ***(G-358)***
Ruscoe Company 330 253-8148
219 E Miller Ave Akron (44301) ***(G-359)***
Rush Graphix Ltd 419 448-7874
30 Riverside Dr Tiffin (44883) ***(G-18079)***
Rush Welding & Machine Inc 740 354-7874
1657 12th St Portsmouth (45662) ***(G-16297)***
Rush, R L Tool & Pattern, Bucyrus *Also called R L Rush Tool & Pattern Inc* ***(G-2342)***
Russel Hunt Total Land Care, Steubenville *Also called Russell Hunt* ***(G-17550)***
Russell Hunt 740 264-1196
175 Detmar Rd Steubenville (43953) ***(G-17550)***
Russell L Garber (PA) 937 548-6224
4891 Clark Station Rd Greenville (45331) ***(G-10394)***
Russell Products Co Inc 330 535-3391
1066 Home Ave Akron (44310) ***(G-360)***
Russell Products Co Inc 330 434-9163
1066 Home Ave Akron (44310) ***(G-361)***
Russell Products Co Inc 216 267-0880
275 N Forge St Ste 2 Akron (44304) ***(G-362)***
Russell Standard Corporation 330 733-9400
990 Hazel St Akron (44305) ***(G-363)***
Russell T Bundy Associates Inc 740 965-3008
601 W Cherry St Sunbury (43074) ***(G-17900)***
Russell T Bundy Associates Inc 419 526-4454
1711 N Main St Mansfield (44903) ***(G-12509)***
Russments Inc 513 602-5035
3714 Church St Cincinnati (45244) ***(G-4290)***

A L P H A B E T I C

Rust Belt Brewing LLC — ALPHABETIC SECTION

Rust Belt Brewing LLC 330 423-3818
  1744 Overlook Ave Youngstown (44509) *(G-21022)*
Ruthie Ann Inc 800 231-3567
  313 New Paris Ave New Paris (45347) *(G-14755)*
Ruthman Pump and Engineering (PA) 513 559-1901
  1212 Streng St Cincinnati (45223) *(G-4291)*
Ruthman Pump and Engineering 937 783-2411
  459 E Fancy St Blanchester (45107) *(G-1706)*
Rutland Plastic Tech Inc 614 846-3055
  777 Dearborn Park Ln N Columbus (43085) *(G-7407)*
Rutland Township 740 742-2805
  33325 Jessie Creek Rd Bidwell (45614) *(G-1669)*
Rutobo Inc 614 236-2948
  4279 E Main St Columbus (43213) *(G-7408)*
Rv Xpress Inc 937 418-0127
  501 East St Piqua (45356) *(G-16161)*
RW Beckett Corporation (PA) 440 327-1060
  38251 Center Ridge Rd North Ridgeville (44039) *(G-15252)*
Rx Frames N Lenses Ltd 513 557-2970
  4270 Boomer Rd Cincinnati (45247) *(G-4292)*
Rxpert Consultants LLC 614 579-9384
  4719 Reed Rd Ste 250 Columbus (43220) *(G-7409)*
Rxscan, Lewis Center Also called Retail Management Products *(G-11776)*
Ryan Development Corp 937 587-2266
  1 Ryan Rd Peebles (45660) *(G-15881)*
Ryans Newark Leader Ex Prtg 740 522-2149
  56 Westgate Dr Newark (43055) *(G-14916)*
Ryanworks Inc 937 438-1282
  175 E Alex Bell Rd # 264 Dayton (45459) *(G-8488)*
Ryder Engraving Inc 740 927-7193
  1029 Hazelton Etna Rd Sw Pataskala (43062) *(G-15842)*
Ryder-Heil Bronze Inc 419 562-2841
  126 E Irving St Bucyrus (44820) *(G-2343)*
Rykon Plating Inc 440 933-3273
  555 Miller Rd Avon Lake (44012) *(G-1006)*
Rykrisp Llc 843 338-0750
  4342 Centennial Dr Apt 33 Cincinnati (45227) *(G-4293)*
Ryman Grinders Inc 330 652-5080
  704 Warren Ave Niles (44446) *(G-15035)*
S & A Industries Corporation (HQ) 330 733-6040
  571 Kennedy Rd Ste R Akron (44305) *(G-364)*
S & A Precision Bearing Inc (PA) 440 930-7600
  1050 Jaycox Rd Avon (44011) *(G-965)*
S & B Metal Products Inc (PA) 330 487-5790
  2060 Case Pkwy Twinsburg (44087) *(G-18852)*
S & D Architectural Metals 440 582-2560
  12955 York Delta Dr North Royalton (44133) *(G-15301)*
S & G Manufacturing Group LLC (PA) 614 529-0100
  4830 Northwest Pkwy Hilliard (43026) *(G-10859)*
S & H Automation & Eqp Co 419 636-0020
  815 Commerce Dr Bryan (43506) *(G-2306)*
S & H Industries Inc 216 831-0550
  5200 Richmond Rd Cleveland (44146) *(G-6018)*
S & H Industries Inc 216 831-0550
  14577 Lorain Ave Cleveland (44111) *(G-6019)*
S & H Industries Inc (PA) 216 831-0550
  5200 Richmond Rd Bedford (44146) *(G-1442)*
S & J Lumber Co 740 245-5804
  3667 Garners Ford Rd Thurman (45685) *(G-18038)*
S & J Precision Inc 937 296-0068
  2015 Dryden Rd Moraine (45439) *(G-14391)*
S & K Metal Polsg & Buffing 513 732-6662
  4194 Taylor Rd Batavia (45103) *(G-1182)*
S & M Products 419 272-2054
  County Rd 5 I Blakeslee (43505) *(G-1697)*
S & N Engineering and Supply, Cleveland Also called S & N Engineering Svcs Corp *(G-6020)*
S & N Engineering Svcs Corp 216 433-1700
  2901 Henninger Rd Cleveland (44109) *(G-6020)*
S & R Egg, Rossburg Also called Fort Recovery Equity Exchange *(G-16582)*
S & R Sheet Metal 937 865-9236
  320 Gargrave Rd Dayton (45449) *(G-8489)*
S & S Aggregates Inc (HQ) 740 453-0721
  3570 S River Rd Zanesville (43701) *(G-21175)*
S & S Aggregates Inc 419 938-5604
  4540 State Route 39 Perrysville (44864) *(G-16031)*
S & S Machining Ltd 419 524-9525
  76 Atenway St Mansfield (44902) *(G-12510)*
S & S Pallets 513 967-7432
  1536 Pointe Dr Milford (45150) *(G-14038)*
S & S Panel 330 412-6735
  3314 S Kohler Rd Orrville (44667) *(G-15617)*
S & S Printing Service Inc 937 228-9411
  505 Hunter Ave Dayton (45404) *(G-8490)*
S & S Sign Co 614 837-1511
  10601 Lithopolis Rd Nw Canal Winchester (43110) *(G-2511)*
S & S Spring Shop 800 619-4652
  1755 Mount Perry Rd Mount Perry (43760) *(G-14458)*
S & S Wldg Fabg Machining Inc 330 392-7878
  2587 Miller Graber Rd Newton Falls (44444) *(G-14993)*

S & W Custom Tops Inc 330 788-2525
  4300 Simon Rd Ste 2 Youngstown (44512) *(G-21023)*
S A E Manufacturing 440 322-9026
  7880 W River Rd S Elyria (44035) *(G-9324)*
S A Langmack Company 216 541-0500
  13400 Glenside Rd Cleveland (44110) *(G-6021)*
S A S Rubber, Painesville Also called Yokohama Tire Corporation *(G-15803)*
S and K Painting 330 505-1910
  1346 Clark St Niles (44446) *(G-15036)*
S and S Tool Inc 440 593-4000
  576 Blair St Conneaut (44030) *(G-7658)*
S Beckman Print & G 614 864-2232
  376 Morrison Rd Ste D Columbus (43213) *(G-7410)*
S C Fastening Systems, Macedonia Also called SC Fire Protection Ltd *(G-12324)*
S C Industries Inc 216 732-9000
  24460 Lakeland Blvd Euclid (44132) *(G-9441)*
S C Johnson & Son Inc 513 665-3600
  36 E 7th St Ste 2450 Cincinnati (45202) *(G-4294)*
S C Machine 419 752-6961
  116 Us Highway 224 W Greenwich (44837) *(G-10408)*
S E Anning Company 513 702-4417
  822 Delta Ave Ste 2 Cincinnati (45226) *(G-4295)*
S E Johnson Companies Inc (HQ) 419 893-8731
  1360 Ford St Maumee (43537) *(G-13142)*
S F C Ltd LLC 419 255-1283
  110 E Woodruff Ave Toledo (43604) *(G-18509)*
S F Mock & Associates LLC 937 438-0196
  105 Westpark Rd Dayton (45459) *(G-8491)*
S F S Stadler Inc 330 239-7100
  5201 Portside Dr Medina (44256) *(G-13332)*
S I Distributing Inc 419 647-4909
  13540 Spencerville Rd Spencerville (45887) *(G-17314)*
S I T Strings Co Inc 330 434-8010
  2493 Romig Rd Akron (44320) *(G-365)*
S J Cox Tool Inc 740 756-1100
  3800 Old Columbus Rd Nw Carroll (43112) *(G-2909)*
S J K Metalworking Inc 440 564-7877
  14940 Cross Creek Pkwy Newbury (44065) *(G-14964)*
S J Roth Enterprises Inc 513 242-8400
  900 Kieley Pl Cincinnati (45217) *(G-4296)*
S J T Enterprises Inc 440 617-1100
  28045 Ranney Pkwy Ste B Westlake (44145) *(G-20153)*
S K Industries, Newbury Also called S J K Metalworking Inc *(G-14964)*
S K M L Inc 330 220-7565
  580 Liverpool Dr Valley City (44280) *(G-19059)*
S K S Manufacturing Corp 330 669-9133
  212 E Eberly St Smithville (44677) *(G-17093)*
S L C Software Services 513 922-4303
  1958 Anderson Ferry Rd Cincinnati (45238) *(G-4297)*
S L M Inc 216 651-0666
  3148 W 32nd St Ste 3 Cleveland (44109) *(G-6022)*
S M C, Upper Sandusky Also called Schmidt Machine Company *(G-18972)*
S O I T A, Dayton Also called Southwestern Ohio Instruction *(G-8513)*
S O S Graphics & Printing Inc 614 846-8229
  445 E Wilson Bridge Rd Worthington (43085) *(G-20702)*
S P I, Xenia Also called Spi Inc *(G-20790)*
S P Z Machine Co 330 848-3286
  2871 Newpark Dr Barberton (44203) *(G-1104)*
S R Door Inc (PA) 740 927-3558
  1120 O Neill Dr Hebron (43025) *(G-10761)*
S R P M Inc 440 248-8440
  30300 Bruce Industrial Pk Cleveland (44139) *(G-6023)*
S R Technologies LLC (PA) 330 523-7184
  2200 N Clvland Mssllon Rd Akron (44333) *(G-366)*
S T A, Oak Harbor Also called Esperia Holdings LLC *(G-15444)*
S T C, Canton Also called Stark Truss Company Inc *(G-2824)*
S T Custom Signs 513 733-4227
  9493 Reading Rd Cincinnati (45215) *(G-4298)*
S T Tool & Design Inc 440 357-1250
  9452 Mercantile Dr Mentor (44060) *(G-13576)*
S Toys Holdings LLC 330 656-0440
  10010 Aurora Hudson Rd Streetsboro (44241) *(G-17693)*
S Wj Llcred 330 938-6173
  1100 N Johnson Rd Sebring (44672) *(G-16892)*
S&G Distribution, Hilliard Also called S & G Manufacturing Group LLC *(G-10859)*
S&R Lumber LLC 740 352-6135
  207 Sugar Run Rd Piketon (45661) *(G-16079)*
S&S Manufactruing, Lancaster Also called Vic Mar Manufacturing Inc *(G-11617)*
S&S Sign Service 614 279-9722
  485 Ternstedt Ln Columbus (43228) *(G-7411)*
S&T Automotive America LLC 614 782-9041
  3900 Gantz Rd Grove City (43123) *(G-10464)*
S&V Industries Inc (PA) 330 666-1986
  5054 Paramount Dr Medina (44256) *(G-13333)*
S-K Mold & Tool Company (PA) 937 339-0299
  955 N 3rd St Tipp City (45371) *(G-18132)*
S-K Mold & Tool Company 937 339-0299
  2120 Corporate Dr Troy (45373) *(G-18701)*

S-P Company Inc (PA)....330 482-0200
400 W Railroad St Ste 1 Columbiana (44408) *(G-6479)*
S-Tek Inc (PA)....440 439-8232
26046 Broadway Ave Bedford (44146) *(G-1443)*
S. C. Manufacturing, Akron *Also called Hawk Manufacturing LLC (G-200)*
S. C. Manufacturing, Akron *Also called Hawk Manufacturing LLC (G-201)*
S. C. Manufacturing, Akron *Also called Hawk Manufacturing LLC (G-202)*
S.E.S., Alliance *Also called Steel Eqp Specialists Inc (G-502)*
Sa-Mor Signs....937 441-4950
185 Kindle St Wapakoneta (45895) *(G-19351)*
Sabatino Cabinet, Salem *Also called Joseph Sabatino (G-16751)*
Sabbagh Tool and Equipment Co, Akron *Also called PC Systems (G-315)*
Sabco Industries Inc....419 531-5347
5242 Angola Rd Ste 150 Toledo (43615) *(G-18510)*
Sabre Energy Corporation....740 685-8266
175 Main St Nw Lore City (43755) *(G-12140)*
Sabre Publishing....440 243-4300
398 W Bagley Rd Ste 210 Berea (44017) *(G-1624)*
Sacks Bruce & Associates....419 537-0623
4959 Damascus Dr Ottawa Hills (43615) *(G-15677)*
Saco Aei Polymers Inc....330 995-1600
1395 Danner Dr Aurora (44202) *(G-906)*
Saco Lowell Parts LLC....330 794-1535
1395 Triplett Blvd Akron (44306) *(G-367)*
Saehwa IMC Na Inc....419 752-4511
2200 Massillon Rd Akron (44312) *(G-368)*
Saehwa IMC Na Inc (PA)....330 645-6653
2200 Massillon Rd Akron (44312) *(G-369)*
Saf-Holland Inc....513 874-7888
246 Circle Freeway Dr West Chester (45246) *(G-19896)*
Safar Machine Company....330 644-0155
905 Brown St Akron (44311) *(G-370)*
Safc Cleveland, Cleveland *Also called Research Organics LLC (G-5978)*
Safe 4 People Inc....419 797-4087
4661 E Woodland Dr Port Clinton (43452) *(G-16257)*
Safe Air Valve Co., Mentor *Also called Aj Fluid Power Sales & Sup Inc (G-13380)*
Safe Auto Systems LLC....216 661-1166
5401 Brookpark Rd Carroll (43112) *(G-2910)*
Safe Grain Max Tronix, Wapakoneta *Also called Safe-Grain Inc (G-19352)*
Safe Rx Pharmacies Inc....740 377-4162
503 4th St E South Point (45680) *(G-17294)*
Safe Systems Inc....216 661-1166
5401 Brookpark Rd Cleveland (44129) *(G-6024)*
Safe-Grain Inc (PA)....513 398-2500
417 Wards Corner Rd Ste B Loveland (45140) *(G-12229)*
Safe-Grain Inc....513 398-2500
902 N Dixie Hwy Wapakoneta (45895) *(G-19352)*
Safecor Health LLC (PA)....781 933-8780
4060 Business Park Dr B Columbus (43204) *(G-7412)*
Safeguard Technology Inc....330 995-5200
1460 Miller Pkwy Streetsboro (44241) *(G-17694)*
Safelite Autoglass, Columbus *Also called Safelite Group Inc (G-7413)*
Safelite Group Inc (HQ)....614 210-9000
7400 Safelite Way Columbus (43235) *(G-7413)*
Safety Sign Company....440 238-7722
19511 Progress Dr Ste 4 Strongsville (44149) *(G-17784)*
Safeway Contact Lens Inc....330 536-6469
1212 Bedford Rd Lowellville (44436) *(G-12256)*
Safeway Packaging Inc (PA)....419 629-3200
300 White Mountain Dr New Bremen (45869) *(G-14660)*
Safeway Safety Step LLC....513 942-7837
5242 Rialto Rd West Chester (45069) *(G-19791)*
Safewhite Inc....614 340-1450
1275 Kinnear Rd Ste 237 Columbus (43212) *(G-7414)*
Safran USA Incorporated....513 247-7000
300 E Business Way Sharonville (45241) *(G-16958)*
Saginomiya America Inc....614 766-7390
655 Metro Pl S Ste 700 Dublin (43017) *(G-8977)*
Sagitta Inc....440 570-5393
1048 Literary Rd Cleveland (44113) *(G-6025)*
Saia-Burgess Lcc....937 898-3621
801 Scholz Dr Vandalia (45377) *(G-19144)*
Sailors Tailor Inc....937 862-7781
1480 Spg Vly Paintrs Rd Spring Valley (45370) *(G-17318)*
Saint Croix Ltd....330 666-1544
3371 W Bath Rd Akron (44333) *(G-371)*
Saint Ctherines Metalworks Inc (PA)....216 409-0576
1985 W 68th St Cleveland (44102) *(G-6026)*
Saint Paris Tool and Grinding....937 526-9800
2270 Russia Versailles Rd Russia (45363) *(G-16613)*
Saint-Gobain Ceramics Plas Inc....330 673-5860
3840 Fishcreek Rd Stow (44224) *(G-17624)*
Saint-Gobain Ceramics Plas Inc....440 834-5600
17900 Great Lakes Pkwy Hiram (44234) *(G-10911)*
Saint-Gobain Hycomp LLC....440 234-2002
17960 Englewood Dr Cleveland (44130) *(G-6027)*
Saint-Gobain Norpro, Stow *Also called Saint-Gobain Ceramics Plas Inc (G-17624)*
Saint-Gobain Norpro (HQ)....330 673-5860
3840 Fishcreek Rd Stow (44224) *(G-17625)*
Saint-Gobain Prfmce Plas Corp....330 296-9948
335 N Diamond St Ravenna (44266) *(G-16400)*
Saint-Gobain Prfmce Plas Corp (HQ)....440 836-6900
31500 Solon Rd Solon (44139) *(G-17227)*
Saint-Gobain Prfmce Plas Corp....330 798-6981
2664 Gilchrist Rd Akron (44305) *(G-372)*
Saint-Gobain Prfmce Plas Corp....614 889-2220
6250 Shier Rings Rd Dublin (43016) *(G-8978)*
Saircorp Ltd....330 669-9099
6020 N Honeytown Rd Smithville (44677) *(G-17094)*
Sajar Plastics, Inc., Middlefield *Also called Universal Plastics - Sajar (G-13863)*
Sakamura USA Inc....740 223-7777
970 Kellogg Pkwy Marion (43302) *(G-12732)*
Sakas Incorporated....740 862-4114
312 Bltmore Smerset Rd Ne Baltimore (43105) *(G-1042)*
Sakrete Inc (PA)....513 242-3644
5155 Fischer Ave Cincinnati (45217) *(G-4299)*
Salco Machine Inc....330 456-8281
3822 Victory Ave Louisville (44641) *(G-12165)*
Salem Industries, Columbus *Also called Salem Manufacturing and Sales (G-7415)*
Salem Manufacturing and Sales....614 572-4242
171 N Hamilton Rd Columbus (43213) *(G-7415)*
Salem Mill & Cabinet Co....330 337-9568
1455 Quaker Cir Salem (44460) *(G-16771)*
Salem Welding & Supply Company....330 332-4517
475 Prospect St Salem (44460) *(G-16772)*
Salem-Republic Rubber Company....877 425-5079
475 W California Ave Sebring (44672) *(G-16893)*
Sales Office Rob Jordan Vp Sls, Hilliard *Also called Textiles Inc (G-10869)*
Salient Systems Inc....614 792-5800
4393 Tuller Rd Ste K Dublin (43017) *(G-8979)*
Salindia LLC....614 501-4799
2756 Eastland Mall Columbus (43232) *(G-7416)*
Salineville Office, Salineville *Also called M3 Midstream LLC (G-16789)*
Salley Tool & Die Co....937 258-3333
3180 Plainfield Rd Ste 1 Dayton (45432) *(G-7989)*
Sally Beauty Supply LLC....330 823-7476
2636 W State St Alliance (44601) *(G-497)*
Salon Styling Concepts Ltd....216 539-0437
20900 Libby Rd Maple Heights (44137) *(G-12579)*
Salsbury Industries Inc....614 409-1600
2300 Rickenbacker Pkwy Columbus (43217) *(G-7417)*
Salt Creek Lumber Company Inc....330 695-3500
11657 Salt Creek Rd Fredericksburg (44627) *(G-9959)*
Saltbox Illustrations....937 319-6434
120 Kenneth Hamilton Way Yellow Springs (45387) *(G-20815)*
Saltcreek Industries....330 674-2816
420 W Jones St Millersburg (44654) *(G-14125)*
Saltillo Corporation (PA)....330 674-6722
2143 Township Road 112 Millersburg (44654) *(G-14126)*
Sam Abdallah....330 532-3900
777 Hamnondsville Rd Hammondsville (43930) *(G-10623)*
Sam Americas Inc....330 628-1118
3555 Gilchrist Rd Mogadore (44260) *(G-14248)*
Sam Dong Ohio Inc....740 363-1985
801 Pittsburgh Dr Delaware (43015) *(G-8721)*
Samco Technologies Inc....216 641-5288
1600 Harvard Ave Newburgh Heights (44105) *(G-14944)*
Sammartino Welding & Auto Sls....330 782-6086
155 W Indianola Ave Youngstown (44507) *(G-21024)*
Sammy S Auto Detail....614 263-2728
3514 Cleveland Ave Columbus (43224) *(G-7418)*
Sample Machining Inc....937 258-3338
220 N Jersey St Dayton (45403) *(G-8492)*
Sams Graphic Industries....330 821-4710
611 Homeworth Rd Alliance (44601) *(G-498)*
Samsco Corp....216 400-8207
837 E 79th St Cleveland (44103) *(G-6028)*
Samsel Rope & Marine Supply Co (PA)....216 241-0333
1285 Old River Rd Uppr Cleveland (44113) *(G-6029)*
Samsel Supply Company, Cleveland *Also called Samsel Rope & Marine Supply Co (G-6029)*
Samson....614 504-8038
772 N High St Ste 101 Columbus (43215) *(G-7419)*
Samuel Clark (PA)....614 855-2263
5037 Babbitt Rd New Albany (43054) *(G-14636)*
Samuel Steel Pickling Company (PA)....330 963-3777
1400 Enterprise Pkwy Twinsburg (44087) *(G-18853)*
Samuel Strapping Systems Inc....740 522-2500
1455 James Pkwy Heath (43056) *(G-10731)*
Samuels Products Inc....513 891-4456
9851 Redhill Dr Blue Ash (45242) *(G-1842)*
San Marco Indiana, Toledo *Also called San Marcos Supermarket LLC (G-18511)*
San Marcos Supermarket LLC....419 469-8963
235 Broadway St Toledo (43604) *(G-18511)*
San Pallet LLC....937 271-5308
1860 State Route 718 Troy (45373) *(G-18702)*
San-Fab Conveyor and Automtn, Sandusky *Also called Sandusky Fabricating & Sls Inc (G-16842)*
Sancap Abrasives, Alliance *Also called Lexington Abrasives Inc (G-482)*

ALPHABETIC

Sancast Inc....740 622-8660
535 Clow Ln Coshocton (43812) ***(G-7750)***
Sanctuary Software Studio Inc....330 666-9690
3560 W Market St Ste 100 Fairlawn (44333) ***(G-9616)***
Sand Hollow Winery....740 323-3959
12558 Sand Hollow Rd Heath (43056) ***(G-10732)***
Sanders Fredrick Excvtg Co Inc....330 297-7980
5858 State Route 14 Ravenna (44266) ***(G-16401)***
Sandra Weddington....740 417-4286
1400 Stratford Rd Delaware (43015) ***(G-8722)***
Sandridge Food Corporation (PA)....330 725-2348
133 Commerce Dr Medina (44256) ***(G-13334)***
Sandridge Food Corporation....330 725-8883
133 Commerce Dr Medina (44256) ***(G-13335)***
Sandridge Gourmet Salads, Medina *Also called Sandridge Food Corporation* ***(G-13334)***
Sandridge Gourmet Salads, Medina *Also called Sandridge Food Corporation* ***(G-13335)***
Sands Hill Coal Hauling Co Inc (PA)....740 384-4211
38701 State Route 160 Hamden (45634) ***(G-10524)***
Sands Hill Mining LLC....740 384-4211
38701 State Route 160 Hamden (45634) ***(G-10525)***
Sandusky Dock Corporation....419 626-1214
2705 W Monroe St Sandusky (44870) ***(G-16841)***
Sandusky Fabricating & Sls Inc (PA)....419 626-4465
2000 Superior St Sandusky (44870) ***(G-16842)***
Sandusky International Inc....419 626-5340
615 W Market St Sandusky (44870) ***(G-16843)***
Sandusky Machine & Tool Inc....419 626-8359
2223 Tiffin Ave Sandusky (44870) ***(G-16844)***
Sandusky Newspaper Group, Sandusky *Also called Sandusky Newspapers Inc* ***(G-16845)***
Sandusky Newspapers Inc (PA)....419 625-5500
314 W Market St Sandusky (44870) ***(G-16845)***
Sandusky Packaging Corporation....419 626-8520
2016 George St Sandusky (44870) ***(G-16846)***
Sandvik Inc....614 438-6579
6325 Huntley Rd Columbus (43229) ***(G-7420)***
Sandvik Hyperion, Columbus *Also called Sandvik Inc* ***(G-7420)***
Sandy Creek Mining Co Inc....419 435-5891
522 S Poplar St Fostoria (44830) ***(G-9857)***
Sandy Smittcamp....937 372-1687
402 W Church St Xenia (45385) ***(G-20788)***
Sanese Services Inc....330 494-5900
2590 Elm Rd Ne Warren (44483) ***(G-19441)***
Sanese Vending Company, Warren *Also called Sanese Services Inc* ***(G-19441)***
Sangraf International Inc....216 543-3288
159 Crocker Park Blvd # 100 Westlake (44145) ***(G-20154)***
Sanoh America Inc (HQ)....419 425-2600
1849 Industrial Dr Findlay (45840) ***(G-9751)***
Sanoh America Inc....740 392-9200
7905 Industrial Park Dr Mount Vernon (43050) ***(G-14505)***
Sanscan Inc....330 332-9365
157 N Ellsworth Ave Salem (44460) ***(G-16773)***
Sansei Showa Co Ltd....440 248-4440
31000 Bainbridge Rd Cleveland (44139) ***(G-6030)***
Sant Sand & Gravel Co....740 397-0000
14220 Parrott Ext Mount Vernon (43050) ***(G-14506)***
Santmyer Coml Fling Netwrk LLC....330 262-2334
2829 Cleveland Rd Wooster (44691) ***(G-20647)***
Santmyer Oil Co of Ashland (HQ)....330 262-6501
1055 W Old Lincoln Way Wooster (44691) ***(G-20648)***
Santmyer Oil Co of Ashland....419 289-8815
1011 Jacobson Ave Ashland (44805) ***(G-746)***
Santos Industrial Ltd (PA)....937 299-7333
3034 Dryden Rd Moraine (45439) ***(G-14392)***
Santos Industrial Ltd....937 299-7333
2960 Springboro W Moraine (45439) ***(G-14393)***
Santrol, Chardon *Also called Technisand Inc* ***(G-3138)***
Sara Hudson....850 890-1455
1632 Wayne Ave Dayton (45410) ***(G-8493)***
Sara Lee Foods....513 204-4941
4680 Parkway Dr Ste 305 Mason (45040) ***(G-12935)***
Sara Wood Pharmaceuticals LLC....513 833-5502
4518 Margaret Ct Mason (45040) ***(G-12936)***
Saras Little Cupcakes....419 305-7914
321 Sturgeon St Saint Marys (45885) ***(G-16699)***
Sarasota Quality Products....440 899-9820
27330 Center Ridge Rd Westlake (44145) ***(G-20155)***
Sarcokinetics LLC....414 477-9585
11000 Cedar Ave Ste 265 Cleveland (44106) ***(G-6031)***
Sardinia Concrete Company (PA)....513 248-0090
911 Us Route 50 Milford (45150) ***(G-14039)***
Sardinia Ready Mix Inc (PA)....937 446-2523
9 Oakdale Ave Sardinia (45171) ***(G-16871)***
Sardinia Ready Mix Inc....937 446-2523
9 Oakdale Ave Sardinia (45171) ***(G-16872)***
Sare Plastics, Alliance *Also called Stuchell Products LLC* ***(G-503)***
Sarica Manufacturing Company....937 484-4030
240 W Twain Ave Urbana (43078) ***(G-19011)***
Sark Technologies LLC....216 932-3171
2270 Tudor Dr Cleveland (44106) ***(G-6032)***
Sarka Bros Machining Inc....419 532-2393
607 Ottawa St Kalida (45853) ***(G-11281)***
Sarka Conveyor, Tiffin *Also called Sarka Shtmtl & Fabrication Inc* ***(G-18080)***
Sarka Shtmtl & Fabrication Inc....419 447-4377
70 Clinton Ave Tiffin (44883) ***(G-18080)***
Sarver Industries LLC....419 455-5509
178 N Sandusky St Tiffin (44883) ***(G-18081)***
Sas Automation LLC....937 372-5255
1200 S Patton St Xenia (45385) ***(G-20789)***
Sash Foam Works Inc....419 522-4074
555 Park Ave E Mansfield (44905) ***(G-12511)***
Sasha Electronics Inc....419 662-8100
135 Dixie Hwy Rossford (43460) ***(G-16593)***
Sat Welding LLC....614 747-2641
308 N Burgess Ave Columbus (43204) ***(G-7421)***
Satco Inc....330 630-8866
59 Industry St Tallmadge (44278) ***(G-18002)***
Satellite, Crestline *Also called PPG Industries Inc* ***(G-7799)***
Satellite Gear Inc....216 514-8668
130 Idlewood Ln Aurora (44202) ***(G-907)***
Satelytics Inc....419 419-5380
1510 N Westwood Ave # 2070 Toledo (43606) ***(G-18512)***
Sattler Companies Inc....330 239-2552
1455 Wolf Creek Trl Wadsworth (44281) ***(G-19276)***
Sattler Machine Products, Inc., Wadsworth *Also called Sattler Companies Inc* ***(G-19276)***
Saturday Knight Ltd (PA)....513 641-1400
4330 Winton Rd Cincinnati (45232) ***(G-4300)***
Saturn Press Inc....440 232-3344
177 Northfield Rd Bedford (44146) ***(G-1444)***
Sauder Machine Ltd....419 896-3722
3071 State Route 603 Plymouth (44865) ***(G-16234)***
Sauder Manufacturing Co (HQ)....419 445-7670
930 W Barre Rd Archbold (43502) ***(G-666)***
Sauder Manufacturing Co....419 682-3061
201 Horton St Stryker (43557) ***(G-17833)***
Sauder Wdwkg Co Welfare Tr....419 446-2711
502 Middle St Archbold (43502) ***(G-667)***
Sauder Woodworking Co (PA)....419 446-2711
502 Middle St Archbold (43502) ***(G-668)***
Sauder Woodworking Co....419 446-2711
330 N Clydes Way Archbold (43502) ***(G-669)***
Sauerwein Welding....513 563-2979
605 Wayne Park Dr Cincinnati (45215) ***(G-4301)***
Saunders Trucking Lcc....419 210-0551
13 Boyd St Fredericktown (43019) ***(G-9976)***
Sausage Shoppe....216 351-5213
1728 S Carpenter Rd Brunswick (44212) ***(G-2237)***
Sausser Steel Company Inc....419 422-9632
230 Crystal Ave Findlay (45840) ***(G-9752)***
Sautter Bros Machine & Fabg, Galion *Also called Sautter Brothers* ***(G-10152)***
Sautter Brothers....419 468-7443
6443 Brandt Rd Galion (44833) ***(G-10152)***
Savanna Tool and Manufacturing....440 327-8330
34395 Mills Rd North Ridgeville (44039) ***(G-15253)***
Savare Specialty Adhesives LLC....614 255-2648
1201 S Houk Rd Delaware (43015) ***(G-8723)***
Save Edge USA, Xenia *Also called File Sharpening Company Inc* ***(G-20772)***
Savko Plastic Pipe & Fittings....614 885-8420
683 E Lincoln Ave Columbus (43229) ***(G-7422)***
Savor Seasonings LLC....513 732-2333
4292 Armstrong Blvd Batavia (45103) ***(G-1183)***
Savory Foods Inc....740 354-6655
2240 6th St Portsmouth (45662) ***(G-16298)***
Sawbrook Steel Castings Co (PA)....513 554-1700
425 Shepherd Ave Cincinnati (45215) ***(G-4302)***
Sawdust....740 862-0612
4799 Refugee Rd Nw Baltimore (43105) ***(G-1043)***
Sawmill Crossing....614 766-1685
6700 Allister Way Columbus (43235) ***(G-7423)***
Sawmill Eye Associates Inc....440 724-0396
8666 Scenicview Dr Broadview Heights (44147) ***(G-2100)***
Sawmill Eye Associates Inc....614 734-2685
6500 Sawmill Rd Columbus (43235) ***(G-7424)***
Sawmill Marathon, Columbus *Also called Marathon At Sawmill* ***(G-7149)***
Sawmill Road Management Co LLC (PA)....937 342-9071
1990 Kingsgate Rd Ste A Springfield (45502) ***(G-17490)***
Sawmill Station....614 434-6147
3062 Sawdust Ln Dublin (43017) ***(G-8980)***
Sawyer Crystal Systems, Willoughby *Also called Sawyer Technical Materials LLC* ***(G-20424)***
Sawyer Research Product....440 951-8770
35400 Lakeland Blvd Eastlake (44095) ***(G-9129)***
Sawyer Technical Materials LLC (HQ)....440 951-8770
35400 Lakeland Blvd Willoughby (44095) ***(G-20424)***
Saxon Jewelers, Cleveland *Also called M B Saxon Co Inc* ***(G-5592)***
Saxon Products Inc....419 241-6771
2283 Fulton St Toledo (43620) ***(G-18513)***
Say Dumpsters....937 578-3744
22665 Drby Pottersburg Rd Marysville (43040) ***(G-12808)***

ALPHABETIC SECTION

Say Security Group USA LLC (PA) 419 634-0004
   520 E Montford Ave Ada (45810) *(G-8)*
Saylor Products Corporation 419 832-2125
   17484 Saylor Ln Grand Rapids (43522) *(G-10320)*
SBC, Columbus Also called Ameritech Publishing Inc *(G-6591)*
SBC, Uniontown Also called Ameritech Publishing Inc *(G-18909)*
SC Campana Inc 440 390-8854
   48201 Rice Rd Amherst (44001) *(G-573)*
SC Fire Protection Ltd 330 468-3300
   8531 Freeway Dr Macedonia (44056) *(G-12324)*
SC Solutions Inc 614 317-7119
   4119 Ashgrove Dr Grove City (43123) *(G-10465)*
Scadatech LLC 614 552-7726
   7821 Taylor Rd Sw Ste C Reynoldsburg (43068) *(G-16452)*
Scallywag Tag 513 922-4999
   5055 Glencrossing Way Cincinnati (45238) *(G-4303)*
Scanacon Incorporated 330 877-7600
   950 Wales Dr Hartville (44632) *(G-10704)*
Scarred Hands Wood Creations 740 975-2835
   8484 Hazelton Etna Rd Sw Etna (43062) *(G-9399)*
Scassa Asphalt Inc 330 830-2039
   4167 Beaumont Ave Nw Massillon (44647) *(G-13046)*
SCC Instruments 513 856-8444
   4436 Hamilton Scipio Rd Hamilton (45013) *(G-10602)*
SCC Wine Company LLC 216 374-3740
   4511 Bates Rd Madison (44057) *(G-12356)*
Scene Magazine, Cleveland Also called Northeast Scene Inc *(G-5776)*
Scenic Ridge Manufacturing LLC 330 674-0557
   5749 County Rd Ste 349 Millersburg (44654) *(G-14127)*
Scenic Screen 419 468-3110
   4463 State Route 309 Galion (44833) *(G-10153)*
Scenic Valley Surplus LLC 330 359-0555
   10258 S Kansas Rd Fredericksburg (44627) *(G-9960)*
Scenic Wood Products, Sugarcreek Also called Pallet Distributors Inc *(G-17856)*
Scentsible Scents Ltd 937 572-6690
   2704 Parklawn Dr Dayton (45440) *(G-8494)*
Schaaf Co Inc 513 241-7044
   2440 Spring Grove Ave Cincinnati (45214) *(G-4304)*
Schaefer Box & Pallet Co 513 738-2500
   11875 Paddys Run Rd Hamilton (45013) *(G-10603)*
Schaefer Equipment Inc 330 372-4006
   1590 Phoenix Rd Ne Warren (44483) *(G-19442)*
Schaefer Group Inc 419 897-2883
   29102 Glenwood Rd Ste A Perrysburg (43551) *(G-16004)*
Schaeffler Group USA Inc 330 273-4383
   5370 Wegman Dr Valley City (44280) *(G-19060)*
Schaeffler Transm Systems LLC 330 264-4383
   3401 Old Airport Rd Wooster (44691) *(G-20649)*
Schaeffler Transmission LLC (HQ) 330 264-4383
   3401 Old Airport Rd Wooster (44691) *(G-20650)*
Schaerer Medical Usa Inc 513 561-2241
   675 Wilmer Ave Cincinnati (45226) *(G-4305)*
Schafer Driveline LLC 614 864-1116
   6635 Taylor Rd Blacklick (43004) *(G-1694)*
Schafer Driveline LLC (HQ) 740 694-2055
   123 Phoenix Pl Fredericktown (43019) *(G-9977)*
Schaffer Grinding Co Inc 323 724-4476
   8470 Chamberlin Rd Twinsburg (44087) *(G-18854)*
Schaffner Publication Inc 419 732-2154
   205 Se Catawba Rd Ste G Port Clinton (43452) *(G-16258)*
Schantz Organ Company (PA) 330 682-6065
   626 S Walnut St Orrville (44667) *(G-15618)*
Scharenberg Sheet Metal 740 664-2431
   2261 Scott Rd New Marshfield (45766) *(G-14744)*
Schauer Battery Chargers, Cincinnati Also called Brookwood Group Inc *(G-3425)*
Scheel Publishing LLC 216 731-8616
   5900 Som Center Rd Willoughby (44094) *(G-20425)*
Schell Scenic Studio Inc 614 444-9550
   841 S Front St 843 Columbus (43206) *(G-7425)*
Schena Company Ltd 419 868-5207
   7710 Hill Ave Ste B Holland (43528) *(G-10955)*
Schenck Process LLC 513 576-9200
   16490 Chillicothe Rd Chagrin Falls (44023) *(G-3074)*
Schenz Theatrical Supply Inc 513 542-6100
   2959 Colerain Ave Cincinnati (45225) *(G-4306)*
Scherba Industries Inc 330 273-3200
   2880 Interstate Pkwy Brunswick (44212) *(G-2238)*
Scherer Industrial Group, Springfield Also called Horner Industrial Services Inc *(G-17421)*
Schien Equipment Company, Akron Also called Heritage Manufacturing Inc *(G-206)*
Schiffer Group Inc 937 694-8185
   1602 Marby Dr Troy (45373) *(G-18703)*
Schilling Graphics Inc (PA) 419 468-1037
   275 Gelsanliter Rd Galion (44833) *(G-10154)*
Schilling Truss Inc 740 984-2396
   230 Stony Run Rd Beverly (45715) *(G-1662)*
Schindler Elevator Corporation 419 861-5900
   1530 Timber Wolf Dr Holland (43528) *(G-10956)*
Schindlers Broad Run Chese Hse 330 343-4108
   6011 Old Route 39 Nw Dover (44622) *(G-8850)*
Schlabach Printers, Sugarcreek Also called Schlabach Printing Ltd *(G-17863)*
Schlabach Printing Ltd 330 852-4687
   798 State Route 93 Nw Sugarcreek (44681) *(G-17863)*
Schlabach Woodworks Ltd 330 674-7488
   6678 State Route 241 Millersburg (44654) *(G-14128)*
Schlessman Seed Co (PA) 419 499-2572
   11513 Us Highway 250 N Milan (44846) *(G-13988)*
Schlezinger Metals, Columbus Also called I H Schlezinger Inc *(G-7016)*
Schloemer, Don Masonry, Willard Also called Donald Schloemer *(G-20239)*
Schloss Media, Cadiz Also called Harrison News Herald Inc *(G-2398)*
Schlumberger Limited 330 878-0794
   211 Zeltman Ave Ne Strasburg (44680) *(G-17652)*
Schmelzer Industries Inc 740 743-2866
   7970 Wesley Chapel Rd Ne Somerset (43783) *(G-17267)*
Schmidt Machine Company 419 294-3814
   7013 State Highway 199 Upper Sandusky (43351) *(G-18972)*
Schmidt Progressive LLC 513 934-2600
   360 Harmon Ave Lebanon (45036) *(G-11693)*
Schmitmeyer Inc 937 295-2091
   195 Ben St Fort Loramie (45845) *(G-9804)*
Schneder Elc Bldngs Amrcas Inc 513 398-9800
   1770 Masn Mrrw Millgrv Rd Lebanon (45036) *(G-11694)*
Schneider Electric Usa Inc 513 755-5503
   5425 Longhunter Chase Dr Liberty Township (45044) *(G-11819)*
Schneider Electric Usa Inc 513 755-5000
   9870 Crescent Park Dr West Chester (45069) *(G-19792)*
Schneider Electric Usa Inc 513 523-4171
   5735 College Corner Pike Oxford (45056) *(G-15700)*
Schneider Electric Usa Inc 513 755-5501
   12000 Mosteller Rd Sharonville (45241) *(G-16959)*
Schneider Electric Usa Inc 513 398-9800
   9928 Windisch Rd West Chester (45069) *(G-19793)*
Schneider Electric Usa Inc 937 258-8426
   1875 Founders Dr Dayton (45420) *(G-8495)*
Schneller LLC (HQ) 330 676-7183
   6019 Powdermill Rd Kent (44240) *(G-11380)*
Schneller LLC 330 673-1299
   6019 Powdermill Rd Kent (44240) *(G-11381)*
Schnider Pallet LLC 440 632-5346
   9782 Bundysburg Rd Middlefield (44062) *(G-13850)*
Schober USA Inc 513 489-7393
   4690 Industry Dr Fairfield (45014) *(G-9561)*
Schodorf Truck Body & Eqp Co 614 228-6793
   885 Harmon Ave Columbus (43223) *(G-7426)*
Schoen Industries Inc 330 533-6659
   290 Southview Rd Canfield (44406) *(G-2544)*
Scholz & Ey Engravers Inc 614 444-8052
   1558 Parsons Ave Columbus (43207) *(G-7427)*
Schomaker Natural Resource 513 741-1370
   2741 Blue Rock Rd Cincinnati (45239) *(G-4307)*
School House Winery LLC 330 602-9463
   455 Schneiders Crssng Rd Dover (44622) *(G-8851)*
School Maintenance Supply Inc (PA) 513 376-8670
   10616 Millington Ct Blue Ash (45242) *(G-1843)*
School Pride Limited 614 568-0697
   3511 Johnny Appleseed Ct Columbus (43231) *(G-7428)*
Schoolbelles, Cleveland Also called Kip-Craft Incorporated *(G-5537)*
Schoonover Industries Inc 419 289-8332
   1440 Simonton Rd Ashland (44805) *(G-747)*
Schott Metal Products Company 330 773-7873
   2225 Lee Dr Akron (44306) *(G-373)*
Schreiner Cstm Stairs & Mllwk 419 435-8935
   1415 Sandusky St Fostoria (44830) *(G-9858)*
Schreiner Manufacturing 419 937-0300
   1997 Township Road 66 New Riegel (44853) *(G-14817)*
Schrock, John 937 544-8457
   61 Poole Rd West Union (45693) *(G-19966)*
Schrock Woodworking 740 489-5229
   71444 Grapevine Rd Freeport (43973) *(G-9986)*
Schuerholz Printing Inc 937 294-5218
   3540 Marshall Rd Dayton (45429) *(G-8496)*
Schulers Bakery Inc (PA) 937 323-4154
   1911 S Limestone St Springfield (45505) *(G-17491)*
Schumann Enterprises Inc 216 267-6850
   12340 Plaza Dr Cleveland (44130) *(G-6033)*
Schupp Advanced Materials LLC 440 488-6416
   10770 Chillicothe Rd Willoughby (44094) *(G-20426)*
Schuster Manufacturing Inc 419 476-5800
   1508 W Laskey Rd Ste 2 Toledo (43612) *(G-18514)*
Schutz Container Systems Inc 419 872-2477
   2105 S Wilkinson Way Perrysburg (43551) *(G-16005)*
Schwab Industries Inc (HQ) 330 364-4411
   2301 Progress St Dover (44622) *(G-8852)*
Schwab Machine Co Inc 419 626-0245
   3120 Venice Rd Sandusky (44870) *(G-16847)*
Schwab Welding Inc 513 353-4262
   7046 Harrison Ave Cincinnati (45247) *(G-4308)*
Schwans Home Service Inc 419 222-9977
   2545 Saint Johns Rd Lima (45804) *(G-11936)*

Schwans Mama Rosass LLC (HQ)....937 498-4511
1910 Fair Rd Sidney (45365) *(G-17072)*
Schwarz Partners Packaging LLC....317 290-1140
2450 Campbell Rd Sidney (45365) *(G-17073)*
Schwebel Baking Co-Solon Bky, Solon *Also called Schwebel Baking Company (G-17228)*
Schwebel Baking Company (PA)....330 783-2860
965 E Midlothian Blvd Youngstown (44502) *(G-21025)*
Schwebel Baking Company....440 846-1921
22626 Royalton Rd Strongsville (44149) *(G-17785)*
Schwebel Baking Company....440 248-1500
6250 Camp Industrial Rd Solon (44139) *(G-17228)*
Schwebel Baking Company....216 481-1880
345 E 200th St Euclid (44119) *(G-9442)*
Schwebel Baking Company....330 783-2860
121 O Neill Dr Hebron (43025) *(G-10762)*
Schweizer Dipple Inc....440 786-8090
7227 Division St Cleveland (44146) *(G-6034)*
Schwieterman Cy Inc....937 548-3965
4240 State Route 49 Arcanum (45304) *(G-633)*
SCI Engineered Materials Inc....614 486-0261
2839 Charter St Columbus (43228) *(G-7429)*
Scicompro - LLC....513 680-8686
4861 Hampton Pond Ln Mason (45040) *(G-12937)*
Science/Electronics Inc....937 224-4444
521 Kiser St Dayton (45404) *(G-8497)*
Scio Laminated Products Inc....740 945-1321
117 Fowler Ave Scio (43988) *(G-16879)*
Scioto Ceramic Products Inc....614 436-0405
854 Curleys Ct Columbus (43235) *(G-7430)*
Scioto Darby Quarter Horses....614 464-7290
8701 Scioto Darby Rd Orient (43146) *(G-15577)*
Scioto Ready Mix LLC....740 924-9273
6214 Taylor Rd Sw Pataskala (43062) *(G-15843)*
Scioto Readymix Co....614 491-0773
1500 Williams Rd Columbus (43207) *(G-7431)*
Scioto Sand & Gravel, Prospect *Also called Fleming Construction Co (G-16350)*
Scioto Sign Co Inc....419 673-1261
6047 Us Highway 68 Kenton (43326) *(G-11422)*
Scioto Voice....740 574-5400
1280 Dogwood Ridge Rd Wheelersburg (45694) *(G-20184)*
Scis Aerospace LLC....216 533-8533
1179 Alexandria Ln Medina (44256) *(G-13336)*
Scorecards Unlimited LLC....614 885-0796
6334 Huntley Rd Columbus (43229) *(G-7432)*
Scorpion Case Mfg LLC....614 274-7246
329 Clover Ln Dublin (43017) *(G-8981)*
Scot Industries Inc....330 262-7585
6578 Ashland Rd Wooster (44691) *(G-20651)*
Scots....215 370-9498
3875 S Elyria Rd Shreve (44676) *(G-17009)*
Scott A Zurbrugg....330 821-9814
6016 Union Ave Ne Alliance (44601) *(G-499)*
Scott Bader Inc....330 920-4410
4280 Hudson Dr Stow (44224) *(G-17626)*
Scott Fetzer Company....216 267-9000
4801 W 150th St Cleveland (44135) *(G-6035)*
Scott Fetzer Company....216 228-2403
1920 W 114th St Cleveland (44102) *(G-6036)*
Scott Fetzer Company....216 252-1190
3881 W 150th St Cleveland (44111) *(G-6037)*
Scott Fetzer Company....440 871-2160
875 Bassett Rd Cleveland (44145) *(G-6038)*
Scott Fetzer Company....216 228-2400
16841 Park Circle Dr Chagrin Falls (44023) *(G-3075)*
Scott Fetzer Company....440 439-1616
101 Production Dr Harrison (45030) *(G-10669)*
Scott Fetzer Company....216 281-1100
10920 Madison Ave Cleveland (44102) *(G-6039)*
Scott Fetzer Company....216 433-7797
4750 W 160th St Cleveland (44135) *(G-6040)*
Scott Fetzer Company....440 871-2160
33672 Pin Oak Pkwy Avon Lake (44012) *(G-1007)*
Scott Fetzer Company (HQ)....440 892-3000
28800 Clemens Rd Westlake (44145) *(G-20156)*
Scott Models Inc....513 771-8005
607 Redna Ter Ste 400 Cincinnati (45215) *(G-4309)*
Scott Molders Incorporated....330 673-5777
7180 State Route 43 Kent (44240) *(G-11382)*
Scott Port-A-Fold, Napoleon *Also called Toy & Sport Trends Inc (G-14562)*
Scott Port-A-Fold Inc....419 748-8880
5963 State Route 110 Napoleon (43545) *(G-14561)*
Scott Process Systems Inc....330 877-2350
1160 Sunnyside St Sw Hartville (44632) *(G-10705)*
Scott Systems Intl Inc....740 383-8383
370 W Fairground St Marion (43302) *(G-12733)*
Scott Thomas Furniture, Twinsburg *Also called R A Hamed International Inc (G-18844)*
Scott-Randall Systems Inc....937 446-2293
5815 Tracy Rd Sardinia (45171) *(G-16873)*
Scottcare Corporation (HQ)....216 362-0550
4791 W 150th St Cleveland (44135) *(G-6041)*
Scottdel Cushion LLC....419 825-0432
400 Church St Swanton (43558) *(G-17921)*
Scottrods LLC....419 499-2705
2512 Higbee Rd Monroeville (44847) *(G-14290)*
Scotts Company LLC....614 863-3920
710 Cross Pointe Rd Gahanna (43230) *(G-10102)*
Scotts Company LLC....937 454-2782
20 Innovation Ct Dayton (45414) *(G-8498)*
Scotts Company LLC (HQ)....937 644-0011
14111 Scottslawn Rd Marysville (43040) *(G-12809)*
Scotts Miracle-Gro Company....330 684-0421
1220 Schrock Rd Orrville (44667) *(G-15619)*
Scotts Miracle-Gro Company (PA)....937 644-0011
14111 Scottslawn Rd Marysville (43040) *(G-12810)*
Scotts Miracle-Gro Company....937 578-5065
14101 Industrial Pkwy Marysville (43040) *(G-12811)*
Scotts Miracle-Gro Products, Marysville *Also called Scotts Company LLC (G-12809)*
Scotts Miracle-Gro Products....937 644-0011
14111 Scottslawn Rd Marysville (43040) *(G-12812)*
Scotts- Hyponex, Marysville *Also called Hyponex Corporation (G-12794)*
Scotts- Hyponex, Shreve *Also called Hyponex Corporation (G-17002)*
Scrambl-Gram Inc....419 635-2321
5225 W Lkshore Dr Ste 340 Port Clinton (43452) *(G-16259)*
Scratch Off Works....440 333-4302
19537 Lake Rd Rocky River (44116) *(G-16556)*
Scratch-Off Systems Inc....216 649-7800
6600 W Snowville Rd Brecksville (44141) *(G-2056)*
Screen Craft Plastics....440 286-4060
695 South St Ste 7 Chardon (44024) *(G-3135)*
Screen Images Inc....440 779-7356
6122 Croton Dr North Olmsted (44070) *(G-15197)*
Screen Machine, Pataskala *Also called SMI Holdings Inc (G-15845)*
Screen Machine Industries LLC....740 927-3464
10685 Columbus Pkwy Pataskala (43062) *(G-15844)*
Screen Printing Show House....614 252-2202
853 N Nelson Rd Columbus (43219) *(G-7433)*
Screen Printing Unlimited....419 621-2335
3410 Tiffin Ave Sandusky (44870) *(G-16848)*
Screen Tech Graphics....740 695-7950
152 Saint Patricks Aly B Saint Clairsville (43950) *(G-16650)*
Screen Works Inc (PA)....937 264-9111
3970 Image Dr Dayton (45414) *(G-8499)*
Screenmobile Inc....614 868-8663
6737 Thomas Rd Radnor (43066) *(G-16358)*
Screenplay Printing, Xenia *Also called Liming Printing Inc (G-20782)*
Scrip-Safe International, Loveland *Also called Scrip-Safe Security Products (G-12230)*
Scrip-Safe Security Products....513 697-7789
136 Commerce Dr Loveland (45140) *(G-12230)*
Scripps Media Inc....513 977-3000
312 Walnut St Fl 28 Cincinnati (45202) *(G-4310)*
Scriptel Corporation....614 276-8402
2174 Dividend Dr Columbus (43228) *(G-7434)*
Scriptype Publishing Inc....330 659-0303
4300 W Streetsboro Rd Richfield (44286) *(G-16485)*
Scs Construction Services Inc....513 929-0260
2130 Western Ave Cincinnati (45214) *(G-4311)*
Scs Gearbox Inc....419 483-7278
739 W Main St Bellevue (44811) *(G-1543)*
Scsrm Concrete Company Ltd....937 533-1001
4723 Hardin Wapakoneta Rd Sidney (45365) *(G-17074)*
SD Ip Holdings Company....513 483-3300
4747 Lake Forest Dr Blue Ash (45242) *(G-1844)*
Sdg News Group Inc....419 929-3411
43 E Main St New London (44851) *(G-14737)*
Sdh Flow Controls LLC....513 624-7001
7437 Wallingford Dr Cincinnati (45244) *(G-4312)*
Sdi Industries....513 561-4032
8561 New England Ct Cincinnati (45236) *(G-4313)*
SDS Logistics Services, Youngstown *Also called SDS National LLC (G-21026)*
SDS National LLC....330 759-8066
19 Colonial Dr Ste 27 Youngstown (44505) *(G-21026)*
Sea Air Spc McG and Mld LLC....440 248-3025
10036 Aurora Hudson Rd Streetsboro (44241) *(G-17695)*
Sea Bird Publications Inc....513 869-2200
311 Nilles Rd Ste B Fairfield (45014) *(G-9562)*
Seabiscuit Motorsports Inc (HQ)....440 951-6600
7201 Industrial Park Blvd Mentor (44060) *(G-13577)*
Seacor Painting Corporation....330 755-6361
98 Creed Cir Campbell (44405) *(G-2469)*
Seaforth Mineral & Ore Co Inc (PA)....216 292-5820
3690 Orange Pl Ste 495 Cleveland (44122) *(G-6042)*
Seagate Plastics Company (PA)....419 878-5010
1110 Disher Dr Waterville (43566) *(G-19505)*
Seal Master Corporation....330 673-8410
340 Martinel Dr Kent (44240) *(G-11383)*
Seal Tite LLC....937 393-4268
120 Moore Rd Hillsboro (45133) *(G-10891)*
Seal-Rite Door, Hebron *Also called S R Door Inc (G-10761)*

ALPHABETIC SECTION

Sealant Solutions 614 599-8000
  947 E Johnstown Rd Columbus (43230) *(G-7435)*
Sealco Inc 740 922-4122
  6566 Superior Rd Se Uhrichsville (44683) *(G-18893)*
Sealmaster, Sandusky *Also called Thorworks Industries Inc (G-16855)*
Sealmaster, Kent *Also called Seal Master Corporation (G-11383)*
Sealy Mattress Company 330 725-4146
  1070 Lake Rd Medina (44256) *(G-13337)*
Sealy Mattress Mfg Co Inc 800 697-3259
  1070 Lake Rd Medina (44256) *(G-13338)*
Seaman Corporation (PA) 330 262-1111
  1000 Venture Blvd Wooster (44691) *(G-20652)*
Seapine Software Inc (HQ) 513 754-1655
  6960 Cintas Blvd Mason (45040) *(G-12938)*
Seaport Mold & Casting Company 419 243-1422
  1309 W Bancroft St Toledo (43606) *(G-18515)*
Seaport Mold and Casting Co, Toledo *Also called Chippewa Industries Inc (G-18231)*
Season of Wreath 330 936-7498
  8347 Market Ave N Canton (44721) *(G-2812)*
Seat Division Bridgestone, Upper Sandusky *Also called Bridgestone APM Company (G-18947)*
Seavival LLC 330 252-1151
  526 S Main St Ste 518 Akron (44311) *(G-374)*
Seaway Enterprises, Toledo *Also called Initial Designs Inc (G-18347)*
Seaway Pattern Mfg Inc 419 865-5724
  5749 Angola Rd Toledo (43615) *(G-18516)*
Seawin Inc 419 355-9111
  728 Graham Dr Fremont (43420) *(G-10050)*
Sebring Fluid Power Corp 330 938-9984
  513 N Johnson Rd Sebring (44672) *(G-16894)*
Sebring Industrial Plating 330 938-6666
  546 W Tennessee Ave Sebring (44672) *(G-16895)*
Sebring Plating, Sebring *Also called Sebring Industrial Plating (G-16895)*
Seco Machine Inc 330 499-2150
  7376 Whipple Ave Nw North Canton (44720) *(G-15116)*
Secondary Machining Services 440 593-1272
  539 Center Rd Conneaut (44030) *(G-7659)*
Secqure Surgical Corp 513 769-1916
  4480 Lake Forest Dr # 414 Blue Ash (45242) *(G-1845)*
Secret Image Promotion, Clayton *Also called Image Industries Inc (G-4575)*
Sectional Stamping Inc 440 647-2100
  350 Maple St Wellington (44090) *(G-19591)*
Securcom Inc 419 628-1049
  307 W 1st St Minster (45865) *(G-14224)*
Secure Medical Mail LLC 216 269-1971
  3257 Mayfield Rd Apt 21 Cleveland (44118) *(G-6043)*
Secure Pak, Perrysburg *Also called Glassline Corporation (G-15958)*
Security Designs, Cleveland *Also called Technlgy Install Partners LLC (G-6156)*
Security Fence Group Inc (PA) 513 681-3700
  4260 Dane Ave Cincinnati (45223) *(G-4314)*
Securtex International Inc 937 312-1414
  982 Senate Dr Dayton (45459) *(G-8500)*
Sedlak 330 908-2200
  4020 Kinross Lakes Pkwy Richfield (44286) *(G-16486)*
Sedona Office, Chagrin Falls *Also called Perennial Software Inc (G-3027)*
See Ya There Inc 614 856-9037
  12710 W Bank Dr Ne Millersport (43046) *(G-14161)*
See Ya There Vacation and Trvl, Millersport *Also called See Ya There Inc (G-14161)*
Seeb Industrial Inc 216 896-9016
  5182 Richmond Rd Bedford (44146) *(G-1445)*
Seebach Inc 937 275-3565
  2622 Keenan Ave Dayton (45414) *(G-8501)*
Seebach Tools & Molds Mfg, Dayton *Also called Seebach Inc (G-8501)*
Seeburger Greenhouse 419 832-1834
  11480 S River Rd Grand Rapids (43522) *(G-10321)*
Seekirk Inc 614 278-9200
  2420 Scioto Harper Dr Columbus (43204) *(G-7436)*
Seelaus Instrument Co 513 733-8222
  422 Alexandersville Rd Miamisburg (45342) *(G-13714)*
Seemless Design & Printing LLC 513 871-2366
  717 Linn St Cincinnati (45203) *(G-4315)*
Seepex Inc 937 864-7150
  511 Speedway Dr Enon (45323) *(G-9386)*
Segna Inc 937 335-6700
  1316 Barnhart Rd Troy (45373) *(G-18704)*
Sei Inc 513 942-6170
  10004 International Blvd West Chester (45246) *(G-19897)*
Seifert Printing Company 330 759-7414
  3200 Belmont Ave Ste 11 Youngstown (44505) *(G-21027)*
Seilkop Industries Inc (PA) 513 761-1035
  425 W North Bend Rd Cincinnati (45216) *(G-4316)*
Seilkop Industries Inc 513 353-3090
  5927 State Route 128 Miamitown (45041) *(G-13751)*
Seilkop Industries Inc 513 679-5680
  7211 Market Pl Cincinnati (45216) *(G-4317)*
Seislove Brial Vlts Sptc Tnks, Tiffin *Also called Seislove Vault & Septic Tanks (G-18082)*
Seislove Vault & Septic Tanks 419 447-5473
  2168 S State Route 100 Tiffin (44883) *(G-18082)*

Sekely Industries Inc (PA) 248 844-9201
  240 Pennsylvania Ave Salem (44460) *(G-16774)*
Selah Paperie 330 755-2759
  130 S Bridge St Struthers (44471) *(G-17824)*
Selas Heat Technology Co LLC 216 662-8800
  11012 Aurora Hudson Rd Streetsboro (44241) *(G-17696)*
Selas Heat Technology Co LLC (HQ) 800 523-6500
  11012 Aurora Hudson Rd Streetsboro (44241) *(G-17697)*
Selbro Inc 419 483-9918
  555 Goodrich Rd Bellevue (44811) *(G-1544)*
Selby Service/Roxy Press Inc 513 241-3445
  2020 Elm St Cincinnati (45202) *(G-4318)*
Selco Industries Inc 419 861-0336
  1590 Albon Rd Ste 1 Holland (43528) *(G-10957)*
Select Industries Corporation 937 233-9191
  60 Heid Ave Dayton (45404) *(G-8502)*
Select International Corp (PA) 937 233-9191
  60 Heid Ave Dayton (45404) *(G-8503)*
Select Logging 419 564-0361
  5739 Township Road 21 Marengo (43334) *(G-12594)*
Select Machine Co Inc 330 678-7676
  4125 Karg Industrial Pkwy Kent (44240) *(G-11384)*
Select Optical, Columbus *Also called Bsa Industries Inc (G-6706)*
Select Seating, Columbus *Also called N Wasserstrom & Sons Inc (G-7207)*
Select Tool & Production, Toledo *Also called Hedges Selective Tool & Prod (G-18329)*
Select Woodworking Inc 513 948-9901
  427c W Seymour Ave Cincinnati (45216) *(G-4319)*
Select-Arc Inc (PA) 937 295-5215
  600 Enterprise Dr Fort Loramie (45845) *(G-9805)*
Selecteon Corporation 614 710-1132
  2041 Arlingate Ln Columbus (43228) *(G-7437)*
Selective Med Components Inc 740 397-7838
  504 Harcourt Rd Ste 3 Mount Vernon (43050) *(G-14507)*
Selective Micro Tech LLC 614 551-5974
  6200 Avery Rd Ste A Dublin (43016) *(G-8982)*
Selectronics Incorporated 440 546-5595
  9771 Forge Dr Brecksville (44141) *(G-2057)*
Selinick Co 440 632-1788
  15879 Madison Rd Middlefield (44062) *(G-13851)*
Selmco Metal Fabricators Inc 937 498-1331
  1615 Ferguson Ct Sidney (45365) *(G-17075)*
Selzer Tool & Die Inc 440 365-4124
  163 Kenwood St Elyria (44035) *(G-9325)*
Sem-Com Company Inc (PA) 419 537-8813
  1040 N Westwood Ave Toledo (43607) *(G-18517)*
Sematic Usa Inc 216 524-0100
  7852 Bavaria Rd Twinsburg (44087) *(G-18855)*
Semco 800 848-5764
  1025 Pole Lane Rd Marion (43302) *(G-12734)*
Semco Carbon, Lorain *Also called Sentinel Management Inc (G-12119)*
Semco Ceramics, Uhrichsville *Also called Stebbins Engineering & Mfg Co (G-18895)*
Seme & Son Automotive Inc 216 261-0066
  1320 E 260th St Euclid (44132) *(G-9443)*
Semper Quality Industry Inc 440 352-8111
  9411 Mercantile Dr Mentor (44060) *(G-13578)*
Semtorq Inc 330 487-0600
  1953 Case Pkwy S Twinsburg (44087) *(G-18856)*
Senator International Inc (PA) 419 887-5806
  4111 N Jerome Rd Maumee (43537) *(G-13143)*
Senco Brands Inc 513 388-2833
  8450 Broadwell Rd Cincinnati (45244) *(G-4320)*
Senco Brands Inc (HQ) 513 388-2000
  4270 Ivy Pointe Blvd Cincinnati (45245) *(G-3262)*
Seneca Label Inc 440 237-1600
  13821 Progress Pkwy Cleveland (44133) *(G-6044)*
Seneca Millwork Inc 419 435-6671
  300 Court Pl Fostoria (44830) *(G-9859)*
Seneca Petroleum Co Inc 419 691-3581
  1441 Woodville Rd Toledo (43605) *(G-18518)*
Seneca Petroleum Co Inc 419 691-3581
  2563 Front St Toledo (43605) *(G-18519)*
Seneca Railroad & Mining Co 419 483-7764
  1075 W Main St Bellevue (44811) *(G-1545)*
Seneca Sheet Metal Company 419 447-8434
  277 Water St Tiffin (44883) *(G-18083)*
Seneca Tiles Inc 419 426-3561
  7100 S County Road 23 Attica (44807) *(G-859)*
Seneca Wire Group Inc (PA) 419 435-9261
  820 Willipie St Wapakoneta (45895) *(G-19353)*
Senior Impact Publication 513 791-8800
  5980 Kugler Mill Rd Cincinnati (45236) *(G-4321)*
Senneca Holdings Inc (HQ) 800 543-4455
  11502 Century Blvd Cincinnati (45246) *(G-4322)*
Senneco Glass Inc (PA) 330 825-7717
  1730 Newberry St Cuyahoga Falls (44221) *(G-7915)*
Sense Diagnostics Inc 513 515-3853
  1776 Mentor Ave Ste 178 Cincinnati (45212) *(G-4323)*
Sensetronics LLC 614 292-2833
  8407 Gleneagles Ct Dublin (43017) *(G-8983)*

Sensible Products Inc 330 659-4212
3857 Brecksville Rd Richfield (44286) ***(G-16487)***
Sensical Inc 216 641-1141
31115 Aurora Rd Solon (44139) ***(G-17229)***
Sensopart USA Inc 419 931-7696
28400 Cedar Park Blvd Perrysburg (43551) ***(G-16006)***
Sensor Technology Systems, Miamisburg *Also called Steiner Eoptics Inc* ***(G-13721)***
Sensorwerks, Hilliard *Also called Sensotec LLC* ***(G-10860)***
Sensory Effects, Defiance *Also called Sensoryeffects Flavor Company* ***(G-8642)***
Sensoryeffects Flavor Company 419 782-5010
136 Fox Run Dr Defiance (43512) ***(G-8642)***
Sensoryffcts Powdr Systems Inc 419 783-5518
136 Fox Run Dr Defiance (43512) ***(G-8643)***
Sensotec LLC 614 481-8616
3450 Cemetery Rd Hilliard (43026) ***(G-10860)***
Sensource Global Sourcing LLC 513 659-8283
4270 Ivy Pointe Blvd Cincinnati (45245) ***(G-3263)***
Sensus, Fairfield Township *Also called Synergy Flavors (oh) LLC* ***(G-9587)***
Sensus LLC 513 892-7100
2991 Hamilton Mason Rd Fairfield Township (45011) ***(G-9585)***
Sentek Corporation 614 586-1123
1300 Memory Ln N Columbus (43209) ***(G-7438)***
Sentinel Consumer Products Inc (PA) 801 825-5671
7750 Tyler Blvd Mentor (44060) ***(G-13579)***
Sentinel Daily 740 992-2155
109 W 2nd St Pomeroy (45769) ***(G-16241)***
Sentinel Management Inc 440 821-7372
3000 Leavitt Rd Lorain (44052) ***(G-12119)***
Sentinel USA Inc 740 345-6412
1285 Granville Rd Newark (43055) ***(G-14917)***
Sentinel Utility Services, Newark *Also called Sentinel USA Inc* ***(G-14917)***
Sentrilock LLC 513 618-5800
7701 Service Center Dr West Chester (45069) ***(G-19794)***
Sentronic, Hinckley *Also called Controlled Access Inc* ***(G-10899)***
Sentry Graphics Inc 440 735-0850
114 Hiram College Dr Northfield (44067) ***(G-15324)***
Sentry Products, Canton *Also called Canton Sterilized Wiping Cloth* ***(G-2618)***
Sentry Protection LLC 216 228-3200
16927 Detroit Ave Ste 3 Lakewood (44107) ***(G-11535)***
Sentry Protection Products, Lakewood *Also called Sentry Protection LLC* ***(G-11535)***
Septic Products Inc 419 282-5933
1378 Township Road 743 Ashland (44805) ***(G-748)***
Serappers Gallery, Newark *Also called M & R Phillips Enterprises* ***(G-14895)***
Sergeant Stone Inc 740 452-7434
1425 State Route 555 Ne Corning (43730) ***(G-7702)***
Sermonix Pharmaceuticals 614 864-4919
142 S Remington Rd Columbus (43209) ***(G-7439)***
Serta Mattress Company, Cincinnati *Also called National Bedding Company LLC* ***(G-4060)***
Sertek LLC 614 504-5828
6399 Shier Rings Rd Dublin (43016) ***(G-8984)***
Serv All Graphics LLC 513 681-8883
10901 Reed Hartman Hwy # 209 Blue Ash (45242) ***(G-1846)***
Serva Tool, Dayton *Also called Milja Inc* ***(G-8359)***
Servatii Inc 513 231-4455
7161 Beechmont Ave Cincinnati (45230) ***(G-4324)***
Servatii Inc 513 271-5040
3774 Paxton Ave Cincinnati (45209) ***(G-4325)***
Servepro of Parma, Valley City *Also called Matthew Koster* ***(G-19048)***
Service Iron & Steel Company, Akron *Also called McMillen Steel LLC* ***(G-274)***
Service Spring Corp (PA) 419 838-6081
1703 Toll Gate Dr Maumee (43537) ***(G-13144)***
Service Stampings Inc 440 946-2330
4700 Hamann Pkwy Willoughby (44094) ***(G-20427)***
Service Station Equipment Co (PA) 216 431-6100
1294 E 55th St Cleveland (44103) ***(G-6045)***
Services Acquisition Co LLC 330 479-9267
4412 Pleasant Vly Rd Se Dennison (44621) ***(G-8786)***
Serving Veterans Mobility Inc 937 746-4788
303 Conover Dr Franklin (45005) ***(G-9918)***
Servo Systems Inc 440 779-2780
31375 Lorain Rd North Olmsted (44070) ***(G-15198)***
SES Fabracating LLC 440 636-5853
17217 Huntley Rd Windsor (44099) ***(G-20528)***
Sesh Communications 513 851-1693
3440 Burnet Ave Ste 130 Cincinnati (45229) ***(G-4326)***
Sest Inc 440 777-9777
24509 Annie Ln Westlake (44145) ***(G-20157)***
Setco Industries Inc 513 941-5110
5880 Hillside Ave Cincinnati (45233) ***(G-4327)***
Setco Sales Company (HQ) 513 941-5110
5880 Hillside Ave Cincinnati (45233) ***(G-4328)***
Setex Inc 419 394-7800
1111 Mckinley Rd Saint Marys (45885) ***(G-16700)***
Seth Enterprises, Zanesville *Also called Buckeye Energy Resources Inc* ***(G-21113)***
Sevan At-Ndustrial Pnt Abr Ltd 614 258-4747
1555 Alum Creek Dr Columbus (43209) ***(G-7440)***
Sevell + Sevell Inc 614 341-9700
692 N High St Ste 306 Columbus (43215) ***(G-7441)***
Seven Hills Reporter 216 524-9515
6817 Parkgate Oval Seven Hills (44131) ***(G-16906)***
Seven Mile Creek Corporation 937 456-3320
315 S Beech St Eaton (45320) ***(G-9165)***
Seven Ranges Mfg Corp 330 627-7155
330 Industrial Dr Sw Carrollton (44615) ***(G-2928)***
Seven-Ogun International LLC 614 888-8939
670 Lkview Plz Blvd Ste K Worthington (43085) ***(G-20703)***
Seventh Son Brewing Co 614 783-4217
1101 N 4th St Columbus (43201) ***(G-7442)***
Seves Glass Block Inc 440 627-6257
10576 Broadview Rd Broadview Heights (44147) ***(G-2101)***
Seville Bronze, Seville *Also called Jj Seville LLC* ***(G-16918)***
Sew It Seams, Woodsfield *Also called J C L S Enterprises LLC* ***(G-20545)***
Sew-Eurodrive Inc 937 335-0036
2001 W Main St Troy (45373) ***(G-18705)***
Sewah Studios Inc 740 373-2087
190 Mill Creek Rd Marietta (45750) ***(G-12666)***
Sewer Rodding Equipment Co 419 991-2065
3434 S Dixie Hwy Lima (45804) ***(G-11937)***
Sewline Products Inc 419 929-1114
30 S Railroad St New London (44851) ***(G-14738)***
Sexton Industrial Inc 513 530-5555
366 Circle Freeway Dr West Chester (45246) ***(G-19898)***
Seyekcub Inc 330 324-1394
615 W 4th St Uhrichsville (44683) ***(G-18894)***
Seymour, Lloyd, Columbus *Also called Buckeye Cstm Screen Print EMB* ***(G-6709)***
Seymours Logging 740 288-1825
1085 Loop Rd Wellston (45692) ***(G-19606)***
Sfc Graphic Arts Div, Toledo *Also called Sfc Graphics Cleveland Ltd* ***(G-18520)***
Sfc Graphics Cleveland Ltd 419 255-1283
110 E Woodruff Ave Toledo (43604) ***(G-18520)***
Sfs Group Usa Inc 330 239-7100
5201 Portside Dr Medina (44256) ***(G-13339)***
Sfs Intec, Medina *Also called Sfs Group Usa Inc* ***(G-13339)***
Sfs Truck Sales & Parts, Gallipolis *Also called King Kutter II Inc* ***(G-10169)***
SGB Usa Inc 330 472-1187
180 South Ave Tallmadge (44278) ***(G-18003)***
Sgi Matrix LLC (PA) 937 438-9033
1041 Byers Rd Miamisburg (45342) ***(G-13715)***
Sgl, Millbury *Also called Spectra Group Limited Inc* ***(G-14052)***
Sgl Technic Inc 440 572-3600
21945 Drake Rd Strongsville (44149) ***(G-17786)***
Sgm Co Inc 440 255-1190
9000 Tyler Blvd Mentor (44060) ***(G-13580)***
Sgo Designer Glass, Dayton *Also called Cadenza Enterprises LLC* ***(G-8073)***
SH Bell Company 412 963-9910
2217 Michigan Ave East Liverpool (43920) ***(G-9068)***
Shade Text Book Service Inc 740 696-1323
401 Gilkey Ridge Rd Shade (45776) ***(G-16921)***
Shade Winery, Shade *Also called Shade Text Book Service Inc* ***(G-16921)***
Shade Youngstown & Aluminum Co 330 782-2373
3335 South Ave Youngstown (44502) ***(G-21028)***
Shadetree Machine 513 727-8771
5994 Kalbfleisch Rd Middletown (45042) ***(G-13951)***
Shadetree Systems LLC 614 844-5990
6317 Busch Blvd Columbus (43229) ***(G-7443)***
Shafer Valve Company, Ontario *Also called Emerson Process Management* ***(G-15541)***
Shaffer Manufacturing Corp 937 652-2151
720 S Edgewood Ave Urbana (43078) ***(G-19012)***
Shaffer Metal Fab Inc 937 492-1384
2031 Commerce Dr Sidney (45365) ***(G-17076)***
Shaffer Mixers & Proc Eqp, Urbana *Also called Shaffer Manufacturing Corp* ***(G-19012)***
Shafts Mfg 440 942-6012
1585 E 361st St Unit G1 Willoughby (44095) ***(G-20428)***
Shagbark Seed & Mill, Athens *Also called Indie-Peasant Enterprises* ***(G-835)***
Shaheen Oriental Rug Co Inc (PA) 330 493-9000
4120 Whipple Ave Nw Canton (44718) ***(G-2813)***
Shaker Numeric Mfg, Euclid *Also called Tech-Med Inc* ***(G-9445)***
Shaker Valley Foods Inc 216 961-8600
3304 W 67th Pl Cleveland (44102) ***(G-6046)***
Shalersville Asphalt Co (PA) 440 834-4294
14376 N Cheshire St Burton (44021) ***(G-2370)***
Shalix Inc 216 941-3546
10910 Briggs Rd Cleveland (44111) ***(G-6047)***
Shallow Lake Corp 614 883-6350
8958 Cotter St Lewis Center (43035) ***(G-11779)***
Shalmet Corporation 440 236-8840
164 Freedom Ct Elyria (44035) ***(G-9326)***
Shamrock Acquisition Company, Westlake *Also called Shamrock Companies Inc* ***(G-20158)***
Shamrock Companies Inc (PA) 440 899-9510
24090 Detroit Rd Westlake (44145) ***(G-20158)***
Shamrock Molded Products, Holland *Also called Doyle Manufacturing Inc* ***(G-10926)***
Shamrock Plastics Inc 740 392-5555
633 Howard St Mount Vernon (43050) ***(G-14508)***
Shanafelt Manufacturing Co (PA) 330 455-0315
2600 Wnfeld Way Ne 2700 Canton (44705) ***(G-2814)***

Shaneway Inc (PA)...330 868-2220
1032 Brush Rd Ne Minerva (44657) ***(G-14201)***
Shannon Tool Inc...513 563-2300
3355 Hill St Cincinnati (45241) ***(G-4329)***
Shannon Ward...330 592-8177
4526 Bunker Ln Stow (44224) ***(G-17627)***
Shape Supply Inc...513 863-6695
700 S Erie Hwy Hamilton (45011) ***(G-10604)***
Sharc Industries...216 272-0668
10600 Bridle Path Columbia Station (44028) ***(G-6448)***
Shark Solar LLC...216 630-7395
4386 Belmont Ct Medina (44256) ***(G-13340)***
Sharon James Cellers...440 739-4065
11303 Kinsman Rd Newbury (44065) ***(G-14965)***
Sharon Printing Co Inc...330 239-1684
4983 Ridge Rd Sharon Center (44274) ***(G-16953)***
Sharon Stone Co...740 374-3236
County Road 10 Dexter City (45727) ***(G-8795)***
Sharon Stone Inc...740 732-7100
44895 Sharon Stone Rd Caldwell (43724) ***(G-2411)***
Sharonco Inc...419 882-3443
5651 Main St Sylvania (43560) ***(G-17960)***
Sharp Enterprises Inc...937 295-2965
400 Enterprise Dr Fort Loramie (45845) ***(G-9806)***
Sharp Tool Service Inc...330 273-4144
4735 W 150th St Frnt B Cleveland (44135) ***(G-6048)***
Sharper Tooling...330 667-2960
9473 Smith Rd Litchfield (44253) ***(G-11987)***
Sharpys Food Systems LLC...440 232-9601
26245 Broadway Ave Oakwood Village (44146) ***(G-15483)***
Shasta Beverages Inc...614 491-5415
4685 Groveport Rd Obetz (43207) ***(G-15513)***
Shasta Beverges, Obetz *Also called National Beverage Corp* ***(G-15512)***
Shatzels Backhoe Service LLC...937 289-9630
4044 Pansy Rd Clarksville (45113) ***(G-4568)***
Shaw Industries Inc...513 942-3692
4436 Muhlhauser Rd # 100 West Chester (45011) ***(G-19795)***
Shaw Pallets & Specialties...740 498-7892
12269 Lick Brown Rd Newcomerstown (43832) ***(G-14981)***
Shaw Wilbert Vaults LLC...740 498-7438
12269 Lick Run Rd Newcomerstown (43832) ***(G-14982)***
Shawcor Inc...513 683-7800
173 Commerce Dr Loveland (45140) ***(G-12231)***
Shawne Springs Winery...740 623-0744
20093 County Road 6 Coshocton (43812) ***(G-7751)***
Shawnee Molds, Eaton *Also called Camden Concrete Products* ***(G-9145)***
Shawnee Systems Inc...513 561-9932
3616 Church St Cincinnati (45244) ***(G-4330)***
Shawnee Wood Products Inc...440 632-1771
8918 Bundysburg Rd Middlefield (44062) ***(G-13852)***
Shear Service Inc...216 341-2700
3175 E 81st St Cleveland (44104) ***(G-6049)***
Shear Service, The, Cleveland *Also called Shear Service Inc* ***(G-6049)***
Shearer Farm Inc (PA)...330 345-9023
7762 Cleveland Rd Wooster (44691) ***(G-20653)***
Shearer's Snacks, Massillon *Also called Shearers Foods LLC* ***(G-13047)***
Shearers Foods LLC (PA)...330 834-4030
100 Lincoln Way E Massillon (44646) ***(G-13047)***
Sheep & Farm Life Inc...419 492-2364
5696 Johnston Rd New Washington (44854) ***(G-14832)***
Sheet Metal Fabricator, Tiffin *Also called Seneca Sheet Metal Company* ***(G-18083)***
Sheet Metal Products Co Inc...440 392-9000
5950 Pinecone Dr Mentor (44060) ***(G-13581)***
Sheffield Bronze Paint Corp...216 481-8330
17814 S Waterloo Rd Cleveland (44119) ***(G-6050)***
Sheffield Metals Cleveland LLC (PA)...800 283-5262
5467 Evergreen Pkwy Sheffield Village (44054) ***(G-16975)***
Sheffield Metals International, Sheffield Village *Also called Sheffield Metals Cleveland LLC* ***(G-16975)***
Sheffield Oldcastle, Sheffield Village *Also called Oldcastle Apg Midwest Inc* ***(G-16973)***
Sheiban Jewelry Inc...440 238-0616
16938 Pearl Rd Strongsville (44136) ***(G-17787)***
Shelburne Corp (PA)...216 321-9177
20001 Shelburne Rd Shaker Heights (44118) ***(G-16936)***
Shelby County Review, Wapakoneta *Also called Horizon Ohio Publications Inc* ***(G-19332)***
Shelby Daily Globe Inc...419 342-4276
37 W Main St Shelby (44875) ***(G-16988)***
Shelby Printing Partners LLC...419 342-3171
325 S Martin Dr Shelby (44875) ***(G-16989)***
Shelby Welded Tube Div, Shelby *Also called Phillips Mfg and Tower Co* ***(G-16985)***
Sheldon On Site Inc...419 339-1381
4848 Gomer Rd Elida (45807) ***(G-9200)***
Shellenbarger Excavating & Log...740 397-9949
9260 Fairview Rd Mount Vernon (43050) ***(G-14509)***
Shelley Company, Maumee *Also called Stoneco Inc* ***(G-13149)***
Shelli R McMurray...614 275-4381
1360 Louvaine Dr Rear Columbus (43223) ***(G-7444)***
Shells Inc (PA)...330 808-5558
1245 S Cleveland Massillo Copley (44321) ***(G-7694)***
Shelly & Sands Zanesville OH, Perrysville *Also called S & S Aggregates Inc* ***(G-16031)***
Shelly and Sands Inc...330 743-8850
2800 Center Rd Youngstown (44514) ***(G-21029)***
Shelly and Sands Inc (PA)...740 453-0721
3570 S River Rd Zanesville (43701) ***(G-21176)***
Shelly and Sands Inc...740 373-6495
Hc 7 Box S Marietta (45750) ***(G-12667)***
Shelly and Sands Inc...740 859-2104
1731 Old State Route 7 Rayland (43943) ***(G-16423)***
Shelly and Sands Inc...740 453-0721
3570 S River Rd Zanesville (43701) ***(G-21177)***
Shelly and Shells, Zanesville *Also called Mansfield Asphalt Paving Inc* ***(G-21154)***
Shelly and Zans, Bethesda *Also called Mar-Zane Inc* ***(G-1657)***
Shelly Company...330 666-1125
3350 Sawmill Rd Copley (44321) ***(G-7695)***
Shelly Company...740 687-4420
3232 Lgan Lancaster Rd Se Lancaster (43130) ***(G-11606)***
Shelly Company...419 422-8854
1700 Fostoria Ave Ste 200 Findlay (45840) ***(G-9753)***
Shelly Company...740 474-6255
24537 Canal Rd Circleville (43113) ***(G-4557)***
Shelly Company...740 246-6315
80 Park Dr Thornville (43076) ***(G-18033)***
Shelly Company, The, Thornville *Also called Shelly Materials Inc* ***(G-18035)***
Shelly Fisher...419 522-6696
449 Newman St Mansfield (44902) ***(G-12512)***
Shelly Liquid Division, Toledo *Also called Shelly Materials Inc* ***(G-18521)***
Shelly Liquid Division...216 781-9264
101 Mahoning Ave Cleveland (44113) ***(G-6051)***
Shelly Materials, East Fultonham *Also called Chesterhill Stone Co* ***(G-9045)***
Shelly Materials, Lancaster *Also called Shelly Company* ***(G-11606)***
Shelly Materials Inc...419 229-2741
600 N Sugar St Lima (45801) ***(G-11938)***
Shelly Materials Inc...740 775-4567
1177 Hopetown Rd Chillicothe (45601) ***(G-3222)***
Shelly Materials Inc...740 246-6315
352 George Hardy Dr Toledo (43605) ***(G-18521)***
Shelly Materials Inc...740 246-5009
8775 Blackbird Ln Thornville (43076) ***(G-18034)***
Shelly Materials Inc...330 274-0802
3943 Beck Rd Mantua (44255) ***(G-12558)***
Shelly Materials Inc...330 722-2190
300 N State Rd Medina (44256) ***(G-13341)***
Shelly Materials Inc...614 871-6704
3300 Jackson Pike Grove City (43123) ***(G-10466)***
Shelly Materials Inc...330 364-4411
2301 Progress St Dover (44622) ***(G-8853)***
Shelly Materials Inc...330 425-7861
8920 Canyon Falls Blvd # 120 Twinsburg (44087) ***(G-18857)***
Shelly Materials Inc...740 446-7789
1248 State Route 7 N Gallipolis (45631) ***(G-10175)***
Shelly Materials Inc...419 622-2101
2364 Richey Rd Convoy (45832) ***(G-7671)***
Shelly Materials Inc...330 673-3646
1181 Cherry St Kent (44240) ***(G-11385)***
Shelly Materials Inc...740 666-5841
8328 Watkins Rd Ostrander (43061) ***(G-15646)***
Shelly Materials Inc...740 745-5965
6824 Mount Vernon Rd Newark (43055) ***(G-14918)***
Shelly Materials Inc (HQ)...740 246-6315
80 Park Dr Thornville (43076) ***(G-18035)***
Shelly Materials Inc...419 273-2510
3798 State Route 53 Forest (45843) ***(G-9788)***
Shenango Valley Sand and Grav (PA)...330 758-9100
7240 Glenwood Ave Youngstown (44512) ***(G-21030)***
Shenet LLC...614 563-9600
50 W Broad St Ste 12000 Columbus (43215) ***(G-7445)***
SHEOGA HARDWOOD FLOORING & PAN, Middlefield *Also called Hardwood Flrg & Paneling Inc* ***(G-13803)***
Shepherd Chemical Company...513 200-6987
2825 Highland Ave Cincinnati (45212) ***(G-4331)***
Shepherd Chemical Company...513 731-1110
2803 Highland Ave Cincinnati (45219) ***(G-4332)***
Shepherd Chemical Company...513 424-7276
3444 Yankee Rd Middletown (45044) ***(G-13952)***
Shepherd Material Science Co (PA)...513 731-1110
4900 Beech St Norwood (45212) ***(G-15428)***
Shepherd Middletown Co, Middletown *Also called Shepherd Chemical Company* ***(G-13952)***
Shepherd, The, New Washington *Also called Sheep & Farm Life Inc* ***(G-14832)***
Sherbrooke Metals...440 942-3520
36490 Reading Ave Willoughby (44094) ***(G-20429)***
Sheridan Mfg, Wauseon *Also called Lear Corporation* ***(G-19526)***
Sheridan One Stop Carryout...740 687-1300
1510 Sheridan Dr Lancaster (43130) ***(G-11607)***
Sheridan Woodworks Inc...216 663-9333
17801 S Miles Rd Cleveland (44128) ***(G-6052)***
Sherwin Software Solutions...440 498-8010
5380 Naiman Pkwy Ste B Solon (44139) ***(G-17230)***

ALPHABETIC

Sherwin-Williams Company (PA) ALPHABETIC SECTION

Sherwin-Williams Company (PA) 216 566-2000
101 W Prospect Ave # 1020 Cleveland (44115) ***(G-6053)***
Sherwin-Williams Company 440 282-2310
2280 Coper Foster Pk Rd W Lorain (44053) ***(G-12120)***
Sherwin-Williams Company 330 253-6625
6483 Dressler Rd Nw North Canton (44720) ***(G-15117)***
Sherwin-Williams Company 330 830-6000
600 Nova Dr Se Massillon (44646) ***(G-13048)***
Sherwin-Williams Company 614 539-8456
3875 Brookham Dr Grove City (43123) ***(G-10467)***
Sherwin-Williams Company 440 846-4328
11410 Alameda Dr Strongsville (44149) ***(G-17788)***
Sherwin-Williams Company 216 662-3300
5020 Turney Rd Cleveland (44125) ***(G-6054)***
Sherwin-Williams Company 330 528-0124
5860 Darrow Rd Hudson (44236) ***(G-11072)***
Sherwin-Williams Mfg Co 216 566-2000
101 W Prospect Ave # 1020 Cleveland (44115) ***(G-6055)***
Sherwn-Wllams Auto Fnshes Corp (HQ) 216 332-8330
4440 Warrensville Ctr Rd Cleveland (44128) ***(G-6056)***
Sherwn-Wllams Intl Hldings Inc (HQ) 216 566-2000
4603 Ledgewood Dr Medina (44256) ***(G-13342)***
Sherwood Refractores, Cleveland *Also called PCC Airfoils LLC* ***(G-5857)***
Sherwood Rtm Corp 330 875-7151
4043 Beck Ave Louisville (44641) ***(G-12166)***
Sherwood Valve LLC 216 264-5023
7900 Hub Pkwy Cleveland (44125) ***(G-6057)***
Sherwood Valve LLC 216 264-5028
7900 Hub Pkwy Cleveland (44125) ***(G-6058)***
Shield Laminating, Columbus *Also called The Guardtower Inc* ***(G-7524)***
Shiffler Equipment Sales Inc (PA) 440 285-9175
745 South St Chardon (44024) ***(G-3136)***
Shilling Transport 330 948-1105
9718 Avon Lake Rd Lodi (44254) ***(G-12019)***
Shiloh Automotive Inc 330 558-2600
880 Steel Dr Valley City (44280) ***(G-19061)***
Shiloh Carriage Shop LLC 419 896-3869
8465 Shiloh Norwalk Rd Shiloh (44878) ***(G-17000)***
Shiloh Corporation (HQ) 330 558-2600
880 Steel Dr Valley City (44280) ***(G-19062)***
Shiloh Industries Inc 937 236-5100
5988 Executive Blvd Ste B Dayton (45424) ***(G-8504)***
Shiloh Industries Inc 330 558-2300
5580 Wegman Dr Valley City (44280) ***(G-19063)***
Shiloh Industries Inc 440 647-2100
350 Maple St Wellington (44090) ***(G-19592)***
Shiloh Industries Inc 330 558-2000
5569 Innovation Dr Valley City (44280) ***(G-19064)***
Shiloh Industries Inc 330 558-2600
880 Steel Dr Valley City (44280) ***(G-19065)***
Shiloh Industries Inc (PA) 330 558-2600
880 Steel Dr Valley City (44280) ***(G-19066)***
Shiloh Industries, Inc., Valley City *Also called Medina Blanking Inc* ***(G-19049)***
Shinagawa Advanced Materials A 330 628-1118
3555 Gilchrist Rd Mogadore (44260) ***(G-14249)***
Ship Print E Sell 614 459-1205
3145 Kingsdale Ctr Columbus (43221) ***(G-7446)***
Shipping Room Products Inc 216 531-4422
19400 Saint Clair Ave Cleveland (44117) ***(G-6059)***
Shirer Brothers Meats 740 796-3214
7805 Adamsville Otsego Rd Adamsville (43802) ***(G-10)***
Shirer Brothers Slaughter Hse, Adamsville *Also called Shirer Brothers Meats* ***(G-10)***
Shirley KS Storage Trays LLC 740 868-8140
1150 Newark Rd Zanesville (43701) ***(G-21178)***
Shirt Family 740 706-1284
23 Garden City Rd Marietta (45750) ***(G-12668)***
Shirt Stop LLC 740 574-4774
11769 Gallia Pike Rd Wheelersburg (45694) ***(G-20185)***
Shockakhan Express LLC 614 432-3133
4953 Bixby Ridge Dr W Groveport (43125) ***(G-10511)***
Shoemaker Electric Company 614 294-5626
831 Bonham Ave Columbus (43211) ***(G-7447)***
Shoemaker Industrial Solutions, Columbus *Also called Shoemaker Electric Company* ***(G-7447)***
Shook Manufactured Pdts Inc (PA) 330 848-9780
1017 Kenmore Blvd Akron (44314) ***(G-375)***
Shook Manufactured Pdts Inc 440 247-9130
3801 Wiltshire Rd Chagrin Falls (44022) ***(G-3029)***
Shook Tool Inc 937 337-6471
405 W High St Ansonia (45303) ***(G-594)***
Shoot A Way Inc 419 294-4654
3305 Township Highway 47 Upper Sandusky (43351) ***(G-18973)***
Shoot-A-Way Inc 419 294-4654
8706 State Highway 67 Upper Sandusky (43351) ***(G-18974)***
Shooters Choice LLC 440 834-8888
66 Windward Way Chagrin Falls (44023) ***(G-3076)***
Shooting Range Supply LLC 440 576-7711
735 Fairway St Jefferson (44047) ***(G-11237)***
Shoppers Compass 419 947-9234
114 Iberia St Mount Gilead (43338) ***(G-14432)***
Shops By Todd Inc (PA) 937 458-3192
2727 Fairfld Comns W273 Beavercreek (45431) ***(G-1340)***
Shopsmith, Dayton *Also called Rlfshop LLC* ***(G-8480)***
Shore To Shore Inc (HQ) 937 866-1908
8170 Washington Vlg Dr Dayton (45458) ***(G-8505)***
Shoreline Machine Products Co (PA) 216 481-8033
19301 Saint Clair Ave Cleveland (44117) ***(G-6060)***
Shoreway Sports, Lorain *Also called Swocat Design Inc* ***(G-12127)***
Shorr Packaging, Cincinnati *Also called Hanchett Paper Company* ***(G-3796)***
Short Run Machine Products Inc 440 969-1313
4744 Kister Ct Ashtabula (44004) ***(G-804)***
Shortstack Printing, Warrensville Heights *Also called Hummingbird Graphics LLC* ***(G-19470)***
Shot Selector, Twinsburg *Also called Golf Marketing Group Inc* ***(G-18788)***
Shot-Force Pro LLC 740 753-3927
13580 Kimberley Rd Nelsonville (45764) ***(G-14597)***
Show What You Know, Dayton *Also called Lorenz Corporation* ***(G-8316)***
Showa Aluminum Corp America 740 895-6422
210 Washington Sq Wshngtn CT Hs (43160) ***(G-20744)***
Showcase Cab Mar Rstoration LL 419 626-6715
5404 Sandy Acres Dr Sandusky (44870) ***(G-16849)***
Showerline Products LLC 614 794-3476
1143 Lori Ln Westerville (43081) ***(G-20074)***
Showplace Inc 419 468-7368
201 S Market St Galion (44833) ***(G-10155)***
Showplace Rental, Galion *Also called Showplace Inc* ***(G-10155)***
Showroom Tracker LLC 888 407-0094
6543 Forestwood St Nw Canton (44718) ***(G-2815)***
Shred Away 740 363-6327
227 Rockmill St Delaware (43015) ***(G-8724)***
Shreiner Sole Co Inc 330 276-6135
1 Taylor Dr Killbuck (44637) ***(G-11454)***
Shreve Printing LLC 330 567-2341
390 E Wood St Shreve (44676) ***(G-17010)***
Shriner Sheet Metal Inc 330 435-6735
196 S Main St Creston (44217) ***(G-7809)***
Shrock Prefab LLC 740 599-9401
23403 College Hill Rd Danville (43014) ***(G-7965)***
Shu Shop, The, Richfield *Also called Gail J Shumaker Originals* ***(G-16472)***
Shuler International, Chagrin Falls *Also called E L Ostendorf Inc* ***(G-3016)***
Shumaker Racing Components 419 238-0801
11037 Van Wert Decatur Rd Van Wert (45891) ***(G-19105)***
Shur Clean Usa LLC 513 341-5486
7568 Wyandot Ln Unit 3 Liberty Township (45044) ***(G-11820)***
Shur Fit Distributors Inc 937 746-0567
221 N Main St Franklin (45005) ***(G-9919)***
Shur-Co LLC 330 297-0888
1100 N Freedom St Ravenna (44266) ***(G-16402)***
Shur-Form Laminates Division, Franklin *Also called Shur Fit Distributors Inc* ***(G-9919)***
Shurtape Technologies LLC 440 937-7000
32150 Just Imagine Dr Avon (44011) ***(G-966)***
Shurtech Brands LLC (HQ) 440 937-7000
32150 Just Imagine Dr Avon (44011) ***(G-967)***
Shutter Expressions 937 626-0462
8460 Heather Ct Franklin (45005) ***(G-9920)***
Shutterbus Ohio LLC 937 726-9634
3590 Smiley Rd Hilliard (43026) ***(G-10861)***
Siata Ds Inc (PA) 216 503-7200
24665 Greenwich Ln Beachwood (44122) ***(G-1278)***
Sibg, Cleveland *Also called Snyder Intl Brewing Group LLC* ***(G-6076)***
Sidaris Italian Foods, Cleveland *Also called Bellissimo Distribution LLC* ***(G-4803)***
Sidley Truck & Equipment, Thompson *Also called R W Sidley Incorporated* ***(G-18028)***
Sidney Alive 937 210-2539
101 S Ohio Ave Sidney (45365) ***(G-17077)***
Sidney Can & Tool LLC 937 492-0977
5670 Cecil Rd Sidney (45365) ***(G-17078)***
Sidney Manufacturing Company 937 492-4154
405 N Main Ave Sidney (45365) ***(G-17079)***
Sidney Plant, Sidney *Also called Advanced Composites Inc* ***(G-17013)***
Sidney Printing Works Inc 513 542-4000
2611 Colerain Ave Cincinnati (45214) ***(G-4333)***
Sidney Stiers 740 454-7368
620 Moxahala Ave Zanesville (43701) ***(G-21179)***
Sidwell Materials Inc 740 849-2394
4200 Maysville Pike Zanesville (43701) ***(G-21180)***
Sidwell Materials Inc 740 968-4313
72607 Gun Club Rd Saint Clairsville (43950) ***(G-16651)***
Sieb & Meyer America Inc 513 563-0860
3975 Port Union Rd Fairfield (45014) ***(G-9563)***
Sieb & Meyer America USA, Fairfield *Also called Sieb & Meyer America Inc* ***(G-9563)***
Siefker Sawmill 419 339-1956
8705 W State Rd Elida (45807) ***(G-9201)***
Siegfried, Akron *Also called Ivan Extruders Co Inc* ***(G-220)***
Siemens Energy Inc 740 393-8897
105 N Sandusky St Mount Vernon (43050) ***(G-14510)***
Siemens Energy Inc 740 393-8464
607 W Chestnut St Mount Vernon (43050) ***(G-14511)***
Siemens Energy Inc 740 504-1947
105 N Sandusky St Mount Vernon (43050) ***(G-14512)***

Siemens Industry Inc ... 513 841-3100
4620 Forest Ave Cincinnati (45212) ***(G-4334)***
Siemens Industry Inc ... 440 526-2770
6930 Treeline Dr Ste A Brecksville (44141) ***(G-2058)***
Siemens Industry Inc ... 937 593-6010
811 N Main St Bellefontaine (43311) ***(G-1525)***
Siemens Industry Inc ... 419 499-4616
21 N Main St Milan (44846) ***(G-13989)***
Siemens Industry Inc ... 513 336-2267
4170 Columbia Rd Lebanon (45036) ***(G-11695)***
Siemens Industry Inc ... 614 573-8212
977 Gahanna Pkwy Columbus (43230) ***(G-7448)***
Siemens Power and Gas, Mount Vernon *Also called Siemens Energy Inc* ***(G-14512)***
Siemer Distributing, New Lexington *Also called Lori Holding Co* ***(G-14717)***
Sietins Plastics Inc ... 440 232-8515
380 Solon Rd Ste 4 Cleveland (44146) ***(G-6061)***
Sietins Precision, Cleveland *Also called Sietins Plastics Inc* ***(G-6061)***
Sifco Applied Srfc Cncepts LLC (PA) ... 216 524-0099
5708 E Schaaf Rd Cleveland (44131) ***(G-6062)***
Sifco ASC, Cleveland *Also called Sifco Applied Srfc Cncepts LLC* ***(G-6062)***
Sifco Industries Inc (PA) ... 216 881-8600
970 E 64th St Cleveland (44103) ***(G-6063)***
Sifted Sweet Shop LLC ... 216 901-7100
4496 Mahoning Ave Ste 905 Youngstown (44515) ***(G-21031)***
Siglent Technologies Amer Inc ... 440 398-5800
6557 Cochran Rd Solon (44139) ***(G-17231)***
Sigma Div, Newburgh Heights *Also called Howmet Aluminum Casting Inc* ***(G-14937)***
Sigma T E K, Cincinnati *Also called Sigmatek Systems LLC* ***(G-4335)***
Sigma-Aldrich, Miamisburg *Also called Aldrich Chemical* ***(G-13638)***
Sigmatek Systems LLC (PA) ... 513 674-0005
1445 Kemper Meadow Dr Cincinnati (45240) ***(G-4335)***
Sign A Rama ... 330 499-4653
435 Applegrove St Nw North Canton (44720) ***(G-15118)***
Sign A Rama ... 614 337-6000
64 Granville St Gahanna (43230) ***(G-10103)***
Sign A Rama Inc ... 614 932-7005
3960 Presidential Pkwy A Powell (43065) ***(G-16335)***
Sign A Rama Inc ... 440 442-5002
731 Beta Dr Ste D Cleveland (44143) ***(G-6064)***
Sign A Rama Inc ... 513 671-2213
2519 Crescentville Rd Cincinnati (45241) ***(G-4336)***
Sign America Incorporated ... 740 765-5555
3887 State Route 43 Richmond (43944) ***(G-16498)***
Sign City Inc ... 614 486-6700
5357 State Route 95 Mount Gilead (43338) ***(G-14433)***
Sign Connection Inc ... 937 435-4070
90 Compark Rd Ste B Dayton (45459) ***(G-8506)***
Sign Design Wooster Inc ... 330 262-8838
1537 W Old Lincoln Way Wooster (44691) ***(G-20654)***
Sign Dynamics, Dayton *Also called Jeffrey L Becht Inc* ***(G-8283)***
Sign Graphics & Design ... 513 576-1639
420 Main St Unit A Milford (45150) ***(G-14040)***
Sign Lady Inc ... 419 476-9191
5981 Telegraph Rd Toledo (43612) ***(G-18522)***
Sign Makers LLC ... 330 455-0909
2417 Cleveland Ave Nw Canton (44709) ***(G-2816)***
Sign Pro of Lima ... 419 222-7767
404 Brower Rd Lima (45801) ***(G-11939)***
Sign Shop ... 740 474-1499
3269 State Route 361 Circleville (43113) ***(G-4558)***
Sign Smith LLC ... 614 519-9144
2760 County Road 26 Marengo (43334) ***(G-12595)***
Sign Source USA Inc ... 419 224-1130
1700 S Dixie Hwy Lima (45804) ***(G-11940)***
Sign Technologies LLC ... 937 439-3970
2001 Kuntz Rd Dayton (45404) ***(G-8507)***
Sign Write ... 937 559-4388
3348 Dayton Xenia Rd Beavercreek (45432) ***(G-1341)***
Sign-A-Rama, Dayton *Also called R & H Signs Unlimited Inc* ***(G-8457)***
Sign-A-Rama, North Canton *Also called Sign A Rama* ***(G-15118)***
Sign-A-Rama, Gahanna *Also called Sign A Rama* ***(G-10103)***
Sign-A-Rama, Powell *Also called Sign A Rama Inc* ***(G-16335)***
Sign-A-Rama, Cleveland *Also called Sign A Rama Inc* ***(G-6064)***
Sign-A-Rama, Columbus *Also called Business Idntification Systems* ***(G-6716)***
Sign-A-Rama, Cincinnati *Also called Sign A Rama Inc* ***(G-4336)***
Signage Consultants Inc ... 614 297-7446
870 E 5th Ave Columbus (43201) ***(G-7449)***
Signal Graphics Printing, Copley *Also called Vision Graphics* ***(G-7698)***
Signal Group, Ashland *Also called Advanced Cylinder Repair Inc* ***(G-675)***
Signalysis Inc ... 513 528-6164
539 Glenrose Ln Cincinnati (45244) ***(G-4337)***
Signarama Worthington, Columbus *Also called Corporate ID Inc* ***(G-6823)***
Signature 4 Image, Coldwater *Also called Signature Partners Inc* ***(G-6420)***
Signature Beef LLC ... 740 468-3579
5500 Canal Rd Ne Pleasantville (43148) ***(G-16230)***
Signature Cabinetry Inc ... 614 252-2227
1285 Alum Creek Dr Columbus (43209) ***(G-7450)***
Signature Control Systems, Columbus *Also called Tiba LLC* ***(G-7528)***
Signature Partners Inc ... 419 678-1400
149 Harvest Dr Coldwater (45828) ***(G-6420)***
Signature Sign Co Inc ... 216 426-1234
1776 E 43rd St Cleveland (44103) ***(G-6065)***
Signature Store Fixtures, Columbus *Also called A-Display Service Corp* ***(G-6517)***
Signature Technologies Inc (HQ) ... 937 859-6323
3728 Benner Rd Miamisburg (45342) ***(G-13716)***
Signcom Incorporated ... 614 228-9999
527 W Rich St Columbus (43215) ***(G-7451)***
Signed By Josette LLC ... 419 796-9632
303 E Sandusky St Findlay (45840) ***(G-9754)***
Signery ... 513 932-1938
1002 W Main St Apt D Lebanon (45036) ***(G-11696)***
Signery2 LLC ... 513 738-3048
2571 Millville Shandon Rd Hamilton (45013) ***(G-10605)***
Signet Group Inc ... 330 668-5901
375 Ghent Rd Fairlawn (44333) ***(G-9617)***
Signetics, Dayton *Also called Sign Technologies LLC* ***(G-8507)***
Significant Impressions Inc ... 513 874-5223
4050 Thunderbird Ln Fairfield (45014) ***(G-9564)***
Signline Graphics & Lettering ... 740 397-5806
114 Clinton Rd Mount Vernon (43050) ***(G-14513)***
Signmaker Shop, The, Coshocton *Also called Steven Mercer Inc* ***(G-7753)***
Signmaster Inc ... 614 777-0670
758 Radio Dr Lewis Center (43035) ***(G-11780)***
Signode Industrial Group LLC ... 513 248-2990
396 Wards Corner Rd # 100 Loveland (45140) ***(G-12232)***
Signpost Games LLC ... 614 467-9025
7108 Starkeys Ct Dublin (43017) ***(G-8985)***
Signs 2 Graphics ... 740 493-2049
746 State Route 220 Piketon (45661) ***(G-16080)***
Signs By George ... 216 394-2095
5815 Warren Sharon Rd Brookfield (44403) ***(G-2109)***
Signs By Tomorrow, West Chester *Also called Meka Signs Enterprises Inc* ***(G-19878)***
Signs By Tomorrow, Dublin *Also called Bambeck Inc* ***(G-8887)***
Signs By Tomorrow, Cleveland *Also called Jalo Inc* ***(G-5492)***
Signs Limited LLC ... 740 282-7715
356 Technology Way Steubenville (43952) ***(G-17551)***
Signs N Ship, Elyria *Also called All Star Group Inc* ***(G-9212)***
Signs N Stuff Inc ... 440 974-3151
9354 Mentor Ave Ste 4 Mentor (44060) ***(G-13582)***
Signs Now, Dayton *Also called Tract Inc* ***(G-7993)***
Signs of The Times, Cleveland *Also called A Sign For The Times Inc* ***(G-4593)***
Signs PDQ Inc ... 440 951-6651
35160 Topps Industrial Pk Willoughby (44094) ***(G-20430)***
Signs To Go, Dover *Also called Kim Phillips Sign Co LLC* ***(G-8834)***
Signs Unlimited The Graphic (PA) ... 614 836-7446
21313 State Route 93 S Logan (43138) ***(G-12043)***
Sika Corporation ... 740 387-9224
1682 Mrn Williamsprt Rd E Marion (43302) ***(G-12735)***
Siler Excavation Services ... 513 400-8628
6025 Catherine Dr Milford (45150) ***(G-14041)***
Silfex Inc ... 937 472-3311
950 S Franklin St Eaton (45320) ***(G-9166)***
Silgan Plastics LLC ... 419 523-3737
690 Woodland Dr Ottawa (45875) ***(G-15664)***
Silica Press Inc ... 419 843-8500
3545 Silica Rd Unit A2 Sylvania (43560) ***(G-17961)***
Silicon USA Inc ... 330 928-6217
1220 Orlen Ave Cuyahoga Falls (44221) ***(G-7916)***
Silicone Solutions Inc ... 330 920-3125
338 Remington Rd Cuyahoga Falls (44224) ***(G-7917)***
Silicone Solutions Intl LLC ... 419 720-8709
3441 South Ave Toledo (43609) ***(G-18523)***
Silk Road Sourcing LLC ... 814 571-5533
161 Charles Ave Amherst (44001) ***(G-574)***
Silk Screen Special TS Inc ... 740 246-4843
9075 Boundaries Rd Thornville (43076) ***(G-18036)***
Silmix Division, Canton *Also called Wacker Chemical Corporation* ***(G-2862)***
Silver Creek Log Homes ... 419 335-3220
5350 County Road 16 Wauseon (43567) ***(G-19532)***
Silver Crest, Madison *Also called SCC Wine Company LLC* ***(G-12356)***
Silver Expressions ... 740 687-0144
1635 River Valley Cir S # 5078 Lancaster (43130) ***(G-11608)***
Silver Machine Co, Elyria *Also called Ultra Machine Inc* ***(G-9340)***
Silver Maple Publications ... 937 767-1259
1308 Corry St Yellow Springs (45387) ***(G-20816)***
Silver Threads Inc ... 614 733-0099
7710 Corporate Blvd Plain City (43064) ***(G-16211)***
Silver Tool Inc ... 937 865-0012
2440 Cross Pointe Dr Miamisburg (45342) ***(G-13717)***
Silver, Burdett & Ginn, Columbus *Also called Simon & Schuster Inc* ***(G-7453)***
Silverado Trucks & Accessories ... 937 492-8862
720 Linden Ave Sidney (45365) ***(G-17080)***
Silvercote LLC ... 330 748-8500
9600b Valley View Rd Macedonia (44056) ***(G-12325)***

ALPHABETIC

(PA)=Parent Co (HQ)=Headquarters (DH)=Div Headquarters
2019 Harris Ohio Industrial Directory
1249

Silvesco Inc.......740 373-6661
2985 State Route 26 Marietta (45750) ***(G-12669)***
Simcote Inc.......740 382-5000
250 N Greenwood St Marion (43302) ***(G-12736)***
Simcote of Ohio Division, Marion *Also called Simcote Inc* ***(G-12736)***
Simet, Hudson *Also called Sintered Metal Industries Inc* ***(G-11073)***
Simex Inc.......304 665-1104
181 Pleasants Indus Park Columbus (43224) ***(G-7452)***
Simmons Company.......614 871-8088
3960 Brookham Dr Grove City (43123) ***(G-10468)***
Simon & Schuster Inc.......614 876-0371
4350 Equity Dr Columbus (43228) ***(G-7453)***
Simon & Simon Blue Pond Inc.......330 928-2298
2211 Harding Rd Cuyahoga Falls (44223) ***(G-7918)***
Simon De Young Corporation.......440 834-3000
15010 Brkshire Indus Pkwy Middlefield (44062) ***(G-13853)***
Simon Ellis Superabrasives.......937 226-0683
501 Progress Rd Dayton (45449) ***(G-8508)***
Simon Roofing and Shtmtl Corp (PA).......330 629-7392
70 Karago Ave Youngstown (44512) ***(G-21032)***
Simona PMC LLC.......419 429-0042
2040 Industrial Dr Findlay (45840) ***(G-9755)***
Simonds International LLC.......978 424-0100
76000 Old Twenty One Rd Kimbolton (43749) ***(G-11457)***
Simple Living, Troy *Also called Wellington Wllams Wrldwide LLC* ***(G-18718)***
Simple Products LLC.......330 674-2448
10336 Township Road 262 Millersburg (44654) ***(G-14129)***
Simple Vms LLC.......888 255-8918
7373 Beechmont Ave # 130 Cincinnati (45230) ***(G-4338)***
Simplex-It LLC.......234 380-1277
4301 Darrow Rd Ste 1200 Stow (44224) ***(G-17628)***
Simply Canvas Inc.......330 436-6500
1479 Exeter Rd Akron (44306) ***(G-376)***
Simply Elegant Formals Inc.......419 738-7722
708 N Dixie Hwy Wapakoneta (45895) ***(G-19354)***
Simply Unique Snacks LLC.......513 223-7736
4420 Haight Ave Cincinnati (45223) ***(G-4339)***
Simpson & Sons Inc.......513 367-0152
10220 Harrison Ave Harrison (45030) ***(G-10670)***
Simpson Brothers Machine Works.......740 353-6870
2204 Gallia St Portsmouth (45662) ***(G-16299)***
Simpson Strong-Tie Company Inc.......614 876-8060
2600 International St Columbus (43228) ***(G-7454)***
Sims-Lohman Inc (PA).......513 651-3510
6325 Este Ave Cincinnati (45232) ***(G-4340)***
Sims-Lohman Inc.......440 799-8285
1500 Valley Belt Rd Brooklyn Heights (44131) ***(G-2131)***
Sims-Lohman Inc.......330 456-8408
6570 Promway Ave Nw North Canton (44720) ***(G-15119)***
Sims-Lohman Fine Kitchens Gran, Cincinnati *Also called Sims-Lohman Inc* ***(G-4340)***
Simxperience, New Franklin *Also called Villers Enterprises Limited* ***(G-14688)***
Sinbon Usa LLC.......937 667-8999
4265 Gibson Dr Tipp City (45371) ***(G-18133)***
Sine Wall LLC.......919 453-2011
7162 Liberty West Chester (45069) ***(G-19796)***
Sinel Company Inc.......937 433-4772
4811 Pamela Sue Dr Dayton (45429) ***(G-8509)***
Sinful Sweets LLC.......330 721-0916
3862 Turnberry Dr Medina (44256) ***(G-13343)***
Singer Press.......216 595-9400
23500 Mercantile Rd Ste A Beachwood (44122) ***(G-1279)***
Single Phase Pwr Solutions LLC (PA).......513 722-5098
1917 Tilden Ave Norwood (45212) ***(G-15429)***
Single Source Technologies LLC.......513 573-7200
7680 Innovation Way Mason (45040) ***(G-12939)***
Singleton Corporation.......216 651-7800
3280 W 67th Pl Cleveland (44102) ***(G-6066)***
Singleton Reels Inc.......330 274-2961
11783 Timber Point Trl Mantua (44255) ***(G-12559)***
Sinico Mtm US Inc.......216 264-8344
8001 Sweet Valley Dr # 6 Cleveland (44125) ***(G-6067)***
Sinners N Saints LLC.......614 231-7467
1515 Alum Creek Dr Columbus (43209) ***(G-7455)***
Sintered Metal Industries Inc.......330 650-4000
1890 Georgetown Rd Hudson (44236) ***(G-11073)***
Sir Speedy, Fairlawn *Also called Tcp Inc* ***(G-9622)***
Sir Speedy, Cleveland *Also called Frank J Prucha & Associates* ***(G-5272)***
Sir Steak Machinery Inc.......419 526-9181
40 Baird Pkwy Mansfield (44903) ***(G-12513)***
Sirio Panel Inc.......937 238-3607
1385 Stonycreek Rd Ste E Troy (45373) ***(G-18706)***
Sirrus Inc.......513 448-0308
422 Wards Corner Rd Loveland (45140) ***(G-12233)***
Sissel Logging LLC.......740 858-4613
69 Pond Lick Rd Portsmouth (45663) ***(G-16300)***
Site Tech (PA).......740 522-0019
75 Central Pkwy Heath (43056) ***(G-10733)***
Siteone Landscape Supply LLC.......330 220-8691
2925 Interstate Pkwy Brunswick (44212) ***(G-2239)***
Sitler Printer Inc.......330 482-4463
707 E Park Ave Columbiana (44408) ***(G-6480)***
Sivon Manufacturing LLC.......440 259-5505
3131 Perry Park Rd Perry (44081) ***(G-15912)***
Sivon Manufacturing Company, Perry *Also called Sivon Manufacturing LLC* ***(G-15912)***
Six C Fabrication Inc.......330 296-5594
5245 S Prospect St Ravenna (44266) ***(G-16403)***
Six-3.......614 260-5610
2514 Summit St Columbus (43202) ***(G-7456)***
Sizetec Inc.......330 492-9682
4825 Higbee Ave Nw # 103 Canton (44718) ***(G-2817)***
Sjbs, Akron *Also called Standard Jig Boring Svc LLC* ***(G-384)***
Sjpm Inc.......614 475-4571
264 Agler Rd Gahanna (43230) ***(G-10104)***
Sk Machinery Corporation.......330 733-7325
487 Wellington Ave Akron (44305) ***(G-377)***
Sk Tech Inc.......937 836-3535
200 Metro Dr Englewood (45315) ***(G-9375)***
Sk Textile Inc.......323 581-8986
1 Knollcrest Dr Cincinnati (45237) ***(G-4341)***
Skeeles Manufacturing Corp.......614 274-4700
4040 Fondorf Dr Columbus (43228) ***(G-7457)***
SKF Machine Tools Service, Cleveland *Also called American Precision Spindles* ***(G-4694)***
SKF Usa Inc.......800 589-5563
670 Alpha Dr Cleveland (44143) ***(G-6068)***
Skid Guard, Cleveland *Also called Sure-Foot Industries Corp* ***(G-6131)***
Skidmore Engineering Div, Chagrin Falls *Also called Buckeye Gear Co* ***(G-3038)***
Skidmore-Wilhelm Manufacturing, Cleveland *Also called Tungsten Capital Partners LLC* ***(G-6221)***
Skidmore-Wilhelm Mfg Company.......216 481-4774
30340 Solon Industrial B Solon (44139) ***(G-17232)***
Skiff Craft, Plain City *Also called W of Ohio Inc* ***(G-16216)***
Skillsoft Corporation.......216 524-5200
6645 Acres Dr Independence (44131) ***(G-11150)***
Skin.......937 222-0222
333 Wayne Ave Dayton (45410) ***(G-8510)***
Skinner Machining Co.......216 486-6636
23574 Saint Clair Ave Cleveland (44117) ***(G-6069)***
Skinner Metal Products, Medina *Also called Skinner Sales Group Inc* ***(G-13344)***
Skinner Powder Coating Inc.......937 606-2188
631 Boone St Piqua (45356) ***(G-16162)***
Skinner Sales Group Inc.......440 572-8455
3860 Deer Lake Dr Medina (44256) ***(G-13344)***
Skinny Piggy Kombucha LLC.......513 646-5753
5510 Glengate Ln Cincinnati (45212) ***(G-4342)***
Skirdle, Blue Ash *Also called Protein Express Laboratories* ***(G-1839)***
Skladany Enterprises Inc.......614 823-6883
695 Mccorkle Blvd Westerville (43082) ***(G-20023)***
Skladany Printing Center, Westerville *Also called Skladany Enterprises Inc* ***(G-20023)***
Skr Enterprises LLC.......419 891-1112
127 W Wayne St Maumee (43537) ***(G-13145)***
Skribs Tool and Die Inc.......440 951-7774
7555 Tyler Blvd Ste 11 Mentor (44060) ***(G-13583)***
Skrl Die Casting Inc.......440 946-7200
34580 Lakeland Blvd Willoughby (44095) ***(G-20431)***
Skuld LLC.......330 423-7339
4324 Bennington Creek Ln Groveport (43125) ***(G-10512)***
Skuttle Indoor Air Qulty Pdts, Marietta *Also called Skuttle Mfg Co* ***(G-12670)***
Skuttle Mfg Co.......740 373-9169
101 Margaret St Marietta (45750) ***(G-12670)***
Sky Climber LLC (PA).......740 203-3900
1800 Pittsburgh Dr Delaware (43015) ***(G-8725)***
Sky Climber Fasteners LLC.......740 816-9830
1600 Pittsburgh Dr Delaware (43015) ***(G-8726)***
Sky Climber Wind Solutions, Delaware *Also called Sky Climber LLC* ***(G-8725)***
Sky Riders Inc.......440 310-6819
3736 Dallas Ave Lorain (44055) ***(G-12121)***
Sky-Tek, East Palestine *Also called Carlson Aircraft Inc* ***(G-9070)***
Skybox Investments Inc.......419 525-6013
1275 Pollock Pkwy Mansfield (44905) ***(G-12514)***
Skybox Packaging LLC.......419 525-7209
1275 Pollock Pkwy Mansfield (44905) ***(G-12515)***
Skybryte Company Inc.......216 771-1590
3125 Perkins Ave Cleveland (44114) ***(G-6070)***
Skylift Inc.......440 960-2100
3000 Leavitt Rd Ste 6 Lorain (44052) ***(G-12122)***
Skyline Chili Inc (PA).......513 874-1188
4180 Thunderbird Ln Fairfield (45014) ***(G-9565)***
Skyline Corporation.......330 852-2483
580 Mill St Nw Sugarcreek (44681) ***(G-17864)***
Skyline Exhibits Grtr Cncnt.......513 671-4460
9850 Prnctn Glndle Rd Ste Cincinnati (45246) ***(G-4343)***
Skyline Trisource Exhibits, Cleveland *Also called Ternion Inc* ***(G-6161)***
Skyliner.......740 738-0874
225 Main St Bridgeport (43912) ***(G-2078)***
Slabe Machine Products Co.......440 946-6555
4659 Hamann Pkwy Willoughby (44094) ***(G-20432)***

Slabe Tool Company 740 439-1647
   1300 Oxford Ave Cambridge (43725) *(G-2456)*
Slade Gardner 440 355-8015
   233 Commerce Dr Unit B Lagrange (44050) *(G-11493)*
Slap N Tickle LLC 419 349-3226
   5645 Angola Rd Ste A Toledo (43615) *(G-18524)*
Slater Builders Supply, The Plains Also called Tyjen Inc *(G-18023)*
Slater Silk Screen 419 755-8337
   323 Lenox Ave Mansfield (44906) *(G-12516)*
Slater's Builders Supplies, Logan Also called Tyjen Inc *(G-12045)*
Slats and Nails Inc 330 866-1008
   10465 Sandyville Ave Se East Sparta (44626) *(G-9095)*
Slice Mfg LLC 330 733-7600
   1800 Triplett Blvd Akron (44306) *(G-378)*
Slice of Heaven Bakery 419 656-6606
   463 N County Road 268 Clyde (43410) *(G-6396)*
Slicksaw.com, Brunswick Also called Rboog Industries LLC *(G-2233)*
Slimans Printery Inc 330 454-9141
   624 5th St Nw Canton (44703) *(G-2818)*
Slimline Surgical Devices LLC 937 335-0496
   1990 W Stanfield Rd Troy (45373) *(G-18707)*
Sloat Inc 440 951-9554
   34099 Melinz Pkwy Unit A Willoughby (44095) *(G-20433)*
Slogans LLC 330 942-9464
   234 W State St Barberton (44203) *(G-1105)*
Slush Puppie 513 771-0940
   44 Carnegie Way West Chester (45246) *(G-19899)*
Sluterbeck Tool & Die Inc 937 836-5736
   7540 Jacks Ln Clayton (45315) *(G-4578)*
Sluterbeck Tool Co, Clayton Also called Sluterbeck Tool & Die Inc *(G-4578)*
Slutzkers Quickprint Center 440 244-0330
   721 Broadway Lorain (44052) *(G-12123)*
Sly Inc (PA) 440 891-3200
   8300 Dow Cir Ste 600 Strongsville (44136) *(G-17789)*
SMA Plastics LLC 330 627-1377
   755 N Lisbon St Carrollton (44615) *(G-2929)*
Small Business Products 800 553-6485
   8603 Winton Rd Cincinnati (45231) *(G-4344)*
Small Dog Printing 614 777-7620
   3972 Brown Park Dr Ste E Hilliard (43026) *(G-10862)*
Small Sand & Gravel Inc 740 427-3130
   10229 Killduff Rd Gambier (43022) *(G-10183)*
Small's Ready-Mixed Concrete, Gambier Also called Smalls Inc *(G-10185)*
Smalls Asphalt Paving Inc 740 427-4096
   10229 Killduff Rd Gambier (43022) *(G-10184)*
Smalls Inc 740 427-3633
   10229 Killduff Rd Gambier (43022) *(G-10185)*
Smart 3d Solutions LLC 330 972-7840
   411 Wolf Ledges Pkwy # 100 Akron (44311) *(G-379)*
Smart Business Magazine, Cleveland Also called Smart Business Network Inc *(G-6071)*
Smart Business Network Inc (PA) 440 250-7000
   835 Sharon Dr Ste 200 Cleveland (44145) *(G-6071)*
Smart Commercialization Center 440 366-4048
   141 Innovation Dr Elyria (44035) *(G-9327)*
Smart Microsystems Ltd 440 366-4257
   141 Innovation Dr Elyria (44035) *(G-9328)*
Smart Papers Holdings LLC 513 869-5583
   601 N B St Hamilton (45013) *(G-10606)*
Smart Snic Stencil Clg Systems, Cleveland Also called Smart Sonic Corporation *(G-6072)*
Smart Solutions, Beachwood Also called Ohio Cllbrtive Lrng Sltons Inc *(G-1255)*
Smart Sonic Corporation 818 610-7900
   837 E 79th St Cleveland (44103) *(G-6072)*
Smart Tooling, Xenia Also called Spintech LLC *(G-20791)*
Smartbill Ltd 740 928-6909
   1050 O Neill Dr Hebron (43025) *(G-10763)*
Smartcopy Inc (PA) 740 392-6162
   50 Parrott St Ste A Mount Vernon (43050) *(G-14514)*
Smartronix Inc 216 378-3300
   416 Apple Hill Dr Northfield (44067) *(G-15325)*
Smashing Events and Baking 513 415-9693
   693 Winding Way Cincinnati (45245) *(G-3264)*
SMC Corporation of America 330 659-2006
   4160 Highlander Pkwy # 200 Richfield (44286) *(G-16488)*
Smead Manufacturing Company 740 385-5601
   851 Smead Rd Logan (43138) *(G-12044)*
Smedleys Bar and Grill 216 941-0124
   17004 Lorain Ave Cleveland (44111) *(G-6073)*
Smg Growing Media Inc (HQ) 937 644-0011
   14111 Scottslawn Rd Marysville (43040) *(G-12813)*
SMH Manufacturing Inc 419 884-0071
   300 S Mill St Lexington (44904) *(G-11806)*
SMI Holdings Inc 740 927-3464
   10685 Columbus Pkwy Pataskala (43062) *(G-15845)*
Smile Brands Inc 440 471-6133
   25102 Brookpark Rd North Olmsted (44070) *(G-15199)*
Smith & Nephew Inc 513 821-5888
   5005 Barrow Ave Ste 100 Cincinnati (45209) *(G-4345)*
Smith & Nephew Inc 614 793-0581
   4360 Tuller Rd Dublin (43017) *(G-8986)*
Smith Brothers Erection Inc 740 373-3575
   101 Industry Rd Marietta (45750) *(G-12671)*
Smith Carl E Cnslting Engneers, Bath Also called Warmus and Associates Inc *(G-1203)*
Smith Concrete Co (PA) 740 373-7441
   2301 Progress St Dover (44622) *(G-8854)*
Smith Electro Chemical Co 513 351-7227
   5936 Carthage Ct Cincinnati (45212) *(G-4346)*
Smith Facing and Supply Co, Cleveland Also called Fleig Enterprises Inc *(G-5249)*
Smith International Inc 330 497-2999
   2616 Country Squire St Nw Uniontown (44685) *(G-18931)*
Smith Machine Inc 330 821-9898
   20651 Lake Park Blvd Alliance (44601) *(G-500)*
Smith Marathon Distributing, West Mansfield Also called M J S Oil Inc *(G-19944)*
Smith P K Woodcarving LLC 513 271-7077
   2021 A Riverside Drv Stea Louisville (44641) *(G-12167)*
Smith Pallets 937 564-6492
   9855 State Route 121 Versailles (45380) *(G-19190)*
Smith Quarter Horses 419 420-0112
   1116 Glen Meadow Dr Findlay (45840) *(G-9756)*
Smith Rn Sheet Metal Shop Inc 740 653-5011
   1312 Campground Rd Lancaster (43130) *(G-11609)*
Smith Security Safes Inc 419 823-1423
   17641 Tontogany Rd Bowling Green (43402) *(G-1999)*
Smith Smith & Deyarman 330 866-5521
   9260 Bachelor Rd Nw Magnolia (44643) *(G-12363)*
Smith Springs Inc 800 619-4652
   1755 Mount Perry Rd Mount Perry (43760) *(G-14459)*
Smith Truck Cranes & Eqp Co 330 929-3303
   307 Munroe Falls Ave Cuyahoga Falls (44221) *(G-7919)*
Smith-Lustig Paper Box Mfg Co 216 621-0453
   22475 Aurora Rd Bedford (44146) *(G-1446)*
Smithers-Oasis Company (PA) 330 945-5100
   295 S Water St Ste 201 Kent (44240) *(G-11386)*
Smithers-Oasis Company 330 673-5831
   919 Marvin St Kent (44240) *(G-11387)*
Smithfield Bioscience Inc 513 772-8130
   12150 Best Pl Cincinnati (45241) *(G-4347)*
Smithfield Packaged Meats Corp (HQ) 513 782-3800
   805 E Kemper Rd Cincinnati (45246) *(G-4348)*
Smithfield Packaged Meats Corp 513 782-3805
   801 E Kemper Rd Cincinnati (45246) *(G-4349)*
Smithfoods Inc (PA) 330 683-8710
   1381 Dairy Ln Orrville (44667) *(G-15620)*
Smiths Medical Asd Inc 800 796-8701
   5200 Upper Metro Pl # 200 Dublin (43017) *(G-8987)*
Smiths Medical Asd Inc 614 889-2220
   6250 Shier Rings Rd Dublin (43016) *(G-8988)*
Smiths Medical Asd Inc 614 210-6431
   5200 Upper Metro Pl # 200 Dublin (43017) *(G-8989)*
Smiths Medical North America 614 210-7300
   5200 Upper Metro Pl Dublin (43017) *(G-8990)*
Smiths Medical Pm Inc (PA) 614 210-7300
   5200 Upper Metro Pl # 200 Dublin (43017) *(G-8991)*
Smiths Sawdust Studio 740 484-4656
   206 Maple Ave Bethesda (43719) *(G-1658)*
Smithville Mfg Co 330 345-5818
   6563 Cleveland Rd Wooster (44691) *(G-20655)*
Smitten Enterprises LLC 937 267-6963
   205 S Main St Springboro (45066) *(G-17353)*
Sml Inc (PA) 330 668-6555
   4083 Embassy Pkwy Akron (44333) *(G-380)*
Smoke Rings Inc 419 420-9966
   1928 Tiffin Ave Findlay (45840) *(G-9757)*
Smokeheal Inc 216 255-5119
   5247 Wilson Mills Rd # 421 Cleveland (44143) *(G-6074)*
Smokin Guns LLC 440 324-4003
   41458 Griswold Rd Elyria (44035) *(G-9329)*
Smokin TS Smokehouse 440 577-1117
   1550 Stnhpe Kllggsvlle Jefferson (44047) *(G-11238)*
Smolic Machine Co 440 946-1747
   37127 Ben Hur Ave Willoughby (44094) *(G-20434)*
Smoothie Creations Inc 817 313-8212
   17137 Misty Lake Dr Strongsville (44136) *(G-17790)*
Smoothie-Licious 513 742-2260
   1325 Quail Ridge Rd Batavia (45103) *(G-1184)*
Smp Welding LLC 440 205-9353
   8171 Tyler Blvd Mentor (44060) *(G-13584)*
SMS Communications Inc 216 374-6686
   20116 Chagrin Blvd Shaker Heights (44122) *(G-16937)*
SMS Technologies Inc 419 465-4175
   3531 Everingin Rd Monroeville (44847) *(G-14291)*
Smucker International Inc (HQ) 330 682-3000
   1 Strawberry Ln Orrville (44667) *(G-15621)*
Smucker Manufacturing Inc 888 550-9555
   1 Strawberry Ln Orrville (44667) *(G-15622)*
Smucker Natural Foods Inc 330 682-3000
   Strawberry Ln Orrville (44667) *(G-15623)*
SMUCKER'S, Orrville Also called J M Smucker Company *(G-15596)*
Smucker's, Orrville Also called Smucker International Inc *(G-15621)*
Smurfit Stone, Cincinnati Also called Westrock Cp LLC *(G-4504)*

Smurfit-Stone, Blue Ash | ALPHABETIC SECTION

Smurfit-Stone, Blue Ash *Also called Westrock Cp LLC* ***(G-1868)***
Smurfit-Stone Container, Coshocton *Also called Westrock Cp LLC* ***(G-7757)***
Snack Alliance Inc (HQ).....330 767-3426
100 Lincoln Way E Massillon (44646) ***(G-13049)***
Snair Co.....614 873-7020
8163 Business Way Plain City (43064) ***(G-16212)***
Snakebite Snaps.....520 227-5442
2642 Archwood Pl Cuyahoga Falls (44221) ***(G-7920)***
Snap Rite Manufacturing Inc.....910 897-4080
14300 Darley Ave Cleveland (44110) ***(G-6075)***
Snap-On Business Solutions (HQ).....330 659-1600
4025 Kinross Lakes Pkwy Richfield (44286) ***(G-16489)***
Snappskin Inc.....440 318-4879
534 Manor Brook Dr Chagrin Falls (44022) ***(G-3030)***
Snaps Inc.....419 477-5100
2557 Township Road 35 Mount Cory (45868) ***(G-14418)***
Sneaky Pete Band.....419 933-6251
4418 N Greenfield Rd Willard (44890) ***(G-20245)***
Sneller Machine Tool Division, Cleveland *Also called Grand Harbor Yacht Sales & Svc* ***(G-5339)***
Sni Inc.....937 427-9447
75 Harbert Dr Ste A Beavercreek (45440) ***(G-1363)***
Snook Advertising Al Publisher.....614 866-3333
1567 Alar Ave Reynoldsburg (43068) ***(G-16453)***
Snook Al Advertising/Publisher, Reynoldsburg *Also called Snook Advertising Al Publisher* ***(G-16453)***
Snow Aviation Intl Inc.....614 588-2452
949 Creek Dr Gahanna (43230) ***(G-10105)***
Snow Metal Products Co, Solon *Also called Swagelok* ***(G-17239)***
Snow Printing Co Inc.....419 229-7669
1000 W Grand Ave Frnt Lima (45801) ***(G-11941)***
Snows Wood Shop Inc (PA).....419 836-3805
7220 Brown Rd Oregon (43616) ***(G-15567)***
Sns Nano Fiber Technology LLC.....330 655-0030
5633 Hudson Indus Pkwy Hudson (44236) ***(G-11074)***
Snyder Brick and Block, Moraine *Also called Snyder Concrete Products Inc* ***(G-14394)***
Snyder Brick and Block, Monroe *Also called Snyder Concrete Products Inc* ***(G-14276)***
Snyder Brick and Block, Dayton *Also called Snyder Concrete Products Inc* ***(G-8511)***
Snyder Concrete Products Inc (PA).....937 885-5176
2301 W Dorothy Ln Moraine (45439) ***(G-14394)***
Snyder Concrete Products Inc.....513 539-7686
233 Senate Dr Monroe (45050) ***(G-14276)***
Snyder Concrete Products Inc.....937 224-1433
1433 S Euclid Ave Dayton (45417) ***(G-8511)***
Snyder Electronics.....513 738-7200
5501 Lawrenceburg Rd # 100 Harrison (45030) ***(G-10671)***
Snyder Fabrication LLC.....419 946-6616
6145 County Road 30 Mount Gilead (43338) ***(G-14434)***
Snyder Hot Shot, Wooster *Also called H & H Equipment Inc* ***(G-20601)***
Snyder Intl Brewing Group LLC (PA).....216 619-7424
1940 E 6th St Ste 200 Cleveland (44114) ***(G-6076)***
Snyder Machine Co Inc.....419 526-1527
256 N Diamond St Mansfield (44902) ***(G-12517)***
Snyder Manufacturing Inc.....330 343-4456
3001 Progress St Dover (44622) ***(G-8855)***
Snyder Manufacturing Co Ltd.....330 343-4456
3001 Progress St Dover (44622) ***(G-8856)***
Snyder Printing LLC.....740 353-3947
1552 Gallia St Portsmouth (45662) ***(G-16301)***
Snyder Printing & Signs, Portsmouth *Also called Snyder Printing LLC* ***(G-16301)***
Snyders Tool & Die Inc.....614 878-2205
6481 W Broad St Galloway (43119) ***(G-10180)***
Snyders-Lance Inc.....614 856-4616
4000 Gantz Rd Ste E Grove City (43123) ***(G-10469)***
So-Low Environmental Eqp Co.....513 772-9410
10310 Spartan Dr Cincinnati (45215) ***(G-4350)***
Soam Seal, Cleveland *Also called Novagard Solutions Inc* ***(G-5789)***
Sober Sand & Gravel Co.....330 325-7088
2908 Tallmadge Rd Ravenna (44266) ***(G-16404)***
Socar of Ohio Inc (PA).....419 596-3100
21739 Road E16 Continental (45831) ***(G-7668)***
Soccer Centre Owners Ltd.....419 893-5425
1620 Market Place Dr Maumee (43537) ***(G-13146)***
Soccer First Inc (PA).....614 889-1115
6490 Dublin Park Dr Dublin (43016) ***(G-8992)***
Social Supper, Dresden *Also called Dresden Specialties Inc* ***(G-8868)***
Society of The Precious Blood.....419 925-4516
2860 Us Route 127 Celina (45822) ***(G-2984)***
Soda Pig LLC.....646 241-7126
790 Kerr St Columbus (43215) ***(G-7458)***
Soffseal Inc.....513 934-0815
2175 Deerfield Rd Lebanon (45036) ***(G-11697)***
Sofie, Oakwood Village *Also called N-Molecular Inc* ***(G-15481)***
Soft Touch Wood LLC.....330 545-4204
1560 S State St Girard (44420) ***(G-10266)***
Soft Tuch Furn Repr Rfinishing, Girard *Also called Soft Touch Wood LLC* ***(G-10266)***
Soft-Lite LLC (HQ).....330 528-3400
10250 Philipp Pkwy Streetsboro (44241) ***(G-17698)***
Soft-Lite Windows, Streetsboro *Also called Soft-Lite LLC* ***(G-17698)***
Softchoice Corporation.....614 224-4123
300 Marconi Blvd Ste 303 Columbus (43215) ***(G-7459)***
Softpoint Industries.....330 668-2645
988 Traci Ln Copley (44321) ***(G-7696)***
Softura Legal Solutions LLC.....614 220-5611
1555 Lake Shore Dr Columbus (43204) ***(G-7460)***
Software Authority Inc.....216 236-0200
6001 W Creek Rd Cleveland (44131) ***(G-6077)***
Software Management Group.....513 618-2165
1128 Main St Fl 6 Cincinnati (45202) ***(G-4351)***
Software Solutions Inc (PA).....513 932-6667
420 E Main St Lebanon (45036) ***(G-11698)***
Software To Systems Inc.....513 893-4367
640 Glenna Dr Fairfield (45014) ***(G-9566)***
Sojourners Truth.....419 243-0007
1811 Adams St Toledo (43604) ***(G-18525)***
Sol-Fly Technologies LLC.....330 465-8883
3098 Tamarack Ln Wooster (44691) ***(G-20656)***
Solae Central Soya, Bellevue *Also called Solae LLC* ***(G-1546)***
Solae LLC.....419 483-0400
300 Great Lakes Pkwy Bellevue (44811) ***(G-1546)***
Solae LLC.....419 483-5340
605 Goodrich Rd Bellevue (44811) ***(G-1547)***
Solar Arts Graphic Designs.....330 744-0535
824 Tod Ave Youngstown (44502) ***(G-21033)***
Solar Con Inc.....419 865-5877
7134 Railroad St Holland (43528) ***(G-10958)***
Soldier Tech & Armor RES LLC.....330 896-5217
3300 Massillon Rd Akron (44312) ***(G-381)***
Sole Choice Inc.....740 354-2813
830 Murray St Portsmouth (45662) ***(G-16302)***
Soleo Health Inc.....844 467-8200
6185 Shamrock Ct Ste A Dublin (43016) ***(G-8993)***
Solid Dimensions Inc.....419 663-1134
720 Townline Road 151 Norwalk (44857) ***(G-15415)***
Solid Dimensions Line, Norwalk *Also called Solid Dimensions Inc* ***(G-15415)***
Solid Light Company Inc.....740 548-1219
7750 Green Meadows Dr A Lewis Center (43035) ***(G-11781)***
Solmet Technologies Inc.....330 915-4160
2716 Shepler Ch Ave Sw Canton (44706) ***(G-2819)***
Solo Products Inc.....513 321-7884
838 Reedy St Cincinnati (45202) ***(G-4352)***
Solomon Industries LLC.....937 558-5334
3365 Peebles Rd Troy (45373) ***(G-18708)***
Solomons Mines Inc.....330 337-0123
7219 Salem Unity Rd Salem (44460) ***(G-16775)***
Solon.....440 498-1798
38235 Mcdowell Dr Solon (44139) ***(G-17233)***
Solon Glass Center Inc.....440 248-5018
33001 Station St Cleveland (44139) ***(G-6078)***
Solon Glass Ctr, Cleveland *Also called Solon Glass Center Inc* ***(G-6078)***
Solon Manufacturing Company.....440 286-7149
425 Center St Chardon (44024) ***(G-3137)***
Solon Specialty 0537, Solon *Also called Solon Specialty Wire Co* ***(G-17234)***
Solon Specialty Wire Co.....440 248-7600
30000 Solon Rd Solon (44139) ***(G-17234)***
Solstice Sleep Products, Columbus *Also called SSP Tennessee LLC* ***(G-7483)***
Solstreme, Cincinnati *Also called X-3-5 LLC* ***(G-4526)***
Solsys Inc.....419 886-4683
96 Vanderbilt Rd Mansfield (44904) ***(G-12518)***
Solut, Lewis Center *Also called Duracorp LLC* ***(G-11758)***
Solution Industries LLC.....440 816-9500
17830 Englewood Dr Ste 11 Middleburg Heights (44130) ***(G-13770)***
Solution Ventures Inc.....440 242-1658
31728 Commodore Ct Avon Lake (44012) ***(G-1008)***
Solutions In Polycarbonate LLC.....330 572-2860
6353 Norwalk Rd Medina (44256) ***(G-13345)***
Solutions Plus Inc.....513 943-9600
3907 Bach Buxton Rd Amelia (45102) ***(G-547)***
Solvay Advanced Polymers LLC.....740 373-9242
17005 State Route 7 Marietta (45750) ***(G-12672)***
Solvay Spclty Polymers USA LLC.....740 373-9242
17005 State Route 7 Marietta (45750) ***(G-12673)***
Solvay USA Inc.....513 482-5700
4775 Paddock Rd Cincinnati (45229) ***(G-4353)***
Solvent Recovery Division, Columbus *Also called Durr Megtec LLC* ***(G-6877)***
Somerset Commercial Prtg Co.....740 536-7187
9050 Pleasantville Rd Ne Rushville (43150) ***(G-16597)***
Somerset Galleries Inc.....614 443-0003
1144 S 4th St Columbus (43206) ***(G-7461)***
Somerville Manufacturing Inc.....740 336-7847
15 Townhall Rd Marietta (45750) ***(G-12674)***
Sommers Wood N Door Company.....614 873-3506
7802 Amish Pike Plain City (43064) ***(G-16213)***
Sonalysts Inc.....937 429-9711
2940 Presidential Dr # 160 Beavercreek (45324) ***(G-1342)***
Sonoco Products Company.....330 688-8247
59 N Main St Munroe Falls (44262) ***(G-14527)***

Sonoco Products Company ...740 927-2525
8865 Smiths Mill Rd N Johnstown (43031) *(G-11271)*
Sonoco Products Company ...937 429-0040
761 Space Dr Beavercreek Township (45434) *(G-1374)*
Sonoco Products Company ...513 870-3985
4633 Dues Dr West Chester (45246) *(G-19900)*
Sonoco Products Company ...419 448-4428
60 Heritage Dr Tiffin (44883) *(G-18084)*
Sonoco Products Company ...614 759-8470
444 Mccormick Blvd Columbus (43213) *(G-7462)*
Sonoco Prtective Solutions Inc...419 420-0029
1900 Industrial Dr Findlay (45840) *(G-9758)*
Sonoco Prtective Solutions Inc...419 420-0029
1900 Industrial Dr Findlay (45840) *(G-9759)*
Sonogage Inc ...216 464-1119
26650 Rnohance Pkwy Ste 3 Cleveland (44128) *(G-6079)*
Sonoma Grinding Machining Inc ...440 918-7990
37195 Ben Hur Ave Ste E Willoughby (44094) *(G-20435)*
Sonoran Salsa Company LLC...216 513-3596
25456 Hilliard Blvd Westlake (44145) *(G-20159)*
Sontek / Ysi, Yellow Springs *Also called Sontek Corporation* *(G-20817)*
Sontek Corporation...937 767-7241
1725 Brannum Ln Yellow Springs (45387) *(G-20817)*
Sonus-Usa Inc...419 474-9324
3829 Woodley Rd Bldg B Toledo (43606) *(G-18526)*
Soondook LLC...614 389-5757
6344 Nicholas Dr Columbus (43235) *(G-7463)*
Soprema USA Inc ...330 334-0066
310 Quadral Dr Wadsworth (44281) *(G-19277)*
Sorbothane Inc (PA)...330 678-9444
2144 State Route 59 Kent (44240) *(G-11388)*
Sorta 4 U LLC...440 365-0091
267 Bon Air Ave Elyria (44035) *(G-9330)*
Sotto ...513 977-6886
118 E 6th St Cincinnati (45202) *(G-4354)*
Soulsby, John, Mentor *Also called Mentor Signs & Graphics Inc* *(G-13516)*
Sound and Vibration, Bay Village *Also called Acoustical Publications Inc* *(G-1204)*
Sound Communications Inc...614 875-8500
3474 Park St Grove City (43123) *(G-10470)*
Sound Concepts LLC...513 703-0147
1233 Castle Dr Ste A5 Mason (45040) *(G-12940)*
Sound Solutions Cnstr Svcs, Bedford *Also called Baswa Acoustics North Amer LLC* *(G-1388)*
Soundproof...440 864-8864
15400 Highland Dr Grafton (44044) *(G-10310)*
Soundwich Inc (PA)...216 486-2666
881 Wayside Rd Cleveland (44110) *(G-6080)*
Source3media Inc...330 467-9003
9085 Freeway Dr Macedonia (44056) *(G-12326)*
Sourcelink Ohio LLC...937 885-8000
3303 W Tech Blvd Miamisburg (45342) *(G-13718)*
South Akron Awning Co (PA)...330 848-7611
763 Kenmore Blvd Akron (44314) *(G-382)*
South Central Industrial LLC...740 333-5401
1629 S Fayette St Washington Court Hou (43160) *(G-19477)*
South End Printing Co ...216 341-0669
3558 E 80th St Cleveland (44105) *(G-6081)*
South Shore Controls Inc ...440 259-2500
4485 N Ridge Rd Perry (44081) *(G-15913)*
South Shore Gas & Oil, Portsmouth *Also called Delmar E Hicks* *(G-16281)*
South Side Audio LLC...614 453-0757
2501 S High St Frnt Frnt Columbus (43207) *(G-7464)*
South Side Drive Thru...937 295-2927
9204 Hilgefort Rd Fort Loramie (45845) *(G-9807)*
Southast Diesl Acquisition Sub, Greenville *Also called Stateline Power Corp* *(G-10397)*
Southeast Health Center, Cleveland *Also called Northeast OH Neighborhood Heal* *(G-5774)*
Southeast Ohio Timber Pdts Co ...740 344-2570
67 Beech Rock Dr Zanesville (43701) *(G-21181)*
Southeast Publications Inc...740 732-2341
309 Main St Caldwell (43724) *(G-2412)*
Southeastern Container Inc...419 352-6300
307 Industrial Pkwy Bowling Green (43402) *(G-2000)*
Southeastern Shafting Mfg...740 342-4629
402 W Broadway St New Lexington (43764) *(G-14723)*
Southern Adhesive Coatings...513 561-8440
8121 Camargo Rd Cincinnati (45243) *(G-4355)*
Southern Bag, Wilmington *Also called Hood Packaging Corporation* *(G-20498)*
Southern Cabinetry Inc...740 245-5992
41 International Blvd Bidwell (45614) *(G-1670)*
Southern Division, Perrysburg *Also called Ohio Table Pad Company* *(G-15985)*
Southern Ohio Kitchens, Dayton *Also called C-Link Enterprises LLC* *(G-8071)*
Southern Ohio Lumber LLC ...614 436-4472
11855 State Route 73 Peebles (45660) *(G-15882)*
Southern Ohio Materials...937 386-3200
800 Nathan Denton Rd Seaman (45679) *(G-16884)*
Southern Ohio Mfg Inc...513 943-2555
1147 Clough Pike Batavia (45103) *(G-1185)*
Southern Ohio Wood...740 288-1825
1085 Loop Rd Wellston (45692) *(G-19607)*
Southern Ornamental Iron Co (PA)...937 278-4319
4267 Salem Ave Dayton (45416) *(G-8512)*
Southern Wholesale, Millersburg *Also called Affordable Barn Co Ltd* *(G-14055)*
Southpaw Enterprises Inc ...937 252-7676
2350 Dryden Rd Moraine (45439) *(G-14395)*
Southside Wolfies...419 422-5450
546 6th St Findlay (45840) *(G-9760)*
Southstern Machining Field Svc (PA)...740 689-1147
500 Lincoln Ave Lancaster (43130) *(G-11610)*
Southwest Electric Co...330 875-7000
609 Enterprise Cir Louisville (44641) *(G-12168)*
Southwest Greens Ohio LLC...614 389-6042
1781 Westbelt Dr Columbus (43228) *(G-7465)*
Southwest Ohio Computer Assn, Fairfield Township *Also called Butler Tech Career Dev Schools* *(G-9580)*
Southwest Tire Molds, Akron *Also called Northeast Tire Molds Inc* *(G-302)*
Southwestern Ohio Instruction...937 746-6333
1205 E 5th St Dayton (45402) *(G-8513)*
Southwire Avon Lake Plant, Avon Lake *Also called Southwire Company LLC* *(G-1009)*
Southwire Company LLC ...440 933-6110
567 Miller Rd Avon Lake (44012) *(G-1009)*
Southworth Wood Products, Beaver *Also called Ramona Southworth* *(G-1293)*
Sovereign Circuits Inc...330 538-3900
12080 Debartolo Dr North Jackson (44451) *(G-15154)*
Sovereign Stitch ...440 829-0678
701 Jockeys Cir Avon Lake (44012) *(G-1010)*
Sp Medical, Cleveland *Also called Superior Products Llc* *(G-6125)*
SP Mount Printing Company...216 881-3316
1306 E 55th St Cleveland (44103) *(G-6082)*
Sp3 Cutting Tools Inc (PA)...937 667-4476
835 N Hyatt St Tipp City (45371) *(G-18134)*
Spa Pool Covers Inc...440 235-9981
7806 Royalton Rd North Royalton (44133) *(G-15302)*
Space Age Coatings LLC ...937 275-5117
4825 Wolf Creek Pike Dayton (45417) *(G-8514)*
Space Age Concepts, Dayton *Also called Space Age Coatings LLC* *(G-8514)*
Space Dynamics Corp...513 792-9800
10080 Alliance Rd Blue Ash (45242) *(G-1847)*
Space-Links Inc ...330 788-2401
1110 Thalia Ave Youngstown (44512) *(G-21034)*
Spacelinks Enterprises Inc...330 788-2401
1110 Thalia Ave Youngstown (44512) *(G-21035)*
Spall Autoc Syste / US Millwr, Lima *Also called Spallinger Millwright Svc Co* *(G-11942)*
Spallinger Millwright Svc Co...419 225-5830
1155 E Hanthorn Rd Lima (45804) *(G-11942)*
Spang & Company...440 350-6108
9305 Progress Pkwy Mentor (44060) *(G-13585)*
Spanish Lngage Productions Inc...614 737-3424
3017 Mounts Rd Alexandria (43001) *(G-443)*
Spanish Portugese Translation, Westlake *Also called Advanced Translation/Cnsltng* *(G-20087)*
SPAOS Inc (PA)...937 890-0783
6012 N Dixie Dr Dayton (45414) *(G-8515)*
Spark LLC...513 924-1559
10760 Chester Rd Cincinnati (45246) *(G-4356)*
Sparks Belting Company Inc...216 398-7774
4653 Spring Rd Cleveland (44131) *(G-6083)*
Spartan Chemical Company Inc (PA) ...419 897-5551
1110 Spartan Dr Maumee (43537) *(G-13147)*
Spartan Fabrication...330 758-3512
230 Mcclurg Rd Youngstown (44512) *(G-21036)*
Spartech LLC ...937 548-1395
1050 Landsdowne Ave Greenville (45331) *(G-10395)*
Spartech LLC ...419 399-4050
925 W Gasser Rd Paulding (45879) *(G-15871)*
Spartech Plastics, Greenville *Also called Polyone Corporation* *(G-10388)*
Spartech Plastics, Paulding *Also called Spartech LLC* *(G-15871)*
Sparton Enterprises Inc...330 745-6088
3717 Clark Mill Rd Norton (44203) *(G-15375)*
Sparton Medical Systems Inc...440 878-4630
22740 Lunn Rd Strongsville (44149) *(G-17791)*
Spb Global LLC...419 931-6559
26611 Nawash Dr Perrysburg (43551) *(G-16007)*
Spc Specialty Products LLC...844 475-5414
520 E Woodruff Ave Toledo (43604) *(G-18527)*
Spear USA Inc (HQ)...513 459-1100
5510 Courseview Dr Mason (45040) *(G-12941)*
Spearfysh Inc...330 487-0300
60 W Streetsboro St Ste 5 Hudson (44236) *(G-11075)*
Spec Mask Ohio LLC...440 522-3055
7899 Euclid Chardon Rd Kirtland (44094) *(G-11470)*
Specgrade Led, Columbus *Also called Lighting Solutions Group LLC* *(G-7127)*
Special Design Products Inc ...614 272-6700
520 Industrial Mile Rd Columbus (43228) *(G-7466)*
Special Mtls RES & Tech Inc...440 777-4024
27390 Lusandra Cir North Olmsted (44070) *(G-15200)*
Special t Foods LLC...330 533-9493
5529 W Middletown Rd Canfield (44406) *(G-2545)*

ALPHABETIC

Special Way 2 ....740 282-8281
1592 State Route 213 Steubenville (43952) ***(G-17552)***
Specialized Business Sftwr Inc 440 542-9145
6240 Som Center Rd # 230 Solon (44139) ***(G-17235)***
Specialized Pharmaceuticals 419 371-2081
799 S Main St Lima (45804) ***(G-11943)***
Specialtee Sportswear & Design 614 877-0976
9819 Us Highway 62 Orient (43146) ***(G-15578)***
Specialties Mds Induction Ltd 330 394-3338
762 E Market St Warren (44481) ***(G-19443)***
Specialties Unlimited, Mentor *Also called J & P Products Inc* ***(G-13482)***
Specialty Adhesive Film Co 513 353-1885
5838 Hamilton Cleves Rd Cleves (45002) ***(G-6375)***
Specialty Ceramics Inc 330 482-0800
41995 State Route 344 Columbiana (44408) ***(G-6481)***
Specialty Drapery Workroom 330 864-4190
50 S Frank Blvd Akron (44313) ***(G-383)***
Specialty Fab, North Lima *Also called Bird Equipment LLC* ***(G-15166)***
Specialty Films Inc 614 471-9100
2887 Johnstown Rd Columbus (43219) ***(G-7467)***
Specialty Gas Publishing Inc 216 226-3796
12550 Lake Ave Apt 1312 Cleveland (44107) ***(G-6084)***
Specialty Gas Report, Cleveland *Also called Specialty Gas Publishing Inc* ***(G-6084)***
Specialty Hose Aerospace Corp 330 497-9650
7802 Freedom Ave Nw Canton (44720) ***(G-2820)***
Specialty Lithographing Co 513 621-0222
1035 W 7th St Cincinnati (45203) ***(G-4357)***
Specialty Magnetics LLC 330 468-8834
440 Highland Rd E Macedonia (44056) ***(G-12327)***
Specialty Metals Processing 330 656-2767
837 Seasons Rd Hudson (44224) ***(G-11076)***
Specialty Pallet & Design Ltd 330 857-0257
2600 Kidron Rd Orrville (44667) ***(G-15624)***
Specialty Pallet Entps LLC 419 673-0247
18031 State Route 309 Kenton (43326) ***(G-11423)***
Specialty Pipe & Tube Inc (HQ) 330 505-8262
3600 Union St Mineral Ridge (44440) ***(G-14171)***
Specialty Plas Fabrications 513 856-9475
1600 Irma Ave Hamilton (45011) ***(G-10607)***
Specialty Printing LLC 937 335-4046
1202 Archer Dr Troy (45373) ***(G-18709)***
Specialty Printing and Proc 614 322-9035
4670 Groves Rd Columbus (43232) ***(G-7468)***
Specialty Products, Cleveland *Also called Gortons Inc* ***(G-5333)***
Specialty Services Inc 614 421-1599
1382 Ohlen Ave Columbus (43211) ***(G-7469)***
Specialty Steel Solutions 567 674-0011
14574 State Route 292 Kenton (43326) ***(G-11424)***
Specialty Switch Co 330 427-3000
525 Mcclurg Rd Youngstown (44512) ***(G-21037)***
Specialty Systems Electric LLC 304 529-3861
1853 County Road 411 Proctorville (45669) ***(G-16345)***
Specialty Technology & Res 614 870-0744
1150 Milepost Dr Columbus (43228) ***(G-7470)***
Specialty Wood Products, Cincinnati *Also called Wjf Enterprises LLC* ***(G-4514)***
Specified Structures Inc 330 753-0693
643 Holmes Ave Barberton (44203) ***(G-1106)***
Specilty Fbrics Converting Inc (HQ) 706 637-3000
703 S Clvland Mssillon Rd Fairlawn (44333) ***(G-9618)***
Specmat, North Olmsted *Also called Special Mtls RES & Tech Inc* ***(G-15200)***
Spectra Group Limited Inc 419 837-9783
27800 Lemoyne Rd Ste J Millbury (43447) ***(G-14052)***
Spectra Photopolymers Inc., Millbury *Also called Formlabs Ohio Inc* ***(G-14049)***
Spectra-Tech Manufacturing Inc 513 735-9300
4013 Borman Dr Batavia (45103) ***(G-1186)***
Spectracam Ltd 937 223-3805
1112 E Race Dr Dayton (45404) ***(G-8516)***
Spectral Uv Systems, Amherst *Also called Nordson Uv Inc* ***(G-568)***
Spectramed Inc 740 263-3059
275 W Johnstown Rd Gahanna (43230) ***(G-10106)***
Spectre EDM 513 469-7700
6082 Interstate Cir Blue Ash (45242) ***(G-1848)***
Spectre Sensors Inc (PA) 440 250-0372
2392 Georgia Dr Westlake (44145) ***(G-20160)***
Spectroglass Corp 614 297-0412
1380 Holly Ave Columbus (43212) ***(G-7471)***
Spectron Inc 937 461-5590
132 S Terry St Dayton (45403) ***(G-8517)***
Spectrum Adhesives Inc 740 763-2886
11047 Lambs Ln Newark (43055) ***(G-14919)***
Spectrum Brands Inc 440 357-2600
447 Lexington Ave Painesville (44077) ***(G-15783)***
Spectrum Dispersions Inc 330 296-0600
225 W Lake St Ravenna (44266) ***(G-16405)***
Spectrum Dynamics Inc 614 486-3223
1951 Hampshire Rd Columbus (43221) ***(G-7472)***
Spectrum Embroidery Inc 937 847-9905
332 Gargrave Rd Dayton (45449) ***(G-8518)***
Spectrum Image LLC 614 954-0102
374 Morrison Rd Ste F Columbus (43213) ***(G-7473)***
Spectrum Inc 440 951-6061
800 Resource Dr Ste 8 Brooklyn Heights (44131) ***(G-2132)***
Spectrum Infared, Brooklyn Heights *Also called Spectrum Inc* ***(G-2132)***
Spectrum Machine Inc (PA) 330 626-3666
1668 Frost Rd Streetsboro (44241) ***(G-17699)***
Spectrum Metal Finishing Inc 330 758-8358
535 Bev Rd Youngstown (44512) ***(G-21038)***
Spectrum Mfg & Sls Inc (PA) 614 486-3223
1951 Hampshire Rd Columbus (43221) ***(G-7474)***
Spectrum Plastics Corporation 330 926-9766
99 E Ascot Ln Cuyahoga Falls (44223) ***(G-7921)***
Spectrum Printing & Design, Dayton *Also called Eugene Stewart* ***(G-8189)***
Spectrum Surgical Instruments, Stow *Also called Steris Instrument MGT Svcs Inc* ***(G-17632)***
Speed City LLC 440 975-1969
12361 Kinsman Rd Ste A Newbury (44065) ***(G-14966)***
Speed North America Inc 330 202-7775
1700a Old Mansfield Rd Wooster (44691) ***(G-20657)***
Speed Selector Inc 440 543-8233
17050 Munn Rd Chagrin Falls (44023) ***(G-3077)***
Speed-O-Print, Crooksville *Also called Temple Oil & Gas Company* ***(G-7820)***
Speedline Corporation (PA) 440 914-1122
6810 Cochran Rd Solon (44139) ***(G-17236)***
Speedway LLC 330 874-4616
11099 State Route 212 Ne Bolivar (44612) ***(G-1928)***
Speedway LLC 440 943-0044
29201 Euclid Ave Wickliffe (44092) ***(G-20231)***
Speedway LLC (HQ) 937 864-3000
500 Speedway Dr Enon (45323) ***(G-9387)***
Speedway LLC 937 653-6840
725 N Main St Urbana (43078) ***(G-19013)***
Speedway LLC 614 418-9325
2875 Stelzer Rd Columbus (43219) ***(G-7475)***
Speedway LLC 937 390-6651
2040 N Bechtle Ave Springfield (45504) ***(G-17492)***
Speedway LLC 614 861-6397
7881 E Main St Reynoldsburg (43068) ***(G-16454)***
Speedway LLC 330 339-7770
1260 W High Ave New Philadelphia (44663) ***(G-14800)***
Speedway LLC 937 372-7129
1455 Brush Row Rd Wilberforce (45384) ***(G-20237)***
Speedway LLC 513 683-2034
12184 Mason Rd Cincinnati (45249) ***(G-4358)***
Speedway LLC 330 468-3320
757 E Aurora Rd Macedonia (44056) ***(G-12328)***
Speedway LLC 330 343-9469
225 S Wooster Ave Dover (44622) ***(G-8857)***
Speedway LLC 419 468-9773
746 Harding Way W Galion (44833) ***(G-10156)***
Speedway LLC 440 988-8014
712 N Leavitt Rd Amherst (44001) ***(G-575)***
Speedway Superamerica, Urbana *Also called Speedway LLC* ***(G-19013)***
Speedway Superamerica 1848, Macedonia *Also called Speedway LLC* ***(G-12328)***
Speedway Superamerica 2034, Columbus *Also called Speedway LLC* ***(G-7475)***
Speedway Superamerica 3027, Wickliffe *Also called Speedway LLC* ***(G-20231)***
Speedway Superamerica 3187, Galion *Also called Speedway LLC* ***(G-10156)***
Speedway Superamerica 4131, Springfield *Also called Speedway LLC* ***(G-17492)***
Speedway Superamerica 4487, Reynoldsburg *Also called Speedway LLC* ***(G-16454)***
Speedway Superamerica 5110, Cincinnati *Also called Speedway LLC* ***(G-4358)***
Speedway Superamerica 5839, Wilberforce *Also called Speedway LLC* ***(G-20237)***
Speedway Superamerica 6241, Bolivar *Also called Speedway LLC* ***(G-1928)***
Speedway Superamerica 6243, Dover *Also called Speedway LLC* ***(G-8857)***
Speedway Superamerica 6246, New Philadelphia *Also called Speedway LLC* ***(G-14800)***
Speedway Superamerica 9975, Amherst *Also called Speedway LLC* ***(G-575)***
Speelman Electric Inc 330 633-1410
358 Commerce St Tallmadge (44278) ***(G-18004)***
Spence Technologies Inc 440 946-3035
4752 Topps Indus Pkwy Willoughby (44094) ***(G-20436)***
Spencer Forge & Manufacturing, Spencer *Also called Spencer Manufacturing Company* ***(G-17306)***
Spencer Forge & Manufacturing, Spencer *Also called Alta Mira Corporation* ***(G-17303)***
Spencer Manufacturing Company 330 648-2461
225 N Main St Spencer (44275) ***(G-17306)***
Spencer-Walker Press Inc (PA) 740 344-6110
1433 Amesbury Ln Newark (43055) ***(G-14920)***
Spencer-Walker Press Inc 740 345-4494
44 S 4th St Newark (43055) ***(G-14921)***
Sperco, Cleveland *Also called Sperzel Inc* ***(G-6085)***
Sperling Railway Services Inc 330 479-2004
4313 Southway St Sw Canton (44706) ***(G-2821)***
Sperzel Inc 216 281-6868
15728 Industrial Pkwy Cleveland (44135) ***(G-6085)***
Sphon Associates Inc 614 741-4002
962 Bryn Mawr Dr Gahanna (43230) ***(G-10107)***
Spi Inc 937 374-2700
1170 S Patton St Xenia (45385) ***(G-20790)***

SPI Mailing, Canton *Also called Slimans Printery Inc* ***(G-2818)***
Spicy Olive LLC (PA)....513 847-4397
7671 Cox Ln West Chester (45069) ***(G-19797)***
Spicy Olive LLC....513 376-9061
2736 Erie Ave Cincinnati (45208) ***(G-4359)***
Spiegelberg Manufacturing Inc (PA)....440 324-3042
12200 Alameda Dr Strongsville (44149) ***(G-17792)***
Spiegler Brake Systems USA LLC....937 291-1735
1699 Thomas Paine Pkwy Dayton (45459) ***(G-8519)***
Spillman Company....614 444-2184
1701 Moler Rd Columbus (43207) ***(G-7476)***
Spinal Balance Inc....419 530-5935
11360 S Airfield Rd Swanton (43558) ***(G-17922)***
Spinnaker Coating LLC....937 332-6300
518 E Water St Troy (45373) ***(G-18710)***
Spinnaker Coating LLC (PA)....937 332-6500
518 E Water St Troy (45373) ***(G-18711)***
Spinnaker Coatings....937 332-6619
130 Marybill Dr S Troy (45373) ***(G-18712)***
Spintech LLC....937 912-3250
1150 S Patton St Xenia (45385) ***(G-20791)***
Spiral Brushes Inc....330 686-2861
1355 Commerce Dr Stow (44224) ***(G-17629)***
Spiralcool Company....419 483-2510
186 Sheffield St Ste 188 Bellevue (44811) ***(G-1548)***
Spirit Aeronautics, Columbus *Also called Spirit Avionics Ltd* ***(G-7477)***
Spirit Avionics Ltd....614 237-4271
4808 E 5th Ave Columbus (43219) ***(G-7477)***
Spirol International Corp....330 920-3655
321 Remington Rd Stow (44224) ***(G-17630)***
Spitfire Technologies LLC....937 463-7729
110 N Main St Dayton (45402) ***(G-8520)***
Splendid LLC....614 396-6481
1415 E Dubln Grnvl Rd 2 Columbus (43229) ***(G-7478)***
Splicenet Inc....513 563-3533
9624 Cincinnati Columbus West Chester (45241) ***(G-19901)***
Spoerr Precast Concrete Inc....419 625-9132
2020 Caldwell St Sandusky (44870) ***(G-16850)***
Sponseller Group Inc (PA)....419 861-3000
1600 Timber Wolf Dr Holland (43528) ***(G-10959)***
Sponseller Group Inc....937 492-9949
808 W Russell Rd Ste A Sidney (45365) ***(G-17081)***
Sports & Sports, Ashtabula *Also called Peska Inc* ***(G-797)***
Sports Art, Nashport *Also called B D P Services Inc* ***(G-14564)***
Sports Care Products Inc....216 663-8110
4310 Cranwood Pkwy Cleveland (44128) ***(G-6086)***
Sports Express....330 297-1112
956 E Main St Ravenna (44266) ***(G-16406)***
Sports Loft, Delphos *Also called Lion Clothing Inc* ***(G-8751)***
Sports Monster Corp....614 443-0190
1553 Parsons Ave Columbus (43207) ***(G-7479)***
Sportsales, Columbus *Also called Great Oppurtunities Inc* ***(G-6969)***
Sportsartcom....330 903-0895
939 Traci Ln Copley (44321) ***(G-7697)***
Sportsco Imprinting....513 641-5111
8277 Wicklow Ave Cincinnati (45236) ***(G-4360)***
Sportsguard Laboratories Inc....330 673-3932
821 W Main St Kent (44240) ***(G-11389)***
Sportsmaster....440 257-3900
9140 Lake Shore Blvd Mentor (44060) ***(G-13586)***
Sportwing, Cleveland *Also called Dawn Enterprises Inc* ***(G-5072)***
Sposie LLC....888 977-2229
4064 Technology Dr Maumee (43537) ***(G-13148)***
Spotted Horse Studio Inc....330 533-2391
6385 State Rte 165 Greenford (44422) ***(G-10355)***
SPR Machine Inc....513 737-8040
2130 Tuley Rd Fairfield Township (45015) ***(G-9586)***
Spradlin Bros Welding Co....800 219-2182
2131 Quality Ln Springfield (45505) ***(G-17493)***
Sprague Products, Brecksville *Also called Curtiss-Wright Flow Ctrl Corp* ***(G-2028)***
Spring Grove Manufacturing....513 542-0185
2838 Spring Grove Ave Cincinnati (45225) ***(G-4361)***
Spring Grove Manufacturing....513 542-6900
2838 Spring Grove Ave Cincinnati (45225) ***(G-4362)***
Spring Team Inc....440 275-5981
2851 Industrial Park Dr Austinburg (44010) ***(G-926)***
Spring Works Inc....614 351-9345
3201 Alberta St Columbus (43204) ***(G-7480)***
Springco Metal Coatings Inc (PA)....216 941-0020
12500 Elmwood Ave Cleveland (44111) ***(G-6087)***
Springdale Bindery LLC....513 772-8500
11411 Landan Ln Cincinnati (45246) ***(G-4363)***
Springdale Ice Cream Beverage....513 699-4984
11801 Chesterdale Rd Cincinnati (45246) ***(G-4364)***
Springdot Inc....513 542-4000
2611 Colerain Ave Cincinnati (45214) ***(G-4365)***
Springfield Metal Finishing....937 324-2353
1108 Robin Rd Springfield (45503) ***(G-17494)***
Springfield News Sun, Springfield *Also called Springfield Newspapers Inc* ***(G-17495)***
Springfield Newspapers Inc (HQ)....937 323-5533
137 E Main St Springfield (45502) ***(G-17495)***
Springfield Plastics Inc....937 322-6071
15 N Bechtle Ave Springfield (45504) ***(G-17496)***
Springseal Inc....330 626-0673
800 Enterprise Pkwy Ravenna (44266) ***(G-16407)***
Springtime Manufacturing....419 697-3720
1121 Hazelwood St Toledo (43605) ***(G-18528)***
Sprint Print Inc....740 622-4429
520 Main St Coshocton (43812) ***(G-7752)***
Sprint Signs & Graphics, Youngstown *Also called R T Communications Inc* ***(G-21011)***
Sprinter Marking Inc....740 453-1000
1805 Chandlersville Rd Zanesville (43701) ***(G-21182)***
SPS International Inc....216 671-9911
9321 Pheasant Run Pl Strongsville (44149) ***(G-17793)***
Spsi, Hartville *Also called Scott Process Systems Inc* ***(G-10705)***
Spunfab, Cuyahoga Falls *Also called Keuchel & Associates Inc* ***(G-7888)***
Spunfab Ltd (PA)....330 945-9455
175 Muffin Ln Cuyahoga Falls (44223) ***(G-7922)***
Spurlino Materials LLC (PA)....513 705-0111
4000 Oxford State Rd Middletown (45044) ***(G-13953)***
Spurlino Materials LLC....513 202-1111
6600 Dry Fork Rd Cleves (45002) ***(G-6376)***
Square One Solutions LLC....419 425-5445
105 Jefferson St Findlay (45840) ***(G-9761)***
Squire Shoppe Bakery....440 964-3303
511 Lake Ave Ashtabula (44004) ***(G-805)***
Sr Products....330 998-6500
1380 Highland Rd E Macedonia (44056) ***(G-12329)***
SRC Liquidation LLC (HQ)....937 221-1000
600 Albany St Dayton (45417) ***(G-8521)***
SRC Worldwide Inc (HQ)....216 941-6115
3425 Service Rd Cleveland (44111) ***(G-6088)***
Sreco Flexible, Lima *Also called Sewer Rodding Equipment Co* ***(G-11937)***
SRI, Toledo *Also called Structural Radar Imaging Inc* ***(G-18532)***
SRI Ohio Inc....740 653-5800
1061 Mill Park Dr Lancaster (43130) ***(G-11611)***
Srico Inc....614 799-0664
2724 Sawbury Blvd Columbus (43235) ***(G-7481)***
Srm Concrete LLC....937 773-0841
8395 Piqua Lockington Rd Piqua (45356) ***(G-16163)***
Srm Concrete LLC....937 698-7229
555 Old Springfield Rd Vandalia (45377) ***(G-19145)***
Srm Graphics Inc....614 263-4433
950 Oakland Park Ave Columbus (43224) ***(G-7482)***
Sro Prints LLC....865 604-0420
4430 Yakima Ct Cincinnati (45236) ***(G-4366)***
Sroka Inc....440 572-2811
21265 Westwood Dr Strongsville (44149) ***(G-17794)***
Sroka Industries Inc....440 572-2811
21265 Westwood Dr Strongsville (44149) ***(G-17795)***
Sroufe Healthcare Products LLC....260 894-4171
961 Seville Rd Wadsworth (44281) ***(G-19278)***
SRS Die Casting Holdings LLC (HQ)....330 467-0750
635 Highland Rd E Macedonia (44056) ***(G-12330)***
SRS Light Metals Inc (PA)....330 467-0750
635 Highland Rd E Macedonia (44056) ***(G-12331)***
SRS Manufacturing Corp....937 746-3086
395 Industrial Dr Franklin (45005) ***(G-9921)***
SRS Worldwide, Amherst *Also called Silk Road Sourcing LLC* ***(G-574)***
Ss Defense LLC....937 407-0659
22160 State Route 198 Cridersville (45806) ***(G-7812)***
Ss Industries, Dayton *Also called Stanco Precision Manufacturing* ***(G-8524)***
Ss Metal Fabricators Inc....937 226-9957
423 Rita St Dayton (45404) ***(G-8522)***
SSC Controls Company, Mentor *Also called Peloton Manufacturing Corp* ***(G-13546)***
Sseco Solutions, Cleveland *Also called Service Station Equipment Co* ***(G-6045)***
Ssi Manufacturing Inc....513 761-7757
9615 Inter Ocean Dr West Chester (45246) ***(G-19902)***
Ssi Tiles, Minerva *Also called Kepcor Inc* ***(G-14186)***
Ssk Industries, Wintersville *Also called Johndavid D Jones* ***(G-20539)***
Sso Inc....440 235-3500
27064 Dogwood Ln Olmsted Twp (44138) ***(G-15536)***
SSP Fittings Corp (PA)....330 425-4250
8250 Boyle Pkwy Twinsburg (44087) ***(G-18858)***
SSP Industrial Group Inc....330 665-2900
3560 W Market St Ste 300 Fairlawn (44333) ***(G-9619)***
SSP Tennessee LLC....614 279-8850
2652 Fisher Rd Ste A Columbus (43204) ***(G-7483)***
Sst Conveyor Components Inc....513 583-5500
185 Commerce Dr Loveland (45140) ***(G-12234)***
Sst Precision Manufacturing....513 583-5500
154 Commerce Dr Loveland (45140) ***(G-12235)***
St Anthony Messenger Press, Cincinnati *Also called Province of St John The Baptis* ***(G-4219)***
St Bernard Insulation LLC....513 266-2158
8703 Pippin Rd Cincinnati (45251) ***(G-4367)***

ALPHABETIC

(PA)=Parent Co (HQ)=Headquarters (DH)=Div Headquarters
2019 Harris Ohio Industrial Directory
1255

St Bernard Soap Company — ALPHABETIC SECTION

St Bernard Soap Company 513 242-2227
5177 Spring Grove Ave Cincinnati (45217) *(G-4368)*

St Clairsville Dairy Queen 740 635-1800
178 E Main St Saint Clairsville (43950) *(G-16652)*

St Henry Tile Co Inc (PA) 419 678-4841
281 W Washington St Saint Henry (45883) *(G-16667)*

St Henry Tile Co Inc 937 548-1101
5410 S State Route 49 Greenville (45331) *(G-10396)*

St John Chemical Dist Co, Galloway Also called St John Ltd Inc *(G-10181)*

St John Ltd Inc (PA) 614 851-8153
6299 George Fox Dr Galloway (43119) *(G-10181)*

St Lawrence Holdings LLC 330 562-9000
16500 Rockside Rd Maple Heights (44137) *(G-12580)*

St Marys Cement Inc (us) 937 642-4573
14531 Industrial Pkwy Marysville (43040) *(G-12814)*

St Marys Foundry Inc (PA) 419 394-3346
405 E South St Saint Marys (45885) *(G-16701)*

St Marys Iron Works Inc 419 300-6300
1880 Celina Rd Saint Marys (45885) *(G-16702)*

St Media Group Intl Inc 513 421-2050
11262 Cornell Park Dr Blue Ash (45242) *(G-1849)*

STA-Warm Electric Company 330 296-6461
553 N Chestnut St Ravenna (44266) *(G-16408)*

Staber Industries Inc 614 836-5995
4800 Homer Ohio Ln Groveport (43125) *(G-10513)*

Stable Step LLC 513 825-1888
8930 Global Way West Chester (45069) *(G-19798)*

Staceys Kitchen Limited 614 921-1290
4350 Kerr Dr Ste B Hilliard (43026) *(G-10863)*

Staci Lagrange, Lagrange Also called Inservco Inc *(G-11483)*

Staco Energy Products Co (HQ) 937 253-1191
2425 Technical Dr Miamisburg (45342) *(G-13719)*

Stacy Equipment Co. 419 447-6903
325 Hall St Tiffin (44883) *(G-18085)*

Stadco Inc 937 878-0911
632 Yllow Sprng Frfeld Rd Fairborn (45324) *(G-9468)*

Stadco Automatics, Fairborn Also called Stadco Inc *(G-9468)*

Stadvec Inc 330 644-7724
579 W Tuscarawas Ave Barberton (44203) *(G-1107)*

Staely Custom Crating, Conover Also called Conover Lumber Company Inc *(G-7663)*

Stafast Products Inc (PA) 440 357-5546
505 Lakeshore Blvd Painesville (44077) *(G-15784)*

Stafast West, Painesville Also called Stafast Products Inc *(G-15784)*

Stafford Gage & Tool Inc 937 277-9944
4606 Webster St Dayton (45414) *(G-8523)*

Stafford Gravel Inc 419 298-2440
4225 Co Rd 79 Edgerton (43517) *(G-9180)*

Stagecraft Costuming Inc 513 541-7150
3950 Spring Grove Ave Cincinnati (45223) *(G-4369)*

Stagecraft Theatrical, Cincinnati Also called Stagecraft Costuming Inc *(G-4369)*

Stahl Cranesystems Inc 843 767-1951
4401 Gateway Blvd Springfield (45502) *(G-17497)*

Stahl Farm Market 330 325-0640
4560 State Route 14 Ravenna (44266) *(G-16409)*

Stahl Gear & Machine Co 216 431-2820
3901 Hamilton Ave Cleveland (44114) *(G-6089)*

Stahl/Scott Fetzer Company 419 864-8045
201 Cunard St Cardington (43315) *(G-2876)*

Stahl/Scott Fetzer Company (HQ) 800 277-8245
3201 W Old Lincoln Way Wooster (44691) *(G-20658)*

Stainless Automation 216 961-4550
1978 W 74th St Cleveland (44102) *(G-6090)*

Stainless Machine Engineering 330 501-1992
5275 Woodville Rd Leetonia (44431) *(G-11721)*

Stainless Specialties Inc 440 942-4242
33240 Lakeland Blvd Eastlake (44095) *(G-9130)*

Stainless Works, Streetsboro Also called Ohio Classic Street Rods Inc *(G-17686)*

Stainwood Products 440 244-1352
2803 Toledo Ave Lorain (44055) *(G-12124)*

Stalder Spring Works Inc 937 322-6120
2345 Springfield Xenia Rd Springfield (45506) *(G-17498)*

Staley & Sons Powerwashing LLC 937 843-2713
6732 Wisharte Russells Point (43348) *(G-16601)*

Stallion Oilfield Cnstr LLC 330 868-2083
3361 Baird Ave Se Paris (44669) *(G-15809)*

Stam Inc 440 974-2500
7350 Production Dr Mentor (44060) *(G-13587)*

Stamco Industries Inc 216 731-9333
26650 Lakeland Blvd Cleveland (44132) *(G-6091)*

Stamm Contracting Co Inc 330 274-8230
4566 Orchard St Mantua (44255) *(G-12560)*

Stamped Steel Products Inc 330 538-3951
151 S Bailey Rd North Jackson (44451) *(G-15155)*

Stamtex, Niles Also called Metal Products Company *(G-15022)*

Stamtex Metal Stampings, Niles Also called Metal Products Company *(G-15021)*

Stan Rileys Custom Draperies 513 821-3732
7041 Vine St Cincinnati (45216) *(G-4370)*

Stanco Precision Manufacturing 937 274-1785
1 Walbrook Ave Dayton (45405) *(G-8524)*

Stancorp Inc 330 545-6615
712 Trumbull Ave Girard (44420) *(G-10267)*

Standard Advertising Co, Coshocton Also called Beach Company *(G-7722)*

Standard Bariatrics Inc 513 620-7751
4362 Glendale Milford Rd Blue Ash (45242) *(G-1850)*

Standard Car Truck Company 740 775-6450
387 Wetzel Dr Chillicothe (45601) *(G-3223)*

Standard Die Supply, Dayton Also called Ready Technology Inc *(G-8465)*

Standard Energy Company 614 885-1901
1105 Schrock Rd Ste 602 Columbus (43229) *(G-7484)*

Standard Engineering Group Inc 330 494-4300
3516 Highland Park Nw North Canton (44720) *(G-15120)*

Standard Jig Boring Svc LLC (HQ) 330 896-9530
3360 Miller Park Rd Akron (44312) *(G-384)*

Standard Jig Boring Svc LLC 330 644-5405
3194 Massillon Rd Akron (44312) *(G-385)*

Standard Machine Inc 216 631-4440
1952 W 93rd St Cleveland (44102) *(G-6092)*

Standard Oil Company 419 698-6200
4001 Cedar Point Rd Oregon (43616) *(G-15568)*

Standard Oil Company 419 691-2460
4151 Cedar Point Rd Oregon (43616) *(G-15569)*

Standard Printing Co Inc 419 586-2371
123 E Market St Celina (45822) *(G-2985)*

Standard Prototyping Ideals 614 837-9180
70 Cross St 100 Pickerington (43147) *(G-16060)*

Standard Publishing LLC 513 931-4050
8805 Governors Hill Dr # 400 Cincinnati (45249) *(G-4371)*

Standard Register, Coldwater Also called Taylor Communications Inc *(G-6422)*

Standard Signs Incorporated (PA) 330 467-2030
9115 Freeway Dr Macedonia (44056) *(G-12332)*

Standard Technologies LLC 419 332-6434
2641 Hayes Ave Fremont (43420) *(G-10051)*

Standard Textile Co Inc (PA) 513 761-9256
1 Knollcrest Dr Cincinnati (45237) *(G-4372)*

Standard Welding & Lift Truck, Lorain Also called Perkins Motor Service Ltd *(G-12112)*

Standard Welding & Steel Pdts 330 273-2777
260 S State Rd Medina (44256) *(G-13346)*

Standards Testing Labs Inc (PA) 330 833-8548
1845 Harsh Ave Se Massillon (44646) *(G-13050)*

Standby Screw Machine Pdts Co 440 243-8200
1122 W Bagley Rd Berea (44017) *(G-1625)*

Standing Rock Designery 330 650-9089
5194 Darrow Rd Hudson (44236) *(G-11077)*

Standing Rock Gallery, Hudson Also called Standing Rock Designery *(G-11077)*

Standout Stickers Inc 877 449-7703
4930 Chippewa Rd Unit A Medina (44256) *(G-13347)*

Stanek E F & Assoc Inc 216 341-7700
700 Highland Rd E Macedonia (44056) *(G-12333)*

Stanek Windows, Macedonia Also called Stanek E F and Assoc Inc *(G-12333)*

Stanley Access Tech LLC 440 461-5500
5335 Avion Park Dr Cleveland (44143) *(G-6093)*

Stanley Bittinger 740 942-4302
81331 Hines Rd Cadiz (43907) *(G-2401)*

Stanley Electric US Co Inc (HQ) 740 852-5200
420 E High St London (43140) *(G-12069)*

Stanley Industrial & Auto LLC 614 755-7089
505 N Cleveland Ave # 200 Westerville (43082) *(G-20024)*

Stanley Industrial & Auto LLC (HQ) 614 755-7000
505 N Cleveland Ave Westerville (43082) *(G-20025)*

Stanley Industries Inc 216 475-4000
19120 Cranwood Pkwy Cleveland (44128) *(G-6094)*

Stanley Proctor & Company Inc 330 425-7814
2016 Midway Dr Twinsburg (44087) *(G-18859)*

Stanley Steemer Carpet Cleaner, Dublin Also called Stanley Steemer Intl Inc *(G-8994)*

Stanley Steemer Intl Inc (PA) 614 764-2007
5800 Innovation Dr Dublin (43016) *(G-8994)*

Stansley Mineral Resources Inc (PA) 419 843-2813
3793 Silica Rd B Sylvania (43560) *(G-17962)*

Stapins Qick Cpy/Print Ctr LLC 330 296-0123
253 W Main St Ravenna (44266) *(G-16410)*

Star, Columbus Also called Specialty Technology & Res *(G-7470)*

Star, Marion Also called Steam Turb Alte Reso *(G-12737)*

Star Beverage Corporation Ohio 216 991-4799
3277 Lee Rd Shaker Heights (44120) *(G-16938)*

Star Brite Express Car WA 330 674-0062
887 S Washington St Millersburg (44654) *(G-14130)*

Star Calendar & Printing Co 216 741-3223
4354 Pearl Rd Cleveland (44109) *(G-6095)*

Star City Art Co 937 865-9792
421 S 9th St Miamisburg (45342) *(G-13720)*

Star Combustion Systems LLC 513 282-0810
6506 Castle Dr Mason (45040) *(G-12942)*

Star Door & Sash Co Inc 419 841-3396
4815 Kilburn Rd Berkey (43504) *(G-1636)*

Star Dynamics Corporation (PA) 614 334-4510
4455 Reynolds Dr Hilliard (43026) *(G-10864)*

Star Engineering Inc 740 342-3514
701 Madison St New Lexington (43764) *(G-14724)*

Star Extruded Shapes Inc 330 533-9863
7055 Herbert Rd Canfield (44406) ***(G-2546)***
Star Fab Inc (PA) 330 533-9863
7055 Herbert Rd Canfield (44406) ***(G-2547)***
Star Fab Inc 330 482-1601
400 W Railroad St Ste 8 Columbiana (44408) ***(G-6482)***
Star Fire Distributing, Akron *Also called Thermo-Rite Mfg Company* ***(G-403)***
Star Forming Manufacturing LL 330 740-8300
1775 Logan Ave Youngstown (44505) ***(G-21039)***
Star Jet LLC 614 338-4379
4130 E 5th Ave Columbus (43219) ***(G-7485)***
Star Metal Products Co Inc (PA) 440 899-7000
30405 Clemens Rd Westlake (44145) ***(G-20161)***
Star Newspaper 614 622-5930
1472 Dobson Sq N Columbus (43229) ***(G-7486)***
Star Precision Tech LLC 440 266-7700
6989 Lindsay Dr Mentor (44060) ***(G-13588)***
Star Printing, Steubenville *Also called Ogden Newspapers Inc* ***(G-17547)***
Star Printing Company Inc 330 376-0514
125 N Union St Akron (44304) ***(G-386)***
Star Screw Machine Products 216 361-0307
1531 E 41st St Cleveland (44103) ***(G-6096)***
Star Seal of Ohio Inc 614 870-1590
1400 Walcutt Rd Columbus (43228) ***(G-7487)***
Star Spangled Spectacular Inc 419 879-3502
4230 Elida Rd Lima (45807) ***(G-11944)***
Star Wipers Inc (PA) 724 695-2721
1125 E Main St Newark (43055) ***(G-14922)***
Starbringer Media Group Ltd 440 871-5448
871 Canterbury Rd Ste B Westlake (44145) ***(G-20162)***
Starchem Inc (PA) 513 458-8262
3000 Disney St Cincinnati (45209) ***(G-4373)***
Starecasing Systems Inc 312 203-5632
2822 Fisher Rd Columbus (43204) ***(G-7488)***
Stark Airways 330 526-6416
5430 Lauby Rd Bldg 27 North Canton (44720) ***(G-15121)***
Stark Forest Products, Canton *Also called Stark Truss Company Inc* ***(G-2825)***
Stark Industrial LLC 330 493-9773
5103 Stoneham Rd North Canton (44720) ***(G-15122)***
Stark Materials Inc 330 497-1648
7345 Sunset Strip Ave Nw Canton (44720) ***(G-2822)***
Stark Ready Mix & Supply Co 330 580-4307
2905 Columbus Rd Ne Canton (44705) ***(G-2823)***
Stark Truss Beach City Lumber, Beach City *Also called Stark Truss Company Inc* ***(G-1215)***
Stark Truss Company Inc (PA) 330 478-2100
109 Miles Ave Sw Canton (44710) ***(G-2824)***
Stark Truss Company Inc 330 478-2100
4933 Southway St Sw Canton (44706) ***(G-2825)***
Stark Truss Company Inc 740 335-4156
2000 Landmark Blvd Washington Court Hou (43160) ***(G-19478)***
Stark Truss Company Inc 419 298-3777
400 Component Dr Edgerton (43517) ***(G-9181)***
Stark Truss Company Inc 330 756-3050
6855 Chestnut Ridge Rd Nw Beach City (44608) ***(G-1215)***
Starkey Machinery Inc 419 468-2560
254 S Washington St Galion (44833) ***(G-10157)***
Starks Plastics LLC 513 541-4591
11236 Sebring Dr Cincinnati (45240) ***(G-4374)***
Starpoint Extrusions LLC 330 825-2373
3985 Eastern Rd C Norton (44203) ***(G-15376)***
Starr Fabricating Inc 330 394-9891
4175 Warren Sharon Rd Vienna (44473) ***(G-19210)***
Starr Machine Inc 740 753-0009
226 Sylvania Ave Nelsonville (45764) ***(G-14598)***
Starr Printing Services Inc 513 241-7708
3625 Spring Grove Ave Cincinnati (45223) ***(G-4375)***
Starr Trophy & Awards, London *Also called John C Starr* ***(G-12063)***
Start Printing 513 424-2121
3140 Cincinnati Dayton Rd Middletown (45044) ***(G-13954)***
Starwin Industries LLC 937 293-8568
3387 Woodman Dr Dayton (45429) ***(G-8525)***
Starwin Industries, Inc., Dayton *Also called Starwin Industries LLC* ***(G-8525)***
Starwood, Middlefield *Also called Norstar Aluminum Molds Inc* ***(G-13841)***
Stat Index Tab, Chillicothe *Also called Stat Industries Inc* ***(G-3224)***
Stat Index Tab Company, Chillicothe *Also called Stat Industries Inc* ***(G-3225)***
Stat Industries Inc 513 860-4482
3269 Profit Dr Hamilton (45014) ***(G-10608)***
Stat Industries Inc (PA) 740 779-6561
137 Stone Rd Chillicothe (45601) ***(G-3224)***
Stat Industries Inc 740 779-6561
137 Stone Rd Chillicothe (45601) ***(G-3225)***
State 8 Motorcycle & Atv, Peninsula *Also called Wholecycle Inc* ***(G-15902)***
State Chemical Manufacturing, Cleveland *Also called State Industrial Products Corp* ***(G-6097)***
State Farm Insurance, West Chester *Also called Johnny Chin Insurance Agency* ***(G-19871)***
State Industrial Products Corp (PA) 877 747-6986
5915 Landerbrook Dr # 300 Cleveland (44124) ***(G-6097)***
State Machine Co Inc 440 248-1050
30400 Solon Indus Pkwy Cleveland (44139) ***(G-6098)***
State Metal Hose Inc 614 527-4700
4171 Lyman Dr Hilliard (43026) ***(G-10865)***
State Molded Plastics Division, Cleveland *Also called State Tool and Die Inc* ***(G-6099)***
State of Ohio Dayton Raceway 937 237-7802
777 Hollywood Blvd Dayton (45414) ***(G-8526)***
State Tool and Die Inc 216 267-6030
4780 Briar Rd Cleveland (44135) ***(G-6099)***
Stateline Power Corp 937 547-1006
650 Pine St Greenville (45331) ***(G-10397)***
Stationery Shop Inc 330 376-2033
30 N Summit St Akron (44308) ***(G-387)***
Status Mens Accessories 440 232-6700
7781 First Pl Cleveland (44146) ***(G-6100)***
Stays Lighting Inc 440 328-3254
936 Taylor St Elyria (44035) ***(G-9331)***
STC International Co Ltd (PA) 561 308-6002
1499 Shaker Run Blvd Lebanon (45036) ***(G-11699)***
Std Specialty Filters Inc 216 881-3727
837 E 79th St Cleveland (44103) ***(G-6101)***
Steam Engine Works LLC 513 813-3690
2364 Heather Hill Blvd N Cincinnati (45244) ***(G-4376)***
Steam Turb Alte Reso 740 387-5535
116 Latourette St Marion (43302) ***(G-12737)***
Stebbins Engineering & Mfg Co 740 922-3012
4778 Belden Dr Se Uhrichsville (44683) ***(G-18895)***
Steck Manufacturing Co Inc 937 222-0062
1115 S Broadway St Ste 1 Dayton (45417) ***(G-8527)***
Steel & Alloy Utility Pdts Inc 330 530-2220
110 Ohio Ave Mc Donald (44437) ***(G-13202)***
Steel Aviation Aircraft Sales 937 332-7587
4433 E State Route 55 Casstown (45312) ***(G-2934)***
Steel City Corporation (PA) 330 792-7663
1000 Hedstrom Dr Ashland (44805) ***(G-749)***
Steel Eqp Specialists Inc 330 829-2626
22623 Lake Park Blvd Alliance (44601) ***(G-501)***
Steel Eqp Specialists Inc (PA) 330 823-8260
1507 Beeson St Ne Alliance (44601) ***(G-502)***
Steel It LLC 513 253-3111
11793 Enyart Rd Loveland (45140) ***(G-12236)***
Steel Products Corp Akron 330 688-6633
2288 Samira Rd Stow (44224) ***(G-17631)***
Steel Quest Inc 513 772-5030
8180 Corp Pk Dr Ste 250 Cincinnati (45242) ***(G-4377)***
Steel Service Plus Ltd 216 391-9000
6515 Juniata Ave Cleveland (44103) ***(G-6102)***
Steel Services Inc 513 353-4173
3150 State Line Rd North Bend (45052) ***(G-15055)***
Steel Structures of Ohio LLC 330 374-9900
1324 Firestone Pkwy A Akron (44301) ***(G-388)***
Steel Technologies LLC 440 946-8666
220 Joseph Lloyd Pkwy Willoughby (44094) ***(G-20437)***
Steel Technologies LLC 419 523-5199
740 E Williamstown Rd Ottawa (45875) ***(G-15665)***
Steel Valley Sign 330 755-7446
616 Youngstown Poland Rd Struthers (44471) ***(G-17825)***
Steel Valley Tank & Welding 740 598-4994
24 County Road 7e Brilliant (43913) ***(G-2080)***
Steel Warehouse Division, Columbus *Also called Columbus Pipe and Equipment Co* ***(G-6798)***
Steelastic Company LLC 330 633-0505
1 Vision Ln Cuyahoga Falls (44223) ***(G-7923)***
Steelcon LLC 330 457-4003
47287 State Route 558 New Waterford (44445) ***(G-14843)***
Steeles 5 Acre Mill Inc 419 542-9363
10860 State Route 2 Hicksville (43526) ***(G-10782)***
Steeles Display Cases 740 965-6426
5665 State Route 605 S Westerville (43082) ***(G-20026)***
Steelial Cnstr Met Fabrication, Vinton *Also called Steelial Wldg Met Fbrction Inc* ***(G-19216)***
Steelial Wldg Met Fbrction Inc 740 669-5300
70764 State Route 124 Vinton (45686) ***(G-19216)***
Steeltec Products LLC 216 681-1114
13000 Saint Clair Ave Cleveland (44108) ***(G-6103)***
Steer & Gear Inc 614 231-4064
1000 Barnett Rd Columbus (43227) ***(G-7489)***
Steer & Geer, Columbus *Also called Steer & Gear Inc* ***(G-7489)***
Steer America, Uniontown *Also called Steeramerica Inc* ***(G-18932)***
Steeramerica Inc 330 563-4407
1525 Corporate Woods Pkwy Uniontown (44685) ***(G-18932)***
Steere Enterprises Inc 330 633-4926
303 Tacoma Ave Tallmadge (44278) ***(G-18005)***
Stefan Restoration, Cleveland *Also called Keban Industries Inc* ***(G-5522)***
Stefra Inc 440 846-8240
18021 Cliffside Dr Strongsville (44136) ***(G-17796)***
Stegemeyer Machine 513 321-5651
212 Mccullough St Cincinnati (45226) ***(G-4378)***
Stehlin, John & Sons Meats, Cincinnati *Also called John Stehlin & Sons Co Inc* ***(G-3881)***

Stein Inc (PA) ALPHABETIC SECTION

Stein Inc (PA).....440 526-9301
1929 E Royalton Rd Ste C Cleveland (44147) ***(G-6104)***
Stein Inc.....216 883-7444
2032 Campbell Rd Cleveland (44105) ***(G-6105)***
Stein Inc.....419 747-2611
1490 Old Bowman St Mansfield (44903) ***(G-12519)***
Stein Steel Mill Services Inc.....440 526-9301
1929 E Royalton Rd Broadview Heights (44147) ***(G-2102)***
Stein-Palmer Printing Co.....740 633-3894
1 Westwood Dr Unit 202 Saint Clairsville (43950) ***(G-16653)***
Stein-Way Equipment.....330 857-8700
12335 Emerson Rd Apple Creek (44606) ***(G-619)***
Steinbarger Precision Cnc Inc.....937 252-0322
3100 Plainfield Rd Ste A Dayton (45432) ***(G-7990)***
Steinbarger Precision Cnc Inc.....937 376-0322
634 Cincinnati Ave Xenia (45385) ***(G-20792)***
Steiner Eoptics Inc (PA).....937 426-2341
3475 Newmark Dr Miamisburg (45342) ***(G-13721)***
Steinert Industries Inc.....330 678-0028
1507 Franklin Ave Kent (44240) ***(G-11390)***
Stelfast Inc (HQ).....440 879-0077
22979 Stelfast Pkwy Strongsville (44149) ***(G-17797)***
Stella Lou LLC.....937 935-9536
3939 Hickory Rock Dr Powell (43065) ***(G-16336)***
Stellar I T Co, Lancaster *Also called Stellar Industrial Tech Co* ***(G-11612)***
Stellar Industrial Tech Co.....740 654-7052
1918 York Town Ct Lancaster (43130) ***(G-11612)***
Stellar Systems Inc.....513 921-8748
1944 Harrison Ave Cincinnati (45214) ***(G-4379)***
Stelter and Brinck Inc.....513 367-9300
201 Sales Ave Harrison (45030) ***(G-10672)***
Stemco Air Springs.....234 466-7200
3524 Southwestern Blvd Fairlawn (44333) ***(G-9620)***
Stencilsmith LLC.....614 876-4350
3001 Stouenburgh Dr Hilliard (43026) ***(G-10866)***
Step 2, Streetsboro *Also called Step2 Company LLC* ***(G-17700)***
Step It Up LLC.....720 289-1520
580 N 4th St Columbus (43215) ***(G-7490)***
Step2 Company LLC (PA).....866 429-5200
10010 Aurora Hudson Rd Streetsboro (44241) ***(G-17700)***
Step2 Company LLC.....419 938-6343
2 Step 2 Dr 2nd Perrysville (44864) ***(G-16032)***
Stephen Andrews Inc.....330 725-2672
7634 Lafayette Rd Lodi (44254) ***(G-12020)***
Stephen J Page.....865 951-3316
143 Winding Trails Dr Williamsburg (45176) ***(G-20255)***
Stephen M Trudick.....440 834-1891
13813 Station Rd Burton (44021) ***(G-2371)***
Stephen R Lilley.....513 899-4400
2900 S Waynesville Rd Morrow (45152) ***(G-14415)***
Stephen R White.....740 522-1512
800 Hebron Rd Newark (43056) ***(G-14923)***
Stephen Radecky.....440 232-2132
659 Broadway Ave Bedford (44146) ***(G-1447)***
Stephens Pipe & Steel LLC.....740 869-2257
10732 Schadel Ln Mount Sterling (43143) ***(G-14465)***
Stepp Sewing Service, Milford *Also called Chris Stepp* ***(G-14002)***
Stepping Stone Enterprises Inc.....419 472-0505
5847 Secor Rd Toledo (43623) ***(G-18529)***
Sterilite Corporation.....330 830-2204
4495 Sterilite St Se Massillon (44646) ***(G-13051)***
Steris Corporation.....440 354-2600
5900 Heisley Rd Mentor (44060) ***(G-13589)***
Steris Corporation (HQ).....440 354-2600
5960 Heisley Rd Mentor (44060) ***(G-13590)***
Steris Corporation.....440 354-2600
6100 Heisley Rd Mentor (44060) ***(G-13591)***
Steris Corporation.....440 354-2600
6515 Hopkins Rd Mentor (44060) ***(G-13592)***
Steris Corporation.....440 354-2600
9325 Pinecone Dr Mentor (44060) ***(G-13593)***
Steris Instrument MGT Svcs Inc.....800 783-9251
4575 Hudson Dr Stow (44224) ***(G-17632)***
Sterling Associates Inc.....330 630-3500
1783 Brittain Rd Akron (44310) ***(G-389)***
Sterling Coating.....513 942-4900
9048 Port Union Rialto Rd West Chester (45069) ***(G-19799)***
Sterling Collectables Inc.....419 892-5708
862 Pugh Rd Mansfield (44903) ***(G-12520)***
Sterling Grinding Company Inc.....614 836-3412
62 High St Carroll (43112) ***(G-2911)***
Sterling Industries, Cincinnati *Also called Richard B Linneman* ***(G-4266)***
Sterling Industries Inc.....419 523-3788
740 E Main St Ottawa (45875) ***(G-15666)***
Sterling Jewelers Inc.....614 799-8000
5043 Tutle Crosng Blvd Ste 165 Dublin (43016) ***(G-8995)***
Sterling Media, Willoughby *Also called A & D Printing Co* ***(G-20263)***
Sterling Mining Corporation (HQ).....330 549-2165
10900 South Ave North Lima (44452) ***(G-15178)***
Sterling Pipe & Tube Inc (PA).....419 729-9756
5335 Enterprise Blvd Toledo (43612) ***(G-18530)***
Steubenville Bakery.....740 282-6851
525 South St Steubenville (43952) ***(G-17553)***
Steubenville Truck Center Inc.....740 282-2711
620 South St Steubenville (43952) ***(G-17554)***
Stevco, Wellsville *Also called Stevenson Mfg Co* ***(G-19614)***
Steve Henderson.....419 738-6999
1311 Lincoln Hwy Wapakoneta (45895) ***(G-19355)***
Steve Schaefer.....513 792-9911
9200 Montgomery Rd 23a Cincinnati (45242) ***(G-4380)***
Steve Vore Welding and Steel.....419 375-4087
3234 State Route 49 Fort Recovery (45846) ***(G-9827)***
Steven Douglas Corp.....440 564-5200
10420 Kinsman Rd Newbury (44065) ***(G-14967)***
Steven L Lones.....740 452-8851
3275 Carnation Rd Zanesville (43701) ***(G-21183)***
Steven Mercer Inc.....740 623-0033
801 Walnut St Coshocton (43812) ***(G-7753)***
Steven Nickel.....419 732-3377
3117 E Shore Dr Port Clinton (43452) ***(G-16260)***
Steven Yant.....937 596-0497
103 Jerry Dr Jackson Center (45334) ***(G-11216)***
Stevens Auto Glaze and SEC LL.....440 953-2900
36250 Lkeland Blvd Unit 3 Eastlake (44095) ***(G-9131)***
Stevens Auto Parts & Towng.....740 988-2260
2848 Big Rock Rd Jackson (45640) ***(G-11195)***
Stevens Oil & Gas LLC.....740 374-4542
110 Lynch Church Rd Marietta (45750) ***(G-12675)***
Stevens, Mel U-Cart & Rental, Toledo *Also called Mel Stevens U-Cart Concrete* ***(G-18406)***
Stevenson Color Inc.....513 321-7500
535 Wilmer Ave Cincinnati (45226) ***(G-4381)***
Stevenson Machine Inc.....513 761-4121
7666 Production Dr Cincinnati (45237) ***(G-4382)***
Stevenson Mfg Co.....330 532-1581
1 1st St Wellsville (43968) ***(G-19614)***
Steves Sports Inc.....440 735-0044
10333 Northfield Rd # 136 Northfield (44067) ***(G-15326)***
Steves Vans & Accessories LLC.....740 374-3154
221 Pike St Marietta (45750) ***(G-12676)***
Stewardship Technology Inc.....866 604-8880
201 W High St Mount Vernon (43050) ***(G-14515)***
Stewart Acquisition LLC.....800 376-4466
7955 Euclid Chardon Rd Kirtland (44094) ***(G-11471)***
Stewart Acquisition LLC (PA).....330 963-0322
2146 Enterprise Pkwy Twinsburg (44087) ***(G-18860)***
Stewart Filmscreen Corp.....513 753-0800
3919 Bach Buxton Rd Amelia (45102) ***(G-548)***
Stewart Manufacturing Corp.....937 390-3333
5230 Prosperity Dr Springfield (45502) ***(G-17499)***
Stewart McDnalds Guitar Sp Sup, Athens *Also called Stewart-Macdonald Mfg Co* ***(G-849)***
Stewart-Macdonald Mfg Co (PA).....740 592-3021
21 N Shafer St Athens (45701) ***(G-849)***
Stewarts Machining Inc.....513 422-5000
960 Holman Dr Monroe (45050) ***(G-14277)***
Stick-It Graphics LLC.....330 407-0142
3161 Egypt Rd Ne New Philadelphia (44663) ***(G-14801)***
Sticker Corporation (PA).....440 946-2100
37877 Elm St Willoughby (44094) ***(G-20438)***
Sticky Petes Maple Syrup.....740 662-2726
18216 S Canaan Rd Athens (45701) ***(G-850)***
Stiers Countertop Sales, Zanesville *Also called Sidney Stiers* ***(G-21179)***
Stiger Pre Cast Inc.....740 482-2313
17793 State Highway 231 Nevada (44849) ***(G-14601)***
Stiglers Woodworks.....513 733-3009
9358 Opal Ct Blue Ash (45242) ***(G-1851)***
Stillwater Technologies LLC.....937 440-2505
1040 S Dorset Rd Troy (45373) ***(G-18713)***
Stillwell Equipment Co Inc.....330 650-1029
5398 Akron Cleveland Rd Peninsula (44264) ***(G-15898)***
Stillwrights Distillery.....937 879-4447
5380 Intrastate Dr Fairborn (45324) ***(G-9469)***
Stine Consulting Inc.....513 723-4800
120 W 7th St Cincinnati (45202) ***(G-4383)***
Stingray Pressure Pumping LLC (PA).....405 648-4177
42739 National Rd Belmont (43718) ***(G-1567)***
Stirling Ultracold, Athens *Also called Global Cooling Inc* ***(G-833)***
Stitches & Stuff.....330 426-9500
39 N Market St East Palestine (44413) ***(G-9084)***
Stock Equipment Company, Chagrin Falls *Also called Stock Fairfield Corporation* ***(G-3078)***
Stock Fairfield Corporation.....440 543-6000
16490 Chillicothe Rd Chagrin Falls (44023) ***(G-3078)***
Stock Mfg & Design Co Inc (PA).....513 353-3600
10040 Cilley Rd Cleves (45002) ***(G-6377)***
Stocker & Sitler Oil Company (HQ).....614 888-9588
4770 Indianola Ave Columbus (43214) ***(G-7491)***
Stocker Concrete Company.....740 254-4626
7574 Us Hwy 36 Se Gnadenhutten (44629) ***(G-10283)***
Stocker Sand & Gravel Co (PA).....740 254-4635
Rr 36 Gnadenhutten (44629) ***(G-10284)***

Stoepfel Drilling Co 419 532-3307
12245 State Route 115 Ottawa (45875) ***(G-15667)***
Stoett Industries Inc 419 542-0247
600 Defiance Ave Hicksville (43526) ***(G-10783)***
Stofiel Aerospace LLC 216 389-0084
11115 Lake Ave Apt 309 Cleveland (44102) ***(G-6106)***
Stolle Machinery Company LLC 937 497-5400
2900 Campbell Rd Sidney (45365) ***(G-17082)***
Stolle Machinery-Sidney, Sidney *Also called Stolle Machinery Company LLC* ***(G-17082)***
Stolle Milk Biologics Inc 513 489-7997
4735 Devitt Dr West Chester (45246) ***(G-19903)***
Stolle Properties Inc 513 932-8664
6954 Cornell Rd Ste 100 Blue Ash (45242) ***(G-1852)***
Stoller Custom Cabinetry 330 939-6555
12573 Frick Rd Sterling (44276) ***(G-17524)***
Stone Center of Dayton, Moraine *Also called 3jd Inc* ***(G-14327)***
Stone Statements Incorporated 513 489-7866
7451 Fields Ertel Rd Cincinnati (45241) ***(G-4384)***
Stonebridge Operating Co LLC 740 373-6134
1635 Warren Chapel Rd Fleming (45729) ***(G-9781)***
Stonebrook Machine 440 951-5013
1572 E 365th St Eastlake (44095) ***(G-9132)***
Stoneco Inc (HQ) 419 422-8854
1700 Fostoria Ave Ste 200 Findlay (45840) ***(G-9762)***
Stoneco Inc 419 393-2555
13762 Road 179 Oakwood (45873) ***(G-15474)***
Stoneco Inc 419 893-7645
1360 Ford St Maumee (43537) ***(G-13149)***
Stoneco Inc 419 693-3933
352 George Hardy Dr Toledo (43605) ***(G-18531)***
Stoneco Inc 419 686-3311
11580 S Dixie Hwy Portage (43451) ***(G-16274)***
Stonecote, Norton *Also called E L Stone Company* ***(G-15365)***
Stonefruit Coffee Co 330 509-2787
410 W Main St Canfield (44406) ***(G-2548)***
Stoneman Welding, Eastlake *Also called C Stoneman Corporation* ***(G-9100)***
Stoneridge Inc 419 884-1219
345 S Mill St Lexington (44904) ***(G-11807)***
Stoneware Palace Ltd 614 529-6974
3560 Mountshannon Rd Columbus (43221) ***(G-7492)***
Stoneworkd 740 920-4099
1050 Harris Ave Newark (43055) ***(G-14924)***
Stoney Acres Woodworking Llc 440 834-0717
14575 Patch Rd Burton (44021) ***(G-2372)***
Stoney Ridge Farm & Winery, Bryan *Also called Stoney Ridge Winery Ltd* ***(G-2307)***
Stoney Ridge Winery Ltd 419 636-3500
7144 County Road 16 Bryan (43506) ***(G-2307)***
Stony Point Hardwoods 330 852-4512
7842 Stony Point Rd Nw Sugarcreek (44681) ***(G-17865)***
Stony Point Metals LLC 330 852-7100
7820 Stony Point Rd Nw Sugarcreek (44681) ***(G-17866)***
Stop Stick Ltd 513 202-5500
365 Industrial Dr Harrison (45030) ***(G-10673)***
Stopol Equipment Sales LLC 440 499-0030
1321 Industrial Pkwy N # 600 Brunswick (44212) ***(G-2240)***
Storad Label Co 740 382-6440
126 Blaine Ave Marion (43302) ***(G-12738)***
Storage Buildings Unlimited 216 731-0010
12321 Hollow Ridge Rd Doylestown (44230) ***(G-8866)***
Storetek Engineering Inc 330 294-0678
399 Commerce St Tallmadge (44278) ***(G-18006)***
Storopack Inc (HQ) 513 874-0314
4758 Devitt Dr West Chester (45246) ***(G-19904)***
Stouffer Corporation (HQ) 440 349-5757
30003 Bainbridge Rd Solon (44139) ***(G-17237)***
Straight 72 Inc 740 943-5730
20078 State Route 4 Marysville (43040) ***(G-12815)***
Straight Creek Bushman LLC 513 732-1698
202 E Main St Batavia (45103) ***(G-1187)***
Straight Razor Designes 330 598-1414
4307 Belmont Ct Medina (44256) ***(G-13348)***
Straightaway Fabrications Ltd 419 281-9440
481 Us Highway 250 E Ashland (44805) ***(G-750)***
Strasburg Provision Inc 330 878-1059
172 Rosanna Ave Strasburg (44680) ***(G-17653)***
Strassells Machine Inc 419 747-1088
1015 Springmill St Mansfield (44906) ***(G-12521)***
Strata Mine Services Inc 740 695-6880
68000 Bayberry Dr Bldg 2 Saint Clairsville (43950) ***(G-16654)***
Stratagraph Ne Inc 740 373-3091
116 Ellsworth Ave Marietta (45750) ***(G-12677)***
Strategic Materials Inc 740 349-9523
101 S Arch St Newark (43055) ***(G-14925)***
Strategic Technology Entp 440 354-2600
5960 Heisley Rd Mentor (44060) ***(G-13594)***
Stratos Seating,, New Albany *Also called Mayflower Vehicle Systems LLC* ***(G-14630)***
Stratton Creek Wood Works LLC 330 876-0005
5915 Burnett East Rd Kinsman (44428) ***(G-11466)***
Strawn Oil Field Service, Salem *Also called Everflow Eastern Partners LP* ***(G-16736)***
Streamsavvy LLC 614 256-7955
629 N High St Fl 4 Columbus (43215) ***(G-7493)***
Streamside Materials Llc 419 423-1290
7440 Township Road 95 Findlay (45840) ***(G-9763)***
Streetsboro Operations, Twinsburg *Also called Facil North America Inc* ***(G-18774)***
Streicher's Quickprint, Findlay *Also called Streichers Enterprises Inc* ***(G-9764)***
Streichers Enterprises Inc 419 423-8606
109 S Main St Findlay (45840) ***(G-9764)***
Stress Con Industries Inc (PA) 586 731-1628
1321 Industrial Pkwy N # 500 Brunswick (44212) ***(G-2241)***
Stress-Crete Company 440 576-9073
1153 State Route 46 N Jefferson (44047) ***(G-11239)***
Stresscrete, Jefferson *Also called King Luminaire Company Inc* ***(G-11233)***
Stretcher Pad Company, The, Valley City *Also called S K M L Inc* ***(G-19059)***
Stretchtape Inc 216 486-9400
3100 Hamilton Ave Cleveland (44114) ***(G-6107)***
Strib Industries Inc 216 281-1155
6400 Herman Ave Cleveland (44102) ***(G-6108)***
Stricker Refinishing Inc 216 696-2906
2060 Hamilton Ave Cleveland (44114) ***(G-6109)***
Strictly Stitchery Inc 440 543-7128
13801 Shaker Blvd Apt 4a Cleveland (44120) ***(G-6110)***
Stride Tool LLC 440 247-4600
30333 Emerald Valley Pkwy Solon (44139) ***(G-17238)***
Striker Hydraulic Breakers, Willoughby *Also called Toku America Inc* ***(G-20449)***
Stripmatic Products Inc 216 241-7143
5301 Grant Ave Ste 200 Cleveland (44125) ***(G-6111)***
Strohecker Incorporated 330 426-9496
213 N Pleasant Dr East Palestine (44413) ***(G-9085)***
Strong Bindery 216 231-0001
13015 Larchmere Blvd Cleveland (44120) ***(G-6112)***
Strong M Llc 614 329-8025
2046 Leonard Ave Columbus (43219) ***(G-7494)***
Strongbasics LLC 716 903-6151
35 E Gay St Ste 322 Columbus (43215) ***(G-7495)***
Stronghold Coating Ltd 937 704-4020
3495 Mustafa Dr Cincinnati (45241) ***(G-4385)***
Stronghold Coating Systems, Cincinnati *Also called Stronghold Coating Ltd* ***(G-4385)***
Stronghold Construction, Powell *Also called Success Technologies Inc* ***(G-16337)***
Strouse Industries Inc 440 257-2520
8090 Danbury Ct Mentor (44060) ***(G-13595)***
Structural Radar Imaging Inc 425 970-3890
5217 Monroe St Ste A Toledo (43623) ***(G-18532)***
Structural Steel Fabrication, Pataskala *Also called Ohio Steel Industries Inc* ***(G-15836)***
Struers Inc (HQ) 440 871-0071
24766 Detroit Rd Westlake (44145) ***(G-20163)***
Struggle Grind Success LLC 330 834-6738
6414 Market St Boardman (44512) ***(G-1903)***
Strutt Products LLC 330 889-2727
6340 State Route 45 Cd Bristolville (44402) ***(G-2084)***
Stryker Orthopedic 614 766-2990
4420 Tuller Rd Dublin (43017) ***(G-8996)***
Stryker Plant, Stryker *Also called Sauder Manufacturing Co* ***(G-17833)***
Stryker Steel Tube LLC (PA) 419 682-4527
100 Railroad Ave Stryker (43557) ***(G-17834)***
Stryker Welding 419 682-2301
104 W Mulberry St Stryker (43557) ***(G-17835)***
Stryver Mfg Inc 937 854-3048
15 N Broadway St Trotwood (45426) ***(G-18630)***
Stuart Burial Vault Company 740 569-4158
527 Ford St Bremen (43107) ***(G-2064)***
Stuart Company 513 621-9462
2160 Patterson St Cincinnati (45214) ***(G-4386)***
Stuchell Products LLC 330 821-4299
12240 Rockhill Ave Ne Alliance (44601) ***(G-503)***
Stud Welding Associates, Strongsville *Also called Spiegelberg Manufacturing Inc* ***(G-17792)***
Studio Arts & Glass Inc 330 494-9779
7495 Strauss Ave Nw Canton (44720) ***(G-2826)***
Studio Eleven Inc (PA) 937 295-2225
301 S Main St Fort Loramie (45845) ***(G-9808)***
Studio Foundry, Cleveland *Also called Foundry Artist Inc* ***(G-5268)***
Studio Vertu Inc 513 241-9038
1208 Central Pkwy 1 Cincinnati (45202) ***(G-4387)***
Studium LLC 614 402-0359
4158 Bright Rd Dublin (43016) ***(G-8997)***
Studs N Hip Hop 614 477-0786
2032 E Hudson St Columbus (43211) ***(G-7496)***
Stuebing Automatic Machine Co 513 771-8028
2518 Leslie Ave Cincinnati (45212) ***(G-4388)***
Stumbo Publishing Co 419 529-2847
347 Allen Dr Ontario (44906) ***(G-15548)***
Stumps Converting Inc 419 492-2542
742 W Mansfield St New Washington (44854) ***(G-14833)***
Stumptown Lbr Pallet Mills Ltd 740 757-2275
55613 Washington St Somerton (43713) ***(G-17269)***
Stuntronics LLC 216 780-1413
23020 Miles Rd Bedford Heights (44128) ***(G-1480)***
Stutzman Brothers Sawmill 440 272-5179
15991 Nauvoo Rd Middlefield (44062) ***(G-13854)***

ALPHABETIC

Stutzman Manufacturing Ltd — ALPHABETIC SECTION

Stutzman Manufacturing Ltd 330 674-4359
  7727 Township Road 604 Millersburg (44654) *(G-14131)*
Style Crest Inc (HQ) 419 332-7369
  2450 Enterprise St Fremont (43420) *(G-10052)*
Style Crest Enterprises Inc (PA) 419 355-8586
  2450 Enterprise St Fremont (43420) *(G-10053)*
Style-Line Incorporated (PA) 614 291-0600
  901 W 3rd Ave Ste A Columbus (43212) *(G-7497)*
Suarez Corporation Industries 330 494-4282
  7800 Whipple Ave Nw Canton (44767) *(G-2827)*
Suarez Corporation Industries 330 494-5504
  7800 Whipple Ave Nw Canton (44767) *(G-2828)*
Sub of Manitowoc Company, Cleveland *Also called Cleveland Range LLC (G-4971)*
Subaru of A 614 793-2358
  565 Metro Pl S Ste 150 Dublin (43017) *(G-8998)*
Subtropolis Mining Co 330 549-2165
  10900 South Ave North Lima (44452) *(G-15179)*
Suburban Communications Inc 440 632-0130
  14905 N State Ave Middlefield (44062) *(G-13855)*
Suburban Electronics Assembly 330 483-4077
  7877 Grafton Rd Valley City (44280) *(G-19067)*
Suburban Manufacturing Co 440 953-2024
  1924 E 337th St Eastlake (44095) *(G-9133)*
Suburban Marble and Granite Co 216 281-5557
  7818 Lake Ave Cleveland (44102) *(G-6113)*
Suburban Metal Products Inc 740 474-4237
  1050 Tarlton Rd Circleville (43113) *(G-4559)*
Suburban Press Inc 216 961-0766
  3818 Lorain Ave Cleveland (44113) *(G-6114)*
Suburban Steel of Indiana, Columbus *Also called Suburban Stl Sup Co Ltd Partnr (G-7498)*
Suburban Stl Sup Co Ltd Partnr 317 783-6555
  1900 Deffenbaugh Ct Columbus (43230) *(G-7498)*
Subway, Circleville *Also called Circleville Oil Co (G-4539)*
Success Pro Publications 614 886-9922
  3137 Houston Dr Columbus (43207) *(G-7499)*
Success Technologies Inc 614 761-0008
  35 Grace Dr Powell (43065) *(G-16337)*
Sucurtex Digital, Dayton *Also called Securtex International Inc (G-8500)*
Suds 937 273-6007
  160 Main Cross Eldorado (45321) *(G-9191)*
Suever Stone Company (PA) 419 331-1945
  706 E Main St Lima (45807) *(G-11945)*
Suez Wts Usa Inc 330 339-2292
  2118 Reiser Ave Se New Philadelphia (44663) *(G-14802)*
Sugar Creek Packing Co (PA) 740 335-3586
  2101 Kenskill Ave Wshngtn CT Hs (43160) *(G-20745)*
Sugar Creek Packing Co 937 268-6601
  1241 N Gettysburg Ave Dayton (45417) *(G-8528)*
Sugar Creek Packing Co 513 874-4422
  4235 Thunderbird Ln West Chester (45014) *(G-19800)*
Sugar Creek Packing Co 513 874-4422
  4585 Muhlhauser Rd West Chester (45011) *(G-19801)*
Sugar Foods Corporation 513 336-9748
  4398 Wilderness Way Mason (45040) *(G-12943)*
Sugar Memories LLC 216 472-0206
  6770 Brookpark Rd Cleveland (44129) *(G-6115)*
Sugar Shack 419 961-4016
  4703 Flowers Rd Mansfield (44903) *(G-12522)*
Sugar Showcase 330 792-9154
  1725 S Raccoon Rd Youngstown (44515) *(G-21040)*
Sugarbush Creek Farm 440 636-5371
  13034 Madison Rd Middlefield (44062) *(G-13856)*
Sugarcreek Budget Publishers 330 852-4634
  134 Factory St Ne Sugarcreek (44681) *(G-17867)*
Sugarcreek Lime Service 330 364-4460
  2068 Gordon Rd Nw Dover (44622) *(G-8858)*
Sugarcreek Pallett 330 852-9812
  681 Belden Pkwy Ne Sugarcreek (44681) *(G-17868)*
Sugarcreek Ready Mix, Bellbrook *Also called Ernst Enterprises Inc (G-1493)*
Sugarcreek Shavings LLC 330 763-4239
  3121 Winklepleck Rd Nw Sugarcreek (44681) *(G-17869)*
Sugartree Square Mercantile 740 345-3882
  5541 Grumms Ln Ne Newark (43055) *(G-14926)*
Sulecki Precision Products 440 255-5454
  8785 East Ave Mentor (44060) *(G-13596)*
Sullivan Company, The, Westerville *Also called Bluelogos Inc (G-20038)*
Sulo Enterprises Inc 440 926-3322
  1017 Commerce Dr Grafton (44044) *(G-10311)*
Sumiriko Ohio Inc (HQ) 419 358-2121
  320 Snider Rd Bluffton (45817) *(G-1893)*
Sumitomo Elc Carbide Mfg Inc (HQ) 440 354-0600
  210 River St Grand River (44045) *(G-10326)*
Sumitomo Elc Wirg Systems Inc 937 642-7579
  14800 Industrial Pkwy Marysville (43040) *(G-12816)*
Summa Holdings Inc (PA) 440 838-4700
  8223 Brecksville Rd # 100 Cleveland (44141) *(G-6116)*
Summco Inc 330 965-7446
  6981 Southern Blvd Ste D Youngstown (44512) *(G-21041)*
Summer Garden Food Mfg, Boardman *Also called Zidian Manufacturing Inc (G-1905)*

Summer Global Systems LLC 330 397-1653
  115 Creed Cir Campbell (44405) *(G-2470)*
Summers Acquisition Corp (HQ) 216 941-7700
  12555 Berea Rd Cleveland (44111) *(G-6117)*
Summers Acquisition Corp 419 526-5800
  10 W Piper Rd Mansfield (44903) *(G-12523)*
Summers Acquisition Corp 419 423-5800
  16406 E Us Route 224 Findlay (45840) *(G-9765)*
Summers Acquisition Corp 740 373-0303
  100 Tennis Center Dr Marietta (45750) *(G-12678)*
Summers Acquisition Corp 440 946-5611
  1857 E 337th St Unit B Eastlake (44095) *(G-9134)*
Summers Rubber Co Branch 06, Marietta *Also called Summers Acquisition Corp (G-12678)*
Summers Rubber Company, Cleveland *Also called Summers Acquisition Corp (G-6117)*
Summit Aerospace Products 330 612-7341
  159 Ballantrae Dr Northfield (44067) *(G-15327)*
Summit Arms, Stow *Also called Apex Alliance LLC (G-17569)*
Summit Avionics Inc 330 425-1440
  2225 E Entp Pkwy 1a 1 A Twinsburg (44087) *(G-18861)*
Summit Container Corporation (PA) 719 481-8400
  8080 Beckett Center Dr # 203 West Chester (45069) *(G-19802)*
Summit Custom Cabinets 740 345-1734
  10430 Hoover Rd Ne Newark (43055) *(G-14927)*
Summit Diagnostic Imaging LLC 513 233-3320
  7755 5 Mile Rd Cincinnati (45230) *(G-4389)*
Summit Drilling Company Inc 800 775-5537
  152 W Dartmore Ave Akron (44301) *(G-390)*
Summit Engineered Products 330 854-5388
  516 Elm Ridge Ave Canal Fulton (44614) *(G-2493)*
Summit Ethanol LLC 419 943-7447
  3875 State Rd 65 Leipsic (45856) *(G-11737)*
Summit Finishing Technologies 937 424-5512
  2490 Arbor Blvd Unit B Moraine (45439) *(G-14396)*
Summit Machine Ltd 330 628-2663
  3991 Mogadore Rd Mogadore (44260) *(G-14250)*
Summit Millwork LLC 330 920-4000
  1619 Main St Cuyahoga Falls (44221) *(G-7924)*
Summit Online Products LLC 800 326-1972
  3982 Powell Rd Ste 137 Powell (43065) *(G-16338)*
Summit Packaging Solutions LLC (PA) 719 481-8400
  8080 Beckett Center Dr # 203 West Chester (45069) *(G-19803)*
Summit Petroleum Inc 330 487-5494
  9345 Ravenna Rd Twinsburg (44087) *(G-18862)*
Summit Plastic Company 330 633-3668
  3175 Gilchrist Rd Mogadore (44260) *(G-14251)*
Summit Printing & Graphics 330 645-7644
  1265 W Waterloo Rd Akron (44314) *(G-391)*
Summit Printing and Graphics, Akron *Also called Summit Printing & Graphics (G-391)*
Summit Research Group 330 689-1778
  4466 Darrow Rd Ste 15 Stow (44224) *(G-17633)*
Summit Resources Group Inc 330 653-3992
  7476 Whitemarsh Way Hudson (44236) *(G-11078)*
Summit Street News Inc 330 609-5600
  645 Summit St Nw Warren (44485) *(G-19444)*
Summit Tool Company (HQ) 330 535-7177
  768 E North St Akron (44305) *(G-392)*
Summit Trailer Sales & Svcs, Coventry Township *Also called Friess Welding Inc (G-7770)*
Summit Valley Lumber 330 698-7781
  6086 Fountain Nook Rd Apple Creek (44606) *(G-620)*
Summit Well Services Inc 330 223-1074
  28050 Speidel Rd East Rochester (44625) *(G-9091)*
Summitville Lab, Minerva *Also called Summitville Tiles Inc (G-14203)*
Summitville Tiles Inc 330 868-6771
  1310 Alliance Rd Nw Minerva (44657) *(G-14202)*
Summitville Tiles Inc 330 868-6463
  81 Arbor Rd Ne Minerva (44657) *(G-14203)*
Sun & Soil LLC 513 575-5900
  1357 State Route 28 Loveland (45140) *(G-12237)*
Sun Art Decals Inc 440 234-9045
  83 Dorland Ave Berea (44017) *(G-1626)*
Sun Chemical Corporation 513 671-0407
  12049 Centron Pl Cincinnati (45246) *(G-4390)*
Sun Chemical Corporation 513 681-5950
  4526 Chickering Ave Cincinnati (45232) *(G-4391)*
Sun Chemical Corporation 419 891-3514
  1380 Ford St Maumee (43537) *(G-13150)*
Sun Chemical Corporation 513 753-9550
  3922 Bach Buxton Rd Amelia (45102) *(G-549)*
Sun Chemical Corporation 513 681-5950
  5020 Spring Grove Ave Cincinnati (45232) *(G-4392)*
Sun Chemical Corporation 937 743-8055
  125 Jaygee Dr Franklin (45005) *(G-9922)*
Sun Chemical Corporation 513 771-4030
  600 Redna Ter Cincinnati (45215) *(G-4393)*
Sun Chemical Corporation 513 681-5950
  5020 Spring Grove Ave Cincinnati (45232) *(G-4394)*
Sun Chemical Corporation 513 830-8667
  5000 Spring Grove Ave Cincinnati (45232) *(G-4395)*
Sun Cleaners & Laundry Inc 740 756-4749
  3739 Old Columbus Rd Nw Carroll (43112) *(G-2912)*

ALPHABETIC SECTION

Sun Color Corporation 330 499-7010
  1325 Irondale Cir Ne North Canton (44720) (G-15123)
Sun Communities Inc 740 548-1942
  5277 Columbus Pike Lewis Center (43035) (G-11782)
Sun Microsystems, Beachwood Also called Oracle America Inc (G-1260)
Sun Newspaper Div, Cleveland Also called Comcorp Inc (G-5000)
Sun Polishing Corp 440 237-5525
  13800 Progress Pkwy Ste E Cleveland (44133) (G-6118)
Sun Shine Awards 740 425-2504
  36099 Bethesda Street Ext Barnesville (43713) (G-1119)
Sun State Plastics Inc 330 494-5220
  4045 Kevin St Nw Canton (44720) (G-2829)
Sunamericaconverting LLC 330 821-6300
  46 N Rockhill Ave Alliance (44601) (G-504)
Sunbeam Products Co LLC 419 691-1551
  623 Main St Toledo (43605) (G-18533)
Sunbright Usa Inc 440 205-0600
  8909 East Ave Mentor (44060) (G-13597)
Suncoke Energy Nc 513 727-5571
  3353 Yankee Rd Middletown (45044) (G-13955)
Sunday School Software 614 527-8776
  4369 Brickwood Dr Hilliard (43026) (G-10867)
Sunfield Inc 740 928-0404
  116 Enterprise Dr Hebron (43025) (G-10764)
Sunforest Vision Center Inc 419 475-4646
  3915 Sunforest Ct Ste A Toledo (43623) (G-18534)
Sunless Inc (PA) 440 836-0199
  8909 Freeway Dr Ste A Macedonia (44056) (G-12334)
Sunny Brook Pressed Con Co 330 673-7667
  3586 Sunnybrook Rd Kent (44240) (G-11391)
Sunny Delight Beverage Co (HQ) 513 483-3300
  10300 Alliance Rd Ste 500 Blue Ash (45242) (G-1853)
Sunny Olive LLC 513 996-4091
  9901 Montgomery Rd Cincinnati (45242) (G-4396)
Sunny Side Feeds LLC 330 635-1455
  6371 W Pleasant Home Rd West Salem (44287) (G-19958)
Sunoco Inc 216 912-2579
  1375 Home Ave Akron (44310) (G-393)
Sunpower Inc 740 594-2221
  2005 E State St Ste 104 Athens (45701) (G-851)
Sunprene Company 330 666-3751
  3550 W Market St Fairlawn (44333) (G-9621)
Sunrise Cooperative Inc 419 929-1568
  1981 Fitchville River Rd Wakeman (44889) (G-19289)
Sunrise Cooperative Inc 419 628-4705
  292 W 4th St Minster (45865) (G-14225)
Sunrise Cooperative Inc 419 683-4600
  3000 W Bucyrus St Crestline (44827) (G-7801)
Sunrise Foods Inc 614 276-2880
  2097 Corvair Blvd Columbus (43207) (G-7500)
Sunset Golf LLC 419 994-5563
  71 West Ave Ste 6 Tallmadge (44278) (G-18007)
Sunset Industries Inc 216 731-8131
  1272 E 286th St Euclid (44132) (G-9444)
Sunshine Farms Dairy, Elyria Also called Consun Food Industries Inc (G-9238)
Sunsong North America Inc 919 365-3825
  3535 Kettering Blvd Moraine (45439) (G-14397)
Sunstar Engrg Americas Inc 937 743-9049
  700 Watkins Glen Dr Franklin (45005) (G-9923)
Sunstar Engrg Americas Inc (HQ) 937 746-8575
  85 S Pioneer Blvd Springboro (45066) (G-17354)
Sunstar Sprockets, Franklin Also called Sunstar Engrg Americas Inc (G-9923)
Suntan Supply, Avon Also called JLW - TW Corp (G-952)
Suntwist Corp 800 935-3534
  5461 Dunham Rd Maple Heights (44137) (G-12581)
Sup-R-Die Inc (PA) 216 252-3930
  10003 Memphis Ave Cleveland (44144) (G-6119)
Sup-R-Die Inc 330 688-7600
  1337 Commerce Dr Ste 3 Stow (44224) (G-17634)
Super Fine Shine Inc 740 774-1700
  2806 Patton Hill Rd Lot 6 Chillicothe (45601) (G-3226)
Super Inn.com, Cleveland Also called Sark Technologies LLC (G-6032)
Super Sheet Metal 330 482-9045
  40811 Bonesville Schl Rd Leetonia (44431) (G-11722)
Super Sign Guys LLC 330 477-3887
  5060 Navarre Rd Sw Ste C Canton (44706) (G-2830)
Super Signs Inc 480 968-2200
  9890 Mount Nebo Rd North Bend (45052) (G-15056)
Super Systems Inc (PA) 513 772-0060
  7205 Edington Dr Cincinnati (45249) (G-4397)
Superalloy Mfg Solutions Corp 513 489-9800
  11230 Deerfield Rd Blue Ash (45242) (G-1854)
Superb Industries Inc 330 852-0500
  100 Innovation Plz Nw Sugarcreek (44681) (G-17870)
Superb Industries Supplier, Sugarcreek Also called Superb Industries Inc (G-17870)
Supercharger Systems Inc 216 676-5800
  5300 W 140th St Brookpark (44142) (G-2156)
Superfine Manufacturing Inc 330 897-9024
  33715 County Road 10 Fresno (43824) (G-10071)

Superfinishers Inc 330 467-2125
  380 Highland Rd E Macedonia (44056) (G-12335)
Superion Inc 937 374-0033
  1285 S Patton St Xenia (45385) (G-20793)
Superior Ag-Patoka Vlly Feed 419 294-3838
  7148 State Highway 199 Upper Sandusky (43351) (G-18975)
Superior Bar Products Inc 419 784-2590
  1710 Spruce St Defiance (43512) (G-8644)
Superior Clay Corp 740 922-4122
  6566 Superior Rd Se Uhrichsville (44683) (G-18896)
Superior Coffee & Foods, Youngstown Also called Hillshire Brands Company (G-20931)
Superior Cup Inc 330 393-6187
  448 E Market St Warren (44481) (G-19445)
Superior Energy Systems LLC 440 236-6009
  13660 Station Rd Columbia Station (44028) (G-6449)
Superior Fibers Inc 740 394-2491
  9702 Iron Point Rd Se Shawnee (43782) (G-16962)
Superior Flux & Mfg Co 440 349-3000
  6615 Parkland Blvd Cleveland (44139) (G-6120)
Superior Forge & Steel Corp (PA) 419 222-4412
  1820 Mcclain Rd Lima (45804) (G-11946)
Superior Hardwoods Cambridge, Cambridge Also called Superior Hardwoods Ohio Inc (G-2457)
Superior Hardwoods of Ohio 740 596-2561
  62581 Us Highway 50 Mc Arthur (45651) (G-13184)
Superior Hardwoods of Ohio 740 384-6862
  78 Jackson Hill Rd Jackson (45640) (G-11196)
Superior Hardwoods Ohio Inc (PA) 740 384-5677
  134 Wellston Indus Pk Rd Wellston (45692) (G-19608)
Superior Hardwoods Ohio Inc 740 439-2727
  9911 Ohio Ave Cambridge (43725) (G-2457)
Superior Holding LLC (HQ) 216 651-9400
  3786 Ridge Rd Cleveland (44144) (G-6121)
Superior Impressions Inc 419 244-8676
  327 12th St Toledo (43604) (G-18535)
Superior Label Systems Inc (HQ) 513 336-0825
  7500 Industrial Row Dr Mason (45040) (G-12944)
Superior Machine and Tool 937 308-5771
  7726 Crowl Rd De Graff (43318) (G-8606)
Superior Machine Co, Canton Also called Robert Smart Inc (G-2809)
Superior Machine Systems, Mason Also called Superior Label Systems Inc (G-12944)
Superior Machine Tool Inc 419 675-2363
  13606 Us Highway 68 Kenton (43326) (G-11425)
Superior Marine Ways Inc (PA) 740 894-6224
  5852 County Road 1 South Point (45680) (G-17295)
Superior Marine Ways Inc 740 894-6224
  5852 County Rd 1 Suoth Pt Proctorville (45669) (G-16346)
Superior Metal Products, Lima Also called American Trim LLC (G-11837)
Superior Metal Products Inc (PA) 419 228-1145
  1005 W Grand Ave Lima (45801) (G-11947)
Superior Metal Worx LLC 614 879-9400
  1239 Alum Creek Dr Columbus (43209) (G-7501)
Superior Mold & Die Co 330 688-8251
  449 N Main St Munroe Falls (44262) (G-14528)
Superior Packaging 419 380-3335
  2930 Airport Hwy Toledo (43609) (G-18536)
Superior Pneumatic & Mfg Inc 440 871-8780
  855 Canterbury Rd Cleveland (44145) (G-6122)
Superior Precision Products 216 881-3696
  968 E 69th Pl Cleveland (44103) (G-6123)
Superior Printing Ink Co Inc 513 221-4707
  10861 Millington Ct Ste B Blue Ash (45242) (G-1855)
Superior Printing Ink Co Inc 216 328-1720
  7655 Hub Pkwy Ste 205 Cleveland (44125) (G-6124)
Superior Products Llc 216 651-9400
  3786 Ridge Rd Cleveland (44144) (G-6125)
Superior Products LLC 216 651-9400
  3786 Ridge Rd Cleveland (44144) (G-6126)
Superior Quality Machine Co 330 527-7146
  10500 Industrial Dr Garrettsville (44231) (G-10202)
Superior Soda Service LLC 937 657-9700
  3626 Napanee Dr Beavercreek (45430) (G-1364)
Superior Steel Service LLC 513 724-0437
  2760 Old State Route 32 Batavia (45103) (G-1188)
Superior Steel Stamp Co 216 431-6460
  3200 Lakeside Ave E Cleveland (44114) (G-6127)
Superior Structures Inc 513 942-5954
  320 N State St Harrison (45030) (G-10674)
Superior Tasting Products Inc 614 442-0622
  2555 Bethel Rd Columbus (43220) (G-7502)
Superior Trim, Findlay Also called Pieco Inc (G-9741)
Superior Trim Formed Products, Findlay Also called Radar Love Co (G-9744)
Superior Trims Springfield Div, Springfield Also called Pieco Inc (G-17472)
Superior Water Conditioning Co, Moraine Also called Enting Water Conditioning Inc (G-14350)
Superior Weld and Fabg Co Inc 216 249-5122
  15002 Woodworth Rd Cleveland (44110) (G-6128)
Superior Welding Co 614 252-8539
  906 S Nelson Rd Columbus (43205) (G-7503)

(PA)=Parent Co (HQ)=Headquarters (DH)=Div Headquarters

Superior's Brand Meats, Massillon *Also called Fresh Mark Inc* ***(G-12983)***
Superkids Reading Program, Columbus *Also called Zaner-Bloser Inc* ***(G-7624)***
Supermedia LLC 614 216-6566
470 Olde Worthington Rd Westerville (43082) ***(G-20027)***
Superprinter Inc 440 277-0787
1925 N Ridge Rd E Lorain (44055) ***(G-12125)***
Superprinter Ltd 440 277-0787
1901 N Ridge Rd E Lorain (44055) ***(G-12126)***
Supertrapp Industries Inc 216 265-8400
4540 W 160th St Cleveland (44135) ***(G-6129)***
Supplier Inspection Svcs Inc (PA) 937 263-7097
2941 S Gettysburg Ave Dayton (45439) ***(G-8529)***
Supply Dynamics Inc 513 965-2000
6279 Tr Rdge Blvd Ste 310 Loveland (45140) ***(G-12238)***
Supply International Inc 740 282-8604
602 Kingsdale Rd Ste 1 Steubenville (43952) ***(G-17555)***
Supply Technologies LLC 614 759-9939
590 Claycraft Rd Columbus (43230) ***(G-7504)***
Supply Technologies LLC (HQ) 440 947-2100
6065 Parkland Blvd Ste 2 Cleveland (44124) ***(G-6130)***
Supply Technologies LLC 937 898-5795
4704 Wadsworth Rd Dayton (45414) ***(G-8530)***
Supply Technologies LLC 740 363-1971
700 London Rd Delaware (43015) ***(G-8727)***
Support Service, Lexington *Also called Support Svc LLC* ***(G-11808)***
Support Svc LLC 419 617-0660
25 Walnut St Rear Lexington (44904) ***(G-11808)***
Supreme Fan/Industrial Air, Dayton *Also called Lau Industries Inc* ***(G-7983)***
Supro Spring & Wire Forms Inc 330 722-5628
6440 Norwalk Rd Ste N Medina (44256) ***(G-13349)***
Sur-Seal LLC (HQ) 513 574-8500
6156 Wesselman Rd Cincinnati (45248) ***(G-4398)***
Sur-Seal Corporation 513 574-8500
10053 Simonson Rd Harrison (45030) ***(G-10675)***
Sur-Seal Gasket & Packing, Cincinnati *Also called Sur-Seal LLC* ***(G-4398)***
Sure To Grow, Beachwood *Also called 6062 Holdings LLC* ***(G-1216)***
Sure Tool & Manufacturing Co 937 253-9111
429 Winston Ave Dayton (45403) ***(G-8531)***
Sure-Foot Industries Corp 440 234-4446
20260 1st Ave Cleveland (44130) ***(G-6131)***
Surenergy LLC 419 626-8000
319 Howard Dr Sandusky (44870) ***(G-16851)***
Surface Combustion Inc (PA) 419 891-7150
1700 Indian Wood Cir Maumee (43537) ***(G-13151)***
Surface Dynamics Inc 513 772-6635
231 Northland Blvd Cincinnati (45246) ***(G-4399)***
Surface Enhancement Tech LLC 513 561-1520
3929 Virginia Ave Cincinnati (45227) ***(G-4400)***
Surface Enterprises Inc 419 476-5670
1465 W Alexis Rd Toledo (43612) ***(G-18537)***
Surface Recovery Tech LLC 937 879-5864
833 Zapata Dr Fairborn (45324) ***(G-9470)***
Surface Systems, Akron *Also called Cto Inc* ***(G-126)***
Surface-All Inc 440 428-2233
745 N Hidden Harbor Dr Port Clinton (43452) ***(G-16261)***
Surftech, Austinburg *Also called Euclid Refinishing Compnay Inc* ***(G-920)***
Surftech Inc 440 275-3356
2937 Industrial Park Dr Austinburg (44010) ***(G-927)***
Surgeye, Powell *Also called Actis Ltd* ***(G-16306)***
Surgical Appliance Inds Inc (PA) 513 271-4594
3960 Rosslyn Dr Cincinnati (45209) ***(G-4401)***
Surgical Appliance Inds Inc 937 392-4301
1311 S 2nd St Ripley (45167) ***(G-16518)***
Surgical Theater LLC (PA) 216 452-2177
781 Beta Dr Ste A Mayfield Village (44143) ***(G-13177)***
Surgical Theater LLC 216 496-7884
4541 Greenwold Rd Cleveland (44121) ***(G-6132)***
Surgrx Inc 650 482-2400
4545 Creek Rd Blue Ash (45242) ***(G-1856)***
Surili Couture LLC 440 600-1456
29961 Persimmon Dr Westlake (44145) ***(G-20164)***
Surplus Freight Inc (PA) 614 235-7660
501 Morrison Rd Ste 100 Gahanna (43230) ***(G-10108)***
Surtec Inc 440 239-9710
3097 Interstate Pkwy Brunswick (44212) ***(G-2242)***
Surveying Cannon Land 740 342-2835
7945 Township Road 114 Ne New Lexington (43764) ***(G-14725)***
Survitec Group (usa) Inc (HQ) 330 239-4331
1420 Wolfcreek Trl Sharon Center (44274) ***(G-16954)***
Susan Products, Cleveland *Also called Mystic Chemical Products Co* ***(G-5718)***
Sushi On The Roll, Medina *Also called Jroll LLC* ***(G-13283)***
Suspension Feeder, Fort Recovery *Also called Roessner Holdings Inc* ***(G-9826)***
Suspension Feeder Corporation 419 763-1377
482 State Route 119 Fort Recovery (45846) ***(G-9828)***
Suspension Technology Inc 330 458-3058
1424 Scales St Sw Canton (44706) ***(G-2831)***
Sutphen Corporation (PA) 800 726-7030
6450 Eiterman Rd Dublin (43016) ***(G-8999)***
Sutphen Corporation 937 969-8851
1701 W County Line Rd Springfield (45502) ***(G-17500)***
Sutterlin Machine & Tool Co 440 357-0817
9445 Pineneedle Dr Mentor (44060) ***(G-13598)***
Suzin L Chocolatiers 440 323-3372
230 Broad St Elyria (44035) ***(G-9332)***
Suzuki of Toleda, Toledo *Also called Customers Car Care Center* ***(G-18247)***
Svm America Ltd 937 218-7591
1004 River Forest Dr Maineville (45039) ***(G-12377)***
Swagelok (HQ) 440 349-5657
29500 Solon Rd Solon (44139) ***(G-17239)***
Swagelok Biopharm Services Co, Willoughby Hills *Also called Swagelok Company* ***(G-20476)***
Swagelok Company (PA) 440 248-4600
29500 Solon Rd Solon (44139) ***(G-17240)***
Swagelok Company 440 349-5652
6100 Cochran Rd Solon (44139) ***(G-17241)***
Swagelok Company 440 248-4600
26653 Curtiss Wright Pkwy Willoughby Hills (44092) ***(G-20475)***
Swagelok Company 440 944-8988
26651 Curtiss Wright Pkwy Willoughby Hills (44092) ***(G-20476)***
Swagelok Company 440 442-6611
328 Bishop Rd Cleveland (44143) ***(G-6133)***
Swagelok Company 440 473-1050
318 Bishop Rd Cleveland (44143) ***(G-6134)***
Swagelok Company 440 461-7714
358 Bishop Rd Cleveland (44143) ***(G-6135)***
Swagelok Company 440 349-5934
31400 Aurora Rd Solon (44139) ***(G-17242)***
Swagelok Company 440 349-5836
6262 Cochran Rd Solon (44139) ***(G-17243)***
Swagelok Hy-Level Company (PA) 440 238-1260
15400 Foltz Pkwy Strongsville (44149) ***(G-17798)***
Swagelok Manufacturing Co LLC 440 248-4600
29500 Solon Rd Solon (44139) ***(G-17244)***
Swagg Productions2015llc 614 815-1173
2003 Chalfield Ct Reynoldsburg (43068) ***(G-16455)***
Swanson Orthotic & Prosthetic 419 690-0026
3048 Navarre Ave Oregon (43616) ***(G-15570)***
Swanson Prosthetic Center Inc 419 472-8910
3102 W Sylvania Ave Toledo (43613) ***(G-18538)***
Swanton Wldg Machining Co Inc (PA) 419 826-4816
407 Broadway Ave Swanton (43558) ***(G-17923)***
Swarovski North America Ltd 216 292-9737
26300 Cedar Rd Cleveland (44122) ***(G-6136)***
Swartz Audie 740 820-2341
527 Flower Ison Rd Minford (45653) ***(G-14207)***
Swartz Manufacturing Inc 440 284-0297
820 Walnut St Elyria (44035) ***(G-9333)***
Swartz Race Cars, Minford *Also called Swartz Audie* ***(G-14207)***
Swartz Woodworking 330 359-6359
7136 Township Road 654 Millersburg (44654) ***(G-14132)***
Sweaty Bands LLC 513 871-1222
3802 Ford Cir Cincinnati (45227) ***(G-4402)***
Sweet GS Cupcakery Ltd 419 610-8507
3820 Turnock Gln Columbus (43230) ***(G-7505)***
Sweet Manufacturing Company 937 325-1511
2000 E Leffel Ln Springfield (45505) ***(G-17501)***
Sweet Melissas 440 333-6357
19337 Detroit Rd Rocky River (44116) ***(G-16557)***
Sweet Mobile Cupcakery 440 465-7333
428 Walmar Rd Bay Village (44140) ***(G-1210)***
Sweet Persuasions LLC 614 216-9052
9636 Circle Dr Pickerington (43147) ***(G-16061)***
Swift Filters Inc (PA) 440 735-0995
24040 Forbes Rd Oakwood Village (44146) ***(G-15484)***
Swift Manufacturing Co Inc 740 237-4405
700 Lorain St Ironton (45638) ***(G-11173)***
Swift Print, Cleveland *Also called D M J F Inc* ***(G-5057)***
Swift Tool Inc 330 945-6973
1420 Ritchie St Cuyahoga Falls (44221) ***(G-7925)***
Swigart Electric, Englewood *Also called Kent Swigart* ***(G-9365)***
Swiger Coil Systems Ltd 216 362-7500
4677 Manufacturing Ave Cleveland (44135) ***(G-6137)***
Swimmer Printing Inc 216 623-1005
1701 E 12th St Cleveland (44114) ***(G-6138)***
Swingle Drilling, Crooksville *Also called Petro Ware Inc* ***(G-7819)***
Swisher Hygiene Inc 513 870-4830
5579 Spellmire Dr West Chester (45246) ***(G-19905)***
Swiss Woodcraft Inc 330 925-1807
15 Industrial St Rittman (44270) ***(G-16529)***
Switchback Group Inc (PA) 330 523-5200
3778 Timberlake Dr Richfield (44286) ***(G-16490)***
Switzer Performance Engrg 440 774-4219
44800 Us Highway 20 Oberlin (44074) ***(G-15505)***
Switzer Performance Innovation, Oberlin *Also called Switzer Performance Engrg* ***(G-15505)***
Swivel-Tek Industries LLC 419 636-7770
417 N Lynn St Bryan (43506) ***(G-2308)***

Swocat Design Inc....440 282-4700
4325 Oberlin Ave Uppr Lorain (44053) *(G-12127)*
Sword Furs....440 249-5001
25112 Center Ridge Rd Westlake (44145) *(G-20165)*
Swp Legacy Ltd....330 340-9663
10143 Copperhead Rd Nw Sugarcreek (44681) *(G-17871)*
Sylvan Forge Inc....440 237-3626
7420 James Dr North Royalton (44133) *(G-15303)*
Sylvan Studio, Sylvania *Also called Sharonco Inc (G-17960)*
Sylvan Studio Inc....419 882-3423
5651 Main St Sylvania (43560) *(G-17963)*
Sylvania Moose Lodge 1579, Sylvania *Also called Sylvania Moose Lodge No (G-17964)*
Sylvania Moose Lodge No....419 885-4953
6072 Main St Sylvania (43560) *(G-17964)*
Symantec Corporation....614 793-3060
545 Metro Pl S Ste 100 Dublin (43017) *(G-9000)*
Symantec Corporation....216 643-6700
6100 Oak Tree Blvd Independence (44131) *(G-11151)*
Symatic Inc....330 225-1510
2831 Center Rd Brunswick (44212) *(G-2243)*
Symbol Tool & Die Inc....440 582-5989
11000 Industrial First Av North Royalton (44133) *(G-15304)*
Syme Inc (PA)....330 723-6000
300 Lake Rd Medina (44256) *(G-13350)*
Symmetry Oes....614 890-1758
4528 Ravine Dr Westerville (43081) *(G-20075)*
Symrise Inc....440 324-6060
110 Liberty Ct Elyria (44035) *(G-9334)*
Synagro Midwest Inc....937 384-0669
4515 Infirmary Rd Miamisburg (45342) *(G-13722)*
Syndicate Printers Inc....513 779-3625
7291 Saint Ives Pl West Chester (45069) *(G-19804)*
Synergy Flavors (oh) LLC....513 892-7100
2991 Hamilton Mason Rd Fairfield Township (45011) *(G-9587)*
Synergy Grinding Inc....216 447-4000
1994 Coes Post Run Westlake (44145) *(G-20166)*
Synergy Health North Amer Inc....513 398-6406
7086 Industrial Row Dr Mason (45040) *(G-12945)*
Synsei Medical....609 759-1101
6474 Weston Cir W Dublin (43016) *(G-9001)*
Syntec LLC....440 229-6262
20525 Center Ridge Rd # 512 Rocky River (44116) *(G-16558)*
Synthetic Body Parts Inc....440 838-0985
6099 Warblers Roost Brecksville (44141) *(G-2059)*
Synthetic Rubber Technology....330 494-2221
11021 Wright Rd Nw Uniontown (44685) *(G-18933)*
Syracuse China Company (HQ)....419 727-2100
300 Madison Ave Toledo (43604) *(G-18539)*
Sysco Guest Supply LLC....440 960-2515
7395 Lorain Indus Pkwy Lorain (44052) *(G-12128)*
Syscom Advanced Materials Inc....614 487-3626
1305 Kinnear Rd Columbus (43212) *(G-7506)*
Systech Environmental Corp (HQ)....800 888-8011
3085 Woodman Dr Ste 300 Dayton (45420) *(G-8532)*
Systech Handling Inc....419 445-8226
120 Taylor Pkwy Archbold (43502) *(G-670)*
Systecon LLC....513 777-7722
6121 Schumacher Park Dr West Chester (45069) *(G-19805)*
System Controls Inc....216 351-9121
4549 State Rd Cleveland (44109) *(G-6139)*
System EDM of Ohio, Mason *Also called Hi-Tek Manufacturing Inc (G-12886)*
System Packaging of Glassline....419 666-9712
28905 Glenwood Rd Perrysburg (43551) *(G-16008)*
System Seals Inc (HQ)....440 735-0200
9505 Midwest Ave Cleveland (44125) *(G-6140)*
Systematic Machine Corp....440 877-9884
12955 York Delta Dr Ste F North Royalton (44133) *(G-15305)*
Systemax Manufacturing Inc....937 368-2300
6450 Poe Ave Ste 200 Dayton (45414) *(G-8533)*
Systems Jay LLC Nanogate....419 747-1096
1555 W Longview Ave Mansfield (44906) *(G-12524)*
Systems Jay LLC Nanogate....419 522-7745
515 Newman St Mansfield (44902) *(G-12525)*
Systems Pack Inc....330 467-5729
649 Highland Rd E Macedonia (44056) *(G-12336)*
Systems Specialty Ctrl Co Inc....419 478-4156
1550 Coining Dr Toledo (43612) *(G-18540)*
Szpak Manufacturing Co Inc....440 236-5233
27500 Royalton Rd Unit 5 Columbia Station (44028) *(G-6450)*
T & B Foundry Company....216 391-4200
2469 E 71st St Cleveland (44104) *(G-6141)*
T & D Fabricating Inc....440 951-5646
1489 E 363rd St Eastlake (44095) *(G-9135)*
T & D Thompson Inc....740 332-8515
15952 State Route 56 E Laurelville (43135) *(G-11627)*
T & K Heins Corporation....740 452-6006
1326 Brandywine Blvd Zanesville (43701) *(G-21184)*
T & K Welding Co Inc....216 432-0221
1405 E 39th St Cleveland (44114) *(G-6142)*
T & L Custom Screening Inc....937 237-3121
3464 Successful Way Dayton (45414) *(G-8534)*
T & L Welding LLC....937 498-9170
211 E Russell Rd Sidney (45365) *(G-17083)*
T & M Machine Products Inc....740 753-2960
14265 State Route 691 Nelsonville (45764) *(G-14599)*
T & R Noodles LLC....614 537-4710
11400 State Route 37 E New Lexington (43764) *(G-14726)*
T & R Welding Systems Inc....937 228-7517
1 Janney Rd Dayton (45404) *(G-8535)*
T & S Discount Tires Inc....440 951-9084
36525 Reading Ave Willoughby (44094) *(G-20439)*
T & S Enterprises....419 424-1122
1616 Bliss Ave Findlay (45840) *(G-9766)*
T & S Machine Inc....419 453-2101
712 Maple St Wapakoneta (45895) *(G-19356)*
T & T Machine Inc....440 354-0605
892 Callendar Blvd Painesville (44077) *(G-15785)*
T & W Tool & Machine Inc....937 667-2039
467 N 5th St Tipp City (45371) *(G-18135)*
T A Bacon Co....216 851-1404
11655 Chillicothe Rd Chesterland (44026) *(G-3169)*
T A C, Hilliard *Also called Thermoplastic Accessories Corp (G-10870)*
T and D Industries LLC....937 321-3424
1325 Foxglen Cir Dayton (45429) *(G-8536)*
T and D Washers LLC....419 562-5500
255 E Warren St Bucyrus (44820) *(G-2344)*
T and W Stamping Acquisition....330 821-5777
930 W Ely St Alliance (44601) *(G-505)*
T C F C, Cleveland *Also called Those Charc From Cleve Inc (G-6172)*
T C I, Greenville *Also called Treaty City Industries Inc (G-10398)*
T C Redi Mix Youngstown Inc (PA)....330 755-2143
2400 Poland Ave Youngstown (44502) *(G-21042)*
T C Woodworking, New Lexington *Also called R Carney Thomas (G-14722)*
T D Dynamics Inc....216 881-0800
4101 Commerce Ave Cleveland (44103) *(G-6143)*
T D Group Holdings LLC....216 706-2939
1301 E 9th St Ste 3710 Cleveland (44114) *(G-6144)*
T E Hubler Inc....419 476-2552
236 New Towne Square Dr 1b Toledo (43612) *(G-18541)*
T E Martindale Enterprises....614 253-6826
2840 E 5th Ave Columbus (43219) *(G-7507)*
T E S, Milford *Also called Tactical Envmtl Systems Inc (G-14042)*
T F O, Jeffersonville *Also called Tfo Tech Co Ltd (G-11248)*
T H E B Inc....216 391-4800
3700 Kelley Ave Cleveland (44114) *(G-6145)*
T J Davies Company Inc....440 248-5510
30745 Solon Rd Ste 1 Solon (44139) *(G-17245)*
T J Ellis Enterprises Inc....419 224-1969
1505 Neubrecht Rd Lima (45801) *(G-11948)*
T J F Inc....419 878-4400
1070 Disher Dr Waterville (43566) *(G-19506)*
T J Target....330 658-3057
235 Bailey Ct Doylestown (44230) *(G-8867)*
T JS Oil & Gas Inc....740 623-0192
23191 County Road 621 Coshocton (43812) *(G-7754)*
T K Holdings, Piqua *Also called Tk Holdings Inc (G-16166)*
T K L Lettering....937 832-2091
300 W National Rd Ste C Englewood (45322) *(G-9376)*
T M D, Toledo *Also called Toledo Molding & Die Inc (G-18564)*
T M Industries Inc....330 627-4410
4082 Thrasher Rd Sw Carrollton (44615) *(G-2930)*
T N T Technologies Inc....330 448-4744
7848 Locust St Masury (44438) *(G-13063)*
T P F Inc....513 761-9968
313 S Wayne Ave Cincinnati (45215) *(G-4403)*
T R C, Frankfort *Also called Jay Tackett (G-9862)*
T S I, Englewood *Also called Tom Smith Industries Inc (G-9378)*
T Shirts & Soccer Wearhouse, Twinsburg *Also called Custom Screen Printing (G-18759)*
T T Machine Tool, Willoughby *Also called McTt Machine Tool Inc (G-20375)*
T V Specialties Inc....330 364-6678
320 W 3rd St Dover (44622) *(G-8859)*
T&A Pallets Inc....330 968-4743
2849 Denny Rd Ravenna (44266) *(G-16411)*
T&K Laser Works Inc....937 693-3783
401 N Main St Botkins (45306) *(G-1938)*
T&M Plastics Co Inc....216 651-7700
1249 W 78th St Cleveland (44102) *(G-6146)*
T&R Logging LLC....740 288-1825
1085 Loop Rd Wellston (45692) *(G-19609)*
T&R Wood Products, Middle Point *Also called Traveling & Recycle Wood Pdts (G-13757)*
T&T Welding....513 615-1156
1469 State Route 28 Loveland (45140) *(G-12239)*
T-Fab, Willoughby *Also called Tkr Metal Fabricating LLC (G-20448)*
T-N-T Concrete Inc....540 480-4040
6032 W Valleyview Ct Mentor (44060) *(G-13599)*
T-Top Shoppe....330 343-3481
138 E High Ave New Philadelphia (44663) *(G-14803)*

ALPHABETIC

Ta Die For Gourmet Cupcakes 740 751-4586
2094 Harding Hwy E Marion (43302) *(G-12739)*
Taasi, Delaware *Also called Attia Applied Sciences Inc (G-8656)*
Tabco, Chesterland *Also called T A Bacon Co (G-3169)*
Tablox Inc 440 953-1951
4821 E 345th St Willoughby (44094) *(G-20440)*
Tabtronics Inc 937 222-9969
2153 Winners Cir Dayton (45404) *(G-8537)*
TAC Enterprises, Springfield *Also called TAC Industries Inc (G-17502)*
TAC Industries Inc (PA) 937 328-5200
2160 Old Selma Rd Springfield (45505) *(G-17502)*
Tachometer Press, Cincinnati *Also called Micropress America LLC (G-4024)*
Tack-Anew Inc 419 734-4212
451 W Lakeshore Dr Port Clinton (43452) *(G-16262)*
Tacpack, Dublin *Also called Brass Tacks Corporation Ltd (G-8891)*
Tactical Envmtl Systems Inc 513 831-2663
1156 Us Route 50 Milford (45150) *(G-14042)*
Tactical Revolution LLC 419 348-9526
10436 Country Acres Dr # 7 Ottawa (45875) *(G-15668)*
Tadd Spring Co Inc 440 572-1313
15060 Foltz Pkwy Strongsville (44149) *(G-17799)*
Tadlock Trailer Sales, West Union *Also called Jerry Tadlock (G-19963)*
Taft Tool & Production Co 419 385-2576
756 S Byrne Rd Ste 1 Toledo (43609) *(G-18542)*
Tag 614 921-1732
2226 Wilson Rd Columbus (43228) *(G-7508)*
Tag Sportswear LLC 330 456-8867
1300 Market Ave N Canton (44714) *(G-2832)*
Tahoe Interactive Systems Inc 614 891-2323
60 Nadine Pl N Westerville (43081) *(G-20076)*
Tahoma Enterprises Inc (PA) 330 745-9016
255 Wooster Rd N Barberton (44203) *(G-1108)*
Tahoma Rubber & Plastics Inc (HQ) 330 745-9016
255 Wooster Rd N Barberton (44203) *(G-1109)*
Taiho Corporation of America 419 443-1645
194 Heritage Dr Tiffin (44883) *(G-18086)*
Tailored Systems Inc 937 299-3900
2853 Springboro W Moraine (45439) *(G-14398)*
Tailspin Brewing Company 419 852-9366
626 S 2nd St Coldwater (45828) *(G-6421)*
Tailwind Technologies Inc (PA) 937 778-4200
1 Propeller Pl Piqua (45356) *(G-16164)*
Taiyo America Inc (HQ) 419 300-8811
1702 E Spring St Saint Marys (45885) *(G-16703)*
Take It For Granite LLC 513 735-0555
3898 Mcmann Rd Cincinnati (45245) *(G-3265)*
Takeda Pharmaceuticals USA Inc 440 238-0872
19495 Trotwood Park Strongsville (44149) *(G-17800)*
Takeya USA Corporation 714 374-9900
265 N Hamilton Rd Columbus (43213) *(G-7509)*
Takk Industries Inc 513 353-4306
5838a Hamilton Cleves Rd Cleves (45002) *(G-6378)*
Talan Products Inc 216 458-0170
18800 Cochran Ave Cleveland (44110) *(G-6147)*
Talbot Drake & Co, Cleveland *Also called Talbot Drake Incorporated (G-6148)*
Talbot Drake Incorporated 216 441-5600
5808 Grant Ave Cleveland (44105) *(G-6148)*
Talent Tool & Die Inc 440 239-8777
777 Berea Industrial Pkwy Berea (44017) *(G-1627)*
Talisman Racing, Cincinnati *Also called All Craft Manufacturing Co (G-3321)*
Talk of Town Silkscreen & EMB, Akron *Also called B Richardson Inc (G-76)*
Tallmadge Finishing Co Inc 330 633-7466
879 Moe Dr Ste C20 Akron (44310) *(G-394)*
Tallmadge Spinning & Metal Co 330 794-2277
2783 Gilchrist Rd Unit A Akron (44305) *(G-395)*
Talon Defense 419 236-7695
408 S Main St Columbus Grove (45830) *(G-7638)*
Tamarkin Company 330 634-0688
205 West Ave Tallmadge (44278) *(G-18008)*
Tamarkin Company 614 878-8942
4780 W Broad St Columbus (43228) *(G-7510)*
Tamarron Technology Inc 800 277-3207
8044 Montgomery Rd Cincinnati (45236) *(G-4404)*
Tambrands Sales Corp (HQ) 513 983-1100
1 Procter And Gamble Plz Cincinnati (45202) *(G-4405)*
Tampax, Cincinnati *Also called Tambrands Sales Corp (G-4405)*
Tangent Air Inc 740 474-1114
127 Edison Ave Circleville (43113) *(G-4560)*
Tangent Company LLC 440 543-2775
10175 Queens Way Ste 1 Chagrin Falls (44023) *(G-3079)*
Tangible Solutions Inc 937 912-4603
678 Yllow Sprng Frfeld Rd Fairborn (45324) *(G-9471)*
Tango Echo Bravo Mfg Inc 440 937-3800
4915 Mills Indus Pkwy North Ridgeville (44039) *(G-15254)*
Tank Services, Dennison *Also called Services Acquisition Co LLC (G-8786)*
Tanning 937 233-4554
7109 Taylorsville Rd Dayton (45424) *(G-8538)*
Tap Packaging Solutions, Cleveland *Also called Chilcote Company (G-4922)*
Tapco Holdings Inc 800 771-4486
200 Shotwell Dr Franklin (45005) *(G-9924)*
Tapestry Inc 419 471-9033
5001 Monroe St Ste 1743 Toledo (43623) *(G-18543)*
Tarahill Inc 706 864-0808
3985 Groves Rd Columbus (43232) *(G-7511)*
Tarantula Performance Racg LLC 330 273-3456
1669 W 130th St Ste 301 Hinckley (44233) *(G-10906)*
Targa Enterprises, Cleveland *Also called Darryl Smith (G-5068)*
Target Business Services, Pickerington *Also called Our Fifth Street LLC (G-16055)*
Target Printing & Graphics 937 228-0170
233 Leo St Dayton (45404) *(G-8539)*
Target Thompson Technology 330 699-8000
3651 Apache St Nw Uniontown (44685) *(G-18934)*
Targeted Cmpund Monitoring LLC 513 461-3535
2790 Indian Ripple Rd A Beavercreek (45440) *(G-1365)*
Targeting Customer Safety Inc 330 865-9593
1021 Galsworthy Dr Akron (44313) *(G-396)*
Tarigma Corporation 614 436-3734
6161 Busch Blvd Ste 110 Columbus (43229) *(G-7512)*
Tark Inc (PA) 937 434-6766
420 Congress Park Dr Dayton (45459) *(G-8540)*
Tarkett Inc 440 708-9366
16910 Munn Rd Chagrin Falls (44023) *(G-3080)*
Tarkett Inc (HQ) 800 899-8916
30000 Aurora Rd Solon (44139) *(G-17246)*
Tarkett North America, Solon *Also called Tarkett Inc (G-17246)*
Tarkett USA Inc (HQ) 440 543-8916
30000 Aurora Rd Solon (44139) *(G-17247)*
Tarman Machine Company Inc 614 834-4010
8215 Dove Pkwy Canal Winchester (43110) *(G-2512)*
Tarpco, Kent *Also called Hapco Inc (G-11331)*
Tarpco Inc 330 677-8277
390 Portage Blvd Kent (44240) *(G-11392)*
Tarped Out Inc 330 325-7722
4442 State Route 14 Ravenna (44266) *(G-16412)*
Tarpstop LLC (PA) 419 873-7867
12000 Williams Rd Perrysburg (43551) *(G-16009)*
Tarrier Foods Corp 614 876-8594
2700 International St # 100 Columbus (43228) *(G-7513)*
Tarrier Steel Company Inc 614 444-4000
1379 S 22nd St Columbus (43206) *(G-7514)*
Tasi Group, Harrison *Also called Tasi Holdings Inc (G-10676)*
Tasi Holdings Inc (PA) 513 202-5182
10100 Progress Way Harrison (45030) *(G-10676)*
Taste of Belgium LLC 513 381-3280
1801 Race St Ste 30 Cincinnati (45202) *(G-4406)*
Taste of Heaven Original Gourm, Akron *Also called Waymakers Inc (G-432)*
Tastemorr Snacks, Coldwater *Also called Basic Grain Products Inc (G-6402)*
Tat Engineering, Nelsonville *Also called Tat Pumps Inc (G-14600)*
Tat Machine and Tool Ltd 419 836-7706
1313 S Cousino Rd Curtice (43412) *(G-7827)*
Tat Pumps Inc 740 385-0008
398 Poplar St Nelsonville (45764) *(G-14600)*
Tata America Intl Corp 513 677-6500
1000 Summit Dr Unit 1 Milford (45150) *(G-14043)*
Tata Consultancy Services, Milford *Also called Tata America Intl Corp (G-14043)*
Tate Lyle Ingrdnts Amricas LLC 937 236-5906
5600 Brentlinger Dr Dayton (45414) *(G-8541)*
Tate Lyle Ingrdnts Amricas LLC 937 235-4074
5584 Webster St Dayton (45414) *(G-8542)*
Tater Tool & Die Inc 330 648-1148
11145 Old Mill Rd Spencer (44275) *(G-17307)*
Tatham Schulz Incorporated 216 861-4431
836 Broadway Ave Cleveland (44115) *(G-6149)*
Tatum Landscaping & Lawncare, Columbus *Also called Frankie Tatum (G-6934)*
Tatum Petroleum Corporation 740 819-6810
667 Lkview Plz Blvd Ste E Worthington (43085) *(G-20704)*
Taupe Holdings Co 614 330-4600
7758 Deercrest Ct Dublin (43016) *(G-9002)*
Tavens Container Inc 216 883-3333
22475 Aurora Rd Bedford (44146) *(G-1448)*
Tavens Packg Display Solutions, Bedford *Also called Tavens Container Inc (G-1448)*
Taylor & Moore Co 513 733-5530
807 Wachendorf St Cincinnati (45215) *(G-4407)*
Taylor - Winfield Corporation (PA) 330 259-8500
3200 Innovation Pl Hubbard (44425) *(G-11010)*
Taylor Communications Inc 419 678-6000
515 W Sycamore St Coldwater (45828) *(G-6422)*
Taylor Communications Inc 440 974-1611
7200 Justin Way Mentor (44060) *(G-13600)*
Taylor Communications Inc 937 221-1000
600 Albany St Dayton (45417) *(G-8543)*
Taylor Communications Inc 216 265-1800
4125 Highlander Pkwy # 230 Richfield (44286) *(G-16491)*
Taylor Communications Inc 614 351-6868
3950 Business Park Dr Columbus (43204) *(G-7515)*
Taylor Communications Inc 614 277-7500
3125 Lewis Centre Way Grove City (43123) *(G-10471)*

Taylor Communications Inc...732 356-0081
7755 Paragon Rd Ste 101 Dayton (45459) ***(G-8544)***
Taylor Communications Inc...937 221-3347
3545 Urbancrest Indus Grove City (43123) ***(G-10472)***
Taylor Communications Inc...937 228-5800
220 E Monument Ave Dayton (45402) ***(G-8545)***
Taylor Communications Inc...866 541-0937
2222 Philadcelphia Dr Dayton (45406) ***(G-8546)***
Taylor Company (PA)...513 271-2550
5721 Dragon Way Ste 117 Cincinnati (45227) ***(G-4408)***
Taylor Lumber Worldwide Inc...740 259-6222
18253 State Route 73 Mc Dermott (45652) ***(G-13194)***
Taylor Made Glass Systems, Payne *Also called Taylor Products Inc* ***(G-15875)***
Taylor Manufacturing Company...937 322-8622
1101 W Main St Springfield (45504) ***(G-17503)***
Taylor Metal Products Co...419 522-3471
700 Springmill St Mansfield (44903) ***(G-12526)***
Taylor Mtl Hdlg & Conveyor, Toledo *Also called Bobco Enterprises Inc* ***(G-18208)***
Taylor Products Inc...419 263-2313
230 S Laura St Payne (45880) ***(G-15874)***
Taylor Products Inc...419 263-2313
407 N Maple St Payne (45880) ***(G-15875)***
Taylor Quick Print...740 439-2208
1008 Woodlawn Ave A Cambridge (43725) ***(G-2458)***
Taylor Tool & Die Inc...937 845-1491
306 N Main St New Carlisle (45344) ***(G-14678)***
Taylor Winfield Indus Wldg Eqp, Youngstown *Also called Taylor-Winfield Tech Inc* ***(G-21043)***
Taylor-Winfield Tech Inc (HQ)...330 259-8500
3200 Innovation Pl Youngstown (44509) ***(G-21043)***
Tbec, Painesville *Also called Thirion Brothers Eqp Co LLC* ***(G-15790)***
Tbh International...440 323-4651
150 Ridge Circle Ln Apt A Elyria (44035) ***(G-9335)***
Tbone Sales LLC...330 897-6131
410 N Ray St Baltic (43804) ***(G-1033)***
Tc Precision Machine Inc...937 278-3334
2540 Ashcraft Rd Dayton (45414) ***(G-8547)***
TC Service Co...440 954-7500
38285 Pelton Rd Willoughby (44094) ***(G-20441)***
Tca Graphics, Fairborn *Also called Tee Creations* ***(G-9472)***
Tcb Automation LLC...330 556-6444
601 W 15th St Dover (44622) ***(G-8860)***
Tce International Ltd...800 962-2376
4843 N Ridge Rd Perry (44081) ***(G-15914)***
Tcp Inc...330 836-4239
2747 Crawfis Blvd Ste 108 Fairlawn (44333) ***(G-9622)***
TCS, Akron *Also called Targeting Customer Safety Inc* ***(G-396)***
TD Landscape Inc...740 694-0244
16780 Pinkley Rd Fredericktown (43019) ***(G-9978)***
Tdc Systems Inc...440 953-5918
38296 Western Pkwy Willoughby (44094) ***(G-20442)***
Tdl Tool Inc...937 374-0055
1296 S Patton St Xenia (45385) ***(G-20794)***
Tdm LLC...440 969-1442
1303 W 38th St Ashtabula (44004) ***(G-806)***
Tdm Fuelcell LLC Tdm LLC...440 969-1442
12144 W Shiloh Dr Chesterland (44026) ***(G-3170)***
TDS Custom Cabinets LLC...614 517-2220
1819 Walcutt Rd Ste A Columbus (43228) ***(G-7516)***
TE Brown LLC (PA)...937 223-2241
1205 Lamar St Dayton (45404) ***(G-8548)***
Te Connectivity Corporation...419 521-9500
175 N Diamond St Mansfield (44902) ***(G-12527)***
TE Signs and Ship LLC...440 281-9340
810 Taylor St Elyria (44035) ***(G-9336)***
Te-Co Manufacturing LLC...937 836-0961
100 Quinter Farm Rd Englewood (45322) ***(G-9377)***
Teachers Publishing Group...614 486-0631
4200 Parkway Ct Hilliard (43026) ***(G-10868)***
Team Inc...614 263-1808
3005 Silver Dr Columbus (43224) ***(G-7517)***
Team Amity Molds & Plastic...937 667-7856
1435 Commerce Park Dr Tipp City (45371) ***(G-18136)***
Team Cooperheat Mqs...614 501-7304
5764 Westbourne Ave Columbus (43213) ***(G-7518)***
Team Plastics Inc...216 251-8270
3901 W 150th St Cleveland (44111) ***(G-6150)***
Team Systems, Toledo *Also called Decoma Systems Integration Gro* ***(G-18257)***
Team Wendy LLC...216 738-2518
17000 Saint Clair Ave # 5 Cleveland (44110) ***(G-6151)***
Tebben Rubber Stamp Company, Elida *Also called Ulrich Rubber Stamp Company* ***(G-9202)***
TEC Design & Manufacturing Inc...937 435-2147
4549 Gateway Cir Dayton (45440) ***(G-8549)***
TEC Design and Mfg LLC...216 362-8962
5240 Smith Rd Ste 4 Cleveland (44142) ***(G-6152)***
TEC Line Inc...740 881-5948
8020 Strawberry Hill Rd Lewis Center (43035) ***(G-11783)***
Teca, Dayton *Also called Troy Engineered Components and* ***(G-8569)***
Tech Art Productions, Columbus *Also called Technical Artistry Inc* ***(G-7520)***
Tech Dynamics Inc...419 666-1666
361 D St Ste B Perrysburg (43551) ***(G-16010)***
Tech Group, Norton *Also called Buckeye Field Machining Inc* ***(G-15362)***
Tech II Inc...937 969-7000
1765 W County Line Rd Urbana (43078) ***(G-19014)***
Tech Industries Inc...216 861-7337
1313 Washington Ave Cleveland (44113) ***(G-6153)***
Tech International, Johnstown *Also called Technical Rubber Company Inc* ***(G-11272)***
Tech Mold & Tool Co Inc...937 667-8851
4333 Lisa Dr Tipp City (45371) ***(G-18137)***
Tech Pro Inc...330 923-3546
3030 Gilchrist Rd Akron (44305) ***(G-397)***
Tech Products Corporation (HQ)...937 438-1100
2215 Lyons Rd Miamisburg (45342) ***(G-13723)***
Tech Ready Mix Inc...216 361-5000
5000 Crayton Ave Cleveland (44104) ***(G-6154)***
Tech Solutions LLC...419 852-7190
658 N Main St Celina (45822) ***(G-2986)***
Tech Systems Inc...419 878-2100
1070 Disher Dr Waterville (43566) ***(G-19507)***
Tech Tool Inc...330 674-1176
2901 County Road 150 Millersburg (44654) ***(G-14133)***
Tech Wear Embroidery Company...740 344-1276
738 W Main St Newark (43055) ***(G-14928)***
Tech-Bond Solutions...614 327-8884
3775 Columbus Lancaster Carroll (43112) ***(G-2913)***
Tech-E-Z LLC...419 692-1700
446 E Cleveland St Delphos (45833) ***(G-8755)***
Tech-Med Inc...216 486-0900
1080 E 222nd St Euclid (44117) ***(G-9445)***
Tech-Sonic Inc...614 792-3117
2710 Sawbury Blvd Columbus (43235) ***(G-7519)***
Tech-Way Industries Inc...937 746-1004
301 Industrial Dr Franklin (45005) ***(G-9925)***
Tech/III Inc (PA)...513 482-7500
1330 Tennessee Ave Cincinnati (45229) ***(G-4409)***
Techalloy Inc...216 481-8100
22801 Saint Clair Ave Euclid (44117) ***(G-9446)***
Techbrite LLC...800 246-9977
1000 Kieley Pl Cincinnati (45217) ***(G-4410)***
Techneglas Inc (HQ)...419 873-2000
2100 N Wilkinson Way Perrysburg (43551) ***(G-16011)***
Techneglas Inc...419 873-2000
25875 Dixie Hwy Bldg 52 Perrysburg (43551) ***(G-16012)***
Technibus Inc...330 479-4202
1501 Raff Rd Sw Ste 6 Canton (44710) ***(G-2833)***
Technical Artistry Inc...614 299-7777
1945 Corvair Ave Columbus (43207) ***(G-7520)***
Technical Glass Products Inc...425 396-8420
7460 Ponderosa Rd Perrysburg (43551) ***(G-16013)***
Technical Glass Products Inc (PA)...440 639-6399
881 Callendar Blvd Painesville (44077) ***(G-15786)***
Technical Rubber Company Inc (PA)...740 967-9015
200 E Coshocton St Johnstown (43031) ***(G-11272)***
Technical Sales & Solution...614 793-9612
4361 Wyandotte Woods Blvd Dublin (43016) ***(G-9003)***
Technical Tool & Gauge Inc...330 273-1778
2914 Westway Dr Brunswick (44212) ***(G-2244)***
Technical Translation Services (PA)...440 942-3130
37841 Euclid Ave Ste 7 Willoughby (44094) ***(G-20443)***
Technicolor Usa Inc...614 474-8821
155 E Circle Ln Circleville (43113) ***(G-4561)***
Technicote Inc (PA)...800 358-4448
222 Mound Ave Miamisburg (45342) ***(G-13724)***
Technicote Inc...330 928-1476
70 Marc Dr Cuyahoga Falls (44223) ***(G-7926)***
Technicote Westfield Inc...937 859-4448
222 Mound Ave Miamisburg (45342) ***(G-13725)***
Technidrill Systems Inc...330 678-9980
429 Portage Blvd Kent (44240) ***(G-11393)***
Technifab Inc...440 934-8324
38600 Chester Rd Avon (44011) ***(G-968)***
Technifab Inc...440 934-8324
1300 Chester Indus Pkwy Avon (44011) ***(G-969)***
Technifab Inc (PA)...440 934-8324
1355 Chester Indus Pkwy Avon (44011) ***(G-970)***
Technifab Engineered Products, Avon *Also called Technifab Inc* ***(G-970)***
Techniform Industries Inc...419 332-8484
2107 Hayes Ave Fremont (43420) ***(G-10054)***
Technimold Plus Inc...937 492-4077
102 Wall St Port Jefferson (45360) ***(G-16266)***
Techniplate Inc...216 486-8825
700 E 163rd St Cleveland (44110) ***(G-6155)***
Techniques Surfaces Usa Inc...937 323-2556
2015 Progress Rd Springfield (45505) ***(G-17504)***
Technisand Inc (HQ)...440 285-3132
11833 Ravenna Rd Chardon (44024) ***(G-3138)***
Technlogy Install Partners LLC...888 586-7040
13701 Enterprise Ave Cleveland (44135) ***(G-6156)***
Technofab, Wellington *Also called Forest City Technologies Inc* ***(G-19582)***

ALPHABETIC

Technoform GL Insul N Amer Inc 330 487-6600
1755 Entp Pkwy Ste 300 Twinsburg (44087) *(G-18863)*
Technologies Inc Arlington VA, Beavercreek Also called Drs Advanced Isr LLC *(G-1311)*
Technology and Services Inc 740 626-2020
1336 Baum Hill Rd Chillicothe (45601) *(G-3227)*
Technology Exploritation Pdts, Mentor Also called Gdj Inc *(G-13455)*
Technology House Ltd 440 248-3025
30555 Solon Indus Pkwy Solon (44139) *(G-17248)*
Technology House Ltd (PA) 440 248-3025
10036 Aurora Hudson Rd Streetsboro (44241) *(G-17701)*
Technology Products Inc 937 652-3412
2423 Barger Rd Urbana (43078) *(G-19015)*
Technology Resources Inc 419 241-9248
916 N Summit St Toledo (43604) *(G-18544)*
Technoprint Inc 614 899-1403
515 S State St Westerville (43081) *(G-20077)*
Technosoft Inc 513 985-9877
11180 Reed Hartman Hwy # 200 Blue Ash (45242) *(G-1857)*
Techtron Systems Inc 440 505-2990
29500 Fountain Pkwy Solon (44139) *(G-17249)*
Tecmark Corporation (PA) 440 205-7600
7745 Metric Dr Mentor (44060) *(G-13601)*
Tecmark Corporation 440 205-9188
7335 Production Dr Mentor (44060) *(G-13602)*
Tecnocap LLC 330 392-7222
2100 Griswold St Ne Warren (44483) *(G-19446)*
Teco, Toledo Also called Toledo Engineering Co Inc *(G-18558)*
Tecsis LP 614 430-0683
771 Dearborn Park Ln F Worthington (43085) *(G-20705)*
Tectum Inc 740 345-9691
105 S 6th St Newark (43055) *(G-14929)*
Tecumseh Packg Solutions Inc 419 238-1122
1275 Industrial Dr Van Wert (45891) *(G-19106)*
Tecumseh Redevelopment Inc 330 659-9100
4020 Kinross Lakes Pkwy Richfield (44286) *(G-16492)*
Ted Tipple 740 432-3263
6176 Simmons Rd Cambridge (43725) *(G-2459)*
Tedia Company Inc 513 874-5340
1000 Tedia Way Fairfield (45014) *(G-9567)*
Tee Creations 937 878-2822
701 N Broad St Ste C Fairborn (45324) *(G-9472)*
Tegam Inc (PA) 440 466-6100
10 Tegam Way Geneva (44041) *(G-10229)*
Tegratek 513 742-5100
500 Northland Blvd Cincinnati (45240) *(G-4411)*
Tek Gear & Machine Inc 330 455-3331
1220 Camden Ave Sw Canton (44706) *(G-2834)*
Tek Group International Inc 330 706-0000
567 Elm Ridge Ave Canal Fulton (44614) *(G-2494)*
Tek Manufacturing, Canal Fulton Also called Tek Group International Inc *(G-2494)*
Tekdog Inc 614 737-3743
4813 Granview Rd Granville (43023) *(G-10338)*
Tekfor Inc 330 202-7420
3690 Long Rd Wooster (44691) *(G-20659)*
Tekfor USA, Wooster Also called Tekfor Inc *(G-20659)*
Tekmar-Dohrmann, Mason Also called Teledyne Tekmar Company *(G-12948)*
Tekni-Plex Inc 419 491-2399
1445 Timber Wolf Dr Holland (43528) *(G-10960)*
Teknol Inc (PA) 937 264-0190
5751 Webster St Dayton (45414) *(G-8550)*
Tekraft Industries Inc 440 352-8321
244 Latimore St Painesville (44077) *(G-15787)*
Tektronix Inc 513 870-4729
9639 Inter Ocean Dr Dr2 West Chester (45246) *(G-19906)*
Tektronix Inc 440 248-0400
28775 Aurora Rd Solon (44139) *(G-17250)*
Tekus, L Sweater Design, Cleveland Also called Fine Points Inc *(G-5239)*
Tekworx LLC 513 533-4777
4538 Cornell Rd Blue Ash (45241) *(G-1858)*
Telcon LLC 330 562-5566
1677 Miller Pkwy Streetsboro (44241) *(G-17702)*
Teledoor LLC 419 227-3000
1075 Prosperity Rd Lima (45801) *(G-11949)*
Teledyne Brown Engineering Inc 419 470-3000
1330 W Laskey Rd Toledo (43612) *(G-18545)*
Teledyne Instruments Inc 513 229-7000
4736 Scialville Foster Rd Mason (45040) *(G-12946)*
Teledyne Instruments Inc 603 886-8400
4736 Scialville Foster Rd Mason (45040) *(G-12947)*
Teledyne Leeman Labs, Mason Also called Teledyne Instruments Inc *(G-12947)*
Teledyne Tekmar, Mason Also called Teledyne Instruments Inc *(G-12946)*
Teledyne Tekmar Company (HQ) 513 229-7000
4736 Scialville Foster Rd Mason (45040) *(G-12948)*
Telefast Industries Inc 440 826-0011
777 W Bagley Rd Berea (44017) *(G-1628)*
Telegram 740 286-3604
920 Veterans Dr Unit C Jackson (45640) *(G-11197)*
Telemecanique Sensors 800 435-2121
1875 Founders Dr Dayton (45420) *(G-8551)*

Telempu N Hayashi Amer Corp 513 932-9319
1500 Kingsview Dr Lebanon (45036) *(G-11700)*
Telesis Marking Systems, Circleville Also called Telesis Technologies Inc *(G-4562)*
Telesis Technologies Inc (HQ) 740 477-5000
28181 River Dr Circleville (43113) *(G-4562)*
Telex Communications Inc 419 865-0972
5660 Southwyck Blvd # 150 Toledo (43614) *(G-18546)*
Telling Industries LLC (PA) 440 974-3370
4420 Sherwin Rd Willoughby (44094) *(G-20444)*
Telling Industries LLC 928 681-2010
4420 Sherwin Rd Ste 3 Willoughby (44094) *(G-20445)*
Telling Industries LLC 740 435-8900
2105 Larrick Rd Cambridge (43725) *(G-2460)*
Telos Alliance, The, Cleveland Also called Tls Corp *(G-6177)*
Telos Systems, Cleveland Also called Cutting Edge Technologies Inc *(G-5051)*
Tema Isenmann Inc (HQ) 859 252-0613
7806 Redsky Dr Cincinnati (45249) *(G-4412)*
Tema Systems Inc 513 489-7811
7806 Redsky Dr Cincinnati (45249) *(G-4413)*
Tembec Btlsr Inc 419 244-5856
2112 Sylvan Ave Toledo (43606) *(G-18547)*
Tempac LLC 513 505-9700
7370 Avenel Ct West Chester (45069) *(G-19806)*
Tempcraft Corporation 216 391-3885
3960 S Marginal Rd Cleveland (44114) *(G-6157)*
Temperature Controls Company 330 773-6633
661 Anderson Ave Akron (44306) *(G-398)*
Tempest Inc 216 883-6500
12750 Berea Rd Cleveland (44111) *(G-6158)*
Temple Architectural Products, Spencer Also called John Baird *(G-17305)*
Temple Inland 513 425-0830
912 Nelbar St Middletown (45042) *(G-13956)*
Temple Israel 330 762-8617
91 Springside Dr Akron (44333) *(G-399)*
Temple Oil & Gas Company 740 452-7878
6626 Ceramic Rd Ne Crooksville (43731) *(G-7820)*
Temple-Inland Inc 614 221-1522
1600 Cascade Dr Marion (43302) *(G-12740)*
Tempo Manufacturing Company 937 773-6613
727 E Ash St Piqua (45356) *(G-16165)*
Tempo Trophy Mfg, Piqua Also called Tempo Manufacturing Company *(G-16165)*
Ten Dogs Global Industries LLC 513 752-9000
4400 Glen Willow Lake Ln Batavia (45103) *(G-1189)*
Ten Mfg LLC 440 487-1100
7675 Saint Clair Ave A Mentor (44060) *(G-13603)*
Tenacity Manufacturing Company 513 821-0201
4455 Muhlhauser Rd West Chester (45011) *(G-19807)*
Tenan Machine & Fabricating 440 997-5100
6002 State Rd Bldg A Ashtabula (44004) *(G-807)*
Tencate Advanced Armor USA Inc 740 928-0326
1051 Oneill Dr Hebron (43025) *(G-10765)*
Tenda Horse Products LLC 740 694-8836
18400 N Liberty Rd Fredericktown (43019) *(G-9979)*
Tendon Manufacturing Inc 216 663-3200
20805 Aurora Rd Cleveland (44146) *(G-6159)*
Tenk Machine, Strongsville Also called Cleveland Jsm Inc *(G-17729)*
Tenkotte Tops Inc 513 738-7300
11029 State Route 128 Harrison (45030) *(G-10677)*
Tenneco, Napoleon Also called Pullman Company *(G-14556)*
Tenneco, Milan Also called Pullman Company *(G-13987)*
Tenneco Automotive Oper Co Inc 937 781-4940
2555 Woodman Dr Kettering (45420) *(G-11442)*
Tennessee Coatings Inc (HQ) 513 770-4900
8093 Columbia Rd Ste 201 Mason (45040) *(G-12949)*
Tenney Tool & Supply Co 330 666-2807
973 Wooster Rd N Barberton (44203) *(G-1110)*
Tenpoint Crossbow Technologies, Mogadore Also called Hunters Manufacturing Co Inc *(G-14240)*
Tep Bedding Grp Inc 440 437-7700
161 Grand Valley Ave Orwell (44076) *(G-15635)*
Teradata Operations Inc 937 866-0032
2461 Rosina Dr Miamisburg (45342) *(G-13726)*
Teradata Operations Inc (HQ) 937 242-4030
10000 Innovation Dr Miamisburg (45342) *(G-13727)*
Teradyne Inc 937 427-1280
2689 Commons Blvd Ste 201 Beavercreek (45431) *(G-1343)*
Terewell Inc 216 334-6897
2683 W 14th St Cleveland (44113) *(G-6160)*
Terex USA, Solon Also called Demag Cranes & Components Corp *(G-17132)*
Terex Utilities Inc 513 539-9770
920 Deneen Ave Monroe (45050) *(G-14278)*
Terex Utilities Inc 440 262-3200
6400 W Snowville Rd Ste 1 Brecksville (44141) *(G-2060)*
Terminal Equipment Industries 330 468-0322
64 Privet Ln Northfield (44067) *(G-15328)*
Terminal Optical Lab 216 289-7722
26215 Tungsten Rd Euclid (44132) *(G-9447)*
Terminal Ready-Mix Inc 440 288-0181
524 Colorado Ave Lorain (44052) *(G-12129)*

ALPHABETIC SECTION Therm-O-Link Inc (PA)

Ternion Inc (PA) 216 642-6180
7635 Hub Pkwy Ste A Cleveland (44125) ***(G-6161)***
Teron Lighting Inc 513 858-6004
33 Donald Dr Uppr Fairfield (45014) ***(G-9568)***
Terra Comp Technology 330 745-8912
449 4th St Nw Barberton (44203) ***(G-1111)***
Terra Sonic International LLC 740 374-6608
27825 State Route 7 Marietta (45750) ***(G-12679)***
Terra Star Inc 405 200-1336
111 N Main St Waynesburg (44688) ***(G-19566)***
Terrasource Global Corporation 330 923-5254
601-607 Munroe Falls Ave Cuyahoga Falls (44221) ***(G-7927)***
Terreal North America LLC 888 582-9052
4757 Tile Plant Rd Se New Lexington (43764) ***(G-14727)***
Terrene Labs LLC 513 445-3539
5939 Deerfield Blvd Mason (45040) ***(G-12950)***
Terry & Jack Neon Sign Co 419 229-0674
225 S Collins Ave Lima (45804) ***(G-11950)***
Terry A Johnson 614 561-0706
15094 Palmer Rd Sw Etna (43068) ***(G-9389)***
Terry Asphalt Materials Inc (HQ) 513 874-6192
8600 Bilstein Blvd Hamilton (45015) ***(G-10609)***
Terry G Sickles 740 286-8880
2207 Boy Scout Rd Ray (45672) ***(G-16422)***
Terry Lumber and Supply Co 330 659-6800
1710 Mill St W Peninsula (44264) ***(G-15899)***
Tersus Pharmaceuticals 440 951-2451
5966 Heisley Rd Mentor (44060) ***(G-13604)***
Terydon Inc 330 879-2448
7260 Erie Ave Sw Navarre (44662) ***(G-14588)***
Tesa Inc 614 847-8200
544 Enterprise Dr Ste A Lewis Center (43035) ***(G-11784)***
Tesla Inc 614 532-5060
4005 The Strand W Columbus (43219) ***(G-7521)***
Tesla Inc 513 745-9111
9111 Blue Ash Rd Blue Ash (45242) ***(G-1859)***
Tesla Motors, Blue Ash *Also called Tesla Inc* ***(G-1859)***
Tessa Precision Product Inc 440 392-3470
850 Callendar Blvd Painesville (44077) ***(G-15788)***
Tessec LLC 937 985-3552
5679 Webster St Dayton (45414) ***(G-8552)***
Tessec Manufacturing Svcs LLC 937 985-3552
5679 Webster St Dayton (45414) ***(G-8553)***
Test Mark Industries Inc 330 426-2200
995 N Market St East Palestine (44413) ***(G-9086)***
Test-Fuchs Corporation 440 708-3505
10325 Brecksville Rd Brecksville (44141) ***(G-2061)***
Testlink USA 513 272-1081
11445 Century Cir W Cincinnati (45246) ***(G-4414)***
Tetra Mold & Tool Inc 937 845-1651
51 Quick Rd New Carlisle (45344) ***(G-14679)***
Tetra Tech Inc 330 286-3683
6715 Tippecanoe Rd C201 Canfield (44406) ***(G-2549)***
Tetrad Electronics Inc (PA) 440 946-6443
2048 Joseph Lloyd Pkwy Willoughby (44094) ***(G-20446)***
Teva Pharmaceuticals Inc 800 225-6878
5040 Duramed Rd Cincinnati (45213) ***(G-4415)***
Teva Womens Health Inc (HQ) 513 731-9900
5040 Duramed Rd Cincinnati (45213) ***(G-4416)***
Tewell & Associates 440 543-5190
10260 Washington St Chagrin Falls (44023) ***(G-3081)***
Tex-Tyler Corporation 419 729-4951
5148 Stickney Ave Toledo (43612) ***(G-18548)***
Tex-Vent Co 614 299-1902
6100 Huntley Rd Columbus (43229) ***(G-7522)***
Texas Tile Manufacturing LLC 713 869-5811
30000 Aurora Rd Solon (44139) ***(G-17251)***
Texmaster Tools Inc 740 965-8778
143 Tuttle Ave Fredericktown (43019) ***(G-9980)***
Texstone Industries 419 722-4664
433 Oak Ave Findlay (45840) ***(G-9767)***
Textiles Inc (PA) 740 852-0782
23 Old Springfield Rd London (43140) ***(G-12070)***
Textiles Inc 614 529-8642
5892 Heritage Lakes Dr Hilliard (43026) ***(G-10869)***
Textron Inc 330 626-7800
555 Mondial Pkwy Streetsboro (44241) ***(G-17703)***
Tez Tool & Fabrication Inc 440 323-2300
115 Buckeye St Elyria (44035) ***(G-9337)***
Tfo Tech Co Ltd 740 426-6381
221 State St Jeffersonville (43128) ***(G-11248)***
Tfr Printing, Marion *Also called Tree Free Resources LLC* ***(G-12744)***
Tgm Holdings Company 419 885-3769
5439 Roan Rd Sylvania (43560) ***(G-17965)***
Tgs International Inc 330 893-4828
4464 State Route 39 Millersburg (44654) ***(G-14134)***
Th Magnesium Inc 513 285-7568
9435 Waterstone Blvd Cincinnati (45249) ***(G-4417)***
Th Manufacturing Inc 330 893-3572
4674 County Road 120 Millersburg (44654) ***(G-14135)***
Th Plastics Inc 419 352-2770
843 Miller Dr Bowling Green (43402) ***(G-2001)***
Th Plastics Inc 419 425-5825
1640 Westfield Dr Findlay (45840) ***(G-9768)***
Th Plastics Inc 419 425-5825
101 Bentley Ct Findlay (45840) ***(G-9769)***
Thaler Machine Company 937 550-2400
216 Tahlequah Trl Springboro (45066) ***(G-17355)***
Thanks Mom Designs, Cincinnati *Also called Apparel Impressions Inc* ***(G-3351)***
Thatcher Enterprises Co Ltd 614 228-2013
205 E Broad St Columbus (43215) ***(G-7523)***
The Beacon Journal Pubg Co 330 996-3000
44 E Exchange St Akron (44308) ***(G-400)***
The Blind Factory, Hilliard *Also called Blind Factory Showroom* ***(G-10814)***
The Bookseller Inc 330 865-5831
39 Westgate Cir Akron (44313) ***(G-401)***
The Cleveland Jewish Publ Co 216 454-8300
23880 Commerce Park Ste 1 Beachwood (44122) ***(G-1280)***
The Cleveland-Cliffs Iron Co 216 694-5700
1100 Superior Ave E # 1500 Cleveland (44114) ***(G-6162)***
The County Classified's, Bellefontaine *Also called County Classifieds* ***(G-1510)***
The Defiance Publishing Co 419 784-5441
624 W 2nd St Defiance (43512) ***(G-8645)***
The Delo Screw Products Co 740 363-1971
700 London Rd Delaware (43015) ***(G-8728)***
The Fischer & Jirouch Company 216 361-3840
4821 Superior Ave Cleveland (44103) ***(G-6163)***
The Florand Company 330 747-8986
1776 Cherry St Ste A Youngstown (44506) ***(G-21044)***
The Fremont Kraut Company 419 332-6481
724 N Front St Fremont (43420) ***(G-10055)***
The Gazette Printing Co Inc (PA) 440 576-9125
46 W Jefferson St Jefferson (44047) ***(G-11240)***
The Gazette Printing Co Inc 440 593-6030
218 Washington St Conneaut (44030) ***(G-7660)***
The General's Books, Columbus *Also called Generals Books* ***(G-6946)***
The Great Lakes Brewing Co 216 771-4404
2516 Market Ave Cleveland (44113) ***(G-6164)***
The Guardtower Inc 614 488-4311
3600 Trabue Rd Columbus (43204) ***(G-7524)***
The Hartman Corp 614 475-5035
3216 Morse Rd Columbus (43231) ***(G-7525)***
The Hc Companies Inc (HQ) 440 632-3333
15150 Madison Rd Middlefield (44062) ***(G-13857)***
The Holtkamp Organ Co 216 741-5180
2909 Meyer Ave Cleveland (44109) ***(G-6165)***
The Label Team Inc 330 332-1067
1251 Quaker Cir Salem (44460) ***(G-16776)***
The Mansfield Strl & Erct Co (PA) 419 522-5911
429 Park Ave E Mansfield (44905) ***(G-12528)***
The Mansfield Strl & Erct Co 419 747-6571
817 Belmont Ave Mansfield (44906) ***(G-12529)***
The Max 440 357-0036
759 Lakeshore Blvd Painesville (44077) ***(G-15789)***
The Metal Marker Mfg Co 440 327-2300
6225 Lear Nagle Rd North Ridgeville (44039) ***(G-15255)***
The Mobility Store, Westerville *Also called Columbus Prescr Rehabilitation* ***(G-20040)***
The National Lime and Stone Co 330 455-5722
5377 Lauby Rd Ste 201 North Canton (44720) ***(G-15124)***
The Printed Image, Columbus *Also called Printed Image* ***(G-7350)***
The Q-P Manufacturing Co Inc 440 946-2120
215 5th Ave Chardon (44024) ***(G-3139)***
THE QUIKRETE COMPANIES INC, Columbus *Also called Quikrete Companies Inc* ***(G-7369)***
The Reliable Spring Wire Frms 440 365-7400
300 Abbe Rd S Elyria (44035) ***(G-9338)***
The Rubber Stamp Shop 419 478-4444
4418 Lewis Ave Toledo (43612) ***(G-18549)***
The Shelby Co 440 871-9901
865 Canterbury Rd Westlake (44145) ***(G-20167)***
The W L Jenkins Company 330 477-3407
1445 Whipple Ave Sw Canton (44710) ***(G-2835)***
The Wood Shed 937 429-3355
2665 Trebein Rd Xenia (45385) ***(G-20795)***
The-Fischer-Group 513 285-1281
20282052 Bohlke Blvd Fairfield (45014) ***(G-9569)***
Thees Machine & Tool Co 419 586-4766
2007 State Route 703 Celina (45822) ***(G-2987)***
Theiss Uav Solutions LLC 330 584-2070
10881 Johnson Rd North Benton (44449) ***(G-15062)***
Theken Companies LLC 330 733-7600
1800 Triplett Blvd Akron (44306) ***(G-402)***
Therapedic Mattress, Orwell *Also called Tep Bedding Grp Inc* ***(G-15635)***
Therm-All Inc (PA) 440 779-9494
31387 Industrial Pkwy North Olmsted (44070) ***(G-15201)***
Therm-O-Disc Incorporated (HQ) 419 525-8500
1320 S Main St Mansfield (44907) ***(G-12530)***
Therm-O-Link Inc (PA) 330 527-2124
10513 Freedom St Garrettsville (44231) ***(G-10203)***

ALPHABETIC

Therm-O-Link Inc 330 393-7600
621 Dana St Ne Ste 5 Warren (44483) *(G-19447)*
Therm-O-Link of Texas Inc 330 393-4300
621 Dana St Ne Ste V Warren (44483) *(G-19448)*
Therm-O-Packaging Suppliers 440 543-5188
16815 Park Circle Dr Chagrin Falls (44023) *(G-3082)*
Therm-O-Vent, Medina Also called Thermo Vent Manufacturing Inc *(G-13351)*
Therma-Tru Corp 419 740-5193
6214 Monclova Rd Maumee (43537) *(G-13152)*
Thermacal Inc 440 498-1005
30325 Binbridge Rd Ste 2a Solon (44139) *(G-17252)*
Thermafab Alloy Inc 216 861-0540
25367 Water St Olmsted Falls (44138) *(G-15531)*
Thermal Industries Inc 216 464-0674
4920 Commerce Pkwy Ste 4 Cleveland (44128) *(G-6166)*
Thermal Solutions Inc 614 263-1808
3005 Silver Dr Columbus (43224) *(G-7526)*
Thermal Treatment Center Inc (HQ) 216 881-8100
1101 E 55th St Cleveland (44103) *(G-6167)*
Thermal Treatment Center Inc 216 883-4820
11116 Avon Ave Cleveland (44105) *(G-6168)*
Thermal Treatment Center Inc 440 943-4555
28910 Lakeland Blvd Wickliffe (44092) *(G-20232)*
Thermal Treatment Center Inc 216 941-0440
10601 Briggs Rd Cleveland (44111) *(G-6169)*
Thermal Visions Inc (PA) 740 587-4025
83 Stone Henge Dr Granville (43023) *(G-10339)*
Thermalgraphics, Cincinnati Also called Agnone-Kelly Enterprises Inc *(G-3310)*
Thermeq Co, Waterville Also called T J F Inc *(G-19506)*
Thermo Eberline LLC 440 703-1400
1 Thermo Fisher Way Oakwood Village (44146) *(G-15485)*
Thermo Fisher Scientific, Oakwood Village Also called Thermo Eberline LLC *(G-15485)*
Thermo Fisher Scientific 740 373-4763
401 Mill Creek Rd Marietta (45750) *(G-12680)*
Thermo Fisher Scientific Inc 800 871-8909
1 Thermo Fisher Way Oakwood Village (44146) *(G-15486)*
Thermo Fisher Scientific Inc 513 489-2926
8761 Arcturus Dr Montgomery (45249) *(G-14299)*
Thermo Fisher Scientific Inc 440 703-1400
1 Thermo Fisher Way Bedford (44146) *(G-1449)*
Thermo King Corporation 478 625-7241
13 Orchard Cir Chagrin Falls (44022) *(G-3031)*
Thermo Systems Technology 216 292-8250
2000 Auburn Dr Ste 200 Cleveland (44122) *(G-6170)*
Thermo Vent Manufacturing Inc 330 239-0239
1213 Medina Rd Medina (44256) *(G-13351)*
Thermo-Rite Mfg Company 330 633-8680
1355 Evans Ave Akron (44305) *(G-403)*
Thermocolor LLC (HQ) 419 626-5677
2901 W Monroe St Sandusky (44870) *(G-16852)*
Thermocolor LLC 419 626-5677
2108 Superior St Sandusky (44870) *(G-16853)*
Thermodyn Corporation 419 874-5100
12265 Williams Rd Ste B Perrysburg (43551) *(G-16014)*
Thermogenics Corp 513 247-7963
300 E Bus Way Ste 200 Cincinnati (45241) *(G-4418)*
Thermoplastic Accessories Corp 614 771-4777
3949 Lyman Dr Hilliard (43026) *(G-10870)*
Thermotion Corp 440 639-8325
6520 Hopkins Rd Mentor (44060) *(G-13605)*
Thermotion-Madison, Mentor Also called Thermotion Corp *(G-13605)*
Thermtrol Corporation (PA) 330 497-4148
8914 Pleasantwood Ave Nw North Canton (44720) *(G-15125)*
Thickemz Entertainment LLC 404 399-4255
1268 Wellingshire Cir Cuyahoga Falls (44221) *(G-7928)*
Thiels Replacement Systems Inc 419 289-6139
419 E 8th St Ashland (44805) *(G-751)*
Thieman Machine 419 628-2474
5395 State Route 119 Minster (45865) *(G-14226)*
Thieman Quality Metal Fab Inc 419 629-2612
05140 Dicke Rd New Bremen (45869) *(G-14661)*
Thieman Tailgates Inc 419 586-7727
600 E Wayne St Celina (45822) *(G-2988)*
Think Signs LLC 614 384-0333
689 Radio Dr Lewis Center (43035) *(G-11785)*
Thinkware Incorporated 513 598-3300
7611 Cheviot Rd Ste 2 Cincinnati (45247) *(G-4419)*
Third Party Service Ltd 419 872-2312
1205 Louisiana Ave Perrysburg (43552) *(G-16015)*
Third Wave Water LLC 855 590-4500
83 N Main St Cedarville (45314) *(G-2947)*
Thirion Brothers Eqp Co LLC 440 357-8004
340 W Prospect St Painesville (44077) *(G-15790)*
Thirsty Dog Brewing Co 330 252-8740
529 Grant St Ste 103 Akron (44311) *(G-404)*
This Week, Columbus Also called Consumers News Services Inc *(G-6811)*
Thk Manufacturing America Inc 740 928-1415
471 N High St Hebron (43025) *(G-10766)*
Thogus Products Company 440 933-8850
33490 Pin Oak Pkwy Avon Lake (44012) *(G-1011)*

Thomas Allen Co 330 823-8487
1062 Parkside Dr Alliance (44601) *(G-506)*
Thomas Cabinet Shop Inc 937 847-8239
321 Gargrave Rd Dayton (45449) *(G-8554)*
Thomas Creative Apparel Inc 419 929-1506
1 Harmony Pl New London (44851) *(G-14739)*
Thomas D Epperson 937 855-3300
7440 Weaver Rd Germantown (45327) *(G-10246)*
Thomas Do-It Center Inc (PA) 740 446-2002
176 Mccormick Rd Gallipolis (45631) *(G-10176)*
Thomas Entps of Georgetown 937 378-6300
933 S Main St Georgetown (45121) *(G-10238)*
Thomas J Raffa DDS Inc 440 997-5208
355 W Prospect Rd Ste 120 Ashtabula (44004) *(G-808)*
Thomas J Weaver Inc (PA) 740 622-2040
1501 Kenilworth Ave Coshocton (43812) *(G-7755)*
Thomas Products Co Inc (PA) 513 756-9009
3625 Spring Grove Ave Cincinnati (45223) *(G-4420)*
Thomas Rental, Gallipolis Also called Thomas Do-It Center Inc *(G-10176)*
Thomas Ross Associates Inc 330 723-1110
303 N Broadway St Medina (44256) *(G-13352)*
Thomas Steel Inc 419 483-7540
305 Elm St Bellevue (44811) *(G-1549)*
Thomas Tape and Supply Company 937 325-6414
1713 Sheridan Ave Springfield (45505) *(G-17505)*
Thomas Tool & Mold Company 614 890-4978
271 Broad St Westerville (43081) *(G-20078)*
Thomas Welding & Repair, Georgetown Also called Thomas Entps of Georgetown *(G-10238)*
Thomas-Wilbert Vault Co Inc 740 695-5671
49132 Randall Dr Saint Clairsville (43950) *(G-16655)*
Thompson Aluminum Casting Co 216 206-2781
5161 Canal Rd Cleveland (44125) *(G-6171)*
Thompson Assoc Hudson Ohio 330 655-2142
5771 Sunset Dr Hudson (44236) *(G-11079)*
Thompson Brothers Mining Co 330 549-3979
3379 E Garfield Rd New Springfield (44443) *(G-14821)*
Thompson Castings, Cleveland Also called Thompson Aluminum Casting Co *(G-6171)*
Thompson Distributing Co Inc 513 422-9011
3227 Seneca St Middletown (45044) *(G-13957)*
Thompson Partners Inc 866 475-2500
82 Mill St Ste A Gahanna (43230) *(G-10109)*
Thor Industries Inc 937 596-6111
419 W Pike St Jackson Center (45334) *(G-11217)*
Thorfood LLC (HQ) 419 626-4375
2520 Campbell St Sandusky (44870) *(G-16854)*
Thorncreek Winery & Garden 330 562-9245
155 Treat Rd Aurora (44202) *(G-908)*
Thornton Powder Coatings Inc 419 522-7183
2300 N Main St Mansfield (44903) *(G-12531)*
Thoroughbred Gt Mfg LLC 330 533-0048
6145 State Route 446 Canfield (44406) *(G-2550)*
Thorwald Holdings Inc 740 756-9271
866 Mill Park Dr Lancaster (43130) *(G-11613)*
Thorworks Industries Inc (PA) 419 626-4375
2520 Campbell St Sandusky (44870) *(G-16855)*
Those Charc From Cleve Inc 216 252-7300
1 American Rd Cleveland (44144) *(G-6172)*
Thoughts That Count, Millersburg Also called Broty Enterprises Inc *(G-14069)*
Thread Works Custom Embroidery 937 478-5231
2630 Colonel Glenn Hwy Beavercreek (45324) *(G-1344)*
Thread-Rite Tool & Mfg Inc 937 222-2836
1200 E 1st St Dayton (45403) *(G-8555)*
Three AS Inc 419 227-4240
1605 E 4th St Lima (45804) *(G-11951)*
Three Bond International Inc 937 610-3000
101 Daruma Pkwy Dayton (45439) *(G-8556)*
Three Bond International Inc (HQ) 513 779-7300
6184 Schumacher Park Dr West Chester (45069) *(G-19808)*
Three Cord LLC 419 445-2673
203 E Lugbill Rd Archbold (43502) *(G-671)*
Three Leaf Inc 888 308-1007
3189 Princeton Rd Ste 123 Fairfield Township (45011) *(G-9588)*
Three Peaks Wellness LLC 216 438-3334
818 E 185th St Cleveland (44119) *(G-6173)*
Three Sons Minerva Hardware 330 868-7709
16400 Bayard Rd Minerva (44657) *(G-14204)*
Threshhold, Granville Also called Thermal Visions Inc *(G-10339)*
Thrift Tool Inc 937 275-3600
5916 Milo Rd Dayton (45414) *(G-8557)*
Thriverx, Cincinnati Also called Biorx LLC *(G-3394)*
Tht Presses, Dayton Also called THT Presses Inc *(G-8558)*
THT Presses Inc 937 898-2012
7475 Webster St Dayton (45414) *(G-8558)*
Thundawear LLC 419 787-2675
1709 Spielbusch Ave # 100 Toledo (43604) *(G-18550)*
Thundawear Skull Caps, Toledo Also called Thundawear LLC *(G-18550)*
Thunder Dreamer Publishing 419 424-2004
2500 Crystal Ave Findlay (45840) *(G-9770)*

Thurns Bakery & Deli 614 221-9246
541 S 3rd St Columbus (43215) *(G-7527)*
Thycurb, Akron *Also called Burt Manufacturing Company Inc* *(G-100)*
Thyssenkrupp Bilstein Amer Inc (HQ) 513 881-7600
8685 Bilstein Blvd Hamilton (45015) *(G-10610)*
Thyssenkrupp Bilstein Amer Inc 513 881-7600
4440 Muhlhauser Rd West Chester (45011) *(G-19809)*
Thyssenkrupp Materials NA Inc 216 883-8100
6050 Oak Tree Blvd # 110 Independence (44131) *(G-11152)*
TI Group Auto Systems LLC 740 929-2049
3600 Hebron Rd Hebron (43025) *(G-10767)*
Tia Marie & Company 513 521-8694
8694 Long Ln Cincinnati (45231) *(G-4421)*
Tiama Americas Inc 269 274-3107
6500 Weatherfield Ct Maumee (43537) *(G-13153)*
Tiba LLC 614 328-2040
2228 Citygate Dr Columbus (43219) *(G-7528)*
Tidewater Products Inc 419 873-0223
12305 Williams Rd Perrysburg (43551) *(G-16016)*
Tidewater Products Inc 419 534-9870
4520 Brookside Rd Ottawa Hills (43615) *(G-15678)*
Tierra-Derco International LLC 419 929-2240
40 S Main St New London (44851) *(G-14740)*
Tiffin Foundry & Machine Inc 419 447-3991
423 W Adams St Tiffin (44883) *(G-18087)*
Tiffin Metal Products Co (PA) 419 447-8414
450 Wall St Tiffin (44883) *(G-18088)*
Tiffin Scenic Studios Inc (PA) 800 445-1546
146 Riverside Dr Tiffin (44883) *(G-18089)*
Tig Welding Specialties Inc 216 621-1763
13616 Enterprise Ave Cleveland (44135) *(G-6174)*
Tig Wood & Die Inc 937 849-6741
1760 Dalton Dr New Carlisle (45344) *(G-14680)*
Tiger Cat Furniture 330 220-7232
294 Marks Rd Brunswick (44212) *(G-2245)*
Tiger Construction, Canal Winchester *Also called Tiger Oil Inc* *(G-2513)*
Tiger General LLC 330 239-4949
6867 Wooster Pike Medina (44256) *(G-13353)*
Tiger Mirror Corporation 419 855-3146
465 Main St Clay Center (43408) *(G-4569)*
Tiger Oil Inc (PA) 614 837-5552
650 Winchester Pike Canal Winchester (43110) *(G-2513)*
Tiger Sand & Gravel LLC 330 833-6325
411 Oberlin Ave Sw Massillon (44647) *(G-13052)*
Tiger Sul Products LLC 203 451-3305
7361 Township Road 163 West Liberty (43357) *(G-19938)*
Tigerpoly Manufacturing Inc 614 871-0045
6231 Enterprise Pkwy Grove City (43123) *(G-10473)*
Tii Treeman Industries, Boardman *Also called Treemen Industries Inc* *(G-1904)*
Tilden Mining Company LC (HQ) 216 694-5700
200 Public Sq Ste 3300 Cleveland (44114) *(G-6175)*
Tiller Foods, Dayton *Also called Instantwhip-Dayton Inc* *(G-8269)*
Tiller Foods, Dayton *Also called Instantwhip-Dayton Inc* *(G-8270)*
Tilt 15 Inc 330 239-4192
1440 Wolf Creek Trl Sharon Center (44274) *(G-16955)*
Tilt-Or-Lift Inc (PA) 419 893-6944
124 E Dudley St Maumee (43537) *(G-13154)*
Tilton Corporation 419 227-6421
330 S Pine St Lima (45804) *(G-11952)*
Tim Boutwell 419 358-4653
902 N Main St Bluffton (45817) *(G-1894)*
Tim Calvin Access Controls 740 494-4200
7585 Taway Rd Radnor (43066) *(G-16359)*
Tim Calvin Enterprises, Radnor *Also called Tim Calvin Access Controls* *(G-16359)*
Tim Crabtree 740 286-4535
117 Athens St Jackson (45640) *(G-11198)*
Tim L Humbert 330 497-4944
6535 Promler St Nw Canton (44720) *(G-2836)*
Tim's Woodshop, Jackson *Also called Tim Crabtree* *(G-11198)*
Timac Manufacturing Company 937 372-3305
825 Bellbrook Ave Xenia (45385) *(G-20796)*
Timber Products Inc 440 693-4098
8652 Parkman Mespo Rd Middlefield (44062) *(G-13858)*
Timberlane Woodworking 419 895-9945
8425 Olvsburg Ftchvlle Rd Greenwich (44837) *(G-10409)*
Timbermill Ltd 740 862-3426
11015 Stoudertown Rd Nw Baltimore (43105) *(G-1044)*
Timbertech, Wilmington *Also called Cpg International LLC* *(G-20492)*
Timbertech Limited 614 443-4891
2141 Fairwood Ave Columbus (43207) *(G-7529)*
Timco Inc 740 685-2594
57051 Marietta Rd Byesville (43723) *(G-2393)*
Timco Rubber Products Inc (PA) 216 267-6242
125 Blaze Industrial Pkwy Berea (44017) *(G-1629)*
Time 4 You 614 593-2695
5938 Sedgwick Rd Columbus (43235) *(G-7530)*
Time Is Money 419 701-6098
1280 North Dr Fostoria (44830) *(G-9860)*
Timekap Inc 330 747-2122
2315 Belmont Ave Youngstown (44505) *(G-21045)*
Timekap Indus Sls Svc & Mch, Youngstown *Also called Timekap Inc* *(G-21045)*
Timekeeping Systems Inc (PA) 216 595-0890
30700 Bainbridge Rd Ste H Solon (44139) *(G-17253)*
Timely Tours Inc 419 734-3751
141 Maple St Ste A Port Clinton (43452) *(G-16263)*
Times Bulletin Media 419 238-2285
700 Fox Rd Van Wert (45891) *(G-19107)*
Times Recorder, The, Zanesville *Also called Gannett Co Inc* *(G-21141)*
Times Reporter, New Philadelphia *Also called Mansfield Journal Co* *(G-14782)*
Times Reporter/Midwest Offset, New Philadelphia *Also called Copley Ohio Newspapers Inc* *(G-14765)*
Timet, Warrensville Heights *Also called Titanium Metals Corporation* *(G-19473)*
Timet Toronto, Toronto *Also called Titanium Metals Corporation* *(G-18612)*
Timken Aircraft Operation, Canton *Also called Timken Company* *(G-2837)*
Timken Company (PA) 234 262-3000
4500 Mount Pleasant St Nw North Canton (44720) *(G-15126)*
Timken Company 419 563-2200
2325 E Mansfield St Bucyrus (44820) *(G-2345)*
Timken Company 330 339-1151
1957 E High Ave New Philadelphia (44663) *(G-14804)*
Timken Company 330 471-4300
5430 Lauby Rd Bldg 7 Canton (44720) *(G-2837)*
Timken Company 614 836-3337
3782 Potomac St Groveport (43125) *(G-10514)*
Timken Company 330 471-5028
20th & Dueber Ave Sw Canton (44706) *(G-2838)*
Timken Company 234 262-3000
4500 Mount Pleasant St Nw North Canton (44720) *(G-15127)*
Timken Company 330 471-4791
22261 Margaret Ln Alliance (44601) *(G-507)*
Timken Company 330 471-5043
786 Whipple Ave Sw Canton (44710) *(G-2839)*
Timken Foundation 330 452-1144
200 Market Ave N Ste 210 Canton (44702) *(G-2840)*
Timken Receivables Corporation 234 262-3000
4500 Mount Pleasant St Nw North Canton (44720) *(G-15128)*
Timkensteel Corporation (PA) 330 471-7000
1835 Dueber Ave Sw Canton (44706) *(G-2841)*
Timkensteel Corporation 330 471-7000
4511 Faircrest St Sw Canton (44706) *(G-2842)*
Timmys Sandwich Shop 419 350-8267
5426 Cresthaven Ln Toledo (43614) *(G-18551)*
Timon J Reinhart 419 476-1990
1560 W Laskey Rd Ste B Toledo (43612) *(G-18552)*
Timon Tool & Die, Toledo *Also called Timon J Reinhart* *(G-18552)*
Timothy A. Lyons, New Marshfield *Also called Diesel Fltrtion Spcialists LLC* *(G-14743)*
Timothy Allen Jewelers Inc 440 974-8885
8925 Mentor Ave Ste D Mentor (44060) *(G-13606)*
Timothy C Georges 330 933-9114
4900 Massillon Rd Apt 6 North Canton (44720) *(G-15129)*
Timothy Sasser 740 260-9499
59538 Lost Rd Byesville (43723) *(G-2394)*
Timothy Sinfield 740 685-3684
54962 Marietta Rd Pleasant City (43772) *(G-16223)*
Tin Indian Performance 216 214-5485
2656 Watervale Dr Uniontown (44685) *(G-18935)*
Tin Shed LLC 330 636-2524
6 S Myrtle Ave Willard (44890) *(G-20246)*
Tin Wizard Heating and Cooling 330 468-7884
8853 Robinwood Ter Macedonia (44056) *(G-12337)*
Tin-Sau LLC 419 586-8886
1406 Canterbury Dr Celina (45822) *(G-2989)*
Tinker Omega Manufacturing LLC 937 322-2272
2424 Columbus Rd Springfield (45503) *(G-17506)*
Tinnerman Palnut Engineered PR 330 220-5100
1060 W 130th St Brunswick (44212) *(G-2246)*
Tiny Lion Music Groups 419 874-7353
144 E 5th St Perrysburg (43551) *(G-16017)*
Tinycircuits 330 329-5753
540 S Main St Akron (44311) *(G-405)*
Tip Products Inc 216 252-2535
15411 Chatfield Ave Ste 5 Cleveland (44111) *(G-6176)*
Tip Top Canning Co (PA) 937 667-3713
505 S 2nd St Tipp City (45371) *(G-18138)*
Tipco Punch Inc 513 874-9140
6 Rowe Ct Hamilton (45015) *(G-10611)*
Tipp Stone Inc 937 890-4051
8172 Meeker Rd Dayton (45414) *(G-8559)*
Tipton Environmental Intl Inc 513 735-2777
4446 State Route 132 Batavia (45103) *(G-1190)*
Tisch Environmental Inc 513 467-9000
145 S Miami Ave Cleves (45002) *(G-6379)*
Titan Bus LLC 419 523-3593
804 N Pratt St Ottawa (45875) *(G-15669)*
Titan Chemical, Milford *Also called Jeff Pendergrass* *(G-14021)*
Titan Manufacturing LLC 440 942-2258
4730 Beidler Rd Willoughby (44094) *(G-20447)*

ALPHABETIC

(PA)=Parent Co (HQ)=Headquarters (DH)=Div Headquarters

2019 Harris Ohio
Industrial Directory

1269

Titan Tire Corporation — ALPHABETIC SECTION

Titan Tire Corporation 419 633-4221
  927 S Union St Bryan (43506) *(G-2309)*
Titan Tire Corporation Bryan, Bryan Also called Titan Tire Corporation *(G-2309)*
Titanium Contractors Ltd 513 256-2152
  9400 Reading Rd Cincinnati (45215) *(G-4422)*
Titanium Lacrosse LLC 614 562-8082
  2671 Coltsbridge Dr Lewis Center (43035) *(G-11786)*
Titanium Metals Corporation (HQ) 610 968-1300
  4832 Richmond Rd Ste 100 Warrensville Heights (44128) *(G-19473)*
Titanium Metals Corporation 740 537-1571
  100 Titanium Way Toronto (43964) *(G-18612)*
Titanium Sales Group LLC 614 204-6098
  7905 Melrue Ct Dublin (43016) *(G-9004)*
Titanium Trout LLC 440 543-3187
  18060 Birch Hill Dr Chagrin Falls (44023) *(G-3083)*
Tite Seal Case Company Inc 440 647-2371
  299 Clay St Wellington (44090) *(G-19593)*
Tj Bell Inc 330 633-3644
  1340 Home Ave Ste E Akron (44310) *(G-406)*
Tj Metzgers Inc 419 861-8611
  207 Arco Dr Toledo (43607) *(G-18553)*
Tjar Innovations LLC 937 347-1999
  1004 Cincinnati Ave Xenia (45385) *(G-20797)*
Tk America, Cincinnati Also called Toyobo Kureha America Co Ltd *(G-4427)*
Tk Gas Services Inc 740 826-0303
  2303 John Glenn Hwy New Concord (43762) *(G-14687)*
Tk Holdings Inc 937 778-9713
  1401 Innovation Pkwy Piqua (45356) *(G-16166)*
Tk Machining Specialties LLC 513 368-3963
  2677 Morgan Ln Hamilton (45013) *(G-10612)*
Tkf Conveyor Systems LLC 513 621-5260
  5298 River Rd Cincinnati (45233) *(G-4423)*
Tkn Oilfield Services LLC 740 516-2583
  108 Woodcrest Dr Marietta (45750) *(G-12681)*
Tko Mfg Services Inc 937 299-1637
  2360 W Dorothy Ln Ste 111 Moraine (45439) *(G-14399)*
Tkr Metal Fabricating LLC 440 221-2770
  37552 N Industrial Pkwy Willoughby (44094) *(G-20448)*
Tks Industrial Company 614 444-5602
  1939 Refugee Rd Columbus (43207) *(G-7531)*
TL Industries Inc (PA) 419 666-8144
  2541 Tracy Rd Northwood (43619) *(G-15346)*
TL Krieg Offset Inc 513 542-1522
  10600 Chester Rd Cincinnati (45215) *(G-4424)*
Tla Designs, New Lexington Also called C S A Enterprises *(G-14713)*
Tls Corp (PA) 216 574-4759
  1241 Superior Ave E Cleveland (44114) *(G-6177)*
Tlt-Turbo Inc 330 776-5115
  2693 Wingate Ave Akron (44314) *(G-407)*
Tm Machine & Tool Inc 419 478-0310
  521 Mel Simon Dr Toledo (43612) *(G-18554)*
Tmac Machine Inc 330 673-0621
  924 Overholt Rd Kent (44240) *(G-11394)*
Tmarzetti Company 614 268-3722
  380 Polaris Pkwy Ste 400 Westerville (43082) *(G-20028)*
Tmarzetti Company (HQ) 614 846-2232
  380 Polaris Pkwy Ste 400 Westerville (43082) *(G-20029)*
Tmarzetti Company 614 277-3577
  5800 N Meadows Dr Grove City (43123) *(G-10474)*
Tmarzetti Company 330 674-2993
  7445 County Road 68 Millersburg (44654) *(G-14136)*
Tmarzetti Company 614 279-8673
  1709 Frank Rd Columbus (43223) *(G-7532)*
Tmarzetti Company 216 292-5655
  25900 Fargo Ave Bedford (44146) *(G-1450)*
Tmb Enterprises LLC 419 243-2189
  6509 Angola Rd Holland (43528) *(G-10961)*
Tmd Wek North LLC 440 576-6940
  1085 Jffrsn Eagleville Rd Jefferson (44047) *(G-11241)*
Tmh Industries LLC 954 232-7938
  5795 Baronscourt Way Dublin (43016) *(G-9005)*
TMI Inc 330 270-9780
  6475 Victoria East Rd Youngstown (44515) *(G-21046)*
Tmk Farm Service, Sugarcreek Also called Mullet Enterprises Inc *(G-17855)*
Tmk Ipsco, Brookfield Also called Ultra Premium Oilfld Svcs Ltd *(G-2110)*
Tms International LLC 513 425-6462
  1801 Crawford St Middletown (45044) *(G-13958)*
Tms International LLC 419 747-5500
  1344 Bowman St Mansfield (44903) *(G-12532)*
Tms International LLC 513 422-4572
  3018 Oxford State Rd Middletown (45044) *(G-13959)*
Tms International LLC 216 441-9702
  4300 E 49th St Cleveland (44125) *(G-6178)*
Tms International LLC 330 847-0844
  4000 Mahoning Ave Nw Warren (44483) *(G-19449)*
Tms International Corporation 740 223-0091
  912 Cheney Ave Marion (43302) *(G-12741)*
Tmsi LLC 888 867-4872
  9073 Pleasantwood Ave Nw North Canton (44720) *(G-15130)*

Tmt Inc 419 592-1041
  655 D St Perrysburg (43551) *(G-16018)*
Tmt Logistics, Perrysburg Also called Tmt Inc *(G-16018)*
Tmw Systems Inc 615 986-1900
  6085 Parkland Blvd Cleveland (44124) *(G-6179)*
Tmw Systems Inc (HQ) 216 831-6606
  6085 Parkland Blvd Mayfield Heights (44124) *(G-13171)*
Toagosei America Inc 614 718-3855
  1450 W Main St West Jefferson (43162) *(G-19928)*
Toastmasters International 937 429-2680
  1854 Redleaf Ct Dayton (45432) *(G-7991)*
Toccata Technologies Inc 614 430-9888
  50 E Olentangy St Ste 204 Powell (43065) *(G-16339)*
Tod Thin Brushes Inc 440 576-6859
  1152 State Route 46 N Jefferson (44047) *(G-11242)*
Today's Bride Magazine, Akron Also called Jadlyn Inc *(G-221)*
Todco, Upper Sandusky Also called Overhead Door Corporation *(G-18970)*
Todco 740 223-2542
  1295 E Fairground Rd Marion (43302) *(G-12742)*
Todd W Goings 740 389-5842
  360 Summit St Marion (43302) *(G-12743)*
Toft Dairy Inc 419 625-4376
  3717 Venice Rd Sandusky (44870) *(G-16856)*
Toibox Structuretures, Carrollton Also called All Steel Structures Inc *(G-2915)*
Tokin America Corporation 513 644-9743
  9844 Windisch Rd West Chester (45069) *(G-19810)*
Toku America Inc 440 954-9923
  3900 Ben Hur Ave Ste 3 Willoughby (44094) *(G-20449)*
Tolco Corporation 419 241-1113
  1920 Linwood Ave Toledo (43604) *(G-18555)*
Toledo Alfalfa Mills Inc 419 836-3705
  861 S Stadium Rd Oregon (43616) *(G-15571)*
Toledo Automatic Screw Co 419 726-3441
  2114 Champlain St Toledo (43611) *(G-18556)*
Toledo Blade Company 419 724-6000
  541 N Superior St Toledo (43660) *(G-18557)*
Toledo Business Journals, Toledo Also called Telex Communications Inc *(G-18546)*
Toledo City Paper, Toledo Also called Adams Street Publishing Co *(G-18156)*
Toledo Cutting Tools, Perrysburg Also called Imco Carbide Tool Inc *(G-15965)*
Toledo Deburring Co, Northwood Also called Toledo Metal Finishing Inc *(G-15347)*
Toledo Driveline, Toledo Also called Dana Light Axle Mfg LLC *(G-18253)*
Toledo Driveline, Fremont Also called Certified Power Inc *(G-10006)*
Toledo Electromotive Inc 419 874-7751
  28765 White Rd Perrysburg (43551) *(G-16019)*
Toledo Engineering Co Inc (PA) 419 537-9711
  3400 Executive Pkwy Ste 4 Toledo (43606) *(G-18558)*
Toledo Express, Swanton Also called Toledo Jet Center LLC *(G-17924)*
Toledo Fiber Products Corp 419 720-0303
  1245 E Manhattan Blvd Toledo (43608) *(G-18559)*
Toledo Grmtor Blffton Mtr Wrks, Sylvania Also called Tgm Holdings Company *(G-17965)*
Toledo Integrated Systems, Holland Also called Toledo Transducers Inc *(G-10962)*
Toledo Jet Center LLC (PA) 419 866-9050
  11591 W Airport Svc Rd Swanton (43558) *(G-17924)*
Toledo Journal 419 472-4521
  3021 Douglas Rd Toledo (43606) *(G-18560)*
Toledo Metal Finishing Inc 419 661-1422
  7880 Caple Blvd Northwood (43619) *(G-15347)*
Toledo Metal Spinning Company 419 535-5931
  1819 Clinton St Toledo (43607) *(G-18561)*
Toledo Mobile Media LLC (PA) 419 389-0687
  757 Warehouse Rd Ste D Toledo (43615) *(G-18562)*
Toledo Molding & Die Inc 419 354-6050
  515 E Gypsy Lane Rd Bowling Green (43402) *(G-2002)*
Toledo Molding & Die Inc 419 476-0581
  4 E Laskey Rd Toledo (43612) *(G-18563)*
Toledo Molding & Die Inc 419 443-9031
  1441 Maule Rd Tiffin (44883) *(G-18090)*
Toledo Molding & Die Inc (HQ) 419 470-3950
  1429 Coining Dr Toledo (43612) *(G-18564)*
Toledo Molding & Die Inc 419 692-6022
  900 Gressel Dr Delphos (45833) *(G-8756)*
Toledo Molding & Die Inc 419 692-6022
  24086 State Route 697 Delphos (45833) *(G-8757)*
Toledo Optical Laboratory Inc 419 248-3384
  1201 Jefferson Ave Toledo (43604) *(G-18565)*
Toledo Paint & Chemical Co 419 244-3726
  33 Blucher St Toledo (43607) *(G-18566)*
Toledo Pro Fiberglass Inc 419 241-9390
  210 Wade St Toledo (43604) *(G-18567)*
Toledo Scales & Systems, Worthington Also called Mettler-Toledo LLC *(G-20695)*
Toledo Screw Products, Toledo Also called D L Salkil LLC *(G-18251)*
Toledo Screw Products Inc 419 841-3341
  8261 W Bancroft St Toledo (43617) *(G-18568)*
Toledo Signs & Designs Ltd 419 843-1073
  6636 W Bancroft St Ste 2 Toledo (43615) *(G-18569)*
Toledo Streets Newspaper 419 214-3460
  913 Madison Ave Toledo (43604) *(G-18570)*

Toledo Sword Newspaper 419 932-0767
3332 Stanhope Dr Toledo (43606) ***(G-18571)***
Toledo Tape and Label Company 419 536-8316
114 Dulton Dr Toledo (43615) ***(G-18572)***
Toledo Ticket Company 419 476-5424
3963 Catawba St Toledo (43612) ***(G-18573)***
Toledo Tool and Die Co Inc 419 476-4422
105 W Alexis Rd Toledo (43612) ***(G-18574)***
Toledo Transducers Inc 419 724-4170
6834 Spring Valley Dr # 3 Holland (43528) ***(G-10962)***
Toledo Window & Awning Inc 419 474-3396
3035 W Sylvania Ave Toledo (43613) ***(G-18575)***
Tolento's Family Restaurant, Cleveland *Also called Adkins Marlena* ***(G-4617)***
Toll Compaction Group LLC 740 376-0511
721 Farson St Belpre (45714) ***(G-1584)***
Tolloti Pipe LLC 330 364-6627
102 Barnhill Rd Se New Philadelphia (44663) ***(G-14805)***
Tolloti Plastic Pipe Inc (PA) 330 364-6627
102 Barnhill Rd Se New Philadelphia (44663) ***(G-14806)***
Tolloti Plastic Pipe Inc 740 922-6911
1830 Barbour Dr Se Uhrichsville (44683) ***(G-18897)***
Tolson Pallet Mfg Inc 937 787-3511
10240 State Rte 122 Gratis (45330) ***(G-10340)***
Tom Bad Brewing LLC 513 871-4677
4720 Eastern Ave Cincinnati (45226) ***(G-4425)***
Tom Barbour Auto Parts Inc (PA) 740 354-4654
915 11th St Portsmouth (45662) ***(G-16303)***
Tom Fucito Inc 513 273-2092
21 Lynn Ave Oxford (45056) ***(G-15701)***
Tom James Company 614 488-8400
1156 Dublin Rd Ste 101 Columbus (43215) ***(G-7533)***
Tom Richards Inc (PA) 440 974-1300
7010 Lindsay Dr Mentor (44060) ***(G-13607)***
Tom Smith Industries Inc 937 832-1555
500 Smith Dr Englewood (45315) ***(G-9378)***
Tom Thumb Clip Co Inc 440 953-9606
36300 Lkeland Blvd Unit 2 Willoughby (44095) ***(G-20450)***
Tom's Print Shop, Zanesville *Also called Dresden Specialties Inc* ***(G-21131)***
Tomahawk Entertainment Group 216 505-0548
6501 Marsol Rd Apt 108 Cleveland (44124) ***(G-6180)***
Tomahawk Printing Inc 419 335-3161
229 N Fulton St Wauseon (43567) ***(G-19533)***
Tomahawk Printing LLC (PA) 419 335-3161
229 N Fulton St Wauseon (43567) ***(G-19534)***
Tomahawk Tool Supply 419 485-8737
1604 Magda Dr Montpelier (43543) ***(G-14319)***
Tomak Precision, Lebanon *Also called Aws Industries Inc* ***(G-11635)***
Tomco Industries 330 652-7531
1660 E County Line Rd Mineral Ridge (44440) ***(G-14172)***
Tomco Machining Inc 937 264-1943
4962 Riverton Dr Dayton (45414) ***(G-8560)***
Tomco Tool Inc 937 322-5768
203 S Wittenberg Ave Springfield (45506) ***(G-17507)***
Tomlinson Industries, Cleveland *Also called Meyer Company* ***(G-5663)***
Tomlinson Industries LLC 216 587-3400
13700 Brdwy Ave Cleveland (44125) ***(G-6181)***
Toms Country Place Inc 440 934-4553
3442 Stoney Ridge Rd Avon (44011) ***(G-971)***
Tomson Steel Company 513 420-8600
1400 Made Industrial Dr Middletown (45044) ***(G-13960)***
Tonys Wldg & Fabrication LLC 740 333-4000
2305 Robinson Rd Se Wshngtn CT Hs (43160) ***(G-20746)***
Tool & Die Systems Inc 440 327-5800
38900 Taylor Indus Pkwy North Ridgeville (44039) ***(G-15256)***
Tool Service Co Inc 937 254-4000
4620 Tall Oaks Dr Dayton (45432) ***(G-7992)***
Tool Systems Inc 440 461-6363
71 Alpha Park Cleveland (44143) ***(G-6182)***
Tool Technologies Van Dyke 937 349-4900
639 Clymer Rd Marysville (43040) ***(G-12817)***
Toolbold Corporation (PA) 216 676-9840
5330 Commerce Pkwy W Cleveland (44130) ***(G-6183)***
Toolbold Corporation 440 543-1660
5330 Commerce Pkwy W Cleveland (44130) ***(G-6184)***
Toolco Inc 419 667-3462
16913 Wren Landeck Rd Van Wert (45891) ***(G-19108)***
Toolcomp, Toledo *Also called Tooling & Components Corp* ***(G-18576)***
Toolcraft Products Inc 937 223-8271
1265 Mccook Ave Dayton (45404) ***(G-8561)***
Tooling & Components Corp 419 478-9122
5261 Tractor Rd Toledo (43612) ***(G-18576)***
Tooling Components Division, Cleveland *Also called Jergens Inc* ***(G-5495)***
Tooling Connection Inc 419 594-3339
N Ste 12603 Hc 66 Oakwood (45873) ***(G-15475)***
Tooling Tech Group, Fort Loramie *Also called Tooling Technology LLC* ***(G-9810)***
Tooling Tech Holdings LLC (HQ) 937 295-3672
100 Enterprise Dr Fort Loramie (45845) ***(G-9809)***
Tooling Technology LLC (PA) 937 295-3672
100 Enterprise Dr Fort Loramie (45845) ***(G-9810)***
Tooling Zone Inc 937 550-4180
285 S Pioneer Blvd Springboro (45066) ***(G-17356)***
Toolovation LLC 216 514-3022
23980 Mercantile Rd Uppr Cleveland (44122) ***(G-6185)***
Toolrite Manufacturing Inc 937 278-1962
5370 Wadsworth Rd Dayton (45414) ***(G-8562)***
Tools Plus, Troy *Also called Gary Compton* ***(G-18660)***
Tooltex Inc 614 539-3222
6160 Seeds Rd Grove City (43123) ***(G-10475)***
Toomey Inc 513 831-4771
914 Lila Ave Milford (45150) ***(G-14044)***
Toomey Natural Foods, Milford *Also called Toomey Inc* ***(G-14044)***
Top Cat Air Tools, Willoughby *Also called TC Service Co* ***(G-20441)***
Top Drilling Corporation (PA) 304 477-3333
107 Lancaster St 301 Marietta (45750) ***(G-12682)***
Top Hat Designs 614 898-1962
776 Autumn Branch Rd Westerville (43081) ***(G-20079)***
Top Knotch Products Inc 419 543-2266
819 Colonel Dr Cleveland (44109) ***(G-6186)***
Top Network, Columbus *Also called Essilor Laboratories Amer Inc* ***(G-6906)***
Top Notch Fleet Services LLC 419 260-4057
801 Wall St Maumee (43537) ***(G-13155)***
Top Notch Logging 330 466-1780
8242 Secrest Rd Apple Creek (44606) ***(G-621)***
Top Shelf Embroidery 440 209-8566
9450 Mentor Ave Mentor (44060) ***(G-13608)***
Top Shot Ammunition, Mount Gilead *Also called TS Sales LLC* ***(G-14435)***
Top Tool & Die Inc 216 267-5878
15500 Brookpark Rd Cleveland (44135) ***(G-6187)***
Tope Printing Inc 330 674-4993
1056 S Washington St Millersburg (44654) ***(G-14137)***
Topkote Inc 440 428-0525
404 N Lake St Madison (44057) ***(G-12357)***
Topps Products Inc 216 271-2550
3201 E 66th St Cleveland (44127) ***(G-6188)***
Tops Auto Interiors, Mentor *Also called Tops Inc* ***(G-13609)***
Tops Inc 440 954-9451
7564 Tyler Blvd Ste A Mentor (44060) ***(G-13609)***
Torbot Group Inc 419 724-1475
5030 Advantage Dr Ste 101 Toledo (43612) ***(G-18577)***
Tormaxx Co 513 721-6299
1150 W 8th St Ste 111 Cincinnati (45203) ***(G-4426)***
Torok Supply Company 330 799-6677
52 S Meridian Rd Youngstown (44509) ***(G-21047)***
Torq Corporation 440 232-4100
32 W Monroe Ave Bedford (44146) ***(G-1451)***
Torque Transmission, Fairport Harbor *Also called Rampe Manufacturing Company* ***(G-9629)***
Torr Metal Products Inc 216 671-1616
12125 Bennington Ave Cleveland (44135) ***(G-6189)***
Torsion Control Product 248 597-9997
840 W Spring Valley Pike Dayton (45458) ***(G-8563)***
Torsion Plastics 812 453-9645
1133 Windward Ln Kent (44240) ***(G-11395)***
Torso 614 421-7663
772 N High St Ste 100 Columbus (43215) ***(G-7534)***
Tortilla 614 557-3367
8134 E Broad St Reynoldsburg (43068) ***(G-16456)***
Tortilla Factory, Toledo *Also called La Perla Inc* ***(G-18374)***
Tortilleria El Maizal LLP 330 209-9344
1895 Greentree Pl Se Massillon (44646) ***(G-13053)***
Tortilleria La Bamba LLC 216 469-0410
1849 W 24th St Cleveland (44113) ***(G-6190)***
Tortilleria La Bamba LLC 216 515-1600
12119 Bennington Ave Cleveland (44135) ***(G-6191)***
Tosoh America Inc (HQ) 614 539-8622
3600 Gantz Rd Grove City (43123) ***(G-10476)***
Tosoh SMD Inc 614 875-7912
2050 Southpark Pl Grove City (43123) ***(G-10477)***
Tosoh SMD Inc (HQ) 614 875-7912
3600 Gantz Rd Grove City (43123) ***(G-10478)***
Total Automation, Columbia Station *Also called Columbia Stamping Inc* ***(G-6433)***
Total Cable Solutions Inc 513 457-7013
475 Victory Ln Springboro (45066) ***(G-17357)***
Total Lubrication MGT Co (HQ) 888 478-6996
3713 Progress St Ne Canton (44705) ***(G-2843)***
Total Maintenance Management 513 228-2345
320 Harmon Ave Lebanon (45036) ***(G-11701)***
Total Manufacturing Co Inc 440 205-9700
7777 Saint Clair Ave Mentor (44060) ***(G-13610)***
Total Plastics Resources LLC 440 891-1140
17851 Englewood Dr Ste A Cleveland (44130) ***(G-6192)***
Total Quality Machining Inc 937 746-7765
10 Shotwell Dr Franklin (45005) ***(G-9926)***
Total Repair Express Mich LLC 248 690-9410
4575 Hudson Dr Stow (44224) ***(G-17635)***
Total Self Defense Toledo LLC 419 466-5882
5921 Therfield Dr Sylvania (43560) ***(G-17966)***
Total Tennis Inc 614 488-5004
1733 Cardiff Rd Columbus (43221) ***(G-7535)***

ALPHABETIC

Total Voice Technologies, Broadview Heights *Also called Cleveland Business Supply LLC* ***(G-2091)***
Totally Promotional, Coldwater *Also called Casad Company Inc* ***(G-6404)***
Totes Isotoner Corporation (HQ)....513 682-8200
9655 International Blvd West Chester (45246) ***(G-19907)***
Totes Isotoner Holdings Corp (PA)....513 682-8200
9655 International Blvd West Chester (45246) ***(G-19908)***
Toth Industries Inc....419 729-4669
5102 Enterprise Blvd Toledo (43612) ***(G-18578)***
Toth Mold & Die Inc....440 232-8530
380 Solon Rd Ste 7 Cleveland (44146) ***(G-6193)***
Touch Life Centers LLC....614 388-8075
3455 Mill Run Dr Ste 310 Hilliard (43026) ***(G-10871)***
Touch of Glass....419 861-2888
908 Jean Rd Toledo (43615) ***(G-18579)***
Touch Print Solution, Cincinnati *Also called Onetouchpoint East Corp* ***(G-4113)***
Touchmark, Dublin *Also called Advanced Prgrm Resources Inc* ***(G-8874)***
Touchstone Woodworks....330 297-1313
7820 Cooley Rd Ravenna (44266) ***(G-16413)***
Tow Path Materials, Lucasville *Also called Tow Path Ready Mix* ***(G-12268)***
Tow Path Ready Mix....740 286-2131
1668 Kessinger School Rd Jackson (45640) ***(G-11199)***
Tow Path Ready Mix (PA)....740 259-3222
12360 State Route 104 Lucasville (45648) ***(G-12268)***
Tower Automotive Operations I....419 358-8966
18717 County Road 15 Bluffton (45817) ***(G-1895)***
Tower Automotive Operations I....419 483-1500
630 Southwest St Bellevue (44811) ***(G-1550)***
Tower Industries Ltd....330 837-2216
2101 9th St Sw Massillon (44647) ***(G-13054)***
Tower Manufacturing Company, Springfield *Also called Robertson Incorporated* ***(G-17488)***
Tower Tool & Manufacturing Co....330 425-1623
2057 E Aurora Rd Ste No Twinsburg (44087) ***(G-18864)***
Town Cntry Technical Svcs Inc....614 866-7700
6200 Eastgreen Blvd Reynoldsburg (43068) ***(G-16457)***
Town Crier, The, Warren *Also called Ogden Newspapers Inc* ***(G-19425)***
Town Planner, The, Richfield *Also called Pauler Communications Inc* ***(G-16480)***
Townsend Machinery, Montville *Also called Ray Townsend* ***(G-14325)***
Toxco Inc....740 653-6290
265 Quarry Rd Se Lancaster (43130) ***(G-11614)***
Toy & Sport Trends Inc....419 748-8880
5963 State Route 110 Napoleon (43545) ***(G-14562)***
Toyo Seiki Usa Inc....513 546-9657
11130 Luschek Dr Blue Ash (45241) ***(G-1860)***
Toyobo Kureha America Co Ltd....513 771-6788
11630 Mosteller Rd Cincinnati (45241) ***(G-4427)***
Tpi Medical, Gahanna *Also called Thompson Partners Inc* ***(G-10109)***
Tpr, Hinckley *Also called Tarantula Performance Racg LLC* ***(G-10906)***
Tpr Plasma Center....419 244-3910
625 Dorr St Toledo (43604) ***(G-18580)***
Tpsc Inc....440 439-9320
25801 Solon Rd Bedford Heights (44146) ***(G-1481)***
Tq Manufacturing Company Inc....440 255-9000
7345 Production Dr Mentor (44060) ***(G-13611)***
Tracer Specialties Inc....216 696-2363
1842 Columbus Rd Cleveland (44113) ***(G-6194)***
Tracewell Power Inc....614 846-6175
567 Enterprise Dr Westerville (43081) ***(G-20080)***
Tracewell Systems Inc (PA)....614 846-6175
567 Enterprise Dr Lewis Center (43035) ***(G-11787)***
Track-It Systems....513 522-0083
1776 Mentor Ave Ste 560 Cincinnati (45212) ***(G-4428)***
Tracker Machine Inc....330 482-4086
1370 Kauffman Ave Columbiana (44408) ***(G-6483)***
Tract Inc....937 427-3431
3197 Beaver Vu Dr Dayton (45434) ***(G-7993)***
Trademark Designs Inc....419 628-3897
17 Jackson St Minster (45865) ***(G-14227)***
Tradewinds Prin Twear....740 214-5005
35 E Athens Rd Roseville (43777) ***(G-16580)***
Trading Corp of America, Columbus *Also called Marfo Company* ***(G-7150)***
Trading Post....740 922-1199
202 N Water St Uhrichsville (44683) ***(G-18898)***
Traditional Marble & Gran Ltd....419 625-3966
10105 Us Highway 250 N Milan (44846) ***(G-13990)***
Traditions Sauces LLC....419 704-4506
606 Durango Dr Toledo (43609) ***(G-18581)***
Tradye Machine & Tool Inc....740 625-7550
3116a Wilson Rd Centerburg (43011) ***(G-2994)***
Traffic Cntrl Sgnls Signs & MA....740 670-7763
1195 E Main St Newark (43055) ***(G-14930)***
Traffic Detectors & Signs Inc....330 707-9060
7521 Forest Hill Ave Youngstown (44514) ***(G-21048)***
Traffic Engineering Department, Canton *Also called City of Canton* ***(G-2625)***
Traichal Construction Company (PA)....800 255-3667
332 Plant St Niles (44446) ***(G-15037)***
Trail Cabinet....330 893-3791
2270 Township Road 415 Dundee (44624) ***(G-9027)***
Trail Mix....330 657-2277
1565 Boston Mills Rd W Peninsula (44264) ***(G-15900)***
Trailer Component Mfg Inc....440 255-2888
8120 Tyler Blvd Mentor (44060) ***(G-13612)***
Trailer One Inc....330 723-7474
6378 Norwalk Rd Medina (44256) ***(G-13354)***
Trailex Inc....330 533-6814
1 Industrial Park Dr Canfield (44406) ***(G-2551)***
Trailway Wood....330 893-9966
3173 Township Road 414 Dundee (44624) ***(G-9028)***
Tramec Sloan LLC....419 468-9122
1310 Freese Works Pl Galion (44833) ***(G-10158)***
Trane Company....419 491-2278
1001 Hamilton Dr Holland (43528) ***(G-10963)***
Trane National Account Service, Columbus *Also called Trane US Inc* ***(G-7537)***
Trane US Inc....513 771-8884
10300 Springfield Pike Cincinnati (45215) ***(G-4429)***
Trane US Inc....614 473-3131
2300 Citygate Dr Ste 100 Columbus (43219) ***(G-7536)***
Trane US Inc....614 497-6300
6600 Port Rd Ste 200 Groveport (43125) ***(G-10515)***
Trane US Inc....614 473-8701
2300 Citygate Dr Ste 250 Columbus (43219) ***(G-7537)***
Tranquility, Bowling Green *Also called Principle Business Entps Inc* ***(G-1992)***
Trans Ash Inc....859 341-1528
360 S Wayne Ave Cincinnati (45215) ***(G-4430)***
Trans Foam Inc....330 630-9444
281 Southwest Ave Tallmadge (44278) ***(G-18009)***
Trans-Acc Inc (PA)....513 793-6410
11167 Deerfield Rd Blue Ash (45242) ***(G-1861)***
Transcendia Inc....740 929-5100
3700 Hebron Rd Hebron (43025) ***(G-10768)***
Transcendia Inc....440 638-2000
22889 Lunn Rd Strongsville (44149) ***(G-17801)***
Transco Railway Products Inc....330 872-0934
2310 S Center St Newton Falls (44444) ***(G-14994)***
Transco Railway Products Inc....419 726-3383
4800 Schwartz Rd Toledo (43611) ***(G-18582)***
Transcon Conveyor, Mentor *Also called New Transcon LLC* ***(G-13526)***
Transcontinental Electric LLC....614 496-4379
3155 Wareham Rd Columbus (43221) ***(G-7538)***
Transcontinental Oil & Gas....330 995-0777
1509 Page Rd Aurora (44202) ***(G-909)***
Transdermal Inc....440 241-1846
938 Chestnut Run Gates Mills (44040) ***(G-10209)***
Transdigm Inc....216 291-6025
4223 Monticello Blvd Cleveland (44121) ***(G-6195)***
Transdigm Inc....440 352-6182
313 Gillett St Painesville (44077) ***(G-15791)***
Transdigm Inc (HQ)....216 706-2939
4223 Monticello Blvd Cleveland (44121) ***(G-6196)***
Transdigm Group Incorporated (PA)....216 706-2960
1301 E 9th St Ste 3000 Cleveland (44114) ***(G-6197)***
Transducers Direct Llc....513 583-7597
112 Lakeview Ct Loveland (45140) ***(G-12240)***
Transducers Direct Llc....513 247-0601
12115 Ellington Ct Cincinnati (45249) ***(G-4431)***
Transel Corporation....513 897-3442
123 E South St Harveysburg (45032) ***(G-10706)***
Transel Technologies, Harveysburg *Also called Transel Corporation* ***(G-10706)***
Transfer Express Inc....440 918-1900
7650 Tyler Blvd Mentor (44060) ***(G-13613)***
Transformer Associates Limited....330 430-0750
831 Market Ave N Canton (44702) ***(G-2844)***
Transglobal Inc (PA)....419 396-9079
225 N Patterson St Carey (43316) ***(G-2890)***
Transimage Inc....937 293-0261
314 Spirea Dr Oakwood (45419) ***(G-15466)***
Transit Sittings of NA....330 797-2516
295 S Meridian Rd Youngstown (44509) ***(G-21049)***
Transitworks LLC....855 337-9543
1090 W Wilbeth Rd Akron (44314) ***(G-408)***
Transmet Corporation....614 276-5522
4290 Perimeter Dr Columbus (43228) ***(G-7539)***
Transmit Identity LLC....330 576-4732
3916 Clk Pnte Trl Ste 101 Stow (44224) ***(G-17636)***
Transport Container Corp....614 459-8140
950 Augusta Glen Dr Columbus (43235) ***(G-7540)***
Transportation Group, Mantua *Also called Mantaline Corporation* ***(G-12551)***
Transportation Ohio Department....740 927-2285
318 S Township Rd Pataskala (43062) ***(G-15846)***
Transtar Holding Company (PA)....800 359-3339
7350 Young Dr Walton Hills (44146) ***(G-19315)***
Transue & Williams Stampg Corp (PA)....330 821-5777
930 W Ely St Alliance (44601) ***(G-508)***
Transue & Williams Stampg Corp....330 270-0891
207 N Four Mile Run Rd Youngstown (44515) ***(G-21050)***
Transue Williams Stamping Inc....330 270-0891
207 N Four Mile Run Rd Austintown (44515) ***(G-935)***

Transue Williams Stamping Inc (HQ).....330 829-5007
930 W Ely St Alliance (44601) *(G-509)*
Tranzonic Acquisition Corp.....216 535-4300
26301 Curtiss Wright Pkwy Richmond Heights (44143) *(G-16505)*
Tranzonic Companies, Richmond Heights *Also called Tranzonic Acquisition Corp (G-16505)*
Tranzonic Companies (PA).....216 535-4300
26301 Curtiss Wright Pkwy # 200 Richmond Heights (44143) *(G-16506)*
Tranzonic Companies.....216 535-4300
26301 Curtiss Wright Pkwy # 200 Richmond Heights (44143) *(G-16507)*
Tranzonic Companies.....440 446-0643
26301 Curtiss Wright Pkwy # 200 Cleveland (44143) *(G-6198)*
Trapeze Software Group Inc.....905 629-8727
23215 Commerce Park # 200 Beachwood (44122) *(G-1281)*
Travelers Custom Case Inc.....216 621-8447
2261 E 14th St Cleveland (44115) *(G-6199)*
Travelers Vacation Guide.....440 582-4949
10143 Royalton Rd North Royalton (44133) *(G-15306)*
Traveling & Recycle Wood Pdts.....419 968-2649
19590 Bellis Rd Middle Point (45863) *(G-13757)*
Traxium LLC.....330 572-8200
4246 Hudson Dr Stow (44224) *(G-17637)*
Traxler Printing.....614 593-1270
3029 Silver Dr Columbus (43224) *(G-7541)*
Trd Leathers.....216 631-6233
6321 Detroit Ave Cleveland (44102) *(G-6200)*
Treadstone Company.....216 410-3435
1565 Landsdale Cir Twinsburg (44087) *(G-18865)*
Treasured Times Enterprises, West Alexandria *Also called John M Hand (G-19619)*
Treaty City Industries Inc.....937 548-9000
945 Sater St Greenville (45331) *(G-10398)*
Trebnick Systems Inc.....937 743-1550
215 S Pioneer Blvd Springboro (45066) *(G-17358)*
Trebnick Tags and Labels, Springboro *Also called Trebnick Systems Inc (G-17358)*
Trec Industries Inc.....216 741-4114
4713 Spring Rd Cleveland (44131) *(G-6201)*
Tree City Mold & Machine Co.....330 673-9807
6752 State Route 43 Kent (44240) *(G-11396)*
Tree Free Resources LLC.....740 751-4844
175 Park Blvd Marion (43302) *(G-12744)*
Treehouse Private Brands Inc.....740 654-8880
3775 Lanc New Lex Rd Se Lancaster (43130) *(G-11615)*
Treehouse Private Brands Inc.....740 654-8880
276 Bremen Rd Lancaster (43130) *(G-11616)*
Treemen Industries Inc.....330 965-3777
691 Mcclurg Rd Boardman (44512) *(G-1904)*
Trellborg Sling Prfiles US Inc.....330 995-5125
285 Lena Dr Aurora (44202) *(G-910)*
Trellborg Sling Prfiles US Inc (HQ).....330 995-9725
285 Lena Dr Aurora (44202) *(G-911)*
Trelleborg Wheel Systems Ameri (HQ).....866 633-8473
1501 Exeter Rd Akron (44306) *(G-409)*
Tremac Corporation.....937 372-8662
550 Bellbrook Ave Xenia (45385) *(G-20798)*
Tremcar USA Inc.....330 878-7708
436 12th St Ne Strasburg (44680) *(G-17654)*
Tremco Glazing Solutions Group, Ashland *Also called Tremco Incorporated (G-752)*
Tremco Inc.....216 514-7783
23150 Commerce Park Beachwood (44122) *(G-1282)*
Tremco Incorporated.....216 752-4401
4475 E 175th St Cleveland (44128) *(G-6202)*
Tremco Incorporated (HQ).....216 292-5000
3735 Green Rd Beachwood (44122) *(G-1283)*
Tremco Incorporated.....419 289-2050
1451 Jacobson Ave Ashland (44805) *(G-752)*
Tremont Electric Incorporated.....888 214-3137
2112 W 7th St Cleveland (44113) *(G-6203)*
Trend Consulting Services, Solon *Also called Netsmart Technologies Inc (G-17207)*
Trend Curve, The, Cleveland *Also called Marketing Directions Inc (G-5621)*
Trendco Inc (PA).....216 661-6903
8043 Corporate Cir Ste 1 North Royalton (44133) *(G-15307)*
Trent Manufacturing Company.....216 391-1551
6212 Carnegie Ave Cleveland (44103) *(G-6204)*
Tresco International Ltd Co.....330 757-8131
1637 Bluebell Trl Youngstown (44514) *(G-21051)*
Tresslers Plumbing LLC.....419 784-2142
9170 State Route 15 Defiance (43512) *(G-8646)*
Treved Exteriors.....513 771-3888
10235 Spartan Dr Ste T Cincinnati (45215) *(G-4432)*
Trevi Technology Inc.....614 754-7175
1029 Dublin Rd Columbus (43215) *(G-7542)*
Trexler Rubber Co Inc (PA).....330 296-9677
503 N Diamond St Ravenna (44266) *(G-16414)*
Trey Corrugated Inc.....513 942-4800
9048 Port Union Rialto Rd West Chester (45069) *(G-19811)*
Tri - Flex of Ohio Inc (PA).....330 705-7084
2701 Applegrove St Nw North Canton (44720) *(G-15131)*
Tri Cast Limited Partnership.....330 733-8718
2128 Killian Rd Akron (44312) *(G-410)*
Tri Con Distribution LLC.....937 399-3312
776 Deerfield Trl Springfield (45503) *(G-17508)*
Tri County Asphalt Materials.....330 549-2852
405 Andrews Ave Youngstown (44505) *(G-21052)*
Tri County Concrete Inc (PA).....330 425-4464
9423 Darrow Rd Twinsburg (44087) *(G-18866)*
Tri County Concrete Inc.....330 425-4464
10155 Royalton Rd Cleveland (44133) *(G-6205)*
Tri County Door Service Inc.....216 531-2245
21701 Tungsten Rd Euclid (44117) *(G-9448)*
Tri County Eggs, Versailles *Also called Weaver Bros Inc (G-19193)*
Tri County Locksmith, Cincinnati *Also called AB Bonded Locksmiths Inc (G-3286)*
Tri County Marble & Granite, Fostoria *Also called Fostoria Monument Co (G-9844)*
Tri County Quality Wtr Systems.....740 751-4764
659 N Main St Marion (43302) *(G-12745)*
Tri County Ready Mixed Con Co, Cleveland *Also called Tri County Concrete Inc (G-6205)*
Tri County Tarp LLC (PA).....419 288-3350
13100 State Rte 23 Bradner (43406) *(G-2016)*
Tri County Wheel and Rim Ltd.....419 666-1760
6943 Wales Rd Ste A Northwood (43619) *(G-15348)*
Tri Dlta Metal Fabrication LLC.....937 499-4315
643 Dunraven Pass Miamisburg (45342) *(G-13728)*
Tri R Tooling Inc.....419 522-8665
220 Piper Rd Mansfield (44905) *(G-12533)*
Tri State Countertop Service.....740 354-3663
3350 Indian Dr Portsmouth (45662) *(G-16304)*
Tri State Dairy LLC.....419 542-8788
210 Wendell Ave Hicksville (43526) *(G-10784)*
Tri State Dairy LLC.....330 897-5555
115 S Mill St Baltic (43804) *(G-1034)*
Tri State Equipment Company.....513 738-7227
5009 Cncnnt Brookville Rd Shandon (45063) *(G-16942)*
Tri State Media LLC.....513 933-0101
325 Davids Dr Wilmington (45177) *(G-20509)*
Tri State Pallet Inc.....937 323-5210
854 Sherman Ave Springfield (45503) *(G-17509)*
Tri State Pallet Inc (PA).....937 746-8702
8401 Claude Thomas Rd # 57 Franklin (45005) *(G-9927)*
Tri-America Contractors Inc (PA).....740 574-0148
1664 State Route 522 Wheelersburg (45694) *(G-20186)*
Tri-America Contractors Inc.....740 574-0148
1664 State Route 522 Wheelersburg (45694) *(G-20187)*
Tri-Cast Inc (PA).....330 733-8718
2128 Killian Rd Akron (44312) *(G-411)*
Tri-Co Industries.....740 927-1928
13804 Refugee Rd Sw Pataskala (43062) *(G-15847)*
Tri-County Block and Brick Inc.....419 826-7060
1628 Us 20 Alternate Swanton (43558) *(G-17925)*
Tri-Craft Inc.....440 826-1050
17941 Englewood Dr Cleveland (44130) *(G-6206)*
Tri-Fab Inc.....330 337-3425
10372 W South Range Rd Salem (44460) *(G-16777)*
Tri-K Enterprises Inc.....330 832-7380
935 Mckinley Ave Sw Canton (44707) *(G-2845)*
Tri-Mac Mfg & Serv, Hamilton *Also called Tri-Mac Mfg & Svcs Co (G-10613)*
Tri-Mac Mfg & Svcs Co.....513 896-4445
860 Belle Ave Hamilton (45015) *(G-10613)*
Tri-R Dies Inc.....330 758-8050
556 Bev Rd Youngstown (44512) *(G-21053)*
Tri-Seal LLC.....330 821-1166
16125 Armour St Ne Alliance (44601) *(G-510)*
Tri-State Asphalt Co, Rayland *Also called Shelly and Sands Inc (G-16423)*
Tri-State Beef Co Inc.....513 579-1722
2124 Baymiller St Cincinnati (45214) *(G-4433)*
Tri-State Belting Ltd.....800 330-2358
5525 Vine St Cincinnati (45217) *(G-4434)*
Tri-State Fabricators Inc.....513 752-5005
1146 Ferris Rd Amelia (45102) *(G-550)*
Tri-State Fasteners LLC.....937 442-1904
2875 Gath North Rd Sardinia (45171) *(G-16874)*
Tri-State Garden Supply Inc.....419 445-6561
56 State Rte 66 Archbold (43502) *(G-672)*
Tri-State Jet Mfg LLC.....513 896-4538
1480 Beissinger Rd Hamilton (45013) *(G-10614)*
Tri-State Machining LLC.....513 257-9442
6088 Hamilton Cleves Rd # 2 Cleves (45002) *(G-6380)*
Tri-State Model Flyers Inc.....740 886-8429
358 Township Road 1161 Proctorville (45669) *(G-16347)*
Tri-State Plating & Polishing.....304 529-2579
187 Township Road 1204 Proctorville (45669) *(G-16348)*
Tri-State Printing, Steubenville *Also called Tri-State Publishing Company (G-17556)*
Tri-State Publishing Company (PA).....740 283-3686
157 N 3rd St Steubenville (43952) *(G-17556)*
Tri-State Special Events Inc.....513 221-2962
614 Tafel St Cincinnati (45225) *(G-4435)*
Tri-State Supply Co Inc.....614 272-6767
3840 Fisher Rd Columbus (43228) *(G-7543)*
Tri-State Tool & Die Inc.....330 655-2536
1396 Norton Rd Stow (44224) *(G-17638)*
Tri-State Tool Grinding Inc.....513 347-0100
5311 Robert Ave Ste A Cincinnati (45248) *(G-4436)*

ALPHABETIC

Tri-State Wilbert Vault Co, Ironton *Also called Allen Enterprises Inc* **(G-11159)**
Tri-State Wire Rope Supply Inc (HQ).....513 871-8623
5246 Wooster Pike Cincinnati (45226) **(G-4437)**
Tri-Tech Laboratories Inc.....614 656-1130
8825 Smiths Mill Rd New Albany (43054) **(G-14637)**
Tri-Tech Led Systems.....614 593-2868
600 W Market St Baltimore (43105) **(G-1045)**
Tri-Tech Machining LLC.....513 575-3959
1885 Seven Lands Dr Milford (45150) **(G-14045)**
Tri-Tech Medical Inc.....800 253-8692
35401 Avon Commerce Pkwy Avon (44011) **(G-972)**
Tri-Tech Mfg LLC.....419 238-0140
7404 State Route 66 Delphos (45833) **(G-8758)**
Tri-Tech Research LLC.....440 946-6122
34099 Melinz Pkwy Unit K Eastlake (44095) **(G-9136)**
Tri-Way Rebar Inc (PA).....330 296-9662
625 S Walnut St Ravenna (44266) **(G-16415)**
Tri-Weld Inc.....216 281-6009
4411 Detroit Ave Cleveland (44113) **(G-6207)**
Triad Capital Aat LLC.....440 236-4163
13676 Station Rd Columbia Station (44028) **(G-6451)**
Triad Energy Corporation.....740 374-2940
125 Putnam St Marietta (45750) **(G-12683)**
Triad Governmental Systems.....937 376-5446
358 S Monroe St Xenia (45385) **(G-20799)**
Triad Hunter LLC (HQ).....740 374-2940
125 Putnam St Marietta (45750) **(G-12684)**
Triad Hunter LLC.....740 374-2940
125 Putnam St Marietta (45750) **(G-12685)**
Triad Metal Products Company.....216 676-6505
12990 Snow Rd Chagrin Falls (44023) **(G-3084)**
Triage Ortho Group.....937 653-6431
132 Lafayette Ave Urbana (43078) **(G-19016)**
Triangle Adhesives LLC.....330 670-9722
3616 Torrey Pines Dr Akron (44333) **(G-412)**
Triangle Label Inc.....513 242-2822
6392 Gano Rd West Chester (45069) **(G-19812)**
Triangle Machine Products Co.....216 524-5872
6055 Hillcrest Dr Cleveland (44125) **(G-6208)**
Triangle Precision Industries.....937 299-6776
1650 Delco Park Dr Dayton (45420) **(G-8564)**
Triangle Sign Co.....513 863-2578
221 N B St Hamilton (45013) **(G-10615)**
Triaxis Machine & Tool LLC.....440 230-0303
11941 Abbey Rd Ste H North Royalton (44133) **(G-15308)**
Tribco Incorporated.....216 486-2000
18901 Cranwood Pkwy Cleveland (44128) **(G-6209)**
Triboro Quilt Mfg Corp.....937 222-2132
303 Corporate Center Dr # 108 Vandalia (45377) **(G-19146)**
Tribotech Composites Inc.....216 901-1300
7800 Exchange St Cleveland (44125) **(G-6210)**
Tribune , The, Jefferson *Also called The Gazette Printing Co Inc* **(G-11240)**
Tribune Chronicle, Warren *Also called Ogden Newspapers Inc* **(G-19426)**
Tribune Courier, Ontario *Also called Stumbo Publishing Co* **(G-15548)**
Tribune Printing Inc.....419 542-7764
147 E High St Hicksville (43526) **(G-10785)**
Tribune Shopping News, The, New Lexington *Also called Perry County Tribune* **(G-14720)**
Tribus Enterprises, Englewood *Also called Tribus Innovations LLC* **(G-9379)**
Tribus Innovations LLC.....509 992-4743
155 Haas Dr Englewood Oh Englewood (45322) **(G-9379)**
Trico Corporation.....216 642-3223
9700 Rockside Rd Ste 430 Cleveland (44125) **(G-6211)**
Trico Enterprises LLC.....330 674-1157
6430 Township Road 348 Millersburg (44654) **(G-14138)**
Trico Group LLC (HQ).....216 589-0198
127 Public Sq Ste 5110 Cleveland (44114) **(G-6212)**
Trico Group Holdings LLC (PA).....216 274-9027
127 Public Sq Ste 5110 Cleveland (44114) **(G-6213)**
Trico Machine Products Corp.....216 662-4194
5081 Corbin Dr Cleveland (44128) **(G-6214)**
Tricor Industrial Inc (PA).....330 264-3299
3225 W Old Lincoln Way Wooster (44691) **(G-20660)**
Tricor Metals, Wooster *Also called Tricor Industrial Inc* **(G-20660)**
Trident Polymer Solutions, Green *Also called Next Design & Build LLC* **(G-10343)**
Tridico Silk Screen & Sign Co.....419 526-1695
162 N Diamond St Mansfield (44902) **(G-12534)**
Trifecta Tool & Engrg LLC.....937 291-0933
4648 Gateway Cir Dayton (45440) **(G-8565)**
Trigon Industries Inc.....937 299-1350
1616 Delaine Ave Oakwood (45419) **(G-15467)**
Trillium Health Care Products.....513 242-2227
5177 Spring Grove Ave Cincinnati (45217) **(G-4438)**
Trilogy Plastics Inc (PA).....330 821-4700
2290 W Main St Alliance (44601) **(G-511)**
Trilogy Plastics Inc.....440 893-5522
7160 Chagrin Rd Chagrin Falls (44023) **(G-3085)**
Trim Parts Inc.....513 934-0815
2175 Deerfield Rd Lebanon (45036) **(G-11702)**
Trim Systems Operating Corp (HQ).....614 289-5360
7800 Walton Pkwy New Albany (43054) **(G-14638)**
Trim Systems Operating Corp.....614 289-5360
7800 Walton Pkwy New Albany (43054) **(G-14639)**
Trim Systems Operating Corp.....740 772-5998
75 Chamber Dr Chillicothe (45601) **(G-3228)**
Trim Tool & Machine Inc.....216 889-1916
3431 Service Rd Cleveland (44111) **(G-6215)**
Trimble Inc.....937 233-8921
5475 Kellenburger Rd Dayton (45424) **(G-8566)**
Trimline Die Corporation.....440 355-6900
421 Commerce Dr E Lagrange (44050) **(G-11494)**
Trimold LLC.....740 474-7591
200 Pittsburgh Rd Circleville (43113) **(G-4563)**
Trinel Inc.....216 265-9190
5251 W 137th St Cleveland (44142) **(G-6216)**
Trinity Door Systems.....877 603-2018
13886 Woodworth Rd New Springfield (44443) **(G-14822)**
Trinity Highway Products Llc.....419 227-1296
425 E O Connor Ave Lima (45801) **(G-11953)**
Trinity Printing Co.....513 469-1000
2300 E Kemper Rd Ste A19 Cincinnati (45241) **(G-4439)**
Trio Insulated Glass Inc.....614 276-1647
1094 Mckinley Ave Columbus (43222) **(G-7544)**
Trionetics Inc.....216 812-3570
4924 Schaaf Ln Brooklyn Heights (44131) **(G-2133)**
Trionix Research Laboratory.....330 425-9055
8037 Bavaria Rd Twinsburg (44087) **(G-18867)**
Trip Transport LLC.....773 969-1402
2905 Sunbury Sq Columbus (43219) **(G-7545)**
Triple Arrow Industries Inc.....614 437-5588
13311 Industrial Pkwy Marysville (43040) **(G-12818)**
Triple Diamond Plastics LLC.....419 533-0085
405 N Pleasantview Dr Liberty Center (43532) **(G-11810)**
Triple J Oilfield Services LLC.....740 483-9030
42722 State Route 7 Hannibal (43931) **(G-10625)**
Triple T Fabricating, Byesville *Also called Timothy Sasser* **(G-2394)**
Triplett Bluffton Corporation.....419 358-8750
1 Triplett Dr Bluffton (45817) **(G-1896)**
Tripoint Instruments Inc.....513 702-9217
7513 Hamilton Ave Cincinnati (45231) **(G-4440)**
Tristan Rubber Molding Inc (PA).....330 499-4055
7255 Whipple Ave Nw North Canton (44720) **(G-15132)**
Triton Products LLC.....440 248-5480
30700 Carter St Ste D Solon (44139) **(G-17254)**
Triumph Signs & Consulting Inc.....513 576-8090
480 Milford Pkwy Milford (45150) **(G-14046)**
Triumph Thermal Systems LLC (HQ).....419 273-2511
200 Railroad St Forest (45843) **(G-9789)**
Triumph Tool LLC.....937 222-6885
229 Leo St Dayton (45404) **(G-8567)**
Triumphant Enterprises Inc.....513 617-1668
7096 Hill Station Rd Goshen (45122) **(G-10290)**
Trixies Pickles Inc.....817 658-6648
1978 Tiffin Ave Findlay (45840) **(G-9771)**
TRM Manufacturing Inc.....330 769-2600
601 Munroe Falls Ave Cuyahoga Falls (44221) **(G-7929)**
Trogdon Publishing Inc.....330 721-7678
5164 Normandy Park Dr # 100 Medina (44256) **(G-13355)**
Trojon Gear Inc.....937 254-1737
418 San Jose St Dayton (45403) **(G-8568)**
Trolios Silk Screening & EMB, Youngstown *Also called K & J Holdings Inc* **(G-20951)**
Tronair Inc (HQ).....419 866-6301
1 Air Cargo Pkwy E Swanton (43558) **(G-17926)**
Tronair Parent Inc (HQ).....419 866-6301
1 Air Cargo Pkwy E Swanton (43558) **(G-17927)**
Troo Clean Enviromental LLC.....304 215-4501
47096 Magee Rd Saint Clairsville (43950) **(G-16656)**
Trophy Nut Co (PA).....937 667-8478
320 N 2nd St Tipp City (45371) **(G-18139)**
Trophy Nut Co.....937 669-5513
1567 Harmony Dr Tipp City (45371) **(G-18140)**
Tropical Ohio Smoothie Inc.....937 673-6218
988 Miamisburg Centerville (45459) **(G-3006)**
Tropical Smoothie Cafe, Centerville *Also called Tropical Ohio Smoothie Inc* **(G-3006)**
Trotwood Corporation.....937 854-3047
11 N Broadway St Trotwood (45426) **(G-18631)**
Troy Daily News, Troy *Also called Aim Media Midwest Oper LLC* **(G-18633)**
Troy Engineered Components and.....937 335-8070
4900 Webster St Dayton (45414) **(G-8569)**
Troy Filters Ltd.....614 777-8222
1680 Westbelt Dr Columbus (43228) **(G-7546)**
Troy Innovative Instrs Inc.....440 834-9567
15111 White Rd Middlefield (44062) **(G-13859)**
Troy Laminating & Coating Inc.....937 335-5611
421 Union St Troy (45373) **(G-18714)**
Troy Manufacturing Co.....440 834-8262
17090 Rapids Rd Burton (44021) **(G-2373)**
Troy Precision Carbide Die.....440 834-4477
17720 Claridon Troy Rd Burton (44021) **(G-2374)**

ALPHABETIC SECTION
Tungsten Sltons Group Intl Inc

Troy Sand and Gravel, Troy *Also called Marietta Martin Materials Inc* ***(G-18686)***
Troy Screw Products 440 946-3381
7455 Clover Ave Mentor (44060) ***(G-13614)***
Troy Valley Petroleum 937 604-0012
201 Valley St Dayton (45404) ***(G-8570)***
Troy Water Treatment Plant, Troy *Also called City of Troy* ***(G-18641)***
Troy West LLC 937 339-2192
650 Olympic Dr Troy (45373) ***(G-18715)***
Troyer Cheese Inc 330 893-2479
6597 County Road 625 Millersburg (44654) ***(G-14139)***
Troyers Pallet Shop 330 897-1038
31052 Township Road 227 Fresno (43824) ***(G-10072)***
Troyers Trail Bologna Inc 330 893-2414
6552 State Route 515 Dundee (44624) ***(G-9029)***
Troyke Manufacturing Company 513 769-4242
11294 Orchard St Cincinnati (45241) ***(G-4441)***
Troymill Manufacturing Inc (PA) 440 632-5580
17055 Kinsman Rd Middlefield (44062) ***(G-13860)***
Troymill Wood Products, Middlefield *Also called Troymill Manufacturing Inc* ***(G-13860)***
Tru Comfort Mattress 614 595-8600
8994 Mediterra Pl Dublin (43016) ***(G-9006)***
Tru Form Metal Products Inc 216 252-3700
12305 Grimsby Ave Cleveland (44135) ***(G-6217)***
Tru-Chem Company Inc 614 888-2436
6645 Singletree Dr Columbus (43229) ***(G-7547)***
Tru-Edge Grinding Inc 419 678-4991
752 Jim Lachey Dr Saint Henry (45883) ***(G-16668)***
Tru-Fab Inc 937 435-1733
4751 Gateway Cir Dayton (45440) ***(G-8571)***
Tru-Fab Technology Inc 440 954-9760
34820 Lakeland Blvd Willoughby (44095) ***(G-20451)***
Tru-Form Steel & Wire Inc 765 348-5001
5509 Telegraph Rd Toledo (43612) ***(G-18583)***
Tru-Har Products 330 338-6826
7946 Darrow Rd Unit 334 Hudson (44236) ***(G-11080)***
Tru-Tex International Corp 513 825-8844
11050 Southland Rd Cincinnati (45240) ***(G-4442)***
Truax Printing Inc 419 994-4166
425 E Haskell St Loudonville (44842) ***(G-12149)***
Trucast Inc 440 942-4923
4382 Hamann Pkwy Willoughby (44094) ***(G-20452)***
Truck Fax Inc 216 921-8866
17700 S Woodland Rd Cleveland (44120) ***(G-6218)***
Truck Stop Embroidery (PA) 419 257-2860
12906 Deshler Rd North Baltimore (45872) ***(G-15048)***
Truck Stop Embroidery 419 257-2860
12906 Deshler Rd North Baltimore (45872) ***(G-15049)***
Truco Inc 216 631-1000
3033 W 44th St Cleveland (44113) ***(G-6219)***
Trucut Incorporated (PA) 330 938-9806
1145 Allied Dr Sebring (44672) ***(G-16896)***
True Defense Solutions LLC 330 325-1695
3265 State Route 44 Rootstown (44272) ***(G-16573)***
True Dinero Records & Tech LLC 513 428-4610
2611 Kemper Ln Uppr Lv1 Cincinnati (45206) ***(G-4443)***
True Grinding 440 786-7608
20502 Krick Rd Bedford (44146) ***(G-1452)***
True Industries Inc 330 296-4342
666 Pratt St Ravenna (44266) ***(G-16416)***
True Kote Inc 419 334-8813
2132 E Cole Rd Fremont (43420) ***(G-10056)***
True North Energy LLC 440 442-0060
6411 Mayfield Rd Mayfield Heights (44124) ***(G-13172)***
True Torq, Blanchester *Also called Fulflo Specialties Company* ***(G-1703)***
True Turn Industries 440 355-6256
233 Commerce Dr Unit D Lagrange (44050) ***(G-11495)***
True Value, North Baltimore *Also called Mid-Wood Inc* ***(G-15046)***
Truechoicepack Corp 937 630-3832
5155 Financial Way Ste 6 Mason (45040) ***(G-12951)***
Truenorth Energy, Mayfield Heights *Also called True North Energy LLC* ***(G-13172)***
Truex Tool & Die Div, Youngstown *Also called Jamen Tool & Die Co* ***(G-20945)***
Trufast, Bryan *Also called Altenloh Brinck & Co US Inc* ***(G-2263)***
Truflex Rubber Products Co 740 967-9015
200 E Coshocton St Johnstown (43031) ***(G-11273)***
Trugreen Cleaners LLC 740 703-1063
1733 Anderson Station Rd Chillicothe (45601) ***(G-3229)***
Truline Industries Inc 440 729-0140
11685 Chillicothe Rd Chesterland (44026) ***(G-3171)***
Trulite GL Alum Solutions LLC 614 876-1057
2395 Setterlin Dr Columbus (43228) ***(G-7548)***
Trumbull Cement Products Co 330 372-4342
2185 Larchmont Ave Ne Warren (44483) ***(G-19450)***
Trumbull County Hardwoods 440 632-0555
9446 Bundysburg Rd Middlefield (44062) ***(G-13861)***
Trumbull County Legal News 330 392-7112
108 Main Ave Sw Ste 700 Warren (44481) ***(G-19451)***
Trumbull Industries Inc 330 434-6174
209 Perkins St Akron (44304) ***(G-413)***
Trumbull Locker Plant Inc 440 474-4631
3393 State Route 534 Rock Creek (44084) ***(G-16534)***
Trumbull Manufacturing Inc 330 393-6624
400 Dietz Rd Ne Warren (44483) ***(G-19452)***
Trumbull Mobile Meals Inc 330 394-2538
323 E Market St Warren (44481) ***(G-19453)***
Trunk Show 330 565-5326
339 Imperial St Youngstown (44509) ***(G-21054)***
Trupoint Products 330 204-3302
Uknown Sugarcreek (44681) ***(G-17872)***
Truseal Technologies Inc (HQ) 216 910-1500
388 S Main St Ste 700 Akron (44311) ***(G-414)***
Truss Worx LLC 419 363-2100
12412 Frysinger Rd Rockford (45882) ***(G-16541)***
Trust Manufacturing LLC 216 531-8787
20080 Saint Clair Ave Euclid (44117) ***(G-9449)***
Trust Technologies, Eastlake *Also called Kilroy Company* ***(G-9117)***
Trutech Cabinetry 614 338-0680
2121 S James Rd Columbus (43232) ***(G-7549)***
Trv Incorporated 440 951-7722
4860 E 345th St Willoughby (44094) ***(G-20453)***
TRW Automotive Fayette Plant, Fayette *Also called TRW Automotive Inc* ***(G-9637)***
TRW Automotive Inc 419 237-2511
705 N Fayette St Fayette (43521) ***(G-9637)***
TRW Automotive Inc 216 750-2400
8333 Rockside Rd Cleveland (44125) ***(G-6220)***
TRW Shared Services, Cleveland *Also called TRW Automotive Inc* ***(G-6220)***
TS Defense LLC 740 446-7716
214 Buck Ridge Rd Bidwell (45614) ***(G-1671)***
TS Engineering, Washingtonville *Also called Turvey Engineering* ***(G-19481)***
TS Sales LLC 727 804-8060
255 Neal Ave Mount Gilead (43338) ***(G-14435)***
TS Tech USA Corporation (HQ) 614 577-1088
8400 E Broad St Reynoldsburg (43068) ***(G-16458)***
TS Trim Industries Inc 614 837-4114
6380 Canal St Canal Winchester (43110) ***(G-2514)***
TS Trim Industries Inc 740 593-5958
10 Kenny Dr Athens (45701) ***(G-852)***
Tsjmedia, Blue Ash *Also called Gate West Coast Ventures LLC* ***(G-1781)***
Tsk America Co Ltd 513 942-4002
9668 Inter Ocean Dr West Chester (45246) ***(G-19909)***
Tsp Inc 513 732-8900
2009 Glenn Pkwy Batavia (45103) ***(G-1191)***
TSR Machinery Services Inc 513 874-9697
100 Security Dr Fairfield (45014) ***(G-9570)***
TSS Acquisition Company 513 772-7000
1201 Hill Smith Dr Cincinnati (45215) ***(G-4444)***
Tsw Industries Inc 440 572-7200
14960 Foltz Pkwy Strongsville (44149) ***(G-17802)***
TTI Floor Care North Amer Inc (HQ) 440 996-2000
7005 Cochran Rd Solon (44139) ***(G-17255)***
TTI Sports Equipment, Columbus *Also called Total Tennis Inc* ***(G-7535)***
Ttm, North Jackson *Also called Cleveland Coretec Inc* ***(G-15144)***
Ttm Technologies Inc 330 538-3900
12080 Debartolo Dr North Jackson (44451) ***(G-15156)***
Ttr Manufacturing 440 366-5005
740 Sugar Ln Elyria (44035) ***(G-9339)***
Tubar Eureka Industrial Group, Sugarcreek *Also called Belden Brick Company* ***(G-17842)***
Tube Fitting, Lewisburg *Also called Parker-Hannifin Corporation* ***(G-11796)***
Tube Fittings Division, Columbus *Also called Parker-Hannifin Corporation* ***(G-7294)***
Tube Fittings Division, Lewisburg *Also called Parker-Hannifin Corporation* ***(G-11797)***
Tubetech Inc (PA) 330 426-9476
900 E Taggart St East Palestine (44413) ***(G-9087)***
Tubetech North America, East Palestine *Also called Tubetech Inc* ***(G-9087)***
Tuboscope Pipeline Svcs Inc 530 695-3569
2199 E 28th St Lorain (44055) ***(G-12130)***
Tubular Techniques Inc 614 529-4130
3025 Scioto Darby Exec Ct Hilliard (43026) ***(G-10872)***
Tuckers Mold Polishing 937 339-3063
3225 E Peterson Rd Troy (45373) ***(G-18716)***
Tuf-N-Lite, Liberty Twp *Also called Feather Lite Innovations Inc* ***(G-11825)***
Tuf-N-Lite, Springboro *Also called Feather Lite Innovations Inc* ***(G-17327)***
Tuf-Tex, Norwalk *Also called Maple City Rubber Company* ***(G-15405)***
Tuf-Tug Products Div, Moraine *Also called Deuer Developments Inc* ***(G-14345)***
Tuff Stuff Performance, Cleveland *Also called Hurst Auto-Truck Electric* ***(G-5426)***
Tuffy Manufacturing 330 940-2356
140 Ascot Pkwy Cuyahoga Falls (44223) ***(G-7930)***
Tuffy Pad Company Inc 330 688-0043
454 Seasons Rd Stow (44224) ***(G-17639)***
Tune Town Car Audio 419 627-1100
2345 E Perkins Ave Sandusky (44870) ***(G-16857)***
Tungsten and Capital, Solon *Also called Bowes Manufacturing Inc* ***(G-17117)***
Tungsten Capital Partners LLC 216 481-4774
30340 Solon Industrial Pk Cleveland (44139) ***(G-6221)***
Tungsten Sltons Group Intl Inc 440 708-3096
17523 Merry Oaks Trl Chagrin Falls (44023) ***(G-3086)***

ALPHABETIC

Tunnel Vision Hoops LLC 440 487-0939
3558 Lee Rd Shaker Heights (44120) ***(G-16939)***
Tunnell Hill Reclamation, New Lexington *Also called Oxford Mining Company Inc* ***(G-14719)***
Tuppas Software Corporation 419 897-7902
1690 Woodlands Dr Maumee (43537) ***(G-13156)***
Turbine Eng Cmpnents Tech Corp 216 692-6173
23555 Euclid Ave Cleveland (44117) ***(G-6222)***
Turbine Standard Ltd (PA) 419 865-0355
10550 Industrial St Holland (43528) ***(G-10964)***
Turbo Machine & Tool Inc 216 651-1940
2151 W 117th St Cleveland (44111) ***(G-6223)***
Turbo-Mold Inc 440 352-2530
440 Blackbrook Rd Painesville (44077) ***(G-15792)***
Turbos FBC LLC 614 245-4840
1050 Beecher Xing N Columbus (43230) ***(G-7550)***
Turf Care Supply Corp (HQ) 877 220-1014
50 Pearl Rd Ste 200 Brunswick (44212) ***(G-2247)***
Turk+hillinger Usa Inc 440 781-1900
6650 W Snowville Rd Ste W Brecksville (44141) ***(G-2062)***
Turkeyfoot Creek Creamery 419 335-0224
11313 County Road D Wauseon (43567) ***(G-19535)***
Turkeyfoot Hill Sand & Gravel 330 899-1997
465 E Turkeyfoot Lake Rd Akron (44319) ***(G-415)***
Turkeyfoot Printing, Napoleon *Also called Mustang Printing* ***(G-14551)***
Turn-All Machine & Gear Co 937 342-8710
5499 Tremont Ln Springfield (45502) ***(G-17510)***
Turn-Key Industrial Svcs LLC 614 274-1128
820 Distribution Dr Columbus (43228) ***(G-7551)***
Turn-Key Tunneling Inc 614 275-4832
1247 Stimmel Rd Columbus (43223) ***(G-7552)***
Turner Lightning Protection Co 614 738-6225
5193 Dry Creek Dr Dublin (43016) ***(G-9007)***
Turner Machine Co 330 332-5821
1433 Salem Pkwy Salem (44460) ***(G-16778)***
Turner Pressure 614 871-7775
3997 Thistlewood Dr Grove City (43123) ***(G-10479)***
Turner Vault Co 419 537-1133
2121 Tracy Rd Northwood (43619) ***(G-15349)***
Turning Technologies LLC (PA) 330 746-3015
255 W Federal St Youngstown (44503) ***(G-21055)***
Turnkey Technology Sales, Cincinnati *Also called Ela Holding Corporation* ***(G-3631)***
Turnwood Industries Inc 330 278-2421
365 State Rd Hinckley (44233) ***(G-10907)***
Turtlecreek Township 513 932-4080
670 N Rte 123 Lebanon (45036) ***(G-11703)***
Turvey Engineering 330 427-0125
240 High St Washingtonville (44490) ***(G-19481)***
Tusco Hardwoods LLC 330 852-4281
10887 Gerber Valley Rd Nw Sugarcreek (44681) ***(G-17873)***
Tutto Vino, Dublin *Also called Muirfield Wine Company LLC* ***(G-8949)***
Tvh Parts Co 877 755-7311
8756 Global Way West Chester (45069) ***(G-19813)***
TW Corporation 440 461-3234
99 S Seiberling St Akron (44305) ***(G-416)***
TW Tank LLC 419 334-2664
721 Graham Dr Fremont (43420) ***(G-10057)***
TW Tank LLC 419 334-2664
721 Graham Dr Fremont (43420) ***(G-10058)***
Tween Brands Inc 937 435-6928
2700 Mmsburg Cntrville Rd Dayton (45459) ***(G-8572)***
Twenty Second Cntury Foods LLC 419 866-6343
6546 Weatherfield Ct C Maumee (43537) ***(G-13157)***
Twg Noodle Company LLC 419 560-2033
1151 State Route 61 Marengo (43334) ***(G-12596)***
Twin Cities Concrete Co (HQ) 330 343-4491
141 S Tuscarawas Ave Dover (44622) ***(G-8861)***
Twin Cities Concrete Co 330 627-2158
1031 Kensington Rd Ne Carrollton (44615) ***(G-2931)***
Twin Design AP Promotions Ltd 937 732-6798
5785 Far Hills Ave Dayton (45429) ***(G-8573)***
Twin Fin, Austinburg *Also called Multi-Design Inc* ***(G-923)***
Twin Oaks Barn 330 893-3126
3337 Us Route 62 Dundee (44624) ***(G-9030)***
Twin Point Inc (PA) 419 923-7525
11955 County Road 10 2 Delta (43515) ***(G-8778)***
Twin Rivers Technologies Mfg, Painesville *Also called Twin Rvers Tech - Pnsville LLC* ***(G-15793)***
Twin Rvers Tech - Pnsville LLC 440 350-6300
679 Hardy Rd Painesville (44077) ***(G-15793)***
Twin Tool LLC 937 435-8946
4648 Gateway Cir Dayton (45440) ***(G-8574)***
Twin Valley Metalcraft Asm LLC 937 787-4634
4739 Enterprise Rd West Alexandria (45381) ***(G-19622)***
Twin Ventures Inc 330 405-3838
2457 Edison Blvd Twinsburg (44087) ***(G-18868)***
Twinsburg Development Corp (PA) 440 357-5562
20389 1st Ave Cleveland (44130) ***(G-6224)***
Twinsource LLC 440 248-6800
32333 Aurora Rd Ste 50 Solon (44139) ***(G-17256)***

Twist Inc (PA) 937 675-9581
47 S Limestone St Jamestown (45335) ***(G-11221)***
Twist Inc 937 675-9581
5100 Waynesville Jamestown (45335) ***(G-11222)***
Twister Displays, East Liverpool *Also called Delta Manufacturing Inc* ***(G-9056)***
Two Bandits Brewing Co LLC 419 636-4045
206 Scott Dr Bryan (43506) ***(G-2310)***
Two Grandmothers Gourmet Kit 614 746-0888
9127 Firstgate Dr Reynoldsburg (43068) ***(G-16459)***
Two M Precision Co Inc 440 946-2120
1747 Joseph Lloyd Pkwy # 3 Willoughby (44094) ***(G-20454)***
Two Tin Cans LLC 419 692-2027
21623 Lehman Rd Delphos (45833) ***(G-8759)***
Tyjen Inc (PA) 740 380-3215
35255 Hocking Dr Logan (43138) ***(G-12045)***
Tyjen Inc 740 797-4064
8 Slater Dr The Plains (45780) ***(G-18023)***
Tykma Inc 877 318-9562
370 Gateway Dr Chillicothe (45601) ***(G-3230)***
Tykma Electrox, Chillicothe *Also called Tykma Inc* ***(G-3230)***
Tyler Electric Motor Repair 330 836-5537
1888 Copley Rd Akron (44320) ***(G-417)***
Tyler Elevator Products, Twinsburg *Also called Sematic Usa Inc* ***(G-18855)***
Tyler Grain & Fertilizer Co 330 669-2341
3388 Eby Rd Smithville (44677) ***(G-17095)***
Tyler Haver Inc (HQ) 440 974-1047
8570 Tyler Blvd Mentor (44060) ***(G-13615)***
Tyler Haver Inc 800 255-1259
8570 Tyler Blvd Mentor (44060) ***(G-13616)***
Tylok International Inc 216 261-7310
1061 E 260th St Cleveland (44132) ***(G-6225)***
Tymex Plastics Inc 216 429-8950
5300 Harvard Ave Cleveland (44105) ***(G-6226)***
Tymoca Partners LLC 440 946-4327
33220 Lakeland Blvd Eastlake (44095) ***(G-9137)***
Tyseka 419 860-9585
1021 Brower Rd Lima (45801) ***(G-11954)***
Tytek Industries Inc (PA) 513 874-7326
4700 Ashwood Dr Ste 445 Blue Ash (45241) ***(G-1862)***
U C Printing Service, Cincinnati *Also called University of Cincinnati* ***(G-4454)***
U C Signs, Unionville Center *Also called Unionville Center Sign Co* ***(G-18938)***
U C X, Cleveland *Also called Undercar Express LLC* ***(G-6229)***
U D F, Cincinnati *Also called United Dairy Farmers Inc* ***(G-4447)***
U M D Automated Systems Inc 740 694-8614
9855 Salem Rd Fredericktown (43019) ***(G-9981)***
U S Alloy Die Corp 216 749-9700
4007 Brookpark Rd Cleveland (44134) ***(G-6227)***
U S Army Corps of Engineers 740 537-2571
29501 State Rte 7 Toronto (43964) ***(G-18613)***
U S Chemical & Plastics 740 254-4311
600 Nova Dr Se Massillon (44646) ***(G-13055)***
U S Chrome Corporation Ohio 877 872-7716
107 Westboro St Dayton (45417) ***(G-8575)***
U S Development Corp 570 966-5990
900 W Main St Kent (44240) ***(G-11397)***
U S Development Corp (PA) 330 673-6900
900 W Main St Kent (44240) ***(G-11398)***
U S Fuel Development Co (PA) 614 486-0614
1445 Goodale Blvd Columbus (43212) ***(G-7553)***
U S Graphics, Urbana *Also called David Brandeberry* ***(G-18988)***
U S Hair Inc 614 235-5190
3727 E Broad St Columbus (43213) ***(G-7554)***
U S M, Wickliffe *Also called Usm Precision Products Inc* ***(G-20236)***
U S Terminals Inc 513 561-8145
7504 Camargo Rd Cincinnati (45243) ***(G-4445)***
U S Thermal Inc 513 777-7763
9846 Crescent Park Dr West Chester (45069) ***(G-19814)***
U S Weatherford L P 330 746-2502
1100 Performance Pl Youngstown (44502) ***(G-21056)***
U-Sonico 423 348-7117
543 Cookston Ave Springfield (45503) ***(G-17511)***
U.S. Bridge, Cambridge *Also called Ohio Bridge Corporation* ***(G-2451)***
Uc Trailer Co., Sunbury *Also called Universal Composite LLC* ***(G-17901)***
UCAR Carbon, Brooklyn Heights *Also called Graftech Intl Holdings Inc* ***(G-2125)***
Ucg Technologies, Independence *Also called United Computer Group Inc* ***(G-11153)***
UCI, North Canton *Also called United Components LLC* ***(G-15133)***
Udderly Smooth, Salem *Also called Redex Industries Inc* ***(G-16770)***
Udecx LLC 877 698-3329
320 N 4th St Tipp City (45371) ***(G-18141)***
Ufp Blanchester LLC 937 783-2443
940 Cherry St Blanchester (45107) ***(G-1707)***
Ufp Hamilton LLC 513 285-7190
115 Distribution Dr Hamilton (45014) ***(G-10616)***
Ugn Inc 513 360-3500
201 Exploration Dr Lebanon (45036) ***(G-11704)***
Uhrichsville Carbide Inc 740 922-9197
410 N Water St Uhrichsville (44683) ***(G-18899)***
UIC West Chester Plant, West Chester *Also called Usui International Corporation* ***(G-19817)***

Ulrich Rubber Stamp Company ... 419 339-9939
2130 Larkspur Dr Elida (45807) *(G-9202)*
Ultimate Chem Solutions Inc ... 440 998-6751
1800 E 21st St Ashtabula (44004) *(G-809)*
Ultimate Cloth, Plain City *Also called Advanced Cleaning Tech LLC* *(G-16169)*
Ultimate Pallet & Trucking LLC ... 440 693-4090
4774 Parks West Rd Middlefield (44062) *(G-13862)*
Ultimate Printing Co Inc ... 330 847-2941
6090 Mahoning Ave Nw C Warren (44481) *(G-19454)*
Ultimate Rb Inc (HQ) ... 419 692-3000
1430 N Main St Delphos (45833) *(G-8760)*
Ultimate Signs and Graphics ... 740 633-8928
904 Indiana St Martins Ferry (43935) *(G-12762)*
Ultra Graphics, Cleveland *Also called Gail Zeilmann* *(G-5286)*
Ultra Impressions Inc ... 440 951-4777
7533 Tyler Blvd Ste D Mentor (44060) *(G-13617)*
Ultra Machine Inc ... 440 323-7632
530 Lowell St Elyria (44035) *(G-9340)*
Ultra Premium Oilfld Svcs Ltd ... 330 448-3683
6880 Parkway Dr Brookfield (44403) *(G-2110)*
Ultra Printing & Design Inc ... 440 887-0393
707 Brookpark Rd Ste 3 Cleveland (44109) *(G-6228)*
Ultra Tech Machinery Inc ... 330 929-5544
297 Ascot Pkwy Cuyahoga Falls (44223) *(G-7931)*
Ultra-Met Company ... 937 653-7133
720 N Main St Urbana (43078) *(G-19017)*
Ultra-Met Company ... 937 653-7133
120 Fyffe St Urbana (43078) *(G-19018)*
Ultrabuilt Play Systems Inc ... 419 652-2294
1114 Us Highway 224 Nova (44859) *(G-15436)*
Ultratech Polymers Inc ... 330 945-9410
280 Ascot Pkwy Cuyahoga Falls (44223) *(G-7932)*
Umami Seasonings LLC ... 614 687-0315
4996 Tamarack Blvd Columbus (43229) *(G-7555)*
Umd Contractors Inc ... 740 694-8614
9855 Salem Rd Fredericktown (43019) *(G-9982)*
Umecc, West Chester *Also called Mecc-Usa LLC* *(G-19742)*
Umicore Spclty Mtls Recycl LLC ... 440 833-3000
28960 Lakeland Blvd Wickliffe (44092) *(G-20233)*
Unarco Material Handling Inc ... 419 384-3211
407 E Washington St Pandora (45877) *(G-15807)*
Unbridled Brewing Company LLC ... 937 361-2573
3387 Cincinnati Dayton Rd Middletown (45044) *(G-13961)*
Uncle Jesters Fine Foods LLC ... 937 550-1025
2564 Kohnle Dr Miamisburg (45342) *(G-13729)*
Under Armour Inc ... 330 995-9557
549 S Chillicothe Rd # 355 Aurora (44202) *(G-912)*
Under Hill Water Well ... 740 852-0858
1789 Itawamba Trl London (43140) *(G-12071)*
Under Pressure Systems Inc ... 330 602-4466
322 North Ave Ne New Philadelphia (44663) *(G-14807)*
Undercar Express LLC ... 216 531-7004
18451 Euclid Ave Cleveland (44112) *(G-6229)*
Underground Sport Shop Inc ... 513 751-1662
1233 Findlay St Ste Frnt Cincinnati (45214) *(G-4446)*
Undiscovered Radio Network ... 740 533-1032
621 S 6th St Ironton (45638) *(G-11174)*
Unger Kosher Bakery Inc ... 216 321-7176
1831 S Taylor Rd Cleveland Heights (44118) *(G-6352)*
Ungers Bakery, Cleveland Heights *Also called Unger Kosher Bakery Inc* *(G-6352)*
UNI-Facs, Columbus *Also called Universal Fabg Cnstr Svcs Inc* *(G-7561)*
Unibat, Cleveland *Also called Cleanlife Energy LLC* *(G-4941)*
Unibilt Industries Inc ... 937 890-7570
8005 Johnson Station Rd Vandalia (45377) *(G-19147)*
Unican Ohio LLC ... 419 636-5461
4600 Oak Harbor Rd Fremont (43420) *(G-10059)*
Unicontrol Inc (PA) ... 216 398-0330
1111 Brookpark Rd Cleveland (44109) *(G-6230)*
Unified Screening & Crushing ... 937 836-3201
200 Cass Dr Englewood (45315) *(G-9380)*
Unifin Chesapeake, Salem *Also called Cardinal Pumps Exchangers Inc* *(G-16723)*
Uniloy Milacron Inc ... 513 487-5000
4165 Half Acre Rd Batavia (45103) *(G-1192)*
Uninterrupted LLC ... 216 771-2323
3800 Embassy Pkwy Ste 360 Akron (44333) *(G-418)*
Union America, Cincinnati *Also called United Precision Services Inc* *(G-4449)*
Union Camp Corp ... 330 343-7701
875 Harger St Dover (44622) *(G-8862)*
Union Carbide Corporation ... 216 529-3784
11709 Madison Ave Cleveland (44107) *(G-6231)*
Union Enterprises Division, Plain City *Also called Gold Metal Machining Inc* *(G-16195)*
Union Fabricating & Machine Co ... 419 626-5963
3427 Venice Rd Sandusky (44870) *(G-16858)*
Union Flonetics, Salem *Also called Hunt Valve Company Inc* *(G-16749)*
Union Gospel Press Division, Cleveland *Also called Incorporated Trst Gspl Wk Scty* *(G-5448)*
Union Metal Industries Corp ... 330 456-7653
1432 Maple Ave Ne Canton (44705) *(G-2846)*
Union Process Inc ... 330 929-3333
1925 Akron Peninsula Rd Akron (44313) *(G-419)*
Union Sewing Company, Akron *Also called Jordan E Armour* *(G-226)*
Uniontown Septic Tanks Inc ... 330 699-3386
2781 Raber Rd Uniontown (44685) *(G-18936)*
Unionville Center Sign Co ... 614 873-5834
110 W Main St Unionville Center (43077) *(G-18938)*
Unipac Inc ... 740 929-2000
2109 National Rd Sw Hebron (43025) *(G-10769)*
Unique Awards & Signs, Saint Marys *Also called Behrco Inc* *(G-16676)*
Unique Covers ... 419 925-9600
8758 State Route 119 Maria Stein (45860) *(G-12601)*
UNIQUE EXPRESSIONS, Gallipolis *Also called Riverview Productions Inc* *(G-10174)*
Unique Fabrications Inc ... 419 355-1700
2520 Hayes Ave Fremont (43420) *(G-10060)*
Unique Led Products LLC ... 440 520-4959
200 Chestnut Ave Northfield (44067) *(G-15329)*
Unique Packaging & Printing ... 440 785-6730
9086 Goldfinch Ct Mentor (44060) *(G-13618)*
Unique Paving Materials Corp ... 216 341-7711
3993 E 93rd St Cleveland (44105) *(G-6232)*
Unique Plastics LLC ... 419 352-0066
13350 Bishop Rd Bowling Green (43402) *(G-2003)*
Unique Solutions, Newark *Also called Holophane Corporation* *(G-14883)*
Unique Straight Line & Sfety S ... 740 452-2724
2776 Coopermill Rd Zanesville (43701) *(G-21185)*
Unique Woodmasters LLC ... 419 268-9663
6750 Guadalupe Rd Celina (45822) *(G-2990)*
Unique-Chardan Inc ... 419 636-6900
705 S Union St Bryan (43506) *(G-2311)*
Unisand Incorporated ... 330 722-0222
1097 Industrial Pkwy Medina (44256) *(G-13356)*
Unison Industries LLC ... 937 426-0621
2070 Heller Rd Alpha (45301) *(G-517)*
Unison Industries LLC ... 904 667-9904
2455 Dayton Xenia Rd Dayton (45434) *(G-7994)*
Unison Industries LLC ... 937 426-4676
530 Orchard Ln Alpha (45301) *(G-518)*
Unison Industries LLC ... 937 427-0550
2070 Heller Dr Beavercreek (45434) *(G-1345)*
Unison Industries LLC ... 937 426-0621
2156 Heller Dr Beavercreek (45434) *(G-1346)*
Unisport Inc ... 419 529-4727
2254 Stumbo Rd Ontario (44906) *(G-15549)*
Unit Dle, Eastlake *Also called Lange Equipment* *(G-9120)*
Unit Sets Inc ... 937 840-6123
835 S High St Hillsboro (45133) *(G-10892)*
United Auto Worker AFL CIO ... 419 592-0434
410 Fillmore St Napoleon (43545) *(G-14563)*
United Buff & Supply Co Inc ... 419 738-2417
2 E Harrison St Wapakoneta (45895) *(G-19357)*
United Chart Processors Inc ... 740 373-5801
1461 Masonic Park Rd Marietta (45750) *(G-12686)*
United Circuits Inc ... 440 926-1000
1000 Commerce Dr Grafton (44044) *(G-10312)*
United Components LLC (HQ) ... 812 867-4516
2100 International Pkwy North Canton (44720) *(G-15133)*
United Computer Group Inc (PA) ... 216 520-1333
7100 E Pleasant Valley Rd # 250 Independence (44131) *(G-11153)*
United Controls Group Inc ... 740 936-0005
400 Lazelle Rd Ste 14 Columbus (43240) *(G-6507)*
United Converting Inc ... 614 863-9972
3960 Groves Rd Unit B Columbus (43232) *(G-7556)*
United Dairy Inc (PA) ... 740 633-1451
300 N 5th St Martins Ferry (43935) *(G-12763)*
United Dairy Farmers Inc (PA) ... 513 396-8700
3955 Montgomery Rd Cincinnati (45212) *(G-4447)*
United Dental Laboratories (PA) ... 330 253-1810
261 South Ave Tallmadge (44278) *(G-18010)*
United Die & Mfg Co ... 330 938-6141
100 S 17th St Sebring (44672) *(G-16897)*
United Engineering & Fndry Co ... 330 456-2761
1400 Grace Ave Ne Canton (44705) *(G-2847)*
United Engraving, Cincinnati *Also called Wood Graphics Inc* *(G-4516)*
United Envelope LLC ... 513 542-4700
4890 Spring Grove Ave Cincinnati (45232) *(G-4448)*
United Extrusion Dies Inc ... 330 533-2915
5171 W Western Reserve Rd Canfield (44406) *(G-2552)*
United Feed Screws Ltd ... 330 798-5532
487 Wellington Ave Akron (44305) *(G-420)*
United Fiberglass America Inc ... 937 325-7305
2145 Airpark Dr Springfield (45502) *(G-17512)*
United Finshg & Die Cutng Inc ... 216 881-0239
3875 King Ave Cleveland (44114) *(G-6233)*
United Fire Apparatus Corp ... 419 645-4083
204 S Gay St Cridersville (45806) *(G-7813)*
United Graphics, Cincinnati *Also called Cns Inc* *(G-3533)*
United Grinding and Machine Co ... 330 453-7402
2315 Ellis Ave Ne Canton (44705) *(G-2848)*

ALPHABETIC

(PA)=Parent Co (HQ)=Headquarters (DH)=Div Headquarters
2019 Harris Ohio Industrial Directory
1277

United Grinding North Amer Inc (HQ)....937 859-1975
2100 United Grinding Blvd Miamisburg (45342) ***(G-13730)***
United Group Services Inc (PA)....800 633-9690
9740 Near Dr West Chester (45246) ***(G-19910)***
United Hard Chrome Corporation....330 453-2786
2202 Gilbert Ave Ne Canton (44705) ***(G-2849)***
United Hardwoods Ltd....330 878-9510
5508 Hilltop Dr Nw Strasburg (44680) ***(G-17655)***
United Hydraulics, Willoughby *Also called Two M Precision Co Inc* ***(G-20454)***
United Hydraulics....440 585-0906
29627 Lakeland Blvd Wickliffe (44092) ***(G-20234)***
United Ignition Wire Corp....216 898-1112
15620 Industrial Pkwy Cleveland (44135) ***(G-6234)***
United Initiators Inc (HQ)....440 326-2416
555 Garden St Elyria (44035) ***(G-9341)***
United Machine and Tool Inc....440 946-7677
1956 E 337th St Eastlake (44095) ***(G-9138)***
United McGill....614 829-1226
1777 Refugee Rd Columbus (43207) ***(G-7557)***
United McGill Corporation (HQ)....614 829-1200
1 Mission Park Groveport (43125) ***(G-10516)***
United Medical Supply Company....866 678-8633
708 Marks Rd Ste 308 Valley City (44280) ***(G-19068)***
United Metal Fabricators Inc....216 662-2000
14301 Industrial Ave S Maple Heights (44137) ***(G-12582)***
United Packaging Supply Co Div, Bedford *Also called Overseas Packing LLC* ***(G-1434)***
United Precast Inc....740 393-1121
400 Howard St Mount Vernon (43050) ***(G-14516)***
United Precision Services Inc....513 851-6900
11180 Southland Rd Cincinnati (45240) ***(G-4449)***
United Prtrs & Lithographers....216 771-2759
1045 French St Cleveland (44113) ***(G-6235)***
United Quality Chekd Dairy, Martins Ferry *Also called United Dairy Inc* ***(G-12763)***
United Ready Mix Inc....216 696-1600
7820 Carnegie Ave Cleveland (44103) ***(G-6236)***
United Rolls Inc (HQ)....330 456-2761
1400 Grace Ave Ne Canton (44705) ***(G-2850)***
United Rotary Brush Inc....937 644-3515
8150 Business Way Plain City (43064) ***(G-16214)***
United Safety Authority, Warren *Also called D M V Supply Corporation* ***(G-19393)***
United Seal Company, Columbus *Also called United Security Seals Inc* ***(G-7558)***
United Security Seals Inc (PA)....614 443-7633
2000 Fairwood Ave Columbus (43207) ***(G-7558)***
United Sport Apparel....330 722-0818
229 Harding St Ste B Medina (44256) ***(G-13357)***
United State Pltg Bumper Svc....614 403-4666
1937 W Dblin Granville Rd Worthington (43085) ***(G-20706)***
United States Dept of Army....419 221-9500
1155 Buckeye Rd Lima (45804) ***(G-11955)***
United States Dept of Army....330 358-7311
8451 State Route 5 Ravenna (44266) ***(G-16417)***
United States Drill Head Co....513 941-0300
5298 River Rd Cincinnati (45233) ***(G-4450)***
United States Endoscopy....440 639-4494
6091 Heisley Rd Mentor (44060) ***(G-13619)***
United States Gypsum Company....419 734-3161
121 S Lake St Gypsum (43433) ***(G-10521)***
United States Steel Corp....440 240-2500
2199 E 28th St Lorain (44055) ***(G-12131)***
United Surface Finishing Inc....330 453-2786
2202 Gilbert Ave Ne Canton (44705) ***(G-2851)***
United Taconite LLC (HQ)....218 744-7800
1100 Superior Ave E # 1500 Cleveland (44114) ***(G-6237)***
United Titanium Inc (PA)....330 264-2111
3450 Old Airport Rd Wooster (44691) ***(G-20661)***
United Tool and Machine Inc....937 843-5603
490 N Main St Lakeview (43331) ***(G-11505)***
United Tool Supply Inc....513 752-6000
851 Ohio Pike Ste 101 Cincinnati (45245) ***(G-3266)***
United Tube Corporation....330 725-4196
960 Lake Rd Medina (44256) ***(G-13358)***
United Wire Edm Inc....440 239-8777
777 Berea Industrial Pkwy Berea (44017) ***(G-1630)***
United Wood Products, Youngstown *Also called Ictm Inc* ***(G-20936)***
United-Maier Signs Inc....513 681-6600
1030 Straight St Cincinnati (45214) ***(G-4451)***
Unitherm Inc....937 278-1900
601 Norgal Dr Lebanon (45036) ***(G-11705)***
Unitus, Solon *Also called Sensical Inc* ***(G-17229)***
Unity Cable Technologies Inc....419 322-4118
1811 Adams St Toledo (43604) ***(G-18584)***
Unity Defense Systems, Toledo *Also called Unity Cable Technologies Inc* ***(G-18584)***
Unity Enterprises Inc....614 231-1370
3757 Courtright Ct Columbus (43227) ***(G-7559)***
Unity Tube Inc....330 426-4282
1862 State Route 165 East Palestine (44413) ***(G-9088)***
Univar USA Inc....513 714-5264
4600 Dues Dr West Chester (45246) ***(G-19911)***
Universal Bindery, Toledo *Also called Fergusons Finishing Inc* ***(G-18293)***
Universal Black Oxiding, Cleveland *Also called Universal Heat Treating Inc* ***(G-6238)***
Universal Cargo, Cleveland *Also called Acme Lifting Products Inc* ***(G-4606)***
Universal Coatings Division, Twinsburg *Also called Universal Rack & Equipment Co* ***(G-18870)***
Universal Composite LLC....614 507-1646
200 Kintner Pkwy Sunbury (43074) ***(G-17901)***
Universal Drect Flfllment Corp....330 650-5000
5581 Hudson Indus Pkwy Hudson (44236) ***(G-11081)***
Universal Dsign Fbrication LLC....419 359-1794
5619 Skadden Rd Sandusky (44870) ***(G-16859)***
Universal Electronics Inc....330 487-1110
1864 Entp Pkwy Ste B Twinsburg (44087) ***(G-18869)***
Universal Equipment Mfg....614 586-1780
2140 Advance Ave Columbus (43207) ***(G-7560)***
Universal Fabg Cnstr Svcs Inc....614 274-1128
1241 Mckinley Ave Columbus (43222) ***(G-7561)***
Universal Fabrication Assembly, Cleveland *Also called Wire Products Company Inc* ***(G-6315)***
Universal Forest Products, Dayton *Also called Idx Dayton LLC* ***(G-8260)***
Universal Forest Products, Blanchester *Also called Ufp Blanchester LLC* ***(G-1707)***
Universal Forest Products, Hamilton *Also called Ufp Hamilton LLC* ***(G-10616)***
Universal Heat Treating Inc....216 641-2000
3878 E 93rd St Cleveland (44105) ***(G-6238)***
Universal Hydraulik USA Corp....419 873-6340
25651 Fort Meigs Rd Ste A Perrysburg (43551) ***(G-16020)***
Universal Industrial Pdts Inc....419 737-9584
1 Coreway Dr Pioneer (43554) ***(G-16097)***
Universal J&Z Machine LLC....216 486-2220
4781 E 355th St Willoughby (44094) ***(G-20455)***
Universal Lettering Company, Van Wert *Also called Universal Lettering Inc* ***(G-19109)***
Universal Lettering Inc....419 238-9320
1197 Grill Rd B Van Wert (45891) ***(G-19109)***
Universal Machine, Willoughby *Also called Usm Acquisition Corporation* ***(G-20457)***
Universal Machine Products....513 860-4530
9060 Goldpark Dr West Chester (45011) ***(G-19815)***
Universal Metal Products Inc (PA)....440 943-3040
29980 Lakeland Blvd Wickliffe (44092) ***(G-20235)***
Universal Metal Products Inc....419 287-3223
850 W Front St Pemberville (43450) ***(G-15887)***
Universal Metals Cutting Inc....330 580-5192
2656 Harrison Ave Sw Canton (44706) ***(G-2852)***
Universal Oil Inc....216 771-4300
265 Jefferson Ave Cleveland (44113) ***(G-6239)***
Universal Packg Systems Inc....513 732-2000
5055 State Route 276 Batavia (45103) ***(G-1193)***
Universal Packg Systems Inc....513 674-9400
470 Northland Blvd Cincinnati (45240) ***(G-4452)***
Universal Packg Systems Inc....513 735-4777
5069 State Route 276 Batavia (45103) ***(G-1194)***
Universal Pallets Inc (PA)....614 444-1095
659 Marion Rd Columbus (43207) ***(G-7562)***
Universal Pallets Inc....614 444-1095
611 Marion Rd Columbus (43207) ***(G-7563)***
Universal Percussion Inc....330 482-5750
1431 Heck Rd Columbiana (44408) ***(G-6484)***
Universal Plastics, North Canton *Also called Upl International Inc* ***(G-15134)***
Universal Plastics - Sajar....440 632-5203
15285 S State Ave Middlefield (44062) ***(G-13863)***
Universal Polymer & Rubber Ltd....330 633-1666
165 Northeast Ave Tallmadge (44278) ***(G-18011)***
Universal Polymer & Rubber Ltd (PA)....440 632-1691
15730 Madison Rd Middlefield (44062) ***(G-13864)***
Universal Precision Products....330 633-6128
1480 Industrial Pkwy Akron (44310) ***(G-421)***
Universal Prototype Product Co....440 953-3550
36781 Lake Shore Blvd Eastlake (44095) ***(G-9139)***
Universal Rack & Equipment Co....330 963-6776
8511 Tower Dr Twinsburg (44087) ***(G-18870)***
Universal Rubber & Plastics, Tallmadge *Also called Universal Polymer & Rubber Ltd* ***(G-18011)***
Universal Scientific Inc....440 428-1777
6210 Campbell Dr Madison (44057) ***(G-12358)***
Universal Stainless, North Jackson *Also called North Jckson Specialty Stl LLC* ***(G-15150)***
Universal Steel Company....216 883-4972
6600 Grant Ave Cleveland (44105) ***(G-6240)***
Universal Tire Molds Inc....330 253-5101
5127 Boyer Pkwy Akron (44312) ***(G-422)***
Universal Tool Technology, Dayton *Also called Mdf Enterprises LLC* ***(G-8336)***
Universal Tool Technology LLC....937 222-4608
3488 Stop 8 Rd Dayton (45414) ***(G-8576)***
Universal Urethane Pdts Inc....419 693-7400
410 1st St Toledo (43605) ***(G-18585)***
Universal Veneer Production....740 522-1147
1776 Tamarack Rd Newark (43055) ***(G-14931)***
Universal Veneer Sales Corp (PA)....740 522-1147
1776 Tamarack Rd Newark (43055) ***(G-14932)***
Universal Well Services Inc....814 333-2656
11 S Washington St Millersburg (44654) ***(G-14140)***

ALPHABETIC SECTION V Collection

University Accessories Inc 440 327-4151
5152 Mills Indus Pkwy North Ridgeville (44039) ***(G-15257)***
University Hring Aid Assctions, Cincinnati *Also called Communications Aid Inc* ***(G-3537)***
University of Cincinnati 513 558-1243
3130 Highland Ave Fl 3 Cincinnati (45219) ***(G-4453)***
University of Cincinnati 513 556-5042
5121 Fishwick Dr Ste 120 Cincinnati (45216) ***(G-4454)***
University Sports Publications 614 291-6416
1265 Indianola Ave Columbus (43201) ***(G-7564)***
Uniwall Manufacturing Co (HQ) 330 875-1444
3750 Beck Ave Louisville (44641) ***(G-12169)***
Unlimited Machine and Tool LLC 419 269-1730
5139 Tractor Rd Ste C Toledo (43612) ***(G-18586)***
Unmanned Solutions Tech LLC 937 771-7023
3908 Eagle Point Dr Beavercreek (45430) ***(G-1366)***
Unocal, Danville *Also called Carol Mickley* ***(G-7960)***
Unverferth Mfg Co Inc (PA) 419 532-3121
601 S Broad St Kalida (45853) ***(G-11282)***
Unverferth Mfg Co Inc 419 695-2060
24325 State Route 697 Delphos (45833) ***(G-8761)***
UPA Technology Inc 513 755-1380
8963 Cncnnati Columbus Rd West Chester (45069) ***(G-19816)***
Upcreek Productions Inc 740 208-8124
1513 Upcreek Rd Bidwell (45614) ***(G-1672)***
Updegraff Inc 216 621-7600
1335 Main Ave Cleveland (44113) ***(G-6241)***
Updike Supply Company (PA) 937 482-4000
8241 Expansion Way Huber Heights (45424) ***(G-11024)***
Upl International Inc 330 433-2860
7661 Freedom Ave Nw North Canton (44720) ***(G-15134)***
Upm Inc 419 595-2600
4777 S Us Highway 23 Alvada (44802) ***(G-520)***
Upper Echelon Bar LLC 513 531-2814
1747 Avonlea Ave Cincinnati (45237) ***(G-4455)***
Upper Monument 419 310-2387
436 N Sandusky Ave Upper Sandusky (43351) ***(G-18976)***
Upper Sarahsville LLC 740 732-2071
48726 Sarahsville Rd Caldwell (43724) ***(G-2413)***
Upright Steel LLC 216 923-0852
1335 E 171st St Cleveland (44110) ***(G-6242)***
UPS, New Philadelphia *Also called Allen Green Enterprises LLC* ***(G-14757)***
UPS Store 4862, Delaware *Also called J&B Postal and Print Svcs LLC* ***(G-8698)***
UPS Stores, The, Medina *Also called Robloc Inc* ***(G-13329)***
Upside Innovations LLC 513 889-2492
5470 Spellmire Dr West Chester (45246) ***(G-19912)***
Uptivity, Columbus *Also called Callcopy Inc* ***(G-6725)***
Uptown Dog The Inc 740 592-4600
9 W Union St Athens (45701) ***(G-853)***
Uptown Graphics, Norwood *Also called Blt Inc* ***(G-15424)***
Urbn Timber LLC 614 981-3043
29 Kingston Ave Columbus (43207) ***(G-7565)***
Urc, Chagrin Falls *Also called Utility Relay Co Ltd* ***(G-3087)***
Us Inc 513 791-1162
10937 Reed Hartman Hwy Blue Ash (45242) ***(G-1863)***
US 261 Corp 216 531-7143
341 E 131st St Cleveland (44108) ***(G-6243)***
US Aeroteam Inc 937 458-0344
2601 W Stroop Rd Ste 60 Dayton (45439) ***(G-8577)***
US Coexcell Inc 419 897-9110
400 W Dussel Dr Ste C Maumee (43537) ***(G-13158)***
US Corrugated of Massillon 216 663-3344
16645 Granite Rd Maple Heights (44137) ***(G-12583)***
US Cotton LLC 216 676-6400
15501 Industrial Pkwy Cleveland (44135) ***(G-6244)***
US Die & Mold, Canal Winchester *Also called Manifold & Phalor Inc* ***(G-2506)***
US Filter, Pickerington *Also called Evoqua Water Technologies LLC* ***(G-16047)***
US Fittings Inc 234 212-9420
2182 E Aurora Rd Twinsburg (44087) ***(G-18871)***
US Foam Corporation (PA) 513 528-9800
7412 Jager Ct Cincinnati (45230) ***(G-4456)***
US Government Publishing Off 614 469-5657
200 N High St Rm 207 Columbus (43215) ***(G-7566)***
US Greentech 513 371-5520
3607 Church St Cincinnati (45244) ***(G-4457)***
US Group, East Palestine *Also called E R Advanced Ceramics Inc* ***(G-9077)***
US Industrial Lubricants Inc 513 541-2225
3330 Beekman St Cincinnati (45223) ***(G-4458)***
US Machine Prcsion Grnding LLC 440 284-0711
880 Taylor St Elyria (44035) ***(G-9342)***
US Metalcraft Inc 419 692-4962
101 S Franklin St Delphos (45833) ***(G-8762)***
US Mold Machine Tool Company, Painesville *Also called J & H Corporation* ***(G-15751)***
US Molding Machinery Co Inc 440 918-1701
38294 Pelton Rd Willoughby (44094) ***(G-20456)***
US Powder Coating Inc 440 255-3090
8665 Tyler Blvd Mentor (44060) ***(G-13620)***
US Refractory Products LLC 440 386-4580
7660 Race Rd North Ridgeville (44039) ***(G-15258)***
US Screen Co 419 736-2400
462 County Road 40 Sullivan (44880) ***(G-17882)***
US Technology Corporation 330 455-1181
4200 Munson St Nw Canton (44718) ***(G-2853)***
US Technology Media Inc 330 874-3094
509 Water St Sw Bolivar (44612) ***(G-1929)***
US Tsubaki Power Transm LLC 419 626-4560
1010 Edgewater Ave Sandusky (44870) ***(G-16860)***
US Tubular Products Inc 330 832-1734
14852 Lincoln Way W North Lawrence (44666) ***(G-15163)***
US Video 440 734-6463
23551 Westchester Dr North Olmsted (44070) ***(G-15202)***
US Water Company LLC 740 453-0604
1115 Newark Rd Zanesville (43701) ***(G-21186)***
US Yachiyo Inc 740 375-4687
1177 Kellogg Pkwy Marion (43302) ***(G-12746)***
USA Heat Treating Inc 216 587-4700
4500 Lee Rd Ste B Cleveland (44128) ***(G-6245)***
USA Instruments Inc 330 562-1000
1515 Danner Dr Aurora (44202) ***(G-913)***
USA Label Express Inc 330 874-1001
11206 Industrial Pkwy Nw Bolivar (44612) ***(G-1930)***
USA Precast Concrete Limited 330 854-9600
801 Elm Ridge Ave Canal Fulton (44614) ***(G-2495)***
USA Quickprint Inc (PA) 330 455-5119
409 3rd St Sw Canton (44702) ***(G-2854)***
USA Rolls, Canfield *Also called Alstart Enterprises LLC* ***(G-2521)***
Usalco, Fairfield *Also called Dpa Investments Inc* ***(G-9495)***
Usalco LLC 440 993-2721
3050 Lake Rd E Ashtabula (44004) ***(G-810)***
Usalco Fairfield Plant LLC 513 737-7100
3700 Dixie Hwy Fairfield (45014) ***(G-9571)***
USB Corporation 216 765-5000
26111 Miles Rd Cleveland (44128) ***(G-6246)***
Usc Metal Fabricators, Grand Rapids *Also called Seeburger Greenhouse* ***(G-10321)***
User Friendly Phone Book LLC 216 674-6500
2 Summit Park Dr Ste 105 Independence (44131) ***(G-11154)***
Usm Acquisition Corporation (PA) 440 975-8600
2002 Joseph Lloyd Pkwy Willoughby (44094) ***(G-20457)***
Usm Precision Products Inc 440 975-8600
1340 Lloyd Rd Ste D Wickliffe (44092) ***(G-20236)***
Ustek Incorporated 614 538-8000
4663 Executive Dr Ste 3 Columbus (43220) ***(G-7567)***
Usui International Corporation 513 448-0410
88 Partnership Way Sharonville (45241) ***(G-16960)***
Usui International Corporation 734 354-3626
8748 Jacquemin Dr Ste 100 West Chester (45069) ***(G-19817)***
Usui International Corporation 513 448-0410
88 Partnership Way Cincinnati (45241) ***(G-4459)***
UTAC, Cleveland *Also called United Taconite LLC* ***(G-6237)***
UTC Aerospace Systems, Troy *Also called Goodrich Corporation* ***(G-18663)***
UTC Aerospace Systems 330 374-3040
1555 Corporate Woods Pkwy Uniontown (44685) ***(G-18937)***
UTC Fire SEC Americas Corp Inc 513 821-7945
14 Knollcrest Dr Cincinnati (45237) ***(G-4460)***
Utica E Ohio Midstream 330 679-2295
70 E Main St Salineville (43945) ***(G-16790)***
Utica East Ohio Midstream 330 223-1766
8194 Trout Rd Ne Kensington (44427) ***(G-11286)***
Utica East Ohio Midstream LLC 740 945-2226
117 Fowler Ave Scio (43988) ***(G-16880)***
Utica Herald 740 892-2771
60 N Main St Utica (43080) ***(G-19028)***
Utility Relay Co Ltd 440 708-1000
10100 Queens Way Chagrin Falls (44023) ***(G-3087)***
Utility Solutions Inc 740 369-4300
327 Curtis St Delaware (43015) ***(G-8729)***
Utility Wire Products Inc 216 441-2180
3302 E 87th St Cleveland (44127) ***(G-6247)***
Utv Hitchworks LLC 513 615-8568
1295 W Us Highway 22 & 3 Maineville (45039) ***(G-12378)***
Uvisir Inc 216 374-9376
23600 Merc Rd Ste 102 Beachwood (44122) ***(G-1284)***
V & A Process Inc 440 288-8137
2345 E 28th St Lorain (44055) ***(G-12132)***
V & C Enterprises Co 614 221-1412
41 S Grant Ave Columbus (43215) ***(G-7568)***
V & M Star LP 330 742-6300
2669 Mrtn Luthr Kg Jr Bld Youngstown (44510) ***(G-21057)***
V & R Molded Products Inc 419 752-4171
181 Us Highway 224 W Willard (44890) ***(G-20247)***
V & S Columbus Galanizing LLC 614 449-8281
987 Buckeye Park Rd Columbus (43207) ***(G-7569)***
V & S Schuler Engineering Inc (HQ) 330 452-5200
2240 Allen Ave Se Canton (44707) ***(G-2855)***
V & W Woodcraft 330 674-0073
5071 Township Road 353 Millersburg (44654) ***(G-14141)***
V Collection 419 517-0508
5630 Main St Sylvania (43560) ***(G-17967)***

ALPHABETIC

(PA)=Parent Co (HQ)=Headquarters (DH)=Div Headquarters
2019 Harris Ohio
Industrial Directory
1279

V H Cooper & Co Inc ALPHABETIC SECTION

V H Cooper & Co Inc......419 678-4853
1 Cooper Farm Dr Saint Henry (45883) ***(G-16669)***
V H Cooper & Co Inc......419 678-4853
1 Cooper Farm Dr Saint Henry (45883) ***(G-16670)***
V H Cooper & Co Inc (HQ)......419 375-4116
2321 State Route 49 Fort Recovery (45846) ***(G-9829)***
V I E W I N G, Cleveland *Also called Visualy Imp Exp Wm Isues Fr Gr* ***(G-6265)***
V I I Craft, Xenia *Also called Visual Information Institute* ***(G-20801)***
V I P Printing & Design......513 777-7468
4836 Duff Dr Ste A West Chester (45246) ***(G-19913)***
V K C Inc......440 951-9634
7667 Jenther Dr Mentor (44060) ***(G-13621)***
V M Machine Co Inc......216 281-4569
9607 Clinton Rd Cleveland (44144) ***(G-6248)***
V M Systems Inc......419 535-1044
3125 Hill Ave Toledo (43607) ***(G-18587)***
V Mast Manufacturing Inc......330 409-8116
1712 Kimball Rd Se Canton (44707) ***(G-2856)***
V Metro, Fairborn *Also called Vmetro Inc* ***(G-9473)***
V P, Newton Falls *Also called Venture Plastics Inc* ***(G-14995)***
V R I, Franklin *Also called Valued Relationships Inc* ***(G-9928)***
V S I, Massillon *Also called Vehicle Systems Inc* ***(G-13056)***
V T S, Aurora *Also called Vibration Test Systems Inc* ***(G-914)***
V&P Group International LLC......703 349-6432
1931 Lawn Ave Cincinnati (45237) ***(G-4461)***
V-Ash Machine Company......216 267-3400
1220 Orlen Ave Cuyahoga Falls (44221) ***(G-7933)***
VA Technology, Brunswick *Also called Versatile Automation Tech Ltd* ***(G-2248)***
Vacalon Company Inc......614 577-1945
12960 Stonecreek Dr Ste D Pickerington (43147) ***(G-16062)***
Vacca Inc (PA)......513 697-0270
9501 Union Cemetery Rd # 100 Loveland (45140) ***(G-12241)***
Vacono America LLC......216 938-7428
1163 E 40th St Ste 301 Cleveland (44114) ***(G-6249)***
Vacuflo Factory......330 875-2450
512 W Gorgas St Louisville (44641) ***(G-12170)***
Vacuform Inc......330 938-9674
500 Courtney Rd Sebring (44672) ***(G-16898)***
Vacupanel, Dayton *Also called Energy Storage Technologies* ***(G-8183)***
Vacuum Electric Switch Co Inc (PA)......330 374-5156
2390 Romig Rd Akron (44320) ***(G-423)***
Vacuum Finishing Company......440 286-4386
10275 Old State Rd Chardon (44024) ***(G-3140)***
Vadose Syn Fuels Inc......330 564-0545
323 S Main St Munroe Falls (44262) ***(G-14529)***
Vail Rubber Works Inc......513 705-2060
605 Clark St Middletown (45042) ***(G-13962)***
Val Casting Inc......419 562-2499
108 E Rensselaer St Bucyrus (44820) ***(G-2346)***
Val Products, Coldwater *Also called Val-Co Pax Inc* ***(G-6423)***
Val-Co Pax Inc (HQ)......717 354-4586
210 E Main St Coldwater (45828) ***(G-6423)***
Val-Con Inc......440 357-1898
7201 Hermitage Rd Painesville (44077) ***(G-15794)***
Valco Cincinnati Inc (PA)......513 874-6550
497 Circle Freeway Dr # 490 West Chester (45246) ***(G-19914)***
Valco Cincinnati Inc......513 874-6550
411 Circle Freeway Dr West Chester (45246) ***(G-19915)***
Valco Division, North Royalton *Also called Valley Tool & Die Inc* ***(G-15309)***
Valco Industries Inc......937 399-7400
625 Burt St Springfield (45505) ***(G-17513)***
Valco Melton, West Chester *Also called Valco Cincinnati Inc* ***(G-19914)***
Valco Melton Inc......513 874-6550
411 Circle Freeway Dr West Chester (45246) ***(G-19916)***
Valensil Technologies LLC......440 937-8181
34910 Commerce Way Avon (44011) ***(G-973)***
Valentine Research Inc......513 984-8900
10280 Alliance Rd Blue Ash (45242) ***(G-1864)***
Valentino Industries LLC......330 523-7216
3615 Southern Rd Richfield (44286) ***(G-16493)***
Valfilm LLC......419 423-6500
3441 N Main St Findlay (45840) ***(G-9772)***
Valley Asphalt, Morrow *Also called Morrow Gravel Company Inc* ***(G-14413)***
Valley Asphalt Corporation......513 381-0652
4850 Stubbs Mills Rd Morrow (45152) ***(G-14416)***
Valley Asphalt Corporation......937 426-7682
782 N Valley Rd Xenia (45385) ***(G-20800)***
Valley Asphalt Corporation......937 335-3664
250 Dye Mill Rd Troy (45373) ***(G-18717)***
Valley Asphalt Corporation......513 353-2171
5073 Kilby Rd Cleves (45002) ***(G-6381)***
Valley Asphalt Corporation......513 561-1551
7940 Main St Cincinnati (45244) ***(G-4462)***
Valley Asphalt Corporation......513 784-1476
612 W Mehring Way Cincinnati (45202) ***(G-4463)***
Valley Concrete, Carrollton *Also called Ernst Enterprises Inc* ***(G-2919)***
Valley Concrete Division, Fairborn *Also called Ernst Enterprises Inc* ***(G-9458)***

Valley Containers Inc......330 544-2244
3515 Union St Mineral Ridge (44440) ***(G-14173)***
Valley Converting Co Inc (PA)......740 537-2152
405 Daniels St Toronto (43964) ***(G-18614)***
Valley Converting Co Inc......740 537-2152
310 Loretta Ave Toronto (43964) ***(G-18615)***
Valley Electric Company......419 332-6405
432 N Wood St Fremont (43420) ***(G-10061)***
Valley Graphics......330 652-0484
1494 Salt Springs Rd Niles (44446) ***(G-15038)***
Valley Machine Tool Co Inc......513 899-2737
9773 Morrow Cozaddale Rd Morrow (45152) ***(G-14417)***
Valley Metal Works Inc......513 554-1022
698 W Columbia Ave Cincinnati (45215) ***(G-4464)***
Valley Petroleum Inc......740 668-4901
25010 Divan Rd Utica (43080) ***(G-19029)***
Valley Plastics Company Inc......419 666-2349
399 Phillips Ave Toledo (43612) ***(G-18588)***
Valley Rubber Mixing Inc......330 434-4442
4478 Regal Dr Akron (44321) ***(G-424)***
Valley Tool & Die Inc......440 237-0160
10020 York Theta Dr North Royalton (44133) ***(G-15309)***
Valley Trailers, Leesburg *Also called Creative Fab & Welding LLC* ***(G-11709)***
Valley View Pallets LLC......740 599-0010
22414 Hostetler Rd Danville (43014) ***(G-7966)***
Valley View Pallets Partners, Danville *Also called Valley View Pallets LLC* ***(G-7966)***
Valley View Woodcraft......330 852-3000
1190 Shutt Valley Rd Nw Sugarcreek (44681) ***(G-17874)***
Valley View Woodcraft & Finshg, Sugarcreek *Also called Valley View Woodcraft* ***(G-17874)***
Valley Vitamins II Inc......330 533-0051
4449 Easton Way Fl 2 Columbus (43219) ***(G-7570)***
Valley Welding Service, Harrison *Also called Robert E Moore* ***(G-10668)***
Valleyview Wood Turning Co......330 763-0407
8260 Township Road 652 Millersburg (44654) ***(G-14142)***
Vallourec Star LP (HQ)......330 742-6300
2669 M L K J Blvd Youngstown (44510) ***(G-21058)***
Vallourec Star LP......330 742-6227
706 S State St Girard (44420) ***(G-10268)***
Valtris, Independence *Also called Polymer Additives Holdings Inc* ***(G-11147)***
Valtris Specialty Chemical, Cleveland *Also called Polymer Additives Inc* ***(G-5895)***
Valtris Specialty Chemicals, Independence *Also called Polymer Additives Inc* ***(G-11146)***
Valtris Specialty Chemicals......216 875-7200
7050 Krick Rd Walton Hills (44146) ***(G-19316)***
Valtronic Technology Inc......440 349-1239
29200 Fountain Pkwy Solon (44139) ***(G-17257)***
Value Added Business Svcs Co (PA)......614 854-9755
120 Twin Oaks Dr Jackson (45640) ***(G-11200)***
Value Added Packaging Inc......937 832-9595
44 Lau Pkwy Englewood (45315) ***(G-9381)***
Value Stream Systems Inc......330 907-0064
2575 Medina Rd Ste B Medina (44256) ***(G-13359)***
Value-Rooter, Elyria *Also called Personal Plumber Service Corp* ***(G-9311)***
Valued Relationships Inc (PA)......800 860-4230
1400 Commerce Center Dr B Franklin (45005) ***(G-9928)***
Valutex Reinforcements Inc......800 251-2507
2000 Kenskill Ave Wshngtn CT Hs (43160) ***(G-20747)***
Valv-Trol Company......330 686-2800
1340 Commerce Dr Stow (44224) ***(G-17640)***
Valve Related Controls Inc......513 677-8724
143 Commerce Dr Loveland (45140) ***(G-12242)***
Valveco Inc (PA)......330 337-9535
1913 E State St Salem (44460) ***(G-16779)***
Valvole America LLC......330 464-8872
2550 Medina Rd Medina (44256) ***(G-13360)***
Valvoline, West Chester *Also called Ashland LLC* ***(G-19652)***
Valvsys LLC......513 539-1234
421 Breaden Dr Ste 15 Monroe (45050) ***(G-14279)***
Vam Usa Llc......330 742-3130
1053 Ohio Works Dr Youngstown (44510) ***(G-21059)***
Vampire Optical Coatings Inc......740 919-4596
63 E Mill St Unit B Pataskala (43062) ***(G-15848)***
Van Burens Welding & Machine......740 787-2636
11496 Cherry Hill Rd Glenford (43739) ***(G-10273)***
Van Deleigh Industries LLC......419 467-2244
5611 Bent Oak Rd Sylvania (43560) ***(G-17968)***
Van Dyke Custom Iron Inc......614 860-9300
311 Outerbelt St Columbus (43213) ***(G-7571)***
Van Engineering Co, Cincinnati *Also called R Vandewalle Inc* ***(G-4245)***
Van Heusen, Aurora *Also called Pvh Corp* ***(G-900)***
Van Orders Pallet Company Inc......419 875-6932
2452 County Road 2 Swanton (43558) ***(G-17928)***
Van Wert Division, Van Wert *Also called Tecumseh Packg Solutions Inc* ***(G-19106)***
Van Wert Machine Inc......419 692-6836
210 E Cleveland St Delphos (45833) ***(G-8763)***
Van Wert Memorials LLC......419 238-9067
625 S Shannon St Van Wert (45891) ***(G-19110)***
Van Wert Pallets LLC......419 203-1823
9042 John Brown Rd Van Wert (45891) ***(G-19111)***

ALPHABETIC SECTION — Vermilion Dock Masters

Van-Griner LLC 419 733-7951
 1009 Delta Ave Cincinnati (45208) *(G-4465)*
Vanamatic Company 419 692-6085
 701 Ambrose Dr Delphos (45833) *(G-8764)*
Vance Adams 330 424-9670
 123 E Lincoln Way Lisbon (44432) *(G-11981)*
Vance's Wonder Store, Manchester Also called Vances Department Store *(G-12397)*
Vances Department Store (PA) 937 549-2188
 37 E 2nd St Manchester (45144) *(G-12397)*
Vances Department Store 937 549-3033
 600 Washington St Manchester (45144) *(G-12398)*
Vandalia Machining Inc 937 264-9155
 884 Center Dr Vandalia (45377) *(G-19148)*
Vandalia Massage Therapy 937 890-8660
 147 W National Rd Vandalia (45377) *(G-19149)*
Vanderpool Motor Sports 513 424-2166
 6315 Howe Rd Middletown (45042) *(G-13963)*
Vanguard Die & Machine Inc 330 394-4170
 2070 Mcmyler St Nw Warren (44485) *(G-19455)*
Vanguard Fabrication Division, Mantua Also called Aetna Plastics Corp *(G-12541)*
Vanguard Oil & Gas 330 223-1074
 28050 Speidel Rd East Rochester (44625) *(G-9092)*
Vanity Classics, Cincinnati Also called Custom Cast Marbleworks Inc *(G-3564)*
Vanner Holdings Inc 614 771-2718
 4282 Reynolds Dr Hilliard (43026) *(G-10873)*
Vanni Wang Couture, Rocky River Also called Lucio Vanni LLC *(G-16549)*
Vans Inc 419 471-1541
 5001 Monroe St Ste 1560 Toledo (43623) *(G-18589)*
Vanscoyk Sheet Metal Corp 937 845-0581
 475 Quick Rd New Carlisle (45344) *(G-14681)*
Vantage Athletic 419 680-5274
 325 Cottage St Fremont (43420) *(G-10062)*
Vantage Specialty Ingredients 937 264-1222
 707 Harco Dr Englewood (45315) *(G-9382)*
Vapen8r LLC 440 934-8273
 5220 Cobblestone Rd Sheffield Village (44035) *(G-16976)*
Vapor Cast, Sheffield Village Also called Vapen8r LLC *(G-16976)*
Vapor Vault 513 400-8089
 2601 1/2 Short Vine St Cincinnati (45219) *(G-4466)*
Varbros LLC 216 267-5200
 16025 Brookpark Rd Cleveland (44142) *(G-6250)*
Varco LP 440 277-8696
 1807 E 28th St Lorain (44055) *(G-12133)*
Vari-Wall Tube Specialists Inc 330 482-0000
 1350 Wardingsley Ave Columbiana (44408) *(G-6485)*
Variety Glass Inc 740 432-3643
 201 Foster Ave Cambridge (43725) *(G-2461)*
Variety Printing 216 676-9815
 5707 Van Wert Ave Brookpark (44142) *(G-2157)*
Variflow Equipment Inc 513 245-0420
 3834 Ridgedale Dr Cincinnati (45247) *(G-4467)*
Varmland Inc 216 741-1510
 1200 Brookpark Rd Cleveland (44109) *(G-6251)*
Varsity Sporting Goods, Grove City Also called Joe Sestito *(G-10437)*
Vasil Co Inc 419 562-2901
 119 E Mary St Bucyrus (44820) *(G-2347)*
Vasil Fashions, Bucyrus Also called Vasil Co Inc *(G-2347)*
Vast Mold & Tool Co Inc 440 942-7585
 7154 Industrial Park Blvd Mentor (44060) *(G-13622)*
Ve Global Vending Inc 216 785-2611
 8700 Brookpark Rd Cleveland (44129) *(G-6252)*
Vector Chemicals, Youngstown Also called Howard Grant Corp *(G-20932)*
Vector Electromagnetics LLC 937 478-5904
 2670b Indian Ripple Rd Beavercreek (45440) *(G-1367)*
Vector International Corp 440 942-2002
 7404 Tyler Blvd Mentor (44060) *(G-13623)*
Vector Mechanical LLC 216 337-4042
 5240 Smith Rd Brookpark (44142) *(G-2158)*
Vector Screenprinting & EMB, Mentor Also called Vector International Corp *(G-13623)*
Vectron Inc 440 323-3369
 201 Perry Ct Elyria (44035) *(G-9343)*
Vedda Printing, Cleveland Also called Phil Vedda & Sons Inc *(G-5870)*
Vee Gee Enterprise Corporation 330 493-9780
 4897 Fulton Dr Nw Canton (44718) *(G-2857)*
Veeam Software Corporation (PA) 614 339-8200
 8800 Lyra Dr Ste 350 Columbus (43240) *(G-6508)*
Veeders Mailbox Inc 513 984-8749
 10050 Montgomery Rd # 324 Cincinnati (45242) *(G-4468)*
Veelo Technologies LLC 513 309-5947
 10340 Julian Dr Cincinnati (45215) *(G-4469)*
Vega Americas Inc (HQ) 513 272-0131
 4170 Rosslyn Dr Ste A Cincinnati (45209) *(G-4470)*
Vega Technology Group LLC 216 772-1434
 412 Sheraton Dr Nw North Canton (44720) *(G-15135)*
Veggie Valley Farm LLC 330 866-2712
 3444 Dueber Rd Ne Sandyville (44671) *(G-16864)*
Vegv, Cleveland Also called Ve Global Vending Inc *(G-6252)*
Vehicle Systems Inc 330 854-0535
 7130 Lutz Ave Nw Massillon (44646) *(G-13056)*

Vehtek Systems Inc 419 373-8741
 2125 Wood Bridge Blvd Bowling Green (43402) *(G-2004)*
Vein Center and Medspa 330 629-9400
 965 Windham Ct Ste 2 Youngstown (44512) *(G-21060)*
Vein Center, The, Youngstown Also called Vein Center and Medspa *(G-21060)*
Veitsch-Radex America LLC 440 969-2300
 4741 Kister Ct Ashtabula (44004) *(G-811)*
Vela 614 500-0150
 58560 Kennonsburg Rd Salesville (43778) *(G-16784)*
Vellus Products Inc 614 889-2391
 64906490 Fiesta Dr Columbus (43235) *(G-7572)*
Velocity Concept Dev Group LLC (PA) 513 204-2100
 4393 Digital Way Mason (45040) *(G-12952)*
Velocity Concept Dev Group LLC 740 685-2637
 8824 Clay Pike Byesville (43723) *(G-2395)*
Velocys Inc 614 733-3300
 7950 Corporate Blvd Plain City (43064) *(G-16215)*
Velvet Ice Cream Company 419 562-2009
 1233 Whetstone St Bucyrus (44820) *(G-2348)*
Vemuri International LLC (PA) 513 483-6300
 10600 Evendale Dr Cincinnati (45241) *(G-4471)*
Venco Manufacturing Inc (HQ) 513 772-8448
 12110 Best Pl Cincinnati (45241) *(G-4472)*
Venco Venturo Industries LLC (PA) 513 772-8448
 12110 Best Pl Cincinnati (45241) *(G-4473)*
Venco/Venturo Div, Cincinnati Also called Venco Venturo Industries LLC *(G-4473)*
Vendfriend, Dublin Also called Neil Barton *(G-8953)*
Venice Cornerstone Newspaper 513 738-7151
 2640 Cncnnati Brkville Rd Hamilton (45014) *(G-10617)*
Venom Exterminating LLC 330 637-3366
 40 Monte Ln Cortland (44410) *(G-7716)*
Ventari Corporation 937 278-4269
 8641 Washington Church Rd Miamisburg (45342) *(G-13731)*
Ventco Inc 440 834-8888
 66 Windward Way Chagrin Falls (44023) *(G-3088)*
Ventra Sandusky LLC 419 627-3600
 3020 Tiffin Ave Sandusky (44870) *(G-16861)*
Vents US, Blue Ash Also called Bodor Vents LLC *(G-1739)*
Venture Medical, Plain City Also called Bahler Medical Inc *(G-16174)*
Venture Packaging Inc 419 465-2534
 311 Monroe St Monroeville (44847) *(G-14292)*
Venture Packaging Midwest Inc 419 465-2534
 311 Monroe St Monroeville (44847) *(G-14293)*
Venture Plastics Inc (PA) 330 872-5774
 4000 Warren Rd Newton Falls (44444) *(G-14995)*
Venture Plastics Inc 330 872-6262
 4325 Warren Ravenna Rd Newton Falls (44444) *(G-14996)*
Venture Therapeutics Inc 614 430-3300
 10739 Johnstown Rd New Albany (43054) *(G-14640)*
Venturemedgroup Ltd 567 661-0768
 2865 N Reynolds Rd 220a Toledo (43615) *(G-18590)*
Venturo Manufacturing Inc 513 772-8448
 12110 Best Pl Cincinnati (45241) *(G-4474)*
Venu On 3rd 937 222-2891
 905 E 3rd St Dayton (45402) *(G-8578)*
Venue Lifestyle & Event Guide 513 405-6822
 11959 Tramway Dr Cincinnati (45241) *(G-4475)*
Venus Trading LLC 513 374-0066
 10965 Rednor Ct Loveland (45140) *(G-12243)*
Veolia NA Regeneration Srvcs 513 941-4121
 11215 Brower Rd North Bend (45052) *(G-15057)*
Veolia Water Technologies Inc 937 890-4075
 945 S Brown School Rd Vandalia (45377) *(G-19150)*
Veoneer Nissin Brake 419 425-6725
 2001 Industrial Dr Findlay (45840) *(G-9773)*
Ver Mich Ltd 330 493-7330
 4210 Cleveland Ave Nw Canton (44709) *(G-2858)*
Ver-Mac Industries Inc 740 397-6511
 100 Progress Dr Mount Vernon (43050) *(G-14517)*
Verantis Corporation (HQ) 440 243-0700
 7251 Engle Rd Ste 300 Middleburg Heights (44130) *(G-13771)*
Verdin Company, Cincinnati Also called I T Verdin Co *(G-3833)*
Veressa Medical Inc 614 591-4201
 1375 Perry St Columbus (43201) *(G-7573)*
Vergeline LLC 419 730-0300
 1301 N Summit St Toledo (43604) *(G-18591)*
Verhoff Alfalfa Mills Inc (PA) 419 523-4767
 1188 Sugar Mill Dr Ottawa (45875) *(G-15670)*
Verhoff Alfalfa Mills Inc 419 653-4161
 1577 Henry Y New Bavaria (43548) *(G-14643)*
Verhoff Machine & Welding Inc 419 596-3202
 7300 Road 18 Continental (45831) *(G-7669)*
Veriano Fine Foods Spirits Ltd 614 745-7705
 5175 Zarley St Ste A New Albany (43054) *(G-14641)*
Veritas, Kent Also called Schneller LLC *(G-11380)*
Veritrack Inc 513 202-0790
 9487 Dry Fork Rd Harrison (45030) *(G-10678)*
Vermilion Dock Masters 440 244-5370
 858 Vermilion Rd Vermilion (44089) *(G-19171)*

(PA)=Parent Co (HQ)=Headquarters (DH)=Div Headquarters

Vernay Manufacturing Inc (HQ)......937 767-7261
120 E South College St Yellow Springs (45387) ***(G-20818)***
Vero Security Group Ltd......513 731-8376
5296 Montgomery Rd Cincinnati (45212) ***(G-4476)***
Verona Agriculture Center, Verona *Also called Harvest Land Co-Op Inc (G-19172)*
Versa-Pak Ltd......419 586-5466
500 Staeger Rd Celina (45822) ***(G-2991)***
Versailles Building Supply......937 526-3238
741 N Center St Versailles (45380) ***(G-19191)***
Versalift East Inc......610 866-1400
4884 Corporate St Sw Canton (44706) ***(G-2859)***
Versatile Automation Tech Ltd......330 220-2600
2853 Westway Dr Brunswick (44212) ***(G-2248)***
Versatile Machine......330 618-9895
402 Commerce St Tallmadge (44278) ***(G-18012)***
Versitec Manufacturing Inc......440 354-4283
152 Elevator Ave Painesville (44077) ***(G-15795)***
Versitech Mold, Akron *Also called Saehwa IMC Na Inc (G-368)*
Versitech Mold Div, Akron *Also called Saehwa IMC Na Inc (G-369)*
Verso Corporation (PA)......877 855-7243
8540 Gander Creek Dr Miamisburg (45342) ***(G-13732)***
Verso Corporation......901 369-4105
8540 Gander Creek Dr Miamisburg (45342) ***(G-13733)***
Verso Corporation......901 369-4100
8540 Gander Creek Dr Miamisburg (45342) ***(G-13734)***
Verso Paper, Miamisburg *Also called Verso Corporation (G-13733)*
Verso Paper Holding LLC (HQ)......877 855-7243
8540 Gander Creek Dr Miamisburg (45342) ***(G-13735)***
Verso Paper Holding LLC......901 369-4100
8540 Gander Creek Dr Miamisburg (45342) ***(G-13736)***
Verstraete In Mold Lab......513 943-0080
4101 Founders Blvd Batavia (45103) ***(G-1195)***
Vertebration Inc......614 395-3346
3982 Powell Rd 220 Powell (43065) ***(G-16340)***
Vertex Inc......330 628-6230
3956 Mogadore Indus Pkwy Mogadore (44260) ***(G-14252)***
Vertex Computer Systems Inc......513 662-6888
11260 Chester Rd Ste 300 Cincinnati (45246) ***(G-4477)***
Vertex Refining OH LLC......614 441-4001
4001 E 5th Ave Columbus (43219) ***(G-7574)***
Vertex Refining OH LLC (HQ)......281 486-4182
4376 State Route 601 Norwalk (44857) ***(G-15416)***
Vertical Data LLC......330 289-0313
2169 Chuckery Ln Akron (44333) ***(G-425)***
Vertical Runner......330 262-3000
148 W Liberty St Wooster (44691) ***(G-20662)***
Vertiflo Pump Company......513 530-0888
7807 Redsky Dr Cincinnati (45249) ***(G-4478)***
Vertiv, Columbus *Also called Liebert North America Inc (G-7125)*
Vertiv Co., Columbus *Also called Vertiv Group Corporation (G-7576)*
Vertiv Corporation (HQ)......614 888-0246
1050 Dearborn Dr Columbus (43085) ***(G-7575)***
Vertiv Corporation......740 547-5100
3040 S 9th St Ironton (45638) ***(G-11175)***
Vertiv Energy Systems Inc......440 288-1122
1510 Kansas Ave Lorain (44052) ***(G-12134)***
Vertiv Group Corporation (HQ)......614 888-0246
1050 Dearborn Dr Columbus (43085) ***(G-7576)***
Vertiv Group Corporation......440 288-1122
1510 Kansas Ave Lorain (44052) ***(G-12135)***
Vertiv Group Corporation......440 460-3600
5900 Landerbrook Dr # 300 Cleveland (44124) ***(G-6253)***
Vertiv Holdings LLC (HQ)......614 888-0246
1050 Dearborn Dr Columbus (43085) ***(G-7577)***
Vertiv North America Inc......614 888-0246
1050 Dearborn Dr Columbus (43085) ***(G-7578)***
Vertiv Solutions Inc (HQ)......614 888-0246
1050 Dearborn Dr Columbus (43085) ***(G-7579)***
Vervasi Vineyard & Itln Bistro......330 497-1000
1700 55th St Ne Canton (44721) ***(G-2860)***
Vesco Medical LLC......614 914-5991
1039 Kingsmill Pkwy Columbus (43229) ***(G-7580)***
Vesco Oil Corporation......419 335-8871
247 N Brunell St Wauseon (43567) ***(G-19536)***
Vesi Incorporated......513 563-6002
16 Techview Dr Cincinnati (45215) ***(G-4479)***
Vestcom Retail Solutions, Lewis Center *Also called Electronic Imaging Svcs Inc (G-11759)*
Vesuvius U S A Corporation......440 593-1161
1100 Maple Ave Conneaut (44030) ***(G-7661)***
Vesuvius U S A Corporation......440 816-3051
20200 Sheldon Rd Cleveland (44142) ***(G-6254)***
Veteran Industries LLC......937 751-2133
147 Lake Bluff Dr Columbus (43235) ***(G-7581)***
Veterans Representative Co LLC......330 779-0768
1584 Tamarisk Trl Youngstown (44514) ***(G-21061)***
Veterans Steel Inc......216 938-7476
900 E 69th St Cleveland (44103) ***(G-6255)***
Vetgraft LLC......614 203-0603
7590 Brandon Rd New Albany (43054) ***(G-14642)***
Vexos Electronic Mfg Svcs......855 711-3227
110 Commerce Dr Lagrange (44050) ***(G-11496)***
Vf Outdoor LLC......614 337-1147
4025 Gramercy St Columbus (43219) ***(G-7582)***
Vgs Inc......216 431-7800
2239 E 55th St Cleveland (44103) ***(G-6256)***
Vgu Industries Inc......216 676-9093
4747 Manufacturing Ave Cleveland (44135) ***(G-6257)***
Viasat Inc......216 706-7800
5990 W Creek Rd Ste 1 Independence (44131) ***(G-11155)***
Vibra Finish Co......513 870-6300
8411 Seward Rd Fairfield (45011) ***(G-9572)***
Vibration Test Systems Inc......330 562-5729
10246 Clipper Cv Aurora (44202) ***(G-914)***
Vibrodyne Division, Moraine *Also called Tailored Systems Inc (G-14398)*
Vibronic......937 274-1114
5208 Wadsworth Rd Dayton (45414) ***(G-8579)***
Vic Mar Manufacturing Inc......740 687-5434
730 Lawrence St Lancaster (43130) ***(G-11617)***
Vic Maroscher......330 332-4958
36135 Salem Grange Rd Salem (44460) ***(G-16780)***
Vicart Prcsion Fabricators Inc......614 771-0080
4101 Leap Rd Hilliard (43026) ***(G-10874)***
Vicas Manufacturing Co Inc......513 791-7741
8407 Monroe Ave Cincinnati (45236) ***(G-4480)***
Vici Defense Ltd......330 669-3735
7147 N Honeytown Rd Smithville (44677) ***(G-17096)***
Vickers International Inc (HQ)......419 867-2200
3000 Strayer Rd Maumee (43537) ***(G-13159)***
Vicon Fabricating Company Ltd......440 205-6700
7200 Justin Way Mentor (44060) ***(G-13624)***
Vicrobiz, Westerville *Also called World Development & Conslt LLC (G-20083)*
Vics Turning Co Inc......216 531-5016
16911 Saint Clair Ave Cleveland (44110) ***(G-6258)***
Victor McKenzie Drilling Co......740 453-0834
3596 Maple Ave Ste A Zanesville (43701) ***(G-21187)***
Victor Organ Company......330 792-1321
5340 Mahoning Ave Youngstown (44515) ***(G-21062)***
Victoria Ventures Inc (PA)......330 793-9321
425 Victoria Rd Ste 427 Youngstown (44515) ***(G-21063)***
Victorian Farms......330 628-9188
1375 Aberagg Rd Atwater (44201) ***(G-864)***
Victory Athletics Inc......330 274-2854
10702 Second St Mantua (44255) ***(G-12561)***
Victory Direct LLC......614 626-0000
750 Cross Pointe Rd Ste M Gahanna (43230) ***(G-10110)***
Victory Postcards & Souvenirs, Columbus *Also called Victory Postcards Inc (G-7583)*
Victory Postcards Inc......614 764-8975
1005 Old Henderson Rd Columbus (43220) ***(G-7583)***
Victory Store Fixtures Inc......740 499-3494
3153 Winnemac Pike S La Rue (43332) ***(G-11477)***
Victory White Metal Company......216 641-2575
7930 Jones Rd Cleveland (44105) ***(G-6259)***
Victory White Metal Company (PA)......216 271-1400
6100 Roland Ave Cleveland (44127) ***(G-6260)***
Victory White Metal Company......216 271-1400
3027 E 55th St Cleveland (44127) ***(G-6261)***
Vida Ve Corp......614 203-2607
8210 Timber Mist Ct Dublin (43017) ***(G-9008)***
Video Products Inc......330 562-2622
1275 Danner Dr Aurora (44202) ***(G-915)***
Vidonish Stained Glass Studio, Mansfield *Also called Vidonish Studios (G-12535)*
Vidonish Studios......419 884-1119
20 E Main St Mansfield (44904) ***(G-12535)***
Viewpoint Graphic Design......419 447-6073
132 S Washington St Tiffin (44883) ***(G-18091)***
Viewray Technologies Inc......440 703-3210
2 Thermo Fisher Way Oakwood Village (44146) ***(G-15487)***
Viking Explosives LLC......218 263-8845
25800 Science Park Dr Cleveland (44122) ***(G-6262)***
Viking Fabricators Inc......740 374-5246
2021 Hanna Rd Marietta (45750) ***(G-12687)***
Viking Group Inc (PA)......937 443-0433
2806 Wayne Ave Dayton (45420) ***(G-8580)***
Viking Intl Resources Co Inc......304 628-3878
125 Putnam St Marietta (45750) ***(G-12688)***
Viking Paper, Toledo *Also called Tex-Tyler Corporation (G-18548)*
Viking Paper Company (PA)......419 729-4951
5148 Stickney Ave Toledo (43612) ***(G-18592)***
Village Cabinet Shop Inc......704 966-0801
1820 Loisview Ln Cincinnati (45255) ***(G-4481)***
Village of Dupont......419 596-3061
105 Liberty St Dupont (45837) ***(G-9037)***
Village of Somerset......740 743-1986
1672 Big Inch Rd Nw Somerset (43783) ***(G-17268)***
Village of West Alexandria (PA)......937 839-4168
16 N Main St Unit 2 West Alexandria (45381) ***(G-19623)***
Village Outdoors......440 256-1172
7875 Euclid Chardon Rd Kirtland (44094) ***(G-11472)***

Village Plastics Co....330 753-0100
100 16th St Sw Barberton (44203) *(G-1112)*
Village Reporter....419 485-4851
115 Broad St Montpelier (43543) *(G-14320)*
Village Square Antique Mall, Sunbury *Also called Indian River Industries (G-17890)*
Village Voice of Ottawa Hills, Toledo *Also called Village Voice Publishing Ltd (G-18593)*
Village Voice Publishing Ltd....419 537-0286
4041 W Central Ave Ste 6 Toledo (43606) *(G-18593)*
Villager Newspaper, The, Bay Village *Also called Robert Tuneberg (G-1209)*
Villers Enterprises Limited....330 818-9838
980 Dunning Rd Bldg B New Franklin (44614) *(G-14688)*
Vinco Machine Products Inc....216 475-6708
17601 Pennsylvania Ave Cleveland (44137) *(G-6263)*
Vindicator....330 755-0135
3770 Wilson Ave Campbell (44405) *(G-2471)*
Vindicator Boardman Office....330 259-1732
8075 Southern Blvd Youngstown (44512) *(G-21064)*
Vindicator Printing Company....330 744-8611
101 W Boardman St Youngstown (44503) *(G-21065)*
Vindicator Printing Company....330 392-0176
135 Pine Ave Se Ste 208 Warren (44481) *(G-19456)*
Vinnies Drive Thru....419 225-5272
864 W North St Lima (45801) *(G-11956)*
Vintage Machine Supply Inc....330 723-0800
650 W Smith Rd Ste 9 Medina (44256) *(G-13361)*
Vintage Vault....330 607-0136
832 Elmore Ave Akron (44302) *(G-426)*
Vinyl Building Products LLC....513 539-4444
351 N Garver Rd Monroe (45050) *(G-14280)*
Vinyl Design Corporation....419 283-4009
7856 Hill Ave Holland (43528) *(G-10965)*
Vinyl Graphics, Cleveland *Also called Vgu Industries Inc (G-6257)*
Vinyl Profiles Acquisition LLC....330 538-0660
11675 Mahoning Ave North Jackson (44451) *(G-15157)*
Vinyl Tech Storage Barn....330 674-5670
5930 State Route 39 Millersburg (44654) *(G-14143)*
Vinyl Tool & Die Company Inc....330 782-0254
1144 Meadowbrook Ave Youngstown (44512) *(G-21066)*
Vinylmax Corporation....800 847-3736
2921 Mcbride Ct Hamilton (45011) *(G-10618)*
Vinyltech Inc....330 538-0369
11635 Mahoning Ave North Jackson (44451) *(G-15158)*
Vinylume Products Inc....330 799-2000
3745 Hendricks Rd Youngstown (44515) *(G-21067)*
Viotec LLC....614 596-2054
5970 Pirthshire St Dublin (43016) *(G-9009)*
VIP-Scs, West Chester *Also called VIP-Supply Chain Solutions LLC (G-19818)*
VIP-Supply Chain Solutions LLC (PA)....513 454-2020
9166 Sutton Pl West Chester (45011) *(G-19818)*
Viral Antigens, Cincinnati *Also called Meridian Life Science Inc (G-4007)*
Virant Family Winery Inc....440 466-6279
541 Atkins Rd Geneva (44041) *(G-10230)*
Virco, Marietta *Also called Viking Intl Resources Co Inc (G-12688)*
Virco Virlon Industries Corp....216 410-4872
24700 Aurora Rd Ste 3 Bedford Heights (44146) *(G-1482)*
Virgail Industries Inc....740 928-6001
145 S High St Hebron (43025) *(G-10770)*
Virgils Kitchens Inc....440 355-5058
18800 Whitehead Rd Lagrange (44050) *(G-11497)*
Virginia Air Distributors Inc....614 262-1129
2821 Silver Dr Columbus (43211) *(G-7584)*
Virtual Boss Inc....419 872-7686
517 Prairie Rose Dr Perrysburg (43551) *(G-16021)*
Virtual Hold Technology LLC (PA)....330 670-2200
3875 Embassy Pkwy Ste 350 Akron (44333) *(G-427)*
Virtus Stunts LLC....440 543-0472
16320 Snyder Rd Chagrin Falls (44023) *(G-3089)*
Visi-Trak Worldwide LLC (PA)....216 524-2363
8400 Sweet Valley Dr # 406 Cleveland (44125) *(G-6264)*
Visible Solutions Inc (PA)....440 925-2810
1991 Crocker Rd Ste 222 Westlake (44145) *(G-20168)*
Visimax Technologies Inc....330 405-8330
9177 Dutton Dr Twinsburg (44087) *(G-18872)*
Vision Color LLC....419 924-9450
214 S Defiance St West Unity (43570) *(G-19975)*
Vision Graphics....330 665-4451
3545 Copley Rd Copley (44321) *(G-7698)*
Vision Graphix Inc....440 835-6540
29260 Clemens Rd Ste A Westlake (44145) *(G-20169)*
Vision Press Inc....440 357-6362
1634 W Jackson St Painesville (44077) *(G-15796)*
Vision Projects Inc....937 667-8648
1350 Commerce Park Dr Tipp City (45371) *(G-18142)*
Vision Quest, Elmore *Also called Alvin L Roepke (G-9203)*
Visionary Signs LLC....614 504-5899
6155 Huntley Rd Ste C Columbus (43229) *(G-7585)*
Visionmark, Sidney *Also called Riverside Mfg LLC (G-17067)*
Visionmark Nameplate Co LLC....419 977-3131
100 White Mountain Dr New Bremen (45869) *(G-14662)*
Visiontech Automation LLC....614 554-2013
6682 Weston Cir W Dublin (43016) *(G-9010)*
Vista Industrial Packaging LLC....800 454-6117
4700 Fisher Rd Columbus (43228) *(G-7586)*
Vista Packaging & Logistics, Columbus *Also called Vista Industrial Packaging LLC (G-7586)*
Vista Research Group LLC....419 281-3927
1554 Township Road 805 Ashland (44805) *(G-753)*
Vistanet, Ashland *Also called Vista Research Group LLC (G-753)*
Vistech Mfg Solutions LLC....513 860-1408
4274 Thunderbird Ln Fairfield (45014) *(G-9573)*
Vistech Mfg Solutions LLC....513 933-9300
265 S West St Lebanon (45036) *(G-11706)*
Visual Advantage LLC....714 671-0988
13010 Five Point Rd Perrysburg (43551) *(G-16022)*
Visual Art Graphic Services....330 274-2775
5244 Goodell Rd Mantua (44255) *(G-12562)*
Visual Expressions Sign Co....440 245-6660
901 Broadway Lorain (44052) *(G-12136)*
Visual Information Institute....937 376-4361
1065 Lower Bellbrook Rd Xenia (45385) *(G-20801)*
Visualy Imp Exp Wm Isues Fr Gr....216 561-6864
3041 E 121st St Cleveland (44120) *(G-6265)*
Vitakraft Sun Seed Inc....419 832-1641
20584 Long Judson Rd Weston (43569) *(G-20178)*
Vital Connections Incorporated....937 667-3880
955 N 3rd St Tipp City (45371) *(G-18143)*
Vital Signs & Advertising LLC....937 292-7967
224 S Madriver St Bellefontaine (43311) *(G-1526)*
Vitalrock LLC....888 596-8892
19885 Detroit Rd Ste 108 Rocky River (44116) *(G-16559)*
Vitamin Lac....440 548-5294
17642 Tavern Rd Middlefield (44062) *(G-13865)*
Vitec Inc....216 464-4670
26901 Cannon Rd Bedford (44146) *(G-1453)*
Vitex Corporation....216 883-0920
2960 Broadway Ave Cleveland (44115) *(G-6266)*
Vivid Graphix, Bellaire *Also called Charles Wisvari (G-1484)*
Vivid Wraps LLC....513 515-8386
12130 Royal Point Dr Cincinnati (45249) *(G-4482)*
Vivo Brothers LLC....330 629-8686
8420 South Ave Poland (44514) *(G-16239)*
Vlchek Plastics....440 632-1631
15981 Valplast St Middlefield (44062) *(G-13866)*
Vmaxx Inc....419 738-4044
323 Commerce Rd Wapakoneta (45895) *(G-19358)*
Vmetro Inc (HQ)....281 584-0728
2600 Paramount Pl Ste 200 Fairborn (45324) *(G-9473)*
Vmi Americas Inc (HQ)....330 929-6800
4670 Allen Rd Stow (44224) *(G-17641)*
Vocational Services Inc....216 431-8085
2239 E 55th St Cleveland (44103) *(G-6267)*
Voci, Pataskala *Also called Vampire Optical Coatings Inc (G-15848)*
Vogelsang Brazil Comercio E, Ravenna *Also called Hugo Vglsang Maschinenbau GMBH (G-16382)*
Voice Media Group Inc....216 241-7550
1468 W 9th St Ste 805 Cleveland (44113) *(G-6268)*
Voice Products Inc....216 360-0433
23715 Merc Rd Ste A200 Cleveland (44122) *(G-6269)*
Voigt & Schweitzer LLC (HQ)....614 449-8281
987 Buckeye Park Rd Columbus (43207) *(G-7587)*
Voisard Tool LLC....937 526-5451
2700 Russia Versailles Rd Russia (45363) *(G-16614)*
Volk Corporation....513 621-1052
635 Main St Ste 1 Cincinnati (45202) *(G-4483)*
Volk Optical Inc....440 942-6161
7893 Enterprise Dr Mentor (44060) *(G-13625)*
Voll Hockey Inc....216 521-4625
11820 Edgewater Dr # 418 Lakewood (44107) *(G-11536)*
Volpe Millwork Inc....216 581-0200
4500 Lee Rd Cleveland (44128) *(G-6270)*
Voltage Regulator Sales & Svcs....937 878-0673
590 E Dayton Dr Fairborn (45324) *(G-9474)*
Von Roll Isola, Cleveland *Also called Von Roll Usa Inc (G-6271)*
Von Roll Usa Inc....216 433-7474
4853 W 130th St Cleveland (44135) *(G-6271)*
Voodoo Industries....440 653-5333
33640 Pin Oak Pkwy Ste 4 Avon Lake (44012) *(G-1012)*
Vores Steve Welding & Steel, Fort Recovery *Also called Steve Vore Welding and Steel (G-9827)*
Vorhees Logging LLC....740 385-0216
15275 Mount Olive Rd Rockbridge (43149) *(G-16538)*
Vorlage Special Tool....419 697-1201
205 Utah St Oregon (43605) *(G-15572)*
Vortec and Paxton Products....513 891-7474
10125 Carver Rd Blue Ash (45242) *(G-1865)*
Vortec Corporation....513 891-7485
10125 Carver Rd Blue Ash (45242) *(G-1866)*
Vortec-An Illinois Tl Works Co, Blue Ash *Also called Vortec Corporation (G-1866)*
Vorti-Siv, Salem *Also called M M Industries Inc (G-16758)*

ALPHABETIC

Voss Clamp Technology Division, Cleveland *Also called Voss Industries Inc* ***(G-6272)***
Voss Industries Inc.....216 771-7655
2168 W 25th St Cleveland (44113) ***(G-6272)***
Voss Industries LLC (HQ).....216 771-7655
2168 W 25th St Cleveland (44113) ***(G-6273)***
Voyale Minority Enterprise LLC.....216 271-3661
5855 Grant Ave Cleveland (44105) ***(G-6274)***
VPI, Aurora *Also called Video Products Inc* ***(G-915)***
Vpp Industries Inc.....937 526-3775
960 E Main St Versailles (45380) ***(G-19192)***
Vr Waverly Inc., Waverly *Also called Kirchhoff Auto Waverly Inc* ***(G-19550)***
Vrc, Loveland *Also called Valve Related Controls Inc* ***(G-12242)***
Vrc Inc.....440 243-6666
696 W Bagley Rd Berea (44017) ***(G-1631)***
Vrc Manufacturers, Berea *Also called Vrc Inc* ***(G-1631)***
Vscorp LLC.....937 305-3562
4754 Us Route 40 Tipp City (45371) ***(G-18144)***
Vsp Lab Columbus.....614 409-8900
2605 Rohr Rd Lockbourne (43137) ***(G-11999)***
Vss Store Operations LLC.....800 411-5116
4 Limited Pkwy E Reynoldsburg (43068) ***(G-16460)***
Vtd Systems Inc.....440 323-4122
7600 W River Rd S Elyria (44035) ***(G-9344)***
Vti Instruments Corporation.....216 447-8950
7525 Granger Rd Ste 7 Cleveland (44125) ***(G-6275)***
Vts Co Ltd.....419 273-4010
607 E Lima St Forest (45843) ***(G-9790)***
Vulcan International Corp.....513 621-2850
30 Garfield Pl Ste 1000 Cincinnati (45202) ***(G-4484)***
Vulcan Machinery Corporation.....330 376-6025
20 N Case Ave Akron (44305) ***(G-428)***
Vulcan Oil Company, Cincinnati *Also called New Vulco Mfg & Sales Co LLC* ***(G-4072)***
Vulcan Products Co Inc.....419 468-1039
208 S Washington St Galion (44833) ***(G-10159)***
Vulcan Tool Company.....937 253-6194
730 Lorain Ave Dayton (45410) ***(G-8581)***
Vulkor, Warren *Also called Therm-O-Link Inc* ***(G-19447)***
Vulkor Incorporated (PA).....330 393-7600
621 Dana St Ne Ste V Warren (44483) ***(G-19457)***
Vvi Dispensers, Bedford Heights *Also called Virco Virlon Industries Corp* ***(G-1482)***
Vwm Republic Metals, Cleveland *Also called Victory White Metal Company* ***(G-6259)***
Vwm-Republic Inc.....216 271-1400
6100 Roland Ave Cleveland (44127) ***(G-6276)***
VWR Chemicals LLC (HQ).....800 448-4442
28600 Fountain Pkwy Solon (44139) ***(G-17258)***
Vya Inc.....513 772-5400
1325 Glendale Milford Rd Cincinnati (45215) ***(G-4485)***
W & W Automotive, Beavercreek Township *Also called W&W Automotive & Towing Inc* ***(G-1375)***
W & W Custom Fabrication Inc.....513 353-4617
4801 Hamilton Cleves Rd Cleves (45002) ***(G-6382)***
W & W Custom Fabrication Inc (PA).....513 353-4617
143 E Fairway Dr Hamilton (45013) ***(G-10619)***
W A S P Inc.....740 439-2398
59100 Claysville Rd Cambridge (43725) ***(G-2462)***
W B, Marion *Also called Wilson Bohannan Company* ***(G-12750)***
W B Becherer Inc.....330 758-6616
7905 Southern Blvd Youngstown (44512) ***(G-21068)***
W B Mason Co Inc.....888 926-2766
12985 Snow Rd Cleveland (44130) ***(G-6277)***
W C Heller & Co Inc.....419 485-3176
201 W Wabash St Montpelier (43543) ***(G-14321)***
W C R, Fairborn *Also called Wcr Inc* ***(G-9475)***
W C Sims Co Inc (PA).....937 325-7035
3845 W National Rd Springfield (45504) ***(G-17514)***
W G Lockhart Construction Co.....330 745-6520
800 W Waterloo Rd Akron (44314) ***(G-429)***
W G Machine Tool Service Co.....330 723-3428
7735 Spieth Rd Medina (44256) ***(G-13362)***
W H K Company.....937 372-3368
1720 State Route 380 Xenia (45385) ***(G-20802)***
W H Patten Drilling Co Inc.....330 674-3046
6336 County Road 207 Millersburg (44654) ***(G-14144)***
W J Egli Company Inc (PA).....330 823-3666
205 E Columbia St Alliance (44601) ***(G-512)***
W L Arehart Computing Systems.....937 383-4710
555 Fife Rd Wilmington (45177) ***(G-20510)***
W L Beck Printing & Design.....330 762-3020
1326 S Main St Akron (44301) ***(G-430)***
W M Inc.....330 427-6115
275 High St Washingtonville (44490) ***(G-19482)***
W M Dauch Concrete Inc.....419 562-6917
900 Nevada Rd Bucyrus (44820) ***(G-2349)***
W N Albums and Frames Inc.....800 325-5179
2160 Superior Ave E Cleveland (44114) ***(G-6278)***
W O Hardwoods Inc.....740 425-1588
58098 Wright Rd Barnesville (43713) ***(G-1120)***
W of Ohio Inc (PA).....614 873-4664
225 Guy St Plain City (43064) ***(G-16216)***
W P Brown Enterprises Inc.....740 685-2594
57051 Marietta Rd Byesville (43723) ***(G-2396)***
W Pole Contracting Inc.....330 325-7177
4188 State Route 14 Ravenna (44266) ***(G-16418)***
W Productions, Urbana *Also called Wright John* ***(G-19020)***
W R G Inc.....216 351-8494
3961 Pearl Rd Cleveland (44109) ***(G-6279)***
W S Tyler, Mentor *Also called Tyler Haver Inc* ***(G-13615)***
W T Inc.....419 224-6942
606 N Jackson St Lima (45801) ***(G-11957)***
W W Cross Industries Inc.....330 588-8400
2510 Allen Ave Se Canton (44707) ***(G-2861)***
W W F, Fayetteville *Also called Wiederhold Wldg & Fabrication* ***(G-9642)***
W W Williams Company LLC.....330 659-3084
2920 Brecksville Rd B1 Richfield (44286) ***(G-16494)***
W&W Automotive & Towing Inc.....937 429-1699
680 Orchard Ln Beavercreek Township (45434) ***(G-1375)***
W&W Rock Sand and Gravel.....513 266-3708
1451 Maple Grove Rd Williamsburg (45176) ***(G-20256)***
W-J Inc.....440 248-8282
34180 Solon Rd Solon (44139) ***(G-17259)***
W.T.nickell Co., Batavia *Also called D&D Design Concepts Inc* ***(G-1135)***
W/S Packaging Group Inc.....740 929-2210
1720 James Pkwy Heath (43056) ***(G-10734)***
W/S Packaging Group Inc.....513 459-2400
7500 Industrial Row Dr Mason (45040) ***(G-12953)***
W3 Ultrasonics LLC.....330 284-3667
5288 Huckleberry St Nw North Canton (44720) ***(G-15136)***
WA Hammond Drierite Co Ltd.....937 376-2927
138 Dayton Ave Xenia (45385) ***(G-20803)***
Wabash National Corporation.....419 434-9409
2000 Fostoria Ave Findlay (45840) ***(G-9774)***
Wabash River Conservancy.....419 375-2577
14574 State Route 49 Fort Recovery (45846) ***(G-9830)***
Wabash River Conservancy Dst, Fort Recovery *Also called Wabash River Conservancy* ***(G-9830)***
Wabtec Corporation.....440 238-5350
12312 Alameda Dr Strongsville (44149) ***(G-17803)***
Wabtec Corporation.....216 362-7500
4677 Manufacturing Ave Cleveland (44135) ***(G-6280)***
Wabush Mines Cliffs Mining Co.....216 694-5700
200 Public Sq Ste 3300 Cleveland (44114) ***(G-6281)***
Wacker Chemical Corporation.....330 899-0847
2215 International Pkwy Canton (44720) ***(G-2862)***
Waddell A Div GMI Companies, Greenfield *Also called GMI Companies Inc* ***(G-10349)***
Waddell Manufacturing Company, Stow *Also called Baker McMillen Co* ***(G-17573)***
Wade Dynamics Inc.....216 431-8484
1411 E 39th St Cleveland (44114) ***(G-6282)***
Wades Woodworking Inc.....937 374-6470
1427 Bellbrook Ave Xenia (45385) ***(G-20804)***
Wadsworth Brewing Company LLC.....330 475-4935
186 Humbolt Ave Wadsworth (44281) ***(G-19279)***
Wadsworth Excavating Inc.....419 898-0771
7869 W State Route 163 Oak Harbor (43449) ***(G-15448)***
Waeco Valve Division, Salem *Also called Hunt Valve Company Inc* ***(G-16748)***
Waffle House Inc.....937 746-6830
6840 Franklin Lebanon Rd Franklin (45005) ***(G-9929)***
Waffle House Inc.....513 539-8372
1225 Hamilton Lebanon Rd Monroe (45050) ***(G-14281)***
Wagers Inc.....513 825-6300
2464 California Rd Okeana (45053) ***(G-15520)***
Wagner Farms & Sawmill LLC.....419 653-4126
13201 Road X Leipsic (45856) ***(G-11738)***
Wagner Machine Inc.....330 706-0700
5151 Wooster Rd W Norton (44203) ***(G-15377)***
Wagner Quarries Company.....419 625-8141
4203 Milan Rd Sandusky (44870) ***(G-16862)***
Wagner Rustproofing Co Inc.....216 361-4930
7708 Quincy Ave Cleveland (44104) ***(G-6283)***
Wagoner Stores Inc (PA).....937 836-3636
324 Union Blvd Englewood (45322) ***(G-9383)***
Wagoners Red Wing Shs Fabrics, Englewood *Also called Wagoner Stores Inc* ***(G-9383)***
Wagram, Etna *Also called Alice Beougher* ***(G-9388)***
Wahconah Group Inc.....216 923-0570
2930 Euclid Ave Cleveland (44115) ***(G-6284)***
Wahl Refractory Solutions LLC.....419 334-2658
767 S State Route 19 Fremont (43420) ***(G-10063)***
Wahlies Cstm Cft Drapery Uphl.....419 229-1731
605 W Kibby St Lima (45804) ***(G-11958)***
Waibel Electric Co Inc.....740 964-2956
133 Humphries Dr Etna (43068) ***(G-9390)***
Waino Sheet Metal Inc.....330 945-4226
4198 Ellsworth Rd Stow (44224) ***(G-17642)***
Waits Instruments LLC.....513 600-5996
1337 Karahill Dr Cincinnati (45240) ***(G-4486)***
Wake Nation.....513 887-9253
201 Joe Nuxhall Way Fairfield (45014) ***(G-9574)***

Wake Robin Fermented Foods LLC 216 961-9944
1303 W 103rd St Cleveland (44102) *(G-6285)*
Wal Plax, Bedford *Also called Walton Plastics Inc (G-1454)*
Wal-Bon of Ohio Inc (PA) 740 423-6351
210 Main St Belpre (45714) *(G-1585)*
Wal-Bon of Ohio Inc 740 423-8178
708 Main St Belpre (45714) *(G-1586)*
Walbridge Coatings, Walbridge *Also called MSC Walbridge Coatings Inc (G-19297)*
Walden Industries Inc 740 633-5971
101 Walden Ave Tiltonsville (43963) *(G-18094)*
Waldo & Associates Inc 419 666-3662
28214 Glenwood Rd Perrysburg (43551) *(G-16023)*
Waldock Eqp Sls & Svc Inc (PA) 419 426-7771
12178 E County Road 6 Attica (44807) *(G-860)*
Waldorf Marking Devices, New London *Also called Monode Marking Products Inc (G-14731)*
Waldorf Marking Devices Div, Mentor *Also called Monode Marking Products Inc (G-13522)*
Walest Incorporated 216 362-8110
15500 Commerce Park Dr Cleveland (44142) *(G-6286)*
Walker Magnetics Group Inc 614 492-1614
2195 Wright Brothers Ave Columbus (43217) *(G-7588)*
Walker National, Columbus *Also called Walker Magnetics Group Inc (G-7588)*
Walker National Inc 614 492-1614
2195 Wright Brothers Ave Columbus (43217) *(G-7589)*
Walker Tool & Machine Co 419 661-8000
7700 Ponderosa Rd Perrysburg (43551) *(G-16024)*
Wall Colmonoy Corporation 937 278-9111
940 Redna Ter Cincinnati (45215) *(G-4487)*
Wall Colmonoy Corporation 513 842-4200
940 Redna Ter Cincinnati (45215) *(G-4488)*
Wall Polishing LLC 937 698-1330
1953 S State Route 48 Ludlow Falls (45339) *(G-12270)*
Wall Technology Inc 715 532-5548
1 Owens Corning Pkwy Toledo (43659) *(G-18594)*
Wallace Forge Company 330 488-1203
3700 Georgetown Rd Ne Canton (44704) *(G-2863)*
Wallen Commercial Hardware 937 426-5711
832 Space Dr Beavercreek Township (45434) *(G-1376)*
Waller Brothers Stone Company 740 858-1948
744 Mcdermott Rushtown Rd Mc Dermott (45652) *(G-13195)*
Wallingford Coffee Mills Inc (PA) 513 771-3131
11401 Rockfield Ct Cincinnati (45241) *(G-4489)*
Wallover Enterprises Inc (HQ) 440 238-9250
21845 Drake Rd Strongsville (44149) *(G-17804)*
Wallover Oil Company Inc 440 238-9250
21845 Drake Rd Strongsville (44149) *(G-17805)*
Wallover Oil Company Inc (HQ) 440 238-9250
21845 Drake Rd Strongsville (44149) *(G-17806)*
Wallover Oil Hamilton Inc 513 896-6692
1000 Forest Ave Hamilton (45015) *(G-10620)*
Walls Asphalt Manufacturing, Greenville *Also called Walls Bros Asphalt Co Inc (G-10399)*
Walls Bros Asphalt Co Inc (PA) 937 548-7158
3690 Hllnsburg Sampson Rd Greenville (45331) *(G-10399)*
Wallseye Concrete Corp (PA) 440 235-1800
26000 Sprague Rd Cleveland (44138) *(G-6287)*
Wallseye Concrete Corp 419 483-2738
8802 Portland Rd Castalia (44824) *(G-2941)*
Walnut Creek Cart Shop 330 893-1097
3309 State Route 39 Millersburg (44654) *(G-14145)*
Walnut Creek Chocolate Company 330 893-2995
4917 State Rte 515 Walnut Creek (44687) *(G-19308)*
Walnut Creek Lumber Co Ltd 330 852-4559
10433 Pleasant Hill Rd Nw Dundee (44624) *(G-9031)*
Walnut Creek Planing Ltd 330 893-3244
5778 State Route 515 Millersburg (44654) *(G-14146)*
Walnut Creek Wood Design 330 852-9663
1689 State Route 39 Sugarcreek (44681) *(G-17875)*
Walnut Creek Woodworking LLC 513 504-3520
1878 Jones Florer Rd Bethel (45106) *(G-1656)*
Walnut Hill Shop 740 828-3346
17388a Frampton Rd Frazeysburg (43822) *(G-9942)*
Walsh Manufacturing, Cleveland *Also called Herman Manufacturing LLC (G-5398)*
Walt Myers 937 325-0313
303 N Greenmount Ave Springfield (45503) *(G-17515)*
Waltco Lift Corp (HQ) 330 633-9191
285 Northeast Ave Tallmadge (44278) *(G-18013)*
Walter F Stephens Jr Inc 937 746-0521
415 South Ave Franklin (45005) *(G-9930)*
Walter Graphics Inc 419 522-5261
850 Oak St Mansfield (44907) *(G-12536)*
Walter Grinders Inc 937 859-1975
510 Earl Blvd Miamisburg (45342) *(G-13737)*
Walter H Drane Co Inc 216 514-1022
23811 Chagrin Blvd # 344 Beachwood (44122) *(G-1285)*
Walter North 937 204-6050
900 Pimlico Dr Apt 2a Dayton (45459) *(G-8582)*
Walters Buildings, Urbana *Also called Jack Walters & Sons Corp (G-18999)*
Walther EMC, Franklin *Also called Walther Engrg & Mfg Co Inc (G-9931)*
Walther Engrg & Mfg Co Inc 937 743-8125
3501 Shotwell Dr Franklin (45005) *(G-9931)*
Walton Hills, Walton Hills *Also called Controllix Corporation (G-19309)*
Walton Plastics Inc 440 786-7711
20493 Hannan Pkwy Bedford (44146) *(G-1454)*
Walton, Rego and Roy, West Chester *Also called Wrr Creative Concepts LLC (G-19822)*
Wanashab Inc 330 606-6675
1768 E 25th St Ste 308 Cleveland (44114) *(G-6288)*
Wannemacher Enterprises Inc 419 771-1101
422 W Guthrie Dr Upper Sandusky (43351) *(G-18977)*
Wannemacher Packaging, Upper Sandusky *Also called Wannemacher Enterprises Inc (G-18977)*
Wanner Metal Worx Inc 740 369-4034
525 London Rd Delaware (43015) *(G-8730)*
Wapak Tool & Die Inc 419 738-6215
732 Keller Dr Wapakoneta (45895) *(G-19359)*
Wapakoneta Daily News, Wapakoneta *Also called Horizon Publications Inc (G-19333)*
Wapakoneta Plant, Wapakoneta *Also called General Aluminum Mfg Company (G-19330)*
Wappoo Wood Products Inc 937 492-1166
12877 Kirkwood Rd Sidney (45365) *(G-17084)*
Ward Construction Co (PA) 419 943-2450
385 Oak St Leipsic (45856) *(G-11739)*
Ward Mold & Machine 740 472-5303
317 Fairground Rd Woodsfield (43793) *(G-20549)*
Ward/Kraft Forms of Ohio Inc 740 694-0015
700 Salem Ave Ext Fredericktown (43019) *(G-9983)*
Warehouse, Mansfield *Also called Gorman-Rupp Company (G-12449)*
Warfighter Fcsed Logistics Inc (PA) 740 513-4692
3894 Worthington Rd Galena (43021) *(G-10117)*
Warlock Inc 614 471-4055
2179 Citygate Dr Columbus (43219) *(G-7590)*
Warmus and Associates Inc 330 659-4440
2324 N Clvland Msslln Rd Bath (44210) *(G-1203)*
Warner Chlcott Phrmcticals Inc (PA) 513 983-1100
1 Procter And Gamble Plz Cincinnati (45202) *(G-4490)*
Warner Fabricating Inc 330 848-3191
7812 Hartman Rd Wadsworth (44281) *(G-19280)*
Warner Hildebrant 740 286-1903
714 Bear Run Rd South Webster (45682) *(G-17300)*
Warner Vess Inc 740 585-2481
12 Warner Second St Lower Salem (45745) *(G-12259)*
Warped Wing Brewing Co LLC 937 222-7003
26 Wyandot St Dayton (45402) *(G-8583)*
Warren Castings Inc 216 883-2520
2934 E 55th St Cleveland (44127) *(G-6289)*
Warren Concrete and Supply Co 330 393-1581
1113 Parkman Rd Nw Warren (44485) *(G-19458)*
Warren Door, Niles *Also called Traichal Construction Company (G-15037)*
Warren Drilling Co Inc 740 783-2775
305 Smithson St Dexter City (45727) *(G-8796)*
Warren Enterprises 330 836-6119
1067 Winhurst Dr Akron (44313) *(G-431)*
Warren Fabricating Corporation (PA) 330 534-5017
7845 Chestnut Ridge Rd Hubbard (44425) *(G-11011)*
Warren Fabricating Corporation 330 544-4101
907 S Main St Niles (44446) *(G-15039)*
Warren Fire Equipment Inc (PA) 330 824-3523
6880 Tod Ave Sw Warren (44481) *(G-19459)*
Warren Fire Equipment Inc 937 866-8918
2240 E Central Ave Miamisburg (45342) *(G-13738)*
Warren Metal Lithography, Warren *Also called Tecnocap LLC (G-19446)*
Warren Printing & Off Pdts Inc 419 523-3635
250 E Main St Ottawa (45875) *(G-15671)*
Warren Rupp Inc 419 524-8388
800 N Main St Mansfield (44902) *(G-12537)*
Warren Screw Machine Inc 330 609-6020
3869 Niles Rd Se Warren (44484) *(G-19460)*
Warren Steel Specialties Corp 330 399-8360
1309 Niles Rd Se Warren (44484) *(G-19461)*
Warren Trucking, Dexter City *Also called Warren Drilling Co Inc (G-8796)*
Warren Welding and Fabrication, Lebanon *Also called Kirbys Auto & Truck Repair (G-11669)*
Warren Zachman Contracting 740 389-4503
5005 Marion Edison Rd Marion (43302) *(G-12747)*
Warrenton Copper LLC 636 456-3488
1240 Marquette St Cleveland (44114) *(G-6290)*
Warrior Technologies Inc 937 438-0279
7320 Kings Run Rd Dayton (45459) *(G-8584)*
Warthman Drilling Inc 740 746-9950
7525 Lancaster Logan Rd Sugar Grove (43155) *(G-17840)*
Warwick Products Company 216 334-1200
5350 Tradex Pkwy Cleveland (44102) *(G-6291)*
Washing Systems LLC (HQ) 800 272-1974
167 Commerce Dr Loveland (45140) *(G-12244)*
Washington Crt Hse Converting, Wshngtn CT Hs *Also called Weyerhaeuser Company (G-20751)*
Washington Group, Oregon *Also called Aecom Energy & Cnstr Inc (G-15553)*
Washington Products Inc 330 837-5101
1875 Harsh Ave Se Ste 1 Massillon (44646) *(G-13057)*
Washita Valley Enterprises Inc 330 510-1568
3707 Tulane Ave Bldg 9 Louisville (44641) *(G-12171)*

(PA)=Parent Co (HQ)=Headquarters (DH)=Div Headquarters

ALPHABETIC

Wasserstrom Company (PA) 614 228-6525
4500 E Broad St Columbus (43213) ***(G-7591)***
Wasserstrom Company 614 228-2233
2777 Silver Dr Columbus (43211) ***(G-7592)***
Wasserstrom Marketing Division, Columbus *Also called N Wasserstrom & Sons Inc* ***(G-7206)***
Waste King, North Olmsted *Also called Anaheim Manufacturing Company* ***(G-15181)***
Waste Parchment Inc 330 674-6868
4510 Township Road 307 Millersburg (44654) ***(G-14147)***
Waste Water Plant, The, Ravenna *Also called City of Ravenna* ***(G-16372)***
Waste Water Pollution Control 330 263-5290
1123 Columbus Rd Wooster (44691) ***(G-20663)***
Waste Water Treatment Plant, Madison *Also called County of Lake* ***(G-12345)***
Wastequip Manufacturing Co LLC 330 674-1119
930 Massillon Rd Millersburg (44654) ***(G-14148)***
Watch-Us Inc 513 829-8870
4450 Dixie Hwy Fairfield (45014) ***(G-9575)***
Water & Sewer, Chardon *Also called City of Chardon* ***(G-3105)***
Water & Waste Water Dept., Mount Vernon *Also called City of Mount Vernon* ***(G-14475)***
Water & Waste Water Eqp Co 440 542-0972
32100 Solon Rd Ste 101a Solon (44139) ***(G-17260)***
Water Drop Media Inc 234 600-5817
289 Youngstown Kingsvl Se Vienna (44473) ***(G-19211)***
Water Ink Technologies, Blue Ash *Also called Actega North America Inc* ***(G-1720)***
Water Star Inc 440 996-0800
7590 Discovery Ln Painesville (44077) ***(G-15797)***
Water Systems Services 513 523-6766
4164 Miami Western Dr Oxford (45056) ***(G-15702)***
Water Treatment, Middletown *Also called City of Middletown* ***(G-13894)***
Water Treatment Plant, Marietta *Also called City of Marietta* ***(G-12615)***
Water Warriors Inc 513 288-5669
1776 Mentor Ave Ste 400f Cincinnati (45212) ***(G-4491)***
Waterford Signs Inc 740 362-7446
288 S Sandusky St Ste C Delaware (43015) ***(G-8731)***
Waterford Tank Fabrication Ltd 740 984-4100
203 State Route 83 Beverly (45715) ***(G-1663)***
Waterloo Industries Inc 800 833-8851
12487 Plaza Dr Cleveland (44130) ***(G-6292)***
Waterloo Manufacturing Co Inc 330 947-2917
6298 Waterloo Rd Atwater (44201) ***(G-865)***
Waterlox Coatings Corporation 216 641-4877
9808 Meech Ave Cleveland (44105) ***(G-6293)***
Waterpro 330 372-3565
2926 Commonwealth Ave Ne Warren (44483) ***(G-19462)***
Watershed Mangement LLC 740 852-5607
10460 State Route 56 Se Mount Sterling (43143) ***(G-14466)***
Watersource LLC 419 747-9552
1225 W Longview Ave Mansfield (44906) ***(G-12538)***
Waterville Sheet Metal Company 419 878-5050
1210 Wtrville Monclova Rd Waterville (43566) ***(G-19508)***
Watkins Auto Body Shop, Holland *Also called Custom Color Match and Spc* ***(G-10921)***
Watkins Printing Company 614 297-8270
1401 E 17th Ave Columbus (43211) ***(G-7593)***
Watson Electric Motor Svc Inc 614 836-9904
536 Stockbridge Rd Columbus (43207) ***(G-7594)***
Watson Gravel Inc 513 422-3781
2100 S Main St Middletown (45044) ***(G-13964)***
Watson Gravel Inc (PA) 513 863-0070
2728 Hamilton Cleves Rd Hamilton (45013) ***(G-10621)***
Watson Haran & Company Inc 937 436-1414
1500 Yankee Park Pl Dayton (45458) ***(G-8585)***
Watson Meeks and Company 937 378-2355
10402 W Fork Rd Georgetown (45121) ***(G-10239)***
Watson's, Cincinnati *Also called Entertrainment Junction* ***(G-3644)***
Watt Printers, Cleveland *Also called Gergel-Kellem Company Inc* ***(G-5318)***
Watteredge LLC (HQ) 440 933-6110
567 Miller Rd Avon Lake (44012) ***(G-1013)***
Watters Manufacturing Co Inc 216 281-8600
1931 W 47th St Cleveland (44102) ***(G-6294)***
Watts Acquisition Company II, Eastlake *Also called Tri-Tech Research LLC* ***(G-9136)***
Watts Antenna Company 740 797-9380
70 N Plains Rd Ste H The Plains (45780) ***(G-18024)***
Waugs Inc 440 315-4851
956 State Route 302 Ashland (44805) ***(G-754)***
Wausau Mosinee Paper, Middletown *Also called Wausau Paper Corp* ***(G-13965)***
Wausau Paper Corp 513 217-3623
700 Columbia Ave Middletown (45042) ***(G-13965)***
Wausau Ppr Towel & Tissue LLC 513 424-2999
700 Columbia Ave Middletown (45042) ***(G-13966)***
Wauseon Machine & Mfg Inc 419 337-0940
2495 Technical Dr Miamisburg (45342) ***(G-13739)***
Wauseon Machine & Mfg Inc (PA) 419 337-0940
995 Enterprise Ave Wauseon (43567) ***(G-19537)***
Wauseon Precast, Wauseon *Also called Wauseon Silo & Coal Company* ***(G-19538)***
Wauseon Silo & Coal Company 419 335-6041
535 Wood St Wauseon (43567) ***(G-19538)***
Waverly Tool Co Ltd 740 988-4831
2596 Glade Rd Beaver (45613) ***(G-1294)***
Waxco International Inc 937 746-4845
727 Dayton Oxford Rd Miamisburg (45342) ***(G-13740)***
Waxman Industries Inc (PA) 440 439-1830
24460 Aurora Rd Cleveland (44146) ***(G-6295)***
Waymakers Inc 330 352-1096
628 Roscoe Ave Akron (44306) ***(G-432)***
Wayne - Dalton Plastics, Conneaut *Also called Hrh Door Corp* ***(G-7649)***
Wayne - Dalton Rolling Doors, Dalton *Also called Hrh Door Corp* ***(G-7943)***
Wayne Builders Supply, Greenville *Also called St Henry Tile Co Inc* ***(G-10396)***
Wayne Concrete Company 937 545-9919
223 Western Dr Medway (45341) ***(G-13367)***
Wayne County Rubber Inc 330 264-5553
1205 E Bowman St Wooster (44691) ***(G-20664)***
Wayne Dalton, Mount Hope *Also called Hrh Door Corp* ***(G-14438)***
Wayne Frame Products Inc 419 726-7715
5832 Lakeside Ave Toledo (43611) ***(G-18595)***
Wayne Manufacturing, Zanesville *Also called New Wayne Inc* ***(G-21162)***
Wayne Pak Ltd 440 323-8744
214 Brace Ave Elyria (44035) ***(G-9345)***
Wayne Signer Enterprises Inc 513 841-1351
6545 Wiehe Rd Cincinnati (45237) ***(G-4492)***
Wayne Sporting Goods 937 236-6665
7101 Taylorsville Rd Dayton (45424) ***(G-8586)***
Wayne Trail Technologies Inc 937 295-2120
407 S Main St Fort Loramie (45845) ***(G-9811)***
Wayne Water Systems, Harrison *Also called Wayne/Scott Fetzer Company* ***(G-10679)***
Wayne's Precision Mach Shop, East Palestine *Also called Waynes Precision Machine Inc* ***(G-9089)***
Wayne/Scott Fetzer Company 800 237-0987
101 Production Dr Harrison (45030) ***(G-10679)***
Waynedale Truss & Panel Co 330 683-4471
93 Lake Dr Dalton (44618) ***(G-7953)***
Waynedale Truss and Panel Co 330 698-7373
8971 Dover Rd Apple Creek (44606) ***(G-622)***
Waynes Precision Machine Inc 330 426-4626
354 N Liberty St East Palestine (44413) ***(G-9089)***
Waytek Corporation 937 743-6142
400 Shotwell Dr Franklin (45005) ***(G-9932)***
Wbc Group LLC (PA) 866 528-2144
6333 Hudson Crossing Pkwy Hudson (44236) ***(G-11082)***
Wc Sales Inc 419 836-2300
5732 Woodville Rd Ste C Northwood (43619) ***(G-15350)***
Wccv Floor Coverings LLC (PA) 330 688-0114
4535 State Rd Peninsula (44264) ***(G-15901)***
Wch Molding LLC 740 335-6320
1850 Lowes Blvd Wshngtn CT Hs (43160) ***(G-20748)***
Wcho AM, Wshngtn CT Hs *Also called Iheartcommunications Inc* ***(G-20728)***
Wcm Holdings Inc 513 705-2100
11500 Canal Rd Cincinnati (45241) ***(G-4493)***
Wcr Inc (PA) 937 223-0703
2377 Commerce Center Blvd B Fairborn (45324) ***(G-9475)***
Wcr Incorporated 740 333-3448
809 Delaware St Wshngtn CT Hs (43160) ***(G-20749)***
We Grind Muzik 614 670-4142
4000 Andrus Ct Apt D Columbus (43227) ***(G-7595)***
Wear Magic, Cincinnati *Also called Cincinnati Advg Pdts LLC* ***(G-3479)***
Wear Technology, Batavia *Also called Milacron Marketing Company LLC* ***(G-1167)***
Weastec Incorporated 937 393-6800
1600 N High St Hillsboro (45133) ***(G-10893)***
Weastec Incorporated 614 734-9645
6195 Enterprise Ct Dublin (43016) ***(G-9011)***
Weastec Incorporated (HQ) 937 393-6800
1600 N High St Hillsboro (45133) ***(G-10894)***
Weatherproofing Tech Inc 281 480-7900
3735 Green Rd Beachwood (44122) ***(G-1286)***
Weaver Barns Ltd 330 852-2103
1696 State Route 39 Sugarcreek (44681) ***(G-17876)***
Weaver Boos Consultants Inc 419 933-5216
1145 S Conwell Ave Willard (44890) ***(G-20248)***
Weaver Bros Inc (PA) 937 526-3907
895 E Main St Versailles (45380) ***(G-19193)***
Weaver Craft of Sugarcreek, Sugarcreek *Also called Weavers Furniture Ltd* ***(G-17877)***
Weaver Fab & Finishing, Akron *Also called Bogie Industries Inc Ltd* ***(G-92)***
Weaver Lumber Co 330 359-5091
1925 Us Route 62 Wilmot (44689) ***(G-20517)***
Weaver Pallet Ltd 330 682-4022
9380 Ely Rd Apple Creek (44606) ***(G-623)***
Weaver Woodcraft L L C 330 695-2150
9652 Harrison Rd Apple Creek (44606) ***(G-624)***
Weavers Furniture Ltd 330 852-2701
7011 Old Route 39 Nw Sugarcreek (44681) ***(G-17877)***
Web3box Software LLC 330 794-7397
34 Merz Blvd Ste D Tallmadge (44278) ***(G-18014)***
Webb Machine & Fab Inc 330 717-5745
15262 Hoyle Rd Berlin Center (44401) ***(G-1651)***
Webb-Stiles Company (PA) 330 225-7761
675 Liverpool Dr Valley City (44280) ***(G-19069)***
WEBB-STILES OF ALABAMA, Valley City *Also called Webb-Stiles Company* ***(G-19069)***

Weber Jewelers Incorporated 937 643-9200
3155 Far Hills Ave Dayton (45429) ***(G-8587)***
Weber Orthopedic Inc 440 934-1812
1324 Chester Indus Pkwy Avon (44011) ***(G-974)***
Weber Ready Mix Inc 419 394-9097
16672 County Road 66a Saint Marys (45885) ***(G-16704)***
Weber Sand & Gravel Inc 419 298-2388
2702 County Road 3b Edgerton (43517) ***(G-9182)***
Weber Sand & Gravel Inc 419 636-7920
14586 Us Highway 127 Ew Bryan (43506) ***(G-2312)***
Weber Technologies Inc 440 946-8833
34000 Melinz Pkwy Eastlake (44095) ***(G-9140)***
Weber Tool & Mfg Inc 440 786-0221
7761 First Pl Oakwood Village (44146) ***(G-15488)***
Webers Body & Frame 937 839-5946
2017 State Route 503 N West Alexandria (45381) ***(G-19624)***
Webster Industries Inc (PA) 419 447-8232
325 Hall St Tiffin (44883) ***(G-18092)***
Webster Manufacturing Company, Tiffin *Also called Webster Industries Inc* ***(G-18092)***
Wecall Inc 440 437-8202
64 Penniman Rd Orwell (44076) ***(G-15636)***
Wecan Fabricators LLC 740 667-0731
49425 E Park Dr Tuppers Plains (45783) ***(G-18721)***
Wedco LLC 513 309-0781
716 N High St Mount Orab (45154) ***(G-14452)***
Wedding Pages, Canton *Also called Brahler Inc* ***(G-2597)***
Wedding Plantation, Columbus *Also called Beverly Snider* ***(G-6665)***
Wedge Hardwood Products 330 525-7775
2137 Knox School Rd Alliance (44601) ***(G-513)***
Wedge Products Inc 330 405-4477
2181 Enterprise Pkwy Twinsburg (44087) ***(G-18873)***
Wedgeworks Mch Tl & Boring Co 216 441-1200
3169 E 80th St Cleveland (44104) ***(G-6296)***
Weed Instrument Company Inc 800 321-0796
6133 Rockside Rd Ste 300 Independence (44131) ***(G-11156)***
Weekly Brothers Cnty Line Far 330 674-4195
1533 Township Road 110 Millersburg (44654) ***(G-14149)***
Weekly Chatter 740 336-4704
1564 Calder Ridge Rd Belpre (45714) ***(G-1587)***
Weekly Juicery 513 321-0680
2727 Erie Ave Cincinnati (45208) ***(G-4494)***
Weekly Villager Inc 330 527-5761
8088 Main St Garrettsville (44231) ***(G-10204)***
Weekly Villager, The, Garrettsville *Also called Weekly Villager Inc* ***(G-10204)***
Weenk Labs LLC 614 448-0160
221 N 4th St Columbus (43215) ***(G-7596)***
Weidmann Electrical Tech Inc 937 652-1220
700 W Court St Urbana (43078) ***(G-19019)***
Weighing Division, Columbus *Also called Interface Logic Systems Inc* ***(G-7041)***
Weirton Daily Times 740 283-4711
401 Herald Sq Steubenville (43952) ***(G-17557)***
Weirton Daily Times, The, Steubenville *Also called Ogden Newspapers Inc* ***(G-17546)***
Weiskopf Industries Corp 440 442-4400
54 Alpha Park Cleveland (44143) ***(G-6297)***
Weiss Construction & Sewer, Mentor *Also called L B Weiss Construction Inc* ***(G-13492)***
Weiss Industries Inc 419 526-2480
2480 N Main St Mansfield (44903) ***(G-12539)***
Weiss Metallurgical Services, Mansfield *Also called Weiss Industries Inc* ***(G-12539)***
Weiss Motors 330 678-5585
4554 State Route 43 Kent (44240) ***(G-11399)***
Wek Industries, Jefferson *Also called Tmd Wek North LLC* ***(G-11241)***
Welage Corporation 513 681-2300
1925 Powers St Cincinnati (45223) ***(G-4495)***
Welch Foods Inc A Cooperative 513 632-5610
720 E Pete Rose Way Cincinnati (45202) ***(G-4496)***
Welch Holdings Inc 513 353-3220
8953 E Miami River Rd Cincinnati (45247) ***(G-4497)***
Welch Packaging Columbus, Columbus *Also called Welch Packaging Group Inc* ***(G-7597)***
Welch Packaging Group Inc 614 870-2000
4700 Alkire Rd Columbus (43228) ***(G-7597)***
Welch Publishing Co (PA) 419 874-2528
117 E 2nd St Perrysburg (43551) ***(G-16025)***
Welch Publishing Co 419 666-5344
215 Osborne St Rossford (43460) ***(G-16594)***
Weld-Action Company Inc 330 372-1063
2100 N River Rd Ne Warren (44483) ***(G-19463)***
Welded Ring Products Co (PA) 216 961-3800
2180 W 114th St Cleveland (44102) ***(G-6298)***
Welded Tube Pros LLC 330 854-2966
215 Market St W Canal Fulton (44614) ***(G-2496)***
Welded Tubes Inc (PA) 216 378-2092
135 Penniman Rd Orwell (44076) ***(G-15637)***
Welded Tubes Inc 440 437-5144
135 Penniman Rd Orwell (44076) ***(G-15638)***
Welded Tubes LLC 210 278-3757
135 Penniman Rd Orwell (44076) ***(G-15639)***
Welders Supply Inc (HQ) 216 241-1696
2020 Train Ave Cleveland (44113) ***(G-6299)***
Weldfab Inc 440 563-3310
2642 E Water St Rock Creek (44084) ***(G-16535)***
Welding Consultants Inc 614 258-7018
889 N 22nd St Columbus (43219) ***(G-7598)***
Welding Equipment Repair Co 330 536-2125
142 E Water St Lowellville (44436) ***(G-12257)***
Welding Improvement Company 330 424-9666
10070 Stookesberry Rd Lisbon (44432) ***(G-11982)***
Weldments Inc 937 235-9261
167 Heid Ave Dayton (45404) ***(G-8588)***
Weldon 330 263-9533
3834 Zane Trace Dr Columbus (43228) ***(G-7599)***
Weldon Ice Cream Company 740 467-2400
2887 Canal Dr Millersport (43046) ***(G-14162)***
Weldon Plastics Corporation 330 425-9660
1962 Case Pkwy Twinsburg (44087) ***(G-18874)***
Weldon Pump, Cleveland *Also called Bergstrom Company Ltd Partnr* ***(G-4805)***
Weldon Pump Acquition LLC 440 232-2282
640 Golden Oak Pkwy Oakwood Village (44146) ***(G-15489)***
Weldon Technologies, Columbus *Also called Akron Brass Company* ***(G-6557)***
Weldon West, Akron *Also called West Motorsports Inc* ***(G-434)***
Weldparts Inc 513 530-0064
6500 Corporate Dr Blue Ash (45242) ***(G-1867)***
Weldtec Inc 419 586-1200
8319 Us Route 127 Celina (45822) ***(G-2992)***
Welker Machine & Grinding Co 216 481-1360
718 E 163rd St Cleveland (44110) ***(G-6300)***
Well Service Group Inc 330 308-0880
1490 Truss Rd Sw New Philadelphia (44663) ***(G-14808)***
Wellington Manufacturing 440 647-1162
200 Erie St Wellington (44090) ***(G-19594)***
Wellington Stamping, Wellington *Also called Sectional Stamping Inc* ***(G-19591)***
Wellington Wllams Wrldwide LLC 423 805-6198
305 S Market St U871 Troy (45373) ***(G-18718)***
Wellnitz, Columbus *Also called Hazelbaker Industries Ltd* ***(G-6984)***
Wells Group LLC 740 532-9240
487 Gallia Pike Ironton (45638) ***(G-11176)***
Wells Inc 419 457-2611
8176 Us Highway 23 Risingsun (43457) ***(G-16519)***
Wells Manufacturing Co Llc 937 987-2481
280 W Main St New Vienna (45159) ***(G-14826)***
Wellsgroup 740 289-1000
3293 Us Highway 23 Piketon (45661) ***(G-16081)***
Wellsgroup 937 382-4003
1481 S Us Highway 68 Wilmington (45177) ***(G-20511)***
Wellston Aerosol Mfg Co Inc 740 384-2320
105 W A St Wellston (45692) ***(G-19610)***
Welsh Farms LLC 513 723-4487
221 E 4th St Ste 2000 Cincinnati (45202) ***(G-4498)***
Wendell Machine Shop 330 627-3480
2076 Mobile Rd Ne Carrollton (44615) ***(G-2932)***
Wengerd Cabinets 330 231-0879
6605 Township Road 362 Millersburg (44654) ***(G-14150)***
Wengerd Wood Inc 330 359-4300
1760 County Road 200 Dundee (44624) ***(G-9032)***
Wengerd's Machine, Dalton *Also called Pioneer Equipment Company* ***(G-7951)***
Wenrick Machine and Tool Corp 937 667-7307
4685 Us Route 40 Tipp City (45371) ***(G-18145)***
Wentworth Mold Inc Electra 937 898-8460
852 Scholz Dr Vandalia (45377) ***(G-19151)***
Wentworth Solutions 440 212-7696
2868 Westway Dr Ste B Brunswick (44212) ***(G-2249)***
Wentworth Technologies LLC 440 212-7696
2868 Westway Dr Brunswick (44212) ***(G-2250)***
Weprintquick.com, Cleveland *Also called Eveready Printing Inc* ***(G-5200)***
Were Rolling Pretzle Company 419 784-0762
2500 W State St Ste 82 Alliance (44601) ***(G-514)***
Wereb Metal Fabricating, Willoughby *Also called James L Wereb* ***(G-20347)***
Werk-Brau Company 419 422-2912
2800 Fostoria Ave Findlay (45840) ***(G-9775)***
Werling and Sons Inc 937 338-3281
100 Plum St Burkettsville (45310) ***(G-2356)***
Werlor Inc 419 784-4285
1420 Ralston Ave Defiance (43512) ***(G-8647)***
Werlor Waste Control, Defiance *Also called Werlor Inc* ***(G-8647)***
Wernke Wldg & Stl Erection Co 513 353-4173
3150 State Line Rd North Bend (45052) ***(G-15058)***
Wernli Realty Inc 937 258-7878
1300 Grange Hall Rd Beavercreek (45430) ***(G-1368)***
Wersell's Bike & Ski Shop, Toledo *Also called Wersells Bike Shop Co* ***(G-18596)***
Wersells Bike Shop Co 419 474-7412
2860 W Central Ave Toledo (43606) ***(G-18596)***
Wes-Garde Components Group Inc 614 885-0319
300 Enterprise Dr Westerville (43081) ***(G-20081)***
Weschler Instruments, Strongsville *Also called Hughes Corporation* ***(G-17751)***
Wesco Distribution Inc 419 666-1670
6519 Fairfield Dr Northwood (43619) ***(G-15351)***
Wesco Machine Inc 330 688-6973
918 N Main St Akron (44310) ***(G-433)***

ALPHABETIC

West & Barker Inc — ALPHABETIC SECTION

West & Barker Inc 330 652-9923
 950 Summit Ave Niles (44446) *(G-15040)*
West Bend Printing & Pubg Inc 419 258-2000
 101 N Main St Antwerp (45813) *(G-600)*
West Carrollton Converting Inc 937 859-3621
 400 E Dixie Dr West Carrollton (45449) *(G-19633)*
West Carrollton Parchment 513 594-3341
 400 E Dixie Dr West Carrollton (45449) *(G-19634)*
West Chester Holdings LLC 800 647-1900
 11500 Canal Rd Cincinnati (45241) *(G-4499)*
West Chester Lock Co LLC 513 777-6486
 6847 Lakota Plaza Dr West Chester (45069) *(G-19819)*
West Chester Protective Gear, Cincinnati Also called West Chester Holdings LLC *(G-4499)*
West Equipment Company Inc (PA) 419 698-1601
 1545 E Broadway St Toledo (43605) *(G-18597)*
West Erie Fuel 440 282-3493
 4935 W Erie Ave Lorain (44053) *(G-12137)*
West Extrusion LLC 330 744-0625
 75 Mccartney Rd Campbell (44405) *(G-2472)*
West Liberty Commons, Medina Also called Al Root Company *(G-13219)*
West Motorsports Inc 330 350-0375
 1018 Ironwood Rd Ste A Akron (44306) *(G-434)*
West Ohio Tool & Mfg LLC 419 678-4745
 3965 Lange Rd Saint Henry (45883) *(G-16671)*
West Ohio Tool Company 937 842-6688
 7311 World Class Dr Russells Point (43348) *(G-16602)*
West Pharmaceutical Svcs Inc 513 741-3004
 3309 Wheatcroft Dr Cincinnati (45239) *(G-4500)*
West Point Optical Group LLC 614 395-9775
 4680 Parkway Dr Ste 455 Mason (45040) *(G-12954)*
West Ridge Resources Inc (PA) 740 338-3100
 46226 National Rd Saint Clairsville (43950) *(G-16657)*
West Side Leader, Fairlawn Also called Leader Publications Inc *(G-9612)*
West Troy, Troy Also called Troy West LLC *(G-18715)*
West-Camp Press Inc (PA) 614 882-2378
 39 Collegeview Rd Westerville (43081) *(G-20082)*
West-Camp Press Inc 614 895-0233
 5178 Sinclair Rd Columbus (43229) *(G-7600)*
West-Camp Press Inc 216 426-2660
 1538 E 41st St Cleveland (44103) *(G-6301)*
Westar Plastics Llc 419 636-1333
 4271 County Road 15d Bryan (43506) *(G-2313)*
Westend Brewing LLC 513 922-0289
 5091 Orangelawn Dr Cincinnati (45238) *(G-4501)*
Westerhaus Metals LLC 513 240-9441
 3965 Delmar Ave Cincinnati (45211) *(G-4502)*
Westerman Inc (HQ) 740 569-4143
 245 N Broad St Bremen (43107) *(G-2065)*
Westerman Inc 330 262-6946
 899 Venture Blvd Wooster (44691) *(G-20665)*
Westerman Acquisition Co LLC 330 264-2447
 776 Kemrow Ave Wooster (44691) *(G-20666)*
Western & Southern Lf Insur Co (HQ) 513 629-1800
 400 Broadway St Cincinnati (45202) *(G-4503)*
Western Branch Diesel Inc 330 454-8800
 1616 Metric Ave Sw Canton (44706) *(G-2864)*
Western Digital Corporation 440 684-1331
 2635 Butternut Ln Cleveland (44124) *(G-6302)*
Western Enterprises, Westlake Also called Western/Scott Fetzer Company *(G-20170)*
Western Entps A Scott Fetzer, Avon Lake Also called Scott Fetzer Company *(G-1007)*
Western KY Coal Resources LLC 740 338-3100
 46226 National Rd Saint Clairsville (43950) *(G-16658)*
Western Ohio Cut Stone Ltd 937 492-4722
 1130 Dingman Slagle Rd Sidney (45365) *(G-17085)*
Western Ohio Graphics, Troy Also called Painted Hill Inv Group Inc *(G-18691)*
Western Ohio Graphics 937 335-8769
 402 E Main St Troy (45373) *(G-18719)*
Western Reserve Distillers LLC 330 780-9599
 14221 Madison Ave Lakewood (44107) *(G-11537)*
Western Reserve Foods LLC 330 770-0885
 325 Bell St Chagrin Falls (44022) *(G-3032)*
Western Reserve Furniture Co 440 235-6216
 29701 Wellington Dr North Olmsted (44070) *(G-15203)*
Western Reserve Graphics 440 729-9527
 13404 Caves Rd Chesterland (44026) *(G-3172)*
Western Reserve Industries LLC 330 238-1800
 25933 State Route 62 Beloit (44609) *(G-1572)*
Western Reserve Lubricants 440 951-5700
 13981 Leroy Center Rd Painesville (44077) *(G-15798)*
Western Reserve Metals Inc 330 448-4092
 7775 Addison Rd Masury (44438) *(G-13064)*
Western Reserve Mfg Co 216 641-0500
 9200 Inman Ave Cleveland (44105) *(G-6303)*
Western Reserve Sleeve Inc 440 238-8750
 22360 Royalton Rd Strongsville (44149) *(G-17807)*
Western Reserve Wire Products, Twinsburg Also called Wrwp LLC *(G-18875)*
Western Roto Engravers Inc 330 336-7636
 668 Seville Rd Wadsworth (44281) *(G-19281)*
Western Star Newspaper, Liberty Township Also called Cox Newspapers LLC *(G-11812)*
Western Star Rail Services, Newark Also called Dennis Lavender *(G-14867)*
Western States Envelope Co 419 666-7480
 6859 Commodore Dr Walbridge (43465) *(G-19300)*
Western States Envelope Label, Walbridge Also called Western States Envelope Co *(G-19300)*
Western Stress, Northwood Also called Analytic Stress Relieving Inc *(G-15332)*
Western-Southern Life, Cincinnati Also called Western & Southern Lf Insur Co *(G-4503)*
Western/Scott Fetzer Company 440 871-2160
 875 Bassett Rd Westlake (44145) *(G-20170)*
Western/Scott Fetzer Company (HQ) 440 892-3000
 28800 Clemens Rd Westlake (44145) *(G-20171)*
Westerville Endoscopy Ctr LLC 614 568-1666
 300 Polaris Pkwy Ste 1500 Westerville (43082) *(G-20030)*
Westfield Steel Inc 937 322-2414
 1120 S Burnett Rd Springfield (45505) *(G-17516)*
Westgate Machine Co Inc 216 889-9745
 10665 Knights Way North Royalton (44133) *(G-15310)*
Westgerdes Cabinets 419 375-2113
 2664 Sawmill Rd Fort Recovery (45846) *(G-9831)*
Westinghouse A Brake Tech Corp 419 526-5323
 472 Rembrandt St Mansfield (44902) *(G-12540)*
Westmont Inc 330 862-3080
 3035 Union Ave Ne Minerva (44657) *(G-14205)*
Westmoreland Resources Gp LLC 740 622-6302
 544 Chestnut St Coshocton (43812) *(G-7756)*
Westmount Technology Inc 216 328-2011
 6100 Oak Tree Blvd Independence (44131) *(G-11157)*
Westrock Commercial LLC 419 476-9101
 1635 Coining Dr Toledo (43612) *(G-18598)*
Westrock Converting Company 513 860-0225
 9266 Meridian Way West Chester (45069) *(G-19820)*
Westrock Cp LLC 513 745-2400
 9960 Alliance Rd Blue Ash (45242) *(G-1868)*
Westrock Cp LLC 740 622-0581
 500 N 4th St Coshocton (43812) *(G-7757)*
Westrock Cp LLC 770 448-2193
 1010 Mead St Wshngtn CT Hs (43160) *(G-20750)*
Westrock Cp LLC 330 297-0841
 975 N Freedom St Ravenna (44266) *(G-16419)*
Westrock Cp LLC 937 898-2115
 7032 N Dixie Dr Dayton (45414) *(G-8589)*
Westrock Cp LLC 614 445-6850
 1015 Marion Rd Columbus (43207) *(G-7601)*
Westrock Cp LLC 513 745-2586
 414 S Cooper Ave Cincinnati (45215) *(G-4504)*
Westrock Mwv LLC 937 495-6323
 10 W 2nd St Dayton (45402) *(G-8590)*
Westrock Mwv LLC 937 495-6323
 4751 Hempstead Station Dr Kettering (45429) *(G-11443)*
Westrock Rkt LLC 513 860-5546
 9245 Meridian Way West Chester (45069) *(G-19821)*
Westrock Rkt Company 330 296-5155
 975 N Freedom St Ravenna (44266) *(G-16420)*
Westrock Usc Inc 740 681-1600
 1290 Campground Rd Lancaster (43130) *(G-11618)*
Westrock Usc Inc 740 484-1000
 41298 Brown Rd Bethesda (43719) *(G-1659)*
Westside Supply Co Inc 216 267-9353
 5010 W 140th St Brookpark (44142) *(G-2159)*
Westview Concrete Corp 440 458-5800
 40105 Butternut Ridge Rd Elyria (44035) *(G-9346)*
Westwood Fvrication Shtmtl Inc 937 837-0494
 1752 Stanley Ave Dayton (45404) *(G-8591)*
Wetsu Group Inc 937 324-9353
 125 W North St Springfield (45504) *(G-17517)*
Wettle Corporation 419 865-6923
 952 Holland Park Blvd Holland (43528) *(G-10966)*
Weyerhaeuser Co Containeerboar 740 397-5215
 8800 Granville Rd Mount Vernon (43050) *(G-14518)*
Weyerhaeuser Company 740 335-4480
 1803 Lowes Blvd Wshngtn CT Hs (43160) *(G-20751)*
Wfmj-Tv21, Youngstown Also called Vindicator Printing Company *(G-21065)*
Wfs Filter Co, Cleveland Also called Micropure Filtration Inc *(G-5669)*
Wfsr Holdings LLC 877 735-4966
 220 E Monument Ave Dayton (45402) *(G-8592)*
Wg Mobile Welding LLC 440 720-1940
 6151 Wilson Mills Rd # 210 Highland Heights (44143) *(G-10800)*
WH Fetzer & Sons Mfg Inc 419 687-8237
 500 Donnenwirth Dr Plymouth (44865) *(G-16235)*
Whatifsportscom Inc 513 333-0313
 10200 Alliance Rd Ste 301 Blue Ash (45242) *(G-1869)*
Wheat Ridge Pallet & Lumber, West Union Also called Schrock John *(G-19966)*
Wheatland Tube Company, Cambridge Also called Zekelman Industries Inc *(G-2463)*
Wheatland Tube Company, Niles Also called John Maneely Company *(G-15019)*
Wheatley Electric Service Co 513 531-4951
 2046 Ross Ave Cincinnati (45212) *(G-4505)*
Wheel Group Holdings LLC 614 253-6247
 2901 E 4th Ave Ste 3 Columbus (43219) *(G-7602)*
Wheel One, Columbus Also called Wheel Group Holdings LLC *(G-7602)*

Wheeler Embroidery....740 550-9751
1007 N 2nd St Ironton (45638) *(G-11177)*
Wheeler Manufacturing, Ashtabula *Also called Rex International USA Inc (G-803)*
Wheeler Sheet Metal Inc....419 668-0481
4640 Plank Rd Norwalk (44857) *(G-15417)*
Whelco Industrial Ltd (PA)....419 385-4627
28210 Cedar Park Blvd Perrysburg (43551) *(G-16026)*
Whelco Industrial Ltd....419 873-6134
28210 Cedar Park Blvd Perrysburg (43551) *(G-16027)*
Whemco, Canton *Also called United Rolls Inc (G-2850)*
Whemco-Ohio Foundry Inc....419 222-2111
1600 Mcclain Rd Lima (45804) *(G-11959)*
Whempys Corp....614 888-6670
6969 Worth Galena Rd P Worthington (43085) *(G-20707)*
Whip Appeal Inc....216 288-6201
13405 Graham Rd Cleveland (44112) *(G-6304)*
Whip Guide Co....440 543-5151
16829 Park Circle Dr Chagrin Falls (44023) *(G-3090)*
Whirlaway Corporation (HQ)....440 647-4711
720 Shiloh Ave Wellington (44090) *(G-19595)*
Whirlaway Corporation....440 647-4711
125 Bennett St Wellington (44090) *(G-19596)*
Whirlaway Corporation....440 647-4711
720 Shiloh Ave Wellington (44090) *(G-19597)*
Whirlpool Corporation....937 548-4126
1701 Kitchen Aid Way Greenville (45331) *(G-10400)*
Whirlpool Corporation....740 383-7122
1300 Marion Agosta Rd Marion (43302) *(G-12748)*
Whirlpool Corporation....419 547-7711
119 Birdseye St Clyde (43410) *(G-6397)*
Whirlpool Corporation....419 423-8123
4901 N Main St Findlay (45840) *(G-9776)*
Whirlpool Corporation....937 547-0773
1301 Sater St Greenville (45331) *(G-10401)*
Whirlpool Corporation....614 409-4340
6241 Shook Rd Lockbourne (43137) *(G-12000)*
Whirlpool Corporation....419 523-5100
677 Woodland Dr Ottawa (45875) *(G-15672)*
Whiskey Fox Corporation....440 779-6767
1060 W Bagley Rd Ste 102 Berea (44017) *(G-1632)*
Whitacre Enterprises Inc....740 934-2331
35651 State Route 537 Graysville (45734) *(G-10342)*
Whitacre Greer Company (PA)....330 823-1610
1400 S Mahoning Ave Alliance (44601) *(G-515)*
Whitaker Finishing LLC....419 666-7746
2707 Tracy Rd Northwood (43619) *(G-15352)*
White Castle System Inc (PA)....614 228-5781
555 W Goodale St Columbus (43215) *(G-7603)*
White Castle System Inc....513 563-2290
3126 Exon Ave Cincinnati (45241) *(G-4506)*
White Co David....440 247-2920
10161 Music St Novelty (44072) *(G-15440)*
White Dove Mattress, Newburgh Heights *Also called H Goodman Inc (G-14936)*
White Dove Mattress Ltd....216 341-0200
3201 Harvard Ave Newburgh Heights (44105) *(G-14945)*
White Feather Foods Inc....419 738-8975
13845 Cemetery Rd Wapakoneta (45895) *(G-19360)*
White Industrial Tool Inc....330 773-6889
102 W Wilbeth Rd Akron (44301) *(G-435)*
White Jewelers....330 264-3324
211 E Liberty St Wooster (44691) *(G-20667)*
White Machine & Mfg Co (PA)....740 453-3444
120 Graham St Zanesville (43701) *(G-21188)*
White Machine Inc....440 237-3282
9621 York Alpha Dr North Royalton (44133) *(G-15311)*
White Mule Company....740 382-9008
2420 W 4th St Ontario (44906) *(G-15550)*
White Rock Quarry L P....419 855-8388
3800 Bolander Rd Clay Center (43408) *(G-4570)*
White Tool, Akron *Also called White Industrial Tool Inc (G-435)*
White Water Forest, Batavia *Also called Whitewater Forest Products LLC (G-1196)*
Whitefeather Foods, Wapakoneta *Also called White Feather Foods Inc (G-19360)*
Whiteford Industries Inc....419 381-1155
3323 South Ave Toledo (43609) *(G-18599)*
Whitehouse, Tiffin *Also called Bradleys Beacons Ltd (G-18052)*
Whitehouse Bros Inc....513 621-2259
4393 Creek Rd Blue Ash (45241) *(G-1870)*
Whiterock Pigments Inc....216 391-7765
1768 E 25th St Cleveland (44114) *(G-6305)*
Whiteside Manufacturing Co....740 363-1179
309 Hayes St Delaware (43015) *(G-8732)*
Whitewater Forest Products LLC....513 673-7596
2720 Moraine Way Batavia (45103) *(G-1196)*
Whitewater Processing Co....513 367-4133
10964 Campbell Rd Harrison (45030) *(G-10680)*
Whiteys Food Systems Inc....330 659-4070
3600 Brecksville Rd Ofc Richfield (44286) *(G-16495)*
Whitman Corporation....513 541-3223
2530 Joyce Ln Okeana (45053) *(G-15521)*
Whitmer Woodworks Inc....614 873-1196
8490 Carters Mill Rd Plain City (43064) *(G-16217)*
Whitmore Productions Inc....216 752-3960
20209 Harvard Ave Warrensville Heights (44122) *(G-19474)*
Whitmore's Bbq, Warrensville Heights *Also called Whitmore Productions Inc (G-19474)*
Whitney Company, Northwood *Also called Wc Sales Inc (G-15350)*
Whitney House....614 396-7846
666 High St Ste 102 Worthington (43085) *(G-20708)*
Whitney Stained Glass Studio....216 348-1616
5939 Broadway Ave Cleveland (44127) *(G-6306)*
Whits Frozen Custard....740 965-1427
101 W Cherry St Unit A Sunbury (43074) *(G-17902)*
Whitt Machine Inc....513 423-7624
806 Central Ave Middletown (45044) *(G-13967)*
Whitten Studios....419 368-8366
1180 County Road 30a Ashland (44805) *(G-755)*
Whitworth Knife Company....513 321-9177
508 Missouri Ave Cincinnati (45226) *(G-4507)*
Whole Shop Inc....330 630-5305
181 S Thomas Rd Tallmadge (44278) *(G-18015)*
Whole Solutions....330 652-1725
1217 Salt Springs Rd Mineral Ridge (44440) *(G-14174)*
Wholecycle Inc....330 929-8123
100 Cyhoga Fls Indus Pkwy Peninsula (44264) *(G-15902)*
Wholesale Bait Co Inc (PA)....513 863-2380
2619 Bobmeyer Rd Fairfield (45014) *(G-9576)*
Wholesale Channel Letters....440 256-3200
8603 Euclid Chardon Rd Kirtland (44094) *(G-11473)*
Wholesale Fairy Gardenscom LLC....614 504-5304
8400 Industrial Pkwy F Plain City (43064) *(G-16218)*
Wholesale Imprints Inc....440 224-3527
6259 Hewitt Ln North Kingsville (44068) *(G-15161)*
Wholesale Printers Ltd....440 354-5788
195 N Doan Ave Painesville (44077) *(G-15799)*
Wico Products Inc....937 783-0000
311 E Fancy St Blanchester (45107) *(G-1708)*
Wide Area Media LLC....440 356-3133
24500 Center Ridge Rd # 205 Westlake (44145) *(G-20172)*
Wiederhold Wldg & Fabrication....513 875-3755
1843 Us Highway 50 Fayetteville (45118) *(G-9642)*
Wieland, Archbold *Also called Sauder Manufacturing Co (G-666)*
Wifi-Plus Inc....877 838-4195
2950 Westway Dr Ste 101 Brunswick (44212) *(G-2251)*
Wififace LLC....419 754-4816
5424 Westcastle Dr Apt D Toledo (43615) *(G-18600)*
Wikoff Color Corporation....216 271-2300
3650 E 93rd St Cleveland (44105) *(G-6307)*
Wikoff Color Corporation....513 423-0727
1330 Hook Dr Middletown (45042) *(G-13968)*
Wil-Mark Froyo LLC....330 421-6043
124 Joshua Dr Rittman (44270) *(G-16530)*
Wilbert Inc....419 483-2300
635 Southwest St Bellevue (44811) *(G-1551)*
Wilbert Plastic Services, Bellevue *Also called Wilbert Inc (G-1551)*
Wilbert Shaw Valts, Newcomerstown *Also called Shaw Wilbert Vaults LLC (G-14982)*
Wilcoxon, James H Jr, Columbus *Also called Johnsons Real Ice Cream Co (G-7074)*
Wild Berry Incense Inc....513 523-8583
5475 College Corner Pike Oxford (45056) *(G-15703)*
Wild Berry Incense Factory, Oxford *Also called Wild Berry Incense Inc (G-15703)*
Wild Fire Systems....440 442-8999
535 Ransome Rd Cleveland (44143) *(G-6308)*
Wild Joe's Beef Jerky, Cincinnati *Also called Wild Joes Inc (G-4508)*
Wild Joes Inc....513 681-9200
2905 Jessamine St Cincinnati (45225) *(G-4508)*
Wild Oak LLC....513 769-0526
35 Lenore Dr Cincinnati (45215) *(G-4509)*
Wildcat Creek Farms Inc....419 263-2549
4633 Road 94 Payne (45880) *(G-15876)*
Wildcat Creek Popcorn, Payne *Also called Wildcat Creek Farms Inc (G-15876)*
Wiley Farms....937 537-0676
29984 State Route 739 Richwood (43344) *(G-16509)*
Wiley Organics Inc....740 622-0755
1245 S 6th St Coshocton (43812) *(G-7758)*
Wileys Finest LLC....740 622-1072
545 Walnut St Ste B Coshocton (43812) *(G-7759)*
Wilguss Automotive Machine....937 465-0043
216 Runkle St West Liberty (43357) *(G-19939)*
Wilkes Energy Inc....330 252-4560
17 S Main St Ste 101a Akron (44308) *(G-436)*
Wilkett Enterprises LLC....740 384-2890
109 Mitchell Dr 4 Wellston (45692) *(G-19611)*
Wilks Industries....330 868-5105
4010 Robertsville Ave Se Minerva (44657) *(G-14206)*
Wilkshire Dry Cleaners LLC....330 674-7696
5660 County Road 203 Millersburg (44654) *(G-14151)*
Will-Burt Advnced Cmpsites Inc....330 684-5286
356 Collins Blvd Orrville (44667) *(G-15625)*
Will-Burt Company (PA)....330 682-7015
169 S Main St Orrville (44667) *(G-15626)*

ALPHABETIC

Will-Burt Company — **ALPHABETIC SECTION**

Will-Burt Company 330 683-9991
  150 Allen Ave Orrville (44667) *(G-15627)*
Will-Burt Company 330 682-7015
  312 Collins Blvd Orrville (44667) *(G-15628)*
Willard Kelsey Solar Group LLC 419 931-2001
  1775 Progress Dr Perrysburg (43551) *(G-16028)*
Willard Machine & Welding Inc 330 467-0642
  556 Highland Rd E Ste 3 Macedonia (44056) *(G-12338)*
Willard Times Junction 419 935-0184
  211 S Myrtle Ave Willard (44890) *(G-20249)*
William A Selz, Dayton Also called S & S Printing Service Inc *(G-8490)*
William Darling Company Inc 614 878-0085
  615 Hilliard Rome Rd A Columbus (43228) *(G-7604)*
William Dauch Concrete Company (PA) 419 668-4458
  84 Cleveland Rd Norwalk (44857) *(G-15418)*
William Dauch Concrete Company 419 562-6917
  900 Nevada Wynford Rd Bucyrus (44820) *(G-2350)*
William Evanko Dgs, Wadsworth Also called Evanko Wm/Barringer Richd DDS *(G-19238)*
William Exline Inc 216 941-0800
  12301 Bennington Ave Cleveland (44135) *(G-6309)*
William F Kelly, North Olmsted Also called Western Reserve Furniture Co *(G-15203)*
William Harding 513 738-3344
  5359 Jenkins Rd Hamilton (45013) *(G-10622)*
William J Bergen & Co 440 248-6132
  32520 Arthur Rd Solon (44139) *(G-17261)*
William J Dupps 419 734-2126
  126 Madison St Port Clinton (43452) *(G-16264)*
William J Minneman Family LP 937 890-7461
  3370 Obco Ct Dayton (45414) *(G-8593)*
William Oeder Ready Mix Inc 513 899-3901
  8807 State Route 134 Martinsville (45146) *(G-12768)*
William Powell Company (PA) 513 852-2000
  2503 Spring Grove Ave Cincinnati (45214) *(G-4510)*
William S Miller Inc 330 223-1794
  11250 Montgomery Rd Kensington (44427) *(G-11287)*
William Thompson 440 232-4363
  11304 Chamberlain Rd Aurora (44202) *(G-916)*
Williams Carrier Transicold, Richfield Also called W W Williams Company LLC *(G-16494)*
Williams Concrete Inc 419 893-3251
  1350 Ford St Maumee (43537) *(G-13160)*
Williams County Publishing, Montpelier Also called Advance Reporter *(G-14301)*
Williams Executive Entps Inc 440 887-1000
  13367 Smith Rd Cleveland (44130) *(G-6310)*
Williams Grgory Martin Fnrl HM, Steubenville Also called Martin M Hardin *(G-17543)*
Williams Industrial Svc Inc 419 353-2120
  2120 Wood Bridge Blvd Bowling Green (43402) *(G-2005)*
Williams John F Oil Field Svcs 740 622-7692
  20669 Coshocton Co Rd 6 Jackson (45640) *(G-11201)*
Williams Leather Products Inc 740 223-1604
  1476 Likens Rd Ste 104 Marion (43302) *(G-12749)*
Williams Machine Co Inc 330 534-3058
  461 N Main St Hubbard (44425) *(G-11012)*
Williams Partners LP 330 966-3674
  7235 Whipple Ave Nw North Canton (44720) *(G-15137)*
Williams Pork Co Op 419 682-9022
  18487 County Road F Stryker (43557) *(G-17836)*
Williams Precision Tool Inc 937 384-0608
  6855 Gillen Ln Miamisburg (45342) *(G-13741)*
Williams Steel Rule Die Co 216 431-3232
  1633 E 40th St Cleveland (44103) *(G-6311)*
Williamson Safe Inc 937 393-9919
  5631 State Route 73 Hillsboro (45133) *(G-10895)*
Willis Cnc 440 926-0434
  1008 Commerce Dr Grafton (44044) *(G-10313)*
Willis Music Company 513 671-3288
  11700 Princeton Pike E209 Cincinnati (45246) *(G-4511)*
Willmac Enterprises Inc 740 967-1979
  12200 Johnstown Utica Rd Johnstown (43031) *(G-11274)*
Willoughby Brewing Company 440 975-0202
  4057 Erie St Willoughby (44094) *(G-20458)*
Willoughby Manufacturing Inc 330 402-8217
  47415 Heck Rd New Waterford (44445) *(G-14844)*
Willow Frog LLC 513 861-4834
  9 Briarwood Ln Cincinnati (45218) *(G-4512)*
Willow Hill Industries LLC 440 942-3003
  37611 Euclid Ave Willoughby (44094) *(G-20459)*
Willow Tool & Machining Ltd 440 572-2288
  15110 Foltz Pkwy Ste 1 Strongsville (44149) *(G-17808)*
Willow Water Treatment Inc 440 254-6313
  7855 Jennings Dr Painesville (44077) *(G-15800)*
Willowwood, Mount Sterling Also called Ohio Willow Wood Company *(G-14464)*
Willy's Fresh Salsa, Swanton Also called Willys Inc *(G-17929)*
Willys Inc 419 823-3200
  11305 W Airport Svc Rd Swanton (43558) *(G-17929)*
Wilmer 419 678-6000
  515 W Sycamore St Coldwater (45828) *(G-6424)*
Wilmington Forest Products 937 382-5013
  5562 S Us Highway 68 Wilmington (45177) *(G-20512)*
Wilmington Precision Machining, Wilmington Also called Cliffco Stands Inc *(G-20489)*

Wilson Blacktop Corporation 740 635-3566
  915 Carlisle St Rear Martins Ferry (43935) *(G-12764)*
Wilson Bohannan Company 740 382-3639
  621 Buckeye St Marion (43302) *(G-12750)*
Wilson Cabinet Co 330 276-8711
  Straits Industrial Park Killbuck (44637) *(G-11455)*
Wilson Concrete Products Inc (PA) 937 885-7965
  10075 Sheehan Rd Dayton (45458) *(G-8594)*
Wilson Electronic Displays, Dayton Also called Wilson Sign Co Inc *(G-8595)*
Wilson Mobility LLC 216 921-9457
  17602 Deforest Ave Cleveland (44128) *(G-6312)*
Wilson Optical Laboratory Inc 440 357-7000
  9450 Pineneedle Dr Mentor (44060) *(G-13626)*
Wilson Prtg Graphics of London (PA) 740 852-5934
  158 S Main St London (43140) *(G-12072)*
Wilson Seat Company Inc 513 732-2460
  199 Foundry Ave Batavia (45103) *(G-1197)*
Wilson Sign Co Inc 937 253-2246
  300 Hamilton Ave Dayton (45403) *(G-8595)*
Wilson Specialties, North Jackson Also called Canfield Manufacturing Co Inc *(G-15143)*
Wilson Well Service, Malta Also called Wolfe Creek Farms *(G-12384)*
Wilsonart LLC 614 876-1515
  2500 International St Columbus (43228) *(G-7605)*
Wilsons Country Creations 330 377-4190
  13248 County Road 6 Killbuck (44637) *(G-11456)*
Win Cd Inc 330 929-1999
  3333 Win St Cuyahoga Falls (44223) *(G-7934)*
Win Plex, Cuyahoga Falls Also called Win Cd Inc *(G-7934)*
Winans Chocolate and Coffee, Piqua Also called Piqua Chocolate Company Inc *(G-16151)*
Windsor Airmotive, West Chester Also called Barnes Group Inc *(G-19656)*
Windsor Mold Inc 419 484-2400
  122 Hirt Dr Bellevue (44811) *(G-1552)*
Windsor Mold USA Inc 419 483-0653
  560 Goodrich Rd Bellevue (44811) *(G-1553)*
Windsor Tool Inc 216 671-1900
  10714 Bellaire Rd Cleveland (44111) *(G-6313)*
Wine Cellar Innovations LLC 513 321-3733
  4575 Eastern Ave Cincinnati (45226) *(G-4513)*
Winery At Spring Hill Inc 440 466-0626
  6062 S Ridge Rd W Geneva (44041) *(G-10231)*
Winery At Wolf Creek 330 666-9285
  2637 Clvland Massillon Rd Barberton (44203) *(G-1113)*
Wines For You 440 946-1420
  7344 Mentor Ave Mentor (44060) *(G-13627)*
Winesburg Hardwood Lumber Co 330 893-2705
  2871 Us Route 62 Dundee (44624) *(G-9033)*
Winesburg Meats Inc 330 359-5092
  2181 Us Rte 62 Winesburg (44690) *(G-20535)*
Wingate Packaging Inc (PA) 513 745-8600
  4347 Indeco Ct Blue Ash (45241) *(G-1871)*
Wingate Packaging South, Blue Ash Also called Wingate Packaging Inc *(G-1871)*
Wings Way Drive Thru Inc 330 533-2788
  9194 Salem Warren Rd Salem (44460) *(G-16781)*
Wings Way Ice, Salem Also called Wings Way Drive Thru Inc *(G-16781)*
Winkle Industries Inc 330 823-9730
  2080 W Main St Alliance (44601) *(G-516)*
Winkler Co Inc 937 294-2662
  435 Patterson Rd Dayton (45419) *(G-8596)*
Winner Welding Fabricating, New Weston Also called Fred Winner *(G-14845)*
Winner's Meat Service, Yorkshire Also called Robert Winner Sons Inc *(G-20826)*
Winners Meat Farm, Greenville Also called Robert Winner Sons Inc *(G-10393)*
Winsell Incorporated 330 836-7421
  1720 Merriman Rd Unit J Akron (44313) *(G-437)*
Winspec Inc 440 834-9068
  15470 Chipmunk Ln Middlefield (44062) *(G-13867)*
Winston Campbell LLC 614 274-7015
  1777 Mckinley Ave Columbus (43222) *(G-7606)*
Winston Heat Treating Inc 937 226-0110
  711 E 2nd St Dayton (45402) *(G-8597)*
Winston Oil Co Inc 740 373-9664
  1 Court House Ln Ste 3 Marietta (45750) *(G-12689)*
Winston Products LLC 440 478-1418
  30339 Diamond Pkwy # 105 Cleveland (44139) *(G-6314)*
Winsupply Inc 937 346-0600
  2187 W 1st St Springfield (45504) *(G-17518)*
Winters Concrete, Jackson Also called Winters Products Inc *(G-11202)*
Winters Products Inc 740 286-4149
  109 Athens St Jackson (45640) *(G-11202)*
Winzeler Stamping Co 419 485-3147
  129 W Wabash St Montpelier (43543) *(G-14322)*
Wipe Out Enterprises 937 497-9473
  6523 Dawson Rd Sidney (45365) *(G-17086)*
Wire Lab Company, Cleveland Also called Omni Technical Products Inc *(G-5814)*
Wire Products Company Inc (PA) 216 267-0777
  14601 Industrial Pkwy Cleveland (44135) *(G-6315)*
Wire Products Company Inc 216 267-0777
  14700 Industrial Pkwy Cleveland (44135) *(G-6316)*

Wire Shop Inc..........440 354-6842
5959 Pinecone Dr Mentor (44060) ***(G-13628)***
Wired Inc..........440 567-8379
38849 Courtland Dr Willoughby (44094) ***(G-20460)***
Wireless Retail LLC..........614 657-5182
6750 Commerce Court Dr Blacklick (43004) ***(G-1695)***
Wiremax Ltd..........419 531-9500
705 Wamba Ave Toledo (43607) ***(G-18601)***
Wirick Press Inc..........330 273-3488
839 Pearl Rd Brunswick (44212) ***(G-2252)***
Wisco Products Incorporated..........937 228-2101
109 Commercial St Dayton (45402) ***(G-8598)***
Wise Consumer Products Company..........513 484-6530
4729 Cornell Rd Blue Ash (45241) ***(G-1872)***
Wise Contracts, Berea *Also called Wise Window Treatment Inc* ***(G-1633)***
Wise Enterprises Inc..........330 568-7095
1911 Wick Campbell Rd Hubbard (44425) ***(G-11013)***
Wise Window Treatment Inc..........216 676-4080
353 Race St Berea (44017) ***(G-1633)***
Wiseco, Mentor *Also called Race Winning Brands Inc* ***(G-13572)***
Wiseco Piston Company, Inc., Mentor *Also called Seabiscuit Motorsports Inc* ***(G-13577)***
Wiseman Bros Fabg & Stl Ltd..........740 988-5121
2598 Glade Rd Beaver (45613) ***(G-1295)***
Witt Enterprises Inc..........440 992-8333
2024 Aetna Rd Ashtabula (44004) ***(G-812)***
Witt Industries Inc (HQ)..........513 871-5700
4600 N Masn Montgomery Rd Mason (45040) ***(G-12955)***
Witt Products, Mason *Also called Witt Industries Inc* ***(G-12955)***
Witt-Gor Inc..........419 659-2151
108 S High St 110 Columbus Grove (45830) ***(G-7639)***
Wittich's Candy Shop, Circleville *Also called Wittichs Candies Inc* ***(G-4564)***
Wittichs Candies Inc..........740 474-3313
117 W High St Circleville (43113) ***(G-4564)***
Wittrock Wdwkg & Mfg Co Inc..........513 891-5800
4201 Malsbary Rd Blue Ash (45242) ***(G-1873)***
Wiwa LLC..........419 757-0141
107 N Main St Alger (45812) ***(G-444)***
Wiwa LP..........419 757-0141
107 N Main St Alger (45812) ***(G-445)***
Wizard Graphics Inc..........419 354-3098
112 S Main St Bowling Green (43402) ***(G-2006)***
Wizard Publications Inc..........808 821-1214
1979 Wilshire Ln Nw Lancaster (43130) ***(G-11619)***
Wjf Enterprises LLC..........513 871-7320
1347 Custer Ave Cincinnati (45208) ***(G-4514)***
Wk Brick Company..........614 416-6700
970 Claycraft Rd Columbus (43230) ***(G-7607)***
WLS Fabricating Co..........440 449-0543
5405 Avion Park Dr Cleveland (44143) ***(G-6317)***
WLS Stamping Co (PA)..........216 271-5100
3292 E 80th St Cleveland (44104) ***(G-6318)***
Wm Caxton Printing, Westerville *Also called Mc Vay Ventures Inc* ***(G-20064)***
Wm Lang & Sons Company..........513 541-3304
3280 Beekman St Cincinnati (45223) ***(G-4515)***
Wm Plotz Machine and Forge Co..........216 861-0441
2514 Center St Cleveland (44113) ***(G-6319)***
Wm Software Inc..........330 558-0501
3660 Center Rd Ste 371 Brunswick (44212) ***(G-2253)***
Wmt, Independence *Also called Westmount Technology Inc* ***(G-11157)***
Wober Muster, Springfield *Also called Crowning Food Company* ***(G-17381)***
Woco, Strongsville *Also called Wallover Oil Company Inc* ***(G-17805)***
Woco, Strongsville *Also called Wallover Oil Company Inc* ***(G-17806)***
Wodin Inc..........440 439-4222
5441 Perkins Rd Cleveland (44146) ***(G-6320)***
Woeber Mustard Mfg Co..........937 323-6281
1966 Commerce Cir Springfield (45504) ***(G-17519)***
Woebkenberg Starting Gates..........937 696-2446
8011 Kinsey Rd West Alexandria (45381) ***(G-19625)***
Wolf Composite Solutions, Columbus *Also called Wolfden Products Inc* ***(G-7609)***
Wolf G T Awning & Tent Co..........937 548-4161
3352 State Route 571 Greenville (45331) ***(G-10402)***
Wolf Machine Company (PA)..........513 791-5194
5570 Creek Rd Blue Ash (45242) ***(G-1874)***
Wolf Metals Inc..........614 461-6361
1625 W Mound St Columbus (43223) ***(G-7608)***
Wolfden Products Inc..........614 219-6990
3991 Fondorf Dr Columbus (43228) ***(G-7609)***
Wolfe Associates Inc..........614 461-5000
34 S 3rd St Columbus (43215) ***(G-7610)***
Wolfe Creek Farms..........740 962-4563
433 Wilson Dr Malta (43758) ***(G-12384)***
Wolfe Grinding Inc..........330 929-6677
4582 Allen Rd Stow (44224) ***(G-17643)***
Wolfe Oil Company LLC..........513 732-6220
2944 Quitter Rd Williamsburg (45176) ***(G-20257)***
Wolfe Paper Co, Fremont *Also called JMJ Paper Inc* ***(G-10029)***
Wolfe Paper Co., Avon Lake *Also called JMJ Paper Inc* ***(G-990)***
Wolff House Art Papers Inc..........740 501-3766
133 S Main St Mount Vernon (43050) ***(G-14519)***
Wolff Tool & Manufacturing Co..........440 933-7797
139 Lear Rd Avon Lake (44012) ***(G-1014)***
Wolters Kluwer Clinical Drug..........330 650-6506
1100 Terex Rd Hudson (44236) ***(G-11083)***
Wonder Machine Services Inc..........440 937-7500
35340 Avon Commerce Pkwy Avon (44011) ***(G-975)***
Wonder Weld Inc..........614 875-1447
6127 Harrisburg Pike Orient (43146) ***(G-15579)***
Wonder-Shirts Inc..........917 679-2336
7695 Crawley Dr Dublin (43017) ***(G-9012)***
Wood County Ohio..........419 353-1227
991 S Main St Bowling Green (43402) ***(G-2007)***
Wood Graphics Inc (HQ)..........513 771-6300
8075 Reading Rd Ste 301 Cincinnati (45237) ***(G-4516)***
Wood Kraft..........440 487-4634
8928 Ely Rd Garrettsville (44231) ***(G-10205)***
Wood Recovery, Newark *Also called Hope Timber & Marketing Group* ***(G-14884)***
Wood Specialists..........440 639-9797
9485 Pinecone Dr Mentor (44060) ***(G-13629)***
Wood Stove Shed..........419 562-1545
4602 Stetzer Rd Bucyrus (44820) ***(G-2351)***
Wood Works..........330 674-0333
9210 Township Road 304 Millersburg (44654) ***(G-14152)***
Wood-Sebring Corporation..........216 267-3191
13800 Enterprise Ave Cleveland (44135) ***(G-6321)***
Woodbine Products Company..........330 725-0165
915 W Smith Rd Medina (44256) ***(G-13363)***
Woodbridge Group..........419 334-3666
827 Graham Dr Fremont (43420) ***(G-10064)***
Woodburn Press LLC..........937 293-9245
405 Littell Ave Dayton (45419) ***(G-8599)***
Woodbury Vineyards Inc (PA)..........440 835-2828
2001 Crocker Rd Ste 440 Westlake (44145) ***(G-20173)***
Woodbury Welding Inc..........937 968-3573
10393 Oh In State Line Rd Union City (45390) ***(G-18906)***
Woodcor America Inc (PA)..........614 277-2930
625 Crescent Rd Columbus (43204) ***(G-7611)***
Woodcraft, Dayton *Also called Ryanworks Inc* ***(G-8488)***
Woodcraft Industries Inc..........440 437-7811
131 Grand Valley Ave Orwell (44076) ***(G-15640)***
Woodcraft Industries Inc..........440 632-9655
15351 S State Ave Middlefield (44062) ***(G-13868)***
Woodcraft Pattern Works Inc..........330 630-2158
210 Southwest Ave Tallmadge (44278) ***(G-18016)***
Wooden Horse..........740 503-5243
204 N Main St Baltimore (43105) ***(G-1046)***
Wooden Horse Corporation..........419 663-1472
819 Dublin Rd Norwalk (44857) ***(G-15419)***
Woodford Logistics..........513 417-8453
15 Sprague Rd South Charleston (45368) ***(G-17274)***
Woodhill Plating Works Company..........216 883-1344
9114 Reno Ave Cleveland (44105) ***(G-6322)***
Woodland Woodworking..........330 897-7282
2586 Township Road 183 Baltic (43804) ***(G-1035)***
Woodlawn Rubber Co..........513 489-1718
11268 Williamson Rd Blue Ash (45241) ***(G-1875)***
Woodman Agitator Inc..........440 937-9865
1404 Lear Industrial Pkwy Avon (44011) ***(G-976)***
Woodrow Corp..........937 322-7696
105 N Thompson Ave Springfield (45504) ***(G-17520)***
Woodrow Manufacturing Co..........937 399-9333
4300 River Rd Springfield (45502) ***(G-17521)***
Woodsage Corporation..........419 476-3553
7400 Airport Hwy Holland (43528) ***(G-10967)***
Woodsage Industries LLC..........419 866-8000
7400 Airport Hwy Holland (43528) ***(G-10968)***
Woodsage LLC..........419 866-8000
7400 Airport Hwy Holland (43528) ***(G-10969)***
Woodsfeld True Vlue HM Ctr Inc..........740 472-1651
218 State Rte 78 Woodsfield (43793) ***(G-20550)***
Woodsmiths Design & Mfg, Bowerston *Also called L J Smith Inc* ***(G-1940)***
Woodspirits Limited Inc (PA)..........937 663-5025
1920 Apple Rd Saint Paris (43072) ***(G-16712)***
Woodstock Products Inc..........216 641-3811
2914 Broadway Ave Cleveland (44115) ***(G-6323)***
Woodworks Design..........440 693-4414
9005 N Girdle Rd Middlefield (44062) ***(G-13869)***
Woodworks For You..........440 277-8147
465 W River Rd Wakeman (44889) ***(G-19290)***
Woodworks Unlimited..........740 574-4523
330 Lambro Ln Franklin Furnace (45629) ***(G-9936)***
Wooldridge Lumber Co..........740 289-4912
3264 Laurel Ridge Rd Piketon (45661) ***(G-16082)***
Woosco, Wooster *Also called Westerman Acquisition Co LLC* ***(G-20666)***
Wooster, Wooster *Also called Waste Water Pollution Control* ***(G-20663)***
Wooster Book Company, The, Wooster *Also called Ketman Corporation* ***(G-20613)***
Wooster Brush Company..........440 322-8081
870 Infirmary Rd Elyria (44035) ***(G-9347)***

A L P H A B E T I C

(PA)=Parent Co (HQ)=Headquarters (DH)=Div Headquarters

Wooster Daily Record Inc LLC (HQ)....330 264-1125
212 E Liberty St Wooster (44691) **(G-20668)**
Wooster Products Inc (PA)....330 264-2844
1000 Spruce St Wooster (44691) **(G-20669)**
Wooster Products Inc....330 264-2844
3503 Old Airport Rd Wooster (44691) **(G-20670)**
Wooster Products Inc....330 264-2854
1000 Spruce St Wooster (44691) **(G-20671)**
Wooster Tool and Supply Co, Wooster *Also called Westerman Inc* **(G-20665)**
Wordcross Enterprises Inc....614 410-4140
735 Taylor Rd Ste 230 Columbus (43230) **(G-7612)**
Workflex Solutions LLC (HQ)....513 257-0215
7872 Cooper Rd Cincinnati (45242) **(G-4517)**
Workhorse Group Inc (PA)....513 297-3640
100 Commerce Dr Loveland (45140) **(G-12245)**
Working Professionals LLC....833 244-6299
3353 Oak Bend Blvd Canal Winchester (43110) **(G-2515)**
Workman Electronic Pdts Inc....419 923-7525
11955 County Road 10 2 Delta (43515) **(G-8779)**
Workman Electronics, Delta *Also called Twin Point Inc* **(G-8778)**
Works International Inc....513 631-6111
3825 Edwards Rd Ste 400 Cincinnati (45209) **(G-4518)**
Workshop Wire Cut and Mch Inc....330 995-6404
100 Francis D Kenneth Dr Aurora (44202) **(G-917)**
Workspeed Management LLC....917 369-9025
28925 Fountain Pkwy Solon (44139) **(G-17262)**
Workstream Inc (HQ)....513 870-4400
3158 Production Dr Fairfield (45014) **(G-9577)**
World Class Plastics Inc....937 843-3003
7695 State Route 708 Russells Point (43348) **(G-16603)**
World Connections Corps....419 363-2681
10803 Erastus Durbin Rd Rockford (45882) **(G-16542)**
World Development & Conslt LLC....614 805-4450
855 S Sunbury Rd Westerville (43081) **(G-20083)**
World Express Packaging Corp....216 634-9000
3607 W 56th St Cleveland (44102) **(G-6324)**
World Harvest Church Inc (PA)....614 837-1990
4595 Gender Rd Canal Winchester (43110) **(G-2516)**
World Journal....216 458-0988
1735 E 36th St Cleveland (44114) **(G-6325)**
World Prep Inc....419 843-3869
8432 Central Ave Ste 10 Sylvania (43560) **(G-17969)**
World Resource Solutons Corp....614 733-3737
8485 Estates Ct Plain City (43064) **(G-16219)**
World Wide Medical Physics Inc....419 266-7530
26302 Thompson Rd Perrysburg (43551) **(G-16029)**
World Wide Recyclers Inc....614 554-3296
3755 S High St Columbus (43207) **(G-7613)**
Worldwide Graphics and Sign, Blue Ash *Also called Beebe Worldwide Graphics Sign* **(G-1733)**
Worldwide Machine Tool LLC....614 496-9414
9000 Cotter St Lewis Center (43035) **(G-11788)**
Worldwide Machining & Mfg LLC....937 902-5629
2300 Arbor Blvd Moraine (45439) **(G-14400)**
Worleys Machine & Fab Inc....740 532-3337
1003 State Rr 650 Hanging Rock (45638) **(G-10624)**
Wornick Company (HQ)....800 860-4555
4700 Creek Rd Blue Ash (45242) **(G-1876)**
Wornick Company....513 552-7463
4700 Creek Rd Blue Ash (45242) **(G-1877)**
Wornick Foods, Blue Ash *Also called Wornick Company* **(G-1876)**
Wornick Holding Company Inc....513 794-9800
4700 Creek Rd Blue Ash (45242) **(G-1878)**
Worthignton Products Inc....330 452-7400
3405 Kuemerle Ct Ne Canton (44705) **(G-2865)**
Worthington, Beachwood *Also called RSI Company* **(G-1277)**
Worthington Cnstr Group Inc....216 472-1511
3100 E 45th St Ste 400 Cleveland (44127) **(G-6326)**
Worthington Cylinder Corp....740 569-4143
245 N Broad St Bremen (43107) **(G-2066)**
Worthington Cylinder Corp....330 262-1762
899 Venture Blvd Wooster (44691) **(G-20672)**
Worthington Cylinder Corp (HQ)....614 840-3210
200 W Old Wlson Bridge Rd Worthington (43085) **(G-20709)**
Worthington Cylinder Corp....440 576-5847
863 State Route 307 E Jefferson (44047) **(G-11243)**
Worthington Cylinder Corp....614 438-7900
1085 Dearborn Dr Columbus (43085) **(G-7614)**
Worthington Cylinder Corp....614 840-3800
333 Maxtown Rd Westerville (43082) **(G-20031)**
Worthington Energy Innovations, Fremont *Also called Professional Supply Inc* **(G-10046)**
Worthington Foods Inc....740 453-5501
1675 Fairview Rd Zanesville (43701) **(G-21189)**
Worthington Industries, Cleveland *Also called Worthington Mid-Rise Cnstr Inc* **(G-6327)**
Worthington Industries Inc (PA)....614 438-3210
200 W Old Wlson Bridge Rd Worthington (43085) **(G-20710)**
Worthington Industries Inc....937 556-6111
200 W Old Wlson Bridge Rd Worthington (43085) **(G-20711)**
Worthington Industries Inc....513 539-9291
350 Lawton Ave Monroe (45050) **(G-14282)**
Worthington Industries Inc....614 438-3113
2170 West Case Rd Columbus (43235) **(G-7615)**
Worthington Industries Inc....614 438-3190
1127 Dearborn Dr Columbus (43085) **(G-7616)**
Worthington Industries Inc....419 822-2500
6303 County Road 10 Delta (43515) **(G-8780)**
Worthington Industries Inc (HQ)....614 438-3077
200 W Old Wlson Bridge Rd Worthington (43085) **(G-20712)**
Worthington Industries Lsg LLC....614 438-3210
200 W Old Wlson Bridge Rd Worthington (43085) **(G-20713)**
Worthington Mid-Rise Cnstr Inc (HQ)....216 472-1511
3100 E 45th St Ste 400 Cleveland (44127) **(G-6327)**
Worthington Pallet....614 888-1573
160 Tucker Dr Worthington (43085) **(G-20714)**
Worthington Steel, Worthington *Also called Precision Specialty Metals Inc* **(G-20700)**
Worthington Steel Company (HQ)....614 438-3210
200 W Old Wlson Bridge Rd Worthington (43085) **(G-20715)**
Worthington Steel Company....216 441-8300
4310 E 49th St Cleveland (44125) **(G-6328)**
Worthington Steel Company....513 702-0130
1501 Made Dr Middletown (45044) **(G-13969)**
Worthington Steel Div, Columbus *Also called Worthington Industries Inc* **(G-7616)**
Worthmore Food Products Co....513 559-1473
1021 Ludlow Ave Cincinnati (45223) **(G-4519)**
Worthngton Stelpac Systems LLC....937 747-2370
5256 Burton Rd North Lewisburg (43060) **(G-15165)**
Worthngton Stelpac Systems LLC (HQ)....614 438-3205
1205 Dearborn Dr Columbus (43085) **(G-7617)**
Wray Precision Products Inc....513 228-5000
3650 Turtlecreek Rd Lebanon (45036) **(G-11707)**
Wre Color Tech, Wadsworth *Also called Western Roto Engravers Inc* **(G-19281)**
Wreaths & Masn Jars By Krissi....419 250-6606
332 Saint James Cir Holland (43528) **(G-10970)**
Wrena LLC....937 667-4403
265 Lightner Rd Tipp City (45371) **(G-18146)**
Wright Brothers Inc (PA)....513 731-2222
1930 Losantiville Ave Cincinnati (45237) **(G-4520)**
Wright Brothers Global Gas LLC....513 731-2222
7825 Cooper Rd Cincinnati (45242) **(G-4521)**
Wright Buffing Wheel Company....330 424-7887
300 S Market St Lisbon (44432) **(G-11983)**
Wright Designs Inc (PA)....216 524-6662
5099 Valley Woods Dr Cleveland (44131) **(G-6329)**
Wright John....937 653-4570
935 N Main St Urbana (43078) **(G-19020)**
Wright Leather Works....567 314-0019
2789 Hayes Ave Fremont (43420) **(G-10065)**
Wright Solutions LLC....937 938-8745
1085 Redbluff Dr Dayton (45449) **(G-8600)**
Wright Tool Company....330 848-0600
1 Wright Pl Barberton (44203) **(G-1114)**
Wright Way Patterns....513 574-5776
6109 W Fork Rd Cincinnati (45247) **(G-4522)**
Wrights Saw Mill....937 773-2546
9018 Piqua Lockington Rd Piqua (45356) **(G-16167)**
Wrights Well Service....740 380-9602
37940 Scout Rd Logan (43138) **(G-12046)**
Writely Sew LLC....513 728-2682
3862 Race Rd Cincinnati (45211) **(G-4523)**
Wrp Energy Inc....330 533-1921
12 W Main St Canfield (44406) **(G-2553)**
Wrr Creative Concepts LLC....513 659-2284
6082 Ash Hill Ct West Chester (45069) **(G-19822)**
Wrwp LLC....330 425-3421
1920 Case Pkwy S Twinsburg (44087) **(G-18875)**
Ws Thermal Process Tech Inc....440 385-6829
8301 W Erie Ave Lorain (44053) **(G-12138)**
Ws Trading LLC....800 830-4547
2623 S State Route 605 Galena (43021) **(G-10118)**
WS Tyler Screening Inc....440 974-1047
8570 Tyler Blvd Mentor (44060) **(G-13630)**
Wsny FM, Columbus *Also called Franklin Communications Inc* **(G-6936)**
Wt Tool & Die Inc....330 332-2254
1300 Pennsylvania Ave Salem (44460) **(G-16782)**
Wtd Real Estate Inc....440 934-5305
1280 Moore Rd Avon (44011) **(G-977)**
Wtp Engineering, Canal Fulton *Also called Welded Tube Pros LLC* **(G-2496)**
Wulco Inc....513 679-2600
6900 Steger Dr Cincinnati (45237) **(G-4524)**
Wulco Inc (PA)....513 679-2600
6899 Steger Dr Ste A Cincinnati (45237) **(G-4525)**
Wurms Woodworking Company....419 492-2184
725 W Mansfield St New Washington (44854) **(G-14834)**
Wurtec Manufacturing Service....419 726-1066
6200 Brent Dr Toledo (43611) **(G-18602)**
Wurth Elecktronik, Dayton *Also called Wurth Electronics Ics Inc* **(G-8601)**
Wurth Electronics Ics Inc....937 415-7700
7496 Webster St Dayton (45414) **(G-8601)**

ALPHABETIC SECTION

Yes Press Printing Co

Www Boat Services Inc...419 626-0883
2218 River Ave Sandusky (44870) *(G-16863)*
Www.groovycandies.com, Cleveland *Also called Sugar Memories LLC (G-6115)*
Wyandot Inc...740 383-4031
135 Wyandot Ave Marion (43302) *(G-12751)*
Wyandotte Wine Cellar Inc...614 476-3624
4640 Wyandotte Dr Columbus (43230) *(G-7618)*
Wyatt Industries LLC...330 954-1790
1790 Miller Pkwy Streetsboro (44241) *(G-17704)*
Wyatt Printing, Mentor *Also called Bill Wyatt Inc (G-13403)*
Wyatt Specialties Inc...614 989-5362
4761 State Route 361 Circleville (43113) *(G-4565)*
Wyeth-Scott Company...740 345-4528
85 Dayton Rd Ne Newark (43055) *(G-14933)*
Wyman Gordon, Cleveland *Also called Wyman-Gordon Company (G-6330)*
Wyman Woodworking...614 338-0615
389 Robinwood Ave Columbus (43213) *(G-7619)*
Wyman-Gordon Company...216 341-0085
3097 E 61st St Cleveland (44127) *(G-6330)*
Wyoming Casing Service Inc...330 479-8785
1414 Raff Rd Sw Canton (44710) *(G-2866)*
Wyse Electric Motor Repair...419 445-5921
2101 S Defiance St Archbold (43502) *(G-673)*
Wyse Industrial Carts Inc...419 923-7353
10510 County Road 12 Wauseon (43567) *(G-19539)*
Wysong Concrete Products LLC...513 874-3109
2138 Resor Rd Fairfield (45014) *(G-9578)*
Wysong Gravel Co Inc (PA)...937 456-4539
2332 State Route 503 N West Alexandria (45381) *(G-19626)*
Wysong Gravel Co Inc...937 452-1523
120 Cmden Cllege Cornr Rd Camden (45311) *(G-2467)*
Wysong Gravel Co Inc...937 839-5497
2032 State Route 503 N West Alexandria (45381) *(G-19627)*
Wysong Stone Co...937 962-2559
5897 State Route 503 N Lewisburg (45338) *(G-11799)*
X L Sand and Gravel Co...330 426-9876
9289 Jackman Rd Negley (44441) *(G-14592)*
X M C, Sylvania *Also called Don-Ell Corporation (G-17937)*
X M C Division, Sylvania *Also called Don-Ell Corporation (G-17936)*
X Press Printing Services Inc...440 951-8848
4405 Glenbrook Rd Willoughby (44094) *(G-20461)*
X-3-5 LLC...513 489-5477
7621 E Kemper Rd Cincinnati (45249) *(G-4526)*
X-Mil Inc...937 444-1323
220 Homan Way Mount Orab (45154) *(G-14453)*
X-Press Tool Inc...330 225-8748
2845 Interstate Pkwy Brunswick (44212) *(G-2254)*
X-Treme Finishes Inc...330 474-0614
387 Medina Rd Ste 1000 Medina (44256) *(G-13364)*
X-Treme Shooting Products LLC...513 313-3464
2008 Glenn Pkwy Batavia (45103) *(G-1198)*
Xact Genomics LLC...216 956-0957
9022 White Oak Dr Twinsburg (44087) *(G-18876)*
Xact Spec Industries LLC...440 543-8157
16959 Munn Rd Chagrin Falls (44023) *(G-3091)*
Xact Spec Industries LLC (PA)...440 543-8157
16959 Munn Rd Chagrin Falls (44023) *(G-3092)*
Xapc Co (PA)...216 362-4100
15583 Brookpark Rd Cleveland (44142) *(G-6331)*
XCEL Mold and Machine Inc...330 499-8450
7661 Freedom Ave Nw Canton (44720) *(G-2867)*
Xcite Systems Corporation...513 965-0300
675 Cncnnati Batavia Pike Cincinnati (45245) *(G-3267)*
Xellia Pharmaceuticals USA LLC...847 986-7984
200 Northfield Rd Bedford (44146) *(G-1455)*
Xenia City Water Treatment Div, Xenia *Also called City of Xenia (G-20762)*
Xenotronix/Tli Inc...407 331-4793
2541 Tracy Rd Northwood (43619) *(G-15353)*
Xerion Advanced Battery Corp...720 229-0697
3100 Res Blvd Ste 320 Kettering (45420) *(G-11444)*
Xerox Corporation...513 539-4858
6500 Hamilton Lebanon Rd Monroe (45044) *(G-14283)*
Xerox Corporation...513 539-4808
6490 Hamilton Lebanon Rd Monroe (45044) *(G-14284)*
Xerox Corporation...513 554-3200
10560 Ashview Pl Blue Ash (45242) *(G-1879)*
Xerox Corporation C/O Genco...503 582-6059
6290 Opus Dr Groveport (43125) *(G-10517)*
Xgs.it, West Chester *Also called It XCEL Consulting LLC (G-19728)*
Xim Products Inc...440 871-4737
1169 Bassett Rd Westlake (44145) *(G-20174)*
Xl Pattern Shop Inc...330 682-2981
242 N Kansas Rd Orrville (44667) *(G-15629)*
Xomox Corporation...513 947-1200
4576 Helmsdale Ct Batavia (45103) *(G-1199)*
Xomox Corporation...936 271-6500
4444 Cooper Rd Cincinnati (45242) *(G-4527)*
Xomox Corporation...513 745-6000
4477 Malsbary Rd Blue Ash (45242) *(G-1880)*
Xorb Corporation...419 354-6021
455 W Woodland Cir Bowling Green (43402) *(G-2008)*
Xpedx National Accounts...513 870-0711
4225 Dues Dr West Chester (45246) *(G-19917)*
Xperion E&E USA LLC...740 788-9560
1475 James Pkwy Heath (43056) *(G-10735)*
Xponet Inc...440 354-6617
20 Elberta Rd Painesville (44077) *(G-15801)*
Xpress Print & Bus Systems, Louisville *Also called Xpress Print Inc (G-12172)*
Xpress Print Inc...330 494-7246
6424 Easton St Louisville (44641) *(G-12172)*
Xray Media Ltd...513 751-9641
445 Mcgregor Ave Cincinnati (45206) *(G-4528)*
XS Smith Inc (PA)...252 940-5060
5513 Vine St Ste 1 Cincinnati (45217) *(G-4529)*
Xt Innovations Ltd...419 562-1989
4799 Stetzer Rd Bucyrus (44820) *(G-2352)*
Xtek Inc (PA)...513 733-7800
11451 Reading Rd Cincinnati (45241) *(G-4530)*
Xth Industries, Cleveland *Also called Kusakabe America Corporation (G-5547)*
Xto Energy Inc...740 671-9901
2358 W 23rd St Bellaire (43906) *(G-1489)*
Xxx Intrntional Amusements Inc (PA)...216 671-6900
3313 W 140th St Ste D Cleveland (44111) *(G-6332)*
Xylem Inc...937 767-7241
1700 Brannum Ln 1725 Yellow Springs (45387) *(G-20819)*
XYZ Plastics Inc...440 632-5281
15760 Madison Rd Middlefield (44062) *(G-13870)*
Y City Recycling LLC...740 452-2500
4005 All American Way Zanesville (43701) *(G-21190)*
Y Z Enterprises Inc...419 893-8777
1930 Indian Wood Cir # 100 Maumee (43537) *(G-13161)*
Y&B Logging...440 437-1053
3647 Montgomery Rd Orwell (44076) *(G-15641)*
Yachiyo of America Inc (HQ)...614 876-3220
2285 Walcutt Rd Columbus (43228) *(G-7620)*
Yagoot...513 791-6600
7875 Montgomery Rd # 1241 Cincinnati (45236) *(G-4531)*
Yale Industries, Dayton *Also called Otter Group LLC (G-8410)*
Yamada North America Inc...937 462-7111
9000 Clmbus Cincinnati Rd South Charleston (45368) *(G-17275)*
Yanfeng US Automotive...419 662-4905
7560 Arbor Dr Northwood (43619) *(G-15354)*
Yanfeng US Automotive...419 636-4211
918 S Union St Bryan (43506) *(G-2314)*
Yanke Bionics Inc (PA)...330 762-6411
303 W Exchange St Akron (44302) *(G-438)*
Yanke Bionics Inc...330 833-0955
2400 Wales Ave Nw Massillon (44646) *(G-13058)*
Yanke Bionics Inc...330 668-4070
3975 Embassy Pkwy Ste 1 Akron (44333) *(G-439)*
Yankee Wire Cloth Products Inc...740 545-9129
221 W Main St West Lafayette (43845) *(G-19934)*
Yant Beef Jerky, Jackson Center *Also called Steven Yant (G-11216)*
YAR Corporation...330 652-1222
406 S Main St Niles (44446) *(G-15041)*
Yarder Manufacturing Company (PA)...419 476-3933
722 Phillips Ave Toledo (43612) *(G-18603)*
Yarder Manufacturing Company...419 269-3474
730 Phillips Ave Toledo (43612) *(G-18604)*
Yarn Shop Inc...614 457-7836
1125 Kenny Centre Mall Columbus (43220) *(G-7621)*
Yarnell Bros Inc...419 278-2831
103 E North St Deshler (43516) *(G-8790)*
Yaskawa America Inc...614 733-3200
8628 Industrial Pkwy A Plain City (43064) *(G-16220)*
Yaskawa America Inc...937 847-6200
100 Automation Way Miamisburg (45342) *(G-13742)*
Yaugher Enterprizes Inc...440 968-0151
9755 Plank Rd Ste A Montville (44064) *(G-14326)*
Yaya's, Kent *Also called Mark Grzianis St Treats Ex Inc (G-11349)*
Yeager Sports, Cincinnati *Also called R L Y Inc (G-4244)*
Yellow Creek Casting Company...330 532-4608
18141 Fife Coal Rd Wellsville (43968) *(G-19615)*
Yellow Springs Brewery LLC...937 767-0222
305 N Walnut St Ste B Yellow Springs (45387) *(G-20820)*
Yellow Springs International, Yellow Springs *Also called Ysi Incorporated (G-20825)*
Yellow Springs News Inc...937 767-7373
253 And A Half Xenia Ave Yellow Springs (45387) *(G-20821)*
Yellow Springs Pottery...937 767-1666
222 Xenia Ave Ste 1 Yellow Springs (45387) *(G-20822)*
Yellow Tang Interiors LLC...330 629-9279
1255 Barbie Dr Youngstown (44512) *(G-21069)*
Yemaneh Musie...614 506-3687
2734 Rosedale Ave Columbus (43204) *(G-7622)*
Yes Management Inc (PA)...330 747-8593
44612 State Route 14 Columbiana (44408) *(G-6486)*
Yes Press Printing Co...330 535-8398
720 E Glenwood Ave Front Akron (44310) *(G-440)*

ALPHABETIC

Yespress Graphics LLC..........614 899-1403
515 S State St Westerville (43081) **(G-20084)**
Yi Xing Inc..........614 785-9631
850 Busch Ct Columbus (43229) **(G-7623)**
Yizumi-HPM Corporation..........740 382-5600
3424 State Rt 309 Iberia (43325) **(G-11115)**
YKK AP America Inc..........513 942-7200
8748 Jacquemin Dr Ste 400 West Chester (45069) **(G-19823)**
YKK USA, West Chester *Also called YKK AP America Inc* **(G-19823)**
Yockey Group Inc..........513 860-9053
9053 Le Saint Dr West Chester (45014) **(G-19824)**
Yoder & Frey Inc..........419 445-2070
3649 County Road 24 Archbold (43502) **(G-674)**
Yoder Cabinets Ltd..........614 873-5186
9996 Amish Pike Plain City (43064) **(G-16221)**
Yoder Industries Inc (PA)..........937 278-5769
2520 Needmore Rd Dayton (45414) **(G-8602)**
Yoder Industries Inc..........937 890-4322
3009 Production Ct Dayton (45414) **(G-8603)**
Yoder Logging..........740 679-2635
22144 Oxford Rd Quaker City (43773) **(G-16354)**
Yoder Lumber Co Inc (PA)..........330 893-3121
4515 Township Road 367 Millersburg (44654) **(G-14153)**
Yoder Lumber Co Inc..........330 674-1435
7100 County Road 407 Millersburg (44654) **(G-14154)**
Yoder Lumber Co Inc..........330 893-3131
3799 County Road 70 Sugarcreek (44681) **(G-17878)**
Yoder Manufacturing..........740 504-5028
7679 Flack Rd Howard (43028) **(G-10998)**
Yoder Window & Siding Ltd..........330 857-4530
7165 Fredericksburg Rd Fredericksburg (44627) **(G-9961)**
Yoder Window & Siding Ltd (PA)..........330 695-6960
7846 Harrison Rd Fredericksburg (44627) **(G-9962)**
Yoder Window and Siding, Fredericksburg *Also called Yoder Window & Siding Ltd* **(G-9962)**
Yoder Woodworking..........740 399-9400
21198 Swendal Rd Butler (44822) **(G-2378)**
Yoder's Cider Barn, Gambier *Also called Yoders Cider Barn* **(G-10186)**
Yoders Cider Barn..........740 668-4961
3361 Martinsburg Rd Gambier (43022) **(G-10186)**
Yoders Harness Shop..........440 632-1505
14698 Bundysburg Rd Middlefield (44062) **(G-13871)**
Yoders Nylon Halter Shop..........330 893-3479
7682 Township Road 652 Millersburg (44654) **(G-14155)**
Yoders Woodworking..........888 818-0568
2249 Township Road 112 Millersburg (44654) **(G-14156)**
Yokohama Inds Amricas Ohio Inc..........440 352-3321
474 Newell St Painesville (44077) **(G-15802)**
Yokohama Tire Corporation..........440 352-3321
474 Newell St Painesville (44077) **(G-15803)**
Yonezawa USA Inc..........614 799-2210
7920 Corporate Blvd Ste A Plain City (43064) **(G-16222)**
York Fabrication & Machine..........419 483-6275
6964 County Road 191 Bellevue (44811) **(G-1554)**
York Paving Co (PA)..........740 594-3600
758 W Union St Athens (45701) **(G-854)**
Yost & Son Inc..........440 779-8025
5502 Barton Rd North Olmsted (44070) **(G-15204)**
Yost Candy Co..........330 828-2777
51 N Cochran St Dalton (44618) **(G-7954)**
Yost Foods Inc..........330 273-4420
2795 Westway Dr Brunswick (44212) **(G-2255)**
Yost Labs Inc..........740 876-4936
630 2nd St Portsmouth (45662) **(G-16305)**
Yost Superior Co..........937 323-7591
300 S Center St Ste 1 Springfield (45506) **(G-17522)**
Yotec, South Charleston *Also called Yamada North America Inc* **(G-17275)**
You Dough Girl LLC..........330 207-5031
12725 Kent Rd Salem (44460) **(G-16783)**
Young & Bertke Air Systems, Cincinnati *Also called Pcy Enterprises Inc* **(G-4143)**
Young Regulator Company Inc..........440 232-9452
7100 Krick Rd Ste A Bedford (44146) **(G-1456)**
Young Sand & Gravel Co Inc..........419 994-3040
689 State Route 39 Loudonville (44842) **(G-12150)**
Youngs Jersey Dairy Inc..........937 325-0629
6880 Springfield Xenia Rd Yellow Springs (45387) **(G-20823)**
Youngs Locker Serv & Meat Proc, Danville *Also called Youngs Locker Service Inc* **(G-7967)**
Youngs Locker Service Inc..........740 599-6833
16201 Nashville Rd Danville (43014) **(G-7967)**
Youngs Publishing Inc..........937 259-6575
2171 N Fairfield Rd Beavercreek (45431) **(G-1347)**
Youngs Screenprinting & Embro..........330 922-5777
1245 Munroe Falls Ave Cuyahoga Falls (44221) **(G-7935)**
Youngstown ARC Engraving Co..........330 793-2471
380 Victoria Rd Youngstown (44515) **(G-21070)**
Youngstown Bending Rolling..........330 799-2227
3710 Hendricks Rd Bldg 2b Youngstown (44515) **(G-21071)**
Youngstown Bolt & Supply Co..........330 799-3201
340 N Meridian Rd Youngstown (44509) **(G-21072)**
Youngstown Burial Vault Co..........330 782-0015
546 E Indianola Ave Youngstown (44502) **(G-21073)**
Youngstown Casket Co Inc..........330 758-2008
450 Melbourne Ave Youngstown (44512) **(G-21074)**
Youngstown Curve Form Inc..........330 744-3028
1102 Rigby St Youngstown (44506) **(G-21075)**
Youngstown Die Development..........330 755-0722
137 Walton Ave Struthers (44471) **(G-17826)**
Youngstown Electric Supply, Columbiana *Also called Yes Management Inc* **(G-6486)**
Youngstown Fence Inc..........330 788-8110
235 E Indianola Ave Youngstown (44507) **(G-21076)**
Youngstown Hard Chrome Plating..........330 758-9721
8451 Southern Blvd Youngstown (44512) **(G-21077)**
Youngstown Heat Treating..........330 788-3025
1118 Meadowbrook Ave Youngstown (44512) **(G-21078)**
Youngstown Letter Shop Inc..........330 793-4935
615 N Meridian Rd Youngstown (44509) **(G-21079)**
Youngstown Lithographing Co, Youngstown *Also called Youngstown ARC Engraving Co* **(G-21070)**
Youngstown Metal Fabricating, Youngstown *Also called M F Y Inc* **(G-20963)**
Youngstown Plant, Struthers *Also called Munroe Incorporated* **(G-17821)**
Youngstown Plastic Tooling (PA)..........330 782-7222
1209 Velma Ct Youngstown (44512) **(G-21080)**
Youngstown Pre-Press Inc..........330 793-3690
3691 Leharps Dr Youngstown (44515) **(G-21081)**
Youngstown Rubber Products, Youngstown *Also called Mid-State Sales Inc* **(G-20971)**
Youngstown Specialty Mtls Inc..........330 259-1110
571 Andrews Ave Youngstown (44505) **(G-21082)**
Youngstown Tool & Die Company..........330 747-4464
1261 Poland Ave Youngstown (44502) **(G-21083)**
Youngstown Tube Co..........330 743-7414
401 Andrews Ave Youngstown (44505) **(G-21084)**
Youngstown-Kenworth Inc (PA)..........330 534-9761
7255 Hubbard Masury Rd Hubbard (44425) **(G-11014)**
Your Cabinetry..........440 638-4925
16488 Pearl Rd Strongsville (44136) **(G-17809)**
Your Carpenter Inc..........216 241-6434
2403 Saint Clair Ave Ne Cleveland (44114) **(G-6333)**
Your Daily Motivation Ydm Fitn..........440 954-1038
6631 Vrooman Rd Painesville (44077) **(G-15804)**
Yrp Industries Inc..........330 533-2524
854 Mahoning Ave Youngstown (44502) **(G-21085)**
Ysd Industries Inc..........330 792-6521
3710 Henricks Rd Youngstown (44515) **(G-21086)**
Ysi, Yellow Springs *Also called Xylem Inc* **(G-20819)**
Ysi Environmental Inc..........937 767-7241
1725 Brannum Ln Yellow Springs (45387) **(G-20824)**
Ysi Incorporated (HQ)..........937 767-7241
1700 Brannum Ln 1725 Yellow Springs (45387) **(G-20825)**
Ysie, Yellow Springs *Also called Ysi Environmental Inc* **(G-20824)**
Ysk Corporation..........740 774-7315
1 Colomet Rd Chillicothe (45601) **(G-3231)**
Yuckon International Corp..........216 361-2103
1400 E 34th St Cleveland (44114) **(G-6334)**
Yugo Mold Inc..........330 606-0710
1733 Wadsworth Rd Akron (44320) **(G-441)**
Yusa Corporation (HQ)..........740 335-0335
151 Jamison Rd Sw Washington Court Hou (43160) **(G-19479)**
Yutec LLC (PA)..........440 725-5353
3940 Ellendale Rd Chagrin Falls (44022) **(G-3033)**
Yutzy Woodworking Ltd..........330 359-6166
6995 Township Road 654 Millersburg (44654) **(G-14157)**
Yxlon..........234 284-7862
5675 Hudson Indus Pkwy Hudson (44236) **(G-11084)**
Yxlon International, Hudson *Also called Comet Technologies USA Inc* **(G-11038)**
Z & Z Manufacturing Inc..........440 953-2800
4765 E 355th St Willoughby (44094) **(G-20462)**
Z and M Screw Machine Products..........330 467-5822
10232 Hopkins Rd Garrettsville (44231) **(G-10206)**
Z Line Kitchen and Bath LLC (PA)..........614 777-5004
916 Delaware Ave Marysville (43040) **(G-12819)**
Z M O Company Inc (PA)..........614 875-0230
4188 Alkire Rd Grove City (43123) **(G-10480)**
Z M O Oil, Grove City *Also called Z M O Company Inc* **(G-10480)**
Z Track Magazine..........614 764-1703
6142 Northcliff Blvd Dublin (43016) **(G-9013)**
Z3 Controls LLC..........419 261-2654
27962 E Broadway St Walbridge (43465) **(G-19301)**
Zaclon LLC..........216 271-1601
2981 Independence Rd Cleveland (44115) **(G-6335)**
Zaenkert Surveying Essentials..........513 738-2917
7461a Cncnnati Brkvlle Rd Okeana (45053) **(G-15522)**
Zagar Inc..........216 731-0500
24000 Lakeland Blvd Cleveland (44132) **(G-6336)**
Zak Box Co Inc..........216 961-5636
7100 Clark Ave Cleveland (44102) **(G-6337)**
Zal Air Products Inc..........440 237-7155
1687 W Royalton Rd Cleveland (44147) **(G-6338)**
Zane Casket Company Inc..........740 452-4680
1201 Hall Ave Zanesville (43701) **(G-21191)**

ALPHABETIC SECTION

Zaner-Bloser Inc (HQ) 614 486-0221
1400 Goodale Blvd Ste 200 Columbus (43212) *(G-7624)*

Zaner-Bloser Inc 608 441-5555
1400 Goodale Blvd Ste 200 Columbus (43212) *(G-7625)*

Zanesville Bearing Div, Zanesville *Also called H & R Tool & Machine Co Inc (G-21143)*

Zanesville Newspaper 740 452-4561
34 S 4th St Zanesville (43701) *(G-21192)*

Zanesville Pallet Co Inc 740 454-3700
2235 Licking Rd Zanesville (43701) *(G-21193)*

Zanesville Terminal Warehouse, Zanesville *Also called Porto Pump Inc (G-21170)*

Zanesville Tool Grinding 740 453-9356
624 Main St Zanesville (43701) *(G-21194)*

Zap, Cleveland *Also called Zal Air Products Inc (G-6338)*

Zarbana Alum Extrusions LLC 330 482-5092
41738 Esterly Dr Columbiana (44408) *(G-6487)*

Zaromet Inc 513 891-0773
10851 Millington Ct Blue Ash (45242) *(G-1881)*

Zaytran Corporation 440 324-2814
41535 Schadden Rd Elyria (44035) *(G-9348)*

Zebco Industries Inc 740 654-4510
211 N Columbus St Lancaster (43130) *(G-11620)*

Zebec of North America Inc 513 829-5533
210 Donald Dr Fairfield (45014) *(G-9579)*

Zech Printing Industries Inc 937 748-2776
6310 Este Ave Cincinnati (45232) *(G-4532)*

Zed Digital, Columbus *Also called IPA Ltd (G-7048)*

Zed Industries Inc 937 667-8407
3580 Lightner Rd Vandalia (45377) *(G-19152)*

Zeeco Equipment Commodity 440 838-1102
6581 Glen Coe Dr Brecksville (44141) *(G-2063)*

Zehrco-Giancola Composites Inc (PA) 440 994-6317
1501 W 47th St Ashtabula (44004) *(G-813)*

Zehrco-Giancola Composites Inc 440 576-9941
382 E Erie St Jefferson (44047) *(G-11244)*

Zeiger Industries 330 484-4413
4704 Wiseland Ave Se Canton (44707) *(G-2868)*

Zekelman Industries Inc 740 432-2146
9208 Jeffrey Dr Cambridge (43725) *(G-2463)*

Zen Industries Inc 216 432-3240
6200 Harvard Ave Cleveland (44105) *(G-6339)*

Zenex International 440 232-4155
7777 First Pl Bedford (44146) *(G-1457)*

Zenos Activewear Inc 614 443-0070
1354 Parsons Ave Columbus (43206) *(G-7626)*

Zephyr Industries Inc 419 281-4485
600 Township Road 1500 Ashland (44805) *(G-756)*

Zero-D Products Inc (PA) 440 417-1843
37939 Stevens Blvd Willoughby (44094) *(G-20463)*

Zerust Consumer Products LLC 330 405-1965
9345 Ravenna Rd Unit E Twinsburg (44087) *(G-18877)*

Zeus Electronics LLC 330 220-1571
5083 Creekside Blvd Brunswick (44212) *(G-2256)*

ZF North America Inc 419 726-5599
5915 Jason St Toledo (43611) *(G-18605)*

ZF North America Inc 216 750-2400
8333 Rockside Rd Cleveland (44125) *(G-6340)*

ZF North America Inc 216 332-7100
19501 Emery Rd Cleveland (44128) *(G-6341)*

Zhai Hui Filters & Home Pdts, Beachwood *Also called Zhao Hui Filters (us) Inc (G-1287)*

Zhao Hui Filters (us) Inc (PA) 440 519-9301
24400 Highpoint Rd Ste 5 Beachwood (44122) *(G-1287)*

Zide Screen Printing, Marietta *Also called Zide Sport Shop of Ohio Inc (G-12690)*

Zide Sport Shop of Ohio Inc 740 373-8199
118 Industry Rd Marietta (45750) *(G-12690)*

Zidian Manufacturing Inc (PA) 330 965-8455
500 Mcclurg Rd Boardman (44512) *(G-1905)*

Zie Bart Rhino Linings Toledo, Toledo *Also called Zie Bart Rhino Linings Toledo (G-18606)*

Zie Bart Rhino Linings Toledo 419 841-2886
3343 N Hlland Sylvania Rd Toledo (43615) *(G-18606)*

Ziegler Bros Tool & Mch Inc 419 738-6048
13790 Infirmary Rd Wapakoneta (45895) *(G-19361)*

Ziegler Brothers Tool & Mch, Wapakoneta *Also called Ziegler Bros Tool & Mch Inc (G-19361)*

Ziegler Engineering Inc 440 582-8715
9840 York Alpha Dr Ste F North Royalton (44133) *(G-15312)*

Zimcom Internet Solutions, Cincinnati *Also called One Cloud Services LLC (G-4112)*

Zimmer Inc 614 508-6000
6816 Lauffer Rd Columbus (43231) *(G-7627)*

Zimmer Enterprises Inc (PA) 937 428-1057
911 Senate Dr Dayton (45459) *(G-8604)*

Zimmer Orthopaedic Surgical, Dover *Also called Zimmer Surgical Inc (G-8863)*

Zimmer Surgical Inc 800 321-5533
200 W Ohio Ave Dover (44622) *(G-8863)*

Zimmerman Shtmtl Stl & Wldg 419 335-3806
1179 N Ottokee St Wauseon (43567) *(G-19540)*

Zimmerman Steel & Sup Co LLC 330 828-1010
18543 Davis Rd Dalton (44618) *(G-7955)*

Zing Pac Inc 440 248-7997
30300 Solon Indus Pkwy Cleveland (44139) *(G-6342)*

Zinkan Enterprises Inc (PA) 330 487-1500
1919 Case Pkwy Twinsburg (44087) *(G-18878)*

Zion Industries Inc (PA) 330 225-3246
6229 Grafton Rd Valley City (44280) *(G-19070)*

Zip Center, The-Division, Marietta *Also called Richardson Printing Corp (G-12663)*

Zip Graphics, Cincinnati *Also called Margaret Trentman (G-3980)*

Zip Laser Systems Inc 740 286-6613
345 E Main St Ste H Jackson (45640) *(G-11203)*

Zip Systems of Jackson, Jackson *Also called Zip Laser Systems Inc (G-11203)*

Zip Tool & Die Inc 216 267-1117
12200 Sprecher Ave Cleveland (44135) *(G-6343)*

Zipper Manufacturing LLC 937 444-0904
16698 Edgington Rd Williamsburg (45176) *(G-20258)*

Zippitycom Print LLC 216 438-0001
1600 E 23rd St Cleveland (44114) *(G-6344)*

Zipscene LLC 513 201-5174
615 Main St Fl 5 Cincinnati (45202) *(G-4533)*

Zircoa Inc (PA) 440 248-0500
31501 Solon Rd Cleveland (44139) *(G-6345)*

Zircoa Inc 440 349-7237
31501 Solon Rd Solon (44139) *(G-17263)*

Zircon Industries Inc 216 595-0200
4920 Commerce Pkwy Ste 9 Cleveland (44128) *(G-6346)*

Zitello Fine Art LLC 330 792-8894
1221 N Meridian Rd Ste 16 Youngstown (44509) *(G-21087)*

Zitnik Enterprises Inc 440 951-0089
35530 Lakeland Blvd Willoughby (44095) *(G-20464)*

Znode Inc 888 755-5541
8415 Pulsar Pl Ste 200 Columbus (43240) *(G-6509)*

Zoia, Cleveland *Also called Artistic Metal Spinning Inc (G-4741)*

Zoo Publishing Inc 513 824-8297
11258 Cornell Park Dr # 608 Blue Ash (45242) *(G-1882)*

Zook Enterprises LLC (PA) 440 543-1010
16809 Park Circle Dr Chagrin Falls (44023) *(G-3093)*

Zorbx Inc 440 238-1847
17647 Foltz Pkwy Strongsville (44149) *(G-17810)*

Zorich Industries Inc 330 482-9803
1400 Wardingsley Ave Columbiana (44408) *(G-6488)*

ZS Cream & Bean 440 652-6369
2706 Boston Rd Hinckley (44233) *(G-10908)*

Zshot Inc 800 385-8581
6155 Huntley Rd Ste D Columbus (43229) *(G-7628)*

Zsi Manufacturing Inc 440 266-0701
8059 Crile Rd Painesville (44077) *(G-15805)*

Zts Inc 513 271-2557
5628 Wooster Pike Cincinnati (45227) *(G-4534)*

Zukowski Rack Co 440 942-5889
1647 E 361st St Willoughby (44095) *(G-20465)*

Zurbrugg Machine, Alliance *Also called Scott A Zurbrugg (G-499)*

Zurn Industries LLC 814 455-0921
4501 Sutphen Ct Hilliard (43026) *(G-10875)*

Zwf Golf LLC 937 767-5621
920 N Broad St Fairborn (45324) *(G-9476)*

Zygo Inc 513 281-0888
2832 Jefferson Ave Cincinnati (45219) *(G-4535)*

Zyvex Performance Mtls Inc (HQ) 614 481-2222
1255 Kinnear Rd Ste 100 Columbus (43212) *(G-7629)*

Zyvex Technologies, Columbus *Also called Zyvex Performance Mtls Inc (G-7629)*

PRODUCT INDEX

• Product categories are listed in alphabetical order.

A

ABRASIVE STONES, EXC GRINDING STONES: Ground Or Whole
ABRASIVES
ABRASIVES: Coated
ABRASIVES: Grains
ABRASIVES: Synthetic
ACCELERATION INDICATORS & SYSTEM COMPONENTS: Aerospace
ACCELERATORS, RUBBER PROCESSING: Cyclic or Acyclic
ACCELERATORS: Electron Linear
ACCELERATORS: Linear
ACCOUNTING MACHINES & CASH REGISTERS
ACCOUNTING SVCS, NEC
ACCOUNTING SVCS: Certified Public
ACIDS
ACIDS: Hydrochloric
ACIDS: Inorganic
ACIDS: Sulfuric, Oleum
ACOUSTICAL BOARD & TILE
ACRYLIC RESINS
ACTUATORS: Indl, NEC
ADAPTERS: Well
ADDITIVE BASED PLASTIC MATERIALS: Plasticizers
ADDRESSING SVCS
ADDRESSOGRAPHING SVCS
ADHESIVES
ADHESIVES & SEALANTS
ADHESIVES & SEALANTS WHOLESALERS
ADHESIVES: Adhesives, plastic
ADHESIVES: Epoxy
ADVERTISING AGENCIES
ADVERTISING AGENCIES: Consultants
ADVERTISING DISPLAY PRDTS
ADVERTISING REPRESENTATIVES: Electronic Media
ADVERTISING REPRESENTATIVES: Media
ADVERTISING REPRESENTATIVES: Newspaper
ADVERTISING SPECIALTIES, WHOLESALE
ADVERTISING SVCS, NEC
ADVERTISING SVCS: Billboards
ADVERTISING SVCS: Direct Mail
ADVERTISING SVCS: Display
ADVERTISING SVCS: Outdoor
ADVERTISING SVCS: Poster, Exc Outdoor
ADVERTISING SVCS: Poster, Outdoor
AERIAL WORK PLATFORMS
AEROSOLS
AGENTS, BROKERS & BUREAUS: Personal Service
AGRICULTURAL EQPT: BARN, SILO, POULTRY, DAIRY/LIVESTOCK MACH
AGRICULTURAL EQPT: Combine, Digger, Packer/Thresher, Peanut
AGRICULTURAL EQPT: Elevators, Farm
AGRICULTURAL EQPT: Fertilizing Machinery
AGRICULTURAL EQPT: Fillers & Unloaders, Silo
AGRICULTURAL EQPT: Grounds Mowing Eqpt
AGRICULTURAL EQPT: Loaders, Manure & General Utility
AGRICULTURAL EQPT: Shakers, Tree, Nuts, Fruits, Etc
AGRICULTURAL EQPT: Turf & Grounds Eqpt
AGRICULTURAL LIMESTONE: Ground
AGRICULTURAL MACHINERY & EQPT REPAIR
AGRICULTURAL MACHINERY & EQPT: Wholesalers
AIR CLEANING SYSTEMS
AIR CONDITIONING & VENTILATION EQPT & SPLYS: Wholesales
AIR CONDITIONING EQPT
AIR CONDITIONING REPAIR SVCS
AIR CONDITIONING UNITS: Complete, Domestic Or Indl
AIR DUCT CLEANING SVCS
AIR MATTRESSES: Plastic
AIR POLLUTION CONTROL EQPT & SPLYS WHOLESALERS
AIR PURIFICATION EQPT
AIR TRAFFIC CONTROL SVCS
AIR, WATER & SOLID WASTE PROGRAMS ADMINISTRATION SVCS
AIR-CONDITIONING SPLY SVCS
AIRCRAFT & AEROSPACE FLIGHT INSTRUMENTS & GUIDANCE SYSTEMS
AIRCRAFT & HEAVY EQPT REPAIR SVCS
AIRCRAFT ASSEMBLY PLANTS
AIRCRAFT CLEANING & JANITORIAL SVCS
AIRCRAFT CONTROL SYSTEMS:
AIRCRAFT CONTROL SYSTEMS: Electronic Totalizing Counters
AIRCRAFT ELECTRICAL EQPT REPAIR SVCS
AIRCRAFT ENGINES & ENGINE PARTS: Airfoils
AIRCRAFT ENGINES & ENGINE PARTS: Lubrication Systems
AIRCRAFT ENGINES & ENGINE PARTS: Pumps
AIRCRAFT ENGINES & ENGINE PARTS: Research & Development, Mfr
AIRCRAFT ENGINES & ENGINE PARTS: Rocket Motors
AIRCRAFT ENGINES & PARTS
AIRCRAFT EQPT & SPLYS WHOLESALERS
AIRCRAFT FLIGHT INSTRUMENTS
AIRCRAFT HANGAR OPERATION SVCS
AIRCRAFT MAINTENANCE & REPAIR SVCS
AIRCRAFT PARTS & AUX EQPT: Governors, Propeller Feathering
AIRCRAFT PARTS & AUXILIARY EQPT: Assys, Subassemblies/Parts
AIRCRAFT PARTS & AUXILIARY EQPT: Blades, Prop, Metal Or Wood
AIRCRAFT PARTS & AUXILIARY EQPT: Body & Wing Assys & Parts
AIRCRAFT PARTS & AUXILIARY EQPT: Body Assemblies & Parts
AIRCRAFT PARTS & AUXILIARY EQPT: Brakes
AIRCRAFT PARTS & AUXILIARY EQPT: Landing Assemblies & Brakes
AIRCRAFT PARTS & AUXILIARY EQPT: Lighting/Landing Gear Assy
AIRCRAFT PARTS & AUXILIARY EQPT: Military Eqpt & Armament
AIRCRAFT PARTS & AUXILIARY EQPT: Refueling Eqpt, In Flight
AIRCRAFT PARTS & AUXILIARY EQPT: Research & Development, Mfr
AIRCRAFT PARTS & EQPT, NEC
AIRCRAFT PARTS WHOLESALERS
AIRCRAFT PROPELLERS & PARTS
AIRCRAFT SERVICING & REPAIRING
AIRCRAFT TURBINES
AIRCRAFT WHEELS
AIRCRAFT: Airplanes, Fixed Or Rotary Wing
AIRCRAFT: Motorized
AIRCRAFT: Research & Development, Manufacturer
AIRPORTS, FLYING FIELDS & SVCS
ALARM SYSTEMS WHOLESALERS
ALARMS: Burglar
ALARMS: Fire
ALCOHOL: Ethyl & Ethanol
ALCOHOL: Methyl & Methanol, Synthetic
ALKALIES & CHLORINE
ALLOYS: Additive, Exc Copper Or Made In Blast Furnaces
ALTERNATORS: Automotive
ALUMINUM
ALUMINUM PRDTS
ALUMINUM: Coil & Sheet
ALUMINUM: Ingots & Slabs
ALUMINUM: Pigs
ALUMINUM: Rolling & Drawing
ALUMINUM: Slabs, Primary
AMMUNITION
AMMUNITION: Arming & Fusing Devices
AMMUNITION: Jet Propulsion Projectiles
AMMUNITION: Pellets & BB's, Pistol & Air Rifle
AMMUNITION: Shot, Steel
AMMUNITION: Small Arms
AMPLIFIERS
AMPLIFIERS: RF & IF Power
AMUSEMENT & REC SVCS: Baseball Club, Exc Pro & Semi-Pro
AMUSEMENT & REC SVCS: Cake/Pastry Decorating Instruction
AMUSEMENT & RECREATION SVCS: Arts & Crafts Instruction
AMUSEMENT & RECREATION SVCS: Exhibition Operation
AMUSEMENT & RECREATION SVCS: Exposition Operation
AMUSEMENT & RECREATION SVCS: Golf Svcs & Professionals
AMUSEMENT & RECREATION SVCS: Gun Club, Membership
AMUSEMENT & RECREATION SVCS: Ice Skating Rink
AMUSEMENT & RECREATION SVCS: Indoor Court Clubs
AMUSEMENT & RECREATION SVCS: Juke Box
AMUSEMENT & RECREATION SVCS: Outfitters, Recreation
AMUSEMENT & RECREATION SVCS: Physical Fitness Instruction
AMUSEMENT & RECREATION SVCS: Racquetball Club, Non-Member
AMUSEMENT & RECREATION SVCS: Shooting Range
AMUSEMENT & RECREATION SVCS: Video Game Arcades
AMUSEMENT & RECREATION SVCS: Zoological Garden, Commercial
AMUSEMENT PARK DEVICES & RIDES
AMUSEMENT PARK DEVICES & RIDES Carousels Or Merry-Go-Rounds
AMUSEMENT PARK DEVICES & RIDES: Carnival Mach & Eqpt, NEC
ANALYZERS: Network
ANALYZERS: Respiratory
ANESTHESIA EQPT
ANIMAL BASED MEDICINAL CHEMICAL PRDTS
ANIMAL FEED & SUPPLEMENTS: Livestock & Poultry
ANIMAL FEED: Wholesalers
ANIMAL FOOD & SUPPLEMENTS: Alfalfa Or Alfalfa Meal
ANIMAL FOOD & SUPPLEMENTS: Bird Food, Prepared
ANIMAL FOOD & SUPPLEMENTS: Bone Meal
ANIMAL FOOD & SUPPLEMENTS: Cat
ANIMAL FOOD & SUPPLEMENTS: Dog
ANIMAL FOOD & SUPPLEMENTS: Dog & Cat
ANIMAL FOOD & SUPPLEMENTS: Feed Concentrates
ANIMAL FOOD & SUPPLEMENTS: Feed Premixes
ANIMAL FOOD & SUPPLEMENTS: Feed Supplements
ANIMAL FOOD & SUPPLEMENTS: Livestock
ANIMAL FOOD & SUPPLEMENTS: Mineral feed supplements
ANIMAL FOOD & SUPPLEMENTS: Pet, Exc Dog & Cat, Dry
ANIMAL FOOD & SUPPLEMENTS: Poultry
ANIMAL FOOD & SUPPLEMENTS: Specialty, Mice & Other Pets
ANIMAL FOOD & SUPPLEMENTS: Stock Feeds, Dry
ANIMAL FOOD/SUPPLEMENTS: Feeds Fm Meat/Meat/Veg Combnd Meals
ANNEALING: Metal
ANNUNCIATORS
ANODIZING EQPT
ANODIZING SVC
ANTENNA REPAIR & INSTALLATION SVCS
ANTENNAS: Radar Or Communications
ANTENNAS: Receiving
ANTIBIOTICS
ANTIQUE & CLASSIC AUTOMOBILE RESTORATION
ANTIQUE FURNITURE RESTORATION & REPAIR
ANTIQUE REPAIR & RESTORATION SVCS, EXC FURNITURE & AUTOS
ANTIQUE SHOPS
ANTIQUES, WHOLESALE
APPAREL ACCESS STORES
APPAREL DESIGNERS: Commercial
APPAREL PRESSING SVCS
APPAREL: Hand Woven
APPLIANCE PARTS: Porcelain Enameled
APPLIANCES, HOUSEHOLD OR COIN OPERATED: Laundry Dryers
APPLIANCES, HOUSEHOLD: Kitchen, Major, Exc Refrigs & Stoves
APPLIANCES, HOUSEHOLD: Laundry Machines, Incl Coin-Operated
APPLIANCES, HOUSEHOLD: Refrigs, Mechanical & Absorption

PRODUCT INDEX

APPLIANCES: Household, NEC
APPLIANCES: Household, Refrigerators & Freezers
APPLIANCES: Major, Cooking
APPLIANCES: Small, Electric
APPLICATIONS SOFTWARE PROGRAMMING
APPRAISAL SVCS, EXC REAL ESTATE
APRONS: Rubber, Vulcanized Or Rubberized Fabric
AQUARIUMS & ACCESS: Glass
AQUARIUMS & ACCESS: Plastic
ARCHITECTURAL PANELS OR PARTS: Porcelain Enameled
ARCHITECTURAL SVCS
ARMATURE REPAIRING & REWINDING SVC
ARMORED CAR SVCS
ART & ORNAMENTAL WARE: Pottery
ART DEALERS & GALLERIES
ART DESIGN SVCS
ART MARBLE: Concrete
ART RELATED SVCS
ART RESTORATION SVC
ART SPLY STORES
ARTISTS' AGENTS & BROKERS
ARTISTS' MATERIALS: Brushes, Air
ARTISTS' MATERIALS: Canvas, Prepared On Frames
ARTISTS' MATERIALS: Ink, Drawing, Black & Colored
ARTISTS' MATERIALS: Pencil Holders
ARTISTS' MATERIALS: Water Colors
ARTISTS' MATERIALS: Wax
ARTS & CRAFTS SCHOOL
ASBESTOS PRDTS: Roofing, Felt Roll
ASBESTOS PRDTS: Textiles, Exc Insulating Material
ASPHALT & ASPHALT PRDTS
ASPHALT COATINGS & SEALERS
ASPHALT MINING & BITUMINOUS STONE QUARRYING SVCS
ASPHALT MINING SVCS
ASPHALT MIXTURES WHOLESALERS
ASPHALT PLANTS INCLUDING GRAVEL MIX TYPE
ASSEMBLING SVC: Plumbing Fixture Fittings, Plastic
ASSOCIATION FOR THE HANDICAPPED
ASSOCIATIONS: Business
ASSOCIATIONS: Fraternal
ASSOCIATIONS: Manufacturers'
ASSOCIATIONS: Real Estate Management
ASSOCIATIONS: Trade
ATOMIZERS
AUCTION SVCS: Motor Vehicle
AUDIO & VIDEO EQPT, EXC COMMERCIAL
AUDIO COMPONENTS
AUDIO ELECTRONIC SYSTEMS
AUDIO-VISUAL PROGRAM PRODUCTION SVCS
AUDIOLOGICAL EQPT: Electronic
AUDIOLOGISTS' OFFICES
AUTO & HOME SUPPLY STORES: Auto & Truck Eqpt & Parts
AUTO & HOME SUPPLY STORES: Automotive Access
AUTO & HOME SUPPLY STORES: Automotive parts
AUTO & HOME SUPPLY STORES: Batteries, Automotive & Truck
AUTO & HOME SUPPLY STORES: Trailer Hitches, Automotive
AUTO & HOME SUPPLY STORES: Truck Eqpt & Parts
AUTOMATED TELLER MACHINE OR ATM REPAIR SVCS
AUTOMATIC REGULATING CNTRLS: Liq Lvl, Residential/Comm Heat
AUTOMATIC REGULATING CNTRLS: Steam Press, Residential/ Comm
AUTOMATIC REGULATING CONTROL: Building Svcs Monitoring, Auto
AUTOMATIC REGULATING CONTROLS: AC & Refrigeration
AUTOMATIC REGULATING CONTROLS: Appliance, Exc Air-Cond/Refr
AUTOMATIC REGULATING CONTROLS: Energy Cutoff, Residtl/Comm
AUTOMATIC REGULATING CONTROLS: Hardware, Environmental Reg
AUTOMATIC REGULATING CONTROLS: Refrigeration, Pressure
AUTOMATIC REGULATING CONTROLS: Surface Burner, Temperature
AUTOMATIC REGULATING CTRLS: Damper, Pneumatic Or Electric
AUTOMATIC TELLER MACHINES
AUTOMOBILE RECOVERY SVCS
AUTOMOBILE STORAGE GARAGE
AUTOMOBILES & OTHER MOTOR VEHICLES WHOLESALERS
AUTOMOBILES: Off-Road, Exc Recreational Vehicles
AUTOMOTIVE & TRUCK GENERAL REPAIR SVC
AUTOMOTIVE BATTERIES WHOLESALERS
AUTOMOTIVE BODY SHOP
AUTOMOTIVE BODY, PAINT & INTERIOR REPAIR & MAINTENANCE SVC
AUTOMOTIVE BRAKE REPAIR SHOPS
AUTOMOTIVE CUSTOMIZING SVCS, NONFACTORY BASIS
AUTOMOTIVE GLASS REPLACEMENT SHOPS
AUTOMOTIVE PAINT SHOP
AUTOMOTIVE PARTS, ACCESS & SPLYS
AUTOMOTIVE PARTS: Plastic
AUTOMOTIVE PRDTS: Rubber
AUTOMOTIVE RADIATOR REPAIR SHOPS
AUTOMOTIVE REPAIR SHOPS: Alternators/Generator, Rebuild/Rpr
AUTOMOTIVE REPAIR SHOPS: Diesel Engine Repair
AUTOMOTIVE REPAIR SHOPS: Electrical Svcs
AUTOMOTIVE REPAIR SHOPS: Engine Rebuilding
AUTOMOTIVE REPAIR SHOPS: Engine Repair
AUTOMOTIVE REPAIR SHOPS: Machine Shop
AUTOMOTIVE REPAIR SHOPS: Trailer Repair
AUTOMOTIVE REPAIR SHOPS: Truck Engine Repair, Exc Indl
AUTOMOTIVE REPAIR SVC
AUTOMOTIVE REPAIR SVCS, MISCELLANEOUS
AUTOMOTIVE RUSTPROOFING & UNDERCOATING SHOPS
AUTOMOTIVE SPLYS & PARTS, NEW, WHOL: Auto Servicing Eqpt
AUTOMOTIVE SPLYS & PARTS, NEW, WHOL: Testing Eqpt, Electric
AUTOMOTIVE SPLYS & PARTS, NEW, WHOLESALE: Bumpers
AUTOMOTIVE SPLYS & PARTS, NEW, WHOLESALE: Clutches
AUTOMOTIVE SPLYS & PARTS, NEW, WHOLESALE: Engines/Eng Parts
AUTOMOTIVE SPLYS & PARTS, NEW, WHOLESALE: Filters, Air & Oil
AUTOMOTIVE SPLYS & PARTS, NEW, WHOLESALE: Pumps, Oil & Gas
AUTOMOTIVE SPLYS & PARTS, NEW, WHOLESALE: Seat Covers
AUTOMOTIVE SPLYS & PARTS, NEW, WHOLESALE: Splys
AUTOMOTIVE SPLYS & PARTS, NEW, WHOLESALE: Stampings
AUTOMOTIVE SPLYS & PARTS, NEW, WHOLESALE: Tools & Eqpt
AUTOMOTIVE SPLYS & PARTS, NEW, WHOLESALE: Trailer Parts
AUTOMOTIVE SPLYS & PARTS, NEW, WHOLESALE: Wheels
AUTOMOTIVE SPLYS & PARTS, USED, RETAIL ONLY: Tires, Used
AUTOMOTIVE SPLYS & PARTS, USED, WHOLESALE
AUTOMOTIVE SPLYS & PARTS, WHOLESALE, NEC
AUTOMOTIVE SPLYS, USED, WHOLESALE & RETAIL
AUTOMOTIVE SPLYS/PART, NEW, WHOL: Spring, Shock Absorb/Strut
AUTOMOTIVE SPLYS/PARTS, NEW, WHOL: Body Rpr/Paint Shop Splys
AUTOMOTIVE SVCS, EXC REPAIR & CARWASHES: Customizing
AUTOMOTIVE SVCS, EXC REPAIR & CARWASHES: Maintenance
AUTOMOTIVE SVCS, EXC REPAIR & CARWASHES: Road Svc
AUTOMOTIVE SVCS, EXC REPAIR & CARWASHES: Trailer Maintenance
AUTOMOTIVE TOPS INSTALLATION OR REPAIR: Canvas Or Plastic
AUTOMOTIVE TOWING & WRECKING SVC
AUTOMOTIVE TOWING SVCS
AUTOMOTIVE TRANSMISSION REPAIR SVC
AUTOMOTIVE WELDING SVCS
AUTOMOTIVE: Bodies
AUTOMOTIVE: Seat Frames, Metal
AUTOMOTIVE: Seating
AUTOTRANSFORMERS: Electric
AWNINGS & CANOPIES
AWNINGS & CANOPIES: Awnings, Fabric, From Purchased Matls
AWNINGS & CANOPIES: Fabric
AWNINGS: Fiberglass
AWNINGS: Metal
AXLES
Ammunition Loading & Assembling Plant

B

BACKHOES
BADGES: Identification & Insignia
BAFFLES
BAGS & CONTAINERS: Textile, Exc Sleeping
BAGS: Canvas
BAGS: Cellophane
BAGS: Food Storage & Frozen Food, Plastic
BAGS: Food Storage & Trash, Plastic
BAGS: Garment Storage Exc Paper Or Plastic Film
BAGS: Paper, Made From Purchased Materials
BAGS: Plastic
BAGS: Plastic & Pliofilm
BAGS: Plastic, Made From Purchased Materials
BAGS: Pliofilm, Made From Purchased Materials
BAGS: Rubber Or Rubberized Fabric
BAGS: Shipping
BAGS: Shopping, Made From Purchased Materials
BAGS: Textile
BAGS: Trash, Plastic Film, Made From Purchased Materials
BAGS: Vacuum cleaner, Made From Purchased Materials
BAIT, FISHING, WHOLESALE
BAKERIES, COMMERCIAL: On Premises Baking Only
BAKERIES: On Premises Baking & Consumption
BAKERY FOR HOME SVC DELIVERY
BAKERY MACHINERY
BAKERY PRDTS, FROZEN: Wholesalers
BAKERY PRDTS: Bagels, Fresh Or Frozen
BAKERY PRDTS: Bakery Prdts, Partially Cooked, Exc frozen
BAKERY PRDTS: Biscuits, Dry
BAKERY PRDTS: Bread, All Types, Fresh Or Frozen
BAKERY PRDTS: Buns, Bread Type, Fresh Or Frozen
BAKERY PRDTS: Cakes, Bakery, Exc Frozen
BAKERY PRDTS: Cakes, Bakery, Frozen
BAKERY PRDTS: Cones, Ice Cream
BAKERY PRDTS: Cookies
BAKERY PRDTS: Cookies & crackers
BAKERY PRDTS: Doughnuts, Exc Frozen
BAKERY PRDTS: Dry
BAKERY PRDTS: Frozen
BAKERY PRDTS: Pastries, Exc Frozen
BAKERY PRDTS: Pies, Exc Frozen
BAKERY PRDTS: Pretzels
BAKERY PRDTS: Rice Cakes
BAKERY PRDTS: Wholesalers
BAKERY: Wholesale Or Wholesale & Retail Combined
BALLOONS: Toy & Advertising, Rubber
BANDS: Plastic
BANNERS: Fabric
BANQUET HALL FACILITIES
BAR
BAR JOISTS & CONCRETE REINFORCING BARS: Fabricated
BARBECUE EQPT
BARBER SHOP SELLING WIGS
BARGES BUILDING & REPAIR
BARRELS: Shipping, Metal
BARS & BAR SHAPES: Copper & Copper Alloy
BARS & BAR SHAPES: Steel, Cold-Finished, Own Hot-Rolled
BARS & BAR SHAPES: Steel, Hot-Rolled
BARS, COLD FINISHED: Steel, From Purchased Hot-Rolled
BARS, PIPES, PLATES & SHAPES: Lead/Lead Alloy Bars, Pipe
BARS: Concrete Reinforcing, Fabricated Steel
BARS: Iron, Made In Steel Mills
BARS: Rolled, Aluminum
BASALT: Crushed & Broken
BASEMENT WINDOW AREAWAYS: Concrete
BASES, BEVERAGE
BASKETS, WHOLESALE
BASKETS: Steel Wire
BATCHING PLANTS: Bituminous
BATH SALTS
BATH SHOPS
BATHMATS: Rubber
BATHROOM ACCESS & FITTINGS: Vitreous China & Earthenware
BATHROOM FIXTURES: Plastic
BATTERIES, EXC AUTOMOTIVE: Wholesalers
BATTERIES: Alkaline, Cell Storage
BATTERIES: Dry

PRODUCT INDEX

BATTERIES: Lead Acid, Storage
BATTERIES: Rechargeable
BATTERIES: Storage
BATTERIES: Wet
BATTERY CASES: Plastic Or Plastics Combination
BATTERY CHARGERS
BATTERY CHARGERS: Storage, Motor & Engine Generator Type
BATTERY CHARGING GENERATORS
BATTERY REPAIR & SVCS
BEADS: Unassembled
BEARINGS
BEARINGS & PARTS Ball
BEARINGS: Ball & Roller
BEARINGS: Railroad Car Journal
BEARINGS: Roller & Parts
BEAUTY & BARBER SHOP EQPT
BEAUTY SALONS
BED & BREAKFAST INNS
BEDDING & BEDSPRINGS STORES
BEDDING, BEDSPREADS, BLANKETS & SHEETS
BEDDING, BEDSPREADS, BLANKETS & SHEETS: Comforters & Quilts
BEDS & ACCESS STORES
BEDS: Hospital
BEDS: Institutional
BEDSPREADS & BED SETS, FROM PURCHASED MATERIALS
BEDSPREADS, COTTON
BEER & ALE WHOLESALERS
BEER, WINE & LIQUOR STORES: Beer, Packaged
BEER, WINE & LIQUOR STORES: Wine
BEER, WINE & LIQUOR STORES: Wine & Beer
BELLOWS
BELLOWS ASSEMBLIES: Missiles, Metal
BELLS: Electric
BELTING: Plastic
BELTING: Rubber
BELTS & BELT PRDTS
BELTS: Conveyor, Made From Purchased Wire
BELTS: Seat, Automotive & Aircraft
BENTONITE MINING
BERYLLIUM
BEVERAGE BASES & SYRUPS
BEVERAGE PRDTS: Brewers' Grain
BEVERAGES, ALCOHOLIC: Ale
BEVERAGES, ALCOHOLIC: Beer
BEVERAGES, ALCOHOLIC: Beer & Ale
BEVERAGES, ALCOHOLIC: Bourbon Whiskey
BEVERAGES, ALCOHOLIC: Cocktails
BEVERAGES, ALCOHOLIC: Distilled Liquors
BEVERAGES, ALCOHOLIC: Liquors, Malt
BEVERAGES, ALCOHOLIC: Near Beer
BEVERAGES, ALCOHOLIC: Neutral Spirits, Fruit
BEVERAGES, ALCOHOLIC: Rye Whiskey
BEVERAGES, ALCOHOLIC: Wines
BEVERAGES, MALT
BEVERAGES, NONALCOHOLIC: Bottled & canned soft drinks
BEVERAGES, NONALCOHOLIC: Carbonated
BEVERAGES, NONALCOHOLIC: Carbonated, Canned & Bottled, Etc
BEVERAGES, NONALCOHOLIC: Cider
BEVERAGES, NONALCOHOLIC: Flavoring extracts & syrups, nec
BEVERAGES, NONALCOHOLIC: Fruit Drnks, Under 100% Juice, Can
BEVERAGES, NONALCOHOLIC: Soft Drinks, Canned & Bottled, Etc
BEVERAGES, NONALCOHOLIC: Tea, Iced, Bottled & Canned, Etc
BEVERAGES, WINE & DISTILLED ALCOHOLIC, WHOLESALE: Liquor
BEVERAGES, WINE & DISTILLED ALCOHOLIC, WHOLESALE: Wine
BIBS: Rubber, Vulcanized Or Rubberized Fabric
BICYCLE REPAIR SHOP
BICYCLE SHOPS
BICYCLES, PARTS & ACCESS
BILLFOLD INSERTS: Plastic
BILLIARD & POOL TABLES & SPLYS
BILLING & BOOKKEEPING SVCS
BINDING SVC: Books & Manuals
BINDING SVC: Pamphlets
BINDING SVC: Trade
BINDINGS: Bias, Made From Purchased Materials
BINDINGS: Cap & Hat, Made From Purchased Materials
BINGO HALL
BINOCULARS
BINS: Prefabricated, Sheet Metal
BIOLOGICAL PRDTS: Bacteriological Media
BIOLOGICAL PRDTS: Exc Diagnostic
BIOLOGICAL PRDTS: Serums
BIOLOGICAL PRDTS: Toxin, Viruses/Simlr Substncs, Incl Venom
BIOLOGICAL PRDTS: Vaccines
BIOLOGICAL PRDTS: Vaccines & Immunizing
BIOLOGICAL PRDTS: Venoms
BIOLOGICAL PRDTS: Veterinary
BLACKBOARDS & CHALKBOARDS
BLACKBOARDS: Slate
BLADES: Knife
BLADES: Saw, Hand Or Power
BLANKBOOKS
BLANKBOOKS & LOOSELEAF BINDERS
BLANKBOOKS: Account
BLANKBOOKS: Albums
BLANKBOOKS: Passbooks, Bank, Etc
BLANKETS & BLANKETING, COTTON
BLAST FURNACE & RELATED PRDTS
BLASTING SVC: Sand, Metal Parts
BLINDS & SHADES: Vertical
BLINDS : Window
BLINDS, WOOD
BLOCK & BRICK: Sand Lime
BLOCKS & BRICKS: Concrete
BLOCKS: Insulating, Concrete
BLOCKS: Landscape Or Retaining Wall, Concrete
BLOCKS: Paving
BLOCKS: Paving, Composition
BLOCKS: Paving, Concrete
BLOCKS: Standard, Concrete Or Cinder
BLOOD BANK
BLOWERS & FANS
BLOWERS & FANS
BLUEPRINTING SVCS
BOAT BUILDING & REPAIR
BOAT BUILDING & REPAIRING: Dories
BOAT BUILDING & REPAIRING: Iceboats
BOAT BUILDING & REPAIRING: Kits, Not Models
BOAT BUILDING & REPAIRING: Lifeboats
BOAT BUILDING & REPAIRING: Motorized
BOAT BUILDING & REPAIRING: Tenders, Small Motor Craft
BOAT DEALERS
BOAT DEALERS: Marine Splys & Eqpt
BOAT DEALERS: Motor
BOAT LIFTS
BOAT REPAIR SVCS
BOAT YARD: Boat yards, storage & incidental repair
BOATS & OTHER MARINE EQPT: Plastic
BODIES: Truck & Bus
BODY PARTS: Automobile, Stamped Metal
BOILER & HEATING REPAIR SVCS
BOILER GAGE COCKS
BOILER REPAIR SHOP
BOILERS: Low-Pressure Heating, Steam Or Hot Water
BOLTS: Metal
BONDERIZING: Bonderizing, Metal Or Metal Prdts
BONDS, RAIL: Electric, Propulsion & Signal Circuit Uses
BOOK STORES
BOOK STORES: Comic
BOOK STORES: Religious
BOOKS, WHOLESALE
BOOTHS: Spray, Sheet Metal, Prefabricated
BORING MILL
BOTTLE CAPS & RESEALERS: Plastic
BOTTLED GAS DEALERS: Propane
BOTTLED WATER DELIVERY
BOTTLES: Plastic
BOWL COVERS: Plastic
BOWLING CENTERS
BOWLING EQPT & SPLY STORES
BOWLING EQPT & SPLYS
BOXES & CRATES: Rectangular, Wood
BOXES & SHOOK: Nailed Wood
BOXES: Corrugated
BOXES: Filing, Paperboard Made From Purchased Materials
BOXES: Fuse, Electric
BOXES: Mail Or Post Office, Collection/Storage, Sheet Metal
BOXES: Packing & Shipping, Metal
BOXES: Paperboard, Folding
BOXES: Paperboard, Set-Up
BOXES: Plastic
BOXES: Stamped Metal
BOXES: Tool Chests, Wood
BOXES: Wooden
BRAKES & BRAKE PARTS
BRAKES: Bicycle, Friction Clutch & Other
BRAKES: Electromagnetic
BRAKES: Metal Forming
BRASS & BRONZE PRDTS: Die-casted
BRASS FOUNDRY, NEC
BRAZING SVCS
BRAZING: Metal
BRIC-A-BRAC
BRICK, STONE & RELATED PRDTS WHOLESALERS
BRICKS & BLOCKS: Structural
BRICKS : Ceramic Glazed, Clay
BRICKS : Paving, Clay
BRICKS: Clay
BRICKS: Concrete
BRIDAL SHOPS
BRIDGE COMPONENTS: Bridge sections, prefabricated, highway
BROACHING MACHINES
BROADCASTING & COMMS EQPT: Antennas, Transmitting/Comms
BROADCASTING & COMMS EQPT: Rcvr-Transmitter Unt, Transceiver
BROADCASTING & COMMUNICATIONS EQPT: Cellular Radio Telephone
BROADCASTING & COMMUNICATIONS EQPT: Light Comms Eqpt
BROADCASTING STATIONS, RADIO: Music Format
BROKERS' SVCS
BROKERS, MARINE TRANSPORTATION
BROKERS: Contract Basis
BROKERS: Food
BROKERS: Log & Lumber
BROKERS: Printing
BRONZE FOUNDRY, NEC
BRONZE ROLLING & DRAWING
BROOMS & BRUSHES
BROOMS & BRUSHES: Household Or Indl
BROOMS & BRUSHES: Paint & Varnish
BROOMS & BRUSHES: Street Sweeping, Hand Or Machine
BRUSH BLOCKS: Carbon Or Molded Graphite
BRUSHES & BRUSH STOCK CONTACTS: Electric
BUCKETS: Plastic
BUFFING FOR THE TRADE
BUILDING & OFFICE CLEANING SVCS
BUILDING & STRUCTURAL WOOD MEMBERS
BUILDING & STRUCTURAL WOOD MEMBERS: Arches, Laminated Lumber
BUILDING CLEANING & MAINTENANCE SVCS
BUILDING CLEANING SVCS
BUILDING COMPONENT CLEANING SVCS
BUILDING COMPONENTS: Structural Steel
BUILDING ITEM REPAIR SVCS, MISCELLANEOUS
BUILDING MAINTENANCE SVCS, EXC REPAIRS
BUILDING PRDTS & MATERIALS DEALERS
BUILDING PRDTS: Concrete
BUILDING PRDTS: Stone
BUILDING SCALES MODELS
BUILDING STONE, ARTIFICIAL: Concrete
BUILDINGS & COMPONENTS: Prefabricated Metal
BUILDINGS, PREFABRICATED: Wholesalers
BUILDINGS: Farm & Utility
BUILDINGS: Farm, Prefabricated Or Portable, Wood
BUILDINGS: Portable
BUILDINGS: Prefabricated, Metal
BUILDINGS: Prefabricated, Plastic
BUILDINGS: Prefabricated, Wood
BUILDINGS: Prefabricated, Wood
BULLETIN BOARDS: Cork
BULLETIN BOARDS: Wood
BULLETPROOF VESTS
BUOYS: Metal
BUOYS: Plastic
BURGLAR ALARM MAINTENANCE & MONITORING SVCS
BURIAL VAULTS, FIBERGLASS
BURIAL VAULTS: Concrete Or Precast Terrazzo
BURIAL VAULTS: Stone
BURLAP & BURLAP PRDTS
BURNERS: Gas, Domestic

PRODUCT INDEX

BURNERS: Gas, Indl
BURNERS: Oil, Domestic Or Indl
BUS BARS: Electrical
BUSHINGS & BEARINGS
BUSHINGS & BEARINGS: Brass, Exc Machined
BUSHINGS & BEARINGS: Bronze, Exc Machined
BUSINESS ACTIVITIES: Non-Commercial Site
BUSINESS FORMS WHOLESALERS
BUSINESS FORMS: Printed, Continuous
BUSINESS FORMS: Printed, Manifold
BUSINESS FORMS: Unit Sets, Manifold
BUSINESS MACHINE REPAIR, ELECTRIC
BUSINESS SUPPORT SVCS
BUSINESS TRAINING SVCS
BUTTER WHOLESALERS

C

CABINETS & CASES: Show, Display & Storage, Exc Wood
CABINETS: Bathroom Vanities, Wood
CABINETS: Entertainment
CABINETS: Entertainment Units, Household, Wood
CABINETS: Factory
CABINETS: Filing, Wood
CABINETS: Kitchen, Metal
CABINETS: Kitchen, Wood
CABINETS: Office, Metal
CABINETS: Office, Wood
CABINETS: Show, Display, Etc, Wood, Exc Refrigerated
CABLE & OTHER PAY TELEVISION DISTRIBUTION
CABLE TELEVISION
CABLE WIRING SETS: Battery, Internal Combustion Engines
CABLE: Fiber
CABLE: Fiber Optic
CABLE: Noninsulated
CABLE: Ropes & Fiber
CABLE: Steel, Insulated Or Armored
CABS: Indl Trucks & Tractors
CAFETERIAS
CAFFEINE & DERIVATIVES
CAGES: Wire
CALCULATING & ACCOUNTING EQPT
CALENDARS, WHOLESALE
CALIBRATING SVCS, NEC
CAMERAS & RELATED EQPT: Photographic
CAMPGROUNDS
CAMSHAFTS
CANDLE SHOPS
CANDLES
CANDLES: Wholesalers
CANDY & CONFECTIONS: Cake Ornaments
CANDY & CONFECTIONS: Candy Bars, Including Chocolate Covered
CANDY & CONFECTIONS: Chocolate Candy, Exc Solid Chocolate
CANDY & CONFECTIONS: Chocolate Covered Dates
CANDY & CONFECTIONS: Cough Drops, Exc Pharmaceutical Preps
CANDY & CONFECTIONS: Fudge
CANDY & CONFECTIONS: Nuts, Glace
CANDY & CONFECTIONS: Popcorn Balls/Other Trtd Popcorn Prdts
CANDY, NUT & CONFECTIONERY STORE: Popcorn, Incl Caramel Corn
CANDY, NUT & CONFECTIONERY STORES: Candy
CANDY, NUT & CONFECTIONERY STORES: Confectionery
CANDY, NUT & CONFECTIONERY STORES: Nuts
CANDY: Chocolate From Cacao Beans
CANDY: Hard
CANNED SPECIALTIES
CANOPIES: Sheet Metal
CANS & CASES: Capacitor Or Condenser, Stamped Metal
CANS & TUBES: Ammunition, Board Laminated With Metal Foil
CANS: Aluminum
CANS: Beer, Metal
CANS: Composite Foil-Fiber, Made From Purchased Materials
CANS: Fiber
CANS: Garbage, Stamped Or Pressed Metal
CANS: Metal
CANS: Tin
CANVAS PRDTS
CANVAS PRDTS: Air Cushions & Mattresses
CANVAS PRDTS: Convertible Tops, Car/Boat, Fm Purchased Mtrl
CANVAS PRDTS: Shades, Made From Purchased Materials

CAPACITORS: NEC
CAPS & PLUGS: Electric, Attachment
CAPS: Plastic
CAR LOADING SVCS
CAR WASH EQPT
CAR WASH EQPT & SPLYS WHOLESALERS
CAR WASHES
CARBIDES
CARBON & GRAPHITE PRDTS, NEC
CARBON BLACK
CARBON DISULFIDE
CARBON PAPER & INKED RIBBONS
CARDIOVASCULAR SYSTEM DRUGS, EXC DIAGNOSTIC
CARDS: Beveled
CARDS: Color
CARDS: Greeting
CARDS: Identification
CARDS: Playing
CARNIVAL & AMUSEMENT PARK EQPT WHOLESALERS
CARNIVAL SPLYS, WHOLESALE
CARPET & UPHOLSTERY CLEANING SVCS
CARPET & UPHOLSTERY CLEANING SVCS: Carpet/Furniture, On Loc
CARPETS & RUGS: Tufted
CARPETS, RUGS & FLOOR COVERING
CARRIAGES: Horse Drawn
CARRIERS: Infant, Textile
CARS: Electric
CARTONS: Egg, Molded Pulp, Made From Purchased Materials
CARVING SETS, STAINLESS STEEL
CASES, WOOD
CASES: Carrying
CASES: Plastic
CASES: Shipping, Nailed Or Lock Corner, Wood
CASH REGISTERS & PARTS
CASINGS: Rocket Transportation
CASINGS: Sheet Metal
CASINGS: Storage, Missile & Missile Components
CASKETS & ACCESS
CASKETS WHOLESALERS
CAST STONE: Concrete
CASTERS
CASTINGS GRINDING: For The Trade
CASTINGS: Aerospace Investment, Ferrous
CASTINGS: Aerospace, Aluminum
CASTINGS: Aerospace, Nonferrous, Exc Aluminum
CASTINGS: Aluminum
CASTINGS: Brass, NEC, Exc Die
CASTINGS: Bronze, NEC, Exc Die
CASTINGS: Commercial Investment, Ferrous
CASTINGS: Copper & Copper-Base Alloy, NEC, Exc Die
CASTINGS: Die, Aluminum
CASTINGS: Die, Copper & Copper Alloy
CASTINGS: Die, Magnesium & Magnesium-Base Alloy
CASTINGS: Die, Nonferrous
CASTINGS: Die, Zinc
CASTINGS: Ductile
CASTINGS: Gray Iron
CASTINGS: Machinery, Aluminum
CASTINGS: Machinery, Nonferrous, Exc Die or Aluminum Copper
CASTINGS: Magnesium
CASTINGS: Precision
CASTINGS: Steel
CASTINGS: Zinc
CATALOG & MAIL-ORDER HOUSES
CATALOG SALES
CATALYSTS: Chemical
CATAPULTS
CATCH BASIN COVERS: Concrete
CATERERS
CATTLE WHOLESALERS
CAULKING COMPOUNDS
CEILING SYSTEMS: Luminous, Commercial
CELLULOSE ACETATE
CELLULOSE DERIVATIVE MATERIALS
CEMENT & CONCRETE RELATED PRDTS & EQPT: Bituminous
CEMENT ROCK: Crushed & Broken
CEMENT, EXC LINOLEUM & TILE
CEMENT: Heat Resistant
CEMENT: Hydraulic
CEMENT: Masonry
CEMENT: Natural

CEMENT: Portland
CEMENT: Rubber
CEMETERIES: Real Estate Operation
CEMETERY & FUNERAL DIRECTOR'S EQPT & SPLYS WHOLESALERS
CEMETERY MEMORIAL DEALERS
CERAMIC FIBER
CERAMIC FLOOR & WALL TILE WHOLESALERS
CHAIN: Wire
CHAINS: Power Transmission
CHALK MINING: Crushed & Broken
CHANDELIERS: Residential
CHARCOAL
CHARCOAL, WHOLESALE
CHARCOAL: Activated
CHASSIS: Motor Vehicle
CHEESE WHOLESALERS
CHEMICAL CLEANING SVCS
CHEMICAL ELEMENTS
CHEMICAL PROCESSING MACHINERY & EQPT
CHEMICAL SPLYS FOR FOUNDRIES
CHEMICALS & ALLIED PRDTS WHOLESALERS, NEC
CHEMICALS & ALLIED PRDTS, WHOLESALE: Anti-Corrosion Prdts
CHEMICALS & ALLIED PRDTS, WHOLESALE: Caustic Soda
CHEMICALS & ALLIED PRDTS, WHOLESALE: Chemical Additives
CHEMICALS & ALLIED PRDTS, WHOLESALE: Chemicals, Indl
CHEMICALS & ALLIED PRDTS, WHOLESALE: Chemicals, Indl & Heavy
CHEMICALS & ALLIED PRDTS, WHOLESALE: Concrete Additives
CHEMICALS & ALLIED PRDTS, WHOLESALE: Detergent/Soap
CHEMICALS & ALLIED PRDTS, WHOLESALE: Detergents
CHEMICALS & ALLIED PRDTS, WHOLESALE: Dry Ice
CHEMICALS & ALLIED PRDTS, WHOLESALE: Glue
CHEMICALS & ALLIED PRDTS, WHOLESALE: Indl Gases
CHEMICALS & ALLIED PRDTS, WHOLESALE: Oxygen
CHEMICALS & ALLIED PRDTS, WHOLESALE: Plastics Materials, NEC
CHEMICALS & ALLIED PRDTS, WHOLESALE: Plastics Prdts, NEC
CHEMICALS & ALLIED PRDTS, WHOLESALE: Plastics Sheets & Rods
CHEMICALS & ALLIED PRDTS, WHOLESALE: Plastics, Basic Shapes
CHEMICALS & ALLIED PRDTS, WHOLESALE: Resins
CHEMICALS & ALLIED PRDTS, WHOLESALE: Rubber, Synthetic
CHEMICALS & ALLIED PRDTS, WHOLESALE: Sealants
CHEMICALS & ALLIED PRDTS, WHOLESALE: Syn Resin, Rub/Plastic
CHEMICALS & ALLIED PRDTS, WHOLESALE: Waxes, Exc Petroleum
CHEMICALS & OTHER PRDTS DERIVED FROM COKING
CHEMICALS, AGRICULTURE: Wholesalers
CHEMICALS: Agricultural
CHEMICALS: Alcohols
CHEMICALS: Alkalies
CHEMICALS: Aluminum Compounds
CHEMICALS: Aluminum Oxide
CHEMICALS: Aluminum Sulfate
CHEMICALS: Bauxite, Refined
CHEMICALS: Bleaching Powder, Lime Bleaching Compounds
CHEMICALS: Calcium & Calcium Compounds
CHEMICALS: Caustic Potash & Potassium Hydroxide
CHEMICALS: Caustic Soda
CHEMICALS: Copper Compounds Or Salts, Inorganic
CHEMICALS: Fire Retardant
CHEMICALS: High Purity Grade, Organic
CHEMICALS: High Purity, Refined From Technical Grade
CHEMICALS: Inorganic, NEC
CHEMICALS: Isotopes, Radioactive
CHEMICALS: Lead Compounds/Salts, Inorganic, Not Pigments
CHEMICALS: Lithium Compounds, Inorganic
CHEMICALS: Luminous Compounds, Radium
CHEMICALS: Medicinal
CHEMICALS: Medicinal, Organic, Uncompounded, Bulk
CHEMICALS: Metal Salts/Compounds, Exc Sodium, Potassium/Alum
CHEMICALS: NEC
CHEMICALS: Nonmetallic Compounds

PRODUCT INDEX

CHEMICALS: Organic, NEC
CHEMICALS: Phenol
CHEMICALS: Phosphates, Defluorinated/Ammoniated, Exc Fertlr
CHEMICALS: Reagent Grade, Refined From Technical Grade
CHEMICALS: Sodium Bicarbonate
CHEMICALS: Sulfur Chloride
CHEMICALS: Tin, Stannic/Stannous, Compounds/Salts, Inorganic
CHEMICALS: Water Treatment
CHEMICALS: Zinc Chloride
CHICKEN SLAUGHTERING & PROCESSING
CHILD DAY CARE SVCS
CHILD RESTRAINT SEATS, AUTOMOTIVE, WHOLESALE
CHILDREN'S WEAR STORES
CHIMNEY CAPS: Concrete
CHIMNEY CLEANING SVCS
CHINA: Fired & Decorated
CHINAWARE WHOLESALERS
CHIROPRACTORS' OFFICES
CHLORINE
CHOCOLATE, EXC CANDY FROM BEANS: Chips, Powder, Block, Syrup
CHOCOLATE, EXC CANDY FROM PURCH CHOC: Chips, Powder, Block
CHRISTMAS NOVELTIES, WHOLESALE
CHRISTMAS TREE LIGHTING SETS: Electric
CHUCKS
CHUTES & TROUGHS
CIGAR STORES
CIGARETTE & CIGAR PRDTS & ACCESS
CIGARETTE LIGHTERS
CIRCUIT BOARD REPAIR SVCS
CIRCUIT BOARDS, PRINTED: Television & Radio
CIRCUIT BOARDS: Wiring
CIRCUIT BREAKERS
CIRCUITS: Electronic
CLAMPS & COUPLINGS: Hose
CLAMPS: Metal
CLAY MINING, COMMON
CLAY: Ground Or Treated
CLEANING & DESCALING SVC: Metal Prdts
CLEANING COMPOUNDS: Rifle Bore
CLEANING EQPT: Blast, Dustless
CLEANING EQPT: Commercial
CLEANING EQPT: Floor Washing & Polishing, Commercial
CLEANING EQPT: High Pressure
CLEANING EQPT: Janitors' Carts
CLEANING OR POLISHING PREPARATIONS, NEC
CLEANING PRDTS: Automobile Polish
CLEANING PRDTS: Degreasing Solvent
CLEANING PRDTS: Deodorants, Nonpersonal
CLEANING PRDTS: Disinfectants, Household Or Indl Plant
CLEANING PRDTS: Drain Pipe Solvents Or Cleaners
CLEANING PRDTS: Drycleaning Preparations
CLEANING PRDTS: Dusting Cloths, Chemically Treated
CLEANING PRDTS: Floor Waxes
CLEANING PRDTS: Indl Plant Disinfectants Or Deodorants
CLEANING PRDTS: Laundry Preparations
CLEANING PRDTS: Metal Polish
CLEANING PRDTS: Paint & Wallpaper
CLEANING PRDTS: Polishing Preparations & Related Prdts
CLEANING PRDTS: Rug, Upholstery/Dry Clng Detergents/Spotters
CLEANING PRDTS: Sanitation Preparations
CLEANING PRDTS: Sanitation Preps, Disinfectants/Deodorants
CLEANING PRDTS: Specialty
CLEANING PRDTS: Stain Removers
CLEANING SVCS
CLEANING SVCS: Industrial Or Commercial
CLIPS & FASTENERS, MADE FROM PURCHASED WIRE
CLOCKS
CLOSURES: Closures, Stamped Metal
CLOSURES: Plastic
CLOTHING & ACCESS STORES
CLOTHING & ACCESS, WOMEN, CHILD & INFANT, WHSLE: Sportswear
CLOTHING & ACCESS, WOMEN, CHILDREN & INFANT, WHOL: Sweaters
CLOTHING & ACCESS, WOMEN, CHILDREN & INFANT, WHOL: Uniforms
CLOTHING & ACCESS, WOMEN, CHILDREN/INFANT, WHOL: Outerwear
CLOTHING & ACCESS: Costumes, Lodge
CLOTHING & ACCESS: Costumes, Theatrical
CLOTHING & ACCESS: Garter Belts
CLOTHING & ACCESS: Hospital Gowns
CLOTHING & ACCESS: Men's Miscellaneous Access
CLOTHING & ACCESS: Regalia
CLOTHING & APPAREL STORES: Custom
CLOTHING & FURNISHINGS, MEN'S & BOYS', WHOLESALE: Shirts
CLOTHING & FURNISHINGS, MEN'S & BOYS', WHOLESALE: Uniforms
CLOTHING ACCESS STORES: Umbrellas
CLOTHING STORES, NEC
CLOTHING STORES: Formal Wear
CLOTHING STORES: Leather
CLOTHING STORES: T-Shirts, Printed, Custom
CLOTHING STORES: Uniforms & Work
CLOTHING STORES: Unisex
CLOTHING/ACCESS, WOMEN, CHILDREN/INFANT, WHOL: Hosp Gowns
CLOTHING: Access
CLOTHING: Access, Women's & Misses'
CLOTHING: Aprons, Exc Rubber/Plastic, Women, Misses, Junior
CLOTHING: Aprons, Harness
CLOTHING: Aprons, Work, Exc Rubberized & Plastic, Men's
CLOTHING: Athletic & Sportswear, Men's & Boys'
CLOTHING: Baker, Barber, Lab/Svc Ind Apparel, Washable, Men
CLOTHING: Belts
CLOTHING: Bibs, Waterproof, From Purchased Materials
CLOTHING: Blouses, Women's & Girls'
CLOTHING: Blouses, Womens & Juniors, From Purchased Mtrls
CLOTHING: Bras & Corsets, Maternity
CLOTHING: Bridal Gowns
CLOTHING: Caps, Baseball
CLOTHING: Children & Infants'
CLOTHING: Coats & Suits, Men's & Boys'
CLOTHING: Costumes
CLOTHING: Disposable
CLOTHING: Dresses
CLOTHING: Foundation Garments, Women's
CLOTHING: Gowns & Dresses, Wedding
CLOTHING: Gowns, Plastic
CLOTHING: Hats & Caps, NEC
CLOTHING: Hosiery, Men's & Boys'
CLOTHING: Hospital, Men's
CLOTHING: Jackets, Field, Military
CLOTHING: Leather
CLOTHING: Lounge, Bed & Leisurewear
CLOTHING: Men's & boy's clothing, nec
CLOTHING: Men's & boy's underwear & nightwear
CLOTHING: Outerwear, Knit
CLOTHING: Outerwear, Lthr, Wool/Down-Filled, Men, Youth/Boy
CLOTHING: Outerwear, Women's & Misses' NEC
CLOTHING: Robes & Dressing Gowns
CLOTHING: Shirts, Dress, Men's & Boys'
CLOTHING: Socks
CLOTHING: Sportswear, Women's
CLOTHING: Suits, Men's & Boys', From Purchased Materials
CLOTHING: Sweaters & Sweater Coats, Knit
CLOTHING: Sweatshirts & T-Shirts, Men's & Boys'
CLOTHING: T-Shirts & Tops, Knit
CLOTHING: Tuxedos, From Purchased Materials
CLOTHING: Underwear, Women's & Children's
CLOTHING: Uniforms & Vestments
CLOTHING: Uniforms, Ex Athletic, Women's, Misses' & Juniors'
CLOTHING: Uniforms, Firemen's, From Purchased Materials
CLOTHING: Uniforms, Men's & Boys'
CLOTHING: Uniforms, Military, Men/Youth, Purchased Materials
CLOTHING: Uniforms, Work
CLOTHING: Vests, Sport, Suede, Leatherette, Etc, Mens & Boys
CLOTHING: Work Apparel, Exc Uniforms
CLOTHING: Work, Men's
CLOTHING: Work, Waterproof, Exc Raincoats
CLUTCHES OR BRAKES: Electromagnetic
CLUTCHES, EXC VEHICULAR
COAL & OTHER MINERALS & ORES WHOLESALERS
COAL MINING SERVICES
COAL MINING SVCS: Bituminous, Contract Basis
COAL MINING: Anthracite
COAL MINING: Bituminous & Lignite Surface
COAL MINING: Bituminous Coal & Lignite-Surface Mining
COAL MINING: Bituminous Underground
COAL MINING: Bituminous, Auger
COAL MINING: Bituminous, Strip
COAL MINING: Bituminous, Surface, NEC
COAL MINING: Lignite, Surface, NEC
COAL PREPARATION PLANT: Bituminous or Lignite
COAL PYROLYSIS
COAL, MINERALS & ORES, WHOLESALE: Coal
COAL, MINERALS & ORES, WHOLESALE: Iron Ore
COATED OR PLATED PRDTS
COATING COMPOUNDS: Tar
COATING OR WRAPPING SVC: Steel Pipe
COATING SVC
COATING SVC: Aluminum, Metal Prdts
COATING SVC: Electrodes
COATING SVC: Hot Dip, Metals Or Formed Prdts
COATING SVC: Metals & Formed Prdts
COATING SVC: Metals, With Plastic Or Resins
COATING SVC: Rust Preventative
COATING SVC: Silicon
COATINGS: Epoxy
COATINGS: Polyurethane
COILS & TRANSFORMERS
COILS, WIRE: Aluminum, Made In Rolling Mills
COILS: Electric Motors Or Generators
COIN COUNTERS
COINS & TOKENS: Non-Currency
COLLECTION AGENCY, EXC REAL ESTATE
COLLEGES, UNIVERSITIES & PROFESSIONAL SCHOOLS
COLLETS
COLOR LAKES OR TONERS
COLOR PIGMENTS
COLOR SEPARATION: Photographic & Movie Film
COLORS IN OIL, EXC ARTISTS'
COLORS: Pigments, Inorganic
COLORS: Pigments, Organic
COMBINED ELEMENTARY & SECONDARY SCHOOLS, PUBLIC
COMBS, EXC HARD RUBBER
COMMERCIAL & OFFICE BUILDINGS RENOVATION & REPAIR
COMMERCIAL ART & GRAPHIC DESIGN SVCS
COMMERCIAL ART & ILLUSTRATION SVCS
COMMERCIAL CONTAINERS WHOLESALERS
COMMERCIAL EQPT & SPLYS, WHOLESALE: Price Marking
COMMERCIAL EQPT WHOLESALERS, NEC
COMMERCIAL EQPT, WHOLESALE: Bakery Eqpt & Splys
COMMERCIAL EQPT, WHOLESALE: Comm Cooking & Food Svc Eqpt
COMMERCIAL EQPT, WHOLESALE: Display Eqpt, Exc Refrigerated
COMMERCIAL EQPT, WHOLESALE: Food Warming
COMMERCIAL EQPT, WHOLESALE: Neon Signs
COMMERCIAL EQPT, WHOLESALE: Restaurant, NEC
COMMERCIAL EQPT, WHOLESALE: Scales, Exc Laboratory
COMMERCIAL EQPT, WHOLESALE: Store Eqpt
COMMERCIAL EQPT, WHOLESALE: Store Fixtures & Display Eqpt
COMMERCIAL PRINTING & NEWSPAPER PUBLISHING COMBINED
COMMODITY CONTRACT TRADING COMPANIES
COMMON SAND MINING
COMMUNICATION HEADGEAR: Telephone
COMMUNICATIONS CARRIER: Wired
COMMUNICATIONS EQPT & SYSTEMS, NEC
COMMUNICATIONS EQPT REPAIR & MAINTENANCE
COMMUNICATIONS EQPT WHOLESALERS
COMMUNICATIONS SVCS
COMMUNICATIONS SVCS: Data
COMMUNICATIONS SVCS: Internet Connectivity Svcs
COMMUNICATIONS SVCS: Online Svc Providers
COMMUNICATIONS SVCS: Radio Pager Or Beeper
COMMUNICATIONS SVCS: Signal Enhancement Network Svcs
COMMUNICATIONS SVCS: Telephone Or Video
COMMUNICATIONS SVCS: Telephone, Local & Long Distance
COMMUNICATIONS SVCS: Telephone, Long Distance
COMMUNITY ACTION AGENCY
COMMUNITY DEVELOPMENT GROUPS
COMMUTATORS: Electric Motors
COMMUTATORS: Electronic
COMPACT DISCS OR CD'S, WHOLESALE

PRODUCT INDEX

COMPACT LASER DISCS: Prerecorded
COMPARATORS: Machinists
COMPOST
COMPRESSORS, AIR CONDITIONING: Wholesalers
COMPRESSORS: Air & Gas
COMPRESSORS: Air & Gas, Including Vacuum Pumps
COMPRESSORS: Refrigeration & Air Conditioning Eqpt
COMPRESSORS: Repairing
COMPRESSORS: Wholesalers
COMPUTER & COMPUTER SOFTWARE STORES
COMPUTER & COMPUTER SOFTWARE STORES: Computer Tapes
COMPUTER & COMPUTER SOFTWARE STORES: Peripheral Eqpt
COMPUTER & COMPUTER SOFTWARE STORES: Printers & Plotters
COMPUTER & COMPUTER SOFTWARE STORES: Software & Access
COMPUTER & COMPUTER SOFTWARE STORES: Software, Bus/Non-Game
COMPUTER & COMPUTER SOFTWARE STORES: Software, Computer Game
COMPUTER & DATA PROCESSING EQPT REPAIR & MAINTENANCE
COMPUTER & OFFICE MACHINE MAINTENANCE & REPAIR
COMPUTER FORMS
COMPUTER GRAPHICS SVCS
COMPUTER INTERFACE EQPT: Indl Process
COMPUTER PERIPHERAL EQPT REPAIR & MAINTENANCE
COMPUTER PERIPHERAL EQPT, NEC
COMPUTER PERIPHERAL EQPT, WHOLESALE
COMPUTER PERIPHERAL EQPT: Decoders
COMPUTER PERIPHERAL EQPT: Graphic Displays, Exc Terminals
COMPUTER PERIPHERAL EQPT: Input Or Output
COMPUTER PROCESSING SVCS
COMPUTER PROGRAMMING SVCS
COMPUTER PROGRAMMING SVCS: Custom
COMPUTER RELATED MAINTENANCE SVCS
COMPUTER RELATED SVCS, NEC
COMPUTER SERVICE BUREAU
COMPUTER SOFTWARE DEVELOPMENT
COMPUTER SOFTWARE DEVELOPMENT & APPLICATIONS
COMPUTER SOFTWARE SYSTEMS ANALYSIS & DESIGN: Custom
COMPUTER SOFTWARE WRITERS
COMPUTER SOFTWARE WRITERS: Freelance
COMPUTER STORAGE DEVICES, NEC
COMPUTER SYSTEM SELLING SVCS
COMPUTER SYSTEMS ANALYSIS & DESIGN
COMPUTER TERMINALS
COMPUTER TERMINALS: CRT
COMPUTER TIME-SHARING
COMPUTER-AIDED DESIGN SYSTEMS SVCS
COMPUTER-AIDED ENGINEERING SYSTEMS SVCS
COMPUTERS, NEC
COMPUTERS, NEC, WHOLESALE
COMPUTERS, PERIPH & SOFTWARE, WHLSE: Personal & Home Entrtn
COMPUTERS, PERIPHERALS & SOFTWARE, WHOLESALE: Software
COMPUTERS, PERIPHERALS/SFTWR, WHOL: Anti-Static Eqpt/Devices
COMPUTERS: Mainframe
COMPUTERS: Mini
COMPUTERS: Personal
CONCENTRATES, DRINK
CONCENTRATES, FLAVORING, EXC DRINK
CONCRETE BUILDING PRDTS WHOLESALERS
CONCRETE CURING & HARDENING COMPOUNDS
CONCRETE PLANTS
CONCRETE PRDTS
CONCRETE PRDTS, PRECAST, NEC
CONCRETE: Asphaltic, Not From Refineries
CONCRETE: Bituminous
CONCRETE: Dry Mixture
CONCRETE: Ready-Mixed
CONDENSERS & CONDENSING UNITS: Air Conditioner
CONDENSERS: Heat Transfer Eqpt, Evaporative
CONDENSERS: Refrigeration
CONDUITS & FITTINGS: Electric
CONES, PYROMETRIC: Earthenware
CONFECTIONS & CANDY
CONNECTORS & TERMINALS: Electrical Device Uses
CONNECTORS: Cord, Electric
CONNECTORS: Electrical
CONNECTORS: Electronic
CONNECTORS: Power, Electric
CONSTRUCTION & MINING MACHINERY WHOLESALERS
CONSTRUCTION EQPT REPAIR SVCS
CONSTRUCTION EQPT: Airport
CONSTRUCTION EQPT: Attachments
CONSTRUCTION EQPT: Attachments, Snow Plow
CONSTRUCTION EQPT: Backhoes, Tractors, Cranes & Similar Eqpt
CONSTRUCTION EQPT: Blade, Grader, Scraper, Dozer/Snow Plow
CONSTRUCTION EQPT: Bucket Or Scarifier Teeth
CONSTRUCTION EQPT: Buckets, Excavating, Clamshell, Etc
CONSTRUCTION EQPT: Crane Carriers
CONSTRUCTION EQPT: Cranes
CONSTRUCTION EQPT: Crushers, Portable
CONSTRUCTION EQPT: Entrenching Machines
CONSTRUCTION EQPT: Grinders, Stone, Portable
CONSTRUCTION EQPT: Rock Crushing Machinery, Portable
CONSTRUCTION EQPT: Roofing Eqpt
CONSTRUCTION EQPT: Tunneling
CONSTRUCTION MATERIALS, WHOL: Concrete/Cinder Bldg Prdts
CONSTRUCTION MATERIALS, WHOLESALE: Architectural Metalwork
CONSTRUCTION MATERIALS, WHOLESALE: Block, Concrete & Cinder
CONSTRUCTION MATERIALS, WHOLESALE: Brick, Exc Refractory
CONSTRUCTION MATERIALS, WHOLESALE: Building Stone
CONSTRUCTION MATERIALS, WHOLESALE: Building Stone, Granite
CONSTRUCTION MATERIALS, WHOLESALE: Building Stone, Marble
CONSTRUCTION MATERIALS, WHOLESALE: Building, Exterior
CONSTRUCTION MATERIALS, WHOLESALE: Building, Interior
CONSTRUCTION MATERIALS, WHOLESALE: Ceiling Systems & Prdts
CONSTRUCTION MATERIALS, WHOLESALE: Cement
CONSTRUCTION MATERIALS, WHOLESALE: Door Frames
CONSTRUCTION MATERIALS, WHOLESALE: Drywall Materials
CONSTRUCTION MATERIALS, WHOLESALE: Fiberglass Building Mat
CONSTRUCTION MATERIALS, WHOLESALE: Glass
CONSTRUCTION MATERIALS, WHOLESALE: Gravel
CONSTRUCTION MATERIALS, WHOLESALE: Joists
CONSTRUCTION MATERIALS, WHOLESALE: Limestone
CONSTRUCTION MATERIALS, WHOLESALE: Masons' Materials
CONSTRUCTION MATERIALS, WHOLESALE: Molding, All Materials
CONSTRUCTION MATERIALS, WHOLESALE: Pallets, Wood
CONSTRUCTION MATERIALS, WHOLESALE: Particleboard
CONSTRUCTION MATERIALS, WHOLESALE: Paving Materials
CONSTRUCTION MATERIALS, WHOLESALE: Prefabricated Structures
CONSTRUCTION MATERIALS, WHOLESALE: Roof, Asphalt/Sheet Metal
CONSTRUCTION MATERIALS, WHOLESALE: Roofing & Siding Material
CONSTRUCTION MATERIALS, WHOLESALE: Sand
CONSTRUCTION MATERIALS, WHOLESALE: Septic Tanks
CONSTRUCTION MATERIALS, WHOLESALE: Sewer Pipe, Clay
CONSTRUCTION MATERIALS, WHOLESALE: Siding, Exc Wood
CONSTRUCTION MATERIALS, WHOLESALE: Stone, Crushed Or Broken
CONSTRUCTION MATERIALS, WHOLESALE: Tile & Clay Prdts
CONSTRUCTION MATERIALS, WHOLESALE: Tile, Clay/Other Ceramic
CONSTRUCTION MATERIALS, WHOLESALE: Trim, Sheet Metal
CONSTRUCTION MATERIALS, WHOLESALE: Windows
CONSTRUCTION MATL, WHOLESALE: Structural Assy, Prefab, Wood
CONSTRUCTION MATLS, WHOL: Composite Board Prdts, Woodboard
CONSTRUCTION MATLS, WHOL: Doors, Combination, Screen-Storm
CONSTRUCTION MATLS, WHOL: Lumber, Rough, Dressed/Finished
CONSTRUCTION MATLS, WHOLESALE: Soil Erosion Cntrl Fabrics
CONSTRUCTION MTRLS, WHOL: Exterior Flat Glass, Plate/Window
CONSTRUCTION SAND MINING
CONSTRUCTION SITE PREPARATION SVCS
CONSTRUCTION: Agricultural Building
CONSTRUCTION: Aqueduct
CONSTRUCTION: Athletic & Recreation Facilities
CONSTRUCTION: Bridge
CONSTRUCTION: Commercial & Institutional Building
CONSTRUCTION: Commercial & Office Building, New
CONSTRUCTION: Concrete Patio
CONSTRUCTION: Dams, Waterways, Docks & Other Marine
CONSTRUCTION: Factory
CONSTRUCTION: Food Prdts Manufacturing or Packing Plant
CONSTRUCTION: Foundation & Retaining Wall
CONSTRUCTION: Garage
CONSTRUCTION: Golf Course
CONSTRUCTION: Grain Elevator
CONSTRUCTION: Greenhouse
CONSTRUCTION: Guardrails, Highway
CONSTRUCTION: Heavy Highway & Street
CONSTRUCTION: Hospital
CONSTRUCTION: Indl Building & Warehouse
CONSTRUCTION: Indl Building, Prefabricated
CONSTRUCTION: Indl Buildings, New, NEC
CONSTRUCTION: Indl Plant
CONSTRUCTION: Institutional Building
CONSTRUCTION: Land Preparation
CONSTRUCTION: Oil & Gas Line & Compressor Station
CONSTRUCTION: Oil & Gas Pipeline Construction
CONSTRUCTION: Pipeline, NEC
CONSTRUCTION: Power Plant
CONSTRUCTION: Residential, Nec
CONSTRUCTION: Roads, Gravel or Dirt
CONSTRUCTION: Sewer Line
CONSTRUCTION: Single-Family Housing
CONSTRUCTION: Single-family Housing, New
CONSTRUCTION: Street Sign Installation & Mntnce
CONSTRUCTION: Street Surfacing & Paving
CONSTRUCTION: Swimming Pools
CONSTRUCTION: Telephone & Communication Line
CONSTRUCTION: Tennis Court
CONSTRUCTION: Utility Line
CONSTRUCTION: Water Main
CONSULTING SVC: Business, NEC
CONSULTING SVC: Computer
CONSULTING SVC: Data Processing
CONSULTING SVC: Educational
CONSULTING SVC: Engineering
CONSULTING SVC: Human Resource
CONSULTING SVC: Management
CONSULTING SVC: Marketing Management
CONSULTING SVC: Online Technology
CONSULTING SVC: Sales Management
CONSULTING SVC: Telecommunications
CONSULTING SVCS, BUSINESS: Agricultural
CONSULTING SVCS, BUSINESS: Communications
CONSULTING SVCS, BUSINESS: Energy Conservation
CONSULTING SVCS, BUSINESS: Environmental
CONSULTING SVCS, BUSINESS: Safety Training Svcs
CONSULTING SVCS, BUSINESS: Sys Engnrg, Exc Computer/Prof
CONSULTING SVCS, BUSINESS: Systems Analysis & Engineering
CONSULTING SVCS, BUSINESS: Systems Analysis Or Design
CONSULTING SVCS, BUSINESS: Testing, Educational Or Personnel
CONSULTING SVCS, BUSINESS: Traffic
CONSULTING SVCS: Geological
CONSULTING SVCS: Oil
CONTACT LENSES
CONTACTS: Electrical
CONTAINERS, GLASS: Food
CONTAINERS: Air Cargo, Metal

PRODUCT INDEX

CONTAINERS: Cargo, Wood
CONTAINERS: Cargo, Wood & Metal Combination
CONTAINERS: Cargo, Wood & Wood With Metal
CONTAINERS: Corrugated
CONTAINERS: Foil, Bakery Goods & Frozen Foods
CONTAINERS: Food & Beverage
CONTAINERS: Food, Folding, Made From Purchased Materials
CONTAINERS: Food, Liquid Tight, Including Milk
CONTAINERS: Food, Metal
CONTAINERS: Food, Wood Wirebound
CONTAINERS: Glass
CONTAINERS: Ice Cream, Made From Purchased Materials
CONTAINERS: Metal
CONTAINERS: Plastic
CONTAINERS: Plywood & Veneer, Wood
CONTAINERS: Sanitary, Food
CONTAINERS: Shipping & Mailing, Fiber
CONTAINERS: Shipping, Bombs, Metal Plate
CONTAINERS: Shipping, Metal, Milk, Fluid
CONTAINERS: Shipping, Wood
CONTAINERS: Wood
CONTAINMENT VESSELS: Reactor, Metal Plate
CONTRACTOR: Dredging
CONTRACTOR: Rigging & Scaffolding
CONTRACTORS: Access Control System Eqpt
CONTRACTORS: Access Flooring System Installation
CONTRACTORS: Acoustical & Insulation Work
CONTRACTORS: Artificial Turf Installation
CONTRACTORS: Asbestos Removal & Encapsulation
CONTRACTORS: Asphalt
CONTRACTORS: Awning Installation
CONTRACTORS: Bathtub Refinishing
CONTRACTORS: Blasting, Exc Building Demolition
CONTRACTORS: Boiler & Furnace
CONTRACTORS: Boiler Maintenance Contractor
CONTRACTORS: Boiler Setting
CONTRACTORS: Building Eqpt & Machinery Installation
CONTRACTORS: Building Sign Installation & Mntnce
CONTRACTORS: Cable Laying
CONTRACTORS: Cable TV Installation
CONTRACTORS: Carpentry Work
CONTRACTORS: Carpentry, Cabinet & Finish Work
CONTRACTORS: Carpentry, Cabinet Building & Installation
CONTRACTORS: Chimney Construction & Maintenance
CONTRACTORS: Closet Organizers, Installation & Design
CONTRACTORS: Coating, Caulking & Weather, Water & Fire
CONTRACTORS: Commercial & Office Building
CONTRACTORS: Communications Svcs
CONTRACTORS: Computer Installation
CONTRACTORS: Computerized Controls Installation
CONTRACTORS: Concrete
CONTRACTORS: Concrete Block Masonry Laying
CONTRACTORS: Concrete Pumping
CONTRACTORS: Concrete Reinforcement Placing
CONTRACTORS: Concrete Structure Coating, Plastic
CONTRACTORS: Construction Caulking
CONTRACTORS: Construction Site Metal Structure Coating
CONTRACTORS: Core Drilling & Cutting
CONTRACTORS: Corrosion Control Installation
CONTRACTORS: Countertop Installation
CONTRACTORS: Demolition, Building & Other Structures
CONTRACTORS: Diamond Drilling & Sawing
CONTRACTORS: Directional Oil & Gas Well Drilling Svc
CONTRACTORS: Dock Eqpt Installation, Indl
CONTRACTORS: Drapery Track Installation
CONTRACTORS: Driveway
CONTRACTORS: Earthmoving
CONTRACTORS: Electric Power Systems
CONTRACTORS: Electrical
CONTRACTORS: Electronic Controls Installation
CONTRACTORS: Elevator Front Installation, Metal
CONTRACTORS: Energy Management Control
CONTRACTORS: Epoxy Application
CONTRACTORS: Excavating
CONTRACTORS: Exterior Painting
CONTRACTORS: Fence Construction
CONTRACTORS: Fiber Optic Cable Installation
CONTRACTORS: Fire Detection & Burglar Alarm Systems
CONTRACTORS: Floor Laying & Other Floor Work
CONTRACTORS: Flooring
CONTRACTORS: Foundation & Footing
CONTRACTORS: Foundation Building
CONTRACTORS: Fountain Installation
CONTRACTORS: Garage Doors
CONTRACTORS: Gas Field Svcs, NEC
CONTRACTORS: Gasoline Condensation Removal Svcs
CONTRACTORS: General Electric
CONTRACTORS: Glass Tinting, Architectural & Automotive
CONTRACTORS: Glass, Glazing & Tinting
CONTRACTORS: Gutters & Downspouts
CONTRACTORS: Heating & Air Conditioning
CONTRACTORS: Heating Systems Repair & Maintenance Svc
CONTRACTORS: Highway & Street Construction, General
CONTRACTORS: Highway & Street Paving
CONTRACTORS: Highway Sign & Guardrail Construction & Install
CONTRACTORS: Home & Office Intrs Finish, Furnish/Remodel
CONTRACTORS: Hotel, Motel/Multi-Famly Home Renovtn/Remodel
CONTRACTORS: Hydraulic Eqpt Installation & Svcs
CONTRACTORS: Hydraulic Well Fracturing Svcs
CONTRACTORS: Indl Building Renovation, Remodeling & Repair
CONTRACTORS: Insulation Installation, Building
CONTRACTORS: Kitchen & Bathroom Remodeling
CONTRACTORS: Kitchen Cabinet Installation
CONTRACTORS: Lighting Syst
CONTRACTORS: Lightweight Steel Framing Installation
CONTRACTORS: Machine Rigging & Moving
CONTRACTORS: Machinery Installation
CONTRACTORS: Maintenance, Parking Facility Eqpt
CONTRACTORS: Marble Installation, Interior
CONTRACTORS: Masonry & Stonework
CONTRACTORS: Mechanical
CONTRACTORS: Metal Ceiling Construction & Repair Work
CONTRACTORS: Millwrights
CONTRACTORS: Nonresidential Building Design & Construction
CONTRACTORS: Oil & Gas Aerial Geophysical Exploration Svcs
CONTRACTORS: Oil & Gas Building, Repairing & Dismantling Svc
CONTRACTORS: Oil & Gas Field Fire Fighting Svcs
CONTRACTORS: Oil & Gas Field Geological Exploration Svcs
CONTRACTORS: Oil & Gas Field Geophysical Exploration Svcs
CONTRACTORS: Oil & Gas Field Tools Fishing Svcs
CONTRACTORS: Oil & Gas Well Casing Cement Svcs
CONTRACTORS: Oil & Gas Well Drilling Svc
CONTRACTORS: Oil & Gas Well Flow Rate Measurement Svcs
CONTRACTORS: Oil & Gas Well Foundation Grading Svcs
CONTRACTORS: Oil & Gas Well On-Site Foundation Building Svcs
CONTRACTORS: Oil & Gas Well Plugging & Abandoning Svcs
CONTRACTORS: Oil & Gas Well Redrilling
CONTRACTORS: Oil & Gas Wells Pumping Svcs
CONTRACTORS: Oil & Gas Wells Svcs
CONTRACTORS: Oil Field Haulage Svcs
CONTRACTORS: Oil Field Mud Drilling Svcs
CONTRACTORS: Oil Field Pipe Testing Svcs
CONTRACTORS: Oil Sampling Svcs
CONTRACTORS: Oil/Gas Field Casing,Tube/Rod Running,Cut/Pull
CONTRACTORS: Oil/Gas Well Construction, Rpr/Dismantling Svcs
CONTRACTORS: On-Site Welding
CONTRACTORS: Ornamental Metal Work
CONTRACTORS: Painting & Wall Covering
CONTRACTORS: Painting, Commercial
CONTRACTORS: Painting, Commercial, Interior
CONTRACTORS: Painting, Indl
CONTRACTORS: Painting, Residential
CONTRACTORS: Parking Lot Maintenance
CONTRACTORS: Patio & Deck Construction & Repair
CONTRACTORS: Petroleum Storage Tanks, Pumping & Draining
CONTRACTORS: Pipe & Boiler Insulating
CONTRACTORS: Pipe Laying
CONTRACTORS: Plumbing
CONTRACTORS: Pollution Control Eqpt Installation
CONTRACTORS: Post Disaster Renovations
CONTRACTORS: Power Generating Eqpt Installation
CONTRACTORS: Prefabricated Window & Door Installation
CONTRACTORS: Process Piping
CONTRACTORS: Pulpwood, Engaged In Cutting
CONTRACTORS: Refrigeration
CONTRACTORS: Rigging, Theatrical
CONTRACTORS: Roof Repair
CONTRACTORS: Roofing
CONTRACTORS: Roustabout Svcs
CONTRACTORS: Sandblasting Svc, Building Exteriors
CONTRACTORS: Screening, Window & Door
CONTRACTORS: Septic System
CONTRACTORS: Sheet Metal Work, NEC
CONTRACTORS: Sheet metal Work, Architectural
CONTRACTORS: Siding
CONTRACTORS: Single-Family Home Fire Damage Repair
CONTRACTORS: Single-family Home General Remodeling
CONTRACTORS: Skylight Installation
CONTRACTORS: Solar Energy Eqpt
CONTRACTORS: Sound Eqpt Installation
CONTRACTORS: Specialized Public Building
CONTRACTORS: Storage Tank Erection, Metal
CONTRACTORS: Store Fixture Installation
CONTRACTORS: Structural Iron Work, Structural
CONTRACTORS: Structural Steel Erection
CONTRACTORS: Svc Station Eqpt Installation, Maint & Repair
CONTRACTORS: Svc Well Drilling Svcs
CONTRACTORS: Tile Installation, Ceramic
CONTRACTORS: Trenching
CONTRACTORS: Tuck Pointing & Restoration
CONTRACTORS: Underground Utilities
CONTRACTORS: Ventilation & Duct Work
CONTRACTORS: Warm Air Heating & Air Conditioning
CONTRACTORS: Water Well Drilling
CONTRACTORS: Water Well Servicing
CONTRACTORS: Waterproofing
CONTRACTORS: Well Bailing, Cleaning, Swabbing & Treating Svc
CONTRACTORS: Well Casings Perforating Svcs
CONTRACTORS: Well Logging Svcs
CONTRACTORS: Well Swabbing Svcs
CONTRACTORS: Windows & Doors
CONTRACTORS: Wood Floor Installation & Refinishing
CONTRACTORS: Wrecking & Demolition
CONTROL EQPT: Electric
CONTROL EQPT: Electric Buses & Locomotives
CONTROL EQPT: Noise
CONTROL PANELS: Electrical
CONTROLS & ACCESS: Indl, Electric
CONTROLS & ACCESS: Motor
CONTROLS: Access, Motor
CONTROLS: Adjustable Speed Drive
CONTROLS: Air Flow, Refrigeration
CONTROLS: Automatic Temperature
CONTROLS: Crane & Hoist, Including Metal Mill
CONTROLS: Electric Motor
CONTROLS: Environmental
CONTROLS: Hydronic
CONTROLS: Numerical
CONTROLS: Positioning, Electric
CONTROLS: Relay & Ind
CONTROLS: Resistance Welder
CONTROLS: Thermostats
CONTROLS: Thermostats, Built-in
CONTROLS: Voice
CONVENIENCE STORES
CONVENTION & TRADE SHOW SVCS
CONVERTERS: Data
CONVERTERS: Frequency
CONVERTERS: Phase Or Rotary, Electrical
CONVERTERS: Power, AC to DC
CONVEYOR SYSTEMS
CONVEYOR SYSTEMS: Belt, General Indl Use
CONVEYOR SYSTEMS: Bucket Type
CONVEYOR SYSTEMS: Bulk Handling
CONVEYOR SYSTEMS: Pneumatic Tube
CONVEYOR SYSTEMS: Robotic
CONVEYORS & CONVEYING EQPT
CONVEYORS: Overhead
COOKING & FOOD WARMING EQPT: Commercial
COOKING & FOODWARMING EQPT: Coffee Brewing
COOKING & FOODWARMING EQPT: Commercial
COOLING TOWERS: Metal
COOPERAGE STOCK PRODUCTS
COPINGS: Concrete
COPPER ORE MINING
COPPER: Blocks

PRODUCT INDEX

COPPER: Rolling & Drawing
COPY MACHINES WHOLESALERS
CORRECTION FLUID
CORRESPONDENCE SCHOOLS
CORRUGATED PRDTS: Boxes, Partition, Display Items, Sheet/Pad
CORRUGATING MACHINES
COSMETIC PREPARATIONS
COSMETICS & TOILETRIES
COSMETICS WHOLESALERS
COSTUME JEWELRY & NOVELTIES: Apparel, Exc Precious Metals
COSTUME JEWELRY STORES
COUNTER & SINK TOPS
COUNTERS & COUNTER DISPLAY CASES: Refrigerated
COUNTERS & COUNTING DEVICES
COUNTERS OR COUNTER DISPLAY CASES, EXC WOOD
COUNTERS OR COUNTER DISPLAY CASES, WOOD
COUNTING DEVICES: Controls, Revolution & Timing
COUNTING DEVICES: Predetermining
COUNTING DEVICES: Tachometer, Centrifugal
COUNTRY CLUBS
COUPLINGS, EXC PRESSURE & SOIL PIPE
COUPLINGS: Hose & Tube, Hydraulic Or Pneumatic
COUPLINGS: Pipe
COUPLINGS: Shaft
COURIER SVCS: Air
COURIER SVCS: Ground
COURTS OF LAW: County Government
COVERS & PADS Chair, Made From Purchased Materials
COVERS: Automobile Seat
COVERS: Metal Plate
COVERS: Slip Made Of Fabric, Plastic, Etc.
CRANE & AERIAL LIFT SVCS
CRANES & MONORAIL SYSTEMS
CRANES: Indl Plant
CRANES: Indl Truck
CRANES: Locomotive
CRANES: Overhead
CRANKSHAFTS & CAMSHAFTS: Machining
CRANKSHAFTS: Motor Vehicle
CREATIVE SVCS: Advertisers, Exc Writers
CREMATORIES
CROWNS & CLOSURES
CRUCIBLES
CRUDE PETROLEUM & NATURAL GAS PRODUCTION
CRUDE PETROLEUM & NATURAL GAS PRODUCTION
CRUDE PETROLEUM PRODUCTION
CRYOGENIC COOLING DEVICES: Infrared Detectors, Masers
CRYSTALS
CULTURE MEDIA
CULVERTS: Metal Plate
CULVERTS: Sheet Metal
CUPS: Paper, Made From Purchased Materials
CUPS: Plastic Exc Polystyrene Foam
CURBING: Granite Or Stone
CURTAIN & DRAPERY FIXTURES: Poles, Rods & Rollers
CURTAIN WALLS: Building, Steel
CURTAINS: Shower
CURTAINS: Window, From Purchased Materials
CUSHIONS & PILLOWS
CUSHIONS & PILLOWS: Bed, From Purchased Materials
CUSHIONS: Carpet & Rug, Foamed Plastics
CUSHIONS: Textile, Exc Spring & Carpet
CUSTOM COMPOUNDING OF RUBBER MATERIALS
CUSTOMIZING SVCS
CUT STONE & STONE PRODUCTS
CUTLERY
CUTOUTS: Cardboard, Die-Cut, Made From Purchased Materials
CUTOUTS: Distribution
CUTTING EQPT: Glass Cutters
CUTTING SVC: Paper, Exc Die-Cut
CUTTING SVC: Paperboard
CYCLIC CRUDES & INTERMEDIATES
CYLINDER & ACTUATORS: Fluid Power
CYLINDERS: Pressure
CYLINDERS: Pump

D

DAIRY EQPT
DAIRY PRDTS STORE: Cheese
DAIRY PRDTS STORE: Ice Cream, Packaged
DAIRY PRDTS STORES
DAIRY PRDTS WHOLESALERS: Fresh
DAIRY PRDTS: Butter
DAIRY PRDTS: Canned Cream
DAIRY PRDTS: Canned Milk, Whole
DAIRY PRDTS: Cheese
DAIRY PRDTS: Cheese, Cottage
DAIRY PRDTS: Concentrated Milk
DAIRY PRDTS: Condensed Milk
DAIRY PRDTS: Cream Substitutes
DAIRY PRDTS: Cream, Whipped
DAIRY PRDTS: Dietary Supplements, Dairy & Non-Dairy Based
DAIRY PRDTS: Dips & Spreads, Cheese Based
DAIRY PRDTS: Evaporated Milk
DAIRY PRDTS: Frozen Desserts & Novelties
DAIRY PRDTS: Half & Half
DAIRY PRDTS: Ice Cream & Ice Milk
DAIRY PRDTS: Ice Cream, Bulk
DAIRY PRDTS: Ice Cream, Packaged, Molded, On Sticks, Etc.
DAIRY PRDTS: Ice milk, Bulk
DAIRY PRDTS: Milk, Condensed & Evaporated
DAIRY PRDTS: Milk, Fluid
DAIRY PRDTS: Milk, Processed, Pasteurized, Homogenized/Btld
DAIRY PRDTS: Natural Cheese
DAIRY PRDTS: Powdered Milk
DAIRY PRDTS: Processed Cheese
DAIRY PRDTS: Sour Cream
DAIRY PRDTS: Whipped Topping, Exc Frozen Or Dry Mix
DAIRY PRDTS: Yogurt, Exc Frozen
DAIRY PRDTS: Yogurt, Frozen
DATA ENTRY SVCS
DATA PROCESSING & PREPARATION SVCS
DATA PROCESSING SVCS
DATABASE INFORMATION RETRIEVAL SVCS
DECALS, WHOLESALE
DECORATIVE WOOD & WOODWORK
DEFENSE SYSTEMS & EQPT
DEGREASING MACHINES
DEHUMIDIFIERS: Electric
DEHYDRATION EQPT
DEICING OR DEFROSTING FLUID
DENTAL EQPT
DENTAL EQPT & SPLYS
DENTAL EQPT & SPLYS WHOLESALERS
DENTAL EQPT & SPLYS: Enamels
DENTAL EQPT & SPLYS: Impression Materials
DENTAL EQPT & SPLYS: Orthodontic Appliances
DENTAL EQPT & SPLYS: Teeth, Artificial, Exc In Dental Labs
DENTISTS' OFFICES & CLINICS
DEODORANTS: Personal
DEPARTMENT STORES
DEPARTMENT STORES: Army-Navy Goods
DEPARTMENT STORES: Country General
DERMATOLOGICALS
DERRICKS
DESALTER KITS: Sea Water
DESIGN SVCS, NEC
DESIGN SVCS: Commercial & Indl
DESIGN SVCS: Computer Integrated Systems
DESIGN SVCS: Hand Tools
DETECTION APPARATUS: Electronic/Magnetic Field, Light/Heat
DETECTION EQPT: Magnetic Field
DETECTIVE & ARMORED CAR SERVICES
DETECTORS: Water Leak
DIAGNOSTIC SUBSTANCES
DIAGNOSTIC SUBSTANCES OR AGENTS: In Vitro
DIAGNOSTIC SUBSTANCES OR AGENTS: Microbiology & Virology
DIAGNOSTIC SUBSTANCES OR AGENTS: Radioactive
DIAGNOSTIC SUBSTANCES OR AGENTS: Veterinary
DIAMOND SETTER SVCS
DIAPERS: Disposable
DICE & DICE CUPS
DIE CUTTING SVC: Paper
DIE SETS: Presses, Metal Stamping
DIE SPRINGS
DIES & TOOLS: Special
DIES: Cutting, Exc Metal
DIES: Extrusion
DIES: Paper Cutting
DIES: Plastic Forming
DIES: Steel Rule
DIES: Wire Drawing & Straightening
DIFFERENTIAL ASSEMBLIES & PARTS
DIMENSION STONE: Buildings
DIODES: Light Emitting
DIODES: Solid State, Germanium, Silicon, Etc
DIRECT SELLING ESTABLISHMENTS: Beverage Svcs
DIRECT SELLING ESTABLISHMENTS: Food Svcs
DIRECT SELLING ESTABLISHMENTS: Home Related Prdts
DIRECT SELLING ESTABLISHMENTS: Snacks
DISCS & TAPE: Optical, Blank
DISHWASHING EQPT: Commercial
DISHWASHING EQPT: Household
DISK & DISKETTE CONVERSION SVCS
DISK DRIVES: Computer
DISPENSING EQPT & PARTS, BEVERAGE: Beer
DISPENSING EQPT & PARTS, BEVERAGE: Coolers, Milk/Water, Elec
DISPENSING EQPT & PARTS, BEVERAGE: Fountain/Other Beverage
DISPLAY FIXTURES: Showcases, Wood, Exc Refrigerated
DISPLAY FIXTURES: Wood
DISPLAY ITEMS: Corrugated, Made From Purchased Materials
DISPLAY ITEMS: Solid Fiber, Made From Purchased Materials
DISPLAY LETTERING SVCS
DISPLAY STANDS: Merchandise, Exc Wood
DISTILLATION PRDTS: Wood
DISTILLERS DRIED GRAIN & SOLUBLES
DISTRIBUTORS: Motor Vehicle Engine
DOCK EQPT & SPLYS, INDL
DOCKS: Prefabricated Metal
DOCUMENT DESTRUCTION SVC
DOGS, WHOLESALE
DOLLIES: Industrial
DOLLIES: Mechanics'
DOLOMITE: Crushed & Broken
DOOR & WINDOW REPAIR SVCS
DOOR FRAMES: Wood
DOOR OPERATING SYSTEMS: Electric
DOORS & WINDOWS WHOLESALERS: All Materials
DOORS & WINDOWS: Screen & Storm
DOORS & WINDOWS: Storm, Metal
DOORS: Combination Screen & Storm, Wood
DOORS: Fiberglass
DOORS: Folding, Plastic Or Plastic Coated Fabric
DOORS: Garage, Overhead, Metal
DOORS: Garage, Overhead, Wood
DOORS: Glass
DOORS: Hangar, Metal
DOORS: Louver, Wood
DOORS: Rolling, Indl Building Or Warehouse, Metal
DOORS: Screen, Metal
DOORS: Wooden
DOWELS & DOWEL RODS
DRAFTING SPLYS WHOLESALERS
DRAFTING SVCS
DRAINAGE PRDTS: Concrete
DRAPERIES & CURTAINS
DRAPERIES & DRAPERY FABRICS, COTTON
DRAPERIES: Plastic & Textile, From Purchased Materials
DRAPERY & UPHOLSTERY STORES: Draperies
DRAPES & DRAPERY FABRICS, FROM MANMADE FIBER
DRIED FRUITS WHOLESALERS
DRILL BITS
DRILLING MACHINERY & EQPT: Oil & Gas
DRILLS & DRILLING EQPT: Mining
DRINK MIXES, NONALCOHOLIC: Cocktail
DRINKING FOUNTAINS: Metal, Nonrefrigerated
DRINKING PLACES: Alcoholic Beverages
DRINKING PLACES: Bars & Lounges
DRINKING PLACES: Beer Garden
DRINKING PLACES: Tavern
DRIVE SHAFTS
DRIVES: High Speed Indl, Exc Hydrostatic
DRUG STORES
DRUG TESTING KITS: Blood & Urine
DRUGS & DRUG PROPRIETARIES, WHOLESALE
DRUGS & DRUG PROPRIETARIES, WHOLESALE: Antiseptics
DRUGS & DRUG PROPRIETARIES, WHOLESALE: Druggists' Sundries
DRUGS & DRUG PROPRIETARIES, WHOLESALE: Medicinals/Botanicals

PRODUCT INDEX

DRUGS & DRUG PROPRIETARIES, WHOLESALE: Patent Medicines
DRUGS & DRUG PROPRIETARIES, WHOLESALE: Pharmaceuticals
DRUGS & DRUG PROPRIETARIES, WHOLESALE: Vitamins & Minerals
DRUGS ACTING ON THE CENTRAL NERVOUS SYSTEM & SENSE ORGANS
DRUMS: Fiber
DRUMS: Shipping, Metal
DRYCLEANING EQPT & SPLYS: Commercial
DRYCLEANING PLANTS
DRYERS & REDRYERS: Indl
DUCTING: Plastic
DUCTS: Sheet Metal
DUMPSTERS: Garbage
DURABLE GOODS WHOLESALERS, NEC
DUST OR FUME COLLECTING EQPT: Indl
DYES & PIGMENTS: Organic
DYES OR COLORS: Food, Synthetic
DYES: Synthetic Organic

E

EARTH SCIENCE SVCS
EATING PLACES
EDUCATIONAL SVCS
EDUCATIONAL SVCS, NONDEGREE GRANTING: Continuing Education
EGG WHOLESALERS
ELASTOMERS
ELECTRIC & OTHER SERVICES COMBINED
ELECTRIC FENCE CHARGERS
ELECTRIC MOTOR & GENERATOR AUXILIARY PARTS
ELECTRIC MOTOR REPAIR SVCS
ELECTRIC SERVICES
ELECTRIC SVCS, NEC Power Transmission
ELECTRICAL APPARATUS & EQPT WHOLESALERS
ELECTRICAL APPLIANCES, TELEVISIONS & RADIOS WHOLESALERS
ELECTRICAL CURRENT CARRYING WIRING DEVICES
ELECTRICAL DEVICE PARTS: Porcelain, Molded
ELECTRICAL DISCHARGE MACHINING, EDM
ELECTRICAL EQPT & SPLYS
ELECTRICAL EQPT FOR ENGINES
ELECTRICAL EQPT REPAIR & MAINTENANCE
ELECTRICAL EQPT REPAIR SVCS
ELECTRICAL EQPT REPAIR SVCS: High Voltage
ELECTRICAL EQPT: Automotive, NEC
ELECTRICAL EQPT: Household
ELECTRICAL GOODS, WHOL: Antennas, Receiving/Satellite Dishes
ELECTRICAL GOODS, WHOLESALE: Alarms & Signaling Eqpt
ELECTRICAL GOODS, WHOLESALE: Boxes & Fittings
ELECTRICAL GOODS, WHOLESALE: Cable Conduit
ELECTRICAL GOODS, WHOLESALE: Connectors
ELECTRICAL GOODS, WHOLESALE: Electronic Parts
ELECTRICAL GOODS, WHOLESALE: Generators
ELECTRICAL GOODS, WHOLESALE: Ground Fault Interrupters
ELECTRICAL GOODS, WHOLESALE: Household Appliances, NEC
ELECTRICAL GOODS, WHOLESALE: Insulators
ELECTRICAL GOODS, WHOLESALE: Motor Ctrls, Starters & Relays
ELECTRICAL GOODS, WHOLESALE: Motors
ELECTRICAL GOODS, WHOLESALE: Radio & TV Or TV Eqpt & Parts
ELECTRICAL GOODS, WHOLESALE: Radio Parts & Access, NEC
ELECTRICAL GOODS, WHOLESALE: Security Control Eqpt & Systems
ELECTRICAL GOODS, WHOLESALE: Sound Eqpt
ELECTRICAL GOODS, WHOLESALE: Switchboards
ELECTRICAL GOODS, WHOLESALE: Switches, Exc Electronic, NEC
ELECTRICAL GOODS, WHOLESALE: Telephone Eqpt
ELECTRICAL GOODS, WHOLESALE: Transformers
ELECTRICAL GOODS, WHOLESALE: Washing Machines
ELECTRICAL GOODS, WHOLESALE: Wire & Cable
ELECTRICAL GOODS, WHOLESALE: Wire & Cable, Ctrl & Sig
ELECTRICAL INDL APPARATUS, NEC
ELECTRICAL MEASURING INSTRUMENT REPAIR & CALIBRATION SVCS

ELECTRICAL SPLYS
ELECTRICAL SUPPLIES: Porcelain
ELECTRODES: Indl Process
ELECTRODES: Thermal & Electrolytic
ELECTROMEDICAL EQPT
ELECTROMEDICAL EQPT WHOLESALERS
ELECTROMETALLURGICAL PRDTS
ELECTRONIC COMPONENTS
ELECTRONIC DEVICES: Solid State, NEC
ELECTRONIC EQPT REPAIR SVCS
ELECTRONIC PARTS & EQPT WHOLESALERS
ELECTRONIC SHOPPING
ELECTRONIC TRAINING DEVICES
ELECTROPLATING & PLATING SVC
ELEMENTARY & SECONDARY SCHOOLS, PRIVATE NEC
ELEMENTARY & SECONDARY SCHOOLS, SPECIAL EDUCATION
ELEVATOR: Grain, Storage Only
ELEVATORS & EQPT
ELEVATORS: Automobile
ELEVATORS: Installation & Conversion
EMBALMING FLUID
EMBLEMS: Embroidered
EMBOSSING SVC: Paper
EMBROIDERING & ART NEEDLEWORK FOR THE TRADE
EMBROIDERING SVC
EMBROIDERING: Swiss Loom
EMBROIDERY ADVERTISING SVCS
EMERGENCY & RELIEF SVCS
EMERGENCY ALARMS
EMERGENCY SHELTERS
EMPLOYMENT SVCS: Labor Contractors
ENAMELING SVC: Metal Prdts, Including Porcelain
ENAMELS
ENCLOSURES: Electronic
ENCLOSURES: Screen
ENCODERS: Digital
ENERGY MEASUREMENT EQPT
ENGINE PARTS & ACCESS: Internal Combustion
ENGINE REBUILDING: Diesel
ENGINE REBUILDING: Gas
ENGINEERING SVCS
ENGINEERING SVCS: Acoustical
ENGINEERING SVCS: Aviation Or Aeronautical
ENGINEERING SVCS: Civil
ENGINEERING SVCS: Construction & Civil
ENGINEERING SVCS: Electrical Or Electronic
ENGINEERING SVCS: Energy conservation
ENGINEERING SVCS: Fire Protection
ENGINEERING SVCS: Heating & Ventilation
ENGINEERING SVCS: Industrial
ENGINEERING SVCS: Machine Tool Design
ENGINEERING SVCS: Mechanical
ENGINEERING SVCS: Pollution Control
ENGINEERING SVCS: Professional
ENGINES: Diesel & Semi-Diesel Or Duel Fuel
ENGINES: Gasoline, NEC
ENGINES: Internal Combustion, NEC
ENGINES: Jet Propulsion
ENGINES: Marine
ENGINES: Steam
ENGRAVING SVC, NEC
ENGRAVING SVC: Jewelry & Personal Goods
ENGRAVING SVCS
ENGRAVING: Steel line, For The Printing Trade
ENGRAVINGS: Plastic
ENTERTAINERS
ENTERTAINERS & ENTERTAINMENT GROUPS
ENTERTAINMENT GROUP
ENTERTAINMENT SVCS
ENVELOPES
ENVELOPES WHOLESALERS
ENZYMES
EPOXY RESINS
EQUIPMENT: Pedestrian Traffic Control
EQUIPMENT: Rental & Leasing, NEC
ETCHING & ENGRAVING SVC
ETCHING SVC: Metal
ETHYLENE GLYCOL TEREPHTHALIC ACID: Mylar
ETHYLENE-PROPYLENE RUBBERS: EPDM Polymers
EXERCISE EQPT STORES
EXHAUST SYSTEMS: Eqpt & Parts
EXPLOSIVES
EXPLOSIVES, EXC AMMO & FIREWORKS WHOLESALERS
EXPLOSIVES, FUSES & DETONATORS: Primary explosives

EXTENSION CORDS
EXTRACTS, FLAVORING
EXTRACTS: Dying Or Tanning, Natural
EYEGLASSES
EYES: Artificial
Ethylene Glycols

F

FABRIC SOFTENERS
FABRIC STORES
FABRICATED METAL PRODUCTS, NEC
FABRICS & CLOTHING: Rubber Coated
FABRICS: Apparel & Outerwear, Cotton
FABRICS: Broadwoven, Cotton
FABRICS: Broadwoven, Synthetic Manmade Fiber & Silk
FABRICS: Canvas
FABRICS: Chemically Coated & Treated
FABRICS: Cotton, Narrow
FABRICS: Decorative Trim & Specialty, Including Twist Weave
FABRICS: Denims
FABRICS: Diaper, NEC
FABRICS: Duck, Cotton
FABRICS: Fiberglass, Broadwoven
FABRICS: Flannels, Cotton
FABRICS: Glass & Fiberglass, Broadwoven
FABRICS: Laminated
FABRICS: Manmade Fiber, Narrow
FABRICS: Metallized
FABRICS: Moleskins
FABRICS: Nonwoven
FABRICS: Nylon, Broadwoven
FABRICS: Osnaburgs
FABRICS: Polyethylene, Broadwoven
FABRICS: Print, Cotton
FABRICS: Resin Or Plastic Coated
FABRICS: Rubber & Elastic Yarns & Fabrics
FABRICS: Rubberized
FABRICS: Scrub Cloths
FABRICS: Shoe Laces, Exc Leather
FABRICS: Sleeving, Textile, Saturated
FABRICS: Tracing Cloth, Cotton
FABRICS: Trimmings
FABRICS: Umbrella Cloth, Cotton
FABRICS: Upholstery, Wool
FABRICS: Varnished Glass & Coated Fiberglass
FABRICS: Wall Covering, From Manmade Fiber Or Silk
FABRICS: Waterproofed, Exc Rubberized
FABRICS: Woven, Narrow Cotton, Wool, Silk
FACILITIES SUPPORT SVCS
FACILITY RENTAL & PARTY PLANNING SVCS
FAMILY CLOTHING STORES
FAMILY PLANNING CENTERS
FANS, BLOWING: Indl Or Commercial
FANS, EXHAUST: Indl Or Commercial
FANS, VENTILATING: Indl Or Commercial
FANS: Ceiling
FARM & GARDEN MACHINERY WHOLESALERS
FARM MACHINERY REPAIR SVCS
FARM PRDTS, RAW MATERIALS, WHOLESALE: Hides
FARM PRDTS, RAW MATERIALS, WHOLESALE: Nuts & Nut By-Prdts
FARM SPLY STORES
FARM SPLYS WHOLESALERS
FARM SPLYS, WHOLESALE: Feed
FARM SPLYS, WHOLESALE: Fertilizers & Agricultural Chemicals
FARM SPLYS, WHOLESALE: Garden Splys
FARM SPLYS, WHOLESALE: Greenhouse Eqpt & Splys
FARM SPLYS, WHOLESALE: Harness Eqpt
FARM SPLYS, WHOLESALE: Limestone, Agricultural
FASTENERS: Metal
FASTENERS: Metal
FASTENERS: Notions, NEC
FASTENERS: Notions, Zippers
FASTENERS: Wire, Made From Purchased Wire
FAUCETS & SPIGOTS: Metal & Plastic
FEATHERS & FEATHER PRODUCTS
FELT PARTS
FELT: Automotive
FENCE POSTS: Iron & Steel
FENCES OR POSTS: Ornamental Iron Or Steel
FENCING DEALERS
FENCING MADE IN WIREDRAWING PLANTS
FENCING MATERIALS: Docks & Other Outdoor Prdts, Wood
FENCING MATERIALS: Plastic

PRODUCT INDEX

FENCING MATERIALS: Wood
FENCING: Chain Link
FENDERS: Automobile, Stamped Or Pressed Metal
FERRALLOY ORES, EXC VANADIUM
FERROALLOYS
FERROALLOYS: Produced In Blast Furnaces
FERROMANGANESE, NOT MADE IN BLAST FURNACES
FERROSILICON, EXC MADE IN BLAST FURNACES
FERROUS METALS: Reclaimed From Clay
FERTILIZER MINERAL MINING
FERTILIZER, AGRICULTURAL: Wholesalers
FERTILIZERS: NEC
FERTILIZERS: Nitrogen Solutions
FERTILIZERS: Nitrogenous
FERTILIZERS: Phosphatic
FIBER & FIBER PRDTS: Acrylic
FIBER & FIBER PRDTS: Acrylonitrile
FIBER & FIBER PRDTS: Cuprammonium
FIBER & FIBER PRDTS: Elastomeric
FIBER & FIBER PRDTS: Organic, Noncellulose
FIBER & FIBER PRDTS: Polyester
FIBER & FIBER PRDTS: Synthetic Cellulosic
FIBER & FIBER PRDTS: Vinyl
FIBER OPTICS
FIBER: Vulcanized
FIBERS: Carbon & Graphite
FIELD WAREHOUSING SVCS
FILE FOLDERS
FILM & SHEET: Unsuppported Plastic
FILM BASE: Cellulose Acetate Or Nitrocellulose Plastics
FILM DEVELOPING & PRINTING SVCS
FILM: Rubber
FILTER ELEMENTS: Fluid & Hydraulic Line
FILTERS
FILTERS & SOFTENERS: Water, Household
FILTERS & STRAINERS: Pipeline
FILTERS: Air
FILTERS: Air Intake, Internal Combustion Engine, Exc Auto
FILTERS: General Line, Indl
FILTERS: Motor Vehicle
FILTERS: Oil, Internal Combustion Engine, Exc Auto
FILTRATION DEVICES: Electronic
FINANCIAL SVCS
FINDINGS & TRIMMINGS: Fabric
FINGERNAILS, ARTIFICIAL
FINGERPRINT EQPT
FINISHING AGENTS
FIRE ARMS, SMALL: Guns Or Gun Parts, 30 mm & Below
FIRE ARMS, SMALL: Machine Guns & Grenade Launchers
FIRE ARMS, SMALL: Machine Guns/Machine Gun Parts, 30mm/below
FIRE ARMS, SMALL: Rifles Or Rifle Parts, 30 mm & below
FIRE ARMS, SMALL: Shotguns Or Shotgun Parts, 30 mm & Below
FIRE CLAY MINING
FIRE CONTROL EQPT REPAIR SVCS, MILITARY
FIRE CONTROL OR BOMBING EQPT: Electronic
FIRE DETECTION SYSTEMS
FIRE EXTINGUISHER CHARGES
FIRE EXTINGUISHER SVC
FIRE EXTINGUISHERS, WHOLESALE
FIRE EXTINGUISHERS: Portable
FIRE OR BURGLARY RESISTIVE PRDTS
FIRE PROTECTION EQPT
FIREARMS & AMMUNITION, EXC SPORTING, WHOLESALE
FIREARMS: Small, 30mm or Less
FIREFIGHTING APPARATUS
FIREPLACE & CHIMNEY MATERIAL: Concrete
FIREPLACE EQPT & ACCESS
FIREWORKS
FIREWORKS SHOPS
FISH & SEAFOOD PROCESSORS: Canned Or Cured
FISH & SEAFOOD WHOLESALERS
FISH FOOD
FISH, PACKAGED FROZEN: Wholesalers
FISHING EQPT: Lures
FITTINGS & ASSEMBLIES: Hose & Tube, Hydraulic Or Pneumatic
FITTINGS: Pipe
FITTINGS: Pipe, Fabricated
FIXTURES & EQPT: Kitchen, Metal, Exc Cast Aluminum
FIXTURES & EQPT: Kitchen, Porcelain Enameled
FIXTURES: Cut Stone
FLAGS: Fabric
FLAGSTONES
FLAKES: Metal
FLARES
FLAT GLASS: Building
FLAT GLASS: Construction
FLAT GLASS: Float
FLAT GLASS: Picture
FLAT GLASS: Plate, Polished & Rough
FLAT GLASS: Tempered
FLAT GLASS: Window, Clear & Colored
FLAVORS OR FLAVORING MATERIALS: Synthetic
FLIGHT RECORDERS
FLOATING DRY DOCKS
FLOCKING SVC: Fabric
FLOOR COVERING STORES
FLOOR COVERING STORES: Carpets
FLOOR COVERING STORES: Rugs
FLOOR COVERING: Plastic
FLOOR COVERINGS WHOLESALERS
FLOOR COVERINGS: Asphalted-Felt Base, Linoleum Or Carpet
FLOOR COVERINGS: Rubber
FLOOR COVERINGS: Tile, Support Plastic
FLOOR COVERINGS: Twisted Paper, Grass, Reed, Coir, Etc
FLOORING & SIDING: Metal
FLOORING: Hard Surface
FLOORING: Hardwood
FLOORING: Rubber
FLOORING: Tile
FLORIST: Flowers, Fresh
FLORISTS
FLOWER POTS Plastic
FLOWERS, FRESH, WHOLESALE
FLUID METERS & COUNTING DEVICES
FLUID POWER PUMPS & MOTORS
FLUID POWER VALVES & HOSE FITTINGS
FLUORSPAR MINING
FLUSH TANKS: Vitreous China
FLUXES
FOAM RUBBER
FOAMS & RUBBER, WHOLESALE
FOIL & LEAF: Metal
FOLDERS: Manila
FOOD PRDTS, BREAKFAST: Cereal, Granola & Muesli
FOOD PRDTS, BREAKFAST: Cereal, Oatmeal
FOOD PRDTS, BREAKFAST: Cereal, Wheat Flakes
FOOD PRDTS, CANNED OR FRESH PACK: Fruit Juices
FOOD PRDTS, CANNED OR FRESH PACK: Vegetable Juices
FOOD PRDTS, CANNED, NEC
FOOD PRDTS, CANNED: Baby Food
FOOD PRDTS, CANNED: Barbecue Sauce
FOOD PRDTS, CANNED: Beans, Without Meat
FOOD PRDTS, CANNED: Catsup
FOOD PRDTS, CANNED: Chili
FOOD PRDTS, CANNED: Chili Sauce, Tomato
FOOD PRDTS, CANNED: Ethnic
FOOD PRDTS, CANNED: Fruit Juices, Fresh
FOOD PRDTS, CANNED: Fruit Pie Mixes & Fillings
FOOD PRDTS, CANNED: Fruits
FOOD PRDTS, CANNED: Fruits
FOOD PRDTS, CANNED: Italian
FOOD PRDTS, CANNED: Jams, Including Imitation
FOOD PRDTS, CANNED: Jams, Jellies & Preserves
FOOD PRDTS, CANNED: Jellies, Edible, Including Imitation
FOOD PRDTS, CANNED: Mexican, NEC
FOOD PRDTS, CANNED: Pizza Sauce
FOOD PRDTS, CANNED: Puddings, Exc Meat
FOOD PRDTS, CANNED: Ravioli
FOOD PRDTS, CANNED: Soups
FOOD PRDTS, CANNED: Soups, Exc Seafood
FOOD PRDTS, CANNED: Spaghetti
FOOD PRDTS, CANNED: Spaghetti & Other Pasta Sauce
FOOD PRDTS, CANNED: Tomato Sauce.
FOOD PRDTS, CANNED: Tomatoes
FOOD PRDTS, CANNED: Vegetables
FOOD PRDTS, CONFECTIONERY, WHOLESALE: Candy
FOOD PRDTS, CONFECTIONERY, WHOLESALE: Nuts, Salted/Roasted
FOOD PRDTS, CONFECTIONERY, WHOLESALE: Potato Chips
FOOD PRDTS, CONFECTIONERY, WHOLESALE: Snack Foods
FOOD PRDTS, CONFECTIONERY, WHOLESALE: Syrups, Fountain
FOOD PRDTS, DAIRY, WHOLESALE: Milk & Cream, Fluid
FOOD PRDTS, FISH & SEAFOOD, WHOLESALE: Seafood
FOOD PRDTS, FROZEN: Breakfasts, Packaged
FOOD PRDTS, FROZEN: Dinners, Packaged
FOOD PRDTS, FROZEN: Ethnic Foods, NEC
FOOD PRDTS, FROZEN: Fruit Juice, Concentrates
FOOD PRDTS, FROZEN: Fruit Juices
FOOD PRDTS, FROZEN: Fruits
FOOD PRDTS, FROZEN: Fruits & Vegetables
FOOD PRDTS, FROZEN: Fruits, Juices & Vegetables
FOOD PRDTS, FROZEN: NEC
FOOD PRDTS, FROZEN: Pizza
FOOD PRDTS, FROZEN: Potato Prdts
FOOD PRDTS, FROZEN: Snack Items
FOOD PRDTS, FROZEN: Vegetables, Exc Potato Prdts
FOOD PRDTS, FRUITS & VEGETABLES, FRESH, WHOLESALE
FOOD PRDTS, FRUITS & VEGETABLES, FRESH, WHOLESALE: Vegetable
FOOD PRDTS, FRUITS & VEGETABLES, FRESH, WHOLESALE: Vegetable
FOOD PRDTS, MEAT & MEAT PRDTS, WHOLESALE: Cured Or Smoked
FOOD PRDTS, MEAT & MEAT PRDTS, WHOLESALE: Fresh
FOOD PRDTS, WHOL: Canned Goods, Fruit, Veg, Seafood/Meats
FOOD PRDTS, WHOLESALE: Baking Splys
FOOD PRDTS, WHOLESALE: Beverages, Exc Coffee & Tea
FOOD PRDTS, WHOLESALE: Chocolate
FOOD PRDTS, WHOLESALE: Coffee, Green Or Roasted
FOOD PRDTS, WHOLESALE: Condiments
FOOD PRDTS, WHOLESALE: Corn
FOOD PRDTS, WHOLESALE: Dried or Canned Foods
FOOD PRDTS, WHOLESALE: Flour
FOOD PRDTS, WHOLESALE: Grain Elevators
FOOD PRDTS, WHOLESALE: Grains
FOOD PRDTS, WHOLESALE: Health
FOOD PRDTS, WHOLESALE: Juices
FOOD PRDTS, WHOLESALE: Salt, Edible
FOOD PRDTS, WHOLESALE: Specialty
FOOD PRDTS, WHOLESALE: Starch
FOOD PRDTS, WHOLESALE: Syrups, Exc Fountain Use
FOOD PRDTS, WHOLESALE: Water, Mineral Or Spring, Bottled
FOOD PRDTS: Animal & marine fats & oils
FOOD PRDTS: Baking Powder, Soda, Yeast & Leavenings
FOOD PRDTS: Bread Crumbs, Exc Made In Bakeries
FOOD PRDTS: Cake Fillings, Exc Fruit
FOOD PRDTS: Cereals
FOOD PRDTS: Chicken, Processed, Cooked
FOOD PRDTS: Chicken, Processed, Fresh
FOOD PRDTS: Chicken, Processed, NEC
FOOD PRDTS: Chocolate Bars, Solid
FOOD PRDTS: Cocoa, Powdered
FOOD PRDTS: Coffee
FOOD PRDTS: Coffee Roasting, Exc Wholesale Grocers
FOOD PRDTS: Corn Chips & Other Corn-Based Snacks
FOOD PRDTS: Corn Oil Prdts
FOOD PRDTS: Dips, Exc Cheese & Sour Cream Based
FOOD PRDTS: Dough, Pizza, Prepared
FOOD PRDTS: Doughs, Frozen Or Refrig From Purchased Flour
FOOD PRDTS: Dressings, Salad, Raw & Cooked Exc Dry Mixes
FOOD PRDTS: Dried & Dehydrated Fruits, Vegetables & Soup Mix
FOOD PRDTS: Edible fats & oils
FOOD PRDTS: Eggs, Processed
FOOD PRDTS: Eggs, Processed, Frozen
FOOD PRDTS: Emulsifiers
FOOD PRDTS: Flour & Other Grain Mill Products
FOOD PRDTS: Flour Mixes & Doughs
FOOD PRDTS: Flour, Blended From Purchased Flour
FOOD PRDTS: Fruit Juices
FOOD PRDTS: Fruits & Vegetables, Pickled
FOOD PRDTS: Fruits, Dried Or Dehydrated, Exc Freeze-Dried
FOOD PRDTS: Gelatin Dessert Preparations
FOOD PRDTS: Granola & Energy Bars, Nonchocolate
FOOD PRDTS: Honey
FOOD PRDTS: Ice, Blocks
FOOD PRDTS: Ice, Cubes
FOOD PRDTS: Macaroni, Noodles, Spaghetti, Pasta, Etc
FOOD PRDTS: Mayonnaise & Dressings, Exc Tomato Based
FOOD PRDTS: Mixes, Bread & Bread-Type Roll
FOOD PRDTS: Mixes, Bread & Roll From Purchased Flour

PRODUCT INDEX

FOOD PRDTS: Mixes, Cake, From Purchased Flour
FOOD PRDTS: Mixes, Doughnut From Purchased Flour
FOOD PRDTS: Mixes, Flour
FOOD PRDTS: Mixes, Sauces, Dry
FOOD PRDTS: Mustard, Prepared
FOOD PRDTS: Nuts & Seeds
FOOD PRDTS: Oils & Fats, Animal
FOOD PRDTS: Olive Oil
FOOD PRDTS: Oriental Noodles
FOOD PRDTS: Pasta, Rice/Potatoes, Uncooked, Pkgd
FOOD PRDTS: Pasta, Uncooked, Packaged With Other Ingredients
FOOD PRDTS: Peanut Butter
FOOD PRDTS: Pickles, Vinegar
FOOD PRDTS: Pizza Doughs From Purchased Flour
FOOD PRDTS: Popcorn, Unpopped
FOOD PRDTS: Pork Rinds
FOOD PRDTS: Potato & Corn Chips & Similar Prdts
FOOD PRDTS: Potato Chips & Other Potato-Based Snacks
FOOD PRDTS: Potatoes, Dried
FOOD PRDTS: Poultry, Processed, Frozen
FOOD PRDTS: Preparations
FOOD PRDTS: Prepared Sauces, Exc Tomato Based
FOOD PRDTS: Salad Oils, Refined Vegetable, Exc Corn
FOOD PRDTS: Salads
FOOD PRDTS: Sandwiches
FOOD PRDTS: Sausage, Poultry
FOOD PRDTS: Seasonings & Spices
FOOD PRDTS: Shortening & Solid Edible Fats
FOOD PRDTS: Soup Powders
FOOD PRDTS: Soybean Protein Concentrates & Isolates
FOOD PRDTS: Spices, Including Ground
FOOD PRDTS: Starch, Corn
FOOD PRDTS: Sugar
FOOD PRDTS: Sugar, Beet
FOOD PRDTS: Syrup, Maple
FOOD PRDTS: Syrups
FOOD PRDTS: Tea
FOOD PRDTS: Tortillas
FOOD PRDTS: Turkey, Processed, Canned
FOOD PRDTS: Turkey, Processed, NEC
FOOD PRDTS: Turkey, Slaughtered & Dressed
FOOD PRODUCTS MACHINERY
FOOD STORES: Convenience, Chain
FOOD STORES: Convenience, Independent
FOOD STORES: Delicatessen
FOOD STORES: Grocery, Independent
FOOD STORES: Supermarkets, Chain
FOOTWEAR, WHOLESALE: Athletic
FOOTWEAR, WHOLESALE: Boots
FOOTWEAR, WHOLESALE: Shoes
FOOTWEAR: Custom Made
FOOTWEAR: Cut Stock
FORESTRY RELATED EQPT
FORGINGS
FORGINGS: Aircraft, Ferrous
FORGINGS: Aluminum
FORGINGS: Armor Plate, Iron Or Steel
FORGINGS: Automotive & Internal Combustion Engine
FORGINGS: Construction Or Mining Eqpt, Ferrous
FORGINGS: Internal Combustion Engine, Ferrous
FORGINGS: Iron & Steel
FORGINGS: Machinery, Ferrous
FORGINGS: Metal, Ornamental, Ferrous
FORGINGS: Nonferrous
FORGINGS: Plumbing Fixture, Nonferrous
FORMS: Concrete, Sheet Metal
FOUNDRIES: Aluminum
FOUNDRIES: Brass, Bronze & Copper
FOUNDRIES: Gray & Ductile Iron
FOUNDRIES: Iron
FOUNDRIES: Nonferrous
FOUNDRIES: Steel
FOUNDRIES: Steel Investment
FOUNDRY MACHINERY & EQPT
FOUNDRY MATERIALS: Insulsleeves
FOUNDRY SAND MINING
FOUNTAINS, METAL, EXC DRINKING
FOUNTAINS: Concrete
FRACTIONATION PRDTS OF CRUDE PETROLEUM, HYDROCARBONS, NEC
FRANCHISES, SELLING OR LICENSING
FREEZERS: Household
FREIGHT FORWARDING ARRANGEMENTS
FREIGHT TRANSPORTATION ARRANGEMENTS

FREON
FRICTION MATERIAL, MADE FROM POWDERED METAL
FRITS
FRUIT & VEGETABLE MARKETS
FRUIT STANDS OR MARKETS
FRUITS & VEGETABLES WHOLESALERS: Fresh
FUEL ADDITIVES
FUEL CELLS: Solid State
FUEL DEALERS: Coal
FUEL OIL DEALERS
FUEL TREATING
FUELS: Diesel
FUELS: Ethanol
FUELS: Jet
FUELS: Oil
FUNDRAISING SVCS
FUNERAL HOME
FUNERAL HOMES & SVCS
FUNGICIDES OR HERBICIDES
FUR: Hats
FURNACES & OVENS: Fuel-Fired
FURNACES & OVENS: Indl
FURNACES: Indl, Electric
FURNACES: Warm Air, Electric
FURNITURE & CABINET STORES: Cabinets, Custom Work
FURNITURE & CABINET STORES: Custom
FURNITURE & FIXTURES Factory
FURNITURE PARTS: Metal
FURNITURE REFINISHING SVCS
FURNITURE REPAIR & MAINTENANCE SVCS
FURNITURE STOCK & PARTS: Carvings, Wood
FURNITURE STOCK & PARTS: Chair Seats, Hardwood
FURNITURE STOCK/PARTS: Chair Stk, Hardwd, Turnd, Shapd/Carvd
FURNITURE STORES
FURNITURE STORES: Cabinets, Kitchen, Exc Custom Made
FURNITURE STORES: Custom Made, Exc Cabinets
FURNITURE STORES: Office
FURNITURE STORES: Outdoor & Garden
FURNITURE WHOLESALERS
FURNITURE, BARBER & BEAUTY SHOP
FURNITURE, CHURCH: Concrete
FURNITURE, MATTRESSES: Wholesalers
FURNITURE, OFFICE: Wholesalers
FURNITURE, WHOLESALE: Bedsprings
FURNITURE, WHOLESALE: Chairs
FURNITURE, WHOLESALE: Filing Units
FURNITURE, WHOLESALE: Racks
FURNITURE, WHOLESALE: Tables, Occasional
FURNITURE, WHOLESALE: Unfinished
FURNITURE: Bar furniture
FURNITURE: Bed Frames & Headboards, Wood
FURNITURE: Bedroom, Wood
FURNITURE: Beds, Household, Incl Folding & Cabinet, Metal
FURNITURE: Bookcases & Partitions, Office, Exc Wood
FURNITURE: Cabinets & Filing Drawers, Office, Exc Wood
FURNITURE: Cabinets & Vanities, Medicine, Metal
FURNITURE: Chairs, Bentwood
FURNITURE: Chairs, Dental
FURNITURE: Chairs, Folding
FURNITURE: Chairs, Household Upholstered
FURNITURE: Chairs, Household Wood
FURNITURE: Chairs, Office Exc Wood
FURNITURE: Chairs, Office Wood
FURNITURE: Church
FURNITURE: Club Room, Wood
FURNITURE: Console Tables, Wood
FURNITURE: Desks & Tables, Office, Exc Wood
FURNITURE: Dining Room, Wood
FURNITURE: Fiberglass & Plastic
FURNITURE: Foundations & Platforms
FURNITURE: Frames, Box Springs Or Bedsprings, Metal
FURNITURE: Hospital
FURNITURE: Hotel
FURNITURE: Household, Metal
FURNITURE: Household, NEC
FURNITURE: Household, Upholstered, Exc Wood Or Metal
FURNITURE: Household, Wood
FURNITURE: Hydraulic Barber & Beauty Shop Chairs
FURNITURE: Institutional, Exc Wood
FURNITURE: Juvenile, Metal
FURNITURE: Juvenile, Wood
FURNITURE: Kitchen & Dining Room
FURNITURE: Lawn & Garden, Except Wood & Metal
FURNITURE: Lawn, Exc Wood, Metal, Stone Or Concrete

FURNITURE: Living Room, Upholstered On Wood Frames
FURNITURE: Mattresses & Foundations
FURNITURE: Mattresses, Box & Bedsprings
FURNITURE: Mattresses, Innerspring Or Box Spring
FURNITURE: Novelty, Wood
FURNITURE: Office Panel Systems, Exc Wood
FURNITURE: Office Panel Systems, Wood
FURNITURE: Office, Exc Wood
FURNITURE: Office, Wood
FURNITURE: Outdoor, Wood
FURNITURE: Picnic Tables Or Benches, Park
FURNITURE: Play Pens, Children's, Wood
FURNITURE: Restaurant
FURNITURE: School
FURNITURE: Silverware Chests, Wood
FURNITURE: Stools, Household, Wood
FURNITURE: Table Tops, Marble
FURNITURE: Tables & Table Tops, Wood
FURNITURE: Unfinished, Wood
FURNITURE: Upholstered
FURNITURE: Vehicle
FUSE MOUNTINGS: Electric Power
Furs

G

GAMES & TOYS: Banks
GAMES & TOYS: Baskets
GAMES & TOYS: Bingo Boards
GAMES & TOYS: Board Games, Children's & Adults'
GAMES & TOYS: Cars, Play, Children's Vehicles
GAMES & TOYS: Child Restraint Seats, Automotive
GAMES & TOYS: Craft & Hobby Kits & Sets
GAMES & TOYS: Dollhouses & Furniture
GAMES & TOYS: Dolls, Exc Stuffed Toy Animals
GAMES & TOYS: Electronic
GAMES & TOYS: Game Machines, Exc Coin-Operated
GAMES & TOYS: Kits, Science, Incl Microscopes/Chemistry Sets
GAMES & TOYS: Miniature Dolls, Collectors'
GAMES & TOYS: Models, Airplane, Toy & Hobby
GAMES & TOYS: Models, Automobile & Truck, Toy & Hobby
GAMES & TOYS: Models, Railroad, Toy & Hobby
GAMES & TOYS: Strollers, Baby, Vehicle
GAMES & TOYS: Structural Toy Sets
GAMES & TOYS: Wagons, Coaster, Express & Play, Children's
GARAGE DOOR REPAIR SVCS
GARBAGE CONTAINERS: Plastic
GARBAGE DISPOSALS: Household
GARBAGE DISPOSERS & COMPACTORS: Commercial
GAS & OIL FIELD EXPLORATION SVCS
GAS & OIL FIELD SVCS, NEC
GAS & OTHER COMBINED SVCS
GAS FIELD MACHINERY & EQPT
GAS STATIONS
GAS SYSTEM CONVERSION SVCS
GASES: Acetylene
GASES: Argon
GASES: Carbon Dioxide
GASES: Hydrogen
GASES: Indl
GASES: Neon
GASES: Nitrogen
GASES: Oxygen
GASKET MATERIALS
GASKETS
GASKETS & SEALING DEVICES
GASOLINE BLENDING PLANT
GASOLINE FILLING STATIONS
GASOLINE WHOLESALERS
GATES: Ornamental Metal
GAUGE BLOCKS
GAUGES
GEARS
GEARS & GEAR UNITS: Reduction, Exc Auto
GEARS: Power Transmission, Exc Auto
GEMSTONE & INDL DIAMOND MINING SVCS
GENERAL MERCHANDISE, NONDURABLE, WHOLESALE
GENERATING APPARATUS & PARTS: Electrical
GENERATION EQPT: Electronic
GENERATORS: Automotive & Aircraft
GENERATORS: Electric
GENERATORS: Gas
GENERATORS: Ultrasonic
GIFT SHOP

PRODUCT INDEX

GIFT WRAP: Paper, Made From Purchased Materials
GIFT, NOVELTY & SOUVENIR STORES: Artcraft & carvings
GIFT, NOVELTY & SOUVENIR STORES: Gift Baskets
GIFT, NOVELTY & SOUVENIR STORES: Gifts & Novelties
GIFT, NOVELTY & SOUVENIR STORES: Party Favors
GIFT, NOVELTY & SOUVENIR STORES: Trading Cards, Sports
GIFTS & NOVELTIES: Wholesalers
GLACE, FOR GLAZING FOOD
GLASS & GLASS CERAMIC PRDTS, PRESSED OR BLOWN: Tableware
GLASS FABRICATORS
GLASS PRDTS, FROM PURCHASED GLASS: Glass Beads, Reflecting
GLASS PRDTS, FROM PURCHASED GLASS: Glassware
GLASS PRDTS, FROM PURCHASED GLASS: Insulating
GLASS PRDTS, FROM PURCHASED GLASS: Mirrored
GLASS PRDTS, FROM PURCHASED GLASS: Novelties, Fruit, Etc
GLASS PRDTS, FROM PURCHASED GLASS: Ornaments, Christmas Tree
GLASS PRDTS, FROM PURCHASED GLASS: Reflecting
GLASS PRDTS, FROM PURCHASED GLASS: Sheet, Bent
GLASS PRDTS, FROM PURCHASED GLASS: Windshields
GLASS PRDTS, FROM PURCHD GLASS: Strengthened Or Reinforced
GLASS PRDTS, PRESSED OR BLOWN: Blocks & Bricks
GLASS PRDTS, PRESSED OR BLOWN: Bulbs, Electric Lights
GLASS PRDTS, PRESSED OR BLOWN: Furnishings & Access
GLASS PRDTS, PRESSED OR BLOWN: Glass Fibers, Textile
GLASS PRDTS, PRESSED OR BLOWN: Glassware, Art Or Decorative
GLASS PRDTS, PRESSED OR BLOWN: Glassware, Novelty
GLASS PRDTS, PRESSED OR BLOWN: Lantern Globes
GLASS PRDTS, PRESSED OR BLOWN: Scientific Glassware
GLASS PRDTS, PRESSED OR BLOWN: Tubing
GLASS PRDTS, PRESSED OR BLOWN: Yarn, Fiberglass
GLASS PRDTS, PRESSED/BLOWN: Glassware, Art, Decor/Novelty
GLASS PRDTS, PURCHSD GLASS: Ornamental, Cut, Engraved/Décor
GLASS STORE: Leaded Or Stained
GLASS STORES
GLASS, AUTOMOTIVE: Wholesalers
GLASS: Fiber
GLASS: Flat
GLASS: Indl Prdts
GLASS: Insulating
GLASS: Laminated
GLASS: Leaded
GLASS: Pressed & Blown, NEC
GLASS: Safety
GLASS: Stained
GLASS: Structural
GLASS: Tempered
GLASSWARE STORES
GLASSWARE WHOLESALERS
GLASSWARE, NOVELTY, WHOLESALE
GLASSWARE: Cut & Engraved
GLOBAL POSITIONING SYSTEMS & EQPT
GLOVES: Fabric
GLOVES: Leather
GLOVES: Linings, Exc Fur
GLOVES: Safety
GLOVES: Work
GLOVES: Woven Or Knit, From Purchased Materials
GLUE
GLYCERIN
GLYCOL ETHERS
GOLF CARTS: Powered
GOLF COURSES: Public
GOLF DRIVING RANGES
GOLF EQPT
GOLF GOODS & EQPT
GOURMET FOOD STORES
GOVERNMENT, EXECUTIVE OFFICES: City & Town Managers' Offices
GOVERNMENT, EXECUTIVE OFFICES: County Supervisor/Exec Office
GOVERNMENT, EXECUTIVE OFFICES: Mayors'
GOVERNMENT, GENERAL: Administration
GOVERNMENT, GENERAL: Administration, Federal
GOVERNORS: Diesel Engine

GRADING SVCS
GRANITE: Crushed & Broken
GRANITE: Cut & Shaped
GRANITE: Dimension
GRAPHIC ARTS & RELATED DESIGN SVCS
GRAPHIC LAYOUT SVCS: Printed Circuitry
GRAPHITE MINING SVCS
GRATINGS: Open Steel Flooring
GRATINGS: Tread, Fabricated Metal
GRAVE MARKERS: Concrete
GRAVE VAULTS, METAL
GRAVEL MINING
GREASES & INEDIBLE FATS, RENDERED
GREASES: Lubricating
GREENHOUSES: Prefabricated Metal
GREETING CARD SHOPS
GRILLES & REGISTERS: Ornamental Metal Work
GRINDING MEDIA: Pottery
GRINDING SVC: Precision, Commercial Or Indl
GRIPS OR HANDLES: Rubber
GRITS: Crushed & Broken
GROCERIES WHOLESALERS, NEC
GROCERIES, GENERAL LINE WHOLESALERS
GUARD SVCS
GUARDRAILS
GUARDS: Machine, Sheet Metal
GUIDED MISSILES & SPACE VEHICLES
GUIDED MISSILES/SPACE VEHICLE PARTS/AUX EQPT: Research/Devel
GUN SIGHTS: Optical
GUN SVCS
GUTTERS: Sheet Metal
GYPSUM PRDTS
GYROSCOPES

H

HAIR & HAIR BASED PRDTS
HAIR CARE PRDTS
HAIR CARE PRDTS: Hair Coloring Preparations
HAIR CURLERS: Beauty Shop
HAND TOOLS, NEC: Wholesalers
HANDBAGS
HANDBAGS: Women's
HANDLES: Wood
HANGERS: Garment, Wire
HARD RUBBER PRDTS, NEC
HARDWARE
HARDWARE & BUILDING PRDTS: Plastic
HARDWARE & EQPT: Stage, Exc Lighting
HARDWARE CLOTH: Woven Wire, Made From Purchased Wire
HARDWARE STORES
HARDWARE STORES: Builders'
HARDWARE STORES: Chainsaws
HARDWARE STORES: Pumps & Pumping Eqpt
HARDWARE STORES: Snowblowers
HARDWARE STORES: Tools
HARDWARE STORES: Tools, Power
HARDWARE WHOLESALERS
HARDWARE, WHOLESALE: Bolts
HARDWARE, WHOLESALE: Builders', NEC
HARDWARE, WHOLESALE: Nuts
HARDWARE, WHOLESALE: Power Tools & Access
HARDWARE, WHOLESALE: Saw Blades
HARDWARE, WHOLESALE: Screws
HARDWARE: Aircraft
HARDWARE: Aircraft & Marine, Incl Pulleys & Similar Items
HARDWARE: Builders'
HARDWARE: Casket
HARDWARE: Furniture, Builders' & Other Household
HARDWARE: Hangers, Wall
HARDWARE: Padlocks
HARDWARE: Piano
HARDWARE: Plastic
HARDWARE: Rubber
HARNESS ASSEMBLIES: Cable & Wire
HARNESS REPAIR SHOP
HARNESS WIRING SETS: Internal Combustion Engines
HEALTH & ALLIED SERVICES, NEC
HEALTH AIDS: Exercise Eqpt
HEALTH FOOD & SUPPLEMENT STORES
HEALTH SYSTEMS AGENCY
HEARING AIDS
HEAT EMISSION OPERATING APPARATUS
HEAT EXCHANGERS

HEAT EXCHANGERS: After Or Inter Coolers Or Condensers, Etc
HEAT TREATING: Metal
HEATERS: Room & Wall, Including Radiators
HEATING & AIR CONDITIONING EQPT & SPLYS WHOLESALERS
HEATING & AIR CONDITIONING UNITS, COMBINATION
HEATING APPARATUS: Steam
HEATING EQPT & SPLYS
HEATING EQPT: Complete
HEATING EQPT: Dielectric
HEATING EQPT: Induction
HEATING PADS: Nonelectric
HEATING UNITS & DEVICES: Indl, Electric
HEATING UNITS: Gas, Infrared
HEAVY DISTILLATES
HELMETS: Steel
HELP SUPPLY SERVICES
HISTORICAL SOCIETY
HITCHES: Trailer
HOBBY, TOY & GAME STORES: Arts & Crafts & Splys
HOBBY, TOY & GAME STORES: Ceramics Splys
HOBBY, TOY & GAME STORES: Children's Toys & Games, Exc Dolls
HOBBY, TOY & GAME STORES: Dolls & Access
HOBBY, TOY & GAME STORES: Toys & Games
HOGS WHOLESALERS
HOISTING SLINGS
HOISTS
HOISTS: Mine
HOLDING COMPANIES: Banks
HOLDING COMPANIES: Investment, Exc Banks
HOLDING COMPANIES: Personal, Exc Banks
HOME ENTERTAINMENT EQPT: Electronic, NEC
HOME ENTERTAINMENT REPAIR SVCS
HOME FOR THE MENTALLY HANDICAPPED
HOME FURNISHINGS WHOLESALERS
HOME HEALTH CARE SVCS
HOME IMPROVEMENT & RENOVATION CONTRACTOR AGENCY
HOMEBUILDERS & OTHER OPERATIVE BUILDERS
HOMEFURNISHING STORE: Bedding, Sheet, Blanket,Spread/Pillow
HOMEFURNISHING STORES: Brushes
HOMEFURNISHING STORES: Cutlery
HOMEFURNISHING STORES: Metalware
HOMEFURNISHING STORES: Mirrors
HOMEFURNISHING STORES: Pictures, Wall
HOMEFURNISHING STORES: Pottery
HOMEFURNISHING STORES: Venetian Blinds
HOMEFURNISHING STORES: Vertical Blinds
HOMEFURNISHING STORES: Window Furnishings
HOMEFURNISHING STORES: Window Shades, NEC
HOMEFURNISHINGS & SPLYS, WHOLESALE: Decorative
HOMEFURNISHINGS, WHOLESALE: Blankets
HOMEFURNISHINGS, WHOLESALE: Blinds, Venetian
HOMEFURNISHINGS, WHOLESALE: Blinds, Vertical
HOMEFURNISHINGS, WHOLESALE: Decorating Splys
HOMEFURNISHINGS, WHOLESALE: Draperies
HOMEFURNISHINGS, WHOLESALE: Grills, Barbecue
HOMEFURNISHINGS, WHOLESALE: Kitchenware
HOMEFURNISHINGS, WHOLESALE: Linens, Table
HOMEFURNISHINGS, WHOLESALE: Mirrors/Pictures, Framed/Unframd
HOMEFURNISHINGS, WHOLESALE: Pottery
HOMEFURNISHINGS, WHOLESALE: Window Covering Parts & Access
HOMEFURNISHINGS, WHOLESALE: Wood Flooring
HOMES, MODULAR: Wooden
HOMES: Log Cabins
HONING & LAPPING MACHINES
HOODS: Range, Sheet Metal
HOOKS: Crane, Laminated Plate
HOPPERS: End Dump
HOPPERS: Sheet Metal
HORSE & PET ACCESSORIES: Textile
HORSE ACCESS: Harnesses & Riding Crops, Etc, Exc Leather
HOSE: Automobile, Rubber
HOSE: Flexible Metal
HOSE: Plastic
HOSE: Rubber
HOSES & BELTING: Rubber & Plastic
HOSPITALS: Medical & Surgical
HOTELS & MOTELS

PRODUCT INDEX

HOUSEHOLD APPLIANCE STORES
HOUSEHOLD APPLIANCE STORES: Air Cond Rm Units, Self-Contnd
HOUSEHOLD APPLIANCE STORES: Ranges, Gas
HOUSEHOLD APPLIANCE STORES: Suntanning Eqpt & Splys
HOUSEHOLD ARTICLES, EXC KITCHEN: Pottery
HOUSEHOLD ARTICLES: Metal
HOUSEHOLD FURNISHINGS, NEC
HOUSEWARES, ELECTRIC, EXC COOKING APPLIANCES & UTENSILS
HOUSEWARES, ELECTRIC: Air Purifiers, Portable
HOUSEWARES, ELECTRIC: Cooking Appliances
HOUSEWARES, ELECTRIC: Fans, Exhaust & Ventilating
HOUSEWARES, ELECTRIC: Heating, Bsbrd/Wall, Radiant Heat
HOUSEWARES, ELECTRIC: Humidifiers, Household
HOUSEWARES, ELECTRIC: Toasters
HOUSEWARES: Dishes, China
HOUSEWARES: Dishes, Earthenware
HOUSEWARES: Dishes, Plastic
HOUSEWARES: Food Dishes & Utensils, Pressed & Molded Pulp
HOUSEWARES: Plates, Pressed/Molded Pulp, From Purchased Mtrl
HOUSING COMPONENTS: Prefabricated, Concrete
HOUSINGS: Business Machine, Sheet Metal
HOUSINGS: Pressure
HUMIDIFIERS & DEHUMIDIFIERS
HYDRAULIC EQPT REPAIR SVC
HYDRAULIC FLUIDS: Synthetic Based
HYDROPONIC EQPT
Hard Rubber & Molded Rubber Prdts

I

ICE
ICE CREAM & ICES WHOLESALERS
ICE WHOLESALERS
IDENTIFICATION PLATES
IGNEOUS ROCK: Crushed & Broken
IGNITERS: Jet Fuel
IGNITION SYSTEMS: High Frequency
IGNITION SYSTEMS: Internal Combustion Engine
INCENSE
INCUBATORS & BROODERS: Farm
INDL & PERSONAL SVC PAPER WHOLESALERS
INDL & PERSONAL SVC PAPER, WHOL: Bags, Paper/Disp Plastic
INDL & PERSONAL SVC PAPER, WHOL: Boxes, Corrugtd/Solid Fiber
INDL & PERSONAL SVC PAPER, WHOL: Paper, Wrap/Coarse/Prdts
INDL & PERSONAL SVC PAPER, WHOLESALE: Boxes & Containers
INDL & PERSONAL SVC PAPER, WHOLESALE: Disposable
INDL & PERSONAL SVC PAPER, WHOLESALE: Paper Tubes & Cores
INDL & PERSONAL SVC PAPER, WHOLESALE: Shipping Splys
INDL & PERSONAL SVC PAPER, WHOLESALE: Towels, Paper
INDL CONTRACTORS: Exhibit Construction
INDL DIAMONDS WHOLESALERS
INDL EQPT CLEANING SVCS
INDL EQPT SVCS
INDL GASES WHOLESALERS
INDL HELP SVCS
INDL MACHINERY & EQPT WHOLESALERS
INDL MACHINERY REPAIR & MAINTENANCE
INDL PATTERNS: Foundry Cores
INDL PATTERNS: Foundry Patternmaking
INDL PROCESS INSTRUMENTS: Absorp Analyzers, Infrared, X-Ray
INDL PROCESS INSTRUMENTS: Chromatographs
INDL PROCESS INSTRUMENTS: Control
INDL PROCESS INSTRUMENTS: Controllers, Process Variables
INDL PROCESS INSTRUMENTS: Data Loggers
INDL PROCESS INSTRUMENTS: Digital Display, Process Variables
INDL PROCESS INSTRUMENTS: Draft Gauges
INDL PROCESS INSTRUMENTS: Fluidic Devices, Circuit & Systems
INDL PROCESS INSTRUMENTS: Indl Flow & Measuring
INDL PROCESS INSTRUMENTS: Manometers

INDL PROCESS INSTRUMENTS: Moisture Meters
INDL PROCESS INSTRUMENTS: Temperature
INDL PROCESS INSTRUMENTS: Water Quality Monitoring/Cntrl Sys
INDL SPLYS WHOLESALERS
INDL SPLYS, WHOL: Fasteners, Incl Nuts, Bolts, Screws, Etc
INDL SPLYS, WHOLESALE: Abrasives
INDL SPLYS, WHOLESALE: Abrasives & Adhesives
INDL SPLYS, WHOLESALE: Adhesives, Tape & Plasters
INDL SPLYS, WHOLESALE: Barrels, New Or Reconditioned
INDL SPLYS, WHOLESALE: Bearings
INDL SPLYS, WHOLESALE: Bins & Containers, Storage
INDL SPLYS, WHOLESALE: Bottler Splys
INDL SPLYS, WHOLESALE: Brushes, Indl
INDL SPLYS, WHOLESALE: Clean Room Splys
INDL SPLYS, WHOLESALE: Drums, New Or Reconditioned
INDL SPLYS, WHOLESALE: Fasteners & Fastening Eqpt
INDL SPLYS, WHOLESALE: Filters, Indl
INDL SPLYS, WHOLESALE: Fittings
INDL SPLYS, WHOLESALE: Gaskets
INDL SPLYS, WHOLESALE: Gaskets & Seals
INDL SPLYS, WHOLESALE: Gears
INDL SPLYS, WHOLESALE: Hydraulic & Pneumatic Pistons/Valves
INDL SPLYS, WHOLESALE: Knives, Indl
INDL SPLYS, WHOLESALE: Plastic, Pallets
INDL SPLYS, WHOLESALE: Power Transmission, Eqpt & Apparatus
INDL SPLYS, WHOLESALE: Rubber Goods, Mechanical
INDL SPLYS, WHOLESALE: Seals
INDL SPLYS, WHOLESALE: Signmaker Eqpt & Splys
INDL SPLYS, WHOLESALE: Tools
INDL SPLYS, WHOLESALE: Tools, NEC
INDL SPLYS, WHOLESALE: Valves & Fittings
INDL TOOL GRINDING SVCS
INDUSTRIAL & COMMERCIAL EQPT INSPECTION SVCS
INFORMATION RETRIEVAL SERVICES
INGOT, EXTRUSION: Extrusion ingot, aluminum: rolling mills
INGOT: Aluminum
INK OR WRITING FLUIDS
INK: Gravure
INK: Lithographic
INK: Printing
INSECTICIDES & PESTICIDES
INSPECTION & TESTING SVCS
INSTRUMENTS & METERS: Measuring, Electric
INSTRUMENTS, LAB: Refractometers, Exc Indl Process Types
INSTRUMENTS, LAB: Spectroscopic/Optical Properties Measuring
INSTRUMENTS, LABORATORY: Analyzers, Automatic Chemical
INSTRUMENTS, LABORATORY: Blood Testing
INSTRUMENTS, LABORATORY: Gas Analyzing
INSTRUMENTS, LABORATORY: Infrared Analytical
INSTRUMENTS, LABORATORY: Spectrometers
INSTRUMENTS, LABORATORY: Ultraviolet Analytical
INSTRUMENTS, MEASURING & CNTRL: Gauges, Auto, Computer
INSTRUMENTS, MEASURING & CNTRL: Geophysical & Meteorological
INSTRUMENTS, MEASURING & CNTRL: Radiation & Testing, Nuclear
INSTRUMENTS, MEASURING & CNTRL: Testing, Abrasion, Etc
INSTRUMENTS, MEASURING & CNTRL: Whole Body Counters, Nuclear
INSTRUMENTS, MEASURING & CNTRLG: Aircraft & Motor Vehicle
INSTRUMENTS, MEASURING & CNTRLG: Electrogamma Ray Loggers
INSTRUMENTS, MEASURING & CNTRLG: Stress, Strain & Measure
INSTRUMENTS, MEASURING & CNTRLG: Tensile Strength Testing
INSTRUMENTS, MEASURING & CNTRLG: Thermometers/Temp Sensors
INSTRUMENTS, MEASURING & CNTRLNG: Nuclear Instrument Modules
INSTRUMENTS, MEASURING & CONTROLLING: Anamometers
INSTRUMENTS, MEASURING & CONTROLLING: Breathalyzers
INSTRUMENTS, MEASURING & CONTROLLING: Cable Testing

INSTRUMENTS, MEASURING & CONTROLLING: Gas Detectors
INSTRUMENTS, MEASURING & CONTROLLING: Magnetometers
INSTRUMENTS, MEASURING & CONTROLLING: Surveying & Drafting
INSTRUMENTS, MEASURING & CONTROLLING: Torsion Testing
INSTRUMENTS, MEASURING & CONTROLLING: Transits, Surveyors'
INSTRUMENTS, MEASURING & CONTROLLING: Ultrasonic Testing
INSTRUMENTS, MEASURING/CNTRL: Gauging, Ultrasonic Thickness
INSTRUMENTS, MEASURING/CNTRLG: Fare Registers, St Cars/Buses
INSTRUMENTS, MEASURING/CNTRLG: Fire Detect Sys, Non-Electric
INSTRUMENTS, MEASURING/CNTRLNG: Med Diagnostic Sys, Nuclear
INSTRUMENTS, OPTICAL: Lenses, All Types Exc Ophthalmic
INSTRUMENTS, OPTICAL: Test & Inspection
INSTRUMENTS, SURGICAL & MEDICAL: Blood & Bone Work
INSTRUMENTS, SURGICAL & MEDICAL: Forceps
INSTRUMENTS, SURGICAL & MEDICAL: IV Transfusion
INSTRUMENTS, SURGICAL & MEDICAL: Inhalation Therapy
INSTRUMENTS, SURGICAL & MEDICAL: Lasers, Surgical
INSTRUMENTS, SURGICAL & MEDICAL: Operating Tables
INSTRUMENTS, SURGICAL & MEDICAL: Optometers
INSTRUMENTS, SURGICAL & MEDICAL: Physiotherapy, Electrical
INSTRUMENTS, SURGICAL & MEDICAL: Probes, Surgical
INSTRUMENTS, SURGICAL/MED: Microsurgical, Exc Electromedical
INSTRUMENTS: Airspeed
INSTRUMENTS: Analytical
INSTRUMENTS: Analyzers, Radio Apparatus, NEC
INSTRUMENTS: Combustion Control, Indl
INSTRUMENTS: Differential Pressure, Indl
INSTRUMENTS: Electrocardiographs
INSTRUMENTS: Endoscopic Eqpt, Electromedical
INSTRUMENTS: Eye Examination
INSTRUMENTS: Flow, Indl Process
INSTRUMENTS: Gastroscopes, Electromedical
INSTRUMENTS: Indicating, Electric
INSTRUMENTS: Indl Process Control
INSTRUMENTS: Infrared, Indl Process
INSTRUMENTS: Laser, Scientific & Engineering
INSTRUMENTS: Measurement, Indl Process
INSTRUMENTS: Measuring & Controlling
INSTRUMENTS: Measuring Electricity
INSTRUMENTS: Measuring, Current, NEC
INSTRUMENTS: Measuring, Electrical Energy
INSTRUMENTS: Measuring, Electrical Power
INSTRUMENTS: Measuring, Electrical Quantities
INSTRUMENTS: Medical & Surgical
INSTRUMENTS: Particle Size Analyzers
INSTRUMENTS: Power Measuring, Electrical
INSTRUMENTS: Pressure Measurement, Indl
INSTRUMENTS: Radar Testing, Electric
INSTRUMENTS: Radio Frequency Measuring
INSTRUMENTS: Recorders, Oscillographic
INSTRUMENTS: Refractometers, Indl Process
INSTRUMENTS: Signal Generators & Averagers
INSTRUMENTS: Surface Area Analyzers
INSTRUMENTS: Temperature Measurement, Indl
INSTRUMENTS: Test, Electrical, Engine
INSTRUMENTS: Test, Electronic & Electric Measurement
INSTRUMENTS: Test, Electronic & Electrical Circuits
INSTRUMENTS: Thermal Conductive, Indl
INSTRUMENTS: Transducers, Volts, Amperes, Watts, VARs & Freq
INSTRUMENTS: Vibration
INSULATING COMPOUNDS
INSULATION & CUSHIONING FOAM: Polystyrene
INSULATION & ROOFING MATERIALS: Wood, Reconstituted
INSULATION MATERIALS WHOLESALERS
INSULATION: Fiberglass
INSULATORS & INSULATION MATERIALS: Electrical
INSURANCE AGENTS, NEC
INSURANCE BROKERS, NEC
INSURANCE CARRIERS: Life
INSURANCE CLAIM PROCESSING, EXC MEDICAL
INSURANCE PATROL SVCS

PRODUCT INDEX

INSURANCE RESEARCH SVCS
INTEGRATED CIRCUITS, SEMICONDUCTOR NETWORKS, ETC
INTERCOMMUNICATION EQPT REPAIR SVCS
INTERCOMMUNICATIONS SYSTEMS: Electric
INTERIOR DECORATING SVCS
INTERIOR DESIGN SVCS, NEC
INTERIOR DESIGNING SVCS
INTERIOR REPAIR SVCS
INTERMEDIATE CARE FACILITY
INTRAVENOUS SOLUTIONS
INVERTERS: Nonrotating Electrical
INVESTMENT ADVISORY SVCS
INVESTMENT FIRM: General Brokerage
INVESTMENT FUNDS: Open-Ended
INVESTORS, NEC
INVESTORS: Real Estate, Exc Property Operators
IRON & STEEL PRDTS: Hot-Rolled
IRON ORE MINING
IRON ORE PELLETIZING
IRON ORES
IRON OXIDES
IRRADIATION EQPT: Nuclear

J

JACKETS: Indl, Metal Plate
JACKS: Hydraulic
JANITORIAL & CUSTODIAL SVCS
JANITORIAL EQPT & SPLYS WHOLESALERS
JEWELERS' FINDINGS & MATERIALS
JEWELERS' FINDINGS & MATERIALS: Castings
JEWELERS' FINDINGS & MATERIALS: Pin Stems
JEWELERS' FINDINGS & MTLS: Jewel Prep, Instr, Tools, Watches
JEWELRY & PRECIOUS STONES WHOLESALERS
JEWELRY APPAREL
JEWELRY FINDINGS & LAPIDARY WORK
JEWELRY REPAIR SVCS
JEWELRY STORES
JEWELRY STORES: Precious Stones & Precious Metals
JEWELRY STORES: Silverware
JEWELRY, PRECIOUS METAL: Bracelets
JEWELRY, PRECIOUS METAL: Buttons, Precious Or Semi Or Stone
JEWELRY, PRECIOUS METAL: Cigar & Cigarette Access
JEWELRY, PRECIOUS METAL: Medals, Precious Or Semi-precious
JEWELRY, PRECIOUS METAL: Mountings & Trimmings
JEWELRY, PRECIOUS METAL: Pearl, Natural Or Cultured
JEWELRY, PRECIOUS METAL: Pins
JEWELRY, PRECIOUS METAL: Rings, Finger
JEWELRY, WHOLESALE
JEWELRY: Decorative, Fashion & Costume
JEWELRY: Precious Metal
JIGS & FIXTURES
JOB PRINTING & NEWSPAPER PUBLISHING COMBINED
JOB TRAINING & VOCATIONAL REHABILITATION SVCS
JOB TRAINING SVCS
JOINTS OR FASTENINGS: Rail
JOINTS: Expansion
JOINTS: Expansion, Pipe
JOISTS: Long-Span Series, Open Web Steel

K

KEYS, KEY BLANKS
KILNS & FURNACES: Ceramic
KITCHEN & COOKING ARTICLES: Pottery
KITCHEN CABINET STORES, EXC CUSTOM
KITCHEN CABINETS WHOLESALERS
KITCHEN TOOLS & UTENSILS WHOLESALERS
KITCHEN UTENSILS: Food Handling & Processing Prdts, Wood
KITCHEN UTENSILS: Wooden
KITCHENWARE STORES
KITCHENWARE: Plastic
KITS: Plastic
KNIVES: Agricultural Or indl

L

LABELS: Cotton, Printed
LABELS: Paper, Made From Purchased Materials
LABELS: Woven
LABORATORIES, TESTING: Food
LABORATORIES, TESTING: Hazardous Waste
LABORATORIES, TESTING: Hydrostatic
LABORATORIES, TESTING: Metallurgical
LABORATORIES, TESTING: Pollution
LABORATORIES, TESTING: Product Testing
LABORATORIES, TESTING: Product Testing, Safety/Performance
LABORATORIES, TESTING: Water
LABORATORIES: Biological Research
LABORATORIES: Biotechnology
LABORATORIES: Commercial Nonphysical Research
LABORATORIES: Dental
LABORATORIES: Dental, Crown & Bridge Production
LABORATORIES: Dental, Denture Production
LABORATORIES: Electronic Research
LABORATORIES: Medical
LABORATORIES: Noncommercial Research
LABORATORIES: Physical Research, Commercial
LABORATORIES: Testing
LABORATORIES: Testing
LABORATORIES: Ultrasound
LABORATORY APPARATUS & FURNITURE
LABORATORY APPARATUS, EXC HEATING & MEASURING
LABORATORY APPARATUS: Calibration Tapes, Phy Testing Mach
LABORATORY APPARATUS: Crushing & Grinding
LABORATORY APPARATUS: Freezers
LABORATORY APPARATUS: Furnaces
LABORATORY APPARATUS: Particle Size Reduction
LABORATORY APPARATUS: Pipettes, Hemocytometer
LABORATORY CHEMICALS: Organic
LABORATORY EQPT, EXC MEDICAL: Wholesalers
LABORATORY EQPT: Chemical
LABORATORY EQPT: Clinical Instruments Exc Medical
LABORATORY EQPT: Incubators
LABORATORY EQPT: Measuring
LABORATORY INSTRUMENT REPAIR SVCS
LADDERS: Metal
LADLE BRICK: Clay
LADLES: Metal Plate
LAMINATED PLASTICS: Plate, Sheet, Rod & Tubes
LAMINATING MATERIALS
LAMINATING SVCS
LAMP & LIGHT BULBS & TUBES
LAMP BULBS & TUBES, ELECTRIC: Filaments
LAMP BULBS & TUBES, ELECTRIC: For Specialized Applications
LAMP BULBS & TUBES, ELECTRIC: Sealed Beam
LAMP BULBS & TUBES/PARTS, ELECTRIC: Generalized Applications
LAMP FIXTURES: Ultraviolet
LAMP REPAIR & MOUNTING SVCS
LAMP SHADES: Plastic
LAMP STORES
LAMPS: Desk, Residential
LAMPS: Fluorescent
LAMPS: Incandescent, Filament
LAMPS: Table, Residential
LAND SUBDIVISION & DEVELOPMENT
LANTERNS
LAPIDARY WORK: Contract Or Other
LAPIDARY WORK: Jewel Cut, Drill, Polish, Recut/Setting
LASER SYSTEMS & EQPT
LASERS: Welding, Drilling & Cutting Eqpt
LATEX: Foamed
LATH: Expanded Metal
LATH: Snow Fence
LATHES
LAUNDRY & GARMENT SVCS, NEC: Garment Alteration & Repair
LAUNDRY EQPT: Commercial
LAUNDRY EQPT: Household
LAUNDRY SVCS: Indl
LAWN & GARDEN EQPT
LAWN & GARDEN EQPT STORES
LAWN & GARDEN EQPT: Grass Catchers, Lawn Mower
LAWN & GARDEN EQPT: Lawnmowers, Residential, Hand Or Power
LAWN & GARDEN EQPT: Rototillers
LAWN & GARDEN EQPT: Tractors & Eqpt
LAWN & GARDEN EQPT: Trimmers
LAWN MOWER REPAIR SHOP
LEAD & ZINC
LEAD PENCILS & ART GOODS
LEAD-IN WIRES: Electric Lamp
LEASING & RENTAL SVCS: Cranes & Aerial Lift Eqpt
LEASING & RENTAL SVCS: Oil Field Eqpt
LEASING & RENTAL SVCS: Oil Well Drilling
LEASING & RENTAL: Construction & Mining Eqpt
LEASING & RENTAL: Medical Machinery & Eqpt
LEASING & RENTAL: Mobile Home Sites
LEASING & RENTAL: Office Machines & Eqpt
LEASING & RENTAL: Other Real Estate Property
LEASING & RENTAL: Trucks, Indl
LEASING & RENTAL: Trucks, Without Drivers
LEATHER & CANVAS GOODS: Leggings Or Chaps, NEC
LEATHER GOODS, EXC FOOTWEAR, GLOVES, LUGGAGE/BELTING, WHOL
LEATHER GOODS: Coin Purses
LEATHER GOODS: Corners, Luggage
LEATHER GOODS: Feed Bags, Horse
LEATHER GOODS: Garments
LEATHER GOODS: Harnesses Or Harness Parts
LEATHER GOODS: Holsters
LEATHER GOODS: NEC
LEATHER GOODS: Personal
LEATHER GOODS: Razor Strops
LEATHER GOODS: Saddles Or Parts
LEATHER GOODS: Safety Belts
LEATHER GOODS: Stirrups, Wood Or Metal
LEATHER GOODS: Wallets
LEATHER TANNING & FINISHING
LEATHER, CHAMOIS, WHOLESALE
LEGAL OFFICES & SVCS
LEGAL SVCS: General Practice Attorney or Lawyer
LENS COATING: Ophthalmic
LENSES: Plastic, Exc Optical
LESSORS: Farm Land
LICENSE TAGS: Automobile, Stamped Metal
LIFE INSURANCE AGENTS
LIFE INSURANCE CARRIERS
LIGHTING EQPT: Flashlights
LIGHTING EQPT: Floodlights
LIGHTING EQPT: Miners' Lamps
LIGHTING EQPT: Motor Vehicle
LIGHTING EQPT: Motor Vehicle, Headlights
LIGHTING EQPT: Motor Vehicle, NEC
LIGHTING EQPT: Outdoor
LIGHTING EQPT: Searchlights
LIGHTING EQPT: Spotlights
LIGHTING FIXTURES WHOLESALERS
LIGHTING FIXTURES, NEC
LIGHTING FIXTURES: Airport
LIGHTING FIXTURES: Fluorescent, Commercial
LIGHTING FIXTURES: Indl & Commercial
LIGHTING FIXTURES: Motor Vehicle
LIGHTING FIXTURES: Ornamental, Commercial
LIGHTING FIXTURES: Residential
LIGHTING FIXTURES: Residential, Electric
LIGHTING FIXTURES: Street
LIGHTING FIXTURES: Underwater
LIGHTS: Trouble lights
LIME
LIME ROCK: Ground
LIMESTONE & MARBLE: Dimension
LIMESTONE: Crushed & Broken
LIMESTONE: Cut & Shaped
LIMESTONE: Dimension
LIMESTONE: Ground
LINEN SPLY SVC
LINEN SPLY SVC: Apron
LINEN SPLY SVC: Table Cover
LINERS & COVERS: Fabric
LINERS & LINING
LINIMENTS
LININGS: Fabric, Apparel & Other, Exc Millinery
LININGS: Vulcanizable Rubber
LINTELS: Steel, Light Gauge
LIP BALMS
LIQUEFIED PETROLEUM GAS DEALERS
LIQUEFIED PETROLEUM GAS WHOLESALERS
LIQUID CRYSTAL DISPLAYS
LITHOGRAPHIC PLATES
LIVESTOCK WHOLESALERS, NEC
LOADS: Electronic
LOCKERS
LOCKS
LOCKS & LOCK SETS, WHOLESALE
LOCKS: Safe & Vault, Metal
LOCKSMITHS
LOCOMOTIVES & PARTS

PRODUCT INDEX

LOGGING
LOGGING CAMPS & CONTRACTORS
LOGGING: Saw Logs
LOGGING: Stump Harvesting
LOGGING: Timber, Cut At Logging Camp
LOGGING: Veneer Logs
LOGGING: Wood Chips, Produced In The Field
LOGGING: Wooden Logs
LOGS: Gas, Fireplace
LOOSELEAF BINDERS
LOTIONS OR CREAMS: Face
LUBRICANTS: Corrosion Preventive
LUBRICATING EQPT: Indl
LUBRICATING OIL & GREASE WHOLESALERS
LUBRICATING SYSTEMS: Centralized
LUBRICATION SYSTEMS & EQPT
LUGGAGE & BRIEFCASES
LUGGAGE & LEATHER GOODS STORES
LUGGAGE & LEATHER GOODS STORES: Leather, Exc Luggage & Shoes
LUGGAGE: Traveling Bags
LUMBER & BLDG MATLS DEALER, RET: Garage Doors, Sell/Install
LUMBER & BLDG MATRLS DEALERS, RET: Bath Fixtures, Eqpt/Sply
LUMBER & BLDG MATRLS DEALERS, RETAIL: Doors, Wood/Metal
LUMBER & BLDG MTRLS DEALERS, RET: Closets, Interiors/Access
LUMBER & BLDG MTRLS DEALERS, RET: Doors, Storm, Wood/Metal
LUMBER & BLDG MTRLS DEALERS, RET: Planing Mill Prdts/Lumber
LUMBER & BLDG MTRLS DEALERS, RET: Windows, Storm, Wood/Metal
LUMBER & BUILDING MATERIAL DEALERS, RETAIL: Roofing Material
LUMBER & BUILDING MATERIALS DEALER, RET: Door & Window Prdts
LUMBER & BUILDING MATERIALS DEALER, RET: Masonry Matls/Splys
LUMBER & BUILDING MATERIALS DEALERS, RET: Solar Heating Eqpt
LUMBER & BUILDING MATERIALS DEALERS, RETAIL: Brick
LUMBER & BUILDING MATERIALS DEALERS, RETAIL: Cement
LUMBER & BUILDING MATERIALS DEALERS, RETAIL: Countertops
LUMBER & BUILDING MATERIALS DEALERS, RETAIL: Flooring, Wood
LUMBER & BUILDING MATERIALS DEALERS, RETAIL: Jalousies
LUMBER & BUILDING MATERIALS DEALERS, RETAIL: Modular Homes
LUMBER & BUILDING MATERIALS DEALERS, RETAIL: Sand & Gravel
LUMBER & BUILDING MATERIALS DEALERS, RETAIL: Siding
LUMBER & BUILDING MATERIALS DEALERS, RETAIL: Tile, Ceramic
LUMBER & BUILDING MATERIALS RET DEALERS: Millwork & Lumber
LUMBER & BUILDING MATLS DEALERS, RET: Concrete/Cinder Block
LUMBER & BUILDING MTRLS DEALERS, RET: Insulation Mtrl, Bldg
LUMBER: Dimension, Hardwood
LUMBER: Fiberboard
LUMBER: Flooring, Dressed, Softwood
LUMBER: Furniture Dimension Stock, Softwood
LUMBER: Hardwood Dimension
LUMBER: Hardwood Dimension & Flooring Mills
LUMBER: Kiln Dried
LUMBER: Plywood, Hardwood
LUMBER: Plywood, Hardwood or Hardwood Faced
LUMBER: Plywood, Prefinished, Hardwood
LUMBER: Plywood, Softwood
LUMBER: Plywood, Softwood
LUMBER: Rails, Fence, Round Or Split
LUMBER: Treated
LUMBER: Veneer, Hardwood
LUMBER: Veneer, Softwood

M

MACHINE PARTS: Stamped Or Pressed Metal

MACHINE SHOPS
MACHINE TOOL ACCESS: Broaches
MACHINE TOOL ACCESS: Cams
MACHINE TOOL ACCESS: Collars
MACHINE TOOL ACCESS: Cutting
MACHINE TOOL ACCESS: Diamond Cutting, For Turning, Etc
MACHINE TOOL ACCESS: Dies, Thread Cutting
MACHINE TOOL ACCESS: Dressing/Wheel Crushing Attach, Diamond
MACHINE TOOL ACCESS: Drill Bushings, Drilling Jig
MACHINE TOOL ACCESS: Drills
MACHINE TOOL ACCESS: End Mills
MACHINE TOOL ACCESS: Hopper Feed Devices
MACHINE TOOL ACCESS: Knives, Metalworking
MACHINE TOOL ACCESS: Knives, Shear
MACHINE TOOL ACCESS: Machine Attachments & Access, Drilling
MACHINE TOOL ACCESS: Milling Machine Attachments
MACHINE TOOL ACCESS: Rotary Tables
MACHINE TOOL ACCESS: Shaping Tools
MACHINE TOOL ACCESS: Sockets
MACHINE TOOL ACCESS: Threading Tools
MACHINE TOOL ACCESS: Tool Holders
MACHINE TOOL ACCESS: Tools & Access
MACHINE TOOL ACCESS: Wheel Turning Eqpt, Diamond Point, Etc
MACHINE TOOL ATTACHMENTS & ACCESS
MACHINE TOOLS & ACCESS
MACHINE TOOLS, METAL CUTTING: Chucking, Automatic
MACHINE TOOLS, METAL CUTTING: Die Sinking
MACHINE TOOLS, METAL CUTTING: Drilling
MACHINE TOOLS, METAL CUTTING: Drilling & Boring
MACHINE TOOLS, METAL CUTTING: Electron-Discharge
MACHINE TOOLS, METAL CUTTING: Exotic, Including Explosive
MACHINE TOOLS, METAL CUTTING: Grind, Polish, Buff, Lapp
MACHINE TOOLS, METAL CUTTING: Home Workshop
MACHINE TOOLS, METAL CUTTING: Lathes
MACHINE TOOLS, METAL CUTTING: Numerically Controlled
MACHINE TOOLS, METAL CUTTING: Pipe Cutting & Threading
MACHINE TOOLS, METAL CUTTING: Plasma Process
MACHINE TOOLS, METAL CUTTING: Regrinding, Crankshaft
MACHINE TOOLS, METAL CUTTING: Sawing & Cutoff
MACHINE TOOLS, METAL CUTTING: Tool Replacement & Rpr Parts
MACHINE TOOLS, METAL CUTTING: Ultrasonic
MACHINE TOOLS, METAL FORMING: Bending
MACHINE TOOLS, METAL FORMING: Crimping, Metal
MACHINE TOOLS, METAL FORMING: Die Casting & Extruding
MACHINE TOOLS, METAL FORMING: Electroforming
MACHINE TOOLS, METAL FORMING: Forging Machinery & Hammers
MACHINE TOOLS, METAL FORMING: Gear Rolling
MACHINE TOOLS, METAL FORMING: Headers
MACHINE TOOLS, METAL FORMING: Magnetic Forming
MACHINE TOOLS, METAL FORMING: Marking
MACHINE TOOLS, METAL FORMING: Mechanical, Pneumatic Or Hyd
MACHINE TOOLS, METAL FORMING: Nail Heading
MACHINE TOOLS, METAL FORMING: Presses, Hyd & Pneumatic
MACHINE TOOLS, METAL FORMING: Rebuilt
MACHINE TOOLS, METAL FORMING: Spinning, Spline Rollg/Windg
MACHINE TOOLS: Metal Cutting
MACHINE TOOLS: Metal Forming
MACHINERY & EQPT, AGRICULTURAL, WHOL: Farm Eqpt Parts/Splys
MACHINERY & EQPT, AGRICULTURAL, WHOLESALE: Farm Implements
MACHINERY & EQPT, AGRICULTURAL, WHOLESALE: Hydroponic
MACHINERY & EQPT, AGRICULTURAL, WHOLESALE: Lawn & Garden
MACHINERY & EQPT, AGRICULTURAL, WHOLESALE: Livestock Eqpt
MACHINERY & EQPT, AGRICULTURAL, WHOLESALE: Tractors
MACHINERY & EQPT, INDL, WHOL: Controlling Instruments/Access
MACHINERY & EQPT, INDL, WHOL: Environ Pollution Cntrl, Water

MACHINERY & EQPT, INDL, WHOL: Meters, Consumption Registerng
MACHINERY & EQPT, INDL, WHOLESALE: Cement Making
MACHINERY & EQPT, INDL, WHOLESALE: Chemical Process
MACHINERY & EQPT, INDL, WHOLESALE: Conveyor Systems
MACHINERY & EQPT, INDL, WHOLESALE: Cranes
MACHINERY & EQPT, INDL, WHOLESALE: Engines & Parts, Diesel
MACHINERY & EQPT, INDL, WHOLESALE: Engines, Gasoline
MACHINERY & EQPT, INDL, WHOLESALE: Engs & Parts, Air-Cooled
MACHINERY & EQPT, INDL, WHOLESALE: Fans
MACHINERY & EQPT, INDL, WHOLESALE: Food Manufacturing
MACHINERY & EQPT, INDL, WHOLESALE: Heat Exchange
MACHINERY & EQPT, INDL, WHOLESALE: Hydraulic Systems
MACHINERY & EQPT, INDL, WHOLESALE: Indl Machine Parts
MACHINERY & EQPT, INDL, WHOLESALE: Instruments & Cntrl Eqpt
MACHINERY & EQPT, INDL, WHOLESALE: Lift Trucks & Parts
MACHINERY & EQPT, INDL, WHOLESALE: Machine Tools & Access
MACHINERY & EQPT, INDL, WHOLESALE: Machine Tools & Metalwork
MACHINERY & EQPT, INDL, WHOLESALE: Measure/Test, Electric
MACHINERY & EQPT, INDL, WHOLESALE: Metal Refining
MACHINERY & EQPT, INDL, WHOLESALE: Noise Control
MACHINERY & EQPT, INDL, WHOLESALE: Packaging
MACHINERY & EQPT, INDL, WHOLESALE: Paint Spray
MACHINERY & EQPT, INDL, WHOLESALE: Paper Manufacturing
MACHINERY & EQPT, INDL, WHOLESALE: Petroleum Industry
MACHINERY & EQPT, INDL, WHOLESALE: Plastic Prdts Machinery
MACHINERY & EQPT, INDL, WHOLESALE: Pneumatic Tools
MACHINERY & EQPT, INDL, WHOLESALE: Processing & Packaging
MACHINERY & EQPT, INDL, WHOLESALE: Pulverizing
MACHINERY & EQPT, INDL, WHOLESALE: Robots
MACHINERY & EQPT, INDL, WHOLESALE: Safety Eqpt
MACHINERY & EQPT, INDL, WHOLESALE: Tool & Die Makers
MACHINERY & EQPT, INDL, WHOLESALE: Trailers, Indl
MACHINERY & EQPT, INDL, WHOLESALE: Woodworking
MACHINERY & EQPT, TEXTILE: Fabric Forming
MACHINERY & EQPT, WHOLESALE: Concrete Processing
MACHINERY & EQPT, WHOLESALE: Construction & Mining, Ladders
MACHINERY & EQPT, WHOLESALE: Construction, General
MACHINERY & EQPT, WHOLESALE: Contractors Materials
MACHINERY & EQPT, WHOLESALE: Logging & Forestry
MACHINERY & EQPT, WHOLESALE: Masonry
MACHINERY & EQPT, WHOLESALE: Oil Field Eqpt
MACHINERY & EQPT, WHOLESALE: Road Construction & Maintenance
MACHINERY & EQPT: Electroplating
MACHINERY & EQPT: Farm
MACHINERY & EQPT: Gas Producers, Generators/Other Rltd Eqpt
MACHINERY & EQPT: Liquid Automation
MACHINERY & EQPT: Metal Finishing, Plating Etc
MACHINERY & EQPT: Petroleum Refinery
MACHINERY & EQPT: Silver Recovery
MACHINERY & EQPT: Smelting & Refining
MACHINERY & EQPT: Vibratory Parts Handling Eqpt
MACHINERY BASES
MACHINERY, CALCULATING: Calculators & Adding
MACHINERY, COMMERCIAL LAUNDRY & Drycleaning: Ironers
MACHINERY, COMMERCIAL LAUNDRY: Dryers, Incl Coin-Operated
MACHINERY, EQPT & SUPPLIES: Parking Facility
MACHINERY, FOOD PRDTS: Beverage
MACHINERY, FOOD PRDTS: Choppers, Commercial
MACHINERY, FOOD PRDTS: Cutting, Chopping, Grinding, Mixing
MACHINERY, FOOD PRDTS: Food Processing, Smokers

PRODUCT INDEX

MACHINERY, FOOD PRDTS: Mixers, Commercial
MACHINERY, FOOD PRDTS: Presses, Cheese, Beet, Cider & Sugar
MACHINERY, FOOD PRDTS: Processing, Poultry
MACHINERY, FOOD PRDTS: Slicers, Commercial
MACHINERY, LUBRICATION: Automatic
MACHINERY, MAILING: Mailing
MACHINERY, MAILING: Postage Meters
MACHINERY, METALWORKING: Assembly, Including Robotic
MACHINERY, METALWORKING: Coil Winding, For Springs
MACHINERY, METALWORKING: Coiling
MACHINERY, METALWORKING: Cutting & Slitting
MACHINERY, METALWORKING: Cutting-Up Lines
MACHINERY, METALWORKING: Drawing
MACHINERY, METALWORKING: Rotary Slitters, Metalworking
MACHINERY, METALWORKING: Screw Driving
MACHINERY, OFFICE: Paper Handling
MACHINERY, OFFICE: Perforators
MACHINERY, OFFICE: Time Clocks &Time Recording Devices
MACHINERY, PACKAGING: Aerating, Beverages
MACHINERY, PACKAGING: Canning, Food
MACHINERY, PACKAGING: Packing & Wrapping
MACHINERY, PACKAGING: Vacuum
MACHINERY, PACKAGING: Wrapping
MACHINERY, PAPER INDUSTRY: Converting, Die Cutting & Stampng
MACHINERY, PAPER INDUSTRY: Fourdrinier
MACHINERY, PAPER INDUSTRY: Paper Mill, Plating, Etc
MACHINERY, PAPER INDUSTRY: Pulp Mill
MACHINERY, PAPER INDUSTRY: Sandpaper
MACHINERY, PRINTING TRADES: Mats, Advertising & Newspaper
MACHINERY, PRINTING TRADES: Plates
MACHINERY, PRINTING TRADES: Plates, Engravers' Metal
MACHINERY, PRINTING TRADES: Plates, Offset
MACHINERY, PRINTING TRADES: Type Casting, Founding/Melting
MACHINERY, TEXTILE: Braiding
MACHINERY, TEXTILE: Embroidery
MACHINERY, TEXTILE: Printing
MACHINERY, TEXTILE: Silk Screens
MACHINERY, WOODWORKING: Cabinet Makers'
MACHINERY, WOODWORKING: Furniture Makers
MACHINERY, WOODWORKING: Lathes, Wood Turning Includes Access
MACHINERY, WOODWORKING: Pattern Makers'
MACHINERY/EQPT, INDL, WHOL: Cleaning, High Press, Sand/Steam
MACHINERY/EQPT, INDL, WHOL: Machinist Precision Measrng Tool
MACHINERY: Ammunition & Explosives Loading
MACHINERY: Assembly, Exc Metalworking
MACHINERY: Automobile Garage, Frame Straighteners
MACHINERY: Automotive Maintenance
MACHINERY: Automotive Related
MACHINERY: Binding
MACHINERY: Blasting, Electrical
MACHINERY: Bottle Washing & Sterilzing
MACHINERY: Bottling & Canning
MACHINERY: Brewery & Malting
MACHINERY: Bridge Or Gate, Hydraulic
MACHINERY: Centrifugal
MACHINERY: Clay Working & Tempering
MACHINERY: Concrete Prdts
MACHINERY: Construction
MACHINERY: Cryogenic, Industrial
MACHINERY: Custom
MACHINERY: Deburring
MACHINERY: Die Casting
MACHINERY: Electrical Discharge Erosion
MACHINERY: Electronic Component Making
MACHINERY: Engraving
MACHINERY: Extruding
MACHINERY: Fiber Optics Strand Coating
MACHINERY: Folding
MACHINERY: Gas Separators
MACHINERY: Gear Cutting & Finishing
MACHINERY: General, Industrial, NEC
MACHINERY: Glassmaking
MACHINERY: Grinding
MACHINERY: Ice Cream
MACHINERY: Industrial, NEC
MACHINERY: Jewelers
MACHINERY: Kilns
MACHINERY: Knitting
MACHINERY: Labeling
MACHINERY: Logging Eqpt
MACHINERY: Marking, Metalworking
MACHINERY: Metalworking
MACHINERY: Milling
MACHINERY: Mining
MACHINERY: Pack-Up Assemblies, Wheel Overhaul
MACHINERY: Packaging
MACHINERY: Paint Making
MACHINERY: Paper Industry Miscellaneous
MACHINERY: Pharmaciutical
MACHINERY: Plastic Working
MACHINERY: Polishing & Buffing
MACHINERY: Printing Presses
MACHINERY: Recycling
MACHINERY: Riveting
MACHINERY: Road Construction & Maintenance
MACHINERY: Robots, Molding & Forming Plastics
MACHINERY: Rubber Working
MACHINERY: Saw & Sawing
MACHINERY: Screening Eqpt, Electric
MACHINERY: Semiconductor Manufacturing
MACHINERY: Separation Eqpt, Magnetic
MACHINERY: Service Industry, NEC
MACHINERY: Sheet Metal Working
MACHINERY: Sifting & Screening
MACHINERY: Specialty
MACHINERY: Stone Working
MACHINERY: Tapping
MACHINERY: Textile
MACHINERY: Tire Retreading
MACHINERY: Tire Shredding
MACHINERY: Wire Drawing
MACHINERY: Woodworking
MACHINES: Forming, Sheet Metal
MACHINISTS' TOOLS & MACHINES: Measuring, Metalworking Type
MACHINISTS' TOOLS: Measuring, Precision
MACHINISTS' TOOLS: Precision
MAGAZINE STAND
MAGNESIUM
MAGNESIUM
MAGNETIC INK & OPTICAL SCANNING EQPT
MAGNETIC RESONANCE IMAGING DEVICES: Nonmedical
MAGNETIC TAPE, AUDIO: Prerecorded
MAGNETS: Permanent
MAIL-ORDER HOUSE, NEC
MAIL-ORDER HOUSES: Books, Exc Book Clubs
MAIL-ORDER HOUSES: Cards
MAIL-ORDER HOUSES: Cheese
MAIL-ORDER HOUSES: Computers & Peripheral Eqpt
MAIL-ORDER HOUSES: Educational Splys & Eqpt
MAIL-ORDER HOUSES: Fitness & Sporting Goods
MAIL-ORDER HOUSES: Food
MAIL-ORDER HOUSES: Furniture & Furnishings
MAIL-ORDER HOUSES: General Merchandise
MAIL-ORDER HOUSES: Gift Items
MAIL-ORDER HOUSES: Novelty Merchandise
MAIL-ORDER HOUSES: Record & Tape, Music Or Video Club
MAIL-ORDER HOUSES: Tools & Hardware
MAILBOX RENTAL & RELATED SVCS
MAILING & MESSENGER SVCS
MAILING LIST: Compilers
MAILING MACHINES WHOLESALERS
MAILING SVCS, NEC
MANAGEMENT CONSULTING SVCS: Automation & Robotics
MANAGEMENT CONSULTING SVCS: Business
MANAGEMENT CONSULTING SVCS: Construction Project
MANAGEMENT CONSULTING SVCS: Corporation Organizing
MANAGEMENT CONSULTING SVCS: General
MANAGEMENT CONSULTING SVCS: Industrial
MANAGEMENT CONSULTING SVCS: Industry Specialist
MANAGEMENT CONSULTING SVCS: New Products & Svcs
MANAGEMENT CONSULTING SVCS: Public Utilities
MANAGEMENT CONSULTING SVCS: Real Estate
MANAGEMENT CONSULTING SVCS: Training & Development
MANAGEMENT CONSULTING SVCS: Transportation
MANAGEMENT SERVICES
MANAGEMENT SVCS, FACILITIES SUPPORT: Environ Remediation
MANAGEMENT SVCS: Administrative
MANAGEMENT SVCS: Business
MANAGEMENT SVCS: Construction
MANAGEMENT SVCS: Financial, Business
MANHOLES & COVERS: Metal
MANICURE PREPARATIONS
MANIFOLDS: Pipe, Fabricated From Purchased Pipe
MANNEQUINS
MANUFACTURED & MOBILE HOME DEALERS
MANUFACTURING INDUSTRIES, NEC
MAPS
MAPS & CHARTS, WHOLESALE
MARBLE, BUILDING: Cut & Shaped
MARINAS
MARINE CARGO HANDLING SVCS
MARINE HARDWARE
MARINE PROPELLER REPAIR SVCS
MARINE SPLY DEALERS
MARINE SPLYS WHOLESALERS
MARKETS: Meat & fish
MARKING DEVICES
MARKING DEVICES: Canceling Stamps, Hand, Rubber Or Metal
MARKING DEVICES: Date Stamps, Hand, Rubber Or Metal
MARKING DEVICES: Embossing Seals & Hand Stamps
MARKING DEVICES: Embossing Seals, Corporate & Official
MARKING DEVICES: Figures, Metal
MARKING DEVICES: Letters, Metal
MARKING DEVICES: Numbering Stamps, Hand, Rubber Or Metal
MARKING DEVICES: Pads, Inking & Stamping
MARKING DEVICES: Screens, Textile Printing
MARKING DEVICES: Stationary Embossers, Personal
MARKING DEVICES: Textile Making Stamps, Hand, Rubber/Metal
MASQUERADE OR THEATRICAL COSTUMES STORES
MASSAGE MACHINES, ELECTRIC: Barber & Beauty Shops
MASSAGE PARLORS
MASTIC ROOFING COMPOSITION
MASTS: Cast Aluminum
MATERIAL GRINDING & PULVERIZING SVCS NEC
MATERIALS HANDLING EQPT WHOLESALERS
MATS & MATTING, MADE FROM PURCHASED WIRE
MATS OR MATTING, NEC: Rubber
MATS, MATTING & PADS: Auto, Floor, Exc Rubber Or Plastic
MATS, MATTING & PADS: Nonwoven
MATS: Table, Plastic & Textile
MATTRESS STORES
MEAL DELIVERY PROGRAMS
MEAT & FISH MARKETS: Food & Freezer Plans, Meat
MEAT & FISH MARKETS: Freezer Provisioners, Meat
MEAT & MEAT PRDTS WHOLESALERS
MEAT CUTTING & PACKING
MEAT MARKETS
MEAT PRDTS: Bacon, Side & Sliced, From Purchased Meat
MEAT PRDTS: Cooked Meats, From Purchased Meat
MEAT PRDTS: Corned Beef, From Slaughtered Meat
MEAT PRDTS: Cured, From Slaughtered Meat
MEAT PRDTS: Frozen
MEAT PRDTS: Luncheon Meat, From Purchased Meat
MEAT PRDTS: Pork, Cured, From Purchased Meat
MEAT PRDTS: Pork, From Slaughtered Meat
MEAT PRDTS: Prepared Beef Prdts From Purchased Beef
MEAT PRDTS: Prepared Pork Prdts, From Purchased Meat
MEAT PRDTS: Sausages, From Purchased Meat
MEAT PRDTS: Sausages, From Slaughtered Meat
MEAT PRDTS: Snack Sticks, Incl Jerky, From Purchased Meat
MEAT PRDTS: Veal, From Slaughtered Meat
MEAT PROCESSED FROM PURCHASED CARCASSES
MEATS, PACKAGED FROZEN: Wholesalers
MECHANICAL INSTRUMENT REPAIR SVCS
MEDIA BUYING AGENCIES
MEDIA: Magnetic & Optical Recording
MEDICAL & HOSPITAL EQPT WHOLESALERS
MEDICAL & HOSPITAL SPLYS: Radiation Shielding Garments
MEDICAL & SURGICAL SPLYS: Atomizers, Medical
MEDICAL & SURGICAL SPLYS: Bandages & Dressings
MEDICAL & SURGICAL SPLYS: Braces, Elastic
MEDICAL & SURGICAL SPLYS: Braces, Orthopedic
MEDICAL & SURGICAL SPLYS: Canes, Orthopedic
MEDICAL & SURGICAL SPLYS: Clothing, Fire Resistant & Protect
MEDICAL & SURGICAL SPLYS: Cosmetic Restorations
MEDICAL & SURGICAL SPLYS: Foot Appliances, Orthopedic

PRODUCT INDEX

MEDICAL & SURGICAL SPLYS: Grafts, Artificial
MEDICAL & SURGICAL SPLYS: Hosiery, Support
MEDICAL & SURGICAL SPLYS: Limbs, Artificial
MEDICAL & SURGICAL SPLYS: Live Preservers, Exc Cork & Inflat
MEDICAL & SURGICAL SPLYS: Orthopedic Appliances
MEDICAL & SURGICAL SPLYS: Personal Safety Eqpt
MEDICAL & SURGICAL SPLYS: Prosthetic Appliances
MEDICAL & SURGICAL SPLYS: Respiratory Protect Eqpt, Personal
MEDICAL & SURGICAL SPLYS: Splints, Pneumatic & Wood
MEDICAL & SURGICAL SPLYS: Stretchers
MEDICAL & SURGICAL SPLYS: Technical Aids, Handicapped
MEDICAL & SURGICAL SPLYS: Welders' Hoods
MEDICAL CENTERS
MEDICAL EQPT REPAIR SVCS, NON-ELECTRIC
MEDICAL EQPT: CAT Scanner Or Computerized Axial Tomography
MEDICAL EQPT: Diagnostic
MEDICAL EQPT: Electromedical Apparatus
MEDICAL EQPT: Electrotherapeutic Apparatus
MEDICAL EQPT: Laser Systems
MEDICAL EQPT: MRI/Magnetic Resonance Imaging Devs, Nuclear
MEDICAL EQPT: Pacemakers
MEDICAL EQPT: Patient Monitoring
MEDICAL EQPT: Sterilizers
MEDICAL EQPT: Ultrasonic Scanning Devices
MEDICAL EQPT: X-Ray Apparatus & Tubes, Radiographic
MEDICAL FIELD ASSOCIATION
MEDICAL INSURANCE CLAIM PROCESSING: Contract Or Fee Basis
MEDICAL SUNDRIES: Rubber
MEDICAL TRAINING SERVICES
MEDICAL, DENTAL & HOSP EQPT, WHOLESALE: X-ray Film & Splys
MEDICAL, DENTAL & HOSPITAL EQPT, WHOL: Dentists' Prof Splys
MEDICAL, DENTAL & HOSPITAL EQPT, WHOL: Hospital Eqpt & Splys
MEDICAL, DENTAL & HOSPITAL EQPT, WHOL: Hosptl Eqpt/Furniture
MEDICAL, DENTAL & HOSPITAL EQPT, WHOL: Surgical Eqpt & Splys
MEDICAL, DENTAL & HOSPITAL EQPT, WHOLESALE: Diagnostic, Med
MEDICAL, DENTAL & HOSPITAL EQPT, WHOLESALE: Med Eqpt & Splys
MEDICAL, DENTAL & HOSPITAL EQPT, WHOLESALE: Orthopedic
MEDICAL, DENTAL & HOSPITAL EQPT, WHOLESALE: Safety
MEDICAL, DENTAL & HOSPITAL EQPT, WHOLESALE: Therapy
MEDICAL, DENTAL/HOSPITAL EQPT, WHOL: Veterinarian Eqpt/Sply
MELAMINE RESINS: Melamine-Formaldehyde
MEMBERSHIP HOTELS
MEMBERSHIP ORGANIZATIONS, BUSINESS: Contractors' Association
MEMBERSHIP ORGANIZATIONS, CIVIC, SOCIAL/FRAT: Social Assoc
MEMBERSHIP ORGANIZATIONS, NEC: Bowling club
MEMBERSHIP ORGANIZATIONS, NEC: Flying Club
MEMBERSHIP ORGANIZATIONS, NEC: Personal Interest
MEMBERSHIP ORGANIZATIONS, REL: Christian & Reformed Church
MEMBERSHIP ORGANIZATIONS, REL: Churches, Temples & Shrines
MEMBERSHIP ORGANIZATIONS, RELIGIOUS: Brethren Church
MEMBERSHIP ORGANIZATIONS, RELIGIOUS: Nonchurch
MEMBERSHIP ORGS, BUSINESS: Shipping/Steamship Co Assoc
MEMBERSHIP ORGS, RELIGIOUS: Non-Denominational Church
MEMORIALS, MONUMENTS & MARKERS
MEN'S & BOYS' CLOTHING STORES
MEN'S & BOYS' CLOTHING WHOLESALERS, NEC
MEN'S & BOYS' SPORTSWEAR CLOTHING STORES
MEN'S & BOYS' SPORTSWEAR WHOLESALERS
MEN'S & BOYS' WORK CLOTHING WHOLESALERS
METAL & STEEL PRDTS: Abrasive
METAL COMPONENTS: Prefabricated
METAL CUTTING SVCS
METAL DETECTORS
METAL FABRICATORS: Architechtural
METAL FABRICATORS: Plate
METAL FABRICATORS: Sheet
METAL FABRICATORS: Structural, Ship
METAL FINISHING SVCS
METAL MINING SVCS
METAL RESHAPING & REPLATING SVCS
METAL SERVICE CENTERS & OFFICES
METAL SLITTING & SHEARING
METAL SPINNING FOR THE TRADE
METAL STAMPING, FOR THE TRADE
METAL STAMPINGS: Ornamental
METAL STAMPINGS: Patterned
METAL TREATING COMPOUNDS
METAL TREATING: Cryogenic
METAL, TITANIUM: Sponge & Granules
METAL: Battery
METALS SVC CENTERS & WHOL: Structural Shapes, Iron Or Steel
METALS SVC CENTERS & WHOLESALERS: Bars, Metal
METALS SVC CENTERS & WHOLESALERS: Cable, Wire
METALS SVC CENTERS & WHOLESALERS: Casting, Rough,Iron/Steel
METALS SVC CENTERS & WHOLESALERS: Copper
METALS SVC CENTERS & WHOLESALERS: Ferroalloys
METALS SVC CENTERS & WHOLESALERS: Ferrous Metals
METALS SVC CENTERS & WHOLESALERS: Flat Prdts, Iron Or Steel
METALS SVC CENTERS & WHOLESALERS: Foundry Prdts
METALS SVC CENTERS & WHOLESALERS: Iron & Steel Prdt, Ferrous
METALS SVC CENTERS & WHOLESALERS: Lead
METALS SVC CENTERS & WHOLESALERS: Misc Nonferrous Prdts
METALS SVC CENTERS & WHOLESALERS: Pipe & Tubing, Steel
METALS SVC CENTERS & WHOLESALERS: Plates, Metal
METALS SVC CENTERS & WHOLESALERS: Rope, Wire, Exc Insulated
METALS SVC CENTERS & WHOLESALERS: Sheets, Metal
METALS SVC CENTERS & WHOLESALERS: Stampings, Metal
METALS SVC CENTERS & WHOLESALERS: Steel
METALS SVC CENTERS & WHOLESALERS: Tubing, Metal
METALS SVC CTRS & WHOLESALERS: Aluminum Bars, Rods, Etc
METALS: Precious NEC
METALS: Precious, Secondary
METALS: Primary Nonferrous, NEC
METALWORK: Miscellaneous
METALWORK: Ornamental
METALWORKING MACHINERY WHOLESALERS
METEOROLOGICAL INSTRUMENT REPAIR SVCS
METER READERS: Remote
METERING DEVICES: Flow Meters, Impeller & Counter Driven
METERING DEVICES: Gasoline Dispensing
METERING DEVICES: Water Quality Monitoring & Control Systems
METERS: Liquid
METERS: Pyrometers, Indl Process
MGMT CONSULTING SVCS: Matls, Incl Purch, Handle & Invntry
MICA PRDTS
MICROCIRCUITS, INTEGRATED: Semiconductor
MICROPHONES
MICROPROCESSORS
MICROPUBLISHER
MICROSCOPES
MICROWAVE COMPONENTS
MILITARY INSIGNIA
MILL PRDTS: Structural & Rail
MILLINERY SUPPLIES: Sweat Bands, Hat/Cap, From Purchsd Mtrls
MILLINERY SUPPLIES: Veils & Veiling, Bridal, Funeral, Etc
MILLING: Cereal Flour, Exc Rice
MILLING: Chemical
MILLING: Grains, Exc Rice
MILLS: Ferrous & Nonferrous
MILLWORK
MINE & QUARRY SVCS: Nonmetallic Minerals
MINE DEVELOPMENT SVCS: Nonmetallic Minerals
MINE EXPLORATION SVCS: Nonmetallic Minerals
MINE PUMPING OR DRAINING SVCS: Nonmetallic Minerals
MINERAL MINING: Nonmetallic
MINERAL WOOL
MINERAL WOOL INSULATION PRDTS
MINERALS: Ground Or Otherwise Treated
MINERALS: Ground or Treated
MINIATURES
MINING EXPLORATION & DEVELOPMENT SVCS
MINING MACHINERY & EQPT WHOLESALERS
MINING MACHINES & EQPT: Augers
MINING MACHINES & EQPT: Bits, Rock, Exc Oil/Gas Field Tools
MINING MACHINES & EQPT: Cages, Mine Shaft
MINING MACHINES & EQPT: Crushers, Stationary
MINING MACHINES & EQPT: Rock Crushing, Stationary
MINING MACHINES & EQPT: Shuttle Cars, Underground
MINING MACHINES/EQPT: Mine Car, Plow, Loader, Feeder/Eqpt
MINING SVCS, NEC: Bituminous
MIRRORS: Motor Vehicle
MISSILES: Ballistic, Complete
MIXERS: Hot Metal
MIXING EQPT
MIXTURES & BLOCKS: Asphalt Paving
MOBILE COMMUNICATIONS EQPT
MOBILE HOME & TRAILER REPAIR
MOBILE HOMES
MOBILE HOMES, EXC RECREATIONAL
MODELS
MODELS: General, Exc Toy
MODULES: Computer Logic
MOLDED RUBBER PRDTS
MOLDING COMPOUNDS
MOLDING SAND MINING
MOLDINGS & TRIM: Metal, Exc Automobile
MOLDINGS & TRIM: Wood
MOLDINGS OR TRIM: Automobile, Stamped Metal
MOLDINGS, ARCHITECTURAL: Plaster Of Paris
MOLDINGS: Picture Frame
MOLDS: Gray, Ingot, Cast Iron
MOLDS: Indl
MOLDS: Plastic Working & Foundry
MOLYBDENUM SILICON, EXC MADE IN BLAST FURNACES
MONORAIL SYSTEMS
MONUMENTS & GRAVE MARKERS, EXC TERRAZZO
MONUMENTS: Concrete
MONUMENTS: Cut Stone, Exc Finishing Or Lettering Only
MOPS: Floor & Dust
MORTAR
MOTION PICTURE & VIDEO PRODUCTION SVCS
MOTION PICTURE EQPT
MOTION PICTURE PRODUCTION & DISTRIBUTION: Television
MOTOR & GENERATOR PARTS: Electric
MOTOR HOMES
MOTOR REBUILDING SVCS, EXC AUTOMOTIVE
MOTOR REPAIR SVCS
MOTOR SCOOTERS & PARTS
MOTOR VEHICLE ASSEMBLY, COMPLETE: Ambulances
MOTOR VEHICLE ASSEMBLY, COMPLETE: Autos, Incl Specialty
MOTOR VEHICLE ASSEMBLY, COMPLETE: Bus/Large Spclty Vehicles
MOTOR VEHICLE ASSEMBLY, COMPLETE: Buses, All Types
MOTOR VEHICLE ASSEMBLY, COMPLETE: Cars, Armored
MOTOR VEHICLE ASSEMBLY, COMPLETE: Fire Department Vehicles
MOTOR VEHICLE ASSEMBLY, COMPLETE: Hearses
MOTOR VEHICLE ASSEMBLY, COMPLETE: Military Motor Vehicle
MOTOR VEHICLE ASSEMBLY, COMPLETE: Mobile Lounges
MOTOR VEHICLE ASSEMBLY, COMPLETE: Snow Plows
MOTOR VEHICLE ASSEMBLY, COMPLETE: Truck & Tractor Trucks
MOTOR VEHICLE ASSEMBLY, COMPLETE: Truck Tractors, Highway
MOTOR VEHICLE ASSEMBLY, COMPLETE: Wreckers, Tow Truck
MOTOR VEHICLE DEALERS: Automobiles, New & Used
MOTOR VEHICLE DEALERS: Cars, Used Only
MOTOR VEHICLE DEALERS: Pickups & Vans, Used
MOTOR VEHICLE DEALERS: Pickups, New & Used
MOTOR VEHICLE DEALERS: Trucks, Tractors/Trailers, New & Used
MOTOR VEHICLE DEALERS: Vans, New & Used
MOTOR VEHICLE PARTS & ACCESS: Acceleration Eqpt

PRODUCT INDEX

MOTOR VEHICLE PARTS & ACCESS: Air Conditioner Parts
MOTOR VEHICLE PARTS & ACCESS: Axel Housings & Shafts
MOTOR VEHICLE PARTS & ACCESS: Bearings
MOTOR VEHICLE PARTS & ACCESS: Body Components & Frames
MOTOR VEHICLE PARTS & ACCESS: Booster Cables, Jump-Start
MOTOR VEHICLE PARTS & ACCESS: Brakes, Air
MOTOR VEHICLE PARTS & ACCESS: Clutches
MOTOR VEHICLE PARTS & ACCESS: Connecting Rods
MOTOR VEHICLE PARTS & ACCESS: Cylinder Heads
MOTOR VEHICLE PARTS & ACCESS: Electrical Eqpt
MOTOR VEHICLE PARTS & ACCESS: Engines & Parts
MOTOR VEHICLE PARTS & ACCESS: Frames
MOTOR VEHICLE PARTS & ACCESS: Fuel Pumps
MOTOR VEHICLE PARTS & ACCESS: Fuel Systems & Parts
MOTOR VEHICLE PARTS & ACCESS: Gas Tanks
MOTOR VEHICLE PARTS & ACCESS: Gears
MOTOR VEHICLE PARTS & ACCESS: Heaters
MOTOR VEHICLE PARTS & ACCESS: Ice Scrapers & Window Brushes
MOTOR VEHICLE PARTS & ACCESS: Instrument Board Assemblies
MOTOR VEHICLE PARTS & ACCESS: Manifolds
MOTOR VEHICLE PARTS & ACCESS: Mufflers, Exhaust
MOTOR VEHICLE PARTS & ACCESS: Oil Strainers
MOTOR VEHICLE PARTS & ACCESS: Power Steering Eqpt
MOTOR VEHICLE PARTS & ACCESS: Propane Conversion Eqpt
MOTOR VEHICLE PARTS & ACCESS: Pumps, Hydraulic Fluid Power
MOTOR VEHICLE PARTS & ACCESS: Sanders, Safety
MOTOR VEHICLE PARTS & ACCESS: Tie Rods
MOTOR VEHICLE PARTS & ACCESS: Tire Valve Cores
MOTOR VEHICLE PARTS & ACCESS: Trailer Hitches
MOTOR VEHICLE PARTS & ACCESS: Transmission Housings Or Parts
MOTOR VEHICLE PARTS & ACCESS: Transmissions
MOTOR VEHICLE PARTS & ACCESS: Water Pumps
MOTOR VEHICLE PARTS & ACCESS: Wheel rims
MOTOR VEHICLE PARTS & ACCESS: Wind Deflectors
MOTOR VEHICLE PARTS & ACCESS: Wiring Harness Sets
MOTOR VEHICLE SPLYS & PARTS WHOLESALERS: New
MOTOR VEHICLE SPLYS & PARTS WHOLESALERS: Used
MOTOR VEHICLE: Hardware
MOTOR VEHICLE: Radiators
MOTOR VEHICLE: Shock Absorbers
MOTOR VEHICLE: Wheels
MOTOR VEHICLES & CAR BODIES
MOTOR VEHICLES, WHOLESALE: Ambulances
MOTOR VEHICLES, WHOLESALE: Fire Trucks
MOTOR VEHICLES, WHOLESALE: Trailers for passenger vehicles
MOTOR VEHICLES, WHOLESALE: Trailers, Truck, New & Used
MOTOR VEHICLES, WHOLESALE: Truck bodies
MOTOR VEHICLES, WHOLESALE: Truck tractors
MOTOR VEHICLES, WHOLESALE: Trucks, commercial
MOTORCYCLE & BICYCLE PARTS: Frames
MOTORCYCLE ACCESS
MOTORCYCLE DEALERS
MOTORCYCLE DEALERS
MOTORCYCLE PARTS & ACCESS DEALERS
MOTORCYCLE PARTS: Wholesalers
MOTORCYCLE REPAIR SHOPS
MOTORCYCLES & RELATED PARTS
MOTORCYCLES: Wholesalers
MOTORS: Electric
MOTORS: Generators
MOTORS: Pneumatic
MOTORS: Starting, Automotive & Aircraft
MOTORS: Torque
MOUNTING RINGS, MOTOR Rubber Covered Or Bonded
MOUTHWASHES
MOVING SVC: Local
MOWERS & ACCESSORIES
MUSEUMS
MUSIC DISTRIBUTION APPARATUS
MUSIC RECORDING PRODUCER
MUSICAL INSTRUMENT REPAIR
MUSICAL INSTRUMENTS & ACCESS: Carrying Cases
MUSICAL INSTRUMENTS & ACCESS: NEC
MUSICAL INSTRUMENTS & ACCESS: Pipe Organs
MUSICAL INSTRUMENTS & PARTS: Brass
MUSICAL INSTRUMENTS & PARTS: Percussion
MUSICAL INSTRUMENTS & PARTS: String
MUSICAL INSTRUMENTS & SPLYS STORES
MUSICAL INSTRUMENTS & SPLYS STORES: String instruments
MUSICAL INSTRUMENTS WHOLESALERS
MUSICAL INSTRUMENTS: Banjos & Parts
MUSICAL INSTRUMENTS: Bells
MUSICAL INSTRUMENTS: Carillon Bells
MUSICAL INSTRUMENTS: Fretted Instruments & Parts
MUSICAL INSTRUMENTS: Guitars & Parts, Electric & Acoustic
MUSICAL INSTRUMENTS: Keyboards
MUSICAL INSTRUMENTS: Keyboards & Parts|
MUSICAL INSTRUMENTS: Organ Parts & Materials
MUSICAL INSTRUMENTS: Organs
MUSICAL INSTRUMENTS: Recorders, Musical

N

NAIL SALONS
NAME PLATES: Engraved Or Etched
NAMEPLATES
NATIONAL SECURITY FORCES
NATIONAL SECURITY, GOVERNMENT: Air Force
NATIONAL SECURITY, GOVERNMENT: Army
NATURAL GAS DISTRIBUTION TO CONSUMERS
NATURAL GAS LIQUIDS PRODUCTION
NATURAL GAS POWER BROKER
NATURAL GAS PRODUCTION
NATURAL GAS TRANSMISSION
NATURAL GAS TRANSMISSION & DISTRIBUTION
NATURAL GASOLINE PRODUCTION
NATURAL PROPANE PRODUCTION
NAUTICAL REPAIR SVCS
NAVIGATIONAL SYSTEMS & INSTRUMENTS
NEPHELINE SYENITE MINING
NET & NETTING PRDTS
NETS: Launderers & Dyers
NETTING: Cargo
NEW & USED CAR DEALERS
NEWS DEALERS & NEWSSTANDS
NEWS SYNDICATES
NEWSSTAND
NICKEL ALLOY
NIPPLES: Rubber
NONCURRENT CARRYING WIRING DEVICES
NONDURABLE GOODS WHOLESALERS, NEC
NONFERROUS: Rolling & Drawing, NEC
NONMETALLIC MINERALS & CONCENTRATE WHOLESALERS
NONMETALLIC MINERALS DEVELOPMENT & TEST BORING SVC
NONMETALLIC MINERALS: Support Activities, Exc Fuels
NOTEBOOKS, MADE FROM PURCHASED MATERIALS
NOTIONS: Pins, Straight, Steel Or Brass
NOVELTIES
NOVELTIES, DURABLE, WHOLESALE
NOVELTIES: Leather
NOVELTIES: Plastic
NOVELTY SHOPS
NOZZLES: Fire Fighting
NOZZLES: Spray, Aerosol, Paint Or Insecticide
NUCLEAR DETECTORS: Solid State
NUCLEAR FUELS SCRAP REPROCESSING
NUCLEAR REACTORS: Military Or Indl
NUCLEAR SHIELDING: Metal Plate
NURSERIES & LAWN & GARDEN SPLY STORE, RET: Fountain, Outdoor
NURSERIES & LAWN & GARDEN SPLY STORE, RET: Lawn/Garden Splys
NURSERIES & LAWN & GARDEN SPLY STORES, RETAIL
NURSERIES & LAWN & GARDEN SPLY STORES, RETAIL: Fertilizer
NURSERIES & LAWN & GARDEN SPLY STORES, RETAIL: Lawn Ornament
NURSERIES & LAWN & GARDEN SPLY STORES, RETAIL: Top Soil
NURSERIES & LAWN/GARDEN SPLY STORE, RET: Lawnmowers/Tractors
NURSERY & GARDEN CENTERS
NURSING CARE FACILITIES: Skilled
NUTRITION SVCS
NUTS: Metal
NYLON FIBERS

O

OFCS & CLINICS,MEDICAL DRS: Specl, Physician Or Surgn, ENT
OFFICE EQPT WHOLESALERS
OFFICE EQPT, WHOL: Check Writing, Signing/Endorsing Mach
OFFICE EQPT, WHOLESALE: Blueprinting
OFFICE EQPT, WHOLESALE: Duplicating Machines
OFFICE EQPT, WHOLESALE: Typewriter & Dictation
OFFICE EQPT, WHOLESALE: Typewriters
OFFICE FIXTURES: Exc Wood
OFFICE FIXTURES: Wood
OFFICE FURNITURE REPAIR & MAINTENANCE SVCS
OFFICE SPLY & STATIONERY STORES
OFFICE SPLY & STATIONERY STORES: Office Forms & Splys
OFFICE SPLY & STATIONERY STORES: School Splys
OFFICE SPLYS, NEC, WHOLESALE
OFFICES & CLINICS OF DOCTORS OF MEDICINE: Dermatologist
OFFICES & CLINICS OF DOCTORS OF MEDICINE: Surgeon
OFFICES & CLINICS OF DRS OF MED: Cardiologist & Vascular
OFFICES & CLINICS OF DRS OF MED: Physician/Surgeon, Int Med
OFFICES & CLINICS OF DRS OF MEDICINE: Med Clinic, Pri Care
OIL & GAS FIELD EQPT: Drill Rigs
OIL & GAS FIELD MACHINERY
OIL ABSORPTION Eqpt
OIL FIELD MACHINERY & EQPT
OIL FIELD SVCS, NEC
OIL ROYALTY TRADERS
OIL TREATING COMPOUNDS
OILS & ESSENTIAL OILS
OILS & GREASES: Blended & Compounded
OILS & GREASES: Lubricating
OILS: Cutting
OILS: Lubricating
OILS: Lubricating
OILS: Mineral, Natural
OILS: Road
OINTMENTS
OLEFINS
ON-LINE DATABASE INFORMATION RETRIEVAL SVCS
OPENERS, BOTTLE Stamped Metal
OPERATOR TRAINING, COMPUTER
OPERATOR: Apartment Buildings
OPERATOR: Nonresidential Buildings
OPHTHALMIC GOODS
OPHTHALMIC GOODS WHOLESALERS
OPHTHALMIC GOODS, NEC, WHOLESALE: Contact Lenses
OPHTHALMIC GOODS, NEC, WHOLESALE: Lenses
OPHTHALMIC GOODS: Lenses, Ophthalmic
OPTICAL GOODS STORES
OPTICAL GOODS STORES: Eyeglasses, Prescription
OPTICAL INSTRUMENTS & APPARATUS
OPTICAL INSTRUMENTS & LENSES
OPTICAL SCANNING SVCS
OPTOMETRIC EQPT & SPLYS WHOLESALERS
OPTOMETRISTS' OFFICES
ORAL PREPARATIONS
ORDNANCE
ORGAN TUNING & REPAIR SVCS
ORGANIZATIONS: Civic & Social
ORGANIZATIONS: Medical Research
ORGANIZATIONS: Physical Research, Noncommercial
ORGANIZATIONS: Religious
ORGANIZATIONS: Scientific Research Agency
ORNAMENTS: Christmas Tree, Exc Electrical & Glass
ORNAMENTS: Lawn
ORTHOPEDIC SUNDRIES: Molded Rubber
OUTBOARD MOTORS & PARTS
OUTLETS: Electric, Convenience
OVENS: Core Baking & Mold Drying
OVENS: Laboratory

P

PACKAGE DESIGN SVCS
PACKAGED FROZEN FOODS WHOLESALERS, NEC
PACKAGING & LABELING SVCS
PACKAGING MATERIALS, WHOLESALE
PACKAGING MATERIALS: Paper
PACKAGING MATERIALS: Paper, Coated Or Laminated

PRODUCT INDEX

PACKAGING MATERIALS: Paperboard Backs For Blister/Skin Pkgs
PACKAGING MATERIALS: Plastic Film, Coated Or Laminated
PACKAGING MATERIALS: Polystyrene Foam
PACKAGING: Blister Or Bubble Formed, Plastic
PACKING & CRATING SVC
PACKING MATERIALS: Mechanical
PACKING SVCS: Shipping
PACKING: Metallic
PADDING: Foamed Plastics
PADS: Athletic, Protective
PAILS: Shipping, Metal
PAINT & PAINTING SPLYS STORE
PAINT DRIERS
PAINT STORE
PAINTING SVC: Metal Prdts
PAINTS & ADDITIVES
PAINTS & ALLIED PRODUCTS
PAINTS, VARNISHES & SPLYS WHOLESALERS
PAINTS, VARNISHES & SPLYS, WHOLESALE: Paints
PAINTS, VARNISHES & SPLYS, WHOLESALE: Stain
PAINTS, VARNISHES & SPLYS, WHOLESALE: Thinner
PAINTS: Asphalt Or Bituminous
PAINTS: Marine
PAINTS: Oil Or Alkyd Vehicle Or Water Thinned
PALLET REPAIR SVCS
PALLETIZERS & DEPALLETIZERS
PALLETS
PALLETS & SKIDS: Wood
PALLETS: Corrugated
PALLETS: Metal
PALLETS: Plastic
PALLETS: Wooden
PAN GLAZING SVC
PANEL & DISTRIBUTION BOARDS & OTHER RELATED APPARATUS
PANEL & DISTRIBUTION BOARDS: Electric
PANELS & SECTIONS: Prefabricated, Concrete
PANELS: Building, Metal
PANELS: Building, Plastic, NEC
PANELS: Building, Wood
PAPER & BOARD: Die-cut
PAPER CONVERTING
PAPER MANUFACTURERS: Exc Newsprint
PAPER NAPKINS WHOLESALERS
PAPER PRDTS: Book Covers
PAPER PRDTS: Infant & Baby Prdts
PAPER PRDTS: Napkins, Made From Purchased Materials
PAPER PRDTS: Napkins, Sanitary, Made From Purchased Material
PAPER PRDTS: Sanitary
PAPER PRDTS: Sanitary Tissue Paper
PAPER PRDTS: Tampons, Sanitary, Made From Purchased Material
PAPER PRDTS: Towels, Napkins/Tissue Paper, From Purchd Mtrls
PAPER PRDTS: Wrappers, Blank, Made From Purchased Materials
PAPER, WHOLESALE: Printing
PAPER: Adding Machine Rolls, Made From Purchased Materials
PAPER: Adhesive
PAPER: Art
PAPER: Book
PAPER: Building, Insulating & Packaging
PAPER: Building, Insulation
PAPER: Cardboard
PAPER: Chemically Treated, Made From Purchased Materials
PAPER: Cloth, Lined, Made From Purchased Materials
PAPER: Coated & Laminated, NEC
PAPER: Coated, Exc Photographic, Carbon Or Abrasive
PAPER: Enameled, Made From Purchased Materials
PAPER: Fine
PAPER: Gummed, Made From Purchased Materials
PAPER: Milk Filter
PAPER: Newsprint
PAPER: Packaging
PAPER: Parchment
PAPER: Printer
PAPER: Specialty
PAPER: Specialty Or Chemically Treated
PAPER: Tissue
PAPER: Wallpaper
PAPER: Waterproof
PAPER: Waxed, Made From Purchased Materials
PAPER: Wrapping
PAPER: Wrapping & Packaging
PAPERBOARD
PAPERBOARD CONVERTING
PAPERBOARD PRDTS: Container Board
PAPERBOARD PRDTS: Folding Boxboard
PAPERBOARD PRDTS: Packaging Board
PAPERBOARD PRDTS: Specialty Board
PAPERBOARD PRDTS: Stencil Board
PAPERBOARD: Corrugated
PAPETERIES & WRITING PAPER SETS
PARKING GARAGE
PARKING METERS
PARTICLEBOARD: Laminated, Plastic
PARTITIONS & FIXTURES: Except Wood
PARTITIONS WHOLESALERS
PARTITIONS: Nonwood, Floor Attached
PARTITIONS: Solid Fiber, Made From Purchased Materials
PARTITIONS: Wood & Fixtures
PARTS: Metal
PARTY & SPECIAL EVENT PLANNING SVCS
PASTES, FLAVORING
PASTES: Metal
PATIENT MONITORING EQPT WHOLESALERS
PATTERNS: Indl
PAVERS
PAVING MATERIALS: Coal Tar, Not From Refineries
PAVING MATERIALS: Prefabricated, Concrete
PAVING MIXTURES
PAYROLL SVCS
PENCILS & PENS WHOLESALERS
PENS & PARTS: Ball Point
PENS & PENCILS: Mechanical, NEC
PERFUME: Perfumes, Natural Or Synthetic
PERIODICALS, WHOLESALE
PERSONAL APPEARANCE SVCS
PERSONAL CREDIT INSTITUTIONS: Financing, Autos, Furniture
PERSONAL DEVELOPMENT SCHOOL
PERSONAL SVCS, NEC
PEST CONTROL IN STRUCTURES SVCS
PEST CONTROL SVCS
PESTICIDES
PESTICIDES WHOLESALERS
PET COLLARS, LEASHES, MUZZLES & HARNESSES: Leather
PET SPLYS
PET SPLYS WHOLESALERS
PETROLEUM & PETROLEUM PRDTS, WHOLESALE Crude Oil
PETROLEUM & PETROLEUM PRDTS, WHOLESALE Diesel Fuel
PETROLEUM & PETROLEUM PRDTS, WHOLESALE Engine Fuels & Oils
PETROLEUM & PETROLEUM PRDTS, WHOLESALE Fuel Oil
PETROLEUM & PETROLEUM PRDTS, WHOLESALE: Bulk Stations
PETROLEUM PRDTS WHOLESALERS
PETS & PET SPLYS, WHOLESALE
PEWTER WARE
PHARMACEUTICAL PREPARATIONS: Adrenal
PHARMACEUTICAL PREPARATIONS: Druggists' Preparations
PHARMACEUTICAL PREPARATIONS: Emulsions
PHARMACEUTICAL PREPARATIONS: Medicines, Capsule Or Ampule
PHARMACEUTICAL PREPARATIONS: Pills
PHARMACEUTICAL PREPARATIONS: Proprietary Drug PRDTS
PHARMACEUTICAL PREPARATIONS: Solutions
PHARMACEUTICAL PREPARATIONS: Tablets
PHARMACEUTICALS
PHARMACEUTICALS: Medicinal & Botanical Prdts
PHARMACIES & DRUG STORES
PHOSPHATES
PHOTOCOPY MACHINE REPAIR SVCS
PHOTOCOPY MACHINES
PHOTOCOPYING & DUPLICATING SVCS
PHOTOELECTRIC DEVICES: Magnetic
PHOTOENGRAVING SVC
PHOTOFINISHING LABORATORIES
PHOTOGRAPHIC EQPT & SPLYS
PHOTOGRAPHIC EQPT & SPLYS WHOLESALERS
PHOTOGRAPHIC EQPT & SPLYS, WHOLESALE: Project, Motion/Slide
PHOTOGRAPHIC EQPT & SPLYS: Blueprint Reproduction Mach/Eqpt
PHOTOGRAPHIC EQPT & SPLYS: Film, Cloth & Paper, Sensitized
PHOTOGRAPHIC EQPT & SPLYS: Graphic Arts Plates, Sensitized
PHOTOGRAPHIC EQPT & SPLYS: Lens Shades, Camera
PHOTOGRAPHIC EQPT & SPLYS: Paper & Cloth, All Types, NEC
PHOTOGRAPHIC EQPT & SPLYS: Plates, Sensitized
PHOTOGRAPHIC EQPT & SPLYS: Printing Eqpt
PHOTOGRAPHIC EQPT & SPLYS: Processing Eqpt
PHOTOGRAPHIC EQPT & SPLYS: Toners, Prprd, Not Chem Plnts
PHOTOGRAPHIC EQPT & SPLYS: Tripods, Camera & Projector
PHOTOGRAPHIC EQPT REPAIR SVCS
PHOTOGRAPHY SVCS: Commercial
PHOTOGRAPHY SVCS: Still Or Video
PHOTOGRAPHY: Aerial
PHOTOTYPESETTING SVC
PHOTOVOLTAIC Solid State
PHYSICAL FITNESS CENTERS
PHYSICIANS' OFFICES & CLINICS: Medical
PHYSICIANS' OFFICES & CLINICS: Medical doctors
PICTURE FRAMES: Metal
PICTURE FRAMES: Wood
PICTURE FRAMING SVCS, CUSTOM
PIECE GOODS & NOTIONS WHOLESALERS
PIECE GOODS, NOTIONS & DRY GOODS, WHOL: Fabrics Broadwoven
PIECE GOODS, NOTIONS & DRY GOODS, WHOL: Textile Converters
PIECE GOODS, NOTIONS & DRY GOODS, WHOLESALE: Fabrics, Lace
PIECE GOODS, NOTIONS & DRY GOODS, WHOLESALE: Sewing Access
PIECE GOODS, NOTIONS & DRY GOODS, WHOLESALE: Tape, Textile
PIECE GOODS, NOTIONS & OTHER DRY GOODS, WHOL: Flags/Banners
PIECE GOODS, NOTIONS/DRY GOODS, WHOL: Drapery Mtrl, Woven
PIGMENTS, INORGANIC: Metallic & Mineral, NEC
PILOT SVCS: Aviation
PINS
PINS: Dowel
PIPE & FITTING: Fabrication
PIPE & FITTINGS: Cast Iron
PIPE & TUBES: Seamless
PIPE FITTINGS: Plastic
PIPE JOINT COMPOUNDS
PIPE SECTIONS, FABRICATED FROM PURCHASED PIPE
PIPE, CULVERT: Concrete
PIPE, CYLINDER: Concrete, Prestressed Or Pretensioned
PIPE, SEWER: Concrete
PIPE: Concrete
PIPE: Plastic
PIPE: Seamless Steel
PIPE: Sheet Metal
PIPE: Water, Cast Iron
PIPELINES: Crude Petroleum
PIPELINES: Natural Gas
PIPES & TUBES
PIPES & TUBES: Steel
PIPES & TUBES: Welded
PIPES OR FITTINGS: Sewer, Clay
PIPES: Steel & Iron
PISTONS & PISTON RINGS
PLACER GOLD MINING
PLANING MILL, NEC
PLANING MILLS: Millwork
PLANTERS: Plastic
PLANTS, POTTED, WHOLESALE
PLANTS: Artificial & Preserved
PLAQUES: Clay, Plaster/Papier-Mache, Factory Production
PLAQUES: Picture, Laminated
PLASMAS
PLASTER WORK: Ornamental & Architectural
PLASTER, ACOUSTICAL: Gypsum
PLASTIC COLORING & FINISHING
PLASTIC PRDTS
PLASTICIZERS, ORGANIC: Cyclic & Acyclic

PRODUCT INDEX

PLASTICS FILM & SHEET
PLASTICS FILM & SHEET: Polyethylene
PLASTICS FILM & SHEET: Polypropylene
PLASTICS FILM & SHEET: Polyvinyl
PLASTICS FILM & SHEET: Vinyl
PLASTICS FINISHED PRDTS: Laminated
PLASTICS MATERIAL & RESINS
PLASTICS MATERIALS, BASIC FORMS & SHAPES WHOLESALERS
PLASTICS PROCESSING
PLASTICS SHEET: Packing Materials
PLASTICS: Blow Molded
PLASTICS: Cast
PLASTICS: Extruded
PLASTICS: Finished Injection Molded
PLASTICS: Injection Molded
PLASTICS: Molded
PLASTICS: Polystyrene Foam
PLASTICS: Protein
PLASTICS: Thermoformed
PLATE WORK: For Nuclear Industry
PLATE WORK: Metalworking Trade
PLATEMAKING SVC: Color Separations, For The Printing Trade
PLATEMAKING SVC: Embossing, For The Printing Trade
PLATENS, EXC PRINTERS': Rubber, Solid Or Covered
PLATES
PLATES: Paper, Made From Purchased Materials
PLATES: Plastic Exc Polystyrene Foam
PLATES: Sheet & Strip, Exc Coated Prdts
PLATES: Steel
PLATING & FINISHING SVC: Decorative, Formed Prdts
PLATING & POLISHING SVC
PLATING COMPOUNDS
PLATING SVC: Chromium, Metals Or Formed Prdts
PLATING SVC: Electro
PLATING SVC: NEC
PLAYGROUND EQPT
PLEATING & STITCHING FOR THE TRADE: Decorative & Novelty
PLEATING & STITCHING SVC
PLUMBERS' GOODS: Rubber
PLUMBING & HEATING EQPT & SPLY, WHOL: Htg Eqpt/Panels, Solar
PLUMBING & HEATING EQPT & SPLY, WHOLESALE: Hydronic Htg Eqpt
PLUMBING & HEATING EQPT & SPLYS WHOLESALERS
PLUMBING & HEATING EQPT & SPLYS, WHOL: Fireplaces, Prefab
PLUMBING & HEATING EQPT & SPLYS, WHOL: Pipe/Fitting, Plastic
PLUMBING & HEATING EQPT & SPLYS, WHOL: Plumbing Fitting/Sply
PLUMBING & HEATING EQPT & SPLYS, WHOL: Plumbng/Heatng Valves
PLUMBING & HEATING EQPT & SPLYS, WHOL: Water Purif Eqpt
PLUMBING & HEATING EQPT, WHOLESALE: Water Heaters/Purif
PLUMBING & HEATING EQPT/SPLYS, WHOL: Boilers, Hot Water Htg
PLUMBING FIXTURES
PLUMBING FIXTURES: Brass, Incl Drain Cocks, Faucets/Spigots
PLUMBING FIXTURES: Plastic
PLUMBING FIXTURES: Vitreous
PLUMBING FIXTURES: Vitreous China
POINT OF SALE DEVICES
POLE LINE HARDWARE
POLICE PROTECTION
POLISHING SVC: Metals Or Formed Prdts
POLYESTERS
POLYETHYLENE CHLOROSULFONATED RUBBER
POLYETHYLENE RESINS
POLYMETHYL METHACRYLATE RESINS: Plexiglas
POLYPROPYLENE RESINS
POLYSTYRENE RESINS
POLYTETRAFLUOROETHYLENE RESINS
POLYURETHANE RESINS
POLYVINYL CHLORIDE RESINS
POLYVINYLIDENE CHLORIDE RESINS
PONTOONS: Rubber
POPCORN & SUPPLIES WHOLESALERS
PORCELAIN ENAMELED PRDTS & UTENSILS
POSTERS, WHOLESALE

POSTS: Floor, Adjustable, Metal
POTPOURRI
POTTERY
POTTING SOILS
POULTRY & POULTRY PRDTS WHOLESALERS
POULTRY & SMALL GAME SLAUGHTERING & PROCESSING
POULTRY SLAUGHTERING & PROCESSING
POWDER: Iron
POWDER: Metal
POWDER: Silver
POWER GENERATORS
POWER SPLY CONVERTERS: Static, Electronic Applications
POWER SUPPLIES: All Types, Static
POWER SUPPLIES: Transformer, Electronic Type
POWER SWITCHING EQPT
POWER TOOLS, HAND: Drills, Port, Elec/Pneumatic, Exc Rock
POWER TOOLS, HAND: Hammers, Portable, Elec/Pneumatic, Chip
POWER TRANSMISSION EQPT WHOLESALERS
POWER TRANSMISSION EQPT: Mechanical
POWER TRANSMISSION EQPT: Vehicle
POWERED GOLF CART DEALERS
PRECAST TERRAZZO OR CONCRETE PRDTS
PRECIOUS STONES & METALS, WHOLESALE
PRECIPITATORS: Electrostatic
PRECISION INSTRUMENT REPAIR SVCS
PRERECORDED TAPE, COMPACT DISC & RECORD STORES: Records
PRESSED FIBER & MOLDED PULP PRDTS, EXC FOOD PRDTS
PRESSES
PRESSURIZERS OR AUXILIARY EQPT: Nuclear, Metal Plate
PRESTRESSED CONCRETE PRDTS
PRIMARY FINISHED OR SEMIFINISHED SHAPES
PRIMARY METAL PRODUCTS
PRIMARY ROLLING MILL EQPT
PRINT CARTRIDGES: Laser & Other Computer Printers
PRINTED CIRCUIT BOARDS
PRINTERS & PLOTTERS
PRINTERS' SVCS: Folding, Collating, Etc
PRINTERS: Computer
PRINTERS: Magnetic Ink, Bar Code
PRINTING & BINDING: Books
PRINTING & BINDING: Pamphlets
PRINTING & BINDING: Textbooks
PRINTING & EMBOSSING: Plastic Fabric Articles
PRINTING & ENGRAVING: Financial Notes & Certificates
PRINTING & ENGRAVING: Invitation & Stationery
PRINTING & STAMPING: Fabric Articles
PRINTING & WRITING PAPER WHOLESALERS
PRINTING INKS WHOLESALERS
PRINTING MACHINERY
PRINTING MACHINERY, EQPT & SPLYS: Wholesalers
PRINTING TRADES MACHINERY & EQPT REPAIR SVCS
PRINTING, COMMERCIAL Newspapers, NEC
PRINTING, COMMERCIAL: Bags, Plastic, NEC
PRINTING, COMMERCIAL: Business Forms, NEC
PRINTING, COMMERCIAL: Calendars, NEC
PRINTING, COMMERCIAL: Cards, Visiting, Incl Business, NEC
PRINTING, COMMERCIAL: Circulars, NEC
PRINTING, COMMERCIAL: Decals, NEC
PRINTING, COMMERCIAL: Envelopes, NEC
PRINTING, COMMERCIAL: Imprinting
PRINTING, COMMERCIAL: Invitations, NEC
PRINTING, COMMERCIAL: Labels & Seals, NEC
PRINTING, COMMERCIAL: Letterpress & Screen
PRINTING, COMMERCIAL: Literature, Advertising, NEC
PRINTING, COMMERCIAL: Magazines, NEC
PRINTING, COMMERCIAL: Menus, NEC
PRINTING, COMMERCIAL: Music, Sheet, NEC
PRINTING, COMMERCIAL: Post Cards, Picture, NEC
PRINTING, COMMERCIAL: Promotional
PRINTING, COMMERCIAL: Publications
PRINTING, COMMERCIAL: Screen
PRINTING, COMMERCIAL: Tickets, NEC
PRINTING, LITHOGRAPHIC: Calendars
PRINTING, LITHOGRAPHIC: Calendars & Cards
PRINTING, LITHOGRAPHIC: Catalogs
PRINTING, LITHOGRAPHIC: Color
PRINTING, LITHOGRAPHIC: Decals
PRINTING, LITHOGRAPHIC: Forms & Cards, Business
PRINTING, LITHOGRAPHIC: Forms, Business

PRINTING, LITHOGRAPHIC: Letters, Circular Or Form
PRINTING, LITHOGRAPHIC: Offset & photolithographic printing
PRINTING, LITHOGRAPHIC: On Metal
PRINTING, LITHOGRAPHIC: Posters
PRINTING, LITHOGRAPHIC: Publications
PRINTING, LITHOGRAPHIC: Tags
PRINTING, LITHOGRAPHIC: Tickets
PRINTING, LITHOGRAPHIC: Transfers, Decalcomania Or Dry
PRINTING: Book Music
PRINTING: Books
PRINTING: Books
PRINTING: Broadwoven Fabrics. Cotton
PRINTING: Commercial, NEC
PRINTING: Engraving & Plate
PRINTING: Flexographic
PRINTING: Gravure, Business Form & Card
PRINTING: Gravure, Color
PRINTING: Gravure, Coupons
PRINTING: Gravure, Envelopes
PRINTING: Gravure, Forms, Business
PRINTING: Gravure, Invitations
PRINTING: Gravure, Job
PRINTING: Gravure, Labels
PRINTING: Gravure, Rotogravure
PRINTING: Laser
PRINTING: Letterpress
PRINTING: Lithographic
PRINTING: Offset
PRINTING: Pamphlets
PRINTING: Photo-Offset
PRINTING: Photolithographic
PRINTING: Rotary Photogravure
PRINTING: Rotogravure
PRINTING: Screen, Broadwoven Fabrics, Cotton
PRINTING: Screen, Fabric
PRINTING: Screen, Manmade Fiber & Silk, Broadwoven Fabric
PRINTING: Thermography
PRODUCTS: Petroleum & coal, NEC
PROFESSIONAL EQPT & SPLYS, WHOLESALE: Analytical Instruments
PROFESSIONAL EQPT & SPLYS, WHOLESALE: Bank
PROFESSIONAL EQPT & SPLYS, WHOLESALE: Engineers', NEC
PROFESSIONAL EQPT & SPLYS, WHOLESALE: Optical Goods
PROFESSIONAL EQPT & SPLYS, WHOLESALE: Precision Tools
PROFESSIONAL EQPT & SPLYS, WHOLESALE: Scientific & Engineerg
PROFESSIONAL INSTRUMENT REPAIR SVCS
PROFILE SHAPES: Unsupported Plastics
PROGRAM ADMINISTRATION, GOVT: Workers' Compensation Office
PROPELLERS: Boat & Ship, Cast
PROPERTY & CASUALTY INSURANCE AGENTS
PROPRIETARY STORES, NON-PRESCRIPTION MEDICINE
PROTECTION EQPT: Lightning
PROTECTIVE FOOTWEAR: Rubber Or Plastic
PUBLIC RELATIONS & PUBLICITY SVCS
PUBLISHERS: Atlases
PUBLISHERS: Book
PUBLISHERS: Books, No Printing
PUBLISHERS: Catalogs
PUBLISHERS: Directories, NEC
PUBLISHERS: Directories, Telephone
PUBLISHERS: Guides
PUBLISHERS: Magazines, No Printing
PUBLISHERS: Maps
PUBLISHERS: Miscellaneous
PUBLISHERS: Music Book
PUBLISHERS: Music Book & Sheet Music
PUBLISHERS: Music, Sheet
PUBLISHERS: Newsletter
PUBLISHERS: Newspaper
PUBLISHERS: Newspapers, No Printing
PUBLISHERS: Pamphlets, No Printing
PUBLISHERS: Periodical, With Printing
PUBLISHERS: Periodicals, Magazines
PUBLISHERS: Periodicals, No Printing
PUBLISHERS: Sheet Music
PUBLISHERS: Technical Manuals
PUBLISHERS: Technical Manuals & Papers
PUBLISHERS: Telephone & Other Directory

PRODUCT INDEX

PUBLISHERS: Television Schedules, No Printing
PUBLISHERS: Textbooks, No Printing
PUBLISHERS: Trade journals, No Printing
PUBLISHING & BROADCASTING: Internet Only
PUBLISHING & PRINTING: Art Copy
PUBLISHING & PRINTING: Book Music
PUBLISHING & PRINTING: Books
PUBLISHING & PRINTING: Directories, NEC
PUBLISHING & PRINTING: Directories, Telephone
PUBLISHING & PRINTING: Guides
PUBLISHING & PRINTING: Magazines: publishing & printing
PUBLISHING & PRINTING: Newsletters, Business Svc
PUBLISHING & PRINTING: Newspapers
PUBLISHING & PRINTING: Pamphlets
PUBLISHING & PRINTING: Periodical Statistical Reports
PUBLISHING & PRINTING: Posters
PUBLISHING & PRINTING: Shopping News
PUBLISHING & PRINTING: Technical Papers
PUBLISHING & PRINTING: Textbooks
PUBLISHING & PRINTING: Trade Journals
PULLEYS: Metal
PULLEYS: Power Transmission
PULP MILLS
PULP MILLS: Mechanical & Recycling Processing
PUMP SLEEVES: Rubber
PUMPS
PUMPS & PARTS: Indl
PUMPS & PUMPING EQPT REPAIR SVCS
PUMPS & PUMPING EQPT WHOLESALERS
PUMPS: Domestic, Water Or Sump
PUMPS: Fluid Power
PUMPS: Gasoline, Measuring Or Dispensing
PUMPS: Hydraulic Power Transfer
PUMPS: Measuring & Dispensing
PUMPS: Oil Well & Field
PUMPS: Oil, Measuring Or Dispensing
PUNCHES: Forming & Stamping
PURCHASING SVCS
PURIFICATION & DUST COLLECTION EQPT
PURLINS: Steel, Light Gauge

Q

QUARTZ CRYSTAL MINING SVCS
QUARTZ CRYSTALS: Electronic
QUILTING SVC & SPLYS, FOR THE TRADE

R

RABBIT SLAUGHTERING & PROCESSING
RACEWAYS
RACKS & SHELVING: Household, Wood
RACKS: Display
RACKS: Railroad Car, Vehicle Transportation, Steel
RADAR SYSTEMS & EQPT
RADIO & TELEVISION COMMUNICATIONS EQUIPMENT
RADIO BROADCASTING & COMMUNICATIONS EQPT
RADIO BROADCASTING STATIONS
RADIO COMMUNICATIONS: Airborne Eqpt
RADIO COMMUNICATIONS: Carrier Eqpt
RADIO RECEIVER NETWORKS
RADIO REPAIR & INSTALLATION SVCS
RADIO, TELEVISION & CONSUMER ELECTRONICS STORES: Eqpt, NEC
RADIO, TV & CONSUMER ELEC STORES: Automotive Sound Eqpt
RADIO, TV & CONSUMER ELEC STORES: High Fidelity Stereo Eqpt
RADIO, TV/CONSUMER ELEC STORES: Antennas, Satellite Dish
RADIOS WHOLESALERS
RAILINGS: Prefabricated, Metal
RAILINGS: Wood
RAILROAD CAR CUSTOMIZING SVCS
RAILROAD CAR RENTING & LEASING SVCS
RAILROAD CAR REPAIR SVCS
RAILROAD CARGO LOADING & UNLOADING SVCS
RAILROAD CROSSINGS: Steel Or Iron
RAILROAD EQPT
RAILROAD EQPT & SPLYS WHOLESALERS
RAILROAD EQPT: Brakes, Air & Vacuum
RAILROAD EQPT: Cars & Eqpt, Dining
RAILROAD EQPT: Cars & Eqpt, Interurban
RAILROAD EQPT: Cars & Eqpt, Train, Freight Or Passenger
RAILROAD EQPT: Cars, Rebuilt
RAILROAD EQPT: Locomotives & Parts, Indl
RAILROAD MAINTENANCE & REPAIR SVCS
RAILROAD RELATED EQPT
RAILROAD RELATED EQPT: Railway Track
RAILROAD TIES: Concrete
RAILROAD TIES: Wood
RAILS: Rails, Rerolled Or Renewed
RAILS: Rails, rolled & drawn, aluminum
RAMPS: Prefabricated Metal
RAZORS, RAZOR BLADES
REACTORS: Current Limiting
REACTORS: Saturable
REAL ESTATE AGENCIES & BROKERS
REAL ESTATE AGENCIES: Buying
REAL ESTATE AGENCIES: Commercial
REAL ESTATE AGENCIES: Leasing & Rentals
REAL ESTATE AGENCIES: Residential
REAL ESTATE AGENTS & MANAGERS
REAL ESTATE INVESTMENT TRUSTS
REAL ESTATE OPERATORS, EXC DEVELOPERS: Commercial/Indl Bldg
REAL ESTATE OPERATORS, EXC DEVELOPERS: Property, Retail
REALTY INVESTMENT TRUSTS
RECEIVERS: Radio Communications
RECHROMING SVC: Automobile Bumpers
RECLAIMED RUBBER: Reworked By Manufacturing Process
RECORD BLANKS: Phonographic
RECORDING TAPE: Video, Blank
RECORDS & TAPES: Prerecorded
RECORDS OR TAPES: Masters
RECOVERY SVC: Iron Ore, From Open Hearth Slag
RECOVERY SVC: Silver, From Used Photographic Film
RECOVERY SVCS: Metal
RECREATIONAL & SPORTING CAMPS
RECREATIONAL DEALERS: Camper & Travel Trailers
RECREATIONAL SPORTING EQPT REPAIR SVCS
RECREATIONAL VEHICLE PARTS & ACCESS STORES
RECREATIONAL VEHICLE REPAIR SVCS
RECTIFIERS: Electronic, Exc Semiconductor
RECYCLABLE SCRAP & WASTE MATERIALS WHOLESALERS
RECYCLING: Paper
REELS: Cable, Metal
REELS: Fiber, Textile, Made From Purchased Materials
REELS: Wood
REFINERS & SMELTERS: Aluminum
REFINERS & SMELTERS: Brass, Secondary
REFINERS & SMELTERS: Copper
REFINERS & SMELTERS: Copper, Secondary
REFINERS & SMELTERS: Gold
REFINERS & SMELTERS: Gold, Secondary
REFINERS & SMELTERS: Lead, Secondary
REFINERS & SMELTERS: Nonferrous Metal
REFINERS & SMELTERS: Rhenium, Primary
REFINERS & SMELTERS: Silicon, Primary, Over 99% Pure
REFINERS & SMELTERS: Zirconium
REFINING LUBRICATING OILS & GREASES, NEC
REFINING: Petroleum
REFLECTIVE ROAD MARKERS, WHOLESALE
REFRACTORIES: Brick
REFRACTORIES: Cement
REFRACTORIES: Clay
REFRACTORIES: Graphite, Carbon Or Ceramic Bond
REFRACTORIES: Nonclay
REFRIGERATION & HEATING EQUIPMENT
REFRIGERATION EQPT & SPLYS WHOLESALERS
REFRIGERATION EQPT & SPLYS, WHOLESALE: Beverage Dispensers
REFRIGERATION EQPT & SPLYS, WHOLESALE: Commercial Eqpt
REFRIGERATION EQPT: Complete
REFRIGERATION REPAIR SVCS
REFRIGERATORS & FREEZERS WHOLESALERS
REFUGEE SVCS
REFUSE SYSTEMS
REGISTERS: Air, Metal
REGULATION & ADMIN, GOVT: Facility Licensing & Inspection
REGULATORS: Generator Voltage
REGULATORS: Power
REHABILITATION SVCS
RELAYS & SWITCHES: Indl, Electric
RELAYS: Control Circuit, Ind
RELAYS: Electronic Usage
RELIGIOUS SPLYS WHOLESALERS
REMOVERS & CLEANERS
REMOVERS: Paint
RENT-A-CAR SVCS
RENTAL SVCS: Business Machine & Electronic Eqpt
RENTAL SVCS: Costume
RENTAL SVCS: Eqpt, Theatrical
RENTAL SVCS: Home Cleaning & Maintenance Eqpt
RENTAL SVCS: Motor Home
RENTAL SVCS: Musical Instrument
RENTAL SVCS: Office Facilities & Secretarial Svcs
RENTAL SVCS: Pallet
RENTAL SVCS: Saddle Horse
RENTAL SVCS: Sign
RENTAL SVCS: Sound & Lighting Eqpt
RENTAL SVCS: Sporting Goods, NEC
RENTAL SVCS: Stores & Yards Eqpt
RENTAL SVCS: Tent & Tarpaulin
RENTAL SVCS: Trailer
RENTAL SVCS: Tuxedo
RENTAL SVCS: Vending Machine
RENTAL SVCS: Work Zone Traffic Eqpt, Flags, Cones, Etc
RENTAL: Portable Toilet
RENTAL: Trucks, With Drivers
RENTAL: Video Tape & Disc
REPAIR SERVICES, NEC
REPAIR TRAINING, COMPUTER
REPOSSESSION SVCS
REPRODUCTION SVCS: Video Tape Or Disk
RESEARCH & DEVELOPMENT SVCS, COMMERCIAL: Engineering Lab
RESEARCH, DEV & TESTING SVCS, COMM: Chem Lab, Exc Testing
RESEARCH, DEVEL & TEST SVCS, COMM: Sociological & Education
RESEARCH, DEVELOPMENT & TEST SVCS, COMM: Cmptr Hardware Dev
RESEARCH, DEVELOPMENT & TEST SVCS, COMM: Research, Exc Lab
RESEARCH, DEVELOPMENT & TESTING SVCS, COMM: Agricultural
RESEARCH, DEVELOPMENT & TESTING SVCS, COMM: Research Lab
RESEARCH, DEVELOPMENT & TESTING SVCS, COMMERCIAL: Business
RESEARCH, DEVELOPMENT & TESTING SVCS, COMMERCIAL: Education
RESEARCH, DEVELOPMENT & TESTING SVCS, COMMERCIAL: Energy
RESEARCH, DEVELOPMENT & TESTING SVCS, COMMERCIAL: Medical
RESEARCH, DEVELOPMENT & TESTING SVCS, COMMERCIAL: Physical
RESEARCH, DVLPT & TEST SVCS, COMM: Mkt Analysis or Research
RESEARCH, DVLPT & TESTING SVCS, COMM: Mkt, Bus & Economic
RESIDENTIAL MENTAL HEALTH & SUBSTANCE ABUSE FACILITIES
RESIDENTIAL REMODELERS
RESINS: Custom Compound Purchased
RESISTORS
RESISTORS & RESISTOR UNITS
RESOLVERS
RESPIRATORS
RESTAURANT EQPT REPAIR SVCS
RESTAURANT EQPT: Carts
RESTAURANT EQPT: Sheet Metal
RESTAURANTS:Full Svc, American
RESTAURANTS:Full Svc, Barbecue
RESTAURANTS:Full Svc, Chinese
RESTAURANTS:Full Svc, Family, Chain
RESTAURANTS:Full Svc, Family, Independent
RESTAURANTS:Full Svc, Italian
RESTAURANTS:Limited Svc, Chili Stand
RESTAURANTS:Limited Svc, Coffee Shop
RESTAURANTS:Limited Svc, Fast-Food, Chain
RESTAURANTS:Limited Svc, Grill
RESTAURANTS:Limited Svc, Ice Cream Stands Or Dairy Bars
RESTAURANTS:Limited Svc, Lunch Counter
RESTAURANTS:Limited Svc, Pizza
RESTAURANTS:Limited Svc, Pizzeria, Chain
RESTAURANTS:Limited Svc, Pizzeria, Independent
RESTAURANTS:Limited Svc, Sandwiches & Submarines Shop
RESTAURANTS:Limited Svc, Snack Shop

PRODUCT INDEX

RESTROOM CLEANING SVCS
RETAIL BAKERY: Bread
RETAIL BAKERY: Cakes
RETAIL BAKERY: Cookies
RETAIL BAKERY: Doughnuts
RETAIL BAKERY: Pastries
RETAIL BAKERY: Pies
RETAIL BAKERY: Pretzels
RETAIL FIREPLACE STORES
RETAIL LUMBER YARDS
RETAIL STORES, NEC
RETAIL STORES: Air Purification Eqpt
RETAIL STORES: Alcoholic Beverage Making Eqpt & Splys
RETAIL STORES: Aquarium Splys
RETAIL STORES: Architectural Splys
RETAIL STORES: Art & Architectural Splys
RETAIL STORES: Artificial Limbs
RETAIL STORES: Audio-Visual Eqpt & Splys
RETAIL STORES: Awnings
RETAIL STORES: Banners
RETAIL STORES: Batteries, Non-Automotive
RETAIL STORES: Business Machines & Eqpt
RETAIL STORES: Cake Decorating Splys
RETAIL STORES: Children's Furniture, NEC
RETAIL STORES: Christmas Lights & Decorations
RETAIL STORES: Cleaning Eqpt & Splys
RETAIL STORES: Communication Eqpt
RETAIL STORES: Concrete Prdts, Precast
RETAIL STORES: Cosmetics
RETAIL STORES: Decals
RETAIL STORES: Drafting Eqpt & Splys
RETAIL STORES: Educational Aids & Electronic Training Mat
RETAIL STORES: Electronic Parts & Eqpt
RETAIL STORES: Engine & Motor Eqpt & Splys
RETAIL STORES: Farm Eqpt & Splys
RETAIL STORES: Farm Tractors
RETAIL STORES: Fiberglass Materials, Exc Insulation
RETAIL STORES: Fire Extinguishers
RETAIL STORES: Flags
RETAIL STORES: Gravestones, Finished
RETAIL STORES: Hair Care Prdts
RETAIL STORES: Hearing Aids
RETAIL STORES: Hospital Eqpt & Splys
RETAIL STORES: Ice
RETAIL STORES: Medical Apparatus & Splys
RETAIL STORES: Monuments, Finished To Custom Order
RETAIL STORES: Motors, Electric
RETAIL STORES: Orthopedic & Prosthesis Applications
RETAIL STORES: Pet Splys
RETAIL STORES: Photocopy Machines
RETAIL STORES: Picture Frames, Ready Made
RETAIL STORES: Plumbing & Heating Splys
RETAIL STORES: Police Splys
RETAIL STORES: Religious Goods
RETAIL STORES: Rock & Stone Specimens
RETAIL STORES: Rubber Stamps
RETAIL STORES: Safety Splys & Eqpt
RETAIL STORES: Sunglasses
RETAIL STORES: Swimming Pools, Above Ground
RETAIL STORES: Technical Aids For The Handicapped
RETAIL STORES: Telephone & Communication Eqpt
RETAIL STORES: Telephone Eqpt & Systems
RETAIL STORES: Tents
RETAIL STORES: Theatrical Eqpt & Splys
RETAIL STORES: Typewriters & Business Machines
RETAIL STORES: Vaults & Safes
RETAIL STORES: Water Purification Eqpt
RETAIL STORES: Welding Splys
RETREADING MATERIALS: Tire
REUPHOLSTERY & FURNITURE REPAIR
REUPHOLSTERY SVCS
RIBBONS & BOWS
RIBBONS: Machine, Inked Or Carbon
RIVETS: Metal
ROAD CONSTRUCTION EQUIPMENT WHOLESALERS
ROAD MATERIALS: Bituminous, Not From Refineries
ROBOTS: Assembly Line
ROBOTS: Indl Spraying, Painting, Etc
ROD & BAR Aluminum
RODS: Extruded, Aluminum
RODS: Plastic
RODS: Rolled, Aluminum
RODS: Steel & Iron, Made In Steel Mills
RODS: Welding
ROLL COVERINGS: Rubber
ROLL FORMED SHAPES: Custom
ROLLING MILL EQPT: Finishing
ROLLING MILL EQPT: Galvanizing Lines
ROLLING MILL MACHINERY
ROLLING MILL ROLLS: Cast Steel
ROLLS & ROLL COVERINGS: Rubber
ROOFING MATERIALS: Asphalt
ROOFING MATERIALS: Sheet Metal
ROOFING MEMBRANE: Rubber
ROOM COOLERS: Portable
ROTORS: Motor
RUBBER
RUBBER BANDS
RUBBER PRDTS
RUBBER PRDTS REPAIR SVCS
RUBBER PRDTS: Appliance, Mechanical
RUBBER PRDTS: Automotive, Mechanical
RUBBER PRDTS: Mechanical
RUBBER PRDTS: Medical & Surgical Tubing, Extrudd & Lathe-Cut
RUBBER PRDTS: Oil & Gas Field Machinery, Mechanical
RUBBER PRDTS: Reclaimed
RUBBER PRDTS: Sheeting
RUBBER PRDTS: Silicone
RUBBER PRDTS: Sponge
RUBBER STAMP, WHOLESALE
RUBBER STRUCTURES: Air-Supported
RUST ARRESTING COMPOUNDS: Animal Or Vegetable Oil Based
RUST PROOFING SVC: Hot Dipping, Metals & Formed Prdts
RUST REMOVERS
RUST RESISTING

S

SADDLERY STORES
SAFE DEPOSIT BOXES
SAFES & VAULTS: Metal
SAFETY EQPT & SPLYS WHOLESALERS
SAILBOAT BUILDING & REPAIR
SAILS
SALES PROMOTION SVCS
SALT
SALT & SULFUR MINING
SALT MINING: Common
SALT: Packers'
SAND & GRAVEL
SAND LIME PRDTS
SAND MINING
SAND: Hygrade
SAND: Silica
SANDBLASTING EQPT
SANDBLASTING SVC: Building Exterior
SANDSTONE: Dimension
SANITARY SVC, NEC
SANITARY SVCS: Chemical Detoxification
SANITARY SVCS: Environmental Cleanup
SANITARY SVCS: Hazardous Waste, Collection & Disposal
SANITARY SVCS: Liquid Waste Collection & Disposal
SANITARY SVCS: Refuse Collection & Disposal Svcs
SANITARY SVCS: Rubbish Collection & Disposal
SANITARY SVCS: Waste Materials, Recycling
SANITARY WARE: Metal
SANITATION CHEMICALS & CLEANING AGENTS
SASHES: Door Or Window, Metal
SATELLITES: Communications
SAW BLADES
SAWDUST & SHAVINGS
SAWING & PLANING MILLS
SAWING & PLANING MILLS: Custom
SAWMILL MACHINES
SAWS & SAWING EQPT
SAWS: Hand, Metalworking Or Woodworking
SCAFFOLDS: Mobile Or Stationary, Metal
SCALE REPAIR SVCS
SCALES & BALANCES, EXC LABORATORY
SCALES: Indl
SCALES: Truck
SCHOOL SPLYS, EXC BOOKS: Wholesalers
SCHOOLS & EDUCATIONAL SVCS, NEC
SCHOOLS: Vocational, NEC
SCIENTIFIC EQPT REPAIR SVCS
SCIENTIFIC INSTRUMENTS WHOLESALERS
SCRAP & WASTE MATERIALS, WHOLESALE: Ferrous Metal
SCRAP & WASTE MATERIALS, WHOLESALE: Junk & Scrap
SCRAP & WASTE MATERIALS, WHOLESALE: Lumber Scrap
SCRAP & WASTE MATERIALS, WHOLESALE: Metal
SCRAP & WASTE MATERIALS, WHOLESALE: Nonferrous Metals Scrap
SCRAP & WASTE MATERIALS, WHOLESALE: Rubber Scrap
SCRAP STEEL CUTTING
SCREENS: Door, Metal Covered Wood
SCREENS: Door, Wood Frame
SCREENS: Projection
SCREENS: Window, Metal
SCREENS: Window, Wood Framed
SCREENS: Woven Wire
SCREW MACHINE PRDTS
SCREW MACHINES
SCREWS: Metal
SCREWS: Wood
SEALANTS
SEALING COMPOUNDS: Sealing, synthetic rubber or plastic
SEALS: Hermetic
SEARCH & DETECTION SYSTEMS, EXC RADAR
SEARCH & NAVIGATION SYSTEMS
SEAT BELTS: Automobile & Aircraft
SEATING: Chairs, Table & Arm
SEATING: Stadium
SEATING: Transportation
SECRETARIAL & COURT REPORTING
SECRETARIAL SVCS
SECURITY CONTROL EQPT & SYSTEMS
SECURITY DEVICES
SECURITY EQPT STORES
SECURITY PROTECTIVE DEVICES MAINTENANCE & MONITORING SVCS
SECURITY SYSTEMS SERVICES
SEMICONDUCTOR CIRCUIT NETWORKS
SEMICONDUCTORS & RELATED DEVICES
SENSORS: Infrared, Solid State
SENSORS: Radiation
SENSORS: Temperature, Exc Indl Process
SENSORS: Ultraviolet, Solid State
SEPARATORS: Metal Plate
SEPTIC TANK CLEANING SVCS
SEPTIC TANKS: Concrete
SEPTIC TANKS: Plastic
SEWAGE & WATER TREATMENT EQPT
SEWAGE FACILITIES
SEWAGE TREATMENT SYSTEMS & EQPT
SEWER CLEANING & RODDING SVC
SEWER CLEANING EQPT: Power
SEWING CONTRACTORS
SEWING MACHINES & PARTS: Indl
SEWING, NEEDLEWORK & PIECE GOODS STORE: Quilting Matls/Splys
SEWING, NEEDLEWORK & PIECE GOODS STORES: Knitting Splys
SEWING, NEEDLEWORK & PIECE GOODS STORES: Notions, Incl Trim
SEWING, NEEDLEWORK & PIECE GOODS STORES: Sewing & Needlework
SHADES: Window
SHAFTS: Shaft Collars
SHALE MINING, COMMON
SHAPES & PILINGS, STRUCTURAL: Steel
SHAPES: Extruded, Aluminum, NEC
SHAVING PREPARATIONS
SHEARS
SHEET METAL SPECIALTIES, EXC STAMPED
SHEETING: Laminated Plastic
SHEETS & STRIPS: Aluminum
SHEETS: Hard Rubber
SHELLAC
SHELTERED WORKSHOPS
SHELVES & SHELVING: Wood
SHELVING ANGLES OR SLOTTED BARS, EXC WOOD
SHELVING, MADE FROM PURCHASED WIRE
SHELVING: Office & Store, Exc Wood
SHIMS: Metal
SHIP BUILDING & REPAIRING: Cargo Vessels
SHIP BUILDING & REPAIRING: Lighthouse Tenders
SHIP BUILDING & REPAIRING: Tankers
SHIP BUILDING & REPAIRING: Tugboats
SHIP COMPONENTS: Metal, Prefabricated
SHIPBUILDING & REPAIR
SHOE MATERIALS: Counters
SHOE MATERIALS: Inner Soles
SHOE MATERIALS: Quarters
SHOE MATERIALS: Rands

PRODUCT INDEX

SHOE MATERIALS: Rubber
SHOE MATERIALS: Uppers
SHOE REPAIR SHOP
SHOE STORES
SHOE STORES: Boots, Men's
SHOE STORES: Men's
SHOE STORES: Women's
SHOES & BOOTS WHOLESALERS
SHOES: Athletic, Exc Rubber Or Plastic
SHOES: Canvas, Rubber Soled
SHOES: Men's
SHOES: Plastic Or Rubber
SHOES: Women's
SHOES: Women's, Dress
SHOT PEENING SVC
SHOWCASES & DISPLAY FIXTURES: Office & Store
SHOWER STALLS: Plastic & Fiberglass
SHREDDERS: Indl & Commercial
SHUTTERS, DOOR & WINDOW: Metal
SHUTTERS, DOOR & WINDOW: Plastic
SIDING & STRUCTURAL MATERIALS: Wood
SIDING MATERIALS
SIDING: Plastic
SIDING: Precast Stone
SIDING: Sheet Metal
SIGN LETTERING & PAINTING SVCS
SIGN PAINTING & LETTERING SHOP
SIGNALS: Traffic Control, Electric
SIGNALS: Transportation
SIGNS & ADVERTISING SPECIALTIES
SIGNS & ADVERTISING SPECIALTIES: Artwork, Advertising
SIGNS & ADVERTISING SPECIALTIES: Displays, Paint Process
SIGNS & ADVERTISING SPECIALTIES: Letters For Signs, Metal
SIGNS & ADVERTISING SPECIALTIES: Novelties
SIGNS & ADVERTISING SPECIALTIES: Scoreboards, Electric
SIGNS & ADVERTISING SPECIALTIES: Signs
SIGNS & ADVERTSG SPECIALTIES: Displays/Cutouts Window/Lobby
SIGNS, ELECTRICAL: Wholesalers
SIGNS, EXC ELECTRIC, WHOLESALE
SIGNS: Electrical
SIGNS: Neon
SILICA MINING
SILICON WAFERS: Chemically Doped
SILICON: Pure
SILICONE RESINS
SILICONES
SILK SCREEN DESIGN SVCS
SILVERWARE & PLATED WARE
SIMULATORS: Flight
SINK TOPS, PLASTIC LAMINATED
SINTER: Iron
SIZES: Indl
SKIDS
SKIDS: Wood
SKYLIGHTS
SLAB & TILE: Precast Concrete, Floor
SLAG PRDTS
SLAG: Crushed Or Ground
SLAUGHTERING & MEAT PACKING
SLINGS: Lifting, Made From Purchased Wire
SLIPPERS: House
SLOT MACHINES
SMOKE DETECTORS
SNOW PLOWING SVCS
SNOW REMOVAL EQPT: Residential
SOAP DISHES: Vitreous China
SOAPS & DETERGENTS
SOCIAL SERVICES, NEC
SOCIAL SVCS: Individual & Family
SOCKETS: Electric
SOFT DRINKS WHOLESALERS
SOFTWARE PUBLISHERS: Application
SOFTWARE PUBLISHERS: Business & Professional
SOFTWARE PUBLISHERS: Computer Utilities
SOFTWARE PUBLISHERS: Education
SOFTWARE PUBLISHERS: Home Entertainment
SOFTWARE PUBLISHERS: NEC
SOFTWARE PUBLISHERS: Operating Systems
SOFTWARE PUBLISHERS: Publisher's
SOFTWARE TRAINING, COMPUTER
SOLAR CELLS
SOLAR HEATING EQPT
SOLDERING EQPT: Electrical, Exc Handheld
SOLDERING EQPT: Electrical, Handheld
SOLDERS
SOLENOIDS
SOLES, BOOT OR SHOE: Rubber, Composition Or Fiber
SOLVENTS
SOLVENTS: Organic
SONAR SYSTEMS & EQPT
SOUND EFFECTS & MUSIC PRODUCTION: Motion Picture
SOUND EQPT: Electric
SOUND RECORDING STUDIOS
SOUVENIR SHOPS
SOUVENIRS, WHOLESALE
SOYBEAN PRDTS
SPACE RESEARCH & TECHNOLOGY PROGRAMS ADMINISTRATION
SPACE VEHICLE EQPT
SPARK PLUGS: Internal Combustion Engines
SPARK PLUGS: Porcelain
SPEAKER SYSTEMS
SPECIALIZED LIBRARIES
SPECIALTY FOOD STORES: Coffee
SPECIALTY FOOD STORES: Dried Fruit
SPECIALTY FOOD STORES: Eggs & Poultry
SPECIALTY FOOD STORES: Health & Dietetic Food
SPECIALTY FOOD STORES: Soft Drinks
SPEED CHANGERS
SPICE & HERB STORES
SPINDLES: Textile
SPONGES, ANIMAL, WHOLESALE
SPONGES: Bleached & Dyed
SPOOLS: Indl
SPORTING & ATHLETIC GOODS: Bases, Baseball
SPORTING & ATHLETIC GOODS: Basketball Eqpt & Splys, NEC
SPORTING & ATHLETIC GOODS: Bows, Archery
SPORTING & ATHLETIC GOODS: Camping Eqpt & Splys
SPORTING & ATHLETIC GOODS: Cases, Gun & Rod
SPORTING & ATHLETIC GOODS: Crossbows
SPORTING & ATHLETIC GOODS: Darts & Table Sports Eqpt & Splys
SPORTING & ATHLETIC GOODS: Driving Ranges, Golf, Electronic
SPORTING & ATHLETIC GOODS: Dumbbells & Other Weight Eqpt
SPORTING & ATHLETIC GOODS: Fishing Bait, Artificial
SPORTING & ATHLETIC GOODS: Fishing Eqpt
SPORTING & ATHLETIC GOODS: Fishing Tackle, General
SPORTING & ATHLETIC GOODS: Flies, Fishing, Artificial
SPORTING & ATHLETIC GOODS: Hooks, Fishing
SPORTING & ATHLETIC GOODS: Hunting Eqpt
SPORTING & ATHLETIC GOODS: Indian Clubs
SPORTING & ATHLETIC GOODS: Masks, Hockey, Baseball, Etc
SPORTING & ATHLETIC GOODS: Pigeons, Clay Targets
SPORTING & ATHLETIC GOODS: Pools, Swimming, Exc Plastic
SPORTING & ATHLETIC GOODS: Pools, Swimming, Plastic
SPORTING & ATHLETIC GOODS: Reels, Fishing
SPORTING & ATHLETIC GOODS: Shafts, Golf Club
SPORTING & ATHLETIC GOODS: Shooting Eqpt & Splys, General
SPORTING & ATHLETIC GOODS: Skateboards
SPORTING & ATHLETIC GOODS: Soccer Eqpt & Splys
SPORTING & ATHLETIC GOODS: Target Shooting Eqpt
SPORTING & ATHLETIC GOODS: Targets, Archery & Rifle Shooting
SPORTING & ATHLETIC GOODS: Team Sports Eqpt
SPORTING & ATHLETIC GOODS: Tennis Eqpt & Splys
SPORTING & ATHLETIC GOODS: Water Sports Eqpt
SPORTING & RECREATIONAL GOODS & SPLYS WHOLESALERS
SPORTING & RECREATIONAL GOODS, WHOL: Sharpeners, Sporting
SPORTING & RECREATIONAL GOODS, WHOLESALE: Athletic Goods
SPORTING & RECREATIONAL GOODS, WHOLESALE: Bowling
SPORTING & RECREATIONAL GOODS, WHOLESALE: Fitness
SPORTING & RECREATIONAL GOODS, WHOLESALE: Golf
SPORTING & RECREATIONAL GOODS, WHOLESALE: Gymnasium
SPORTING & RECREATIONAL GOODS, WHOLESALE: Hot Tubs
SPORTING & RECREATIONAL GOODS, WHOLESALE: Hunting
SPORTING & RECREATIONAL GOODS, WHOLESALE: Spa
SPORTING GOODS
SPORTING GOODS STORES, NEC
SPORTING GOODS STORES: Ammunition
SPORTING GOODS STORES: Baseball Eqpt
SPORTING GOODS STORES: Camping Eqpt
SPORTING GOODS STORES: Firearms
SPORTING GOODS STORES: Hockey Eqpt, Exc Skates
SPORTING GOODS STORES: Hunting Eqpt
SPORTING GOODS STORES: Playground Eqpt
SPORTING GOODS STORES: Soccer Splys
SPORTING GOODS STORES: Team sports Eqpt
SPORTING GOODS: Archery
SPORTING GOODS: Fishing Nets
SPORTING/ATHLETIC GOODS: Gloves, Boxing, Handball, Etc
SPORTS APPAREL STORES
SPOUTING: Plastic & Fiberglass Reinforced
SPRAYING & DUSTING EQPT
SPRAYS: Self-Defense
SPRINGS: Coiled Flat
SPRINGS: Cold Formed
SPRINGS: Leaf, Automobile, Locomotive, Etc
SPRINGS: Mechanical, Precision
SPRINGS: Precision
SPRINGS: Steel
SPRINGS: Torsion Bar
SPRINGS: Wire
SPRINKLER SYSTEMS: Field
SPRINKLING SYSTEMS: Fire Control
SPROCKETS: Power Transmission
STACKING MACHINES: Automatic
STAGE LIGHTING SYSTEMS
STAINED GLASS ART SVCS
STAINLESS STEEL
STAINLESS STEEL WARE
STAIR TREADS: Rubber
STAIRCASES & STAIRS, WOOD
STAMPED ART GOODS FOR EMBROIDERING
STAMPING: Fabric Articles
STAMPINGS: Automotive
STAMPINGS: Metal
STANDS & RACKS: Engine, Metal
STARTERS & CONTROLLERS: Motor, Electric
STARTERS: Electric Motor
STARTERS: Motor
STATIC ELIMINATORS: Ind
STATIONARY & OFFICE SPLYS, WHOL: Albums, Scrapbooks/Binders
STATIONARY & OFFICE SPLYS, WHOLESALE: Inked Ribbons
STATIONARY & OFFICE SPLYS, WHOLESALE: Marking Devices
STATIONARY & OFFICE SPLYS, WHOLESALE: Office Filing Splys
STATIONER'S SUNDRIES: Rubber
STATIONERY & OFFICE SPLYS WHOLESALERS
STATIONERY ARTICLES: Pottery
STATIONERY PRDTS
STATIONERY: Made From Purchased Materials
STATUARY & OTHER DECORATIVE PRDTS: Nonmetallic
STATUARY GOODS, EXC RELIGIOUS: Wholesalers
STATUES: Nonmetal
STEAM SPLY SYSTEMS SVCS INCLUDING GEOTHERMAL
STEEL & ALLOYS: Tool & Die
STEEL Electrometallurgical
STEEL FABRICATORS
STEEL MILLS
STEEL, COLD-ROLLED: Flat Bright, From Purchased Hot-Rolled
STEEL, COLD-ROLLED: Sheet Or Strip, From Own Hot-Rolled
STEEL, COLD-ROLLED: Strip NEC, From Purchased Hot-Rolled
STEEL, COLD-ROLLED: Strip Or Wire
STEEL, COLD-ROLLED: Strip, Razor Blade, Purchd Hot-Rld Steel
STEEL, HOT-ROLLED: Sheet Or Strip
STEEL: Cold-Rolled
STEEL: Galvanized
STEERING SYSTEMS & COMPONENTS

PRODUCT INDEX

STENCILS
STEREOGRAPHS: Photographic Message Svcs
STITCHING SVCS
STITCHING SVCS: Custom
STONE: Cast Concrete
STONE: Dimension, NEC
STONE: Quarrying & Processing, Own Stone Prdts
STONES, SYNTHETIC: Gem Stone & Indl Use
STONEWARE PRDTS: Pottery
STORE FIXTURES, EXC REFRIGERATED: Wholesalers
STORE FIXTURES: Exc Wood
STORE FIXTURES: Wood
STORE FRONTS: Prefabricated, Metal
STORES: Auto & Home Supply
STORES: Drapery & Upholstery
STRAINERS: Line, Piping Systems
STRAPPING
STRAPS: Bindings, Textile
STRAPS: Braids, Textile
STRAPS: Spindle Banding
STRAPS: Webbing, Woven
STRUCTURAL SUPPORT & BUILDING MATERIAL: Concrete
STUDIOS: Artist
STUDIOS: Artists & Artists' Studios
STUDS & JOISTS: Sheet Metal
SUBDIVIDERS & DEVELOPERS: Real Property, Cemetery Lots Only
SUBMARINE BUILDING & REPAIR
SUBPRESSES, METALWORKING
SUGAR SUBSTITUTES: Organic
SUNDRIES & RELATED PRDTS: Medical & Laboratory, Rubber
SUNROOFS: Motor Vehicle
SUNROOMS: Prefabricated Metal
SUPERMARKETS & OTHER GROCERY STORES
SURFACE ACTIVE AGENTS
SURFACE ACTIVE AGENTS: Emulsifiers, Exc Food & Pharmaceuticl
SURGICAL & MEDICAL INSTRUMENTS WHOLESALERS
SURGICAL APPLIANCES & SPLYS
SURGICAL APPLIANCES & SPLYS
SURGICAL EQPT: See Also Instruments
SURGICAL IMPLANTS
SURVEYING & MAPPING: Land Parcels
SURVEYING INSTRUMENTS WHOLESALERS
SUSPENSION SYSTEMS: Acoustical, Metal
SVC ESTABLISH EQPT, WHOLESALE: Carpet/Rug Clean Eqpt & Sply
SVC ESTABLISHMENT EQPT & SPLYS WHOLESALERS
SVC ESTABLISHMENT EQPT, WHOL: Cleaning & Maint Eqpt & Splys
SVC ESTABLISHMENT EQPT, WHOL: Concrete Burial Vaults & Boxes
SVC ESTABLISHMENT EQPT, WHOLESALE: Beauty Parlor Eqpt & Sply
SVC ESTABLISHMENT EQPT, WHOLESALE: Firefighting Eqpt
SVC ESTABLISHMENT EQPT, WHOLESALE: Restaurant Splys
SVC ESTABLISHMENT EQPT, WHOLESALE: Shredders, Indl & Comm
SWEEPING COMPOUNDS
SWIMMING POOL ACCESS: Leaf Skimmers Or Pool Rakes
SWIMMING POOL EQPT: Filters & Water Conditioning Systems
SWIMMING POOLS, EQPT & SPLYS: Wholesalers
SWITCHBOARDS & PARTS: Power
SWITCHES
SWITCHES: Electric Power
SWITCHES: Electric Power, Exc Snap, Push Button, Etc
SWITCHES: Electronic
SWITCHES: Electronic Applications
SWITCHES: Flow Actuated, Electrical
SWITCHES: Knife, Electric
SWITCHES: Thermostatic
SWITCHES: Time, Electrical Switchgear Apparatus
SWITCHGEAR & SWITCHBOARD APPARATUS
SWITCHGEAR & SWITCHGEAR ACCESS, NEC
SWITCHING EQPT: Radio & Television Communications
SYNAGOGUES
SYNCHROS
SYNTHETIC RESIN FINISHED PRDTS, NEC
SYRUPS, DRINK
SYRUPS, FLAVORING, EXC DRINK
SYRUPS: Pharmaceutical

SYSTEMS ENGINEERING: Computer Related
SYSTEMS INTEGRATION SVCS
SYSTEMS INTEGRATION SVCS: Local Area Network
SYSTEMS INTEGRATION SVCS: Office Computer Automation
SYSTEMS SOFTWARE DEVELOPMENT SVCS

T

TABLE OR COUNTERTOPS, PLASTIC LAMINATED
TABLETS & PADS: Newsprint, Made From Purchased Materials
TABLETS: Bronze Or Other Metal
TABLEWARE OR KITCHEN ARTICLES: Commercial, Fine Earthenware
TABLEWARE: Vitreous China
TACKS: Steel, Wire Or Cut
TAGS & LABELS: Paper
TAGS: Paper, Blank, Made From Purchased Paper
TANK & BOILER CLEANING SVCS
TANK REPAIR & CLEANING SVCS
TANK REPAIR SVCS
TANKS & OTHER TRACKED VEHICLE CMPNTS
TANKS: Concrete
TANKS: Cryogenic, Metal
TANKS: For Tank Trucks, Metal Plate
TANKS: Fuel, Including Oil & Gas, Metal Plate
TANKS: Lined, Metal
TANKS: Military, Including Factory Rebuilding
TANKS: Plastic & Fiberglass
TANKS: Standard Or Custom Fabricated, Metal Plate
TANKS: Storage, Farm, Metal Plate
TANNING SALON EQPT & SPLYS, WHOLESALE
TANNING SALONS
TAPE DRIVES
TAPES, ADHESIVE: MedicaL
TAPES: Fabric
TAPES: Insulating
TAPES: Magnetic
TAPES: Plastic Coated
TAPES: Pressure Sensitive
TARPAULINS
TARPAULINS, WHOLESALE
TATTOO PARLORS
TAX RETURN PREPARATION SVCS
TECHNICAL INSTITUTE
TECHNICAL MANUAL PREPARATION SVCS
TELECOMMUNICATION EQPT REPAIR SVCS, EXC TELEPHONES
TELECOMMUNICATION SYSTEMS & EQPT
TELECOMMUNICATIONS CARRIERS & SVCS: Wired
TELEMETERING EQPT
TELEPHONE BOOTHS, EXC WOOD
TELEPHONE CENTRAL OFFICE EQPT: Dial Or Manual
TELEPHONE EQPT INSTALLATION
TELEPHONE EQPT: Modems
TELEPHONE EQPT: NEC
TELEPHONE SET REPAIR SVCS
TELEPHONE STATION EQPT & PARTS: Wire
TELEPHONE SWITCHING EQPT: Toll Switching
TELEPHONE: Fiber Optic Systems
TELEPHONE: Headsets
TELEPHONE: Sets, Exc Cellular Radio
TELEVISION BROADCASTING & COMMUNICATIONS EQPT
TELEVISION BROADCASTING STATIONS
TELEVISION REPAIR SHOP
TELEVISION: Closed Circuit Eqpt
TEMPORARY HELP SVCS
TENT REPAIR SHOP
TENTS: All Materials
TERMINAL BOARDS
TEST BORING SVCS: Nonmetallic Minerals
TEST BORING, METAL MINING
TESTERS: Battery
TESTERS: Environmental
TESTERS: Gas, Exc Indl Process
TESTERS: Liquid, Exc Indl Process
TESTERS: Physical Property
TESTERS: Water, Exc Indl Process
TESTING SVCS
TEXTILE BAGS WHOLESALERS
TEXTILE FABRICATORS
TEXTILE FINISHING: Chem Coat/Treat, Man, Broadwoven, Cotton
TEXTILE FINISHING: Chemical Coating Or Treating, Narrow

TEXTILE FINISHING: Decorative, Man Fiber & Silk, Broadwoven
TEXTILE FINISHING: Napping, Manmade Fiber & Silk, Broadwoven
TEXTILE: Finishing, Cotton Broadwoven
TEXTILE: Finishing, Raw Stock NEC
TEXTILES
TEXTILES: Flock
TEXTILES: Jute & Flax Prdts
TEXTILES: Tops & Top Processing, Manmade Or Other Fiber
TEXTILES: Tops, Combing & Converting
THEATRICAL LIGHTING SVCS
THEATRICAL PRODUCTION SVCS
THEATRICAL SCENERY
THEATRICAL TALENT & BOOKING AGENCIES
THERMISTORS, EXC TEMPERATURE SENSORS
THERMOCOUPLES
THERMOCOUPLES: Indl Process
THERMOMETERS: Indl
THERMOMETERS: Medical, Digital
THERMOPLASTIC MATERIALS
THERMOPLASTICS
THERMOSETTING MATERIALS
THREAD: Embroidery
THREAD: Rubber
TIES, FORM: Metal
TILE: Brick & Structural, Clay
TILE: Clay, Drain & Structural
TILE: Clay, Roof
TILE: Drain, Clay
TILE: Vinyl, Asbestos
TILE: Wall & Floor, Ceramic
TILE: Wall, Ceramic
TIMING DEVICES: Electronic
TIN
TIN-BASE ALLOYS, PRIMARY
TIRE & INNER TUBE MATERIALS & RELATED PRDTS
TIRE & TUBE REPAIR MATERIALS, WHOLESALE
TIRE CORD & FABRIC
TIRE CORD & FABRIC: Indl, Reinforcing
TIRE DEALERS
TIRE INNER-TUBES
TIRE RECAPPING & RETREADING
TIRE SUNDRIES OR REPAIR MATERIALS: Rubber
TIRES & INNER TUBES
TIRES & TUBES WHOLESALERS
TIRES: Auto
TIRES: Indl Vehicles
TIRES: Plastic
TITANIUM MILL PRDTS
TOBACCO & PRDTS, WHOLESALE: Cigars
TOBACCO & TOBACCO PRDTS WHOLESALERS
TOBACCO STORES & STANDS
TOBACCO: Chewing & Snuff
TOBACCO: Cigarettes
TOBACCO: Cigars
TOBACCO: Smoking
TOILET PREPARATIONS
TOILETRIES, COSMETICS & PERFUME STORES
TOILETRIES, WHOLESALE: Toiletries
TOMBSTONES: Cut Stone, Exc Finishing Or Lettering Only
TOMBSTONES: Terrazzo Or Concrete, Precast
TOOL & DIE STEEL
TOOL REPAIR SVCS
TOOLS & EQPT: Used With Sporting Arms
TOOLS: Carpenters', Including Levels & Chisels, Exc Saws
TOOLS: Hand
TOOLS: Hand, Engravers'
TOOLS: Hand, Jewelers'
TOOLS: Hand, Masons'
TOOLS: Hand, Mechanics
TOOLS: Hand, Plumbers'
TOOLS: Hand, Power
TOOLS: Soldering
TOOTHPASTES, GELS & TOOTHPOWDERS
TOWELS: Fabric & Nonwoven, Made From Purchased Materials
TOWELS: Paper
TOWERS, SECTIONS: Transmission, Radio & Television
TOWERS: Cooling, Sheet Metal
TOWING & TUGBOAT SVC
TOWING SVCS: Marine
TOYS
TOYS & HOBBY GOODS & SPLYS, WHOLESALE: Arts/Crafts Eqpt/Sply

PRODUCT INDEX

TOYS & HOBBY GOODS & SPLYS, WHOLESALE: Balloons, Novelty
TOYS & HOBBY GOODS & SPLYS, WHOLESALE: Dolls
TOYS & HOBBY GOODS & SPLYS, WHOLESALE: Educational Toys
TOYS & HOBBY GOODS & SPLYS, WHOLESALE: Playing Cards
TOYS & HOBBY GOODS & SPLYS, WHOLESALE: Toys & Games
TOYS & HOBBY GOODS & SPLYS, WHOLESALE: Toys, NEC
TOYS & HOBBY GOODS & SPLYS, WHOLESALE: Video Games
TOYS, HOBBY GOODS & SPLYS WHOLESALERS
TOYS: Dolls, Stuffed Animals & Parts
TOYS: Kites
TOYS: Rubber
TRADE SHOW ARRANGEMENT SVCS
TRAILERS & PARTS: Boat
TRAILERS & PARTS: Truck & Semi's
TRAILERS & TRAILER EQPT
TRAILERS OR VANS: Horse Transportation, Fifth-Wheel Type
TRAILERS: Bodies
TRAILERS: Camping, Tent-Type
TRAILERS: Semitrailers, Missile Transportation
TRAILERS: Semitrailers, Truck Tractors
TRANSDUCERS: Electrical Properties
TRANSDUCERS: Pressure
TRANSFORMERS: Distribution
TRANSFORMERS: Distribution, Electric
TRANSFORMERS: Electric
TRANSFORMERS: Furnace, Electric
TRANSFORMERS: Ignition, Domestic Fuel Burners
TRANSFORMERS: Machine Tool
TRANSFORMERS: Meters, Electronic
TRANSFORMERS: Power Related
TRANSFORMERS: Specialty
TRANSFORMERS: Voltage Regulating
TRANSLATION & INTERPRETATION SVCS
TRANSMISSION FLUID, MADE FROM PURCHASED MATERIALS
TRANSMISSIONS: Motor Vehicle
TRANSPORTATION EPQT & SPLYS, WHOLESALE: Boats, Non-Rec
TRANSPORTATION EPQT & SPLYS, WHOLESALE: Combat Vehicles
TRANSPORTATION EPQT & SPLYS, WHOLESALE: Tanks & Tank Compnts
TRANSPORTATION EQPT & SPLYS WHOLESALERS, NEC
TRANSPORTATION EQUIPMENT, NEC
TRANSPORTATION PROGRAM REGULATION & ADMIN, GOVT: State
TRANSPORTATION SVCS, AIR, NONSCHEDULED: Air Cargo Carriers
TRANSPORTATION SVCS, NEC
TRANSPORTATION SVCS: Railroads, Steam
TRANSPORTATION: Air, Scheduled Passenger
TRANSPORTATION: Deep Sea Foreign Freight
TRANSPORTATION: Horse-Drawn
TRAPS: Animal, Iron Or Steel
TRAVEL TRAILERS & CAMPERS
TRAVELER ACCOMMODATIONS, NEC
TRAYS: Plastic
TRAYS: Rubber
TROPHIES, NEC
TROPHIES, PLATED, ALL METALS
TROPHIES, STAINLESS STEEL
TROPHIES, WHOLESALE
TROPHIES: Metal, Exc Silver
TROPHY & PLAQUE STORES
TRUCK & BUS BODIES: Ambulance
TRUCK & BUS BODIES: Automobile Wrecker Truck
TRUCK & BUS BODIES: Bus Bodies
TRUCK & BUS BODIES: Car Carrier
TRUCK & BUS BODIES: Cement Mixer
TRUCK & BUS BODIES: Dump Truck
TRUCK & BUS BODIES: Garbage Or Refuse Truck
TRUCK & BUS BODIES: Motor Vehicle, Specialty
TRUCK & BUS BODIES: Tank Truck
TRUCK & BUS BODIES: Truck Beds
TRUCK & BUS BODIES: Truck Cabs, Motor Vehicles
TRUCK & BUS BODIES: Truck, Motor Vehicle
TRUCK & BUS BODIES: Utility Truck
TRUCK & BUS BODIES: Van Bodies
TRUCK BODIES: Body Parts

TRUCK BODY SHOP
TRUCK DRIVER SVCS
TRUCK GENERAL REPAIR SVC
TRUCK PAINTING & LETTERING SVCS
TRUCK PARTS & ACCESSORIES: Wholesalers
TRUCKING & HAULING SVCS: Animal & Farm Prdt
TRUCKING & HAULING SVCS: Contract Basis
TRUCKING & HAULING SVCS: Garbage, Collect/Transport Only
TRUCKING & HAULING SVCS: Hazardous Waste
TRUCKING & HAULING SVCS: Heavy Machinery, Local
TRUCKING & HAULING SVCS: Liquid, Local
TRUCKING & HAULING SVCS: Machinery, Heavy
TRUCKING & HAULING SVCS: Mail Carriers, Contract
TRUCKING, ANIMAL
TRUCKING, AUTOMOBILE CARRIER
TRUCKING, DUMP
TRUCKING: Except Local
TRUCKING: Local, With Storage
TRUCKING: Local, Without Storage
TRUCKS & TRACTORS: Industrial
TRUCKS, INDL: Wholesalers
TRUCKS: Forklift
TRUCKS: Indl
TRUNKS
TRUSSES & FRAMING: Prefabricated Metal
TRUSSES: Wood, Floor
TRUSSES: Wood, Roof
TRUST MANAGEMENT SVC, EXC EDUCATIONAL, RELIGIOUS & CHARITY
TUB CONTAINERS: Plastic
TUBE & PIPE MILL EQPT
TUBE & TUBING FABRICATORS
TUBES: Finned, For Heat Transfer
TUBES: Generator, Electron Beam, Beta Ray
TUBES: Hard Rubber
TUBES: Paper
TUBES: Paper Or Fiber, Chemical Or Electrical Uses
TUBES: Steel & Iron
TUBES: Wrought, Welded Or Lock Joint
TUBING: Copper
TUBING: Electrical Use, Quartz
TUBING: Flexible, Metallic
TUBING: Glass
TUBING: Plastic
TUBING: Rubber
TUBING: Seamless
TUGBOAT SVCS
TUNGSTEN CARBIDE POWDER
TUNGSTEN MILL PRDTS
TURBINE GENERATOR SET UNITS: Hydraulic, Complete
TURBINES & TURBINE GENERATOR SET UNITS, COMPLETE
TURBINES & TURBINE GENERATOR SETS
TURBINES & TURBINE GENERATOR SETS & PARTS
TURBINES: Gas, Mechanical Drive
TURBINES: Hydraulic, Complete
TURBINES: Steam
TURBO-SUPERCHARGERS: Aircraft
TURNSTILES
TWINE PRDTS
TYPE: Rubber
TYPESETTING SVC
TYPESETTING SVC: Computer

U

ULTRASONIC EQPT: Cleaning, Exc Med & Dental
UMBRELLAS & CANES
UNDERCOATINGS: Paint
UNIFORM SPLY SVCS: Indl
UNIFORM STORES
UNISEX HAIR SALONS
UNIVERSITY
UNSUPPORTED PLASTICS: Floor Or Wall Covering
UPHOLSTERY WORK SVCS
USED CAR DEALERS
USED MERCHANDISE STORES: Musical Instruments
USED MERCHANDISE STORES: Rare Books
UTENSILS: Cast Aluminum
UTENSILS: Cast Aluminum, Cooking Or Kitchen
UTENSILS: Household, Cooking & Kitchen, Metal
UTILITY TRAILER DEALERS

V

VACUUM CLEANER STORES

VACUUM CLEANERS: Household
VACUUM CLEANERS: Indl Type
VALUE-ADDED RESELLERS: Computer Systems
VALVE REPAIR SVCS, INDL
VALVES
VALVES & PARTS: Gas, Indl
VALVES & PIPE FITTINGS
VALVES & REGULATORS: Pressure, Indl
VALVES: Aerosol, Metal
VALVES: Aircraft
VALVES: Aircraft, Fluid Power
VALVES: Aircraft, Hydraulic
VALVES: Control, Automatic
VALVES: Engine
VALVES: Fluid Power, Control, Hydraulic & pneumatic
VALVES: Gas Cylinder, Compressed
VALVES: Hard Rubber
VALVES: Indl
VALVES: Nuclear Power Plant, Ferrous
VALVES: Plumbing & Heating
VALVES: Regulating & Control, Automatic
VALVES: Regulating, Process Control
VALVES: Water Works
VAN CONVERSIONS
VANADIUM ORE MINING, NEC
VARIETY STORES
VARNISHES, NEC
VASES: Pottery
VAULTS & SAFES WHOLESALERS
VEHICLES: All Terrain
VEHICLES: Recreational
VENDING MACHINE OPERATORS: Cigarette
VENDING MACHINE OPERATORS: Sandwich & Hot Food
VENDING MACHINES & PARTS
VENETIAN BLIND REPAIR SHOP
VENETIAN BLINDS & SHADES
VENTILATING EQPT: Metal
VENTILATING EQPT: Sheet Metal
VENTURE CAPITAL COMPANIES
VESSELS: Process, Indl, Metal Plate
VETERINARY PHARMACEUTICAL PREPARATIONS
VETERINARY PRDTS: Instruments & Apparatus
VIBRATORS, ELECTRIC: Beauty & Barber Shop
VIBRATORS: Concrete Construction
VIBRATORS: Interrupter
VIDEO & AUDIO EQPT, WHOLESALE
VIDEO TAPE PRODUCTION SVCS
VIDEO TRIGGERS EXC REMOTE CONTROL TV DEVICES
VIDEO TRIGGERS: Remote Control TV Devices
VINYL RESINS, NEC
VISES: Machine
VISUAL COMMUNICATIONS SYSTEMS
VITAMINS: Pharmaceutical Preparations
VOCATIONAL REHABILITATION AGENCY
VOCATIONAL TRAINING AGENCY

W

WALL & CEILING SQUARES: Concrete
WALL COVERINGS: Rubber
WALLPAPER & WALL COVERINGS
WALLS: Curtain, Metal
WAREHOUSING & STORAGE FACILITIES, NEC
WAREHOUSING & STORAGE, REFRIGERATED: Cold Storage Or Refrig
WAREHOUSING & STORAGE, REFRIGERATED: Frozen Or Refrig Goods
WAREHOUSING & STORAGE: Farm Prdts
WAREHOUSING & STORAGE: General
WAREHOUSING & STORAGE: General
WAREHOUSING & STORAGE: Self Storage
WARM AIR HEATING & AC EQPT & SPLYS, WHOL: Dust Collecting
WARM AIR HEATING & AC EQPT & SPLYS, WHOL: Elec Heating Eqpt
WARM AIR HEATING & AC EQPT & SPLYS, WHOLESALE Air Filters
WARM AIR HEATING & AC EQPT & SPLYS, WHOLESALE Furnaces, Elec
WARM AIR HEATING/AC EQPT/SPLYS, WHOL Warm Air Htg Eqpt/Splys
WASHCLOTHS & BATH MITTS, FROM PURCHASED MATERIALS
WASHERS
WASHERS: Metal
WASHERS: Rubber

INDEX

PRODUCT INDEX

WASHERS: Spring, Metal
WASHING MACHINES: Household
WATCH & CLOCK STORES
WATCH REPAIR SVCS
WATER HEATERS
WATER PURIFICATION EQPT: Household
WATER PURIFICATION PRDTS: Chlorination Tablets & Kits
WATER SOFTENER SVCS
WATER SOFTENING WHOLESALERS
WATER SPLY: Irrigation
WATER SUPPLY
WATER TREATMENT EQPT: Indl
WATER: Distilled
WATER: Pasteurized & Mineral, Bottled & Canned
WATER: Pasteurized, Canned & Bottled, Etc
WATERPROOFING COMPOUNDS
WEATHER STRIP: Sponge Rubber
WEATHER STRIPS: Metal
WEIGHING MACHINERY & APPARATUS
WELDING & CUTTING APPARATUS & ACCESS, NEC
WELDING EQPT
WELDING EQPT & SPLYS WHOLESALERS
WELDING EQPT & SPLYS: Gas
WELDING EQPT & SPLYS: Generators, Arc Welding, AC & DC
WELDING EQPT & SPLYS: Resistance, Electric
WELDING EQPT & SPLYS: Spot, Electric
WELDING EQPT & SPLYS: Wire, Bare & Coated
WELDING EQPT REPAIR SVCS
WELDING EQPT: Electric
WELDING EQPT: Electrical
WELDING MACHINES & EQPT: Ultrasonic
WELDING REPAIR SVC
WELDING SPLYS, EXC GASES: Wholesalers
WELDING TIPS: Heat Resistant, Metal
WELDMENTS
WELL CURBING: Concrete
WET CORN MILLING
WHEELCHAIR LIFTS
WHEELCHAIRS
WHEELS
WHEELS & BRAKE SHOES: Railroad, Cast Iron
WHEELS & GRINDSTONES, EXC ARTIFICIAL: Abrasive
WHEELS & PARTS
WHEELS, GRINDING: Artificial
WHEELS: Abrasive
WHEELS: Buffing & Polishing
WHEELS: Disc, Wheelbarrow, Stroller, Etc, Stamped Metal
WHEELS: Iron & Steel, Locomotive & Car
WHEELS: Railroad Car, Cast Steel

WHEELS: Water
WHITING MINING: Crushed & Broken
WICKING
WINCHES
WINDINGS: Coil, Electronic
WINDMILLS: Electric Power Generation
WINDMILLS: Farm Type
WINDOW & DOOR FRAMES
WINDOW FRAMES & SASHES: Plastic
WINDOW FRAMES, MOLDING & TRIM: Vinyl
WINDOW FURNISHINGS WHOLESALERS
WINDOW SCREENING: Plastic
WINDOWS: Frames, Wood
WINDOWS: Wood
WINDSHIELD WIPER SYSTEMS
WINDSHIELDS: Plastic
WINE & DISTILLED ALCOHOLIC BEVERAGES WHOLESALERS
WINE CELLARS, BONDED: Wine, Blended
WIRE
WIRE & CABLE: Aluminum
WIRE & CABLE: Nonferrous, Aircraft
WIRE & CABLE: Nonferrous, Building
WIRE & WIRE PRDTS
WIRE CLOTH & WOVEN WIRE PRDTS, MADE FROM PURCHASED WIRE
WIRE FABRIC: Welded Steel
WIRE FENCING & ACCESS WHOLESALERS
WIRE MATERIALS: Aluminum
WIRE MATERIALS: Copper
WIRE MATERIALS: Steel
WIRE PRDTS: Ferrous Or Iron, Made In Wiredrawing Plants
WIRE PRDTS: Steel & Iron
WIRE WINDING OF PURCHASED WIRE
WIRE, FLAT: Strip, Cold-Rolled, Exc From Hot-Rolled Mills
WIRE: Barbed
WIRE: Communication
WIRE: Magnet
WIRE: Mesh
WIRE: Nonferrous
WIRE: Steel, Insulated Or Armored
WIRE: Wire, Ferrous Or Iron
WIRING DEVICES WHOLESALERS
WOMEN'S & CHILDREN'S CLOTHING WHOLESALERS, NEC
WOMEN'S & GIRLS' SPORTSWEAR WHOLESALERS
WOMEN'S SPORTSWEAR STORES
WOOD & WOOD BY-PRDTS, WHOLESALE
WOOD CHIPS, PRODUCED AT THE MILL
WOOD EXTRACT PRDTS

WOOD PRDTS
WOOD PRDTS: Applicators
WOOD PRDTS: Door Trim
WOOD PRDTS: Engraved
WOOD PRDTS: Furniture Inlays, Veneers
WOOD PRDTS: Ladders & Stepladders
WOOD PRDTS: Laundry
WOOD PRDTS: Moldings, Unfinished & Prefinished
WOOD PRDTS: Mulch Or Sawdust
WOOD PRDTS: Mulch, Wood & Bark
WOOD PRDTS: Novelties, Fiber
WOOD PRDTS: Panel Work
WOOD PRDTS: Plugs
WOOD PRDTS: Reed, Rattan, Wicker & Willow ware, Exc Furnitr
WOOD PRDTS: Saddle Trees
WOOD PRDTS: Signboards
WOOD PRDTS: Survey Stakes
WOOD PRDTS: Trophy Bases
WOOD PRDTS: Veneer Work, Inlaid
WOOD PRDTS: Washboards, Wood & Part Wood
WOOD PRDTS: Weather Strip, Wood
WOOD PRDTS: Wrappers, Excelsior
WOOD PRODUCTS: Reconstituted
WOOD TREATING: Millwork
WOOD TREATING: Structural Lumber & Timber
WOODWORK & TRIM: Exterior & Ornamental
WOODWORK & TRIM: Interior & Ornamental
WOODWORK: Carved & Turned
WOODWORK: Interior & Ornamental, NEC
WOODWORK: Ornamental, Cornices, Mantels, Etc.
WOOL: Felted
WORD PROCESSING EQPT
WORK EXPERIENCE CENTER
WOVEN WIRE PRDTS, NEC
WREATHS: Artificial
WRENCHES

X

X-RAY EQPT & TUBES
X-RAY EQPT REPAIR SVCS

Y

YARN & YARN SPINNING
YARN: Manmade & Synthetic Fiber, Twisting Or Winding

PRODUCT SECTION

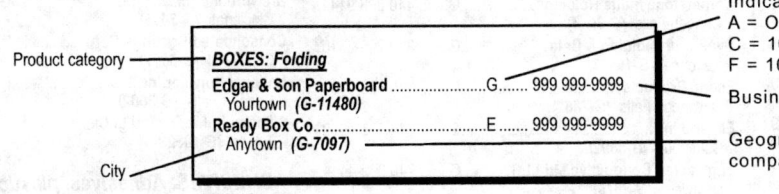

Indicates approximate employment figure
A = Over 500 employees, B = 251-500
C = 101-250, D = 51-100, E = 20-50
F = 10-19, G = 3-9

Product category → BOXES: Folding
Edgar & Son Paperboard ....G...... 999 999-9999
  Yourtown (G-11480)
Ready Box Co..E...... 999 999-9999
  Anytown (G-7097)
City

Business phone

Geographic Section entry number where full company information appears.

See footnotes for symbols and codes identification.
- Refer to the Industrial Product Index preceding this section to locate product headings.

ABRASIVE STONES, EXC GRINDING STONES: Ground Or Whole

Abrasive Technology Inc ....C....... 740 548-4100
  Lewis Center (G-11740)

ABRASIVES

Abrasive Source Inc ....F....... 937 526-9753
  Russia (G-16605)
Abrasive Supply Company Inc ....F....... 330 894-2818
  Minerva (G-14175)
Ali Industries Inc ....C....... 937 878-3946
  Fairborn (G-9450)
ARC Abrasives Inc ....D....... 800 888-4885
  Troy (G-18638)
Baaron Abrasives Inc ....G....... 330 263-7737
  Wooster (G-20568)
Buffalo Abrasives Inc ....G....... 614 891-6450
  Westerville (G-20039)
Coastal Diamond Incorporated.......G....... 440 946-7171
  Mentor (G-13417)
Diamond Innovations Inc ....B....... 614 438-2000
  Columbus (G-6863)
Hec Investments Inc ....C....... 937 278-9123
  Dayton (G-8247)
Inner City Abrasives LLC ....G....... 216 391-4402
  Cleveland (G-5459)
Jason Incorporated ....F....... 513 860-3400
  Hamilton (G-10576)
Lawrence Industries Inc ....C....... 216 518-7000
  Cleveland (G-5566)
Mill-Rose Company ....C....... 440 255-9171
  Mentor (G-13520)
National Lime and Stone Co ....C....... 419 396-7671
  Carey (G-2884)
Ohio Slitting & Storage ....E....... 937 452-1108
  Camden (G-2465)
Park-Hio Frged McHned Pdts LLC ..F....... 216 692-7200
  Euclid (G-9432)
Performance Abrasives Inc ....G....... 513 733-9283
  Cincinnati (G-4147)
Sure-Foot Industries Corp ....E....... 440 234-4446
  Cleveland (G-6131)
US Technology Corporation ....E....... 330 455-1181
  Canton (G-2853)
US Technology Media Inc ....F....... 330 874-3094
  Bolivar (G-1929)
Vibra Finish Co.................................E....... 513 870-6300
  Fairfield (G-9572)

ABRASIVES: Coated

Lexington Abrasives Inc ....D....... 330 821-1166
  Alliance (G-482)
Nanolap Technologies LLC..............E....... 877 658-4949
  Englewood (G-9370)
Premier Coatings Ltd ....F....... 513 942-1070
  West Chester (G-19766)

ABRASIVES: Grains

Golden Dynamic Inc ....G....... 614 575-1222
  Columbus (G-6959)

ABRASIVES: Synthetic

Noritake Co Inc................................E....... 513 234-0770
  Mason (G-12915)

ACCELERATION INDICATORS & SYSTEM COMPONENTS: Aerospace

Eaton Aerospace LLC......................F....... 216 523-5000
  Cleveland (G-5144)
Eaton Aerospace LLC......................E....... 216 523-5000
  Cleveland (G-5145)
Midwest Precision Holdings Inc ......D....... 440 497-4086
  Eastlake (G-9121)
Nhvs International Inc ....B....... 440 527-8610
  Mentor (G-13527)

ACCELERATORS, RUBBER PROCESSING: Cyclic or Acyclic

Image Armor LLC ....G....... 877 673-4377
  Midvale (G-13979)

ACCELERATORS: Electron Linear

Spang & Company ....E....... 440 350-6108
  Mentor (G-13585)

ACCELERATORS: Linear

Ci Disposition Co ....E....... 216 587-5200
  Brooklyn Heights (G-2118)

ACCOUNTING MACHINES & CASH REGISTERS

Cambridge Ohio Production & As ...F....... 740 432-6383
  Cambridge (G-2429)

ACCOUNTING SVCS, NEC

Patterson Colburne..........................G....... 419 866-5544
  Holland (G-10949)
St John Ltd Inc ....G....... 614 851-8153
  Galloway (G-10181)

ACCOUNTING SVCS: Certified Public

Patrick J Burke & Co ....E....... 513 455-8200
  Cincinnati (G-4137)
Watson Haran & Company Inc.......G....... 937 436-1414
  Dayton (G-8585)

ACIDS

Emery Oleochemicals LLC..............B....... 513 762-2500
  Cincinnati (G-3636)

ACIDS: Hydrochloric

Jones-Hamilton Co ....D....... 419 666-9838
  Walbridge (G-19296)

ACIDS: Inorganic

Capital Resin Corporation................D....... 614 445-7177
  Columbus (G-6733)
Detrex Corporation ....F....... 216 749-2605
  Cleveland (G-5087)

ACIDS: Sulfuric, Oleum

Veolia NA Regeneration Srvcs.......F....... 513 941-4121
  North Bend (G-15057)

ACOUSTICAL BOARD & TILE

Essi Acoustical Products ....F....... 216 251-7888
  Cleveland (G-5192)

Mpc Inc...F....... 440 835-1405
  Cleveland (G-5707)

ACRYLIC RESINS

Capital Resin Corporation................D....... 614 445-7177
  Columbus (G-6733)
Plaskolite LLC ....D....... 740 450-1109
  Zanesville (G-21168)
Plaskolite LLC ....B....... 614 294-3281
  Columbus (G-7321)

ACTUATORS: Indl, NEC

Automation Technology Inc ....E....... 937 233-6084
  Dayton (G-8045)
Kz Solutions Inc ....G....... 513 942-9378
  West Chester (G-19733)
Moog Inc ....D....... 330 682-0010
  Orrville (G-15603)
Norgren Inc ....C....... 937 833-4033
  Brookville (G-2179)
SMC Corporation of America ....E....... 330 659-2006
  Richfield (G-16488)
Thermotion Corp ....F....... 440 639-8325
  Mentor (G-13605)

ADAPTERS: Well

Grip Force LLC ....G....... 440 497-7014
  Eastlake (G-9112)
Wells Inc ....F....... 419 457-2611
  Risingsun (G-16519)

ADDITIVE BASED PLASTIC MATERIALS: Plasticizers

Mum Industries Inc ....E....... 440 269-4966
  Mentor (G-13525)
Sun Color Corporation ....G....... 330 499-7010
  North Canton (G-15123)

ADDRESSING SVCS

Cleveland Letter Service Inc ....E....... 216 781-8300
  Chagrin Falls (G-3013)
Franklins Printing Company ....F....... 740 452-6375
  Zanesville (G-21138)
Gerald L Hermann Co Inc ....F....... 513 661-1818
  Cincinnati (G-3750)
Hecks Direct Mail & Prtg Svc ....E....... 419 697-3505
  Toledo (G-18327)

ADDRESSOGRAPHING SVCS

Selby Service/Roxy Press Inc.........G....... 513 241-3445
  Cincinnati (G-4318)

ADHESIVES

Adchem Adhesives Inc...................F....... 440 526-1976
  Cleveland (G-4614)
Akzo Nobel Paints LLC....................G....... 513 242-0530
  Cincinnati (G-3316)
Certon Technologies Inc ....F....... 440 786-7185
  Bedford (G-1395)
Choice Brands Adhesives Ltd ....G....... 800 330-5566
  Cincinnati (G-3472)
Conversion Tech Intl Inc ....E....... 419 924-5566
  West Unity (G-19967)
CP Industries Inc.............................F....... 740 763-2886
  Newark (G-14865)
Elaston Company ....F....... 330 863-2865
  Malvern (G-12389)

ADHESIVES

PRODUCT SECTION

Engineered Mtls Systems Inc ....E		740 362-4444
Delaware *(G-8677)*		
Entrochem Inc ....F		614 946-7602
Columbus *(G-6900)*		
Evans Adhesive Corporation ....E		614 451-2665
Columbus *(G-6908)*		
Fairmount Santrol Inc ....G		440 214-3200
Independence *(G-11127)*		
Har Equipment Sales Inc ....G		440 786-7189
Bedford *(G-1411)*		
HB Fuller Company ....E		513 719-3600
Blue Ash *(G-1786)*		
HB Fuller Company ....E		513 719-3600
Blue Ash *(G-1787)*		
Henkel Adhesive Corporation ....E		513 677-5800
Maineville *(G-12370)*		
Henkel Corporation C		216 475-3600
Cleveland *(G-5392)*		
Henkel US Operations Corp ....E		440 255-8900
Mentor *(G-13464)*		
Henkel US Operations Corp ....D		513 830-0260
Cincinnati *(G-3808)*		
Imperial Adhesives ....G		513 351-1300
Cincinnati *(G-3841)*		
Invisible Repair Products Inc ....G		330 798-0441
Akron *(G-219)*		
Millennium Adhesive Products ....G		440 708-1212
Chagrin Falls *(G-3060)*		
Mitsubishi Chls Perf Plyrs Inc ....D		419 483-2931
Bellevue *(G-1540)*		
Morgan Adhesives Company LLC ....B		330 688-1111
Stow *(G-17606)*		
Nova Films and Foils Inc ....G		440 201-1300
Bedford *(G-1431)*		
Ohio Valley Adhesives ....G		513 454-1800
Cincinnati *(G-4106)*		
Paramet Arguesо Kindt Inc ....G		216 252-4122
Cleveland *(G-5839)*		
Premier Building Solutions Inc ....D		330 244-2907
Massillon *(G-13042)*		
RPM Consumer Holding Company ....G		330 273-5090
Medina *(G-13330)*		
Savare Specialty Adhesives LLC ....E		614 255-2648
Delaware *(G-8723)*		
Shelli R McMurray ....G		614 275-4381
Columbus *(G-7444)*		
Southern Adhesive Coatings ....G		513 561-8440
Cincinnati *(G-4355)*		
Spectra Group Limited Inc ....G		419 837-9783
Millbury *(G-14052)*		
Sunstar Engrg Americas Inc C		937 746-8575
Springboro *(G-17354)*		
Technicote Inc ....E		330 928-1476
Cuyahoga Falls *(G-7926)*		
Three Bond International Inc ....E		937 610-3000
Dayton *(G-8556)*		
Three Bond International Inc ....D		513 779-7300
West Chester *(G-19808)*		
Toagosei America Inc ....D		614 718-3855
West Jefferson *(G-19928)*		
Triangle Adhesives LLC ....G		330 670-9722
Akron *(G-412)*		

ADHESIVES & SEALANTS

Akron Coating & Adhesives Inc ....F		330 724-4716
Akron *(G-35)*		
Akron Paint & Varnish Inc ....D		330 773-8911
Akron *(G-46)*		
Alpha Coatings Inc C		419 435-5111
Fostoria *(G-9832)*		
Arclin USA LLC ....E		419 726-5013
Toledo *(G-18190)*		
Avery Dennison Corporation ....B		440 358-3700
Painesville *(G-15716)*		
Boltaron Inc ....D		740 498-5900
Newcomerstown *(G-14970)*		
Brewer Company ....G		513 576-6300
Cincinnati *(G-3414)*		
Brewer Company ....E		614 279-8688
Columbus *(G-6694)*		
Cardinal Rubber Company Inc ....E		330 745-2191
Barberton *(G-1069)*		
Cemedine North America LLC ....G		513 618-4652
Cincinnati *(G-3454)*		
Chemspec Ltd ....F		330 896-0355
Uniontown *(G-18915)*		
Cincinnati Assn For The Blind C		513 221-8558
Cincinnati *(G-3481)*		
Consolidated Coatings Corp ....E		216 514-7596
Cleveland *(G-5017)*		
Continental Products Company ....E		216 531-0710
Cleveland *(G-5024)*		
Cornerstone Indus Holdings ....G		440 893-9144
Chagrin Falls *(G-3014)*		
Dyna Tech Molding & Beta ....G		330 296-2315
Ravenna *(G-16377)*		
Econo Products Inc ....F		330 923-4101
Cuyahoga Falls *(G-7862)*		
Elmer S Inc ....G		614 225-4000
Columbus *(G-6892)*		
Engineered Conductive Mtl LLC ....G		740 362-4444
Delaware *(G-8676)*		
Gdc Inc ....G		574 533-3128
Wooster *(G-20596)*		
Gold Key Processing Inc C		440 632-0901
Middlefield *(G-13800)*		
Henkel US Operations Corp C		440 250-7700
Westlake *(G-20122)*		
Hexpol Compounding LLC C		440 834-4644
Burton *(G-2360)*		
Hoover & Wells Inc C		419 691-9220
Toledo *(G-18335)*		
Illinois Tool Works Inc C		513 489-7600
Blue Ash *(G-1791)*		
Illinois Tool Works Inc ....D		440 914-3100
Solon *(G-17166)*		
Kcg Inc ....G		614 238-9450
Columbus *(G-7084)*		
Laird Technologies Inc ....E		216 939-2300
Cleveland *(G-5554)*		
Laminate Technologies Inc ....D		419 448-0812
Tiffin *(G-18064)*		
Lubrizol Global Management ....F		216 447-5000
Brecksville *(G-2048)*		
Mameco International Inc ....F		216 752-4400
Cleveland *(G-5611)*		
Marlen Manufacturing & Dev Co ....E		216 292-7546
Bedford *(G-1425)*		
Millennium Adhesive Pdts Inc ....F		440 708-1212
Chagrin Falls *(G-3024)*		
Nac Products ....G		330 644-3117
Coventry Township *(G-7774)*		
National Adhesives Inc ....F		513 683-8650
Cincinnati *(G-4059)*		
National Starch Chemical ....G		513 830-0260
Cincinnati *(G-4062)*		
Polymerics Inc ....E		330 434-6665
Cuyahoga Falls *(G-7906)*		
PRC - Desoto International Inc C		800 772-9378
Chillicothe *(G-3216)*		
Priest Services Inc ....E		440 333-1123
Mayfield Heights *(G-13170)*		
Quest Solutions Group LLC ....G		513 703-4520
Liberty Township *(G-11818)*		
Republic Powdered Metals Inc ....D		330 225-3192
Medina *(G-13327)*		
RPM International Inc ....D		330 273-5090
Medina *(G-13331)*		
Rubex Inc ....F		614 875-6343
Grove City *(G-10463)*		
Ruscoe Company ....E		330 253-8148
Akron *(G-358)*		
Sem-Com Company Inc ....F		419 537-8813
Toledo *(G-18517)*		
Sherwin-Williams Company C		330 830-6000
Massillon *(G-13048)*		
Silicone Solutions Inc ....G		330 920-3125
Cuyahoga Falls *(G-7917)*		
Sirrus Inc ....E		513 448-0308
Loveland *(G-12233)*		
Sonoco Products Company ....D		937 429-0040
Beavercreek Township *(G-1374)*		
Spinnaker Coating LLC C		937 332-6300
Troy *(G-18710)*		
Sportsmaster ....F		440 257-3900
Mentor *(G-13586)*		
Thorworks Industries Inc ....E		419 626-4375
Sandusky *(G-16855)*		
Tremco Inc ....E		216 514-7783
Beachwood *(G-1282)*		
Tremco Incorporated ....D		419 289-2050
Ashland *(G-752)*		
United McGill Corporation ....E		614 829-1200
Groveport *(G-10516)*		
Waytek Corporation ....E		937 743-6142
Franklin *(G-9932)*		
Weatherproofing Tech Inc ....G		281 480-7900
Beachwood *(G-1286)*		

ADHESIVES & SEALANTS WHOLESALERS

Brewpro Inc ....G		513 577-7200
Cincinnati *(G-3415)*		
Consolidated Coatings Corp ....E		216 514-7596
Cleveland *(G-5017)*		
National Polymer Inc ....F		440 708-1245
Chagrin Falls *(G-3062)*		
Silicone Solutions Intl LLC ....G		419 720-8709
Toledo *(G-18523)*		

ADHESIVES: Adhesives, plastic

Durez Corporation C		567 295-6400
Kenton *(G-11404)*		
National Polymer Inc ....F		440 708-1245
Chagrin Falls *(G-3062)*		

ADHESIVES: Epoxy

Nanosperse LLC ....G		937 296-5030
Kettering *(G-11435)*		
Renegade Materials Corporation ....E		508 579-7888
Miamisburg *(G-13711)*		
Sivon Manufacturing LLC ....G		440 259-5505
Perry *(G-15912)*		
Summitville Tiles Inc ....E		330 868-6463
Minerva *(G-14203)*		

ADVERTISING AGENCIES

Aardvark Screen Prtg & EMB LLC ....F		419 354-6686
Bowling Green *(G-1948)*		
Applied Graphics Ltd ....G		419 756-6882
Mansfield *(G-12407)*		
Black River Group Inc ....E		419 524-6699
Mansfield *(G-12411)*		
Buckeye Business Forms Inc ....G		614 882-1890
Westerville *(G-19982)*		
Dee Printing Inc ....E		614 777-8700
Columbus *(G-6856)*		
International Advg Concepts ....G		440 331-4733
Cleveland *(G-5467)*		
Job News ....G		513 984-5724
Blue Ash *(G-1795)*		
L M Berry and Company ....A		937 296-2121
Moraine *(G-14364)*		
Mark Advertising Agency Inc ....F		419 626-9000
Sandusky *(G-16827)*		
McQueen Advertising Inc ....G		440 967-1137
Vermilion *(G-19168)*		
Paul/Jay Associates ....G		740 676-8776
Bellaire *(G-1488)*		
Pixslap Inc ....G		937 559-2671
Middletown *(G-13942)*		
Propress Inc ....F		216 631-8200
Cleveland *(G-5929)*		

ADVERTISING AGENCIES: Consultants

Airmate Company ....D		419 636-3184
Bryan *(G-2258)*		
David Esrati ....G		937 228-4433
Dayton *(G-8126)*		
Just Business Inc ....F		866 577-3303
Dayton *(G-8287)*		
Penca Design Group Ltd ....G		440 210-4422
Painesville *(G-15774)*		

ADVERTISING DISPLAY PRDTS

Aster Industries Inc ....F		330 762-7965
Akron *(G-72)*		
On Display Ltd ....E		513 841-1600
Batavia *(G-1174)*		
Power Media Inc ....G		330 475-0500
Akron *(G-325)*		
Skr Enterprises LLC ....G		419 891-1112
Maumee *(G-13145)*		
Toledo Mobile Media LLC ....G		419 389-0687
Toledo *(G-18562)*		

ADVERTISING REPRESENTATIVES: Electronic Media

Moments To Remember USA LLC ....G		330 830-0839
Massillon *(G-13027)*		

ADVERTISING REPRESENTATIVES: Media

Agri Communicators Inc ....E		614 273-0465
Columbus *(G-6551)*		

(G-0000) Company's Geographic Section entry number

PRODUCT SECTION

AGRICULTURAL EQPT: Grounds Mowing Eqpt

ADVERTISING REPRESENTATIVES: Newspaper

American City Bus Journals Inc .... E 937 528-4400
  Dayton *(G-8024)*
B G News .... E 419 372-2601
  Bowling Green *(G-1952)*
Copley Ohio Newspapers Inc .... C 330 364-5577
  New Philadelphia *(G-14765)*
Gazette Publishing Company .... F 419 335-2010
  Wauseon *(G-19517)*
News Watchman & Paper .... F 740 947-2149
  Waverly *(G-19553)*
Ohio Newspaper Services Inc .... G 614 486-6677
  Columbus *(G-7252)*
Progressor Times .... G 419 396-7567
  Carey *(G-2887)*
Trumbull County Legal News .... G 330 392-7112
  Warren *(G-19451)*

ADVERTISING SPECIALTIES, WHOLESALE

Ace Plastics Co .... G 330 928-7720
  Stow *(G-17566)*
Akos Promotions Inc .... G 513 398-6324
  Mason *(G-12822)*
Auto Dealer Designs Inc .... E 330 374-7666
  Akron *(G-74)*
Baker Plastics Inc .... G 330 743-3142
  Youngstown *(G-20851)*
Benchmark Prints .... F 419 332-7640
  Fremont *(G-9997)*
Bluelogos Inc .... F 614 898-9971
  Westerville *(G-20038)*
Bottomline Ink Corporation .... E 419 897-8000
  Perrysburg *(G-15923)*
Cal Sales Embroidery .... G 440 236-3820
  Columbia Station *(G-6431)*
Capehart Enterprises LLC .... F 614 769-7746
  Columbus *(G-6730)*
Charizma Corp .... G 216 621-2220
  Cleveland *(G-4909)*
Cnr Marketing Ltd .... G 937 293-1030
  Dayton *(G-8094)*
Custom Sportswear Imprints LLC .... G 330 335-8326
  Wadsworth *(G-19231)*
Echographics Inc .... G 440 846-2330
  North Ridgeville *(G-15222)*
Evolution Crtive Solutions LLC .... E 513 681-4450
  Cincinnati *(G-3660)*
F & K Concepts Inc .... G 937 426-6843
  Springboro *(G-17326)*
Flashions Sportswear Ltd .... G 937 323-5885
  Springfield *(G-17403)*
G Q Business Products .... G 513 792-4750
  Blue Ash *(G-1780)*
Gail Berner .... G 937 322-0314
  Springfield *(G-17406)*
Galaxy Balloons Incorporated .... C 216 476-3360
  Cleveland *(G-5287)*
Gary Lawrence Enterprises Inc .... G 330 833-7181
  Massillon *(G-12986)*
Gauntlet Awards & Engraving .... G 937 890-5811
  Dayton *(G-8214)*
Harris Hawk .... G 800 459-4295
  Mason *(G-12885)*
In-Touch Corp .... G 440 268-0881
  Cleveland *(G-5447)*
Madison Group Inc .... G 216 362-9000
  Cleveland *(G-5602)*
Marathon Mfg & Sup Co .... D 330 343-2656
  New Philadelphia *(G-14783)*
Mr Emblem Inc .... G 419 697-1888
  Oregon *(G-15561)*
Novelty Advertising Co Inc .... E 740 622-3113
  Coshocton *(G-7745)*
Ohio State Institute of Fin .... G 614 861-8811
  Reynoldsburg *(G-16445)*
P S Superior Inc .... F 216 587-1000
  Cleveland *(G-5833)*
Peter Graham Dunn Inc .... E 330 816-0035
  Dalton *(G-7950)*
Publishing Group Ltd .... F 614 572-1240
  Columbus *(G-7356)*
Randd Assoc Prtg & Promotions .... G 937 294-1874
  Dayton *(G-8464)*
Screen Works Inc .... E 937 264-9111
  Dayton *(G-8499)*
Shamrock Companies Inc .... D 440 899-9510
  Westlake *(G-20158)*
Silk Screen Special TS Inc .... G 740 246-4843
  Thornville *(G-18036)*
Solar Arts Graphic Designs .... G 330 744-0535
  Youngstown *(G-21033)*
Specialtee Sportswear & Design .... G 614 877-0976
  Orient *(G-15578)*
Star Calendar & Printing Co .... G 216 741-3223
  Cleveland *(G-6095)*
Supply International Inc .... G 740 282-8604
  Steubenville *(G-17555)*
T & L Custom Screening Inc .... G 937 237-3121
  Dayton *(G-8534)*
Traichal Construction Company .... E 800 255-3667
  Niles *(G-15037)*
Underground Sport Shop Inc .... F 513 751-1662
  Cincinnati *(G-4446)*
W C Sims Co Inc .... G 937 325-7035
  Springfield *(G-17514)*

ADVERTISING SVCS, NEC

Gibbs E & Associates LLC .... G 614 939-1672
  New Albany *(G-14625)*

ADVERTISING SVCS: Billboards

Barnes Advertising Corp .... F 740 453-6836
  Zanesville *(G-21103)*
Bench Billboard Company Inc .... G 513 271-2222
  Cincinnati *(G-3388)*
Hart Advertising Inc .... F 419 668-1194
  Norwalk *(G-15397)*

ADVERTISING SVCS: Direct Mail

Advanced Fitness Inc .... G 513 563-1000
  Cincinnati *(G-3299)*
Angstrom Graphics Inc Midwest .... B 216 271-5300
  Cleveland *(G-4717)*
Cap City Direct LLC .... F 614 252-6245
  Columbus *(G-6729)*
Consoldated Graphics Group Inc .... C 216 881-9191
  Cleveland *(G-5015)*
Digital Color Intl LLC .... E 330 762-6959
  Akron *(G-143)*
Hecks Direct Mail & Prtg Svc .... E 419 661-6028
  Toledo *(G-18328)*
Jscs Group Inc .... G 513 563-4900
  Cincinnati *(G-3886)*
Laipplys Prtg Mktg Sltions Inc .... G 740 387-9282
  Marion *(G-12715)*
Moments To Remember USA LLC .... G 330 830-0839
  Massillon *(G-13027)*
Network Printing & Graphics .... F 614 230-2084
  Columbus *(G-7214)*
Our Fifth Street LLC .... G 614 866-4065
  Pickerington *(G-16055)*
Quez Media Marketing Inc .... F 216 910-0202
  Independence *(G-11149)*
Sevell + Sevell Inc .... G 614 341-9700
  Columbus *(G-7441)*
Sourcelink Ohio LLC .... C 937 885-8000
  Miamisburg *(G-13718)*
Traxium LLC .... E 330 572-8200
  Stow *(G-17637)*

ADVERTISING SVCS: Display

Cgs Signs LLC .... F 419 897-3000
  Holland *(G-10919)*
Design Masters Inc .... G 513 772-7175
  Cincinnati *(G-3584)*
Digital Color Intl LLC .... E 330 762-6959
  Akron *(G-143)*
Display Dynamics Inc .... F 937 832-2830
  Englewood *(G-9355)*
Jordan Reed LLC .... G 678 956-1222
  Columbus *(G-7076)*
Performance Packaging Inc .... F 419 478-8805
  Toledo *(G-18465)*
Schiffer Group Inc .... G 937 694-8185
  Troy *(G-18703)*

ADVERTISING SVCS: Outdoor

Kessler Sign Company .... E 740 453-0668
  Zanesville *(G-21153)*
Kessler Sign Company .... G 937 898-0633
  Dayton *(G-8295)*
Ohio Shelterall Inc .... F 614 882-1110
  Westerville *(G-20068)*
Orange Barrel Media LLC .... E 614 294-4898
  Columbus *(G-7275)*

ADVERTISING SVCS: Poster, Exc Outdoor

Hollywood Imprints LLC .... F 614 501-6040
  Gahanna *(G-10083)*
Sprint Print Inc .... G 740 622-4429
  Coshocton *(G-7752)*

ADVERTISING SVCS: Poster, Outdoor

Norton Outdoor Advertising .... E 513 631-4864
  Cincinnati *(G-4089)*

AERIAL WORK PLATFORMS

G & T Manufacturing Co .... F 440 639-7777
  Mentor *(G-13453)*
Haulotte US Inc .... E 419 445-8915
  Archbold *(G-652)*
Kenn Feld Group LLC .... F 419 238-1299
  Van Wert *(G-19098)*

AEROSOLS

C A P Industries Inc .... F 937 773-1824
  Piqua *(G-16105)*
Eveready Products Corporation .... F 216 661-2755
  Cleveland *(G-5201)*
Wellston Aerosol Mfg Co Inc .... E 740 384-2320
  Wellston *(G-19610)*
Zenex International .... E 440 232-4155
  Bedford *(G-1457)*

AGENTS, BROKERS & BUREAUS: Personal Service

Finastra USA Corporation .... E 937 435-2335
  Miamisburg *(G-13668)*
Loroco Industries Inc .... E 513 554-0356
  Cincinnati *(G-3951)*
Matly Digital Solutions LLC .... G 513 860-3435
  Fairfield *(G-9526)*
Tema Isenmann Inc .... G 859 252-0613
  Cincinnati *(G-4412)*

AGRICULTURAL EQPT: BARN, SILO, POULTRY, DAIRY/LIVESTOCK MACH

Fort Recovery Equipment Inc .... E 419 375-1006
  Fort Recovery *(G-9816)*
Stein-Way Equipment .... F 330 857-8700
  Apple Creek *(G-619)*

AGRICULTURAL EQPT: Combine, Digger, Packer/Thresher, Peanut

Birds Eye Foods Inc .... E 330 854-0818
  Canal Fulton *(G-2477)*

AGRICULTURAL EQPT: Elevators, Farm

Afs Technology LLC .... F 937 669-3548
  Ansonia *(G-592)*
Gerald Grain Center Inc .... F 419 445-2451
  Archbold *(G-650)*
Hord Elevator LLC .... F 419 562-5934
  Bucyrus *(G-2335)*
Keynes Brothers Inc .... G 740 426-6332
  Jeffersonville *(G-11247)*
Sweet Manufacturing Company .... F 937 325-1511
  Springfield *(G-17501)*

AGRICULTURAL EQPT: Fertilizing Machinery

Shearer Farm Inc .... E 330 345-9023
  Wooster *(G-20653)*

AGRICULTURAL EQPT: Fillers & Unloaders, Silo

Flying Dutchman Inc .... G 740 694-1734
  Smithville *(G-17088)*

AGRICULTURAL EQPT: Grounds Mowing Eqpt

Landscape Group LLC .... G 614 302-4537
  Mount Sterling *(G-14463)*
R L Parsons & Son Equipment Co .... G 614 879-7601
  West Jefferson *(G-19927)*
TD Landscape Inc .... F 740 694-0244
  Fredericktown *(G-9978)*

Employee Codes: A=Over 500 employees, B=251-500
C=101-250, D=51-100, E=20-50, F=10-19, G=3-9

AGRICULTURAL EQPT: Loaders, Manure & General Utility

END Separation LLC .... G 419 438-0879
  Oakwood *(G-15470)*

AGRICULTURAL EQPT: Shakers, Tree, Nuts, Fruits, Etc

Kriss Kreations .... G 330 405-6102
  Twinsburg *(G-18803)*

AGRICULTURAL EQPT: Turf & Grounds Eqpt

Randall Richard & Moore LLC .... F 330 455-8873
  Canton *(G-2802)*
Rhinestahl Corporation .... D 513 229-5300
  Mason *(G-12933)*

AGRICULTURAL LIMESTONE: Ground

Carmeuse Lime Inc .... G 419 986-2000
  Tiffin *(G-18055)*

AGRICULTURAL MACHINERY & EQPT REPAIR

Friesen Fab and Equipment .... G 614 873-4354
  Plain City *(G-16192)*
Jayron Fabrication LLC .... G 740 335-3184
  Leesburg *(G-11710)*
MCS Midwest LLC .... F 513 217-0805
  Franklin *(G-9898)*

AGRICULTURAL MACHINERY & EQPT: Wholesalers

Buckeye Companies .... E 740 452-3641
  Zanesville *(G-21112)*
R J Cox Co .... G 937 548-4699
  Arcanum *(G-631)*
Reberland Equipment Inc .... F 330 698-5883
  Apple Creek *(G-618)*
S I Distributing Inc .... F 419 647-4909
  Spencerville *(G-17314)*
Yoder & Frey Inc .... G 419 445-2070
  Archbold *(G-674)*

AIR CLEANING SYSTEMS

Radon Be Gone Inc .... G 614 268-4440
  Columbus *(G-7375)*

AIR CONDITIONING & VENTILATION EQPT & SPLYS: Wholesales

Tactical Envmtl Systems Inc .... G 513 831-2663
  Milford *(G-14042)*

AIR CONDITIONING EQPT

Duro Dyne Midwest Corp .... B 513 870-6000
  Hamilton *(G-10551)*
Hydro-Thrift Corporation .... E 330 837-5141
  Massillon *(G-13001)*
J D Indoor Comfort Inc .... F 440 949-8758
  Sheffield Village *(G-16968)*
Rs Pro Sales LLC .... G 513 699-5329
  Cincinnati *(G-4286)*
Snap Rite Manufacturing Inc .... E 910 897-4080
  Cleveland *(G-6075)*
Tactical Envmtl Systems Inc .... G 513 831-2663
  Milford *(G-14042)*
Vertiv Corporation .... A 614 888-0246
  Columbus *(G-7575)*

AIR CONDITIONING REPAIR SVCS

Air-Rite Inc .... E 216 228-8200
  Cleveland *(G-4645)*

AIR CONDITIONING UNITS: Complete, Domestic Or Indl

BMC Holdings Inc .... G 419 636-1194
  Bryan *(G-2269)*
Ecu Corporation .... E 513 898-9294
  Cincinnati *(G-3630)*
Electrolux Professional Inc .... E 216 898-1800
  Cleveland *(G-5167)*
Ellis & Watts Intl LLC .... G 513 752-9000
  Batavia *(G-1143)*
Fred D Pfening Company .... E 614 294-5361
  Columbus *(G-6938)*
Hdt Expeditionary Systems Inc .... E 440 466-6640
  Geneva *(G-10222)*
Lintern Corporation .... E 440 255-9333
  Mentor *(G-13501)*
Taylor & Moore Co .... F 513 733-5530
  Cincinnati *(G-4407)*
Vertiv Group Corporation .... A 614 888-0246
  Columbus *(G-7576)*
Vertiv Holdings LLC .... G 614 888-0246
  Columbus *(G-7577)*
Whirlpool Corporation .... C 614 409-4340
  Lockbourne *(G-12000)*

AIR DUCT CLEANING SVCS

Indoor Envmtl Specialists Inc .... F 937 433-5202
  Dayton *(G-8262)*

AIR MATTRESSES: Plastic

7 Rowe Court Properties LLC .... G 513 874-7236
  Hamilton *(G-10526)*
American Mobile Fitness LLC .... G 419 351-1381
  Toledo *(G-18177)*
Dester Corporation .... F 419 362-8020
  Lima *(G-11855)*
Fiber-Tech Industries Inc .... D 740 335-9400
  Wshngtn CT Hs *(G-20725)*
J & B Rogers Inc .... G 937 669-2677
  Tipp City *(G-18118)*
Plastic Fabrication Svcs Inc .... G 440 953-9990
  Willoughby *(G-20402)*
Plastic Materials Inc .... E 330 468-5706
  Macedonia *(G-12315)*
Plastic Materials Inc .... E 330 468-0184
  Macedonia *(G-12316)*
Polimeros Usa LLC .... G 216 591-0175
  Warrensville Heights *(G-19472)*

AIR POLLUTION CONTROL EQPT & SPLYS WHOLESALERS

Verantis Corporation .... E 440 243-0700
  Middleburg Heights *(G-13771)*

AIR PURIFICATION EQPT

Adwest Technologies Inc .... G 513 458-2600
  Cincinnati *(G-3304)*
Airecon Manufacturing Corp .... E 513 561-5522
  Cincinnati *(G-3313)*
Allied Separation Tech Inc .... E 704 736-0420
  Twinsburg *(G-18732)*
Bha Altair LLC .... G 717 285-8040
  Blue Ash *(G-1734)*
Clearflite Inc .... G 440 281-7368
  Sheffield Lake *(G-16963)*
Durr Megtec LLC .... C 614 258-9501
  Columbus *(G-6876)*
Guardian Technologies LLC .... E 216 706-2250
  Euclid *(G-9415)*
Indoor Envmtl Specialists Inc .... F 937 433-5202
  Dayton *(G-8262)*
Met-Pro Technologies LLC .... C 513 458-2600
  Cincinnati *(G-4011)*
Verantis Corporation .... E 440 243-0700
  Middleburg Heights *(G-13771)*

AIR TRAFFIC CONTROL SVCS

Arges .... G 440 574-1305
  Oberlin *(G-15490)*

AIR, WATER & SOLID WASTE PROGRAMS ADMINISTRATION SVCS

City of Columbus .... E 614 645-3152
  Lockbourne *(G-11993)*
X-3-5 LLC .... G 513 489-5477
  Cincinnati *(G-4526)*

AIR-CONDITIONING SPLY SVCS

Marketing Comm Resource Inc .... D 440 484-3010
  Willoughby *(G-20371)*

AIRCRAFT & AEROSPACE FLIGHT INSTRUMENTS & GUIDANCE SYSTEMS

Ball Aerospace & Tech Corp .... C 303 939-4000
  Beavercreek *(G-1303)*
Hi Tech Aero Spares .... G 513 942-4150
  West Chester *(G-19721)*
Kaman Corporation .... E 614 871-1893
  Grove City *(G-10438)*
Tri-State Jet Mfg LLC .... G 513 896-4538
  Hamilton *(G-10614)*

AIRCRAFT & HEAVY EQPT REPAIR SVCS

Carlson Aircraft Inc .... G 330 426-3934
  East Palestine *(G-9070)*
Grimes Aerospace Company .... B 937 484-2001
  Urbana *(G-18990)*
K & J Machine Inc .... F 740 425-3282
  Barnesville *(G-1117)*
McNational Inc .... E 740 377-4391
  South Point *(G-17287)*
Pas Technologies Inc .... D 937 840-1000
  Hillsboro *(G-10889)*
Tri State Equipment Company .... G 513 738-7227
  Shandon *(G-16942)*

AIRCRAFT ASSEMBLY PLANTS

Aero Composites Inc .... G 937 849-0244
  Medway *(G-13365)*
Air One Jet Center .... G 513 867-9500
  Hamilton *(G-10530)*
Boeing Company .... F 937 427-1767
  Fairborn *(G-9453)*
Boeing Company .... A 740 788-5805
  Newark *(G-14855)*
Boeing Company .... B 937 431-3503
  Wright Patterson Afb *(G-20717)*
Carlson Aircraft Inc .... G 330 426-3934
  East Palestine *(G-9070)*
Edward S Eveland .... G 937 233-6568
  Dayton *(G-8178)*
Executive Wings Inc .... G 440 254-1812
  Painesville *(G-15736)*
Flightlogix LLC .... G 513 321-1200
  Cincinnati *(G-3694)*
Goodrich Corporation .... A 937 339-3811
  Troy *(G-18663)*
Hexacrafter Ltd .... G 330 929-0989
  Cuyahoga Falls *(G-7879)*
Hyfast Aerospace LLC .... G 216 712-4158
  Parma *(G-15823)*
Lockheed Martin Corporation .... B 330 796-2800
  Akron *(G-256)*
Nextant Aerospace Holdings LLC ..... D 216 261-9000
  Cleveland *(G-5752)*
Ruhe Sales Inc .... F 419 943-3357
  Leipsic *(G-11736)*
Sea Air Spc McG and Mld LLC .... F 440 248-3025
  Streetsboro *(G-17695)*
Sky Riders Inc .... G 440 310-6819
  Lorain *(G-12121)*
Snow Aviation Intl Inc .... C 614 588-2452
  Gahanna *(G-10105)*
Star Jet LLC .... F 614 338-4379
  Columbus *(G-7485)*
Stark Airways .... G 330 526-6416
  North Canton *(G-15121)*
Summit Aerospace Products .... G 330 612-7341
  Northfield *(G-15327)*
Tessec Manufacturing Svcs LLC ...... E 937 985-3552
  Dayton *(G-8553)*
Textron Inc .... F 330 626-7800
  Streetsboro *(G-17703)*
Theiss Uav Solutions LLC .... G 330 584-2070
  North Benton *(G-15062)*
Toledo Jet Center LLC .... F 419 866-9050
  Swanton *(G-17924)*
Tri-State Model Flyers Inc .... D 740 886-8429
  Proctorville *(G-16347)*

AIRCRAFT CLEANING & JANITORIAL SVCS

Aero Jet Wash Llc .... F 866 381-7955
  West Carrollton *(G-19628)*

AIRCRAFT CONTROL SYSTEMS:

Saircorp Ltd .... G 330 669-9099
  Smithville *(G-17094)*

PRODUCT SECTION

AIRCRAFT PARTS & AUXILIARY EQPT: Military Eqpt & Armament

AIRCRAFT CONTROL SYSTEMS: Electronic Totalizing Counters

- 3gc LLC .... G 740 703-0580
  Cardington (G-2869)
- GE Aviation Systems LLC .... E 937 898-9600
  Dayton (G-8217)
- GE Aviation Systems LLC .... F 513 470-2889
  Cincinnati (G-3732)
- GE Aviation Systems LLC .... C 513 552-4278
  West Chester (G-19711)
- GE Aviation Systems LLC .... G 937 898-9600
  Cincinnati (G-3736)
- Honeywell International Inc .... A 937 484-2000
  Urbana (G-18995)

AIRCRAFT ELECTRICAL EQPT REPAIR SVCS

- General Electric Company .... B 513 977-1500
  Cincinnati (G-3741)
- Spirit Avionics Ltd .... F 614 237-4271
  Columbus (G-7477)
- Stephen Radecky .... G 440 232-2132
  Bedford (G-1447)

AIRCRAFT ENGINES & ENGINE PARTS: Airfoils

- Certech Inc .... G 330 405-1033
  Twinsburg (G-18750)
- PCC Airfoils LLC .... C 440 255-9770
  Mentor (G-13545)
- Turbine Eng Cmpnents Tech Corp .... E 216 692-6173
  Cleveland (G-6222)

AIRCRAFT ENGINES & ENGINE PARTS: Lubrication Systems

- Warfighter Fcsed Logistics Inc .... G 740 513-4692
  Galena (G-10117)

AIRCRAFT ENGINES & ENGINE PARTS: Pumps

- At Holdings Corporation .... A 216 692-6000
  Cleveland (G-4755)
- Eaton Industrial Corporation .... B 216 523-4205
  Cleveland (G-5152)

AIRCRAFT ENGINES & ENGINE PARTS: Research & Development, Mfr

- Aerospace Co Inc .... D 413 998-1637
  Cleveland (G-4635)
- Parker Aircraft Sales .... G 937 833-4820
  Brookville (G-2180)
- Scis Aerospace LLC .... G 216 533-8533
  Medina (G-13336)

AIRCRAFT ENGINES & ENGINE PARTS: Rocket Motors

- Stofiel Aerospace LLC .... G 216 389-0084
  Cleveland (G-6106)

AIRCRAFT ENGINES & PARTS

- Advanced Ground Systems .... F 513 402-7226
  Cincinnati (G-3300)
- Aero Jet Wash Llc .... F 866 381-7955
  West Carrollton (G-19628)
- American Aero Components LLC .... G 937 367-5068
  Dayton (G-8022)
- Avion Tool Corporation .... F 937 278-0779
  Dayton (G-8046)
- Barnes Group Inc .... A 513 759-3528
  West Chester (G-19655)
- Barnes Group Inc .... A 513 779-6888
  West Chester (G-19656)
- CFM International Inc .... D 513 552-2787
  West Chester (G-19667)
- CFM International Inc .... E 513 563-4180
  Cincinnati (G-3460)
- Challenger Aviation Products .... G 937 387-6500
  Vandalia (G-19119)
- Enginetics Corporation .... G 937 878-3800
  Huber Heights (G-11017)
- Ferrotherm Corporation .... C 216 883-9350
  Cleveland (G-5233)
- GE Aircraft Engines .... E 513 243-2000
  Cincinnati (G-3731)
- GE Aviation Systems LLC .... B 937 898-5881
  Vandalia (G-19124)
- GE Aviation Systems LLC .... C 513 977-1500
  Cincinnati (G-3733)
- GE Military Systems .... A 513 243-2000
  Cincinnati (G-3738)
- General Electric Company .... G 513 948-4170
  Cincinnati (G-3742)
- General Electric Company .... C 513 552-5364
  West Chester (G-19713)
- General Electric Company .... A 513 552-2000
  Cincinnati (G-3743)
- Henry Tools Inc .... G 216 291-1011
  Cleveland (G-5395)
- Hi-Tek Manufacturing Inc .... C 513 459-1094
  Mason (G-12886)
- Honeywell .... G 614 850-8228
  Columbus (G-7005)
- Honeywell Automation Control .... F 937 264-2662
  Urbana (G-18994)
- Honeywell International Inc .... A 440 349-7330
  Solon (G-17162)
- Lsp Technologies Inc .... E 614 718-3000
  Dublin (G-8944)
- Magellan Arospc Middletown Inc .... D 513 422-2751
  Middletown (G-13923)
- Metro Mech Inc .... G 216 641-6262
  Cleveland (G-5662)
- Meyer Tool Inc .... A 513 681-7362
  Cincinnati (G-4020)
- Otto Konigslow Mfg Co .... F 216 851-7900
  Cleveland (G-5826)
- Parker-Hannifin Corporation .... C 440 284-6277
  Elyria (G-9309)
- Pas Technologies Inc .... D 937 840-1000
  Hillsboro (G-10889)
- Polycraft Products Inc .... G 513 353-3334
  Cleves (G-6373)
- Sifco Industries Inc .... B 216 881-8600
  Cleveland (G-6063)
- Snow Aviation Intl Inc .... C 614 588-2452
  Gahanna (G-10105)
- Spirit Avionics Ltd .... F 614 237-4271
  Columbus (G-7477)
- Trojon Gear Inc .... G 937 254-1737
  Dayton (G-8568)
- Turbine Standard Ltd .... F 419 865-0355
  Holland (G-10964)
- US Aeroteam Inc .... G 937 458-0344
  Dayton (G-8577)
- Welded Ring Products Co .... D 216 961-3800
  Cleveland (G-6298)

AIRCRAFT EQPT & SPLYS WHOLESALERS

- Aerovent Inc .... G 937 473-3789
  Covington (G-7779)
- Cleveland Wheels .... D 440 937-6211
  Avon (G-944)
- Integrated Aircraft Systems .... G 330 686-2982
  Stow (G-17596)
- Transdigm Inc .... G 216 706-2939
  Cleveland (G-6196)
- Transdigm Group Incorporated .... C 216 706-2960
  Cleveland (G-6197)

AIRCRAFT FLIGHT INSTRUMENTS

- General Plastics North Corp .... E 800 542-2466
  Cincinnati (G-3746)
- L3 Aviation Products Inc .... D 614 825-2001
  Columbus (G-7108)

AIRCRAFT HANGAR OPERATION SVCS

- General Electric Company .... A 513 552-2000
  Cincinnati (G-3743)
- Swagelok Company .... F 440 442-6611
  Cleveland (G-6133)

AIRCRAFT MAINTENANCE & REPAIR SVCS

- Malta Dynamics LLC .... F 740 749-3512
  Waterford (G-19488)
- Toledo Jet Center LLC .... F 419 866-9050
  Swanton (G-17924)

AIRCRAFT PARTS & AUX EQPT: Governors, Propeller Feathering

- Hartzell Propeller Inc .... F 937 778-4200
  Piqua (G-16125)

AIRCRAFT PARTS & AUXILIARY EQPT: Assys, Subassemblies/Parts

- Ctl-Aerospace Inc .... C 513 874-7900
  West Chester (G-19845)
- Electronic Concepts Engrg Inc .... F 419 861-9000
  Holland (G-10930)
- Master Swaging Inc .... G 937 596-6171
  Jackson Center (G-11211)
- Parker-Hannifin Corporation .... C 440 284-6277
  Elyria (G-9309)
- Pitco Products Inc .... F 513 228-7245
  Dayton (G-8427)
- Snow Aviation Intl Inc .... C 614 588-2452
  Gahanna (G-10105)
- Summa Holdings Inc .... G 440 838-4700
  Cleveland (G-6116)

AIRCRAFT PARTS & AUXILIARY EQPT: Blades, Prop, Metal Or Wood

- Meak Solutions Llc .... G 440 796-8209
  Mentor (G-13513)
- Triaxis Machine & Tool LLC .... G 440 230-0303
  North Royalton (G-15308)

AIRCRAFT PARTS & AUXILIARY EQPT: Body & Wing Assys & Parts

- Achilles Aerospace Pdts Inc .... E 330 425-8444
  Twinsburg (G-18725)
- Industrial Mfg Co LLC .... F 440 838-4700
  Brecksville (G-2041)

AIRCRAFT PARTS & AUXILIARY EQPT: Body Assemblies & Parts

- Jeff Cales Customer AVI LLC .... G 330 298-9479
  Ravenna (G-16384)
- Magellan Arospc Middletown Inc .... D 513 422-2751
  Middletown (G-13923)
- Milan Tool Corp .... E 216 661-1078
  Cleveland (G-5685)

AIRCRAFT PARTS & AUXILIARY EQPT: Brakes

- Meggitt Aircraft Braking .... A 330 796-4400
  Akron (G-278)

AIRCRAFT PARTS & AUXILIARY EQPT: Landing Assemblies & Brakes

- Friction Products Co .... B 330 725-4941
  Medina (G-13265)

AIRCRAFT PARTS & AUXILIARY EQPT: Lighting/Landing Gear Assy

- Goodrich Corporation .... B 216 429-4018
  Independence (G-11133)
- Hdi Landing Gear Usa Inc .... D 937 325-1586
  Springfield (G-17413)
- Hdi Landing Gear Usa Inc .... E 440 783-5255
  Strongsville (G-17748)

AIRCRAFT PARTS & AUXILIARY EQPT: Military Eqpt & Armament

- Air Force US Dept of .... G 937 245-1962
  Wright Patterson Afb (G-20716)
- Dircksen and Associates Inc .... G 614 238-0413
  Columbus (G-6865)
- Salley Tool & Die Co .... F 937 258-3333
  Dayton (G-7989)
- Scis Aerospace LLC .... G 216 533-8533
  Medina (G-13336)
- Test-Fuchs Corporation .... G 440 708-3505
  Brecksville (G-2061)

Employee Codes: A=Over 500 employees, B=251-500
C=101-250, D=51-100, E=20-50, F=10-19, G=3-9

2019 Harris Ohio Industrial Directory

AIRCRAFT PARTS & AUXILIARY EQPT: Refueling Eqpt, In Flight

AIRCRAFT PARTS & AUXILIARY EQPT: Refueling Eqpt, In Flight

Garsite/Progress LLC .... F 419 424-1100
   Findlay *(G-9692)*
Proflo Industries LLC .... E 419 436-6008
   Alvada *(G-519)*

AIRCRAFT PARTS & AUXILIARY EQPT: Research & Development, Mfr

Airwolf Aerospace LLC .... G 440 632-1687
   Middlefield *(G-13774)*
Drt Aerospace LLC .... E 937 298-7391
   West Chester *(G-19695)*
Weldon Pump Acquition LLC .... E 440 232-2282
   Oakwood Village *(G-15489)*

AIRCRAFT PARTS & EQPT, NEC

8888 Butler Investments Inc .... G 440 748-0810
   North Ridgeville *(G-15205)*
Ace Products Co of Toledo Inc .... G 419 472-1247
   Toledo *(G-18155)*
Advanced Fuel Systems Inc .... G 614 252-8422
   Columbus *(G-6545)*
Aero Tube & Connector Company .... G 614 885-2514
   Worthington *(G-20673)*
Aerocontrolex Group Inc .... D 440 352-6182
   Painesville *(G-15707)*
Aeroquip-Vickers Inc .... G 216 523-5000
   Cleveland *(G-4633)*
Aerospace Maint Solutions LLC .... E 440 729-7703
   Chesterland *(G-3150)*
Airtug LLC .... G 440 829-2167
   Avon *(G-940)*
Allen Aircraft Products Inc .... E 330 296-9621
   Ravenna *(G-16365)*
American Aero Components LLC .... G 937 367-5068
   Dayton *(G-8022)*
At Holdings Corporation .... A 216 692-6000
   Cleveland *(G-4755)*
Aviation Cmpnent Solutions Inc .... F 440 295-6590
   Richmond Heights *(G-16501)*
Aviation Technologies Inc .... G 216 706-2960
   Cleveland *(G-4776)*
Avtron Aerospace Inc .... C 216 750-5152
   Cleveland *(G-4778)*
Aws Industries Inc .... E 513 932-7941
   Lebanon *(G-11635)*
Cleveland Instrument Corp .... G 440 826-1800
   Brookpark *(G-2138)*
Columbus Jack Corporation .... D 614 747-1596
   Swanton *(G-17909)*
Ctl-Aerospace Inc .... D 513 874-7900
   West Chester *(G-19846)*
Cuda Composites LLC .... G 937 499-0360
   Dayton *(G-8117)*
Drt Holdings Inc .... D 937 298-7391
   Dayton *(G-8169)*
Dukes Aerospace Inc .... D 818 998-9811
   Painesville *(G-15732)*
Eaton Aeroquip LLC .... C 216 523-5000
   Cleveland *(G-5143)*
Eaton Hydraulics LLC .... E 419 232-7777
   Van Wert *(G-19088)*
Eaton Industrial Corporation .... B 216 523-4205
   Cleveland *(G-5152)*
Enginetics Corporation .... C 937 878-3800
   Huber Heights *(G-11017)*
Eti Tech LLC .... F 937 832-4200
   Englewood *(G-9358)*
Exito Manufacturing .... G 937 291-9871
   Beavercreek *(G-1355)*
Federal Equipment Company .... D 513 621-5260
   Cincinnati *(G-3680)*
Ferco Tech LLC .... C 937 746-6696
   Franklin *(G-9883)*
Field Aviation Inc .... G 513 792-2282
   Cincinnati *(G-3686)*
General Electric Company .... B 513 977-1500
   Cincinnati *(G-3741)*
Goodrich Corporation .... A 937 339-3811
   Troy *(G-18663)*
Goodrich Corporation 216 706-2530
   Cleveland *(G-5331)*
Grimes Aerospace Company .... C 937 484-2000
   Urbana *(G-18991)*
GSE Production and Support LLC .... G 972 329-2646
   Swanton *(G-17914)*

Heico Aerospace Parts Corp .... B 954 987-6101
   Highland Heights *(G-10793)*
Heller Machine Products Inc .... G 216 281-2951
   Cleveland *(G-5390)*
Heroux-Devtek Inc .... F 937 325-1586
   Springfield *(G-17417)*
Hydro-Aire Inc .... C 440 323-3211
   Elyria *(G-9267)*
JCB Arrowhead Products Inc .... G 440 546-4288
   Brecksville *(G-2043)*
Jonathan Bishop .... G 330 836-6947
   Akron *(G-225)*
L&E Engineering LLC .... E 937 746-6696
   Franklin *(G-9894)*
Lawrence Technologies Inc .... G 937 274-7771
   Dayton *(G-8308)*
Lockheed Martin Integ .... D 330 796-2800
   Akron *(G-257)*
Logan Machine Company .... G 330 633-6163
   Akron *(G-259)*
M & L Machine .... G 937 386-2604
   Seaman *(G-16883)*
Mar-Con Tool Company Inc .... E 937 299-2244
   Moraine *(G-14367)*
Maverick Molding Co .... F 513 387-6100
   Blue Ash *(G-1817)*
Meggitt Polymers & Composites .... G 513 851-5550
   Cincinnati *(G-4001)*
Microweld Engineering Inc .... F 614 847-9410
   Worthington *(G-20697)*
Midwest Aircraft Products Co .... F 419 884-2164
   Mansfield *(G-12481)*
Nextant Aerospace LLC .... E 216 898-4800
   Cleveland *(G-5751)*
Nona Composites LLC .... G 937 490-4814
   Miamisburg *(G-13700)*
Pako Inc .... C 440 946-8030
   Mentor *(G-13540)*
PCC Airfoils LLC .... B 740 982-6025
   Crooksville *(G-7818)*
Schneller LLC .... D 330 673-1299
   Kent *(G-11381)*
Sirio Panel Inc .... G 937 238-3607
   Troy *(G-18706)*
Skidmore-Wilhelm Mfg Company .... E 216 481-4774
   Solon *(G-17232)*
Summit Avionics Inc .... F 330 425-1440
   Twinsburg *(G-18861)*
Taylor Manufacturing Company .... E 937 322-8622
   Springfield *(G-17503)*
Tracewell Systems Inc .... D 614 846-6175
   Lewis Center *(G-11787)*
Transdigm Group Incorporated .... C 216 706-2960
   Cleveland *(G-6197)*
Triumph Thermal Systems LLC .... D 419 273-2511
   Forest *(G-9789)*
Tronair Inc .... D 419 866-6301
   Swanton *(G-17926)*
Tronair Parent Inc .... G 419 866-6301
   Swanton *(G-17927)*
Truline Industries Inc .... D 440 729-0140
   Chesterland *(G-3171)*
Turbine Eng Cmpnents Tech Corp .... E 216 692-6173
   Cleveland *(G-6222)*
Unison Industries LLC .... B 904 667-9904
   Dayton *(G-7994)*
Unison Industries LLC .... B 937 427-0550
   Beavercreek *(G-1345)*
Unison Industries LLC .... C 937 426-0621
   Beavercreek *(G-1346)*
Unison Industries LLC .... D 937 426-4676
   Alpha *(G-518)*
US Aeroteam Inc .... E 937 458-0344
   Dayton *(G-8577)*
US Technology Corporation .... E 330 455-1181
   Canton *(G-2853)*
Wayne Trail Technologies Inc .... D 937 295-2120
   Fort Loramie *(G-9811)*
White Machine Inc .... G 440 237-3282
   North Royalton *(G-15311)*

AIRCRAFT PARTS WHOLESALERS

Grimes Aerospace Company .... B 937 484-2001
   Urbana *(G-18990)*

AIRCRAFT PROPELLERS & PARTS

Hartzell Propeller Inc .... C 937 778-4200
   Piqua *(G-16126)*

AIRCRAFT SERVICING & REPAIRING

Spirit Avionics Ltd .... F 614 237-4271
   Columbus *(G-7477)*
Unison Industries LLC .... B 904 667-9904
   Dayton *(G-7994)*
Unison Industries LLC .... B 937 427-0550
   Beavercreek *(G-1345)*

AIRCRAFT TURBINES

Honeywell International Inc .... A 216 459-6048
   Independence *(G-11135)*

AIRCRAFT WHEELS

Jay-Em Aerospace Corporation .... E 330 923-0333
   Cuyahoga Falls *(G-7884)*
Parker-Hannifin Corporation .... C 440 937-6211
   Avon *(G-956)*

AIRCRAFT: Airplanes, Fixed Or Rotary Wing

Steel Aviation Aircraft Sales .... G 937 332-7587
   Casstown *(G-2934)*

AIRCRAFT: Motorized

Tessec LLC .... E 937 985-3552
   Dayton *(G-8552)*

AIRCRAFT: Research & Development, Manufacturer

E Star Aerospace Corporation .... G 614 396-6868
   Westerville *(G-19989)*
Tdc Systems Inc .... E 440 953-5918
   Willoughby *(G-20442)*
Unmanned Solutions Tech LLC .... G 937 771-7023
   Beavercreek *(G-1366)*
Wanashab Inc .... G 330 606-6675
   Cleveland *(G-6288)*

AIRPORTS, FLYING FIELDS & SVCS

Grand Aire Inc .... E 419 861-6700
   Swanton *(G-17913)*
Ruhe Sales Inc .... F 419 943-3357
   Leipsic *(G-11736)*

ALARM SYSTEMS WHOLESALERS

Ademco Inc .... F 513 772-1851
   Blue Ash *(G-1721)*

ALARMS: Burglar

Alert Safety Products Inc .... G 513 791-4790
   Blue Ash *(G-1725)*
David Boswell .... E 614 441-2497
   Columbus *(G-6852)*
Safe Systems Inc .... G 216 661-1166
   Cleveland *(G-6024)*

ALARMS: Fire

Honeywell International Inc .... A 937 484-2000
   Urbana *(G-18995)*
Honeywell International Inc .... D 937 754-4134
   Fairborn *(G-9461)*
Viking Group Inc .... G 937 443-0433
   Dayton *(G-8580)*

ALCOHOL: Ethyl & Ethanol

Andersons Clymers Ethanol LLC .... E 574 722-2627
   Maumee *(G-13074)*
Coshocton Ethanol LLC .... E 740 623-3046
   Coshocton *(G-7727)*
Fostoria Ethanol LLC .... E 419 436-0954
   Fostoria *(G-9841)*
Greater Ohio Ethanol LLC .... G 567 940-9500
   Lima *(G-11870)*
Guardian Lima LLC .... E 567 940-9500
   Lima *(G-11872)*
Harrison 20 Mtd Borefinery LLC .... G 740 796-4797
   Adamsville *(G-9)*
Marion Ethanol LLC .... E 740 383-4400
   Marion *(G-12717)*
Summit Ethanol LLC .... E 419 943-7447
   Leipsic *(G-11737)*

PRODUCT SECTION — AMUSEMENT & RECREATION SVCS: Exposition Operation

ALCOHOL: Methyl & Methanol, Synthetic
Es Manufacturing Inc .... G 888 331-3443
Newark *(G-14873)*

ALKALIES & CHLORINE
GFS Chemicals Inc .... E 740 881-5501
Powell *(G-16322)*
National Colloid Company .... E 740 282-1171
Steubenville *(G-17545)*
National Lime and Stone Co .... C 419 396-7671
Carey *(G-2884)*
Occidental Chemical Corp .... E 513 242-2900
Cincinnati *(G-4097)*
Occidental Chemical Corp .... E 330 764-3441
Medina *(G-13309)*
PPG Industries Inc .... E 419 683-2400
Crestline *(G-7799)*

ALLOYS: Additive, Exc Copper Or Made In Blast Furnaces
GE Aviation Systems LLC .... C 513 733-1611
Cincinnati *(G-3734)*
GE Aviation Systems LLC .... F 513 889-5150
West Chester *(G-19710)*
GE Aviation Systems LLC .... G 513 552-5663
Cincinnati *(G-3735)*
Morris Technologies Inc .... C 513 733-1611
Cincinnati *(G-4047)*
Slice Mfg LLC .... G 330 733-7600
Akron *(G-378)*

ALTERNATORS: Automotive
Cuyahoga Rebuilders Inc .... G 440 846-0532
Cleveland *(G-5054)*
M W Solutions LLC .... F 419 782-1611
Defiance *(G-8633)*

ALUMINUM
Arconic Inc .... G 216 391-3885
Cleveland *(G-4730)*
Benjamin Steel Company Inc .... E 937 233-1212
Springfield *(G-17368)*
Boggs Recycling Inc .... G 800 837-8101
Newbury *(G-14946)*
Fabrication Group LLC .... E 216 251-1125
Cleveland *(G-5213)*
Kaiser Aluminum Fab Pdts LLC .... C 740 522-1151
Heath *(G-10723)*
Wagner Rustproofing Co Inc .... F 216 361-4930
Cleveland *(G-6283)*

ALUMINUM PRDTS
Accu-Tek Tool & Die Inc .... G 330 726-1946
Salem *(G-16713)*
Alanod Westlake Metal Ind Inc .... E 440 327-8184
North Ridgeville *(G-15206)*
Aleris Corporation .... G 216 910-3400
Cleveland *(G-4654)*
Aluminum Extruded Shapes Inc .... C 513 563-2205
Cincinnati *(G-3328)*
American Aluminum Extrusions .... C 330 458-0300
Canton *(G-2572)*
Arem Co .... F 440 974-6740
Mentor *(G-13393)*
Astro Aluminum Enterprises Inc .... E 330 755-1414
Struthers *(G-17813)*
Astro Shapes LLC .... C 330 755-1414
Struthers *(G-17814)*
Astro Shapes LLC .... F 330 755-1414
Struthers *(G-17815)*
BRT Extrusions Inc .... C 330 544-0177
Niles *(G-15001)*
Central Aluminum Company LLC .... E 614 491-5700
Obetz *(G-15508)*
Compliant Access Products LLC .... G 513 518-4525
Cleves *(G-6358)*
Datco Mfg Company Inc .... D 330 781-6100
Youngstown *(G-20887)*
Exal Corporation .... E 330 744-9505
Youngstown *(G-20901)*
Extrudex Aluminum Inc .... C 330 538-4444
North Jackson *(G-15146)*
Gdic Group LLC .... G 330 468-0700
Cleveland *(G-5297)*
Hydro Aluminum Fayetteville .... G 937 492-9194
Sidney *(G-17044)*
Industrial Mold Inc .... E 330 425-7374
Twinsburg *(G-18796)*
Isaiah Industries Inc .... E 937 773-9840
Piqua *(G-16131)*
Klb Industries Inc .... E 937 592-9010
Bellefontaine *(G-1521)*
Knoble Glass & Metal Inc .... E 513 753-1246
Cincinnati *(G-3919)*
L & L Ornamental Iron Co .... F 513 353-1930
Cleves *(G-6369)*
Langstons Ultimate Clg Svcs Inc .... E 330 298-9150
Ravenna *(G-16387)*
Loxcreen Company Inc .... F 513 539-2255
Middletown *(G-13921)*
Magnode Corporation .... C 513 988-6351
Trenton *(G-18623)*
Magnode Corporation .... D 317 243-3553
Trenton *(G-18624)*
National Metal Shapes Inc .... E 740 363-9559
Delaware *(G-8709)*
Navarre Industries Inc .... E 330 767-3003
Navarre *(G-14582)*
Northern States Metals Company .... D 860 521-6001
Youngstown *(G-20978)*
Orrvilon Inc .... C 330 684-9400
Orrville *(G-15610)*
Owens Corning Sales LLC .... G 740 983-1300
Ashville *(G-819)*
Precision of Ohio Inc .... F 330 793-0900
Youngstown *(G-21004)*
Star Extruded Shapes Inc .... B 330 533-9863
Canfield *(G-2546)*
Star Fab Inc .... C 330 533-9863
Canfield *(G-2547)*
Star Fab Inc .... G 330 482-1601
Columbiana *(G-6482)*
T & D Fabricating Inc .... E 440 951-5646
Eastlake *(G-9135)*
Tecnocap LLC .... D 330 392-7222
Warren *(G-19446)*
Tri County Tarp LLC .... E 419 288-3350
Bradner *(G-2016)*
Youngstown Tool & Die Company .... D 330 747-4464
Youngstown *(G-21083)*
Zarbana Alum Extrusions LLC .... E 330 482-5092
Columbiana *(G-6487)*

ALUMINUM: Coil & Sheet
Monarch Steel Company Inc .... E 216 587-8000
Cleveland *(G-5703)*

ALUMINUM: Ingots & Slabs
Homan Metals LLC .... G 513 721-5010
Cincinnati *(G-3821)*

ALUMINUM: Pigs
Real Alloy Specialty Pdts LLC .... A 216 755-8836
Beachwood *(G-1273)*
Real Alloy Specification LLC .... G 216 755-8900
Beachwood *(G-1275)*

ALUMINUM: Rolling & Drawing
Aleris Rm Inc .... C 216 910-3400
Beachwood *(G-1220)*
Aleris Rolled Products LLC .... E 216 910-3400
Cleveland *(G-4657)*
Arconic Inc .... G 330 544-7633
Niles *(G-14998)*
Eastman Kodak Company .... E 937 259-3000
Dayton *(G-8175)*
Novelis Corporation .... D 330 841-3456
Warren *(G-19423)*
Nuvox .... G 614 232-9115
Columbus *(G-7234)*
Real Alloy Specialty Pdts LLC .... G 440 322-0072
Elyria *(G-9317)*
Real Alloy Specialty Products .... C 216 755-8836
Beachwood *(G-1274)*
Southwire Company LLC .... G 440 933-6110
Avon Lake *(G-1009)*

ALUMINUM: Slabs, Primary
Imperial Alum - Minerva LLC .... D 330 868-7765
Minerva *(G-14184)*

AMMUNITION
United States Dept of Army .... G 330 358-7311
Ravenna *(G-16417)*
Vergeline LLC .... G 419 730-0300
Toledo *(G-18591)*

AMMUNITION: Arming & Fusing Devices
L3 Fuzing and Ord Systems Inc .... A 513 943-2000
Cincinnati *(G-3257)*

AMMUNITION: Jet Propulsion Projectiles
Marine Jet Power Inc .... G 614 759-9000
Blacklick *(G-1689)*

AMMUNITION: Pellets & BB's, Pistol & Air Rifle
Johndavid D Jones .... G 740 264-0176
Wintersville *(G-20539)*
Toll Compaction Group LLC .... E 740 376-0511
Belpre *(G-1584)*

AMMUNITION: Shot, Steel
Premier Shot Company Inc .... G 330 405-0583
Twinsburg *(G-18838)*

AMMUNITION: Small Arms
Ares Inc .... D 419 635-2175
Port Clinton *(G-16242)*
Center Mass Ammo LLC .... G 440 796-6207
Madison *(G-12342)*
Galion LLC .... C 419 468-5214
Galion *(G-10138)*
Jmr Enterprises LLC .... G 937 618-1736
Maineville *(G-12371)*
National Bullet Co .... G 800 317-9506
Eastlake *(G-9125)*
R & S Monitions Inc .... G 614 846-0597
Columbus *(G-7371)*

AMPLIFIERS
Dare Electronics Inc .... E 937 335-0031
Troy *(G-18645)*
Dr Z Amps Inc .... F 216 475-1444
Maple Heights *(G-12571)*

AMPLIFIERS: RF & IF Power
Rf Linx Inc .... G 513 777-2774
Lebanon *(G-11690)*

AMUSEMENT & REC SVCS: Baseball Club, Exc Pro & Semi-Pro
Lake Township Trustees .... G 419 836-1143
Millbury *(G-14050)*

AMUSEMENT & REC SVCS: Cake/Pastry Decorating Instruction
Cake Decor .... G 614 836-5533
Groveport *(G-10487)*
Sugar Showcase .... G 330 792-9154
Youngstown *(G-21040)*

AMUSEMENT & RECREATION SVCS: Arts & Crafts Instruction
Crawford County Arts Council .... G 419 834-4133
Bucyrus *(G-2323)*
Frame Depot Inc .... G 330 652-7865
Niles *(G-15009)*

AMUSEMENT & RECREATION SVCS: Exhibition Operation
Asm International .... D 440 338-5151
Novelty *(G-15438)*

AMUSEMENT & RECREATION SVCS: Exposition Operation
Park Corporation .... B 216 267-4870
Cleveland *(G-5841)*
Relx Inc .... E 937 865-6800
Miamisburg *(G-13708)*

AMUSEMENT & RECREATION SVCS: Golf Svcs & Professionals
X-Press Tool Inc .... E 330 225-8748
Brunswick *(G-2254)*

AMUSEMENT & RECREATION SVCS: Gun Club, Membership
Smokin Guns LLC .... G 440 324-4003
Elyria *(G-9329)*

AMUSEMENT & RECREATION SVCS: Ice Skating Rink
Jmac Inc .... E 614 436-2418
Columbus *(G-7069)*

AMUSEMENT & RECREATION SVCS: Indoor Court Clubs
Soccer Centre Owners Ltd .... E 419 893-5425
Maumee *(G-13146)*

AMUSEMENT & RECREATION SVCS: Juke Box
Glenn Michael Brick .... F 740 391-5735
Flushing *(G-9783)*

AMUSEMENT & RECREATION SVCS: Outfitters, Recreation
Reelflyrodcom .... G 937 434-8472
Dayton *(G-8469)*

AMUSEMENT & RECREATION SVCS: Physical Fitness Instruction
Building Block Performance LLC .... G 614 918-7476
Plain City *(G-16179)*

AMUSEMENT & RECREATION SVCS: Racquetball Club, Non-Member
Melinz Industries Inc .... F 440 946-3512
Willoughby *(G-20378)*

AMUSEMENT & RECREATION SVCS: Shooting Range
Black Wing Shooting Center LLC .... G 740 363-7555
Delaware *(G-8658)*
Kelblys Rifle Range Inc .... G 330 683-0070
North Lawrence *(G-15162)*

AMUSEMENT & RECREATION SVCS: Video Game Arcades
Practice Center Inc .... G 513 489-5229
Cincinnati *(G-4183)*

AMUSEMENT & RECREATION SVCS: Zoological Garden, Commercial
Kabler Farms .... G 513 732-0501
Batavia *(G-1156)*

AMUSEMENT PARK DEVICES & RIDES
Advanced Indus Machining Inc .... F 614 596-4183
Powell *(G-16307)*
Alpha Machining LLC .... G 330 889-2207
West Farmington *(G-19919)*
ARM (usa) Inc .... F 740 264-6599
Steubenville *(G-17527)*
Delta Manufacturing Inc .... F 330 386-1270
East Liverpool *(G-9056)*
Happy Time Adventures .... G 419 407-6409
Toledo *(G-18323)*
Hearn Plating Co Ltd .... F 419 473-9773
Toledo *(G-18325)*
OReilly Precision Products .... G 937 526-4677
Russia *(G-16610)*
Quality Design Machining Inc .... G 440 352-7290
Mentor *(G-13564)*
Reeces Las Vegas Supplies .... G 937 274-5000
Dayton *(G-8467)*

AMUSEMENT PARK DEVICES & RIDES: Carousels Or Merry-Go-Rounds
Carousel Magic LLC .... G 419 522-6456
Mansfield *(G-12420)*
Carousel Works Inc .... E 419 522-7558
Mansfield *(G-12421)*

AMUSEMENT PARK DEVICES & RIDES: Carnival Mach & Eqpt, NEC
Majestic Manufacturing Inc .... E 330 457-2447
New Waterford *(G-14841)*

ANALYZERS: Network
Community Care Network Inc .... E 216 671-0977
Cleveland *(G-5007)*
Simplex-It LLC .... G 234 380-1277
Stow *(G-17628)*

ANALYZERS: Respiratory
Health Care Solutions Inc .... G 419 636-4189
Bryan *(G-2285)*
Medical Equipment Provider .... G 937 778-2190
Piqua *(G-16141)*
Medinvent LLC .... G 330 247-0921
Medina *(G-13299)*

ANESTHESIA EQPT
Lababidi Enterprises Inc .... E 330 733-2907
Akron *(G-245)*

ANIMAL BASED MEDICINAL CHEMICAL PRDTS
Badizo LLC .... G 844 344-3833
Stow *(G-17571)*

ANIMAL FEED & SUPPLEMENTS: Livestock & Poultry
Archer-Daniels-Midland Company .... G 330 852-3025
Sugarcreek *(G-17841)*
Archer-Daniels-Midland Company .... G 419 705-3292
Toledo *(G-18189)*
Cargill Incorporated .... G 330 745-0031
Akron *(G-104)*
Cargill Incorporated .... E 419 394-3374
Saint Marys *(G-16681)*
Cooper Hatchery Inc .... C 419 594-3325
Oakwood *(G-15469)*
Csa Nutrition Services Inc .... F 800 257-3788
Brookville *(G-2164)*
Granville Milling Co .... G 740 345-1305
Newark *(G-14881)*
Hamlet Protein Inc .... E 567 525-5627
Findlay *(G-9698)*
Hartz Mountain Corporation .... D 513 877-2131
Pleasant Plain *(G-16227)*
IAMS Company .... B 800 675-3849
Mason *(G-12887)*
J & B Feed Co Inc .... G 419 335-5821
Wauseon *(G-19523)*
Legacy Farmers Cooperative .... F 419 423-2611
Findlay *(G-9713)*
Magnus International Group Inc .... G 216 592-8355
Chagrin Falls *(G-3056)*
Mid-Wood Inc .... F 419 257-3331
North Baltimore *(G-15046)*
Occidental Chemical Corp .... E 513 242-2900
Cincinnati *(G-4097)*
Ohio Blenders Inc .... F 419 726-2655
Toledo *(G-18435)*
Pettisville Grain Co .... E 419 446-2547
Pettisville *(G-16035)*
Premier Feeds LLC .... G 937 584-2411
Sabina *(G-16618)*
Pro-Pet LLC .... G 419 394-3374
Saint Marys *(G-16695)*
Provimi North America Inc .... D 937 770-2400
Lewisburg *(G-11798)*
Provimi North America Inc .... B 937 770-2400
Brookville *(G-2182)*
Psd Partners LLC .... G 419 294-3838
Carey *(G-2888)*
Purina Animal Nutrition LLC .... F 740 335-0207
Wshngtn CT Hs *(G-20737)*
Purina Animal Nutrition LLC .... E 419 224-2015
Lima *(G-11923)*
Purina Animal Nutrition LLC .... E 330 682-1951
Orrville *(G-15611)*
Purina Animal Nutrition LLC .... E 330 879-2158
Massillon *(G-13043)*
Purina Mills LLC .... G 330 682-1951
Orrville *(G-15612)*
Quality Liquid Feeds Inc .... F 330 532-4635
Wellsville *(G-19613)*
Rek Associates LLC .... F 419 294-3838
Upper Sandusky *(G-18971)*
Rogers Mill Inc .... G 330 227-3214
Rogers *(G-16561)*
Terry A Johnson .... G 614 561-0706
Etna *(G-9389)*

ANIMAL FEED: Wholesalers
Gerald Grain Center Inc .... F 419 445-2451
Archbold *(G-650)*
Granville Milling Co .... G 740 345-1305
Newark *(G-14881)*
J & B Feed Co Inc .... G 419 335-5821
Wauseon *(G-19523)*
Land OLakes Inc .... G 330 879-2158
Massillon *(G-13013)*
Provimi North America Inc .... B 937 770-2400
Brookville *(G-2182)*
Ridley USA Inc .... F 800 837-8222
Botkins *(G-1936)*

ANIMAL FOOD & SUPPLEMENTS: Alfalfa Or Alfalfa Meal
Toledo Alfalfa Mills Inc .... G 419 836-3705
Oregon *(G-15571)*
Verhoff Alfalfa Mills Inc .... G 419 653-4161
New Bavaria *(G-14643)*
Verhoff Alfalfa Mills Inc .... G 419 523-4767
Ottawa *(G-15670)*
Yarnell Bros Inc .... G 419 278-2831
Deshler *(G-8790)*

ANIMAL FOOD & SUPPLEMENTS: Bird Food, Prepared
Centerra Co-Op .... E 800 362-9598
Jefferson *(G-11226)*
Centerra Co-Op .... E 419 281-2153
Ashland *(G-690)*
Four Natures Keepers Inc .... F 740 363-8007
Delaware *(G-8679)*
Lakeshore Feed & Seed Inc .... G 216 961-5729
Cleveland *(G-5555)*
Lizzie Maes Birdseed & Dg Co .... G 330 927-1795
Rittman *(G-16524)*
Sunny Side Feeds LLC .... G 330 635-1455
West Salem *(G-19958)*
Vitakraft Sun Seed Inc .... D 419 832-1641
Weston *(G-20178)*

ANIMAL FOOD & SUPPLEMENTS: Bone Meal
Manco Inc .... G 937 962-2661
Lewisburg *(G-11795)*

ANIMAL FOOD & SUPPLEMENTS: Cat
Hartz Mountain Corporation .... D 513 877-2131
Pleasant Plain *(G-16227)*
Pro-Pet LLC .... G 419 394-3374
Saint Marys *(G-16695)*

ANIMAL FOOD & SUPPLEMENTS: Dog
Bil-Jac Foods Inc .... E 330 722-7888
Medina *(G-13229)*
G & C Raw LLC .... G 937 827-0010
Versailles *(G-19181)*
IAMS Company .... B 800 675-3849
Mason *(G-12887)*
IAMS Company .... C 419 943-4267
Leipsic *(G-11726)*
IAMS Company .... D 937 962-7782
Lewisburg *(G-11793)*
Lakeshore Feed & Seed Inc .... G 216 961-5729
Cleveland *(G-5555)*
Lucky Paws LLC .... G 859 620-2525
Cincinnati *(G-3954)*
Mars Petcare Us Inc .... E 614 878-7242
Columbus *(G-7153)*

PRODUCT SECTION

APPLIANCES, HOUSEHOLD: Laundry Machines, Incl Coin-Operated

Nom Nom Nom .... G 614 302-4815
  Columbus *(G-7222)*
Ohio Pet Foods Inc .... E 330 424-1431
  Lisbon *(G-11977)*

ANIMAL FOOD & SUPPLEMENTS: Dog & Cat

About Cats & Dogs LLC .... G 440 263-8989
  Hudson *(G-11025)*
Cargill Incorporated .... E 419 394-3374
  Saint Marys *(G-16681)*
In Good Hlth & Animal Wellness ..... G 330 908-1234
  Northfield *(G-15319)*
Kelly Foods Corporation .... E 330 722-8855
  Medina *(G-13285)*
Land OLakes Inc .... E 330 879-2158
  Massillon *(G-13013)*
Nestle Purina Petcare Company ..... D 740 454-8575
  Zanesville *(G-21160)*
Ohio Blenders Inc .... F 419 726-2655
  Toledo *(G-18435)*
Vitakraft Sun Seed Inc .... D 419 832-1641
  Weston *(G-20178)*

ANIMAL FOOD & SUPPLEMENTS: Feed Concentrates

Woodstock Products Inc .... G 216 641-3811
  Cleveland *(G-6323)*

ANIMAL FOOD & SUPPLEMENTS: Feed Premixes

Rowe Premix Inc .... F 937 678-9015
  West Manchester *(G-19941)*

ANIMAL FOOD & SUPPLEMENTS: Feed Supplements

Agri-Products Inc .... G 216 831-5890
  Cleveland *(G-4642)*
Direct Action Co Inc .... F 330 364-3219
  Dover *(G-8816)*

ANIMAL FOOD & SUPPLEMENTS: Livestock

Edward Keiter & Sons .... G 937 382-3249
  Wilmington *(G-20494)*
Geauga Feed and Grain Supply ...... G 440 564-5000
  Newbury *(G-14953)*
Gerber & Sons Inc .... E 330 897-6201
  Baltic *(G-1030)*
Hanby Farms Inc .... E 740 763-3554
  Nashport *(G-14567)*
International Multifoods Corp .... E 330 682-3000
  Orrville *(G-15595)*
Kalmbach Feeds Inc .... C 419 294-3838
  Upper Sandusky *(G-18957)*
Land OLakes Inc .... E 330 879-2158
  Massillon *(G-13013)*
Le Summer Kidron Inc .... E 330 857-2031
  Apple Creek *(G-610)*
Republic Mills Inc .... F 419 758-3511
  Okolona *(G-15523)*
Ridley USA Inc .... F 800 837-8222
  Botkins *(G-1936)*
Ridley USA Inc .... E 937 693-6393
  Botkins *(G-1937)*
Superior Ag-Patoka Vlly Feed .... F 419 294-3838
  Upper Sandusky *(G-18975)*

ANIMAL FOOD & SUPPLEMENTS: Mineral feed supplements

Tenda Horse Products LLC .... G 740 694-8836
  Fredericktown *(G-9979)*

ANIMAL FOOD & SUPPLEMENTS: Pet, Exc Dog & Cat, Dry

Kelly Foods Corporation .... E 330 722-8855
  Medina *(G-13285)*

ANIMAL FOOD & SUPPLEMENTS: Poultry

2nd Roe LLC .... G 419 499-3031
  Monroeville *(G-14285)*
Cooper Farms Inc .... D 419 375-4116
  Fort Recovery *(G-9813)*
Cooper Farms Inc .... D 419 375-4119
  Fort Recovery *(G-9814)*

Cooper Farms Inc .... F 419 375-4619
  Fort Recovery *(G-9815)*
Nature Pure LLC .... E 937 358-2364
  Raymond *(G-16424)*

ANIMAL FOOD & SUPPLEMENTS: Specialty, Mice & Other Pets

Ohio Pet Foods Inc .... E 330 424-1431
  Lisbon *(G-11977)*

ANIMAL FOOD & SUPPLEMENTS: Stock Feeds, Dry

Stahl Farm Market .... F 330 325-0640
  Ravenna *(G-16409)*

ANIMAL FOOD/SUPPLEMENTS: Feeds Fm Meat/Meat/Veg Combnd Meals

G A Wintzer and Son Company ...... D 419 739-4913
  Wapakoneta *(G-19329)*

ANNEALING: Metal

Atmosphere Annealing LLC .... D 330 478-0314
  Kenton *(G-11402)*
Northlake Steel Corporation .... D 330 220-7717
  Valley City *(G-19056)*
Ohio Coatings Company .... D 740 859-5500
  Yorkville *(G-20827)*
Pro-TEC Coating Company LLC ..... D 419 943-1100
  Leipsic *(G-11733)*
Youngstown Heat Treating .... E 330 788-3025
  Youngstown *(G-21078)*

ANNUNCIATORS

Seekirk Inc .... F 614 278-9200
  Columbus *(G-7436)*

ANODIZING EQPT

Singleton Corporation .... F 216 651-7800
  Cleveland *(G-6066)*

ANODIZING SVC

Amac Enterprises Inc .... D 216 362-1880
  Cleveland *(G-4681)*
Anomatic Corporation .... B 740 522-2203
  Johnstown *(G-11255)*
Anomatic Corporation .... B 740 522-2203
  Newark *(G-14851)*
Bedford Anodizing Co .... E 330 650-6052
  Hudson *(G-11034)*
Commercial Anodizing Co .... E 440 942-8384
  Willoughby *(G-20298)*
Custom Powdercoating LLC .... G 937 972-3516
  Dayton *(G-8122)*
Electrolizing Corporation Ohio .... E 216 451-3153
  Cleveland *(G-5165)*
Electrolizing Corporation Ohio .... E 216 451-8653
  Cleveland *(G-5166)*
K-B Plating Inc .... F 216 341-1115
  Cleveland *(G-5514)*
Luke Engineering & Mfg Corp .... E 330 335-1501
  Wadsworth *(G-19252)*
Luke Engineering & Mfg Corp .... E 330 925-3344
  Rittman *(G-16525)*
Sifco Industries Inc .... B 216 881-8600
  Cleveland *(G-6063)*

ANTENNA REPAIR & INSTALLATION SVCS

Central USA Wireless LLC .... E 513 469-1500
  Cincinnati *(G-3459)*

ANTENNAS: Radar Or Communications

Circle Prime Manufacturing .... E 330 923-0019
  Cuyahoga Falls *(G-7850)*
Quasonix Inc .... E 513 942-1287
  West Chester *(G-19775)*

ANTENNAS: Receiving

Sinbon Usa LLC .... G 937 667-8999
  Tipp City *(G-18133)*
Solar Con Inc .... E 419 865-5877
  Holland *(G-10958)*
Wifi-Plus Inc .... G 877 838-4195
  Brunswick *(G-2251)*

ANTIBIOTICS

Pfizer Inc .... C 937 746-3603
  Franklin *(G-9908)*

ANTIQUE & CLASSIC AUTOMOBILE RESTORATION

Cincinnati Woodworks Inc .... G 513 241-6412
  Cincinnati *(G-3512)*

ANTIQUE FURNITURE RESTORATION & REPAIR

Mark Rasche .... G 614 882-1810
  Westerville *(G-20009)*
Todd W Goings .... G 740 389-5842
  Marion *(G-12743)*

ANTIQUE REPAIR & RESTORATION SVCS, EXC FURNITURE & AUTOS

Carousel Magic LLC .... G 419 522-6456
  Mansfield *(G-12420)*

ANTIQUE SHOPS

Indian River Industries .... G 740 965-4377
  Sunbury *(G-17890)*
John Purdum .... G 513 897-9686
  Waynesville *(G-19569)*

ANTIQUES, WHOLESALE

Indian River Industries .... G 740 965-4377
  Sunbury *(G-17890)*

APPAREL ACCESS STORES

Indra Holdings Corp .... G 513 682-8200
  West Chester *(G-19867)*

APPAREL DESIGNERS: Commercial

Heather B Moore Inc .... G 216 932-5430
  Cleveland *(G-5387)*
Struggle Grind Success LLC .... G 330 834-6738
  Boardman *(G-1903)*

APPAREL PRESSING SVCS

Graphix Junction .... G 234 284-8392
  Hudson *(G-11049)*

APPAREL: Hand Woven

Specilty Fbrics Converting Inc .... E 706 637-3000
  Fairlawn *(G-9618)*

APPLIANCE PARTS: Porcelain Enameled

Destiny Manufacturing Inc .... E 330 273-9000
  Brunswick *(G-2199)*
Ice Industries Columbus Inc .... G 419 842-3600
  Sylvania *(G-17944)*
Whirlaway Corporation .... C 440 647-4711
  Wellington *(G-19595)*

APPLIANCES, HOUSEHOLD OR COIN OPERATED: Laundry Dryers

Carly Co LLC .... G 937 477-6411
  Centerville *(G-3000)*
Junebugs Wash N Dry .... G 513 988-5863
  Trenton *(G-18621)*
Whirlpool Corporation .... C 740 383-7122
  Marion *(G-12748)*

APPLIANCES, HOUSEHOLD: Kitchen, Major, Exc Refrigs & Stoves

ABC Appliance Inc .... E 419 693-4414
  Oregon *(G-15552)*
New Path International LLC .... E 614 410-3974
  Powell *(G-16331)*

APPLIANCES, HOUSEHOLD: Laundry Machines, Incl Coin-Operated

Whirlpool Corporation .... C 937 547-0773
  Greenville *(G-10401)*
Whirlpool Corporation .... C 419 523-5100
  Ottawa *(G-15672)*

Employee Codes: A=Over 500 employees, B=251-500
C=101-250, D=51-100, E=20-50, F=10-19, G=3-9

APPLIANCES, HOUSEHOLD: Laundry Machines, Incl Coin-Operated

Whirlpool Corporation .... C 614 409-4340
  Lockbourne *(G-12000)*

APPLIANCES, HOUSEHOLD: Refrigs, Mechanical & Absorption

Norcold Inc .... B 937 497-3080
  Sidney *(G-17057)*
Whirlpool Corporation .... C 614 409-4340
  Lockbourne *(G-12000)*
Whirlpool Corporation .... C 419 523-5100
  Ottawa *(G-15672)*

APPLIANCES: Household, NEC

JC and Associates Sylvania LLC .... G 419 824-0011
  Sylvania *(G-17947)*

APPLIANCES: Household, Refrigerators & Freezers

Cold Storage Services LLC .... G 740 837-0858
  London *(G-12054)*
Dover Corporation .... F 513 870-3206
  West Chester *(G-19694)*
Norcold Inc .... C 937 447-2241
  Gettysburg *(G-10247)*
Whirlpool Corporation .... D 419 423-8123
  Findlay *(G-9776)*
Whirlpool Corporation .... C 740 383-7122
  Marion *(G-12748)*

APPLIANCES: Major, Cooking

Nacco Industries Inc .... E 440 229-5151
  Cleveland *(G-5719)*
Royalton Food Service Eqp Co .... E 440 237-0806
  North Royalton *(G-15299)*

APPLIANCES: Small, Electric

Ces Nationwide .... G 937 322-0771
  Springfield *(G-17373)*
Cleveland Range LLC .... C 216 481-4900
  Cleveland *(G-4972)*
Driven Innovations LLC .... G 330 818-7681
  Englewood *(G-9356)*
Dyoung Enterprise Inc .... D 440 918-0505
  Willoughby *(G-20312)*
Glo-Quartz Electric Heater Co .... E 440 255-9701
  Mentor *(G-13459)*
Johnson Bros Rubber Co Inc .... E 419 752-4814
  Greenwich *(G-10404)*
Qualtek Electronics Corp .... C 440 951-3300
  Mentor *(G-13567)*

APPLICATIONS SOFTWARE PROGRAMMING

Analytica Usa Inc .... G 513 348-2333
  Dayton *(G-8031)*
B-Tek Scales LLC .... E 330 471-8900
  Canton *(G-2582)*
Foundation Software Inc .... D 330 220-8383
  Strongsville *(G-17744)*
Pwi Inc .... F 732 212-8110
  New Albany *(G-14635)*

APPRAISAL SVCS, EXC REAL ESTATE

Amos Media Company .... C 937 498-2111
  Sidney *(G-17015)*
Jaffe & Gross Jewelry Company .... G 937 461-9450
  Dayton *(G-8276)*
Pughs Designer Jewelers Inc .... G 740 344-9259
  Newark *(G-14914)*

APRONS: Rubber, Vulcanized Or Rubberized Fabric

Ansell Healthcare Products LLC .... C 740 295-5414
  Coshocton *(G-7720)*

AQUARIUMS & ACCESS: Glass

Frigid Units Inc .... G 419 478-4000
  Toledo *(G-18297)*

AQUARIUMS & ACCESS: Plastic

Acrylic Arts .... G 440 537-0300
  West Farmington *(G-19918)*
Th Plastics Inc .... C 419 425-5825
  Findlay *(G-9769)*

ARCHITECTURAL PANELS OR PARTS: Porcelain Enameled

Eurocase Architectural Cabinet .... F 330 674-0681
  Millersburg *(G-14081)*

ARCHITECTURAL SVCS

Barr Engineering Incorporated .... F 614 892-0162
  Columbus *(G-6649)*
Ceso Inc .... D 937 435-8584
  Miamisburg *(G-13649)*
Dlz Ohio Inc .... C 614 888-0040
  Columbus *(G-6871)*
Garland Industries Inc .... G 216 641-7500
  Cleveland *(G-5294)*
Garland/Dbs Inc .... C 216 641-7500
  Cleveland *(G-5295)*

ARMATURE REPAIRING & REWINDING SVC

City Machine Technologies Inc .... F 330 747-2639
  Youngstown *(G-20870)*
City Machine Technologies Inc .... E 330 740-8186
  Youngstown *(G-20871)*
Diversified Air Systems Inc .... E 216 741-1700
  Brooklyn Heights *(G-2121)*
Dolin Supply Co .... E 304 529-4171
  South Point *(G-17282)*
Econ-O-Machine Products Inc .... G 937 882-6307
  Donnelsville *(G-8801)*
Horner Industrial Services Inc .... F 513 874-8722
  West Chester *(G-19865)*
Integrated Power Services LLC .... E 216 433-7808
  Cleveland *(G-5463)*
K C N Technologies LLC .... G 440 439-4219
  Bedford *(G-1419)*
Setco Sales Company .... D 513 941-5110
  Cincinnati *(G-4328)*

ARMORED CAR SVCS

Garda CL Technical Svcs Inc .... E 937 294-4099
  Moraine *(G-14355)*

ART & ORNAMENTAL WARE: Pottery

All Fired Up Pnt Your Own Pot .... G 330 865-5858
  Copley *(G-7677)*
Carruth Studio Inc .... F 419 878-3060
  Waterville *(G-19491)*
J-Vac Industries Inc .... D 740 384-2155
  Wellston *(G-19603)*
Marchione Studio Inc .... G 330 454-7408
  Canton *(G-2742)*
Strictly Stitchery Inc .... F 440 543-7128
  Cleveland *(G-6110)*

ART DEALERS & GALLERIES

Fenwick Gallery of Fine Arts .... G 419 475-1651
  Toledo *(G-18292)*
Lazars Art Gllery Crtive Frmng .... G 330 477-8351
  Canton *(G-2731)*

ART DESIGN SVCS

Ddg Incorporated .... G 440 343-5060
  Medina *(G-13250)*
Eugene Stewart .... G 937 898-1117
  Dayton *(G-8189)*
Graphicsource Inc .... G 440 248-9200
  Solon *(G-17154)*
Meridian Arts and Graphics .... F 330 759-9099
  Youngstown *(G-20969)*
Rapid Signs & More Inc .... G 513 553-4040
  New Richmond *(G-14814)*
Shamrock Companies Inc .... D 440 899-9510
  Westlake *(G-20158)*
Youngstown Pre-Press Inc .... F 330 793-3690
  Youngstown *(G-21081)*

ART MARBLE: Concrete

Agean Marble Manufacturing .... F 513 874-1475
  West Chester *(G-19829)*
Artistic Rock LLC .... G 216 291-8856
  Cleveland *(G-4742)*
Marblelife of Central Ohio .... G 614 837-6146
  Pickerington *(G-16053)*

ART RELATED SVCS

Smartcopy Inc .... G 740 392-6162
  Mount Vernon *(G-14514)*
Those Charc From Cleve Inc .... F 216 252-7300
  Cleveland *(G-6172)*

ART RESTORATION SVC

Bonfoey Co .... F 216 621-0178
  Cleveland *(G-4831)*

ART SPLY STORES

Print Craft Inc .... G 513 931-6828
  Cincinnati *(G-4191)*

ARTISTS' AGENTS & BROKERS

Thickemz Entertainment LLC .... G 404 399-4255
  Cuyahoga Falls *(G-7928)*

ARTISTS' MATERIALS: Brushes, Air

RPM Consumer Holding Company .... G 330 273-5090
  Medina *(G-13330)*

ARTISTS' MATERIALS: Canvas, Prepared On Frames

Whitten Studios .... G 419 368-8366
  Ashland *(G-755)*

ARTISTS' MATERIALS: Ink, Drawing, Black & Colored

Modern Ink Technology LLC .... F 419 738-9664
  Lima *(G-11908)*

ARTISTS' MATERIALS: Pencil Holders

Pen Pal LLC .... G 614 348-2517
  New Albany *(G-14633)*

ARTISTS' MATERIALS: Water Colors

Crawford County Arts Council .... G 419 834-4133
  Bucyrus *(G-2323)*

ARTISTS' MATERIALS: Wax

Puracera 3 LLC .... F 513 231-7555
  Cincinnati *(G-4222)*

ARTS & CRAFTS SCHOOL

Studio Arts & Glass Inc .... F 330 494-9779
  Canton *(G-2826)*
Wooden Horse .... G 740 503-5243
  Baltimore *(G-1046)*

ASBESTOS PRDTS: Roofing, Felt Roll

American Way Exteriors LLC .... G 855 766-3293
  Dayton *(G-8028)*

ASBESTOS PRDTS: Textiles, Exc Insulating Material

Pop/Pos Advantage .... G 440 543-9452
  Chagrin Falls *(G-3067)*

ASPHALT & ASPHALT PRDTS

Asphalt Materials Inc .... G 740 373-3040
  Marietta *(G-12606)*
Asphalt Materials Inc .... F 740 374-5100
  Marietta *(G-12607)*
Central Oil Asphalt Corp .... G 614 224-8111
  Columbus *(G-6754)*
D & R Supply Inc .... G 330 855-3781
  Marshallville *(G-12752)*
Full Circle Technologies LLC .... G 216 650-0007
  Cleveland *(G-5276)*
Glenn O Hawbaker Inc .... G 330 308-0533
  New Philadelphia *(G-14772)*
Grand River Asphalt .... G 440 352-2254
  Grand River *(G-10322)*
Hanson Aggregates Midwest LLC .... G 419 878-2006
  Waterville *(G-19497)*
Kokosing Materials Inc .... F 419 522-2715
  Mansfield *(G-12467)*
Kokosing Materials Inc .... G 614 891-5090
  Westerville *(G-20061)*

PRODUCT SECTION

Kokosing Materials Inc ....E 614 491-1199
Columbus *(G-7098)*
Koski Construction Co ....G 440 997-5337
Ashtabula *(G-782)*
Lucas County Asphalt Inc ....E 419 476-0705
Toledo *(G-18389)*
Lynn James Contracting LLC ....G 419 467-4505
Delta *(G-8775)*
Maintenance + Inc ....F 330 264-6262
Wooster *(G-20618)*
Morrow Gravel Company Inc ....E 513 771-0820
Cincinnati *(G-4048)*
Mt Pleasant Blacktopping Inc ....G 513 874-3777
Fairfield *(G-9532)*
S E Johnson Companies Inc ....F 419 893-8731
Maumee *(G-13142)*
Seneca Petroleum Co Inc ....F 419 691-3581
Toledo *(G-18518)*
Shalersville Asphalt Co ....E 440 834-4294
Burton *(G-2370)*
Shelly and Sands Inc ....F 740 373-6495
Marietta *(G-12667)*
Shelly and Sands Inc ....G 740 453-0721
Zanesville *(G-21177)*
Shelly and Sands Inc ....F 740 453-0721
Zanesville *(G-21176)*
Shelly Materials Inc ....G 740 446-7789
Gallipolis *(G-10175)*
Shelly Materials Inc ....E 740 666-5841
Ostrander *(G-15646)*
Stoneco Inc ....D 419 422-8854
Findlay *(G-9762)*
Unique Paving Materials Corp ....E 216 341-7711
Cleveland *(G-6232)*
Valley Asphalt Corporation ....G 937 426-7682
Xenia *(G-20800)*
Valley Asphalt Corporation ....G 513 353-2171
Cleves *(G-6381)*
Valley Asphalt Corporation ....G 513 784-1476
Cincinnati *(G-4463)*
Valley Asphalt Corporation ....G 513 561-1551
Cincinnati *(G-4462)*
Walls Bros Asphalt Co Inc ....G 937 548-7158
Greenville *(G-10399)*
Wilson Blacktop Corporation ....E 740 635-3566
Martins Ferry *(G-12764)*

ASPHALT COATINGS & SEALERS

Aluminum Coating Manufacturers ....E 216 341-2000
Cleveland *(G-4680)*
Atlas Roofing Corporation ....C 937 746-9941
Franklin *(G-9870)*
Brewer Company ....E 614 279-8688
Columbus *(G-6694)*
Century Industries Corporation ....E 330 457-2367
New Waterford *(G-14838)*
Hy-Grade Corporation ....E 216 341-7711
Cleveland *(G-5429)*
Hyload Inc ....F 330 336-6604
Seville *(G-16916)*
Ipm Inc ....E 419 248-8000
Toledo *(G-18351)*
Isaiah Industries Inc ....E 937 773-9840
Piqua *(G-16131)*
Kettering Roofing & Shtmtl ....E 513 281-6413
Cincinnati *(G-3906)*
Metal Sales Manufacturing Corp ....E 440 319-3779
Jefferson *(G-11234)*
Midwest Industrial Products ....G 216 771-8555
Cleveland *(G-5681)*
National Tool & Equipment Inc ....F 330 629-8665
Youngstown *(G-20973)*
Owens Corning ....A 419 248-8000
Toledo *(G-18446)*
Owens Corning Sales LLC ....A 419 248-8000
Toledo *(G-18448)*
Qualico Inc ....G 216 271-2550
Cleveland *(G-5938)*
Simon Roofing and Shtmtl Corp ....C 330 629-7392
Youngstown *(G-21032)*
Sr Products ....G 330 998-6500
Macedonia *(G-12329)*
State Industrial Products Corp ....B 877 747-6986
Cleveland *(G-6097)*
Surface-All Inc ....G 440 428-2233
Port Clinton *(G-16261)*
Terry Asphalt Materials Inc ....E 513 874-6192
Hamilton *(G-10609)*
Thorworks Industries Inc ....E 419 626-4375
Sandusky *(G-16855)*

Transtar Holding Company ....G 800 359-3339
Walton Hills *(G-19315)*

ASPHALT MINING & BITUMINOUS STONE QUARRYING SVCS

Kellstone ....G 419 621-8140
Sandusky *(G-16820)*
Shelly Liquid Division ....G 216 781-9264
Cleveland *(G-6051)*

ASPHALT MINING SVCS

Mar-Zane Inc ....G 419 529-2086
Ontario *(G-15543)*
National Lime and Stone Co ....G 330 339-2144
New Philadelphia *(G-14790)*
National Lime and Stone Co ....G 216 883-9840
Cleveland *(G-5726)*

ASPHALT MIXTURES WHOLESALERS

Barrett Paving Materials Inc ....C 513 271-6200
Middletown *(G-13970)*
Hy-Grade Corporation ....E 216 341-7711
Cleveland *(G-5429)*
Russell Standard Corporation ....G 330 733-9400
Akron *(G-363)*

ASPHALT PLANTS INCLUDING GRAVEL MIX TYPE

G & J Asphalt & Material Inc ....F 740 773-6358
Chillicothe *(G-3186)*
Rls Parts & Equipment LLC ....G 440 498-1843
Solon *(G-17223)*

ASSEMBLING SVC: Plumbing Fixture Fittings, Plastic

Langenau Manufacturing Company ....F 216 651-3400
Cleveland *(G-5558)*

ASSOCIATION FOR THE HANDICAPPED

Cincinnati Assn For The Blind ....C 513 221-8558
Cincinnati *(G-3481)*

ASSOCIATIONS: Business

Americanhort Services Inc ....F 614 884-1203
Columbus *(G-6588)*
Diversifd OH Vlly Eqpt & Srvcs ....F 740 458-9881
Clarington *(G-4567)*
Hirzel Canning Company ....D 419 693-0531
Northwood *(G-15338)*
Interstate Contractors LLC ....E 513 372-5393
Mason *(G-12897)*
Superior Clay Corp ....D 740 922-4122
Uhrichsville *(G-18896)*

ASSOCIATIONS: Fraternal

Sylvania Moose Lodge No ....F 419 885-4953
Sylvania *(G-17964)*

ASSOCIATIONS: Manufacturers'

Albin Sales Inc ....G 740 927-7210
Pataskala *(G-15827)*
James J Fairbanks Company Inc ....G 330 534-1374
Hubbard *(G-11003)*

ASSOCIATIONS: Real Estate Management

Ajami Holdings Group LLC ....G 216 396-6089
Richmond Heights *(G-16500)*
Elite Property Group LLC ....F 216 356-7469
Elyria *(G-9250)*
Nesco Inc ....E 440 461-6000
Cleveland *(G-5741)*

ASSOCIATIONS: Trade

Ohio Association Realtors Inc ....E 614 228-6675
Columbus *(G-7241)*
Precision Metalforming Assn ....E 216 241-1482
Independence *(G-11148)*

ATOMIZERS

11am Industries LLC ....F 330 730-3177
Barberton *(G-1047)*

AUDIO ELECTRONIC SYSTEMS

AT&f Nuclear Inc ....G 216 252-1500
Cleveland *(G-4757)*
Bison USA Corp ....G 513 713-0513
Hamilton *(G-10541)*
Centaur Inc ....G 419 469-8000
Toledo *(G-18225)*
Cr Brands Inc ....D 513 860-5039
West Chester *(G-19686)*
Datco Mfg Company Inc ....E 330 787-1127
Youngstown *(G-20886)*
Ferguson Fire Fabrication Inc ....F 614 299-2070
Columbus *(G-6918)*
H Rosen Usa LLC ....C 614 354-6707
Columbus *(G-6973)*
Henry-Griffitts Limited ....G 419 482-9095
Maumee *(G-13117)*
Jrb Industries LLC ....E 567 825-7022
Greenville *(G-10377)*
MD Solutions Inc ....G 866 637-6588
Plain City *(G-16201)*
Sunsong North America Inc ....G 919 365-3825
Moraine *(G-14397)*
Triboro Quilt Mfg Corp ....F 937 222-2132
Vandalia *(G-19146)*
Truck Fax Inc ....G 216 921-8866
Cleveland *(G-6218)*
Velocity Concept Dev Group LLC ....G 513 204-2100
Mason *(G-12952)*
Woodsage Industries LLC ....G 419 866-8000
Holland *(G-10968)*
Zorich Industries Inc ....F 330 482-9803
Columbiana *(G-6488)*

AUCTION SVCS: Motor Vehicle

Rikenkaki America Corporation ....G 614 336-2744
Dublin *(G-8974)*
Subaru of A ....G 614 793-2358
Dublin *(G-8998)*

AUDIO & VIDEO EQPT, EXC COMMERCIAL

DIng Products ....G 440 442-7777
Cleveland *(G-5096)*
E3 Diagnostics Inc ....G 937 435-2250
Dayton *(G-8174)*
Eprad Inc ....E 419 666-3266
Perrysburg *(G-15948)*
Eq Technologies LLC ....G 216 548-3684
Cleveland *(G-5185)*
Gadgets Manufacturing Co ....G 937 686-5371
Huntsville *(G-11087)*
Greyfield Industries Inc ....F 513 860-1785
Trenton *(G-18620)*
Hudson Access Group II ....G 330 283-6214
Hudson *(G-11052)*
Knukonceptzcom Ltd ....G 216 310-6555
Windham *(G-20525)*
Markeys Audio/Visual Inc ....G 419 244-8844
Toledo *(G-18399)*
Mitsubishi Elc Auto Amer Inc ....B 513 573-6614
Mason *(G-12911)*
Pioneer Automotive Tech Inc ....C 937 746-2293
Springboro *(G-17344)*
R L Drake Company ....D 937 746-4556
Franklin *(G-9914)*
Rs Pro Sales LLC ....G 513 699-5329
Cincinnati *(G-4286)*
Soundproof ....G 440 864-8864
Grafton *(G-10310)*
Tech Products Corporation ....E 937 438-1100
Miamisburg *(G-13723)*
Technicolor Usa Inc ....A 614 474-8821
Circleville *(G-4561)*
Tls Corp ....E 216 574-4759
Cleveland *(G-6177)*
Tune Town Car Audio ....G 419 627-1100
Sandusky *(G-16857)*

AUDIO COMPONENTS

Avtek International Inc ....G 330 633-7500
Tallmadge *(G-17973)*
Bose Corporation ....G 614 475-8565
Columbus *(G-6688)*
China Enterprises Inc ....G 419 885-1485
Toledo *(G-18230)*

AUDIO ELECTRONIC SYSTEMS

Advanced Custom Sound ....G 330 372-9900
Warren *(G-19363)*

Employee Codes: A=Over 500 employees, B=251-500
C=101-250, D=51-100, E=20-50, F=10-19, G=3-9

AUDIO ELECTRONIC SYSTEMS

Andersound PA Service .... G 216 561-2636
  Cleveland *(G-4713)*
Digital Media Integration LLC .... G 937 305-5582
  Dayton *(G-8160)*
House of Hindenach .... G 419 422-0392
  Findlay *(G-9707)*
Pro Audio .... G 513 752-7500
  Cincinnati *(G-3261)*
Snyder Electronics .... G 513 738-7200
  Harrison *(G-10671)*
Sound Concepts LLC .... G 513 703-0147
  Mason *(G-12940)*
South Side Audio LLC .... G 614 453-0757
  Columbus *(G-7464)*
Undiscovered Radio Network .... G 740 533-1032
  Ironton *(G-11174)*

AUDIO-VISUAL PROGRAM PRODUCTION SVCS

Technical Translation Services .... F 440 942-3130
  Willoughby *(G-20443)*

AUDIOLOGICAL EQPT: Electronic

E3 Diagnostics Inc .... G 937 435-2250
  Dayton *(G-8174)*

AUDIOLOGISTS' OFFICES

Akron Ent Hearing Services Inc .... G 330 762-8959
  Akron *(G-38)*

AUTO & HOME SUPPLY STORES: Auto & Truck Eqpt & Parts

Tbone Sales LLC .... E 330 897-6131
  Baltic *(G-1033)*

AUTO & HOME SUPPLY STORES: Automotive Access

Bucyrus Precision Tech Inc .... C 419 563-9950
  Bucyrus *(G-2320)*
Epix Tube Co Inc .... D 937 529-4858
  Dayton *(G-8184)*
Horizon Global Americas Inc .... D 440 498-0001
  Solon *(G-17163)*
Kemper Automotive .... G 800 783-8004
  Franklin *(G-9892)*
Rex Manufacturing Co .... G 419 224-5751
  Lima *(G-11931)*
Stevens Auto Glaze and SEC LL .... G 440 953-2900
  Eastlake *(G-9131)*
Steves Vans & Accessories LLC .... G 740 374-3154
  Marietta *(G-12676)*

AUTO & HOME SUPPLY STORES: Automotive parts

ABC Inoac Exterior Systems LLC .... C 419 334-8951
  Fremont *(G-9988)*
American Cold Forge LLC .... E 419 836-1062
  Northwood *(G-15331)*
Center Automotive Parts Co .... G 330 434-2174
  Akron *(G-109)*
Crown Dielectric Inds Inc .... C 614 224-5161
  Columbus *(G-6839)*
Gellner Engineering Inc .... G 216 398-8500
  Cleveland *(G-5301)*
General Parts Inc .... G 614 891-6014
  Westerville *(G-20055)*
III Williams LLC .... G 440 721-8191
  Chardon *(G-3118)*
Jenkins Motor Parts .... G 330 525-4011
  Beloit *(G-1570)*
K-M-S Industries Inc .... E 440 243-6680
  Brookpark *(G-2150)*
Ken Veney Industries LLC .... G 330 336-5825
  Wadsworth *(G-19248)*
Liber Limited LLC .... G 440 427-0647
  Olmsted Twp *(G-15533)*
M Technologies Inc .... F 330 477-9009
  Canton *(G-2739)*
Mader Automotive Center Inc .... F 937 339-2681
  Troy *(G-18685)*
Ohio Auto Supply Company .... E 330 454-5105
  Canton *(G-2771)*
Performance Motorsports .... G 513 931-9999
  Cincinnati *(G-4149)*
R4 Holdings LLC .... G 614 873-6499
  Plain City *(G-16210)*
Speed City LLC .... G 440 975-1969
  Newbury *(G-14966)*
Stevens Auto Parts & Towng .... G 740 988-2260
  Jackson *(G-11195)*
Supercharger Systems Inc .... G 216 676-5800
  Brookpark *(G-2156)*
Tom Barbour Auto Parts Inc .... F 740 354-4654
  Portsmouth *(G-16303)*

AUTO & HOME SUPPLY STORES: Batteries, Automotive & Truck

B W T Inc .... G 330 928-9107
  Akron *(G-77)*
Battery Unlimited .... G 740 452-5030
  Zanesville *(G-21104)*
Interstate Batteries Inc .... G 740 968-2211
  Saint Clairsville *(G-16634)*
N S T Battery .... G 937 433-9222
  Bellbrook *(G-1496)*

AUTO & HOME SUPPLY STORES: Trailer Hitches, Automotive

Custom Hitch and Trailer/ Over .... G 740 289-3925
  Piketon *(G-16068)*

AUTO & HOME SUPPLY STORES: Truck Eqpt & Parts

Ace Truck Equipment Co .... E 740 453-0551
  Zanesville *(G-21091)*
Galion-Godwin Truck Bdy Co LLC .... D 330 359-5495
  Millersburg *(G-14084)*
H & H Truck Parts LLC .... G 216 642-4540
  Cleveland *(G-5362)*
Jerry Tadlock .... G 937 544-2851
  West Union *(G-19963)*
Kaffenbarger Truck Eqp Co .... E 513 772-6800
  Cincinnati *(G-3892)*
Marlow-2000 Inc .... F 216 362-8500
  Cleveland *(G-5625)*
Martin Diesel Inc .... E 419 782-9911
  Defiance *(G-8636)*
Perkins Motor Service Ltd .... E 440 277-1256
  Lorain *(G-12112)*
River City Body Company .... F 513 772-9317
  Cincinnati *(G-4271)*
Shur-Co LLC .... G 330 297-0888
  Ravenna *(G-16402)*
Western Branch Diesel Inc .... E 330 454-8800
  Canton *(G-2864)*

AUTOMATED TELLER MACHINE OR ATM REPAIR SVCS

American Merchant Servic .... G 216 598-3100
  Westlake *(G-20093)*
Glenn Michael Brick .... F 740 391-5735
  Flushing *(G-9783)*

AUTOMATIC REGULATING CNTRLS: Liq Lvl, Residential/Comm Heat

Cfrc Wtr & Enrgy Solutions Inc .... G 216 479-0290
  Cleveland *(G-4906)*
Conery Manufacturing Inc .... F 419 289-1444
  Ashland *(G-696)*

AUTOMATIC REGULATING CNTRLS: Steam Press, Residential/ Comm

Turner Pressure .... G 614 871-7775
  Grove City *(G-10479)*

AUTOMATIC REGULATING CONTROL: Building Svcs Monitoring, Auto

A & P Tool Inc .... E 419 542-6681
  Hicksville *(G-10773)*
Evokes LLC .... E 513 947-8433
  Mason *(G-12868)*
Qleanair Scandinavia Inc .... G 614 323-1756
  Columbus *(G-7360)*

AUTOMATIC REGULATING CONTROLS: AC & Refrigeration

Fes-Ohio Inc .... G 513 772-8566
  Cincinnati *(G-3683)*
Siemens Industry Inc .... D 513 336-2267
  Lebanon *(G-11695)*
Siemens Industry Inc .... D 614 573-8212
  Columbus *(G-7448)*
Young Regulator Company Inc .... E 440 232-9452
  Bedford *(G-1456)*

AUTOMATIC REGULATING CONTROLS: Appliance, Exc Air-Cond/Refr

K Davis Inc .... G 419 637-2859
  Gibsonburg *(G-10249)*
Melink Corporation .... F 513 685-0958
  Milford *(G-14026)*
Portage Electric Products Inc .... C 330 499-2727
  North Canton *(G-15111)*

AUTOMATIC REGULATING CONTROLS: Energy Cutoff, Residtl/Comm

Action Air & Hydraulics Inc .... G 937 372-8614
  Xenia *(G-20753)*
Estabrook Assembly Svcs Inc .... F 440 243-3350
  Berea *(G-1606)*
Sasha Electronics Inc .... F 419 662-8100
  Rossford *(G-16593)*

AUTOMATIC REGULATING CONTROLS: Hardware, Environmental Reg

Mestek Inc .... D 419 288-2703
  Bradner *(G-2015)*

AUTOMATIC REGULATING CONTROLS: Refrigeration, Pressure

Etc Enterprises LLC .... G 417 262-6382
  Delphos *(G-8743)*
Norcold Inc .... C 937 447-2241
  Gettysburg *(G-10247)*

AUTOMATIC REGULATING CONTROLS: Surface Burner, Temperature

Ohio Coatings Company .... D 740 859-5500
  Yorkville *(G-20827)*

AUTOMATIC REGULATING CTRLS: Damper, Pneumatic Or Electric

Howden North America Inc .... D 330 867-8540
  Medina *(G-13274)*
Mader Machine Co Inc .... E 440 355-4505
  Lagrange *(G-11488)*

AUTOMATIC TELLER MACHINES

American Merchant Servic .... G 216 598-3100
  Westlake *(G-20093)*
Diebold Nixdorf Incorporated .... A 330 490-4000
  North Canton *(G-15078)*
Diebold Nixdorf Incorporated .... D 330 490-4000
  North Canton *(G-15079)*
Diebold Nixdorf Incorporated .... B 330 490-4000
  Canton *(G-2659)*
Ginko Voting Systems LLC .... G 937 291-4060
  Dayton *(G-8222)*
Glenn Michael Brick .... F 740 391-5735
  Flushing *(G-9783)*
Peoples Bancorp Inc .... C 740 685-1500
  Byesville *(G-2391)*
Testlink USA .... F 513 272-1081
  Cincinnati *(G-4414)*

AUTOMOBILE RECOVERY SVCS

D & D Classic Auto Restoration .... E 937 473-2229
  Covington *(G-7784)*

AUTOMOBILE STORAGE GARAGE

Dasher Lawless Automation LLC .... E 855 755-7275
  Warren *(G-19394)*

PRODUCT SECTION

AUTOMOTIVE PARTS, ACCESS & SPLYS

AUTOMOBILES & OTHER MOTOR VEHICLES WHOLESALERS

Btw LLC	G	419 382-4443
Toledo *(G-18217)*		
Diversifd OH Vlly Eqpt & Srvcs	F	740 458-9881
Clarington *(G-4567)*		
Doug Marine Motors Inc	E	740 335-3700
Wshngtn CT Hs *(G-20724)*		
Interstate Truckway Inc	E	614 771-1220
Columbus *(G-7047)*		
Sevan At-Ndustrial Pnt Abr Ltd	G	614 258-4747
Columbus *(G-7440)*		
Warren Fire Equipment Inc	G	937 866-8918
Miamisburg *(G-13738)*		

AUTOMOBILES: Off-Road, Exc Recreational Vehicles

Mx Spring Inc	G	330 426-4600
East Palestine *(G-9081)*		
Swartz Audie	G	740 820-2341
Minford *(G-14207)*		

AUTOMOTIVE & TRUCK GENERAL REPAIR SVC

Diesel Recon Service Inc	G	513 625-1887
Pleasant Plain *(G-16225)*		
Doug Marine Motors Inc	E	740 335-3700
Wshngtn CT Hs *(G-20724)*		
Goodyear Tire & Rubber Company	A	330 796-2121
Akron *(G-191)*		
Gregory Auto Service	G	513 248-0423
Loveland *(G-12194)*		
Hutter Racing Engines Ltd	F	440 285-2175
Chardon *(G-3117)*		
Johnson Engine & Machine	G	614 876-0724
Hilliard *(G-10835)*		
Kennedy Mint Inc	D	440 572-3222
Cleveland *(G-5528)*		
Kirbys Auto & Truck Repair	G	513 934-3999
Lebanon *(G-11669)*		
Ohio Trailer Inc	F	330 392-4444
Warren *(G-19428)*		
Pattons Truck & Heavy Eqp Svc	F	740 385-4067
Logan *(G-12039)*		
Prestons Repair & Welding	F	937 947-1883
Laura *(G-11625)*		
Sammartino Welding & Auto Sls	G	330 782-6086
Youngstown *(G-21024)*		
Sammy S Auto Detail	F	614 263-2728
Columbus *(G-7418)*		
Wilguss Automotive Machine	G	937 465-0043
West Liberty *(G-19939)*		
Youngstown-Kenworth Inc	E	330 534-9761
Hubbard *(G-11014)*		

AUTOMOTIVE BATTERIES WHOLESALERS

All Power Battery Inc	G	330 453-5236
Canton *(G-2567)*		
Exide Technologies	G	614 863-3866
Gahanna *(G-10081)*		

AUTOMOTIVE BODY SHOP

Johns Body Shop	G	419 358-1200
Bluffton *(G-1890)*		
Obs Inc	F	330 453-3725
Canton *(G-2769)*		
W&W Automotive & Towing Inc	F	937 429-1699
Beavercreek Township *(G-1375)*		
Webers Body & Frame	G	937 839-5946
West Alexandria *(G-19624)*		

AUTOMOTIVE BODY, PAINT & INTERIOR REPAIR & MAINTENANCE SVC

Bobbart Industries Inc	E	419 350-5477
Sylvania *(G-17934)*		
Weiss Motors	G	330 678-5585
Kent *(G-11399)*		
Willard Machine & Welding Inc	F	330 467-0642
Macedonia *(G-12338)*		

AUTOMOTIVE BRAKE REPAIR SHOPS

Circleville Oil Co	G	740 477-3341
Circleville *(G-4539)*		

AUTOMOTIVE CUSTOMIZING SVCS, NONFACTORY BASIS

Aerotech Styling Inc	G	419 923-6970
Lyons *(G-12272)*		
Silverado Trucks & Accessories	G	937 492-8862
Sidney *(G-17080)*		

AUTOMOTIVE GLASS REPLACEMENT SHOPS

A Service Glass Inc	F	937 426-4920
Beavercreek *(G-1297)*		
J W Goss Co Inc	F	330 395-0739
Warren *(G-19413)*		
Mentor Glass Supplies and Repr	G	440 255-9444
Mentor *(G-13515)*		
Safelite Group Inc	A	614 210-9000
Columbus *(G-7413)*		
Support Svc LLC	G	419 617-0660
Lexington *(G-11808)*		
Webers Body & Frame	G	937 839-5946
West Alexandria *(G-19624)*		

AUTOMOTIVE PAINT SHOP

L & N Olde Car Co	G	440 564-7204
Newbury *(G-14959)*		
Precision Coatings Systems	E	937 642-4727
Marysville *(G-12806)*		

AUTOMOTIVE PARTS, ACCESS & SPLYS

1 A Lifesafer Hawaii Inc	F	513 651-9560
Blue Ash *(G-1717)*		
A G Parts Inc	F	937 596-6448
Jackson Center *(G-11204)*		
Accel Performance Group LLC	C	216 658-6413
Independence *(G-11117)*		
Access 2 Communications Inc	G	800 561-1110
Steubenville *(G-17525)*		
Ach LLC	G	419 621-5748
Sandusky *(G-16791)*		
Adient US LLC	C	937 383-5200
Greenfield *(G-10345)*		
Adient US LLC	C	419 662-4950
Northwood *(G-15330)*		
Aerotech Styling Inc	G	419 923-6970
Lyons *(G-12272)*		
Airstream Inc	B	937 596-6111
Jackson Center *(G-11205)*		
Airtex Industries LLC	G	330 899-0340
North Canton *(G-15068)*		
Alex Products Inc	C	419 399-4500
Paulding *(G-15855)*		
AM General LLC	G	937 704-0160
Franklin *(G-9868)*		
American Manufacturing & Eqp	G	513 829-2248
Fairfield *(G-9482)*		
AMP Electric Vehicles Inc	F	513 360-4704
Loveland *(G-12177)*		
Amsoil Inc	G	614 274-9851
Columbus *(G-6593)*		
Amsted Industries Incorporated	C	614 836-2323
Groveport *(G-10481)*		
Aptiv Services Us LLC	C	330 367-6000
Vienna *(G-19196)*		
Arlington Rack & Packaging Co	G	419 476-7700
Toledo *(G-18191)*		
Atc Lighting & Plastics Inc	C	440 466-7670
Andover *(G-580)*		
Atlas Industries Inc	B	419 637-2117
Tiffin *(G-18046)*		
Atwood Mobile Products LLC	E	419 258-5531
Antwerp *(G-597)*		
Auria Fremont LLC	B	419 332-1587
Fremont *(G-9994)*		
Auria Holmesville LLC	B	330 279-4505
Holmesville *(G-10973)*		
Auria Sidney LLC	G	937 492-1225
Sidney *(G-17017)*		
Auria Sidney LLC	E	937 492-1225
Sidney *(G-17018)*		
Autoneum North America Inc	E	419 690-8924
Oregon *(G-15555)*		
Autoneum North America Inc	B	419 693-0511
Oregon *(G-15556)*		
B A Malcuit Racing Inc	G	330 878-7111
Strasburg *(G-17645)*		
B&C Machine Co LLC	G	330 745-4013
Barberton *(G-1058)*		
Beach Manufacturing Co	C	937 882-6372
Donnelsville *(G-8800)*		
Bobbart Industries Inc	E	419 350-5477
Sylvania *(G-17934)*		
Bores Manufacturing Co Inc	F	419 465-2606
Monroeville *(G-14287)*		
Buyers Products Company	G	440 974-8888
Mentor *(G-13408)*		
Buyers Products Company	G	440 974-8888
Mentor *(G-13410)*		
Bwi Chassis Dynamics NA Inc	F	937 455-5100
Kettering *(G-11427)*		
Bwi North America Inc	C	937 455-5190
Kettering *(G-11428)*		
Bwi North America Inc	E	937 253-1130
Kettering *(G-11429)*		
Cadillac Products Inc	E	248 813-8255
Lebanon *(G-11639)*		
Certified Power Inc	D	419 355-1200
Fremont *(G-10006)*		
Cleveland Ignition Co Inc	G	440 439-3688
Cleveland *(G-4964)*		
Comprehensive Logistics Co Inc	E	330 793-0504
Youngstown *(G-20877)*		
Continental Strl Plas Inc	B	419 396-1980
Carey *(G-2880)*		
Continental Strl Plas Inc	C	419 257-2231
North Baltimore *(G-15043)*		
Continental Strl Plas Inc	B	419 238-4628
Van Wert *(G-19082)*		
Cosma International Amer Inc	E	419 409-7350
Bowling Green *(G-1966)*		
Cummins Inc	G	614 604-6004
Grove City *(G-10424)*		
Custer Products Limited	F	330 490-3158
Massillon *(G-12972)*		
Custom Cltch Jint Hydrlics Inc	G	330 455-1202
Canton *(G-2642)*		
D-Terra Solutions LLC	G	614 450-1040
Powell *(G-16320)*		
Dana Auto Systems Group LLC	D	419 887-3000
Maumee *(G-13086)*		
Dana Automotive Aftermarket	G	419 887-3000
Maumee *(G-13087)*		
Dana Brazil Holdings I LLC	G	419 887-3000
Maumee *(G-13088)*		
Dana Commercial Vhcl Mfg LLC	G	419 887-3000
Maumee *(G-13089)*		
Dana Commercial Vhcl Pdts LLC	D	419 887-3000
Maumee *(G-13090)*		
Dana Drive Shaft Pdts Group	G	419 227-2001
Lima *(G-11852)*		
Dana Driveshaft Mfg LLC	C	419 222-9708
Lima *(G-11853)*		
Dana Driveshaft Mfg LLC	D	419 887-3000
Maumee *(G-13091)*		
Dana Driveshaft Products LLC	D	419 887-3000
Maumee *(G-13092)*		
Dana Global Products Inc	G	419 887-3000
Maumee *(G-13093)*		
Dana Heavy Vehicle Systems	G	419 887-3000
Maumee *(G-13094)*		
Dana Incorporated	B	419 887-3000
Maumee *(G-13095)*		
Dana Light Axle Mfg LLC	B	419 887-3000
Toledo *(G-18253)*		
Dana Light Axle Mfg LLC	B	419 887-3000
Maumee *(G-13096)*		
Dana Limited	G	419 887-3000
Maumee *(G-13097)*		
Dana Limited	D	419 482-2000
Maumee *(G-13098)*		
Dana Limited	B	419 887-3000
Maumee *(G-13099)*		
Dana Off Highway Products LLC	E	614 864-1116
Blacklick *(G-1683)*		
Dana Off Highway Products LLC	E	419 887-3000
Maumee *(G-13100)*		
Dana Sealing Manufacturing LLC	D	419 887-3000
Maumee *(G-13101)*		
Dana Sealing Products LLC	E	419 887-3000
Maumee *(G-13102)*		
Dana Structural Products LLC	G	419 887-3000
Maumee *(G-13103)*		
Dana Thermal Products LLC	E	419 887-3000
Maumee *(G-13104)*		
Dana World Trade Corporation	G	419 887-3000
Maumee *(G-13105)*		
Dayton Clutch & Joint Inc	F	937 236-9770
Dayton *(G-8130)*		

Employee Codes: A=Over 500 employees, B=251-500 C=101-250, D=51-100, E=20-50, F=10-19, G=3-9

AUTOMOTIVE PARTS, ACCESS & SPLYS — PRODUCT SECTION

Dcm Manufacturing Inc .... E 216 265-8006
Cleveland *(G-5078)*
Denso Automotive Ohio .... G 614 336-1261
Dublin *(G-8906)*
Doug Marine Motors Inc .... E 740 335-3700
Wshngtn CT Hs *(G-20724)*
Dove Machine Inc .... F 440 864-2645
Columbia Station *(G-6437)*
Dove Manufacturing LLC .... G 440 506-7935
Grafton *(G-10298)*
Driveline 1 Inc .... G 614 279-7734
Columbus *(G-6875)*
Dti Molded Products Inc .... F 937 492-5008
Sidney *(G-17033)*
Ebog Legacy Inc .... D 330 239-4933
Sharon Center *(G-16949)*
Edgerton Forge Inc .... F 419 298-2333
Edgerton *(G-9171)*
Egr Products Company Inc .... F 330 833-6554
Dalton *(G-7941)*
Exito Manufacturing .... G 937 291-9871
Beavercreek *(G-1355)*
Falls Stamping & Welding Co .... C 330 928-1191
Cuyahoga Falls *(G-7867)*
Farin Industries Inc .... F 440 275-2755
Austinburg *(G-921)*
Federal-Mogul Powertrain LLC .... C 740 432-2393
Cambridge *(G-2437)*
Flex N Gate .... G 330 332-6363
Salem *(G-16738)*
Flex Technologies Inc .... D 330 359-5415
Mount Eaton *(G-14420)*
Florida Production Engrg Inc .... D 937 996-4361
New Madison *(G-14741)*
Force Control Industries Inc .... D 513 868-0900
Fairfield *(G-9498)*
Ford Motor Company .... A 216 676-7918
Brookpark *(G-8746)*
Fram Group Operations LLC .... A 419 436-5827
Fostoria *(G-9845)*
Ftech R&D North America Inc .... D 937 339-2777
Troy *(G-18659)*
Gellner Engineering Inc .... G 216 398-8500
Cleveland *(G-5301)*
General Aluminum Mfg Company .... C 419 739-9300
Wapakoneta *(G-19330)*
General Metals Powder Co .... G 330 633-1226
Akron *(G-186)*
General Motors LLC .... B 330 824-5840
Warren *(G-19406)*
General Motors LLC .... A 216 265-5000
Cleveland *(G-5312)*
GKN Driveline North Amer Inc .... D 419 354-3955
Bowling Green *(G-1974)*
Grand-Rock Company Inc .... E 440 639-2000
Painesville *(G-15742)*
Green Rdced Emssons Netwrk LLC .... G 330 340-0941
Strasburg *(G-17648)*
Green Tokai Co Ltd .... G 937 237-1630
Dayton *(G-8237)*
Gt Motorsports .... G 937 763-7272
Lynchburg *(G-12271)*
H O Fibertrends .... G 740 983-3864
Ashville *(G-818)*
Hall-Toledo Inc .... F 419 893-4334
Maumee *(G-13114)*
Hendrickson International Corp .... D 740 929-5600
Hebron *(G-10747)*
Hendrickson Usa LLC .... C 330 456-7288
Canton *(G-2696)*
Hfi LLC .... B 614 491-0700
Columbus *(G-6995)*
Hi-Tek Manufacturing Inc .... C 513 459-1094
Mason *(G-12886)*
Hirschvogel Incorporated .... C 614 340-5657
Columbus *(G-7002)*
Hit & Miss Enterprises .... G 440 272-5335
Orwell *(G-15632)*
Honda of America Mfg Inc .... C 937 644-0724
Marysville *(G-12792)*
Horizon Global Americas Inc .... D 440 498-0001
Solon *(G-17163)*
Hot Shot Motor Works M LLC .... F 419 294-1997
Upper Sandusky *(G-18956)*
Hp2g LLC .... F 419 906-1525
Napoleon *(G-14544)*
Hurst Auto-Truck Electric .... G 216 961-1800
Cleveland *(G-5426)*
Igw USA .... G 740 588-1722
Zanesville *(G-21149)*

Illinois Tool Works Inc .... C 513 489-7600
Blue Ash *(G-1791)*
Illinois Tool Works Inc .... C 262 248-8277
Bryan *(G-2289)*
Imasen Bucyrus Technology Inc .... C 419 563-9590
Bucyrus *(G-2336)*
Industry Products Co .... B 937 778-0585
Piqua *(G-16130)*
International Automotive Compo .... A 419 335-1000
Wauseon *(G-19522)*
International Automotive Compo .... A 419 433-5653
Huron *(G-11099)*
Inteva Products LLC .... F 937 280-8500
Vandalia *(G-19129)*
Ishikawa Gasket America Inc .... C 419 353-7300
Bowling Green *(G-1976)*
Johnson Power Ltd .... G 419 866-6692
Holland *(G-10939)*
Joseph Industries Inc .... D 330 528-0091
Streetsboro *(G-17680)*
Jr Engineering Inc .... C 330 848-0960
Barberton *(G-1079)*
Julie Maynard Inc .... F 937 443-0408
Dayton *(G-8286)*
K Wm Beach Mfg Co Inc .... C 937 399-3838
Springfield *(G-17429)*
Kalida Manufacturing Inc .... C 419 532-2026
Kalida *(G-11278)*
Kasai North America Inc .... E 419 209-0470
Upper Sandusky *(G-18958)*
Kasai North America Inc .... F 614 356-1494
Dublin *(G-8936)*
Kenley Enterprises LLC .... E 419 630-0921
Bryan *(G-2293)*
Kilar Manufacturing Inc .... E 330 534-8961
Hubbard *(G-11004)*
Knippen Chrysler Dodge Jeep .... E 419 695-4976
Delphos *(G-8746)*
Kongsberg Actuation Systems .... F 440 639-8778
Grand River *(G-10324)*
Kth Parts Industries Inc .... A 937 663-5941
Saint Paris *(G-16709)*
Ktri Holdings Inc .... G 216 371-1700
Cleveland *(G-5546)*
Kurts Auto Parts LLC .... G 330 723-0166
Medina *(G-13286)*
Lacal Equipment Inc .... E 800 543-6161
Jackson Center *(G-11210)*
Lawrence Technologies Inc .... G 937 274-7771
Dayton *(G-8308)*
Leadec Corp .... E 513 731-3590
Blue Ash *(G-1804)*
Lear Corp .... G 614 850-8630
Columbus *(G-7118)*
Lear Corporation .... E 740 928-4358
Hebron *(G-10750)*
Lear Corporation .... C 419 335-6010
Wauseon *(G-19526)*
Lear Corporation .... F 614 850-8630
Columbus *(G-7119)*
Leggett & Platt Incorporated .... G 330 262-6010
Apple Creek *(G-611)*
Linde Hydraulics Corporation .... E 330 533-6801
Canfield *(G-2532)*
Lynn Truck Parts & Service .... G 330 966-1470
North Canton *(G-15100)*
M-Tek Inc .... A 419 209-0399
Upper Sandusky *(G-18961)*
Maags Automotive & Machine .... G 419 626-1539
Sandusky *(G-16824)*
Magna Seating America Inc .... C 330 824-3101
Warren *(G-19420)*
Magnaco Industries Inc .... E 216 961-3636
Lodi *(G-12016)*
Mahle Behr Dayton LLC .... B 937 356-2001
Vandalia *(G-19134)*
Mahle Behr Dayton LLC .... D 937 369-2900
Dayton *(G-8325)*
Mahle Behr USA Inc .... G 937 369-2900
Dayton *(G-8326)*
Mahle Behr USA Inc .... C 937 356-2001
Vandalia *(G-19135)*
Mahle Industries Incorporated .... E 937 890-2739
Dayton *(G-8328)*
Marmon Highway Tech LLC .... E 330 878-5595
Dover *(G-8839)*
Maxion Wheels Akron LLC .... E 330 794-2310
Akron *(G-272)*
Maxion Wheels Sedalia LLC .... G 330 794-2300
Akron *(G-273)*

Millat Industries Corp .... E 937 535-1500
Dayton *(G-8361)*
Millat Industries Corp .... D 937 434-6666
Dayton *(G-8360)*
Mitec Powertrain Inc .... C 567 525-5606
Findlay *(G-9727)*
Mitsubishi Elc Auto Amer Inc .... B 513 573-6614
Mason *(G-12911)*
Multi-Design Inc .... G 440 275-2255
Austinburg *(G-923)*
Navistar Inc .... D 937 390-5653
Springfield *(G-17457)*
Navistar Inc .... D 937 390-5704
Springfield *(G-17459)*
Nebraska Industries Corp .... E 419 335-6010
Wauseon *(G-19529)*
Norlake Manufacturing Company .... D 440 353-3200
North Ridgeville *(G-15241)*
Norplas Industries Inc .... B 419 662-3317
Northwood *(G-15341)*
North Coast Exotics Inc .... G 216 651-5512
Cleveland *(G-5765)*
Northern Stamping Co .... G 216 642-8081
Cleveland *(G-5784)*
Norton Manufacturing Co Inc .... F 419 435-0411
Fostoria *(G-9853)*
Ohio Auto Supply Company .... E 330 454-5105
Canton *(G-2771)*
Ohta Press US Inc .... F 937 374-3382
Xenia *(G-20785)*
Pacific Manufacturing Ohio Inc .... B 513 860-3900
Fairfield *(G-9542)*
Pako Inc .... C 440 946-8030
Mentor *(G-13540)*
Parker-Hannifin Corporation .... B 440 943-5700
Wickliffe *(G-20224)*
Parker-Hannifin Corporation .... A 216 531-3000
Cleveland *(G-5849)*
Pioneer Automotive Tech Inc .... C 937 746-2293
Springboro *(G-17344)*
Piston Automotive LLC .... D 419 464-0250
Toledo *(G-18471)*
Powers and Sons LLC .... C 419 485-3151
Montpelier *(G-14314)*
Powers and Sons LLC .... G 419 737-2373
Pioneer *(G-16091)*
Production Turning LLC .... G 937 424-0034
Moraine *(G-14386)*
Quality Reproductions Inc .... G 330 335-5000
Wadsworth *(G-19269)*
Race Winning Brands Inc .... B 440 951-6600
Mentor *(G-13572)*
Radar Love Co .... F 419 951-4750
Findlay *(G-9744)*
Ramco Specialties Inc .... C 330 653-5135
Hudson *(G-11069)*
Reactive Resin Products Co .... E 419 666-6119
Perrysburg *(G-16003)*
Reineke Company LLC .... F 419 281-5800
Ashland *(G-743)*
Resinoid Engineering Corp .... E 740 928-2220
Heath *(G-10730)*
Riverside Engines Inc .... G 419 927-6838
Tiffin *(G-18077)*
Rubberduck 4x4 .... G 513 889-1735
Hamilton *(G-10601)*
Safe Auto Systems LLC .... G 216 661-1166
Carroll *(G-2910)*
Saia-Burgess Lcc .... D 937 898-3621
Vandalia *(G-19144)*
Sanoh America Inc .... C 740 392-9200
Mount Vernon *(G-14505)*
Schaeffler Transm Systems LLC .... A 330 264-4383
Wooster *(G-20649)*
Schott Metal Products Company .... D 330 773-7873
Akron *(G-373)*
Seabiscuit Motorsports Inc .... B 440 951-6600
Mentor *(G-13577)*
Senneco Glass Inc .... G 330 825-7717
Cuyahoga Falls *(G-7915)*
Sew-Eurodrive Inc .... D 937 335-0036
Troy *(G-18705)*
Sfs Group Usa Inc .... C 330 239-7100
Medina *(G-13339)*
Spectrum Brands Inc .... F 440 357-2600
Painesville *(G-15783)*
SPS International Inc .... G 216 671-9911
Strongsville *(G-17793)*
Std Specialty Filters Inc .... F 216 881-3727
Cleveland *(G-6101)*

PRODUCT SECTION — AUTOMOTIVE REPAIR SVCS, MISCELLANEOUS

Steck Manufacturing Co Inc............F...... 937 222-0062
  Dayton *(G-8527)*
Sumiriko Ohio Inc...........................C...... 419 358-2121
  Bluffton *(G-1893)*
Sutphen Corporation......................D...... 937 969-8851
  Springfield *(G-17500)*
Systems Jay LLC Nanogate..............C...... 419 522-7745
  Mansfield *(G-12525)*
Tetra Mold & Tool Inc....................E...... 937 845-1651
  New Carlisle *(G-14679)*
Tfo Tech Co Ltd............................C...... 740 426-6381
  Jeffersonville *(G-11248)*
Thyssenkrupp Bilstein Amer Inc......E...... 513 881-7600
  West Chester *(G-19809)*
TI Group Auto Systems LLC............C...... 740 929-2049
  Hebron *(G-10767)*
Tigerpoly Manufacturing Inc...........B...... 614 871-0045
  Grove City *(G-10473)*
Tko Mfg Services Inc......................E...... 937 299-1637
  Moraine *(G-14399)*
Toledo Molding & Die Inc...............C...... 419 692-6022
  Delphos *(G-8756)*
Toledo Molding & Die Inc...............D...... 419 692-6022
  Delphos *(G-8757)*
Toledo Pro Fiberglass Inc................G...... 419 241-9390
  Toledo *(G-18567)*
Tom Smith Industries Inc................F...... 937 832-1555
  Englewood *(G-9378)*
Trailer Component Mfg Inc.............C...... 440 255-2888
  Mentor *(G-13612)*
Tramec Sloan LLC...........................F...... 419 468-9122
  Galion *(G-10158)*
Tri-Mac Mfg & Svcs Co....................F...... 513 896-4445
  Hamilton *(G-10613)*
Trim Parts Inc................................E...... 513 934-0815
  Lebanon *(G-11702)*
Trim Systems Operating Corp.........D...... 614 289-5360
  New Albany *(G-14638)*
TRW Automotive Inc......................C...... 419 237-2511
  Fayette *(G-9637)*
TS Trim Industries Inc....................B...... 740 593-5958
  Athens *(G-852)*
Ugn Inc...C...... 513 360-3500
  Lebanon *(G-11704)*
Unique-Chardan Inc......................C...... 419 636-6900
  Bryan *(G-2311)*
Unison Industries LLC...................B...... 904 667-9904
  Dayton *(G-7994)*
United Components LLC................C...... 812 867-4516
  North Canton *(G-15133)*
US Tsubaki Power Transm LLC.........C...... 419 626-4560
  Sandusky *(G-16860)*
Usui International Corporation.......D...... 734 354-3626
  West Chester *(G-19817)*
Varbros LLC..................................C...... 216 267-5200
  Cleveland *(G-6250)*
Vari-Wall Tube Specialists Inc.........D...... 330 482-0000
  Columbiana *(G-6485)*
Venco Manufacturing Inc...............C...... 513 772-8448
  Cincinnati *(G-4472)*
Venco Venturo Industries LLC........E...... 513 772-8448
  Cincinnati *(G-4473)*
Ventra Sandusky LLC....................C...... 419 627-3600
  Sandusky *(G-16861)*
Walther Engrg & Mfg Co Inc...........E...... 937 743-8125
  Franklin *(G-9931)*
West & Barker Inc..........................E...... 330 652-9923
  Niles *(G-15040)*
Western Branch Diesel Inc.............E...... 330 454-8800
  Canton *(G-2864)*
Whirlaway Corporation..................C...... 440 647-4711
  Wellington *(G-19596)*
Whirlaway Corporation..................E...... 440 647-4711
  Wellington *(G-19597)*
Woodbridge Group........................C...... 419 334-3666
  Fremont *(G-10064)*
Workhorse Group Inc....................D...... 513 297-3640
  Loveland *(G-12225)*

AUTOMOTIVE PARTS: Plastic

A & A Discount Tire.......................G...... 330 863-1936
  Carrollton *(G-2914)*
Bta Enterprises Inc........................E...... 937 277-0881
  Dayton *(G-8067)*
Clark Prfmce Fabrication LLC.........G...... 701 721-1378
  Dayton *(G-8093)*
Daddy Katz LLC.............................G...... 937 296-0347
  Moraine *(G-14341)*
Greenville Technology Inc..............G...... 937 642-6744
  Marysville *(G-12785)*
Hematite Inc..................................G...... 937 540-9889
  Englewood *(G-9362)*
Ken Veney Industries LLC...............G...... 330 336-5825
  Wadsworth *(G-19248)*
M W Solutions LLC........................F...... 419 782-1611
  Defiance *(G-8633)*
Milkmen Design LLC.....................G...... 440 590-5788
  Cleveland *(G-5687)*
Molten North America Corp..........C...... 419 425-2700
  Findlay *(G-9728)*
Mos International Inc....................F...... 330 329-0905
  Stow *(G-17607)*
National Fleet Svcs Ohio LLC..........F...... 440 930-5177
  Avon Lake *(G-997)*
Nifco America Corporation............B...... 614 920-6800
  Canal Winchester *(G-2507)*
Nifco America Corporation............C...... 614 836-3808
  Canal Winchester *(G-2508)*
Nifco America Corporation............C...... 614 836-8691
  Groveport *(G-10507)*
Polyfill LLC...................................E...... 937 493-0041
  Sidney *(G-17061)*
S&T Automotive America LLC........G...... 614 782-9041
  Grove City *(G-10464)*
Speed City LLC.............................G...... 440 975-1969
  Newbury *(G-14966)*
Th Plastics Inc...............................F...... 419 425-5825
  Findlay *(G-9768)*
Toledo Molding & Die Inc..............B...... 419 443-9031
  Tiffin *(G-18090)*
Trifecta Tool & Engrg LLC..............G...... 937 291-0933
  Dayton *(G-8565)*

AUTOMOTIVE PRDTS: Rubber

Ds Technologies Group Ltd............G...... 419 841-5388
  Toledo *(G-18270)*
Enterprise / Ameriseal Inc..............G...... 937 284-3003
  Springfield *(G-17396)*
Green Tokai Co Ltd.......................A...... 937 833-5444
  Brookville *(G-2170)*
Kn Rubber LLC..............................C...... 419 739-4200
  Wapakoneta *(G-19338)*
Myers Industries Inc......................C...... 330 336-6621
  Wadsworth *(G-19255)*
Myers Industries Inc......................E...... 330 253-5592
  Akron *(G-292)*
Performance Additives Amer LLC....G...... 330 365-9256
  New Philadelphia *(G-14793)*
Soffseal Inc...................................E...... 513 934-0815
  Lebanon *(G-11697)*

AUTOMOTIVE RADIATOR REPAIR SHOPS

Albright Radiator Inc....................G...... 330 264-8886
  Wooster *(G-20561)*
Brock RAD & Wldg Fabrication......G...... 740 773-2540
  Chillicothe *(G-3178)*
D & M Welding & Radiator............G...... 740 947-9032
  Waverly *(G-19544)*
Friess Welding Inc.........................F...... 330 644-8160
  Coventry Township *(G-7770)*
Perkins Motor Service Ltd..............E...... 440 277-1256
  Lorain *(G-12112)*

AUTOMOTIVE REPAIR SHOPS: Alternators/Generator, Rebuild/Rpr

Hurst Auto-Truck Electric...............G...... 216 961-1800
  Cleveland *(G-5426)*
Support Svc LLC............................G...... 419 617-0660
  Lexington *(G-11808)*

AUTOMOTIVE REPAIR SHOPS: Diesel Engine Repair

Cummins Inc.................................E...... 614 771-1000
  Hilliard *(G-10823)*
Power Acquisition LLC..................G...... 614 228-5000
  Dublin *(G-8966)*
W W Williams Company LLC.........F...... 330 659-3084
  Richfield *(G-16494)*

AUTOMOTIVE REPAIR SHOPS: Electrical Svcs

C RC Automotive...........................G...... 513 422-4775
  Middletown *(G-13889)*
Entratech Systems LLC..................F...... 419 433-7683
  Sandusky *(G-16809)*

AUTOMOTIVE REPAIR SHOPS: Engine Rebuilding

Done Right Engine & Machine........G...... 440 582-1366
  Cleveland *(G-5107)*
H & R Tool & Machine Co Inc.........G...... 740 452-0784
  Zanesville *(G-21143)*
Jenkins Motor Parts.......................G...... 330 525-4011
  Beloit *(G-1570)*
Maags Automotive & Machine.......G...... 419 626-1539
  Sandusky *(G-16824)*
Seme & Son Automotive Inc..........G...... 216 261-0066
  Euclid *(G-9443)*

AUTOMOTIVE REPAIR SHOPS: Engine Repair

Deer Creek Custom Canvas LLC.....G...... 740 495-9239
  New Holland *(G-14701)*
Joe Baker Equipment Sales............G...... 513 451-1327
  Cincinnati *(G-3875)*

AUTOMOTIVE REPAIR SHOPS: Machine Shop

B K Fabrication & Machine Shop....G...... 740 695-4164
  Saint Clairsville *(G-16622)*
Debolt Machine Inc.......................G...... 740 454-8082
  Zanesville *(G-21127)*
Deuer Developments Inc...............F...... 937 299-1213
  Moraine *(G-14345)*
Engine Machine Service Inc...........G...... 330 505-1804
  Niles *(G-15007)*
Gellner Engineering Inc.................G...... 216 398-8500
  Cleveland *(G-5301)*
RL Best Company..........................E...... 330 758-8601
  Boardman *(G-1902)*

AUTOMOTIVE REPAIR SHOPS: Trailer Repair

Capitol City Trailers Inc.................D...... 614 491-2616
  Obetz *(G-15507)*
Greggs Specialty Services..............F...... 419 478-0803
  Toledo *(G-18313)*
J & L Body Inc...............................F...... 216 661-2323
  Brooklyn Heights *(G-2126)*
M & W Trailers Inc........................F...... 419 453-3331
  Ottoville *(G-15682)*
Mac Trailer Manufacturing Inc.......C...... 330 823-9900
  Alliance *(G-485)*
Marmon Highway Tech LLC...........E...... 330 878-5595
  Dover *(G-8839)*
Nelson Manufacturing Company....D...... 419 523-5321
  Ottawa *(G-15660)*

AUTOMOTIVE REPAIR SHOPS: Truck Engine Repair, Exc Indl

Carl E Oeder Sons Sand & Grav......E...... 513 494-1555
  Lebanon *(G-11640)*
Kaffenbarger Truck Eqp Co............E...... 513 772-6800
  Cincinnati *(G-3892)*
Kinstle Truck & Auto Svc Inc..........F...... 419 738-7493
  Wapakoneta *(G-19337)*
Steubenville Truck Center Inc........E...... 740 282-2711
  Steubenville *(G-17554)*

AUTOMOTIVE REPAIR SVC

Certified Power Inc.......................D...... 419 355-1200
  Fremont *(G-10006)*
East Manufacturing Corporation...B...... 330 325-9921
  Randolph *(G-16360)*
Goodyear Tire & Rubber Company..A...... 330 796-2121
  Akron *(G-191)*
Jordon Auto Service & Tire Inc......G...... 216 214-6528
  Cleveland *(G-5505)*
Maags Automotive & Machine.......G...... 419 626-1539
  Sandusky *(G-16824)*
Mikes Automotive LLC..................G...... 937 233-1433
  Dayton *(G-8358)*
Sanoh America Inc........................C...... 740 392-9200
  Mount Vernon *(G-14505)*
Smith Springs Inc.........................G...... 800 619-4652
  Mount Perry *(G-14459)*

AUTOMOTIVE REPAIR SVCS, MISCELLANEOUS

North Coast Exotics Inc.................G...... 216 651-5512
  Cleveland *(G-5765)*

Employee Codes: A=Over 500 employees, B=251-500
C=101-250, D=51-100, E=20-50, F=10-19, G=3-9

AUTOMOTIVE RUSTPROOFING & UNDERCOATING SHOPS

AUTOMOTIVE RUSTPROOFING & UNDERCOATING SHOPS

X-Treme Finishes Inc..................F...... 330 474-0614
  Medina (G-13364)

AUTOMOTIVE SPLYS & PARTS, NEW, WHOL: Auto Servicing Eqpt

C RC Automotive..........................G...... 513 422-4775
  Middletown (G-13889)
D & J Electric Motor Repair Co ....F...... 330 336-4343
  Wadsworth (G-19232)
Tuffy Manufacturing.....................G...... 330 940-2356
  Cuyahoga Falls (G-7930)

AUTOMOTIVE SPLYS & PARTS, NEW, WHOL: Testing Eqpt, Electric

Nu-Di Products Co Inc...................D...... 216 251-9070
  Cleveland (G-5793)
Tmsi LLC..................................F...... 888 867-4872
  North Canton (G-15130)

AUTOMOTIVE SPLYS & PARTS, NEW, WHOLESALE: Bumpers

Durable Corporation.....................D...... 800 537-1603
  Norwalk (G-15389)

AUTOMOTIVE SPLYS & PARTS, NEW, WHOLESALE: Clutches

All Wright Enterprises LLC ....G...... 440 259-5656
  Perry (G-15903)

AUTOMOTIVE SPLYS & PARTS, NEW, WHOLESALE: Engines/Eng Parts

Ds Technologies Group Ltd ....G...... 419 841-5388
  Toledo (G-18270)
Interstate Diesel Service Inc ....B...... 216 881-0015
  Cleveland (G-5470)
Keihin Thermal Tech Amer Inc ....B...... 740 869-3000
  Mount Sterling (G-14462)
Mantapart................................G...... 330 549-2389
  New Springfield (G-14820)
Ultra-Met Company......................G...... 937 653-7133
  Urbana (G-19018)

AUTOMOTIVE SPLYS & PARTS, NEW, WHOLESALE: Filters, Air & Oil

Oil Skimmers Inc.........................E...... 440 237-4600
  North Royalton (G-15291)

AUTOMOTIVE SPLYS & PARTS, NEW, WHOLESALE: Pumps, Oil & Gas

Motionsource International LLC........F...... 440 287-7037
  Solon (G-17198)

AUTOMOTIVE SPLYS & PARTS, NEW, WHOLESALE: Seat Covers

School Maintenance Supply Inc........G...... 513 376-8670
  Blue Ash (G-1843)

AUTOMOTIVE SPLYS & PARTS, NEW, WHOLESALE: Splys

Finishmaster Inc ....D...... 614 228-4328
  Columbus (G-6924)
Winston Products LLC ....D...... 440 478-1418
  Cleveland (G-6314)

AUTOMOTIVE SPLYS & PARTS, NEW, WHOLESALE: Stampings

Bear Diversified Inc ....G...... 216 883-5494
  Cleveland (G-4799)
T A Bacon Co.............................F...... 216 851-1404
  Chesterland (G-3169)

AUTOMOTIVE SPLYS & PARTS, NEW, WHOLESALE: Tools & Eqpt

Cedar Elec Holdings Corp...............D...... 773 804-6288
  West Chester (G-19666)
Matco Tools Corporation................B...... 330 929-4949
  Stow (G-17605)
Myers Industries Inc ....E...... 330 253-5592
  Akron (G-292)

AUTOMOTIVE SPLYS & PARTS, NEW, WHOLESALE: Trailer Parts

Frontier Tank Center Inc................E...... 330 659-3888
  Richfield (G-16471)
Ohio Trailer Supply Inc..................G...... 614 471-9121
  Columbus (G-7263)

AUTOMOTIVE SPLYS & PARTS, NEW, WHOLESALE: Wheels

Chestnut Holdings Inc...................G...... 330 849-6503
  Akron (G-114)
Herbert E Orr Company.................C...... 419 399-4866
  Paulding (G-15860)
Rocknstarr Holdings LLC................E...... 330 509-9086
  Youngstown (G-21020)

AUTOMOTIVE SPLYS & PARTS, USED, RETAIL ONLY: Tires, Used

A & A Discount Tire.....................G...... 330 863-1936
  Carrollton (G-2914)

AUTOMOTIVE SPLYS & PARTS, USED, WHOLESALE

Stevens Auto Parts & Towng ....G...... 740 988-2260
  Jackson (G-11195)

AUTOMOTIVE SPLYS & PARTS, WHOLESALE, NEC

A & H Automotive Industries ....G...... 614 235-1759
  Columbus (G-6514)
Accel Performance Group LLC........C...... 216 658-6413
  Independence (G-11117)
Alegre Inc..................................F...... 937 885-6786
  Miamisburg (G-13639)
Alex Products Inc ....C...... 419 399-4500
  Paulding (G-15855)
Atlas Industries Inc ....B...... 419 637-2117
  Tiffin (G-18046)
Brookville Roadster Inc..................E...... 937 833-4605
  Brookville (G-2162)
Certified Power Inc ....D...... 419 355-1200
  Fremont (G-10006)
Crown Dielectric Inds Inc...............C...... 614 224-5161
  Columbus (G-6839)
D-G Custom Chrome LLC ....D...... 513 531-1881
  Cincinnati (G-3571)
Florence Alloys Inc......................G...... 330 745-9141
  Barberton (G-1071)
General Parts Inc ....G...... 614 891-6014
  Westerville (G-20055)
Gmelectric Inc............................G...... 330 477-3392
  Canton (G-2685)
H & R Tool & Machine Co Inc ....G...... 740 452-0784
  Zanesville (G-21143)
H O Fibertrends..........................G...... 740 983-3864
  Ashville (G-818)
Hebco Products Inc ....A...... 419 562-7987
  Bucyrus (G-2333)
Hite Parts Exchange Inc ....E...... 614 272-5115
  Columbus (G-7003)
Interstate Batteries Inc ....G...... 740 968-2211
  Saint Clairsville (G-16634)
Jenkins Motor Parts.....................G...... 330 525-4011
  Beloit (G-1570)
Mader Automotive Center Inc ....F...... 937 339-2681
  Troy (G-18685)
Martin Diesel Inc.........................E...... 419 782-9911
  Defiance (G-8636)
Ohashi Technica USA Inc...............E...... 740 965-5115
  Sunbury (G-17894)
Ohio Auto Supply Company ....E...... 330 454-5105
  Canton (G-2771)
Ohio Classic Street Rods Inc ....G...... 440 543-6593
  Streetsboro (G-17686)
R S C Sales Company ....E...... 423 581-4916
  Dayton (G-8460)
Rex Manufacturing Co..................G...... 419 224-5751
  Lima (G-11931)
Satco Inc..................................G...... 330 630-8866
  Tallmadge (G-18002)
Stevens Auto Glaze and SEC LL ......G...... 440 953-2900
  Eastlake (G-9131)
Thyssenkrupp Bilstein Amer Inc ......E...... 513 881-7600
  West Chester (G-19809)

AUTOMOTIVE SPLYS, USED, WHOLESALE & RETAIL

Cedar Elec Holdings Corp...............D...... 773 804-6288
  West Chester (G-19666)

AUTOMOTIVE SPLYS/PART, NEW, WHOL: Spring, Shock Absorb/Strut

Thyssenkrupp Bilstein Amer Inc ......C...... 513 881-7600
  Hamilton (G-10610)

AUTOMOTIVE SPLYS/PARTS, NEW, WHOL: Body Rpr/Paint Shop Splys

ABRA Auto Body & Glass LP..........G...... 513 367-9200
  Harrison (G-10627)
ABRA Auto Body & Glass LP..........G...... 513 247-3400
  Cincinnati (G-3289)
ABRA Auto Body & Glass LP..........G...... 513 755-7709
  West Chester (G-19635)
Midwest Spray Booths ....G...... 937 439-6600
  Dayton (G-8355)

AUTOMOTIVE SVCS, EXC REPAIR & CARWASHES: Customizing

AGC Automotive Americas ....D...... 937 599-3131
  Bellefontaine (G-1501)

AUTOMOTIVE SVCS, EXC REPAIR & CARWASHES: Maintenance

Tbone Sales LLC ....E...... 330 897-6131
  Baltic (G-1033)

AUTOMOTIVE SVCS, EXC REPAIR & CARWASHES: Road Svc

Top Notch Fleet Services LLC ....G...... 419 260-4057
  Maumee (G-13155)

AUTOMOTIVE SVCS, EXC REPAIR & CARWASHES: Trailer Maintenance

J & L Body Inc............................F...... 216 661-2323
  Brooklyn Heights (G-2126)

AUTOMOTIVE TOPS INSTALLATION OR REPAIR: Canvas Or Plastic

D & D Classic Auto Restoration ....E...... 937 473-2229
  Covington (G-7784)

AUTOMOTIVE TOWING & WRECKING SVC

Johns Welding & Towing Inc ....F...... 419 447-8937
  Tiffin (G-18063)
Precision Coatings Systems ....E...... 937 642-4727
  Marysville (G-12806)

AUTOMOTIVE TOWING SVCS

Stevens Auto Parts & Towng ....G...... 740 988-2260
  Jackson (G-11195)

AUTOMOTIVE TRANSMISSION REPAIR SVC

Power Acquisition LLC..................G...... 614 228-5000
  Dublin (G-8966)
Rumpke Transportation Co LLC ....F...... 513 851-0122
  Cincinnati (G-4288)
Selinick Co.................................G...... 440 632-1788
  Middlefield (G-13851)
W W Williams Company LLC ....F...... 330 659-3084
  Richfield (G-16494)

AUTOMOTIVE WELDING SVCS

Bridgetown Welders LLC ....G...... 513 574-4851
  Cincinnati (G-3416)
Brock RAD & Wldg Fabrication ....G...... 740 773-2540
  Chillicothe (G-3178)
Brown Industrial Inc ....E...... 937 693-3838
  Botkins (G-1934)
Central Ohio Fabrication LLC ....G...... 740 969-2976
  Amanda (G-524)

PRODUCT SECTION

Industry Products Co .... B 937 778-0585
  Piqua *(G-16130)*
Jatdco LLC .... G 440 238-6570
  Strongsville *(G-17757)*
Perkins Motor Service Ltd .... E 440 277-1256
  Lorain *(G-12112)*
Prestons Repair & Welding .... G 937 947-1883
  Laura *(G-11625)*
R K Industries Inc .... D 419 523-5001
  Ottawa *(G-15663)*
Rose City Manufacturing Inc .... D 937 325-5561
  Springfield *(G-17489)*
Sammartino Welding & Auto Sls .... G 330 782-6086
  Youngstown *(G-21024)*
Top Notch Fleet Services LLC .... G 419 260-4057
  Maumee *(G-13155)*
Turn-Key Industrial Svcs LLC .... D 614 274-1128
  Columbus *(G-7551)*

AUTOMOTIVE: Bodies

Biggys Auto Buffet .... G 740 455-4663
  Zanesville *(G-21106)*
Johns Body Shop .... G 419 358-1200
  Bluffton *(G-1890)*
Kps NAPA .... F 740 522-9445
  Heath *(G-10725)*
Scottrods LLC .... G 419 499-2705
  Monroeville *(G-14290)*

AUTOMOTIVE: Seat Frames, Metal

Alex Products Inc .... C 419 399-4500
  Paulding *(G-15855)*
Camaco LLC .... A 440 288-4444
  Lorain *(G-12082)*
Cctm Inc .... G 513 934-3533
  Lebanon *(G-11641)*
Jay Mid-South LLC .... C 256 439-6600
  Mansfield *(G-12462)*
Pfi USA .... F 937 547-0413
  Greenville *(G-10386)*

AUTOMOTIVE: Seating

Gra-Mag Truck Intr Systems LLC .... E 740 490-1000
  London *(G-12061)*
Gramag LLC .... E 614 875-8435
  Grove City *(G-10431)*
Jay Industries Inc .... A 419 747-4161
  Mansfield *(G-12461)*
Johnson Controls Inc .... D 419 636-4211
  Bryan *(G-2292)*
Johnson Controls Inc .... D 216 587-0100
  Cleveland *(G-5504)*
Johnson Controls Inc .... F 513 671-6338
  Cincinnati *(G-3882)*
Magna International Amer Inc .... E 905 853-3604
  Ridgeville Corners *(G-16512)*
Magna Seating America Inc .... C 330 824-3101
  Warren *(G-19420)*
Setex Inc .... B 419 394-7800
  Saint Marys *(G-16700)*

AUTOTRANSFORMERS: Electric

SGB Usa Inc .... E 330 472-1187
  Tallmadge *(G-18003)*

AWNINGS & CANOPIES

Patio Room Factory Inc .... G 614 449-7900
  Columbus *(G-7296)*
Rex Burnett .... G 740 927-4669
  Etna *(G-9397)*

AWNINGS & CANOPIES: Awnings, Fabric, From Purchased Matls

A B C Sign Inc .... F 513 241-8884
  Cincinnati *(G-3278)*
Awning Fabri Caters Inc .... G 216 476-4888
  Cleveland *(G-4781)*
Canvas Specialty Mfg Co .... G 216 881-0647
  Cleveland *(G-4868)*
Capital City Awning Company .... E 614 221-5404
  Columbus *(G-6731)*
Glawe Manufacturing Co Inc .... E 937 754-0064
  Fairborn *(G-9460)*
Independent Awning & Canvas Co .... G 937 223-9661
  Dayton *(G-8261)*
Main Awning & Tent Inc .... G 513 621-6947
  Cincinnati *(G-3974)*

Odyssey Canvas Works Inc .... G 937 392-4422
  Ripley *(G-16515)*
Ohio Awning & Manufacturing Co ...... E 216 861-2400
  Cleveland *(G-5799)*
ONeals Tarpaulin & Awning Co .... F 330 788-6504
  Youngstown *(G-20985)*
Phillips Awning Co .... G 740 653-2433
  Lancaster *(G-11596)*
Queen City Awning & Tent Co .... E 513 530-9660
  Cincinnati *(G-4234)*
Schaaf Co Inc .... G 513 241-7044
  Cincinnati *(G-4304)*
South Akron Awning Co .... F 330 848-7611
  Akron *(G-382)*
Tarped Out Inc .... F 330 325-7722
  Ravenna *(G-16412)*

AWNINGS & CANOPIES: Fabric

P C R Restorations Inc .... F 419 747-7957
  Mansfield *(G-12501)*

AWNINGS: Fiberglass

Mor-Lite Co Inc .... G 513 661-8587
  Cincinnati *(G-4045)*
P C R Restorations Inc .... F 419 747-7957
  Mansfield *(G-12501)*
Superior Fibers Inc .... B 740 394-2491
  Shawnee *(G-16962)*

AWNINGS: Metal

Alumetal Manufacturing Company ...... E 419 268-2311
  Coldwater *(G-6399)*
Color Brite Company Inc .... G 216 441-4117
  Cleveland *(G-4998)*
Crest Awning & Home Imprv Co .... G 440 942-3092
  Willoughby *(G-20303)*
Crest Products Inc .... F 440 942-5770
  Mentor *(G-13427)*
General Awning Company Inc .... F 216 749-0110
  Cleveland *(G-5305)*
Joyce Manufacturing Co .... D 440 239-9100
  Berea *(G-1615)*
Mor-Lite Co Inc .... G 513 661-8587
  Cincinnati *(G-4045)*
Shade Youngstown & Aluminum Co ... G 330 782-2373
  Youngstown *(G-21028)*
Toledo Window & Awning Inc .... G 419 474-3396
  Toledo *(G-18575)*

AXLES

Alta Mira Corporation .... D 330 648-2461
  Spencer *(G-17303)*
Axle Surgeons of NW Ohio .... G 419 822-5775
  Delta *(G-8765)*
Meritor Inc .... C 740 348-3498
  Granville *(G-10333)*
Schafer Driveline LLC .... G 614 864-1116
  Blacklick *(G-1694)*
Schafer Driveline LLC .... D 740 694-2055
  Fredericktown *(G-9977)*
Spencer Manufacturing Company .... D 330 648-2461
  Spencer *(G-17306)*

Ammunition Loading & Assembling Plant

Center Mass Ammo LLC .... G 440 796-6207
  Madison *(G-12342)*

BACKHOES

Donald E Dornon .... G 740 926-9144
  Beallsville *(G-1290)*
Shatzels Backhoe Service LLC .... G 937 289-9630
  Clarksville *(G-4568)*

BADGES: Identification & Insignia

ID Card Systems Inc .... G 330 963-7446
  Twinsburg *(G-18795)*

BAFFLES

Dynamic Control North Amer Inc .... F 513 860-5094
  Hamilton *(G-10552)*

BAGS & CONTAINERS: Textile, Exc Sleeping

Baggallini Inc .... G 800 628-0321
  Pickerington *(G-16040)*

BAGS: Plastic, Made From Purchased Materials

BAGS: Canvas

American Made Bags LLC .... F 330 475-1385
  Akron *(G-62)*
Capital City Awning Company .... E 614 221-5404
  Columbus *(G-6731)*
Hdt Expeditionary Systems Inc .... B 216 438-6111
  Solon *(G-17161)*

BAGS: Cellophane

Buckeye Boxes Inc .... C 614 274-8484
  Columbus *(G-6707)*
Vee Gee Enterprise Corporation .... G 330 493-9780
  Canton *(G-2857)*

BAGS: Food Storage & Frozen Food, Plastic

Global Plastic Tech Inc .... G 440 879-6045
  Lorain *(G-12093)*

BAGS: Food Storage & Trash, Plastic

Accutech Films Inc .... F 419 678-8700
  Coldwater *(G-6398)*
American Plastics LLC .... C 419 423-1213
  Findlay *(G-9650)*

BAGS: Garment Storage Exc Paper Or Plastic Film

Db Redihead Inc .... E 216 361-0530
  Cleveland *(G-5075)*
Henty USA .... F 513 984-5590
  Cincinnati *(G-3809)*

BAGS: Paper, Made From Purchased Materials

Greif Inc .... E 740 549-6000
  Delaware *(G-8681)*
Greif Inc .... E 740 657-6500
  Delaware *(G-8682)*

BAGS: Plastic

Automated Packg Systems Inc .... D 330 342-2000
  Bedford *(G-1386)*
Automated Packg Systems Inc .... C 216 663-2000
  Cleveland *(G-4770)*
Command Plastic Corporation .... F 800 321-8001
  Tallmadge *(G-17977)*
Dayton Industrial Drum Inc .... E 937 253-8933
  Dayton *(G-7977)*
Flavorseal LLC .... D 440 937-3900
  Avon *(G-949)*
Hood Packaging Corporation .... C 937 382-6681
  Wilmington *(G-20498)*
Kennedy Group Incorporated .... D 440 951-7660
  Willoughby *(G-20352)*
Multiplast Systems Inc .... F 440 349-0800
  Solon *(G-17200)*
Packaging Materials Inc .... E 740 432-6337
  Cambridge *(G-2452)*
Pitt Plastics Inc .... D 614 868-8660
  Columbus *(G-7317)*
Safeway Packaging Inc .... D 419 629-3200
  New Bremen *(G-14660)*

BAGS: Plastic & Pliofilm

Advanced Poly-Packaging Inc .... G 330 785-4000
  Akron *(G-32)*
Charter Nex Films - Del OH Inc .... E 740 369-2770
  Delaware *(G-8663)*
Charter Nex Holding Company .... E 740 369-2770
  Delaware *(G-8664)*
General Films Inc .... D 888 436-3456
  Covington *(G-7786)*
Next Generation Films Inc .... C 419 884-8150
  Lexington *(G-11805)*
North American Plas Chem Inc .... E 216 531-3400
  Euclid *(G-9430)*

BAGS: Plastic, Made From Purchased Materials

Ampac Holdings LLC .... A 513 671-1777
  Cincinnati *(G-3340)*
Atlapac Corp .... D 614 252-2121
  Columbus *(G-6625)*
B K Plastics Inc .... G 937 473-2087
  Covington *(G-7783)*

Employee Codes: A=Over 500 employees, B=251-500
C=101-250, D=51-100, E=20-50, F=10-19, G=3-9

BAGS: Plastic, Made From Purchased Materials

Cpg - Ohio LLC .... D 513 825-4800
  Cincinnati *(G-3555)*
Inpaco Corporation .... F 614 888-9288
  Worthington *(G-20691)*
L & C Plastic Bags Inc .... F 937 473-2968
  Covington *(G-7789)*
Liqui-Box Corporation .... C 419 289-9696
  Ashland *(G-721)*
Mid-West Poly Pak Inc .... E 330 658-2921
  Doylestown *(G-8865)*
Next Generation Bag Inc .... B 419 884-1327
  Mansfield *(G-12492)*
Pexco Packaging Corp .... G 419 470-5935
  Toledo *(G-18468)*
Poly Works .... G 419 678-3758
  Coldwater *(G-6418)*
Primary Packaging Incorporated .... D 330 874-3131
  Bolivar *(G-1924)*

BAGS: Pliofilm, Made From Purchased Materials

Ampac Packaging LLC .... G 513 671-1777
  Cincinnati *(G-3341)*

BAGS: Rubber Or Rubberized Fabric

Midwestern Bag Co Inc .... E 419 241-3112
  Toledo *(G-18411)*
Timco Rubber Products Inc .... E 216 267-6242
  Berea *(G-1629)*

BAGS: Shipping

Hood Packaging Corporation .... C 937 382-6681
  Wilmington *(G-20498)*

BAGS: Shopping, Made From Purchased Materials

Ampac Holdings LLC .... A 513 671-1777
  Cincinnati *(G-3340)*

BAGS: Textile

Cleveland Canvas Goods Mfg Co .... D 216 361-4567
  Cleveland *(G-4948)*
DCW Acquisition Inc .... F 216 451-0666
  Cleveland *(G-5079)*
Jordan E Armour .... E 330 252-0290
  Akron *(G-226)*
King Bag and Manufacturing Co .... E 513 541-5440
  Cincinnati *(G-3910)*
Lamports Filter Media Inc .... F 216 881-2050
  Cleveland *(G-5557)*
Loctote LLC .... G 614 407-0882
  Blacklick *(G-1688)*
Nyp Corp (frmr Ny-Pters Corp) .... G 440 428-0129
  Madison *(G-12354)*
Rich Industries Inc .... E 330 339-4113
  New Philadelphia *(G-14797)*
Sailors Tailor Inc .... G 937 862-7781
  Spring Valley *(G-17318)*
Seven Mile Creek Corporation .... F 937 456-3320
  Eaton *(G-9165)*

BAGS: Trash, Plastic Film, Made From Purchased Materials

Heritage Bag Company .... D 513 874-3311
  West Chester *(G-19720)*

BAGS: Vacuum cleaner, Made From Purchased Materials

Cleveland Canvas Goods Mfg Co .... D 216 361-4567
  Cleveland *(G-4948)*
Home Care Products LLC .... F 919 693-1002
  Chagrin Falls *(G-3050)*

BAIT, FISHING, WHOLESALE

Wholesale Bait Co Inc .... F 513 863-2380
  Fairfield *(G-9576)*

BAKERIES, COMMERCIAL: On Premises Baking Only

614 Cupcakes LLC .... G 614 245-8800
  New Albany *(G-14602)*
Alfred Nickles Bakery Inc .... B 330 879-5635
  Navarre *(G-14571)*
Amish Door Inc .... B 330 359-5464
  Wilmot *(G-20513)*
An Baiceir Bakery .... G 740 739-0501
  Etna *(G-9391)*
Angry Cupcakes Productions LLC .... C 216 229-2394
  Cleveland *(G-4715)*
Auntie Annes .... G 330 652-1939
  Niles *(G-15000)*
B L F Enterprises Inc .... F 937 642-6425
  Westerville *(G-20036)*
Bimbo Bakeries USA Cleveland .... F 216 641-5700
  Cleveland *(G-4814)*
Bites Baking Company LLC .... G 614 457-6092
  Dublin *(G-8889)*
Blue Cottage Bakery LLC .... G 216 221-9733
  Lakewood *(G-11513)*
Bread Kneads Inc .... G 419 422-3863
  Findlay *(G-9661)*
Breaking Bread Pizza Company .... E 614 754-4777
  Lewis Center *(G-11752)*
Buns of Delaware Inc .... G 740 363-2867
  Delaware *(G-8659)*
Campbell Soup Company .... D 419 592-1010
  Napoleon *(G-14534)*
Cjr Desserts .... G 513 549-6403
  Maineville *(G-12365)*
Cora Cupcakes .... G 440 227-7145
  Painesville *(G-15726)*
Country Crust Bakery .... G 888 860-2940
  Bainbridge *(G-1015)*
Cupcake Divaz .... G 216 509-3850
  North Ridgeville *(G-15217)*
Cupcake Wishes .... G 440 315-3856
  North Ridgeville *(G-15218)*
Cupcakes For A Cure .... G 419 764-1719
  Perrysburg *(G-15936)*
Danis Sweet Cupcakes .... G 614 581-8978
  Centerburg *(G-2993)*
Dulcelicious Cupcakes and More .... G 440 385-7706
  Cleveland *(G-5118)*
Eat Moore Cupcakes .... G 513 713-8139
  Batavia *(G-1138)*
Flowers Bakeries LLC .... E 330 724-1604
  Akron *(G-174)*
Four Generations Inc .... G 330 784-2243
  Lakemore *(G-11499)*
Fragapane Bakeries Inc .... G 440 779-6050
  North Olmsted *(G-15190)*
Garys Chesecakes Fine Desserts .... G 513 574-1700
  Cincinnati *(G-3728)*
Geyers Markets Inc .... D 419 468-9477
  Galion *(G-10141)*
Glorious Cupcakes .... G 216 544-2325
  Medina *(G-13268)*
Go Cupcake .... G 937 299-4985
  Dayton *(G-8232)*
Graeters Manufacturing Co .... D 513 721-3323
  Cincinnati *(G-3774)*
Hazel and Rye Artisan Bkg Co .... G 330 454-6658
  Canton *(G-2695)*
Heinens Inc .... D 330 562-5297
  Aurora *(G-882)*
Hot Mama Foods Inc .... F 419 474-3402
  Toledo *(G-18337)*
I Heart Cupcakes .... G 614 787-3896
  Columbus *(G-7017)*
J M Smucker Company .... E 440 323-5100
  Elyria *(G-9280)*
K Cupcakes .... G 440 576-3464
  Jefferson *(G-11230)*
Kellogg Company .... B 513 271-3500
  Cincinnati *(G-3902)*
Kennedys Bakery Inc .... E 740 432-2301
  Cambridge *(G-2444)*
Klosterman Baking Co .... F 937 743-9021
  Springboro *(G-17334)*
Klosterman Baking Co .... D 513 242-1004
  Cincinnati *(G-3917)*
Kroger Co .... C 513 742-9500
  Cincinnati *(G-3924)*
Kroger Co .... C 937 743-5900
  Springboro *(G-17335)*
Kroger Co .... C 740 335-4030
  Wshngtn CT Hs *(G-20731)*
Kroger Co .... C 740 264-5057
  Steubenville *(G-17540)*
Kroger Co .... D 419 423-2065
  Findlay *(G-9711)*
Kroger Co .... C 614 263-1766
  Columbus *(G-7103)*
Kroger Co .... C 614 575-3742
  Columbus *(G-7104)*
Kroger Co .... C 740 671-5164
  Bellaire *(G-1487)*
Kroger Co .... D 513 683-4001
  Maineville *(G-12372)*
Kroger Co .... C 937 277-0950
  Dayton *(G-8302)*
Kroger Co .... C 740 374-2523
  Marietta *(G-12638)*
M Mazzone & Sons Bakery Inc .... G 216 631-6511
  Cleveland *(G-5593)*
Main Street Gourmet LLC .... C 330 929-0000
  Cuyahoga Falls *(G-7895)*
Martans Foods .... G 330 483-9009
  Valley City *(G-19047)*
Meeks Pastry Shop .... E 419 782-4871
  Defiance *(G-8637)*
Morselicious Cupcakes .... E 216 408-7508
  Brookpark *(G-2152)*
Mustard Seed Health Fd Mkt Inc .... C 440 519-3663
  Solon *(G-17201)*
My Lady Muffins LLC .... G 937 854-5317
  Dayton *(G-8374)*
Nanak Bakery .... G 614 882-0882
  Westerville *(G-20067)*
New Bakery of Zanesville LLC .... B 614 764-3100
  Dublin *(G-8955)*
Osmans Pies Inc .... G 330 607-9083
  Stow *(G-17616)*
P&S Bakery Inc .... G 330 707-4141
  Youngstown *(G-20989)*
Perkins & Marie Callenders LLC .... C 513 881-7900
  Fairfield *(G-9548)*
Pesce Baking Company Ltd .... E 330 746-6537
  Youngstown *(G-20999)*
Pf Management Inc .... G 513 874-8741
  West Chester *(G-19885)*
Pierre Holding Corp .... G 513 874-8741
  West Chester *(G-19886)*
Quality Bakery Company Inc .... G 614 846-2232
  Westerville *(G-20019)*
Quality Bakery Company Inc .... E 614 224-1424
  Columbus *(G-7364)*
Rich Products Corporation .... C 614 771-1117
  Hilliard *(G-10858)*
Riesbeck Food Markets Inc .... C 740 695-3401
  Saint Clairsville *(G-16649)*
Saras Little Cupcakes .... G 419 305-7914
  Saint Marys *(G-16699)*
Schulers Bakery Inc .... E 937 323-4154
  Springfield *(G-17491)*
Schwebel Baking Company .... E 216 481-1880
  Euclid *(G-9442)*
Schwebel Baking Company .... D 330 783-2860
  Hebron *(G-10762)*
Schwebel Baking Company .... C 440 248-1500
  Solon *(G-17228)*
Servatii Inc .... F 513 271-5040
  Cincinnati *(G-4325)*
Smashing Events and Baking .... G 513 415-9693
  Cincinnati *(G-3264)*
Squire Shoppe Bakery .... G 440 964-3303
  Ashtabula *(G-805)*
Sweet GS Cupcakery Ltd .... G 419 610-8507
  Columbus *(G-7505)*
Sweet Mobile Cupcakery .... G 440 465-7333
  Bay Village *(G-1210)*
Taste of Belgium LLC .... G 513 381-3280
  Cincinnati *(G-4406)*
Thurns Bakery & Deli .... E 614 221-9246
  Columbus *(G-7527)*
Unger Kosher Bakery Inc .... E 216 321-7176
  Cleveland Heights *(G-6352)*
White Castle System Inc .... B 614 228-5781
  Columbus *(G-7603)*

BAKERIES: On Premises Baking & Consumption

Alfred Nickles Bakery Inc .... E 740 453-6522
  Zanesville *(G-21096)*
Buns of Delaware Inc .... E 740 363-2867
  Delaware *(G-8659)*
Crumbs Inc .... F 740 592-3803
  Athens *(G-826)*
Fields Associates Inc .... G 513 426-8652
  Cincinnati *(G-3688)*
Fragapane Bakeries Inc .... G 440 779-6050
  North Olmsted *(G-15190)*

PRODUCT SECTION — BAKERY: Wholesale Or Wholesale & Retail Combined

Giminetti Baking Company .... E 513 751-7655
Cincinnati *(G-3753)*
Osmans Pies Inc .... E 330 607-9083
Stow *(G-17616)*
Thurns Bakery & Deli .... E 614 221-9246
Columbus *(G-7527)*
Wal-Bon of Ohio Inc .... D 740 423-8178
Belpre *(G-1586)*

BAKERY FOR HOME SVC DELIVERY

Alfred Nickles Bakery Inc .... F 937 256-3762
Dayton *(G-8015)*
Trumbull Mobile Meals Inc .... F 330 394-2538
Warren *(G-19453)*

BAKERY MACHINERY

Fred D Pfening Company .... G 614 294-5361
Columbus *(G-6939)*
Ingredient Masters Inc .... G 513 231-7432
Batavia *(G-1154)*
Magna Machine Co .... C 513 851-6900
Cincinnati *(G-3972)*
Peerless Foods Inc .... C 937 492-4158
Sidney *(G-17058)*
Shaffer Manufacturing Corp .... E 937 652-2151
Urbana *(G-19012)*
Tpsc Inc .... F 440 439-9320
Bedford Heights *(G-1481)*

BAKERY PRDTS, FROZEN: Wholesalers

Bake ME Happy LLC .... G 614 477-3642
Columbus *(G-6643)*

BAKERY PRDTS: Bagels, Fresh Or Frozen

Fields Associates Inc .... G 513 426-8652
Cincinnati *(G-3688)*

BAKERY PRDTS: Bakery Prdts, Partially Cooked, Exc frozen

Champa Ventures LLC .... G 614 726-1801
Dublin *(G-8900)*

BAKERY PRDTS: Biscuits, Dry

Consolidated Biscuit Company .... F 419 293-2911
Mc Comb *(G-13187)*
Kellogg Company .... B 513 271-3500
Cincinnati *(G-3902)*

BAKERY PRDTS: Bread, All Types, Fresh Or Frozen

New York Frozen Foods Inc .... B 216 292-5655
Bedford *(G-1430)*
Orlando Baking Company .... C 216 361-1872
Cleveland *(G-5820)*
Perfection Bakeries Inc .... E 513 942-1442
West Chester *(G-19884)*

BAKERY PRDTS: Buns, Bread Type, Fresh Or Frozen

B & J Baking Company Inc .... F 513 541-2386
Cincinnati *(G-3374)*
Bimbo Qsr Ohio LLC .... F 740 454-6876
Zanesville *(G-21108)*
Bimbo Qsr Ohio LLC .... F 740 454-6876
Zanesville *(G-21109)*
Jtm Provisions Company Inc .... B 513 367-4900
Harrison *(G-10653)*
New Horizons Baking Company .... B 419 668-8226
Norwalk *(G-15407)*

BAKERY PRDTS: Cakes, Bakery, Exc Frozen

A Cupcake A Day LLC .... G 330 389-1247
Stow *(G-17565)*
Beckers Bakeshop Inc .... F 216 752-4161
Cleveland *(G-4800)*
Cake Arts Supplies .... G 419 472-4959
Toledo *(G-18221)*
Caryns Cuisine .... G 614 237-4143
Columbus *(G-6749)*
Destination Donuts LLC .... G 614 370-0754
Columbus *(G-6861)*
George Weston Co .... G 614 868-7565
Columbus *(G-6948)*

Gluten-Free Expressions .... G 740 928-0338
Hebron *(G-10746)*
Sifted Sweet Shop LLC .... G 216 901-7100
Youngstown *(G-21031)*
Sinful Sweets LLC .... G 330 721-0916
Medina *(G-13343)*

BAKERY PRDTS: Cakes, Bakery, Frozen

Atk2 Inc .... G 513 661-5869
Cincinnati *(G-3366)*
Bartells Cupcakery .... G 330 957-1793
Austintown *(G-929)*
Cleveland Bagel Company LLC .... G 216 385-7723
Cleveland *(G-4946)*
Kissicakes - N-Sweets LLC .... G 614 940-2779
Columbus *(G-7096)*
Mammas Mandel .... G 513 827-2457
Mason *(G-12906)*

BAKERY PRDTS: Cones, Ice Cream

Frischco Inc .... G 740 363-7537
Delaware *(G-8680)*
Jagger Cone Company Inc .... G 419 682-1816
Stryker *(G-17830)*
Norse Dairy Systems LP .... B 614 421-5297
Columbus *(G-7225)*

BAKERY PRDTS: Cookies

Beckers Bakeshop Inc .... F 216 752-4161
Cleveland *(G-4800)*
Cheryl & Co .... C 614 776-1500
Westerville *(G-19985)*
Cleveland Bean Sprout Inc .... F 216 881-2112
Cleveland *(G-4947)*
CTB Consulting LLC .... F 216 712-7764
Rocky River *(G-16545)*
Great American Cookie Company .... F 419 474-9417
Toledo *(G-18311)*
Hearthside Food Solutions LLC .... A 419 293-2911
Mc Comb *(G-13189)*
Keebler Company .... E 513 271-3500
Cincinnati *(G-3901)*
Pepperidge Farm Incorporated .... G 614 457-4800
Columbus *(G-7309)*
Pepperidge Farm Incorporated .... G 419 933-2611
Willard *(G-20244)*
Snyders-Lance Inc .... G 614 856-4616
Grove City *(G-10469)*
Y Z Enterprises Inc .... E 419 893-8777
Maumee *(G-13161)*

BAKERY PRDTS: Cookies & crackers

B L F Enterprises Inc .... F 937 642-6425
Westerville *(G-20036)*
Campbell Soup Company .... D 419 592-1010
Napoleon *(G-14534)*
Cheryl & Co .... D 614 776-1500
Obetz *(G-15509)*
Cookie Bouquets Inc .... G 614 888-2171
Columbus *(G-6817)*
Hen of Woods LLC .... G 513 833-7357
Cincinnati *(G-3807)*
Kennedys Bakery Inc .... E 740 432-2301
Cambridge *(G-2444)*
Kroger Co .... C 740 671-5164
Bellaire *(G-1487)*
Kroger Co .... D 513 683-4001
Maineville *(G-12372)*
Kroger Co .... C 937 277-0950
Dayton *(G-8302)*
Kroger Co .... D 740 374-2523
Marietta *(G-12638)*
Lenas Amish Granola .... G 330 600-1599
Shreve *(G-17005)*
Main Street Gourmet LLC .... G 330 929-0000
Cuyahoga Falls *(G-7895)*
Norcia Bakery .... G 330 454-1077
Canton *(G-2763)*
Osmans Pies Inc .... E 330 607-9083
Stow *(G-17616)*
Patjim Holdings Company .... G 419 727-1298
Toledo *(G-18458)*
Rudys Strudel Shop .... G 440 886-4430
Cleveland *(G-6016)*
Rykrisp Llc .... G 843 338-0750
Cincinnati *(G-4293)*
Schulers Bakery Inc .... E 937 323-4154
Springfield *(G-17491)*

BAKERY PRDTS: Doughnuts, Exc Frozen

Crispie Creme of Chillicothe .... E 740 774-3770
Chillicothe *(G-3183)*
Dandi Enterprises Inc .... F 419 516-9070
Solon *(G-17131)*
Georges Donuts Inc .... G 330 963-9902
Twinsburg *(G-18784)*
Jims Donut Shop .... G 937 898-4222
Vandalia *(G-19131)*
Mary Ann Donut Shoppe Inc .... E 330 478-1655
Canton *(G-2745)*
McHappys Donuts of Parkersburg .... G 740 593-8744
Athens *(G-838)*
Servatii Inc .... F 513 231-4455
Cincinnati *(G-4324)*
Wal-Bon of Ohio Inc .... D 740 423-8178
Belpre *(G-1586)*

BAKERY PRDTS: Dry

Brand Castle LLC .... F 216 292-7700
Bedford Heights *(G-1462)*
Good Fortunes Inc .... F 440 942-2888
Willoughby *(G-20333)*

BAKERY PRDTS: Frozen

Chefs Pantry Inc .... G 440 288-0146
Amherst *(G-557)*
Main Street Gourmet LLC .... C 330 929-0000
Cuyahoga Falls *(G-7895)*
Pepperidge Farm Incorporated .... G 614 457-4800
Columbus *(G-7309)*
Pepperidge Farm Incorporated .... G 419 933-2611
Willard *(G-20244)*

BAKERY PRDTS: Pastries, Exc Frozen

Krispy Kreme Doughnut Corp .... F 614 798-0812
Columbus *(G-7101)*
Royal Gateau .... G 216 351-3553
Cleveland *(G-6011)*

BAKERY PRDTS: Pies, Exc Frozen

Bake ME Happy LLC .... G 614 477-3642
Columbus *(G-6643)*
K & B Acquisitions Inc .... F 937 253-1163
Dayton *(G-8288)*

BAKERY PRDTS: Pretzels

Annes Auntie Pretzels .... E 614 418-7021
Columbus *(G-6605)*
Ditsch Usa LLC .... E 513 782-8888
Cincinnati *(G-3591)*
J & J Snack Foods Corp .... G 440 248-2084
Solon *(G-17173)*
K & R Pretzel Co .... G 937 299-2231
Dayton *(G-8289)*
Mar Chele Inc .... F 937 429-2300
Beavercreek *(G-1330)*
Mar Chele Inc .... G 937 833-3400
Brookville *(G-2174)*

BAKERY PRDTS: Rice Cakes

Basic Grain Products Inc .... D 419 678-2304
Coldwater *(G-6402)*

BAKERY PRDTS: Wholesalers

Brownie Points Inc .... G 614 860-8470
Columbus *(G-6705)*
Ditsch Usa LLC .... E 513 782-8888
Cincinnati *(G-3591)*
Klosterman Baking Co .... D 513 242-1004
Cincinnati *(G-3917)*
Osmans Pies Inc .... E 330 607-9083
Stow *(G-17616)*
Thurns Bakery & Deli .... E 614 221-9246
Columbus *(G-7527)*
Unger Kosher Bakery Inc .... E 216 321-7176
Cleveland Heights *(G-6352)*

BAKERY: Wholesale Or Wholesale & Retail Combined

7 Little Cupcakes .... G 419 252-0858
Perrysburg *(G-15915)*
A Bun In Oven .... G 419 559-3056
Fremont *(G-9987)*

Employee Codes: A=Over 500 employees, B=251-500
C=101-250, D=51-100, E=20-50, F=10-19, G=3-9

BAKERY: Wholesale Or Wholesale & Retail Combined

Alfred Nickles Bakery Inc .... E 740 453-6522
  Zanesville (G-21096)
Atlas Produce LLC .... G 937 223-1446
  Dayton (G-8042)
Berlin Natural Bakery Inc .... E 330 893-2734
  Berlin (G-1638)
Bimbo Bakeries Usa Inc .... E 740 797-4449
  The Plains (G-18019)
Bimbo Bakeries Usa Inc .... E 740 797-4449
  The Plains (G-18020)
Bonbonneri Inc .... F 513 321-3399
  Cincinnati (G-3401)
Borden Bakers Inc .... G 614 457-9800
  Columbus (G-6687)
Calvary Christian Ch of Ohio .... E 740 828-9000
  Frazeysburg (G-9937)
Crumbs Inc .... F 740 592-3803
  Athens (G-826)
DUrso Bakery Inc .... F 330 652-4741
  Niles (G-15006)
Empire Bakery Commissary LLC ...... G 513 793-6241
  Blue Ash (G-1764)
Evans Bakery Inc .... G 937 228-4151
  Dayton (G-8190)
Gibson Bros Inc .... E 440 774-2401
  Oberlin (G-15496)
Giminetti Baking Company .... E 513 751-7655
  Cincinnati (G-3753)
Home Bakery .... F 419 678-3018
  Coldwater (G-6413)
International Multifoods Corp .... G 440 323-5100
  Elyria (G-9268)
Jeffs Bakery .... G 937 890-9703
  Dayton (G-8284)
Killer Brownie Ltd .... F 937 535-5690
  Dayton (G-8296)
Klosterman Baking Co .... E 513 242-5667
  Cincinnati (G-3916)
Klosterman Baking Co .... F 937 322-9588
  Springfield (G-17432)
Klosterman Baking Co .... F 513 398-2707
  Mason (G-12899)
Kneading Dough LLC .... G 719 310-5774
  Mason (G-12900)
Kustom Cases LLC .... G 240 380-6275
  Dayton (G-8303)
McL Inc .... D 614 861-6259
  Columbus (G-7167)
Nikkicakes .... G 330 606-5745
  Cuyahoga Falls (G-7901)
Norcia Bakery .... E 330 454-1077
  Canton (G-2763)
Olde Home Market LLC .... G 614 738-3975
  Grove City (G-10454)
Perfection Bakeries Inc .... D 614 866-8171
  Blacklick (G-1691)
Perfection Bakeries Inc .... D 419 221-2359
  Lima (G-11916)
Reineckers Bakery Ltd .... G 330 467-2221
  Macedonia (G-12323)
Rudys Strudel Shop .... G 440 886-4430
  Cleveland (G-6016)
Schwebel Baking Company .... B 330 783-2860
  Youngstown (G-21025)
Schwebel Baking Company .... C 440 846-1921
  Strongsville (G-17785)
Skyliner .... G 740 738-0874
  Bridgeport (G-2078)
Slice of Heaven Bakery .... G 419 656-6606
  Clyde (G-6396)
Steubenville Bakery .... G 740 282-6851
  Steubenville (G-17553)
Sweet Persuasions LLC .... G 614 216-9052
  Pickerington (G-16061)
Ta Die For Gourmet Cupcakes .... G 740 751-4586
  Marion (G-12739)
Turbos FBC LLC .... G 614 245-4840
  Columbus (G-7550)
Wal-Bon of Ohio Inc .... F 740 423-6451
  Belpre (G-1585)
You Dough Girl LLC .... G 330 207-5031
  Salem (G-16783)

BALLOONS: Toy & Advertising, Rubber

Maple City Rubber Company .... E 419 668-8261
  Norwalk (G-15405)
Scherba Industries Inc .... D 330 273-3200
  Brunswick (G-2238)

BANDS: Plastic

Chica Bands LLC .... G 513 871-4300
  Cincinnati (G-3470)

BANNERS: Fabric

Party Animal Inc .... G 440 471-1030
  Westlake (G-20139)

BANQUET HALL FACILITIES

Buns of Delaware Inc .... E 740 363-2867
  Delaware (G-8659)
Mustard Seed Health Fd Mkt Inc ..... E 440 519-3663
  Solon (G-17201)
Todd W Goings .... G 740 389-5842
  Marion (G-12743)
Vulcan Machinery Corporation .... E 330 376-6025
  Akron (G-428)

BAR

The Great Lakes Brewing Co .... D 216 771-4404
  Cleveland (G-6164)

BAR JOISTS & CONCRETE REINFORCING BARS: Fabricated

Foundation Systems Anchors Inc .... F 330 454-1700
  Canton (G-2675)
Worthington Industries Inc .... C 614 438-3210
  Worthington (G-20710)

BARBECUE EQPT

Gosun Inc .... F 888 868-6154
  Cincinnati (G-3772)
Lapa Lowe Enterprises LLC .... G 440 944-9410
  Willoughby (G-20360)

BARBER SHOP SELLING WIGS

Mels Life Like Hair .... G 937 278-9486
  Dayton (G-8339)

BARGES BUILDING & REPAIR

McGinnis Inc .... C 740 377-4391
  South Point (G-17286)
McNational Inc .... E 740 377-4391
  South Point (G-17287)
O-Kan Marine Repair Inc .... E 740 446-4686
  Gallipolis (G-10172)
Superior Marine Ways Inc .... C 740 894-6224
  Proctorville (G-16346)

BARRELS: Shipping, Metal

Cleveland Steel Container Corp .... E 330 544-2271
  Niles (G-15003)
Mauser Usa LLC .... E 614 856-5982
  Mount Vernon (G-14491)

BARS & BAR SHAPES: Copper & Copper Alloy

Avtron Aerospace Inc .... C 216 750-5152
  Cleveland (G-4778)

BARS & BAR SHAPES: Steel, Cold-Finished, Own Hot-Rolled

Bertin Steel Processing Inc .... E 440 943-0094
  Wickliffe (G-20202)
Republic Steel Inc .... C 330 438-5533
  Canton (G-2805)

BARS & BAR SHAPES: Steel, Hot-Rolled

J & L Steel Bar LLC .... G 440 526-0050
  Broadview Heights (G-2093)
McDonald Steel Corporation .... C 330 530-9118
  Mc Donald (G-13201)

BARS, COLD FINISHED: Steel, From Purchased Hot-Rolled

Columbia Steel and Wire Inc .... G 330 468-2709
  Northfield (G-15315)
New Dimension Metals Corp .... E 937 299-2233
  Moraine (G-14373)
Nucor Bright Bar Orville LLC .... F 330 682-5555
  Orrville (G-15607)

BARS, PIPES, PLATES & SHAPES: Lead/Lead Alloy Bars, Pipe

G A Avril Company .... F 513 731-5133
  Cincinnati (G-3720)

BARS: Concrete Reinforcing, Fabricated Steel

Action Group Inc .... D 614 868-8868
  Blacklick (G-1676)
Akron Rebar Co .... E 330 745-7100
  Akron (G-50)
Alpha Control LLC .... E 740 377-3400
  South Point (G-17278)
Austintown Metal Works Inc .... F 330 259-4673
  Youngstown (G-20848)
Bridge Components Incorporated ... G 614 873-0777
  Columbus (G-6697)
Falcon Fab and Finishes LLC .... E 740 820-4458
  Lucasville (G-12263)
Gateway Concrete Forming Svcs .... D 513 353-2000
  Miamitown (G-13746)
Genesis Services LLC .... G 740 896-3734
  Beverly (G-1661)
Hartford Steel Sales .... G 513 275-1744
  Hamilton (G-10570)
J & L Welding Fabricating Inc .... F 330 393-9353
  Warren (G-19412)
Mound Steel Corp .... E 937 748-2937
  Springboro (G-17337)
Ohio Bridge Corporation .... C 740 432-6334
  Cambridge (G-2451)
Smith Brothers Erection Inc .... E 740 373-3575
  Marietta (G-12671)
Steel Structures of Ohio LLC .... E 330 374-9900
  Akron (G-388)
Superior Steel Service LLC .... E 513 724-0437
  Batavia (G-1188)
Telling Industries LLC .... F 440 974-3370
  Willoughby (G-20444)
Telling Industries LLC .... F 928 681-2010
  Willoughby (G-20445)
Telling Industries LLC .... D 740 435-8900
  Cambridge (G-2460)
Veterans Steel Inc .... F 216 938-7476
  Cleveland (G-6255)

BARS: Iron, Made In Steel Mills

Republic Engineered Products .... E 440 277-2000
  Lorain (G-12116)
Republic Steel .... B 330 438-5435
  Canton (G-2804)

BARS: Rolled, Aluminum

Aleris Corporation .... G 216 910-3400
  Cleveland (G-4654)
Aleris International Inc .... C 216 910-3400
  Beachwood (G-1218)

BASALT: Crushed & Broken

Riverrock Recycl Crushing LLC .... G 937 325-2052
  Springfield (G-17485)

BASEMENT WINDOW AREAWAYS: Concrete

Bilco Company .... E 740 455-9020
  Zanesville (G-21107)

BASES, BEVERAGE

Bayswater Beverages LLC .... G 312 224-8012
  Cincinnati (G-3383)
Third Wave Water LLC .... G 855 590-4500
  Cedarville (G-2947)

BASKETS, WHOLESALE

Buhi Imports .... G 440 224-0013
  North Kingsville (G-15159)

BASKETS: Steel Wire

Sunrise Cooperative Inc .... E 419 683-4600
  Crestline (G-7801)

BATCHING PLANTS: Bituminous

Allied Construction Pdts LLC .... E 216 431-2600
  Cleveland (G-4671)

PRODUCT SECTION

BATH SALTS
Ashland Specialty Ingredients.............D....... 614 529-3311
 Columbus (G-6619)

BATH SHOPS
Savko Plastic Pipe & Fittings.............F....... 614 885-8420
 Columbus (G-7422)

BATHMATS: Rubber
Innocor Foam Tech - Acp Inc.............F....... 419 647-4172
 Spencerville (G-17309)

BATHROOM ACCESS & FITTINGS: Vitreous China & Earthenware
A C Products Co ....D....... 330 698-1105
 Apple Creek (G-601)

BATHROOM FIXTURES: Plastic
Marble Arch Products Inc ....F....... 937 746-8388
 Franklin (G-9897)

BATTERIES, EXC AUTOMOTIVE: Wholesalers
Ametek Inc ....F....... 937 440-0800
 Troy (G-18637)
B W T Inc.............G....... 330 928-9107
 Akron (G-77)
Battery Unlimited ....G....... 740 452-5030
 Zanesville (G-21104)
D C Systems Inc.............F....... 330 273-3030
 Brunswick (G-2198)
Forklifts of Americas LLC.............G....... 440 821-5143
 Highland Heights (G-10790)
Interstate Batteries Inc ....G....... 740 968-2211
 Saint Clairsville (G-16634)
N S T Battery.............G....... 937 433-9222
 Bellbrook (G-1496)
One Wish LLC.............F....... 800 505-6883
 Beachwood (G-1259)

BATTERIES: Alkaline, Cell Storage
Energizer Manufacturing Inc.............D....... 440 835-7866
 Westlake (G-20112)
Transdigm Inc.............F....... 216 291-6025
 Cleveland (G-6195)
Transdigm Inc.............G....... 216 706-2939
 Cleveland (G-6196)

BATTERIES: Dry
D C Systems Inc.............F....... 330 273-3030
 Brunswick (G-2198)
Rus Power Storage LLC.............G....... 937 999-8121
 Middletown (G-13950)

BATTERIES: Lead Acid, Storage
All Power Battery Inc.............G....... 330 453-5236
 Canton (G-2567)
Enersys.............C....... 513 737-2268
 West Chester (G-19698)

BATTERIES: Rechargeable
Graywacke Inc.............F....... 419 884-7014
 Mansfield (G-12453)
Johnson Contrls Btry Group Inc.............A....... 419 865-0542
 Holland (G-10938)
Retriev Technologies Inc.............D....... 740 653-6290
 Lancaster (G-11602)
Toxco Inc.............G....... 740 653-6290
 Lancaster (G-11614)
Xerion Advanced Battery Corp.............F....... 720 229-0697
 Kettering (G-11444)

BATTERIES: Storage
B W T Inc.............G....... 330 928-9107
 Akron (G-77)
Crown Battery Manufacturing Co.............B....... 419 334-7181
 Fremont (G-10009)
Crown Battery Manufacturing Co.............G....... 330 425-3308
 Twinsburg (G-18758)
Dynalite Corp.............G....... 419 873-1706
 Perrysburg (G-15942)
Edgewell Per Care Brands LLC.............D....... 330 527-2191
 Garrettsville (G-10188)
Innovative Weld Solutions Ltd.............G....... 937 545-7695
 Beavercreek (G-1356)
Interstate Batteries Inc.............G....... 740 968-2211
 Saint Clairsville (G-16634)
Lithchem Intl Toxco Inc.............G....... 740 653-6290
 Lancaster (G-11584)
Ovonic Energy Products Inc.............C....... 937 743-1001
 Springboro (G-17341)
Robert Bosch Btry Systems LLC.............D....... 937 743-1001
 Springboro (G-17352)
Rus Power Storage LLC.............G....... 937 999-8121
 Middletown (G-13950)

BATTERIES: Wet
N S T Battery.............G....... 937 433-9222
 Bellbrook (G-1496)

BATTERY CASES: Plastic Or Plastics Combination
Koroseal Interior Products LLC.............C....... 330 668-7600
 Fairlawn (G-9611)

BATTERY CHARGERS
Asg Division Jergens Inc.............G....... 888 486-6163
 Cleveland (G-4749)
Brookwood Group Inc.............F....... 513 791-3030
 Cincinnati (G-3425)
D C Systems Inc.............F....... 330 273-3030
 Brunswick (G-2198)
Ecotec Ltd LLC.............G....... 937 606-2793
 Troy (G-18652)
Exide Technologies.............G....... 614 863-3866
 Gahanna (G-10081)
Japlar Group Inc.............F....... 513 791-7192
 Cincinnati (G-3870)
TL Industries Inc.............C....... 419 666-8144
 Northwood (G-15346)
Xenotronix/Tli Inc.............G....... 407 331-4793
 Northwood (G-15353)

BATTERY CHARGERS: Storage, Motor & Engine Generator Type
Brinkley Technology Group LLC.............F....... 330 830-2498
 Massillon (G-12963)
Charger Connection ....G....... 888 427-5829
 Cincinnati (G-3464)
Design Flux Technologies LLC.............G....... 216 543-6066
 Akron (G-139)
Lesch Btry & Pwr Solution LLC.............G....... 419 884-0219
 Mansfield (G-12469)

BATTERY CHARGING GENERATORS
Design Flux Technologies LLC.............G....... 216 543-6066
 Akron (G-139)

BATTERY REPAIR & SVCS
All Power Battery Inc.............G....... 330 453-5236
 Canton (G-2567)
Battery Unlimited.............G....... 740 452-5030
 Zanesville (G-21104)
D C Systems Inc.............F....... 330 273-3030
 Brunswick (G-2198)

BEADS: Unassembled
Bead Shoppe At Home.............G....... 330 479-9598
 Canton (G-2587)

BEARINGS
Erie Shore Industrial Svc Co.............G....... 440 933-4301
 Avon Lake (G-985)

BEARINGS & PARTS Ball
Bearings Manufacturing Company.............E....... 440 846-5517
 Strongsville (G-17718)
Federal-Mogul Powertrain LLC.............C....... 740 432-2393
 Cambridge (G-2437)
Jay Dee Service Corporation.............G....... 330 425-1546
 Macedonia (G-12307)
Miller Bearing Company Inc.............E....... 330 678-8844
 Kent (G-11356)
Nn Inc.............C....... 440 647-4711
 Wellington (G-19587)
Rotek Incorporated.............G....... 330 562-4000
 Aurora (G-904)
Tsk America Co Ltd.............F....... 513 942-4002
 West Chester (G-19909)

BEARINGS: Ball & Roller
FAg Bearings Corporation.............C....... 513 398-1139
 Mason (G-12869)
Gt Technologies Inc.............C....... 419 782-8955
 Defiance (G-8625)
Randolph Research Co.............G....... 330 666-1667
 Akron (G-341)
Schaeffler Group USA Inc.............B....... 330 273-4383
 Valley City (G-19060)
Timken Company.............A....... 419 563-2200
 Bucyrus (G-2345)
Timken Company.............C....... 330 339-1151
 New Philadelphia (G-14804)
Timken Company.............G....... 330 471-4300
 Canton (G-2837)
Timken Company.............F....... 614 836-3337
 Groveport (G-10514)
Timken Company.............G....... 330 471-5028
 Canton (G-2838)
Timken Company.............G....... 234 262-3000
 North Canton (G-15127)
Timken Company.............G....... 330 471-4791
 Alliance (G-507)
Timken Company.............A....... 330 471-5043
 Canton (G-2839)

BEARINGS: Railroad Car Journal
Rail Bearing Service LLC.............B....... 234 262-3000
 North Canton (G-15113)

BEARINGS: Roller & Parts
HMS Industries LLC.............G....... 440 899-0001
 Westlake (G-20124)
Timken Company.............A....... 234 262-3000
 North Canton (G-15126)

BEAUTY & BARBER SHOP EQPT
Aluminum Line Products Company.............D....... 440 835-8880
 Westlake (G-20091)
Anderson Co Mfg LLC.............G....... 419 230-7332
 Carey (G-2877)
Beauty Systems Group LLC.............G....... 740 456-5434
 New Boston (G-14646)
Carroll Hills Industries Inc.............D....... 330 627-5524
 Carrollton (G-2917)
Columbus Industries Inc.............F....... 937 544-6896
 West Union (G-19960)
Country Clippins.............G....... 740 472-5228
 Woodsfield (G-20543)
Duraflow Industries Inc.............G....... 440 965-5047
 Wakeman (G-19284)
Exikon Industries LLC.............F....... 216 485-2947
 Cleveland (G-5207)
Firelands Manufacturing LLC.............F....... 419 687-8237
 Plymouth (G-16231)
Francis Industries LLC.............G....... 330 333-3352
 Youngstown (G-20910)
Gibraltar Industries Inc.............G....... 440 617-9230
 Westlake (G-20118)
GKN Driveline Bowl Green Inc.............E....... 419 373-7700
 Bowling Green (G-1973)
Goodwill Inds NW Ohio Inc.............E....... 419 255-0070
 Toledo (G-18308)
James J Fairbanks Company Inc.............G....... 330 534-1374
 Hubbard (G-11003)
Mab Fabrication Inc.............G....... 855 622-3221
 Harrison (G-10656)
Medline Industries Inc.............G....... 330 484-1450
 Canton (G-2752)
Pinnacle Sales Inc.............G....... 440 734-9195
 Westlake (G-20143)
Production TI Co Cleveland Inc.............F....... 330 425-4466
 Twinsburg (G-18841)
Quick Tech Business Forms Inc.............G....... 937 743-5952
 Springboro (G-17347)
Rbs Manufacturing Inc.............E....... 330 426-9486
 East Palestine (G-9082)
Reiser Manufacturing.............G....... 330 846-8003
 New Waterford (G-14842)
Rowend Industries Inc.............G....... 419 333-8300
 Fremont (G-10049)
Schreiner Manufacturing.............G....... 419 937-0300
 New Riegel (G-14817)
Shaw Industries Inc.............G....... 513 942-3692
 West Chester (G-19795)

Employee Codes: A=Over 500 employees, B=251-500
C=101-250, D=51-100, E=20-50, F=10-19, G=3-9

BEAUTY & BARBER SHOP EQPT

Tango Echo Bravo Mfg Inc .... G 440 937-3800
  North Ridgeville *(G-15254)*
Virco Virlon Industries Corp .... G 216 410-4872
  Bedford Heights *(G-1482)*

BEAUTY SALONS

James C Robinson .... G 513 969-7482
  Cincinnati *(G-3869)*

BED & BREAKFAST INNS

Breitenbach Wine Cellar Inc .... G 330 343-3603
  Dover *(G-8810)*

BEDDING & BEDSPRINGS STORES

Ahmf Inc .... E 614 921-1223
  Columbus *(G-6553)*
Original Mattress Factory Inc .... G 216 661-8388
  Cleveland *(G-5819)*
Original Mattress Factory Inc .... G 513 752-6600
  Cincinnati *(G-3260)*

BEDDING, BEDSPREADS, BLANKETS & SHEETS

Fluvitex USA Inc .... G 614 610-1199
  Groveport *(G-10490)*
Sewline Products Inc .... F 419 929-1114
  New London *(G-14738)*

BEDDING, BEDSPREADS, BLANKETS & SHEETS: Comforters & Quilts

Aunties Attic .... E 740 548-5059
  Lewis Center *(G-11748)*

BEDS & ACCESS STORES

Green Acres Furniture Ltd .... F 330 359-6251
  Navarre *(G-14574)*

BEDS: Hospital

Belmont Community Hospital .... B 740 671-1216
  Bellaire *(G-1483)*

BEDS: Institutional

Success Technologies Inc .... G 614 761-0008
  Powell *(G-16337)*

BEDSPREADS & BED SETS, FROM PURCHASED MATERIALS

Wise Window Treatment Inc .... F 216 676-4080
  Berea *(G-1633)*

BEDSPREADS, COTTON

Sk Textile Inc .... C 323 581-8986
  Cincinnati *(G-4341)*

BEER & ALE WHOLESALERS

Flat Rocks Brewing Company .... G 419 270-3582
  Napoleon *(G-14538)*
Victoria Ventures Inc .... E 330 793-9321
  Youngstown *(G-21063)*

BEER, WINE & LIQUOR STORES: Beer, Packaged

Csv Inc .... F 937 438-1142
  Dayton *(G-8115)*
Currier Richard & James .... G 440 988-4132
  Amherst *(G-559)*
Millersburg Ice Co .... E 330 674-3016
  Millersburg *(G-14114)*
Wings Way Drive Thru Inc .... G 330 533-2788
  Salem *(G-16781)*

BEER, WINE & LIQUOR STORES: Wine

CWC Partners LLC .... G 567 208-1573
  Findlay *(G-9676)*
Kelleys Island Wine Co .... G 419 746-2678
  Kelleys Island *(G-11283)*
Sandra Weddington .... G 740 417-4286
  Delaware *(G-8722)*

BEER, WINE & LIQUOR STORES: Wine & Beer

Ohio Eagle Distributing LLC .... E 513 539-8483
  West Chester *(G-19753)*

BELLOWS

Alloy Bllows Prcision Wldg Inc .... D 440 684-3000
  Cleveland *(G-4674)*
Xorb Corporation .... G 419 354-6021
  Bowling Green *(G-2008)*

BELLOWS ASSEMBLIES: Missiles, Metal

Shelburne Corp .... G 216 321-9177
  Shaker Heights *(G-16936)*

BELLS: Electric

I T Verdin Co .... E 513 241-4010
  Cincinnati *(G-3833)*
I T Verdin Co .... E 513 559-3947
  Cincinnati *(G-3834)*
S R Technologies LLC .... G 330 523-7184
  Akron *(G-366)*

BELTING: Plastic

Engineered Plastics Corp .... E 330 376-7700
  Akron *(G-155)*
Polychem Corporation .... D 419 547-1400
  Clyde *(G-6392)*

BELTING: Rubber

Fenner Dunlop (toledo) LLC .... E 419 531-5300
  Toledo *(G-18291)*
Novex Inc .... F 330 335-2371
  Wadsworth *(G-19257)*

BELTS & BELT PRDTS

C H R Industries Inc .... G 440 361-0744
  Geneva *(G-10215)*

BELTS: Conveyor, Made From Purchased Wire

Akron Belting & Supply Company .... G 330 633-8212
  Akron *(G-33)*
American Pennekamp Mfg Inc .... G 740 687-0096
  Lancaster *(G-11539)*
Contitech Usa Inc .... E 937 644-8900
  Marysville *(G-12776)*
May Conveyor Inc .... F 440 237-8012
  North Royalton *(G-15286)*
Seven-Ogun International LLC .... G 614 888-8939
  Worthington *(G-20703)*
Tri-State Belting Ltd .... G 800 330-2358
  Cincinnati *(G-4434)*

BELTS: Seat, Automotive & Aircraft

Tk Holdings Inc .... E 937 778-9713
  Piqua *(G-16166)*

BENTONITE MINING

American Colloid Company .... G 419 445-9085
  Archbold *(G-635)*

BERYLLIUM

Materion Brush Inc .... A 419 862-2745
  Elmore *(G-9208)*
Materion Brush Inc .... D 216 486-4200
  Mayfield Heights *(G-13167)*
Materion Corporation .... C 216 486-4200
  Mayfield Heights *(G-13168)*

BEVERAGE BASES & SYRUPS

Ancient Infusions LLC .... G 419 659-5110
  Columbus Grove *(G-7630)*
J M Smucker Company .... A 330 682-3000
  Orrville *(G-15596)*
Mapledale Farm Inc .... F 440 286-3389
  Chardon *(G-3125)*
Nu Pet Company .... C 330 682-3000
  Orrville *(G-15606)*

BEVERAGE PRDTS: Brewers' Grain

Hansa Bewery LLC .... G 216 631-6585
  Cleveland *(G-5372)*
Rivertown Brewing Company LLC .... E 513 827-9280
  Monroe *(G-14275)*
Wedco LLC .... G 513 309-0781
  Mount Orab *(G-14452)*

BEVERAGES, ALCOHOLIC: Ale

Seventh Son Brewing Co .... G 614 783-4217
  Columbus *(G-7442)*
Tom Bad Brewing LLC .... F 513 871-4677
  Cincinnati *(G-4425)*

BEVERAGES, ALCOHOLIC: Beer

Actual Brewing Company LLC .... F 614 636-3825
  Columbus *(G-6540)*
Anheuser-Busch LLC .... B 614 847-6213
  Columbus *(G-6604)*
Bar 25 LLC .... G 216 621-4000
  Cleveland *(G-4789)*
Birdfish Brewing Company LLC .... G 330 397-4010
  Columbiana *(G-6454)*
Black Cloister Brewing Co LLC .... G 419 481-3891
  Toledo *(G-18205)*
Brew Kettle Inc .... F 440 234-8788
  Strongsville *(G-17721)*
Brewery Real Estate Partnr .... G 614 224-9023
  Columbus *(G-6695)*
Brufist LLC .... G 330 221-4472
  Bowling Green *(G-1957)*
Carry Grandview Out .... G 614 487-0305
  Columbus *(G-6748)*
Dayton Heidelberg Distrg Co .... D 440 989-1027
  Lorain *(G-12088)*
Dinos Drive Thru LLC .... G 330 263-1111
  Wooster *(G-20584)*
District Brewing Co Inc .... G 614 224-3626
  Columbus *(G-6870)*
Eagles Club .... G 740 962-6490
  McConnelsville *(G-13203)*
Hill James R & Hill Earley W .... G 740 591-4203
  Albany *(G-442)*
Jackie Os Pub Brewery LLC .... D 740 274-0777
  Athens *(G-836)*
Larrys Drive Thru & Mini Mart .... G 330 953-0512
  Youngstown *(G-20958)*
Marios Drive Thru .... G 330 452-8793
  Canton *(G-2743)*
Marks Brew Thru .... G 330 699-1755
  Akron *(G-271)*
Miiler Brewing Company .... F 513 896-9200
  Trenton *(G-18625)*
Millercoors LLC .... D 513 896-9200
  Trenton *(G-18626)*
Minnicks Drive-Thru .... G 513 868-6126
  Hamilton *(G-10587)*
Pop A Top Cruise Thru .... G 419 947-5855
  Mount Gilead *(G-14430)*
Snyder Intl Brewing Group LLC .... E 216 619-7424
  Cleveland *(G-6076)*
South Side Drive Thru .... G 937 295-2927
  Fort Loramie *(G-9807)*
The Great Lakes Brewing Co .... D 216 771-4404
  Cleveland *(G-6164)*
Thirsty Dog Brewing Co .... G 330 252-8740
  Akron *(G-404)*
Unbridled Brewing Company LLC .... F 937 361-2573
  Middletown *(G-13961)*
Willoughby Brewing Company .... D 440 975-0202
  Willoughby *(G-20458)*

BEVERAGES, ALCOHOLIC: Beer & Ale

Barnstorm Brewing Company LLC ...... G 419 852-9366
  Coldwater *(G-6400)*
Brew Kettle Strongsville LLC .... G 440 915-7074
  Medina *(G-13233)*
Brew Monkeys LLC .... G 513 330-8806
  Cincinnati *(G-3413)*
Brewpub Restaurant Corp .... D 614 228-2537
  Columbus *(G-6696)*
Brick and Barrel .... G 503 927-0629
  Cleveland *(G-4837)*
Burgie Brauerei Inc .... G 740 344-1620
  Newark *(G-14858)*
Columbus Kombucha Company LLC ... G 614 262-0000
  Columbus *(G-6795)*

PRODUCT SECTION

BEVERAGES, NONALCOHOLIC: Bottled & canned soft drinks

Commissary Brewing ....G...... 614 636-3164
  Columbus *(G-6807)*
Earnest Brew Works ....G...... 419 340-2589
  Toledo *(G-18274)*
Flat Rocks Brewing Company ....G...... 419 270-3582
  Napoleon *(G-14538)*
Guys Brewing Gear ....G...... 330 554-9362
  Kent *(G-11327)*
Homestead Beer Company ....G...... 740 522-8018
  Heath *(G-10720)*
McKinleys Meadery LLC ....G...... 740 928-0229
  Hebron *(G-10751)*
Moeller Brew Barn LLC ....G...... 419 925-3005
  Maria Stein *(G-12600)*
Municipal Brew Works LLC ....G...... 513 889-8369
  Hamilton *(G-10588)*
Nine Giant Brewing LLC ....G...... 510 220-5104
  Cincinnati *(G-4081)*
Rocky River Brewing Co ....E...... 440 895-2739
  Rocky River *(G-16555)*
Rust Belt Brewing LLC ....G...... 330 423-3818
  Youngstown *(G-21022)*
Tailspin Brewing Company ....G...... 419 852-9366
  Coldwater *(G-6421)*
Two Bandits Brewing Co LLC ....G...... 419 636-4045
  Bryan *(G-2310)*
Victoria Ventures Inc ....E...... 330 793-9321
  Youngstown *(G-21063)*
Wadsworth Brewing Company LLC ....G...... 330 475-4935
  Wadsworth *(G-19279)*
Warped Wing Brewing Co LLC ....F...... 937 222-7003
  Dayton *(G-8583)*
Westend Brewing LLC ....G...... 513 922-0289
  Cincinnati *(G-4501)*
Wright Designs Inc ....G...... 216 524-6662
  Cleveland *(G-6329)*
Yellow Springs Brewery LLC ....E...... 937 767-0222
  Yellow Springs *(G-20820)*

BEVERAGES, ALCOHOLIC: Bourbon Whiskey

Luxco Inc ....E...... 216 671-6300
  Cleveland *(G-5588)*

BEVERAGES, ALCOHOLIC: Cocktails

Catawba Island Brewing Co ....G...... 419 960-7764
  Port Clinton *(G-16244)*

BEVERAGES, ALCOHOLIC: Distilled Liquors

Black Swamp Distillery ....G...... 419 344-4347
  Fremont *(G-9999)*
Cleveland Whiskey LLC ....G...... 216 881-8481
  Cleveland *(G-4984)*
Doc Howards Distillery ....G...... 440 488-9463
  Mentor *(G-13430)*
Iron Vault Distillery LLC ....G...... 419 747-7560
  Ontario *(G-15542)*
John McCulloch Distillery ....G...... 937 725-5588
  Martinsville *(G-12766)*
Killbuck Creek Distillery LLC ....G...... 740 502-2880
  Warsaw *(G-19475)*
Klivlend Cask Distilling LLC ....G...... 216 926-1682
  Painesville *(G-15754)*
Smedleys Bar and Grill ....G...... 216 941-0124
  Cleveland *(G-6073)*
Stillwrights Distillery ....G...... 937 879-4447
  Fairborn *(G-9469)*
Veriano Fine Foods Spirits Ltd ....F...... 614 745-7705
  New Albany *(G-14641)*
Western Reserve Distillers LLC ....G...... 330 780-9599
  Lakewood *(G-11537)*

BEVERAGES, ALCOHOLIC: Liquors, Malt

AEC Brews LLC DBA Old Frhuse B ....G...... 513 536-9071
  Williamsburg *(G-20250)*

BEVERAGES, ALCOHOLIC: Near Beer

Georgetown Vineyards Inc ....E...... 740 435-3222
  Cambridge *(G-2440)*
Green Room Brewing LLC ....G...... 614 596-3655
  Columbus *(G-6970)*
North High Brewing LLC ....F...... 614 407-5278
  Columbus *(G-7227)*
Platform Beers LLC ....F...... 440 539-3245
  Cleveland *(G-5889)*

BEVERAGES, ALCOHOLIC: Neutral Spirits, Fruit

Four Fires Meadery LLC ....G...... 419 704-9573
  Maumee *(G-13110)*

BEVERAGES, ALCOHOLIC: Rye Whiskey

Five Points Distillery LLC ....G...... 937 776-4634
  Dayton *(G-8197)*

BEVERAGES, ALCOHOLIC: Wines

Autumn Rush Vineyard LLC ....G...... 614 312-5748
  Johnstown *(G-11258)*
Belvino LLC ....G...... 440 715-0076
  Chagrin Falls *(G-3010)*
Breitenbach Wine Cellar Inc ....G...... 330 343-3603
  Dover *(G-8810)*
Camelot Cellars Winery ....G...... 614 441-8860
  Columbus *(G-6726)*
Chalet Debonne Vineyards Inc ....F...... 440 466-3485
  Madison *(G-12343)*
CWC Partners LLC ....G...... 567 208-1573
  Findlay *(G-9676)*
Deluca Vineyards ....G...... 440 685-4242
  North Bloomfield *(G-15064)*
Deodora Vineyards & Winery LLC ....G...... 513 238-1167
  Cincinnati *(G-3582)*
Drake Brothers Ltd ....G...... 415 819-4941
  Columbus *(G-6874)*
E & J Gallo Winery ....E...... 513 381-4050
  Cincinnati *(G-3615)*
Emerine Estates Inc ....G...... 440 293-8199
  Jefferson *(G-11229)*
Ferrante Wine Farm Inc ....E...... 440 466-8466
  Geneva *(G-10219)*
Filia ....G...... 330 322-1200
  Wadsworth *(G-19239)*
Firelands Winery ....E...... 419 625-5474
  Sandusky *(G-16811)*
Flint Ridge Vineyard LLC ....G...... 740 787-2116
  Hopewell *(G-10992)*
Gillig Custom Winery Inc ....G...... 419 202-6057
  Findlay *(G-9693)*
Glenn Ravens Winery ....E...... 740 545-1000
  West Lafayette *(G-19930)*
Hanover Winery Inc ....G...... 513 304-9702
  Hamilton *(G-10569)*
High Low Winery ....G...... 844 466-4456
  Medina *(G-13273)*
Hillside Winery ....G...... 419 456-3108
  Gilboa *(G-10250)*
Hundley Cellars LLC ....G...... 843 368-5016
  Geneva *(G-10223)*
John Christ Winery Inc ....G...... 440 933-9672
  Avon Lake *(G-991)*
Kelleys Island Wine Co ....G...... 419 746-2678
  Kelleys Island *(G-11283)*
King Vineyards ....G...... 440 967-4191
  Vermilion *(G-19165)*
Klingshirn Winery Inc ....G...... 440 933-6666
  Avon Lake *(G-992)*
Larrys Drive Thru & Mini Mart ....G...... 330 953-0512
  Youngstown *(G-20958)*
Laurentia Winery ....G...... 440 296-9170
  Madison *(G-12353)*
Markko Vineyard ....G...... 440 593-3197
  Conneaut *(G-7655)*
Mastropietro Winery Inc ....G...... 330 547-2151
  Berlin Center *(G-1647)*
Meiers Wine Cellars Inc ....E...... 513 891-2900
  Cincinnati *(G-4003)*
Meranda Nixon Estate Wine LLC ....G...... 937 515-8013
  Ripley *(G-16514)*
Mio Vino ....G...... 513 407-0486
  Cincinnati *(G-4033)*
Moyer Vineyards Inc ....E...... 937 549-2957
  Manchester *(G-12395)*
Mt Carmel Brewing Company ....G...... 513 519-7161
  Cincinnati *(G-4052)*
Odyssey Cellars Inc ....G...... 330 782-0177
  Youngstown *(G-20980)*
Old Mason Winery Inc ....G...... 937 698-1122
  West Milton *(G-19951)*
Old Mill Winery Inc ....F...... 440 466-5560
  Geneva *(G-10227)*
Olde Schlhuse Vnyrd Winery LLC ....G...... 937 273-6023
  Eldorado *(G-9190)*
Paper Moon Winery ....G...... 440 967-2500
  Vermilion *(G-19169)*
Powell Village Winery LLC ....G...... 614 290-5898
  Powell *(G-16333)*
Rainbow Hills Vineyards Inc ....G...... 740 545-9305
  Newcomerstown *(G-14980)*
Renee Barrett Winery ....G...... 513 471-1340
  Cincinnati *(G-4259)*
Rockside Winery & Vineyards LL ....G...... 740 687-4414
  Lancaster *(G-11605)*
Sand Hollow Winery ....G...... 740 323-3959
  Heath *(G-10732)*
Sandra Weddington ....G...... 740 417-4286
  Delaware *(G-8722)*
SCC Wine Company LLC ....G...... 216 374-3740
  Madison *(G-12356)*
Shade Text Book Service Inc ....G...... 740 696-1323
  Shade *(G-16921)*
Sharon James Cellers ....G...... 440 739-4065
  Newbury *(G-14965)*
Shawne Springs Winery ....G...... 740 623-0744
  Coshocton *(G-7751)*
Stoney Ridge Winery Ltd ....G...... 419 636-3500
  Bryan *(G-2307)*
Thorncreek Winery & Garden ....G...... 330 562-9245
  Aurora *(G-908)*
Vervasi Vineyard & Itln Bistro ....E...... 330 497-1000
  Canton *(G-2860)*
Virant Family Winery Inc ....G...... 440 466-6279
  Geneva *(G-10230)*
Winery At Spring Hill Inc ....F...... 440 466-0626
  Geneva *(G-10231)*
Winery At Wolf Creek ....F...... 330 666-9285
  Barberton *(G-1113)*
Wines For You ....G...... 440 946-1420
  Mentor *(G-13627)*
Woodbury Vineyards Inc ....G...... 440 835-2828
  Westlake *(G-20173)*
Wyandotte Wine Cellar Inc ....G...... 614 476-3624
  Columbus *(G-7618)*

BEVERAGES, MALT

Fifty West Brewing Company ....D...... 513 834-8789
  Cincinnati *(G-3689)*

BEVERAGES, NONALCOHOLIC: Bottled & canned soft drinks

7 Up of Marietta Inc ....E...... 740 423-9230
  Little Hocking *(G-11988)*
Abbott Laboratories ....A...... 614 624-3191
  Columbus *(G-6519)*
American Bottling Company ....D...... 937 236-0333
  Dayton *(G-8023)*
American Bottling Company ....E...... 740 922-5253
  Midvale *(G-13974)*
American Bottling Company ....D...... 740 423-9230
  Little Hocking *(G-11990)*
American Bottling Company ....E...... 419 229-7777
  Lima *(G-11836)*
American Bottling Company ....D...... 419 535-0777
  Toledo *(G-18171)*
American Bottling Company ....C...... 513 242-5151
  Cincinnati *(G-3330)*
Belton Foods ....E...... 937 890-7768
  Dayton *(G-8053)*
Borden Dairy Co Cincinnati LLC ....C...... 513 948-8811
  Cincinnati *(G-3404)*
Cadbury Schweppes Bottling ....G...... 614 238-0469
  Columbus *(G-6722)*
Central Coca-Cola Btlg Co Inc ....D...... 330 783-1982
  Youngstown *(G-20867)*
Central Coca-Cola Btlg Co Inc ....D...... 614 863-7200
  Columbus *(G-6751)*
Central Coca-Cola Btlg Co Inc ....E...... 419 522-2653
  Mansfield *(G-12424)*
Central Coca-Cola Btlg Co Inc ....D...... 440 324-3335
  Elyria *(G-9235)*
Central Coca-Cola Btlg Co Inc ....E...... 740 452-3608
  Zanesville *(G-21118)*
Central Coca-Cola Btlg Co Inc ....D...... 330 425-4401
  Twinsburg *(G-18749)*
Central Coca-Cola Btlg Co Inc ....D...... 440 269-1433
  Willoughby *(G-20295)*
Cleveland Coca-Cola Btlg Inc ....D...... 216 690-2653
  Bedford Heights *(G-1465)*
Coca-Cola ....G...... 937 446-4644
  Sardinia *(G-16867)*
Coca-Cola Bottling Co Cnsld ....E...... 740 353-3133
  Portsmouth *(G-16280)*
Coca-Cola Company ....C...... 614 491-6305
  Columbus *(G-6779)*

Employee Codes: A=Over 500 employees, B=251-500
C=101-250, D=51-100, E=20-50, F=10-19, G=3-9

BEVERAGES, NONALCOHOLIC: Bottled & canned soft drinks

Csv Inc .... F 937 438-1142
  Dayton *(G-8115)*
Currier Richard & James .... G 440 988-4132
  Amherst *(G-559)*
Delite Fruit Juices .... G 614 470-4333
  Columbus *(G-6858)*
Dr Pepper Snapple Group .... G 419 223-0072
  Lima *(G-11856)*
Dragon Beverage Inc .... G 614 506-5592
  Columbus *(G-6873)*
Fbg Bottling Group LLC .... F 614 554-4646
  Columbus *(G-6914)*
G & J Pepsi-Cola Bottlers Inc .... E 740 774-2148
  Chillicothe *(G-3187)*
Gordon Brothers Btlg Group Inc ...... G 330 337-8754
  Salem *(G-16742)*
Haus Mathias .... G 330 533-5305
  Canfield *(G-2529)*
Hornell Brewing Co Inc .... G 516 812-0384
  Cincinnati *(G-3827)*
Keurig Dr Pepper Inc .... G 419 535-0777
  Toledo *(G-18366)*
L & F Lauch LLC .... G 513 732-5805
  Batavia *(G-1161)*
Medi Home Health Agency Inc .... G 740 472-3220
  Woodsfield *(G-20546)*
Meiers Wine Cellars Inc .... E 513 891-2900
  Cincinnati *(G-4003)*
Niagara Bottling LLC .... F 614 751-7420
  Gahanna *(G-10096)*
Nurture Brands LLC .... G 513 307-2338
  Cincinnati *(G-4093)*
P-Americas LLC .... E 419 227-3541
  Lima *(G-11913)*
Pepsi-Cola Metro Btlg Co Inc .... B 330 963-0426
  Twinsburg *(G-18833)*
Smucker International Inc .... G 330 682-3000
  Orrville *(G-15621)*
Smucker Natural Foods Inc .... E 330 682-3000
  Orrville *(G-15623)*
Vinnies Drive Thru .... G 419 225-5272
  Lima *(G-11956)*

BEVERAGES, NONALCOHOLIC: Carbonated

G & J Pepsi-Cola Bottlers Inc .... B 740 354-9191
  Franklin Furnace *(G-9934)*
G & J Pepsi-Cola Bottlers Inc .... C 513 896-3700
  Hamilton *(G-10560)*
P-Americas LLC .... E 740 266-6121
  Wintersville *(G-20540)*
P-Americas LLC .... B 513 948-5100
  Cincinnati *(G-4129)*
P-Americas LLC .... C 614 253-8771
  Columbus *(G-7283)*
P-Americas LLC .... C 330 336-3553
  Wadsworth *(G-19259)*
P-Americas LLC .... C 330 837-4224
  Massillon *(G-13036)*
P-Americas LLC .... E 330 963-0090
  Twinsburg *(G-18827)*
P-Americas LLC .... C 330 746-7652
  Youngstown *(G-20990)*
Pepsi-Cola Metro Btlg Co Inc .... C 614 261-8193
  Columbus *(G-7310)*
Pepsi-Cola Metro Btlg Co Inc .... E 330 963-5300
  Twinsburg *(G-18834)*
Pepsi-Cola Metro Btlg Co Inc .... E 419 534-2186
  Toledo *(G-18463)*
SD Ip Holdings Company .... G 513 483-3300
  Blue Ash *(G-1844)*

BEVERAGES, NONALCOHOLIC: Carbonated, Canned & Bottled, Etc

Bawls Acquisition LLC .... G 888 731-9708
  Twinsburg *(G-18739)*
Central Coca-Cola Btlg Co Inc .... C 419 476-6622
  Toledo *(G-18226)*
Coca-Cola Bottling Co Cnsld .... D 937 878-5000
  Dayton *(G-8096)*
Dominion Liquid Tech LLC .... E 513 272-2824
  Cincinnati *(G-3600)*
G & J Pepsi-Cola Bottlers Inc .... D 740 593-3366
  Athens *(G-831)*
Gehm & Sons Limited .... G 330 724-8423
  Akron *(G-185)*
L & J Drive Thru .... G 330 767-2185
  Brewster *(G-2069)*

BEVERAGES, NONALCOHOLIC: Cider

Beckwith Orchards Inc .... F 330 673-6433
  Kent *(G-11299)*
Fuhrmann Orchards LLC .... G 740 776-6406
  Wheelersburg *(G-20181)*
Haus Mathias .... G 330 533-5305
  Canfield *(G-2529)*
Hays Orchard & Cider Mill LLC .... F 330 482-2924
  Columbiana *(G-6468)*

BEVERAGES, NONALCOHOLIC: Flavoring extracts & syrups, nec

Abbott Laboratories .... A 614 624-3191
  Columbus *(G-6519)*
Agrana Fruit Us Inc .... C 937 693-3821
  Botkins *(G-1932)*
Cargill Incorporated .... E 937 236-1971
  Dayton *(G-8075)*
Flavor Systems Intl Inc .... E 513 870-4900
  West Chester *(G-19854)*
Givaudan Flavors Corporation .... G 513 948-8000
  Cincinnati *(G-3756)*
Givaudan Flvors Fragrances Inc ...... G 513 948-8000
  Cincinnati *(G-3757)*
Givaudan Fragrances Corp .... B 513 948-3428
  Cincinnati *(G-3759)*
Givaudan Roure US Inc .... G 513 948-8000
  Cincinnati *(G-3760)*
Joseph Adams Corp .... F 330 225-9125
  Valley City *(G-19042)*
Mane Inc .... D 513 248-9876
  Lebanon *(G-11672)*
Tate Lyle Ingrdnts Amricas LLC ...... G 937 236-5906
  Dayton *(G-8541)*

BEVERAGES, NONALCOHOLIC: Fruit Drnks, Under 100% Juice, Can

Country Pure Foods Inc .... C 330 848-6875
  Akron *(G-123)*
Life Support Development Ltd .... G 614 221-1765
  Columbus *(G-7126)*
Ohio Beverage Systems Inc .... F 216 475-3900
  Cleveland *(G-5800)*
Ohio Pure Foods Inc .... D 330 753-2293
  Akron *(G-309)*
Our Heart Health Care Svcs LLC ..... G 614 943-5216
  Columbus *(G-7279)*
Recov Beverages LLC .... G 513 518-9794
  Cincinnati *(G-4255)*
Sunny Delight Beverage Co .... G 513 483-3300
  Blue Ash *(G-1853)*

BEVERAGES, NONALCOHOLIC: Soft Drinks, Canned & Bottled, Etc

American Bottling Company .... D 614 237-4201
  Columbus *(G-6580)*
American Bottling Company .... E 740 377-4371
  South Point *(G-17279)*
American Bottling Company .... D 614 237-4201
  Columbus *(G-6581)*
American Bottling Company .... D 513 381-4891
  Cincinnati *(G-3329)*
Central Coca-Cola Btlg Co Inc .... G 740 474-2180
  Circleville *(G-4538)*
Central Coca-Cola Btlg Co Inc .... G 330 875-1487
  Akron *(G-110)*
Central Coca-Cola Btlg Co Inc .... G 330 487-0212
  Macedonia *(G-12282)*
Cincinnati Marlins Inc .... G 513 761-3320
  Cincinnati *(G-3500)*
Coca-Cola Bottling Co Cnsld .... G 419 422-3743
  Lima *(G-11849)*
Coca-Cola Bottling Co Cnsld .... B 513 527-6600
  Cincinnati *(G-3535)*
Coca-Cola Company .... F 937 446-4644
  Sardinia *(G-16868)*
Dr Pepper Bottlers Associates .... G 330 746-7651
  Youngstown *(G-20894)*
Dr Pepper Bottling Company .... G 740 452-2721
  Zanesville *(G-21130)*
Dr Pepper Snapple Group .... G 513 242-5151
  Cincinnati *(G-3608)*
Dr Pepper/Seven Up Inc .... D 419 229-7777
  Lima *(G-11857)*
G & J Pepsi-Cola Bottlers Inc .... F 513 785-6060
  Cincinnati *(G-3718)*
G & J Pepsi-Cola Bottlers Inc .... D 937 392-4937
  Ripley *(G-16513)*
G & J Pepsi-Cola Bottlers Inc .... A 614 253-8771
  Columbus *(G-6942)*
G & J Pepsi-Cola Bottlers Inc .... D 740 452-2721
  Zanesville *(G-21140)*
Gem Beverages Inc .... F 740 384-2411
  Wellston *(G-19600)*
Keurig Dr Pepper Inc .... D 614 237-4201
  Columbus *(G-7089)*
Keurig Dr Pepper Inc .... D 614 237-4201
  Columbus *(G-7090)*
National Beverage Corp .... E 614 491-5415
  Obetz *(G-15512)*
P-Americas LLC .... C 440 323-5524
  Elyria *(G-9307)*
Pepsi-Cola Metro Btlg Co Inc .... B 937 461-4664
  Dayton *(G-8421)*
Shasta Beverages Inc .... E 614 491-5415
  Obetz *(G-15513)*
Skinny Piggy Kombucha LLC .... G 513 646-5753
  Cincinnati *(G-4342)*
Star Beverage Corporation Ohio ..... G 216 991-4799
  Shaker Heights *(G-16938)*

BEVERAGES, NONALCOHOLIC: Tea, Iced, Bottled & Canned, Etc

Ohio Eagle Distributing LLC .... E 513 539-8483
  West Chester *(G-19753)*

BEVERAGES, WINE & DISTILLED ALCOHOLIC, WHOLESALE: Liquor

Veriano Fine Foods Spirits Ltd .... F 614 745-7705
  New Albany *(G-14641)*

BEVERAGES, WINE & DISTILLED ALCOHOLIC, WHOLESALE: Wine

CWC Partners LLC .... G 567 208-1573
  Findlay *(G-9676)*
Sandra Weddington .... G 740 417-4286
  Delaware *(G-8722)*
Wedco LLC .... G 513 309-0781
  Mount Orab *(G-14452)*

BIBS: Rubber, Vulcanized Or Rubberized Fabric

Okamoto Sandusky Mfg LLC .... D 419 626-1633
  Sandusky *(G-16832)*

BICYCLE REPAIR SHOP

Wersells Bike Shop Co .... G 419 474-7412
  Toledo *(G-18596)*

BICYCLE SHOPS

Wersells Bike Shop Co .... G 419 474-7412
  Toledo *(G-18596)*

BICYCLES, PARTS & ACCESS

Edge Cycling Technologies LLC .... G 937 532-3891
  Xenia *(G-20768)*
Old Mill Power Equipment .... G 740 982-3246
  Crooksville *(G-7817)*
Wersells Bike Shop Co .... G 419 474-7412
  Toledo *(G-18596)*

BILLFOLD INSERTS: Plastic

Armeton US Co .... F 419 660-9296
  Norwalk *(G-15381)*

BILLIARD & POOL TABLES & SPLYS

American Heritage Billd LLC .... D 330 626-3710
  Streetsboro *(G-17660)*
Bullseye Dart Shoppe Inc .... G 440 951-9277
  Willoughby *(G-20290)*
Clark & Son Pool Table Company .... G 330 454-9153
  Canton *(G-2626)*

BILLING & BOOKKEEPING SVCS

C S A Enterprises .... G 740 342-9367
  New Lexington *(G-14713)*

PRODUCT SECTION

BIOLOGICAL PRDTS: Exc Diagnostic

BINDING SVC: Books & Manuals

21st Century Printers Inc .... G 513 771-4150
  Cincinnati *(G-3268)*
A-A Blueprint Co Inc .... E 330 794-8803
  Akron *(G-23)*
AAA Laminating and Bindery Inc .... G 513 860-2680
  Fairfield *(G-9477)*
Activities Press Inc .... E 440 953-1200
  Mentor *(G-13374)*
AGS Custom Graphics Inc .... D 330 963-7770
  Macedonia *(G-12275)*
Allen Graphics Inc .... G 440 349-4100
  Solon *(G-17102)*
Anderson Graphics Inc .... E 330 745-2165
  Barberton *(G-1052)*
Baise Enterprises Inc .... G 614 444-3171
  Columbus *(G-6642)*
Barnhart Printing Corp .... F 330 456-2279
  Canton *(G-2585)*
Beck & Orr Inc .... G 614 276-8809
  Columbus *(G-6656)*
Bill Wyatt Inc .... G 330 535-1113
  Mentor *(G-13403)*
Bindery & Spc Pressworks Inc .... D 614 873-4623
  Plain City *(G-16178)*
Black River Group Inc .... D 419 524-6699
  Mansfield *(G-12411)*
Bock & Pierce Enterprises .... G 513 474-9500
  Cincinnati *(G-3398)*
Boldman Printing LLC .... G 937 653-3431
  Urbana *(G-18980)*
Bookbinders Incorporated .... G 330 848-4980
  Barberton *(G-1066)*
Bookfactory LLC .... E 937 226-7100
  Dayton *(G-8059)*
Century Graphics Inc .... E 614 895-7698
  Westerville *(G-19983)*
Cincinnati Bindery & Packg Inc .... G 859 816-0282
  Cincinnati *(G-3484)*
Classic Laminations Inc .... E 440 735-1333
  Cleveland *(G-4939)*
Cleveland Letter Service Inc .... E 216 781-8300
  Chagrin Falls *(G-3013)*
Clints Printing Inc .... G 937 426-2771
  Beavercreek *(G-1354)*
Consolidated Graphics Group Inc ...... C 216 881-9191
  Cleveland *(G-5015)*
Copley Ohio Newspapers Inc .... G 330 364-5577
  New Philadelphia *(G-14765)*
COS Blueprint Inc .... F 330 376-0022
  Akron *(G-122)*
Cox Printing Co .... G 937 382-2312
  Wilmington *(G-20491)*
Debandale Printing Inc .... G 330 725-5122
  Medina *(G-13251)*
Delphos Herald Inc .... D 419 695-0015
  Delphos *(G-8739)*
Earl D Arnold Printing Company .... E 513 533-6900
  Cincinnati *(G-3624)*
Easterdays Printing Center .... G 330 726-1182
  Youngstown *(G-20895)*
Eugene Stewart .... G 937 898-1117
  Dayton *(G-8189)*
Fedex Office & Print Svcs Inc .... E 937 436-0677
  Dayton *(G-8192)*
Fedex Office & Print Svcs Inc .... F 614 575-0800
  Reynoldsburg *(G-16439)*
Fedex Office & Print Svcs Inc .... E 216 573-1511
  Cleveland *(G-5228)*
Folks Creative Printers Inc .... E 740 383-6326
  Marion *(G-12702)*
Frank J Prucha & Associates .... G 216 642-3838
  Cleveland *(G-5272)*
Franklins Printing Company .... F 740 452-6375
  Zanesville *(G-21138)*
Ganger Enterprises Inc .... G 614 776-3985
  Westerville *(G-19993)*
Golden Graphics Ltd .... F 419 673-6260
  Kenton *(G-11406)*
Grant John .... G 937 298-0633
  Dayton *(G-8234)*
Great Lakes Integrated Inc .... D 216 651-1500
  Cleveland *(G-5347)*
Greg Blume .... G 740 574-2308
  Wheelersburg *(G-20182)*
Harris Paper Crafts Inc .... F 614 299-2141
  Columbus *(G-6983)*
Hecks Direct Mail & Prtg Svc .... E 419 697-3505
  Toledo *(G-18327)*

Henry Bussman .... G 614 224-0417
  Columbus *(G-6988)*
Hf Group .... E 440 729-9411
  Chesterland *(G-3158)*
Hf Group LLC .... F 440 729-2445
  Chesterland *(G-3159)*
Homewood Press Inc .... E 419 478-0695
  Toledo *(G-18334)*
Hopewell Industries Inc .... D 740 622-3563
  Coshocton *(G-7737)*
Icibinding Corporation .... E 440 729-2445
  Chesterland *(G-3162)*
Innomark Communications LLC .... E 937 454-5555
  Miamisburg *(G-13679)*
Jack Walker Printing Co .... F 440 352-4222
  Mentor *(G-13483)*
Kad Holdings Inc .... G 614 792-3399
  Dublin *(G-8935)*
Kehl-Kolor Inc .... E 419 281-3107
  Ashland *(G-717)*
Kenwel Printers Inc .... E 614 261-1011
  Columbus *(G-7088)*
Kevin K Tidd .... G 419 885-5603
  Sylvania *(G-17948)*
Keystone Press Inc .... G 419 243-7326
  Toledo *(G-18367)*
Keystone Printing & Copy Cat .... G 740 354-6542
  Portsmouth *(G-16286)*
Laipplys Prtg Mktg Sltions Inc .... G 740 387-9282
  Marion *(G-12715)*
Lam Pro Inc .... F 216 426-0661
  Cleveland *(G-5556)*
Lee Corporation .... G 513 771-3602
  Cincinnati *(G-3937)*
Legal News Publishing Co .... E 216 696-3322
  Cleveland *(G-5572)*
Lilienthal Southeastern Inc .... F 740 439-1640
  Cambridge *(G-2446)*
Lund Printing Co .... G 330 628-4047
  Akron *(G-262)*
Mmp Printing Inc .... E 513 381-0990
  Cincinnati *(G-4035)*
Monco Enterprises Inc .... A 937 461-0034
  Dayton *(G-8366)*
Montview Corporation .... G 330 723-3409
  Medina *(G-13304)*
Multi-Craft Litho Inc .... E 859 581-2754
  Blue Ash *(G-1824)*
Nari Inc .... G 440 960-2280
  Monroeville *(G-14289)*
Network Printing & Graphics .... F 614 230-2084
  Columbus *(G-7214)*
Newfax Corporation .... F 419 241-5157
  Toledo *(G-18423)*
North End Press Incorporated .... E 740 653-6514
  Lancaster *(G-11591)*
Ohio Laminating & Binding Inc .... E 614 771-4868
  Hilliard *(G-10846)*
Old Trail Printing Company .... C 614 443-4852
  Columbus *(G-7269)*
Onetouchpoint East Corp .... D 513 421-1600
  Cincinnati *(G-4113)*
Orrville Printing Co Inc .... G 330 682-5066
  Orrville *(G-15608)*
Painesville Publishing Co .... G 440 354-4142
  Austinburg *(G-924)*
Patricia Lee Burd .... G 513 302-4860
  Cincinnati *(G-4136)*
Penguin Enterprises Inc .... E 440 899-5112
  Westlake *(G-20140)*
Pooles Printing & Office Svcs .... F 419 475-9000
  Toledo *(G-18474)*
Prime Printing Inc .... E 937 438-3707
  Dayton *(G-8442)*
Print-Digital Incorporated .... G 330 686-5945
  Stow *(G-17621)*
Printed Image .... F 614 221-1412
  Columbus *(G-7350)*
Promatch Solutions LLC .... F 937 299-0185
  Springboro *(G-17346)*
Quick Tab II Inc .... D 419 448-6622
  Tiffin *(G-18076)*
R T Industries Inc .... G 937 335-5784
  Troy *(G-18695)*
R W Michael Printing Co .... G 330 923-9277
  Akron *(G-340)*
Repro Acquisition Company LLC ...... E 216 738-3800
  Cleveland *(G-5977)*
Ricci Anthony .... G 330 758-5761
  Youngstown *(G-21015)*

Robert Esterman .... G 513 541-3311
  Cincinnati *(G-4277)*
Robert H Shackelford .... G 330 364-2221
  New Philadelphia *(G-14799)*
Robin Enterprises Company .... C 614 891-0250
  Westerville *(G-20073)*
Ryans Newark Leader Ex Prtg .... F 740 522-2149
  Newark *(G-14916)*
Sandy Smittcamp .... G 937 372-1687
  Xenia *(G-20788)*
Slutzkers Quickprint Center .... G 440 244-0330
  Lorain *(G-12123)*
Spencer-Walker Press Inc .... F 740 344-6110
  Newark *(G-14920)*
Star Printing Company Inc .... E 330 376-0514
  Akron *(G-386)*
Strong Bindery .... G 216 231-0001
  Cleveland *(G-6112)*
Suburban Press Inc .... E 216 961-0766
  Cleveland *(G-6114)*
Target Printing & Graphics .... G 937 228-0170
  Dayton *(G-8539)*
Taylor Communications Inc .... G 937 228-5800
  Dayton *(G-8545)*
Tj Metzgers Inc .... D 419 861-8611
  Toledo *(G-18553)*
TL Krieg Offset Inc .... E 513 542-1522
  Cincinnati *(G-4424)*
Traxium LLC .... E 330 572-8200
  Stow *(G-17637)*
Watkins Printing Company .... G 614 297-8270
  Columbus *(G-7593)*
West-Camp Press Inc .... D 614 882-2378
  Westerville *(G-20082)*
Wfsr Holdings LLC .... A 877 735-4966
  Dayton *(G-8592)*
William J Dupps .... G 419 734-2126
  Port Clinton *(G-16264)*
Youngstown ARC Engraving Co .... E 330 793-2471
  Youngstown *(G-21070)*

BINDING SVC: Pamphlets

Fergusons Finishing Inc .... E 419 241-9123
  Toledo *(G-18293)*
Macke Brothers Inc .... D 513 771-7500
  Cincinnati *(G-3969)*

BINDING SVC: Trade

Bip Printing Solutions LLC .... F 216 832-5673
  Beachwood *(G-1225)*

BINDINGS: Bias, Made From Purchased Materials

National Bias Fabric Co .... E 216 361-0530
  Cleveland *(G-5722)*

BINDINGS: Cap & Hat, Made From Purchased Materials

Elken Co .... G 513 459-7207
  Maineville *(G-12368)*

BINGO HALL

Access To Independence Inc .... G 330 296-8111
  Ravenna *(G-16363)*

BINOCULARS

Vance Adams .... G 330 424-9670
  Lisbon *(G-11981)*

BINS: Prefabricated, Sheet Metal

Beacon Metal Fabricators Inc .... F 216 391-7444
  Cleveland *(G-4798)*
Metal Fabricating Corporation .... D 216 631-8121
  Cleveland *(G-5658)*

BIOLOGICAL PRDTS: Bacteriological Media

Envirozyme LLC .... G 800 232-2847
  Bowling Green *(G-1972)*
General Environmental Science .... G 216 464-0680
  Beachwood *(G-1239)*

BIOLOGICAL PRDTS: Exc Diagnostic

ABI Inc .... F 216 378-1336
  Bedford *(G-1378)*

BIOLOGICAL PRDTS: Exc Diagnostic

Bio-Blood Components Inc .... E 614 294-3183
  Columbus (G-6669)
Carbogene USA LLC .... G 215 378-4306
  Columbus (G-6738)
Copernicus Therapeutics Inc .... F 216 707-1776
  Cleveland (G-5029)
EMD Millipore Corporation .... C 513 631-0445
  Norwood (G-15426)
Ferro Corporation .... D 216 577-7144
  Bedford (G-1405)
Microbiological Labs Inc .... G 330 626-2264
  Streetsboro (G-17682)
Perkinelmer Hlth Sciences Inc .... E 330 825-4525
  Akron (G-318)
Safewhite Inc .... G 614 340-1450
  Columbus (G-7414)
Supply Dynamics Inc .... E 513 965-2000
  Loveland (G-12238)

BIOLOGICAL PRDTS: Serums

Columbus Serum Co .... G 614 793-0615
  Columbus (G-6801)

BIOLOGICAL PRDTS: Toxin, Viruses/Simlr Substncs, Incl Venom

Protein Express Laboratories .... G 513 769-9654
  Blue Ash (G-1839)

BIOLOGICAL PRDTS: Vaccines

Global Health Services Inc .... G 513 777-8111
  Hamilton (G-10564)

BIOLOGICAL PRDTS: Vaccines & Immunizing

Decaria Brothers Inc .... G 330 385-0825
  East Liverpool (G-9055)
Phagevax Inc .... G 740 502-9010
  Newark (G-14910)
Tamarkin Company .... G 330 634-0688
  Tallmadge (G-18008)
Tamarkin Company .... G 614 878-8942
  Columbus (G-7510)

BIOLOGICAL PRDTS: Venoms

Venom Exterminating LLC .... G 330 637-3366
  Cortland (G-7716)

BIOLOGICAL PRDTS: Veterinary

No Rinse Laboratories LLC .... G 937 746-7457
  Springboro (G-17339)

BLACKBOARDS & CHALKBOARDS

GMI Companies Inc .... C 513 932-3445
  Lebanon (G-11657)
GMI Companies Inc .... G 937 981-0244
  Greenfield (G-10348)
Tri-State Supply Co Inc .... F 614 272-6767
  Columbus (G-7543)

BLACKBOARDS: Slate

Michael Kaufman Companies Inc .... F 330 673-4881
  Kent (G-11353)
Michael Kaufman Companies Inc .... F 330 673-4881
  Kent (G-11354)

BLADES: Knife

A & P Tech Services Inc .... G 330 535-1700
  Akron (G-17)
Advetech Inc .... E 330 533-2227
  Canfield (G-2517)
American Quicksilver Co .... G 513 871-4517
  Cincinnati (G-3337)
Busse Knife Co .... E 419 923-6471
  Wauseon (G-19511)
Cut Off Blades Inc .... G 440 543-2947
  Chagrin Falls (G-3043)
Evolution Resources LLC .... G 937 438-2390
  Centerville (G-3002)

BLADES: Saw, Hand Or Power

Blade Manufacturing Co Inc .... F 614 294-1649
  Columbus (G-6679)
M K Morse Company .... B 330 453-8187
  Canton (G-2737)

Peerless Saw Company .... C 614 836-5790
  Groveport (G-10509)

BLANKBOOKS

Lilienthal Southeastern Inc .... F 740 439-1640
  Cambridge (G-2446)

BLANKBOOKS & LOOSELEAF BINDERS

Deluxe Corporation .... C 330 342-1500
  Hudson (G-11041)
Dupli-Systems Inc .... C 440 234-9415
  Strongsville (G-17738)
Elken Co .... E 513 459-7207
  Maineville (G-12368)
Quick Tech Graphics Inc .... E 937 743-5952
  Springboro (G-17348)

BLANKBOOKS: Account

Gotta Groove Records Inc .... E 216 431-7373
  Cleveland (G-5334)

BLANKBOOKS: Albums

W N Albums and Frames Inc .... G 800 325-5179
  Cleveland (G-6278)

BLANKBOOKS: Passbooks, Bank, Etc

William Exline Inc .... E 216 941-0800
  Cleveland (G-6309)

BLANKETS & BLANKETING, COTTON

Grow With Me- Creations .... G 800 850-1889
  Hartville (G-10691)

BLAST FURNACE & RELATED PRDTS

Custom Blast & Coat Inc .... G 419 225-6024
  Lima (G-11851)
Rmi Titanium Company LLC .... D 330 471-1844
  Canton (G-2807)

BLASTING SVC: Sand, Metal Parts

American Indus Maintenance .... G 937 254-3400
  Dayton (G-8026)
Badboy Blasters Incorporated .... F 330 454-2699
  Canton (G-2583)
Boville Indus Coatings Inc .... G 330 669-8558
  Smithville (G-17087)
Derrick Company Inc .... E 513 321-8122
  Cincinnati (G-3583)
Industrial Mill Maintenance .... E 330 746-1155
  Youngstown (G-20939)
L & N Olde Car Co .... G 440 564-7204
  Newbury (G-14959)
Lima Sandblasting & Pntg Co .... G 419 331-2939
  Lima (G-11892)
Newsome & Work Metalizing Co .... G 330 376-7144
  Akron (G-296)
Pki Inc .... F 513 832-8749
  Cincinnati (G-4164)
Witt Enterprises Inc .... E 440 992-8333
  Ashtabula (G-812)

BLINDS & SHADES: Vertical

11 92 Holdings LLC .... E 216 920-7790
  Chagrin Falls (G-3008)
Blind Factory Showroom .... E 614 771-6549
  Hilliard (G-10814)
Blind Outlet .... G 614 895-2002
  Westerville (G-20037)
Optimun Blinds Inc .... G 740 598-5808
  Brilliant (G-2079)
Vertical Runner .... G 330 262-3000
  Wooster (G-20662)

BLINDS : Window

ARC Blinds Inc .... G 513 889-4864
  Mason (G-12825)
Cascade Group of Ohio Limited .... G 440 572-2480
  Strongsville (G-17723)
E W Perry Service Co Inc .... G 419 473-1231
  Toledo (G-18273)
M C L Window Coverings Inc .... G 513 868-6000
  Fairfield Township (G-9584)
Mag Resources LLC .... G 330 294-0494
  Barberton (G-1083)

BLINDS, WOOD

Mag Resources LLC .... G 330 294-0494
  Barberton (G-1083)

BLOCK & BRICK: Sand Lime

Kent Paverbrick LLC .... G 330 995-7000
  Aurora (G-888)
R W Sidley Incorporated .... E 440 352-9343
  Painesville (G-15777)

BLOCKS & BRICKS: Concrete

Charles Svec Inc .... E 216 662-5200
  Maple Heights (G-12568)
K & L Ready Mix Inc .... F 419 532-3585
  Kalida (G-11277)
Mapes Concrete Construction .... G 513 245-2631
  Cincinnati (G-3978)
Midwest Specialties Inc .... F 419 738-8147
  Wapakoneta (G-19346)
Oberfields LLC .... F 614 252-0955
  Columbus (G-7237)
R W Sidley Incorporated .... E 440 564-2221
  Newbury (G-14962)
RE Connors Construction Ltd .... G 740 644-0261
  Thornville (G-18031)
S & S Aggregates Inc .... G 740 453-0721
  Zanesville (G-21175)
Stocker Concrete Company .... F 740 254-4626
  Gnadenhutten (G-10283)
William Dauch Concrete Company .... F 419 668-4458
  Norwalk (G-15418)

BLOCKS: Insulating, Concrete

ICC Safety Service Inc .... G 614 261-4557
  Columbus (G-7020)
North Central Concrete Design .... F 419 606-1908
  Wooster (G-20632)

BLOCKS: Landscape Or Retaining Wall, Concrete

Benchmark Land Management LLC ...... G 513 310-7850
  West Chester (G-19658)
Bryce Hill Inc .... E 937 663-4152
  Saint Paris (G-16705)
Frankie Tatum .... G 614 216-1556
  Columbus (G-6934)
Green Vision Materials Inc .... F 440 564-5500
  Newbury (G-14954)
Kathy Edie .... G 740 763-4887
  Newark (G-14890)
Meridienne International Inc .... G 330 274-8317
  Mantua (G-12554)
Ready Field Solutions LLC .... G 330 562-0550
  Streetsboro (G-17692)
Simon & Simon Blue Pond Inc .... G 330 928-2298
  Cuyahoga Falls (G-7918)
T-N-T Concrete Inc .... G 540 480-4040
  Mentor (G-13599)

BLOCKS: Paving

B & S Blacktop Co .... G 513 797-5759
  New Richmond (G-14810)
Husac Paving .... G 513 200-2818
  Harrison (G-10650)
La Rose Paving Co Inc .... G 440 632-0330
  Middlefield (G-13813)

BLOCKS: Paving, Composition

T-N-T Concrete Inc .... G 540 480-4040
  Mentor (G-13599)

BLOCKS: Paving, Concrete

B & S Blacktop Co .... G 513 797-5759
  New Richmond (G-14810)
E C S Corp .... F 440 323-1707
  Elyria (G-9247)
Gennaro Pavers .... G 330 536-6825
  Lowellville (G-12252)

BLOCKS: Standard, Concrete Or Cinder

American Concrete Products .... F 937 224-1433
  Dayton (G-8025)
Cantelli Block and Brick Inc .... E 419 433-0102
  Huron (G-11091)

Cement Products Inc .... E 419 524-4342
   Mansfield *(G-12423)*
Dearth Resources Inc .... G 937 325-0651
   Springfield *(G-17384)*
Dearth Resources Inc .... G 937 663-4171
   Springfield *(G-17385)*
Hanson Aggregates East LLC .... E 740 773-2172
   Chillicothe *(G-3191)*
Hazelbaker Industries Ltd .... E 614 276-2631
   Columbus *(G-6984)*
J P Sand & Gravel Company .... E 614 497-0083
   Lockbourne *(G-11995)*
Koltcz Concrete Block Co .... E 440 232-3630
   Bedford *(G-1421)*
Martin Block Company .... G 740 286-7507
   Jackson *(G-11190)*
National Lime and Stone Co .... E 614 497-0083
   Lockbourne *(G-11998)*
Oberfields LLC .... E 614 491-7643
   Columbus *(G-7236)*
Osborne Inc .... E 440 942-7000
   Mentor *(G-13539)*
Portsmouth Block Inc .... F 740 353-4113
   Portsmouth *(G-16295)*
Quality Block & Supply Inc .... E 330 364-4411
   Mount Eaton *(G-14421)*
Reading Rock Inc .... C 513 874-2345
   West Chester *(G-19893)*
Snyder Concrete Products Inc .... E 937 885-5176
   Moraine *(G-14394)*
Snyder Concrete Products Inc .... G 937 224-1433
   Dayton *(G-8511)*
St Henry Tile Co Inc .... E 419 678-4841
   Saint Henry *(G-16667)*
St Henry Tile Co Inc .... F 937 548-1101
   Greenville *(G-10396)*
Stiger Pre Cast Inc .... G 740 482-2313
   Nevada *(G-14601)*
Stocker Sand & Gravel Co .... E 740 254-4635
   Gnadenhutten *(G-10284)*
Tri-County Block and Brick Inc .... E 419 826-7060
   Swanton *(G-17925)*
Trumbull Cement Products Co .... G 330 372-4342
   Warren *(G-19450)*
Tyjen Inc .... G 740 380-3215
   Logan *(G-12045)*
Tyjen Inc .... G 740 797-4064
   The Plains *(G-18023)*
Walden Industries Inc .... E 740 633-5971
   Tiltonsville *(G-18094)*

BLOOD BANK

Bio-Blood Components Inc .... E 614 294-3183
   Columbus *(G-6669)*

BLOWERS & FANS

A A S Amels Sheet Meta L Inc .... E 330 793-9326
   Youngstown *(G-20830)*
Air Cleaning Systems Inc .... G 440 285-3565
   Chardon *(G-3096)*
Air-Rite Inc .... E 216 228-8200
   Cleveland *(G-4645)*
American Manufacturing & Eqp .... G 513 829-2248
   Fairfield *(G-9482)*
Beckett Air Incorporated .... D 440 327-9999
   North Ridgeville *(G-15209)*
Bry-Air Inc .... E 740 965-2974
   Sunbury *(G-17883)*
Burt Manufacturing Company Inc .... C 330 762-0061
   Akron *(G-100)*
Ceco Group Inc .... G 513 458-2600
   Cincinnati *(G-3452)*
Diamond Power Intl Inc .... B 740 687-6500
   Lancaster *(G-11566)*
Ellis & Watts Intl LLC .... E 513 752-9000
   Batavia *(G-1143)*
Famous Industries Inc .... D 740 685-2592
   Byesville *(G-2384)*
Flex Technologies Inc .... D 330 359-5415
   Mount Eaton *(G-14420)*
Howden American Fan Company .... E 513 874-2400
   Fairfield *(G-9507)*
Howden North America Inc .... E 330 721-7374
   Medina *(G-13275)*
Howden North America Inc .... C 513 874-2400
   Fairfield *(G-9508)*
Illinois Tool Works Inc .... C 262 248-8277
   Bryan *(G-2289)*
Kirk Williams Company Inc .... D 614 875-9023
   Grove City *(G-10440)*

Langdon Inc .... E 513 733-5955
   Cincinnati *(G-3930)*
Link-O-Matic Company Inc .... F 765 962-1538
   Brookville *(G-2173)*
Mestek Inc .... D 419 288-2703
   Bradner *(G-2015)*
Midwestern Industries Inc .... C 330 837-4203
   Massillon *(G-13026)*
Minova USA Inc .... D 740 377-9146
   South Point *(G-17289)*
Nupro Company .... C 440 951-9729
   Willoughby *(G-20392)*
Ohio Blow Pipe Company .... E 216 681-7379
   Cleveland *(G-5801)*
Oil Skimmers Inc .... E 440 237-4600
   North Royalton *(G-15291)*
Pcy Enterprises Inc .... E 513 241-5566
   Cincinnati *(G-4143)*
Plas-Tanks Industries Inc .... E 513 942-3800
   Hamilton *(G-10596)*
Qualtek Electronics Corp .... C 440 951-3300
   Mentor *(G-13567)*
Quickdraft Inc .... E 330 477-4574
   Canton *(G-2799)*
Selas Heat Technology Co LLC .... E 800 523-6500
   Streetsboro *(G-17697)*
Starr Fabricating Inc .... D 330 394-9891
   Vienna *(G-19210)*
Stelter and Brinck Inc .... E 513 367-9300
   Harrison *(G-10672)*
Thermo Vent Manufacturing Inc .... F 330 239-0239
   Medina *(G-13351)*
Tisch Environmental Inc .... F 513 467-9000
   Cleves *(G-6379)*
Tosoh America Inc .... B 614 539-8622
   Grove City *(G-10476)*

BLOWERS & FANS

Americraft Mfg Co Inc .... F 513 489-1047
   Cincinnati *(G-3338)*
Buckeye BOP LLC .... G 740 498-9898
   Newcomerstown *(G-14971)*
Hartzell Fan Inc .... C 937 773-7411
   Piqua *(G-16122)*
Howden North America Inc .... D 330 867-8540
   Medina *(G-13274)*
OEM Corporation .... F 937 859-7492
   Miamisburg *(G-13702)*
Vortec and Paxton Products .... F 513 891-7474
   Blue Ash *(G-1865)*

BLUEPRINTING SVCS

Fedex Office & Print Svcs Inc .... F 937 335-3816
   Troy *(G-18657)*
Instant Impressions Inc .... G 614 538-9844
   Columbus *(G-7030)*
Northeast Blueprint & Sup Co .... E 216 261-7500
   Cleveland *(G-5773)*
Profile Digital Printing LLC .... E 937 866-4241
   Dayton *(G-8448)*
Queen City Reprographics .... C 513 326-2300
   Cincinnati *(G-4240)*
Richland Blue Printcom Inc .... E 419 524-2781
   Mansfield *(G-12505)*
Robert Becker Impressions Inc .... F 419 385-5303
   Toledo *(G-18504)*

BOAT BUILDING & REPAIR

Checkmate Marine Inc .... F 419 562-3881
   Bucyrus *(G-2321)*
Don Wartko Construction Co .... D 330 673-5252
   Kent *(G-11315)*
Extreme Marine .... G 330 963-7800
   Twinsburg *(G-18772)*
Jacks Marine Inc .... G 440 997-5060
   Ashtabula *(G-781)*
Marinemax Inc .... C 918 782-3277
   Port Clinton *(G-16252)*
Mariners Landing Inc .... F 513 941-3625
   Cincinnati *(G-3981)*
O-Kan Marine Repair Inc .... E 740 446-4686
   Gallipolis *(G-10172)*
Racelite South Coast Inc .... F 216 581-4600
   Maple Heights *(G-12578)*
W of Ohio Inc .... G 614 873-4664
   Plain City *(G-16216)*
William Thompson .... G 440 232-4363
   Aurora *(G-916)*

Www Boat Services Inc .... G 419 626-0883
   Sandusky *(G-16863)*

BOAT BUILDING & REPAIRING: Dories

Mentor Inc .... G 440 255-1250
   Mentor On The Lake *(G-13632)*

BOAT BUILDING & REPAIRING: Iceboats

Duck Water Boats Inc .... G 330 602-9008
   Dover *(G-8824)*

BOAT BUILDING & REPAIRING: Kits, Not Models

Brewster Sugarcreek Twp Histo .... F 330 767-0045
   Brewster *(G-2068)*

BOAT BUILDING & REPAIRING: Lifeboats

Healthcare Benefits Inc .... G 419 433-4499
   Huron *(G-11095)*

BOAT BUILDING & REPAIRING: Motorized

Nauticus Inc .... G 440 746-1290
   Brecksville *(G-2051)*

BOAT BUILDING & REPAIRING: Tenders, Small Motor Craft

Gallagher Wood & Crafts .... G 513 523-2748
   Oxford *(G-15693)*

BOAT DEALERS

Duck Water Boats Inc .... G 330 602-9008
   Dover *(G-8824)*
Dynamic Plastics Inc .... G 937 437-7261
   New Paris *(G-14753)*
Mariners Landing Inc .... F 513 941-3625
   Cincinnati *(G-3981)*
Www Boat Services Inc .... G 419 626-0883
   Sandusky *(G-16863)*

BOAT DEALERS: Marine Splys & Eqpt

Hydromotive Engineering Co .... G 330 425-4266
   Twinsburg *(G-18793)*
Minderman Marine Products Inc .... G 419 732-2626
   Port Clinton *(G-16253)*
Sailors Tailor Inc .... G 937 862-7781
   Spring Valley *(G-17318)*

BOAT DEALERS: Motor

Marinemax Inc .... C 918 782-3277
   Port Clinton *(G-16252)*

BOAT LIFTS

American Power Hoist Inc .... G 740 964-2035
   Pataskala *(G-15828)*
Cincinnati Recreation Comm .... G 513 921-5657
   Cincinnati *(G-3505)*
Indian Lake Boat Lift .... G 937 539-2868
   Russells Point *(G-16599)*
Westerman Inc .... D 330 262-6946
   Wooster *(G-20665)*

BOAT REPAIR SVCS

Duck Water Boats Inc .... G 330 602-9008
   Dover *(G-8824)*
Superior Marine Ways Inc .... C 740 894-6224
   Proctorville *(G-16346)*

BOAT YARD: Boat yards, storage & incidental repair

Jacks Marine Inc .... G 440 997-5060
   Ashtabula *(G-781)*
Mariners Landing Inc .... F 513 941-3625
   Cincinnati *(G-3981)*
Tack-Anew Inc .... E 419 734-4212
   Port Clinton *(G-16262)*

BOATS & OTHER MARINE EQPT: Plastic

Mustang Aerial Services Inc .... G 740 373-9262
   Reno *(G-16426)*

BODIES: Truck & Bus

BODIES: Truck & Bus

Ace Truck Equipment Co ....E 740 453-0551
   Zanesville *(G-21091)*
Airstream Inc ....B 937 596-6111
   Jackson Center *(G-11205)*
Atc Lighting & Plastics Inc............................C 440 466-7670
   Andover *(G-580)*
Bores Manufacturing Co Inc ....F 419 465-2606
   Monroeville *(G-14287)*
Cascade Corporation......................................C 937 327-0300
   Springfield *(G-17370)*
Cleveland Hdwr & Forging Co ....E 216 641-5200
   Cleveland *(G-4962)*
Columbus McKinnon Corporation ....D 330 424-7248
   Lisbon *(G-11965)*
Field Gymmy Inc ....G 419 538-6511
   Glandorf *(G-10269)*
Galion-Godwin Truck Bdy Co LLC 330 359-5495
   Millersburg *(G-14084)*
Hendrickson International Corp ....D 740 929-5600
   Hebron *(G-10747)*
International Brake Inds Inc ....C 419 227-4421
   Lima *(G-11879)*
Johns Body Shop 419 358-1200
   Bluffton *(G-1890)*
Joseph Industries Inc ....D 330 528-0091
   Streetsboro *(G-17680)*
King Kutter II Inc ....E 740 446-0351
   Gallipolis *(G-10169)*
Kuka Toledo Production ....C 419 727-5500
   Toledo *(G-18372)*
Leyman Manufacturing Corp 513 891-6210
   Cincinnati *(G-3939)*
Martin Sheet Metal Inc ....D 216 377-8200
   Cleveland *(G-5627)*
Meritor Inc.. 740 348-3498
   Granville *(G-10333)*
Paccar Inc ....A 740 774-5111
   Chillicothe *(G-3205)*
Radar Love Co..F 419 951-4750
   Findlay *(G-9744)*
Tarpstop LLC ....E 419 873-7867
   Perrysburg *(G-16009)*
Trim Systems Operating Corp ....C 614 289-5360
   New Albany *(G-14639)*
Wallace Forge Company ....D 330 488-1203
   Canton *(G-2863)*
Youngstown-Kenworth Inc ....E 330 534-9761
   Hubbard *(G-11014)*

BODY PARTS: Automobile, Stamped Metal

Antique Auto Sheet Metal Inc ....E 937 833-4422
   Brookville *(G-2161)*
Artiflex Manufacturing LLC.................B 330 262-2015
   Wooster *(G-20564)*
Buyers Products Company...........................G 440 974-8888
   Mentor *(G-13409)*
Custom Floaters LLC...........................G 216 937-9118
   Brookpark *(G-2140)*
Decoma Systems Integration Gro ....D 419 324-3387
   Toledo *(G-18257)*
Fuserashi Intl Tech Inc ....F 330 273-0140
   Valley City *(G-19038)*
General Motors LLC......................................A 216 265-5000
   Cleveland *(G-5312)*
Ksi Distribution Inc 440 256-2500
   Mentor *(G-13491)*
Liber Limited LLC ....G 440 427-0647
   Olmsted Twp *(G-15533)*
Lwb/ISE LP ....F 937 778-3828
   Piqua *(G-16139)*
Matsu Ohio Inc ....C 419 298-2394
   Edgerton *(G-9176)*
Murotech Ohio Corporation..........................C 419 394-6529
   Saint Marys *(G-16690)*
Transitworks LLC ....G 855 337-9543
   Akron *(G-408)*
Trellborg Sling Prfiles US Inc ....E 330 995-9725
   Aurora *(G-911)*
Valco Industries Inc ....F 937 399-7400
   Springfield *(G-17513)*
Vehtek Systems Inc ....A 419 373-8741
   Bowling Green *(G-2004)*
Wrena LLC ....E 937 667-4403
   Tipp City *(G-18146)*

BOILER & HEATING REPAIR SVCS

Air-Rite Inc..E 216 228-8200
   Cleveland *(G-4645)*

Babcock & Wilcox Company ....A 330 753-4511
   Barberton *(G-1059)*
Lim Services LLC..F 513 217-0801
   Middletown *(G-13920)*
Nbw Inc ....E 216 377-1700
   Cleveland *(G-5732)*

BOILER GAGE COCKS

Cfrc Wtr & Enrgy Solutions Inc ....G 216 479-0290
   Cleveland *(G-4906)*
Xomox Corporation ....E 936 271-6500
   Cincinnati *(G-4527)*

BOILER REPAIR SHOP

Acme Boiler Co Inc................................G 216 961-2471
   Cleveland *(G-4605)*
Gurina Company ....G 614 279-3891
   Columbus *(G-6971)*
Manitowoc Company Inc ....G 920 746-3332
   Cleveland *(G-5612)*

BOILERS: Low-Pressure Heating, Steam Or Hot Water

Abbott Mechanical Services LLC ....G 419 460-4315
   Maumee *(G-13065)*
Nbbi ....G 614 888-8320
   Columbus *(G-7212)*

BOLTS: Metal

Agrati - Medina LLC ....G 740 467-3199
   Millersport *(G-14158)*
Airfasco Inc ....E 330 430-6190
   Canton *(G-2561)*
Auto Bolt Company ....D 216 881-3913
   Cleveland *(G-4767)*
Bowes Manufacturing Inc ....F 216 378-2110
   Solon *(G-17117)*
Cold Headed Fas Assemblies Inc.........F 330 833-0800
   Massillon *(G-12968)*
Cold Heading Co ....D 216 581-3000
   Cleveland *(G-4996)*
Consolidated Metal Pdts Inc ....C 513 251-2624
   Cincinnati *(G-3542)*
Curtiss-Wright Flow Ctrl Corp ....D 216 267-3200
   Cleveland *(G-5045)*
Elgin Fastener Group LLC ....E 440 717-7650
   Brecksville *(G-2031)*
Elgin Fastener Group LLC ....F 812 689-8990
   Brecksville *(G-2032)*
Ferry Cap & Set Screw Company ....C 216 649-7400
   Lakewood *(G-11517)*
Iwata Bolt USA Inc ....F 513 942-5050
   Fairfield *(G-9512)*
Jacodar Inc ....F 330 832-9557
   Massillon *(G-13005)*
Jacodar Fsa LLC ....E 330 454-1832
   Canton *(G-2715)*
Keystone Bolt & Nut Company ....D 216 524-9626
   Cleveland *(G-5532)*
Matdan Corporation ....E 513 794-0500
   Blue Ash *(G-1815)*
Mid-West Fabricating Co ....E 740 277-7021
   Lancaster *(G-11587)*
Mid-West Fabricating Co ....G 740 681-4411
   Lancaster *(G-11588)*
Mid-West Fabricating Co ....C 740 969-4411
   Amanda *(G-526)*
Nova Machine Products Inc ....D 216 267-3200
   Middleburg Heights *(G-13767)*
R S Manufacturing Inc ....F 440 946-8002
   Mentor *(G-13570)*
Ronson Manufacturing Inc....................F 440 256-1463
   Willoughby *(G-20423)*
Stelfast Inc..E 440 879-0077
   Strongsville *(G-17797)*

BONDERIZING: Bonderizing, Metal Or Metal Prdts

Cardinal Rubber Company Inc ....E 330 745-2191
   Barberton *(G-1069)*
High Tech Elastomers Inc ....E 937 236-6575
   Vandalia *(G-19128)*
Kecamm LLC ....G 330 527-2918
   Garrettsville *(G-10194)*
Metaltek Industries Inc ....F 937 323-4933
   Springfield *(G-17447)*

BONDS, RAIL: Electric, Propulsion & Signal Circuit Uses

Omnithruster Inc ....F 330 963-6310
   Twinsburg *(G-18825)*

BOOK STORES

Bookfactory LLC ....E 937 226-7100
   Dayton *(G-8059)*
Province of St John The Baptis ....D 513 241-5615
   Cincinnati *(G-4219)*
US Government Publishing Off ....G 614 469-5657
   Columbus *(G-7566)*

BOOK STORES: Comic

Ketman Corporation ....G 330 262-1688
   Wooster *(G-20613)*

BOOK STORES: Religious

Incorporated Trst Gspl Wk Scty ....D 216 749-2100
   Cleveland *(G-5448)*

BOOKS, WHOLESALE

CSS Publishing Co Inc ....E 419 227-1818
   Lima *(G-11850)*
Hubbard Company ....E 419 784-4455
   Defiance *(G-8627)*
Wellington Wllams Wrldwide LLC ....G 423 805-6198
   Troy *(G-18718)*
Zaner-Bloser Inc.....................................D 614 486-0221
   Columbus *(G-7624)*
Zaner-Bloser Inc.....................................E 608 441-5555
   Columbus *(G-7625)*

BOOTHS: Spray, Sheet Metal, Prefabricated

Midwest Spray Booths ....G 937 439-6600
   Dayton *(G-8355)*
Paint Booth Pros Inc ....G 440 653-3982
   Amherst *(G-569)*

BORING MILL

Tri-State Tool Grinding Inc ....E 513 347-0100
   Cincinnati *(G-4436)*

BOTTLE CAPS & RESEALERS: Plastic

6s Products LLC ....G 937 394-7440
   Anna *(G-587)*
Berry Global Inc ....F 419 887-1602
   Maumee *(G-13080)*
Berry Global Inc ....F 330 896-6700
   Streetsboro *(G-17664)*
Takeya USA Corporation ....F 714 374-9900
   Columbus *(G-7509)*
Venture Packaging Midwest Inc ....F 419 465-2534
   Monroeville *(G-14293)*

BOTTLED GAS DEALERS: Propane

Brightstar Propane & Fuels ....G 614 891-8395
   Westerville *(G-19981)*
Jomac Ltd ....G 330 627-7727
   Carrollton *(G-2922)*
Ngo Development Corporation ....F 740 622-9560
   Coshocton *(G-7743)*

BOTTLED WATER DELIVERY

Bayswater Beverages LLC...................G 312 224-8012
   Cincinnati *(G-3383)*
Pro-Kleen Industrial Svcs Inc ....E 740 689-1886
   Lancaster *(G-11599)*

BOTTLES: Plastic

Al Root Company ....C 330 723-4359
   Medina *(G-13219)*
Al Root Company ....C 330 725-6677
   Medina *(G-13220)*
Alpha Packaging Holdings Inc ....B 216 252-5595
   Cleveland *(G-4675)*
Alpla Inc ....F 419 991-9484
   Lima *(G-11960)*
Eco-Groupe Inc ....F 937 898-2603
   Dayton *(G-8176)*
GK Packaging Inc ....D 614 873-3900
   Plain City *(G-16194)*

PRODUCT SECTION

BOXES: Corrugated

Graham Packaging Company LP ....E....... 419 334-4197
   Fremont *(G-10024)*
Graham Packaging Company LP ....E....... 513 874-1770
   West Chester *(G-19861)*
Graham Packaging Pet Tech Inc ....C....... 419 334-4197
   Fremont *(G-10025)*
Graham Packg Plastic Pdts Inc ....C....... 419 421-8037
   Findlay *(G-9695)*
Kirtland Cpitl Partners III LP ....G....... 440 585-9010
   Willoughby Hills *(G-20470)*
Novatex North America Inc ....D....... 419 282-4264
   Ashland *(G-728)*
Phoenix Technologies Intl LLC ....E....... 419 353-7738
   Bowling Green *(G-1990)*
Plastipak Packaging Inc ....B....... 937 596-6142
   Jackson Center *(G-11212)*
Plastipak Packaging Inc ....C....... 937 596-5166
   Jackson Center *(G-11213)*
Plastipak Packaging Inc ....C....... 740 928-4435
   Hebron *(G-10757)*
Pure Water Global Inc ....G....... 419 737-2352
   Pioneer *(G-16093)*
Quality-Service Products Inc ....F....... 614 447-9522
   Columbus *(G-7367)*
Rexam PLC ....G....... 330 893-2451
   Millersburg *(G-14122)*
Ring Container Tech LLC ....E....... 937 492-0961
   Sidney *(G-17066)*
Southeastern Container Inc ....D....... 419 352-6300
   Bowling Green *(G-2000)*

BOWL COVERS: Plastic

Mon-Say Corp ....G....... 419 720-0163
   Toledo *(G-18415)*

BOWLING CENTERS

Greater Cincinnati Bowl Assn ....E....... 513 761-7387
   Cincinnati *(G-3780)*

BOWLING EQPT & SPLY STORES

The Hartman Corp ....G....... 614 475-5035
   Columbus *(G-7525)*

BOWLING EQPT & SPLYS

Done-Rite Bowling Service Co ....E....... 440 232-3280
   Bedford *(G-1402)*
Forrest Enterprises Inc ....G....... 937 773-1714
   Piqua *(G-16116)*

BOXES & CRATES: Rectangular, Wood

Cima Inc ....E....... 513 382-8976
   Hamilton *(G-10546)*
Custom Built Crates Inc ....E....... 513 248-4422
   Milford *(G-14006)*
Dp Products LLC ....G....... 440 834-9663
   Burton *(G-2357)*
J & L Wood Products Inc ....E....... 937 667-4064
   Tipp City *(G-18119)*
Schaefer Box & Pallet Co ....E....... 513 738-2500
   Hamilton *(G-10603)*
Silvesco Inc ....F....... 740 373-6661
   Marietta *(G-12669)*
Terry Lumber and Supply Co ....F....... 330 659-6800
   Peninsula *(G-15899)*
VIP-Supply Chain Solutions LLC ....G....... 513 454-2020
   West Chester *(G-19818)*

BOXES & SHOOK: Nailed Wood

Caravan Packaging Inc ....F....... 440 243-4100
   Cleveland *(G-4875)*
Cassady Woodworks Inc ....F....... 937 256-7948
   Dayton *(G-7974)*
Clark Rm Inc ....E....... 419 425-9889
   Findlay *(G-9669)*
Dp Products LLC ....G....... 440 834-9663
   Burton *(G-2357)*
Hann Manufacturing Inc ....E....... 740 962-3752
   McConnelsville *(G-13206)*
Hines Builders Inc ....F....... 937 335-4586
   Troy *(G-18665)*
J & L Wood Products Inc ....E....... 937 667-4064
   Tipp City *(G-18119)*
Kennedy Group Incorporated ....D....... 440 951-7660
   Willoughby *(G-20352)*
Lima Pallet Company Inc ....E....... 419 229-5736
   Lima *(G-11889)*
Quadco Rehabilitation Ctr Inc ....B....... 419 682-1011
   Stryker *(G-17832)*
Schaefer Box & Pallet Co ....E....... 513 738-2500
   Hamilton *(G-10603)*
Van Orders Pallet Company Inc ....F....... 419 875-6932
   Swanton *(G-17928)*

BOXES: Corrugated

A-Kobak Container Company ....F....... 330 225-7791
   Hinckley *(G-10896)*
Adapt-A-Pak Inc ....E....... 937 845-0386
   Tipp City *(G-18098)*
Akers Packaging Service Inc ....C....... 513 422-6312
   Middletown *(G-13879)*
Akers Packaging Solutions Inc ....D....... 513 422-6312
   Middletown *(G-13880)*
Akers Packaging Solutions Inc ....E....... 304 525-0342
   Middletown *(G-13881)*
Alpha Container Co Inc ....F....... 937 644-5511
   Marysville *(G-12769)*
American Made Corrugated Packg ....F....... 937 981-2111
   Greenfield *(G-10346)*
Archbold Container Corp ....C....... 800 446-2520
   Archbold *(G-637)*
Argrov Box Co ....F....... 937 898-1700
   Dayton *(G-8036)*
B & B Box Company Inc ....F....... 419 872-5600
   Perrysburg *(G-15922)*
Basic Packaging Ltd ....F....... 330 634-9665
   Lima *(G-11961)*
BDS Packaging Inc ....D....... 937 643-0530
   Moraine *(G-14333)*
Bruce Box Co Inc ....G....... 740 533-0670
   Ironton *(G-11162)*
Bryan Packaging Inc ....F....... 419 636-2600
   Bryan *(G-2273)*
Buckeye Boxes Inc ....C....... 614 274-8484
   Columbus *(G-6707)*
Buckeye Boxes Inc ....F....... 937 599-2551
   Bellefontaine *(G-1508)*
Buckeye Corrugated Inc ....G....... 330 576-0590
   Fairlawn *(G-9599)*
Buckeye Corrugated Inc ....D....... 330 264-6336
   Wooster *(G-20575)*
Cambridge Packaging Inc ....E....... 740 432-3351
   Cambridge *(G-2430)*
Cameron Packaging Inc ....G....... 419 222-9404
   Lima *(G-11848)*
Cardinal Container Corporation ....E....... 614 497-3033
   Columbus *(G-6741)*
Chillicothe Packaging Corp ....E....... 740 773-5800
   Chillicothe *(G-3180)*
Clecorr Inc ....E....... 216 961-5500
   Cleveland *(G-4944)*
Container King Inc ....G....... 937 652-3087
   Urbana *(G-18986)*
Creative Packaging LLC ....E....... 740 452-8497
   Zanesville *(G-21124)*
Family Packaging Inc ....G....... 937 325-4106
   Springfield *(G-17401)*
Gatton Packaging Inc ....G....... 419 886-2577
   Bellville *(G-1556)*
Georgia-Pacific LLC ....C....... 740 477-3347
   Circleville *(G-4546)*
Graphic Paper Products Corp ....G....... 937 325-5503
   Springfield *(G-17407)*
Green Bay Packaging Inc ....F....... 419 332-5593
   Fremont *(G-10027)*
Green Bay Packaging Inc ....D....... 513 228-5560
   Lebanon *(G-11660)*
Greif Inc ....F....... 740 657-6500
   Delaware *(G-8682)*
Greif Inc ....E....... 740 549-6000
   Delaware *(G-8681)*
International Paper Company ....F....... 330 264-1322
   Wooster *(G-20607)*
International Paper Company ....C....... 740 363-9882
   Delaware *(G-8696)*
International Paper Company ....C....... 740 369-7691
   Delaware *(G-8697)*
International Paper Company ....D....... 740 522-3123
   Newark *(G-14888)*
Jet Container Company ....E....... 614 444-2133
   Columbus *(G-7066)*
JIT Packaging Inc ....G....... 513 934-0905
   Lebanon *(G-11665)*
Lewisburg Container Company ....C....... 937 962-2681
   Lewisburg *(G-11794)*
Menasha Packaging Company LLC ...F....... 740 773-8204
   Groveport *(G-10505)*
Miami Vly Packg Solutions Inc ....F....... 937 224-1800
   Dayton *(G-8348)*
Mid Ohio Packaging LLC ....E....... 740 383-9200
   Marion *(G-12719)*
Midwest Box Company ....E....... 216 281-9021
   Cleveland *(G-5678)*
Midwest Container Corporation ....E....... 513 870-3000
   Fairfield *(G-9529)*
Mount Vernon Packaging Inc ....F....... 740 397-3221
   Mount Vernon *(G-14494)*
N-Stock Box Inc ....E....... 513 423-0319
   Middletown *(G-13934)*
Northeast Box Company ....D....... 440 992-5500
   Ashtabula *(G-793)*
Novolex Holdings Inc ....B....... 937 746-1933
   Franklin *(G-9905)*
Omer J Smith Inc ....E....... 513 921-4717
   West Chester *(G-19754)*
Orora Packaging Solutions ....G....... 513 539-8274
   Monroe *(G-14274)*
Packaging Corporation America ....D....... 513 424-3542
   Middletown *(G-13939)*
Packaging Corporation America ....C....... 419 282-5809
   Ashland *(G-733)*
Packaging Corporation America ....G....... 513 860-1145
   Fairfield *(G-9543)*
Packaging Corporation America ....E....... 513 582-0690
   Cincinnati *(G-4130)*
Packaging Corporation America ....C....... 740 344-1126
   Newark *(G-14908)*
Packaging Corporation America ....E....... 330 644-9542
   Coventry Township *(G-7776)*
Pallet & Cont Corp of Amer ....G....... 419 255-1256
   Toledo *(G-18457)*
Pax Corrugated Products Inc ....D....... 513 932-9855
   Lebanon *(G-11682)*
Phillips Packaging Inc ....G....... 937 484-4702
   Urbana *(G-19008)*
Piqua Paper Box Company ....E....... 937 773-0313
   Piqua *(G-16155)*
Pjs Corrugated Inc ....F....... 419 644-3383
   Swanton *(G-17918)*
Pratt (jet Corr) Inc ....E....... 937 390-7100
   Springfield *(G-17473)*
Pro-Pak Industries Inc ....C....... 419 729-0751
   Maumee *(G-13139)*
R and D Incorporated ....E....... 216 581-6328
   Maple Heights *(G-12577)*
Riblet Packaging Co ....F....... 937 652-3087
   Urbana *(G-19009)*
Riverview Packaging Inc ....E....... 937 743-9530
   Franklin *(G-9915)*
Safeway Packaging Inc ....D....... 419 629-3200
   New Bremen *(G-14660)*
Schwarz Partners Packaging LLC ......F....... 317 290-1140
   Sidney *(G-17073)*
Skybox Investments Inc ....E....... 419 525-6013
   Mansfield *(G-12514)*
Smith-Lustig Paper Box Mfg Co ....E....... 216 621-0453
   Bedford *(G-1446)*
Square One Solutions LLC ....F....... 419 425-5445
   Findlay *(G-9761)*
Summit Container Corporation ....E....... 719 481-8400
   West Chester *(G-19802)*
Tavens Container Inc ....D....... 216 883-3333
   Bedford *(G-1448)*
Tecumseh Packg Solutions Inc ....E....... 419 238-1122
   Van Wert *(G-19106)*
Unipac Inc ....E....... 740 929-2000
   Hebron *(G-10769)*
US Corrugated of Massillon ....F....... 216 663-3344
   Maple Heights *(G-12583)*
Value Added Packaging Inc ....F....... 937 832-9595
   Englewood *(G-9381)*
Verso Corporation ....D....... 901 369-4105
   Miamisburg *(G-13733)*
Westrock Cp LLC ....B....... 513 745-2400
   Blue Ash *(G-1868)*
Westrock Cp LLC ....D....... 770 448-2193
   Wshngtn CT Hs *(G-20750)*
Westrock Cp LLC ....C....... 330 297-0841
   Ravenna *(G-16419)*
Westrock Rkt LLC ....E....... 513 860-5546
   West Chester *(G-19821)*
Westrock Usc Inc ....C....... 740 681-1600
   Lancaster *(G-11618)*
Westrock Usc Inc ....G....... 740 484-1000
   Bethesda *(G-1659)*
Weyerhaeuser Co Containeerboar ....E....... 740 397-5215
   Mount Vernon *(G-14518)*

Employee Codes: A=Over 500 employees, B=251-500
C=101-250, D=51-100, E=20-50, F=10-19, G=3-9

BOXES: Corrugated

Weyerhaeuser Company .... D 740 335-4480
   Wshngtn CT Hs *(G-20751)*

BOXES: Filing, Paperboard Made From Purchased Materials

A To Z Paper Box Co .... G 330 325-8722
   Rootstown *(G-16565)*

BOXES: Fuse, Electric

Tri-Fab Inc .... E 330 337-3425
   Salem *(G-16777)*

BOXES: Mail Or Post Office, Collection/Storage, Sheet Metal

Salsbury Industries Inc .... C 614 409-1600
   Columbus *(G-7417)*

BOXES: Packing & Shipping, Metal

Karyall-Telday Inc .... E 216 281-4063
   Cleveland *(G-5516)*
Yarder Manufacturing Company .... D 419 476-3933
   Toledo *(G-18603)*
Yarder Manufacturing Company .... G 419 269-3474
   Toledo *(G-18604)*

BOXES: Paperboard, Folding

B & L Labels and Packg Co Inc .... G 937 773-9080
   Piqua *(G-16103)*
Bell Ohio Inc .... F 605 332-6721
   Groveport *(G-10485)*
Boxit Corporation .... G 216 416-9475
   Cleveland *(G-4835)*
Boxit Corporation .... D 216 631-6900
   Cleveland *(G-4834)*
Carton Service Incorporated .... B 419 342-5010
   Shelby *(G-16980)*
Chilcote Company .... C 216 781-6000
   Cleveland *(G-4922)*
Graphic Packaging Intl Inc .... C 513 424-4200
   Middletown *(G-13911)*
Graphic Packaging Intl Inc .... C 440 248-4370
   Solon *(G-17153)*
Graphic Packaging Intl LLC .... C 740 387-6543
   Marion *(G-12707)*
Jefferson Smurfit Corporation .... G 440 248-4370
   Solon *(G-17175)*
Oak Hills Carton Co .... E 513 948-4200
   Cincinnati *(G-4095)*
RR Donnelley & Sons Company .... G 513 870-4040
   West Chester *(G-19789)*
Sandusky Packaging Corporation .... E 419 626-8520
   Sandusky *(G-16846)*
The Shelby Co .... E 440 871-9901
   Westlake *(G-20167)*
Therm-O-Packaging Suppliers .... F 440 543-5188
   Chagrin Falls *(G-3082)*
Unipac Inc .... E 740 929-2000
   Hebron *(G-10769)*
Yuckon International Corp .... G 216 361-2103
   Cleveland *(G-6334)*

BOXES: Paperboard, Set-Up

Boxit Corporation .... D 216 631-6900
   Cleveland *(G-4834)*
Boxit Corporation .... G 216 416-9475
   Cleveland *(G-4835)*
Chilcote Company .... C 216 781-6000
   Cleveland *(G-4922)*
Clarke-Boxit Corporation .... G 716 487-1950
   Cleveland *(G-4938)*
Graphic Paper Products Corp .... D 937 325-5503
   Springfield *(G-17407)*
R and D Incorporated .... E 216 581-6328
   Maple Heights *(G-12577)*
Sandusky Packaging Corporation .... E 419 626-8520
   Sandusky *(G-16846)*

BOXES: Plastic

Chatelain Plastics Inc .... G 419 422-4323
   Findlay *(G-9667)*
Metro Recycling Company .... G 513 251-1800
   Cincinnati *(G-4017)*
Oldcastle Precast Inc .... E 419 592-2309
   Napoleon *(G-14554)*

Triple Diamond Plastics LLC .... G 419 533-0085
   Liberty Center *(G-11810)*

BOXES: Stamped Metal

Roper Lockbox LLC .... G 330 656-5148
   Hudson *(G-11071)*

BOXES: Tool Chests, Wood

H Gerstner & Sons Inc .... E 937 228-1662
   Dayton *(G-8241)*

BOXES: Wooden

Aslan Worldwide .... F 513 671-0671
   West Chester *(G-19653)*
Boxes & Such .... G 440 237-7122
   Wooster *(G-20574)*
Buckeye Diamond Logistics Inc .... C 937 462-8361
   South Charleston *(G-17271)*
Built-Rite Box & Crate Inc .... E 330 263-0936
   Wooster *(G-20577)*
Cedar Craft Products Inc .... E 614 759-1600
   Blacklick *(G-1681)*
Damar Products Inc .... F 937 492-9023
   Sidney *(G-17025)*
Damar Products Inc .... F 937 492-9023
   Sidney *(G-17026)*
Forest City Companies Inc .... E 216 586-5279
   Cleveland *(G-5261)*
Lefco Worthington LLC .... E 216 432-4422
   Cleveland *(G-5571)*
Ohio Box & Crate Inc .... F 440 526-3133
   Burton *(G-2366)*
Sterling Industries Inc .... F 419 523-3788
   Ottawa *(G-15666)*
Thomas J Weaver Inc .... F 740 622-2040
   Coshocton *(G-7755)*
Traveling & Recycle Wood Pdts .... F 419 968-2649
   Middle Point *(G-13757)*
World Express Packaging Corp .... G 216 634-9000
   Cleveland *(G-6324)*
Zak Box Co Inc .... G 216 961-5636
   Cleveland *(G-6337)*

BRAKES & BRAKE PARTS

Advics Manufacturing Ohio Inc .... A 513 932-7878
   Lebanon *(G-11631)*
Buckeye Brake Manufacturing .... F 740 782-1379
   Morristown *(G-14406)*
Carlisle Brake & Friction Inc .... F 440 528-4000
   Solon *(G-17123)*
Cooper-Standard Automotive Inc .... B 740 342-3523
   New Lexington *(G-14714)*
Friction Products Co .... B 330 725-4941
   Medina *(G-13265)*
Harco Manufacturing Group LLC .... B 937 528-5000
   Moraine *(G-14359)*
Harco Manufacturing Group LLC .... C 937 528-5000
   Moraine *(G-14360)*
Hebco Products Inc .... A 419 562-7987
   Bucyrus *(G-2333)*
International Brake Inds Inc .... C 419 227-4421
   Lima *(G-11879)*
Kerr Friction Products Inc .... E 330 455-3983
   Canton *(G-2723)*
Nissin Brake Ohio Inc .... A 419 420-3800
   Findlay *(G-9731)*
Nissin Brake Ohio Inc .... E 937 642-7556
   East Liberty *(G-9049)*
Undercar Express LLC .... E 216 531-7004
   Cleveland *(G-6229)*
Vehicle Systems Inc .... G 330 854-0535
   Massillon *(G-13056)*
Veoneer Nissin Brake .... B 419 425-6725
   Findlay *(G-9773)*
Whirlaway Corporation .... C 440 647-4711
   Wellington *(G-19595)*

BRAKES: Bicycle, Friction Clutch & Other

Carlisle Brake & Friction Inc .... E 330 725-4941
   Medina *(G-13234)*
Carlisle Brake & Friction Inc .... C 440 528-4000
   Solon *(G-17124)*
Multi-Design Inc .... G 440 275-2255
   Austinburg *(G-923)*

BRAKES: Electromagnetic

Beckworth Industries Inc .... G 216 268-5557
   Cleveland *(G-4801)*

BRAKES: Metal Forming

Ata Tools Inc .... D 330 928-7744
   Cuyahoga Falls *(G-7844)*
Eaton Corporation .... C 216 281-2211
   Cleveland *(G-5147)*
Ebog Legacy Inc .... D 330 239-4933
   Sharon Center *(G-16949)*

BRASS & BRONZE PRDTS: Die-casted

Akron Brass Company .... E 309 444-4440
   Wooster *(G-20556)*
Hamilton Brass & Alum Castings .... E 513 867-0400
   Hamilton *(G-10567)*
Model Pattern & Foundry Co .... E 513 542-2322
   Cincinnati *(G-4036)*
Ryder-Heil Bronze Inc .... E 419 562-2841
   Bucyrus *(G-2343)*

BRASS FOUNDRY, NEC

Anchor Bronze and Metals Inc .... E 440 549-5653
   Cleveland *(G-4705)*
Brost Foundry Company .... F 419 522-1133
   Mansfield *(G-12415)*
Bunting Bearings LLC .... D 419 866-7000
   Holland *(G-10917)*
Maass Midwest Mfg Inc .... G 419 894-6424
   Arcadia *(G-625)*
National Brass Company Inc .... E 216 651-8530
   Cleveland *(G-5723)*
Non-Ferrous Casting Co .... G 937 228-1162
   Dayton *(G-8382)*

BRAZING SVCS

Braze Solutions LLC .... F 440 349-5100
   Solon *(G-17119)*
Paulo Products Company .... E 440 942-0153
   Willoughby *(G-20399)*

BRAZING: Metal

Advanced Flame Hardening Inc .... G 216 431-0370
   Cleveland *(G-4625)*
American Metal Treating Co .... E 216 431-4492
   Cleveland *(G-4692)*
Brazing Service Inc .... G 440 871-1120
   Westlake *(G-20104)*
Fbf Limited .... E 513 541-6300
   Cincinnati *(G-3679)*
HI Tecmetal Group Inc .... E 216 881-8100
   Cleveland *(G-5402)*
HI Tecmetal Group Inc .... E 440 946-2280
   Willoughby *(G-20337)*
J W Harris Co Inc .... F 216 481-8100
   Euclid *(G-9421)*
Kando of Cincinnati Inc .... E 513 459-7782
   Lebanon *(G-11668)*
Ohio Flame Hardening Company .... G 513 336-6160
   Lebanon *(G-11678)*
Ohio Flame Hardening Company .... E 513 733-5162
   Cincinnati *(G-4102)*
Surface Enhancement Tech LLC .... F 513 561-1520
   Cincinnati *(G-4400)*
Wall Colmonoy Corporation .... F 937 278-9111
   Cincinnati *(G-4487)*
Zion Industries Inc .... D 330 225-3246
   Valley City *(G-19070)*

BRIC-A-BRAC

CM Paula Company .... E 513 759-7473
   Mason *(G-12849)*

BRICK, STONE & RELATED PRDTS WHOLESALERS

Grafton Ready Mix Concrete Inc .... E 440 926-2911
   Grafton *(G-10302)*
Kuhlman Corporation .... C 419 897-6000
   Maumee *(G-13124)*
Lancaster West Side Coal Co .... F 740 862-4713
   Lancaster *(G-11582)*
Modern Builders Supply Inc .... F 419 526-0002
   Mansfield *(G-12485)*

PRODUCT SECTION — BUILDING & STRUCTURAL WOOD MEMBERS

Modern Builders Supply Inc ....C...... 419 241-3961
  Toledo (G-18414)
Myko Industries ....G...... 216 431-0900
  Cleveland (G-5717)
Ohio Beauty Inc ....G...... 330 644-2241
  Akron (G-305)
R W Sidley Incorporated ....E...... 330 793-7374
  Youngstown (G-21012)
Sidwell Materials Inc ....C...... 740 849-2394
  Zanesville (G-21180)
Stamm Contracting Co Inc ....E...... 330 274-8230
  Mantua (G-12560)
Trumbull Cement Products Co ....G...... 330 372-4342
  Warren (G-19450)
Wallseye Concrete Corp ....F...... 419 483-2738
  Castalia (G-2941)
Warren Concrete and Supply Co .....F...... 330 393-1581
  Warren (G-19458)
William Dauch Concrete Company ...F...... 419 668-4458
  Norwalk (G-15418)

BRICKS & BLOCKS: Structural

Belden Brick Company LLC ....C...... 330 456-0031
  Sugarcreek (G-17843)
Belden Brick Company LLC ....E...... 330 265-2030
  Sugarcreek (G-17844)
Glen-Gery Corporation ....E...... 419 468-5002
  Iberia (G-11113)
Meridian Brick LLC ....G...... 937 294-1548
  Franklin (G-9899)

BRICKS : Ceramic Glazed, Clay

Afc Company ....F...... 330 533-5581
  Canfield (G-2519)
Nutro Inc ....E...... 440 572-3800
  Strongsville (G-17773)
Wk Brick Company ....G...... 614 416-6700
  Columbus (G-7607)

BRICKS : Paving, Clay

Whitacre Greer Company ....E...... 330 823-1610
  Alliance (G-515)

BRICKS : Clay

Bowerston Shale Company ....E...... 740 763-3921
  Newark (G-14856)
Bowerston Shale Company ....E...... 740 269-2921
  Bowerston (G-1939)
Glen-Gery Corporation ....D...... 419 845-3321
  Caledonia (G-2416)

BRICKS: Concrete

Belden Brick Company LLC ....C...... 330 456-0031
  Sugarcreek (G-17843)
Belden Brick Company LLC ....E...... 330 265-2030
  Sugarcreek (G-17844)

BRIDAL SHOPS

Beverly Snider ....G...... 614 837-5817
  Columbus (G-6665)
Brahler Inc ....G...... 330 966-7730
  Canton (G-2597)

BRIDGE COMPONENTS: Bridge sections, prefabricated, highway

DS Techstar Inc ....G...... 419 424-0888
  Findlay (G-9681)

BROACHING MACHINES

Accurate Machining & Welding ....G...... 937 584-4518
  Sabina (G-16615)
Ohio Broach & Machine Company ....E...... 440 946-1040
  Willoughby (G-20393)

BROADCASTING & COMMS EQPT: Antennas, Transmitting/Comms

AG Antenna Group LLC ....F...... 513 289-6521
  Cincinnati (G-3309)
Central USA Wireless LLC ....E...... 513 469-1500
  Cincinnati (G-3459)
Electro-Magwave Inc ....G...... 216 453-1160
  Cleveland (G-5164)
Watts Antenna Company ....G...... 740 797-9380
  The Plains (G-18024)

BROADCASTING & COMMS EQPT: Rcvr-Transmitter Unt, Transceiver

Control Industries Inc ....G...... 937 653-7694
  Findlay (G-9671)

BROADCASTING & COMMUNICATIONS EQPT: Cellular Radio Telephone

Radio Hospital ....G...... 419 679-1103
  Kenton (G-11419)

BROADCASTING & COMMUNICATIONS EQPT: Light Comms Eqpt

Armada Power LLC ....G...... 614 204-9341
  Columbus (G-6615)
LSI Industries Inc ....B...... 513 793-3200
  Blue Ash (G-1811)

BROADCASTING STATIONS, RADIO: Music Format

Tomahawk Entertainment Group ......G...... 216 505-0548
  Cleveland (G-6180)

BROKERS' SVCS

Shamrock Companies Inc ....D...... 440 899-9510
  Westlake (G-20158)

BROKERS, MARINE TRANSPORTATION

Ogc Industries Inc ....F...... 330 456-1500
  Canton (G-2770)

BROKERS: Contract Basis

Tewell & Associates ....G...... 440 543-5190
  Chagrin Falls (G-3081)

BROKERS: Food

General Mills Inc ....D...... 513 770-0558
  Mason (G-12876)
Homestat Farm Ltd ....E...... 614 718-3060
  Dublin (G-8924)
Shaker Valley Foods Inc ....E...... 216 961-8600
  Cleveland (G-6046)

BROKERS: Log & Lumber

Hochstetler Milling LLC ....E...... 419 368-0004
  Loudonville (G-12143)
Kenneth Schrock ....G...... 937 544-7566
  West Union (G-19964)
Ned A Shreve ....G...... 740 732-6465
  Sarahsville (G-16866)

BROKERS: Printing

C Massouh Printing Co Inc ....G...... 330 832-6334
  Massillon (G-12964)
Scrip-Safe Security Products ....E...... 513 697-7789
  Loveland (G-12230)

BRONZE FOUNDRY, NEC

Advance Bronzehubco Div ....E...... 304 232-4414
  Lodi (G-12004)
Foundry Artist Inc ....G...... 216 391-9030
  Cleveland (G-5268)
Meierjohan-Wengler Inc ....F...... 513 771-6074
  Cincinnati (G-4002)

BRONZE ROLLING & DRAWING

Jj Seville LLC ....E...... 330 769-2071
  Seville (G-16918)

BROOMS & BRUSHES

Deco Tools Inc ....E...... 419 476-9321
  Toledo (G-18256)
Demel Enterprises Inc ....G...... 740 331-1400
  Athens (G-827)
Designetics Inc ....D...... 419 866-0700
  Holland (G-10925)
Fimm USA Inc ....F...... 253 243-1522
  Columbus (G-6922)
Hoge Lumber Company ....F...... 419 753-2351
  New Knoxville (G-14704)
Mill Rose Laboratories Inc ....E...... 440 974-6730
  Mentor (G-13519)
Stephen M Trudick ....E...... 440 834-1891
  Burton (G-2371)
Unique Packaging & Printing ....F...... 440 785-6730
  Mentor (G-13618)

BROOMS & BRUSHES: Household Or Indl

Brushes Inc ....E...... 216 267-8084
  Cleveland (G-4847)
Malish Corporation ....C...... 440 951-5356
  Mentor (G-13509)
Mill-Rose Company ....C...... 440 255-9171
  Mentor (G-13520)
Ohio Brush Company ....F...... 216 791-3265
  Cleveland (G-5802)
Ohio Carbon Company ....G...... 216 251-7274
  Ashland (G-729)
Precision Brush Co ....F...... 440 542-9600
  Solon (G-17218)
Spiral Brushes Inc ....E...... 330 686-2861
  Stow (G-17629)
Tod Thin Brushes Inc ....F...... 440 576-6859
  Jefferson (G-11242)
Trent Manufacturing Company ....F...... 216 391-1551
  Cleveland (G-6204)
United Rotary Brush Inc ....D...... 937 644-3515
  Plain City (G-16214)

BROOMS & BRUSHES: Paint & Varnish

D A L E S Corporation ....F...... 419 255-5335
  Toledo (G-18250)
Wooster Brush Company ....G...... 440 322-8081
  Elyria (G-9347)

BROOMS & BRUSHES: Street Sweeping, Hand Or Machine

Public Works Dept Street Div ....E...... 740 283-6013
  Steubenville (G-17549)
Taupe Holdings Co ....G...... 614 330-4600
  Dublin (G-9002)

BRUSH BLOCKS: Carbon Or Molded Graphite

Buckeye Molded Products Ltd ....F...... 440 323-2244
  Elyria (G-9226)

BRUSHES & BRUSH STOCK CONTACTS: Electric

Ohio Power Tool Brush Co ....G...... 419 736-3010
  Ashland (G-731)

BUCKETS: Plastic

Graham Packaging Co Europe LLC ..C...... 513 398-5000
  Mason (G-12882)
Impact Products LLC ....C...... 419 841-2891
  Toledo (G-18342)

BUFFING FOR THE TRADE

Anchor Fabricators Inc ....E...... 937 836-5117
  Clayton (G-4571)
Buffex Metal Finishing Inc ....F...... 216 631-2202
  Cleveland (G-4851)
Reliable Buffing Co Inc ....G...... 419 647-4432
  Spencerville (G-17312)
S & K Metal Polsg & Buffing ....G...... 513 732-6662
  Batavia (G-1182)

BUILDING & OFFICE CLEANING SVCS

Cbr Industrial Llc ....G...... 419 645-6447
  Wapakoneta (G-19326)
High-TEC Industrial Services ....C...... 937 667-1772
  Tipp City (G-18115)
Image By J & K LLC ....B...... 888 667-6929
  Maumee (G-13118)
Taupe Holdings Co ....G...... 614 330-4600
  Dublin (G-9002)

BUILDING & STRUCTURAL WOOD MEMBERS

Baker McMillen Co ....E...... 330 923-3303
  Stow (G-17573)
Byler Truss ....G...... 330 465-5412
  Ashland (G-688)

Employee Codes: A=Over 500 employees, B=251-500
C=101-250, D=51-100, E=20-50, F=10-19, G=3-9

BUILDING & STRUCTURAL WOOD MEMBERS — PRODUCT SECTION

Carter-Jones Lumber Company ....C 330 674-9060
  Millersburg (G-14077)
Holmes Lumber & Bldg Ctr Inc ....C 330 674-9060
  Millersburg (G-14098)
Laminate Technologies Inc ....D 419 448-0812
  Tiffin (G-18064)
Minova USA Inc ....D 740 377-9146
  South Point (G-17289)
Socar of Ohio Inc ....D 419 596-3100
  Continental (G-7668)

BUILDING & STRUCTURAL WOOD MEMBERS: Arches, Laminated Lumber

Richland Laminated Columns LLC ....F 419 895-0036
  Greenwich (G-10407)

BUILDING CLEANING & MAINTENANCE SVCS

All Pack Services LLC ....F 614 935-0964
  Grove City (G-10413)
City of Kent ....F 330 673-8897
  Kent (G-11304)
Contract Lumber Inc ....D 614 751-1109
  Columbus (G-6814)
Hopewell Industries Inc ....D 740 622-3563
  Coshocton (G-7737)
Obersons Nurs & Landscapes Inc ....F 513 894-0669
  Fairfield (G-9538)
Phase II Enterprises Inc ....G 330 484-2113
  Canton (G-2784)
Richland Newhope Industries ....F 419 774-4400
  Mansfield (G-12506)
Rossi Machinery Services Inc ....G 419 281-4488
  Ashland (G-744)

BUILDING CLEANING SVCS

Leadec Corp ....E 513 731-3590
  Blue Ash (G-1804)

BUILDING COMPONENT CLEANING SVCS

Cincinnati A Flter Sls Svc Inc ....E 513 242-3400
  Cincinnati (G-3478)

BUILDING COMPONENTS: Structural Steel

American Qulty Fabrication Inc ....G 937 742-7001
  Vandalia (G-19116)
Applied Engneered Surfaces Inc ....F 440 366-0440
  Elyria (G-9218)
Boardman Steel Inc ....D 330 758-0951
  Columbiana (G-6455)
Dietrich Industries Inc ....C 330 372-4014
  Warren (G-19395)
Dietrich Industries Inc ....F 614 438-3210
  Worthington (G-20683)
Dietrich Industries Inc ....D 216 472-1511
  Cleveland (G-5095)
Dietrich Industries Inc ....E 614 438-3210
  Worthington (G-20684)
Frederick Steel Company LLC ....D 513 821-6400
  Cincinnati (G-3712)
Fwt LLC ....G 419 542-1420
  Hicksville (G-10778)
GL Nause Co Inc ....E 513 722-9500
  Loveland (G-12192)
J A McMahon Incorporated ....E 330 652-2588
  Niles (G-15017)
J&J Precision Machine Ltd ....E 330 923-5783
  Cuyahoga Falls (G-7883)
Kirwan Industries Inc ....G 513 333-0766
  Cincinnati (G-3913)
Louis Arthur Steel Company ....G 440 997-5545
  Geneva (G-10224)
M & M Fabrication Inc ....F 740 779-3071
  Chillicothe (G-3199)
Mad River Steel Ltd ....G 937 845-4046
  New Carlisle (G-14671)
Mc Elwain Industries Inc ....F 419 532-3126
  Ottawa (G-15658)
Minova USA Inc ....B 740 269-8100
  Bowerston (G-1941)
Mound Technologies Inc ....E 937 748-2937
  Springboro (G-17338)
Northeast Ohio Contractors LLC ....G 216 269-7881
  Cleveland (G-5775)
Nova Structural Steel Inc ....F 216 938-7476
  Cleveland (G-5788)
Rol- Fab Inc ....E 216 662-2500
  Cleveland (G-6001)
Steelcon LLC ....G 330 457-4003
  New Waterford (G-14843)
Thomas Steel Inc ....E 419 483-7540
  Bellevue (G-1549)
Turn-Key Industrial Svcs LLC ....D 614 274-1128
  Columbus (G-7551)
Unique Fabrications Inc ....F 419 355-1700
  Fremont (G-10060)
Universal Fabg Cnstr Svcs Inc ....D 614 274-1128
  Columbus (G-7561)
Waterford Tank Fabrication Ltd ....D 740 984-4100
  Beverly (G-1663)
Wernli Realty Inc ....F 937 258-7878
  Beavercreek (G-1368)
Wm Lang & Sons Company ....F 513 541-3304
  Cincinnati (G-4515)

BUILDING ITEM REPAIR SVCS, MISCELLANEOUS

IV J Telecommunications LLC ....G 606 694-1762
  South Point (G-17284)

BUILDING MAINTENANCE SVCS, EXC REPAIRS

Lima Sheet Metal Machine & Mfg ....E 419 229-1161
  Lima (G-11893)

BUILDING PRDTS & MATERIALS DEALERS

Adams Brothers Inc ....F 740 819-0323
  Zanesville (G-21093)
Avon Concrete Corporation ....G 440 937-6264
  Avon (G-941)
Building Concepts Inc ....F 419 298-2371
  Edgerton (G-9169)
Carter-Jones Lumber Company ....C 330 674-9060
  Millersburg (G-14077)
Consumeracq Inc ....C 440 277-9305
  Lorain (G-12084)
Consumers Builders Supply Co ....E 440 277-9306
  Lorain (G-12085)
Contract Lumber Inc ....D 614 751-1109
  Columbus (G-6814)
Counter Concepts Inc ....F 330 848-4848
  Doylestown (G-8864)
Dearth Resources Inc ....G 937 325-0651
  Springfield (G-17384)
Dnl Oil Corp ....G 740 342-4970
  New Lexington (G-14715)
Fort Loramie Cast Stone Pdts ....G 937 420-2257
  Fort Loramie (G-9798)
Friends Ornamental Iron Co ....E 216 431-6710
  Cleveland (G-5275)
Great Lakes Window Inc ....A 419 666-5555
  Walbridge (G-19294)
Holmes Lumber & Bldg Ctr Inc ....C 330 674-9060
  Millersburg (G-14098)
Holmes Panel ....G 330 897-5040
  Baltic (G-1031)
Hull Builders Supply Inc ....E 440 967-3159
  Vermilion (G-19161)
Judy Mills Company Inc ....E 513 271-4241
  Cincinnati (G-3887)
K M B Inc ....E 330 889-3451
  Bristolville (G-2082)
Khempco Bldg Sup Co Ltd Partnr ....D 740 549-0465
  Delaware (G-8700)
Lancaster West Side Coal Co ....F 740 862-4713
  Lancaster (G-11582)
Lang Stone Company Inc ....D 614 235-4099
  Columbus (G-7114)
Martin Block Company ....G 740 286-7507
  Jackson (G-11190)
Menard Inc ....C 513 583-1444
  Loveland (G-12214)
Osborne Inc ....E 440 942-7000
  Mentor (G-13539)
Portsmouth Block Inc ....F 740 353-4113
  Portsmouth (G-16295)
Stamm Contracting Co Inc ....E 330 274-8230
  Mantua (G-12560)
T C Redi Mix Youngstown Inc ....E 330 755-2143
  Youngstown (G-21042)
Terry Lumber and Supply Co ....F 330 659-6800
  Peninsula (G-15899)
Tri-County Block and Brick Inc ....E 419 826-7060
  Swanton (G-17925)
Trumbull Cement Products Co ....G 330 372-4342
  Warren (G-19450)
Tyjen Inc ....G 740 380-3215
  Logan (G-12045)
Vances Department Store ....G 937 549-2188
  Manchester (G-12397)
Vances Department Store ....F 937 549-3033
  Manchester (G-12398)
Warren Concrete and Supply Co ....F 330 393-1581
  Warren (G-19458)
Wilson Concrete Products Inc ....E 937 885-7965
  Dayton (G-8594)
Zaenkert Surveying Essentials ....G 513 738-2917
  Okeana (G-15522)

BUILDING PRDTS: Concrete

Baswa Acoustics North Amer LLC ....F 216 475-7197
  Bedford (G-1388)
Evan Ragouzis Co ....G 513 242-5900
  Hamilton (G-10555)
Kcg Inc ....G 614 238-9450
  Columbus (G-7084)
Motz Mobile Containers Inc ....G 513 772-6689
  Cincinnati (G-4050)
Olde Wood Ltd ....E 330 866-1441
  Magnolia (G-12361)
One Wish LLC ....G 800 505-6883
  Beachwood (G-1259)
Patriot Holdings Unlimited LLC ....G 740 574-2112
  Wheelersburg (G-20183)
Tamarron Technology Inc ....F 800 277-3207
  Cincinnati (G-4404)

BUILDING PRDTS: Stone

Davids Stone Company LLC ....G 740 373-1996
  Marietta (G-12618)
Jalco Industries Inc ....F 740 286-3808
  Jackson (G-11188)

BUILDING SCALES MODELS

3-D Technical Services Company ....E 937 746-2901
  Franklin (G-9866)

BUILDING STONE, ARTIFICIAL: Concrete

Provia LLC ....F 330 852-4711
  Sugarcreek (G-17860)

BUILDINGS & COMPONENTS: Prefabricated Metal

Benchmark Archtectural Systems ....E 614 444-0110
  Columbus (G-6662)
Benko Products Inc ....E 440 934-2180
  Sheffield Village (G-16966)
Better Built Barns ....G 606 348-6146
  Winchester (G-20518)
Cdc Fab Co ....F 419 866-7705
  Maumee (G-13082)
Consolidatd Analytical Sys Inc ....E 513 542-1200
  Cleves (G-6359)
Cover Up Building Systems ....G 740 668-8985
  Martinsburg (G-12765)
Haz-Safe LLC ....F 330 793-0900
  Austintown (G-933)
Hoge Lumber Company ....E 419 753-2263
  New Knoxville (G-14703)
Lab-Pro Inc ....G 937 434-9600
  Dayton (G-8304)
Morton Buildings Inc ....G 419 399-4549
  Paulding (G-15866)
ONeals Tarpaulin & Awning Co ....F 330 788-6504
  Youngstown (G-20985)
R L Torbeck Industries Inc ....D 513 367-0080
  Harrison (G-10667)
Rebsco Inc ....F 937 548-2246
  Greenville (G-10390)
Reliable Metal Buildings LLC ....G 419 737-1300
  Pioneer (G-16096)
Skyline Corporation ....C 330 852-2483
  Sugarcreek (G-17864)
Sorta 4 U LLC ....G 440 365-0091
  Elyria (G-9330)
Storage Buildings Unlimited ....G 216 731-0010
  Doylestown (G-8866)
Will-Burt Advnced Cmpsites Inc ....F 330 684-5286
  Orrville (G-15625)

BUILDINGS, PREFABRICATED: Wholesalers

Lab-Pro Inc		G	937 434-9600
Dayton (G-8304)			

BUILDINGS: Farm & Utility

Barncraft Storage Buildings		G	513 738-5654
Hamilton (G-10537)			
Morton Buildings Inc		D	419 675-2311
Kenton (G-11415)			
Vinyl Tech Storage Barn		G	330 674-5670
Millersburg (G-14143)			

BUILDINGS: Farm, Prefabricated Or Portable, Wood

Millers Storage Barns LLC		E	330 893-3293
Millersburg (G-14113)			

BUILDINGS: Portable

Affordable Barn Co Ltd		F	330 674-3001
Millersburg (G-14055)			
Golden Giant Inc		E	419 674-4038
Kenton (G-11405)			
Jack Walters & Sons Corp		F	937 653-8986
Urbana (G-18999)			
Mobile Mini Inc		E	303 305-9515
Canton (G-2756)			
Mobile Mini Inc		F	614 449-8655
Columbus (G-7188)			
Morton Buildings Inc		F	330 345-6188
Wooster (G-20628)			

BUILDINGS: Prefabricated, Metal

Enclosure Suppliers LLC		E	513 782-3900
Cincinnati (G-3637)			
Great Day Improvements LLC		G	330 468-0700
Macedonia (G-12300)			
Joyce Manufacturing Co		D	440 239-9100
Berea (G-1615)			
Nci Building Systems Inc		C	937 584-3300
Middletown (G-13936)			
Rayhaven Group Inc		F	330 659-3183
Richfield (G-16484)			
Rupcol Inc		G	419 924-5215
West Unity (G-19974)			

BUILDINGS: Prefabricated, Plastic

J & M Construction LLP		G	740 454-8986
Hopewell (G-10993)			

BUILDINGS: Prefabricated, Wood

Americraft Stor Buildings Ltd		G	330 877-6900
Hartville (G-10684)			
Beachy Barns Ltd		F	614 873-4193
Plain City (G-16177)			
Fifth Avenue Lumber Co		D	614 833-6655
Canal Winchester (G-2503)			
J Aaron Weaver		G	440 474-9185
Rome (G-16562)			
Morton Buildings Inc		D	419 675-2311
Kenton (G-11415)			
Patio Enclosures		F	513 733-4646
Cincinnati (G-4135)			
Rona Enterprises Inc		G	740 927-9971
Pataskala (G-15841)			
Skyline Corporation		C	330 852-2483
Sugarcreek (G-17864)			
Vinyl Design Corporation		E	419 283-4009
Holland (G-10965)			

BUILDINGS: Prefabricated, Wood

Carter-Jones Lumber Company		F	440 834-8164
Middlefield (G-13782)			
Consolidatd Analytical Sys Inc		F	513 542-1200
Cleves (G-6359)			
Hershbergers Dutch Market LLP		E	740 489-5322
Old Washington (G-15526)			
Nef Ltd		G	419 445-6696
Archbold (G-661)			
Smiths Sawdust Studio		G	740 484-4656
Bethesda (G-1658)			
Twin Oaks Barn		F	330 893-3126
Dundee (G-9030)			
Weaver Barns Ltd		F	330 852-2103
Sugarcreek (G-17876)			

BULLETIN BOARDS: Cork

GMI Companies Inc		G	937 981-0244
Greenfield (G-10348)			
Michael Kaufman Companies Inc		F	330 673-4881
Kent (G-11353)			
Michael Kaufman Companies Inc		F	330 673-4881
Kent (G-11354)			
Mpc Inc		F	440 835-1405
Cleveland (G-5707)			

BULLETIN BOARDS: Wood

GMI Companies Inc		C	513 932-3445
Lebanon (G-11657)			
Tri-State Supply Co Inc		F	614 272-6767
Columbus (G-7543)			

BULLETPROOF VESTS

Forceone LLC		E	513 939-1018
Hebron (G-10743)			

BUOYS: Metal

Worthington Products Inc		G	330 452-7400
Canton (G-2865)			

BUOYS: Plastic

Worthignton Products Inc		G	330 452-7400
Canton (G-2865)			

BURGLAR ALARM MAINTENANCE & MONITORING SVCS

Area Wide Protective Inc		E	513 321-9889
Fairfield (G-9483)			

BURIAL VAULTS, FIBERGLASS

McCord Products Inc		F	419 352-3691
Bowling Green (G-1985)			

BURIAL VAULTS: Concrete Or Precast Terrazzo

Akron Vault Company Inc		F	330 784-5475
Akron (G-55)			
Alexander Wilbert Vault Co		F	419 468-3477
Galion (G-10122)			
Andras Corp		G	440 323-2528
Elyria (G-9217)			
Bell Burial Vault Co		G	513 896-9044
Hamilton (G-10539)			
Bell Vault & Monument Works		E	937 866-2444
Miamisburg (G-13643)			
Brock Burial Vault Inc		G	740 894-5246
South Point (G-17280)			
Buckeye Vault Service Inc		G	419 747-1976
Mansfield (G-12416)			
Coate Concrete Products Inc		G	937 698-4181
West Milton (G-19948)			
Crummitt & Son Vault Corp		G	304 281-2420
Martins Ferry (G-12759)			
Fithian-Wilbert Burial Vlt Co		F	330 758-2327
Youngstown (G-20907)			
Fort Stben Burial Estates Assn		G	740 266-6101
Steubenville (G-17534)			
Galena Vault Ltd		G	740 965-2200
Galena (G-10112)			
Harn Vault Service Inc		F	330 832-1995
Minerva (G-14182)			
Hilles Burial Vaults Inc		G	330 823-2251
Alliance (G-473)			
Landon Vault Company		F	614 443-5505
Columbus (G-7113)			
Mack Industries		C	419 353-7081
Bowling Green (G-1983)			
Mack Industries Inc		G	330 460-7005
Brunswick (G-2219)			
Money Jewelry Vaults		G	937 366-6391
Wilmington (G-20500)			
Neher Burial Vault Company		F	937 399-4494
Springfield (G-17460)			
Paper Vault		G	614 859-5538
Columbus (G-7291)			
Paws & Remember Nwo		G	419 662-9000
Northwood (G-15343)			
Seislove Vault & Septic Tanks		G	419 447-5473
Tiffin (G-18082)			
Shaw Wilbert Vaults LLC		G	740 498-7438
Newcomerstown (G-14982)			
Stuart Burial Vault Company		F	740 569-4158
Bremen (G-2064)			
Thomas-Wilbert Vault Co Inc		G	740 695-5671
Saint Clairsville (G-16655)			
Turner Vault Co		E	419 537-1133
Northwood (G-15349)			
Vapor Vault		G	513 400-8089
Cincinnati (G-4466)			
Vintage Vault		G	330 607-0136
Akron (G-426)			
Youngstown Burial Vault Co		G	330 782-0015
Youngstown (G-21073)			

BURIAL VAULTS: Stone

Bell Burial Vault Co		G	513 896-9044
Hamilton (G-10539)			

BURLAP & BURLAP PRDTS

Dayton Bag & Burlap Co		F	937 253-1722
Dayton (G-8128)			

BURNERS: Gas, Domestic

BMC Holdings Inc		G	419 636-1194
Bryan (G-2269)			

BURNERS: Gas, Indl

Burner Tech Unlimited Inc		G	440 232-3200
Twinsburg (G-18744)			
Selas Heat Technology Co LLC		G	216 662-8800
Streetsboro (G-17696)			
Ws Thermal Process Tech Inc		G	440 385-6829
Lorain (G-12138)			

BURNERS: Oil, Domestic Or Indl

Es Thermal Inc		E	440 323-3291
Elyria (G-9260)			
RW Beckett Corporation		C	440 327-1060
North Ridgeville (G-15252)			

BUS BARS: Electrical

Crown Electric Engrg & Mfg LLC		E	513 539-7394
Middletown (G-13898)			
Schneider Electric Usa Inc		B	513 523-4171
Oxford (G-15700)			
Schneider Electric Usa Inc		D	513 755-5000
West Chester (G-19792)			

BUSHINGS & BEARINGS

Advance Bronze Inc		D	330 948-1231
Lodi (G-12003)			
Climax Metal Products Company		D	440 943-8898
Mentor (G-13416)			
Connell Limited Partnership		D	877 534-8986
Northfield (G-15316)			
Daido Metal Bellefontaine LLC		C	937 592-5010
Bellefontaine (G-1511)			
Dupont Specialty Pdts USA LLC		C	216 901-3600
Cleveland (G-5120)			
McNeil Industries Inc		E	440 951-7756
Painesville (G-15762)			
S C Industries Inc		E	216 732-9000
Euclid (G-9441)			

BUSHINGS & BEARINGS: Brass, Exc Machined

A & H Automotive Industries		G	614 235-1759
Columbus (G-6514)			

BUSHINGS & BEARINGS: Bronze, Exc Machined

Bunting Bearings LLC		E	419 522-3323
Mansfield (G-12417)			

BUSINESS ACTIVITIES: Non-Commercial Site

AG Designs LLC		G	614 506-2849
Delaware (G-8652)			
Aja Industries LLC		G	614 216-9566
Gahanna (G-10074)			
Apex Alliance LLC		G	234 200-5930
Stow (G-17569)			
Apostrophe Apps LLC		G	513 608-4399
Liberty Twp (G-11821)			

BUSINESS ACTIVITIES: Non-Commercial Site PRODUCT SECTION

Aqua Lily Products LLC ....F 951 246-9610
Willoughby *(G-20279)*
Big Bills Trucking LLC ....G 614 850-0626
Hilliard *(G-10813)*
Bjond Inc ....G 614 537-7246
Columbus *(G-6674)*
Bridgits Bath LLC ....G 937 259-1960
Dayton *(G-8061)*
Calvin Lanier ....E 937 952-4221
Dayton *(G-8074)*
Canvas 123 Inc ....G 312 805-0563
Coventry Township *(G-7766)*
Casentric LLC ....G 216 233-6300
Shaker Heights *(G-16928)*
Cbr Industrial Llc ....G 419 645-6447
Wapakoneta *(G-19326)*
Cedar Products LLC ....G 937 892-0070
Peebles *(G-15877)*
CFC Startec LLC ....G 330 688-8316
Stow *(G-17575)*
Coffing Corporation ....F 513 919-2813
Liberty Twp *(G-11822)*
Collaborative For Adaptive Lif ....G 216 513-0572
Fairlawn *(G-9601)*
Corcadence Inc ....G 216 702-6371
Beachwood *(G-1231)*
Country Lane Custom Buildings ....G 740 485-8481
Danville *(G-7961)*
Creative Fabrication Ltd ....G 740 262-5789
Richwood *(G-16508)*
Cult Couture LLC ....G 330 801-9475
Cuyahoga Falls *(G-7855)*
Custom Built Crates Inc ....E 513 248-4422
Milford *(G-14006)*
Custom Machining Solutions LLC ....G 330 221-1523
Rootstown *(G-16567)*
D&M Fencing LLC ....G 419 604-0698
Spencerville *(G-17308)*
Digionyx LLC ....G 614 594-9897
London *(G-12058)*
Eae Logistics Company LLC ....G 440 417-4788
Madison *(G-12348)*
Earth Anatomy Fabrication LLC ....G 740 244-5316
Norton *(G-15366)*
Echo Mobile Solutions LLC ....G 614 282-3756
Pickerington *(G-16046)*
Elite Biomedical Solutions LLC ....F 513 207-0602
Cincinnati *(G-3248)*
Enerchem Incorporated ....G 513 745-0580
Cincinnati *(G-3639)*
Eq Technologies LLC ....G 216 548-3684
Cleveland *(G-5185)*
Ergo Desktop LLC ....E 567 890-3746
Celina *(G-2960)*
Erik V Lamb ....G 330 962-1540
Copley *(G-7684)*
Essential Pathways Ohio LLC ....G 330 518-3091
Youngstown *(G-20900)*
Everykey Inc ....G 855 666-5006
Cleveland *(G-5202)*
Everything In America ....G 347 871-6872
Cleveland *(G-5203)*
Fabstar Tanks Inc ....F 419 587-3639
Grover Hill *(G-10518)*
Fgm Media Inc ....G 440 376-0487
North Royalton *(G-15272)*
Fun-In-Games Inc ....G 866 587-1004
Mason *(G-12874)*
Garden of Delight LLC ....G 513 300-7205
Cincinnati *(G-3725)*
Garys Classic Guitars ....G 513 891-0555
Loveland *(G-12190)*
Gdw Woodworking LLC ....G 513 494-3041
South Lebanon *(G-17276)*
Gro2 Bags & Accessories LLC ....G 740 622-0928
Coshocton *(G-7736)*
Groundhogs 2000 LLC ....G 440 653-1647
Bedford *(G-1407)*
Hands On International LLC ....G 513 502-9000
Mason *(G-12884)*
Harvey Whitney Books Company ....G 513 793-3555
Cincinnati *(G-3801)*
Health Nuts Media LLC ....G 818 802-5222
Cleveland *(G-5384)*
Hebraic Way Press Company ....G 330 614-4872
Alliance *(G-472)*
Hundley Cellars LLC ....G 843 368-5016
Geneva *(G-10223)*
Immersus Health Company LLC ....G 855 994-4325
Cincinnati *(G-3838)*
Innovative Integrations Inc ....G 216 533-5353
Mesopotamia *(G-13633)*
Instruction & Design Concepts ....G 937 439-2698
Dayton *(G-8271)*
J Com Data Inc ....G 614 304-1455
Pataskala *(G-15833)*
Jason Wilson ....E 937 604-8209
Tipp City *(G-18120)*
Jeff Pendergrass ....G 513 575-1226
Milford *(G-14021)*
Jls Funeral Home ....F 614 625-1220
Columbus *(G-7068)*
Joseph G Pappas ....G 330 383-2917
East Liverpool *(G-9061)*
Kick Salsa LLC ....G 614 330-2499
Columbus *(G-7094)*
Ksn Clearing LLC ....F 304 269-3306
Gallipolis *(G-10170)*
Kustom Cases LLC ....G 240 380-6275
Dayton *(G-8303)*
Kw River Hydroelectric I LLC ....G 513 673-2251
Cincinnati *(G-3927)*
Leap Publishing Services Inc ....F 234 738-0082
Stow *(G-17600)*
Lifo Enterprises Inc ....G 513 225-8801
Loveland *(G-12210)*
M&M Great Adventures LLC ....G 937 344-1415
Westerville *(G-20008)*
Manifest Productions LLC ....G 614 806-3054
Columbus *(G-7147)*
Mark Grzianis St Treats Ex Inc ....F 330 414-6266
Kent *(G-11349)*
Mbenztech ....G 937 291-1527
Centerville *(G-3003)*
Micropress America LLC ....G 513 746-0689
Cincinnati *(G-4024)*
Midwest Exposure Magazine ....G 937 626-6738
Dayton *(G-8352)*
Minnie Hanmons Catering Inc ....G 216 815-7744
Cleveland *(G-5694)*
Monitored Therapeutics Inc ....G 614 761-3555
Dublin *(G-8948)*
Morris Clean It N Sweep Clean ....G 513 200-8222
Cincinnati *(G-4046)*
Nanbrands LLC ....G 513 313-9581
Cincinnati *(G-4057)*
Neurorescue LLC ....G 614 354-6453
Lewis Center *(G-11769)*
Olde Man Granola LLC ....F 419 819-9576
Findlay *(G-9735)*
Park Press Direct ....G 419 626-4426
Sandusky *(G-16835)*
Pentagear Products LLC ....F 937 660-8182
Dayton *(G-8420)*
Pilot Production Solutions LLC ....G 513 602-1467
Mason *(G-12921)*
Pmj Partners LLC ....G 201 360-1914
Columbus *(G-7330)*
Popped ....F 330 678-1893
Kent *(G-11365)*
Qleanair Scandinavia Inc ....G 614 323-1756
Columbus *(G-7360)*
Quality Durable Indus Floors ....F 937 696-2833
Farmersville *(G-9631)*
Quayle Consulting Inc ....G 614 868-1363
Pickerington *(G-16058)*
R & H Enterprises Llc ....G 216 702-4449
Richmond Heights *(G-16504)*
Rageon Inc ....E 617 633-0544
Cleveland *(G-5958)*
RE Connors Construction Ltd ....G 740 644-0261
Thornville *(G-18031)*
Red Barakuda LLC ....G 614 596-5432
Columbus *(G-7380)*
Resource Exchange Company Inc ....G 440 773-8915
Akron *(G-347)*
Ricers Residential Svcs LLC ....G 567 203-7414
Shelby *(G-16987)*
Riverrock Recycl Crushing LLC ....G 937 325-2052
Springfield *(G-17485)*
Roboworld Molded Products LLC ....G 513 720-6900
West Chester *(G-19784)*
Rock Iron Corporation ....G 419 529-9411
Crestline *(G-7800)*
Scottrods LLC ....G 419 499-2705
Monroeville *(G-14290)*
Shade Text Book Service Inc ....G 740 696-1323
Shade *(G-16921)*
Shot-Force Pro LLC ....G 740 753-3927
Nelsonville *(G-14597)*
Signalysis Inc ....F 513 528-6164
Cincinnati *(G-4337)*
Simply Unique Snacks LLC ....G 513 223-7736
Cincinnati *(G-4339)*
Sro Prints LLC ....G 865 604-0420
Cincinnati *(G-4366)*
Star Newspaper ....G 614 622-5930
Columbus *(G-7486)*
Stephen J Page ....G 865 951-3316
Williamsburg *(G-20255)*
Steven L Lones ....G 740 452-8851
Zanesville *(G-21183)*
Stronghold Coating Ltd ....G 937 704-4020
Cincinnati *(G-4385)*
Stutzman Manufacturing Ltd ....G 330 674-4359
Millersburg *(G-14131)*
Swagg Productions2015llc ....F 614 815-1173
Reynoldsburg *(G-16455)*
TE Signs and Ship LLC ....G 440 281-9340
Elyria *(G-9336)*
Time Is Money ....G 419 701-6098
Fostoria *(G-9860)*
Timmys Sandwich Shop ....G 419 350-8267
Toledo *(G-18551)*
Ulrich Rubber Stamp Company ....G 419 339-9939
Elida *(G-9202)*
Valley View Pallets LLC ....G 740 599-0010
Danville *(G-7966)*
Vela ....G 614 500-0150
Salesville *(G-16784)*
Walter North ....F 937 204-6050
Dayton *(G-8582)*
Warfighter Fcsed Logistics Inc ....G 740 513-4692
Galena *(G-10117)*
Wellington Wllams Wrldwide LLC ....G 423 805-6198
Troy *(G-18718)*
Wild Oak LLC ....G 513 769-0526
Cincinnati *(G-4509)*

BUSINESS FORMS WHOLESALERS

Anthony Business Forms Inc ....F 937 253-0072
Dayton *(G-7971)*
Bay Business Forms Inc ....F 937 322-3000
Springfield *(G-17367)*
Bloch Printing Company ....G 330 576-6760
Copley *(G-7678)*
Delores E OBeirn ....G 440 582-3610
Cleveland *(G-5082)*
G A Spring Advertising ....G 330 343-9030
Dover *(G-8827)*
G Q Business Products ....G 513 792-4750
Blue Ash *(G-1780)*
GBS Corp ....C 330 494-5330
North Canton *(G-15085)*
Lindsey Graphics Inc ....G 330 995-9241
Aurora *(G-891)*
Optimum System Products Inc ....E 614 885-4464
Westerville *(G-20069)*
Rotary Printing Company ....G 419 668-4821
Norwalk *(G-15414)*
Sentry Graphics Inc ....G 440 735-0850
Northfield *(G-15324)*
Shamrock Companies Inc ....D 440 899-9510
Westlake *(G-20158)*
Taylor Communications Inc ....G 937 228-5800
Dayton *(G-8545)*
William J Bergen & Co ....G 440 248-6132
Solon *(G-17261)*

BUSINESS FORMS: Printed, Continuous

Highland Computer Forms Inc ....C 937 393-4215
Hillsboro *(G-10879)*
Rotary Forms Press Inc ....E 937 393-3426
Hillsboro *(G-10890)*

BUSINESS FORMS: Printed, Manifold

Anderson Graphics Inc ....E 330 745-2165
Barberton *(G-1052)*
Anthony Business Forms Inc ....F 937 253-0072
Dayton *(G-7971)*
Crabar/Gbf Inc ....F 419 943-2141
Leipsic *(G-11724)*
Custom Products Corporation ....D 440 528-7100
Solon *(G-17129)*
Delores E OBeirn ....G 440 582-3610
Cleveland *(G-5082)*
Dupli-Systems Inc ....C 440 234-9415
Strongsville *(G-17738)*

PRODUCT SECTION

Eleet Cryogenics Inc .... E 330 874-4009
  Bolivar (G-1913)
GBS Corp .... C 330 863-1828
  Malvern (G-12391)
GBS Corp .... C 330 494-5330
  North Canton (G-15085)
Geygan Enterprises Inc .... F 513 932-4222
  Lebanon (G-11656)
Hubert Enterprises Inc .... G 513 367-8600
  Harrison (G-10648)
Kroy LLC .... C 216 426-5600
  Cleveland (G-5544)
Lakeshore Graphic Industries .... F 419 626-8631
  Sandusky (G-16821)
Little Printing Company .... G 937 773-4595
  Piqua (G-16137)
Misato Computer Products Inc .... G 937 890-8410
  Vandalia (G-19139)
P H Glatfelter Company .... D 419 333-6700
  Fremont (G-10043)
Print-Digital Incorporated .... G 330 686-5945
  Stow (G-17621)
Quick Tech Graphics Inc .... E 937 743-5952
  Springboro (G-17348)
Reynolds and Reynolds Company .... F 419 584-7000
  Celina (G-2983)
Reynolds and Reynolds Company .... F 937 449-4039
  Dayton (G-8476)
Reynolds and Reynolds Company .... F 937 485-2805
  Beavercreek (G-1362)
S F Mock & Associates LLC .... F 937 438-0196
  Dayton (G-8491)
Shawnee Systems Inc .... D 513 561-9932
  Cincinnati (G-4330)
SRC Liquidation LLC .... A 937 221-1000
  Dayton (G-8521)
Taylor Communications Inc .... G 440 974-1611
  Mentor (G-13600)
Taylor Communications Inc .... E 937 221-1000
  Dayton (G-8543)
Taylor Communications Inc .... D 216 265-1800
  Richfield (G-16491)
Taylor Communications Inc .... F 732 356-0081
  Dayton (G-8544)
Taylor Communications Inc .... D 937 221-3347
  Grove City (G-10472)
Taylor Communications Inc .... G 937 228-5800
  Dayton (G-8545)
Tcp Inc .... G 330 836-4239
  Fairlawn (G-9622)
Thomas Products Co Inc .... E 513 756-9009
  Cincinnati (G-4420)
Wfsr Holdings LLC .... A 877 735-4966
  Dayton (G-8592)

BUSINESS FORMS: Unit Sets, Manifold

Unit Sets Inc .... E 937 840-6123
  Hillsboro (G-10892)

BUSINESS MACHINE REPAIR, ELECTRIC

Queen City Office Machine .... F 513 251-7200
  Cincinnati (G-4238)

BUSINESS SUPPORT SVCS

Advanced Propeller Systems .... G 937 409-1038
  Dayton (G-7968)
Gardella Jewelry LLC .... G 440 877-9261
  North Royalton (G-15273)
Industrial Application Svs .... F 419 875-5093
  Grand Rapids (G-10315)
Jrg Performance Technologies .... F 216 408-5974
  Cleveland (G-5508)
Lesch Btry & Pwr Solution LLC .... G 419 884-0219
  Mansfield (G-12469)

BUSINESS TRAINING SVCS

Pakra LLC .... F 614 477-6965
  Columbus (G-7286)
Wellington Wllams Wrldwide LLC .... G 423 805-6198
  Troy (G-18718)

BUTTER WHOLESALERS

Frank L Harter & Son Inc .... G 513 574-1330
  Cincinnati (G-3709)

CABINETS & CASES: Show, Display & Storage, Exc Wood

Bedford Cabinet Inc .... G 440 439-4830
  Cleveland (G-4802)
D Lewis Inc .... G 740 695-2615
  Saint Clairsville (G-16630)
GMR Furniture Services Ltd .... F 216 244-5072
  Parma (G-15820)
Metal Fabricating Corporation .... D 216 631-8121
  Cleveland (G-5658)
Paul Yoder .... G 740 439-5811
  Senecaville (G-16900)

CABINETS: Bathroom Vanities, Wood

Cabinetry By Ebbing .... G 419 678-2191
  Celina (G-2952)
East Oberlin Cabinets .... G 440 775-1166
  Oberlin (G-15493)
Hampshire Co .... E 937 773-3493
  Piqua (G-16119)
Malco Laminated Inc .... G 513 541-8300
  Cincinnati (G-3975)
Masco Cbinetry Middlefield LLC .... A 440 632-5333
  Middlefield (G-13818)
Old Mill Custom Cabinetry Co .... G 419 423-8897
  Findlay (G-9734)
Profiles In Design Inc .... F 513 751-2212
  Cincinnati (G-4217)
S & G Manufacturing Group LLC .... C 614 529-0100
  Hilliard (G-10859)
Tenkotte Tops Inc .... G 513 738-7300
  Harrison (G-10677)
Wilson Cabinet Co .... E 330 276-8711
  Killbuck (G-11455)
Yoder Cabinets Ltd .... G 614 873-5186
  Plain City (G-16221)

CABINETS: Entertainment

Cabinetworks Unlimited LLC .... G 234 320-4107
  Salem (G-16722)
Innerwood & Company .... F 513 677-2229
  Loveland (G-12199)
Kraftmaid Trucking Inc .... D 440 632-2531
  Middlefield (G-13812)
Xxx Intrntional Amusements Inc .... E 216 671-6900
  Cleveland (G-6332)

CABINETS: Entertainment Units, Household, Wood

Progressive Furniture Inc .... E 419 446-4500
  Archbold (G-664)

CABINETS: Factory

Bolons Custom Kitchens Inc .... F 330 499-0092
  Canton (G-2595)
Columbia Cabinets Inc .... G 440 748-1010
  Columbia Station (G-6432)
Custom Surroundings Inc .... F 330 483-9020
  Valley City (G-19035)
Don Walter Kitchen Distrs Inc .... G 330 793-9338
  Youngstown (G-20893)
Home Idea Center Inc .... F 419 375-4951
  Fort Recovery (G-9821)
Kinnemyers Cornerstone Cab Inc .... G 513 353-3030
  Cleves (G-6367)
Mro Built Inc .... D 330 526-0555
  North Canton (G-15104)
The Wood Shed .... G 937 429-3355
  Xenia (G-20795)
Tri-Co Industries .... G 740 927-1928
  Pataskala (G-15847)
Vivo Brothers LLC .... F 330 629-8686
  Poland (G-16239)
Wades Woodworking Inc .... F 937 374-6470
  Xenia (G-20804)

CABINETS: Filing, Wood

Innerwood & Company .... F 513 677-2229
  Loveland (G-12199)
Innovative Woodworking Inc .... G 513 531-1940
  Cincinnati (G-3850)

CABINETS: Kitchen, Metal

C-Link Enterprises LLC .... F 937 222-2829
  Dayton (G-8071)

Cabintpak Kitchens of Columbus .... G 614 294-4646
  Columbus (G-6721)

CABINETS: Kitchen, Wood

4-B Wood Specialties Inc .... F 330 769-2188
  Seville (G-16909)
A & J Woodworking Inc .... G 419 695-5655
  Delphos (G-8734)
Affordable Cabinet Doors .... G 513 734-9663
  Bethel (G-1655)
Agean Marble Manufacturing .... F 513 874-1475
  West Chester (G-19829)
Ailes Millwork Inc .... F 330 678-4300
  Kent (G-11290)
Al-Co Products Inc .... F 419 399-3867
  Latty (G-11624)
Alpine Cabinets Inc .... G 330 273-2131
  Hinckley (G-10897)
Apex Cabinetry .... G 859 581-5300
  Cincinnati (G-3350)
Approved Plumbing Co .... F 216 663-5063
  Cleveland (G-4722)
As America Inc .... E 419 522-4211
  Mansfield (G-12408)
Bauman Custom Woodworking LLC .... G 330 482-4330
  Salem (G-16720)
Bear Cabinetry LLC .... G 216 481-9282
  Euclid (G-9404)
Benchmark Cabinets .... E 740 397-4615
  Mount Vernon (G-14470)
Benchmark Cabinets .... E 740 694-1144
  Fredericktown (G-9963)
Bestway Cabinets LLC .... G 614 306-3518
  Hilliard (G-10811)
Bowes Mill and Cabinet LLC .... G 440 236-3255
  Columbia Station (G-6430)
Bowman Cabinet Shop .... G 419 331-8209
  Elida (G-9194)
Breits Inc .... G 216 651-5800
  Cleveland (G-4836)
Bricolage Inc .... F 614 853-6789
  Grove City (G-10418)
Brower Products Inc .... D 937 563-1111
  Cincinnati (G-3426)
Bruewer Woodwork Mfg Co .... D 513 353-3505
  Cleves (G-6355)
Cabinet Source .... G 330 336-5600
  Wadsworth (G-19229)
Cabinet Specialties Inc .... E 330 695-3463
  Fredericksburg (G-9944)
Cabinet Systems Inc .... G 440 237-1924
  Cleveland (G-4861)
Canton Cabinet Co .... G 330 455-2585
  Canton (G-2607)
Cardinal Custom Cabinets Ltd .... G 216 281-1570
  Cleveland (G-4876)
Care Cabinetry Inc .... G 216 481-7445
  Euclid (G-9407)
Carnegie Plas Cabinetry Inc .... G 216 451-3300
  Cleveland (G-4880)
Carter-Jones Lumber Company .... C 330 674-9060
  Millersburg (G-14077)
Cedee Cedar Inc .... F 740 363-3148
  Delaware (G-8662)
Chesterland Cabinet Company .... G 440 564-1157
  Newbury (G-14947)
Clancys Cabinet Shop .... E 419 445-4455
  Archbold (G-641)
Clark Son Actn Liquidation Inc .... G 330 866-9330
  East Sparta (G-9094)
Cleveland Custom Cabinets LLC .... G 213 663-0606
  Cleveland (G-4955)
Colonial Cabinets Inc .... F 440 355-9663
  Lagrange (G-11478)
Commercial Bar & Cabinetry .... G 330 743-1420
  Youngstown (G-20876)
Creative Cabinets Ltd .... F 740 689-0603
  Lancaster (G-11557)
Crowes Cabinets Inc .... E 330 729-9911
  Youngstown (G-20881)
Custom Woodworking Inc .... G 419 456-3330
  Ottawa (G-15649)
D Lewis Inc .... G 740 695-2615
  Saint Clairsville (G-16630)
Danny Cabinet Co .... G 440 667-6635
  Cleveland (G-5062)
Distinct Cbntry Innvations LLC .... G 937 661-1051
  New Lebanon (G-14708)
Distinctive Surfaces LLC .... F 614 431-0898
  Columbus (G-6869)

Employee Codes: A=Over 500 employees, B=251-500
C=101-250, D=51-100, E=20-50, F=10-19, G=3-9

Dover Cabinet Inc ....F 330 343-9074
Dover (G-8818)
Dutch Valley Woodworking Inc........F 330 852-4319
Sugarcreek (G-17848)
E J Skok Industries........E 216 292-7533
Bedford (G-1403)
Easyfit Products Inc ....G....... 740 362-9900
Delaware (G-8674)
Ernst Custom Cabinets LLC ....G....... 513 376-9554
Cincinnati (G-3652)
Fairfield Woodworks Ltd ....G....... 740 689-1953
Lancaster (G-11571)
Fdi Cabinetry LLC ....G....... 513 353-4500
Cleves (G-6362)
Fine Wood Design Inc ....G....... 440 327-0751
North Ridgeville (G-15225)
Fleetwood Custom Countertops ....F 740 965-9833
Johnstown (G-11265)
Flottemesch Anthony & Son........F 513 561-1212
Cincinnati (G-3696)
Formware Inc........G....... 614 231-9387
Columbus (G-6930)
Forum III Inc........F 513 961-5123
Cincinnati (G-3706)
Franklin Cabinet Company Inc ....E 937 743-9606
Franklin (G-9884)
Gillard Construction Inc ....F 740 376-9744
Marietta (G-12627)
Gross & Sons Custom Millwork ....G....... 419 227-0214
Lima (G-11871)
Harold Flory........G....... 937 473-3030
Covington (G-7787)
Hattenbach Company ....E 330 744-2732
Youngstown (G-20929)
Hattenbach Company ....D....... 216 881-5200
Cleveland (G-5380)
Heartland Home Cabinetry Ltd ....G....... 740 936-5100
Sunbury (G-17888)
Holmes Lumber & Bldg Ctr Inc........C 330 674-9060
Millersburg (G-14098)
Idx Corporation ....C 937 401-3225
Dayton (G-8259)
Inter Cab Corporation........G....... 216 351-0770
Cleveland (G-5464)
J & K Cabinetry Incorporated ....G....... 513 860-3461
West Chester (G-19870)
J & L Door........G....... 330 684-1496
Dalton (G-7944)
James F Seme........G....... 440 759-6455
Berea (G-1614)
Johannings Inc........G....... 330 875-1706
Louisville (G-12159)
Kellogg Cabinets Inc ....G....... 614 833-9596
Canal Winchester (G-2504)
Kelly Cabinet Company LLC........G....... 614 563-2971
Powell (G-16324)
Kinnemyers Cornerstone Cab Inc........G....... 513 353-3030
Cleves (G-6367)
Kinsella Manufacturing Co Inc ....F 513 561-5285
Cincinnati (G-3911)
Kitchen Designs Plus Inc ....E 419 536-6605
Toledo (G-18368)
Kitchen Works Inc........G....... 440 353-0939
North Ridgeville (G-15236)
Kitchens By Rutenschroer Inc........F 513 251-8333
Cincinnati (G-3914)
Knapke Custom Cabinetry Ltd ....F 937 459-8866
Versailles (G-19185)
Lima Millwork Inc........E 419 331-3303
Elida (G-9195)
M A Miller........G....... 440 636-5697
Middlefield (G-13814)
Marsh Industries Inc........E 330 308-8667
New Philadelphia (G-14784)
Masco Cabinetry LLC ....A 440 632-2547
Middlefield (G-13817)
Masco Cbinetry Middlefield LLC ....D....... 440 632-5058
Middlefield (G-13819)
Masco Cbinetry Middlefield LLC ....B 440 437-8537
Orwell (G-15634)
Midwest Woodworking Co Inc ....E 513 631-6684
Cincinnati (G-4028)
Miller Cabinet Ltd........E 614 873-4221
Plain City (G-16203)
Millwork Design Solutions Inc........G....... 440 946-8837
Willoughby (G-20384)
Mock Woodworking Company LLC........E 740 452-2701
Zanesville (G-21157)
Mro Built Inc ....D....... 330 526-0555
North Canton (G-15104)
N C W Nicoloff Cab Works LLC ....G....... 513 821-1400
Fairfield (G-9534)
Navigator Construction LLC ....G....... 330 244-0221
North Canton (G-15106)
Northeast Cabinet Co LLC ....G....... 614 759-0800
Columbus (G-7229)
Northpointe Cabinetry LLC ....G....... 740 455-4045
Zanesville (G-21163)
Oakwood Furniture Inc........G....... 740 896-3162
Lowell (G-12247)
Oen Custom Cabinets Inc ....G....... 419 738-8115
Wapakoneta (G-19348)
Ohio River Valley Cabinet ....G....... 740 975-8846
Newark (G-14906)
Online Mega Sellers Corp ....D....... 888 384-6468
Toledo (G-18439)
Peters Cabinetry ....G....... 937 884-7514
Brookville (G-2181)
Phil D De Mint........G....... 740 474-7777
Circleville (G-4551)
Pleasant Valley Wdwkg LLC ....G....... 440 636-5860
Middlefield (G-13847)
R Carney Thomas ....G....... 740 342-3388
New Lexington (G-14722)
Red Barn Cabinet Co ....G....... 937 884-9800
Arcanum (G-632)
Regal Cabinet Inc........G....... 419 865-3932
Toledo (G-18500)
Reserve Millwork Inc ....E 216 531-6982
Bedford (G-1441)
Rheaco Builders Inc ....G....... 330 425-3090
Twinsburg (G-18846)
Riceland Cabinet Inc........D....... 330 601-1071
Wooster (G-20644)
Riceland Cabinet Corporation ....F 330 601-1071
Wooster (G-20645)
Richard Benhase & Associates ....F 513 772-1896
Cincinnati (G-4267)
Riggenbach Kitchens ....G....... 330 669-2113
Smithville (G-17091)
River East Custom Cabinets........E 419 244-3226
Toledo (G-18502)
Riverside Cnstr Svcs Inc........E 513 723-0900
Cincinnati (G-4273)
Rn Cabinets & More Ltd ....G....... 330 275-0203
Fredericksburg (G-9957)
Roettger Hardwood Inc ....F....... 937 693-6811
Kettlersville (G-11445)
Royal Cabinet Design Co Inc........F 216 267-5330
Cleveland (G-6010)
S & W Custom Tops Inc........G....... 330 788-2525
Youngstown (G-21023)
Salem Mill & Cabinet Co........G....... 330 337-9568
Salem (G-16771)
Schrock Woodworking ....G....... 740 489-5229
Freeport (G-9986)
Shawnee Wood Products Inc........G....... 440 632-1771
Middlefield (G-13852)
Showcase Cab Mar Rstoration LL........G....... 419 626-6715
Sandusky (G-16849)
Sidney Stiers ....G....... 740 454-7368
Zanesville (G-21179)
Signature Cabinetry Inc........F 614 252-2227
Columbus (G-7450)
Snows Wood Shop Inc ....E 419 836-3805
Oregon (G-15567)
Specified Structures Inc........G....... 330 753-0693
Barberton (G-1106)
Summit Custom Cabinets ....G....... 740 345-1734
Newark (G-14927)
Surface Enterprises Inc........G....... 419 476-5670
Toledo (G-18537)
TDS Custom Cabinets LLC ....G....... 614 517-2220
Columbus (G-7516)
Thomas Cabinet Shop Inc........F 937 847-8239
Dayton (G-8554)
Tiffin Metal Products Co........C 419 447-8414
Tiffin (G-18088)
Timberlane Woodworking........G....... 419 895-9945
Greenwich (G-10409)
Trail Cabinet ....G....... 330 893-3791
Dundee (G-9027)
Trutech Cabinetry ....G....... 614 338-0680
Columbus (G-7549)
Turnwood Industries Inc ....E 330 278-2421
Hinckley (G-10907)
Unique Woodmasters LLC........G....... 419 268-9663
Celina (G-2990)
Virgils Kitchens Inc........G....... 440 355-5058
Lagrange (G-11497)
Wengerd Cabinets ....G....... 330 231-0879
Millersburg (G-14150)
Westgerdes Cabinets ....G....... 419 375-2113
Fort Recovery (G-9831)
Woodcraft Industries Inc........D....... 440 437-7811
Orwell (G-15640)
Woodcraft Industries Inc........C 440 632-9655
Middlefield (G-13868)
Wurms Woodworking Company........E 419 492-2184
New Washington (G-14834)
Xxx Intrntional Amusements Inc ....E 216 671-6900
Cleveland (G-6332)
Your Cabinetry ....G....... 440 638-4925
Strongsville (G-17809)

CABINETS: Office, Metal

Edsal Sandusky Corporation........C 419 626-5465
Sandusky (G-16806)
Kitchen Works Inc........G....... 440 353-0939
North Ridgeville (G-15236)

CABINETS: Office, Wood

Cabinet Systems Inc........G....... 440 237-1924
Cleveland (G-4861)
Custom Millcraft Corp ....E 513 874-7080
West Chester (G-19690)
East Woodworking Company ....G....... 216 791-5950
Cleveland (G-5140)
Geograph Industries Inc........E 513 202-9200
Harrison (G-10643)
Hoge Lumber Company ....E 419 753-2263
New Knoxville (G-14703)
Interior Products Co Inc ....F 216 641-1919
Cleveland (G-5466)
Macwood Inc ....G....... 614 279-7676
Columbus (G-7143)
Mel Heitkamp Builders Ltd........G....... 419 375-0405
Fort Recovery (G-9825)
R Carney Thomas ....G....... 740 342-3388
New Lexington (G-14722)
Richard Benhase & Associates ....F 513 772-1896
Cincinnati (G-4267)
Specialty Services Inc ....G....... 614 421-1599
Columbus (G-7469)

CABINETS: Show, Display, Etc, Wood, Exc Refrigerated

A J Construction Co ....G....... 330 539-9544
Girard (G-10251)
Amtekco Industries LLC........D....... 614 228-6590
Columbus (G-6596)
Case Crafters Inc ....G....... 937 667-9473
Tipp City (G-18107)
Custom Design Cabinets & Tops ....G....... 440 639-9900
Painesville (G-15728)
Designer Cntemporary Laminates ....G....... 440 946-8207
Willoughby (G-20309)
Gary L Gast........G....... 419 626-5915
Sandusky (G-16812)
Hattenbach Company........D....... 216 881-5200
Cleveland (G-5380)
Hattenbach Company........E 330 744-2732
Youngstown (G-20929)
Kellogg Cabinets Inc ....G....... 614 833-9596
Canal Winchester (G-2504)
Macwood Inc ....G....... 614 279-7676
Columbus (G-7143)
Mespo Woodworking........G....... 440 693-4041
Middlefield (G-13821)
Miller Cabinet Ltd........E 614 873-4221
Plain City (G-16203)
R D Cook Company LLC ....G....... 614 262-0550
Columbus (G-7372)
Rinos Woodworking Shop Inc........F 440 946-1718
Willoughby (G-20421)
Robertson Cabinets Inc........E 937 698-3755
West Milton (G-19952)
Stoller Custom Cabinetry........G....... 330 939-6555
Sterling (G-17524)
Vances Department Store ....G....... 937 549-2188
Manchester (G-12397)
Vances Department Store ....F 937 549-3033
Manchester (G-12398)
Village Cabinet Shop Inc ....G....... 704 966-0801
Cincinnati (G-4481)
Woodworks For You ....G....... 440 277-8147
Wakeman (G-19290)

PRODUCT SECTION

CABLE & OTHER PAY TELEVISION DISTRIBUTION

EW Scripps Company ....E 513 977-3000
  Cincinnati *(G-3663)*
Ohio News Network ....D 614 460-3700
  Columbus *(G-7251)*

CABLE TELEVISION

Block Communications Inc ....F 419 724-6212
  Toledo *(G-18206)*

CABLE WIRING SETS: Battery, Internal Combustion Engines

Empire Power Systems Co ....G 440 796-4401
  Madison *(G-12349)*
Noco Company ....B 216 464-8131
  Solon *(G-17208)*

CABLE: Fiber

Connect Television ....G 614 876-4402
  Hilliard *(G-10820)*

CABLE: Fiber Optic

Integrated Systems Professiona ....G 614 875-0104
  Grove City *(G-10436)*
Syscom Advanced Materials Inc ....F 614 487-3626
  Columbus *(G-7506)*

CABLE: Noninsulated

Assembly Specialty Pdts Inc ....E 216 676-5600
  Cleveland *(G-4752)*
Cable and Ctrl Solutions LLC ....G 937 254-2227
  Dayton *(G-7972)*
Cable Mfg & Assembly Inc ....C 330 874-2900
  Bolivar *(G-1908)*
Microplex Inc ....G 330 498-0600
  North Canton *(G-15101)*

CABLE: Ropes & Fiber

Phoenix/Electrotek LLC ....E 740 681-1412
  Lancaster *(G-11597)*
Radix Wire & Cable LLC ....G 216 731-9191
  Cleveland *(G-5955)*

CABLE: Steel, Insulated Or Armored

Electroduct LLC ....E 330 220-9300
  Brunswick *(G-2202)*
Murphy Industries Inc ....E 740 387-7890
  Marion *(G-12722)*

CABS: Indl Trucks & Tractors

Martin Sheet Metal Inc ....D 216 377-8200
  Cleveland *(G-5627)*

CAFETERIAS

Mark Grzianis St Treats Ex Inc ....F 330 414-6266
  Kent *(G-11349)*

CAFFEINE & DERIVATIVES

Goosefoot Acres Inc ....G 330 225-7184
  Valley City *(G-19039)*

CAGES: Wire

Darryl Smith ....G 216 991-5468
  Cleveland *(G-5068)*
Mason Company LLC ....E 937 780-2321
  Leesburg *(G-11713)*
Precision Wire Products Inc ....G 216 265-7580
  Cleveland *(G-5913)*
Royal Wire Products Inc ....D 440 237-8787
  North Royalton *(G-15297)*

CALCULATING & ACCOUNTING EQPT

NCR International Inc ....G 937 445-5000
  Kettering *(G-11437)*
North American Research Corp ....G 937 445-5000
  Kettering *(G-11438)*

CALENDARS, WHOLESALE

Gordon Bernard Company LLC ....E 513 248-7600
  Milford *(G-14013)*

CALIBRATING SVCS, NEC

Continental Testing Inc ....F 937 832-3322
  Union *(G-18900)*
Measurement Specialties Inc ....F 937 885-0800
  Dayton *(G-8337)*
Tungsten Capital Partners LLC ....G 216 481-4774
  Cleveland *(G-6221)*

CAMERAS & RELATED EQPT: Photographic

Sensopart USA Inc ....G 419 931-7696
  Perrysburg *(G-16006)*

CAMPGROUNDS

Caskeys Inc ....G 330 683-0249
  Orrville *(G-15586)*

CAMSHAFTS

Mahle Industries Incorporated ....C 740 962-2040
  McConnelsville *(G-13207)*
North Coast Camshaft Inc ....G 216 671-3700
  Cleveland *(G-5761)*
Park-Ohio Industries Inc ....C 216 341-2300
  Newburgh Heights *(G-14942)*

CANDLE SHOPS

Candle Cottage ....G 937 526-4041
  Versailles *(G-19176)*

CANDLES

Al Root Company ....C 330 723-4359
  Medina *(G-13219)*
Al Root Company ....C 330 725-6677
  Medina *(G-13220)*
Ambrosia Inc ....G 419 825-1151
  Swanton *(G-17904)*
Back Rd Candles & HM Decor LLC ....G 330 461-6075
  Lodi *(G-12007)*
Candle Cottage ....G 937 526-4041
  Versailles *(G-19176)*
Candle-Lite Company LLC ....E 937 780-2711
  Leesburg *(G-11708)*
Candle-Lite Company LLC ....D 513 563-1113
  Blue Ash *(G-1747)*
Candles By Joyce ....G 740 886-6355
  Proctorville *(G-16343)*
Cleveland Plant and Flower Co ....E 614 478-9900
  Columbus *(G-6773)*
Connies Candles ....G 740 574-1224
  Wheelersburg *(G-20179)*
Dano Jr LLC ....G 440 781-5774
  Cleveland *(G-5063)*
Faith Guiding Cafe LLC ....F 614 245-8451
  New Albany *(G-14623)*
Fallen Oak Candles Inc ....G 419 204-8162
  Celina *(G-2962)*
Glasslight Candles LLC ....G 443 509-5505
  Mason *(G-12878)*
Gorant Chocolatier LLC ....C 330 726-8821
  Boardman *(G-1899)*
Heart Warming Candles ....G 937 456-2720
  Eaton *(G-9151)*
Kendee Candles LLC ....G 330 899-9898
  Uniontown *(G-18923)*
Lincoln Candle Company Inc ....G 419 749-4224
  Convoy *(G-7670)*
Lumi-Lite Candle Company ....D 740 872-3248
  Norwich *(G-15421)*
Ohio Candle Co Inc ....G 740 289-8000
  Waverly *(G-19555)*
Willoughby Manufacturing Inc ....G 330 402-8217
  New Waterford *(G-14844)*

CANDLES: Wholesalers

Scentsible Scents Ltd ....G 937 572-6690
  Dayton *(G-8494)*

CANDY & CONFECTIONS: Cake Ornaments

Decko Products Inc ....D 419 626-5757
  Sandusky *(G-16804)*

CANDY & CONFECTIONS: Candy Bars, Including Chocolate Covered

69 Taps ....G 330 253-4554
  Akron *(G-16)*

CANDY, NUT & CONFECTIONERY STORES: Candy

Gwen Rosenberg Enterprises LLC ....G 330 678-1893
  Kent *(G-11328)*
Malleys Candies ....C 216 362-8700
  Lakewood *(G-11528)*
Maries Candies ....E 937 465-3061
  West Liberty *(G-19937)*
Rcs Brewhouse ....G 440 984-3103
  Amherst *(G-572)*
Snyders-Lance Inc ....G 614 856-4616
  Grove City *(G-10469)*

CANDY & CONFECTIONS: Chocolate Candy, Exc Solid Chocolate

Al Meda Chocolates Inc ....G 419 446-2676
  Archbold *(G-634)*
Daffins Candies ....G 330 545-0325
  Girard *(G-10256)*
New Bloomer Candy Company LLC .....E 740 452-7501
  Zanesville *(G-21161)*
Suzin L Chocolatiers ....F 440 323-3372
  Elyria *(G-9332)*

CANDY & CONFECTIONS: Chocolate Covered Dates

Walnut Creek Chocolate Company ......E 330 893-2995
  Walnut Creek *(G-19308)*

CANDY & CONFECTIONS: Cough Drops, Exc Pharmaceutical Preps

Amerisource Health Svcs LLC ....D 614 492-8177
  Columbus *(G-6590)*

CANDY & CONFECTIONS: Fudge

Gift Cove Inc ....G 419 285-2920
  Put In Bay *(G-16352)*

CANDY & CONFECTIONS: Nuts, Glace

Great Lakes Popcorn Company ....G 419 732-3080
  Port Clinton *(G-16248)*

CANDY & CONFECTIONS: Popcorn Balls/Other Trtd Popcorn Prdts

Crawford Acquisition Corp ....F 216 486-0702
  Cleveland *(G-5038)*
Humphrey Popcorn Company ....F 216 662-6629
  Strongsville *(G-17752)*
Jml Holdings Inc ....F 419 866-7500
  Holland *(G-10937)*

CANDY, NUT & CONFECTIONERY STORE: Popcorn, Incl Caramel Corn

Gwen Rosenberg Enterprises LLC ....G 330 678-1893
  Kent *(G-11328)*

CANDY, NUT & CONFECTIONERY STORES: Candy

Becky Knapp ....G 330 854-4400
  Canal Fulton *(G-2476)*
Brandts Candies ....G 440 942-1016
  Willoughby *(G-20286)*
Campbells Candies ....G 330 493-1805
  Canton *(G-2606)*
Coffelt Candy Inc ....G 937 399-8772
  Springfield *(G-17376)*
Coons Homemade Candies ....G 740 496-4141
  Harpster *(G-10626)*
E R B Enterprises Inc ....G 740 948-9174
  Jeffersonville *(G-11246)*
Fannie May Confections Inc ....A 330 494-0833
  North Canton *(G-15082)*
Fawn Confectionery ....F 513 574-9612
  Cincinnati *(G-3675)*
Gorant Chocolatier LLC ....C 330 726-8821
  Boardman *(G-1899)*
Harry London Candies Inc ....D 330 494-0833
  North Canton *(G-15092)*
Hartville Chocolates Inc ....F 330 877-1999
  Hartville *(G-10692)*
Haute Chocolate Inc ....G 513 793-9999
  Montgomery *(G-14294)*
Island Delights Inc ....G 866 887-4100
  Seville *(G-16917)*

Employee Codes: A=Over 500 employees, B=251-500
C=101-250, D=51-100, E=20-50, F=10-19, G=3-9

CANDY, NUT & CONFECTIONERY STORES: Candy

Malleys Candies ....C 216 362-8700
  Lakewood (G-11528)
Maries Candies LLC ....E 937 465-3061
  West Liberty (G-19937)
Neumeisters Candy Shoppe LLC ....G 419 294-3647
  Upper Sandusky (G-18966)
Normant Candy Co ....F 419 886-4214
  Mansfield (G-12494)
Piqua Chocolate Company Inc ....G 937 773-1981
  Piqua (G-16151)
Robert E McGrath Inc ....E 440 572-7747
  Strongsville (G-17783)
Suzin L Chocolatiers ....F 440 323-3372
  Elyria (G-9332)
Walnut Creek Chocolate Company .....E 330 893-2995
  Walnut Creek (G-19308)
Wittichs Candies Inc ....E 740 474-3313
  Circleville (G-4564)

CANDY, NUT & CONFECTIONERY STORES: Confectionery

Dietsch Brothers Incorporated ....D 419 422-4474
  Findlay (G-9677)

CANDY, NUT & CONFECTIONERY STORES: Nuts

Jml Holdings Inc ....F 419 866-7500
  Holland (G-10937)
Krema Products Inc ....G 614 889-4824
  Dublin (G-8939)
Trophy Nut Co ....D 937 667-8478
  Tipp City (G-18139)

CANDY: Chocolate From Cacao Beans

American Confections Co LLC ....G 614 888-8838
  Coventry Township (G-7765)
Campbells Candies ....G 330 493-1805
  Canton (G-2606)
Giannios Candy Co Inc ....E 330 755-7000
  Struthers (G-17817)
L C F Inc ....F 330 877-3322
  Hartville (G-10700)
Walnut Creek Chocolate Company .....E 330 893-2995
  Walnut Creek (G-19308)

CANDY: Hard

Lollipop Stop ....G 614 991-5192
  Grove City (G-10442)
Yost Candy Co ....E 330 828-2777
  Dalton (G-7954)

CANNED SPECIALTIES

Abbott Laboratories ....A 614 624-3191
  Columbus (G-6519)
Bittersweet Inc ....D 419 875-6986
  Whitehouse (G-20189)
Hayden Valley Foods Inc ....F 614 539-7233
  Urbancrest (G-19021)
JES Foods/Celina Inc ....E 419 586-7446
  Celina (G-2971)
L J Minor Corp ....G 216 861-8350
  Cleveland (G-5550)
Milnot Company ....G 888 656-3245
  Gahanna (G-10091)
Oasis Mediterranean Cuisine ....E 419 269-1459
  Toledo (G-18432)
P3 Secure LLC ....E 937 610-5500
  Dayton (G-8415)
Robert Rothschild Farm LLC ....F 937 653-7397
  Cincinnati (G-4279)
Skyline Chili Inc ....C 513 874-1188
  Fairfield (G-9565)
Wornick Company ....A 513 552-7463
  Blue Ash (G-1877)
Wornick Holding Company Inc ....A 513 794-9800
  Blue Ash (G-1878)

CANOPIES: Sheet Metal

Geist Co Inc ....F 216 771-2200
  Cleveland (G-5300)
Shadetree Systems LLC ....F 614 844-5990
  Columbus (G-7443)
Upside Innovations LLC ....G 513 889-2492
  West Chester (G-19912)

CANS & CASES: Capacitor Or Condenser, Stamped Metal

Select Industries Corporation ....C 937 233-9191
  Dayton (G-8502)

CANS & TUBES: Ammunition, Board Laminated With Metal Foil

Greif Bros Corp Ohio Inc ....F 740 549-6000
  Delaware (G-8687)

CANS: Aluminum

Busch Properties Inc ....G 614 888-0946
  Columbus (G-6714)
Crown Cork & Seal Usa Inc ....B 330 833-1011
  Massillon (G-12971)
Exal Corporation ....E 330 744-9505
  Youngstown (G-20901)
Sidney Can & Tool LLC ....G 937 492-0977
  Sidney (G-17078)

CANS: Beer, Metal

Ball Metal Beverage Cont Corp ....C 419 423-3071
  Findlay (G-9654)
Container Manufacturing Ltd ....G 937 264-2370
  Dayton (G-8102)

CANS: Composite Foil-Fiber, Made From Purchased Materials

Artistic Composite & Mold Co ....G 330 352-6632
  Litchfield (G-11984)
Companies of North Coast LLC ....G 216 398-8550
  Cleveland (G-5008)
Hpc Holdings LLC ....F 330 666-3751
  Fairlawn (G-9608)
North Coast Composites Inc ....G 216 398-8550
  Cleveland (G-5762)
Sonoco Products Company ....E 513 870-3985
  West Chester (G-19900)

CANS: Fiber

Sonoco Products Company ....D 937 429-0040
  Beavercreek Township (G-1374)

CANS: Garbage, Stamped Or Pressed Metal

Witt Industries Inc ....D 513 871-5700
  Mason (G-12955)

CANS: Metal

Anchor Hocking LLC ....A 740 681-6478
  Lancaster (G-11541)
Anchor Hocking LLC ....G 740 687-2500
  Lancaster (G-11542)
Ball Corporation ....D 614 771-9112
  Columbus (G-6645)
Buckeye Stamping Company ....D 614 445-0059
  Columbus (G-6712)
BWAY Corporation ....E 513 388-2200
  Cincinnati (G-3433)
Cardinal Welding Inc ....G 330 426-2404
  East Palestine (G-9069)
Cleveland Steel Container Corp ....E 330 656-5600
  Streetsboro (G-17666)
Crown Cork & Seal Usa Inc ....E 419 727-8201
  Toledo (G-18243)
Crown Cork & Seal Usa Inc ....C 937 299-2027
  Moraine (G-14339)
Crown Cork & Seal Usa Inc ....E 740 681-6593
  Lancaster (G-11561)
Crown Cork & Seal Usa Inc ....E 740 681-3000
  Lancaster (G-11560)
Eisenhauer Mfg Co LLC ....D 419 238-0081
  Van Wert (G-19090)
Encore Plastics Corporation ....C 419 626-8000
  Sandusky (G-16808)
Ghp II LLC ....C 740 687-2500
  Lancaster (G-11575)
Industrial Container Svcs LLC ....E 513 921-8811
  Cincinnati (G-3844)
Industrial Container Svcs LLC ....D 614 864-1900
  Blacklick (G-1687)
Organized Living Inc ....E 513 489-9300
  Cincinnati (G-4118)
Packaging Specialties Inc ....E 330 723-6000
  Medina (G-13316)
Witt Industries Inc ....D 513 871-5700
  Mason (G-12955)

CANS: Tin

Independent Can Company ....E 440 593-5300
  Conneaut (G-7650)
Two Tin Cans LLC ....G 419 692-2027
  Delphos (G-8759)

CANVAS PRDTS

Advantage Tent Fittings Inc ....F 740 773-3015
  Chillicothe (G-3173)
Canvas Exchange Inc ....G 216 749-2233
  Cleveland (G-4867)
Chalfant Sew Fabricators Inc ....E 216 521-7922
  Cleveland (G-4907)
Cleveland Canvas Goods Mfg Co .....D 216 361-4567
  Cleveland (G-4948)
Columbus Canvas Products Inc ....F 614 375-1397
  Columbus (G-6785)
DCW Acquisition Inc ....E 216 451-0666
  Cleveland (G-5079)
Deer Creek Custom Canvas LLC ......G 740 495-9239
  New Holland (G-14701)
Delphos Tent and Awning Inc ....E 419 692-5776
  Delphos (G-8740)
Forest City Companies Inc ....E 216 586-5279
  Cleveland (G-5261)
Galion Canvas Products ....F 419 468-5333
  Galion (G-10139)
Hdt Expeditionary Systems Inc ....B 216 438-6111
  Solon (G-17161)
J & W Canvas Company ....G 330 652-7678
  Mineral Ridge (G-14167)
National Bias Fabric Co ....E 216 361-0530
  Cleveland (G-5722)
Raven Industries Inc ....G 937 323-4625
  Springfield (G-17480)
Samsel Rope & Marine Supply Co ....E 216 241-0333
  Cleveland (G-6029)
Scherba Industries Inc ....D 330 273-3200
  Brunswick (G-2238)
Shade Youngstown & Aluminum Co ..G 330 782-2373
  Youngstown (G-21028)
Shur-Co LLC ....G 330 297-0888
  Ravenna (G-16402)
Stan Rileys Custom Draperies ....E 513 821-3732
  Cincinnati (G-4370)
Wolf G T Awning & Tent Co ....F 937 548-4161
  Greenville (G-10402)

CANVAS PRDTS: Air Cushions & Mattresses

Rainbow Bedding ....G 330 852-3127
  Sugarcreek (G-17861)

CANVAS PRDTS: Convertible Tops, Car/Boat, Fm Purchased Mtrl

Allen Zahradnik Inc ....G 419 729-1201
  Toledo (G-18163)
American Canvas Products Inc ....F 419 382-8450
  Toledo (G-18172)
Crown Dielectric Inds Inc ....C 614 224-5161
  Columbus (G-6839)
Griffin Fisher Co Inc ....G 513 961-2110
  Cincinnati (G-3785)
Rex Manufacturing Co ....E 419 224-5751
  Lima (G-11931)
William Thompson ....G 440 232-4363
  Aurora (G-916)

CANVAS PRDTS: Shades, Made From Purchased Materials

Lumenomics Inc ....E 614 798-3500
  Lewis Center (G-11766)

CAPACITORS: NEC

CPI Group Limited ....G 216 525-0046
  Cleveland (G-5035)
Elliott Oren Products Inc ....E 419 298-2306
  Edgerton (G-9173)

CAPS & PLUGS: Electric, Attachment

Knappco Corporation ....C 816 741-0786
  West Chester (G-19731)

CAPS: Plastic

Bprex Halthcare Brookville Inc................C....... 847 541-9700
  Perrysburg *(G-15924)*
Electro-Cap International Inc.................F....... 937 456-6099
  Eaton *(G-9148)*
Wisco Products Incorporated................G....... 937 228-2101
  Dayton *(G-8598)*

CAR LOADING SVCS

Yemaneh Musie..G....... 614 506-3687
  Columbus *(G-7622)*

CAR WASH EQPT

Car-Nation Inc..G....... 330 862-9001
  Paris *(G-15808)*
Chiefs Manufacturing & Eqp Co.............G....... 216 291-3200
  Cleveland *(G-4921)*
Eastern Ohio Investments Inc................G....... 740 266-2228
  Steubenville *(G-17532)*
Giant Industries Inc................................E....... 419 531-4600
  Toledo *(G-18305)*
Hilo Tech Inc...G....... 440 979-1155
  North Olmsted *(G-15192)*
L A Express...G....... 513 752-6999
  Batavia *(G-1162)*
Majic Touch...G....... 330 923-8259
  Cuyahoga Falls *(G-7896)*
National Pride Equipment Inc................G....... 419 289-2886
  Ashland *(G-727)*
Powerwash of Ohio..................................G....... 614 260-2756
  Lewis Center *(G-11773)*
Sammy S Auto Detail..............................F....... 614 263-2728
  Columbus *(G-7418)*

CAR WASH EQPT & SPLYS WHOLESALERS

National Pride Equipment Inc................G....... 419 289-2886
  Ashland *(G-727)*
Service Station Equipment Co................F....... 216 431-6100
  Cleveland *(G-6045)*

CAR WASHES

Clearly Visible Mobile Wash....................G....... 440 543-9299
  Chagrin Falls *(G-3040)*
Lawnview Industries Inc.........................C....... 937 653-5217
  Urbana *(G-19003)*
Tops Inc..G....... 440 954-9451
  Mentor *(G-13609)*

CARBIDES

Nap Asset Holdings Ltd...........................F....... 330 633-0599
  Tallmadge *(G-17995)*
Ohio Metal Working Products.................E....... 330 455-2009
  Canton *(G-2773)*

CARBON & GRAPHITE PRDTS, NEC

Albemarle Corporation............................G....... 330 425-2354
  Twinsburg *(G-18729)*
American Spring Wire Corp....................C....... 216 292-4620
  Bedford Heights *(G-1460)*
Angstron Materials Inc...........................G....... 937 331-9884
  Dayton *(G-8032)*
Applied Sciences Inc..............................E....... 937 766-2020
  Cedarville *(G-2943)*
Cammann Inc..F....... 440 965-4051
  Wakeman *(G-19282)*
Durr Megtec LLC....................................C....... 614 258-9501
  Columbus *(G-6876)*
GE Aviation Systems LLC.......................B....... 937 898-5881
  Vandalia *(G-19125)*
Graftech Holdings Inc.............................B....... 216 676-2000
  Independence *(G-11134)*
Graftech International Ltd......................D....... 216 676-2000
  Brooklyn Heights *(G-2123)*
Graftech Intl Holdings Inc......................C....... 216 529-3777
  Cleveland *(G-5337)*
Graftech Intl Holdings Inc......................B....... 216 676-2000
  Brooklyn Heights *(G-2124)*
Graphite Sales Inc..................................E....... 419 652-3388
  Nova *(G-15434)*
Mill-Rose Company.................................C....... 440 255-9171
  Mentor *(G-13520)*
Morgan Advanced Materials...................C....... 419 435-8182
  Fostoria *(G-9849)*
National Elec Carbn Pdts Inc.................D....... 419 435-8182
  Fostoria *(G-9850)*

Ohio Carbon Blank Inc...........................E....... 440 953-9302
  Willoughby *(G-20394)*
Ohio Carbon Industries Inc....................E....... 419 496-2530
  Ashland *(G-730)*
Pyrograf Products Inc.............................F....... 937 766-2020
  Cedarville *(G-2946)*
Pyrotek Incorporated..............................C....... 440 349-8800
  Aurora *(G-901)*
R&S Carbon Trading LLC........................G....... 614 264-3083
  Gahanna *(G-10099)*
Randall Bearings Inc..............................D....... 419 223-1075
  Lima *(G-11927)*
Randall Bearings Inc..............................E....... 419 678-2486
  Coldwater *(G-6419)*
Sentinel Management Inc.......................E....... 440 821-7372
  Lorain *(G-12119)*
Zyvex Performance Mtls Inc...................E....... 614 481-2222
  Columbus *(G-7629)*

CARBON BLACK

Jacobi Carbons Inc................................E....... 215 546-3900
  Columbus *(G-7057)*
North Central Processing Inc.................G....... 216 623-1090
  Cleveland *(G-5760)*

CARBON DISULFIDE

New Mulch In A Bottle Limited..............G....... 724 290-2341
  Marietta *(G-12648)*

CARBON PAPER & INKED RIBBONS

Adaptive Data Inc..................................F....... 937 436-2343
  Dayton *(G-8007)*
Kroy LLC...C....... 216 426-5600
  Cleveland *(G-5544)*
Nanotechlabs Inc....................................F....... 937 297-9518
  Kettering *(G-11436)*
Pubco Corporation..................................D....... 216 881-5300
  Cleveland *(G-5932)*

CARDIOVASCULAR SYSTEM DRUGS, EXC DIAGNOSTIC

Pfizer Inc...C....... 937 746-3603
  Franklin *(G-9908)*

CARDS: Beveled

Cott Systems Inc....................................D....... 614 847-4405
  Columbus *(G-6827)*

CARDS: Color

Coloramic Process Inc............................F....... 440 275-1199
  Austinburg *(G-919)*
Golf Marketing Group Inc.......................G....... 330 963-5155
  Twinsburg *(G-18788)*

CARDS: Greeting

American Greetings Corporation............A....... 216 252-7300
  Cleveland *(G-4688)*
Frogs In Bloom..G....... 330 678-9508
  Kent *(G-11323)*
Kim Brauer & Company LLC...................G....... 330 540-9152
  Youngstown *(G-20952)*
Naptime Productions LLC.......................F....... 419 662-9521
  Rossford *(G-16587)*
Plus Mark LLC..E....... 216 252-6770
  Cleveland *(G-5891)*
Those Charc From Cleve Inc..................F....... 216 252-7300
  Cleveland *(G-6172)*

CARDS: Identification

Octsys Security Corp..............................G....... 614 470-4510
  Columbus *(G-7239)*
Plasticards Inc..E....... 330 896-5555
  Uniontown *(G-18930)*

CARDS: Playing

Fun-In-Games Inc....................................G....... 866 587-1004
  Mason *(G-12874)*

CARNIVAL & AMUSEMENT PARK EQPT WHOLESALERS

Majestic Manufacturing Inc....................E....... 330 457-2447
  New Waterford *(G-14841)*

CARNIVAL SPLYS, WHOLESALE

Jackpot Festival & Gaming......................G....... 216 531-3500
  Cleveland *(G-5491)*

CARPET & UPHOLSTERY CLEANING SVCS

Image By J & K LLC...............................B....... 888 667-6929
  Maumee *(G-13118)*

CARPET & UPHOLSTERY CLEANING SVCS: Carpet/Furniture, On Loc

Downey Enterprises Inc..........................G....... 740 587-4258
  Granville *(G-10329)*
Shaheen Oriental Rug Co Inc.................F....... 330 493-9000
  Canton *(G-2813)*
Stanley Steemer Intl Inc.........................C....... 614 764-2007
  Dublin *(G-8994)*

CARPETS & RUGS: Tufted

Mohawk Industries Inc...........................C....... 800 837-3812
  Grove City *(G-10447)*

CARPETS, RUGS & FLOOR COVERING

Alliance Carpet Cushion Co....................D....... 740 966-5001
  Johnstown *(G-11254)*
Boardman Molded Products Inc.............D....... 330 788-2400
  Youngstown *(G-20854)*
Buckeye Volleyball Center LLC..............G....... 614 764-1075
  Powell *(G-16309)*
Davies Since 1900..................................G....... 419 756-4212
  Mansfield *(G-12432)*
Johns Manville Corporation...................B....... 419 878-8111
  Waterville *(G-19498)*
Kadee Industries Newco Inc...................F....... 440 439-8650
  Bedford *(G-1420)*
Lapchi LLC...G....... 216 360-0104
  Cleveland *(G-5561)*
Mat Basics Incorporated.........................G....... 513 793-0313
  Blue Ash *(G-1814)*
Mini Graphics Inc....................................G....... 513 563-8600
  Cincinnati *(G-4030)*
Remnant Room.......................................G....... 937 938-7350
  Dayton *(G-8471)*
Xt Innovations Ltd..................................G....... 419 562-1989
  Bucyrus *(G-2352)*

CARRIAGES: Horse Drawn

Burkholder Buggy Shop..........................G....... 330 674-5891
  Millersburg *(G-14074)*
Farmerstown Axle Co..............................G....... 330 897-2711
  Baltic *(G-1028)*
London Coach Shop................................G....... 419 347-4803
  Shelby *(G-16983)*
Shiloh Carriage Shop LLC.......................G....... 419 896-3869
  Shiloh *(G-17000)*
Victorian Farms......................................G....... 330 628-9188
  Atwater *(G-864)*
Walnut Creek Cart Shop.........................G....... 330 893-1097
  Millersburg *(G-14145)*

CARRIERS: Infant, Textile

Sewline Products Inc..............................F....... 419 929-1114
  New London *(G-14738)*

CARS: Electric

American Honda Motor Co Inc...............G....... 937 339-0157
  Troy *(G-18635)*
Mobile Solutions LLC..............................F....... 614 286-3944
  Columbus *(G-7189)*
Myers Motors LLC..................................G....... 330 630-7000
  Tallmadge *(G-17994)*

CARTONS: Egg, Molded Pulp, Made From Purchased Materials

Tekni-Plex Inc..E....... 419 491-2399
  Holland *(G-10960)*

CARVING SETS, STAINLESS STEEL

Ahner Fabricating & Shtmtl Inc.............E....... 419 626-6641
  Sandusky *(G-16793)*

CASES, WOOD

Aerocase Incorporated...........................F....... 440 617-9294
  Westlake *(G-20088)*

Employee Codes: A=Over 500 employees, B=251-500
C=101-250, D=51-100, E=20-50, F=10-19, G=3-9

CASES, WOOD

Custom Displays LLC .... G 330 454-8850
  Bolivar *(G-1910)*
Fca LLC .... F 309 644-2424
  Clayton *(G-4573)*
Global Packaging & Exports Inc ... G 513 454-2020
  West Chester *(G-19716)*

CASES: Carrying

Clipper Products Inc .... G 513 688-7300
  Cincinnati *(G-3243)*
Professional Case Inc .... F 513 682-2520
  West Chester *(G-19890)*
Travelers Custom Case Inc .... F 216 621-8447
  Cleveland *(G-6199)*
Whitman Corporation .... G 513 541-3223
  Okeana *(G-15521)*

CASES: Plastic

Aerocase Incorporated .... F 440 617-9294
  Westlake *(G-20088)*
Checkpoint Systems Inc .... C 330 456-7776
  Canton *(G-2622)*
Warwick Products Company .... E 216 334-1200
  Cleveland *(G-6291)*
William J Minneman Family LP .... E 937 890-7461
  Dayton *(G-8593)*

CASES: Shipping, Nailed Or Lock Corner, Wood

Scorpion Case Mfg LLC .... F 614 274-7246
  Dublin *(G-8981)*

CASH REGISTERS & PARTS

Allied Retail Solutions .... G 330 332-8141
  Salem *(G-16716)*
Bartek Systems .... G 614 759-6014
  Columbus *(G-6652)*

CASINGS: Rocket Transportation

Ds Express Carriers Inc .... G 419 433-6200
  Norwalk *(G-15388)*

CASINGS: Sheet Metal

Art Fremont Iron Co .... G 419 332-5554
  Fremont *(G-9992)*

CASINGS: Storage, Missile & Missile Components

Tdm Fuelcell LLC Tdm LLC .... G 440 969-1442
  Chesterland *(G-3170)*

CASKETS & ACCESS

Case Ohio Burial Co .... F 440 779-1992
  Cleveland *(G-4885)*
Youngstown Casket Co Inc .... G 330 758-2008
  Youngstown *(G-21074)*
Zane Casket Company Inc .... E 740 452-4680
  Zanesville *(G-21191)*

CASKETS WHOLESALERS

Allen Enterprises Inc .... E 740 532-5913
  Ironton *(G-11159)*
Case Ohio Burial Co .... F 440 779-1992
  Cleveland *(G-4885)*

CAST STONE: Concrete

Fibreboard Corporation .... C 419 248-8000
  Toledo *(G-18294)*

CASTERS

Cleveland Caster LLC .... G 440 333-1443
  Cleveland *(G-4949)*
Western Reserve Mfg Co .... G 216 641-0500
  Cleveland *(G-6203)*

CASTINGS GRINDING: For The Trade

Able Grinding Co Inc .... E 216 961-6455
  Cleveland *(G-4600)*
Axis Tool & Grinding LLC .... G 330 535-4713
  Akron *(G-75)*
Brockman Jig Grinding Service .... G 937 220-9780
  Dayton *(G-8064)*

Centerless Grinding Solutions ..... G 216 520-4612
  Twinsburg *(G-18748)*
Combine Grinding Co Inc .... G 440 439-6148
  Bedford *(G-1397)*
F & J Grinding Inc .... G 440 942-4430
  Willoughby *(G-20318)*
Grandview Grind .... G 614 485-9005
  Columbus *(G-6967)*
Hr Parts N Stuff .... G 330 947-2433
  Atwater *(G-861)*
Jamar Precision Grinding Co .... E 330 220-0099
  Hinckley *(G-10903)*
M L Grinding Co .... G 440 975-9111
  Willoughby *(G-20364)*
Micro Lapping & Grinding Co .... E 216 267-6500
  Cleveland *(G-5667)*
Ohio Engineering and Mfg Sls ..... G 937 855-6971
  Germantown *(G-10244)*
Owen S Precision Grinding .... G 513 745-9335
  Cincinnati *(G-4126)*
P & L Heat Trting Grinding Inc .... G 330 746-1339
  Youngstown *(G-20986)*
Performance Point Grinding .... G 330 220-0871
  Hinckley *(G-10905)*
Trinel Inc .... F 216 265-9190
  Cleveland *(G-6216)*
True Grinding .... G 440 786-7608
  Bedford *(G-1452)*
V M Machine Co Inc .... G 216 281-4569
  Cleveland *(G-6248)*
We Grind Muzik .... G 614 670-4142
  Columbus *(G-7595)*
Youngstown Hard Chrome Plating .. E 330 758-9721
  Youngstown *(G-21077)*

CASTINGS: Aerospace Investment, Ferrous

Bescast Inc .... C 440 946-5300
  Willoughby *(G-20285)*
Caspa Home Page Inc .... G 216 781-0748
  Cleveland *(G-4886)*
General Aluminum Mfg Company . C 419 739-9300
  Wapakoneta *(G-19330)*
International Precision .... G 330 342-0407
  Hudson *(G-11056)*

CASTINGS: Aerospace, Aluminum

Howmet Aluminum Casting Inc ... E 216 641-4340
  Newburgh Heights *(G-14937)*
Htci Co .... F 937 845-1204
  New Carlisle *(G-14667)*
Lockheed Martin Investments ..... F 937 429-0100
  Beavercreek *(G-1329)*
Mpe Aeroengines Inc .... G 937 878-3800
  Huber Heights *(G-11022)*
TW Corporation .... E 440 461-3234
  Akron *(G-416)*

CASTINGS: Aerospace, Nonferrous, Exc Aluminum

Computational Engineering Svcs .. G 513 745-0313
  Blue Ash *(G-1752)*
Microweld Engineering Inc .... F 614 847-9410
  Worthington *(G-20697)*
Voss Industries LLC .... C 216 771-7655
  Cleveland *(G-6273)*

CASTINGS: Aluminum

Accro-Cast Corporation .... F 937 228-0497
  Dayton *(G-8001)*
Boscott Metals Inc .... F 937 448-2018
  Bradford *(G-2009)*
Brost Foundry Company .... E 216 641-1131
  Cleveland *(G-4842)*
Cast Metals Technology Inc .... G 740 363-1690
  Delaware *(G-8661)*
Cushman Foundry LLC .... F 513 984-5570
  Blue Ash *(G-1757)*
General Aluminum Mfg Company . B 330 297-1225
  Cleveland *(G-5304)*
General Aluminum Mfg Company . E 330 297-1020
  Ravenna *(G-16381)*
General Aluminum Mfg Company . B 440 593-6225
  Conneaut *(G-7646)*
General Motors LLC .... A 419 782-7010
  Defiance *(G-8623)*
Iabf Inc .... G 614 279-4498
  Columbus *(G-7018)*

Merit Foundry Co Inc .... G 216 741-4282
  Cleveland *(G-5656)*
Morris Bean & Company .... C 937 767-7301
  Yellow Springs *(G-20812)*
Multi Cast LLC .... E 419 335-0010
  Wauseon *(G-19528)*
New London Foundry Inc .... F 419 929-2073
  New London *(G-14733)*
New Mansfield Brass & Alum Co .. E 419 492-2166
  New Washington *(G-14830)*
OKeefe Casting Co .... G 440 277-5427
  Lorain *(G-12110)*
P C M Co .... D 330 336-8040
  Wadsworth *(G-19258)*
Palmer Engineered Products Inc .. G 937 322-1481
  Springfield *(G-17466)*
Piqua Emery Cutter & Fndry Co .. D 937 773-4134
  Piqua *(G-16152)*
Pride Cast Metals Inc .... D 513 541-1295
  Cincinnati *(G-4189)*
Ross Aluminum Castings LLC .... G 937 492-4134
  Sidney *(G-17069)*
Rotocast Technologies Inc .... G 330 798-9091
  Akron *(G-354)*
Sawbrook Steel Castings Co ...... D 513 554-1700
  Cincinnati *(G-4302)*
US Metalcraft Inc .... E 419 692-4962
  Delphos *(G-8762)*

CASTINGS: Brass, NEC, Exc Die

Accurate Products Company .... G 740 498-7202
  Newcomerstown *(G-14969)*

CASTINGS: Bronze, NEC, Exc Die

Brost Foundry Company .... E 216 641-1131
  Cleveland *(G-4842)*
Oakes Foundry Inc .... E 330 372-4010
  Warren *(G-19424)*
OKeefe Casting Co .... G 440 277-5427
  Lorain *(G-12110)*
Piqua Emery Cutter & Fndry Co .. D 937 773-4134
  Piqua *(G-16152)*
Pride Cast Metals Inc .... D 513 541-1295
  Cincinnati *(G-4189)*

CASTINGS: Commercial Investment, Ferrous

B W Grinding Co .... E 419 923-1376
  Lyons *(G-12273)*
Dd Foundry Inc .... D 216 362-4100
  Brookpark *(G-2143)*
Howmet Castings & Services Inc . B 216 641-4400
  Newburgh Heights *(G-14938)*
Howmet Corporation .... E 757 825-7086
  Newburgh Heights *(G-14939)*
Kovatch Castings Inc .... C 330 896-9944
  Uniontown *(G-18924)*
Rimer Enterprises Inc .... E 419 878-8156
  Waterville *(G-19504)*

CASTINGS: Copper & Copper-Base Alloy, NEC, Exc Die

Falcon Foundry Company .... D 330 536-6221
  Lowellville *(G-12250)*
M A Harrison Mfg Co Inc .... E 440 965-4306
  Wakeman *(G-19287)*

CASTINGS: Die, Aluminum

Ahresty Wilmington Corporation .. B 937 382-6112
  Wilmington *(G-20484)*
Akron Foundry Co .... C 330 745-3101
  Akron *(G-40)*
Alliance Castings Company LLC .. E 330 829-5600
  Alliance *(G-452)*
Alumacast LLC .... G 419 584-1473
  Celina *(G-2949)*
American Light Metals LLC .... C 330 908-3065
  Macedonia *(G-12277)*
Apex Aluminum Die Cast Co Inc .. E 937 773-0432
  Piqua *(G-16099)*
Cast Specialties Inc .... E 216 292-7393
  Cleveland *(G-4888)*
CSM Horvath Ledgebrook .... G 419 522-1133
  Mansfield *(G-12430)*
Custom Industries Inc .... G 216 251-2804
  Cleveland *(G-5047)*
Destin Die Casting LLC .... E 937 347-1111
  Xenia *(G-20766)*

PRODUCT SECTION

CATALYSTS: Chemical

Fort Recovery Industries Inc .... B 419 375-4121
  Fort Recovery *(G-9818)*
General Aluminum Mfg Company .... C 419 739-9300
  Wapakoneta *(G-19330)*
General Die Casters Inc .... D 330 467-6700
  Northfield *(G-15318)*
General Die Casters Inc .... E 330 678-2528
  Twinsburg *(G-18781)*
Krengel Equipment LLC .... C 440 946-3570
  Eastlake *(G-9118)*
Matalco (us) Inc .... E 330 452-4760
  Canton *(G-2746)*
Model Pattern & Foundry Co .... E 513 542-2322
  Cincinnati *(G-4036)*
Ohio Aluminum Industries Inc .... C 216 641-8865
  Cleveland *(G-5798)*
Ohio Decorative Products LLC .... C 419 647-9033
  Spencerville *(G-17311)*
Omni Die Casting Inc .... E 330 830-5500
  Massillon *(G-13033)*
Park-Ohio Holdings Corp .... F 440 947-2000
  Cleveland *(G-5842)*
Park-Ohio Industries Inc .... C 440 947-2000
  Cleveland *(G-5843)*
Plaster Process Castings Co .... E 216 663-1814
  Cleveland *(G-5885)*
Ramco Electric Motors Inc .... D 937 548-2525
  Greenville *(G-10389)*
Ravana Industries Inc .... G 330 536-4015
  Lowellville *(G-12254)*
Reliable Castings Corporation .... D 937 497-5217
  Sidney *(G-17065)*
Ross Casting & Innovation LLC .... B 937 497-4500
  Sidney *(G-17070)*
Seilkop Industries Inc .... E 513 761-1035
  Cincinnati *(G-4316)*
Seilkop Industries Inc .... F 513 679-5680
  Cincinnati *(G-4317)*
Seyekcub Inc .... G 330 324-1394
  Uhrichsville *(G-18894)*
SRS Die Casting Holdings LLC .... G 330 467-0750
  Macedonia *(G-12330)*
SRS Light Metals Inc .... G 330 467-0750
  Macedonia *(G-12331)*
Thompson Aluminum Casting Co .... D 216 206-2781
  Cleveland *(G-6171)*
Tooling Technology LLC .... D 937 295-3672
  Fort Loramie *(G-9810)*
United States Drill Head Co .... E 513 941-0300
  Cincinnati *(G-4450)*
Yoder Industries Inc .... C 937 278-5769
  Dayton *(G-8602)*

CASTINGS: Die, Copper & Copper Alloy

D Picking & Co .... G 419 562-5016
  Bucyrus *(G-2324)*
Federal Metal Company .... D 440 232-8700
  Bedford *(G-1404)*

CASTINGS: Die, Magnesium & Magnesium-Base Alloy

Magnesium Elektron North Amer .... E 419 424-8878
  Findlay *(G-9716)*
Thompson Aluminum Casting Co .... D 216 206-2781
  Cleveland *(G-6171)*

CASTINGS: Die, Nonferrous

Certech Inc .... G 330 405-1033
  Twinsburg *(G-18750)*
Custom Industries Inc .... G 216 251-2804
  Cleveland *(G-5047)*
Dd Foundry Inc .... D 216 362-4100
  Brookpark *(G-2143)*
Empire Brass Co .... E 216 431-6565
  Cleveland *(G-5173)*
M & M Dies Inc .... G 216 883-6628
  Cleveland *(G-5590)*
Martina Metal LLC .... E 614 291-9700
  Columbus *(G-7155)*
Oakwood Industries Inc .... D 440 232-8700
  Bedford *(G-1433)*
Support Svc LLC .... G 419 617-0660
  Lexington *(G-11808)*
Teledyne Brown Engineering Inc .... D 419 470-3000
  Toledo *(G-18545)*
Tessec LLC .... E 937 985-3552
  Dayton *(G-8552)*
Yoder Industries Inc .... E 937 890-4322
  Dayton *(G-8603)*

Yoder Industries Inc .... C 937 278-5769
  Dayton *(G-8602)*

CASTINGS: Die, Zinc

American Light Metals LLC .... C 330 908-3065
  Macedonia *(G-12277)*
Cast Specialties Inc .... E 216 292-7393
  Cleveland *(G-4888)*
General Die Casters Inc .... E 330 678-2528
  Twinsburg *(G-18781)*
General Die Casters Inc .... D 330 467-6700
  Northfield *(G-15318)*
Omni USA Inc .... D 330 830-5500
  Massillon *(G-13034)*
Plaster Process Castings Co .... E 216 663-1814
  Cleveland *(G-5885)*
Ray Lewis & Son Incorporated .... E 937 644-4015
  Marysville *(G-12807)*
Reebar Die Casting Inc .... F 419 878-7591
  Waterville *(G-19503)*
SRS Die Casting Holdings LLC .... G 330 467-0750
  Macedonia *(G-12330)*
SRS Light Metals Inc .... G 330 467-0750
  Macedonia *(G-12331)*

CASTINGS: Ductile

Sancast Inc .... E 740 622-8660
  Coshocton *(G-7750)*

CASTINGS: Gray Iron

A C Williams Co Inc .... E 330 296-6110
  Ravenna *(G-16362)*
Blanchester Foundry Co Inc .... F 937 783-2091
  Blanchester *(G-1700)*
Cast Metals Incorporated .... F 419 278-2010
  Deshler *(G-8787)*
Casting Solutions LLC .... C 740 452-9371
  Zanesville *(G-21117)*
Castings Usa Inc .... G 330 339-3611
  New Philadelphia *(G-14764)*
Chris Erhart Foundry & Mch Co .... E 513 421-6550
  Cincinnati *(G-3473)*
Col-Pump Company Inc .... D 330 482-1029
  Columbiana *(G-6459)*
Domestic Casting Company LLC .... C 717 532-6615
  Delaware *(G-8673)*
Ej Usa Inc .... E 216 692-3001
  Cleveland *(G-5159)*
Foote Foundry LLC .... D 740 694-1595
  Fredericktown *(G-9969)*
General Motors LLC .... A 419 782-7010
  Defiance *(G-8623)*
Knapp Foundry Co Inc .... F 330 434-0916
  Akron *(G-240)*
Liberty Casting Company LLC .... C 740 363-1941
  Delaware *(G-8702)*
Miami-Cast Inc .... E 937 866-2951
  Miamisburg *(G-13692)*
Osco Industries Inc .... B 740 354-3183
  Portsmouth *(G-16293)*
Osco Industries Inc .... C 740 286-5004
  Jackson *(G-11193)*
Pioneer City Casting Company .... E 740 423-7533
  Belpre *(G-1582)*
Piqua Champion Foundry Inc .... E 937 773-3375
  Piqua *(G-16150)*
Quality Castings Company .... B 330 682-6871
  Orrville *(G-15613)*
St Marys Foundry Inc .... C 419 394-3346
  Saint Marys *(G-16701)*
T & B Foundry Company .... D 216 391-4200
  Cleveland *(G-6141)*
Tri Cast Limited Partnership .... E 330 733-8718
  Akron *(G-410)*
Tri-Cast Inc .... E 330 733-8718
  Akron *(G-411)*
Whemco-Ohio Foundry Inc .... C 419 222-2111
  Lima *(G-11959)*
Yellow Creek Casting Company .... E 330 532-4608
  Wellsville *(G-19615)*

CASTINGS: Machinery, Aluminum

Enprotech Industrial Tech LLC .... C 216 883-3220
  Cleveland *(G-5179)*
General Precision Corporation .... G 440 951-9380
  Willoughby *(G-20331)*
Nelson Aluminum Foundry Inc .... G 440 543-1941
  Chagrin Falls *(G-3063)*

Tri - Flex of Ohio Inc .... F 330 705-7084
  North Canton *(G-15131)*
Zephyr Industries Inc .... G 419 281-4485
  Ashland *(G-756)*

CASTINGS: Machinery, Nonferrous, Exc Die or Aluminum Copper

Rossborough Supply Co .... C 216 941-6115
  Cleveland *(G-6005)*

CASTINGS: Magnesium

A C Williams Co Inc .... E 330 296-6110
  Ravenna *(G-16362)*
Garfield Alloys Inc .... F 216 587-4843
  Cleveland *(G-5292)*
Thompson Aluminum Casting Co .... D 216 206-2781
  Cleveland *(G-6171)*

CASTINGS: Precision

Akron Foundry Co .... C 330 745-3101
  Akron *(G-40)*
Consoldted Precision Pdts Corp .... D 440 953-0053
  Eastlake *(G-9102)*
McM Precision Castings Inc .... E 419 669-3226
  Weston *(G-20177)*
PCC Airfoils LLC .... B 740 982-6025
  Crooksville *(G-7818)*
PCC Airfoils LLC .... C 216 692-7900
  Cleveland *(G-5857)*
PCC Airfoils LLC .... C 440 255-9770
  Mentor *(G-13545)*
Sam Americas Inc .... E 330 628-1118
  Mogadore *(G-14248)*
Sandusky International Inc .... C 419 626-5340
  Sandusky *(G-16843)*
Warren Castings Inc .... C 216 883-2520
  Cleveland *(G-6289)*

CASTINGS: Steel

Alcon Industries Inc .... D 216 961-1100
  Cleveland *(G-4653)*
Aza Enterprises LLC .... G 740 678-8482
  Fleming *(G-9778)*
Precision Polymer Casting LLC .... G 440 343-0461
  Moreland Hills *(G-14402)*
Rampp Company .... E 740 373-7886
  Marietta *(G-12662)*
Sandusky International Inc .... C 419 626-5340
  Sandusky *(G-16843)*
Sawbrook Steel Castings Co .... D 513 554-1700
  Cincinnati *(G-4302)*
Sns Nano Fiber Technology LLC .... G 330 655-0030
  Hudson *(G-11074)*
Worthington Industries Inc .... C 614 438-3210
  Worthington *(G-20710)*

CASTINGS: Zinc

Castmor Products Inc .... G 440 953-1103
  Willoughby *(G-20293)*
Custom Industries Inc .... G 216 251-2804
  Cleveland *(G-5047)*
Liberty Die Casting Company .... G 419 636-3971
  Bryan *(G-2297)*
Ohio Decorative Products LLC .... C 419 647-9033
  Spencerville *(G-17311)*

CATALOG & MAIL-ORDER HOUSES

Universal Drect Flfllment Corp .... C 330 650-5000
  Hudson *(G-11081)*

CATALOG SALES

Jmr Enterprises LLC .... G 937 618-1736
  Maineville *(G-12371)*

CATALYSTS: Chemical

BASF Catalysts LLC .... B 440 322-3741
  Elyria *(G-9222)*
BASF Catalysts LLC .... D 216 360-5005
  Cleveland *(G-4794)*
BLaster Corporation .... E 216 901-5800
  Cleveland *(G-4819)*
Johnson Mtthey Prcess Tech Inc .... E 330 298-7005
  Ravenna *(G-16385)*
Solvay USA Inc .... E 513 482-5700
  Cincinnati *(G-4353)*

Employee Codes: A=Over 500 employees, B=251-500
C=101-250, D=51-100, E=20-50, F=10-19, G=3-9

CATALYSTS: Chemical

United Initiators Inc ....D...... 440 326-2416
  Elyria *(G-9341)*

CATAPULTS

Leader Engnrng-Fabrication Inc..............G...... 419 636-1731
  Bryan *(G-2296)*
Universal Fabg Cnstr Svcs Inc ....D...... 614 274-1128
  Columbus *(G-7561)*

CATCH BASIN COVERS: Concrete

Wauseon Silo & Coal Company................F...... 419 335-6041
  Wauseon *(G-19538)*

CATERERS

American Showa Inc ....A...... 937 783-4961
  Blanchester *(G-1698)*
Country Caterers Inc ....G...... 740 389-1013
  Marion *(G-12700)*
Disalvos Deli & Italian Store ....G...... 937 298-5053
  Dayton *(G-8163)*
Mustard Seed Health Fd Mkt Inc..............E...... 440 519-3663
  Solon *(G-17201)*
Reineckers Bakery Ltd ....G...... 330 467-2221
  Macedonia *(G-12323)*
Todd W Goings..G...... 740 389-5842
  Marion *(G-12743)*

CATTLE WHOLESALERS

Gardner Lumber Co Inc............................F...... 740 254-4664
  Tippecanoe *(G-18148)*

CAULKING COMPOUNDS

Dap Products Inc ....C...... 937 667-4461
  Tipp City *(G-18110)*

CEILING SYSTEMS: Luminous, Commercial

Eaton Electric Holdings LLC....................B...... 440 523-5000
  Cleveland *(G-5151)*
M-Boss Inc ....E...... 216 441-6080
  Cleveland *(G-5594)*
Nordic Light America Inc ....F...... 614 981-9497
  Columbus *(G-7223)*
Norton Industries Inc ....E...... 888 357-2345
  Lakewood *(G-11532)*

CELLULOSE ACETATE

Aviles Construction Company.................E...... 216 939-1084
  Cleveland *(G-4777)*

CELLULOSE DERIVATIVE MATERIALS

Advanced Fiber LLC ....E...... 419 562-1337
  Bucyrus *(G-2317)*
Oak View Enterprises Inc ....E...... 513 860-4446
  Bucyrus *(G-2340)*

CEMENT & CONCRETE RELATED PRDTS & EQPT: Bituminous

Koski Construction Co ....G...... 440 964-8171
  Ashtabula *(G-783)*
Mesa Industries Inc..................................D...... 513 321-2950
  Cincinnati *(G-4009)*

CEMENT ROCK: Crushed & Broken

R W Sidley Incorporated ....E...... 440 352-9343
  Painesville *(G-15778)*

CEMENT, EXC LINOLEUM & TILE

Hartline Products Coinc...........................G...... 216 291-2303
  Cleveland *(G-5377)*
Hartline Products Coinc...........................G...... 216 851-7189
  Cleveland *(G-5378)*

CEMENT: Heat Resistant

Refractory Coating Tech Inc ....E...... 330 683-2200
  Orrville *(G-15614)*

CEMENT: Hydraulic

Asphalt Services Ohio Inc........................G...... 614 864-4600
  Columbus *(G-6621)*
Cincinnati Blacktop Company..................F...... 513 681-0952
  Cincinnati *(G-3486)*

Hartline Products Coinc...........................G...... 216 851-7189
  Cleveland *(G-5378)*
Huron Cement Products Company ....E...... 419 433-4161
  Huron *(G-11096)*
Lafarge North America Inc ....C...... 419 399-4861
  Paulding *(G-15864)*
Lafarge North America Inc ....G...... 216 781-9330
  Cleveland *(G-5553)*
Lafarge North America Inc ....G...... 419 241-5256
  Toledo *(G-18375)*
Lafarge North America Inc ....F...... 419 897-7656
  Maumee *(G-13125)*
Lafarge North America Inc ....G...... 740 423-5900
  Belpre *(G-1579)*
Myko Industries...G...... 216 431-0900
  Cleveland *(G-5717)*
Quikrete Companies Inc ....E...... 614 885-4406
  Columbus *(G-7369)*
Quikrete Companies LLC ....G...... 419 241-1148
  Toledo *(G-18491)*
Quikrete Companies LLC ....E...... 330 296-6080
  Ravenna *(G-16397)*
St Marys Cement Inc (us).........................G...... 937 642-4573
  Marysville *(G-12814)*

CEMENT: Masonry

Lozinak & Sons Inc ....G...... 440 877-1819
  North Royalton *(G-15284)*
Murphy James Construction LLC ....E...... 740 667-3626
  Coolville *(G-7675)*

CEMENT: Natural

Fairborn Cement Company LLC.............C...... 937 879-8393
  Xenia *(G-20771)*

CEMENT: Portland

Lehigh Hanson Ecc Inc ....G...... 614 497-2001
  Columbus *(G-7121)*
RC Lonestar Inc ....G...... 513 467-0430
  Cincinnati *(G-4251)*
Wallseye Concrete Corp..........................F...... 440 235-1800
  Cleveland *(G-6287)*
Wallseye Concrete Corp..........................F...... 419 483-2738
  Castalia *(G-2941)*

CEMENT: Rubber

LMI Custom Mixing LLC ....D...... 740 435-0444
  Cambridge *(G-2447)*

CEMETERIES: Real Estate Operation

Fort Stben Burial Estates Assn ....G...... 740 266-6101
  Steubenville *(G-17534)*

CEMETERY & FUNERAL DIRECTOR'S EQPT & SPLYS WHOLESALERS

Jls Funeral Home......................................F...... 614 625-1220
  Columbus *(G-7068)*

CEMETERY MEMORIAL DEALERS

3-G Incorporated......................................G...... 513 921-4515
  Cincinnati *(G-3269)*
Artistic Memorials Ltd ....G...... 419 873-0433
  Perrysburg *(G-15921)*
Linden Monuments...................................G...... 419 468-4130
  Galion *(G-10148)*

CERAMIC FIBER

Astro Met Inc ....E...... 513 772-1242
  Cincinnati *(G-3364)*
Maverick Corporation ....F...... 513 469-9919
  Blue Ash *(G-1816)*
Scioto Ceramic Products Inc ....E...... 614 436-0405
  Columbus *(G-7430)*

CERAMIC FLOOR & WALL TILE WHOLESALERS

Artfinders..G...... 330 264-7706
  Wooster *(G-20563)*
Clay Burley Products Co.........................E...... 740 452-3633
  Roseville *(G-16576)*

CHAIN: Wire

Manufacturers Equipment Co.................F...... 513 424-3573
  Middletown *(G-13924)*

CHAINS: Power Transmission

US Tsubaki Power Transm LLC ....C...... 419 626-4560
  Sandusky *(G-16860)*

CHALK MINING: Crushed & Broken

Chalk Outline Pictures.............................G...... 216 291-3944
  Cleveland *(G-4908)*

CHANDELIERS: Residential

Country Tin ....G...... 937 746-7229
  Franklin *(G-9877)*
Degaetano Sales.......................................G...... 440 729-8877
  Chesterland *(G-3156)*

CHARCOAL

Kingsford Ink LLC ....G...... 216 507-4032
  Cleveland Heights *(G-6349)*

CHARCOAL, WHOLESALE

Nucon International Inc ....F...... 614 846-5710
  Columbus *(G-7232)*

CHARCOAL: Activated

Calgon Carbon Corporation....................C...... 614 258-9501
  Columbus *(G-6723)*

CHASSIS: Motor Vehicle

Allen Morgan Trucking & Repair ....G...... 330 336-5192
  Norton *(G-15361)*
American Race Cars.................................G...... 419 836-5070
  Sandusky *(G-16795)*
Custom Chassis Inc.................................G...... 440 839-5574
  Wakeman *(G-19283)*
Falls Stamping & Welding Co ....C...... 330 928-1191
  Cuyahoga Falls *(G-7867)*
Jefferson Industries Corp ....G...... 614 879-5300
  West Jefferson *(G-19923)*
Mobis North America LLC ....E...... 419 729-6700
  Toledo *(G-18413)*
Progressive Automotive Inc ....G...... 740 862-4696
  Baltimore *(G-1040)*
Sutphen Corporation................................D...... 937 969-8851
  Springfield *(G-17500)*
W&W Automotive & Towing Inc..............F...... 937 429-1699
  Beavercreek Township *(G-1375)*

CHEESE WHOLESALERS

Great Lakes Cheese Co Inc....................B...... 440 834-2500
  Hiram *(G-10910)*
International Multifoods Corp.................G...... 330 682-3000
  Orrville *(G-15595)*
Lori Holding Co ....E...... 740 342-3230
  New Lexington *(G-14717)*
Troyer Cheese Inc ....E...... 330 893-2479
  Millersburg *(G-14139)*

CHEMICAL CLEANING SVCS

Bleachtech LLC...E...... 216 921-1980
  Seville *(G-16913)*
Chemical Solvents Inc ....E...... 216 741-9310
  Cleveland *(G-4919)*
Ozone Systems Svcs Group Inc.............G...... 513 899-4131
  Morrow *(G-14414)*

CHEMICAL ELEMENTS

Artistic Elements Salon LLC...................G...... 330 626-2114
  Streetsboro *(G-17661)*
Distinctive Building Elem........................G...... 419 420-5528
  Findlay *(G-9678)*
Earthganic Elements LLC ....G...... 513 430-0503
  Batavia *(G-1137)*
Element One Home Staging ....G...... 740 972-4714
  Dublin *(G-8913)*
Essential Earth Elements LLC................G...... 740 632-0682
  Toronto *(G-18607)*
Four Elements Integratve Cnsel ....G...... 216 381-8584
  Cleveland Heights *(G-6348)*
M & G Polymers Usa LLC ....E...... 330 239-7400
  Sharon Center *(G-16951)*
Motorcarbon Elements LLC....................G...... 304 617-4047
  South Point *(G-17290)*
Perstorp Polyols Inc ....C...... 419 729-5448
  Toledo *(G-18467)*

PRODUCT SECTION

CHEMICALS & ALLIED PRDTS, WHOLESALE: Sealants

CHEMICAL PROCESSING MACHINERY & EQPT

- Aquila Pharmatech LLC .... G 419 386-2527
  Waterville (G-19490)
- Cammann Inc .... F 440 965-4051
  Wakeman (G-19282)
- Cold Jet LLC .... C 513 831-3211
  Loveland (G-12183)
- Design Fabricators of Mantua .... G 330 274-5353
  Mantua (G-12545)
- Guild Associates Inc .... D 614 798-8215
  Dublin (G-8919)
- Guild Associates Inc .... G 843 573-0095
  Dublin (G-8920)
- Heil Engneered Process Eqp Inc .... F 440 327-6051
  North Ridgeville (G-15228)
- Jbw Systems Inc .... F 614 882-5008
  Westerville (G-20000)
- Processall Inc .... F 513 771-2266
  Cincinnati (G-4196)
- Regal Industries Inc .... G 440 352-9600
  Painesville (G-15780)
- Yost & Son Inc .... G 440 779-8025
  North Olmsted (G-15204)
- Zeeco Equipment Commodity .... G 440 838-1102
  Brecksville (G-2063)

CHEMICAL SPLYS FOR FOUNDRIES

- Atotech USA Inc .... D 216 398-0550
  Cleveland (G-4762)
- Global Chemical Inc .... G 419 242-1004
  Toledo (G-18306)
- Lynx Chemical .... G 513 856-9161
  Franklin (G-9896)
- Merry X-Ray Chemical Corp .... G 614 219-2011
  Hilliard (G-10839)

CHEMICALS & ALLIED PRDTS WHOLESALERS, NEC

- AIN Industries Inc .... G 440 781-0950
  Cleveland (G-4643)
- Airgas Usa LLC .... G 614 308-3730
  Columbus (G-6554)
- American Metal Cleaning Inc .... G 419 255-1828
  Toledo (G-18175)
- Aquablue Inc .... G 330 343-0220
  New Philadelphia (G-14758)
- Ashland LLC .... C 614 790-3333
  Dublin (G-8883)
- Ashland LLC .... G 513 557-3100
  Cincinnati (G-3361)
- Bleachtech LLC .... E 216 921-1980
  Seville (G-16913)
- Calvary Industries Inc .... D 513 874-1113
  Fairfield (G-9487)
- Chem-Sales Inc .... F 419 531-4292
  Toledo (G-18228)
- Chemmasters Inc .... E 440 428-2105
  Madison (G-12344)
- Corrugated Chemicals Inc .... G 513 561-7773
  Cincinnati (G-3553)
- Cs Products .... G 330 452-8566
  Canton (G-2640)
- Formlabs Ohio Inc .... E 419 837-9783
  Millbury (G-14049)
- Inceptor Inc .... G 419 726-8804
  Toledo (G-18343)
- Koch Knight LLC .... D 330 488-1651
  East Canton (G-9041)
- Leverett A Anderson Co Inc .... G 330 670-1363
  Akron (G-253)
- Netherland Rubber Company .... F 513 733-0883
  Cincinnati (G-4068)
- Polymer Additives Inc .... G 216 262-7016
  Walton Hills (G-19313)
- Polymer Additives Holdings Inc .... C 216 875-7200
  Independence (G-11147)
- PVS Chemical Solutions Inc .... F 330 666-0888
  Copley (G-7693)
- Quality Borate Co LLC .... F 216 896-1949
  Cleveland (G-5940)
- Qumont Chemical Co .... G 419 241-1057
  Toledo (G-18492)
- St John Ltd Inc .... G 614 851-8153
  Galloway (G-10181)
- Stevens Auto Glaze and SEC LL .... G 440 953-2900
  Eastlake (G-9131)

- Tricor Industrial Inc .... D 330 264-3299
  Wooster (G-20660)

CHEMICALS & ALLIED PRDTS, WHOLESALE: Anti-Corrosion Prdts

- Electro Prime Group LLC .... D 419 476-0100
  Toledo (G-18278)
- Mesocoat Inc .... F 216 453-0866
  Euclid (G-9427)
- Singleton Corporation .... F 216 651-7800
  Cleveland (G-6066)

CHEMICALS & ALLIED PRDTS, WHOLESALE: Caustic Soda

- National Colloid Company .... E 740 282-1171
  Steubenville (G-17545)

CHEMICALS & ALLIED PRDTS, WHOLESALE: Chemical Additives

- Chemcore Inc .... F 937 228-6118
  Dayton (G-8088)

CHEMICALS & ALLIED PRDTS, WHOLESALE: Chemicals, Indl

- Jamtek Enterprises Inc .... G 513 738-4700
  Harrison (G-10652)
- Lanxess Corporation .... C 440 279-2367
  Chardon (G-3123)
- Nexeo Solutions LLC .... F 800 531-7106
  Dublin (G-8956)
- Polar Inc .... F 937 297-0911
  Moraine (G-14380)
- Rotech Products Incorporated .... G 216 476-3722
  Cleveland (G-6006)
- Tembec Btlsr Inc .... E 419 244-5856
  Toledo (G-18547)
- Tosoh America Inc .... B 614 539-8622
  Grove City (G-10476)
- Univar USA Inc .... C 513 714-5264
  West Chester (G-19911)

CHEMICALS & ALLIED PRDTS, WHOLESALE: Chemicals, Indl & Heavy

- J & K Wade Ltd .... G 419 352-6163
  Bowling Green (G-1977)

CHEMICALS & ALLIED PRDTS, WHOLESALE: Concrete Additives

- Sika Corporation .... D 740 387-9224
  Marion (G-12735)

CHEMICALS & ALLIED PRDTS, WHOLESALE: Detergent/Soap

- Anatrace Products LLC .... E 419 740-6600
  Maumee (G-13071)
- Chemical Solvents Inc .... E 216 741-9310
  Cleveland (G-4919)
- Cr Brands Inc .... D 513 860-5039
  West Chester (G-19686)
- Jeff Pendergrass .... G 513 575-1226
  Milford (G-14021)

CHEMICALS & ALLIED PRDTS, WHOLESALE: Detergents

- Cleaning Lady Inc .... F 419 589-5566
  Mansfield (G-12426)
- Jabco & Associates Inc .... G 513 752-0600
  Amelia (G-542)
- Washing Systems LLC .... C 800 272-1974
  Loveland (G-12244)

CHEMICALS & ALLIED PRDTS, WHOLESALE: Dry Ice

- Gehm & Sons Limited .... G 330 724-8423
  Akron (G-185)

CHEMICALS & ALLIED PRDTS, WHOLESALE: Glue

- Tech-Bond Solutions .... G 614 327-8884
  Carroll (G-2913)

CHEMICALS & ALLIED PRDTS, WHOLESALE: Indl Gases

- Airgas Usa LLC .... E 937 228-8594
  Dayton (G-8013)

CHEMICALS & ALLIED PRDTS, WHOLESALE: Oxygen

- Jerrys Welding Supply Inc .... G 937 364-1500
  Hillsboro (G-10883)

CHEMICALS & ALLIED PRDTS, WHOLESALE: Plastics Materials, NEC

- Alro Steel Corporation .... E 419 720-5300
  Toledo (G-18166)
- Alro Steel Corporation .... E 614 878-7271
  Columbus (G-6578)
- Chatelain Plastics Inc .... G 419 422-4323
  Findlay (G-9667)
- Hillman Group Inc .... G 800 800-4900
  Parma (G-15822)
- Laird Plastics Inc .... F 614 272-0777
  Columbus (G-7110)
- Plastics R Unique Inc .... E 330 334-4820
  Wadsworth (G-19264)

CHEMICALS & ALLIED PRDTS, WHOLESALE: Plastics Prdts, NEC

- Carney Plastics Inc .... G 330 746-8273
  Youngstown (G-20866)
- Inno-Pak Holding Inc .... G 740 363-0090
  Delaware (G-8695)
- Polymer Packaging Inc .... D 330 832-2000
  Massillon (G-13040)
- Queen City Polymers Inc .... G 937 236-2710
  Dayton (G-8456)
- Queen City Polymers Inc .... E 513 779-0990
  West Chester (G-19776)
- Tahoma Enterprises Inc .... D 330 745-9016
  Barberton (G-1108)
- Tahoma Rubber & Plastics Inc .... D 330 745-9016
  Barberton (G-1109)
- Upl International Inc .... E 330 433-2860
  North Canton (G-15134)

CHEMICALS & ALLIED PRDTS, WHOLESALE: Plastics Sheets & Rods

- HP Manufacturing Company Inc .... D 216 361-6500
  Cleveland (G-5421)
- Ilpea Industries Inc .... C 330 562-2916
  Aurora (G-884)
- Total Plastics Resources LLC .... G 440 891-1140
  Cleveland (G-6192)

CHEMICALS & ALLIED PRDTS, WHOLESALE: Plastics, Basic Shapes

- Meridian Machine Inc .... G 330 308-0296
  New Philadelphia (G-14785)

CHEMICALS & ALLIED PRDTS, WHOLESALE: Resins

- Hexpol Compounding LLC .... C 440 834-4644
  Burton (G-2360)
- Polyone Corporation .... D 440 930-1000
  Avon Lake (G-1001)

CHEMICALS & ALLIED PRDTS, WHOLESALE: Rubber, Synthetic

- Goldsmith & Eggleton LLC .... F 203 855-6000
  Wadsworth (G-19243)
- Mantaline Corporation .... D 330 274-2264
  Mantua (G-12551)

CHEMICALS & ALLIED PRDTS, WHOLESALE: Sealants

- McGill Corporation .... F 614 829-1200
  Groveport (G-10504)
- United McGill Corporation .... E 614 829-1200
  Groveport (G-10516)

Employee Codes: A=Over 500 employees, B=251-500
C=101-250, D=51-100, E=20-50, F=10-19, G=3-9

CHEMICALS & ALLIED PRDTS, WHOLESALE: Syn Resin, Rub/Plastic

CHEMICALS & ALLIED PRDTS, WHOLESALE: Syn Resin, Rub/Plastic

Flex Technologies Inc	E	330 897-6311
Baltic (G-1029)		
Kraton Polymers US LLC	B	740 423-7571
Belpre (G-1578)		
Phoenix Technologies Intl LLC	E	419 353-7738
Bowling Green (G-1990)		
Polyone Corporation	D	440 930-1000
North Baltimore (G-15047)		

CHEMICALS & ALLIED PRDTS, WHOLESALE: Waxes, Exc Petroleum

K2 Petroleum & Supply LLC	G	937 503-2614
Cincinnati (G-3891)		

CHEMICALS & OTHER PRDTS DERIVED FROM COKING

Chemwise	G	419 425-3604
Findlay (G-9668)		
FBC Chemical Corporation	G	216 341-2000
Cleveland (G-5223)		
Geauga Coatings LLC	G	440 286-5571
Chardon (G-3113)		

CHEMICALS, AGRICULTURE: Wholesalers

Harvest Land Co-Op Inc	G	937 884-5526
Verona (G-19172)		
Helena Agri-Enterprises LLC	G	614 275-4200
Columbus (G-6986)		
Tyler Grain & Fertilizer Co	F	330 669-2341
Smithville (G-17095)		

CHEMICALS: Agricultural

Harvest Land Co-Op Inc	G	937 884-5526
Verona (G-19172)		
Hawthorne Hydroponics LLC	D	480 777-2000
Marysville (G-12787)		
Isky North America Inc	G	937 823-9595
Vandalia (G-19130)		
Mercer Landmark Inc	G	419 363-3391
Rockford (G-16540)		
Modern AG Supply Inc	G	419 753-3484
New Knoxville (G-14705)		
Monsanto Company	F	937 548-7858
Greenville (G-10384)		
Quality Borate Co LLC	F	216 896-1949
Cleveland (G-5940)		
Village of Dupont	G	419 596-3061
Dupont (G-9037)		

CHEMICALS: Alcohols

Catholic Charity Hispanic Off	F	216 696-2197
Cleveland (G-4891)		

CHEMICALS: Alkalies

Valvsys LLC	G	513 539-1234
Monroe (G-14279)		

CHEMICALS: Aluminum Compounds

Drs Industries Inc	D	419 861-0334
Holland (G-10928)		
Gayston Corporation	C	937 743-6050
Miamisburg (G-13672)		
Pennex Aluminum	D	330 427-6704
Leetonia (G-11719)		

CHEMICALS: Aluminum Oxide

Custom Metal Shearing Inc	F	937 233-6950
Dayton (G-8120)		

CHEMICALS: Aluminum Sulfate

Chemtrade Chemicals US LLC	G	513 422-6319
Middletown (G-13893)		
Dpa Investments Inc	F	440 992-7039
Ashtabula (G-772)		

CHEMICALS: Bauxite, Refined

Porocel Industries LLC	G	513 733-8519
Cincinnati (G-4172)		

CHEMICALS: Bleaching Powder, Lime Bleaching Compounds

Bleachtech LLC	E	216 921-1980
Seville (G-16913)		

CHEMICALS: Calcium & Calcium Compounds

New Eezy-Gro Inc	F	419 927-6110
Upper Sandusky (G-18967)		
Omya Distribution LLC	G	513 387-4600
Blue Ash (G-1827)		

CHEMICALS: Caustic Potash & Potassium Hydroxide

Ashta Chemicals Inc	D	440 997-5221
Ashtabula (G-762)		

CHEMICALS: Caustic Soda

Gbc Metals LLC	E	330 823-1700
Alliance (G-469)		

CHEMICALS: Copper Compounds Or Salts, Inorganic

Three Leaf Inc	G	888 308-1007
Fairfield Township (G-9588)		

CHEMICALS: Fire Retardant

No Burn Inc	G	330 336-1500
Wadsworth (G-19256)		
No Burn North America Inc	F	419 841-6055
Toledo (G-18426)		
Polymer Additives Inc	G	216 875-5840
Cleveland (G-5895)		
Pyro-Chem Corporation	F	740 377-2244
South Point (G-17292)		
Viking Group Inc	G	937 443-0433
Dayton (G-8580)		

CHEMICALS: High Purity Grade, Organic

Enzyme Catalyzed Polymers LLC	G	330 310-1072
Akron (G-158)		
Ronald T Dodge Co	F	937 439-4497
Dayton (G-8484)		

CHEMICALS: High Purity, Refined From Technical Grade

Arboris LLC	E	740 522-9350
Newark (G-14852)		
Gabriel Performance Pdts LLC	F	866 800-2436
Akron (G-180)		
Gabriel Performance Pdts LLC	G	440 992-3200
Ashtabula (G-778)		
Helena Agri-Enterprises LLC	G	419 596-3806
Continental (G-7666)		
Helena Agri-Enterprises LLC	G	614 275-4200
Columbus (G-6986)		
Heraeus Precious Metals North	E	937 264-1000
Vandalia (G-19127)		

CHEMICALS: Inorganic, NEC

Airgas Usa LLC	G	440 232-6397
Oakwood Village (G-15477)		
Akron Dispersions Inc	E	330 666-0045
Copley (G-7676)		
Alchem Corporation	G	330 725-2436
Medina (G-13221)		
Allyn Corp	G	614 442-3900
Columbus (G-6575)		
Alpha Zeta Holdings Inc	G	216 271-1601
Cleveland (G-4677)		
Aluchem Inc	E	513 733-8519
Cincinnati (G-3327)		
Aluchem of Jackson Inc	E	740 286-2455
Jackson (G-11180)		
Americhem Inc	A	330 929-4213
Cuyahoga Falls (G-7835)		
Amresco LLC	C	440 349-2805
Cleveland (G-4701)		
Arizona Chemical Company LLC	C	330 343-7701
Dover (G-8804)		
Bio-Systems Corporation	D	608 365-9550
Bowling Green (G-1956)		
Blue Cube Operations LLC	G	440 248-1223
Macedonia (G-12280)		
Bond Chemicals Inc	F	330 725-5935
Medina (G-13230)		
Borchers Americas Inc	D	440 899-2950
Westlake (G-20103)		
C T Chemicals Inc	G	513 459-9744
Lebanon (G-11638)		
Calvary Industries Inc	D	513 874-1113
Fairfield (G-9487)		
Chem Technologies Ltd	E	440 632-9311
Middlefield (G-13783)		
Chemtrade Refinery Svcs Inc	F	419 641-4151
Cairo (G-2402)		
Cil Isotope Separations LLC	F	937 376-5413
Xenia (G-20761)		
Cincinnati Specialties LLC	C	513 242-3300
Cincinnati (G-3507)		
Coolant Control Inc	E	513 471-8770
Cincinnati (G-3548)		
Cristal USA Inc	C	440 994-1400
Ashtabula (G-769)		
Curtis Chemical Inc	G	330 656-2514
Hudson (G-11040)		
Db Parent Inc	G	513 475-3265
Cincinnati (G-3578)		
Diverseylever Inc	G	513 554-4200
Cincinnati (G-3593)		
Diversified Brands	G	216 595-8777
Bedford (G-1401)		
Dover Chemical Corporation	C	330 343-7711
Dover (G-8819)		
Dpa Investments Inc	G	440 992-3377
Ashtabula (G-771)		
Dpa Investments Inc	G	513 737-7100
Fairfield (G-9495)		
Elco Corporation	E	440 997-6131
Ashtabula (G-773)		
Elements LLC	G	937 663-5837
Saint Paris (G-16708)		
Enerchem Incorporated	G	513 745-0580
Cincinnati (G-3639)		
Engelhard Corp	G	440 322-3741
Elyria (G-9258)		
Evonik Corporation	D	513 554-8969
Cincinnati (G-3661)		
Ferro Corporation	D	216 577-7144
Bedford (G-1405)		
General Electric Company	D	216 268-3846
Cleveland (G-5310)		
Globe Metallurgical Inc	C	740 984-2361
Waterford (G-19484)		
Gnrl Chemical L	G	419 255-0193
Toledo (G-18307)		
Graphite Sales Inc	E	419 652-3388
Nova (G-15434)		
Hilltop Energy Inc	E	330 859-2108
Mineral City (G-14164)		
Illinois Tool Works Inc	D	440 914-3100
Solon (G-17166)		
Kerry Flavor Systems Us LLC	E	513 539-7373
Monroe (G-14270)		
Kingscote Chemicals Inc	G	330 523-5300
Richfield (G-16475)		
Littlern Corporation		330 848-8847
Barberton (G-1081)		
McGean-Rohco Inc	D	216 441-4900
Newburgh Heights (G-14941)		
Molecular Research Center	F	513 841-0900
Cincinnati (G-4040)		
Nachurs Alpine Solutions Corp	E	740 382-5701
Marion (G-12723)		
National Colloid Company	E	740 282-1171
Steubenville (G-17545)		
Nutrien AG Solutions Inc	E	513 941-4100
North Bend (G-15053)		
Occidental Chemical Corp	E	513 242-2900
Cincinnati (G-4097)		
Occidental Chemical Durez	G	419 675-5300
Kenton (G-11417)		
Ohio Oxide Corporation Del	F	740 654-6555
Pleasantville (G-16229)		
Omnova Solutions Inc	D	330 734-1237
Akron (G-311)		
Omnova Solutions Inc	C	216 682-7000
Beachwood (G-1257)		
Omnova Wallcovering USA Inc	G	216 682-7000
Beachwood (G-1258)		
Pickett Enterprises Inc	G	937 428-6747
Dayton (G-8425)		

PRODUCT SECTION — CHEMICALS: NEC

Company	Code	Phone
PMC Specialties Group Inc	E	513 242-3300
Cincinnati (G-4169)		
PMC Specialties Group Inc	G	513 242-3300
Cincinnati (G-4170)		
Polymerics Inc	E	330 434-6665
Cuyahoga Falls (G-7906)		
PQ Corporation	G	216 341-2578
Newburgh Heights (G-14943)		
Press Chemical & Phrm Lab	G	614 863-2802
Columbus (G-7345)		
Process Sltions For Indust Inc	G	330 702-1685
Canfield (G-2541)		
Rtprocess LLC	G	937 366-6215
Wilmington (G-20508)		
Saint-Gobain Ceramics Plas Inc	A	330 673-5860
Stow (G-17624)		
Saint-Gobain Ceramics Plas Inc	C	440 834-5600
Hiram (G-10911)		
Selective Micro Tech LLC	G	614 551-5974
Dublin (G-8982)		
Shepherd Chemical Company	F	513 200-6987
Cincinnati (G-4331)		
Tate Lyle Ingrdnts Amricas LLC	D	937 236-5906
Dayton (G-8541)		
TEC Line Inc	G	740 881-5948
Lewis Center (G-11783)		
Tiger Sul Products LLC	G	203 451-3305
West Liberty (G-19938)		
Tru-Chem Company Inc	F	614 888-2436
Columbus (G-7547)		
Union Camp Corp	G	330 343-7701
Dover (G-8862)		
Univar USA Inc	C	513 714-5264
West Chester (G-19911)		
VWR Chemicals LLC	E	800 448-4442
Solon (G-17258)		
WA Hammond Drierite Co Ltd	E	937 376-2927
Xenia (G-20803)		
Zaclon LLC	E	216 271-1601
Cleveland (G-6335)		

CHEMICALS: Isotopes, Radioactive

Company	Code	Phone
Aldrich Chemical	D	937 859-1808
Miamisburg (G-13638)		

CHEMICALS: Lead Compounds/Salts, Inorganic, Not Pigments

Company	Code	Phone
Metals and Additives Corp Inc	F	740 654-6555
Pleasantville (G-16228)		

CHEMICALS: Lithium Compounds, Inorganic

Company	Code	Phone
Lithium Innovations Co LLC	G	419 843-6051
Toledo (G-18386)		

CHEMICALS: Luminous Compounds, Radium

Company	Code	Phone
Solvay Advanced Polymers LLC	F	740 373-9242
Marietta (G-12672)		

CHEMICALS: Medicinal

Company	Code	Phone
Amresco LLC	D	440 349-2805
Solon (G-17107)		
Pharmacia Hepar LLC	D	937 746-3603
Franklin (G-9909)		
Polar Products Inc	G	330 253-9973
Stow (G-17619)		
Proctoer & Gamble	G	513 983-1100
Blue Ash (G-1837)		

CHEMICALS: Medicinal, Organic, Uncompounded, Bulk

Company	Code	Phone
Nutritional Medicinals LLC	F	937 433-4673
West Chester (G-19750)		
Press Chemical & Phrm Lab	G	614 863-2802
Columbus (G-7345)		

CHEMICALS: Metal Salts/Compounds, Exc Sodium, Potassium/Alum

Company	Code	Phone
Shepherd Chemical Company	F	513 731-1110
Cincinnati (G-4332)		
Shepherd Chemical Company	F	513 424-7276
Middletown (G-13952)		
Shepherd Material Science Co	F	513 731-1110
Norwood (G-15428)		

CHEMICALS: NEC

Company	Code	Phone
Additive Technology Inc	G	419 968-2777
Middle Point (G-13754)		
Advanced Chem Solutions Inc	G	216 692-3005
Orrville (G-15582)		
Akron Dispersions Inc	E	330 666-0045
Copley (G-7676)		
Akzo Nobel Chemicals LLC	E	419 229-0088
Lima (G-11833)		
Aldrich Chemical	D	937 859-1808
Miamisburg (G-13638)		
Allyn Corp	G	614 442-3900
Columbus (G-6575)		
Amresco LLC	C	440 349-2805
Cleveland (G-4701)		
Aps-Materials Inc	G	937 278-6547
Dayton (G-8034)		
Ashland LLC	C	614 790-3333
Dublin (G-8883)		
Ashland LLC	G	513 682-2405
West Chester (G-19652)		
Ashland LLC	E	419 998-8728
Lima (G-11844)		
Ask Chemicals	F	216 961-4690
Cleveland (G-4751)		
Ask Chemicals LLC	E	800 848-7485
Dublin (G-8885)		
Attia Applied Sciences Inc	G	740 369-1891
Delaware (G-8656)		
Bernard Laboratories Inc	E	513 681-7373
Cincinnati (G-3391)		
Bird Control International	E	330 425-2377
Twinsburg (G-18741)		
BLaster Corporation	E	216 901-5800
Cleveland (G-4819)		
Bond Distributing LLC	E	440 461-7920
Cleveland (G-4830)		
Borchers Americas Inc	D	440 899-2950
Westlake (G-20103)		
Brewer Industries LLC	G	216 469-0808
Chagrin Falls (G-3011)		
Bulk Molding Compounds Inc	D	419 874-7941
Perrysburg (G-15926)		
Capital Chemical Co	E	330 494-9535
Canton (G-2619)		
Cargill Incorporated	F	513 941-7400
Cincinnati (G-3443)		
Cargill Incorporated	C	216 651-7200
Cleveland (G-4877)		
Chem Technologies Ltd	E	440 632-9311
Middlefield (G-13783)		
Chemical Methods Inc	E	216 476-8400
Strongsville (G-17725)		
Cinchempro Inc	C	513 724-6111
Batavia (G-1129)		
Cincinnati - Vulcan Company	E	513 242-5300
Cincinnati (G-3477)		
Coolant Control Inc	E	513 471-8770
Cincinnati (G-3548)		
CP Chemicals Group LP	D	440 833-3000
Wickliffe (G-20208)		
Creative Commercial Finishing	G	513 722-9393
Loveland (G-12184)		
Cresset Chemical Co Inc	F	419 669-2041
Weston (G-20175)		
Cresset Chemical Co Inc	F	419 669-2041
Weston (G-20176)		
Dayton Superior Corporation	C	937 866-0711
Miamisburg (G-13655)		
Dover Chemical Corporation	C	330 343-7711
Dover (G-8819)		
Durr Megtec LLC	C	614 258-9501
Columbus (G-6876)		
Elco Corporation	E	440 997-6131
Ashtabula (G-773)		
EMD Millipore Corporation	C	513 631-0445
Norwood (G-15426)		
Emerald Performance Mtls LLC	D	513 841-4000
Cincinnati (G-3634)		
Emerald Performance Mtls LLC	D	330 374-2418
Akron (G-152)		
Ensign Product Company Inc	G	216 341-5911
Cleveland (G-5180)		
Envirnmntal Prtctive Ctngs LLC	G	740 363-6180
Ostrander (G-15643)		
Environment Chemical Corp	G	330 453-5200
Uniontown (G-18918)		
Etna Products Incorporated	E	440 543-9845
Chagrin Falls (G-3046)		
Euclid Chemical Company	E	800 321-7628
Cleveland (G-5193)		
Euclid Chemical Company	F	216 292-5000
Beachwood (G-1238)		
Euclid Chemical Company	D	216 531-9222
Cleveland (G-5194)		
Ferro Corporation	D	216 875-5600
Cleveland (G-5232)		
Flexsys America LP	D	330 666-4111
Akron (G-173)		
Formlabs Ohio Inc	E	419 837-9783
Millbury (G-14049)		
Fort Amanda Specialties LLC	D	419 229-0088
Lima (G-11865)		
Fuchs Lubricants Co	E	330 963-0400
Twinsburg (G-18777)		
Fusion Automation Inc	G	440 602-5595
Willoughby (G-20326)		
Fusion Ceramics Inc	E	330 627-5821
Carrollton (G-2920)		
Galapagos Inc	G	937 890-3068
Dayton (G-8213)		
General Electric Company	D	216 268-3846
Cleveland (G-5310)		
GFS Chemicals Inc	E	740 881-5501
Powell (G-16322)		
GFS Chemicals Inc	D	614 224-5345
Columbus (G-6950)		
Global Bioprotect LLC	F	336 861-0162
Columbus (G-6495)		
Grean Technologies LLC	G	513 510-7116
Monroe (G-14265)		
Harsco Corporation	D	330 372-1781
Warren (G-19408)		
Hexion LLC	G	614 225-4000
Columbus (G-6993)		
Hexpol Compounding LLC	C	440 834-4644
Burton (G-2360)		
Hill & Griffith Company	G	513 921-1075
Cincinnati (G-3812)		
Hunt Imaging LLC	E	440 826-0433
Berea (G-1611)		
Illinois Tool Works Inc	D	440 914-3100
Solon (G-17166)		
Ineos LLC	D	419 226-1200
Lima (G-11877)		
Ink Factory Inc	G	330 799-0888
Youngstown (G-20940)		
Jay Tackett	G	740 779-1715
Frankfort (G-9862)		
Jeff Pendergrass	G	513 575-1226
Milford (G-14021)		
Joules Angstrom UV Printing	E	740 964-9113
Etna (G-9395)		
Leonhardt Plating Company	E	513 242-1410
Cincinnati (G-3938)		
Liquid Development Company	G	216 641-9366
Independence (G-11141)		
Lubrizol Advanced Mtls Inc	E	419 352-5565
Bowling Green (G-1982)		
Lubrizol Advanced Mtls Inc	C	440 933-0400
Avon Lake (G-993)		
Lubrizol Corporation	E	440 357-7064
Painesville (G-15758)		
Lubrizol Corporation	G	216 447-6212
Akron (G-261)		
Lubrizol Global Management	F	216 447-5000
Brecksville (G-2048)		
McGean-Rohco Inc	D	216 441-4900
Newburgh Heights (G-14941)		
Momentive Performance	G	281 325-3536
Columbus (G-7192)		
Momentive Performance Mtls Inc	G	614 986-2495
Columbus (G-7193)		
Monarch Engraving Inc	E	440 638-1500
Strongsville (G-17766)		
Morgan Advanced Ceramics Inc	G	330 405-1033
Twinsburg (G-18822)		
Morton Salt Inc	C	330 925-3015
Rittman (G-16526)		
National Colloid Company	E	740 282-1171
Steubenville (G-17545)		
New Vulco Mfg & Sales Co LLC	D	513 242-2672
Cincinnati (G-4072)		
Noco Company	B	216 464-8131
Solon (G-17208)		
Nof Metal Coatings N Amer Inc	E	440 285-2231
Chardon (G-3128)		
Noveon Fcc Inc	G	440 943-4200
Wickliffe (G-20219)		

Employee Codes: A=Over 500 employees, B=251-500
C=101-250, D=51-100, E=20-50, F=10-19, G=3-9

CHEMICALS: NEC

Ohio Aluminum Chemicals LLC	G	513 860-3842
West Chester (G-19752)		
Oliver Chemical Co Inc	G	513 541-4540
Cincinnati (G-4110)		
Parker Trutec Incorporated	D	937 653-8500
Urbana (G-19007)		
Polymer Additives Inc	D	216 875-7200
Independence (G-11146)		
Polymer Additives Inc	G	216 262-7016
Walton Hills (G-19313)		
Polymer Additives Holdings Inc	C	216 875-7200
Independence (G-11147)		
Polymerics Inc	E	330 677-1131
Kent (G-11364)		
Premier Ink Systems Inc	F	513 367-2300
Harrison (G-10664)		
Quaker Chemical Corporation	D	513 422-9600
Middletown (G-13947)		
Quikrete Companies Inc	E	614 885-4406
Columbus (G-7369)		
Railtech Matweld Inc	G	419 592-5050
Napoleon (G-14558)		
Railtech Matweld Inc	G	419 591-3770
Napoleon (G-14559)		
Research Organics LLC	D	216 883-8025
Cleveland (G-5978)		
Rhenium Alloys Inc	D	440 365-7388
North Ridgeville (G-15251)		
Rozzi Company Inc	F	513 683-0620
Martinsville (G-12767)		
Smithfield Bioscience Inc	E	513 772-8130
Cincinnati (G-4347)		
Solvay USA Inc	E	513 482-5700
Cincinnati (G-4353)		
State Industrial Products Corp	B	877 747-6986
Cleveland (G-6097)		
Summitville Tiles Inc	E	330 868-6463
Minerva (G-14203)		
Sun & Soil LLC	G	513 575-5900
Loveland (G-12237)		
Tate Lyle Ingrdnts Amricas LLC	D	937 236-5906
Dayton (G-8541)		
Teknol Inc	D	937 264-0190
Dayton (G-8550)		
U S Chemical & Plastics	C	740 254-4311
Massillon (G-13055)		
Univar USA Inc	C	513 714-5264
West Chester (G-19911)		
Valtris Specialty Chemicals	G	216 875-7200
Walton Hills (G-19316)		
Vesuvius U S A Corporation	D	440 593-1161
Conneaut (G-7661)		
Vesuvius U S A Corporation	E	440 816-3051
Cleveland (G-6254)		
Zinkan Enterprises Inc	F	330 487-1500
Twinsburg (G-18878)		

CHEMICALS: Nonmetallic Compounds

Baerlocher Production Usa LLC	E	513 482-6300
Cincinnati (G-3377)		
Baerlocher Usa LLC	F	330 364-6000
Dover (G-8805)		

CHEMICALS: Organic, NEC

1803 Bacon Ltd	G	740 398-7644
Columbus (G-6510)		
Abitec Corporation	E	614 429-6464
Columbus (G-6527)		
ABS Materials Inc	D	330 234-7999
Wooster (G-20553)		
Akzo Nobel Chemicals LLC	F	419 229-0088
Lima (G-11833)		
Alco-Chem Inc	E	330 253-3535
Akron (G-56)		
Aldrich Chemical	D	937 859-1808
Miamisburg (G-13638)		
Alpha Zeta Holdings Inc	G	216 271-1601
Cleveland (G-4677)		
Ampacet Corporation	C	740 929-5521
Newark (G-14850)		
BASF Corporation	C	937 547-6700
Greenville (G-10360)		
BASF Corporation	C	419 877-5308
Whitehouse (G-20188)		
BASF Corporation	C	513 482-3000
Cincinnati (G-3381)		
Borchers Americas Inc	D	440 899-2950
Westlake (G-20103)		
Cargill Incorporated	F	513 941-7400
Cincinnati (G-3443)		
Chem-Sales Inc	F	419 531-4292
Toledo (G-18228)		
Chemcore Inc	F	937 228-6118
Dayton (G-8088)		
Clariant Corporation	G	513 791-2964
Blue Ash (G-1751)		
Controlled Release Society Inc	E	513 948-8000
Cincinnati (G-3545)		
Corrugated Chemicals Inc	C	513 561-7773
Cincinnati (G-3553)		
Dnd Emulsions Inc	G	419 525-4988
Mansfield (G-12433)		
Dover Chemical Corporation	C	330 343-7711
Dover (G-8819)		
Dow Chemical Company	D	937 839-4612
West Alexandria (G-19618)		
Elco Corporation	E	440 997-6131
Ashtabula (G-773)		
Elco Corporation	D	800 321-0467
Cleveland (G-5160)		
Emerald Polymer Additives LLC	D	330 374-2424
Akron (G-153)		
Eqm Technologies & Energy Inc	F	513 825-7500
Cincinnati (G-3650)		
Equistar Chemicals LP	F	513 530-4000
Cincinnati (G-3651)		
Ferro Corporation	D	216 577-7144
Bedford (G-1405)		
Geo Specialty Chemical	G	330 650-0237
Hudson (G-11045)		
GFS Chemicals Inc	E	740 881-5501
Powell (G-16322)		
GFS Chemicals Inc	D	614 224-5345
Columbus (G-6950)		
Green Harvest Energy LLC	F	330 716-3068
Columbiana (G-6467)		
Ha-International LLC	E	419 537-0096
Toledo (G-18317)		
Heraeus Precious Metals North	E	937 264-1000
Vandalia (G-19127)		
Hill & Griffith Company	G	513 921-1075
Cincinnati (G-3812)		
Hunt Imaging LLC	F	440 826-0433
Berea (G-1611)		
Ibidltd-Blue Green Energy	F	909 547-5160
Toledo (G-18339)		
Ineos Nitriles USA LLC	F	419 226-1200
Lima (G-11878)		
Insightfuel LLC	F	330 998-7380
Macedonia (G-12304)		
J R M Chemical Inc	F	216 475-8488
Cleveland (G-5487)		
Jatrodiesel Inc	F	937 847-8050
Miamisburg (G-13681)		
K & E Chemical Co Inc	F	216 341-0500
Cleveland (G-5511)		
Karl Industries Inc	G	330 562-4100
Aurora (G-887)		
Littlern Corporation	G	330 848-8847
Barberton (G-1081)		
Lubrizol Corporation	A	440 943-4200
Wickliffe (G-20215)		
Lyondell Chemical Company	E	440 352-9393
Fairport Harbor (G-9625)		
Momentive Specialty Chem Inc	F	740 452-5451
Zanesville (G-21158)		
Nachurs Alpine Solutions Corp	E	740 382-5701
Marion (G-12723)		
National Colloid Company	E	740 282-1171
Steubenville (G-17545)		
Nease Co LLC	F	513 587-2800
West Chester (G-19747)		
Novation Solutions LLC	G	330 620-1189
Barberton (G-1090)		
Noveon Fcc Inc	C	440 943-4200
Wickliffe (G-20219)		
Occidental Chemical Corp	E	513 242-2900
Cincinnati (G-4097)		
Ohio Biosystems Coop Inc	G	419 980-7663
Loudonville (G-12146)		
Orion Engineered Carbons LLC	D	740 423-9571
Belpre (G-1581)		
Pen Brands LLC	E	216 674-1430
Brooklyn Heights (G-2129)		
Polychem Dispersions Inc	E	800 545-3530
Middlefield (G-13848)		
Polymer Additives Inc	G	216 875-7273
Cleveland (G-5894)		
Research Organics LLC	D	216 883-8025
Cleveland (G-5978)		
Shepherd Chemical Company	F	513 200-6987
Cincinnati (G-4331)		
Shepherd Material Science Co	F	513 731-1110
Norwood (G-15428)		
Trugreen Cleaners LLC	G	740 703-1063
Chillicothe (G-3229)		
Twin Rvers Tech - Pnsville LLC	D	440 350-6300
Painesville (G-15793)		
Ultimate Chem Solutions Inc	C	440 998-6751
Ashtabula (G-809)		
Union Carbide Corporation	D	216 529-3784
Cleveland (G-6231)		
United Initiators Inc	D	440 326-2416
Elyria (G-9341)		
Univar USA Inc	C	513 714-5264
West Chester (G-19911)		
Vantage Specialty Ingredients	F	937 264-1222
Englewood (G-9382)		
Zaclon LLC	E	216 271-1601
Cleveland (G-6335)		

CHEMICALS: Phenol

Altivia Petrochemicals LLC	E	740 532-3420
Haverhill (G-10707)		

CHEMICALS: Phosphates, Defluorinated/Ammoniated, Exc Fertlr

Pcs Phosphate Company Inc	C	513 738-1261
Harrison (G-10662)		

CHEMICALS: Reagent Grade, Refined From Technical Grade

Adna Inc	G	614 397-4974
Dublin (G-8873)		
GFS Chemicals Inc	E	740 881-5501
Powell (G-16322)		
GFS Chemicals Inc	D	614 224-5345
Columbus (G-6950)		
GFS Chemicals Inc	D	614 351-5347
Columbus (G-6951)		
Rapid Blanket Restorer Corp	G	330 821-6326
Willoughby (G-20418)		

CHEMICALS: Sodium Bicarbonate

Church & Dwight Co Inc	D	740 852-3621
London (G-12053)		
Church & Dwight Co Inc	F	419 992-4244
Old Fort (G-15524)		

CHEMICALS: Sulfur Chloride

PVS Chemical Solutions Inc	F	330 666-0888
Copley (G-7693)		

CHEMICALS: Tin, Stannic/Stannous, Compounds/Salts, Inorganic

Ohio Coatings Company	D	740 859-5500
Yorkville (G-20827)		

CHEMICALS: Water Treatment

Anchor Corporation	G	614 836-9590
Columbus (G-6600)		
Aqua Science Inc	E	614 252-5000
Columbus (G-6611)		
Aquablue Inc	G	330 343-0220
New Philadelphia (G-14758)		
Bond Chemicals Inc	F	330 725-5935
Medina (G-13230)		
City of Mount Vernon	G	740 393-9508
Mount Vernon (G-14475)		
Enviro Polymers & Chemicals	G	937 427-1315
Beavercreek (G-1314)		
Ques Industries Inc	F	216 267-8989
Cleveland (G-5946)		
Qumont Chemical Co	G	419 241-1057
Toledo (G-18492)		
Suez Wts Usa Inc	E	330 339-2292
New Philadelphia (G-14802)		
Tidewater Products Inc	G	419 873-0223
Perrysburg (G-16016)		
Tidewater Products Inc	G	419 534-9870
Ottawa Hills (G-15678)		
US Water Company LLC	G	740 453-0604
Zanesville (G-21186)		
Usalco Fairfield Plant LLC	E	513 737-7100
Fairfield (G-9571)		

PRODUCT SECTION

CIRCUITS: Electronic

CHEMICALS: Zinc Chloride
Columbia Chemical Corporation ....E 330 225-3200
  Brunswick *(G-2196)*

CHICKEN SLAUGHTERING & PROCESSING
Pf Management Inc ....G 513 874-8741
  West Chester *(G-19885)*
Pierre Holding Corp ....G 513 874-8741
  West Chester *(G-19886)*
V H Cooper & Co Inc ....C 419 375-4116
  Fort Recovery *(G-9829)*

CHILD DAY CARE SVCS
L & H Printing ....G 937 855-4512
  Germantown *(G-10243)*

CHILD RESTRAINT SEATS, AUTOMOTIVE, WHOLESALE
Recaro Child Safety LLC ....E 248 904-1570
  Cincinnati *(G-4253)*

CHILDREN'S WEAR STORES
L Brands Inc ....C 614 479-2000
  Columbus *(G-7106)*
Locker Room Lettering Ltd ....G 419 359-1761
  Castalia *(G-2940)*

CHIMNEY CAPS: Concrete
Day Pre-Cast Products Co ....G 419 536-2909
  Toledo *(G-18254)*
Whempys Corp ....G 614 888-6670
  Worthington *(G-20707)*

CHIMNEY CLEANING SVCS
Whempys Corp ....G 614 888-6670
  Worthington *(G-20707)*

CHINA: Fired & Decorated
Kiln of Hyde Park Inc ....F 513 321-3307
  Cincinnati *(G-3908)*
Potter House ....G 419 584-1705
  Celina *(G-2981)*

CHINAWARE WHOLESALERS
Ghp II LLC ....B 740 681-6825
  Lancaster *(G-11576)*

CHIROPRACTORS' OFFICES
A&M Woodworking ....G 513 722-5415
  Loveland *(G-12173)*
Polar Products Inc ....G 330 253-9973
  Stow *(G-17619)*

CHLORINE
Clorox Company ....F 513 445-1840
  Mason *(G-12848)*
Clorox Sales Company ....E 440 892-1700
  Westlake *(G-20106)*
Jci Jones Chemicals Inc ....F 330 825-2531
  New Franklin *(G-14692)*

CHOCOLATE, EXC CANDY FROM BEANS: Chips, Powder, Block, Syrup
Anthony-Thomas Candy Company ....C 614 274-8405
  Columbus *(G-6606)*
Becky Knapp ....G 330 854-4400
  Canal Fulton *(G-2476)*
Brandts Candies ....G 440 942-1016
  Willoughby *(G-20286)*
Brownie Points Inc ....G 614 860-8470
  Columbus *(G-6705)*
Cheryl & Co ....D 614 776-1500
  Obetz *(G-15509)*
Chocolate Pig Inc ....E 440 461-4511
  Cleveland *(G-4923)*
Dietsch Brothers Incorporated ....D 419 422-4474
  Findlay *(G-9677)*
E R B Enterprises Inc ....G 740 948-9174
  Jeffersonville *(G-11246)*
Fawn Confectionery ....F 513 574-9612
  Cincinnati *(G-3675)*

Gorant Chocolatier LLC ....C 330 726-8821
  Boardman *(G-1899)*
Graeters Manufacturing Co ....D 513 721-3323
  Cincinnati *(G-3774)*
Harry London Candies Inc ....D 330 494-0833
  North Canton *(G-15092)*
Haute Chocolate Inc ....G 513 793-9999
  Montgomery *(G-14294)*
Malleys Candies ....C 216 362-8700
  Lakewood *(G-11528)*
Malleys Candies Inc ....E 216 529-6262
  Cleveland *(G-5609)*
Milk & Honey ....F 330 492-5884
  Canton *(G-2755)*
Neumeisters Candy Shoppe LLC .....G 419 294-3647
  Upper Sandusky *(G-18966)*
Robert E McGrath Inc ....E 440 572-7747
  Strongsville *(G-17783)*

CHOCOLATE, EXC CANDY FROM PURCH CHOC: Chips, Powder, Block
Golden Turtle Chocolate Fctry ....G 513 932-1990
  Lebanon *(G-11658)*
Hartville Chocolates Inc ....F 330 877-1999
  Hartville *(G-10692)*

CHRISTMAS NOVELTIES, WHOLESALE
Sterling Collectables Inc ....G 419 892-5708
  Mansfield *(G-12520)*

CHRISTMAS TREE LIGHTING SETS: Electric
Christmas Ranch LLC ....E 513 505-3865
  Morrow *(G-14409)*

CHUCKS
Ajax Industries Inc ....E 614 272-6944
  Columbus *(G-6556)*
Dillon Manufacturing Inc ....F 937 325-8482
  Springfield *(G-17388)*
Flex-E-On Inc ....F 330 928-4496
  Cuyahoga Falls *(G-7868)*
Hammill Manufacturing Co ....D 419 476-0789
  Maumee *(G-13115)*
Jerry Tools Inc ....F 513 242-3211
  Cincinnati *(G-3871)*
Shook Manufactured Pdts Inc ....G 330 848-9780
  Akron *(G-375)*
Shook Manufactured Pdts Inc ....G 440 247-9130
  Chagrin Falls *(G-3029)*

CHUTES & TROUGHS
Cbr Industrial Llc ....G 419 645-6447
  Wapakoneta *(G-19326)*
Chute Source LLC ....F 330 475-0377
  Akron *(G-117)*

CIGAR STORES
Moosehead Cigar Company Llc ....G 513 266-7207
  Fairfield *(G-9530)*

CIGARETTE & CIGAR PRDTS & ACCESS
Gumbys LLC ....G 740 671-0818
  Bellaire *(G-1486)*
Priority Vending Inc ....G 216 361-4100
  Cleveland *(G-5923)*

CIGARETTE LIGHTERS
Hunters Manufacturing Co Inc ....E 330 628-9245
  Mogadore *(G-14240)*

CIRCUIT BOARD REPAIR SVCS
Mid-Ohio Electric Co ....E 614 274-8000
  Columbus *(G-7178)*

CIRCUIT BOARDS, PRINTED: Television & Radio
Neo Technology Solutions ....G 513 234-5725
  Mason *(G-12914)*

CIRCUIT BOARDS: Wiring
Parlex USA LLC ....D 937 898-3621
  Vandalia *(G-19142)*

R-K Electronics Inc ....F 513 204-6060
  Mason *(G-12929)*

CIRCUIT BREAKERS
Eaton Corporation ....E 513 387-2000
  West Chester *(G-19696)*

CIRCUITS: Electronic
Accurate Electronics Inc ....C 330 682-7015
  Orrville *(G-15581)*
Advanced Quartz Fabrication ....F 440 350-4567
  Chardon *(G-3095)*
Advantage Circuits Ltd ....G 330 256-7768
  Rootstown *(G-16566)*
Astro Industries Inc ....G 937 429-5900
  Beavercreek *(G-1301)*
B5 Systems Inc ....G 937 372-4768
  Xenia *(G-20757)*
Bionetics Corporation ....E 740 788-3800
  Heath *(G-10718)*
C E Electronics Inc ....D 419 636-6705
  Bryan *(G-2275)*
Captor Corporation ....D 937 667-8484
  Tipp City *(G-18106)*
CEC Electronics Corp ....G 330 916-8100
  Akron *(G-107)*
Channel Products Inc ....D 440 423-0113
  Solon *(G-17126)*
Cleveland Circuits Corp ....E 216 267-9020
  Cleveland *(G-4950)*
CMC Electronics Cincinn ....G 513 573-6316
  Mason *(G-12850)*
Commercial Mfg Svcs Inc ....G 440 953-2701
  Mentor *(G-13420)*
Cutting Edge Technologies Inc ....E 216 574-4759
  Cleveland *(G-5051)*
Dynalab Ems Inc ....C 614 866-9999
  Reynoldsburg *(G-16436)*
Educational Electronics Inc ....G 234 301-9077
  Millersburg *(G-14080)*
Electro-Line Inc ....F 937 461-5683
  Dayton *(G-8181)*
Epic Technologies LLC ....D 513 683-5455
  Mason *(G-12867)*
Eti Tech LLC ....F 937 832-4200
  Englewood *(G-9358)*
Great Lakes Glasswerks Inc ....F 440 358-0460
  Painesville *(G-15743)*
Inductive Components Mfg ....E 513 752-4731
  Amelia *(G-541)*
Ingram Products Inc ....F 904 778-1010
  Ashland *(G-714)*
Inservco Inc ....D 847 855-9600
  Lagrange *(G-11483)*
J & C Group Inc of Ohio ....E 440 205-9658
  Mentor *(G-13478)*
John B Allen ....G 614 488-7122
  Columbus *(G-7072)*
Laird Technologies Inc ....F 330 434-7929
  Akron *(G-247)*
Lintech Electronics LLC ....F 513 528-6190
  Cincinnati *(G-3259)*
Mc Gregor & Associates Inc ....C 937 833-6768
  Brookville *(G-2178)*
Mitchell Electronics Inc ....F 740 594-8532
  Athens *(G-842)*
Niktec LLC ....G 513 282-3747
  Franklin *(G-9904)*
Parker-Hannifin Corporation ....C 937 644-3915
  Marysville *(G-12805)*
Performance Electronics Ltd ....F 513 777-5233
  Cincinnati *(G-4148)*
Precision Manufacturing Co Inc ....D 937 236-2170
  Dayton *(G-8433)*
Qlog Corp ....G 513 874-1211
  Hamilton *(G-10599)*
Rct Industries Inc ....F 937 602-1100
  Springboro *(G-17351)*
Rpa Electronic Distributors ....F 937 223-7001
  Dayton *(G-8486)*
Sawyer Research Product ....G 440 951-8770
  Eastlake *(G-9129)*
Shiloh Industries Inc ....F 937 236-5100
  Dayton *(G-8504)*
Showplace Inc ....G 419 468-7368
  Galion *(G-10155)*
Sovereign Circuits Inc ....G 330 538-3900
  North Jackson *(G-15154)*
Spectron Inc ....G 937 461-5590
  Dayton *(G-8517)*

Employee Codes: A=Over 500 employees, B=251-500
C=101-250, D=51-100, E=20-50, F=10-19, G=3-9

CIRCUITS: Electronic

The W L Jenkins Company .... F 330 477-3407
  Canton *(G-2835)*
Tinycircuits .... G 330 329-5753
  Akron *(G-405)*
Tk Machining Specialties LLC .... G 513 368-3963
  Hamilton *(G-10612)*
Tls Corp .... E 216 574-4759
  Cleveland *(G-6177)*
Twin Point Inc .... F 419 923-7525
  Delta *(G-8778)*
U S Terminals Inc .... G 513 561-8145
  Cincinnati *(G-4445)*
Valley Electric Company .... G 419 332-6405
  Fremont *(G-10061)*
Workman Electronic Pdts Inc .... F 419 923-7525
  Delta *(G-8779)*
Zeus Electronics LLC .... G 330 220-1571
  Brunswick *(G-2256)*

CLAMPS & COUPLINGS: Hose

Aeroquip-Vickers Inc .... G 216 523-5000
  Cleveland *(G-4633)*
Bowes Manufacturing Inc .... F 216 378-2110
  Solon *(G-17117)*
Eaton Aeroquip LLC .... C 216 523-5000
  Cleveland *(G-5143)*
Eaton Corporation .... A 419 238-1190
  Van Wert *(G-19087)*
Eaton-Aeroquip Llc .... D 419 238-1190
  Van Wert *(G-19089)*
Voss Industries Inc .... D 216 771-7655
  Cleveland *(G-6272)*
Voss Industries LLC .... C 216 771-7655
  Cleveland *(G-6273)*
Winzeler Stamping Co .... D 419 485-3147
  Montpelier *(G-14222)*

CLAMPS: Metal

Case-Maul Clamps Inc .... F 419 668-6563
  Norwalk *(G-15384)*
Clampco Products Inc .... C 330 336-8857
  Wadsworth *(G-19230)*
Etl Performance Products Inc .... G 234 575-7226
  Salem *(G-16735)*
Herman Machine Inc .... F 330 633-3261
  Tallmadge *(G-17984)*
Ottawa Products Co .... G 419 836-5115
  Curtice *(G-7826)*

CLAY MINING, COMMON

L & M Mineral Co .... G 330 852-3696
  Sugarcreek *(G-17851)*

CLAY: Ground Or Treated

J R Goslee Co .... F 330 723-4904
  Medina *(G-13282)*

CLEANING & DESCALING SVC: Metal Prdts

American Metal Cleaning Inc .... G 419 255-1828
  Toledo *(G-18175)*
American Mtal Clg Cncnnati Inc .... G 513 825-1171
  Cincinnati *(G-3336)*
Auto Core Systems .... G 740 362-5599
  Delaware *(G-8657)*
Carpe Diem Industries LLC .... E 419 358-0129
  Bluffton *(G-1887)*
Carpe Diem Industries LLC .... D 419 659-5639
  Columbus Grove *(G-7632)*
Chemical Solvents Inc .... E 216 741-9310
  Cleveland *(G-4919)*
Roberts Demand No 3 Corp .... F 216 641-0460
  Cleveland *(G-5992)*

CLEANING COMPOUNDS: Rifle Bore

Sports Care Products Inc .... G 216 663-8110
  Cleveland *(G-6086)*

CLEANING EQPT: Blast, Dustless

Cleaning Tech Group LLC .... E 513 870-0100
  West Chester *(G-19843)*
Nmgg Ctg LLC .... G 419 447-5211
  Tiffin *(G-18072)*

CLEANING EQPT: Commercial

American Plastics LLC .... C 419 423-1213
  Findlay *(G-9650)*
Aurand Manufacturing & Eqp Co .... G 513 541-7200
  Cincinnati *(G-3371)*
Detrex Corporation .... F 216 749-2605
  Cleveland *(G-5087)*
Environmental Closure Systems .... F 614 759-9186
  Reynoldsburg *(G-16437)*
Evers Enterprises Inc .... G 513 541-7200
  Cincinnati *(G-3657)*
Friess Equipment Inc .... G 330 945-9440
  Akron *(G-178)*
Holdren Brothers Inc .... F 937 465-7050
  West Liberty *(G-19936)*
Kaivac Inc .... E 513 887-4600
  Hamilton *(G-10577)*
Metal Equipment Co .... E 440 835-3100
  Westlake *(G-20130)*
MPW Industrial Svcs Group Inc .... D 740 927-8790
  Hebron *(G-10754)*
Oh-LI Commercial Cleaning LLC .... G 614 390-3628
  Grove City *(G-10453)*
Reid Asset Management Company ..... G 216 642-3223
  Cleveland *(G-5970)*
Staley & Sons Powerwashing LLC ...... G 937 843-2713
  Russells Point *(G-16601)*
W3 Ultrasonics LLC .... G 330 284-3667
  North Canton *(G-15136)*

CLEANING EQPT: Floor Washing & Polishing, Commercial

Image By J & K LLC .... B 888 667-6929
  Maumee *(G-13118)*
Nss Enterprises Inc .... C 419 531-2121
  Toledo *(G-18430)*
Powerbuff Inc .... F 419 241-2156
  Toledo *(G-18475)*

CLEANING EQPT: High Pressure

Complete Dry Flood .... G 513 200-9274
  Cincinnati *(G-3539)*
Mork Process Inc .... E 330 928-3700
  Worthington *(G-20698)*

CLEANING EQPT: Janitors' Carts

Flexcart LLC .... G 614 348-2517
  New Albany *(G-14624)*

CLEANING OR POLISHING PREPARATIONS, NEC

American Chemical Products .... F 216 267-7722
  Cleveland *(G-4685)*
Aromair Fine Fragrance Company ...... B 614 984-2896
  New Albany *(G-14605)*
Canberra Corporation .... C 419 724-4300
  Toledo *(G-18222)*
Chem 1 Inc .... G 216 475-7443
  Warrensville Heights *(G-19466)*
Chemical Methods Inc .... E 216 476-8400
  Strongsville *(G-17725)*
Chempace Corporation .... F 419 535-0101
  Toledo *(G-18229)*
Clayton Manufacturing Company .... F 513 563-1300
  Cincinnati *(G-3526)*
Diversey Inc .... F 513 326-8300
  Cincinnati *(G-3592)*
Emes Supply LLC .... G 216 400-8025
  Willowick *(G-20478)*
EZ Brite Brands Inc .... F 440 871-7817
  Cleveland *(G-5211)*
Inceptor Inc .... G 419 726-8804
  Toledo *(G-18343)*
Kleen Test Products Corp .... F 330 878-5586
  Strasburg *(G-17649)*
Morris Clean It N Sweep Clean .... G 513 200-8222
  Cincinnati *(G-4046)*
Ohio Auto Supply Company .... E 330 454-5105
  Canton *(G-2771)*
Paro Services Co .... F 330 467-1300
  Twinsburg *(G-18828)*
Strib Industries Inc .... E 216 281-1155
  Cleveland *(G-6108)*
Ventco Inc .... F 440 834-8888
  Chagrin Falls *(G-3088)*
Vitex Corporation .... F 216 883-0920
  Cleveland *(G-6266)*
Wise Consumer Products Company ... G 513 484-6530
  Blue Ash *(G-1872)*
Woodbine Products Company .... F 330 725-0165
  Medina *(G-13363)*

CLEANING PRDTS: Automobile Polish

BLaster Corporation .... E 216 901-5800
  Cleveland *(G-4819)*
Custom Chemical Packaging LLC ...... E 330 331-7416
  Medina *(G-13247)*
James C Robinson .... G 513 969-7482
  Cincinnati *(G-3869)*
Jax Wax Inc .... F 614 476-6769
  Columbus *(G-7064)*
Sevan At-Ndustrial Pnt Abr Ltd .... G 614 258-4747
  Columbus *(G-7440)*

CLEANING PRDTS: Degreasing Solvent

Leesburg Modern Sales Inc .... G 937 780-2613
  Leesburg *(G-11712)*

CLEANING PRDTS: Deodorants, Nonpersonal

Fresh Products LLC .... D 419 531-9741
  Perrysburg *(G-15955)*
Nilodor Inc .... E 800 443-4321
  Bolivar *(G-1919)*

CLEANING PRDTS: Disinfectants, Household Or Indl Plant

Malco Products Inc .... E 330 753-0361
  Alliance *(G-487)*

CLEANING PRDTS: Drain Pipe Solvents Or Cleaners

Personal Plumber Service Corp .... F 440 324-4321
  Elyria *(G-9311)*

CLEANING PRDTS: Drycleaning Preparations

All Prem Cleaners Inc .... G 440 349-3649
  Solon *(G-17100)*
Pats Nu-Style Cleaners Inc .... G 216 676-4855
  Cleveland *(G-5854)*
Wilkshire Dry Cleaners LLC .... G 330 674-7696
  Millersburg *(G-14151)*

CLEANING PRDTS: Dusting Cloths, Chemically Treated

Ohio Mills Corporation .... G 216 431-3979
  Cleveland *(G-5807)*

CLEANING PRDTS: Floor Waxes

S C Johnson & Son Inc .... E 513 665-3600
  Cincinnati *(G-4294)*
Spartan Chemical Company Inc .... E 419 897-5551
  Maumee *(G-13147)*

CLEANING PRDTS: Indl Plant Disinfectants Or Deodorants

Solutions Plus Inc .... E 513 943-9600
  Amelia *(G-547)*
Trigon Industries Inc .... G 937 299-1350
  Oakwood *(G-15467)*

CLEANING PRDTS: Laundry Preparations

Cedar Point Laundry .... G 419 627-2274
  Sandusky *(G-16801)*
Clorox Company .... F 513 445-1840
  Mason *(G-12848)*
Procter & Gamble Far East Inc .... C 513 983-1100
  Cincinnati *(G-4210)*

CLEANING PRDTS: Metal Polish

Aman & Co Inc .... G 330 854-1122
  Canal Fulton *(G-2473)*
Easy Care Products Inc .... G 330 405-1380
  Twinsburg *(G-18767)*
Saint Ctherines Metalworks Inc .... G 216 409-0576
  Cleveland *(G-6026)*

PRODUCT SECTION

CLOTHING STORES, NEC

CLEANING PRDTS: Paint & Wallpaper

Advanced Cleaning Tech LLC ....G....... 614 504-2014
  Plain City *(G-16169)*

CLEANING PRDTS: Polishing Preparations & Related Prdts

Mix-Masters Inc ....F 513 228-2800
  Lebanon *(G-11673)*

CLEANING PRDTS: Rug, Upholstery/Dry Clng Detergents/Spotters

Carolyn Chemical Company ....F 614 252-5000
  Columbus *(G-6746)*
Jackson Deluxe Cleaners Ltd ....G 419 592-2826
  Napoleon *(G-14547)*

CLEANING PRDTS: Sanitation Preparations

L-Mor Inc ....F 216 541-2224
  Cleveland *(G-5551)*
New Waste Concepts Inc ....F 877 736-6924
  Perrysburg *(G-15981)*
Oliver Chemical Co Inc ....G 513 541-4540
  Cincinnati *(G-4110)*

CLEANING PRDTS: Sanitation Preps, Disinfectants/Deodorants

D & J Distributing & Mfg ....E 419 865-2552
  Holland *(G-10923)*
Dem Technology LLC ....G 937 223-1317
  Dayton *(G-8155)*
Ecolab Inc ....G 513 932-0830
  Lebanon *(G-11649)*
Sara Hudson ....G 850 890-1455
  Dayton *(G-8493)*
Tranzonic Acquisition Corp ....A 216 535-4300
  Richmond Heights *(G-16505)*
Tranzonic Companies ....C 216 535-4300
  Richmond Heights *(G-16506)*
Tranzonic Companies ....C 440 446-0643
  Cleveland *(G-6198)*

CLEANING PRDTS: Specialty

Carbonklean Llc ....G 614 980-9515
  Powell *(G-16313)*
Cleaning By Sndra Msters Touch ....F 216 524-6827
  Seven Hills *(G-16902)*
Kinzua Environmental Inc ....E 216 881-4040
  Cleveland *(G-5536)*
Orchem Corporation ....E 513 874-9700
  Dayton *(G-8406)*
Procter & Gamble Company ....B 513 983-1100
  Cincinnati *(G-4198)*
Procter & Gamble Company ....C 513 983-1100
  Cincinnati *(G-4199)*
Procter & Gamble Company ....E 513 266-4375
  Cincinnati *(G-4200)*
Procter & Gamble Company ....E 513 871-7557
  Cincinnati *(G-4201)*
Procter & Gamble Company ....B 419 998-5891
  Lima *(G-11920)*
Procter & Gamble Company ....F 513 482-6789
  Cincinnati *(G-4203)*
Procter & Gamble Company ....B 513 672-4044
  West Chester *(G-19767)*
Procter & Gamble Company ....B 513 627-7115
  Cincinnati *(G-4205)*
Procter & Gamble Company ....C 513 634-9600
  West Chester *(G-19768)*
Procter & Gamble Company ....C 513 634-9110
  West Chester *(G-19769)*
Procter & Gamble Company ....C 513 934-3406
  Oregonia *(G-15573)*
Procter & Gamble Company ....G 513 627-7779
  Cincinnati *(G-4207)*
Procter & Gamble Company ....B 513 945-0340
  Cincinnati *(G-4208)*
Procter & Gamble Company ....C 513 622-1000
  Mason *(G-12926)*
Republic Powdered Metals Inc ....D 330 225-3192
  Medina *(G-13327)*
Rose Products and Services Inc ....E 614 443-7647
  Columbus *(G-7402)*
RPM International Inc ....D 330 273-5090
  Medina *(G-13331)*
Shur Clean Usa LLC ....G 513 341-5486
  Liberty Township *(G-11820)*

US Industrial Lubricants Inc ....E 513 541-2225
  Cincinnati *(G-4458)*

CLEANING PRDTS: Stain Removers

Sherwin-Williams Company ....C 330 830-6000
  Massillon *(G-13048)*

CLEANING SVCS

Cleaning By Sndra Msters Touch ....F 216 524-6827
  Seven Hills *(G-16902)*
Langstons Ultmate Clg Svcs Inc ....F 330 298-9150
  Ravenna *(G-16387)*
Liberty Casting Company LLC ....E 740 363-1941
  Delaware *(G-8703)*
Sara Hudson ....G 850 890-1455
  Dayton *(G-8493)*
Stein Co ....F 440 526-9301
  Cleveland *(G-6104)*

CLEANING SVCS: Industrial Or Commercial

MPW Industrial Svcs Group Inc ....D 740 927-8790
  Hebron *(G-10754)*
Omega Cementing Co ....G 330 695-7147
  Apple Creek *(G-616)*
Paro Services Co ....F 330 467-1300
  Twinsburg *(G-18828)*

CLIPS & FASTENERS, MADE FROM PURCHASED WIRE

Tom Thumb Clip Co Inc ....F 440 953-9606
  Willoughby *(G-20450)*

CLOCKS

I T Verdin Co ....E 513 241-4010
  Cincinnati *(G-3833)*
I T Verdin Co ....E 513 559-3947
  Cincinnati *(G-3834)*

CLOSURES: Closures, Stamped Metal

Crown Cork & Seal Usa Inc ....D 740 681-3000
  Lancaster *(G-11560)*

CLOSURES: Plastic

Crown Cork & Seal Usa Inc ....D 740 681-3000
  Lancaster *(G-11560)*

CLOTHING & ACCESS STORES

Joe Sestito ....G 614 871-7778
  Grove City *(G-10437)*

CLOTHING & ACCESS, WOMEN, CHILD & INFANT, WHSLE: Sportswear

K Ventures Inc ....F 419 678-2308
  Coldwater *(G-6415)*

CLOTHING & ACCESS, WOMEN, CHILDREN & INFANT, WHOL: Sweaters

Majestic Sportswear Company ....G 937 773-1144
  Piqua *(G-16140)*

CLOTHING & ACCESS, WOMEN, CHILDREN & INFANT, WHOL: Uniforms

Cintas Sales Corporation ....B 513 459-1200
  Cincinnati *(G-3520)*
Digitek Corp ....F 513 794-3190
  Blue Ash *(G-1758)*
Impact Sports Wear Inc ....G 513 922-7406
  North Bend *(G-15051)*

CLOTHING & ACCESS, WOMEN, CHILDREN/INFANT, WHOL: Outerwear

Swocat Design Inc ....G 440 282-4700
  Lorain *(G-12127)*

CLOTHING & ACCESS: Costumes, Lodge

Thomas Creative Apparel Inc ....E 419 929-1506
  New London *(G-14739)*

CLOTHING & ACCESS: Costumes, Theatrical

Costume Specialists Inc ....E 614 464-2115
  Columbus *(G-6825)*
Costume Specialists Inc ....G 614 464-2115
  Columbus *(G-6826)*
Schenz Theatrical Supply Inc ....F 513 542-6100
  Cincinnati *(G-4306)*
Snaps Inc ....G 419 477-5100
  Mount Cory *(G-14418)*
Stagecraft Costuming Inc ....F 513 541-7150
  Cincinnati *(G-4369)*
Top Hat Designs ....G 614 898-1962
  Westerville *(G-20079)*

CLOTHING & ACCESS: Garter Belts

Golda Inc ....B 216 464-5490
  Cleveland *(G-5328)*

CLOTHING & ACCESS: Hospital Gowns

Standard Textile Co Inc ....B 513 761-9256
  Cincinnati *(G-4372)*

CLOTHING & ACCESS: Men's Miscellaneous Access

Indra Holdings Corp ....G 513 682-8200
  West Chester *(G-19867)*
Inner Fire Sports LLC ....G 719 244-6622
  Cincinnati *(G-3849)*
L Brands Inc ....C 614 479-2000
  Columbus *(G-7106)*
Rocky Brands Inc ....B 740 753-1951
  Nelsonville *(G-14595)*
Salindia LLC ....G 614 501-4799
  Columbus *(G-7416)*
Status Mens Accessories ....G 440 232-6700
  Cleveland *(G-6100)*

CLOTHING & ACCESS: Regalia

New London Regalia Mfg Co ....F 419 929-1516
  New London *(G-14734)*

CLOTHING & APPAREL STORES: Custom

Bluelogos Inc ....F 614 898-9971
  Westerville *(G-20038)*
Carols Ultra Stitch & Variety ....G 419 935-8991
  Willard *(G-20238)*
Charles Wisvari ....F 740 671-9960
  Bellaire *(G-1484)*
Dpi Inc ....G 419 273-1400
  Forest *(G-9786)*
Indra Holdings Corp ....G 513 682-8200
  West Chester *(G-19867)*
Pelz Lettering Inc ....G 419 625-3567
  Sandusky *(G-16838)*

CLOTHING & FURNISHINGS, MEN'S & BOYS', WHOLESALE: Shirts

Swocat Design Inc ....G 440 282-4700
  Lorain *(G-12127)*

CLOTHING & FURNISHINGS, MEN'S & BOYS', WHOLESALE: Uniforms

Cintas Sales Corporation ....B 513 459-1200
  Cincinnati *(G-3520)*
Digitek Corp ....F 513 794-3190
  Blue Ash *(G-1758)*
Impact Sports Wear Inc ....G 513 922-7406
  North Bend *(G-15051)*
Standard Textile Co Inc ....B 513 761-9256
  Cincinnati *(G-4372)*
Walter F Stephens Jr Inc ....E 937 746-0521
  Franklin *(G-9930)*

CLOTHING ACCESS STORES: Umbrellas

Totes Isotoner Corporation ....F 513 682-8200
  West Chester *(G-19907)*
Totes Isotoner Holdings Corp ....C 513 682-8200
  West Chester *(G-19908)*

CLOTHING STORES, NEC

Owl Be Sweatin ....G 513 260-2026
  Cincinnati *(G-4127)*

Employee Codes: A=Over 500 employees, B=251-500
C=101-250, D=51-100, E=20-50, F=10-19, G=3-9

CLOTHING STORES: Formal Wear
Dresden Specialties Inc............G...... 740 754-2451
  Dresden (G-8868)

CLOTHING STORES: Leather
LLC Bowman Leather...............G...... 330 893-1954
  Millersburg (G-14107)

CLOTHING STORES: T-Shirts, Printed, Custom
Cotton Pickin Tees & Caps.........G...... 419 636-3595
  Bryan (G-2277)
Jones & Assoc Advg & Design......G...... 330 799-6876
  Youngstown (G-20949)
Odyssey Spirits Inc..................F...... 330 562-1523
  Aurora (G-896)
Robs Creative Screen Printing.....G...... 740 264-6383
  Wintersville (G-20541)

CLOTHING STORES: Uniforms & Work
Appleheart............................G...... 937 384-0430
  Miamisburg (G-13641)
Markt..................................G...... 740 397-5900
  Mount Vernon (G-14490)

CLOTHING STORES: Unisex
Chris Stepp...........................G...... 513 248-0822
  Milford (G-14002)
Ohio Mills Corporation..............G...... 216 431-3979
  Cleveland (G-5807)

CLOTHING/ACCESS, WOMEN, CHILDREN/INFANT, WHOL: Hosp Gowns
Philips Medical Systems Clevel....B...... 440 247-2652
  Cleveland (G-5871)

CLOTHING: Access
Rageon Inc...........................E...... 617 633-0544
  Cleveland (G-5958)
Ralphie Gianni Mfg & Co............F...... 216 507-3873
  Euclid (G-9439)
Tactical Revolution LLC.............G...... 419 348-9526
  Ottawa (G-15668)
V Collection..........................G...... 419 517-0508
  Sylvania (G-17967)

CLOTHING: Access, Women's & Misses'
Indra Holdings Corp.................G...... 513 682-8200
  West Chester (G-19867)
Lena Fiore Inc.......................F...... 330 659-0020
  Akron (G-252)
Lettermans LLC.....................G...... 330 345-2628
  Wooster (G-20616)
Rocky Brands Inc...................B...... 740 753-1951
  Nelsonville (G-14595)

CLOTHING: Aprons, Exc Rubber/Plastic, Women, Misses, Junior
Carrera Holdings Inc................G...... 216 687-1311
  Cleveland (G-4883)
Geauga Group LLC..................G...... 440 543-8797
  Chagrin Falls (G-3047)

CLOTHING: Aprons, Harness
Seven Mile Creek Corporation......F...... 937 456-3320
  Eaton (G-9165)
Watershed Mangement LLC.........F...... 740 852-5607
  Mount Sterling (G-14466)

CLOTHING: Aprons, Work, Exc Rubberized & Plastic, Men's
Geauga Group LLC..................G...... 440 543-8797
  Chagrin Falls (G-3047)

CLOTHING: Athletic & Sportswear, Men's & Boys'
Afi Brands LLC.......................G...... 614 999-6426
  Dublin (G-8875)
Dunhams Sports.....................F...... 330 334-3257
  Wadsworth (G-19235)

Fanz Stop.............................G...... 937 310-1436
  Bellbrook (G-1494)
Gametime Apparel & Dezigns LLC...G...... 740 255-5254
  Cambridge (G-2439)
Hilliard Cat Shack LLC...............G...... 614 527-9711
  Hilliard (G-10829)
Inner Fire Sports LLC................G...... 719 244-6622
  Cincinnati (G-3849)
J America LLC.......................G...... 614 914-2091
  Columbus (G-7054)
Kam Manufacturing Inc..............C...... 419 238-6037
  Van Wert (G-19096)
Lettermans LLC.....................G...... 330 345-2628
  Wooster (G-20616)
Rocky Brands Inc...................B...... 740 753-1951
  Nelsonville (G-14595)
Torso..................................G...... 614 421-7663
  Columbus (G-7534)
Under Armour Inc...................G...... 330 995-9557
  Aurora (G-912)
Vesi Incorporated....................E...... 513 563-6002
  Cincinnati (G-4479)
Whip Appeal Inc.....................G...... 216 288-6201
  Cleveland (G-6304)

CLOTHING: Baker, Barber, Lab/Svc Ind Apparel, Washable, Men
All-Bilt Uniform Corp.................E...... 513 793-5400
  Blue Ash (G-1728)

CLOTHING: Belts
Peregrine Outdoor Products LLC...G...... 800 595-3850
  Lebanon (G-11683)

CLOTHING: Bibs, Waterproof, From Purchased Materials
Grow With Me- Creations...........G...... 800 850-1889
  Hartville (G-10691)

CLOTHING: Blouses, Women's & Girls'
Afi Brands LLC.......................G...... 614 999-6426
  Dublin (G-8875)
Kam Manufacturing Inc..............C...... 419 238-6037
  Van Wert (G-19096)
Quality Sewing Inc...................G...... 216 475-0411
  Cleveland (G-5944)
Rocky Brands Inc...................B...... 740 753-1951
  Nelsonville (G-14595)
Smitten Enterprises LLC............G...... 937 267-6963
  Springboro (G-17353)

CLOTHING: Blouses, Womens & Juniors, From Purchased Mtrls
J C L S Enterprises LLC............G...... 740 472-0314
  Woodsfield (G-20545)

CLOTHING: Bras & Corsets, Maternity
Golda Inc.............................B...... 216 464-5490
  Cleveland (G-5328)

CLOTHING: Bridal Gowns
Lavander Bridal Salon................F...... 330 602-0333
  Dover (G-8836)
Surili Couture LLC...................F...... 440 600-1456
  Westlake (G-20164)

CLOTHING: Caps, Baseball
Barbs Graffiti Inc....................E...... 216 881-5550
  Cleveland (G-4790)

CLOTHING: Children & Infants'
Tween Brands Inc..................F...... 937 435-6928
  Dayton (G-8572)

CLOTHING: Coats & Suits, Men's & Boys'
Bea-Ecc Apparels Inc...............G...... 216 650-6336
  Cleveland (G-4797)
Wahconah Group Inc..............F...... 216 923-0570
  Cleveland (G-6284)

CLOTHING: Costumes
Akron Design & Costume Co......G...... 330 644-4849
  Coventry Township (G-7762)
Promo Costumes Inc...............F...... 740 383-5176
  Marion (G-12728)

CLOTHING: Disposable
Direct Disposables LLC.............G...... 440 717-3335
  Brecksville (G-2029)
Rich Industries Inc..................E...... 330 339-4113
  New Philadelphia (G-14797)

CLOTHING: Dresses
Quality Sewing Inc...................G...... 216 475-0411
  Cleveland (G-5944)

CLOTHING: Foundation Garments, Women's
Laura Dawson.......................G...... 513 777-2513
  West Chester (G-19735)

CLOTHING: Gowns & Dresses, Wedding
Finishing Touch......................F...... 440 263-9264
  Cleveland (G-5241)
Polished Pearl LLP..................G...... 513 659-8824
  Montgomery (G-14298)

CLOTHING: Gowns, Plastic
Paradigm International Inc.........G...... 740 370-2428
  Piketon (G-16078)

CLOTHING: Hats & Caps, NEC
Genesco Inc.........................G...... 330 633-8179
  Akron (G-187)
Wagoner Stores Inc.................G...... 937 836-3636
  Englewood (G-9383)

CLOTHING: Hosiery, Men's & Boys'
Forepleasure.........................G...... 330 821-1293
  Alliance (G-468)

CLOTHING: Hospital, Men's
Pearl Healthwear Inc................G...... 440 446-0265
  Cleveland (G-5859)
Standard Textile Co Inc............B...... 513 761-9256
  Cincinnati (G-4372)

CLOTHING: Jackets, Field, Military
Pantac Usa Ltd......................G...... 614 423-6743
  Columbus (G-7289)

CLOTHING: Leather
Fionas Fineries......................G...... 440 796-7426
  Willoughby (G-20322)

CLOTHING: Lounge, Bed & Leisurewear
Heritage Inc..........................G...... 614 860-1185
  Reynoldsburg (G-16443)

CLOTHING: Men's & boy's clothing, nec
Promotions Plus Inc................G...... 440 582-2855
  Broadview Heights (G-2098)
Sacks Bruce & Associates.........G...... 419 537-0623
  Ottawa Hills (G-15677)

CLOTHING: Men's & boy's underwear & nightwear
Tranzonic Companies...............B...... 216 535-4300
  Richmond Heights (G-16507)

CLOTHING: Outerwear, Knit
Okm LLC.............................G...... 216 272-6375
  Cleveland (G-5808)

CLOTHING: Outerwear, Lthr, Wool/Down-Filled, Men, Youth/Boy
Universal Lettering Inc..............E...... 419 238-9320
  Van Wert (G-19109)

PRODUCT SECTION

COAL MINING SERVICES

CLOTHING: Outerwear, Women's & Misses' NEC

Barton-Carey Medical Products .... E 419 887-1285
  Maumee (G-13078)
Fechheimer Brothers Company .... C 513 793-5400
  Blue Ash (G-1772)
Inner Fire Sports LLC .... G 719 244-6622
  Cincinnati (G-3849)
Kip-Craft Incorporated .... D 216 898-5500
  Cleveland (G-5537)

CLOTHING: Robes & Dressing Gowns

Thomas Creative Apparel Inc .... E 419 929-1506
  New London (G-14739)

CLOTHING: Shirts, Dress, Men's & Boys'

Pvh Corp .... G 330 562-4440
  Aurora (G-900)

CLOTHING: Socks

Agile Socks LLC .... G 614 440-2812
  Columbus (G-6550)
Broken Spinning Wheel .... G 419 825-1609
  Swanton (G-17907)
Disante Socks .... G 614 481-3243
  Columbus (G-6866)
Hype Socks LLC .... F 855 497-3769
  Columbus (G-6497)
Next Step Socks LLC .... G 216 534-8077
  Lakewood (G-11531)

CLOTHING: Sportswear, Women's

Fanz Stop .... G 937 310-1436
  Bellbrook (G-1494)
Vesi Incorporated .... E 513 563-6002
  Cincinnati (G-4479)
Whip Appeal Inc .... G 216 288-6201
  Cleveland (G-6304)

CLOTHING: Suits, Men's & Boys', From Purchased Materials

Hugo Boss Usa Inc .... B 216 671-8100
  Cleveland (G-5425)
Tom James Company .... F 614 488-8400
  Columbus (G-7533)

CLOTHING: Sweaters & Sweater Coats, Knit

Fine Points Inc .... F 216 229-6644
  Cleveland (G-5239)

CLOTHING: Sweatshirts & T-Shirts, Men's & Boys'

Fun-In-Games Inc .... G 866 587-1004
  Mason (G-12874)
J C L S Enterprises LLC .... G 740 472-0314
  Woodsfield (G-20545)

CLOTHING: T-Shirts & Tops, Knit

Digitek Corp .... F 513 794-3190
  Blue Ash (G-1758)
E Retailing Associates LLC .... D 614 300-5785
  Columbus (G-6880)
Gibbs E & Associates LLC .... G 614 939-1672
  New Albany (G-14625)
Pjs Wholesale Inc .... G 614 402-9363
  Columbus (G-7318)
Wonder-Shirts Inc .... G 917 679-2336
  Dublin (G-9012)

CLOTHING: Tuxedos, From Purchased Materials

American Commodore Tuxedos .... G 440 324-2889
  Elyria (G-9214)
Cinderella .... G 937 312-9969
  Dayton (G-8089)
Simply Elegant Formals Inc .... G 419 738-7722
  Wapakoneta (G-19354)

CLOTHING: Underwear, Women's & Children's

Tranzonic Companies .... B 216 535-4300
  Richmond Heights (G-16507)

CLOTHING: Uniforms & Vestments

Alma Mater Sportswear LLC .... G 614 260-8222
  Columbus (G-6576)
Fire-Dex LLC .... D 330 723-0000
  Medina (G-13262)
Novak Supply LLC .... G 216 741-5112
  Cleveland (G-5791)
Walter F Stephens Jr Inc .... E 937 746-0521
  Franklin (G-9930)

CLOTHING: Uniforms, Ex Athletic, Women's, Misses' & Juniors'

Cintas Corporation .... A 513 459-1200
  Cincinnati (G-3518)
Cintas Corporation .... D 513 631-5750
  Cincinnati (G-3519)
Cintas Corporation No 2 .... D 330 966-7800
  Canton (G-2624)
Pearl Healthwear Inc .... G 440 446-0265
  Cleveland (G-5859)
Standard Textile Co Inc .... B 513 761-9256
  Cincinnati (G-4372)

CLOTHING: Uniforms, Firemen's, From Purchased Materials

Lion Apparel Inc .... C 937 898-1949
  Dayton (G-8313)

CLOTHING: Uniforms, Men's & Boys'

Fechheimer Brothers Company .... C 513 793-5400
  Blue Ash (G-1772)

CLOTHING: Uniforms, Military, Men/Youth, Purchased Materials

Contingncy Prcrement Group LLC .... G 513 204-9590
  Maineville (G-12366)
Global Gear LLC .... G 941 830-0531
  Chagrin Falls (G-3048)
Government Specialty Pdts LLC .... G 937 672-9473
  Dayton (G-8233)
Vgs Inc .... C 216 431-7800
  Cleveland (G-6256)

CLOTHING: Uniforms, Work

Cintas Corporation .... D 513 631-5750
  Cincinnati (G-3519)
Cintas Corporation .... A 513 459-1200
  Cincinnati (G-3518)
Cintas Corporation No 2 .... D 330 966-7800
  Canton (G-2624)
Cintas Sales Corporation .... B 513 459-1200
  Cincinnati (G-3520)
Lawft .... G 419 422-5293
  Findlay (G-9712)
Rons Texstyles LLC .... G 513 936-9975
  Columbus (G-7400)
Vgs Inc .... C 216 431-7800
  Cleveland (G-6256)
Whip Appeal Inc .... G 216 288-6201
  Cleveland (G-6304)

CLOTHING: Vests, Sport, Suede, Leatherette, Etc, Mens & Boys

Noxgear LLC .... G 937 248-1860
  Columbus (G-7231)

CLOTHING: Work Apparel, Exc Uniforms

Hall Safety Apparel Inc .... F 740 922-3671
  Uhrichsville (G-18887)
Hands On International LLC .... G 513 502-9000
  Mason (G-12884)

CLOTHING: Work, Men's

3n1 Mens Fashion .... G 513 851-3610
  Cincinnati (G-3272)
Alsico Usa Inc .... D 330 673-7413
  Kent (G-11292)
Ansell Healthcare Products LLC .... C 740 295-5414
  Coshocton (G-7720)
Barton-Carey Medical Products .... E 419 887-1285
  Maumee (G-13078)
Bello Verde LLC .... G 614 365-3000
  Columbus (G-6661)
Carhartt Inc .... G 513 657-7130
  Cincinnati (G-3444)
Cleveland Canvas Goods Mfg Co .... G 216 361-4567
  Cleveland (G-4948)
DCW Acquisition Inc .... F 216 451-0666
  Cleveland (G-5079)
Epluno Inc .... F 800 249-5275
  Miamisburg (G-13664)
Kip-Craft Incorporated .... D 216 898-5500
  Cleveland (G-5537)
Morning Pride Mfg LLC .... A 937 264-2662
  Dayton (G-8367)
Rich Industries Inc .... E 330 339-4113
  New Philadelphia (G-14797)
Samson .... G 614 504-8038
  Columbus (G-7419)
Seven Mile Creek Corporation .... F 937 456-3320
  Eaton (G-9165)
Wagoner Stores Inc .... G 937 836-3636
  Englewood (G-9383)

CLOTHING: Work, Waterproof, Exc Raincoats

Linsalata Capital Partners Fun .... G 440 684-1400
  Cleveland (G-5579)
Tranzonic Acquisition Corp .... A 216 535-4300
  Richmond Heights (G-16505)
Tranzonic Companies .... C 440 446-0643
  Cleveland (G-6198)

CLUTCHES OR BRAKES: Electromagnetic

Eaton Corporation .... C 216 281-2211
  Cleveland (G-5147)

CLUTCHES, EXC VEHICULAR

Cook Bonding & Mfg Co Inc .... G 216 661-1698
  Cleveland (G-5027)
Eaton Corporation .... C 216 281-2211
  Cleveland (G-5147)
Ebog Legacy Inc .... D 330 239-4933
  Sharon Center (G-16949)
Force Control Industries Inc .... D 513 868-0900
  Fairfield (G-9498)
Logan Clutch Corporation .... E 440 808-4258
  Cleveland (G-5582)

COAL & OTHER MINERALS & ORES WHOLESALERS

B & S Transport Inc .... F 330 767-4319
  Navarre (G-14572)
Graphel Corporation .... C 513 779-6166
  West Chester (G-19718)
Tosoh America Inc .... B 614 539-8622
  Grove City (G-10476)

COAL MINING SERVICES

Airtite Mine Products LLC .... F 740 894-8778
  Proctorville (G-16342)
American Energy Corporation .... F 740 926-9152
  Beallsville (G-1289)
Anthony Mining Co Inc .... G 740 266-8100
  Wintersville (G-20537)
Appalachian Fuels LLC .... G 606 928-0460
  Dublin (G-8880)
Boich Companies LLC .... G 614 221-0101
  Columbus (G-6685)
Coal Resources Inc .... F 740 338-3100
  Saint Clairsville (G-16627)
Coal Services Inc .... D 740 795-5220
  Powhatan Point (G-16341)
Consol Energy .... G 740 232-2140
  Saint Clairsville (G-16629)
D & D Mining Co Inc .... F 330 549-3127
  New Springfield (G-14819)
Don Gamertsfelder .... G 740 797-4495
  The Plains (G-18021)
Global Coal Sales Group LLC .... G 614 221-0101
  Columbus (G-6956)
Global Mining Holding Co LLC .... G 614 221-0101
  Columbus (G-6957)

Employee Codes: A=Over 500 employees, B=251-500 C=101-250, D=51-100, E=20-50, F=10-19, G=3-9

COAL MINING SERVICES

Harrison County Coal Company .... E 740 338-3100
  Saint Clairsville *(G-16633)*
Kurtz Bros Inc .... E 614 491-0868
  Groveport *(G-10500)*
North American Auger Mining .... G 740 622-8782
  Coshocton *(G-7744)*
Ohio Valley Resources Inc .... E 740 795-5220
  Saint Clairsville *(G-16645)*
Oxford Mining Company Inc .... G 330 878-5120
  Strasburg *(G-17651)*
Oxford Mining Company Inc .... G 740 622-6302
  Coshocton *(G-7747)*
Oxford Mining Company LLC .... E 740 622-6302
  Coshocton *(G-7748)*
Oxford Mining Inc .... G 330 339-4546
  Stone Creek *(G-17563)*
Peabody Coal Company .... B 740 450-2420
  Zanesville *(G-21167)*
Resource Fuels LLC .... G 614 221-0101
  Columbus *(G-7389)*
Sandusky Dock Corporation .... F 419 626-1214
  Sandusky *(G-16841)*
Strata Mine Services Inc .... F 740 695-6880
  Saint Clairsville *(G-16654)*
Suncoke Energy Nc .... E 513 727-5571
  Middletown *(G-13955)*

COAL MINING SVCS: Bituminous, Contract Basis

Ohio Valley Transloading Co .... A 740 795-4967
  Saint Clairsville *(G-16646)*

COAL MINING: Anthracite

Coal Services Inc .... D 740 795-5220
  Powhatan Point *(G-16341)*

COAL MINING: Bituminous & Lignite Surface

Commercial Minerals Inc .... G 330 549-2165
  North Lima *(G-15168)*
East Fairfield Coal Co .... E 330 542-1010
  Petersburg *(G-16033)*
Ivi Mining Group Ltd .... G 740 418-7745
  Vinton *(G-19215)*
J & D Mining Inc .... E 330 339-4935
  New Philadelphia *(G-14776)*
Kenneth Mc Beth .... G 740 922-9494
  Dennison *(G-8784)*
Murray American Energy Inc .... A 740 338-3100
  Saint Clairsville *(G-16638)*
Oxford Mining Company Inc .... F 740 588-0190
  Zanesville *(G-21166)*
PM Coal Company LLC .... G 440 256-7624
  Willoughby *(G-20403)*

COAL MINING: Bituminous Coal & Lignite- Surface Mining

Coal Services Inc .... D 740 795-5220
  Powhatan Point *(G-16341)*
King Quarries Inc .... G 740 732-2923
  Caldwell *(G-2408)*
L & M Mineral Co .... G 330 852-3696
  Sugarcreek *(G-17851)*
Morning Sun Technologies Inc .... G 513 461-1417
  Oxford *(G-15698)*
Ohio Valley Coal Company .... B 740 926-1351
  Saint Clairsville *(G-16644)*
Rosebud Mining Company .... E 740 768-2097
  Bergholz *(G-1635)*
Straight Creek Bushman LLC .... G 513 732-1698
  Batavia *(G-1187)*
Subtropolis Mining Co .... G 330 549-2165
  North Lima *(G-15179)*
Ted Tipple .... G 740 432-3263
  Cambridge *(G-2459)*
Westmoreland Resources Gp LLC .... F 740 622-6302
  Coshocton *(G-7756)*

COAL MINING: Bituminous Underground

American Energy Corporation .... F 740 926-9152
  Beallsville *(G-1289)*
Coal Services Inc .... D 740 795-5220
  Powhatan Point *(G-16341)*
Ivi Mining Group Ltd .... G 740 418-7745
  Vinton *(G-19215)*
Kenamerican Resources Inc .... G 740 338-3100
  Saint Clairsville *(G-16635)*
Maple Creek Mining Inc .... G 740 926-9205
  Alledonia *(G-446)*
Murray Energy Corporation .... G 740 338-3100
  Saint Clairsville *(G-16639)*
Murray Kentucky Energy Inc .... G 740 338-3100
  Saint Clairsville *(G-16640)*
Rosebud Mining Company .... E 740 658-4217
  Freeport *(G-9985)*
Rosebud Mining Company .... E 740 768-2097
  Bergholz *(G-1635)*
Rosebud Mining Company .... E 740 922-9122
  Uhrichsville *(G-18892)*
Sterling Mining Corporation .... F 330 549-2165
  North Lima *(G-15178)*
West Ridge Resources Inc .... G 740 338-3100
  Saint Clairsville *(G-16657)*
Western KY Coal Resources LLC .... B 740 338-3100
  Saint Clairsville *(G-16658)*

COAL MINING: Bituminous, Auger

CAM Co Inc .... G 740 922-4533
  Dennison *(G-8783)*

COAL MINING: Bituminous, Strip

B&N Coal Inc .... D 740 783-3575
  Dexter City *(G-8792)*
F & M Coal Company .... G 740 544-5203
  Toronto *(G-18609)*
Holmes Limestone Co .... G 330 893-2721
  Berlin *(G-1642)*
Oxford Mining Company Inc .... D 740 342-7666
  New Lexington *(G-14719)*
Oxford Mining Company - KY LLC .... G 740 622-6302
  Coshocton *(G-7749)*
Rosebud Mining Company .... E 740 922-9122
  Uhrichsville *(G-18892)*
Sands Hill Coal Hauling Co Inc .... C 740 384-4211
  Hamden *(G-10524)*
Thompson Brothers Mining Co .... F 330 549-3979
  New Springfield *(G-14821)*

COAL MINING: Bituminous, Surface, NEC

Marietta Coal Co .... E 740 695-2197
  Saint Clairsville *(G-16637)*
Rayle Coal Co .... F 740 695-2197
  Saint Clairsville *(G-16648)*

COAL MINING: Lignite, Surface, NEC

Nacco Industries Inc .... E 440 229-5151
  Cleveland *(G-5719)*

COAL PREPARATION PLANT: Bituminous or Lignite

Cliffs Logan County Coal LLC .... G 216 694-5700
  Cleveland *(G-4989)*

COAL PYROLYSIS

Enrevo Pyro LLC .... G 203 517-5002
  Brookfield *(G-2106)*

COAL, MINERALS & ORES, WHOLESALE: Coal

Johnson Energy Company .... G 937 435-5401
  Oakwood *(G-15462)*

COAL, MINERALS & ORES, WHOLESALE: Iron Ore

Masters Group Inc .... G 440 893-1900
  Chagrin Falls *(G-3059)*

COATED OR PLATED PRDTS

Ohio Coatings Company .... D 740 859-5500
  Yorkville *(G-20827)*

COATING COMPOUNDS: Tar

Brewer Company .... G 800 394-0017
  Milford *(G-13999)*
Brewer Company .... E 440 944-3800
  Wickliffe *(G-20206)*
Brewer Company .... G 513 576-6300
  Cincinnati *(G-3414)*
Dnd Emulsions Inc .... G 419 525-4988
  Mansfield *(G-12433)*

COATING OR WRAPPING SVC: Steel Pipe

Imperial Metal Solutions LLC .... F 216 781-4094
  Cleveland *(G-5444)*

COATING SVC

Bogden Industrial Coatings LLC .... G 513 267-5101
  Middletown *(G-13887)*

COATING SVC: Aluminum, Metal Prdts

E L Stone Company .... E 330 825-4565
  Norton *(G-15365)*
Emt Trading Company LLC .... G 888 352-8000
  Chagrin Falls *(G-3019)*
Epco Extrusion Painting Co .... E 330 781-6100
  Youngstown *(G-20899)*
Hardline International Inc .... F 419 924-9556
  West Unity *(G-19969)*
SH Bell Company .... F 412 963-9910
  East Liverpool *(G-9068)*
Treemen Industries Inc .... E 330 965-3777
  Boardman *(G-1904)*
Vacono America LLC .... E 216 938-7428
  Cleveland *(G-6249)*
Vacuum Finishing Company .... F 440 286-4386
  Chardon *(G-3140)*

COATING SVC: Electrodes

Advanced Coatings Intl .... G 330 794-6361
  Akron *(G-30)*
De Nora North America Inc .... F 440 357-4000
  Painesville *(G-15730)*
Visimax Technologies Inc .... F 330 405-8330
  Twinsburg *(G-18872)*

COATING SVC: Hot Dip, Metals Or Formed Prdts

AAA Galvanizing - Joliet Inc .... E 513 871-5700
  Cincinnati *(G-3285)*
Azz Incorporated .... E 330 445-2170
  Canton *(G-2581)*
Poly-Met Inc .... F 330 630-9006
  Akron *(G-323)*
Rack Coating Service Inc .... E 330 854-2869
  Canal Fulton *(G-2491)*

COATING SVC: Metals & Formed Prdts

A & E Powder Coating Ltd .... G 937 525-3750
  Springfield *(G-17359)*
A Class Coatings Inc .... F 440 960-6869
  Lorain *(G-12076)*
A Plus Powder Coaters Inc .... F 330 482-4389
  Columbiana *(G-6452)*
Advanced Technical Pdts Sup Co .... F 513 851-6858
  West Chester *(G-19638)*
Advantage Powder Coating Inc .... D 419 782-2363
  Defiance *(G-8611)*
Aesthetic Finishers Inc .... E 937 778-8777
  Piqua *(G-16098)*
Alpha Coatings Inc .... C 419 435-5111
  Fostoria *(G-9832)*
American Tchnical Coatings Inc .... G 440 401-2270
  Westlake *(G-20096)*
American Utility Proc LLC .... E 330 535-3000
  Akron *(G-65)*
Aps-Materials Inc .... D 937 278-6547
  Dayton *(G-8034)*
Aps-Materials Inc .... G 937 278-6547
  Dayton *(G-8035)*
Architectural and Industrial .... F 440 963-0410
  Vermilion *(G-19156)*
Armoloy of Ohio Inc .... F 937 323-8702
  Springfield *(G-17365)*
Bekaert Corporation .... C 330 683-5060
  Orrville *(G-15583)*
Boville Indus Coatings Inc .... E 330 669-8558
  Smithville *(G-17087)*
Cast Plus Inc .... E 937 743-7278
  Franklin *(G-9873)*
Cincinnati Thermal Spray Inc .... C 513 793-1037
  Blue Ash *(G-1750)*
Coat All .... G 419 659-2757
  Columbus Grove *(G-7634)*
Coating Systems Inc .... F 513 367-5600
  Harrison *(G-10637)*
Custom Powdercoating LLC .... G 937 972-3516
  Dayton *(G-8122)*

Ellison Srfc Tech - Mexico LLC............E....... 513 770-4900
  Mason (G-12862)
Ellison Surface Tech Inc............F....... 513 770-4922
  Mason (G-12864)
Ferro Corporation............D....... 216 875-5600
  Mayfield Heights (G-13163)
Greber Machine Tool Inc............G....... 440 322-3685
  Elyria (G-9264)
Greenkote Usa Inc............G....... 440 243-2865
  Brookpark (G-2148)
Hardcoating Technologies Ltd............E....... 330 686-2136
  Munroe Falls (G-14523)
Hartzell Mfg Co............E....... 937 859-5955
  Miamisburg (G-13674)
Howmet Corporation............E....... 757 825-7086
  Newburgh Heights (G-14939)
Inter-Ion Inc............E....... 330 928-9655
  Cuyahoga Falls (G-7882)
Ionbond LLC............F....... 216 831-0880
  Cleveland (G-5474)
Ivac Technologies Corp............F....... 216 662-4987
  Cleveland (G-5479)
Logan Coatings LLC............F....... 740 380-0047
  Logan (G-12032)
Medina Powder Coating Corp............G....... 330 952-1977
  Medina (G-13295)
Medina Powder Group............G....... 330 952-2711
  Medina (G-13296)
Mesocoat Inc............F....... 216 453-0866
  Euclid (G-9427)
Metokote Corporation............D....... 440 934-4686
  Sheffield Village (G-16971)
Metokote Corporation............E....... 270 889-9907
  Lima (G-11902)
Metokote Corporation............B....... 419 996-7800
  Lima (G-11903)
Metokote Corporation............D....... 419 227-1100
  Lima (G-11904)
Metokote Corporation............C....... 937 235-2811
  Dayton (G-8343)
Miamisburg Coating............F....... 937 866-1323
  Miamisburg (G-13693)
Mmf Inc............F....... 614 252-0078
  Columbus (G-7186)
Nation Coating Systems Inc............G....... 937 746-7632
  Franklin (G-9902)
Niles Manufacturing & Finshg............C....... 330 544-0402
  Niles (G-15024)
Northeast Coatings Inc............F....... 330 784-7773
  Tallmadge (G-17996)
Oerlikon Blzers Cating USA Inc............G....... 330 343-9892
  Dover (G-8846)
Ohio Coatings Company............D....... 740 859-5500
  Yorkville (G-20827)
Omni Manufacturing Inc............D....... 419 394-7424
  Saint Marys (G-16693)
Omni Manufacturing Inc............F....... 419 394-7424
  Saint Marys (G-16694)
Pioneer Custom Coating LLC............G....... 419 737-3152
  Pioneer (G-16087)
Pki Inc............F....... 513 832-8749
  Cincinnati (G-4164)
Precision Coatings Inc............F....... 216 441-0805
  Cleveland (G-5908)
Progressive Powder Coating Inc............F....... 440 974-3478
  Mentor (G-13559)
Raf Acquisition Co............F....... 440 572-5999
  Valley City (G-19058)
Reifel Industries Inc............F....... 419 737-2138
  Pioneer (G-16095)
Russell Products Co Inc............G....... 330 434-9163
  Akron (G-361)
Russell T Bundy Associates Inc............F....... 740 965-3008
  Sunbury (G-17900)
Semper Quality Industry Inc............G....... 440 352-8111
  Mentor (G-13578)
Skinner Powder Coating Inc............G....... 937 606-2188
  Piqua (G-16162)
Tennessee Coatings Inc............F....... 513 770-4900
  Mason (G-12949)
Thornton Powder Coatings Inc............F....... 419 522-7183
  Mansfield (G-12531)
Trans-Acc Inc............E....... 513 793-6410
  Blue Ash (G-1861)
Venus Trading LLC............G....... 513 374-0066
  Loveland (G-12243)
Water Star Inc............F....... 440 996-0800
  Painesville (G-15797)

COATING SVC: Metals, With Plastic Or Resins

Corrotec Inc............E....... 937 325-3585
  Springfield (G-17379)
Gem Coatings Ltd............E....... 740 589-2998
  Athens (G-832)
Godfrey & Wing Inc............E....... 330 562-1440
  Aurora (G-881)
Harwood Rubber Products Inc............E....... 330 923-3256
  Cuyahoga Falls (G-7878)
Master Vac Incorporated............G....... 419 335-7796
  Wauseon (G-19527)
Metokote Corporation............C....... 419 221-2754
  Lima (G-11905)
Metokote Corporation............D....... 319 232-6994
  Lima (G-11906)
Perfection Finishers Inc............E....... 419 337-8015
  Wauseon (G-19531)
Rack Processing Company Inc............E....... 937 294-1911
  Moraine (G-14388)
Surftech Inc............G....... 440 275-3356
  Austinburg (G-927)
Techneglas Inc............E....... 419 873-2000
  Perrysburg (G-16011)
Universal Rack & Equipment Co............E....... 330 963-6776
  Twinsburg (G-18870)

COATING SVC: Rust Preventative

Anotex Industries Inc............E....... 513 860-1165
  West Chester (G-19645)

COATING SVC: Silicon

Momentive Performance Mtls Inc............C....... 740 928-7010
  Hebron (G-10753)
Momentive Performance Mtls Inc............A....... 440 878-5705
  Richmond Heights (G-16503)
Momentive Prfmce Mtls Qrtz Inc............C....... 440 878-5700
  Strongsville (G-17765)

COATINGS: Epoxy

CPI Industrial Co............E....... 614 445-0800
  Columbus (G-6833)
Diamant Coating Systems Ltd............G....... 513 515-3078
  Sharonville (G-16956)
Dynafloor Systems Inc............F....... 330 467-6005
  Solon (G-17134)
Epoxy Systems Blstg Cating Inc............E....... 513 924-1800
  Cleves (G-6361)
Master Builders LLC............E....... 216 831-5500
  Beachwood (G-1247)
Nanosperse LLC............G....... 937 296-5030
  Kettering (G-11435)
Postle Industries Inc............E....... 216 265-9000
  Cleveland (G-5897)
Quality Durable Indus Floors............F....... 937 696-2833
  Farmersville (G-9631)
X-Treme Finishes Inc............F....... 330 474-0614
  Medina (G-13364)

COATINGS: Polyurethane

Baker Built Products Inc............G....... 419 965-2646
  Ohio City (G-15514)
Stronghold Coating Ltd............G....... 937 704-4020
  Cincinnati (G-4385)
Trexler Rubber Co Inc............E....... 330 296-9677
  Ravenna (G-16414)

COILS & TRANSFORMERS

Barnes International Inc............D....... 419 352-7501
  Bowling Green (G-1953)
Canfield Industries Inc............G....... 800 554-5071
  Youngstown (G-20864)
Custom Coil & Transformer Co............E....... 740 452-5211
  Zanesville (G-21126)
Electromotive Inc............F....... 330 688-6494
  Stow (G-17581)
Industrial Quartz Corp............F....... 440 942-0909
  Mentor (G-13469)
Kurz-Kasch Inc............D....... 740 498-8343
  Newcomerstown (G-14977)
Nexjen Technologies Ltd............G....... 781 572-5737
  Avon Lake (G-998)
PCC Airfoils LLC............C....... 216 692-7900
  Cleveland (G-5857)
Precision Switching Inc............G....... 800 800-8143
  Mansfield (G-12502)
Rapid Mr International LLC............G....... 614 486-6300
  Columbus (G-7378)
Schneider Electric Usa Inc............B....... 513 523-4171
  Oxford (G-15700)
Staco Energy Products Co............G....... 937 253-1191
  Miamisburg (G-13719)
Standard Car Truck Company............D....... 740 775-6450
  Chillicothe (G-3223)
Swiger Coil Systems Ltd............C....... 216 362-7500
  Cleveland (G-6137)
USA Instruments Inc............C....... 330 562-1000
  Aurora (G-913)
Wabtec Corporation............G....... 216 362-7500
  Cleveland (G-6280)
Wonder Weld Inc............G....... 614 875-1447
  Orient (G-15579)

COILS, WIRE: Aluminum, Made In Rolling Mills

Amh Holdings LLC............A....... 330 929-1811
  Cuyahoga Falls (G-7836)
Amh Holdings II Inc............B....... 330 929-1811
  Cuyahoga Falls (G-7837)

COILS: Electric Motors Or Generators

Custom Coil & Transformer Co............E....... 740 452-5211
  Zanesville (G-21126)
High Performance Servo LLC............G....... 440 541-3529
  Westlake (G-20123)
Single Phase Pwr Solutions LLC............G....... 513 722-5098
  Norwood (G-15429)

COIN COUNTERS

Garda CL Technical Svcs Inc............E....... 937 294-4099
  Moraine (G-14355)

COINS & TOKENS: Non-Currency

Osborne Coinage Company............D....... 513 681-5424
  Cincinnati (G-4120)

COLLECTION AGENCY, EXC REAL ESTATE

C & S Associates Inc............E....... 440 461-9661
  Highland Heights (G-10786)

COLLEGES, UNIVERSITIES & PROFESSIONAL SCHOOLS

Cold Control LLC............G....... 614 564-7011
  Westerville (G-19986)

COLLETS

Advanced Holding Designs Inc............F....... 330 928-4456
  Cuyahoga Falls (G-7831)

COLOR LAKES OR TONERS

Ferro Corporation............C....... 216 875-6178
  Cleveland (G-5231)

COLOR PIGMENTS

Ferro Corporation............D....... 216 875-5600
  Mayfield Heights (G-13163)
Ferro International Svcs Inc............G....... 216 875-5600
  Mayfield Heights (G-13164)
General Color Investments Inc............D....... 330 868-4161
  Minerva (G-14180)
Spectrum Dispersions Inc............F....... 330 296-0600
  Ravenna (G-16405)

COLOR SEPARATION: Photographic & Movie Film

Tj Metzgers Inc............D....... 419 861-8611
  Toledo (G-18553)

COLORS IN OIL, EXC ARTISTS'

Robert Raack............G....... 216 932-6127
  Cleveland Heights (G-6351)

COLORS: Pigments, Inorganic

Americhem Inc............E....... 330 926-3185
  Cuyahoga Falls (G-7834)
Americhem Inc............A....... 330 929-4213
  Cuyahoga Falls (G-7835)

COLORS: Pigments, Inorganic

Ampacet Corporation .... C 740 929-5521
  Newark (G-14850)
BASF Corporation .... G 440 329-2525
  Elyria (G-9223)
Chromaflo Technologies Corp .... C 440 997-0081
  Ashtabula (G-764)
Chromaflo Technologies Corp .... C 513 733-5111
  Cincinnati (G-3474)
Chromaflo Technologies Corp .... C 440 997-5137
  Ashtabula (G-765)
Colormatrix Group Inc .... G 216 622-0100
  Berea (G-1598)
Colormatrix Holdings Inc .... G 440 930-3162
  Berea (G-1599)
Day-Glo Color Corp .... G 216 391-7070
  Cleveland (G-5073)
Day-Glo Color Corp .... C 216 391-7070
  Cleveland (G-5074)
Day-Glo Color Corp .... F 216 391-7070
  Twinsburg (G-18761)
Degussa Incorporated .... G 513 733-5111
  Cincinnati (G-3580)
Eckart America Corporation .... D 440 954-7600
  Painesville (G-15734)
Leonhardt Plating Company .... E 513 242-1410
  Cincinnati (G-3938)
Lightstab Ltd Co .... G 216 751-5800
  Shaker Heights (G-16933)
PMC Specialties Group Inc .... E 513 242-3300
  Cincinnati (G-4169)
PMC Specialties Group Inc .... G 513 242-3300
  Cincinnati (G-4170)
Polyone Corporation .... C 419 668-4844
  Norwalk (G-15412)
Revlis Corporation .... E 330 535-2108
  Barberton (G-1101)
Rti Niles .... G 330 455-4010
  Niles (G-15034)
Sun Chemical Corporation .... C 513 681-5950
  Cincinnati (G-4391)
Thorworks Industries Inc .... E 419 626-4375
  Sandusky (G-16855)

COLORS: Pigments, Organic

Americhem Inc .... E 330 926-3185
  Cuyahoga Falls (G-7834)
Americhem Inc .... A 330 929-4213
  Cuyahoga Falls (G-7835)
Chromaflo Technologies Corp .... C 513 733-5111
  Cincinnati (G-3474)
Chromaflo Technologies Corp .... C 440 997-0081
  Ashtabula (G-764)
Flint Group US LLC .... D 513 771-1900
  Cincinnati (G-3695)
Ruscoe Company .... E 330 253-8148
  Akron (G-359)
Spectrum Dispersions Inc .... F 330 296-0600
  Ravenna (G-16405)

COMBINED ELEMENTARY & SECONDARY SCHOOLS, PUBLIC

Butler Tech Career Dev Schools .... F 513 867-1028
  Fairfield Township (G-9580)

COMBS, EXC HARD RUBBER

Sunbright Usa Inc .... G 440 205-0600
  Mentor (G-13597)

COMMERCIAL & OFFICE BUILDINGS RENOVATION & REPAIR

Shade Youngstown & Aluminum Co .... G 330 782-2373
  Youngstown (G-21028)
Thomas Cabinet Shop Inc .... F 937 847-8239
  Dayton (G-8554)

COMMERCIAL ART & GRAPHIC DESIGN SVCS

AG Designs LLC .... G 614 506-2849
  Delaware (G-8652)
Am Graphics .... G 330 799-7319
  Youngstown (G-20842)
Converters/Prepress Inc .... F 937 743-0935
  Carlisle (G-2891)
Creatia Inc .... G 937 368-3100
  Fletcher (G-9782)
Echographics Inc .... G 440 846-2330
  North Ridgeville (G-15222)
Enlarging Arts Inc .... G 330 434-3433
  Akron (G-156)
Fire Ball Press .... G 614 280-0100
  Columbus (G-6925)
Fx Digital Media Inc .... E 216 241-4040
  Cleveland (G-5282)
General Theming Contrs LLC .... C 614 252-6342
  Columbus (G-6945)
Graphic Touch Inc .... G 330 337-3341
  Salem (G-16744)
Hardmagic .... F 415 390-6232
  Marietta (G-12631)
Heartland Design Concepts .... G 419 774-0199
  Mansfield (G-12456)
Innovtive Crtive Solutions LLC .... E 614 491-9638
  Groveport (G-10494)
Instruction & Design Concepts .... G 937 439-2698
  Dayton (G-8271)
Johnson Brothers Holdings LLC .... G 614 868-5273
  Columbus (G-7073)
Jscs Group Inc .... G 513 563-4900
  Cincinnati (G-3886)
La Dua Inc .... G 440 243-9600
  Lakewood (G-11524)
Maximum Graphix Inc .... G 440 353-3301
  North Ridgeville (G-15240)
Middlefield Sign Co .... G 440 632-0708
  Middlefield (G-13827)
Mlp Interent Enterprises LLC .... E 614 917-8705
  Mansfield (G-12483)
Morse Enterprises Inc .... G 513 229-3600
  Mason (G-12912)
Our Fifth Street LLC .... G 614 866-4065
  Pickerington (G-16055)
Penca Design Group Ltd .... G 440 210-4422
  Painesville (G-15774)
Quez Media Marketing Inc .... F 216 910-0202
  Independence (G-11149)
Stick-It Graphics LLC .... G 330 407-0142
  New Philadelphia (G-14801)
Sylvan Studio Inc .... G 419 882-3423
  Sylvania (G-17963)
True Dinero Records & Tech LLC .... G 513 428-4610
  Cincinnati (G-4443)
Visual Art Graphic Services .... E 330 274-2775
  Mantua (G-12562)

COMMERCIAL ART & ILLUSTRATION SVCS

ONeil & Associates Inc .... B 937 865-0800
  Miamisburg (G-13704)

COMMERCIAL CONTAINERS WHOLESALERS

Askia Inc .... G 513 828-7443
  Cincinnati (G-3362)
Kaufman Container Company .... C 216 898-2000
  Cleveland (G-5519)

COMMERCIAL EQPT & SPLYS, WHOLESALE: Price Marking

Century Marketing Corporation .... C 419 354-2591
  Bowling Green (G-1961)

COMMERCIAL EQPT WHOLESALERS, NEC

Bar Codes Unlimited Inc .... G 937 434-2633
  Dayton (G-8051)
CMC Daymark Corporation .... C 419 354-2591
  Bowling Green (G-1963)
Cummins - Allison Corp .... G 614 529-1940
  Columbus (G-6841)
Cummins - Allison Corp .... G 440 824-5050
  Cleveland (G-5042)
Cummins - Allison Corp .... G 513 469-2924
  Blue Ash (G-1756)
General Data Company Inc .... C 513 752-7978
  Cincinnati (G-3252)
National Pride Equipment Inc .... G 419 289-2886
  Ashland (G-727)
Precision Equipment Llc .... G 330 220-7600
  Brunswick (G-2228)
Preferred Pump & Equipment LP .... G 937 322-4000
  Springfield (G-17475)
Rayhaven Group Inc .... F 330 659-3183
  Richfield (G-16484)

COMMERCIAL EQPT, WHOLESALE: Bakery Eqpt & Splys

Ervan Guttman Co .... G 513 791-0767
  Cincinnati (G-3653)

COMMERCIAL EQPT, WHOLESALE: Comm Cooking & Food Svc Eqpt

Harry C Lobalzo & Sons Inc .... E 330 666-6758
  Akron (G-199)
Wasserstrom Company .... B 614 228-6525
  Columbus (G-7591)

COMMERCIAL EQPT, WHOLESALE: Display Eqpt, Exc Refrigerated

Abstract Displays Inc .... G 513 985-9700
  Blue Ash (G-1719)
Ternion Inc .... E 216 642-6180
  Cleveland (G-6161)

COMMERCIAL EQPT, WHOLESALE: Food Warming

Joneszylon Company LLC .... G 740 545-6341
  West Lafayette (G-19933)

COMMERCIAL EQPT, WHOLESALE: Neon Signs

Behrco Inc .... G 419 394-1612
  Saint Marys (G-16676)

COMMERCIAL EQPT, WHOLESALE: Restaurant, NEC

International Beverage Works .... G 614 798-5398
  Columbus (G-7043)
ITW Food Equipment Group LLC .... A 937 332-2396
  Troy (G-18679)
Joseph Knapp .... F 330 832-3515
  Massillon (G-13006)
N Wasserstrom & Sons Inc .... C 614 228-5550
  Columbus (G-7206)
Rightway Food Service .... G 419 223-4075
  Lima (G-11932)

COMMERCIAL EQPT, WHOLESALE: Scales, Exc Laboratory

Kanawha Scales & Systems Inc .... F 513 576-0700
  Milford (G-14023)
Perfect Measuring Tape Company .... G 419 243-6811
  Toledo (G-18464)

COMMERCIAL EQPT, WHOLESALE: Store Eqpt

Hubert Enterprises Inc .... G 513 367-8600
  Harrison (G-10648)

COMMERCIAL EQPT, WHOLESALE: Store Fixtures & Display Eqpt

Baker Plastics Inc .... G 330 743-3142
  Youngstown (G-20851)
Possible Plastics Inc .... G 614 277-2100
  Grove City (G-10457)

COMMERCIAL PRINTING & NEWSPAPER PUBLISHING COMBINED

Advance Reporter .... G 419 485-4851
  Montpelier (G-14301)
Bellefontaine Examiner .... G 937 592-3060
  Bellefontaine (G-1507)
Brown Publishing Co .... F 937 544-2391
  West Union (G-19959)
Cameco Communications .... G 937 840-9490
  Hillsboro (G-10877)
Carrollton Publishing Company .... F 330 627-5591
  Carrollton (G-2918)
Cincinnati Crt Index Press Inc .... F 513 241-1450
  Cincinnati (G-3488)
Clermont Sun Publishing Co .... G 937 444-3441
  Mount Orab (G-14441)
Copley Ohio Newspapers Inc .... D 585 598-0030
  Canton (G-2636)

PRODUCT SECTION

COMPRESSORS: Air & Gas

Copley Ohio Newspapers Inc ....C....... 330 364-5577
  New Philadelphia *(G-14765)*
Copley Ohio Newspapers Inc ....D....... 330 833-2631
  Massillon *(G-12969)*
Cox Media Group Ohio Inc ....A....... 937 225-2000
  Dayton *(G-8105)*
Daily Chief Union ....F....... 419 294-2331
  Upper Sandusky *(G-18950)*
Dayton Dailey News ....F....... 937 743-2387
  Franklin *(G-9878)*
Delaware Gazette Company ....D....... 740 363-1161
  Delaware *(G-8670)*
Digicom Inc ....G....... 216 642-3838
  Brooklyn Heights *(G-2120)*
Dispatch Printing Company ....C....... 740 548-5331
  Lewis Center *(G-11757)*
Dispatch Printing Company ....E....... 614 885-6020
  Columbus *(G-6868)*
Gannett Publishing Svcs LLC ....G....... 419 522-3311
  Mansfield *(G-12444)*
Hamilton Journal News Inc ....D....... 513 863-8200
  Liberty Township *(G-11815)*
Herald Reflector Inc ....D....... 419 668-3771
  Norwalk *(G-15399)*
Hirt Publishing Co Inc ....G....... 419 523-5709
  Ottawa *(G-15652)*
Horizon Ohio Publications Inc ....F....... 419 394-7414
  Saint Marys *(G-16686)*
Horizon Ohio Publications Inc ....E....... 419 738-2128
  Wapakoneta *(G-19332)*
Hubbard Publishing Co ....E....... 937 592-3060
  Bellefontaine *(G-1518)*
King Media Enterprises Inc ....E....... 216 588-6700
  Cleveland *(G-5535)*
Knowles Press Inc ....G....... 330 877-9345
  Hartville *(G-10699)*
Knox County Printing Co ....G....... 740 848-4032
  Galion *(G-10147)*
Kroner Publications Inc ....E....... 330 544-5500
  Niles *(G-15020)*
Mirror ....E....... 419 893-8135
  Maumee *(G-13134)*
New Urban Distributors LLC ....G....... 216 373-2349
  Cleveland *(G-5749)*
Progressive Communications ....D....... 740 397-5333
  Mount Vernon *(G-14503)*
Register Herald Office ....F....... 937 456-5553
  Eaton *(G-9164)*
Sentinel Daily ....G....... 740 992-2155
  Pomeroy *(G-16241)*
Southeast Publications Inc ....F....... 740 732-2341
  Caldwell *(G-2412)*
Standard Printing Co Inc ....E....... 419 586-2371
  Celina *(G-2985)*
The Defiance Publishing Co ....A....... 419 784-5441
  Defiance *(G-8645)*
Toledo Blade Company ....B....... 419 724-6000
  Toledo *(G-18557)*
Truax Printing Inc ....E....... 419 994-4166
  Loudonville *(G-12149)*
Wooster Daily Record Inc LLC ....C....... 330 264-1125
  Wooster *(G-20668)*

COMMODITY CONTRACT TRADING COMPANIES

Cac Energy Ltd ....G....... 937 867-5593
  Dayton *(G-8072)*
Meak Solutions Llc ....G....... 440 796-8209
  Mentor *(G-13513)*

COMMON SAND MINING

De Milta Sand and Gravel Inc ....F....... 440 942-2015
  Willoughby *(G-20307)*
Feikert Sand & Gravel Co Inc ....E....... 330 674-0038
  Millersburg *(G-14082)*
FML Sand LLC ....G....... 440 214-3200
  Independence *(G-11130)*
Kirby and Sons Inc ....F....... 419 927-2260
  Upper Sandusky *(G-18959)*
Nelson Sand & Gravel Inc ....F....... 440 224-0198
  Kingsville *(G-11461)*
Shenango Valley Sand and Grav ......G....... 330 758-9100
  Youngstown *(G-21030)*
Stocker Sand & Gravel Co ....E....... 740 254-4635
  Gnadenhutten *(G-10284)*
Weber Sand & Gravel Inc ....F....... 419 298-2388
  Edgerton *(G-9182)*
Welch Holdings Inc ....E....... 513 353-3220
  Cincinnati *(G-4497)*
X L Sand and Gravel Co ....F....... 330 426-9876
  Negley *(G-14592)*

COMMUNICATION HEADGEAR: Telephone

Commtech Solutions Inc ....G....... 440 458-4870
  Grafton *(G-10294)*

COMMUNICATIONS CARRIER: Wired

Protech Electric LLC ....F....... 937 427-0813
  Beavercreek *(G-1337)*

COMMUNICATIONS EQPT & SYSTEMS, NEC

Robert F Sams ....G....... 330 990-0477
  Akron *(G-351)*
Special Way 2 ....G....... 740 282-8281
  Steubenville *(G-17552)*

COMMUNICATIONS EQPT REPAIR & MAINTENANCE

Cattron Holdings Inc ....E....... 234 806-0018
  Warren *(G-19381)*
House of Hindenach ....G....... 419 422-0392
  Findlay *(G-9707)*

COMMUNICATIONS EQPT WHOLESALERS

Cattron Holdings Inc ....E....... 234 806-0018
  Warren *(G-19381)*
Cota International Inc ....F....... 937 526-5520
  Versailles *(G-19177)*
Quasonix Inc ....E....... 513 942-1287
  West Chester *(G-19775)*
Ray Communications Inc ....G....... 330 686-0226
  Stow *(G-17623)*
Securcom Inc ....E....... 419 628-1049
  Minster *(G-14224)*

COMMUNICATIONS SVCS

Harris Hawk ....G....... 800 459-4295
  Mason *(G-12885)*
S T Custom Signs ....G....... 513 733-4227
  Cincinnati *(G-4298)*

COMMUNICATIONS SVCS: Data

Springdot Inc ....D....... 513 542-4000
  Cincinnati *(G-4365)*
Water Drop Media Inc ....G....... 234 600-5817
  Vienna *(G-19211)*

COMMUNICATIONS SVCS: Internet Connectivity Svcs

Great Lakes Telcom Ltd ....E....... 330 629-8848
  Youngstown *(G-20924)*
Revolution Group Inc ....D....... 614 212-1111
  Westerville *(G-20020)*

COMMUNICATIONS SVCS: Online Svc Providers

F+w Media Inc ....B....... 513 531-2690
  Blue Ash *(G-1770)*
Vista Research Group LLC ....G....... 419 281-3927
  Ashland *(G-753)*

COMMUNICATIONS SVCS: Radio Pager Or Beeper

Airwave Communications Cons ....G....... 419 331-1526
  Lima *(G-11832)*

COMMUNICATIONS SVCS: Signal Enhancement Network Svcs

Alanax Technologies Inc ....G....... 216 469-1545
  Belmont *(G-1564)*

COMMUNICATIONS SVCS: Telephone Or Video

J Com Data Inc ....G....... 614 304-1455
  Pataskala *(G-15833)*

COMMUNICATIONS SVCS: Telephone, Local & Long Distance

Airwave Communications Cons ....G....... 419 331-1526
  Lima *(G-11832)*
AT&T Corp ....G....... 513 792-9300
  Cincinnati *(G-3365)*

COMMUNICATIONS SVCS: Telephone, Long Distance

Mitel (delaware) Inc ....E....... 513 733-8000
  West Chester *(G-19745)*

COMMUNITY ACTION AGENCY

Community Action Program Corp ....F....... 740 374-8501
  Marietta *(G-12617)*

COMMUNITY DEVELOPMENT GROUPS

Access To Independence Inc ....G....... 330 296-8111
  Ravenna *(G-16363)*
News Reel Inc ....G....... 614 469-0700
  Columbus *(G-7218)*

COMMUTATORS: Electric Motors

Kirkwood Holding Inc ....C....... 216 267-6200
  Cleveland *(G-5539)*

COMMUTATORS: Electronic

Ra Consultants LLC ....E....... 513 469-6600
  Blue Ash *(G-1840)*

COMPACT DISCS OR CD'S, WHOLESALE

CD Solutions Inc ....G....... 937 676-2376
  Pleasant Hill *(G-16224)*
Upcreek Productions Inc ....G....... 740 208-8124
  Bidwell *(G-1672)*

COMPACT LASER DISCS: Prerecorded

Jk Digital Publishing LLC ....E....... 937 299-0185
  Springboro *(G-17331)*

COMPARATORS: Machinists

Certified Comparator Products ....G....... 937 426-9677
  Beavercreek *(G-1353)*

COMPOST

Charles Daniel Young ....G....... 937 968-3423
  Union City *(G-18903)*
City of Columbus ....E....... 614 645-3152
  Lockbourne *(G-11993)*
Compost Cincy ....G....... 513 278-8178
  Cincinnati *(G-3540)*
Hyponex Corporation ....E....... 330 262-1300
  Shreve *(G-17002)*
Kurtz Bros Compost Services ....E....... 330 864-2621
  Akron *(G-242)*
Midwest Compost Inc ....F....... 419 547-7979
  Clyde *(G-6391)*
Opal Diamond LLC ....G....... 330 653-5876
  Rocky River *(G-16550)*
Price Farms Organics Ltd ....F....... 740 369-1000
  Delaware *(G-8717)*
Werlor Inc ....E....... 419 784-4285
  Defiance *(G-8647)*

COMPRESSORS, AIR CONDITIONING: Wholesalers

Diversified Air Systems Inc ....E....... 216 741-1700
  Brooklyn Heights *(G-2121)*

COMPRESSORS: Air & Gas

Airtech ....G....... 419 269-1000
  Walbridge *(G-19291)*
Airtx International Ltd ....F....... 513 631-0660
  Cincinnati *(G-3314)*
Arete Innovative Solutions LLC ....G....... 513 503-2712
  Morrow *(G-14408)*
Ariel Corporation ....G....... 740 397-0311
  Mount Vernon *(G-14468)*
Ariel Corporation ....F....... 740 397-0311
  Mount Vernon *(G-14469)*
Atlas Machine and Supply Inc ....G....... 614 351-1603
  Hilliard *(G-10807)*

Employee Codes: A=Over 500 employees, B=251-500
C=101-250, D=51-100, E=20-50, F=10-19, G=3-9

COMPRESSORS: Air & Gas

Dresser-Rand Company .... E 513 874-8388
 Fairfield *(G-9496)*
Eaton Comprsr Fabrication Inc .... E 877 283-7614
 Englewood *(G-9357)*
Ecowise LLC .... G 216 692-3700
 Cleveland *(G-5156)*
Edwards Vacuum LLC .... G 440 248-4453
 Solon *(G-17135)*
Ernest Industries Inc .... F 937 325-9851
 Springfield *(G-17397)*
Field Gymmy Inc .... G 419 538-6511
 Glandorf *(G-10269)*
Gardner Denver Nash LLC .... F 440 871-9505
 Cleveland *(G-5291)*
General Fabrications Corp .... E 419 625-6055
 Sandusky *(G-16813)*
Giti Tech Group Ltd .... G 866 381-7955
 West Carrollton *(G-19632)*
Kingsly Compression Inc .... G 740 439-0772
 Cambridge *(G-2445)*
Lsq Manufacturing Inc .... F 330 725-4905
 Medina *(G-13287)*
Mack Industrial LLC .... G 800 918-9986
 Perrysburg *(G-15974)*
Optimair Ltd .... G 419 661-9568
 Perrysburg *(G-15992)*
Optime Air MSP Ltd .... F 419 661-9568
 Perrysburg *(G-15993)*
Powerex-Iwata Air Tech Inc .... D 888 769-7979
 Harrison *(G-10663)*
Rotary Compression Tech Inc .... G 937 498-2555
 Sidney *(G-17071)*
T D Group Holdings LLC .... G 216 706-2939
 Cleveland *(G-6144)*
Transdigm Inc .... G 216 706-2939
 Cleveland *(G-6196)*
Transdigm Inc .... F 216 291-6025
 Cleveland *(G-6195)*

COMPRESSORS: Air & Gas, Including Vacuum Pumps

Aci Services Inc .... E 740 435-0240
 Cambridge *(G-2421)*
Campbell Hausfeld LLC .... C 513 367-4811
 Cincinnati *(G-3439)*
Finishmaster Inc .... D 614 228-4328
 Columbus *(G-6924)*
Potemkin Industries Inc .... E 740 397-4888
 Mount Vernon *(G-14501)*

COMPRESSORS: Refrigeration & Air Conditioning Eqpt

Certified Service Inc .... G 937 643-0393
 Dayton *(G-8085)*
Emerson Climate Tech Inc .... A 937 498-3011
 Sidney *(G-17036)*
Hanon Systems Usa LLC .... C 313 920-0583
 Carey *(G-2882)*
IV J Telecommunications LLC .... F 606 694-1762
 South Point *(G-17284)*
Midwest Compressor Co Inc .... G 216 941-9200
 Cleveland *(G-5679)*

COMPRESSORS: Repairing

Fmh Electric Inc .... F 419 782-0671
 Lima *(G-11863)*

COMPRESSORS: Wholesalers

A P O Holdings Inc .... E 330 455-8925
 Canton *(G-2556)*
Atlas Machine and Supply Inc .... E 502 584-7262
 West Chester *(G-19834)*
Diversified Air Systems Inc .... E 216 741-1700
 Brooklyn Heights *(G-2121)*
General Electric Intl Inc .... G 330 963-2066
 Twinsburg *(G-18783)*
Harbor Freight Tools Usa Inc .... G 937 415-0770
 Dayton *(G-8244)*

COMPUTER & COMPUTER SOFTWARE STORES

Copier Resources Inc .... G 614 268-1100
 Columbus *(G-6818)*
Gordons Graphics Inc .... G 330 863-2322
 Malvern *(G-12392)*

Journey Systems LLC .... F 513 831-6200
 Milford *(G-14022)*
Tech-E-Z LLC .... G 419 692-1700
 Delphos *(G-8755)*

COMPUTER & COMPUTER SOFTWARE STORES: Computer Tapes

Ohio Graphic Supply Inc .... G 937 433-7537
 Dayton *(G-8397)*

COMPUTER & COMPUTER SOFTWARE STORES: Peripheral Eqpt

B W T Inc .... G 330 928-9107
 Akron *(G-77)*
Computer Zoo Inc .... G 937 310-1474
 Bellbrook *(G-1490)*
Golubitsky Corporation .... G 800 552-4204
 Cleveland *(G-5329)*
Lazer Action Inc .... G 330 630-9200
 Akron *(G-249)*
PC Systems .... G 330 825-7966
 Akron *(G-315)*
T E Hubler Inc .... G 419 476-2552
 Toledo *(G-18541)*

COMPUTER & COMPUTER SOFTWARE STORES: Printers & Plotters

Kehler Enterprises Inc .... G 614 889-8488
 Dublin *(G-8937)*
Nickum Enterprises Inc .... G 513 561-2292
 Cincinnati *(G-4077)*

COMPUTER & COMPUTER SOFTWARE STORES: Software & Access

Ezshred LLC .... G 440 256-7640
 Kirtland *(G-11468)*
Lantek Systems Inc .... G 513 988-8708
 Mason *(G-12903)*
Merkur Group Inc .... G 937 429-4288
 Beavercreek *(G-1331)*

COMPUTER & COMPUTER SOFTWARE STORES: Software, Bus/Non-Game

A Graphic Solution .... F 216 228-7223
 Cleveland *(G-4587)*
Delores E OBeirn .... G 440 582-3610
 Cleveland *(G-5082)*
Retalix Inc .... C 937 384-2277
 Miamisburg *(G-13712)*

COMPUTER & COMPUTER SOFTWARE STORES: Software, Computer Game

Lasermark LLC .... G 513 312-9889
 Dayton *(G-8306)*
Moonstruck Games Inc .... G 513 721-3900
 Cincinnati *(G-4044)*

COMPUTER & DATA PROCESSING EQPT REPAIR & MAINTENANCE

P C Power Inc .... G 440 779-4080
 North Olmsted *(G-15195)*
Thomas Ross Associates Inc .... G 330 723-1110
 Medina *(G-13352)*

COMPUTER & OFFICE MACHINE MAINTENANCE & REPAIR

Davis Laser Products .... G 614 252-7711
 Columbus *(G-6853)*
Eaj Services LLC .... F 513 792-3400
 Blue Ash *(G-1762)*
Freedom Usa Inc .... F 216 503-6374
 Twinsburg *(G-18776)*
Government Acquisitions Inc .... E 513 721-8700
 Cincinnati *(G-3773)*
ID Card Systems Inc .... G 330 963-7446
 Twinsburg *(G-18795)*
Magnum Computers Inc .... F 216 781-1757
 Cleveland *(G-5605)*
Newwave Technologies Inc .... G 513 683-1211
 Loveland *(G-12218)*
Programmable Control Service .... F 740 927-0744
 Pataskala *(G-15838)*

T E Hubler Inc .... G 419 476-2552
 Toledo *(G-18541)*
Tech-E-Z LLC .... G 419 692-1700
 Delphos *(G-8755)*
Terra Comp Technology .... G 330 745-8912
 Barberton *(G-1111)*

COMPUTER FORMS

Crabar/Gbf Inc .... E 419 269-1720
 Toledo *(G-18242)*
R R Donnelley & Sons Company .... E 440 774-2101
 Oberlin *(G-15504)*

COMPUTER GRAPHICS SVCS

Bob King Sign Company Inc .... G 330 753-2679
 Akron *(G-90)*
Columbus Advnced Mfg Sftwr Inc .... G 614 410-2300
 Delaware *(G-8668)*
Datatex Media Dolls .... G 216 598-1000
 Cleveland *(G-5070)*
Great Lakes Publishing Company .... D 216 771-2833
 Cleveland *(G-5350)*
IPA Ltd .... F 614 523-3974
 Columbus *(G-7048)*
Jjkb Enterprises LLC .... G 513 731-4332
 Cincinnati *(G-3873)*
M Grafix LLC .... F 419 528-8665
 Mansfield *(G-12471)*
Quez Media Marketing Inc .... F 216 910-0202
 Independence *(G-11149)*
R T Communications Inc .... G 330 726-7892
 Youngstown *(G-21011)*
Sevell + Sevell Inc .... G 614 341-9700
 Columbus *(G-7441)*

COMPUTER INTERFACE EQPT: Indl Process

Comtec Incorporated .... F 330 425-8102
 Twinsburg *(G-18756)*
Keithley Instruments LLC .... C 440 248-0400
 Solon *(G-17182)*
Measurement Computing Corp .... E 440 439-4091
 Cleveland *(G-5650)*
Technology Resources Inc .... G 419 241-9248
 Toledo *(G-18544)*
Vertiv North America Inc .... A 614 888-0246
 Columbus *(G-7578)*
Wild Fire Systems .... G 440 442-8999
 Cleveland *(G-6308)*

COMPUTER PERIPHERAL EQPT REPAIR & MAINTENANCE

Ascendtech Inc .... E 216 458-1101
 Willoughby *(G-20282)*
Lazer Action Inc .... G 330 630-9200
 Akron *(G-249)*
PC Systems .... G 330 825-7966
 Akron *(G-315)*
Smartronix Inc .... F 216 378-3300
 Northfield *(G-15325)*

COMPUTER PERIPHERAL EQPT, NEC

Adaptive Data Inc .... F 937 436-2343
 Dayton *(G-8007)*
Advanced Microbeam Inc .... G 330 394-1255
 Vienna *(G-19195)*
Airwave Communications Cons .... G 419 331-1526
 Lima *(G-11832)*
AT&T Corp .... G 513 792-9300
 Cincinnati *(G-3365)*
Black Box Corporation .... G 800 837-7777
 Dublin *(G-8890)*
Black Box Corporation .... F 800 676-8850
 Brecksville *(G-2023)*
Black Box Corporation .... G 800 837-7777
 Westlake *(G-20101)*
Black Box Corporation .... F 614 825-7400
 Lewis Center *(G-11751)*
Cisco Systems Inc .... A 419 977-2404
 New Bremen *(G-14648)*
Dataq Instruments .... F 330 668-1444
 Akron *(G-133)*
Eastman Kodak Company .... E 937 259-3000
 Dayton *(G-8175)*
Embedded Planet Inc .... F 216 245-4180
 Warrensville Heights *(G-19467)*
Enterasys Networks Inc .... B 330 245-0240
 Akron *(G-157)*

PRODUCT SECTION

COMPUTER SOFTWARE DEVELOPMENT

Epic Technologies LLC ....D...... 513 683-5455
  Mason (G-12867)
Esterline Georgia US LLC ....E...... 937 372-7579
  Xenia (G-20770)
Gleason Metrology Systems Corp ....E...... 937 384-8901
  Dayton (G-8223)
Government Acquisitions Inc 513 721-8700
  Cincinnati (G-3773)
Intermec Inc ....G...... 513 874-5882
  West Chester (G-19724)
Intermec Technologies Corp ....G...... 513 874-5882
  West Chester (G-19725)
Intermec Technologies Corp ....F...... 513 874-5882
  West Chester (G-19726)
Kern Inc ....E...... 614 317-2600
  Grove City (G-10439)
Kern Inc ....G...... 440 930-7315
  Cleveland (G-5531)
Lazer Action Inc ....G...... 330 630-9200
  Akron (G-249)
Parker-Hannifin Corporation ....D...... 513 831-2340
  Milford (G-14031)
Phase Array Company LLC ....G...... 513 785-0801
  West Chester (G-19759)
Prentke Romich Company ....C...... 330 262-1984
  Wooster (G-20641)
Qualtek Electronics Corp ....G...... 440 951-3300
  Mentor (G-13567)
Scriptel Corporation ....F...... 614 276-8402
  Columbus (G-7434)
Signature Technologies Inc ....E...... 937 859-6323
  Miamisburg (G-13716)
Stellar Systems Inc ....G...... 513 921-8748
  Cincinnati (G-4379)
Superior Label Systems Inc ....B...... 513 336-0825
  Mason (G-12944)
Systemax Manufacturing Inc ....C...... 937 368-2300
  Dayton (G-8533)
T E Hubler Inc ....G...... 419 476-2552
  Toledo (G-18541)
Tech Pro Inc ....E...... 330 923-3546
  Akron (G-397)
Timekeeping Systems Inc ....F...... 216 595-0890
  Solon (G-17253)
University Accessories Inc ....G...... 440 327-4151
  North Ridgeville (G-15257)
Video Products Inc ....D...... 330 562-2622
  Aurora (G-915)
Vmetro Inc ....G...... 281 584-0728
  Fairborn (G-9473)
Xerox Corporation ....D...... 513 539-4858
  Monroe (G-14283)
Xerox Corporation ....G...... 513 539-4808
  Monroe (G-14284)
Xponet Inc ....E...... 440 354-6617
  Painesville (G-15801)
Yonezawa USA Inc ....G...... 614 799-2210
  Plain City (G-16222)

COMPUTER PERIPHERAL EQPT, WHOLESALE

Ascendtech Inc ....E...... 216 458-1101
  Willoughby (G-20282)
Eagle Wright Innovations Inc ....G...... 937 640-8093
  Moraine (G-14348)
Legrand North America LLC ....B...... 937 224-0639
  Dayton (G-8309)
Microplex Inc ....E...... 330 498-0600
  North Canton (G-15101)
PC Systems ....G...... 330 825-7966
  Akron (G-315)
Systemax Manufacturing Inc ....C...... 937 368-2300
  Dayton (G-8533)

COMPUTER PERIPHERAL EQPT: Decoders

Harris Mackessy & Brennan ....C...... 614 221-6831
  Westerville (G-19996)

COMPUTER PERIPHERAL EQPT: Graphic Displays, Exc Terminals

Abstract Displays Inc ....G...... 513 985-9700
  Blue Ash (G-1719)
AGE Graphics LLC ....F...... 740 989-0006
  Little Hocking (G-11989)
Penca Design Group Ltd ....G...... 440 210-4422
  Painesville (G-15774)
Star City Art Co ....F...... 937 865-9792
  Miamisburg (G-13720)

COMPUTER PERIPHERAL EQPT: Input Or Output

Computer Zoo Inc ....G...... 937 310-1474
  Bellbrook (G-1490)

COMPUTER PROCESSING SVCS

List Media Inc ....G...... 330 995-0864
  Chagrin Falls (G-3023)

COMPUTER PROGRAMMING SVCS

Aclara Technologies LLC ....C...... 440 528-7200
  Solon (G-17098)
Advanced Prgrm Resources Inc ....E...... 614 761-9994
  Dublin (G-8874)
Application Link Inc ....F...... 614 934-1735
  Columbus (G-6609)
Brown Dave Products Inc ....F...... 513 738-1576
  Hamilton (G-10543)
Cimx LLC ....E...... 513 248-7700
  Cincinnati (G-3476)
Command Alkon Incorporated ....D...... 614 799-0600
  Dublin (G-8901)
Computer Workshop Inc ....E...... 614 798-9505
  Dublin (G-8902)
Drb Systems LLC ....C...... 330 645-3299
  Akron (G-147)
Drs Signal Technologies Inc ....E...... 937 429-7470
  Beavercreek (G-1312)
Eclipse Blind Systems Inc ....C...... 330 296-0112
  Ravenna (G-16378)
Gb Liquidating Company Inc ....E...... 513 248-7600
  Milford (G-14010)
Gracie Plum Investments Inc ....E...... 740 355-9029
  Portsmouth (G-16284)
Immigration Law Systems Inc ....E...... 614 252-3078
  Columbus (G-7023)
Intelligrated Inc ....E...... 513 874-0788
  West Chester (G-19868)
Mapsys Inc ....E...... 614 255-7258
  Columbus (G-7148)
NCR International Inc ....E...... 937 445-5000
  Kettering (G-11437)
North Coast Security Group LLC ....G...... 614 887-7255
  Columbus (G-7226)
Pathfinder Computer Systems ....G...... 330 928-1961
  Barberton (G-1094)
Pdmb Inc ....G...... 513 522-7362
  Cincinnati (G-4144)
Pixslap Inc ....G...... 937 559-2671
  Middletown (G-13942)
Proficient Information Tech ....G...... 937 470-1300
  Dayton (G-8447)
Quayle Consulting Inc ....G...... 614 868-1363
  Pickerington (G-16058)
Reichard Software Corp ....E...... 614 537-8598
  Dublin (G-8972)
Reynolds and Reynolds Company ....F...... 937 485-2805
  Beavercreek (G-1362)
Seapine Software Inc ....E...... 513 754-1655
  Mason (G-12938)
Tahoe Interactive Systems Inc ....F...... 614 891-2323
  Westerville (G-20076)
Tata America Intl Corp ....B...... 513 677-6500
  Milford (G-14043)
Technology and Services Inc ....G...... 740 626-2020
  Chillicothe (G-3227)
Technosoft Inc ....F...... 513 985-9877
  Blue Ash (G-1857)

COMPUTER PROGRAMMING SVCS: Custom

Avasax Ltd ....G...... 937 694-0807
  Beavercreek (G-1350)
Corporate Elevator LLC ....F...... 614 288-1847
  Columbus (G-6822)
Fgm Media Inc ....G...... 440 376-0487
  North Royalton (G-15272)
Jasstek Inc ....F...... 614 808-3600
  Dublin (G-8932)
Sentinel USA Inc ....F...... 740 345-6412
  Newark (G-14917)
Teachers Publishing Group ....F...... 614 486-0631
  Hilliard (G-10868)
Timekeeping Systems Inc ....F...... 216 595-0890
  Solon (G-17253)

COMPUTER RELATED MAINTENANCE SVCS

Ascendtech Inc ....E...... 216 458-1101
  Willoughby (G-20282)
Digital Controls Corporation ....D...... 513 746-8118
  Miamisburg (G-13659)
Lync Corp ....E...... 513 655-7286
  Cincinnati (G-3959)
Proficient Information Tech ....G...... 937 470-1300
  Dayton (G-8447)
Wolters Kluwer Clinical Drug ....D...... 330 650-6506
  Hudson (G-11083)

COMPUTER RELATED SVCS, NEC

Brakers Publishing & Prtg Svc ....G...... 440 576-0136
  Jefferson (G-11225)

COMPUTER SERVICE BUREAU

CD Solutions Inc ....G...... 937 676-2376
  Pleasant Hill (G-16224)

COMPUTER SOFTWARE DEVELOPMENT

Agent Technologies Inc ....G...... 513 942-9444
  West Chester (G-19639)
Alanax Technologies Inc ....G...... 216 469-1545
  Belmont (G-1564)
Applied Systems Inc ....E...... 513 943-0000
  Milford (G-13994)
Auto Des Sys Inc ....E...... 614 488-7984
  Upper Arlington (G-18943)
Brainmaster Technologies Inc ....G...... 440 232-6000
  Bedford (G-1391)
Coso Media LLC ....G...... 330 904-5889
  Hudson (G-11039)
Eci Macola/Max LLC ....C...... 978 539-6186
  Dublin (G-8911)
Einstruction Corporation ....D...... 330 746-3015
  Youngstown (G-20897)
Electronic Concepts Engrg Inc ....F...... 419 861-9000
  Holland (G-10930)
Elynx Holdings LLC ....G...... 513 612-5969
  Cincinnati (G-3633)
Embedded Planet Inc ....F...... 216 245-4180
  Warrensville Heights (G-19467)
Ganymede Technologies Corp ....G...... 419 562-5522
  Bucyrus (G-2330)
Intelligrated Systems Inc ....A...... 866 936-7300
  Mason (G-12894)
Intelligrated Systems LLC ....A...... 513 701-7300
  Mason (G-12895)
IPA Ltd ....F...... 614 523-3974
  Columbus (G-7048)
John B Allen ....G...... 614 488-7122
  Columbus (G-7072)
Keithley Instruments LLC ....C...... 440 248-0400
  Solon (G-17182)
Leidos Inc ....D...... 937 431-2270
  Beavercreek (G-1326)
Navistone Inc ....G...... 844 677-3667
  Cincinnati (G-4065)
Omniboom LLC ....G...... 833 675-3987
  Hamilton (G-10594)
P3labs LLC ....G...... 800 259-8059
  North Canton (G-15108)
Parker-Hannifin Corporation ....D...... 513 831-2340
  Milford (G-14031)
Qc Software LLC ....G...... 513 469-1424
  Cincinnati (G-4224)
Queen City Technologies ....F...... 513 253-1312
  West Chester (G-19892)
Rawhide Software Inc ....G...... 419 878-0857
  Bowling Green (G-1993)
Sanctuary Software Studio Inc ....E...... 330 666-9690
  Fairlawn (G-9616)
Stellar Systems Inc ....G...... 513 921-8748
  Cincinnati (G-4379)
Strongbasics LLC ....G...... 716 903-6151
  Columbus (G-7495)
Thinkware Incorporated ....E...... 513 598-3300
  Cincinnati (G-4419)
Triad Governmental Systems ....G...... 937 376-5446
  Xenia (G-20799)
Truck Fax Inc ....G...... 216 921-8866
  Cleveland (G-6218)
Virtual Hold Technology LLC ....D...... 330 670-2200
  Akron (G-427)

Employee Codes: A=Over 500 employees, B=251-500
C=101-250, D=51-100, E=20-50, F=10-19, G=3-9

2019 Harris Ohio Industrial Directory

COMPUTER SOFTWARE DEVELOPMENT & APPLICATIONS

COMPUTER SOFTWARE DEVELOPMENT & APPLICATIONS

Alonovus Corp .... D 330 674-2300
  Millersburg *(G-14057)*
Callcopy Inc .... G 614 340-3346
  Columbus *(G-6725)*
Computer Allied Technology Co .... G 614 457-2292
  Columbus *(G-6808)*
Cott Systems Inc .... D 614 847-4405
  Columbus *(G-6827)*
Data Genomix Inc .... F 216 860-4770
  Cleveland *(G-5069)*
Deemsys Inc .... G 614 322-9928
  Gahanna *(G-10079)*
Ezshred LLC .... G 440 256-7640
  Kirtland *(G-11468)*
Forcam Inc .... F 513 878-2780
  Cincinnati *(G-3702)*
Gatesair Inc .... D 513 459-3400
  Mason *(G-12875)*
Generic Systems Inc .... G 419 841-8460
  Holland *(G-10932)*
Hab Inc .... E 608 785-7650
  Solon *(G-17158)*
Lantek Systems Inc .... G 513 988-8708
  Mason *(G-12903)*
List Media Inc .... G 330 995-0864
  Chagrin Falls *(G-3023)*
Lync Corp .... E 513 655-7286
  Cincinnati *(G-3959)*
Mamsys Consulting Services .... G 440 287-6824
  Solon *(G-17187)*
Pearl Tech Corporation .... G 614 284-8357
  Dublin *(G-8960)*
Sest Inc .... F 440 777-9777
  Westlake *(G-20157)*
Signalysis Inc .... F 513 528-6164
  Cincinnati *(G-4337)*
Simple Vms LLC .... G 888 255-8918
  Cincinnati *(G-4338)*
Tech Solutions LLC .... G 419 852-7190
  Celina *(G-2986)*
Value Stream Systems Inc .... G 330 907-0064
  Medina *(G-13359)*
Westmount Technology Inc .... G 216 328-2011
  Independence *(G-11157)*

COMPUTER SOFTWARE SYSTEMS ANALYSIS & DESIGN: Custom

Airwave Communications Cons .... G 419 331-1526
  Lima *(G-11832)*
Armada Power LLC .... G 614 204-9341
  Columbus *(G-6615)*
Associated Software Cons Inc .... F 440 826-1010
  Middleburg Heights *(G-13761)*
Eighty Six Inc .... G 800 760-0722
  Huber Heights *(G-11016)*
Empyracom Inc .... E 330 744-5570
  Canfield *(G-2526)*
Facts Inc .... E 330 928-2332
  Cuyahoga Falls *(G-7866)*
Lockheed Martin Corporation .... G 614 418-1930
  Columbus *(G-7133)*
Microstrategy Incorporated .... G 513 792-2253
  Cincinnati *(G-4027)*
Nvision Technology Inc .... G 412 254-4668
  Norton *(G-15374)*
Online Mega Sellers Corp .... D 888 384-6468
  Toledo *(G-18439)*
Quez Media Marketing Inc .... F 216 910-0202
  Independence *(G-11149)*
Technology Resources Inc .... G 419 241-9248
  Toledo *(G-18544)*

COMPUTER SOFTWARE WRITERS

Health Nuts Media LLC .... G 818 802-5222
  Cleveland *(G-5384)*
Wentworth Solutions .... F 440 212-7696
  Brunswick *(G-2249)*

COMPUTER SOFTWARE WRITERS: Freelance

Curt Harler Inc .... G 440 238-4556
  Cleveland *(G-5044)*

COMPUTER STORAGE DEVICES, NEC

Capsa Solutions LLC .... D 800 437-6633
  Canal Winchester *(G-2500)*
EMC Corporation .... E 216 606-2000
  Independence *(G-11125)*
Expansion Programs Intl .... G 216 631-8544
  Cleveland *(G-5208)*
Magnext Ltd .... F 614 433-0011
  Columbus *(G-7145)*
Quantem Fbo Services .... G 603 647-6763
  Cincinnati *(G-4230)*
Quantum 740 328-2548
  Newark *(G-14915)*
Quantum Commerce LLC .... G 513 777-0737
  West Chester *(G-19774)*
Quantum Integration Llc 330 609-0355
  Cortland *(G-7715)*
Quantum Sails 567 283-5335
  Sandusky *(G-16840)*
Quantum World Technologies 937 747-3018
  Zanesfield *(G-21089)*
Solsys Inc .... G 419 886-4683
  Mansfield *(G-12518)*
Town Cntry Technical Svcs Inc .... F 614 866-7700
  Reynoldsburg *(G-16457)*
Tracewell Systems Inc .... D 614 846-6175
  Lewis Center *(G-11787)*

COMPUTER SYSTEM SELLING SVCS

Lantek Systems Inc .... G 513 988-8708
  Mason *(G-12903)*

COMPUTER SYSTEMS ANALYSIS & DESIGN

Honeywell International Inc .... D 513 745-7200
  Cincinnati *(G-3826)*

COMPUTER TERMINALS

Fivepoint LLC .... F 937 374-3193
  Xenia *(G-20773)*
NCR International Inc .... G 937 445-5000
  Kettering *(G-11437)*
Parker-Hannifin Corporation .... D 513 831-2340
  Milford *(G-14031)*

COMPUTER TERMINALS: CRT

Copier Resources Inc .... G 614 268-1100
  Columbus *(G-6818)*

COMPUTER TIME-SHARING

Miami Valley Eductl Cmpt Assn .... F 937 767-1468
  Yellow Springs *(G-20811)*

COMPUTER-AIDED DESIGN SYSTEMS SVCS

Industrial Screen Process .... F 419 255-4900
  Toledo *(G-18346)*

COMPUTER-AIDED ENGINEERING SYSTEMS SVCS

Sest Inc .... F 440 777-9777
  Westlake *(G-20157)*

COMPUTERS, NEC

3d Systems Inc .... C 215 757-9611
  Columbus *(G-6512)*
Analog Bridge Inc .... G 937 901-4832
  Beavercreek *(G-1299)*
Ascendtech Inc .... E 216 458-1101
  Willoughby *(G-20282)*
AT&T Corp .... G 513 792-9300
  Cincinnati *(G-3365)*
Cardinal Health Tech LLC .... G 614 757-5000
  Dublin *(G-8896)*
Chaos Matrix Ltd 614 638-4748
  Oberlin *(G-15492)*
Codonics Inc .... C 216 226-1066
  Cincinnati *(G-4995)*
Computer Zoo Inc .... G 937 310-1474
  Bellbrook *(G-1490)*
Dapsco .... F 937 294-5331
  Moraine *(G-14342)*
Davis Laser Products .... G 614 252-7711
  Columbus *(G-6853)*
Dell Inc 513 644-1700
  West Chester *(G-19693)*
Delohio Tech .... F 740 816-5628
  Delaware *(G-8671)*
Dupont Electronic Polymers LP .... D 937 268-3411
  Dayton *(G-8172)*
Eaj Services LLC .... F 513 792-3400
  Blue Ash *(G-1762)*
First Product Technologies LLC ...... G 440 364-0664
  Independence *(G-11128)*
Golubitsky Corporation .... G 800 552-4204
  Cleveland *(G-5329)*
Hardware Exchange Inc 440 449-8006
  Solon *(G-17159)*
International Products .... G 614 334-1500
  Columbus *(G-7044)*
Journey Systems LLC .... F 513 831-6200
  Milford *(G-14022)*
Kenneth Hickman Co 513 348-0016
  Batavia *(G-1158)*
Lab Electronics Inc .... G 330 674-9818
  Millersburg *(G-14104)*
Magnum Computers Inc .... F 216 781-1757
  Cleveland *(G-5605)*
Mbenztech 937 291-1527
  Centerville *(G-3003)*
North American Research Corp 937 445-5000
  Kettering *(G-11438)*
Parker-Hannifin Corporation .... D 513 831-2340
  Milford *(G-14031)*
Potential Labs LLC .... G 740 590-0009
  Athens *(G-845)*
Powersonic Industries LLC .... E 513 429-2329
  West Chester *(G-19887)*
Site Tech .... G 740 522-0019
  Heath *(G-10733)*
Smartronix Inc .... F 216 378-3300
  Northfield *(G-15325)*
Systemax Manufacturing Inc .... C 937 368-2300
  Dayton *(G-8533)*
Teradata Operations Inc .... G 937 866-0032
  Miamisburg *(G-13726)*
Teradata Operations Inc .... D 937 242-4030
  Miamisburg *(G-13727)*
Thomas Ross Associates Inc .... G 330 723-1110
  Medina *(G-13352)*
Town Cntry Technical Svcs Inc .... F 614 866-7700
  Reynoldsburg *(G-16457)*
Tracewell Systems Inc .... D 614 846-6175
  Lewis Center *(G-11787)*
Walter North .... F 937 204-6050
  Dayton *(G-8582)*

COMPUTERS, NEC, WHOLESALE

Tech-E-Z LLC .... G 419 692-1700
  Delphos *(G-8755)*
Thomas Ross Associates Inc .... G 330 723-1110
  Medina *(G-13352)*

COMPUTERS, PERIPH & SOFTWARE, WHLSE: Personal & Home Entrtn

Clark Associates Inc 419 334-3838
  Fremont *(G-10008)*
Reynolds and Reynolds Company ... G 937 485-4771
  Dayton *(G-8475)*

COMPUTERS, PERIPHERALS & SOFTWARE, WHOLESALE: Software

A Graphic Solution .... F 216 228-7223
  Cleveland *(G-4587)*
Callcopy Inc .... G 614 340-3346
  Columbus *(G-6725)*
Columbus Advnced Mfg Sftwr Inc ... G 614 410-2300
  Delaware *(G-8668)*
Data Genomix Inc .... F 216 860-4770
  Cleveland *(G-5069)*
Eci Macola/Max LLC .... C 978 539-6186
  Dublin *(G-8911)*
Federal Barcode Label Systems ..... G 440 748-8060
  North Ridgeville *(G-15224)*
Government Acquisitions Inc .... E 513 721-8700
  Cincinnati *(G-3773)*
Investment Systems Company .... G 440 247-2865
  Chagrin Falls *(G-3022)*
Mitel (delaware) Inc .... E 513 733-8000
  West Chester *(G-19745)*
Software Solutions Inc .... E 513 932-6667
  Lebanon *(G-11698)*
T E Hubler Inc .... G 419 476-2552
  Toledo *(G-18541)*

PRODUCT SECTION

COMPUTERS, PERIPHERALS/SFTWR, WHOL: Anti-Static Eqpt/Devices

Pemro Corporation ....F 800 440-5441
　Cleveland *(G-5863)*

COMPUTERS: Mainframe

Freedom Usa Inc ....F 216 503-6374
　Twinsburg *(G-18776)*

COMPUTERS: Mini

G2 Digital Solutions ....F 937 951-1530
　Xenia *(G-20774)*

COMPUTERS: Personal

Accurate Insulation LLC ....G 302 241-0940
　Columbus *(G-6533)*
Apple Seed LLC ....G 330 606-1776
　Akron *(G-67)*
Eaton Corporation ....B 440 523-5000
　Cleveland *(G-5146)*

CONCENTRATES, DRINK

Belton Foods ....E 937 890-7768
　Dayton *(G-8053)*
Inter American Products Inc ....E 800 645-2233
　Cincinnati *(G-3853)*

CONCENTRATES, FLAVORING, EXC DRINK

Givaudan Flavors Corporation ....B 513 948-4933
　Cincinnati *(G-3755)*
Wiley Organics Inc ....C 740 622-0755
　Coshocton *(G-7758)*

CONCRETE BUILDING PRDTS WHOLESALERS

CMA Supply Company Inc ....F 513 942-6663
　West Chester *(G-19844)*
Jalco Industries Inc ....E 740 286-3808
　Jackson *(G-11188)*
Michaels Pre-Cast Con Pdts ....F 513 683-1292
　Loveland *(G-12215)*
Moritz Materials Inc ....E 419 281-0575
　Ashland *(G-726)*
Stocker Concrete Company ....F 740 254-4626
　Gnadenhutten *(G-10283)*
Tamarron Technology Inc ....F 800 277-3207
　Cincinnati *(G-4404)*

CONCRETE CURING & HARDENING COMPOUNDS

Blackthorn LLC ....F 937 836-9296
　Clayton *(G-4572)*
Chemmasters Inc ....E 440 428-2105
　Madison *(G-12344)*
Dayton Superior Corporation ....E 815 732-3136
　Miamisburg *(G-13656)*
I P Specrete Inc ....G 216 721-2050
　Cleveland *(G-5434)*
Master Builders LLC ....E 216 831-5500
　Beachwood *(G-1247)*
Sika Corporation ....D 740 387-9224
　Marion *(G-12735)*

CONCRETE PLANTS

McNeilus Truck and Mfg Inc ....E 513 874-2022
　Fairfield *(G-9528)*
McTech Corp ....F 216 391-7700
　Cleveland *(G-5649)*

CONCRETE PRDTS

9/10 Castings Inc ....G 216 406-8907
　Chardon *(G-3094)*
American Spring Wire Corp ....C 216 292-4620
　Bedford Heights *(G-1460)*
B & B Cast Stone Co Inc ....G 740 697-0008
　Roseville *(G-16574)*
Baxter Burial Vault Service ....E 513 641-1010
　Cincinnati *(G-3382)*
Carruth Studio Inc ....F 419 878-3060
　Waterville *(G-19491)*
Cement Products Inc ....E 419 524-4342
　Mansfield *(G-12423)*

Cemex Materials LLC ....D 937 268-6706
　Dayton *(G-8081)*
Charles Svec Inc ....E 216 662-5200
　Maple Heights *(G-12568)*
Concrete Material Supply LLC ....G 419 261-6404
　Toledo *(G-18237)*
Contech Bridge Solutions LLC ....F 937 878-2170
　Dayton *(G-8103)*
Dalaco Materials LLC ....F 513 893-5483
　Liberty Twp *(G-11824)*
Douglas Industries LLC ....E 740 775-2400
　Chillicothe *(G-3185)*
Fort Loramie Cast Stone Pdts ....G 937 420-2257
　Fort Loramie *(G-9798)*
Forterra Pipe & Precast LLC ....F 614 445-3830
　Columbus *(G-6931)*
Forterra Pipe & Precast LLC ....G 937 268-6707
　Dayton *(G-8204)*
Forterra Pipe & Precast LLC ....G 937 268-6707
　Dayton *(G-8203)*
Growco Inc ....G 419 886-4628
　Mansfield *(G-12454)*
Hanson Aggregates East LLC ....E 740 773-2172
　Chillicothe *(G-3191)*
Hanson Concrete Products Ohio .....E 614 443-4846
　Columbus *(G-6980)*
Hazelbaker Industries Ltd ....E 614 276-2631
　Columbus *(G-6984)*
Hilltop Basic Resources Inc ....E 513 621-1500
　Cincinnati *(G-3814)*
Hilltop Stone Llc ....G 513 651-5000
　Cincinnati *(G-3816)*
Huron Cement Products Company ...E 419 433-4161
　Huron *(G-11096)*
Janell Inc ....G 740 532-9111
　Ironton *(G-11168)*
K M B Inc ....E 330 889-3451
　Bristolville *(G-2082)*
Koppers Industries Inc ....E 740 776-3238
　Portsmouth *(G-16288)*
Lang Stone Company Inc ....D 614 235-4099
　Columbus *(G-7114)*
Mack Industries PA Inc ....F 330 638-7680
　Vienna *(G-19202)*
Metro Mech Inc ....G 216 641-6262
　Cleveland *(G-5662)*
Michaels Pre-Cast Con Pdts ....F 513 683-1292
　Loveland *(G-12215)*
O K Brugmann Jr & Sons Inc ....F 330 274-2106
　Mantua *(G-12555)*
Oberfields LLC ....F 614 252-0955
　Columbus *(G-7237)*
Oberfields LLC ....E 614 491-7643
　Columbus *(G-7236)*
Ohio Cast Stone Co LLC ....G 614 444-2278
　Columbus *(G-7242)*
Oldcastle Companies ....G 800 899-8455
　Oakwood *(G-15472)*
Orrville Trucking & Grading Co ....E 330 682-4010
　Orrville *(G-15609)*
Pawnee Maintenance Inc ....D 740 373-6861
　Marietta *(G-12652)*
Premiere Con Solutions LLC ....F 419 737-9808
　Pioneer *(G-16092)*
Prestress Services Inds LLC ....C 859 299-0461
　Columbus *(G-7346)*
R W Sidley Incorporated ....F 440 564-2221
　Newbury *(G-14962)*
S & S Aggregates Inc ....G 740 453-0721
　Zanesville *(G-21175)*
Snyder Concrete Products Inc ....E 937 885-5176
　Moraine *(G-14394)*
Tri County Concrete Inc ....E 330 425-4464
　Twinsburg *(G-18866)*
William Dauch Concrete Company ...F 419 668-4458
　Norwalk *(G-15418)*
Wilson Concrete Products Inc ....E 937 885-7965
　Dayton *(G-8594)*
Wilsons Country Creations ....F 330 377-4190
　Killbuck *(G-11456)*
Wysong Concrete Products LLC ......G 513 874-3109
　Fairfield *(G-9578)*

CONCRETE PRDTS, PRECAST, NEC

Aco Polymer Products Inc ....E 440 285-7000
　Mentor *(G-13373)*
Ald Precast Corp ....G 614 449-3366
　Columbus *(G-6562)*
Carey Precast Concrete Company ...G 419 396-7142
　Carey *(G-2879)*

Cox Inc ....F 740 858-4400
　Lucasville *(G-12261)*
Donald Schloemer ....G 419 933-2002
　Willard *(G-20239)*
E Pompili & Sons Inc ....G 216 581-8080
　Cleveland *(G-5130)*
Everly Concrete Products ....G 740 635-1415
　Bridgeport *(G-2074)*
Fin Pan Inc ....F 513 870-9200
　Hamilton *(G-10558)*
Jim Bumen Construction Company ...G 740 663-2659
　Chillicothe *(G-3197)*
Mack Industries PA Inc ....D 330 483-3111
　Valley City *(G-19045)*
Mansfield Brick & Supply Co ....G 419 526-1191
　Mansfield *(G-12475)*
McGill Septic Tank Co ....E 330 876-2171
　Kinsman *(G-11465)*
North American Cast Stone Inc ......G 440 286-1999
　Chardon *(G-3129)*
Norwalk Concrete Inds Inc ....E 419 668-8167
　Norwalk *(G-15408)*
Norwalk Concrete Inds Inc ....E 419 668-8167
　Norwalk *(G-15409)*
Oberfields LLC ....D 740 369-7644
　Delaware *(G-8712)*
Oberfields LLC ....E 740 369-7644
　Sunbury *(G-17893)*
Oberfields LLC ....G 937 885-3711
　Dayton *(G-8393)*
Oberfields Holdings LLC ....G 740 369-7644
　Delaware *(G-8713)*
Oldcastle Apg Midwest Inc ....D 440 949-1815
　Sheffield Village *(G-16973)*
Poland Concrete Products Inc ....G 330 757-1241
　Poland *(G-16238)*
Precast Services Inc ....G 614 428-4541
　Reynoldsburg *(G-16447)*
Resco Products Inc ....E 330 372-3716
　Warren *(G-19438)*
Snyder Concrete Products Inc ....F 513 539-7686
　Monroe *(G-14276)*
Spoerr Precast Concrete Inc ....F 419 625-9132
　Sandusky *(G-16850)*
St Henry Tile Co Inc ....F 937 548-1101
　Greenville *(G-10396)*
United Precast Inc ....C 740 393-1121
　Mount Vernon *(G-14516)*
USA Precast Concrete Limited ....G 330 854-9600
　Canal Fulton *(G-2495)*

CONCRETE: Asphaltic, Not From Refineries

H P Streicher Inc ....G 419 841-4715
　Toledo *(G-18315)*
Robert Gorey ....G 330 725-7272
　Medina *(G-13328)*
Shelly Materials Inc ....G 330 673-3646
　Kent *(G-11385)*
Shelly Materials Inc ....D 740 246-6315
　Thornville *(G-18035)*

CONCRETE: Bituminous

Russell Standard Corporation ....G 330 733-9400
　Akron *(G-363)*
Shelly Company ....G 740 474-6255
　Circleville *(G-4557)*

CONCRETE: Dry Mixture

Quikrete Companies Inc ....E 614 885-4406
　Columbus *(G-7369)*
Quikrete Companies Inc ....E 513 367-6135
　Harrison *(G-10666)*
Quikrete Companies LLC ....E 419 241-1148
　Toledo *(G-18491)*
Quikrete Companies LLC ....E 330 296-6080
　Ravenna *(G-16397)*
Smith Concrete Co ....E 740 373-7441
　Dover *(G-8854)*

CONCRETE: Ready-Mixed

A K Ready Mix LLC ....F 740 286-8900
　Jackson *(G-11179)*
ACE Ready Mix LLC ....G 330 745-8125
　Norton *(G-15356)*
Ace Ready Mix Concrete Co Inc ......F 330 745-8125
　Norton *(G-15357)*
Adams Bros Concrete Pdts Ltd ....F 740 452-7566
　Zanesville *(G-21092)*

Employee Codes: A=Over 500 employees, B=251-500
C=101-250, D=51-100, E=20-50, F=10-19, G=3-9

Adams Brothers Inc....F....740 819-0323
Zanesville *(G-21093)*
Alexis Concrete Enterprise Inc....F....440 366-0031
Elyria *(G-9211)*
All Ohio Ready Mix Concrete....G....419 841-3838
Perrysburg *(G-15918)*
All-Rite Rdymx Miami Vly LLC....G....513 738-1933
Harrison *(G-10630)*
Allega Concrete Corp....E....216 447-0814
Cleveland *(G-4670)*
Anderson Concrete Corp....C....614 443-0123
Columbus *(G-6602)*
Arrow Coal Grove Inc....F....740 532-6143
Ironton *(G-11160)*
ASAP Ready Mix Inc....G....513 797-1774
Amelia *(G-532)*
Associated Associates Inc....E....330 626-3300
Mantua *(G-12542)*
Avon Concrete Corporation....G....440 937-6264
Avon *(G-941)*
Baird Concrete Products Inc....F....740 623-8600
Coshocton *(G-7721)*
Baker-Shindler Contracting Co....G....419 399-4841
Cecil *(G-2942)*
Baker-Shindler Contracting Co....E....419 782-5080
Defiance *(G-8615)*
Bellbrook Transport Inc....G....937 233-5555
Dayton *(G-8052)*
Bryce Hill Inc....G....937 325-0651
Springfield *(G-17369)*
Buckeye Ready-Mix....G....419 294-2389
Upper Sandusky *(G-18948)*
Buckeye Ready-Mix LLC....G....740 967-4801
Johnstown *(G-11260)*
Buckeye Ready-Mix LLC....G....614 879-6316
West Jefferson *(G-19921)*
Buckeye Ready-Mix LLC....F....740 387-8846
Marion *(G-12696)*
Buckeye Ready-Mix LLC....E....614 575-2132
Reynoldsburg *(G-16431)*
Buckeye Ready-Mix LLC....E....937 642-2951
Marysville *(G-12773)*
Buckeye Ready-Mix LLC....F....740 654-4423
Lancaster *(G-11549)*
C F Poeppelman Inc....G....937 526-5137
Versailles *(G-19175)*
C F Poeppelman Inc....E....937 448-2191
Bradford *(G-2010)*
Caldwell Lumber & Supply Co....E....740 732-2306
Caldwell *(G-2404)*
Caldwell Redi Mix Company....G....740 732-2906
Caldwell *(G-2405)*
Caldwell Redi Mix Company....G....740 685-6554
Byesville *(G-2379)*
Camden Ready Mix Co....F....937 456-4539
Camden *(G-2464)*
Car Bros Inc....G....440 232-1840
Bedford *(G-1393)*
Carr Bros Inc....E....440 232-3700
Bedford *(G-1394)*
Carr Bros Bldrs Sup & Coal Co....E....440 232-3700
Cleveland *(G-4882)*
Castalia Trenching & Ready Mix....F....419 684-5502
Castalia *(G-2936)*
Cement Products Inc....E....419 524-4342
Mansfield *(G-12423)*
Cemex Cnstr Mtls ATL LLC....D....937 878-8651
Xenia *(G-20760)*
Cemex Construction Corporation....G....440 449-0872
Mentor *(G-13411)*
Cemex Construction Mtls Inc....G....440 449-0872
Cleveland *(G-4898)*
Cemex Materials LLC....E....937 268-6706
Dayton *(G-8082)*
Cemex USA Inc....F....937 879-8350
Fairborn *(G-9455)*
Center Concrete Inc....F....800 453-4224
Edgerton *(G-9170)*
Central Ready Mix LLC....E....513 402-5001
Cincinnati *(G-3457)*
Central Ready Mix LLC....G....513 367-1939
Cleves *(G-6356)*
Central Ready-Mix of Ohio LLC....E....614 252-3452
Cincinnati *(G-3458)*
Chappell-Zimmerman Inc....F....330 337-8711
Salem *(G-16725)*
Christman Supply Co Inc....G....740 472-0046
Woodsfield *(G-20542)*
Citywide Materials Inc....E....513 533-1111
Cincinnati *(G-3522)*

Cleveland Ready Mix....G....216 399-6688
Cleveland *(G-4973)*
Consumeracq Inc....C....440 277-9305
Lorain *(G-12084)*
Consumers Builders Supply Co....E....440 277-9306
Lorain *(G-12085)*
Cremeans Concrete and Sup Co....G....740 446-1142
Gallipolis *(G-10162)*
D W Dickey and Son Inc....D....330 424-1441
Lisbon *(G-11966)*
Dan K Williams Inc....E....419 893-3251
Maumee *(G-13085)*
Dan Shrock Cement....G....440 548-2498
Parkman *(G-15811)*
Dearth Resources Inc....G....937 325-0651
Springfield *(G-17384)*
Dearth Resources Inc....G....937 663-4171
Springfield *(G-17385)*
Diano Construction and Sup Co....E....330 456-7229
Canton *(G-2658)*
Diversified Ready Mix Ltd....G....330 628-3355
Tallmadge *(G-17980)*
Eci....G....419 483-2738
Castalia *(G-2937)*
Ernst Enterprises Inc....F....937 878-9378
Fairborn *(G-9458)*
Ernst Enterprises Inc....E....937 233-5555
Dayton *(G-8186)*
Ernst Enterprises Inc....E....513 874-8300
Lebanon *(G-11651)*
Ernst Enterprises Inc....E....937 848-6811
Bellbrook *(G-1493)*
Ernst Enterprises Inc....E....937 866-9441
Carrollton *(G-2919)*
Ernst Enterprises Inc....G....614 308-0063
Columbus *(G-6905)*
Ernst Enterprises Inc....E....937 339-6249
Troy *(G-18653)*
Ernst Enterprises Inc....F....513 422-3651
Middletown *(G-13905)*
Ernst Enterprises Inc....E....614 443-9456
Columbus *(G-6904)*
Feikert Sand & Gravel Co Inc....E....330 674-0038
Millersburg *(G-14082)*
G Big Inc....E....740 867-5758
Chesapeake *(G-3145)*
G Big Inc....G....740 532-9123
Ironton *(G-11165)*
Geauga Concrete Inc....F....440 338-4915
Newbury *(G-14952)*
Grafton Ready Mix Concret Inc....E....440 926-2911
Grafton *(G-10302)*
Hanson Aggregates East LLC....E....740 773-2172
Chillicothe *(G-3191)*
Hanson Aggregates East LLC....E....937 587-2671
Peebles *(G-15878)*
Hanson Ready Mix Inc....D....614 221-5345
Columbus *(G-6981)*
Hensel Ready Mix....G....419 253-9200
Marengo *(G-12592)*
Hensel Ready Mix Inc....F....419 675-1808
Kenton *(G-11409)*
Hensel Ready Mix Inc....G....614 755-6365
Columbus *(G-6989)*
Hilltop Basic Resources Inc....F....937 795-2020
Aberdeen *(G-1)*
Hilltop Basic Resources Inc....E....513 621-1500
Cincinnati *(G-3814)*
Hilltop Basic Resources Inc....F....513 651-5000
Cincinnati *(G-3813)*
Hilltop Big Bend Quarry LLC....G....513 651-5000
Cincinnati *(G-3815)*
Hocking Valley Concrete Inc....E....740 385-2165
Logan *(G-12027)*
Hocking Valley Concrete Inc....G....740 342-1948
New Lexington *(G-14716)*
Hocking Valley Concrete Inc....G....740 385-2165
Logan *(G-12028)*
Hull Builders Supply Inc....E....440 967-3159
Vermilion *(G-19161)*
Hull Ready Mix Concrete Inc....F....419 625-8070
Sandusky *(G-16815)*
Huron Cement Products Company....G....419 433-4161
Sandusky *(G-16816)*
Huron Cement Products Company....E....419 433-4161
Huron *(G-11096)*
Huron Products....G....419 483-5608
Bellevue *(G-1536)*
Huth Ready Mix & Supply Co....F....330 833-4191
Massillon *(G-12999)*

IMI-Irving Materials Inc....G....513 844-8444
Hamilton *(G-10571)*
Ioppolo Concrete Corporation....E....440 439-6606
Bedford *(G-1418)*
Irving Materials Inc....F....513 523-7127
Oxford *(G-15695)*
Irving Materials Inc....F....513 844-8444
Hamilton *(G-10573)*
Joe McClelland Inc....E....740 452-3036
Zanesville *(G-21151)*
K & L Ready Mix Inc....G....419 943-2200
Leipsic *(G-11727)*
K & L Ready Mix Inc....F....419 523-4376
Ottawa *(G-15656)*
K & L Ready Mix Inc....F....419 532-3585
Kalida *(G-11277)*
K & L Ready Mix Inc....F....419 293-2937
Mc Comb *(G-13190)*
K M B Inc....E....330 889-3451
Bristolville *(G-2082)*
Kuhlman Corporation....E....419 321-1670
Toledo *(G-18370)*
Kuhlman Corporation....C....419 897-6000
Maumee *(G-13124)*
Lafarge North America Inc....D....419 798-4486
Marblehead *(G-12586)*
Lafarge North America Inc....E....330 393-5656
Warren *(G-19415)*
Lancaster West Side Coal Co....F....740 862-4713
Lancaster *(G-11582)*
Lehigh Cement Company LLC....G....330 499-9100
Middlebranch *(G-13759)*
Lehigh Hanson Ecc Inc....F....330 499-9100
Middlebranch *(G-13760)*
M & R Redi Mix Inc....E....419 445-7771
Pettisville *(G-16034)*
M & R Redi Mix Inc....G....419 748-8442
Mc Clure *(G-13186)*
Mack Concrete Industries Inc....F....330 483-3111
Valley City *(G-19044)*
Mack Concrete Industries Inc....F....330 784-7008
Akron *(G-264)*
Market Ready....G....513 289-9231
Maineville *(G-12374)*
Marvin Mix....G....614 774-9337
Columbus *(G-7156)*
McConnell Ready Mix....G....440 458-4325
Elyria *(G-9292)*
McGovney Ready Mix Inc....E....740 353-4111
Portsmouth *(G-16290)*
Mecco Inc....E....513 422-3651
Middletown *(G-13926)*
Medina Supply Company....E....330 425-0752
Twinsburg *(G-18816)*
Medina Supply Company....E....330 723-3681
Medina *(G-13298)*
Mel Stevens U-Cart Concrete....G....419 478-2600
Toledo *(G-18406)*
Miami Valley Ready Mix Inc....E....513 738-2616
Harrison *(G-10659)*
Mini Mix Inc....F....513 353-3811
Cleves *(G-6371)*
Moritz Concrete Inc....E....419 529-3232
Mansfield *(G-12486)*
Moritz Materials Inc....E....419 281-0575
Ashland *(G-726)*
Nalcon Ready Mix Inc....G....419 422-4341
Kenton *(G-11416)*
National Lime and Stone Co....E....419 423-3400
Findlay *(G-9729)*
National Lime and Stone Co....G....330 339-2144
New Philadelphia *(G-14790)*
National Lime and Stone Co....G....216 883-9840
Cleveland *(G-5726)*
Nissen Lumber & Coal Co Inc....G....419 836-8035
Oregon *(G-15562)*
O K Brugmann Jr & Sons Inc....F....330 274-2106
Mantua *(G-12555)*
Olen Corporation....F....419 294-2611
Upper Sandusky *(G-18969)*
Orrville Trucking & Grading Co....E....330 682-4010
Orrville *(G-15609)*
Osborne Inc....F....440 232-1440
Cleveland *(G-5822)*
Osborne Inc....E....440 942-7000
Mentor *(G-13539)*
Osborne Inc....E....216 771-0010
Cleveland *(G-5821)*
Pahl Ready Mix Concrete Inc....F....419 636-4238
Bryan *(G-2303)*

Pahl Ready Mix Concrete Inc................F 419 636-4238
Waterville *(G-19502)*
Palmer Bros Transit Mix Con.................F 419 332-6363
Fremont *(G-10044)*
Palmer Bros Transit Mix Con.................F 419 352-4681
Bowling Green *(G-1989)*
Palmer Bros Transit Mix Con.................G....... 419 447-2018
Tiffin *(G-18075)*
Palmer Bros Transit Mix Con.................F 419 686-2366
Portage *(G-16273)*
Paul H Rohe Company Inc.....................G....... 513 326-6789
Cincinnati *(G-4140)*
Paul R Lipp & Son Inc...........................F 330 227-9614
Rogers *(G-16560)*
Petros Concrete Inc...............................G....... 330 868-6130
Waynesburg *(G-19565)*
Philip Armbrust.......................................G....... 740 335-7285
Wshngtn CT Hs *(G-20735)*
Phillips Companies.................................E 937 426-5461
Beavercreek Township *(G-1371)*
Phillips Ready Mix Co............................D....... 937 426-5151
Beavercreek Township *(G-1372)*
Placecrete Inc...F 937 298-2121
Moraine *(G-14379)*
Pleasant Valley Ready Mix Inc..............F 330 852-2613
Sugarcreek *(G-17858)*
Quadcast...G....... 330 854-4511
Canal Fulton *(G-2490)*
Quality Block & Supply Inc....................E 330 364-4411
Mount Eaton *(G-14421)*
Quality Ready Mix Inc............................F 419 394-8870
Saint Marys *(G-16696)*
Quikrete Companies Inc........................E 513 367-6135
Harrison *(G-10666)*
Quikrete Companies LLC.......................E 330 296-6080
Ravenna *(G-16397)*
R W Sidley Inc..F 440 224-2664
Kingsville *(G-11462)*
R W Sidley Incorporated........................E 440 298-3232
Thompson *(G-18028)*
R W Sidley Incorporated........................E 440 564-2221
Newbury *(G-14962)*
R W Sidley Incorporated........................F 330 499-5616
Canton *(G-2801)*
R W Sidley Incorporated........................F 330 392-2721
Warren *(G-19435)*
R W Sidley Incorporated........................E 330 793-7374
Youngstown *(G-21012)*
Ready To Go LLC....................................G....... 216 862-8572
Cleveland *(G-5964)*
Rinker Materials.....................................G....... 330 654-2511
Diamond *(G-8799)*
Rockport Cnstr & Mtls Inc.....................E 216 432-9465
Cleveland *(G-5997)*
Ross Co Redi Mix Co Inc.......................G....... 740 333-6833
Wshngtn CT Hs *(G-20743)*
Ross-Co Redi-Mix Co Inc.......................E 740 775-4466
Chillicothe *(G-3221)*
S J Roth Enterprises Inc........................E 513 242-8400
Cincinnati *(G-4296)*
Sakrete Inc..E 513 242-3644
Cincinnati *(G-4299)*
Sardinia Concrete Company..................E 513 248-0090
Milford *(G-14039)*
Sardinia Ready Mix Inc..........................G....... 937 446-2523
Sardinia *(G-16871)*
Sardinia Ready Mix Inc..........................F 937 446-2523
Sardinia *(G-16872)*
Schwab Industries Inc...........................F........ 330 364-4411
Dover *(G-8852)*
Scioto Ready Mix LLC...........................D....... 740 924-9273
Pataskala *(G-15843)*
Scioto Readymix Co...............................G....... 614 491-0773
Columbus *(G-7431)*
Scsrm Concrete Company Ltd..............E 937 533-1001
Sidney *(G-17074)*
Shelly Company......................................G....... 740 246-6315
Thornville *(G-18033)*
Shelly Materials Inc................................G....... 614 871-6704
Grove City *(G-10466)*
Sidwell Materials Inc..............................F 740 968-4313
Saint Clairsville *(G-16651)*
Smalls Inc..F 740 427-3633
Gambier *(G-10185)*
Smith Concrete Co..................................E 740 373-7441
Dover *(G-8854)*
Spurlino Materials LLC..........................E........ 513 705-0111
Middletown *(G-13953)*
Spurlino Materials LLC..........................G 513 202-1111
Cleves *(G-6376)*

Srm Concrete LLC..................................D....... 937 773-0841
Piqua *(G-16163)*
Srm Concrete LLC..................................F 937 698-7229
Vandalia *(G-19145)*
St Henry Tile Co Inc...............................E 419 678-4841
Saint Henry *(G-16667)*
Stamm Contracting Co Inc....................E 330 274-8230
Mantua *(G-12560)*
Stark Ready Mix & Supply Co................E 330 580-4307
Canton *(G-2823)*
Stocker Concrete Company...................F 740 254-4626
Gnadenhutten *(G-10283)*
T C Redi Mix Youngstown Inc...............E 330 755-2143
Youngstown *(G-21042)*
Tech Ready Mix Inc.................................E 216 361-5000
Cleveland *(G-6154)*
Ten Mfg LLC..F........ 440 487-1100
Mentor *(G-13603)*
Terminal Ready-Mix Inc.........................E 440 288-0181
Lorain *(G-12129)*
Tow Path Ready Mix...............................F 740 286-2131
Jackson *(G-11199)*
Tow Path Ready Mix...............................G....... 740 259-3222
Lucasville *(G-12268)*
Trail Mix...G....... 330 657-2277
Peninsula *(G-15900)*
Tri County Concrete Inc.........................E 330 425-4464
Twinsburg *(G-18866)*
Tri County Concrete Inc.........................F 330 425-4464
Cleveland *(G-6205)*
Twin Cities Concrete Co.........................F 330 343-4491
Dover *(G-8861)*
Twin Cities Concrete Co.........................G....... 330 627-2158
Carrollton *(G-2931)*
United Ready Mix Inc..............................E 216 696-1600
Cleveland *(G-6236)*
W G Lockhart Construction Co.............D....... 330 745-6520
Akron *(G-429)*
W M Dauch Concrete Inc........................G....... 419 562-6917
Bucyrus *(G-2349)*
Warren Concrete and Supply Co...........F 330 393-1581
Warren *(G-19458)*
Weber Ready Mix Inc..............................E 419 394-9097
Saint Marys *(G-16704)*
Wells Group LLC.....................................F 740 532-9240
Ironton *(G-11176)*
Wellsgroup...G....... 740 289-1000
Piketon *(G-16081)*
Wellsgroup...G....... 937 382-4003
Wilmington *(G-20511)*
Westview Concrete Corp........................E 440 458-5800
Elyria *(G-9346)*
William Dauch Concrete Company.......F 419 562-6917
Bucyrus *(G-2350)*
William Dauch Concrete Company.......F 419 668-4458
Norwalk *(G-15418)*
William Oeder Ready Mix Inc................E 513 899-3901
Martinsville *(G-12768)*
Williams Concrete Inc.............................F 419 893-3251
Maumee *(G-13160)*
Winters Products Inc..............................F 740 286-4149
Jackson *(G-11202)*

CONDENSERS & CONDENSING UNITS: Air Conditioner

Cleveland Smacna...................................G....... 440 877-3500
Cleveland *(G-4976)*

CONDENSERS: Heat Transfer Eqpt, Evaporative

Hydro-Dyne Inc..E 330 832-5076
Massillon *(G-13000)*
Lfg Specialties LLC.................................E 419 424-4999
Findlay *(G-9715)*

CONDENSERS: Refrigeration

Emerson Climate Tech Inc......................C 937 498-3011
Sidney *(G-17037)*
Emerson Climate Tech Inc......................E 937 498-3587
Sidney *(G-17038)*

CONDUITS & FITTINGS: Electric

Allied Tube & Conduit Corp....................F 740 928-1018
Hebron *(G-10737)*
Emco Electric International....................G....... 440 878-1199
Strongsville *(G-17742)*

Madison Electric Products Inc...............E 216 391-7776
Bedford Heights *(G-1473)*
Saylor Products Corporation..................F 419 832-2125
Grand Rapids *(G-10320)*
Treadstone Company...............................G....... 216 410-3435
Twinsburg *(G-18865)*
United Fiberglass America Inc...............F 937 325-7305
Springfield *(G-17512)*

CONES, PYROMETRIC: Earthenware

Orton Edward Jr Crmic Fndation...........E 614 895-2663
Westerville *(G-20014)*

CONFECTIONS & CANDY

Albanese Concessions LLC....................G....... 614 402-4937
Canal Winchester *(G-2498)*
Anthony-Thomas Candy Company.......C....... 614 274-8405
Columbus *(G-6606)*
Anthony-Thomas Candy Company.......G....... 614 870-8899
Columbus *(G-6607)*
Arnolds Candies Inc................................G....... 330 733-4022
Akron *(G-70)*
Becky Knapp..G....... 330 854-4400
Canal Fulton *(G-2476)*
Cake Decor...G....... 614 836-5533
Groveport *(G-10487)*
Celebrations...G....... 419 381-8088
Toledo *(G-18224)*
Chocolate Pig Inc.....................................E 440 461-4511
Cleveland *(G-4923)*
Cincinnati Premier Candy LLC..............E 513 253-0079
Cincinnati *(G-3513)*
Coffelt Candy Inc.....................................G....... 937 399-8772
Springfield *(G-17376)*
Coons Homemade Candies...................G....... 740 496-4141
Harpster *(G-10626)*
Doschers Candies LLC...........................F 513 381-8656
Cincinnati *(G-3603)*
E R B Enterprises Inc..............................G....... 740 948-9174
Jeffersonville *(G-11246)*
Ervan Guttman Co...................................G....... 513 791-0767
Cincinnati *(G-3653)*
Fawn Confectionery.................................F 513 574-9612
Cincinnati *(G-3675)*
Giannios Candy Co Inc............................E 330 755-7000
Struthers *(G-17817)*
Gibson Bros Inc..E 440 774-2401
Oberlin *(G-15496)*
Graeters Manufacturing Co.....................D....... 513 721-3323
Cincinnati *(G-3774)*
Hake Head LLC...E 614 291-2244
Columbus *(G-6976)*
Island Delights Inc...................................G....... 866 887-4100
Seville *(G-16917)*
Kevin G Ryba Inc......................................G....... 419 627-2010
Huron *(G-11101)*
Light Vision...E 513 351-9444
Cincinnati *(G-3942)*
Mageros Candies......................................G....... 330 534-1146
Hubbard *(G-11005)*
Malleys Candies Inc.................................E 216 529-6262
Cleveland *(G-5609)*
Marshas Buckeyes LLC............................E 419 872-7666
Perrysburg *(G-15975)*
McJak Candy Company LLC...................E 330 722-3531
Medina *(G-13292)*
Milk & Honey...F 330 492-5884
Canton *(G-2755)*
Nestle Usa Inc...E 513 576-4930
Loveland *(G-12217)*
Neumeisters Candy Shoppe LLC...........G....... 419 294-3647
Upper Sandusky *(G-18966)*
Normant Candy Co....................................F 419 886-4214
Mansfield *(G-12494)*
Piqua Chocolate Company Inc................G....... 937 773-1981
Piqua *(G-16151)*
Popped..F 330 678-1893
Kent *(G-11365)*
Richards Maple Products Inc..................G....... 440 286-4160
Chardon *(G-3134)*
Sugar Memories LLC...............................G....... 216 472-0206
Cleveland *(G-6115)*
Sweet Melissas..G....... 440 333-6357
Rocky River *(G-16557)*
Witttichs Candies Inc................................G....... 740 474-3313
Circleville *(G-4564)*

CONNECTORS & TERMINALS: Electrical Device Uses

Alcon Inc .... E 513 722-1037
  Loveland *(G-12175)*
Brumall Mfg Coroporation .... E 440 974-2622
  Mentor *(G-13406)*
Connectronics Corp .... D 419 537-0020
  Toledo *(G-18239)*
Hermetic Seal Technology Inc .... F 513 851-4899
  Cincinnati *(G-3810)*
Mdfritz Technologies Inc .... G 937 314-1234
  Centerville *(G-3004)*
T & S Enterprises .... E 419 424-1122
  Findlay *(G-9766)*

CONNECTORS: Cord, Electric

Tip Products Inc .... E 216 252-2535
  Cleveland *(G-6176)*

CONNECTORS: Electrical

Bardes Corporation .... B 513 533-6200
  Cincinnati *(G-3379)*
Connector Manufacturing Co .... C 513 860-4455
  Hamilton *(G-10548)*
Cooper Interconnect Inc .... G 800 386-1911
  Cleveland *(G-5028)*
Ericson Manufacturing Co .... D 440 951-8000
  Willoughby *(G-20315)*
International Hydraulics Inc .... E 440 951-7186
  Mentor *(G-13474)*
Newact Inc .... F 513 321-5177
  Batavia *(G-1173)*
Ohio Associated Entps LLC .... C 440 354-3148
  Painesville *(G-15769)*
P C Power Inc .... G 440 779-4080
  North Olmsted *(G-15195)*

CONNECTORS: Electronic

Ankim Enterprises Incorporated .... E 937 599-1121
  Sidney *(G-17016)*
Associated Enterprises .... G 440 354-2106
  Painesville *(G-15712)*
Astro Industries Inc .... E 937 429-5900
  Beavercreek *(G-1301)*
Aviation Technologies Inc .... G 216 706-2960
  Cleveland *(G-4776)*
Canadus Power Systems LLC .... F 216 831-6600
  Twinsburg *(G-18746)*
Canfield Industries Inc .... G 800 554-5071
  Youngstown *(G-20864)*
Connective Design Incorporated .... F 937 746-8252
  Miamisburg *(G-13651)*
Connectors Unlimited Inc .... E 440 357-1161
  Painesville *(G-15724)*
Connectronics Corp .... D 419 537-0020
  Toledo *(G-18239)*
Cooper Interconnect Inc .... G 800 386-1911
  Cleveland *(G-5028)*
D C M Industries Inc .... F 937 254-8500
  Dayton *(G-8124)*
HCC Industries .... G 513 334-5585
  Cincinnati *(G-3804)*
HCC/Sealtron .... E 513 733-8400
  Cincinnati *(G-3805)*
Mueller Electric Company Inc .... E 614 888-8855
  New Albany *(G-14631)*
Ohio Associated Entps LLC .... E 440 354-2106
  Painesville *(G-15768)*
Ohio Associated Entps LLC .... E 440 354-3148
  Painesville *(G-15770)*
Ortronics Inc .... G 937 224-0639
  Dayton *(G-8408)*
Plcc2 LLC .... G 614 279-1796
  Columbus *(G-7328)*
Powell Electrical Systems Inc .... D 330 966-1750
  Canton *(G-2787)*
Servo Systems Inc .... G 440 779-2780
  North Olmsted *(G-15198)*
Spi Inc .... G 937 374-2700
  Xenia *(G-20790)*
U S Terminals Inc .... G 513 561-8145
  Cincinnati *(G-4445)*
Xponet Inc .... E 440 354-6617
  Painesville *(G-15801)*

CONNECTORS: Power, Electric

Nolan Manufacturing LLC .... G 614 859-2302
  Westerville *(G-20012)*

CONSTRUCTION & MINING MACHINERY WHOLESALERS

Advanced Specialty Products .... D 419 882-6528
  Bowling Green *(G-1950)*
Columbus Pipe and Equipment Co .... F 614 444-7871
  Columbus *(G-6798)*
Great Lakes Power Service Co .... G 440 259-0025
  Perry *(G-15905)*
JD Power Systems LLC .... F 614 317-9394
  Hilliard *(G-10833)*
Koenig Equipment Inc .... F 937 653-5281
  Urbana *(G-19002)*
La Mfg Inc .... G 513 577-7200
  Cincinnati *(G-3928)*
Mesa Industries Inc .... D 513 321-2950
  Cincinnati *(G-4009)*
Murphy Tractor & Eqp Co Inc .... G 614 876-1141
  Columbus *(G-7201)*
Murphy Tractor & Eqp Co Inc .... G 937 898-4198
  Vandalia *(G-19140)*
Murphy Tractor & Eqp Co Inc .... G 419 221-3666
  Lima *(G-11909)*
Murphy Tractor & Eqp Co Inc .... G 330 477-9304
  Canton *(G-2759)*
Murphy Tractor & Eqp Co Inc .... G 330 220-4999
  Brunswick *(G-2221)*
Shearer Farm Inc .... E 330 345-9023
  Wooster *(G-20653)*
Simpson Strong-Tie Company Inc ..... C 614 876-8060
  Columbus *(G-7454)*

CONSTRUCTION EQPT REPAIR SVCS

Mine Equipment Services LLC .... E 740 936-5427
  Sunbury *(G-17891)*
Morris Material Handling Inc .... G 937 525-5520
  Springfield *(G-17452)*
West Equipment Company Inc .... F 419 698-1601
  Toledo *(G-18597)*

CONSTRUCTION EQPT: Airport

Brewpro Inc .... G 513 577-7200
  Cincinnati *(G-3415)*

CONSTRUCTION EQPT: Attachments

Aim Attachments .... E 614 539-3030
  Grove City *(G-10412)*
Jrb Attachments LLC .... G 330 734-3000
  Akron *(G-227)*
New River Equipment Corp .... G 330 669-0040
  North Canton *(G-15107)*

CONSTRUCTION EQPT: Attachments, Snow Plow

H Y O Inc .... F 614 488-2861
  Columbus *(G-6974)*

CONSTRUCTION EQPT: Backhoes, Tractors, Cranes & Similar Eqpt

Mazzella Lifting Tech Inc .... D 440 239-5700
  Cleveland *(G-5639)*

CONSTRUCTION EQPT: Blade, Grader, Scraper, Dozer/Snow Plow

ARM Opco Inc .... E 330 868-7724
  Canton *(G-2575)*
Bucyrus Blades Inc .... C 419 562-6015
  Bucyrus *(G-2318)*
Jennmar McSweeney LLC .... C 740 377-3354
  South Point *(G-17285)*
Meyer Products LLC .... D 216 486-1313
  Steubenville *(G-17544)*

CONSTRUCTION EQPT: Bucket Or Scarifier Teeth

Fabco Inc .... E 419 421-4740
  Findlay *(G-9682)*

CONSTRUCTION EQPT: Buckets, Excavating, Clamshell, Etc

D & L Excavating Ltd .... G 419 271-0635
  Port Clinton *(G-16246)*
Werk-Brau Company .... D 419 422-2912
  Findlay *(G-9775)*

CONSTRUCTION EQPT: Crane Carriers

Rnm Holdings Inc .... E 937 704-9900
  Franklin *(G-9916)*
Splendid LLC .... F 614 396-6481
  Columbus *(G-7478)*

CONSTRUCTION EQPT: Cranes

Rogue Manufacturing Inc .... G 937 839-4026
  West Alexandria *(G-19621)*
Terex Utilities Inc .... D 513 539-9770
  Monroe *(G-14278)*

CONSTRUCTION EQPT: Crushers, Portable

Toku America Inc .... F 440 954-9923
  Willoughby *(G-20449)*

CONSTRUCTION EQPT: Entrenching Machines

M S K Partnership .... G 419 394-4444
  Celina *(G-2972)*

CONSTRUCTION EQPT: Grinders, Stone, Portable

Ryman Grinders Inc .... F 330 652-5080
  Niles *(G-15035)*

CONSTRUCTION EQPT: Rock Crushing Machinery, Portable

Hudco Manufacturing Inc .... G 440 951-4040
  Willoughby *(G-20338)*

CONSTRUCTION EQPT: Roofing Eqpt

Dimensional Metals Inc .... D 740 927-3633
  Reynoldsburg *(G-16435)*
JC Roofing Supply .... G 937 258-9999
  Dayton *(G-8281)*
Ohio Restoration Group LLC .... G 330 568-5815
  Youngstown *(G-20983)*
Stony Point Metals LLC .... G 330 852-7100
  Sugarcreek *(G-17866)*

CONSTRUCTION EQPT: Tunneling

Barbco Inc .... E 330 488-9400
  East Canton *(G-9038)*
Robbins Company .... C 440 248-3303
  Solon *(G-17224)*
Turn-Key Tunneling Inc .... E 614 275-4832
  Columbus *(G-7552)*

CONSTRUCTION MATERIALS, WHOL: Concrete/Cinder Bldg Prdts

Encore Precast LLC .... F 513 726-5678
  Seven Mile *(G-16907)*
O K Brugmann Jr & Sons Inc .... F 330 274-2106
  Mantua *(G-12555)*

CONSTRUCTION MATERIALS, WHOLESALE: Architectural Metalwork

Charles Mfg Co .... F 330 395-3490
  Warren *(G-19383)*

CONSTRUCTION MATERIALS, WHOLESALE: Block, Concrete & Cinder

Basetek LLC .... F 877 712-2273
  Middlefield *(G-13779)*
Quality Block & Supply Inc .... E 330 364-4411
  Mount Eaton *(G-14421)*
Schwab Industries Inc .... F 330 364-4411
  Dover *(G-8852)*

CONSTRUCTION MATERIALS, WHOLESALE: Brick, Exc Refractory

Company	Code	Phone
Mansfield Brick & Supply Co	G	419 526-1191
Mansfield (G-12475)		
Snyder Concrete Products Inc	E	937 885-5176
Moraine (G-14394)		
Snyder Concrete Products Inc	G	937 224-1433
Dayton (G-8511)		

CONSTRUCTION MATERIALS, WHOLESALE: Building Stone

Company	Code	Phone
Lang Stone Company Inc	D	614 235-4099
Columbus (G-7114)		

CONSTRUCTION MATERIALS, WHOLESALE: Building Stone, Granite

Company	Code	Phone
Mayfair Granite Co Inc	G	216 382-8150
Cleveland (G-5636)		
Piqua Granite & Marble Co Inc	G	937 773-2000
Piqua (G-16153)		

CONSTRUCTION MATERIALS, WHOLESALE: Building Stone, Marble

Company	Code	Phone
Castelli Marble Inc	G	216 361-2410
Cleveland (G-4890)		
Earth Anatomy Fabrication LLC	E	740 244-5316
Norton (G-15366)		
Helmart Company Inc	G	513 941-3095
Cincinnati (G-3806)		

CONSTRUCTION MATERIALS, WHOLESALE: Building, Exterior

Company	Code	Phone
Christman Supply Co Inc	G	740 472-0046
Woodsfield (G-20542)		
Francis-Schulze Co	E	937 295-3941
Russia (G-16608)		
Orrville Trucking & Grading Co	E	330 682-4010
Orrville (G-15609)		
Style Crest Inc	B	419 332-7369
Fremont (G-10052)		

CONSTRUCTION MATERIALS, WHOLESALE: Building, Interior

Company	Code	Phone
Youngstown Curve Form Inc	F	330 744-3028
Youngstown (G-21075)		

CONSTRUCTION MATERIALS, WHOLESALE: Ceiling Systems & Prdts

Company	Code	Phone
Eger Products Inc	D	513 753-4200
Amelia (G-539)		

CONSTRUCTION MATERIALS, WHOLESALE: Cement

Company	Code	Phone
Huron Cement Products Company	E	419 433-4161
Huron (G-11096)		
Lehigh Hanson Ecc Inc	G	614 497-2001
Columbus (G-7121)		

CONSTRUCTION MATERIALS, WHOLESALE: Door Frames

Company	Code	Phone
Provia Holdings Inc	C	330 852-4711
Sugarcreek (G-17859)		

CONSTRUCTION MATERIALS, WHOLESALE: Drywall Materials

Company	Code	Phone
Kcg Inc	G	614 238-9450
Columbus (G-7084)		

CONSTRUCTION MATERIALS, WHOLESALE: Fiberglass Building Mat

Company	Code	Phone
Day Industries Inc	G	216 577-6674
Grafton (G-10297)		

CONSTRUCTION MATERIALS, WHOLESALE: Glass

Company	Code	Phone
A Service Glass Inc	F	937 426-4920
Beavercreek (G-1297)		
Dale Kestler	G	513 871-9000
Cincinnati (G-3574)		
Global Glass Block Inc	G	216 731-2333
Euclid (G-9414)		
Machined Glass Specialist Inc	F	937 743-6166
Springboro (G-17336)		

CONSTRUCTION MATERIALS, WHOLESALE: Gravel

Company	Code	Phone
Hilltop Basic Resources Inc	F	937 859-3616
Miamisburg (G-13676)		

CONSTRUCTION MATERIALS, WHOLESALE: Joists

Company	Code	Phone
Marysville Steel Inc	E	937 642-5971
Marysville (G-12801)		

CONSTRUCTION MATERIALS, WHOLESALE: Limestone

Company	Code	Phone
Hull Builders Supply Inc	E	440 967-3159
Vermilion (G-19161)		
Pinney Dock & Transport LLC	E	440 964-7186
Ashtabula (G-798)		

CONSTRUCTION MATERIALS, WHOLESALE: Masons' Materials

Company	Code	Phone
Koltcz Concrete Block Co	E	440 232-3630
Bedford (G-1421)		

CONSTRUCTION MATERIALS, WHOLESALE: Molding, All Materials

Company	Code	Phone
A & B Wood Design Assoc Inc	G	330 721-2789
Wadsworth (G-19218)		
Toledo Molding & Die Inc	D	419 692-6022
Delphos (G-8757)		

CONSTRUCTION MATERIALS, WHOLESALE: Pallets, Wood

Company	Code	Phone
Mulch World	G	419 873-6852
Perrysburg (G-15978)		
Universal Pallets Inc	E	614 444-1095
Columbus (G-7563)		

CONSTRUCTION MATERIALS, WHOLESALE: Particleboard

Company	Code	Phone
Litco International Inc	E	330 539-5433
Vienna (G-19201)		

CONSTRUCTION MATERIALS, WHOLESALE: Paving Materials

Company	Code	Phone
Erie Materials Inc	G	419 483-4648
Castalia (G-2938)		

CONSTRUCTION MATERIALS, WHOLESALE: Prefabricated Structures

Company	Code	Phone
Morton Buildings Inc	F	330 345-6188
Wooster (G-20628)		
Morton Buildings Inc	D	419 675-2311
Kenton (G-11415)		
Patio Enclosures	F	513 733-4646
Cincinnati (G-4135)		
Will-Burt Company	B	330 682-7015
Orrville (G-15626)		
Will-Burt Company	E	330 682-7015
Orrville (G-15628)		

CONSTRUCTION MATERIALS, WHOLESALE: Roof, Asphalt/Sheet Metal

Company	Code	Phone
Modern Builders Supply Inc	F	419 526-0002
Mansfield (G-12485)		

CONSTRUCTION MATERIALS, WHOLESALE: Roofing & Siding Material

Company	Code	Phone
Associated Materials LLC	B	330 929-1811
Cuyahoga Falls (G-7841)		
Associated Materials Group Inc	E	330 929-1811
Cuyahoga Falls (G-7842)		
Associated Mtls Holdings LLC	A	330 929-1811
Cuyahoga Falls (G-7843)		
Midwest Industrial Products	G	216 771-8555
Cleveland (G-5681)		

CONSTRUCTION MATERIALS, WHOLESALE: Sand

Company	Code	Phone
Acme Company	D	330 758-2313
Poland (G-16236)		
Allied Corporation Inc	G	330 425-7861
Twinsburg (G-18730)		
Phoenix Asphalt Company Inc	G	330 339-4935
Magnolia (G-12362)		

CONSTRUCTION MATERIALS, WHOLESALE: Septic Tanks

Company	Code	Phone
Allen Enterprises Inc	E	740 532-5913
Ironton (G-11159)		

CONSTRUCTION MATERIALS, WHOLESALE: Sewer Pipe, Clay

Company	Code	Phone
Sewer Rodding Equipment Co	E	419 991-2065
Lima (G-11937)		

CONSTRUCTION MATERIALS, WHOLESALE: Siding, Exc Wood

Company	Code	Phone
O A R Vinyl Windows & Siding	G	440 636-5573
Middlefield (G-13842)		
Stony Point Metals LLC	G	330 852-7100
Sugarcreek (G-17866)		
Vinyl Design Corporation	E	419 283-4009
Holland (G-10965)		

CONSTRUCTION MATERIALS, WHOLESALE: Stone, Crushed Or Broken

Company	Code	Phone
Olen Corporation	F	419 294-2611
Upper Sandusky (G-18969)		
Palmer Bros Transit Mix Con	F	419 686-2366
Portage (G-16273)		
Ridge Township Stone Quarry	G	419 968-2222
Van Wert (G-19104)		
Sharon Stone Co	G	740 374-3236
Dexter City (G-8795)		
Sims-Lohman Inc	G	330 456-8408
North Canton (G-15119)		
Stoneco Inc	F	419 893-7645
Maumee (G-13149)		

CONSTRUCTION MATERIALS, WHOLESALE: Tile & Clay Prdts

Company	Code	Phone
Hess & Gault Lumber Co	G	419 281-3105
Ashland (G-710)		

CONSTRUCTION MATERIALS, WHOLESALE: Tile, Clay/Other Ceramic

Company	Code	Phone
Ohio Tile & Marble Co	E	513 541-4211
Cincinnati (G-4105)		

CONSTRUCTION MATERIALS, WHOLESALE: Trim, Sheet Metal

Company	Code	Phone
Dublin Millwork Co Inc	E	614 889-7776
Dublin (G-8908)		

CONSTRUCTION MATERIALS, WHOLESALE: Windows

Company	Code	Phone
Associated Materials LLC	B	330 929-1811
Cuyahoga Falls (G-7841)		
Associated Materials Group Inc	E	330 929-1811
Cuyahoga Falls (G-7842)		
Associated Mtls Holdings LLC	A	330 929-1811
Cuyahoga Falls (G-7843)		
Blockamerica Corporation	G	614 274-0700
Columbus (G-6680)		
Roofing Annex LLC	G	513 942-0555
West Chester (G-19895)		

CONSTRUCTION MATL, WHOLESALE: Structural Assy, Prefab, Wood

Company	Code	Phone
Custom Sink Top Mfg	F	440 245-6220
Lorain (G-12087)		

Employee Codes: A=Over 500 employees, B=251-500 C=101-250, D=51-100, E=20-50, F=10-19, G=3-9

CONSTRUCTION MATLS, WHOL: Composite Board Prdts, Woodboard

BAC Technologies Ltd..................G...... 937 465-2228
  West Liberty *(G-19935)*

CONSTRUCTION MATLS, WHOL: Doors, Combination, Screen-Storm

Otter Group LLC............................F...... 937 315-1199
  Dayton *(G-8410)*

CONSTRUCTION MATLS, WHOL: Lumber, Rough, Dressed/Finished

Appalachia Wood Inc.....................E...... 740 596-2551
  Mc Arthur *(G-13178)*
Baillie Lumber Co LP.....................E...... 419 462-2000
  Galion *(G-10123)*
Berea Hardwood Co Inc..................G...... 216 898-8956
  Cleveland *(G-4804)*
Cabot Lumber Inc...........................G...... 740 545-7109
  West Lafayette *(G-19929)*
Clarksville Stave & Lumber Co........G...... 937 376-4618
  Xenia *(G-20763)*
Contract Lumber Inc.......................D...... 614 751-1109
  Columbus *(G-6814)*
Gross Lumber Inc..........................E...... 330 683-2055
  Apple Creek *(G-606)*
Hartzell Hardwoods Inc..................E...... 937 773-7054
  Piqua *(G-16123)*
J McCoy Lumber Co Ltd.................E...... 937 587-3423
  Peebles *(G-15879)*
J McCoy Lumber Co Ltd.................E...... 937 544-2968
  West Union *(G-19962)*
Khempco Bldg Sup Co Ltd Partnr....D...... 740 549-0465
  Delaware *(G-8700)*
Premier Construction Company.......E...... 513 874-2611
  Fairfield *(G-9550)*
Salt Creek Lumber Company Inc....G...... 330 695-3500
  Fredericksburg *(G-9959)*
Stephen M Trudick..........................E...... 440 834-1891
  Burton *(G-2371)*
Walnut Creek Lumber Co Ltd..........E...... 330 852-4559
  Dundee *(G-9031)*
Wappoo Wood Products Inc............E...... 937 492-1166
  Sidney *(G-17084)*

CONSTRUCTION MATLS, WHOLESALE: Soil Erosion Cntrl Fabrics

Johnston-Morehouse-Dickey Co......G...... 330 405-6050
  Macedonia *(G-12308)*

CONSTRUCTION MTRLS, WHOL: Exterior Flat Glass, Plate/Window

Anderson Glass Co Inc...................E...... 614 476-4877
  Columbus *(G-6603)*

CONSTRUCTION SAND MINING

Arden J Neer Sr.............................F...... 937 585-6733
  Bellefontaine *(G-1504)*
Central Allied Enterprises Inc..........G...... 330 879-2132
  Navarre *(G-14573)*
Columbus Equipment Company......G...... 740 455-4036
  Zanesville *(G-21122)*
Hilltop Basic Resources Inc............F...... 513 651-5000
  Cincinnati *(G-3813)*
Hocking Valley Concrete Inc...........E...... 740 385-2165
  Logan *(G-12027)*
Hugo Sand Company......................G...... 216 570-1212
  Kent *(G-11333)*
J P Sand & Gravel Company...........G...... 614 497-0083
  Lockbourne *(G-11995)*
Lakeside Sand & Gravel Inc............E...... 330 274-2569
  Mantua *(G-12550)*
Masons Sand and Gravel Co..........G...... 614 491-3611
  Obetz *(G-15510)*
Mecco Inc.......................................E...... 513 422-3651
  Middletown *(G-13926)*
Mechanicsburg Sand & Gravel........G...... 937 834-2606
  Mechanicsburg *(G-13211)*
Morrow Gravel Company Inc...........G...... 513 771-0820
  Cincinnati *(G-4048)*
National Lime and Stone Co............E...... 614 497-0083
  Lockbourne *(G-11998)*
Olen Corporation............................G...... 740 745-5865
  Saint Louisville *(G-16674)*

Oscar Brugmann Sand & Gravel.....F...... 330 274-8224
  Mantua *(G-12556)*
S & S Aggregates Inc.....................F...... 419 938-5604
  Perrysville *(G-16031)*
Shelly and Sands Inc.....................F...... 740 453-0721
  Zanesville *(G-21176)*
Shelly Company.............................F...... 740 687-4420
  Lancaster *(G-11606)*
Sober Sand & Gravel Co.................G...... 330 325-7088
  Ravenna *(G-16404)*

CONSTRUCTION SITE PREPARATION SVCS

C & L Erectors & Riggers Inc..........E...... 740 332-7185
  Laurelville *(G-11626)*
Great Lakes Crushing Ltd................E...... 440 944-5500
  Wickliffe *(G-20211)*
L&L Excavating & Land Clearing.....G...... 740 682-7823
  Oak Hill *(G-15454)*
Miller Logging Inc............................E...... 330 279-4721
  Holmesville *(G-10983)*

CONSTRUCTION: Agricultural Building

Barncraft Storage Buildings.............G...... 513 738-5654
  Hamilton *(G-10537)*

CONSTRUCTION: Aqueduct

Neptune Equipment Company.........F...... 513 851-8008
  Cincinnati *(G-4067)*

CONSTRUCTION: Athletic & Recreation Facilities

MGM Construction Inc....................F...... 440 234-7660
  Berea *(G-1617)*

CONSTRUCTION: Bridge

Ashland LLC...................................G...... 513 557-3100
  Cincinnati *(G-3361)*
Ohio Bridge Corporation..................C...... 740 432-6334
  Cambridge *(G-2451)*
S E Johnson Companies Inc...........F...... 419 893-8731
  Maumee *(G-13142)*

CONSTRUCTION: Commercial & Institutional Building

A Metalcraft Associates Inc............G...... 937 693-4008
  Botkins *(G-1931)*
Aecom Energy & Cnstr Inc..............C...... 419 698-6277
  Oregon *(G-15553)*
Bud Corp..G...... 740 967-9992
  Johnstown *(G-11261)*
Falls Metal Fabricators Ind..............F...... 330 253-7181
  Akron *(G-164)*
Jim Nier Construction Inc................F...... 740 289-3925
  Piketon *(G-16072)*
Jjs3 Foundation..............................G...... 513 751-3292
  Cincinnati *(G-3874)*
Kellys Welding & Fabricating..........G...... 440 593-6040
  Conneaut *(G-7651)*
Shelly and Sands Inc.....................D...... 740 859-2104
  Rayland *(G-16423)*

CONSTRUCTION: Commercial & Office Building, New

A W S Incorporated........................G...... 419 352-5397
  Bowling Green *(G-1944)*
Fleming Construction Co.................E...... 740 494-2177
  Prospect *(G-16350)*
Ingle-Barr Inc..................................C...... 740 702-6117
  Chillicothe *(G-3195)*
Jim Bumen Construction Company..G...... 740 663-2659
  Chillicothe *(G-3197)*
Rebsco Inc......................................F...... 937 548-2246
  Greenville *(G-10390)*
Scs Construction Services Inc.........E...... 513 929-0260
  Cincinnati *(G-4311)*
Thomas J Weaver Inc.....................F...... 740 622-2040
  Coshocton *(G-7755)*

CONSTRUCTION: Concrete Patio

Morel Landscaping LLC..................F...... 216 551-4395
  Richfield *(G-16476)*

CONSTRUCTION: Dams, Waterways, Docks & Other Marine

Cincinnati Barge Rail Trml LLC........G...... 513 227-3611
  Cincinnati *(G-3482)*

CONSTRUCTION: Factory

Falls Metal Fabricators Ind..............F...... 330 253-7181
  Akron *(G-164)*

CONSTRUCTION: Food Prdts Manufacturing or Packing Plant

Iron Bean Inc..................................G...... 518 641-9917
  Toledo *(G-18353)*
Milos Whole World Gourmet LLC....G...... 740 589-6456
  Athens *(G-840)*

CONSTRUCTION: Foundation & Retaining Wall

Motz Mobile Containers Inc............G...... 513 772-6689
  Cincinnati *(G-4050)*

CONSTRUCTION: Garage

Beachy Barns Ltd...........................F...... 614 873-4193
  Plain City *(G-16177)*
Overhead Door of Salem Inc..........G...... 330 332-9530
  Salem *(G-16765)*

CONSTRUCTION: Golf Course

Bay Island Company Inc.................G...... 513 248-0356
  Loveland *(G-12180)*

CONSTRUCTION: Grain Elevator

Agridry LLC....................................E...... 419 459-4399
  Edon *(G-9183)*

CONSTRUCTION: Greenhouse

Ludy Greenhouse Mfg Corp............D...... 800 255-5839
  New Madison *(G-14742)*
Rough Brothers Mfg Inc..................D...... 513 242-0310
  Cincinnati *(G-4283)*

CONSTRUCTION: Guardrails, Highway

Paul Peterson Company..................E...... 614 486-4375
  Columbus *(G-7299)*
Security Fence Group Inc...............E...... 513 681-3700
  Cincinnati *(G-4314)*

CONSTRUCTION: Heavy Highway & Street

Hull Ready Mix Concrete Inc...........F...... 419 625-8070
  Sandusky *(G-16815)*
Seneca Petroleum Co Inc...............F...... 419 691-3581
  Toledo *(G-18519)*
Smalls Asphalt Paving Inc..............E...... 740 427-4096
  Gambier *(G-10184)*
W G Lockhart Construction Co.......D...... 330 745-6520
  Akron *(G-429)*

CONSTRUCTION: Hospital

Healthcare Benefits Inc...................G...... 419 433-4499
  Huron *(G-11095)*

CONSTRUCTION: Indl Building & Warehouse

Diversifd OH Vlly Eqpt & Srvcs........F...... 740 458-9881
  Clarington *(G-4567)*
Enerfab Inc.....................................B...... 513 641-0500
  Cincinnati *(G-3640)*
Jim Nier Construction Inc................F...... 740 289-3925
  Piketon *(G-16072)*
Pawnee Maintenance Inc................D...... 740 373-6861
  Marietta *(G-12652)*
Stamm Contracting Co Inc..............E...... 330 274-8230
  Mantua *(G-12560)*

CONSTRUCTION: Indl Building, Prefabricated

Rupcol Inc.......................................G...... 419 924-5215
  West Unity *(G-19974)*

CONSTRUCTION: Indl Buildings, New, NEC

Baker-Shindler Contracting Co .... E 419 782-5080
  Defiance *(G-8615)*
Fleming Construction Co .... E 740 494-2177
  Prospect *(G-16350)*
Hines Builders Inc .... F 937 335-4586
  Troy *(G-18665)*
Jim Bumen Construction Company ...... G 740 663-2659
  Chillicothe *(G-3197)*
Thomas J Weaver Inc .... F 740 622-2040
  Coshocton *(G-7755)*

CONSTRUCTION: Indl Plant

Advanced Indus Machining Inc .... F 614 596-4183
  Powell *(G-16307)*
Babcock & Wilcox Company .... A 330 753-4511
  Barberton *(G-1059)*
Htec Systems Inc .... F 937 438-3010
  Dayton *(G-8255)*
Tri-America Contractors Inc .... E 740 574-0148
  Wheelersburg *(G-20186)*

CONSTRUCTION: Institutional Building

Consoldted Grnhse Slutions LLC .... G 330 844-8598
  Strongsville *(G-17732)*

CONSTRUCTION: Land Preparation

Intrusion-Prepakt Inc .... G 440 238-6950
  Cleveland *(G-5472)*

CONSTRUCTION: Oil & Gas Line & Compressor Station

Don Wartko Construction Co .... D 330 673-5252
  Kent *(G-11315)*
Global Oilfield Services LLC .... G 419 756-8027
  Mansfield *(G-12446)*

CONSTRUCTION: Oil & Gas Pipeline Construction

Bluefoot Industrial LLC .... E 740 314-5299
  Steubenville *(G-17528)*
IV J Telecommunications LLC .... G 606 694-1762
  South Point *(G-17284)*
Terra Sonic International LLC .... E 740 374-6608
  Marietta *(G-12679)*

CONSTRUCTION: Pipeline, NEC

Eastern Automated Piping .... G 740 535-8184
  Mingo Junction *(G-14208)*

CONSTRUCTION: Power Plant

Enerfab Inc .... B 513 641-0500
  Cincinnati *(G-3640)*
Siemens Energy Inc .... B 740 393-8897
  Mount Vernon *(G-14510)*

CONSTRUCTION: Residential, Nec

Bearcat Construction Inc .... G 513 314-0867
  Mason *(G-12832)*
Byrd Prcurement Specialist Inc .... G 419 936-0019
  Swanton *(G-17908)*
Kim Phillips Sign Co LLC .... G 330 364-4280
  Dover *(G-8834)*
M J Coates Construction Co .... G 937 886-9546
  Dayton *(G-8318)*
Mohican Log Homes Inc .... G 419 994-4088
  Loudonville *(G-12144)*

CONSTRUCTION: Roads, Gravel or Dirt

Road Maintenance Products .... G 740 465-7181
  Morral *(G-14405)*

CONSTRUCTION: Sewer Line

Connolly Construction Co Inc .... G 937 644-8831
  Marysville *(G-12775)*
Fleming Construction Co .... E 740 494-2177
  Prospect *(G-16350)*
Mack Ready Mix Concrete Inc .... G 330 483-3111
  Valley City *(G-19046)*
Mt Pleasant Blacktopping Inc .... G 513 874-3777
  Fairfield *(G-9532)*
Robert Gorey .... G 330 725-7272
  Medina *(G-13328)*

CONSTRUCTION: Single-Family Housing

A W S Incorporated .... G 419 352-5397
  Bowling Green *(G-1944)*
Building Concepts Inc .... F 419 298-2371
  Edgerton *(G-9169)*
Community RE Group-Comvet .... G 440 319-6714
  Ashtabula *(G-767)*
Elite Mill Service & Cnstr .... G 513 422-4234
  Trenton *(G-18617)*
Gutter Topper Ltd .... G 513 797-5800
  Batavia *(G-1150)*
Humble Construction Co .... E 614 888-8960
  Columbus *(G-7010)*
Manufactured Housing Entps Inc .... C 419 636-4511
  Bryan *(G-2298)*
Silver Creek Log Homes .... G 419 335-3220
  Wauseon *(G-19532)*
Volpe Millwork Inc .... G 216 581-0200
  Cleveland *(G-6270)*

CONSTRUCTION: Single-family Housing, New

Al Yoder Construction Company .... G 330 359-5726
  Millersburg *(G-14056)*
Cabinet Systems Inc .... G 440 237-1924
  Cleveland *(G-4861)*
Connolly Construction Co Inc .... G 937 644-8831
  Marysville *(G-12775)*
Hoge Lumber Company .... E 419 753-2263
  New Knoxville *(G-14703)*
Mohican Log Homes Inc .... G 419 994-4088
  Loudonville *(G-12144)*
Thomas J Weaver Inc .... F 740 622-2040
  Coshocton *(G-7755)*
Wright Designs Inc .... G 216 524-6662
  Cleveland *(G-6329)*

CONSTRUCTION: Street Sign Installation & Mntnce

A & A Safety Inc .... F 937 567-9781
  Beavercreek *(G-1348)*
A & A Safety Inc .... E 513 943-6100
  Amelia *(G-527)*

CONSTRUCTION: Street Surfacing & Paving

Action Blacktop Sealcoating & .... G 937 667-4769
  Tipp City *(G-18097)*
Ashland LLC .... G 513 557-3100
  Cincinnati *(G-3361)*
Baileys Asphalt Sealing .... F 740 453-9409
  South Zanesville *(G-17301)*
Barrett Paving Materials Inc .... C 513 271-6200
  Middletown *(G-13970)*
Image Pavement Maintenance .... E 937 833-9200
  Brookville *(G-2172)*
John R Jurgensen Co .... G 937 293-3112
  Springfield *(G-17427)*
Koski Construction Co .... G 440 997-5337
  Ashtabula *(G-782)*
Mar-Zane Inc .... G 330 626-2079
  Mantua *(G-12552)*
Morlock Asphalt Ltd .... F 419 686-4601
  Portage *(G-16271)*
Shelly Materials Inc .... G 740 666-5841
  Ostrander *(G-15646)*
Suever Stone Company .... F 419 331-1945
  Lima *(G-11945)*

CONSTRUCTION: Swimming Pools

Imperial On-Pece Fibrgls Pools .... F 740 747-2971
  Ashley *(G-757)*
Spa Pool Covers Inc .... G 440 235-9981
  North Royalton *(G-15302)*

CONSTRUCTION: Telephone & Communication Line

Fishel Company .... D 614 850-4400
  Columbus *(G-6926)*
Parallel Technologies Inc .... D 614 798-9700
  Dublin *(G-8958)*

CONSTRUCTION: Tennis Court

Image Pavement Maintenance .... E 937 833-9200
  Brookville *(G-2172)*

CONSTRUCTION: Utility Line

Groundhogs 2000 LLC .... G 440 653-1647
  Bedford *(G-1407)*

CONSTRUCTION: Water Main

Coleman Machine Inc .... G 740 695-3006
  Saint Clairsville *(G-16628)*

CONSULTING SVC: Business, NEC

Biorx LLC .... C 866 442-4679
  Cincinnati *(G-3394)*
D M L Steel Tech .... F 513 737-9911
  Liberty Twp *(G-11823)*
Deemsys Inc .... D 614 322-9928
  Gahanna *(G-10079)*
E Retailing Associates LLC .... D 614 300-5785
  Columbus *(G-6880)*
Ktsdi LLC .... G 330 783-2000
  North Lima *(G-15173)*
Lake Publishing Inc .... G 440 299-8500
  Mentor *(G-13495)*
Magnum Computers Inc .... F 216 781-1757
  Cleveland *(G-5605)*
Mamsys Consulting Services .... G 440 287-6824
  Solon *(G-17187)*
Metal-Mation Inc .... F 216 651-1083
  Cleveland *(G-5660)*
Petro Evaluation Services Inc .... G 330 264-4454
  Wooster *(G-20636)*
Ponderosa Consulting Services .... G 330 264-2298
  Wooster *(G-20637)*
Rapid Blanket Restorer Corp .... G 330 821-6326
  Willoughby *(G-20418)*
Ream and Haager Laboratory .... F 330 343-3711
  Dover *(G-8849)*
Rxpert Consultants LLC .... G 614 579-9384
  Columbus *(G-7409)*
Simple Vms LLC .... G 888 255-8918
  Cincinnati *(G-4338)*
Truechoicepack Corp .... E 937 630-3832
  Mason *(G-12951)*
Vista Research Group LLC .... G 419 281-3927
  Ashland *(G-753)*

CONSULTING SVC: Computer

Advanced Prgrm Resources Inc .... E 614 761-9994
  Dublin *(G-8874)*
Akron Council of Engineering .... G 330 535-8835
  Akron *(G-37)*
Albert Bickel .... G 513 530-5700
  Cincinnati *(G-3317)*
Argentifex LLC .... G 440 990-1108
  Ashtabula *(G-761)*
Carey Color Llc/Cincinnati .... G 513 241-5210
  Cincinnati *(G-3442)*
Casentric LLC .... G 216 233-6300
  Shaker Heights *(G-16928)*
Concept Xxi Inc .... F 216 831-2121
  Beachwood *(G-1230)*
Einstruction Corporation .... D 330 746-3015
  Youngstown *(G-20897)*
Empyracom Inc .... E 330 744-5570
  Canfield *(G-2526)*
It XCEL Consulting LLC .... F 513 847-8261
  West Chester *(G-19728)*
Netsmart Technologies Inc .... E 440 942-4040
  Solon *(G-17207)*
Onx Holdings LLC .... F 866 587-2287
  Cincinnati *(G-4114)*
Onx USA LLC .... D 440 569-2300
  Cleveland *(G-5815)*
Phase Array Company LLC .... G 513 785-0801
  West Chester *(G-19759)*
Quayle Consulting Inc .... G 614 868-1363
  Pickerington *(G-16058)*
Rawhide Software Inc .... G 419 878-0857
  Bowling Green *(G-1993)*
Revolution Group Inc .... D 614 212-1111
  Westerville *(G-20020)*
S L C Software Services .... G 513 922-4303
  Cincinnati *(G-4297)*
Strongbasics LLC .... G 716 903-6151
  Columbus *(G-7495)*
Teradata Operations Inc .... D 937 242-4030
  Miamisburg *(G-13727)*
Value Stream Systems Inc .... G 330 907-0064
  Medina *(G-13359)*

CONSULTING SVC: Computer

Wild Fire Systems .... G 440 442-8999
  Cleveland (G-6308)

CONSULTING SVC: Data Processing

Image Integrations Systems .... F 419 872-0003
  Perrysburg (G-15964)
Mamsys Consulting Services .... G 440 287-6824
  Solon (G-17187)
W L Arehart Computing Systems .... G 937 383-4710
  Wilmington (G-20510)

CONSULTING SVC: Educational

Align Assess Achieve LLC .... G 614 505-6820
  Columbus (G-6563)
Instruction & Design Concepts .... G 937 439-2698
  Dayton (G-8271)

CONSULTING SVC: Engineering

4r Enterprises Incorporated .... G 330 923-9799
  Cuyahoga Falls (G-7829)
ACC Automation Co Inc .... E 330 928-3821
  Akron (G-26)
Advanced Engrg Solutions Inc .... D 937 743-6900
  Springboro (G-17319)
Aero Composites Inc .... G 937 849-0244
  Medway (G-13365)
Amcan Productions Ltd .... G 330 332-9129
  Salem (G-16717)
BSK Industries Inc .... F 440 230-9299
  North Royalton (G-15264)
Consolidatd Analytical Sys Inc .... F 513 542-1200
  Cleves (G-6359)
Curtiss-Wright Controls .... E 937 252-5601
  Fairborn (G-9456)
Dlz Ohio Inc .... C 614 888-0040
  Columbus (G-6871)
Empire Systems Inc .... F 440 653-9300
  Avon Lake (G-984)
Fluid Equipment Corp .... G 419 636-0777
  Bryan (G-2281)
Forte Indus Eqp Systems Inc .... E 513 398-2800
  Mason (G-12871)
Halliday Technologies Inc .... G 614 504-4150
  Delaware (G-8691)
Independent Digital Consulting .... G 330 753-0777
  Norton (G-15370)
James Engineering Inc .... G 740 373-9521
  Marietta (G-12636)
Keuchel & Associates Inc .... E 330 945-9455
  Cuyahoga Falls (G-7888)
Maval Industries LLC .... C 330 405-1600
  Twinsburg (G-18813)
On-Power Inc .... E 513 228-2100
  Lebanon (G-11679)
Ozone Systems Svcs Group Inc .... G 513 899-4131
  Morrow (G-14414)
P G M Diversified Industries .... G 440 885-3500
  Cleveland (G-5830)
Reliance Design Inc .... F 216 267-5450
  Rocky River (G-16554)
Sest Inc .... F 440 777-9777
  Westlake (G-20157)
Signalysis Inc .... F 513 528-6164
  Cincinnati (G-4337)
Sponseller Group Inc .... E 419 861-3000
  Holland (G-10959)
Sponseller Group Inc .... G 937 492-9949
  Sidney (G-17081)
Storetek Engineering Inc .... E 330 294-0678
  Tallmadge (G-18006)
Tetra Tech Inc .... F 330 286-3683
  Canfield (G-2549)
Visiontech Automation LLC .... G 614 554-2013
  Dublin (G-9010)
Warmus and Associates Inc .... F 330 659-4440
  Bath (G-1203)
Watson Meeks and Company .... G 937 378-2455
  Georgetown (G-10239)
Welded Tube Pros LLC .... G 330 854-2966
  Canal Fulton (G-2496)

CONSULTING SVC: Human Resource

360water Inc .... G 614 294-3600
  Columbus (G-6511)
Avesta Systems Inc .... G 330 650-1800
  Hudson (G-11032)
Delphia Consulting LLC .... G 614 421-2000
  Columbus (G-6860)
Simple Vms LLC .... G 888 255-8918
  Cincinnati (G-4338)

CONSULTING SVC: Management

A C Knox Inc .... G 513 921-5028
  Cincinnati (G-3279)
Advanced Prgrm Resources Inc .... E 614 761-9994
  Dublin (G-8874)
Amerihua Intl Entps Inc .... G 740 549-0300
  Lewis Center (G-11744)
AT&T Government Solutions Inc .... D 937 306-3030
  Beavercreek (G-1302)
Cac Energy Ltd .... G 937 867-5593
  Dayton (G-8072)
Digital Controls Corporation .... D 513 746-8118
  Miamisburg (G-13659)
Enerchem Incorporated .... G 513 745-0580
  Cincinnati (G-3639)
EP Ferris & Associates Inc .... G 614 299-2999
  Columbus (G-6902)
Frisbie Engine & Machine Co .... F 513 542-1770
  Cincinnati (G-3714)
Harris Mackessy & Brennan .... C 614 221-6831
  Westerville (G-19996)
Instruction & Design Concepts .... G 937 439-2698
  Dayton (G-8271)
International Trade Group Inc .... G 614 486-4634
  Columbus (G-7045)
Pakra LLC .... F 614 477-6965
  Columbus (G-7286)
Power Management Inc .... E 937 222-2909
  Dayton (G-8430)
SSP Industrial Group Inc .... G 330 665-2900
  Fairlawn (G-9619)
Transel Corporation .... G 513 897-3442
  Harveysburg (G-10706)
Value Added Business Svcs Co .... G 614 854-9755
  Jackson (G-11200)
Vehicle Systems Inc .... G 330 854-0535
  Massillon (G-13056)
Welding Consultants Inc .... G 614 258-7018
  Columbus (G-7598)
Wide Area Media LLC .... G 440 356-3133
  Westlake (G-20172)
Wild Oak LLC .... G 513 769-0526
  Cincinnati (G-4509)

CONSULTING SVC: Marketing Management

Alonovus Corp .... D 330 674-2300
  Millersburg (G-14057)
Applied Marketing Services .... E 440 716-9962
  Westlake (G-20098)
Capehart Enterprises LLC .... F 614 769-7746
  Columbus (G-6730)
David Esrati .... G 937 228-4433
  Dayton (G-8126)
Dsk Imaging LLC .... F 513 554-1797
  Blue Ash (G-1759)
Electronic Imaging Svcs Inc .... G 740 549-2487
  Lewis Center (G-11759)
Eltool Corporation .... G 513 723-1772
  Mansfield (G-12436)
Frankes Wood Products LLC .... E 937 642-0706
  Marysville (G-12783)
Green Willow Inc .... G 937 436-5290
  Dayton (G-8238)
International Advg Concepts .... G 440 331-4733
  Cleveland (G-5467)
Just Business Inc .... F 866 577-3303
  Dayton (G-8287)
Kitto Katsu Inc .... G 818 256-6997
  Clayton (G-4576)
Minor Corporation .... G 216 291-8723
  Cleveland (G-5695)
Nsa Technologies LLC .... C 330 576-4600
  Akron (G-304)
Nurdcon LLC .... G 614 208-5898
  Canal Winchester (G-2509)
One Wish LLC .... G 800 505-6883
  Beachwood (G-1259)
Page One Group .... G 740 397-4240
  Mount Vernon (G-14499)
Peloton Manufacturing Corp .... F 440 205-1600
  Mentor (G-13546)
Proficient Information Tech .... G 937 470-1300
  Dayton (G-8447)
Quez Media Marketing Inc .... F 216 910-0202
  Independence (G-11149)
Sagitta Inc .... G 440 570-5393
  Cleveland (G-6025)
Tomahawk Entertainment Group .... G 216 505-0548
  Cleveland (G-6180)

CONSULTING SVC: Online Technology

Cisco Systems Inc .... A 937 427-4264
  Beavercreek (G-1306)
Estreamz Inc .... E 513 278-7836
  Cincinnati (G-3654)
Jasstek Inc .... F 614 808-3600
  Dublin (G-8932)
Sns Nano Fiber Technology LLC .... G 330 655-0030
  Hudson (G-11074)
Wentworth Technologies LLC .... F 440 212-7696
  Brunswick (G-2250)
Westmount Technology Inc .... G 216 328-2011
  Independence (G-11157)

CONSULTING SVC: Sales Management

Chemigon LLC .... G 330 592-1875
  Akron (G-113)

CONSULTING SVC: Telecommunications

Digital Automation Associates .... G 419 352-6977
  Bowling Green (G-1969)
J Com Data Inc .... G 614 304-1455
  Pataskala (G-15833)

CONSULTING SVCS, BUSINESS: Agricultural

Advancing Eco-Agriculture LLC .... G 800 495-6603
  Middlefield (G-13773)
Tyler Grain & Fertilizer Co .... F 330 669-2341
  Smithville (G-17095)

CONSULTING SVCS, BUSINESS: Communications

Telex Communications Inc .... F 419 865-0972
  Toledo (G-18546)

CONSULTING SVCS, BUSINESS: Energy Conservation

Melink Corporation .... F 513 685-0958
  Milford (G-14026)

CONSULTING SVCS, BUSINESS: Environmental

Alpha Omega Bioremediation LLC ...... F 614 287-2600
  Columbus (G-6577)
Summit Drilling Company Inc .... F 800 775-5537
  Akron (G-390)

CONSULTING SVCS, BUSINESS: Safety Training Svcs

American Apex Corporation .... F 614 652-2000
  Plain City (G-16171)
Stuntronics LLC .... G 216 780-1413
  Bedford Heights (G-1480)

CONSULTING SVCS, BUSINESS: Sys Engnrg, Exc Computer/Prof

A Graphic Solution .... F 216 228-7223
  Cleveland (G-4587)
Das Consulting Services Inc .... F 330 896-4064
  Canton (G-2650)
Fluid Equipment Corp .... G 419 636-0777
  Bryan (G-2281)
Jasstek Inc .... F 614 808-3600
  Dublin (G-8932)
Mv Designlabs LLC .... G 724 355-7986
  Cleveland (G-5715)
North Coast Security Group LLC .... G 614 887-7255
  Columbus (G-7226)
Tangible Solutions Inc .... G 937 912-4603
  Fairborn (G-9471)

CONSULTING SVCS, BUSINESS: Systems Analysis & Engineering

Great Lakes Mfg Group Ltd .... G 440 391-8266
  Rocky River (G-16548)
Interactive Engineering Corp .... E 330 239-6888
  Medina (G-13280)
Nvision Technology Inc .... G 412 254-4668
  Norton (G-15374)

PRODUCT SECTION

CONTAINERS: Metal

Sentek Corporation ....G........ 614 586-1123
  Columbus *(G-7438)*
Tekworx LLC ....F........ 513 533-4777
  Blue Ash *(G-1858)*

CONSULTING SVCS, BUSINESS: Systems Analysis Or Design

Akers Identity LLC ....G........ 330 493-0055
  Canton *(G-2566)*
Architctral Identification Inc ....E........ 614 868-8400
  Gahanna *(G-10076)*
Qlog Corp ....G........ 513 874-1211
  Hamilton *(G-10599)*

CONSULTING SVCS, BUSINESS: Testing, Educational Or Personnel

Community RE Group-Comvet ....G........ 440 319-6714
  Ashtabula *(G-767)*
Terewell Inc ....G........ 216 334-6897
  Cleveland *(G-6160)*

CONSULTING SVCS, BUSINESS: Traffic

Athens Technical Specialists ....F........ 740 592-2874
  Athens *(G-824)*
Barr Engineering Incorporated ....F........ 614 892-0162
  Columbus *(G-6649)*

CONSULTING SVCS: Geological

David A Waldron & Associates ....G........ 330 264-7275
  Wooster *(G-20583)*

CONSULTING SVCS: Oil

Diamond Oilfield Tech LLC ....F........ 234 806-4185
  Vienna *(G-19198)*
Washita Valley Enterprises Inc ....F........ 330 510-1568
  Louisville *(G-12171)*

CONTACT LENSES

Albright Albright & Schn ....G........ 614 825-4829
  Worthington *(G-20674)*
Brunswick Eye & Contact Lens C ....G........ 419 439-3381
  Defiance *(G-8617)*
Diversified Ophthalmics Inc ....F........ 803 783-3454
  Cincinnati *(G-3594)*
Safeway Contact Lens Inc ....G........ 330 536-6469
  Lowellville *(G-12256)*

CONTACTS: Electrical

Aviation Technologies Inc ....G........ 216 706-2960
  Cleveland *(G-4776)*

CONTAINERS, GLASS: Food

Bprex Plastic Packaging Inc ....F........ 419 247-5000
  Toledo *(G-18213)*

CONTAINERS: Air Cargo, Metal

Shanafelt Manufacturing Co ....E........ 330 455-0315
  Canton *(G-2814)*

CONTAINERS: Cargo, Wood

Frankes Wood Products LLC ....E........ 937 642-0706
  Marysville *(G-12783)*
Riverview Indus WD Pdts Inc ....D........ 330 669-8509
  Wooster *(G-20646)*
Riverview Indus WD Pdts Inc ....F........ 330 669-8509
  Smithville *(G-17092)*
Universal Pallets Inc ....E........ 614 444-1095
  Columbus *(G-7563)*

CONTAINERS: Cargo, Wood & Metal Combination

Schutz Container Systems Inc ....D........ 419 872-2477
  Perrysburg *(G-16005)*

CONTAINERS: Cargo, Wood & Wood With Metal

Findlay Pallet Inc ....G........ 419 423-0511
  Findlay *(G-9685)*
Kmak Group LLC ....F........ 937 308-1023
  London *(G-12064)*

Ohio Specialty Mfg Co ....G........ 419 531-5402
  Toledo *(G-18437)*

CONTAINERS: Corrugated

1923 W 25th St Inc ....G........ 216 696-7529
  Cleveland *(G-4579)*
3d Corrugated LLC ....G........ 513 241-8126
  Cincinnati *(G-3270)*
Buckeye Boxes Inc ....E........ 614 274-8484
  Columbus *(G-6708)*
Charles Messina ....D........ 216 663-3344
  Cleveland *(G-4911)*
Gbc International LLC ....G........ 513 943-7283
  Cincinnati *(G-3251)*
Georgia-Pacific LLC ....C........ 513 536-3020
  Batavia *(G-1149)*
Honeymoon Paper Products Inc ....D........ 513 755-7200
  Fairfield *(G-9505)*
JIT Packaging Inc ....E........ 330 562-8080
  Aurora *(G-885)*
Joseph T Snyder Industries ....G........ 216 883-6900
  Cleveland *(G-5506)*
Marshalltown Packaging Inc ....E........ 641 753-5272
  Columbus *(G-7154)*
Midwest Filtration LLC ....E........ 513 874-6510
  West Chester *(G-19880)*
Nicofibers Inc ....G........ 740 394-2491
  Shawnee *(G-16961)*
Packaging Tech LLC ....E........ 216 374-7308
  Cleveland *(G-5836)*
Pactiv LLC ....E........ 330 644-9542
  Coventry Township *(G-7777)*
Sonoco Products Company ....E........ 614 759-8470
  Columbus *(G-7462)*
Systems Pack Inc ....E........ 330 467-5729
  Macedonia *(G-12336)*
Temple Inland ....G........ 513 425-0830
  Middletown *(G-13956)*
Temple-Inland Inc ....F........ 614 221-1522
  Marion *(G-12740)*
Westrock Rkt Company ....G........ 330 296-5155
  Ravenna *(G-16420)*

CONTAINERS: Foil, Bakery Goods & Frozen Foods

CC Investors Management Co LLC ......G........ 740 374-8129
  Marietta *(G-12614)*

CONTAINERS: Food & Beverage

Amcor Rigid Plastics Usa LLC ....G........ 419 483-4343
  Bellevue *(G-1528)*
Ball Corporation ....C........ 419 423-3071
  Findlay *(G-9653)*
Ball Corporation ....F........ 330 244-2313
  North Canton *(G-15072)*
Broodle Brands LLC ....F........ 855 276-6353
  Cincinnati *(G-3424)*
G&M Media Packaging Inc ....F........ 419 636-5461
  Bryan *(G-2282)*
Seven-Ogun International LLC ....G........ 614 888-8939
  Worthington *(G-20703)*
SSP Industrial Group Inc ....G........ 330 665-2900
  Fairlawn *(G-9619)*

CONTAINERS: Food, Folding, Made From Purchased Materials

Americraft Carton Inc ....E........ 419 668-1006
  Norwalk *(G-15380)*

CONTAINERS: Food, Liquid Tight, Including Milk

Kerry Inc ....G........ 760 685-2548
  Byesville *(G-2389)*
Ohio State Plastics ....F........ 614 299-5618
  Columbus *(G-7258)*
Verso Corporation ....D........ 901 369-4105
  Miamisburg *(G-13733)*

CONTAINERS: Food, Metal

G W Cobb Co ....F........ 216 341-0100
  Cleveland *(G-5285)*

CONTAINERS: Food, Wood Wirebound

Patriotic Buildings LLC ....G........ 740 853-3970
  Patriot *(G-15853)*

CONTAINERS: Glass

Anchor Glass Container Corp ....C........ 740 452-2743
  Zanesville *(G-21099)*
Anchor Hocking LLC ....A........ 740 681-6478
  Lancaster *(G-11541)*
Anchor Hocking LLC ....G........ 740 687-2500
  Lancaster *(G-11542)*
Chantilly Development Corp ....F........ 419 243-8109
  Toledo *(G-18227)*
Custom Deco LLC ....G........ 419 698-2900
  Toledo *(G-18245)*
Dura Temp Corporation ....F........ 419 866-4348
  Holland *(G-10929)*
Ghp II LLC ....C........ 740 687-2500
  Lancaster *(G-11575)*
Owens-Brockway Glass Cont Inc ....C........ 740 336-8449
  Perrysburg *(G-15995)*
Owens-Brockway Packaging Inc ....G........ 567 336-5000
  Perrysburg *(G-15996)*
Owens-Illinois Inc ....B........ 567 336-5000
  Perrysburg *(G-15997)*
Owens-Illinois De Puerto Rico ....D........ 419 874-9708
  Toledo *(G-18451)*
Owens-Illinois General Inc ....B........ 567 336-5000
  Perrysburg *(G-15998)*
Owens-Illinois Group Inc ....E........ 567 336-5000
  Perrysburg *(G-15999)*
Pyromatics Corp ....F........ 440 352-3500
  Mentor *(G-13561)*
Tiama Americas Inc ....G........ 269 274-3107
  Maumee *(G-13153)*

CONTAINERS: Ice Cream, Made From Purchased Materials

Huhtamaki Inc ....B........ 937 746-9700
  Franklin *(G-9890)*
Huhtamaki Inc ....B........ 513 201-1525
  Batavia *(G-1153)*
Norse Dairy Systems LP ....B........ 614 421-5297
  Columbus *(G-7225)*

CONTAINERS: Metal

Champion Company ....D........ 937 324-5681
  Springfield *(G-17375)*
Champion Company ....D........ 937 324-5681
  Springfield *(G-17374)*
Deufol Worldwide Packaging LLC ....E........ 440 232-1100
  Bedford *(G-1400)*
Eisenhauer Mfg Co LLC ....D........ 419 238-0081
  Van Wert *(G-19090)*
Georgia-Pacific LLC ....C........ 740 477-3347
  Circleville *(G-4546)*
Green Bay Packaging Inc ....C........ 419 332-5593
  Fremont *(G-10027)*
Green Bay Packaging Inc ....D........ 513 228-5560
  Lebanon *(G-11660)*
Horwitz & Pintis Co ....F........ 419 666-2220
  Toledo *(G-18336)*
Industrial Container Svcs LLC ....E........ 513 921-8811
  Cincinnati *(G-3844)*
Industrial Container Svcs LLC ....D........ 614 864-1900
  Blacklick *(G-1687)*
Mauser USA LLC ....E........ 614 856-5982
  Mount Vernon *(G-14492)*
Mobile Mini Inc ....F........ 614 449-8655
  Columbus *(G-7188)*
Overseas Packing LLC ....F........ 440 232-2917
  Bedford *(G-1434)*
Packaging Specialties Inc ....E........ 330 723-6000
  Medina *(G-13316)*
Sabco Industries Inc ....E........ 419 531-5347
  Toledo *(G-18510)*
Schwarz Partners Packaging LLC ....F........ 317 290-1140
  Sidney *(G-17073)*
SSP Industrial Group Inc ....G........ 330 665-2900
  Fairlawn *(G-9619)*
Syme Inc ....E........ 330 723-6000
  Medina *(G-13350)*
Tavens Container Inc ....D........ 216 883-3333
  Bedford *(G-1448)*
Unican Ohio LLC ....G........ 419 636-5461
  Fremont *(G-10059)*
Werk-Brau Company ....D........ 419 422-2912
  Findlay *(G-9775)*
Westrock Cp LLC ....C........ 330 297-0841
  Ravenna *(G-16419)*
Westrock Cp LLC ....B........ 513 745-2400
  Blue Ash *(G-1868)*

Employee Codes: A=Over 500 employees, B=251-500
C=101-250, D=51-100, E=20-50, F=10-19, G=3-9

CONTAINERS: Metal

Westrock Cp LLC .... D 770 448-2193
  Wshngtn CT Hs (G-20750)
Witt Industries Inc .... D 513 871-5700
  Mason (G-12955)

CONTAINERS: Plastic

Amcor Rigid Plastics Usa LLC .... D 419 483-4343
  Bellevue (G-1527)
Amcor Rigid Plastics Usa LLC .... E 419 592-1998
  Napoleon (G-14531)
Bakelite N Sumitomo Amer Inc .... G 419 675-1282
  Kenton (G-11403)
Bkhn Inc .... D 513 831-4402
  Milford (G-13998)
Bprex Plastic Packaging Inc .... F 419 247-5000
  Toledo (G-18213)
Buckhorn Inc .... E 513 831-4402
  Milford (G-14000)
Buckhorn Material Hdlg Group .... D 513 831-4402
  Milford (G-14001)
Century Container LLC .... E 330 457-2367
  New Waterford (G-14837)
Century Container LLC .... G 330 457-2367
  Columbiana (G-6457)
CK Technologies LLC .... B 419 485-1110
  Montpelier (G-14305)
Composite Technologies Co LLC .... D 937 228-2880
  Dayton (G-8101)
Consolidated Container Co .... G 330 394-0905
  Warren (G-19389)
Dadco Inc .... F 513 489-2244
  Cincinnati (G-3573)
Dadco Inc .... F 513 489-2244
  Cincinnati (G-3572)
Dester Corporation .... F 419 362-8020
  Lima (G-11854)
Dometic Sanitation Corporation .... D 330 439-5550
  Big Prairie (G-1673)
Eaton Corporation .... C 330 274-0743
  Aurora (G-877)
Eliason Corporation .... G 800 828-3655
  West Chester (G-19851)
Enpac LLC .... E 440 975-0070
  Eastlake (G-9108)
Environmental Sampling Sup Inc .... E 330 497-9396
  North Canton (G-15080)
Fabohio Inc .... E 740 922-4233
  Uhrichsville (G-18886)
Flambeau Inc .... D 440 632-6131
  Middlefield (G-13799)
Genpak LLC .... E 614 276-5156
  Columbus (G-6947)
Graham Packaging Company LP .... E 740 439-4242
  Cambridge (G-2441)
Graham Packaging Company LP .... E 513 874-1770
  West Chester (G-19861)
Graham Packaging Company LP .... E 419 334-4197
  Fremont (G-10024)
Graham Packg Plastic Pdts Inc .... E 717 849-8500
  Toledo (G-18310)
Greif Inc .... E 740 549-6000
  Delaware (G-8681)
Greif Inc .... E 740 657-6500
  Delaware (G-8682)
Hamilton Custom Molding Inc .... G 513 844-6643
  Hamilton (G-10568)
Hendrickson International Corp .... D 740 929-5600
  Hebron (G-10747)
Hinkle Manufacturing LLC .... F 313 584-0400
  Perrysburg (G-15962)
Hub Plastics Inc .... D 614 861-1791
  Blacklick (G-1686)
Huhtamaki Inc .... B 937 987-3078
  New Vienna (G-14824)
Hydrant Hat LLC .... G 440 224-1007
  Kingsville (G-11459)
Ilpea Industries Inc .... C 330 562-2916
  Aurora (G-884)
Iml Containers Ohio Inc .... F 330 754-1066
  Canton (G-2705)
Kennedy Group Incorporated .... D 440 951-7660
  Willoughby (G-20352)
Klockner Pentaplast Amer Inc .... D 937 548-7272
  Greenville (G-10378)
Klw Plastics Inc .... G 678 674-2990
  Monroe (G-14271)
Landmark Plastic Corporation .... C 330 785-2200
  Akron (G-248)
Mastic Home Exteriors Inc .... C 937 497-7008
  Sidney (G-17050)

Med Center Systems LLC .... G 513 942-6066
  West Chester (G-19877)
Midwest Plastic Systems Inc .... G 513 553-4380
  New Richmond (G-14813)
Olan Plastics Inc .... E 614 834-6526
  Canal Winchester (G-2510)
Orbis Corporation .... G 513 737-9489
  Hamilton (G-10595)
Patrick Products Inc .... C 419 943-4137
  Leipsic (G-11730)
Philpott Indus Plas Entps Ltd .... G 330 225-3344
  Brunswick (G-2224)
Plastics R Unique Inc .... E 330 334-4820
  Wadsworth (G-19264)
Plastipak Packaging Inc .... C 740 928-4435
  Hebron (G-10757)
Polymer & Steel Tech Inc .... E 440 510-0108
  Eastlake (G-9128)
Pretium Packaging LLC .... C 419 943-3733
  Leipsic (G-11732)
Resource Mtl Hdlg & Recycl Inc .... E 440 834-0727
  Middlefield (G-13849)
Roswell Inc .... G 419 433-4709
  Huron (G-11111)
S Toys Holdings LLC .... A 330 656-0440
  Streetsboro (G-17693)
Shirley KS Storage Trays LLC .... G 740 868-8140
  Zanesville (G-21178)
Silgan Plastics LLC .... C 419 523-3737
  Ottawa (G-15664)
Southeastern Container Inc .... D 419 352-6300
  Bowling Green (G-2000)
Spartech LLC .... D 937 548-1395
  Greenville (G-10395)
Specialty Plas Fabrications .... G 513 856-9475
  Hamilton (G-10607)
US Coexcell Inc .... E 419 897-9110
  Maumee (G-13158)
Versa-Pak Ltd .... E 419 586-5466
  Celina (G-2991)
Wayne Pak Ltd .... F 440 323-8744
  Elyria (G-9345)

CONTAINERS: Plywood & Veneer, Wood

Pallet & Cont Corp of Amer .... G 419 255-1256
  Toledo (G-18457)

CONTAINERS: Sanitary, Food

Duracorp LLC .... D 740 549-3336
  Lewis Center (G-11758)
Novolex Holdings Inc .... B 937 746-1933
  Franklin (G-9905)
Sonoco Products Company .... E 513 870-3985
  West Chester (G-19900)
Washington Products Inc .... F 330 837-5101
  Massillon (G-13057)

CONTAINERS: Shipping & Mailing, Fiber

Operational Support Svcs LLC .... F 419 425-0889
  Findlay (G-9736)
Shockakhan Express LLC .... G 614 432-3133
  Groveport (G-10511)

CONTAINERS: Shipping, Bombs, Metal Plate

Buckeye Stamping Company .... D 614 445-0059
  Columbus (G-6712)
Industrial Repair & Mfg Inc .... D 419 822-4232
  Delta (G-8774)

CONTAINERS: Shipping, Metal, Milk, Fluid

Fluid-Bag LLC .... G 513 310-9550
  West Chester (G-19705)

CONTAINERS: Shipping, Wood

Frankes Wood Products LLC .... E 937 642-0706
  Marysville (G-12783)
Greif Inc .... E 740 549-6000
  Delaware (G-8681)
Greif Inc .... E 740 657-6500
  Delaware (G-8682)

CONTAINERS: Wood

A-Z Packaging Company .... F 614 444-8441
  Columbus (G-6518)
Brown-Forman Corporation .... E 740 384-3027
  Wellston (G-19598)

Cima Inc .... E 513 382-8976
  Hamilton (G-10545)
Clark Rm Inc .... E 419 425-9889
  Findlay (G-9669)
Denoon Lumber Company LLC .... D 740 768-2220
  Bergholz (G-1634)
Haessly Lumber Sales Co .... D 740 373-6681
  Marietta (G-12630)
Hann Box Works .... E 740 962-3752
  McConnelsville (G-13205)
Joe Gonda Company Inc .... F 440 458-6000
  Grafton (G-10305)
Ohio Plywood Box .... E 513 242-9125
  Cincinnati (G-4104)
Overseas Packing LLC .... F 440 232-2917
  Bedford (G-1434)
T & D Thompson Inc .... E 740 332-8515
  Laurelville (G-11627)
Traveling & Recycle Wood Pdts .... F 419 968-2649
  Middle Point (G-13757)

CONTAINMENT VESSELS: Reactor, Metal Plate

FSRc Tanks Inc .... E 234 221-2015
  Bolivar (G-1914)

CONTRACTOR: Dredging

Cappco Tubular Products Inc .... G 216 641-2218
  North Olmsted (G-15183)

CONTRACTOR: Rigging & Scaffolding

AM Industrial Group LLC .... E 216 433-7171
  Brookpark (G-2134)
Janson Industries .... D 330 455-7029
  Canton (G-2716)

CONTRACTORS: Access Control System Eqpt

Safe Systems Inc .... G 216 661-1166
  Cleveland (G-6024)

CONTRACTORS: Access Flooring System Installation

X-Treme Finishes Inc .... F 330 474-0614
  Medina (G-13364)

CONTRACTORS: Acoustical & Insulation Work

Holland Assocts LLC DBA Archou .... F 513 891-0006
  Cincinnati (G-3818)
One Wish LLC .... F 800 505-6883
  Beachwood (G-1259)

CONTRACTORS: Artificial Turf Installation

Trendco Inc .... G 216 661-6903
  North Royalton (G-15307)

CONTRACTORS: Asbestos Removal & Encapsulation

American Way Exteriors LLC .... G 855 766-3293
  Dayton (G-8028)

CONTRACTORS: Asphalt

Asphalt Services Ohio Inc .... G 614 864-4600
  Columbus (G-6621)
H P Streicher Inc .... G 419 841-4715
  Toledo (G-18315)
Lucas County Asphalt Inc .... E 419 476-0705
  Toledo (G-18389)
Massillon Asphalt Co .... G 330 833-6330
  Massillon (G-13019)
Morrow Gravel Company Inc .... E 513 771-0820
  Cincinnati (G-4048)
Mt Pleasant Blacktopping Inc .... G 513 874-3777
  Fairfield (G-9532)
Smalls Asphalt Paving Inc .... E 740 427-4096
  Gambier (G-10184)
Wilson Blacktop Corporation .... E 740 635-3566
  Martins Ferry (G-12764)
York Paving Co .... F 740 594-3600
  Athens (G-854)

PRODUCT SECTION

CONTRACTORS: Concrete

CONTRACTORS: Awning Installation
Color Brite Company Inc ....G....... 216 441-4117
  Cleveland *(G-4998)*
South Akron Awning Co ....F....... 330 848-7611
  Akron *(G-382)*

CONTRACTORS: Bathtub Refinishing
Thiels Replacement Systems Inc ....D....... 419 289-6139
  Ashland *(G-751)*

CONTRACTORS: Blasting, Exc Building Demolition
Kars Ohio LLC ....G....... 614 655-1099
  Pataskala *(G-15834)*

CONTRACTORS: Boiler & Furnace
E & M Liberty Welding Inc ....G....... 330 866-2338
  Waynesburg *(G-19563)*

CONTRACTORS: Boiler Maintenance Contractor
Dalton Combustion Systems Inc ....G....... 216 447-0647
  Cleveland *(G-5060)*
Holgate Metal Fab Inc ....F....... 419 599-2000
  Napoleon *(G-14543)*
Park Corporation ....B....... 216 267-4870
  Cleveland *(G-5841)*
Prout Boiler Htg & Wldg Inc ....E....... 330 744-0293
  Youngstown *(G-21008)*

CONTRACTORS: Boiler Setting
Gurina Company ....G....... 614 279-3891
  Columbus *(G-6971)*
Nbw Inc ....E....... 216 377-1700
  Cleveland *(G-5732)*

CONTRACTORS: Building Eqpt & Machinery Installation
Cincinnati Crane & Hoist LLC ....F....... 513 202-1408
  Harrison *(G-10634)*
Edmonds Elevator Company ....F....... 216 781-9135
  Thompson *(G-18025)*
Fmt Repair Service Co ....G....... 330 347-7374
  Mentor *(G-13444)*
Nbw Inc ....E....... 216 377-1700
  Cleveland *(G-5732)*
Terex Utilities Inc ....F....... 440 262-3200
  Brecksville *(G-2060)*
Trinity Door Systems ....G....... 877 603-2018
  New Springfield *(G-14822)*

CONTRACTORS: Building Sign Installation & Mntnce
A B C Sign Inc ....F....... 513 241-8884
  Cincinnati *(G-3278)*
All Signs of Chillicothe Inc ....G....... 740 773-5016
  Chillicothe *(G-3174)*
Archer Corporation ....E....... 330 455-9995
  Canton *(G-2574)*
Bird Corporation ....G....... 419 424-3095
  Findlay *(G-9656)*
Bob King Sign Company Inc ....G....... 330 753-2679
  Akron *(G-90)*
Boyer Signs & Graphics Inc ....E....... 216 383-7242
  Columbus *(G-6691)*
Brilliant Electric Sign Co Ltd ....D....... 216 741-3800
  Brooklyn Heights *(G-2116)*
Danite Holdings Ltd ....E....... 614 444-3333
  Columbus *(G-6849)*
Exchange Signs ....G....... 330 644-4552
  Coventry Township *(G-7769)*
Gus Holthaus Signs Inc ....E....... 513 861-0060
  Cincinnati *(G-3790)*
Identitek Systems Inc ....D....... 330 832-9844
  Massillon *(G-13002)*
Kessler Sign Company ....G....... 937 898-0633
  Dayton *(G-8295)*
Macray Co LLC ....G....... 937 325-1726
  Springfield *(G-17440)*
Mel Wacker Sign Inc ....G....... 330 832-1726
  Massillon *(G-13024)*
R M Davis Inc ....G....... 419 756-6719
  Mansfield *(G-12503)*

Signature Sign Co Inc ....F....... 216 426-1234
  Cleveland *(G-6065)*
United-Maier Signs Inc ....D....... 513 681-6600
  Cincinnati *(G-4451)*

CONTRACTORS: Cable Laying
Cambridge Cable Service Co ....G....... 740 685-5775
  Byesville *(G-2380)*

CONTRACTORS: Cable TV Installation
Xxx Intrntional Amusements Inc ....E....... 216 671-6900
  Cleveland *(G-6332)*

CONTRACTORS: Carpentry Work
AK Fabrication Inc ....F....... 330 458-1037
  Canton *(G-2565)*
Custom Hitch and Trailer/ Over ....G....... 740 289-3925
  Piketon *(G-16068)*
Finelli Ornamental Iron Co ....F....... 440 248-0050
  Cleveland *(G-5240)*
Joseph Sabatino ....G....... 330 332-5879
  Salem *(G-16751)*
Millwood Wholesale Inc ....F....... 330 359-6109
  Dundee *(G-9023)*
N C W Nicoloff Cab Works LLC ....G....... 513 821-1400
  Fairfield *(G-9534)*
Premier Construction Company ....E....... 513 874-2611
  Fairfield *(G-9550)*
Riverside Cnstr Svcs Inc ....G....... 513 723-0900
  Cincinnati *(G-4273)*
Tri County Door Service Inc ....F....... 216 531-2245
  Euclid *(G-9448)*

CONTRACTORS: Carpentry, Cabinet & Finish Work
Bobs Custom Str Interiors LLC ....G....... 567 316-7490
  Toledo *(G-18209)*
Cabintpak Kitchens of Columbus ....G....... 614 294-4646
  Columbus *(G-6721)*
Case Crafters Inc ....G....... 937 667-9473
  Tipp City *(G-18107)*
Chesterland Cabinet Company ....G....... 440 564-1157
  Newbury *(G-14947)*
Display Dynamics Inc ....G....... 937 832-2830
  Englewood *(G-9355)*
Kbi Group Inc ....G....... 614 873-5825
  Plain City *(G-16198)*
Modern Designs Inc ....G....... 330 644-1771
  Coventry Township *(G-7773)*
Oakwood Furniture Inc ....G....... 740 896-3162
  Lowell *(G-12247)*
Snows Wood Shop Inc ....E....... 419 836-3805
  Oregon *(G-15567)*
Summit Custom Cabinets ....G....... 740 345-1734
  Newark *(G-14927)*

CONTRACTORS: Carpentry, Cabinet Building & Installation
A & J Woodworking Inc ....G....... 419 695-5655
  Delphos *(G-8734)*
Accent Manufacturing Inc ....F....... 330 724-7704
  Norton *(G-15355)*
Battershell Cabinets ....G....... 419 542-6448
  Hicksville *(G-10777)*
Colby Woodworking Inc ....G....... 937 224-7676
  Dayton *(G-8097)*
East Woodworking Company ....G....... 216 791-5950
  Cleveland *(G-5140)*
Murray Display Fixtures Ltd ....F....... 614 875-1594
  Grove City *(G-10448)*
R Carney Thomas ....G....... 740 342-3388
  New Lexington *(G-14722)*
S & W Custom Tops Inc ....G....... 330 788-2525
  Youngstown *(G-21023)*
Sheridan Woodworks Inc ....F....... 216 663-9333
  Cleveland *(G-6052)*
Ssi Manufacturing Inc ....F....... 513 761-7757
  West Chester *(G-19902)*
Thomas Cabinet Shop Inc ....F....... 937 847-8239
  Dayton *(G-8554)*
Wades Woodworking Inc ....F....... 937 374-6470
  Xenia *(G-20804)*

CONTRACTORS: Chimney Construction & Maintenance
Donald Schloemer ....G....... 419 933-2002
  Willard *(G-20239)*
Whempys Corp ....G....... 614 888-6670
  Worthington *(G-20707)*

CONTRACTORS: Closet Organizers, Installation & Design
Ptmj Enterprises ....C....... 440 543-8000
  Solon *(G-17220)*

CONTRACTORS: Coating, Caulking & Weather, Water & Fire
Asb Industries Inc ....E....... 330 753-8458
  Barberton *(G-1054)*

CONTRACTORS: Commercial & Office Building
Arrow Coal Grove Inc ....F....... 740 532-6143
  Ironton *(G-11160)*
Bent Wood Solutions LLC ....G....... 330 674-1454
  Millersburg *(G-14065)*
Brenmar Construction Inc ....D....... 740 286-2151
  Jackson *(G-11183)*
MGM Construction Inc ....F....... 440 234-7660
  Berea *(G-1617)*
Stamm Contracting Co Inc ....E....... 330 274-8230
  Mantua *(G-12560)*

CONTRACTORS: Communications Svcs
Gatesair Inc ....D....... 513 459-3400
  Mason *(G-12875)*
Legrand North America LLC ....B....... 937 224-0639
  Dayton *(G-8309)*
Vertiv Group Corporation ....F....... 440 460-3600
  Cleveland *(G-6253)*

CONTRACTORS: Computer Installation
Data Power Solutions ....G....... 614 471-1911
  Columbus *(G-6851)*
Thomas Ross Associates Inc ....G....... 330 723-1110
  Medina *(G-13352)*
Town Cntry Technical Svcs Inc ....F....... 614 866-7700
  Reynoldsburg *(G-16457)*

CONTRACTORS: Computerized Controls Installation
Computer Enterprise Inc ....F....... 216 228-7156
  Lakewood *(G-11515)*

CONTRACTORS: Concrete
Concrete Material Supply LLC ....G....... 419 261-6404
  Toledo *(G-18237)*
Dan Shrock Cement ....G....... 440 548-2498
  Parkman *(G-15811)*
Forterra Pipe & Precast LLC ....G....... 937 268-6707
  Dayton *(G-8203)*
G Big Inc ....E....... 740 867-5758
  Chesapeake *(G-3145)*
Gennaro Pavers ....G....... 330 536-6825
  Lowellville *(G-12252)*
Hanson Concrete Products Ohio ....E....... 614 443-4846
  Columbus *(G-6980)*
Hilltop Basic Resources Inc ....F....... 937 882-6357
  Springfield *(G-17418)*
Koski Construction Co ....G....... 440 997-5337
  Ashtabula *(G-782)*
Lynn James Contracting LLC ....G....... 419 467-4505
  Delta *(G-8775)*
Mack Industries Inc ....G....... 330 460-7005
  Brunswick *(G-2219)*
Precast Services Inc ....G....... 614 428-4541
  Reynoldsburg *(G-16447)*
R W Sidley Incorporated ....E....... 440 352-9343
  Painesville *(G-15777)*
RE Connors Construction Ltd ....G....... 740 644-0025
  Thornville *(G-18031)*
Shelly and Sands Inc ....E....... 740 453-0721
  Zanesville *(G-21177)*
Spillman Company ....E....... 614 444-2184
  Columbus *(G-7476)*

Employee Codes: A=Over 500 employees, B=251-500
C=101-250, D=51-100, E=20-50, F=10-19, G=3-9

CONTRACTORS: Concrete

Stamm Contracting Co Inc .... E 330 274-8230
  Mantua *(G-12560)*
T-N-T Concrete Inc .... G 540 480-4040
  Mentor *(G-13599)*
W M Dauch Concrete Inc .... G 419 562-6917
  Bucyrus *(G-2349)*
Ward Construction Co .... F 419 943-2450
  Leipsic *(G-11739)*

CONTRACTORS: Concrete Block Masonry Laying

North Central Concrete Design .... F 419 606-1908
  Wooster *(G-20632)*
Pierce GL Inc .... G 513 772-7202
  Cincinnati *(G-4158)*
T-N-T Concrete Inc .... G 540 480-4040
  Mentor *(G-13599)*

CONTRACTORS: Concrete Pumping

Phillips Companies .... E 937 426-5461
  Beavercreek Township *(G-1371)*
Phillips Ready Mix Co .... D 937 426-5151
  Beavercreek Township *(G-1372)*

CONTRACTORS: Concrete Reinforcement Placing

Upright Steel LLC .... E 216 923-0852
  Cleveland *(G-6242)*

CONTRACTORS: Concrete Structure Coating, Plastic

Custom Powdercoating LLC .... G 937 972-3516
  Dayton *(G-8122)*
Paulo Products Company .... E 440 942-0153
  Willoughby *(G-20399)*

CONTRACTORS: Construction Caulking

Master Builders LLC .... E 216 831-5500
  Beachwood *(G-1247)*

CONTRACTORS: Construction Site Metal Structure Coating

Bogie Industries Inc Ltd .... E 330 745-3105
  Akron *(G-92)*
Carpe Diem Industries LLC .... D 419 659-5639
  Columbus Grove *(G-7632)*
Carpe Diem Industries LLC .... E 419 358-0129
  Bluffton *(G-1887)*
L B Foster Company .... E 330 652-1461
  Mineral Ridge *(G-14168)*

CONTRACTORS: Core Drilling & Cutting

Barr Engineering Incorporated .... F 614 892-0162
  Columbus *(G-6649)*
Barr Engineering Incorporated .... E 614 714-0299
  Columbus *(G-6650)*

CONTRACTORS: Corrosion Control Installation

Mesocoat Inc .... F 216 453-0866
  Euclid *(G-9427)*

CONTRACTORS: Countertop Installation

Brad Snoderly .... F 419 476-0184
  Toledo *(G-18214)*
Classic Countertops LLC .... G 330 882-4220
  Akron *(G-119)*
Columbia Cabinets Inc .... G 440 748-1010
  Columbia Station *(G-6432)*
Crafted Surface and Stone LLC .... E 440 658-3799
  Bedford Heights *(G-1467)*
Dell Fixtures Inc .... E 614 449-1750
  Columbus *(G-6859)*
Imperial Countertops .... F 216 851-0888
  Cleveland *(G-5443)*
Laminate Shop .... F 740 749-3536
  Waterford *(G-19486)*
Pietra Naturale Inc .... F 937 438-8882
  Franklin *(G-9911)*
Stone Statements Incorporated .... G 513 489-7866
  Cincinnati *(G-4384)*

CONTRACTORS: Demolition, Building & Other Structures

Js Fabrications Inc .... G 419 333-0323
  Fremont *(G-10031)*
Sidwell Materials Inc .... C 740 849-2394
  Zanesville *(G-21180)*

CONTRACTORS: Diamond Drilling & Sawing

Curtiss-Wright Flow Control .... D 513 735-2538
  Batavia *(G-1134)*

CONTRACTORS: Directional Oil & Gas Well Drilling Svc

Brendel Producing Company .... G 330 854-4151
  Canton *(G-2598)*
Camphire Drilling Inc .... G 740 599-6928
  Danville *(G-7959)*
Clearpath Utlity Solutions LLC .... F 740 661-4240
  Zanesville *(G-21119)*
D Anderson Corp .... G 330 433-0606
  Canton *(G-2646)*
Directional One Svcs Inc USA .... G 740 371-5031
  Marietta *(G-12620)*
Future Productions Inc .... G 330 478-0477
  Canton *(G-2677)*
Groundhogs 2000 LLC .... G 440 653-1647
  Bedford *(G-1407)*
J Valtier Gas and Oil Co Inc .... G 740 342-2839
  Malta *(G-12383)*
JAC Construction Ohio Llc .... G 440 564-5005
  Newbury *(G-14958)*
Kirk Excavating & Construction .... E 614 444-4008
  Columbus *(G-7095)*
Ngo Development Corporation .... F 740 344-3790
  Newark *(G-14903)*
Oak Dale Drilling Inc .... G 740 385-5888
  Logan *(G-12037)*
R & J Drilling Company Inc .... G 740 763-3991
  Frazeysburg *(G-9941)*
Temple Oil & Gas Company .... G 740 452-7878
  Crooksville *(G-7820)*
Top Drilling Corporation .... F 304 477-3333
  Marietta *(G-12682)*
Warren Drilling Co Inc .... C 740 783-2775
  Dexter City *(G-8796)*

CONTRACTORS: Dock Eqpt Installation, Indl

Vector Mechanical LLC .... G 216 337-4042
  Brookpark *(G-2158)*

CONTRACTORS: Drapery Track Installation

Carmens Installation Co .... F 216 321-4040
  Cleveland *(G-4879)*
E W Perry Service Co Inc .... G 419 473-1231
  Toledo *(G-18273)*
M C L Window Coverings Inc .... G 513 868-6000
  Fairfield Township *(G-9584)*
Nancys Draperies .... F 330 855-7751
  Marshallville *(G-12754)*
Style-Line Incorporated .... E 614 291-0600
  Columbus *(G-7497)*

CONTRACTORS: Driveway

Action Blacktop Sealcoating & .... G 937 667-4769
  Tipp City *(G-18097)*
Baileys Asphalt Sealing .... F 740 453-9409
  South Zanesville *(G-17301)*
Image Pavement Maintenance .... E 937 833-9200
  Brookville *(G-2172)*
Parkins Asphalt Sealing .... G 419 422-2399
  Findlay *(G-9739)*

CONTRACTORS: Earthmoving

Biedenbach Logging .... G 740 732-6477
  Sarahsville *(G-16865)*

CONTRACTORS: Electric Power Systems

Asg Division Jergens Inc .... G 888 486-6163
  Cleveland *(G-4749)*
Columbia Energy Group .... A 614 460-4683
  Columbus *(G-6781)*

CONTRACTORS: Electrical

Akron Foundry Co .... E 330 745-3101
  Barberton *(G-1050)*
Atlas Industrial Contrs LLC .... B 614 841-4500
  Columbus *(G-6627)*
Connor Electric Inc .... G 513 932-5798
  Lebanon *(G-11643)*
Electric Ctrl & Mtr Repr Svc .... G 216 881-3143
  Cleveland *(G-5162)*
Fishel Company .... D 614 850-4400
  Columbus *(G-6926)*
Gould Group LLC .... G 740 807-4294
  Hilliard *(G-10825)*
Graham Electric .... G 614 231-8500
  Columbus *(G-6964)*
Hess Advanced Solutions Llc .... G 937 829-4794
  Dayton *(G-8249)*
JC Electric .... G 330 760-2915
  Garrettsville *(G-10193)*
Jobap Assembly Inc .... F 440 632-5393
  Middlefield *(G-13810)*
Mirus Adapted Tech LLC .... G 614 402-4585
  Dublin *(G-8946)*
Mr Electric .... G 419 289-7474
  Mansfield *(G-12488)*
Schneder Elc Bldngs Amrcas Inc .... D 513 398-9800
  Lebanon *(G-11694)*

CONTRACTORS: Electronic Controls Installation

Control Associates Inc .... G 440 708-1770
  Chagrin Falls *(G-3042)*
Controls Inc .... E 330 239-4345
  Medina *(G-13240)*
Industrial Electronic Service .... F 937 746-9750
  Carlisle *(G-2893)*
Safe-Grain Inc .... G 513 398-2500
  Loveland *(G-12229)*

CONTRACTORS: Elevator Front Installation, Metal

Architectural Products Dev .... G 216 631-6260
  Cleveland *(G-4728)*

CONTRACTORS: Energy Management Control

Siemens Energy Inc .... B 740 393-8897
  Mount Vernon *(G-14510)*
Tekworx LLC .... F 513 533-4777
  Blue Ash *(G-1858)*

CONTRACTORS: Epoxy Application

Flow-Liner Systems Ltd .... E 800 348-0020
  Zanesville *(G-21136)*
Hy-Blast Inc .... F 513 424-0704
  Middletown *(G-13912)*

CONTRACTORS: Excavating

Alden Sand & Gravel Co Inc .... F 330 928-3249
  Cuyahoga Falls *(G-7832)*
Arrow Coal Grove Inc .... F 740 532-6143
  Ironton *(G-11160)*
Castalia Trenching & Ready Mix .... F 419 684-5502
  Castalia *(G-2936)*
David Cox .... G 740 254-4858
  Gnadenhutten *(G-10277)*
Don Wartko Construction Co .... D 330 673-5252
  Kent *(G-11315)*
H & S Drilling Co Inc .... G 740 828-2411
  Frazeysburg *(G-9940)*
Ingles Logging .... G 740 379-2760
  Patriot *(G-15852)*
Kelchner Inc .... C 937 704-9890
  Springboro *(G-17333)*
Kipps Gravel Company Inc .... F 513 732-1024
  Batavia *(G-1160)*
Koski Construction Co .... G 440 997-5337
  Ashtabula *(G-782)*
Liebrecht Manufacturing LLC .... F 419 596-3501
  Continental *(G-7667)*
Personal Plumber Service Corp .... F 440 324-4321
  Elyria *(G-9311)*
Phillips Companies .... E 937 426-5461
  Beavercreek Township *(G-1370)*
Phillips Ready Mix Co .... D 937 426-5151
  Beavercreek Township *(G-1372)*

PRODUCT SECTION

CONTRACTORS: Home & Office Intrs Finish, Furnish/Remodel

Pipelines Inc .... G 330 448-0000
  Masury *(G-13061)*
R & B Enterprises USA Inc .... G 330 674-2227
  Millersburg *(G-14121)*
R J Dobay Enterprises Inc .... G 440 227-1005
  Burton *(G-2367)*
Rbm Environmental and Cnstr .... E 419 693-5840
  Oregon *(G-15566)*
Sanders Fredrick Excvtg Co Inc .... G 330 297-7980
  Ravenna *(G-16401)*
Siler Excavation Services .... E 513 400-8628
  Milford *(G-14041)*
T-N-T Concrete Inc .... G 540 480-4040
  Mentor *(G-13599)*
Wadsworth Excavating Inc .... G 419 898-0771
  Oak Harbor *(G-15448)*

CONTRACTORS: Exterior Painting

All Ohio Companies Inc .... F 216 420-9274
  Cleveland *(G-4664)*

CONTRACTORS: Fence Construction

Connaughton Wldg & Fence LLC ...... G 513 867-0230
  Hamilton *(G-10547)*
Fence One Inc .... F 216 441-2600
  Cleveland *(G-5229)*
Security Fence Group Inc .... E 513 681-3700
  Cincinnati *(G-4314)*
Youngstown Fence Inc .... G 330 788-8110
  Youngstown *(G-21076)*

CONTRACTORS: Fiber Optic Cable Installation

JAC Construction Ohio Llc .... G 440 564-5005
  Newbury *(G-14958)*

CONTRACTORS: Fire Detection & Burglar Alarm Systems

Independent Protection Systems ...... G 330 832-7992
  Massillon *(G-13003)*

CONTRACTORS: Floor Laying & Other Floor Work

Done-Rite Bowling Service Co .... E 440 232-3280
  Bedford *(G-1402)*
Dynafloor Systems Inc .... F 330 467-6005
  Solon *(G-17134)*
Forsvara Engineering LLC .... G 937 254-9711
  Dayton *(G-8202)*
Myko Industries .... G 216 431-0900
  Cleveland *(G-5717)*
Tremco Incorporated .... B 216 292-5000
  Beachwood *(G-1283)*
True Kote Inc .... G 419 334-8813
  Fremont *(G-10056)*
Western Reserve Furniture Co .... G 440 235-6216
  North Olmsted *(G-15203)*

CONTRACTORS: Flooring

Mount Hope Planing .... F 330 359-0538
  Millersburg *(G-14115)*
Protective Industrial Polymers .... F 440 327-0015
  North Ridgeville *(G-15246)*

CONTRACTORS: Foundation & Footing

Byedak Construction Ltd .... G 937 414-6153
  New Paris *(G-14752)*
Gateway Concrete Forming Svcs ..... D 513 353-2000
  Miamitown *(G-13746)*
Intrusion-Prepakt Inc .... G 440 238-6950
  Cleveland *(G-5472)*

CONTRACTORS: Foundation Building

Cappco Tubular Products Inc .... G 216 641-2218
  North Olmsted *(G-15183)*
North Central Insulation Inc .... F 419 886-2030
  Bellville *(G-1561)*

CONTRACTORS: Fountain Installation

Meridienne International Inc .... G 330 274-8317
  Mantua *(G-12554)*

CONTRACTORS: Garage Doors

Division Overhead Door Inc .... F 513 872-0888
  Cincinnati *(G-3597)*
Nofziger Door Sales Inc .... C 419 337-9900
  Wauseon *(G-19530)*

CONTRACTORS: Gas Field Svcs, NEC

Catress LLC .... G 740 695-0918
  Saint Clairsville *(G-16626)*
Clearfield Ohio Holdings Inc .... D 740 947-5121
  Waverly *(G-19542)*
Exelon Energy Company .... F 614 797-4377
  Westerville *(G-19991)*
Gas Analytical Services Inc .... G 330 539-4267
  Girard *(G-10260)*
James L Williams .... G 740 865-3382
  Wingett Run *(G-20536)*
Natural Gas Construction Inc .... G 330 364-9240
  Dover *(G-8844)*
OS Power Tong Inc .... G 330 866-3815
  Waynesburg *(G-19564)*
Standard Oil Company .... G 419 691-2460
  Oregon *(G-15569)*
Stingray Pressure Pumping LLC ...... E 405 648-4177
  Belmont *(G-1567)*
United Chart Processors Inc .... G 740 373-5801
  Marietta *(G-12686)*

CONTRACTORS: Gasoline Condensation Removal Svcs

Heckmann Wtr Resources Cvr Inc ... G 740 844-0045
  Norwich *(G-15420)*

CONTRACTORS: General Electric

Burkett Industries Inc .... G 419 332-4391
  Fremont *(G-10002)*
Commercial Electric Pdts Corp .... E 216 241-2886
  Cleveland *(G-5002)*
D & E Electric Inc .... F 513 738-1172
  Okeana *(G-15518)*
D & J Electric Motor Repair Co .... F 330 336-4343
  Wadsworth *(G-19232)*
Franks Electric Inc .... E 513 313-5883
  Cincinnati *(G-3711)*
Instrmntation Ctrl Systems Inc .... E 513 662-2600
  Cincinnati *(G-3851)*
Jeff Bonham Electric Inc .... E 937 233-7662
  Dayton *(G-8282)*
Magnum Computers Inc .... F 216 781-1757
  Cleveland *(G-5605)*
P S C Inc .... G 216 531-3375
  Cleveland *(G-5832)*
Security Fence Group Inc .... E 513 681-3700
  Cincinnati *(G-4314)*
Speelman Electric Inc .... D 330 633-1410
  Tallmadge *(G-18004)*
Tcb Automation LLC .... E 330 556-6444
  Dover *(G-8860)*
Valley Electric Company .... G 419 332-6405
  Fremont *(G-10061)*
Waibel Electric Co Inc .... F 740 964-2956
  Etna *(G-9390)*

CONTRACTORS: Glass Tinting, Architectural & Automotive

AGC Automotive Americas .... D 937 599-3131
  Bellefontaine *(G-1501)*

CONTRACTORS: Glass, Glazing & Tinting

A Service Glass Inc .... F 937 426-4920
  Beavercreek *(G-1297)*
AGC Automotive Americas .... D 937 599-3131
  Bellefontaine *(G-1501)*
All State GL Block Fctry Inc .... F 440 205-8410
  Mentor *(G-13384)*
Kimmatt Corp .... G 937 228-3811
  Dayton *(G-8297)*
Mentor Glass Supplies and Repr ...... F 440 255-9444
  Mentor *(G-13515)*
Pentagon Protection Usa LLC .... F 614 734-7240
  Dublin *(G-8964)*
Pioneer Cldding Glzing Systems ..... E 216 816-4242
  Cleveland *(G-5879)*
Solon Glass Center Inc .... F 440 248-5018
  Cleveland *(G-6078)*

Trinity Door Systems .... G 877 603-2018
  New Springfield *(G-14822)*

CONTRACTORS: Gutters & Downspouts

Barnett Spouting Inc .... G 330 644-0853
  Akron *(G-80)*
Cincinnati Gutter Supply Inc .... G 513 825-0500
  West Chester *(G-19672)*
Thiels Replacement Systems Inc ..... D 419 289-6139
  Ashland *(G-751)*
Yoder Window & Siding Ltd .... F 330 695-6960
  Fredericksburg *(G-9962)*

CONTRACTORS: Heating & Air Conditioning

A A A Professional Htg & Coolg .... G 513 933-0564
  Lebanon *(G-11628)*
Abbott Mechanical Services LLC ..... G 419 460-4315
  Maumee *(G-13065)*
BT Investments II Inc .... G 937 434-4321
  Dayton *(G-8066)*
Carrier Corporation .... E 937 275-0645
  Dayton *(G-8077)*
Cartwright Construction Inc .... G 330 929-3020
  Cuyahoga Falls *(G-7846)*
Hess Advanced Solutions Llc .... G 937 829-4794
  Dayton *(G-8249)*
IV J Telecommunications LLC .... G 606 694-1762
  South Point *(G-17284)*
J Feldkamp Design Build Ltd .... E 513 870-0601
  Cincinnati *(G-3863)*
Northeastern Rfrgn Corp .... E 440 942-7676
  Willoughby *(G-20390)*
Us Inc .... G 513 791-1162
  Blue Ash *(G-1863)*
Vector Mechanical LLC .... G 216 337-4042
  Brookpark *(G-2158)*

CONTRACTORS: Heating Systems Repair & Maintenance Svc

Whempys Corp .... G 614 888-6670
  Worthington *(G-20707)*
Wood Stove Shed .... G 419 562-1545
  Bucyrus *(G-2351)*

CONTRACTORS: Highway & Street Construction, General

Kenmore Construction Co Inc .... E 330 832-8888
  Massillon *(G-13009)*
S E Johnson Companies Inc .... F 419 893-8731
  Maumee *(G-13142)*
Valley Asphalt Corporation .... G 513 561-1551
  Cincinnati *(G-4462)*
Walls Bros Asphalt Co Inc .... G 937 548-7158
  Greenville *(G-10399)*
Ward Construction Co .... F 419 943-2450
  Leipsic *(G-11739)*

CONTRACTORS: Highway & Street Paving

Able Industries Inc .... G 614 252-1050
  Columbus *(G-6528)*
Shelly and Sands Inc .... F 740 453-0721
  Zanesville *(G-21176)*
Shelly and Sands Inc .... F 740 453-0721
  Zanesville *(G-21177)*
Shelly Company .... G 740 474-6255
  Circleville *(G-4557)*
Terminal Ready-Mix Inc .... E 440 288-0181
  Lorain *(G-12129)*
Wilson Blacktop Corporation .... E 740 635-3566
  Martins Ferry *(G-12764)*

CONTRACTORS: Highway Sign & Guardrail Construction & Install

Traffic Detectors & Signs Inc .... G 330 707-9060
  Youngstown *(G-21048)*

CONTRACTORS: Home & Office Intrs Finish, Furnish/Remodel

Boyce Ltd .... G 614 236-8901
  Columbus *(G-6690)*
Distinct Cbntry Innvations LLC .... G 937 661-1051
  New Lebanon *(G-14708)*
Fdi Cabinetry LLC .... G 513 353-4500
  Cleves *(G-6362)*

Employee Codes: A=Over 500 employees, B=251-500
C=101-250, D=51-100, E=20-50, F=10-19, G=3-9

2019 Harris Ohio
Industrial Directory

CONTRACTORS: Hotel, Motel/Multi-Famly Home Renovtn/Remodel

Cardinal Builders Inc .... E 614 237-1000
  Columbus (G-6739)
Northpointe Cabinetry LLC .... G 740 455-4045
  Zanesville (G-21163)

CONTRACTORS: Hydraulic Eqpt Installation & Svcs

Jani Auto Parts Inc .... G 330 494-2975
  North Canton (G-15095)
K C N Technologies LLC .... G 440 439-4219
  Bedford (G-1419)
Pakk Systems LLC .... G 440 839-9999
  Wakeman (G-19288)

CONTRACTORS: Hydraulic Well Fracturing Svcs

PSC Holdings Inc .... G 740 454-6253
  Zanesville (G-21174)
Universal Well Services Inc .... E 814 333-2656
  Millersburg (G-14140)

CONTRACTORS: Indl Building Renovation, Remodeling & Repair

Herbert Wood Products Inc .... G 440 834-1410
  Middlefield (G-13805)
Ingle-Barr Inc .... C 740 702-6117
  Chillicothe (G-3195)
Universal Fabg Cnstr Svcs Inc .... D 614 274-1128
  Columbus (G-7561)

CONTRACTORS: Insulation Installation, Building

North Central Insulation Inc .... F 419 886-2030
  Bellville (G-1561)

CONTRACTORS: Kitchen & Bathroom Remodeling

Cardinal Builders Inc .... E 614 237-1000
  Columbus (G-6739)
James F Seme .... G 440 759-6455
  Berea (G-1614)
Kitchen Works Inc .... G 440 353-0939
  North Ridgeville (G-15236)

CONTRACTORS: Kitchen Cabinet Installation

Old Mill Custom Cabinetry Co .... G 419 423-8897
  Findlay (G-9734)

CONTRACTORS: Lighting Syst

Pearlwind LLC .... G 216 591-9463
  Beachwood (G-1264)

CONTRACTORS: Lightweight Steel Framing Installation

J N Linrose Mfg LLC .... G 513 867-5500
  Hamilton (G-10574)

CONTRACTORS: Machine Rigging & Moving

Atlas Industrial Contrs LLC .... B 614 841-4500
  Columbus (G-6627)
Chagrin Vly Stl Erectors Inc .... F 440 975-1556
  Willoughby Hills (G-20468)

CONTRACTORS: Machinery Installation

Camton Mechanical Inc .... G 614 864-7620
  Columbus (G-6727)
De-Ko Inc .... G 440 951-2585
  Willoughby (G-20308)
Expert Crane Inc .... E 216 451-9900
  Cleveland (G-5209)
Hilo Tech Inc .... G 440 979-1155
  North Olmsted (G-15192)
Intertec Corporation .... B 419 537-9711
  Toledo (G-18350)
Molding Machine Services Inc .... G 330 461-2270
  Medina (G-13303)
Northwest Installations Inc .... E 419 423-5738
  Findlay (G-9732)

Spallinger Millwright Svc Co .... D 419 225-5830
  Lima (G-11942)

CONTRACTORS: Maintenance, Parking Facility Eqpt

Parking & Traffic Control SEC .... F 440 243-7565
  Cleveland (G-5851)

CONTRACTORS: Marble Installation, Interior

Cutting Edge Countertops Inc .... E 419 873-9500
  Perrysburg (G-15937)
Davies Since 1900 .... G 419 756-4212
  Mansfield (G-12432)
Distinctive Marble & Gran Inc .... F 614 760-0003
  Plain City (G-16187)

CONTRACTORS: Masonry & Stonework

Albert Freytag Inc .... E 419 628-2018
  Minster (G-14209)
North Hill Marble & Granite Co .... F 330 253-2179
  Akron (G-301)
Pioneer Cldding Glzing Systems .... E 216 816-4242
  Cleveland (G-5879)
Rmi Titanium Company LLC .... E 330 652-9952
  Niles (G-15028)

CONTRACTORS: Mechanical

Debra-Kuempel Inc .... D 513 271-6500
  Cincinnati (G-3579)
Edwards Electrical & Mech .... E 614 485-2003
  Columbus (G-6885)
Enerfab Inc .... B 513 641-0500
  Cincinnati (G-3640)
Greer & Whitehead Cnstr Inc .... E 513 202-1757
  Harrison (G-10644)
Jan Squires Inc .... G 440 988-7859
  Amherst (G-563)
Kirk Williams Company Inc .... D 614 875-9023
  Grove City (G-10440)
Schweizer Dipple Inc .... D 440 786-8090
  Cleveland (G-6034)
Sexton Industrial Inc .... C 513 530-5555
  West Chester (G-19898)
Temperature Controls Company .... F 330 773-6633
  Akron (G-398)
Tilton Corporation .... C 419 227-6421
  Lima (G-11952)

CONTRACTORS: Metal Ceiling Construction & Repair Work

Andy Russo Jr Inc .... F 440 585-1456
  Wickliffe (G-20198)

CONTRACTORS: Millwrights

D & G Welding Inc .... G 419 445-5751
  Archbold (G-643)
K F T Inc .... D 513 241-5910
  Cincinnati (G-3890)

CONTRACTORS: Nonresidential Building Design & Construction

McDannald Welding & Machining .... G 937 644-0300
  Marysville (G-12802)

CONTRACTORS: Oil & Gas Aerial Geophysical Exploration Svcs

Global Oil & Gas Services LLC .... G 330 807-1490
  Mc Donald (G-13200)

CONTRACTORS: Oil & Gas Building, Repairing & Dismantling Svc

Dow Cameron Oil & Gas LLC .... G 740 452-1568
  Zanesville (G-21129)
Dp2 Energy LLC .... G 330 376-5068
  Akron (G-146)
Elsaan Energy LLC .... G 740 294-9399
  Walhonding (G-19306)
Formation Cementing Inc .... G 740 453-6926
  Zanesville (G-21137)
Hill & Associates Inc .... G 740 685-5168
  Byesville (G-2386)
Interden Industries Inc .... G 419 368-9011
  Lakeville (G-11506)

Ralph Robinson Inc .... G 740 385-2747
  Logan (G-12042)

CONTRACTORS: Oil & Gas Field Fire Fighting Svcs

Cgh-Global Emerg Mngmt Strateg .... E 800 376-0655
  Cincinnati (G-3242)

CONTRACTORS: Oil & Gas Field Geological Exploration Svcs

Clarence Tussel Jr .... G 440 576-3415
  Jefferson (G-11228)
David R Hill Inc .... G 740 685-5168
  Byesville (G-2381)
New World Energy Resources .... B 740 344-4087
  Newark (G-14901)

CONTRACTORS: Oil & Gas Field Geophysical Exploration Svcs

Dlz Ohio Inc .... C 614 888-0040
  Columbus (G-6871)
Hocking Hills Energy & Well SE .... G 740 385-6690
  Logan (G-12026)

CONTRACTORS: Oil & Gas Field Tools Fishing Svcs

Lakeside Sport Shop Inc .... G 330 637-2862
  Cortland (G-7711)

CONTRACTORS: Oil & Gas Well Casing Cement Svcs

Purple Land Management LLC .... G 740 238-4259
  Saint Clairsville (G-16647)
Terra Star Inc .... E 405 200-1336
  Waynesburg (G-19566)

CONTRACTORS: Oil & Gas Well Drilling Svc

Anderson Energy Inc .... G 740 678-8608
  Fleming (G-9777)
Artex Oil Company .... E 740 373-3313
  Marietta (G-12605)
Bancequity Petroleum Corp .... G 330 468-5935
  Macedonia (G-12278)
Buckeye Oil Producing Co .... F 330 264-8847
  Wooster (G-20576)
Clarence Tussel Jr .... G 440 576-3415
  Jefferson (G-11228)
Columbus Oilfield Exploration .... G 614 895-9520
  Powell (G-16317)
Dnl Oil Corp .... G 740 342-4970
  New Lexington (G-14715)
Domestic Oil & Gas Co Inc .... G 440 232-3150
  Cleveland (G-5104)
Doris Kimble .... E 330 343-1226
  Dover (G-8817)
Dugan Drilling Incorporated .... G 740 668-3811
  Walhonding (G-19305)
Echo Drilling Inc .... G 740 254-4127
  Gnadenhutten (G-10278)
Eclipse Resources - Ohio LLC .... E 740 452-4503
  Zanesville (G-21132)
Frank Csapo .... G 330 435-4458
  Creston (G-7805)
Gills Petroleum LLC .... G 740 702-2600
  Chillicothe (G-3189)
H & D Drilling Co Inc .... G 740 745-2236
  Frazeysburg (G-9939)
Hocking Hills Energy & Well SE .... G 740 385-6690
  Logan (G-12026)
Interden Industries Inc .... G 419 368-9011
  Lakeville (G-11506)
J D Drilling Co .... E 740 949-2512
  Racine (G-16356)
James R Smail Inc .... G 330 264-7500
  Wooster (G-20610)
Kilbarger Construction Inc .... C 740 385-6019
  Logan (G-12030)
King Energy Inc .... G 330 297-5508
  Ravenna (G-16386)
Lee Oil & Gas Inc .... G 937 223-8891
  Oakwood (G-15463)
Maric Drilling Company Inc .... F 330 830-8178
  Winesburg (G-20532)
Moore Well Services Inc .... E 330 650-4443
  Mogadore (G-14244)

PRODUCT SECTION

Nomac Drilling LLC .... G 330 476-7040
  Carrollton (G-2926)
Nomac Drilling LLC .... F 724 324-2205
  Saint Clairsville (G-16641)
Ohio Valley Energy Systems .... G 330 799-2268
  Youngstown (G-20984)
Oogeep .... G 740 587-0410
  Granville (G-10335)
Osair Inc .... G 440 974-6500
  Mentor (G-13537)
P & S Energy Inc .... G 330 652-2525
  Mineral Ridge (G-14170)
PAC Drilling O & G LLC .... G 330 874-3781
  Bolivar (G-1921)
Parrot Energy Company .... G 330 637-0151
  Cortland (G-7714)
Paul A Grim Inc .... G 740 385-9637
  Logan (G-12040)
Petro Quest Inc .... G 740 593-3800
  Athens (G-844)
Ponderosa Consulting Services .... G 330 264-2298
  Wooster (G-20637)
Portage Resources Inc .... G 330 856-2622
  Warren (G-19432)
Professional Oilfield Services .... G 740 685-5168
  Byesville (G-2392)
Qes Pressure Control LLC .... E 740 489-5721
  Lore City (G-12139)
Rj Drilling Company Inc .... G 740 763-3991
  Nashport (G-14570)
Rockbottom Oil & Gas .... G 740 374-2478
  Marietta (G-12664)
Sabre Energy Corporation .... G 740 685-8266
  Lore City (G-12140)
Smith Smith & Deyarman .... G 330 866-5521
  Magnolia (G-12363)
Stratagraph Ne Inc .... E 740 373-3091
  Marietta (G-12677)
Summit Drilling Company Inc .... F 800 775-5537
  Akron (G-390)
Tiger Oil Inc .... G 614 837-5552
  Canal Winchester (G-2513)
Timco Inc .... F 740 685-2594
  Byesville (G-2393)
Transcontinental Oil & Gas .... G 330 995-0777
  Aurora (G-909)
U S Fuel Development Co .... G 614 486-0614
  Columbus (G-7553)
Victor McKenzie Drilling Co .... E 740 453-0834
  Zanesville (G-21187)
Warthman Drilling Inc .... G 740 746-9950
  Sugar Grove (G-17840)

CONTRACTORS: Oil & Gas Well Flow Rate Measurement Svcs

Fts International Inc .... A 330 754-2375
  East Canton (G-9040)

CONTRACTORS: Oil & Gas Well Foundation Grading Svcs

Ksn Clearing LLC .... F 304 269-3306
  Gallipolis (G-10170)

CONTRACTORS: Oil & Gas Well On-Site Foundation Building Svcs

Atlas Growth Eagle Ford LLC .... G 330 896-8510
  Uniontown (G-18911)
Bearcat Construction Inc .... G 513 314-0867
  Mason (G-12832)
Greer & Whitehead Cnstr Inc .... E 513 202-1757
  Harrison (G-10644)

CONTRACTORS: Oil & Gas Well Plugging & Abandoning Svcs

Omega Cementing Co .... G 330 695-7147
  Apple Creek (G-616)
Pluggers Inc .... G 330 383-7692
  Niles (G-15027)

CONTRACTORS: Oil & Gas Well Redrilling

Decker Drilling Inc .... E 740 749-3939
  Vincent (G-19213)

CONTRACTORS: Oil & Gas Wells Pumping Svcs

Ottawa Oil Co Inc .... F 419 425-3301
  Findlay (G-9737)
Performance Technologies LLC .... G 330 875-1216
  Louisville (G-12164)
Pettigrew Pumping Inc .... G 330 297-7900
  Ravenna (G-16396)
Stocker & Sitler Oil Company .... G 614 888-9588
  Columbus (G-7491)

CONTRACTORS: Oil & Gas Wells Svcs

A W Tipka Oil & Gas Inc .... G 330 364-4333
  Dover (G-8802)
Bakerwell Inc .... E 330 276-2161
  Killbuck (G-11448)
Hackworth Oil Field Electric .... G 330 345-6504
  Wooster (G-20603)
Harmon John .... G 740 934-2032
  Graysville (G-10341)
J Valtier Gas and Oil Co Inc .... G 740 342-2839
  Malta (G-12383)
Karlco Oilfield Services Inc .... F 440 576-3415
  Jefferson (G-11231)
Pyramid Treating Inc .... G 330 325-2811
  Atwater (G-863)
Renegade Well Services LLC .... G 330 488-6055
  Canton (G-2803)
Wrights Well Service .... G 740 380-9602
  Logan (G-12046)

CONTRACTORS: Oil Field Haulage Svcs

Fishburn Tank Truck Service .... D 419 253-6031
  Marengo (G-12591)

CONTRACTORS: Oil Field Mud Drilling Svcs

Kelchner Inc .... C 937 704-9890
  Springboro (G-17333)

CONTRACTORS: Oil Field Pipe Testing Svcs

Ream and Haager Laboratory .... F 330 343-3711
  Dover (G-8849)

CONTRACTORS: Oil Sampling Svcs

Bdi Inc .... C 216 642-9100
  Cleveland (G-4796)
Predict Inc .... F 216 642-3223
  Cleveland (G-5914)

CONTRACTORS: Oil/Gas Field Casing,Tube/Rod Running,Cut/Pull

Varco LP .... E 440 277-8696
  Lorain (G-12133)

CONTRACTORS: Oil/Gas Well Construction, Rpr/Dismantling Svcs

A1 Industrial Painting Inc .... G 330 750-9441
  Struthers (G-17811)
Acer Contracting LLC .... G 702 236-5917
  Columbus (G-6537)
Ajami Holdings Group LLC .... G 216 396-6089
  Richmond Heights (G-16500)
Barnes Services LLC .... G 440 319-2088
  Maple Heights (G-12565)
Boyce Ltd .... G 614 236-8901
  Columbus (G-6690)
Brightstar Propane & Fuels .... G 614 891-8395
  Westerville (G-19981)
Byrd Prcurement Specialist Inc .... G 419 936-0019
  Swanton (G-17908)
Carper Well Service Inc .... F 740 374-2567
  Marietta (G-12613)
Circleville Oil Co .... G 740 477-3341
  Circleville (G-4539)
Collier Well Eqp & Sup Inc .... F 330 345-3968
  Wooster (G-20580)
Elite Property Group LLC .... F 216 356-7469
  Elyria (G-9250)
Homestead Landscapers .... G 740 435-8480
  Cambridge (G-2443)
Ingle-Barr Inc .... C 740 702-6117
  Chillicothe (G-3195)
Kbc Services .... F 513 693-3743
  Loveland (G-12203)
MGM Construction Inc .... F 440 234-7660
  Berea (G-1617)
Naw Petroleum Service .... G 740 464-7988
  Chillicothe (G-3202)
P & M Enterprises Group Inc .... G 330 316-0387
  Canton (G-2777)
R Anthony Enterprises LLC .... F 419 341-0961
  Marion (G-12729)
Scassa Asphalt Inc .... F 330 830-2039
  Massillon (G-13046)
Siler Excavation Services .... E 513 400-8628
  Milford (G-14041)

CONTRACTORS: On-Site Welding

Accurate Machining & Welding .... G 937 584-4518
  Sabina (G-16615)
Bob Lanes Welding Inc .... F 740 373-3567
  Marietta (G-12609)
Burdens Machine & Welding .... E 740 345-9246
  Newark (G-14857)
C Stoneman Corporation .... G 440 942-3325
  Eastlake (G-9100)
D & M Welding & Radiator .... G 740 947-9032
  Waverly (G-19544)
Dennis Corso Co Inc .... G 330 673-2411
  Kent (G-11312)
DMC Welding Incorporated .... G 330 877-1935
  Hartville (G-10689)
Dover Fabrication and Burn Inc .... G 330 339-1057
  Dover (G-8820)
G & R Welding & Machining .... G 937 323-9353
  Springfield (G-17405)
Geyer Transport & Mfg .... F 740 382-9008
  Marion (G-12706)
Halls Welding & Supplies Inc .... G 330 385-9353
  East Liverpool (G-9058)
Holdsworth Industrial Fabg .... G 330 874-3945
  Bolivar (G-1916)
Jackson Machine & Fabrication .... G 740 682-3994
  Oak Hill (G-15452)
Kellys Welding & Fabricating .... G 440 593-6040
  Conneaut (G-7651)
Kent Swigart .... G 937 836-5292
  Englewood (G-9365)
Knowlton Machine Inc .... G 419 281-6802
  Ashland (G-719)
Lefeld Welding & Stl Sups Inc .... E 419 678-2397
  Coldwater (G-6416)
Leon Newswanger .... F 419 896-3336
  Shiloh (G-16996)
Lim Services LLC .... F 513 217-0801
  Middletown (G-13920)
M & M Certified Welding Inc .... F 330 467-1729
  Macedonia (G-12311)
M M I Services Inc .... F 440 259-2939
  Perry (G-15908)
Marsam Metalfab Inc .... E 330 405-1520
  Twinsburg (G-18811)
Massillon Machine & Die Inc .... G 330 833-8913
  Massillon (G-13020)
McDannald Welding & Machining .... G 937 644-0300
  Marysville (G-12802)
Mh & Son Machining & Wldg Co .... G 419 621-0690
  Sandusky (G-16829)
P & S Welding Co .... G 330 274-2850
  Mantua (G-12557)
Quality Fabricated Metals Inc .... E 330 332-7008
  Salem (G-16769)
Robs Welding Technologies Ltd .... G 937 890-4963
  Dayton (G-8483)
Select International Corp .... G 937 233-9191
  Dayton (G-8503)
Steve Vore Welding and Steel .... F 419 375-4087
  Fort Recovery (G-9827)
Warrior Technologies Inc .... G 937 438-0279
  Dayton (G-8584)
Weldments Inc .... F 937 235-9261
  Dayton (G-8588)

CONTRACTORS: Ornamental Metal Work

Custom Way Welding Inc .... F 937 845-9469
  New Carlisle (G-14665)
Fabrication Group LLC .... E 216 251-1125
  Cleveland (G-5213)
Friends Ornamental Iron Co .... G 216 431-6710
  Cleveland (G-5275)
Spradlin Bros Welding Co .... F 800 219-2182
  Springfield (G-17493)

Employee Codes: A=Over 500 employees, B=251-500
C=101-250, D=51-100, E=20-50, F=10-19, G=3-9

CONTRACTORS: Painting & Wall Covering

A & A Safety Inc .... F 937 567-9781
  Beavercreek (G-1348)
A & A Safety Inc .... E 513 943-6100
  Amelia (G-527)
National Electro-Coatings Inc .... D 216 898-0080
  Cleveland (G-5724)
Premier Coatings Ltd .... F 513 942-1070
  West Chester (G-19766)
Procoat Painting Inc .... G 513 735-2500
  Batavia (G-1179)

CONTRACTORS: Painting, Commercial

Napoleon Machine LLC .... E 419 591-7010
  Napoleon (G-14553)

CONTRACTORS: Painting, Commercial, Interior

Davies Since 1900 .... G 419 756-4212
  Mansfield (G-12432)

CONTRACTORS: Painting, Indl

A1 Industrial Painting Inc .... G 330 750-9441
  Struthers (G-17811)
Banks Manufacturing Company .... F 440 458-8661
  Grafton (G-10293)
Industrial Mill Maintenance .... E 330 746-1155
  Youngstown (G-20939)
Js Fabrications Inc .... G 419 333-0323
  Fremont (G-10031)
Kars Ohio LLC .... G 614 655-1099
  Pataskala (G-15834)
Semper Quality Industry Inc .... G 440 352-8111
  Mentor (G-13578)

CONTRACTORS: Painting, Residential

Lim Services LLC .... F 513 217-0801
  Middletown (G-13920)

CONTRACTORS: Parking Lot Maintenance

Action Blacktop Sealcoating & .... G 937 667-4769
  Tipp City (G-18097)
Baileys Asphalt Sealing .... F 740 453-9409
  South Zanesville (G-17301)
Image Pavement Maintenance .... E 937 833-9200
  Brookville (G-2172)

CONTRACTORS: Patio & Deck Construction & Repair

Americraft Stor Buildings Ltd .... G 330 877-6900
  Hartville (G-10684)
Better Living Sunrooms NW Ohio .... G 419 692-4526
  Delphos (G-8737)
Byrd Prcurement Specialist Inc .... G 419 936-0019
  Swanton (G-17908)
Patio Enclosures .... F 513 733-4646
  Cincinnati (G-4135)

CONTRACTORS: Petroleum Storage Tanks, Pumping & Draining

Envirnmntal Cmpliance Tech LLC .... G 216 634-0400
  North Royalton (G-15271)

CONTRACTORS: Pipe & Boiler Insulating

BT Investments II Inc .... G 937 434-4321
  Dayton (G-8066)

CONTRACTORS: Pipe Laying

Bob Lanes Welding Inc .... F 740 373-3567
  Marietta (G-12609)
Steelial Wldg Met Fbrction Inc .... E 740 669-5300
  Vinton (G-19216)

CONTRACTORS: Plumbing

Approved Plumbing Co .... F 216 663-5063
  Cleveland (G-4722)
Mansfield Plumbing Pdts LLC .... E 330 496-2301
  Big Prairie (G-1675)
Northeast Ohio Contractors LLC .... G 216 269-7881
  Cleveland (G-5775)
Personal Plumber Service Corp .... F 440 324-4321
  Elyria (G-9311)

Pioneer Pipe Inc .... A 740 376-2400
  Marietta (G-12653)

CONTRACTORS: Pollution Control Eqpt Installation

Corro-Tech Equipment Corp .... G 216 941-1552
  Cleveland (G-5031)
L Haberny Co Inc .... F 440 543-5999
  Chagrin Falls (G-3054)
McGill Airclean LLC .... D 614 829-1200
  Columbus (G-7163)

CONTRACTORS: Post Disaster Renovations

Complete Dry Flood .... G 513 200-9274
  Cincinnati (G-3539)

CONTRACTORS: Power Generating Eqpt Installation

Clopay Corporation .... C 800 282-2260
  Mason (G-12847)
John McHael Priester Assoc Inc .... G 513 761-8605
  Wyoming (G-20752)

CONTRACTORS: Prefabricated Window & Door Installation

General Awning Company Inc .... F 216 749-0110
  Cleveland (G-5305)
Midwest Curtainwalls Inc .... D 216 641-7900
  Cleveland (G-5680)
Mor-Lite Co Inc .... G 513 661-8587
  Cincinnati (G-4045)
Thiels Replacement Systems Inc .... D 419 289-6139
  Ashland (G-751)
Yoder Window & Siding Ltd .... F 330 695-6960
  Fredericksburg (G-9962)

CONTRACTORS: Process Piping

United Group Services Inc .... C 800 633-9690
  West Chester (G-19910)

CONTRACTORS: Pulpwood, Engaged In Cutting

Brown Forest Products .... G 937 544-1515
  Otway (G-15686)

CONTRACTORS: Refrigeration

Hattenbach Company .... D 216 881-5200
  Cleveland (G-5380)
Hattenbach Company .... E 330 744-2732
  Youngstown (G-20929)
Integrated Development & Mfg .... F 440 247-5100
  Chagrin Falls (G-3021)

CONTRACTORS: Rigging, Theatrical

Beck Studios Inc .... E 513 831-6650
  Milford (G-13997)

CONTRACTORS: Roof Repair

Boyce Ltd .... G 614 236-8901
  Columbus (G-6690)

CONTRACTORS: Roofing

Celcore Inc .... F 440 234-7888
  Cleveland (G-4897)
Four Js Bldg Components LLC .... F 740 886-6112
  Scottown (G-16881)
Home Sheet Metal & Roofing Co .... G 419 562-7806
  Bucyrus (G-2334)
Maines Brothers Tin Shop .... G 937 393-1633
  Hillsboro (G-10885)
MGM Construction Inc .... F 440 234-7660
  Berea (G-1617)
Nr Lee Restoration Ltd .... G 419 692-2233
  Delphos (G-8752)
Related Metals Inc .... G 330 799-4866
  Canfield (G-2543)
Simon Roofing and Shtmtl Corp .... C 330 629-7392
  Youngstown (G-21032)
Tremco Incorporated .... B 216 292-5000
  Beachwood (G-1283)

CONTRACTORS: Roustabout Svcs

R & B Enterprises USA Inc .... G 330 674-2227
  Millersburg (G-14121)
Ruscilli Real Estate Services .... F 614 923-6400
  Dublin (G-8976)

CONTRACTORS: Sandblasting Svc, Building Exteriors

Banks Manufacturing Company .... F 440 458-8661
  Grafton (G-10293)
Universal Fabg Cnstr Svcs Inc .... D 614 274-1128
  Columbus (G-7561)

CONTRACTORS: Screening, Window & Door

Screenmobile Inc .... G 614 868-8663
  Radnor (G-16358)

CONTRACTORS: Septic System

Accurate Mechanical Inc .... E 740 681-1332
  Lancaster (G-11538)
Mack Industries .... C 419 353-7081
  Bowling Green (G-1983)

CONTRACTORS: Sheet Metal Work, NEC

All-Type Welding & Fabrication .... E 440 439-3990
  Cleveland (G-4669)
Anchor Metal Processing Inc .... F 216 362-6463
  Cleveland (G-4707)
Anchor Metal Processing Inc .... E 216 362-1850
  Cleveland (G-4708)
Avon Lake Sheet Metal Co .... E 440 933-3505
  Avon Lake (G-980)
Budde Sheet Metal Works Inc .... E 937 224-0868
  Dayton (G-8068)
Cmt Machining & Fabg LLC .... F 937 652-3740
  Urbana (G-18983)
Dimensional Metals Inc .... D 740 927-3633
  Reynoldsburg (G-16435)
Ducts Inc .... E 216 391-2400
  Cleveland (G-5117)
Franck and Fric Incorporated .... D 216 524-4451
  Cleveland (G-5271)
Holgate Metal Fab Inc .... F 419 599-2000
  Napoleon (G-14543)
Jim Nier Construction Inc .... F 740 289-3925
  Piketon (G-16072)
Kettering Roofing & Shtmtl .... F 513 281-6413
  Cincinnati (G-3906)
Kirk & Blum Manufacturing Co .... C 513 458-2600
  Cincinnati (G-3912)
Martina Metal LLC .... E 614 291-9700
  Columbus (G-7155)
Metrodeck Inc .... F 513 541-4370
  Cincinnati (G-4018)
Ontario Mechanical LLC .... E 419 529-2578
  Ontario (G-15544)
Pcy Enterprises Inc .... E 513 241-5566
  Cincinnati (G-4143)
Seneca Sheet Metal Company .... F 419 447-8434
  Tiffin (G-18083)
Tendon Manufacturing Inc .... E 216 663-3200
  Cleveland (G-6159)
Tilton Corporation .... C 419 227-6421
  Lima (G-11952)

CONTRACTORS: Sheet metal Work, Architectural

Ameridian Specialty Services .... E 513 769-0150
  Cincinnati (G-3339)
Federal Iron Works Company .... E 330 482-5910
  Columbiana (G-6465)

CONTRACTORS: Siding

Cardinal Builders Inc .... E 614 237-1000
  Columbus (G-6739)
Champion Opco LLC .... B 513 327-7338
  Cincinnati (G-3463)
Color Brite Company Inc .... G 216 441-4117
  Cleveland (G-4998)
General Awning Company Inc .... F 216 749-0110
  Cleveland (G-5305)
Mor-Lite Co Inc .... G 513 661-8587
  Cincinnati (G-4045)
O A R Vinyl Windows & Siding .... G 440 636-5573
  Middlefield (G-13842)

PRODUCT SECTION

CONTROL EQPT: Electric

Waxco International Inc.................F....... 937 746-4845
  Miamisburg (G-13740)

CONTRACTORS: Single-Family Home Fire Damage Repair

Ohio Restoration Group LLC................G....... 330 568-5815
  Youngstown (G-20983)

CONTRACTORS: Single-family Home General Remodeling

C-Link Enterprises LLC...................F....... 937 222-2829
  Dayton (G-8071)
Cardinal Builders Inc....................E....... 614 237-1000
  Columbus (G-6739)
Fence One Inc............................F....... 216 441-2600
  Cleveland (G-5229)
Gillard Construction Inc.................F....... 740 376-9744
  Marietta (G-12627)
Henderson Builders Inc...................G....... 419 665-2684
  Gibsonburg (G-10248)
Ingle-Barr Inc...........................C....... 740 702-6117
  Chillicothe (G-3195)
Kitchen Works Inc........................G....... 440 353-0939
  North Ridgeville (G-15236)
Mikes Mill Shop Inc......................G....... 419 538-6091
  Ottawa (G-15659)
RE Connors Construction Ltd..............G....... 740 644-0261
  Thornville (G-18031)
Van Dyke Custom Iron Inc.................G....... 614 860-9300
  Columbus (G-7571)
Waxco International Inc..................F....... 937 746-4845
  Miamisburg (G-13740)

CONTRACTORS: Skylight Installation

Scs Construction Services Inc............E....... 513 929-0260
  Cincinnati (G-4311)

CONTRACTORS: Solar Energy Eqpt

Edison Solar Inc.........................F....... 419 499-0000
  Milan (G-13982)
Hunters Hightech Energy Systm............G....... 614 275-4777
  Columbus (G-7012)
Shark Solar LLC..........................G....... 216 630-7395
  Medina (G-13340)

CONTRACTORS: Sound Eqpt Installation

House of Hindenach.......................G....... 419 422-0392
  Findlay (G-9707)
Importers Direct LLC.....................E....... 330 436-3260
  Akron (G-214)
Tri-Tech Machining LLC...................G....... 513 575-3959
  Milford (G-14045)

CONTRACTORS: Specialized Public Building

Baker-Shindler Contracting Co............E....... 419 782-5080
  Defiance (G-8615)

CONTRACTORS: Storage Tank Erection, Metal

Columbiana Boiler Company LLC............E....... 330 482-3373
  Columbiana (G-6460)
FSRc Tanks Inc...........................E....... 234 221-2015
  Bolivar (G-1914)

CONTRACTORS: Store Fixture Installation

Couch Business Development Inc...........F....... 937 253-1099
  Dayton (G-8104)

CONTRACTORS: Structural Iron Work, Structural

Wernke Wldg & Stl Erection Co............F....... 513 353-4173
  North Bend (G-15058)
White Mule Company.......................E....... 740 382-9008
  Ontario (G-15550)

CONTRACTORS: Structural Steel Erection

Chagrin Vly Stl Erectors Inc.............F....... 440 975-1556
  Willoughby Hills (G-20468)
Concord Fabricators Inc..................E....... 614 875-2500
  Grove City (G-10421)
Evers Welding Co Inc.....................E....... 513 385-7352
  Cincinnati (G-3658)

Frederick Steel Company LLC..............D....... 513 821-6400
  Cincinnati (G-3712)
GL Nause Co Inc..........................E....... 513 722-9500
  Loveland (G-12192)
Henderson Fabricating Co Inc.............F....... 216 432-0404
  Cleveland (G-5391)
Marysville Steel Inc.....................E....... 937 642-5971
  Marysville (G-12801)
Mound Technologies Inc...................E....... 937 748-2937
  Springboro (G-17338)
Ontario Mechanical LLC...................E....... 419 529-2578
  Ontario (G-15544)
Pro-Fab Inc..............................E....... 330 644-0044
  Akron (G-332)
Rittman Inc..............................D....... 330 927-6855
  Rittman (G-16528)
Smith Brothers Erection Inc..............E....... 740 373-3575
  Marietta (G-12671)
Tri-Way Rebar Inc........................G....... 330 296-9662
  Ravenna (G-16415)

CONTRACTORS: Svc Station Eqpt Installation, Maint & Repair

Industrial Fiberglass Spc Inc............E....... 937 222-9000
  Dayton (G-8263)

CONTRACTORS: Svc Well Drilling Svcs

Bakerwell Service Rigs Inc...............F....... 330 276-2161
  Killbuck (G-11449)
G & H Drilling Inc.......................E....... 330 674-4868
  Millersburg (G-14083)
Geocore Drilling Inc.....................G....... 419 864-4011
  Cardington (G-2872)
Jackson Wells Services...................E....... 419 886-2017
  Bellville (G-1558)
Well Service Group Inc...................F....... 330 308-0880
  New Philadelphia (G-14808)

CONTRACTORS: Tile Installation, Ceramic

Prints & Paints Flr Cvg Co Inc...........E....... 419 462-5663
  Galion (G-10151)

CONTRACTORS: Trenching

Breaker Technology Inc...................E....... 440 248-7168
  Solon (G-17120)

CONTRACTORS: Tuck Pointing & Restoration

Nr Lee Restoration Ltd...................G....... 419 692-2233
  Delphos (G-8752)

CONTRACTORS: Underground Utilities

Great Lakes Crushing Ltd.................E....... 440 944-5500
  Wickliffe (G-20211)

CONTRACTORS: Ventilation & Duct Work

A A S Amels Sheet Meta L Inc.............E....... 330 793-9326
  Youngstown (G-20830)
Franck and Fric Incorporated.............D....... 216 524-4451
  Cleveland (G-5271)
Jacobs Mechanical Co.....................C....... 513 681-6800
  Cincinnati (G-3866)
Scharenberg Sheet Metal..................G....... 740 664-2431
  New Marshfield (G-14744)

CONTRACTORS: Warm Air Heating & Air Conditioning

Cincinnati Air Conditioning Co...........D....... 513 721-5622
  Cincinnati (G-3480)
Columbus Heating & Vent Co...............C....... 614 274-1177
  Columbus (G-6790)
Gundlach Sheet Metal Works Inc...........D....... 419 626-4525
  Sandusky (G-16814)
Hvac Inc.................................F....... 330 343-5511
  Dover (G-8830)
Kitts Heating & AC.......................G....... 330 755-9242
  Struthers (G-17818)
Langdon Inc..............................E....... 513 733-5955
  Cincinnati (G-3930)
Lowry Furnace Company Inc................G....... 330 745-4822
  Akron (G-260)
S L M Inc................................G....... 216 651-0666
  Cleveland (G-6022)

Shriner Sheet Metal Inc..................F....... 330 435-6735
  Creston (G-7809)
V M Systems Inc..........................D....... 419 535-1044
  Toledo (G-18587)
Wheeler Sheet Metal Inc..................G....... 419 668-0481
  Norwalk (G-15417)

CONTRACTORS: Water Well Drilling

Layne Heavy Civil Inc....................E....... 513 424-7287
  Middletown (G-13919)
Stoepfel Drilling Co.....................G....... 419 532-3307
  Ottawa (G-15667)

CONTRACTORS: Water Well Servicing

Warthman Drilling Inc....................G....... 740 746-9950
  Sugar Grove (G-17840)

CONTRACTORS: Waterproofing

Indoor Envmtl Specialists Inc............F....... 937 433-5202
  Dayton (G-8262)
Paul Peterson Company....................E....... 614 486-4375
  Columbus (G-7299)
Richtech Industries Inc..................G....... 440 937-4401
  Avon (G-964)

CONTRACTORS: Well Bailing, Cleaning, Swabbing & Treating Svc

Diesel Fltrtion Spcialists LLC...........G....... 740 698-0255
  New Marshfield (G-14743)
Troo Clean Enviromental LLC..............G....... 304 215-4501
  Saint Clairsville (G-16656)

CONTRACTORS: Well Casings Perforating Svcs

Appalachian Well Surveys Inc.............G....... 740 255-7652
  Cambridge (G-2425)

CONTRACTORS: Well Logging Svcs

Oaktree Wireline LLC.....................G....... 330 352-7250
  New Philadelphia (G-14791)

CONTRACTORS: Well Swabbing Svcs

Bill Hall Well Service...................G....... 330 695-4671
  Fredericksburg (G-9943)
Martz Well Service.......................G....... 330 323-7417
  Canton (G-2744)

CONTRACTORS: Windows & Doors

3-G Incorporated.........................G....... 513 921-4515
  Cincinnati (G-3269)
Bert Radebaugh...........................G....... 740 382-8134
  Marion (G-12695)
Traichal Construction Company............E....... 800 255-3667
  Niles (G-15037)

CONTRACTORS: Wood Floor Installation & Refinishing

Attractive Kitchens & Flrg LLC...........G....... 440 406-9299
  Elyria (G-9220)
Hoover & Wells Inc.......................C....... 419 691-9220
  Toledo (G-18335)

CONTRACTORS: Wrecking & Demolition

Allgeier & Son Inc.......................E....... 513 574-3735
  Cincinnati (G-3324)
Rnw Holdings Inc.........................E....... 330 792-0600
  Youngstown (G-21018)

CONTROL EQPT: Electric

Asco Valve Inc...........................F....... 216 360-0366
  Cleveland (G-4746)
Central Systems & Control................G....... 440 835-0015
  Cleveland (G-4901)
Cincinnati Ctrl Dynamics Inc.............G....... 513 242-7300
  Cincinnati (G-3489)
Controls Inc.............................E....... 330 239-4345
  Medina (G-13240)
Das Consulting Services Inc..............F....... 330 896-4064
  Canton (G-2650)
Davis Technologies Inc...................F....... 330 823-2544
  Alliance (G-464)

CONTROL EQPT: Electric

Lake Shore Electric Corp ....E..... 440 232-0200
  Bedford *(G-1422)*
Positive Safety Mfr Co ....F..... 440 951-2130
  Willoughby *(G-20407)*
R-K Electronics Inc ....E..... 513 204-6060
  Mason *(G-12929)*
Rockwell Automation Inc ....B..... 330 425-3211
  Twinsburg *(G-18848)*
Spang & Company ....E..... 440 350-6108
  Mentor *(G-13585)*
Superb Industries Inc ....D..... 330 852-0500
  Sugarcreek *(G-17870)*

CONTROL EQPT: Electric Buses & Locomotives

Precision Design Inc ....G..... 419 289-1553
  Ashland *(G-737)*

CONTROL EQPT: Noise

Acon Inc ....G..... 513 276-2111
  Tipp City *(G-18096)*
Bost & Filtrex Inc ....F..... 301 206-9466
  Columbus *(G-6689)*
Hueston Industries Inc ....G..... 937 264-8163
  Dayton *(G-8256)*
Noise Suppression Technologies ......F..... 614 275-1818
  Columbus *(G-7221)*
Tech Products Corporation ....E..... 937 438-1100
  Miamisburg *(G-13723)*

CONTROL PANELS: Electrical

Adgo Incorporated ....E..... 513 752-6880
  Cincinnati *(G-3239)*
Advanced Controls Inc ....E..... 440 354-5413
  Eastlake *(G-9097)*
Agent Technologies Inc ....G..... 513 942-9444
  West Chester *(G-19639)*
Altronic LLC ....C..... 330 545-9768
  Girard *(G-10252)*
Apex Circuits Inc ....G..... 513 942-4400
  West Chester *(G-19647)*
Auto-Tronic Control Co ....F..... 419 666-5100
  Northwood *(G-15333)*
Bentronix Corp ....G..... 440 632-0606
  Middlefield *(G-13780)*
City Machine Technologies Inc ....E..... 330 747-2639
  Youngstown *(G-20872)*
City Machine Technologies Inc ....G..... 330 747-2639
  Youngstown *(G-20873)*
Control Craft LLC ....F..... 513 674-0056
  Cincinnati *(G-3544)*
Control Interface Inc ....G..... 513 874-2062
  West Chester *(G-19683)*
Custom Craft Controls Inc ....F..... 330 630-9599
  Akron *(G-128)*
Cutler Richard DBA Ohio Contro ......G..... 440 892-1858
  Cleveland *(G-5050)*
DRDC Realty Inc ....G..... 419 478-7091
  Toledo *(G-18269)*
Dynamics Research & Dev ....F..... 419 478-7091
  Toledo *(G-18271)*
Electrical Control Systems ....G..... 937 859-7136
  Dayton *(G-8179)*
Electro Controls Inc ....E..... 866 497-1717
  Sidney *(G-17035)*
Emt Inc ....G..... 330 399-6939
  Warren *(G-19399)*
Epanel Plus Ltd ....F..... 513 772-0888
  Cincinnati *(G-3647)*
Etched Metal Company ....E..... 440 248-0240
  Solon *(G-17142)*
Industrial and Mar Eng Svc Co ....F..... 740 694-0791
  Fredericktown *(G-9971)*
Industrial Ctrl Dsign Mint Inc ....F..... 330 785-9840
  Tallmadge *(G-17987)*
Industrial Thermal Systems Inc ....F..... 513 561-2100
  Cincinnati *(G-3845)*
Innovative Control Systems ....G..... 513 894-3712
  Fairfield Township *(G-9582)*
Innovative Controls Corp ....D..... 419 691-6684
  Toledo *(G-18348)*
Instrmntation Ctrl Systems Inc ....E..... 513 662-2600
  Cincinnati *(G-3851)*
Koester Corporation ....D..... 419 599-0291
  Napoleon *(G-14548)*
Matrix Cable and Mould ....G..... 513 832-2577
  Cincinnati *(G-3987)*
Myers Controlled Power LLC ....C..... 330 834-3200
  North Canton *(G-15105)*

Otr Controls LLC ....G..... 513 621-2197
  Cincinnati *(G-4123)*
Panel Control Inc ....G..... 937 394-2201
  Anna *(G-591)*
Panel Master LLC ....E..... 440 355-4442
  Lagrange *(G-11491)*
Panel-Fab Inc ....D..... 513 771-1462
  Cincinnati *(G-4132)*
Panelmatic Inc ....E..... 513 829-3666
  Fairfield *(G-9544)*
Panelmatic Inc ....E..... 330 782-8007
  Youngstown *(G-20991)*
Panelmatic Cincinnati Inc ....E..... 513 829-1960
  Fairfield *(G-9545)*
Panelmatic Youngstown Inc ....E..... 330 782-8007
  Youngstown *(G-20992)*
Primex ....E..... 513 831-9959
  Milford *(G-14035)*
Scott Fetzer Company ....C..... 216 267-9000
  Cleveland *(G-6035)*
System Controls Inc ....G..... 216 351-9121
  Cleveland *(G-6139)*
Systems Specialty Ctrl Co Inc ....E..... 419 478-4156
  Toledo *(G-18540)*
Tcb Automation LLC ....E..... 330 556-6444
  Dover *(G-8860)*
Trucut Incorporated ....D..... 330 938-9806
  Sebring *(G-16896)*
United Rolls Inc ....D..... 330 456-2761
  Canton *(G-2850)*

CONTROLS & ACCESS: Indl, Electric

Avtron Holdings LLC ....B..... 216 642-1230
  Cleveland *(G-4779)*
Barry Brothers Electric ....G..... 614 299-8187
  Columbus *(G-6651)*
Corrotec Inc ....E..... 937 325-3585
  Springfield *(G-17379)*
Electrical Control Design Inc ....G..... 419 443-9290
  Perrysburg *(G-15943)*
Filnor Inc ....E..... 330 821-8731
  Alliance *(G-465)*
Filnor Inc ....G..... 330 829-3180
  Alliance *(G-466)*
Filnor Inc ....F..... 330 821-7667
  Alliance *(G-467)*
Fuse Chicken Llc ....G..... 330 338-7108
  Cuyahoga Falls *(G-7871)*
Miami Control Systems Inc ....G..... 937 698-5725
  West Milton *(G-19949)*
PMC Systems Limited ....E..... 330 538-2268
  North Jackson *(G-15153)*
Rockwell Automation Inc ....D..... 440 646-5000
  Cleveland *(G-5999)*
Tekworx LLC ....F..... 513 533-4777
  Blue Ash *(G-1858)*
Tri-Tech Research LLC ....F..... 440 946-6122
  Eastlake *(G-9136)*

CONTROLS & ACCESS: Motor

Eaton Corporation ....B..... 440 523-5000
  Cleveland *(G-5146)*
Eaton Corporation ....C..... 888 328-6677
  Cleveland *(G-5148)*
Eaton Corporation ....G..... 440 748-2236
  Grafton *(G-10299)*
Grill ....G..... 937 673-6768
  Eaton *(G-9150)*
James R Eaton ....G..... 937 435-7767
  Dayton *(G-8278)*
Parkside & Eaton Estate ....G..... 330 467-2995
  Northfield *(G-15321)*

CONTROLS: Access, Motor

Quality Controls Inc ....F..... 513 272-3900
  Cincinnati *(G-4225)*

CONTROLS: Adjustable Speed Drive

Axel Austin LLC ....G..... 440 237-1610
  North Royalton *(G-15261)*
Lincoln Electric Company ....C..... 216 524-8800
  Cleveland *(G-5576)*

CONTROLS: Air Flow, Refrigeration

Cool Times ....G..... 513 608-5201
  Cincinnati *(G-3547)*
Mestek Inc ....D..... 419 288-2703
  Holland *(G-10944)*

CONTROLS: Automatic Temperature

Acutemp Thermal Systems ....F..... 937 312-0114
  Moraine *(G-14329)*
Building Ctrl Integrators LLC ....E..... 614 334-3300
  Powell *(G-16310)*
Building Ctrl Integrators LLC ....G..... 513 247-6154
  Cincinnati *(G-3430)*
Building Ctrl Integrators LLC ....G..... 440 526-6660
  Brecksville *(G-2025)*
Building Ctrl Integrators LLC ....G..... 513 860-9600
  West Chester *(G-19836)*
Honeywell International Inc ....D..... 937 754-4134
  Fairborn *(G-9461)*
Ignio Systems LLC ....F..... 419 708-0503
  Toledo *(G-18340)*

CONTROLS: Crane & Hoist, Including Metal Mill

Konecranes Inc ....F..... 937 328-5123
  Columbus *(G-7099)*
Midwest Minicranes Inc ....G..... 330 332-3700
  Salem *(G-16761)*
Morris Material Handling Inc ....G..... 937 525-5520
  Springfield *(G-17452)*

CONTROLS: Electric Motor

Ignio Systems LLC ....F..... 419 708-0503
  Toledo *(G-18340)*
Toledo Electromotive Inc ....G..... 419 874-7751
  Perrysburg *(G-16019)*

CONTROLS: Environmental

Ademco Inc ....F..... 513 772-1851
  Blue Ash *(G-1721)*
Ademco Inc ....G..... 440 439-7002
  Bedford *(G-1379)*
Alan Manufacturing Inc ....E..... 330 262-1555
  Wooster *(G-20560)*
Babcock & Wilcox Company ....A..... 330 753-4511
  Barberton *(G-1059)*
Balta Technology Inc ....G..... 513 724-0247
  Batavia *(G-1126)*
Bry-Air Inc ....E..... 740 965-2974
  Sunbury *(G-17883)*
Channel Products Inc ....G..... 440 423-0113
  Solon *(G-17126)*
Cincinnati Air Conditioning Co ....D..... 513 721-5622
  Cincinnati *(G-3480)*
Data Analysis Technologies ....G..... 614 873-0710
  Plain City *(G-16186)*
Doan/Pyramid Solutions LLC ....F..... 216 587-9510
  Cleveland *(G-5102)*
Dyoung Enterprise Inc ....D..... 440 918-0505
  Willoughby *(G-20312)*
Follow River Designs LLC ....G..... 614 325-9954
  McConnelsville *(G-13204)*
Future Controls Corporation ....E..... 440 275-3191
  Austinburg *(G-922)*
Helm Instrument Company Inc ....E..... 419 893-4356
  Maumee *(G-13116)*
Honeywell International Inc ....A..... 937 484-2000
  Urbana *(G-18995)*
Hunter Defense Tech Inc ....E..... 216 438-6111
  Solon *(G-17164)*
Integrated Development & Mfg ....F..... 440 247-5100
  Chagrin Falls *(G-3021)*
Integrated Development & Mfg ....E..... 440 543-2423
  Chagrin Falls *(G-3053)*
Kanawha Scales & Systems Inc ......F..... 513 576-0700
  Milford *(G-14023)*
Karman Rubber Company ....E..... 330 864-2161
  Akron *(G-232)*
Midwest Energy Emissions Corp .....F..... 614 505-6115
  Lewis Center *(G-11768)*
Peco II Inc ....D..... 614 431-0694
  Columbus *(G-7305)*
Pepperl + Fuchs Inc ....G..... 330 425-3555
  Twinsburg *(G-18830)*
Pepperl + Fuchs Entps Inc ....G..... 330 425-3555
  Twinsburg *(G-18831)*
Prentke Romich Company ....G..... 330 262-1984
  Wooster *(G-20641)*
Schneder Elc Bldngs Amrcas Inc ....D..... 513 398-9800
  Lebanon *(G-11694)*
Skuttle Mfg Co ....F..... 740 373-9169
  Marietta *(G-12670)*
Tetra Tech Inc ....G..... 330 286-3683
  Canfield *(G-2549)*

PRODUCT SECTION

CONVEYOR SYSTEMS: Bulk Handling

Ventra Sandusky LLC .... C 419 627-3600
  Sandusky *(G-16861)*
Vortec Corporation .... E 513 891-7485
  Blue Ash *(G-1866)*

CONTROLS: Hydronic

Certified Labs & Service Inc .... G 419 289-7462
  Ashland *(G-691)*

CONTROLS: Numerical

GE Intelligent Platforms Inc .... G 937 459-5404
  Greenville *(G-10372)*

CONTROLS: Positioning, Electric

Valve Related Controls Inc .... F 513 677-8724
  Loveland *(G-12242)*

CONTROLS: Relay & Ind

Altronic LLC .... C 330 545-9768
  Girard *(G-10252)*
Amano Cincinnati Incorporated .... D 513 697-9000
  Loveland *(G-12176)*
Autoneum North America Inc .... B 419 693-0511
  Oregon *(G-15556)*
BV Thermal Systems LLC .... F 209 522-3701
  Willoughby *(G-20291)*
Cattron Holdings Inc .... E 234 806-0018
  Warren *(G-19381)*
Cattron North America Inc .... D 234 806-0018
  Warren *(G-19382)*
Chandler Systems Incorporated .... F 888 363-9434
  Ashland *(G-693)*
Channel Products Inc .... D 440 423-0113
  Solon *(G-17126)*
Clark Substations LLC .... E 330 452-5200
  Canton *(G-2628)*
Cleveland Hdwr & Forging Co .... E 216 641-5200
  Cleveland *(G-4962)*
Command Alkon Incorporated .... D 614 799-0600
  Dublin *(G-8901)*
Comtec Incorporated .... F 330 425-8102
  Twinsburg *(G-18756)*
Control Associates Inc .... G 440 708-1770
  Chagrin Falls *(G-3042)*
Creative Electronic Design .... G 937 256-5106
  Beavercreek *(G-1308)*
Curtiss-Wright Controls .... E 937 252-5601
  Fairborn *(G-9456)*
Delta Systems Inc .... C 330 626-2811
  Streetsboro *(G-17671)*
Dimcogray Corporation .... G 937 433-7600
  Centerville *(G-3001)*
Divelbiss Corporation .... E 800 245-2327
  Fredericktown *(G-9966)*
Eaton Corporation .... C 440 826-1115
  Cleveland *(G-5150)*
Electrocraft Ohio Inc .... C 740 441-6200
  Gallipolis *(G-10164)*
Electrodynamics Inc .... C 847 259-0740
  Cincinnati *(G-3247)*
Ellis & Watts Intl LLC .... G 513 752-9000
  Batavia *(G-1143)*
Energy Technologies Inc .... D 419 522-4444
  Mansfield *(G-12437)*
Fabriweld Corporation .... E 419 668-3358
  Norwalk *(G-15393)*
Future Controls Corporation .... E 440 275-3191
  Austinburg *(G-922)*
GE Aviation Systems LLC .... B 937 898-5881
  Vandalia *(G-19125)*
Harris Instrument Corporation .... G 740 369-3580
  Delaware *(G-8692)*
Helm Instrument Company Inc .... E 419 893-4356
  Maumee *(G-13116)*
Hite Parts Exchange Inc .... E 614 272-5115
  Columbus *(G-7003)*
Hurst Auto-Truck Electric .... G 216 961-1800
  Cleveland *(G-5426)*
Ideal Electric Power Co .... F 419 522-3611
  Mansfield *(G-12460)*
Independent Digital Consulting .... G 330 753-0777
  Norton *(G-15370)*
Innovative Controls Corp .... D 419 691-6684
  Toledo *(G-18348)*
Job One Control Services .... G 216 347-0133
  Cleveland *(G-5500)*
Kahle Technologies Inc .... E 419 523-3951
  Ottawa *(G-15657)*

Maags Automotive & Machine .... G 419 626-1539
  Sandusky *(G-16824)*
Ohio Magnetics Inc .... E 216 662-8484
  Maple Heights *(G-12575)*
Ohio Semitronics Inc .... D 614 777-1005
  Hilliard *(G-10847)*
Opw Engineered Systems Inc .... G 888 771-9438
  Lebanon *(G-11680)*
Panel Master LLC .... E 440 355-4442
  Lagrange *(G-11491)*
Peco II Inc .... D 614 431-0694
  Columbus *(G-7305)*
Peloton Manufacturing Corp .... F 440 205-1600
  Mentor *(G-13546)*
Pepperl + Fuchs Inc .... C 330 425-3555
  Twinsburg *(G-18830)*
Pepperl + Fuchs Entps Inc .... G 330 425-3555
  Twinsburg *(G-18831)*
Precision Switching Inc .... G 800 800-8143
  Mansfield *(G-12502)*
Prime Controls Inc .... G 937 435-8659
  Dayton *(G-8440)*
Primex .... E 513 831-9959
  Milford *(G-14035)*
Ramco Electric Motors Inc .... D 937 548-2525
  Greenville *(G-10389)*
Rbb Systems Inc .... D 330 263-4502
  Wooster *(G-20643)*
Regal Beloit America Inc .... C 608 364-8800
  Lima *(G-11928)*
Resinoid Engineering Corp .... E 740 928-2220
  Heath *(G-10730)*
Rex Automation Inc .... G 614 766-4672
  Columbus *(G-7391)*
Rockwell Automation Inc .... D 513 942-9828
  West Chester *(G-19785)*
Rockwell Automation Inc .... E 440 604-8410
  Cleveland *(G-5998)*
Rockwell Automation Inc .... E 513 943-1145
  Batavia *(G-1180)*
Rockwell Automation Inc .... D 614 776-3021
  Westerville *(G-20022)*
Rockwell Automation Inc .... F 440 646-7900
  Cleveland *(G-6000)*
Satco Inc .... G 330 630-8866
  Tallmadge *(G-18002)*
Schneider Electric Usa Inc .... D 513 755-5000
  West Chester *(G-19792)*
Sieb & Meyer America Inc .... F 513 563-0860
  Fairfield *(G-9563)*
Stock Fairfield Corporation .... C 440 543-6000
  Chagrin Falls *(G-3078)*
T D Group Holdings LLC .... G 216 706-2939
  Cleveland *(G-6144)*
Technology Products Inc .... G 937 652-3412
  Urbana *(G-19015)*
Toledo Transducers Inc .... C 419 724-4170
  Holland *(G-10962)*
Tramec Sloan LLC .... F 419 468-9122
  Galion *(G-10158)*
Transdigm Inc .... G 216 706-2939
  Cleveland *(G-6196)*
Transdigm Inc .... E 216 291-6025
  Cleveland *(G-6195)*
Tvh Parts Co .... F 877 755-7311
  West Chester *(G-19813)*
Z3 Controls LLC .... G 419 261-2654
  Walbridge *(G-19301)*

CONTROLS: Resistance Welder

Retek Inc .... G 440 937-6282
  Avon *(G-963)*

CONTROLS: Thermostats

Grid Sentry LLC .... F 937 490-2101
  Beavercreek *(G-1320)*
Thermtrol Corporation .... E 330 497-4148
  North Canton *(G-15125)*

CONTROLS: Thermostats, Built-in

Therm-O-Disc Incorporated .... A 419 525-8500
  Mansfield *(G-12530)*

CONTROLS: Voice

Innocomp .... G 440 248-5104
  Solon *(G-17170)*

CONVENIENCE STORES

Delmar E Hicks .... G 740 354-4333
  Portsmouth *(G-16281)*
Tbone Sales LLC .... E 330 897-6131
  Baltic *(G-1033)*

CONVENTION & TRADE SHOW SVCS

Columbus Bride .... D 614 888-4567
  Columbus *(G-6784)*

CONVERTERS: Data

Cisco Systems Inc .... A 937 427-4264
  Beavercreek *(G-1306)*
Electrodynamics Inc .... C 847 259-0740
  Cincinnati *(G-3247)*

CONVERTERS: Frequency

R E Smith Inc .... F 513 771-0645
  Cincinnati *(G-4243)*

CONVERTERS: Phase Or Rotary, Electrical

Electric Service Co Inc .... E 513 271-6387
  Cincinnati *(G-3632)*
Pace Converting Eqp Co Inc .... F 216 631-4555
  Cleveland *(G-5834)*

CONVERTERS: Power, AC to DC

10155 Broadview Business .... G 440 546-1901
  Broadview Heights *(G-2085)*
Core Technology Inc .... F 440 934-9935
  Avon *(G-946)*

CONVEYOR SYSTEMS

Hostar International Inc .... F 440 564-5362
  Newbury *(G-14957)*
Metal Equipment Co .... E 440 835-3100
  Westlake *(G-20130)*
Power-Pack Conveyor Company .... E 440 975-9955
  Willoughby *(G-20408)*

CONVEYOR SYSTEMS: Belt, General Indl Use

Almo Process Technology Inc .... G 513 402-2566
  West Chester *(G-19642)*
Blair Rubber Company .... D 330 769-5583
  Seville *(G-16912)*
Conveyor Solutions LLC .... G 513 367-4845
  Cleves *(G-6360)*
Manufacturers Equipment Co .... F 513 424-3573
  Middletown *(G-13924)*
Martin Rubber Company .... F 330 336-6604
  Seville *(G-16920)*
Mayfran International Inc .... C 440 461-4100
  Cleveland *(G-5637)*
Mfh Partners Inc .... F 440 461-4100
  Cleveland *(G-5664)*
Midwest Conveyor Products Inc .... E 419 281-1235
  Ashland *(G-725)*
Mine Equipment Services LLC .... E 740 936-5427
  Sunbury *(G-17891)*
New Transcon LLC .... E 440 255-7600
  Mentor *(G-13526)*
Nkc of America Inc .... G 937 642-4033
  Marysville *(G-12804)*
T J Davies Company Inc .... G 440 248-5510
  Solon *(G-17245)*

CONVEYOR SYSTEMS: Bucket Type

Fenner Dunlop Port Clinton Inc .... C 419 635-2191
  Port Clinton *(G-16247)*
Joy Global Underground Min LLC .... F 440 248-7970
  Cleveland *(G-5507)*

CONVEYOR SYSTEMS: Bulk Handling

Air Technical Industries Inc .... E 440 951-5191
  Mentor *(G-13378)*
Bulk Handling Equipment Co .... G 330 468-5703
  Northfield *(G-15314)*
Lewco Inc .... C 419 625-4014
  Sandusky *(G-16822)*
Webster Industries Inc .... B 419 447-8232
  Tiffin *(G-18092)*

CONVEYOR SYSTEMS: Pneumatic Tube

CONVEYOR SYSTEMS: Pneumatic Tube

American Solving Inc ....G...... 440 234-7373
   Brookpark *(G-2135)*
Fred D Pfening Company ....E...... 614 294-5361
   Columbus *(G-6938)*
Hamilton Air Products Inc ....G...... 513 874-4030
   Fairfield *(G-9503)*
Schenck Process LLC ....F...... 513 576-9200
   Chagrin Falls *(G-3074)*

CONVEYOR SYSTEMS: Robotic

Automation Systems Designs Inc ....E...... 937 387-0351
   Dayton *(G-8044)*
Grob Systems Inc ....C...... 419 358-9015
   Bluffton *(G-1889)*
Ins Robotics Inc ....G...... 888 293-5325
   Hilliard *(G-10830)*
Ka Wanner Inc ....E...... 740 251-4636
   Marion *(G-12714)*
Rhino Robotics Ltd ....G...... 513 353-9772
   Miamitown *(G-13750)*
Scott-Randall Systems Inc ....F...... 937 446-2293
   Sardinia *(G-16873)*

CONVEYORS & CONVEYING EQPT

Advanced Equipment Systems LLC ....G...... 216 289-6505
   Euclid *(G-9400)*
Alba Manufacturing Inc ....D...... 513 874-0551
   Fairfield *(G-9480)*
Allied Consolidated Industries ....C...... 330 744-0808
   Youngstown *(G-20841)*
Allied Fabricating & Wldg Co ....E...... 614 751-6664
   Columbus *(G-6572)*
Ambaflex Inc ....E...... 330 478-1858
   Canton *(G-2571)*
Ashtech Corporation 440 646-9911
   Gates Mills *(G-10207)*
Barth Industries Co LP ....D...... 216 267-0531
   Cleveland *(G-4793)*
Belden Brick Company ....E...... 330 852-2411
   Sugarcreek *(G-17842)*
Bobco Enterprises Inc ....F...... 419 867-3560
   Toledo *(G-18208)*
Bry-Air Inc ....E...... 740 965-2974
   Sunbury *(G-17883)*
Building & Conveyer Maint LLC ....G...... 303 882-0912
   Ravenna *(G-16371)*
C S Bell Co ....F...... 419 448-0791
   Tiffin *(G-18054)*
CA Litzler Co Inc ....E...... 216 267-8020
   Cleveland *(G-4859)*
Cincinnati Mine Machinery Co ....D...... 513 522-7777
   Cincinnati *(G-3501)*
Coating Systems Group Inc ....F...... 440 816-9306
   Middleburg Heights *(G-13763)*
Con-Belt Inc ....E...... 330 273-2003
   Valley City *(G-19032)*
Conveyor Metal Works Inc ....E...... 740 477-8700
   Frankfort *(G-9861)*
Conveyor Technologies Ltd ....G...... 513 248-0663
   Milford *(G-14005)*
Daifuku America Corporation ....C...... 614 863-1888
   Reynoldsburg *(G-16434)*
Decision Systems Inc ....E...... 330 456-7600
   Canton *(G-2653)*
Dillin Engineered Systems Corp ....E...... 419 666-6789
   Perrysburg *(G-15940)*
Dover Conveyor Inc ....E...... 740 922-9390
   Midvale *(G-13976)*
Duplex Mill & Manufacturing Co ....E...... 937 325-5555
   Springfield *(G-17392)*
E S Industries Inc ....G...... 419 643-2625
   Lima *(G-11859)*
Eagle Crusher Co Inc ....C...... 419 468-2288
   Galion *(G-10135)*
Esco Turbine Tech Cleveland ....F...... 440 953-0053
   Eastlake *(G-9110)*
Ethos Inc ....E...... 513 242-6336
   Cincinnati *(G-3655)*
Fabacraft Inc 513 677-0500
   Maineville *(G-12369)*
Fabco Inc 419 421-4740
   Findlay *(G-9682)*
Falcon Industries Inc 330 723-0099
   Medina *(G-13260)*
Federal Equipment Company ....D...... 513 621-5260
   Cincinnati *(G-3680)*
Feedall Inc ....F...... 440 942-8100
   Willoughby *(G-20321)*

Formtek Inc ....D...... 216 292-6300
   Cleveland *(G-5263)*
Formtek Inc ....D...... 216 292-4460
   Cleveland *(G-5264)*
Glassline Corporation ....C...... 419 666-9712
   Perrysburg *(G-15958)*
Grasan Equipment Company Inc ....D...... 419 526-4440
   Mansfield *(G-12452)*
Gray-Eering Ltd ....G...... 740 498-8816
   Tippecanoe *(G-18149)*
Harsco Corporation ....E...... 740 387-1150
   Marion *(G-12710)*
Hawthorne-Seving Inc ....E...... 419 643-5531
   Cridersville *(G-7810)*
Ibiza Holdings Inc ....E...... 513 701-7300
   Mason *(G-12888)*
Imperial Technologies Inc ....F...... 330 491-3200
   Canton *(G-2706)*
Innovative Controls Corp ....D...... 419 691-6684
   Toledo *(G-18348)*
Innovative Hdlg & Metalfab LLC ....E...... 419 882-7480
   Sylvania *(G-17945)*
Intelligrated Inc ....E...... 866 936-7300
   Mason *(G-12891)*
Intelligrated Inc ....E...... 513 874-0788
   West Chester *(G-19868)*
Intelligrated Headquarters LLC ....E...... 866 936-7300
   Mason *(G-12892)*
Intelligrated Products LLC ....E...... 740 490-0300
   London *(G-12062)*
Intelligrated Sub Holdings Inc ....E...... 513 701-7300
   Mason *(G-12893)*
Intelligrated Systems Inc ....A...... 866 936-7300
   Mason *(G-12894)*
Intelligrated Systems LLC ....A...... 513 701-7300
   Mason *(G-12895)*
Intelligrated Systems Ohio LLC ....A...... 513 701-7300
   Mason *(G-12896)*
Intelligrated Systems Ohio LLC 513 682-6600
   West Chester *(G-19869)*
Kleenline LLC ....G...... 800 259-5973
   Loveland *(G-12205)*
Kolinahr Systems Inc ....F...... 513 745-9401
   Blue Ash *(G-1801)*
Laser Automation Inc ....F...... 440 543-9291
   Chagrin Falls *(G-3055)*
Ledow Company Inc ....G...... 330 657-2837
   Peninsula *(G-15895)*
Logitech Inc ....E...... 614 871-2822
   Grove City *(G-10441)*
Martin Sprocket & Gear Inc ....D...... 419 485-5515
   Montpelier *(G-14312)*
Met Fab Fabrication and Mch ....E...... 513 724-3715
   Batavia *(G-1164)*
Midwest Industrial Rubber Inc ....F...... 614 876-3110
   Hilliard *(G-10841)*
Miller Products Inc ....E...... 330 308-5934
   New Philadelphia *(G-14786)*
Mountaineer Mining Corp ....G...... 740 418-1817
   Jackson *(G-11192)*
Mulhern Belting Inc ....E...... 201 337-5700
   Fairfield *(G-9533)*
Nesco Inc ....E...... 440 461-6000
   Cleveland *(G-5741)*
Ocs Intellitrak Inc ....F...... 513 742-5600
   Fairfield *(G-9539)*
Ohio Magnetics Inc ....E...... 216 662-8484
   Maple Heights *(G-12575)*
Opw Engineered Systems Inc ....G...... 888 771-9438
   Lebanon *(G-11680)*
P B Fabrication Mech Contr ....E...... 419 478-4869
   Toledo *(G-18454)*
Parker-Hannifin Corporation ....F...... 330 336-3511
   Wadsworth *(G-19262)*
Pfpc Enterprises Inc ....B...... 513 941-6200
   Cincinnati *(G-4155)*
Pneumatic Scale Corporation ....C...... 330 923-0491
   Cuyahoga Falls *(G-7905)*
Pomacon Inc 330 273-1576
   Brunswick *(G-2226)*
Precision Conveyor Technology ....F...... 440 352-3601
   Perry *(G-15911)*
Quickdraft Inc 330 477-4574
   Canton *(G-2799)*
Richmond Machine Co ....E...... 419 485-5740
   Montpelier *(G-14318)*
Robbins Company ....C...... 440 248-3303
   Solon *(G-17224)*
Rolcon Inc ....F...... 513 821-7259
   Cincinnati *(G-4281)*

Sandusky Fabricating & Sls Inc ....E...... 419 626-4465
   Sandusky *(G-16842)*
Siemens Industry Inc 440 526-2770
   Brecksville *(G-2058)*
Sparks Belting Company Inc ....G...... 216 398-7774
   Cleveland *(G-6083)*
Sst Conveyor Components Inc ....E...... 513 583-5500
   Loveland *(G-12234)*
Stacy Equipment Co 419 447-6903
   Tiffin *(G-18085)*
Stock Fairfield Corporation 440 543-6000
   Chagrin Falls *(G-3078)*
Sweet Manufacturing Company ....E...... 937 325-1511
   Springfield *(G-17501)*
Tkf Conveyor Systems LLC ....C...... 513 621-5260
   Cincinnati *(G-4423)*
Webb-Stiles Company ....D...... 330 225-7761
   Valley City *(G-19069)*

CONVEYORS: Overhead

Hoist Equipment Co Inc ....E...... 440 232-0300
   Bedford Heights *(G-1472)*
K F T Inc ....D...... 513 241-5910
   Cincinnati *(G-3890)*

COOKING & FOOD WARMING EQPT: Commercial

Cleveland Range LLC ....C...... 216 481-4900
   Cleveland *(G-4972)*
High-TEC Industrial Services ....C...... 937 667-1772
   Tipp City *(G-18115)*
Lima Sheet Metal Machine & Mfg ....E...... 419 229-1161
   Lima *(G-11893)*
Tema Systems Inc ....E...... 513 489-7811
   Cincinnati *(G-4413)*

COOKING & FOODWARMING EQPT: Coffee Brewing

American Craft Hardware LLC ....G...... 440 746-0098
   Cleveland *(G-4686)*

COOKING & FOODWARMING EQPT: Commercial

Frontline International Inc ....F...... 330 861-1100
   Cuyahoga Falls *(G-7870)*
Henny Penny Corporation ....A...... 937 456-8400
   Eaton *(G-9152)*
JE Grote Company Inc ....D...... 614 868-8414
   Columbus *(G-7065)*
Peerless Stove & Mfg Co Inc ....F...... 419 625-4514
   Sandusky *(G-16836)*

COOLING TOWERS: Metal

Airtech Mechanical Inc ....F...... 419 292-0074
   Toledo *(G-18161)*

COOPERAGE STOCK PRODUCTS

Brown-Forman Corporation ....E...... 740 384-3027
   Wellston *(G-19598)*

COPINGS: Concrete

Douglas S Kutz ....G...... 440 238-8426
   Strongsville *(G-17737)*

COPPER ORE MINING

Warrenton Copper LLC ....E...... 636 456-3488
   Cleveland *(G-6290)*

COPPER: Blocks

Bryan Metals LLC ....G...... 419 636-4571
   Bryan *(G-2272)*
Hildreth Mfg LLC ....E...... 740 375-5832
   Marion *(G-12712)*

COPPER: Rolling & Drawing

Chase Brass and Copper Co LLC ....B...... 419 485-3193
   Montpelier *(G-14304)*
T & D Fabricating Inc ....E...... 440 951-5646
   Eastlake *(G-9135)*

PRODUCT SECTION

COUPLINGS: Pipe

COPY MACHINES WHOLESALERS
D and D Business Equipment Inc...........G....... 440 777-5441
　Cleveland (G-5056)

CORRECTION FLUID
Milacron LLC ....E 513 487-5000
　Blue Ash (G-1822)

CORRESPONDENCE SCHOOLS
Zaner-Bloser Inc....................................D....... 614 486-0221
　Columbus (G-7624)
Zaner-Bloser Inc....................................G....... 608 441-5555
　Columbus (G-7625)

CORRUGATED PRDTS: Boxes, Partition, Display Items, Sheet/Pad
International Paper Company ....C....... 330 626-7300
　Streetsboro (G-17678)
Jamestown Cont Cleveland Inc ....B....... 216 831-3700
　Cleveland (G-5493)
Kennedy Mint Inc..................................D....... 440 572-3222
　Cleveland (G-5528)
Martin Paper Products Inc ....E 740 756-9271
　Carroll (G-2907)
Orbis Corporation ....D....... 262 560-5000
　Perrysburg (G-15994)
Prestige Display and Packg LLC ....F 513 285-1040
　Fairfield (G-9551)
Valley Containers Inc ....F 330 544-2244
　Mineral Ridge (G-14173)
Wood Specialists ....G....... 440 639-9797
　Mentor (G-13629)

CORRUGATING MACHINES
Rebiltco Inc...G....... 513 424-2024
　Middletown (G-13948)

COSMETIC PREPARATIONS
Argentifex LLC ....G....... 440 990-1108
　Ashtabula (G-761)
Art of Beauty Company Inc ....F 216 438-6363
　Bedford (G-1385)
B & P Company Inc ....G....... 937 298-0265
　Dayton (G-8048)
Bonne Bell LLC ....G....... 440 835-2440
　Westlake (G-20102)
Galleria Co ....G....... 513 983-1490
　Cincinnati (G-3722)
House of Delara Fragrances ....G....... 216 651-5803
　Cleveland (G-5420)
KAO USA Inc ....B....... 513 421-1400
　Cincinnati (G-3897)
Natural Essentials Inc ....E 330 562-8022
　Aurora (G-895)
Naturally Smart Labs LLC ....G....... 216 503-9398
　Independence (G-11143)
Oils By Nature Incorporated ....G....... 330 468-8897
　Hudson (G-11064)
Olay LLC ....G....... 787 535-2191
　Blue Ash (G-1826)
Universal Packg Systems Inc ....B....... 513 732-2000
　Batavia (G-1193)
Universal Packg Systems Inc ....B....... 513 674-9400
　Cincinnati (G-4452)
Universal Packg Systems Inc ....E 513 735-4777
　Batavia (G-1194)
Vein Center and Medspa ....G....... 330 629-9400
　Youngstown (G-21060)

COSMETICS & TOILETRIES
Abitec Corporation ....E 614 429-6464
　Columbus (G-6527)
Bath & Body Works LLC ....B....... 614 856-6000
　Reynoldsburg (G-16430)
Cameo Inc ....E 419 661-9611
　Perrysburg (G-15930)
Cashmere & Twig LLC ....F 740 404-8468
　New Concord (G-14684)
Colgate-Palmolive Company ....A....... 212 310-2000
　Cambridge (G-2432)
Columbus Kdc ....F 614 656-1130
　New Albany (G-14614)
Edgewell Per Care Brands LLC ....D....... 937 228-0105
　Dayton (G-8177)
Eileen Musser Shiela ....G....... 937 295-4212
　Fort Loramie (G-9796)

Erik V Lamb ....G....... 330 962-1540
　Copley (G-7684)
Estee Lauder Companies Inc ....G....... 310 994-9651
　Loveland (G-12186)
Facial Sensation Products ....G....... 937 293-2280
　Oakwood (G-15461)
Garden Art Innovations LLC ....G....... 330 697-0007
　Barberton (G-1072)
Gojo Industries Inc ....C....... 330 255-6000
　Akron (G-189)
Gojo Industries Inc ....C....... 330 255-6525
　Stow (G-17593)
Gojo Industries Inc ....C....... 330 922-4522
　Cuyahoga Falls (G-7874)
Honey Sweetie Acres LLC ....G....... 513 456-6090
　Goshen (G-10288)
KAO USA Inc ....G....... 513 421-1400
　Hamilton (G-10578)
LS Bombshelles ....G....... 513 254-6898
　Cincinnati (G-3953)
Luminex Home Decor ....A....... 513 563-1113
　Blue Ash (G-1812)
Meridian Industries Inc ....E 330 359-5809
　Beach City (G-1212)
Nehemiah Manufacturing Co LLC ....E 513 351-5700
　Cincinnati (G-4066)
Oil Bar LLC ....F 614 880-3950
　Columbus (G-6504)
Olfactorium Corp Inc ....G....... 216 663-8831
　Cleveland (G-5811)
Primal Life Organics LLC ....F 419 356-3843
　Akron (G-330)
Procter & Gamble Mfg Co ....C....... 419 226-5500
　Lima (G-11921)
Sally Beauty Supply LLC.......................G....... 330 823-7476
　Alliance (G-497)
Sentinel Consumer Products Inc ....D....... 801 825-5671
　Mentor (G-13579)
Sysco Guest Supply LLC ....F 440 960-2515
　Lorain (G-12128)
US Cotton LLC ....B....... 216 676-6400
　Cleveland (G-6244)
Woodbine Products Company ....G....... 330 725-0165
　Medina (G-13363)

COSMETICS WHOLESALERS
Safe 4 People Inc ....G....... 419 797-4087
　Port Clinton (G-16257)

COSTUME JEWELRY & NOVELTIES: Apparel, Exc Precious Metals
Gardella Jewelry LLC ....G....... 440 877-9261
　North Royalton (G-15273)
Prosperity On Payne Inc ....G....... 216 431-7677
　Cleveland (G-5930)

COSTUME JEWELRY STORES
Elizabeths Closet ....G....... 513 646-5025
　Maineville (G-12367)

COUNTER & SINK TOPS
3jd Inc ....F 513 324-9655
　Moraine (G-14327)
American Countertops Inc ....G....... 330 877-0343
　Hartville (G-10683)
Benchmark Cabinets ....E 740 694-1144
　Fredericktown (G-9963)
Brad Snoderly ....F 419 476-0184
　Toledo (G-18214)
C & D Counters ....G....... 740 259-5529
　Lucasville (G-12260)
Cameo Countertops Inc ....G....... 419 865-6371
　Holland (G-10918)
Counter- Advice Inc ....F 937 291-1600
　Franklin (G-9876)
Countertop Sales ....F 614 626-4476
　Columbus (G-6830)
Countertop Xpress ....G....... 440 358-0500
　Painesville (G-15727)
Crafted Surface and Stone LLC ....E 440 658-3799
　Bedford Heights (G-1467)
Formica Corporation ....E 513 786-3400
　Cincinnati (G-3705)
Gross & Sons Custom Millwork ....G....... 419 227-0214
　Lima (G-11871)
Imperial Countertops ....F 216 851-0888
　Cleveland (G-5443)

Kbi Group Inc ....G....... 614 873-5825
　Plain City (G-16198)
Kitchen & Bath Factory Inc ....G....... 440 510-8111
　Mentor (G-13490)
Miami Valley Counters & Spc ....G....... 937 865-0562
　Miamisburg (G-13690)
Sidney Stiers ....G....... 740 454-7368
　Zanesville (G-21179)
Skeeles Manufacturing Corp ....F 614 274-4700
　Columbus (G-7457)

COUNTERS & COUNTER DISPLAY CASES: Refrigerated
Florline Display Products Corp ....G....... 440 975-9449
　Willoughby (G-20324)

COUNTERS & COUNTING DEVICES
Aclara Technologies LLC ....C....... 440 528-7200
　Solon (G-17098)
Commercial Electric Pdts Corp ....E 216 241-2886
　Cleveland (G-5002)
Eaton Corporation ....B....... 440 523-5000
　Beachwood (G-1233)
Westmont Inc ....G....... 330 862-3080
　Minerva (G-14205)

COUNTERS OR COUNTER DISPLAY CASES, EXC WOOD
Formatech Inc ....E 330 273-2800
　Brunswick (G-2205)

COUNTERS OR COUNTER DISPLAY CASES, WOOD
Counter Concepts Inc ....F 330 848-4848
　Doylestown (G-8864)
Custom Counter Tops & Spc Co ....G....... 330 637-4856
　Cortland (G-7709)
Formatech Inc ....E 330 273-2800
　Brunswick (G-2205)
Kinsella Manufacturing Co Inc ....F 513 561-5285
　Cincinnati (G-3911)
Randys Countertops Inc ....F 740 881-5831
　Powell (G-16334)

COUNTING DEVICES: Controls, Revolution & Timing
Electrodynamics Inc ....C....... 847 259-0740
　Cincinnati (G-3247)

COUNTING DEVICES: Predetermining
Graco Ohio Inc ....D....... 330 494-1313
　North Canton (G-15088)

COUNTING DEVICES: Tachometer, Centrifugal
Lake Shore Cryotronics Inc ....C....... 614 891-2243
　Westerville (G-20003)

COUNTRY CLUBS
Cincinnati Marlins Inc ....G....... 513 761-3320
　Cincinnati (G-3500)

COUPLINGS, EXC PRESSURE & SOIL PIPE
Eaton Corporation ....C....... 440 826-1115
　Berea (G-1604)
Fulflo Specialties Company ....E 937 783-2411
　Blanchester (G-1703)

COUPLINGS: Hose & Tube, Hydraulic Or Pneumatic
Custom Cltch Jint Hydrlics Inc ....F 216 431-1630
　Cleveland (G-5046)
Dyna-Flex Inc ....F 440 946-9424
　Mentor (G-13434)

COUPLINGS: Pipe
B S F Inc ....F 937 890-6121
　Dayton (G-8050)
B S F Inc ....F 937 890-6121
　Tipp City (G-18100)

COUPLINGS: Shaft

COUPLINGS: Shaft
- B S F Inc .... F 937 890-6121
  Dayton (G-8050)
- B S F Inc .... F 937 890-6121
  Tipp City (G-18100)
- Bowes Manufacturing Inc .... F 216 378-2110
  Solon (G-17117)
- Climax Metal Products Company .... D 440 943-8898
  Mentor (G-13416)
- Eicom Corporation .... E 937 294-5692
  Moraine (G-14349)

COURIER SVCS: Air
- Garda CL Technical Svcs Inc .... E 937 294-4099
  Moraine (G-14355)

COURIER SVCS: Ground
- Asb Industries Inc .... E 330 753-8458
  Barberton (G-1054)
- Grand Aire Inc .... E 419 861-6700
  Swanton (G-17913)

COURTS OF LAW: County Government
- Belmont County of Ohio .... G 740 699-2140
  Saint Clairsville (G-16625)

COVERS & PADS Chair, Made From Purchased Materials
- Cvg National Seating Co LLC .... D 219 872-7295
  New Albany (G-14621)

COVERS: Automobile Seat
- Besi Manufacturing Inc .... E 513 874-0232
  West Chester (G-19659)
- Buckeye Seating LLC .... F 330 473-2379
  Millersburg (G-14071)
- Crown Dielectric Inds Inc .... C 614 224-5161
  Columbus (G-6839)
- Griffin Fisher Co Inc .... G 513 961-2110
  Cincinnati (G-3785)
- Rex Manufacturing Co .... E 419 224-5751
  Lima (G-11931)
- School Maintenance Supply Inc .... G 513 376-8670
  Blue Ash (G-1843)
- TS Trim Industries Inc .... B 740 593-5958
  Athens (G-852)

COVERS: Metal Plate
- Ayling and Reichert Co Consent .... E 419 898-2471
  Oak Harbor (G-15441)

COVERS: Slip Made Of Fabric, Plastic, Etc.
- Eastern Slipcover Company Inc .... G 440 951-2310
  Mentor (G-13436)

CRANE & AERIAL LIFT SVCS
- Ibi Brake Products Inc .... G 440 543-7962
  Chagrin Falls (G-3052)
- J & A Machine .... G 330 424-5235
  Lisbon (G-11970)
- Konecranes Inc .... F 440 461-8400
  Brecksville (G-2046)
- Pollock Research & Design Inc .... E 330 332-3300
  Salem (G-16767)

CRANES & MONORAIL SYSTEMS
- Emh Inc .... E 330 220-8600
  Valley City (G-19036)

CRANES: Indl Plant
- Delta Crane Systems Inc .... F 937 324-7425
  Springfield (G-17387)
- Demag Cranes & Components Corp ..... C 440 248-2400
  Solon (G-17132)
- Hiab USA Inc .... D 419 482-6000
  Perrysburg (G-15961)
- Kci Holding USA Inc .... C 937 525-5533
  Springfield (G-17430)
- Konecranes Inc .... E 937 328-5100
  Springfield (G-17433)
- Konecranes Inc .... B 937 525-5533
  Springfield (G-17434)
- Radocy Inc .... F 419 666-4400
  Rossford (G-16591)

CRANES: Indl Truck
- Hoist Equipment Co Inc .... E 440 232-0300
  Bedford Heights (G-1472)
- Skylift Inc .... G 440 960-2100
  Lorain (G-12122)
- Venturo Manufacturing Inc .... E 513 772-8448
  Cincinnati (G-4474)

CRANES: Locomotive
- Ers Industries Inc .... E 419 562-6010
  Bucyrus (G-2328)

CRANES: Overhead
- ACC Automation Co Inc .... E 330 928-3821
  Akron (G-26)
- Altec Industries Inc .... F 205 408-2341
  Cuyahoga Falls (G-7833)
- Mmh Americas Inc .... G 414 764-6200
  Springfield (G-17449)
- Mmh Holdings Inc .... G 937 525-5533
  Springfield (G-17450)
- Morgan Engineering Systems Inc .... E 330 821-4721
  Alliance (G-491)
- Ohio Mechanical Handling Co .... F 330 773-5165
  Akron (G-308)
- Rnm Holdings Inc .... F 614 444-5556
  Columbus (G-7397)

CRANKSHAFTS & CAMSHAFTS: Machining
- Atlas Industries Inc .... C 419 355-1000
  Fremont (G-9993)
- Atlas Industries Inc .... B 419 637-2117
  Tiffin (G-18046)
- Atlas Industries Inc .... D 419 447-4730
  Tiffin (G-18047)
- Custom Crankshaft Inc .... E 330 382-1200
  East Liverpool (G-9054)
- Ellwood Group Inc .... G 216 862-6341
  Cleveland (G-5169)
- Galactic Precision Mfg LLC .... G 937 540-1800
  Englewood (G-9360)
- Napoleon Machine LLC .... E 419 591-7010
  Napoleon (G-14553)
- Nippon Stl Smkin Crnkshaft LLC .... F 419 435-0411
  Fostoria (G-9852)
- Sst Precision Manufacturing .... F 513 583-5500
  Loveland (G-12235)

CRANKSHAFTS: Motor Vehicle
- Nippon Stl Smkin Crnkshaft LLC .... F 419 435-0411
  Fostoria (G-9852)

CREATIVE SVCS: Advertisers, Exc Writers
- Digital Color Intl LLC .... E 330 762-6959
  Akron (G-143)

CREMATORIES
- Martin M Hardin .... G 740 282-1234
  Steubenville (G-17543)

CROWNS & CLOSURES
- American Flange & Mfg Co Inc .... G 740 549-6073
  Delaware (G-8653)
- Boardman Molded Products Inc .... D 330 788-2400
  Youngstown (G-20854)
- Eisenhauer Mfg Co LLC .... D 419 238-0081
  Van Wert (G-19090)

CRUCIBLES
- General Electric Company .... G 740 928-7010
  Hebron (G-10745)

CRUDE PETROLEUM & NATURAL GAS PRODUCTION
- AB Resources LLC .... E 440 922-1098
  Brecksville (G-2017)
- Broad Street Financial Company .... G 614 228-0326
  Columbus (G-6704)
- Exco Resources LLC .... G 740 254-4061
  Tippecanoe (G-18147)
- Hunter Eureka Pipeline LLC .... G 740 374-2940
  Marietta (G-12633)
- John D Oil and Gas Company .... G 440 255-6325
  Mentor (G-13486)
- Kenoil Inc .... E 330 262-1144
  Wooster (G-20612)
- Lee A Williams Jr .... G 419 225-6751
  Lima (G-11886)
- Pin Oak Energy Partners LLC .... G 888 748-0763
  Akron (G-320)
- Stocker & Sitler Oil Company .... G 614 888-9588
  Columbus (G-7491)
- Viking Intl Resources Co Inc .... G 304 628-3878
  Marietta (G-12688)

CRUDE PETROLEUM & NATURAL GAS PRODUCTION
- A S Nf Producing Inc .... G 330 933-0622
  Hartville (G-10682)
- American Rodpump Ltd .... G 440 987-9457
  Dublin (G-8879)
- Blaze Oil & Gas Inc .... G 330 345-6700
  Wooster (G-20572)
- Brendel Producing Company .... G 330 854-4151
  Canton (G-2598)
- Buckeye Energy Resources Inc .... G 740 452-9506
  Zanesville (G-21113)
- Cac Energy Ltd .... G 937 867-5593
  Dayton (G-8072)
- City of Lancaster .... E 740 687-6670
  Lancaster (G-11554)
- Columbia Gas Meter Shop .... F 614 460-5519
  Columbus (G-6782)
- Equity Oil & Gas Funds Inc .... G 234 231-1004
  Stow (G-17582)
- Everflow Eastern Partners LP .... E 330 533-2692
  Canfield (G-2528)
- General Electric Company .... F 330 425-3755
  Twinsburg (G-18782)
- Hanini Seven Oil .... G 216 857-0172
  Cleveland (G-5370)
- James R Bernhardt Producing .... G 330 345-5306
  Wooster (G-20609)
- Killbuck Creek Oil Co .... G 330 601-0921
  Wooster (G-20614)
- Lagc Ltd .... G 419 886-2141
  Fredericktown (G-9972)
- M3 Midstream LLC .... D 740 945-1170
  Scio (G-16878)
- Mason Producing Inc .... G 740 913-0686
  Galena (G-10115)
- MRC Global (us) Inc .... F 614 475-4033
  Gahanna (G-10092)
- P & S Energy Inc .... G 330 652-2525
  Mineral Ridge (G-14170)
- Purvi Oil Inc .... G 419 207-8234
  Ashland (G-739)
- R D Holder Oil Co Inc .... G 740 522-3136
  Heath (G-10728)
- Sheridan One Stop Carryout .... G 740 687-1300
  Lancaster (G-11607)
- Triad Hunter Inc .... G 740 374-2940
  Marietta (G-12685)
- U S Fuel Development Co .... G 614 486-0614
  Columbus (G-7553)
- Ultra-Met Company .... G 937 653-7133
  Urbana (G-19018)
- Utica E Ohio Midstream .... G 330 679-2295
  Salineville (G-16790)
- Utica East Ohio Midstream LLC .... G 740 945-2226
  Scio (G-16880)
- Valley Petroleum Inc .... G 740 668-4901
  Utica (G-19029)
- Vesco Oil Corporation .... G 419 335-8871
  Wauseon (G-19536)

CRUDE PETROLEUM PRODUCTION
- A P Production & Service .... G 740 745-5317
  Utica (G-19023)
- Alliance Petroleum Corporation .... D 330 493-0440
  Canton (G-2569)
- Bakerwell Inc .... E 330 276-2161
  Killbuck (G-11448)
- Belden & Blake Corporation .... E 330 602-5551
  Dover (G-8808)
- Beucler Brothers Inc .... G 330 735-2267
  Dellroy (G-8733)
- BT Energy Corporation .... G 740 373-6134
  Fleming (G-9779)

Buckeye Oil Producing Co .... F 330 264-8847
  Wooster (G-20576)
Cameron Drilling Co Inc .... F 740 453-3300
  Zanesville (G-21114)
Carlton Oil Corp .... G 740 473-2629
  Newport (G-14983)
Carol Mickley .... G 740 599-7870
  Danville (G-7960)
Cgas Exploration Inc .... G 614 436-4631
  Worthington (G-20679)
Cgas Inc .... G 614 975-4697
  Worthington (G-20680)
Chevron Ae Resources LLC .... E 330 654-4343
  Deerfield (G-8607)
Columbia Energy Group .... A 614 460-4683
  Columbus (G-6781)
Crude Oil Company .... G 740 452-3335
  Zanesville (G-21125)
David A Waldron & Associates .... G 330 264-7275
  Wooster (G-20583)
Derrick Petroleum Inc .... G 740 668-5711
  Bladensburg (G-1696)
Dome Drilling Co .... G 440 892-9434
  Westlake (G-20109)
Dome Drilling Co .... G 330 262-5113
  Wooster (G-20585)
Dp Operating Company Inc .... G 330 938-2172
  Beloit (G-1569)
Elkhead Gas & Oil Co .... G 740 763-3966
  Newark (G-14870)
Excalibur Exploration Inc .... G 330 966-7003
  Greentown (G-10358)
Franklin Gas & Oil Company LLC ...... G 330 264-8739
  Wooster (G-20593)
Geopetro LLC .... G 614 885-9350
  Worthington (G-20686)
Green Energy Inc .... G 330 262-5112
  Wooster (G-20599)
Gulfport Energy Corporation .... E 740 251-0407
  Saint Clairsville (G-16632)
H & S Drilling Co Inc .... G 740 828-2411
  Frazeysburg (G-9940)
H I Smith Oil & Gas Inc .... G 330 279-2361
  Holmesville (G-10975)
Hopco Resources Inc .... G 614 882-8533
  Columbus (G-7008)
Jerry Moore Inc .... G 330 877-1155
  Hartville (G-10697)
Kilbarger Investments Inc .... G 740 385-6019
  Logan (G-12031)
King Drilling Co .... G 330 769-3434
  Seville (G-16919)
Koch Knight LLC .... D 330 488-1651
  East Canton (G-9041)
Konoil Inc .... G 330 499-9811
  Canton (G-2729)
Lake Region Oil Inc .... G 330 828-8420
  Dalton (G-7946)
Marietta Resources Corporation .... F 740 373-6305
  Marietta (G-12643)
MFC Drilling Inc .... F 740 622-5600
  Coshocton (G-7740)
Midland Oil Co .... G 740 787-2557
  Brownsville (G-2184)
Northwood Energy Corporation .... E 614 457-1024
  Columbus (G-7230)
Oil & Go LLC .... G 330 854-6345
  Canal Fulton (G-2488)
Penick Gas & Oil .... G 740 323-3040
  Newark (G-14909)
Petro Evaluation Services Inc .... G 330 264-4454
  Wooster (G-20636)
Profit Energy Company Inc .... G 740 472-1018
  Jerusalem (G-11251)
R C Poling Company Inc .... G 740 939-0023
  Junction City (G-11275)
Robert Barr .... F 740 826-7325
  New Concord (G-14686)
Rodco Petroleum Inc .... G 330 477-9823
  Canton (G-2810)
Saint Croix Ltd .... G 330 666-1544
  Akron (G-371)
Speedway LLC .... F 330 874-4616
  Bolivar (G-1928)
Speedway LLC .... G 440 943-0044
  Wickliffe (G-20231)
Speedway LLC .... G 937 653-6840
  Urbana (G-19013)
Speedway LLC .... F 614 418-9325
  Columbus (G-7475)
Speedway LLC .... F 937 390-6651
  Springfield (G-17492)
Speedway LLC .... F 614 861-6397
  Reynoldsburg (G-16454)
Speedway LLC .... G 330 339-7770
  New Philadelphia (G-14800)
Speedway LLC .... F 937 372-7129
  Wilberforce (G-20237)
Speedway LLC .... F 513 683-2034
  Cincinnati (G-4358)
Speedway LLC .... F 330 468-3320
  Macedonia (G-12328)
Speedway LLC .... G 330 343-9469
  Dover (G-8857)
Speedway LLC .... F 419 468-9773
  Galion (G-10156)
Speedway LLC .... F 440 988-8014
  Amherst (G-575)
Standard Energy Company .... G 614 885-1901
  Columbus (G-7484)
Stonebridge Operating Co LLC .... G 740 373-6134
  Fleming (G-9781)
Summit Petroleum Inc .... G 330 487-5494
  Twinsburg (G-18862)
T JS Oil & Gas Inc .... G 740 623-0192
  Coshocton (G-7754)
Tatum Petroleum Corporation .... G 740 819-6810
  Worthington (G-20704)
Triad Hunter LLC .... F 740 374-2940
  Marietta (G-12684)
W H Patten Drilling Co Inc .... G 330 674-3046
  Millersburg (G-14144)
W P Brown Enterprises Inc .... G 740 685-2594
  Byesville (G-2396)
William S Miller Inc .... G 330 223-1794
  Kensington (G-11287)
Xto Energy Inc .... D 740 671-9901
  Bellaire (G-1489)

CRYOGENIC COOLING DEVICES: Infrared Detectors, Masers

Advanced Cryogenic Entps LLC .... F 330 922-0750
  Akron (G-31)
Drivetrain USA Inc .... F 614 733-0940
  Plain City (G-16189)
Lake Shore Cryotronics Inc .... C 614 891-2243
  Westerville (G-20003)
Philips Medical Systems Mr .... C 440 483-2499
  Highland Heights (G-10798)

CRYSTALS

Saint-Gobain Ceramics Plas Inc .... A 330 673-5860
  Stow (G-17624)

CULTURE MEDIA

Sneaky Pete Band .... G 419 933-6251
  Willard (G-20245)
Star Spangled Spectacular Inc .... G 419 879-3502
  Lima (G-11944)

CULVERTS: Metal Plate

Contech Engnered Solutions LLC ...... F 513 425-5337
  Middletown (G-13897)

CULVERTS: Sheet Metal

Contech Engnered Solutions Inc .... F 513 645-7000
  West Chester (G-19680)
Contech Engnered Solutions LLC ...... D 513 645-7000
  Middletown (G-13896)
Discount Drainage Supplies LLC .... G 513 563-8616
  Cincinnati (G-3590)
Edwards Sheet Metal Works Inc .... F 740 694-0010
  Fredericktown (G-9967)

CUPS: Paper, Made From Purchased Materials

American Greetings Corporation .... A 216 252-7300
  Cleveland (G-4688)
Graphic Packaging Intl LLC .... B 419 673-0711
  Kenton (G-11407)
Ricking Paper and Specialty Co .... E 513 825-3551
  Cincinnati (G-4269)
Superior Cup Inc .... E 330 393-6187
  Warren (G-19445)

CUPS: Plastic Exc Polystyrene Foam

Anchor Hocking LLC .... A 740 681-6478
  Lancaster (G-11541)
Anchor Hocking LLC .... G 740 687-2500
  Lancaster (G-11542)
Ghp II LLC .... C 740 687-2500
  Lancaster (G-11575)

CURBING: Granite Or Stone

Distinctive Marble & Gran Inc .... F 614 760-0003
  Plain City (G-16187)
Granex Industries Inc .... F 440 248-4915
  Solon (G-17152)

CURTAIN & DRAPERY FIXTURES: Poles, Rods & Rollers

Astra Products of Ohio Ltd .... C 330 296-0112
  Ravenna (G-16367)
Desinger Window Treatment Inc .... G 419 822-4967
  Delta (G-8768)
Gannons Discount Blinds .... G 216 398-2761
  Cleveland (G-5289)
Hang-UPS Instllation Group Inc .... F 614 239-7004
  Columbus (G-6978)
Lumenomics Inc .... E 614 798-3500
  Lewis Center (G-11766)

CURTAIN WALLS: Building, Steel

Scs Construction Services Inc .... E 513 929-0260
  Cincinnati (G-4311)

CURTAINS: Shower

Seven Mile Creek Corporation .... F 937 456-3320
  Eaton (G-9165)

CURTAINS: Window, From Purchased Materials

Anthony Decorative Fabrics and .... G 937 299-4637
  Moraine (G-14331)
Style-Line Incorporated .... E 614 291-0600
  Columbus (G-7497)

CUSHIONS & PILLOWS

Easy Way Leisure Corporation .... E 513 731-5640
  Cincinnati (G-3627)
Greendale Home Fashions LLC .... D 859 916-5475
  Cincinnati (G-3782)
Innocor Foam Tech - Acp Inc .... F 419 647-4172
  Spencerville (G-17309)

CUSHIONS & PILLOWS: Bed, From Purchased Materials

Brentwood Originals Inc .... B 330 793-2255
  Youngstown (G-20856)
Down-Lite International Inc .... C 513 229-3696
  Mason (G-12858)
Downhome Inc .... E 513 921-3373
  Cincinnati (G-3607)

CUSHIONS: Carpet & Rug, Foamed Plastics

Johnsonite Inc .... B 440 632-3441
  Middlefield (G-13811)
Scottdel Cushion LLC .... E 419 825-0432
  Swanton (G-17921)
Solo Products Inc .... F 513 321-7884
  Cincinnati (G-4352)

CUSHIONS: Textile, Exc Spring & Carpet

Columbus Canvas Products Inc .... F 614 375-1397
  Columbus (G-6785)
Luxaire Cushion Co .... F 330 872-0995
  Newton Falls (G-14989)
Polka DOT Pin Cushion Inc .... G 330 659-0233
  Richfield (G-16481)
Queen City Carpets LLC .... F 513 823-8238
  Cincinnati (G-4235)

CUSTOM COMPOUNDING OF RUBBER MATERIALS

Killian Latex Inc .... F 330 644-6746
  Akron (G-236)

Employee Codes: A=Over 500 employees, B=251-500
C=101-250, D=51-100, E=20-50, F=10-19, G=3-9

CUSTOM COMPOUNDING OF RUBBER MATERIALS

Kiltex Corporation .... E 330 644-6746
   Akron *(G-237)*
Maine Rubber Preforms LLC .... G 216 210-2094
   Middlefield *(G-13815)*
Polymerics Inc .... E 330 434-6665
   Cuyahoga Falls *(G-7906)*
Prcc Holdings Inc .... C 330 798-4790
   Copley *(G-7691)*
Preferred Compounding Corp .... C 330 798-4790
   Copley *(G-7692)*
Wayne County Rubber Inc .... E 330 264-5553
   Wooster *(G-20664)*

CUSTOMIZING SVCS

Architectural Art Glass Studio .... G 513 731-7336
   Cincinnati *(G-3355)*
Handcrafted Jewelry Inc .... G 330 650-9011
   Hudson *(G-11051)*

CUT STONE & STONE PRODUCTS

Agean Marble Manufacturing .... F 513 874-1475
   West Chester *(G-19829)*
As America Inc .... E 419 522-4211
   Mansfield *(G-12408)*
Bell Vault & Monument Works .... E 937 866-2444
   Miamisburg *(G-13643)*
Bella Stone Cincinnati .... G 513 772-3552
   Cincinnati *(G-3387)*
Brower Products Inc .... D 937 563-1111
   Cincinnati *(G-3426)*
Cascade Cut Stone .... E 419 422-4341
   Findlay *(G-9664)*
Castelli Marble Inc .... G 216 361-2410
   Cleveland *(G-4890)*
Classic Stone Company Inc .... F 614 833-3946
   Columbus *(G-6770)*
Creative Design Marble Inc .... G 937 434-8892
   Dayton *(G-8110)*
Cumberland Limestone LLC .... F 740 638-3942
   Cumberland *(G-7823)*
Drake Monument Company .... G 937 399-7941
   Springfield *(G-17391)*
Dutch Quality Stone Inc .... E 877 359-7866
   Mount Eaton *(G-14419)*
Etched In Stone .... G 614 302-8924
   Sugar Grove *(G-17838)*
Jack Huffman .... G 740 384-5178
   Wellston *(G-19604)*
Lang Stone Company Inc .... D 614 235-4099
   Columbus *(G-7114)*
Lima Millwork Inc .... E 419 331-3303
   Elida *(G-9195)*
Marble Works .... G 216 496-7745
   Cleveland *(G-5615)*
Marsh Industries Inc .... E 330 308-8667
   New Philadelphia *(G-14784)*
Maumee Valley Memorials Inc .... F 419 878-9030
   Waterville *(G-19501)*
Medina Supply Company .... E 330 723-3681
   Medina *(G-13298)*
Melvin Stone Co LLC .... G 513 771-0820
   Cincinnati *(G-4004)*
National Lime and Stone Co .... D 419 562-0771
   Bucyrus *(G-2339)*
National Lime and Stone Co .... C 419 396-7671
   Carey *(G-2884)*
North Hill Marble & Granite Co .... F 330 253-2179
   Akron *(G-301)*
OBrien Cut Stone Company .... E 216 663-7800
   Cleveland *(G-5796)*
OBrien Cut Stone Company .... E 216 663-7800
   Cleveland *(G-5797)*
Ohio Beauty Inc .... G 330 644-2241
   Akron *(G-305)*
Ohio Centech .... G 513 477-8779
   Cincinnati *(G-4100)*
Pavestone LLC .... D 513 474-3783
   Cincinnati *(G-4142)*
Riceland Cabinet Inc .... D 330 601-1071
   Wooster *(G-20644)*
Sims-Lohman Inc .... E 440 799-8285
   Brooklyn Heights *(G-2131)*
Studio Vertu Inc .... E 513 241-9038
   Cincinnati *(G-4387)*
Transtar Holding Company .... G 800 359-3339
   Walton Hills *(G-19215)*
Western Ohio Cut Stone Ltd .... E 937 492-4722
   Sidney *(G-17085)*

CUTLERY

Air Technical Industries Inc .... E 440 951-5191
   Mentor *(G-13378)*
American Punch Co Inc .... E 216 731-4501
   Euclid *(G-9403)*
Dan Wilzynski .... G 800 531-3343
   Columbus *(G-6848)*
Fred Marvin and Associates Inc .... G 330 784-9211
   Stow *(G-17590)*
General Cutlery Inc .... E 419 332-2316
   Fremont *(G-10023)*
Libbey Glass Inc .... A 419 729-7272
   Toledo *(G-18383)*
Npk Construction Equipment Inc .... D 440 232-7900
   Bedford *(G-1432)*

CUTOUTS: Cardboard, Die-Cut, Made From Purchased Materials

Alliance Indus Masking Inc .... G 937 681-5569
   Dayton *(G-8018)*

CUTOUTS: Distribution

International Bus Mchs Corp .... B 513 826-1001
   Cincinnati *(G-3857)*

CUTTING EQPT: Glass Cutters

Crystal Carvers Inc .... G 800 365-9782
   Powell *(G-16319)*
Glass Medic Inc .... G 800 356-4009
   Westerville *(G-19994)*

CUTTING SVC: Paper, Exc Die-Cut

Customformed Products Inc .... F 937 388-0480
   Miamisburg *(G-13653)*
D and D Business Equipment Inc .... G 440 777-5441
   Cleveland *(G-5056)*
Rmt Holdings Inc .... F 419 221-1168
   Lima *(G-11933)*

CUTTING SVC: Paperboard

Loroco Industries Inc .... E 513 891-9544
   Blue Ash *(G-1807)*

CYCLIC CRUDES & INTERMEDIATES

Cleveland FP Inc .... D 216 249-4900
   Cleveland *(G-4959)*
Ferro Corporation .... F 330 682-8015
   Orrville *(G-15590)*
Kingscote Chemicals Inc .... G 937 886-9100
   Miamisburg *(G-13683)*
Marathon Petroleum Company LP .... F 419 422-2121
   Findlay *(G-9719)*
Polymerics Inc .... E 330 434-6665
   Cuyahoga Falls *(G-7906)*
Sun Chemical Corporation .... C 513 681-5950
   Cincinnati *(G-4391)*
Sun Chemical Corporation .... D 513 753-9550
   Amelia *(G-549)*
Thermocolor LLC .... E 419 626-5677
   Sandusky *(G-16852)*
Thermocolor LLC .... F 419 626-5677
   Sandusky *(G-16853)*

CYLINDER & ACTUATORS: Fluid Power

Cascade Corporation .... C 937 327-0300
   Springfield *(G-17370)*
Control Line Equipment Inc .... F 216 433-7766
   Cleveland *(G-5025)*
Custom Hoists Inc .... C 419 368-4721
   Ashland *(G-699)*
Cylinders & Valves Inc .... G 440 238-7343
   Strongsville *(G-17736)*
Eaton Leasing Corporation .... G 216 382-2292
   Beachwood *(G-1235)*
Eaton-Aeroquip Llc .... D 419 891-7775
   Maumee *(G-13109)*
Hydraulic Parts Store Inc .... E 330 364-6667
   New Philadelphia *(G-14774)*
Hydraulic Specialists Inc .... E 740 922-3343
   Midvale *(G-13978)*
Nook Industries Inc .... C 216 271-7900
   Cleveland *(G-5756)*
North Coast Instruments Inc .... E 216 251-2353
   Cleveland *(G-5766)*
Northcoast Process Controls .... G 440 498-0542
   Cleveland *(G-5771)*
Parker-Hannifin Corporation .... B 216 896-3000
   Cleveland *(G-5848)*
Parker-Hannifin Corporation .... C 330 336-3511
   Wadsworth *(G-19260)*
Robeck Fluid Power Co .... D 330 562-1140
   Aurora *(G-903)*
Sebring Fluid Power Corp .... G 330 938-9984
   Sebring *(G-16894)*
Skidmore-Wilhelm Mfg Company .... E 216 481-4774
   Solon *(G-17232)*
Steel Eqp Specialists Inc .... E 330 829-2626
   Alliance *(G-501)*
Steel Eqp Specialists Inc .... D 330 823-8260
   Alliance *(G-502)*
Suburban Manufacturing Co .... D 440 953-2024
   Eastlake *(G-9133)*
Swagelok Company .... D 440 349-5934
   Solon *(G-17242)*

CYLINDERS: Pressure

Enk Tenofour LLC .... G 419 661-1465
   Northwood *(G-15336)*
Gayston Corporation .... C 937 743-6050
   Miamisburg *(G-13672)*
Hutnik Company .... G 330 336-9700
   Wadsworth *(G-19246)*
Toledo Metal Spinning Company .... E 419 535-5931
   Toledo *(G-18561)*
Worthington Cylinder Corp .... C 740 569-4143
   Bremen *(G-2066)*
Worthington Cylinder Corp .... C 330 262-1762
   Wooster *(G-20672)*
Worthington Cylinder Corp .... C 614 840-3210
   Worthington *(G-20709)*
Worthington Cylinder Corp .... C 440 576-5847
   Jefferson *(G-11243)*
Worthington Cylinder Corp .... C 614 438-7900
   Columbus *(G-7614)*
Worthington Cylinder Corp .... C 614 840-3800
   Westerville *(G-20031)*
Worthington Industries Inc .... C 614 438-3210
   Worthington *(G-20710)*

CYLINDERS: Pump

Custom Cltch Jint Hydrlics Inc .... F 216 431-1630
   Cleveland *(G-5046)*
Eric Allshouse LLC .... G 330 533-4258
   Canfield *(G-2527)*
Hr Parts N Stuff .... G 330 947-2433
   Atwater *(G-861)*
Rolcon Inc .... F 513 821-7259
   Cincinnati *(G-4281)*

DAIRY EQPT

Hollmann Inc .... G 513 522-1800
   Cincinnati *(G-3819)*

DAIRY PRDTS STORE: Cheese

Bunker Hill Cheese Co Inc .... D 330 893-2131
   Millersburg *(G-14073)*
Guggisberg Cheese Inc .... E 330 893-2550
   Millersburg *(G-14086)*
Schindlers Broad Run Chese Hse .... F 330 343-4108
   Dover *(G-8850)*

DAIRY PRDTS STORE: Ice Cream, Packaged

Malleys Candies .... C 216 362-8700
   Lakewood *(G-11528)*
Milk & Honey .... F 330 492-5884
   Canton *(G-2755)*
Superior Tasting Products Inc .... E 614 442-0622
   Columbus *(G-7502)*

DAIRY PRDTS STORES

Broughton Foods Company .... C 740 373-4121
   Marietta *(G-12610)*
Hans Rothenbuhler & Son Inc .... E 440 632-6000
   Middlefield *(G-13802)*
United Dairy Farmers Inc .... C 513 396-8700
   Cincinnati *(G-4447)*
Youngs Jersey Dairy Inc .... B 937 325-0629
   Yellow Springs *(G-20823)*

DAIRY PRDTS WHOLESALERS: Fresh

Company	Code	Phone
Acme Steak & Seafood Inc	F	330 270-8000
Youngstown (G-20836)		
Auburn Dairy Products Inc	E	614 488-2536
Columbus (G-6628)		
Barkett Fruit Co Inc	E	330 364-6645
Dover (G-8807)		
Borden Dairy Co Cincinnati LLC	C	513 948-8811
Cincinnati (G-3404)		
Country Parlour Ice Cream Co	F	440 237-4040
Cleveland (G-5032)		
Dallas Instantwhip Inc		614 488-2536
Columbus (G-6847)		
Hans Rothenbuhler & Son Inc		440 632-6000
Middlefield (G-13802)		
Instantwhip Connecticut Inc		614 488-2536
Columbus (G-7031)		
Instantwhip Detroit Inc		800 544-9447
Columbus (G-7033)		
Instantwhip Foods Inc	F	614 488-2536
Columbus (G-7034)		
Instantwhip of Buffalo Inc	F	614 488-2536
Columbus (G-7035)		
Instantwhip Products Co PA	F	614 488-2536
Columbus (G-7036)		
Instantwhip-Columbus Inc	E	614 871-9447
Grove City (G-10435)		
Instantwhip-Dayton Inc	F	937 235-5930
Dayton (G-8269)		
Johnsons Real Ice Cream Co	E	614 231-0014
Columbus (G-7074)		
Louis Instantwhip-St Inc	F	614 488-2536
Columbus (G-7138)		
Ohio Processors Inc	G	740 852-9243
Columbus (G-7255)		
Philadelphia Instantwhip Inc	F	614 488-2536
Columbus (G-7314)		
Weaver Bros Inc	D	937 526-3907
Versailles (G-19193)		

DAIRY PRDTS: Butter

Company	Code	Phone
Black Radish Creamery Ltd	G	614 323-6016
New Albany (G-14608)		
California Creamery Operators	G	440 264-5351
Solon (G-17122)		
Dairy Farmers America Inc	E	330 670-7800
Medina (G-13249)		
Fairmont Creamery LLC	G	216 357-2560
Cleveland (G-5216)		
Minerva Dairy Inc	D	330 868-4196
Minerva (G-14193)		
Turkeyfoot Creek Creamery	G	419 335-0224
Wauseon (G-19535)		

DAIRY PRDTS: Canned Cream

Company	Code	Phone
Tmarzetti Company	C	614 279-8673
Columbus (G-7532)		

DAIRY PRDTS: Canned Milk, Whole

Company	Code	Phone
J M Smucker Company	A	330 682-3000
Orrville (G-15596)		
Nu Pet Company	C	330 682-3000
Orrville (G-15606)		

DAIRY PRDTS: Cheese

Company	Code	Phone
9444 Ohio Holding Co	E	330 359-6291
Winesburg (G-20529)		
Amish Wedding Foods Inc	E	330 674-9199
Millersburg (G-14060)		
Dairy Farmers America Inc	E	330 670-7800
Medina (G-13249)		
Es Steiner Dairy LLC	F	330 897-5555
Baltic (G-1027)		
Lake Erie Frozen Foods Mfg Co	E	419 289-9204
Ashland (G-720)		
Lakeview Farms LLC	C	419 695-9925
Delphos (G-8750)		
Land OLakes Inc	C	330 678-1578
Kent (G-11346)		
Oakvale Farm Cheese Inc	E	740 857-1230
London (G-12067)		
Tri State Dairy LLC	G	419 542-8788
Hicksville (G-10784)		
Tri State Dairy LLC	F	330 897-5555
Baltic (G-1034)		

DAIRY PRDTS: Cheese, Cottage

Company	Code	Phone
Broughton Foods Company	C	740 373-4121
Marietta (G-12610)		
Broughton Foods Company	F	800 598-7545
South Point (G-17281)		

DAIRY PRDTS: Concentrated Milk

Company	Code	Phone
L & F Lauch LLC	G	513 732-5805
Batavia (G-1161)		

DAIRY PRDTS: Condensed Milk

Company	Code	Phone
Eagle Family Foods Group LLC	E	330 382-3725
Richfield (G-16468)		
Milnot Company	G	888 656-3245
Gahanna (G-10091)		

DAIRY PRDTS: Cream Substitutes

Company	Code	Phone
Instantwhip-Dayton Inc	F	937 235-5930
Dayton (G-8269)		
Instantwhip-Dayton Inc	G	937 435-4371
Dayton (G-8270)		

DAIRY PRDTS: Cream, Whipped

Company	Code	Phone
Instantwhip Detroit Inc	F	800 544-9447
Columbus (G-7033)		
Instantwhip-Chicago Inc	E	614 488-2536
Columbus (G-7037)		

DAIRY PRDTS: Dietary Supplements, Dairy & Non-Dairy Based

Company	Code	Phone
Aggregate Tersonrance LLC	G	330 418-4751
Canton (G-2560)		
Alifet USA Inc	G	513 793-8033
Blue Ash (G-1726)		
Freedom Health LLC	E	330 562-0888
Aurora (G-880)		
Healthy Living	G	937 962-4705
Lewisburg (G-11792)		
Infinit Nutrition LLC	F	513 791-3500
Blue Ash (G-1793)		
Innovated Health LLC	G	330 858-0651
Cuyahoga Falls (G-7881)		
Instantwhip-Columbus Inc	E	614 871-9447
Grove City (G-10435)		
Lifestyle Nutraceuticals Ltd	F	513 376-7218
Cincinnati (G-3941)		
Muscle Feast LLC	F	740 877-8808
Nashport (G-14568)		
Toomey Inc	G	513 831-4771
Milford (G-14044)		
Wileys Finest LLC	C	740 622-1072
Coshocton (G-7759)		

DAIRY PRDTS: Dips & Spreads, Cheese Based

Company	Code	Phone
Lakeview Farms LLC	E	419 695-9925
Delphos (G-8749)		

DAIRY PRDTS: Evaporated Milk

Company	Code	Phone
Nestle Usa Inc	C	216 524-7738
Cleveland (G-5742)		
Nestle Usa Inc	C	216 524-3397
Cleveland (G-5743)		
Nestle Usa Inc	C	440 349-5757
Solon (G-17205)		

DAIRY PRDTS: Frozen Desserts & Novelties

Company	Code	Phone
Archies Too	D	419 427-2663
Findlay (G-9651)		
B M DS Fish N More LLC	F	419 238-2722
Van Wert (G-19078)		
Better Than Sex Ice Cream LLC		614 444-5505
Columbus (G-6664)		
CTB Consulting LLC	F	216 712-7764
Rocky River (G-16545)		
Dietsch Brothers Incorporated	D	419 422-4474
Findlay (G-9677)		
Home City Ice Company	F	419 562-4953
Delaware (G-8694)		
Honeybaked Ham Company	E	513 583-9700
Cincinnati (G-3824)		
ICEE USA	F	513 771-0630
West Chester (G-19866)		
Jim H Niemeyer	F	419 422-2465
Findlay (G-9709)		
Johnsons Real Ice Cream Co	E	614 231-0014
Columbus (G-7074)		
Joshua Leigh Enterprises Inc	G	330 244-9200
Canton (G-2720)		
Louis Trauth Dairy LLC	B	859 431-7553
West Chester (G-19873)		
R D Lucky LLC		614 570-8005
Columbus (G-7373)		
Robert E McGrath Inc	E	440 572-7747
Strongsville (G-17783)		
Smithfoods Inc	G	330 683-8710
Orrville (G-15620)		
Springdale Ice Cream Beverage	E	513 699-4984
Cincinnati (G-4364)		
St Clairsville Dairy Queen	G	740 635-1800
Saint Clairsville (G-16652)		
Stella Lou LLC	F	937 935-9536
Powell (G-16336)		
Welsh Farms LLC		513 723-4487
Cincinnati (G-4498)		
Youngs Jersey Dairy Inc	B	937 325-0629
Yellow Springs (G-20823)		

DAIRY PRDTS: Half & Half

Company	Code	Phone
Instantwhip-Dayton Inc	F	937 235-5930
Dayton (G-8269)		
Instantwhip-Dayton Inc	G	937 435-4371
Dayton (G-8270)		

DAIRY PRDTS: Ice Cream & Ice Milk

Company	Code	Phone
Double Dippin Inc	G	937 847-2572
Miamisburg (G-13660)		
Gibson Bros Inc	E	440 774-2401
Oberlin (G-15496)		
International Brand Services	F	513 376-8209
Cincinnati (G-3856)		
Malleys Candies	C	216 362-8700
Lakewood (G-11528)		
Toft Dairy Inc	D	419 625-4376
Sandusky (G-16856)		
United Dairy Farmers Inc	C	513 396-8700
Cincinnati (G-4447)		

DAIRY PRDTS: Ice Cream, Bulk

Company	Code	Phone
Bacconis Lickety Split	G	330 924-0418
Cortland (G-7703)		
Bojos Cream	G	330 270-3332
Austintown (G-930)		
Country Caterers Inc	G	740 389-1013
Marion (G-12700)		
Country Maid Ice Cream Inc	G	330 659-6830
Richfield (G-16466)		
Country Parlour Ice Cream Co	F	440 237-4040
Cleveland (G-5032)		
Dairy Shed	G	937 848-3504
Bellbrook (G-1492)		
Fritzie Freeze Inc	G	419 727-0818
Toledo (G-18298)		
Mitchell Bros Ice Cream Inc	F	216 861-2799
Cleveland (G-5697)		
Pierres French Ice Cream Inc	E	216 431-2555
Cleveland (G-5876)		
Reiter Dairy of Akron Inc	E	419 424-5060
Findlay (G-9746)		
Royal Ice Cream Co	D	216 432-1144
Cleveland (G-6012)		
United Dairy Inc	C	740 633-1451
Martins Ferry (G-12763)		
Weldon Ice Cream Company	G	740 467-2400
Millersport (G-14162)		
Whits Frozen Custard	G	740 965-1427
Sunbury (G-17902)		
Yagoot	G	513 791-6600
Cincinnati (G-4531)		
ZS Cream & Bean	G	440 652-6369
Hinckley (G-10908)		

DAIRY PRDTS: Ice Cream, Packaged, Molded, On Sticks, Etc.

Company	Code	Phone
Broughton Foods Company	C	740 373-4121
Marietta (G-12610)		
Graeters Manufacturing Co	D	513 721-3323
Cincinnati (G-3774)		
Schwans Home Service Inc	E	419 222-9977
Lima (G-11936)		

Employee Codes: A=Over 500 employees, B=251-500
C=101-250, D=51-100, E=20-50, F=10-19, G=3-9

DAIRY PRDTS: Ice milk, Bulk

Superior Tasting Products Inc .... E 614 442-0622
  Columbus (G-7502)

DAIRY PRDTS: Milk, Condensed & Evaporated

Hans Rothenbuhler & Son Inc .... E 440 632-6000
  Middlefield (G-13802)
Ingredia Inc .... E 419 738-4060
  Wapakoneta (G-19334)
Minerva Dairy Inc .... D 330 868-4196
  Minerva (G-14193)
Moo Technologies Inc .... G 513 732-5805
  Batavia (G-1169)
Nestle Usa Inc .... D 216 861-8350
  Cleveland (G-5744)
Rich Products Corporation .... C 614 771-1117
  Hilliard (G-10858)

DAIRY PRDTS: Milk, Fluid

Consun Food Industries Inc .... D 440 322-6301
  Elyria (G-9238)
Dairy Farmers America Inc .... E 330 670-7800
  Medina (G-13249)
Dean Foods Co .... G 419 473-9621
  Toledo (G-18255)
Instantwhip Foods Inc .... F 614 488-2536
  Columbus (G-7034)
Louis Trauth Dairy LLC .... B 859 431-7553
  West Chester (G-19873)
Reiter Dairy of Akron Inc .... E 513 795-6962
  West Chester (G-19894)
Smithfoods Inc .... G 330 683-8710
  Orrville (G-15620)

DAIRY PRDTS: Milk, Processed, Pasteurized, Homogenized/Btld

Borden Dairy Co Cincinnati LLC .... C 513 948-8811
  Cincinnati (G-3404)
Borden Dairy Company Ohio LLC .... C 216 671-2300
  Cleveland (G-4832)
Daisy Brand LLC .... F 330 202-4376
  Wooster (G-20582)
Reiter Dairy of Akron Inc .... E 937 323-5777
  Springfield (G-17483)
Reiter Dairy of Akron Inc .... E 419 424-5060
  Findlay (G-9746)
Toft Dairy Inc .... D 419 625-4376
  Sandusky (G-16856)
United Dairy Inc .... C 740 633-1451
  Martins Ferry (G-12763)
United Dairy Farmers Inc .... C 513 396-8700
  Cincinnati (G-4447)

DAIRY PRDTS: Natural Cheese

Biery Cheese Co .... C 330 875-3381
  Louisville (G-12152)
Brewster Cheese Company .... C 330 767-3492
  Brewster (G-2067)
Bunker Hill Cheese Co Inc .... D 330 893-2131
  Millersburg (G-14073)
Great Lakes Cheese Co Inc .... B 440 834-2500
  Hiram (G-10910)
Guggisberg Cheese Inc .... E 330 893-2550
  Millersburg (G-14086)
Hans Rothenbuhler & Son Inc .... E 440 632-6000
  Middlefield (G-13802)
Holmes Cheese Co .... E 330 674-6451
  Millersburg (G-14096)
Miceli Dairy Products Co .... D 216 791-6222
  Cleveland (G-5666)
Middlefield Cheese House Inc .... E 440 632-5228
  Middlefield (G-13822)
Middlefield Mix Inc .... F 440 632-0157
  Middlefield (G-13824)
Middlfeld Original Cheese Coop .... E 440 632-5567
  Middlefield (G-13828)
Pearl Valley Cheese Inc .... E 740 545-6002
  Fresno (G-10068)
Schindlers Broad Run Chese Hse .... F 330 343-4108
  Dover (G-8850)

DAIRY PRDTS: Powdered Milk

Stolle Milk Biologics Inc .... C 513 489-7997
  West Chester (G-19903)

DAIRY PRDTS: Processed Cheese

A & M Cheese Co .... D 419 476-8369
  Toledo (G-18152)
Christina A Kraft PHD .... G 330 375-7474
  Akron (G-115)
Inter American Products Inc .... E 800 645-2233
  Cincinnati (G-3853)
Kathys Krafts and Kollectibles .... G 423 787-3709
  Medina (G-13284)
Kraft House No 5 .... G 614 396-9091
  Powell (G-16325)
Kraft of Writing 614 620-2476
  Columbus (G-7100)
Minerva Dairy Inc .... D 330 868-4196
  Minerva (G-14193)
Wood Kraft .... G 440 487-4634
  Garrettsville (G-10205)

DAIRY PRDTS: Sour Cream

Lakeview Farms Inc .... D 419 695-9925
  Delphos (G-8748)
Lakeview Farms LLC .... E 419 695-9925
  Delphos (G-8749)
Lakeview Farms LLC .... C 419 695-9925
  Delphos (G-8750)

DAIRY PRDTS: Whipped Topping, Exc Frozen Or Dry Mix

Auburn Dairy Products Inc .... E 614 488-2536
  Columbus (G-6628)
Dallas Instantwhip Inc .... F 614 488-2536
  Columbus (G-6847)
Instantwhip Connecticut Inc .... F 614 488-2536
  Columbus (G-7031)
Instantwhip Detroit Inc .... F 614 488-2536
  Columbus (G-7032)
Instantwhip of Buffalo Inc .... F 614 488-2536
  Columbus (G-7035)
Instantwhip Products Co PA .... F 614 488-2536
  Columbus (G-7036)
Instantwhip-Columbus Inc .... E 614 871-9447
  Grove City (G-10435)
Instantwhip-Syracuse Inc .... F 614 488-2536
  Columbus (G-7038)
Louis Instantwhip-St Inc .... F 614 488-2536
  Columbus (G-7138)
Ohio Processors Inc .... G 740 852-9243
  Columbus (G-7255)
Peak Foods Llc .... D 937 440-0707
  Troy (G-18692)
Philadelphia Instantwhip Inc .... G 614 488-2536
  Columbus (G-7314)

DAIRY PRDTS: Yogurt, Exc Frozen

American Confections Co LLC .... G 614 888-8838
  Coventry Township (G-7765)

DAIRY PRDTS: Yogurt, Frozen

Awesome Yogurt LLC .... G 937 643-0879
  Dayton (G-8047)
Danone Us LLC .... B 513 229-0092
  Mason (G-12854)
Danone Us LLC .... B 419 628-3861
  Minster (G-14211)
Tmarzetti Company .... C 614 279-8673
  Columbus (G-7532)
Wil-Mark Froyo LLC .... G 330 421-6043
  Rittman (G-16530)

DATA ENTRY SVCS

J Com Data Inc .... G 614 304-1455
  Pataskala (G-15833)

DATA PROCESSING & PREPARATION SVCS

3dlt LLC .... F 513 452-3358
  Cincinnati (G-3271)
Datatrak International Inc .... E 440 443-0082
  Mayfield Heights (G-13162)
Gracie Plum Investments Inc .... E 740 355-9029
  Portsmouth (G-16284)
NCR International Inc .... G 937 445-5000
  Kettering (G-11437)
Thinkware Incorporated .... E 513 598-3300
  Cincinnati (G-4419)

DATA PROCESSING SVCS

Aero Fulfillment Services Corp .... D 800 225-7145
  Mason (G-12820)
Capitol Citicom Inc .... E 614 472-2679
  Columbus (G-6735)
Cpmm Services Group Inc .... F 614 447-0165
  Columbus (G-6834)
Image Integrations Systems .... F 419 872-0003
  Perrysburg (G-15964)
Sourcelink Ohio LLC .... C 937 885-8000
  Miamisburg (G-13718)

DATABASE INFORMATION RETRIEVAL SVCS

Lexisnexis Group .... C 937 865-6800
  Miamisburg (G-13684)

DECALS, WHOLESALE

Blang Acquisition LLC .... F 937 223-2155
  Dayton (G-8058)

DECORATIVE WOOD & WOODWORK

77 Coach Supply Ltd .... E 330 674-1454
  Millersburg (G-14053)
Adroit Thinking Inc .... E 419 542-9363
  Hicksville (G-10774)
Barkman Products LLC .... G 330 893-2520
  Millersburg (G-14063)
Brown Wood Products Company .... G 330 339-8000
  New Philadelphia (G-14761)
Buckeye Dimensions LLC .... G 330 857-0223
  Dalton (G-7936)
Cado Door & Design Inc .... G 330 343-4288
  New Philadelphia (G-14763)
Cedar Chest .... G 937 878-9097
  Fairborn (G-9454)
CM Paula Company .... E 513 759-7473
  Mason (G-12849)
Colby Woodworking Inc .... G 937 224-7676
  Dayton (G-8097)
Family Woodworks LLC 740 289-4071
  Piketon (G-16070)
G R K Manufacturing Co Inc .... E 513 863-3131
  Hamilton (G-10563)
Handicraft LLC .... G 216 295-1950
  Bedford (G-1410)
Hardwood Solutions .... G 330 359-5755
  Wilmot (G-20516)
Hardwood Store Inc .... G 937 864-2899
  Enon (G-9384)
Herbert Wood Products Inc .... G 440 834-1410
  Middlefield (G-13805)
Homestead Collections .... G 419 422-8286
  Findlay (G-9705)
Insta Plak Inc .... F 419 537-1555
  Toledo (G-18349)
J & R Woodworking .... G 330 893-0713
  Millersburg (G-14101)
J R Custom Unlimited .... F 513 894-9800
  Hamilton (G-10575)
Judith C Zell .... G 740 385-0386
  Logan (G-12029)
Marcum Crew Cut Inc .... G 740 862-3400
  Baltimore (G-1039)
Mikes Mill Shop Inc .... G 419 538-6091
  Ottawa (G-15659)
Miller Manufacturing Inc .... E 330 852-0689
  Sugarcreek (G-17854)
Millwork Designs Inc .... G 740 335-5203
  Wshngtn CT Hs (G-20733)
Newbury Woodworks .... G 440 564-5273
  Newbury (G-14960)
P & T Millwork Inc .... E 440 543-2151
  Chagrin Falls (G-3064)
Revonoc Inc .... G 440 548-3491
  Parkman (G-15813)
Ryanworks Inc .... F 937 438-1282
  Dayton (G-8488)
Steeles 5 Acre Mill Inc .... F 419 542-9363
  Hicksville (G-10782)
W H K Company .... G 937 372-3368
  Xenia (G-20802)
Walnut Creek Planing Ltd .... D 330 893-3244
  Millersburg (G-14146)
Walnut Creek Wood Design .... G 330 852-9663
  Sugarcreek (G-17875)
Wengerd Wood Inc .... G 330 359-4300
  Dundee (G-9032)

Woodcraft Pattern Works Inc..................G...... 330 630-2158
  Tallmadge (G-18016)

DEFENSE SYSTEMS & EQPT

232 Defense LLC..............................G...... 419 348-4343
  Custar (G-7828)
Action Defense LLC...........................G...... 440 503-7886
  Cleveland (G-4611)
Advanced Defense Products LLC...........G...... 440 571-2277
  Painesville (G-15705)
Alternate Defense LLC.......................G...... 216 225-5889
  Maple Heights (G-12564)
American Icon Defense Ltd.................G...... 216 233-5184
  Lakewood (G-11510)
Center Mass Defense.........................G...... 513 314-8401
  Hamilton (G-10544)
Central Ohio Defense LLC..................G...... 614 668-6527
  Columbus (G-6752)
Citizens Defense LLC........................G...... 740 645-1101
  Thurman (G-18037)
Damsel In Defense............................G...... 561 307-4177
  North Olmsted (G-15184)
Damsel In Defense Diva....................G...... 330 874-2068
  Bolivar (G-1911)
Defense Surplus LLC.........................G...... 419 460-9906
  Maumee (G-13106)
Easy Defense Products......................G...... 513 258-2897
  Cincinnati (G-3626)
En Garde Deer Defense LLC..............G...... 440 334-7271
  Brecksville (G-2033)
Freedom Road Defense.....................G...... 740 541-7467
  Cambridge (G-2438)
Front Line Defense...........................G...... 419 516-7992
  Ada (G-6)
Guardian Strategic Defense LLC.........G...... 937 707-8985
  Marysville (G-12786)
HM Defense....................................G...... 513 260-6200
  Mount Orab (G-14445)
Hot Brass Personal Defense...............G...... 419 733-7400
  Celina (G-2969)
IMT Defense Corp.............................G...... 614 891-8812
  Westerville (G-19998)
JP Self Defense LLC........................G...... 330 356-1541
  Massillon (G-13007)
K & M Home Defense LLC................G...... 313 258-6142
  Fairborn (G-9462)
Koroshi School of Defense.................G...... 740 323-3582
  Heath (G-10724)
Landis Defense Solutions..................G...... 937 938-0688
  Moraine (G-14366)
Linx Defense LLC...........................G...... 805 233-2472
  Canton (G-2734)
MCO Solutions Inc...........................G...... 937 205-9512
  Dayton (G-8335)
Means of Defense............................G...... 740 513-6210
  Mount Gilead (G-14429)
Modern Defense...............................G...... 614 505-9338
  Columbus (G-7190)
Ohio Defense Services Inc.................G...... 937 608-2371
  Dayton (G-8396)
Ohio First Defense............................G...... 513 571-9461
  Maineville (G-12376)
On Guard Defense LLC......................G...... 740 596-1984
  New Plymouth (G-14809)
Outlier Solutions LLC......................G...... 330 947-2678
  Alliance (G-494)
Phase Line Defense LLC..................G...... 440 219-0046
  Medina (G-13317)
Primary Defense LLC.........................G...... 937 673-5703
  Toledo (G-18483)
Ss Defense LLC................................G...... 937 407-0659
  Cridersville (G-7812)
Talon Defense..................................G...... 419 236-7695
  Columbus Grove (G-7638)
Total Self Defense Toledo LLC............G...... 419 466-5882
  Sylvania (G-17966)
True Defense Solutions LLC...............G...... 330 325-1695
  Rootstown (G-16573)
TS Defense LLC................................G...... 740 446-7716
  Bidwell (G-1671)
Vector Electromagnetics LLC............G...... 937 478-5904
  Beavercreek (G-1367)
Vici Defense Ltd...............................G...... 330 669-3735
  Smithville (G-17096)

DEGREASING MACHINES

Auto-Tap Inc...................................G...... 216 671-1043
  Cleveland (G-4769)
Crowne Group LLC..........................D...... 216 589-0198
  Cleveland (G-5040)

Findlay Machine & Tool Inc..............E...... 419 434-3100
  Findlay (G-9684)

DEHUMIDIFIERS: Electric

Bry-Air Inc.....................................E...... 740 965-2974
  Sunbury (G-17883)

DEHYDRATION EQPT

Cleveland Range LLC.......................G...... 216 481-4900
  Cleveland (G-4971)

DEICING OR DEFROSTING FLUID

Visible Solutions Inc.........................G...... 440 925-2810
  Westlake (G-20168)
Zircon Industries Inc.........................G...... 216 595-0200
  Cleveland (G-6346)

DENTAL EQPT

Coltene/Whaledent Inc......................C...... 330 916-8800
  Cuyahoga Falls (G-7851)
Metz Dental Laboratory Inc..............G...... 614 252-4444
  Columbus (G-7175)

DENTAL EQPT & SPLYS

Asch-Klaassen Sonics LLC................G...... 513 671-3226
  Cincinnati (G-3360)
Chicago Dental Supply Inc................G...... 800 571-5211
  Harrison (G-10633)
Dental Ceramics Inc..........................E...... 330 523-5240
  Richfield (G-16467)
Dresch Tolson Dental Labs................D...... 419 842-6730
  Sylvania (G-17938)
Duncan Dental Lab LLC...................G...... 614 793-0330
  Dublin (G-8909)
Midmark Corporation.........................A...... 937 526-3662
  Kettering (G-11434)
Obsidian Biodent..............................G...... 937 938-9244
  Oakwood (G-15465)
Precision Swiss LLC..........................G...... 513 716-7000
  Cincinnati (G-4185)
Smile Brands Inc..............................G...... 440 471-6133
  North Olmsted (G-15199)
Sportsguard Laboratories Inc.............G...... 330 673-3932
  Kent (G-11389)
United Dental Laboratories................E...... 330 253-1810
  Tallmadge (G-18010)
Vacalon Company Inc.......................G...... 614 577-1945
  Pickerington (G-16062)
Wbc Group LLC..............................D...... 866 528-2144
  Hudson (G-11082)

DENTAL EQPT & SPLYS WHOLESALERS

Dentronix Inc..................................E...... 330 916-7300
  Cuyahoga Falls (G-7860)

DENTAL EQPT & SPLYS: Enamels

Absolute Smile LLC..........................G...... 937 293-9866
  Dayton (G-8000)

DENTAL EQPT & SPLYS: Impression Materials

Dentsply Sirona Inc..........................D...... 419 865-9497
  Maumee (G-13108)

DENTAL EQPT & SPLYS: Orthodontic Appliances

Dentronix Inc..................................E...... 330 916-7300
  Cuyahoga Falls (G-7860)
Mark Dental Laboratory....................G...... 216 464-6424
  Cleveland (G-5618)
Thomas J Raffa DDS Inc...................G...... 440 997-5208
  Ashtabula (G-808)

DENTAL EQPT & SPLYS: Teeth, Artificial, Exc In Dental Labs

Dentsply Sirona Inc..........................E...... 419 893-5672
  Maumee (G-13107)

DENTISTS' OFFICES & CLINICS

Thomas J Raffa DDS Inc...................G...... 440 997-5208
  Ashtabula (G-808)

DEODORANTS: Personal

Dover Wipes Company.......................G...... 513 983-1100
  Cincinnati (G-3606)
Procter & Gamble Company...............C...... 513 983-1100
  Cincinnati (G-4199)
Procter & Gamble Company...............E...... 513 266-4375
  Cincinnati (G-4200)
Procter & Gamble Company...............E...... 513 871-7557
  Cincinnati (G-4201)
Procter & Gamble Company...............E...... 513 983-1100
  Cincinnati (G-4202)
Procter & Gamble Company...............B...... 419 998-5891
  Lima (G-11920)
Procter & Gamble Company...............F...... 513 482-6789
  Cincinnati (G-4203)
Procter & Gamble Company...............B...... 513 672-4044
  West Chester (G-19767)
Procter & Gamble Company...............B...... 513 634-5069
  Cincinnati (G-4204)
Procter & Gamble Company...............B...... 513 627-7115
  Cincinnati (G-4205)
Procter & Gamble Company...............C...... 513 634-9600
  West Chester (G-19768)
Procter & Gamble Company...............C...... 513 634-9110
  West Chester (G-19769)
Procter & Gamble Company...............B...... 513 983-1100
  Cincinnati (G-4206)
Procter & Gamble Company...............C...... 513 934-3406
  Oregonia (G-15573)
Procter & Gamble Company...............G...... 513 627-7779
  Cincinnati (G-4207)
Procter & Gamble Company...............B...... 513 945-0340
  Cincinnati (G-4208)
Procter & Gamble Company...............C...... 513 626-2500
  Blue Ash (G-1836)
Procter & Gamble Company...............G...... 513 622-1000
  Mason (G-12926)
Procter & Gamble Company...............F...... 513 242-5752
  Cincinnati (G-4209)
Procter & Gamble Company...............C...... 410 527-5735
  Grove City (G-10460)

DEPARTMENT STORES

Wagoner Stores Inc..........................G...... 937 836-3636
  Englewood (G-9383)

DEPARTMENT STORES: Army-Navy Goods

Raven Concealment Systems LLC........F...... 440 508-9000
  North Ridgeville (G-15249)

DEPARTMENT STORES: Country General

John Purdum...................................G...... 513 897-9686
  Waynesville (G-19569)
Rubys Country Store.........................G...... 330 359-0406
  Dundee (G-9026)

DERMATOLOGICALS

Chester Packaging LLC.....................C...... 513 458-3840
  Cincinnati (G-3469)
Essence Maker................................G...... 440 729-3894
  Chesterland (G-3157)
Family Medical Clinic & Laser.............G...... 740 345-2767
  Newark (G-14874)

DERRICKS

Altec Industries Inc..........................F...... 205 408-2341
  Cuyahoga Falls (G-7833)

DESALTER KITS: Sea Water

Luxfer Magtech Inc..........................E...... 513 772-3066
  Cincinnati (G-3958)
Natures Own Source LLC..................G...... 440 838-5135
  Brecksville (G-2050)

DESIGN SVCS, NEC

A & B Wood Design Assoc Inc............G...... 330 721-2789
  Wadsworth (G-19218)
B C Wilson Inc...............................G...... 937 439-1866
  Dayton (G-8049)
Bollin & Sons Inc............................E...... 419 693-6573
  Toledo (G-18210)
Controls Inc....................................E...... 330 239-4345
  Medina (G-13240)
Dasher Lawless Automation LLC........E...... 855 755-7275
  Warren (G-19394)

DESIGN SVCS, NEC

Heartland Design Concepts .... G 419 774-0199
  Mansfield (G-12456)
Htec Systems Inc .... F 937 438-3010
  Dayton (G-8255)
IEC Infrared Systems LLC .... E 440 234-8000
  Middleburg Heights (G-13766)
Laura Dawson .... G 513 777-2513
  West Chester (G-19735)
Manchik Engineering & Co .... G 740 927-4454
  Dublin (G-8945)
Signs Unlimited The Graphic .... G 614 836-7446
  Logan (G-12043)
Twin Design AP Promotions Ltd .... G 937 732-6798
  Dayton (G-8573)
Universal Dsign Fbrication LLC .... G 419 359-1794
  Sandusky (G-16859)

DESIGN SVCS: Commercial & Indl

Acreo Inc .... G 513 734-3327
  Amelia (G-528)
David Wolfe Design Inc .... F 330 633-6124
  Akron (G-134)
Electrovations Inc .... E 330 274-3558
  Aurora (G-878)
Hutnik Company .... G 330 336-9700
  Wadsworth (G-19246)
Ies Systems Inc .... E 330 533-6683
  Canfield (G-2530)
Joseph B Stinson Co .... G 419 334-4151
  Fremont (G-10030)
Military Resources LLC .... E 330 263-1040
  Wooster (G-20626)
Military Resources LLC .... D 330 309-9970
  Wooster (G-20627)
New Path International LLC .... E 614 410-3974
  Powell (G-16331)
Precision Inc .... G 330 897-8860
  Fresno (G-10070)
R and J Corporation .... E 440 871-6009
  Westlake (G-20147)
R J K Enterprises Inc .... F 440 257-6018
  Mentor (G-13569)
Ultra Tech Machinery Inc .... E 330 929-5544
  Cuyahoga Falls (G-7931)

DESIGN SVCS: Computer Integrated Systems

Aclara Technologies LLC .... C 440 528-7200
  Solon (G-17098)
Applied Experience LLC .... G 614 943-2970
  Columbus (G-6610)
Cott Systems Inc .... D 614 847-4405
  Columbus (G-6827)
Eaj Services LLC .... F 513 792-3400
  Blue Ash (G-1762)
Electronic Concepts Engrg Inc .... F 419 861-9000
  Holland (G-10930)
IPA Ltd .... F 614 523-3974
  Columbus (G-7048)
M T Systems Inc .... G 330 453-4646
  Canton (G-2738)
Matrix Management Solutions .... G 330 470-3700
  Canton (G-2747)
New ERA Controls Inc .... G 216 641-8683
  Cleveland (G-5747)
Sgi Matrix LLC .... D 937 438-9033
  Miamisburg (G-13715)
Software Solutions Inc .... E 513 932-6667
  Lebanon (G-11698)
Tata America Intl Corp .... B 513 677-6500
  Milford (G-14043)

DESIGN SVCS: Hand Tools

Harbor Freight Tools Usa Inc .... G 937 415-0770
  Dayton (G-8244)

DETECTION APPARATUS: Electronic/Magnetic Field, Light/Heat

L3 Cincinnati Electronics Corp .... A 513 573-6100
  Mason (G-12902)

DETECTION EQPT: Magnetic Field

Ceia Usa Ltd .... E 330 405-3190
  Twinsburg (G-18747)
Peerless-Winsmith Inc .... G 614 526-7000
  Dublin (G-8963)

DETECTIVE & ARMORED CAR SERVICES

Contingncy Prcrement Group LLC .... G 513 204-9590
  Maineville (G-12366)

DETECTORS: Water Leak

Fluid Conservation Systems .... F 513 831-9335
  Milford (G-14008)
Robert J & Cindy K Hartz .... G 513 521-6215
  Cincinnati (G-4278)
Tegratek .... G 513 742-5100
  Cincinnati (G-4411)

DIAGNOSTIC SUBSTANCES

Core Quantum Technologies Inc ...... G 614 214-7210
  Columbus (G-6821)
Diagnostic Hybrids Inc .... C 740 593-1784
  Athens (G-828)
Diramed LLC .... F 614 487-3660
  Columbus (G-6864)
Enlyton Ltd .... G 614 888-9220
  Columbus (G-6897)
GE Healthcare Inc .... F 513 241-5955
  Cincinnati (G-3737)
John P Ellis Clinic Podiatry .... G 440 460-0444
  Cleveland (G-5503)
Meridian Bioscience Inc .... B 513 271-3700
  Cincinnati (G-4006)
Nanofiber Solutions Inc .... G 614 453-5877
  Hilliard (G-10843)
Perkinelmer Hlth Sciences Inc .... E 330 825-4525
  Akron (G-318)
Quidel Corporation .... D 740 589-3300
  Athens (G-847)
Sarcokinetics LLC .... G 414 477-9585
  Cleveland (G-6031)
Thermo Fisher Scientific Inc .... C 800 871-8909
  Oakwood Village (G-15486)

DIAGNOSTIC SUBSTANCES OR AGENTS: In Vitro

Apollo Medical Devices LLC .... G 440 935-5027
  Cleveland (G-4721)
Filament LLC .... G 614 732-0754
  Columbus (G-6921)
Molecular Theranostics LLC .... G 216 595-1968
  Cleveland (G-5701)

DIAGNOSTIC SUBSTANCES OR AGENTS: Microbiology & Virology

Xact Genomics LLC .... G 216 956-0957
  Twinsburg (G-18876)

DIAGNOSTIC SUBSTANCES OR AGENTS: Radioactive

Cardinal Health 414 LLC .... G 614 473-0786
  Columbus (G-6742)
Cardinal Health 414 LLC .... C 614 757-5000
  Dublin (G-8895)
Cardinal Health 414 LLC .... G 513 759-1900
  West Chester (G-19664)
Petnet Solutions Inc .... G 865 218-2000
  Cincinnati (G-4154)
Petnet Solutions Inc .... G 865 218-2000
  Cleveland (G-5867)
USB Corporation .... D 216 765-5000
  Cleveland (G-6246)

DIAGNOSTIC SUBSTANCES OR AGENTS: Veterinary

Cleveland AEC West LLC .... G 216 362-6000
  Cleveland (G-4945)
Meridian Life Science Inc .... D 513 271-3700
  Cincinnati (G-4007)
Vetgraft LLC .... G 614 203-0603
  New Albany (G-14642)

DIAMOND SETTER SVCS

Jewels By Img Inc .... F 440 461-4464
  Cleveland (G-5498)

DIAPERS: Disposable

Absorbent Products Company Inc .... E 419 352-5353
  Bowling Green (G-1949)

Principle Business Entps Inc .... C 419 352-1551
  Bowling Green (G-1992)

DICE & DICE CUPS

Container Graphics Corp .... D 419 531-5133
  Toledo (G-18241)

DIE CUTTING SVC: Paper

Forest Converting Company Inc ...... G 513 631-4190
  Cincinnati (G-3703)
P & R Specialty Inc .... E 937 773-0263
  Piqua (G-16147)
Williams Steel Rule Die Co .... F 216 431-3232
  Cleveland (G-6311)

DIE SETS: Presses, Metal Stamping

Centaur Tool & Die Inc .... F 419 352-7704
  Bowling Green (G-1959)
Columbia Stamping Inc .... F 440 236-6677
  Columbia Station (G-6433)
Connell Limited Partnership .... D 877 534-8986
  Northfield (G-15316)
Kurtz Tool & Die Co Inc .... G 330 755-7723
  Struthers (G-17819)
McAfee Tool & Die Inc .... G 330 896-9555
  Uniontown (G-18927)
Misumi Investment USA Corp .... G 937 859-5111
  Dayton (G-8363)
Producto Dieco Corporation .... F 440 542-0000
  Solon (G-17219)
Rock Iron Corporation .... G 419 529-9411
  Crestline (G-7800)
Toolcraft Products Inc .... D 937 223-8271
  Dayton (G-8561)

DIE SPRINGS

Fremont Cutting Dies Inc .... G 419 334-5153
  Fremont (G-10017)

DIES & TOOLS: Special

A & B Tool & Manufacturing .... G 419 382-0215
  Toledo (G-18151)
Accu Tool Inc .... G 937 667-5878
  Tipp City (G-18095)
Accu-Rite Tool & Die Co Corp .... G 330 497-9959
  Canton (G-2557)
Accu-Tek Tool & Die Inc .... G 330 726-1946
  Salem (G-16713)
Accurate Machining & Welding .... G 937 584-4518
  Sabina (G-16615)
Accurate Tool Co Inc .... G 330 332-9448
  Salem (G-16714)
Ace American Wire Die Co .... F 330 425-7269
  Twinsburg (G-18723)
Acro Tool & Die Company .... D 330 773-5173
  Akron (G-29)
Allen Tool Co Inc .... G 937 987-2037
  New Vienna (G-14823)
Allied Tool & Die Inc .... F 216 941-6196
  Cleveland (G-4673)
Aluminum Fence & Mfg Co .... G 330 755-5323
  Aurora (G-868)
Amcraft Inc .... G 419 729-7900
  Toledo (G-18170)
Amtech Tool and Machine Inc .... F 330 758-8215
  Youngstown (G-20844)
Apollo Products Inc .... F 440 269-8551
  Willoughby (G-20275)
Argo Tool Corporation .... F 330 425-2407
  Twinsburg (G-18735)
Arken Manufacturing Inc .... G 216 883-6628
  Cleveland (G-4733)
Artisan Tool & Die Corp .... E 216 883-2769
  Cleveland (G-4740)
Athens Mold and Machine Inc .... D 740 593-6613
  Athens (G-823)
Atlantic Tool & Die Company .... C 330 239-3700
  Sharon Center (G-16945)
Atlantic Tool & Die Company .... C 330 769-4500
  Seville (G-16910)
Automation Tool & Die Inc .... D 330 225-8336
  Valley City (G-19030)
Banco Die Inc .... F 330 821-8511
  Alliance (G-456)
Banner Metals Group Inc .... D 614 291-3105
  Columbus (G-6646)
Bk Tool Company Inc .... F 513 870-9622
  Fairfield (G-9485)

Blick Tool & Die Inc......G....... 330 343-1277
Dover *(G-8809)*

Blitz Tool & Die Inc......G....... 440 237-1177
Cleveland *(G-4821)*

Brainin-Advance Industries LLC......E....... 513 874-9760
West Chester *(G-19663)*

Brinkman Tool & Die Inc......E....... 937 222-1161
Dayton *(G-8062)*

Browder Tool Co Inc......G....... 937 233-6731
Dayton *(G-8065)*

Brw Tool Inc......F....... 419 394-3371
Saint Marys *(G-16679)*

C-H Tool & Die......G....... 740 397-7214
Mount Vernon *(G-14471)*

Capital Precision Machine & Tl......G....... 937 258-1176
Dayton *(G-7973)*

Capital Tool Company......E....... 216 661-5750
Cleveland *(G-4871)*

Chippewa Tool & Mfg Co......F....... 419 849-2790
Woodville *(G-20551)*

Claridon Tool & Die Inc......G....... 740 389-1944
Caledonia *(G-2414)*

Classic Tool Inc......G....... 330 922-1933
Stow *(G-17578)*

Cleveland Metal Processing Inc......C....... 440 243-3404
Cleveland *(G-4968)*

Cleveland Roll Forming Co......G....... 216 281-0202
Cleveland *(G-4975)*

Cliffco Stands Inc......E....... 937 382-3700
Wilmington *(G-20489)*

Clyde Tool & Die Inc......F....... 419 547-9574
Clyde *(G-6387)*

Coach Tool & Die Inc......G....... 937 890-4716
Dayton *(G-8095)*

Cole Tool & Die Company......E....... 419 522-1272
Ontario *(G-15540)*

Colonial Machine Company Inc......D....... 330 673-5859
Kent *(G-11305)*

Companies of North Coast LLC......G....... 216 398-8550
Cleveland *(G-5008)*

Concord Design Inc......G....... 330 722-5133
Medina *(G-13239)*

Conison Tool and Die Inc......G....... 330 758-1574
Youngstown *(G-20878)*

Conti Tool & Die Inc......G....... 330 633-1414
Akron *(G-121)*

Contour Tool Inc......E....... 440 365-7333
North Ridgeville *(G-15216)*

Cornerstone Manufacturing Inc......G....... 937 456-5930
Eaton *(G-9146)*

Custom Machine Inc......E....... 419 986-5122
Tiffin *(G-18057)*

D A Fitzgerald Co Inc......G....... 937 548-0511
Greenville *(G-10367)*

D J Metro Mold & Die Inc......G....... 440 237-1130
North Royalton *(G-15268)*

Dayton Lamina Corporation......G....... 937 859-5111
Dayton *(G-8136)*

Dayton Tool Co Inc......E....... 937 222-5501
Dayton *(G-8146)*

Defiance Metal Products Co......B....... 419 784-5332
Defiance *(G-8619)*

Die Cast Division......G....... 330 769-2013
Seville *(G-16915)*

Die Craft Machining & Engineer......G....... 513 771-1290
Cincinnati *(G-3588)*

Die-Mension Corporation......F....... 330 273-5872
Brunswick *(G-2200)*

Die-Namic Tool & Die Inc......G....... 330 296-6923
Ravenna *(G-16375)*

Direct Wire Service LLP......G....... 937 526-4447
Versailles *(G-19178)*

Dove Die and Stamping Company......E....... 216 267-3720
Cleveland *(G-5109)*

Dreier Tool & Die Corp......G....... 513 521-8200
Cincinnati *(G-3610)*

Drt Mfg Co......C....... 937 297-6670
Dayton *(G-8171)*

Duco Tool & Die Inc......F....... 419 628-2031
Minster *(G-14212)*

Duncan Tool Inc......F....... 937 667-9364
Tipp City *(G-18111)*

Dyco Manufacturing Inc......F....... 419 485-5525
Montpelier *(G-14307)*

Dynamic Tool Die......G....... 440 834-0007
Middlefield *(G-13795)*

E D M Fastar Inc......G....... 216 676-0100
Cleveland *(G-5129)*

Eagle Precision Products LLC......G....... 440 582-9393
North Royalton *(G-15270)*

Eagle Tool & Die Inc......G....... 216 671-5055
Cleveland *(G-5135)*

Edco Inc......E....... 419 726-1595
Toledo *(G-18275)*

Euclid Design & Manufacturing......F....... 440 942-0066
Willoughby *(G-20316)*

F & G Tool and Die Co......E....... 937 294-1405
Moraine *(G-14352)*

Fabrication Shop Inc......F....... 419 435-7934
Fostoria *(G-9837)*

Fargo Toolite Incorporated......F....... 440 997-2442
Ashtabula *(G-775)*

Faull & Son LLC......F....... 330 652-4341
Niles *(G-15008)*

Feller Tool Co Inc......F....... 440 324-6277
Lorain *(G-12092)*

Fostoria Machine Products......G....... 419 435-4262
Fostoria *(G-9843)*

G & G Header Die Inc......G....... 330 468-3458
Macedonia *(G-12297)*

G & S Custom Tooling LLC......G....... 419 286-2888
Fort Jennings *(G-9792)*

Garvin Tool & Die Inc......G....... 419 334-2392
Fremont *(G-10022)*

Gasdorf Tool and Mch Co Inc......E....... 419 227-0103
Lima *(G-11867)*

Gem City Engineering Co......C....... 937 223-5544
Dayton *(G-8219)*

General Tool Company......C....... 513 733-5500
Cincinnati *(G-3747)*

Gentzler Tool & Die Corp......E....... 330 896-1941
Akron *(G-188)*

Gokoh Corporation......F....... 937 339-4977
Troy *(G-18662)*

Gottschall Tool & Die Inc......E....... 330 332-1544
Salem *(G-16743)*

Grandon Mfg Co Inc......G....... 614 294-2694
Columbus *(G-6966)*

H K K Machining Co......E....... 419 924-5116
West Unity *(G-19968)*

H Machining Inc......F....... 419 636-6890
Bryan *(G-2283)*

Hardin Creek Machine & Tool......F....... 419 678-4913
Coldwater *(G-6410)*

Hedges Selective Tool & Prod......F....... 419 478-8670
Toledo *(G-18329)*

Herd Manufacturing Inc......E....... 216 651-4221
Cleveland *(G-5397)*

Hess Industries Ltd......F....... 419 525-4000
Mansfield *(G-12458)*

Hofacker Prcsion Machining LLC......F....... 937 832-7712
Clayton *(G-4574)*

Holland Engraving Company......F....... 419 865-2765
Toledo *(G-18332)*

Honda Engineering N Amer Inc......B....... 937 642-5000
Marysville *(G-12789)*

Honda Engineering NA Inc......F....... 937 707-5357
Marysville *(G-12790)*

Horizon Industries Corp......G....... 937 323-0801
Springfield *(G-17420)*

Hunter Tool and Die Company......G....... 937 256-9798
Dayton *(G-8257)*

I-Dee-X Inc......G....... 330 788-2186
Youngstown *(G-20935)*

Ibycorp......G....... 330 425-8226
Twinsburg *(G-18794)*

Impact Industries Inc......E....... 440 327-2360
North Ridgeville *(G-15230)*

Imperial Die & Mfg Co......F....... 440 268-9080
Strongsville *(G-17753)*

Independent Stamping Inc......E....... 216 251-3500
Cleveland *(G-5451)*

Innovative Tool & Die Inc......G....... 419 599-0492
Napoleon *(G-14545)*

Ishmael Precision Tool Corp......E....... 937 335-8070
Troy *(G-18677)*

J & J Tool & Die Inc......G....... 330 343-4721
Dover *(G-8833)*

J P Tool Inc......G....... 419 354-8696
Bowling Green *(G-1978)*

J W Harwood Co......F....... 216 531-6230
Cleveland *(G-5489)*

JB Products Co......G....... 330 342-0223
Streetsboro *(G-17679)*

Jena Tool Inc......D....... 937 296-1122
Moraine *(G-14361)*

Jet Tool and Prototype Co......G....... 419 666-1199
Walbridge *(G-19295)*

Johnston Manufacturing Inc......G....... 440 269-1420
Mentor *(G-13487)*

K & L Die & Manufacturing......G....... 419 895-1301
Greenwich *(G-10405)*

K & L Tool Inc......F....... 419 258-2086
Antwerp *(G-598)*

K B Machine & Tool Inc......G....... 937 773-1624
Piqua *(G-16136)*

K K Tool Co......E....... 937 325-1373
Springfield *(G-17428)*

K P Precision Tool and Mch Co......G....... 419 237-2596
Fayette *(G-9633)*

Kalt Manufacturing Company......D....... 440 327-2102
North Ridgeville *(G-15235)*

Ken Forging Inc......C....... 440 993-8091
Jefferson *(G-11232)*

Knous Tool & Machine Inc......G....... 419 394-3541
Saint Marys *(G-16687)*

Knowlton Manufacturing Co Inc......F....... 513 631-7353
Cincinnati *(G-3920)*

L C G Machine & Tool Inc......G....... 614 261-1651
Columbus *(G-7107)*

La Ganke & Sons Stamping Co......F....... 216 451-0278
Columbia Station *(G-6439)*

Lab Quality Machining Inc......G....... 513 625-0219
Goshen *(G-10289)*

Larosa Die Engineering Inc......G....... 513 284-9195
Cincinnati *(G-3931)*

Laspina Tool & Die Inc......F....... 330 923-9996
Stow *(G-17599)*

Line Tool & Die Inc......G....... 419 332-2931
Fremont *(G-10035)*

Lowry Tool & Die Inc......F....... 330 332-1722
Salem *(G-16755)*

Lrb Tool & Die Ltd......F....... 330 898-5783
Warren *(G-19418)*

Lukens Inc......D....... 937 440-2500
Troy *(G-18684)*

Lunar Tool & Mold Inc......F....... 440 237-2141
North Royalton *(G-15285)*

M & M Dies Inc......G....... 216 883-6628
Cleveland *(G-5590)*

M S K Tool & Die Inc......G....... 440 930-8100
Avon Lake *(G-994)*

Machine Tek Systems Inc......E....... 330 527-4450
Garrettsville *(G-10197)*

Magnum Tool Corp......G....... 937 228-0900
Dayton *(G-8323)*

Mar-Vel Tool Co Inc......E....... 937 223-2137
Dayton *(G-8331)*

Martin Machine & Tool Inc......F....... 419 373-1711
Bowling Green *(G-1984)*

Master Craft Products Inc......F....... 216 281-5910
Cleveland *(G-5631)*

MD Tool & Die Inc......G....... 440 647-6456
Wellington *(G-19586)*

Mdf Enterprises LLC......G....... 937 640-3436
Dayton *(G-8336)*

Mdf Tool Corporation......F....... 440 237-2277
North Royalton *(G-15287)*

Metro Tool & Die Co Inc......G....... 937 836-8242
Englewood *(G-9368)*

Meyer Machine Tool Company......G....... 614 235-0039
Columbus *(G-7176)*

Midwest Tool & Engineering Co......E....... 937 224-0756
Dayton *(G-8356)*

Mikan Die and Tool LLC......G....... 216 265-2811
Cleveland *(G-5684)*

Mold Shop Inc......F....... 419 829-2041
Sylvania *(G-17951)*

Moldmakers Inc......F....... 419 673-0902
Kenton *(G-11414)*

MOM Tools LLC......G....... 216 283-4014
Cleveland *(G-5702)*

Monarch Products Co......E....... 330 868-7717
Minerva *(G-14195)*

Mtd Holdings Inc......B....... 330 225-2600
Valley City *(G-19052)*

National Roller Die Inc......F....... 440 951-3850
Willoughby *(G-20386)*

New Bremen Machine & Tool Co......E....... 419 629-3295
New Bremen *(G-14657)*

New Die Inc......E....... 419 726-7581
Toledo *(G-18422)*

Noble Tool Corp......E....... 937 461-4040
Dayton *(G-8381)*

Ohio Specialty Dies LLC......F....... 330 538-3396
North Jackson *(G-15151)*

Omni Manufacturing Inc......D....... 419 394-7424
Saint Marys *(G-16693)*

Omni Manufacturing Inc......F....... 419 394-7424
Saint Marys *(G-16694)*

PRODUCT

Employee Codes: A=Over 500 employees, B=251-500
C=101-250, D=51-100, E=20-50, F=10-19, G=3-9

2019 Harris Ohio
Industrial Directory

1409

DIES & TOOLS: Special

PA MA Inc ....G 440 846-3799
  Strongsville (G-17776)
Paramount Stamping & Wldg Co ....D 216 631-1755
  Cleveland (G-5840)
Phillips Mch & Stamping Corp ....G 330 882-6714
  New Franklin (G-14696)
Pier Tool & Die Inc ....F 440 236-3188
  Columbia Station (G-6443)
Pioneer Precision Tool Inc ....G 513 932-8805
  Lebanon (G-11684)
Pitco Products Inc ....F 513 228-7245
  Dayton (G-8427)
Positool Technologies Inc ....G 330 220-4002
  Brunswick (G-2227)
Precise Tool Inc......................................G 937 778-3441
  Piqua (G-16156)
Precision Component Inds LLC ....E 330 477-1052
  Canton (G-2790)
Precision Die Masters.............................F 440 255-1204
  Mentor (G-13552)
Prime Time Machine Inc ....G 440 942-7410
  Willoughby (G-20411)
Progress Tool & Stamping Inc ....E 419 628-2384
  Minster (G-14223)
PSK Steel Corp ....E 330 759-1251
  Hubbard (G-11009)
Puehler Tool Co......................................G 216 447-0101
  Cleveland (G-5934)
Pyramid Mold Inc ....F 330 673-5200
  Kent (G-11370)
Quality Tooling Systems Inc ....F 330 722-5025
  Medina (G-13326)
Queen City Tool Works Inc ....G 513 874-0111
  Fairfield (G-9555)
R & R Machine & Tool Co ....G 216 281-7609
  Cleveland (G-5948)
R K S Tool & Die Inc..............................G 513 870-0225
  Fairfield (G-9557)
R M Tool & Die Inc................................F 440 238-6459
  Strongsville (G-17780)
Ram Tool Inc ....G 937 277-0717
  Dayton (G-8463)
Rapid Mold Repair & Machine ....G 330 253-1000
  Akron (G-343)
Raymath Company ....C 937 335-1860
  Troy (G-18697)
Raymonds Tool & Gauge LLC ....G 419 485-8340
  Montpelier (G-14317)
Regal Metal Products Co ....F 330 868-6343
  Minerva (G-14199)
Renco Mold Inc ....G 937 233-3233
  Dayton (G-8472)
Reserve Industries Inc............................E 440 871-2796
  Bay Village (G-1208)
Rme Machining Co.................................G 513 541-3328
  Cincinnati (G-4275)
Rmt Corporation ....F 513 942-8308
  Dayton (G-8481)
Rockstedt Tool & Die Inc ....F 330 273-9000
  Brunswick (G-2235)
Ronlen Industries Inc ....E 330 273-6468
  Brunswick (G-2236)
Royer Technologies Inc ....G 937 743-6114
  Saint Marys (G-16698)
RPM Carbide Die Inc.............................E 419 894-6426
  Arcadia (G-626)
Rural Products Inc ....G 419 298-2677
  Edgerton (G-9179)
S-K Mold & Tool Company ....E 937 339-0299
  Tipp City (G-18132)
S-K Mold & Tool Company ....E 937 339-0299
  Troy (G-18701)
Saint-Gobain Ceramics Plas Inc ....A 330 673-5860
  Stow (G-17624)
Schmitmeyer Inc.....................................G 937 295-2091
  Fort Loramie (G-9804)
Seilkop Industries Inc ....E 513 761-1035
  Cincinnati (G-4316)
Sekely Industries Inc..............................C 248 844-9201
  Salem (G-16774)
Shiloh Corporation ....B 330 558-2600
  Valley City (G-19062)
Shiloh Industries Inc...............................A 330 558-2600
  Valley City (G-19065)
Shiloh Industries Inc...............................G 330 558-2600
  Valley City (G-19066)
Skrl Die Casting Inc ....D 440 946-7200
  Willoughby (G-20431)
Smithville Mfg Co...................................E 330 345-5818
  Wooster (G-20655)
Sni Inc ....G 937 427-9447
  Beavercreek (G-1363)
Snyders Tool & Die Inc..........................G 614 878-2205
  Galloway (G-10180)
Sroka Industries Inc ....E 440 572-2811
  Strongsville (G-17795)
Stanco Precision Manufacturing ....G 937 274-1785
  Dayton (G-8524)
Sup-R-Die Inc ....E 216 252-3930
  Cleveland (G-6119)
Sup-R-Die Inc ....G 330 688-7600
  Stow (G-17634)
Sure Tool & Manufacturing Co ....G 937 253-9111
  Dayton (G-8531)
Sutterlin Machine & Tool Co ....F 440 357-0817
  Mentor (G-13598)
Symbol Tool & Die Inc ....G 440 582-5989
  North Royalton (G-15304)
T & W Tool & Machine Inc ....G 937 667-2039
  Tipp City (G-18135)
Taft Tool & Production Co ....F 419 385-2576
  Toledo (G-18542)
Tater Tool & Die Inc...............................G 330 648-1148
  Spencer (G-17307)
Taylor Tool & Die Inc.............................G 937 845-1491
  New Carlisle (G-14678)
Tech Industries Inc ....E 216 861-7337
  Cleveland (G-6153)
Tm Machine & Tool Inc ....G 419 478-0310
  Toledo (G-18554)
Tomahawk Tool Supply ....G 419 485-8737
  Montpelier (G-14319)
Tooling Connection Inc ....G 419 594-3339
  Oakwood (G-15475)
Tooling Zone Inc ....G 937 550-4180
  Springboro (G-17356)
Top Tool & Die Inc.................................F 216 267-5878
  Cleveland (G-6187)
Tradye Machine & Tool Inc ....G 740 625-7550
  Centerburg (G-2994)
Trim Tool & Machine Inc ....G 216 889-1916
  Cleveland (G-6215)
Trimline Die Corporation ....E 440 355-6900
  Lagrange (G-11494)
True Industries Inc ....E 330 296-4342
  Ravenna (G-16416)
U S Alloy Die Corp.................................F 216 749-9700
  Cleveland (G-6227)
United Extrusion Dies Inc ....F 330 533-2915
  Canfield (G-2552)
United Finshg & Die Cutng Inc ....F 216 881-0239
  Cleveland (G-6233)
Universal Tool Technology LLC ....E 937 222-4608
  Dayton (G-8576)
Unlimited Machine and Tool LLC ....F 419 269-1730
  Toledo (G-18586)
Valley Tool & Die Inc ....D 440 237-0160
  North Royalton (G-15309)
Van Wert Machine Inc ....F 419 692-6836
  Delphos (G-8763)
Voisard Tool LLC ....E 937 526-5451
  Russia (G-16614)
Vulcan Tool Company ....G 937 253-6194
  Dayton (G-8581)
Walest Incorporated ....G 216 362-8110
  Cleveland (G-6286)
Walker Tool & Machine Co ....F 419 661-8000
  Perrysburg (G-16024)
Wapak Tool & Die Inc............................G 419 738-6215
  Wapakoneta (G-19359)
Waverly Tool Co Ltd...............................G 740 988-4831
  Beaver (G-1294)
Weiss Industries Inc ....E 419 526-2480
  Mansfield (G-12539)
Windsor Tool Inc ....F 216 671-1900
  Cleveland (G-6313)
Wire Shop Inc ....G 440 354-6842
  Mentor (G-13628)
WLS Stamping Co...................................D 216 271-5100
  Cleveland (G-6318)
Wrena LLC ....E 937 667-4403
  Tipp City (G-18146)
Youngstown Die Development ....G 330 755-0722
  Struthers (G-17826)
Youngstown Tool & Die Company ....D 330 747-4464
  Youngstown (G-21083)

DIES: Cutting, Exc Metal

Ashco Manufacturing Inc ....G 419 838-7193
  Toledo (G-18193)

D & M Saw & Tool Inc ....G 513 871-5433
  Cincinnati (G-3568)
Jbc Technologies Inc ....D 440 327-4522
  North Ridgeville (G-15234)

DIES: Extrusion

American Extrusion Svcs Inc ....G 937 743-1210
  Springboro (G-17322)
Amex Dies Inc ....F 330 545-9766
  Girard (G-10253)
B V Mfg Inc ....F 330 549-5331
  New Springfield (G-14818)
International Dies Co Inc ....G 330 744-7951
  Diamond (G-8798)
Jamen Tool & Die Co ....F 330 788-6521
  Youngstown (G-20945)
Tomco Industries ....G 330 652-7531
  Mineral Ridge (G-14172)
Tri-R Dies Inc ....F 330 758-8050
  Youngstown (G-21053)
Village Plastics Co ....G 330 753-0100
  Barberton (G-1112)
Vinyl Tool & Die Company Inc ....F 330 782-0254
  Youngstown (G-21066)

DIES: Paper Cutting

Tig Wood & Die Inc ....G 937 849-6741
  New Carlisle (G-14680)
Williams Steel Rule Die Co....................F 216 431-3232
  Cleveland (G-6311)

DIES: Plastic Forming

Fremar Industries Inc ....E 330 220-3700
  Brunswick (G-2207)
Kelch Manufacturing Corp ....G 440 366-5060
  Elyria (G-9282)
Liberty Mold & Machine Company ....G 330 278-7825
  Hinckley (G-10904)
National Pattern Mfg Co ....F 330 682-6871
  Orrville (G-15605)
Progrssive Molding Bolivar Inc ....C 330 874-3000
  Bolivar (G-1925)
Trico Machine Products Corp ....F 216 662-4194
  Cleveland (G-6214)

DIES: Steel Rule

Aukerman J F Steel Rule Die ....G 937 456-4498
  Eaton (G-9142)
Container Graphics Corp ....E 937 746-5666
  Franklin (G-9875)
Csw of Ny Inc ....F 413 589-1311
  Sylvania (G-17935)
Customformed Products Inc ....F 937 388-0480
  Miamisburg (G-13653)
D A Stirling Inc ....G 330 923-3195
  Cuyahoga Falls (G-7857)
Die Guys Inc ....E 330 239-3437
  Medina (G-13252)
Hedalloy Die Corp ....F 216 341-3768
  Cleveland (G-5388)
Lorain Ruled Die Products Inc...............E 440 281-8607
  North Ridgeville (G-15239)
Loroco Industries Inc ....E 513 891-9544
  Blue Ash (G-1807)
True Kote Inc ....G 419 334-8813
  Fremont (G-10056)

DIES: Wire Drawing & Straightening

Carbide Specialist Inc............................F 440 951-4027
  Willoughby (G-20292)
Lanko Industries Inc ....G 440 269-1641
  Mentor (G-13496)

DIFFERENTIAL ASSEMBLIES & PARTS

Adelmans Truck Parts Corp...................F 216 362-0500
  Canton (G-2559)

DIMENSION STONE: Buildings

Cleveland Granite & Marble LLC ....E 216 291-7637
  Cleveland (G-4961)

DIODES: Light Emitting

Bestlight Led Corporation......................G 440 205-1552
  Mentor (G-13402)
Bright Focus Sales Inc ....F 216 751-8384
  Cleveland (G-4838)

PRODUCT SECTION

Ceso Inc .... D 937 435-8584
  Miamisburg (G-13649)
Energy Focus Inc .... C 440 715-1300
  Solon (G-17137)
Tri-Tech Led Systems .... G 614 593-2868
  Baltimore (G-1045)

DIODES: Solid State, Germanium, Silicon, Etc

Measurement Specialties Inc .... F 937 427-1231
  Beavercreek (G-1358)

DIRECT SELLING ESTABLISHMENTS: Beverage Svcs

Superior Soda Service LLC .... G 937 657-9700
  Beavercreek (G-1364)

DIRECT SELLING ESTABLISHMENTS: Food Svcs

Schwans Home Service Inc .... E 419 222-9977
  Lima (G-11936)

DIRECT SELLING ESTABLISHMENTS: Home Related Prdts

P & M Enterprises Group Inc .... G 330 316-0387
  Canton (G-2777)

DIRECT SELLING ESTABLISHMENTS: Snacks

Conns Potato Chip Co Inc .... E 740 452-4615
  Zanesville (G-21123)

DISCS & TAPE: Optical, Blank

Folio Photonics LLC .... G 440 420-4500
  Solon (G-17145)

DISHWASHING EQPT: Commercial

Hobart Corporation .... E 937 332-3000
  Troy (G-18671)
Hobart Corporation .... C 937 332-2797
  Piqua (G-16128)
Illinois Tool Works Inc .... E 937 335-7171
  Troy (G-18673)

DISHWASHING EQPT: Household

Whirlpool Corporation .... D 419 423-8123
  Findlay (G-9776)
Whirlpool Corporation .... B 419 547-7711
  Clyde (G-6397)
Whirlpool Corporation .... C 419 523-5100
  Ottawa (G-15672)

DISK & DISKETTE CONVERSION SVCS

J Com Data Inc .... G 614 304-1455
  Pataskala (G-15833)

DISK DRIVES: Computer

Western Digital Corporation .... G 440 684-1331
  Cleveland (G-6302)

DISPENSING EQPT & PARTS, BEVERAGE: Beer

Boston Beer Company .... F 267 240-4429
  Cincinnati (G-3405)
Rack Draft Service Inc .... F 513 353-5520
  North Bend (G-15054)

DISPENSING EQPT & PARTS, BEVERAGE: Coolers, Milk/Water, Elec

Brookpark Laboratories Inc .... G 216 267-7140
  Cleveland (G-4841)
DTE Cool Co .... G 513 579-0160
  Cincinnati (G-3611)

DISPENSING EQPT & PARTS, BEVERAGE: Fountain/Other Beverage

Dj Beverage Innovations Inc .... G 614 769-1569
  Plain City (G-16188)

International Beverage Works .... G 614 798-5398
  Columbus (G-7043)

DISPLAY FIXTURES: Showcases, Wood, Exc Refrigerated

GMI Companies Inc .... E 937 981-7724
  Greenfield (G-10349)
GMI Companies Inc .... C 513 932-3445
  Lebanon (G-11657)
GMI Companies Inc .... G 937 981-0244
  Greenfield (G-10348)
Indian River Industries .... G 740 965-4377
  Sunbury (G-17890)
Roy L Bayes .... G 614 274-6729
  Columbus (G-7404)

DISPLAY FIXTURES: Wood

7d Marketing Inc .... F 330 721-8822
  Medina (G-13215)
A-Display Service Corp .... F 614 469-1230
  Columbus (G-6517)
Cassady Woodworks Inc .... F 937 256-7948
  Dayton (G-7974)
Couch Business Development Inc .. F 937 253-1099
  Dayton (G-8104)
Gabriel Logan LLC .... D 740 380-6809
  Logan (G-12024)
Kdm Signs Inc .... E 513 769-3900
  Cincinnati (G-3899)
Midwest Woodworking Co Inc .... E 513 631-6684
  Cincinnati (G-4028)
Murray Display Fixtures Ltd .... F 614 875-1594
  Grove City (G-10448)
Ohio Woodworking Co Inc .... G 513 631-0870
  Cincinnati (G-4107)
Ptmj Enterprises .... C 440 543-8000
  Solon (G-17220)
Tim Crabtree .... G 740 286-4535
  Jackson (G-11198)
Ultrabuilt Play Systems Inc .... F 419 652-2294
  Nova (G-15436)
W J Egli Company Inc .... F 330 823-3666
  Alliance (G-512)
Witt-Gor Inc .... G 419 659-2151
  Columbus Grove (G-7639)

DISPLAY ITEMS: Corrugated, Made From Purchased Materials

Pratt Industries Inc .... D 513 770-0851
  Mason (G-12924)
The Shelby Co .... E 440 871-9901
  Westlake (G-20167)

DISPLAY ITEMS: Solid Fiber, Made From Purchased Materials

Acrylicon Inc .... G 614 263-2086
  Columbus (G-6539)
Digital Color Intl LLC .... E 330 762-6959
  Akron (G-143)

DISPLAY LETTERING SVCS

P S Superior Inc .... F 216 587-1000
  Cleveland (G-5833)

DISPLAY STANDS: Merchandise, Exc Wood

Warren Steel Specialties Corp .... F 330 399-8360
  Warren (G-19461)

DISTILLATION PRDTS: Wood

Arizona Chemical Company LLC .... C 330 343-7701
  Dover (G-8804)

DISTILLERS DRIED GRAIN & SOLUBLES

Buckeye Distillery .... G 937 877-1901
  Tipp City (G-18103)
Indian Creek Distillery .... G 937 846-1443
  New Carlisle (G-14668)

DISTRIBUTORS: Motor Vehicle Engine

Brinkley Technology Group LLC .... F 330 830-2498
  Massillon (G-12963)
Industrial Systems & Solutions ...... G 440 205-1658
  Mentor (G-13470)

DOOR OPERATING SYSTEMS: Electric

Legacy Supplies Inc .... F 330 405-4565
  Twinsburg (G-18805)
Power Acquisition LLC .... G 614 228-5000
  Dublin (G-8966)
Stellar Industrial Tech Co .... G 740 654-7052
  Lancaster (G-11612)
Thirion Brothers Eqp Co LLC .... G 440 357-8004
  Painesville (G-15790)
Weldon Pump Acquition LLC .... E 440 232-2282
  Oakwood Village (G-15489)

DOCK EQPT & SPLYS, INDL

Heartland Engineered Pdts LLC .... F 513 367-0080
  Harrison (G-10645)
Tmt Inc .... C 419 592-1041
  Perrysburg (G-16018)

DOCKS: Prefabricated Metal

American Tower Acquisition .... F 419 347-1185
  Shelby (G-16977)
Commercial Dock & Door Inc .... E 440 951-1210
  Mentor (G-13419)
Genesis Services LLC .... G 740 896-3734
  Beverly (G-1661)
Jet Dock Systems Inc .... E 216 750-2264
  Cleveland (G-5497)
Metal Craft Docks Inc .... G 440 286-7135
  Painesville (G-15763)

DOCUMENT DESTRUCTION SVC

P C Workshop Inc .... D 419 399-4805
  Paulding (G-15869)

DOGS, WHOLESALE

Dog Depot .... G 513 771-9274
  Cincinnati (G-3599)

DOLLIES: Industrial

R B Mfg Co .... F 419 626-9464
  Wadsworth (G-19270)

DOLLIES: Mechanics'

Pegasus Products Company Inc ... G 330 677-1123
  Kent (G-11361)

DOLOMITE: Crushed & Broken

Covia Holdings Corporation .... D 440 214-3284
  Independence (G-11123)
Drummond Dolomite Inc .... F 440 942-7000
  Mentor (G-13432)

DOOR & WINDOW REPAIR SVCS

Bert Radebaugh .... G 740 382-8134
  Marion (G-12695)
Pickens Window Service Inc .... F 513 931-4432
  Cincinnati (G-4157)
Screenmobile Inc .... G 614 868-8663
  Radnor (G-16358)

DOOR FRAMES: Wood

All Pro Ovrhd Door Systems LLC ... G 614 444-3667
  Columbus (G-6567)
Architectural Door Systems LLC ... G 513 808-9900
  Norwood (G-15422)

DOOR OPERATING SYSTEMS: Electric

A L Callahan Door Sales .... G 419 884-3667
  Mansfield (G-12399)
Action Industries Ltd .... F 216 252-7800
  Strongsville (G-17705)
Bert Radebaugh .... G 740 382-8134
  Marion (G-12695)
Bonham Enterprsises .... G 740 333-0501
  Wshngtn CT Hs (G-20719)
GMI Holdings Inc .... B 330 821-5360
  Mount Hope (G-14437)
JC Electric .... E 330 760-2915
  Garrettsville (G-10193)
Oakes Door Serv .... G 937 323-6188
  Springfield (G-17463)
Overhead Door of Salem Inc .... G 330 332-9530
  Salem (G-16765)
Trinity Door Systems .... G 877 603-2018
  New Springfield (G-14822)

Employee Codes: A=Over 500 employees, B=251-500
C=101-250, D=51-100, E=20-50, F=10-19, G=3-9

DOORS & WINDOWS WHOLESALERS: All Materials

DOORS & WINDOWS WHOLESALERS: All Materials

Bert Radebaugh	G	740 382-8134	
Marion (G-12695)			
Gorell Enterprises Inc	B	724 465-1800	
Streetsboro (G-17675)			
Great Lakes Stair & Mllwk Co	G	330 225-2005	
Hinckley (G-10900)			
Mason Structural Steel Inc	D	440 439-1040	
Walton Hills (G-19312)			
Rockwood Products Ltd	F	330 893-2392	
Millersburg (G-14124)			
Toledo Window & Awning Inc		419 474-3396	
Toledo (G-18575)			
Traichal Construction Company	E	800 255-3667	
Niles (G-15037)			

DOORS & WINDOWS: Screen & Storm

- Duo-Corp ..... E 330 549-2149
  North Lima (G-15170)
- Euclid Jalousies Inc ..... G 440 953-1112
  Cleveland (G-5196)
- Quanex Screens LLC ..... G 419 662-5001
  Perrysburg (G-16002)
- Stoett Industries Inc ..... E 419 542-0247
  Hicksville (G-10783)

DOORS & WINDOWS: Storm, Metal

- Angel Window Mfg Corp ..... G 440 891-1006
  Berea (G-1590)
- Champion Opco LLC ..... B 513 327-7338
  Cincinnati (G-3463)
- Champion Win Co Cleveland LLC ..... E 440 899-2562
  Macedonia (G-12283)
- Otter Group LLC ..... F 937 315-1199
  Dayton (G-8410)

DOORS: Combination Screen & Storm, Wood

- R C Moore Lumber Co ..... F 740 732-4950
  Caldwell (G-2410)

DOORS: Fiberglass

- Schmidt Progressive LLC ..... E 513 934-2600
  Lebanon (G-11693)
- Toledo Pro Fiberglass Inc ..... G 419 241-9390
  Toledo (G-18567)

DOORS: Folding, Plastic Or Plastic Coated Fabric

- Clear Fold Door Inc ..... G 440 735-1351
  Cleveland (G-4942)
- Eckel Industries Inc ..... E 978 772-0480
  West Chester (G-19850)
- Modern Builders Supply Inc ..... F 419 526-0002
  Mansfield (G-12485)
- National Access Design LLC ..... F 513 351-3400
  Cincinnati (G-4058)
- Pease Industies Inc ..... B 513 870-3600
  Fairfield (G-9546)

DOORS: Garage, Overhead, Metal

- All Around Garage Door Inc ..... G 440 759-5079
  North Ridgeville (G-15207)
- Amarr Company ..... G 216 573-7100
  Independence (G-11119)
- Anderson Door Co ..... E 216 475-5700
  Cleveland (G-4712)
- Clopay Building Pdts Co Inc ..... E 513 770-4800
  Mason (G-12846)
- Clopay Building Pdts Co Inc ..... G 937 526-4301
  Russia (G-16606)
- Clopay Building Pdts Co Inc ..... G 937 440-6403
  Troy (G-18642)
- Clopay Corporation ..... C 800 282-2260
  Mason (G-12847)
- Custom Hitch and Trailer/ Over ..... G 740 289-3925
  Piketon (G-16068)
- Division Overhead Door Inc ..... F 513 872-0888
  Cincinnati (G-3597)
- Haas Door Company ..... C 419 337-9900
  Wauseon (G-19519)
- Hrh Door Corp ..... A 850 208-3400
  Mount Hope (G-14438)
- Hrh Door Corp 330 828-2291
  Dalton (G-7943)
- Overhead Door Corporation ..... D 740 383-6376
  Marion (G-12727)
- Overhead Door Corporation ..... F 419 294-3874
  Upper Sandusky (G-18970)
- Tri County Door Service Inc ..... F 216 531-2245
  Euclid (G-9448)

DOORS: Garage, Overhead, Wood

- All Around Garage Door Inc ..... G 440 759-5079
  North Ridgeville (G-15207)
- Amarr Company ..... G 216 573-7100
  Independence (G-11119)
- Anderson Door Co 216 475-5700
  Cleveland (G-4712)
- Clopay Building Pdts Co Inc ..... E 513 770-4800
  Mason (G-12846)
- Clopay Building Pdts Co Inc ..... G 937 526-4301
  Russia (G-16606)
- Clopay Building Pdts Co Inc ..... G 937 440-6403
  Troy (G-18642)
- Clopay Corporation ..... C 800 282-2260
  Mason (G-12847)
- Division Overhead Door Inc 513 872-0888
  Cincinnati (G-3597)
- Hrh Door Corp ..... A 850 208-3400
  Mount Hope (G-14438)

DOORS: Glass

- A Service Glass Inc ..... F 937 426-4920
  Beavercreek (G-1297)
- Basco Manufacturing Company ..... C 513 573-1900
  Mason (G-12831)
- Scs Construction Services Inc ..... E 513 929-0260
  Cincinnati (G-4311)

DOORS: Hangar, Metal

- Machine Tool & Fab Corp ..... F 419 435-7676
  Fostoria (G-9846)

DOORS: Louver, Wood

- C Square Lumber Products ..... F 740 557-3129
  Stockport (G-17559)

DOORS: Rolling, Indl Building Or Warehouse, Metal

- Dynaco Usa Inc ..... G 419 227-3000
  Lima (G-11858)

DOORS: Screen, Metal

- Central Ohio Rtrctable Screens ..... G 614 868-5080
  Radnor (G-16357)

DOORS: Wooden

- Courthouse Manufacturing LLC ..... E 740 335-2727
  Washington Court Hou (G-19476)
- Creative Millwork Ohio Inc 440 992-3566
  Ashtabula (G-768)
- Darby Creek Millwork Co ..... G 614 873-3267
  Plain City (G-16185)
- Designer Doors Inc ..... E 330 772-6391
  Burghill (G-2354)
- Jeld-Wen Inc ..... B 740 397-1144
  Mount Vernon (G-14485)
- Jeld-Wen Inc ..... C 740 964-1431
  Etna (G-9394)
- Jeld-Wen Inc ..... E 740 397-3403
  Mount Vernon (G-14486)
- Khempco Bldg Sup Co Ltd Partnr ..... D 740 549-0465
  Delaware (G-8700)
- Masco Cbinetry Middlefield LLC ..... B 440 437-8537
  Orwell (G-15634)
- Masonite Corporation ..... D 937 454-9207
  Vandalia (G-19136)
- Oak Front Inc 330 948-4500
  Lodi (G-12017)
- Overhead Door Corporation ..... D 740 383-6376
  Marion (G-12727)
- Overhead Door Corporation ..... F 419 294-3874
  Upper Sandusky (G-18970)
- Pease Industies Inc ..... B 513 870-3600
  Fairfield (G-9546)
- Precision Wood Products Inc ..... E 937 787-3523
  Camden (G-2466)
- S R Door Inc ..... C 740 927-3558
  Hebron (G-10761)
- Sommers Wood N Door Company ..... G 614 873-3506
  Plain City (G-16213)
- Star Door & Sash Co Inc ..... F 419 841-3396
  Berkey (G-1636)
- Swiss Woodcraft Inc ..... E 330 925-1807
  Rittman (G-16529)
- Teledoor LLC ..... G 419 227-3000
  Lima (G-11949)

DOWELS & DOWEL RODS

- Berlin Wood Products Inc 330 893-3281
  Berlin (G-1639)
- Cincinnati Dowel & WD Pdts Co ..... E 937 444-2502
  Mount Orab (G-14439)
- Puttmann Industries Inc ..... F 513 202-9444
  Harrison (G-10665)

DRAFTING SPLYS WHOLESALERS

- J C Equipment Sales & Leasing ..... G 513 772-7612
  Cincinnati (G-3862)
- Queen City Reprographics ..... C 513 326-2300
  Cincinnati (G-4240)

DRAFTING SVCS

- Applied Experience LLC ..... G 614 943-2970
  Columbus (G-6610)

DRAINAGE PRDTS: Concrete

- Hanson Aggregates East LLC ..... E 330 467-7890
  Macedonia (G-12301)
- Mack Ready Mix Concrete Inc ..... G 330 483-3111
  Valley City (G-19046)

DRAPERIES & CURTAINS

- A Designers Workroom ..... G 513 251-7396
  Cincinnati (G-3280)
- Accent Drapery Co Inc ..... E 614 488-0741
  Columbus (G-6531)
- Biaginis Draperies ..... G 614 876-1706
  Hilliard (G-10812)
- Carter Drapery Service Inc ..... G 419 289-2530
  Ashland (G-689)
- Drapery Stitch Cincinnati Inc ..... F 513 561-2443
  Cincinnati (G-3609)
- Janson Industries ..... D 330 455-7029
  Canton (G-2716)
- Silver Threads Inc ..... E 614 733-0099
  Plain City (G-16211)
- Sk Textile Inc ..... C 323 581-8986
  Cincinnati (G-4341)
- Vocational Services Inc ..... C 216 431-8085
  Cleveland (G-6267)
- Wise Window Treatment Inc ..... F 216 676-4080
  Berea (G-1633)

DRAPERIES & DRAPERY FABRICS, COTTON

- Carmens Installation Co ..... F 216 321-4040
  Cleveland (G-4879)
- Cleveland Drapery Stitch Inc ..... F 216 252-3857
  Cleveland (G-4957)
- Custom Craft Drap Inc ..... G 330 929-5728
  Cuyahoga Falls (G-7856)
- Lumenomics Inc ..... E 614 798-3500
  Lewis Center (G-11766)
- Nancys Draperies ..... F 330 855-7751
  Marshallville (G-12754)
- Silver Threads Inc ..... E 614 733-0099
  Plain City (G-16211)
- Winspec Inc ..... G 440 834-9068
  Middlefield (G-13867)

DRAPERIES: Plastic & Textile, From Purchased Materials

- Drapery Stitch of Delphos ..... E 419 692-3921
  Delphos (G-8741)
- E W Perry Service Co Inc ..... G 419 473-1231
  Toledo (G-18273)
- Elden Draperies of Toledo Inc 419 535-1909
  Toledo (G-18277)
- Specialty Drapery Workroom ..... G 330 864-4190
  Akron (G-383)
- Stan Rileys Custom Draperies ..... G 513 821-3732
  Cincinnati (G-4370)
- Standard Textile Co Inc ..... B 513 761-9256
  Cincinnati (G-4372)

PRODUCT SECTION — DUMPSTERS: Garbage

Tiffin Scenic Studios Inc ....D....... 800 445-1546
  Tiffin (G-18089)
Wahlies Cstm Cft Drapery Uphl ....G....... 419 229-1731
  Lima (G-11958)

DRAPERY & UPHOLSTERY STORES: Draperies

Accent Drapery Co Inc ....E....... 614 488-0741
  Columbus (G-6531)
Custom Craft Drap Inc ....G....... 330 929-5728
  Cuyahoga Falls (G-7856)
Elden Draperies of Toledo Inc ....F....... 419 535-1909
  Toledo (G-18277)
Nancys Draperies ....F....... 330 855-7751
  Marshallville (G-12754)

DRAPES & DRAPERY FABRICS, FROM MANMADE FIBER

Cleveland Drapery Stitch Inc ....F....... 216 252-3857
  Cleveland (G-4957)
Lumenomics Inc ....E....... 614 798-3500
  Lewis Center (G-11766)

DRIED FRUITS WHOLESALERS

Ohio Hickory Harvest Brand Pro ....E....... 330 644-6266
  Coventry Township (G-7775)

DRILL BITS

Custom Carbide Cutter Inc ....F....... 513 851-6363
  West Chester (G-19847)

DRILLING MACHINERY & EQPT: Oil & Gas

Arete Innovative Solutions LLC ....G....... 513 503-2712
  Morrow (G-14408)
Dynamic Leasing Ltd ....G....... 330 892-0164
  New Waterford (G-14839)
Monroe Drilling Operations ....G....... 740 472-0866
  Woodsfield (G-20548)
Rmi Titanium Company LLC ....E....... 330 652-9952
  Niles (G-15028)
Terra Sonic International LLC ....E....... 740 374-6608
  Marietta (G-12679)
Tiger General LLC ....D....... 330 239-4949
  Medina (G-13353)

DRILLS & DRILLING EQPT: Mining

Davey Kent Inc ....E....... 330 673-5400
  Kent (G-11310)

DRINK MIXES, NONALCOHOLIC: Cocktail

Great Western Juice Company ....F....... 216 475-5770
  Cleveland (G-5352)

DRINKING FOUNTAINS: Metal, Nonrefrigerated

Murdock Inc ....F....... 513 471-7700
  Cincinnati (G-4055)

DRINKING PLACES: Alcoholic Beverages

Rocky River Brewing Co ....E....... 440 895-2739
  Rocky River (G-16555)

DRINKING PLACES: Bars & Lounges

Green Room Brewing LLC ....G....... 614 596-3655
  Columbus (G-6970)
Tom Bad Brewing LLC ....F....... 513 871-4677
  Cincinnati (G-4425)

DRINKING PLACES: Beer Garden

Bar 25 LLC ....G....... 216 621-4000
  Cleveland (G-4789)

DRINKING PLACES: Tavern

Railroad Brewing Company ....G....... 440 723-8234
  Avon (G-961)

DRIVE SHAFTS

Cincinnati Drveline Hydraulics ....G....... 513 651-2406
  Cincinnati (G-3490)

DRIVES: High Speed Indl, Exc Hydrostatic

Jamtek Enterprises Inc ....G....... 513 738-4700
  Harrison (G-10652)
Nidec Indus Automtn USA LLC ....E....... 216 901-2400
  Cleveland (G-5753)
Speed Selector Inc ....F....... 440 543-8233
  Chagrin Falls (G-3077)

DRUG STORES

Omnicare Phrm of Midwest LLC ....D....... 513 719-2600
  Cincinnati (G-4111)

DRUG TESTING KITS: Blood & Urine

Aufbackgroundscreeningcom ....G....... 216 831-4113
  Beachwood (G-1224)
University of Cincinnati ....F....... 513 558-1243
  Cincinnati (G-4453)

DRUGS & DRUG PROPRIETARIES, WHOLESALE

Buderer Drug Co ....G....... 419 626-3429
  Sandusky (G-16798)
Buderer Drug Company Inc ....F....... 419 627-2800
  Sandusky (G-16799)
Buderer Drug Company Inc ....F....... 419 873-2800
  Perrysburg (G-15925)
Buderer Drug Company Inc ....G....... 440 934-3100
  Avon (G-943)
Omnicare Phrm of Midwest LLC ....D....... 513 719-2600
  Cincinnati (G-4111)

DRUGS & DRUG PROPRIETARIES, WHOLESALE: Antiseptics

Beiersdorf Inc ....C....... 513 682-7300
  West Chester (G-19835)

DRUGS & DRUG PROPRIETARIES, WHOLESALE: Druggists' Sundries

Samuels Products Inc ....E....... 513 891-4456
  Blue Ash (G-1842)

DRUGS & DRUG PROPRIETARIES, WHOLESALE: Medicinals/Botanicals

Goosefoot Acres Inc ....G....... 330 225-7184
  Valley City (G-19039)

DRUGS & DRUG PROPRIETARIES, WHOLESALE: Patent Medicines

Teva Womens Health Inc ....C....... 513 731-9900
  Cincinnati (G-4416)

DRUGS & DRUG PROPRIETARIES, WHOLESALE: Pharmaceuticals

American Regent Inc ....D....... 614 436-2222
  Hilliard (G-10804)
Amerisourcebergen Corporation ....D....... 614 497-3665
  Lockbourne (G-11992)
Biorx LLC ....C....... 866 442-4679
  Cincinnati (G-3394)
Cardinal Health Inc ....G....... 614 553-3830
  Dublin (G-8893)
Cardinal Health Inc ....A....... 614 757-5000
  Dublin (G-8894)
Markethatch Co Inc ....F....... 330 376-6363
  Akron (G-269)
River City Pharma ....D....... 513 870-1680
  Fairfield (G-9558)

DRUGS & DRUG PROPRIETARIES, WHOLESALE: Vitamins & Minerals

Direct Action Co Inc ....F....... 330 364-3219
  Dover (G-8816)
Suarez Corporation Industries ....D....... 330 494-4282
  Canton (G-2827)
Wbc Group LLC ....D....... 866 528-2144
  Hudson (G-11082)

DRUGS ACTING ON THE CENTRAL NERVOUS SYSTEM & SENSE ORGANS

Allergan Inc ....D....... 614 623-8140
  Powell (G-16308)

DRUMS: Fiber

Greif Inc ....E....... 419 238-0565
  Van Wert (G-19094)
Greif Inc ....E....... 740 657-6500
  Delaware (G-8682)

DRUMS: Shipping, Metal

Greif Inc ....E....... 740 549-6000
  Delaware (G-8681)
Greif Inc ....E....... 740 657-6500
  Delaware (G-8682)
Mauser Usa LLC ....D....... 513 398-1300
  Mason (G-12908)
North Coast Container Corp ....D....... 216 441-6214
  Cleveland (G-5763)

DRYCLEANING EQPT & SPLYS: Commercial

Thompson Distributing Co Inc ....G....... 513 422-9011
  Middletown (G-13957)

DRYCLEANING PLANTS

Jackson Deluxe Cleaners Ltd ....G....... 419 592-2826
  Napoleon (G-14547)

DRYERS & REDRYERS: Indl

Agridry LLC ....E....... 419 459-4399
  Edon (G-9183)

DUCTING: Plastic

Aetna Plastics Corp ....G....... 330 274-2855
  Mantua (G-12541)

DUCTS: Sheet Metal

A A A Professional Htg & Coolg ....G....... 513 933-0564
  Lebanon (G-11628)
Controls and Sheet Metal Inc ....E....... 513 721-3610
  Cincinnati (G-3546)
Custom Duct & Supply Co Inc ....G....... 937 228-2058
  Dayton (G-8118)
Eastern Sheet Metal Inc ....D....... 513 793-3440
  Blue Ash (G-1763)
Kerber Sheetmetal Works Inc ....F....... 937 339-6366
  Troy (G-18681)
Langdon Inc ....E....... 513 733-5955
  Cincinnati (G-3930)
Lukjan Metal Products Inc ....C....... 440 599-8127
  Conneaut (G-7654)
McGill Airflow LLC ....F....... 614 829-1200
  Columbus (G-7164)
McGill Airflow LLC ....G....... 614 829-1200
  Groveport (G-10503)
McGill Corporation ....F....... 614 829-1200
  Groveport (G-10504)
Ohio Fabricators Inc ....E....... 216 391-2400
  Akron (G-306)
Scharenberg Sheet Metal ....G....... 740 664-2431
  New Marshfield (G-14744)
Technibus Inc ....D....... 330 479-4202
  Canton (G-2833)
United McGill Corporation ....E....... 614 829-1200
  Groveport (G-10516)

DUMPSTERS: Garbage

Cheap Dumpsters LLC ....G....... 614 285-5865
  Columbus (G-6760)
Cincy-Dumpster Inc ....G....... 513 941-3063
  Cleves (G-6357)
Dumpsters Inc ....G....... 440 241-6927
  Seven Hills (G-16903)
E-Pak Manufacturing LLC ....D....... 800 235-1632
  Wooster (G-20588)
Gerald H Smith ....G....... 740 446-3455
  Bidwell (G-1666)
Gorilla Dumpsters ....G....... 614 344-4677
  Dublin (G-8917)
Heights Dumpster Services LLC ....G....... 937 321-0096
  Huber Heights (G-11019)
North Coast Dumpster Svcs LLC ......G....... 216 644-5647
  Cleveland (G-5764)

Employee Codes: A=Over 500 employees, B=251-500
C=101-250, D=51-100, E=20-50, F=10-19, G=3-9

DUMPSTERS: Garbage

Porter Dumpsters LLC ....G...... 330 659-0043
  Richfield (G-16482)
Say Dumpsters ....G...... 937 578-3744
  Marysville (G-12808)
Wastequip Manufacturing Co LLC ....E...... 330 674-1119
  Millersburg (G-14148)

DURABLE GOODS WHOLESALERS, NEC

Aerovent Inc ....G...... 937 473-3789
  Covington (G-7779)
Assoc Talents Inc ....G...... 440 716-1265
  Westlake (G-20100)

DUST OR FUME COLLECTING EQPT: Indl

Camfil USA Inc ....G...... 937 773-0866
  Piqua (G-16106)
Envirofab Inc ....F...... 216 651-1767
  Cleveland (G-5182)
Herman Manufacturing LLC ....F...... 216 251-6400
  Cleveland (G-5398)
Jacp Inc ....G...... 513 353-3660
  Miamitown (G-13747)
Process Automation Specialists ....G...... 330 247-1384
  Canal Fulton (G-2489)
Schenck Process LLC ....F...... 513 576-9200
  Chagrin Falls (G-3074)
Sly Inc ....F...... 440 891-3200
  Strongsville (G-17789)

DYES & PIGMENTS: Organic

Accel Corporation ....F...... 440 327-7418
  Avon (G-937)
Colormatrix Group Inc ....G...... 216 622-0100
  Berea (G-1598)
Colormatrix Holdings Inc ....G...... 440 930-3162
  Berea (G-1599)
Dorum Color Co Inc ....G...... 330 773-1900
  Coventry Township (G-7768)
Hexpol Compounding LLC ....G...... 440 834-4644
  Burton (G-2360)
Norlab Inc ....G...... 440 282-5265
  Lorain (G-12107)
Polyone Corporation ....G...... 419 668-4844
  Norwalk (G-15412)
Republic Powdered Metals Inc ....D...... 330 225-3192
  Medina (G-13327)
RPM International Inc ....D...... 330 273-5090
  Medina (G-13331)
Sun Chemical Corporation ....E...... 513 830-8667
  Cincinnati (G-4395)

DYES OR COLORS: Food, Synthetic

Berghausen Corporation ....E...... 513 541-5631
  Cincinnati (G-3389)

DYES: Synthetic Organic

Inceptor Inc ....G...... 419 726-8804
  Toledo (G-18343)

EARTH SCIENCE SVCS

Nucon International Inc ....F...... 614 846-5710
  Columbus (G-7232)

EATING PLACES

Auntie Annes ....G...... 330 652-1939
  Niles (G-15000)
Ball Corp ....G...... 419 483-4343
  Bellevue (G-1530)
Breitenbach Wine Cellar Inc ....G...... 330 343-3603
  Dover (G-8810)
Brewpub Restaurant Corp ....D...... 614 228-2537
  Columbus (G-6696)
Buns of Delaware Inc ....E...... 740 363-2867
  Delaware (G-8659)
Ferrante Wine Farm Inc ....E...... 440 466-8466
  Geneva (G-10219)
Guggisberg Cheese Inc ....G...... 330 893-2550
  Millersburg (G-14086)
John Purdum ....G...... 513 897-9686
  Waynesville (G-19569)
Kroger Co ....C...... 740 671-5164
  Bellaire (G-1487)
Kroger Co ....D...... 740 374-2523
  Marietta (G-12638)
Old World Foods Inc ....G...... 216 341-5665
  Cleveland (G-5810)

Rocky River Brewing Co ....E...... 440 895-2739
  Rocky River (G-16555)
Sausage Shoppe ....G...... 216 351-5213
  Brunswick (G-2237)
Trixies Pickles Inc ....E...... 817 658-6648
  Findlay (G-9771)
Willoughby Brewing Company ....D...... 440 975-0202
  Willoughby (G-20458)

EDUCATIONAL SVCS

Dietrich Von Hildebrand Legacy ....G...... 703 496-7821
  Steubenville (G-17530)
International Cntr Artfcial or ....G...... 440 358-1102
  Painesville (G-15749)
Tangible Solutions Inc ....G...... 937 912-4603
  Fairborn (G-9471)

EDUCATIONAL SVCS, NONDEGREE GRANTING: Continuing Education

360water Inc ....G...... 614 294-3600
  Columbus (G-6511)
Deemsys Inc ....D...... 614 322-9928
  Gahanna (G-10079)
Toastmasters International ....F...... 937 429-2680
  Dayton (G-7991)

EGG WHOLESALERS

Ballas Egg Products Corp ....D...... 614 453-0386
  Zanesville (G-21102)
Barkett Fruit Co Inc ....E...... 330 364-6645
  Dover (G-8807)
Frank L Harter & Son Inc ....G...... 513 574-1330
  Cincinnati (G-3709)
Ohio Fresh Eggs LLC ....C...... 740 893-7200
  Croton (G-7822)
Ohio Fresh Eggs LLC ....E...... 937 354-2233
  Mount Victory (G-14520)

ELASTOMERS

Advanced Elastomer Systems LP ....D...... 330 336-7641
  Wadsworth (G-19221)
Altera Polymers LLC ....G...... 864 973-7000
  Jefferson (G-11224)
Asi Investment Holding Co ....D...... 330 666-3751
  Fairlawn (G-9593)
Sunprene Company ....C...... 330 666-3751
  Fairlawn (G-9621)

ELECTRIC & OTHER SERVICES COMBINED

Cliffs Minnesota Minerals Co ....A...... 216 694-5700
  Cleveland (G-4992)
Northshore Mining Company ....G...... 216 694-5700
  Cleveland (G-5785)

ELECTRIC FENCE CHARGERS

Agratronix LLC ....E...... 330 562-2222
  Streetsboro (G-17657)
D&M Fencing LLC ....G...... 419 604-0698
  Spencerville (G-17308)

ELECTRIC MOTOR & GENERATOR AUXILIARY PARTS

Mv Designlabs LLC ....G...... 724 355-7986
  Cleveland (G-5715)

ELECTRIC MOTOR REPAIR SVCS

3-D Service Ltd ....C...... 330 830-3500
  Massillon (G-12956)
A E Ruston Electric LLC ....G...... 740 286-3022
  Jackson (G-11178)
Akron Indus Mtr Sls & Svc Inc ....G...... 330 753-7624
  Norton (G-15359)
Al Bradshaw Jr ....G...... 513 422-8870
  Middletown (G-13882)
Allan A Irish ....G...... 419 394-3284
  Saint Marys (G-16675)
Als High Tech Inc ....F...... 440 232-7090
  Bedford (G-1380)
B W Electrical & Maint Svc ....G...... 330 534-7870
  Hubbard (G-10999)
Barry Brothers Electric ....G...... 614 299-8187
  Columbus (G-6651)
Bay Electric Co ....G...... 419 625-1046
  Sandusky (G-16796)

Bennett Electric Inc ....F...... 800 874-5405
  Norwalk (G-15382)
Big River Electric Inc ....G...... 740 446-4360
  Gallipolis (G-10161)
Bornhorst Motor Service Inc ....G...... 937 773-0426
  Piqua (G-16104)
Brian Franks Electric Inc ....G...... 330 821-5457
  Alliance (G-458)
C and O Electric Motor Service ....G...... 614 491-6387
  Columbus (G-6718)
C P Electric Motor Repair Inc ....G...... 330 425-9593
  Twinsburg (G-18745)
Campton Electric Sales & Svc ....G...... 740 826-4429
  New Concord (G-14682)
Cardinal Electric LLC ....G...... 740 366-6850
  Newark (G-14860)
Carnation Elc Mtr Repr Sls Inc ....G...... 330 823-7116
  Alliance (G-460)
Clark-Fowler Enterprises Inc ....E...... 330 262-0906
  Wooster (G-20578)
Columbus Electrical Works Co ....F...... 614 294-4651
  Columbus (G-6787)
D & J Electric Motor Repair Co ....F...... 330 336-4343
  Wadsworth (G-19232)
E-Z Electric Motor Svc Corp ....E...... 216 581-8820
  Cleveland (G-5132)
Electric Ctrl & Mtr Repr Svc ....G...... 216 881-3143
  Cleveland (G-5162)
Electric Motor Svc of Athens ....E...... 740 592-1682
  The Plains (G-18022)
Electro Torque ....G...... 614 297-1600
  Columbus (G-6890)
Fenton Bros Electric Co ....E...... 330 343-0093
  New Philadelphia (G-14768)
Fmh Electric Inc ....F...... 419 782-0671
  Lima (G-11863)
Franks Electric Inc ....G...... 513 313-5883
  Cincinnati (G-3711)
Hackworth Electric Motors Inc ....G...... 330 345-6049
  Wooster (G-20602)
Hannon Company ....E...... 740 453-0527
  Zanesville (G-21146)
Hannon Company ....F...... 330 343-7758
  Dover (G-8829)
Hennings Quality Service Inc ....F...... 216 941-9120
  Cleveland (G-5393)
Horner Industrial Services Inc ....E...... 937 390-6667
  Springfield (G-17421)
Hunnell Electric Co Inc ....G...... 330 773-8278
  Akron (G-209)
Integrated Power Services LLC ....E...... 513 863-8816
  Hamilton (G-10572)
James W Cunningham ....F...... 419 639-2111
  Green Springs (G-10344)
K B Electric Motor Service ....G...... 740 537-1346
  Toronto (G-18610)
Kent Swigart ....G...... 937 836-5292
  Englewood (G-9365)
Kiemle-Hankins Company ....E...... 419 661-2430
  Perrysburg (G-15972)
Kw Services LLC ....G...... 419 636-3438
  Bryan (G-2294)
Kw Services LLC ....G...... 419 228-1325
  Lima (G-11884)
Lebanon Electric Motor Svc LLC ....G...... 513 932-2889
  Lebanon (G-11670)
Lemsco Inc ....G...... 419 242-4005
  Toledo (G-18381)
Lima Armature Works Inc ....G...... 419 222-4010
  Lima (G-11887)
Lorain Armature & Mtr Repr Inc ....G...... 440 967-2620
  Vermilion (G-19166)
M & R Electric Motor Svc Inc ....E...... 937 222-6282
  Dayton (G-8317)
Mac Electric Inc ....G...... 419 782-0671
  Lima (G-11896)
Machine Doctors Inc ....G...... 513 422-3060
  Cincinnati (G-3966)
Mader Electr Motor & Power Tra ....G...... 937 325-5576
  Springfield (G-17442)
Magnetech Industrial Svcs Inc ....C...... 330 830-3500
  Massillon (G-13016)
Matlock Electric Co Inc ....E...... 513 731-9600
  Cincinnati (G-3986)
Mid-Ohio Electric Co ....E...... 614 274-8000
  Columbus (G-7178)
Moto-Electric Inc ....G...... 419 668-7894
  Norwalk (G-15406)
National Electric Coil Inc ....B...... 614 488-1151
  Columbus (G-7209)

PRODUCT SECTION — ELECTRICAL EQPT & SPLYS

Ohio Electric Motor Svc LLC ....F 614 444-1451
  Columbus *(G-7247)*
Ohio Electric Motor Svc LLC ....G...... 419 525-2225
  Mansfield *(G-12496)*
Oliver Pool and Spa Inc........................G...... 740 264-5368
  Steubenville *(G-17548)*
Phillips Electric Co ....F 216 361-0014
  Cleveland *(G-5873)*
Sheldon On Site Inc................................G...... 419 339-1381
  Elida *(G-9200)*
Shoemaker Electric Company ....E 614 294-5626
  Columbus *(G-7447)*
Southwest Electric Co ....F 330 875-7000
  Louisville *(G-12168)*
Total Maintenance Management...........G...... 513 228-2345
  Lebanon *(G-11701)*
Tyler Electric Motor Repair ....G...... 330 836-5537
  Akron *(G-417)*
Watson Electric Motor Svc Inc ....F 614 836-9904
  Columbus *(G-7594)*
Wheatley Electric Service Co ....G...... 513 531-4951
  Cincinnati *(G-4505)*
Whelco Industrial Ltd ....F 419 385-4627
  Perrysburg *(G-16026)*
Whelco Industrial Ltd ....E 419 873-6134
  Perrysburg *(G-16027)*
Wyse Electric Motor Repair ....G...... 419 445-5921
  Archbold *(G-673)*

ELECTRIC SERVICES

National Gas & Oil Corporation ....E 740 344-2102
  Newark *(G-14900)*

ELECTRIC SVCS, NEC Power Transmission

Gould Group LLC ....G...... 740 807-4294
  Hilliard *(G-10825)*

ELECTRICAL APPARATUS & EQPT WHOLESALERS

Acorn Technology Corporation ....E 216 663-1244
  Cleveland *(G-4610)*
Ademco Inc...G...... 440 439-7002
  Bedford *(G-1379)*
Allen Fields Assoc Inc ....G...... 513 228-1010
  Lebanon *(G-11632)*
Als High Tech Inc ....F 440 232-7090
  Bedford *(G-1380)*
Best Lighting Products Inc ....D...... 740 964-0063
  Etna *(G-9392)*
Controllix Corporation............................F 440 232-8757
  Walton Hills *(G-19309)*
Filnor Inc ....E 330 821-8731
  Alliance *(G-465)*
Hughes Corporation ....E 440 238-2550
  Strongsville *(G-17751)*
Kirk Key Interlock Company LLC ....E 330 833-8223
  North Canton *(G-15096)*
Peak Electric Inc ....G...... 419 726-4848
  Toledo *(G-18460)*
Powell Electrical Systems Inc................D...... 330 966-1750
  Canton *(G-2787)*
S L C Software Services..........................G...... 513 922-4303
  Cincinnati *(G-4297)*
Schneider Electric Usa Inc ....D...... 513 755-5000
  West Chester *(G-19792)*
Sieb & Meyer America Inc ....F 513 563-0860
  Fairfield *(G-9563)*
Spb Global LLC ....G...... 419 931-6559
  Perrysburg *(G-16007)*
Specialty Switch Co................................F 330 427-3000
  Youngstown *(G-21037)*
Spi Inc...G...... 937 374-2700
  Xenia *(G-20790)*
Tesa Inc...G...... 614 847-8200
  Lewis Center *(G-11784)*
Warmus and Associates Inc ....F 330 659-4440
  Bath *(G-1203)*

ELECTRICAL APPLIANCES, TELEVISIONS & RADIOS WHOLESALERS

Spb Global LLC ....G...... 419 931-6559
  Perrysburg *(G-16007)*

ELECTRICAL CURRENT CARRYING WIRING DEVICES

Accurate Electronics Inc ....C...... 330 682-7015
  Orrville *(G-15581)*
Bud Industries Inc ....G...... 440 946-3200
  Willoughby *(G-20289)*
Cambridge Ohio Production & As ....F 740 432-6383
  Cambridge *(G-2429)*
Chalfant Manufacturing Company ....G...... 330 273-3510
  Brunswick *(G-2195)*
Chalfant Manufacturing Company ....F 440 323-9870
  Elyria *(G-9236)*
Channel Products Inc ....D...... 440 423-0113
  Solon *(G-17126)*
D & E Electric Inc ....F 513 738-1172
  Okeana *(G-15518)*
Desco Corporation..................................G...... 614 888-8855
  New Albany *(G-14622)*
Dreison International Inc ....C...... 216 362-0755
  Cleveland *(G-5113)*
Electric Cord Sets Inc ....G...... 216 261-1000
  Cleveland *(G-5161)*
Erie Copper Works Inc ....G...... 330 725-5590
  Medina *(G-13257)*
Filnor Inc ....F 330 821-7667
  Alliance *(G-467)*
GE Aviation Systems LLC ....B...... 937 898-5881
  Vandalia *(G-19125)*
General Plug and Mfg Co ....C...... 440 926-2411
  Grafton *(G-10301)*
Hubbell Incorporated ....E 330 335-2361
  Wadsworth *(G-19245)*
I Sq R Power Cable Co ....F 330 588-3000
  Canton *(G-2704)*
Kathom Manufacturing Co Inc..............E 513 868-8890
  Hamilton *(G-10579)*
Lake Shore Electric Corp ....E 440 232-0200
  Bedford *(G-1422)*
Legrand AV Inc ....E 574 267-8101
  Blue Ash *(G-1805)*
Legrand North America LLC ....B...... 937 224-0639
  Dayton *(G-8309)*
MJM Industries Inc.................................D...... 440 350-1230
  Fairport Harbor *(G-9626)*
Mueller Electric Company Inc..............E 216 771-5225
  Akron *(G-290)*
Parker-Hannifin Corporation ....C...... 330 336-3511
  Wadsworth *(G-19260)*
Pave Technology Co................................E 937 890-1100
  Dayton *(G-8417)*
Power Grounding Solutions LLC ....G...... 440 926-3219
  Grafton *(G-10309)*
Qualtek Electronics Corp ....C...... 440 951-3300
  Mentor *(G-13567)*
Rogers Industrial Products Inc.............E 330 535-3331
  Akron *(G-353)*
Royal Plastics Inc ....G...... 440 352-1357
  Mentor *(G-13575)*
Siemens Industry Inc..............................D...... 937 593-6010
  Bellefontaine *(G-1525)*
Simpson Strong-Tie Company Inc ....C...... 614 876-8060
  Columbus *(G-7454)*
SMH Manufacturing Inc.........................F 419 884-0071
  Lexington *(G-11806)*
Solon Manufacturing Company ....E 440 286-7149
  Chardon *(G-3137)*
Tecmark Corporation..............................D...... 440 205-7600
  Mentor *(G-13601)*
Torq Corporation.....................................E 440 232-4100
  Bedford *(G-1451)*
Turner Lightning Protection Co ....G...... 614 738-6225
  Dublin *(G-9007)*
Vital Connections Incorporated ....E 937 667-3880
  Tipp City *(G-18143)*
Vulcan Tool Company ....G...... 937 253-6194
  Dayton *(G-8581)*
Watteredge LLC ....D...... 440 933-6110
  Avon Lake *(G-1013)*
Weastec Incorporated ....C...... 937 393-6800
  Hillsboro *(G-10893)*
Wedge Products Inc ....B...... 330 405-4477
  Twinsburg *(G-18873)*
Wiremax Ltd ....G...... 419 531-9500
  Toledo *(G-18601)*
Xponet Inc...E 440 354-6617
  Painesville *(G-15801)*

ELECTRICAL DEVICE PARTS: Porcelain, Molded

Materion Brush Inc ....D...... 216 486-4200
  Mayfield Heights *(G-13167)*

ELECTRICAL DISCHARGE MACHINING, EDM

Detroit Diesl Specialty TI Inc..................E 740 435-4452
  Byesville *(G-2383)*
E D M Services Inc ....G...... 216 486-2068
  Euclid *(G-9411)*
Max Daetwyler Corp................................F 937 428-1781
  Miamisburg *(G-13687)*
Morris Technologies Inc ....C...... 513 733-1611
  Cincinnati *(G-4047)*
Precision Inc...G...... 330 897-8860
  Fresno *(G-10070)*
Skinner Machining Co ....G...... 216 486-6636
  Cleveland *(G-6069)*
Superalloy Mfg Solutions Corp ....C...... 513 489-9800
  Blue Ash *(G-1854)*
U S Alloy Die Corp ....F 216 749-9700
  Cleveland *(G-6227)*

ELECTRICAL EQPT & SPLYS

Akron Brass Company ....E 614 529-7230
  Columbus *(G-6557)*
Akron Brass Company ....B...... 330 264-5678
  Wooster *(G-20558)*
Akron Brass Holding Corp......................G...... 330 264-5678
  Wooster *(G-20559)*
Akron Foundry Co ....E 330 745-3101
  Barberton *(G-1050)*
Allen Fields Assoc Inc ....G...... 513 228-1010
  Lebanon *(G-11632)*
Allied Moulded Products Inc................C...... 419 636-4217
  Bryan *(G-2259)*
Ametek Inc...F 937 440-0800
  Troy *(G-18637)*
Azz Inc...E 330 456-3241
  Canton *(G-2580)*
Barth Industries Co LP ....D...... 216 267-0531
  Cleveland *(G-4793)*
Beta Industries Inc..................................E 937 299-7385
  Dayton *(G-8056)*
Bos Electric Supply LLC ....G...... 937 426-0578
  Moraine *(G-14335)*
Buckeye Electrical Products...................E 937 693-7519
  Botkins *(G-1935)*
Ces Nationwide ....G...... 937 322-0771
  Springfield *(G-17373)*
Chandler Systems Incorporated ....G...... 419 281-6829
  Ashland *(G-692)*
Circle Prime Manufacturing ....E 330 923-0019
  Cuyahoga Falls *(G-7850)*
Clark Substations LLC ....G...... 330 452-5200
  Canton *(G-2628)*
Commercial Electric Pdts Corp ....E 216 241-2886
  Cleveland *(G-5002)*
Control System Manufacturing.............E 330 542-0000
  New Middletown *(G-14749)*
Corrpro Companies Inc ....E 330 723-5082
  Medina *(G-13242)*
Corrpro Companies Inc ....F 330 725-6681
  Medina *(G-13243)*
Corrpro Companies Intl Inc...................G...... 330 723-5082
  Medina *(G-13244)*
Debra Harbour ....G...... 937 440-9618
  Troy *(G-18647)*
Elcor Inc ....E 440 365-5941
  Elyria *(G-9249)*
Emega Technologies LLC ....G...... 740 407-3712
  Zanesville *(G-21134)*
Engineered Mfg & Eqp Co ....G...... 937 642-7776
  Marysville *(G-12781)*
Erico Global Company ....G...... 440 248-0100
  Solon *(G-17139)*
Federal Equipment Company ....D...... 513 621-5260
  Cincinnati *(G-3680)*
General Electric Company ....C...... 216 266-2357
  Cleveland *(G-5311)*
Graham Electric ....G...... 614 231-8500
  Columbus *(G-6964)*
Halex/Scott Fetzer Company ....D...... 440 439-1616
  Bedford Heights *(G-1471)*
Halls Welding & Supplies Inc................G...... 330 385-9353
  East Liverpool *(G-9058)*
Hannon Company ....D...... 330 456-4728
  Canton *(G-2693)*

ELECTRICAL EQPT & SPLYS

Heat Exchange Institute Inc ....G.... 216 241-7333
  Cleveland *(G-5385)*
Hess Advanced Solutions Llc ....G.... 937 829-4794
  Dayton *(G-8249)*
Insource Technologies Inc ....C.... 419 399-3600
  Paulding *(G-15863)*
Jech Technologies Inc ....G.... 740 927-3495
  Pickerington *(G-16050)*
Jobap Assembly Inc ....F.... 440 632-5393
  Middlefield *(G-13810)*
Juggerbot 3d LLC ....G.... 330 406-6900
  Youngstown *(G-20950)*
Kiemle-Hankins Company ....E.... 419 661-2430
  Perrysburg *(G-15972)*
Kraft Electrical Contg Inc ....E.... 614 836-9300
  Groveport *(G-10498)*
Levans Electric & Hvac ....G.... 937 468-2269
  Rushsylvania *(G-16596)*
Libra Industries Inc ....C.... 440 974-7770
  Mentor *(G-13498)*
Liebert North America Inc ....E.... 614 888-0246
  Columbus *(G-7125)*
Lockheed Martin Integ ....D.... 330 796-2800
  Akron *(G-257)*
Matlock Electric Co Inc ....E.... 513 731-9600
  Cincinnati *(G-3986)*
Mitsubishi Elc Automtn Inc ....G.... 937 492-3058
  Sidney *(G-17054)*
Mr Electric..G.... 419 289-7474
  Mansfield *(G-12488)*
Mueller Electric Company Inc ....E.... 216 771-5225
  Akron *(G-290)*
Mv Innovative Technologies LLC ....G.... 301 661-0951
  Dayton *(G-8373)*
Nabco Entrances Inc ....G.... 419 842-0484
  Sylvania *(G-17954)*
Niftech Inc..F.... 440 257-6018
  Mentor *(G-13528)*
Nook Industries Inc ....C.... 216 271-7900
  Cleveland *(G-5756)*
Ohio Electric Motor Svc LLC ....G.... 419 525-2225
  Mansfield *(G-12496)*
Overly Hautz Motor Base Co ....E.... 513 932-0025
  Lebanon *(G-11681)*
P & B Electric..G.... 937 754-4695
  Fairborn *(G-9465)*
Pepperl + Fuchs Mfg Inc ....C.... 330 425-3555
  Twinsburg *(G-18832)*
Philips Medical Systems Clevel ....B.... 440 247-2652
  Cleveland *(G-5871)*
Powell Electrical Systems Inc ....D.... 330 966-1750
  Canton *(G-2787)*
Primex ....E.... 513 831-9959
  Milford *(G-14035)*
Qualtech Technologies Inc ....E.... 440 946-8081
  Willoughby *(G-20416)*
Rexel Inc ....G.... 330 468-1122
  Northfield *(G-15323)*
Riverside Drives Inc ....E.... 216 362-1211
  Cleveland *(G-5988)*
RPS America Inc ....G.... 937 231-9339
  West Chester *(G-19788)*
Schneider Electric Usa Inc ....E.... 513 398-9800
  West Chester *(G-19793)*
Schneider Electric Usa Inc ....F.... 937 258-8426
  Dayton *(G-8495)*
Schneider Electric Usa Inc ....B.... 513 523-4171
  Oxford *(G-15700)*
Sew-Eurodrive Inc ....D.... 937 335-0036
  Troy *(G-18705)*
Tip Products Inc ....E.... 216 252-2535
  Cleveland *(G-6176)*
Vanner Holdings Inc ....D.... 614 771-2718
  Hilliard *(G-10873)*
Vortec Corporation ....E.... 513 891-7485
  Blue Ash *(G-1866)*
Vti Instruments Corporation ....G.... 216 447-8950
  Cleveland *(G-6275)*
Wesco Distribution Inc ....E.... 419 666-1670
  Northwood *(G-15351)*
Yaskawa America Inc ....F.... 614 733-3200
  Plain City *(G-16220)*

ELECTRICAL EQPT FOR ENGINES

Aptiv Services Us LLC ....C.... 330 505-3150
  Warren *(G-19373)*
Cummins Inc ....G.... 614 604-6004
  Grove City *(G-10424)*
Ewh Spectrum LLC ....D.... 937 593-8010
  Bellefontaine *(G-1515)*

Exact-Tool & Die Inc ....E.... 216 676-9140
  Cleveland *(G-5204)*
Ferrotherm Corporation ....C.... 216 883-9350
  Cleveland *(G-5233)*
Flex Technologies Inc ....D.... 330 359-5415
  Mount Eaton *(G-14420)*
Gmelectric Inc ....G.... 330 477-3392
  Canton *(G-2685)*
GSW Manufacturing Inc ....B.... 419 423-7111
  Findlay *(G-9696)*
Hurst Auto-Truck Electric........................G.... 216 961-1800
  Cleveland *(G-5426)*
Machine Products Company ....G.... 937 890-6600
  Dayton *(G-8320)*
Per-Tech Inc...E.... 330 833-8824
  Massillon *(G-13038)*
Satco Inc ....G.... 330 630-8866
  Tallmadge *(G-18002)*
Sk Tech Inc ....C.... 937 836-3535
  Englewood *(G-9375)*
Sumitomo Elc Wirg Systems Inc ....E.... 937 642-7579
  Marysville *(G-12816)*
United Controls Group Inc ....G.... 740 936-0005
  Columbus *(G-6507)*
Unity Cable Technologies Inc ....E.... 419 322-4118
  Toledo *(G-18584)*

ELECTRICAL EQPT REPAIR & MAINTENANCE

Allied Machine Works Inc ....G.... 740 454-2534
  Zanesville *(G-21097)*
Amko Service Company ....E.... 330 364-8857
  Midvale *(G-13975)*
Ascendtech Inc ....E.... 216 458-1101
  Willoughby *(G-20282)*
Boeing Company ....E.... 740 788-4000
  Newark *(G-14854)*
Brocks Welding & Repair Svc...............G.... 740 453-3943
  Zanesville *(G-21111)*
Carlton Natco ....E.... 216 451-5588
  Cleveland *(G-4878)*
Copier Resources Inc ....G.... 614 268-1100
  Columbus *(G-6818)*
Emerson Network Power.........................E.... 614 841-8054
  Ironton *(G-11164)*
Enprotech Industrial Tech LLC ....C.... 216 883-3220
  Cleveland *(G-5179)*
Exchange Signs ....G.... 330 644-4552
  Coventry Township *(G-7769)*
Fosbel Inc ....C.... 216 362-3900
  Cleveland *(G-5265)*
General Electric Company ....D.... 216 883-1000
  Cleveland *(G-5306)*
Greggs Specialty Services ....F.... 419 478-0803
  Toledo *(G-18313)*
Hannon Company ....F.... 330 343-7758
  Dover *(G-8829)*
J-C-R Tech Inc ....E.... 937 783-2296
  Blanchester *(G-1704)*
K C N Technologies LLC ....G.... 440 439-4219
  Bedford *(G-1419)*
Metaltek Industries Inc ....F.... 937 323-4933
  Springfield *(G-17447)*
Narrow Way Custom Technology ....E.... 937 743-1611
  Carlisle *(G-2895)*
Niktec LLC ....G.... 513 282-3747
  Franklin *(G-9904)*
Oaks Welding Inc ....G.... 330 482-4216
  Columbiana *(G-6475)*
Rubber City Machinery Corp ....E.... 330 434-3500
  Akron *(G-356)*
Steel Eqp Specialists Inc........................D.... 330 823-8260
  Alliance *(G-502)*
Stein Inc ....F.... 440 526-9301
  Cleveland *(G-6104)*
Terex Utilities Inc ....D.... 513 539-9770
  Monroe *(G-14278)*
Voltage Regulator Sales & Svcs ....G.... 937 878-0673
  Fairborn *(G-9474)*
Wauseon Machine & Mfg Inc ....D.... 419 337-0940
  Wauseon *(G-19537)*

ELECTRICAL EQPT REPAIR SVCS

D & J Electric Motor Repair Co ....F.... 330 336-4343
  Wadsworth *(G-19232)*
General Electric Intl Inc ....G.... 410 737-7228
  Cincinnati *(G-3744)*
Kiemle-Hankins Company ....E.... 419 661-2430
  Perrysburg *(G-15972)*

PRODUCT SECTION

Palesh & Associates Inc ....G.... 440 942-9168
  Willoughby *(G-20398)*

ELECTRICAL EQPT REPAIR SVCS: High Voltage

Delta Transformer Inc ....G.... 513 242-9400
  Cincinnati *(G-3581)*
Wilson Sign Co Inc ....F.... 937 253-2246
  Dayton *(G-8595)*

ELECTRICAL EQPT: Automotive, NEC

Electra Sound Inc ....D.... 216 433-9600
  Parma *(G-15817)*
Stanley Electric US Co Inc ....B.... 740 852-5200
  London *(G-12069)*

ELECTRICAL EQPT: Household

Romanoff Elc Residential LLC ....D.... 614 755-4500
  Gahanna *(G-10101)*

ELECTRICAL GOODS, WHOL: Antennas, Receiving/Satellite Dishes

Wifi-Plus Inc ....G.... 877 838-4195
  Brunswick *(G-2251)*

ELECTRICAL GOODS, WHOLESALE: Alarms & Signaling Eqpt

Cattron Holdings Inc ....E.... 234 806-0018
  Warren *(G-19381)*

ELECTRICAL GOODS, WHOLESALE: Boxes & Fittings

Akron Foundry Co ....C.... 330 745-3101
  Akron *(G-40)*
Ignio Systems LLC ....F.... 419 708-0503
  Toledo *(G-18340)*
Osburn Associates Inc ....E.... 740 385-5732
  Logan *(G-12038)*

ELECTRICAL GOODS, WHOLESALE: Cable Conduit

Legrand North America LLC ....B.... 937 224-0639
  Dayton *(G-8309)*

ELECTRICAL GOODS, WHOLESALE: Connectors

Spi Inc ....G.... 937 374-2700
  Xenia *(G-20790)*

ELECTRICAL GOODS, WHOLESALE: Electronic Parts

C P Electric Motor Repair Inc ....G.... 330 425-9593
  Twinsburg *(G-18745)*
Creative Electronic Design ....G.... 937 256-5106
  Beavercreek *(G-1308)*
Foxtronix Inc ....G.... 937 866-2112
  Miamisburg *(G-13670)*
Pemro Corporation ....F.... 800 440-5441
  Cleveland *(G-5863)*
Rixan Associates Inc ....E.... 937 438-3005
  Dayton *(G-8479)*
Rpa Electronic Distributors ....F.... 937 223-7001
  Dayton *(G-8486)*
Wes-Garde Components Group Inc ....G.... 614 885-0319
  Westerville *(G-20081)*

ELECTRICAL GOODS, WHOLESALE: Generators

Lima Equipment Co ....G.... 419 222-4181
  Lima *(G-11888)*
Mr Electric..G.... 419 289-7474
  Mansfield *(G-12488)*
Western Branch Diesel Inc ....E.... 330 454-8800
  Canton *(G-2864)*

ELECTRICAL GOODS, WHOLESALE: Ground Fault Interrupters

Askia Inc ....G.... 513 828-7443
  Cincinnati *(G-3362)*

PRODUCT SECTION

ELECTROMEDICAL EQPT

ELECTRICAL GOODS, WHOLESALE: Household Appliances, NEC

World Wide Recyclers Inc .... F 614 554-3296
  Columbus *(G-7613)*

ELECTRICAL GOODS, WHOLESALE: Insulators

Unity Cable Technologies Inc .... G 419 322-4118
  Toledo *(G-18584)*

ELECTRICAL GOODS, WHOLESALE: Motor Ctrls, Starters & Relays

Servo Systems Inc .... G 440 779-2780
  North Olmsted *(G-15198)*

ELECTRICAL GOODS, WHOLESALE: Motors

Akron Indus Mtr Sls & Svc Inc .... G 330 753-7624
  Norton *(G-15359)*
Allan A Irish .... G 419 394-3284
  Saint Marys *(G-16675)*
Ametek Tchnical Indus Pdts Inc .... D 330 677-3754
  Kent *(G-11294)*
Bay Electric Co .... G 419 625-1046
  Sandusky *(G-16796)*
Bennett Electric Inc .... F 800 874-5405
  Norwalk *(G-15382)*
Big River Electric Inc .... G 740 446-4360
  Gallipolis *(G-10161)*
Bornhorst Motor Service Inc .... G 937 773-0426
  Piqua *(G-16104)*
C P Electric Motor Repair Inc .... G 330 425-9593
  Twinsburg *(G-18745)*
Campton Electric Sales & Svc .... G 740 826-4429
  New Concord *(G-14682)*
Cardinal Electric LLC .... G 740 366-6850
  Newark *(G-14860)*
Clark-Fowler Enterprises Inc .... E 330 262-0906
  Wooster *(G-20578)*
Columbus Electrical Works Co .... F 614 294-4651
  Columbus *(G-6787)*
Electro Torque .... G 614 297-1600
  Columbus *(G-6890)*
Fmh Electric Inc .... F 419 782-0671
  Lima *(G-11863)*
Hackworth Electric Motors Inc .... G 330 345-6049
  Wooster *(G-20602)*
Hannon Company .... F 330 343-7758
  Dover *(G-8829)*
Hannon Company .... E 740 453-0527
  Zanesville *(G-21146)*
Horner Industrial Services Inc .... E 937 390-6667
  Springfield *(G-17421)*
Hunnell Electric Co Inc .... G 330 773-8278
  Akron *(G-209)*
Lebanon Electric Motor Svc LLC .... G 513 932-2889
  Lebanon *(G-11670)*
Lima Armature Works Inc .... G 419 222-4010
  Lima *(G-11887)*
M & R Electric Motor Svc Inc .... E 937 222-6282
  Dayton *(G-8317)*
Mader Electr Motor & Power Tra .... G 937 325-5576
  Springfield *(G-17442)*
Matlock Electric Co Inc .... E 513 731-9600
  Cincinnati *(G-3986)*
Mid-Ohio Electric Co .... E 614 274-8000
  Columbus *(G-7178)*
Moto-Electric Inc .... G 419 668-7894
  Norwalk *(G-15406)*
Palesh & Associates Inc .... G 440 942-9168
  Willoughby *(G-20398)*
Phillips Electric Co .... F 216 361-0014
  Cleveland *(G-5873)*
Shoemaker Electric Company .... E 614 294-5626
  Columbus *(G-7447)*
Tyler Electric Motor Repair .... G 330 836-5537
  Akron *(G-417)*
Watson Electric Motor Svc Inc .... F 614 836-9904
  Columbus *(G-7594)*
Wheatley Electric Service Co .... G 513 531-4951
  Cincinnati *(G-4505)*

ELECTRICAL GOODS, WHOLESALE: Radio & TV Or TV Eqpt & Parts

S-Tek Inc .... G 440 439-8232
  Bedford *(G-1443)*

ELECTRICAL GOODS, WHOLESALE: Radio Parts & Access, NEC

T V Specialties Inc .... F 330 364-6678
  Dover *(G-8859)*

ELECTRICAL GOODS, WHOLESALE: Security Control Eqpt & Systems

Aysco Security Consultants Inc .... E 330 733-8183
  Kent *(G-11297)*
Mace Personal Def & SEC Inc .... E 440 424-5321
  Cleveland *(G-5597)*
MAI Media Group Llc .... G 513 779-0604
  West Chester *(G-19875)*
Modular Security Systems Inc .... G 740 532-7822
  Ironton *(G-11169)*
P3labs LLC .... G 800 259-8059
  North Canton *(G-15108)*

ELECTRICAL GOODS, WHOLESALE: Sound Eqpt

Electra Sound Inc .... D 216 433-9600
  Parma *(G-15817)*
Holland Assocts LLC DBA Archou .... F 513 891-0006
  Cincinnati *(G-3818)*

ELECTRICAL GOODS, WHOLESALE: Switchboards

Industrial Ctrl Dsign Mnt Inc .... F 330 785-9840
  Tallmadge *(G-17987)*

ELECTRICAL GOODS, WHOLESALE: Switches, Exc Electronic, NEC

Etc Enterprises LLC .... G 417 262-6382
  Delphos *(G-8743)*
Wes-Garde Components Group Inc ... G 614 885-0319
  Westerville *(G-20081)*

ELECTRICAL GOODS, WHOLESALE: Telephone Eqpt

ABC Appliance Inc .... E 419 693-4414
  Oregon *(G-15552)*
Famous Industries Inc .... E 330 535-1811
  Akron *(G-166)*
Mitel (delaware) Inc .... E 513 733-8000
  West Chester *(G-19745)*
Pro Oncall Technologies LLC .... F 614 761-1400
  Dublin *(G-8967)*

ELECTRICAL GOODS, WHOLESALE: Transformers

Etc Enterprises LLC .... G 417 262-6382
  Delphos *(G-8743)*

ELECTRICAL GOODS, WHOLESALE: Washing Machines

Whirlpool Corporation .... C 740 383-7122
  Marion *(G-12748)*

ELECTRICAL GOODS, WHOLESALE: Wire & Cable

Associated Mtls Holdings LLC .... A 330 929-1811
  Cuyahoga Falls *(G-7843)*
Max Mighty Inc .... F 937 862-9530
  Spring Valley *(G-17317)*
Multilink Inc .... C 440 366-6966
  Elyria *(G-9298)*
Noco Company .... B 216 464-8131
  Solon *(G-17208)*
Scott Fetzer Company .... C 216 267-9000
  Cleveland *(G-6035)*
Sumitomo Elc Wirg Systems Inc .... E 937 642-7579
  Marysville *(G-12816)*

ELECTRICAL GOODS, WHOLESALE: Wire & Cable, Ctrl & Sig

Winkle Industries Inc .... D 330 823-9730
  Alliance *(G-516)*

ELECTRICAL INDL APPARATUS, NEC

Amplified Solar Inc .... G 216 236-4225
  Lakewood *(G-11511)*
Avtron Inc .... E 216 642-1230
  Independence *(G-11120)*
Graftech Global Entps Inc .... G 216 676-2000
  Cleveland *(G-5336)*
Industrial Application Svs .... G 419 875-5093
  Grand Rapids *(G-10315)*
Wired Inc .... G 440 567-8379
  Willoughby *(G-20460)*

ELECTRICAL MEASURING INSTRUMENT REPAIR & CALIBRATION SVCS

Instrmntation Ctrl Systems Inc .... E 513 662-2600
  Cincinnati *(G-3851)*
Interface Logic Systems Inc .... G 614 236-8388
  Columbus *(G-7041)*
Tegam Inc .... E 440 466-6100
  Geneva *(G-10229)*

ELECTRICAL SPLYS

Accurate Mechanical Inc .... E 740 681-1332
  Lancaster *(G-11538)*
Ces Nationwide .... G 937 322-0771
  Springfield *(G-17373)*
Creative Electronic Design .... G 937 256-5106
  Beavercreek *(G-1308)*
Fenton Bros Electric Co .... E 330 343-0093
  New Philadelphia *(G-14768)*
Ohio Electric Motor Svc LLC .... G 419 525-2225
  Mansfield *(G-12496)*
Yes Management Inc .... G 330 747-8593
  Columbiana *(G-6486)*

ELECTRICAL SUPPLIES: Porcelain

Akron Porcelain & Plastics Co .... C 330 745-2159
  Akron *(G-49)*
CAM-Lem Inc .... G 216 391-7750
  Cleveland *(G-4863)*
Channel Products Inc .... D 440 423-0113
  Solon *(G-17126)*
Electrodyne Company Inc .... F 513 732-2822
  Batavia *(G-1140)*
Ferro Corporation .... C 216 875-6178
  Cleveland *(G-5231)*
Fram Group Operations LLC .... A 419 436-5827
  Fostoria *(G-9845)*
Petro Ware Inc .... D 740 982-1302
  Crooksville *(G-7819)*

ELECTRODES: Indl Process

Mettler-Toledo Intl Fin Inc .... G 614 438-4511
  Columbus *(G-6500)*
Selective Med Components Inc .... E 740 397-7838
  Mount Vernon *(G-14507)*

ELECTRODES: Thermal & Electrolytic

De Nora Tech LLC .... D 440 710-5300
  Painesville *(G-15731)*
Graftech Intl Holdings Inc .... C 330 239-3023
  Parma *(G-15821)*
Graftech Intl Holdings Inc .... C 216 676-2000
  Brooklyn Heights *(G-2125)*
Graphel Corporation .... C 513 779-6166
  West Chester *(G-19718)*
Graphite Sales Inc .... F 419 652-3388
  Nova *(G-15433)*
Neograf Solutions LLC .... C 216 529-3777
  Lakewood *(G-11530)*
Sangraf International Inc .... F 216 543-3288
  Westlake *(G-20154)*
Sherbrooke Metals .... E 440 942-3520
  Willoughby *(G-20429)*
Spectramed Inc .... F 740 263-3059
  Gahanna *(G-10106)*

ELECTROMEDICAL EQPT

Brainmaster Technologies Inc .... G 440 232-6000
  Bedford *(G-1391)*
Cardiac Analytics LLC .... F 614 314-1332
  Powell *(G-16314)*
Checkpoint Surgical Inc .... G 216 378-9107
  Cleveland *(G-4917)*
Critical Patient Care Inc .... G 937 434-5455
  Dayton *(G-8114)*

Employee Codes: A=Over 500 employees, B=251-500
C=101-250, D=51-100, E=20-50, F=10-19, G=3-9

ELECTROMEDICAL EQPT

Ctl Analyzers LLC .... F 216 791-5084
  Shaker Heights *(G-16930)*
Eoi Inc .... F 740 201-3300
  Lewis Center *(G-11760)*
Gyrus Acmi LP .... C 419 668-8201
  Norwalk *(G-15396)*
Lumitex Inc .... D 440 243-8401
  Strongsville *(G-17763)*
Mercury Biomed LLC .... G 216 777-1492
  Cleveland *(G-5655)*
Monitored Therapeutics Inc .... G 614 761-3555
  Dublin *(G-8948)*
Mrpicker 440 354-6497
  Cleveland *(G-5712)*
Nano Mark LLC .... G 216 409-3104
  Cleveland *(G-5720)*
Ndi Medical LLC .... E 216 378-9106
  Cleveland *(G-5733)*
Neuros Medical Inc 440 951-2565
  Willoughby Hills *(G-20472)*
Nxstage Medical Inc .... G 513 712-1300
  Cincinnati *(G-4094)*
Osteodynamics .... G 405 921-9271
  Cincinnati *(G-4122)*
Pemco Inc .... E 216 524-2990
  Cleveland *(G-5862)*
Philips Healthcare Cleveland .... E 440 483-3235
  Highland Heights *(G-10797)*
Rapiscan Systems High Energy I .... G 937 879-4200
  Fairborn *(G-9466)*
Sensetronics LLC 614 292-2833
  Dublin *(G-8983)*
Veressa Medical Inc .... F 614 591-4201
  Columbus *(G-7573)*
Viewray Technologies Inc .... D 440 703-3210
  Oakwood Village *(G-15487)*

ELECTROMEDICAL EQPT WHOLESALERS

Relevium Labs Inc 614 568-7000
  Oxford *(G-15699)*
Smiths Medical Pm Inc .... F 614 210-7300
  Dublin *(G-8991)*

ELECTROMETALLURGICAL PRDTS

Rhenium Alloys Inc .... D 440 365-7388
  North Ridgeville *(G-15251)*

ELECTRONIC COMPONENTS

Acoh Inc .... G 419 741-3195
  Ottawa *(G-15647)*
Autosyte .... G 440 858-3226
  Painesville *(G-15713)*
Networked Cmmnctons Sltons LLC .... G 440 374-4990
  Bedford Heights *(G-1477)*
Sol-Fly Technologies LLC .... G 330 465-8883
  Wooster *(G-20656)*
Suburban Electronics Assembly .... G 330 483-4077
  Valley City *(G-19067)*
Weldon .... G 330 263-9533
  Columbus *(G-7599)*

ELECTRONIC DEVICES: Solid State, NEC

Burke Products Inc .... E 937 372-3516
  Xenia *(G-20759)*
D F Electronics Inc .... D 513 772-7792
  Cincinnati *(G-3569)*
Dan-Mar Company Inc .... E 419 660-8830
  Norwalk *(G-15386)*

ELECTRONIC EQPT REPAIR SVCS

Bentronix Corp .... G 440 632-0606
  Middlefield *(G-13780)*
Electric Service Co Inc .... E 513 271-6387
  Cincinnati *(G-3632)*
Sasha Electronics Inc .... F 419 662-8100
  Rossford *(G-16593)*
Vacuum Electric Switch Co Inc .... G 330 374-5156
  Akron *(G-423)*
Vertiv Corporation .... A 614 888-0246
  Columbus *(G-7575)*

ELECTRONIC PARTS & EQPT WHOLESALERS

Cartessa Corporation .... F 513 738-4477
  Shandon *(G-16940)*
Certified Comparator Products .... G 937 426-9677
  Beavercreek *(G-1353)*

Electro-Line Inc .... F 937 461-5683
  Dayton *(G-8181)*
Element14 US Holdings Inc .... G 330 523-4280
  Richfield *(G-16469)*
John F Kilfoil Co .... G 513 791-6150
  Cincinnati *(G-3878)*
Keithley Instruments Intl Corp .... B 440 248-0400
  Cleveland *(G-5525)*
Pepperl + Fuchs Inc .... C 330 425-3555
  Twinsburg *(G-18830)*
Pepperl + Fuchs Entps Inc .... G 330 425-3555
  Twinsburg *(G-18831)*
Premier Farnell Holding Inc .... E 330 523-4273
  Richfield *(G-16483)*
Spirit Avionics Ltd .... F 614 237-4271
  Columbus *(G-7477)*
University Accessories Inc .... G 440 327-4151
  North Ridgeville *(G-15257)*
Vmetro Inc .... G 281 584-0728
  Fairborn *(G-9473)*

ELECTRONIC SHOPPING

E Retailing Associates LLC .... D 614 300-5785
  Columbus *(G-6880)*

ELECTRONIC TRAINING DEVICES

E-Beam Services Inc .... E 513 933-0031
  Lebanon *(G-11648)*

ELECTROPLATING & PLATING SVC

Automation Finishing Inc .... E 216 251-8805
  Cleveland *(G-4774)*
Krendl Rack Co Inc .... G 419 667-4800
  Venedocia *(G-19154)*
Sifco Applied Srfc Cncepts LLC .... E 216 524-0099
  Cleveland *(G-6062)*
Swagelok .... G 440 349-5657
  Solon *(G-17239)*
Twist Inc 937 675-9581
  Jamestown *(G-11221)*

ELEMENTARY & SECONDARY SCHOOLS, PRIVATE NEC

Society of The Precious Blood .... E 419 925-4516
  Celina *(G-2984)*

ELEMENTARY & SECONDARY SCHOOLS, SPECIAL EDUCATION

Community RE Group-Comvet 440 319-6714
  Ashtabula *(G-767)*

ELEVATOR: Grain, Storage Only

E S Industries Inc .... G 419 643-2625
  Lima *(G-11859)*

ELEVATORS & EQPT

Aimco Mfg Inc .... G 419 476-6572
  Toledo *(G-18160)*
Canton Elevator Inc .... D 330 833-3600
  North Canton *(G-15076)*
Elevator Cncepts By Wurtec LLC .... F 734 246-4700
  Toledo *(G-18280)*
Fujitec America Inc .... C 513 755-6100
  Mason *(G-12873)*
Gray-Eering Ltd .... G 740 498-8816
  Tippecanoe *(G-18149)*
Otis Elevator Company .... D 216 573-2333
  Cleveland *(G-5825)*
Schindler Elevator Corporation .... E 419 861-5900
  Holland *(G-10956)*
Sematic Usa Inc .... E 216 524-0100
  Twinsburg *(G-18855)*
Sweet Manufacturing Company .... E 937 325-1511
  Springfield *(G-17501)*

ELEVATORS: Automobile

Dasher Lawless Automation LLC .... E 855 755-7275
  Warren *(G-19394)*

ELEVATORS: Installation & Conversion

Otis Elevator Company .... D 216 573-2333
  Cleveland *(G-5825)*

EMBALMING FLUID

Champion Company .... D 937 324-5681
  Springfield *(G-17374)*
Martin M Hardin .... G 740 282-1234
  Steubenville *(G-17543)*

EMBLEMS: Embroidered

Atlantis Sportswear Inc .... E 937 773-0680
  Piqua *(G-16101)*
Craco Embroidery Inc 513 563-6999
  Cincinnati *(G-3556)*
Glorias .... G 330 264-8963
  Wooster *(G-20598)*
Lion Clothing Inc .... G 419 692-9981
  Delphos *(G-8751)*
Novak J F Manufacturing Co LLC .... G 216 741-5112
  Cleveland *(G-5790)*
Pelz Lettering Inc 419 625-3567
  Sandusky *(G-16838)*
Randy Gray .... G 513 533-3200
  Cincinnati *(G-4248)*
Sportsco Imprinting .... G 513 641-5111
  Cincinnati *(G-4360)*

EMBOSSING SVC: Paper

Precision Graphic Services .... F 419 241-5189
  Toledo *(G-18478)*

EMBROIDERING & ART NEEDLEWORK FOR THE TRADE

A & S Inc .... G 866 209-1574
  Arcanum *(G-627)*
All For Show Inc .... G 440 729-7186
  Chesterland *(G-3152)*
Alphabet Soup Inc .... G 330 467-4418
  Macedonia *(G-12276)*
Assoc Talents Inc .... G 440 716-1265
  Westlake *(G-20100)*
Aubrey Rose Apparel LLC .... G 513 728-2681
  Cincinnati *(G-3370)*
Avina Specialties Inc .... G 419 592-5646
  Napoleon *(G-14533)*
Barbs Custom Embroidery 419 393-2226
  Defiance *(G-8616)*
Barbs Embroidery .... G 614 875-9933
  Grove City *(G-10416)*
Campbell Signs & Apparel LLC .... F 330 386-4768
  East Liverpool *(G-9052)*
Carter Evans Enterprises Inc 614 920-2276
  Granville *(G-10327)*
Cheryl A Lucas .... G 614 755-2100
  Columbus *(G-6762)*
Chris Stepp 513 248-0822
  Milford *(G-14002)*
Creative Stitches Monogramming .... G 740 667-3592
  Little Hocking *(G-11991)*
Eastgate Custom Graphics Ltd .... G 513 528-7922
  Cincinnati *(G-3625)*
Embroidme .... G 330 484-8484
  Canton *(G-2668)*
Emroid ME .... G 614 789-1898
  Westerville *(G-20051)*
Expert TS 330 263-4588
  Wooster *(G-20589)*
Fcs Graphics Inc .... G 216 771-5177
  Cleveland *(G-5225)*
Fine Line Embroidery Company .... G 330 788-9070
  Youngstown *(G-20904)*
Got Graphix Llc .... F 330 703-9047
  Fairlawn *(G-9606)*
H & H Screen Process Inc .... G 937 253-7520
  Dayton *(G-8240)*
Hang Time Group Inc .... G 216 771-5885
  Cleveland *(G-5369)*
Heller Acquisitions Inc .... G 937 833-2676
  Brookville *(G-2171)*
Hometown Threads 440 779-6053
  North Olmsted *(G-15193)*
Initial Designs Inc .... G 419 475-3900
  Toledo *(G-18347)*
Jetts Embroideries 937 981-3716
  Greenfield *(G-10353)*
Just Name It Inc .... G 614 626-8662
  Pickerington *(G-16052)*
K Ventures Inc .... F 419 678-2308
  Coldwater *(G-6415)*
Kathy Simecek .... G 440 886-2468
  Cleveland *(G-5518)*

PRODUCT SECTION

ENGINE PARTS & ACCESS: Internal Combustion

Kens His & Hers Shop Inc ....G....... 330 872-3190
  Newton Falls *(G-14988)*
Kts Cstm Lgs/Xclsvely You Inc..........G....... 440 285-9803
  Chardon *(G-3120)*
Kts Custom Logos ....G....... 440 285-9803
  Chardon *(G-3121)*
Markt ....G....... 740 397-5900
  Mount Vernon *(G-14490)*
McCc Sportswear Inc ....E....... 513 583-9210
  West Chester *(G-19876)*
Mr Emblem Inc ....G....... 419 697-1888
  Oregon *(G-15561)*
National Ntwrk EMB Prfssionals ....G....... 502 212-7500
  Stow *(G-17613)*
Our Family Mall ....G....... 216 761-8669
  Cleveland *(G-5827)*
Permanent Impressions ....G....... 740 892-3045
  Utica *(G-19027)*
Phantasm Designs ....G....... 419 538-6737
  Ottawa *(G-15662)*
Qualitee Design Sportswear Co ....E....... 740 333-8337
  Wshngtn CT Hs *(G-20739)*
Quality Rubber Stamp Inc ....G....... 614 235-2700
  Columbus *(G-7365)*
R Sportswear LLC ....G....... 937 748-3507
  Springboro *(G-17350)*
Red Barn Screen Printing & EMB......F....... 740 474-6657
  Circleville *(G-4556)*
Stitches & Stuff ....G....... 330 426-9500
  East Palestine *(G-9084)*
Sun Shine Awards ....F....... 740 425-2504
  Barnesville *(G-1119)*
Thompson Assoc Hudson Ohio ....G....... 330 655-2142
  Hudson *(G-11079)*
Thread Works Custom Embroidery.....G....... 937 478-5231
  Beavercreek *(G-1344)*
Twin Design AP Promotions Ltd..........G....... 937 732-6798
  Dayton *(G-8573)*
Vector International Corp ....G....... 440 942-2002
  Mentor *(G-13623)*
Walnut Hill Shop ....G....... 740 828-3346
  Frazeysburg *(G-9942)*
Wholesale Imprints Inc ....E....... 440 224-3527
  North Kingsville *(G-15161)*
Writely Sew LLC ....G....... 513 728-2682
  Cincinnati *(G-4523)*

EMBROIDERING SVC

5 BS Inc ....C....... 740 454-8453
  Zanesville *(G-21090)*
A To Z Wear Ltd ....G....... 513 923-4662
  Cincinnati *(G-3281)*
Aardvark Sportswear Inc ....G....... 330 793-9428
  Youngstown *(G-20832)*
Alley Cat Designs Inc ....G....... 937 291-8803
  Dayton *(G-8017)*
Alphabet Embroidery Studios ....F....... 937 372-6557
  Xenia *(G-20755)*
Apparel Impressions Inc ....G....... 513 247-0555
  Cincinnati *(G-3351)*
Appleheart ....G....... 937 384-0430
  Miamisburg *(G-13641)*
B D P Services Inc ....D....... 740 828-9685
  Nashport *(G-14564)*
Cal Sales Embroidery ....G....... 440 236-3820
  Columbia Station *(G-6431)*
Carols Ultra Stitch & Variety ....G....... 419 935-8991
  Willard *(G-20238)*
Charles Wisvari ....F....... 740 671-9960
  Bellaire *(G-1484)*
CNG Business Group ....G....... 614 771-0877
  Hilliard *(G-10818)*
Color 3 Embroidery Inc ....G....... 330 652-9495
  Warren *(G-19385)*
Computer Stitch Designs Inc.............G....... 330 856-7826
  Warren *(G-19386)*
Elegant Embroidery Llc ....G....... 440 878-0904
  Strongsville *(G-17741)*
Embroid ME ....G....... 216 459-9250
  Cleveland *(G-5171)*
Embroidered ID Inc ....G....... 440 974-8113
  Mentor *(G-13439)*
Embroidery Design Group LLC ....G....... 614 798-8152
  Columbus *(G-6894)*
Ems/Hooptech ....G....... 513 829-7768
  West Chester *(G-19697)*
Ernst Sporting Gds Minster LLC ......G....... 937 526-9822
  Versailles *(G-19179)*
Fastpatch Ltd ....F....... 513 367-1838
  Harrison *(G-10640)*

Fine Line Embroidery Company ....G....... 440 331-7030
  Rocky River *(G-16547)*
Gail Berner ....G....... 937 322-0314
  Springfield *(G-17406)*
Garment Specialties Inc ....G....... 330 425-2928
  Twinsburg *(G-18779)*
Good JP ....G....... 419 207-8484
  Ashland *(G-706)*
Graphic Stitch Inc ....G....... 937 642-6707
  Marysville *(G-12784)*
Great Oppurtunities Inc ....G....... 614 868-1899
  Columbus *(G-6969)*
J America LLC ....G....... 614 914-2091
  Columbus *(G-7054)*
Jane Valentine ....G....... 330 452-3154
  North Canton *(G-15094)*
Jaquas Monogramming & Design ....G....... 419 422-2244
  Findlay *(G-9708)*
Judy Dubois ....G....... 419 738-6979
  Wapakoneta *(G-19336)*
Kiwi Promotional AP & Prtg Co ....E....... 330 487-5115
  Twinsburg *(G-18801)*
Kuhls Hot Sportspot ....F....... 513 474-2282
  Cincinnati *(G-3926)*
Locker Room Lettering Ltd ....G....... 419 359-1761
  Castalia *(G-2940)*
Logo This ....G....... 419 445-1355
  Archbold *(G-657)*
Lynns Logos Inc ....G....... 440 786-1156
  Cleveland *(G-5589)*
M & Y Marketing ....G....... 937 322-3423
  Springfield *(G-17439)*
Oasis Embroidery ....G....... 614 785-7266
  Columbus *(G-7235)*
Personal Stitch Monogramming.........G....... 440 282-7707
  Amherst *(G-570)*
Precision Imprint ....G....... 740 592-5916
  Athens *(G-846)*
Quality Image Embroidery & AP ....G....... 440 230-1109
  Broadview Heights *(G-2099)*
Quality Stitch Embroidery Inc ....G....... 614 237-0480
  Columbus *(G-7366)*
Quickstitch Plus LLC ....G....... 614 476-3186
  Columbus *(G-7368)*
Route 14 Storage Inc ....G....... 330 296-0084
  Ravenna *(G-16399)*
Sovereign Stitch ....G....... 440 829-0678
  Avon Lake *(G-1010)*
Spectrum Embroidery Inc ....G....... 937 847-9905
  Dayton *(G-8518)*
T & L Custom Screening Inc ....G....... 937 237-3121
  Dayton *(G-8534)*
Tag Sportswear LLC ....G....... 330 456-8867
  Canton *(G-2832)*
Tech Wear Embroidery Company .....G....... 740 344-1276
  Newark *(G-14928)*
Top Shelf Embroidery ....G....... 440 209-8566
  Mentor *(G-13608)*
Truck Stop Embroidery ....G....... 419 257-2860
  North Baltimore *(G-15049)*
Unisport Inc ....F....... 419 529-4727
  Ontario *(G-15549)*
United Sport Apparel ....G....... 330 722-0818
  Medina *(G-13357)*
Zimmer Enterprises Inc ....E....... 937 428-1057
  Dayton *(G-8604)*

EMBROIDERING: Swiss Loom

Quali-Tee Design Sports ....F....... 937 382-7997
  Wilmington *(G-20505)*

EMBROIDERY ADVERTISING SVCS

Centennial Screen Printing ....G....... 419 422-5548
  Findlay *(G-9665)*
Custom Sportswear Imprints LLC ....G....... 330 335-8326
  Wadsworth *(G-19231)*
Evolution Crtive Solutions LLC ....E....... 513 681-4450
  Cincinnati *(G-3660)*
Heller Acquisitions Inc ....G....... 937 833-2676
  Brookville *(G-2171)*
Madison Group Inc ....G....... 216 362-9000
  Cleveland *(G-5602)*
Rossi Concept Arts ....G....... 330 453-6366
  Canton *(G-2811)*
Screen Works Inc ....E....... 937 264-9111
  Dayton *(G-8499)*
Underground Sport Shop Inc............F....... 513 751-1662
  Cincinnati *(G-4446)*

EMERGENCY & RELIEF SVCS

Cgh-Global Emerg Mngmt Strateg .....E....... 800 376-0655
  Cincinnati *(G-3242)*

EMERGENCY ALARMS

Ademco Inc..F....... 513 772-1851
  Blue Ash *(G-1721)*
Ademco Inc..G....... 440 439-7002
  Bedford *(G-1379)*
Cincinnati Bell Any Dstnce Inc ....A....... 513 397-9900
  Cincinnati *(G-3483)*
Johnson Controls ....E....... 419 861-0662
  Maumee *(G-13123)*
Offendaway LLC ....G....... 937 232-3933
  Centerville *(G-3005)*
UTC Fire SEC Americas Corp Inc ....G....... 513 821-7945
  Cincinnati *(G-4460)*

EMERGENCY SHELTERS

Lighthouse Youth Services Inc..........F....... 513 961-4080
  Cincinnati *(G-3943)*

EMPLOYMENT SVCS: Labor Contractors

Shaneway Inc ....G....... 330 868-2220
  Minerva *(G-14201)*

ENAMELING SVC: Metal Prdts, Including Porcelain

Cto Inc ....G....... 330 785-1130
  Akron *(G-126)*
Erie Ceramic Arts Company LLC .....G....... 419 228-1145
  Lima *(G-11860)*

ENAMELS

Ferro Corporation ....D....... 216 875-5600
  Mayfield Heights *(G-13163)*
North Shore Strapping Inc ....D....... 216 661-5200
  Brooklyn Heights *(G-2128)*
RPM Consumer Holding Company ...G....... 330 273-5090
  Medina *(G-13330)*

ENCLOSURES: Electronic

American Rugged Enclosures...........F....... 513 942-3004
  Hamilton *(G-10533)*
Brooks Utility Products Group ....F....... 330 455-0301
  Canton *(G-2599)*
Buckeye Stamping Company ....D....... 614 445-0059
  Columbus *(G-6712)*
Bud Industries Inc ....G....... 440 946-3200
  Willoughby *(G-20289)*
Ecp Corporation ....F....... 440 934-0444
  Avon *(G-948)*
Electrical Control Systems ....G....... 937 859-7136
  Dayton *(G-8179)*
N N Metal Stampings Inc ....E....... 419 737-2311
  Pioneer *(G-16086)*
Rittal Corp..C....... 440 572-4999
  Strongsville *(G-17782)*

ENCLOSURES: Screen

Patton Aluminum Products Inc ....F....... 937 845-9404
  New Carlisle *(G-14676)*

ENCODERS: Digital

Liquid Image Corp of America...........G....... 216 458-9800
  Cleveland *(G-5580)*

ENERGY MEASUREMENT EQPT

Val-Con Inc ....G....... 440 357-1898
  Painesville *(G-15794)*

ENGINE PARTS & ACCESS: Internal Combustion

American Fine Sinter Co Ltd............C....... 419 443-8880
  Tiffin *(G-18042)*
DW Hercules LLC..............................E....... 330 830-2498
  Massillon *(G-12977)*
Industrial Parts Depot LLC ....G....... 440 237-9164
  North Royalton *(G-15278)*
Mantapart ....G....... 330 549-2389
  New Springfield *(G-14820)*
Metaldyne Pwrtrain Cmpnnts Inc .....C....... 330 486-3200
  Twinsburg *(G-18818)*

Employee Codes: A=Over 500 employees, B=251-500
C=101-250, D=51-100, E=20-50, F=10-19, G=3-9

ENGINE REBUILDING: Diesel

ENGINE REBUILDING: Diesel

Chemequip Sales Inc	E	330 724-8300
Coventry Township *(G-7767)*		
Detroit Desl Rmnfacturing Corp	F	740 439-7701
Cambridge *(G-2434)*		
Detroit Desl Rmnfctrng-Ast Inc	B	740 439-7701
Byesville *(G-2382)*		
General Engine Products LLC	D	937 704-0160
Franklin *(G-9886)*		
Jatrodiesel Inc	F	937 847-8050
Miamisburg *(G-13681)*		
Maags Automotive & Machine	G	419 626-1539
Sandusky *(G-16824)*		
Navistar Inc	E	937 390-5704
Springfield *(G-17459)*		
Performace Diesel Inc	F	740 392-3693
Mount Vernon *(G-14500)*		

ENGINE REBUILDING: Gas

Rozevink Engines LLC	G	419 789-1159
Holgate *(G-10913)*		

ENGINEERING SVCS

A C Knox Inc	G	513 921-5028
Cincinnati *(G-3279)*		
A+ Engineering Fabrication Inc	F	419 832-0748
Grand Rapids *(G-10314)*		
Alfons Haar Inc	E	937 560-2031
Springboro *(G-17321)*		
Applied Experience LLC	G	614 943-2970
Columbus *(G-6610)*		
B&N Coal Inc	D	740 783-3575
Dexter City *(G-8792)*		
Bender Engineering Company	G	330 938-2355
Beloit *(G-1568)*		
Beringer Plating Inc	G	330 633-8409
Akron *(G-84)*		
Bison USA Corp	G	513 713-0513
Hamilton *(G-10541)*		
Braze Solutions LLC	G	440 349-5100
Solon *(G-17119)*		
Ceco Group Inc	G	513 458-2600
Cincinnati *(G-3452)*		
Circle Prime Manufacturing	E	330 923-0019
Cuyahoga Falls *(G-7850)*		
Clarkwestern Dietrich Building	F	330 372-5564
Warren *(G-19384)*		
Clarkwestern Dietrich Building	F	513 870-1100
West Chester *(G-19677)*		
Coal Services Inc	D	740 795-5220
Powhatan Point *(G-16341)*		
Coating Systems Group Inc	F	440 816-9306
Middleburg Heights *(G-13763)*		
Comtec Incorporated	F	330 425-8102
Twinsburg *(G-18756)*		
Control Electric Co	E	216 671-8010
Columbia Station *(G-6434)*		
Corrpro Companies Inc	F	330 723-5082
Medina *(G-13242)*		
Corrpro Companies Inc	F	330 725-6681
Medina *(G-13243)*		
Custom Craft Controls Inc	F	330 630-9599
Akron *(G-128)*		
Dante Solutions Inc	G	440 234-8477
Cleveland *(G-5064)*		
Davis Technologies Inc	F	330 823-2544
Alliance *(G-464)*		
Decision Systems Inc	E	330 456-7600
Canton *(G-2653)*		
Delta Control Inc	G	937 277-3444
Dayton *(G-8154)*		
Dlhbowles Inc	B	330 478-2503
Canton *(G-2661)*		
Donald E Didion II	E	419 483-2226
Bellevue *(G-1535)*		
Emh Inc	E	330 220-8600
Valley City *(G-19036)*		
Enprotech Industrial Tech LLC	C	216 883-3220
Cleveland *(G-5179)*		
Eti Tech LLC	F	937 832-4200
Englewood *(G-9358)*		
Fishel Company	D	614 850-4400
Columbus *(G-6926)*		
Frost Engineering Inc	E	513 541-6330
Cincinnati *(G-3715)*		
General Electric Intl Inc	G	410 737-7228
Cincinnati *(G-3744)*		
General Precision Corporation	G	440 951-9380
Willoughby *(G-20331)*		
Htec Systems Inc	F	937 438-3010
Dayton *(G-8255)*		
Hunter Defense Tech Inc	E	216 438-6111
Solon *(G-17164)*		
Hydro-Dyne Inc	E	330 832-5076
Massillon *(G-13000)*		
Imax Industries Inc	F	440 639-0242
Painesville *(G-15747)*		
Innovative Controls Corp	D	419 691-6684
Toledo *(G-18348)*		
Jotco Inc	G	513 721-4943
Mansfield *(G-12465)*		
Kendall Holdings Ltd	E	614 486-4750
Columbus *(G-7086)*		
L3 Aviation Products Inc	G	614 825-2001
Columbus *(G-7108)*		
Majestic Engineering & TI LLC	G	937 845-1079
New Carlisle *(G-14672)*		
Matrix Research Inc	D	937 427-8433
Beavercreek *(G-1357)*		
Micro Industries Corporation	D	740 548-7878
Westerville *(G-20065)*		
Mitchell Electronics Inc	G	740 594-8532
Athens *(G-842)*		
Nesco Inc	E	440 461-6000
Cleveland *(G-5741)*		
New Path International LLC	E	614 410-3974
Powell *(G-16331)*		
Nona Composites LLC	G	937 490-4814
Miamisburg *(G-13700)*		
Ohio Blow Pipe Company	E	216 681-7379
Cleveland *(G-5801)*		
Ohio Structures Inc	G	330 533-0084
Canfield *(G-2539)*		
Owens Corning Sales LLC	F	330 633-6735
Tallmadge *(G-17999)*		
Peco II Inc	D	614 431-0694
Columbus *(G-7305)*		
Plate-All Metal Company Inc	G	330 633-6166
Akron *(G-322)*		
Plcc2 LLC	G	614 279-1796
Columbus *(G-7328)*		
Process Innovations Inc	G	330 856-5192
Vienna *(G-19207)*		
Providence Rees Inc	G	614 833-6231
Columbus *(G-7355)*		
Quality Plating Co	G	216 361-0151
Cleveland *(G-5942)*		
RAD-Con Inc	E	440 871-5720
Lakewood *(G-11534)*		
Sgi Matrix LLC	D	937 438-9033
Miamisburg *(G-13715)*		
Sizetec Inc	G	330 492-9682
Canton *(G-2817)*		
Sunpower Inc	D	740 594-2221
Athens *(G-851)*		
Support Svc LLC	G	419 617-0660
Lexington *(G-11808)*		
Systech Handling Inc	F	419 445-8226
Archbold *(G-670)*		
Tangent Company LLC	G	440 543-2775
Chagrin Falls *(G-3079)*		
Tangible Solutions Inc	G	937 912-4603
Fairborn *(G-9471)*		
Thermal Treatment Center Inc	E	216 881-8100
Cleveland *(G-6167)*		
Timekeeping Systems Inc	F	216 595-0890
Solon *(G-17253)*		
Tri-Tech Research LLC	F	440 946-6122
Eastlake *(G-9136)*		
Trumbull Industries Inc	E	330 434-6174
Akron *(G-413)*		
U S Army Corps of Engineers	F	740 537-2571
Toronto *(G-18613)*		
Updegraff Inc	G	216 621-7600
Cleveland *(G-6241)*		
V&P Group International LLC	F	703 349-6432
Cincinnati *(G-4461)*		
Weastec Incorporated	E	614 734-9645
Dublin *(G-9011)*		
Welding Consultants Inc	G	614 258-7018
Columbus *(G-7598)*		
Xcite Systems Corporation	G	513 965-0300
Cincinnati *(G-3267)*		

ENGINEERING SVCS: Acoustical

Straight 72 Inc	D	740 943-5730
Marysville *(G-12815)*		

ENGINEERING SVCS: Aviation Or Aeronautical

GE Aviation Systems LLC	B	937 898-5881
Vandalia *(G-19125)*		
Ultra-Met Company	G	937 653-7133
Urbana *(G-19018)*		

ENGINEERING SVCS: Civil

Barr Engineering Incorporated	E	614 714-0299
Columbus *(G-6650)*		
Ceso Inc	D	937 435-8584
Miamisburg *(G-13649)*		
JBI Corporation	F	419 855-3389
Genoa *(G-10233)*		
Pollock Research & Design Inc	E	330 332-3300
Salem *(G-16767)*		
Ra Consultants LLC	E	513 469-6600
Blue Ash *(G-1840)*		

ENGINEERING SVCS: Construction & Civil

Barr Engineering Incorporated	F	614 892-0162
Columbus *(G-6649)*		
EP Ferris & Associates Inc	G	614 299-2999
Columbus *(G-6902)*		

ENGINEERING SVCS: Electrical Or Electronic

CPI Group Limited	G	216 525-0046
Cleveland *(G-5035)*		
Digital Automation Associates	G	419 352-6977
Bowling Green *(G-1969)*		
Electrovations Inc	E	330 274-3558
Aurora *(G-878)*		
Field Apparatus Service & Tstg	G	513 353-9399
Cincinnati *(G-3685)*		
L-3 Cmmncations Nova Engrg Inc	C	877 282-1168
Mason *(G-12901)*		
Lintech Electronics LLC	F	513 528-6190
Cincinnati *(G-3259)*		
Mid-Ohio Electric Co	G	614 274-8000
Columbus *(G-7178)*		
Midwest Telemetry Inc	G	440 725-5718
Kirtland *(G-11469)*		
PMC Systems Limited	E	330 538-2268
North Jackson *(G-15153)*		
Quayle Consulting Inc	G	614 868-1363
Pickerington *(G-16058)*		
Stock Fairfield Corporation	C	440 543-6000
Chagrin Falls *(G-3078)*		
TL Industries Inc	C	419 666-8144
Northwood *(G-15346)*		
Vector Electromagnetics LLC	G	937 478-5904
Beavercreek *(G-1367)*		

ENGINEERING SVCS: Energy conservation

Albemarle Corporation	G	330 425-2354
Twinsburg *(G-18729)*		
Tekworx LLC	F	513 533-4777
Blue Ash *(G-1858)*		

ENGINEERING SVCS: Fire Protection

Cgh-Global Emerg Mngmt Strateg	E	800 376-0655
Cincinnati *(G-3242)*		

ENGINEERING SVCS: Heating & Ventilation

Cetek Ltd	E	216 362-3900
Cleveland *(G-4905)*		
Hess Advanced Solutions Llc	G	937 829-4794
Dayton *(G-8249)*		
Melink Corporation	F	513 685-0958
Milford *(G-14026)*		

ENGINEERING SVCS: Industrial

Control Associates Inc	G	440 708-1770
Chagrin Falls *(G-3042)*		
Crowne Group LLC	D	216 589-0198
Cleveland *(G-5040)*		
Imds Corporation	F	330 747-4637
Youngstown *(G-20937)*		
JB Industries Ltd	F	330 856-4587
Warren *(G-19414)*		
Mercury Iron and Steel Co	F	440 349-1500
Solon *(G-17190)*		
Production Design Services Inc	D	937 866-3377
Dayton *(G-8446)*		

PRODUCT SECTION

EQUIPMENT: Pedestrian Traffic Control

Spark LLC .... G 513 924-1559
  Cincinnati *(G-4356)*
Technology House Ltd .... E 440 248-3025
  Streetsboro *(G-17701)*

ENGINEERING SVCS: Machine Tool Design

Guardian Engineering & Mfg Co .... G 419 335-1784
  Wauseon *(G-19518)*
Invotec Engineering Inc .... D 937 886-3232
  Miamisburg *(G-13680)*
Magna Group LLC .... G 513 388-9463
  Cincinnati *(G-3971)*
Mound Manufacturing Center Inc .... F 937 236-8387
  Dayton *(G-8370)*
Terydon Inc .... F 330 879-2448
  Navarre *(G-14588)*
Youngstown Plastic Tooling .... E 330 782-7222
  Youngstown *(G-21080)*

ENGINEERING SVCS: Mechanical

Chipmatic Tool & Machine Inc .... D 419 862-2737
  Elmore *(G-9205)*
Dillin Engineered Systems Corp .... E 419 666-6789
  Perrysburg *(G-15940)*
Johnson Machining Services LLC .... G 937 866-4744
  Miamisburg *(G-13682)*
Markley Enterprises LLC .... E 513 771-1290
  Cincinnati *(G-3982)*
Morris Technologies Inc .... C 513 733-1611
  Cincinnati *(G-4047)*
Performnce Plymr Solutions Inc .... F 937 298-3713
  Moraine *(G-14375)*
Qcsm LLC .... G 216 531-5960
  Cleveland *(G-5937)*

ENGINEERING SVCS: Pollution Control

Neundorfer Inc .... E 440 942-8990
  Willoughby *(G-20387)*
Nucon International Inc .... F 614 846-5710
  Columbus *(G-7232)*

ENGINEERING SVCS: Professional

Eaton-Aeroquip Llc .... D 419 891-7775
  Maumee *(G-13109)*
Inovent Engineering Inc .... G 330 468-0005
  Macedonia *(G-12303)*
Lawrence Technologies Inc .... G 937 274-7771
  Dayton *(G-8308)*

ENGINES: Diesel & Semi-Diesel Or Duel Fuel

Country Sales & Service LLC .... F 330 683-2500
  Orrville *(G-15588)*
Dmax Ltd .... D 937 425-9700
  Moraine *(G-14346)*
Hy-Production Inc .... C 330 273-2400
  Valley City *(G-19040)*
Kinstle Truck & Auto Svc Inc .... F 419 738-7493
  Wapakoneta *(G-19237)*

ENGINES: Gasoline, NEC

Graham Ford Power Products .... G 614 801-0049
  Columbus *(G-6965)*

ENGINES: Internal Combustion, NEC

B A Malcuit Racing Inc .... G 330 878-7111
  Strasburg *(G-17645)*
Cameron International Corp .... G 740 397-4888
  Mount Vernon *(G-14472)*
Cricket Engines .... G 513 532-2145
  Blanchester *(G-1701)*
Cummins - Allison Corp .... G 614 529-1940
  Columbus *(G-6841)*
Cummins - Allison Corp .... G 513 469-2924
  Blue Ash *(G-1756)*
Cummins - Allison Corp .... G 440 824-5050
  Cleveland *(G-5042)*
Cummins Bridgeway Columbus LLC .. D 614 771-1000
  Hilliard *(G-10822)*
Cummins Bridgeway Toledo LLC .... G 419 893-8711
  Maumee *(G-13084)*
Cummins Inc .... G 614 604-6004
  Grove City *(G-10424)*
Cummins Inc .... E 614 771-1000
  Hilliard *(G-10823)*
Debolt Machine Inc .... G 740 454-8082
  Zanesville *(G-21127)*

Draime Enterprises Inc .... G 330 837-2254
  Massillon *(G-12976)*
Ford Motor Company .... A 419 226-7000
  Lima *(G-11864)*
Gellner Engineering Inc .... G 216 398-8500
  Cleveland *(G-5301)*
Jjb Engineer .... G 330 807-0671
  Cuyahoga Falls *(G-7885)*
Kenworth of Dayton .... F 937 235-2589
  Dayton *(G-8294)*
Western Branch Diesel Inc .... E 330 454-8800
  Canton *(G-2864)*

ENGINES: Jet Propulsion

Enginetics Corporation .... C 937 878-3800
  Huber Heights *(G-11017)*
GE Rolls Royce Fighter .... G 513 243-2787
  Cincinnati *(G-3739)*

ENGINES: Marine

Performance Research Inc .... G 614 475-8300
  Columbus *(G-7312)*

ENGINES: Steam

Steam Engine Works LLC .... G 513 813-3690
  Cincinnati *(G-4376)*

ENGRAVING SVC, NEC

Gordons Graphics Inc .... G 330 863-2322
  Malvern *(G-12392)*
Handcrafted Jewelry Inc .... G 330 650-9011
  Hudson *(G-11051)*
Irwin Engraving & Printing Co .... G 216 391-7300
  Cleveland *(G-5477)*
Sams Graphic Industries .... F 330 821-4710
  Alliance *(G-498)*

ENGRAVING SVC: Jewelry & Personal Goods

F & K Concepts Inc .... G 937 426-6843
  Springboro *(G-17326)*
Scholz & Ey Engravers Inc .... F 614 444-8052
  Columbus *(G-7427)*

ENGRAVING SVCS

Canton Graphic Arts Service .... G 330 456-9868
  Canton *(G-2611)*
Designer Awards Inc .... G 937 339-4444
  Troy *(G-18650)*
Engravers Gallery & Sign Co .... G 330 830-1271
  Massillon *(G-12980)*
Gauntlet Awards & Engraving .... G 937 890-5811
  Dayton *(G-8214)*
Hafner Hardwood Connection LLC ..... G 419 726-4828
  Toledo *(G-18318)*
John C Starr .... G 740 852-5592
  London *(G-12063)*
Plastic Products and Supply .... G 330 744-5076
  Youngstown *(G-21000)*
Professional Award Service .... G 513 389-3600
  Cincinnati *(G-4216)*
Raschke Engraving Inc .... G 330 677-5544
  Kent *(G-11373)*
Ryder Engraving Inc .... G 740 927-7193
  Pataskala *(G-15842)*

ENGRAVING: Steel line, For The Printing Trade

Bomen Marking Products Inc .... G 440 582-0053
  Cleveland *(G-4829)*

ENGRAVINGS: Plastic

Foundation Industries Inc .... D 330 564-1250
  Akron *(G-176)*
Hathaway Stamp Co .... F 513 621-1052
  Cincinnati *(G-3803)*
Minotas Trophies & Awards .... G 440 720-1288
  Cleveland *(G-5696)*
Plate Engraving Corporation .... F 330 239-2155
  Medina *(G-13320)*

ENTERTAINERS

Amcan Productions Ltd .... G 330 332-9129
  Salem *(G-16717)*

ENTERTAINERS & ENTERTAINMENT GROUPS

American Guild of English Hand .... G 937 438-0085
  Cincinnati *(G-3333)*
Swagg Productions2015llc .... F 614 815-1173
  Reynoldsburg *(G-16455)*
Tomahawk Entertainment Group .... G 216 505-0548
  Cleveland *(G-6180)*

ENTERTAINMENT GROUP

Club 513 LLC .... G 800 530-2574
  Cincinnati *(G-3531)*

ENTERTAINMENT SVCS

Technical Artistry Inc .... G 614 299-7777
  Columbus *(G-7520)*

ENVELOPES

Access Envelope Inc .... F 513 889-0888
  Hamilton *(G-10528)*
Ampac Holdings LLC .... A 513 671-1777
  Cincinnati *(G-3340)*
Bayley Envelope Inc .... G 330 821-2150
  Alliance *(G-457)*
Church Budget Monthly Inc .... D 330 337-1122
  Salem *(G-16726)*
Church-Budget Envelope Company .... E 800 446-9780
  Salem *(G-16727)*
Envelope 1 Inc .... D 330 482-3900
  Columbiana *(G-6464)*
Envelope Mart of Ohio Inc .... E 440 365-8177
  Elyria *(G-9259)*
Ohio Envelope Manufacturing Co .... E 216 267-2920
  Cleveland *(G-5805)*
Pac Worldwide Corporation .... D 800 610-9367
  Middletown *(G-13938)*
Quality Envelope Inc .... G 513 942-7578
  West Chester *(G-19891)*
SRC Liquidation LLC .... A 937 221-1000
  Dayton *(G-8521)*
Tcp Inc .... G 330 836-4239
  Fairlawn *(G-9622)*
United Envelope LLC .... B 513 542-4700
  Cincinnati *(G-4448)*
Western States Envelope Co .... D 419 666-7480
  Walbridge *(G-19300)*

ENVELOPES WHOLESALERS

Envelope Mart of Ohio Inc .... E 440 365-8177
  Elyria *(G-9259)*
Pac Worldwide Corporation .... D 800 610-9367
  Middletown *(G-13938)*
Western States Envelope Co .... D 419 666-7480
  Walbridge *(G-19300)*

ENZYMES

Biowish Technologies Inc .... G 312 572-6700
  Cincinnati *(G-3395)*
Enzyme Industries of The U S A .... G 740 929-4975
  Newark *(G-14871)*
Mp Biomedicals LLC .... C 440 337-1200
  Solon *(G-17199)*
Oxyrase Inc .... F 419 589-8800
  Ontario *(G-15545)*

EPOXY RESINS

Key Resin Company .... F 513 943-4225
  Batavia *(G-1159)*
Nanosperse LLC .... G 937 296-5030
  Kettering *(G-11435)*
Nona Composites LLC .... G 937 490-4814
  Miamisburg *(G-13700)*
Renegade Materials Corporation .... E 508 579-7888
  Miamisburg *(G-13711)*

EQUIPMENT: Pedestrian Traffic Control

Area Wide Protective Inc .... E 330 644-0655
  Kent *(G-11296)*
Area Wide Protective Inc .... G 419 221-2997
  Lima *(G-11842)*
Lightle Enterprises Ohio LLC .... G 740 998-5363
  Frankfort *(G-9863)*

Employee Codes: A=Over 500 employees, B=251-500
C=101-250, D=51-100, E=20-50, F=10-19, G=3-9

2019 Harris Ohio Industrial Directory

EQUIPMENT: Rental & Leasing, NEC

Aircraft Dynamics Corporation	F	419 331-0371
Elida (G-9193)		
Askia Inc	G	513 828-7443
Cincinnati (G-3362)		
Brinkman LLC	F	419 204-5934
Lima (G-11846)		
Cattron Holdings Inc	E	234 806-0018
Warren (G-19381)		
De Nora Tech LLC	D	440 710-5300
Painesville (G-15731)		
Diversifd OH Vlly Eqpt & Srvcs	F	740 458-9881
Clarington (G-4567)		
DRDC Realty Inc	G	419 478-7091
Toledo (G-18269)		
Eaton Leasing Corporation	G	216 382-2292
Beachwood (G-1235)		
Elliott Tool Technologies Ltd	D	937 253-6133
Dayton (G-8182)		
Glawe Manufacturing Co Inc	E	937 754-0064
Fairborn (G-9460)		
Great Lakes Crushing Ltd	E	440 944-5500
Wickliffe (G-20211)		
Hansen Scaffolding LLC	F	513 574-9000
West Chester (G-19863)		
M C L Window Coverings Inc	G	513 868-6000
Fairfield Township (G-9584)		
Mitel (delaware) Inc	E	513 733-8000
West Chester (G-19745)		
Mobile Mini Inc	F	614 449-8655
Columbus (G-7188)		
Powerclean Equipment Company	F	513 202-0001
Cleves (G-6374)		
Snyder Manufacturing Co Ltd	G	330 343-4456
Dover (G-8856)		
Summa Holdings Inc	G	440 838-4700
Cleveland (G-6116)		
Thomas Do-It Center Inc	D	740 446-2002
Gallipolis (G-10176)		
Trailer One Inc	F	330 723-7474
Medina (G-13354)		
Tri State Equipment Company	G	513 738-7227
Shandon (G-16942)		
West Equipment Company Inc	F	419 698-1601
Toledo (G-18597)		

ETCHING & ENGRAVING SVC

Carved Stone LLC	G	614 778-9855
Powell (G-16315)		
Cubbison Company	D	330 793-2481
Youngstown (G-20882)		
Dayton Coating Tech LLC	G	937 278-2060
Dayton (G-8131)		
Doak Laser	G	740 374-0090
Marietta (G-12621)		
Georgia Metal Coatings Company	F	770 446-3930
Chardon (G-3115)		
Hadronics Inc	D	513 321-9350
Cincinnati (G-3792)		
M & M Engraving	G	216 749-7166
Cleveland (G-5591)		
Mark True Engraving Company	G	216 252-7422
Cleveland (G-5620)		
Play All LLC	G	440 992-7529
Ashtabula (G-799)		
Rite Way Black & Deburr Inc	G	937 224-7762
Dayton (G-8478)		
Sterling Coating	G	513 942-4900
West Chester (G-19799)		
T&K Laser Works Inc	G	937 693-3783
Botkins (G-1938)		
Tce International Ltd	F	800 962-2376
Perry (G-15914)		
X-Treme Finishes Inc	F	330 474-0614
Medina (G-13364)		

ETCHING SVC: Metal

Akron Metal Etching Co	G	330 762-7687
Akron (G-44)		
Great Lakes Etching Finshg Co	F	440 439-3624
Cleveland (G-5344)		
Master Marking Company Inc	F	330 688-6797
Stow (G-17604)		
Roban Inc	G	330 794-1059
Lakemore (G-11500)		
Woodrow Manufacturing Co	E	937 399-9333
Springfield (G-17521)		

ETHYLENE GLYCOL TEREPHTHALIC ACID: Mylar

Global Biochem	G	513 792-2218
Cincinnati (G-3762)		

ETHYLENE-PROPYLENE RUBBERS: EPDM Polymers

Alan L Grant Polymer Inc	G	757 627-4000
Uniontown (G-18908)		
Canton OH Rubber Speclty Prods	G	330 454-3847
Canton (G-2612)		
Cephas Enterprises LLC	G	513 317-5685
West Chester (G-19839)		
East West Copolymer & Rbr LLC	F	225 267-3713
Cleveland (G-5138)		
Key Resin Company	G	513 943-4225
Batavia (G-1159)		
Lyondellbasell	G	513 530-4000
Cincinnati (G-3961)		
Matterworks	G	740 200-0071
Heath (G-10726)		
Mexichem Specialty Resins Inc	E	440 930-1435
Avon Lake (G-996)		
Nova Polymers Inc	G	888 484-6682
Bryan (G-2300)		
Polyshield Corporation	F	614 755-7674
Pickerington (G-16056)		
Protective Industrial Polymers	F	440 327-0015
North Ridgeville (G-15246)		
Toyo Seiki Usa Inc	G	513 546-9657
Blue Ash (G-1860)		

EXERCISE EQPT STORES

R T H Processing Inc	D	419 692-3000
Delphos (G-8754)		

EXHAUST SYSTEMS: Eqpt & Parts

Cardington Yutaka Tech Inc	A	419 864-8777
Cardington (G-2871)		
Classic Exhaust	G	440 466-5460
Geneva (G-10216)		
Fabberge LLC		614 365-0056
Plain City (G-16191)		
Faurecia Exhaust Systems Inc	B	937 339-0551
Troy (G-18656)		
Faurecia Exhaust Systems Inc	B	937 743-0551
Franklin (G-9882)		
Ohio Classic Street Rods Inc	G	440 543-6593
Streetsboro (G-17686)		

EXPLOSIVES

Austin Powder Company	D	216 464-2400
Cleveland (G-4765)		
Austin Powder Company	C	740 596-5286
Mc Arthur (G-13179)		
Austin Powder Company	G	419 299-3347
Findlay (G-9652)		
Austin Powder Company	E	740 968-1555
Saint Clairsville (G-16621)		
Austin Powder Holdings Company	D	216 464-2400
Cleveland (G-4766)		
Hilltop Energy Inc	E	330 859-2108
Mineral City (G-14164)		
Viking Explosives LLC	E	218 263-8845
Cleveland (G-6262)		

EXPLOSIVES, EXC AMMO & FIREWORKS WHOLESALERS

D W Dickey and Son Inc	D	330 424-1441
Lisbon (G-11966)		
Viking Explosives LLC	E	218 263-8845
Cleveland (G-6262)		

EXPLOSIVES, FUSES & DETONATORS: Primary explosives

Sloat Inc	G	440 951-9554
Willoughby (G-20433)		

EXTENSION CORDS

Alert Stamping & Mfg Co Inc	E	440 232-5020
Bedford Heights (G-1458)		
Electra - Cord Inc	D	330 832-8124
Massillon (G-12979)		

EXTRACTS, FLAVORING

Berghausen Corporation	E	513 541-5631
Cincinnati (G-3389)		
Bickford Laboratories Inc	G	440 354-7747
Wickliffe (G-20204)		
Flavor Systems International		513 870-0420
West Chester (G-19853)		
Frutarom USA Inc	C	513 870-4900
West Chester (G-19856)		
Mane Inc	D	513 248-9876
Lebanon (G-11671)		
Sensoryeffects Flavor Company		419 782-5010
Defiance (G-8642)		
Synergy Flavors (oh) LLC		513 892-7100
Fairfield Township (G-9587)		

EXTRACTS: Dying Or Tanning, Natural

Tanning	G	937 233-4554
Dayton (G-8538)		

EYEGLASSES

Central Optical Inc	E	330 783-9660
Youngstown (G-20869)		
Essilor Laboratories Amer Inc	G	330 425-3003
Twinsburg (G-18771)		
Essilor Laboratories Amer Inc	E	614 274-0840
Columbus (G-6906)		
Hollywood Family Eye Care	G	740 264-1220
Steubenville (G-17537)		
Libbey Inc	F	419 244-5697
Toledo (G-18384)		
Nexus Vision Group LLC	E	866 492-6499
Grove City (G-10452)		
Optical Distribution Corp	F	937 405-7280
Columbus (G-7273)		
Rooney Optical Inc	E	216 267-5600
Twinsburg (G-18849)		
Toledo Optical Laboratory Inc	D	419 248-3384
Toledo (G-18565)		

EYES: Artificial

Sunforest Vision Center Inc		419 475-4646
Toledo (G-18534)		

Ethylene Glycols

Global Biochem	G	513 792-2218
Cincinnati (G-3762)		

FABRIC SOFTENERS

Edmar Chemical Company	G	440 247-9560
Chagrin Falls (G-3018)		

FABRIC STORES

Fabric Square Shop	G	330 752-3044
Stow (G-17585)		

FABRICATED METAL PRODUCTS, NEC

A&E Machine & Fabrication Inc	F	740 820-4701
Beaver (G-1291)		
Buckeye Metals	G	740 446-9590
Bidwell (G-1665)		
Cpmg		440 263-2780
North Royalton (G-15267)		
Eastern Automated Piping	G	740 535-8184
Mingo Junction (G-14208)		
Fisher Metal Fabricating	F	419 838-7200
Walbridge (G-19293)		
GCI Metals Inc	G	937 262-7500
Dayton (G-8215)		
Ksm Metal Fabrication	G	937 339-6366
Troy (G-18683)		
Lam Welding & Met Fabrication	G	304 839-2404
Carrollton (G-2924)		
Mills Aluminum Fab	G	330 821-4108
Alliance (G-489)		
Rework Furnishings LLC	F	614 300-5021
Columbus (G-7390)		
SES Fabracating LLC	G	440 636-5853
Windsor (G-20528)		
Universal Design Fbrication LLC	G	419 359-1794
Sandusky (G-16859)		

FABRICS & CLOTHING: Rubber Coated

Ansell Healthcare Products LLC	D	740 622-4311
Coshocton (G-7719)		

PRODUCT SECTION — FABRICS: Trimmings

FABRICS: Apparel & Outerwear, Cotton
Fabric Square Shop ....G....... 330 752-3044
  Stow *(G-17585)*
Gillz LLC ....G....... 904 330-1094
  Westlake *(G-20119)*
Mary James Inc ....E....... 419 599-2941
  Napoleon *(G-14550)*
Struggle Grind Success LLC ....G....... 330 834-6738
  Boardman *(G-1903)*
Twin Design AP Promotions Ltd............G....... 937 732-6798
  Dayton *(G-8573)*
Wonder-Shirts Inc ....G....... 917 679-2336
  Dublin *(G-9012)*

FABRICS: Broadwoven, Cotton
Compass Energy LLC...............................D....... 866 665-2225
  Cleveland *(G-5009)*

FABRICS: Broadwoven, Synthetic Manmade Fiber & Silk
Detroit Technologies Inc ....E....... 937 492-2708
  Sidney *(G-17030)*
Mini Graphics Inc ....G....... 513 563-8600
  Cincinnati *(G-4030)*
Old Es LLC ....E....... 330 468-6600
  Macedonia *(G-12312)*
Owens Corning Sales LLC ....B....... 740 587-3562
  Granville *(G-10336)*
Snyder Manufacturing Co Ltd................G....... 330 343-4456
  Dover *(G-8856)*

FABRICS: Canvas
Canvas Salon and Skin Bar ....G....... 614 336-3942
  Powell *(G-16311)*
Custom Marine Canvas Training ....G....... 419 732-8362
  Port Clinton *(G-16245)*

FABRICS: Chemically Coated & Treated
Omnova Overseas Inc ....C....... 330 869-4200
  Fairlawn *(G-9614)*

FABRICS: Cotton, Narrow
US Cotton LLC ....B....... 216 676-6400
  Cleveland *(G-6244)*

FABRICS: Decorative Trim & Specialty, Including Twist Weave
I-Group Technologies LLC......................G....... 877 622-3477
  New Philadelphia *(G-14775)*
Omnova Solutions Inc ....C....... 216 682-7000
  Beachwood *(G-1257)*

FABRICS: Denims
Noble Denim Workshop ....G....... 513 560-5640
  Cincinnati *(G-4084)*

FABRICS: Diaper, NEC
Associated Hygienic Pdts LLC ....B....... 770 497-9800
  Delaware *(G-8655)*

FABRICS: Duck, Cotton
Mmi Textiles Inc ....F....... 440 899-8050
  Westlake *(G-20131)*

FABRICS: Fiberglass, Broadwoven
Chautauqua Fiberglass & Plasti..............G....... 513 423-8840
  Middletown *(G-13892)*
Schmelzer Industries Inc........................E....... 740 743-2866
  Somerset *(G-17267)*

FABRICS: Flannels, Cotton
Franjinhas Inc...G....... 440 463-1523
  Strongsville *(G-17745)*

FABRICS: Glass & Fiberglass, Broadwoven
Architectural Fiberglass Inc....................E....... 216 641-8300
  Cleveland *(G-4727)*

FABRICS: Laminated
Lintec USA Holding Inc ....G....... 781 935-7850
  Stow *(G-17602)*

Prints & Paints Flr Cvg Co Inc................E....... 419 462-5663
  Galion *(G-10151)*
Trim Systems Operating Corp ....C....... 614 289-5360
  New Albany *(G-14639)*

FABRICS: Manmade Fiber, Narrow
Spunfab Ltd ....G....... 330 945-9455
  Cuyahoga Falls *(G-7922)*

FABRICS: Metallized
Alron..G....... 330 477-3405
  Strasburg *(G-17644)*
Laserflex Corporation.............................D....... 614 850-9600
  Hilliard *(G-10837)*
Ohio Metalizing LLC ....G....... 330 830-1092
  Massillon *(G-13030)*

FABRICS: Moleskins
Moleman ....G....... 513 662-3017
  Cincinnati *(G-4041)*

FABRICS: Nonwoven
Autoneum North America Inc ....B....... 419 693-0511
  Oregon *(G-15556)*
Intrusion-Prepakt Inc ....G....... 440 238-6950
  Cleveland *(G-5472)*
Polyflex LLC ....F....... 440 946-0758
  Willoughby *(G-20406)*
Toyobo Kureha America Co Ltd ....E....... 513 771-6788
  Cincinnati *(G-4427)*

FABRICS: Nylon, Broadwoven
Seaman Corporation...............................C....... 330 262-1111
  Wooster *(G-20652)*
Yoders Nylon Halter Shop ....G....... 330 893-3479
  Millersburg *(G-14155)*

FABRICS: Osnaburgs
Osnaburg Quilt Fibr Art Guild................G....... 330 488-2591
  East Canton *(G-9042)*

FABRICS: Polyethylene, Broadwoven
King Bag and Manufacturing Co ....E....... 513 541-5440
  Cincinnati *(G-3910)*

FABRICS: Print, Cotton
The Max...G....... 440 357-0036
  Painesville *(G-15789)*

FABRICS: Resin Or Plastic Coated
Biothane Coated Webbing Corp ....E....... 440 327-0485
  North Ridgeville *(G-15212)*
Duracote Corporation............................E....... 330 296-9600
  Ravenna *(G-16376)*
Durez Corporation ....C....... 567 295-6400
  Kenton *(G-11404)*
Gvc Plastics & Metals LLC ....G....... 440 232-9360
  Bedford *(G-1409)*
Petfiber LLC ....C....... 216 767-4482
  Cleveland *(G-5866)*
Schneller LLC..C....... 330 676-7183
  Kent *(G-11380)*

FABRICS: Rubber & Elastic Yarns & Fabrics
Murrubber Technologies Inc..................E....... 330 688-4881
  Stow *(G-17609)*

FABRICS: Rubberized
Salem-Republic Rubber Company ....E....... 877 425-5079
  Sebring *(G-16893)*

FABRICS: Scrub Cloths
Akron Cotton Products Inc ....G....... 330 434-7171
  Akron *(G-36)*
Canton Sterilized Wiping Cloth ....G....... 330 455-5179
  Canton *(G-2618)*
Linsalata Capital Partners Fun ....G....... 440 684-1400
  Cleveland *(G-5579)*
Star Wipers Inc.......................................G....... 724 695-2721
  Newark *(G-14922)*
Tranzonic Acquisition Corp ....A....... 216 535-4300
  Richmond Heights *(G-16505)*

Tranzonic Companies.............................C....... 440 446-0643
  Cleveland *(G-6198)*

FABRICS: Shoe Laces, Exc Leather
Joe Busby ....G....... 513 821-1716
  Cincinnati *(G-3876)*
Mitchellace Inc ....E....... 740 354-2813
  Portsmouth *(G-16291)*
Sole Choice Inc ....E....... 740 354-2813
  Portsmouth *(G-16302)*

FABRICS: Sleeving, Textile, Saturated
Bexley Fabrics Inc ....G....... 614 231-7272
  Columbus *(G-6666)*

FABRICS: Tracing Cloth, Cotton
Weiskopf Industries Corp ....E....... 440 442-4400
  Cleveland *(G-6297)*

FABRICS: Trimmings
A C Hadley - Printing Inc ....G....... 937 426-0952
  Beavercreek *(G-1296)*
ABC Inoac Exterior Systems LLC ....C....... 419 334-8951
  Fremont *(G-9988)*
Adcraft Decals Inc..................................E....... 216 524-2934
  Cleveland *(G-4615)*
Am Graphics..G....... 330 799-7319
  Youngstown *(G-20842)*
Anomatic Corporation ....B....... 740 522-2203
  Johnstown *(G-11255)*
Art Tees Inc...G....... 614 338-8337
  Columbus *(G-6617)*
Atlantis Sportswear Inc ....E....... 937 773-0680
  Piqua *(G-16101)*
Bates Metal Products Inc ....D....... 740 498-8371
  Port Washington *(G-16267)*
Brass Bull 1 LLC ....G....... 740 335-8030
  Wshngtn CT Hs *(G-20720)*
Brown Cnty Bd Mntal Rtardation..........E....... 937 378-4891
  Georgetown *(G-10237)*
Crabar/Gbf Inc ....F....... 419 943-2141
  Leipsic *(G-11724)*
Design Original Inc ....F....... 937 596-5121
  Jackson Center *(G-11207)*
Dresden Specialties Inc..........................G....... 740 754-2451
  Dresden *(G-8868)*
Dupli-Systems Inc ....C....... 440 234-9415
  Strongsville *(G-17738)*
Fedex Office & Print Svcs Inc ....E....... 614 898-0000
  Westerville *(G-20054)*
Fried Daddy ....G....... 937 854-4542
  Dayton *(G-8207)*
Gail Berner ....G....... 937 322-0314
  Springfield *(G-17406)*
Gail Zeilmann ....G....... 440 888-4858
  Cleveland *(G-5286)*
General Theming Contrs LLC ....C....... 614 252-6342
  Columbus *(G-6945)*
Hall Company ....E....... 937 652-1376
  Urbana *(G-18992)*
Hayes Reconditioning Group ....G....... 937 299-8013
  Dayton *(G-8246)*
Hunt Products Inc..................................E....... 440 667-2457
  Newburgh Heights *(G-14940)*
J America LLC ....G....... 614 914-2091
  Columbus *(G-7054)*
Jerry Pulfer ....G....... 937 778-1861
  Piqua *(G-16134)*
Kemper Automotive................................G....... 800 783-8004
  Franklin *(G-9892)*
Kent Stow Screen Printing Inc...............F....... 330 923-5118
  Akron *(G-235)*
Logan Screen Printing............................G....... 740 385-3303
  Logan *(G-12033)*
Lund Printing Co ....G....... 330 628-4047
  Akron *(G-262)*
Northeastern Plastics Inc ....G....... 330 453-5925
  Canton *(G-2768)*
Plus Mark LLC ....E....... 216 252-6770
  Cleveland *(G-5891)*
Randy Gray ....G....... 513 533-3200
  Cincinnati *(G-4248)*
Schilling Graphics Inc ....E....... 419 468-1037
  Galion *(G-10154)*
Screen Works Inc....................................E....... 937 264-9111
  Dayton *(G-8499)*
Standard Prototyping Ideals ....G....... 614 837-9180
  Pickerington *(G-16060)*

Employee Codes: A=Over 500 employees, B=251-500 C=101-250, D=51-100, E=20-50, F=10-19, G=3-9

FABRICS: Trimmings

T & L Custom Screening Inc ....G....... 937 237-3121
Dayton (G-8534)
Tendon Manufacturing Inc ....E....... 216 663-3200
Cleveland (G-6159)
Trim Systems Operating Corp ....C....... 740 772-5998
Chillicothe (G-3228)
Universal Drect Flfllment Corp ....C....... 330 650-5000
Hudson (G-11081)
Vgu Industries Inc ....E....... 216 676-9093
Cleveland (G-6257)
W J Egli Company Inc ....F....... 330 823-3666
Alliance (G-512)
West & Barker Inc ....E....... 330 652-9923
Niles (G-15040)
Woodrow Manufacturing Co ....E....... 937 399-9333
Springfield (G-17521)
Yi Xing Inc ....G....... 614 785-9631
Columbus (G-7623)
Zenos Activewear Inc ....G....... 614 443-0070
Columbus (G-7626)

FABRICS: Umbrella Cloth, Cotton

Totes Isotoner Corporation ....F....... 513 682-8200
West Chester (G-19907)
Totes Isotoner Holdings Corp ....C....... 513 682-8200
West Chester (G-19908)

FABRICS: Upholstery, Wool

Midwest Composites LLC ....E....... 419 738-2431
Wapakoneta (G-19342)

FABRICS: Varnished Glass & Coated Fiberglass

Spectroglass Corp ....G....... 614 297-0412
Columbus (G-7471)

FABRICS: Wall Covering, From Manmade Fiber Or Silk

C S A Enterprises ....G....... 740 342-9367
New Lexington (G-14713)

FABRICS: Waterproofed, Exc Rubberized

Excello Fabric Finishers Inc ....G....... 740 622-7444
Coshocton (G-7732)

FABRICS: Woven, Narrow Cotton, Wool, Silk

A & P Technology Inc ....D....... 513 688-3200
Cincinnati (G-3235)
A & P Technology Inc ....D....... 513 688-3200
Cincinnati (G-3236)
A & P Technology Inc ....E....... 513 688-3200
Cincinnati (G-3237)
Keuchel & Associates Inc ....E....... 330 945-9455
Cuyahoga Falls (G-7888)
Paxar Corporation ....F....... 937 681-4541
Dayton (G-8418)
Samsel Rope & Marine Supply Co ....E....... 216 241-0333
Cleveland (G-6029)
Shurtape Technologies LLC ....B....... 440 937-7000
Avon (G-966)

FACILITIES SUPPORT SVCS

MPW Industrial Svcs Group Inc ....D....... 740 927-8790
Hebron (G-10754)
Taylor Communications Inc ....E....... 937 221-1000
Dayton (G-8543)

FACILITY RENTAL & PARTY PLANNING SVCS

Loris Printing Inc ....G....... 419 626-6648
Sandusky (G-16823)
Skyliner ....G....... 740 738-0874
Bridgeport (G-2078)

FAMILY CLOTHING STORES

Cotton Pickin Tees & Caps ....G....... 419 636-3595
Bryan (G-2277)
Odyssey Spirits Inc ....F....... 330 562-1523
Aurora (G-896)
Vances Department Store ....G....... 937 549-2188
Manchester (G-12397)
Vances Department Store ....F....... 937 549-3033
Manchester (G-12398)

FAMILY PLANNING CENTERS

Community Action Program Corp ....F....... 740 374-8501
Marietta (G-12617)

FANS, BLOWING: Indl Or Commercial

Halifax-Fan USA LLC ....G....... 262 257-9779
Cuyahoga Falls (G-7876)

FANS, EXHAUST: Indl Or Commercial

ARI Phoenix Inc ....E....... 513 229-3750
Lebanon (G-11634)
Criticalaire LLC ....F....... 513 475-3800
Columbus (G-6838)
Criticalaire LLC ....G....... 614 499-7744
Cincinnati (G-3559)
Howden American Fan Company ....C....... 513 874-2400
Fairfield (G-9506)
Multi-Wing America Inc ....E....... 440 834-9400
Middlefield (G-13834)

FANS, VENTILATING: Indl Or Commercial

Duro Dyne Midwest Corp ....B....... 513 870-6000
Hamilton (G-10551)
Lau Industries Inc ....C....... 937 476-6500
Dayton (G-7983)
Tlt-Turbo Inc ....G....... 330 776-5115
Akron (G-407)
Usui International Corporation ....E....... 513 448-0410
Cincinnati (G-4459)
Vector Mechanical LLC ....G....... 216 337-4042
Brookpark (G-2158)

FANS: Ceiling

Acorn Technology Corporation ....E....... 216 663-1244
Cleveland (G-4610)

FARM & GARDEN MACHINERY WHOLESALERS

All Power Equipment LLC ....F....... 740 593-3279
Athens (G-822)
J L Wannemacher Sales & Svc ....F....... 419 453-3445
Ottoville (G-15681)
Smg Growing Media Inc ....G....... 937 644-0011
Marysville (G-12813)

FARM MACHINERY REPAIR SVCS

Dalin Auto Service ....G....... 440 997-3301
Ashtabula (G-770)
J L Wannemacher Sales & Svc ....F....... 419 453-3445
Ottoville (G-15681)
Reberland Equipment Inc ....F....... 330 698-5883
Apple Creek (G-618)

FARM PRDTS, RAW MATERIALS, WHOLESALE: Hides

Inland Products Inc ....E....... 614 443-3425
Columbus (G-7027)

FARM PRDTS, RAW MATERIALS, WHOLESALE: Nuts & Nut By-Prdts

Krema Products Inc ....G....... 614 889-4824
Dublin (G-8939)

FARM SPLY STORES

Centerra Co-Op ....E....... 419 281-2153
Ashland (G-690)
Dinsmore Inc ....G....... 937 544-3332
West Union (G-19961)
Farmers Commission Company ....E....... 419 294-2371
Upper Sandusky (G-18954)
J & B Feed Co Inc ....G....... 419 335-5821
Wauseon (G-19523)
Pettisville Grain Co ....E....... 419 446-2547
Pettisville (G-16035)
RJR & Associates Inc ....G....... 419 237-2220
Fayette (G-9636)
Sunrise Cooperative Inc ....F....... 419 929-1568
Wakeman (G-19289)

FARM SPLYS WHOLESALERS

Andersons Inc ....C....... 419 893-5050
Maumee (G-13072)
Andersons Inc ....G....... 419 536-0460
Toledo (G-18184)
Centerra Co-Op ....E....... 800 362-9598
Jefferson (G-11226)
Countyline Co-Op Inc ....F....... 419 287-3241
Pemberville (G-15883)
Darling International Inc ....E....... 216 651-9300
Cleveland (G-5066)
Legacy Farmers Cooperative ....F....... 419 423-2611
Findlay (G-9713)
Luckey Farmers Inc ....G....... 419 287-3275
Bradner (G-2013)
Phillips Ready Mix Co ....D....... 937 426-5151
Beavercreek Township (G-1372)
Rogers Mill Inc ....G....... 330 227-3214
Rogers (G-16561)
Rural Farm Distributors Co ....G....... 419 747-6807
Mansfield (G-12508)

FARM SPLYS, WHOLESALE: Feed

Cooper Farms Inc ....D....... 419 375-4116
Fort Recovery (G-9813)
Cooper Farms Inc ....F....... 419 375-4619
Fort Recovery (G-9815)
K M B Inc ....E....... 330 889-3451
Bristolville (G-2082)
Mennel Milling Company ....E....... 740 385-6824
Logan (G-12035)
Mennel Milling Company ....D....... 740 385-6824
Logan (G-12036)
Republic Mills Inc ....F....... 419 758-3511
Okolona (G-15523)
Sunrise Cooperative Inc ....F....... 419 628-4705
Minster (G-14225)

FARM SPLYS, WHOLESALE: Fertilizers & Agricultural Chemicals

Helena Agri-Enterprises LLC ....G....... 419 596-3806
Continental (G-7666)
Hoopes Fertilizer Works Inc ....G....... 330 894-2121
East Rochester (G-9090)
Naturym LLC ....G....... 614 284-3068
Gahanna (G-10093)
Nutrien AG Solutions Inc ....G....... 614 873-4253
Milford Center (G-14047)

FARM SPLYS, WHOLESALE: Garden Splys

Wholesale Fairy Gardenscom LLC ....G....... 614 504-5304
Plain City (G-16218)

FARM SPLYS, WHOLESALE: Greenhouse Eqpt & Splys

XS Smith Inc ....E....... 252 940-5060
Cincinnati (G-4529)

FARM SPLYS, WHOLESALE: Harness Eqpt

Yoders Harness Shop ....G....... 440 632-1505
Middlefield (G-13871)

FARM SPLYS, WHOLESALE: Limestone, Agricultural

Lesco Inc ....F....... 740 633-6366
Martins Ferry (G-12761)

FASTENERS: Metal

Aerotech Industries Inc ....G....... 216 881-6660
Cleveland (G-4636)
Bricolage Inc ....F....... 614 853-6789
Grove City (G-10418)
CP Metals Inc ....G....... 724 510-4293
Warren (G-19390)
Elgin Fastener Group LLC ....F....... 812 689-8990
Brecksville (G-2032)
Midwest Motor Supply Co ....C....... 800 233-1294
Columbus (G-7181)
National Fasteners Inc ....G....... 216 771-6473
Brooklyn Heights (G-2127)
Robert A Reich Company ....G....... 440 808-0033
Westlake (G-20151)
Stonebrook Machine ....G....... 440 951-5013
Eastlake (G-9132)
Tru-Har Products ....G....... 330 338-6826
Hudson (G-11080)

FASTENERS: Metal

Hudson Fasteners Inc .... G 330 270-9500
 Youngstown *(G-20933)*
Sky Climber Fasteners LLC .... G 740 816-9830
 Delaware *(G-8726)*
Supply International Inc .... G 740 282-8604
 Steubenville *(G-17555)*
Wecall Inc .... G 440 437-8202
 Orwell *(G-15636)*

FASTENERS: Notions, NEC

A Raymond Tinnerman Indus Inc ..... D 330 220-5100
 Brunswick *(G-2186)*
Cardinal Fstener Specialty Inc .... E 216 831-3800
 Bedford Heights *(G-1464)*
Dimcogray Corporation .... D 937 433-7600
 Centerville *(G-3001)*
Dubose Energy Fasteners & Mach ..... F 216 362-1700
 Middleburg Heights *(G-13764)*
Eaglehead Manufacturing Co .... E 216 692-1240
 Euclid *(G-9412)*
Elgin Fastener Group .... G 440 325-4337
 Berea *(G-1605)*
Erico International Corp .... B 440 248-0100
 Solon *(G-17140)*
ET&f Fastening Systems Inc .... F 800 248-2376
 Solon *(G-17141)*
Global Specialties Inc .... G 800 338-0814
 Brunswick *(G-2210)*
Interfast Inc .... G 216 581-3000
 Cleveland *(G-5465)*
Midwest Motor Supply Co .... C 800 233-1294
 Columbus *(G-7181)*
Ohashi Technica USA Mfg Inc .... E 740 965-9002
 Sunbury *(G-17895)*
Phillips Contractors Sup LLC .... F 216 861-5730
 Cleveland *(G-5872)*
R L Technologies Inc .... G 937 321-5544
 Dayton *(G-8459)*
Ramco Specialties Inc .... C 330 653-5135
 Hudson *(G-11069)*
Silicon USA Inc .... G 330 928-6217
 Cuyahoga Falls *(G-7916)*
Stelfast Inc .... E 440 879-0077
 Strongsville *(G-17797)*
Tri-State Fasteners LLC .... G 937 442-1904
 Sardinia *(G-16874)*
W W Cross Industries Inc .... F 330 588-8400
 Canton *(G-2861)*
Wodin Inc .... G 440 439-4222
 Cleveland *(G-6320)*
Youngstown Bolt & Supply Co .... G 330 799-3201
 Youngstown *(G-21072)*

FASTENERS: Notions, Zippers

Zipper Manufacturing LLC .... G 937 444-0904
 Williamsburg *(G-20258)*

FASTENERS: Wire, Made From Purchased Wire

Fastener Industries Inc .... F 216 267-2240
 Cleveland *(G-5221)*

FAUCETS & SPIGOTS: Metal & Plastic

Toolbold Corporation .... E 440 543-1660
 Cleveland *(G-6184)*

FEATHERS & FEATHER PRODUCTS

Ohio Feather Company Inc .... G 513 921-3373
 Cincinnati *(G-4101)*

FELT PARTS

Ohio Table Pad Company .... D 419 872-6400
 Perrysburg *(G-15986)*

FELT: Automotive

NC Works Inc .... E 937 514-7781
 Franklin *(G-9903)*

FENCE POSTS: Iron & Steel

Msls Group LLC .... E 330 723-4431
 Medina *(G-13305)*

FENCES OR POSTS: Ornamental Iron Or Steel

Akron Products Company .... F 330 576-1750
 Wadsworth *(G-19223)*
City Iron LLC .... G 513 721-5678
 Cincinnati *(G-3521)*
Randy Lewis Inc .... F 330 784-0456
 Akron *(G-342)*

FENCING DEALERS

Bugh Vinyl Products Inc .... G 330 305-0978
 Canton *(G-2601)*
Randy Lewis Inc .... F 330 784-0456
 Akron *(G-342)*
Youngstown Fence Inc .... G 330 788-8110
 Youngstown *(G-21076)*

FENCING MADE IN WIREDRAWING PLANTS

Hsm Wire International Inc .... G 330 244-8501
 North Canton *(G-15093)*

FENCING MATERIALS: Docks & Other Outdoor Prdts, Wood

Cornerstone Spclty WD Pdts LLC ..... D 513 772-5560
 Cincinnati *(G-3550)*
Lucius Fence Decking Irrigat .... G 419 450-9907
 New Riegel *(G-14815)*

FENCING MATERIALS: Plastic

All Around Garage Door Inc .... G 440 759-5079
 North Ridgeville *(G-15207)*
American Way Manufacturing Inc ..... E 330 824-2353
 Warren *(G-19369)*
Bugh Vinyl Products Inc .... G 330 305-0978
 Canton *(G-2601)*
Customized Vinyl Sales .... G 330 518-3238
 East Palestine *(G-9072)*
Doglok Inc .... G 440 223-1836
 Perry *(G-15904)*
Randy Lewis Inc .... F 330 784-0456
 Akron *(G-342)*

FENCING MATERIALS: Wood

Greenes Fence Co Inc .... G 216 464-3160
 Solon *(G-17157)*
Kalinich Fence Company Inc .... F 440 238-6127
 Strongsville *(G-17759)*
Mi-Lar Fence Co Inc .... G 216 464-3160
 Solon *(G-17193)*
Randy Lewis Inc .... F 330 784-0456
 Akron *(G-342)*
Youngstown Fence Inc .... G 330 788-8110
 Youngstown *(G-21076)*

FENCING: Chain Link

Aluminum Fence & Mfg Co .... G 330 755-3323
 Aurora *(G-868)*
D&M Fencing LLC .... G 419 604-0698
 Spencerville *(G-17308)*
Randy Lewis Inc .... F 330 784-0456
 Akron *(G-342)*
Richards Whl Fence Co Inc .... E 330 773-0423
 Akron *(G-348)*
Stephens Pipe & Steel LLC .... C 740 869-2257
 Mount Sterling *(G-14465)*

FENDERS: Automobile, Stamped Or Pressed Metal

Fiberglass Link Inc .... G 216 531-5515
 Cleveland *(G-5236)*
Ltf Acquisition LLC .... F 330 533-0111
 Canfield *(G-2533)*

FERRALLOY ORES, EXC VANADIUM

Rhenium Alloys Inc .... D 440 365-7388
 North Ridgeville *(G-15251)*

FERROALLOYS

International Metal Supply LLC .... F 330 764-1004
 Medina *(G-13281)*
Marietta Eramet Inc .... C 740 374-1000
 Marietta *(G-12642)*

FERROALLOYS: Produced In Blast Furnaces

Pelletier Brothers Mfg .... F 740 774-4704
 Chillicothe *(G-3208)*

FERROMANGANESE, NOT MADE IN BLAST FURNACES

Real Alloy Specialty Pdts LLC .... A 216 755-8836
 Beachwood *(G-1273)*
Real Alloy Specification LLC .... G 216 755-8900
 Beachwood *(G-1275)*

FERROSILICON, EXC MADE IN BLAST FURNACES

Globe Metallurgical Inc .... C 740 984-2361
 Waterford *(G-19484)*

FERROUS METALS: Reclaimed From Clay

A-Gas US Holdings Inc .... F 419 867-8990
 Bowling Green *(G-1945)*

FERTILIZER MINERAL MINING

Everris NA Inc .... E 614 726-7100
 Dublin *(G-8914)*

FERTILIZER, AGRICULTURAL: Wholesalers

Farmers Commission Company .... E 419 294-2371
 Upper Sandusky *(G-18954)*
Hanby Farms Inc .... E 740 763-3554
 Nashport *(G-14567)*
Ohigro Inc .... E 740 726-2429
 Waldo *(G-19304)*

FERTILIZERS: NEC

All Ways Green Lawn & Turf LLC ..... G 937 763-4766
 Seaman *(G-16882)*
Countyline Co-Op Inc .... F 419 287-3241
 Pemberville *(G-15883)*
Growmark Fs LLC .... F 330 386-7626
 East Liverpool *(G-9057)*
Hoopes Fertilizer Works Inc .... G 330 894-2121
 East Rochester *(G-9090)*
Hoopes Fertilizer Works Inc .... G 330 821-3550
 Alliance *(G-476)*
Hyponex Corporation .... D 937 644-0011
 Marysville *(G-12794)*
Insta-Gro Manufacturing Inc .... G 419 845-3046
 Caledonia *(G-2417)*
Legacy Farmers Cooperative .... F 419 423-2611
 Findlay *(G-9713)*
Lesco Inc .... F 740 633-6366
 Martins Ferry *(G-12761)*
LLC Kurtz Bros Central Ohio .... G 614 733-3074
 Dublin *(G-8943)*
Luckey Farmers Inc .... G 419 287-3275
 Bradner *(G-2013)*
Nachurs Alpine Solutions Corp .... E 740 382-5701
 Marion *(G-12723)*
Nutrien AG Solutions Inc .... E 513 941-4100
 North Bend *(G-15053)*
Nutrien AG Solutions Inc .... G 614 873-4253
 Milford Center *(G-14047)*
Ohigro Inc .... E 740 726-2429
 Waldo *(G-19304)*
Ottokee Group Inc .... G 419 636-1932
 Bryan *(G-2302)*
Rural Farm Distributors Co .... G 419 747-6807
 Mansfield *(G-12508)*
Tri-State Garden Supply Inc .... E 419 445-6561
 Archbold *(G-672)*
Tyler Grain & Fertilizer Co .... F 330 669-2341
 Smithville *(G-17095)*

FERTILIZERS: Nitrogen Solutions

Naturym LLC .... G 614 284-3068
 Gahanna *(G-10093)*
Pcs Nitrogen Inc .... B 419 226-1200
 Lima *(G-11914)*

FERTILIZERS: Nitrogenous

Agrium Advanced Tech US Inc .... G 614 276-5103
 Columbus *(G-6552)*
Andersons Plant Nutrient LLC .... G 419 396-3501
 Carey *(G-2878)*

FERTILIZERS: Nitrogenous

Harvest Land Co-Op Inc ....G...... 937 884-5526
  Verona (G-19172)
Nutrien AG Solutions Inc ....E...... 513 941-4100
  North Bend (G-15053)
Pcs Nitrogen Ohio LP 419 879-8989
  Lima (G-11915)
R & J AG Manufacturing Inc ....F...... 419 962-4707
  Ashland (G-741)
Scotts Miracle-Gro Company ....D...... 330 684-0421
  Orrville (G-15619)
Scotts Miracle-Gro Products 937 644-0011
  Marysville (G-12812)
Synagro Midwest Inc ....F...... 937 384-0669
  Miamisburg (G-13722)
Turf Care Supply Corp ....B...... 877 220-1014
  Brunswick (G-2247)

FERTILIZERS: Phosphatic

Andersons Inc ....C...... 419 893-5050
  Maumee (G-13072)
Andersons Inc ....G...... 419 536-0460
  Toledo (G-18184)
Occidental Chemical Corp ....E...... 513 242-2900
  Cincinnati (G-4097)

FIBER & FIBER PRDTS: Acrylic

Success Technologies Inc ....G...... 614 761-0008
  Powell (G-16337)

FIBER & FIBER PRDTS: Acrylonitrile

Buckeye Polymers Inc ....E...... 330 948-3007
  Lodi (G-12008)
Ineos Nitriles USA LLC ....C...... 419 226-1200
  Lima (G-11878)

FIBER & FIBER PRDTS: Cuprammonium

Laser Horizons ....G...... 330 208-0575
  Norton (G-15373)

FIBER & FIBER PRDTS: Elastomeric

Bridge Components Incorporated ....G...... 614 873-0777
  Columbus (G-6697)

FIBER & FIBER PRDTS: Organic, Noncellulose

Ecm Biofilms Inc ....G...... 440 350-1400
  Painesville (G-15735)
Omnova Solutions Inc ....C...... 330 628-6550
  Mogadore (G-14246)
Organic Roots Horticulture LLC ....G...... 330 620-1108
  Ravenna (G-16393)

FIBER & FIBER PRDTS: Polyester

Fft Sidney LLC ....D...... 937 492-2709
  Sidney (G-17040)

FIBER & FIBER PRDTS: Synthetic Cellulosic

Advanced Fiber LLC ....E...... 419 562-1337
  Bucyrus (G-2317)
Fft Sidney LLC ....D...... 937 492-2709
  Sidney (G-17040)
Flexsys America LP ....D...... 330 666-4111
  Akron (G-173)
J Rettenmaier USA LP 440 385-6701
  Oberlin (G-15500)
J Rettenmaier USA LP ....D...... 937 652-2101
  Urbana (G-18997)
J Rettenmaier USA LP ....D...... 937 652-2101
  Urbana (G-18998)
Mfg Composite Systems Company ....B...... 440 997-5851
  Ashtabula (G-786)
Morgan Adhesives Company LLC ....B...... 330 688-1111
  Stow (G-17606)

FIBER & FIBER PRDTS: Vinyl

Mytee Products Inc ....F...... 440 591-4301
  Aurora (G-894)

FIBER OPTICS

Jason Wilson ....E...... 937 604-8209
  Tipp City (G-18120)
Nextgen Fiber Optics LLC ....D...... 513 549-4691
  Cincinnati (G-4075)

PLC Connections LLC ....F...... 614 279-1796
  Columbus (G-7327)
Sem-Com Company Inc ....F...... 419 537-8813
  Toledo (G-18517)
Srico Inc ....G...... 614 799-0664
  Columbus (G-7481)

FIBER: Vulcanized

Fft Sidney LLC ....D...... 937 492-2709
  Sidney (G-17040)

FIBERS: Carbon & Graphite

Wolfden Products Inc ....G...... 614 219-6990
  Columbus (G-7609)
Xperion E&E USA LLC ....E...... 740 788-9560
  Heath (G-10735)

FIELD WAREHOUSING SVCS

Truechoicepack Corp ....E...... 937 630-3832
  Mason (G-12951)

FILE FOLDERS

GBS Corp ....C...... 330 863-1828
  Malvern (G-12391)
GBS Corp ....C...... 330 494-5330
  North Canton (G-15085)
Keeler Enterprises Inc ....G...... 330 336-7601
  Wadsworth (G-19247)
Smead Manufacturing Company ....C...... 740 385-5601
  Logan (G-12044)

FILM & SHEET: Unsuppported Plastic

Ampac Holdings LLC ....A...... 513 671-1777
  Cincinnati (G-3340)
Avery Dennison Corporation ....D...... 440 358-3408
  Painesville (G-15717)
Berry Global Inc ....F...... 419 887-1602
  Maumee (G-13080)
CCL Label Inc 216 676-2703
  Cleveland (G-4894)
CCL Label Inc ....E...... 440 878-7000
  Brunswick (G-2194)
Charter Nex Films - Del OH Inc ....E...... 740 369-2770
  Delaware (G-8663)
Clopay Corporation ....G...... 440 542-9215
  Solon (G-17127)
Command Plastic Corporation ....F...... 800 321-8001
  Tallmadge (G-17977)
DJM Plastics Ltd ....F...... 419 424-5250
  Findlay (G-9679)
Dupont Specialty Pdts USA LLC 740 474-0220
  Circleville (G-4543)
General Data Company Inc ....C...... 513 752-7978
  Cincinnati (G-3252)
Industry Products Co ....B...... 937 778-0585
  Piqua (G-16130)
James McGuire ....G...... 614 483-9825
  Columbus (G-7061)
Liqui-Box Corporation ....C...... 419 289-9696
  Ashland (G-721)
Mar-Bal Inc ....D...... 440 543-7526
  Chagrin Falls (G-3057)
Mar-Bal Inc ....D...... 440 543-7526
  Chagrin Falls (G-3058)
North Shore Strapping Inc ....D...... 216 661-5200
  Brooklyn Heights (G-2128)
North Shore Strapping Inc ....D...... 216 661-5200
  Cleveland (G-5770)
Omnova Solutions Inc ....C...... 216 682-7000
  Beachwood (G-1257)
Orbis Rpm LLC ....G...... 419 307-8511
  Columbus (G-7276)
Orbis Rpm LLC 740 772-6355
  Chillicothe (G-3203)
Orbis Rpm LLC ....F...... 419 355-8310
  Fremont (G-10042)
Packaging Materials Inc 740 432-6337
  Cambridge (G-2452)
Pexco Packaging Corp ....E...... 419 470-5935
  Toledo (G-18468)
Plastic Suppliers Inc 614 471-9100
  Columbus (G-7323)
Plastic Suppliers Inc ....E...... 214 467-3700
  Columbus (G-7324)
Polyone Corporation ....D...... 440 930-1000
  Avon Lake (G-1001)
Priority Custom Molding Inc ....F...... 937 431-8770
  Beavercreek Township (G-1373)

Profusion Industries LLC ....G...... 800 938-2858
  Fairlawn (G-9615)
Profusion Industries LLC ....E...... 740 374-6400
  Marietta (G-12660)
Quality Poly Corp ....F...... 330 453-9559
  Canton (G-2796)
Rotary Products Inc ....F...... 740 747-2623
  Ashley (G-760)
Snyder Manufacturing Co Ltd ....G...... 330 343-4456
  Dover (G-8856)
Spartech LLC ....D...... 937 548-1395
  Greenville (G-10395)
Spartech LLC 419 399-4050
  Paulding (G-15871)
Summit Plastic Company ....D...... 330 633-3668
  Mogadore (G-14251)
Team Plastics Inc ....F...... 216 251-8270
  Cleveland (G-6150)
Transcendia Inc ....C...... 740 929-5100
  Hebron (G-10768)
Transcendia Inc 440 638-2000
  Strongsville (G-17801)

FILM BASE: Cellulose Acetate Or Nitrocellulose Plastics

American Insulation Tech LLC ....F...... 513 733-4248
  Milford (G-13993)
Boltaron Inc ....D...... 740 498-5900
  Newcomerstown (G-14970)

FILM DEVELOPING & PRINTING SVCS

SMS Communications Inc ....E...... 216 374-6686
  Shaker Heights (G-16937)

FILM: Rubber

B D G Wrap-Tite Inc ....D...... 440 349-5400
  Solon (G-17110)

FILTER ELEMENTS: Fluid & Hydraulic Line

Parker-Hannifin Corporation ....B...... 216 896-3000
  Cleveland (G-5848)
Parker-Hannifin Corporation ....F...... 216 896-3000
  Cleveland (G-5850)
Two M Precision Co Inc ....E...... 440 946-2120
  Willoughby (G-20454)

FILTERS

Abanaki Corporation ....F...... 440 543-7400
  Chagrin Falls (G-3034)
Allied Separation Tech Inc 704 732-8034
  Twinsburg (G-18731)
Aronit Machine LLC ....F...... 419 782-4740
  Defiance (G-8613)
Barney Corporation Inc ....G...... 614 274-9069
  Hilliard (G-10810)
Columbus Industries Inc ....A...... 740 983-2552
  Ashville (G-816)
Diamondback Filters 419 494-1156
  Bowling Green (G-1968)
E R Advanced Ceramics Inc ....E...... 330 426-9433
  East Palestine (G-9077)
Evoqua Water Technologies LLC ....E...... 614 861-5440
  Pickerington (G-16047)
Filter Factory-Ttn Inc ....G...... 440 963-2034
  Vermilion (G-19159)
Foseco Inc ....G...... 440 826-4548
  Cleveland (G-5267)
Hdt Expeditionary Systems Inc ....G...... 216 438-6111
  Solon (G-17160)
Hunter Defense Tech Inc 216 438-6111
  Solon (G-17164)
Kc Robotics Inc ....F...... 513 860-4442
  West Chester (G-19729)
Lawrence Technologies Inc ....G...... 937 274-7771
  Dayton (G-8308)
Oil Skimmers Inc ....E...... 440 237-4600
  North Royalton (G-15291)
Process Machinery Inc ....E...... 614 278-1055
  Columbus (G-7352)
Raymond W Reisiger 740 400-4090
  Baltimore (G-1041)
Swift Filters Inc ....E...... 440 735-0995
  Oakwood Village (G-15484)
Zhao Hui Filters (us) Inc 440 519-9301
  Beachwood (G-1287)

FILTERS & SOFTENERS: Water, Household

Company	Code	Phone
Amsoil Inc	G	614 274-9851
Columbus (G-6593)		
Enting Water Conditioning Inc	E	937 294-5100
Moraine (G-14350)		
Monarch Water Systems Inc	F	937 426-5773
Beavercreek (G-1333)		
Mountain Filtration Systems	G	419 395-2526
Defiance (G-8640)		
New Aqua LLC	G	614 265-9000
Columbus (G-7215)		
Tri County Quality Wtr Systems	G	740 751-4764
Marion (G-12745)		
United McGill	G	614 829-1226
Columbus (G-7557)		
Water Systems Services	G	513 523-6766
Oxford (G-15702)		

FILTERS & STRAINERS: Pipeline

Company	Code	Phone
City of Mansfield	F	419 884-3310
Mansfield (G-12425)		
Hellan Strainer Company	G	216 206-4200
Cleveland (G-5389)		

FILTERS: Air

Company	Code	Phone
Air Cleaning Solutions	G	937 832-3600
Dayton (G-8012)		
Ceco Filters Inc	G	513 458-2600
Cincinnati (G-3451)		
Cincinnati A Flter Sls Svc Inc	E	513 242-3400
Cincinnati (G-3478)		
Complete Filter Media LLC	E	740 438-0929
Lancaster (G-11555)		
First Filter LLC	G	419 666-5260
Perrysburg (G-15951)		
Glasfloss Industries Inc	C	740 687-1100
Lancaster (G-11577)		
Hdt Expeditionary Systems Inc	E	440 466-6640
Geneva (G-10222)		
Hunter Environmental Corp	G	440 248-6111
Solon (G-17165)		
Skuttle Mfg Co	F	740 373-9169
Marietta (G-12670)		
Std Specialty Filters Inc	F	216 881-3727
Cleveland (G-6101)		
Troy Filters Ltd	E	614 777-8222
Columbus (G-7546)		

FILTERS: Air Intake, Internal Combustion Engine, Exc Auto

Company	Code	Phone
Donaldson Company Inc	D	330 928-4100
Stow (G-17580)		
Engine Machine Service Inc	G	330 505-1804
Niles (G-15007)		
Lariat Machine Inc	G	330 297-5765
Ravenna (G-16388)		
Norwood Medical	G	937 228-4101
Dayton (G-8385)		
Plas-Mac Corp	D	440 349-3222
Solon (G-17216)		

FILTERS: General Line, Indl

Company	Code	Phone
D C Filter & Chemical Inc	G	419 626-3967
Sandusky (G-16802)		
Edjean Technical Services Inc	G	440 647-3300
Sullivan (G-17881)		
Falls Filtration Tech Inc	E	330 928-4100
Stow (G-17586)		
Gvs Filtration Inc	B	419 423-9040
Findlay (G-9697)		
Membrane Specialists LLC	G	513 860-9490
Hamilton (G-10586)		
Midwest Filtration LLC	E	513 874-6510
West Chester (G-19880)		
Nupro Company	C	440 951-9729
Willoughby (G-20392)		
Petro Ware Inc	D	740 982-1302
Crooksville (G-7819)		
Pyrotek Incorporated	G	440 349-8800
Aurora (G-901)		
S A Langmack Company	F	216 541-0500
Cleveland (G-6021)		
Tungsten Capital Partners LLC	G	216 481-4774
Cleveland (G-6221)		

FILTERS: Motor Vehicle

Company	Code	Phone
Bellevue Manufacturing Company	D	419 483-3190
Bellevue (G-1531)		
Bellevue Manufacturing Company	G	419 483-3190
Bellevue (G-1532)		
Entratech Systems LLC	F	419 423-7683
Sandusky (G-16809)		
Fram Group Operations LLC	G	937 316-3000
Greenville (G-10369)		
Roki America Co Ltd	B	419 424-9713
Findlay (G-9747)		

FILTERS: Oil, Internal Combustion Engine, Exc Auto

Company	Code	Phone
Brinkley Technology Group LLC	F	330 830-2498
Massillon (G-12963)		

FILTRATION DEVICES: Electronic

Company	Code	Phone
Chicopee Engineering Assoc Inc	E	413 592-2273
Twinsburg (G-18751)		
Contech Strmwter Solutions LLC	G	513 645-7000
West Chester (G-19682)		
Crawford Resources Inc	G	419 624-8400
Lorain (G-12086)		
Illinois Tool Works Inc	C	262 248-8277
Bryan (G-2289)		
Micropure Filtration Inc	F	952 472-2323
Cleveland (G-5669)		
Nu Stream Filtration Inc	G	937 949-3174
Dayton (G-8390)		

FINANCIAL SVCS

Company	Code	Phone
International Supply Corp	G	513 793-0393
Cincinnati (G-3858)		

FINDINGS & TRIMMINGS: Fabric

Company	Code	Phone
Detroit Technologies Inc	E	937 492-2708
Sidney (G-17030)		
Eisenhauer Mfg Co LLC	D	419 238-0081
Van Wert (G-19090)		
Greenfield Research Inc	G	937 876-9224
Greenfield (G-10351)		
Griffin Fisher Co Inc	G	513 961-2110
Cincinnati (G-3785)		
Hfi LLC	B	614 491-0700
Columbus (G-6995)		
Lesch Boat Cover Canvas Co LLC	G	419 668-6374
Norwalk (G-15404)		
Pieco Inc	E	419 422-5335
Findlay (G-9741)		
Pieco Inc	D	937 399-5100
Springfield (G-17472)		
Spirit Avionics Ltd	F	614 237-4271
Columbus (G-7477)		
Telempu N Hayashi Amer Corp	G	513 932-9319
Lebanon (G-11700)		

FINGERNAILS, ARTIFICIAL

Company	Code	Phone
Hung Pham	G	614 850-9695
Columbus (G-7011)		
Nail Art	G	614 899-7155
Westerville (G-20066)		
Nail Secret	G	513 459-3373
Maineville (G-12375)		

FINGERPRINT EQPT

Company	Code	Phone
Advanced Livescan Technologies	G	440 759-7028
Cleveland (G-4628)		

FINISHING AGENTS

Company	Code	Phone
Pilot Chemical Company Ohio	E	513 326-0600
Cincinnati (G-4159)		
Pilot Chemical Company Ohio	E	513 733-4880
Cincinnati (G-4160)		

FIRE ARMS, SMALL: Guns Or Gun Parts, 30 mm & Below

Company	Code	Phone
762mm Firearms LLC	G	440 655-8572
Wadsworth (G-19217)		
Faxon Firearms LLC	G	513 674-2580
Cincinnati (G-3677)		
Highpoint Firearms	E	419 747-9444
Mansfield (G-12459)		
Iberia Firearms Inc	G	419 468-3746
Galion (G-10145)		
Jmr Enterprises LLC	G	937 618-1736
Maineville (G-12371)		
Ohio Ordnance Works Inc	E	440 285-3481
Chardon (G-3130)		
Smokin Guns LLC	G	440 324-4003
Elyria (G-9329)		
TS Sales LLC	F	727 804-8060
Mount Gilead (G-14435)		
X-Treme Shooting Products LLC	G	513 313-3464
Batavia (G-1198)		

FIRE ARMS, SMALL: Machine Guns & Grenade Launchers

Company	Code	Phone
Reloading Supplies Corp	G	440 228-0367
Ashtabula (G-802)		

FIRE ARMS, SMALL: Machine Guns/Machine Gun Parts, 30mm/below

Company	Code	Phone
Apex Alliance LLC	G	234 200-5930
Stow (G-17569)		
Parabellum Armament Co LLC	G	614 557-5987
Grove City (G-10456)		

FIRE ARMS, SMALL: Rifles Or Rifle Parts, 30 mm & below

Company	Code	Phone
Inland Manufacturing LLC	G	937 835-0220
Dayton (G-8264)		
Kelblys Rifle Range Inc	G	330 683-0070
North Lawrence (G-15162)		
Zshot Inc	G	800 385-8581
Columbus (G-7628)		

FIRE ARMS, SMALL: Shotguns Or Shotgun Parts, 30 mm & Below

Company	Code	Phone
Quality Replacement Parts Inc	G	216 674-0200
Cleveland (G-5943)		

FIRE CLAY MINING

Company	Code	Phone
E J Bognar Inc	F	330 426-9292
East Palestine (G-9076)		

FIRE CONTROL EQPT REPAIR SVCS, MILITARY

Company	Code	Phone
Fire Foe Corp	E	330 759-9834
Girard (G-10258)		

FIRE CONTROL OR BOMBING EQPT: Electronic

Company	Code	Phone
Fire-End & Croker Corp	G	513 870-0517
West Chester (G-19852)		
Highcom Global Security Inc	F	727 592-9400
Columbus (G-6997)		

FIRE DETECTION SYSTEMS

Company	Code	Phone
Hyq Technologies LLC	G	513 225-6911
Oxford (G-15694)		

FIRE EXTINGUISHER CHARGES

Company	Code	Phone
SC Fire Protection Ltd	G	330 468-3300
Macedonia (G-12324)		
Warren Fire Equipment Inc	E	330 824-3523
Warren (G-19459)		

FIRE EXTINGUISHER SVC

Company	Code	Phone
Antram Fire Equipment	G	330 525-7171
North Georgetown (G-15139)		
Fire Safety Services Inc	F	937 686-2000
Huntsville (G-11086)		
L-Mor Inc	F	216 541-2224
Cleveland (G-5551)		
Warren Fire Equipment Inc	G	937 866-8918
Miamisburg (G-13738)		

FIRE EXTINGUISHERS, WHOLESALE

Company	Code	Phone
A-Gas US Holdings Inc	F	419 867-8990
Bowling Green (G-1945)		
Fire Safety Services Inc	F	937 686-2000
Huntsville (G-11086)		

Employee Codes: A=Over 500 employees, B=251-500 C=101-250, D=51-100, E=20-50, F=10-19, G=3-9

FIRE EXTINGUISHERS: Portable

FIRE EXTINGUISHERS: Portable
Fire Safety Services Inc................F....... 937 686-2000
  Huntsville (G-11086)

FIRE OR BURGLARY RESISTIVE PRDTS
Alchemical Transmutation................C....... 216 313-8674
  Cleveland (G-4651)
B K Fabrication & Machine Shop........G....... 740 695-4164
  Saint Clairsville (G-16622)
Donald E Didion II................E....... 419 483-2226
  Bellevue (G-1535)
Fabricating Solutions Inc................F....... 330 486-0998
  Twinsburg (G-18773)
M A K Fabricating Inc................F....... 330 747-0040
  Youngstown (G-20962)
Mast Farm Service Ltd................E....... 330 893-2972
  Walnut Creek (G-19307)
MTS Enterprises LLC................F....... 937 324-7510
  Springfield (G-17453)
Quest Technologies Inc................F....... 937 743-1200
  Franklin (G-9913)
Smith Security Safes Inc................G....... 419 823-1423
  Bowling Green (G-1999)

FIRE PROTECTION EQPT
A-1 Sprinkler Company Inc................D....... 937 859-6198
  Miamisburg (G-13636)
Action Coupling & Eqp Inc................D....... 330 279-4242
  Holmesville (G-10972)
Akron Brass Company................E....... 309 444-4440
  Wooster (G-20556)
Akron Brass Company................B....... 330 264-5678
  Wooster (G-20557)
All-American Fire Eqp Inc................F....... 800 972-6035
  Wshngtn CT Hs (G-20718)
American Rescue Technology................F....... 937 293-6240
  Dayton (G-8027)
E S H Inc................G....... 330 345-1010
  Wooster (G-20587)
Elite Fire Services LLC................F....... 614 586-4255
  Columbus (G-6891)
Globe Pipe Hanger Products Inc................E....... 216 362-6300
  Cleveland (G-5326)
Red Head Brass Inc................G....... 330 567-2903
  Shreve (G-17007)
Rhba Acquisitions LLC................D....... 330 567-2903
  Shreve (G-17008)
Warren Fire Equipment Inc................G....... 937 866-8918
  Miamisburg (G-13738)
Zephyr Industries Inc................G....... 419 281-4485
  Ashland (G-756)

FIREARMS & AMMUNITION, EXC SPORTING, WHOLESALE
Fedex Office & Print Svcs Inc................F....... 937 335-3816
  Troy (G-18657)
Hanger Prsthetcs & Ortho Inc................G....... 330 374-9544
  Akron (G-198)

FIREARMS: Small, 30mm or Less
Acme Machine Automatics Inc................D....... 419 453-0010
  Ottoville (G-15679)
American Apex Corporation................F....... 614 652-2000
  Plain City (G-16171)
Ares Inc................D....... 419 635-2175
  Port Clinton (G-16242)
Beech Armament LLC................G....... 330 962-4694
  Cuyahoga Falls (G-7845)
Kaeper Machine Inc................E....... 440 974-1010
  Mentor (G-13488)
Nicana Consulting Inc................G....... 419 615-9703
  Kalida (G-11279)

FIREFIGHTING APPARATUS
United Fire Apparatus Corp................G....... 419 645-4083
  Cridersville (G-7813)

FIREPLACE & CHIMNEY MATERIAL: Concrete
Ohio Flame................G....... 330 953-0863
  Youngstown (G-20981)

FIREPLACE EQPT & ACCESS
Doan Machinery & Eqp Co Inc................G....... 216 932-6243
  University Heights (G-18941)

Strutt Products LLC................G....... 330 889-2727
  Bristolville (G-2084)
Thermo-Rite Mfg Company................E....... 330 633-8680
  Akron (G-403)

FIREWORKS
Alan BJ Company................G....... 330 372-1201
  Warren (G-19365)
Diamond Sparkler Mfg Co................G....... 330 746-1064
  Youngstown (G-20890)
Eagle Fireworks Co................G....... 740 373-3357
  Marietta (G-12622)
Midwest Fireworks Mfg Co II................G....... 330 584-7000
  Deerfield (G-8610)
Phantom Fireworks Inc................G....... 419 237-2185
  Fayette (G-9635)
Prestige Fireworks LLC................F....... 513 492-7726
  Mason (G-12925)
Rozzi Company Inc................E....... 513 683-0620
  Loveland (G-12228)
Sam Abdallah................E....... 330 532-3900
  Hammondsville (G-10623)

FIREWORKS SHOPS
Eagle Fireworks Co................G....... 740 373-3357
  Marietta (G-12622)
Phantom Fireworks Inc................G....... 419 237-2185
  Fayette (G-9635)

FISH & SEAFOOD PROCESSORS: Canned Or Cured
Strasburg Provision Inc................E....... 330 878-1059
  Strasburg (G-17653)

FISH & SEAFOOD WHOLESALERS
Jroll LLC................F....... 330 661-0600
  Medina (G-13283)

FISH FOOD
Jroll LLC................F....... 330 661-0600
  Medina (G-13283)
Ocean Providence Columbus LLC................G....... 614 272-5973
  Columbus (G-7238)

FISH, PACKAGED FROZEN: Wholesalers
King Kold Inc................E....... 937 836-2731
  Englewood (G-9366)

FISHING EQPT: Lures
AC Shiners Inc................G....... 513 738-1573
  Okeana (G-15515)
Drowned Lure................G....... 330 548-5873
  Tallmadge (G-17982)
Lure Inc................E....... 440 951-8862
  Willoughby (G-20363)
N Bass Bait Co................G....... 419 647-4501
  Spencerville (G-17310)
Ouchless Lures Inc................G....... 330 653-3867
  Hudson (G-11066)
Reef Runner Tackle Co Inc................G....... 419 798-9125
  Marblehead (G-12587)

FITTINGS & ASSEMBLIES: Hose & Tube, Hydraulic Or Pneumatic
Ace Manufacturing Company................E....... 513 541-2490
  West Chester (G-19825)
Aeroquip-Vickers Inc................G....... 216 523-5000
  Cleveland (G-4633)
Air-Way Manufacturing Company................C....... 419 298-2366
  Edgerton (G-9167)
Eaton Aeroquip LLC................C....... 216 523-5000
  Cleveland (G-5143)
Eaton Hydraulics LLC................E....... 419 232-7777
  Van Wert (G-19088)
Eaton-Aeroquip Llc................D....... 419 238-1190
  Van Wert (G-19089)
Industrial Connections Inc................G....... 330 274-2155
  Mantua (G-12549)
Integrated Aircraft Systems................G....... 330 686-2982
  Stow (G-17596)
Kaman Fluid Power LLC................G....... 330 315-3100
  Akron (G-230)
Malone Specialty Inc................F....... 440 255-4200
  Mentor (G-13510)

Maverick Industries Inc................F....... 440 838-5335
  Brecksville (G-2049)
Mid-State Sales Inc................G....... 330 744-2158
  Youngstown (G-20971)
Netherland Rubber Company................F....... 513 733-0883
  Cincinnati (G-4068)
Ohio Hydraulics Inc................E....... 513 771-2590
  Cincinnati (G-4103)
Parker-Hannifin Corporation................E....... 440 943-5700
  Wickliffe (G-20225)
Parker-Hannifin Corporation................C....... 937 962-5566
  Lewisburg (G-11797)
State Metal Hose Inc................G....... 614 527-4700
  Hilliard (G-10865)
Summers Acquisition Corp................G....... 740 373-0303
  Marietta (G-12678)
Tylok International Inc................D....... 216 261-7310
  Cleveland (G-6225)

FITTINGS: Pipe
Adaptall America Inc................F....... 330 425-4114
  Twinsburg (G-18727)
Amaltech Inc................G....... 440 248-7500
  Solon (G-17105)
Drainage Pipe & Fitting................G....... 419 538-6337
  Ottawa (G-15651)
General Plug and Mfg Co................C....... 440 926-2411
  Grafton (G-10301)
Greater Cleve Pipe Ftting Fund................F....... 216 524-8334
  Cleveland (G-5353)
Parker-Hannifin Corporation................B....... 937 456-5571
  Eaton (G-9163)
Parker-Hannifin Corporation................C....... 614 279-7070
  Columbus (G-7294)
PHD Manufacturing Inc................C....... 330 482-9256
  Columbiana (G-6476)
Richards Industries Inc................C....... 513 533-5600
  Cincinnati (G-4268)
SSP Fittings Corp................C....... 330 425-4250
  Twinsburg (G-18858)
Steven L Lones................G....... 740 452-8851
  Zanesville (G-21183)
Swagelok Company................A....... 440 248-4600
  Solon (G-17240)
Swagelok Company................D....... 440 349-5652
  Solon (G-17241)
Swagelok Company................E....... 440 473-1050
  Cleveland (G-6134)
Swagelok Company................E....... 440 349-5836
  Solon (G-17243)
US Fittings Inc................F....... 234 212-9420
  Twinsburg (G-18871)

FITTINGS: Pipe, Fabricated
Cleveland Coppersmithing Works................G....... 330 607-3998
  Richfield (G-16465)
Phoenix Forge Group LLC................C....... 800 848-6125
  West Jefferson (G-19926)
Pipe Line Development Company................D....... 440 871-5700
  Westlake (G-20144)

FIXTURES & EQPT: Kitchen, Metal, Exc Cast Aluminum
Amtekco Industries LLC................D....... 614 228-6590
  Columbus (G-6596)
Washington Products Inc................F....... 330 837-5101
  Massillon (G-13057)

FIXTURES & EQPT: Kitchen, Porcelain Enameled
Oneida Group Inc................C....... 740 687-2500
  Lancaster (G-11595)
Schoen Industries Inc................G....... 330 533-6659
  Canfield (G-2544)

FIXTURES: Cut Stone
Rainbow Cultured Marble................F....... 330 225-3400
  Brunswick (G-2232)

FLAGS: Fabric
Annin & Co................D....... 740 622-4447
  Coshocton (G-7718)
Flag Lady Inc................G....... 614 263-1776
  Columbus (G-6927)

FLAGSTONES
Brocks Chimney .... G 740 819-2489
  Nashport *(G-14565)*

FLAKES: Metal
Ohio Valley Manufacturing Inc .... D 419 522-5818
  Mansfield *(G-12497)*
Premar Manufacturing Ltd .... G 440 250-0373
  Westlake *(G-20145)*
Transmet Corporation .... G 614 276-5522
  Columbus *(G-7539)*

FLARES
Lfg Specialties LLC .... E 419 424-4999
  Findlay *(G-9715)*

FLAT GLASS: Building
Therm-All Inc .... E 440 779-9494
  North Olmsted *(G-15201)*

FLAT GLASS: Construction
Imaging Sciences LLC .... G 440 975-9640
  Willoughby *(G-20342)*
Kaaa/Hamilton Enterprises Inc .... E 513 874-5874
  Fairfield *(G-9516)*
Pilkington North America Inc .... C 419 247-3731
  Urbancrest *(G-19022)*
Pilkington North America Inc .... B 419 247-3731
  Toledo *(G-18470)*
S R Door Inc .... C 740 927-3558
  Hebron *(G-10761)*

FLAT GLASS: Float
Pilkington North America Inc .... B 419 247-3211
  Rossford *(G-16589)*

FLAT GLASS: Picture
Knight Industries Corp .... E 419 478-8550
  Toledo *(G-18369)*

FLAT GLASS: Plate, Polished & Rough
Custom GL Sltions Millbury LLC .... C 419 855-7706
  Millbury *(G-14048)*

FLAT GLASS: Tempered
Cardinal CT Company .... E 740 892-2324
  Utica *(G-19024)*
Cardinal Glass Industries Inc .... E 740 892-2324
  Utica *(G-19025)*
Glasstech Inc .... E 419 661-9500
  Perrysburg *(G-15959)*
Machined Glass Specialist Inc .... F 937 743-6166
  Springboro *(G-17336)*

FLAT GLASS: Window, Clear & Colored
Sonalysts Inc .... E 937 429-9711
  Beavercreek *(G-1342)*

FLAVORS OR FLAVORING MATERIALS: Synthetic
Frutarom USA Holding Inc .... G 201 861-9500
  West Chester *(G-19855)*
Givaudan .... F 513 482-2536
  Cincinnati *(G-3754)*
Givaudan Flavors Corporation .... B 513 948-4933
  Cincinnati *(G-3755)*
Givaudan Flvors Fragrances Inc .... G 513 948-8000
  Cincinnati *(G-3757)*
Givaudan Fragrances Corp .... B 513 948-3428
  Cincinnati *(G-3759)*
Kerry Flavor Systems Us LLC .... E 513 539-7373
  Monroe *(G-14270)*

FLIGHT RECORDERS
Electrodynamics Inc .... C 847 259-0740
  Cincinnati *(G-3247)*

FLOATING DRY DOCKS
Pinney Dock & Transport LLC .... E 440 964-7186
  Ashtabula *(G-798)*

FLOCKING SVC: Fabric
Ohio Flock-Cote Company Inc .... E 440 914-1122
  Solon *(G-17210)*

FLOOR COVERING STORES
Armstrong World Industries Inc .... D 614 771-9307
  Hilliard *(G-10806)*
Davies Since 1900 .... G 419 756-4212
  Mansfield *(G-12432)*
Witt-Gor Inc .... G 419 659-2151
  Columbus Grove *(G-7639)*

FLOOR COVERING STORES: Carpets
Dpi Inc .... G 419 273-1400
  Forest *(G-9786)*
Stanley Steemer Intl Inc .... C 614 764-2007
  Dublin *(G-8994)*
Wccv Floor Coverings LLC .... E 330 688-0114
  Peninsula *(G-15901)*

FLOOR COVERING STORES: Rugs
Shaheen Oriental Rug Co Inc .... F 330 493-9000
  Canton *(G-2813)*

FLOOR COVERING: Plastic
Armaly LLC .... E 740 852-3621
  London *(G-12049)*
Next Generation Films Inc .... C 419 884-8150
  Lexington *(G-11805)*
Udecx LLC .... G 877 698-3329
  Tipp City *(G-18141)*

FLOOR COVERINGS WHOLESALERS
Pfpc Enterprises Inc .... B 513 941-6200
  Cincinnati *(G-4155)*

FLOOR COVERINGS: Asphalted-Felt Base, Linoleum Or Carpet
Prints & Paints Flr Cvg Co Inc .... E 419 462-5663
  Galion *(G-10151)*

FLOOR COVERINGS: Rubber
Champion Manufacturing Inc .... G 419 253-7930
  Marengo *(G-12588)*
Dandy Products Inc .... F 513 625-3000
  Goshen *(G-10286)*
Mameco International Inc .... P 216 752-4400
  Cleveland *(G-5611)*

FLOOR COVERINGS: Tile, Support Plastic
Flowcrete North America Inc .... E 936 539-6700
  Cleveland *(G-5253)*

FLOOR COVERINGS: Twisted Paper, Grass, Reed, Coir, Etc
B and L Sales Inc .... G 330 279-2007
  Millersburg *(G-14061)*

FLOORING & SIDING: Metal
Americas Best Siding Co .... G 419 589-5900
  Mansfield *(G-12406)*
Associated Materials LLC .... G 937 236-5679
  Dayton *(G-8040)*

FLOORING: Hard Surface
Armstrong World Industries Inc .... D 614 771-9307
  Hilliard *(G-10806)*
Schlabach Woodworks Ltd .... E 330 674-7488
  Millersburg *(G-14128)*

FLOORING: Hardwood
Hardwood Flrg & Paneling Inc .... D 440 834-1710
  Middlefield *(G-13803)*
Kelco Hardwood Floors Inc .... G 440 354-0974
  Painesville *(G-15753)*
Marsh Valley Forest Pdts Ltd .... G 440 632-1889
  Middlefield *(G-13816)*
Prestige Enterprise Intl Inc .... D 513 469-6044
  Blue Ash *(G-1835)*
Property Assist Inc .... G 419 480-1700
  Toledo *(G-18487)*

FLUID POWER PUMPS & MOTORS
Robbins Inc .... E 513 871-8988
  Cincinnati *(G-4276)*
Silk Road Sourcing LLC .... G 814 571-5533
  Amherst *(G-574)*

FLOORING: Rubber
Roppe Corporation .... B 419 435-8546
  Fostoria *(G-9855)*
Tarkett Inc .... G 440 708-9366
  Chagrin Falls *(G-3080)*
Tarkett Inc .... D 800 899-8916
  Solon *(G-17246)*

FLOORING: Tile
PCC Ceramic Group 1 .... G 440 516-3672
  Wickliffe *(G-20226)*
Summitville Tiles Inc .... C 330 868-6771
  Minerva *(G-14202)*

FLORIST: Flowers, Fresh
Cleveland Plant and Flower Co .... E 614 478-9900
  Columbus *(G-6773)*
Huston Gifts Dolls and Flowers .... G 740 775-9141
  Chillicothe *(G-3193)*

FLORISTS
Kroger Co .... D 513 683-4001
  Maineville *(G-12372)*
Kroger Co .... D 740 374-2523
  Marietta *(G-12638)*
Kroger Co .... C 937 277-0950
  Dayton *(G-8302)*

FLOWER POTS Plastic
Janorpot LLC .... E 330 564-0232
  Mogadore *(G-14241)*

FLOWERS, FRESH, WHOLESALE
Cleveland Plant and Flower Co .... E 614 478-9900
  Columbus *(G-6773)*
Huston Gifts Dolls and Flowers .... G 740 775-9141
  Chillicothe *(G-3193)*

FLUID METERS & COUNTING DEVICES
Aqua Technology Group LLC .... G 513 298-1183
  West Chester *(G-19648)*
Automatic Timing & Controls .... G 614 888-8855
  New Albany *(G-14606)*
Exact Equipment Corporation .... F 215 295-2000
  Columbus *(G-6491)*
Flow Line Options Corp .... G 330 331-7331
  Wadsworth *(G-19242)*
K-Hill Signal Co Inc .... G 740 922-0421
  Uhrichsville *(G-18890)*
Triplett Bluffton Corporation .... G 419 358-8750
  Bluffton *(G-1896)*

FLUID POWER PUMPS & MOTORS
Aerocontrolex Group Inc .... D 440 352-6182
  Painesville *(G-15706)*
Ban-Fam Industries Inc .... G 216 265-9588
  Cleveland *(G-4788)*
Bergstrom Company Ltd Partnr .... E 440 232-2282
  Cleveland *(G-4805)*
Eaton Leasing Corporation .... G 216 382-2292
  Beachwood *(G-1235)*
Eaton-Aeroquip Llc .... D 419 891-7775
  Maumee *(G-13109)*
Emerson Process Management .... E 419 529-4311
  Ontario *(G-15541)*
Force Control Industries Inc .... D 513 868-0900
  Fairfield *(G-9498)*
Furukawa Rock Drill USA Co Ltd .... E 330 673-5826
  Kent *(G-11325)*
Giant Industries Inc .... E 419 531-4600
  Toledo *(G-18305)*
Gorman-Rupp Company .... B 419 755-1011
  Mansfield *(G-12403)*
Gorman-Rupp Company .... E 419 755-1011
  Mansfield *(G-12450)*
H Y O Inc .... F 614 488-2861
  Columbus *(G-6974)*
Hite Parts Exchange Inc .... E 614 272-5115
  Columbus *(G-7003)*
Hy-Production Inc .... C 330 273-2400
  Valley City *(G-19040)*

FLUID POWER PUMPS & MOTORS

Hydraulic Parts Store Inc .... E 330 364-6667
  New Philadelphia (G-14774)
Hydraulic Products Inc .... G 440 946-4575
  Willoughby (G-20339)
Ingersoll-Rand Company .... E 419 633-6800
  Bryan (G-2291)
Midwest Tool & Engineering Co .... G 937 224-0756
  Dayton (G-8356)
Parker Hannifin Partner B LLC .... G 216 896-3000
  Cleveland (G-5845)
Parker Royalty Partnership .... D 216 896-3000
  Cleveland (G-5846)
Parker-Hannifin Corporation .... C 330 963-0601
  Macedonia (G-12313)
Parker-Hannifin Corporation .... C 937 962-5301
  Lewisburg (G-11796)
Parker-Hannifin Corporation .... C 513 847-1758
  West Chester (G-19757)
Parker-Hannifin Corporation .... B 440 366-5100
  Elyria (G-9308)
Parker-Hannifin Corporation .... G 330 261-1618
  Berlin Center (G-1650)
Parker-Hannifin Corporation .... C 440 205-8230
  Mentor (G-13543)
Parker-Hannifin Corporation .... F 330 743-6893
  Youngstown (G-20995)
Pfpc Enterprises Inc .... B 513 941-6200
  Cincinnati (G-4155)
Quad Fluid Dynamics Inc .... G 330 220-3005
  Brunswick (G-2231)
Radocy Inc .... F 419 666-4400
  Rossford (G-16591)
Robeck Fluid Power Co .... D 330 562-1140
  Aurora (G-903)
Semtorq Inc .... F 330 487-0600
  Twinsburg (G-18856)
Starkey Machinery Inc .... E 419 468-2560
  Galion (G-10157)
Sunset Industries Inc .... E 216 731-8131
  Euclid (G-9444)
Swagelok Company .... E 440 349-5836
  Solon (G-17243)
Toth Industries Inc .... D 419 729-4669
  Toledo (G-18578)

FLUID POWER VALVES & HOSE FITTINGS

Alkon Corporation .... D 419 355-9111
  Fremont (G-9990)
Canfield Industries Inc .... G 800 554-5071
  Youngstown (G-20864)
Commercial Honing Ohio Inc .... D 330 343-8896
  Dover (G-8812)
Dixon Valve & Coupling Co LLC .... F 330 425-3000
  Twinsburg (G-18765)
Eaton-Aeroquip Llc .... D 419 891-7775
  Maumee (G-13109)
Encore Distributing Inc .... G 513 948-1242
  Cincinnati (G-3638)
Freudenberg-Nok General Partnr .... C 419 427-5221
  Findlay (G-9689)
Hydraulic Parts Store Inc .... E 330 364-6667
  New Philadelphia (G-14774)
Kirtland Capital Partners LP .... E 216 593-0100
  Beachwood (G-1244)
Parker-Hannifin Corporation .... B 440 943-5700
  Wickliffe (G-20224)
Parker-Hannifin Corporation .... B 937 456-5571
  Eaton (G-9163)
SSP Fittings Corp .... C 330 425-4250
  Twinsburg (G-18858)
Superior Holding LLC .... E 216 651-9400
  Cleveland (G-6121)
Superior Products LLC .... D 216 651-9400
  Cleveland (G-6126)
Superior Products Llc .... D 216 651-9400
  Cleveland (G-6125)
Swagelok .... G 440 349-5657
  Solon (G-17239)
Swagelok Company .... E 440 349-5836
  Solon (G-17243)
T D Group Holdings LLC .... G 216 706-2939
  Cleveland (G-6144)
Thogus Products Company .... D 440 933-8850
  Avon Lake (G-1011)
Transdigm Inc .... F 216 291-6025
  Cleveland (G-6195)
Transdigm Inc .... G 216 706-2939
  Cleveland (G-6196)
Winzeler Stamping Co .... D 419 485-3147
  Montpelier (G-14322)

Zaytran Corporation .... E 440 324-2814
  Elyria (G-9348)

FLUORSPAR MINING

Glf International Inc .... F 216 621-6901
  Cleveland (G-5324)

FLUSH TANKS: Vitreous China

Dittmar Sales and Service .... G 740 653-7933
  Lancaster (G-11567)

FLUXES

American Metal Chemical Corp .... G 440 244-1800
  Lorain (G-12078)
Bluefoot Industrial LLC .... E 740 314-5299
  Steubenville (G-17528)
Gasflux Company .... G 440 365-1941
  Elyria (G-9262)
Morgan Advanced Ceramics Inc .... C 440 232-8604
  Bedford (G-1428)
Pemro Corporation .... F 800 440-5441
  Cleveland (G-5863)
SRC Worldwide Inc .... F 216 941-6115
  Cleveland (G-6088)
Superior Flux & Mfg Co .... F 440 349-3000
  Cleveland (G-6120)
Worthington Industries Inc .... E 937 556-6111
  Worthington (G-20711)

FOAM RUBBER

ISO Technologies Inc .... E 740 344-9554
  Hebron (G-10749)
Ohio Foam Corporation .... G 614 252-4877
  Columbus (G-7248)
Ohio Foam Corporation .... E 330 799-4553
  Youngstown (G-20982)
Ohio Foam Corporation .... F 419 492-2151
  New Washington (G-14831)
Precision Fab Products Inc .... G 937 526-5681
  Versailles (G-19189)

FOAMS & RUBBER, WHOLESALE

Global Manufacturing Solutions .... F 937 236-8315
  Dayton (G-8225)
Johnson Bros Rubber Co Inc .... D 419 853-4122
  West Salem (G-19955)
Johnson Bros Rubber Co Inc .... E 419 752-4814
  Greenwich (G-10404)
Tahoma Enterprises Inc .... D 330 745-9016
  Barberton (G-1108)
Tahoma Rubber & Plastics Inc .... D 330 745-9016
  Barberton (G-1109)

FOIL & LEAF: Metal

A J Oster Foils LLC .... D 330 823-1700
  Alliance (G-447)
CCL Label Inc .... C 216 676-2703
  Cleveland (G-4894)
CCL Label Inc .... E 440 878-7000
  Brunswick (G-2194)

FOLDERS: Manila

R D Thompson Paper Pdts Co Inc ...... E 419 994-3614
  Loudonville (G-12147)

FOOD PRDTS, BREAKFAST: Cereal, Granola & Muesli

Olde Man Granola LLC .... F 419 819-9576
  Findlay (G-9735)

FOOD PRDTS, BREAKFAST: Cereal, Oatmeal

Niese Farms .... G 419 347-1204
  Crestline (G-7797)

FOOD PRDTS, BREAKFAST: Cereal, Wheat Flakes

General Mills Inc .... F 419 269-3100
  Toledo (G-18303)

FOOD PRDTS, CANNED OR FRESH PACK: Fruit Juices

Fremont Company .... E 419 363-2924
  Rockford (G-16539)

FOOD PRDTS, CANNED OR FRESH PACK: Vegetable Juices

Garden of Flavor LLC .... G 216 702-7991
  Cleveland (G-5290)

FOOD PRDTS, CANNED, NEC

Conagra Brands Inc .... B 419 445-8015
  Archbold (G-642)

FOOD PRDTS, CANNED: Baby Food

Wornick Company .... B 800 860-4555
  Blue Ash (G-1876)

FOOD PRDTS, CANNED: Barbecue Sauce

Dominion Liquid Tech LLC .... E 513 272-2824
  Cincinnati (G-3600)
Guys Barbeque Inc .... G 330 872-7256
  Newton Falls (G-14987)
Uncle Jesters Fine Foods LLC .... G 937 550-1025
  Miamisburg (G-13729)

FOOD PRDTS, CANNED: Beans, Without Meat

Beckman & Gast Company .... F 419 678-4195
  Saint Henry (G-16659)
Randall Foods Inc .... E 513 793-6525
  Cincinnati (G-4247)

FOOD PRDTS, CANNED: Catsup

Portion Pac Inc .... B 513 398-0400
  Mason (G-12922)

FOOD PRDTS, CANNED: Chili

D & A Rofael Enterprises Inc .... G 513 751-4929
  Cincinnati (G-3567)
Gold Star Chili Inc .... E 513 231-4541
  Cincinnati (G-3767)
Whiteys Food Systems Inc .... G 330 659-4070
  Richfield (G-16495)

FOOD PRDTS, CANNED: Chili Sauce, Tomato

Traditions Sauces LLC .... G 419 704-4506
  Toledo (G-18581)

FOOD PRDTS, CANNED: Ethnic

Magic Wok Inc .... G 419 531-1818
  Toledo (G-18394)
Troyer Cheese Inc .... E 330 893-2479
  Millersburg (G-14139)

FOOD PRDTS, CANNED: Fruit Juices, Fresh

Country Pure Foods Inc .... C 330 848-6875
  Akron (G-123)
Great Western Juice Company .... F 216 475-5770
  Cleveland (G-5352)
Meiers Wine Cellars Inc .... E 513 891-2900
  Cincinnati (G-4003)
Natural Country Farms Inc .... G 330 753-2293
  Akron (G-294)
Ohio Pure Foods Inc .... D 330 753-2293
  Akron (G-309)

FOOD PRDTS, CANNED: Fruit Pie Mixes & Fillings

Cincinnati Preserving Company .... F 513 771-2000
  Cincinnati (G-3504)

FOOD PRDTS, CANNED: Fruits

Clovervale Farms Inc .... D 440 960-0146
  Amherst (G-558)
Landec Corporation .... C 419 931-1095
  Bowling Green (G-1980)

PRODUCT SECTION

FOOD PRDTS, FROZEN: Fruits, Juices & Vegetables

FOOD PRDTS, CANNED: Fruits

Campbell Soup Company	D	419 592-1010	
Napoleon *(G-14534)*			
Fry Foods Inc	E	419 448-0831	
Tiffin *(G-18061)*			
Gofast LLC	G	419 562-8027	
Bucyrus *(G-2332)*			
J M Smucker Company	F	330 684-1500	
Orrville *(G-15597)*			
J M Smucker Company	G	330 497-0073	
Canton *(G-2714)*			
JES Foods/Celina Inc	E	419 586-7446	
Celina *(G-2971)*			
Kraft Heinz Foods Company	E	419 332-7357	
Fremont *(G-10032)*			
Louis Trauth Dairy LLC	B	859 431-7553	
West Chester *(G-19873)*			
Milos Whole World Gourmet LLC	G	740 589-6456	
Athens *(G-840)*			
Ocean Spray Cranberries Inc	G	513 455-5770	
Loveland *(G-12219)*			
Pillsbury Company LLC	F	740 286-2170	
Wellston *(G-19605)*			
Pillsbury Company LLC	D	419 845-3751	
Caledonia *(G-2420)*			
Robert Rothschild Farm LLC	F	937 653-7397	
Cincinnati *(G-4279)*			
Smucker International Inc	G	330 682-3000	
Orrville *(G-15621)*			
The Fremont Kraut Company	D	419 332-6481	
Fremont *(G-10055)*			
Two Grandmothers Gourmet Kit	G	614 746-0888	
Reynoldsburg *(G-16459)*			
Welch Foods Inc A Cooperative	G	513 632-5610	
Cincinnati *(G-4496)*			

FOOD PRDTS, CANNED: Italian

Disalvos Deli & Italian Store ....G....... 937 298-5053
 Dayton *(G-8163)*
Gia Russa ....F....... 330 743-6050
 Youngstown *(G-20921)*

FOOD PRDTS, CANNED: Jams, Including Imitation

Yoders Cider Barn..............................F....... 740 668-4961
 Gambier *(G-10186)*

FOOD PRDTS, CANNED: Jams, Jellies & Preserves

Amys Beauty Jams LLC ....G....... 330 869-8317
 Akron *(G-66)*
Coopers Mill Inc ....F....... 419 562-4215
 Bucyrus *(G-2322)*
J M Smucker Company ....A....... 330 682-3000
 Orrville *(G-15596)*
Nu Pet Company ....C....... 330 682-3000
 Orrville *(G-15606)*
OSister Jams & Jellies ....G....... 419 968-2505
 Delphos *(G-8753)*
Smucker Manufacturing Inc.................G....... 888 550-9555
 Orrville *(G-15622)*

FOOD PRDTS, CANNED: Jellies, Edible, Including Imitation

Inter American Products Inc ....E....... 800 645-2233
 Cincinnati *(G-3853)*

FOOD PRDTS, CANNED: Mexican, NEC

Elizabeths Closet ....G....... 513 646-5025
 Maineville *(G-12367)*
Kick Salsa LLC ....G....... 614 330-2499
 Columbus *(G-7094)*
Lifo Enterprises Inc ....G....... 513 225-8801
 Loveland *(G-12210)*
San Marcos Supermarket LLC.............G....... 419 469-8963
 Toledo *(G-18511)*

FOOD PRDTS, CANNED: Pizza Sauce

Worthmore Food Products Co..............F....... 513 559-1473
 Cincinnati *(G-4519)*

FOOD PRDTS, CANNED: Puddings, Exc Meat

Clovervale Farms Inc..........................D....... 440 960-0146
 Amherst *(G-558)*

FOOD PRDTS, CANNED: Ravioli

Food Designs Inc ....F....... 216 651-9221
 Cleveland *(G-5259)*

FOOD PRDTS, CANNED: Soups

More Than Gourmet Inc......................E....... 330 762-6652
 Akron *(G-286)*

FOOD PRDTS, CANNED: Soups, Exc Seafood

Worthmore Food Products Co..............F....... 513 559-1473
 Cincinnati *(G-4519)*

FOOD PRDTS, CANNED: Spaghetti

Campbell Soup Company ....D....... 419 592-1010
 Napoleon *(G-14534)*

FOOD PRDTS, CANNED: Spaghetti & Other Pasta Sauce

Bellisio Foods Inc ....C....... 740 286-5505
 Jackson *(G-11182)*
RC Industries Inc ....E....... 330 879-5486
 Navarre *(G-14586)*

FOOD PRDTS, CANNED: Tomato Sauce.

Kraft Heinz Company..........................A....... 330 837-8331
 Massillon *(G-13012)*

FOOD PRDTS, CANNED: Tomatoes

Beckman & Gast Company ....F....... 419 678-4195
 Saint Henry *(G-16659)*
Hirzel Canning Company ....E....... 419 287-3288
 Pemberville *(G-15885)*
Hirzel Canning Company ....D....... 419 693-0531
 Northwood *(G-15338)*
Hirzel Canning Company ....F....... 419 523-3225
 Ottawa *(G-15654)*
Tip Top Canning Co ....E....... 937 667-3713
 Tipp City *(G-18138)*

FOOD PRDTS, CANNED: Vegetables

Fremont Company ....C....... 419 334-8995
 Fremont *(G-10015)*
Fremont Company ....E....... 419 334-8995
 Fremont *(G-10016)*

FOOD PRDTS, CONFECTIONERY, WHOLESALE: Candy

Gorant Chocolatier LLC ....C....... 330 726-8821
 Boardman *(G-1899)*
International Multifoods Corp...............G....... 330 682-3000
 Orrville *(G-15595)*
Robert E McGrath Inc ....E....... 440 572-7747
 Strongsville *(G-17783)*

FOOD PRDTS, CONFECTIONERY, WHOLESALE: Nuts, Salted/Roasted

Jml Holdings Inc ....F....... 419 866-7500
 Holland *(G-10937)*
Nuts Are Good Inc ....F....... 586 619-2400
 Columbus *(G-7233)*
Ohio Hickory Harvest Brand Pro ....E....... 330 644-6266
 Coventry Township *(G-7775)*
Tarrier Foods Corp.............................E....... 614 876-8594
 Columbus *(G-7513)*

FOOD PRDTS, CONFECTIONERY, WHOLESALE: Potato Chips

Jones Potato Chip Co.........................E....... 419 529-9424
 Mansfield *(G-12464)*

FOOD PRDTS, CONFECTIONERY, WHOLESALE: Snack Foods

J & J Snack Foods Corp.....................G....... 440 248-2084
 Solon *(G-17173)*
Katies Snack Foods LLC ....G....... 614 440-0780
 Hilliard *(G-10836)*
Mike-Sells Potato Chip Co ....E....... 937 228-9400
 Dayton *(G-8357)*

Pepperidge Farm Incorporated............G....... 614 457-4800
 Columbus *(G-7309)*
Pepperidge Farm Incorporated............G....... 419 933-2611
 Willard *(G-20244)*
Shearers Foods LLC ....A....... 330 834-4030
 Massillon *(G-13047)*
Waffle House Inc ....G....... 937 746-6830
 Franklin *(G-9929)*
Waffle House Inc ....F....... 513 539-8372
 Monroe *(G-14281)*

FOOD PRDTS, CONFECTIONERY, WHOLESALE: Syrups, Fountain

Gehm & Sons Limited........................G....... 330 724-8423
 Akron *(G-185)*

FOOD PRDTS, DAIRY, WHOLESALE: Milk & Cream, Fluid

Louis Trauth Dairy LLC ....B....... 859 431-7553
 West Chester *(G-19873)*

FOOD PRDTS, FISH & SEAFOOD, WHOLESALE: Seafood

Acme Steak & Seafood Inc.................F....... 330 270-8000
 Youngstown *(G-20836)*

FOOD PRDTS, FROZEN: Breakfasts, Packaged

Richelieu Foods Inc............................F....... 740 335-4813
 Wshngtn CT Hs *(G-20741)*

FOOD PRDTS, FROZEN: Dinners, Packaged

Bellisio Foods Inc ....C....... 740 286-5505
 Jackson *(G-11182)*
Classic Recipe Chili Inc......................G....... 513 771-1441
 Cincinnati *(G-3525)*
Nestle Prepared Foods Company ....A....... 440 248-3600
 Solon *(G-17203)*
Stouffer Corporation...........................G....... 440 349-5757
 Solon *(G-17237)*

FOOD PRDTS, FROZEN: Ethnic Foods, NEC

Lopaus Point Inc ....G....... 614 302-7242
 Columbus *(G-7137)*
Sunrise Foods Inc..............................E....... 614 276-2880
 Columbus *(G-7500)*

FOOD PRDTS, FROZEN: Fruit Juice, Concentrates

Country Pure Foods Inc ....C....... 330 848-6875
 Akron *(G-123)*
Natural Country Farms Inc..................G....... 330 753-2293
 Akron *(G-294)*
Schwans Home Service Inc ....E....... 419 222-9977
 Lima *(G-11936)*

FOOD PRDTS, FROZEN: Fruit Juices

Simply Unique Snacks LLC ....G....... 513 223-7736
 Cincinnati *(G-4339)*

FOOD PRDTS, FROZEN: Fruits

National Fruit Vegetable Tech..............E....... 740 400-4055
 Columbus *(G-7210)*

FOOD PRDTS, FROZEN: Fruits & Vegetables

Heinz Foreign Investment Co ....F....... 330 837-8331
 Massillon *(G-12994)*
HJ Heinz Company LP ....A....... 330 837-8331
 Massillon *(G-12997)*

FOOD PRDTS, FROZEN: Fruits, Juices & Vegetables

Creek Smoothies LLC.........................G....... 937 429-1519
 Beavercreek *(G-1309)*
Cwm Smoothie LLC ....G....... 419 283-6387
 Toledo *(G-18248)*
Nestle Prepared Foods Company ....D....... 440 349-5757
 Solon *(G-17204)*
NRG Smoothies LLC..........................G....... 972 800-1002
 Vienna *(G-19206)*

Employee Codes: A=Over 500 employees, B=251-500 C=101-250, D=51-100, E=20-50, F=10-19, G=3-9

FOOD PRDTS, FROZEN: Fruits, Juices & Vegetables

Smoothie Creations Inc .... G 817 313-8212
  Strongsville *(G-17790)*
Smoothie-Licious .... G 513 742-2260
  Batavia *(G-1184)*
Tri-State Special Events Inc .... G 513 221-2962
  Cincinnati *(G-4435)*
Tropical Ohio Smoothie Inc .... E 937 673-6218
  Centerville *(G-3006)*

FOOD PRDTS, FROZEN: NEC

Athens Foods Inc .... C 216 676-8500
  Cleveland *(G-4758)*
Bellisio .... G 740 286-5505
  Jackson *(G-11181)*
Campbell Soup Company .... D 419 592-1010
  Napoleon *(G-14534)*
Chef 2 Chef Foods .... G 216 696-0080
  Cleveland *(G-4918)*
Chieffos Frozen Foods Inc .... G 330 652-1222
  Niles *(G-15002)*
Clovervale Farms Inc .... D 440 960-0146
  Amherst *(G-558)*
Frozen Specialties Inc .... C 419 445-9015
  Archbold *(G-647)*
FSI/Mfp Inc .... G 419 445-9015
  Archbold *(G-648)*
Kahiki Foods Inc .... C 614 322-3180
  Gahanna *(G-10087)*
King Kold Inc .... E 937 836-2731
  Englewood *(G-9366)*
Lancaster Colony Corporation .... E 614 224-7141
  Westerville *(G-20004)*
Nestle Prepared Foods Company .... D 440 349-5757
  Solon *(G-17204)*
Rsw Distributors LLC .... D 502 587-8877
  Blue Ash *(G-1841)*
Skyline Chili Inc .... C 513 874-1188
  Fairfield *(G-9565)*
Worthington Foods Inc .... D 740 453-5501
  Zanesville *(G-21189)*

FOOD PRDTS, FROZEN: Pizza

Frozen Specialties Inc .... E 419 445-9015
  Perrysburg *(G-15956)*
Hudson Village Pizza Inc .... G 330 968-4563
  Stow *(G-17595)*
Paleomd LLC 248 854-0031
  Bedford *(G-1435)*
Schwans Mama Rosass LLC .... C 937 498-4511
  Sidney *(G-17072)*

FOOD PRDTS, FROZEN: Potato Prdts

Old World Foods Inc .... G 216 341-5665
  Cleveland *(G-5810)*

FOOD PRDTS, FROZEN: Snack Items

Ascot Valley Foods LLC .... G 330 376-9411
  Cuyahoga Falls *(G-7840)*
Brilista Foods Company Inc .... G 614 299-4132
  Columbus *(G-6700)*
Fry Foods Inc .... E 419 448-0831
  Tiffin *(G-18061)*
Lake Erie Frozen Foods Mfg Co .... E 419 289-9204
  Ashland *(G-720)*

FOOD PRDTS, FROZEN: Vegetables, Exc Potato Prdts

Big Gus Onion Rings Inc .... E 216 883-9045
  Cleveland *(G-4812)*
Lake Erie Frozen Foods Mfg Co 419 289-9204
  Ashland *(G-720)*
Nestle Prepared Foods Company .... A 440 248-3600
  Solon *(G-17203)*

FOOD PRDTS, FRUITS & VEGETABLES, FRESH, WHOLESALE

Big Gus Onion Rings Inc .... E 216 883-9045
  Cleveland *(G-4812)*
C J Kraft Enterprises Inc .... E 740 653-9606
  Lancaster *(G-11551)*
Dno Inc .... D 614 231-3601
  Columbus *(G-6872)*
Dole Fresh Vegetables Inc .... C 937 525-4300
  Springfield *(G-17390)*

FOOD PRDTS, FRUITS & VEGETABLES, FRESH, WHOLESALE: Vegetable

Barkett Fruit Co Inc .... E 330 364-6645
  Dover *(G-8807)*

FOOD PRDTS, FRUITS & VEGETABLES, FRESH, WHOLESALE: Vegetable

Freshway Foods Inc .... C 937 498-4664
  Sidney *(G-17041)*

FOOD PRDTS, MEAT & MEAT PRDTS, WHOLESALE: Cured Or Smoked

Mama Mias Foods Inc 216 281-2188
  Cleveland *(G-5610)*
Troyer Cheese Inc .... E 330 893-2479
  Millersburg *(G-14139)*

FOOD PRDTS, MEAT & MEAT PRDTS, WHOLESALE: Fresh

Acme Steak & Seafood Inc .... F 330 270-8000
  Youngstown *(G-20836)*
Caven and Sons Meat Packing Co .... F 937 368-3841
  Conover *(G-7662)*
Fink Meat Company Inc .... G 937 390-2750
  Springfield *(G-17402)*
John Krusinski .... F 216 441-0100
  Cleveland *(G-5502)*
Kenosha Beef International Ltd .... C 614 771-1330
  Columbus *(G-7087)*
Links Country Meats .... G 419 683-2195
  Crestline *(G-7796)*
Lori Holding Co .... E 740 342-3230
  New Lexington *(G-14717)*
Marshallville Packing Co Inc .... E 330 855-2871
  Marshallville *(G-12753)*

FOOD PRDTS, WHOL: Canned Goods, Fruit, Veg, Seafood/Meats

Acme Steak & Seafood Inc .... F 330 270-8000
  Youngstown *(G-20836)*

FOOD PRDTS, WHOLESALE: Baking Splys

Marble Works .... G 216 496-7745
  Cleveland *(G-5615)*

FOOD PRDTS, WHOLESALE: Beverages, Exc Coffee & Tea

Ancient Infusions LLC .... G 419 659-5110
  Columbus Grove *(G-7630)*
G & J Pepsi-Cola Bottlers Inc .... D 740 593-3366
  Athens *(G-831)*
Louis Trauth Dairy LLC .... B 859 431-7553
  West Chester *(G-19873)*

FOOD PRDTS, WHOLESALE: Chocolate

Walnut Creek Chocolate Company .... E 330 893-2995
  Walnut Creek *(G-19308)*

FOOD PRDTS, WHOLESALE: Coffee, Green Or Roasted

Crooked River Coffee Co .... G 440 442-8330
  Cleveland *(G-5039)*
International Multifoods Corp .... G 330 682-3000
  Orrville *(G-15595)*
Iron Bean Co .... G 518 641-9917
  Toledo *(G-18353)*

FOOD PRDTS, WHOLESALE: Condiments

Kerry .... G 760 685-2548
  Byesville *(G-2389)*

FOOD PRDTS, WHOLESALE: Corn

Hanby Farms Inc .... E 740 763-3554
  Nashport *(G-14567)*
Pioneer Hi-Bred Intl Inc .... E 419 748-8051
  Grand Rapids *(G-10318)*

FOOD PRDTS, WHOLESALE: Dried or Canned Foods

James C Robinson .... G 513 969-7482
  Cincinnati *(G-3869)*
Tarrier Foods Corp .... E 614 876-8594
  Columbus *(G-7513)*

FOOD PRDTS, WHOLESALE: Flour

Cleveland Syrup Corp .... G 330 963-1900
  Twinsburg *(G-18755)*

FOOD PRDTS, WHOLESALE: Grain Elevators

Fort Recovery Equity Inc .... C 419 375-4119
  Fort Recovery *(G-9817)*
Harvest Land Co-Op Inc .... G 937 884-5526
  Verona *(G-19172)*
Mullet Enterprises Inc .... G 330 852-4681
  Sugarcreek *(G-17855)*
Mullet Enterprises Inc .... G 330 897-3911
  Bakersville *(G-1021)*
Pettisville Grain Co .... E 419 446-2547
  Pettisville *(G-16035)*
Sunrise Cooperative Inc .... E 419 628-4705
  Minster *(G-14225)*

FOOD PRDTS, WHOLESALE: Grains

Andersons Inc .... C 419 893-5050
  Maumee *(G-13072)*
Andersons Inc .... G 419 536-0460
  Toledo *(G-18184)*
Cooper Farms Inc .... F 419 375-4619
  Fort Recovery *(G-9815)*
Cooper Hatchery Inc .... C 419 594-3325
  Oakwood *(G-15469)*
Countyline Co-Op Inc .... F 419 287-3241
  Pemberville *(G-15883)*
Geauga Feed and Grain Supply .... G 440 564-5000
  Newbury *(G-14953)*
Hansen-Mueller Co .... E 419 729-5535
  Toledo *(G-18322)*
Legacy Farmers Cooperative .... F 419 423-2611
  Findlay *(G-9713)*
Mid-Wood Inc .... F 419 257-3331
  North Baltimore *(G-15046)*
Premier Feeds LLC .... G 937 584-2411
  Sabina *(G-16618)*

FOOD PRDTS, WHOLESALE: Health

Lifestyle Nutraceuticals Ltd .... F 513 376-7218
  Cincinnati *(G-3941)*
Muscle Feast LLC .... F 740 877-8808
  Nashport *(G-14568)*

FOOD PRDTS, WHOLESALE: Juices

Alacwin Nutrition Corporation .... G 614 961-6479
  Columbus *(G-6561)*

FOOD PRDTS, WHOLESALE: Salt, Edible

Morton Salt Inc .... C 330 925-3015
  Rittman *(G-16526)*

FOOD PRDTS, WHOLESALE: Specialty

Amerihua Intl Entps Inc .... G 740 549-0300
  Lewis Center *(G-11744)*
Good Earth Good Eating LLC .... G 513 256-5935
  Cincinnati *(G-3771)*
Troyer Cheese Inc .... E 330 893-2479
  Millersburg *(G-14139)*

FOOD PRDTS, WHOLESALE: Starch

G & J Pepsi-Cola Bottlers Inc .... E 740 774-2148
  Chillicothe *(G-3187)*

FOOD PRDTS, WHOLESALE: Syrups, Exc Fountain Use

Richards Maple Products Inc .... G 440 286-4160
  Chardon *(G-3134)*
Stumps Converting Inc .... F 419 492-2542
  New Washington *(G-14833)*

PRODUCT SECTION

FOOD PRDTS: Flour & Other Grain Mill Products

FOOD PRDTS, WHOLESALE: Water, Mineral Or Spring, Bottled

Distillata Company .... D 216 771-2900
Cleveland (G-5098)

FOOD PRDTS: Animal & marine fats & oils

Archer-Daniels-Midland Company .... E 419 435-6633
Fostoria (G-9833)
Cargill Incorporated .... D 937 498-4555
Sidney (G-17020)
Darling Ingredients Inc .... G 972 717-0300
Cincinnati (G-3576)
Darling Ingredients Inc .... G 216 351-3440
Cleveland (G-5065)
Darling International Inc .... F 216 651-9300
Cleveland (G-5066)
Fiske Brothers Refining Co .... D 419 691-2491
Toledo (G-18295)
Holmes By Products Co .... E 330 893-2322
Millersburg (G-14095)

FOOD PRDTS: Baking Powder, Soda, Yeast & Leavenings

Coalescence LLC .... E 614 861-3639
Columbus (G-6778)

FOOD PRDTS: Bread Crumbs, Exc Made In Bakeries

Pepperidge Farm Incorporated .... G 614 457-4800
Columbus (G-7309)
Pepperidge Farm Incorporated .... G 419 933-2611
Willard (G-20244)

FOOD PRDTS: Cake Fillings, Exc Fruit

Pfizer Inc .... C 937 746-3603
Franklin (G-9908)

FOOD PRDTS: Cereals

General Mills Inc .... D 513 771-8200
Cincinnati (G-3745)
General Mills Inc .... E 740 286-2170
Wellston (G-19601)
Kellogg Company .... B 614 879-9659
West Jefferson (G-19924)
Kellogg Company .... B 513 792-2700
Cincinnati (G-3903)
Kellogg Company .... A 614 855-3437
Delaware (G-8699)
Kellogg Company .... C 740 453-5501
Zanesville (G-21152)
Treehouse Private Brands Inc .... B 740 654-8880
Lancaster (G-11615)
Treehouse Private Brands Inc .... G 740 654-8880
Lancaster (G-11616)

FOOD PRDTS: Chicken, Processed, Cooked

Roots Poultry Inc .... F 419 332-0041
Fremont (G-10048)

FOOD PRDTS: Chicken, Processed, Fresh

Gerber Farm Division Inc .... G 800 362-7381
Kidron (G-11446)
Nutrifresh Eggs .... G 567 224-7676
Willard (G-20243)
Rcf Kitchens Indiana LLC .... C 765 478-6600
Beavercreek (G-1361)

FOOD PRDTS: Chicken, Processed, NEC

Advancepierre Foods Inc .... B 513 874-8741
West Chester (G-19826)

FOOD PRDTS: Chocolate Bars, Solid

Fannie May Confections Inc .... A 330 494-0833
North Canton (G-15082)

FOOD PRDTS: Cocoa, Powdered

Benjamin P Forbes Company .... F 440 838-4400
Broadview Heights (G-2088)

FOOD PRDTS: Coffee

Altraserv LLC .... G 614 889-2500
Plain City (G-16170)

Dunkin Donuts .... G 330 336-2500
Wadsworth (G-19236)
Essential Wonders Inc .... G 888 525-5282
Cuyahoga Falls (G-7863)
Generations Coffee Company LLC ...... G 440 546-0901
Brecksville (G-2038)
Good Beans Coffee Roasters LLC .... G 513 310-9516
Milford (G-14012)
Inter American Products Inc .... E 800 645-2233
Cincinnati (G-3853)
Iron Bean Inc .... G 518 641-9917
Toledo (G-18353)
Little Ghost Roasters .... G 614 325-2065
Columbus (G-7132)
Mc Concepts Llc .... G 330 933-6402
Canton (G-2748)
Raptis Coffee Inc .... G 330 399-7011
Warren (G-19436)
Rezas Roast LLC .... G 937 823-1193
Fairborn (G-9467)
Stonefruit Coffee Co .... G 330 509-2787
Canfield (G-2548)

FOOD PRDTS: Coffee Roasting, Exc Wholesale Grocers

Boston Stoker Inc .... G 937 890-6401
Vandalia (G-19118)
Crooked River Coffee Co .... G 440 442-8330
Cleveland (G-5039)
Euclid Coffee Co Inc .... G 216 481-3330
Cleveland (G-5195)
Folger Coffee Company .... F 800 937-9745
Orrville (G-15591)
Millstone Coffee Inc .... D 513 983-1100
Cincinnati (G-4029)
Pmd Enterprises Inc .... F 440 546-0901
Brecksville (G-2055)
Wallingford Coffee Mills Inc .... D 513 771-3131
Cincinnati (G-4489)

FOOD PRDTS: Corn Chips & Other Corn-Based Snacks

Basic Grain Products Inc .... E 614 408-3091
Coldwater (G-6401)
Wyandot Inc .... B 740 383-4031
Marion (G-12751)

FOOD PRDTS: Corn Oil Prdts

Marion Ethanol LLC .... E 740 383-4400
Marion (G-12717)

FOOD PRDTS: Dips, Exc Cheese & Sour Cream Based

Gomez Salsa LLC .... F 513 314-1978
Cincinnati (G-3769)
Lakeview Farms LLC .... C 419 695-9925
Delphos (G-8750)
Oasis Mediterranean Cuisine .... E 419 269-1459
Toledo (G-18432)
Sonoran Salsa Company LLC .... G 216 513-3596
Westlake (G-20159)

FOOD PRDTS: Dough, Pizza, Prepared

Crestar Crusts Inc .... B 740 335-4813
Wshngtn CT Hs (G-20722)
International Multifoods Corp .... G 330 682-3000
Orrville (G-15595)

FOOD PRDTS: Doughs, Frozen Or Refrig From Purchased Flour

Mid American Ventures Inc .... F 216 524-0974
Cleveland (G-5673)

FOOD PRDTS: Dressings, Salad, Raw & Cooked Exc Dry Mixes

Consumer Guild Foods Inc .... E 419 726-3406
Toledo (G-18240)
Lancaster Colony Corporation .... E 614 224-7141
Westerville (G-20004)
Lancaster Colony Corporation .... F 614 792-9774
Westerville (G-20005)
Lancaster Colony Corporation .... D 614 224-7141
Westerville (G-20006)

Mark Grzianis St Treats Ex Inc .... F 330 414-6266
Kent (G-11349)
Tmarzetti Company .... C 614 268-3722
Westerville (G-20028)
Tmarzetti Company .... C 614 846-2232
Westerville (G-20029)

FOOD PRDTS: Dried & Dehydrated Fruits, Vegetables & Soup Mix

Hirzel Canning Company .... D 419 693-0531
Northwood (G-15338)

FOOD PRDTS: Edible fats & oils

Cincinnati Biorefining Corp .... G 513 482-8800
Cincinnati (G-3485)
Cincinnati Renewable Fuels LLC .... D 513 482-8800
Cincinnati (G-3506)
Garden of Delight LLC .... G 513 300-7205
Cincinnati (G-3725)
Wileys Finest LLC .... C 740 622-1072
Coshocton (G-7759)

FOOD PRDTS: Eggs, Processed

Ballas Egg Products Corp .... D 614 453-0386
Zanesville (G-21102)
BE Products Inc .... D 740 453-0386
Zanesville (G-21105)
Fort Recovery Equity Inc .... C 419 375-4119
Fort Recovery (G-9817)
Fort Recovery Equity Exchange .... E 937 338-8901
Rossburg (G-16582)
Hemmelgarn & Sons Inc .... D 419 678-2351
Coldwater (G-6412)
Nature Pure LLC .... F 937 358-2364
West Mansfield (G-19945)
Ohio Fresh Eggs LLC .... C 740 893-7200
Croton (G-7822)

FOOD PRDTS: Eggs, Processed, Frozen

Cal-Maine Foods Inc .... E 937 968-4874
Union City (G-18901)

FOOD PRDTS: Emulsifiers

Feinkost Ingredient Co U S A .... G 330 948-3006
Lodi (G-12011)
Lanxess Solutions US Inc .... E 440 324-6060
Elyria (G-9284)
Staceys Kitchen Limited .... G 614 921-1290
Hilliard (G-10863)

FOOD PRDTS: Flour & Other Grain Mill Products

Archer-Daniels-Midland Company .... G 419 705-3292
Toledo (G-18189)
Archer-Daniels-Midland Company .... E 419 435-6633
Fostoria (G-9833)
Archer-Daniels-Midland Company .... F 740 702-6179
Chillicothe (G-3175)
Bunge North America Foundation .... G 419 483-5340
Bellevue (G-1533)
Cargill Incorporated .... E 937 236-1971
Dayton (G-8075)
Countyline Co-Op Inc .... F 419 287-3241
Pemberville (G-15283)
Dik Jaxon Products Co .... G 937 890-7350
Dayton (G-8162)
Farmers Commission Company .... E 419 294-2371
Upper Sandusky (G-18954)
Hansen-Mueller Co .... E 419 729-5535
Toledo (G-18322)
I Dream of Cakes .... G 937 533-6024
Eaton (G-9153)
Indie-Peasant Enterprises .... G 740 590-8240
Athens (G-835)
Legacy Farmers Cooperative .... F 419 423-2611
Findlay (G-9713)
Mennel Milling Company .... D 419 436-5130
Fostoria (G-9848)
Mondelez Global LLC .... D 419 691-5200
Toledo (G-18416)
Mullet Enterprises Inc .... G 330 852-4681
Sugarcreek (G-17855)
Mullet Enterprises Inc .... G 330 897-3911
Bakersville (G-1021)
Pettisville Grain Co .... E 419 446-2547
Pettisville (G-16035)

Employee Codes: A=Over 500 employees, B=251-500
C=101-250, D=51-100, E=20-50, F=10-19, G=3-9

FOOD PRDTS: Flour & Other Grain Mill Products

Pillsbury Company LLC ....F 740 286-2170
  Wellston (G-19605)
Pillsbury Company LLC ....D 419 845-3751
  Caledonia (G-2420)
Pioneer Hi-Bred Intl Inc ....E 419 748-8051
  Grand Rapids (G-10318)
Premier Feeds LLC ....G 937 584-2411
  Sabina (G-16618)
Sunrise Cooperative Inc ....F 419 628-4705
  Minster (G-14225)

FOOD PRDTS: Flour Mixes & Doughs

Abitec Corporation ....E 614 429-6464
  Columbus (G-6527)
Athens Foods Inc ....C 216 676-8500
  Cleveland (G-4758)
Hometown Food Company ....G 419 470-7914
  Toledo (G-18333)
Rich Products Corporation ....C 614 771-1117
  Hilliard (G-10858)

FOOD PRDTS: Flour, Blended From Purchased Flour

Fleetchem LLC ....F 513 539-1111
  Monroe (G-14262)

FOOD PRDTS: Fruit Juices

Griffin Cider Works LLC ....G 440 785-7418
  Westlake (G-20120)

FOOD PRDTS: Fruits & Vegetables, Pickled

Kaiser Pickles LLC ....E 513 621-2053
  Cincinnati (G-3896)
Trixies Pickles Inc ....E 817 658-6648
  Findlay (G-9771)

FOOD PRDTS: Fruits, Dried Or Dehydrated, Exc Freeze-Dried

Kanan Enterprises Inc ....C 440 248-8484
  Solon (G-17179)
Kanan Enterprises Inc ....F 440 349-0719
  Solon (G-17180)

FOOD PRDTS: Gelatin Dessert Preparations

Clovervale Farms Inc ....D 440 960-0146
  Amherst (G-558)

FOOD PRDTS: Granola & Energy Bars, Nonchocolate

Good Nutrition LLC ....F 216 534-6617
  Oakwood Village (G-15480)

FOOD PRDTS: Honey

Deer Creek Honey Farms Ltd ....G 740 852-0899
  London (G-12057)

FOOD PRDTS: Ice, Blocks

Donahues Hilltop Ice Company ....F 740 432-3348
  Cambridge (G-2435)
Luc Ice Inc ....G 419 734-2201
  Port Clinton (G-16251)

FOOD PRDTS: Ice, Cubes

Home City Ice Company ....E 513 851-4040
  Cincinnati (G-3823)
Zygo Inc ....G 513 281-0888
  Cincinnati (G-4535)

FOOD PRDTS: Macaroni, Noodles, Spaghetti, Pasta, Etc

Lariccias Italian Foods ....F 330 729-0222
  Youngstown (G-20957)
Twg Noodle Company LLC ....G 419 560-2033
  Marengo (G-12596)
YAR Corporation ....G 330 652-1222
  Niles (G-15041)

FOOD PRDTS: Mayonnaise & Dressings, Exc Tomato Based

Food Specialties Co ....G 513 761-1242
  Cincinnati (G-3701)

FOOD PRDTS: Mixes, Bread & Bread-Type Roll

Jaz Foods Inc ....G 800 456-7115
  Canton (G-2717)

FOOD PRDTS: Mixes, Bread & Roll From Purchased Flour

B O K Inc ....C 937 322-9588
  Springfield (G-17366)

FOOD PRDTS: Mixes, Cake, From Purchased Flour

J M Smucker Company ....E 440 323-5100
  Elyria (G-9280)
Procter & Gamble Mfg Co ....F 513 983-1100
  Cincinnati (G-4212)

FOOD PRDTS: Mixes, Doughnut From Purchased Flour

Bigmouth Donut Company LLC ....G 216 264-0250
  Cleveland (G-4813)

FOOD PRDTS: Mixes, Flour

1-2-3 Gluten Free Inc ....G 216 378-9233
  Chagrin Falls (G-3007)
Fowlers Milling Co Inc ....G 440 286-2024
  Chardon (G-3112)
General Mills Inc ....D 513 770-0558
  Mason (G-12876)

FOOD PRDTS: Mixes, Sauces, Dry

Whitmore Productions Inc ....F 216 752-3960
  Warrensville Heights (G-19474)

FOOD PRDTS: Mustard, Prepared

Woeber Mustard Mfg Co ....C 937 323-6281
  Springfield (G-17519)

FOOD PRDTS: Nuts & Seeds

Anthony-Thomas Candy Company .....C 614 274-8405
  Columbus (G-6606)
Back Development LLC ....G 937 671-7896
  Cleveland (G-4787)
Nuts Are Good Inc ....F 586 619-2400
  Columbus (G-7233)
Simply Unique Snacks LLC ....G 513 223-7736
  Cincinnati (G-4339)
Southside Wolfies ....G 419 422-5450
  Findlay (G-9760)
Thorfood LLC ....E 419 626-4375
  Sandusky (G-16854)

FOOD PRDTS: Oils & Fats, Animal

Wileys Finest LLC ....C 740 622-1072
  Coshocton (G-7759)

FOOD PRDTS: Olive Oil

A Twist On Olives LLC ....G 614 823-8800
  Westerville (G-20032)
III Olive LLC Spicy ....G 937 247-5969
  Miamisburg (G-13678)
Motts Oils & More ....G 330 601-1645
  Wooster (G-20629)
Olivamed LLC ....F 937 401-0821
  Franklin (G-9906)
Olive Branch ....G 614 563-3139
  London (G-12068)
Olive Smuckers Oil ....G 513 646-7103
  Cincinnati (G-4109)
Olive Tap ....G 330 721-6500
  Medina (G-13311)
Spicy Olive LLC ....F 513 847-4397
  West Chester (G-19797)
Spicy Olive LLC ....G 513 376-9061
  Cincinnati (G-4359)
Sunny Olive LLC ....G 513 996-4091
  Cincinnati (G-4396)

FOOD PRDTS: Oriental Noodles

Best Bite Grill LLC ....F 419 344-7462
  Versailles (G-19174)

FOOD PRDTS: Pasta, Rice/Potatoes, Uncooked, Pkgd

Bellissimo Distribution LLC ....F 216 431-3344
  Cleveland (G-4803)
Three Peaks Wellness LLC ....G 216 438-3334
  Cleveland (G-6173)

FOOD PRDTS: Pasta, Uncooked, Packaged With Other Ingredients

Food Designs Inc ....F 216 651-9221
  Cleveland (G-5259)
Rossi Pasta Factory Inc ....F 740 376-2065
  Marietta (G-12665)

FOOD PRDTS: Peanut Butter

J M Smucker Company ....D 513 482-8000
  Cincinnati (G-3865)
Krema Group Inc ....F 614 889-4824
  Plain City (G-16200)
Krema Products Inc ....G 614 889-4824
  Dublin (G-8939)
Procter & Gamble Mfg Co ....F 513 983-1100
  Cincinnati (G-4212)

FOOD PRDTS: Pickles, Vinegar

Kaiser Foods Inc ....F 513 241-6833
  Cincinnati (G-3895)

FOOD PRDTS: Pizza Doughs From Purchased Flour

B & D Commissary LLC ....E 740 743-3890
  Mount Perry (G-14454)

FOOD PRDTS: Popcorn, Unpopped

Great Lakes Popcorn Company ....G 419 732-3080
  Port Clinton (G-16248)
Wildcat Creek Farms Inc ....F 419 263-2549
  Payne (G-15876)

FOOD PRDTS: Pork Rinds

Rudolph Foods Company Inc ....C 909 383-7463
  Lima (G-11935)
Savory Foods Inc ....D 740 354-6655
  Portsmouth (G-16298)
White Feather Foods Inc ....F 419 738-8975
  Wapakoneta (G-19360)

FOOD PRDTS: Potato & Corn Chips & Similar Prdts

Basic Grain Products Inc ....D 419 678-2304
  Coldwater (G-6402)
Birds Eye Foods Inc ....E 330 854-0818
  Canal Fulton (G-2477)
Campbell Soup Company ....D 419 592-1010
  Napoleon (G-14534)
Frito-Lay North America Inc ....C 614 508-3004
  Columbus (G-6940)
Frito-Lay North America Inc ....C 513 229-3000
  Mason (G-12872)
Frito-Lay North America Inc ....C 972 334-7000
  Wooster (G-20594)
Pats Delicious LLC ....G 614 441-7047
  Columbus (G-7298)
Poppees Popcorn Inc ....E 440 327-0775
  North Ridgeville (G-15245)
Robert E McGrath Inc ....E 440 572-7747
  Strongsville (G-17783)
Shearers Foods LLC ....A 330 834-4030
  Massillon (G-13047)
Snack Alliance Inc ....E 330 767-3426
  Massillon (G-13049)
Waffle House Inc ....E 937 746-6830
  Franklin (G-9929)
Waffle House Inc ....F 513 539-8372
  Monroe (G-14281)

FOOD PRDTS: Potato Chips & Other Potato-Based Snacks

Ballreich Bros Inc ....C 419 447-1814
  Tiffin (G-18050)
Conns Potato Chip Co Inc ....E 740 452-4615
  Zanesville (G-21123)

PRODUCT SECTION

FOOD PRDTS: Shortening & Solid Edible Fats

Daniel Meenan .... G 330 756-2818
   Beach City *(G-1211)*
Frito-Lay North America Inc .... D 330 477-7009
   Canton *(G-2676)*
Gold N Krisp Chips & Pretzels .... G 330 832-8395
   Massillon *(G-12988)*
Grippo Potato Chip Co Inc .... D 513 923-1900
   Cincinnati *(G-3786)*
Herr Foods Incorporated .... E 740 773-8282
   Chillicothe *(G-3192)*
Jones Potato Chip Co .... E 419 529-9424
   Mansfield *(G-12464)*
Mike-Sells Potato Chip Co .... E 937 228-9400
   Dayton *(G-8357)*
Mumfords Potato Chips & Deli .... E 937 653-3491
   Urbana *(G-19005)*

FOOD PRDTS: Potatoes, Dried

Green Gourmet Foods LLC .... E 740 400-4212
   Baltimore *(G-1038)*

FOOD PRDTS: Poultry, Processed, Frozen

Martin-Brower Company LLC .... B 513 773-2301
   West Chester *(G-19741)*

FOOD PRDTS: Preparations

Agrana Fruit Us Inc .... C 937 693-3821
   Botkins *(G-1932)*
Alacwin Nutrition Corporation .... G 614 961-6479
   Columbus *(G-6561)*
Alamarra Inc .... G 800 336-3007
   Mentor *(G-13381)*
Allenbaugh Foods LLC .... E 216 952-3984
   Lakewood *(G-11509)*
American Sweet Bean Co LLC .... G 888 995-0007
   Tiffin *(G-18043)*
Amir International Foods Inc .... G 614 332-1742
   Grove City *(G-10415)*
Amish Wedding Foods Inc .... E 330 674-9199
   Millersburg *(G-14060)*
Andys Mdterranean Fd Pdts LLC ..... G 513 281-9791
   Cincinnati *(G-3347)*
Apf Legacy Subs LLC .... G 513 682-7173
   West Chester *(G-19833)*
Artistic Foods Incorporated .... G 330 401-1313
   Lodi *(G-12006)*
Atlantic Investment .... G 440 567-5054
   Lorain *(G-12079)*
Ballreich Bros Inc .... C 419 447-1814
   Tiffin *(G-18050)*
Basic Grain Products Inc .... D 419 678-2304
   Coldwater *(G-6402)*
Beatty Foods LLC .... G 330 327-2442
   Canton *(G-2588)*
Big Gus Onion Rings Inc .... E 216 883-9045
   Cleveland *(G-4812)*
Bread Kneads Inc .... G 419 422-3863
   Findlay *(G-9661)*
Chez Rama Restaurant .... G 614 237-9315
   Columbus *(G-6763)*
Cincinnatti Premier Candy LLC .... E 513 253-0079
   Cincinnati *(G-3513)*
Classic Delight Inc .... E 419 394-7955
   Saint Marys *(G-16682)*
Conagra Brands Inc .... C 513 229-0305
   Mason *(G-12853)*
Conagra Brands Inc .... F 740 465-3912
   Morral *(G-14403)*
Conagra Brands Inc .... B 419 445-8015
   Archbold *(G-642)*
Conagra Fods Pckaged Foods LLC . B 937 440-2800
   Troy *(G-18643)*
Country Parlour Ice Cream Co .... F 440 237-4040
   Cleveland *(G-5032)*
Curation Foods Inc .... G 419 931-1029
   Bowling Green *(G-1967)*
Cuyahoga Vending Co Inc .... F 440 353-9595
   North Ridgeville *(G-15219)*
Daniel Meenan .... G 330 756-2818
   Beach City *(G-1211)*
Dole Fresh Vegetables Inc .... C 937 525-4300
   Springfield *(G-17390)*
Food 4 Your Soul .... F 330 402-4073
   Youngstown *(G-20908)*
Fremont Company .... E 419 363-2924
   Rockford *(G-16539)*
Fresh Table LLC .... G 513 381-3774
   Cincinnati *(G-3713)*

Freshway Foods Inc .... C 937 498-4664
   Sidney *(G-17041)*
Frito-Lay North America Inc .... C 972 334-7000
   Wooster *(G-20594)*
Frito-Lay North America Inc .... D 330 477-7009
   Canton *(G-2676)*
Frog Ranch Foods Ltd .... F 740 767-3705
   Glouster *(G-10276)*
Gaslamp Popcorn Company .... G 951 684-6767
   Lima *(G-11868)*
General Mills Inc .... D 513 771-8200
   Cincinnati *(G-3745)*
Gold Star Chili Inc .... E 513 231-4541
   Cincinnati *(G-3767)*
Gold Star Chili Inc .... E 513 631-1990
   Cincinnati *(G-3768)*
Graffiti Foods Limited .... F 513 759-1921
   Columbus *(G-6963)*
Grippo Potato Chip Co Inc .... D 513 923-1900
   Cincinnati *(G-3786)*
Hiland Group Incorporated .... G 330 499-8404
   Canton *(G-2699)*
Homestat Farm Ltd .... E 614 718-3060
   Dublin *(G-8924)*
Hometown Food Company .... G 419 470-7914
   Toledo *(G-18333)*
Honeybaked Ham Company .... E 513 583-9700
   Cincinnati *(G-3824)*
Hydrofresh Ltd .... G 419 785-3221
   Delphos *(G-8745)*
Infant Food Project Inc .... G 614 239-5763
   Columbus *(G-7025)*
Ingredient Innovations Intl Co .... G 330 262-4440
   Wooster *(G-20606)*
J M Smucker Company .... E 440 323-5100
   Elyria *(G-9280)*
JM Smucker Co .... G 330 684-8274
   Orrville *(G-15600)*
John Krusinski .... F 216 441-0100
   Cleveland *(G-5502)*
Koch Foods of Cincinnati LLC .... C 513 874-3500
   Fairfield *(G-9518)*
Kraft Heinz Company .... A 330 837-8331
   Massillon *(G-13012)*
Main Street Gourmet LLC .... C 330 929-0000
   Cuyahoga Falls *(G-7895)*
Mane Inc .... D 513 248-9876
   Lebanon *(G-11671)*
Miami Valley Pizza Hut Inc .... E 419 586-5900
   Celina *(G-2976)*
Micah Specialty Foods .... G 405 320-3325
   Warrensville Heights *(G-19471)*
Mid American Ventures Inc .... F 216 524-0974
   Cleveland *(G-5673)*
Minnie Hanmons Catering Inc .... G 216 815-7744
   Cleveland *(G-5694)*
Nestle Brands Company .... F 440 264-6600
   Solon *(G-17202)*
Nija Foods LLC .... G 513 377-7495
   Cincinnati *(G-4079)*
Oceanside Foods .... G 440 554-7810
   Avon Lake *(G-999)*
Ohio Hickory Harvest Brand Pro ..... E 330 644-6266
   Coventry Township *(G-7775)*
Peer Pantry LLC .... G 216 236-4087
   Willowick *(G-20480)*
Pita Wrap LLC .... G 330 886-8091
   Boardman *(G-1900)*
Pure Foods LLC .... G 303 358-8375
   Highland Heights *(G-10799)*
Purushealth LLC .... F 800 601-0580
   Shaker Heights *(G-16935)*
Rich Products Corporation .... C 614 771-1117
   Hilliard *(G-10858)*
Ritchie Foods LLC .... G 440 354-7474
   Fairport Harbor *(G-9630)*
Roare-Q LLC .... G 419 801-4040
   Bowling Green *(G-1997)*
Rudolph Foods Company Inc .... C 909 383-7463
   Lima *(G-11935)*
Sanese Services Inc .... E 330 494-5900
   Warren *(G-19441)*
SC Campana Inc .... C 440 390-8854
   Amherst *(G-573)*
Sensoryffcts Powdr Systems Inc .... D 419 783-5518
   Defiance *(G-8643)*
Sharpys Food Systems LLC .... G 440 232-9601
   Oakwood Village *(G-15483)*
Solae LLC .... G 419 483-5340
   Bellevue *(G-1547)*

Special t Foods LLC .... G 330 533-9493
   Canfield *(G-2545)*
Sunrise Foods Inc .... E 614 276-2880
   Columbus *(G-7500)*
Tarrier Foods Corp .... E 614 876-8594
   Columbus *(G-2676)*
Toms Country Place Inc .... E 440 934-4553
   Avon *(G-971)*
Twenty Second Cntury Foods LLC .. G 419 866-6343
   Maumee *(G-13157)*
Umami Seasonings LLC .... G 614 687-0315
   Columbus *(G-7555)*
Unger Kosher Bakery Inc .... E 216 321-7176
   Cleveland Heights *(G-6352)*
Wake Robin Fermented Foods LLC . G 216 961-9944
   Cleveland *(G-6285)*
Wal-Bon of Ohio Inc .... D 740 423-8178
   Belpre *(G-1586)*
Wannemacher Enterprises Inc .... F 419 771-1101
   Upper Sandusky *(G-18977)*
Western Reserve Foods LLC .... G 330 770-0885
   Chagrin Falls *(G-3032)*
White Feather Foods Inc .... F 419 738-8975
   Wapakoneta *(G-19360)*
Willys Inc .... F 419 823-3200
   Swanton *(G-17929)*
Woeber Mustard Mfg Co .... C 937 323-6281
   Springfield *(G-17519)*
Yost Foods Inc .... G 330 273-4420
   Brunswick *(G-2255)*

FOOD PRDTS: Prepared Sauces, Exc Tomato Based

Hinkle Fine Foods Inc .... G 937 836-3665
   Dayton *(G-8250)*
Portion Pac Inc .... B 513 398-0400
   Mason *(G-12922)*
Ribs King Inc .... G 513 791-1942
   Cincinnati *(G-4265)*

FOOD PRDTS: Salad Oils, Refined Vegetable, Exc Corn

Inter American Products Inc .... E 800 645-2233
   Cincinnati *(G-3853)*

FOOD PRDTS: Salads

Barkett Fruit Co Inc .... E 330 364-6645
   Dover *(G-8807)*
Bob Evans Farms Inc .... B 614 491-2225
   New Albany *(G-14609)*
Dno Inc .... D 614 231-3601
   Columbus *(G-6872)*
Frank L Harter & Son Inc .... G 513 574-1330
   Cincinnati *(G-3709)*
Herold Salads Inc .... E 216 991-7500
   Cleveland *(G-5399)*
Sandridge Food Corporation .... G 330 725-2348
   Medina *(G-13334)*
Sandridge Food Corporation .... C 330 725-8883
   Medina *(G-13335)*

FOOD PRDTS: Sandwiches

Advancperre Foods Holdings Inc .... E 800 969-2747
   West Chester *(G-19828)*
White Castle System Inc .... E 513 563-2290
   Cincinnati *(G-4506)*

FOOD PRDTS: Sausage, Poultry

Freak-N-Fries Inc .... G 440 453-1877
   Lagrange *(G-11480)*

FOOD PRDTS: Seasonings & Spices

Blue Point Capitl Partners LLC .... F 216 535-4700
   Cleveland *(G-4824)*
Midwest Spray Drying Company ..... G 419 294-4221
   Upper Sandusky *(G-18964)*
Savor Seasonings LLC .... G 513 732-2333
   Batavia *(G-1183)*

FOOD PRDTS: Shortening & Solid Edible Fats

Procter & Gamble Mfg Co .... F 513 983-1100
   Cincinnati *(G-4212)*

FOOD PRDTS: Soup Powders
Dismat Corporation .... G 419 531-8963
  Toledo (G-18264)

FOOD PRDTS: Soybean Protein Concentrates & Isolates
Bunge North America Foundation .... G 740 426-6332
  Jeffersonville (G-11245)

FOOD PRDTS: Spices, Including Ground
Frutarom USA Inc .... C 513 870-4900
  West Chester (G-19856)
Frutarom USA Inc .... F 513 870-4900
  West Chester (G-19857)
Frutarom USA Inc .... G 513 870-4900
  West Chester (G-19858)
Inter American Products Inc .... E 800 645-2233
  Cincinnati (G-3853)

FOOD PRDTS: Starch, Corn
Cargill Incorporated .... E 937 236-1971
  Dayton (G-8075)

FOOD PRDTS: Sugar
Domino Foods Inc .... D 216 432-3222
  Cleveland (G-5106)

FOOD PRDTS: Sugar, Beet
Michigan Sugar Company .... F 419 332-9931
  Fremont (G-10040)
Michigan Sugar Company .... G 419 423-1666
  Findlay (G-9724)

FOOD PRDTS: Syrup, Maple
Goodell Farms .... G 330 274-2161
  Mantua (G-12547)
Sticky Petes Maple Syrup .... G 740 662-2726
  Athens (G-850)
Sugarbush Creek Farm .... G 440 636-5371
  Middlefield (G-13856)

FOOD PRDTS: Syrups
J M Smucker Company .... A 330 682-3000
  Orrville (G-15596)
National Foods Packaging Inc .... F 216 415-7102
  Cleveland (G-5725)
Nu Pet Company .... C 330 682-3000
  Orrville (G-15606)
Simple Products LLC .... G 330 674-2448
  Millersburg (G-14129)
Smucker International Inc .... G 330 682-3000
  Orrville (G-15621)

FOOD PRDTS: Tea
Ancient Infusions LLC .... G 419 659-5110
  Columbus Grove (G-7630)
Wallingford Coffee Mills Inc .... D 513 771-3131
  Cincinnati (G-4489)

FOOD PRDTS: Tortillas
Indie-Peasant Enterprises .... G 740 590-8240
  Athens (G-835)
La Perla Inc .... F 419 534-2074
  Toledo (G-18374)
Perez Foods LLC .... G 419 264-0303
  Holgate (G-10912)
Tortilla .... G 614 557-3367
  Reynoldsburg (G-16456)
Tortilleria El Maizal LLP .... G 330 209-9344
  Massillon (G-13053)
Tortilleria La Bamba LLC .... G 216 469-0410
  Cleveland (G-6190)
Tortilleria La Bamba LLC .... E 216 515-1600
  Cleveland (G-6191)

FOOD PRDTS: Turkey, Processed, Canned
Brinkman Turkey Farms Inc .... F 419 365-5127
  Findlay (G-9662)

FOOD PRDTS: Turkey, Processed, NEC
Cooper Hatchery Inc .... C 419 594-3325
  Oakwood (G-15469)

V H Cooper & Co Inc .... B 419 678-4853
  Saint Henry (G-16669)

FOOD PRDTS: Turkey, Slaughtered & Dressed
Whitewater Processing Co .... D 513 367-4133
  Harrison (G-10680)

FOOD PRODUCTS MACHINERY
Abj Equipfix .... E 419 684-5236
  Castalia (G-2935)
Acreo Inc .... G 513 734-3327
  Amelia (G-528)
American Pan Company .... C 937 652-3232
  Urbana (G-18978)
Ashco .... G 330 385-2400
  East Liverpool (G-9050)
Avure Technologies Inc .... D 513 433-2500
  Middletown (G-13885)
Biro Manufacturing Company .... F 419 798-4451
  North Canton (G-15073)
Christy Machine Company .... F 419 332-6451
  Fremont (G-10007)
Cleveland Gas Systems LLC .... G 216 391-7780
  Streetsboro (G-17665)
Cleveland Range LLC .... C 216 481-4900
  Cleveland (G-4972)
Crescent Metal Products Inc .... C 440 350-1100
  Mentor (G-13426)
E S Industries Inc .... G 419 643-2625
  Lima (G-11859)
G F Frank and Sons Inc .... F 513 870-9075
  West Chester (G-19709)
Grice Equipment Repair Inc .... G 937 440-8343
  Troy (G-18664)
Harry C Lobalzo & Sons Inc .... E 330 666-6758
  Akron (G-199)
Hawthorne-Seving Inc .... E 419 643-5531
  Cridersville (G-7810)
Hobart Corporation .... E 937 332-3000
  Troy (G-18671)
Hobart Corporation .... C 937 332-2797
  Piqua (G-16128)
Hobart International Holdings .... C 937 332-3000
  Troy (G-18672)
Innovative Controls Corp .... D 419 691-6684
  Toledo (G-18348)
ITW Food Equipment Group LLC .... F 937 332-3000
  Troy (G-18678)
ITW Food Equipment Group LLC .... G 937 393-4271
  Hillsboro (G-10882)
ITW Food Equipment Group LLC .... A 937 332-2396
  Troy (G-18679)
JE Grote Company Inc .... D 614 868-8414
  Columbus (G-7065)
John Bean Technologies Corp .... B 419 627-4349
  Sandusky (G-16819)
Lima Sheet Metal Machine & Mfg .... E 419 229-1161
  Lima (G-11893)
Maverick Corp Partners LLC .... G 330 669-2631
  Smithville (G-17090)
Maverick Innvtive Slutions LLC .... E 419 281-7944
  Ashland (G-722)
Meyer Company .... C 216 587-3400
  Cleveland (G-5663)
N Wasserstrom & Sons Inc .... C 614 228-5550
  Columbus (G-7206)
National Oilwell Varco LP .... D 937 454-3200
  Dayton (G-8377)
Nemco Food Equipment Ltd .... D 419 542-7751
  Hicksville (G-10780)
Norse Dairy Systems Inc .... C 614 294-4931
  Columbus (G-7224)
Omar Associates LLC .... G 419 426-0610
  Attica (G-858)
Premier Industries Inc .... E 513 271-2550
  Cincinnati (G-4187)
Probake Inc .... F 330 425-4427
  Twinsburg (G-18840)
Processall Inc .... F 513 771-2266
  Cincinnati (G-4196)
R and J Corporation .... E 440 871-6009
  Westlake (G-20147)
Richard B Linneman .... G 513 922-5537
  Cincinnati (G-4266)
Royalton Food Service Eqp Co .... E 440 237-0806
  North Royalton (G-15299)
Sarka Bros Machining Inc .... G 419 532-2393
  Kalida (G-11281)

Sidney Manufacturing Company .... E 937 492-4154
  Sidney (G-17079)
Tomlinson Industries LLC .... C 216 587-3400
  Cleveland (G-6181)
Winston Products LLC .... D 440 478-1418
  Cleveland (G-6314)
Wolf Machine Company .... C 513 791-5194
  Blue Ash (G-1874)

FOOD STORES: Convenience, Chain
Speedway LLC .... A 937 864-3000
  Enon (G-9387)
United Dairy Farmers Inc .... C 513 396-8700
  Cincinnati (G-4447)

FOOD STORES: Convenience, Independent
Larrys Drive Thru & Mini Mart .... G 330 953-0512
  Youngstown (G-20958)
Whitacre Enterprises Inc .... F 740 934-2331
  Graysville (G-10342)

FOOD STORES: Delicatessen
Baltic Country Meats .... G 330 897-7025
  Baltic (G-1023)
Bread Kneads Inc .... G 419 422-3863
  Findlay (G-9661)
Fragapane Bakeries Inc 440 779-6050
  North Olmsted (G-15190)
Mumfords Potato Chips & Deli .... G 937 653-3491
  Urbana (G-19005)
Zygo Inc .... G 513 281-0888
  Cincinnati (G-4535)

FOOD STORES: Grocery, Independent
Brinkman Turkey Farms Inc .... F 419 365-5127
  Findlay (G-9662)
C J Kraft Enterprises Inc .... E 740 653-9606
  Lancaster (G-11551)
Geyers Markets Inc .... D 419 468-9477
  Galion (G-10141)
Gibson Bros Inc .... E 440 774-2401
  Oberlin (G-15496)
Lariccias Italian Foods .... F 330 729-0222
  Youngstown (G-20957)
Troyers Trail Bologna Inc .... E 330 893-2414
  Dundee (G-9029)
Unger Kosher Bakery Inc .... E 216 321-7176
  Cleveland Heights (G-6352)

FOOD STORES: Supermarkets, Chain
Heinens Inc .... D 330 562-5297
  Aurora (G-882)
Kroger Co .... C 740 671-5164
  Bellaire (G-1487)
Kroger Co .... C 740 335-4030
  Wshngtn CT Hs (G-20731)
Kroger Co .... C 740 264-5057
  Steubenville (G-17540)
Kroger Co .... D 513 683-4001
  Maineville (G-12372)
Kroger Co .... C 513 742-9500
  Cincinnati (G-3924)
Kroger Co .... D 740 374-2523
  Marietta (G-12638)
Kroger Co .... D 419 423-2065
  Findlay (G-9711)
Kroger Co .... C 937 277-0950
  Dayton (G-8302)
Kroger Co .... C 614 263-1766
  Columbus (G-7103)
Kroger Co .... C 937 743-5900
  Springboro (G-17335)
Kroger Co .... C 614 575-3742
  Columbus (G-7104)
Riesbeck Food Markets Inc .... C 740 695-3401
  Saint Clairsville (G-16649)

FOOTWEAR, WHOLESALE: Athletic
NTS Enterprises Ltd .... G 513 531-1166
  Cincinnati (G-4092)

FOOTWEAR, WHOLESALE: Boots
Hudson Leather Ltd .... G 419 485-8531
  Pioneer (G-16085)

PRODUCT SECTION

FOOTWEAR, WHOLESALE: Shoes

Georgia-Boot Inc ....D....... 740 753-1951
 Nelsonville *(G-14593)*

FOOTWEAR: Custom Made

Cobblers Corner LLC ....F....... 330 482-4005
 Columbiana *(G-6458)*

FOOTWEAR: Cut Stock

Hudson Leather Ltd ....G....... 419 485-8531
 Pioneer *(G-16085)*
Remington Products Co ....C....... 330 335-1571
 Wadsworth *(G-19274)*

FORESTRY RELATED EQPT

Rayco Manufacturing LLC ....G....... 330 264-8699
 Wooster *(G-20642)*

FORGINGS

Akron Gear & Engineering Inc ....E....... 330 773-6608
 Akron *(G-41)*
Alta Mira Corporation ....D....... 330 648-2461
 Spencer *(G-17303)*
Brooker Bros Forging Co Inc ....E....... 419 668-2535
 Norwalk *(G-15383)*
Buckeye Gear Co ....F....... 216 292-7998
 Chagrin Falls *(G-3038)*
Bula Forge & Machine Inc ....E....... 216 252-7600
 Cleveland *(G-4852)*
Cailin Dev Ltd Lblty Co ....F....... 216 408-6261
 Cleveland *(G-4862)*
Canton Drop Forge Inc ....B....... 330 477-4511
 Canton *(G-2608)*
Carbo Forge Inc ....E....... 419 334-9788
 Fremont *(G-10004)*
Cleveland Hdwr & Forging Co ....E....... 216 641-5200
 Cleveland *(G-4962)*
Cleveland Hollow Boring Inc ....G....... 216 883-1926
 Cleveland *(G-4963)*
Colfor Manufacturing Inc ....A....... 330 863-7500
 Malvern *(G-12387)*
Cordier Group Holdings Inc ....B....... 330 477-4511
 Canton *(G-2637)*
Edgerton Forge Inc ....E....... 419 298-2333
 Edgerton *(G-9171)*
Edward W Daniel LLC ....E....... 440 647-1960
 Wellington *(G-19577)*
For Call Inc ....B....... 330 863-0404
 Malvern *(G-12390)*
Forge Products Corporation ....D....... 216 231-2600
 Cleveland *(G-5262)*
Forging Eqp Solutions Inc ....G....... 330 239-2222
 Medina *(G-13263)*
Geneva Gear & Machine Inc ....F....... 937 866-0318
 Dayton *(G-8221)*
GKN PLC ....G....... 740 446-9211
 Gallipolis *(G-10165)*
GKN Sinter Metals LLC ....C....... 740 441-3203
 Gallipolis *(G-10166)*
J & H Manufacturing LLC ....F....... 330 482-2636
 Columbiana *(G-6471)*
Ken Forging Inc ....C....... 440 993-8091
 Jefferson *(G-11232)*
King-Indiana Forge Inc ....F....... 330 425-4250
 Twinsburg *(G-18800)*
Lange Precision Inc ....F....... 513 530-9500
 Blue Ash *(G-1802)*
Lextech Industries Ltd ....C....... 216 883-7900
 Cleveland *(G-5574)*
Martin Sprocket & Gear Inc ....D....... 419 485-5515
 Montpelier *(G-14312)*
Metal Forming & Coining Corp ....D....... 419 897-9530
 Maumee *(G-13132)*
Mid-West Forge Corporation ....C....... 216 481-3030
 Cleveland *(G-5677)*
Ohio Chain Company LLC ....E....... 419 843-9476
 Sylvania *(G-17958)*
Ohio Star Forge Co ....D....... 330 847-6360
 Warren *(G-19427)*
Park-Ohio Industries Inc ....C....... 440 947-2000
 Cleveland *(G-5843)*
Penn Machine Company ....E....... 814 288-1547
 Twinsburg *(G-18829)*
Powers and Sons LLC ....D....... 419 737-2373
 Pioneer *(G-16091)*
Presrite Corporation ....C....... 440 576-0015
 Jefferson *(G-11236)*
Queen City Forging Company ....F....... 513 321-2003
 Cincinnati *(G-4237)*
Rose Metal Industries LLC ....F....... 216 881-3355
 Cleveland *(G-6002)*
Rotek Incorporated ....C....... 330 562-4000
 Aurora *(G-904)*
Sakamura USA Inc ....F....... 740 223-7777
 Marion *(G-12732)*
Solmet Technologies Inc ....E....... 330 915-4160
 Canton *(G-2819)*
Stahl Gear & Machine Co ....E....... 216 431-2820
 Cleveland *(G-6089)*
T & S Discount Tires Inc ....G....... 440 951-9084
 Willoughby *(G-20439)*
TRM Manufacturing Inc ....E....... 330 769-2600
 Cuyahoga Falls *(G-7929)*
US Tsubaki Power Transm LLC ....C....... 419 626-4560
 Sandusky *(G-16860)*
Wallace Forge Company ....D....... 330 488-1203
 Canton *(G-2863)*
Wright Tool Company ....C....... 330 848-0600
 Barberton *(G-1114)*
Wyman-Gordon Company ....E....... 216 341-0085
 Cleveland *(G-6330)*

FORGINGS: Aircraft, Ferrous

Sifco Industries Inc ....B....... 216 881-8600
 Cleveland *(G-6063)*

FORGINGS: Aluminum

Arconic Inc ....A....... 216 641-3600
 Newburgh Heights *(G-14934)*
Arconic Inc ....A....... 216 641-3600
 Newburgh Heights *(G-14935)*
Arconic Inc ....G....... 330 544-7633
 Niles *(G-14998)*
Gateway Industries ....G....... 330 633-3700
 Akron *(G-182)*

FORGINGS: Armor Plate, Iron Or Steel

Shot-Force Pro LLC ....G....... 740 753-3927
 Nelsonville *(G-14597)*

FORGINGS: Automotive & Internal Combustion Engine

American Cold Forge LLC ....E....... 419 836-1062
 Northwood *(G-15331)*
Cliffs High Performance ....G....... 740 397-2921
 Mount Vernon *(G-14476)*
Ohio Metal Technologies Inc ....D....... 740 928-8288
 Hebron *(G-10756)*
Performance Motorsports ....G....... 513 931-9999
 Cincinnati *(G-4149)*
Presrite Corporation ....B....... 216 441-5990
 Cleveland *(G-5918)*

FORGINGS: Construction Or Mining Eqpt, Ferrous

Dayton Superior Corporation ....C....... 937 866-0711
 Miamisburg *(G-13655)*
Dependable Gear Corp ....G....... 440 942-4969
 Eastlake *(G-9103)*
Rudd Equipment Company Inc ....E....... 513 321-7833
 Cincinnati *(G-4287)*

FORGINGS: Internal Combustion Engine, Ferrous

Park-Ohio Holdings Corp ....F....... 440 947-2000
 Cleveland *(G-5842)*

FORGINGS: Iron & Steel

Forge Products Corporation ....D....... 216 231-2600
 Cleveland *(G-5262)*
Pilgrim-Harp Co ....G....... 440 249-4185
 Avon *(G-957)*
S&V Industries Inc ....E....... 330 666-1986
 Medina *(G-13333)*

FORGINGS: Machinery, Ferrous

Dayton Forging Heat Treating ....D....... 937 253-4126
 Dayton *(G-8132)*
Wodin Inc ....E....... 440 439-4222
 Cleveland *(G-6320)*

FORGINGS: Metal, Ornamental, Ferrous

Alliance Forging Group LLC ....G....... 330 680-4861
 Akron *(G-60)*

FORGINGS: Nonferrous

Canton Drop Forge Inc ....B....... 330 477-4511
 Canton *(G-2608)*
Cleveland Hdwr & Forging Co ....E....... 216 641-5200
 Cleveland *(G-4962)*
Colfor Manufacturing Inc ....A....... 330 863-7500
 Malvern *(G-12387)*
Edward W Daniel LLC ....E....... 440 647-1960
 Wellington *(G-19577)*
Forge Products Corporation ....D....... 216 231-2600
 Cleveland *(G-5262)*
Powers and Sons LLC ....D....... 419 737-2373
 Pioneer *(G-16091)*
Rotek Incorporated ....C....... 330 562-4000
 Aurora *(G-904)*
Turbine Eng Cmpnents Tech Corp ....E....... 216 692-6173
 Cleveland *(G-6222)*
Wallace Forge Company ....D....... 330 488-1203
 Canton *(G-2863)*
Wodin Inc ....E....... 440 439-4222
 Cleveland *(G-6320)*

FORGINGS: Plumbing Fixture, Nonferrous

Guarantee Specialties Inc ....D....... 216 451-9744
 Strongsville *(G-17747)*
Mansfield Plumbing Pdts LLC ....A....... 419 938-5211
 Perrysville *(G-16030)*

FORMS: Concrete, Sheet Metal

Adjustable Kicker LLC ....G....... 740 362-9170
 Delaware *(G-8650)*
C L W Inc ....G....... 740 374-8443
 Marietta *(G-12611)*
C M L Concrete Construction ....G....... 330 758-8314
 Youngstown *(G-20863)*
Carroll Distrg & Cnstr Sup Inc ....G....... 513 422-3327
 Middletown *(G-13890)*
Carroll Distrg & Cnstr Sup Inc ....G....... 614 564-9799
 Columbus *(G-6747)*
CMA Supply Company Inc ....F....... 513 942-6663
 West Chester *(G-19844)*
Creative Concepts ....G....... 216 513-6463
 Medina *(G-13246)*
Efco Corp ....E....... 614 876-1226
 Columbus *(G-6886)*
Feather Lite Innovations Inc ....F....... 513 893-5483
 Liberty Twp *(G-11825)*
Feather Lite Innovations Inc ....E....... 937 743-9008
 Springboro *(G-17327)*

FOUNDRIES: Aluminum

Acuity Brands Lighting Inc ....B....... 740 349-4343
 Newark *(G-14848)*
Air Craft Wheels LLC ....G....... 440 937-7903
 Ravenna *(G-16364)*
Akron Foundry Co ....C....... 330 745-3101
 Akron *(G-40)*
Akron Foundry Co ....E....... 330 745-3101
 Barberton *(G-1050)*
Aluminum Line Products Company ....D....... 440 835-8880
 Westlake *(G-20091)*
Aztec Manufacturing Inc ....E....... 330 783-9747
 Youngstown *(G-20850)*
C M M S - Re LLC ....F....... 513 489-5111
 Blue Ash *(G-1745)*
Cast Metals Technology Inc ....E....... 937 968-5460
 Union City *(G-18902)*
Castek Aluminum Inc ....E....... 440 365-2333
 Elyria *(G-9234)*
Consoldted Precision Pdts Corp ....C....... 216 453-4800
 Cleveland *(G-5016)*
Dd Foundry Inc ....D....... 216 362-4100
 Brookpark *(G-2143)*
Durivage Pattern & Mfg Co ....E....... 419 836-8655
 Williston *(G-20262)*
Euclid Products Co Inc ....G....... 440 942-7310
 Willoughby *(G-20317)*
Francis Manufacturing Company ....C....... 937 526-4551
 Russia *(G-16607)*
General Die Casters Inc ....E....... 330 678-2528
 Twinsburg *(G-18781)*
Globe Motors Inc ....C....... 937 228-3171
 Dayton *(G-8227)*

Employee Codes: A=Over 500 employees, B=251-500
C=101-250, D=51-100, E=20-50, F=10-19, G=3-9

Kovatch Castings Inc ....C 330 896-9944
Uniontown (G-18924)
Lite Metals Company ....E 330 296-6110
Ravenna (G-16389)
Lodi Foundry Co Inc ....E 330 948-1516
Lodi (G-12014)
Metal-Mation Inc ....F 216 651-1083
Cleveland (G-5660)
Miller Casting Inc ....F 330 482-2923
Columbiana (G-6473)
Model Pattern & Foundry Co ....E 513 542-2322
Cincinnati (G-4036)
Myron D Budd ....G 330 682-5866
Orrville (G-15604)
Reliable Castings Corporation ....D 937 497-5217
Sidney (G-17065)
Seilkop Industries Inc ....F 513 679-5680
Cincinnati (G-4317)
Skuld LLC ....G 330 423-7339
Groveport (G-10512)
Stripmatic Products Inc ....E 216 241-7143
Cleveland (G-6111)
Thompson Aluminum Casting Co ....D 216 206-2781
Cleveland (G-6171)
Tooling Technology LLC ....D 937 295-3672
Fort Loramie (G-9810)
Yoder Industries Inc ....E 937 890-4322
Dayton (G-8603)
Yoder Industries Inc ....C 937 278-5769
Dayton (G-8602)

FOUNDRIES: Brass, Bronze & Copper

American Bronze Corporation ....E 216 341-7800
Cleveland (G-4684)
Buckeye Aluminum Foundry Inc ....G 440 428-7180
Madison (G-12340)
Calmego Specialized Pdts LLC ....F 937 669-5620
Greenville (G-10362)
D Picking & Co ....G 419 562-5016
Bucyrus (G-2324)
Hadronics Inc ....D 513 321-9350
Cincinnati (G-3792)
Kovatch Castings Inc ....C 330 896-9944
Uniontown (G-18924)
Model Pattern & Foundry Co ....E 513 542-2322
Cincinnati (G-4036)
National Bronze Mtls Ohio Inc ....E 440 277-1226
Lorain (G-12106)
Randall Bearings Inc ....D 419 223-1075
Lima (G-11927)
Randall Bearings Inc ....F 419 678-2486
Coldwater (G-6419)
Santos Industrial Ltd ....E 937 299-7333
Moraine (G-14392)
Semco ....D 800 848-5764
Marion (G-12734)
Snair Co ....F 614 873-7020
Plain City (G-16212)
Stripmatic Products Inc ....E 216 241-7143
Cleveland (G-6111)
Whip Guide Co ....F 440 543-5151
Chagrin Falls (G-3090)

FOUNDRIES: Gray & Ductile Iron

Akron Gear & Engineering Inc ....E 330 773-6608
Akron (G-41)
Arcelormittal Tubular Products ....A 419 347-2424
Shelby (G-16978)
Arconic Inc ....A 216 641-3600
Newburgh Heights (G-14934)
Barberton Steel Industries Inc ....E 330 745-6837
Barberton (G-1065)
Castco Inc ....E 440 365-2333
Elyria (G-9233)
D Picking & Co ....G 419 562-5016
Bucyrus (G-2324)
Dd Foundry Inc ....D 216 362-4100
Brookpark (G-2143)
Ford Motor Company ....A 216 676-7918
Brookpark (G-2147)
Hamilton Brass & Alum Castings ....E 513 867-0400
Hamilton (G-10567)
Hobart Corporation ....E 937 332-3000
Troy (G-18671)
Hobart Corporation ....C 937 332-2797
Piqua (G-16128)
Korff Holdings LLC ....C 330 332-1566
Salem (G-16752)
OS Kelly Corporation ....E 937 322-4921
Springfield (G-17465)
Rotek Incorporated ....C 330 562-4000
Aurora (G-904)
Skuld LLC ....G 330 423-7339
Groveport (G-10512)
Tiffin Foundry & Machine Inc ....E 419 447-3991
Tiffin (G-18087)
Wallace Forge Company ....D 330 488-1203
Canton (G-2863)

FOUNDRIES: Iron

Ej Usa Inc ....E 216 692-3001
Cleveland (G-5159)
Ellwood Engineered Castings Co ....C 330 568-3000
Hubbard (G-11001)
General Aluminum Mfg Company ....C 419 739-9300
Wapakoneta (G-19330)
General Motors LLC ....A 419 782-7010
Defiance (G-8623)
Kenton Iron Products Inc ....D 419 674-4178
Kenton (G-11411)
Osco Industries Inc ....C 740 286-5004
Jackson (G-11193)
Pioneer City Casting Company ....E 740 423-7533
Belpre (G-1582)
Sancast Inc ....E 740 622-8660
Coshocton (G-7750)
St Marys Foundry Inc ....C 419 394-3346
Saint Marys (G-16701)
T & B Foundry Company ....D 216 391-4200
Cleveland (G-6141)
Tiffin Foundry & Machine Inc ....E 419 447-3991
Tiffin (G-18087)
Tooling Technology LLC ....D 937 295-3672
Fort Loramie (G-9810)
Whemco-Ohio Foundry Inc ....C 419 222-2111
Lima (G-11959)
Yellow Creek Casting Company ....E 330 532-4608
Wellsville (G-19615)

FOUNDRIES: Nonferrous

Air Craft Wheels LLC ....G 440 937-7903
Ravenna (G-16364)
Alcon Industries Inc ....D 216 961-1100
Cleveland (G-4653)
Apex Aluminum Die Cast Co Inc ....E 937 773-0432
Piqua (G-16099)
Brost Foundry Company ....E 216 641-1131
Cleveland (G-4842)
Bunting Bearings LLC ....E 419 522-3323
Mansfield (G-12417)
Catania Medallic Specialty ....E 440 933-9595
Avon Lake (G-981)
Concorde Castings Inc ....G 440 953-0053
Willoughby (G-20299)
Curtiss-Wright Flow Ctrl Corp ....D 216 267-3200
Cleveland (G-5045)
Dd Foundry Inc ....D 216 362-4100
Brookpark (G-2143)
Dmk Industries Inc ....F 513 727-4549
Middletown (G-13901)
Durivage Pattern & Mfg Co ....E 419 836-8655
Williston (G-20262)
Ellwood Engineered Castings Co ....C 330 568-3000
Hubbard (G-11001)
Francis Manufacturing Company ....C 937 526-4551
Russia (G-16607)
General Aluminum Mfg Company ....B 330 297-1225
Cleveland (G-5304)
General Aluminum Mfg Company ....E 330 297-1020
Ravenna (G-16381)
General Aluminum Mfg Company ....B 440 593-6225
Conneaut (G-7646)
General Die Casters Inc ....E 330 678-2528
Twinsburg (G-18781)
General Motors LLC ....A 419 782-7010
Defiance (G-8623)
Globe Motors Inc ....C 937 228-3171
Dayton (G-8227)
Harbor Castings Inc ....E 330 499-7178
Cuyahoga Falls (G-7877)
Iabf Inc ....G 614 279-4498
Columbus (G-7018)
Kovatch Castings Inc ....C 330 896-9944
Uniontown (G-18924)
Kse Manufacturing ....G 937 409-9831
Sidney (G-17048)
Lite Metals Company ....E 330 296-6110
Ravenna (G-16389)
Materion Brush Inc ....A 419 862-2745
Elmore (G-9208)
Morris Bean & Company ....C 937 767-7301
Yellow Springs (G-20812)
Nelson Aluminum Foundry Inc ....G 440 543-1941
Chagrin Falls (G-3063)
New London Foundry Inc ....F 419 929-2073
New London (G-14733)
Nova Machine Products Inc ....D 216 267-3200
Middleburg Heights (G-13767)
PCC Airfoils LLC ....C 330 868-6441
Minerva (G-14196)
PCC Airfoils LLC ....F 440 350-6150
Painesville (G-15773)
PCC Airfoils LLC ....F 216 766-6206
Beachwood (G-1263)
PCC Airfoils LLC ....E 216 831-3590
Cleveland (G-5856)
Piqua Emery Cutter & Fndry Co ....D 937 773-4134
Piqua (G-16152)
Ray Lewis & Son Incorporated ....E 937 644-4015
Marysville (G-12807)
Reliable Castings Corporation ....D 937 497-5217
Sidney (G-17065)
Ross Aluminum Castings LLC ....C 937 492-4134
Sidney (G-17069)
Sawbrook Steel Castings Co ....D 513 554-1700
Cincinnati (G-4302)
Seaport Mold & Casting Company ....F 419 243-1422
Toledo (G-18515)
Seilkop Industries Inc ....F 513 679-5680
Cincinnati (G-4317)
St Marys Foundry Inc ....C 419 394-3346
Saint Marys (G-16701)
Symmetry Oes ....G 614 890-1758
Westerville (G-20075)
T & B Foundry Company ....D 216 391-4200
Cleveland (G-6141)
Technology House Ltd ....D 440 248-3025
Solon (G-17248)
Technology House Ltd ....E 440 248-3025
Streetsboro (G-17701)
Telcon LLC ....D 330 562-5566
Streetsboro (G-17702)
Yoder Industries Inc ....C 937 278-5769
Dayton (G-8602)

FOUNDRIES: Steel

Anointed Design & Technologies ....G 330 826-1493
Massillon (G-12959)
B-Tek Scales LLC ....E 330 471-8900
Canton (G-2582)
Brost Foundry Company ....E 216 641-1131
Cleveland (G-4842)
Castings Usa Inc ....G 330 339-3611
New Philadelphia (G-14764)
Dd Foundry Inc ....D 216 362-4100
Brookpark (G-2143)
Durivage Pattern & Mfg Co ....E 419 836-8655
Williston (G-20262)
Evertz Technology Service Usa ....E 513 422-8400
Middletown (G-13907)
Harbor Castings Inc ....E 330 499-7178
Cuyahoga Falls (G-7877)
Jmac Inc ....E 614 436-2418
Columbus (G-7069)
Korff Holdings LLC ....C 330 332-1566
Salem (G-16752)
Kovatch Castings Inc ....C 330 896-9944
Uniontown (G-18924)
Lakeway Mfg Inc ....E 419 433-3030
Huron (G-11103)
Medina Blanking Inc ....C 330 558-2300
Valley City (G-19049)
Munroe Incorporated ....G 330 755-7216
Struthers (G-17821)
Premier Inv Cast Group LLC ....E 937 299-7333
Moraine (G-14381)
Steel Service Plus Ltd ....F 216 391-9000
Cleveland (G-6102)
Tecumseh Redevelopment Inc ....G 330 659-9100
Richfield (G-16492)
Tiffin Foundry & Machine Inc ....E 419 447-3991
Tiffin (G-18087)
Whemco-Ohio Foundry Inc ....C 419 222-2111
Lima (G-11959)
Worthington Industries Inc ....C 513 539-9291
Monroe (G-14282)
Worthngton Stelpac Systems LLC ....C 614 438-3205
Columbus (G-7617)

PRODUCT SECTION

FUELS: Ethanol

FOUNDRIES: Steel Investment

Brost Foundry Company................E....... 216 641-1131
  Cleveland *(G-4842)*
Castalloy Inc................................D....... 216 961-7990
  Cleveland *(G-4889)*
Consoldted Precision Pdts Corp..........C....... 216 453-4800
  Cleveland *(G-5016)*
Harbor Castings Inc......................E....... 330 499-7178
  Cuyahoga Falls *(G-7877)*
Mercury Machine Co.....................D....... 440 349-3222
  Solon *(G-17191)*
Mold Masters Intl Inc....................C....... 440 953-0220
  Eastlake *(G-9123)*
PCC Airfoils LLC..........................C....... 330 868-6441
  Minerva *(G-14196)*
PCC Airfoils LLC..........................C....... 440 255-9770
  Mentor *(G-13545)*
Premier Inv Cast Group LLC............E....... 413 727-2860
  Moraine *(G-14382)*
Skuld LLC.................................G....... 330 423-7339
  Groveport *(G-10512)*
Summit Resources Group Inc..........G....... 330 653-3992
  Hudson *(G-11078)*
Xapc Co..................................D....... 216 362-4100
  Cleveland *(G-6331)*

FOUNDRY MACHINERY & EQPT

Empire Systems Inc......................F....... 440 653-9300
  Avon Lake *(G-984)*
Equipment Manufacturers Intl..........E....... 216 651-6700
  Cleveland *(G-5186)*
Fremont Flask Co........................F....... 419 332-2231
  Fremont *(G-10019)*
Gokoh Corporation......................F....... 937 339-4977
  Troy *(G-18662)*
Mark Carpenter Industries Inc..........G....... 419 294-4568
  Fremont *(G-10039)*
Mosbro Machine and Tool Inc...........G....... 330 467-0913
  Northfield *(G-15320)*
Palmer Klein Inc..........................G....... 937 323-6339
  Springfield *(G-17467)*
Palmer Mfg and Supply Inc............E....... 937 323-6339
  Springfield *(G-17468)*

FOUNDRY MATERIALS: Insulsleeves

Exochem Corporation..................D....... 800 807-7464
  Lorain *(G-12091)*

FOUNDRY SAND MINING

C E D Process Minerals Inc............F....... 330 666-5500
  Akron *(G-101)*

FOUNTAINS, METAL, EXC DRINKING

Fountain Specialists Inc................G....... 513 831-5717
  Milford *(G-14009)*
Manufacturing Futures Inc............G....... 216 903-7993
  Cleveland *(G-5613)*

FOUNTAINS: Concrete

Fountain Specialists Inc................G....... 513 831-5717
  Milford *(G-14009)*

FRACTIONATION PRDTS OF CRUDE PETROLEUM, HYDROCARBONS, NEC

Arizona Chemical Company LLC......C....... 330 343-7701
  Dover *(G-8804)*
Enrevo Pyro LLC..........................G....... 203 517-5002
  Brookfield *(G-2106)*

FRANCHISES, SELLING OR LICENSING

Gold Star Chili Inc......................E....... 513 231-4541
  Cincinnati *(G-3767)*
Instantwhip Foods Inc..................F....... 614 488-2536
  Columbus *(G-7034)*
R&D Marketing Group Inc..............G....... 216 398-9100
  Brooklyn Heights *(G-2130)*
Rascal House Inc........................G....... 216 781-0904
  Cleveland *(G-5961)*
Skyline Chili Inc..........................C....... 513 874-1188
  Fairfield *(G-9565)*
Stanley Steemer Intl Inc................C....... 614 764-2007
  Dublin *(G-8994)*

FREEZERS: Household

Whirlpool Corporation..................B....... 419 547-7711
  Clyde *(G-6397)*

FREIGHT FORWARDING ARRANGEMENTS

Tgs International Inc....................E....... 330 893-4828
  Millersburg *(G-14134)*

FREIGHT TRANSPORTATION ARRANGEMENTS

Ds Express Carriers Inc................G....... 419 433-6200
  Norwalk *(G-15388)*
Eae Logistics Company LLC............G....... 440 417-4788
  Madison *(G-12348)*
Faircosa LLC.............................G....... 216 577-9909
  Cleveland *(G-5215)*
Kendall & Sons Company..............G....... 937 222-6996
  Dayton *(G-8292)*
Millwood Natural LLC..................C....... 330 393-4400
  Vienna *(G-19205)*
SDS National LLC......................G....... 330 759-8066
  Youngstown *(G-21026)*
Taupe Holdings Co......................G....... 614 330-4600
  Dublin *(G-9002)*
VIP-Supply Chain Solutions LLC......G....... 513 454-2020
  West Chester *(G-19818)*

FREON

A-Gas US Holdings Inc..................F....... 419 867-8990
  Bowling Green *(G-1945)*
A-Gas US Inc............................G....... 800 372-1301
  Bowling Green *(G-1946)*
Reclamation Technologies Inc........E....... 800 372-1301
  Bowling Green *(G-1994)*
Reclamation Technologies Inc........G....... 419 867-8990
  Bowling Green *(G-1995)*

FRICTION MATERIAL, MADE FROM POWDERED METAL

General Metals Powder Co............D....... 330 633-1226
  Akron *(G-186)*
Lewark Metal Spinning Inc............E....... 937 275-3303
  Dayton *(G-8312)*
Miscellnous Mtals Fbrction Inc........G....... 740 779-3071
  Chillicothe *(G-3200)*
Rmi Titanium Company LLC..........D....... 330 455-4010
  Canton *(G-2806)*
Tribco Incorporated....................E....... 216 486-2000
  Cleveland *(G-6209)*
US Powder Coating Inc................G....... 440 255-3090
  Mentor *(G-13620)*

FRITS

Ferro Corporation......................C....... 216 875-6178
  Cleveland *(G-5231)*

FRUIT & VEGETABLE MARKETS

Country Maid Ice Cream Inc..........G....... 330 659-6830
  Richfield *(G-16466)*

FRUIT STANDS OR MARKETS

Beckwith Orchards Inc................F....... 330 673-6433
  Kent *(G-11299)*
Coopers Mill Inc........................F....... 419 562-4215
  Bucyrus *(G-2322)*

FRUITS & VEGETABLES WHOLESALERS: Fresh

Frank L Harter & Son Inc..............G....... 513 574-1330
  Cincinnati *(G-3709)*

FUEL ADDITIVES

BLaster Corporation....................E....... 216 901-5800
  Cleveland *(G-4819)*

FUEL CELLS: Solid State

Firstfuelcellscom LLC..................G....... 440 884-2503
  Cleveland *(G-5243)*
Hydrogen 411 Technology LLC......G....... 440 941-6760
  Cleveland *(G-5430)*

FUEL DEALERS: Coal

Cliffs Logan County Coal LLC........G....... 216 694-5700
  Cleveland *(G-4989)*

FUEL OIL DEALERS

Centerra Co-Op..........................E....... 419 281-2153
  Ashland *(G-690)*
Cincinnati - Vulcan Company..........D....... 513 242-5300
  Cincinnati *(G-3477)*
New Vulco Mfg & Sales Co LLC......D....... 513 242-2672
  Cincinnati *(G-4072)*
Santmyer Oil Co of Ashland..........G....... 330 262-6501
  Wooster *(G-20648)*
Santmyer Oil Co of Ashland..........G....... 419 289-8815
  Ashland *(G-746)*

FUEL TREATING

Opw Fueling Components Inc........E....... 800 422-2525
  West Chester *(G-19756)*

FUELS: Diesel

Appal Energy............................G....... 740 448-4605
  Amesville *(G-551)*
Bloom Center Biodiesel LLC..........G....... 937 585-6412
  Lewistown *(G-11800)*
Diesel Recon Service Inc..............G....... 513 625-1887
  Pleasant Plain *(G-16225)*
Santmyer Oil Co of Ashland..........G....... 419 289-8815
  Ashland *(G-746)*

FUELS: Ethanol

Adr Fuel Inc..............................G....... 419 872-2178
  Perrysburg *(G-15917)*
AMA Fuel Services LLC................G....... 513 836-3800
  Lebanon *(G-11633)*
B P Oil Company........................G....... 513 671-4107
  Cincinnati *(G-3376)*
Bam Fuel Inc............................G....... 740 397-6674
  Howard *(G-10995)*
Beloit Fuel LLC..........................G....... 330 584-1915
  North Benton *(G-15060)*
Brightstar Propane & Fuels............G....... 614 891-8395
  Westerville *(G-19981)*
Canton Fuel..............................G....... 330 455-3400
  Canton *(G-2609)*
Creative Fuels LLC......................F....... 330 923-2222
  Cuyahoga Falls *(G-7854)*
East Side Fuel Plus Operations........G....... 419 563-0777
  Bucyrus *(G-2327)*
Eco Chem Alternative Fuels LLC......G....... 614 764-3835
  Dublin *(G-8912)*
Eco Fuel Solution LLC..................G....... 440 282-8592
  Amherst *(G-562)*
Exp Fuels Inc............................G....... 419 382-7713
  Toledo *(G-18287)*
Fitness Fuel Training..................G....... 330 807-7353
  Tallmadge *(G-17983)*
Fly Race Fuels LLC......................G....... 419 744-9402
  North Fairfield *(G-15138)*
Franklin..................................G....... 419 699-5757
  Waterville *(G-19495)*
Fuel America............................G....... 419 586-5609
  Celina *(G-2963)*
Fuel G USA LLC..........................G....... 440 617-0950
  Westlake *(G-20115)*
Greene Fuel Plaza Inc..................G....... 937 532-4826
  Kettering *(G-11432)*
Hardy Industrial Tech LLC............D....... 440 350-6300
  Painesville *(G-15745)*
Homeland AG Fuels LLC..............G....... 216 763-1004
  Cleveland *(G-5415)*
Ishos Bros Fuel Ventures Inc..........G....... 586 634-0187
  Maumee *(G-13119)*
Ishos Bros Fuel Ventures Inc..........G....... 419 913-5718
  Toledo *(G-18355)*
L and S Express Fuel Center..........G....... 330 549-9566
  North Lima *(G-15174)*
Leaf Lono Earth Alterntv Fuels........G....... 614 829-7159
  Canal Winchester *(G-2505)*
Lost Nation Fuel........................G....... 440 951-9088
  Willoughby *(G-20362)*
M J S Oil Inc............................G....... 937 982-3519
  West Mansfield *(G-19944)*
Mart Plus Fuel..........................G....... 216 261-0420
  Euclid *(G-9425)*
North East Fuel Inc....................G....... 330 264-4454
  Wooster *(G-20633)*

FUELS: Ethanol

P S P Inc .... E 330 283-5635
  Kent *(G-11359)*
Patriot Energy LLC .... D 330 923-4442
  Cuyahoga Falls *(G-7903)*
Rex American Resources Corp .... C 937 276-3931
  Dayton *(G-8474)*
Santmyer Coml Fling Netwrk LLC .... G 330 262-2334
  Wooster *(G-20647)*
Speedway LLC .... A 937 864-3000
  Enon *(G-9387)*
Systech Environmental Corp .... E 800 888-8011
  Dayton *(G-8532)*
Vadose Syn Fuels Inc .... G 330 564-0545
  Munroe Falls *(G-14529)*
West Erie Fuel .... G 440 282-3493
  Lorain *(G-12137)*

FUELS: Jet

Jetfuel Sports Inc .... G 614 327-3300
  New Albany *(G-14629)*

FUELS: Oil

Capital City Oil Inc .... G 740 397-4483
  Mount Vernon *(G-14473)*
Husky Lima Refinery .... D 419 226-2300
  Lima *(G-11875)*
Knox Energy Inc .... F 740 927-6731
  Pataskala *(G-15835)*
Usalco LLC .... G 440 993-2721
  Ashtabula *(G-810)*

FUNDRAISING SVCS

Clovernook Center For The Bli .... C 513 522-3860
  Cincinnati *(G-3530)*

FUNERAL HOME

Van Wert Memorials LLC .... G 419 238-9067
  Van Wert *(G-19110)*

FUNERAL HOMES & SVCS

Bell Vault & Monument Works .... E 937 866-2444
  Miamisburg *(G-13643)*

FUNGICIDES OR HERBICIDES

Dow Chemical Company .... F 937 254-1550
  Dayton *(G-8166)*
Scotts Company LLC .... B 937 644-0011
  Marysville *(G-12809)*
Scotts Miracle-Gro Company .... E 937 578-5065
  Marysville *(G-12811)*

FUR: Hats

Blonde Swan .... F 419 307-8591
  Fremont *(G-10000)*

FURNACES & OVENS: Fuel-Fired

Facultatieve Tech Americas Inc .... E 330 723-6339
  Medina *(G-13259)*

FURNACES & OVENS: Indl

A Jacks Manufacturing Co .... E 216 531-1010
  Cleveland *(G-4591)*
Abp Induction LLC .... F 330 830-6252
  Massillon *(G-12958)*
Ajax Tocco Magnethermic Corp .... C 440 278-7200
  Wickliffe *(G-20197)*
Ajax Tocco Magnethermic Corp .... D 330 818-8080
  Canton *(G-2564)*
Armature Coil Equipment Inc .... F 216 267-6366
  Cleveland *(G-4734)*
Benko Products Inc .... E 440 934-2180
  Sheffield Village *(G-16966)*
CA Litzler Co Inc .... E 216 267-8020
  Cleveland *(G-4859)*
CA Litzler Holding Company .... D 216 267-8020
  Cleveland *(G-4860)*
Crescent Metal Products Inc .... C 440 350-1100
  Mentor *(G-13426)*
Delta H Technologies LLC .... E 740 756-7676
  Carroll *(G-2903)*
Delta H Technologies LLC .... G 614 561-8860
  Pickerington *(G-16045)*
Ebner Furnaces Inc .... D 330 335-2311
  Wadsworth *(G-19237)*
Hannon Company .... D 330 456-4728
  Canton *(G-7733)*
Haynn Construction Co Inc .... G 419 853-4747
  West Salem *(G-19954)*
I Cerco Inc .... D 740 982-2050
  Crooksville *(G-7816)*
Kaufman Engineered Systems Inc .... D 419 878-9727
  Waterville *(G-19499)*
Komar Industries Inc .... E 614 836-2366
  Groveport *(G-10497)*
L Haberny Co Inc .... G 440 543-5999
  Chagrin Falls *(G-3054)*
Lakeway Mfg Inc .... G 419 433-3030
  Huron *(G-11103)*
Lewco Inc .... C 419 625-4014
  Sandusky *(G-16822)*
Micropyretics Heaters Intl Inc .... F 513 772-0404
  Cincinnati *(G-4025)*
Pillar Induction .... G 262 317-5300
  Warren *(G-19431)*
R K Combustion & Controls .... G 937 444-9700
  Mount Orab *(G-14451)*
RAD-Con Inc .... E 440 871-5720
  Lakewood *(G-11534)*
Resilience Fund III LP .... F 216 292-0200
  Cleveland *(G-5979)*
Robbins Furnace Works Inc .... F 440 949-2292
  Sheffield Village *(G-16974)*
Selas Heat Technology Co LLC 800 523-6500
  Streetsboro *(G-17697)*
Stelter and Brinck Inc .... E 513 367-9300
  Harrison *(G-10672)*
Strohecker Incorporated .... E 330 426-9496
  East Palestine *(G-9085)*
Surface Combustion Inc 419 891-7150
  Maumee *(G-13151)*
T J F Inc .... F 419 878-4400
  Waterville *(G-19506)*
United McGill Corporation .... E 614 829-1200
  Groveport *(G-10516)*

FURNACES: Indl, Electric

Ajax Tocco Magnethermic Corp .... C 330 372-8511
  Warren *(G-19364)*
CMI Industry Americas Inc .... D 330 332-4661
  Salem *(G-16728)*

FURNACES: Warm Air, Electric

Columbus Heating & Vent Co .... C 614 274-1177
  Columbus *(G-6790)*

FURNITURE & CABINET STORES: Cabinets, Custom Work

Bobs Custom Str Interiors LLC .... G 567 316-7490
  Toledo *(G-18209)*
Kitchen Works Inc .... G 440 353-0939
  North Ridgeville *(G-15236)*
Newbury Woodworks .... G 440 564-5273
  Newbury *(G-14960)*
River East Custom Cabinets .... E 419 244-3226
  Toledo *(G-18502)*
Virgils Kitchens Inc .... G 440 355-5058
  Lagrange *(G-11497)*

FURNITURE & CABINET STORES: Custom

Fine Wood Design Inc .... G 440 327-0751
  North Ridgeville *(G-15225)*
Mel Heitkamp Builders Ltd .... G 419 375-0405
  Fort Recovery *(G-9825)*

FURNITURE & FIXTURES Factory

Custom Sink Top Mfg .... F 440 245-6220
  Lorain *(G-12087)*
Epix Tube Co Inc .... D 937 529-4858
  Dayton *(G-8184)*
Master Mfg Co Inc .... E 216 641-0500
  Cleveland *(G-5632)*

FURNITURE PARTS: Metal

Pucel Enterprises Inc .... D 216 881-4604
  Cleveland *(G-5933)*

FURNITURE REFINISHING SVCS

Dura Bilt Drapery & Upholstery .... F 440 269-8438
  Willoughby *(G-20311)*
Feslers Refinishing .... G 740 622-4849
  Coshocton *(G-7733)*
Mielke Furniture Repair Inc .... G 419 625-4572
  Sandusky *(G-16830)*
Soft Touch Wood LLC .... E 330 545-4204
  Girard *(G-10266)*

FURNITURE REPAIR & MAINTENANCE SVCS

Furniture Concepts Inc .... F 216 292-9100
  Cleveland *(G-5280)*
Joseph G Betz & Sons .... G 513 481-0322
  Cincinnati *(G-3884)*

FURNITURE STOCK & PARTS: Carvings, Wood

Plank and Hide Co .... F 888 462-6852
  Cincinnati *(G-4165)*
Urbn Timber LLC .... G 614 981-3043
  Columbus *(G-7565)*

FURNITURE STOCK & PARTS: Chair Seats, Hardwood

Hillcrest .... G 740 824-4849
  Brinkhaven *(G-2081)*
Hillside Wood Ltd 330 359-5991
  Millersburg *(G-14092)*

FURNITURE STOCK/PARTS: Chair Stk, Hardwd, Turnd, Shapd/Carvd

Valleyview Wood Turning Co .... F 330 763-0407
  Millersburg *(G-14142)*

FURNITURE STORES

Archbold Furniture Co .... E 567 444-4666
  Archbold *(G-638)*
Bruening Glass Works Inc .... G 440 333-4768
  Cleveland *(G-4846)*
Eoi Inc .... F 740 201-3300
  Lewis Center *(G-11760)*
Fortner Upholstering Inc 614 475-8282
  Columbus *(G-6933)*
Furniture By Otmar Inc .... F 937 435-2039
  Dayton *(G-8211)*
Furniture By Otmar Inc 513 891-5141
  Cincinnati *(G-3717)*
Hallmark Industries Inc .... E 937 864-7378
  Springfield *(G-17410)*
Home Stor & Off Solutions Inc .... F 216 362-4660
  Cleveland *(G-5414)*
J-J Berlin Woodcraft Inc .... G 330 893-9171
  Berlin *(G-1643)*
Oakwood Furniture Inc .... G 740 896-3162
  Lowell *(G-12247)*
Ohio Table Pad Company .... D 419 872-6400
  Perrysburg *(G-15986)*
Precision Fab Products Inc .... G 937 526-5681
  Versailles *(G-19189)*
Sailors Tailor Inc .... G 937 862-7781
  Spring Valley *(G-17318)*
Stiglers Woodworks .... G 513 733-3009
  Blue Ash *(G-1851)*
Wahlies Cstm Cft Drapery Uphl 419 229-1731
  Lima *(G-11958)*

FURNITURE STORES: Cabinets, Kitchen, Exc Custom Made

American Craft Hardware LLC .... G 440 746-0098
  Cleveland *(G-4686)*

FURNITURE STORES: Custom Made, Exc Cabinets

Kennewegs Wood Products .... G 330 832-1540
  Massillon *(G-13010)*
Urbn Timber LLC .... G 614 981-3043
  Columbus *(G-7565)*

FURNITURE STORES: Office

COS Blueprint Inc .... F 330 376-0022
  Akron *(G-122)*
Recycled Systems Furniture Inc .... E 614 880-9110
  Worthington *(G-20701)*
Senator International Inc .... E 419 887-5806
  Maumee *(G-13143)*

PRODUCT SECTION

FURNITURE: Household, Wood

W B Mason Co Inc .... E 888 926-2766
  Cleveland *(G-6277)*

FURNITURE STORES: Outdoor & Garden

Great Day Improvements LLC .... G 330 468-0700
  Macedonia *(G-12300)*
Queen City Awning & Tent Co .... E 513 530-9660
  Cincinnati *(G-4234)*

FURNITURE WHOLESALERS

Friends Service Co Inc .... F 800 427-1704
  Dayton *(G-8208)*
Friends Service Co Inc .... G 800 427-1704
  Kent *(G-11322)*
Friends Service Co Inc .... D 419 427-1704
  Findlay *(G-9690)*
Sauder Woodworking Co .... A 419 446-2711
  Archbold *(G-668)*
Sauder Woodworking Co .... G 419 446-2711
  Archbold *(G-669)*
Urbn Timber LLC .... G 614 981-3043
  Columbus *(G-7565)*

FURNITURE, BARBER & BEAUTY SHOP

Natural Beauty Hc Express .... G 440 459-1776
  Mayfield Heights *(G-13169)*

FURNITURE, CHURCH: Concrete

Gdy Installations Inc .... E 419 467-0036
  Toledo *(G-18302)*

FURNITURE, MATTRESSES: Wholesalers

Ahmf Inc .... E 614 921-1223
  Columbus *(G-6553)*
Bailey & Jensen Inc .... F 937 272-1784
  Centerville *(G-2998)*

FURNITURE, OFFICE: Wholesalers

Furniture Concepts Inc .... F 216 292-9100
  Cleveland *(G-5280)*
Wasserstrom Company .... B 614 228-6525
  Columbus *(G-7591)*
Wasserstrom Company .... F 614 228-2233
  Columbus *(G-7592)*
William J Dupps .... G 419 734-2126
  Port Clinton *(G-16264)*

FURNITURE, WHOLESALE: Bedsprings

Mantua Manufacturing Co .... C 800 333-8333
  Solon *(G-17188)*

FURNITURE, WHOLESALE: Chairs

Gasser Chair Co Inc .... F 330 534-2234
  Youngstown *(G-20913)*
Millwood Wholesale Inc .... F 330 359-6109
  Dundee *(G-9023)*

FURNITURE, WHOLESALE: Filing Units

Jsc Employee Leasing Corp .... F 330 773-8971
  Akron *(G-228)*

FURNITURE, WHOLESALE: Racks

Partitions Plus LLC .... F 419 422-2600
  Findlay *(G-9740)*

FURNITURE, WHOLESALE: Tables, Occasional

Progressive Furniture Inc .... E 419 446-4500
  Archbold *(G-664)*

FURNITURE, WHOLESALE: Unfinished

J & F Furniture Shop .... G 330 852-2478
  Sugarcreek *(G-17850)*

FURNITURE: Bar furniture

Lasting Impression Llc .... G 614 806-1186
  Columbus *(G-7117)*
Wood Works .... G 330 674-0333
  Millersburg *(G-14152)*

FURNITURE: Bed Frames & Headboards, Wood

Progressive Furniture Inc .... E 419 446-4500
  Archbold *(G-664)*
Yoders Woodworking .... G 888 818-0568
  Millersburg *(G-14156)*

FURNITURE: Bedroom, Wood

Andal Woodworking .... F 330 897-8059
  Baltic *(G-1022)*
Farmside Wood .... G 330 695-5100
  Apple Creek *(G-605)*
Simmons Company .... G 614 871-8088
  Grove City *(G-10468)*

FURNITURE: Beds, Household, Incl Folding & Cabinet, Metal

Invacare Corporation .... A 440 329-6000
  Elyria *(G-9272)*
Invacare Corporation .... D 800 333-6900
  Elyria *(G-9273)*
Invacare Holdings Corporation .... G 440 329-6000
  Elyria *(G-9276)*
Invacare International Corp .... G 440 329-6000
  Elyria *(G-9277)*

FURNITURE: Bookcases & Partitions, Office, Exc Wood

Hobart Cabinet Company .... G 937 335-4666
  Troy *(G-18670)*
Innovative Woodworking Inc .... G 513 531-1940
  Cincinnati *(G-3850)*

FURNITURE: Cabinets & Filing Drawers, Office, Exc Wood

East Woodworking Company .... G 216 791-5950
  Cleveland *(G-5140)*
Jsc Employee Leasing Corp .... F 330 773-8971
  Akron *(G-228)*

FURNITURE: Cabinets & Vanities, Medicine, Metal

Installed Building Pdts LLC .... E 614 308-9900
  Columbus *(G-7029)*

FURNITURE: Chairs, Bentwood

Hochstetler Wood .... F 330 893-2384
  Millersburg *(G-14093)*

FURNITURE: Chairs, Dental

Dental Pure Water Inc .... F 440 234-0890
  Berea *(G-1601)*

FURNITURE: Chairs, Folding

Gasser Chair Co Inc .... F 330 534-2234
  Youngstown *(G-20913)*
Sauder Manufacturing Co .... C 419 682-3061
  Stryker *(G-17833)*

FURNITURE: Chairs, Household Upholstered

Gasser Chair Co Inc .... F 330 534-2234
  Youngstown *(G-20913)*

FURNITURE: Chairs, Household Wood

Colonial Woodcraft Inc .... F 513 779-8088
  Lebanon *(G-11642)*

FURNITURE: Chairs, Office Exc Wood

Gasser Chair Co Inc .... F 330 534-2234
  Youngstown *(G-20913)*
Geograph Industries Inc .... E 513 202-9200
  Harrison *(G-10643)*
Veterans Representative Co LLC .... F 330 779-0768
  Youngstown *(G-21061)*

FURNITURE: Chairs, Office Wood

Buzz Seating Inc .... F 877 263-5737
  Cincinnati *(G-3432)*
Gasser Chair Co Inc .... E 330 534-2234
  Youngstown *(G-20912)*

FURNITURE: Church

Sauder Manufacturing Co .... C 419 445-7670
  Archbold *(G-666)*

FURNITURE: Club Room, Wood

Paradise Inc .... G 330 928-3789
  Cuyahoga Falls *(G-7902)*

FURNITURE: Console Tables, Wood

Dorel Home Furnishings Inc .... C 419 447-7448
  Tiffin *(G-18058)*

FURNITURE: Desks & Tables, Office, Exc Wood

Office Magic Inc .... F 510 782-6100
  Medina *(G-13310)*

FURNITURE: Dining Room, Wood

Canal Dover Furniture LLC .... D 330 359-5375
  Millersburg *(G-14076)*

FURNITURE: Fiberglass & Plastic

Evenflo Company Inc .... D 937 773-3971
  Troy *(G-18654)*
Evenflo Company Inc .... C 937 415-3300
  Miamisburg *(G-13666)*
Office Magic Inc .... F 510 782-6100
  Medina *(G-13310)*
Sauder Woodworking Co .... G 419 446-2711
  Archbold *(G-669)*

FURNITURE: Foundations & Platforms

Timken Foundation .... G 330 452-1144
  Canton *(G-2840)*

FURNITURE: Frames, Box Springs Or Bedsprings, Metal

Albion Industries Inc .... E 440 238-1955
  Strongsville *(G-17707)*
Mantua Manufacturing Co .... C 800 333-8333
  Solon *(G-17188)*

FURNITURE: Hospital

Brodwill LLC .... G 513 258-2716
  Cincinnati *(G-3423)*

FURNITURE: Hotel

Textiles Inc .... G 614 529-8642
  Hilliard *(G-10869)*

FURNITURE: Household, Metal

Bailey & Jensen Inc .... F 937 272-1784
  Centerville *(G-2998)*
Medallion Lighting Corporation .... E 440 255-8383
  Mentor *(G-13514)*
Metal Fabricating Corporation .... D 216 631-8121
  Cleveland *(G-5658)*
Pine Acres Woodcraft .... G 330 852-0190
  Sugarcreek *(G-17857)*

FURNITURE: Household, NEC

Entertainment Junction .... D 513 326-1100
  Cincinnati *(G-3644)*

FURNITURE: Household, Upholstered, Exc Wood Or Metal

Bulk Carrier Trnsp Eqp Co .... E 330 339-3333
  New Philadelphia *(G-14762)*
John Purdum .... G 513 897-9686
  Waynesville *(G-19569)*
Kitchens By Rutenschroer Inc .... F 513 251-8333
  Cincinnati *(G-3914)*
Sailors Tailor Inc .... G 937 862-7781
  Spring Valley *(G-17318)*

FURNITURE: Household, Wood

Allied Plastic Co Inc .... G 419 389-1688
  Toledo *(G-18165)*
Andy Raber .... G 740 622-1386
  Fresno *(G-10066)*

Employee Codes: A=Over 500 employees, B=251-500
C=101-250, D=51-100, E=20-50, F=10-19, G=3-9

Ariels Oak Inc ....E 330 343-7453
Sherrodsville (G-16990)
Armada Fortress LLC ....G 330 953-2185
Youngstown (G-20847)
Artistic Finishes Inc ....F 440 951-7850
Willoughby (G-20281)
Basic Cases Inc ....G 216 662-3900
Cleveland (G-4795)
Battershell Cabinets ....G 419 542-6448
Hicksville (G-10777)
Benners Custom Woodworking ....G 513 932-9159
Lebanon (G-11636)
Berlin Gardens Gazebos Ltd ....E 330 893-3411
Berlin (G-1637)
Briar Hill Furniture ....G 330 223-2109
Kensington (G-11284)
Cabinet Systems Inc ....G 440 237-1924
Cleveland (G-4861)
Carlisle Oak ....G 330 852-8734
Sugarcreek (G-17845)
Clearwater Wood Group LLC ....G 567 644-9951
Hebron (G-10739)
Criswell Furniture LLC ....F 330 695-2082
Fredericksburg (G-9947)
Diversified Products & Svcs ....C 740 393-6202
Mount Vernon (G-14478)
Dutch Heritage Woodcraft ....E 330 893-2211
Berlin (G-1641)
Dutch Legacy LLC ....G 330 359-0270
Dundee (G-9018)
Dutch Valley Woodcraft Ltd ....G 330 695-2364
Fredericksburg (G-9949)
Fleetwood Custom Countertops ....F 740 965-9833
Johnstown (G-11265)
Flottemesch Anthony & Son ....F 513 561-1212
Cincinnati (G-3696)
Furniture By Otmar Inc ....F 937 435-2039
Dayton (G-8211)
Furniture By Otmar Inc ....G 513 891-5141
Cincinnati (G-3717)
G R K Manufacturing Co Inc ....E 513 863-3131
Hamilton (G-10563)
Gasser Chair Co Inc ....D 330 759-2234
Youngstown (G-20914)
Grabo Interiors Inc ....G 216 391-6677
Cleveland (G-5335)
Green Acres Furniture Ltd ....F 330 359-6251
Navarre (G-14574)
Hill Finishing ....G 740 623-0650
Millersburg (G-14091)
Hochstetler Wood Ltd ....F 330 893-1601
Millersburg (G-14094)
Holmes Panel ....G 330 897-5040
Baltic (G-1031)
Hopewood Inc ....E 330 359-5656
Millersburg (G-14100)
Idx Corporation ....C 937 401-3225
Dayton (G-8259)
Integral Design Inc ....F 216 524-0555
Cleveland (G-5462)
J & F Furniture Shop ....G 330 852-2478
Sugarcreek (G-17850)
J-J Berlin Woodcraft Inc ....G 330 893-9171
Berlin (G-1643)
Jeffco Sheltered Workshop ....E 740 264-4608
Steubenville (G-17539)
Joe P Fischer Woodcraft ....G 513 474-4316
Cincinnati (G-3877)
Ken Harper ....C 740 439-4452
Byesville (G-2388)
Kencraft Co Inc ....G 419 536-0333
Toledo (G-18364)
Kenway Corp ....G 937 767-1660
Yellow Springs (G-20809)
Kitchens By Rutenschroer Inc ....F 513 251-8333
Cincinnati (G-3914)
Lauber Manufacturing Co ....G 419 446-2450
Archbold (G-654)
Legacy Oak and Hardwoods LLC ....F 330 859-2656
Zoarville (G-21196)
Lima Millwork Inc ....E 419 331-3303
Elida (G-9195)
Mark Rasche ....G 614 882-1810
Westerville (G-20009)
Masco Cbinetry Middlefield LLC ....D 440 632-5058
Middlefield (G-13819)
Michaels Pre-Cast Con Pdts ....F 513 683-1292
Loveland (G-12215)
Mielke Furniture Repair Inc ....G 419 625-4572
Sandusky (G-16830)
Miller Cabinet Ltd ....E 614 873-4221
Plain City (G-16203)
Mini Graphics Inc ....G 513 563-8600
Cincinnati (G-4030)
N Wasserstrom & Sons Inc ....D 614 737-5410
Columbus (G-7207)
P Graham Dunn Inc ....D 330 828-2105
Dalton (G-7949)
Patrician Furniture Builders ....G 330 746-6354
Youngstown (G-20996)
Penwood Mfg ....G 330 359-5600
Fresno (G-10069)
R A Hamed International Inc ....F 330 247-0190
Twinsburg (G-18844)
R D Cook Company LLC ....G 614 262-0550
Columbus (G-7372)
Regal Cabinet Inc ....G 419 865-3932
Toledo (G-18500)
Richard Benhase & Associates ....F 513 772-1896
Cincinnati (G-4267)
Rnr Enterprises LLC ....F 330 852-3022
Sugarcreek (G-17862)
Specialty Services Inc ....G 614 421-1599
Columbus (G-7469)
Stark Truss Company Inc ....D 330 478-2100
Canton (G-2825)
Stark Truss Company Inc ....D 419 298-3777
Edgerton (G-9181)
Stephen J Page ....G 865 951-3316
Williamsburg (G-20255)
Textiles Inc ....C 740 852-0782
London (G-12070)
Textiles Inc ....G 614 529-8642
Hilliard (G-10869)
Vocational Services Inc ....C 216 431-8085
Cleveland (G-6267)
Waller Brothers Stone Company ....E 740 858-1948
Mc Dermott (G-13195)
Weaver Woodcraft L L C ....G 330 695-2150
Apple Creek (G-624)
Western Reserve Furniture Co ....G 440 235-6216
North Olmsted (G-15203)
Wine Cellar Innovations LLC ....C 513 321-3733
Cincinnati (G-4513)

FURNITURE: Hydraulic Barber & Beauty Shop Chairs

Global Manufacturing Inds ....G 513 271-2180
Cincinnati (G-3764)

FURNITURE: Institutional, Exc Wood

Absolutely Paper Established ....G 216 932-4822
Cleveland (G-4602)
Bell Vault & Monument Works ....E 937 866-2444
Miamisburg (G-13643)
Franklin Cabinet Company Inc ....E 937 743-9606
Franklin (G-9884)
General Motors LLC ....A 216 265-5000
Cleveland (G-5312)
Global Furnishings Inc ....G 216 595-0901
Cleveland (G-5325)
Grand-Rock Company Inc ....E 440 639-2000
Painesville (G-15742)
Granite Industries Inc ....D 419 445-4733
Archbold (G-651)
Hann Manufacturing Inc ....E 740 962-3752
McConnelsville (G-13206)
McGill Septic Tank Co ....E 330 876-2171
Kinsman (G-11465)
Michaels Pre-Cast Con Pdts ....F 513 683-1292
Loveland (G-12215)
Mock Woodworking Company LLC ....E 740 452-2701
Zanesville (G-21157)
Modern Manufacturing Inc ....F 513 251-3600
Cincinnati (G-4039)
N Wasserstrom & Sons Inc ....D 614 737-5410
Columbus (G-7207)
Oberfields LLC ....F 614 252-0955
Columbus (G-7237)
Quality Seating Company Inc ....E 330 747-0181
Youngstown (G-21009)
Soft Touch Wood LLC ....E 330 545-4204
Girard (G-10266)
Tiffin Metal Products Co ....C 419 447-8414
Tiffin (G-18088)
Trim Systems Operating Corp ....C 614 289-5360
New Albany (G-14639)
Yanfeng US Automotive ....D 419 662-4905
Northwood (G-15354)

FURNITURE: Juvenile, Metal

Angels Landing Inc ....G 513 687-3681
Moraine (G-14330)

FURNITURE: Juvenile, Wood

Foundations Worldwide Inc ....E 330 722-5033
Medina (G-13264)

FURNITURE: Kitchen & Dining Room

Millwood Wholesale Inc ....F 330 359-6109
Dundee (G-9023)
Tri State Countertop Service ....G 740 354-3663
Portsmouth (G-16304)

FURNITURE: Lawn & Garden, Except Wood & Metal

G Keener & Co ....G 937 846-1210
New Carlisle (G-14666)
Poly Concepts LLC ....G 419 678-3300
Saint Henry (G-16666)
Valley View Woodcraft ....G 330 852-3000
Sugarcreek (G-17874)

FURNITURE: Lawn, Exc Wood, Metal, Stone Or Concrete

Hershy Way Ltd ....G 330 893-2809
Millersburg (G-14090)

FURNITURE: Living Room, Upholstered On Wood Frames

Hallmark Industries Inc ....E 937 864-7378
Springfield (G-17410)
Quality Fabrications LLC ....G 330 695-2478
Fredericksburg (G-9956)

FURNITURE: Mattresses & Foundations

Ahmf Inc ....E 614 921-1223
Columbus (G-6553)
H Goodman Inc ....D 216 341-0200
Newburgh Heights (G-14936)
Homecare Mattress Inc ....F 937 746-2556
Franklin (G-9889)
Innocor Foam Tech - Acp Inc ....F 419 647-4172
Spencerville (G-17309)
Ohio Mattress ....G 740 739-8219
Lancaster (G-11593)
Original Mattress Factory Inc ....G 216 661-8388
Cleveland (G-5819)
Original Mattress Factory Inc ....G 513 752-6600
Cincinnati (G-3260)
Tep Bedding Grp Inc ....E 440 437-7700
Orwell (G-15635)
Tru Comfort Mattress ....G 614 595-8600
Dublin (G-9006)
Walter F Stephens Jr Inc ....E 937 746-0521
Franklin (G-9930)
White Dove Mattress Ltd ....E 216 341-0200
Newburgh Heights (G-14945)

FURNITURE: Mattresses, Box & Bedsprings

Banner Mattress Co Inc ....G 419 324-7181
Toledo (G-18198)
Heritage Sleep Products LLC ....E 440 437-4425
Orwell (G-15631)
Midwest Quality Bedding Inc ....G 614 504-5971
Columbus (G-7182)
National Bedding Company LLC ....G 513 825-4172
Cincinnati (G-4060)
SSP Tennessee LLC ....G 614 279-8850
Columbus (G-7483)

FURNITURE: Mattresses, Innerspring Or Box Spring

Quilting Inc ....D 614 504-5971
Plain City (G-16209)
Sealy Mattress Mfg Co Inc ....D 800 697-3259
Medina (G-13338)

FURNITURE: Novelty, Wood

Feslers Refinishing ....G 740 622-4849
Coshocton (G-7733)

FURNITURE: Office Panel Systems, Exc Wood

GMI Companies Inc	C	513 932-3445	
Lebanon *(G-11657)*			
GMI Companies Inc	G	937 981-0244	
Greenfield *(G-10348)*			
H S Morgan Limited Partnership		513 870-4400	
Fairfield *(G-9502)*			
Workstream Inc	D	513 870-4400	
Fairfield *(G-9577)*			

FURNITURE: Office Panel Systems, Wood

GMI Companies Inc	C	513 932-3445	
Lebanon *(G-11657)*			
GMI Companies Inc	G	937 981-0244	
Greenfield *(G-10348)*			
H S Morgan Limited Partnership		513 870-4400	
Fairfield *(G-9502)*			
Workstream Inc	D	513 870-4400	
Fairfield *(G-9577)*			

FURNITURE: Office, Exc Wood

Axess International LLC	G	330 460-4840	
Brunswick *(G-2189)*			
Casco Mfg Solutions Inc	D	513 681-0003	
Cincinnati *(G-3447)*			
Custom Millcraft Corp	E	513 874-7080	
West Chester *(G-19690)*			
Design Trac Inc	G	330 759-3131	
Youngstown *(G-20889)*			
Ergo Desktop LLC	E	567 890-3746	
Celina *(G-2960)*			
Frontier Signs & Displays Inc	G	513 367-0813	
Harrison *(G-10642)*			
Furniture Concepts Inc	F	216 292-9100	
Cleveland *(G-5280)*			
Gasser Chair Co Inc	D	330 759-2234	
Youngstown *(G-20914)*			
Infinium Wall Systems Inc	E	440 572-5000	
Strongsville *(G-17754)*			
M/W International Inc	F	440 526-6900	
Broadview Heights *(G-2094)*			
Mark Rasche	G	614 882-1810	
Westerville *(G-20009)*			
Marsh Industries Inc	E	330 308-8667	
New Philadelphia *(G-14784)*			
Metal Fabricating Corporation	D	216 631-8121	
Cleveland *(G-5658)*			
National Electro-Coatings Inc	D	216 898-0080	
Cleveland *(G-5724)*			
Patriot Seating Inc	F	330 779-0768	
Youngstown *(G-20997)*			
Pucel Enterprises Inc	D	216 881-4604	
Cleveland *(G-5933)*			
R B Mfg Co	F	419 626-9464	
Wadsworth *(G-19270)*			
Recycled Systems Furniture Inc	E	614 880-9110	
Worthington *(G-20701)*			
Senator International Inc	E	419 887-5806	
Maumee *(G-13143)*			
Starr Fabricating Inc	D	330 394-9891	
Vienna *(G-19210)*			
Tiffin Metal Products Co	C	419 447-8414	
Tiffin *(G-18088)*			

FURNITURE: Office, Wood

Basic Cases Inc	G	216 662-3900	
Cleveland *(G-4795)*			
Creative Woodworks	G	440 355-8155	
Grafton *(G-10295)*			
Crow Works LLC	E	888 811-2769	
Killbuck *(G-11450)*			
DIng Products	G	440 442-7777	
Cleveland *(G-5096)*			
Dutch Design Products LLC	E	330 674-1167	
Fredericksburg *(G-9948)*			
Dvuv LLC	F	216 741-5511	
Cleveland *(G-5124)*			
Frontier Signs & Displays Inc	G	513 367-0813	
Harrison *(G-10642)*			
Gasser Chair Co Inc	D	330 759-2234	
Youngstown *(G-20914)*			
Global Design Factory LLC	G	330 322-8775	
Hudson *(G-11047)*			
Idx Corporation	C	937 401-3225	
Dayton *(G-8259)*			
LAtelier Custom Woodworking	G	234 759-3359	
North Lima *(G-15175)*			
Lima Millwork Inc	E	419 331-3303	
Elida *(G-9195)*			
Mark Rasche	G	614 882-1810	
Westerville *(G-20009)*			
Miller Cabinet Ltd	E	614 873-4221	
Plain City *(G-16203)*			
National Electro-Coatings Inc	D	216 898-0080	
Cleveland *(G-5724)*			
Sauder Manufacturing Co	C	419 682-3061	
Stryker *(G-17833)*			
Senator International Inc	E	419 887-5806	
Maumee *(G-13143)*			
Stephen J Page	G	865 951-3316	
Williamsburg *(G-20255)*			
Symatic Inc	E	330 225-1510	
Brunswick *(G-2243)*			
Tiffin Metal Products Co	C	419 447-8414	
Tiffin *(G-18088)*			
Yellow Tang Interiors LLC	G	330 629-9279	
Youngstown *(G-21069)*			

FURNITURE: Outdoor, Wood

Cedar Outdoor Furniture Inc	G	330 863-2580	
Malvern *(G-12386)*			

FURNITURE: Picnic Tables Or Benches, Park

City of Conneaut	G	440 599-7071	
Conneaut *(G-7643)*			
City of Kent	F	330 673-8897	
Kent *(G-11304)*			
County of Summit	G	330 865-8065	
Akron *(G-124)*			

FURNITURE: Play Pens, Children's, Wood

Western & Southern Lf Insur Co	A	513 629-1800	
Cincinnati *(G-4503)*			

FURNITURE: Restaurant

Joseph Knapp	F	330 832-3515	
Massillon *(G-13006)*			
Quality Seating Company Inc	E	330 747-0181	
Youngstown *(G-21009)*			
Rightway Food Service	G	419 223-4075	
Lima *(G-11932)*			

FURNITURE: School

Shiffler Equipment Sales Inc	E	440 285-9175	
Chardon *(G-3136)*			
W C Heller & Co Inc	F	419 485-3176	
Montpelier *(G-14321)*			

FURNITURE: Silverware Chests, Wood

East Oberlin Cabinets	G	440 775-1166	
Oberlin *(G-15493)*			

FURNITURE: Stools, Household, Wood

Hen House Inc	E	419 663-3377	
Norwalk *(G-15398)*			

FURNITURE: Table Tops, Marble

Accent Manufacturing Inc	F	330 724-7704	
Norton *(G-15355)*			

FURNITURE: Tables & Table Tops, Wood

Richmonds Woodworks Inc	F	330 343-8184	
New Philadelphia *(G-14798)*			
Trailway Wood	F	330 893-9966	
Dundee *(G-9028)*			

FURNITURE: Unfinished, Wood

Archbold Furniture Co	E	567 444-4666	
Archbold *(G-638)*			
Chris Haughey	G	937 652-3338	
Urbana *(G-18982)*			

FURNITURE: Upholstered

Central Design Services	G	513 829-7027	
Fairfield *(G-9489)*			
Dura Bilt Drapery & Upholstery	F	440 269-8438	
Willoughby *(G-20311)*			
Fortner Upholstering Inc	F	614 475-8282	
Columbus *(G-6933)*			
Franklin Cabinet Company Inc	E	937 743-9606	
Franklin *(G-9884)*			
G R K Manufacturing Co Inc	E	513 863-3131	
Hamilton *(G-10563)*			
H Goodman Inc	D	216 341-0200	
Newburgh Heights *(G-14936)*			
Hopewood Inc	E	330 359-5656	
Millersburg *(G-14100)*			
Joseph G Betz & Sons	G	513 481-0322	
Cincinnati *(G-3884)*			
Kenneth Shannon	G	513 777-8888	
Liberty Twp *(G-11826)*			
Kroehler Furniture Mfg Co Inc	B	828 459-9865	
Columbus *(G-7102)*			
LAtelier Custom Woodworking	G	234 759-3359	
North Lima *(G-15175)*			
Mastercraft Mfg Inc	E	330 893-3366	
Youngstown *(G-20967)*			
Njm Furniture Outlet Inc	F	330 893-3514	
Millersburg *(G-14118)*			
Robert Mayo Industries	G	330 426-2587	
East Palestine *(G-9083)*			
Sauder Woodworking Co	A	419 446-2711	
Archbold *(G-668)*			
Stiglers Woodworks	G	513 733-3009	
Blue Ash *(G-1851)*			
Weavers Furniture Ltd	F	330 852-2701	
Sugarcreek *(G-17877)*			

FURNITURE: Vehicle

Mayflower Vehicle Systems LLC	G	419 668-8132	
New Albany *(G-14630)*			
Wurms Woodworking Company	E	419 492-2184	
New Washington *(G-14834)*			

FUSE MOUNTINGS: Electric Power

Regal Beloit America Inc	C	419 352-8441	
Bowling Green *(G-1996)*			

Furs

Fin Feather Fur	G	330 493-8300	
Canton *(G-2671)*			
Sword Furs	G	440 249-5001	
Westlake *(G-20165)*			

GAMES & TOYS: Banks

First Merit	G	330 849-8750	
Akron *(G-172)*			
Mag-Nif Inc	D	440 255-9366	
Mentor *(G-13508)*			

GAMES & TOYS: Baskets

American Traditions Basket Co	E	330 854-0900	
Canal Fulton *(G-2474)*			

GAMES & TOYS: Bingo Boards

Cowells - Arrow Bingo Company	G	216 961-3500	
Cleveland *(G-5034)*			

GAMES & TOYS: Board Games, Children's & Adults'

Late For Sky Production Co	E	513 531-4400	
Cincinnati *(G-3932)*			

GAMES & TOYS: Cars, Play, Children's Vehicles

Brp Inc	G	440 988-4398	
Amherst *(G-556)*			

GAMES & TOYS: Child Restraint Seats, Automotive

Evenflo Company Inc	D	937 773-3971	
Troy *(G-18654)*			
Evenflo Company Inc	C	937 415-3300	
Miamisburg *(G-13666)*			
Recaro Child Safety LLC	E	248 904-1570	
Cincinnati *(G-4253)*			
Rockys Hinge Co	G	330 539-6296	
Girard *(G-10265)*			

GAMES & TOYS: Craft & Hobby Kits & Sets

Gingerbread N Bows	G	740 945-1027	
Scio *(G-16877)*			
Larose Industries LLC	E	419 237-1600	
Fayette *(G-9634)*			

GAMES & TOYS: Craft & Hobby Kits & Sets

Michaels Stores Inc ....E 330 505-1168
  Niles *(G-15023)*
Ramon Robinson ....G 330 883-3244
  Vienna *(G-19208)*

GAMES & TOYS: Dollhouses & Furniture

Lawbre Co ....G 330 637-3363
  Cortland *(G-7712)*

GAMES & TOYS: Dolls, Exc Stuffed Toy Animals

Eboni Corner ....G 724 518-3065
  Cleveland *(G-5154)*
Gail J Shumaker Originals ....G 330 659-0680
  Richfield *(G-16472)*
Huston Gifts Dolls and Flowers ....G 740 775-9141
  Chillicothe *(G-3193)*
Middleton Llyd Dolls Inc ....G 740 989-2082
  Coolville *(G-7674)*
Middleton Lee Original Dolls ....F
  Columbus *(G-7180)*

GAMES & TOYS: Electronic

Moonstruck Games Inc ....G 513 721-3900
  Cincinnati *(G-4044)*
Weenk Labs LLC ....G 614 448-0160
  Columbus *(G-7596)*

GAMES & TOYS: Game Machines, Exc Coin-Operated

Applied Concepts Inc ....F 440 229-5033
  Willoughby *(G-20277)*

GAMES & TOYS: Kits, Science, Incl Microscopes/Chemistry Sets

Dunecraft Inc ....E 800 306-4168
  Cleveland *(G-5119)*
M G 3d ....F 614 262-0956
  Columbus *(G-7140)*
Molecular Dimensions Inc ....G 419 740-6600
  Maumee *(G-13137)*

GAMES & TOYS: Miniature Dolls, Collectors'

Alice Beougher ....G 740 927-2470
  Etna *(G-9388)*

GAMES & TOYS: Models, Airplane, Toy & Hobby

Brown Dave Products Inc ....F 513 738-1576
  Hamilton *(G-10543)*
Erockets LLC ....G 616 460-2678
  Dayton *(G-8187)*
Ready Made Rc LLC ....G 740 936-4500
  Lewis Center *(G-11775)*

GAMES & TOYS: Models, Automobile & Truck, Toy & Hobby

Parma International Inc ....E 440 237-8650
  North Royalton *(G-15293)*
Watch-Us Inc ....E 513 829-8870
  Fairfield *(G-9575)*

GAMES & TOYS: Models, Railroad, Toy & Hobby

D L H Locomotive Works ....G 937 629-0321
  Springfield *(G-17383)*

GAMES & TOYS: Strollers, Baby, Vehicle

Foundations Worldwide Inc ....E 330 722-5033
  Medina *(G-13264)*
Mahoning Valley Manufacturing ....G 330 537-4492
  Beloit *(G-1571)*

GAMES & TOYS: Structural Toy Sets

Hershberger Lawn Structures ....F 330 674-3900
  Millersburg *(G-14088)*

GAMES & TOYS: Wagons, Coaster, Express & Play, Children's

Berlin Wood Products Inc ....E 330 893-3281
  Berlin *(G-1639)*

GARAGE DOOR REPAIR SVCS

A L Callahan Door Sales ....G 419 884-3667
  Mansfield *(G-12399)*
Division Overhead Door Inc ....F 513 872-0888
  Cincinnati *(G-3597)*

GARBAGE CONTAINERS: Plastic

1 888 U Pitch It ....G 440 796-9028
  Mentor *(G-13368)*
MCS Midwest LLC ....F 513 217-0805
  Franklin *(G-9898)*

GARBAGE DISPOSALS: Household

Anaheim Manufacturing Company ....E 800 767-6293
  North Olmsted *(G-15181)*

GARBAGE DISPOSERS & COMPACTORS: Commercial

City of Ashland ....G 419 289-8728
  Ashland *(G-694)*
Knight Manufacturing Co Inc ....G 740 676-5516
  Shadyside *(G-16923)*
Master Disposers Inc ....F 513 553-2289
  New Richmond *(G-14812)*

GAS & OIL FIELD EXPLORATION SVCS

Alliance Petroleum Corporation ....D 330 493-0440
  Canton *(G-2569)*
Alteirs Oil Inc ....G 740 347-4335
  Corning *(G-7699)*
Antero Resources Corporation ....D 740 760-1000
  Marietta *(G-12603)*
Atlas America Inc ....E 330 339-3155
  New Philadelphia *(G-14759)*
Bakerwell Inc ....D 614 898-7590
  Westerville *(G-19979)*
Bands Company Inc ....G 330 674-0446
  Millersburg *(G-14062)*
Beck Energy Corp ....F 330 297-6891
  Ravenna *(G-16368)*
Belden & Blake Corporation ....E 330 602-5551
  Dover *(G-8808)*
Bergstein Oil & Gas Partnr ....G 513 771-6220
  Cincinnati *(G-3390)*
Blue Racer Midstream LLC ....F 740 630-7556
  Cambridge *(G-2428)*
Bocor Holdings LLC ....G 330 494-1221
  Canton *(G-2594)*
Canton Oil Well Service Inc ....F 330 494-1221
  Canton *(G-2613)*
Capital City Energy Group Inc ....G 614 485-3110
  Powell *(G-16312)*
Capital Oil & Gas Inc ....G 330 533-1828
  Austintown *(G-931)*
Cgas Exploration Inc ....G 614 436-4631
  Worthington *(G-20679)*
Chevron Ae Resources LLC ....E 330 654-4343
  Deerfield *(G-8607)*
Columbus Oilfield Exploration ....G 614 895-9520
  Powell *(G-16317)*
Delmar E Hicks ....G 740 354-4333
  Portsmouth *(G-16281)*
Dome Drilling Co ....G 440 892-9434
  Westlake *(G-20109)*
Dome Drilling Co ....G 330 262-5113
  Wooster *(G-20585)*
Dome Energicorp ....G 440 892-4900
  Westlake *(G-20110)*
Dunn S Tank Service Inc ....G 330 863-2200
  Malvern *(G-12388)*
Eastern Reserve Development ....G 614 319-3179
  Columbus *(G-6883)*
Elkhead Gas & Oil Co ....G 740 763-3966
  Newark *(G-14870)*
Enervest Ltd ....D 330 877-6747
  Hartville *(G-10690)*
Everflow Eastern Partners LP ....E 330 533-2692
  Canfield *(G-2528)*
Gonzoil Inc ....G 330 497-5888
  Canton *(G-2686)*
H & S Drilling Co Inc ....G 740 828-2411
  Frazeysburg *(G-9940)*
Husky Marketing and Supply Co ....E 614 210-2300
  Dublin *(G-8927)*
John D Oil and Gas Company ....G 440 255-6325
  Mentor *(G-13486)*
K Petroleum Inc ....F 614 532-5420
  Gahanna *(G-10086)*
Mori Shuji ....G 614 459-1296
  Columbus *(G-7196)*
Ngo Development Corporation ....F 740 622-9560
  Coshocton *(G-7743)*
Ohio Valley Energy Systems ....G 330 799-2268
  Youngstown *(G-20984)*
Precision Geophysical Inc ....G 330 674-2198
  Millersburg *(G-14120)*
Precision Geophysical Inc ....F 740 849-3044
  Mount Perry *(G-14457)*
Quantum Energy LLC ....G 440 285-7381
  Chardon *(G-3133)*
Range Rsurces - Appalachia LLC ....E 330 866-3301
  Dover *(G-8848)*
Reserve Energy Exploration Co ....G 440 543-0770
  Chagrin Falls *(G-3072)*
Santmyer Oil Co of Ashland ....G 330 262-6501
  Wooster *(G-20648)*
Standard Energy Company ....G 614 885-1901
  Columbus *(G-7484)*
Standard Oil Company ....G 419 691-2460
  Oregon *(G-15569)*
Summit Well Services Inc ....G 330 223-1074
  East Rochester *(G-9091)*
Triad Energy Corporation ....E 740 374-2940
  Marietta *(G-12683)*
True North Energy LLC ....G 440 442-0060
  Mayfield Heights *(G-13172)*
Utica East Ohio Midstream ....G 330 223-1766
  Kensington *(G-11286)*
Whitacre Enterprises Inc ....F 740 934-2331
  Graysville *(G-10342)*
Wilkes Energy Inc ....G 330 252-4560
  Akron *(G-436)*
Wrp Energy Inc ....G 330 533-1921
  Canfield *(G-2553)*

GAS & OIL FIELD SVCS, NEC

Altheirs Oil Inc ....G 740 347-4335
  Corning *(G-7700)*
Bradner Oil Company Inc ....G 419 288-2945
  Wayne *(G-19560)*
Buckeye Brine LLC ....F 740 575-4482
  Coshocton *(G-7724)*
D & D Energy Co ....G 330 495-1631
  Canton *(G-2644)*
Joseph G Pappas ....G 330 383-2917
  East Liverpool *(G-9061)*
Stevens Oil & Gas LLC ....G 740 374-4542
  Marietta *(G-12675)*
Timothy Sinfield ....E 740 685-3684
  Pleasant City *(G-16223)*
Vanguard Oil & Gas ....G 330 223-1074
  East Rochester *(G-9092)*

GAS & OTHER COMBINED SVCS

National Gas & Oil Corporation ....E 740 344-2102
  Newark *(G-14900)*

GAS FIELD MACHINERY & EQPT

Jet Rubber Company ....E 330 325-1821
  Rootstown *(G-16569)*
Westerman Inc ....D 330 262-6946
  Wooster *(G-20665)*

GAS STATIONS

J & A Auto Service ....G 614 837-6820
  Pickerington *(G-16049)*
Northeast Tubular Service Inc ....G 330 262-1881
  Wooster *(G-20634)*
Standard Oil Company ....E 419 698-6200
  Oregon *(G-15568)*

GAS SYSTEM CONVERSION SVCS

Compliant Healthcare Tech LLC ....E 216 255-9607
  Cleveland *(G-5011)*

GASES: Acetylene

Delille Oxygen Company........................E....... 614 444-1177
Columbus *(G-6857)*

GASES: Argon

Airgas Usa LLC........................F....... 419 228-2828
Lima *(G-11831)*

GASES: Carbon Dioxide

Praxair Distribution Inc........................G....... 419 422-1353
Lima *(G-11918)*
Praxair Distribution Inc........................G....... 513 821-2192
Cincinnati *(G-4184)*
Praxair Distribution Inc........................F....... 937 283-3400
Wilmington *(G-20504)*

GASES: Hydrogen

Hydrogen Energy Systems LLC............G....... 330 236-0358
Akron *(G-211)*
Ihod USA LLC........................G....... 216 459-7179
Cleveland *(G-5436)*
William Harding........................G....... 513 738-3344
Hamilton *(G-10622)*

GASES: Indl

Air Products and Chemicals Inc............F....... 216 781-2801
Cleveland *(G-4644)*
Airgas Usa LLC........................G....... 937 237-0621
Dayton *(G-8014)*
Airgas Usa LLC........................E....... 937 228-8594
Dayton *(G-8013)*
Airgas Usa LLC........................G....... 440 232-6397
Oakwood Village *(G-15477)*
Delille Oxygen Company........................G....... 937 325-9595
Springfield *(G-17386)*
Endurance Manufacturing Inc..............G....... 330 628-2600
Mogadore *(G-14236)*
Gsf Energy LLC........................G....... 513 825-0504
Cincinnati *(G-3787)*
Invacare Corporation........................A....... 440 329-6000
Elyria *(G-9272)*
Invacare Corporation........................D....... 800 333-6900
Elyria *(G-9273)*
Linde Gas USA LLC........................F....... 330 425-3989
Twinsburg *(G-18808)*
Matheson Tri-Gas Inc........................F....... 330 425-4407
Twinsburg *(G-18812)*
Messer LLC........................E....... 330 608-3008
Uniontown *(G-18928)*
Messer LLC........................E....... 419 227-9585
Lima *(G-11900)*
Messer LLC........................G....... 614 539-2259
Grove City *(G-10445)*
Messer LLC........................G....... 419 822-3909
Delta *(G-8776)*
National Gas & Oil Corporation............E....... 740 344-2102
Newark *(G-14900)*
Nyeco Gas Inc........................G....... 419 447-2712
Sandusky *(G-16831)*
Praxair Inc........................E....... 216 778-5555
Cleveland *(G-5903)*
Praxair Inc........................E....... 440 237-8690
Cleveland *(G-5904)*
Praxair Inc........................G....... 419 698-8005
Oregon *(G-15564)*
Praxair Inc........................G....... 419 729-7732
Toledo *(G-18476)*
Praxair Inc........................G....... 740 453-0346
Zanesville *(G-21171)*
Praxair Inc........................G....... 937 323-6408
Springfield *(G-17474)*
Praxair Inc........................G....... 740 373-6449
Marietta *(G-12656)*
Praxair Inc........................G....... 419 422-1353
Lima *(G-11917)*
Praxair Inc........................F....... 330 264-6633
Wooster *(G-20640)*
Praxair Inc........................E....... 419 652-3562
Cleveland *(G-5905)*
Praxair Inc........................G....... 440 944-8844
Cleveland *(G-5906)*
Praxair Inc........................F....... 740 374-5525
Marietta *(G-12657)*
Praxair Inc........................E....... 330 453-9904
Canton *(G-2789)*
Praxair Inc........................D....... 419 666-5206
Rossford *(G-16590)*
Praxair Inc........................G....... 330 747-4126
Youngstown *(G-21002)*
Praxair Inc........................G....... 330 825-4449
Barberton *(G-1098)*
Praxair Distribution Inc........................F....... 614 443-7687
Columbus *(G-7341)*
Praxair Distribution Inc........................E....... 419 476-0738
Toledo *(G-18477)*
Reliable Mfg Co LLC........................G....... 740 756-9373
Carroll *(G-2908)*
Wright Brothers Inc........................E....... 513 731-2222
Cincinnati *(G-4520)*
Wright Brothers Global Gas LLC..........G....... 513 731-2222
Cincinnati *(G-4521)*

GASES: Neon

GSC Neon........................G....... 216 310-6243
Mayfield Hts *(G-13173)*
Neo Tech........................G....... 937 845-0999
New Carlisle *(G-14674)*
Neon........................G....... 216 761-4782
Cleveland *(G-5735)*
Neon Beach Tan........................G....... 440 933-3051
Amherst *(G-565)*
Neon By Deon LLC........................G....... 440 292-5626
Cleveland *(G-5736)*
Neon City........................G....... 440 301-2000
Cleveland *(G-5737)*
Neon Goldfish Mktg Solutions..............G....... 419 842-4462
Holland *(G-10946)*
Neon Health Services Inc........................E....... 216 231-7700
Cleveland *(G-5738)*
Neon Hussy LLC........................G....... 513 374-7644
Columbus *(G-7213)*
Neon Paintbrush........................G....... 419 436-1202
Fostoria *(G-9851)*
Northeast OH Neighborhood Heal.........D....... 216 751-3100
Cleveland *(G-5774)*

GASES: Nitrogen

Linde Gas North America LLC..............F....... 614 846-7048
Columbus *(G-7129)*
Matheson Tri-Gas Inc........................F....... 513 727-9638
Middletown *(G-13925)*
Matheson Tri-Gas Inc........................F....... 419 865-8881
Holland *(G-10943)*
Messer LLC........................E....... 513 831-4742
Miamiville *(G-13753)*
Messer LLC........................G....... 330 394-4541
Warren *(G-19422)*
Messer LLC........................E....... 419 221-5043
Lima *(G-11901)*
Osair Inc........................G....... 440 974-6500
Mentor *(G-13537)*

GASES: Oxygen

Air Products and Chemicals Inc............D....... 513 420-3663
Middletown *(G-13876)*
Air Products and Chemicals Inc............G....... 513 242-9215
Cincinnati *(G-3312)*
Airgas Usa LLC........................E....... 330 454-1330
Canton *(G-2563)*
Messer LLC........................E....... 216 533-7256
Cleveland *(G-5657)*
Praxair Inc........................D....... 440 994-1000
Ashtabula *(G-800)*
Welders Supply Inc........................F....... 216 241-1696
Cleveland *(G-6299)*

GASKET MATERIALS

Flow Dry Technology Inc........................C....... 937 833-2161
Brookville *(G-2168)*
Forest City Technologies Inc...............C....... 440 647-2115
Wellington *(G-19580)*
Forest City Technologies Inc...............C....... 440 647-2115
Wellington *(G-19581)*

GASKETS

Ace Gasket Manufacturing Co..............G....... 513 271-6321
Cincinnati *(G-3292)*
Akron Gasket & Packg Entps Inc.........F....... 330 633-3742
Tallmadge *(G-17971)*
Ashtabula Rubber Co........................C....... 440 992-2195
Ashtabula *(G-763)*
Blackthorn LLC........................F....... 937 836-9296
Clayton *(G-4572)*
Chestnut Holdings Inc........................G....... 330 849-6503
Akron *(G-114)*
Cincinnati Gasket Pkg Mfg Inc............E....... 513 761-3458
Cincinnati *(G-3492)*
Columbus Gasket Co Inc........................G....... 614 878-6041
Columbus *(G-6789)*
Durox Company........................D....... 440 238-5350
Strongsville *(G-17739)*
Epg Inc........................D....... 330 995-5125
Aurora *(G-879)*
Epg Inc........................F....... 330 995-9725
Streetsboro *(G-17673)*
Essential Sealing Products Inc.............F....... 440 543-8108
Chagrin Falls *(G-3045)*
Forest City Technologies Inc...............B....... 440 647-2115
Wellington *(G-19578)*
Fouty & Company Inc........................E....... 419 693-0017
Oregon *(G-15560)*
Freudenberg-Nok General Partnr..........C....... 419 427-5221
Findlay *(G-9689)*
Gasko Fabricated Products LLC...........E....... 330 239-1781
Medina *(G-13266)*
Industry Products Co........................B....... 937 778-0585
Piqua *(G-16130)*
Ishikawa Gasket America Inc...............F....... 419 353-7300
Bowling Green *(G-1975)*
K Wm Beach Mfg Co Inc........................C....... 937 399-3838
Springfield *(G-17429)*
May Lin Silicone Products Inc...............G....... 330 825-9019
Barberton *(G-1085)*
Miami Valley Gasket Co Inc..................E....... 937 228-0781
Dayton *(G-8346)*
Netherland Rubber Company...............F....... 513 733-0883
Cincinnati *(G-4068)*
Newman International Inc...................D....... 513 932-7379
Lebanon *(G-11674)*
Newman Sanitary Gasket Company......E....... 513 932-7379
Lebanon *(G-11675)*
Ohio Gasket and Shim Co Inc...............E....... 330 630-0626
Akron *(G-307)*
P & E Sales Ltd........................G....... 330 829-0100
Alliance *(G-495)*
P & R Specialty Inc........................E....... 937 773-0263
Piqua *(G-16147)*
Paul J Tatulinski Ltd........................F....... 330 584-8251
North Benton *(G-15061)*
Phoenix Associates........................E....... 440 543-9701
Chagrin Falls *(G-3066)*
Sur-Seal LLC........................C....... 513 574-8500
Cincinnati *(G-4398)*
Sur-Seal Corporation........................G....... 513 574-8500
Harrison *(G-10675)*

GASKETS & SEALING DEVICES

Cornerstone Indus Holdings..................G....... 440 893-9144
Chagrin Falls *(G-3014)*
Dana Limited........................B....... 419 887-3000
Maumee *(G-13099)*
Federal-Mogul Powertrain LLC.............C....... 740 432-2393
Cambridge *(G-2437)*
Federal-Mogul Powertrain LLC.............A....... 419 238-1053
Van Wert *(G-19091)*
Forest City Technologies Inc...............B....... 440 647-2115
Wellington *(G-19579)*
Forest City Technologies Inc...............G....... 440 647-2115
Wellington *(G-19582)*
Freudenberg-Nok General Partnr..........E....... 937 335-3306
Troy *(G-18658)*
G-M-I Inc........................G....... 440 953-8811
Willoughby *(G-20329)*
Ishikawa Gasket America Inc...............C....... 419 353-7300
Bowling Green *(G-1976)*
Jbm Technologies Inc........................G....... 419 368-4362
Hayesville *(G-10715)*
Nitto Inc........................C....... 937 773-4820
Piqua *(G-16146)*
Parker-Hannifin Corporation...............B....... 216 896-3000
Cleveland *(G-5848)*
Parker-Hannifin Corporation...............F....... 216 896-3000
Cleveland *(G-5850)*
SKF Usa Inc........................F....... 800 589-5563
Cleveland *(G-6068)*
Thermodyn Corporation........................G....... 419 874-5100
Perrysburg *(G-16014)*
Tri-Seal LLC........................G....... 330 821-1166
Alliance *(G-510)*

GASOLINE BLENDING PLANT

Certified Oil Company Inc....................C....... 614 421-7500
Columbus *(G-6755)*
Lavy Inc........................G....... 937 692-8189
Arcanum *(G-630)*

Employee Codes: A=Over 500 employees, B=251-500
C=101-250, D=51-100, E=20-50, F=10-19, G=3-9
2019 Harris Ohio Industrial Directory
1445

GASOLINE FILLING STATIONS

GASOLINE FILLING STATIONS
Calvary Christian Ch of Ohio .... E 740 828-9000
  Frazeysburg *(G-9937)*
N M R Inc .... G 513 530-9075
  Cincinnati *(G-4056)*
Speedway LLC .... A 937 864-3000
  Enon *(G-9387)*
Tbone Sales LLC .... E 330 897-6131
  Baltic *(G-1033)*
True North Energy LLC .... E 440 442-0060
  Mayfield Heights *(G-13172)*
United Dairy Farmers Inc .... C 513 396-8700
  Cincinnati *(G-4447)*

GASOLINE WHOLESALERS
Lavy Inc .... G 937 692-8189
  Arcanum *(G-630)*
Marathon Petroleum Company LP .... F 419 422-2121
  Findlay *(G-9719)*
Marathon Petroleum Corporation .... B 419 422-2121
  Findlay *(G-9721)*
Mplx Terminals LLC .... B 330 479-5539
  Canton *(G-2757)*

GATES: Ornamental Metal
All Ohio Companies Inc .... F 216 420-9274
  Cleveland *(G-4664)*
Autogate Inc .... E 419 588-2796
  Berlin Heights *(G-1652)*
Mound Technologies Inc .... F 937 748-2937
  Springboro *(G-17338)*
Quality Security Door & Mfg Co .... G 440 246-0770
  Lorain *(G-12114)*

GAUGE BLOCKS
Blue Ash Tool & Die Co Inc .... F 513 793-4530
  Blue Ash *(G-1737)*
LS Starrett Company .... D 440 835-0005
  Westlake *(G-20129)*

GAUGES
Angstrom Corp .... G 330 405-0524
  Twinsburg *(G-18733)*
Chart Tech Tool Inc .... E 937 667-3543
  Tipp City *(G-18108)*
Jones Industrial Service LLC .... G 419 287-4553
  Pemberville *(G-15886)*
PMC Mercury .... G 440 953-3300
  Willoughby *(G-20405)*
Precision Gage & Tool Company .... E 937 866-9666
  Dayton *(G-8432)*
Silver Tool Inc .... E 937 865-0012
  Miamisburg *(G-13717)*
Taft Tool & Production Co .... F 419 385-2576
  Toledo *(G-18542)*

GEARS
Cincinnati Gearing Systems Inc .... C 513 527-8634
  Cincinnati *(G-3494)*
Gear Company of America Inc .... D 216 671-5400
  Cleveland *(G-5298)*
Landerwood Industries Inc .... E 440 233-4234
  Willoughby *(G-20358)*
Satellite Gear Inc .... F 216 514-8668
  Aurora *(G-907)*
Summa Holdings Inc .... G 440 838-4700
  Cleveland *(G-6116)*

GEARS & GEAR UNITS: Reduction, Exc Auto
Hefty Hoist Inc .... E 740 467-2515
  Millersport *(G-14160)*
Tgm Holdings Company .... F 419 885-3769
  Sylvania *(G-17965)*
Westerman Inc .... C 740 569-4143
  Bremen *(G-2065)*
Westerman Inc .... D 330 262-6946
  Wooster *(G-20665)*

GEARS: Power Transmission, Exc Auto
Accurate Gear Manufacturing Co .... G 513 761-3220
  Cincinnati *(G-3290)*
Akron Gear & Engineering Inc .... E 330 773-6608
  Akron *(G-41)*
B & B Gear & Machine Co Inc .... F 937 687-1771
  New Lebanon *(G-14707)*
Buckeye Gear Co .... F 216 292-7998
  Chagrin Falls *(G-3038)*
Cage Gear & Machine LLC .... F 330 452-1532
  Canton *(G-2604)*
Canton Gear Mfg Design Co Inc .... F 330 455-2771
  Canton *(G-2610)*
Dayton Gear & Tool Co Inc .... E 937 866-4327
  Dayton *(G-8134)*
Forge Industries Inc .... A 330 782-8301
  Youngstown *(G-20909)*
Gear Company of America Inc .... D 216 671-5400
  Cleveland *(G-5298)*
Geartec Inc .... E 440 953-3900
  Willoughby *(G-20330)*
Geneva Gear & Machine Inc .... F 937 866-0318
  Dayton *(G-8221)*
Horsburgh & Scott Co .... C 216 432-5858
  Cleveland *(G-5418)*
Horsburgh & Scott Co .... G 216 383-2909
  Cleveland *(G-5419)*
Jonmar Gear and Machine Inc .... G 330 854-6500
  Canal Fulton *(G-2481)*
Linde Hydraulics Corporation .... E 330 533-6801
  Canfield *(G-2532)*
Martin Sprocket & Gear Inc .... D 419 485-5515
  Montpelier *(G-14312)*
Petro Gear Corporation .... F 216 431-2820
  Cleveland *(G-5868)*
Robertson Manufacturing Co .... F 216 531-8222
  Cleveland *(G-5994)*
Sew-Eurodrive Inc .... D 937 335-0036
  Troy *(G-18705)*
Stahl Gear & Machine Co .... E 216 431-2820
  Cleveland *(G-6089)*

GEMSTONE & INDL DIAMOND MINING SVCS
Massillon Metaphysics .... G 330 837-1653
  Massillon *(G-13021)*

GENERAL MERCHANDISE, NONDURABLE, WHOLESALE
M&M Great Adventures LLC .... G 937 344-1415
  Westerville *(G-20008)*

GENERATING APPARATUS & PARTS: Electrical
Turk+hillinger Usa Inc .... G 440 781-1900
  Brecksville *(G-2062)*
Turtlecreek Township .... F 513 932-4080
  Lebanon *(G-11703)*
Visiontech Automation LLC .... G 614 554-2013
  Dublin *(G-9010)*

GENERATION EQPT: Electronic
Cable and Ctrl Solutions LLC .... G 937 254-2227
  Dayton *(G-7972)*
Cvc Limited 1 LLC .... G 740 605-3853
  Lebanon *(G-11645)*
Energy Technologies Inc .... D 419 522-4444
  Mansfield *(G-12437)*
Eti Tech LLC .... F 937 832-4200
  Englewood *(G-9358)*
Liebert Field Services Inc .... D 614 841-5763
  Westerville *(G-20007)*
Lubrizol Global Management .... F 216 447-5000
  Brecksville *(G-2048)*
Power Source Service LLC .... G 513 607-4555
  Batavia *(G-1177)*
Proteus Electronics Inc .... F 419 886-2296
  Bellville *(G-1563)*
Sarica Manufacturing Company .... E 937 484-4030
  Urbana *(G-19011)*
Spirit Avionics Ltd .... F 614 237-4271
  Columbus *(G-7477)*
Superior Packaging .... F 419 380-3335
  Toledo *(G-18536)*
Tasi Holdings Inc .... E 513 202-5182
  Harrison *(G-10676)*
Tecmark Corporation .... D 440 205-7600
  Mentor *(G-13601)*

GENERATORS: Automotive & Aircraft
Charles Auto Electric Co Inc .... G 330 535-6269
  Akron *(G-111)*
Cycle Electric Inc .... F 937 884-7300
  Brookville *(G-2165)*
Egr Products Company Inc .... F 330 833-6554
  Dalton *(G-7941)*

GENERATORS: Electric
Accurate Electronics Inc .... C 330 682-7015
  Orrville *(G-15581)*
Ideal Electric Power Co .... F 419 522-3611
  Mansfield *(G-12460)*
Martin Diesel Inc .... E 419 782-9911
  Defiance *(G-8636)*

GENERATORS: Gas
Rexarc International Inc .... E 937 839-4604
  West Alexandria *(G-19620)*

GENERATORS: Ultrasonic
Tech-Sonic Inc .... F 614 792-3117
  Columbus *(G-7519)*

GIFT SHOP
Amish Door Inc .... B 330 359-5464
  Wilmot *(G-20513)*
Beckwith Orchards Inc .... F 330 673-6433
  Kent *(G-11299)*
Broty Enterprises Inc .... G 330 674-6900
  Millersburg *(G-14069)*
Crystal Art Imports Inc .... F 614 430-8180
  Columbus *(G-6840)*
Custom Engraving & Screen Prtg .... G 440 933-2902
  Avon Lake *(G-983)*
Daffins Candies .... G 330 545-0325
  Girard *(G-10256)*
Down Home .... G 740 393-1186
  Mount Vernon *(G-14479)*
Dresden Specialties Inc .... G 740 754-2451
  Dresden *(G-8868)*
Friends of Bears Mill Inc .... G 937 548-5112
  Greenville *(G-10370)*
Handcrafted Jewelry Inc .... G 330 650-9011
  Hudson *(G-11051)*
Huston Gifts Dolls and Flowers .... G 740 775-9141
  Chillicothe *(G-3193)*
John C Starr .... G 740 852-5592
  London *(G-12063)*
Odyssey Spirits Inc .... E 330 562-1523
  Aurora *(G-896)*
S-P Company Inc .... F 330 482-0200
  Columbiana *(G-6479)*
Schindlers Broad Run Chese Hse .... E 330 343-4108
  Dover *(G-8850)*
Scholz & Ey Engravers Inc .... F 614 444-8052
  Columbus *(G-7427)*
Shops By Todd Inc .... G 937 458-3192
  Beavercreek *(G-1340)*
Suzin L Chocolatiers .... E 440 323-3372
  Elyria *(G-9332)*
Youngs Jersey Dairy Inc .... B 937 325-0629
  Yellow Springs *(G-20823)*

GIFT WRAP: Paper, Made From Purchased Materials
American Greetings Corporation .... A 216 252-7300
  Cleveland *(G-4688)*

GIFT, NOVELTY & SOUVENIR STORES: Artcraft & carvings
Ohio Designer Craftsmen Entps .... F 614 486-7119
  Columbus *(G-7245)*

GIFT, NOVELTY & SOUVENIR STORES: Gift Baskets
American Traditions Basket Co .... E 330 854-0900
  Canal Fulton *(G-2474)*
Cookie Bouquets Inc .... G 614 888-2171
  Columbus *(G-6817)*
Fowlers Milling Co Inc .... G 440 286-2024
  Chardon *(G-3112)*

GIFT, NOVELTY & SOUVENIR STORES: Gifts & Novelties
Global Manufacturing Solutions .... F 937 236-8315
  Dayton *(G-8225)*
Golden Turtle Chocolate Fctry .... G 513 932-1990
  Lebanon *(G-11658)*

PRODUCT SECTION

GLASS PRDTS, PRESSED OR BLOWN: Scientific Glassware

Middleton Lee Original Dolls .... F .....
  Columbus *(G-7180)*
Rubys Country Store .... G 330 359-0406
  Dundee *(G-9026)*

GIFT, NOVELTY & SOUVENIR STORES: Party Favors

Adyl Inc .... G 330 797-8700
  Austintown *(G-928)*

GIFT, NOVELTY & SOUVENIR STORES: Trading Cards, Sports

Baseball Card Corner .... G 513 677-0464
  Loveland *(G-12179)*
The Hartman Corp .... G 614 475-5035
  Columbus *(G-7525)*

GIFTS & NOVELTIES: Wholesalers

Aunties Attic .... E 740 548-5059
  Lewis Center *(G-11748)*
Scholz & Ey Engravers Inc .... F 614 444-8052
  Columbus *(G-7427)*

GLACE, FOR GLAZING FOOD

Roare-Q LLC .... G 419 801-4040
  Bowling Green *(G-1997)*

GLASS & GLASS CERAMIC PRDTS, PRESSED OR BLOWN: Tableware

Anchor Hocking LLC .... A 740 681-6478
  Lancaster *(G-11541)*
Anchor Hocking LLC .... G 740 687-2500
  Lancaster *(G-11542)*
Custom Deco South Inc .... E 419 698-2900
  Toledo *(G-18246)*
Ghp II LLC .... C 740 687-2500
  Lancaster *(G-11575)*
Libbey Glass Inc .... C 419 325-2100
  Toledo *(G-18382)*
Libbey Glass Inc .... A 419 729-7272
  Toledo *(G-18383)*

GLASS FABRICATORS

A & B Iron & Metal Company .... F 937 228-1561
  Dayton *(G-7997)*
Addis Glass Fabricating Inc .... F 513 860-3340
  West Chester *(G-19637)*
Adria Scientific GL Works Co .... G 440 474-6691
  Geneva *(G-10211)*
AGC Automotive Americas .... D 937 599-3131
  Bellefontaine *(G-1501)*
American Woodwork Specialty Co .... E 937 263-1053
  Dayton *(G-8029)*
Anchi Inc .... A 740 653-2527
  Lancaster *(G-11540)*
Anderson Glass Co Inc .... E 614 476-4877
  Columbus *(G-6603)*
Atc Lighting & Plastics Inc .... C 440 466-7670
  Andover *(G-580)*
Cadenza Enterprises LLC .... G 937 428-6058
  Dayton *(G-8073)*
Champion Window Co of Toledo .... E 419 841-0154
  Perrysburg *(G-15933)*
Custom GL Sltions Millbury LLC .... C 419 855-7706
  Millbury *(G-14048)*
Enclosure Suppliers LLC .... E 513 782-3900
  Cincinnati *(G-3637)*
Environmental Sampling Sup Inc .... E 330 497-9396
  North Canton *(G-15080)*
Fuyao Glass America Inc .... C 937 496-5777
  Dayton *(G-8212)*
General Electric Company .... D 740 385-2114
  Logan *(G-12025)*
General Glass & Screen Inc .... G 440 350-9033
  Mentor *(G-13456)*
Ghp II LLC .... B 740 681-6825
  Lancaster *(G-11576)*
Great Day Improvements LLC .... G 330 468-0700
  Macedonia *(G-12300)*
Libbey Glass Inc .... C 419 325-2100
  Toledo *(G-18382)*
North Central Insulation Inc .... F 419 886-2030
  Bellville *(G-1561)*
Ohio Mirror Technologies Inc .... F 419 399-5903
  Paulding *(G-15867)*

Ohio Mirror Technologies Inc .... F 419 399-5903
  Paulding *(G-15868)*
Pilkington North America Inc .... B 419 247-3211
  Rossford *(G-16589)*
Pyromatics Corp .... F 440 352-3500
  Mentor *(G-13561)*
R M Yates Co Inc .... G 216 441-0900
  Cleveland *(G-5953)*
Rumpke Transportation Co LLC .... C 513 242-4600
  Cincinnati *(G-4289)*
Sem-Com Company Inc .... F 419 537-8813
  Toledo *(G-18517)*
Solon Glass Center Inc .... F 440 248-5018
  Cleveland *(G-6078)*
Strategic Materials Inc .... G 740 349-9523
  Newark *(G-14925)*
Taylor Products Inc .... E 419 263-2313
  Payne *(G-15874)*
Taylor Products Inc .... E 419 263-2313
  Payne *(G-15875)*
Technicolor Usa Inc .... A 614 474-8821
  Circleville *(G-4561)*
XS Smith Inc .... E 252 940-5060
  Cincinnati *(G-4529)*

GLASS PRDTS, FROM PURCHASED GLASS: Glass Beads, Reflecting

Potters Industries LLC .... E 216 621-0840
  Cleveland *(G-5898)*

GLASS PRDTS, FROM PURCHASED GLASS: Glassware

Dresden Specialties Inc .... G 740 754-2451
  Dresden *(G-8868)*
East Palestine Decorating LLC .... F 330 426-9600
  East Palestine *(G-9078)*
Etching Concepts .... G 419 691-9086
  Rossford *(G-16585)*
Jafe Decorating Co Inc .... E 937 547-1888
  Greenville *(G-10375)*

GLASS PRDTS, FROM PURCHASED GLASS: Insulating

Intigral Inc .... C 440 439-0980
  Walton Hills *(G-19311)*
Intigral Inc .... E 440 439-0980
  Youngstown *(G-20942)*
Trio Insulated Glass Inc .... G 614 276-1647
  Columbus *(G-7544)*

GLASS PRDTS, FROM PURCHASED GLASS: Mirrored

Bruening Glass Works Inc .... G 440 333-4768
  Cleveland *(G-4846)*
Chantilly Development Corp .... F 419 243-8109
  Toledo *(G-18227)*
Installed Building Pdts LLC .... E 614 308-9900
  Columbus *(G-7029)*
R G C Inc .... F 513 683-3110
  Loveland *(G-12225)*

GLASS PRDTS, FROM PURCHASED GLASS: Novelties, Fruit, Etc

Colleen D Turner .... G 419 886-4810
  Bellville *(G-1555)*

GLASS PRDTS, FROM PURCHASED GLASS: Ornaments, Christmas Tree

Amerihua Intl Entps Inc .... G 740 549-0300
  Lewis Center *(G-11744)*

GLASS PRDTS, FROM PURCHASED GLASS: Reflecting

Macpherson Engineering Inc .... E 440 243-6565
  Berea *(G-1616)*

GLASS PRDTS, FROM PURCHASED GLASS: Sheet, Bent

Glasstech Inc .... C 419 661-9500
  Perrysburg *(G-15959)*

GLASS PRDTS, FROM PURCHASED GLASS: Windshields

Safelite Group Inc .... A 614 210-9000
  Columbus *(G-7413)*

GLASS PRDTS, FROM PURCHD GLASS: Strengthened Or Reinforced

Glass Surface Systems Inc .... D 330 745-8500
  Barberton *(G-1075)*
Kimmatt Corp .... G 937 228-3811
  Dayton *(G-8297)*
PPG Industries Inc .... E 419 683-2400
  Crestline *(G-7799)*

GLASS PRDTS, PRESSED OR BLOWN: Blocks & Bricks

All State GL Block Fctry Inc .... G 440 205-8410
  Mentor *(G-13384)*
Blockamerica Corporation .... G 614 274-0700
  Columbus *(G-6680)*
Global Glass Block Inc .... G 216 731-2333
  Euclid *(G-9414)*
Pierce GL Inc .... G 513 772-7202
  Cincinnati *(G-4158)*

GLASS PRDTS, PRESSED OR BLOWN: Bulbs, Electric Lights

Katies Light House LLC .... E 419 645-5451
  Cridersville *(G-7811)*
Leveck Lighting Products Inc .... E 937 667-4421
  Tipp City *(G-18121)*

GLASS PRDTS, PRESSED OR BLOWN: Furnishings & Access

Angel Glass Lost .... G 419 353-2831
  Bowling Green *(G-1951)*
Libbey Inc .... C 419 325-2100
  Toledo *(G-18385)*

GLASS PRDTS, PRESSED OR BLOWN: Glass Fibers, Textile

Ipm Inc .... G 419 248-8000
  Toledo *(G-18351)*
Knoble Glass & Metal Inc .... G 513 753-1246
  Cincinnati *(G-3919)*
Owens Corning .... A 419 248-8000
  Toledo *(G-18446)*
Owens Corning Ht Inc .... A 419 248-8000
  Toledo *(G-18447)*
Owens Corning Sales LLC .... A 419 248-8000
  Toledo *(G-18448)*

GLASS PRDTS, PRESSED OR BLOWN: Glassware, Art Or Decorative

Anchor Hocking Consmr GL Corp .... G 740 653-2527
  Lancaster *(G-11543)*
Glass Axis .... G 614 291-4250
  Columbus *(G-6952)*
Modern China Inc .... E 330 938-6104
  Sebring *(G-16889)*

GLASS PRDTS, PRESSED OR BLOWN: Glassware, Novelty

Mosser Glass Incorporated .... E 740 439-1827
  Cambridge *(G-2449)*

GLASS PRDTS, PRESSED OR BLOWN: Lantern Globes

Brubaker Metalcrafts Inc .... G 937 456-5834
  Eaton *(G-9143)*

GLASS PRDTS, PRESSED OR BLOWN: Scientific Glassware

Technical Glass Products Inc .... G 425 396-8420
  Perrysburg *(G-16013)*
Variety Glass Inc .... F 740 432-3643
  Cambridge *(G-2461)*

Employee Codes: A=Over 500 employees, B=251-500
C=101-250, D=51-100, E=20-50, F=10-19, G=3-9

GLASS PRDTS, PRESSED OR BLOWN: Tubing

Echo EMR Inc ....F 937 322-4972
  Springfield (G-17394)

GLASS PRDTS, PRESSED OR BLOWN: Yarn, Fiberglass

Tencate Advanced Armor USA Inc ....D 740 928-0326
  Hebron (G-10765)

GLASS PRDTS, PRESSED/BLOWN: Glassware, Art, Decor/Novelty

John Krizay Inc ....E 330 332-5607
  Salem (G-16750)

GLASS PRDTS, PURCHSD GLASS: Ornamental, Cut, Engraved/Décor

Crystal Art Imports Inc ....F 614 430-8180
  Columbus (G-6840)
Marchione Studio Inc ....G 330 454-7408
  Canton (G-2742)

GLASS STORE: Leaded Or Stained

Franklin Art Glass Studios ....E 614 221-2972
  Columbus (G-6935)
Middlefield Glass Incorporated ....E 440 632-5699
  Middlefield (G-13823)
Standing Rock Designery ....G 330 650-9089
  Hudson (G-11077)

GLASS STORES

A Service Glass Inc ....F 937 426-4920
  Beavercreek (G-1297)
All State GL Block Fctry Inc ....G 440 205-8410
  Mentor (G-13384)
Blockamerica Corporation ....G 614 274-0700
  Columbus (G-6680)
Dale Kestler ....G 513 871-9000
  Cincinnati (G-3574)
General Glass & Screen Inc ....G 440 350-9033
  Mentor (G-13456)
Glass Mirror Awards Inc ....G 419 638-2221
  Helena (G-10772)
Oldcastle Buildingenvelope Inc ....D 419 661-5079
  Perrysburg (G-15988)

GLASS, AUTOMOTIVE: Wholesalers

Fuyao Glass America Inc ....C 937 496-5777
  Dayton (G-8212)
Pittsburgh Glass Works LLC ....F 740 774-8762
  Chillicothe (G-3211)

GLASS: Fiber

Celstar Group Inc ....G 937 224-1730
  Dayton (G-8080)
Dal-Little Fabricating Inc ....G 216 883-3323
  Cleveland (G-5059)
Industrial Fiberglass Spc Inc ....E 937 222-9000
  Dayton (G-8263)
Mfg Composite Systems Company ....B 440 997-5851
  Ashtabula (G-786)
Midwest Composites LLC ....E 419 738-2431
  Wapakoneta (G-19342)
Molded Fiber Glass Research ....E 440 994-5100
  Ashtabula (G-791)
PPG Industries Inc ....E 419 683-2400
  Crestline (G-7799)
Scottrods LLC ....G 419 499-2705
  Monroeville (G-14290)

GLASS: Flat

Addis Glass Fabricating Inc ....F 513 860-3340
  West Chester (G-19637)
AGC Flat Glass North Amer Inc ....F 937 292-7784
  Bellefontaine (G-1502)
AGC Flat Glass North Amer Inc ....G 330 965-1000
  Youngstown (G-20839)
AGC Flat Glass North Amer Inc ....G 330 965-1000
  Boardman (G-1897)
AGC Flat Glass North Amer Inc ....G 937 599-3131
  Bellefontaine (G-1503)
Custom Glass Solutions LLC ....F 248 340-1800
  Worthington (G-20682)
Glass Fabricators Inc ....G 216 529-1919
  Lakewood (G-11518)
Guardian Industries LLC ....E 614 431-6309
  Worthington (G-20688)
Nsg Glass North America Inc ....C 419 247-4800
  Toledo (G-18429)
Pilkington Holdings Inc ....B 419 247-3731
  Toledo (G-18469)
Pilkington North America Inc ....C 800 547-9280
  Northwood (G-15344)
Pittsburgh Glass Works LLC ....F 740 774-8762
  Chillicothe (G-3211)
PPG Industries Inc ....E 419 683-2400
  Crestline (G-7799)
Schodorf Truck Body & Eqp Co ....E 614 228-6793
  Columbus (G-7426)
Taylor Products Inc ....E 419 263-2313
  Payne (G-15875)
Vinylume Products Inc ....D 330 799-2000
  Youngstown (G-21067)
Yoder Window & Siding Ltd ....G 330 857-4530
  Fredericksburg (G-9961)

GLASS: Indl Prdts

Cincinnati Gasket Pkg Mfg Inc ....E 513 761-3458
  Cincinnati (G-3492)

GLASS: Insulating

3-G Incorporated ....G 513 921-4515
  Cincinnati (G-3269)
Dela-Glassware Ltd LLC ....G 740 369-6737
  Delaware (G-8669)
Mentor Glass Supplies and Repr ....G 440 255-9444
  Mentor (G-13515)
Poma GL Specialty Windows Inc ....G 330 965-1000
  Boardman (G-1901)

GLASS: Laminated

Custom Glass Solutions Upper S ....B 419 294-4921
  Upper Sandusky (G-18949)

GLASS: Leaded

Fergusons Cut Glass Works ....G 419 734-0808
  Marblehead (G-12585)

GLASS: Pressed & Blown, NEC

Anderson Glass Co Inc ....E 614 476-4877
  Columbus (G-6603)
Eagle Laboratory Glass Co LLC ....G 440 354-8350
  Painesville (G-15733)
Eye Lighting Intl N Amer Inc ....C 440 350-7000
  Mentor (G-13442)
General Electric Company ....D 740 385-2114
  Logan (G-12025)
General Electric Company ....A 330 373-1400
  Mc Donald (G-13199)
International Automotive Compo ....A 419 433-5653
  Huron (G-11099)
Jjs3 Foundation ....G 513 751-3292
  Cincinnati (G-3874)
Johns Manville Corporation ....B 419 878-8111
  Waterville (G-19498)
Matthews Art Glass ....G 419 335-2448
  Archbold (G-658)
R G C Inc ....F 513 683-3110
  Loveland (G-12225)
Touch of Glass ....G 419 861-2888
  Toledo (G-18579)
Wilson Optical Laboratory Inc ....E 440 357-7000
  Mentor (G-13626)

GLASS: Safety

AGC Flat Glass North Amer Inc ....G 937 599-3131
  Bellefontaine (G-1503)

GLASS: Stained

Architectural Art Glass Studio ....G 513 731-7336
  Cincinnati (G-3355)
Franklin Art Glass Studios ....E 614 221-2972
  Columbus (G-6935)
Glass Seale Ltd ....G 513 733-1464
  Cincinnati (G-3761)
Kessler Studios Inc ....G 513 683-7500
  Loveland (G-12204)
Middlefield Glass Incorporated ....E 440 632-5699
  Middlefield (G-13823)
Standing Rock Designery ....G 330 650-9089
  Hudson (G-11077)
Studio Arts & Glass Inc ....F 330 494-9779
  Canton (G-2826)
Vidonish Studios ....G 419 884-1119
  Mansfield (G-12535)
Whitney Stained Glass Studio ....G 216 348-1616
  Cleveland (G-6306)

GLASS: Structural

Continental GL Sls & Inv Group ....B 614 679-1201
  Powell (G-16318)

GLASS: Tempered

Auto Temp Inc ....C 513 732-6969
  Batavia (G-1123)
Oldcastle Buildingenvelope Inc ....D 419 661-5079
  Perrysburg (G-15988)

GLASSWARE STORES

Eagle Laboratory Glass Co LLC ....G 440 354-8350
  Painesville (G-15733)
Mosser Glass Incorporated ....E 740 439-1827
  Cambridge (G-2449)

GLASSWARE WHOLESALERS

Anchor Hocking Glass Company ....G 740 681-6025
  Lancaster (G-11544)
Eagle Laboratory Glass Co LLC ....G 440 354-8350
  Painesville (G-15733)

GLASSWARE, NOVELTY, WHOLESALE

Etching Concepts ....G 419 691-9086
  Rossford (G-16585)
Mosser Glass Incorporated ....E 740 439-1827
  Cambridge (G-2449)

GLASSWARE: Cut & Engraved

Tyseka ....G 419 860-9585
  Lima (G-11954)

GLOBAL POSITIONING SYSTEMS & EQPT

Hyq Technologies LLC ....G 513 225-6911
  Oxford (G-15694)

GLOVES: Fabric

C & G Associates Inc ....G 419 756-6583
  Mansfield (G-12418)
Hillman Group Inc ....G 440 248-7000
  Cleveland (G-5409)

GLOVES: Leather

Hillman Group Inc ....G 440 248-7000
  Cleveland (G-5409)
Totes Isotoner Corporation ....F 513 682-8200
  West Chester (G-19907)
Totes Isotoner Holdings Corp ....C 513 682-8200
  West Chester (G-19908)

GLOVES: Linings, Exc Fur

Independent Protection Systems ....G 330 832-7992
  Massillon (G-13003)

GLOVES: Safety

Ansell Healthcare Products LLC ....D 740 622-4311
  Coshocton (G-7719)
Ansell Healthcare Products LLC ....C 740 295-5414
  Coshocton (G-7720)
Hillman Group Inc ....G 440 248-7000
  Cleveland (G-5409)

GLOVES: Work

Hall Safety Apparel Inc ....F 740 922-3671
  Uhrichsville (G-18887)
Wcm Holdings Inc ....G 513 705-2100
  Cincinnati (G-4493)
West Chester Holdings LLC ....C 800 647-1900
  Cincinnati (G-4499)

PRODUCT SECTION

GLOVES: Woven Or Knit, From Purchased Materials

Totes Isotoner Corporation ....F 513 682-8200
  West Chester (G-19907)
Totes Isotoner Holdings Corp ....C 513 682-8200
  West Chester (G-19908)

GLUE

Spectrum Adhesives Inc ....F 740 763-2886
  Newark (G-14919)
Tech-Bond Solutions ....G 614 327-8884
  Carroll (G-2913)

GLYCERIN

Coil Specialty Chemicals LLC ....G 740 236-2407
  Marietta (G-12616)

GLYCOL ETHERS

Nease Co LLC ....D 513 738-1255
  Harrison (G-10661)

GOLF CARTS: Powered

B & B Industries Inc ....G 614 871-3883
  Orient (G-15574)
Kmj Leasing Ltd ....E 614 871-3883
  Orient (G-15575)

GOLF COURSES: Public

Carol Mickley ....G 740 599-7870
  Danville (G-7960)
Joe McClelland Inc ....E 740 452-3036
  Zanesville (G-21151)
Practice Center Inc ....G 513 489-5229
  Cincinnati (G-4183)

GOLF DRIVING RANGES

Hole Hunter Golf Inc ....G 937 339-5833
  Piqua (G-16129)
Practice Center Inc ....G 513 489-5229
  Cincinnati (G-4183)
Youngs Jersey Dairy Inc ....B 937 325-0629
  Yellow Springs (G-20823)

GOLF EQPT

Bay Island Company Inc ....G 513 248-0356
  Loveland (G-12180)
Dayton Stencil Works Company ....E 937 223-3233
  Dayton (G-8145)
Golf Ball Manufacturers LLC ....G 419 994-5563
  Loudonville (G-12142)
Golf Galaxy Golfworks Inc ....C 740 328-4193
  Newark (G-14880)
Hole Hunter Golf Inc ....G 937 339-5833
  Piqua (G-16129)
Jason Stuller Pro Shop LLC ....G 419 882-3197
  Sylvania (G-17946)
Sunset Golf LLC ....E 419 994-5563
  Tallmadge (G-18007)

GOLF GOODS & EQPT

Hole Hunter Golf Inc ....G 937 339-5833
  Piqua (G-16129)

GOURMET FOOD STORES

Disalvos Deli & Italian Store ....G 937 298-5053
  Dayton (G-8163)
Mustard Seed Health Fd Mkt Inc .....E 440 519-3663
  Solon (G-17201)
Rossi Pasta Factory Inc ....F 740 376-2065
  Marietta (G-12665)

GOVERNMENT, EXECUTIVE OFFICES: City & Town Managers' Offices

Lake Township Trustees ....G 419 836-1143
  Millbury (G-14050)

GOVERNMENT, EXECUTIVE OFFICES: County Supervisor/Exec Office

County of Summit ....G 330 865-8065
  Akron (G-124)

GOVERNMENT, EXECUTIVE OFFICES: Mayors'

City of Canton ....E 330 489-3370
  Canton (G-2625)
City of Marietta ....E 740 374-6864
  Marietta (G-12615)

GOVERNMENT, GENERAL: Administration

City of Cleveland ....F 216 664-3013
  Cleveland (G-4930)
Turtlecreek Township ....F 513 932-4080
  Lebanon (G-11703)

GOVERNMENT, GENERAL: Administration, Federal

US Government Publishing Off ....G 614 469-5657
  Columbus (G-7566)

GOVERNORS: Diesel Engine

Brinkley Technology Group LLC .....F 330 830-2498
  Massillon (G-12963)
HK Engine Components LLC ....G 330 830-3500
  Massillon (G-12998)

GRADING SVCS

Great Lakes Crushing Ltd ....E 440 944-5500
  Wickliffe (G-20211)

GRANITE: Crushed & Broken

Bradley Stone Industries LLC ....F 440 519-3277
  Solon (G-17118)
Martin Marietta Materials Inc ....F 513 701-1120
  Mason (G-12907)
Martin Marietta Materials Inc ....E 513 701-1140
  West Chester (G-19740)
Martin Marietta Materials Inc ....E 937 766-2351
  Cedarville (G-2945)
National Lime and Stone Co ....E 419 294-3049
  Upper Sandusky (G-18965)
National Lime and Stone Co ....G 330 339-2144
  New Philadelphia (G-14790)
National Lime and Stone Co ....G 216 883-9840
  Cleveland (G-5726)

GRANITE: Cut & Shaped

Angelina Stone & Marble Ltd ....G 740 633-3360
  Bridgeport (G-2072)
Barta Viorel ....G 440 735-1699
  Bedford (G-1387)
Bartan Design Inc ....G 216 267-6474
  North Royalton (G-15262)
Creative Countertops Ohio LLC ....F 937 540-9450
  Englewood (G-9352)
Cutting Edge Countertops Inc ....E 419 873-9500
  Perrysburg (G-15937)
Granite Fabricators Inc ....G 216 228-3669
  Cleveland (G-5340)
HBK Stoneworks ....G 740 817-2244
  Johnstown (G-11268)
Lind Stoneworks Ltd ....F 614 866-9733
  Columbus (G-7128)
Quarrymasters Inc ....G 330 612-0474
  Canton (G-2797)
Schena Company Ltd ....G 419 868-5207
  Holland (G-10955)
Take It For Granite LLC ....F 513 735-0555
  Cincinnati (G-3265)
Traditional Marble & Gran Ltd ....F 419 625-3966
  Milan (G-13990)

GRANITE: Dimension

Designer Stone Co ....G 740 492-1300
  Port Washington (G-16268)
Helmart Company Inc ....G 513 941-3095
  Cincinnati (G-3806)
Stone Statements Incorporated ....G 513 489-7866
  Cincinnati (G-4384)

GRAPHIC ARTS & RELATED DESIGN SVCS

A Graphic Solution ....F 216 228-7223
  Cleveland (G-4587)
Abstract Displays Inc ....G 513 985-9700
  Blue Ash (G-1719)

GRATINGS: Open Steel Flooring

Academy Graphic Comm Inc ....E 216 661-2550
  Cleveland (G-4603)
Alfacomp Inc ....G 216 459-1790
  Cleveland (G-4659)
Art-American Printing Plates ....E 216 241-4420
  Cleveland (G-4738)
Container Graphics Corp ....D 419 531-5133
  Toledo (G-18241)
David Esrati ....G 937 228-4433
  Dayton (G-8126)
Design Avenue Inc ....G 330 487-5280
  Twinsburg (G-18763)
Envoi Design Inc ....G 513 651-4229
  Cincinnati (G-3645)
Evolution Crtive Solutions LLC ....E 513 681-4450
  Cincinnati (G-3660)
Golden Graphics Ltd ....F 419 673-6260
  Kenton (G-11406)
Graphic Image ....G 937 320-0302
  Beavercreek (G-1318)
Graphic Publications Inc ....E 330 674-2300
  Millersburg (G-14085)
Great Lakes Graphics Inc ....E 216 391-0077
  Cleveland (G-5345)
Gregg Macmillan ....G 513 248-2121
  Milford (G-14014)
Insignia Signs Inc ....G 937 866-2341
  Dayton (G-8268)
Jeffrey A Clark ....G 419 866-8775
  Holland (G-10936)
Key Marketing Group ....G 440 748-3479
  Grafton (G-10306)
King Retail Solutions Inc ....F 513 729-5858
  Hamilton (G-10580)
Laipplys Prtg Mktg Sltions Inc ....G 740 387-9282
  Marion (G-12715)
ML Advertising & Design LLC ....G 419 447-6523
  Tiffin (G-18069)
Mueller Art Cover & Binding Co ....E 440 238-3303
  Strongsville (G-17768)
Northeast Scene Inc ....G 216 241-7550
  Cleveland (G-5776)
Nova Creative Group Inc ....F 937 291-8653
  Dayton (G-8388)
Painted Hill Inv Group Inc ....F 937 339-1756
  Troy (G-18691)
Perrons Printing Company ....E 440 236-8870
  Columbia Station (G-6442)
Phantasm Designs ....G 419 538-6737
  Ottawa (G-15662)
Rba Inc ....G 330 336-6700
  Wadsworth (G-19273)
Roberts Graphic Center ....G 330 788-4642
  Youngstown (G-21019)
Schiffer Group Inc ....G 937 694-8185
  Troy (G-18703)
Schuerholz Printing Inc ....G 937 294-5218
  Dayton (G-8496)
Sevell + Sevell Inc ....G 614 341-9700
  Columbus (G-7441)
Sign City Inc ....G 614 486-6700
  Mount Gilead (G-14433)
Signage Consultants Inc ....G 614 297-7446
  Columbus (G-7449)
Sjpm Inc ....G 614 475-4571
  Gahanna (G-10104)
Ultra Printing & Design Inc ....G 440 887-0393
  Cleveland (G-6228)
Vivid Wraps LLC ....G 513 515-8386
  Cincinnati (G-4482)
Wordcross Enterprises Inc ....F 614 410-4140
  Columbus (G-7612)

GRAPHIC LAYOUT SVCS: Printed Circuitry

Atchley Signs & Graphics ....G 614 421-7446
  Columbus (G-6624)

GRAPHITE MINING SVCS

Graftech Holdings Inc ....B 216 676-2000
  Independence (G-11134)

GRATINGS: Open Steel Flooring

Brown-Campbell Company ....F 216 332-0101
  Maple Heights (G-12567)
Ohio Gratings Inc ....B 330 477-6707
  Canton (G-2772)

GRATINGS: Tread, Fabricated Metal

Final Touch Metal Fabricating .... G 216 348-1750
Cleveland *(G-5238)*

GRAVE MARKERS: Concrete

Ashland Monument Company Inc .... G 419 281-2688
Ashland *(G-678)*

GRAVE VAULTS, METAL

Clark Grave Vault Company .... C 614 294-3761
Columbus *(G-6769)*

GRAVEL MINING

Beck Sand & Gravel Inc .... G 330 626-3863
Ravenna *(G-16369)*
Fleming Construction Co .... E 740 494-2177
Prospect *(G-16350)*
Fouremans Sand & Gravel Inc .... G 937 547-1005
Greenville *(G-10368)*
Haueter Construction Co .... G 440 834-8220
Newbury *(G-14956)*
John L Garber Materials Corp .... F 419 884-1567
Mansfield *(G-12463)*
Kipps Gravel Company Inc .... F 513 732-1024
Batavia *(G-1160)*
M J Coates Construction Co .... G 937 886-9546
Dayton *(G-8318)*
Morrow Gravel Company Inc .... F 513 899-2000
Morrow *(G-14413)*
Oster Sand and Gravel Inc .... G 330 494-5472
Canton *(G-2776)*
Shelly Materials Inc .... F 740 775-4567
Chillicothe *(G-3222)*
Stansley Mineral Resources Inc .... E 419 843-2813
Sylvania *(G-17962)*
Watson Gravel Inc .... E 513 422-3781
Middletown *(G-13964)*
Watson Gravel Inc .... D 513 863-0070
Hamilton *(G-10621)*
Weber Sand & Gravel Inc .... G 419 636-7920
Bryan *(G-2312)*
Wysong Gravel Co Inc .... F 937 456-4539
West Alexandria *(G-19626)*
Wysong Gravel Co Inc .... G 937 452-1523
Camden *(G-2467)*
Wysong Gravel Co Inc .... G 937 839-5497
West Alexandria *(G-19627)*

GREASES & INEDIBLE FATS, RENDERED

Inland Products Inc .... E 614 443-3425
Columbus *(G-7027)*

GREASES: Lubricating

Foam Seal Inc .... D 216 881-8111
Cleveland *(G-5256)*

GREENHOUSES: Prefabricated Metal

Consoldted Grnhse Slutions LLC .... G 330 844-8598
Strongsville *(G-17732)*
Cropking Incorporated .... F 330 302-4203
Lodi *(G-12009)*
Ludy Greenhouse Mfg Corp .... D 800 255-5839
New Madison *(G-14742)*
Rough Brothers Mfg Inc .... D 513 242-0310
Cincinnati *(G-4283)*
Superior Structures Inc .... F 513 942-5954
Harrison *(G-10674)*
XS Smith Inc .... E 252 940-5060
Cincinnati *(G-4529)*

GREETING CARD SHOPS

Gorant Chocolatier LLC .... C 330 726-8821
Boardman *(G-1899)*
Naptime Productions LLC .... F 419 662-9521
Rossford *(G-16587)*
Piqua Chocolate Company Inc .... G 937 773-1981
Piqua *(G-16151)*

GRILLES & REGISTERS: Ornamental Metal Work

E C S Corp .... F 440 323-1707
Elyria *(G-9247)*

GRINDING MEDIA: Pottery

E R Advanced Ceramics Inc .... E 330 426-9433
East Palestine *(G-9077)*

GRINDING SVC: Precision, Commercial Or Indl

Advanced Cryogenic Entps LLC .... F 330 922-0750
Akron *(G-31)*
Afc Company .... F 330 533-5581
Canfield *(G-2519)*
Blade Manufacturing Co Inc .... F 614 294-1649
Columbus *(G-6679)*
Brockman Jig Grinding Service .... G 937 220-9780
Dayton *(G-8064)*
G H Cutter Services Inc .... G 419 476-0476
Toledo *(G-18300)*
Herman Machine Inc .... F 330 633-3261
Tallmadge *(G-17984)*
Micro Products Co Inc .... D 440 943-0258
Willoughby Hills *(G-20471)*
P & J Manufacturing Inc .... F 419 241-7369
Toledo *(G-18453)*
P & L Precision Grinding LLC .... F 330 746-8081
Youngstown *(G-20988)*
S C Industries Inc .... E 216 732-9000
Euclid *(G-9441)*
Tc Precision Machine Inc .... G 937 278-3334
Dayton *(G-8547)*
Thread-Rite Tool & Mfg Inc .... G 937 222-2836
Dayton *(G-8555)*
Triaxis Machine & Tool LLC .... G 440 230-0303
North Royalton *(G-15308)*
Wright Buffing Wheel Company .... G 330 424-7887
Lisbon *(G-11983)*

GRIPS OR HANDLES: Rubber

US 261 Corp .... G 216 531-7143
Cleveland *(G-6243)*

GRITS: Crushed & Broken

Sands Hill Mining LLC .... F 740 384-4211
Hamden *(G-10525)*
Southern Ohio Materials .... G 937 386-3200
Seaman *(G-16884)*

GROCERIES WHOLESALERS, NEC

American Bottling Company .... D 614 237-4201
Columbus *(G-6581)*
Bread Kneads Inc .... G 419 422-3863
Findlay *(G-9661)*
Brew Kettle Inc .... F 440 234-8788
Strongsville *(G-17721)*
Central Coca-Cola Btlg Co Inc .... C 419 476-6622
Toledo *(G-18226)*
Ervan Guttman Co .... G 513 791-0767
Cincinnati *(G-3653)*
G & J Pepsi-Cola Bottlers Inc .... B 740 354-9191
Franklin Furnace *(G-9934)*
G & J Pepsi-Cola Bottlers Inc .... D 740 452-2721
Zanesville *(G-21140)*
Generations Coffee Company LLC .... G 440 546-0901
Brecksville *(G-2038)*
Hiland Group Incorporated .... D 330 499-8404
Canton *(G-2699)*
Luxfer Magtech Inc .... E 513 772-3066
Cincinnati *(G-3958)*
Norcia Bakery .... E 330 454-1077
Canton *(G-2763)*
P-Americas LLC .... C 330 746-7652
Youngstown *(G-20990)*
Pepsi-Cola Metro Btlg Co Inc .... B 937 461-4664
Dayton *(G-8421)*
Pepsi-Cola Metro Btlg Co Inc .... B 330 963-0426
Twinsburg *(G-18833)*
Schwebel Baking Company .... C 440 248-1500
Solon *(G-17228)*
Skyline Chili Inc .... C 513 874-1188
Fairfield *(G-9565)*

GROCERIES, GENERAL LINE WHOLESALERS

La Perla Inc .... F 419 534-2074
Toledo *(G-18374)*
Nestle Usa Inc .... E 513 576-4930
Loveland *(G-12217)*

Ricking Paper and Specialty Co .... E 513 825-3551
Cincinnati *(G-4269)*
Sandridge Food Corporation .... C 330 725-8883
Medina *(G-13335)*
Uncle Jesters Fine Foods LLC .... G 937 550-1025
Miamisburg *(G-13729)*

GUARD SVCS

Area Wide Protective Inc .... E 513 321-9889
Fairfield *(G-9483)*

GUARDRAILS

Highway Safety Corp .... F 740 387-6991
Marion *(G-12711)*

GUARDS: Machine, Sheet Metal

Custom Enclosures Corp .... G 330 786-9000
Akron *(G-129)*
Hennig Inc .... G 513 247-0838
Blue Ash *(G-1788)*
Tkr Metal Fabricating LLC .... G 440 221-2770
Willoughby *(G-20448)*

GUIDED MISSILES & SPACE VEHICLES

Daniel Malek .... G 330 701-5760
Cuyahoga Falls *(G-7858)*
Tessec Manufacturing Svcs LLC .... E 937 985-3552
Dayton *(G-8553)*

GUIDED MISSILES/SPACE VEHICLE PARTS/AUX EQPT: Research/Devel

Defense Co Inc .... D 413 998-1637
Cleveland *(G-5081)*

GUN SIGHTS: Optical

Mbm Industries Ltd .... G 937 522-0719
Beavercreek Township *(G-1369)*

GUN SVCS

J & J Performance Inc .... F 330 567-2455
Shreve *(G-17004)*

GUTTERS: Sheet Metal

Aba Gutters Inc .... G 440 729-2177
Chesterland *(G-3149)*
Gutter Topper Ltd .... G 513 797-5800
Batavia *(G-1150)*
J O Y Aluminum Products Inc .... F 513 797-1100
Batavia *(G-1155)*
Matteo Aluminum Inc .... E 440 585-5213
Wickliffe *(G-20217)*
Roofing Annex LLC .... G 513 942-0555
West Chester *(G-19895)*

GYPSUM PRDTS

California Ceramic Supply Co .... G 216 531-9185
Euclid *(G-9406)*
Caraustar Industries Inc .... E 330 665-7700
Copley *(G-7679)*
Ernst Enterprises Inc .... F 419 222-2015
Lima *(G-11861)*
Mineral Processing Company .... G 419 396-3501
Carey *(G-2883)*
Owens Corning Sales LLC .... C 330 634-0460
Tallmadge *(G-17998)*
Priest Services Inc .... E 440 333-1123
Mayfield Heights *(G-13170)*
Priest Services Inc .... F 440 333-1123
Rocky River *(G-16552)*
United States Gypsum Company .... B 419 734-3161
Gypsum *(G-10521)*
Wall Technology Inc .... E 715 532-5548
Toledo *(G-18594)*

GYROSCOPES

Atlantic Inertial Systems Inc .... E 740 788-3800
Heath *(G-10717)*

HAIR & HAIR BASED PRDTS

Mels Life Like Hair .... G 937 278-9486
Dayton *(G-8339)*
Safe 4 People Inc .... G 419 797-4087
Port Clinton *(G-16257)*

PRODUCT SECTION

HARDWARE & BUILDING PRDTS: Plastic

U S Hair Inc ....G 614 235-5190
  Columbus (G-7554)

HAIR CARE PRDTS

John Frieda Prof Hair Care Inc ....E 800 521-3189
  Cincinnati (G-3879)
LOreal Usa Inc ....A 440 248-3700
  Cleveland (G-5584)
Mantra Haircare LLC ....F 440 526-3304
  Broadview Heights (G-2095)
Natural Beauty Products Inc ....F 513 420-9400
  Middletown (G-13935)
Pfizer Inc ....C 937 746-3603
  Franklin (G-9908)
Procter & Gamble Company ....B 513 983-1100
  Cincinnati (G-4198)

HAIR CARE PRDTS: Hair Coloring Preparations

Fantastic Sams Hair Care Salon ....G 740 456-4296
  Portsmouth (G-16282)

HAIR CURLERS: Beauty Shop

Salon Styling Concepts Ltd ....E 216 539-0437
  Maple Heights (G-12579)

HAND TOOLS, NEC: Wholesalers

CR Laurence Co Inc ....G 440 248-0003
  Cleveland (G-5036)
Elliott Tool Technologies Ltd ....D 937 253-6133
  Dayton (G-8182)
National Tool & Equipment Inc ....F 330 629-8665
  Youngstown (G-20973)
Norbar Torque Tools Inc ....F 440 953-1175
  Willoughby (G-20389)

HANDBAGS

Gro2 Bags & Accessories LLC ....G 740 622-0928
  Coshocton (G-7736)
Judith Leiber LLC ....D 614 449-4217
  Columbus (G-7080)
Ravenworks Deer Skin ....G 937 354-5151
  Mount Victory (G-14521)

HANDBAGS: Women's

Hugo Bosca Company Inc ....E 937 323-5523
  Springfield (G-17423)
Tapestry Inc ....F 419 471-9033
  Toledo (G-18543)

HANDLES: Wood

Canfield Manufacturing Co Inc ....G 330 533-3333
  North Jackson (G-15143)

HANGERS: Garment, Wire

Wire Products Company Inc ....C 216 267-0777
  Cleveland (G-6316)

HARD RUBBER PRDTS, NEC

Dacon Industries Co ....E 330 298-9491
  Ravenna (G-16374)
International Automotive ....F 330 279-6557
  Holmesville (G-10982)

HARDWARE

AB Bonded Locksmiths Inc ....G 513 531-7334
  Cincinnati (G-3286)
Action Coupling & Eqp Inc ....D 330 279-4242
  Holmesville (G-10972)
Aluminum Bearing Co of America ....G 216 267-8560
  Cleveland (G-4679)
Ampex Metal Products Company .....E 216 267-9242
  Brookpark (G-2136)
Annin & Co ....D 740 622-4447
  Coshocton (G-7718)
Architectural Door Systems LLC ......G 513 808-9900
  Norwood (G-15422)
Arnco Corporation ....C 800 847-7661
  Elyria (G-9219)
Baker McMillen Co ....E 330 923-3303
  Stow (G-17573)
Boardman Molded Products Inc ......D 330 788-2400
  Youngstown (G-20854)

Brass Accents Inc ....F 330 332-9500
  Salem (G-16721)
Chantilly Development Corp ....F 419 243-8109
  Toledo (G-18227)
Cleveland Hdwr & Forging Co ....E 216 641-5200
  Cleveland (G-4962)
Curtiss-Wright Flow Ctrl Corp ....D 216 267-3200
  Cleveland (G-5045)
Custom Metal Works Inc ....F 419 668-7831
  Norwalk (G-15385)
Dayton Superior Corporation ....F 937 682-4015
  Rushsylvania (G-16595)
Desco Corporation ....G 614 888-8855
  New Albany (G-14622)
Detroit Technologies Inc ....E 937 492-2708
  Sidney (G-17030)
Die Co Inc ....F 440 942-8856
  Eastlake (G-9104)
Eaton Corporation ....C 330 274-0743
  Aurora (G-877)
Edward W Daniel LLC ....E 440 647-1960
  Wellington (G-19577)
Elster Perfection Corporation ....D 440 428-1171
  Geneva (G-10218)
Exact Pipe Tools ....G 330 922-8150
  Cuyahoga Falls (G-7865)
Fastenal Company ....G 419 629-3024
  New Bremen (G-14654)
Faull & Son LLC ....F 330 652-4341
  Niles (G-15008)
Federal Equipment Company ....G 513 621-5260
  Cincinnati (G-3680)
First Francis Company Inc ....E 440 352-8927
  Painesville (G-15739)
Flex-Strut Inc ....G 330 372-9999
  Warren (G-19403)
Florida Production Engrg Inc ....D 937 996-4361
  New Madison (G-14741)
Fort Recovery Industries Inc ....B 419 375-4121
  Fort Recovery (G-9818)
Gateway Concrete Forming Svcs ....D 513 353-2000
  Miamiburg (G-13746)
Group Industries Inc ....E 216 271-0702
  Cleveland (G-5355)
Hawthorne Bolt Works Corp ....G 330 723-0555
  Medina (G-13270)
Hbd/Thermoid Inc ....F 937 593-5010
  Bellefontaine (G-1517)
Hbd/Thermoid Inc ....C 614 526-7000
  Dublin (G-8922)
Hebco Products Inc ....A 419 562-7987
  Bucyrus (G-2333)
Heller Machine Products Inc ....E 216 281-2951
  Cleveland (G-5390)
Hfi LLC ....B 614 491-0700
  Columbus (G-6995)
Hoffman Hinge and Hardware LLC ..G 330 935-2240
  Alliance (G-474)
International Automotive Compo .....A 419 433-5653
  Huron (G-11099)
J B Kepple Sheet Metal ....G 740 393-2971
  Mount Vernon (G-14484)
John Stieg & Associates ....G 614 889-7954
  Dublin (G-8933)
Kasai North America Inc ....F 614 356-1494
  Dublin (G-8936)
L & W Inc ....D 734 397-6300
  Avon (G-953)
Lake Park Tool & Machine LLC ....F 330 788-2437
  Youngstown (G-20956)
Matdan Corporation ....E 513 794-0500
  Blue Ash (G-1815)
Mecc-Usa LLC ....G 513 891-0301
  West Chester (G-19742)
Meese Inc ....D 440 998-1202
  Ashtabula (G-785)
Midlake Products & Mfg Co ....D 330 875-4202
  Louisville (G-12161)
Miller Studio Inc ....D 330 339-1100
  New Philadelphia (G-14787)
Morgal Machine Tool Co ....D 937 325-5561
  Springfield (G-17451)
Netherland Rubber Company ....F 513 733-0883
  Cincinnati (G-4068)
Nova Machine Products Inc ....D 216 267-3200
  Middleburgh Heights (G-13767)
Ohio Hydraulics Inc ....E 513 771-2590
  Cincinnati (G-4103)
Progressive Machine Die Inc ....E 330 405-6600
  Macedonia (G-12321)

R & R Tool Inc ....E 937 783-8665
  Blanchester (G-1705)
Samsel Rope & Marine Supply Co ...E 216 241-0333
  Cleveland (G-6029)
Sarasota Quality Products ....G 440 899-9820
  Westlake (G-20155)
Sheet Metal Products Co Inc ....E 440 392-9000
  Mentor (G-13581)
Summers Acquisition Corp ....E 216 941-7700
  Cleveland (G-6117)
Summers Acquisition Corp ....G 419 526-5800
  Mansfield (G-12523)
Summers Acquisition Corp ....E 440 946-5611
  Eastlake (G-9134)
Summers Acquisition Corp ....E 419 423-5800
  Findlay (G-9765)
Superior Metal Products Inc ....E 419 228-1145
  Lima (G-11947)
Te-Co Manufacturing LLC ....D 937 836-0961
  Englewood (G-9377)
Technoform GL Insul N Amer Inc ....E 330 487-6600
  Twinsburg (G-18863)
Texmaster Tools Inc ....F 740 965-8778
  Fredericktown (G-9980)
Three Sons Minerva Hardware ....F 330 868-7709
  Minerva (G-14204)
Trim Parts Inc ....E 513 934-0815
  Lebanon (G-11702)
Trim Systems Operating Corp ....C 614 289-5360
  New Albany (G-14639)
Trust Manufacturing LLC ....F 216 531-8787
  Euclid (G-9449)
United Die & Mfg Co ....E 330 938-6141
  Sebring (G-16897)
Universal Industrial Pdts Inc ....F 419 737-9584
  Pioneer (G-16097)
Verhoff Machine & Welding Inc ....C 419 596-3202
  Continental (G-7669)
Wallen Commercial Hardware ....G 937 426-5711
  Beavercreek Township (G-1376)
Washington Products Inc ....F 330 837-5101
  Massillon (G-13057)
Whiteside Manufacturing Co ....E 740 363-1179
  Delaware (G-8732)

HARDWARE & BUILDING PRDTS: Plastic

Ames Lock Specialties Inc ....G 419 474-2995
  Toledo (G-18183)
Ametek Inc ....C 419 739-3202
  Wapakoneta (G-19320)
Associated Materials LLC ....B 330 929-1811
  Cuyahoga Falls (G-7841)
Associated Materials Group Inc ....E 330 929-1811
  Cuyahoga Falls (G-7842)
Associated Mtls Holdings LLC ....A 330 929-1811
  Cuyahoga Falls (G-7843)
Blackthorn LLC ....E 937 836-9296
  Clayton (G-4572)
Buckeye Stamping Company ....D 614 445-0059
  Columbus (G-6712)
Cpg International LLC ....E 937 655-8766
  Wilmington (G-20492)
Dayton Superior Corporation ....C 937 866-0711
  Miamisburg (G-13655)
Deflecto LLC ....E 330 602-0840
  Dover (G-8815)
Fox Lite Inc ....E 937 864-1966
  Fairborn (G-9459)
Fypon Ltd ....C 800 446-3040
  Maumee (G-13112)
Gilkey Window Company Inc ....G 513 769-9663
  Cincinnati (G-3751)
Gilkey Window Company Inc ....D 513 769-4527
  Cincinnati (G-3752)
Gorell Enterprises Inc ....B 724 465-1800
  Streetsboro (G-17675)
Harbor Industrial Corp ....F 440 599-8366
  Conneaut (G-7647)
Interntnal Plstic Cmpnents Inc ....F 330 744-0625
  Campbell (G-2468)
Johnston-Morehouse-Dickey Co .....G 614 866-0452
  Columbus (G-7075)
Johnston-Morehouse-Dickey Co .....G 330 405-6050
  Macedonia (G-12308)
MTI Acquisition LLC ....E 740 929-2065
  Hebron (G-10755)
Protec Industries Incorporated ....G 440 937-4142
  Avon (G-959)
Resinoid Engineering Corp ....E 740 928-2220
  Heath (G-10730)

Employee Codes: A=Over 500 employees, B=251-500
C=101-250, D=51-100, E=20-50, F=10-19, G=3-9

2019 Harris Ohio Industrial Directory

1451

HARDWARE & BUILDING PRDTS: Plastic

Style Crest Enterprises Inc ....D....... 419 355-8586
  Fremont *(G-10053)*
Timbertech Limited ....F....... 614 443-4891
  Columbus *(G-7529)*
West & Barker Inc ....E....... 330 652-9923
  Niles *(G-15040)*

HARDWARE & EQPT: Stage, Exc Lighting

Beck Studios Inc ....E....... 513 831-6650
  Milford *(G-13997)*
Janson Industries ....D....... 330 455-7029
  Canton *(G-2716)*
Tiffin Scenic Studios Inc ....D....... 800 445-1546
  Tiffin *(G-18089)*

HARDWARE CLOTH: Woven Wire, Made From Purchased Wire

Cleveland Wire Cloth & Mfg Co ....E....... 216 341-1832
  Cleveland *(G-4985)*

HARDWARE STORES

Caldwell Lumber & Supply Co ....E....... 740 732-2306
  Caldwell *(G-2404)*
Cambridge Cable Service Co ....G....... 740 685-5775
  Byesville *(G-2380)*
Hershbergers Dutch Market LLP ......E....... 740 489-5322
  Old Washington *(G-15526)*
Matco Tools Corporation ....B....... 330 929-4949
  Stow *(G-17605)*
Mid-Wood Inc ....F....... 419 257-3331
  North Baltimore *(G-15046)*
Rockys Hinge Co ....G....... 330 539-6296
  Girard *(G-10265)*
Terry Lumber and Supply Co ....F....... 330 659-6800
  Peninsula *(G-15899)*
Thomas Do-It Center Inc ....D....... 740 446-2002
  Gallipolis *(G-10176)*
Woodsfeld True Vlue HM Ctr Inc ......F....... 740 472-1651
  Woodsfield *(G-20550)*

HARDWARE STORES: Builders'

Wauseon Silo & Coal Company ....F....... 419 335-6041
  Wauseon *(G-19538)*

HARDWARE STORES: Chainsaws

D & M Saw & Tool Inc ....G....... 513 871-5433
  Cincinnati *(G-3568)*
Dittmar Sales and Service ....F....... 740 653-7933
  Lancaster *(G-11567)*

HARDWARE STORES: Pumps & Pumping Eqpt

Fountain Specialists Inc ....E....... 513 831-5717
  Milford *(G-14009)*
Graco Ohio Inc ....D....... 330 494-1313
  North Canton *(G-15088)*
Layne Heavy Civil Inc ....E....... 513 424-7287
  Middletown *(G-13919)*

HARDWARE STORES: Snowblowers

Mapledale Farm Inc ....F....... 440 286-3389
  Chardon *(G-3125)*

HARDWARE STORES: Tools

Cammel Saw Company Inc ....F....... 330 477-3764
  Canton *(G-2605)*
Gordon Tool Inc ....F....... 419 263-3151
  Payne *(G-15872)*
Mataco ....G....... 440 546-8355
  Broadview Heights *(G-2096)*
National Tool & Equipment Inc ....F....... 330 629-8665
  Youngstown *(G-20973)*
Royer Technologies Inc ....G....... 937 743-6114
  Saint Marys *(G-16698)*
Simonds International LLC ....F....... 978 424-0100
  Kimbolton *(G-11457)*
Stanley Industrial & Auto LLC ....C....... 614 755-7089
  Westerville *(G-20024)*
Triaxis Machine & Tool LLC ....G....... 440 230-0303
  North Royalton *(G-15308)*

HARDWARE STORES: Tools, Power

Gary Compton ....G....... 937 339-6829
  Troy *(G-18660)*

Lees Machinery Inc ....G....... 440 259-2222
  Perry *(G-15907)*

HARDWARE WHOLESALERS

Atlas Bolt & Screw Company LLC ....C....... 419 289-6171
  Ashland *(G-681)*
Barnes Group Inc ....E....... 419 891-9292
  Maumee *(G-13077)*
Chrisnik Inc ....G....... 513 738-2920
  Okeana *(G-15516)*
Custer Products Limited ....F....... 330 490-3158
  Massillon *(G-12972)*
Diy Holster LLC ....G....... 419 921-2168
  Elyria *(G-9244)*
Khempco Bldg Sup Co Ltd Partnr ...D....... 740 549-0465
  Delaware *(G-8700)*
Matco Tools Corporation ....B....... 330 929-4949
  Stow *(G-17605)*
Ohashi Technica USA Inc ....F....... 740 965-5115
  Sunbury *(G-17894)*
Ohio Power Tool Brush Co ....G....... 419 736-3010
  Ashland *(G-731)*
Paulin Industries Inc ....E....... 216 433-7633
  Parma *(G-15826)*
Shook Manufactured Pdts Inc ....G....... 330 848-9780
  Akron *(G-375)*
Texmaster Tools Inc ....F....... 740 965-8778
  Fredericktown *(G-9980)*
Twin Ventures Inc ....F....... 330 405-3838
  Twinsburg *(G-18868)*
Waxman Industries Inc ....C....... 440 439-1830
  Cleveland *(G-6295)*

HARDWARE, WHOLESALE: Bolts

Akko Fastener Inc ....F....... 513 489-8300
  Blue Ash *(G-1724)*
Hudson Fasteners Inc ....G....... 330 270-9500
  Youngstown *(G-20933)*

HARDWARE, WHOLESALE: Builders', NEC

LE Smith Company ....D....... 419 636-4555
  Bryan *(G-2295)*
Twin Cities Concrete Co ....F....... 330 343-4491
  Dover *(G-8861)*

HARDWARE, WHOLESALE: Nuts

Facil North America Inc ....C....... 330 487-2500
  Twinsburg *(G-18774)*

HARDWARE, WHOLESALE: Power Tools & Access

Form-A-Chip Inc ....G....... 937 223-4135
  Dayton *(G-8201)*
Noco Company ....B....... 216 464-8131
  Solon *(G-17208)*
TTI Floor Care North Amer Inc ....B....... 440 996-2000
  Solon *(G-17255)*

HARDWARE, WHOLESALE: Saw Blades

Cammel Saw Company Inc ....F....... 330 477-3764
  Canton *(G-2605)*
Uhrichsville Carbide Inc ....F....... 740 922-9197
  Uhrichsville *(G-18899)*

HARDWARE, WHOLESALE: Screws

Maumee Machine & Tool Corp ....E....... 419 385-2501
  Toledo *(G-18402)*

HARDWARE: Aircraft

Twin Valley Metalcraft Asm LLC ......G....... 937 787-4634
  West Alexandria *(G-19622)*

HARDWARE: Aircraft & Marine, Incl Pulleys & Similar Items

Acorn Technology Corporation ....E....... 216 663-1244
  Cleveland *(G-4610)*

HARDWARE: Builders'

Allfasteners Usa LLC ....E....... 440 232-6060
  Medina *(G-13222)*
Arrow Tru-Line Inc ....D....... 419 636-7013
  Bryan *(G-2265)*
Cleveland Steel Specialty Co ....E....... 216 464-9400
  Bedford Heights *(G-1466)*

Leetonia Tool Company ....F....... 330 427-6944
  Leetonia *(G-11718)*
Napoleon Spring Works Inc ....C....... 419 445-1010
  Archbold *(G-660)*
Stanley Industrial & Auto LLC ....D....... 614 755-7000
  Westerville *(G-20025)*

HARDWARE: Casket

Langenau Manufacturing Company ..F....... 216 651-3400
  Cleveland *(G-5558)*

HARDWARE: Furniture, Builders' & Other Household

Fortner Upholstering Inc ....F....... 614 475-8282
  Columbus *(G-6933)*
Master Mfg Co Inc ....E....... 216 641-0500
  Cleveland *(G-5632)*
PA Stratton & Co Inc ....E....... 419 660-9979
  Collins *(G-6425)*

HARDWARE: Hangers, Wall

Design Magnetics Ltd ....G....... 234 380-5500
  Hudson *(G-11042)*
J W Goss Co Inc ....F....... 330 395-0739
  Warren *(G-19413)*
Triton Products LLC ....C....... 440 248-5480
  Solon *(G-17254)*

HARDWARE: Padlocks

Hercules Industries Inc ....E....... 740 494-2620
  Prospect *(G-16351)*
Wilson Bohannan Company ....D....... 740 382-3639
  Marion *(G-12750)*

HARDWARE: Piano

Marlboro Manufacturing Inc ....E....... 330 935-2221
  Alliance *(G-488)*

HARDWARE: Plastic

Chuck Meadors Plastics Co ....F....... 440 813-4466
  Jefferson *(G-11227)*

HARDWARE: Rubber

Reynolds Industries Inc ....E....... 330 889-9466
  West Farmington *(G-19920)*

HARNESS ASSEMBLIES: Cable & Wire

Adcura Mfg ....G....... 937 222-3800
  Dayton *(G-8008)*
Alphabet Inc ....D....... 330 856-3366
  Warren *(G-19366)*
American Advnced Assmblies LLC .E....... 937 339-6267
  Troy *(G-18634)*
Ankim Enterprises Incorporated ......E....... 937 599-1121
  Sidney *(G-17016)*
Co- Ax Technology Inc ....E....... 440 914-9200
  Solon *(G-17128)*
Connective Design Incorporated ......F....... 937 746-8252
  Miamisburg *(G-13651)*
Empire Power Systems Co ....G....... 440 796-4401
  Madison *(G-12349)*
Ewh Spectrum LLC ....D....... 937 593-8010
  Bellefontaine *(G-1515)*
Gmelectric Inc ....G....... 330 477-3392
  Canton *(G-2685)*
Inventus Power (ohio) Inc ....F....... 614 351-2191
  Dublin *(G-8931)*
L & J Cable Inc ....E....... 937 526-9445
  Russia *(G-16609)*
La Grange Elec Assemblies Co ....E....... 440 355-5388
  Lagrange *(G-11486)*
Malabar Properties LLC ....F....... 419 884-0071
  Mansfield *(G-12473)*
Microplex Inc ....E....... 330 498-0600
  North Canton *(G-15101)*
Mk Enterprises Inc ....E....... 440 632-0121
  Middlefield *(G-13832)*
Mueller Electric Company Inc ....E....... 614 888-8855
  New Albany *(G-14631)*
Ogc Industries Inc ....F....... 330 456-1500
  Canton *(G-2770)*
Ohio Wire Harness LLC ....F....... 937 292-7355
  Bellefontaine *(G-1523)*
Otr Controls LLC ....G....... 513 621-2197
  Cincinnati *(G-4123)*

Per-Tech Inc..........E....... 330 833-8824
Massillon *(G-13038)*
RTD Electronics Inc..........F....... 330 487-0716
Twinsburg *(G-18851)*
SMH Manufacturing Inc..........F....... 419 884-0071
Lexington *(G-11806)*
Spi Inc..........G....... 937 374-2700
Xenia *(G-20790)*
Thermtrol Corporation..........E....... 330 497-4148
North Canton *(G-15125)*
Total Cable Solutions Inc..........G....... 513 457-7013
Springboro *(G-17357)*
Valtronic Technology Inc..........D....... 440 349-1239
Solon *(G-17257)*
Wetsu Group Inc..........F....... 937 324-9353
Springfield *(G-17517)*

HARNESS REPAIR SHOP

Charm Harness and Boot Ltd..........F....... 330 893-0402
Charm *(G-3141)*
Maysville Harness Shop Ltd..........G....... 330 695-9977
Apple Creek *(G-612)*

HARNESS WIRING SETS: Internal Combustion Engines

Elcor Inc..........E....... 440 365-5941
Elyria *(G-9249)*
Electripack Inc..........E....... 937 433-2602
Miamisburg *(G-13663)*
Mueller Electric Company Inc..........E....... 216 771-5225
Akron *(G-290)*

HEALTH & ALLIED SERVICES, NEC

Kapios LLC..........G....... 567 661-0772
Toledo *(G-18361)*

HEALTH AIDS: Exercise Eqpt

Balbo Industries Inc..........G....... 440 333-0630
Rocky River *(G-16543)*
Elite Ftscom Inc..........G....... 740 845-0987
London *(G-12059)*
Wooden Horse Corporation..........G....... 419 663-1472
Norwalk *(G-15419)*

HEALTH FOOD & SUPPLEMENT STORES

Nestle Usa Inc..........D....... 216 861-8350
Cleveland *(G-5744)*
Wileys Finest LLC..........C....... 740 622-1072
Coshocton *(G-7759)*

HEALTH SYSTEMS AGENCY

American Heart Association Inc..........F....... 419 740-6180
Maumee *(G-13070)*

HEARING AIDS

Akron Ent Hearing Services Inc..........G....... 330 762-8959
Akron *(G-38)*
Bills Sports Center..........G....... 419 335-2405
Wauseon *(G-19510)*
Communications Aid Inc..........F....... 513 475-8453
Cincinnati *(G-3537)*
Ear Medical Center Inc..........F....... 812 537-0031
Cincinnati *(G-3623)*
Hearing Aid Center of NW Ohio..........G....... 419 636-8959
Bryan *(G-2286)*
Morris Maico Hearing Aid Svc..........G....... 419 232-6200
Van Wert *(G-19103)*
Phonak LLC..........G....... 513 420-4568
Middletown *(G-13940)*
Sonus-Usa Inc..........E....... 419 474-9324
Toledo *(G-18526)*

HEAT EMISSION OPERATING APPARATUS

Electrowarmth Products LLC..........G....... 740 599-7222
Danville *(G-7963)*
Hanon Systems Usa LLC..........C....... 313 920-0583
Carey *(G-2882)*

HEAT EXCHANGERS

Chart Asia Inc..........D....... 440 753-1490
Cleveland *(G-4913)*
Chart Industries Inc..........B....... 440 753-1490
Cleveland *(G-4914)*
Chart International Inc..........E....... 440 753-1490
Cleveland *(G-4915)*
Ross Hx LLC..........G....... 513 217-1565
Middletown *(G-13949)*
Wcr Incorporated..........E....... 740 333-3448
Wshngtn CT Hs *(G-20749)*

HEAT EXCHANGERS: After Or Inter Coolers Or Condensers, Etc

Ohio Heat Transfer Ltd..........F....... 740 695-0635
Saint Clairsville *(G-16643)*
Sgl Technic Inc..........E....... 440 572-3600
Strongsville *(G-17786)*
Universal Hydraulik USA Corp..........G....... 419 873-6340
Perrysburg *(G-16020)*

HEAT TREATING: Metal

Accuphase Metal Treating LLC..........G....... 937 610-5934
Moraine *(G-14328)*
Akron Steel Treating Co..........E....... 330 773-8211
Akron *(G-53)*
Al Fe Heat Treating-Ohio Inc..........E....... 330 336-0211
Wadsworth *(G-19224)*
Al-Fe Heat Treating Inc..........E....... 419 782-7200
Defiance *(G-8612)*
Allegheny Ludlum LLC..........E....... 330 875-2244
Louisville *(G-12151)*
Alternative Flash Inc..........E....... 330 334-6111
Wadsworth *(G-19225)*
AM Castle & Co..........D....... 330 425-7000
Bedford *(G-1381)*
Amac Enterprises Inc..........C....... 216 362-1880
Parma *(G-15814)*
American Quality Stripping..........E....... 419 625-6288
Sandusky *(G-16794)*
American Steel Treating Inc..........E....... 419 874-2044
Perrysburg *(G-15919)*
Analytic Stress Relieving Inc..........G....... 804 271-7198
Northwood *(G-15332)*
Arcelormittal Columbus LLC..........C....... 614 492-6800
Columbus *(G-6613)*
B&C Machine Co LLC..........B....... 330 745-4013
Barberton *(G-1058)*
Bekaert Corporation..........C....... 330 683-5060
Orrville *(G-15583)*
Bob Lanes Welding Inc..........F....... 740 373-3567
Marietta *(G-12609)*
Bodycote Imt Inc..........E....... 740 852-5000
London *(G-12050)*
Bodycote Thermal Proc Inc..........E....... 614 444-1181
Columbus *(G-6683)*
Bodycote Thermal Proc Inc..........E....... 513 921-2300
Cincinnati *(G-3399)*
Bodycote Thermal Proc Inc..........F....... 440 473-2020
Cleveland *(G-4827)*
Bodycote Thermal Proc Inc..........E....... 216 475-0400
Cleveland *(G-4828)*
Bodycote Thermal Proc Inc..........G....... 740 852-4955
London *(G-12051)*
Bowdil Company..........F....... 800 356-8663
Canton *(G-2596)*
Carpe Diem Industries LLC..........E....... 419 358-0129
Bluffton *(G-1887)*
Carpe Diem Industries LLC..........D....... 419 659-5639
Columbus Grove *(G-7632)*
Certified Heat Treating Inc..........E....... 937 866-0245
Dayton *(G-8084)*
Cincinnati Gearing Systems Inc..........D....... 513 527-8600
Cincinnati *(G-3493)*
Cincinnati Gearing Systems Inc..........D....... 513 527-8600
Cincinnati *(G-3495)*
Cleveland Hollow Boring Inc..........G....... 216 883-1926
Cleveland *(G-4963)*
Clifton Steel Company..........D....... 216 662-6111
Maple Heights *(G-12569)*
Columbus Coatings Company..........D....... 614 492-6800
Columbus *(G-6786)*
Commercial Steel Treating Co..........F....... 216 431-8204
Cleveland *(G-5004)*
Dayton Forging Heat Treating..........D....... 937 253-4126
Dayton *(G-8132)*
Derrick Company Inc..........E....... 513 321-8122
Cincinnati *(G-3583)*
Detroit Flame Hardening Co..........G....... 216 531-4273
Euclid *(G-9410)*
Detroit Flame Hardening Co..........F....... 513 942-1400
Fairfield *(G-9494)*
Dewitt Inc..........G....... 216 662-0800
Maple Heights *(G-12570)*
Die Co Inc..........E....... 440 942-8856
Eastlake *(G-9104)*
Dowa Tht America Inc..........E....... 419 354-4144
Bowling Green *(G-1971)*
Erie Steel Ltd..........E....... 419 478-3743
Toledo *(G-18285)*
Euclid Heat Treating Co..........D....... 216 481-8444
Euclid *(G-9413)*
Flynn Inc..........B....... 419 478-3743
Toledo *(G-18296)*
Franklin Field Service..........G....... 614 885-1779
Columbus *(G-6937)*
Fusion Automation Inc..........G....... 440 602-5595
Willoughby *(G-20326)*
General Steel Corporation..........F....... 216 883-4200
Cleveland *(G-5314)*
Gerdau Macsteel Atmosphere Ann..........D....... 330 478-0314
Canton *(G-2683)*
Gt Technologies Inc..........C....... 419 782-8955
Defiance *(G-8625)*
H & M Metal Processing Co..........E....... 330 745-3075
Akron *(G-194)*
H & S Steel Treating Inc..........F....... 330 678-5245
Kent *(G-11329)*
Heat Treating Inc..........E....... 937 325-3121
Springfield *(G-17414)*
Heat Treating Inc..........F....... 937 325-3121
Springfield *(G-17415)*
Heat Treating Inc..........G....... 614 759-9963
Gahanna *(G-10082)*
Heat Treating Technologies..........E....... 419 224-8324
Lima *(G-11873)*
Hl Tecmetal Group Inc..........E....... 440 373-5101
Wickliffe *(G-20213)*
Hl Tecmetal Group Inc..........F....... 216 941-0440
Cleveland *(G-5403)*
Hl Tecmetal Group Inc..........F....... 216 881-8100
Cleveland *(G-5404)*
Hmt Inc..........G....... 440 599-7005
Conneaut *(G-7648)*
Induction Hrdning Spclists Inc..........G....... 234 678-6820
Peninsula *(G-15894)*
Induction Management Svcs LLC..........G....... 440 947-2000
Warren *(G-19410)*
Isostatic Pressing Svcs LLC..........G....... 614 370-2140
Columbus *(G-7051)*
Kowalski Heat Treating Co..........F....... 216 631-4411
Cleveland *(G-5543)*
Lapham-Hickey Steel Corp..........D....... 419 399-4803
Paulding *(G-15865)*
Lapham-Hickey Steel Corp..........E....... 614 443-4881
Columbus *(G-7116)*
Mannings USA..........G....... 614 836-0021
Groveport *(G-10502)*
Metallurgical Service Inc..........E....... 937 294-2681
Moraine *(G-14368)*
Miller Consolidated Industries..........C....... 937 294-2681
Moraine *(G-14370)*
Moore Mc Millen Holdings..........D....... 330 745-3075
Cuyahoga Falls *(G-7899)*
Neturen America Corporation..........F....... 513 863-1900
Hamilton *(G-10589)*
Northwind Industries Inc..........E....... 216 433-0666
Cleveland *(G-5787)*
Ohio Metallurgical Service Inc..........D....... 440 365-4104
Elyria *(G-9304)*
P & L Heat Trting Grinding Inc..........E....... 330 746-1339
Youngstown *(G-20986)*
P & L Precision Grinding LLC..........F....... 330 746-8081
Youngstown *(G-20988)*
Parker Trutec Incorporated..........D....... 937 323-8833
Springfield *(G-17469)*
Pike Machine Products Co..........E....... 216 731-1880
Euclid *(G-9433)*
Pressure Technology Ohio Inc..........E....... 215 628-1975
Painesville *(G-15776)*
Pride Investments LLC..........F....... 937 461-1121
Dayton *(G-8439)*
Quality Metal Treating Company..........G....... 931 432-7467
Cincinnati *(G-4227)*
Ridge Machine & Welding Co..........G....... 740 537-2821
Toronto *(G-18611)*
Ropama Inc..........F....... 440 358-1304
Painesville *(G-15781)*
Samuel Steel Pickling Company..........D....... 330 963-3777
Twinsburg *(G-18853)*
Team Inc..........F....... 614 263-1808
Columbus *(G-7517)*
Team Cooperheat Mqs..........G....... 614 501-7304
Columbus *(G-7518)*
Techniques Surfaces Usa Inc..........G....... 937 323-2556
Springfield *(G-17504)*

PRODUCT

Employee Codes: A=Over 500 employees, B=251-500
C=101-250, D=51-100, E=20-50, F=10-19, G=3-9
2019 Harris Ohio
Industrial Directory
1453

HEAT TREATING: Metal

Thermal Solutions Inc ....G....... 614 263-1808
  Columbus *(G-7526)*
Thermal Treatment Center Inc ....E....... 216 881-8100
  Cleveland *(G-6167)*
Thermal Treatment Center Inc ....G....... 216 883-4820
  Cleveland *(G-6168)*
Thermal Treatment Center Inc ....E....... 440 943-4555
  Wickliffe *(G-20232)*
Thermal Treatment Center Inc ....F....... 216 941-0440
  Cleveland *(G-6169)*
Universal Heat Treating Inc ....E....... 216 641-2000
  Cleveland *(G-6238)*
USA Heat Treating Inc ....E....... 216 587-4700
  Cleveland *(G-6245)*
Vicon Fabricating Company Ltd ....E....... 440 205-6700
  Mentor *(G-13624)*
Weiss Industries Inc ....E....... 419 526-2480
  Mansfield *(G-12539)*
Winston Heat Treating Inc ....E....... 937 226-0110
  Dayton *(G-8597)*
Xtek Inc ....B....... 513 733-7800
  Cincinnati *(G-4530)*

HEATERS: Room & Wall, Including Radiators

Hunter Defense Tech Inc ....E....... 216 438-6111
  Solon *(G-17164)*
Suarez Corporation Industries ....E....... 330 494-5504
  Canton *(G-2828)*

HEATING & AIR CONDITIONING EQPT & SPLYS WHOLESALERS

Controls and Sheet Metal Inc ....E....... 513 721-3610
  Cincinnati *(G-3546)*
Custom Duct & Supply Co Inc ....G....... 937 228-2058
  Dayton *(G-8118)*
Daikin Applied Americas Inc ....G....... 614 351-9862
  Westerville *(G-20045)*
Reynolds & Co Inc ....G....... 937 592-8300
  Bellefontaine *(G-1524)*
Style Crest Inc ....B....... 419 332-7369
  Fremont *(G-10052)*
Style Crest Enterprises Inc ....D....... 419 355-8586
  Fremont *(G-10053)*
Yanfeng US Automotive ....D....... 419 662-4905
  Northwood *(G-15354)*

HEATING & AIR CONDITIONING UNITS, COMBINATION

Albin Sales Inc ....G....... 740 927-7210
  Pataskala *(G-15827)*
Aquapro Systems LLC ....F....... 877 278-2797
  West Chester *(G-19650)*
Cartwright Construction Inc ....G....... 330 929-3020
  Cuyahoga Falls *(G-7846)*
Famous Realty Cleveland Inc ....F....... 740 685-2533
  Byesville *(G-2385)*
Goodman Distribution Inc ....E....... 440 324-4071
  Avon Lake *(G-987)*
Hickok Ae LLC ....D....... 330 794-9770
  Akron *(G-207)*
Insource Tech Inc ....E....... 419 399-3600
  Paulding *(G-15862)*
J&I Duct Fab LLC ....F....... 937 473-2121
  Covington *(G-7788)*
R & R Comfort Experts LLC ....G....... 216 475-3995
  Cleveland *(G-5947)*

HEATING APPARATUS: Steam

Grid Industrial Heating Inc ....G....... 330 332-9931
  Salem *(G-16745)*

HEATING EQPT & SPLYS

Accent Manufacturing Inc ....F....... 330 724-7704
  Norton *(G-15355)*
Airtech Mechanical Inc ....F....... 419 292-0074
  Toledo *(G-18161)*
Beckett Air Incorporated ....D....... 440 327-9999
  North Ridgeville *(G-15209)*
Data Cooling Technologies LLC ....C....... 330 954-3800
  Cleveland Heights *(G-6347)*
Dcm Manufacturing Inc ....E....... 216 265-8006
  Cleveland *(G-5078)*
Duro Dyne Midwest Corp ....B....... 513 870-6000
  Hamilton *(G-10551)*
Ebner Furnaces Inc ....D....... 330 335-2311
  Wadsworth *(G-19237)*
Ets Schaefer LLC ....G....... 330 468-6600
  Macedonia *(G-12292)*
Ets Schaefer LLC ....G....... 330 468-6600
  Beachwood *(G-1237)*
Famous Industries Inc ....D....... 740 685-2592
  Byesville *(G-2384)*
First Solar Inc ....B....... 419 661-1478
  Perrysburg *(G-15952)*
Fives N Amercn Combustn Inc ....C....... 216 271-6000
  Cleveland *(G-5244)*
Fives N Amercn Combustn Inc ....G....... 734 207-7008
  Cleveland *(G-5245)*
Fives N Amercn Combustn Inc ....E....... 412 655-0101
  Cleveland *(G-5246)*
Glo-Quartz Electric Heater Co ....E....... 440 255-9701
  Mentor *(G-13459)*
Hartzell Fan Inc ....C....... 937 773-7411
  Piqua *(G-16122)*
Hdt Expeditionary Systems Inc ....E....... 440 466-6640
  Geneva *(G-10222)*
Lakeway Mfg Inc ....G....... 419 433-3030
  Huron *(G-11103)*
Mid-Ohio Regional Plg Comm ....E....... 614 351-9210
  Columbus *(G-7179)*
North Amrcn Sstnable Enrgy Ltd ....G....... 440 539-7133
  Parma *(G-15824)*
Old Es LLC ....E....... 330 468-6600
  Macedonia *(G-12312)*
Onix Corporation ....E....... 800 844-0076
  Perrysburg *(G-15990)*
Qual-Fab Inc ....E....... 440 327-5000
  Avon *(G-960)*
Selas Heat Technology Co LLC ....E....... 800 523-6500
  Streetsboro *(G-17697)*
Sgm Co Inc ....G....... 440 255-1190
  Mentor *(G-13580)*
Stelter and Brinck Inc ....E....... 513 367-9300
  Harrison *(G-10672)*
Sticker Corporation ....F....... 440 946-2100
  Willoughby *(G-20438)*
Swagelok Company ....E....... 440 349-5836
  Solon *(G-17243)*
T J F Inc ....F....... 419 878-4400
  Waterville *(G-19506)*
Thermo Systems Technology ....E....... 216 292-8250
  Cleveland *(G-6170)*
Trumbull Manufacturing Inc ....D....... 330 393-6624
  Warren *(G-19452)*

HEATING EQPT: Complete

Adams Manufacturing Company ....E....... 216 662-1600
  Cleveland *(G-4613)*
Briskheat Corporation ....C....... 614 294-3376
  Columbus *(G-6702)*
Chilltex LLC ....F....... 937 710-3308
  Anna *(G-588)*
Edison Solar Inc ....F....... 419 499-0000
  Milan *(G-13982)*
Hatfield Industries LLC ....G....... 513 225-0456
  West Chester *(G-19719)*
Hbb Pro Sales ....G....... 216 901-7900
  Cleveland *(G-5381)*
Sticker Corporation ....F....... 440 946-2100
  Willoughby *(G-20438)*
Trane Company ....F....... 419 491-2278
  Holland *(G-10963)*

HEATING EQPT: Dielectric

P S C Inc ....G....... 216 531-3375
  Cleveland *(G-5832)*

HEATING EQPT: Induction

Custom Coils ....G....... 330 426-3797
  Negley *(G-14589)*
Induction Services Inc ....G....... 330 652-4494
  Niles *(G-15013)*
Induction Tooling Inc ....E....... 440 237-0711
  North Royalton *(G-15277)*
Inter-Power Corporation ....G....... 330 652-4494
  Niles *(G-15014)*
Magneforce Inc ....F....... 330 856-9300
  Warren *(G-19421)*
Park-Ohio Holdings Corp ....F....... 440 947-2000
  Cleveland *(G-5842)*
Park-Ohio Industries Inc ....C....... 440 947-2000
  Cleveland *(G-5843)*
Specialties Mds Induction Ltd ....G....... 330 394-3338
  Warren *(G-19443)*
Taylor - Winfield Corporation ....D....... 330 259-8500
  Hubbard *(G-11010)*

HEATING PADS: Nonelectric

Vacca Inc ....G....... 513 697-0270
  Loveland *(G-12241)*

HEATING UNITS & DEVICES: Indl, Electric

Briskheat Corporation ....E....... 614 429-3232
  Columbus *(G-6703)*
Euclid Products Co Inc ....G....... 440 942-7310
  Willoughby *(G-20317)*
Furnace Technologies Inc ....D....... 419 878-2100
  Waterville *(G-19496)*
Glo-Quartz Electric Heater Co ....E....... 440 255-9701
  Mentor *(G-13459)*
Heat and Sensor Tech LLC ....D....... 513 228-0481
  Lebanon *(G-11661)*
James Thomas Shiveley ....G....... 330 468-2601
  Macedonia *(G-12306)*
Lanly Company ....E....... 216 731-1115
  Cleveland *(G-5560)*
Sivon Manufacturing LLC ....G....... 440 259-5505
  Perry *(G-15912)*
STA-Warm Electric Company ....F....... 330 296-6461
  Ravenna *(G-16408)*
Tegratek ....G....... 513 742-5100
  Cincinnati *(G-4411)*
Thermo Systems Technology ....E....... 216 292-8250
  Cleveland *(G-6170)*
Williams Industrial Svc Inc ....E....... 419 353-2120
  Bowling Green *(G-2005)*

HEATING UNITS: Gas, Infrared

Aitken Products Inc ....G....... 440 466-5711
  Geneva *(G-10213)*
Enerco Group Inc ....C....... 216 916-3000
  Cleveland *(G-5177)*
Enerco Technical Products Inc ....C....... 216 916-3000
  Cleveland *(G-5178)*
Mr Heater Inc ....E....... 216 916-3000
  Cleveland *(G-5711)*
Panelbloc Inc ....G....... 440 974-8877
  Mentor *(G-13541)*
Spectrum Inc ....F....... 440 951-6061
  Brooklyn Heights *(G-2132)*

HEAVY DISTILLATES

Ashland LLC ....G....... 513 557-3100
  Cincinnati *(G-3361)*

HELMETS: Steel

Armorsource LLC ....E....... 740 928-0070
  Hebron *(G-10738)*

HELP SUPPLY SERVICES

CPC Logistics Inc ....D....... 513 874-5787
  Fairfield *(G-9492)*

HISTORICAL SOCIETY

Baptist Heritage Revival Soc ....G....... 915 526-2832
  Goshen *(G-10285)*

HITCHES: Trailer

Geyer Transport & Mfg ....F....... 740 382-9008
  Marion *(G-12706)*

HOBBY, TOY & GAME STORES: Arts & Crafts & Splys

Crawford County Arts Council ....G....... 419 834-4133
  Bucyrus *(G-2323)*
Our Family Mall ....G....... 216 761-8669
  Cleveland *(G-5827)*

HOBBY, TOY & GAME STORES: Ceramics Splys

California Ceramic Supply Co ....G....... 216 531-9185
  Euclid *(G-9406)*

PRODUCT SECTION — HOMEFURNISHINGS, WHOLESALE: Decorating Splys

HOBBY, TOY & GAME STORES: Children's Toys & Games, Exc Dolls

Ready Made Rc LLC ....G....... 740 936-4500
  Lewis Center (G-11775)

HOBBY, TOY & GAME STORES: Dolls & Access

Middleton Lee Original Dolls ....F
  Columbus (G-7180)

HOBBY, TOY & GAME STORES: Toys & Games

Ohio Art Company ....D....... 419 636-3141
  Bryan (G-2301)
Rubys Country Store ....G....... 330 359-0406
  Dundee (G-9026)

HOGS WHOLESALERS

Robert Winner Sons Inc ....E....... 419 582-4321
  Yorkshire (G-20826)

HOISTING SLINGS

Acme Lifting Products Inc ....G....... 440 838-4430
  Cleveland (G-4606)

HOISTS

American Climber & Mch Corp ....G....... 330 420-0019
  Lisbon (G-11964)
ARI Phoenix Inc..E....... 513 229-3750
  Lebanon (G-11634)
Columbus McKinnon Corporation ....D....... 330 332-5769
  Salem (G-16729)
David Round Company Inc ....E....... 330 656-1600
  Streetsboro (G-17668)
Hoist Equipment Co Inc ....E....... 440 232-0300
  Bedford Heights (G-1472)
Lisbon Hoist Inc.......................................F....... 330 424-7283
  Lisbon (G-11974)

HOISTS: Mine

Gray-Eering Ltd..G....... 740 498-8816
  Tippecanoe (G-18149)

HOLDING COMPANIES: Banks

Black McCuskey Souers ....G....... 330 456-8341
  Canton (G-2593)

HOLDING COMPANIES: Investment, Exc Banks

Ajami Holdings Group LLC ....G....... 216 396-6089
  Richmond Heights (G-16500)
Akron Brass Holding Corp ....G....... 330 264-5678
  Wooster (G-20559)
Ampac Holdings LLC ....A....... 513 671-1777
  Cincinnati (G-3340)
Armor Consolidated Inc ....G....... 513 923-5260
  Mason (G-12826)
Companies of North Coast LLC ....G....... 216 398-8550
  Cleveland (G-5008)
Dayton Lamina Corporation ....G....... 937 859-5111
  Dayton (G-8136)
Dcc Corp ....F....... 330 494-0494
  Canton (G-2651)
Drt Holdings Inc ....D....... 937 298-7391
  Dayton (G-8169)
Elite Property Group LLC ....F....... 216 356-7469
  Elyria (G-9250)
Esperia Holdings LLC ....G....... 714 249-7888
  Oak Harbor (G-15444)
Hexpol Holding Inc ....F....... 440 834-4644
  Burton (G-2362)
Indra Holdings Corp ....G....... 513 682-8200
  West Chester (G-19867)
Misumi Investment USA Corp................G....... 937 859-5111
  Dayton (G-8363)
Mmh Americas Inc ....G....... 414 764-6200
  Springfield (G-17449)
Norse Dairy Systems Inc ....C....... 614 294-4931
  Columbus (G-7224)
Oberfields Holdings LLC ....G....... 740 369-7644
  Delaware (G-8713)
PMC Acquisitions Inc ....D....... 419 429-0042
  Findlay (G-9742)
Real Alloy Holding LLC ....G....... 216 755-8900
  Beachwood (G-1270)
Sp3 Cutting Tools Inc ....G....... 937 667-4476
  Tipp City (G-18134)
Tronair Parent Inc ....G....... 419 866-6301
  Swanton (G-17927)

HOLDING COMPANIES: Personal, Exc Banks

Gdic Group LLC ....G....... 330 468-0700
  Cleveland (G-5297)
Hartzell Industries Inc............................D....... 937 773-6295
  Piqua (G-16124)

HOME ENTERTAINMENT EQPT: Electronic, NEC

Beacon Audio Video Systems Inc ....G....... 937 723-9587
  Centerville (G-2999)
Custom Automation Technologies.........G....... 614 939-4228
  New Albany (G-14618)
Daca Vending Wholesale LLC................G....... 513 753-1600
  Amelia (G-535)
Electrimotion Inc.....................................G....... 740 362-0251
  Delaware (G-8675)

HOME ENTERTAINMENT REPAIR SVCS

Markeys Audio/Visual Inc......................G....... 419 244-8844
  Toledo (G-18399)

HOME FOR THE MENTALLY HANDICAPPED

Bittersweet Inc ....D....... 419 875-6986
  Whitehouse (G-20189)
R T Industries Inc....................................C....... 937 335-5784
  Troy (G-18695)

HOME FURNISHINGS WHOLESALERS

American Frame Corporation ....E....... 419 893-5595
  Maumee (G-13069)
V&P Group International LLC ....F....... 703 349-6432
  Cincinnati (G-4461)
Weavers Furniture Ltd ....F....... 330 852-2701
  Sugarcreek (G-17877)

HOME HEALTH CARE SVCS

Terewell Inc...G....... 216 334-6897
  Cleveland (G-6160)

HOME IMPROVEMENT & RENOVATION CONTRACTOR AGENCY

Ricers Residential Svcs LLC ....G....... 567 203-7414
  Shelby (G-16987)

HOMEBUILDERS & OTHER OPERATIVE BUILDERS

Superior Structures Inc ....F....... 513 942-5954
  Harrison (G-10674)

HOMEFURNISHING STORE: Bedding, Sheet, Blanket, Spread/Pillow

Down-Lite International Inc...................C....... 513 229-3696
  Mason (G-12858)

HOMEFURNISHING STORES: Brushes

Buckeye BOP LLC ....G....... 740 498-9898
  Newcomerstown (G-14971)

HOMEFURNISHING STORES: Cutlery

Handy Twine Knife Co ....G....... 419 294-3424
  Upper Sandusky (G-18955)

HOMEFURNISHING STORES: Metalware

Scs Construction Services Inc ....E....... 513 929-0260
  Cincinnati (G-4311)
Stainless Machine Engineering ....G....... 330 501-1992
  Leetonia (G-11721)

HOMEFURNISHING STORES: Mirrors

Bruening Glass Works Inc ....G....... 440 333-4768
  Cleveland (G-4846)
Dale Kestler ....G....... 513 871-9000
  Cincinnati (G-3574)

HOMEFURNISHING STORES: Pictures, Wall

Bonfoey Co...F....... 216 621-0178
  Cleveland (G-4831)
House of 10000 Picture Frames.............G....... 937 254-5541
  Dayton (G-8253)

HOMEFURNISHING STORES: Pottery

All Fired Up Pnt Your Own Pot ....G....... 330 865-5858
  Copley (G-7677)
Annies Mud Pie Shop LLC ....G....... 513 871-2529
  Cincinnati (G-3348)
Crawford County Arts Council ....G....... 419 834-4133
  Bucyrus (G-2323)
Kiln of Hyde Park Inc ....F....... 513 321-3307
  Cincinnati (G-3908)

HOMEFURNISHING STORES: Venetian Blinds

Mag Resources LLC ....G....... 330 294-0494
  Barberton (G-1083)
Miles Pk Vntian Blind Shds Mfg ....G....... 216 239-0850
  Beachwood (G-1248)

HOMEFURNISHING STORES: Vertical Blinds

Blind Factory Showroom ....E....... 614 771-6549
  Hilliard (G-10814)
Blind Outlet...G....... 614 895-2002
  Westerville (G-20037)
Optimun Blinds Inc ....G....... 740 598-5808
  Brilliant (G-2079)

HOMEFURNISHING STORES: Window Furnishings

Great Day Improvements LLC ....G....... 330 468-0700
  Macedonia (G-12300)

HOMEFURNISHING STORES: Window Shades, NEC

Cincinnati Window Shade Inc...............G....... 513 398-8510
  Mason (G-12844)
Cincinnati Window Shade Inc...............F....... 513 631-7200
  Cincinnati (G-3510)
Gotcha Covered ....G....... 513 829-7555
  Fairfield (G-9500)

HOMEFURNISHINGS & SPLYS, WHOLESALE: Decorative

Lena Fiore Inc..F....... 330 659-0020
  Akron (G-252)
Luminex Home Decor ....A....... 513 563-1113
  Blue Ash (G-1812)

HOMEFURNISHINGS, WHOLESALE: Blankets

Watershed Mangement LLC..................F....... 740 852-5607
  Mount Sterling (G-14466)

HOMEFURNISHINGS, WHOLESALE: Blinds, Venetian

Mag Resources LLC ....G....... 330 294-0494
  Barberton (G-1083)
Style-Line Incorporated..........................E....... 614 291-0600
  Columbus (G-7497)

HOMEFURNISHINGS, WHOLESALE: Blinds, Vertical

Blind Factory Showroom ....E....... 614 771-6549
  Hilliard (G-10814)
Blind Outlet...G....... 614 895-2002
  Westerville (G-20037)

HOMEFURNISHINGS, WHOLESALE: Decorating Splys

Rhc Inc ....G....... 330 874-3750
  Bolivar (G-1927)

Employee Codes: A=Over 500 employees, B=251-500
C=101-250, D=51-100, E=20-50, F=10-19, G=3-9

HOMEFURNISHINGS, WHOLESALE: Draperies

Accent Drapery Co Inc .... E 614 488-0741
  Columbus *(G-6531)*
Lumenomics Inc .... E 614 798-3500
  Lewis Center *(G-11766)*

HOMEFURNISHINGS, WHOLESALE: Grills, Barbecue

S I Distributing Inc .... F 419 647-4909
  Spencerville *(G-17314)*

HOMEFURNISHINGS, WHOLESALE: Kitchenware

Brighteye Innovations LLC 800 573-0052
  Akron *(G-96)*
Us Inc .... G 513 791-1162
  Blue Ash *(G-1863)*
Walter F Stephens Jr Inc 937 746-0521
  Franklin *(G-9930)*

HOMEFURNISHINGS, WHOLESALE: Linens, Table

Rons Texstyles LLC .... G 513 936-9975
  Columbus *(G-7400)*

HOMEFURNISHINGS, WHOLESALE: Mirrors/Pictures, Framed/Unframd

Dale Kestler .... G 513 871-9000
  Cincinnati *(G-3574)*

HOMEFURNISHINGS, WHOLESALE: Pottery

Annies Mud Pie Shop LLC .... G 513 871-2529
  Cincinnati *(G-3348)*
Yellow Springs Pottery .... F 937 767-1666
  Yellow Springs *(G-20822)*

HOMEFURNISHINGS, WHOLESALE: Window Covering Parts & Access

Cincinnati Window Shade Inc .... G 513 398-8510
  Mason *(G-12844)*
E W Perry Service Co Inc .... G 419 473-1231
  Toledo *(G-18273)*

HOMEFURNISHINGS, WHOLESALE: Wood Flooring

Silk Road Sourcing LLC .... G 814 571-5533
  Amherst *(G-574)*

HOMES, MODULAR: Wooden

Everything In America .... G 347 871-6872
  Cleveland *(G-5203)*
J L Wannemacher Sales & Svc .... F 419 453-3445
  Ottoville *(G-15681)*
Unibilt Industries Inc .... E 937 890-7570
  Vandalia *(G-19147)*

HOMES: Log Cabins

Al Yoder Construction Company .... G 330 359-5726
  Millersburg *(G-14056)*
Duffy Family Partner .... G 330 650-6716
  Peninsula *(G-15892)*
Gillard Construction Inc .... F 740 376-9744
  Marietta *(G-12627)*
Hochstetler Milling LLC .... E 419 368-0004
  Loudonville *(G-12143)*
Mohican Log Homes Inc 419 994-4088
  Loudonville *(G-12144)*
Silver Creek Log Homes 419 335-3220
  Wauseon *(G-19532)*

HONING & LAPPING MACHINES

Diversified Honing Inc .... E 330 874-4663
  Bolivar *(G-1912)*
Precision Honing Inc 440 942-7339
  Willoughby *(G-20410)*

HOODS: Range, Sheet Metal

Z Line Kitchen and Bath LLC .... F 614 777-5004
  Marysville *(G-12819)*

HOOKS: Crane, Laminated Plate

Morris Material Handling Inc .... G 937 525-5520
  Springfield *(G-17452)*
Rampp Company .... E 740 373-7886
  Marietta *(G-12662)*

HOPPERS: End Dump

McCullough Industries Inc .... E 419 673-0767
  Kenton *(G-11412)*
Mcl Inc .... E 216 292-3800
  Cleveland *(G-5643)*
Working Professionals LLC .... G 833 244-6299
  Canal Winchester *(G-2515)*

HOPPERS: Sheet Metal

Apex Welding Incorporated .... F 440 232-6770
  Bedford *(G-1384)*

HORSE & PET ACCESSORIES: Textile

Vitamin Lac .... F 440 548-5294
  Middlefield *(G-13865)*

HORSE ACCESS: Harnesses & Riding Crops, Etc, Exc Leather

Scenic Ridge Manufacturing LLC .... G 330 674-0557
  Millersburg *(G-14127)*
Woebkenberg Starting Gates .... G 937 696-2446
  West Alexandria *(G-19625)*

HOSE: Automobile, Rubber

Cooper-Standard Automotive Inc .... B 419 352-3533
  Bowling Green *(G-1965)*
Mm Outsourcing LLC .... F 937 661-4300
  Leesburg *(G-11714)*
Myers Industries Inc .... C 330 336-6621
  Wadsworth *(G-19255)*
Myers Industries Inc .... E 330 253-5592
  Akron *(G-292)*
Sumiriko Ohio Inc .... C 419 358-2121
  Bluffton *(G-1893)*

HOSE: Flexible Metal

Ace Manufacturing Company .... E 513 541-2490
  West Chester *(G-19825)*
First Francis Company Inc .... E 440 352-8927
  Painesville *(G-15739)*
Specialty Hose Aerospace Corp .... F 330 497-9650
  Canton *(G-2820)*
Swagelok Manufacturing Co LLC 440 248-4600
  Solon *(G-17244)*

HOSE: Plastic

Kentak Products Company .... D 330 386-3700
  East Liverpool *(G-9062)*
Kentak Products Company .... E 330 382-2000
  East Liverpool *(G-9063)*
Kentak Products Company 330 532-6211
  East Liverpool *(G-9064)*
Klockner Pentaplast Amer Inc .... G 937 743-8040
  Franklin *(G-9893)*

HOSE: Rubber

Aeroquip-Vickers Inc .... G 216 523-5000
  Cleveland *(G-4633)*
Eaton Aeroquip LLC .... C 216 523-5000
  Cleveland *(G-5143)*
Eaton Corporation .... A 419 238-1190
  Van Wert *(G-19087)*
Eaton Hydraulics LLC .... E 419 232-7777
  Van Wert *(G-19088)*
Eaton-Aeroquip Llc .... D 419 238-1190
  Van Wert *(G-19089)*
Salem-Republic Rubber Company .... E 877 425-5079
  Sebring *(G-16893)*
Summers Acquisition Corp .... G 740 373-0303
  Marietta *(G-12678)*

HOSES & BELTING: Rubber & Plastic

Aeroquip Corp .... G 419 238-1190
  Van Wert *(G-19074)*
Allied Fabricating & Wldg Co .... E 614 751-6664
  Columbus *(G-6572)*
Cmt Machining & Fabg LLC .... F 937 652-3740
  Urbana *(G-18983)*

PRODUCT SECTION

Crushproof Tubing Co .... E 419 293-2111
  Mc Comb *(G-13188)*
Eaton Corporation .... C 330 274-0743
  Aurora *(G-877)*
Eaton-Aeroquip Llc .... D 419 891-7775
  Maumee *(G-13109)*
Goodyear Tire & Rubber Company .... A 330 796-2121
  Akron *(G-191)*
Hbd/Thermoid Inc .... G 937 593-5010
  Bellefontaine *(G-1517)*
Hbd/Thermoid Inc .... C 614 526-7000
  Dublin *(G-8922)*
Kent Elastomer Products Inc .... G 800 331-4762
  Mogadore *(G-14242)*
Kent Elastomer Products Inc .... C 330 673-1011
  Kent *(G-11341)*
Mechanical Elastomerics Inc .... G 330 863-1014
  Malvern *(G-12393)*
Parker-Hannifin Corporation .... C 330 296-2871
  Ravenna *(G-16394)*
Parker-Hannifin Corporation .... E 330 296-2871
  Ravenna *(G-16395)*
Roller Source Inc .... F 440 748-4033
  Columbia Station *(G-6445)*
Summers Acquisition Corp .... G 419 526-5800
  Mansfield *(G-12523)*
Summers Acquisition Corp .... G 419 423-5800
  Findlay *(G-9765)*
Watteredge LLC .... D 440 933-6110
  Avon Lake *(G-1013)*

HOSPITALS: Medical & Surgical

Optoquest Corporation .... G 216 445-3637
  Cleveland *(G-5816)*

HOTELS & MOTELS

Continental GL Sls & Inv Group .... B 614 679-1201
  Powell *(G-16318)*

HOUSEHOLD APPLIANCE STORES

Carr Supply Co .... G 937 276-2555
  Dayton *(G-8076)*

HOUSEHOLD APPLIANCE STORES: Air Cond Rm Units, Self-Contnd

Carr Supply Co .... G 937 316-6300
  Greenville *(G-10363)*
Winsupply Inc .... F 937 346-0600
  Springfield *(G-17518)*

HOUSEHOLD APPLIANCE STORES: Ranges, Gas

Z Line Kitchen and Bath LLC .... F 614 777-5004
  Marysville *(G-12819)*

HOUSEHOLD APPLIANCE STORES: Suntanning Eqpt & Splys

Success Technologies Inc .... G 614 761-0008
  Powell *(G-16337)*

HOUSEHOLD ARTICLES, EXC KITCHEN: Pottery

Bodycote Imt Inc .... E 740 852-5000
  London *(G-12050)*

HOUSEHOLD ARTICLES: Metal

Hoffman Machining & Repair LLC .... G 419 547-9204
  Clyde *(G-6389)*
R L Torbeck Industries Inc .... D 513 367-0080
  Harrison *(G-10667)*
Voyale Minority Enterprise LLC .... E 216 271-3661
  Cleveland *(G-6274)*

HOUSEHOLD FURNISHINGS, NEC

Casco Mfg Solutions Inc .... D 513 681-0003
  Cincinnati *(G-3447)*
Columbus Canvas Products Inc .... F 614 375-1397
  Columbus *(G-6785)*
DCW Acquisition Inc .... F 216 451-0666
  Cleveland *(G-5079)*
Master Mfg Co Inc .... E 216 641-0500
  Cleveland *(G-5632)*

Ohio Table Pad Company....................D..... 419 872-6400
  Perrysburg (G-15986)
Pen Brands LLC.....................................E..... 216 674-1430
  Brooklyn Heights (G-2129)
Silver Threads Inc..................................E..... 614 733-0099
  Plain City (G-16211)
Stan Rileys Custom Draperies..............G..... 513 821-3732
  Cincinnati (G-4370)

HOUSEWARES, ELECTRIC, EXC COOKING APPLIANCES & UTENSILS

Klawhorn Industries Inc........................G..... 330 335-8191
  Wadsworth (G-19249)

HOUSEWARES, ELECTRIC: Air Purifiers, Portable

Hmi Industries Inc................................E..... 440 846-7800
  Brooklyn (G-2113)

HOUSEWARES, ELECTRIC: Cooking Appliances

Didonato Products Inc..........................G..... 330 535-1119
  Akron (G-142)
Nacco Industries Inc.............................E..... 740 773-9150
  Chillicothe (G-3201)
Nacco Industries Inc.............................E..... 440 229-5151
  Cleveland (G-5719)
Whirlpool Corporation..........................B..... 937 548-4126
  Greenville (G-10400)

HOUSEWARES, ELECTRIC: Fans, Exhaust & Ventilating

Anson Co..G..... 216 524-8838
  Bedford (G-1383)
Broan-Nutone LLC................................G..... 888 336-3948
  Blue Ash (G-1741)

HOUSEWARES, ELECTRIC: Heating, Bsbrd/Wall, Radiant Heat

Aitken Products Inc..............................G..... 440 466-5711
  Geneva (G-10213)

HOUSEWARES, ELECTRIC: Humidifiers, Household

Skuttle Mfg Co......................................F..... 740 373-9169
  Marietta (G-12670)

HOUSEWARES, ELECTRIC: Toasters

Kitchen Collection LLC........................D..... 740 773-9150
  Chillicothe (G-3198)

HOUSEWARES: Dishes, China

Libbey Glass Inc...................................A..... 419 729-7272
  Toledo (G-18383)

HOUSEWARES: Dishes, Earthenware

Added Touch Decorating Gallery..........G..... 419 747-3146
  Ontario (G-15537)
Modern China Inc.................................E..... 330 938-6104
  Sebring (G-16889)

HOUSEWARES: Dishes, Plastic

Fukuvi Usa Inc......................................D..... 937 236-7288
  Dayton (G-8210)
Joneszylon Company LLC....................G..... 740 545-6341
  West Lafayette (G-19933)
Newell Brands Inc................................F..... 330 733-7771
  Mogadore (G-14245)
Oneida Group Inc.................................C..... 740 687-2500
  Lancaster (G-11595)
Riotech International Ltd....................D..... 513 779-0990
  West Chester (G-19782)
Rubys Country Store............................G..... 330 359-0406
  Dundee (G-9026)
Sterilite Corporation............................B..... 330 830-2204
  Massillon (G-13051)

HOUSEWARES: Food Dishes & Utensils, Pressed & Molded Pulp

Aloterra Packaging LLC........................G..... 281 547-0568
  Andover (G-578)

HOUSEWARES: Plates, Pressed/Molded Pulp, From Purchased Mtrl

J and N Inc...F..... 234 759-3741
  North Lima (G-15172)

HOUSING COMPONENTS: Prefabricated, Concrete

Ramp Creek III Ltd...............................G..... 740 522-0660
  Heath (G-10729)

HOUSINGS: Business Machine, Sheet Metal

Custom Metal Products Inc..................G..... 614 855-2263
  New Albany (G-14619)
Samuel Clark...F..... 614 855-2263
  New Albany (G-14636)

HOUSINGS: Pressure

Hyq Technologies LLC.........................G..... 513 225-6911
  Oxford (G-15694)

HUMIDIFIERS & DEHUMIDIFIERS

Guardian Technologies LLC.................E..... 216 706-2250
  Euclid (G-9415)

HYDRAULIC EQPT REPAIR SVC

Advanced Cylinder Repair Inc..............G..... 419 289-0538
  Ashland (G-675)
Fluid System Service Inc......................G..... 216 651-2450
  Cleveland (G-5254)
Hhi Company Inc..................................G..... 330 455-3983
  Canton (G-2698)
Hunger Hydraulics CC Ltd...................F..... 419 666-4510
  Rossford (G-16586)
Hunter Hydraulics Inc..........................G..... 330 455-3983
  Canton (G-2701)
Hydraulic Products Inc........................G..... 440 946-4575
  Willoughby (G-20339)
Hydraulic Specialists Inc......................E..... 740 922-3343
  Midvale (G-13978)
Jrs Hydraulic & Welding......................G..... 614 497-1100
  Columbus (G-7079)
Perkins Motor Service Ltd...................E..... 440 277-1256
  Lorain (G-12112)
Quad Fluid Dynamics Inc....................F..... 330 220-3005
  Brunswick (G-2231)
R & L Hydraulics Inc............................G..... 937 399-3407
  Springfield (G-17478)

HYDRAULIC FLUIDS: Synthetic Based

Permco Inc..C..... 330 626-2801
  Streetsboro (G-17687)

HYDROPONIC EQPT

Cropking Incorporated..........................F..... 330 302-4203
  Lodi (G-12009)

Hard Rubber & Molded Rubber Prdts

Ashtabula Rubber Co............................C..... 440 992-2195
  Ashtabula (G-763)
Cep Holdings LLC................................C..... 330 665-2900
  Fairlawn (G-9600)
Colonial Rubber Company....................D..... 330 296-2831
  Ravenna (G-16373)
Eckel Industries Inc..............................E..... 978 772-0480
  West Chester (G-19850)
Foxtronix Inc..G..... 937 866-2112
  Miamisburg (G-13670)
G Grafton Machine & Rubber...............F..... 330 297-1062
  Ravenna (G-16380)
Lexington Rubber Group Inc...............E..... 330 425-8472
  Twinsburg (G-18807)
Martin Industries Inc............................F..... 419 862-2694
  Elmore (G-9207)
Master Mfg Co Inc...............................F..... 216 641-0500
  Cleveland (G-5632)
Merrico Inc...G..... 419 525-2711
  Mansfield (G-12479)
Spiralcool Company.............................F..... 419 483-2510
  Bellevue (G-1548)
Starpoint Extrusions LLC....................E..... 330 825-2373
  Norton (G-15376)
Tallmadge Finishing Co Inc..................E..... 330 633-7466
  Akron (G-394)

Woodbridge Group................................C..... 419 334-3666
  Fremont (G-10064)

ICE

Brady A Lantz Enterprises....................G..... 513 742-4921
  Cincinnati (G-3408)
Haller Enterprises Inc..........................F..... 330 733-9693
  Akron (G-195)
Home City Ice Company.......................F..... 513 353-9346
  Harrison (G-10647)
Home City Ice Company.......................G..... 513 941-0340
  Cincinnati (G-3822)
Home City Ice Company.......................F..... 937 461-6028
  Dayton (G-8252)
Home City Ice Company.......................F..... 419 562-4953
  Delaware (G-8694)
Home City Ice Company.......................F..... 440 439-5001
  Bedford (G-1413)
Home City Ice Company.......................E..... 614 836-2877
  Groveport (G-10493)
Lori Holding Co....................................E..... 740 342-3230
  New Lexington (G-14717)
Millersburg Ice Co................................E..... 330 674-3016
  Millersburg (G-14114)
Olmsted Ice Inc....................................E..... 440 235-8411
  Olmsted Twp (G-15535)
Penguin Serv Ice...................................G..... 614 848-6511
  Worthington (G-20699)
Velvet Ice Cream Company..................F..... 419 562-2009
  Bucyrus (G-2348)
Wings Way Drive Thru Inc...................G..... 330 533-2788
  Salem (G-16781)

ICE CREAM & ICES WHOLESALERS

Country Maid Ice Cream Inc................G..... 330 659-6830
  Richfield (G-16466)
United Dairy Farmers Inc....................C..... 513 396-8700
  Cincinnati (G-4447)
Velvet Ice Cream Company..................F..... 419 562-2009
  Bucyrus (G-2348)

ICE WHOLESALERS

Home City Ice Company.......................E..... 614 836-2877
  Groveport (G-10493)
Lori Holding Co....................................E..... 740 342-3230
  New Lexington (G-14717)

IDENTIFICATION PLATES

API Machining Fabrication Inc............G..... 740 369-0455
  Delaware (G-8654)
Partners In Recognition Inc................E..... 937 420-2150
  Fort Loramie (G-9801)
Trademark Designs Inc........................E..... 419 628-3897
  Minster (G-14227)

IGNEOUS ROCK: Crushed & Broken

Great Lakes Crushing Ltd....................E..... 440 944-5500
  Wickliffe (G-20211)
Stoneco Inc...G..... 419 686-3311
  Portage (G-16274)

IGNITERS: Jet Fuel

K2 Petroleum & Supply LLC................G..... 937 503-2614
  Cincinnati (G-3891)

IGNITION SYSTEMS: High Frequency

Altronic LLC...C..... 330 545-9768
  Girard (G-10252)

IGNITION SYSTEMS: Internal Combustion Engine

United Ignition Wire Corp....................G..... 216 898-1112
  Cleveland (G-6234)

INCENSE

Wild Berry Incense Inc........................F..... 513 523-8583
  Oxford (G-15703)

INCUBATORS & BROODERS: Farm

Chick Master Incubator Company.......C..... 330 722-5591
  Medina (G-13235)

INDL & PERSONAL SVC PAPER WHOLESALERS

INDL & PERSONAL SVC PAPER WHOLESALERS

Buckeye Boxes Inc .... E .... 614 274-8484 Columbus (G-6708)		
Buckeye Paper Co Inc .... E .... 330 477-5925 Canton (G-2600)		
Dayton Industrial Drum Inc .... E .... 937 253-8933 Dayton (G-7977)		
Fox Supply LLC .... G .... 419 628-3051 Minster (G-14214)		
Gt Industrial Supply Inc .... F .... 513 771-7000 Blue Ash (G-1783)		
Gvs Industries Inc .... G .... 513 851-3606 Hamilton (G-10565)		
Millcraft Group LLC .... D .... 216 441-5500 Cleveland (G-5689)		
Putnam Plastics Inc .... G .... 937 866-6261 Dayton (G-8452)		
Zebco Industries Inc .... F .... 740 654-4510 Lancaster (G-11620)		

INDL & PERSONAL SVC PAPER, WHOL: Bags, Paper/Disp Plastic

- A To Z Paper Box Co .... G 330 325-8722
  Rootstown (G-16565)
- Atlapac Corp .... D 614 252-2121
  Columbus (G-6625)
- Qumont Chemical Co .... G 419 241-1057
  Toledo (G-18492)
- Ricking Paper and Specialty Co .... E 513 825-3551
  Cincinnati (G-4269)

INDL & PERSONAL SVC PAPER, WHOL: Boxes, Corrugtd/Solid Fiber

- American Made Corrugated Packg .... F 937 981-2111
  Greenfield (G-10346)
- JIT Packaging Inc .... E 330 562-8080
  Aurora (G-885)
- Westrock Cp LLC .... D 770 448-2193
  Wshngtn CT Hs (G-20750)

INDL & PERSONAL SVC PAPER, WHOL: Paper, Wrap/Coarse/Prdts

- Millcraft Paper Company .... G 216 429-9860
  Cleveland (G-5690)
- Orora Packaging Solutions .... G 513 539-8274
  Monroe (G-14274)
- Polymer Packaging Inc .... D 330 832-2000
  Massillon (G-13040)

INDL & PERSONAL SVC PAPER, WHOLESALE: Boxes & Containers

- Argrov Box Co .... F 937 898-1700
  Dayton (G-8036)
- Deufol Worldwide Packaging LLC .... E 440 232-1100
  Bedford (G-1400)

INDL & PERSONAL SVC PAPER, WHOLESALE: Disposable

- Acme Steak & Seafood Inc .... F 330 270-8000
  Youngstown (G-20836)

INDL & PERSONAL SVC PAPER, WHOLESALE: Paper Tubes & Cores

- Sonoco Products Company .... D 937 429-0040
  Beavercreek Township (G-1374)

INDL & PERSONAL SVC PAPER, WHOLESALE: Shipping Splys

- Adapt-A-Pak Inc .... E 937 845-0386
  Tipp City (G-18098)
- Systems Pack Inc .... E 330 467-5729
  Macedonia (G-12336)

INDL & PERSONAL SVC PAPER, WHOLESALE: Towels, Paper

- Aci Industries Converting Ltd .... E 740 368-4160
  Delaware (G-8649)

INDL CONTRACTORS: Exhibit Construction

- Abstract Displays Inc .... G 513 985-9700
  Blue Ash (G-1719)
- Benchmark Craftsman Inc .... E 330 975-4214
  Seville (G-16911)
- Display Dynamics Inc .... F 937 832-2830
  Englewood (G-9355)

INDL DIAMONDS WHOLESALERS

- Chardon Tool & Supply Co Inc .... E 440 286-6440
  Chardon (G-3104)

INDL EQPT CLEANING SVCS

- Hy-Blast Inc .... F 513 424-0704
  Middletown (G-13912)

INDL EQPT SVCS

- 3-D Service Ltd .... C 330 830-3500
  Massillon (G-12956)
- Commercial Electric Pdts Corp .... E 216 241-2886
  Cleveland (G-5002)
- Dayton Industrial Drum Inc .... E 937 253-8933
  Dayton (G-7977)
- E E Controls Inc .... G 440 585-5554
  Willowick (G-20477)
- Forge Industries Inc .... A 330 782-8301
  Youngstown (G-20909)
- GL Nause Co Inc .... E 513 722-9500
  Loveland (G-12192)
- Graphic Systems Services Inc .... E 937 746-0708
  Springboro (G-17329)
- Grob Systems Inc .... G 419 358-9015
  Bluffton (G-1889)
- Jani Auto Parts Inc .... G 330 494-2975
  North Canton (G-15095)
- L M Equipment & Design Inc .... E 330 332-9951
  Salem (G-16754)
- Magnetech Industrial Svcs Inc .... C 330 830-3500
  Massillon (G-13016)
- Mesocoat Inc .... F 216 453-0866
  Euclid (G-9427)
- Miami Valley Punch & Mfg .... E 937 237-0533
  Dayton (G-8347)
- Midwest Metrology LLC .... G 937 832-0965
  Englewood (G-9369)
- Northwood Industries Inc .... F 419 666-2100
  Perrysburg (G-15983)
- Obr Cooling Towers Inc .... E 419 243-3443
  Rossford (G-16588)
- Quintus Technologies LLC .... E 614 891-2732
  Lewis Center (G-11774)
- Sunbeam Products Co LLC .... G 419 691-1551
  Toledo (G-18533)
- TE Brown LLC .... G 937 223-2241
  Dayton (G-8548)
- US Molding Machinery Co Inc .... E 440 918-1701
  Willoughby (G-20456)
- Walker National Inc .... E 614 492-1614
  Columbus (G-7589)

INDL GASES WHOLESALERS

- Airgas Usa LLC .... G 440 232-6397
  Oakwood Village (G-15477)

INDL HELP SVCS

- Aqua Technology Group LLC .... G 513 298-1183
  West Chester (G-19648)

INDL MACHINERY & EQPT WHOLESALERS

- Addisonmckee Inc .... C 513 228-7000
  Lebanon (G-11629)
- Aerocontrolex Group Inc .... D 440 352-6182
  Painesville (G-15706)
- Alkon Corporation .... D 419 355-9111
  Fremont (G-9990)
- Alkon Corporation .... E 614 799-6650
  Dublin (G-8876)
- Amtech Inc .... G 440 238-2141
  Strongsville (G-17711)
- Ashtech Corporation .... G 440 646-9911
  Gates Mills (G-10207)
- Atlas Machine and Supply Inc .... G 614 351-1603
  Hilliard (G-10807)
- Ats Systems Oregon Inc .... B 541 738-0932
  Lewis Center (G-11747)
- Automation Solutions Inc .... G 614 235-4060
  Columbus (G-6633)
- Avure Autoclave Systems Inc .... E 614 891-2732
  Columbus (G-6637)
- Bionix Safety Technologies Ltd .... E 419 727-0552
  Toledo (G-18202)
- Brown Industrial Inc .... E 937 693-3838
  Botkins (G-1934)
- Carlton Natco .... G 216 451-5588
  Cleveland (G-4878)
- Cortest Inc .... F 440 942-1235
  Willoughby (G-20301)
- Country Sales & Service LLC .... G 330 683-2500
  Orrville (G-15588)
- Ctm Integration Incorporated .... E 330 332-1800
  Salem (G-16732)
- Dengensha America Corporation .... F 440 439-8081
  Bedford (G-1399)
- Dinkmar Inc .... G 419 468-8516
  Galion (G-10132)
- Dura Magnetics Inc .... E 419 882-0591
  Sylvania (G-17939)
- Dynamics Research & Dev .... E 419 478-7091
  Toledo (G-18271)
- Edjean Technical Services Inc .... E 440 647-3300
  Sullivan (G-17881)
- Eltool Corporation .... G 513 723-1772
  Mansfield (G-12436)
- EMI Corp .... D 937 596-5511
  Jackson Center (G-11209)
- Equipment Guys Inc .... E 614 871-9220
  Newark (G-14872)
- Equipment Manufacturers Intl .... E 216 651-6700
  Cleveland (G-5186)
- Freeman Manufacturing & Sup Co .... E 440 934-1902
  Avon (G-950)
- G W Cobb Co .... F 216 341-0100
  Cleveland (G-5285)
- Ged Holdings Inc .... C 330 963-5401
  Twinsburg (G-18780)
- Glavin Industries Inc .... E 440 349-0049
  Solon (G-17149)
- Gokoh Corporation .... F 937 339-4977
  Troy (G-18662)
- Grand Harbor Yacht Sales & Svc .... G 440 442-2919
  Cleveland (G-5339)
- Grenga Machine & Welding .... F 330 743-1113
  Youngstown (G-20925)
- Hannon Company .... D 330 456-4728
  Canton (G-2693)
- Hendrickson International Corp .... D 740 929-5600
  Hebron (G-10747)
- Hirons Memorial Works Inc .... G 937 444-2917
  Mount Orab (G-14444)
- Hug Manufacturing Corporation .... G 419 668-5086
  Norwalk (G-15400)
- Ibi Brake Products Inc .... E 440 543-7962
  Chagrin Falls (G-3052)
- Industrial Machine Tool Svc .... G 216 651-1122
  Cleveland (G-5452)
- Intelligrated Inc .... E 513 874-0788
  West Chester (G-19868)
- Intelligrated Systems Inc .... A 866 936-7300
  Mason (G-12894)
- Intelligrated Systems Ohio LLC .... A 513 701-7300
  Mason (G-12896)
- International Trade Group Inc .... G 614 486-4634
  Columbus (G-7045)
- Interntnal Plstic Cmpnents Inc .... F 330 744-0625
  Campbell (G-2468)
- J McCaman Enterprises Inc .... F 330 825-2401
  New Franklin (G-14691)
- Jcl Equipment Co Inc .... G 937 374-1010
  Xenia (G-20779)
- Jed Industries Inc .... E 440 639-9973
  Grand River (G-10323)
- Jones Industrial Service LLC .... G 419 287-4553
  Pemberville (G-15886)
- JPS Technologies Inc .... F 513 984-6400
  Blue Ash (G-1797)
- JPS Technologies Inc .... F 513 984-6400
  Blue Ash (G-1798)
- Kolinahr Systems Inc .... F 513 745-9401
  Blue Ash (G-1801)
- Kyocera SGS Precision Tools .... E 330 688-6667
  Munroe Falls (G-14524)
- Linden Industries Inc .... E 330 928-4064
  Cuyahoga Falls (G-7893)
- Mataco .... G 440 546-8355
  Broadview Heights (G-2096)

PRODUCT SECTION   INDL PROCESS INSTRUMENTS: Draft Gauges

Mc Kinley Machinery Inc ....E .... 440 937-6300 Avon (G-954)	Custom Metal Works Inc ....F ...... 419 668-7831 Norwalk (G-15385)	Seilkop Industries Inc ....F ...... 513 679-5680 Cincinnati (G-4317)
Mfh Partners Inc ....F ...... 440 461-4100 Cleveland (G-5664)	Cuyahoga Machine Company LLC ....F ...... 216 267-3560 Brookpark (G-2142)	Wright Way Patterns ....G ...... 513 574-5776 Cincinnati (G-4522)
Mine Equipment Services LLC ....E .... 740 936-5427 Sunbury (G-17891)	DNC Hydraulics LLC ....F ...... 419 963-2800 Rawson (G-16421)	**INDL PROCESS INSTRUMENTS: Absorp**
Minerva Welding and Fabg Inc ....E .... 330 868-7731 Minerva (G-14194)	Equipment Spcalists Dayton LLC ....G....... 937 415-2151 Dayton (G-8185)	**Analyzers, Infrared, X-Ray**
Monaghan & Associates Inc ....E .... 937 253-7706 Dayton (G-8365)	Expert Crane Inc ....E .... 216 451-9900 Cleveland (G-5209)	Godfrey & Wing Inc ....F ...... 419 980-4616 Defiance (G-8624)
Multi Products Company ....G....... 330 674-5981 Millersburg (G-14117)	Fawcett Co Inc ....G....... 330 659-4187 Richfield (G-16470)	**INDL PROCESS INSTRUMENTS:**
Neil R Scholl Inc ....F ...... 740 653-6593 Lancaster (G-11590)	General Plastex Inc ....E .... 330 745-7775 Barberton (G-1073)	**Chromatographs**
Off Contact Inc ....F ...... 419 255-5546 Toledo (G-18434)	Hydro Supply Co ....F ...... 740 454-3842 Zanesville (G-21147)	Consolidatd Analytical Sys Inc ....F ...... 513 542-1200 Cleves (G-6359)
Park Corporation ....B .... 216 267-4870 Cleveland (G-5841)	Industrial Repair & Mfg Inc ....D ...... 419 822-4232 Delta (G-8774)	**INDL PROCESS INSTRUMENTS: Control**
Pfpc Enterprises Inc ....B .... 513 941-6200 Cincinnati (G-4155)	Ivan Extruders Co Inc ....G....... 330 644-7400 Akron (G-220)	Aqua Technology Group LLC ....G....... 513 298-1183 West Chester (G-19648)
Pines Manufacturing Inc ....E .... 440 835-5553 Westlake (G-20141)	J&J Precision Machine Ltd ....E .... 330 923-5783 Cuyahoga Falls (G-7883)	Avure Technologies Inc ....F ...... 614 891-2732 Lewis Center (G-11750)
Plastic Process Equipment Inc ....E .... 216 367-7000 Macedonia (G-12317)	Jack Gruber ....G....... 740 408-2718 Cardington (G-2874)	Brighton Technologies LLC ....E .... 513 469-1800 Saint Bernard (G-16620)
Plastran Inc ....G....... 440 237-8404 Cleveland (G-5888)	JF Martt and Associates Inc ....F ...... 330 938-4000 Sebring (G-16887)	Brighton Technologies Group ....G....... 513 469-1800 Cincinnati (G-3417)
Power-Pack Conveyor Company ....E .... 440 975-9955 Willoughby (G-20408)	Jonmar Gear and Machine Inc ....G....... 330 854-6500 Canal Fulton (G-2481)	BSK Industries Inc ....F ...... 440 230-9299 North Royalton (G-15264)
Progressive Manufacturing Co ....G....... 330 784-4717 Akron (G-333)	Justin P Straub LLC ....G....... 513 761-0282 Cincinnati (G-3888)	Clark-Reliance Corporation ....C ...... 440 572-1500 Strongsville (G-17726)
Prospect Mold & Die Company ....D ...... 330 929-3311 Cuyahoga Falls (G-7909)	Laserflex Corporation ....D ...... 614 850-9600 Hilliard (G-10837)	Control Associates Inc ....G....... 440 708-1770 Chagrin Falls (G-3042)
Reid Asset Management Company ....E .... 216 642-3223 Cleveland (G-5971)	Lees Machinery Inc ....G....... 440 259-2222 Perry (G-15907)	Corro-Tech Equipment Corp ....G....... 216 941-1552 Cleveland (G-5031)
Rhino Robotics Ltd ....G....... 513 353-9772 Miamitown (G-13750)	Machine Tool Rebuilders Inc ....E .... 614 228-1070 Columbus (G-7142)	Dynetech LLC ....E .... 419 690-4281 Toledo (G-18272)
Rubber City Machinery Corp ....E .... 330 434-3500 Akron (G-356)	McGuire Machine LLC ....E .... 330 868-3072 Minerva (G-14192)	E E Controls Inc ....G....... 440 585-5554 Willowick (G-20477)
Samuel Strapping Systems Inc ....D ...... 740 522-2500 Heath (G-10731)	Measurement Specialties Inc ....F ...... 937 885-0800 Dayton (G-8337)	Facts Inc ....E .... 330 928-2332 Cuyahoga Falls (G-7866)
Screen Machine Industries LLC ....E .... 740 927-3464 Pataskala (G-15844)	Mechanical Dynamics Analis Ltd ....E .... 440 946-0082 Euclid (G-9426)	John McHael Priester Assoc Inc ....G....... 513 761-8605 Wyoming (G-20752)
Siemens Industry Inc ....E .... 440 526-2770 Brecksville (G-2058)	Odyssey Machine Company Ltd ....G....... 419 455-6621 Perrysburg (G-15984)	Journey Electronics Corp ....G....... 513 539-9836 Monroe (G-14269)
Stanley Bittinger ....G....... 740 942-4302 Cadiz (G-2401)	OKL Can Line Inc ....E .... 513 825-1655 Cincinnati (G-4108)	Monitortech Corp ....G....... 614 231-0500 Columbus (G-7194)
Starkey Machinery Inc ....E .... 419 468-2560 Galion (G-10157)	Palesh & Associates Inc ....G....... 440 942-9168 Willoughby (G-20398)	Nanostatics Corporation ....F ...... 740 477-5900 Circleville (G-4550)
Super Systems Inc ....E .... 513 772-0060 Cincinnati (G-4397)	Qpmr Inc ....F ...... 330 723-1739 Medina (G-13325)	Nidec Indus Automtn USA LLC ....E .... 216 901-2400 Cleveland (G-5753)
Taiyo America Inc ....F ...... 419 300-8811 Saint Marys (G-16703)	Rossi Machinery Services Inc ....G....... 419 281-4488 Ashland (G-744)	Production Control Units Inc ....D ...... 937 299-5594 Moraine (G-14385)
Tilt-Or-Lift Inc ....G....... 419 893-6944 Maumee (G-13154)	Steel Eqp Specialists Inc ....D ...... 330 823-8260 Alliance (G-502)	**INDL PROCESS INSTRUMENTS: Controllers,**
Tj Bell Inc ....G....... 330 633-3644 Akron (G-406)	T P F Inc ....G....... 513 761-9968 Cincinnati (G-4403)	**Process Variables**
Tri State Equipment Company ....G....... 513 738-7227 Shandon (G-16942)	Taft Tool & Production Co ....F ...... 419 385-2576 Toledo (G-18542)	Hunkar Technologies Inc ....C ...... 513 272-1010 Cincinnati (G-3829)
Unarco Material Handling Inc ....G....... 419 384-3211 Pandora (G-15807)	Terex Utilities Inc ....F ...... 440 262-3200 Brecksville (G-2060)	Overhoff Technology Corp ....F ...... 513 248-2400 Milford (G-14030)
United Hydraulics ....F ...... 440 585-0906 Wickliffe (G-20234)	Winkle Industries Inc ....D ...... 330 823-9730 Alliance (G-516)	Quad/Graphics Inc ....A ...... 513 932-1064 Lebanon (G-11687)
Valv-Trol Company ....F ...... 330 686-2800 Stow (G-17640)	Wood Graphics Inc ....E .... 513 771-6300 Cincinnati (G-4516)	Schneider Electric Usa Inc ....D ...... 513 755-5000 West Chester (G-19792)
Valve Related Controls Inc ....F ...... 513 677-8724 Loveland (G-12242)	**INDL PATTERNS: Foundry Cores**	**INDL PROCESS INSTRUMENTS: Data**
Venturo Manufacturing Inc ....E .... 513 772-8448 Cincinnati (G-4474)	Founder Service & Mfg Co ....F ...... 330 584-7759 Deerfield (G-8609)	**Loggers**
W W Williams Company LLC ....F ...... 330 659-3084 Richfield (G-16494)	Humtown Pattern Company ....D ...... 330 482-5555 Columbiana (G-6470)	Computer Aided Solutions LLC ....E .... 440 729-2570 Chesterland (G-3155)
Waterloo Manufacturing Co Inc ....G....... 330 947-2917 Atwater (G-865)	PCC Airfoils LLC ....C ...... 216 692-7900 Cleveland (G-5857)	**INDL PROCESS INSTRUMENTS: Digital**
Welded Tube Pros LLC ....G....... 330 854-2966 Canal Fulton (G-2496)	Sinel Company Inc ....F ...... 937 433-4772 Dayton (G-8509)	**Display, Process Variables**
William Darling Company Inc ....G....... 614 878-0085 Columbus (G-7604)	**INDL PATTERNS: Foundry Patternmaking**	Gem Instrument Co ....F ...... 330 273-6117 Brunswick (G-2209)
Zal Air Products Inc ....G....... 440 237-7155 Cleveland (G-6338)	Accuform Manufacturing Inc ....E .... 330 797-9291 Youngstown (G-20834)	Snappskin Inc ....G....... 440 318-4879 Chagrin Falls (G-3030)
INDL MACHINERY REPAIR & MAINTENANCE	Case Pattern Co Inc ....G....... 216 531-0744 Madison (G-12341)	**INDL PROCESS INSTRUMENTS: Draft**
Abj Equipfix ....E .... 419 684-5236 Castalia (G-2935)	Cincinnati Pattern Company ....F ...... 513 241-9872 Cincinnati (G-3503)	**Gauges**
Ajax Tocco Magnethermic Corp ....C ...... 330 372-8511 Warren (G-19364)	Morcast Precision Inc ....G....... 614 258-5071 Columbus (G-7195)	Indev Gauging Systems Inc ....E .... 815 282-4463 Dublin (G-8929)
Boneng Transmissions (usa) LLC ....G....... 330 425-1516 Twinsburg (G-18743)	National Pattern Mfg Co ....F ...... 330 682-6871 Orrville (G-15605)	Pride Gage Associates LLC ....F ...... 419 318-3793 Toledo (G-18482)
Bradford Neal Machinery Inc ....G....... 440 632-1393 Middlefield (G-13781)	North Coast Pattern Inc ....G....... 440 322-5064 Strongsville (G-17771)	
Cleveland Jsm Inc ....D ...... 440 876-3050 Strongsville (G-17729)	Plas-Mac Corp ....D ...... 440 349-3222 Solon (G-17216)	

Employee Codes: A=Over 500 employees, B=251-500
C=101-250, D=51-100, E=20-50, F=10-19, G=3-9

INDL PROCESS INSTRUMENTS: Fluidic Devices, Circuit & Systems

PRODUCT SECTION

INDL PROCESS INSTRUMENTS: Fluidic Devices, Circuit & Systems

Fluid Equipment Corp ....G....... 419 636-0777
  Bryan *(G-2281)*

INDL PROCESS INSTRUMENTS: Indl Flow & Measuring

Air Logic Power Systems LLC ......G....... 513 202-5130
  Harrison *(G-10629)*
Intek Inc ....E....... 614 895-0301
  Westerville *(G-19999)*
Tasi Holdings Inc ....E....... 513 202-5182
  Harrison *(G-10676)*

INDL PROCESS INSTRUMENTS: Manometers

Rosemount Inc ....F....... 513 851-5555
  West Chester *(G-19786)*

INDL PROCESS INSTRUMENTS: Moisture Meters

GE Infrastructure Sensing Inc ....B....... 740 928-7010
  Hebron *(G-10744)*

INDL PROCESS INSTRUMENTS: Temperature

Altronic LLC ....C....... 330 545-9768
  Girard *(G-10252)*
Automatic Timing & Controls ....G....... 614 888-8855
  New Albany *(G-14606)*
Caron Products and Svcs Inc ....E....... 740 373-6809
  Marietta *(G-12612)*
Doubleday Acquisitions LLC ....C....... 937 242-6768
  Moraine *(G-14347)*
Dyoung Enterprise Inc ....D....... 440 918-0505
  Willoughby *(G-20312)*
Future Controls Corporation ....E....... 440 275-3191
  Austinburg *(G-922)*
Honeywell International Inc ....A....... 937 484-2000
  Urbana *(G-18995)*
Logan Enterprises Inc ....G....... 937 465-8170
  Conover *(G-7664)*
Ram Sensors Inc.............................F....... 440 835-3540
  Cleveland *(G-5959)*

INDL PROCESS INSTRUMENTS: Water Quality Monitoring/Cntrl Sys

American Water Services Inc ....G....... 440 243-9840
  Strongsville *(G-17709)*
C H Washington Water Plan ....G....... 740 636-2382
  Wshngtn CT Hs *(G-20721)*
Danaher Corporation ....C....... 440 995-3003
  Cleveland *(G-5061)*
Danaher Corporation ....C....... 440 995-3025
  Mentor *(G-13428)*
Wabash River Conservancy ....G....... 419 375-2577
  Fort Recovery *(G-9830)*
Ysi Environmental Inc ....C....... 937 767-7241
  Yellow Springs *(G-20824)*

INDL SPLYS WHOLESALERS

Alkon Corporation ....E....... 614 799-6650
  Dublin *(G-8876)*
All Ohio Threaded Rod Co Inc ....E....... 216 426-1800
  Cleveland *(G-4665)*
Alro Steel Corporation ....E....... 419 720-5300
  Toledo *(G-18166)*
Alro Steel Corporation ....E....... 614 878-7271
  Columbus *(G-6578)*
Aqua Technology Group LLC ....G....... 513 298-1183
  West Chester *(G-19648)*
Baaron Abrasives Inc ....G....... 330 263-7737
  Wooster *(G-20568)*
Ci Disposition Co ....E....... 216 587-5200
  Brooklyn Heights *(G-2118)*
Cleveland Plastic Fabricat ....F....... 216 797-7300
  Euclid *(G-9409)*
Cmt Machining & Fabg LLC ....F....... 937 652-3740
  Urbana *(G-18983)*
Coastal Diamond Incorporated .....G....... 440 946-7171
  Mentor *(G-13417)*
Computer System Enhancement ...G....... 513 251-6791
  Cincinnati *(G-3541)*
Cornwell Quality Tools Company ..D....... 330 628-2627
  Mogadore *(G-14232)*

Dan Wilzynski..................................G....... 800 531-3443
  Columbus *(G-6848)*
Dayton Stencil Works Company ....E....... 937 223-3233
  Dayton *(G-8145)*
Dexport Tool Manufacturing Co ....G....... 513 625-1600
  Loveland *(G-12185)*
Dolin Supply Co ....G....... 304 529-4171
  South Point *(G-17282)*
Dynatech Systems Inc ....E....... 440 365-1774
  Elyria *(G-9246)*
Eagle Industrial Truck Mfg LLC .....E....... 734 442-1000
  Swanton *(G-17912)*
Edward W Daniel LLC......................E....... 440 647-1960
  Wellington *(G-19577)*
Fastener Industries Inc ....F....... 216 267-2240
  Cleveland *(G-5221)*
Fcx Performance Inc ....E....... 614 324-6050
  Columbus *(G-6916)*
General Machine & Supply Co ......G....... 740 453-4804
  Zanesville *(G-21142)*
Gokoh Corporation ....F....... 937 339-4977
  Troy *(G-18662)*
Great Lakes Textiles Inc ....E....... 440 914-1122
  Solon *(G-17156)*
GSE Production and Support LLC .G....... 972 329-2646
  Swanton *(G-17914)*
H3d Tool Corporation ....G....... 740 498-5181
  Newcomerstown *(G-14974)*
HMS Industries LLC........................G....... 440 899-0001
  Westlake *(G-20124)*
I-Dee-X Inc ....G....... 330 788-2186
  Youngstown *(G-20935)*
Industrial Mold Inc..........................G....... 330 425-7374
  Twinsburg *(G-18796)*
Jamtek Enterprises Inc...................G....... 513 738-4700
  Harrison *(G-10652)*
JIT Packaging Inc............................E....... 330 562-8080
  Aurora *(G-885)*
Lancaster Commercial Pdts LLC...E....... 740 286-5081
  Columbus *(G-7112)*
Lapcraft Inc......................................E....... 614 764-8993
  Powell *(G-16327)*
Lawrence Industries Inc ....C....... 216 518-7000
  Cleveland *(G-5566)*
Liberty Casting Company LLC ......E....... 740 363-1941
  Delaware *(G-8703)*
Lima Equipment Co ....G....... 419 222-4181
  Lima *(G-11888)*
Logan Clutch Corporation ....E....... 440 808-4258
  Cleveland *(G-5582)*
Maintenance Repair Supply Inc ....E....... 740 922-3006
  Midvale *(G-13980)*
McWane Inc ....B....... 740 622-6651
  Coshocton *(G-7739)*
Metzger Machine Co ....F....... 513 241-3360
  Cincinnati *(G-4019)*
Mill-Rose Company.........................C....... 440 255-9171
  Mentor *(G-13520)*
Newact Inc ....F....... 513 321-5177
  Batavia *(G-1173)*
Orbytel Print and Packg Inc ....G....... 216 267-8734
  Cleveland *(G-5818)*
Pinnacle Sales Inc...........................G....... 440 734-9195
  Westlake *(G-20143)*
Plastic Process Equipment Inc .....E....... 216 367-7000
  Macedonia *(G-12317)*
S & N Engineering Svcs Corp ....G....... 216 433-1700
  Cleveland *(G-6020)*
Samsel Rope & Marine Supply Co .E....... 216 241-0333
  Cleveland *(G-6029)*
Samuel Strapping Systems Inc ....D....... 740 522-2500
  Heath *(G-10731)*
SSP Fittings Corp............................C....... 330 425-4250
  Twinsburg *(G-18858)*
Stark Industrial LLC ....E....... 330 493-9773
  North Canton *(G-15122)*
Superior Holding LLC ....G....... 216 651-9400
  Cleveland *(G-6121)*
United Tool Supply Inc ....G....... 513 752-6000
  Cincinnati *(G-3266)*
Watteredge LLC ....D....... 440 933-6110
  Avon Lake *(G-1013)*
Wesco Distribution Inc ....E....... 419 666-1670
  Northwood *(G-15351)*
Wulco Inc ....D....... 513 679-2600
  Cincinnati *(G-4525)*
Zal Air Products Inc ....G....... 440 237-7155
  Cleveland *(G-6338)*

INDL SPLYS, WHOL: Fasteners, Incl Nuts, Bolts, Screws, Etc

Andre Corporation ....E....... 574 293-0207
  Mason *(G-12824)*
Atlas Bolt & Screw Company LLC..C....... 419 289-6171
  Ashland *(G-681)*
Crawford Products Inc ....E....... 614 890-1822
  Columbus *(G-6837)*
ET&f Fastening Systems Inc ....F....... 800 248-2376
  Solon *(G-17141)*
Facil North America Inc ....C....... 330 487-2500
  Twinsburg *(G-18774)*
RB&w Manufacturing LLC ....G....... 740 363-1971
  Delaware *(G-8718)*
RB&w Manufacturing LLC ....F....... 234 380-8540
  Streetsboro *(G-17691)*
Stafast Products Inc ....E....... 440 357-5546
  Painesville *(G-15784)*
Supply Technologies LLC ....C....... 440 947-2100
  Cleveland *(G-6130)*
Supply Technologies LLC ....G....... 937 898-5795
  Dayton *(G-8530)*
Tricor Industrial Inc ....D....... 330 264-3299
  Wooster *(G-20660)*
Youngstown Bolt & Supply Co ....G....... 330 799-3201
  Youngstown *(G-21072)*

INDL SPLYS, WHOLESALE: Abrasives

ARC Abrasives Inc ....D....... 800 888-4885
  Troy *(G-18638)*
Sevan At-Ndustrial Pnt Abr Ltd .....G....... 614 258-4747
  Columbus *(G-7440)*

INDL SPLYS, WHOLESALE: Abrasives & Adhesives

Evans Adhesive Corporation ....E....... 614 451-2665
  Columbus *(G-6908)*

INDL SPLYS, WHOLESALE: Adhesives, Tape & Plasters

National Adhesives Inc ....F....... 513 683-8650
  Cincinnati *(G-4059)*

INDL SPLYS, WHOLESALE: Barrels, New Or Reconditioned

Sabco Industries Inc ....E....... 419 531-5347
  Toledo *(G-18510)*

INDL SPLYS, WHOLESALE: Bearings

Federal-Mogul Powertrain LLC .....C....... 740 432-2393
  Cambridge *(G-2437)*
Forge Industries Inc ....A....... 330 782-8301
  Youngstown *(G-20909)*

INDL SPLYS, WHOLESALE: Bins & Containers, Storage

Creative Plastic Concepts LLC .....D....... 419 927-9588
  Sycamore *(G-17930)*
Dadco Inc ....F....... 513 489-2244
  Cincinnati *(G-3572)*
Dadco Inc ....F....... 513 489-2244
  Cincinnati *(G-3573)*
Modroto ....G....... 800 772-7659
  Ashtabula *(G-787)*

INDL SPLYS, WHOLESALE: Bottler Splys

Pure Water Global Inc ....G....... 419 737-2352
  Pioneer *(G-16093)*
Tolco Corporation ....D....... 419 241-1113
  Toledo *(G-18555)*

INDL SPLYS, WHOLESALE: Brushes, Indl

Trent Manufacturing Company .....F....... 216 391-1551
  Cleveland *(G-6204)*

INDL SPLYS, WHOLESALE: Clean Room Splys

Precision Environments Inc ....E....... 513 847-1510
  West Chester *(G-19765)*

PRODUCT SECTION
INK: Printing

INDL SPLYS, WHOLESALE: Drums, New Or Reconditioned
Dayton Industrial Drum Inc ....E 937 253-8933
  Dayton (G-7977)
Horwitz & Pintis Co ....F 419 666-2220
  Toledo (G-18336)

INDL SPLYS, WHOLESALE: Fasteners & Fastening Eqpt
Fastenal Company ....G 419 629-3024
  New Bremen (G-14654)
McFeelys Inc ....F 800 443-7937
  Harrison (G-10658)

INDL SPLYS, WHOLESALE: Filters, Indl
Ken AG Inc ....E 419 281-1204
  Ashland (G-718)

INDL SPLYS, WHOLESALE: Fittings
Industrial Connections Inc ....G 330 274-2155
  Mantua (G-12549)
Superior Products LLC ....D 216 651-9400
  Cleveland (G-6126)
Superior Products Llc ....D 216 651-9400
  Cleveland (G-6125)

INDL SPLYS, WHOLESALE: Gaskets
Ishikawa Gasket America Inc ....C 419 353-7300
  Bowling Green (G-1976)

INDL SPLYS, WHOLESALE: Gaskets & Seals
P & E Sales Ltd ....G 330 829-0100
  Alliance (G-495)

INDL SPLYS, WHOLESALE: Gears
Ig Watteeuw Usa LLC ....F 740 588-1722
  Zanesville (G-21148)

INDL SPLYS, WHOLESALE: Hydraulic & Pneumatic Pistons/Valves
Alkon Corporation ....D 419 355-9111
  Fremont (G-9990)

INDL SPLYS, WHOLESALE: Knives, Indl
Alliance Knife Inc ....E 513 367-9000
  Harrison (G-10631)
C B Mfg & Sls Co Inc ....D 937 866-5986
  Miamisburg (G-13647)

INDL SPLYS, WHOLESALE: Plastic, Pallets
San Pallet LLC ....G 937 271-5308
  Troy (G-18702)

INDL SPLYS, WHOLESALE: Power Transmission, Eqpt & Apparatus
Commercial Electric Pdts Corp ....E 216 241-2886
  Cleveland (G-5002)
Great Lakes Power Products Inc ....D 440 951-5111
  Mentor (G-13462)
Siglent Technologies Amer Inc ....G 440 398-5800
  Solon (G-17231)
Stevenson Machine Inc ....F 513 761-4121
  Cincinnati (G-4382)

INDL SPLYS, WHOLESALE: Rubber Goods, Mechanical
Fouty & Company Inc ....E 419 693-0017
  Oregon (G-15560)
Jet Rubber Company ....E 330 325-1821
  Rootstown (G-16569)
Mid-State Sales Inc ....G 330 744-2158
  Youngstown (G-20971)
Netherland Rubber Company ....F 513 733-0883
  Cincinnati (G-4068)
R C Musson Rubber Co ....G 330 773-7651
  Akron (G-339)
Solo Products Inc ....F 513 321-7884
  Cincinnati (G-4352)
Summers Acquisition Corp ....E 216 941-7700
  Cleveland (G-6117)

Summers Acquisition Corp ....G 419 526-5800
  Mansfield (G-12523)
Summers Acquisition Corp ....G 419 423-5800
  Findlay (G-9765)
Summers Acquisition Corp ....G 440 946-5611
  Eastlake (G-9134)
Treadstone Company ....G 216 410-3435
  Twinsburg (G-18865)

INDL SPLYS, WHOLESALE: Seals
Datwyler Sling Sltions USA Inc ....D 937 387-2800
  Vandalia (G-19122)
McNeil Industries Inc ....E 440 951-7756
  Painesville (G-15762)

INDL SPLYS, WHOLESALE: Signmaker Eqpt & Splys
Interstate Sign Products Inc ....G 419 683-1962
  Crestline (G-7795)
Sign Source USA Inc ....D 419 224-1130
  Lima (G-11940)

INDL SPLYS, WHOLESALE: Tools
B W Grinding Co ....E 419 923-1376
  Lyons (G-12273)
Bluelevel Technologies Inc ....G 330 523-5215
  Richfield (G-16463)
File Sharpening Company Inc ....E 937 376-8268
  Xenia (G-20772)
H & D Steel Service Inc ....G 440 237-3390
  North Royalton (G-15275)
High Quality Tools Inc ....F 440 975-9684
  Eastlake (G-9113)
Ohio Drill & Tool Co ....E 330 525-7717
  Homeworth (G-10989)
Tenney Tool & Supply Co ....F 330 666-2807
  Barberton (G-1110)

INDL SPLYS, WHOLESALE: Tools, NEC
F & B Engraving Tls & Sup LLC ....G 937 332-7994
  Piqua (G-16114)
T M Industries Inc ....G 330 627-4410
  Carrollton (G-2930)

INDL SPLYS, WHOLESALE: Valves & Fittings
Crane Pumps & Systems Inc ....B 937 773-2442
  Piqua (G-16107)
Quad Fluid Dynamics Inc ....F 330 220-3005
  Brunswick (G-2231)
Ruthman Pump and Engineering ....E 937 783-2411
  Blancherster (G-1706)
Victory White Metal Company ....D 216 271-1400
  Cleveland (G-6260)

INDL TOOL GRINDING SVCS
Seilkop Industries Inc ....E 513 761-1035
  Cincinnati (G-4316)
Sst Precision Manufacturing ....F 513 583-5500
  Loveland (G-12235)
Triumph Tool LLC ....G 937 222-6885
  Dayton (G-8567)

INDUSTRIAL & COMMERCIAL EQPT INSPECTION SVCS
4r Enterprises Incorporated ....G 330 923-9799
  Cuyahoga Falls (G-7829)
Quintus Technologies LLC ....E 614 891-2732
  Lewis Center (G-11774)
Reid Asset Management Company .....E 216 642-3223
  Cleveland (G-5971)

INFORMATION RETRIEVAL SERVICES
Advant-E Corporation ....F 937 429-4288
  Beavercreek (G-1298)
AGS Custom Graphics Inc ....D 330 963-7770
  Macedonia (G-12275)
Hkm Drect Mkt Cmmnications Inc ......C 216 651-9500
  Cleveland (G-5412)
Promatch Solutions LLC ....F 937 299-0185
  Springboro (G-17346)
Repro Acquisition Company LLC ....E 216 738-3800
  Cleveland (G-5977)
Sevell + Sevell Inc ....G 614 341-9700
  Columbus (G-7441)

Tahoe Interactive Systems Inc ....F 614 891-2323
  Westerville (G-20076)
Welch Publishing Co ....E 419 874-2528
  Perrysburg (G-16025)

INGOT, EXTRUSION: Extrusion ingot, aluminum: rolling mills
Aluminum Extrusion Tech LLC ....G 330 533-3994
  Canfield (G-2522)
Powermount Systems Inc ....G 740 499-4330
  La Rue (G-11476)

INGOT: Aluminum
Homan Metals LLC ....G 513 721-5010
  Cincinnati (G-3821)

INK OR WRITING FLUIDS
International Paper Company ....C 740 363-9882
  Delaware (G-8696)
Sun Chemical Corporation ....D 513 671-0407
  Cincinnati (G-4390)
Wagers Inc ....G 513 825-6300
  Okeana (G-15520)

INK: Gravure
Superior Printing Ink Co Inc ....G 216 328-1720
  Cleveland (G-6124)

INK: Lithographic
Sun Chemical Corporation ....E 513 771-4030
  Cincinnati (G-4393)

INK: Printing
Actega North America Inc ....G 800 426-4657
  Blue Ash (G-1720)
American Inks and Coatings Co ....F 513 552-7200
  Fairfield (G-9481)
Eckart America Corporation ....D 440 954-7600
  Painesville (G-15734)
Erie Laser Ink LLC ....G 419 346-0600
  Toledo (G-18284)
Ferro Corporation ....C 216 875-6178
  Cleveland (G-5231)
Flint Group US LLC ....G 513 934-6500
  Lebanon (G-11652)
Flint Group US LLC ....D 513 771-1900
  Cincinnati (G-3695)
Glass Coatings & Concepts LLC ....E 513 539-5300
  Monroe (G-14264)
Grand Rapids Printing Ink Co ....G 859 261-4530
  Cincinnati (G-3775)
Ink Factory Inc ....G 330 799-0888
  Youngstown (G-20940)
Ink Production Services Inc ....F 513 733-9338
  Cincinnati (G-3848)
Ink Technology Corporation ....E 216 486-6720
  Cleveland (G-5458)
INX International Ink Co ....F 707 693-2990
  Lebanon (G-11663)
INX International Ink Co ....F 513 282-2920
  Lebanon (G-11664)
INX International Ink Co ....G 440 239-1766
  Cleveland (G-5473)
Kennedy Ink Company Inc ....F 513 871-2515
  Cincinnati (G-3905)
Kennedy Ink Company Inc ....G 937 461-5600
  Dayton (G-8293)
L A Machine ....G 216 651-1712
  Cleveland (G-5549)
Magnum Magnetics Corporation ....F 740 516-6237
  Caldwell (G-2409)
Premier Ink Systems Inc ....F 513 367-2300
  Harrison (G-10664)
Red Tie Group Inc ....C 216 271-2300
  Cleveland (G-5968)
Red Tie Group Inc ....G 614 443-9100
  Columbus (G-7381)
Sun Chemical Corporation ....D 513 671-0407
  Cincinnati (G-4390)
Sun Chemical Corporation ....D 419 891-3514
  Maumee (G-13150)
Sun Chemical Corporation ....D 513 753-9550
  Amelia (G-549)
Sun Chemical Corporation ....E 513 681-5950
  Cincinnati (G-4392)
Sun Chemical Corporation ....E 937 743-8055
  Franklin (G-9922)

INK: Printing

Sun Chemical Corporation..............B....... 513 681-5950
Cincinnati *(G-4394)*
Sun Chemical Corporation..............E....... 513 830-8667
Cincinnati *(G-4395)*
Superior Printing Ink Co Inc..........F....... 513 221-4707
Blue Ash *(G-1855)*
Wikoff Color Corporation................D....... 216 271-2300
Cleveland *(G-6307)*
Wikoff Color Corporation................G....... 513 423-0727
Middletown *(G-13968)*

INSECTICIDES & PESTICIDES

A Best Trmt & Pest Ctrl Sups..........G....... 330 434-5555
Akron *(G-18)*
Advanced Biological Mktg Inc.........F....... 419 232-2461
Van Wert *(G-19073)*
Scotts Miracle-Gro Company..........B....... 937 644-0011
Marysville *(G-12810)*
Waldo & Associates Inc.................E....... 419 666-3662
Perrysburg *(G-16023)*

INSPECTION & TESTING SVCS

Brown Company of Findlay Ltd......E....... 419 425-3002
Findlay *(G-9663)*
Cleveland Specialty Insptn Svc......F....... 440 578-1046
Mentor *(G-13415)*
Fluid Conservation Systems............F....... 513 831-9335
Milford *(G-14008)*
National Welding & Tanker Repr....G....... 614 875-3399
Grove City *(G-10449)*
Supplier Inspection Svcs Inc...........E....... 937 263-7097
Dayton *(G-8529)*
Vista Industrial Packaging LLC.......D....... 800 454-6117
Columbus *(G-7586)*

INSTRUMENTS & METERS: Measuring, Electric

FT Group Inc..................................E....... 937 746-6439
Cincinnati *(G-3716)*
Lake Shore Cryotronics Inc.............C....... 614 891-2243
Westerville *(G-20003)*
Lawhorn Machine & Tool Inc..........G....... 937 884-5674
Phillipsburg *(G-16037)*
P G M Diversified Industries............G....... 440 885-3500
Cleveland *(G-5830)*

INSTRUMENTS, LAB: Refractometers, Exc Indl Process Types

Mettler-Toledo Intl Fin Inc...............G....... 614 438-4511
Columbus *(G-6500)*

INSTRUMENTS, LAB: Spectroscopic/Optical Properties Measuring

Akron Council of Engineering.........G....... 330 535-8835
Akron *(G-37)*
Innovative Lab Services LLC............G....... 614 554-6446
Pataskala *(G-15832)*

INSTRUMENTS, LABORATORY: Analyzers, Automatic Chemical

Targeted Cmpund Monitoring LLC...G....... 513 461-3535
Beavercreek *(G-1365)*

INSTRUMENTS, LABORATORY: Blood Testing

C D C At Cityview...........................E....... 216 426-2020
Cleveland *(G-4856)*

INSTRUMENTS, LABORATORY: Gas Analyzing

Elkins Earthworks LLC....................G....... 330 725-7766
Medina *(G-13254)*

INSTRUMENTS, LABORATORY: Infrared Analytical

IEC Infrared Systems Inc..................E....... 440 234-8000
Middleburg Heights *(G-13765)*
IEC Infrared Systems LLC................E....... 440 234-8000
Middleburg Heights *(G-13766)*

INSTRUMENTS, LABORATORY: Spectrometers

Teledyne Instruments Inc...............D....... 603 886-8400
Mason *(G-12947)*

INSTRUMENTS, LABORATORY: Ultraviolet Analytical

Filament LLC..................................G....... 614 732-0754
Columbus *(G-6921)*
Nordson Uv Inc...............................F....... 440 985-4573
Amherst *(G-568)*

INSTRUMENTS, MEASURING & CNTRL: Gauges, Auto, Computer

Lawhorn Machine & Tool Inc..........G....... 937 884-5674
Phillipsburg *(G-16037)*

INSTRUMENTS, MEASURING & CNTRL: Geophysical & Meteorological

Electric Speed Indicator Co.............F....... 216 251-2540
Cleveland *(G-5163)*

INSTRUMENTS, MEASURING & CNTRL: Radiation & Testing, Nuclear

Fluke Biomedical LLC.....................C....... 440 248-9300
Cleveland *(G-5255)*
Nucon International Inc..................F....... 614 846-5710
Columbus *(G-7232)*
Reuter-Stokes LLC..........................B....... 330 425-3755
Twinsburg *(G-18845)*

INSTRUMENTS, MEASURING & CNTRL: Testing, Abrasion, Etc

American Cube Mold Inc.................G....... 330 558-0044
Hinckley *(G-10898)*
Gilson Screen Incorporated.............E....... 419 256-7711
Malinta *(G-12379)*
Magnetic Analysis Corporation.......F....... 330 758-1367
Youngstown *(G-20965)*
MB Dynamics Inc............................E....... 216 292-5850
Cleveland *(G-5641)*
Nanologix Inc.................................G....... 330 534-0800
Hubbard *(G-11006)*
Saginomiya America Inc.................G....... 614 766-7390
Dublin *(G-8977)*
Standards Testing Labs Inc.............D....... 330 833-8548
Massillon *(G-13050)*

INSTRUMENTS, MEASURING & CNTRL: Whole Body Counters, Nuclear

Multi Lapping Service Inc...............F....... 440 944-7592
Wickliffe *(G-20218)*

INSTRUMENTS, MEASURING & CNTRLG: Aircraft & Motor Vehicle

Nidec Motor Corporation................C....... 216 642-1230
Independence *(G-11144)*
Parker-Hannifin Corporation...........B....... 216 896-3000
Cleveland *(G-5848)*
Parker-Hannifin Corporation...........F....... 216 896-3000
Cleveland *(G-5850)*

INSTRUMENTS, MEASURING & CNTRLG: Electrogamma Ray Loggers

P H Glatfelter Company..................G....... 740 289-5100
Piketon *(G-16077)*

INSTRUMENTS, MEASURING & CNTRLG: Stress, Strain & Measure

Fiomet LLC....................................G....... 513 519-7622
Cincinnati *(G-3691)*
Xcite Systems Corporation.............G....... 513 965-0300
Cincinnati *(G-3267)*

INSTRUMENTS, MEASURING & CNTRLG: Tensile Strength Testing

Fischer Engineering Company........G....... 937 754-1750
Dayton *(G-8196)*

INSTRUMENTS, MEASURING & CNTRLG: Thermometers/Temp Sensors

Excelitas Technologies Corp...........C....... 866 539-5916
Miamisburg *(G-13667)*

INSTRUMENTS, MEASURING & CNTRLNG: Nuclear Instrument Modules

Babcock & Wilcox Entps Inc............A....... 330 753-4511
Barberton *(G-1061)*
Overhoff Technology Corp..............F....... 513 248-2400
Milford *(G-14030)*

INSTRUMENTS, MEASURING & CONTROLLING: Anamometers

General Pump & Eqp Compnay......G....... 330 455-2100
Canton *(G-2682)*

INSTRUMENTS, MEASURING & CONTROLLING: Breathalyzers

1 A Lifesafer Hawaii Inc..................F....... 513 651-9560
Blue Ash *(G-1717)*
National Patent Analytical Sys........E....... 419 526-6727
Mansfield *(G-12489)*

INSTRUMENTS, MEASURING & CONTROLLING: Cable Testing

Multilink Inc...................................C....... 440 366-6966
Elyria *(G-9298)*

INSTRUMENTS, MEASURING & CONTROLLING: Gas Detectors

Rae Systems Inc.............................G....... 440 232-0555
Walton Hills *(G-19314)*

INSTRUMENTS, MEASURING & CONTROLLING: Magnetometers

Ceia Usa Ltd..................................E....... 330 405-3190
Twinsburg *(G-18747)*

INSTRUMENTS, MEASURING & CONTROLLING: Surveying & Drafting

J C Equipment Sales & Leasing......G....... 513 772-7612
Cincinnati *(G-3862)*

INSTRUMENTS, MEASURING & CONTROLLING: Torsion Testing

Skidmore-Wilhelm Mfg Company....E....... 216 481-4774
Solon *(G-17232)*

INSTRUMENTS, MEASURING & CONTROLLING: Transits, Surveyors'

Novitran LLC..................................G....... 513 792-2727
Cincinnati *(G-4091)*

INSTRUMENTS, MEASURING & CONTROLLING: Ultrasonic Testing

Advanced OEM Solutions LLC........G....... 513 846-5755
Cincinnati *(G-3301)*
Amron LLC.....................................G....... 330 457-8570
New Waterford *(G-14836)*

INSTRUMENTS, MEASURING/CNTRL: Gauging, Ultrasonic Thickness

Global Gauge Corporation..............F....... 937 254-3500
Moraine *(G-14356)*
Rickly Hydrological Company.........G....... 614 297-9877
Columbus *(G-7394)*

INSTRUMENTS, MEASURING/CNTRLG: Fare Registers, St Cars/Buses

Euclid Products Co Inc....................G....... 440 942-7310
Willoughby *(G-20317)*

PRODUCT SECTION

INSTRUMENTS: Indl Process Control

INSTRUMENTS, MEASURING/CNTRLG: Fire Detect Sys, Non-Electric

Tripoint Instruments Inc .... G 513 702-9217
  Cincinnati *(G-4440)*

INSTRUMENTS, MEASURING/CNTRLNG: Med Diagnostic Sys, Nuclear

GLC Biotechnology Inc .... G 440 349-2193
  Hudson *(G-11046)*
Quidel Dhi .... E 740 589-3300
  Athens *(G-848)*
Tuppas Software Corporation .... C 419 897-7902
  Maumee *(G-13156)*

INSTRUMENTS, OPTICAL: Lenses, All Types Exc Ophthalmic

Bsa Industries Inc .... D 614 846-5515
  Columbus *(G-6706)*

INSTRUMENTS, OPTICAL: Test & Inspection

Lear Engineering Corp .... F 937 429-0534
  Beavercreek *(G-1325)*
Ncrx Optical Solutions Inc .... F 330 239-5353
  Hudson *(G-11063)*
Vampire Optical Coatings Inc .... G 740 919-4596
  Pataskala *(G-15848)*
Welded Tube Pros LLC .... G 330 854-2966
  Canal Fulton *(G-2496)*

INSTRUMENTS, SURGICAL & MEDICAL: Blood & Bone Work

Advanced Medical Solutions Inc .... G 937 291-0069
  Centerville *(G-2995)*
Findlay American Prosthetic & .... G 419 424-1622
  Findlay *(G-9683)*
Nervive Inc .... F 847 274-1790
  Cleveland *(G-5740)*
Neurorescue LLC .... G 614 354-6453
  Lewis Center *(G-11769)*
Resonetics LLC .... D 937 865-4070
  Kettering *(G-11440)*
Troy Innovative Instrs Inc .... E 440 834-9567
  Middlefield *(G-13859)*

INSTRUMENTS, SURGICAL & MEDICAL: Forceps

Dayton Hawker Corporation .... F 937 293-8147
  Dayton *(G-8135)*

INSTRUMENTS, SURGICAL & MEDICAL: IV Transfusion

Smiths Medical Asd Inc .... C 614 889-2220
  Dublin *(G-8988)*

INSTRUMENTS, SURGICAL & MEDICAL: Inhalation Therapy

Invacare Holdings Corporation .... G 440 329-6000
  Elyria *(G-9276)*
Invacare International Corp .... G 440 329-6000
  Elyria *(G-9277)*
Pediavascular Inc .... F 216 236-5533
  Chagrin Falls *(G-3065)*
Rhinosystems Inc .... F 216 351-6262
  Brooklyn *(G-2114)*

INSTRUMENTS, SURGICAL & MEDICAL: Lasers, Surgical

Olentangy Eye and Laser A .... G 614 267-4122
  Columbus *(G-7270)*

INSTRUMENTS, SURGICAL & MEDICAL: Operating Tables

Midmark Corporation .... A 937 526-3662
  Kettering *(G-11434)*

INSTRUMENTS, SURGICAL & MEDICAL: Optometers

Ellen L Ellsworth .... G 440 352-8031
  Mentor *(G-13438)*

INSTRUMENTS, SURGICAL & MEDICAL: Physiotherapy, Electrical

Grimm Scientific Industries .... F 740 374-3412
  Marietta *(G-12629)*

INSTRUMENTS, SURGICAL & MEDICAL: Probes, Surgical

Mac Dhui Probe of America Inc .... G 440 942-5597
  Mentor *(G-13505)*
Morrison Medical .... E 614 461-4400
  Columbus *(G-7197)*

INSTRUMENTS, SURGICAL/MED: Microsurgical, Exc Electromedical

3d Systems Inc .... D 216 229-2040
  Cleveland *(G-4580)*
Norman Noble Inc .... B 216 761-5387
  Highland Heights *(G-10794)*
Norman Noble Inc .... E 216 851-4007
  Euclid *(G-9429)*

INSTRUMENTS: Airspeed

John Wolf & Co Inc .... G 440 942-0083
  Willoughby *(G-20348)*

INSTRUMENTS: Analytical

Affymetrix Inc .... C 216 765-5000
  Cleveland *(G-4640)*
Affymetrix Inc .... F 419 887-1233
  Maumee *(G-13067)*
Bionix Safety Technologies Ltd .... E 419 727-0552
  Toledo *(G-18202)*
Bridge Analyzers Incorporated .... G 216 332-0592
  Bedford Heights *(G-1463)*
Columbus Instruments Intl Corp .... E 614 276-0593
  Columbus *(G-6793)*
Consolidatd Analytical Sys Inc .... F 513 542-1200
  Cleves *(G-6359)*
Dentronix Inc .... E 330 916-7300
  Cuyahoga Falls *(G-7860)*
Diascopic LLC .... G 312 282-1800
  Cleveland *(G-5091)*
Fertility Solutions Inc .... G 216 491-0030
  Cleveland *(G-5234)*
Health Bridge Imaging LLC .... G 740 423-3300
  Belpre *(G-1576)*
Isotopx Inc .... G 508 337-8467
  Hudson *(G-11057)*
Laserlinc Inc .... E 937 318-2440
  Fairborn *(G-9463)*
Measurenet Technology Ltd .... F 513 396-6765
  Cincinnati *(G-3992)*
Metron Instruments Inc .... G 216 332-0592
  Bedford Heights *(G-1474)*
Mettler-Toledo Intl Inc .... B 614 438-4511
  Columbus *(G-6501)*
Mettlr-Tledo Globl Hldings LLC .... F 614 438-4511
  Columbus *(G-6502)*
Nanotronics Imaging Inc .... G 330 926-9809
  Cuyahoga Falls *(G-7900)*
NDC Technologies Inc .... C 937 233-9935
  Dayton *(G-8379)*
Ohio Lumex Co Inc .... G 440 264-2500
  Solon *(G-17211)*
Omnitech Electronics Inc .... F 800 822-1344
  Columbus *(G-7271)*
Orton Edward Jr Crmic Fndation .... E 614 895-2663
  Westerville *(G-20014)*
PMC Gage Inc .... E 440 953-1672
  Willoughby *(G-20404)*
Precision Anlytical Instrs Inc .... G 513 984-1600
  Blue Ash *(G-1834)*
Pts Prfssnal Technical Svc Inc .... D 513 642-0111
  West Chester *(G-19771)*
Q-Lab Corporation .... D 440 835-8700
  Westlake *(G-20146)*
Reid Asset Management Company .... E 216 642-3223
  Cleveland *(G-5971)*
Teledyne Instruments Inc .... E 513 229-7000
  Mason *(G-12946)*
Teledyne Tekmar Company .... E 513 229-7000
  Mason *(G-12948)*
Test-Fuchs Corporation .... G 440 708-3505
  Brecksville *(G-2061)*
Thermo Fisher Scientific .... A 740 373-4763
  Marietta *(G-12680)*
Thermo Fisher Scientific Inc .... F 513 489-2926
  Montgomery *(G-14299)*
Thermo Fisher Scientific Inc .... G 440 703-1400
  Bedford *(G-1449)*

INSTRUMENTS: Analyzers, Radio Apparatus, NEC

Analytica Usa Inc .... G 513 348-2333
  Dayton *(G-8031)*

INSTRUMENTS: Combustion Control, Indl

Burner Tech Unlimited Inc .... G 440 232-3200
  Twinsburg *(G-18744)*
Cleveland Controls Inc .... G 216 398-0330
  Cleveland *(G-4952)*
Maxon Corporation .... G 216 459-6056
  Independence *(G-11142)*
R K Combustion & Controls .... G 937 444-9700
  Mount Orab *(G-14451)*
Star Combustion Systems LLC .... G 513 282-0810
  Mason *(G-12942)*
Unicontrol Inc .... D 216 398-0330
  Cleveland *(G-6230)*

INSTRUMENTS: Differential Pressure, Indl

Stewart Manufacturing Corp .... E 937 390-3333
  Springfield *(G-17499)*

INSTRUMENTS: Electrocardiographs

Cardioinsight Technologies Inc .... G 216 274-2221
  Independence *(G-11121)*
Synsei Medical .... G 609 759-1101
  Dublin *(G-9001)*

INSTRUMENTS: Endoscopic Eqpt, Electromedical

Clear Image Technology LLC .... G 440 366-4330
  Westlake *(G-20105)*
Steris Corporation .... A 440 354-2600
  Mentor *(G-13590)*

INSTRUMENTS: Eye Examination

Eye Surgery Center Ohio Inc .... E 614 228-3937
  Columbus *(G-6912)*

INSTRUMENTS: Flow, Indl Process

Aquacalc LLC .... G 916 372-0534
  Columbus *(G-6612)*
Ernst Flow Industries LLC .... F 732 938-5641
  Strongsville *(G-17743)*
L J Star Incorporated .... E 330 405-3040
  Twinsburg *(G-18804)*
Manico Inc .... G 440 946-5333
  Willoughby *(G-20367)*
Poi Holdings Inc .... G 937 253-7377
  Dayton *(G-7988)*
Westerman Inc .... D 330 262-6946
  Wooster *(G-20665)*

INSTRUMENTS: Gastroscopes, Electromedical

Westerville Endoscopy Ctr LLC .... F 614 568-1666
  Westerville *(G-20030)*

INSTRUMENTS: Indicating, Electric

Aqua Technology Group LLC .... G 513 298-1183
  West Chester *(G-19648)*

INSTRUMENTS: Indl Process Control

ABB Inc .... G 440 585-8500
  Beachwood *(G-1217)*
Airmate Company .... D 419 636-3184
  Bryan *(G-2258)*
Alpha Technologies Svcs LLC .... D 330 745-1641
  Hudson *(G-11027)*
Appleton Grp LLC .... C 330 689-1904
  Cuyahoga Falls *(G-7838)*
Arzel Technology Inc .... E 216 831-6068
  Cleveland *(G-4743)*
Ascon Tecnologic N Amer LLC .... G 216 485-8350
  Cleveland *(G-4747)*
Ats Atmtion Globl Svcs USA Inc .... G 519 653-4483
  Lewis Center *(G-11745)*

Employee Codes: A=Over 500 employees, B=251-500
C=101-250, D=51-100, E=20-50, F=10-19, G=3-9

Automation and Ctrl Tech Inc ....E 614 495-1120
Dublin *(G-8886)*
Automation Technology Inc ....E 937 233-6084
Dayton *(G-8045)*
Bry-Air Inc ....E 740 965-2974
Sunbury *(G-17883)*
Cammann Inc ....F 440 965-4051
Wakeman *(G-19282)*
Chandler Systems Incorporated ....D 888 363-9434
Ashland *(G-693)*
Cleveland Instrument Corp ....G 440 826-1800
Brookpark *(G-2138)*
Combustion Process System ....G 330 922-4161
Cuyahoga Falls *(G-7852)*
Data Control Systems Inc ....G 330 877-4497
Hartville *(G-10688)*
Deban Enterprises Inc ....G 937 426-4235
Dayton *(G-8152)*
Diamond Power Intl Inc ....F 740 687-4001
Lancaster *(G-11565)*
Dynamic Temperature Sups LLC ....G 216 767-5799
Parma *(G-15816)*
Electrodynamics Inc ....C 847 259-0740
Cincinnati *(G-3247)*
Elpro Services Inc ....G 740 568-9900
Marietta *(G-12623)*
Emerson Electric Co ....C 513 731-2020
Cincinnati *(G-3635)*
Emerson Electric Co ....E 440 288-1122
Lorain *(G-12089)*
Emerson Electric Co ....E 440 248-9400
Solon *(G-17136)*
Emerson Process MGT Lllp ....E 877 468-6384
Columbus *(G-6490)*
Encompass Automation & ....F 419 873-0000
Perrysburg *(G-15947)*
Furnace Parts LLC ....E 216 916-9601
Cleveland *(G-5278)*
Gleason Metrology Systems Corp ....E 937 384-8901
Dayton *(G-8223)*
Glo-Quartz Electric Heater Co ....E 440 255-9701
Mentor *(G-13459)*
Gooch & Housego (ohio) LLC ....D 216 486-6100
Highland Heights *(G-10792)*
H W Fairway International Inc ....E 330 678-2540
Kent *(G-11330)*
Harris Corporation ....C 973 284-2866
Beavercreek *(G-1322)*
Harris Instrument Corporation ....G 740 369-3580
Delaware *(G-8692)*
Helm Instrument Company Inc ....E 419 893-4356
Maumee *(G-13116)*
Henry & Wright Corporation ....F 216 851-3750
Cleveland *(G-5394)*
Homeworth Fabrications & Mchs ....F 330 525-5459
Homeworth *(G-10988)*
Huntington Instruments Inc ....G 937 767-7001
Yellow Springs *(G-20808)*
Indy Resolutions Ltd ....G 513 475-6625
Cincinnati *(G-3847)*
Ingersoll-Rand Company ....E 419 633-6800
Bryan *(G-2291)*
Innovative Controls Corp ....D 419 691-6684
Toledo *(G-18348)*
Instrument & Valve Services Co ....G 513 942-1118
West Chester *(G-19722)*
Kuhlman Instrument Company ....G 419 668-9533
Norwalk *(G-15402)*
Lake Shore Cryotronics Inc ....C 614 891-2243
Westerville *(G-20003)*
Lincoln Electric Company ....C 216 524-8800
Cleveland *(G-5576)*
LS Starrett Company ....D 440 835-0005
Westlake *(G-20129)*
M T Systems Inc ....G 330 453-4646
Canton *(G-2738)*
Machine Applications Corp ....G 419 621-2322
Sandusky *(G-16825)*
Mettler-Toledo Intl Inc ....B 614 438-4511
Columbus *(G-6501)*
Newtech Materials & Analytical ....G 330 329-1080
Copley *(G-7690)*
Nidec Motor Corporation ....C 216 642-1230
Independence *(G-11144)*
Noramar Company Inc ....G 440 338-5740
Novelty *(G-15439)*
Noshok Inc ....E 440 243-0888
Berea *(G-1620)*
Onevision Corporation ....G 614 794-1144
Westerville *(G-20013)*
Parker-Hannifin Corporation ....A 216 531-3000
Cleveland *(G-5849)*
Prime Instruments Inc ....D 216 651-0400
Cleveland *(G-5921)*
Primex ....E 513 831-9959
Milford *(G-14035)*
Production Design Services Inc ....D 937 866-3377
Dayton *(G-8446)*
Prosys Sampling Systems Ltd ....G 937 717-4600
Springfield *(G-17477)*
Q-Lab Corporation ....D 440 835-8700
Westlake *(G-20146)*
Quality Metrology Sys & Sol LL ....G 937 431-1800
Beavercreek *(G-1338)*
Rainin Instrument LLC ....G 510 564-1600
Columbus *(G-6505)*
Refractory Specialties Inc ....E 330 938-2101
Sebring *(G-16891)*
Reuter-Stokes LLC ....B 330 425-3755
Twinsburg *(G-18845)*
Richards Industries Inc ....C 513 533-5600
Cincinnati *(G-4268)*
Roto Tech Inc ....E 937 859-8503
Dayton *(G-8485)*
Rsw Technologies LLC ....F 419 662-8100
Rossford *(G-16592)*
Sansei Showa Co Ltd ....E 440 248-4440
Cleveland *(G-6030)*
Scadatech LLC ....G 614 552-7726
Reynoldsburg *(G-16452)*
Selas Heat Technology Co LLC ....E 800 523-6500
Streetsboro *(G-17697)*
Sherbrooke Metals ....E 440 942-3520
Willoughby *(G-20429)*
Stancorp Inc ....G 330 545-6615
Girard *(G-10267)*
Stock Fairfield Corporation ....C 440 543-6000
Chagrin Falls *(G-3078)*
Tecmark Corporation ....E 440 205-9188
Mentor *(G-13602)*
Tecmark Corporation ....D 440 205-7600
Mentor *(G-13601)*
Tecsis LP ....E 614 430-0683
Worthington *(G-20705)*
Telemecanique Sensors ....G 800 435-2121
Dayton *(G-8551)*
Therm-O-Disc Incorporated ....A 419 525-8500
Mansfield *(G-12530)*
Thk Manufacturing America Inc ....C 740 928-1415
Hebron *(G-10766)*
Tls Corp ....E 216 574-4759
Cleveland *(G-6177)*
Toledo Transducers Inc ....E 419 724-4170
Holland *(G-10962)*
United Tool Supply Inc ....G 513 752-6000
Cincinnati *(G-3266)*
Vanner Holdings Inc ....D 614 771-2718
Hilliard *(G-10873)*
Vega Americas Inc ....C 513 272-0131
Cincinnati *(G-4470)*
Vertiv Corporation ....B 740 547-5100
Ironton *(G-11175)*
Vertiv Solutions Inc ....E 614 888-0246
Columbus *(G-7579)*
Visi-Trak Worldwide LLC ....F 216 524-2363
Cleveland *(G-6264)*
Vitec Inc ....F 216 464-4670
Bedford *(G-1453)*
Weed Instrument Company Inc ....E 800 321-0796
Independence *(G-11156)*
Xylem Inc ....D 937 767-7241
Yellow Springs *(G-20819)*
Ysi Incorporated ....D 937 767-7241
Yellow Springs *(G-20825)*

INSTRUMENTS: Infrared, Indl Process

Infrared Imaging Systems Inc ....G 614 989-1148
Marysville *(G-12795)*
L3 Cincinnati Electronics Corp ....A 513 573-6100
Mason *(G-12902)*

INSTRUMENTS: Laser, Scientific & Engineering

Astro Instrumentation LLC ....D 440 238-2005
Strongsville *(G-17712)*
Nvision Technology Inc ....G 412 254-4668
Norton *(G-15374)*

INSTRUMENTS: Measurement, Indl Process

Automation Metrology Intl LLC ....G 440 354-6436
Mentor *(G-13395)*
Beaumont Machine LLC ....F 513 701-0421
Mason *(G-12833)*
Command Alkon Incorporated ....D 614 799-0600
Dublin *(G-8901)*
Hickok Incorporated ....D 216 541-8060
Cleveland *(G-5407)*
Meech Sttic Elminators USA Inc ....F 330 564-2000
Copley *(G-7688)*
Northern Instruments Corp LLC ....G 216 450-5073
Cleveland *(G-5779)*
Rickly Hydrological Co ....E 614 297-9877
Columbus *(G-7393)*
Seelaus Instrument Co ....G 513 733-8222
Miamisburg *(G-13714)*

INSTRUMENTS: Measuring & Controlling

1 A Lifesafer Inc ....G 513 651-9560
Blue Ash *(G-1716)*
Aclara Technologies LLC ....C 440 528-7200
Solon *(G-17098)*
Advanced Industrial Measuremnt ....E 937 320-4930
Miamisburg *(G-13637)*
Amano Cincinnati Incorporated ....D 513 697-9000
Loveland *(G-12176)*
Arnco Corporation ....C 800 847-7661
Elyria *(G-9219)*
AT&T Government Solutions Inc ....D 937 306-3030
Beavercreek *(G-1302)*
Automation and Ctrl Tech Inc ....E 614 495-1120
Dublin *(G-8886)*
Automation Technology Inc ....E 937 233-6084
Dayton *(G-8045)*
Bionetics Corporation ....E 740 788-3800
Heath *(G-10718)*
Bionix Development Corporation ....E 419 727-8421
Toledo *(G-18201)*
Bionix Safety Technologies Ltd ....E 419 727-0552
Toledo *(G-18202)*
Cincinnati Ctrl Dynamics Inc ....G 513 242-7300
Cincinnati *(G-3489)*
Continental Testing Inc ....F 937 832-3322
Union *(G-18900)*
Control Measurement Inc ....G 440 639-0020
Painesville *(G-15725)*
Cooper-Atkins Corporation ....G 513 793-5366
Cincinnati *(G-3549)*
David Boswell ....E 614 441-2497
Columbus *(G-6852)*
Daytronic Corporation ....F 937 866-3300
Miamisburg *(G-13658)*
Denton Atd Inc ....E 567 265-5200
Huron *(G-11093)*
Ets Solutions Usa LLC ....G 330 666-8696
Bath *(G-1200)*
Ferry Industries Inc ....D 330 920-9200
Stow *(G-17587)*
Fowler Products Inc ....F 419 683-4057
Crestline *(G-7794)*
Gem Instrument Co ....F 330 273-6117
Brunswick *(G-2209)*
Gleason Metrology Systems Corp ....E 937 384-8901
Dayton *(G-8223)*
Grale Technologies Inc ....G 724 683-8141
Youngstown *(G-20923)*
Halliday Technologies Inc ....G 614 504-4150
Delaware *(G-8691)*
Harris Instrument Corporation ....G 740 369-3580
Delaware *(G-8692)*
Helm Instrument Company Inc ....E 419 893-4356
Maumee *(G-13116)*
Henry & Wright Corporation ....F 216 851-3750
Cleveland *(G-5394)*
Hickok Incorporated ....D 216 541-8060
Cleveland *(G-5407)*
Honeywell Lebow Products ....C 614 850-5000
Columbus *(G-7006)*
Indicator Shop ....G 513 897-0055
Waynesville *(G-19568)*
Industrial Masurement Ctrl Inc ....G 440 877-1140
Cleveland *(G-5453)*
Instrumentors Inc ....G 440 238-3430
Strongsville *(G-17755)*
Jz Technologies LLC ....G 937 252-5800
Blue Ash *(G-1799)*
Karman Rubber Company ....E 330 864-2161
Akron *(G-232)*

PRODUCT SECTION

INSTRUMENTS: Medical & Surgical

Company	Code	Phone
Kicher and Company	G	440 266-1663
Mentor (G-13489)		
LH Marshall Company	F	614 294-6433
Columbus (G-7124)		
Low Stress Grind Inc	F	513 771-7977
Cincinnati (G-3952)		
LS Starrett Company	D	440 835-0005
Westlake (G-20129)		
Matrix Research Inc	D	937 427-8433
Beavercreek (G-1357)		
Measurement Specialties Inc	D	330 659-3312
Akron (G-277)		
Micro Laboratories Inc	G	440 918-0001
Mentor (G-13518)		
Micro Systems Development Inc	G	937 438-3567
Dayton (G-8349)		
Nebulatronics Inc	E	440 243-2370
Olmsted Twp (G-15534)		
Newall Electronics Inc	F	614 771-0213
Columbus (G-7216)		
Perfect Measuring Tape Company	E	419 243-6811
Toledo (G-18464)		
PMC Gage Inc	E	440 953-1672
Willoughby (G-20404)		
Portage Electric Products Inc	C	330 499-2727
North Canton (G-15111)		
Precision Environments Inc	E	513 847-1510
West Chester (G-19765)		
Prentke Romich Company	C	330 262-1984
Wooster (G-20641)		
Production Control Units Inc	E	937 299-5594
Moraine (G-14385)		
Q-Lab Corporation	D	440 835-8700
Westlake (G-20146)		
Quality Controls Inc	F	513 272-3900
Cincinnati (G-4225)		
R J Engineering Company Inc	G	419 843-8651
Toledo (G-18494)		
Ralston Instruments LLC	E	440 564-1430
Newbury (G-14963)		
Roto Tech Inc	E	937 859-8503
Dayton (G-8485)		
Science/Electronics Inc	F	937 224-4444
Dayton (G-8497)		
Struers Inc	D	440 871-0071
Westlake (G-20163)		
Sumiriko Ohio Inc	C	419 358-2121
Bluffton (G-1893)		
Super Systems Inc	E	513 772-0060
Cincinnati (G-4397)		
Te-Co Manufacturing LLC	D	937 836-0961
Englewood (G-9377)		
Tech Pro Inc	E	330 923-3546
Akron (G-397)		
Tech Products Corporation	E	937 438-1100
Miamisburg (G-13723)		
Tegam Inc	E	440 466-6100
Geneva (G-10229)		
Teledyne Instruments Inc	E	513 229-7000
Mason (G-12946)		
Teledyne Tekmar Company	E	513 229-7000
Mason (G-12948)		
Teradyne Inc	F	937 427-1280
Beavercreek (G-1343)		
Test-Fuchs Corporation	G	440 708-3505
Brecksville (G-2061)		
Thermo Eberline LLC	C	440 703-1400
Oakwood Village (G-15485)		
Tmw Systems Inc	F	615 986-1900
Cleveland (G-6179)		
Toledo Transducers Inc	E	419 724-4170
Holland (G-10962)		
Tool Technologies Van Dyke	F	937 349-4900
Marysville (G-12817)		
UPA Technology Inc	F	513 755-1380
West Chester (G-19816)		
Welding Consultants Inc	E	614 258-7018
Columbus (G-7598)		

INSTRUMENTS: Measuring Electricity

Company	Code	Phone
Aclara Technologies LLC	C	440 528-7200
Solon (G-17098)		
Avtron Holdings LLC	B	216 642-1230
Cleveland (G-4779)		
CDI Industries Inc	E	440 243-1100
Cleveland (G-4895)		
Contact Industries Inc	E	419 884-9788
Lexington (G-11804)		
Data Power Solutions	G	614 471-1911
Columbus (G-6851)		
Desco Corporation	G	614 888-8855
New Albany (G-14622)		
Fisher Testers LLC	G	937 416-6554
Huber Heights (G-11018)		
Hana Microdisplay Tech Inc	D	330 405-4600
Twinsburg (G-18791)		
Helm Instrument Company Inc	E	419 893-4356
Maumee (G-13116)		
Hughes Corporation	E	440 238-2550
Strongsville (G-17751)		
Japlar Group Inc	F	513 791-7192
Cincinnati (G-3870)		
Machine Products Company	E	937 890-6600
Dayton (G-8320)		
Midwest Telemetry Inc	G	440 725-5718
Kirtland (G-11469)		
Omega Engineering Inc	E	740 965-9340
Sunbury (G-17896)		
Opw Engineered Systems Inc	G	888 771-9438
Lebanon (G-11680)		
Orton Edward Jr Crmic Fndation	E	614 895-2663
Westerville (G-20014)		
P P M Inc	F	216 701-0419
Chagrin Falls (G-3026)		
Pressco Technology Inc	D	440 498-2600
Cleveland (G-5919)		
Skidmore-Wilhelm Mfg Company	E	216 481-4774
Solon (G-17232)		
Tech Pro Inc	E	330 923-3546
Akron (G-397)		
Tektronix Inc	E	513 870-4729
West Chester (G-19906)		
Tektronix Inc	E	440 248-0400
Solon (G-17250)		
Tmsi LLC	F	888 867-4872
North Canton (G-15130)		
Visual Information Institute	F	937 376-4361
Xenia (G-20801)		

INSTRUMENTS: Measuring, Current, NEC

Company	Code	Phone
Dynamp LLC	E	614 871-6900
Grove City (G-10427)		

INSTRUMENTS: Measuring, Electrical Energy

Company	Code	Phone
Drs Signal Technologies Inc	E	937 429-7470
Beavercreek (G-1312)		

INSTRUMENTS: Measuring, Electrical Power

Company	Code	Phone
F Squared Inc	G	419 752-7273
Greenwich (G-10403)		

INSTRUMENTS: Measuring, Electrical Quantities

Company	Code	Phone
Alpine Gage Inc	G	937 669-8665
Tipp City (G-18099)		

INSTRUMENTS: Medical & Surgical

Company	Code	Phone
21stcentury Medical Tech LLC	G	732 310-9367
Akron (G-13)		
Acouflow Therapeutics LLC	G	513 558-0073
Cincinnati (G-3293)		
Actis Ltd	G	614 436-0600
Powell (G-16306)		
Altitude Medical Inc	G	440 799-7701
Chardon (G-3097)		
Applied Medical Technology Inc	E	440 717-4000
Brecksville (G-2020)		
Apto Orthopaedics Corporation	E	330 572-7544
Akron (G-68)		
Atc Group Inc	D	440 293-4064
Andover (G-579)		
Avalign Technologies Inc	F	419 542-7743
Hicksville (G-10776)		
Aws Industries Inc	E	513 932-7941
Lebanon (G-11635)		
Axon Medical LLC	E	216 276-0262
Medina (G-13226)		
Beam Technologies Inc	G	800 648-1179
Columbus (G-6655)		
Becton Dickinson and Company	G	858 617-4272
Groveport (G-10484)		
Bionix Development Corporation	E	419 727-8421
Toledo (G-18201)		
Blue Bell Bio-Medical Inc	G	419 238-4442
Van Wert (G-19079)		
Boston Scntfic Nrmdlation Corp	E	513 377-6160
Mason (G-12836)		
Boston Scntfic Nrmdlation Corp	G	419 720-9510
Toledo (G-18211)		
Boston Scntfic Nrmdlation Corp	C	330 372-2652
Warren (G-19378)		
Buckeye Medical Tech LLC	G	330 719-9868
Warren (G-19379)		
Bulk Molding Compounds Inc	D	419 874-7941
Perrysburg (G-15926)		
C&W Swiss Inc	F	937 832-2889
Englewood (G-9350)		
Casco Mfg Solutions Inc	D	513 681-0003
Cincinnati (G-3447)		
Clevex Inc	E	614 675-3757
Columbus (G-6774)		
Cmd Medtech LLC	G	614 364-4243
Columbus (G-6777)		
Collaborative For Adaptive Lif	G	216 513-0572
Fairlawn (G-9601)		
Columbus Vsclar Intrvntion LLC	E	614 917-0696
Westerville (G-20041)		
Cordis Corporation	A	614 757-5000
Dublin (G-8903)		
Covidien Holding Inc	F	513 948-7219
Cincinnati (G-3554)		
Cqt Kennedy LLC	D	419 238-2442
Van Wert (G-19086)		
Dentronix Inc	E	330 916-7300
Cuyahoga Falls (G-7860)		
Devicor Med Pdts Holdings Inc	A	513 864-9000
Cincinnati (G-3586)		
Devicor Medical Products Inc	G	513 864-9000
Cincinnati (G-3587)		
Drt Aerospace LLC	D	937 492-6121
Sidney (G-17031)		
Drt Medical LLC	G	937 387-0880
Dayton (G-8170)		
Elite Biomedical Solutions LLC	F	513 207-0602
Cincinnati (G-3248)		
Em Innovations Inc	G	614 853-1504
Galloway (G-10178)		
Encore Plastics Corporation	C	419 626-8000
Sandusky (G-16808)		
Estech Inc	G	805 895-1263
West Chester (G-19700)		
Falls Welding & Fabg Inc	G	330 253-3437
Akron (G-165)		
Frantz Medical Development Ltd	C	440 255-1155
Mentor (G-13447)		
Frantz Medical Development Ltd	D	440 205-9026
Mentor (G-13448)		
Frantz Medical Group	E	440 974-8522
Mentor (G-13449)		
General Data Company Inc	C	513 752-7978
Cincinnati (G-3252)		
Goal Medical LLC	E	541 654-5951
Mentor (G-13461)		
Gyrus Acmi LP	C	419 668-8201
Norwalk (G-15396)		
Haag-Streit Holding Us Inc	E	513 336-7255
Mason (G-12883)		
Hammill Manufacturing Co	E	419 724-5702
Toledo (G-18320)		
Howmedica Osteonics Corp	F	937 291-3900
Dayton (G-8254)		
Immersus Health Company LLC	G	855 994-4325
Cincinnati (G-3838)		
Immersus Health Company LLC	G	855 994-4325
Blue Ash (G-1792)		
Intellirod Spine Inc	G	234 678-8965
Akron (G-217)		
Klarity Medical Products LLC	F	740 788-8107
Newark (G-14891)		
Liquid Logic LLC	G	937 865-3068
Miamisburg (G-13685)		
Lumoptik Inc	G	216 577-3905
Shaker Heights (G-16934)		
Markethatch Co Inc	F	330 376-6363
Akron (G-269)		
Medinvent LLC	G	330 247-0921
Medina (G-13299)		
Medtronic Inc	F	216 642-1977
Cleveland (G-5652)		
Meridian LLC	F	330 995-0371
Aurora (G-892)		
Minimally Invasive Devices Inc	E	614 484-5036
Columbus (G-7184)		
Morris Technologies Inc	C	513 733-1611
Cincinnati (G-4047)		
National Biological Corp	E	216 831-0600
Beachwood (G-1252)		

Employee Codes: A=Over 500 employees, B=251-500
C=101-250, D=51-100, E=20-50, F=10-19, G=3-9

INSTRUMENTS: Medical & Surgical

Neptune Aquatic Systems Inc ....G....... 513 575-2989
  Loveland *(G-12216)*
New Leaf Medical Inc 216 391-7749
  Cleveland *(G-5748)*
North Coast Medi-Tek Inc ....F....... 440 974-0750
  Mentor *(G-13529)*
Nuevue Solutions Inc ....G....... 440 836-4772
  Rootstown *(G-16572)*
Office Bsed Ansthesia Svcs LLC ....G....... 513 582-5170
  Montgomery *(G-14297)*
Optoquest Corporation ....G....... 216 445-3637
  Cleveland *(G-5816)*
Patriot Products Inc ....F....... 419 865-9712
  Holland *(G-10948)*
Pemco Inc 216 524-2990
  Cleveland *(G-5862)*
Percuvision LLC ....F....... 614 891-4800
  Columbus *(G-7311)*
Perfusion Solutions Inc ....G....... 216 848-1610
  Cleveland *(G-5864)*
PMC Smart Solutions LLC ....F....... 513 921-5040
  Blue Ash *(G-1831)*
Premiere Farnell Corp ....G....... 937 424-1204
  Dayton *(G-8437)*
Prentke Romich Company ....G....... 330 262-1984
  Wooster *(G-20641)*
Pulse Worldwide Ltd ....G....... 513 234-7829
  Mason *(G-12928)*
Quality Electrodynamics LLC ....C....... 440 638-5106
  Mayfield Village *(G-13176)*
R-Med Inc ....G....... 419 693-7481
  Oregon *(G-15565)*
Reliance Medical Products Inc ....D....... 513 398-3937
  Mason *(G-12930)*
RJR Surgical Inc ....G....... 216 241-2804
  Cleveland *(G-5990)*
Sagitta Inc ....G....... 440 570-5393
  Cleveland *(G-6025)*
Secqure Surgical Corp ....G....... 513 769-1916
  Blue Ash *(G-1845)*
Smiths Medical Asd Inc ....E....... 800 796-8701
  Dublin *(G-8987)*
Smiths Medical Asd Inc ....F....... 614 210-6431
  Dublin *(G-8989)*
Smiths Medical North America ....G....... 614 210-7300
  Dublin *(G-8990)*
Sparton Medical Systems Inc ....D....... 440 878-4630
  Strongsville *(G-17791)*
Standard Bariatrics Inc ....G....... 513 620-7751
  Blue Ash *(G-1850)*
Steris Instrument MGT Svcs Inc ....E....... 800 783-9251
  Stow *(G-17632)*
Stryker Orthopedic ....G....... 614 766-2990
  Dublin *(G-8996)*
Summit Online Products LLC ....G....... 800 326-1972
  Powell *(G-16338)*
Surgical Theater LLC ....G....... 216 452-2177
  Mayfield Village *(G-13177)*
Surgical Theater LLC ....G....... 216 496-7884
  Cleveland *(G-6132)*
Surgrx Inc ....F....... 650 482-2400
  Blue Ash *(G-1856)*
Synergy Health North Amer Inc ....D....... 513 398-6406
  Mason *(G-12945)*
Theken Companies LLC ....E....... 330 733-7600
  Akron *(G-402)*
Thermo Fisher Scientific Inc ....C....... 800 871-8909
  Oakwood Village *(G-15486)*
Thompson Partners Inc ....G....... 866 475-2500
  Gahanna *(G-10109)*
Torbot Group Inc ....E....... 419 724-1475
  Toledo *(G-18577)*
Tri-Tech Medical Inc ....E....... 800 253-8692
  Avon *(G-972)*
United Medical Supply Company ....G....... 866 678-8633
  Valley City *(G-19068)*
Valensil Technologies LLC ....G....... 440 937-8181
  Avon *(G-973)*
Venturemedgroup Ltd ....G....... 567 661-0768
  Toledo *(G-18590)*
Vertebration Inc ....G....... 614 395-3446
  Powell *(G-16340)*
Vesco Medical LLC ....F....... 614 914-5991
  Columbus *(G-7580)*

INSTRUMENTS: Particle Size Analyzers

Rotex Global LLC ....C....... 513 541-1236
  Cincinnati *(G-4282)*

INSTRUMENTS: Power Measuring, Electrical

TTI Floor Care North Amer Inc ....B....... 440 996-2000
  Solon *(G-17255)*

INSTRUMENTS: Pressure Measurement, Indl

Avure Autoclave Systems Inc ....E....... 614 891-2732
  Columbus *(G-6637)*
Cincinnati Test Systems Inc ....C....... 513 202-5100
  Harrison *(G-10635)*
Honeywell Inc ....C....... 513 272-1111
  Cincinnati *(G-3825)*
Koester Corporation ....D....... 419 599-0291
  Napoleon *(G-14548)*
Solon Manufacturing Company ....E....... 440 286-7149
  Chardon *(G-3137)*

INSTRUMENTS: Radar Testing, Electric

Structural Radar Imaging Inc ....G....... 425 970-3890
  Toledo *(G-18532)*

INSTRUMENTS: Radio Frequency Measuring

Strong M Llc ....F....... 614 329-8025
  Columbus *(G-7494)*

INSTRUMENTS: Recorders, Oscillographic

County of Medina ....F....... 330 723-3641
  Medina *(G-13245)*

INSTRUMENTS: Refractometers, Indl Process

Mercury Iron and Steel Co ....F....... 440 349-1500
  Solon *(G-17190)*
Rhi US Ltd ....F....... 513 753-1254
  Cincinnati *(G-4264)*

INSTRUMENTS: Signal Generators & Averagers

Palstar Inc ....F....... 937 773-6255
  Piqua *(G-16148)*

INSTRUMENTS: Surface Area Analyzers

4r Enterprises Incorporated ....G....... 330 923-9799
  Cuyahoga Falls *(G-7829)*
HEF USA Corporation ....F....... 937 323-2556
  Springfield *(G-17416)*

INSTRUMENTS: Temperature Measurement, Indl

Furnace Parts LLC ....G....... 800 321-0796
  Cleveland *(G-5279)*
Shelburne Corp ....G....... 216 321-9177
  Shaker Heights *(G-16936)*
TE Brown LLC ....G....... 937 223-2241
  Dayton *(G-8548)*
Thermacal Inc 440 498-1005
  Solon *(G-17252)*

INSTRUMENTS: Test, Electrical, Engine

Nu-Di Products Co Inc ....D....... 216 251-9070
  Cleveland *(G-5793)*

INSTRUMENTS: Test, Electronic & Electric Measurement

Advanced Kiffer Systems Inc ....F....... 216 267-8181
  Cleveland *(G-4627)*
Automtiq Msurement Systems LLC ....G....... 614 431-2667
  Columbus *(G-6634)*
Bionix Safety Technologies Ltd ....E....... 419 727-0552
  Toledo *(G-18202)*
Bird Electronic Corporation ....C....... 440 248-1200
  Solon *(G-17115)*
Bird Technologies Group Inc ....G....... 440 248-1200
  Solon *(G-17116)*
Field Apparatus Service & Tstg ....G....... 513 353-9399
  Cincinnati *(G-3685)*
Keithley Instruments LLC ....C....... 440 248-0400
  Solon *(G-17182)*
Keithley Instruments Intl Corp ....B....... 440 248-0400
  Cleveland *(G-5525)*
Midwest Metrology LLC ....F....... 937 832-0965
  Englewood *(G-9369)*
Mueller Electric Company Inc ....E....... 614 888-8855
  New Albany *(G-14631)*
O H Technologies Inc ....G....... 440 354-8780
  Mentor *(G-13531)*
Paneltech LLC ....F....... 440 516-1300
  Wickliffe *(G-20223)*
Speelman Electric Inc ....D....... 330 633-1410
  Tallmadge *(G-18004)*
Vmetro Inc ....G....... 281 584-0728
  Fairborn *(G-9473)*

INSTRUMENTS: Test, Electronic & Electrical Circuits

Andromeda Research ....G....... 513 831-9708
  Cincinnati *(G-3346)*
Automation Technology Inc ....E....... 937 233-6084
  Dayton *(G-8045)*
Hannon Company ....D....... 330 456-4728
  Canton *(G-2693)*
Lomar Enterprises Inc ....F....... 614 409-9104
  Groveport *(G-10501)*
Pile Dynamics Inc 216 831-6131
  Cleveland *(G-5877)*
Triplett Bluffton Corporation ....G....... 419 358-8750
  Bluffton *(G-1896)*

INSTRUMENTS: Thermal Conductive, Indl

Rsa Controls Inc ....G....... 513 476-6277
  West Chester *(G-19790)*

INSTRUMENTS: Transducers, Volts, Amperes, Watts, VARs & Freq

Nebulatronics Inc ....E....... 440 243-2370
  Olmsted Twp *(G-15534)*

INSTRUMENTS: Vibration

Balmac Inc ....F....... 614 873-8222
  Plain City *(G-16175)*
Bilz Vibration Technology Inc ....F....... 330 468-2459
  Macedonia *(G-12279)*
Vibration Test Systems Inc ....G....... 330 562-5729
  Aurora *(G-914)*

INSULATING COMPOUNDS

St Bernard Insulation LLC ....F....... 513 266-2158
  Cincinnati *(G-4367)*

INSULATION & CUSHIONING FOAM: Polystyrene

Astro Shapes LLC ....C....... 330 755-1414
  Struthers *(G-17814)*
Atlas Roofing Corporation ....C....... 937 746-9941
  Franklin *(G-9870)*
Austin Foam Plastics Inc ....E....... 614 921-0824
  Columbus *(G-6632)*
Energy Storage Technologies ....E....... 937 312-0114
  Dayton *(G-8183)*
Jason Incorporated ....D....... 419 668-4474
  Milan *(G-13985)*
Paratus Supply Inc ....F....... 330 745-3600
  Barberton *(G-1093)*
Plymouth Foam LLC ....E....... 740 254-1188
  Gnadenhutten *(G-10282)*
Surface Dynamics Inc ....G....... 513 772-6635
  Cincinnati *(G-4399)*
Technifab Inc ....E....... 440 934-8324
  Avon *(G-968)*
Technifab Inc ....D....... 440 934-8324
  Avon *(G-969)*
Technifab Inc ....E....... 440 934-8324
  Avon *(G-970)*
Trans Foam Inc ....G....... 330 630-9444
  Tallmadge *(G-18009)*

INSULATION & ROOFING MATERIALS: Wood, Reconstituted

Celcore Inc ....F....... 440 234-7888
  Cleveland *(G-4897)*
Commercial Innovations Inc ....G....... 216 641-7500
  Cleveland *(G-5003)*
Ricers Residential Svcs LLC ....G....... 567 203-7414
  Shelby *(G-16987)*

INSULATION MATERIALS WHOLESALERS

Denizen Inc.....................................F 937 615-9561
  Piqua *(G-16111)*
Great Lakes Textiles Inc................E 440 914-1122
  Solon *(G-17156)*

INSULATION: Fiberglass

American Insulation Tech LLC ....F 513 733-4248
  Milford *(G-13993)*
Blackthorn LLC ....F 937 836-9296
  Clayton *(G-4572)*
Cpic Automotive Inc ....G 740 587-3262
  Granville *(G-10328)*
Derby Fabg Solutions LLC................E 937 498-4054
  Sidney *(G-17027)*
Ipm Inc ....F 419 248-8000
  Toledo *(G-18351)*
Johns Manville Corporation..............B 419 878-8111
  Waterville *(G-19498)*
Johns Manville Corporation..............A 419 784-7000
  Defiance *(G-8629)*
Johns Manville Corporation..............C 419 784-7000
  Defiance *(G-8630)*
Johns Manville Corporation..............C 419 467-8189
  Maumee *(G-13122)*
Johns Manville Corporation..............C 419 878-8111
  Defiance *(G-8631)*
Metal Building Intr Pdts Co ....F 440 322-6500
  Elyria *(G-9294)*
Owens Corning ....G 419 248-8000
  Navarre *(G-14584)*
Owens Corning ....C 740 964-1727
  Toledo *(G-18444)*
Owens Corning ....A 419 248-8000
  Toledo *(G-18446)*
Owens Corning Sales LLC ....F 419 248-8000
  Toledo *(G-18448)*
Owens Corning Sales LLC ....C 740 328-2300
  Newark *(G-14907)*
Owens Corning Sales LLC ....F 419 248-5751
  Swanton *(G-17917)*
Owens Corning Sales LLC ....E 614 539-0830
  Grove City *(G-10455)*
Owens Crning Cmposite Mtls LLC ....E 419 248-8000
  Toledo *(G-18449)*
Owens-Corning Capital LLC ....F 419 248-8000
  Toledo *(G-18450)*

INSULATORS & INSULATION MATERIALS: Electrical

Cornerstone Indus Holdings..............G 440 893-9144
  Chagrin Falls *(G-3014)*
Eger Products Inc ....D 513 753-4200
  Amelia *(G-539)*
Glt Fabricators Inc ....G 713 670-9700
  Solon *(G-17151)*
Merrico Inc...G 419 525-2711
  Mansfield *(G-12479)*
Monti Incorporated ....C 513 761-7775
  Cincinnati *(G-4043)*
Mueller Electric Company Inc...........E 216 771-5225
  Akron *(G-290)*
Red Seal Electric Co ....E 216 941-3900
  Cleveland *(G-5967)*
Resource Mechanical Insul LLC.......E 248 577-0200
  Walbridge *(G-19298)*
Von Roll Usa Inc ....E 216 433-7474
  Cleveland *(G-6271)*
Weidmann Electrical Tech Inc ....D 937 652-1220
  Urbana *(G-19019)*

INSURANCE AGENTS, NEC

Johnny Chin Insurance Agency ....G 513 777-8695
  West Chester *(G-19871)*

INSURANCE BROKERS, NEC

Forge Industries Inc ....A 330 782-8301
  Youngstown *(G-20909)*

INSURANCE CARRIERS: Life

Western & Southern Lf Insur Co ......A 513 629-1800
  Cincinnati *(G-4503)*

INSURANCE CLAIM PROCESSING, EXC MEDICAL

Safelite Group Inc ....A 614 210-9000
  Columbus *(G-7413)*

INSURANCE PATROL SVCS

Henderson Partners LLC..................G 614 883-1310
  Columbus *(G-6987)*

INSURANCE RESEARCH SVCS

Frisbie Engine & Machine Co ....F 513 542-1770
  Cincinnati *(G-3714)*

INTEGRATED CIRCUITS, SEMICONDUCTOR NETWORKS, ETC

A M D ....G 440 918-8930
  Willoughby *(G-20264)*
Leidos Inc ....D 937 431-2270
  Beavercreek *(G-1326)*
Philips Medical Systems Mr..............C 440 483-2499
  Highland Heights *(G-10798)*

INTERCOMMUNICATION EQPT REPAIR SVCS

Industrial Electronic Service..............F 937 746-9750
  Carlisle *(G-2893)*

INTERCOMMUNICATIONS SYSTEMS: Electric

Bird Technologies Group Inc.............G 440 248-1200
  Solon *(G-17116)*
Milicom LLC......................................G 216 765-8875
  Beachwood *(G-1249)*
Public Safety Concepts LLC ....G 614 733-0200
  Plain City *(G-16208)*
Quasonix Inc ....E 513 942-1287
  West Chester *(G-19775)*
Saltillo Corporation............................G 330 674-6722
  Millersburg *(G-14126)*
Sound Communications Inc ....F 614 875-8500
  Grove City *(G-10470)*

INTERIOR DECORATING SVCS

Hang-UPS Instllation Group Inc ....G 614 239-7004
  Columbus *(G-6978)*

INTERIOR DESIGN SVCS, NEC

Blue Streak Services Inc ....G 216 223-3282
  Cleveland *(G-4825)*
Nordic Light America Inc ....F 614 981-9497
  Columbus *(G-7223)*

INTERIOR DESIGNING SVCS

Added Touch Decorating Gallery ......G 419 747-3146
  Ontario *(G-15537)*
CIP International Inc.........................D 513 874-9925
  West Chester *(G-19675)*
Silver Threads Inc ....E 614 733-0099
  Plain City *(G-16211)*
Wright Designs Inc ....G 216 524-6662
  Cleveland *(G-6329)*

INTERIOR REPAIR SVCS

Boyce Ltd..G 614 236-8901
  Columbus *(G-6690)*

INTERMEDIATE CARE FACILITY

Bittersweet Inc ....D 419 875-6986
  Whitehouse *(G-20189)*

INTRAVENOUS SOLUTIONS

Clinical Specialties Inc ....D 888 873-7888
  Brecksville *(G-2027)*
Molorokalin Inc..................................F 330 629-1332
  Canfield *(G-2537)*

INVERTERS: Nonrotating Electrical

Myers Controlled Power LLC ....G 909 923-1800
  Canton *(G-2760)*
Vanner Holdings Inc ....D 614 771-2718
  Hilliard *(G-10873)*

INVESTMENT ADVISORY SVCS

Linsalata Capital Partners Fun ....G 440 684-1400
  Cleveland *(G-5579)*

INVESTMENT FIRM: General Brokerage

Western & Southern Lf Insur Co ......A 513 629-1800
  Cincinnati *(G-4503)*

INVESTMENT FUNDS: Open-Ended

Broad Street Financial Company ......G 614 228-0326
  Columbus *(G-6704)*

INVESTORS, NEC

Alpha Zeta Holdings Inc ....G 216 271-1601
  Cleveland *(G-4677)*
NM Group Global LLC ....G 419 447-5211
  Tiffin *(G-18071)*
Resilience Fund III LP ....F 216 292-0200
  Cleveland *(G-5979)*
Taylor Company ....G 513 271-2550
  Cincinnati *(G-4408)*

INVESTORS: Real Estate, Exc Property Operators

Ajami Holdings Group LLC ....G 216 396-6089
  Richmond Heights *(G-16500)*
Broad Street Financial Company ......G 614 228-0326
  Columbus *(G-6704)*
Faircosa LLC ....G 216 577-9909
  Cleveland *(G-5215)*

IRON & STEEL PRDTS: Hot-Rolled

North Star Bluescope Steel LLC.......B 419 822-2200
  Delta *(G-8777)*

IRON ORE MINING

Bloom Lake Iron Ore Mine Ltd..........G 216 694-5700
  Cleveland *(G-4822)*
Cleveland-Cliffs Inc...........................D 216 694-5700
  Cleveland *(G-4986)*
Cliffs Minnesota Minerals Co............A 216 694-5700
  Cleveland *(G-4992)*
Empire Iron Mining Partnership ....G 216 694-5700
  Cleveland *(G-5174)*
Hibbing Taconite A Joint Ventr ....G 216 694-5700
  Cleveland *(G-5406)*
Northshore Mining Company ....G 216 694-5700
  Cleveland *(G-5785)*
The Cleveland-Cliffs Iron Co.............C 216 694-5700
  Cleveland *(G-6162)*
Tilden Mining Company LC ....A 216 694-5700
  Cleveland *(G-6175)*
Wabush Mines Cliffs Mining Co ....A 216 694-5700
  Cleveland *(G-6281)*

IRON ORE PELLETIZING

United Taconite LLC ....G 218 744-7800
  Cleveland *(G-6237)*

IRON ORES

Cliffs & Associates Ltd.....................G 216 694-5700
  Cleveland *(G-4988)*
Cliffs Michigan Operation ....E 216 694-5303
  Cleveland *(G-4990)*
Cliffs Mining Company ....F 216 694-5700
  Cleveland *(G-4991)*
International Steel Group ....C 330 841-2800
  Warren *(G-19411)*

IRON OXIDES

Ironics Inc...G 330 652-0583
  Niles *(G-15016)*

IRRADIATION EQPT: Nuclear

Trionix Research Laboratory ....G 330 425-9055
  Twinsburg *(G-18867)*

JACKETS: Indl, Metal Plate

Austin Engineering Inc......................G 330 848-0815
  Barberton *(G-1055)*

JACKS: Hydraulic

Joyce/Dayton Corp .... E 937 294-6261
Dayton (G-8285)
Marmac Co .... G 937 372-8093
Xenia (G-20784)
Quality Products Inc .... D 614 228-0185
Swanton (G-17920)

JANITORIAL & CUSTODIAL SVCS

Cleaning Lady Inc .... F 419 589-5566
Mansfield (G-12426)
R T Industries Inc .... C 937 335-5784
Troy (G-18695)

JANITORIAL EQPT & SPLYS WHOLESALERS

Alco-Chem Inc .... E 330 253-3535
Akron (G-56)
Chem-Sales Inc .... F 419 531-4292
Toledo (G-18228)
Friends Service Co Inc .... D 419 427-1704
Findlay (G-9690)
Gt Industrial Supply Inc .... F 513 771-7000
Blue Ash (G-1783)
Impact Products LLC .... C 419 841-2891
Toledo (G-18342)
Rose Products and Services Inc .... E 614 443-7647
Columbus (G-7402)
Zircon Industries Inc .... G 216 595-0200
Cleveland (G-6346)

JEWELERS' FINDINGS & MATERIALS

Zero-D Products Inc .... G 440 417-1843
Willoughby (G-20463)

JEWELERS' FINDINGS & MATERIALS: Castings

Dentsply Sirona Inc .... D 419 865-9497
Maumee (G-13108)

JEWELERS' FINDINGS & MATERIALS: Pin Stems

Dayton Hawker Corporation .... F 937 293-8147
Dayton (G-8135)

JEWELERS' FINDINGS & MTLS: Jewel Prep, Instr, Tools, Watches

Lapcraft Inc .... G 614 764-8993
Powell (G-16327)

JEWELRY & PRECIOUS STONES WHOLESALERS

Goyal Enterprises Inc .... F 513 874-9303
West Chester (G-19860)
Jaffe & Gross Jewelry Company .... G 937 461-9450
Dayton (G-8276)
Renoir Visions LLC .... F 419 586-5679
Celina (G-2982)

JEWELRY APPAREL

Bensan Jewelers Inc .... G 216 221-1434
Lakewood (G-11512)
Cambridge Mfg Jewelers .... G 330 528-0207
Hudson (G-11035)
Marfo Company .... D 614 276-3352
Columbus (G-7150)
Stephen R White .... G 740 522-1512
Newark (G-14923)
Timothy Allen Jewelers Inc .... G 440 974-8885
Mentor (G-13606)

JEWELRY FINDINGS & LAPIDARY WORK

Alex and Ani LLC .... G 513 791-1480
Cincinnati (G-3319)
Alex and Ani LLC .... G 216 378-2139
Beachwood (G-1222)

JEWELRY REPAIR SVCS

Barany Jewelry Inc .... G 330 220-4367
Brunswick (G-2191)
Benchworks Jewelers Inc .... G 937 439-4243
Dayton (G-8054)
Bensan Jewelers Inc .... G 216 221-1434
Lakewood (G-11512)
C M Stephanoff Jewelers Inc .... G 440 526-5890
Brecksville (G-2026)
Davidson Jewelers Inc .... G 513 932-3936
Lebanon (G-11647)
Gustave Julian Jewelers Inc .... G 440 888-1100
Cleveland (G-5360)
H P Nielsen Inc .... G 440 244-4255
Lorain (G-12094)
Koop Diamond Cutters Inc .... F 513 621-2838
Cincinnati (G-3923)
Michael W Hyes Desgr Goldsmith .... G 440 519-0889
Solon (G-17194)
Mr 14k Inc .... G 440 234-6661
Berea (G-1618)
Pughs Designer Jewelers Inc .... G 740 344-9259
Newark (G-14914)
Roulet Company .... G 419 241-2988
Toledo (G-18508)

JEWELRY STORES

Benchworks Jewelers Inc .... G 937 439-4243
Dayton (G-8054)
Farah Jewelers Inc .... F 614 438-6140
Columbus (G-6492)
Marcus Jewelers .... G 513 474-4950
Cincinnati (G-3979)
Michael W Hyes Desgr Goldsmith .... G 440 519-0889
Solon (G-17194)
Panama Jewelers LLC .... G 440 376-6987
Painesville (G-15771)
Rita Caz Jwly Studio & Gallery .... G 937 767-7713
Yellow Springs (G-20814)
Rosenfeld Jewelry Inc .... G 440 446-0099
Cleveland (G-6004)
Timothy Allen Jewelers Inc .... G 440 974-8885
Mentor (G-13606)

JEWELRY STORES: Precious Stones & Precious Metals

Barany Jewelry Inc .... G 330 220-4367
Brunswick (G-2191)
Bensan Jewelers Inc .... G 216 221-1434
Lakewood (G-11512)
Cambridge Mfg Jewelers .... G 330 528-0207
Hudson (G-11035)
Davidson Jewelers Inc .... G 513 932-3936
Lebanon (G-11647)
Em Es Be Company LLC .... G 216 761-9500
Cleveland (G-5170)
Goyal Enterprises Inc .... F 513 874-9303
West Chester (G-19860)
H P Nielsen Inc .... G 440 244-4255
Lorain (G-12094)
Handcrafted Jewelry Inc .... G 330 650-9011
Hudson (G-11051)
Jaffe & Gross Jewelry Company .... G 937 461-9450
Dayton (G-8276)
James C Free Inc .... E 937 298-0171
Dayton (G-8277)
James C Free Inc .... G 513 793-0133
Cincinnati (G-3868)
M B Saxon Co Inc .... F 440 229-5006
Cleveland (G-5592)
Ohio Silver Co .... G 937 767-8261
Yellow Springs (G-20813)
Old Village .... F 614 791-8467
Delaware (G-8714)
Pughs Designer Jewelers Inc .... G 740 344-9259
Newark (G-14914)
Robert W Johnson Inc .... D 614 336-4545
Dublin (G-8975)
Roulet Company .... G 419 241-2988
Toledo (G-18508)
Sheiban Jewelry Inc .... F 440 238-0616
Strongsville (G-17787)
Stephen R White .... G 740 522-1512
Newark (G-14923)
White Jewelers .... G 330 264-3324
Wooster (G-20667)

JEWELRY STORES: Silverware

Gustave Julian Jewelers Inc .... G 440 888-1100
Cleveland (G-5360)

JEWELRY, PRECIOUS METAL: Bracelets

C M Stephanoff Jewelers Inc .... G 440 526-5890
Brecksville (G-2026)
Goyal Enterprises Inc .... F 513 874-9303
West Chester (G-19860)

JEWELRY, PRECIOUS METAL: Buttons, Precious Or Semi Or Stone

Puppy Paws Inc .... G 440 461-9667
Cleveland (G-5935)

JEWELRY, PRECIOUS METAL: Cigar & Cigarette Access

Boos Make & Take .... G 440 647-0000
Wellington (G-19573)
M & M Tobacco .... G 330 573-8543
Carrollton (G-2925)
Phantasm Vapors LLC .... G 513 248-2431
Milford (G-14032)
Smokeheal Inc .... G 216 255-5119
Cleveland (G-6074)
Vapen8r LLC .... G 440 934-8273
Sheffield Village (G-16976)

JEWELRY, PRECIOUS METAL: Medals, Precious Or Semiprecious

Crest Craft Company .... F 513 271-4858
Blue Ash (G-1754)

JEWELRY, PRECIOUS METAL: Mountings & Trimmings

Farah Jewelers Inc .... F 614 438-6140
Columbus (G-6492)

JEWELRY, PRECIOUS METAL: Pearl, Natural Or Cultured

Auld Crafters Inc .... G 614 221-6825
Columbus (G-6630)

JEWELRY, PRECIOUS METAL: Pins

O C Tanner Company .... G 513 583-1100
Mason (G-12917)

JEWELRY, PRECIOUS METAL: Rings, Finger

Jostens Inc .... E 419 874-5835
Perrysburg (G-15971)
Jostens Inc .... G 513 731-5900
Cincinnati (G-3885)

JEWELRY, WHOLESALE

Cambridge Mfg Jewelers .... G 330 528-0207
Hudson (G-11035)
M B Saxon Co Inc .... F 440 229-5006
Cleveland (G-5592)
Marfo Company .... D 614 276-3352
Columbus (G-7150)
Ohio Silver Co .... G 937 767-8261
Yellow Springs (G-20813)
Scholz & Ey Engravers Inc .... F 614 444-8052
Columbus (G-7427)
Sheiban Jewelry Inc .... F 440 238-0616
Strongsville (G-17787)

JEWELRY: Decorative, Fashion & Costume

Cult Couture LLC .... G 330 801-9475
Cuyahoga Falls (G-7855)
Johnstons Banks Inc .... G 614 499-4374
Westerville (G-20001)
Pughs Designer Jewelers Inc .... G 740 344-9259
Newark (G-14914)
Swarovski North America Ltd .... G 216 292-9737
Cleveland (G-6136)

JEWELRY: Precious Metal

AR Jester Co .... G 513 241-1465
Cincinnati (G-3353)
Baldwin B AA Design .... G 740 374-5844
Marietta (G-12608)
Barany Jewelry Inc .... G 330 220-4367
Brunswick (G-2191)

PRODUCT SECTION

Benchworks Jewelers Inc ....G...... 937 439-4243
  Dayton *(G-8054)*
Davidson Jewelers Inc ....G...... 513 932-3936
  Lebanon *(G-11647)*
Dimensional Works of Art ....G...... 330 657-2681
  Peninsula *(G-15891)*
Don Basch Jewelers Inc ....F...... 330 467-2116
  Macedonia *(G-12290)*
Em Es Be Company LLC ....G...... 216 761-9500
  Cleveland *(G-5170)*
Ginos Awards Inc ....E...... 216 831-6565
  Warrensville Heights *(G-19469)*
Gold Mine Inc ....G...... 614 378-8308
  Dublin *(G-8916)*
Gold Pro Inc ....G...... 216 241-5143
  Cleveland *(G-5327)*
Gustave Julian Jewelers Inc ....G...... 440 888-1100
  Cleveland *(G-5360)*
H P Nielsen Inc ....G...... 440 244-4255
  Lorain *(G-12094)*
Heather B Moore Inc ....G...... 216 932-5430
  Cleveland *(G-5387)*
J and L Jewelry Manufacturing ....G...... 440 546-9988
  Cleveland *(G-5481)*
Jaffe & Gross Jewelry Company ....G...... 937 461-9450
  Dayton *(G-8276)*
James C Free Inc ....E...... 937 298-0171
  Dayton *(G-8277)*
James C Free Inc ....G...... 513 793-0133
  Cincinnati *(G-3868)*
Jensen & Sons Inc ....F...... 419 471-1000
  Toledo *(G-18358)*
Jewels By Img Inc ....F...... 440 461-4464
  Cleveland *(G-5498)*
Koop Diamond Cutters Inc ....F...... 513 621-2838
  Cincinnati *(G-3923)*
Levit Jewelers Inc ....G...... 440 985-1685
  Lorain *(G-12100)*
M B Saxon Co Inc ....F...... 440 229-5006
  Cleveland *(G-5592)*
Marcus Jewelers ....G...... 513 474-4950
  Cincinnati *(G-3979)*
Michael W Hyes Desgr Goldsmith ....G...... 440 519-0889
  Solon *(G-17194)*
Mr 14k Inc ....G...... 440 234-6661
  Berea *(G-1618)*
Ohio Silver Co ....G...... 937 767-8261
  Yellow Springs *(G-20813)*
Old Village ....F...... 614 791-8467
  Delaware *(G-8714)*
Rita Caz Jwly Studio & Gallery ....G...... 937 767-7713
  Yellow Springs *(G-20814)*
Robert W Johnson Inc ....D...... 614 336-4545
  Dublin *(G-8975)*
Rosenfeld Jewelry Inc ....G...... 440 446-0099
  Cleveland *(G-6004)*
Roulet Company ....G...... 419 241-2988
  Toledo *(G-18508)*
Sheiban Jewelry Inc ....F...... 440 238-0616
  Strongsville *(G-17787)*
Signet Group Inc ....E...... 330 668-5901
  Fairlawn *(G-9617)*
Val Casting Inc ....E...... 419 562-2499
  Bucyrus *(G-2346)*
Weber Jewelers Incorporated ....G...... 937 643-9200
  Dayton *(G-8587)*
White Jewelers ....G...... 330 264-3324
  Wooster *(G-20667)*
Whitehouse Bros Inc ....G...... 513 621-2259
  Blue Ash *(G-1870)*

JIGS & FIXTURES

Cmt Machining & Fabg LLC ....F...... 937 652-3740
  Urbana *(G-18983)*
Delta Tool & Die Stl Block Inc ....F...... 419 822-5939
  Delta *(G-8767)*
First Tool Corp ....E...... 937 254-6197
  Dayton *(G-8195)*
Glendale Machine Inc ....G...... 440 248-8646
  Solon *(G-17150)*
Homeworth Fabrications & Mchs ....F...... 330 525-5459
  Homeworth *(G-10988)*
Hudak Machine & Tool Inc ....G...... 440 366-8955
  Elyria *(G-9266)*
JBI Corporation ....F...... 419 855-3389
  Genoa *(G-10233)*
Jergens Inc ....C...... 216 486-5540
  Cleveland *(G-5495)*
Kilroy Company ....D...... 440 951-8700
  Eastlake *(G-9117)*

Krisdale Industries Inc ....G...... 330 225-2392
  Valley City *(G-19043)*
P O McIntire Company ....E...... 440 269-1848
  Wickliffe *(G-20221)*
Progage Inc ....F...... 440 951-4477
  Mentor *(G-13558)*
Schuster Manufacturing Inc ....G...... 419 476-5800
  Toledo *(G-18514)*

JOB PRINTING & NEWSPAPER PUBLISHING COMBINED

Bluffton News Pubg & Prtg Co ....E...... 419 358-8010
  Bluffton *(G-1884)*
County Classifieds ....G...... 937 592-8847
  Bellefontaine *(G-1510)*
Douthit Communications Inc ....D...... 419 625-5825
  Sandusky *(G-16805)*
First Catholc Slovak Union U S ....F...... 216 642-9406
  Cleveland *(G-5242)*
Hardin County Publishing Co ....E...... 419 674-4066
  Kenton *(G-11408)*
Holland Springfield Journal ....G...... 419 874-2528
  Perrysburg *(G-15963)*
Job News ....G...... 513 984-5724
  Blue Ash *(G-1795)*
Merrill Corporation ....C...... 614 801-4700
  Grove City *(G-10444)*
Ogden Newspapers Ohio Inc ....E...... 330 424-9541
  Lisbon *(G-11976)*
Ray Barnes Newspaper Inc ....G...... 419 674-4066
  Kenton *(G-11420)*
Springfield Newspapers Inc ....E...... 937 323-5533
  Springfield *(G-17495)*
Utica Herald ....G...... 740 892-2771
  Utica *(G-19028)*
Welch Publishing Co ....E...... 419 874-2528
  Perrysburg *(G-16025)*
Yellow Springs News Inc ....F...... 937 767-7373
  Yellow Springs *(G-20821)*

JOB TRAINING & VOCATIONAL REHABILITATION SVCS

County of Lake ....D...... 440 269-2193
  Willoughby *(G-20302)*
Findaway World LLC ....D...... 440 893-0808
  Solon *(G-17143)*
Pakra LLC ....F...... 614 477-6965
  Columbus *(G-7286)*
Richland Newhope Industries ....C...... 419 774-4400
  Mansfield *(G-12506)*
Vgs Inc ....C...... 216 431-7800
  Cleveland *(G-6256)*
Vocational Services Inc ....C...... 216 431-8085
  Cleveland *(G-6267)*

JOB TRAINING SVCS

Tekdog Inc ....G...... 614 737-3743
  Granville *(G-10338)*

JOINTS OR FASTENINGS: Rail

Mc Cully Supply & Sales Inc ....G...... 330 497-2211
  Canton *(G-2749)*
Seneca Railroad & Mining Co ....F...... 419 483-7764
  Bellevue *(G-1545)*

JOINTS: Expansion

Steel Services Inc ....G...... 513 353-4173
  North Bend *(G-15055)*

JOINTS: Expansion, Pipe

Bosch Rexroth Corporation ....B...... 330 263-3300
  Wooster *(G-20573)*

JOISTS: Long-Span Series, Open Web Steel

Promac International Inc ....G...... 440 967-2040
  Vermilion *(G-19170)*
Socar of Ohio Inc ....D...... 419 596-3100
  Continental *(G-7668)*

KEYS, KEY BLANKS

Hillman Group Inc ....G...... 800 800-4900
  Parma *(G-15822)*
Hillman Group Inc ....G...... 440 248-7000
  Cleveland *(G-5409)*

KILNS & FURNACES: Ceramic

I Cerco Inc ....C...... 330 567-2145
  Shreve *(G-17003)*
Star Engineering Inc ....E...... 740 342-3514
  New Lexington *(G-14724)*

KITCHEN & COOKING ARTICLES: Pottery

Grandpas Pottery ....G...... 937 382-6442
  Wilmington *(G-20495)*

KITCHEN CABINET STORES, EXC CUSTOM

Brower Products Inc ....D...... 937 563-1111
  Cincinnati *(G-3426)*
Carl C Andre Inc ....G...... 614 864-0123
  Brice *(G-2071)*
Creative Products Inc ....E...... 419 866-5501
  Holland *(G-10920)*
Custom Counter Tops & Spc Co ....G...... 330 637-4856
  Cortland *(G-7709)*
Don Walter Kitchen Distrs Inc ....G...... 330 793-9338
  Youngstown *(G-20893)*
Gillard Construction Inc ....F...... 740 376-9744
  Marietta *(G-12627)*
Kinsella Manufacturing Co Inc ....F...... 513 561-5285
  Cincinnati *(G-3911)*
Laminate Shop ....F...... 740 749-3536
  Waterford *(G-19486)*
Oakwood Furniture Inc ....G...... 740 896-3162
  Lowell *(G-12247)*
Thiels Replacement Systems Inc ....D...... 419 289-6139
  Ashland *(G-751)*

KITCHEN CABINETS WHOLESALERS

Brower Products Inc ....D...... 937 563-1111
  Cincinnati *(G-3426)*
Clark Wood Specialties Inc ....G...... 330 499-8711
  Clinton *(G-6384)*
Custom Design Cabinets & Tops ....G...... 440 639-9900
  Painesville *(G-15728)*
Greene Street Wholesale LLC ....G...... 740 374-5206
  Marietta *(G-12628)*
Kitchen Designs Plus Inc ....E...... 419 536-6605
  Toledo *(G-18368)*
Modern Builders Supply Inc ....F...... 419 526-0002
  Mansfield *(G-12485)*
Sims-Lohman Inc ....E...... 513 651-3510
  Cincinnati *(G-4340)*

KITCHEN TOOLS & UTENSILS WHOLESALERS

Creative Products Inc ....E...... 419 866-5501
  Holland *(G-10920)*

KITCHEN UTENSILS: Food Handling & Processing Prdts, Wood

AP Tech Group Inc ....F...... 513 761-8111
  West Chester *(G-19646)*
Mt Perry Foods Inc ....D...... 740 743-3890
  Mount Perry *(G-14456)*
Rightway Food Service ....G...... 419 223-4075
  Lima *(G-11932)*

KITCHEN UTENSILS: Wooden

Attractive Kitchens & Flrg LLC ....G...... 440 406-9299
  Elyria *(G-9220)*
Bushworks Incorporated ....G...... 937 767-1713
  Yellow Springs *(G-20805)*
Henly Corporation ....G...... 419 476-0851
  Toledo *(G-18331)*

KITCHENWARE STORES

Added Touch Decorating Gallery ....G...... 419 747-3146
  Ontario *(G-15537)*
Crystal Art Imports Inc ....F...... 614 430-8180
  Columbus *(G-6840)*
Kitchen Collection LLC ....D...... 740 773-9150
  Chillicothe *(G-3198)*
Nacco Industries Inc ....E...... 440 229-5151
  Cleveland *(G-5719)*
Wasserstrom Company ....B...... 614 228-6525
  Columbus *(G-7591)*

KITCHENWARE: Plastic

Brighteye Innovations LLC .... F 800 573-0052
  Akron *(G-96)*
HI Lite Plastic Products .... G 614 235-9050
  Columbus *(G-6996)*
Jr Larry Knight .... G 216 762-3141
  Maple Heights *(G-12574)*

KITS: Plastic

RPM Consumer Holding Company ..... G 330 273-5090
  Medina *(G-13330)*

KNIVES: Agricultural Or indl

Advetech Inc .... E 330 533-2227
  Canfield *(G-2518)*
Advetech Inc .... E 330 533-2227
  Canfield *(G-2517)*
C B Mfg & Sls Co Inc .... G 937 866-5986
  Miamisburg *(G-13647)*
Handy Twine Knife Co .... G 419 294-3424
  Upper Sandusky *(G-18955)*
Randolph Tool Company Inc .... F 330 877-4923
  Hartville *(G-10703)*
Superion Inc .... E 937 374-0033
  Xenia *(G-20793)*

LABELS: Cotton, Printed

Paxar Corporation .... E 845 398-3229
  Mentor *(G-13544)*

LABELS: Paper, Made From Purchased Materials

Adaptive Data Inc .... F 937 436-2343
  Dayton *(G-8007)*
CCL Label Inc .... C 216 676-2703
  Cleveland *(G-4894)*
CMC Daymark Corporation .... C 419 354-2591
  Bowling Green *(G-1963)*
GBS Corp .... E 330 929-8050
  Stow *(G-17591)*
General Data Company Inc .... C 513 752-7978
  Cincinnati *(G-3252)*
Inline Label Company .... F 513 217-5662
  Middletown *(G-13915)*
Joshua Enterprises Inc .... G 419 872-9699
  Perrysburg *(G-15970)*
Keithley Enterprises Inc .... G 937 890-1878
  Dayton *(G-8290)*
Label Aid Inc .... F 419 433-2888
  Huron *(G-11102)*
Label Technique Southeast LLC ...... E 440 951-7660
  Willoughby *(G-20356)*
Maderite LLC .... G 937 570-1042
  Tipp City *(G-18122)*
Model Graphics & Media Inc .... E 513 541-2355
  West Chester *(G-19746)*
Multi-Color Corporation .... G 513 459-3283
  Mason *(G-12913)*
Multi-Color Corporation .... F 513 381-1480
  Batavia *(G-1171)*
Scratch-Off Systems Inc .... E 216 649-7800
  Brecksville *(G-2056)*
Shore To Shore Inc .... D 937 866-1908
  Dayton *(G-8505)*
Tri State Media LLC .... E 513 933-0101
  Wilmington *(G-20509)*
Verstraete In Mold Lab .... F 513 943-0080
  Batavia *(G-1195)*
W/S Packaging Group Inc .... F 740 929-2210
  Heath *(G-10734)*
W/S Packaging Group Inc .... C 513 459-2400
  Mason *(G-12953)*

LABELS: Woven

Shore To Shore Inc .... D 937 866-1908
  Dayton *(G-8505)*

LABORATORIES, TESTING: Food

Agrana Fruit Us Inc .... C 937 693-3821
  Botkins *(G-1932)*

LABORATORIES, TESTING: Hazardous Waste

Emerald Transformer Ppm LLC .... F 800 908-8800
  Twinsburg *(G-18768)*

LABORATORIES, TESTING: Hydrostatic

US Tubular Products Inc .... D 330 832-1734
  North Lawrence *(G-15163)*

LABORATORIES, TESTING: Metallurgical

Metcut Research Associates Inc ..... D 513 271-5100
  Cincinnati *(G-4015)*
Phymet Inc .... F 937 743-8061
  Springboro *(G-17343)*

LABORATORIES, TESTING: Pollution

Data Analysis Technologies .... G 614 873-0710
  Plain City *(G-16186)*
Nucon International Inc .... F 614 846-5710
  Columbus *(G-7232)*

LABORATORIES, TESTING: Product Testing

Wallover Enterprises Inc .... E 440 238-9250
  Strongsville *(G-17804)*

LABORATORIES, TESTING: Product Testing, Safety/Performance

Amron LLC .... G 330 457-8570
  New Waterford *(G-14836)*
Chemsultants International Inc .... E 440 974-3080
  Mentor *(G-13412)*
Global Manufacturing Solutions ...... F 937 236-8315
  Dayton *(G-8225)*
Standards Testing Labs Inc .... D 330 833-8548
  Massillon *(G-13050)*

LABORATORIES, TESTING: Water

American Polymer Standards .... G 440 255-2211
  Mentor *(G-13386)*
R D Baker Enterprises Inc .... G 937 461-5225
  Dayton *(G-8458)*
Ream and Haager Laboratory .... F 330 343-3711
  Dover *(G-8849)*

LABORATORIES: Biological Research

Aeiou Scientific LLC .... G 614 325-2103
  Columbus *(G-6547)*
Mp Biomedicals LLC .... C 440 337-1200
  Solon *(G-17199)*

LABORATORIES: Biotechnology

Elastance Imaging LLC .... G 614 579-9520
  Columbus *(G-6887)*
EMD Millipore Corporation .... C 513 631-0445
  Norwood *(G-15426)*
Sensetronics LLC .... G 614 292-2833
  Dublin *(G-8983)*

LABORATORIES: Commercial Nonphysical Research

Intek Inc .... E 614 895-0301
  Westerville *(G-19999)*
Power Management Inc .... E 937 222-2909
  Dayton *(G-8430)*

LABORATORIES: Dental

Delmar E Hicks .... G 740 354-4333
  Portsmouth *(G-16281)*
Duncan Dental Lab LLC .... G 614 793-0330
  Dublin *(G-8909)*
Mark Dental Laboratory .... G 216 464-6424
  Cleveland *(G-5618)*

LABORATORIES: Dental, Crown & Bridge Production

Dental Ceramics Inc .... E 330 523-5240
  Richfield *(G-16467)*
Doling & Associates Dental Lab ..... E 937 254-0075
  Dayton *(G-8164)*
Dresch Tolson Dental Labs .... D 419 842-6730
  Sylvania *(G-17938)*

LABORATORIES: Dental, Denture Production

United Dental Laboratories .... E 330 253-1810
  Tallmadge *(G-18010)*

LABORATORIES: Electronic Research

Advanced Microbeam Inc .... G 330 394-1255
  Vienna *(G-19195)*
Electronic Concepts Engrg Inc .... F 419 861-9000
  Holland *(G-10930)*
Point Source Inc .... F 937 855-6020
  Germantown *(G-10245)*
Srico Inc .... G 614 799-0664
  Columbus *(G-7481)*
Steiner Eoptics Inc .... D 937 426-2341
  Miamisburg *(G-13721)*

LABORATORIES: Medical

Cellular Technology Limited .... E 216 791-5084
  Shaker Heights *(G-16929)*
Hanger Prsthetcs & Ortho Inc .... G 740 454-6215
  Zanesville *(G-21145)*
Hanger Prsthetcs & Ortho Inc .... G 740 354-4775
  Portsmouth *(G-16285)*
Hanger Prsthetcs & Ortho Inc .... G 419 522-0055
  Marion *(G-12708)*
Mp Biomedicals LLC .... C 440 337-1200
  Solon *(G-17199)*
Standards Testing Labs Inc .... D 330 833-8548
  Massillon *(G-13050)*

LABORATORIES: Noncommercial Research

Tangent Company LLC .... G 440 543-2775
  Chagrin Falls *(G-3079)*

LABORATORIES: Physical Research, Commercial

Albemarle Corporation .... G 330 425-2354
  Twinsburg *(G-18729)*
Arges .... G 440 574-1305
  Oberlin *(G-15490)*
BASF Catalysts LLC .... D 216 360-5005
  Cleveland *(G-4794)*
Borchers Americas Inc .... D 440 899-2950
  Westlake *(G-20103)*
Circle Prime Manufacturing .... E 330 923-0019
  Cuyahoga Falls *(G-7850)*
Copernicus Therapeutics Inc .... G 216 707-1776
  Cleveland *(G-5029)*
Curtiss-Wright Controls .... E 937 252-5601
  Fairborn *(G-9456)*
Farmed Materials Inc .... G 513 680-4046
  Cincinnati *(G-3673)*
Fertility Solutions Inc .... G 216 491-0030
  Cleveland *(G-5234)*
Flexsys America LP .... D 330 666-4111
  Akron *(G-173)*
Fram Group Operations LLC .... D 419 661-6700
  Perrysburg *(G-15953)*
Kf Technologies and Custom Mfg ... G 419 426-0172
  Attica *(G-857)*
Lyondell Chemical Company .... D 513 530-4000
  Cincinnati *(G-3960)*
Medpace Holdings Inc .... F 513 579-9911
  Cincinnati *(G-3998)*
Microweld Engineering Inc .... F 614 847-9410
  Worthington *(G-20697)*
Morris Technologies .... G 330 384-3084
  Akron *(G-288)*
Northcoast Environmental Labs ...... G 330 342-3377
  Streetsboro *(G-17685)*
Nsa Technologies LLC .... C 330 576-4600
  Akron *(G-304)*
Ohio Elastomers .... G 440 354-9750
  Perry *(G-15910)*
Owens Corning Sales LLC .... B 740 587-3562
  Granville *(G-10336)*
Owens Corning Sales LLC .... F 330 633-6735
  Tallmadge *(G-17999)*
Protein Express Inc .... G 513 769-9654
  Blue Ash *(G-1838)*
Schneller LLC .... D 330 673-1299
  Kent *(G-11381)*
Specialty Technology & Res .... G 614 870-0744
  Columbus *(G-7470)*
Sunpower Inc .... D 740 594-2221
  Athens *(G-851)*
Vehicle Systems Inc .... G 330 854-0535
  Massillon *(G-13056)*

PRODUCT SECTION

LABORATORIES: Testing

Personnel Selection Services..............F....... 440 835-3255
Cleveland *(G-5865)*

LABORATORIES: Testing

Akzo Nobel Coatings Inc......................C....... 614 294-3361
Columbus *(G-6559)*
Balancing Company Inc......................E....... 937 898-9111
Vandalia *(G-19117)*
Barr Engineering Incorporated..............F....... 614 892-0162
Columbus *(G-6649)*
Barr Engineering Incorporated..............E....... 614 714-0299
Columbus *(G-6650)*
Ceco Group Inc................................G....... 513 458-2600
Cincinnati *(G-3452)*
Cleveland Instrument Corp..................G....... 440 826-1800
Brookpark *(G-2138)*
Curtiss-Wright Flow Control................D....... 513 528-7900
Cincinnati *(G-3244)*
Curtiss-Wright Flow Ctrl Corp...............D....... 513 528-7900
Cincinnati *(G-3245)*
Fertility Solutions Inc........................G....... 216 491-0030
Cleveland *(G-5234)*
Fram Group Operations LLC................D....... 419 661-6700
Perrysburg *(G-15953)*
Godfrey & Wing Inc..........................E....... 330 562-1440
Aurora *(G-881)*
Hoya Optical Labs............................G....... 440 239-1924
Berea *(G-1610)*
JBI Corporation...............................F....... 419 855-3389
Genoa *(G-10233)*
Jci Jones Chemicals Inc....................G....... 330 825-2531
New Franklin *(G-14692)*
Micro Laboratories Inc......................G....... 440 918-0001
Mentor *(G-13518)*
Microbiological Labs Inc....................G....... 330 626-2264
Streetsboro *(G-17682)*
National Polymer Inc.........................F....... 440 708-1245
Chagrin Falls *(G-3062)*
Ohio Lumex Co Inc...........................G....... 440 264-2500
Solon *(G-17211)*
Reid Asset Management Company........E....... 216 642-3223
Cleveland *(G-5971)*
Sample Machining Inc.......................E....... 937 258-3338
Dayton *(G-8492)*
Tangent Company LLC......................G....... 440 543-2775
Chagrin Falls *(G-3079)*
Welding Consultants Inc....................G....... 614 258-7018
Columbus *(G-7598)*
Yoder Industries Inc..........................C....... 937 278-5769
Dayton *(G-8602)*

LABORATORIES: Ultrasound

John P Ellis Clinic Podiatry.................G....... 440 460-0444
Cleveland *(G-5503)*

LABORATORY APPARATUS & FURNITURE

Amteco Inc.....................................G....... 513 217-4430
Middletown *(G-13884)*
Asbeka Custom Products LLC...............F....... 440 352-0839
Painesville *(G-15711)*
Chemsultants International Inc.............G....... 513 860-1598
West Chester *(G-19670)*
Chemsultants International Inc.............E....... 440 974-3080
Mentor *(G-13412)*
Cortest Inc......................................F....... 440 942-1235
Willoughby *(G-20301)*
Dentronix Inc..................................E....... 330 916-7300
Cuyahoga Falls *(G-7860)*
Eanytime Corporation.......................G....... 714 969-7000
Columbus *(G-6882)*
Ies Systems Inc..............................G....... 330 533-6683
Canfield *(G-2530)*
Northfield......................................G....... 440 949-1815
Sheffield Village *(G-16972)*
Philips Medical Systems Clevel............B....... 440 247-2652
Cleveland *(G-5871)*
Poi Holdings Inc..............................F....... 937 253-7377
Dayton *(G-7988)*
So-Low Environmental Eqp Co............E....... 513 772-9410
Cincinnati *(G-4350)*
Tech Pro Inc....................................E....... 330 923-3546
Akron *(G-397)*
Teledyne Instruments Inc...................E....... 513 229-7000
Mason *(G-12946)*
Teledyne Tekmar Company.................E....... 513 229-7000
Mason *(G-12948)*

Waller Brothers Stone Company...........E....... 740 858-1948
Mc Dermott *(G-13195)*

LABORATORY APPARATUS, EXC HEATING & MEASURING

Accuscan Instruments Inc..................F....... 614 878-6644
Columbus *(G-6535)*
Caron Products and Svcs Inc...............E....... 740 373-6809
Marietta *(G-12612)*

LABORATORY APPARATUS: Calibration Tapes, Phy Testing Mach

Denton Atd Inc................................E....... 567 265-5200
Huron *(G-11093)*
Qualitech Associates Inc....................G....... 216 265-8702
Cleveland *(G-5939)*

LABORATORY APPARATUS: Crushing & Grinding

Powdermet Powder Production............F....... 216 404-0053
Euclid *(G-9435)*
Regal Industries Inc.........................G....... 440 352-9600
Painesville *(G-15780)*

LABORATORY APPARATUS: Freezers

Global Cooling Inc...........................E....... 740 274-7900
Athens *(G-833)*

LABORATORY APPARATUS: Furnaces

American Isostatic Presses Inc............F....... 614 497-3148
Columbus *(G-6583)*

LABORATORY APPARATUS: Particle Size Reduction

E R Advanced Ceramics Inc...............E....... 330 426-9433
East Palestine *(G-9077)*

LABORATORY APPARATUS: Pipettes, Hemocytometer

Mettler-Toledo Intl Fin Inc..................G....... 614 438-4511
Columbus *(G-6500)*

LABORATORY CHEMICALS: Organic

Chempak International LLC................G....... 440 543-8511
Chagrin Falls *(G-3039)*
Nationwide Chemical Products............G....... 419 714-7075
Perrysburg *(G-15979)*
Ohio Chemical Two..........................G....... 614 482-8073
Columbus *(G-7243)*
Ohio State University........................E....... 614 292-7656
Columbus *(G-7259)*
Rezkem Chemicals LLC....................F....... 330 653-9104
Hudson *(G-11070)*

LABORATORY EQPT, EXC MEDICAL: Wholesalers

Perkinelmer Hlth Sciences Inc..............E....... 330 825-4525
Akron *(G-318)*
Teledyne Instruments Inc...................E....... 513 229-7000
Mason *(G-12946)*
Teledyne Tekmar Company.................E....... 513 229-7000
Mason *(G-12948)*
Test Mark Industries Inc....................F....... 330 426-2200
East Palestine *(G-9086)*

LABORATORY EQPT: Chemical

Cheminstruments Inc.......................G....... 513 860-1598
West Chester *(G-19669)*
Continental Hydrodyne Systems..........F....... 330 494-2740
Canton *(G-2635)*
H & N Instruments Inc......................G....... 740 344-4351
Newark *(G-14882)*

LABORATORY EQPT: Clinical Instruments Exc Medical

Ashton Pumpmatic Inc......................G....... 937 424-1380
Dayton *(G-8039)*
Cellular Technology Limited...............E....... 216 791-5084
Shaker Heights *(G-16929)*
Center For Excptonal Practices............G....... 330 523-5240
Richfield *(G-16464)*

Strategic Technology Entp..................E....... 440 354-2600
Mentor *(G-13594)*

LABORATORY EQPT: Incubators

Malta Dynamics LLC.........................F....... 740 749-3512
Waterford *(G-19488)*

LABORATORY EQPT: Measuring

4r Enterprises Incorporated................G....... 330 923-9799
Cuyahoga Falls *(G-7829)*
Mettler-Toledo Intl Inc......................B....... 614 438-4511
Columbus *(G-6501)*

LABORATORY INSTRUMENT REPAIR SVCS

Tech Pro Inc....................................E....... 330 923-3546
Akron *(G-397)*

LADDERS: Metal

American Scaffolding Inc...................G....... 216 524-7733
Cleveland *(G-4697)*
Avenue Fabricating Inc......................E....... 513 752-1911
Batavia *(G-1124)*
B C Composites Corporation...............F....... 330 262-3070
Medina *(G-13228)*
Bauer Corporation............................E....... 800 321-4760
Wooster *(G-20569)*
Bc Investment Corporation.................G....... 330 262-3070
Wooster *(G-20570)*

LADLE BRICK: Clay

Resco Products Inc..........................E....... 740 682-7794
Oak Hill *(G-15459)*

LADLES: Metal Plate

Rimrock Holdings Corporation.............E....... 614 471-5926
Columbus *(G-7395)*
Rose Metal Industries LLC.................F....... 216 881-3355
Cleveland *(G-6002)*

LAMINATED PLASTICS: Plate, Sheet, Rod & Tubes

Advanced Drainage Systems Inc..........D....... 330 264-4949
Wooster *(G-20554)*
Advanced Drainage Systems Inc..........E....... 419 599-9565
Napoleon *(G-14530)*
Advanced Drainage Systems Inc..........E....... 419 424-8324
Findlay *(G-9648)*
Advanced Elastomer Systems LP.........D....... 330 336-7641
Wadsworth *(G-19221)*
Aetna Plastics Corp..........................G....... 330 274-2855
Mantua *(G-12541)*
Amtank Armor.................................G....... 440 268-7735
Strongsville *(G-17710)*
Applied Medical Technology Inc..........E....... 440 717-4000
Brecksville *(G-2020)*
Arthur Corporation...........................D....... 419 433-7202
Huron *(G-11089)*
Biothane Coated Webbing Corp...........E....... 440 327-0485
North Ridgeville *(G-15212)*
Cool Seal Usa LLC...........................F....... 419 666-1111
Perrysburg *(G-15935)*
Duracote Corporation.......................E....... 330 296-9600
Ravenna *(G-16376)*
Durivage Pattern & Mfg Co.................E....... 419 836-8655
Williston *(G-20262)*
Elster Perfection Corporation..............D....... 440 428-1171
Geneva *(G-10218)*
Fowler Products Inc..........................F....... 419 683-4057
Crestline *(G-7794)*
Hancor Inc.....................................B....... 614 658-0050
Hilliard *(G-10827)*
Hrh Door Corp.................................D....... 440 593-5226
Conneaut *(G-7649)*
Iko Production Inc............................E....... 937 746-4561
Franklin *(G-9891)*
Ilpea Industries Inc...........................C....... 330 562-2916
Aurora *(G-884)*
Interntnal Cnvrter Cldwell Inc..............C....... 740 732-5665
Caldwell *(G-2407)*
Laminate Shop................................F....... 740 749-3536
Waterford *(G-19486)*
Meridian Industries Inc......................D....... 330 673-1011
Kent *(G-11351)*
Meridienne International Inc................G....... 330 274-8317
Mantua *(G-12554)*

Employee Codes: A=Over 500 employees, B=251-500
C=101-250, D=51-100, E=20-50, F=10-19, G=3-9

LAMINATED PLASTICS: Plate, Sheet, Rod & Tubes

Monarch Engraving Inc .... E 440 638-1500
  Strongsville *(G-17766)*
Organized Living Inc .... E 513 489-9300
  Cincinnati *(G-4118)*
Plaskolite LLC .... B 614 294-3281
  Columbus *(G-7321)*
Raven Industries Inc 937 323-4625
  Springfield *(G-17480)*
Recto Molded Products Inc .... D 513 871-5544
  Cincinnati *(G-4256)*
Resinoid Engineering Corp .... D 740 928-6115
  Hebron *(G-10759)*
Rowmark LLC .... D 419 425-8974
  Findlay *(G-9748)*
Saint-Gobain Prfmce Plas Corp .... C 330 798-6981
  Akron *(G-372)*
Shurtape Technologies LLC .... B 440 937-7000
  Avon *(G-966)*
Snyder Manufacturing Inc .... D 330 343-4456
  Dover *(G-8855)*
Snyder Manufacturing Co Ltd 330 343-4456
  Dover *(G-8856)*
Somerset Galleries Inc .... G 614 443-0003
  Columbus *(G-7461)*
Spartech LLC .... C 419 399-4050
  Paulding *(G-15871)*
Specialty Adhesive Film Co 513 353-1885
  Cleves *(G-6375)*
Trim Systems Operating Corp .... C 614 289-5360
  New Albany *(G-14639)*
Wurms Woodworking Company .... E 419 492-2184
  New Washington *(G-14834)*

LAMINATING MATERIALS

Specialty Adhesive Film Co .... G 513 353-1885
  Cleves *(G-6375)*

LAMINATING SVCS

Conversion Tech Intl Inc .... E 419 924-5566
  West Unity *(G-19967)*
Kent Adhesive Products Co .... D 330 678-1626
  Kent *(G-11338)*
Ohio Laminating & Binding Inc .... E 614 771-4868
  Hilliard *(G-10846)*

LAMP & LIGHT BULBS & TUBES

Acuity Brands Lighting Inc .... C 740 349-4409
  Newark *(G-14849)*
Carlisle and Finch Company .... E 513 681-6080
  Cincinnati *(G-3445)*
Clare Sky Inc .... B 866 558-5706
  Cleveland *(G-4936)*
Emitted Energy Inc .... G 513 752-9999
  Cincinnati *(G-3249)*
General Electric Company .... C 440 593-1156
  Mc Donald *(G-13197)*
General Electric Company .... A 330 297-0861
  Mc Donald *(G-13198)*
Lumitex Inc .... G 949 250-8557
  Strongsville *(G-17764)*
Lumitex Inc .... D 440 243-8401
  Strongsville *(G-17763)*
Medallion Lighting Corporation 440 255-8383
  Mentor *(G-13514)*

LAMP BULBS & TUBES, ELECTRIC: Filaments

General Electric Company .... C 330 793-3911
  Youngstown *(G-20916)*

LAMP BULBS & TUBES, ELECTRIC: For Specialized Applications

Magenta Incorporated .... E 216 571-4094
  Cleveland *(G-5603)*
Resource Exchange Company Inc ... G 440 773-8915
  Akron *(G-347)*

LAMP BULBS & TUBES, ELECTRIC: Sealed Beam

General Electric Company .... A 330 373-1400
  Mc Donald *(G-13199)*

LAMP BULBS & TUBES/PARTS, ELECTRIC: Generalized Applications

Advanced Lighting Tech LLC .... E 888 440-2358
  Solon *(G-17099)*
Eye Lighting Intl N Amer Inc .... C 440 350-7000
  Mentor *(G-13442)*

LAMP FIXTURES: Ultraviolet

National Biological Corp .... E 216 831-0600
  Beachwood *(G-1252)*

LAMP REPAIR & MOUNTING SVCS

Johnsons Lamp Shop & Antq Co ..... G 937 568-4551
  South Vienna *(G-17297)*

LAMP SHADES: Plastic

Alpha Omega Import Export LLC ..... G 740 885-9155
  Marietta *(G-12602)*

LAMP STORES

Palette Studios Inc .... G 513 961-1316
  Cincinnati *(G-4131)*

LAMPS: Desk, Residential

Microsun Lamps LLC 888 328-8701
  Dayton *(G-8351)*

LAMPS: Fluorescent

Alert Stamping & Mfg Co Inc .... E 440 232-5020
  Bedford Heights *(G-1458)*
Energy Focus Inc .... C 440 715-1300
  Solon *(G-17137)*
General Electric Company .... B 419 563-1200
  Bucyrus *(G-2331)*
Johnsons Lamp Shop & Antq Co 937 568-4551
  South Vienna *(G-17297)*

LAMPS: Incandescent, Filament

General Electric Company .... B 216 391-8741
  Cleveland *(G-5309)*

LAMPS: Table, Residential

J Schrader Co .... F 216 961-2890
  Cleveland *(G-5488)*
Medallion Lighting Corporation .... E 440 255-8383
  Mentor *(G-13514)*

LAND SUBDIVISION & DEVELOPMENT

Phillips Companies .... E 937 426-5461
  Beavercreek Township *(G-1370)*
U S Fuel Development Co .... G 614 486-0614
  Columbus *(G-7553)*
V&P Group International LLC .... F 703 349-6432
  Cincinnati *(G-4461)*

LANTERNS

Lintern Corporation .... E 440 255-9333
  Mentor *(G-13501)*

LAPIDARY WORK: Contract Or Other

The-Fischer-Group .... E 513 285-1281
  Fairfield *(G-9569)*

LAPIDARY WORK: Jewel Cut, Drill, Polish, Recut/Setting

Koop Diamond Cutters Inc .... F 513 621-2838
  Cincinnati *(G-3923)*

LASER SYSTEMS & EQPT

Automation Metrology Intl LLC .... G 440 354-6436
  Mentor *(G-13395)*
Daskal Enterprise LLC .... G 614 848-5700
  Columbus *(G-6850)*
Eagle Wldg & Fabrication Inc .... E 440 946-0692
  Willoughby *(G-20313)*
FM Manufacturing Inc .... G 419 445-0700
  Archbold *(G-646)*
Fortec Medical Lithotripsy LLC .... E 330 656-4301
  Streetsboro *(G-17674)*
Global Laser Tek .... E 513 701-0452
  Mason *(G-12880)*

PRODUCT SECTION

H W Fairway International Inc .... E 330 678-2540
  Kent *(G-11330)*
Northeast Laser Inc .... G 330 633-2897
  Tallmadge *(G-17997)*
Resonetics LLC .... D 937 865-4070
  Kettering *(G-11440)*
Revolaze LLC .... G 440 617-0502
  Westlake *(G-20150)*
Transdermal Inc .... F 440 241-1846
  Gates Mills *(G-10209)*

LASERS: Welding, Drilling & Cutting Eqpt

C L S Inc .... G 216 251-5011
  Cleveland *(G-4857)*
Great Lakes Power Service Co .... G 440 259-0025
  Perry *(G-15905)*
Innovar Systems Limited .... F 330 538-3942
  North Jackson *(G-15147)*
Laser Automation Inc .... F 440 543-9291
  Chagrin Falls *(G-3055)*
Lucky Thirteen Inc .... G 216 631-0013
  Cleveland *(G-5587)*
Peerless Laser Processors Inc .... E 614 836-5790
  Groveport *(G-10508)*

LATEX: Foamed

Firestone Polymers LLC .... D 330 379-7000
  Akron *(G-171)*
Trexler Rubber Co Inc .... E 330 296-9677
  Ravenna *(G-16414)*

LATH: Expanded Metal

Metrodeck Inc .... F 513 541-4370
  Cincinnati *(G-4018)*

LATH: Snow Fence

D&M Fencing LLC .... G 419 604-0698
  Spencerville *(G-17308)*

LATHES

Blairs Cnc Turning Inc .... G 937 461-1100
  Dayton *(G-8057)*

LAUNDRY & GARMENT SVCS, NEC: Garment Alteration & Repair

Quality Sewing Inc .... G 216 475-0411
  Cleveland *(G-5944)*

LAUNDRY EQPT: Commercial

Ha-International LLC .... E 419 537-0096
  Toledo *(G-18317)*
Process Development Corp 937 890-3388
  Dayton *(G-8445)*
Swisher Hygiene Inc .... G 513 870-4830
  West Chester *(G-19905)*
Whirlpool Corporation .... B 419 547-7711
  Clyde *(G-6397)*

LAUNDRY EQPT: Household

CSC Serviceworks Holdings .... G 800 362-3182
  Macedonia *(G-12286)*
Staber Industries Inc .... E 614 836-5995
  Groveport *(G-10513)*

LAUNDRY SVCS: Indl

Linen Care Plus Inc .... F 614 224-1791
  Columbus *(G-7131)*

LAWN & GARDEN EQPT

Albright Saw Company Inc .... G 740 887-2107
  Londonderry *(G-12073)*
Cannon Salt and Supply Inc .... G 440 232-1700
  Bedford *(G-1392)*
Commercial Turf Products Ltd .... C 330 995-7000
  Streetsboro *(G-17667)*
Dinsmore Inc .... G 937 544-3332
  West Union *(G-19961)*
Elan Designs Inc .... G 614 985-5600
  Westerville *(G-20050)*
Extrudex Limited Partnership .... E 440 352-7101
  Painesville *(G-15737)*
Franklin Equipment LLC .... E 614 228-2014
  Groveport *(G-10492)*

PRODUCT SECTION

Jani Auto Parts Inc .... G 330 494-2975
  North Canton *(G-15095)*
Johnson Tool Distributors .... G 740 653-6959
  Lancaster *(G-11581)*
Klawhorn Industries Inc .... G 330 335-8191
  Wadsworth *(G-19249)*
Koenig Equipment Inc .... F 937 653-5281
  Urbana *(G-19002)*
Mm Service .... G 330 474-3098
  Streetsboro *(G-17683)*
Mtd Holdings Inc .... B 330 225-2600
  Valley City *(G-19052)*
Mtd Products Inc .... B 330 225-2600
  Valley City *(G-19053)*
Mtd Products Inc .... C 419 342-6455
  Shelby *(G-16984)*
Mtd Products Inc .... D 330 225-1940
  Valley City *(G-19055)*
Outback Tree Works .... G 937 332-7300
  Troy *(G-18690)*
Power Distributors LLC .... D 614 876-3533
  Columbus *(G-7334)*
Schomaker Natural Resource .... G 513 741-1370
  Cincinnati *(G-4307)*
Scotts Company LLC .... B 937 644-0011
  Marysville *(G-12809)*
Smg Growing Media Inc .... G 937 644-0011
  Marysville *(G-12813)*
Tierra-Derco International LLC .... G 419 929-2240
  New London *(G-14740)*
Village Outdoors .... G 440 256-1172
  Kirtland *(G-11472)*
WH Fetzer & Sons Mfg Inc .... E 419 687-8237
  Plymouth *(G-16235)*

LAWN & GARDEN EQPT STORES

Bortnick Tractor Sales Inc .... F 330 924-2555
  Cortland *(G-7704)*
Ohio Drill & Tool Co .... E 330 525-7717
  Homeworth *(G-10989)*

LAWN & GARDEN EQPT: Grass Catchers, Lawn Mower

Bortnick Tractor Sales Inc .... F 330 924-2555
  Cortland *(G-7704)*

LAWN & GARDEN EQPT: Lawnmowers, Residential, Hand Or Power

Mtd Products Inc .... B 330 225-9127
  Valley City *(G-19054)*

LAWN & GARDEN EQPT: Rototillers

Rotoline USA LLC .... G 330 677-3223
  Kent *(G-11378)*

LAWN & GARDEN EQPT: Tractors & Eqpt

Cub Cadet LLC .... G 330 273-8669
  Valley City *(G-19034)*
Mid-West Fabricating Co .... C 740 969-4411
  Amanda *(G-526)*
Mtd Consumer Group Inc .... F 330 225-2600
  Valley City *(G-19051)*
Park-Ohio Holdings Corp .... F 440 947-2000
  Cleveland *(G-5842)*
Park-Ohio Industries Inc .... C 440 947-2000
  Cleveland *(G-5843)*

LAWN & GARDEN EQPT: Trimmers

Speed North America Inc .... E 330 202-7775
  Wooster *(G-20657)*

LAWN MOWER REPAIR SHOP

Bens Welding Service Inc .... G 937 878-4052
  Fairborn *(G-9452)*
Wilguss Automotive Machine .... G 937 465-0043
  West Liberty *(G-19939)*

LEAD & ZINC

Victory White Metal Company .... F 216 641-2575
  Cleveland *(G-6259)*

LEAD PENCILS & ART GOODS

North Shore Strapping Inc .... D 216 661-5200
  Brooklyn Heights *(G-2128)*

Ramon Robinson .... G 330 883-3244
  Vienna *(G-19208)*

LEAD-IN WIRES: Electric Lamp

Oldaker Manufacturing Corp .... G 419 759-3551
  Dunkirk *(G-9036)*

LEASING & RENTAL SVCS: Cranes & Aerial Lift Eqpt

Rnm Holdings Inc .... F 614 444-5556
  Columbus *(G-7397)*

LEASING & RENTAL SVCS: Oil Field Eqpt

Eleet Cryogenics Inc .... E 330 874-4009
  Bolivar *(G-1913)*
Terra Sonic International LLC .... E 740 374-6608
  Marietta *(G-12679)*

LEASING & RENTAL SVCS: Oil Well Drilling

Dover Fabrication and Burn Inc .... G 330 339-1057
  Dover *(G-8820)*

LEASING & RENTAL: Construction & Mining Eqpt

Bluefoot Industrial LLC .... E 740 314-5299
  Steubenville *(G-17528)*
Brewpro Inc .... G 513 577-7200
  Cincinnati *(G-3415)*
Dolin Supply Co .... E 304 529-4171
  South Point *(G-17282)*
Efco Corp .... E 614 876-1226
  Columbus *(G-6886)*
Ioppolo Concrete Corporation .... E 440 439-6606
  Bedford *(G-1418)*
Lefeld Welding & Stl Sups Inc .... E 419 678-2397
  Coldwater *(G-6416)*
Mel Stevens U-Cart Concrete .... E 419 478-2600
  Toledo *(G-18406)*
Phillips Ready Mix Co .... D 937 426-5151
  Beavercreek Township *(G-1372)*
Pollock Research & Design Inc .... E 330 332-3300
  Salem *(G-16767)*
Stillwell Equipment Co Inc .... G 330 650-1029
  Peninsula *(G-15898)*

LEASING & RENTAL: Medical Machinery & Eqpt

Columbus Prescr Rehabilitation .... G 614 294-1600
  Westerville *(G-20040)*
Kempf Surgical Appliances Inc .... E 513 984-5758
  Montgomery *(G-14295)*

LEASING & RENTAL: Mobile Home Sites

Kedar D Army .... G 419 238-6929
  Van Wert *(G-19097)*
L C Liming & Sons Inc .... G 513 876-2555
  Felicity *(G-9644)*

LEASING & RENTAL: Office Machines & Eqpt

Copier Resources Inc .... G 614 268-1100
  Columbus *(G-6818)*

LEASING & RENTAL: Other Real Estate Property

Lloyd F Helber .... E 740 756-9607
  Carroll *(G-2906)*

LEASING & RENTAL: Trucks, Indl

Bluefoot Industrial LLC .... E 740 314-5299
  Steubenville *(G-17528)*
Hull Ready Mix Concrete Inc .... F 419 625-8070
  Sandusky *(G-16815)*

LEASING & RENTAL: Trucks, Without Drivers

Knippen Chrysler Dodge Jeep .... E 419 695-4976
  Delphos *(G-8746)*
Marlow-2000 Inc .... F 216 362-8500
  Cleveland *(G-5625)*

LEATHER GOODS: Safety Belts

LEATHER & CANVAS GOODS: Leggings Or Chaps, NEC

Trd Leathers .... G 216 631-6233
  Cleveland *(G-6200)*

LEATHER GOODS, EXC FOOTWEAR, GLOVES, LUGGAGE/BELTING, WHOL

B D G Wrap-Tite Inc .... D 440 349-5400
  Solon *(G-17110)*

LEATHER GOODS: Coin Purses

Hamilton Manufacturing Corp .... E 419 867-4858
  Holland *(G-10933)*

LEATHER GOODS: Corners, Luggage

Brighton Collectibles LLC .... E 614 418-7561
  Columbus *(G-6699)*

LEATHER GOODS: Feed Bags, Horse

Lockbourne AG Center Inc .... G 614 491-0635
  Lockbourne *(G-11996)*

LEATHER GOODS: Garments

AM Retail Group Inc .... G 513 539-7837
  Monroe *(G-14254)*

LEATHER GOODS: Harnesses Or Harness Parts

Charm Harness and Boot Ltd .... F 330 893-0402
  Charm *(G-3141)*
Ervin Yoder .... G 330 359-5862
  Mount Hope *(G-14436)*
Hamilton Animal Products LLC .... E 937 293-9994
  Moraine *(G-14357)*
Maysville Harness Shop Ltd .... G 330 695-9977
  Apple Creek *(G-612)*
Rantek Products LLC .... G 419 485-2421
  Montpelier *(G-14315)*
Yoders Harness Shop .... G 440 632-1505
  Middlefield *(G-13871)*

LEATHER GOODS: Holsters

Diy Holster LLC .... G 419 921-2168
  Elyria *(G-9244)*

LEATHER GOODS: NEC

Berlin Custom Leather Ltd .... G 330 674-3768
  Millersburg *(G-14066)*
LLC Bowman Leather .... G 330 893-1954
  Millersburg *(G-14107)*
Wright Leather Works .... G 567 314-0019
  Fremont *(G-10065)*

LEATHER GOODS: Personal

Bison Leather Co .... G 419 517-1737
  Toledo *(G-18203)*
Down Home .... G 740 393-1186
  Mount Vernon *(G-14479)*
Fount .... G 540 810-0594
  Cleveland *(G-5269)*
Nelson Constantinelli Ltd .... G 800 680-1029
  Dublin *(G-8954)*
Ravenworks Deer Skin .... G 937 354-5151
  Mount Victory *(G-14521)*
Williams Leather Products Inc .... G 740 223-1604
  Marion *(G-12749)*

LEATHER GOODS: Razor Strops

Straight Razor Designes .... G 330 598-1414
  Medina *(G-13348)*

LEATHER GOODS: Saddles Or Parts

Dwayne Hall .... G 740 685-5270
  Senecaville *(G-16899)*
Whitman Corporation .... G 513 541-3223
  Okeana *(G-15521)*

LEATHER GOODS: Safety Belts

Dnd Products Inc .... G 440 286-7275
  Chardon *(G-3109)*

LEATHER GOODS: Stirrups, Wood Or Metal

Holmes Wheel Shop Inc .... E 330 279-2891
  Holmesville *(G-10981)*

LEATHER GOODS: Wallets

Hugo Bosca Company Inc .... E 937 323-5523
  Springfield *(G-17423)*

LEATHER TANNING & FINISHING

Old West Industries Inc .... G 513 889-0500
  Hamilton *(G-10592)*
Premier Tanning & Nutrition .... G 419 342-6259
  Shelby *(G-16986)*

LEATHER, CHAMOIS, WHOLESALE

Canton Sterilized Wiping Cloth .... G 330 455-5179
  Canton *(G-2618)*

LEGAL OFFICES & SVCS

Akron Legal News Inc .... F 330 296-7578
  Akron *(G-42)*
Bigmar Inc .... E 740 966-5800
  Johnstown *(G-11259)*
General Bar Inc .... F 440 835-2000
  Westlake *(G-20117)*
Gongwer News Service Inc .... F 614 221-1992
  Columbus *(G-6960)*
Perfect Probate .... G 513 791-4100
  Cincinnati *(G-4146)*

LEGAL SVCS: General Practice Attorney or Lawyer

Petro Quest Inc .... G 740 593-3800
  Athens *(G-844)*

LENS COATING: Ophthalmic

Wilson Optical Laboratory Inc .... E 440 357-7000
  Mentor *(G-13626)*

LENSES: Plastic, Exc Optical

Greenlight Optics LLC .... E 513 247-9777
  Loveland *(G-12193)*

LESSORS: Farm Land

Prairie Lane Corporation .... G 330 262-3322
  Wooster *(G-20639)*

LICENSE TAGS: Automobile, Stamped Metal

Clemens License Agency .... G 614 288-8007
  Pickerington *(G-16043)*
D J Klingler Inc .... G 513 891-2284
  Cincinnati *(G-3570)*
Fairfield License Center Inc .... G 513 829-6224
  Hamilton *(G-10557)*
Heatherdowns License Bureau .... G 419 381-1109
  Toledo *(G-18326)*
Middletown License Agency Inc .... F 513 422-7225
  Middletown *(G-13928)*
Parma Heights License Bureau .... G 440 888-0388
  Cleveland *(G-5852)*
Public Safety Ohio Department .... G 440 943-5545
  Willowick *(G-20481)*
Transportation Ohio Department .... G 740 927-2285
  Pataskala *(G-15846)*

LIFE INSURANCE AGENTS

First Catholc Slovak Union U S .... F 216 642-9406
  Cleveland *(G-5242)*

LIFE INSURANCE CARRIERS

First Merit .... G 330 849-8750
  Akron *(G-172)*

LIGHTING EQPT: Flashlights

Fulton Industries Inc .... D 419 335-3015
  Wauseon *(G-19516)*
Powertech Inc .... F 901 850-9393
  Beachwood *(G-1266)*

LIGHTING EQPT: Floodlights

LSI Industries Inc .... B 513 793-3200
  Blue Ash *(G-1811)*
LSI Industries Inc .... E 513 793-3200
  Blue Ash *(G-1808)*

LIGHTING EQPT: Miners' Lamps

Shelly Company .... G 330 666-1125
  Copley *(G-7695)*

LIGHTING EQPT: Motor Vehicle

Atc Lighting & Plastics Inc .... C 440 466-7670
  Andover *(G-580)*
Federal-Mogul Powertrain LLC .... C 740 432-2393
  Cambridge *(G-2437)*
Lighting Products Inc .... D 440 293-4064
  Andover *(G-584)*

LIGHTING EQPT: Motor Vehicle, Headlights

K D Lamp Company .... E 440 293-4064
  Andover *(G-583)*

LIGHTING EQPT: Motor Vehicle, NEC

Intellitronix Corporation .... E 440 359-7200
  Eastlake *(G-9115)*
Stanley Electric US Co Inc .... B 740 852-5200
  London *(G-12069)*
Washington Products Inc .... F 330 837-5101
  Massillon *(G-13057)*

LIGHTING EQPT: Outdoor

ATI Irrigation LLC .... G 937 750-2976
  Troy *(G-18639)*
Holophane Corporation .... C 866 759-1577
  Granville *(G-10331)*
LSI Industries Inc .... G 513 372-3200
  Blue Ash *(G-1809)*
Moonlighting .... G 330 533-3324
  Canfield *(G-2538)*

LIGHTING EQPT: Searchlights

Carlisle and Finch Company .... E 513 681-6080
  Cincinnati *(G-3445)*

LIGHTING EQPT: Spotlights

Broadview Heights Spotlights .... G 440 526-4404
  Broadview Heights *(G-2089)*

LIGHTING FIXTURES WHOLESALERS

Contract Lighting Inc .... G 614 746-7022
  Columbus *(G-6813)*
Current Lighting Solutions LLC .... E 800 435-4448
  Cleveland *(G-5043)*
Gt Industrial Supply Inc .... F 513 771-7000
  Blue Ash *(G-1783)*
LSI Industries Inc .... C 913 281-1100
  Blue Ash *(G-1810)*
Rexel Inc .... G 330 468-1122
  Northfield *(G-15323)*
Technical Artistry Inc .... G 614 299-7777
  Columbus *(G-7520)*

LIGHTING FIXTURES, NEC

Acuity Brands Lighting Inc .... B 740 349-4343
  Newark *(G-14848)*
Advanced Lighting Tech LLC .... E 888 440-2358
  Solon *(G-17099)*
Akron Brass Company .... G 614 529-7230
  Columbus *(G-6557)*
Atc Lighting & Plastics Inc .... C 440 466-7670
  Andover *(G-580)*
Aviation Technologies Inc .... G 216 706-2960
  Cleveland *(G-4776)*
Brightguy Inc .... G 440 942-8318
  Willoughby *(G-20287)*
Chromacove LLC .... G 216 264-1104
  Cleveland *(G-4925)*
Clare Sky Inc .... B 866 558-5706
  Cleveland *(G-4936)*
Current Lighting Solutions LLC .... E 800 435-4448
  Cleveland *(G-5043)*
Energy Focus Inc .... C 440 715-1300
  Solon *(G-17137)*
Ericson Manufacturing Co .... D 440 951-8000
  Willoughby *(G-20315)*
Fidelux Lighting LLC .... G 614 839-0250
  Columbus *(G-6919)*
General Electric Company .... A 330 373-1400
  Mc Donald *(G-13199)*
Genesis Lamp Corp .... F 440 354-0095
  Painesville *(G-15741)*
Global E-Lumenation Tech .... E 513 821-8687
  Cincinnati *(G-3763)*
Global Lighting Tech Inc .... E 440 922-4584
  Brecksville *(G-2039)*
Hughey & Phillips LLC .... E 937 652-3500
  Urbana *(G-18996)*
Led Lighting Center LLC .... G 888 988-6533
  Toledo *(G-18378)*
Lighting Solutions Group LLC .... F 614 868-5337
  Columbus *(G-7127)*
Lumitex Inc .... D 440 243-8401
  Strongsville *(G-17763)*
Midmark Corporation .... A 937 526-3662
  Kettering *(G-11434)*
Midmark Corporation .... E 937 526-8387
  Versailles *(G-19187)*
Photon Labs LLC .... G 214 455-0727
  Westerville *(G-20017)*
Pro Lighting LLC .... G 614 561-0089
  Hilliard *(G-10855)*
Vanner Holdings Inc .... D 614 771-2718
  Hilliard *(G-10873)*
Will-Burt Company .... B 330 682-7015
  Orrville *(G-15626)*

LIGHTING FIXTURES: Airport

ADB Safegate Americas LLC .... B 614 861-1304
  Columbus *(G-6542)*
Manairco Inc .... G 419 524-2121
  Mansfield *(G-12474)*

LIGHTING FIXTURES: Fluorescent, Commercial

Magnum Asset Acquisition LLC .... E 330 915-2382
  Hudson *(G-11062)*
Techbrite LLC .... E 800 246-9977
  Cincinnati *(G-4410)*
Teron Lighting Inc .... E 513 858-6004
  Fairfield *(G-9568)*

LIGHTING FIXTURES: Indl & Commercial

Acuity Brands Lighting Inc .... B 740 349-4343
  Newark *(G-14848)*
Acuity Brands Lighting Inc .... C 740 349-4409
  Newark *(G-14849)*
Advanced Lighting Tech LLC .... E 888 440-2358
  Solon *(G-17099)*
Besa Lighting Co Inc .... E 614 475-7046
  Blacklick *(G-1679)*
Best Lighting Products Inc .... D 740 964-0063
  Etna *(G-9392)*
Bock Company LLC .... E 216 912-7050
  Twinsburg *(G-18742)*
Etherium Lighting LLC .... G 310 800-8837
  Columbus *(G-6907)*
Evp International LLC .... E 513 761-7614
  Cincinnati *(G-3662)*
General Electric Company .... A 216 266-2121
  Cleveland *(G-5307)*
General Electric Company .... E 330 458-3200
  Canton *(G-2681)*
Genesis Lamp Corp .... F 440 354-0095
  Painesville *(G-15741)*
Holophane Corporation .... F 740 349-4194
  Newark *(G-14883)*
Holophane Corporation .... C 866 759-1577
  Granville *(G-10331)*
Holophane Lighting .... G 330 823-5535
  Alliance *(G-475)*
Importers Direct LLC .... E 330 436-3260
  Akron *(G-214)*
J Schrader Co .... F 216 961-2890
  Cleveland *(G-5488)*
JB Machining Concepts LLC .... G 419 523-0096
  Ottawa *(G-15655)*
Led Lighting Center Inc .... F 714 271-2633
  Toledo *(G-18376)*
Led Lighting Center LLC .... F 888 988-6533
  Toledo *(G-18377)*
Less Cost Lighting Inc .... F 866 633-6883
  Etna *(G-9396)*

PRODUCT SECTION — LIMESTONE: Cut & Shaped

Light Craft Manufacturing Inc .... F 419 332-0536
Fremont *(G-10034)*
LSI Industries Inc .... C 913 281-1100
Blue Ash *(G-1810)*
LSI Industries Inc .... E 513 793-3200
Blue Ash *(G-1808)*
Lumitex Inc .... D 440 243-8401
Strongsville *(G-17763)*
Mega Bright LLC .... G 216 712-4689
Cleveland *(G-5653)*
Mega Bright LLC .... F 330 577-8859
Cuyahoga Falls *(G-7898)*
Mills Led LLC .... G 800 690-6403
Columbus *(G-7183)*
Mills Led LLC .... G 800 690-6403
Springfield *(G-17448)*
Patriot Consulting LLC .... G 614 554-6455
Columbus *(G-7297)*
Pearlwind LLC .... G 216 591-9463
Beachwood *(G-1264)*
Power Source Service LLC .... G 513 607-4555
Batavia *(G-1177)*
Premiere Building Mtls Inc .... G 574 293-5800
Plain City *(G-16207)*
SMS Technologies Inc .... F 419 465-4175
Monroeville *(G-14291)*
Stress-Crete Company .... F 440 576-9073
Jefferson *(G-11239)*
Treemen Industries Inc .... E 330 965-3777
Boardman *(G-1904)*

LIGHTING FIXTURES: Motor Vehicle

Advanced Technology Corp .... C 440 293-4064
Andover *(G-577)*
Akron Brass Company .... E 614 529-7230
Columbus *(G-6557)*
Akron Brass Company .... B 330 264-5678
Wooster *(G-20557)*
Akron Brass Company .... B 330 264-5678
Wooster *(G-20558)*
Akron Brass Holding Corp .... G 330 264-5678
Wooster *(G-20559)*
Atc Group Inc .... D 440 293-4064
Andover *(G-579)*
Flasher Light Barricade .... G 513 554-1111
Fairfield *(G-9497)*
Grimes Aerospace Company .... B 937 484-2001
Urbana *(G-18990)*
Treemen Industries Inc .... E 330 965-3777
Boardman *(G-1904)*

LIGHTING FIXTURES: Ornamental, Commercial

King Luminaire Company Inc .... E 440 576-9073
Jefferson *(G-11233)*

LIGHTING FIXTURES: Residential

Acuity Brands Lighting Inc .... C 740 349-4409
Newark *(G-14849)*
Acuity Brands Lighting Inc .... B 740 349-4343
Newark *(G-14848)*
Advanced Lighting Tech LLC .... E 888 440-2358
Solon *(G-17099)*
Alert Stamping & Mfg Co Inc .... E 440 232-5020
Bedford Heights *(G-1458)*
American Superior Lighting .... G 740 266-2959
Steubenville *(G-17526)*
Besa Lighting Co Inc .... E 614 475-7046
Blacklick *(G-1679)*
Clare Sky Inc .... B 866 558-5706
Cleveland *(G-4936)*
Contract Lighting Inc .... G 614 746-7022
Columbus *(G-6813)*
E L Ostendorf Inc .... G 440 247-7631
Chagrin Falls *(G-3016)*
JB Machining Concepts LLC .... G 419 523-0096
Ottawa *(G-15655)*
Led Lighting Center Inc .... F 714 271-2633
Toledo *(G-18376)*
Led Lighting Center LLC .... F 888 988-6533
Toledo *(G-18377)*
Lighting Concepts & Control .... G 513 761-6360
West Chester *(G-19737)*
LSI Industries Inc .... E 513 793-3200
Blue Ash *(G-1808)*
Manairco Inc .... G 419 524-2121
Mansfield *(G-12474)*
Mega Bright LLC .... F 330 577-8859
Cuyahoga Falls *(G-7898)*

Palette Studios Inc .... G 513 961-1316
Cincinnati *(G-4131)*
Pike Machine Products Co .... E 216 731-1880
Euclid *(G-9433)*
Rexel Inc .... G 330 468-1122
Northfield *(G-15323)*
Shannon Ward .... G 330 592-8177
Stow *(G-17627)*
Tresco International Ltd Co .... G 330 757-8131
Youngstown *(G-21051)*

LIGHTING FIXTURES: Residential, Electric

Specialty Systems Electric LLC .... G 304 529-3861
Proctorville *(G-16345)*

LIGHTING FIXTURES: Street

Miami Valley Lighting LLC .... G 937 224-6000
Dayton *(G-7985)*

LIGHTING FIXTURES: Underwater

Jeff Katz .... G 614 834-0404
Pickerington *(G-16051)*

LIGHTS: Trouble lights

Alert Safety Lite Products Co .... F 440 232-5020
Cleveland *(G-4658)*

LIME

Ayers Limestone Quarry Inc .... F 740 633-2958
Martins Ferry *(G-12757)*
Bluffton Stone Co .... E 419 358-6941
Bluffton *(G-1886)*
Graymont Dolime (oh) Inc .... D 419 855-8682
Genoa *(G-10232)*
Hanson Aggregates East LLC .... E 937 587-2671
Peebles *(G-15878)*
Hanson Aggregates East LLC .... D 419 483-4390
Castalia *(G-2939)*
Mineral Processing Company .... G 419 396-3501
Carey *(G-2883)*
Naked Lime .... D 937 485-1932
Beavercreek *(G-1359)*
National Lime and Stone Co .... C 419 396-7671
Carey *(G-2884)*
Piqua Materials Inc .... G 937 773-4824
Piqua *(G-16154)*
Shelly Materials Inc .... E 740 666-5841
Ostrander *(G-15646)*
Sugarcreek Lime Service .... G 330 364-4460
Dover *(G-8858)*

LIME ROCK: Ground

National Lime and Stone Co .... C 419 396-7671
Carey *(G-2884)*

LIMESTONE & MARBLE: Dimension

Marble Cliff Limestone Inc .... G 614 488-3030
Hilliard *(G-10838)*
North Shore Stone Inc .... F 614 870-7531
Columbus *(G-7228)*

LIMESTONE: Crushed & Broken

Acme Company .... D 330 758-2313
Poland *(G-16236)*
Allgeier & Son Inc .... E 513 574-3735
Cincinnati *(G-3324)*
Bluffton Stone Co .... E 419 358-6941
Bluffton *(G-1886)*
Carmeuse Lime Inc .... E 419 638-2511
Millersville *(G-14163)*
Carmeuse Lime Inc .... E 419 986-5200
Bettsville *(G-1660)*
Chesterhill Stone Co .... E 740 849-2338
East Fultonham *(G-9045)*
Duff Quarry Inc .... E 937 686-2811
Huntsville *(G-11085)*
Duff Quarry Inc .... F 419 273-2518
Forest *(G-9787)*
Feikert Sand & Gravel Co Inc .... E 330 674-0038
Millersburg *(G-14082)*
Gerald Christman .... G 740 838-2475
Lewisville *(G-11803)*
Hanson Aggregates East LLC .... E 937 587-2671
Peebles *(G-15878)*
Hanson Aggregates East LLC .... E 937 442-6009
Winchester *(G-20521)*

Hanson Aggregates LLC .... E 419 841-3413
Sylvania *(G-17941)*
Hanson Aggregates Midwest LLC .... F 419 882-0123
Sylvania *(G-17942)*
King Limestone Inc .... F 740 638-3942
Cumberland *(G-7824)*
Lang Stone Company Inc .... D 614 235-4099
Columbus *(G-7114)*
Mac Ritchie Materials Inc .... F 419 288-2790
West Millgrove *(G-19946)*
Marietta Martin Materials Inc .... F 919 781-4550
Brookville *(G-2175)*
Marietta Martin Materials Inc .... E 937 766-2351
Cedarville *(G-2944)*
Martin Marietta Materials Inc .... G 513 200-2303
Harrison *(G-10657)*
Martin Marietta Materials Inc .... D 513 353-1400
North Bend *(G-15052)*
Martin Marietta Materials Inc .... E 513 871-7152
Cincinnati *(G-3983)*
Martin Marietta Materials Inc .... E 513 701-1140
West Chester *(G-19740)*
Maysville Materials LLC .... G 740 849-0474
Mount Perry *(G-14455)*
Melvin Stone Company LLC .... G 740 998-5016
Wshngtn CT Hs *(G-20732)*
National Lime and Stone Co .... G 419 657-6745
Wapakoneta *(G-19347)*
National Lime and Stone Co .... E 740 548-4206
Delaware *(G-8708)*
National Lime and Stone Co .... E 419 228-3434
Lima *(G-11910)*
National Lime and Stone Co .... G 419 642-6690
Columbus Grove *(G-7636)*
National Lime and Stone Co .... G 216 883-9840
Cleveland *(G-5726)*
National Lime and Stone Co .... E 419 423-3400
Findlay *(G-9729)*
National Lime and Stone Co .... D 419 562-0771
Bucyrus *(G-2339)*
Omya Industries Inc .... D 513 387-4600
Blue Ash *(G-1828)*
Oster Sand and Gravel Inc .... G 330 833-2649
Massillon *(G-13035)*
Quarries LLC .... G 513 306-2924
Cincinnati *(G-4231)*
Ridge Township Stone Quarry .... G 419 968-2222
Van Wert *(G-19104)*
Sergeant Stone Inc .... G 740 452-7434
Corning *(G-7702)*
Shelly Materials Inc .... G 419 229-2741
Lima *(G-11938)*
Shelly Materials Inc .... G 740 246-6315
Toledo *(G-18521)*
Shelly Materials Inc .... G 330 274-0802
Mantua *(G-12558)*
Shelly Materials Inc .... G 330 722-2190
Medina *(G-13341)*
Shelly Materials Inc .... G 330 364-4411
Dover *(G-8853)*
Shelly Materials Inc .... G 330 425-7861
Twinsburg *(G-18857)*
Shelly Materials Inc .... G 330 673-3646
Kent *(G-11385)*
Shelly Materials Inc .... E 740 666-5841
Ostrander *(G-15646)*
Shelly Materials Inc .... G 740 745-5965
Newark *(G-14918)*
Shelly Materials Inc .... D 740 246-6315
Thornville *(G-18035)*
Sidwell Materials Inc .... C 740 849-2394
Zanesville *(G-21180)*
Stoneco Inc .... E 419 393-2555
Oakwood *(G-15474)*
Stoneco Inc .... F 419 893-7645
Maumee *(G-13149)*
Suever Stone Company .... F 419 331-1945
Lima *(G-11945)*
The National Lime and Stone Co .... G 330 455-5722
North Canton *(G-15124)*
White Rock Quarry L P .... A 419 855-8388
Clay Center *(G-4570)*

LIMESTONE: Cut & Shaped

Maple Grove Materials Inc .... G 419 992-4235
Tiffin *(G-18068)*
National Lime and Stone Co .... G 419 657-6745
Wapakoneta *(G-19347)*

Employee Codes: A=Over 500 employees, B=251-500
C=101-250, D=51-100, E=20-50, F=10-19, G=3-9

2019 Harris Ohio Industrial Directory

LIMESTONE: Dimension

C F Poeppelman Inc .... E 937 448-2191
  Bradford (G-2010)
Gerald Christman .... G 740 838-2475
  Lewisville (G-11803)
Gregory Stone Co Inc .... G 937 275-7455
  Dayton (G-8239)
National Lime and Stone Co .... D 419 562-0771
  Bucyrus (G-2339)
S E Johnson Companies Inc .... F 419 893-8731
  Maumee (G-13142)
Stoneco Inc .... E 419 422-8854
  Findlay (G-9762)

LIMESTONE: Ground

Conag Inc .... E 419 394-8870
  Saint Marys (G-16683)
Hanson Aggregates East LLC .... D 419 483-4390
  Castalia (G-2939)
Hanson Aggregates Midwest LLC .... G 419 983-2211
  Bloomville (G-1715)
Latham Limestone LLC .... G 740 493-2677
  Latham (G-11622)
Marietta Martin Materials Inc .... F 937 884-5814
  Brookville (G-2176)
National Lime and Stone Co .... G 330 262-1317
  Wooster (G-20631)
National Lime and Stone Co .... E 740 387-3485
  Marion (G-12724)
Ohio Asphaltic Limestone Corp .... F 937 364-2191
  Hillsboro (G-10886)
Piqua Materials Inc .... E 937 773-4824
  Piqua (G-16154)
Piqua Materials Inc .... D 513 771-0820
  Cincinnati (G-4163)
Sharon Stone Inc .... G 740 732-7100
  Caldwell (G-2411)
Wagner Quarries Company .... E 419 625-8141
  Sandusky (G-16862)
Wysong Stone Co .... F 937 962-2559
  Lewisburg (G-11799)

LINEN SPLY SVC

Linen Care Plus Inc .... F 614 224-1791
  Columbus (G-7131)
Synergy Health North Amer Inc .... D 513 398-6406
  Mason (G-12945)

LINEN SPLY SVC: Apron

Geauga Group LLC .... G 440 543-8797
  Chagrin Falls (G-3047)

LINEN SPLY SVC: Table Cover

Joseph Knapp .... F 330 832-3515
  Massillon (G-13006)

LINERS & COVERS: Fabric

Berlin Boat Covers .... G 330 547-7600
  Berlin Center (G-1645)
Custom Canvas & Boat Repair .... F 419 732-3314
  Lakeside (G-11501)
Sailors Tailor Inc .... G 937 862-7781
  Spring Valley (G-17318)

LINERS & LINING

Ridge Corporation .... D 614 421-7434
  Etna (G-9398)

LINIMENTS

Cloud 9 Naturally Inc .... G 403 348-7704
  Bridgeport (G-2073)
Millers Liniments LLC .... G 440 548-5800
  Middlefield (G-13831)
Nanofiber Solutions Inc .... G 614 453-5877
  Hilliard (G-10843)
Z M O Company Inc .... G 614 875-0230
  Grove City (G-10480)

LININGS: Fabric, Apparel & Other, Exc Millinery

Indra Holdings Corp .... G 513 682-8200
  West Chester (G-19867)

LININGS: Vulcanizable Rubber

Blair Rubber Company .... D 330 769-5583
  Seville (G-16912)
Martin Rubber Company .... F 330 336-6604
  Seville (G-16920)

LINTELS: Steel, Light Gauge

J N Linrose Mfg LLC .... G 513 867-5500
  Hamilton (G-10574)

LIP BALMS

Amish Country Essentials LLC .... G 330 674-3088
  Millersburg (G-14059)

LIQUEFIED PETROLEUM GAS DEALERS

Airgas Usa LLC .... E 937 228-8594
  Dayton (G-8013)
Legacy Farmers Cooperative .... F 419 423-2611
  Findlay (G-9713)

LIQUEFIED PETROLEUM GAS WHOLESALERS

Centerra Co-Op .... E 800 362-9598
  Jefferson (G-11226)
Centerra Co-Op .... E 419 281-2153
  Ashland (G-690)

LIQUID CRYSTAL DISPLAYS

Aviation Technologies Inc .... G 216 706-2960
  Cleveland (G-4776)
Cks Solution Incorporated .... E 513 947-1277
  Fairfield (G-9491)
Cleanlife Energy LLC .... F 800 316-2532
  Cleveland (G-4941)
Ebulent Technologies Corp .... G 925 922-1448
  Cuyahoga Falls (G-7861)
Kent Displays Inc .... C 330 673-8784
  Kent (G-11340)
S-Tek Inc .... G 440 439-8232
  Bedford (G-1443)

LITHOGRAPHIC PLATES

Great Lakes Integrated Inc .... D 216 651-1500
  Cleveland (G-5347)
Kehl-Kolor Inc .... E 419 281-3107
  Ashland (G-717)
Litho-Craft Lithography Inc .... G 513 542-6404
  Cincinnati (G-3947)
R E May Inc .... F 216 771-6332
  Cleveland (G-5950)
South End Printing Co .... G 216 341-0669
  Cleveland (G-6081)

LIVESTOCK WHOLESALERS, NEC

Werling and Sons Inc .... F 937 338-3281
  Burkettsville (G-2356)

LOADS: Electronic

Electronic Solutions Inc .... F 419 666-4700
  Perrysburg (G-15944)
Omega Engineering Inc .... E 740 965-9340
  Sunbury (G-17896)
TL Industries Inc .... C 419 666-8144
  Northwood (G-15346)

LOCKERS

Industrial Mfg Co LLC .... F 440 838-4700
  Brecksville (G-2041)
Summa Holdings Inc .... G 440 838-4700
  Cleveland (G-6116)
Tiffin Metal Products Co .... C 419 447-8414
  Tiffin (G-18088)

LOCKS

Greyfield Industries Inc .... F 513 860-1785
  Trenton (G-18620)

LOCKS & LOCK SETS, WHOLESALE

Roper Lockbox LLC .... G 330 656-5148
  Hudson (G-11071)

LOCKS: Safe & Vault, Metal

National Security Products .... G 216 566-9962
  Cleveland (G-5729)

LOCKSMITHS

AB Bonded Locksmiths Inc .... G 513 531-7334
  Cincinnati (G-3286)
Ames Lock Specialties Inc .... G 419 474-2995
  Toledo (G-18183)

LOCOMOTIVES & PARTS

B&C Machine Co LLC .... B 330 745-4013
  Barberton (G-1058)
Plymouth Locomotive Svc LLC .... G 419 896-2854
  Shiloh (G-16998)

LOGGING

A & M Logging .... G 740 543-3171
  Salineville (G-16785)
Appalachia Wood Inc .... G 740 596-2551
  Mc Arthur (G-13178)
Brett Purdum .... G 740 626-2890
  South Salem (G-17296)
Broty Enterprises Inc .... G 330 674-6900
  Millersburg (G-14069)
Busy Bee Lumber .... G 330 674-1305
  Millersburg (G-14075)
C & L Erectors & Riggers Inc .... E 740 332-7185
  Laurelville (G-11626)
Chili Logging Ltd .... G 740 545-9502
  Fresno (G-10067)
Chipmunk Logging & Lumber LLC .... G 440 537-5124
  Middlefield (G-13785)
Coldwell Family Tree Farm .... G 330 506-9012
  Salineville (G-16786)
Craig Saylor .... G 740 352-8363
  Portland (G-16275)
Crisenbery Logging LLC .... G 740 256-1439
  Patriot (G-15850)
For Every Home .... G 740 710-1253
  Jackson (G-11185)
Gerald D Damron .... G 740 894-3680
  Chesapeake (G-3146)
Giles Logging LLC .... G 406 855-5284
  Spencer (G-17304)
GM Logging .... G 740 501-0819
  Johnstown (G-11267)
Haessly Lumber Sales Co .... D 740 373-6681
  Marietta (G-12630)
HK Logging & Lumber Ltd .... G 440 632-1997
  Middlefield (G-13806)
Huntington Hardwood Lbr Co Inc .... G 440 647-2283
  Wellington (G-19583)
Ingles Logging .... G 740 379-2909
  Patriot (G-15851)
J D Knisley Logging .... G 740 634-3207
  Bainbridge (G-1016)
Jacobs & Sons Logging LLC .... G 419 678-3802
  Saint Henry (G-16665)
Jason C Gibson .... F 740 663-4520
  Chillicothe (G-3196)
Jeffrey Adams Logging Inc .... G 740 634-2286
  Bainbridge (G-1017)
Jlm Logging LLC .... G 330 340-4863
  Millersburg (G-14102)
JM Logging Inc .... G 740 441-0941
  Gallipolis (G-10168)
John Byler .... G 330 627-7635
  Carrollton (G-2921)
John J Yoder Logging .... G 330 749-6324
  Apple Creek (G-609)
L&L Excavating & Land Clearing .... G 740 682-7823
  Oak Hill (G-15454)
Litzinger Logging .... G 740 743-2245
  Somerset (G-17264)
M H Logging & Lumber .... G 740 694-1988
  Fredericktown (G-9973)
McFadden Logging .... G 740 599-6902
  Danville (G-7964)
Michael D Strickland .... G 740 682-6902
  Oak Hill (G-15456)
Miller Logging Inc .... E 330 279-4721
  Holmesville (G-10983)
NY Logging & Lumber .... G 740 679-2085
  Quaker City (G-16353)
Omega Logging Inc .... F 330 534-0378
  Hubbard (G-11008)

PRODUCT SECTION

LUMBER & BLDG MATRLS DEALERS, RET: Bath Fixtures, Eqpt/Sply

Perkins Wood Products .... G 740 884-4046
  Chillicothe *(G-3210)*
Powell Logging .... G 740 372-6131
  Otway *(G-15689)*
Ray L Lute LL .... G 740 372-7703
  Lucasville *(G-12267)*
Robert Ashcraft .... G 740 667-3690
  Guysville *(G-10520)*
Roger L Best .... G 740 590-9133
  Stockport *(G-17560)*
Ross Tmber Harvstg For MGT Inc ... G 513 383-6933
  Batavia *(G-1181)*
Select Logging .... G 419 564-0361
  Marengo *(G-12594)*
Sissel Logging LLC .... G 740 858-4613
  Portsmouth *(G-16300)*
Stark Truss Company Inc .... D 419 298-3777
  Edgerton *(G-9181)*
Steve Henderson .... G 419 738-6999
  Wapakoneta *(G-19355)*
T J Ellis Enterprises Inc .... G 419 224-1969
  Lima *(G-11948)*
Terry G Sickles .... G 740 286-8880
  Ray *(G-16422)*
Top Notch Logging .... G 330 466-1780
  Apple Creek *(G-621)*
Warner Hildebrant .... G 740 286-1903
  South Webster *(G-17300)*
Y&B Logging .... G 440 437-1053
  Orwell *(G-15641)*

LOGGING CAMPS & CONTRACTORS

A & P Wood Products Inc .... G 419 673-1196
  Kenton *(G-11400)*
Alfman Logging LLC .... G 740 982-6227
  Crooksville *(G-7814)*
Art Saylor Logging .... F 740 682-6188
  Oak Hill *(G-15449)*
Baker Logging .... G 740 686-2817
  Belmont *(G-1565)*
Beachs Trees Selective Harvest .... F 513 289-5976
  Cincinnati *(G-3241)*
Beekman Logging .... G 740 493-2763
  Piketon *(G-16067)*
Biedenbach Logging .... G 740 732-6477
  Sarahsville *(G-16865)*
Blair Logging .... G 740 934-2730
  Lower Salem *(G-12258)*
Blankenship Logging LLC .... G 740 372-3833
  Otway *(G-15684)*
Bolon Timber LLC .... G 740 567-4102
  Lewisville *(G-11802)*
C & B Logging Inc .... G 740 347-4844
  Glouster *(G-10275)*
Chester F Hale .... G 740 379-2437
  Patriot *(G-15849)*
Chub Gibsons Logging .... G 740 884-4079
  Chillicothe *(G-3181)*
Custom Material Hdlg Eqp LLC ..... G 513 235-5336
  Cincinnati *(G-3565)*
D&D Logging .... G 740 679-2573
  Woodsfield *(G-20544)*
David Adkins Logging .... G 740 533-0297
  Kitts Hill *(G-11474)*
Denver Adkins .... F 740 682-3123
  Oak Hill *(G-15450)*
Dunagan Logging .... G 740 599-9368
  Danville *(G-7962)*
Ervin Lee Logging .... G 330 771-0039
  Minerva *(G-14179)*
Gadd Logging .... G 513 312-3941
  Trenton *(G-18619)*
Ingles Logging .... G 740 379-2760
  Patriot *(G-15852)*
J & J Logging .... G 740 896-2827
  Lowell *(G-12246)*
Knauff Bros Logging & Lumber ..... F 740 634-2432
  Bainbridge *(G-1018)*
Miller & Son Logging .... G 330 738-2031
  Mechanicstown *(G-13213)*
Miller Logging .... G 440 693-4001
  Middlefield *(G-13829)*
Ned A Shreve .... G 740 732-6465
  Sarahsville *(G-16866)*
Perkins Logging LLC .... G 740 288-7311
  Chillicothe *(G-3209)*
Randy Carter Logging Inc .... G 740 634-2604
  Bainbridge *(G-1020)*
Shellenbarger Excavating & Log ... G 740 397-9949
  Mount Vernon *(G-14509)*

T&R Logging LLC .... G 740 288-1825
  Wellston *(G-19609)*
Vorhees Logging LLC .... G 740 385-0216
  Rockbridge *(G-16538)*
Yoder Logging .... G 740 679-2635
  Quaker City *(G-16354)*

LOGGING: Saw Logs

B Hogenkamp & R Harlamert .... G 419 925-0526
  Celina *(G-2950)*

LOGGING: Stump Harvesting

Affordable Stump Removal LLC .... G 419 841-8331
  Toledo *(G-18159)*

LOGGING: Timber, Cut At Logging Camp

H & H Tree Service LLC .... G 440 632-0551
  Middlefield *(G-13801)*
Oakbridge Timber Framing .... G 419 994-1052
  Loudonville *(G-12145)*
Superior Hardwoods of Ohio .... D 740 384-6862
  Jackson *(G-11196)*

LOGGING: Veneer Logs

Facemyer Lumber Co Inc .... D 740 992-5965
  Pomeroy *(G-16240)*
Milestone Ventures LLC .... G 317 908-2093
  Granville *(G-10334)*

LOGGING: Wood Chips, Produced In The Field

Erichar Inc .... G 216 402-2628
  Cleveland *(G-5188)*
Seymours Logging .... F 740 288-1825
  Wellston *(G-19606)*

LOGGING: Wooden Logs

Lee Saylor Logging LLC .... G 740 682-0479
  Oak Hill *(G-15455)*

LOGS: Gas, Fireplace

Specialty Ceramics Inc .... D 330 482-0800
  Columbiana *(G-6481)*

LOOSELEAF BINDERS

A H Pelz Co .... G 216 861-1882
  Cleveland *(G-4589)*
Art Guild Binders Inc .... E 513 242-3000
  Cincinnati *(G-3358)*
Bell Binders LLC .... F 419 242-3201
  Toledo *(G-18200)*
Mueller Art Cover & Binding Co .... F 440 238-3303
  Strongsville *(G-17768)*
Tenacity Manufacturing Company . E 513 821-0201
  West Chester *(G-19807)*

LOTIONS OR CREAMS: Face

Amish Country Essentials LLC ..... G 330 674-3088
  Millersburg *(G-14059)*
Beiersdorf Inc .... C 513 682-7300
  West Chester *(G-19835)*
Cellera LLC .... G 513 539-1500
  Monroe *(G-14256)*
Kahuna Bay Spray Tan LLC .... G 419 386-2387
  Toledo *(G-18360)*
Redex Industries Inc .... F 330 332-9800
  Salem *(G-16770)*
Skin 937 222-0222
  Dayton *(G-8510)*

LUBRICANTS: Corrosion Preventive

Apex Advanced Technologies LLC ... G 216 898-1595
  Cleveland *(G-4720)*
Dinol US Inc .... G 740 548-1656
  Lewis Center *(G-11756)*

LUBRICATING EQPT: Indl

Koehler Rubber & Supply Co .... F 216 749-5100
  Cleveland *(G-5541)*
Motionsource International LLC ... F 440 287-7037
  Solon *(G-17198)*
Renite Company .... F 800 883-7876
  Columbus *(G-7385)*

LUBRICATING OIL & GREASE WHOLESALERS

American Ultra Specialties Inc ..... F 330 656-5000
  Hudson *(G-11030)*
Commercial Lubricants Inc .... G 614 475-5952
  Columbus *(G-6806)*
Digilube Systems Inc .... F 937 748-2209
  Springboro *(G-17325)*

LUBRICATING SYSTEMS: Centralized

Parker-Hannifin Corporation .... F 330 335-6740
  Wadsworth *(G-19261)*
Summa Holdings Inc .... G 440 838-4700
  Cleveland *(G-6116)*

LUBRICATION SYSTEMS & EQPT

A S Manufacturing Inc .... G 216 476-0656
  Cleveland *(G-4592)*
Cleveland Gear Company Inc .... C 216 641-9000
  Cleveland *(G-4960)*
Digilube Systems Inc .... F 937 748-2209
  Springboro *(G-17325)*
Groeneveld Atlantic South .... F 330 225-4949
  Brunswick *(G-2212)*
Koester Corporation .... D 419 599-0291
  Napoleon *(G-14548)*
Pax Products Inc .... F 419 586-2337
  Celina *(G-2979)*

LUGGAGE & BRIEFCASES

Buckeye Stamping Company .... D 614 445-0059
  Columbus *(G-6712)*
Cleveland Canvas Goods Mfg Co . D 216 361-4567
  Cleveland *(G-4948)*
Kam Manufacturing Inc .... C 419 238-6037
  Van Wert *(G-19096)*
Plastic Forming Company Inc ...... E 330 830-5167
  Massillon *(G-13039)*
Tia Marie & Company .... G 513 521-8694
  Cincinnati *(G-4421)*

LUGGAGE & LEATHER GOODS STORES

Baggallini Inc .... G 800 628-0321
  Pickerington *(G-16040)*
Tia Marie & Company .... G 513 521-8694
  Cincinnati *(G-4421)*
Whip Appeal Inc .... G 216 288-6201
  Cleveland *(G-6304)*

LUGGAGE & LEATHER GOODS STORES: Leather, Exc Luggage & Shoes

Yoders Harness Shop .... G 440 632-1505
  Middlefield *(G-13871)*

LUGGAGE: Traveling Bags

Eagle Creek Inc .... D 513 385-4442
  Cincinnati *(G-3620)*

LUMBER & BLDG MATLS DEALER, RET: Garage Doors, Sell/Install

A L Callahan Door Sales .... G 419 884-3667
  Mansfield *(G-12399)*
Amarr Company .... G 216 573-7100
  Independence *(G-11119)*
Bonham Enterprsises .... G 740 333-0501
  Wshngtn CT Hs *(G-20719)*
Jerry Harolds Doors Unlimited .... G 740 635-4949
  Bridgeport *(G-2076)*
Nofziger Door Sales Inc .... F 419 445-2961
  Archbold *(G-662)*
Overhead Door of Salem Inc .... G 330 332-9530
  Salem *(G-16765)*
Overhead Inc .... G 419 476-0300
  Toledo *(G-18443)*

LUMBER & BLDG MATRLS DEALERS, RET: Bath Fixtures, Eqpt/Sply

Agean Marble Manufacturing .... F 513 874-1475
  West Chester *(G-19829)*
Marble Arch Products Inc .... F 937 746-8388
  Franklin *(G-9897)*

Employee Codes: A=Over 500 employees, B=251-500
C=101-250, D=51-100, E=20-50, F=10-19, G=3-9

LUMBER & BLDG MATRLS DEALERS, RETAIL: Doors, Wood/Metal

LUMBER & BLDG MATRLS DEALERS, RETAIL: Doors, Wood/Metal

Nofziger Door Sales Inc..................C....... 419 337-9900
  Wauseon *(G-19530)*

LUMBER & BLDG MTRLS DEALERS, RET: Closets, Interiors/Access

Home Stor & Off Solutions Inc ....F....... 216 362-4660
  Cleveland *(G-5414)*

LUMBER & BLDG MTRLS DEALERS, RET: Doors, Storm, Wood/Metal

Champion Window Co of Toledo..........E....... 419 841-0154
  Perrysburg *(G-15933)*
Toledo Window & Awning Inc ....G....... 419 474-3396
  Toledo *(G-18575)*

LUMBER & BLDG MTRLS DEALERS, RET: Planing Mill Prdts/Lumber

Cox Wood Product Inc ....F....... 740 372-4735
  Otway *(G-15687)*
Fivecoat Lumber Inc ....F....... 740 254-4681
  Gnadenhutten *(G-10279)*
Marsh Industries Inc ....E....... 330 308-8667
  New Philadelphia *(G-14784)*
Yoder Lumber Co Inc ....D....... 330 893-3131
  Sugarcreek *(G-17878)*

LUMBER & BLDG MTRLS DEALERS, RET: Windows, Storm, Wood/Metal

Euclid Jalousies Inc.................................G....... 440 953-1112
  Cleveland *(G-5196)*
Pickens Window Service Inc...................F....... 513 931-4432
  Cincinnati *(G-4157)*

LUMBER & BUILDING MATERIAL DEALERS, RETAIL: Roofing Material

Stony Point Metals LLC ....G....... 330 852-7100
  Sugarcreek *(G-17866)*

LUMBER & BUILDING MATERIALS DEALER, RET: Door & Window Prdts

Associated Materials LLC ....G....... 937 236-5679
  Dayton *(G-8040)*
Bert Radebaugh ....G....... 740 382-8134
  Marion *(G-12695)*
Clear Fold Door Inc ....G....... 440 735-1351
  Cleveland *(G-4942)*
Dale Kestler ....G....... 513 871-9000
  Cincinnati *(G-3574)*
Dela-Glassware Ltd LLC ....G....... 740 369-6737
  Delaware *(G-8669)*
P & T Millwork Inc ....E....... 440 543-2151
  Chagrin Falls *(G-3064)*
Rockwood Products Ltd ....F....... 330 893-2392
  Millersburg *(G-14124)*
Waxco International Inc ....F....... 937 746-4845
  Miamisburg *(G-13740)*

LUMBER & BUILDING MATERIALS DEALER, RET: Masonry Matls/Splys

Associated Associates Inc......................E....... 330 626-3300
  Mantua *(G-12542)*
Cemex Materials LLC ....D....... 937 268-6706
  Dayton *(G-8081)*
Feather Lite Innovations Inc ....E....... 937 743-9008
  Springboro *(G-17327)*
Forterra Pipe & Precast LLC ....G....... 937 268-6707
  Dayton *(G-8203)*
Grafton Ready Mix Concret Inc ....E....... 440 926-2911
  Grafton *(G-10302)*
Gregory Stone Co Inc ....G....... 937 275-7455
  Dayton *(G-8239)*
Hazelbaker Industries Ltd ....E....... 614 276-2631
  Columbus *(G-6984)*
Koltcz Concrete Block Co ....E....... 440 232-3630
  Bedford *(G-1421)*
Lafarge North America Inc ....G....... 740 423-5900
  Belpre *(G-1579)*
Mack Industries ....C....... 419 353-7081
  Bowling Green *(G-1983)*

Oberfields LLC...E....... 614 491-7643
  Columbus *(G-7236)*
Pleasant Valley Ready Mix Inc ....F....... 330 852-2613
  Sugarcreek *(G-17858)*
Quikrete Companies LLC ....E....... 330 296-6080
  Ravenna *(G-16397)*
St Henry Tile Co Inc ....E....... 419 678-4841
  Saint Henry *(G-16667)*
St Henry Tile Co Inc ....F....... 937 548-1101
  Greenville *(G-10396)*
Stocker Concrete Company ....F....... 740 254-4626
  Gnadenhutten *(G-10283)*
Westview Concrete Corp..........................E....... 440 458-5800
  Elyria *(G-9346)*

LUMBER & BUILDING MATERIALS DEALERS, RET: Solar Heating Eqpt

Gopowerx Inc ....E....... 440 707-6029
  Oberlin *(G-15497)*

LUMBER & BUILDING MATERIALS DEALERS, RETAIL: Brick

American Concrete Products ....F....... 937 224-1433
  Dayton *(G-8025)*
Glen-Gery Corporation ....D....... 419 845-3321
  Caledonia *(G-2416)*
Huth Ready Mix & Supply Co ....F....... 330 833-4191
  Massillon *(G-12999)*
Mansfield Brick & Supply Co ....G....... 419 526-1191
  Mansfield *(G-12475)*
Medina Supply Company ....E....... 330 723-3681
  Medina *(G-13298)*
Snyder Concrete Products Inc ....F....... 513 539-7686
  Monroe *(G-14276)*

LUMBER & BUILDING MATERIALS DEALERS, RETAIL: Cement

Dan Shrock Cement..................................G....... 440 548-2498
  Parkman *(G-15811)*
Ernst Enterprises Inc ....E....... 614 443-9456
  Columbus *(G-6904)*
Hensel Ready Mix Inc ....G....... 614 755-6365
  Columbus *(G-6989)*
Huron Cement Products Company ....E....... 419 433-4161
  Huron *(G-11096)*
Scioto Ready Mix LLC ....D....... 740 924-9273
  Pataskala *(G-15843)*

LUMBER & BUILDING MATERIALS DEALERS, RETAIL: Countertops

Attractive Kitchens & Flrg LLC..............G....... 440 406-9299
  Elyria *(G-9220)*
Greene Street Wholesale LLC ....G....... 740 374-5206
  Marietta *(G-12628)*
Imperial Countertops...............................F....... 216 851-0888
  Cleveland *(G-5443)*

LUMBER & BUILDING MATERIALS DEALERS, RETAIL: Flooring, Wood

Cardinal Building Supply LLC ....G....... 614 706-4499
  Columbus *(G-6740)*

LUMBER & BUILDING MATERIALS DEALERS, RETAIL: Jalousies

Phillips Awning Co....................................G....... 740 653-2433
  Lancaster *(G-11596)*

LUMBER & BUILDING MATERIALS DEALERS, RETAIL: Modular Homes

Everything In America ....G....... 347 871-6872
  Cleveland *(G-5203)*

LUMBER & BUILDING MATERIALS DEALERS, RETAIL: Sand & Gravel

Melvin Stone Company LLC ....G....... 740 998-5016
  Wshngtn CT Hs *(G-20732)*
National Lime and Stone Co ....G....... 419 294-3049
  Upper Sandusky *(G-18965)*
Nissen Lumber & Coal Co Inc................G....... 419 836-8035
  Oregon *(G-15562)*

LUMBER & BUILDING MATERIALS DEALERS, RETAIL: Siding

Dj & Woodies Vinyl Frontier...................G....... 740 623-2818
  Coshocton *(G-7731)*
O A R Vinyl Windows & Siding ....G....... 440 636-5573
  Middlefield *(G-13842)*

LUMBER & BUILDING MATERIALS DEALERS, RETAIL: Tile, Ceramic

Artfinders..G....... 330 264-7706
  Wooster *(G-20563)*
Ohio Tile & Marble Co ....E....... 513 541-4211
  Cincinnati *(G-4105)*
Saint-Gobain Norpro.................................C....... 330 673-5860
  Stow *(G-17625)*

LUMBER & BUILDING MATERIALS RET DEALERS: Millwork & Lumber

Kencraft Co Inc ....G....... 419 536-0333
  Toledo *(G-18364)*
Laborie Enterprises LLC ....G....... 419 686-6245
  Portage *(G-16270)*
Mohler Lumber Company ....G....... 330 499-5461
  North Canton *(G-15102)*
Walnut Creek Planing Ltd ....D....... 330 893-3244
  Millersburg *(G-14146)*

LUMBER & BUILDING MATLS DEALERS, RET: Concrete/Cinder Block

Encore Precast LLC.................................F....... 513 726-5678
  Seven Mile *(G-16907)*
Ernst Enterprises Inc ....F....... 419 222-2015
  Lima *(G-11861)*
Hensel Ready Mix ....G....... 419 253-9200
  Marengo *(G-12592)*
O K Brugmann Jr & Sons Inc ....F....... 330 274-2106
  Mantua *(G-12555)*
Osborne Inc ....E....... 216 771-0010
  Cleveland *(G-5821)*

LUMBER & BUILDING MTRLS DEALERS, RET: Insulation Mtrl, Bldg

St Bernard Insulation LLC ....F....... 513 266-2158
  Cincinnati *(G-4367)*

LUMBER: Dimension, Hardwood

Creative Concepts ....G....... 216 513-6463
  Medina *(G-13246)*
Halliday Holdings Inc ....E....... 740 335-1430
  Wshngtn CT Hs *(G-20727)*
Hinchcliff Lumber Company ....E....... 440 238-5200
  Strongsville *(G-17749)*
J McCoy Lumber Co Ltd ....E....... 937 587-3423
  Peebles *(G-15879)*
J McCoy Lumber Co Ltd ....E....... 937 544-2968
  West Union *(G-19962)*
Stephen M Trudick ....E....... 440 834-1891
  Burton *(G-2371)*
Woodcraft Industries Inc ....D....... 440 437-7811
  Orwell *(G-15640)*
Woodcraft Industries Inc ....C....... 440 632-9655
  Middlefield *(G-13868)*

LUMBER: Fiberboard

Frankes Wood Products LLC................E....... 937 642-0706
  Marysville *(G-12783)*
Tectum Inc ....C....... 740 345-9691
  Newark *(G-14929)*

LUMBER: Flooring, Dressed, Softwood

Conover Lumber Company Inc.............F....... 937 368-3010
  Conover *(G-7663)*

LUMBER: Furniture Dimension Stock, Softwood

Leppert Companies Inc ....G....... 614 889-2818
  Dublin *(G-8941)*

LUMBER: Hardwood Dimension

Canfield Manufacturing Co Inc ....G....... 330 533-3333
  North Jackson *(G-15143)*

PRODUCT SECTION

Cardinal Building Supply LLC	G	614 706-4499
Columbus (G-6740)		
Itl LLC	B	216 831-3140
Beachwood (G-1242)		
McKay-Gross Div	G	330 683-2055
Apple Creek (G-613)		
Ohio Valley Veneer Inc	E	740 493-2901
Piketon (G-16076)		
Siefker Sawmill	G	419 339-1956
Elida (G-9201)		

LUMBER: Hardwood Dimension & Flooring Mills

Armstrong Custom Moulding Inc	G	740 922-5931
Uhrichsville (G-18880)		
Baillie Lumber Co LP	E	419 462-2000
Galion (G-10123)		
Beaver Wood Products	E	740 226-6211
Beaver (G-1292)		
Carter-Jones Lumber Company	C	330 674-9060
Millersburg (G-14077)		
Cherokee Hardwoods Inc	F	440 632-0322
Middlefield (G-13784)		
Crownover Lumber Co Inc	D	740 596-5229
Mc Arthur (G-13180)		
Denoon Lumber Company LLC	D	740 768-2220
Bergholz (G-1634)		
Dutch Heritage Woodcraft	E	330 893-2211
Berlin (G-1641)		
Gross Lumber Inc	E	330 683-2055
Apple Creek (G-606)		
Haessly Lumber Sales Co	D	740 373-6681
Marietta (G-12630)		
Hartzell Hardwoods Inc	D	937 773-7054
Piqua (G-16123)		
Hochstetler Wood	F	330 893-2384
Millersburg (G-14093)		
Holmes Lumber & Bldg Ctr Inc	C	330 674-9060
Millersburg (G-14098)		
Itl Corp	E	216 831-3140
Cleveland (G-5478)		
Knisley Lumber	F	740 634-2935
Bainbridge (G-1019)		
Mid Ohio Wood Products Inc	E	740 323-0427
Newark (G-14897)		
Mohler Lumber Company	E	330 499-5461
North Canton (G-15102)		
Stony Point Hardwoods	F	330 852-4512
Sugarcreek (G-17865)		
Superior Hardwoods of Ohio	E	740 596-2561
Mc Arthur (G-13184)		
Superior Hardwoods Ohio Inc	D	740 384-5677
Wellston (G-19608)		
Superior Hardwoods Ohio Inc	D	740 439-2727
Cambridge (G-2457)		
T & D Thompson Inc	E	740 332-8515
Laurelville (G-11627)		
Trumbull County Hardwoods	F	440 632-0555
Middlefield (G-13861)		
Wagner Farms & Sawmill LLC	F	419 653-4126
Leipsic (G-11738)		
Walnut Creek Planing Ltd	D	330 893-3244
Millersburg (G-14146)		
Wappoo Wood Products Inc	E	937 492-1166
Sidney (G-17084)		
Wooden Horse	G	740 503-5243
Baltimore (G-1046)		
Yoder Lumber Co Inc	D	330 893-3131
Sugarcreek (G-17878)		
Yoder Lumber Co Inc	D	330 893-3121
Millersburg (G-14153)		

LUMBER: Kiln Dried

Blaney Hardwoods Ohio Inc	E	740 678-8288
Vincent (G-19212)		
Itl Corp	E	216 831-3140
Cleveland (G-5478)		
Miller Lumber Co Inc	D	330 674-0273
Millersburg (G-14112)		

LUMBER: Plywood, Hardwood

Automated Bldg Components Inc	E	419 257-2152
North Baltimore (G-15042)		
Beaver Wood Products	E	740 226-6211
Beaver (G-1292)		
Bruewer Woodwork Mfg Co	D	513 353-3505
Cleves (G-6355)		
Carl C Andre Inc	G	614 864-0123
Brice (G-2071)		
Dimension Hardwood Veneers Inc	E	419 272-2445
Edon (G-9184)		
Fifth Avenue Lumber Co	D	614 833-6655
Canal Winchester (G-2503)		
Haessly Lumber Sales Co	D	740 373-6681
Marietta (G-12630)		
Knisley Lumber	F	740 634-2935
Bainbridge (G-1019)		
Lattasburg Lumberworks Co LLC	G	330 202-7671
West Salem (G-19956)		
Miller Manufacturing	E	330 852-0689
Sugarcreek (G-17854)		
Mohler Lumber Company	E	330 499-5461
North Canton (G-15102)		
Ohio Valley Veneer Inc	E	740 493-2901
Piketon (G-16076)		
S & G Manufacturing Group LLC	C	614 529-0100
Hilliard (G-10859)		
Sims-Lohman Inc	E	513 651-3510
Cincinnati (G-4340)		
Stony Point Hardwoods	F	330 852-4512
Sugarcreek (G-17865)		
Wappoo Wood Products Inc	E	937 492-1166
Sidney (G-17084)		
Yoder Lumber Co Inc	D	330 893-3131
Sugarcreek (G-17878)		

LUMBER: Plywood, Hardwood or Hardwood Faced

A & M Kiln Dry Ltd	F	330 852-0505
Dundee (G-9017)		

LUMBER: Plywood, Prefinished, Hardwood

Decorative Panels Intl Inc	D	419 535-5921
Toledo (G-18259)		
Miller Crist	F	330 359-7877
Fredericksburg (G-9953)		
Starecasing Systems Inc	G	312 203-5632
Columbus (G-7488)		

LUMBER: Plywood, Softwood

Clopay Building Pdts Co Inc	E	513 770-4800
Mason (G-12846)		
Clopay Building Pdts Co Inc	G	937 526-4301
Russia (G-16606)		
Clopay Building Pdts Co Inc	G	937 440-6403
Troy (G-18642)		

LUMBER: Plywood, Softwood

Beaver Wood Products	E	740 226-6211
Beaver (G-1292)		
S & G Manufacturing Group LLC	C	614 529-0100
Hilliard (G-10859)		
Ufp Hamilton LLC	F	513 285-7190
Hamilton (G-10616)		
Universal Veneer Production	C	740 522-1147
Newark (G-14931)		
Wappoo Wood Products Inc	E	937 492-1166
Sidney (G-17084)		

LUMBER: Rails, Fence, Round Or Split

D&M Fencing LLC	G	419 604-0698
Spencerville (G-17308)		

LUMBER: Treated

Appalachia Wood Inc	E	740 596-2551
Mc Arthur (G-13178)		
Appalachian Wood Floors Inc	D	740 354-4572
Portsmouth (G-16277)		
ISK Americas Incorporated	E	440 357-4600
Painesville (G-15750)		
Preserving Your Memories	G	614 861-4283
Reynoldsburg (G-16449)		
Ufp Blanchester LLC	E	937 783-2443
Blanchester (G-1707)		

LUMBER: Veneer, Hardwood

American Vneer Edgebanding Inc	G	740 928-2700
Heath (G-10716)		
Arkansas Face Veneer Co Inc	E	937 773-6295
Piqua (G-16100)		
Erath Veneer Corp Virginia	F	540 483-5223
Granville (G-10330)		
Hartzell Industries Inc	D	937 773-6295
Piqua (G-16124)		
Southeast Ohio Timber Pdts Co	G	740 344-2570
Zanesville (G-21181)		
Universal Veneer Sales Corp	C	740 522-1147
Newark (G-14932)		

LUMBER: Veneer, Softwood

American Vneer Edgebanding Inc	G	740 928-2700
Heath (G-10716)		

MACHINE PARTS: Stamped Or Pressed Metal

Abbott Tool Inc	E	419 476-6742
Toledo (G-18153)		
Artisan Equipment Inc	F	740 756-9135
Carroll (G-2898)		
Avion Manufacturing Company	G	330 220-1989
Brunswick (G-2188)		
CA Picard Surface Engrg Inc	F	440 366-5400
Elyria (G-9229)		
Cleveland Hollow Boring Inc	G	216 883-1926
Cleveland (G-4963)		
Compressor Technologies Inc	E	937 492-3711
Sidney (G-17023)		
Coreworth Holdings LLC	G	419 468-7100
Iberia (G-11112)		
Gb Manufacturing Company	D	419 822-5323
Delta (G-8772)		
Global Manufacturing Tech LLC	G	440 205-1001
Mentor (G-13460)		
Hamlin Newco LLC	D	330 753-7791
Akron (G-196)		
Hidaka Usa Inc	E	614 889-8611
Dublin (G-8923)		
Howland Machine Corp	E	330 544-4029
Niles (G-15012)		
Independent Power Consultants	G	419 476-8383
Toledo (G-18344)		
J R Machining Inc	G	330 528-3406
Hudson (G-11058)		
Jebco Machine Company Inc	G	330 452-2909
Canton (G-2718)		
Lowery Industries	G	740 745-5045
Saint Louisville (G-16673)		
M S C Industries Inc	G	440 474-8788
Rome (G-16564)		
Modern Engineering	G	440 593-5414
Conneaut (G-7656)		
Northwood Industries Inc	F	419 666-2100
Perrysburg (G-15983)		
P M Motor Company	F	440 327-9999
North Ridgeville (G-15243)		
PDQ Technologies Inc	F	937 274-4958
Dayton (G-8419)		
Perry Welding Service Inc	F	330 425-2211
Twinsburg (G-18836)		
Plating Technology Inc	D	937 268-6882
Dayton (G-8428)		
Precision Pressed Powdered Met	F	937 433-6802
Dayton (G-8435)		
Project Engineering Company	F	937 743-9114
Miamisburg (G-13706)		
Saco Lowell Parts LLC	E	330 794-1535
Akron (G-367)		
Sakas Incorporated	F	740 862-4114
Baltimore (G-1042)		
Spectrum Machine Inc	E	330 626-3666
Streetsboro (G-17699)		
SPR Machine Inc	G	513 737-8040
Fairfield Township (G-9586)		
Swivel-Tek Industries LLC	G	419 636-7770
Bryan (G-2308)		
TEC Design & Manufacturing Inc	F	937 435-2147
Dayton (G-8549)		
Tech-Med Inc	F	216 486-0900
Euclid (G-9445)		
Tenacity Manufacturing Company	E	513 821-0201
West Chester (G-19807)		
Thk Manufacturing America Inc	C	740 928-1415
Hebron (G-10766)		
True Turn Industries	G	440 355-6256
Lagrange (G-11495)		
Voss Industries LLC	C	216 771-7655
Cleveland (G-6273)		
Ysk Corporation	B	740 774-7315
Chillicothe (G-3231)		

MACHINE SHOPS

Abco Bar & Tube Cutting Svc	E	513 697-9487
Maineville (G-12364)		

Employee Codes: A=Over 500 employees, B=251-500
C=101-250, D=51-100, E=20-50, F=10-19, G=3-9

MACHINE SHOPS

Company	Section	Phone
Advanced Welding Co	E	937 746-6800
Franklin (G-9867)		
All-Type Welding & Fabrication	E	440 439-3990
Cleveland (G-4669)		
Amcan Productions Ltd	G	330 332-9129
Salem (G-16717)		
American Aero Components LLC		937 367-5068
Dayton (G-8022)		
Applied Experience LLC		614 943-2970
Columbus (G-6610)		
ARC Drilling Inc	F	216 525-0920
Cleveland (G-4723)		
Bardons & Oliver Inc	C	440 498-5800
Solon (G-17112)		
Beacon Metal Fabricators Inc	F	216 391-7444
Cleveland (G-4798)		
Berea Manufacturing Inc	F	440 260-0590
Berea (G-1593)		
Black McCuskey Souers	G	330 456-8341
Canton (G-2593)		
C G Egli Inc		937 254-8898
Dayton (G-8070)		
Centerline Tool & Machine		937 222-3600
Dayton (G-8083)		
Circle Machine Rolls Inc	E	330 938-9010
Sebring (G-16885)		
Crowe Manufacturing Services	D	800 831-1893
Troy (G-18644)		
Crum Manufacturing Inc	E	419 878-9779
Waterville (G-19492)		
Cutting Dynamics Inc	C	440 249-4150
Avon (G-947)		
Design Tech Inc	G	937 254-7000
Dayton (G-8158)		
Devault Machine & Mould Co LLC		740 654-5925
Lancaster (G-11563)		
Dimension Industries Inc	F	440 236-3265
Columbia Station (G-6435)		
Eos Technology Inc	E	216 281-2999
Cleveland (G-5183)		
F3 Defense Systems LLC	G	419 982-2020
Lima (G-11862)		
Forsvara Engineering LLC	G	937 254-9711
Dayton (G-8202)		
Fred W Hanks Company	G	216 731-1774
Cleveland (G-5274)		
Glendale Machine Inc		440 248-8646
Solon (G-17150)		
Goodwin Farms	G	513 877-2636
Pleasant Plain (G-16226)		
Hardin Creek Machine & Tool	F	419 678-4913
Coldwater (G-6410)		
Hawk Engine & Machine	G	440 582-0900
North Royalton (G-15276)		
Hawk Manufacturing LLC	D	330 784-3151
Akron (G-201)		
Holdren Brothers Inc	G	937 465-7050
West Liberty (G-19936)		
Innovative Tool & Die Inc	G	419 599-0492
Napoleon (G-14545)		
Izit Cain Sheet Metal Corp	G	937 667-6521
Tipp City (G-18117)		
Jed Industries Inc	E	440 639-9973
Grand River (G-10323)		
Jotco Inc	G	513 721-4943
Mansfield (G-12465)		
Kastler & Reichlin Inc	E	440 322-0970
Elyria (G-9281)		
Knous Tool & Machine Inc		419 394-3541
Saint Marys (G-16687)		
Krdc Inc	G	937 222-2332
Dayton (G-8301)		
Machine Parts International	G	216 251-4334
Cleveland (G-5600)		
Majestic Engineering & TI LLC	G	937 845-1079
New Carlisle (G-14672)		
McIntosh Machine	G	937 687-3936
New Lebanon (G-14712)		
Melinz Industries Inc	F	440 946-3512
Willoughby (G-20378)		
Meridian Machine Inc	G	330 308-0296
New Philadelphia (G-14785)		
Met Fab Fabrication and Mch	G	513 724-3715
Batavia (G-1164)		
Metcut Research Associates Inc	D	513 271-5100
Cincinnati (G-4015)		
Micro Machine Ltd	G	330 438-7078
Brewster (G-2070)		
Mission Industrial Group LLC	F	740 387-2287
Marion (G-12721)		
Munson Sales & Engineering	G	216 496-5436
Chardon (G-3126)		
Mysta Equipment Co	G	330 879-5353
Navarre (G-14581)		
National Aviation Products Inc	F	330 688-6494
Stow (G-17610)		
Nauvod Machine Co		440 632-1990
Middlefield (G-13837)		
Neff Machinery and Supplies	E	740 454-0128
Zanesville (G-21159)		
Northern Machine Tool Co		216 961-0444
Cleveland (G-5780)		
Northshore Mold Inc		440 838-8212
Cleveland (G-5786)		
Oak Industrial Inc		440 263-2780
North Royalton (G-15290)		
Ohio Metalizing LLC		330 830-1092
Massillon (G-13030)		
Performance Services		419 385-1236
Toledo (G-18466)		
Pohl Machining Inc	E	513 353-2929
Cleves (G-6372)		
Precision Dynamics Inc	G	330 697-0611
Akron (G-326)		
Precision Hydraulic Connectors	F	440 953-3778
Euclid (G-9437)		
Process Development Corp	E	937 890-3388
Dayton (G-8445)		
Qcsm LLC	G	216 531-5960
Cleveland (G-5937)		
Queen City Tool Works Inc	G	513 874-0111
Fairfield (G-9555)		
R & J Cylinder & Machine Inc	D	330 364-8263
New Philadelphia (G-14794)		
R and S Technologies Inc	F	419 483-3691
Bellevue (G-1542)		
Rankin Mfg Inc	E	419 929-8338
New London (G-14735)		
Reliance Design Inc	F	216 267-5450
Rocky River (G-16554)		
Remington Engrg Machining Inc	G	513 965-8999
Milford (G-14037)		
S & N Engineering Svcs Corp		216 433-1700
Cleveland (G-6020)		
Spartan Fabrication	G	330 758-3512
Youngstown (G-21036)		
Spectrum Dynamics Inc	G	614 486-3223
Columbus (G-7472)		
Stillwater Technologies LLC	D	937 440-2505
Troy (G-18713)		
Summer Global Systems LLC		330 397-1653
Campbell (G-2470)		
Swanton Wldg Machining Co Inc	D	419 826-4816
Swanton (G-17923)		
T E Martindale Enterprises	G	614 253-6826
Columbus (G-7507)		
Tdl Tool Inc	F	937 374-0055
Xenia (G-20794)		
Trailer Component Mfg Inc	E	440 255-2888
Mentor (G-13612)		
Tri-State Machining LLC		513 257-9442
Cleves (G-6380)		
Trojon Gear Inc	F	937 254-1737
Dayton (G-8568)		
Vandalia Machining Inc		937 264-9155
Vandalia (G-19148)		
Wc Sales Inc	G	419 836-2300
Northwood (G-15350)		
Wendell Machine Shop	G	330 627-3480
Carrollton (G-2932)		
Westerman Acquisition Co LLC	E	330 264-2447
Wooster (G-20666)		
Wire Shop Inc	E	440 354-6842
Mentor (G-13628)		
Xact Spec Industries LLC	G	440 543-8157
Chagrin Falls (G-3091)		

MACHINE TOOL ACCESS: Broaches

Company	Section	Phone
Northeast Broach & Tool	G	440 918-0048
Eastlake (G-9126)		

MACHINE TOOL ACCESS: Cams

Company	Section	Phone
Connell Limited Partnership	D	877 534-8986
Northfield (G-15316)		

MACHINE TOOL ACCESS: Collars

Company	Section	Phone
Preston	F	740 788-8208
Newark (G-14913)		

MACHINE TOOL ACCESS: Cutting

Company	Section	Phone
Advantage Tool Supply Inc	G	330 896-8869
Uniontown (G-18907)		
BAP Manufacturing Inc	E	419 332-5041
Fremont (G-9995)		
Certified Tool & Grinding Inc	G	937 865-5934
Miamisburg (G-13648)		
Cleveland Carbide Tool Co	G	440 974-1155
Mentor (G-13414)		
Container Graphics Corp	D	419 531-5133
Toledo (G-18241)		
Cr Supply LLC		440 759-5408
Mentor (G-13425)		
Edge-Rite Tools Inc	F	216 642-0966
Cleveland (G-5157)		
Electrofuel Industries Inc	G	937 783-2846
Batavia (G-1141)		
Expert Regrind Service Inc	G	937 526-5662
Versailles (G-19180)		
Ferguson Tools Inc	E	419 298-2327
Edgerton (G-9174)		
Fox Tool Co Inc	E	330 928-3402
Cuyahoga Falls (G-7869)		
Gem Tool LLC	G	216 771-8444
Cleveland (G-5303)		
H Duane Leis Acquisitions	E	937 835-5621
New Lebanon (G-14710)		
Herco Inc	E	740 498-5181
Newcomerstown (G-14975)		
HI Tech Tool Corporation	C	513 346-4061
Monroe (G-14266)		
Independent Die & Mfg Co	G	216 362-6778
Cleveland (G-5450)		
Interstate Tool Corporation	E	216 671-1077
Cleveland (G-5471)		
Jump N Sales LLC	G	513 509-7661
Fairfield Township (G-9583)		
Kennametal Inc	C	440 437-5131
Orwell (G-15633)		
Kennametal Inc	C	419 877-5358
Whitehouse (G-20192)		
Knb Tools of America Inc	F	614 733-0400
Plain City (G-16199)		
Kyocera SGS Precision Tools	E	330 688-6667
Munroe Falls (G-14524)		
Kyocera SGS Precision Tools	E	330 688-6667
Cuyahoga Falls (G-7890)		
Kyocera SGS Precision Tools		330 686-4151
Cuyahoga Falls (G-7891)		
Kyocera SGS Precision Tools	C	330 922-1953
Cuyahoga Falls (G-7892)		
Master Carbide Tools Company	F	440 352-1112
Painesville (G-15760)		
Melin Tool Company Inc	D	216 362-4200
Cleveland (G-5654)		
Monaghan & Associates Inc	E	937 253-7706
Dayton (G-8365)		
North-West Tool Co	G	937 278-7995
Dayton (G-8383)		
Osg-Sterling Die Inc	D	216 267-1300
Parma (G-15825)		
P F S Incorporated	G	440 582-1620
Cleveland (G-5829)		
P O McIntire Company	E	440 269-1848
Wickliffe (G-20221)		
Precise Tool & Mfg Corp	F	216 524-1500
Cleveland (G-5907)		
Productive Carbides Inc	G	513 771-7092
Cincinnati (G-4215)		
Quality Cutter Grinding Co	E	216 362-6444
Cleveland (G-5941)		
R & J Tool Inc	F	937 833-3200
Brookville (G-2183)		
R A Heller Company	F	513 771-6100
Cincinnati (G-4242)		
Regal Diamond Products Corp	E	440 944-7700
Wickliffe (G-20229)		
Sharp Tool Service Inc	G	330 273-4144
Cleveland (G-6048)		
T M Industries Inc	G	330 627-4410
Carrollton (G-2930)		
Tool Systems Inc	F	440 461-6363
Cleveland (G-6182)		
Uhrichsville Carbide Inc	F	740 922-9197
Uhrichsville (G-18899)		
United States Drill Head Co	E	513 941-0300
Cincinnati (G-4450)		
William Darling Company Inc	G	614 878-0085
Columbus (G-7604)		

PRODUCT SECTION — MACHINE TOOLS & ACCESS

MACHINE TOOL ACCESS: Diamond Cutting, For Turning, Etc

- Chardon Tool & Supply Co Inc .... E 440 286-6440
  Chardon *(G-3104)*
- Dark Diamond Tools Inc .... G 440 701-6424
  Chardon *(G-3107)*
- Diamond Reserve Inc .... F 440 892-7877
  Westlake *(G-20108)*
- Diamonds Products LLC .... G 440 323-4616
  Elyria *(G-9242)*
- H3d Tool Corporation .... G 740 498-5181
  Newcomerstown *(G-14974)*
- Hapco Inc .... F 330 678-9353
  Kent *(G-11331)*
- Schumann Enterprises Inc .... E 216 267-6850
  Cleveland *(G-6033)*
- Sp3 Cutting Tools Inc .... G 937 667-4476
  Tipp City *(G-18134)*

MACHINE TOOL ACCESS: Dies, Thread Cutting

- Aeroll Engineering Corp .... G 216 481-2266
  Cleveland *(G-4632)*
- National Rolled Thread Die Co .... F 440 232-8101
  Cleveland *(G-5728)*

MACHINE TOOL ACCESS: Dressing/Wheel Crushing Attach, Diamond

- Glassline Corporation .... C 419 666-9712
  Perrysburg *(G-15958)*

MACHINE TOOL ACCESS: Drill Bushings, Drilling Jig

- Jergens Inc .... C 216 486-5540
  Cleveland *(G-5495)*

MACHINE TOOL ACCESS: Drills

- H Machining Inc .... F 419 636-6890
  Bryan *(G-2283)*

MACHINE TOOL ACCESS: End Mills

- Commercial Grinding Services .... E 330 273-5040
  Medina *(G-13238)*

MACHINE TOOL ACCESS: Hopper Feed Devices

- Feedall Inc .... F 440 942-8100
  Willoughby *(G-20321)*

MACHINE TOOL ACCESS: Knives, Metalworking

- Alliance Knife Inc .... E 513 367-9000
  Harrison *(G-10631)*

MACHINE TOOL ACCESS: Knives, Shear

- Precision Component Inds LLC .... E 330 477-1052
  Canton *(G-2790)*
- Whitworth Knife Company .... G 513 321-9177
  Cincinnati *(G-4507)*

MACHINE TOOL ACCESS: Machine Attachments & Access, Drilling

- Whip Guide Co .... F 440 543-5151
  Chagrin Falls *(G-3090)*

MACHINE TOOL ACCESS: Milling Machine Attachments

- JM Performance Products Inc .... F 440 357-1234
  Fairport Harbor *(G-9624)*

MACHINE TOOL ACCESS: Rotary Tables

- Roto Tech Inc .... E 937 859-8503
  Dayton *(G-8485)*
- Troyke Manufacturing Company .... F 513 769-4242
  Cincinnati *(G-4441)*

MACHINE TOOL ACCESS: Shaping Tools

- H E Long Company .... F 513 899-2610
  Morrow *(G-14411)*

MACHINE TOOL ACCESS: Sockets

- National Machine Company .... E 330 688-2584
  Stow *(G-17612)*

MACHINE TOOL ACCESS: Threading Tools

- Cleveland Specialty Insptn Svc .... F 440 578-1046
  Mentor *(G-13415)*
- Reed Machinery Inc .... G 330 220-6668
  Brunswick *(G-2234)*

MACHINE TOOL ACCESS: Tool Holders

- American Truck Equipment Inc .... G 216 362-0400
  Cleveland *(G-4699)*
- George Whalley Company .... E 216 453-0099
  Fairport Harbor *(G-9623)*
- Kennametal Inc .... C 440 349-5151
  Solon *(G-17183)*

MACHINE TOOL ACCESS: Tools & Access

- Cowles Industrial Tool Co LLC .... E 330 799-9100
  Austintown *(G-932)*
- Furukawa Rock Drill USA Co Ltd .... E 330 673-5826
  Kent *(G-11325)*
- H & S Tool Inc .... F 330 335-1536
  Wadsworth *(G-19244)*
- HI Carb Corp .... F 216 486-5000
  Cleveland *(G-5401)*
- High Quality Tools Inc .... F 440 975-9684
  Eastlake *(G-9113)*
- Imco Carbide Tool Inc .... D 419 661-6313
  Perrysburg *(G-15965)*
- M S C Industries Inc .... G 440 474-8788
  Rome *(G-16564)*
- Oakley Die & Mold Co .... E 513 754-8500
  Mason *(G-12918)*
- Polhe Tool Inc .... G 419 476-2433
  Toledo *(G-18473)*
- Red Head Brass Inc .... G 330 567-2903
  Shreve *(G-17007)*
- Rotairtech Inc .... G 937 435-8178
  Kettering *(G-11441)*
- Roto-Die Inc .... G 216 531-4800
  Cleveland *(G-6007)*
- Tomco Tool Inc .... G 937 322-5768
  Springfield *(G-17507)*

MACHINE TOOL ACCESS: Wheel Turning Eqpt, Diamond Point, Etc

- Performance Superabrasives LLC .... G 440 946-7171
  Mentor *(G-13547)*

MACHINE TOOL ATTACHMENTS & ACCESS

- Allied Machine & Engrg Corp .... C 330 343-4283
  Dover *(G-8803)*
- Carbide Probes Inc .... E 937 490-2994
  Beavercreek *(G-1304)*
- Dayton Precision Punch .... G 937 275-8700
  Dayton *(G-8142)*
- Ellison Technologies Inc .... E 513 874-2736
  Hamilton *(G-10553)*
- Frecon Engineering .... G 513 874-8981
  West Chester *(G-19707)*
- Frecon Technologies Inc .... G 513 874-8981
  West Chester *(G-19708)*
- Hydra Air Equipment Inc .... G 330 274-2222
  Mantua *(G-12548)*
- Lear Manufacturing Inc .... G 440 327-4545
  North Ridgeville *(G-15238)*
- Positrol Inc .... E 513 272-0500
  Cincinnati *(G-4175)*
- Retention Knob Supply & Mfg Co .... F 937 686-6405
  Huntsville *(G-11088)*
- Riten Industries Incorporated .... E 740 335-5353
  Wshngtn CT Hs *(G-20742)*
- Star Metal Products Co Inc .... D 440 899-7000
  Westlake *(G-20161)*
- Te-Co Manufacturing LLC .... D 937 836-0961
  Englewood *(G-9377)*

MACHINE TOOLS & ACCESS

- Able Tool Corporation .... E 513 733-8989
  Cincinnati *(G-3288)*
- Akron Gear & Engineering Inc .... F 330 773-6608
  Akron *(G-41)*
- Anchor Lamina America Inc .... F 330 952-1595
  Medina *(G-13224)*
- Antwerp Tool & Die Inc .... F 419 258-5271
  Antwerp *(G-596)*
- Apollo Products Inc .... F 440 269-8551
  Willoughby *(G-20275)*
- Atlantic Tool & Die Company .... C 330 769-4500
  Seville *(G-19810)*
- B & R Machine Co Inc .... F 216 961-7370
  Cleveland *(G-4784)*
- Bender Engineering Company .... G 330 938-2355
  Beloit *(G-1568)*
- Big Chief Manufacturing Ltd .... C 513 934-3888
  Lebanon *(G-11637)*
- Bully Tools Inc .... E 740 282-5834
  Steubenville *(G-17529)*
- Capital Tool Company .... E 216 661-5750
  Cleveland *(G-4871)*
- Carlton Natco .... E 216 451-5588
  Cleveland *(G-4878)*
- Cnc Indexing Feeding Tech LLC .... G 513 770-4200
  Mason *(G-12851)*
- Coleys Inc .... F 440 967-5630
  Vermilion *(G-19158)*
- Contour Tool Inc .... E 440 365-7333
  North Ridgeville *(G-15216)*
- Covert Manufacturing Inc .... B 419 468-1761
  Galion *(G-10130)*
- Dayton Progress Corporation .... A 937 859-5111
  Dayton *(G-8143)*
- Delta Machine & Tool Co .... F 216 524-2477
  Cleveland *(G-5083)*
- Diamond Products Limited .... G 440 323-4616
  Elyria *(G-9241)*
- Drt Mfg Co .... C 937 297-6670
  Dayton *(G-8171)*
- E & J Demark Inc .... E 419 337-5866
  Wauseon *(G-19513)*
- E & J Demark Inc .... G 419 337-5866
  Wauseon *(G-19514)*
- Evandy Co Inc .... E 216 518-9713
  Cleveland *(G-5199)*
- Eversharpe Deburring Tool Co .... G 513 988-6240
  Trenton *(G-18618)*
- Fischer Special Tooling Corp .... F 440 951-8411
  Mentor *(G-13443)*
- Galaxy Products Inc .... G 419 843-7337
  Sylvania *(G-17940)*
- Gleason Metrology Systems Corp .... E 937 384-8901
  Dayton *(G-8223)*
- Greentec Precision Inc .... G 937 431-1840
  Beavercreek *(G-1319)*
- Hudson Supply Company Inc .... G 216 518-3000
  Cleveland *(G-5424)*
- Hyper Tool Company .... F 440 543-5151
  Chagrin Falls *(G-3051)*
- Johnson Bros Rubber Co Inc .... E 419 752-4814
  Greenwich *(G-10404)*
- Kalt Manufacturing Company .... D 440 327-2102
  North Ridgeville *(G-15235)*
- Kennametal Inc .... D 216 898-6120
  Cleveland *(G-5527)*
- Kilroy Company .... D 440 951-8700
  Eastlake *(G-9117)*
- Lange Precision Inc .... F 513 530-9500
  Blue Ash *(G-1802)*
- Lord Corporation .... C 937 278-9431
  Dayton *(G-8315)*
- Matrix Tool & Machine Inc .... E 440 255-0300
  Mentor *(G-13512)*
- Matvest Inc .... E 614 487-8720
  Columbus *(G-7161)*
- Mdf Tool Corporation .... F 440 237-2277
  North Royalton *(G-15287)*
- Medina Blanking Inc .... C 330 558-2300
  Valley City *(G-19049)*
- Medway Tool Corp .... E 937 335-7717
  Troy *(G-18687)*
- Metalex Manufacturing Inc .... C 513 489-0507
  Blue Ash *(G-1820)*
- Midwest Tool & Engineering Co .... G 937 224-0756
  Dayton *(G-8356)*
- Mikan Die and Tool LLC .... G 216 265-2811
  Cleveland *(G-5684)*
- Nook Industries Inc .... C 216 271-7900
  Cleveland *(G-5756)*
- Obars Machine and Tool Company .... E 419 535-6307
  Toledo *(G-18433)*
- Ohio Broach & Machine Company .... E 440 946-1040
  Willoughby *(G-20393)*
- Ohio Drill & Tool Co .... G 330 525-7161
  Homeworth *(G-10990)*

MACHINE TOOLS & ACCESS

Ohio Drill & Tool Co .... E 330 525-7717
  Homeworth *(G-10989)*
Pakk Systems LLC .... G 440 839-9999
  Wakeman *(G-19288)*
Patriot Mfg Group Inc .... D 937 746-2117
  Carlisle *(G-2896)*
Pemco Inc 216 524-2990
  Cleveland *(G-5862)*
Pike Tool & Manufacturing Co .... G 740 947-7462
  Waverly *(G-19558)*
Production Design Services Inc .... D 937 866-3377
  Dayton *(G-8446)*
R T & T Machining Co Inc 440 974-8479
  Mentor *(G-13571)*
Rex International USA Inc .... E 800 321-7950
  Ashtabula *(G-803)*
Ridge Tool Manufacturing Co .... A 440 323-5581
  Elyria *(G-9322)*
Roehlers Machine Products .... G 937 354-4401
  Mount Victory *(G-14522)*
Rol - Tech Inc .... C 214 905-8050
  Fort Loramie *(G-9803)*
Rossi Machinery Services Inc 419 281-4488
  Ashland *(G-744)*
Royer Technologies Inc .... G 937 743-6114
  Saint Marys *(G-16698)*
Setco Sales Company .... D 513 941-5110
  Cincinnati *(G-4328)*
Sharper Tooling .... G 330 667-2960
  Litchfield *(G-11987)*
Skidmore-Wilhelm Mfg Company .... E 216 481-4774
  Solon *(G-17232)*
Sorbothane Inc .... E 330 678-9444
  Kent *(G-11388)*
Spectrum Machine Inc 330 626-3666
  Streetsboro *(G-17699)*
Stanley Bittinger .... G 740 942-4302
  Cadiz *(G-2401)*
Stark Industrial LLC .... E 330 493-9773
  North Canton *(G-15122)*
STC International Co Ltd 561 308-6002
  Lebanon *(G-11699)*
Sumitomo Elc Carbide Mfg Inc .... F 440 354-0600
  Grand River *(G-10326)*
Superion Inc 937 374-0033
  Xenia *(G-20793)*
Supplier Inspection Svcs Inc .... E 937 263-7097
  Dayton *(G-8529)*
Technidrill Systems Inc 330 678-9980
  Kent *(G-11393)*
Tormaxx Co .... G 513 721-6299
  Cincinnati *(G-4426)*
Voisard Tool LLC 937 526-5451
  Russia *(G-16614)*
Wolff Tool & Manufacturing Co 440 933-7797
  Avon Lake *(G-1014)*
Worldwide Machine Tool LLC .... G 614 496-9414
  Lewis Center *(G-11788)*
Wright Buffing Wheel Company 330 424-7887
  Lisbon *(G-11983)*
X-Press Tool Inc .... E 330 225-8748
  Brunswick *(G-2254)*

MACHINE TOOLS, METAL CUTTING: Chucking, Automatic

Applied Automation Enterprise .... F 419 929-2428
  New London *(G-14728)*

MACHINE TOOLS, METAL CUTTING: Die Sinking

Masheen Specialties .... E 330 652-7535
  Mineral Ridge *(G-14169)*

MACHINE TOOLS, METAL CUTTING: Drilling

Cincinnati Gilbert Mch Tl LLC .... E 513 541-4815
  Cincinnati *(G-3497)*
Martin & Marianne Tools Inc .... G 440 255-5107
  Mentor *(G-13511)*

MACHINE TOOLS, METAL CUTTING: Drilling & Boring

Alliance Drilling Inc .... F 330 584-2781
  North Benton *(G-15059)*
Barbco Inc .... E 330 488-9400
  East Canton *(G-9038)*
Bor-It Manufacturing Inc .... E 419 289-6639
  Ashland *(G-687)*

Cappco Tubular Products Inc .... G 216 641-2218
  North Olmsted *(G-15183)*
Grt Utilicorp Inc .... E 330 264-8444
  Wooster *(G-20600)*
Leland-Gifford Inc 330 785-9730
  Akron *(G-251)*
Technidrill Systems Inc .... E 330 678-9980
  Kent *(G-11393)*
Whole Solutions 330 652-1725
  Mineral Ridge *(G-14174)*

MACHINE TOOLS, METAL CUTTING: Electron-Discharge

Global Specialty Machines LLC .... F 513 701-0452
  Mason *(G-12881)*
Republic EDM Services Inc 937 278-7070
  Dayton *(G-8473)*

MACHINE TOOLS, METAL CUTTING: Exotic, Including Explosive

C M M S - Re LLC .... F 513 489-5111
  Blue Ash *(G-1745)*
Fischer Special Tooling Corp 440 951-8411
  Mentor *(G-13443)*
National Machine Tool Company 513 541-6682
  Cincinnati *(G-4061)*
Single Source Technologies LLC .... B 513 573-7200
  Mason *(G-12939)*

MACHINE TOOLS, METAL CUTTING: Grind, Polish, Buff, Lapp

Bud May Inc .... F 216 676-8850
  Cleveland *(G-4850)*
Rapid Machine Inc .... F 419 737-2377
  Pioneer *(G-16094)*
Tool Service Co Inc .... G 937 254-4000
  Dayton *(G-7992)*

MACHINE TOOLS, METAL CUTTING: Home Workshop

H & D Steel Service Inc .... E 440 237-3390
  North Royalton *(G-15275)*

MACHINE TOOLS, METAL CUTTING: Lathes

Bardons & Oliver Inc .... C 440 498-5800
  Solon *(G-17112)*
Monarch Lathes LP .... E 937 492-4111
  Sidney *(G-17056)*

MACHINE TOOLS, METAL CUTTING: Numerically Controlled

Masters Prcision Machining Inc .... F 330 419-1933
  Kent *(G-11350)*

MACHINE TOOLS, METAL CUTTING: Pipe Cutting & Threading

Rex International USA Inc .... E 800 321-7950
  Ashtabula *(G-803)*
Ridge Tool Company .... A 440 323-5581
  Elyria *(G-9320)*

MACHINE TOOLS, METAL CUTTING: Plasma Process

Accurate Metal Sawing Svc Co .... E 440 205-3205
  Mentor *(G-13371)*
Accurate Plasma Cutting Inc .... F 440 943-1655
  Wickliffe *(G-20195)*
Cutting Systems Inc .... F 216 928-0500
  Cleveland *(G-5052)*
Dbcr Inc .... E 330 920-1900
  Cuyahoga Falls *(G-7859)*

MACHINE TOOLS, METAL CUTTING: Regrinding, Crankshaft

Walter Grinders Inc .... G 937 859-1975
  Miamisburg *(G-13737)*

MACHINE TOOLS, METAL CUTTING: Sawing & Cutoff

AM Industrial Group LLC .... E 216 433-7171
  Brookpark *(G-2134)*
Kmi Processing LLC .... G 330 862-2185
  Minerva *(G-14187)*
Kmi Processing LLC .... F 330 862-2185
  Minerva *(G-14188)*
Lawrence Industries Inc .... C 216 518-7000
  Cleveland *(G-5566)*
Lawrence Industries Inc 216 518-1400
  Cleveland *(G-5567)*
Roll-In Saw Inc .... F 216 459-9001
  Brookpark *(G-2155)*

MACHINE TOOLS, METAL CUTTING: Tool Replacement & Rpr Parts

Ald Group LLC .... G 440 942-9800
  Willoughby *(G-20269)*
Bar Tech Service Inc .... G 440 943-5286
  Wickliffe *(G-20201)*
Cardinal Builders Inc .... E 614 237-1000
  Columbus *(G-6739)*
Center Line Machining LLC 216 289-6828
  Euclid *(G-9408)*
Eagle Machinery & Supply Inc .... E 330 852-1300
  Sugarcreek *(G-17849)*
J-C-R Tech Inc 937 783-2296
  Blanchester *(G-1704)*
Mataco .... G 440 546-8355
  Broadview Heights *(G-2096)*
Mk Global Enterprises LLC 440 823-0081
  Beachwood *(G-1251)*
Molding Machine Services Inc 330 461-2270
  Medina *(G-13303)*
More Manufacturing LLC .... G 937 233-3898
  Tipp City *(G-18123)*
Parkn Manufacturing LLC 330 723-8172
  Litchfield *(G-11986)*
Ravana Industries Inc .... G 330 536-4015
  Lowellville *(G-12254)*
Warner Vess Inc .... G 740 585-2481
  Lower Salem *(G-12259)*

MACHINE TOOLS, METAL CUTTING: Ultrasonic

Nmgg Ctg LLC .... G 419 447-5211
  Tiffin *(G-18072)*
U-Sonico .... F 423 348-7117
  Springfield *(G-17511)*

MACHINE TOOLS, METAL FORMING: Bending

Addisonmckee Inc .... C 513 228-7000
  Lebanon *(G-11629)*
American Fluid Power Inc .... G 877 223-8742
  Elyria *(G-9215)*
Bendco Machine & Tool Inc .... F 419 628-3802
  Minster *(G-14210)*
K & L Tool Inc 419 258-2086
  Antwerp *(G-598)*
Pines Manufacturing Inc .... E 440 835-5553
  Westlake *(G-20141)*
R & B Machining Inc 937 382-6710
  Wilmington *(G-20507)*
Ready Technology Inc .... F 937 866-7200
  Dayton *(G-8466)*
S & H Automation & Eqp Co .... E 419 636-0020
  Bryan *(G-2306)*

MACHINE TOOLS, METAL FORMING: Crimping, Metal

Eaton Hydraulics LLC .... E 419 232-7777
  Van Wert *(G-19088)*

MACHINE TOOLS, METAL FORMING: Die Casting & Extruding

American Metal Tech LLC .... D 937 347-1111
  Xenia *(G-20756)*

PRODUCT SECTION MACHINE TOOLS: Metal Cutting

MACHINE TOOLS, METAL FORMING: Electroforming
Allied Mask and Tooling Inc ....G....... 419 470-2555
  Toledo *(G-18164)*

MACHINE TOOLS, METAL FORMING: Forging Machinery & Hammers
Ajax Manufacturing Company ....E....... 440 295-0244
  Wickliffe *(G-20196)*
NM Group Global LLC ....G....... 419 447-5211
  Tiffin *(G-18071)*

MACHINE TOOLS, METAL FORMING: Gear Rolling
Heimann Manufacturing Co ....G....... 937 652-1865
  Urbana *(G-18993)*

MACHINE TOOLS, METAL FORMING: Headers
National Machinery LLC ....B....... 419 447-5211
  Tiffin *(G-18070)*

MACHINE TOOLS, METAL FORMING: Magnetic Forming
Green Corp Magnetic Inc ....E....... 614 801-4000
  Grove City *(G-10432)*

MACHINE TOOLS, METAL FORMING: Marking
Monode Marking Products Inc ....D....... 440 975-8802
  Mentor *(G-13522)*
Monode Marking Products Inc ....F....... 419 929-0346
  New London *(G-14731)*
Monode Steel Stamp Inc ....E....... 419 929-3501
  New London *(G-14732)*
Monode Steel Stamp Inc ....F....... 440 975-8802
  Mentor *(G-13523)*

MACHINE TOOLS, METAL FORMING: Mechanical, Pneumatic Or Hyd
Apeks LLC ....E....... 740 809-1160
  Johnstown *(G-11256)*
Compass Systems & Sales LLC ....D....... 330 733-2111
  Norton *(G-15363)*
Hawk Manufacturing LLC ....D....... 330 784-3151
  Akron *(G-201)*
Omni Technical Products Inc ....F....... 216 433-1970
  Cleveland *(G-5814)*
Recycling Eqp Solutions Corp ....G....... 330 920-1500
  Cuyahoga Falls *(G-7912)*

MACHINE TOOLS, METAL FORMING: Nail Heading
Stutzman Manufacturing Ltd ....G....... 330 674-4359
  Millersburg *(G-14131)*

MACHINE TOOLS, METAL FORMING: Presses, Hyd & Pneumatic
Accurate Manufacturing Company ....E....... 614 878-6510
  Columbus *(G-6534)*
Airam Press Co Ltd ....E....... 937 473-5672
  Covington *(G-7780)*
Asb Industries Inc ....E....... 330 753-8458
  Barberton *(G-1054)*
Columbus Jack Corporation ....D....... 614 747-1596
  Swanton *(G-17909)*
Connell Limited Partnership ....D....... 877 534-8986
  Northfield *(G-15316)*
DRG Hydraulics Inc ....E....... 216 663-9747
  Cleveland *(G-5114)*
Fabriweld Corporation ....E....... 419 668-3358
  Norwalk *(G-15393)*
French Oil Mill Machinery Co ....D....... 937 773-3420
  Piqua *(G-16117)*
Gad-Jets Inc ....G....... 937 274-2111
  Franklin *(G-9885)*
Henry & Wright Corporation ....F....... 216 851-3750
  Cleveland *(G-5394)*
High Production Technology LLC ....F....... 419 591-7000
  Napoleon *(G-14541)*

Hunter Hydraulics Inc ....G....... 330 455-3983
  Canton *(G-2701)*
Multipress Inc ....G....... 614 228-0185
  Columbus *(G-7200)*
Parker-Hannifin Corporation ....C....... 419 644-4311
  Metamora *(G-13634)*
Phoenix Hydraulic Presses Inc ....F....... 614 850-8940
  Hilliard *(G-10852)*
Qpi Multipress Inc ....G....... 614 228-0185
  Columbus *(G-7361)*
Quality Products Inc ....D....... 614 228-0185
  Swanton *(G-17920)*
Ram Products Inc ....F....... 614 443-4634
  Columbus *(G-7377)*
Rogers Industrial Products Inc ....E....... 330 535-3331
  Akron *(G-353)*
Tri-K Enterprises Inc ....G....... 330 832-7380
  Canton *(G-2845)*

MACHINE TOOLS, METAL FORMING: Rebuilt
Advanced Tech Utilization Co ....F....... 440 238-3770
  Strongsville *(G-17706)*
Edwards Machine Service Inc ....F....... 937 295-2929
  Fort Loramie *(G-9795)*
Industrial Machine Tool Svc ....G....... 216 651-1122
  Cleveland *(G-5452)*
Machine Tool Rebuilders Inc ....G....... 614 228-1070
  Columbus *(G-7142)*
Rossi Machinery Services Inc ....G....... 419 281-4488
  Ashland *(G-744)*
W G Machine Tool Service Co ....G....... 330 723-3428
  Medina *(G-13362)*

MACHINE TOOLS, METAL FORMING: Spinning, Spline Rollg/Windg
BAC Technologies Ltd ....G....... 937 465-2228
  West Liberty *(G-19935)*

MACHINE TOOLS: Metal Cutting
3 Brothers Torching Inc ....G....... 419 339-9985
  Lima *(G-11828)*
5 Axis Grinding Inc ....G....... 937 312-9797
  Dayton *(G-7996)*
A & P Tool Inc ....E....... 419 542-6681
  Hicksville *(G-10773)*
Abrasive Technology Lapidary ....F....... 740 548-4855
  Lewis Center *(G-11741)*
Acro Tool & Die Company ....D....... 330 773-5173
  Akron *(G-29)*
Advanced Innovative Mfg Inc ....F....... 330 562-2468
  Aurora *(G-867)*
Advetech Inc ....E....... 330 533-2227
  Canfield *(G-2517)*
Alcon Tool Company ....G....... 330 773-9171
  Akron *(G-57)*
Barth Industries Co LP ....D....... 216 267-0531
  Cleveland *(G-4793)*
Callahan Cutting Tools Inc ....G....... 614 294-1649
  Columbus *(G-6724)*
Cammann Inc ....F....... 440 965-4051
  Wakeman *(G-19282)*
Carlton Natco ....G....... 216 451-5588
  Cleveland *(G-4878)*
Carter Manufacturing Co Inc ....E....... 513 398-7303
  Mason *(G-12838)*
Channel Products Inc ....D....... 440 423-0113
  Solon *(G-17126)*
Chart Tech Tool Inc ....E....... 937 667-3543
  Tipp City *(G-18108)*
Cincinnati Mine Machinery Co ....D....... 513 522-7777
  Cincinnati *(G-3501)*
Coil Technology Inc ....G....... 330 601-1350
  Wooster *(G-20579)*
Commercial Grinding Services ....E....... 330 273-5040
  Medina *(G-13238)*
Competetive Carbide Inc ....E....... 440 350-9393
  Mentor *(G-13421)*
Criterion Tool & Die Inc ....E....... 216 267-1733
  Brookpark *(G-2139)*
Dan Wilzynski ....G....... 800 531-3343
  Columbus *(G-6848)*
Dexport Tool Manufacturing Co ....E....... 513 625-1600
  Loveland *(G-12185)*
Dixie Machinery Inc ....F....... 513 360-0091
  Monroe *(G-14261)*
Elliott Tool Technologies Ltd ....D....... 937 253-6133
  Dayton *(G-8182)*
Falcon Industries Inc ....E....... 330 723-0099
  Medina *(G-13260)*

Falcon Tool & Machine Inc ....G....... 937 534-9999
  Moraine *(G-14353)*
Frazier Machine and Prod Inc ....E....... 419 661-1656
  Perrysburg *(G-15954)*
Gbi Cincinnati Inc ....G....... 513 841-8684
  Cincinnati *(G-3729)*
General Electric Company ....B....... 513 341-0214
  West Chester *(G-19714)*
Genex Tool & Die Inc ....F....... 330 788-2466
  Youngstown *(G-20919)*
George A Mitchell Company ....E....... 330 758-5777
  Youngstown *(G-20920)*
Glassline Corporation ....C....... 419 666-9712
  Perrysburg *(G-15958)*
Glt Inc ....F....... 937 237-0055
  Dayton *(G-8230)*
Gt Machine & Fab ....G....... 740 701-9607
  Kingston *(G-11458)*
Hawk Manufacturing LLC ....D....... 330 784-3151
  Akron *(G-201)*
Hawk Manufacturing LLC ....D....... 330 784-4815
  Akron *(G-202)*
Hesler Machine Tool ....G....... 937 299-3833
  Dayton *(G-8248)*
Houston Machine Products Inc ....E....... 937 322-8022
  Springfield *(G-17422)*
Hyper Tool Company ....F....... 440 543-5151
  Chagrin Falls *(G-3051)*
Interstate Tool Corporation ....E....... 216 671-1077
  Cleveland *(G-5471)*
J and S Tool Incorporated ....E....... 216 676-8330
  Cleveland *(G-5482)*
K L M Manufacturing Company ....G....... 740 666-5171
  Ostrander *(G-15644)*
Kay Capital Company ....E....... 216 531-1010
  Cleveland *(G-5521)*
Kilroy Company ....D....... 440 951-8700
  Eastlake *(G-9117)*
Klawhorn Industries Inc ....G....... 330 335-8191
  Wadsworth *(G-19249)*
Lahm-Trosper Inc ....F....... 937 252-8791
  Dayton *(G-8305)*
Lees Machinery Inc ....G....... 440 259-2222
  Perry *(G-15907)*
Levan Enterprises Inc ....E....... 330 923-9797
  Stow *(G-17601)*
Machine Component Mfg ....F....... 330 454-4566
  Canton *(G-2740)*
Machine Tl Sltons Unlmited LLC ....F....... 513 761-0709
  Cincinnati *(G-3967)*
Makino Inc ....B....... 513 573-7200
  Mason *(G-12905)*
Martindale Electric Company ....E....... 216 521-8567
  Cleveland *(G-5628)*
Melin Tool Company Inc ....D....... 216 362-4200
  Cleveland *(G-5654)*
Metal Cutting Technology LLC ....G....... 419 733-1236
  Celina *(G-2975)*
Micron Manufacturing Inc ....D....... 440 355-4200
  Lagrange *(G-11489)*
Midwest Knife Grinding Inc ....F....... 330 854-1030
  Canal Fulton *(G-2486)*
Midwest Ohio Tool Co ....G....... 419 294-1987
  Upper Sandusky *(G-18963)*
Milacron Marketing Company LLC ....E....... 513 536-2000
  Batavia *(G-1167)*
Monaghan & Associates Inc ....E....... 937 253-7706
  Dayton *(G-8365)*
Mrd Solutions LLC ....G....... 440 942-6969
  Eastlake *(G-9124)*
Nesco Inc ....E....... 440 461-6000
  Cleveland *(G-5741)*
New Holland Engineering Inc ....G....... 740 495-5200
  New Holland *(G-14702)*
Northwood Industries Inc ....F....... 419 666-2100
  Perrysburg *(G-15983)*
Obars Machine and Tool Company ....E....... 419 535-6307
  Toledo *(G-18433)*
Oceco Inc ....F....... 419 447-0916
  Tiffin *(G-18073)*
P M R Inc ....G....... 440 937-6241
  Avon *(G-955)*
P R Racing Engines ....G....... 419 472-2277
  Toledo *(G-18455)*
Page Slotting Saw Co Inc ....F....... 419 476-7475
  Toledo *(G-18456)*
Peerless Saw Company ....C....... 614 836-5790
  Groveport *(G-10509)*
Phillips Manufacturing Co ....D....... 330 652-4335
  Niles *(G-15026)*

Employee Codes: A=Over 500 employees, B=251-500
C=101-250, D=51-100, E=20-50, F=10-19, G=3-9

MACHINE TOOLS: Metal Cutting

Pilgrim-Harp Co .... G 440 249-4185
  Avon (G-957)
Pinnacle Precision Pdts LLC .... G 440 786-0248
  Bedford (G-1436)
Power Engineering LLC .... G 513 793-5800
  Cincinnati (G-4177)
Rafter Equipment Corporation .... E 440 572-3700
  Strongsville (G-17781)
Raymath Company .... C 937 335-1860
  Troy (G-18697)
Reliable Products Co Inc .... G 419 394-5854
  Saint Marys (G-16697)
Ridge Tool Company .... E 440 329-4737
  Elyria (G-9321)
Ridge Tool Company .... D 740 432-8782
  Cambridge (G-2455)
Ridge Tool Manufacturing Co .... A 440 323-5581
  Elyria (G-9322)
Rimrock Holdings Corporation .... E 614 471-5926
  Columbus (G-7395)
Robbins Company .... C 440 248-3303
  Solon (G-17224)
Rossi Machinery Services Inc .... G 419 281-4488
  Ashland (G-744)
Roto Tech Inc .... E 937 859-8503
  Dayton (G-8485)
Shumaker Racing Components .... E 419 238-0801
  Van Wert (G-19105)
Sinico Mtm US Inc .... G 216 264-8344
  Cleveland (G-6067)
Specialty Metals Processing .... E 330 656-2767
  Hudson (G-11076)
Stadco Inc .... E 937 878-0911
  Fairborn (G-9468)
STC International Co Ltd 561 308-6002
  Lebanon (G-11699)
Strouse Industries Inc .... G 440 257-2520
  Mentor (G-13595)
Sumitomo Elc Carbide Mfg Inc .... F 440 354-0600
  Grand River (G-10326)
Superion Inc .... E 937 374-0033
  Xenia (G-20793)
Supply Dynamics Inc .... E 513 965-2000
  Loveland (G-12238)
Swagelok Hy-Level Company .... C 440 238-1260
  Strongsville (G-17798)
Systematic Machine Corp .... G 440 877-9884
  North Royalton (G-15305)
Tooling Connection Inc 419 594-3339
  Oakwood (G-15475)
TSR Machinery Services Inc .... E 513 874-9697
  Fairfield (G-9570)
Tykma Inc .... D 877 318-9562
  Chillicothe (G-3230)
U S Alloy Die Corp .... F 216 749-9700
  Cleveland (G-6227)
Ultra-Met Company .... D 937 653-7133
  Urbana (G-19017)
United Grinding North Amer Inc .... D 937 859-1975
  Miamisburg (G-13730)
Updike Supply Company .... E 937 482-4000
  Huber Heights (G-11024)
Usm Acquisition Corporation .... D 440 975-8600
  Willoughby (G-20457)
Vulcan Tool Company .... G 937 253-6194
  Dayton (G-8581)
West Ohio Tool & Mfg LLC .... G 419 678-4745
  Saint Henry (G-16671)
West Ohio Tool Company .... F 937 842-6688
  Russells Point (G-16602)
Willow Tool & Machining Ltd .... F 440 572-2288
  Strongsville (G-17808)
Wonder Machine Services Inc .... E 440 937-7500
  Avon (G-975)
Zagar Inc .... E 216 731-0500
  Cleveland (G-6336)

MACHINE TOOLS: Metal Forming

Akron Specialized Products .... G 330 762-9269
  Akron (G-52)
American Laser and Machine LLC .... G 419 214-0880
  Toledo (G-18173)
Anderson & Vreeland Inc 419 636-5002
  Bryan (G-2264)
Barclay Machine Inc .... F 330 337-9541
  Salem (G-16719)
Barth Industries Co LP .... D 216 267-0531
  Cleveland (G-4793)
Brilex Industries Inc .... D 330 744-1114
  Youngstown (G-20858)

Brilex Industries Inc .... C 330 744-1114
  Youngstown (G-20859)
Dover Corporation .... F 513 696-1790
  Mason (G-12857)
E Systems Design & Automtn Inc .... G 419 443-0220
  Tiffin (G-18059)
Elliott Tool Technologies Ltd .... D 937 253-6133
  Dayton (G-8182)
Exito Manufacturing .... G 937 291-9871
  Beavercreek (G-1355)
F & G Tool and Die Co .... E 937 746-3658
  Franklin (G-9880)
First Tool Corp .... E 937 254-6197
  Dayton (G-8195)
Gem City Metal Tech LLC 937 252-8998
  Dayton (G-8220)
High Production Technology LLC .... G 419 599-1511
  Napoleon (G-14542)
Hill & Griffith Company 513 921-1075
  Cincinnati (G-3812)
Howmet Corporation .... E 757 825-7086
  Newburgh Heights (G-14939)
J and S Tool Incorporated .... E 216 676-8330
  Cleveland (G-5482)
Kay Capital Company .... G 216 531-1010
  Cleveland (G-5521)
Kiraly Tool and Die Inc .... F 330 744-5773
  Youngstown (G-20954)
Levan Enterprises Inc .... E 330 923-9797
  Stow (G-17601)
McNeil & Nrm Inc .... D 330 761-1855
  Akron (G-275)
Metal & Wire Products Company .... D 330 332-9448
  Salem (G-16760)
Meyer Machine Tool Company .... G 614 235-0039
  Columbus (G-7176)
Nidec Minster Corporation .... G 419 394-7504
  Saint Marys (G-16691)
Rafter Equipment Corporation .... E 440 572-3700
  Strongsville (G-17781)
Ready Technology Inc 937 228-8181
  Dayton (G-8465)
Ritime Incorporated .... F 330 273-3443
  Cleveland (G-5986)
Scotts Miracle-Gro Company .... B 937 644-0011
  Marysville (G-12810)
Semtorq Inc .... F 330 487-0600
  Twinsburg (G-18856)
Slade Gardner 440 355-8015
  Lagrange (G-11493)
Spencer Manufacturing Company .... D 330 648-2461
  Spencer (G-17306)
Standard Engineering Group Inc .... G 330 494-4300
  North Canton (G-15120)
Starkey Machinery Inc .... E 419 468-2560
  Galion (G-10157)
Stolle Machinery Company LLC .... C 937 497-5400
  Sidney (G-17082)
Taylor - Winfield Corporation .... D 330 259-8500
  Hubbard (G-11010)
TEC Design & Manufacturing Inc .... F 937 435-2147
  Dayton (G-8549)
Terminal Equipment Industries .... G 330 468-0322
  Northfield (G-15328)
Trucut Incorporated .... D 330 938-9806
  Sebring (G-16896)
Turner Machine Co .... F 330 332-5821
  Salem (G-16778)
Twist Inc .... C 937 675-9581
  Jamestown (G-11221)
Twist Inc .... E 937 675-9581
  Jamestown (G-11222)
Uhrichsville Carbide Inc .... F 740 922-9197
  Uhrichsville (G-18899)
Valley Tool & Die Inc .... D 440 237-0160
  North Royalton (G-15309)
Van Burens Welding & Machine .... G 740 787-2636
  Glenford (G-10273)
Vulcan Tool Company .... G 937 253-6194
  Dayton (G-8581)

MACHINERY & EQPT, AGRICULTURAL, WHOL: Farm Eqpt Parts/Splys

Schmidt Machine Company .... E 419 294-3814
  Upper Sandusky (G-18972)

MACHINERY & EQPT, AGRICULTURAL, WHOLESALE: Farm Implements

R L Parsons & Son Equipment Co .... G 614 879-7601
  West Jefferson (G-19927)

MACHINERY & EQPT, AGRICULTURAL, WHOLESALE: Hydroponic

Hawthorne Hydroponics LLC .... D 480 777-2000
  Marysville (G-12787)

MACHINERY & EQPT, AGRICULTURAL, WHOLESALE: Lawn & Garden

Johnson Tool Distributors .... G 740 653-6959
  Lancaster (G-11581)
Siteone Landscape Supply LLC .... G 330 220-8691
  Brunswick (G-2239)

MACHINERY & EQPT, AGRICULTURAL, WHOLESALE: Livestock Eqpt

Fort Recovery Equipment Inc .... E 419 375-1006
  Fort Recovery (G-9816)
RJR & Associates Inc .... G 419 237-2220
  Fayette (G-9636)

MACHINERY & EQPT, AGRICULTURAL, WHOLESALE: Tractors

Franklin Equipment LLC .... E 614 228-2014
  Groveport (G-10492)

MACHINERY & EQPT, INDL, WHOL: Controlling Instruments/Access

Russments Inc .... G 513 602-5035
  Cincinnati (G-4290)

MACHINERY & EQPT, INDL, WHOL: Environ Pollution Cntrl, Water

Samsco Corp .... F 216 400-8207
  Cleveland (G-6028)
X-3-5 LLC .... G 513 489-5477
  Cincinnati (G-4526)

MACHINERY & EQPT, INDL, WHOL: Meters, Consumption Registerng

Flow Line Options Corp .... G 330 331-7331
  Wadsworth (G-19242)
MA Flynn Associates LLC .... G 513 893-7873
  Hamilton (G-10584)

MACHINERY & EQPT, INDL, WHOLESALE: Cement Making

Spillman Company .... E 614 444-2184
  Columbus (G-7476)

MACHINERY & EQPT, INDL, WHOLESALE: Chemical Process

Aldrich Chemical .... D 937 859-1808
  Miamisburg (G-13638)

MACHINERY & EQPT, INDL, WHOLESALE: Conveyor Systems

Alba Manufacturing Inc .... D 513 874-0551
  Fairfield (G-9480)
Digilube Systems Inc .... F 937 748-2209
  Springboro (G-17325)
Logitech Inc .... E 614 871-2822
  Grove City (G-10441)
Midwest Conveyor Products Inc .... E 419 281-1235
  Ashland (G-725)
Mitsubishi Elc Automtn Inc .... G 937 492-3058
  Sidney (G-17054)
Pomacon Inc .... F 330 273-1576
  Brunswick (G-2226)

MACHINERY & EQPT, INDL, WHOLESALE: Cranes

De-Ko Inc .... G 440 951-2585
  Willoughby (G-20308)

PRODUCT SECTION

MACHINERY & EQPT, INDL, WHOLESALE: Robots

Expert Crane Inc .... E 216 451-9900
  Cleveland *(G-5209)*
Hiab USA Inc .... D 419 482-6000
  Perrysburg *(G-15961)*
Rnm Holdings Inc .... E 419 867-8712
  Holland *(G-10954)*
Rnm Holdings Inc .... F 614 444-5556
  Columbus *(G-7397)*
Terex Utilities Inc .... F 440 262-3200
  Brecksville *(G-2060)*
Venco Venturo Industries LLC .... E 513 772-8448
  Cincinnati *(G-4473)*

MACHINERY & EQPT, INDL, WHOLESALE: Engines & Parts, Diesel

Cummins Bridgeway Columbus LLC ..... D 614 771-1000
  Hilliard *(G-10822)*
Cummins Bridgeway Toledo LLC .... G 419 893-8711
  Maumee *(G-13084)*
Cummins Inc .... E 614 771-1000
  Hilliard *(G-10823)*
Industrial Parts Depot LLC .... G 440 237-9164
  North Royalton *(G-15278)*
Martin Diesel Inc .... E 419 782-9911
  Defiance *(G-8636)*
Western Branch Diesel Inc .... E 330 454-8800
  Canton *(G-2864)*

MACHINERY & EQPT, INDL, WHOLESALE: Engines, Gasoline

Graham Ford Power Products .... G 614 801-0049
  Columbus *(G-6965)*

MACHINERY & EQPT, INDL, WHOLESALE: Engs & Parts, Air-Cooled

Power Distributors LLC .... D 614 876-3533
  Columbus *(G-7334)*

MACHINERY & EQPT, INDL, WHOLESALE: Fans

National Tool & Equipment Inc .... F 330 629-8665
  Youngstown *(G-20973)*

MACHINERY & EQPT, INDL, WHOLESALE: Food Manufacturing

R and J Corporation .... E 440 871-6009
  Westlake *(G-20147)*

MACHINERY & EQPT, INDL, WHOLESALE: Heat Exchange

Gerow Equipment Company Inc .... G 216 383-8800
  Cleveland *(G-5319)*
Rayhaven Group Inc .... F 330 659-3183
  Richfield *(G-16484)*

MACHINERY & EQPT, INDL, WHOLESALE: Hydraulic Systems

Breaker Technology Inc .... E 440 248-7168
  Solon *(G-17120)*
Control Line Equipment Inc .... F 216 433-7766
  Cleveland *(G-5025)*
Eaton Corporation .... B 216 523-5000
  Beachwood *(G-1234)*
Eaton Corporation .... B 216 920-2000
  Cleveland *(G-5149)*
Hydra Air Equipment Inc .... G 330 274-2222
  Mantua *(G-12548)*
Hydraulic Parts Store Inc .... E 330 364-6667
  New Philadelphia *(G-14774)*
Hydro Supply Co .... F 740 454-3842
  Zanesville *(G-21147)*
Jay Dee Service Corporation .... G 330 425-1546
  Macedonia *(G-12307)*
Modern Design Stamping Div .... G 216 382-6318
  Cleveland *(G-5698)*
Ohio Hydraulics Inc .... E 513 771-2590
  Cincinnati *(G-4103)*
R & M Fluid Power Inc .... E 330 758-2766
  Youngstown *(G-21010)*
Robeck Fluid Power Co .... D 330 562-1140
  Aurora *(G-903)*
Rumpke Transportation Co LLC .... F 513 851-0122
  Cincinnati *(G-4288)*

System Seals Inc .... D 440 735-0200
  Cleveland *(G-6140)*

MACHINERY & EQPT, INDL, WHOLESALE: Indl Machine Parts

F & W Auto Supply .... G 419 445-3350
  Archbold *(G-644)*
Grt Utilicorp Inc .... E 330 264-8444
  Wooster *(G-20600)*
Retek Inc .... G 440 937-6282
  Avon *(G-963)*
Spectrum Mfg & Sls Inc .... G 614 486-3223
  Columbus *(G-7474)*
Transducers Direct Llc .... F 513 247-0601
  Cincinnati *(G-4431)*

MACHINERY & EQPT, INDL, WHOLESALE: Instruments & Cntrl Eqpt

Airgas .... G 330 345-1257
  Wooster *(G-20555)*
Fcx Performance Inc .... E 614 324-6050
  Columbus *(G-6916)*
Instrumentors Inc .... G 440 238-3430
  Strongsville *(G-17755)*
Prime Controls Inc .... G 937 435-8659
  Dayton *(G-8440)*
Process Automation Specialists .... G 330 247-1384
  Canal Fulton *(G-2489)*
South Shore Controls Inc .... E 440 259-2500
  Perry *(G-15913)*

MACHINERY & EQPT, INDL, WHOLESALE: Lift Trucks & Parts

Crown Equipment Corporation .... D 419 629-2311
  New Bremen *(G-14652)*
Fastener Industries Inc .... E 440 891-2031
  Berea *(G-1607)*
Joseph Industries Inc .... D 330 528-0091
  Streetsboro *(G-17680)*
Suspension Technology Inc .... F 330 458-3058
  Canton *(G-2831)*

MACHINERY & EQPT, INDL, WHOLESALE: Machine Tools & Access

AM Industrial Group LLC .... E 216 433-7171
  Brookpark *(G-2134)*
Clear Fold Door Inc .... G 440 735-1351
  Cleveland *(G-4942)*
Evolution Resources LLC .... G 937 438-2390
  Centerville *(G-3002)*
Imco Carbide Tool Inc .... D 419 661-6313
  Perrysburg *(G-15965)*
Interstate Tool Corporation .... E 216 671-1077
  Cleveland *(G-5471)*
J and S Tool Incorporated .... E 216 676-8330
  Cleveland *(G-5482)*
Jergens Inc .... C 216 486-5540
  Cleveland *(G-5495)*
Jett Industries Inc .... G 740 344-4140
  Newark *(G-14889)*
Lees Machinery Inc .... G 440 259-2222
  Perry *(G-15907)*
Neff Machinery and Supplies .... E 740 454-0128
  Zanesville *(G-21159)*
Tool Systems Inc .... F 440 461-6363
  Cleveland *(G-6182)*
Wolf Machine Company .... C 513 791-5194
  Blue Ash *(G-1874)*

MACHINERY & EQPT, INDL, WHOLESALE: Machine Tools & Metalwork

Armeton US Co .... F 419 660-9296
  Norwalk *(G-15381)*
Friess Equipment Inc .... G 330 945-9440
  Akron *(G-178)*
Gbi Cincinnati Inc .... G 513 841-8684
  Cincinnati *(G-3729)*
Northern Machine Tool Co .... E 216 961-0444
  Cleveland *(G-5780)*
Tool Service Co Inc .... G 937 254-4000
  Dayton *(G-7992)*
Tribus Innovations LLC .... E 509 992-4743
  Englewood *(G-9379)*

MACHINERY & EQPT, INDL, WHOLESALE: Measure/Test, Electric

Automation Metrology Intl LLC .... E 440 354-6436
  Mentor *(G-13395)*

MACHINERY & EQPT, INDL, WHOLESALE: Metal Refining

A & B Deburring Company .... F 513 723-0444
  Cincinnati *(G-3274)*
Stanley Industries Inc .... E 216 475-4000
  Cleveland *(G-6094)*

MACHINERY & EQPT, INDL, WHOLESALE: Noise Control

Tech Products Corporation .... E 937 438-1100
  Miamisburg *(G-13723)*

MACHINERY & EQPT, INDL, WHOLESALE: Packaging

Alfons Haar Inc .... E 937 560-2031
  Springboro *(G-17321)*
Bollin & Sons Inc .... E 419 693-6573
  Toledo *(G-18210)*
Millwood Inc .... F 513 860-4567
  West Chester *(G-19744)*
Millwood Inc .... F 404 629-4811
  Vienna *(G-19204)*

MACHINERY & EQPT, INDL, WHOLESALE: Paint Spray

Kecamm LLC .... G 330 527-2918
  Garrettsville *(G-10194)*

MACHINERY & EQPT, INDL, WHOLESALE: Paper Manufacturing

Oak View Enterprises Inc .... E 513 860-4446
  Bucyrus *(G-2340)*

MACHINERY & EQPT, INDL, WHOLESALE: Petroleum Industry

T JS Oil & Gas Inc .... G 740 623-0192
  Coshocton *(G-7754)*

MACHINERY & EQPT, INDL, WHOLESALE: Plastic Prdts Machinery

Grit Guard Inc .... G 937 592-9003
  Bellefontaine *(G-1516)*
Maintenance Repair Supply Inc .... E 740 922-3006
  Midvale *(G-13980)*

MACHINERY & EQPT, INDL, WHOLESALE: Pneumatic Tools

Belle Center Air Tool Co Inc .... G 937 464-7474
  Belle Center *(G-1497)*
Schenck Process LLC .... F 513 576-9200
  Chagrin Falls *(G-3074)*

MACHINERY & EQPT, INDL, WHOLESALE: Processing & Packaging

Esperia Holdings LLC .... G 714 249-7888
  Oak Harbor *(G-15444)*
Kingsly Compression Inc .... G 740 439-0772
  Cambridge *(G-2445)*

MACHINERY & EQPT, INDL, WHOLESALE: Pulverizing

Maag Automatik Inc .... E 330 677-2225
  Kent *(G-11347)*

MACHINERY & EQPT, INDL, WHOLESALE: Robots

Kc Robotics Inc .... F 513 860-4442
  West Chester *(G-19729)*
Programmable Control Service .... F 740 927-0744
  Pataskala *(G-15838)*
Remtec Engineering .... E 513 860-4299
  Mason *(G-12932)*

MACHINERY & EQPT, INDL, WHOLESALE: Robots

Rixan Associates Inc .... E 937 438-3005
  Dayton *(G-8479)*
Versatile Automation Tech Ltd .... G 330 220-2600
  Brunswick *(G-2248)*

MACHINERY & EQPT, INDL, WHOLESALE: Safety Eqpt

A & A Safety Inc .... F 937 567-9781
  Beavercreek *(G-1348)*
A & A Safety Inc .... E 513 943-6100
  Amelia *(G-527)*
American Rescue Technology .... F 937 293-6240
  Dayton *(G-8027)*
Cintas Corporation .... A 513 459-1200
  Cincinnati *(G-3518)*
Cintas Corporation .... D 513 631-5750
  Cincinnati *(G-3519)*
D M V Supply Corporation .... G 330 847-0450
  Warren *(G-19393)*
GSE Production and Support LLC .... G 972 329-2646
  Swanton *(G-17914)*
Impact Products LLC .... C 419 841-2891
  Toledo *(G-18342)*
Paul Peterson Company .... E 614 486-4375
  Columbus *(G-7299)*

MACHINERY & EQPT, INDL, WHOLESALE: Tool & Die Makers

Ready Technology Inc .... F 937 228-8181
  Dayton *(G-8465)*

MACHINERY & EQPT, INDL, WHOLESALE: Trailers, Indl

Martin Allen Trailer LLC .... G 330 942-0217
  Brunswick *(G-2220)*

MACHINERY & EQPT, INDL, WHOLESALE: Woodworking

Ryanworks Inc .... F 937 438-1282
  Dayton *(G-8488)*

MACHINERY & EQPT, TEXTILE: Fabric Forming

Leesburg Looms Incorporated .... G 419 238-2738
  Van Wert *(G-19099)*

MACHINERY & EQPT, WHOLESALE: Concrete Processing

McNeilus Truck and Mfg Inc .... G 614 868-0760
  Gahanna *(G-10089)*
Mini Mix Inc .... F 513 353-3811
  Cleves *(G-6371)*

MACHINERY & EQPT, WHOLESALE: Construction & Mining, Ladders

American Scaffolding Inc .... G 216 524-7733
  Cleveland *(G-4697)*
Bauer Corporation .... E 800 321-4760
  Wooster *(G-20569)*

MACHINERY & EQPT, WHOLESALE: Construction, General

Baswa Acoustics North Amer LLC ... F 216 475-7197
  Bedford *(G-1388)*
Dayton Tractor & Crane .... G 937 317-5014
  Xenia *(G-20765)*
Npk Construction Equipment Inc ..... D 440 232-7900
  Bedford *(G-1432)*
Thirion Brothers Eqp Co LLC .... G 440 357-8004
  Painesville *(G-15790)*
West Equipment Company Inc .... F 419 698-1601
  Toledo *(G-18597)*

MACHINERY & EQPT, WHOLESALE: Contractors Materials

Carroll Distrg & Cnstr Sup Inc .... G 513 422-3467
  Middletown *(G-13890)*
Carroll Distrg & Cnstr Sup Inc .... G 614 564-9799
  Columbus *(G-6747)*
Cincinnati Gutter Supply Inc .... G 513 825-0500
  West Chester *(G-19672)*

Johnston-Morehouse-Dickey Co ..... G 614 866-0452
  Columbus *(G-7075)*

MACHINERY & EQPT, WHOLESALE: Logging & Forestry

L&L Excavating & Land Clearing ..... G 740 682-7823
  Oak Hill *(G-15454)*

MACHINERY & EQPT, WHOLESALE: Masonry

EZ Grout Corporation Inc .... E 740 962-2024
  Malta *(G-12382)*

MACHINERY & EQPT, WHOLESALE: Oil Field Eqpt

Belden & Blake Corporation .... E 330 602-5551
  Dover *(G-8808)*
Global Oilfield Services LLC .... G 419 756-8027
  Mansfield *(G-12446)*
Petrox Inc .... F 330 653-5526
  Streetsboro *(G-17688)*

MACHINERY & EQPT, WHOLESALE: Road Construction & Maintenance

Terry Asphalt Materials Inc .... E 513 874-6192
  Hamilton *(G-10609)*

MACHINERY & EQPT: Electroplating

Corrotec Inc .... E 937 325-3585
  Springfield *(G-17379)*
Liquid Development Company .... G 216 641-9366
  Independence *(G-11141)*
Universal Rack & Equipment Co ..... E 330 963-6776
  Twinsburg *(G-18870)*

MACHINERY & EQPT: Farm

American Baler Co .... D 419 483-5790
  Bellevue *(G-1529)*
Baker Built Products Inc .... G 419 965-2646
  Ohio City *(G-15514)*
Beth Otto Independent Case Exa .... G 513 868-0484
  Fairfield *(G-9484)*
Buckeye Tractor Company Corp ..... G 419 659-2162
  Columbus Grove *(G-7631)*
C & S Turf Care Equipment Inc .... F 330 966-4511
  North Canton *(G-15074)*
Cailin Dev Ltd Lblty Co .... F 216 408-6261
  Cleveland *(G-4862)*
Consolidated Casework Inc .... G 330 618-6951
  Valley City *(G-19033)*
Country Manufacturing Inc .... F 740 694-9926
  Fredericktown *(G-9964)*
Creamer Metal Products .... E 740 852-1752
  London *(G-12056)*
Empire Plow Company Inc .... E 216 641-2290
  Cleveland *(G-5175)*
Field Gymmy Inc .... G 419 538-6511
  Glandorf *(G-10269)*
Garber Co .... G 937 462-8730
  South Charleston *(G-17272)*
H & S Company Inc .... F 419 394-4444
  Celina *(G-2965)*
Intertec Corporation .... B 419 537-9711
  Toledo *(G-18350)*
J & M Manufacturing Co Inc .... C 419 375-2376
  Fort Recovery *(G-9822)*
Komar Industries Inc .... E 614 836-2366
  Groveport *(G-10497)*
Koster Crop Tester Inc .... G 330 220-2116
  Brunswick *(G-2217)*
Kuhns Mfg Llc .... G 440 693-4630
  North Bloomfield *(G-15065)*
Ley Industries Inc .... G 419 238-6742
  Van Wert *(G-19100)*
Liebrecht Manufacturing LLC .... F 419 596-3501
  Continental *(G-7667)*
Motrin Corporation .... G 740 439-2725
  Cambridge *(G-2450)*
Ntech Industries Inc .... F 707 467-3747
  Dayton *(G-8389)*
Pioneer Equipment Company .... F 330 857-6340
  Dalton *(G-7951)*
Safe-Grain Inc .... G 513 398-2500
  Wapakoneta *(G-19352)*
Stephens Pipe & Steel LLC .... C 740 869-2257
  Mount Sterling *(G-14465)*

Universal Equipment Mfg .... G 614 586-1780
  Columbus *(G-7560)*
Unverferth Mfg Co Inc .... C 419 532-3121
  Kalida *(G-11282)*
Unverferth Mfg Co Inc .... D 419 695-2060
  Delphos *(G-8761)*
Warren Zachman Contracting .... G 740 389-4503
  Marion *(G-12747)*
Woodbury Welding Inc .... G 937 968-3573
  Union City *(G-18906)*
Yoder & Frey Inc .... E 419 445-2070
  Archbold *(G-674)*

MACHINERY & EQPT: Gas Producers, Generators/Other Rltd Eqpt

Applied Marketing Services .... E 440 716-9962
  Westlake *(G-20098)*
Stateline Power Corp .... F 937 547-1006
  Greenville *(G-10397)*
Winston Oil Co Inc .... G 740 373-9664
  Marietta *(G-12689)*

MACHINERY & EQPT: Liquid Automation

Dosmatic USA Inc .... F 972 245-9765
  Cincinnati *(G-3604)*
Fluid Automation Inc .... E 248 912-1970
  North Canton *(G-15084)*
Laureate Machine & Automtn LLC ... G 419 615-4601
  Leipsic *(G-11728)*
National Oilwell Varco Inc .... G 978 687-0101
  Dayton *(G-8376)*
Nutro Corporation .... D 440 572-3800
  Strongsville *(G-17772)*

MACHINERY & EQPT: Metal Finishing, Plating Etc

Broco Products Inc .... G 216 531-0880
  Cleveland *(G-4839)*
Burton Metal Finishing Inc .... E 614 252-9523
  Columbus *(G-6713)*
Conforming Matrix Corporation ...... E 419 729-3777
  Toledo *(G-18238)*
Fanuc America Corporation .... E 513 754-2400
  Mason *(G-12870)*
Lange Equipment .... G 440 953-1621
  Eastlake *(G-9120)*
Luke Engineering & Mfg Corp .... E 330 335-1501
  Wadsworth *(G-19252)*
Silver Tool Inc .... E 937 865-0012
  Miamisburg *(G-13717)*
Tks Industrial Company .... D 614 444-5602
  Columbus *(G-7531)*
Tom Richards Inc .... C 440 974-1300
  Mentor *(G-13607)*

MACHINERY & EQPT: Petroleum Refinery

Cantrell Rfinery Sls Trnsp Inc .... F 937 695-0318
  Winchester *(G-20519)*
Service Station Equipment Co .... F 216 431-6100
  Cleveland *(G-6045)*
Wolfe Oil Company LLC .... G 513 732-6220
  Williamsburg *(G-20257)*
Zook Enterprises LLC .... E 440 543-1010
  Chagrin Falls *(G-3093)*

MACHINERY & EQPT: Silver Recovery

Hess Technologies Inc .... G 513 228-0909
  Lebanon *(G-11662)*

MACHINERY & EQPT: Smelting & Refining

High Temperature Systems Inc ...... G 440 543-8271
  Chagrin Falls *(G-3049)*

MACHINERY & EQPT: Vibratory Parts Handling Eqpt

Stainless Automation .... G 216 961-4550
  Cleveland *(G-6090)*

MACHINERY BASES

Blue Chip Machine & Tool Ltd .... G 419 626-9559
  Sandusky *(G-16797)*
COW Industries Inc .... E 614 443-6537
  Columbus *(G-6831)*

G & M Metal Products Inc..................G........ 513 863-3353
 Hamilton *(G-10561)*
Jaguar Medical Supplies Inc...............G........ 440 263-2780
 North Royalton *(G-15279)*
Johnson Machining Services LLC ....G........ 937 866-4744
 Miamisburg *(G-13682)*
Kard Welding Inc...............................E........ 419 628-2598
 Minster *(G-14218)*
Labcraft Inc.......................................E........ 419 878-4400
 Waterville *(G-19500)*
Mansfield Welding Services LLC..........G........ 419 594-2738
 Oakwood *(G-15471)*

MACHINERY, CALCULATING: Calculators & Adding

Ganymede Technologies Corp ....G........ 419 562-5522
 Bucyrus *(G-2330)*

MACHINERY, COMMERCIAL LAUNDRY & Drycleaning: Ironers

Ellis Laundry & Linen Supply ....G........ 330 339-4941
 New Philadelphia *(G-14767)*

MACHINERY, COMMERCIAL LAUNDRY: Dryers, Incl Coin-Operated

Husqvarna US Holding Inc..................D........ 216 898-1800
 Cleveland *(G-5427)*
Linen Care Plus Inc............................F........ 614 224-1791
 Columbus *(G-7131)*

MACHINERY, EQPT & SUPPLIES: Parking Facility

Amano Cincinnati Incorporated ....D........ 513 697-9000
 Loveland *(G-12176)*
City of Cleveland................................G........ 216 664-2711
 Cleveland *(G-4931)*
Tiba LLC..E........ 614 328-2040
 Columbus *(G-7528)*

MACHINERY, FOOD PRDTS: Beverage

Mojonnier Usa LLC ....G........ 844 665-6664
 Streetsboro *(G-17684)*

MACHINERY, FOOD PRDTS: Choppers, Commercial

Biro Manufacturing Company...............D........ 419 798-4451
 Marblehead *(G-12584)*

MACHINERY, FOOD PRDTS: Cutting, Chopping, Grinding, Mixing

Lem Products Holding LLC..................E........ 513 202-1188
 West Chester *(G-19736)*

MACHINERY, FOOD PRDTS: Food Processing, Smokers

Frost Engineering Inc.........................E........ 513 541-6330
 Cincinnati *(G-3715)*

MACHINERY, FOOD PRDTS: Mixers, Commercial

Arbor Foods Inc..................................E........ 419 698-4442
 Toledo *(G-18188)*
Fred D Pfening Company ....E........ 614 294-5361
 Columbus *(G-6938)*

MACHINERY, FOOD PRDTS: Presses, Cheese, Beet, Cider & Sugar

French Oil Mill Machinery Co................D........ 937 773-3420
 Piqua *(G-16117)*

MACHINERY, FOOD PRDTS: Processing, Poultry

Prime Equipment Group Inc ....D........ 614 253-8590
 Columbus *(G-7347)*

MACHINERY, FOOD PRDTS: Slicers, Commercial

C M Slicechief Co...............................G........ 419 241-7647
 Toledo *(G-18220)*
Kasel Engineering LLC........................G........ 937 854-8875
 Trotwood *(G-18629)*

MACHINERY, LUBRICATION: Automatic

Total Lubrication MGT Co ....E........ 888 478-6996
 Canton *(G-2843)*

MACHINERY, MAILING: Mailing

Pitney Bowes Inc................................G........ 216 351-2598
 Cleveland *(G-5880)*

MACHINERY, MAILING: Postage Meters

Pitney Bowes Inc................................D........ 203 426-7025
 Brecksville *(G-2054)*
Pitney Bowes Inc................................D........ 740 374-5535
 Marietta *(G-12655)*

MACHINERY, METALWORKING: Assembly, Including Robotic

Added Edge Assembly Inc...................F........ 216 464-4305
 Cleveland *(G-4616)*
Automated Machinery Solutions ....F........ 419 727-1772
 Toledo *(G-18194)*
Axatronics LLC...................................G........ 513 239-5898
 Loveland *(G-12178)*
Combined Tech Group Inc ....E........ 937 274-4866
 Dayton *(G-8098)*
Flexomation LLC................................F........ 513 825-0555
 Cincinnati *(G-3693)*
Generic Systems Inc..........................F........ 419 841-8460
 Holland *(G-10932)*
Hunter Defense Tech Inc ....E........ 216 438-6111
 Solon *(G-17164)*
Omega Automation Inc.......................D........ 937 890-2350
 Dayton *(G-8402)*
Omega International Inc.....................F........ 937 890-2350
 Dayton *(G-8403)*
Peco Holdings Corp............................F........ 937 667-4451
 Tipp City *(G-18126)*
Precision Metal Products Inc...............F........ 216 447-1900
 Cleveland *(G-5911)*
Process Equipment Co Tipp City ....D........ 937 667-4451
 Tipp City *(G-18128)*
Richard A Limbacher..........................G........ 330 897-4515
 Stone Creek *(G-17564)*
Riverside Mch & Automtn Inc ....G........ 419 855-8308
 Walbridge *(G-19299)*
Scott Systems Intl Inc.........................F........ 740 383-8383
 Marion *(G-12733)*
Semtorq Inc.......................................F........ 330 487-0600
 Twinsburg *(G-18856)*

MACHINERY, METALWORKING: Coil Winding, For Springs

Armature Coil Equipment Inc ....F........ 216 267-6366
 Cleveland *(G-4734)*
Standard Car Truck Company ....D........ 740 775-6450
 Chillicothe *(G-3223)*

MACHINERY, METALWORKING: Coiling

Formtek Inc..D........ 216 292-4460
 Cleveland *(G-5264)*
Guild International Inc........................E........ 440 232-5887
 Bedford *(G-1408)*
Kent Corporation ....E........ 440 582-3400
 North Royalton *(G-15280)*
Perfecto Industries Inc.......................E........ 937 778-1900
 Piqua *(G-16149)*
Pipe Coil Technology Inc ....F........ 330 256-6070
 Burbank *(G-2353)*

MACHINERY, METALWORKING: Cutting & Slitting

Ged Holdings Inc...............................C........ 330 963-5401
 Twinsburg *(G-18780)*

MACHINERY, METALWORKING: Cutting-Up Lines

Automatic Feed Co.............................D........ 419 592-0050
 Napoleon *(G-14532)*

MACHINERY, METALWORKING: Drawing

Steinbarger Precision Cnc Inc.............G........ 937 376-0322
 Xenia *(G-20792)*

MACHINERY, METALWORKING: Rotary Slitters, Metalworking

Portage Machine Concepts Inc............F........ 330 628-2343
 Akron *(G-324)*

MACHINERY, METALWORKING: Screw Driving

Helix Linear Technologies Inc ....E........ 216 485-2263
 Beachwood *(G-1240)*

MACHINERY, OFFICE: Paper Handling

Symatic Inc..E........ 330 225-1510
 Brunswick *(G-2243)*

MACHINERY, OFFICE: Perforators

Central Business Products Inc............G........ 513 385-5899
 Cincinnati *(G-3455)*

MACHINERY, OFFICE: Time Clocks & Time Recording Devices

Advanced Time Systems.....................G........ 440 466-2689
 Geneva *(G-10212)*
Industrial Electronic Service................F........ 937 746-9750
 Carlisle *(G-2893)*
Parallel Solutions ....G........ 440 498-9920
 Cleveland *(G-5838)*

MACHINERY, PACKAGING: Aerating, Beverages

Beckermills Inc...................................G........ 419 738-3450
 Wapakoneta *(G-19324)*

MACHINERY, PACKAGING: Canning, Food

Dayton Systems Group Inc..................D........ 937 885-5665
 Miamisburg *(G-13657)*
Scanacon Incorporated ....G........ 330 877-7600
 Hartville *(G-10704)*

MACHINERY, PACKAGING: Packing & Wrapping

Able Tool Corporation ....E........ 513 733-8989
 Cincinnati *(G-3288)*
Audion Automation Ltd ....E........ 216 267-1911
 Berea *(G-1591)*
Labeldata..G........ 614 891-5858
 Westerville *(G-20063)*

MACHINERY, PACKAGING: Vacuum

Precision Replacement LLC ....G........ 330 908-0410
 Macedonia *(G-12319)*

MACHINERY, PACKAGING: Wrapping

Heat Seal LLC....................................C........ 216 341-2022
 Cleveland *(G-5386)*
Samuel Strapping Systems Inc ....D........ 740 522-2500
 Heath *(G-10731)*

MACHINERY, PAPER INDUSTRY: Converting, Die Cutting & Stampng

Erd Specialty Graphics Inc ....G........ 419 242-9545
 Toledo *(G-18283)*
Mc Kinley Machinery Inc ....E........ 440 937-6300
 Avon *(G-954)*
Nilpeter Usa Inc.................................C........ 513 489-4400
 Cincinnati *(G-4080)*

MACHINERY, PAPER INDUSTRY: Fourdrinier

Klockner Pentaplast Amer Inc ....G........ 937 743-8040
 Franklin *(G-9893)*

MACHINERY, PAPER INDUSTRY: Paper Mill, Plating, Etc

MACHINERY, PAPER INDUSTRY: Paper Mill, Plating, Etc
Press Technology & Mfg Inc .... G 937 327-0755
  Springfield *(G-17476)*

MACHINERY, PAPER INDUSTRY: Pulp Mill
Fluid Quip Inc .... E 937 324-0352
  Springfield *(G-17404)*
French Oil Mill Machinery Co .... D 937 773-3420
  Piqua *(G-16117)*

MACHINERY, PAPER INDUSTRY: Sandpaper
Kadant Black Clawson Inc .... D 251 653-8558
  Lebanon *(G-11666)*
Sso Inc .... F 440 235-3500
  Olmsted Twp *(G-15536)*

MACHINERY, PRINTING TRADES: Mats, Advertising & Newspaper
Moments To Remember USA LLC .... G 330 830-0839
  Massillon *(G-13027)*

MACHINERY, PRINTING TRADES: Plates
E C Shaw Co .... E 513 721-6334
  Cincinnati *(G-3616)*
Flexoplate Inc .... E 513 489-0433
  Blue Ash *(G-1776)*
Flexotech Graphics Inc .... F 330 929-4743
  Stow *(G-17588)*
Klebaum Machinery Inc .... G 330 455-2046
  Canton *(G-2724)*

MACHINERY, PRINTING TRADES: Plates, Engravers' Metal
Hays Fabricating & Welding .... E 937 325-0031
  Springfield *(G-17412)*

MACHINERY, PRINTING TRADES: Plates, Offset
Great Lakes Graphics Inc .... G 216 391-0077
  Cleveland *(G-5345)*

MACHINERY, PRINTING TRADES: Type Casting, Founding/Melting
Tinker Omega Manufacturing LLC ...... E 937 322-2272
  Springfield *(G-17506)*

MACHINERY, TEXTILE: Braiding
Karg Corporation .... F 330 633-4916
  Tallmadge *(G-17988)*
Oma USA Inc .... G 330 487-0602
  Twinsburg *(G-18824)*
Simon De Young Corporation .... G 440 834-3000
  Middlefield *(G-13853)*

MACHINERY, TEXTILE: Embroidery
Barudan America Inc .... F 440 248-8770
  Solon *(G-17113)*
Protofab Manufacturing Inc .... G 937 849-4983
  Medway *(G-13366)*
Truck Stop Embroidery .... G 419 257-2860
  North Baltimore *(G-15048)*
Wayne Sporting Goods .... G 937 236-6665
  Dayton *(G-8586)*

MACHINERY, TEXTILE: Printing
Alley Cat Designs Inc .... G 937 291-8803
  Dayton *(G-8017)*

MACHINERY, TEXTILE: Silk Screens
Impact Sports Wear Inc .... G 513 922-7406
  North Bend *(G-15051)*
R Sportswear LLC .... G 937 748-3507
  Springboro *(G-17350)*
Schilling Graphics Inc .... E 419 468-1037
  Galion *(G-10154)*
Solid Light Company Inc .... E 740 548-1219
  Lewis Center *(G-11781)*

MACHINERY, WOODWORKING: Cabinet Makers'
Closettec of North East Ohio .... G 216 464-0042
  Bedford *(G-1396)*

MACHINERY, WOODWORKING: Furniture Makers
ITR Manufacturing LLC .... F 419 763-1493
  Saint Henry *(G-16664)*
Kyocera Senco Indus Tls Inc .... F 800 543-4596
  Cincinnati *(G-3256)*

MACHINERY, WOODWORKING: Lathes, Wood Turning Includes Access
Dayton Hawker Corporation .... F 937 293-8147
  Dayton *(G-8135)*

MACHINERY, WOODWORKING: Pattern Makers'
Boko Patterns Models & Molds .... G 937 426-9667
  Beavercreek *(G-1352)*
Seilkop Industries Inc .... E 513 761-1035
  Cincinnati *(G-4316)*

MACHINERY/EQPT, INDL, WHOL: Cleaning, High Press, Sand/Steam
Powerclean Equipment Company .... F 513 202-0001
  Cleves *(G-6374)*

MACHINERY/EQPT, INDL, WHOL: Machinist Precision Measrng Tool
Bilz Vibration Technology Inc .... F 330 468-2459
  Macedonia *(G-12279)*

MACHINERY: Ammunition & Explosives Loading
Emco Usa LLC .... F 740 588-1722
  Zanesville *(G-21133)*
Military Resources LLC .... E 330 263-1040
  Wooster *(G-20626)*
Military Resources LLC .... D 330 309-9970
  Wooster *(G-20627)*

MACHINERY: Assembly, Exc Metalworking
Automation Tooling Systems .... C 614 781-8063
  Lewis Center *(G-11749)*
Gem City Engineering Co .... C 937 223-5544
  Dayton *(G-8219)*
Innovative Assembly Svcs LLC .... F 419 399-3886
  Paulding *(G-15861)*
Joseph B Stinson Co .... G 419 334-4151
  Fremont *(G-10030)*
Mac Ltt Inc .... C 330 474-3795
  Kent *(G-11348)*
Phoenix Safety Outfitters LLC .... G 614 361-0544
  Springfield *(G-17471)*
Remtec Corp .... G 513 860-4299
  Mason *(G-12931)*
Remtec Engineering .... E 513 860-4299
  Mason *(G-12932)*
Selecteon Corporation .... E 614 710-1132
  Columbus *(G-7437)*
Steel & Alloy Utility Pdts Inc .... E 330 530-2220
  Mc Donald *(G-13202)*
Steven Douglas Corp .... E 440 564-5200
  Newbury *(G-14967)*
TEC Design and Mfg LLC .... G 216 362-8962
  Cleveland *(G-6152)*

MACHINERY: Automobile Garage, Frame Straighteners
Halifax Industries Inc .... G 216 990-8951
  Hudson *(G-11050)*

MACHINERY: Automotive Maintenance
Automated Mfg Solutions Inc .... F 440 878-3711
  Strongsville *(G-17716)*
Camton Mechanical Inc .... G 614 864-7620
  Columbus *(G-6727)*
Handle Light Inc .... G 330 772-8901
  Kinsman *(G-11464)*

I T W Automotive Finishing .... G 419 470-2000
  Toledo *(G-18338)*
Johndow Industries Inc .... E 330 753-6895
  Barberton *(G-1078)*
Lube Depot .... G 330 758-0570
  Youngstown *(G-20961)*
Micro-Pise Msrment Systems LLC ...... C 330 541-9100
  Streetsboro *(G-17681)*
Ratech .... G 513 742-2111
  Cincinnati *(G-4249)*
Segna Inc .... F 937 335-6700
  Troy *(G-18704)*
Stevens Auto Glaze and SEC LL .... G 440 953-2900
  Eastlake *(G-9131)*

MACHINERY: Automotive Related
Autotool Inc .... E 614 733-0222
  Plain City *(G-16173)*
Beam Machines Inc .... G 513 745-4510
  Blue Ash *(G-1732)*
Buddy Backyard Inc .... G 330 393-9353
  Warren *(G-19380)*
Customers Car Care Center .... G 419 841-6646
  Toledo *(G-18247)*
Dengensha America Corporation .... F 440 439-8081
  Bedford *(G-1399)*
Designetics Inc .... D 419 866-0700
  Holland *(G-10925)*
Freeman Schwabe Machinery LLC ...... E 513 947-2888
  Batavia *(G-1148)*
Ganzcorp Investments Inc .... G 330 963-5400
  Twinsburg *(G-18778)*
Gary Compton .... G 937 339-6829
  Troy *(G-18660)*
M W Solutions LLC .... F 419 782-1611
  Defiance *(G-8633)*
Manufctring Bus Dev Sltons LLC .... D 419 294-1313
  Findlay *(G-9717)*
Modular Assembly Innovations .... G 614 389-4860
  Dublin *(G-8947)*
Process Development Corp .... E 937 890-3388
  Dayton *(G-8445)*
RP Gatta Inc .... G 330 562-2288
  Aurora *(G-905)*
Steelastic Company LLC .... E 330 633-0505
  Cuyahoga Falls *(G-7923)*
Wauseon Machine & Mfg Inc .... D 419 337-0940
  Wauseon *(G-19537)*

MACHINERY: Binding
Baumfolder Corporation .... E 937 492-1281
  Sidney *(G-17019)*
Collated Products Corp .... F 440 946-1950
  Chardon *(G-3106)*

MACHINERY: Blasting, Electrical
Dan-Mar Company Inc .... E 419 660-8830
  Norwalk *(G-15386)*
Waterloo Manufacturing Co Inc .... G 330 947-2917
  Atwater *(G-865)*

MACHINERY: Bottle Washing & Sterilzing
S A Langmack Company .... F 216 541-0500
  Cleveland *(G-6021)*

MACHINERY: Bottling & Canning
OKL Can Line Inc .... E 513 825-1655
  Cincinnati *(G-4108)*

MACHINERY: Brewery & Malting
Ford Piping and Brewry Svc LLC .... G 614 284-2409
  Columbus *(G-6929)*
Listermann Mfg Co Inc .... G 513 731-1130
  Cincinnati *(G-3946)*
Railroad Brewing Company .... G 440 723-8234
  Avon *(G-961)*

MACHINERY: Bridge Or Gate, Hydraulic
Ogden Hydraulics LLC .... G 419 686-1108
  Portage *(G-16272)*

MACHINERY: Centrifugal
Pneumatic Scale Corporation .... C 330 923-0491
  Cuyahoga Falls *(G-7905)*

MACHINERY: Clay Working & Tempering

Starkey Machinery Inc ....E 419 468-2560
Galion *(G-10157)*

MACHINERY: Concrete Prdts

Tegratek ....G 513 742-5100
Cincinnati *(G-4411)*

MACHINERY: Construction

Allied Consolidated Industries ....C 330 744-0808
Youngstown *(G-20841)*
Allied Construction Pdts LLC ....E 216 431-2600
Cleveland *(G-4672)*
Altec Industries ....G 419 289-6066
Ashland *(G-676)*
Ballinger Industries Inc ....F 419 422-4533
Findlay *(G-9655)*
Basetek LLC ....F 877 712-2273
Middlefield *(G-13779)*
Belden Brick Company ....E 330 852-2411
Sugarcreek *(G-17842)*
Caterpillar Inc ....D 614 834-2400
Canal Winchester *(G-2501)*
Cityscapes International Inc ....C 614 850-2540
Hilliard *(G-10816)*
Coe Manufacturing Company ....D 440 352-9381
Painesville *(G-15722)*
Concrete Cnstr McHy Co LLC ....G 330 638-1515
Cortland *(G-7705)*
Concrete Leveling Systems Inc ....G 330 966-8120
Canton *(G-2634)*
Connor Electric Inc ....G 513 932-5798
Lebanon *(G-11643)*
Construction Polymers Co ....G 440 591-9018
Chagrin Falls *(G-3041)*
Crane Pro Services ....G 937 525-5555
Springfield *(G-17380)*
Custom Machining Solutions LLC ....G 330 221-1523
Rootstown *(G-16567)*
CW Machine Worx Ltd ....F 740 654-5304
Carroll *(G-2902)*
Dandy Products Inc ....G 800 591-2284
Mount Vernon *(G-14477)*
Desco Corporation ....G 614 888-8855
New Albany *(G-14622)*
Dover Corporation ....F 513 696-1790
Mason *(G-12857)*
Dragon Products LLC ....E 330 345-3968
Wooster *(G-20586)*
Dynamic Plastics Inc ....G 937 437-7261
New Paris *(G-14753)*
E R Advanced Ceramics Inc ....E 330 426-9433
East Palestine *(G-9077)*
E Z Grout Corporation ....E 740 749-3512
Malta *(G-12381)*
Eagle Crusher Co Inc ....C 419 468-2288
Galion *(G-10135)*
Field Gymmy Inc ....G 419 538-6511
Glandorf *(G-10269)*
Fives St Corp ....E 234 217-9070
Wadsworth *(G-19241)*
Gibson Machinery LLC ....E 440 439-4000
Cleveland *(G-5321)*
Gradall Industries Inc ....C 330 339-2211
New Philadelphia *(G-14773)*
Grand Harbor Yacht Sales & Svc ....G 440 442-2919
Cleveland *(G-5339)*
Grasan Equipment Company Inc ....D 419 526-4440
Mansfield *(G-12452)*
Great Lakes Machine and Tool ....G 419 836-2346
Curtice *(G-7825)*
Harsco Corporation ....E 740 387-1150
Marion *(G-12710)*
Howard & Blake Excavating LLC ....G 740 701-7938
Richmond Dale *(G-16499)*
Indy Eqp Independence Recycl ....C 216 524-0999
Independence *(G-11136)*
Jbw Systems Inc ....F 614 882-5008
Westerville *(G-20000)*
Jlg Industries Inc ....C 330 684-0132
Orrville *(G-15598)*
Jlg Industries Inc ....C 330 684-0200
Orrville *(G-15599)*
Kaffenbarger Truck Eqp Co ....E 513 772-6800
Cincinnati *(G-3892)*
Klumm Bros ....E 419 829-3166
Holland *(G-10942)*
Komar Industries Inc ....E 614 836-2366
Groveport *(G-10497)*
Kubota Tractor Corporation ....F 614 835-3800
Groveport *(G-10499)*
Magna Group LLC ....G 513 388-9463
Cincinnati *(G-3971)*
Metro Mech Inc ....G 216 641-6262
Cleveland *(G-5662)*
Msk Trencher Mfg Inc ....F 419 394-4444
Celina *(G-2977)*
Murphy Tractor & Eqp Co Inc ....G 614 876-1141
Columbus *(G-7201)*
Murphy Tractor & Eqp Co Inc ....G 937 898-4198
Vandalia *(G-19140)*
Murphy Tractor & Eqp Co Inc ....G 419 221-3666
Lima *(G-11909)*
Murphy Tractor & Eqp Co Inc ....G 330 477-9304
Canton *(G-2759)*
Murphy Tractor & Eqp Co Inc ....G 330 220-4999
Brunswick *(G-2221)*
National Oilwell Varco Inc ....E 978 687-0101
Dayton *(G-8376)*
Npk Construction Equipment Inc ....D 440 232-7900
Bedford *(G-1432)*
Pace Consolidated Inc ....D 440 942-1234
Willoughby *(G-20396)*
Pace Engineering Inc ....C 440 942-1234
Willoughby *(G-20397)*
Precision Engineered Tech LLC ....G 330 335-3300
Wadsworth *(G-19266)*
Pubco Corporation ....D 216 881-5300
Cleveland *(G-5932)*
Roadsafe Traffic Systems Inc ....G 614 274-9782
Columbus *(G-7398)*
Scott Port-A-Fold Inc ....E 419 748-8880
Napoleon *(G-14561)*
Screen Machine Industries LLC ....G 740 927-3464
Pataskala *(G-15844)*
Shaffer Manufacturing Corp ....E 937 652-2151
Urbana *(G-19012)*
Sk Machinery Corporation ....G 330 733-7325
Akron *(G-377)*
Stillwell Equipment Co Inc ....G 330 650-1029
Peninsula *(G-15898)*
Thorworks Industries Inc ....E 419 626-4375
Sandusky *(G-16855)*
Tri-Way Rebar Inc ....G 330 296-9662
Ravenna *(G-16415)*
Wilkett Enterprises LLC ....G 740 384-2890
Wellston *(G-19611)*

MACHINERY: Cryogenic, Industrial

Chart International Inc ....E 440 753-1490
Cleveland *(G-4915)*
Eden Cryogenics LLC ....E 614 873-3949
Plain City *(G-16190)*
JC Carter LLC ....G 440 569-1818
Richmond Heights *(G-16502)*

MACHINERY: Custom

A & R Machine Co Inc ....G 330 832-4631
Massillon *(G-12957)*
Aja Industries LLC ....G 614 216-9566
Gahanna *(G-10074)*
Albright Machine ....G 419 483-1088
Monroeville *(G-14286)*
Alfons Haar Inc ....E 937 560-2031
Springboro *(G-17321)*
Alliance Automation LLC ....F 419 238-2520
Van Wert *(G-19076)*
Alpha Omega Dev & Mch Co ....G 440 352-9915
Painesville *(G-15708)*
Amt Machine Systems Ltd ....F 614 635-8050
Columbus *(G-6595)*
Artisan Equipment Inc ....F 740 756-9135
Carroll *(G-2898)*
Autotec Engineering Company ....E 419 885-2529
Toledo *(G-18195)*
Berran Industrial Group Inc ....E 330 253-5800
Akron *(G-85)*
Bomen Marking Products Inc ....G 440 582-0053
Cleveland *(G-4829)*
Bonnot Company ....E 330 896-6544
Akron *(G-93)*
Bowdil Company ....F 800 356-8663
Canton *(G-2596)*
Brandts Custom Machining LLC ....G 419 566-3192
Mansfield *(G-12413)*
Bsm Columbus Llp ....G 740 755-2380
New Albany *(G-14611)*
Cleaning Tech Group LLC ....E 513 870-0100
West Chester *(G-19843)*
Cleveland Jsm Inc ....D 440 876-3050
Strongsville *(G-17729)*
Dale Adams Enterprises Inc ....G 330 524-2800
Twinsburg *(G-18760)*
Dollman Technical Services ....G 419 877-9404
Toledo *(G-18267)*
Dynamic Machine Concepts Inc ....G 216 470-0270
Lagrange *(G-11479)*
East End Welding Company ....C 330 677-6000
Kent *(G-11317)*
Enprotech Industrial Tech LLC ....C 216 883-3220
Cleveland *(G-5179)*
F & G Tool and Die Co ....E 937 294-1405
Moraine *(G-14352)*
Ferry Industries Inc ....D 330 920-9200
Stow *(G-17587)*
Fredon Corporation ....D 440 951-5200
Mentor *(G-13450)*
Friend Engrg & Mch Co Inc ....G 419 589-5066
Mansfield *(G-12442)*
Friess Equipment Inc ....G 330 945-9440
Akron *(G-178)*
Gasdorf Tool and Mch Co Inc ....E 419 227-0103
Lima *(G-11867)*
Givens Lifting Systems Inc ....E 419 724-9001
Perrysburg *(G-15957)*
Global Srcing Support Svcs LLC ....G 800 645-2986
Cincinnati *(G-3765)*
Globe Products Inc ....E 937 233-0233
Dayton *(G-8229)*
Grinding Equipment & McHy LLC ....F 330 747-2313
Youngstown *(G-20926)*
Guardian Engineering & Mfg Co ....G 419 335-1784
Wauseon *(G-19518)*
H2o Mechanics LLC ....G 440 554-9515
Newbury *(G-14955)*
Heisler Tool Company ....F 440 951-2424
Willoughby *(G-20336)*
Herd Manufacturing Inc ....E 216 651-4221
Cleveland *(G-5397)*
Htec Systems Inc ....F 937 438-3010
Dayton *(G-8255)*
Inovent Engineering Inc ....G 330 468-0005
Macedonia *(G-12303)*
Interscope Manufacturing Inc ....E 513 423-8866
Middletown *(G-13917)*
Invotec Engineering Inc ....D 937 886-3232
Miamisburg *(G-13680)*
JF Martt and Associates Inc ....F 330 938-4000
Sebring *(G-16887)*
Keban Industries Inc ....G 216 446-0159
Cleveland *(G-5522)*
Kiley Machine Company Inc ....G 513 875-3223
Fayetteville *(G-9640)*
Kimble Machines Inc ....F 419 485-8449
Montpelier *(G-14311)*
Latanick Equipment Inc ....E 419 433-2200
Huron *(G-11104)*
Lawson Precision Machining Inc ....G 419 562-1543
Bucyrus *(G-2337)*
Lightning Mold & Machine Inc ....F 440 593-6460
Conneaut *(G-7653)*
Logan Machine Company ....D 330 633-6163
Akron *(G-259)*
M L C Technologies Inc ....G 513 874-7792
Hamilton *(G-10583)*
Machine Development Corp ....G 513 825-5885
Cincinnati *(G-3965)*
Machine Tool & Fab Corp ....F 419 435-7676
Fostoria *(G-9846)*
Margo Tool Technology Inc ....F 740 653-8115
Lancaster *(G-11585)*
Markwith Tool Company Inc ....F 937 548-6808
Greenville *(G-10380)*
Massillon Machine & Die Inc ....G 330 833-8913
Massillon *(G-13020)*
Matrix Tool & Machine Inc ....E 440 255-0300
Mentor *(G-13512)*
McNeil & Nrm Inc ....D 330 761-1855
Akron *(G-275)*
McNeil & Nrm Intl Inc ....D 330 253-2525
Akron *(G-276)*
Messerman Corp ....G 419 782-1136
Defiance *(G-8638)*
Metalex Manufacturing Inc ....C 513 489-0507
Blue Ash *(G-1820)*
Metro Design Inc ....F 440 458-4200
Elyria *(G-9295)*
Midwest Laser Systems Inc ....E 419 424-0062
Findlay *(G-9726)*

Employee Codes: A=Over 500 employees, B=251-500
C=101-250, D=51-100, E=20-50, F=10-19, G=3-9
2019 Harris Ohio
Industrial Directory
1489

MACHINERY: Custom

Modern Design Stamping Div ....G....... 216 382-6318
  Cleveland (G-5698)
Narrow Way Custom Technology ....E....... 937 743-1611
  Carlisle (G-2895)
Neil R Scholl Inc ....F....... 740 653-6593
  Lancaster (G-11590)
NM Group Global LLC ....G....... 419 447-5211
  Tiffin (G-18071)
Odawara Automation Inc ....E....... 937 667-8433
  Tipp City (G-18125)
Odyssey Machine Company Ltd ....G....... 419 455-6621
  Perrysburg (G-15984)
Perfecto Industries Inc ....E....... 937 778-1900
  Piqua (G-16149)
Perry Welding Service Inc ....F....... 330 425-2211
  Twinsburg (G-18836)
Pioneer Industrial Systems LLC ....G....... 419 737-9506
  Alvordton (G-522)
Precision Machine & Tool Co ....F....... 419 334-8405
  Fremont (G-10045)
Premier Prod Svc Inds Inc ....G....... 330 527-0333
  Garrettsville (G-10201)
R J K Enterprises Inc ....F....... 440 257-6018
  Mentor (G-13569)
Radco Industries Inc ....F....... 419 531-4731
  Toledo (G-18496)
Rapid Mold Repair & Machine ....G....... 330 253-1000
  Akron (G-343)
Reichard Industries LLC ....G....... 330 482-5511
  Columbiana (G-6478)
Richmond Machine Co ....E....... 419 485-5740
  Montpelier (G-14318)
Royalton Industries Inc ....F....... 440 748-9900
  Columbia Station (G-6446)
RTZ Manufacturing Co ....G....... 614 848-8366
  Columbus (G-7405)
S R P M Inc ....E....... 440 248-8440
  Cleveland (G-6023)
S-P Company Inc ....F....... 330 482-0200
  Columbiana (G-6479)
Sample Machining Inc ....E....... 937 258-3338
  Dayton (G-8492)
Southsern Machining Field Svc ....E....... 740 689-1147
  Lancaster (G-11610)
Spark LLC ....G....... 513 924-1559
  Cincinnati (G-4356)
Steel Eqp Specialists Inc ....E....... 330 829-2626
  Alliance (G-501)
Steel Eqp Specialists Inc ....D....... 330 823-8260
  Alliance (G-502)
Swift Tool Inc ....G....... 330 945-6973
  Cuyahoga Falls (G-7925)
Swivel-Tek Industries LLC ....G....... 419 636-7770
  Bryan (G-2308)
Systech Handling Inc ....F....... 419 445-8226
  Archbold (G-670)
Techniform Industries Inc ....E....... 419 332-8484
  Fremont (G-10054)
Tema Systems Inc ....E....... 513 489-7811
  Cincinnati (G-4413)
Terydon Inc ....F....... 330 879-2448
  Navarre (G-14588)
Tj Bell Inc ....G....... 330 633-3644
  Akron (G-406)
Tower Tool & Manufacturing Co ....F....... 330 425-1623
  Twinsburg (G-18864)
Tru-Fab Technology Inc ....F....... 440 954-9760
  Willoughby (G-20451)

MACHINERY: Deburring

Cleveland Deburring Machine Co ....G....... 216 472-0200
  Cleveland (G-4956)
Tailored Systems Inc ....G....... 937 299-3900
  Moraine (G-14398)

MACHINERY: Die Casting

Columbia Stamping Inc ....F....... 440 236-6677
  Columbia Station (G-6433)
Hendricks Vacuum Forming Inc ....G....... 330 833-8913
  Massillon (G-12996)
L B Machine & Mfg Co Inc ....G....... 513 471-6137
  Okeana (G-15519)
Snair Co ....F....... 614 873-7020
  Plain City (G-16212)
THT Presses Inc ....E....... 937 898-2012
  Dayton (G-8558)
Yizumi-HPM Corporation ....E....... 740 382-5600
  Iberia (G-11115)

MACHINERY: Electrical Discharge Erosion

E D M Electrofying Inc ....G....... 440 322-8900
  Elyria (G-9248)
United Wire Edm Inc ....G....... 440 239-8777
  Berea (G-1630)

MACHINERY: Electronic Component Making

Inpower LLC ....F....... 740 548-0965
  Lewis Center (G-11763)
Mactek Corporation ....F....... 330 487-5477
  Twinsburg (G-18810)
Storetek Engineering Inc ....E....... 330 294-0678
  Tallmadge (G-18006)

MACHINERY: Engraving

Tykma Inc ....D....... 877 318-9562
  Chillicothe (G-3230)
V I P Printing & Design ....G....... 513 777-7468
  West Chester (G-19913)

MACHINERY: Extruding

Diamond America Corporation ....G....... 330 535-3330
  Akron (G-141)
George A Mitchell Company ....E....... 330 758-5777
  Youngstown (G-20920)
Vmaxx Inc ....F....... 419 738-4044
  Wapakoneta (G-19358)

MACHINERY: Fiber Optics Strand Coating

Diptech Systems Inc ....G....... 330 673-4400
  Kent (G-11314)

MACHINERY: Folding

Baumfolder Corporation ....E....... 937 492-1281
  Sidney (G-17019)
G Fordyce Co ....G....... 937 393-3241
  Hillsboro (G-10878)
L B Folding Co Inc ....G....... 216 961-0888
  North Royalton (G-15282)

MACHINERY: Gas Separators

H P E Inc ....F....... 330 833-3161
  Massillon (G-12993)

MACHINERY: Gear Cutting & Finishing

North East Technologies Inc ....G....... 440 327-9278
  North Ridgeville (G-15242)

MACHINERY: General, Industrial, NEC

La Mfg Inc ....G....... 513 577-7200
  Cincinnati (G-3928)
Ohlheiser Corp ....G....... 860 953-7632
  Columbus (G-7266)

MACHINERY: Glassmaking

Dura Temp Corporation ....F....... 419 866-4348
  Holland (G-10929)
Emhart Glass Manufacturing Inc ....D....... 567 336-7733
  Perrysburg (G-15945)
Emhart Glass Manufacturing Inc ....G....... 567 336-8784
  Perrysburg (G-15946)
Ged Holdings Inc ....C....... 330 963-5401
  Twinsburg (G-18780)
Intertec Corporation ....B....... 419 537-9711
  Toledo (G-18350)
J & S Industrial Mch Pdts Inc ....D....... 419 691-1380
  Toledo (G-18356)
J M Hamilton Group Inc ....F....... 419 229-4010
  Lima (G-11881)
Manifold & Phalor Inc ....E....... 614 920-1200
  Canal Winchester (G-2506)
Steinert Industries Inc ....F....... 330 678-0028
  Kent (G-11390)
Technical Glass Products Inc ....F....... 440 639-6399
  Painesville (G-15786)
Toledo Engineering Co Inc ....C....... 419 537-9711
  Toledo (G-18558)

MACHINERY: Grinding

B V Grinding Machining Inc ....G....... 440 918-1884
  Willoughby (G-20283)
C S Bell Co ....F....... 419 448-0791
  Tiffin (G-18054)
Fives Landis Corp ....D....... 440 709-0700
  Painesville (G-15740)
Fredon Corporation ....D....... 440 951-5200
  Mentor (G-13450)
Grind-All Corporation ....E....... 330 220-1600
  Brunswick (G-2211)
Jacp Inc ....G....... 513 353-3660
  Miamitown (G-13747)
Master Grinding Company Inc ....G....... 440 944-3680
  Wickliffe (G-20216)
Milan Tool Corp ....G....... 216 661-1078
  Cleveland (G-5685)
OReilly Precision Products ....E....... 937 526-4677
  Russia (G-16610)
Stevenson Mfg Co ....G....... 330 532-1581
  Wellsville (G-19614)
Synergy Grinding Inc ....F....... 216 447-4000
  Westlake (G-20166)
Union Process Inc ....E....... 330 929-3333
  Akron (G-419)

MACHINERY: Ice Cream

Country Freezer Units LLC ....G....... 740 623-8658
  Baltic (G-1024)
Norse Dairy Systems LP ....B....... 614 421-5297
  Columbus (G-7225)

MACHINERY: Industrial, NEC

Combined Industrial Solutions ....G....... 513 659-3091
  Milford (G-14004)
Mes Material Hdlg Systems LLC ....G....... 740 477-8920
  Circleville (G-4548)
Michaels Tool Service Co Inc ....G....... 330 772-1119
  Burghill (G-2355)
Morning Glory Technologies ....F....... 440 796-5076
  Chesterland (G-3165)
Northcoast Prfmce & Mch Co ....G....... 330 753-7333
  Barberton (G-1089)

MACHINERY: Jewelers

House Silva-Strongsville Inc ....G....... 330 464-6419
  Strongsville (G-17750)

MACHINERY: Kilns

A & M Kiln Dry Ltd ....G....... 330 852-0505
  Dundee (G-9016)
A & M Kiln Dry Ltd ....F....... 330 852-0505
  Dundee (G-9017)
Industrial Thermal Systems Inc ....F....... 513 561-2100
  Cincinnati (G-3845)
Kiln ....G....... 440 717-1880
  Brecksville (G-2044)
Kilnit Ltd ....G....... 330 906-0748
  Stow (G-17598)
Mirion Technologies Ist Corp ....G....... 614 367-2050
  Pickerington (G-16054)

MACHINERY: Knitting

Knitting Machinery Corp ....G....... 216 851-9900
  Cleveland (G-5540)
Knitting Machinery Corp ....F....... 937 548-2338
  Greenville (G-10379)

MACHINERY: Labeling

Dynamic Bar Code Systems Inc ....G....... 330 220-5451
  Brunswick (G-2201)
General Data Healthcare Inc ....G....... 513 752-7978
  Cincinnati (G-3253)
Huhtamaki Inc ....B....... 937 746-9700
  Franklin (G-9890)
Huhtamaki Inc ....B....... 513 201-1525
  Batavia (G-1153)
Hunkar Technologies Inc ....C....... 513 272-1010
  Cincinnati (G-3829)
M PI Label Systems ....G....... 330 938-2134
  Sebring (G-16888)
Morgan Adhesives Company LLC ....E....... 330 688-1111
  Stow (G-17606)
Mpi Labels of Baltimore Inc ....F....... 330 938-2134
  Sebring (G-16890)
Quadrel Inc ....E....... 440 602-4700
  Mentor (G-13562)
Superior Label Systems Inc ....B....... 513 336-0825
  Mason (G-12944)

MACHINERY: Logging Eqpt

Buck Equipment Inc ....E 614 539-3030
  Grove City *(G-10419)*

MACHINERY: Marking, Metalworking

Cauffiel Corporation ....G 419 843-7262
  Toledo *(G-18223)*
Tdm LLC ....G 440 969-1442
  Ashtabula *(G-806)*

MACHINERY: Metalworking

Addisonmckee Inc ....C 513 228-7000
  Lebanon *(G-11629)*
ADS Machinery Corp ....D 330 399-3601
  Warren *(G-19362)*
Advance Manufacturing Corp ....E 216 333-1684
  Cleveland *(G-4622)*
Bardons & Oliver Inc ....C 440 498-5800
  Solon *(G-17112)*
Barth Industries Co LP ....D 216 267-0531
  Cleveland *(G-4793)*
Berran Industrial Group Inc ....E 330 253-5800
  Akron *(G-85)*
Binns Machinery Company ....G 513 242-3388
  Cincinnati *(G-3393)*
Bison USA Corp ....G 513 713-0513
  Hamilton *(G-10541)*
Brilex Industries Inc ....D 330 744-1114
  Youngstown *(G-20858)*
Brilex Industries Inc ....C 330 744-1114
  Youngstown *(G-20859)*
CA Litzler Co Inc ....E 216 267-8020
  Cleveland *(G-4859)*
Cammann Inc ....F 440 965-4051
  Wakeman *(G-19282)*
Coating Control Inc ....G 330 453-9136
  Canton *(G-2631)*
Ctm Integration Incorporated ....E 330 332-1800
  Salem *(G-16732)*
Dango & Dienenthal Inc ....G 330 829-0277
  Alliance *(G-463)*
Econ-O-Machine Products Inc ....G 937 882-6307
  Donnelsville *(G-8801)*
Elite Mfg Solutions LLC ....G 330 612-7434
  Macedonia *(G-12291)*
F L Enterprises ....E 216 898-5551
  Cleveland *(G-5212)*
Fabriweld Corporation ....G 419 668-3358
  Norwalk *(G-15393)*
Forrest Machine Pdts Co Ltd ....E 419 589-3774
  Mansfield *(G-12441)*
Gem City Engineering Co ....C 937 223-5544
  Dayton *(G-8219)*
Gilson Machine & Tool Co Inc ....E 419 592-2911
  Napoleon *(G-14539)*
Glunt Industries Inc ....C 330 399-7585
  Warren *(G-19407)*
Hahn Manufacturing Company ....E 216 391-9300
  Cleveland *(G-5366)*
Heisler Tool Company ....F 440 951-2424
  Willoughby *(G-20236)*
Holdren Brothers Inc ....F 937 465-7050
  West Liberty *(G-19936)*
J Horst Manufacturing Co ....G 330 828-2216
  Dalton *(G-7945)*
Kalt Manufacturing Company ....D 440 327-2102
  North Ridgeville *(G-15235)*
Kay Capital Company ....G 216 531-1010
  Cleveland *(G-5521)*
Kilroy Company ....D 440 951-8700
  Eastlake *(G-9117)*
Master Marking Company Inc ....F 330 688-6797
  Stow *(G-17604)*
Mathew Odonnell ....G 440 969-4054
  Andover *(G-585)*
Midwest Laser Systems Inc ....F 419 424-0062
  Findlay *(G-9726)*
Milacron LLC ....E 513 487-5000
  Blue Ash *(G-1822)*
Pines Manufacturing Inc ....E 440 835-5553
  Westlake *(G-20141)*
Rafter Equipment Corporation ....E 440 572-3700
  Strongsville *(G-17781)*
Riverside Mch & Automtn Inc ....D 419 855-8308
  Genoa *(G-10236)*
Sir Steak Machinery Inc ....E 419 526-9181
  Mansfield *(G-12513)*
South Shore Controls Inc ....E 440 259-2500
  Perry *(G-15913)*

Stainless Automation ....G 216 961-4550
  Cleveland *(G-6090)*
Stein Inc ....D 216 883-7444
  Cleveland *(G-6105)*
Sticker Corporation ....F 440 946-2100
  Willoughby *(G-20438)*
Tri-Mac Mfg & Svcs Co ....F 513 896-4445
  Hamilton *(G-10613)*
Universal Precision Products ....E 330 633-6128
  Akron *(G-421)*

MACHINERY: Milling

L M Equipment & Design Inc ....E 330 332-9951
  Salem *(G-16754)*
Morlock Asphalt Ltd ....F 419 686-4601
  Portage *(G-16271)*
My Catered Table LLC ....G 614 882-7323
  Columbus *(G-7205)*

MACHINERY: Mining

80 Acres Urban Agriculture LLC ....G 513 218-4387
  Cincinnati *(G-3273)*
Belden Brick Company ....E 330 852-2411
  Sugarcreek *(G-17842)*
Bowdil Company ....F 800 356-8663
  Canton *(G-2596)*
Breaker Technology Inc ....E 440 248-7168
  Solon *(G-17120)*
Cailin Dev Ltd Lblty Co ....F 216 408-6261
  Cleveland *(G-4862)*
Carr Tool Company ....E 513 825-2900
  Fairfield *(G-9488)*
Cool Machines Inc ....F 419 232-4871
  Van Wert *(G-19083)*
Deep Springs Technology LLC ....G 419 536-5741
  Toledo *(G-18260)*
Engines Inc of Ohio ....D 740 377-9874
  South Point *(G-17283)*
Esco Group LLC ....F 419 562-6015
  Bucyrus *(G-2329)*
Joy Mining Machinery ....C 440 248-7970
  Solon *(G-17177)*
Kaffenbarger Truck Eqp Co ....E 513 772-6800
  Cincinnati *(G-3892)*
Kennametal Inc ....C 440 349-5151
  Solon *(G-17183)*
Komatsu Mining Corp ....F 216 503-5029
  Independence *(G-11139)*
Mike Suponcic ....G 740 635-0654
  Bridgeport *(G-2077)*
Nolan Company ....G 330 453-7922
  Canton *(G-2762)*
Nolan Company ....G 740 269-1512
  Bowerston *(G-1942)*
Npk Construction Equipment Inc ....D 440 232-7900
  Bedford *(G-1432)*
Penn Machine Company ....E 814 288-1547
  Twinsburg *(G-18829)*
Pneumatic Parts Co ....F 330 923-6063
  Stow *(G-17618)*
SMI Holdings Inc ....D 740 927-3464
  Pataskala *(G-15845)*
Terrasource Global Corporation ....D 330 923-5254
  Cuyahoga Falls *(G-7927)*
Warren Fabricating Corporation ....D 330 534-5017
  Hubbard *(G-11011)*
Zen Industries Inc ....E 216 432-3240
  Cleveland *(G-6339)*

MACHINERY: Pack-Up Assemblies, Wheel Overhaul

Aot Inc ....E 937 323-9669
  Springfield *(G-17363)*
Haeco Inc ....F 513 722-1030
  Loveland *(G-12195)*

MACHINERY: Packaging

Accu Pak Mfg Inc ....G 330 644-3015
  Akron *(G-27)*
Advanced Poly-Packaging Inc ....G 330 785-4000
  Akron *(G-32)*
Andy Pac Inc ....G 440 748-8800
  Columbia Station *(G-6427)*
Ardagh Metal Packaging USA Inc .....E 419 334-4461
  Fremont *(G-9991)*
Atlas Vac Machine LLC ....G 513 407-3513
  Cincinnati *(G-3368)*

Audion Automation Ltd ....E 216 267-1911
  Berea *(G-1592)*
Automated Packg Systems Inc ....D 330 342-2000
  Bedford *(G-1386)*
Automated Packg Systems Inc ....C 330 626-2313
  Streetsboro *(G-17663)*
Automation Solutions Inc ....G 614 235-4060
  Columbus *(G-6633)*
Boggs Graphic Equipment LLC ....G 888 837-8101
  Maple Heights *(G-12566)*
Combi Packaging Systems Llc ....D 330 456-9333
  Canton *(G-2632)*
Crown Closures Machinery ....E 740 681-6593
  Lancaster *(G-11559)*
Ctm Integration Incorporated ....E 330 332-1800
  Salem *(G-16732)*
Ctm Labeling Systems ....E 330 332-1800
  Salem *(G-16733)*
Darifill Inc ....F 614 890-3274
  Westerville *(G-20046)*
Dover Corporation ....F 513 696-1790
  Mason *(G-12857)*
Euclid Products Co Inc ....G 440 942-7310
  Willoughby *(G-20317)*
Exact Equipment Corporation ....F 215 295-2000
  Columbus *(G-6491)*
Food Equipment Mfg Corp ....E 216 672-5859
  Bedford Heights *(G-1470)*
G L Industries Inc ....E 513 874-1233
  Hamilton *(G-10562)*
H & G Equipment Inc ....F 513 761-2060
  Blue Ash *(G-1784)*
Hill & Griffith Company ....G 513 921-1075
  Cincinnati *(G-3812)*
Impackt ....G 513 559-1488
  Cincinnati *(G-3839)*
Kaufman Engineered Systems Inc .....D 419 878-9727
  Waterville *(G-19499)*
Kennedy Group Incorporated ....D 440 951-7660
  Willoughby *(G-20352)*
Kolinahr Systems Inc ....F 513 745-9401
  Blue Ash *(G-1801)*
Madgar Genis Corp ....G 330 848-6950
  Barberton *(G-1082)*
Millwood Inc ....G 614 717-9099
  Powell *(G-16329)*
Millwood Inc ....F 513 860-4567
  West Chester *(G-19744)*
Millwood Inc ....G 330 729-2120
  Vienna *(G-19203)*
Millwood Inc ....F 404 629-4811
  Vienna *(G-19204)*
Millwood Natural LLC ....C 330 393-4400
  Vienna *(G-19205)*
MTS Medication Tech Inc ....G 440 238-0840
  Strongsville *(G-17767)*
Nilpeter Usa Inc ....C 513 489-4400
  Cincinnati *(G-4080)*
Norse Dairy Systems Inc ....C 614 294-4931
  Columbus *(G-7224)*
Pack Line Corp ....F 212 564-0664
  Cleveland *(G-5835)*
Pak Master LLC ....E 330 523-5319
  Richfield *(G-16479)*
Pneumatic Scale ....F 330 923-0491
  Cuyahoga Falls *(G-7904)*
Reactive Resin Products Co ....E 419 666-6119
  Perrysburg *(G-16003)*
Recon Systems LLC ....G 330 488-0368
  East Canton *(G-9043)*
Rpmi Packaging Inc ....F 513 398-4040
  Lebanon *(G-11692)*
Switchback Group Inc ....E 330 523-5200
  Richfield *(G-16490)*
System Packaging of Glassline ....C 419 666-9712
  Perrysburg *(G-16008)*
Unity Enterprises Inc ....G 614 231-1370
  Columbus *(G-7559)*
Vistech Mfg Solutions LLC ....G 513 860-1408
  Fairfield *(G-9573)*
Vistech Mfg Solutions LLC ....F 513 933-9300
  Lebanon *(G-11706)*
Vmi Americas Inc ....E 330 929-6800
  Stow *(G-17641)*
W/S Packaging Group Inc ....C 513 459-2400
  Mason *(G-12953)*

MACHINERY: Paint Making

Bethel Engineering and Eqp Inc ....E 419 568-1100
  New Hampshire *(G-14699)*

MACHINERY: Paint Making

Bethel Engineering and Eqp Inc ....E 419 568-7976
  New Hampshire *(G-14700)*
Cohesant Inc ....E 216 910-1700
  Beachwood *(G-1228)*
Fawcett Co Inc ....G...... 330 659-4187
  Richfield *(G-16470)*
General Fabrications Corp ....E 419 625-6055
  Sandusky *(G-16813)*
Nutro Corporation ....D...... 440 572-3800
  Strongsville *(G-17772)*
Nutro Inc ....E 440 572-3800
  Strongsville *(G-17773)*
Woodman Agitator Inc ....F 440 937-9865
  Avon *(G-976)*

MACHINERY: Paper Industry Miscellaneous

Aleris Recycling Inc ....G...... 216 910-3400
  Beachwood *(G-1219)*
Elite Mill Service & Cnstr 513 422-4234
  Trenton *(G-18617)*
J E Doyle Company 330 564-0743
  Norton *(G-15371)*
Kadant Black Clawson Inc ....D...... 513 229-8100
  Lebanon *(G-11667)*
Loroco Industries Inc ....E 513 554-0356
  Cincinnati *(G-3951)*
Magna Machine Co ....C 513 851-6900
  Cincinnati *(G-3972)*
Mtr Martco LLC ....D...... 513 424-5307
  Middletown *(G-13932)*
National Oilwell Varco LP ....D...... 937 454-3200
  Dayton *(G-8377)*
Tri-Mac Mfg & Svcs Co ....F 513 896-4445
  Hamilton *(G-10613)*
Universal Precision Products ....E 330 633-6128
  Akron *(G-421)*
Vail Rubber Works Inc ....F 513 705-2060
  Middletown *(G-13962)*

MACHINERY: Pharmaciutical

Enerfab Inc ....G...... 513 771-2300
  Cincinnati *(G-3641)*
McFlusion Inc ....G...... 800 341-8616
  Twinsburg *(G-18814)*

MACHINERY: Plastic Working

Alstart Enterprises LLC ....F 330 533-3222
  Canfield *(G-2521)*
American Plastic Tech Inc ....C 440 632-5203
  Middlefield *(G-13777)*
Bradford Neal Machinery Inc ....F 440 632-1393
  Middlefield *(G-13781)*
Budget Molders Supply Inc ....E 216 367-7050
  Macedonia *(G-12281)*
Chardon Plastics Machinery ....G...... 440 564-5360
  Chardon *(G-3103)*
Component Mfg & Design ....F 330 225-8080
  Brunswick *(G-2197)*
DRG Hydraulics Inc ....E 216 663-9747
  Cleveland *(G-5114)*
Encore Plastics Corporation ....C 419 626-8000
  Sandusky *(G-16808)*
Gloucester Engineering Co Inc ....G...... 330 722-5168
  Medina *(G-13269)*
I G Brenner Inc ....F 740 345-8845
  Newark *(G-14887)*
Innovative Plastic Machinery ....G...... 330 478-1825
  Canton *(G-2708)*
J McCaman Enterprises Inc ....F 330 825-2401
  New Franklin *(G-14691)*
Jaco Manufacturing Company ....F 440 234-4000
  Berea *(G-1613)*
Linden Industries Inc ....E 330 928-4064
  Cuyahoga Falls *(G-7893)*
Plastic Process Equipment Inc ....E 216 367-7000
  Macedonia *(G-12317)*
Tooltex Inc ....F 614 539-3222
  Grove City *(G-10475)*
Vulcan Machinery Corporation ....E 330 376-6025
  Akron *(G-428)*
Wentworth Mold Inc Electra ....D...... 937 898-8460
  Vandalia *(G-19151)*
Wesco Machine Inc ....F 330 688-6973
  Akron *(G-433)*
Youngstown Plastic Tooling ....E 330 782-7222
  Youngstown *(G-21080)*
Zed Industries Inc ....D...... 937 667-8407
  Vandalia *(G-19152)*

MACHINERY: Polishing & Buffing

Areway LLC ....D...... 216 651-9022
  Brooklyn *(G-2112)*

MACHINERY: Printing Presses

1st Choice Web Solution Inc ....G...... 330 503-1591
  Youngstown *(G-20828)*
Advanced Web Corporation ....G...... 740 662-6323
  Stewart *(G-17558)*
Allen Green Enterprises LLC ....G...... 330 339-0200
  New Philadelphia *(G-14757)*
Boggs Graphic Equipment LLC ....G...... 888 837-8101
  Maple Heights *(G-12566)*
Desco Equipment Corp ....E 330 405-1581
  Twinsburg *(G-18762)*
Graphic Systems Services Inc ....E 937 746-0708
  Springboro *(G-17329)*
Incorporated Trustees Gospel W ....D...... 216 749-1428
  Cleveland *(G-5449)*
Key Blue Prints Inc ....G...... 614 899-6180
  Columbus *(G-7092)*
Lyle Printing & Publishing Co ....F 330 337-7172
  Salem *(G-16757)*

MACHINERY: Recycling

Agmet Metals Inc ....E 440 439-7400
  Oakwood Village *(G-15476)*
ARS Recycling Systems LLC ....F 330 536-8210
  Lowellville *(G-12249)*
Cbg Biotech Ltd Co ....G...... 440 786-7667
  Solon *(G-17125)*
Glenn Hunter & Associates Inc ....D...... 419 533-0925
  Delta *(G-8773)*
Grasan Equipment Company Inc ....D...... 419 526-4440
  Mansfield *(G-12452)*
Innovative Recycling Systems ....G...... 440 498-9200
  Solon *(G-17171)*
Plastic Partners LLC ....G...... 425 765-2416
  Salem *(G-16766)*
Prodeva Inc ....F 937 596-6713
  Jackson Center *(G-11215)*
RSI Company ....F 216 360-9800
  Beachwood *(G-1277)*
SDS National LLC ....G...... 330 759-8066
  Youngstown *(G-21026)*
Time Is Money ....G...... 419 701-6098
  Fostoria *(G-9860)*

MACHINERY: Riveting

Fluidpower Assembly Inc ....G...... 419 394-7486
  Saint Marys *(G-16685)*

MACHINERY: Road Construction & Maintenance

American Highway Products LLC ....F 330 874-3270
  Bolivar *(G-1906)*
City of Oxford ....F 513 523-8412
  Oxford *(G-15691)*
Concord Road Equipment Mfg Inc ....E 440 357-5344
  Painesville *(G-15723)*
Forge Industries Inc ....A 330 782-8301
  Youngstown *(G-20909)*
Gledhill Road Machinery Co ....E 419 468-4400
  Galion *(G-10143)*
Gradeworks ....G...... 440 487-4201
  Willoughby *(G-20334)*
Hug Manufacturing Corporation ....G...... 419 668-5086
  Norwalk *(G-15400)*
Jcl Equipment Co Inc ....G...... 937 374-1010
  Xenia *(G-20779)*
Lake Township Trustees ....G...... 419 836-1143
  Millbury *(G-14050)*
Miller Curber Company LLC ....F 330 782-8081
  Youngstown *(G-20972)*
Power-Pack Conveyor Company ....E 440 975-9955
  Willoughby *(G-20408)*
Richland Twp Garage ....G...... 419 358-4897
  Bluffton *(G-1892)*

MACHINERY: Robots, Molding & Forming Plastics

CAM-Lem Inc ....G...... 216 391-7750
  Cleveland *(G-4863)*
Lifeformations Inc ....E 419 352-2101
  Bowling Green *(G-1981)*

MACHINERY: Rubber Working

Anderson International Corp ....D...... 216 641-1112
  Stow *(G-17568)*
Conviber Inc ....F 330 723-6006
  Medina *(G-13241)*
French Oil Mill Machinery Co ....D...... 937 773-3420
  Piqua *(G-16117)*
Heintz Manufacturers Inc ....G...... 724 274-6300
  Medina *(G-13271)*
Hydratecs Injection Eqp Co ....G...... 330 773-0491
  Akron *(G-210)*
Kobelco Stewart Bolling Inc ....G...... 330 655-3111
  Hudson *(G-11060)*
McNeil & Nrm Inc ....D...... 330 761-1855
  Akron *(G-275)*
McNeil & Nrm Intl Inc ....D...... 330 253-2525
  Akron *(G-276)*
R A K Machine Inc ....F 216 631-7750
  Cleveland *(G-5949)*
Rhino Rubber LLC ....G...... 877 744-6603
  North Canton *(G-15115)*
RMS Equipment LLC ....E 330 564-1360
  Cuyahoga Falls *(G-7914)*
Rubber City Machinery Corp ....E 330 434-3500
  Akron *(G-356)*

MACHINERY: Saw & Sawing

Bortnick Tractor Sales Inc ....F 330 924-2555
  Cortland *(G-7704)*

MACHINERY: Screening Eqpt, Electric

M M Industries Inc 330 332-5947
  Salem *(G-16758)*
Measurement Specialties Inc ....F 937 885-0800
  Dayton *(G-8337)*
Midwestern Industries Inc ....C 330 837-4203
  Massillon *(G-13026)*
Sizetec Inc ....G...... 330 492-9682
  Canton *(G-2817)*

MACHINERY: Semiconductor Manufacturing

Eaton Corporation ....B 440 523-5000
  Cleveland *(G-5146)*
Lam Research Corporation ....C 937 472-3311
  Eaton *(G-9158)*
Microcvd Corporation ....G...... 937 573-8984
  Dayton *(G-8350)*

MACHINERY: Separation Eqpt, Magnetic

Decision Systems Inc ....E 330 456-7600
  Canton *(G-2653)*
Ohio Magnetics Inc ....E 216 662-8484
  Maple Heights *(G-12575)*
Peerless-Winsmith Inc 614 526-7000
  Dublin *(G-8963)*

MACHINERY: Service Industry, NEC

Askia Inc ....G...... 513 828-7443
  Cincinnati *(G-3362)*
C J Smith Machinery Service ....G...... 614 348-1376
  Columbus *(G-6719)*
Clark Auto Machine Shop ....G...... 216 939-0768
  Cleveland *(G-4937)*
Erichar Inc ....G...... 216 402-2628
  Cleveland *(G-5188)*

MACHINERY: Sheet Metal Working

Diverse Mfg Solutions LLC ....F 740 363-3600
  Delaware *(G-8672)*

MACHINERY: Sifting & Screening

Rotex Global LLC ....C 513 541-1236
  Cincinnati *(G-4282)*
Tyler Haver Inc ....D...... 800 255-1259
  Mentor *(G-13616)*

MACHINERY: Specialty

Besten Inc ....G...... 216 910-2880
  Cleveland *(G-4808)*
Devilbiss Ransburg ....F 419 470-2000
  Toledo *(G-18262)*
Tex-Vent Co ....G...... 614 299-1902
  Columbus *(G-7522)*

PRODUCT SECTION

MAIL-ORDER HOUSES: Tools & Hardware

MACHINERY: Stone Working

Stoneworkd ....F 740 920-4099
  Newark *(G-14924)*

MACHINERY: Tapping

Midwest Specialties Inc.........................F 419 738-8147
  Wapakoneta *(G-19346)*

MACHINERY: Textile

CA Litzler Co Inc ....E 216 267-8020
  Cleveland *(G-4859)*
Randy Gray..G...... 513 533-3200
  Cincinnati *(G-4248)*
Wolf Machine Company ....C...... 513 791-5194
  Blue Ash *(G-1874)*

MACHINERY: Tire Retreading

American Manufacturing & Eqp ....G...... 513 829-2248
  Fairfield *(G-9482)*

MACHINERY: Tire Shredding

Affinity Information Managemet ....G...... 419 517-2055
  Sylvania *(G-17932)*
File 13 Inc..F 937 642-4855
  Marysville *(G-12782)*
Shred Away..G...... 740 363-6327
  Delaware *(G-8724)*

MACHINERY: Wire Drawing

Arku Coil-Systems Inc ....G...... 513 985-0500
  Blue Ash *(G-1730)*
EZ Grout Corporation Inc........................E 740 962-2024
  Malta *(G-12382)*
Filmtec Inc..E 419 435-1819
  Fostoria *(G-9838)*
Fmt Repair Service Co.............................G...... 330 347-7374
  Mentor *(G-13444)*
Kenley Enterprises LLC ....E 419 630-0921
  Bryan *(G-2293)*
Oma USA Inc ....G...... 330 487-0602
  Twinsburg *(G-18824)*
Shadetree Machine ....G...... 513 727-8771
  Middletown *(G-13951)*
Simon De Young Corporation ....G...... 440 834-3000
  Middlefield *(G-13853)*

MACHINERY: Woodworking

Axiom Tool Group Inc..............................G...... 844 642-4902
  Columbus *(G-6638)*
Bent Wood Solutions LLC ....G...... 330 674-1454
  Millersburg *(G-14065)*
Coe Manufacturing Company ....D...... 440 352-9381
  Painesville *(G-15722)*
General Intl Pwr Pdts LLC ....E 419 877-5234
  Whitehouse *(G-20191)*
McFeelys Inc..F 800 443-7937
  Harrison *(G-10658)*
Rlfshop LLC..G...... 937 898-6070
  Dayton *(G-8480)*

MACHINES: Forming, Sheet Metal

Auburn Metal Processing LLC...............E 315 253-2565
  Twinsburg *(G-18736)*
Jones Metal Products Company ....C...... 740 545-6381
  West Lafayette *(G-19931)*

MACHINISTS' TOOLS & MACHINES: Measuring, Metalworking Type

Hykon Manufacturing Company ....G...... 330 821-8889
  Alliance *(G-477)*
Karma Metal Products Inc......................F 419 524-4371
  Mansfield *(G-12466)*
L C Smith Co ....G...... 440 327-1251
  Elyria *(G-9283)*
PMC Gage Inc ....E 440 953-1672
  Willoughby *(G-20404)*

MACHINISTS' TOOLS: Measuring, Precision

Morgan Precision Instrs LLC ....G...... 330 896-0846
  Akron *(G-287)*
Thaler Machine Company ....G...... 937 550-2400
  Springboro *(G-17355)*

MACHINISTS' TOOLS: Precision

A & B Machine Inc....................................E 937 492-8662
  Sidney *(G-17011)*
Angstrom Precision Metals LLC............D...... 440 255-6700
  Mentor *(G-13388)*
Apollo Manufacturing Co LLC ....E 440 951-9972
  Mentor *(G-13390)*
Chippewa Tool & Mfg Co ....F 419 849-2790
  Woodville *(G-20551)*
J and L Manufacturing Inc ....G...... 937 492-0008
  Sidney *(G-17047)*
Kaeper Machine Inc ....E 440 974-1010
  Mentor *(G-13488)*
Keb Industries Inc ....G...... 440 953-4623
  Willoughby *(G-20351)*
Levan Enterprises Inc ....E 330 923-9797
  Stow *(G-17601)*
M A Harrison Mfg Co Inc ....E 440 965-4306
  Wakeman *(G-19287)*
Machining Technologies Inc ....E 419 862-3110
  Elmore *(G-9206)*
R Dunn Mold Inc.......................................G...... 937 773-3388
  Piqua *(G-16158)*
Schober USA Inc ....G...... 513 489-7393
  Fairfield *(G-9561)*

MAGAZINE STAND

Cruisin Times Magazine ....G...... 440 331-4615
  Rocky River *(G-16544)*

MAGNESIUM

Air Craft Wheels LLC ....G...... 440 937-7903
  Ravenna *(G-16364)*
Lite Metals Company...............................E 330 296-6110
  Ravenna *(G-16389)*
Th Magnesium Inc....................................G...... 513 285-7568
  Cincinnati *(G-4417)*

MAGNESIUM

Magnesium Refining Tech Inc ....E 419 483-9199
  Cleveland *(G-5604)*
Magnesium Refining Tech Inc ....E 419 483-9199
  Bellevue *(G-1538)*

MAGNETIC INK & OPTICAL SCANNING EQPT

Applied Vision Corporation ....D...... 330 926-2222
  Cuyahoga Falls *(G-7839)*

MAGNETIC RESONANCE IMAGING DEVICES: Nonmedical

Alliance Healthcare Svcs Inc ....G...... 330 493-6747
  Canton *(G-2568)*
Mansfield Imaging Center LLC ....F 419 756-8899
  Mansfield *(G-12476)*
Medical Imaging Dist LLC ....G...... 800 898-3392
  Mantua *(G-12553)*
S-Tek Inc ....G...... 440 439-8232
  Bedford *(G-1443)*
Summit Diagnostic Imaging LLC...........E 513 233-3320
  Cincinnati *(G-4389)*

MAGNETIC TAPE, AUDIO: Prerecorded

News Reel Inc..G...... 614 469-0700
  Columbus *(G-7218)*

MAGNETS: Permanent

Dura Magnetics Inc..................................F 419 882-0591
  Sylvania *(G-17939)*
Fenix Magnetics Inc.................................G...... 440 455-1142
  Westlake *(G-20113)*
Flexmag Industries Inc ....D...... 740 373-3492
  Marietta *(G-12624)*
Magnum Magnetics Corporation ....G...... 740 373-7770
  Marietta *(G-12641)*
Ohio Magnetics Inc ....E 216 662-8484
  Maple Heights *(G-12575)*
Sulo Enterprises Inc ....F 440 926-3322
  Grafton *(G-10311)*
Walker Magnetics Group Inc..................E 614 492-1614
  Columbus *(G-7588)*
Walker National Inc..................................E 614 492-1614
  Columbus *(G-7589)*
Winkle Industries Inc ....G...... 330 823-9730
  Alliance *(G-516)*

MAIL-ORDER HOUSE, NEC

American Frame Corporation ....E 419 893-5595
  Maumee *(G-13069)*
Communication Concepts Inc ....G...... 937 426-8600
  Beavercreek *(G-1307)*
Kencraft Co Inc ....G...... 419 536-0333
  Toledo *(G-18364)*
Loctote LLC..G...... 614 407-0882
  Blacklick *(G-1688)*
Pardson Inc ....F 740 373-5285
  Marietta *(G-12651)*

MAIL-ORDER HOUSES: Books, Exc Book Clubs

Scott Fetzer Company..............................F 440 892-3000
  Westlake *(G-20156)*
Stadvec Inc ....G...... 330 644-7724
  Barberton *(G-1107)*

MAIL-ORDER HOUSES: Cards

Mantapart..G...... 330 549-2389
  New Springfield *(G-14820)*

MAIL-ORDER HOUSES: Cheese

Guggisberg Cheese Inc ....E 330 893-2550
  Millersburg *(G-14086)*

MAIL-ORDER HOUSES: Computers & Peripheral Eqpt

Systemax Manufacturing Inc ....C...... 937 368-2300
  Dayton *(G-8533)*

MAIL-ORDER HOUSES: Educational Splys & Eqpt

Bendon Inc ....D...... 419 207-3600
  Ashland *(G-685)*
E-Z Grader Company ....G...... 440 247-7511
  Chagrin Falls *(G-3017)*

MAIL-ORDER HOUSES: Fitness & Sporting Goods

Elite Ftscom Inc ....G...... 740 845-0987
  London *(G-12059)*

MAIL-ORDER HOUSES: Food

Coons Homemade Candies ....G...... 740 496-4141
  Harpster *(G-10626)*
Tech Solutions LLC ....G...... 419 852-7190
  Celina *(G-2986)*

MAIL-ORDER HOUSES: Furniture & Furnishings

Sailors Tailor Inc ....G...... 937 862-7781
  Spring Valley *(G-17318)*

MAIL-ORDER HOUSES: General Merchandise

Toccata Technologies Inc ....G...... 614 430-9888
  Powell *(G-16339)*

MAIL-ORDER HOUSES: Gift Items

Krema Products Inc..................................G...... 614 889-4824
  Dublin *(G-8939)*

MAIL-ORDER HOUSES: Novelty Merchandise

Silk Screen Special TS Inc ....G...... 740 246-4843
  Thornville *(G-18036)*

MAIL-ORDER HOUSES: Record & Tape, Music Or Video Club

Dove Cds Inc ....G...... 330 928-9160
  Tallmadge *(G-17981)*

MAIL-ORDER HOUSES: Tools & Hardware

Diy Holster LLC..G...... 419 921-2168
  Elyria *(G-9244)*

MAILBOX RENTAL & RELATED SVCS

Robloc Inc .... G 330 723-5853
　Medina (G-13329)

MAILING & MESSENGER SVCS

A Z Printing Inc .... G 513 745-0700
　Cincinnati (G-3283)
Allen Green Enterprises LLC .... G 330 339-0200
　New Philadelphia (G-14757)
Richardson Printing Corp .... D 740 373-5362
　Marietta (G-12663)

MAILING LIST: Compilers

Brothers Publishing Co LLC .... E 937 548-3330
　Greenville (G-10361)
Cpmm Services Group Inc .... F 614 447-0165
　Columbus (G-6834)
Haines & Company Inc .... C 330 494-9111
　North Canton (G-15090)

MAILING MACHINES WHOLESALERS

Copier Resources Inc .... G 614 268-1100
　Columbus (G-6818)

MAILING SVCS, NEC

Aero Fulfillment Services Corp .... D 800 225-7145
　Mason (G-12820)
Bindery & Spc Pressworks Inc .... D 614 873-4623
　Plain City (G-16178)
Bpm Realty Inc .... E 614 221-6811
　Columbus (G-6692)
Buckeye Business Forms Inc ...... G 614 882-1890
　Westerville (G-19982)
Covap Inc .... F 513 793-1855
　Blue Ash (G-1753)
Dayton Mailing Services Inc .... E 937 222-5056
　Dayton (G-8138)
Directconnectgroup Ltd .... A 216 281-2866
　Cleveland (G-5097)
Eg Enterprise Services Inc .... F 216 431-3300
　Cleveland (G-5158)
Fine Line Graphics Corp .... C 614 486-0276
　Columbus (G-6923)
Hkm Drect Mkt Cmmnications Inc ... C 216 651-9500
　Cleveland (G-5412)
Macke Brothers Inc .... D 513 771-7500
　Cincinnati (G-3969)
Marco Printed Products Co Inc ... G 937 435-3680
　Dayton (G-8333)
Northcoast Pmm LLC .... F 419 540-8667
　Toledo (G-18428)
Porath Business Services Inc ..... F 216 626-0060
　Cleveland (G-5896)
Power Management Inc .... E 937 222-2909
　Dayton (G-8430)
Print All Inc .... G 419 534-2880
　Toledo (G-18484)
Victory Direct LLC .... G 614 626-0000
　Gahanna (G-10110)
Youngstown Letter Shop Inc .... G 330 793-4935
　Youngstown (G-21079)

MANAGEMENT CONSULTING SVCS: Automation & Robotics

Mitsubishi Elc Automtn Inc .... G 937 492-3058
　Sidney (G-17054)
Recognition Robotics Inc .... F 440 590-0499
　Elyria (G-9319)
Scott Systems Intl Inc .... F 740 383-8383
　Marion (G-12733)

MANAGEMENT CONSULTING SVCS: Business

5me LLC .... E 513 719-1600
　Cincinnati (G-3232)
5me Holdings LLC .... G 859 534-4872
　Cincinnati (G-3233)
Crimson Gate Consulting Co ...... G 614 805-0897
　Dublin (G-8904)
Salient Systems Inc .... E 614 792-5800
　Dublin (G-8979)

MANAGEMENT CONSULTING SVCS: Construction Project

Elite Property Group LLC .... F 216 356-7469
　Elyria (G-9250)
Kbc Services .... F 513 693-3743
　Loveland (G-12203)
Mc Cully Supply & Sales Inc .... G 330 497-2211
　Canton (G-2749)

MANAGEMENT CONSULTING SVCS: Corporation Organizing

Comex North America Inc .... D 303 307-2100
　Cleveland (G-5001)
Pwi Inc .... F 732 212-8110
　New Albany (G-14635)

MANAGEMENT CONSULTING SVCS: General

Faith Guiding Cafe LLC .... F 614 245-8451
　New Albany (G-14623)
Quarrymasters Inc .... G 330 612-0474
　Canton (G-2797)

MANAGEMENT CONSULTING SVCS: Industrial

4r Enterprises Incorporated .... G 330 923-9799
　Cuyahoga Falls (G-7829)
Road Maintenance Products .... G 740 465-7181
　Morral (G-14405)
Stellar Industrial Tech Co .... G 740 654-7052
　Lancaster (G-11612)

MANAGEMENT CONSULTING SVCS: Industry Specialist

Bar Codes Unlimited Inc .... G 937 434-2633
　Dayton (G-8051)
Chemsultants International Inc ... E 440 974-3080
　Mentor (G-13412)
Great Lakes Defense Svcs LLC .. G 216 272-3450
　University Heights (G-18942)
Ketman Corporation .... G 330 262-1688
　Wooster (G-20613)
Telex Communications Inc .... F 419 865-0972
　Toledo (G-18546)

MANAGEMENT CONSULTING SVCS: New Products & Svcs

Akron Centl Engrv Mold Mch Inc ... E 330 794-8704
　Akron (G-34)

MANAGEMENT CONSULTING SVCS: Public Utilities

Sabre Energy Corporation .... G 740 685-8266
　Lore City (G-12140)

MANAGEMENT CONSULTING SVCS: Real Estate

Acer Contracting LLC .... G 702 236-5917
　Columbus (G-6537)

MANAGEMENT CONSULTING SVCS: Training & Development

Hard Chrome Plating Consultant ... G 216 631-9090
　Cleveland (G-5374)
Honda of America Mfg Inc .... C 937 644-0724
　Marysville (G-12792)
Leidos Inc .... D 937 431-2270
　Beavercreek (G-1326)

MANAGEMENT CONSULTING SVCS: Transportation

Comprehensive Logistics Co Inc ... E 330 793-0504
　Youngstown (G-20877)
CPC Logistics Inc .... D 513 874-5787
　Fairfield (G-9492)
Ds Express Carriers Inc .... G 419 433-6200
　Norwalk (G-15388)

MANAGEMENT SERVICES

Babcock & Wilcox Company .... A 330 753-4511
　Barberton (G-1059)

Cardinal Health Inc .... G 614 553-3830
　Dublin (G-8893)
Cardinal Health Inc .... A 614 757-5000
　Dublin (G-8894)
Central Coca-Cola Btlg Co Inc ... G 740 474-2180
　Circleville (G-4538)
Central Coca-Cola Btlg Co Inc ... G 330 875-1487
　Akron (G-110)
Central Coca-Cola Btlg Co Inc ... G 330 487-0212
　Macedonia (G-12282)
CFM Religion Pubg Group LLC .. E 513 931-4050
　Cincinnati (G-3461)
Coal Services Inc .... D 740 795-5220
　Powhatan Point (G-16341)
Eleet Cryogenics Inc .... E 330 874-4009
　Bolivar (G-1913)
Instantwhip-Columbus Inc .... G 614 871-9447
　Grove City (G-10435)
Kurtz Bros Compost Services .... G 330 864-2621
　Akron (G-242)
Leadec Corp .... E 513 731-3590
　Blue Ash (G-1804)
Ohio Designer Craftsmen Entps ... G 614 486-7119
　Columbus (G-7245)
Pf Management Inc .... G 513 874-8741
　West Chester (G-19885)
Revolution Group Inc .... D 614 212-1111
　Westerville (G-20020)
Special Mtls RES & Tech Inc ..... G 440 777-4024
　North Olmsted (G-15200)
TAC Industries Inc .... B 937 328-5200
　Springfield (G-17502)

MANAGEMENT SVCS, FACILITIES SUPPORT: Environ Remediation

Alpha Omega Bioremediation LLC ... F 614 287-2600
　Columbus (G-6577)
Indoor Envmtl Specialists Inc ..... F 937 433-5202
　Dayton (G-8262)
Tetra Tech Inc .... F 330 286-3683
　Canfield (G-2549)

MANAGEMENT SVCS: Administrative

Instantwhip Foods Inc .... F 614 488-2536
　Columbus (G-7034)
Media Procurement Services Inc ... G 513 977-3000
　Cincinnati (G-3996)

MANAGEMENT SVCS: Business

Ohio Cllbrtive Lrng Sltons Inc ..... E 216 595-5289
　Beachwood (G-1255)

MANAGEMENT SVCS: Construction

Ameridian Specialty Services ..... E 513 769-0150
　Cincinnati (G-3339)
Elite Property Group LLC .... F 216 356-7469
　Elyria (G-9250)
Eric Allshouse LLC .... G 330 533-4258
　Canfield (G-2527)
Ingle-Barr Inc .... C 740 702-6117
　Chillicothe (G-3195)
Mel Heitkamp Builders Ltd .... G 419 375-0405
　Fort Recovery (G-9825)
Protective Industrial Polymers .... F 440 327-0015
　North Ridgeville (G-15246)

MANAGEMENT SVCS: Financial, Business

Dco LLC .... B 419 931-9086
　Perrysburg (G-15938)
Dome Energicorp .... G 440 892-4900
　Westlake (G-20110)
Jmac Inc .... E 614 436-2418
　Columbus (G-7069)

MANHOLES & COVERS: Metal

Ej Usa Inc .... G 614 871-2436
　Grove City (G-10428)
Ej Usa Inc .... F 330 782-3900
　Youngstown (G-20898)
Knappco Corporation .... C 816 741-0786
　West Chester (G-19731)

MANICURE PREPARATIONS

Hair & Nail Impressions .... G 937 399-0221
　Springfield (G-17409)

PRODUCT SECTION

MANIFOLDS: Pipe, Fabricated From Purchased Pipe

Propipe Technologies Inc .... E 513 424-5311
 Middletown *(G-13945)*
Rexarc International Inc .... E 937 839-4604
 West Alexandria *(G-19620)*

MANNEQUINS

Denton Atd Inc .... E 567 265-5200
 Huron *(G-11093)*

MANUFACTURED & MOBILE HOME DEALERS

Pro Fab Industries Inc .... G 317 297-0461
 Dundee *(G-9025)*

MANUFACTURING INDUSTRIES, NEC

4S Company .... F 330 792-5518
 Youngstown *(G-20829)*
A-Buck Manufacturing Inc .... G 937 687-3738
 New Lebanon *(G-14706)*
Abby Industries LLC .... G 513 502-9865
 Eaton *(G-9141)*
Access Manufacturing Svcs LLC .... G 330 659-9893
 Richfield *(G-16461)*
Accu Pak Mfg Inc .... G 330 644-3015
 Akron *(G-27)*
Ace Assembly Packaging Inc .... E 330 866-9117
 Waynesburg *(G-19561)*
Actual Industries LLC .... G 614 379-2739
 Columbus *(G-6541)*
Aerovent Inc .... G 937 473-3789
 Covington *(G-7779)*
Alk Industries LLC .... G 513 429-3047
 Cincinnati *(G-3320)*
All Points Industries Inc .... G 513 826-0681
 Cincinnati *(G-3322)*
Alliance Mfg Svcs Inc .... G 937 222-3394
 Trotwood *(G-18627)*
Alt Fuel LLC .... G 419 865-4196
 Toledo *(G-18169)*
American Pioneer Manufacturing .... G 330 457-1400
 New Waterford *(G-14835)*
Aquasurtech OEM Corp .... G 614 577-1203
 Gahanna *(G-10075)*
Arrowhead Industries .... G 440 349-2846
 Solon *(G-17108)*
Axalta Coating Systems USA LLC .... D 614 777-7230
 Hilliard *(G-10809)*
Bankhurst Industries LLC .... G 216 272-5775
 Solon *(G-17111)*
Birge Heavy Industries Ltd .... E 440 821-3249
 Elyria *(G-9225)*
Blue Creek Renewables LLC .... G 419 576-7855
 Paulding *(G-15857)*
BMC of Barfield Inc .... G 513 860-4455
 Hamilton *(G-10542)*
Bomb Mfg LLC .... G 419 559-9689
 Fremont *(G-10001)*
C&H Industries .... G 330 899-0001
 Canton *(G-2603)*
CNB Machining and Mfg LLC .... G 330 877-7920
 Hartville *(G-10687)*
Connelly Industries LLC .... G 330 468-0675
 Macedonia *(G-12285)*
Continental Fan Mfg .... G 937 233-5524
 Huber Heights *(G-11015)*
Creation Industries LLC .... G 440 554-6286
 Middlefield *(G-13787)*
Dem Manufacturing LLC .... F 440 564-7160
 Newbury *(G-14951)*
Devault Industries LLC .... G 330 456-6070
 Canton *(G-2656)*
DSI Parts LLC .... G 937 746-4678
 Miamisburg *(G-13661)*
Duramax Marine Industries .... G 419 668-3728
 Norwalk *(G-15390)*
Eaglehead Manufacturing Co .... G 440 951-0400
 Eastlake *(G-9106)*
Elaire Corporation .... G 419 843-2192
 Toledo *(G-18276)*
Elevated Industries LLC .... G 937 608-3325
 Xenia *(G-20769)*
Energizer Battery Mfg Inc .... G 330 527-2191
 Garrettsville *(G-10189)*
Epik Ltd .... G 419 768-2498
 Fredericktown *(G-9968)*

Faw Industries .... G 216 651-9595
 Cleveland *(G-5222)*
Fbr Industries Inc .... G 330 701-7425
 Mineral Ridge *(G-14165)*
Fortress Industries LLC .... G 614 402-3045
 Johnstown *(G-11266)*
Frugal Systems .... G 419 957-7863
 Carey *(G-2881)*
Gdc Industries LLC .... G 937 640-1212
 Dayton *(G-8216)*
Gojo Industries Inc .... F 800 321-9647
 Cuyahoga Falls *(G-7875)*
Grant Solutions .... G 937 344-5558
 Tipp City *(G-18114)*
Green Door Industries LLC .... G 614 558-1663
 Blacklick *(G-1684)*
Groff Industries .... F 216 634-9100
 Cleveland *(G-5354)*
Gsr Industries LLC .... G 440 934-0201
 Cleveland *(G-5357)*
Highland Technologies LLC .... G 513 739-3510
 Mount Orab *(G-14443)*
Housing & Emrgncy Lgstcs Plnnr .... E 209 201-7511
 Lisbon *(G-11969)*
J S Manufacturing LLC .... G 330 815-2136
 Kent *(G-11336)*
J-Fab .... G 740 384-2649
 Wellston *(G-19602)*
Jrf Industries Ltd .... G 330 665-3130
 Copley *(G-7687)*
JW Manufacturing .... G 419 375-5536
 Fort Recovery *(G-9824)*
K-Column LLC .... G 937 269-3696
 Eaton *(G-9155)*
Kf Technologies and Custom Mfg .... G 419 426-0172
 Attica *(G-857)*
Kiser Industries llc .... G 937 332-6723
 Troy *(G-18682)*
Kitto Katsu Inc .... G 818 256-6997
 Clayton *(G-4576)*
Kole Industries .... G 330 353-1751
 Canton *(G-2728)*
L E P D Industries Ltd .... G 614 985-1470
 Powell *(G-16326)*
Lance Industries Inc .... G 740 243-6657
 Lancaster *(G-11583)*
Linebacker Inc .... G 614 340-1446
 Columbus *(G-7130)*
Maca Mold & Machine Co Inc .... G 330 854-0292
 Canal Fulton *(G-2485)*
Manufacturing Company LLC .... G 414 708-7583
 Cincinnati *(G-3977)*
MCS Mfg LLC .... G 419 923-0169
 Lyons *(G-12274)*
Midwest Stamping & Mfg Co .... G 419 298-2394
 Edgerton *(G-9177)*
Morris Technologies .... G 330 384-3084
 Akron *(G-288)*
New Republic Industries LLC .... F 614 580-9927
 Marysville *(G-12803)*
Nexstep Commercial Pdts LLC .... G 937 322-5163
 Springfield *(G-17461)*
Nichols Industries .... G 614 866-8451
 Columbus *(G-7220)*
Njf Manufacturing LLC .... G 419 294-0400
 Upper Sandusky *(G-18968)*
NI Mfg & Distribution Sys In .... G 513 422-5216
 Middletown *(G-13972)*
Norkaam Industries LLC .... G 330 873-9793
 Akron *(G-298)*
Norris North Manufacturing .... G 330 691-0449
 Canton *(G-2764)*
Norstar International LLC .... G 513 404-3543
 Cincinnati *(G-4085)*
OBrien Industries LLC .... G 513 476-0040
 Cincinnati *(G-4096)*
Ohio Manufacturing EXT Partnr .... G 614 644-8788
 Columbus *(G-7250)*
Oveco Industries Electrica .... G 740 381-3326
 Richmond *(G-16497)*
Pdi Constellation LLC .... G 216 271-7344
 Solon *(G-17213)*
Pegasus Industries .... G 740 772-1049
 Chillicothe *(G-3207)*
Phe Manufacturing .... G 937 790-1582
 Franklin *(G-9910)*
Prochaska Industries LLC .... G 440 423-0464
 Gates Mills *(G-10208)*
Proto Prcsion Mfg Slutions LLC .... F 614 771-0080
 Hilliard *(G-10856)*

Pyramid Industries LLC .... F 614 783-1543
 Columbus *(G-7358)*
Quality Compound Mfg .... G 440 353-0150
 North Ridgeville *(G-15248)*
Restless Noggins Mfg LLC .... G 330 526-6908
 North Canton *(G-15114)*
Rmw Industries Inc .... G 440 439-1971
 Bedford Heights *(G-1479)*
Royal Mfg .... G 419 902-8222
 Findlay *(G-9750)*
RPM Industries .... G 440 268-8077
 Elyria *(G-9323)*
S & H Industries Inc .... G 216 831-0550
 Cleveland *(G-6019)*
Saltcreek Industries .... G 330 674-2816
 Millersburg *(G-14125)*
Sarver Industries LLC .... G 419 455-5509
 Tiffin *(G-18081)*
Scentsible Scents Ltd .... G 937 572-6690
 Dayton *(G-8494)*
Sdi Industries .... G 513 561-4032
 Cincinnati *(G-4313)*
Seavival Inc .... G 330 252-1151
 Akron *(G-374)*
Setco Industries Inc .... G 513 941-5110
 Cincinnati *(G-4327)*
Shafts Mfg .... G 440 942-6012
 Willoughby *(G-20428)*
Sharc Industries .... G 216 272-0668
 Columbia Station *(G-6448)*
Softpoint Industries .... G 330 668-2645
 Copley *(G-7696)*
Soldier Tech & Armor RES LLC .... G 330 896-5217
 Akron *(G-381)*
Solomon Industries LLC .... G 937 558-5334
 Troy *(G-18708)*
T and D Industries LLC .... G 937 321-3424
 Dayton *(G-8536)*
Texstone Industries .... G 419 722-4664
 Findlay *(G-9767)*
Thoroughbred Gt Mfg LLC .... F 330 533-0048
 Canfield *(G-2550)*
Tmh Industries LLC .... G 954 232-7938
 Dublin *(G-9005)*
Tri Dlta Metal Fabrication LLC .... G 937 499-4315
 Miamisburg *(G-13728)*
Ttr Manufacturing .... G 440 366-5005
 Elyria *(G-9339)*
Tuffy Manufacturing .... G 330 940-2356
 Cuyahoga Falls *(G-7930)*
Tunnel Vision Hoops LLC .... G 440 487-0939
 Shaker Heights *(G-16939)*
V Mast Manufacturing Inc .... G 330 409-8116
 Canton *(G-2856)*
Valentino Industries LLC .... G 330 523-7216
 Richfield *(G-16493)*
Vermilion Dock Masters .... G 440 244-5370
 Vermilion *(G-19171)*
Vic Maroscher .... F 330 332-4958
 Salem *(G-16780)*
Voodoo Industries .... G 440 653-5333
 Avon Lake *(G-1012)*
Waterloo Industries Inc .... G 800 833-8851
 Cleveland *(G-6292)*
Wellington Manufacturing .... G 440 647-1162
 Wellington *(G-19584)*
Western Reserve Industries LLC .... G 330 238-1800
 Beloit *(G-1572)*
Wheeler Embroidery .... G 740 550-9751
 Ironton *(G-11177)*
Wilks Industries .... G 330 868-5105
 Minerva *(G-14206)*
Worldwide Machining & Mfg LLC .... G 937 902-5629
 Moraine *(G-14400)*
Yoder Manufacturing .... G 740 504-5028
 Howard *(G-10998)*

MAPS

Hampton Publishing Company .... G 513 777-9543
 Liberty Township *(G-11816)*
Sentinel USA Inc .... F 740 345-6412
 Newark *(G-14917)*

MAPS & CHARTS, WHOLESALE

Ckm Ventures LLC .... G 216 623-0370
 Cleveland *(G-4935)*

Employee Codes: A=Over 500 employees, B=251-500
C=101-250, D=51-100, E=20-50, F=10-19, G=3-9

MARBLE, BUILDING: Cut & Shaped

Akron Cultured Marble Pdts LLC ....G....... 330 628-6757
 Mogadore *(G-14228)*
Al-Co Products Inc ....F 419 399-3867
 Latty *(G-11624)*
Custom Cast Marbleworks Inc ....E 513 769-6505
 Cincinnati *(G-3564)*
Engineered Marble Inc ....G....... 614 308-0041
 Columbus *(G-6895)*
Heritage Marble of Ohio Inc ....E 614 436-1464
 Columbus *(G-6990)*
Ohio Tile & Marble Co ....E 513 541-4211
 Cincinnati *(G-4105)*
Pietra Naturale Inc ....F 937 438-8882
 Franklin *(G-9911)*
Piqua Granite & Marble Co Inc ....G....... 937 773-2000
 Piqua *(G-16153)*
Suburban Marble and Granite Co ....G....... 216 281-5557
 Cleveland *(G-6113)*

MARINAS

Wadsworth Excavating Inc ....G....... 419 898-0771
 Oak Harbor *(G-15448)*

MARINE CARGO HANDLING SVCS

Eae Logistics Company LLC ....G....... 440 417-4788
 Madison *(G-12348)*
McGinnis Inc ....C....... 740 377-4391
 South Point *(G-17286)*
McNational Inc ....C....... 740 377-4391
 South Point *(G-17287)*
Rayle Coal Co ....F 740 695-2197
 Saint Clairsville *(G-16648)*

MARINE HARDWARE

Great Midwest Yacht Co ....G....... 740 965-4511
 Sunbury *(G-17887)*
Hydromotive Engineering Co ....G....... 330 425-4266
 Twinsburg *(G-18793)*
Minderman Marine Products Inc ....G....... 419 732-2626
 Port Clinton *(G-16253)*
Racelite South Coast Inc ....F 216 581-4600
 Maple Heights *(G-12578)*
Worthignton Products Inc ....G....... 330 452-7400
 Canton *(G-2865)*

MARINE PROPELLER REPAIR SVCS

Minderman Marine Products Inc ....G....... 419 732-2626
 Port Clinton *(G-16253)*

MARINE SPLY DEALERS

Great Midwest Yacht Co ....G....... 740 965-4511
 Sunbury *(G-17887)*
Jacks Marine Inc ....G....... 440 997-5060
 Ashtabula *(G-781)*

MARINE SPLYS WHOLESALERS

Hydromotive Engineering Co ....G....... 330 425-4266
 Twinsburg *(G-18793)*

MARKETS: Meat & fish

D & H Meats Inc ....G....... 419 387-7767
 Vanlue *(G-19153)*
Riesbeck Food Markets Inc ....C....... 740 695-3401
 Saint Clairsville *(G-16649)*
Strasburg Provision Inc ....E 330 878-1059
 Strasburg *(G-17653)*

MARKING DEVICES

Akron Paint & Varnish Inc ....D....... 330 773-8911
 Akron *(G-46)*
Bishop Machine Tool & Die ....F 740 453-8818
 Zanesville *(G-21110)*
Dayton Stencil Works Company ....E 937 223-3233
 Dayton *(G-8145)*
Dischem International Inc ....G....... 330 494-5210
 Canton *(G-2660)*
E C Shaw Co ....E 513 721-6334
 Cincinnati *(G-3616)*
East Cleveland Rubber Stamp ....G....... 216 851-5050
 Cleveland *(G-5137)*
Hathaway Stamp & Ident Co of C ....F 513 621-1052
 Cincinnati *(G-3802)*
Identity Holding Company LLC ....D....... 216 514-1277
 Cleveland *(G-5435)*
Inner Products Sales Inc ....G....... 216 581-4141
 Bedford *(G-1416)*
Jerry Pulfer ....G....... 937 778-1861
 Piqua *(G-16134)*
Master Marking Company Inc ....F 330 688-6797
 Stow *(G-17604)*
Microcom Corporation ....E 740 548-6262
 Lewis Center *(G-11767)*
Monode Marking Products Inc ....F 419 929-0346
 New London *(G-14731)*
Monode Steel Stamp Inc ....E 419 929-3501
 New London *(G-14732)*
Quick As A Wink Printing Co ....F 419 224-9786
 Lima *(G-11926)*
Raschke Engraving Inc ....G....... 330 677-5544
 Kent *(G-11373)*
REA Elektronik Inc ....F 440 232-0555
 Bedford *(G-1440)*
Superior Steel Stamp Co ....G....... 216 431-6460
 Cleveland *(G-6127)*
Technology and Services Inc ....G....... 740 626-2020
 Chillicothe *(G-3227)*
The Metal Marker Mfg Co ....F 440 327-2300
 North Ridgeville *(G-15255)*
Volk Corporation ....G....... 513 621-1052
 Cincinnati *(G-4483)*

MARKING DEVICES: Canceling Stamps, Hand, Rubber Or Metal

Telesis Technologies Inc ....C....... 740 477-5000
 Circleville *(G-4562)*

MARKING DEVICES: Date Stamps, Hand, Rubber Or Metal

Desmond Engraving Co Inc ....G....... 216 265-8338
 Cleveland *(G-5086)*
Sprinter Marking Inc ....F 740 453-1000
 Zanesville *(G-21182)*

MARKING DEVICES: Embossing Seals & Hand Stamps

Ace Rubber Stamp & Off Sup Co ....E 216 771-8483
 Cleveland *(G-4604)*
Hathaway Stamp Co ....F 513 621-1052
 Cincinnati *(G-3803)*
Marking Devices Inc ....E 216 861-4498
 Cleveland *(G-5622)*
Royal Acme Corporation ....E 216 241-1477
 Cleveland *(G-6009)*
System Seals Inc ....D....... 440 735-0200
 Cleveland *(G-6140)*
Ulrich Rubber Stamp Company ....G....... 419 339-9939
 Elida *(G-9202)*

MARKING DEVICES: Embossing Seals, Corporate & Official

Williams Steel Rule Die Co ....F 216 431-3232
 Cleveland *(G-6311)*

MARKING DEVICES: Figures, Metal

Infosight Corporation ....D....... 740 642-3600
 Chillicothe *(G-3194)*
Lectroetch Co ....F 440 934-1249
 Sheffield Village *(G-16970)*
Mark-All Enterprises LLC ....E 800 433-3615
 Akron *(G-268)*

MARKING DEVICES: Letters, Metal

Rise Holdings LLC ....F 440 946-9646
 Willoughby *(G-20422)*

MARKING DEVICES: Numbering Stamps, Hand, Rubber Or Metal

Quality Rubber Stamp Inc ....G....... 614 235-2700
 Columbus *(G-7365)*

MARKING DEVICES: Pads, Inking & Stamping

Innovative Ceramic Corp ....G....... 330 385-6515
 East Liverpool *(G-9059)*

MARKING DEVICES: Screens, Textile Printing

Marathon Mfg & Sup Co ....D....... 330 343-2656
 New Philadelphia *(G-14783)*
Zitello Fine Art LLC ....G....... 330 792-8894
 Youngstown *(G-21087)*

MARKING DEVICES: Stationary Embossers, Personal

Global Partners USA Co Inc ....G....... 513 276-4981
 West Chester *(G-19717)*

MARKING DEVICES: Textile Making Stamps, Hand, Rubber/Metal

Ccsi Inc ....G....... 800 742-8535
 Akron *(G-106)*
Greg G Wright & Sons LLC ....E 513 721-3310
 Cincinnati *(G-3784)*
Mark Rite Co ....G....... 330 757-7229
 Youngstown *(G-20966)*

MASQUERADE OR THEATRICAL COSTUMES STORES

Adyl Inc ....G....... 330 797-8700
 Austintown *(G-928)*
Costume Specialists Inc ....G....... 614 464-2115
 Columbus *(G-6826)*

MASSAGE MACHINES, ELECTRIC: Barber & Beauty Shops

Vandalia Massage Therapy ....G....... 937 890-8660
 Vandalia *(G-19149)*

MASSAGE PARLORS

Oil Bar LLC ....F 614 880-3950
 Columbus *(G-6504)*

MASTIC ROOFING COMPOSITION

Chemspec Ltd ....F 330 896-0355
 Uniontown *(G-18915)*

MASTS: Cast Aluminum

Non-Ferrous Casting Co ....G....... 937 228-1162
 Dayton *(G-8382)*
Precision Aluminum Inc ....E 330 335-2351
 Wadsworth *(G-19265)*

MATERIAL GRINDING & PULVERIZING SVCS NEC

Ace Grinding Co ....G....... 440 951-6760
 Willoughby *(G-20266)*
Centerless Grinding Service ....G....... 216 251-4100
 Cleveland *(G-4900)*
Erichar Inc ....G....... 216 402-2628
 Cleveland *(G-5188)*
Fleig Enterprises Inc ....G....... 216 361-8020
 Cleveland *(G-5249)*
Melvin Grain Co ....G....... 937 382-1249
 Wilmington *(G-20499)*
Resource Recycling Inc ....F 419 222-2702
 Lima *(G-11929)*
Tangent Company LLC ....G....... 440 543-2775
 Chagrin Falls *(G-3079)*

MATERIALS HANDLING EQPT WHOLESALERS

American Solving Inc ....G....... 440 234-7373
 Brookpark *(G-2135)*
Bobco Enterprises Inc ....F 419 867-3560
 Toledo *(G-18208)*
Bud Corp ....G....... 740 967-9992
 Johnstown *(G-11261)*
Delta Crane Systems Inc ....F 937 324-7425
 Springfield *(G-17387)*
Forte Indus Eqp Systems Inc ....E 513 398-2800
 Mason *(G-12871)*
Great Lakes Power Products Inc ....D....... 440 951-5111
 Mentor *(G-13462)*
Innovative Hdlg & Metalfab LLC ....E 419 882-7480
 Sylvania *(G-17945)*

PRODUCT SECTION

MEAT PRDTS: Luncheon Meat, From Purchased Meat

Intelligrated Systems LLC..................A...... 513 701-7300
  Mason *(G-12895)*
Mes Material Hdlg Systems LLC..........G...... 740 477-8920
  Circleville *(G-4548)*
Midlands Millroom Supply Inc............E...... 330 453-9100
  Canton *(G-2753)*
Mmh Americas Inc................................G...... 414 764-6200
  Springfield *(G-17449)*
Mmh Holdings Inc..................................G...... 937 525-5533
  Springfield *(G-17450)*
Ohio Mechanical Handling Co...............F...... 330 773-5165
  Akron *(G-308)*
Scott-Randall Systems Inc....................F...... 937 446-2293
  Sardinia *(G-16873)*

MATS & MATTING, MADE FROM PURCHASED WIRE

Kadee Industries Newco Inc................F...... 440 439-8650
  Bedford *(G-1420)*

MATS OR MATTING, NEC: Rubber

DTR Equipment Inc...............................F...... 419 692-3000
  Delphos *(G-8742)*
Durable Corporation..............................D...... 800 537-1603
  Norwalk *(G-15389)*
Garro Tread Corporation.......................G...... 330 376-3125
  Akron *(G-181)*
Ludlow Composites Corporation..........C...... 419 332-5531
  Fremont *(G-10038)*
R C Musson Rubber Co.........................E...... 330 773-7651
  Akron *(G-339)*
R T H Processing Inc............................D...... 419 692-3000
  Delphos *(G-8754)*
Space-Links Inc....................................E...... 330 788-2401
  Youngstown *(G-21034)*
Ultimate Rb Inc.....................................E...... 419 692-3000
  Delphos *(G-8760)*

MATS, MATTING & PADS: Auto, Floor, Exc Rubber Or Plastic

Crown Dielectric Inds Inc.....................C...... 614 224-5161
  Columbus *(G-6839)*

MATS, MATTING & PADS: Nonwoven

Absorbcore LLC....................................G...... 440 614-0457
  North Olmsted *(G-15180)*
Durable Corporation..............................D...... 800 537-1603
  Norwalk *(G-15389)*
Spacelinks Enterprises Inc..................D...... 330 788-2401
  Youngstown *(G-21035)*
Tranzonic Companies............................C...... 216 535-4300
  Richmond Heights *(G-16506)*
Tranzonic Companies............................C...... 440 446-0643
  Cleveland *(G-6198)*

MATS: Table, Plastic & Textile

A & W Table Pad Co..............................F...... 800 541-0271
  Cleveland *(G-4582)*

MATTRESS STORES

Banner Mattress Co Inc........................G...... 419 324-7181
  Toledo *(G-18198)*
Homecare Mattress Inc.........................F...... 937 746-2556
  Franklin *(G-9889)*

MEAL DELIVERY PROGRAMS

Trumbull Mobile Meals Inc...................F...... 330 394-2538
  Warren *(G-19453)*

MEAT & FISH MARKETS: Food & Freezer Plans, Meat

Links Country Meats.............................G...... 419 683-2195
  Crestline *(G-7796)*

MEAT & FISH MARKETS: Freezer Provisioners, Meat

Dumas Meats Inc..................................G...... 330 628-3438
  Mogadore *(G-14235)*

MEAT & MEAT PRDTS WHOLESALERS

Fresh Mark Inc.....................................B...... 330 832-7491
  Massillon *(G-12984)*

Fresh Mark Inc.....................................B...... 330 834-3669
  Massillon *(G-12983)*
Robert Winner Sons Inc.......................E...... 419 582-4321
  Yorkshire *(G-20826)*
Tri-State Beef Co Inc............................E...... 513 579-1722
  Cincinnati *(G-4433)*

MEAT CUTTING & PACKING

Acme Steak & Seafood Inc...................F...... 330 270-8000
  Youngstown *(G-20836)*
Baltic Country Meats............................G...... 330 897-7025
  Baltic *(G-1023)*
C J Kraft Enterprises Inc.......................E...... 740 653-9606
  Lancaster *(G-11551)*
Canaan Country Meats.........................G...... 330 435-4778
  Creston *(G-7804)*
Case Farms of Ohio Inc........................C...... 330 359-7141
  Winesburg *(G-20530)*
Caven and Sons Meat Packing Co.......F...... 937 368-3841
  Conover *(G-7662)*
D & H Meats Inc....................................G...... 419 387-7767
  Vanlue *(G-19153)*
Dee-Jays Custom Butchering...............F...... 740 694-7492
  Fredericktown *(G-9965)*
Duma Deer Processing LLC.................G...... 330 805-3429
  Mogadore *(G-14234)*
Empire Packing Company LP..............A...... 901 948-4788
  Mason *(G-12865)*
Fresh Mark Inc.....................................A...... 330 332-8508
  Salem *(G-16741)*
Fresh Mark Inc.....................................B...... 330 834-3669
  Massillon *(G-12983)*
Gortons Inc...E...... 216 362-1050
  Cleveland *(G-5333)*
Hartville Locker Service Inc.................G...... 330 877-9547
  Hartville *(G-10693)*
Horst Packing Inc..................................G...... 330 482-2997
  Columbiana *(G-6469)*
Industrial Packaging Products.............G...... 440 734-2663
  Cleveland *(G-5454)*
J M Meat Processing............................G...... 740 259-3030
  Mc Dermott *(G-13193)*
Jacoby Packing Co................................G...... 419 924-2684
  West Unity *(G-19970)*
Jones Processing..................................G...... 330 772-2193
  Hartford *(G-10681)*
Karn Meats Inc.....................................E...... 614 252-3712
  Columbus *(G-7083)*
King Kold Inc..E...... 937 836-2731
  Englewood *(G-9366)*
Links Country Meats.............................G...... 419 683-2195
  Crestline *(G-7796)*
Mahan Packing Co Inc..........................E...... 330 889-2454
  Bristolville *(G-2083)*
Mannings Packing Co...........................G...... 937 446-3278
  Sardinia *(G-16870)*
Marshallville Packing Co Inc.................E...... 330 855-2871
  Marshallville *(G-12753)*
Mc Connells Market..............................G...... 740 765-4300
  Richmond *(G-16496)*
New Riegel Cafe Inc.............................E...... 419 595-2255
  New Riegel *(G-14816)*
Northside Meat Co Inc..........................G...... 513 681-4111
  Cincinnati *(G-4088)*
Oiler Processing...................................G...... 740 892-2640
  Utica *(G-19026)*
Patrick M Davidson...............................G...... 513 897-2971
  Waynesville *(G-19571)*
Presslers Meats Inc..............................F...... 330 644-5636
  Akron *(G-329)*
R&C Packing & Custom Butcher..........G...... 740 245-9440
  Bidwell *(G-1668)*
Robert Winner Sons Inc........................E...... 419 582-4321
  Yorkshire *(G-20826)*
Rxpert Consultants LLC.......................G...... 614 579-9384
  Columbus *(G-7409)*
Shaker Valley Foods Inc.......................E...... 216 961-8600
  Cleveland *(G-6046)*
Smithfield Packaged Meats Corp.........B...... 513 782-3805
  Cincinnati *(G-4349)*
Smokin TS Smokehouse........................G...... 440 577-1117
  Jefferson *(G-11238)*
Sugar Creek Packing Co.......................B...... 937 268-6601
  Dayton *(G-8528)*
Sugar Creek Packing Co.......................C...... 513 874-4422
  West Chester *(G-19800)*
Sugar Creek Packing Co.......................G...... 513 874-4422
  West Chester *(G-19801)*
Tempac LLC..G...... 513 505-9700
  West Chester *(G-19806)*

Tri-State Beef Co Inc............................E...... 513 579-1722
  Cincinnati *(G-4433)*
Trumbull Locker Plant Inc....................G...... 440 474-4631
  Rock Creek *(G-16534)*
V H Cooper & Co Inc............................B...... 419 678-4853
  Saint Henry *(G-16669)*
Werling and Sons Inc............................F...... 937 338-3281
  Burkettsville *(G-2356)*
Winesburg Meats Inc............................G...... 330 359-5092
  Winesburg *(G-20535)*
Youngs Locker Service Inc...................F...... 740 599-6833
  Danville *(G-7967)*

MEAT MARKETS

Caven and Sons Meat Packing Co.......F...... 937 368-3841
  Conover *(G-7662)*
Dee-Jays Custom Butchering...............F...... 740 694-7492
  Fredericktown *(G-9965)*
Hoffman Meat Processing....................G...... 419 864-3994
  Cardington *(G-2873)*
Honeybaked Ham Company.................E...... 513 583-9700
  Cincinnati *(G-3824)*
John Krusinski......................................F...... 216 441-0100
  Cleveland *(G-5502)*
John Stehlin & Sons Co Inc..................F...... 513 385-6164
  Cincinnati *(G-3881)*
Lee Williams Meats Inc........................E...... 419 729-3893
  Toledo *(G-18379)*
Marshallville Packing Co Inc.................E...... 330 855-2871
  Marshallville *(G-12753)*
Mc Connells Market..............................G...... 740 765-4300
  Richmond *(G-16496)*
Old Country Sausage Kitchen..............G...... 216 662-5988
  Cleveland *(G-5809)*
Pettisville Meats Inc.............................F...... 419 445-0921
  Pettisville *(G-16036)*
Pine Ridge Processing.........................G...... 740 749-3166
  Fleming *(G-9780)*
Trumbull Locker Plant Inc....................G...... 440 474-4631
  Rock Creek *(G-16534)*
Winesburg Meats Inc............................G...... 330 359-5092
  Winesburg *(G-20535)*

MEAT PRDTS: Bacon, Side & Sliced, From Purchased Meat

Sugar Creek Packing Co.......................B...... 740 335-3586
  Wshngtn CT Hs *(G-20745)*
Sugar Creek Packing Co.......................B...... 937 268-6601
  Dayton *(G-8528)*
Sugar Creek Packing Co.......................C...... 513 874-4422
  West Chester *(G-19800)*

MEAT PRDTS: Cooked Meats, From Purchased Meat

Advancepierre Foods Inc.....................G...... 580 616-4403
  Amherst *(G-552)*
King Kold Inc..E...... 937 836-2731
  Englewood *(G-9366)*

MEAT PRDTS: Corned Beef, From Slaughtered Meat

Signature Beef LLC...............................G...... 740 468-3579
  Pleasantville *(G-16230)*

MEAT PRDTS: Cured, From Slaughtered Meat

Troyers Trail Bologna Inc......................E...... 330 893-2414
  Dundee *(G-9029)*

MEAT PRDTS: Frozen

Frank Brunckhorst Company LLC........G...... 614 662-5300
  Groveport *(G-10491)*
Jtm Provisions Company Inc...............B...... 513 367-4900
  Harrison *(G-10653)*
Martin-Brower Company LLC..............B...... 513 773-2301
  West Chester *(G-19741)*
Sunrise Foods Inc.................................E...... 614 276-2880
  Columbus *(G-7500)*

MEAT PRDTS: Luncheon Meat, From Purchased Meat

Fink Meat Company Inc........................G...... 937 390-2750
  Springfield *(G-17402)*

MEAT PRDTS: Pork, Cured, From Purchased Meat

Williams Pork Co Op .... G 419 682-9022
Stryker *(G-17836)*

MEAT PRDTS: Pork, From Slaughtered Meat

Ohio Packing Company .... D 614 445-0627
Columbus *(G-7254)*
Robert Winner Sons Inc .... G 937 548-7513
Greenville *(G-10393)*
Smithfield Packaged Meats Corp ..... C 513 782-3800
Cincinnati *(G-4348)*
V H Cooper & Co Inc .... C 419 375-4116
Fort Recovery *(G-9829)*

MEAT PRDTS: Prepared Beef Prdts From Purchased Beef

Advancepierre Foods Inc .... B 513 874-8741
West Chester *(G-19826)*
Brinkman Turkey Farms Inc .... F 419 365-5127
Findlay *(G-9662)*
Fresh Mark Inc .... B 330 834-3669
Massillon *(G-12983)*
Pierre Holding Corp .... G 513 874-8741
West Chester *(G-19886)*
Wild Joes Inc .... G 513 681-9200
Cincinnati *(G-4508)*

MEAT PRDTS: Prepared Pork Prdts, From Purchased Meat

Brentmoor Hams LLC .... G 513 677-0813
Loveland *(G-12181)*
D D D Hams Inc .... G 440 487-9572
Solon *(G-17130)*

MEAT PRDTS: Sausages, From Purchased Meat

Dirussos Sausage Inc .... E 330 744-1208
Youngstown *(G-20892)*
Edelmann Provision Company .... D 513 881-5800
Harrison *(G-10639)*
Lous Sausage Inc .... F 216 752-5060
Cleveland *(G-5585)*
Mama Mias Foods Inc .... G 216 281-2188
Cleveland *(G-5610)*
Old Country Sausage Kitchen .... G 216 662-5988
Cleveland *(G-5809)*
Queen City Sausage & Provision ... E 513 541-5581
Cincinnati *(G-4241)*
Raddells Sausage .... G 216 486-1944
Cleveland *(G-5954)*
Rays Sausage Inc .... G 216 921-8782
Cleveland *(G-5963)*
Sausage Shoppe .... G 216 351-5213
Brunswick *(G-2237)*

MEAT PRDTS: Sausages, From Slaughtered Meat

Bob Evans Farms Inc .... D 937 372-4493
Xenia *(G-20758)*
Bob Evans Farms Inc .... F 740 245-5305
Bidwell *(G-1664)*
Bob Evans Farms Inc .... B 614 491-2225
New Albany *(G-14609)*
V H Cooper & Co Inc .... E 419 678-4853
Saint Henry *(G-16670)*

MEAT PRDTS: Snack Sticks, Incl Jerky, From Purchased Meat

Johns Jerky & Snack Meats LLC ... G 937 207-7008
South Charleston *(G-17273)*
Simply Unique Snacks LLC .... G 513 223-7736
Cincinnati *(G-4339)*

MEAT PRDTS: Veal, From Slaughtered Meat

Atlantic Veal & Lamb LLC .... G 330 435-6400
Creston *(G-7803)*
Dalton Veal .... G 330 828-8337
Dalton *(G-7939)*
Ohio Farms Packing Co Ltd .... G 330 435-6400
Creston *(G-7808)*

MEAT PROCESSED FROM PURCHASED CARCASSES

A To Z Portion Ctrl Meats Inc .... E 419 358-2926
Bluffton *(G-1883)*
Advancepierre Foods Inc .... G 513 874-8741
West Chester *(G-19827)*
Advancperre Foods Holdings Inc ... E 800 969-2747
West Chester *(G-19828)*
American Foods Group LLC .... E 513 733-8898
Cincinnati *(G-3332)*
Amish Wedding Foods Inc .... E 330 674-9199
Millersburg *(G-14060)*
Carl Rittberger Sr Inc .... E 740 452-2767
Zanesville *(G-21116)*
Caven and Sons Meat Packing Co .. F 937 368-3841
Conover *(G-7662)*
Dumas Meats Inc .... G 330 628-3438
Mogadore *(G-14235)*
Fresh Mark Inc .... G 330 832-7491
Massillon *(G-12984)*
Fresh Mark Inc .... A 330 332-8508
Salem *(G-16741)*
Hillshire Brands Company .... G 330 758-8885
Youngstown *(G-20931)*
Hoffman Meat Processing .... G 419 864-3994
Cardington *(G-2873)*
Honeybaked Ham Company .... E 513 583-9700
Cincinnati *(G-3824)*
John Krusinski .... F 216 441-0100
Cleveland *(G-5502)*
John Stehlin & Sons Co Inc .... F 513 385-6164
Cincinnati *(G-3881)*
Karn Meats Inc .... E 614 252-3712
Columbus *(G-7083)*
Katies Snack Foods LLC .... G 614 440-0780
Hilliard *(G-10836)*
Keith Grimm .... G 419 899-2725
Sherwood *(G-16991)*
Kenosha Beef International Ltd .... C 614 771-1330
Columbus *(G-7087)*
Keystone Foods LLC .... C 419 257-2341
North Baltimore *(G-15044)*
Kings Command Foods LLC .... D 937 526-3553
Versailles *(G-19184)*
Kraft Heinz Foods Company .... B 740 622-0523
Coshocton *(G-7738)*
Lee Williams Meats Inc .... E 419 729-3893
Toledo *(G-18379)*
Marshallville Packing Co Inc .... E 330 855-2871
Marshallville *(G-12753)*
Medina Foods Inc .... E 330 725-1390
Litchfield *(G-11985)*
Patrick M Davidson .... G 513 897-2971
Waynesville *(G-19571)*
Peggys Pride .... G 614 464-2511
Columbus *(G-7307)*
Perfettes Sausage LLC .... G 330 792-0775
Youngstown *(G-20998)*
Pettisville Meats Inc .... F 419 445-0921
Pettisville *(G-16036)*
Robert Winner Sons Inc .... E 419 582-4321
Yorkshire *(G-20826)*
Sara Lee Foods .... G 513 204-4941
Mason *(G-12935)*
Steven Yant .... G 937 596-0497
Jackson Center *(G-11216)*
Strasburg Provision Inc .... E 330 878-1059
Strasburg *(G-17653)*
Sugar Creek Packing Co .... G 513 874-4422
West Chester *(G-19801)*
Tri-State Beef Co Inc .... E 513 579-1722
Cincinnati *(G-4433)*
White Castle System Inc .... B 614 228-5781
Columbus *(G-7603)*
Youngs Locker Service Inc .... F 740 599-6833
Danville *(G-7967)*

MEATS, PACKAGED FROZEN: Wholesalers

A To Z Portion Ctrl Meats Inc .... E 419 358-2926
Bluffton *(G-1883)*
Dee-Jays Custom Butchering .... F 740 694-7492
Fredericktown *(G-9965)*
Frank Brunckhorst Company LLC .. G 614 662-5300
Groveport *(G-10491)*
White Castle System Inc .... B 614 228-5781
Columbus *(G-7603)*

MECHANICAL INSTRUMENT REPAIR SVCS

Fmt Repair Service Co .... G 330 347-7374
Mentor *(G-13444)*

MEDIA BUYING AGENCIES

Pixslap Inc .... G 937 559-2671
Middletown *(G-13942)*

MEDIA: Magnetic & Optical Recording

CD Solutions Inc .... G 937 676-2376
Pleasant Hill *(G-16224)*

MEDICAL & HOSPITAL EQPT WHOLESALERS

Askia Inc .... G 513 828-7443
Cincinnati *(G-3362)*
Biorx LLC .... C 866 442-4679
Cincinnati *(G-3394)*
Ernie Green Industries Inc .... G 614 219-1423
Columbus *(G-6903)*
Homecare Mattress Inc .... F 937 746-2556
Franklin *(G-9889)*
Smiths Medical North America .... G 614 210-7300
Dublin *(G-8990)*
Wbc Group LLC .... D 866 528-2144
Hudson *(G-11082)*

MEDICAL & HOSPITAL SPLYS: Radiation Shielding Garments

Hall Safety Apparel Inc .... F 740 922-3671
Uhrichsville *(G-18887)*

MEDICAL & SURGICAL SPLYS: Atomizers, Medical

Whiteford Industries Inc .... F 419 381-1155
Toledo *(G-18599)*

MEDICAL & SURGICAL SPLYS: Bandages & Dressings

Beiersdorf Inc .... C 513 682-7300
West Chester *(G-19835)*
Jobskin Div of Torbot Group .... E 419 724-1475
Toledo *(G-18359)*

MEDICAL & SURGICAL SPLYS: Braces, Elastic

Daishin Industrial Co .... G 614 766-9535
Dublin *(G-8905)*
Motion Mobility & Design Inc .... F 330 244-9723
North Canton *(G-15103)*

MEDICAL & SURGICAL SPLYS: Braces, Orthopedic

ABI Orthtc/Prosthetic Labs Ltd .... E 330 758-1143
Youngstown *(G-20833)*
Akron Orthotic Solutions Inc .... G 330 253-3002
Akron *(G-45)*
Anatomical Concepts Inc .... F 330 757-3569
Youngstown *(G-20846)*
Arthur W Guilford III Inc .... G 216 362-1350
Cleveland *(G-4739)*
Brace Shop Prosthetic Ortho .... F 513 421-5653
Cincinnati *(G-3407)*
Bracemart LLC .... G 440 353-2830
North Ridgeville *(G-15213)*
Cranial Technologies Inc .... G 844 447-5894
Cincinnati *(G-3557)*
Faretec Inc .... F 440 350-9510
Painesville *(G-15738)*
Findlay American Prosthetic & ..... G 419 424-1622
Findlay *(G-9683)*
North Cast Orthtics Prsthetics ..... F 440 233-4314
Lorain *(G-12108)*
Opc Inc .... G 419 531-2222
Toledo *(G-18440)*
Orthotics & Prosthetics Rehab .... F 330 856-2553
Warren *(G-19429)*
Weber Orthopedic Inc .... G 440 934-1812
Avon *(G-974)*

PRODUCT SECTION

MEDICAL EQPT: Diagnostic

MEDICAL & SURGICAL SPLYS: Canes, Orthopedic

Biocare Orthopedic Prosthetics .... G 614 754-7514
  Columbus *(G-6671)*

MEDICAL & SURGICAL SPLYS: Clothing, Fire Resistant & Protect

Barton-Carey Medical Products .... E 419 887-1285
  Maumee *(G-13078)*
Wcm Holdings Inc .... G 513 705-2100
  Cincinnati *(G-4493)*
West Chester Holdings LLC .... C 800 647-1900
  Cincinnati *(G-4499)*

MEDICAL & SURGICAL SPLYS: Cosmetic Restorations

Anderson Cosmetic & Vein Inst .... G 513 624-7900
  Cincinnati *(G-3345)*

MEDICAL & SURGICAL SPLYS: Foot Appliances, Orthopedic

Northestrn OH Foot & Ankl Asoc .... G 330 633-3445
  Akron *(G-303)*
Stable Step LLC .... E 513 825-1888
  West Chester *(G-19798)*

MEDICAL & SURGICAL SPLYS: Grafts, Artificial

Evanko Wm/Barringer Richd DDS .... G 330 336-6693
  Wadsworth *(G-19238)*
Interplex Medical LLC .... E 513 248-5120
  Milford *(G-14019)*
Osteonovus Inc .... G 617 717-8867
  Toledo *(G-18442)*

MEDICAL & SURGICAL SPLYS: Hosiery, Support

Julius Zorn Inc .... D 330 923-4999
  Cuyahoga Falls *(G-7886)*

MEDICAL & SURGICAL SPLYS: Limbs, Artificial

Capital Prosthetic & .... F 614 451-0446
  Columbus *(G-6732)*
Capital Prosthetic & .... E 567 560-2051
  Mansfield *(G-12419)*
Capital Prosthetic & .... G 740 453-9545
  Zanesville *(G-21115)*
Capital Prosthetic & .... G 740 522-3331
  Newark *(G-14859)*
Comprhnsive Brace Limb Ctr LLC .... G 330 337-8333
  Salem *(G-16730)*
Fidelity Orthopedic Inc .... G 937 228-0682
  Dayton *(G-8194)*
Hanger Prsthetcs & Ortho Inc .... G 330 758-1143
  Youngstown *(G-20928)*
Hanger Prsthetcs & Ortho Inc .... G 330 374-9544
  Akron *(G-198)*
Hanger Prsthetcs & Ortho Inc .... G 937 773-2441
  Piqua *(G-16120)*
Hanger Prsthetcs & Ortho Inc .... G 740 383-2163
  Marion *(G-12709)*
Hanger Prsthetcs & Ortho Inc .... G 419 522-0055
  Marion *(G-12708)*
Hanger Prsthetcs & Ortho Inc .... G 740 454-6215
  Zanesville *(G-21145)*
Kufbag Inc .... G 614 589-8687
  Westerville *(G-20062)*
Lower Limb Centers LLC .... G 440 365-2502
  Elyria *(G-9289)*
Luminaud Inc .... G 440 255-9082
  Mentor *(G-13503)*
Novacare Inc .... G 216 704-4817
  Beachwood *(G-1254)*
Ohio Willow Wood Company .... C 740 869-3377
  Mount Sterling *(G-14464)*
Out On A Limb .... G 513 432-5091
  Cincinnati *(G-4124)*
Prosthetic Design Inc .... G 937 836-1464
  Englewood *(G-9373)*
Swanson Orthotic & Prosthetic .... G 419 690-0026
  Oregon *(G-15570)*

Yanke Bionics Inc .... E 330 762-6411
  Akron *(G-438)*
Yanke Bionics Inc .... G 330 668-4070
  Akron *(G-439)*

MEDICAL & SURGICAL SPLYS: Live Preservers, Exc Cork & Inflat

Beaufort Rfd Inc .... F 330 239-4331
  Sharon Center *(G-16946)*
Greendale Home Fashions LLC .... D 859 916-5475
  Cincinnati *(G-3782)*

MEDICAL & SURGICAL SPLYS: Orthopedic Appliances

Acor Orthopaedic Inc .... D 216 662-4500
  Cleveland *(G-4608)*
Acor Orthopaedic Inc .... G 440 532-0117
  Cleveland *(G-4609)*
Canton Orthotic Laboratory .... G 330 833-0955
  Canton *(G-2614)*
Central Ohio Orthtic Prsthetic .... G 614 659-1580
  Dublin *(G-8898)*
DPM Orthodontics Inc .... G 330 673-0334
  Kent *(G-11316)*
Earthwalk Orthotic .... F 330 837-6569
  Massillon *(G-12978)*
Gaitwell Orthotics Pedorthics .... G 513 829-2217
  Cincinnati *(G-3721)*
Gottfried Medical Inc .... E 419 474-2973
  Toledo *(G-18309)*
Hanger Prsthetcs & Ortho Inc .... G 216 475-4211
  Maple Heights *(G-12573)*
Matplus Ltd .... G 440 352-7201
  Painesville *(G-15761)*
Medical Device Bus Svcs Inc .... E 937 274-5850
  Dayton *(G-8338)*
O P Services Inc .... G 330 723-6679
  Medina *(G-13308)*
Optimus LLC .... G 937 454-1900
  Dayton *(G-8405)*
Orthotic and Prostetic Spc .... F 216 531-2773
  Euclid *(G-9431)*
Orthotic and Prosthetic I .... G 330 723-6679
  Medina *(G-13313)*
Osteo Solution .... G 614 485-9790
  Westerville *(G-20015)*
Prosthetic & Orthotic Services .... G 330 723-6679
  Medina *(G-13324)*
Sroufe Healthcare Products LLC .... E 260 894-4171
  Wadsworth *(G-19278)*
Zimmer Inc .... C 614 508-6000
  Columbus *(G-7627)*
Zimmer Surgical Inc .... B 800 321-5533
  Dover *(G-8863)*

MEDICAL & SURGICAL SPLYS: Personal Safety Eqpt

Beeline Purchasing LLC .... G 513 703-3733
  Mason *(G-12834)*
Ohio Safety Products LLC .... G 216 255-3067
  Highland Heights *(G-10796)*
Targeting Customer Safety Inc .... G 330 865-9593
  Akron *(G-396)*

MEDICAL & SURGICAL SPLYS: Prosthetic Appliances

Ace Prosthetics Inc .... G 614 291-8325
  Columbus *(G-6536)*
Action Prosthetics LLC .... G 937 548-9100
  Greenville *(G-10359)*
American Orthopedics Inc .... E 614 291-6454
  Columbus *(G-6585)*
Hanger Prsthetcs & Ortho Inc .... F 419 841-9852
  Toledo *(G-18321)*
Hanger Prsthetcs & Ortho Inc .... F 937 228-5462
  Dayton *(G-8243)*
Hanger Prsthetcs & Ortho Inc .... G 740 266-6400
  Steubenville *(G-17536)*
Hanger Prsthetcs & Ortho Inc .... G 740 654-1884
  Lancaster *(G-11578)*
Materials Engineering & Dev .... G 937 884-5118
  Brookville *(G-2177)*
Miller Prsthtics Orthotics LLC .... G 740 421-4211
  Belpre *(G-1580)*
Neu Prosthetics & Orthotics .... G 740 363-3522
  Delaware *(G-8710)*

O & P Options LLC .... G 513 791-7767
  Montgomery *(G-14296)*
Optimus LLC .... G 614 263-5462
  Columbus *(G-7274)*
Ortho Prosthetic Center .... G 419 352-8161
  Bowling Green *(G-1988)*
Orthotic Prosthetic Center .... G 419 531-2222
  Toledo *(G-18441)*
Presque Isle Orthotics .... G 216 371-0660
  Beachwood *(G-1268)*
Swanson Prosthetic Center Inc .... G 419 472-8910
  Toledo *(G-18538)*
Synthetic Body Parts Inc .... G 440 838-0985
  Brecksville *(G-2059)*
Touch Life Centers LLC .... G 614 388-8075
  Hilliard *(G-10871)*
Yanke Bionics Inc .... G 330 833-0955
  Massillon *(G-13058)*

MEDICAL & SURGICAL SPLYS: Respiratory Protect Eqpt, Personal

MST Inc .... G 419 542-6645
  Hicksville *(G-10779)*

MEDICAL & SURGICAL SPLYS: Splints, Pneumatic & Wood

Avalign Technologies Inc .... F 419 542-7743
  Hicksville *(G-10776)*

MEDICAL & SURGICAL SPLYS: Stretchers

Midmark Corporation .... A 937 526-3662
  Kettering *(G-11434)*

MEDICAL & SURGICAL SPLYS: Technical Aids, Handicapped

Forbes Rehab Services Inc .... G 419 589-7688
  Mansfield *(G-12440)*
Ohio State University .... G 614 293-3600
  Columbus *(G-7261)*
Southpaw Enterprises Inc .... E 937 252-7676
  Moraine *(G-14395)*
Visualy Imp Exp Wm Isues Fr Gr .... G 216 561-6864
  Cleveland *(G-6265)*

MEDICAL & SURGICAL SPLYS: Welders' Hoods

Kuhlmanns Fabrication .... G 513 967-4617
  Hamilton *(G-10581)*
M-Co Welling .... G 330 897-1374
  Stone Creek *(G-17561)*

MEDICAL CENTERS

Buses International .... F 440 233-4091
  Lorain *(G-12081)*

MEDICAL EQPT REPAIR SVCS, NON-ELECTRIC

Elite Biomedical Solutions LLC .... F 513 207-0602
  Cincinnati *(G-3248)*

MEDICAL EQPT: CAT Scanner Or Computerized Axial Tomography

Deerfield Medical Imaging LLC .... G 513 271-5717
  Mason *(G-12856)*
Imageiq Inc .... F 855 462-4347
  Cleveland *(G-5438)*

MEDICAL EQPT: Diagnostic

Aeiou Scientific LLC .... G 614 325-2103
  Columbus *(G-6547)*
Attention Dsase Diagnstc Group .... G 216 577-3075
  Cleveland *(G-4763)*
Baby Love Prenatal Imaging LLC .... G 419 905-7935
  Delphos *(G-8736)*
Daavlin Distributing Co .... E 419 636-6304
  Bryan *(G-2278)*
Diagnostic Hybrids Inc .... C 740 593-1784
  Athens *(G-828)*
Ebisyn Medical Inc .... G 609 759-1101
  Dublin *(G-8910)*
Ennovea Medical LLC .... G 855 997-2273
  Columbus *(G-6899)*

MEDICAL EQPT: Diagnostic

Eoi Inc .... F 740 201-3300
  Lewis Center *(G-11760)*
Filament LLC .... G 614 732-0754
  Columbus *(G-6921)*
Flotbi Inc .... G 216 619-5928
  Cleveland *(G-5252)*
Hickok Waekon LLC .... D 216 541-8060
  Cleveland *(G-5408)*
Integrated Med Solutions Inc .... D 440 269-6984
  Mentor *(G-13473)*
Sense Diagnostics Inc .... G 513 515-3853
  Cincinnati *(G-4323)*
Smiths Medical Pm Inc .... F 614 210-7300
  Dublin *(G-8991)*
Sonogage Inc .... F 216 464-1119
  Cleveland *(G-6079)*
Steris Corporation .... A 440 354-2600
  Mentor *(G-13590)*
Transdermal Inc .... F 440 241-1846
  Gates Mills *(G-10209)*
World Wide Medical Physics Inc .... G 419 266-7530
  Perrysburg *(G-16029)*
Ysi Incorporated .... D 937 767-7241
  Yellow Springs *(G-20825)*

MEDICAL EQPT: Electromedical Apparatus

Biosense Webster Inc .... G 513 337-3351
  Blue Ash *(G-1735)*
Furniss Corporation Ltd .... F 614 871-1470
  Mount Sterling *(G-14461)*
Great Lkes Nrotechnologies Inc .... E 855 456-3876
  Cleveland *(G-5351)*
Imalux Corporation .... F 216 502-0755
  Cleveland *(G-5440)*
Nasoneb Inc .... G 330 247-0921
  Medina *(G-13306)*
Relevium Labs Inc .... G 614 568-7000
  Oxford *(G-15699)*

MEDICAL EQPT: Electrotherapeutic Apparatus

Ep Technologies LLC .... F 234 208-8967
  Akron *(G-159)*

MEDICAL EQPT: Laser Systems

Hair Science Systems LLC .... G 513 231-8284
  Cincinnati *(G-3793)*
Infinity Trichology Center .... G 937 281-0555
  Kettering *(G-11433)*
Medical Quant USA Inc .... F 440 542-0761
  Solon *(G-17189)*
Scallywag Tag .... G 513 922-4999
  Cincinnati *(G-4303)*

MEDICAL EQPT: MRI/Magnetic Resonance Imaging Devs, Nuclear

Alltech Med Systems Amer Inc .... E 440 424-2240
  Solon *(G-17104)*
Elastance Imaging LLC .... G 614 579-9520
  Columbus *(G-6887)*
Gvi Medical Devices Corp .... F 330 963-4083
  Twinsburg *(G-18789)*
Magnetic Resonance Tech .... G 440 942-2922
  Willoughby *(G-20365)*
Philips Medical Systems Mr .... C 440 483-2499
  Highland Heights *(G-10798)*

MEDICAL EQPT: Pacemakers

Cardiac Arrhythmia Associates .... G 330 759-8169
  Youngstown *(G-20865)*

MEDICAL EQPT: Patient Monitoring

GE Medical Systems Information .... G 216 663-2110
  Warrensville Heights *(G-19468)*
Medforall LLC .... G 614 947-0791
  Columbus *(G-7171)*
Valued Relationships Inc .... C 800 860-4230
  Franklin *(G-9928)*

MEDICAL EQPT: Sterilizers

Steris Corporation .... A 440 354-2600
  Mentor *(G-13590)*
Steris Corporation .... D 440 354-2600
  Mentor *(G-13592)*

MEDICAL EQPT: Ultrasonic Scanning Devices

Century Biotech Partners Inc .... G 614 746-6998
  Dublin *(G-8899)*
Flocel Inc .... G 216 619-5903
  Cleveland *(G-5251)*
Genii Inc .... G 651 501-4810
  Mentor *(G-13458)*
Imaging Center East Main .... G 614 566-8120
  Columbus *(G-7022)*
Neurowave Systems Inc .... G 216 361-1591
  Cleveland *(G-5745)*
Nuvasive Manufacturing LLC .... E 937 343-0400
  Fairborn *(G-9464)*
Open Sided Mri Cleveland LLC .... G 804 217-7114
  Westlake *(G-20138)*

MEDICAL EQPT: X-Ray Apparatus & Tubes, Radiographic

General Electric Company .... D 216 663-2110
  Cleveland *(G-5308)*

MEDICAL FIELD ASSOCIATION

American Ceramic Society .... E 614 890-4700
  Westerville *(G-19977)*

MEDICAL INSURANCE CLAIM PROCESSING: Contract Or Fee Basis

Acu-Serve Corp .... G 330 923-5258
  Cuyahoga Falls *(G-7830)*
Merry X-Ray Chemical Corp .... G 614 219-2011
  Hilliard *(G-10839)*

MEDICAL SUNDRIES: Rubber

Formco Inc .... G 330 966-2111
  Canton *(G-2674)*
Philpott Rubber LLC .... E 330 225-3344
  Brunswick *(G-2225)*
Philpott Rubber LLC .... G 330 225-3344
  Aurora *(G-899)*
Premiere Medical Resources Inc .... F 330 923-5899
  Cuyahoga Falls *(G-7908)*

MEDICAL TRAINING SERVICES

M R I Education Foundation .... C 513 281-3400
  Cincinnati *(G-3964)*

MEDICAL, DENTAL & HOSP EQPT, WHOLESALE: X-ray Film & Splys

Philips Medical Systems Clevel .... B 440 247-2652
  Cleveland *(G-5871)*

MEDICAL, DENTAL & HOSPITAL EQPT, WHOL: Dentists' Prof Splys

Triage Ortho Group .... G 937 653-6431
  Urbana *(G-19016)*

MEDICAL, DENTAL & HOSPITAL EQPT, WHOL: Hospital Eqpt & Splys

Jones Metal Products Company .... E 740 545-6341
  West Lafayette *(G-19932)*
Kempf Surgical Appliances Inc .... E 513 984-5758
  Montgomery *(G-14295)*
United Medical Supply Company .... G 866 678-8633
  Valley City *(G-19068)*

MEDICAL, DENTAL & HOSPITAL EQPT, WHOL: Hosptl Eqpt/Furniture

Access To Independence Inc .... G 330 296-8111
  Ravenna *(G-16363)*
Electro-Cap International Inc .... F 937 456-6099
  Eaton *(G-9148)*

MEDICAL, DENTAL & HOSPITAL EQPT, WHOL: Surgical Eqpt & Splys

Cardinal Health Inc .... G 614 553-3830
  Dublin *(G-8893)*
Cardinal Health Inc .... A 614 757-5000
  Dublin *(G-8894)*

MEDICAL, DENTAL & HOSPITAL EQPT, WHOLESALE: Diagnostic, Med

Thermo Fisher Scientific Inc .... C 800 871-8909
  Oakwood Village *(G-15486)*
Tosoh America Inc .... B 614 539-8622
  Grove City *(G-10476)*

MEDICAL, DENTAL & HOSPITAL EQPT, WHOLESALE: Med Eqpt & Splys

Eoi Inc .... F 740 201-3300
  Lewis Center *(G-11760)*
Ethicon Endo-Surgery Inc .... A 513 337-7000
  Blue Ash *(G-1765)*
Faretec Inc .... F 440 350-9510
  Painesville *(G-15738)*
Julius Zorn Inc .... D 330 923-4999
  Cuyahoga Falls *(G-7886)*
Markethatch Co Inc .... G 330 376-6363
  Akron *(G-269)*
Mill Rose Laboratories Inc .... E 440 974-6730
  Mentor *(G-13519)*

MEDICAL, DENTAL & HOSPITAL EQPT, WHOLESALE: Orthopedic

Stable Step LLC .... E 513 825-1888
  West Chester *(G-19798)*

MEDICAL, DENTAL & HOSPITAL EQPT, WHOLESALE: Safety

Beeline Purchasing LLC .... G 513 703-3733
  Mason *(G-12834)*

MEDICAL, DENTAL & HOSPITAL EQPT, WHOLESALE: Therapy

Viewray Technologies Inc .... D 440 703-3210
  Oakwood Village *(G-15487)*

MEDICAL, DENTAL/HOSPITAL EQPT, WHOL: Veterinarian Eqpt/Sply

Berlin Industries Inc .... F 330 549-2100
  Youngstown *(G-20852)*

Haag-Streit Holding Us Inc .... E 513 336-7255
  Mason *(G-12883)*

MELAMINE RESINS: Melamine-Formaldehyde

Next Specialty Resins Inc .... E 419 843-4600
  Sylvania *(G-17955)*
Plastic Compounders Inc .... E 740 432-7371
  Cambridge *(G-2453)*

MEMBERSHIP HOTELS

American Guild of English Hand .... G 937 438-0085
  Cincinnati *(G-3333)*

MEMBERSHIP ORGANIZATIONS, BUSINESS: Contractors' Association

Heat Exchange Institute Inc .... G 216 241-7333
  Cleveland *(G-5385)*

MEMBERSHIP ORGANIZATIONS, CIVIC, SOCIAL/FRAT: Social Assoc

Family Motor Coach Assn Inc .... C 513 474-3622
  Cincinnati *(G-3671)*

MEMBERSHIP ORGANIZATIONS, NEC: Bowling club

Greater Cincinnati Bowl Assn .... E 513 761-7387
  Cincinnati *(G-3780)*

MEMBERSHIP ORGANIZATIONS, NEC: Flying Club

Institute Mthmtical Statistics .... G 216 295-2340
  Shaker Heights *(G-16932)*

MEMBERSHIP ORGANIZATIONS, NEC: Personal Interest

American Guild of English Hand .... G 937 438-0085
  Cincinnati *(G-3333)*

MEMBERSHIP ORGANIZATIONS, REL: Christian & Reformed Church

Buses International .... F 440 233-4091
  Lorain *(G-12081)*
Calvary Christian Ch of Ohio .... E 740 828-9000
  Frazeysburg *(G-9937)*

MEMBERSHIP ORGANIZATIONS, REL: Churches, Temples & Shrines

C A I R Ohio .... G 513 281-8200
  Blue Ash *(G-1743)*

MEMBERSHIP ORGANIZATIONS, RELIGIOUS: Brethren Church

Society of The Precious Blood .... E 419 925-4516
  Celina *(G-2984)*

MEMBERSHIP ORGANIZATIONS, RELIGIOUS: Nonchurch

Incorporated Trst Gspl Wk Scty .... D 216 749-2100
  Cleveland *(G-5448)*

MEMBERSHIP ORGS, BUSINESS: Shipping/Steamship Co Assoc

M-Fischer Enterprises LLC .... G 419 782-5309
  Defiance *(G-8634)*

MEMBERSHIP ORGS, RELIGIOUS: Non-Denominational Church

New Life Chapel .... F 513 298-2980
  Cincinnati *(G-4070)*

MEMORIALS, MONUMENTS & MARKERS

Artistic Memorials Ltd .... G 419 873-0433
  Perrysburg *(G-15921)*
Fostoria Monument Co .... G 419 435-0373
  Fostoria *(G-9844)*
Linden Monuments .... G 419 468-4130
  Galion *(G-10148)*

MEN'S & BOYS' CLOTHING STORES

Benchmark Prints .... F 419 332-7640
  Fremont *(G-9997)*
S F Mock & Associates LLC .... F 937 438-0196
  Dayton *(G-8491)*

MEN'S & BOYS' CLOTHING WHOLESALERS, NEC

Fine Line Embroidery Company .... G 440 331-7030
  Rocky River *(G-16547)*
McCc Sportswear Inc .... E 513 583-9210
  West Chester *(G-19876)*
Totes Isotoner Corporation .... F 513 682-8200
  West Chester *(G-19907)*
West Chester Holdings LLC .... C 800 647-1900
  Cincinnati *(G-4499)*

MEN'S & BOYS' SPORTSWEAR CLOTHING STORES

Jakes Sportswear Ltd .... G 740 746-8356
  Sugar Grove *(G-17839)*
Lion Clothing Inc .... G 419 692-9981
  Delphos *(G-8751)*
Locker Room Lettering Ltd .... G 419 359-1761
  Castalia *(G-2940)*
Sports Express .... G 330 297-1112
  Ravenna *(G-16406)*

MEN'S & BOYS' SPORTSWEAR WHOLESALERS

Barbs Graffiti Inc .... E 216 881-5550
  Cleveland *(G-4790)*
Design Original Inc .... F 937 596-5121
  Jackson Center *(G-11207)*
Precision Imprint .... G 740 592-5916
  Athens *(G-846)*
R & A Sports Inc .... E 216 289-2254
  Euclid *(G-9438)*
Unisport Inc .... F 419 529-4727
  Ontario *(G-15549)*

MEN'S & BOYS' WORK CLOTHING WHOLESALERS

Hands On International LLC .... G 513 502-9000
  Mason *(G-12884)*

METAL & STEEL PRDTS: Abrasive

Braun Machine Technologies LLC .... G 330 777-5433
  Vienna *(G-19197)*
Cleveland Granite & Marble LLC .... E 216 291-7637
  Cleveland *(G-4961)*
Innovation Sales LLC .... G 330 239-0400
  Medina *(G-13279)*
Tomson Steel Company .... E 513 420-8600
  Middletown *(G-13960)*

METAL COMPONENTS: Prefabricated

Pioneer Cldding Glzing Systems .... E 216 816-4242
  Cleveland *(G-5879)*
St Marys Iron Works Inc .... F 419 300-6300
  Saint Marys *(G-16702)*

METAL CUTTING SVCS

Aetna Plastics Corp .... G 330 274-2855
  Mantua *(G-12541)*
Dbcr Inc .... E 330 920-1900
  Cuyahoga Falls *(G-7859)*
Exact Cutting Service Inc .... E 440 546-1319
  Brecksville *(G-2035)*
Gerdau Macsteel Atmosphere Ann .... D 330 478-0314
  Canton *(G-2683)*
Independent Steel Company LLC .... C 330 225-7741
  Valley City *(G-19041)*
Laserflex Corporation .... D 614 850-9600
  Hilliard *(G-10837)*
Quest Technologies Inc .... E 937 743-1200
  Franklin *(G-9913)*
Scot Industries Inc .... E 330 262-7585
  Wooster *(G-20651)*
Trojon Gear Inc .... F 937 254-1737
  Dayton *(G-8568)*
Whole Shop Inc .... F 330 630-5305
  Tallmadge *(G-18015)*

METAL DETECTORS

Ceia Usa Ltd .... E 330 405-3190
  Twinsburg *(G-18747)*
Ohio Magnetics Inc .... G 216 662-8484
  Maple Heights *(G-12575)*

METAL FABRICATORS: Architechtural

A & E Butscha Co .... G 513 761-1919
  Cincinnati *(G-3275)*
A & G Manufacturing Co Inc .... E 419 468-7433
  Galion *(G-10119)*
Annin & Co .... D 740 622-4447
  Coshocton *(G-7718)*
Armor Consolidated Inc .... G 513 923-5260
  Mason *(G-12826)*
Armor Group Inc .... C 513 923-5260
  Mason *(G-12827)*
Armor Metal Group Mason Inc .... C 513 769-0700
  Mason *(G-12828)*
Art Fremont Iron Co .... G 419 332-5554
  Fremont *(G-9992)*
Bauer Corporation .... E 800 321-4760
  Wooster *(G-20569)*
Blevins Metal Fabrication Inc .... E 419 522-6082
  Mansfield *(G-12412)*
Cramers Inc .... E 330 477-4571
  Canton *(G-2638)*
Debra-Kuempel Inc .... D 513 271-6500
  Cincinnati *(G-3579)*
Decor Architectural Products .... G 419 537-9493
  Toledo *(G-18258)*
Dover Tank and Plate Company .... G 330 343-4443
  Dover *(G-8823)*
E B P Inc .... E 216 241-2550
  Cleveland *(G-5128)*
Federal Iron Works Company .... E 330 482-5910
  Columbiana *(G-6465)*
Friends Ornamental Iron Co .... G 216 431-6710
  Cleveland *(G-5275)*
Geist Co Inc .... F 216 771-2200
  Cleveland *(G-5300)*
Gem City Metal Tech LLC .... E 937 252-8998
  Dayton *(G-8220)*
GL Nause Co Inc .... E 513 722-9500
  Loveland *(G-12192)*
Graber Metal Works Inc .... E 440 237-8422
  North Royalton *(G-15274)*
Granite Industries Inc .... D 419 445-4733
  Archbold *(G-651)*
Gwp Holdings Inc .... D 513 860-4050
  Fairfield *(G-9501)*
Harsco Corporation .... E 740 387-1150
  Marion *(G-12710)*
Hrh Door Corp .... C 330 828-2291
  Dalton *(G-7943)*
Indian Creek Fabricators Inc .... E 937 667-7214
  Tipp City *(G-18116)*
Jerry Harolds Doors Unlimited .... G 740 635-4949
  Bridgeport *(G-2076)*
Jim Denigris & Sons Ldscpg .... G 440 449-5548
  Cleveland *(G-5499)*
Joyce Manufacturing Co .... D 440 239-9100
  Berea *(G-1615)*
Lakeway Mfg Inc .... E 419 433-3030
  Huron *(G-11103)*
Langdon Inc .... E 513 733-5955
  Cincinnati *(G-3930)*
Lifetime Ironworks LLC .... G 419 443-0567
  Tiffin *(G-18065)*
Mataco .... G 440 546-8355
  Broadview Heights *(G-2096)*
Metal Craft Docks Inc .... G 440 286-7135
  Painesville *(G-15763)*
Metal Maintenance Inc .... F 513 661-3300
  Cleves *(G-6370)*
Michaels Pre-Cast Con Pdts .... E 513 683-1292
  Loveland *(G-12215)*
Modern Builders Supply Inc .... C 419 241-3961
  Toledo *(G-18414)*
Momentive Prfmce Mtls Qrtz Inc .... C 440 878-5700
  Strongsville *(G-17765)*
Quality Architectural and Fabr .... F 937 743-2923
  Franklin *(G-9912)*
Rezmann Karoly .... G 216 441-4357
  Cleveland *(G-5982)*
Royalton Archtctral Fbrication .... F 440 582-0400
  North Royalton *(G-15298)*
Rural Iron Works LLC .... G 419 647-4617
  Spencerville *(G-17313)*
Sausser Steel Company Inc .... F 419 422-9632
  Findlay *(G-9752)*
Schwab Welding Inc .... G 513 353-4262
  Cincinnati *(G-4308)*
Sewah Studios Inc .... F 740 373-2087
  Marietta *(G-12666)*
Sine Wall LLC .... G 919 453-2011
  West Chester *(G-19796)*
Southern Ornamental Iron Co .... G 937 278-4319
  Dayton *(G-8512)*
Spillman Company .... E 614 444-2184
  Columbus *(G-7476)*
Stephens Pipe & Steel LLC .... C 740 869-2257
  Mount Sterling *(G-14465)*
Swanton Wldg Machining Co Inc .... D 419 826-4816
  Swanton *(G-17923)*
T E Martindale Enterprises .... G 614 253-6826
  Columbus *(G-7507)*
Tim Calvin Access Controls .... G 740 494-4200
  Radnor *(G-16359)*
Triangle Precision Industries .... D 937 299-6776
  Dayton *(G-8564)*
Van Dyke Custom Iron Inc .... G 614 860-9300
  Columbus *(G-7571)*
Viking Fabricators Inc .... E 740 374-5246
  Marietta *(G-12687)*
Wright Brothers Inc .... E 513 731-2222
  Cincinnati *(G-4520)*

METAL FABRICATORS: Plate

A A S Amels Sheet Meta L Inc .... E 330 793-9326
  Youngstown *(G-20830)*
A & E Butscha Co .... G 513 761-1919
  Cincinnati *(G-3275)*
A & G Manufacturing Co Inc .... E 419 468-7433
  Galion *(G-10119)*
A Metalcraft Associates Inc .... G 937 693-4008
  Botkins *(G-1931)*

A P O Holdings Inc .... E 330 455-8925
Canton *(G-2556)*
Acme Boiler Co Inc .... G 216 961-2471
Cleveland *(G-4605)*
Advance Industrial Mfg Inc .... E 614 871-3333
Grove City *(G-10411)*
Advanced Welding Co .... E 937 746-6800
Franklin *(G-9867)*
AM Castle & Co .... D 330 425-7000
Bedford *(G-1381)*
Apex Welding Incorporated .... F 440 232-6770
Bedford *(G-1384)*
Ares Inc .... D 419 635-2175
Port Clinton *(G-16242)*
Armor Consolidated Inc .... G 513 923-5260
Mason *(G-12826)*
Armor Group Inc .... C 513 923-5260
Mason *(G-12827)*
Armor Metal Group Mason Inc .... C 513 769-0700
Mason *(G-12828)*
Babcock & Wilcox Company .... A 330 753-4511
Barberton *(G-1059)*
Baxter Holdings Inc .... E 513 860-3593
Hamilton *(G-10538)*
Bico Akron Inc .... D 330 794-1716
Mogadore *(G-14231)*
BJ Equipment Ltd .... F 614 497-1776
Columbus *(G-6673)*
Blackwood Sheet Metal Inc .... G 614 291-3115
Columbus *(G-6678)*
Blevins Metal Fabrication Inc .... E 419 522-6082
Mansfield *(G-12412)*
Boochers Inc .... G 937 667-3414
Tipp City *(G-18101)*
Breitinger Company .... C 419 526-4255
Mansfield *(G-12414)*
Brighton Truedge .... G 513 771-2300
Cincinnati *(G-3418)*
Brown-Singer Co .... F 513 422-9619
Middletown *(G-13888)*
C & C Fabrication Inc .... G 419 354-3535
Bowling Green *(G-1958)*
C & R Inc .... E 614 497-1130
Groveport *(G-10486)*
C A Joseph Co .... F 330 532-4646
Irondale *(G-11158)*
C Imperial Inc .... G 937 669-5620
Tipp City *(G-18104)*
CA Litzler Co Inc .... E 216 267-8020
Cleveland *(G-4859)*
Capital Tool Company .... E 216 661-5750
Cleveland *(G-4871)*
Cds Technologies Inc .... G 800 338-1122
West Chester *(G-19665)*
Ceco Environmental Corp .... E 513 874-8915
West Chester *(G-19838)*
Cincinnati Heat Exchangers Inc .... G 513 874-7232
Mason *(G-12842)*
Cleveland Track Material Inc .... F 216 641-4000
Cleveland *(G-4981)*
Commercial Mtal Fbricators Inc .... E 937 233-4911
Dayton *(G-8100)*
Containment Solutions Inc .... C 419 874-8765
Perrysburg *(G-15934)*
Contech Bridge Solutions LLC .... F 513 645-7000
West Chester *(G-19678)*
Contech Cnstr Pdts Hldings Inc .... A 513 645-7000
West Chester *(G-19679)*
Contech Engnered Solutions Inc .... F 513 645-7000
West Chester *(G-19680)*
Contech Engnered Solutions LLC .... G 614 477-1171
Columbus *(G-6812)*
Contech Engnered Solutions LLC .... D 513 645-7000
Middletown *(G-13896)*
Contech Engnered Solutions LLC .... C 513 645-7000
West Chester *(G-19681)*
Cramers Inc .... E 330 477-4571
Canton *(G-2638)*
Curtiss-Wright Flow Ctrl Corp .... D 513 528-7900
Cincinnati *(G-3245)*
Debra-Kuempel Inc .... D 513 271-6500
Cincinnati *(G-3579)*
Defiance Metal Products Co .... B 419 784-5332
Defiance *(G-8619)*
Deibel Manufacturing LLC .... G 330 482-3351
Leetonia *(G-11717)*
Dover Tank and Plate Company .... E 330 343-4443
Dover *(G-8823)*
Eagle Wldg & Fabrication Inc .... E 440 946-0692
Willoughby *(G-20313)*
Eaton Fabricating Company Inc .... E 440 926-3121
Grafton *(G-10300)*
Ebner Furnaces Inc .... D 330 335-2311
Wadsworth *(G-19237)*
Efco Corp .... E 614 876-1226
Columbus *(G-6886)*
Ellis & Watts Intl LLC .... G 513 752-9000
Batavia *(G-1143)*
En-Hanced Products Inc .... G 614 882-7400
Westerville *(G-20052)*
Fabco Inc .... E 419 421-4740
Findlay *(G-9682)*
Fabrication Shop Inc .... F 419 435-7934
Fostoria *(G-9837)*
Falls Welding & Fabg Inc .... G 330 253-3437
Akron *(G-165)*
Fulton Equipment Co .... E 419 290-5393
Toledo *(G-18299)*
General Technologies Inc .... E 419 747-1800
Mansfield *(G-12445)*
General Tool Company .... C 513 733-5500
Cincinnati *(G-3747)*
GL Nause Co Inc .... E 513 722-9500
Loveland *(G-12192)*
Graber Metal Works Inc .... E 440 237-8422
North Royalton *(G-15274)*
Grenga Machine & Welding .... F 330 743-1113
Youngstown *(G-20925)*
H P E Inc .... F 330 833-3161
Massillon *(G-12993)*
Halvorsen Company .... E 216 341-7500
Cleveland *(G-5367)*
Hammelmann Corporation .... F 937 859-8777
Miamisburg *(G-13673)*
Heat Exchange Applied Tech .... F 330 682-4328
Orrville *(G-15594)*
I L R Inc .... G 216 587-2212
Cleveland *(G-5433)*
Indian Creek Fabricators Inc .... E 937 667-7214
Tipp City *(G-18116)*
Industrial Container Svcs LLC .... E 513 921-2056
Cincinnati *(G-3843)*
Industrial Container Svcs LLC .... E 513 921-8811
Cincinnati *(G-3844)*
Industrial Container Svcs LLC .... D 614 864-1900
Blacklick *(G-1687)*
Industrial Tank & Containment .... F 330 448-4876
Brookfield *(G-2107)*
J B Kepple Sheet Metal .... G 740 393-2971
Mount Vernon *(G-14484)*
Jergens Inc .... C 216 486-5540
Cleveland *(G-5495)*
Jh Industries Inc .... E 330 963-4105
Twinsburg *(G-18797)*
Kard Welding Inc .... E 419 628-2598
Minster *(G-14218)*
Kendall Holdings Ltd .... E 614 486-4750
Columbus *(G-7086)*
Kirk & Blum Manufacturing Co .... C 513 458-2600
Cincinnati *(G-3912)*
Langdon Inc .... E 513 733-5955
Cincinnati *(G-3930)*
Lapham-Hickey Steel Corp .... E 614 443-4881
Columbus *(G-7116)*
Lion Industries LLC .... E 740 699-0369
Saint Clairsville *(G-16636)*
Long-Stanton Mfg Company .... E 513 874-8020
West Chester *(G-19738)*
Louis Arthur Steel Company .... G 440 997-5545
Geneva *(G-10224)*
Louis Arthur Steel Company .... G 440 997-5545
Uniontown *(G-18926)*
Mack Iron Works Company .... E 419 626-3712
Sandusky *(G-16826)*
Metal Fabricating Corporation .... D 216 631-8121
Cleveland *(G-5658)*
Midwestern Industries Inc .... C 330 837-4203
Massillon *(G-13026)*
Moore Mr Specialty Company .... G 330 332-1229
Salem *(G-16763)*
Munroe Incorporated .... G 330 755-7216
Struthers *(G-17821)*
Myers Industries Inc .... E 330 253-5592
Akron *(G-293)*
Myers Industries Inc .... C 330 336-6621
Wadsworth *(G-19255)*
Nbw Inc .... E 216 377-1700
Cleveland *(G-5732)*
New Wayne Inc .... G 740 453-3454
Zanesville *(G-21162)*
Northwest Installations Inc .... E 419 423-5738
Findlay *(G-9732)*
Ohio Heat Transfer .... G 513 870-5323
Hamilton *(G-10591)*
Oil Skimmers Inc .... E 440 237-4600
North Royalton *(G-15291)*
P B Fabrication Mech Contr .... F 419 478-4869
Toledo *(G-18454)*
Parker-Hannifin Corporation .... F 330 336-3511
Wadsworth *(G-19262)*
Pcy Enterprises Inc .... E 513 241-5566
Cincinnati *(G-4143)*
Pioneer Pipe Inc .... A 740 376-2400
Marietta *(G-12653)*
Prout Boiler Htg & Wldg Inc .... E 330 744-0293
Youngstown *(G-21008)*
Pucel Enterprises Inc .... D 216 881-4604
Cleveland *(G-5933)*
R B Mfg Co .... F 419 626-9464
Wadsworth *(G-19270)*
Retays Welding Company .... E 440 327-4100
North Ridgeville *(G-15250)*
Sausser Steel Company Inc .... F 419 422-9632
Findlay *(G-9752)*
Schweizer Dipple Inc .... D 440 786-8090
Cleveland *(G-6034)*
Skinner Sales Group Inc .... E 440 572-8455
Medina *(G-13344)*
Snair Co .... F 614 873-7020
Plain City *(G-16212)*
Spradlin Bros Welding Co .... F 800 219-2182
Springfield *(G-17493)*
St Lawrence Holdings LLC .... E 330 562-9000
Maple Heights *(G-12580)*
Steel & Alloy Utility Pdts Inc .... E 330 530-2220
Mc Donald *(G-13202)*
Steve Vore Welding and Steel .... F 419 375-4087
Fort Recovery *(G-9827)*
Sticker Corporation .... F 440 946-2100
Willoughby *(G-20438)*
Swagelok Company .... D 440 349-5934
Solon *(G-17242)*
Swanton Wldg Machining Co Inc .... D 419 826-4816
Swanton *(G-17923)*
Thermogenics Corp .... G 513 247-7963
Cincinnati *(G-4418)*
Triangle Precision Industries .... D 937 299-6776
Dayton *(G-8564)*
TW Tank LLC .... G 419 334-2664
Fremont *(G-10057)*
Universal Rack & Equipment Co .... E 330 963-6776
Twinsburg *(G-18870)*
Val-Co Pax Inc .... D 717 354-4586
Coldwater *(G-6423)*
Verhoff Machine & Welding Inc .... C 419 596-3202
Continental *(G-7669)*
Viking Fabricators Inc .... E 740 374-5246
Marietta *(G-12687)*
Vortec Corporation .... E 513 891-7485
Blue Ash *(G-1866)*
Warren Fabricating Corporation .... D 330 534-5017
Hubbard *(G-11011)*
Washington Products Inc .... F 330 837-5101
Massillon *(G-13057)*
Will-Burt Company .... E 330 682-7015
Orrville *(G-15628)*
Will-Burt Company .... B 330 682-7015
Orrville *(G-15626)*

METAL FABRICATORS: Sheet

A A S Amels Sheet Meta L Inc .... E 330 793-9326
Youngstown *(G-20830)*
A & C Welding Inc .... E 330 762-4777
Peninsula *(G-15888)*
A & G Manufacturing Co Inc .... E 419 468-7433
Galion *(G-10119)*
A C Shutters Inc .... G 216 429-2424
Cleveland *(G-4584)*
Accufab Inc .... G 513 942-1929
West Chester *(G-19636)*
Acro Tool & Die Company .... D 330 773-5173
Akron *(G-29)*
Advance Metal Products Inc .... F 216 741-1800
Cleveland *(G-4623)*
Advanced Welding Co .... E 937 746-6800
Franklin *(G-9867)*
Aerolite Extrusion Company .... D 330 782-1127
Youngstown *(G-20838)*
Akron Foundry Co .... E 330 745-3101
Barberton *(G-1050)*

Alan Manufacturing Inc..........E....... 330 262-1555
Wooster ***(G-20560)***
Aleris Rolled Products Inc..........D....... 740 983-2571
Ashville ***(G-814)***
Allfab Inc..........F....... 614 491-4944
Columbus ***(G-6570)***
Allied Mask and Tooling Inc..........G....... 419 470-2555
Toledo ***(G-18164)***
Alro Steel Corporation..........E....... 419 720-5300
Toledo ***(G-18166)***
Alro Steel Corporation..........E....... 614 878-7271
Columbus ***(G-6578)***
Aluminum Color Industries Inc..........D....... 330 536-6295
Lowellville ***(G-12248)***
Aluminum Extruded Shapes Inc..........C....... 513 563-2205
Cincinnati ***(G-3328)***
AM Castle & Co..........D....... 330 425-7000
Bedford ***(G-1381)***
AMD Fabricators Inc..........E....... 440 946-8855
Willoughby ***(G-20270)***
American Frame Corporation..........E....... 419 893-5595
Maumee ***(G-13069)***
American Truck Equipment Inc..........G....... 216 362-0400
Cleveland ***(G-4699)***
Ampp Incorporated..........C....... 419 666-4747
Perrysburg ***(G-15920)***
Anchor Metal Processing Inc..........F....... 216 362-6463
Cleveland ***(G-4707)***
Anchor Metal Processing Inc..........E....... 216 362-1850
Cleveland ***(G-4708)***
Andy Russo Jr Inc..........F....... 440 585-1456
Wickliffe ***(G-20198)***
Anro Logistics Inc..........G....... 614 428-7490
Westerville ***(G-19978)***
Antique Auto Sheet Metal Inc..........E....... 937 833-4422
Brookville ***(G-2161)***
Armor Group Inc..........C....... 513 923-5260
Mason ***(G-12827)***
Armor Metal Group Mason Inc..........C....... 513 769-0700
Mason ***(G-12828)***
Arsco Custom Metals LLC..........F....... 513 385-0555
Cincinnati ***(G-3356)***
Austintown Metal Works Inc..........F....... 330 259-4673
Youngstown ***(G-20848)***
Autoneum North America Inc..........B....... 419 693-0511
Oregon ***(G-15556)***
Avon Lake Sheet Metal Co..........E....... 440 933-3505
Avon Lake ***(G-980)***
Aztec Manufacturing Inc..........E....... 330 783-9747
Youngstown ***(G-20850)***
B Y G Industries Inc..........G....... 216 961-5436
Cleveland ***(G-4785)***
B-R-O-T Incorporated..........E....... 216 267-5335
Cleveland ***(G-4786)***
Bainter Machining Company..........E....... 740 653-2422
Lancaster ***(G-11547)***
Baltimore Fabricators Inc..........G....... 740 862-6016
Baltimore ***(G-1036)***
Bayloff Stmped Pdts Knsman Inc..........D....... 330 876-4511
Kinsman ***(G-11463)***
Berran Industrial Group Inc..........E....... 330 253-5800
Akron ***(G-85)***
Bickers Metal Products Inc..........E....... 513 353-4000
Miamitown ***(G-13743)***
BJ Equipment Ltd..........F....... 614 497-1776
Columbus ***(G-6673)***
Blesco Services..........G....... 614 871-4900
Mount Sterling ***(G-14460)***
Blevins Metal Fabrication Inc..........E....... 419 522-6082
Mansfield ***(G-12412)***
Bob Lanes Welding Inc..........F....... 740 373-3567
Marietta ***(G-12609)***
Bogie Industries Inc Ltd..........E....... 330 745-3105
Akron ***(G-92)***
Breitinger Company..........C....... 419 526-4255
Mansfield ***(G-12414)***
Bridges Sheet Metal..........G....... 330 339-3185
New Philadelphia ***(G-14760)***
Bud Corp..........G....... 740 967-9992
Johnstown ***(G-11261)***
Budde Sheet Metal Works Inc..........E....... 937 224-0868
Dayton ***(G-8068)***
Busch & Thiem Inc..........E....... 419 625-7515
Sandusky ***(G-16800)***
C A Joseph Co..........F....... 330 532-4646
Irondale ***(G-11158)***
C G C Systems Inc..........G....... 330 678-3261
Kent ***(G-11302)***
C-N-D Industries Inc..........E....... 330 478-8811
Massillon ***(G-12965)***

Canton Fabricators Inc..........G....... 330 830-2900
Massillon ***(G-12966)***
Cbr Industrial Llc..........G....... 419 645-6447
Wapakoneta ***(G-19326)***
Ceco Group Inc..........G....... 513 458-2600
Cincinnati ***(G-3452)***
Centria Inc..........D....... 740 432-7351
Cambridge ***(G-2431)***
Champion Window Co of Toledo..........E....... 419 841-0154
Perrysburg ***(G-15933)***
Chute Source LLC..........F....... 330 475-0377
Akron ***(G-117)***
Cinfab LLC..........C....... 513 396-6100
Cincinnati ***(G-3516)***
Cleveland Steel Specialty Co..........E....... 216 464-9400
Bedford Heights ***(G-1466)***
Collier Well Eqp & Sup Inc..........F....... 330 345-3968
Wooster ***(G-20580)***
Commercial Mtal Fbricators Inc..........E....... 937 233-4911
Dayton ***(G-8100)***
Compco Industries Inc..........D....... 330 482-6488
Columbiana ***(G-6463)***
Contech Engnered Solutions LLC..........C....... 513 645-7000
West Chester ***(G-19681)***
Contour Forming Inc..........E....... 740 345-9777
Newark ***(G-14864)***
COW Industries Inc..........E....... 614 443-6537
Columbus ***(G-6831)***
Custom Crete..........G....... 740 726-2433
Waldo ***(G-19302)***
Custom Metal Shearing Inc..........F....... 937 233-6950
Dayton ***(G-8120)***
Custom Powdercoating LLC..........G....... 937 972-3516
Dayton ***(G-8122)***
Dae Holdings LLC..........E....... 502 589-1445
Swanton ***(G-17911)***
Datco Mfg Company Inc..........D....... 330 781-6100
Youngstown ***(G-20887)***
David Cox..........G....... 740 254-4858
Gnadenhutten ***(G-10277)***
Decor Architectural Products..........G....... 419 537-9493
Toledo ***(G-18258)***
Defiance Metal Products Co..........B....... 419 784-5332
Defiance ***(G-8620)***
Delafoil Pennsylvania Inc..........D....... 610 327-9565
Perrysburg ***(G-15939)***
Di Lorio Sheet Metal Inc..........F....... 216 961-3703
Cleveland ***(G-5088)***
Die-Cut Products Co..........E....... 216 771-6994
Cleveland ***(G-5094)***
Dimensional Metals Inc..........D....... 740 927-3633
Reynoldsburg ***(G-16435)***
Dover Tank and Plate Company..........E....... 330 343-4443
Dover ***(G-8823)***
Duct Fabricators Inc..........G....... 216 391-2400
Cleveland ***(G-5116)***
Ducts Inc..........E....... 216 391-2400
Cleveland ***(G-5117)***
Duro Dyne Midwest Corp..........B....... 513 870-6000
Hamilton ***(G-10551)***
Dynamic Weld Corporation..........E....... 419 582-2900
Osgood ***(G-15642)***
E & K Products Co Inc..........G....... 216 631-2510
Cleveland ***(G-5127)***
E B P Inc..........E....... 216 241-2550
Cleveland ***(G-5128)***
Eagle Wldg & Fabrication Inc..........E....... 440 946-0692
Willoughby ***(G-20313)***
Eaton Fabricating Company Inc..........E....... 440 926-3121
Grafton ***(G-10300)***
Ebner Furnaces Inc..........D....... 330 335-2311
Wadsworth ***(G-19237)***
Elsass Fabricating Ltd..........G....... 937 394-7169
Anna ***(G-589)***
Enterprise Welding & Fabg Inc..........C....... 440 354-4128
Mentor ***(G-13441)***
F M Sheet Metal Fabrication..........G....... 937 362-4357
Quincy ***(G-16355)***
Fabco Inc..........E....... 419 421-4740
Findlay ***(G-9682)***
Fabcraft Inc..........G....... 440 286-6700
Chardon ***(G-3111)***
Fabricating Solutions Inc..........F....... 330 486-0998
Twinsburg ***(G-18773)***
Fabrication Unlimited LLC..........G....... 937 492-3166
Sidney ***(G-17039)***
Fabtech Ohio..........G....... 440 942-0811
Willoughby ***(G-20319)***
Falcon Industries Inc..........E....... 330 723-0099
Medina ***(G-13260)***

Famous Industries Inc..........C....... 740 397-8842
Mount Vernon ***(G-14481)***
Firestone Laser and Mfg LLC..........E....... 330 337-9551
Salem ***(G-16737)***
First Francis Company Inc..........E....... 440 352-8927
Painesville ***(G-15739)***
Franck and Fric Incorporated..........D....... 216 524-4451
Cleveland ***(G-5271)***
Franklin Frames and Cycles..........G....... 740 763-3838
Newark ***(G-14875)***
Fred Winner..........G....... 419 582-2421
New Weston ***(G-14845)***
Freeman Enclosure Systems LLC..........C....... 877 441-8555
Batavia ***(G-1147)***
Fulton Equipment Co..........E....... 419 290-5393
Toledo ***(G-18299)***
Galion LLC..........C....... 419 468-5214
Galion ***(G-10138)***
Galion-Godwin Truck Bdy Co LLC..........D....... 330 359-5495
Millersburg ***(G-14084)***
Gaspar Inc..........D....... 330 477-2222
Canton ***(G-2679)***
Gem City Metal Tech LLC..........E....... 937 252-8998
Dayton ***(G-8220)***
General Technologies Inc..........E....... 419 747-1800
Mansfield ***(G-12445)***
General Tool Company..........C....... 513 733-5500
Cincinnati ***(G-3747)***
George Manufacturing Inc..........E....... 513 932-1067
Lebanon ***(G-11654)***
Gilson Screen Incorporated..........E....... 419 256-7711
Malinta ***(G-12379)***
GL Nause Co Inc..........E....... 513 722-9500
Loveland ***(G-12192)***
Global Body & Equipment Co..........D....... 330 264-6640
Wooster ***(G-20597)***
Glunt Industries Inc..........C....... 330 399-7585
Warren ***(G-19407)***
GNI Erectors..........G....... 614 465-7260
Galloway ***(G-10179)***
Graber Metal Works Inc..........E....... 440 237-8422
North Royalton ***(G-15274)***
Great Day Improvements LLC..........G....... 330 468-0700
Macedonia ***(G-12300)***
Gunderson Rail Services LLC..........E....... 330 792-6521
Youngstown ***(G-20927)***
Gundlach Sheet Metal Works Inc..........D....... 419 626-4525
Sandusky ***(G-16814)***
Gwp Holdings Inc..........D....... 513 860-4050
Fairfield ***(G-9501)***
H B Products Inc..........E....... 937 492-7031
Sidney ***(G-17042)***
Hall Company..........E....... 937 652-1376
Urbana ***(G-18992)***
Halvorsen Company..........E....... 216 341-7500
Cleveland ***(G-5367)***
Harray LLC..........G....... 888 568-8371
Cincinnati ***(G-3799)***
Harrison Mch & Plastic Corp..........E....... 330 527-5641
Garrettsville ***(G-10191)***
Hartley Machine Inc..........G....... 330 821-0343
Alliance ***(G-471)***
Heim Sheet Metal Inc..........G....... 330 424-7820
Lisbon ***(G-11968)***
Hidaka Usa Inc..........E....... 614 889-8611
Dublin ***(G-8923)***
Hoffman Machining & Repair LLC..........G....... 419 547-9204
Clyde ***(G-6389)***
Holgate Metal Fab Inc..........F....... 419 599-2000
Napoleon ***(G-14543)***
Home Sheet Metal & Roofing Co..........G....... 419 562-7806
Bucyrus ***(G-2334)***
Hvac Inc..........F....... 330 343-5511
Dover ***(G-8830)***
Indian Creek Fabricators Inc..........E....... 937 667-7214
Tipp City ***(G-18116)***
Induction Iron Incorporated..........G....... 330 501-8852
Youngstown ***(G-20938)***
Industrial Fabricators Inc..........E....... 614 882-7423
Westerville ***(G-20059)***
Industrial Hanger Conveyor Co..........G....... 419 332-2661
Fremont ***(G-10028)***
Industrial Mill Maintenance..........E....... 330 746-1155
Youngstown ***(G-20939)***
Isaiah Industries Inc..........E....... 937 773-9840
Piqua ***(G-16131)***
J & L Welding Fabricating Inc..........F....... 330 393-9353
Warren ***(G-19412)***
Jacobs Mechanical Co..........C....... 513 681-6800
Cincinnati ***(G-3866)***

PRODUCT

Employee Codes: A=Over 500 employees, B=251-500
C=101-250, D=51-100, E=20-50, F=10-19, G=3-9
2019 Harris Ohio
Industrial Directory
1503

Jeffery A Burns ....G.... 419 845-2129
Caledonia (G-2418)
Jh Industries Inc ....E.... 330 963-4105
Twinsburg (G-18797)
Jim Nier Construction Inc ....F.... 740 289-3925
Piketon (G-16072)
Joining Metals Inc ....F.... 440 259-1790
Perry (G-15906)
Kalron LLC ....E.... 440 647-3039
Wellington (G-19584)
Kettering Roofing & Shtmtl ....F.... 513 281-6413
Cincinnati (G-3906)
Kilroy Company ....D.... 440 951-8700
Eastlake (G-9117)
Kirk Williams Company Inc ....D.... 614 875-9023
Grove City (G-10440)
Kitts Heating & AC ....G.... 330 755-9242
Struthers (G-17818)
Knight Manufacturing Co Inc ....G.... 740 676-5516
Shadyside (G-16923)
Korda Manufacturing Inc ....D.... 330 262-1555
Wooster (G-20615)
Kramer Power Equipment Co ....F.... 937 456-2232
Eaton (G-9157)
L&M Sheet Metal Ltd ....G.... 513 858-6173
Fairfield (G-9521)
Lake Shore Electric Corp ....E.... 440 232-0200
Bedford (G-1422)
Lima Sheet Metal Machine & Mfg ....E.... 419 229-1161
Lima (G-11893)
Locker Konnection Services LLC ....G.... 419 334-3956
Fremont (G-10036)
Long-Stanton Mfg Company ....E.... 513 874-8020
West Chester (G-19738)
Louis Arthur Steel Company ....G.... 440 997-5545
Geneva (G-10224)
Louis Arthur Steel Company ....G.... 440 997-5545
Uniontown (G-18926)
Lowry Furnace Company Inc ....G.... 330 745-4822
Akron (G-260)
LSI Industries Inc ....E.... 513 793-3200
Blue Ash (G-1808)
Lt Enterprises of Ohio LLC ....E.... 330 526-6908
North Canton (G-15099)
Lund Equipment Co Inc ....E.... 330 659-4800
Bath (G-1201)
M H EBY Inc ....E.... 614 879-6901
West Jefferson (G-19925)
Mack Iron Works Company ....E.... 419 626-3712
Sandusky (G-16826)
Magnode Corporation ....D.... 317 243-3553
Trenton (G-18624)
Maines Brothers Tin Shop ....G.... 937 393-1633
Hillsboro (G-10885)
Mantych Metalworking Inc ....E.... 937 258-1373
Dayton (G-7984)
Marsam Metalfab Inc ....E.... 330 405-1520
Twinsburg (G-18811)
Martina Metal LLC ....E.... 614 291-9700
Columbus (G-7155)
McWane Inc ....B.... 740 622-6651
Coshocton (G-7739)
Medway Tool Corp ....E.... 937 335-7717
Troy (G-18687)
Meese Inc ....D.... 440 998-1202
Ashtabula (G-785)
Mestek Inc ....D.... 419 288-2703
Holland (G-10944)
Mestek Inc ....D.... 419 288-2703
Bradner (G-2015)
Met-L-Fab Inc ....F.... 513 561-4289
Cincinnati (G-4010)
Metal Seal Precision Ltd ....D.... 440 255-8888
Mentor (G-13517)
Metal Seal Precision Ltd ....C.... 440 255-8888
Willoughby (G-20380)
Metalworking Group Holdings ....C.... 513 521-4119
Cincinnati (G-4014)
Metrodeck Inc ....F.... 513 541-4370
Cincinnati (G-4018)
Michael Fabricating Inc ....G.... 330 325-8636
Rootstown (G-16570)
Mid-Ohio Products Inc ....D.... 614 771-2795
Hilliard (G-10840)
Midwest Metal Fabricators ....F.... 419 739-7077
Wapakoneta (G-19345)
Mike Loppe ....F.... 937 969-8102
Tremont City (G-18616)
Milton West Fabricators Inc ....G.... 937 547-3069
Greenville (G-10382)

Mings Heating & AC ....G.... 216 721-2007
Cleveland (G-5693)
Modern Ice Equipment & Sup Co ....E.... 513 367-2101
Cincinnati (G-4038)
Modern Sheet Metal Works Inc ....E.... 513 353-3666
Miamitown (G-13749)
MRS Industrial Inc ....E.... 614 308-1070
Columbus (G-7199)
N Wasserstrom & Sons Inc ....C.... 614 228-5550
Columbus (G-7206)
Nel-Ack Sheet Metal Inc ....G.... 440 357-7844
Painesville (G-15765)
Niles Manufacturing & Finshg ....C.... 330 544-0402
Niles (G-15024)
Nissin Precision N Amer Inc ....D.... 937 836-1910
Englewood (G-9372)
Norstar Aluminum Molds Inc ....D.... 440 632-0853
Middlefield (G-13841)
North Coast Profile Inc ....G.... 330 823-7777
Alliance (G-493)
Northwest Installations Inc ....E.... 419 423-5738
Findlay (G-9732)
Northwind Industries Inc ....E.... 216 433-0666
Cleveland (G-5787)
Ohio Blow Pipe Company ....E.... 216 681-7379
Cleveland (G-5801)
Ohio Gratings Inc ....B.... 330 477-6707
Canton (G-2772)
Ohio Steel Sheet & Plate Inc ....E.... 800 827-2401
Hubbard (G-11007)
Ohio Trailer Inc ....F.... 330 392-4444
Warren (G-19428)
Options Plus Incorporated ....F.... 740 694-9811
Fredericktown (G-9975)
P & L Metalcrafts LLC ....F.... 330 793-2178
Youngstown (G-20987)
P B Fabrication Mech Contr ....F.... 419 478-4869
Toledo (G-18454)
Parker-Hannifin Corporation ....F.... 330 336-3511
Wadsworth (G-19262)
Patterson & Sons Inc ....F.... 419 281-0897
Nova (G-15435)
Pcy Enterprises Inc ....E.... 513 241-5566
Cincinnati (G-4143)
Pennant Moldings Inc ....C.... 937 584-5411
Sabina (G-16617)
Phillips Awning Co ....G.... 740 653-2433
Lancaster (G-11596)
Phillips Manufacturing Co ....D.... 330 652-4335
Niles (G-15026)
Phillips Shtmtl Fabrications ....G.... 937 223-2722
Dayton (G-8423)
Pioneer Fabrication ....G.... 419 737-9464
Alvordton (G-521)
Plas-Tanks Industries Inc ....E.... 513 942-3800
Hamilton (G-10596)
Precise Metal Form Inc ....F.... 419 636-5221
Bryan (G-2305)
Precision Mtal Fabrication Inc ....D.... 937 235-9261
Dayton (G-8434)
Precision Steel Services Inc ....D.... 419 476-5702
Toledo (G-18479)
Precision Welding Corporation ....E.... 216 524-6110
Cleveland (G-5912)
Premier Stamping and Assembly ....G.... 440 293-8961
Williamsfield (G-20259)
Priest Millwright Service ....G.... 937 780-3405
Leesburg (G-11715)
Prototype Fabricators Company ....F.... 216 252-0080
Cleveland (G-5931)
Quality Craftsman Inc ....F.... 740 474-9685
Circleville (G-4555)
Quality Steel Fabrication ....F.... 937 492-9503
Sidney (G-17063)
Quass Sheet Metal Inc ....G.... 330 477-4841
Canton (G-2798)
R B Mfg Co ....F.... 419 626-9464
Wadsworth (G-19270)
R L Torbeck Industries Inc ....D.... 513 367-0080
Harrison (G-10667)
Raka Corporation ....D.... 419 476-6572
Toledo (G-18498)
Range One Products & Fabg ....F.... 330 533-1151
Canfield (G-2542)
Rapid Machine Inc ....F.... 419 737-2377
Pioneer (G-16094)
Related Metals Inc ....G.... 330 799-4866
Canfield (G-2543)
Rezmann Karoly ....G.... 216 441-4357
Cleveland (G-5982)

Ridgeview Sheet Metal ....G.... 330 674-3768
Millersburg (G-14123)
Robinson Fin Machines Inc ....E.... 419 674-4152
Kenton (G-11421)
Rockwell Metals Company LLC ....F.... 440 242-2420
Lorain (G-12118)
Roconex Corporation ....F.... 937 339-2616
Troy (G-18699)
Romar Metal Fabricating Inc ....G.... 740 682-7731
Oak Hill (G-15460)
Royalton Archtctral Fbrication ....F.... 440 582-0400
North Royalton (G-15298)
S & D Architectural Metals ....G.... 440 582-2560
North Royalton (G-15301)
S & G Manufacturing Group LLC ....C.... 614 529-0100
Hilliard (G-10859)
Sarka Shtmtl & Fabrication Inc ....E.... 419 447-4377
Tiffin (G-18080)
Sausser Steel Company Inc ....F.... 419 422-9632
Findlay (G-9752)
Schoonover Industries Inc ....E.... 419 289-8332
Ashland (G-747)
Schweizer Dipple Inc ....D.... 440 786-8090
Cleveland (G-6034)
Shaffer Metal Fab Inc ....E.... 937 492-1384
Sidney (G-17076)
Sheffield Metals Cleveland LLC ....F.... 800 283-5262
Sheffield Village (G-16975)
Shriner Sheet Metal Inc ....F.... 330 435-6735
Creston (G-7809)
Sidney Manufacturing Company ....E.... 937 492-4154
Sidney (G-17079)
Smith Rn Sheet Metal Shop Inc ....E.... 740 653-5011
Lancaster (G-11609)
Snair Co ....F.... 614 873-7020
Plain City (G-16212)
Somerville Manufacturing Inc ....E.... 740 336-7847
Marietta (G-12674)
Spradlin Bros Welding Co ....F.... 800 219-2182
Springfield (G-17493)
Ss Metal Fabricators Inc ....G.... 937 226-9957
Dayton (G-8522)
Staber Industries Inc ....E.... 614 836-5995
Groveport (G-10513)
Standard Technologies LLC ....D.... 419 332-6434
Fremont (G-10051)
Starr Fabricating Inc ....D.... 330 394-9891
Vienna (G-19210)
Steel & Alloy Utility Pdts Inc ....E.... 330 530-2220
Mc Donald (G-13202)
Steelial Wldg Met Fbrction Inc ....E.... 740 669-5300
Vinton (G-19216)
Steeltec Products LLC ....E.... 216 681-1114
Cleveland (G-6103)
Steve Vore Welding and Steel ....F.... 419 375-4087
Fort Recovery (G-9827)
Suburban Metal Products Inc ....F.... 740 474-4237
Circleville (G-4559)
Sulecki Precision Products ....F.... 440 255-5454
Mentor (G-13596)
Super Sheet Metal ....G.... 330 482-9045
Leetonia (G-11722)
Superior Metal Worx LLC ....F.... 614 879-9400
Columbus (G-7501)
Swanton Wldg Machining Co Inc ....D.... 419 826-4816
Swanton (G-17923)
Systech Handling Inc ....F.... 419 445-8226
Archbold (G-670)
Tangent Air Inc ....E.... 740 474-1114
Circleville (G-4560)
Tectum Inc ....C.... 740 345-9691
Newark (G-14929)
Tendon Manufacturing Inc ....E.... 216 663-3200
Cleveland (G-6159)
Tex-Tyler Corporation ....E.... 419 729-4951
Toledo (G-18548)
Tilton Corporation ....C.... 419 227-6421
Lima (G-11952)
TL Industries Inc ....C.... 419 666-8144
Northwood (G-15346)
Tool & Die Systems Inc ....E.... 440 327-5800
North Ridgeville (G-15256)
Torok Supply Company ....G.... 330 799-6677
Youngstown (G-21047)
Tower Tool & Manufacturing Co ....F.... 330 425-1623
Twinsburg (G-18864)
Tri-Fab Inc ....E.... 330 337-3425
Salem (G-16777)
Tri-Mac Mfg & Svcs Co ....F.... 513 896-4445
Hamilton (G-10613)

PRODUCT SECTION

METAL STAMPING, FOR THE TRADE

Tri-State Fabricators Inc ....E...... 513 752-5005
  Amelia *(G-550)*
Triangle Precision Industries ....D...... 937 299-6776
  Dayton *(G-8564)*
Tricor Industrial Inc ....D...... 330 264-3299
  Wooster *(G-20660)*
Tru Form Metal Products Inc ....G...... 216 252-3700
  Cleveland *(G-6217)*
Unison Industries LLC ....D...... 937 426-4676
  Alpha *(G-518)*
Universal Steel Company ....D...... 216 883-4972
  Cleveland *(G-6240)*
V & S Schuler Engineering Inc ....D...... 330 452-5200
  Canton *(G-2855)*
V M Systems Inc ....D...... 419 535-1044
  Toledo *(G-18587)*
Verhoff Machine & Welding Inc ....C...... 419 596-3202
  Continental *(G-7669)*
W & W Custom Fabrication Inc ....G...... 513 353-4617
  Hamilton *(G-10619)*
W J Egli Company Inc ....F...... 330 823-3666
  Alliance *(G-512)*
Waino Sheet Metal Inc ....G...... 330 945-4226
  Stow *(G-17642)*
Warner Fabricating Inc ....F...... 330 848-3191
  Wadsworth *(G-19280)*
Warren Fabricating Corporation ......D...... 330 534-5017
  Hubbard *(G-11011)*
Waterville Sheet Metal Company .....G...... 419 878-5050
  Waterville *(G-19508)*
Weber Technologies Inc ....E...... 440 946-8833
  Eastlake *(G-9140)*
Westwood Fvrication Shtmtl Inc ......G...... 937 837-0494
  Dayton *(G-8591)*
Wheeler Sheet Metal Inc ....G...... 419 668-0481
  Norwalk *(G-15417)*
Will-Burt Company ....B...... 330 682-7015
  Orrville *(G-15626)*
Worthington Steel Company ....G...... 513 702-0130
  Middletown *(G-13969)*
Ysd Industries Inc ....G...... 330 792-6521
  Youngstown *(G-21086)*

METAL FABRICATORS: Structural, Ship

Burghardt Manufacturing Inc ....G...... 330 253-7590
  Akron *(G-98)*
Iron Gate Industries LLC ....E...... 330 264-0626
  Wooster *(G-20608)*

METAL FINISHING SVCS

Allen Aircraft Products Inc ....E...... 330 296-1531
  Ravenna *(G-16366)*
Aluminum Color Industries Inc ....D...... 330 536-6295
  Lowellville *(G-12248)*
Amac Enterprises Inc ....C...... 216 362-1880
  Parma *(G-15814)*
American Quality Stripping ....E...... 419 625-6288
  Sandusky *(G-16794)*
Anodizing Specialists Inc ....F...... 440 951-0257
  Mentor *(G-13389)*
Applied Metals Tech Ltd ....E...... 216 741-3236
  Brooklyn Heights *(G-2115)*
Atom Blasting & Finishing Inc ....G...... 440 235-4765
  Columbia Station *(G-6429)*
Autocoat ....G...... 419 636-3830
  Bryan *(G-2266)*
Bar Processing Corporation ....D...... 330 872-0914
  Newton Falls *(G-14986)*
Chrome & Speed Cycle LLC ....G...... 937 429-5656
  Beavercreek *(G-1305)*
Cleveland Finishing Inc ....G...... 440 572-5475
  Strongsville *(G-17728)*
CMF Custom Metal Finishers ....G...... 513 821-8145
  Cincinnati *(G-3532)*
Davro Ltd ....G...... 216 258-0057
  Cleveland *(G-5071)*
Electro Polish Company Inc ....E...... 937 222-3611
  Dayton *(G-8180)*
Equinox Enterprises LLC ....F...... 419 627-0022
  Sandusky *(G-16810)*
Foundry Support Operation ....F...... 440 951-4142
  Mentor *(G-13446)*
Gateway Metal Finishing Inc ....G...... 216 267-2580
  Cleveland *(G-5296)*
H & R Metal Finishing Inc ....G...... 440 942-6656
  Willoughby *(G-20335)*
Hayes Metalfinishing Inc ....G...... 937 228-7550
  Dayton *(G-8245)*
Jotco Inc ....G...... 513 721-4943
  Mansfield *(G-12465)*

Kel-Mar Inc ....E...... 419 806-4600
  Bowling Green *(G-1979)*
M I P Inc ....F...... 330 744-0215
  Youngstown *(G-20964)*
Mechanical Finishing Inc ....E...... 513 641-5419
  Cincinnati *(G-3994)*
Metal Finishers Inc ....F...... 937 492-9175
  Sidney *(G-17052)*
Micro Metal Finishing LLC ....D...... 513 541-3095
  Cincinnati *(G-4022)*
Microfinish Inc ....D...... 937 264-1598
  Vandalia *(G-19138)*
Ohio Anodizing Company Inc ....F...... 614 252-7855
  Columbus *(G-7240)*
P & J Manufacturing Inc ....F...... 419 241-7369
  Toledo *(G-18453)*
Pro Line Collision and Pnt LLC ....F...... 937 223-7611
  Dayton *(G-8444)*
REA Polishing Inc ....D...... 419 470-0216
  Toledo *(G-18499)*
Rite Way Black & Deburr Inc ....G...... 937 224-7762
  Dayton *(G-8478)*
Russell Products Co Inc ....G...... 330 535-3391
  Akron *(G-360)*
Stricker Refinishing Inc ....G...... 216 696-2906
  Cleveland *(G-6109)*
Superfinishers Inc ....G...... 330 467-2125
  Macedonia *(G-12335)*
Tablox Inc ....G...... 440 953-1951
  Willoughby *(G-20440)*
Tatham Schulz Incorporated ....E...... 216 861-4431
  Cleveland *(G-6149)*
Toledo Metal Finishing Inc ....G...... 419 661-1422
  Northwood *(G-15347)*
Trans-Acc Inc ....E...... 513 793-6410
  Blue Ash *(G-1861)*
Weber Technologies Inc ....E...... 440 946-8833
  Eastlake *(G-9140)*

METAL MINING SVCS

Alloy Metal Exchange LLC ....E...... 216 478-0200
  Bedford Heights *(G-1459)*
Hopedale Mining LLC ....E...... 740 937-2225
  Hopedale *(G-10991)*
Metokote Corporation ....G...... 419 996-7800
  Lima *(G-11907)*
Mining Reclamation Inc ....F...... 740 327-5555
  Dresden *(G-8869)*

METAL RESHAPING & REPLATING SVCS

A Metalcraft Associates Inc ....G...... 937 693-4008
  Botkins *(G-1931)*
Machine Tool Design & Fab LLC .....F...... 419 435-7676
  Fostoria *(G-9847)*
Space Age Coatings LLC ....G...... 937 275-5117
  Dayton *(G-8514)*

METAL SERVICE CENTERS & OFFICES

A J Oster Foils LLC ....D...... 330 823-1700
  Alliance *(G-447)*
Aluminum Line Products Company ...D...... 440 835-8880
  Westlake *(G-20091)*
American Ir Met Cleveland LLC ....E...... 216 266-0509
  Cleveland *(G-4690)*
American Tank & Fabricating Co .....C...... 216 252-1500
  Cleveland *(G-4698)*
Atlas Bolt & Screw Company LLC ....C...... 419 289-6171
  Ashland *(G-681)*
Canfield Coating LLC ....G...... 330 533-3311
  Canfield *(G-2524)*
D T Kothera Inc ....F...... 440 632-1651
  Middlefield *(G-13792)*
EPI of Cleveland Inc ....G...... 330 468-2872
  Twinsburg *(G-18769)*
Graber Metal Works Inc ....E...... 440 237-8422
  North Royalton *(G-15274)*
Kirtland Capital Partners LP ....E...... 216 593-0100
  Beachwood *(G-1244)*
Materion Brush Inc ....F...... 440 960-5660
  Lorain *(G-12105)*
Modern Welding Co Ohio Inc ....E...... 740 344-9425
  Newark *(G-14898)*
Ohio Steel Sheet & Plate Inc ....F...... 800 827-2401
  Hubbard *(G-11007)*
Panacea Products Corporation ....E...... 614 850-7000
  Columbus *(G-7287)*
Perfection Metal Co ....G...... 216 641-0949
  Chagrin Falls *(G-3028)*

Samuel Steel Pickling Company ......D...... 330 963-3777
  Twinsburg *(G-18853)*
Springtime Manufacturing ....G...... 419 697-3720
  Toledo *(G-18528)*
Summit Resources Group Inc ....G...... 330 653-3992
  Hudson *(G-11078)*
The Mansfield Strl & Erct Co ....E...... 419 522-5911
  Mansfield *(G-12528)*
Tricor Industrial Inc ....D...... 330 264-3299
  Wooster *(G-20660)*
Tsk America Co Ltd ....F...... 513 942-4002
  West Chester *(G-19909)*
Watteredge LLC ....D...... 440 933-6110
  Avon Lake *(G-1013)*
Worthington Industries Inc ....C...... 513 539-9291
  Monroe *(G-14282)*
Worthngton Stelpac Systems LLC ....C...... 614 438-3205
  Columbus *(G-7617)*

METAL SLITTING & SHEARING

Cctm Inc ....G...... 513 934-3533
  Lebanon *(G-11641)*
Crest Products Inc ....F...... 440 942-5770
  Mentor *(G-13427)*
Custom Metal Shearing Inc ....F...... 937 233-6950
  Dayton *(G-8120)*
Metal Shredders Inc ....E...... 937 866-0777
  Miamisburg *(G-13689)*
Pettit W T & Sons Co Inc ....G...... 330 539-6100
  Girard *(G-10264)*
Samuel Steel Pickling Company ......D...... 330 963-3777
  Twinsburg *(G-18853)*
Shear Service Inc ....G...... 216 341-2700
  Cleveland *(G-6049)*

METAL SPINNING FOR THE TRADE

Artistic Metal Spinning Inc ....G...... 216 961-3336
  Cleveland *(G-4741)*
Deshler Metal Working Co Inc ....G...... 419 278-0472
  Deshler *(G-8788)*
Elyria Metal Spinning Fabg Co ....G...... 440 323-8068
  Elyria *(G-9253)*
Gem City Metal Tech LLC ....E...... 937 252-8998
  Dayton *(G-8220)*
Hukon Manufacturing Company ......G...... 513 721-5562
  Cincinnati *(G-3828)*
Imperial Metal Spinning Co ....G...... 216 524-5020
  Cleveland *(G-5445)*
J Schrader Co ....F...... 216 961-2890
  Cleveland *(G-5488)*
Lewark Metal Spinning Inc ....E...... 937 275-3303
  Dayton *(G-8312)*
McGlennon Metal Products Inc ......F...... 614 252-7114
  Columbus *(G-7166)*
Ottawa Products Co ....E...... 419 836-5115
  Curtice *(G-7826)*
Toledo Metal Spinning Company .....E...... 419 535-5931
  Toledo *(G-18561)*

METAL STAMPING, FOR THE TRADE

A-1 Manufacturing Corp ....G...... 216 475-6084
  Maple Heights *(G-12563)*
A-Stamp Industries LLC ....D...... 419 633-0451
  Bryan *(G-2257)*
AAA Stamping Inc ....E...... 216 749-4494
  Cleveland *(G-4596)*
Abl Products Inc ....F...... 216 281-2400
  Cleveland *(G-4598)*
Accurate Tool Co Inc ....G...... 330 332-9448
  Salem *(G-16714)*
Acro Tool & Die Company ....D...... 330 773-5173
  Akron *(G-29)*
AJD Holding Co ....D...... 330 405-4477
  Twinsburg *(G-18728)*
Allied Tool & Die Inc ....F...... 216 941-6196
  Cleveland *(G-4673)*
Amaroq Inc ....G...... 419 747-2110
  Mansfield *(G-12403)*
Amclo Group Inc ....C...... 216 791-8400
  North Royalton *(G-15259)*
American Tool & Mfg Co ....F...... 419 522-2452
  Mansfield *(G-12405)*
American Tool and Die Inc ....F...... 419 726-5394
  Toledo *(G-18181)*
Ampex Metal Products Company ....E...... 216 267-9242
  Brookpark *(G-2136)*
Andre Corporation ....E...... 574 293-0207
  Mason *(G-12824)*

Employee Codes: A=Over 500 employees, B=251-500
C=101-250, D=51-100, E=20-50, F=10-19, G=3-9

Atlantic Tool & Die Company.......C....... 440 238-6931
Strongsville (G-17714)
Atlantic Tool & Die Company.......C....... 330 769-4500
Seville (G-16910)
Automatic Stamp Products Inc.......F....... 216 781-7933
Cleveland (G-4773)
Banner Metals Group Inc.......D....... 614 291-3105
Columbus (G-6646)
Bayloff Stmped Pdts Knsman Inc.......D....... 330 876-4511
Kinsman (G-11463)
Boehm Pressed Steel Company.......E....... 330 220-8000
Valley City (G-19031)
Brainerd Industries Inc.......E....... 937 228-0488
Miamisburg (G-13644)
Brainin-Advance Industries LLC.......E....... 513 874-9760
West Chester (G-19663)
Buckley Manufacturing Company.......F....... 513 821-4444
Cincinnati (G-3429)
Central Ohio Metal Stampi.......E....... 614 861-3332
Columbus (G-6753)
Cleveland Die & Mfg Co.......E....... 440 243-3404
Middleburg Heights (G-13762)
Cleveland Metal Stamping Co.......F....... 440 234-0010
Berea (G-1596)
Com-Corp Industries Inc.......D....... 216 431-6266
Cleveland (G-4999)
Continental Business Entps Inc.......F....... 440 439-4400
Cleveland (G-5020)
D & L Manufacturing Inc.......G....... 440 428-1627
Madison (G-12346)
Deerfield Manufacturing Inc.......E....... 513 398-2010
Mason (G-12855)
Dependable Stamping Company.......E....... 216 486-5522
Cleveland (G-5084)
Die Co Inc.......E....... 440 942-8856
Eastlake (G-9104)
Die-Matic Corporation.......D....... 216 749-4656
Brooklyn Heights (G-2119)
Dove Die and Stamping Company.......E....... 216 267-3720
Cleveland (G-5109)
Dyco Manufacturing Inc.......F....... 419 485-5525
Montpelier (G-14307)
Eagle Precision Products LLC.......G....... 440 582-9393
North Royalton (G-15270)
Eisenhauer Mfg Co LLC.......D....... 419 238-0081
Van Wert (G-19090)
Ernst Metal Technologies LLC.......E....... 937 434-3133
Moraine (G-14351)
F C Brengman and Assoc LLC.......E....... 740 756-4308
Carroll (G-2904)
Falls Stamping & Welding Co.......C....... 330 928-1191
Cuyahoga Falls (G-7867)
Famous Industries Inc.......D....... 740 685-2592
Byesville (G-2384)
Faull & Son LLC.......F....... 330 652-4341
Niles (G-15008)
Fulton Industries Inc.......D....... 419 335-3015
Wauseon (G-19516)
G & M Metal Products Inc.......G....... 513 863-3353
Hamilton (G-10561)
Gentzler Tool & Die Corp.......E....... 330 896-1941
Akron (G-188)
Guarantee Specialties Inc.......D....... 216 451-9744
Strongsville (G-17747)
H&M Mtal Stamping Assembly Inc.......F....... 216 898-9030
Brookpark (G-2149)
Hamlin Steel Products LLC.......D....... 330 753-7791
Akron (G-197)
Herd Manufacturing Inc.......E....... 216 651-4221
Cleveland (G-5397)
Hill Manufacturing Inc.......E....... 419 335-5006
Wauseon (G-19520)
Ice Industries Inc.......E....... 419 842-3612
Sylvania (G-17943)
Impact Industries Inc.......E....... 440 327-2360
North Ridgeville (G-15230)
Imperial Die & Mfg Co.......F....... 440 268-9080
Strongsville (G-17753)
Independent Stamping Inc.......E....... 216 251-3500
Cleveland (G-5451)
Interlake Industries Inc.......G....... 440 942-0800
Willoughby (G-20345)
Interlake Stamping Ohio Inc.......E....... 440 942-0800
Willoughby (G-20346)
J B Stamping Inc.......E....... 216 631-0013
Cleveland (G-5484)
K & B Stamping & Manufacturing.......G....... 937 778-8875
Piqua (G-16135)
K & H Industries LLC.......F....... 513 921-6770
Cincinnati (G-3889)
K & L Die & Manufacturing.......G....... 419 895-1301
Greenwich (G-10405)
Kg63 LLC.......F....... 216 941-7766
Cleveland (G-5533)
Knowlton Manufacturing Co Inc.......F....... 513 631-7353
Cincinnati (G-3920)
Kreider Corp.......D....... 937 325-8787
Springfield (G-17436)
L & W Inc.......D....... 734 397-6300
Avon (G-953)
L C I Inc.......G....... 330 948-1922
Lodi (G-12013)
La Ganke & Sons Stamping Co.......F....... 216 451-0278
Columbia Station (G-6439)
Lakepark Industries Inc.......C....... 419 752-4471
Greenwich (G-10406)
Lextech Industries Ltd.......G....... 216 883-7900
Cleveland (G-5574)
Mahoning Valley Manufacturing.......E....... 330 537-4492
Beloit (G-1571)
Mansfield Industries Inc.......E....... 419 524-1300
Mansfield (G-12477)
Marc V Concepts Inc.......F....... 419 782-6505
Defiance (G-8635)
Mark True Engraving Co.......G....... 216 651-7700
Cleveland (G-5619)
Master Products Company.......D....... 216 341-1740
Cleveland (G-5634)
Maumee Assembly & Stamping LLC.......D....... 419 304-2887
Maumee (G-13129)
Metal & Wire Products Company.......D....... 330 332-9448
Salem (G-16760)
Metal Fabricating Corporation.......D....... 216 631-8121
Cleveland (G-5658)
Metal Products Company.......E....... 330 652-6201
Niles (G-15022)
Metal Stampings Unlimited.......F....... 937 328-0206
Springfield (G-17445)
Mohawk Manufacturing Inc.......G....... 860 632-2345
Mount Vernon (G-14493)
Morgal Machine Tool Co.......D....... 937 325-5561
Springfield (G-17451)
Nebraska Industries Corp.......E....... 419 335-6010
Wauseon (G-19529)
Neway Stamping & Mfg Inc.......D....... 440 951-8500
Willoughby (G-20388)
Ohio Gasket and Shim Co Inc.......E....... 330 630-0626
Akron (G-307)
Ohio Valley Manufacturing Inc.......D....... 419 522-5818
Mansfield (G-12497)
Omni Manufacturing Inc.......D....... 419 394-7424
Saint Marys (G-16693)
Omni Manufacturing Inc.......F....... 419 394-7424
Saint Marys (G-16694)
Orick Stamping.......D....... 419 331-0600
Elida (G-9197)
Paramount Stamping & Wldg Co.......D....... 216 631-1755
Cleveland (G-5840)
Peerless Metal Products Inc.......E....... 216 431-6905
Cleveland (G-5861)
Pennant Moldings Inc.......C....... 937 584-5411
Sabina (G-16617)
Pentaflex Inc.......C....... 937 325-5551
Springfield (G-17470)
Pfahl Gauge & Manufacturing Co.......G....... 330 633-8402
Akron (G-319)
Phillips Mch & Stamping Corp.......G....... 330 882-6714
New Franklin (G-14696)
Precision Metal Products Inc.......F....... 216 447-1900
Cleveland (G-5911)
Premier Stamping and Assembly.......G....... 440 293-8961
Williamsfield (G-20259)
Quality Stamping Products Co.......F....... 216 441-2700
Cleveland (G-5945)
Quality Tool Company.......E....... 419 476-8228
Toledo (G-18490)
R K Metals Ltd.......E....... 513 874-6055
Fairfield (G-9556)
R L Rush Tool & Pattern Inc.......G....... 419 562-9849
Bucyrus (G-2342)
RB&w Manufacturing LLC.......G....... 740 363-1971
Delaware (G-8718)
RB&w Manufacturing LLC.......F....... 234 380-8540
Streetsboro (G-17691)
Regal Metal Products Co.......E....... 330 868-6343
Minerva (G-14198)
Regal Metal Products Co.......F....... 330 868-6343
Minerva (G-14199)
Rjm Stamping Co.......F....... 614 443-1191
Columbus (G-7396)
Ronfeldt Associates Inc.......D....... 419 382-5641
Toledo (G-18506)
Ronfeldt Manufacturing LLC.......F....... 419 382-5641
Toledo (G-18507)
Ronlen Industries Inc.......E....... 330 273-6468
Brunswick (G-2236)
Schott Metal Products Company.......D....... 330 773-7873
Akron (G-373)
Sectional Stamping Inc.......B....... 440 647-2100
Wellington (G-19591)
Service Stampings Inc.......E....... 440 946-2330
Willoughby (G-20427)
Seven Ranges Mfg Corp.......E....... 330 627-7155
Carrollton (G-2928)
Stamped Steel Products Inc.......F....... 330 538-3951
North Jackson (G-15155)
Stolle Machinery Company LLC.......C....... 937 497-5400
Sidney (G-17082)
Stuebing Automatic Machine Co.......E....... 513 771-8028
Cincinnati (G-4388)
Sunfield Inc.......D....... 740 928-0404
Hebron (G-10764)
Superior Steel Stamp Co.......G....... 216 431-6460
Cleveland (G-6127)
Supply Technologies LLC.......C....... 440 947-2100
Cleveland (G-6130)
Supply Technologies LLC.......G....... 937 898-5795
Dayton (G-8530)
T and W Stamping Acquisition.......F....... 330 821-5777
Alliance (G-505)
Talan Products Inc.......D....... 216 458-0170
Cleveland (G-6147)
Taylor Metal Products Co.......C....... 419 522-3471
Mansfield (G-12526)
Toledo Tool and Die Co Inc.......E....... 419 476-4422
Toledo (G-18574)
Torr Metal Products Inc.......E....... 216 671-1616
Cleveland (G-6189)
Transue & Williams Stampg Corp.......F....... 330 821-5777
Alliance (G-508)
Transue & Williams Stampg Corp.......F....... 330 270-0891
Youngstown (G-21050)
Transue Williams Stamping Inc.......G....... 330 270-0891
Austintown (G-935)
Transue Williams Stamping Inc.......G....... 330 829-5007
Alliance (G-509)
Triad Metal Products Company.......D....... 216 676-6505
Chagrin Falls (G-3084)
United Die & Mfg Co.......E....... 330 938-6141
Sebring (G-16897)
Universal Metal Products Inc.......C....... 440 943-3040
Wickliffe (G-20235)
Universal Metal Products Inc.......E....... 419 287-3223
Pemberville (G-15887)
V K C Inc.......F....... 440 951-9634
Mentor (G-13621)
Varbros LLC.......C....... 216 267-5200
Cleveland (G-6250)
Weber Technologies Inc.......E....... 440 946-8833
Eastlake (G-9140)
Wedge Products Inc.......B....... 330 405-4477
Twinsburg (G-18873)
WLS Fabricating Co.......E....... 440 449-0543
Cleveland (G-6317)
WLS Stamping Co.......D....... 216 271-5100
Cleveland (G-6318)
Wtd Real Estate Inc.......D....... 440 934-5305
Avon (G-977)

METAL STAMPINGS: Ornamental

Catania Medallic Specialty.......E....... 440 933-9595
Avon Lake (G-981)
Connaughton Wldg & Fence LLC.......G....... 513 867-0230
Hamilton (G-10547)
Pacific Manufacturing Tenn Inc.......E....... 513 900-7862
Jackson (G-11194)

METAL STAMPINGS: Patterned

Durivage Pattern & Mfg Co.......E....... 419 836-8655
Williston (G-20262)
Hynes Modern Pattern Co Inc.......G....... 937 322-3451
Springfield (G-17424)
Mallory Pattern Works Inc.......G....... 419 726-8001
Toledo (G-18398)
Q Model Inc.......E....... 330 673-0473
Barberton (G-1100)
Seilkop Industries Inc.......E....... 513 761-1035
Cincinnati (G-4316)

METAL TREATING COMPOUNDS

Advanced Chemical Solutions .... G 330 283-5157
   Medina *(G-13217)*
Broco Products Inc .... G 216 531-0880
   Cleveland *(G-4839)*
Ferrum Industries Inc .... G 440 519-1768
   Twinsburg *(G-18775)*
Foseco Inc .... G 440 826-4548
   Cleveland *(G-5267)*
Northern Chem Blnding Corp Inc .... G 216 781-7799
   Cleveland *(G-5778)*
Opta Minerals (usa) Inc .... G 330 659-3003
   Independence *(G-11145)*
Qualico Inc .... G 216 271-2550
   Cleveland *(G-5938)*

METAL TREATING: Cryogenic

Cryoplus Inc .... G 330 683-3375
   Wooster *(G-20581)*

METAL, TITANIUM: Sponge & Granules

Advanced Materials Products .... G 330 650-4000
   Hudson *(G-11026)*
Hamilton Rti Inc .... G 330 652-9951
   Niles *(G-15011)*

METAL: Battery

Cleanlife Energy LLC .... F 800 316-2532
   Cleveland *(G-4941)*

METALS SVC CENTERS & WHOL: Structural Shapes, Iron Or Steel

Blackburns Fabrication Inc .... E 614 875-0784
   Columbus *(G-6677)*

METALS SVC CENTERS & WHOLESALERS: Bars, Metal

Ambassador Steel Corporation .... F 740 382-9969
   Marion *(G-12692)*

METALS SVC CENTERS & WHOLESALERS: Cable, Wire

Radix Wire Co .... D 216 731-9191
   Cleveland *(G-5956)*

METALS SVC CENTERS & WHOLESALERS: Casting, Rough,Iron/Steel

Ferralloy Inc .... E 440 250-1900
   Cleveland *(G-5230)*

METALS SVC CENTERS & WHOLESALERS: Copper

Anchor Bronze and Metals Inc .... E 440 549-5653
   Cleveland *(G-4705)*
J W Harris Co Inc .... F 216 481-8100
   Euclid *(G-9421)*
National Bronze Mtls Ohio Inc .... E 440 277-1226
   Lorain *(G-12106)*

METALS SVC CENTERS & WHOLESALERS: Ferroalloys

Howmet Corporation .... E 757 825-7086
   Newburgh Heights *(G-14939)*

METALS SVC CENTERS & WHOLESALERS: Ferrous Metals

Masters Group Inc .... G 440 893-1900
   Chagrin Falls *(G-3059)*
Premier Metal Trading LLC .... G 440 247-9494
   Beachwood *(G-1267)*

METALS SVC CENTERS & WHOLESALERS: Flat Prdts, Iron Or Steel

H & D Steel Service Inc .... E 440 237-3390
   North Royalton *(G-15275)*
Major Metals Company .... E 419 886-4600
   Mansfield *(G-12472)*

METALS SVC CENTERS & WHOLESALERS: Foundry Prdts

CA Picard Surface Engrg Inc .... F 440 366-5400
   Elyria *(G-9229)*
Shells Inc .... D 330 808-5558
   Copley *(G-7694)*

METALS SVC CENTERS & WHOLESALERS: Iron & Steel Prdt, Ferrous

Akers America Inc .... G 330 757-4100
   Poland *(G-16237)*
Fpt Cleveland LLC .... E 216 441-3800
   Cleveland *(G-5270)*
Supply Dynamics Inc .... E 513 965-2000
   Loveland *(G-12238)*

METALS SVC CENTERS & WHOLESALERS: Lead

Victory White Metal Company .... F 216 641-2575
   Cleveland *(G-6259)*

METALS SVC CENTERS & WHOLESALERS: Misc Nonferrous Prdts

HM Wire International Inc .... G 330 244-8501
   Canton *(G-2700)*

METALS SVC CENTERS & WHOLESALERS: Pipe & Tubing, Steel

Discount Drainage Supplies LLC .... G 513 563-8616
   Cincinnati *(G-3590)*
L B Industries Inc .... E 330 750-1002
   Struthers *(G-17820)*
M E P Manufacturing Inc .... G 419 855-7723
   Genoa *(G-10234)*
McWane Inc .... B 740 622-6651
   Coshocton *(G-7739)*

METALS SVC CENTERS & WHOLESALERS: Plates, Metal

Krendl Rack Co Inc .... G 419 667-4800
   Venedocia *(G-19154)*
Loveman Steel Corporation .... D 440 232-6200
   Bedford *(G-1423)*

METALS SVC CENTERS & WHOLESALERS: Rope, Wire, Exc Insulated

Cambridge Cable Service Co .... G 740 685-5775
   Byesville *(G-2380)*
Industrial Wire Rope Sup Inc .... G 513 941-2443
   Cincinnati *(G-3846)*
Samsel Rope & Marine Supply Co ..... E 216 241-0333
   Cleveland *(G-6029)*
Tri-State Wire Rope Supply Inc .... F 513 871-8623
   Cincinnati *(G-4437)*

METALS SVC CENTERS & WHOLESALERS: Sheets, Metal

Rockwell Metals Company LLC .... F 440 242-2420
   Lorain *(G-12118)*

METALS SVC CENTERS & WHOLESALERS: Stampings, Metal

Bear Diversified Inc .... G 216 883-5494
   Cleveland *(G-4799)*
Ohio Engineering and Mfg Sls .... G 937 855-6971
   Germantown *(G-10244)*
Stamped Steel Products Inc .... F 330 538-3951
   North Jackson *(G-15155)*
Tig Wood & Die Inc .... F 937 849-6741
   New Carlisle *(G-14680)*
Troy West LLC .... G 937 339-2192
   Troy *(G-18715)*

METALS SVC CENTERS & WHOLESALERS: Steel

Alro Steel Corporation .... E 419 720-5300
   Toledo *(G-18166)*
Alro Steel Corporation .... E 614 878-7271
   Columbus *(G-6578)*
Alro Steel Corporation .... E 937 253-6121
   Dayton *(G-8021)*
AM Castle & Co .... D 330 425-7000
   Bedford *(G-1381)*
American Posts LLC .... E 419 720-0652
   Toledo *(G-18179)*
AT&f Nuclear Inc .... G 216 252-1500
   Cleveland *(G-4757)*
Benjamin Steel Company Inc .... E 937 233-1212
   Springfield *(G-17368)*
Bico Akron Inc .... D 330 794-1716
   Mogadore *(G-14231)*
Buckeye Metals Industries Inc .... F 216 663-4300
   Cleveland *(G-4849)*
Clifton Steel Company .... D 216 662-6111
   Maple Heights *(G-12569)*
Columbia Steel and Wire Inc .... G 330 468-2709
   Northfield *(G-15315)*
Conley Group Inc .... E 330 372-2030
   Warren *(G-19388)*
Contractors Steel Company .... E 330 425-3050
   Twinsburg *(G-18757)*
Coventry Steel Services Inc .... F 216 883-4477
   Cleveland *(G-5033)*
Efco Corp .... E 614 876-1226
   Columbus *(G-6886)*
General Steel Corporation .... F 216 883-4200
   Cleveland *(G-5314)*
Grenga Machine & Welding .... F 330 743-1113
   Youngstown *(G-20925)*
Hynes Industries Inc .... C 330 799-3221
   Youngstown *(G-20934)*
Independent Steel Company LLC ...... E 330 225-7741
   Valley City *(G-19041)*
Lakewood Steel Inc .... F 440 965-4226
   Wakeman *(G-19286)*
Lapham-Hickey Steel Corp .... E 614 443-4881
   Columbus *(G-7116)*
Latrobe Spcialty Mtls Dist Inc .... D 330 609-5137
   Vienna *(G-19199)*
Louis Arthur Steel Company .... G 440 997-5545
   Geneva *(G-10224)*
Louis Arthur Steel Company .... G 440 997-5545
   Uniontown *(G-18926)*
Master-Halco Inc .... E 513 869-7600
   Fairfield *(G-9524)*
Metals USA Crbn Flat Rlled Inc .... D 937 882-6354
   Springfield *(G-17446)*
Metrodeck Inc .... F 513 541-4370
   Cincinnati *(G-4018)*
Mid-America Steel Corp .... E 800 282-3466
   Cleveland *(G-5674)*
Miller Consolidated Industries .... C 937 294-2681
   Moraine *(G-14370)*
Monarch Steel Company Inc .... E 216 587-8000
   Cleveland *(G-5703)*
North American Steel Company .... E 216 475-7300
   Cleveland *(G-5759)*
Precision Steel Services Inc .... D 419 476-5702
   Toledo *(G-18479)*
Sausser Steel Company Inc .... F 419 422-9632
   Findlay *(G-9752)*
Scot Industries Inc .... E 330 262-7585
   Wooster *(G-20651)*
St Lawrence Holdings LLC .... E 330 562-9000
   Maple Heights *(G-12580)*
Thyssenkrupp Materials NA Inc .... D 216 883-8100
   Independence *(G-11152)*
Tomson Steel Company .... E 513 420-8600
   Middletown *(G-13960)*
Universal Steel Company .... D 216 883-4972
   Cleveland *(G-6240)*
Western Reserve Metals Inc .... E 330 448-4092
   Masury *(G-13064)*
Westfield Steel Inc .... D 937 322-2414
   Springfield *(G-17516)*
Worthington Steel Company .... G 513 702-0130
   Middletown *(G-13969)*

METALS SVC CENTERS & WHOLESALERS: Tubing, Metal

Swagelok Company .... D 440 349-5934
   Solon *(G-17242)*
Tubular Techniques Inc .... G 614 529-4130
   Hilliard *(G-10872)*

Employee Codes: A=Over 500 employees, B=251-500
C=101-250, D=51-100, E=20-50, F=10-19, G=3-9

METALS SVC CTRS & WHOLESALERS: Aluminum Bars, Rods, Etc

Alanod Westlake Metal Ind Inc	E	440 327-8184	
North Ridgeville (G-15206)			
Aluminum Bearing Co of America	G	216 267-8560	
Cleveland (G-4679)			
Loxcreen Company Inc	F	513 539-2255	
Middletown (G-13921)			

METALS: Precious NEC

- Metallic Resources Inc .... E 330 425-3155
  Twinsburg (G-18819)
- Pelham Precious Metals LLC .... G 419 708-7975
  Toledo (G-18462)

METALS: Precious, Secondary

- Auris Noble LLC .... F 330 321-6649
  Fairlawn (G-9594)
- Auris Noble LLC .... G 330 685-3748
  Akron (G-73)
- Materion Brush Inc .... D 216 486-4200
  Mayfield Heights (G-13167)
- Materion Corporation .... C 216 486-4200
  Mayfield Heights (G-13168)
- Mek Van Wert Inc .... G 419 203-4902
  Van Wert (G-19102)

METALS: Primary Nonferrous, NEC

- Aci Industries Ltd. .... E 740 368-4160
  Delaware (G-8648)
- American Friction Tech LLC .... D 216 823-0861
  Cleveland (G-4687)
- American Spring Wire Corp .... C 216 292-4620
  Bedford Heights (G-1460)
- Galt Alloys Inc Main Ofc .... G 330 453-4678
  Canton (G-2678)
- H C Starck Inc .... F 216 692-6990
  Euclid (G-9417)
- Rhenium Alloys Inc .... D 440 365-7388
  North Ridgeville (G-15251)
- Rml Tool Inc .... G 216 941-1615
  Cleveland (G-5991)
- Rti Finance Corp .... G 330 652-9952
  Niles (G-15033)
- Swift Manufacturing Co Inc .... G 740 237-4405
  Ironton (G-11173)
- Zircoa Inc .... E 440 349-7237
  Solon (G-17263)

METALWORK: Miscellaneous

- Advance Industrial Mfg Inc .... E 614 871-3333
  Grove City (G-10411)
- Architctral Rfuse Slutions LLC .... G 330 733-3996
  Akron (G-69)
- Arrow Tru-Line Inc .... D 419 636-7013
  Bryan (G-2265)
- BMA Metals Group Inc .... G 513 874-5152
  West Chester (G-19661)
- Buckeye Stamping Company .... D 614 445-0059
  Columbus (G-6712)
- Burghardt Metal Fabg Inc .... F 330 794-1830
  Akron (G-99)
- CMF Custom Metal Finishers .... G 513 821-8145
  Cincinnati (G-3532)
- Custom Control Tech LLC .... G 419 342-5593
  Shelby (G-16981)
- Fabrication Group LLC .... E 216 251-1125
  Cleveland (G-5213)
- Fortin Welding & Mfg Inc .... E 614 291-4342
  Columbus (G-6932)
- Friesingers Inc .... G 740 452-9480
  Zanesville (G-21139)
- Harvey Brothers Inc .... F 513 541-2622
  Cincinnati (G-3800)
- Harvey Miller .... G 440 834-9125
  Burton (G-2359)
- Lwr Enterprises Inc .... G 740 984-0036
  Waterford (G-19487)
- Markley Enterprises LLC .... E 513 771-1290
  Cincinnati (G-3982)
- Matteo Aluminum Inc .... E 440 585-5213
  Wickliffe (G-20217)
- Metal Sales Manufacturing Corp .... E 440 319-3779
  Jefferson (G-11234)
- Nova Metal Products Inc .... E 440 269-1741
  Eastlake (G-9127)
- Omco Holdings Inc .... E 440 944-2100
  Wickliffe (G-20220)
- Simcote Inc .... E 740 382-5000
  Marion (G-12736)
- Skinner Sales Group Inc .... E 440 572-8455
  Medina (G-13344)
- T J F Inc .... F 419 878-4400
  Waterville (G-19506)
- Tallmadge Spinning & Metal Co .... F 330 794-2277
  Akron (G-395)
- Trulite GL Alum Solutions LLC .... D 614 876-1057
  Columbus (G-7548)
- Ventari Corporation .... E 937 278-4269
  Miamisburg (G-13731)
- Ver-Mac Industries Inc .... E 740 397-6511
  Mount Vernon (G-14517)
- Watteredge LLC .... D 440 933-6110
  Avon Lake (G-1013)
- Will-Burt Company .... E 330 682-7015
  Orrville (G-15628)
- Will-Burt Company .... B 330 682-7015
  Orrville (G-15626)

METALWORK: Ornamental

- Cozmyk Enterprises Inc .... F 614 231-1370
  Columbus (G-6832)
- Enginetics Corporation .... F 440 946-8833
  Eastlake (G-9107)
- Finelli Ornamental Iron Co .... F 440 248-0050
  Cleveland (G-5240)
- Fortin Welding & Mfg Inc .... E 614 291-4342
  Columbus (G-6932)
- Jason Incorporated .... F 513 860-3400
  Hamilton (G-10576)
- L & L Ornamental Iron Co .... F 513 353-1930
  Cleves (G-6369)
- Newman Brothers Inc .... E 513 242-0011
  Cincinnati (G-4074)
- P & L Metalcrafts LLC .... F 330 793-2178
  Youngstown (G-20987)
- Tarrier Steel Company Inc .... E 614 444-4000
  Columbus (G-7514)

METALWORKING MACHINERY WHOLESALERS

- Advanced Tech Utilization Co .... F 440 238-3770
  Strongsville (G-17706)
- Analytic Stress Relieving Inc .... G 804 271-7198
  Northwood (G-15332)
- Patton Industries Inc .... G 419 331-5658
  Elida (G-9198)
- Stuebing Automatic Machine Co .... E 513 771-8028
  Cincinnati (G-4388)

METEOROLOGICAL INSTRUMENT REPAIR SVCS

- Electric Speed Indicator Co .... F 216 251-2540
  Cleveland (G-5163)

METER READERS: Remote

- Matvest Inc .... E 614 487-8720
  Columbus (G-7161)

METERING DEVICES: Flow Meters, Impeller & Counter Driven

- Bif Co LLC .... F 330 564-0941
  Akron (G-88)

METERING DEVICES: Gasoline Dispensing

- CNG Fueling LLC .... G 330 772-2403
  Brookfield (G-2103)

METERING DEVICES: Water Quality Monitoring & Control Systems

- Brooks Manufacturing .... G 419 244-1777
  Toledo (G-18216)
- Ernst Flow Industries LLC .... F 732 938-5641
  Strongsville (G-17743)
- Fred W Hanks Company .... G 216 731-1774
  Cleveland (G-5274)

METERS: Liquid

- APS Accurate Products & Svcs .... G 440 353-9353
  North Ridgeville (G-15208)

METERS: Pyrometers, Indl Process

- Marlin Manufacturing Corp .... D 216 676-1340
  Cleveland (G-5623)
- Ralph Felice Inc .... G 330 468-0482
  Macedonia (G-12322)

MGMT CONSULTING SVCS: Matls, Incl Purch, Handle & Invntry

- Midwest Motor Supply Co .... C 800 233-1294
  Columbus (G-7181)
- Streamside Materials Llc .... G 419 423-1290
  Findlay (G-9763)

MICA PRDTS

- Dayton Wright Composite .... G 937 469-3962
  Dayton (G-8150)
- Fillous & Ruppel Inc .... G 216 431-0470
  Cleveland (G-5237)

MICROCIRCUITS, INTEGRATED: Semiconductor

- Crishtronics Llc .... G 440 572-8318
  Strongsville (G-17733)
- Smart Microsystems Ltd .... F 440 366-4257
  Elyria (G-9328)

MICROPHONES

- C T I Audio Inc .... D 440 593-1111
  Brooklyn Heights (G-2117)
- Cad Audio LLC .... F 440 349-4900
  Solon (G-17121)

MICROPROCESSORS

- AT&T Corp .... G 513 792-9300
  Cincinnati (G-3365)
- Intel Industries LLC .... G 614 551-5702
  Cincinnati (G-3852)
- Salient Systems Inc .... E 614 792-5800
  Dublin (G-8979)

MICROPUBLISHER

- Promatch Solutions LLC .... F 937 299-0185
  Springboro (G-17346)

MICROSCOPES

- FT Group Inc .... E 937 746-6439
  Cincinnati (G-3716)

MICROWAVE COMPONENTS

- Berry Investments Inc .... G 937 293-0398
  Moraine (G-14334)
- Idcomm LLC .... G 661 250-4081
  Willoughby Hills (G-20469)

MILITARY INSIGNIA

- Gayston Corporation .... C 937 743-6050
  Miamisburg (G-13672)
- Staco Energy Products Co .... G 937 253-1191
  Miamisburg (G-13719)

MILL PRDTS: Structural & Rail

- Cleveland Track Material Inc .... D 216 641-4000
  Cleveland (G-4980)
- Cleveland Track Material Inc .... F 216 641-4000
  Cleveland (G-4981)

MILLINERY SUPPLIES: Sweat Bands, Hat/Cap, From Purchsd Mtrls

- Sweaty Bands LLC .... E 513 871-1222
  Cincinnati (G-4402)

MILLINERY SUPPLIES: Veils & Veiling, Bridal, Funeral, Etc

- Jls Funeral Home .... F 614 625-1220
  Columbus (G-7068)

MILLING: Cereal Flour, Exc Rice

- Friends of Bears Mill Inc .... G 937 548-5112
  Greenville (G-10370)

Grain Craft Inc....E.... 216 621-3206
Cleveland (G-5338)
Mennel Milling Company....D.... 740 385-6824
Logan (G-12036)
Mennel Milling Company....E.... 740 385-6824
Logan (G-12035)

MILLING: Chemical

Triaxis Machine & Tool LLC....G.... 440 230-0303
North Royalton (G-15308)

MILLING: Grains, Exc Rice

Sunrise Cooperative Inc....F.... 419 929-1568
Wakeman (G-19289)

MILLS: Ferrous & Nonferrous

North Coast Profile Inc....G.... 330 823-7777
Alliance (G-493)
Sentek Corporation....G.... 614 586-1123
Columbus (G-7438)

MILLWORK

7&7 Woodworking....G.... 330 347-6574
Wooster (G-20552)
7d Marketing Inc....F.... 330 721-8822
Medina (G-13215)
A & J Woodworking Inc....G.... 419 695-5655
Delphos (G-8734)
A & M Woodworking....G.... 330 893-1331
Millersburg (G-14054)
A C Shutters Inc....G.... 216 429-2424
Cleveland (G-4584)
A W S Incorporated....G.... 419 352-5397
Bowling Green (G-1944)
A&M Country Woodworking LLC....G.... 330 674-1011
Holmesville (G-10971)
A&M Woodworking....G.... 513 722-5415
Loveland (G-12173)
Ace Lumber Company....F.... 330 744-3167
Youngstown (G-20835)
Adams Custom Woodworking....F.... 513 761-1395
Cincinnati (G-3297)
Advantage Tent Fittings Inc....F.... 740 773-3015
Chillicothe (G-3173)
Ailes Millwork Inc....F.... 330 678-4300
Kent (G-11290)
Aj Stineburg Wdwkg Studio LLC....G.... 614 526-9480
Columbus (G-6555)
Art Woodworking & Mfg Co....E.... 513 681-2986
Cincinnati (G-3359)
Automated Bldg Components Inc....E.... 419 257-2152
North Baltimore (G-15042)
Beechvale Laminating....F.... 330 674-2804
Millersburg (G-14064)
Berlin Woodworking....G.... 330 893-3234
Millersburg (G-14068)
Bomba S Custom Woodworking....G.... 330 699-9075
Uniontown (G-18913)
Brogan Machine Shop....G.... 513 683-9054
Loveland (G-12182)
Bruewer Woodwork Mfg Co....D.... 513 353-3505
Cleves (G-6355)
Buckeye Products....G.... 740 969-4718
Amanda (G-523)
C & W Custom Wdwkg Co Inc....E.... 513 891-6340
Cincinnati (G-3435)
Capital City Millwork Inc....F.... 614 939-0670
New Albany (G-14613)
Carter-Jones Lumber Company....C.... 330 674-9060
Millersburg (G-14077)
Cassady Woodworks Inc....E.... 937 256-7948
Dayton (G-7974)
Cincinnati Woodworks Inc....G.... 513 241-6412
Cincinnati (G-3512)
Cindoco Wood Products Co....G.... 937 444-2504
Mount Orab (G-14440)
Complete Expressions WD Works....G.... 614 245-4152
New Albany (G-14616)
Corns Quality Woodworking LLC....G.... 419 589-4899
Mansfield (G-12428)
Country Comfort Woodworking....G.... 330 695-4408
Fredericksburg (G-9946)
Creative Woodworks....G.... 330 897-1432
Sugarcreek (G-17847)
Curves and More Woodworking....G.... 614 239-7837
Columbus (G-6842)
Decker Custom Wood Llc....G.... 419 332-3464
Fremont (G-10011)
Dendratec Ltd....G.... 330 473-4878
Dalton (G-7940)
Denoon Lumber Company LLC....D.... 740 768-2220
Bergholz (G-1634)
Design-N-Wood LLC....G.... 937 419-0479
Sidney (G-17028)
Display Dynamics Inc....F.... 937 832-2830
Englewood (G-9355)
Dlwoodworking....G.... 740 927-2693
Pataskala (G-15829)
Door Fabrication Services Inc....E.... 937 454-9207
Vandalia (G-19123)
Dublin Millwork Co Inc....E.... 614 889-7776
Dublin (G-8908)
Dutch Heritage Woodcraft....E.... 330 893-2211
Berlin (G-1641)
Farmstead Acres Woodworking....G.... 330 695-6492
Fredericksburg (G-9951)
Fdi Cabinetry LLC....G.... 513 353-4500
Cleves (G-6362)
Fifth Avenue Lumber Co....D.... 614 833-6655
Canal Winchester (G-2503)
Fixture Dimensions Inc....E.... 513 360-7512
Middletown (G-13908)
Flottemesch Anthony & Son....F.... 513 561-1212
Cincinnati (G-3696)
Forum III Inc....F.... 513 961-5123
Cincinnati (G-3706)
Gdw Woodworking LLC....G.... 513 494-3041
South Lebanon (G-17276)
Gerstenslager Construction....G.... 330 832-3604
Massillon (G-12987)
Gross & Sons Custom Millwork....G.... 419 227-0214
Lima (G-11871)
Hawk Engine & Machine....G.... 440 582-0900
North Royalton (G-15276)
Heartland Stairways Inc....G.... 330 279-2554
Holmesville (G-10976)
Hj Systems Inc....F.... 614 351-9777
Columbus (G-7004)
Hoehnes Custom Woodworking....G.... 937 693-8008
Anna (G-590)
Holes Custom Woodworking....G.... 419 586-8171
Celina (G-2968)
Holmes Lumber & Bldg Ctr Inc....C.... 330 674-9060
Millersburg (G-14098)
Hrh Door Corp....D.... 440 593-5226
Conneaut (G-7649)
Huntington Hardwood Lbr Co Inc....G.... 440 647-2283
Wellington (G-19583)
Hyde Park Lumber Company....E.... 513 271-1500
Cincinnati (G-3830)
Idx Corporation....C.... 937 401-3225
Dayton (G-8259)
Inter Cab Corporation....G.... 216 351-0770
Cleveland (G-5464)
J A H Woodworking LLC....G.... 740 266-6949
Bloomingdale (G-1711)
Jh Woodworking LLC....G.... 330 276-7600
Killbuck (G-11452)
John M Hand....G.... 937 902-1327
West Alexandria (G-19619)
Judy Mills Company Inc....E.... 513 271-4241
Cincinnati (G-3887)
L and J Woodworking....F.... 330 359-3216
Dundee (G-9020)
Liechty Specialties Inc....G.... 419 445-6696
Archbold (G-655)
Lima Millwork Inc....E.... 419 331-3303
Elida (G-9195)
M H Woodworking LLC....G.... 330 893-3929
Millersburg (G-14108)
Maple Hill Woodworking....G.... 330 674-2500
Millersburg (G-14110)
Marsh Industries Inc....E.... 330 308-8667
New Philadelphia (G-14784)
Martin Bauder Woodworking LLC....G.... 513 735-0659
Milford (G-14025)
Menard Inc....F.... 513 250-4566
Cincinnati (G-4005)
Menard Inc....C.... 513 583-1444
Loveland (G-12214)
Menard Inc....E.... 419 998-4348
Lima (G-11899)
Midwest Woodworking Co Inc....E.... 513 631-6684
Cincinnati (G-4028)
Miller and Slay Wdwkg LLC....G.... 513 265-3816
Mason (G-12910)
Miller Manufacturing Inc....E.... 330 852-0689
Sugarcreek (G-17854)
Mills Customs Woodworks....G.... 216 407-3600
Cleveland (G-5691)
Millwood Wholesale Inc....F.... 330 359-6109
Dundee (G-9023)
Millwork Designs Inc....G.... 740 335-5203
Wshngtn CT Hs (G-20733)
Millwork Fabricators Inc....G.... 937 299-5452
Moraine (G-14371)
Morey Woodworking LLC....G.... 937 623-5280
Piqua (G-16144)
Mount Hope Planing....F.... 330 359-0538
Millersburg (G-14115)
Nauvoo Custom Woodworking....G.... 440 632-9502
Middlefield (G-13838)
North View Woodworking....G.... 330 359-6286
Dundee (G-9024)
Noteworthy Woodworking....G.... 330 297-0509
Ravenna (G-16392)
Ohio Woodworking Co Inc....G.... 513 631-0870
Cincinnati (G-4107)
P & T Millwork Inc....E.... 440 543-2151
Chagrin Falls (G-3064)
Paragon Woodworking LLC....G.... 614 402-1459
Columbus (G-7293)
Pj Woodwork LLC....G.... 419 886-0008
Bellville (G-1562)
Precision Woodwork Ltd....G.... 440 257-3002
Mentor (G-13553)
Profac Inc....C.... 440 942-0205
Mentor (G-13555)
R Carney Thomas....G.... 740 342-3388
New Lexington (G-14722)
Rebsco Inc....F.... 937 548-2246
Greenville (G-10390)
Renewal By Andersen LLC....G.... 614 781-9600
Columbus (G-6506)
Rinos Woodworking Shop Inc....F.... 440 946-1718
Willoughby (G-20421)
Riverside Cnstr Svcs Inc....E.... 513 723-0900
Cincinnati (G-4273)
Robertson Cabinets Inc....E.... 937 698-3755
West Milton (G-19952)
Roettger Hardwood Inc....F.... 937 693-6811
Kettlersville (G-11445)
Roy Holtzapple John Johns....G.... 419 657-2460
Wapakoneta (G-19350)
Salem Mill & Cabinet Co....G.... 330 337-9568
Salem (G-16771)
Sauder Wdwkg Co Welfare Tr....G.... 419 446-2711
Archbold (G-667)
Scarred Hands Wood Creations....G.... 740 975-2835
Etna (G-9399)
Select Woodworking Inc....G.... 513 948-9901
Cincinnati (G-4319)
Shade Youngstown & Aluminum Co....G.... 330 782-2373
Youngstown (G-21028)
Sheridan Woodworks Inc....F.... 216 663-9333
Cleveland (G-6052)
Stainwood Products....F.... 440 244-1352
Lorain (G-12124)
Stein Inc....F.... 419 747-2611
Mansfield (G-12519)
Stephen M Trudick....E.... 440 834-1891
Burton (G-2371)
Stoney Acres Woodworking Llc....G.... 440 834-0717
Burton (G-2372)
Stony Point Hardwoods....F.... 330 852-4512
Sugarcreek (G-17865)
Stratton Creek Wood Works LLC....F.... 330 876-0005
Kinsman (G-11466)
Summit Millwork LLC....G.... 330 920-4000
Cuyahoga Falls (G-7924)
Swartz Woodworking....G.... 330 359-6359
Millersburg (G-14132)
T & D Thompson Inc....E.... 740 332-8515
Laurelville (G-11627)
Todco....F.... 740 223-2542
Marion (G-12742)
Versailles Building Supply....G.... 937 526-3238
Versailles (G-19191)
Volpe Millwork Inc....G.... 216 581-0200
Cleveland (G-6270)
Walnut Creek Woodworking LLC....G.... 513 504-3520
Bethel (G-1656)
Whitmer Woodworks Inc....G.... 614 873-1196
Plain City (G-16217)
Wittrock Wdwkg & Mfg Co Inc....D.... 513 891-5800
Blue Ash (G-1873)
Woodcraft Industries Inc....C.... 440 632-9655
Middlefield (G-13868)

Employee Codes: A=Over 500 employees, B=251-500
C=101-250, D=51-100, E=20-50, F=10-19, G=3-9
2019 Harris Ohio
Industrial Directory
1509

MILLWORK

PRODUCT SECTION

Woodcraft Industries Inc .... D 440 437-7811
  Orwell (G-15640)
Woodland Woodworking 330 897-7282
  Baltic (G-1035)
Woodworks Design .... G 440 693-4414
  Middlefield (G-13869)
Woodworks Unlimited 740 574-4523
  Franklin Furnace (G-9936)
Wyman Woodworking .... G 614 338-0615
  Columbus (G-7619)
Yoder Lumber Co Inc .... D 330 893-3121
  Millersburg (G-14153)
Yoder Woodworking .... G 740 399-9400
  Butler (G-2378)
Yutzy Woodworking Ltd 330 359-6166
  Millersburg (G-14157)

MINE & QUARRY SVCS: Nonmetallic Minerals

M G Q Inc .... E 419 992-4236
  Tiffin (G-18067)
Stoepfel Drilling Co 419 532-3307
  Ottawa (G-15667)

MINE DEVELOPMENT SVCS: Nonmetallic Minerals

Robin Industries Inc .... E 330 893-3501
  Berlin (G-1644)

MINE EXPLORATION SVCS: Nonmetallic Minerals

Fgb International LLC .... G 440 359-0000
  Cleveland (G-5235)
Sandy Creek Mining Co Inc .... G 419 435-5891
  Fostoria (G-9857)

MINE PUMPING OR DRAINING SVCS: Nonmetallic Minerals

Tresslers Plumbing LLC .... G 419 784-2142
  Defiance (G-8646)

MINERAL MINING: Nonmetallic

Scots .... G 215 370-9498
  Shreve (G-17009)

MINERAL WOOL

Autoneum North America Inc .... B 419 693-0511
  Oregon (G-15556)
Brendons Fiber Works .... G 614 353-6599
  Columbus (G-6693)
Corrosion Resistant Technology .... G 800 245-3769
  Aurora (G-875)
ICP Adhesives and Sealants Inc .... F 330 753-4585
  Norton (G-15369)
Johns Manville Corporation .... B 419 782-0180
  Defiance (G-8628)
Midwest Acoust-A-Fiber Inc .... C 740 369-3624
  Delaware (G-8705)
Midwest Acoust-A-Fiber Inc .... E 740 363-6247
  Delaware (G-8706)
Nitto Inc .... C 937 773-4820
  Piqua (G-16146)
Owens Corning .... G 614 754-4098
  Columbus (G-7281)
Owens Corning .... G 419 248-8000
  Toledo (G-18445)
Owens Corning Sales LLC .... C 330 764-7800
  Medina (G-13315)
Owens Corning Sales LLC .... D 614 399-3915
  Mount Vernon (G-14497)
Premier Manufacturing Corp .... D 216 941-9700
  Cleveland (G-5916)
Refractory Specialties Inc .... E 330 938-2101
  Sebring (G-16891)
Sorbothane Inc 330 678-9444
  Kent (G-11388)
Tectum Inc .... C 740 345-9691
  Newark (G-14929)

MINERAL WOOL INSULATION PRDTS

Fibreboard Corporation .... C 419 248-8000
  Toledo (G-18294)

MINERALS: Ground Or Otherwise Treated

Cimbar Performance Mnrl WV LLC ...... E 330 532-2034
  Wellsville (G-19612)

MINERALS: Ground or Treated

6062 Holdings LLC .... G 216 359-9005
  Beachwood (G-1216)
Acme Company .... D 330 758-2313
  Poland (G-16236)
Alteo Na LLC .... G 440 460-4600
  Hudson (G-11028)
Aquablok Ltd .... F 419 825-1325
  Swanton (G-17906)
Edw C Levy Co .... E 330 484-6328
  Canton (G-2665)
Edw C Levy Co .... E 419 822-8286
  Delta (G-8769)
EMD Millipore Corporation .... C 513 631-0445
  Norwood (G-15426)
GRB Holdings Inc .... D 937 236-3250
  Dayton (G-8235)
Industrial Quartz Corp 440 942-0909
  Mentor (G-13469)
Pioneer Sands LLC .... E 740 659-2241
  Glenford (G-10271)
Pioneer Sands LLC .... E 740 599-7773
  Howard (G-10997)
Seaforth Mineral & Ore Co Inc .... F 216 292-5820
  Cleveland (G-6042)

MINIATURES

Country Lane Custom Buildings .... G 740 485-8481
  Danville (G-7961)

MINING EXPLORATION & DEVELOPMENT SVCS

Omega Cementing Co .... G 330 695-7147
  Apple Creek (G-616)

MINING MACHINERY & EQPT WHOLESALERS

J & A Machine .... G 330 424-5235
  Lisbon (G-11970)
Unified Screening & Crushing .... G 937 836-3201
  Englewood (G-9380)

MINING MACHINES & EQPT: Augers

Brydet Development Corporation .... E 740 623-0455
  Coshocton (G-7723)
Horizontal Eqp Manufacturing .... G 330 264-2229
  Wooster (G-20604)

MINING MACHINES & EQPT: Bits, Rock, Exc Oil/Gas Field Tools

Jennmar McSweeney LLC .... C 740 377-3354
  South Point (G-17285)

MINING MACHINES & EQPT: Cages, Mine Shaft

Dover Conveyor Inc .... E 740 922-9390
  Midvale (G-13976)
Tema Systems Inc .... E 513 489-7811
  Cincinnati (G-4413)

MINING MACHINES & EQPT: Crushers, Stationary

Grasan Equipment Company Inc .... D 419 526-4440
  Mansfield (G-12452)

MINING MACHINES & EQPT: Rock Crushing, Stationary

Irock Crushers LLC .... G 866 240-0201
  Cleveland (G-5475)

MINING MACHINES & EQPT: Shuttle Cars, Underground

Buzz N Shuttle Service .... G 740 223-0567
  Marion (G-12698)

MINING MACHINES/EQPT: Mine Car, Plow, Loader, Feeder/Eqpt

CF Extrusion Technologies LLC .... G 844 439-8783
  Uhrichsville (G-18882)

MINING SVCS, NEC: Bituminous

Duncan Brothers Drilling Inc .... F 330 426-9507
  East Palestine (G-9074)
Duncan Brothers Drilling Inc .... F 330 426-9507
  East Palestine (G-9075)

MIRRORS: Motor Vehicle

Beach Manufacturing Co .... C 937 882-6372
  Donnelsville (G-8800)
Commercial Vehicle Group Inc .... A 614 289-5360
  New Albany (G-14615)
Tiger Mirror Corporation .... G 419 855-3146
  Clay Center (G-4569)

MISSILES: Ballistic, Complete

Lockheed Martin Corporation .... B 330 796-2800
  Akron (G-256)

MIXERS: Hot Metal

CF Extrusion Technologies LLC .... G 844 439-8783
  Uhrichsville (G-18882)

MIXING EQPT

Duplex Mill & Manufacturing Co .... E 937 325-5555
  Springfield (G-17392)
Quikstir Inc .... F 419 732-2601
  Port Clinton (G-16256)

MIXTURES & BLOCKS: Asphalt Paving

A United .... G 330 782-6005
  Youngstown (G-20831)
Action Blacktop Sealcoating & .... G 937 667-4769
  Tipp City (G-18097)
Advanced Fiber LLC .... G 419 562-1337
  Bucyrus (G-2317)
All Coatings Co Inc .... G 330 821-3806
  Alliance (G-451)
Allied Corporation Inc .... G 330 425-7861
  Twinsburg (G-18730)
Aluminum Coating Manufacturers ..... E 216 341-2000
  Cleveland (G-4680)
Asphalt Fabrics & Specialties .... G 440 786-1077
  Solon (G-17109)
Asphalt Materials Inc .... F 419 693-0626
  Oregon (G-15554)
Atlas Roofing Corporation .... C 937 746-9941
  Franklin (G-9870)
Baileys Asphalt Sealing .... F 740 453-9409
  South Zanesville (G-17301)
Barrett Paving Materials Inc .... C 513 271-6200
  Middletown (G-13970)
Bituminous Products Company .... G 419 693-3933
  Toledo (G-18204)
Bluffton Stone Co .... E 419 358-6941
  Bluffton (G-1886)
Bowerston Shale Company .... E 740 269-2921
  Bowerston (G-1939)
Brewer Company .... E 614 279-8688
  Columbus (G-6694)
Brewer Company .... G 800 394-0017
  Milford (G-13999)
Crafco Inc .... F 330 270-3034
  Youngstown (G-20880)
D and D Asp Sealcoating LLC .... G 614 288-3597
  Pickerington (G-16044)
Erie Materials Inc .... G 419 483-4648
  Castalia (G-2938)
Hanson Aggregates Midwest LLC ..... G 419 983-2211
  Bloomville (G-1715)
Holmes Supply Corp .... G 330 279-2634
  Holmesville (G-10980)
Hy-Grade Corporation .... E 216 341-7711
  Cleveland (G-5429)
Image Pavement Maintenance .... E 937 833-9200
  Brookville (G-2172)
John R Jurgensen Co .... G 937 293-3112
  Springfield (G-17427)
Kokosing Materials Inc .... E 740 745-3341
  Saint Louisville (G-16672)
Lake Erie Asphalt Paving Inc .... G 440 526-5191
  Brecksville (G-2047)

M & B Asphalt Company Inc ....G....... 419 992-4235
Tiffin *(G-18066)*
M & B Asphalt Company Inc ....G....... 419 992-4236
Old Fort *(G-15525)*
Mae Materials LLC ....E....... 740 778-2242
South Webster *(G-17298)*
Mansfield Asphalt Paving Inc ....F....... 740 453-0721
Zanesville *(G-21154)*
Mar-Zane Inc ....F....... 740 453-0721
Zanesville *(G-21155)*
Mar-Zane Inc ....G....... 740 782-1240
Bethesda *(G-1657)*
Mar-Zane Inc ....G....... 740 685-5178
Byesville *(G-2390)*
Mar-Zane Inc ....G....... 330 626-2079
Mantua *(G-12552)*
Marathon Petroleum Company LP ....F....... 419 422-2121
Findlay *(G-9719)*
Massillon Asphalt Co ....G....... 330 833-6330
Massillon *(G-13019)*
Miller Bros Paving Inc ....F....... 419 445-1015
Archbold *(G-659)*
Mplx Terminals LLC ....B....... 330 479-5539
Canton *(G-2757)*
Newton Asphalt Paving Inc ....F....... 330 878-5648
Strasburg *(G-17650)*
Reading Rock Inc ....C....... 513 874-2345
West Chester *(G-19893)*
Rub-R-Road Inc ....G....... 330 678-7050
Kent *(G-11379)*
Rutland Township ....G....... 740 742-2805
Bidwell *(G-1669)*
Seal Master Corporation ....E....... 330 673-8410
Kent *(G-11383)*
Shelly and Sands Inc ....G....... 330 743-8850
Youngstown *(G-21029)*
Shelly and Sands Inc ....D....... 740 859-2104
Rayland *(G-16423)*
Shelly Company ....D....... 419 422-8854
Findlay *(G-9753)*
Shelly Company ....G....... 740 246-6315
Thornville *(G-18033)*
Shelly Materials Inc ....E....... 740 246-5009
Thornville *(G-18034)*
Shelly Materials Inc ....G....... 419 622-2101
Convoy *(G-7671)*
Shelly Materials Inc ....G....... 419 273-2510
Forest *(G-9788)*
Sidwell Materials Inc ....C....... 740 849-2394
Zanesville *(G-21180)*
Smalls Asphalt Paving Inc ....E....... 740 427-4096
Gambier *(G-10184)*
Stark Materials Inc ....E....... 330 497-1648
Canton *(G-2822)*
Stoneco Inc ....E....... 419 393-2555
Oakwood *(G-15474)*
Thorworks Industries Inc ....E....... 419 626-4375
Sandusky *(G-16855)*
Tri County Asphalt Materials ....G....... 330 549-2852
Youngstown *(G-21052)*
Valley Asphalt Corporation ....G....... 513 381-0652
Morrow *(G-14416)*
Valley Asphalt Corporation ....G....... 937 335-3664
Troy *(G-18717)*
York Paving Co ....F....... 740 594-3600
Athens *(G-854)*

MOBILE COMMUNICATIONS EQPT

Eei Acquisition Corp ....E....... 440 564-5484
Middlefield *(G-13797)*
Wireless Retail LLC ....F....... 614 657-5182
Blacklick *(G-1695)*

MOBILE HOME & TRAILER REPAIR

Advanced Rv LLC ....G....... 440 283-0405
Willoughby *(G-20267)*

MOBILE HOMES

C & C Mobile Homes LLC ....G....... 740 663-5535
Waverly *(G-19541)*
Colonial Heights Mhp LLC ....G....... 740 314-5182
Wintersville *(G-20538)*
Ellis & Watts Intl LLC ....G....... 513 752-9000
Batavia *(G-1143)*
Holiday Homes Inc ....F....... 513 353-9777
Harrison *(G-10646)*
Mobile Conversions Inc ....F....... 513 797-1991
Amelia *(G-544)*
Skyline Corporation ....C....... 330 852-2483
Sugarcreek *(G-17864)*
Sun Communities Inc ....G....... 740 548-1942
Lewis Center *(G-11782)*

MOBILE HOMES, EXC RECREATIONAL

Manufactured Housing Entps Inc ....C....... 419 636-4511
Bryan *(G-2298)*

MODELS

Advance Products ....F....... 419 882-8117
Sylvania *(G-17931)*
Consolidated Pattern Works Inc ....G....... 330 434-6060
Akron *(G-120)*
Morris Technologies Inc ....C....... 513 733-1611
Cincinnati *(G-4047)*
Scott Models Inc ....F....... 513 771-8005
Cincinnati *(G-4309)*

MODELS: General, Exc Toy

3-D Technical Services Company ....E....... 937 746-2901
Franklin *(G-9866)*
Anza Inc ....G....... 513 542-7337
Cincinnati *(G-3349)*
Debolt Machine Inc ....G....... 740 454-8082
Zanesville *(G-21127)*
King Model Company ....E....... 330 633-0491
Akron *(G-238)*
Model Engineering Company ....G....... 330 644-3450
Barberton *(G-1087)*

MODULES: Computer Logic

John B Allen ....G....... 614 488-7122
Columbus *(G-7072)*
Laird Connectivity Inc ....B....... 330 434-7929
Akron *(G-246)*

MOLDED RUBBER PRDTS

Action Rubber Co Inc ....F....... 937 866-5975
Dayton *(G-8005)*
Aeroquip-Vickers Inc ....G....... 216 523-5000
Cleveland *(G-4633)*
American Pro-Mold Inc ....E....... 330 336-4111
Wadsworth *(G-19226)*
ARC Rubber Inc ....F....... 440 466-4555
Geneva *(G-10214)*
Cardinal Rubber Company Inc ....E....... 330 745-2191
Barberton *(G-1069)*
Chardon Custom Polymers LLC ....F....... 440 285-2161
Chardon *(G-3101)*
Clark Rbr Plastic Intl Sls Inc ....D....... 440 255-9793
Mentor *(G-13413)*
Columbus Gasket Co Inc ....G....... 614 878-6041
Columbus *(G-6789)*
Contitech Usa Inc ....F....... 330 664-7000
Fairlawn *(G-9603)*
Custom Rubber Corporation ....D....... 216 391-2928
Cleveland *(G-5048)*
Datwyler Sling Sltions USA Inc ....D....... 937 387-2800
Vandalia *(G-19122)*
Eaton Aeroquip LLC ....C....... 216 523-5000
Cleveland *(G-5143)*
Enduro Rubber Company ....G....... 330 296-9603
Ravenna *(G-16379)*
Hhi Company Inc ....G....... 330 455-3983
Canton *(G-2698)*
Hytech Silicone Products Inc ....G....... 330 297-1888
Ravenna *(G-16383)*
Ier Fujikura Inc ....C....... 330 425-7121
Macedonia *(G-12302)*
Jet Rubber Company ....E....... 330 325-1821
Rootstown *(G-16569)*
K F D Inc ....G....... 330 773-4300
Coventry Township *(G-7771)*
Karman Rubber Company ....E....... 330 864-2161
Akron *(G-232)*
Lauren International Ltd ....C....... 330 339-3373
New Philadelphia *(G-14780)*
Lauren Manufacturing LLC ....B....... 330 339-3373
New Philadelphia *(G-14781)*
Luxx Ultra-Tech Inc ....G....... 330 483-6051
Medina *(G-13288)*
Macdivitt Rubber Company LLC ....E....... 440 259-5937
Perry *(G-15909)*
May Lin Silicone Products Inc ....G....... 330 825-9019
Barberton *(G-1085)*
MPS Manufacturing Company LLC ....G....... 330 343-1435
New Philadelphia *(G-14788)*
Mullins Rubber Products Inc ....D....... 937 233-4211
Dayton *(G-8372)*
Neff-Perkins Company ....C....... 440 632-1658
Middlefield *(G-13839)*
Newact Inc ....F....... 513 321-5177
Batavia *(G-1173)*
Noster Rubber Company Inc ....F....... 419 299-3387
Van Buren *(G-19072)*
Park-Ohio Holdings Corp ....F....... 440 947-2000
Cleveland *(G-5842)*
Park-Ohio Industries Inc ....C....... 440 947-2000
Cleveland *(G-5843)*
Park-Ohio Products Inc ....D....... 216 961-7200
Cleveland *(G-5844)*
Plabell Rubber Products Corp ....F....... 419 691-5878
Toledo *(G-18472)*
Profile Rubber Corporation ....F....... 330 239-1703
Wadsworth *(G-19267)*
Q Model Inc ....E....... 330 673-0473
Barberton *(G-1100)*
Qualiform Inc ....E....... 330 336-6777
Wadsworth *(G-19268)*
R C A Rubber Company ....D....... 330 784-1291
Akron *(G-338)*
Raydar Inc of Ohio ....G....... 330 334-6111
Wadsworth *(G-19272)*
Robin Industries Inc ....C....... 330 359-5418
Winesburg *(G-20534)*
Robin Industries Inc ....C....... 330 695-9300
Fredericksburg *(G-9958)*
Robin Industries Inc ....E....... 330 893-3501
Berlin *(G-1644)*
Rubber Associates Inc ....D....... 330 745-2186
New Franklin *(G-14698)*
Rubber-Tech Inc ....F....... 937 274-1114
Dayton *(G-8487)*
Rubberite Corp ....G....... 832 457-0654
Columbus *(G-7406)*
Sorbothane Inc ....E....... 330 678-9444
Kent *(G-11388)*
Sumiriko Ohio Inc ....C....... 419 358-2121
Bluffton *(G-1893)*
Sur-Seal LLC ....C....... 513 574-8500
Cincinnati *(G-4398)*
TMI Inc ....E....... 330 270-9780
Youngstown *(G-21046)*
Tristan Rubber Molding Inc ....E....... 330 499-4055
North Canton *(G-15132)*
Universal Polymer & Rubber Ltd ....C....... 440 632-1691
Middlefield *(G-13864)*
Universal Urethane Pdts Inc ....D....... 419 693-7400
Toledo *(G-18585)*
Vernay Manufacturing Inc ....E....... 937 767-7261
Yellow Springs *(G-20818)*
Woodlawn Rubber Co ....F....... 513 489-1718
Blue Ash *(G-1875)*
Yokohama Inds Amricas Ohio Inc ....D....... 440 352-3321
Painesville *(G-15802)*

MOLDING COMPOUNDS

A Schulman Inc ....D....... 330 666-3751
Fairlawn *(G-9589)*
A Schulman Inc ....C....... 330 773-2700
Akron *(G-20)*
A Schulman Inc ....C....... 330 630-0308
Akron *(G-21)*
A Schulman Inc ....F....... 330 630-3315
Akron *(G-22)*
Ada Solutions Inc ....E....... 440 576-0423
Jefferson *(G-11223)*
Buckeye Polymers Inc ....E....... 330 948-3007
Lodi *(G-12008)*
Clyde Tool & Die Inc ....F....... 419 547-9574
Clyde *(G-6387)*
Dentsply Sirona Inc ....D....... 419 865-9497
Maumee *(G-13108)*
Dlhbowles Inc ....F....... 330 478-2503
Canton *(G-2662)*
Flex Technologies Inc ....E....... 330 897-6311
Baltic *(G-1029)*
Hpc Holdings LLC ....F....... 330 666-3751
Fairlawn *(G-9608)*
Incredible Solutions Inc ....F....... 330 898-3878
Warren *(G-19409)*
Jain America Foods Inc ....G....... 614 850-9400
Columbus *(G-7058)*
Jain America Holdings Inc ....D....... 614 850-9400
Columbus *(G-7059)*
JMS Industries Inc ....E....... 937 325-3502
Springfield *(G-17426)*

Employee Codes: A=Over 500 employees, B=251-500
C=101-250, D=51-100, E=20-50, F=10-19, G=3-9

2019 Harris Ohio
Industrial Directory

1511

MOLDING COMPOUNDS

Kiley Mold Company LLC .... G 513 875-3223
  Fayetteville *(G-9641)*
L-K Industry Inc .... E 937 526-3000
  Versailles *(G-19186)*
Meggitt (erlanger) LLC .... D 513 851-5550
  Cincinnati *(G-4000)*
Michael Day Enterprises LLC .... G 330 335-5100
  Wadsworth *(G-19253)*
Pace Mold & Machine LLC .... G 330 879-1777
  Massillon *(G-13037)*
Pro Mold Design Inc .... G 440 352-1212
  Mentor *(G-13554)*
Resinoid Engineering Corp .... D 740 928-6115
  Hebron *(G-10759)*
Rochling Glastic Composites LP .... C 216 486-0100
  Cleveland *(G-5996)*
Stopol Equipment Sales LLC .... G 440 499-0030
  Brunswick *(G-2240)*

MOLDING SAND MINING

Farsight Management Inc .... G 330 602-8338
  Dover *(G-8826)*
Kistler Instrument Corp 937 268-5920
  Dayton *(G-8298)*

MOLDINGS & TRIM: Metal, Exc Automobile

Aluminum Color Industries Inc .... D 330 536-6295
  Lowellville *(G-12248)*
Magnode Corporation .... D 317 243-3553
  Trenton *(G-18624)*

MOLDINGS & TRIM: Wood

A & B Wood Design Assoc Inc .... G 330 721-2789
  Wadsworth *(G-19218)*
Armstrong Custom Moulding Inc .... G 740 922-5931
  Uhrichsville *(G-18880)*
Fairfield Woodworks Ltd .... G 740 689-1953
  Lancaster *(G-11571)*

MOLDINGS OR TRIM: Automobile, Stamped Metal

American Quality Molds LLC .... G 513 276-7345
  Hamilton *(G-10532)*
American Trim LLC .... A 419 228-1145
  Sidney *(G-17014)*
Florida Production Engrg Inc .... G 937 996-4361
  New Madison *(G-14741)*
M-Tek Inc .... A 419 209-0399
  Upper Sandusky *(G-18961)*
Pennant Companies .... B 614 451-1782
  Columbus *(G-7308)*

MOLDINGS, ARCHITECTURAL: Plaster Of Paris

Richtech Industries Inc .... G 440 937-4401
  Avon *(G-964)*
Stephen R Lilley .... G 513 899-4400
  Morrow *(G-14415)*

MOLDINGS: Picture Frame

Frame USA .... E 513 577-7107
  Cincinnati *(G-3708)*
Ginnys Custom Framing Gallery .... G 419 468-7240
  Galion *(G-10142)*
Hackman Frames LLC .... F 614 841-0007
  Columbus *(G-6975)*
House of 10000 Picture Frames .... G 937 254-5541
  Dayton *(G-8253)*

MOLDS: Gray, Ingot, Cast Iron

Anchor Glass Container Corp .... C 740 452-2743
  Zanesville *(G-21099)*
Ellwood Engineered Castings Co .... C 330 568-3000
  Hubbard *(G-11001)*
Kenton Iron Products Inc .... D 419 674-4178
  Kenton *(G-11411)*

MOLDS: Indl

Akron Centl Engrv Mold Mch Inc .... E 330 794-8704
  Akron *(G-34)*
Alpha Tool & Mold Inc .... F 440 473-2343
  Cleveland *(G-4676)*
American Cube Mold Inc .... G 330 558-0044
  Hinckley *(G-10898)*
Amerimold Inc .... G 330 628-2190
  Mogadore *(G-14229)*
Apollo Plastics Inc .... F 440 951-7774
  Mentor *(G-13391)*
Barberton Mold & Machine Co .... G 330 745-8559
  Barberton *(G-1063)*
Borke Mold Specialist Inc .... E 513 870-8000
  West Chester *(G-19662)*
Broadway Companies Inc .... F 937 890-1888
  Dayton *(G-8063)*
C & D Tool Inc .... G 440 942-8463
  Eastlake *(G-9099)*
Caliber Mold and Machine Inc .... G 330 633-8171
  Akron *(G-102)*
Camden Concrete Products .... G 937 456-1229
  Eaton *(G-9145)*
Canton Pattern & Mold Inc .... G 330 455-4316
  Canton *(G-2615)*
Century Die Company LLC .... D 419 332-2693
  Fremont *(G-10005)*
Cincinnati Mold Incorporated .... G 513 922-1888
  Cincinnati *(G-3502)*
Cubic Blue Inc .... G 330 638-2999
  Cortland *(G-7708)*
Diversified Mold Castings LLC .... E 216 663-1814
  Cleveland *(G-5100)*
Durivage Pattern & Mfg Co .... E 419 836-8655
  Williston *(G-20262)*
Dynamic Tool & Mold Inc .... G 440 237-8665
  Cleveland *(G-5125)*
Erickson-Huff Tool and Die .... G 740 596-4036
  Mc Arthur *(G-13181)*
Estee Mold & Die Inc .... G 937 224-7853
  Dayton *(G-8188)*
Esterle Mold & Machine Co Inc .... F 330 686-1685
  Stow *(G-17584)*
Esterle Mold & Machine Co Inc .... G 330 686-1685
  Stow *(G-17583)*
Exodus Mold & Machine Inc .... G 330 854-0282
  Canal Fulton *(G-2479)*
Faith Tool & Manufacturing .... G 440 951-5934
  Willoughby *(G-20320)*
Ferriot Inc .... C 330 786-3000
  Akron *(G-169)*
H&M Machine & Tool LLC .... E 419 776-9220
  Toledo *(G-18316)*
Herbert Usa Inc .... D 330 929-4297
  Akron *(G-204)*
High Tech Mold & Machine Co .... F 330 896-4466
  Uniontown *(G-18921)*
J & H Corporation .... G 440 357-5982
  Painesville *(G-15751)*
Jamen Tool & Die Co .... G 330 782-6731
  Youngstown *(G-20946)*
Kent Mold and Manufacturing Co ...... E 330 673-3469
  Kent *(G-11343)*
Liberty Die Cast Molds Inc .... F 740 666-7492
  Ostrander *(G-15645)*
Lightning Mold & Machine Inc .... F 440 593-6460
  Conneaut *(G-7653)*
M & R Manufacturing Inc .... G 330 633-5725
  Tallmadge *(G-17989)*
Magnum Molding Inc .... G 937 368-3040
  Conover *(G-7665)*
Malabar Properties LLC .... F 419 884-0071
  Mansfield *(G-12473)*
Mallory Pattern Works Inc .... G 419 726-8001
  Toledo *(G-18398)*
Martz Mold & Machine Inc .... G 330 928-2159
  Cuyahoga Falls *(G-7897)*
Maumee Pattern Company .... E 419 693-4968
  Toledo *(G-18403)*
Mercury Machine Co .... D 440 349-3222
  Solon *(G-17191)*
Milacron Holdings Corp .... D 513 487-5000
  Blue Ash *(G-1821)*
Mold Crafters Inc .... G 937 426-3179
  Dayton *(G-8364)*
Mold Solutions .... G 800 948-4947
  Oberlin *(G-15502)*
Mold Surface Textures .... G 330 678-8590
  Kent *(G-11357)*
Mold-Rite Plastics LLC .... G 330 405-7739
  Twinsburg *(G-18821)*
National Mold Remediation .... G 614 231-6653
  Columbus *(G-7211)*
New Castings Inc .... C 330 645-6653
  Akron *(G-295)*
Nichols Mold Inc .... G 330 297-9719
  Ravenna *(G-16391)*
Northeast Tire Molds Inc .... G 330 376-6107
  Akron *(G-302)*
Norwalk Precast Molds Inc .... E 419 668-1639
  Norwalk *(G-15410)*
Numerics Unlimited Inc .... E 937 849-0100
  New Carlisle *(G-14675)*
Oakley Die & Mold Co .... E 513 754-8500
  Mason *(G-12918)*
Paradise Mold & Die LLC .... G 216 362-1945
  Cleveland *(G-5837)*
Penco Tool LLC .... E 440 998-1116
  Ashtabula *(G-795)*
Pendleton Mold & Machine LLC .... G 440 998-0041
  Ashtabula *(G-796)*
Perfection Mold & Machine Co .... F 330 784-5435
  Twinsburg *(G-18835)*
Plastic Mold Technology Inc .... G 330 848-4921
  Barberton *(G-1095)*
Reuther Mold & Mfg Co Inc .... D 330 923-5266
  Cuyahoga Falls *(G-7913)*
Ron-Al Mold & Machine Inc .... F 330 673-7919
  Kent *(G-11377)*
Saehwa IMC Na Inc .... D 330 645-6653
  Akron *(G-369)*
Seaway Pattern Mfg Inc .... E 419 865-5724
  Toledo *(G-18516)*
Shook Tool Inc .... G 937 337-6471
  Ansonia *(G-594)*
Slabe Tool Company .... G 740 439-1647
  Cambridge *(G-2456)*
Superior Mold & Die Co .... G 330 688-8251
  Munroe Falls *(G-14528)*
Tech Mold & Tool Co Inc .... G 937 667-8851
  Tipp City *(G-18137)*
Tempcraft Corporation .... C 216 391-3885
  Cleveland *(G-6157)*
Tom Smith Industries Inc .... C 937 832-1555
  Englewood *(G-9378)*
Tooling Technology LLC .... D 937 295-3672
  Fort Loramie *(G-9810)*
Tracker Machine Inc .... G 330 482-4086
  Columbiana *(G-6483)*
Tree City Mold & Machine Co .... G 330 673-9807
  Kent *(G-11396)*
Turbo-Mold Inc .... G 440 352-2530
  Painesville *(G-15792)*
Velocity Concept Dev Group LLC ...... G 740 685-2637
  Byesville *(G-2395)*
XCEL Mold and Machine Inc .... F 330 499-8450
  Canton *(G-2867)*
Yugo Mold Inc .... F 330 606-0710
  Akron *(G-441)*

MOLDS: Plastic Working & Foundry

Aspec Inc .... G 513 561-9922
  Cincinnati *(G-3363)*
Basilius Inc .... E 419 536-5810
  Toledo *(G-18199)*
Case Pattern Co Inc .... G 216 531-0744
  Madison *(G-12341)*
Catalysis Additive Tooling LLC .... G 614 715-3674
  Powell *(G-16316)*
Centerline Tool & Machine .... G 937 222-3600
  Dayton *(G-8083)*
Circle Mold Incorporated .... E 330 633-7017
  Tallmadge *(G-17976)*
Data Mold and Tool Inc .... G 419 878-9861
  Waterville *(G-19493)*
De-Lux Mold & Machine Inc .... G 330 678-1030
  Kent *(G-11311)*
Delco Corporation .... E 330 896-4220
  Akron *(G-137)*
Diamond Mold & Die Co .... F 330 633-5682
  Tallmadge *(G-17979)*
Diemaster Tool & Mold Inc .... F 330 467-4281
  Macedonia *(G-12289)*
Diversified Tool Systems .... G 419 845-2143
  Caledonia *(G-2415)*
Eger Products Inc .... D 513 753-4200
  Amelia *(G-539)*
Founder Service & Mfg Co .... F 330 584-7759
  Deerfield *(G-8609)*
Green Machine Tool Inc .... F 937 253-0771
  Dayton *(G-7980)*
Hamilton Mold & Machine Co .... E 216 732-8200
  Cleveland *(G-5368)*
Industrial Mold Inc .... E 330 425-7374
  Twinsburg *(G-18796)*
Justin P Straub LLC .... G 513 761-0282
  Cincinnati *(G-3888)*

PRODUCT SECTION

MOTOR VEHICLE ASSEMBLY, COMPLETE: Snow Plows

Liqui-Box Corporation .... C 419 209-9085
  Upper Sandusky (G-18960)
Match Mold & Machine Inc .... E 330 830-5503
  Massillon (G-13022)
McRon Finance Corp .... A 513 487-5000
  Cincinnati (G-3990)
Midwest Mold & Texture Corp .... E 513 732-1300
  Batavia (G-1165)
Milacron Plas Tech Group LLC .... C 513 536-2000
  Batavia (G-1168)
Milacron Plas Tech Group LLC .... C 937 444-2532
  Mount Orab (G-14447)
Nordson Xaloy Incorporated .... C 724 656-5600
  Youngstown (G-20977)
Pace Mold & Machine LLC .... G 330 879-1777
  Massillon (G-13037)
Premiere Mold and Machine Co .... G 330 874-3000
  Bolivar (G-1923)
Preuss Mold & Die .... G 419 729-9100
  Toledo (G-18481)
Promold Inc .... F 330 633-3532
  Tallmadge (G-18001)
Prospect Mold & Die Company .... D 330 929-3311
  Cuyahoga Falls (G-7909)
Ross Special Products Inc .... F 937 335-8406
  Troy (G-18700)
Shelburne Corp .... G 216 321-9177
  Shaker Heights (G-16936)
Skribs Tool and Die Inc .... E 440 951-7774
  Mentor (G-13583)
Universal Tire Molds Inc .... E 330 253-5101
  Akron (G-422)
Vinyltech Inc .... E 330 538-0369
  North Jackson (G-15158)
Ward Mold & Machine .... G 740 472-5303
  Woodsfield (G-20549)
Wentworth Mold Inc Electra .... D 937 898-8460
  Vandalia (G-19151)

MOLYBDENUM SILICON, EXC MADE IN BLAST FURNACES

H C Starck Inc .... B 216 692-3990
  Euclid (G-9418)

MONORAIL SYSTEMS

Webb-Stiles Company .... D 330 225-7761
  Valley City (G-19069)

MONUMENTS & GRAVE MARKERS, EXC TERRAZZO

Flowers & Monuments R US .... G 937 813-8496
  Dayton (G-8199)
Upper Monument .... G 419 310-2387
  Upper Sandusky (G-18976)

MONUMENTS: Concrete

Art Columbus Memorial Inc .... G 614 221-9333
  Columbus (G-6616)
Jackson Monument Inc .... G 740 286-1590
  Jackson (G-11187)

MONUMENTS: Cut Stone, Exc Finishing Or Lettering Only

Dodds Monument Inc .... F 937 372-2736
  Xenia (G-20767)

MOPS: Floor & Dust

Guardian Co Inc .... G 216 721-2262
  Cleveland (G-5359)
Ha-Ste Manufacturing Co Inc .... E 937 968-4858
  Union City (G-18904)
Impact Products LLC .... G 419 841-2891
  Toledo (G-18342)

MORTAR

Wahl Refractory Solutions LLC .... D 419 334-2658
  Fremont (G-10063)

MOTION PICTURE & VIDEO PRODUCTION SVCS

David Esrati .... G 937 228-4433
  Dayton (G-8126)
Musicol Inc .... G 614 267-3133
  Columbus (G-7203)

Province of St John The Baptis .... D 513 241-5615
  Cincinnati (G-4219)

MOTION PICTURE EQPT

Eprad Inc .... G 419 666-3266
  Perrysburg (G-15948)
Legrand AV Inc .... E 574 267-8101
  Blue Ash (G-1805)

MOTION PICTURE PRODUCTION & DISTRIBUTION: Television

Estreamz Inc .... E 513 278-7836
  Cincinnati (G-3654)

MOTOR & GENERATOR PARTS: Electric

Electrocraft Arkansas Inc .... D 501 268-4203
  Gallipolis (G-10163)
Global Innovative Products LLC .... G 513 701-0441
  Mason (G-12879)
Parker-Hannifin Corporation .... C 330 336-3511
  Wadsworth (G-19260)
Swiger Coil Systems Ltd .... C 216 362-7500
  Cleveland (G-6137)
Wabtec Corporation .... G 216 362-7500
  Cleveland (G-6280)

MOTOR HOMES

Advanced Rv LLC .... G 440 283-0405
  Willoughby (G-20267)
Airstream Inc .... B 937 596-6111
  Jackson Center (G-11205)

MOTOR REBUILDING SVCS, EXC AUTOMOTIVE

Joe Baker Equipment Sales .... G 513 451-1327
  Cincinnati (G-3875)

MOTOR REPAIR SVCS

Bar1 Motorsports .... F 614 284-3732
  Marysville (G-12771)
General Electric Intl Inc .... G 410 737-7228
  Cincinnati (G-3744)
Home Service Station Inc .... G 419 678-2612
  Coldwater (G-6414)

MOTOR SCOOTERS & PARTS

Dco LLC .... B 419 931-9086
  Perrysburg (G-15938)

MOTOR VEHICLE ASSEMBLY, COMPLETE: Ambulances

Braun Industries Inc .... B 419 232-7020
  Van Wert (G-19080)
Horton Enterprises Inc .... G 614 539-8181
  Grove City (G-10434)
La Boit Specialty Vehicles .... E 614 231-7640
  Gahanna (G-10088)

MOTOR VEHICLE ASSEMBLY, COMPLETE: Autos, Incl Specialty

Auto Expo USA of Cleveland .... G 216 889-3000
  Cleveland (G-4768)
Brookville Roadster Inc .... E 937 833-4605
  Brookville (G-2162)
Dakkota Integrated Systems LLC .... E 517 694-6500
  Toledo (G-18252)
Farber Specialty Vehicles Inc .... C 614 863-6470
  Reynoldsburg (G-16438)
General Motors LLC .... A 330 824-5000
  Warren (G-19405)
Great Lakes Assemblies LLC .... D 937 645-3900
  East Liberty (G-9047)
Honda of America Mfg Inc .... A 937 642-5000
  Marysville (G-12791)
Honda of America Mfg Inc .... B 937 642-5000
  Marysville (G-12793)
K K Racing Chassis .... G 330 628-2930
  Akron (G-229)
Magic Dragon Machine Inc .... G 614 539-8004
  Grove City (G-10443)
P C Workshop Inc .... D 419 399-4805
  Paulding (G-15869)

Pittsburgh Glass Works LLC .... C 419 569-7521
  Crestline (G-7798)
Star Fab Inc .... E 330 482-1601
  Columbiana (G-6482)
Universal Composite LLC .... E 614 507-1646
  Sunbury (G-17901)
Weastec Incorporated .... E 614 734-9645
  Dublin (G-9011)
Weiss Motors .... G 330 678-5585
  Kent (G-11399)
Wyatt Specialties Inc .... G 614 989-5362
  Circleville (G-4565)

MOTOR VEHICLE ASSEMBLY, COMPLETE: Bus/Large Spclty Vehicles

Buses International .... F 440 233-4091
  Lorain (G-12081)

MOTOR VEHICLE ASSEMBLY, COMPLETE: Buses, All Types

Aftermarket Parts Company LLC .... B 740 369-1056
  Delaware (G-8651)
Eldorado National Kansas Inc .... G 937 596-6849
  Jackson Center (G-11208)
Thor Industries Inc .... E 937 596-6111
  Jackson Center (G-11217)
Titan Bus LLC .... G 419 523-3593
  Ottawa (G-15669)

MOTOR VEHICLE ASSEMBLY, COMPLETE: Cars, Armored

Hyq Technologies LLC .... G 513 225-6911
  Oxford (G-15694)
Svm America Ltd .... E 937 218-7591
  Maineville (G-12377)

MOTOR VEHICLE ASSEMBLY, COMPLETE: Fire Department Vehicles

Antram Fire Equipment .... G 330 525-7171
  North Georgetown (G-15139)
Columbus Fire Fighters Union .... G 614 481-8900
  Columbus (G-6788)
Copley Fire & Rescue Assn .... E 330 666-6464
  Copley (G-7681)
Reberland Equipment Inc .... F 330 698-5883
  Apple Creek (G-618)
Sutphen Corporation .... C 800 726-7030
  Dublin (G-8999)
United Fire Apparatus Corp .... G 419 645-4083
  Cridersville (G-7813)

MOTOR VEHICLE ASSEMBLY, COMPLETE: Hearses

Accubuilt Inc .... C 419 224-3910
  Lima (G-11829)
Accubuilt Inc .... C 419 224-3910
  Lima (G-11830)
Eagle Coach Inc .... D 513 797-4100
  Amelia (G-537)

MOTOR VEHICLE ASSEMBLY, COMPLETE: Military Motor Vehicle

AM General LLC .... G 937 704-0160
  Franklin (G-9868)
Mbm Industries Ltd .... G 937 522-0719
  Beavercreek Township (G-1369)
Warfighter Fcsed Logistics Inc .... G 740 513-4692
  Galena (G-10117)

MOTOR VEHICLE ASSEMBLY, COMPLETE: Mobile Lounges

Gerling and Associates Inc .... D 740 965-6200
  Sunbury (G-17886)
Obs Inc .... F 330 453-3725
  Canton (G-2769)

MOTOR VEHICLE ASSEMBLY, COMPLETE: Snow Plows

Marc Industries Inc .... G 440 944-9305
  Willoughby (G-20369)

Employee Codes: A=Over 500 employees, B=251-500
C=101-250, D=51-100, E=20-50, F=10-19, G=3-9

2019 Harris Ohio Industrial Directory

MOTOR VEHICLE ASSEMBLY, COMPLETE: Truck & Tractor Trucks

PRODUCT SECTION

MOTOR VEHICLE ASSEMBLY, COMPLETE: Truck & Tractor Trucks

Navistar Inc .... C 937 390-5848
  Springfield *(G-17456)*
Navistar Inc .... D 937 390-5653
  Springfield *(G-17457)*
Navistar Inc .... D 937 561-3315
  Springfield *(G-17458)*
Navistar Inc .... G 513 733-8500
  Cincinnati *(G-4064)*
Paccar Inc .... A 740 774-5111
  Chillicothe *(G-3205)*

MOTOR VEHICLE ASSEMBLY, COMPLETE: Truck Tractors, Highway

Navistar Inc .... E 937 390-5704
  Springfield *(G-17459)*

MOTOR VEHICLE ASSEMBLY, COMPLETE: Wreckers, Tow Truck

Lawsons Towing & Auto Wrckg .... F 216 883-9050
  Cleveland *(G-5568)*

MOTOR VEHICLE DEALERS: Automobiles, New & Used

American Honda Motor Co Inc .... C 937 332-6100
  Troy *(G-18636)*
Doug Marine Motors Inc .... E 740 335-3700
  Wshngtn CT Hs *(G-20724)*
Jmac Inc .... E 614 436-2418
  Columbus *(G-7069)*
Subaru of A .... G 614 793-2358
  Dublin *(G-8998)*

MOTOR VEHICLE DEALERS: Cars, Used Only

D & D Classic Auto Restoration .... E 937 473-2229
  Covington *(G-7784)*
Sammartino Welding & Auto Sls .... G 330 782-6086
  Youngstown *(G-21024)*
Tuffy Manufacturing .... G 330 940-2356
  Cuyahoga Falls *(G-7930)*

MOTOR VEHICLE DEALERS: Pickups & Vans, Used

Life Star Rescue Inc .... E 419 238-2507
  Van Wert *(G-19101)*

MOTOR VEHICLE DEALERS: Pickups, New & Used

Knippen Chrysler Dodge Jeep .... E 419 695-4976
  Delphos *(G-8746)*

MOTOR VEHICLE DEALERS: Trucks, Tractors/Trailers, New & Used

Friess Welding Inc .... F 330 644-8160
  Coventry Township *(G-7770)*
Kinstle Truck & Auto Svc Inc .... F 419 738-7493
  Wapakoneta *(G-19337)*
Steubenville Truck Center Inc .... E 740 282-2711
  Steubenville *(G-17554)*
Tbone Sales LLC .... E 330 897-6131
  Baltic *(G-1033)*
Tiger General LLC .... D 330 239-4949
  Medina *(G-13353)*
Trailer One Inc .... F 330 723-7474
  Medina *(G-13354)*

MOTOR VEHICLE DEALERS: Vans, New & Used

Steves Vans & Accessories LLC .... G 740 374-3154
  Marietta *(G-12676)*

MOTOR VEHICLE PARTS & ACCESS: Acceleration Eqpt

Yachiyo of America Inc .... C 614 876-3220
  Columbus *(G-7620)*

MOTOR VEHICLE PARTS & ACCESS: Air Conditioner Parts

Aptiv Services Us LLC .... B 330 306-1000
  Warren *(G-19372)*
Ftd Investments LLC .... C 937 833-2161
  Brookville *(G-2169)*
Hanon Systems Usa LLC .... C 313 920-0583
  Carey *(G-2882)*
Mahle Behr Dayton LLC .... B 937 369-2900
  Dayton *(G-8324)*
Majestic Trailers Inc .... F 330 798-1698
  Akron *(G-265)*
Taiho Corporation of America .... C 419 443-1645
  Tiffin *(G-18086)*

MOTOR VEHICLE PARTS & ACCESS: Axel Housings & Shafts

Angstrom Automotive Group LLC .... G 440 255-6700
  Mentor *(G-13387)*
Jae Tech Inc .... D 330 698-2000
  Apple Creek *(G-608)*
Ktsdi LLC .... G 330 783-2000
  North Lima *(G-15173)*
Omsi Transmissions Inc .... G 330 405-7350
  Twinsburg *(G-18826)*
Pdi Ground Support Systems Inc .... D 216 271-7344
  Solon *(G-17214)*

MOTOR VEHICLE PARTS & ACCESS: Bearings

Green Acquisition LLC .... E 440 930-7600
  Avon *(G-951)*
S & A Precision Bearing Inc .... G 440 930-7600
  Avon *(G-965)*

MOTOR VEHICLE PARTS & ACCESS: Body Components & Frames

Beasley Fiberglass Inc .... G 440 357-6644
  Painesville *(G-15719)*
Classic Reproductions .... G 937 548-9839
  Greenville *(G-10364)*
Core Automotive Tech LLC .... G 614 870-5000
  Columbus *(G-6819)*
David Boswell .... E 614 441-2497
  Columbus *(G-6852)*
Frontier Tank Center Inc .... E 330 659-3888
  Richfield *(G-16471)*
Gerich Fiberglass Inc .... E 419 362-4591
  Mount Gilead *(G-14424)*
Green Tokai Co Ltd .... A 937 833-5444
  Brookville *(G-2170)*
Karg Fiberglass Inc .... G 330 494-2611
  Middlebranch *(G-13758)*
Magna Modular Systems LLC .... D 419 324-3387
  Toledo *(G-18395)*
Oakley Industries Sub Assembly .... E 419 661-8888
  Northwood *(G-15342)*
TS Tech USA Corporation .... C 614 577-1088
  Reynoldsburg *(G-16458)*
Vivid Wraps LLC .... G 513 515-8386
  Cincinnati *(G-4482)*

MOTOR VEHICLE PARTS & ACCESS: Booster Cables, Jump-Start

Noco Company .... B 216 464-8131
  Solon *(G-17208)*
SMH Manufacturing Inc .... F 419 884-0071
  Lexington *(G-11806)*

MOTOR VEHICLE PARTS & ACCESS: Brakes, Air

Bendix Spcer Fndtion Brake LLC .... D 440 329-9709
  Elyria *(G-9224)*
Eaton Corporation .... C 216 281-2211
  Cleveland *(G-5147)*
Johnson Welded Products Inc .... C 937 652-1242
  Urbana *(G-19001)*

MOTOR VEHICLE PARTS & ACCESS: Clutches

Luk Clutch Systems LLC .... E 330 264-4383
  Wooster *(G-20617)*

Ptt Legacy Inc .... D 330 239-4933
  Sharon Center *(G-16952)*
Westfield Steel Inc .... D 937 322-2414
  Springfield *(G-17516)*

MOTOR VEHICLE PARTS & ACCESS: Connecting Rods

TRW Automotive Inc .... E 216 750-2400
  Cleveland *(G-6220)*
Usui International Corporation .... C 513 448-0410
  Sharonville *(G-16960)*

MOTOR VEHICLE PARTS & ACCESS: Cylinder Heads

All Pro Alum Cylinder Heads .... G 740 967-7761
  Johnstown *(G-11253)*
Done Right Engine & Machine .... G 440 582-1366
  Cleveland *(G-5107)*

MOTOR VEHICLE PARTS & ACCESS: Electrical Eqpt

Eaton Corporation .... B 440 523-5000
  Beachwood *(G-1233)*
Enhanced Mfg Solutions LLC .... D 440 476-1244
  Brecksville *(G-2034)*
Mrs Electronic Inc .... F 937 660-6767
  Dayton *(G-8371)*
Showa Aluminum Corp America .... G 740 895-6422
  Wshngtn CT Hs *(G-20744)*
Stoneridge Inc .... A 419 884-1219
  Lexington *(G-11807)*
Utv Hitchworks LLC .... C 513 615-8568
  Maineville *(G-12378)*
Weastec Incorporated .... C 937 393-6800
  Hillsboro *(G-10893)*
Weastec Incorporated .... C 937 393-6800
  Hillsboro *(G-10894)*

MOTOR VEHICLE PARTS & ACCESS: Engines & Parts

Alegre Inc .... F 937 885-6786
  Miamisburg *(G-13639)*
Areway LLC .... D 216 651-9022
  Brooklyn *(G-2112)*
Bucyrus Precision Tech Inc .... C 419 563-9950
  Bucyrus *(G-2320)*
Custom Fab .... G 330 825-3586
  Norton *(G-15364)*
Custom Speed Parts Inc .... F 440 238-3260
  Strongsville *(G-17735)*
Detroit Toledo Fiber LLC .... F 248 647-0400
  Toledo *(G-18261)*
Dexol Industries Inc .... G 330 633-4477
  Akron *(G-140)*
Eaton Corporation .... B 440 523-5000
  Cleveland *(G-5146)*
Flaming River Industries Inc .... F 440 826-4488
  Berea *(G-1608)*
Ford Motor Company .... A 419 226-7000
  Lima *(G-11864)*
Fram Group Operations LLC .... D 419 661-6700
  Perrysburg *(G-15953)*
FT Precision Inc .... A 740 694-1500
  Fredericktown *(G-9970)*
Gregory Auto Service .... G 513 248-0423
  Loveland *(G-12194)*
Gt Technologies Inc .... C 419 782-8955
  Defiance *(G-8625)*
Gt Technologies Inc .... D 419 324-7300
  Toledo *(G-18314)*
Hite Parts Exchange Inc .... E 614 272-5115
  Columbus *(G-7003)*
Keihin Thermal Tech Amer Inc .... B 740 869-3000
  Mount Sterling *(G-14462)*
Lakota Racing .... G 330 627-7255
  Carrollton *(G-2923)*
Lorain County Auto Systems Inc .... D 248 442-6800
  Lorain *(G-12101)*
Lorain County Auto Systems Inc .... E 440 960-7470
  Lorain *(G-12102)*
Neaton Auto Products Mfg Inc .... B 937 456-7103
  Eaton *(G-9162)*
Pullman Company .... C 419 592-2055
  Napoleon *(G-14556)*
Qualitor Inc .... G 248 204-8600
  Lima *(G-11924)*

PRODUCT SECTION

MOTOR VEHICLE SPLYS & PARTS WHOLESALERS: Used

Reynolds Engineered Pdts LLC ....G....... 513 751-4400
  Cincinnati *(G-4263)*
Rochling Automotive USA LLP ....D....... 330 400-5785
  Akron *(G-352)*
Satco Inc ....G....... 330 630-8866
  Tallmadge *(G-18002)*
Schaeffler Transmission LLC ....C....... 330 264-4383
  Wooster *(G-20650)*
Soundwich Inc ....D....... 216 486-2666
  Cleveland *(G-6080)*
Supercharger Systems Inc ....G....... 216 676-5800
  Brookpark *(G-2156)*
Switzer Performance Engrg ....F....... 440 774-4219
  Oberlin *(G-15505)*
Tenneco Automotive Oper Co Inc ....D....... 937 781-4940
  Kettering *(G-11442)*
Vanderpool Motor Sports ....G....... 513 424-2166
  Middletown *(G-13963)*
W W Williams Company LLC ....F....... 330 659-3084
  Richfield *(G-16494)*

MOTOR VEHICLE PARTS & ACCESS: Frames

Chantilly Development Corp ....F....... 419 243-8109
  Toledo *(G-18227)*

MOTOR VEHICLE PARTS & ACCESS: Fuel Pumps

Bergstrom Company Ltd Partnr ....E....... 440 232-2282
  Cleveland *(G-4805)*

MOTOR VEHICLE PARTS & ACCESS: Fuel Systems & Parts

Interstate Diesel Service Inc ....B....... 216 881-0015
  Cleveland *(G-5470)*
Onix Corporation ....E....... 800 844-0076
  Perrysburg *(G-15991)*

MOTOR VEHICLE PARTS & ACCESS: Gas Tanks

Buckley Manufacturing Company ....F....... 513 821-4444
  Cincinnati *(G-3429)*

MOTOR VEHICLE PARTS & ACCESS: Gears

All Wright Enterprises LLC ....G....... 440 259-5656
  Perry *(G-15903)*
Cincinnati Gearing Systems Inc ....C....... 513 527-8600
  Cincinnati *(G-3496)*
Gear Company of America Inc ....D....... 216 671-5400
  Cleveland *(G-5298)*
Ig Watteeuw Usa LLC ....F....... 740 588-1722
  Zanesville *(G-21148)*
Scs Gearbox Inc ....F....... 419 483-7278
  Bellevue *(G-1543)*
Trojon Gear Inc ....F....... 937 254-1737
  Dayton *(G-8568)*

MOTOR VEHICLE PARTS & ACCESS: Heaters

Hdt Expeditionary Systems Inc ....G....... 216 438-6111
  Solon *(G-17160)*
Lintern Corporation ....E....... 440 255-9333
  Mentor *(G-13501)*

MOTOR VEHICLE PARTS & ACCESS: Ice Scrapers & Window Brushes

OReilly Equipment LLC ....G....... 440 564-1234
  Newbury *(G-14961)*

MOTOR VEHICLE PARTS & ACCESS: Instrument Board Assemblies

New Sabina Industries Inc ....C....... 937 584-2433
  Sabina *(G-16616)*

MOTOR VEHICLE PARTS & ACCESS: Manifolds

Atlas Industries Inc ....D....... 419 447-4730
  Tiffin *(G-18047)*
Mueller Gas Products ....D....... 513 424-5311
  Middletown *(G-13933)*

MOTOR VEHICLE PARTS & ACCESS: Mufflers, Exhaust

Chestnut Holdings Inc ....G....... 330 849-6503
  Akron *(G-114)*
Dreison International Inc ....C....... 216 362-0755
  Cleveland *(G-5113)*
Faurecia Automotive Holdings ....A....... 419 727-5000
  Toledo *(G-18288)*
Faurecia Emissions Control Sys ....C....... 812 341-2000
  Toledo *(G-18289)*
Faurecia Exhaust Systems LLC ....C....... 330 824-2807
  Warren *(G-19402)*
Josh L Derksen ....G....... 937 548-0080
  Greenville *(G-10376)*
Newman Technology Inc ....C....... 419 525-1856
  Mansfield *(G-12490)*
Riker Products Inc ....C....... 419 729-1626
  Toledo *(G-18501)*
Supertrapp Industries Inc ....D....... 216 265-8400
  Cleveland *(G-6129)*

MOTOR VEHICLE PARTS & ACCESS: Oil Strainers

Allied Separation Tech Inc ....E....... 704 736-0420
  Twinsburg *(G-18732)*

MOTOR VEHICLE PARTS & ACCESS: Power Steering Eqpt

Maval Industries LLC ....C....... 330 405-1600
  Twinsburg *(G-18813)*
Steer & Gear Inc ....E....... 614 231-4064
  Columbus *(G-7489)*

MOTOR VEHICLE PARTS & ACCESS: Propane Conversion Eqpt

Superior Energy Systems LLC ....F....... 440 236-6009
  Columbia Station *(G-6449)*

MOTOR VEHICLE PARTS & ACCESS: Pumps, Hydraulic Fluid Power

Eaton Corporation ....B....... 216 523-5000
  Beachwood *(G-1234)*
Eaton Corporation ....B....... 216 920-2000
  Cleveland *(G-5149)*

MOTOR VEHICLE PARTS & ACCESS: Sanders, Safety

Doran Mfg LLC ....F....... 513 681-5424
  Cincinnati *(G-3601)*

MOTOR VEHICLE PARTS & ACCESS: Tie Rods

Mid-West Fabricating Co ....C....... 740 969-4411
  Amanda *(G-526)*
Mid-West Fabricating Co ....C....... 740 681-4411
  Lancaster *(G-11588)*

MOTOR VEHICLE PARTS & ACCESS: Tire Valve Cores

31 Inc ....D....... 740 498-8324
  Newcomerstown *(G-14968)*
Haltec Corporation ....C....... 330 222-1501
  Salem *(G-16746)*

MOTOR VEHICLE PARTS & ACCESS: Trailer Hitches

Liberty Outdoors LLC ....F....... 330 791-3149
  Uniontown *(G-18925)*
Saf-Holland Inc ....G....... 513 874-7888
  West Chester *(G-19896)*
White Mule Company ....E....... 740 382-9008
  Ontario *(G-15550)*

MOTOR VEHICLE PARTS & ACCESS: Transmission Housings Or Parts

Oerlikon Friction Systems ....C....... 937 449-4000
  Dayton *(G-8394)*

MOTOR VEHICLE PARTS & ACCESS: Transmissions

Florence Alloys Inc ....G....... 330 745-9141
  Barberton *(G-1071)*
Goodale Auto-Truck Parts Inc ....E....... 614 294-4777
  Columbus *(G-6962)*
Warfighter Fcsed Logistics Inc ....G....... 740 513-4692
  Galena *(G-10117)*

MOTOR VEHICLE PARTS & ACCESS: Water Pumps

ASC Holdco Inc ....G....... 330 899-0340
  North Canton *(G-15069)*
ASC Industries Inc ....C....... 330 899-0340
  North Canton *(G-15070)*
Hytec Automotive Ind LLC ....F....... 614 527-9370
  Columbus *(G-7014)*
Hytec-Debartolo LLC ....F....... 614 527-9370
  Columbus *(G-7015)*

MOTOR VEHICLE PARTS & ACCESS: Wheel rims

Wheel Group Holdings LLC ....G....... 614 253-6247
  Columbus *(G-7602)*

MOTOR VEHICLE PARTS & ACCESS: Wind Deflectors

Beast Carbon Corporation ....G....... 800 909-9051
  Cincinnati *(G-3384)*

MOTOR VEHICLE PARTS & ACCESS: Wiring Harness Sets

Connective Design Incorporated ....F....... 937 746-8252
  Miamisburg *(G-13651)*
Designed Harness Systems Inc ....F....... 937 599-2485
  Bellefontaine *(G-1512)*
G S Wiring Systems Inc ....B....... 419 423-7111
  Findlay *(G-9691)*
GSW Manufacturing Inc ....B....... 419 423-7111
  Findlay *(G-9696)*
Matrix Cable and Mould ....G....... 513 832-2577
  Cincinnati *(G-3987)*
Sumitomo Elc Wirg Systems Inc ......E....... 937 642-7579
  Marysville *(G-12816)*

MOTOR VEHICLE SPLYS & PARTS WHOLESALERS: New

Anest Iwata Usa Inc ....G....... 513 755-3100
  West Chester *(G-19832)*
Custer Products Limited ....F....... 330 490-3158
  Massillon *(G-12972)*
Dexol Industries Inc ....C....... 330 633-4477
  Akron *(G-140)*
Doran Mfg LLC ....F....... 513 681-5424
  Cincinnati *(G-3601)*
Faurecia Emissions Control Sys ....C....... 812 341-2000
  Toledo *(G-18289)*
G S Wiring Systems Inc ....B....... 419 423-7111
  Findlay *(G-9691)*
Gear Star American Performance .....G....... 330 434-5216
  Akron *(G-183)*
Goodyear Tire & Rubber Company ....A....... 330 796-2121
  Akron *(G-191)*
Legacy Supplies Inc ....F....... 330 405-4565
  Twinsburg *(G-18805)*
Mac Trailer Manufacturing Inc ....C....... 330 823-9900
  Alliance *(G-485)*
Neff Machinery and Supplies ....E....... 740 454-0128
  Zanesville *(G-21159)*
Pioneer Automotive Tech Inc ....C....... 937 746-2293
  Springboro *(G-17344)*
Qualitor Inc ....G....... 248 204-8600
  Lima *(G-11924)*
Safe Systems Inc ....G....... 216 661-1166
  Cleveland *(G-6024)*
Tk Holdings Inc ....E....... 937 778-9713
  Piqua *(G-16166)*

MOTOR VEHICLE SPLYS & PARTS WHOLESALERS: Used

Mac Trailer Manufacturing Inc ....C....... 330 823-9900
  Alliance *(G-485)*

Employee Codes: A=Over 500 employees, B=251-500
C=101-250, D=51-100, E=20-50, F=10-19, G=3-9

MOTOR VEHICLE: Hardware

MOTOR VEHICLE: Hardware
R H Industries Inc .... E 216 281-5210
  Cleveland *(G-5952)*

MOTOR VEHICLE: Radiators
Albright Radiator Inc .... G 330 264-8886
  Wooster *(G-20561)*
Mahle Behr Service America LLC .... G 937 369-2610
  Xenia *(G-20783)*

MOTOR VEHICLE: Shock Absorbers
Pullman Company .... E 419 499-2541
  Milan *(G-13987)*
Stemco Air Springs .... E 234 466-7200
  Fairlawn *(G-9620)*
Thyssenkrupp Bilstein Amer Inc .... C 513 881-7600
  Hamilton *(G-10610)*

MOTOR VEHICLE: Wheels
Dayton Wheel Concepts Inc .... E 937 438-0100
  Dayton *(G-8148)*
Forgeline Inc .... F 937 299-0298
  Moraine *(G-14354)*
Goodrich Corporation .... A 937 339-3811
  Troy *(G-18663)*
Honda Transm Mfg Amer Inc .... A 937 843-5555
  Russells Point *(G-16598)*
Kosei St Marys Corporation .... A 419 394-7840
  Saint Marys *(G-16688)*
Oe Exchange LLC .... G 440 266-1639
  Mentor *(G-13532)*

MOTOR VEHICLES & CAR BODIES
Airstream Inc .... B 937 596-6111
  Jackson Center *(G-11205)*
American Honda Motor Co Inc .... C 937 332-6100
  Troy *(G-18636)*
AMP Electric Vehicles Inc .... F 513 360-4704
  Loveland *(G-12177)*
Antique Auto Sheet Metal Inc .... E 937 833-4422
  Brookville *(G-2161)*
Autowax Inc .... G 440 334-4417
  Strongsville *(G-17717)*
Bartley Lawn Service LLC .... G 937 435-8884
  West Carrollton *(G-19630)*
Bobbart Industries Inc .... E 419 350-5477
  Sylvania *(G-17934)*
Comprehensive Logistics Co Inc .... G 330 793-0504
  Youngstown *(G-20877)*
D & D Classic Auto Restoration .... E 937 473-2229
  Covington *(G-7784)*
Ford Motor Company .... A 440 933-1215
  Avon Lake *(G-986)*
Galion-Godwin Truck Bdy Co LLC .... D 330 359-5495
  Millersburg *(G-14084)*
General Motors LLC .... A 216 265-5000
  Cleveland *(G-5312)*
Halcore Group Inc .... C 614 539-8181
  Grove City *(G-10433)*
Honda of America Mfg Inc .... C 937 644-0724
  Marysville *(G-12792)*
JLW - TW Corp .... G 216 361-5940
  Avon *(G-952)*
Ogara Hess Eisenhardt .... G 513 346-1300
  West Chester *(G-19751)*
Oshkosh Corporation .... G 513 745-9436
  Cincinnati *(G-4121)*
Protection Devices Inc .... G 210 399-2273
  West Chester *(G-19770)*
Rikenkaki America Corporation .... G 614 336-2744
  Dublin *(G-8974)*
Subaru of A .... G 614 793-2358
  Dublin *(G-8998)*
Tesla Inc .... G 614 532-5060
  Columbus *(G-7521)*
Tesla Inc .... G 513 745-9111
  Blue Ash *(G-1859)*
Toledo Pro Fiberglass Inc .... G 419 241-9390
  Toledo *(G-18567)*

MOTOR VEHICLES, WHOLESALE: Ambulances
Life Star Rescue Inc .... E 419 238-2507
  Van Wert *(G-19101)*

MOTOR VEHICLES, WHOLESALE: Fire Trucks
Fire Safety Services Inc .... F 937 686-2000
  Huntsville *(G-11086)*

MOTOR VEHICLES, WHOLESALE: Trailers for passenger vehicles
Mr Trailer Sales Inc .... G 330 339-7701
  New Philadelphia *(G-14789)*

MOTOR VEHICLES, WHOLESALE: Trailers, Truck, New & Used
Bulk Carrier Trnsp Eqp Co .... E 330 339-3333
  New Philadelphia *(G-14762)*
M & W Trailers Inc .... F 419 453-3331
  Ottoville *(G-15682)*
M H EBY Inc .... E 614 879-6901
  West Jefferson *(G-19925)*
Mac Manufacturing Inc .... A 330 823-9900
  Alliance *(G-483)*
Mac Manufacturing Inc .... C 330 829-1680
  Salem *(G-16759)*
Mac Trailer Manufacturing Inc .... C 330 823-9900
  Alliance *(G-485)*

MOTOR VEHICLES, WHOLESALE: Truck bodies
Ace Truck Equipment Co .... E 740 453-0551
  Zanesville *(G-21091)*
Brown Industrial Inc .... E 937 693-3838
  Botkins *(G-1934)*
J W Devers & Son Inc .... F 937 854-3040
  Trotwood *(G-18628)*
Schodorf Truck Body & Eqp Co .... E 614 228-6793
  Columbus *(G-7426)*
Venco Venturo Industries LLC .... E 513 772-8448
  Cincinnati *(G-4473)*

MOTOR VEHICLES, WHOLESALE: Truck tractors
Kinstle Truck & Auto Svc Inc .... F 419 738-7493
  Wapakoneta *(G-19337)*

MOTOR VEHICLES, WHOLESALE: Trucks, commercial
United Fire Apparatus Corp .... G 419 645-4083
  Cridersville *(G-7813)*
Youngstown-Kenworth Inc .... E 330 534-9761
  Hubbard *(G-11014)*

MOTORCYCLE & BICYCLE PARTS: Frames
Franklin Frames and Cycles .... G 740 763-3838
  Newark *(G-14875)*

MOTORCYCLE ACCESS
B&D Truck Parts Sls & Svcs LLC .... G 419 701-7041
  Fostoria *(G-9835)*
J Tyler Enterprise LLC .... G 330 774-4490
  Youngstown *(G-20944)*
Newman Technology Inc .... C 419 525-1856
  Mansfield *(G-12490)*
Outback Cycle Shack LLC .... G 513 554-1048
  Cincinnati *(G-4125)*
Thomas D Epperson .... G 937 855-3300
  Germantown *(G-10246)*

MOTORCYCLE DEALERS
Wholecycle Inc .... E 330 929-8123
  Peninsula *(G-15902)*

MOTORCYCLE DEALERS
Hot Shot Motor Works M LLC .... G 419 294-1997
  Upper Sandusky *(G-18956)*

MOTORCYCLE PARTS & ACCESS DEALERS
Gear Star American Performance .... G 330 434-5216
  Akron *(G-183)*
McIntosh Machine .... G 937 687-3936
  New Lebanon *(G-14712)*
Spiegler Brake Systems USA LLC .... G 937 291-1735
  Dayton *(G-8519)*

MOTORCYCLE PARTS: Wholesalers
Behlke Dalene .... G 330 399-6780
  Warren *(G-19376)*
L & R Racing Inc .... E 330 220-3102
  Brunswick *(G-2218)*
McIntosh Machine .... G 937 687-3936
  New Lebanon *(G-14712)*

MOTORCYCLE REPAIR SHOPS
Alvords Yard & Garden Eqp .... G 440 286-2315
  Chardon *(G-3098)*
Outback Cycle Shack LLC .... G 513 554-1048
  Cincinnati *(G-4125)*
Sinners N Saints LLC .... G 614 231-7467
  Columbus *(G-7455)*

MOTORCYCLES & RELATED PARTS
Bandit Choppers LLC .... G 614 556-4416
  Pickerington *(G-16041)*
Beasley Fiberglass Inc .... G 440 357-6644
  Painesville *(G-15719)*
Cherhire Choppers .... G 740 362-0695
  Delaware *(G-8665)*
Cobra Motorcycles Mfg .... E 330 207-3844
  North Lima *(G-15167)*
Heritage Tool .... F 513 753-7300
  Loveland *(G-12197)*
Shumaker Racing Components .... G 419 238-0801
  Van Wert *(G-19105)*
Sinners N Saints LLC .... G 614 231-7467
  Columbus *(G-7455)*
Sunstar Engrg Americas Inc .... C 937 746-8575
  Springboro *(G-17354)*

MOTORCYCLES: Wholesalers
Ktm North America Inc .... D 855 215-6360
  Amherst *(G-564)*
L & R Racing Inc .... E 330 220-3102
  Brunswick *(G-2218)*
Wholecycle Inc .... E 330 929-8123
  Peninsula *(G-15902)*

MOTORS: Electric
ABM Drives Inc .... G 513 576-1300
  Loveland *(G-12174)*
American Mitsuba Corporation .... G 989 779-4962
  Dublin *(G-8877)*
American Mitsuba Corporation .... G 989 779-4962
  Dublin *(G-8878)*
Ametek Florcare Specialty Mtrs .... F 330 677-3786
  Kent *(G-11293)*
Ametek Tchnical Indus Pdts Inc .... D 330 677-3754
  Kent *(G-11294)*
Dcm Manufacturing Inc .... E 216 265-8006
  Cleveland *(G-5078)*
Dreison International Inc .... C 216 362-0755
  Cleveland *(G-5113)*
Franklin Electric Co Inc .... A 614 794-2266
  Dublin *(G-8915)*
Globe Motors Inc .... C 334 983-3542
  Dayton *(G-8226)*
Globe Motors Inc .... C 937 228-3171
  Dayton *(G-8227)*
Globe Motors Inc .... D 937 228-3171
  Dayton *(G-8228)*
Hannon Company .... D 330 456-4728
  Canton *(G-2693)*
Nidec Motor Corporation .... C 575 434-0633
  Akron *(G-297)*
Palesh & Associates Inc .... G 440 942-9168
  Willoughby *(G-20398)*
Ramco Electric Motors Inc .... D 937 548-2525
  Greenville *(G-10389)*
Regal Beloit America Inc .... C 937 667-2431
  Tipp City *(G-18130)*
Reuland Electric Co .... G 513 825-7314
  Cincinnati *(G-4262)*
Siemens Industry Inc .... C 513 841-3100
  Cincinnati *(G-4334)*

MOTORS: Generators
Aadco Instruments Inc .... G 513 467-1477
  Cleves *(G-6354)*
Ametek Inc .... G 302 636-5401
  Worthington *(G-20678)*
Ares Inc .... D 419 635-2175
  Port Clinton *(G-16242)*

Chemequip Sales Inc............................E........330 724-8300
  Coventry Township (G-7767)
City Machine Technologies Inc..............F........330 747-2639
  Youngstown (G-20870)
City Machine Technologies Inc..............E........330 740-8186
  Youngstown (G-20871)
Dayton-Phoenix Group Inc....................C........937 496-3900
  Dayton (G-8151)
Econ-O-Machine Products Inc................G........937 882-6307
  Donnelsville (G-8801)
Energy Technologies Inc........................D........419 522-4444
  Mansfield (G-12437)
GE Aviation Systems LLC.......................B........937 898-5881
  Vandalia (G-19125)
General Electric Company......................D........216 883-1000
  Cleveland (G-5306)
Gleason Metrology Systems Corp..........E........937 384-8901
  Dayton (G-8223)
Grand-Rock Company Inc.....................G........440 639-2000
  Painesville (G-15742)
Hurst Auto-Truck Electric.......................G........216 961-1800
  Cleveland (G-5426)
Industrial and Mar Eng Svc Co...............F........740 694-0791
  Fredericktown (G-9971)
JD Power Systems LLC.........................F........614 317-9394
  Hilliard (G-10833)
Lake Shore Electric Corp........................E........440 232-0200
  Bedford (G-1422)
Linde Hydraulics Corporation.................E........330 533-6801
  Canfield (G-2532)
Ohio Magnetics Inc................................E........216 662-8484
  Maple Heights (G-12575)
Ohio Semitronics Inc..............................D........614 777-1005
  Hilliard (G-10847)
Peerless-Winsmith Inc...........................B........330 399-3651
  Dublin (G-8962)
Peerless-Winsmith Inc...........................G........614 526-7000
  Dublin (G-8963)
R Gordon Jones Inc...............................G........740 986-8381
  Williamsport (G-20260)
Regal Beloit America Inc........................C........608 364-8800
  Lima (G-11928)
Safran USA Incorporated.......................E........513 247-7000
  Sharonville (G-16958)
Stateline Power Corp.............................F........937 547-1006
  Greenville (G-10397)
Tigerpoly Manufacturing Inc...................B........614 871-0045
  Grove City (G-10473)
Tremont Electric Incorporated................G........888 214-3137
  Cleveland (G-6203)
Vanner Holdings Inc..............................D........614 771-2718
  Hilliard (G-10873)
Waibel Electric Co Inc............................F........740 964-2956
  Etna (G-9390)

MOTORS: Pneumatic

Vickers International Inc.........................F........419 867-2200
  Maumee (G-13159)

MOTORS: Starting, Automotive & Aircraft

Mitsubishi Elc Auto Amer Inc.................B........513 573-6614
  Mason (G-12911)

MOTORS: Torque

Alliance Torque Converters Inc..............G........937 222-3394
  Dayton (G-8019)

MOUNTING RINGS, MOTOR Rubber Covered Or Bonded

Yusa Corporation..................................A........740 335-0335
  Washington Court Hou (G-19479)

MOUTHWASHES

Oasis Consumer Healthcare LLC..........G........216 394-0544
  Cleveland (G-5794)

MOVING SVC: Local

C P S Enterprises Inc............................F........216 441-7969
  Cleveland (G-4858)

MOWERS & ACCESSORIES

California Grounds Care LLC.................G........513 207-0244
  Cincinnati (G-3437)
Friesen Fab and Equipment...................G........614 873-4354
  Plain City (G-16192)

Mtd Products Inc...................................A........419 935-6611
  Willard (G-20242)
Norman Knepp.......................................G........740 978-6339
  Mc Arthur (G-13183)
Tri-Tech Mfg LLC....................................G........419 238-0140
  Delphos (G-8758)

MUSEUMS

Brewster Sugarcreek Twp Histo............F........330 767-0045
  Brewster (G-2068)

MUSIC DISTRIBUTION APPARATUS

Musicmax Inc...F........614 732-0777
  Columbus (G-7202)
Q Music USA LLC..................................G........239 995-5888
  North Olmsted (G-15196)

MUSIC RECORDING PRODUCER

Tiny Lion Music Groups.........................G........419 874-7353
  Perrysburg (G-16017)
Tomahawk Entertainment Group............G........216 505-0548
  Cleveland (G-6180)

MUSICAL INSTRUMENT REPAIR

Fifth Avenue Fret Shop LLC..................G........614 481-8300
  Columbus (G-6920)
Loft Violin Shop......................................F........614 267-7221
  Columbus (G-7135)
Paul Bartel...G........513 541-2000
  Cincinnati (G-4139)

MUSICAL INSTRUMENTS & ACCESS: Carrying Cases

L M Engineering Inc..............................E........330 270-2400
  Youngstown (G-20955)

MUSICAL INSTRUMENTS & ACCESS: NEC

Bbb Music LLC......................................G........740 772-2262
  Chillicothe (G-3176)
Belco Works Inc.....................................B........740 695-0500
  Saint Clairsville (G-16624)
D Picking & Co......................................G........419 562-5016
  Bucyrus (G-2324)
Engels Machining LLC..........................G........419 485-1500
  Montpelier (G-14308)
Grover Musical Products Inc................E........216 391-1188
  Cleveland (G-5356)
Hanser Music Group Inc.......................D........859 817-7100
  West Chester (G-19864)
Loft Violin Shop......................................F........614 267-7221
  Columbus (G-7135)
Muller Pipe Organ Co............................F........740 893-1700
  Croton (G-7821)
New Cleveland Group Inc.....................G........216 932-9310
  Cleveland (G-5746)
The W L Jenkins Company...................F........330 477-3407
  Canton (G-2835)

MUSICAL INSTRUMENTS & ACCESS: Pipe Organs

C E Kegg Inc...G........330 877-8800
  Hartville (G-10686)
J Zamberlan & Co.................................G........740 765-9028
  Steubenville (G-17538)
Lima Pipe Organ Co Inc........................G........419 331-5461
  Elida (G-9196)
Peebles - Herzog Inc............................G........614 279-2211
  Columbus (G-7306)
The Holtkamp Organ Co.......................F........216 741-5180
  Cleveland (G-6165)

MUSICAL INSTRUMENTS & PARTS: Brass

Brooks Manufacturing............................G........419 244-1777
  Toledo (G-18216)
Conn-Selmer Inc...................................E........216 391-7723
  Cleveland (G-5014)

MUSICAL INSTRUMENTS & PARTS: Percussion

Universal Percussion Inc.......................F........330 482-5750
  Columbiana (G-6484)

MUSICAL INSTRUMENTS & PARTS: String

McHael D Goronok String Instrs...........G........216 421-4227
  Cleveland (G-5642)
Paul Bartel...G........513 541-2000
  Cincinnati (G-4139)
Sperzel Inc..E........216 281-6868
  Cleveland (G-6085)

MUSICAL INSTRUMENTS & SPLYS STORES

Bbb Music LLC......................................G........740 772-2262
  Chillicothe (G-3176)
Loft Violin Shop......................................F........614 267-7221
  Columbus (G-7135)
Paul Bartel...G........513 541-2000
  Cincinnati (G-4139)
S I T Strings Co Inc...............................E........330 434-8010
  Akron (G-365)
Stewart-Macdonald Mfg Co...................E........740 592-3021
  Athens (G-849)
Universal Percussion Inc.......................F........330 482-5750
  Columbiana (G-6484)
Willis Music Company...........................F........513 671-3288
  Cincinnati (G-4511)

MUSICAL INSTRUMENTS & SPLYS STORES: String instruments

Fifth Avenue Fret Shop LLC..................G........614 481-8300
  Columbus (G-6920)

MUSICAL INSTRUMENTS WHOLESALERS

Hanser Music Group Inc.......................D........859 817-7100
  West Chester (G-19864)
McHael D Goronok String Instrs...........G........216 421-4227
  Cleveland (G-5642)

MUSICAL INSTRUMENTS: Banjos & Parts

Stewart-Macdonald Mfg Co...................E........740 592-3021
  Athens (G-849)

MUSICAL INSTRUMENTS: Bells

Bell Industries.......................................F........513 353-2355
  Harrison (G-10632)
Commercial Music Service Co..............G........740 746-8500
  Sugar Grove (G-17837)
Hisey Bells..G........740 333-7669
  Greenfield (G-10352)

MUSICAL INSTRUMENTS: Carillon Bells

I T Verdin Co...E........513 241-4010
  Cincinnati (G-3833)
I T Verdin Co...E........513 559-3947
  Cincinnati (G-3834)

MUSICAL INSTRUMENTS: Fretted Instruments & Parts

Waits Instruments LLC.........................G........513 600-5996
  Cincinnati (G-4486)

MUSICAL INSTRUMENTS: Guitars & Parts, Electric & Acoustic

Conn-Selmer Inc...................................B........440 946-6100
  Willoughby (G-20300)
Earthquaker Devices LLC....................F........330 252-9220
  Akron (G-148)
Fifth Avenue Fret Shop LLC..................G........614 481-8300
  Columbus (G-6920)
Garys Classic Guitars...........................G........513 891-0555
  Loveland (G-12190)
S I T Strings Co Inc...............................E........330 434-8010
  Akron (G-365)

MUSICAL INSTRUMENTS: Keyboards

D C Ramey Piano Co............................G........708 602-3961
  Marysville (G-12779)

MUSICAL INSTRUMENTS: Keyboards & Parts

Watson Meeks and Company...............G........937 378-2355
  Georgetown (G-10239)

Employee Codes: A=Over 500 employees, B=251-500
C=101-250, D=51-100, E=20-50, F=10-19, G=3-9

2019 Harris Ohio Industrial Directory

MUSICAL INSTRUMENTS: Organ Parts & Materials

A R Schopps Sons Inc .... E 330 821-8406
　Alliance *(G-448)*

MUSICAL INSTRUMENTS: Organs

Schantz Organ Company .... E 330 682-6065
　Orrville *(G-15618)*
Victor Organ Company .... G 330 792-1321
　Youngstown *(G-21062)*

MUSICAL INSTRUMENTS: Recorders, Musical

Belmont County of Ohio .... G 740 699-2140
　Saint Clairsville *(G-16625)*

NAIL SALONS

Nail Art .... G 614 899-7155
　Westerville *(G-20066)*

NAME PLATES: Engraved Or Etched

Auld Company .... E 614 454-1010
　Columbus *(G-6629)*
Etched Metal Company .... E 440 248-0240
　Solon *(G-17142)*
Hathaway Stamp & Ident Co of C .... F 513 621-1052
　Cincinnati *(G-3802)*
Industrial and Mar Eng Svc Co .... F 740 694-0791
　Fredericktown *(G-9971)*
Laserdealer Inc .... G 440 357-8419
　Mentor *(G-13497)*
Roemer Industries Inc .... D 330 448-2000
　Masury *(G-13062)*
Ryder Engraving Inc .... G 740 927-7193
　Pataskala *(G-15842)*
Signature Partners Inc .... D 419 678-1400
　Coldwater *(G-6420)*
Visionmark Nameplate Co LLC .... E 419 977-3131
　New Bremen *(G-14662)*

NAMEPLATES

Auld Company .... E 614 454-1010
　Columbus *(G-6629)*
Brainerd Industries Inc .... E 937 228-0488
　Miamisburg *(G-13644)*
Cubbison Company .... D 330 793-2481
　Youngstown *(G-20882)*
Greg G Wright & Sons LLC .... E 513 721-3310
　Cincinnati *(G-3784)*
Metalphoto of Cincinnati Inc .... E 513 772-8281
　Cincinnati *(G-4013)*

NATIONAL SECURITY FORCES

Dla Document Services .... G 216 522-3535
　Cleveland *(G-5101)*
Dla Document Services .... E 937 257-6014
　Dayton *(G-7978)*

NATIONAL SECURITY, GOVERNMENT: Air Force

Air Force US Dept of .... B 937 656-2354
　Dayton *(G-7969)*

NATIONAL SECURITY, GOVERNMENT: Army

United States Dept of Army .... D 419 221-9500
　Lima *(G-11955)*

NATURAL GAS DISTRIBUTION TO CONSUMERS

City of Lancaster .... E 740 687-6670
　Lancaster *(G-11554)*
National Gas & Oil Company .... G 740 344-2102
　Newark *(G-14899)*
National Gas & Oil Corporation .... E 740 344-2102
　Newark *(G-14900)*

NATURAL GAS LIQUIDS PRODUCTION

H & S Operating Company Inc .... G 330 830-8178
　Winesburg *(G-20531)*
Markwest Energy Partners LP .... G 740 942-0463
　Cadiz *(G-2399)*

Markwest Utica Emg LLC .... G 740 942-4810
　Jewett *(G-11252)*

NATURAL GAS POWER BROKER

Metals Recovery Services LLC .... G 614 870-0364
　Columbus *(G-7173)*

NATURAL GAS PRODUCTION

All American Energy Coop Assn .... G 440 772-4340
　Westlake *(G-20089)*
B & J Drilling Company Inc .... G 740 599-6700
　Danville *(G-7956)*
Buckeye Franklin Co .... F 330 859-2465
　Zoarville *(G-21195)*
Chevron Ae Resources LLC .... E 330 896-8510
　Uniontown *(G-18916)*
Columbia Midstream Group LLC .... F 330 542-1095
　New Middletown *(G-14748)*
D & L Energy Inc .... E 330 270-1201
　Canton *(G-2645)*
Edco Producing .... G 419 947-2515
　Mount Gilead *(G-14423)*
Interstate Gas Supply Inc .... D 614 659-5000
　Dublin *(G-8930)*
M3 Midstream LLC .... E 330 679-5580
　Salineville *(G-16789)*
M3 Midstream LLC .... D 330 223-2220
　Kensington *(G-11285)*
M3 Midstream LLC .... E 740 431-4168
　Dennison *(G-8785)*
National Gas & Oil Company .... G 740 344-2102
　Newark *(G-14899)*
RCM Engineering Company .... G 330 666-0575
　Akron *(G-345)*
Temple Oil & Gas Company .... G 740 452-7878
　Crooksville *(G-7820)*
Williams Partners LP .... C 330 966-3674
　North Canton *(G-15137)*

NATURAL GAS TRANSMISSION

Belden & Blake Corporation .... E 330 602-5551
　Dover *(G-8808)*
Columbia Energy Group .... A 614 460-4683
　Columbus *(G-6781)*
Koch Knight LLC .... D 330 488-1651
　East Canton *(G-9041)*
National Gas & Oil Company .... G 740 344-2102
　Newark *(G-14899)*
National Gas & Oil Corporation .... E 740 344-2102
　Newark *(G-14900)*

NATURAL GAS TRANSMISSION & DISTRIBUTION

Ngo Development Corporation .... F 740 622-9560
　Coshocton *(G-7743)*

NATURAL GASOLINE PRODUCTION

Husky Marketing and Supply Co .... E 614 210-2300
　Dublin *(G-8927)*
RCM Engineering Company .... G 330 666-0575
　Akron *(G-345)*

NATURAL PROPANE PRODUCTION

A Plus Propane LLC .... G 419 399-4445
　Paulding *(G-15854)*
Consolidated Gas Coop Inc .... G 419 946-6600
　Mount Gilead *(G-14422)*
Nimco Inc .... G 740 596-4477
　Mc Arthur *(G-13182)*

NAUTICAL REPAIR SVCS

Canvas Specialty Mfg Co .... G 216 881-0647
　Cleveland *(G-4868)*
Loadmaster Trailer Company .... F 419 732-3434
　Port Clinton *(G-16250)*

NAVIGATIONAL SYSTEMS & INSTRUMENTS

Cedar Elec Holdings Corp .... D 773 804-6288
　West Chester *(G-19666)*
Drs Advanced Isr LLC .... C 937 429-7408
　Beavercreek *(G-1311)*
Tmw Systems Inc .... F 615 986-1900
　Cleveland *(G-6179)*
Trimble Inc .... F 937 233-8921
　Dayton *(G-8566)*

U S Army Corps of Engineers .... F 740 537-2571
　Toronto *(G-18613)*

NEPHELINE SYENITE MINING

Covia Holdings Corporation .... D 440 214-3284
　Independence *(G-11123)*

NET & NETTING PRDTS

Murray Fabrics Inc .... F 216 881-4041
　Cleveland *(G-5713)*

NETS: Launderers & Dyers

TAC Industries Inc .... B 937 328-5200
　Springfield *(G-17502)*

NETTING: Cargo

Patches LLC .... G 513 304-4882
　Williamsburg *(G-20253)*

NEW & USED CAR DEALERS

Bwi North America Inc .... E 937 253-1130
　Kettering *(G-11429)*

NEWS DEALERS & NEWSSTANDS

Advance Reporter .... G 419 485-4851
　Montpelier *(G-14301)*

NEWS SYNDICATES

Ohio News Network .... D 614 460-3700
　Columbus *(G-7251)*
Plain Dealer Publishing Co .... G 614 228-8200
　Columbus *(G-7319)*

NEWSSTAND

Gazette Publishing Company .... F 419 335-2010
　Wauseon *(G-19517)*
Journal Register Company .... C 440 245-6901
　Lorain *(G-12096)*

NICKEL ALLOY

Allied Mask and Tooling Inc .... G 419 470-2555
　Toledo *(G-18164)*
Chris Nckel Cstm Ltherwork LLC .... G 614 262-2672
　Columbus *(G-6764)*
Eric Nickel .... G 614 818-2488
　Westerville *(G-19990)*
Robert Nickel .... G 419 448-8256
　Tiffin *(G-18078)*
Steven Nickel .... G 419 732-3377
　Port Clinton *(G-16260)*

NIPPLES: Rubber

Novatex North America Inc .... D 419 282-4264
　Ashland *(G-728)*
Ppafco Inc .... F 614 488-7259
　Columbus *(G-7335)*

NONCURRENT CARRYING WIRING DEVICES

Akron Foundry Co .... E 330 745-3101
　Barberton *(G-1050)*
Arnco Corporation .... C 800 847-7661
　Elyria *(G-9219)*
Barracuda Technologies Inc .... F 216 469-1566
　Aurora *(G-872)*
Bud Industries Inc .... G 440 946-3200
　Willoughby *(G-20289)*
Eaton Electric Holdings LLC .... B 440 523-5000
　Cleveland *(G-5151)*
Erico Inc .... E 440 248-0100
　Solon *(G-17138)*
Power Shelf LLC .... G 419 775-6125
　Plymouth *(G-16233)*
Regal Beloit America Inc .... C 419 352-8441
　Bowling Green *(G-1996)*
Rochling Glastic Composites LP .... C 216 486-0100
　Cleveland *(G-5996)*
Vertiv Energy Systems Inc .... A 440 288-1122
　Lorain *(G-12134)*
Vertiv Group Corporation .... G 440 288-1122
　Lorain *(G-12135)*
Zekelman Industries Inc .... C 740 432-2146
　Cambridge *(G-2463)*

NONDURABLE GOODS WHOLESALERS, NEC

La Mfg Inc .... G 513 577-7200
  Cincinnati *(G-3928)*

NONFERROUS: Rolling & Drawing, NEC

API Machining Fabrication Inc .... G 740 369-0455
  Delaware *(G-8654)*
BCi and V Investments Inc .... D 330 538-0660
  North Jackson *(G-15141)*
Bunting Bearings LLC .... E 419 522-3323
  Mansfield *(G-12417)*
Canton Drop Forge Inc .... B 330 477-4511
  Canton *(G-2608)*
Consolidated Metal Pdts Inc .... C 513 251-2624
  Cincinnati *(G-3542)*
Contour Forming Inc .... E 740 345-9777
  Newark *(G-14864)*
Curtiss-Wright Flow Ctrl Corp .... D 216 267-3200
  Cleveland *(G-5045)*
Economy Straightening Service .... G 216 432-4410
  Cleveland *(G-5155)*
ESAB Group Incorporated .... G 440 813-2506
  Ashtabula *(G-774)*
Fusion Incorporated .... E 440 946-3300
  Willoughby *(G-20328)*
G A Avril Company .... F 513 641-0566
  Cincinnati *(G-3719)*
Gem City Metal Tech LLC .... E 937 252-8998
  Dayton *(G-8220)*
General Electric Company .... C 330 793-3911
  Youngstown *(G-20916)*
Kilroy Company .... D 440 951-8700
  Eastlake *(G-9117)*
Mestek Inc .... D 419 288-2703
  Bradner *(G-2015)*
Metal Merchants Usa Inc .... G 330 723-3228
  Medina *(G-13300)*
Nova Machine Products Inc .... D 216 267-3200
  Middleburg Heights *(G-13767)*
Patriot Special Metals Inc .... G 330 538-9621
  North Jackson *(G-15152)*
Patriot Special Metals Inc .... G 330 580-9600
  Canton *(G-2781)*
Titanium Metals Corporation .... A 740 537-1571
  Toronto *(G-18612)*

NONMETALLIC MINERALS & CONCENTRATE WHOLESALERS

Seaforth Mineral & Ore Co Inc .... F 216 292-5820
  Cleveland *(G-6042)*

NONMETALLIC MINERALS DEVELOPMENT & TEST BORING SVC

Barr Engineering Incorporated .... F 614 892-0162
  Columbus *(G-6649)*
Barr Engineering Incorporated .... E 614 714-0299
  Columbus *(G-6650)*

NONMETALLIC MINERALS: Support Activities, Exc Fuels

Masters Group Inc .... G 440 893-1900
  Chagrin Falls *(G-3059)*

NOTEBOOKS, MADE FROM PURCHASED MATERIALS

CCL Label Inc .... E 440 878-7000
  Brunswick *(G-2194)*

NOTIONS: Pins, Straight, Steel Or Brass

Cailin Dev Ltd Lblty Co .... F 216 408-6261
  Cleveland *(G-4862)*

NOVELTIES

Mibtach Enterprises Inc .... G 513 941-0387
  Cincinnati *(G-4021)*
Tiger Cat Furniture .... G 330 220-7232
  Brunswick *(G-2245)*

NOVELTIES, DURABLE, WHOLESALE

Argentifex LLC .... G 440 990-1108
  Ashtabula *(G-761)*

Baker Plastics Inc .... G 330 743-3142
  Youngstown *(G-20851)*
Club 513 LLC .... G 800 530-2574
  Cincinnati *(G-3531)*

NOVELTIES: Leather

Cromwell Aleene .... G 937 547-2281
  Greenville *(G-10366)*
Dpi Inc .... G 419 273-1400
  Forest *(G-9786)*

NOVELTIES: Plastic

Baker Plastics Inc .... G 330 743-3142
  Youngstown *(G-20851)*
CM Paula Company .... E 513 759-7473
  Mason *(G-12849)*
Quality Innovative Pdts LLC .... G 330 990-9888
  Akron *(G-335)*
Yachiyo of America Inc .... C 614 876-3220
  Columbus *(G-7620)*

NOVELTY SHOPS

Route 14 Storage Inc .... G 330 296-0084
  Ravenna *(G-16399)*
Silk Screen Special TS Inc .... G 740 246-4843
  Thornville *(G-18036)*
Wild Berry Incense Inc .... F 513 523-8583
  Oxford *(G-15703)*

NOZZLES: Fire Fighting

Element14 US Holdings Inc .... G 330 523-4280
  Richfield *(G-16469)*
Premier Farnell Holding Inc .... E 330 523-4273
  Richfield *(G-16483)*
Sensible Products Inc .... G 330 659-4212
  Richfield *(G-16487)*

NOZZLES: Spray, Aerosol, Paint Or Insecticide

Exair Corporation .... E 513 671-3322
  Cincinnati *(G-3664)*
J & J Performance Inc .... F 330 567-2455
  Shreve *(G-17004)*
M E P Manufacturing Inc .... G 419 855-7723
  Genoa *(G-10234)*
Vortec Corporation .... E 513 891-7485
  Blue Ash *(G-1866)*

NUCLEAR DETECTORS: Solid State

Rexon Components Inc .... F 440 585-7086
  Cleveland *(G-5981)*

NUCLEAR FUELS SCRAP REPROCESSING

C Soltesz Co .... G 614 529-5494
  Columbus *(G-6720)*

NUCLEAR REACTORS: Military Or Indl

Bwxt Nclear Oprtions Group Inc .... F 330 860-1010
  Barberton *(G-1068)*

NUCLEAR SHIELDING: Metal Plate

Laird Technologies Inc .... G 234 806-0105
  Warren *(G-19416)*

NURSERIES & LAWN & GARDEN SPLY STORE, RET: Fountain, Outdoor

Fountain Specialists Inc .... G 513 831-5717
  Milford *(G-14009)*

NURSERIES & LAWN & GARDEN SPLY STORE, RET: Lawn/Garden Splys

Markers Inc .... G 440 933-5927
  Avon Lake *(G-995)*
The Hc Companies Inc .... E 440 632-3333
  Middlefield *(G-13857)*

NURSERIES & LAWN & GARDEN SPLY STORES, RETAIL

Riverview Productions Inc .... G 740 441-1150
  Gallipolis *(G-10174)*

NURSERIES & LAWN & GARDEN SPLY STORES, RETAIL: Fertilizer

Centerra Co-Op .... E 419 281-2153
  Ashland *(G-690)*
Centerra Co-Op .... E 800 362-9598
  Jefferson *(G-11226)*
Harvest Land Co-Op Inc .... G 937 884-5526
  Verona *(G-19172)*
Insta-Gro Manufacturing Inc .... E 419 845-3046
  Caledonia *(G-2417)*
K M B Inc .... E 330 889-3451
  Bristolville *(G-2082)*
Mid-Wood Inc .... F 419 257-3331
  North Baltimore *(G-15046)*
Naturym LLC .... G 614 284-3068
  Gahanna *(G-10093)*
New Eezy-Gro Inc .... F 419 927-6110
  Upper Sandusky *(G-18967)*
Nutrien AG Solutions Inc .... G 614 873-4253
  Milford Center *(G-14047)*
Ohigro Inc .... E 740 726-2429
  Waldo *(G-19304)*
Premier Feeds LLC .... G 937 584-2411
  Sabina *(G-16618)*

NURSERIES & LAWN & GARDEN SPLY STORES, RETAIL: Lawn Ornament

Wilsons Country Creations .... F 330 377-4190
  Killbuck *(G-11456)*

NURSERIES & LAWN & GARDEN SPLY STORES, RETAIL: Top Soil

Kurtz Bros Inc .... E 614 491-0868
  Groveport *(G-10500)*
Mad River Topsoil Inc .... G 937 882-6115
  Springfield *(G-17441)*

NURSERIES & LAWN/GARDEN SPLY STORE, RET: Lawnmowers/Tractors

Albright Saw Company Inc .... G 740 887-2107
  Londonderry *(G-12073)*
All Power Equipment LLC .... F 740 593-3279
  Athens *(G-822)*
Alvords Yard & Garden Eqp .... G 440 286-2315
  Chardon *(G-3098)*
T JS Oil & Gas Inc .... G 740 623-0192
  Coshocton *(G-7754)*

NURSERY & GARDEN CENTERS

Buckeye Tractor Company Corp .... G 419 659-2162
  Columbus Grove *(G-7631)*
Dittmar Sales and Service .... G 740 653-7933
  Lancaster *(G-11567)*
Mel Stevens U-Cart Concrete .... G 419 478-2600
  Toledo *(G-18406)*
Mulch World .... G 419 873-6852
  Perrysburg *(G-15978)*
Tri-State Garden Supply Inc .... E 419 445-6561
  Archbold *(G-672)*

NURSING CARE FACILITIES: Skilled

Biorx LLC .... C 866 442-4679
  Cincinnati *(G-3394)*

NUTRITION SVCS

Abbott Laboratories .... A 614 624-3191
  Columbus *(G-6519)*
Good Earth Good Eating LLC .... G 513 256-5935
  Cincinnati *(G-3771)*

NUTS: Metal

Facil North America Inc .... C 330 487-2500
  Twinsburg *(G-18774)*
Industrial Nut Corp .... D 419 625-8543
  Sandusky *(G-16817)*
Jerry Tools Inc .... F 513 242-3211
  Cincinnati *(G-3871)*
Lear Mfg Co Inc .... F 440 324-1111
  Elyria *(G-9286)*
Ramco Specialties Inc .... C 330 653-5135
  Hudson *(G-11069)*
Telefast Industries Inc .... D 440 826-0011
  Berea *(G-1628)*

NUTS: Metal

Wheel Group Holdings LLC ....G...... 614 253-6247
  Columbus (G-7602)

NYLON FIBERS

Dowco LLC ....E...... 330 773-6654
  Akron (G-145)

OFCS & CLINICS,MEDICAL DRS: Specl, Physician Or Surgn, ENT

Akron Ent Hearing Services Inc ....G...... 330 762-8959
  Akron (G-38)

OFFICE EQPT WHOLESALERS

Friends Service Co Inc ....G...... 800 427-1704
  Kent (G-11322)
Friends Service Co Inc ....D...... 419 427-1704
  Findlay (G-9690)
Friends Service Co Inc ....F...... 800 427-1704
  Dayton (G-8208)
Giesecke & Devrient Amer Inc ....C...... 330 425-1515
  Twinsburg (G-18785)
Media Procurement Services Inc ....G...... 513 977-3000
  Cincinnati (G-3996)
Mpc Inc ....F...... 440 835-1405
  Cleveland (G-5707)
Pinnacle Sales Inc ....G...... 440 734-9195
  Westlake (G-20143)
Symatic Inc ....E...... 330 225-1510
  Brunswick (G-2243)
Wasserstrom Company ....F...... 614 228-2233
  Columbus (G-7592)
William J Dupps ....G...... 419 734-2126
  Port Clinton (G-16264)
Xerox Corporation ....B...... 513 554-3200
  Blue Ash (G-1879)

OFFICE EQPT, WHOL: Check Writing, Signing/Endorsing Mach

Cummins - Allison Corp ....G...... 440 824-5050
  Cleveland (G-5042)

OFFICE EQPT, WHOLESALE: Blueprinting

Robert Becker Impressions Inc ....F...... 419 385-5303
  Toledo (G-18504)

OFFICE EQPT, WHOLESALE: Duplicating Machines

Xpress Print Inc ....F...... 330 494-7246
  Louisville (G-12172)

OFFICE EQPT, WHOLESALE: Typewriter & Dictation

Cleveland Business Supply LLC ....G...... 888 831-0088
  Broadview Heights (G-2091)

OFFICE EQPT, WHOLESALE: Typewriters

Essential Pathways Ohio LLC ....G...... 330 518-3091
  Youngstown (G-20900)

OFFICE FIXTURES: Exc Wood

Acrylicon Inc ....G...... 614 263-2086
  Columbus (G-6539)

OFFICE FIXTURES: Wood

Bruewer Woodwork Mfg Co ....D...... 513 353-3505
  Cleves (G-6355)
M21 Industries LLC ....D...... 937 781-1377
  Dayton (G-8319)
Mock Woodworking Company LLC ....E...... 740 452-2701
  Zanesville (G-21157)

OFFICE FURNITURE REPAIR & MAINTENANCE SVCS

American Office Services Inc ....G...... 440 899-6888
  Westlake (G-20095)
Recycled Systems Furniture Inc ....E...... 614 880-9110
  Worthington (G-20701)

OFFICE SPLY & STATIONERY STORES

Fedex Office & Print Svcs Inc ....E...... 419 866-5464
  Toledo (G-18290)

The Rubber Stamp Shop ....G...... 419 478-4444
  Toledo (G-18549)

OFFICE SPLY & STATIONERY STORES: Office Forms & Splys

Ace Rubber Stamp & Off Sup Co ....E...... 216 771-8483
  Cleveland (G-4604)
Avon Lake Printing ....G...... 440 933-2078
  Avon Lake (G-979)
COS Blueprint Inc ....F...... 330 376-0022
  Akron (G-122)
Gordons Graphics Inc ....G...... 330 863-2322
  Malvern (G-12392)
Hathaway Stamp Co ....F...... 513 621-1052
  Cincinnati (G-3803)
Hubbard Company ....E...... 419 784-4455
  Defiance (G-8627)
Info-Graphics Inc ....G...... 440 498-1640
  Solon (G-17169)
Millcraft Paper Company ....E...... 216 429-9860
  Cleveland (G-5690)
Murr Corporation ....F...... 330 264-2223
  Wooster (G-20630)
O Connor Office Pdts & Prtg ....G...... 740 852-2209
  London (G-12066)
Print Craft Inc ....G...... 513 931-6828
  Cincinnati (G-4191)
Quick Tech Graphics Inc ....E...... 937 743-5952
  Springboro (G-17348)
W B Mason Co Inc ....G...... 888 926-2766
  Cleveland (G-6277)
Warren Printing & Off Pdts Inc ....F...... 419 523-3635
  Ottawa (G-15671)

OFFICE SPLY & STATIONERY STORES: School Splys

ID Card Systems Inc ....G...... 330 963-7446
  Twinsburg (G-18795)
Marsh Industries Inc ....E...... 330 308-8667
  New Philadelphia (G-14784)

OFFICE SPLYS, NEC, WHOLESALE

Dewitt Group Inc ....F...... 614 847-5919
  Columbus (G-6862)
Queen City Office Machine ....F...... 513 251-7200
  Cincinnati (G-4238)
Supply International Inc ....G...... 740 282-8604
  Steubenville (G-17555)
Wasserstrom Company ....F...... 614 228-2233
  Columbus (G-7592)
Wasserstrom Company ....B...... 614 228-6525
  Columbus (G-7591)
William J Dupps ....G...... 419 734-2126
  Port Clinton (G-16264)

OFFICES & CLINICS OF DOCTORS OF MEDICINE: Dermatologist

Vein Center and Medspa ....G...... 330 629-9400
  Youngstown (G-21060)

OFFICES & CLINICS OF DOCTORS OF MEDICINE: Surgeon

Evokes LLC ....E...... 513 947-8433
  Mason (G-12868)

OFFICES & CLINICS OF DRS OF MED: Cardiologist & Vascular

Cardiac Arrhythmia Associates ....G...... 330 759-8169
  Youngstown (G-20865)

OFFICES & CLINICS OF DRS OF MED: Physician/Surgeon, Int Med

Westerville Endoscopy Ctr LLC ....F...... 614 568-1666
  Westerville (G-20030)

OFFICES & CLINICS OF DRS OF MEDICINE: Med Clinic, Pri Care

Presque Isle Orthotics ....G...... 216 371-0660
  Beachwood (G-1268)

OIL & GAS FIELD EQPT: Drill Rigs

Buckeye Companies ....E...... 740 452-3641
  Zanesville (G-21112)

OIL & GAS FIELD MACHINERY

Allied Machine Works Inc ....G...... 740 454-2534
  Zanesville (G-21097)
Appalachian Equipment Co LLC ....G...... 330 345-2251
  Wooster (G-20562)
Baker Hughes A GE Company LLC ....G...... 304 884-6442
  Hubbard (G-11000)
Cameron International Corp ....G...... 740 654-4260
  Lancaster (G-11552)
Cyclone Supply Company Inc ....G...... 330 204-0313
  Dover (G-8814)
Edi Holding Company LLC ....G...... 740 401-4000
  Belpre (G-1574)
Electrnic Dsign For Indust Inc ....E...... 740 401-4000
  Belpre (G-1575)
General Electric Company ....G...... 330 455-2140
  Canton (G-2680)
H P E Inc ....F...... 330 833-3161
  Massillon (G-12993)
Midflow Services LLC ....F...... 330 674-2399
  Millersburg (G-14111)
Midflow Services LLC ....F...... 330 567-3108
  Shreve (G-17006)
N & N Oil ....G...... 740 743-2848
  Somerset (G-17265)
National Oilwell Varco Inc ....E...... 440 577-1225
  Pierpont (G-16066)
Oil Skimmers Inc ....E...... 440 237-4600
  North Royalton (G-15291)
Reberland Equipment Inc ....G...... 330 698-5883
  Apple Creek (G-618)
Robbins & Myers Inc ....F...... 937 454-3200
  Dayton (G-8482)
Saint-Gobain Norpro ....C...... 330 673-5860
  Stow (G-17625)
Tech Tool Inc ....F...... 330 674-1176
  Millersburg (G-14133)
Timco Inc ....F...... 740 685-2594
  Byesville (G-2393)

OIL ABSORPTION Eqpt

Lamor Corporation ....F...... 440 871-8000
  Westlake (G-20128)

OIL FIELD MACHINERY & EQPT

Condition Monitoring Supplies ....G...... 216 941-6868
  Strongsville (G-17731)
H & S Company Inc ....F...... 419 394-4444
  Celina (G-2965)
Multi Products Company ....E...... 330 674-5981
  Millersburg (G-14117)
TEC Design and Mfg LLC ....G...... 216 362-8962
  Cleveland (G-6152)
Ultra Premium Oilfld Svcs Ltd ....F...... 330 448-3683
  Brookfield (G-2110)

OIL FIELD SVCS, NEC

Altier Brothers Inc ....F...... 740 347-4329
  Corning (G-7701)
Appalachian Oilfield Svcs LLC ....G...... 337 216-0066
  Sardis (G-16875)
Atec Diversfd Wldg Fabrication ....G...... 937 546-4399
  Wilmington (G-20486)
Belden & Blake Corporation ....E...... 330 602-5551
  Dover (G-8808)
Bishop Well Service Corp ....G...... 330 264-2023
  Wooster (G-20571)
BJ Oilfield Services Ltd ....G...... 419 768-2408
  Cardington (G-2870)
Complete Energy Services Inc ....G...... 440 577-1070
  Pierpont (G-16064)
Countryside Pumping Inc ....G...... 330 628-0058
  Mogadore (G-14233)
Crescent Services LLC ....G...... 405 603-1200
  Cambridge (G-2433)
Dansco Mfg & Pmpg Unit Svc LP ....G...... 330 452-3677
  Canton (G-2648)
Darin Jordan ....G...... 740 819-3525
  Nashport (G-14566)
Dover Atwood Corp ....G...... 330 809-0630
  Massillon (G-12975)
Echo Drilling Inc ....G...... 740 498-8560
  Newcomerstown (G-14973)

PRODUCT SECTION

Everflow Eastern Partners LP...............G....... 330 537-3863
  Salem *(G-16736)*
Express Energy Svcs Oper LP ....E....... 740 337-4530
  Toronto *(G-18608)*
Franks Casing ....G....... 330 236-4264
  Massillon *(G-12982)*
Full Circle Oil Field Svcs Inc ....G....... 740 371-5422
  Marietta *(G-12625)*
Global Oilfield Services LLC ....G....... 419 756-8027
  Mansfield *(G-12446)*
Granger Pipeline Corporation................G....... 330 454-8095
  Canton *(G-2687)*
Halliburton Energy Svcs Inc ....C....... 740 617-2917
  Zanesville *(G-21144)*
HI Oilfield Services LLC ....G....... 740 783-1156
  Caldwell *(G-2406)*
James Engineering Inc ....G....... 740 373-9521
  Marietta *(G-12636)*
Killbuck Oilfield Services......................G....... 330 276-6706
  Killbuck *(G-11453)*
Loken Oil Field Services LLC ....G....... 740 749-3495
  Marietta *(G-12639)*
Mac Oil Field Service Inc ....F....... 330 674-7371
  Millersburg *(G-14109)*
Northeastern Oilfield Svcs LLC ....G....... 330 581-3304
  Canton *(G-2767)*
Ohio Natural Gas Services Inc..............G....... 740 796-3305
  Zanesville *(G-21165)*
Petrox Inc..F....... 330 653-5526
  Streetsboro *(G-17688)*
R & J Drilling Company Inc ....G....... 740 763-3991
  Frazeysburg *(G-9941)*
Red Bone Services LLC ....G....... 330 364-0022
  New Philadelphia *(G-14795)*
Sanders Fredrick Excvtg Co Inc............G....... 330 297-7980
  Ravenna *(G-16401)*
Schlumberger Limited ....G....... 330 878-0794
  Strasburg *(G-17652)*
Smith International Inc ....G....... 330 497-2999
  Uniontown *(G-18931)*
Stallion Oilfield Cnstr LLC ....E....... 330 868-2083
  Paris *(G-15809)*
Stratagraph Ne Inc.................................E....... 740 373-3091
  Marietta *(G-12677)*
Surveying Cannon Land.........................G....... 740 342-2835
  New Lexington *(G-14725)*
Tk Gas Services Inc ....E....... 740 826-0303
  New Concord *(G-14687)*
Tkn Oilfield Services LLC ....F....... 740 516-2583
  Marietta *(G-12681)*
Trico Corporation...................................E....... 216 642-3223
  Cleveland *(G-6211)*
Triple J Oilfield Services LLC ....G....... 740 483-9030
  Hannibal *(G-10625)*
U S Weatherford L P ....C....... 330 746-2502
  Youngstown *(G-21056)*
Vam Usa Llc ....G....... 330 742-3130
  Youngstown *(G-21059)*
W Pole Contracting Inc...........................F....... 330 325-7177
  Ravenna *(G-16418)*
Williams John F Oil Field Svcs ....G....... 740 622-7692
  Jackson *(G-11201)*
Wolfe Creek Farms ....G....... 740 962-4563
  Malta *(G-12384)*
Wyoming Casing Service Inc................E....... 330 479-8785
  Canton *(G-2866)*

OIL ROYALTY TRADERS

U S Fuel Development Co ....G....... 614 486-0614
  Columbus *(G-7553)*

OIL TREATING COMPOUNDS

Lubrizol Corporation ....A....... 440 943-4200
  Wickliffe *(G-20215)*

OILS & ESSENTIAL OILS

Natural Essentials Inc.............................E....... 330 562-8022
  Aurora *(G-895)*
Oil Bar LLC ....G....... 614 501-9815
  Columbus *(G-7268)*

OILS & GREASES: Blended & Compounded

Blendzall Inc ....G....... 740 633-1333
  Martins Ferry *(G-12758)*
Cambridge Mill Products Inc ....G....... 330 863-1121
  Malvern *(G-12385)*
Chemical Solvents Inc...........................E....... 216 741-9310
  Cleveland *(G-4919)*
Cincinnati - Vulcan Company ....D....... 513 242-5300
  Cincinnati *(G-3477)*
Digilube Systems Inc..............................F....... 937 748-2209
  Springboro *(G-17325)*
Etna Products Incorporated ....E....... 440 543-9845
  Chagrin Falls *(G-3046)*
Into Great Brands Inc ....F....... 888 771-5656
  Gahanna *(G-10085)*
Jtm Products Inc ....E....... 440 287-2302
  Solon *(G-17178)*
New Vulco Mfg & Sales Co LLC...........D....... 513 242-2672
  Cincinnati *(G-4072)*
Phymet Inc ....F....... 937 743-8061
  Springboro *(G-17343)*
Renite Company ....F....... 800 883-7876
  Columbus *(G-7385)*
US Industrial Lubricants Inc ....E....... 513 541-2225
  Cincinnati *(G-4458)*
Wallover Enterprises Inc ....E....... 440 238-9250
  Strongsville *(G-17804)*
Wallover Oil Company Inc......................E....... 440 238-9250
  Strongsville *(G-17806)*

OILS & GREASES: Lubricating

A & M Products ....G....... 419 595-2092
  Tiffin *(G-18039)*
Amsoil Inc..G....... 614 274-9851
  Columbus *(G-6593)*
BLaster Corporation ....E....... 216 901-5800
  Cleveland *(G-4819)*
Borchers Americas Inc ....D....... 440 899-2950
  Westlake *(G-20103)*
Chemical Methods Inc ....E....... 216 476-8400
  Strongsville *(G-17725)*
Commercial Lubricants Inc.....................G....... 614 475-5952
  Columbus *(G-6806)*
Douglas W & B C Richardson.................G....... 440 247-5262
  Chagrin Falls *(G-3015)*
Eni USA R & M Co Inc ....F....... 330 723-6457
  Medina *(G-13256)*
Fuchs Lubricants Co ....E....... 330 963-0400
  Twinsburg *(G-18777)*
G W Smith and Sons Inc ....F....... 937 253-5114
  Dayton *(G-7979)*
Ha-International LLC ....F....... 419 537-0096
  Toledo *(G-18317)*
Illinois Tool Works Inc ....D....... 440 914-3100
  Solon *(G-17166)*
Interlube Corporation..............................F....... 513 531-1777
  Cincinnati *(G-3855)*
Mar Mor Inc...G....... 216 961-6900
  Cleveland *(G-5614)*
McGlaughln Oil Compny/Fas Lube ....E....... 614 231-2518
  Columbus *(G-7165)*
McO Inc ....E....... 216 341-8914
  Cleveland *(G-5648)*
North Shore Strapping Inc ....D....... 216 661-5200
  Brooklyn Heights *(G-2128)*
Nutech Company LLC ....F....... 440 867-8900
  Youngstown *(G-20979)*
Oliver Chemical Co Inc...........................E....... 513 541-4540
  Cincinnati *(G-4110)*
Paramount Products................................G....... 419 832-0235
  Grand Rapids *(G-10317)*
Perma-Fix of Dayton Inc.......................F....... 937 268-6501
  Dayton *(G-8422)*
Petroliance LLC......................................C....... 216 441-7200
  Cleveland *(G-5869)*
Quaker Chemical Corporation ....D....... 513 422-9600
  Middletown *(G-13947)*
R and J Corporation ....E....... 440 871-6009
  Westlake *(G-20147)*
Reladyne Inc...D....... 513 489-6000
  Cincinnati *(G-4258)*
Shooters Choice LLC ....G....... 440 834-8888
  Chagrin Falls *(G-3076)*
Spec Mask Ohio LLC ....E....... 440 522-3055
  Kirtland *(G-11470)*
State Industrial Products Corp ....B....... 877 747-6986
  Cleveland *(G-6097)*
Triad Energy Corporation.......................E....... 740 374-2940
  Marietta *(G-12683)*
Ventco Inc ....F....... 440 834-8888
  Chagrin Falls *(G-3088)*
Wallover Oil Company Inc......................F....... 440 238-9250
  Strongsville *(G-17805)*

OILS: Cutting

Anchor Chemical Co Inc ....G....... 440 871-1660
  Westlake *(G-20097)*
Dnd Emulsions Inc..................................G....... 419 525-4988
  Mansfield *(G-12433)*
M B Industries Inc ....G....... 419 738-4769
  Wapakoneta *(G-19341)*
Master Chemical Corporation ....B....... 419 874-7902
  Perrysburg *(G-15976)*
Starchem Inc ....G....... 513 458-8262
  Cincinnati *(G-4373)*

OILS: Lubricating

Lube Depot ....G....... 330 854-6345
  Canal Fulton *(G-2484)*
Novagard Solutions Inc ....F....... 216 881-3890
  Cleveland *(G-5789)*
Sports Care Products Inc ....G....... 216 663-8110
  Cleveland *(G-6086)*

OILS: Lubricating

Advanced Fluids Inc ....G....... 216 692-3050
  Cleveland *(G-4626)*
Aerospace Lubricants Inc ....F....... 614 878-3600
  Columbus *(G-6549)*
Aml Industries Inc ....E....... 330 399-5000
  Warren *(G-19370)*
Bechem Lubrication Tech LLC ....G....... 440 543-9845
  Chagrin Falls *(G-3037)*
Diversified Technology Inc ....G....... 330 722-4995
  Medina *(G-13253)*
Ensign Product Company Inc.................G....... 216 341-5911
  Cleveland *(G-5180)*
Functional Products Inc ....E....... 330 963-3060
  Macedonia *(G-12296)*
J J Merlin Systems Inc ....G....... 330 666-8609
  Copley *(G-7686)*
Lcp Tech Inc ....G....... 513 271-1389
  Cincinnati *(G-3936)*
M B Industries Inc ....G....... 419 738-4769
  Wapakoneta *(G-19340)*
Melanda Inc ....G....... 330 833-0517
  Massillon *(G-13025)*
Petroliance...G....... 614 475-5952
  Columbus *(G-7313)*
Universal Oil Inc ....E....... 216 771-4300
  Cleveland *(G-6239)*
Western Reserve Lubricants ....G....... 440 951-5700
  Painesville *(G-15798)*

OILS: Mineral, Natural

Vertex Refining OH LLC ....E....... 614 441-4001
  Columbus *(G-7574)*

OILS: Road

Road Maintenance Products...................G....... 740 465-7181
  Morral *(G-14405)*

OINTMENTS

Dr Hess Products LLC ....G....... 800 718-8022
  Ashland *(G-702)*

OLEFINS

Lyondell Chemical Company ....D....... 513 530-4000
  Cincinnati *(G-3960)*

ON-LINE DATABASE INFORMATION RETRIEVAL SVCS

EW Scripps Company.............................E....... 513 977-3000
  Cincinnati *(G-3663)*

OPENERS, BOTTLE Stamped Metal

Doan Machinery & Eqp Co Inc...............G....... 216 932-6243
  University Heights *(G-18941)*

OPERATOR TRAINING, COMPUTER

Computer Workshop Inc ....E....... 614 798-9505
  Dublin *(G-8902)*

OPERATOR: Apartment Buildings

Dela-Glassware Ltd LLC........................G....... 740 369-6737
  Delaware *(G-8669)*
Patriarch Trucking LLC ....G....... 877 875-5402
  Flushing *(G-9784)*
Power Management Inc ....E....... 937 222-2909
  Dayton *(G-8430)*

Employee Codes: A=Over 500 employees, B=251-500
C=101-250, D=51-100, E=20-50, F=10-19, G=3-9

OPERATOR: Nonresidential Buildings

Great Lakes Management Inc	E	216 883-6500
Cleveland (G-5349)		
Kedar D Army	G	419 238-6929
Van Wert (G-19097)		
Power Management Inc	E	937 222-2909
Dayton (G-8430)		
Pubco Corporation	D	216 881-5300
Cleveland (G-5932)		
Wernli Realty Inc	D	937 258-7878
Beavercreek (G-1368)		

OPHTHALMIC GOODS

Bsa Industries Inc	D	614 846-5515
Columbus (G-6706)		
Bulk Molding Compounds Inc	D	419 874-7941
Perrysburg (G-15926)		
Classic Optical Labs Inc	C	330 759-8245
Youngstown (G-20875)		
Cleveland Hoya Corp	D	440 234-5703
Berea (G-1595)		
Diversified Ophthalmics Inc	F	509 324-6364
Cincinnati (G-3595)		
DMV Corporation	G	740 452-4787
Zanesville (G-21128)		
Jerold Optical Inc	G	216 781-4279
Cleveland (G-5496)		
Lake Cable Optical Lab	G	330 497-3022
Canton (G-2730)		
Luxottica of America Inc	G	614 409-9381
Lockbourne (G-11997)		
Malta Dynamics LLC	F	740 749-3512
Waterford (G-19488)		
Mileti Optical Inc	G	440 884-6333
Cleveland (G-5686)		
Oakley Inc	D	949 672-6560
Dayton (G-8392)		
Opti Vision Inc	G	330 650-0919
Hudson (G-11065)		
Rx Frames N Lenses Ltd	G	513 557-2970
Cincinnati (G-4292)		
Steiner Eoptics Inc	D	937 426-2341
Miamisburg (G-13721)		
Terminal Optical Lab	G	216 289-7722
Euclid (G-9447)		

OPHTHALMIC GOODS WHOLESALERS

Diversified Ophthalmics Inc	F	509 324-6364
Cincinnati (G-3595)		

OPHTHALMIC GOODS, NEC, WHOLESALE: Contact Lenses

Diversified Ophthalmics Inc	F	803 783-3454
Cincinnati (G-3594)		

OPHTHALMIC GOODS, NEC, WHOLESALE: Lenses

Toledo Optical Laboratory Inc	D	419 248-3384
Toledo (G-18565)		

OPHTHALMIC GOODS: Lenses, Ophthalmic

Barnett & Ramel Optical Co Neb	E	402 453-4900
Columbus (G-6648)		
Volk Optical Inc	D	440 942-6161
Mentor (G-13625)		

OPTICAL GOODS STORES

Central Optical Inc	E	330 783-9660
Youngstown (G-20869)		
Mileti Optical Inc	G	440 884-6333
Cleveland (G-5686)		

OPTICAL GOODS STORES: Eyeglasses, Prescription

Jerold Optical Inc	G	216 781-4279
Cleveland (G-5496)		
Opti Vision Inc	G	330 650-0919
Hudson (G-11065)		

OPTICAL INSTRUMENTS & APPARATUS

Greenlight Optics LLC	E	513 247-9777
Loveland (G-12193)		
Trevi Technology Inc	G	614 754-7175
Columbus (G-7542)		

OPTICAL INSTRUMENTS & LENSES

Cleveland Hoya Corp	D	440 234-5703
Berea (G-1595)		
Di Walt Optical Inc	F	330 453-8427
Canton (G-2657)		
Genvac Aerospace Corp	F	440 646-9986
Cleveland (G-5317)		
Gooch & Housego (florida) LLC	D	321 242-7818
Cleveland (G-5330)		
Gooch & Housego (ohio) LLC	D	216 486-6100
Highland Heights (G-10792)		
Holte Eyeware		513 321-4000
Cincinnati (G-3820)		
Hoya Optical Labs	G	440 239-1924
Berea (G-1610)		
Krendl Machine Company	D	419 692-3060
Delphos (G-8747)		
Mercury Iron and Steel Co	F	440 349-1500
Solon (G-17190)		
Point Source Inc	F	937 855-6020
Germantown (G-10245)		
Uvisir Inc	G	216 374-9376
Beachwood (G-1284)		
Volk Optical Inc	D	440 942-6161
Mentor (G-13625)		
Vsp Lab Columbus	G	614 409-8900
Lockbourne (G-11999)		
West Point Optical Group LLC	G	614 395-9775
Mason (G-12954)		
Wilson Optical Laboratory Inc	E	440 357-7000
Mentor (G-13626)		

OPTICAL SCANNING SVCS

Contractor Tools Online LLC	G	614 264-9392
New Albany (G-14617)		
Rebiz LLC	E	844 467-3249
Cleveland (G-5965)		

OPTOMETRIC EQPT & SPLYS WHOLESALERS

Hoya Optical Labs	G	440 239-1924
Berea (G-1610)		

OPTOMETRISTS' OFFICES

Holte Eyeware	G	513 321-4000
Cincinnati (G-3820)		

ORAL PREPARATIONS

Biocurv Medical Instruments	G	330 454-6621
Canton (G-2592)		

ORDNANCE

Advanced Innovation & Mfg Inc	G	330 308-6360
New Philadelphia (G-14756)		
American Apex Corporation	F	614 652-2000
Plain City (G-16171)		
Ares Inc	D	419 635-2175
Port Clinton (G-16242)		
Excelitas Technologies Corp	C	866 539-5916
Miamisburg (G-13667)		
General Dynamics-Ots Inc	C	937 746-8500
Springboro (G-17328)		
Hi-Tech Solutions LLC	G	216 331-3050
Cleveland (G-5405)		
Ordnance Cleaning Systems LLC	G	440 205-0677
Mentor (G-13536)		

ORGAN TUNING & REPAIR SVCS

Lima Pipe Organ Co Inc	G	419 331-5461
Elida (G-9196)		
Peebles - Herzog Inc	G	614 279-2211
Columbus (G-7306)		
Victor Organ Company	G	330 792-1321
Youngstown (G-21062)		

ORGANIZATIONS: Civic & Social

Eagles Club	G	740 962-6490
McConnelsville (G-13203)		

ORGANIZATIONS: Medical Research

Mp Biomedicals LLC	C	440 337-1200
Solon (G-17199)		
Valensil Technologies LLC	G	440 937-8181
Avon (G-973)		

ORGANIZATIONS: Physical Research, Noncommercial

Quasonix Inc	E	513 942-1287
West Chester (G-19775)		
Sunpower Inc	D	740 594-2221
Athens (G-851)		

ORGANIZATIONS: Religious

Pines Manufacturing Inc	E	440 835-5553
Westlake (G-20142)		
Saint Ctherines Metalworks Inc	G	216 409-0576
Cleveland (G-6026)		
Sunday School Software	G	614 527-8776
Hilliard (G-10867)		

ORGANIZATIONS: Scientific Research Agency

Innovative Weld Solutions Ltd	G	937 545-7695
Beavercreek (G-1356)		
Performnce Plymr Solutions Inc	F	937 298-3713
Moraine (G-14375)		

ORNAMENTS: Christmas Tree, Exc Electrical & Glass

Rhc Inc	G	330 874-3750
Bolivar (G-1927)		
Sterling Collectables Inc	G	419 892-5708
Mansfield (G-12520)		

ORNAMENTS: Lawn

Twin Oaks Barn	F	330 893-3126
Dundee (G-9030)		

ORTHOPEDIC SUNDRIES: Molded Rubber

Foot Logic Inc	G	330 699-0123
Uniontown (G-18919)		

OUTBOARD MOTORS & PARTS

Hemco Inc	G	419 499-4602
Milan (G-13984)		

OUTLETS: Electric, Convenience

Alert Safety Lite Products Co	F	440 232-5020
Cleveland (G-4658)		

OVENS: Core Baking & Mold Drying

Miller Core 2 Inc	G	330 359-0500
Beach City (G-1213)		

OVENS: Laboratory

Ignio Systems LLC	F	419 708-0503
Toledo (G-18340)		

PACKAGE DESIGN SVCS

Amatech Inc	E	614 252-2506
Columbus (G-6579)		
Austin Foam Plastics Inc	E	614 921-0824
Columbus (G-6632)		
Diversipak Inc	C	513 321-7884
Cincinnati (G-3596)		

PACKAGED FROZEN FOODS WHOLESALERS, NEC

Koch Meat Co Inc	B	513 874-3500
Fairfield (G-9519)		
Lori Holding Co	E	740 342-3230
New Lexington (G-14717)		

PACKAGING & LABELING SVCS

A-Z Packaging Company	F	614 444-8441
Columbus (G-6518)		
Ace Assembly Packaging Inc	E	330 866-9117
Waynesburg (G-19561)		
Advanced Specialty Products	D	419 882-6528
Bowling Green (G-1950)		
Amros Industries Inc	E	216 433-0010
Cleveland (G-4702)		
Baumfolder Corporation	E	937 492-1281
Sidney (G-17019)		
BDS Packaging Inc	D	937 643-0530
Moraine (G-14333)		

Bernard Laboratories Inc .... E 513 681-7373
Cincinnati *(G-3391)*
C A P Industries Inc .... F 937 773-1824
Piqua *(G-16105)*
Cusc International Ltd .... G 513 881-2000
Hamilton *(G-10549)*
Custom Products Corporation .... D 440 528-7100
Solon *(G-17129)*
Domino Foods Inc .... D 216 432-3222
Cleveland *(G-5106)*
Fedex Office & Print Svcs Inc .... F 937 335-3816
Troy *(G-18657)*
First Choice Packaging Inc .... C 419 333-4100
Fremont *(G-10014)*
G L Industries Inc .... E 513 874-1233
Hamilton *(G-10562)*
G S K Inc .... G 937 547-1611
Greenville *(G-10371)*
Groff Industries .... F 216 634-9100
Cleveland *(G-5354)*
Hunt Products Inc .... E 440 667-2457
Newburgh Heights *(G-14940)*
Iron Wind Metals Co LLC .... G 513 870-0606
Cincinnati *(G-3859)*
Joseph T Snyder Industries .... G 216 883-6900
Cleveland *(G-5506)*
Lawnview Industries Inc .... C 937 653-5217
Urbana *(G-19003)*
Magnaco Industries Inc .... E 216 961-3636
Lodi *(G-12016)*
Magnetic Packaging LLC .... G 419 720-4366
Toledo *(G-18396)*
Metzenbaum Sheltered Inds Inc .... C 440 729-1919
Chesterland *(G-3164)*
Ohio Gasket and Shim Co Inc .... E 330 630-0626
Akron *(G-307)*
Pactiv LLC .... C 614 771-5400
Columbus *(G-7285)*
Pro-Pet LLC .... G 419 394-3374
Saint Marys *(G-16695)*
Production Support Inc .... F 937 526-3897
Russia *(G-16611)*
Richland Newhope Industries .... C 419 774-4400
Mansfield *(G-12506)*
Safecor Health LLC .... F 781 933-8780
Columbus *(G-7412)*
Satco Inc .... G 330 630-8866
Tallmadge *(G-18002)*
Stadvec Inc .... G 330 644-7724
Barberton *(G-1107)*
Systems Pack Inc .... E 330 467-5729
Macedonia *(G-12336)*
Tekni-Plex Inc .... E 419 491-2399
Holland *(G-10960)*
Teva Womens Health Inc .... C 513 731-9900
Cincinnati *(G-4416)*
Tko Mfg Services Inc .... E 937 299-1637
Moraine *(G-14399)*
Unique Packaging & Printing .... F 440 785-6730
Mentor *(G-13618)*
Universal Packg Systems Inc .... B 513 732-2000
Batavia *(G-1193)*
Universal Packg Systems Inc .... E 513 735-4777
Batavia *(G-1194)*
Universal Packg Systems Inc .... B 513 674-9400
Cincinnati *(G-4452)*
VIP-Supply Chain Solutions LLC .... G 513 454-2020
West Chester *(G-19818)*
Welch Packaging Group Inc .... C 614 870-2000
Columbus *(G-7597)*

PACKAGING MATERIALS, WHOLESALE

B B Bradley Company Inc .... G 614 777-5600
Columbus *(G-6641)*
Bemis Company Inc .... E 330 923-5281
Akron *(G-83)*
Cambridge Packaging Inc .... E 740 432-3351
Cambridge *(G-2430)*
Century Marketing Corporation .... C 419 354-2591
Bowling Green *(G-1961)*
Custom Products Corporation .... D 440 528-7100
Solon *(G-17129)*
Diversified Products & Svcs .... C 740 393-6202
Mount Vernon *(G-14478)*
Evergreen Packaging Inc .... G 440 235-7200
Olmsted Falls *(G-15530)*
Gt Industrial Supply Inc .... F 513 771-7000
Blue Ash *(G-1783)*
Kapstone Container Corporation .... C 330 562-6111
Aurora *(G-886)*
Magnetic Packaging LLC .... G 419 720-4366
Toledo *(G-18396)*
Ohio Packaging .... E 330 833-2884
Massillon *(G-13031)*
Putnam Plastics Inc .... G 937 866-6261
Dayton *(G-8452)*
Samuel Strapping Systems Inc .... D 740 522-2500
Heath *(G-10731)*
Skybox Packaging LLC .... D 419 525-7209
Mansfield *(G-12515)*
Storopack Inc .... E 513 874-0314
West Chester *(G-19904)*
Systems Pack Inc .... E 330 467-5729
Macedonia *(G-12336)*

PACKAGING MATERIALS: Paper

Adaptive Data Inc .... F 937 436-2343
Dayton *(G-8007)*
Austin Tape and Label Inc .... D 330 928-7999
Stow *(G-17570)*
Bemis Company Inc .... E 419 334-9465
Fremont *(G-9996)*
Bollin & Sons Inc .... E 419 693-6573
Toledo *(G-18210)*
Cole Pak Inc .... D 937 652-3910
Urbana *(G-18984)*
Crabar/Gbf Inc .... F 419 943-2141
Leipsic *(G-11724)*
Creative Packaging LLC .... E 740 452-8497
Zanesville *(G-21124)*
Custom Products Corporation .... D 440 528-7100
Solon *(G-17129)*
Dayton Fruit Tree Label Co .... G 937 223-4650
Dayton *(G-8133)*
E-Z Stop Service Center .... D 330 448-2236
Brookfield *(G-2105)*
Esperia Holdings LLC .... G 714 249-7888
Oak Harbor *(G-15444)*
Euclid Products Co Inc .... G 440 942-7310
Willoughby *(G-20317)*
Gauntlet Awards & Engraving .... G 937 890-5811
Dayton *(G-8214)*
Georgia-Pacific LLC .... C 740 477-3347
Circleville *(G-4546)*
Greenrock Ltd .... G 646 388-4281
Cincinnati *(G-3783)*
Gt Industrial Supply Inc .... F 513 771-7000
Blue Ash *(G-1783)*
Hooven - Dayton Corp .... D 937 233-4473
Miamisburg *(G-13677)*
Hunt Products Inc .... E 440 667-2457
Newburgh Heights *(G-14940)*
Hygient Corporation .... G 440 796-7964
Cleveland *(G-5431)*
International Paper Company .... C 740 363-9882
Delaware *(G-8696)*
Jerry Pulfer .... G 937 778-1861
Piqua *(G-16134)*
Joseph T Snyder Industries .... G 216 883-6900
Cleveland *(G-5506)*
Kapstone Container Corporation .... C 330 562-6111
Aurora *(G-886)*
Kay Toledo Tag Inc .... D 419 729-5479
Toledo *(G-18363)*
Kroy LLC .... C 216 426-5600
Cleveland *(G-5544)*
Liqui-Box Corporation .... C 419 289-9696
Ashland *(G-721)*
Loroco Industries Inc .... E 513 891-9544
Blue Ash *(G-1807)*
Marlen Manufacturing & Dev Co .... E 216 292-7546
Bedford *(G-1425)*
Multi-Color Corporation .... D 513 943-0080
Batavia *(G-1172)*
National Glass Svc Group LLC .... F 614 652-3699
Dublin *(G-8951)*
Nilpeter Usa Inc .... C 513 489-4400
Cincinnati *(G-4080)*
Norse Dairy Systems Inc .... C 614 294-4931
Columbus *(G-7224)*
North American Plas Chem Inc .... D 216 531-3400
Euclid *(G-9430)*
Novacel Inc .... C 937 335-5611
Troy *(G-18688)*
Novacel Inc .... E 413 283-3468
Troy *(G-18689)*
Packaging Tech LLC .... E 216 374-7308
Cleveland *(G-5836)*
Paxar Corporation .... F 937 681-4541
Dayton *(G-8418)*
Perfection Packaging Inc .... G 614 866-8558
Gahanna *(G-10098)*
Plastic Works Inc .... F 440 331-5575
Cleveland *(G-5887)*
Plastipak Packaging Inc .... B 937 596-6142
Jackson Center *(G-11212)*
Prime Industries Inc .... E 440 288-3626
Lorain *(G-12113)*
Raven Industries Inc .... G 937 323-4625
Springfield *(G-17480)*
Safeway Packaging Inc .... D 419 629-3200
New Bremen *(G-14660)*
Schilling Graphics Inc .... E 419 468-1037
Galion *(G-10154)*
Schwarz Partners Packaging LLC .... F 317 290-1140
Sidney *(G-17073)*
Shurtape Technologies LLC .... B 440 937-7000
Avon *(G-966)*
Signode Industrial Group LLC .... E 513 248-2990
Loveland *(G-12232)*
Sonoco Products Company .... E 419 448-4428
Tiffin *(G-18084)*
Sonoco Products Company .... E 614 759-8470
Columbus *(G-7462)*
Springdot Inc .... D 513 542-4000
Cincinnati *(G-4365)*
Storopack Inc .... E 513 874-0314
West Chester *(G-19904)*
Stretchtape Inc .... E 216 486-9400
Cleveland *(G-6107)*
Superior Label Systems Inc .... B 513 336-0825
Mason *(G-12944)*
Tce International Ltd .... F 800 962-2376
Perry *(G-15914)*
Tcp Inc .... G 330 836-4239
Fairlawn *(G-9622)*
Tech/III Inc .... E 513 482-7500
Cincinnati *(G-4409)*
Therm-O-Packaging Suppliers .... F 440 543-5188
Chagrin Falls *(G-3082)*
Thomas Products Co Inc .... E 513 756-9009
Cincinnati *(G-4420)*
Virgail Industries Inc .... G 740 928-6001
Hebron *(G-10770)*
Westrock Cp LLC .... B 513 745-2400
Blue Ash *(G-1868)*
Zebco Industries Inc .... F 740 654-4510
Lancaster *(G-11620)*
Zech Printing Industries Inc .... E 937 748-2776
Cincinnati *(G-4532)*

PACKAGING MATERIALS: Paper, Coated Or Laminated

Central Coated Products Inc .... D 330 821-9830
Alliance *(G-462)*
Central Ohio Paper & Packg Inc .... F 419 621-9239
Huron *(G-11092)*
Inno-Pak Holding Inc .... G 740 363-0090
Delaware *(G-8695)*
Proampac Pg Borrower LLC .... G 513 671-1777
Cincinnati *(G-4195)*
Retterbush Graphic and Packg .... E 513 779-4466
West Chester *(G-19780)*
Verso Paper Holding LLC .... A 901 369-4100
Miamisburg *(G-13736)*

PACKAGING MATERIALS: Paperboard Backs For Blister/Skin Pkgs

Ample Industries Inc .... C 937 746-9700
Franklin *(G-9869)*
Rohrer Corporation .... C 440 542-3100
Solon *(G-17225)*

PACKAGING MATERIALS: Plastic Film, Coated Or Laminated

Amatech Inc .... E 614 252-2506
Columbus *(G-6579)*
Command Plastic Corporation .... F 800 321-8001
Tallmadge *(G-17977)*
Cpg - Ohio LLC .... D 513 825-4800
Cincinnati *(G-3555)*
Future Polytech Inc .... E 419 763-1352
Saint Henry *(G-16661)*
Johnson Energy Company .... G 937 435-5401
Oakwood *(G-15462)*
Level Packaging LLC .... G 614 392-2412
Findlay *(G-9714)*

Employee Codes: A=Over 500 employees, B=251-500
C=101-250, D=51-100, E=20-50, F=10-19, G=3-9

2019 Harris Ohio
Industrial Directory

1523

PACKAGING MATERIALS: Plastic Film, Coated Or Laminated

Next Design & Build LLC ....G....... 330 907-3042
   Green *(G-10343)*
Next Generation Films Inc ....B....... 419 884-8150
   Mansfield *(G-12493)*
Next Generation Films Inc ....C....... 419 884-8150
   Lexington *(G-11805)*
Packaging Material Direct Inc ....G....... 989 482-8400
   Solon *(G-17212)*
Polychem Corporation ....G....... 440 357-1500
   Mentor *(G-13549)*
Polychem Corporation ....G....... 440 357-1500
   Mentor *(G-13550)*
Richards and Simmons Inc ....G....... 614 268-3909
   Columbus *(G-7392)*
Shurtech Brands LLC ....C....... 440 937-7000
   Avon *(G-967)*
Sonoco Prtective Solutions Inc ....D....... 419 420-0029
   Findlay *(G-9758)*
Universal Packg Systems Inc ....B....... 513 732-2000
   Batavia *(G-1193)*
Universal Packg Systems Inc ....B....... 513 674-9400
   Cincinnati *(G-4452)*
Universal Packg Systems Inc ....E....... 513 735-4777
   Batavia *(G-1194)*

PACKAGING MATERIALS: Polystyrene Foam

American Foam Products Inc ....E....... 440 352-3434
   Painesville *(G-15710)*
Archbold Container Corp ....C....... 800 446-2520
   Archbold *(G-637)*
Arlington Rack & Packaging Co ....G....... 419 476-7700
   Toledo *(G-18191)*
B B Bradley Company Inc ....E....... 440 354-2005
   Painesville *(G-15718)*
B B Bradley Company Inc ....G....... 614 777-5600
   Columbus *(G-6641)*
Concept Manufacturing LLC ....G....... 812 677-2043
   Johnstown *(G-11263)*
Cryovac Inc ....F....... 513 771-7770
   West Chester *(G-19689)*
Custom Foam Products Inc ....E....... 937 295-2700
   Fort Loramie *(G-9794)*
Dayton Polymeric Products Inc ....D....... 937 279-9987
   Dayton *(G-8141)*
Eps Specialties Ltd Inc ....E....... 513 489-3676
   Cincinnati *(G-3649)*
Fabricated Packaging Mtls Inc ....G....... 740 681-1750
   Lancaster *(G-11569)*
Fabricated Packaging Mtls Inc ....F....... 740 654-3492
   Lancaster *(G-11570)*
Foam Concepts & Design Inc ....F....... 513 860-5589
   West Chester *(G-19706)*
Greif Packaging LLC ....D....... 740 549-6000
   Delaware *(G-8688)*
Hitti Enterprises Inc ....F....... 440 243-4100
   Cleveland *(G-5410)*
Orbis Corporation ....D....... 262 560-5000
   Perrysburg *(G-15994)*
Plastic Works Inc ....F....... 440 331-5575
   Cleveland *(G-5887)*
Polycel Incorporated ....E....... 614 252-2400
   Columbus *(G-7331)*
Precision Foam Fabrication Inc ....F....... 330 270-2440
   Youngstown *(G-21003)*
Sash Foam Works Inc ....G....... 419 522-4074
   Mansfield *(G-12511)*
Skybox Packaging LLC ....D....... 419 525-7209
   Mansfield *(G-12515)*
Smithers-Oasis Company ....F....... 330 945-5100
   Kent *(G-11386)*
Special Design Products Inc ....E....... 614 272-6700
   Columbus *(G-7466)*
Storopack Inc ....E....... 513 874-0314
   West Chester *(G-19904)*
Thermal Visions Inc ....G....... 740 587-4025
   Granville *(G-10339)*
Truechoicepack Corp ....E....... 937 630-3832
   Mason *(G-12951)*
US Foam Corporation ....G....... 513 528-9800
   Cincinnati *(G-4456)*
Zebco Industries Inc ....F....... 740 654-4510
   Lancaster *(G-11620)*
Zing Pac Inc ....G....... 440 248-7997
   Cleveland *(G-6342)*

PACKAGING: Blister Or Bubble Formed, Plastic

A Aabaco Plastics Inc ....F....... 216 663-9494
   Cleveland *(G-4583)*
MTS Medication Tech Inc ....G....... 440 238-0840
   Strongsville *(G-17767)*
Rohrer Corporation ....C....... 330 335-1541
   Wadsworth *(G-19275)*
Sonoco Prtective Solutions Inc ....D....... 419 420-0029
   Findlay *(G-9759)*
Truechoicepack Corp ....E....... 937 630-3832
   Mason *(G-12951)*

PACKING & CRATING SVC

A Z Printing Inc ....G....... 513 745-0700
   Cincinnati *(G-3283)*
Bates Metal Products Inc ....D....... 740 498-8371
   Port Washington *(G-16267)*
Forrest Enterprises Inc ....G....... 937 773-1714
   Piqua *(G-16116)*
Lefco Worthington LLC ....E....... 216 432-4422
   Cleveland *(G-5571)*
Third Party Service Ltd ....F....... 419 872-2312
   Perrysburg *(G-16015)*
Vista Industrial Packaging LLC ....D....... 800 454-6117
   Columbus *(G-7586)*

PACKING MATERIALS: Mechanical

Excelsior Solutions ....G....... 937 848-2569
   Spring Valley *(G-17316)*
Produce Packaging Inc ....C....... 216 391-6129
   Cleveland *(G-5925)*

PACKING SVCS: Shipping

Amerisource Health Svcs LLC ....D....... 614 492-8177
   Columbus *(G-6590)*
Caravan Packaging Inc ....F....... 440 243-4100
   Cleveland *(G-4875)*
Forest City Companies Inc ....E....... 216 586-5279
   Cleveland *(G-5261)*
Global Packaging & Exports Inc ....G....... 513 454-2020
   West Chester *(G-19716)*
McElroy Contract Packaging ....F....... 330 262-0855
   Wooster *(G-20621)*
McNerney & Associates LLC ....G....... 513 241-9951
   Cincinnati *(G-3989)*
Overseas Packing LLC ....F....... 440 232-2917
   Bedford *(G-1434)*
Reynolds Industries Inc ....E....... 330 889-9466
   West Farmington *(G-19920)*
World Express Packaging Corp ....G....... 216 634-9000
   Cleveland *(G-6324)*

PACKING: Metallic

Magnetic Packaging LLC ....G....... 419 720-4366
   Toledo *(G-18396)*

PADDING: Foamed Plastics

Aqua Lily Products LLC ....F....... 951 246-9610
   Willoughby *(G-20279)*
J P Industrial Products Inc ....E....... 330 424-3388
   Lisbon *(G-11973)*
Team Wendy LLC ....D....... 216 738-2518
   Cleveland *(G-6151)*

PADS: Athletic, Protective

Soccer Centre Owners Ltd ....E....... 419 893-5425
   Maumee *(G-13146)*
Tuffy Pad Company Inc ....F....... 330 688-0043
   Stow *(G-17639)*

PAILS: Shipping, Metal

Cleveland Steel Container Corp ....E....... 330 656-5600
   Streetsboro *(G-17666)*

PAINT & PAINTING SPLYS STORE

American Indus Maintanence ....G....... 937 254-3400
   Dayton *(G-8026)*
Sherwin-Williams Company ....A....... 216 566-2000
   Cleveland *(G-6053)*
Sherwin-Williams Company ....G....... 440 282-2310
   Lorain *(G-12120)*
Sherwn-Wllams Intl Hldings Inc ....G....... 216 566-2000
   Medina *(G-13342)*

PAINT DRIERS

Ferro Corporation ....D....... 216 577-7144
   Bedford *(G-1405)*

PAINT STORE

Comex North America Inc ....D....... 303 307-2100
   Cleveland *(G-5001)*
Fort Loramie Cast Stone Pdts ....G....... 937 420-2257
   Fort Loramie *(G-9798)*
PPG Architectural Finishes Inc ....G....... 330 477-8165
   Canton *(G-2788)*
Prints & Paints Flr Cvg Co Inc ....E....... 419 462-5663
   Galion *(G-10151)*
Sherwin-Williams Company ....G....... 330 253-6625
   North Canton *(G-15117)*
Sherwin-Williams Company ....E....... 614 539-8456
   Grove City *(G-10467)*
Sherwin-Williams Company ....G....... 440 846-4328
   Strongsville *(G-17788)*
Sherwin-Williams Company ....G....... 216 662-3300
   Cleveland *(G-6054)*
Sherwin-Williams Company ....G....... 330 528-0124
   Hudson *(G-11072)*
Sherwn-Wllams Auto Fnshes Corp ....C....... 216 332-8330
   Cleveland *(G-6056)*

PAINTING SVC: Metal Prdts

Alsco Metals Corporation ....E....... 740 983-2571
   Dennison *(G-8781)*
Astro-Coatings Inc ....G....... 330 755-1414
   Struthers *(G-17816)*
Austin Finishing Co Inc ....G....... 216 883-0326
   Cleveland *(G-4764)*
Balser Inc ....G....... 567 444-4737
   Archbold *(G-640)*
Benco Industries Inc ....G....... 440 572-3555
   Strongsville *(G-17719)*
Brilliant Colorworks LLC ....G....... 800 566-4162
   Columbus *(G-6701)*
Bta of Motorcars Inc ....G....... 440 716-1000
   North Olmsted *(G-15182)*
C L S Finishing Inc ....F....... 330 784-4134
   Tallmadge *(G-17974)*
Carpe Diem Industries LLC ....D....... 419 659-5639
   Columbus Grove *(G-7632)*
Carpe Diem Industries LLC ....E....... 419 358-0129
   Bluffton *(G-1887)*
Creative Powder Coatings ....G....... 440 322-8197
   Elyria *(G-9239)*
Duffee Finishing Inc ....G....... 740 965-4848
   Sunbury *(G-17885)*
Fayette Industrial Coatings ....E....... 419 636-1773
   Bryan *(G-2280)*
Final Finish Corp ....G....... 440 439-3303
   Macedonia *(G-12294)*
Herbert E Orr Company ....C....... 419 399-4866
   Paulding *(G-15860)*
Heritage Industrial Finshg Inc ....D....... 330 798-9840
   Akron *(G-205)*
Hydro Extrusion North Amer LLC ....C....... 888 935-5759
   Sidney *(G-17045)*
Kars Ohio LLC ....G....... 614 655-1099
   Pataskala *(G-15834)*
Lima Sandblasting & Pntg Co ....G....... 419 331-2939
   Lima *(G-11892)*
Material Sciences Corporation ....G....... 330 702-3882
   Canfield *(G-2535)*
Parker Trutec Incorporated ....D....... 937 653-8500
   Urbana *(G-19007)*
Precision Coatings Systems ....E....... 937 642-4727
   Marysville *(G-12806)*
Procoat Painting Inc ....G....... 513 735-2500
   Batavia *(G-1179)*
Production Paint Finishers Inc ....D....... 937 448-2627
   Bradford *(G-2011)*
Seacor Painting Corporation ....G....... 330 755-6361
   Campbell *(G-2469)*
Spectrum Metal Finishing Inc ....D....... 330 758-8358
   Youngstown *(G-21038)*
Springco Metal Coatings Inc ....C....... 216 941-0020
   Cleveland *(G-6087)*
Star Fab Inc ....C....... 330 533-9863
   Canfield *(G-2547)*
Tendon Manufacturing Inc ....E....... 216 663-3200
   Cleveland *(G-6159)*
Tool & Die Systems Inc ....E....... 440 327-5800
   North Ridgeville *(G-15256)*
Tri-State Fabricators Inc ....E....... 513 752-5005
   Amelia *(G-550)*

PAINTS & ADDITIVES

Akron Paint & Varnish Inc ....D....... 330 773-8911
   Akron *(G-46)*

All Coatings Co Inc....G....330 821-3806
Alliance *(G-451)*
Aluminum Coating Manufacturers....E....216 341-2000
Cleveland *(G-4680)*
American Paint Recyclers LLC....G....888 978-6558
Middle Point *(G-13755)*
Avion Manufacturing Company....G....330 220-1989
Brunswick *(G-2188)*
Axalt Powde Coati Syste Usa I....F....614 600-4104
Hilliard *(G-10808)*
Brinkman LLC....F....419 204-5934
Lima *(G-11846)*
Cansto Paint and Varnish Co....G....216 231-6115
Cleveland *(G-4866)*
Certon Technologies Inc....F....440 786-7185
Bedford *(G-1395)*
Chemspec Usa LLC....D....330 669-8512
Orrville *(G-15587)*
Coloramics LLC....E....614 876-1171
Hilliard *(G-10819)*
Comex North America Inc....D....303 307-2100
Cleveland *(G-5001)*
Continental Products Company....E....216 383-3932
Cleveland *(G-5023)*
Continental Products Company....E....216 531-0710
Cleveland *(G-5024)*
Dap Products Inc....C....937 667-4461
Tipp City *(G-18110)*
Filament LLC....G....614 732-0754
Columbus *(G-6921)*
Kalcor Coatings Company....E....440 946-4700
Willoughby *(G-20350)*
Karyall-Telday Inc....E....216 281-4063
Cleveland *(G-5516)*
PPG Industries Inc....E....330 825-0831
Barberton *(G-1096)*
PPG Industries Inc....E....419 683-2400
Crestline *(G-7799)*
PPG Industries Ohio Inc....A....216 671-0050
Cleveland *(G-5901)*
Sheffield Bronze Paint Corp....E....216 481-8330
Cleveland *(G-6050)*
Sherwin-Williams Company....C....330 830-6000
Massillon *(G-13048)*
Spectrum Dispersions Inc....F....330 296-0600
Ravenna *(G-16405)*
Sun Color Corporation....G....330 499-7010
North Canton *(G-15123)*
Thorworks Industries Inc....E....419 626-4375
Sandusky *(G-16855)*
Toledo Paint & Chemical Co....G....419 244-3726
Toledo *(G-18566)*

PAINTS & ALLIED PRODUCTS

Akzo Nobel Coatings Inc....C....614 294-3361
Columbus *(G-6558)*
Akzo Nobel Coatings Inc....C....614 294-3361
Columbus *(G-6559)*
Akzo Nobel Inc....E....614 294-3361
Columbus *(G-6560)*
Americhem Inc....A....330 929-4213
Cuyahoga Falls *(G-7835)*
Aps-Materials Inc....D....937 278-6547
Dayton *(G-8034)*
Basic Coatings LLC....E....419 241-2156
Bowling Green *(G-1954)*
Bollin & Sons Inc....E....419 693-6573
Toledo *(G-18210)*
Cansto Coatings Ltd....F....216 231-6115
Cleveland *(G-4865)*
Carboline Company....G....800 848-4645
University Heights *(G-18940)*
Chemmasters Inc....E....440 428-2105
Madison *(G-12344)*
Consolidated Coatings Corp....E....216 514-7596
Cleveland *(G-5017)*
Creative Commercial Finishing....G....513 722-9393
Loveland *(G-12184)*
Deco Plas Properties LLC....E....419 485-0632
Montpelier *(G-14306)*
Envirnmntal Prtctive Ctngs LLC....G....740 363-6180
Ostrander *(G-15643)*
Fuchs Lubricants Co....E....330 963-0400
Twinsburg *(G-18777)*
General Electric Company....D....216 268-3846
Cleveland *(G-5310)*
Genvac Aerospace Corp....F....440 646-9986
Cleveland *(G-5317)*
Harrison Paint Company....E....330 455-5120
Canton *(G-2694)*
Henkel Corporation....C....216 475-3600
Cleveland *(G-5392)*
Hexpol Compounding LLC....C....440 834-4644
Burton *(G-2360)*
Hoover & Wells Inc....C....419 691-9220
Toledo *(G-18335)*
Kardol Quality Products LLC....E....513 933-8206
Blue Ash *(G-1800)*
Leonhardt Plating Company....E....513 242-1410
Cincinnati *(G-3938)*
Mameco International Inc....F....216 752-4400
Cleveland *(G-5611)*
Matrix Sys Auto Finishes LLC....D....248 668-8135
Massillon *(G-13023)*
Meggitt (erlanger) LLC....D....513 851-5550
Cincinnati *(G-4000)*
Mid America Chemical Corp....G....216 749-0100
Cleveland *(G-5672)*
Myko Industries....G....216 431-0900
Cleveland *(G-5717)*
Nextgen Materials LLC....G....513 858-2365
Fairfield *(G-9535)*
Npa Coatings Inc....C....216 651-5900
Cleveland *(G-5792)*
Parker Trutec Incorporated....D....937 653-8500
Urbana *(G-19007)*
Perstorp Polyols Inc....C....419 729-5448
Toledo *(G-18467)*
Polymerics Inc....E....330 434-6665
Cuyahoga Falls *(G-7906)*
Polynt Composites USA Inc....E....816 391-6000
Sandusky *(G-16839)*
Polyone Corporation....C....419 668-4844
Norwalk *(G-15412)*
PPG Architectural Coatings LLC....F....419 433-5664
Huron *(G-11109)*
PPG Architectural Finishes Inc....G....330 477-8165
Canton *(G-2788)*
PPG Industries Inc....G....513 737-1893
Hamilton *(G-10597)*
PPG Industries Inc....D....440 572-2800
Strongsville *(G-17777)*
PPG Industries Inc....G....740 774-8734
Chillicothe *(G-3212)*
PPG Industries Inc....F....440 232-1260
Bedford *(G-1437)*
PPG Industries Inc....E....216 671-7793
Cleveland *(G-5900)*
PPG Industries Inc....G....740 363-9610
Delaware *(G-8715)*
PPG Industries Inc....G....614 252-6384
Columbus *(G-7336)*
PPG Industries Inc....G....330 825-6328
Barberton *(G-1097)*
PPG Industries Inc....C....740 474-3161
Circleville *(G-4553)*
PPG Industries Inc....E....740 774-7600
Chillicothe *(G-3213)*
PPG Industries Inc....F....740 774-7600
Chillicothe *(G-3214)*
PPG Industries Inc....G....740 774-7600
Chillicothe *(G-3215)*
PPG Industries Inc....E....513 231-3200
Cincinnati *(G-4179)*
PPG Industries Inc....E....740 474-3945
Circleville *(G-4554)*
PPG Industries Inc....E....513 829-6006
Fairfield *(G-9549)*
PPG Industries Inc....E....513 661-5220
Cincinnati *(G-4180)*
PPG Industries Inc....G....614 277-0620
Grove City *(G-10458)*
PPG Industries Inc....G....614 921-9228
Hilliard *(G-10854)*
PPG Industries Inc....E....513 424-1241
Middletown *(G-13943)*
PPG Industries Inc....E....513 984-6761
Cincinnati *(G-4181)*
PPG Industries Inc....E....614 939-2365
Columbus *(G-7337)*
PPG Industries Inc....E....614 268-2609
Columbus *(G-7338)*
PPG Industries Inc....E....513 779-2727
West Chester *(G-19888)*
PPG Industries Inc....E....513 242-3050
Cincinnati *(G-4182)*
PPG Industries Inc....E....614 501-7360
Reynoldsburg *(G-16446)*
PPG Industries Inc....E....330 262-9741
Wooster *(G-20638)*
PPG Industries Inc....E....513 576-3100
Milford *(G-14034)*
PPG Industries Inc....E....330 824-2537
Warren *(G-19433)*
PPG Industries Inc....G....614 846-3128
Columbus *(G-7339)*
PPG Industries Ohio Inc....E....740 363-9610
Delaware *(G-8716)*
PPG Industries Ohio Inc....D....216 486-5300
Euclid *(G-9436)*
Priest Services Inc....E....440 333-1123
Mayfield Heights *(G-13170)*
Prism Powder Coatings Ltd....E....330 225-5626
Brunswick *(G-2230)*
Ramon Robinson....G....330 883-3244
Vienna *(G-19208)*
Republic Powdered Metals Inc....D....330 225-3192
Medina *(G-13327)*
Ruscoe Company....E....330 253-8148
Akron *(G-358)*
Sherwin-Williams Company....A....216 566-2000
Cleveland *(G-6053)*
Sherwin-Williams Company....G....440 282-2310
Lorain *(G-12120)*
Sherwin-Williams Company....G....330 253-6625
North Canton *(G-15117)*
Sherwin-Williams Company....E....614 539-8456
Grove City *(G-10467)*
Sherwin-Williams Company....E....440 846-4328
Strongsville *(G-17788)*
Sherwin-Williams Company....G....216 662-3300
Cleveland *(G-6054)*
Sherwin-Williams Company....G....330 528-0124
Hudson *(G-11072)*
Sherwin-Williams Mfg Co....F....216 566-2000
Cleveland *(G-6055)*
Sherwn-Wllams Auto Fnshes Corp....C....216 332-8330
Cleveland *(G-6056)*
Sherwn-Wllams Intl Hldings Inc....G....216 566-2000
Medina *(G-13342)*
Teknol Inc....D....937 264-0190
Dayton *(G-8550)*
Tremco Incorporated....B....216 292-5000
Beachwood *(G-1283)*
Universal Urethane Pdts Inc....D....419 693-7400
Toledo *(G-18585)*
Wooster Products Inc....D....330 264-2844
Wooster *(G-20669)*
Xim Products Inc....E....440 871-4737
Westlake *(G-20174)*
Zircoa Inc....C....440 248-0500
Cleveland *(G-6345)*

PAINTS, VARNISHES & SPLYS WHOLESALERS

Continental Products Company....E....216 531-0710
Cleveland *(G-5024)*
Cto Inc....G....330 785-1130
Akron *(G-126)*
Finishmaster Inc....D....614 228-4328
Columbus *(G-6924)*
Mini Graphics Inc....G....513 563-8600
Cincinnati *(G-4030)*
Myko Industries....G....216 431-0900
Cleveland *(G-5717)*
Teknol Inc....D....937 264-0190
Dayton *(G-8550)*

PAINTS, VARNISHES & SPLYS, WHOLESALE: Paints

C A P Industries Inc....F....937 773-1824
Piqua *(G-16105)*
Comex North America Inc....D....303 307-2100
Cleveland *(G-5001)*
Jmac Inc....E....614 436-2418
Columbus *(G-7069)*
Matrix Sys Auto Finishes LLC....D....248 668-8135
Massillon *(G-13023)*

PAINTS, VARNISHES & SPLYS, WHOLESALE: Stain

Tridico Silk Screen & Sign Co....G....419 526-1695
Mansfield *(G-12534)*

PRODUCT

Employee Codes: A=Over 500 employees, B=251-500
C=101-250, D=51-100, E=20-50, F=10-19, G=3-9
2019 Harris Ohio
Industrial Directory
1525

PAINTS, VARNISHES & SPLYS, WHOLESALE: Thinner

Sherwin-Williams Mfg Co ....F 216 566-2000
Cleveland *(G-6055)*

PAINTS: Asphalt Or Bituminous

Parkins Asphalt Sealing ....G....... 419 422-2399
Findlay *(G-9739)*

PAINTS: Marine

Precisions Paint Systems LLC ....F 740 894-6224
South Point *(G-17291)*

PAINTS: Oil Or Alkyd Vehicle Or Water Thinned

Akzo Nobel Coatings Inc ....F 937 322-2671
Springfield *(G-17361)*

Mansfield Paint Co Inc ....G....... 330 725-2436
Medina *(G-13289)*

Waterlox Coatings Corporation ....F 216 641-4877
Cleveland *(G-6293)*

PALLET REPAIR SVCS

Able Pallet Mfg & Repr ....F....... 614 444-2115
Columbus *(G-6529)*

Langston Pallets ....G....... 937 492-8769
Sidney *(G-17049)*

Lumberjack Pallet Recycl LLC ....G....... 513 821-7543
Cincinnati *(G-3956)*

Martin Pallet Inc ....E 330 832-5309
Massillon *(G-13018)*

PALLETIZERS & DEPALLETIZERS

Intelligrated Systems Ohio LLC ....A....... 513 701-7300
Mason *(G-12896)*

PALLETS

A2z Pallets LLC ....G....... 513 652-9026
Cincinnati *(G-3284)*

American Built Custom Pallets ....G....... 330 532-4780
Lisbon *(G-11963)*

At Pallet ....G....... 330 264-3903
Wooster *(G-20565)*

Carrillo Pallets LLC ....G....... 513 942-2210
Cincinnati *(G-3446)*

CC Pallets LLC ....G....... 513 442-8766
Terrace Park *(G-18018)*

Cleveland Cstm Pllet Crate Inc ....E 216 881-1414
Cleveland *(G-4954)*

Clover Pallet LLC ....G....... 330 454-5592
Canton *(G-2629)*

Crosscreek Pallet Co ....G....... 440 632-1940
Middlefield *(G-13788)*

Daves Pallets ....G....... 740 525-4938
Belpre *(G-1573)*

Diamond Pallets LLC ....G....... 419 281-2908
Ashland *(G-701)*

Dj Pallets ....G....... 216 701-9183
Columbia Station *(G-6436)*

Fisher Pallet ....G....... 440 632-0863
Middlefield *(G-13798)*

H & K Pallet Services ....G....... 937 608-1140
Xenia *(G-20776)*

Harrys Pallets LLC ....G....... 330 704-1056
Navarre *(G-14576)*

Ironhouse Pallets ....G....... 330 635-5218
North Ridgeville *(G-15233)*

J&R Pallet Ltd ....G 740 226-1112
Waverly *(G-19549)*

Joe Barrett ....G....... 216 385-2384
East Liverpool *(G-9060)*

L N S Pallets ....G....... 330 936-7507
Navarre *(G-14579)*

Lawrence Pallets & Solutions ....G....... 740 259-4283
Lucasville *(G-12265)*

Leroy Yutzy ....G....... 937 386-2872
Winchester *(G-20522)*

Melt Inc ....G....... 330 426-3545
Negley *(G-14591)*

Montgomerys Pallet Service ....G....... 330 297-6677
Ravenna *(G-16390)*

Mulch World ....G....... 419 873-6852
Perrysburg *(G-15978)*

Oakmoor Pallet ....G....... 440 385-7340
Westlake *(G-20135)*

Pallet Guys ....G....... 440 897-3001
North Royalton *(G-15292)*

Pallet Pros ....G....... 440 537-9087
Grafton *(G-10308)*

Paul E Cekovich ....G....... 330 424-3213
Lisbon *(G-11979)*

Plains Precut Ltd ....G....... 330 893-3300
Millersburg *(G-14119)*

Quality Pllets Recyclables LLC ....G....... 419 396-3244
Carey *(G-2889)*

Rettig Family Pallets Inc ....F 419 264-1540
Napoleon *(G-14560)*

S & S Pallets ....G....... 513 967-7432
Milford *(G-14038)*

Schnider Pallet LLC ....G....... 440 632-5346
Middlefield *(G-13850)*

Smith Pallets ....G....... 937 564-6492
Versailles *(G-19190)*

T&A Pallets Inc ....G....... 330 968-4743
Ravenna *(G-16411)*

Tri State Pallet Inc ....E....... 937 746-8702
Franklin *(G-9927)*

Troyers Pallet Shop ....G....... 330 897-1038
Fresno *(G-10072)*

Universal Pallets Inc ....G....... 614 444-1095
Columbus *(G-7562)*

Van Wert Pallets LLC ....G....... 419 203-1823
Van Wert *(G-19111)*

Worthington Pallet ....G....... 614 888-1573
Worthington *(G-20714)*

PALLETS & SKIDS: Wood

A W Taylor Lumber Incorporated ....F 440 577-1889
Pierpont *(G-16063)*

AA Pallets LLC ....G....... 216 856-2614
Cleveland *(G-4595)*

Able Pallet Mfg & Repr ....F....... 614 444-2115
Columbus *(G-6529)*

Arrowhead Pallets LLC ....F 440 693-4241
Middlefield *(G-13778)*

Belco Works ....G....... 740 695-0500
Saint Clairsville *(G-16623)*

Belco Works Inc ....B 740 695-0500
Saint Clairsville *(G-16624)*

Brookhill Center Industries ....C....... 419 876-3932
Ottawa *(G-15648)*

Buckeye Pallett ....G....... 330 359-5919
Millersburg *(G-14070)*

Chep (usa) Inc ....E 614 497-9448
Columbus *(G-6761)*

Clark Rm Inc ....E 419 425-9889
Findlay *(G-9669)*

Coshocton Pallet & Door Bldg ....G....... 740 622-9766
Coshocton *(G-7729)*

Cs Products ....G....... 330 452-8566
Canton *(G-2640)*

D P Products Inc ....G....... 440 834-9663
Middlefield *(G-13791)*

Emergency Products & RES Inc ....G....... 330 673-5003
Kent *(G-11319)*

Findlay Pallett Inc ....G....... 419 423-0511
Findlay *(G-9686)*

Grant Street Pallet Inc ....G....... 330 424-0355
Lisbon *(G-11967)*

Hacker Wood Products Inc ....G....... 513 737-4462
Hamilton *(G-10566)*

Haessly Lumber Sales Co ....D 740 373-6681
Marietta *(G-12630)*

Hann Box Works ....E 740 962-3752
McConnelsville *(G-13205)*

Hann Manufacturing Inc ....E 740 962-3752
McConnelsville *(G-13206)*

Hinchcliff Lumber Company ....G....... 440 238-5200
Strongsville *(G-17749)*

Iroquois Pallet ....G....... 513 677-0048
Cincinnati *(G-3860)*

J E Johnson Pallett Inc ....G....... 614 424-9663
Columbus *(G-7055)*

J I T Pallets Inc ....G....... 330 424-0355
Lisbon *(G-11971)*

Ken Harper ....C 740 439-4452
Byesville *(G-2388)*

Kountry Pride Enterprises ....G....... 330 868-3345
Minerva *(G-14189)*

Litco Manufacturing LLC ....F 330 539-5433
Warren *(G-19417)*

Lumberjack Pallet Recycl LLC ....G....... 513 821-7543
Cincinnati *(G-3956)*

Mec ....G....... 419 483-4852
Bellevue *(G-1539)*

Oak Chips Inc ....E 740 947-4159
Waverly *(G-19554)*

P R U Industries Inc ....F 937 746-8702
Franklin *(G-9907)*

Pallet Distributors Inc ....D....... 330 852-3531
Sugarcreek *(G-17856)*

Price Management Services Ltd ....G....... 419 298-5423
Paulding *(G-15870)*

Pymatning Spcialty Pallets LLC ....G....... 440 293-3306
Andover *(G-586)*

Quadco Rehabilitation Center ....D....... 419 445-1950
Archbold *(G-665)*

Quadco Rehabilitation Ctr Inc ....B 419 682-1011
Stryker *(G-17832)*

Richland Newhope Industries ....C....... 419 774-4400
Mansfield *(G-12506)*

Specialty Pallet Entps LLC ....G....... 419 673-0247
Kenton *(G-11423)*

Sugarcreek Pallett ....G....... 330 852-9812
Sugarcreek *(G-17868)*

Three AS Inc ....G....... 419 227-4240
Lima *(G-11951)*

Troymill Manufacturing Inc ....F 440 632-5580
Middlefield *(G-13860)*

Tusco Hardwoods LLC ....F 330 852-4281
Sugarcreek *(G-17873)*

Ultimate Pallet & Trucking LLC ....G....... 440 693-4090
Middlefield *(G-13862)*

Wjf Enterprises LLC ....F 513 871-7320
Cincinnati *(G-4514)*

Yoder Lumber Co Inc ....E....... 330 674-1435
Millersburg *(G-14154)*

Zak Box Co Inc ....G....... 216 961-5636
Cleveland *(G-6337)*

PALLETS: Corrugated

Jordon Auto Service & Tire Inc ....G....... 216 214-6528
Cleveland *(G-5505)*

PALLETS: Metal

American Truck Equipment Inc ....G....... 216 362-0400
Cleveland *(G-4699)*

PALLETS: Plastic

Marcum Development LLC ....G....... 330 466-8231
Wooster *(G-20619)*

Mye Automotive Inc ....G....... 330 253-5592
Akron *(G-291)*

Myers Industries Inc ....E 330 253-5592
Akron *(G-292)*

Quality Frp Fabrications ....G....... 440 942-9067
Willoughby *(G-20414)*

PALLETS: Wooden

A & D Wood Products Inc ....F 419 331-8859
Elida *(G-9192)*

A & M Pallet ....F 937 295-3093
Russia *(G-16604)*

A & M Pallet Shop Inc ....F 440 632-1941
Middlefield *(G-13772)*

A-Z Packaging Company ....F 614 444-8441
Columbus *(G-6518)*

AAA Plastics and Pallets Ltd ....G....... 330 844-2556
Orrville *(G-15580)*

Akron Crate and Pallet LLC ....G....... 330 524-8955
Kent *(G-11291)*

Anderson Pallet & Packg Inc ....E 937 962-2614
Lewisburg *(G-11789)*

B & B Pallet Co ....G....... 419 435-4530
Fostoria *(G-9834)*

B J Pallett ....G....... 419 447-9665
Tiffin *(G-18049)*

Bonded Pallets ....G....... 513 541-1855
Cincinnati *(G-3402)*

Buck Creek Pallet ....G....... 937 653-3098
Urbana *(G-18981)*

Buckeye Diamond Logistics Inc ....C....... 937 462-8361
South Charleston *(G-17271)*

Cabot Lumber Inc ....G....... 740 545-7109
West Lafayette *(G-19929)*

Caesarcreek Pallets Ltd ....F 937 416-4447
Jamestown *(G-11219)*

Cima Inc ....E 513 382-8976
Hamilton *(G-10545)*

Cimino Box Inc ....G....... 216 961-7377
Cleveland *(G-4928)*

Coblentz Brothers Inc ....E 330 857-7211
Apple Creek *(G-602)*

PRODUCT SECTION

PAPER & BOARD: Die-cut

Company	Code	Phone
Cottonwood Pallet Inc	G	419 468-9703
Galion (G-10129)		
Cox Wood Product Inc	F	740 372-4735
Otway (G-15687)		
Custom Palet Manufacturing	G	440 693-4603
Middlefield (G-13789)		
D M Pallet Service Inc	F	614 491-0881
Columbus (G-6845)		
Damar Products Inc	F	937 492-9023
Sidney (G-17025)		
Damar Products Inc	F	937 492-9023
Sidney (G-17026)		
Dan S Miller & David S Miller	G	937 464-9061
Belle Center (G-1498)		
David J Fisher	G	440 636-2256
Middlefield (G-13793)		
Forrest Rawlins	G	740 778-3366
Wheelersburg (G-20180)		
Fox Hollow Pallet	G	937 386-2872
Winchester (G-20520)		
Franks Sawmill Inc	F	419 682-3831
Stryker (G-17829)		
Gallagher Lumber Co	G	330 274-2333
Mantua (G-12546)		
Gardner Lumber Co Inc	F	740 254-4664
Tippecanoe (G-18148)		
Gross Lumber Inc	E	330 683-2055
Apple Creek (G-606)		
Halliday Holdings Inc	E	740 335-1430
Wshngtn CT Hs (G-20727)		
Hershberger Manufacturing	F	440 272-5555
Windsor (G-20526)		
Hillside Pallet	G	440 272-5425
Windsor (G-20527)		
Hines Builders Inc	F	937 335-4586
Troy (G-18665)		
Hope Timber & Marketing Group	F	740 344-1788
Newark (G-14884)		
Hope Timber Pallet Recycl Inc	F	740 344-1788
Newark (G-14886)		
Ictm Inc	G	330 629-6060
Youngstown (G-20936)		
Ifco Systems North America Inc	D	330 669-2726
Smithville (G-17089)		
Ifco Systems Us LLC	E	513 769-0377
Cincinnati (G-3836)		
Inca Presswood-Pallets Ltd	E	330 343-3361
Dover (G-8831)		
Industrial Hardwood Inc	G	419 666-2503
Perrysburg (G-15966)		
Inland Hardwood Corporation	D	740 373-7187
Marietta (G-12635)		
Iron City Wood Products Inc	E	330 755-2772
Youngstown (G-20943)		
J & K Pallet Inc	G	937 526-5117
Versailles (G-19182)		
J & L Wood Products Inc	E	937 667-4064
Tipp City (G-18119)		
J D L Hardwoods	G	440 272-5630
Middlefield (G-13807)		
JIT Packaging Inc	E	330 562-8080
Aurora (G-885)		
Joe Gonda Company Inc	F	440 458-6000
Grafton (G-10305)		
Kamps Inc	D	937 526-9333
Versailles (G-19183)		
Kenneth Schrock	G	937 544-7566
West Union (G-19964)		
Lake Wood Product Inc	G	419 832-0150
Grand Rapids (G-10316)		
Langston Pallets	G	937 492-8769
Sidney (G-17049)		
Lima Pallet Company Inc	E	419 229-5736
Lima (G-11889)		
Litco International Inc	E	330 539-5433
Vienna (G-19201)		
Martin Pallet Inc	E	330 832-5309
Massillon (G-13018)		
Mid Ohio Wood Products Inc	E	740 323-0427
Newark (G-14897)		
Mid Ohio Wood Recycling Inc	G	419 673-8470
Kenton (G-11413)		
Middlefield Pallet Inc	E	440 632-0553
Middlefield (G-13825)		
Midtown Pallet & Recycling	E	419 241-1311
Toledo (G-18410)		
Miller Pallet Company	G	937 464-4483
Belle Center (G-1500)		
Milltree Lumber Holdings	G	740 226-2090
Waverly (G-19551)		
Millwood Inc	E	330 359-5220
Dundee (G-9022)		
Millwood Inc	D	330 857-3075
Apple Creek (G-614)		
Millwood Inc	D	740 226-2090
Waverly (G-19552)		
Millwood Inc	C	440 914-0540
Solon (G-17195)		
Mjc Enterprises Inc	F	330 669-3744
Sterling (G-17523)		
Morgan Wood Products Inc	F	614 336-4000
Powell (G-16330)		
Mt Eaton Pallet Ltd	E	330 893-2986
Millersburg (G-14116)		
Nwp Manufacturing Inc	F	419 894-6871
Waldo (G-19303)		
Oakmoor Pallet	G	216 926-1858
Westlake (G-20134)		
Ohio State Pallet Corp	G	614 332-3961
Homer (G-10985)		
Ohio Wood Recycling Inc	G	614 491-0881
Columbus (G-7265)		
Olympic Forest Products Co	F	216 421-2775
Cleveland (G-5812)		
Pallet & Cont Corp of Amer	F	419 255-1256
Toledo (G-18457)		
Pallet Specs Plus LLC	F	513 351-3200
Norwood (G-15427)		
Pallet World Inc	E	419 874-9333
Perrysburg (G-16000)		
Parks West Pallet Llc	G	440 693-4651
Middlefield (G-13843)		
Pettits Pallets Inc	G	614 351-4920
Orient (G-15576)		
Plastic Pallet & Container Inc	E	330 650-6700
Hudson (G-11067)		
Precise Pallets LLC	G	513 560-8236
Batavia (G-1178)		
Precision Pallet Inc	G	419 381-8191
Ottawa Hills (G-15676)		
Premier Pallet & Recycling	F	330 767-2221
Navarre (G-14585)		
Prime Wood Craft Inc	E	216 738-2222
Brunswick (G-2229)		
Queen City Pallets Inc	E	513 821-6700
Cincinnati (G-4239)		
R C Family Wood Products	G	937 295-2393
Fort Loramie (G-9802)		
Raber Lumber Co	G	330 893-2797
Charm (G-3142)		
Russell L Garber	F	937 548-6224
Greenville (G-10394)		
S & M Products	G	419 272-2054
Blakeslee (G-1697)		
Schaefer Box & Pallet Co	E	513 738-2500
Hamilton (G-10603)		
Schrock John	G	937 544-8457
West Union (G-19966)		
Sealco Inc	G	740 922-4122
Uhrichsville (G-18893)		
Shaw Pallets & Specialties	G	740 498-7892
Newcomerstown (G-14981)		
Silvesco Inc	F	740 373-6661
Marietta (G-12669)		
Slats and Nails Inc	G	330 866-1008
East Sparta (G-9095)		
Southeast Ohio Timber Pdts Co	G	740 344-2570
Zanesville (G-21181)		
Southern Ohio Lumber LLC	E	614 436-4472
Peebles (G-15882)		
Specialty Pallet & Design Ltd	E	330 857-0257
Orrville (G-15624)		
Sterling Industries Inc	F	419 523-3788
Ottawa (G-15666)		
Stony Point Hardwoods	F	330 852-4512
Sugarcreek (G-17865)		
Stumptown Lbr Pallet Mills Ltd	G	740 757-2275
Somerton (G-17269)		
Swp Legacy Ltd	D	330 340-9663
Sugarcreek (G-17871)		
T & D Thompson Inc	E	740 332-8515
Laurelville (G-11627)		
Terry Lumber and Supply Co	F	330 659-6800
Peninsula (G-15899)		
Thomas J Weaver Inc	F	740 622-2040
Coshocton (G-7755)		
Timber Products Inc	E	440 693-4098
Middlefield (G-13858)		
Tolson Pallet Mfg Inc	F	937 787-3511
Gratis (G-10340)		
Traveling & Recycle Wood Pdts	F	419 968-2649
Middle Point (G-13757)		
Tri State Pallet Inc	G	937 323-5210
Springfield (G-17509)		
Valley View Pallets LLC	G	740 599-0010
Danville (G-7966)		
Van Orders Pallet Company Inc	F	419 875-6932
Swanton (G-17928)		
Weaver Pallet Ltd	E	330 682-4022
Apple Creek (G-623)		
Winesburg Hardwood Lumber Co	E	330 893-2705
Dundee (G-9033)		
Woodford Logistics	D	513 417-8453
South Charleston (G-17274)		
Yoder Lumber Co Inc	D	330 893-3121
Millersburg (G-14153)		
Zanesville Pallet Co Inc	G	740 454-3700
Zanesville (G-21193)		

PAN GLAZING SVC

Company	Code	Phone
Russell T Bundy Associates Inc	E	419 526-4454
Mansfield (G-12509)		

PANEL & DISTRIBUTION BOARDS & OTHER RELATED APPARATUS

Company	Code	Phone
Acorn Technology Corporation	E	216 663-1244
Cleveland (G-4610)		
Eaton Electric Holdings LLC	B	440 523-5000
Cleveland (G-5151)		
Hosler Maps Inc	G	937 855-4173
Germantown (G-10242)		
Jeff Bonham Electric Inc	E	937 233-7662
Dayton (G-8282)		

PANEL & DISTRIBUTION BOARDS: Electric

Company	Code	Phone
Assembly Works Inc	G	419 433-5010
Huron (G-11090)		
Industrial Solutions Inc	E	614 431-8118
Lewis Center (G-11762)		
Osborne Coinage Company	D	513 681-5424
Cincinnati (G-4120)		
Spectra-Tech Manufacturing Inc	E	513 735-9300
Batavia (G-1186)		

PANELS & SECTIONS: Prefabricated, Concrete

Company	Code	Phone
Aetna Plastics Corp	G	330 274-2855
Mantua (G-12541)		

PANELS: Building, Metal

Company	Code	Phone
Otter Group LLC	F	937 315-1199
Dayton (G-8410)		

PANELS: Building, Plastic, NEC

Company	Code	Phone
Clearsonic Manufacturing Inc	G	828 772-9809
Hudson (G-11037)		
Fiberglass Technology Inds Inc	G	740 335-9400
Wshngtn CT Hs (G-20726)		
Remram Recovery LLC	F	740 667-0092
Tuppers Plains (G-18720)		
Tema Isenmann Inc	G	859 252-0613
Cincinnati (G-4412)		

PANELS: Building, Wood

Company	Code	Phone
Premier Construction Company	E	513 874-2611
Fairfield (G-9550)		

PAPER & BOARD: Die-cut

Company	Code	Phone
A G Ruff Paper Specialties Co	G	513 891-7990
Blue Ash (G-1718)		
A H Pelz Co	G	216 861-1882
Cleveland (G-4589)		
Art Guild Binders Inc	E	513 242-3000
Cincinnati (G-3358)		
Buckeye Boxes Inc	C	614 274-8484
Columbus (G-6707)		
Chilcote Company	C	216 781-6000
Cleveland (G-4922)		
Commercial Cutng Graphics LLC	D	419 526-4800
Mansfield (G-12427)		
Consuetudo Abscisum Inc	G	419 281-8002
Ashland (G-697)		
Cornerstone Indus Holdings	G	440 893-9144
Chagrin Falls (G-3014)		

Employee Codes: A=Over 500 employees, B=251-500 C=101-250, D=51-100, E=20-50, F=10-19, G=3-9

PAPER & BOARD: Die-cut

D A Stirling Inc .... G 330 923-3195
  Cuyahoga Falls (G-7857)
Georgia-Pacific LLC .... C 740 477-3347
  Circleville (G-4546)
Harris Paper Crafts Inc .... F 614 299-2141
  Columbus (G-6983)
Honeymoon Paper Products Inc .... D 513 755-7200
  Fairfield (G-9505)
Hunt Products Inc .... E 440 667-2457
  Newburgh Heights (G-14940)
Kent Adhesive Products Co .... D 330 678-1626
  Kent (G-11338)
Keyah International Trdg LLC .... E 937 399-3140
  Springfield (G-17431)
Lam Pro Inc .... F 216 426-0661
  Cleveland (G-5556)
McElroy Contract Packaging .... F 330 262-0855
  Wooster (G-20621)
Multi-Craft Litho Inc .... E 859 581-2754
  Blue Ash (G-1824)
Nordec Inc .... D 330 940-3700
  Stow (G-17615)
Paxar Corporation .... F 937 681-4541
  Dayton (G-8418)
Printers Bindery Services Inc .... D 513 821-8039
  Cincinnati (G-4192)
R W Michael Printing Co .... G 330 923-9277
  Akron (G-340)
Rohrer Corporation .... C 330 335-1541
  Wadsworth (G-19275)
Spencer-Walker Press Inc .... F 740 344-6110
  Newark (G-14920)
Springdot Inc .... D 513 542-4000
  Cincinnati (G-4365)
Stuart Company .... F 513 621-9462
  Cincinnati (G-4386)
Vya Inc .... E 513 772-5400
  Cincinnati (G-4485)

PAPER CONVERTING

American Paper Converting LLC .... F 419 729-4782
  Toledo (G-18178)
Buckeye Paper Co Inc .... E 330 477-5925
  Canton (G-2600)
Buschman Corporation .... F 216 431-6633
  Cleveland (G-4853)
Davidson Converting Inc .... G 330 626-2118
  Streetsboro (G-17669)
Fibercorr Mills LLC .... D 330 837-5151
  Massillon (G-12981)
Gemini Fiber Corporation .... F 330 874-4131
  Bolivar (G-1915)
Harris Paper Crafts Inc .... F 614 299-2141
  Columbus (G-6983)
Kent Adhesive Products Co .... D 330 678-1626
  Kent (G-11338)
Media Procurement Services Inc .... G 513 977-3000
  Cincinnati (G-3996)
Millcraft Group LLC .... D 216 441-5500
  Cleveland (G-5689)
Paper Systems Incorporated .... C 937 746-6841
  Springboro (G-17342)
Pmco LLC .... D 513 825-7626
  West Chester (G-19761)
Rivercor LLC .... E 330 784-1113
  Akron (G-350)
Saltbox Illustrations .... G 937 319-6434
  Yellow Springs (G-20815)
Signode Industrial Group LLC .... E 513 248-2990
  Loveland (G-12232)
Stumps Converting Inc .... F 419 492-2542
  New Washington (G-14833)
Van Deleigh Industries LLC .... G 419 467-2244
  Sylvania (G-17968)

PAPER MANUFACTURERS: Exc Newsprint

Appvion Operations Inc .... B 937 859-8261
  West Carrollton (G-19629)
Cheney Pulp and Paper Company .... E 937 746-9991
  Franklin (G-9874)
Domtar Paper Company LLC .... D 740 333-0003
  Wshngtn CT Hs (G-20723)
Essity Prof Hygiene N Amer LLC .... G 513 217-3644
  Middletown (G-13906)
Evergreen Packaging Inc .... G 440 235-7200
  Olmsted Falls (G-15530)
Georgia-Pacific LLC .... F 513 336-4200
  Mason (G-12877)
Georgia-Pacific LLC .... E 614 491-9100
  Columbus (G-6949)
Georgia-Pacific LLC .... C 330 794-4444
  Mogadore (G-14238)
Georgia-Pacific LLC .... E 513 942-4800
  West Chester (G-19715)
Graphic Packaging Intl LLC .... B 419 673-0711
  Kenton (G-11407)
Honey Cell Inc Mid West .... E 513 360-0280
  Monroe (G-14267)
International Paper Company .... F 937 456-4131
  Eaton (G-9154)
International Paper Company .... C 740 397-5215
  Mount Vernon (G-14483)
International Paper Company .... G 937 578-7718
  Marysville (G-12796)
International Paper Company .... C 800 473-0830
  Middletown (G-13916)
International Paper Company .... B 877 447-2737
  Milford (G-14018)
International Paper Company .... G 440 428-5116
  Madison (G-12351)
International Paper Company .... E 740 439-3527
  Byesville (G-2387)
International Paper Company .... G 513 248-6000
  Loveland (G-12201)
JMJ Paper Inc .... F 419 332-6675
  Fremont (G-10029)
Metro Recycling Company .... G 513 251-1800
  Cincinnati (G-4017)
Millcraft Paper Company .... G 216 429-9860
  Cleveland (G-5690)
Mohawk Fine Papers Inc .... E 440 969-2000
  Ashtabula (G-788)
Newpage Group Inc .... A 937 242-9500
  Miamisburg (G-13698)
Resolute FP US Inc .... B 216 961-3900
  Cleveland (G-5980)
Resolute FP US Inc .... B 614 443-6300
  Columbus (G-7388)
Resolute FP US Inc .... B 513 242-3671
  Cincinnati (G-4260)
Rumford Paper Company .... G 937 242-9230
  Miamisburg (G-13713)
Spinnaker Coatings .... G 937 332-6619
  Troy (G-18712)
Verso Corporation .... B 901 369-4100
  Miamisburg (G-13734)
Wausau Paper Corp .... C 513 217-3623
  Middletown (G-13965)
West Carrollton Converting Inc .... D 937 859-3621
  West Carrollton (G-19633)
Westrock Cp LLC .... B 740 622-0581
  Coshocton (G-7757)
Xpedx National Accounts .... E 513 870-0711
  West Chester (G-19917)

PAPER NAPKINS WHOLESALERS

Canton Sterilized Wiping Cloth .... G 330 455-5179
  Canton (G-2618)

PAPER PRDTS: Book Covers

Blue Ash Paper Sales LLC .... G 513 891-9544
  Blue Ash (G-1736)
Unique Covers .... G 419 925-9600
  Maria Stein (G-12601)

PAPER PRDTS: Infant & Baby Prdts

Hygient Corporation .... G 440 796-7964
  Cleveland (G-5431)
Kimberly-Clark Corporation .... C 513 864-3780
  Cincinnati (G-3909)
Kimberly-Clark Corporation .... C 513 794-1005
  West Chester (G-19730)
Qpi Cincinnati LLC .... G 513 755-2670
  West Chester (G-19772)
Sposie LLC .... F 888 977-2229
  Maumee (G-13148)

PAPER PRDTS: Napkins, Made From Purchased Materials

Tri Con Distribution LLC .... G 937 399-3312
  Springfield (G-17508)

PAPER PRDTS: Napkins, Sanitary, Made From Purchased Material

Health Care Products Inc .... E 419 678-9620
  Coldwater (G-6411)
Procter & Gamble Far East Inc .... C 513 983-1100
  Cincinnati (G-4210)
Tranzonic Acquisition Corp .... A 216 535-4300
  Richmond Heights (G-16505)
Tranzonic Companies .... B 216 535-4300
  Richmond Heights (G-16507)
Tranzonic Companies .... C 216 535-4300
  Richmond Heights (G-16506)
Tranzonic Companies .... C 440 446-0643
  Cleveland (G-6198)

PAPER PRDTS: Sanitary

Fox Supply LLC .... G 419 628-3051
  Minster (G-14214)
Giant Industries Inc .... E 419 531-4600
  Toledo (G-18305)
Linsalata Capital Partners Fun .... G 440 684-1400
  Cleveland (G-5579)
Little Busy Bodies LLC .... E 513 351-5700
  Cincinnati (G-3948)
Playtex Manufacturing Inc .... D 937 498-4710
  Sidney (G-17059)
Procter Gamble Co .... C 513 698-7675
  Hamilton (G-10598)
Wausau Ppr Towel & Tissue LLC .... C 513 424-2999
  Middletown (G-13966)

PAPER PRDTS: Sanitary Tissue Paper

Kimberly-Clark Corporation .... C 513 864-3780
  Cincinnati (G-3909)
Kimberly-Clark Corporation .... C 513 794-1005
  West Chester (G-19730)

PAPER PRDTS: Tampons, Sanitary, Made From Purchased Material

Cbl Products .... G 216 321-2599
  Cleveland (G-4893)
Tambrands Sales Corp .... C 513 983-1100
  Cincinnati (G-4405)

PAPER PRDTS: Towels, Napkins/Tissue Paper, From Purchd Mtrls

Aci Industries Converting Ltd .... E 740 368-4160
  Delaware (G-8649)
Novex Products Incorporated .... E 440 244-3330
  Lorain (G-12109)
PGT Healthcare LLP .... G 513 983-1100
  Cincinnati (G-4156)
Procter & Gamble Company .... B 513 983-1100
  Cincinnati (G-4198)
Procter & Gamble Company .... C 513 983-1100
  Cincinnati (G-4199)
Procter & Gamble Company .... E 513 266-4375
  Cincinnati (G-4200)
Procter & Gamble Company .... E 513 871-7557
  Cincinnati (G-4201)
Procter & Gamble Company .... B 419 998-5891
  Lima (G-11920)
Procter & Gamble Company .... F 513 482-6789
  Cincinnati (G-4203)
Procter & Gamble Company .... B 513 672-4044
  West Chester (G-19767)
Procter & Gamble Company .... B 513 627-7115
  Cincinnati (G-4205)
Procter & Gamble Company .... C 513 634-9600
  West Chester (G-19768)
Procter & Gamble Company .... C 513 634-9110
  West Chester (G-19769)
Procter & Gamble Company .... C 513 934-3406
  Oregonia (G-15573)
Procter & Gamble Company .... C 513 627-7779
  Cincinnati (G-4207)
Procter & Gamble Company .... B 513 945-0340
  Cincinnati (G-4208)
Procter & Gamble Company .... C 513 622-1000
  Mason (G-12926)
Procter & Gamble Paper Pdts Co .... F 513 983-1100
  Cincinnati (G-4213)

PAPER PRDTS: Wrappers, Blank, Made From Purchased Materials

Btw LLC .... G 419 382-4443
  Toledo (G-18217)

PRODUCT SECTION

PAPER, WHOLESALE: Printing

Marco Printed Products Co Inc ....G....... 937 433-5680
  Dayton *(G-8333)*
Millcraft Group LLC ....D....... 216 441-5500
  Cleveland *(G-5689)*

PAPER: Adding Machine Rolls, Made From Purchased Materials

Jr Kennel Mfg ....G....... 937 780-6104
  Leesburg *(G-11711)*

PAPER: Adhesive

Ameri-Cal Corporation ....F....... 330 725-7735
  Medina *(G-13223)*
Avery Dennison Corporation ....C....... 440 358-4691
  Painesville *(G-15715)*
Avery Dennison Corporation ....B....... 440 358-3700
  Painesville *(G-15716)*
Avery Dennison Corporation ....G....... 216 267-8700
  Cleveland *(G-4775)*
Avery Dennison Corporation ....D....... 440 358-3408
  Painesville *(G-15717)*
Bollin & Sons Inc ....E....... 419 693-6573
  Toledo *(G-18210)*
CCL Label Inc ....C....... 216 676-2703
  Cleveland *(G-4894)*
CCL Label Inc ....E....... 440 878-7000
  Brunswick *(G-2194)*
GBS Corp ....C....... 330 863-1828
  Malvern *(G-12391)*
ID Images LLC ....D....... 330 220-7300
  Brunswick *(G-2215)*
Kent Adhesive Products Co ....D....... 330 678-1626
  Kent *(G-11338)*
Miller Studio Inc ....D....... 330 339-1100
  New Philadelphia *(G-14787)*
Morgan Adhesives Company LLC ....B....... 330 688-1111
  Stow *(G-17606)*
Stretchtape Inc ....E....... 216 486-9400
  Cleveland *(G-6107)*
Technicote Inc ....E....... 800 358-4448
  Miamisburg *(G-13724)*
Technicote Westfield Inc ....D....... 937 859-4448
  Miamisburg *(G-13725)*

PAPER: Art

Honeycomb Midwest ....E....... 513 360-0280
  Monroe *(G-14268)*

PAPER: Book

P H Glatfelter Company ....D....... 740 772-3111
  Chillicothe *(G-3204)*

PAPER: Building, Insulating & Packaging

Avery Dennison Corporation ....C....... 440 358-4691
  Painesville *(G-15715)*

PAPER: Building, Insulation

Owens Corning Sales LLC ....D....... 614 399-3915
  Mount Vernon *(G-14497)*

PAPER: Cardboard

Derby Fabg Solutions LLC ....E....... 937 498-4054
  Sidney *(G-17027)*
Valley Converting Co Inc ....E....... 740 537-2152
  Toronto *(G-18614)*

PAPER: Chemically Treated, Made From Purchased Materials

Oliver Products Company ....F....... 513 860-6880
  Hamilton *(G-10593)*

PAPER: Cloth, Lined, Made From Purchased Materials

Tekni-Plex Inc ....E....... 419 491-2399
  Holland *(G-10960)*

PAPER: Coated & Laminated, NEC

21st Century Printers Inc ....G....... 513 771-4150
  Cincinnati *(G-3268)*
3 Sigma LLC ....D....... 937 440-3400
  Troy *(G-18632)*
Adcraft Decals Inc ....E....... 216 524-2934
  Cleveland *(G-4615)*
Admiral Products Company Inc ....E....... 216 671-0600
  Cleveland *(G-4619)*
Ahlstrom West Carrollton LLC ....C....... 937 859-3621
  Dayton *(G-8011)*
All-Seasons Paper Company ....E....... 440 826-1700
  Cleveland *(G-4668)*
Avery Dennison ....F....... 937 865-2439
  Miamisburg *(G-13642)*
Avery Dennison Corporation ....E....... 440 358-3466
  Painesville *(G-15714)*
Avery Dennison Corporation ....G....... 440 534-6527
  Mentor *(G-13396)*
Bemis Company Inc ....E....... 419 334-9465
  Fremont *(G-9996)*
Bemis Company Inc ....E....... 330 923-5281
  Akron *(G-83)*
CCL Label Inc ....B....... 440 878-7277
  Strongsville *(G-17724)*
Central Coated Products Inc ....D....... 330 821-9830
  Alliance *(G-462)*
Deco Tools Inc ....E....... 419 476-9321
  Toledo *(G-18256)*
Dermamed Coatin ....G....... 330 474-3786
  Kent *(G-11313)*
Gary I Teach Jr ....G....... 614 582-7483
  London *(G-12060)*
GBS Corp ....E....... 330 929-8050
  Stow *(G-17591)*
Giesecke & Devrient Amer Inc ....C....... 330 425-1515
  Twinsburg *(G-18785)*
Giesecke+devrient ....F....... 330 405-8442
  Twinsburg *(G-18787)*
Hall Company ....E....... 937 652-1376
  Urbana *(G-18992)*
Kardol Quality Products LLC ....E....... 513 933-8206
  Blue Ash *(G-1800)*
Label Technique Southeast LLC ....E....... 440 951-7660
  Willoughby *(G-20356)*
Lam Pro Inc ....F....... 216 426-0661
  Cleveland *(G-5556)*
Laminate Technologies Inc ....D....... 419 448-0812
  Tiffin *(G-18064)*
Loroco Industries Inc ....E....... 513 891-9544
  Blue Ash *(G-1807)*
Marlen Manufacturing & Dev Co ....C....... 216 292-7546
  Bedford *(G-1425)*
Mr Label Inc ....E....... 513 681-2088
  Cincinnati *(G-4051)*
Newpage Holding Corporation ....G....... 877 855-7243
  Miamisburg *(G-13699)*
Nilpeter Usa Inc ....C....... 513 489-4400
  Cincinnati *(G-4080)*
Novolex Holdings Inc ....D....... 740 397-2555
  Mount Vernon *(G-14496)*
Ohio Laminating & Binding Inc ....E....... 614 771-4868
  Hilliard *(G-10846)*
P H Glatfelter Company ....D....... 419 333-6700
  Fremont *(G-10043)*
Paxar Corporation ....F....... 937 681-4541
  Dayton *(G-8418)*
Pilot Production Solutions LLC ....G....... 513 602-1467
  Mason *(G-12921)*
R R Donnelley & Sons Company ....E....... 440 774-2101
  Oberlin *(G-15504)*
Roemer Industries Inc ....D....... 330 448-2000
  Masury *(G-13062)*
Sensical Inc ....E....... 216 641-1141
  Solon *(G-17229)*
Superior Label Systems Inc ....B....... 513 336-0825
  Mason *(G-12944)*
The Rubber Stamp Shop ....G....... 419 478-4444
  Toledo *(G-18549)*
Thomas Products Co Inc ....E....... 513 756-9009
  Cincinnati *(G-4420)*
Waytek Corporation ....E....... 937 743-6142
  Franklin *(G-9932)*

PAPER: Coated, Exc Photographic, Carbon Or Abrasive

Appvion Operations Inc ....B....... 937 859-8261
  West Carrollton *(G-19629)*
Troy Laminating & Coating Inc ....D....... 937 335-5611
  Troy *(G-18714)*

PAPER: Enameled, Made From Purchased Materials

Coating Applications Intl LLC ....G....... 513 956-5222
  Cincinnati *(G-3534)*

PAPER: Fine

Blue Ridge Paper Products Inc ....C....... 440 235-7200
  Olmsted Falls *(G-15529)*
Newpage Holding Corporation ....G....... 877 855-7243
  Miamisburg *(G-13699)*
Smart Papers Holdings LLC ....C....... 513 869-5583
  Hamilton *(G-10606)*
Verso Paper Holding LLC ....B....... 877 855-7243
  Miamisburg *(G-13735)*

PAPER: Gummed, Made From Purchased Materials

Thomas Tape and Supply Company ....F....... 937 325-6414
  Springfield *(G-17505)*

PAPER: Milk Filter

Ken AG Inc ....E....... 419 281-1204
  Ashland *(G-718)*

PAPER: Newsprint

B & B Paper Converters Inc ....F....... 216 941-8100
  Cleveland *(G-4782)*

PAPER: Packaging

Ampac Plastics LLC ....B....... 513 671-1777
  Cincinnati *(G-3342)*
Duracorp LLC ....D....... 740 549-3336
  Lewis Center *(G-11758)*
Graphic Paper Products Corp ....D....... 937 325-5503
  Springfield *(G-17407)*
JMJ Paper Inc ....F....... 216 941-8100
  Avon Lake *(G-990)*

PAPER: Parchment

Ahlstrom West Carrollton LLC ....C....... 937 859-3621
  Dayton *(G-8011)*

PAPER: Printer

Eagle Wright Innovations Inc ....G....... 937 640-8093
  Moraine *(G-14348)*
Kn8designs LLC ....G....... 859 380-5926
  Cincinnati *(G-3918)*
Transmit Identity LLC ....G....... 330 576-4732
  Stow *(G-17636)*
Verso Corporation ....D....... 901 369-4105
  Miamisburg *(G-13733)*

PAPER: Specialty

T J Target ....G....... 330 658-3057
  Doylestown *(G-8867)*
Verso Corporation ....B....... 877 855-7243
  Miamisburg *(G-13732)*

PAPER: Specialty Or Chemically Treated

Gvs Industries Inc ....G....... 513 851-3606
  Hamilton *(G-10565)*

PAPER: Tissue

Novolex Holdings Inc ....D....... 740 397-2555
  Mount Vernon *(G-14496)*
Novolex Holdings Inc ....B....... 937 746-1933
  Franklin *(G-9905)*

PAPER: Wallpaper

Mini Graphics Inc ....G....... 513 563-8600
  Cincinnati *(G-4030)*

PAPER: Waterproof

Quest Solutions Group LLC ....G....... 513 703-4520
  Liberty Township *(G-11818)*

PAPER: Waxed, Made From Purchased Materials

Novolex Holdings Inc ....D....... 740 397-2555
  Mount Vernon *(G-14496)*

PAPER: Wrapping

Plus Mark LLC .... E 216 252-6770
  Cleveland (G-5891)

PAPER: Wrapping & Packaging

Hanchett Paper Company .... D 513 782-4440
  Cincinnati (G-3796)
Polymer Packaging Inc .... D 330 832-2000
  Massillon (G-13040)
Welch Packaging Group Inc .... C 614 870-2000
  Columbus (G-7597)
Westrock Cp LLC .... C 937 898-2115
  Dayton (G-8589)
Westrock Cp LLC .... B 513 745-2586
  Cincinnati (G-4504)

PAPERBOARD

Ball Corporation .... D 330 244-2800
  Canton (G-2584)
Buckeye Boxes Inc .... C 614 274-8484
  Columbus (G-6707)
Caraustar Industries Inc .... E 614 529-5535
  Columbus (G-6737)
Caraustar Industries Inc .... E 513 871-7112
  Cincinnati (G-3441)
Caraustar Industries Inc .... F 216 939-3001
  Cleveland (G-4874)
Caraustar Industries Inc .... D 740 862-4167
  Baltimore (G-1037)
Churmac Industries Inc .... E 740 773-5800
  Chillicothe (G-3182)
Corpad Company Inc .... D 419 522-7818
  Mansfield (G-12429)
Fibercorr Mills LLC .... D 330 837-5151
  Massillon (G-12981)
G S K Inc .... G 937 547-1611
  Greenville (G-10371)
Georgia-Pacific LLC .... C 740 477-3347
  Circleville (G-4546)
Greif Paper Packg & Svcs LLC .... D 740 549-6000
  Delaware (G-8689)
International Paper Company .... C 740 383-4061
  Marion (G-12713)
International Paper Company .... C 740 363-9882
  Delaware (G-8696)
Loroco Industries Inc .... E 513 891-9544
  Blue Ash (G-1807)
Martin Paper Products Inc .... E 740 756-9271
  Carroll (G-2907)
Miami Valley Paper LLC .... F 937 746-6451
  Franklin (G-9900)
National Bias Fabric Co .... E 216 361-0530
  Cleveland (G-5722)
Norse Dairy Systems Inc .... C 614 294-4931
  Columbus (G-7224)
P & R Specialty Inc .... E 937 773-0263
  Piqua (G-16147)
Pactiv LLC .... C 614 771-5400
  Columbus (G-7285)
Safeway Packaging Inc .... D 419 629-3200
  New Bremen (G-14660)
Sonoco Products Company .... C 330 688-8247
  Munroe Falls (G-14527)
Sonoco Products Company .... D 740 927-2525
  Johnstown (G-11271)
Sonoco Products Company .... E 614 759-8470
  Columbus (G-7462)
Valley Converting Co Inc .... D 740 537-2152
  Toronto (G-18615)
Westrock Cp LLC .... E 614 445-6850
  Columbus (G-7601)
Westrock Mwv LLC .... C 937 495-6323
  Kettering (G-11443)

PAPERBOARD CONVERTING

Caraustar Industries Inc .... F 216 961-5060
  Cleveland (G-4873)
Caraustar Industries Inc .... E 330 665-7700
  Copley (G-7679)
Corrchoice Inc .... D 330 833-5705
  Massillon (G-12970)
E-Z Grader Company .... G 440 247-7511
  Chagrin Falls (G-3017)
Formica Corporation .... E 513 786-3400
  Cincinnati (G-3705)
Oak Hills Carton Co .... E 513 948-4200
  Cincinnati (G-4095)

Ohio Packaging .... E 330 833-2884
  Massillon (G-13031)
Outhouse Paper Etc Inc .... G 937 382-2800
  Waynesville (G-19570)
Paper Service Inc .... F 330 227-3546
  Lisbon (G-11978)
Roberds Converting Co Inc .... E 513 683-6667
  Loveland (G-12227)
Vemuri International LLC .... C 513 483-6300
  Cincinnati (G-4471)

PAPERBOARD PRDTS: Container Board

Westrock Converting Company .... C 513 860-0225
  West Chester (G-19820)

PAPERBOARD PRDTS: Folding Boxboard

Caraustar Industries Inc .... E 330 665-7700
  Copley (G-7679)
Custom Aluminum Boxes .... G 440 864-2664
  Amherst (G-560)
Folding Carton Service Inc .... F 419 281-4099
  Ashland (G-705)
Graphic Packaging Intl Inc .... C 513 424-4200
  Middletown (G-13911)
Graphic Packaging Intl Inc .... C 440 248-4370
  Solon (G-17153)
Smith-Lustig Paper Box Mfg Co ...... E 216 621-0453
  Bedford (G-1446)

PAPERBOARD PRDTS: Packaging Board

Graphic Packaging Intl Inc .... D 937 372-8001
  Xenia (G-20775)
Thorwald Holdings Inc .... E 740 756-9271
  Lancaster (G-11613)

PAPERBOARD PRDTS: Specialty Board

Third Party Service Ltd .... F 419 872-2312
  Perrysburg (G-16015)

PAPERBOARD PRDTS: Stencil Board

Quilting Creations Intl .... E 330 874-4741
  Bolivar (G-1926)

PAPERBOARD: Corrugated

Westrock Cp LLC .... B 740 622-0581
  Coshocton (G-7757)

PAPETERIES & WRITING PAPER SETS

Selco Industries Inc .... C 419 861-0336
  Holland (G-10957)

PARKING GARAGE

Youngstown Letter Shop Inc .... G 330 793-4935
  Youngstown (G-21079)

PARKING METERS

Parking & Traffic Control SEC .... F 440 243-7565
  Cleveland (G-5851)

PARTICLEBOARD: Laminated, Plastic

Amerilam Laminating .... G 440 235-4687
  Cleveland (G-4700)
Miller Manufacturing Inc .... E 330 852-0689
  Sugarcreek (G-17854)
Wico Products Inc .... G 937 783-0000
  Blanchester (G-1708)

PARTITIONS & FIXTURES: Except Wood

3-D Technical Services Company ... E 937 746-2901
  Franklin (G-9866)
Accel Group Inc .... D 330 336-0317
  Wadsworth (G-19220)
B-R-O-T Incorporated .... E 216 267-5335
  Cleveland (G-4786)
Benko Products Inc .... E 440 934-2180
  Sheffield Village (G-16966)
Bud Industries Inc .... G 440 946-3200
  Willoughby (G-20289)
Cdc Corporation .... D 715 532-5548
  Maumee (G-13081)
Component Systems Inc .... E 216 252-9292
  Cleveland (G-5012)
Control Electric Co .... E 216 671-8010
  Columbia Station (G-6434)

Conwed Designscape .... F 715 532-5548
  Maumee (G-13083)
Crescent Metal Products Inc .... C 440 350-1100
  Mentor (G-13426)
Custom Millcraft Corp .... E 513 874-7080
  West Chester (G-19690)
Display Dynamics Inc .... F 937 832-2830
  Englewood (G-9355)
Environmental Wall Systems .... G 440 542-6600
  Hudson (G-11043)
Gallo Displays Inc .... E 216 431-9500
  Cleveland (G-5288)
Gwp Holdings Inc .... D 513 860-4050
  Fairfield (G-9501)
HP Manufacturing Company Inc ...... D 216 361-6500
  Cleveland (G-5421)
Idx Dayton LLC .... C 937 401-3460
  Dayton (G-8260)
Integral Design Inc .... F 216 524-0555
  Cleveland (G-5462)
Intelitool Manufacturing Svcs .... G 440 953-1071
  Willoughby (G-20344)
Kellogg Cabinets Inc .... G 614 833-9596
  Canal Winchester (G-2504)
Marlite Inc .... C 330 343-6621
  Dover (G-8837)
Marlite Inc .... C 330 343-6621
  Dover (G-8838)
Midmark Corporation .... A 937 526-3662
  Kettering (G-11434)
Modern Retail Solutions LLC .... E 330 527-4308
  Garrettsville (G-10199)
Mro Built Inc .... D 330 526-0555
  North Canton (G-15104)
Myers Industries Inc .... C 330 336-6621
  Wadsworth (G-19255)
Ohio Displays Inc .... F 216 961-5600
  Elyria (G-9303)
Organized Living Inc .... E 513 489-9300
  Cincinnati (G-4118)
Panacea Products Corporation .... E 614 850-7000
  Columbus (G-7287)
Panacea Products Corporation .... D 614 429-6320
  Columbus (G-7288)
Pfi Displays Inc .... E 330 925-9015
  Rittman (G-16527)
Pucel Enterprises Inc .... D 216 881-4604
  Cleveland (G-5933)
Rack Processing Company Inc .... E 937 294-1911
  Moraine (G-14387)
Stanley Industrial & Auto LLC .... C 614 755-7089
  Westerville (G-20024)
Sunrise Cooperative Inc .... E 419 683-4600
  Crestline (G-7801)
Ternion Inc .... E 216 642-6180
  Cleveland (G-6161)
Valley Plastics Company Inc .... F 419 666-2349
  Toledo (G-18588)
W B Becherer Inc .... G 330 758-6616
  Youngstown (G-21068)
W J Egli Company Inc .... F 330 823-3666
  Alliance (G-512)
Witt-Gor Inc .... G 419 659-2151
  Columbus Grove (G-7639)

PARTITIONS WHOLESALERS

Door Fabrication Services Inc .... E 937 454-9207
  Vandalia (G-19123)
Partitions Plus LLC .... F 419 422-2600
  Findlay (G-9740)
Tri-State Supply Co Inc .... F 614 272-6767
  Columbus (G-7543)

PARTITIONS: Nonwood, Floor Attached

Mills Company .... E 740 375-0770
  Marion (G-12720)
Tri County Tarp LLC .... E 419 288-3350
  Bradner (G-2016)

PARTITIONS: Solid Fiber, Made From Purchased Materials

Cole Pak Inc .... D 937 652-3910
  Urbana (G-18984)

PARTITIONS: Wood & Fixtures

A & J Woodworking Inc .... G 419 695-5655
  Delphos (G-8734)

PRODUCT SECTION

Accent Manufacturing Inc .... F 330 724-7704
  Norton (G-15355)
Action Group Inc .... D 614 868-8868
  Blacklick (G-1676)
Amtekco Industries Inc .... G 614 228-6525
  Columbus (G-6597)
Andy Raber .... G 740 622-1386
  Fresno (G-10066)
As America Inc .... E 419 522-4211
  Mansfield (G-12408)
Automated Bldg Components Inc .... E 419 257-2152
  North Baltimore (G-15042)
Brower Products Inc .... D 937 563-1111
  Cincinnati (G-3426)
Creative Products Inc .... E 419 866-5501
  Holland (G-10920)
D Lewis Inc .... G 740 695-2615
  Saint Clairsville (G-16630)
Diversified Products & Svcs .... C 740 393-6202
  Mount Vernon (G-14478)
Fleetwood Custom Countertops .... F 740 965-9833
  Johnstown (G-11265)
Forum III Inc .... F 513 961-5123
  Cincinnati (G-3706)
Geograph Industries Inc .... E 513 202-9200
  Harrison (G-10643)
Home Stor & Off Solutions Inc .... F 216 362-4660
  Cleveland (G-5414)
Kitchens By Rutenschroer Inc .... F 513 251-8333
  Cincinnati (G-3914)
LE Smith Company .... D 419 636-4555
  Bryan (G-2295)
Lima Millwork Inc .... E 419 331-3303
  Elida (G-9195)
Partitions Plus LLC .... F 419 422-2600
  Findlay (G-9740)
Reserve Millwork Inc .... E 216 531-6982
  Bedford (G-1441)
Riceland Cabinet Inc .... D 330 601-1071
  Wooster (G-20644)
Symatic Inc .... E 330 225-1510
  Brunswick (G-2243)
Thomas Cabinet Shop Inc .... F 937 847-8239
  Dayton (G-8554)
Trumbull Industries Inc .... E 330 434-6174
  Akron (G-413)
Wine Cellar Innovations LLC .... C 513 321-3733
  Cincinnati (G-4513)
Xxx Intrntional Amusements Inc .... E 216 671-6900
  Cleveland (G-6332)

PARTS: Metal

Allpass Corporation .... F 440 998-6300
  Madison (G-12339)
Centerline Machine Inc .... G 937 322-4887
  Springfield (G-17372)
Cleveland Steel Specialty Co .... E 216 464-9400
  Bedford Heights (G-1466)
Clifton Steel Company .... D 216 662-6111
  Maple Heights (G-12569)
Diller Metals Inc .... G 419 943-3364
  Leipsic (G-11725)
Netshape Technologies Mim Inc .... F 440 248-5456
  Solon (G-17206)
Plastran Inc .... G 440 237-8404
  Cleveland (G-5888)
Strohecker Incorporated .... E 330 426-9496
  East Palestine (G-9085)

PARTY & SPECIAL EVENT PLANNING SVCS

Adyl Inc .... G 330 797-8700
  Austintown (G-928)

PASTES, FLAVORING

Sensus LLC .... F 513 892-7100
  Fairfield Township (G-9585)

PASTES: Metal

Ferro Corporation .... D 216 875-5600
  Mayfield Heights (G-13163)

PATIENT MONITORING EQPT WHOLESALERS

Neurowave Systems Inc .... G 216 361-1591
  Cleveland (G-5745)

PATTERNS: Indl

7 Rowe Court Properties LLC .... G 513 874-7236
  Hamilton (G-10526)
Air Power Dynamics LLC .... C 440 701-2100
  Mentor (G-13377)
Anchor Pattern Company .... G 614 443-2221
  Columbus (G-6601)
Anger Pattern Company Inc .... G 330 882-6519
  Clinton (G-6383)
API Pattern Works Inc .... E 440 269-1766
  Willoughby (G-20274)
Boko Patterns Models & Molds .... G 937 426-9667
  Beavercreek (G-1352)
Cascade Pattern Company Inc .... E 440 323-4300
  Elyria (G-9231)
Clinton Foundry Ltd .... F 419 243-6885
  Toledo (G-18234)
Clinton Pattern Works Inc .... F 419 243-0855
  Toledo (G-18235)
Colonial Patterns Inc .... E 330 673-6475
  Kent (G-11306)
Consolidated Pattern Works Inc .... G 330 434-6060
  Akron (G-120)
Dayton Pattern Inc .... G 937 277-0761
  Dayton (G-8140)
Design Pattern Works Inc .... G 937 252-0797
  Dayton (G-8157)
Design Tech Inc .... G 937 254-7000
  Dayton (G-8158)
Elyria Pattern Co Inc .... G 440 323-1526
  Elyria (G-9254)
Feiner Pattern Works Inc .... F 513 851-9800
  Cincinnati (G-3681)
Foster Pattern Works Inc .... G 330 482-3612
  Columbiana (G-6466)
Freeman Manufacturing & Sup Co .... E 440 934-1902
  Avon (G-950)
Geotech Pattern & Mold Inc .... G 513 683-2600
  Loveland (G-12191)
Glazier Pattern & Coach .... G 937 492-7355
  Houston (G-10994)
H&M Machine & Tool LLC .... E 419 776-9220
  Toledo (G-18316)
Hynes Modern Pattern Co Inc .... G 937 322-3451
  Springfield (G-17424)
Industrial Pattern & Mfg Co .... F 614 252-0934
  Columbus (G-7024)
J-Lenco Inc .... D 740 499-2260
  Morral (G-14404)
Ketco Inc .... E 937 426-9331
  Beavercreek (G-1324)
Kohl Patterns .... G 513 353-3831
  Cleves (G-6368)
Lesleys Patterns Ltd .... G 937 554-4674
  Vandalia (G-19132)
Liberty Pattern and Mold Inc .... G 330 788-9463
  Youngstown (G-20959)
Lisbon Pattern Limited .... G 330 424-7676
  Lisbon (G-11975)
Lorain Modern Pattern Inc .... F 440 365-6780
  Elyria (G-9288)
Maumee Pattern Company .... E 419 693-4968
  Toledo (G-18403)
Model Engineering Company .... G 330 644-3450
  Barberton (G-1087)
Mount Union Pattern Works Inc .... G 330 821-2274
  Alliance (G-492)
R L Rush Tool & Pattern Inc .... G 419 562-9849
  Bucyrus (G-2342)
Reliable Pattern Works Inc .... G 440 232-8820
  Cleveland (G-5972)
Ross Aluminum Castings LLC .... C 937 492-4134
  Sidney (G-17069)
Seaport Mold & Casting Company .... F 419 243-1422
  Toledo (G-18515)
Seaway Pattern Mfg Inc .... E 419 865-5724
  Toledo (G-18516)
Shells Inc .... D 330 808-5558
  Copley (G-7694)
Sherwood Rtm Corp .... G 330 875-7151
  Louisville (G-12166)
Spectracam Ltd .... G 937 223-3805
  Dayton (G-8516)
Tempcraft Corporation .... C 216 391-3885
  Cleveland (G-6157)
Th Manufacturing Inc .... G 330 893-3572
  Millersburg (G-14135)
Transducers Direct Llc .... F 513 247-0601
  Cincinnati (G-4431)
United States Drill Head Co .... E 513 941-0300
  Cincinnati (G-4450)
XI Pattern Shop Inc .... G 330 682-2981
  Orrville (G-15629)

PAVERS

Adairs Pavers .... G 937 454-9302
  Vandalia (G-19112)
Mead Paving .... G 937 322-7414
  Springfield (G-17444)

PAVING MATERIALS: Coal Tar, Not From Refineries

Star Seal of Ohio Inc .... G 614 870-1590
  Columbus (G-7487)

PAVING MATERIALS: Prefabricated, Concrete

Adler & Company Inc .... F 513 248-1500
  Cincinnati (G-3298)
P L M Corporation .... G 216 341-8008
  Cleveland (G-5831)
Pavestone LLC .... D 513 474-3783
  Cincinnati (G-4142)

PAVING MIXTURES

Ashland LLC .... G 513 557-3100
  Cincinnati (G-3361)
Specialty Technology & Res .... G 614 870-0744
  Columbus (G-7470)
Stoneco Inc .... G 419 693-3933
  Toledo (G-18531)

PAYROLL SVCS

Fields Associates Inc .... G 513 426-8652
  Cincinnati (G-3688)

PENCILS & PENS WHOLESALERS

Berea Hardwood Co Inc .... G 216 898-8956
  Cleveland (G-4804)

PENS & PARTS: Ball Point

Berea Hardwood Co Inc .... G 216 898-8956
  Cleveland (G-4804)

PENS & PENCILS: Mechanical, NEC

Bexley Pen Company Inc .... G 614 351-9988
  Columbus (G-6667)

PERFUME: Perfumes, Natural Or Synthetic

Aeroscena LLC .... F 800 671-1890
  Cleveland (G-4634)

PERIODICALS, WHOLESALE

Findaway World LLC .... D 440 893-0808
  Solon (G-17143)

PERSONAL APPEARANCE SVCS

Anderson Cosmetic & Vein Inst .... G 513 624-7900
  Cincinnati (G-3345)
D J Klingler Inc .... G 513 891-2284
  Cincinnati (G-3570)

PERSONAL CREDIT INSTITUTIONS: Financing, Autos, Furniture

Mtd Holdings Inc .... B 330 225-2600
  Valley City (G-19052)

PERSONAL DEVELOPMENT SCHOOL

Dialogue House Associates Inc .... G 216 342-5170
  Beachwood (G-1232)

PERSONAL SVCS, NEC

Tanning .... G 937 233-4554
  Dayton (G-8538)

PEST CONTROL IN STRUCTURES SVCS

A Best Trmt & Pest Ctrl Sups .... G 330 434-5555
  Akron (G-18)

Employee Codes: A=Over 500 employees, B=251-500
C=101-250, D=51-100, E=20-50, F=10-19, G=3-9

PEST CONTROL SVCS

PEST CONTROL SVCS
Scotts Miracle-Gro Company .... B 937 644-0011
  Marysville *(G-12810)*

PESTICIDES
Bird Control International .... E 330 425-2377
  Twinsburg *(G-18741)*
Mystic Chemical Products Co .... G 216 251-4416
  Cleveland *(G-5718)*

PESTICIDES WHOLESALERS
A Best Trmt & Pest Ctrl Sups .... G 330 434-5555
  Akron *(G-18)*

PET COLLARS, LEASHES, MUZZLES & HARNESSES: Leather
Cornerstone Brands Inc .... G 866 668-5962
  West Chester *(G-19684)*
Dog Depot .... G 513 771-9274
  Cincinnati *(G-3599)*
In Good Hlth & Animal Wellness .... G 330 908-1234
  Northfield *(G-15319)*
Tarahill Inc .... E 706 864-0808
  Columbus *(G-7511)*

PET SPLYS
Aquatic Technology .... F 440 236-8330
  Columbia Station *(G-6428)*
Bird Loft .... G 440 988-2473
  Amherst *(G-555)*
Boss Pet Products Inc .... F 216 332-0832
  Oakwood Village *(G-15478)*
Canine Creations .... G 937 667-8576
  Tipp City *(G-18105)*
City Dog .... G 614 228-3647
  Columbus *(G-6767)*
Condos and Trees LLC .... G 419 691-2287
  Northwood *(G-15335)*
Hartz Mountain Corporation .... D 513 877-2131
  Pleasant Plain *(G-16227)*
Miraclecorp Products .... D 937 293-9994
  Moraine *(G-14372)*
Ourpets Company .... E 440 354-6500
  Fairport Harbor *(G-9627)*
Slogans LLC .... G 330 942-9464
  Barberton *(G-1105)*

PET SPLYS WHOLESALERS
IAMS Company .... D 937 962-7782
  Lewisburg *(G-11793)*

PETROLEUM & PETROLEUM PRDTS, WHOLESALE Crude Oil
Echo Drilling Inc .... G 740 498-8560
  Newcomerstown *(G-14973)*

PETROLEUM & PETROLEUM PRDTS, WHOLESALE Diesel Fuel
Cac Energy Ltd .... G 937 867-5593
  Dayton *(G-8072)*
K2 Petroleum & Supply LLC .... G 937 503-2614
  Cincinnati *(G-3891)*

PETROLEUM & PETROLEUM PRDTS, WHOLESALE Engine Fuels & Oils
Sunrise Cooperative Inc .... F 419 628-4705
  Minster *(G-14225)*

PETROLEUM & PETROLEUM PRDTS, WHOLESALE Fuel Oil
D W Dickey and Son Inc .... D 330 424-1441
  Lisbon *(G-11966)*
Santmyer Oil Co of Ashland .... G 330 262-6501
  Wooster *(G-20648)*

PETROLEUM & PETROLEUM PRDTS, WHOLESALE: Bulk Stations
Cincinnati - Vulcan Company .... D 513 242-5300
  Cincinnati *(G-3477)*
New Vulco Mfg & Sales Co LLC .... D 513 242-2672
  Cincinnati *(G-4072)*

Universal Oil Inc .... E 216 771-4300
  Cleveland *(G-6239)*

PETROLEUM PRDTS WHOLESALERS
Bradner Oil Company Inc .... G 419 288-2945
  Wayne *(G-19560)*
Eni USA R & M Co Inc .... F 330 723-6457
  Medina *(G-13256)*
Grand Aire Inc .... E 419 861-6700
  Swanton *(G-17913)*
Koch Knight LLC .... D 330 488-1651
  East Canton *(G-9041)*
Polar Inc .... F 937 297-0911
  Moraine *(G-14380)*
Wallover Oil Company Inc .... F 440 238-9250
  Strongsville *(G-17805)*

PETS & PET SPLYS, WHOLESALE
Aquatic Technology .... F 440 236-8330
  Columbia Station *(G-6428)*

PEWTER WARE
Quantum Jewelry Dist .... E 330 678-2222
  Kent *(G-11371)*

PHARMACEUTICAL PREPARATIONS: Adrenal
American Regent Inc .... F 614 436-2222
  New Albany *(G-14604)*
American Regent Inc .... D 614 436-2222
  Columbus *(G-6586)*

PHARMACEUTICAL PREPARATIONS: Druggists' Preparations
Abbott Laboratories .... A 614 624-7677
  Columbus *(G-6521)*
Abbott Laboratories .... D 614 624-6627
  Columbus *(G-6522)*
Abbott Laboratories .... A 614 624-6627
  Columbus *(G-6523)*
Abbott Laboratories .... A 614 624-6088
  Columbus *(G-6525)*
Abbott Nutrition Mfg Inc .... F 614 624-7485
  Columbus *(G-6526)*
Bristol-Myers Squibb Company .... E 800 321-1335
  Columbus *(G-6489)*
CMC Pharmaceuticals Inc .... G 216 600-9430
  Cleveland *(G-4993)*
Flow Dry Technology Inc .... C 937 833-2161
  Brookville *(G-2168)*
Ftd Investments LLC .... C 937 833-2161
  Brookville *(G-2169)*
Hikma Labs Inc .... C 614 276-4000
  Columbus *(G-6999)*
Soleo Health Inc .... F 844 467-8200
  Dublin *(G-8993)*

PHARMACEUTICAL PREPARATIONS: Emulsions
Performanx Specialty Chem LLC .... G 614 300-7001
  Westerville *(G-20016)*
Polynt Composites USA Inc .... E 816 391-6000
  Sandusky *(G-16839)*

PHARMACEUTICAL PREPARATIONS: Medicines, Capsule Or Ampule
Adare Pharmaceuticals Inc .... C 937 898-9669
  Vandalia *(G-19113)*
Advanced Medical Solutions Inc .... G 937 291-0069
  Centerville *(G-2995)*
Aultwrks Occupational Medicine .... F 330 491-9675
  Canton *(G-2578)*
Buderer Drug Co .... G 419 626-3429
  Sandusky *(G-16798)*
Cabell Huntington .... G 740 867-2665
  Chesapeake *(G-3143)*
Casselberry Clinic Inc .... G 440 995-0555
  Cleveland *(G-4887)*
Dayton Laser & Aesthetic Medic .... G 937 208-8282
  Dayton *(G-8137)*

PHARMACEUTICAL PREPARATIONS: Pills
Ennovea LLC .... E 814 838-6664
  Columbus *(G-6898)*

PRODUCT SECTION

Sermonix Pharmaceuticals .... G 614 864-4919
  Columbus *(G-7439)*

PHARMACEUTICAL PREPARATIONS: Proprietary Drug PRDTS
Buderer Drug Company Inc .... F 419 627-2800
  Sandusky *(G-16799)*
Buderer Drug Company Inc .... F 419 873-2800
  Perrysburg *(G-15925)*
Buderer Drug Company Inc .... G 440 934-3100
  Avon *(G-943)*
Camargo Phrm Svcs LLC .... F 513 561-3329
  Blue Ash *(G-1746)*
Ferro Corporation .... D 216 875-5600
  Mayfield Heights *(G-13163)*

PHARMACEUTICAL PREPARATIONS: Solutions
Sara Wood Pharmaceuticals LLC .... G 513 833-5502
  Mason *(G-12936)*

PHARMACEUTICAL PREPARATIONS: Tablets
Exonanorna LLC .... G 614 928-3512
  Columbus *(G-6910)*

PHARMACEUTICALS
Abbott Laboratories .... F 614 624-3192
  Columbus *(G-6520)*
Abbott Laboratories .... D 800 551-5838
  Columbus *(G-6524)*
Abbott Laboratories .... A 614 624-3191
  Columbus *(G-6519)*
Abitec Corporation .... E 614 429-6464
  Columbus *(G-6527)*
Admiral Therapeutics LLC .... G 410 908-8906
  Shaker Heights *(G-16925)*
Aerpio Pharmaceuticals Inc .... G 513 985-1920
  Blue Ash *(G-1723)*
Affinity Therapeutics LLC .... G 216 224-9364
  Cleveland *(G-4639)*
Alkermes Inc .... E 937 382-5642
  Wilmington *(G-20485)*
Allergan Sales LLC .... C 513 271-6800
  Cincinnati *(G-3323)*
American Regent Inc .... D 614 436-2222
  Hilliard *(G-10804)*
Amerisourcebergen Corporation .... D 614 497-3665
  Lockbourne *(G-11992)*
Amerix Nutra-Pharma .... G 567 204-7756
  Lima *(G-11841)*
Amylin Ohio .... F 512 592-8710
  West Chester *(G-19643)*
Analiza Inc .... F 216 432-9050
  Cleveland *(G-4704)*
Andrew M Farnham .... G 419 298-4300
  Edgerton *(G-9168)*
Aprecia Pharmaceuticals LLC .... F 513 864-4107
  Blue Ash *(G-1729)*
Arth LLC .... G 513 293-1646
  West Chester *(G-19651)*
Athersys Inc .... D 216 431-9900
  Cleveland *(G-4759)*
Barr Laboratories Inc .... B 513 731-9900
  Cincinnati *(G-3380)*
Baxters LLC .... G 234 678-5484
  Akron *(G-81)*
Bellwyck Packg Solutions Inc .... G 513 874-1200
  West Chester *(G-19657)*
Bigmar Inc .... E 740 966-5800
  Johnstown *(G-11259)*
Biorx LLC .... C 866 442-4679
  Cincinnati *(G-3394)*
Bnoat Oncology .... G 330 285-2537
  Akron *(G-89)*
Bodyvega Nutrition LLC .... G 708 712-5743
  Akron *(G-91)*
Boehringer Ingelheim USA Corp .... F 440 232-3320
  Bedford *(G-1390)*
Boehrnger Inglheim Phrmcctcals .... G 440 286-5667
  Chardon *(G-3100)*
Bulk Molding Compounds Inc .... D 419 874-7941
  Perrysburg *(G-15926)*
Calcol Inc .... E 216 245-6301
  Shaker Heights *(G-16927)*
Caps .... G 216 524-0418
  Cleveland *(G-4872)*

Cardinal Health 414 LLC........C....... 614 757-5000
Dublin *(G-8895)*
Cardinal Health 414 LLC........G....... 513 759-1900
West Chester *(G-19664)*
Cardinal Health 414 LLC........G....... 614 473-0786
Columbus *(G-6742)*
Catalent Pharma Solutions LLC........G....... 614 757-4757
Dublin *(G-8897)*
Chester Labs Inc........E....... 513 458-3871
Cincinnati *(G-3468)*
Ddnews........G....... 440 331-6600
Rocky River *(G-16546)*
Diasome Pharmaceuticals Inc........G....... 216 444-7110
Cleveland *(G-5092)*
Dow Chemical Company........F....... 937 254-1550
Dayton *(G-8166)*
Eli Lilly and Company........G....... 937 855-3300
Germantown *(G-10241)*
Fluence Therapeutics........G....... 216 780-5220
Akron *(G-175)*
Forest Pharmaceuticals Inc........C....... 513 271-6800
Cincinnati *(G-3704)*
Forrest Pharmaceuticals........G....... 513 791-1701
Blue Ash *(G-1778)*
GE Healthcare Inc........G....... 502 452-4311
Solon *(G-17146)*
Gebauer Company........E....... 216 581-3030
Cleveland *(G-5299)*
Genoa Healthcare........G....... 740 370-0759
Portsmouth *(G-16283)*
Genoa Healthcare LLC........G....... 513 727-0471
Middletown *(G-13909)*
Genoa Healthcare LLC........G....... 567 202-8326
Toledo *(G-18304)*
Genoa Healthcare LLC........G....... 513 541-0164
Cincinnati *(G-3749)*
Glaxosmithkline LLC........E....... 937 623-2680
Columbus *(G-6953)*
Glaxosmithkline LLC........E....... 440 552-2895
North Ridgeville *(G-15227)*
Glaxosmithkline LLC........E....... 330 608-2365
Copley *(G-7685)*
Glaxosmithkline LLC........E....... 614 570-5970
Columbus *(G-6954)*
Glaxosmithkline LLC........E....... 330 241-4447
Medina *(G-13267)*
Hikma Pharmaceuticals USA Inc........G....... 732 542-1191
Lockbourne *(G-11994)*
Hikma Pharmaceuticals USA Inc........F....... 732 542-1191
Bedford *(G-1412)*
Independent Particle Labs........G....... 330 477-2016
Canton *(G-2707)*
Isp Chemicals LLC........D....... 614 876-3637
Columbus *(G-7052)*
J Rettenmaier USA LP........D....... 937 652-2101
Urbana *(G-18998)*
Kdc US Holdings Inc........G....... 740 927-2817
Johnstown *(G-11269)*
Kerry Inc........E....... 440 229-5200
Mayfield Heights *(G-13166)*
Lib Therapeutics LLC........G....... 859 240-7764
Cincinnati *(G-3940)*
Lubrizol Global Management........F....... 216 447-5000
Brecksville *(G-2048)*
M Pharmaceutical USA........G....... 859 868-3131
Cincinnati *(G-3963)*
Mallinckrodt LLC........F....... 513 948-5751
Cincinnati *(G-3976)*
Masters Pharmaceutical Inc........G....... 513 290-2969
Fairfield *(G-9525)*
Medpace Holdings Inc........F....... 513 579-9911
Cincinnati *(G-3998)*
Medpace Research Inc........G....... 513 579-9911
Cincinnati *(G-3999)*
Meridian Bioscience Inc........B....... 513 271-3700
Cincinnati *(G-4006)*
Middletown Pharmacy Inc........G....... 513 705-6252
Middletown *(G-13929)*
Migraine Proof LLC........G....... 330 635-7874
Medina *(G-13301)*
Mp Biomedicals LLC........C....... 440 337-1200
Solon *(G-17199)*
Mvp Pharmacy........G....... 614 449-8000
Columbus *(G-7204)*
N M R Inc........G....... 513 530-9075
Cincinnati *(G-4056)*
N-Molecular Inc........F....... 440 439-5356
Oakwood Village *(G-15481)*
N8 Medical Inc........G....... 614 537-7246
Dublin *(G-8950)*
Navidea Biopharmaceuticals Inc........E....... 614 793-7500
Dublin *(G-8952)*
Nigerian Assn Pharmacists & PH........G....... 513 861-2329
Cincinnati *(G-4078)*
Nitto Denko Avecia Inc........F....... 513 679-3000
Cincinnati *(G-4082)*
Nnodum Pharmaceuticals Corp........F....... 513 861-2329
Cincinnati *(G-4083)*
Norwich Overseas Inc........F....... 513 983-1100
Mason *(G-12916)*
Novartis Corporation........D....... 919 577-5000
Cincinnati *(G-4090)*
Oak Tree Intl Holdings Inc........G....... 702 462-7295
Elyria *(G-9302)*
Oakwood Laboratories LLC........E....... 440 359-0000
Oakwood Village *(G-15482)*
Ohio Lab Pharma LLC........G....... 484 522-2601
Kettering *(G-11439)*
Omnicare Phrm of Midwest LLC........D....... 513 719-2600
Cincinnati *(G-4111)*
Organon Inc........G....... 440 729-2290
Chesterland *(G-3167)*
Patenthealth LLC........G....... 330 208-1111
North Canton *(G-15109)*
Patheon Pharmaceuticals Inc........B....... 513 948-9111
Cincinnati *(G-4134)*
Performanx Specialty Chem LLC........G....... 614 300-7001
Waverly *(G-19556)*
Perrigo........G....... 937 473-2050
Covington *(G-7792)*
Pfizer Inc........G....... 513 342-9056
West Chester *(G-19758)*
Pfizer Inc........C....... 614 496-0990
Dublin *(G-8965)*
Pfizer Inc........D....... 216 591-0642
Beachwood *(G-1265)*
Pharma Tegix LLC........G....... 740 879-4015
Lewis Center *(G-11771)*
Pharmacia Hepar LLC........D....... 937 746-3603
Franklin *(G-9909)*
Pharmcutical Dev Solutions LLC........G....... 732 766-5222
Powell *(G-16332)*
Polgenix Inc........G....... 440 537-9691
Cleveland *(G-5892)*
Prasco LLC........C....... 513 204-1100
Mason *(G-12923)*
Principled Dynamics Inc........G....... 419 351-6303
Holland *(G-10951)*
Propharma Sales LLC........G....... 513 486-3353
Mason *(G-12927)*
Quality Care Products LLC........E....... 734 847-2704
Holland *(G-10952)*
Ranir Dcp........G....... 616 698-8880
Bay Village *(G-1207)*
RC Outsourcing LLC........G....... 330 536-8500
Lowellville *(G-12255)*
River City Pharma........D....... 513 870-1680
Fairfield *(G-9558)*
Roxane Laboratories........G....... 614 276-4000
Columbus *(G-7403)*
Safe Rx Pharmacies Inc........G....... 740 377-4162
South Point *(G-17294)*
Safecor Health LLC........F....... 781 933-8780
Columbus *(G-7412)*
Specialized Pharmaceuticals........G....... 419 371-2081
Lima *(G-11943)*
Summit Research Group........G....... 330 689-1778
Stow *(G-17633)*
Takeda Pharmaceuticals USA Inc........G....... 440 238-0872
Strongsville *(G-17800)*
Tersus Pharmaceuticals........F....... 440 951-2451
Mentor *(G-13604)*
Teva Pharmaceuticals Inc........G....... 800 225-6878
Cincinnati *(G-4415)*
Teva Womens Health Inc........C....... 513 731-9900
Cincinnati *(G-4416)*
Tri-Tech Laboratories Inc........G....... 614 656-1130
New Albany *(G-14637)*
USB Corporation........D....... 216 765-5000
Cleveland *(G-6246)*
Venture Therapeutics Inc........G....... 614 430-3300
New Albany *(G-14640)*
Warner Chlcott Phrmcticals Inc........F....... 513 983-1100
Cincinnati *(G-4490)*
West Pharmaceutical Svcs Inc........G....... 513 741-3004
Cincinnati *(G-4500)*
Xellia Pharmaceuticals USA LLC........E....... 847 986-7984
Bedford *(G-1455)*

PHARMACEUTICALS: Medicinal & Botanical Prdts

Amresco LLC........C....... 440 349-2805
Cleveland *(G-4701)*
Frutarom USA Inc........G....... 513 870-4900
West Chester *(G-19859)*
Galapagos Inc........G....... 937 890-3068
Dayton *(G-8213)*
Graminex LLC........F....... 419 278-1023
Deshler *(G-8789)*
Natural Options Aromatherapy........G....... 419 886-3736
Bellville *(G-1560)*
Patenthealth LLC........G....... 330 208-1111
North Canton *(G-15109)*
Plymouth Healthcare Pdts LLC........F....... 440 542-0762
Solon *(G-17217)*
USB Corporation........D....... 216 765-5000
Cleveland *(G-6246)*
Valley Vitamins II Inc........E....... 330 533-0051
Columbus *(G-7570)*

PHARMACIES & DRUG STORES

Buderer Drug Co........G....... 419 626-3429
Sandusky *(G-16798)*
Kroger Co........C....... 740 671-5164
Bellaire *(G-1487)*
Kroger Co........C....... 740 264-5057
Steubenville *(G-17540)*
Kroger Co........C....... 614 263-1766
Columbus *(G-7103)*
Kroger Co........C....... 614 575-3742
Columbus *(G-7104)*
Kroger Co........D....... 513 683-4001
Maineville *(G-12372)*
Kroger Co........D....... 740 374-2523
Marietta *(G-12638)*
Kroger Co........C....... 937 277-0950
Dayton *(G-8302)*
Riesbeck Food Markets Inc........C....... 740 695-3401
Saint Clairsville *(G-16649)*
Soleo Health Inc........F....... 844 467-8200
Dublin *(G-8993)*
Specialized Pharmaceuticals........G....... 419 371-2081
Lima *(G-11943)*

PHOSPHATES

Scotts Company LLC........B....... 937 644-0011
Marysville *(G-12809)*

PHOTOCOPY MACHINE REPAIR SVCS

D and D Business Equipment Inc........G....... 440 777-5441
Cleveland *(G-5056)*

PHOTOCOPY MACHINES

E-Waste Systems (ohio) Inc........G....... 614 824-3057
Columbus *(G-6881)*
Xerox Corporation........B....... 513 554-3200
Blue Ash *(G-1879)*

PHOTOCOPYING & DUPLICATING SVCS

A Grade Notes Inc........G....... 614 766-9999
Dublin *(G-8871)*
A-A Blueprint Co Inc........E....... 330 794-8803
Akron *(G-23)*
Bethart Enterprises Inc........F....... 513 863-6161
Hamilton *(G-10540)*
Brooke Printers Inc........G....... 614 235-6800
Lancaster *(G-11548)*
Capitol Citicom Inc........E....... 614 472-2679
Columbus *(G-6735)*
Cincinnati Print Solutions LLC........G....... 513 943-9500
Amelia *(G-534)*
Colortech Graphics & Printing........F....... 614 766-2400
Columbus *(G-6780)*
Corporate Dcment Solutions Inc........F....... 513 595-8200
Cincinnati *(G-3552)*
Domicone Printing Inc........G....... 937 878-3080
Fairborn *(G-9457)*
Doug Smith........G....... 740 345-1398
Newark *(G-14868)*
Eg Enterprise Services Inc........F....... 216 431-3300
Cleveland *(G-5158)*
Elyria Copy Center Inc........G....... 440 323-4145
Elyria *(G-9251)*
Fedex Office & Print Svcs Inc........E....... 937 436-0677
Dayton *(G-8192)*

Employee Codes: A=Over 500 employees, B=251-500
C=101-250, D=51-100, E=20-50, F=10-19, G=3-9
2019 Harris Ohio
Industrial Directory
1533
PRODUCT

PHOTOCOPYING & DUPLICATING SVCS

Fedex Office & Print Svcs Inc ....F........ 330 376-6002
  Akron *(G-167)*
Fedex Office & Print Svcs Inc ....E........ 614 621-1100
  Columbus *(G-6917)*
Fedex Office & Print Svcs Inc ....E........ 419 866-5464
  Toledo *(G-18290)*
Fedex Office & Print Svcs Inc ....E........ 614 898-0000
  Westerville *(G-20054)*
Fedex Office & Print Svcs Inc ....F........ 614 575-0800
  Reynoldsburg *(G-16439)*
Fedex Office & Print Svcs Inc ....E........ 216 573-1511
  Cleveland *(G-5228)*
Fremont Quick Print ....G........ 419 334-8808
  Helena *(G-10771)*
Geygan Enterprises Inc ....F........ 513 932-4222
  Lebanon *(G-11656)*
Great Lakes Engraving Corp ....G........ 419 867-1607
  Maumee *(G-13113)*
Henry Bussman ....G........ 614 224-0417
  Columbus *(G-6988)*
Hilleary-Whitaker Inc ....G........ 614 766-4694
  Columbus *(G-7001)*
Hoster Graphics Company Inc ....F........ 614 299-9770
  Columbus *(G-7009)*
Lakota Printing Inc ....G........ 513 755-3666
  West Chester *(G-19734)*
Montview Corporation ....G........ 330 723-3409
  Medina *(G-13304)*
Morse Enterprises Inc ....G........ 513 229-3600
  Mason *(G-12912)*
Print-Digital Incorporated ....G........ 330 686-5945
  Stow *(G-17621)*
Printers Devil Inc ....F........ 330 650-1218
  Hudson *(G-11068)*
Rhoads Printing Center Inc ....G........ 330 678-2042
  Kent *(G-11375)*
Ricci Anthony ....G........ 330 758-5761
  Youngstown *(G-21015)*
Spectrum Image LLC ....G........ 614 954-0102
  Columbus *(G-7473)*
Technoprint Inc ....F........ 614 899-1403
  Westerville *(G-20077)*
Zip Laser Systems Inc ....G........ 740 286-6613
  Jackson *(G-11203)*

PHOTOELECTRIC DEVICES: Magnetic

Tytek Industries Inc ....E........ 513 874-7326
  Blue Ash *(G-1862)*

PHOTOENGRAVING SVC

Linger Photo Engraving Corp ....G........ 513 579-1380
  Cincinnati *(G-3945)*
Youngstown ARC Engraving Co..........E........ 330 793-2471
  Youngstown *(G-21070)*

PHOTOFINISHING LABORATORIES

Enlarging Arts Inc ....G........ 330 434-3433
  Akron *(G-156)*
Simply Canvas Inc ....E........ 330 436-6500
  Akron *(G-376)*
Transimage Inc ....G........ 937 293-0261
  Oakwood *(G-15466)*

PHOTOGRAPHIC EQPT & SPLYS

AGFA Corporation ....C........ 513 829-6292
  Fairfield *(G-9478)*
Dupont Specialty Pdts USA LLC ....E........ 740 474-0220
  Circleville *(G-4543)*
Eastman Kodak Company ....E........ 937 259-3000
  Kettering *(G-11431)*
Horizons Inc Camcode Division ....E........ 216 714-0020
  Cleveland *(G-5416)*
Jay Tackett ....G........ 740 779-1715
  Frankfort *(G-9862)*
Kg63 LLC ....F........ 216 941-7766
  Cleveland *(G-5533)*
Tbh International ....G........ 440 323-4651
  Elyria *(G-9335)*
Xerox Corporation C/O Genco ....G........ 503 582-6059
  Groveport *(G-10517)*

PHOTOGRAPHIC EQPT & SPLYS WHOLESALERS

ID Card Systems Inc ....G........ 330 963-7446
  Twinsburg *(G-18795)*

PHOTOGRAPHIC EQPT & SPLYS, WHOLESALE: Project, Motion/Slide

Eastman Kodak Company ....E........ 937 259-3000
  Dayton *(G-8175)*

PHOTOGRAPHIC EQPT & SPLYS: Blueprint Reproduction Mach/Eqpt

Rightway Fab & Machine Inc ....G........ 937 295-2200
  Russia *(G-16612)*

PHOTOGRAPHIC EQPT & SPLYS: Film, Cloth & Paper, Sensitized

Stretchtape Inc ....E........ 216 486-9400
  Cleveland *(G-6107)*

PHOTOGRAPHIC EQPT & SPLYS: Graphic Arts Plates, Sensitized

Plastigraphics Inc ....F........ 513 771-8848
  Cincinnati *(G-4166)*

PHOTOGRAPHIC EQPT & SPLYS: Lens Shades, Camera

Kay Zee Inc ....G........ 330 339-1268
  New Philadelphia *(G-14777)*

PHOTOGRAPHIC EQPT & SPLYS: Paper & Cloth, All Types, NEC

Transimage Inc ....G........ 937 293-0261
  Oakwood *(G-15466)*

PHOTOGRAPHIC EQPT & SPLYS: Plates, Sensitized

Horizons Incorporated ....C........ 216 475-0555
  Cleveland *(G-5417)*

PHOTOGRAPHIC EQPT & SPLYS: Printing Eqpt

Advanced Litho Systems ....G........ 419 865-2652
  Monclova *(G-14253)*
Ink Again ....G........ 419 232-4465
  Van Wert *(G-19095)*

PHOTOGRAPHIC EQPT & SPLYS: Processing Eqpt

Smartcopy Inc ....G........ 740 392-6162
  Mount Vernon *(G-14514)*

PHOTOGRAPHIC EQPT & SPLYS: Toners, Prprd, Not Chem Plnts

Gvs Industries Inc ....G........ 513 851-3606
  Hamilton *(G-10565)*

PHOTOGRAPHIC EQPT & SPLYS: Tripods, Camera & Projector

Precision Remotes LLC ....E........ 510 215-6474
  Middleburg Heights *(G-13768)*

PHOTOGRAPHIC EQPT REPAIR SVCS

Amtech Inc ....G........ 440 238-2141
  Strongsville *(G-17711)*

PHOTOGRAPHY SVCS: Commercial

David Esrati ....G........ 937 228-4433
  Dayton *(G-8126)*
Golden Graphics Ltd ....F........ 419 673-6260
  Kenton *(G-11406)*
Middlefield Sign Co ....G........ 440 632-0708
  Middlefield *(G-13827)*
Queen City Reprographics ....C........ 513 326-2300
  Cincinnati *(G-4240)*
Youngstown ARC Engraving Co..........E........ 330 793-2471
  Youngstown *(G-21070)*

PHOTOGRAPHY SVCS: Still Or Video

SMS Communications Inc....................E........ 216 374-6886
  Shaker Heights *(G-16937)*

Studs N Hip Hop ....G........ 614 477-0786
  Columbus *(G-7496)*

PHOTOGRAPHY: Aerial

G2 Digital Solutions ....F........ 937 951-1530
  Xenia *(G-20774)*

PHOTOTYPESETTING SVC

DOV Graphics Inc ....E........ 513 241-5150
  Cincinnati *(G-3605)*
HOT Graphic Services Inc ....E........ 419 242-7000
  Northwood *(G-15339)*
Photo-Type Engraving Company ....F........ 614 308-1900
  Columbus *(G-7315)*
Photo-Type Engraving Company ....F........ 614 308-7914
  Columbus *(G-7316)*
Tj Metzgers Inc ....D........ 419 861-8611
  Toledo *(G-18553)*

PHOTOVOLTAIC Solid State

Hunters Hightech Energy Systm ....G........ 614 275-4777
  Columbus *(G-7012)*

PHYSICAL FITNESS CENTERS

Novacare Inc ....G........ 216 704-4817
  Beachwood *(G-1254)*

PHYSICIANS' OFFICES & CLINICS: Medical

Dayton Laser & Aesthetic Medic ....G........ 937 208-8282
  Dayton *(G-8137)*

PHYSICIANS' OFFICES & CLINICS: Medical doctors

Community Action Program Corp ....F........ 740 374-8501
  Marietta *(G-12617)*
Eye Surgery Center Ohio Inc ....E........ 614 228-3937
  Columbus *(G-6912)*
Francisco Jaume ....G........ 740 622-1200
  Coshocton *(G-7734)*
Lababidi Enterprises Inc ....E........ 330 733-2907
  Akron *(G-245)*
Nutritional Medicinals LLC ....F........ 937 433-4673
  West Chester *(G-19750)*
Orthotics & Prosthetics Rehab ....F........ 330 856-2553
  Warren *(G-19429)*
Volk Optical Inc ....D........ 440 942-6161
  Mentor *(G-13625)*

PICTURE FRAMES: Metal

Frame USA ....E........ 513 577-7107
  Cincinnati *(G-3708)*
Frame Warehouse ....G........ 614 861-4582
  Reynoldsburg *(G-16440)*
Nostalgic Images Inc ....E........ 419 784-1728
  Defiance *(G-8641)*

PICTURE FRAMES: Wood

Bonfoey Co ....F........ 216 621-0178
  Cleveland *(G-4831)*
Cass Frames Inc ....G........ 419 468-2863
  Galion *(G-10126)*
Fenwick Gallery of Fine Arts ....G........ 419 475-1651
  Toledo *(G-18292)*
Frame Depot Inc ....G........ 330 652-7865
  Niles *(G-15009)*
Frame Warehouse ....G........ 614 861-4582
  Reynoldsburg *(G-16440)*
Lazars Art Gllery Crtive Frmng ....G........ 330 477-8351
  Canton *(G-2731)*

PICTURE FRAMING SVCS, CUSTOM

American Frame Corporation ....E........ 419 893-5595
  Maumee *(G-13069)*
Frame Depot Inc ....G........ 330 652-7865
  Niles *(G-15009)*

PIECE GOODS & NOTIONS WHOLESALERS

Sysco Guest Supply LLC ....F........ 440 960-2515
  Lorain *(G-12128)*

PRODUCT SECTION

PIPE, CULVERT: Concrete

PIECE GOODS, NOTIONS & DRY GOODS, WHOL: Fabrics Broadwoven

Mmi Textiles Inc ....F 440 899-8050
  Westlake (G-20131)

PIECE GOODS, NOTIONS & DRY GOODS, WHOL: Textile Converters

Db Rediheat Inc ....E 216 361-0530
  Cleveland (G-5075)

PIECE GOODS, NOTIONS & DRY GOODS, WHOLESALE: Fabrics, Lace

Joe Busby ....G 513 821-1716
  Cincinnati (G-3876)

PIECE GOODS, NOTIONS & DRY GOODS, WHOLESALE: Sewing Access

Embroidered ID Inc ....G 440 974-8113
  Mentor (G-13439)

PIECE GOODS, NOTIONS & DRY GOODS, WHOLESALE: Tape, Textile

Great Lakes Textiles Inc ....E 440 914-1122
  Solon (G-17156)

PIECE GOODS, NOTIONS & OTHER DRY GOODS, WHOL: Flags/Banners

Johnson Brothers Holdings LLC ....G 614 868-5273
  Columbus (G-7073)
Pro Companies Inc ....G 614 738-1222
  Pickerington (G-16057)

PIECE GOODS, NOTIONS/DRY GOODS, WHOL: Drapery Mtrl, Woven

Anthony Decorative Fabrics and ....G 937 299-4637
  Moraine (G-14331)
Style-Line Incorporated ....E 614 291-0600
  Columbus (G-7497)

PIGMENTS, INORGANIC: Metallic & Mineral, NEC

Harsco Corporation ....D 330 372-1781
  Warren (G-19408)
Obron Atlantic Corporation ....F 440 954-7600
  Painesville (G-15767)

PILOT SVCS: Aviation

Theiss Uav Solutions LLC ....G 330 584-2070
  North Benton (G-15062)

PINS

Altenloh Brinck & Co Inc ....C 419 636-6715
  Bryan (G-2262)
Dph Discount Pin Inc ....G 740 264-2450
  Steubenville (G-17531)
Express Trading Pins ....G 419 394-2550
  Saint Marys (G-16684)
Lapel Pins Unlimited LLC ....G 614 562-3218
  Lewis Center (G-11765)
Paine Falls Centerpin LLC ....G 440 298-3202
  Thompson (G-18026)
Pin High LLC ....G 216 577-9999
  Avon (G-958)
Pin Oak Development LLC ....G 440 933-9862
  Avon Lake (G-1000)
Pin Point Marketing LLC ....G 330 336-5863
  Wadsworth (G-19263)
S F S Stadler Inc ....G 330 239-7100
  Medina (G-13332)

PINS: Dowel

Dayton Superior Corporation ....C 937 866-0711
  Miamisburg (G-13655)

PIPE & FITTING: Fabrication

Alloy Bllows Prcision Wldg Inc ....D 440 684-3000
  Cleveland (G-4674)
American Roll Formed Pdts Corp ....C 440 352-0753
  Youngstown (G-20843)

Appian Manufacturing Corp ....E 614 445-2230
  Columbus (G-6608)
Arem Co ....F 440 974-6740
  Mentor (G-13393)
Atlas Industrial Contrs LLC ....B 614 841-4500
  Columbus (G-6627)
Carter Machine Company Inc ....G 419 468-3530
  Galion (G-10125)
Contractors Steel Company ....E 330 425-3050
  Twinsburg (G-18757)
Crest Bending Inc ....E 419 492-2108
  New Washington (G-14828)
Defiance Metal Products WI Inc ....C 920 426-9207
  Defiance (G-8621)
Duro Dyne Midwest Corp ....B 513 870-6000
  Hamilton (G-10551)
Eaton Corporation ....C 440 826-1115
  Berea (G-1604)
Ebner Furnaces Inc ....D 330 335-2311
  Wadsworth (G-19237)
Elliott Tool Technologies Ltd ....D 937 253-6133
  Dayton (G-8182)
Elster Perfection Corporation ....D 440 428-1171
  Geneva (G-10218)
Esterle Mold & Machine Co Inc ....E 330 686-1685
  Stow (G-17583)
Famous Industries Inc ....D 740 685-2592
  Byesville (G-2384)
Faull & Son LLC ....F 330 652-4341
  Niles (G-15008)
Franklin Frames and Cycles ....G 740 763-3838
  Newark (G-14875)
Hollaender Manufacturing Co ....D 513 772-8800
  Cincinnati (G-3817)
Industrial Quartz Corp ....F 440 942-0909
  Mentor (G-13469)
Ipsco Tubulars Inc ....G 330 448-6772
  Brookfield (G-2108)
Jan Squires Inc ....G 440 988-7859
  Amherst (G-563)
John H Hosking Inc ....G 513 821-1080
  Middletown (G-13918)
Kings Welding and Fabg Inc ....E 330 738-3592
  Mechanicstown (G-13212)
Kirtland Capital Partners LP ....E 216 593-0100
  Beachwood (G-1244)
Lakewood Steel Inc ....F 440 965-4226
  Wakeman (G-19286)
Lim Services LLC ....F 513 217-0801
  Middletown (G-13920)
Mitchell Piping LLC ....E 330 245-0258
  Hartville (G-10702)
Normandy Products Company ....D 440 632-5050
  Middlefield (G-13840)
Phillips Mfg and Tower Co ....D 419 347-1720
  Shelby (G-16985)
Pines Manufacturing Inc ....C 440 835-5553
  Westlake (G-20142)
Precise Tube Forming Inc ....E 440 237-3956
  North Royalton (G-15296)
Precision Fittings LLC ....E 440 647-4143
  Wellington (G-19589)
Qual-Fab Inc ....E 440 327-5000
  Avon (G-960)
Quality Mechanicals Inc ....E 513 559-0998
  Cincinnati (G-4226)
Rafter Equipment Corporation ....E 440 572-3700
  Strongsville (G-17781)
Rbm Environmental and Cnstr ....E 419 693-5840
  Oregon (G-15566)
Rhenium Alloys Inc ....D 440 365-7388
  North Ridgeville (G-15251)
Riker Products Inc ....C 419 729-1626
  Toledo (G-18501)
Scot Industries Inc ....E 330 262-7585
  Wooster (G-20651)
Seal Tite LLC ....D 937 393-4268
  Hillsboro (G-10891)
Sroka Industries Inc ....E 440 572-2811
  Strongsville (G-17795)
SSP Fittings Corp ....C 330 425-4250
  Twinsburg (G-18858)
Stripmatic Products Inc ....E 216 241-7143
  Cleveland (G-6111)
Summers Acquisition Corp ....F 419 423-5800
  Findlay (G-9765)
Swagelok Company ....D 440 349-5934
  Solon (G-17242)
Swagelok Company ....D 440 349-5652
  Solon (G-17241)

T & D Fabricating Inc ....E 440 951-5646
  Eastlake (G-9135)
Tech Tool Inc ....F 330 674-1176
  Millersburg (G-14133)
TI Group Auto Systems LLC ....C 740 929-2049
  Hebron (G-10767)
Tilton Corporation ....C 419 227-6421
  Lima (G-11952)
Transit Sittings of NA ....G 330 797-2516
  Youngstown (G-21049)
Tri-America Contractors Inc ....E 740 574-0148
  Wheelersburg (G-20186)
Tri-America Contractors Inc ....E 740 574-0148
  Wheelersburg (G-20187)
Tri-State Fabricators Inc ....E 513 752-5005
  Amelia (G-550)
Unison Industries LLC ....B 904 667-9904
  Dayton (G-7994)
United Group Services Inc ....C 800 633-9690
  West Chester (G-19910)
Vortec Corporation ....E 513 891-7485
  Blue Ash (G-1866)
W J Egli Company Inc ....F 330 823-3666
  Alliance (G-512)
Welded Tubes Inc ....F 440 437-5144
  Orwell (G-15638)
Zekelman Industries Inc ....C 740 432-2146
  Cambridge (G-2463)

PIPE & FITTINGS: Cast Iron

General Aluminum Mfg Company ....C 419 739-9300
  Wapakoneta (G-19330)
McWane Inc ....B 740 622-6651
  Coshocton (G-7739)
Tangent Air Inc ....E 740 474-1114
  Circleville (G-4560)

PIPE & TUBES: Seamless

Reliacheck Manufacturing Inc ....E 440 933-6162
  Avon Lake (G-1005)

PIPE FITTINGS: Plastic

Cantex Inc ....D 330 995-3665
  Aurora (G-874)
Cleveland Plastic Fabricat ....F 216 797-7300
  Euclid (G-9409)
Elster Perfection Corporation ....D 440 428-1171
  Geneva (G-10218)
Gad-Jets Inc ....G 937 274-2111
  Franklin (G-9885)
Haviland Plastic Products Co ....E 419 622-3110
  Haviland (G-10712)
Lenz Inc ....E 937 277-9364
  Dayton (G-8311)
Osburn Associates Inc ....E 740 385-5732
  Logan (G-12038)
Parker-Hannifin Corporation ....D 330 673-2700
  Kent (G-11360)
Ppafco Inc ....F 614 488-7259
  Columbus (G-7335)
Qube Corporation ....F 440 543-2393
  Chagrin Falls (G-3071)
Speedline Corporation ....G 440 914-1122
  Solon (G-17236)

PIPE JOINT COMPOUNDS

Hydratech Engineered Pdts LLC ....F 513 827-9169
  Cincinnati (G-3831)

PIPE SECTIONS, FABRICATED FROM PURCHASED PIPE

Excel Loading Systems LLC ....G 513 265-2936
  Blue Ash (G-1769)
John Maneely Company ....E 724 342-6851
  Niles (G-15019)
Kottler Metal Products Co Inc ....E 440 946-7473
  Willoughby (G-20355)
Pioneer Pipe Inc ....A 740 376-2400
  Marietta (G-12653)
Scott Process Systems Inc ....C 330 877-2350
  Hartville (G-10705)

PIPE, CULVERT: Concrete

Forterra Pipe & Precast LLC ....G 330 467-7890
  Macedonia (G-12295)

Employee Codes: A=Over 500 employees, B=251-500
C=101-250, D=51-100, E=20-50, F=10-19, G=3-9

PIPE, CYLINDER: Concrete, Prestressed Or Pretensioned

Complete Cylinder Service Inc ....G....... 513 772-1500
  Cincinnati (G-3538)

PIPE, SEWER: Concrete

Ash Sewer & Drain Service ....G....... 330 376-9714
  Akron (G-71)
L B Weiss Construction Inc ....G....... 440 205-1774
  Mentor (G-13492)

PIPE: Concrete

Haviland Culvert Company ....G....... 419 622-6951
  Haviland (G-10710)
Northern Concrete Pipe Inc ....F....... 419 841-3361
  Sylvania (G-17957)

PIPE: Plastic

ADS ....G....... 419 422-6521
  Findlay (G-9645)
ADS Ventures Inc ....G....... 614 658-0050
  Hilliard (G-10801)
Advanced Drainage of Ohio Inc ....D....... 614 658-0050
  Hilliard (G-10802)
Advanced Drainage Systems Inc ....E....... 740 852-9554
  London (G-12047)
Advanced Drainage Systems Inc ....D....... 513 863-1384
  Hamilton (G-10529)
Advanced Drainage Systems Inc ....F....... 419 384-3140
  Pandora (G-15806)
Advanced Drainage Systems Inc ....D....... 330 264-4949
  Wooster (G-20554)
Advanced Drainage Systems Inc ....D....... 614 658-0050
  Hilliard (G-10803)
Advanced Drainage Systems Inc ....E....... 419 599-9565
  Napoleon (G-14530)
Advanced Drainage Systems Inc ....D....... 740 852-2980
  London (G-12048)
Advanced Drainage Systems Inc ....E....... 419 424-8324
  Findlay (G-9648)
Aetna Plastics Corp ....G....... 330 274-2855
  Mantua (G-12541)
Baughman Tile Company ....D....... 800 837-3160
  Paulding (G-15856)
Cantex Inc ....D....... 330 995-3665
  Aurora (G-874)
Contech Engnered Solutions Inc ....F....... 513 645-7000
  West Chester (G-19680)
Contech Engnered Solutions LLC .....D....... 513 645-7000
  Middletown (G-13896)
Contech Engnered Solutions LLC .....C....... 513 645-7000
  West Chester (G-19681)
Drain Products LLC ....G....... 419 230-4549
  Lakeview (G-11504)
Drainage Products Inc ....E....... 419 622-6951
  Haviland (G-10709)
Dura-Line Corporation ....E....... 440 322-1000
  Elyria (G-9245)
Elster Perfection Corporation ....D....... 440 428-1171
  Geneva (G-10218)
Fowler Products Inc ....F....... 419 683-4057
  Crestline (G-7794)
Hancor Holding Corporation ....B....... 419 422-6521
  Findlay (G-9700)
Hancor Inc ....B....... 614 658-0050
  Hilliard (G-10827)
Hancor Inc ....D....... 419 424-8222
  Findlay (G-9702)
Hancor Inc ....D....... 419 424-8225
  Findlay (G-9701)
Harrison Mch & Plastic Corp ....E....... 330 527-5641
  Garrettsville (G-10191)
Ipex USA LLC ....G....... 513 942-9910
  Fairfield (G-9511)
Nupco Inc ....G....... 419 629-2259
  New Bremen (G-14658)
Plas-Tanks Industries Inc ....G....... 513 942-3800
  Hamilton (G-10596)
Savko Plastic Pipe & Fittings ....F....... 614 885-8420
  Columbus (G-7422)
Tolloti Pipe LLC ....F....... 330 364-6627
  New Philadelphia (G-14805)
Tolloti Plastic Pipe Inc ....E....... 330 364-6627
  New Philadelphia (G-14806)
Tolloti Plastic Pipe Inc ....G....... 740 922-6911
  Uhrichsville (G-18897)
Utility Solutions Inc ....G....... 740 369-4300
  Delaware (G-8729)

PIPE: Seamless Steel

Vallourec Star LP ....B....... 330 742-6300
  Youngstown (G-21058)
Zekelman Industries Inc ....C....... 740 432-2146
  Cambridge (G-2463)

PIPE: Sheet Metal

American Culvert & Fabg Co ....F....... 740 432-6334
  Cambridge (G-2422)
Shape Supply Inc ....G....... 513 863-6695
  Hamilton (G-10604)
Siata Ds Inc ....G....... 216 503-7200
  Beachwood (G-1278)

PIPE: Water, Cast Iron

Monroe Water System ....G....... 740 472-1030
  Sardis (G-16876)

PIPELINES: Crude Petroleum

Bluefoot Industrial LLC ....E....... 740 314-5299
  Steubenville (G-17528)

PIPELINES: Natural Gas

Ngo Development Corporation ....F....... 740 344-3790
  Newark (G-14903)

PIPES & TUBES

George Manufacturing Inc ....E....... 513 932-1067
  Lebanon (G-11654)
Lokring Technology LLC ....D....... 440 942-0880
  Willoughby (G-20361)
Prime Conduit Inc ....F....... 216 464-3400
  Beachwood (G-1269)

PIPES & TUBES: Steel

AK Tube LLC ....C....... 419 661-4150
  Walbridge (G-19292)
All Steel Structures Inc ....G....... 330 312-3131
  Carrollton (G-2915)
Alro Steel Corporation ....E....... 937 253-6121
  Dayton (G-8021)
Arcelormittal Tubular ....D....... 740 382-3979
  Marion (G-12693)
Arcelormittal Tubular Products ....A....... 419 347-2424
  Shelby (G-16978)
Benjamin Steel Company Inc ....E....... 937 233-1212
  Springfield (G-17368)
Bull Moose Tube Company ....G....... 330 448-4878
  Masury (G-13059)
Busch & Thiem Inc ....E....... 419 625-7515
  Sandusky (G-16800)
Chart International Inc ....E....... 440 753-1490
  Cleveland (G-4915)
Cheryl Heintz ....G....... 937 492-3310
  Sidney (G-17022)
Commercial Honing LLC ....D....... 330 343-8896
  Dover (G-8811)
Conduit Pipe Products Company .....D....... 614 879-9114
  West Jefferson (G-19922)
Contech Engnered Solutions Inc ....F....... 513 645-7000
  West Chester (G-19680)
Contech Engnered Solutions LLC .....D....... 513 645-7000
  Middletown (G-13896)
Contech Engnered Solutions LLC .....C....... 513 645-7000
  West Chester (G-19681)
Crest Bending Inc ....E....... 419 492-2108
  New Washington (G-14828)
Fd Rolls Corp ....G....... 216 536-1433
  Highland Heights (G-10789)
Jackson Tube Service Inc ....C....... 937 773-8550
  Piqua (G-16133)
James O Emert Jr ....G....... 330 650-6990
  Hudson (G-11059)
Jmc Steel Group ....E....... 216 910-3700
  Beachwood (G-1243)
John Maneely Company ....E....... 724 342-6851
  Niles (G-15019)
Kirtland Capital Partners LP ....E....... 216 593-0100
  Beachwood (G-1244)
Major Metals Company ....E....... 419 886-4600
  Mansfield (G-12472)
Metal Matic ....G....... 513 422-6007
  Middletown (G-13927)
Munroe Incorporated ....G....... 330 755-7126
  Struthers (G-17821)
Phillips Mfg and Tower Co ....D....... 419 347-1720
  Shelby (G-16985)
PMC Industries Corp ....D....... 440 943-3300
  Wickliffe (G-20227)
Precision Cutoff LLC ....C....... 419 866-8000
  Holland (G-10950)
Shawcor Inc ....E....... 513 683-7800
  Loveland (G-12231)
Sterling Pipe & Tube Inc ....E....... 419 729-9756
  Toledo (G-18530)
Stryker Steel Tube LLC ....E....... 419 682-4527
  Stryker (G-17834)
T & D Fabricating Inc ....E....... 440 951-5646
  Eastlake (G-9135)
TI Group Auto Systems LLC ....C....... 740 929-2049
  Hebron (G-10767)
Timkensteel Corporation ....F....... 330 471-7000
  Canton (G-2842)
Unison Industries LLC ....B....... 904 667-9904
  Dayton (G-7994)
Vallourec Star LP ....F....... 330 742-6227
  Girard (G-10268)
Welded Tubes Inc ....E....... 440 437-5144
  Orwell (G-15638)
Woodsage LLC ....C....... 419 866-8000
  Holland (G-10969)

PIPES & TUBES: Welded

Specialty Pipe & Tube Inc ....F....... 330 505-8262
  Mineral Ridge (G-14171)
Welded Tubes LLC ....E....... 210 278-3757
  Orwell (G-15639)

PIPES OR FITTINGS: Sewer, Clay

Superior Clay Corp ....D....... 740 922-4122
  Uhrichsville (G-18896)

PIPES: Steel & Iron

Youngstown Tube Co ....E....... 330 743-7414
  Youngstown (G-21084)

PISTONS & PISTON RINGS

Ad Piston Ring Company LLC ....F....... 216 781-5200
  Cleveland (G-4612)
Air Conversion Technology Inc ....G....... 419 841-1720
  Sylvania (G-17933)
Celina Alum Precision Tech Inc ....B....... 419 586-2278
  Celina (G-2953)
Dover Corporation ....G....... 440 951-6600
  Mentor (G-13431)
Federal-Mogul Powertrain LLC ....C....... 740 432-2393
  Cambridge (G-2437)
Race Winning Brands Inc ....B....... 440 951-6600
  Mentor (G-13572)
Seabiscuit Motorsports Inc ....B....... 440 951-6600
  Mentor (G-13577)

PLACER GOLD MINING

Ivi Mining Group Ltd ....G....... 740 418-7745
  Vinton (G-19215)

PLANING MILL, NEC

Walnut Creek Planing Ltd ....D....... 330 893-3244
  Millersburg (G-14146)

PLANING MILLS: Millwork

Wedge Hardwood Products ....G....... 330 525-7775
  Alliance (G-513)

PLANTERS: Plastic

Rubbermaid Incorporated ....C....... 330 733-7771
  Mogadore (G-14247)
The Hc Companies Inc ....E....... 440 632-3333
  Middlefield (G-13857)

PLANTS, POTTED, WHOLESALE

Trumbull Locker Plant Inc ....G....... 440 474-4631
  Rock Creek (G-16534)

PLANTS: Artificial & Preserved

Custom Made Palm Trees LLC ....G....... 330 633-0063
  Akron (G-130)

PRODUCT SECTION

PLASTICS MATERIAL & RESINS

PLAQUES: Clay, Plaster/Papier-Mache, Factory Production

Miller Studio Inc ....D....... 330 339-1100
  New Philadelphia *(G-14787)*

PLAQUES: Picture, Laminated

Dcc Corp ....F....... 330 494-0494
  Canton *(G-2651)*
Gerber Wood Products Inc ....G....... 330 857-3901
  Kidron *(G-11447)*
Glass Mirror Awards Inc ....G....... 419 638-2221
  Helena *(G-10772)*
Hafner Hardwood Connection LLC ....G....... 419 726-4828
  Toledo *(G-18318)*
Idx Corporation ....C....... 937 401-3225
  Dayton *(G-8259)*
Lawnview Industries Inc ....C....... 937 653-5217
  Urbana *(G-19003)*

PLASMAS

Csl Plasma Inc ....E....... 937 325-4200
  Springfield *(G-17382)*
Tpr Plasma Center ....G....... 419 244-3910
  Toledo *(G-18580)*

PLASTER WORK: Ornamental & Architectural

Seves Glass Block Inc ....G....... 440 627-6257
  Broadview Heights *(G-2101)*

PLASTER, ACOUSTICAL: Gypsum

Next Sales LLC ....G....... 330 704-4126
  Dover *(G-8845)*

PLASTIC COLORING & FINISHING

Ampacet Corporation ....E....... 513 247-5400
  Cincinnati *(G-3343)*

PLASTIC PRDTS

Achill Island Composites LLC ....G....... 440 838-1746
  Brecksville *(G-2019)*
Ball Corp ....G....... 419 483-4343
  Bellevue *(G-1530)*
Clear One LLC ....G....... 800 279-3724
  Columbus *(G-6772)*
Diversity-Vuteq LLC ....G....... 614 490-5034
  Gahanna *(G-10080)*
Fdi Enterprises ....G....... 440 269-8282
  Cleveland *(G-5226)*
Fibertech Networks ....G....... 614 436-3565
  Worthington *(G-20685)*
Giesecke & Devrient Can ....G....... 330 425-1515
  Twinsburg *(G-18786)*
Holm Industries Inc ....G....... 330 562-2900
  Aurora *(G-883)*
J H Plastics ....G....... 419 937-2035
  Tiffin *(G-18062)*
Jeffrey Brandewie ....G....... 937 726-7765
  Fort Loramie *(G-9800)*
Jjc Products Inc ....G....... 330 666-4582
  Akron *(G-224)*
Louis G Freeman Co ....G....... 513 263-1720
  Batavia *(G-1163)*
Molding Technologies Ltd ....F....... 740 929-2065
  Hebron *(G-10752)*
Showerline Products LLC ....G....... 614 794-3476
  Westerville *(G-20074)*
Solon ....G....... 440 498-1798
  Solon *(G-17233)*
Unique Plastics LLC ....G....... 419 352-0066
  Bowling Green *(G-2003)*
Valutex Reinforcements Inc ....G....... 800 251-2507
  Wshngtn CT Hs *(G-20747)*
White Co David ....G....... 440 247-2920
  Novelty *(G-15440)*
Wrr Creative Concepts LLC ....G....... 513 659-2284
  West Chester *(G-19822)*

PLASTICIZERS, ORGANIC: Cyclic & Acyclic

Chemionics Corporation ....E....... 330 733-8834
  Tallmadge *(G-17975)*

PLASTICS FILM & SHEET

Advanced Polymer Coatings Ltd ....E....... 440 937-6218
  Avon *(G-939)*
Berry Film Products Co Inc ....D....... 800 225-6729
  Mason *(G-12835)*
Berry Plastics Filmco Inc ....D....... 330 562-6111
  Aurora *(G-873)*
Clopay Corporation ....C....... 800 282-2260
  Mason *(G-12847)*
Clopay Corporation ....G....... 513 742-1984
  Cincinnati *(G-3529)*
Dow Chemical Company ....F....... 937 254-1550
  Dayton *(G-8166)*
Entrotech Inc ....F....... 614 946-7602
  Columbus *(G-6901)*
Graphic Art Systems Inc ....E....... 216 581-9050
  Cleveland *(G-5341)*
Plastic Suppliers Inc ....D....... 614 475-8010
  Columbus *(G-7325)*
PMC Acquisitions Inc ....D....... 419 429-0042
  Findlay *(G-9742)*
Renegade Materials Corporation ....E....... 508 579-7888
  Miamisburg *(G-13711)*
Simona PMC LLC ....D....... 419 429-0042
  Findlay *(G-9755)*
Specialty Films Inc ....E....... 614 471-9100
  Columbus *(G-7467)*
Tsp Inc ....E....... 513 732-8900
  Batavia *(G-1191)*
United Converting Inc ....G....... 614 863-9972
  Columbus *(G-7556)*
Valfilm LLC ....D....... 614 423-6500
  Findlay *(G-9772)*

PLASTICS FILM & SHEET: Polyethylene

Blako Industries Inc ....E....... 419 246-6172
  Dunbridge *(G-9014)*
Charter Nex Holding Company ....E....... 740 369-2770
  Delaware *(G-8664)*
Future Poly Tech Inc ....E....... 614 942-1209
  Saint Henry *(G-16660)*
General Films Inc ....D....... 888 436-3456
  Covington *(G-7786)*
Putnam Plastics Inc ....G....... 937 866-6261
  Dayton *(G-8452)*

PLASTICS FILM & SHEET: Polypropylene

Crown Plastics Co ....D....... 513 367-0238
  Harrison *(G-10638)*

PLASTICS FILM & SHEET: Polyvinyl

Jain America Foods Inc ....G....... 614 850-9400
  Columbus *(G-7058)*
Jain America Holdings Inc ....D....... 614 850-9400
  Columbus *(G-7059)*

PLASTICS FILM & SHEET: Vinyl

Champion Win Co Cleveland LLC .....E....... 440 899-2562
  Macedonia *(G-12283)*
Clarkwestern Dietrich Building ....F....... 330 372-5564
  Warren *(G-19384)*
Clarkwestern Dietrich Building ....F....... 513 870-1100
  West Chester *(G-19677)*
Ludlow Composites Corporation ....C....... 419 332-5531
  Fremont *(G-10038)*
Rotary Products Inc ....F....... 740 747-2623
  Ashley *(G-759)*
Scherba Industries Inc ....D....... 330 273-3200
  Brunswick *(G-2238)*
Vinyl Building Products LLC ....B....... 513 539-4444
  Monroe *(G-14280)*
Walton Plastics Inc ....E....... 440 786-7711
  Bedford *(G-1454)*
World Connections Corps ....E....... 419 363-2681
  Rockford *(G-16542)*

PLASTICS FINISHED PRDTS: Laminated

Blt Inc ....F....... 513 631-5050
  Norwood *(G-15424)*
Bruewer Woodwork Mfg Co ....D....... 513 353-3505
  Cleves *(G-6355)*
Counter Concepts Inc ....F....... 330 848-4848
  Doylestown *(G-8864)*
Designer Cntemporary Laminates .....G....... 440 946-8207
  Willoughby *(G-20309)*
Fdi Cabinetry LLC ....G....... 513 353-4500
  Cleves *(G-6362)*
Franklin Cabinet Company Inc ....E....... 937 743-9606
  Franklin *(G-9884)*
General Electric Company ....D....... 740 623-5379
  Coshocton *(G-7735)*
Idx Corporation ....C....... 937 401-3225
  Dayton *(G-8259)*
International Laminating Corp ....E....... 937 254-8181
  Dayton *(G-8274)*
Lintec USA Holding Inc ....G....... 781 935-7850
  Stow *(G-17602)*
Quality Rubber Stamp Inc ....G....... 614 235-2700
  Columbus *(G-7365)*
Southern Cabinetry Inc ....E....... 740 245-5992
  Bidwell *(G-1670)*
Spring Grove Manufacturing ....F....... 513 542-0185
  Cincinnati *(G-4361)*
Victory Store Fixtures Inc ....F....... 740 499-3494
  La Rue *(G-11477)*

PLASTICS MATERIAL & RESINS

A Schulman Inc ....E....... 330 498-4840
  North Canton *(G-15066)*
A Schulman Inc ....G....... 440 224-7544
  Geneva *(G-10210)*
A Schulman Inc ....G....... 419 872-1408
  Perrysburg *(G-15916)*
A Schulman Inc ....G....... 909 356-8091
  Fairlawn *(G-9590)*
A Schulman International Inc ....G....... 330 666-3751
  Fairlawn *(G-9591)*
Al-Co Products Inc ....F....... 419 399-3867
  Latty *(G-11624)*
American Polymer Standards ....G....... 440 255-2211
  Mentor *(G-13386)*
Ametek Inc ....F....... 419 739-3200
  Wapakoneta *(G-19321)*
Ampacet Corp ....G....... 513 247-5403
  Mason *(G-12823)*
Anchor Hocking Glass Company ....G....... 740 681-6025
  Lancaster *(G-11544)*
Arclin USA LLC ....E....... 419 726-5013
  Toledo *(G-18190)*
Arizona Chemical Company LLC ......C....... 330 343-7701
  Dover *(G-8804)*
Ashland LLC ....G....... 513 557-3100
  Cincinnati *(G-3361)*
Biobent Holdings LLC ....G....... 513 658-5560
  Columbus *(G-6670)*
Biothane Coated Webbing Corp ....E....... 440 327-0485
  North Ridgeville *(G-15212)*
Bricolage Inc ....F....... 614 853-6789
  Grove City *(G-10418)*
Cameo Countertops Inc ....G....... 419 865-6371
  Holland *(G-10918)*
Carolina Color Corp Ohio ....E....... 740 363-6622
  Delaware *(G-8660)*
Chemionics Corporation ....G....... 330 733-8834
  Tallmadge *(G-17975)*
Chroma Color Corporation ....E....... 740 363-6622
  Delaware *(G-8666)*
Colormatrix ....G....... 440 930-1000
  Avon Lake *(G-982)*
Concrete Sealants Inc ....E....... 937 845-8776
  Tipp City *(G-18109)*
Cornerstone Indus Holdings ....G....... 440 893-9144
  Chagrin Falls *(G-3014)*
Covestro LLC ....C....... 740 929-2015
  Hebron *(G-10740)*
Crane Plastics Mfg Ltd ....G....... 614 754-3700
  Columbus *(G-6836)*
Crown Plastics Co ....D....... 513 367-0238
  Harrison *(G-10638)*
Dayson Polymers LLC ....G....... 330 335-5237
  Wadsworth *(G-19233)*
Dow Chemical Company ....C....... 419 423-6500
  Findlay *(G-9680)*
Dupont Specialty Pdts USA LLC ....D....... 740 474-0635
  Circleville *(G-4544)*
Durez Corporation ....C....... 567 295-6400
  Kenton *(G-11404)*
E C Shaw Co ....E....... 513 721-6334
  Cincinnati *(G-3616)*
E P S Specialists Ltd Inc ....F....... 513 489-3676
  Cincinnati *(G-3618)*
Eagle Elastomer Inc ....E....... 330 923-7070
  Peninsula *(G-15893)*
Emerald Performance Mtls LLC ....D....... 330 374-2418
  Akron *(G-152)*
Emerald Specialty Polymers LLC ......E....... 330 374-2424
  Akron *(G-154)*

Employee Codes: A=Over 500 employees, B=251-500
C=101-250, D=51-100, E=20-50, F=10-19, G=3-9

2019 Harris Ohio Industrial Directory

Engineered Polymer Systems LLC ....G....... 216 255-2116
Medina *(G-13255)*
Ep Bollinger LLC..................................A 513 941-1101
Cincinnati *(G-3646)*
Farmed Materials Inc..........................G....... 513 680-4046
Cincinnati *(G-3673)*
Ferro Corporation................................D....... 216 875-5600
Mayfield Heights *(G-13163)*
Fibretuff Med Biopolymers LLC ....G....... 419 346-8728
Perrysburg *(G-15950)*
Flexsys America LP..............................D 330 666-4111
Akron *(G-173)*
Freeman Manufacturing & Sup Co........E....... 440 934-1902
Avon *(G-950)*
Geo-Tech Polymers LLC.......................F 614 797-2300
Waverly *(G-19546)*
Goldsmith & Eggleton LLC...................F 203 855-6000
Wadsworth *(G-19243)*
Grit Guard Inc.......................................G....... 937 592-9003
Bellefontaine *(G-1516)*
Hancor Inc...D....... 419 424-8225
Findlay *(G-9701)*
Hexion US Finance Corp......................F 614 225-4000
Columbus *(G-6994)*
Hexpol Holding Inc...............................F 440 834-4644
Burton *(G-2362)*
Hggc Citadel Plas Holdings Inc............G....... 330 666-3751
Fairlawn *(G-9607)*
Huntsman...G....... 614 659-0155
Dublin *(G-8925)*
Ic3d Inc..G....... 614 344-0414
Columbus *(G-7019)*
ICO Holdings LLC.................................G....... 330 666-3751
Fairlawn *(G-9609)*
ICP Adhesives and Sealants Inc............F 330 753-4585
Norton *(G-15369)*
Ier Fujikura Inc......................................C....... 330 425-7121
Macedonia *(G-12302)*
Industrial Thermoset Plas Inc...............F....... 440 975-0411
Mentor *(G-13471)*
Ineos ABS (usa) LLC............................C....... 513 467-2400
Addyston *(G-11)*
Integrated Chem Concepts Inc..............G....... 440 838-5666
Brecksville *(G-2042)*
Intergroup International Ltd..................D....... 216 965-0257
Akron *(G-218)*
International Technical..........................E 330 505-1218
Niles *(G-15015)*
Isochem Incorporated...........................G....... 614 775-9328
New Albany *(G-14627)*
J P Industrial Products Inc....................G 330 424-1110
Lisbon *(G-11972)*
JB Polymers Inc....................................G....... 216 941-7041
Oberlin *(G-15501)*
Jerico Plastic Industries Inc..................E....... 330 868-4600
Minerva *(G-14185)*
Jjc Plastics Ltd......................................G....... 330 334-3637
Norton *(G-15372)*
Kardol Quality Products LLC................E 513 933-8206
Blue Ash *(G-1800)*
Kathom Manufacturing Co Inc..............E 513 868-8890
Hamilton *(G-10579)*
Kraton Polymers US LLC......................B 740 423-7571
Belpre *(G-1578)*
Lrbg Chemicals USA Inc.......................G....... 419 244-5856
Toledo *(G-18388)*
Ltg Polymers Limited............................G....... 330 854-5609
Massillon *(G-13015)*
Lubrizol Advanced Mtls Inc..................E....... 440 933-0400
Avon Lake *(G-993)*
Materion Brush Inc................................E....... 440 960-5660
Lorain *(G-12105)*
Minova USA Inc.....................................D....... 740 377-9146
South Point *(G-17289)*
Mitsubishi Chls Perf Plyrs Inc...............D....... 419 483-2931
Bellevue *(G-1540)*
Mjs Plastics Inc......................................G....... 937 548-1000
Greenville *(G-10383)*
Modern Plastics Recovery Inc...............F....... 419 622-4611
Haviland *(G-10713)*
Multibase Inc...D....... 330 666-0505
Copley *(G-7689)*
Nano Innovations LLC...........................G....... 614 203-5706
Columbus *(G-7208)*
National Polymer Dev Co Inc................F 440 708-1245
Chagrin Falls *(G-3061)*
Nexeo Solutions LLC............................F 800 531-7106
Dublin *(G-8956)*
Next Generation Plastics LLC...............G....... 330 668-1200
Fairlawn *(G-9613)*
Novo Foam Products LLC.....................G....... 440 892-3325
Westlake *(G-20133)*
Occidental Chemical Corp....................E 513 242-2900
Cincinnati *(G-4097)*
Ohio Foam Corporation.........................F 419 492-2151
New Washington *(G-14831)*
Ohio Plastics Belting Co.......................G....... 330 882-6764
New Franklin *(G-14695)*
OK Industries Inc...................................E 419 435-2361
Fostoria *(G-9854)*
Optem Inc...G....... 330 723-5686
Medina *(G-13312)*
OSI Global Sourcing LLC......................C....... 614 471-4800
Columbus *(G-7277)*
Ovation Polymer Technology and.........E....... 330 723-5686
Medina *(G-13314)*
Owens Corning Sales LLC....................F 330 633-6735
Tallmadge *(G-17999)*
Performnce Plymr Solutions Inc............F 937 298-3713
Moraine *(G-14375)*
Perstorp Polyols Inc..............................C....... 419 729-5448
Toledo *(G-18467)*
Plaskolite LLC.......................................C....... 614 294-3281
Columbus *(G-7320)*
Plasti-Kemm Inc....................................G....... 330 239-1555
Medina *(G-13318)*
Plastic Regrinders Inc...........................G....... 740 659-2346
Glenford *(G-10272)*
Plastic Selection Group Inc...................G....... 614 464-2008
Columbus *(G-7322)*
Plastrx Inc..G....... 513 847-4032
West Chester *(G-19760)*
Poly Green Technologies LLC...............G....... 419 529-9909
Ontario *(G-15547)*
Polygroup Inc...E 877 476-5972
Loveland *(G-12222)*
Polymer Packaging Inc..........................D....... 330 832-2000
Massillon *(G-13040)*
Polymerics Inc.......................................E 330 677-1131
Kent *(G-11364)*
Polymerics Inc.......................................E 330 434-6665
Cuyahoga Falls *(G-7906)*
Polynew Inc..G....... 330 897-3202
Baltic *(G-1032)*
Polynt Composites USA Inc...................E 816 391-6000
Sandusky *(G-16839)*
Polyone Corporation..............................G....... 216 622-0100
Berea *(G-1622)*
Polyone Corporation..............................C....... 800 727-4338
Greenville *(G-10387)*
Polyone Corporation..............................E 937 548-2133
Greenville *(G-10388)*
Polyone Corporation..............................D....... 330 834-3812
Massillon *(G-13041)*
Polyone Corporation..............................F 440 930-3817
Avon Lake *(G-1002)*
PPG Industries Inc.................................E 419 683-2400
Crestline *(G-7799)*
Premix Inc...C....... 440 224-2181
North Kingsville *(G-15160)*
Prime Industries Inc...............................E 440 288-3626
Lorain *(G-12113)*
Rauh Polymers Inc.................................F....... 330 376-1120
Akron *(G-344)*
Ravago Americas LLC...........................F 419 924-9090
West Unity *(G-19973)*
Ray Fogg Construction Inc....................F 216 351-7976
Cleveland *(G-5962)*
Rotopolymers..G....... 216 645-0333
Cleveland *(G-6008)*
Saco Aei Polymers Inc...........................F 330 995-1600
Aurora *(G-906)*
Scott Bader Inc.......................................G....... 330 920-4410
Stow *(G-17626)*
Scott Molders Incorporated...................D....... 330 673-5777
Kent *(G-11382)*
Sherwood Rtm Corp...............................G....... 330 875-7151
Louisville *(G-12166)*
Solvay Spclty Polymers USA LLC.........E 740 373-9242
Marietta *(G-12673)*
Sonoco Prtective Solutions Inc..............D....... 419 420-0029
Findlay *(G-9759)*
Sorbothane Inc.......................................E 330 678-9444
Kent *(G-11388)*
STC International Co Ltd......................G....... 561 308-6002
Lebanon *(G-11699)*
Synthetic Rubber Technology................G....... 330 494-2221
Uniontown *(G-18933)*
Tembec Btlsr Inc...................................E 419 244-5856
Toledo *(G-18547)*
Tribotech Composites Inc.......................G....... 216 901-1300
Cleveland *(G-6210)*
Triple Arrow Industries Inc....................G....... 614 437-5588
Marysville *(G-12818)*
Ultratech Polymers Inc...........................F 330 945-9410
Cuyahoga Falls *(G-7932)*
Uniloy Milacron Inc................................E 513 487-5000
Batavia *(G-1192)*
V & A Process Inc...................................F 440 288-8137
Lorain *(G-12132)*
Vinyl Profiles Acquisition LLC...............E 330 538-0660
North Jackson *(G-15157)*
Wilsonart LLC...E 614 876-1515
Columbus *(G-7605)*
Winsell Incorporated...............................G....... 330 836-7421
Akron *(G-437)*

PLASTICS MATERIALS, BASIC FORMS & SHAPES WHOLESALERS

Ampacet Corporation..............................E 513 247-5400
Cincinnati *(G-3343)*
Drain Products LLC.................................G....... 419 230-4549
Lakeview *(G-11504)*
Nexeo Solutions LLC..............................F 800 531-7106
Dublin *(G-8956)*

PLASTICS PROCESSING

AMS Global Ltd.......................................F 937 620-1036
West Alexandria *(G-19616)*
Apollo Plastics Inc...................................F 440 951-7774
Mentor *(G-13391)*
Baldie Corporation...................................G....... 513 503-0953
Cincinnati *(G-3378)*
Ball Bounce and Sport Inc......................B 419 289-9310
Ashland *(G-682)*
Bc Investment Corporation.....................G....... 330 262-3070
Wooster *(G-20570)*
Budd Co Plastics Div..............................G....... 419 238-4332
Van Wert *(G-19081)*
C A Joseph Co...G....... 330 385-6869
East Liverpool *(G-9051)*
Chemigon LLC...G....... 330 592-1875
Akron *(G-113)*
David Wolfe Design Inc...........................F 330 633-6124
Akron *(G-134)*
Dawn Enterprises Inc...............................E 216 642-5506
Cleveland *(G-5072)*
Dyna Vac Plastics Inc..............................G....... 937 773-0092
Piqua *(G-16112)*
Eger Products Inc....................................E 513 735-1400
Batavia *(G-1139)*
Encore Plastics Corporation...................D....... 740 432-1652
Cambridge *(G-2436)*
Flambeau Inc...C....... 330 239-0202
Sharon Center *(G-16950)*
Fountain Specialists Inc...........................G....... 513 831-5717
Milford *(G-14009)*
G I Plastek Inc..G....... 440 230-1942
Westlake *(G-20116)*
H P Manufacturing Co..............................D....... 216 361-6500
Cleveland *(G-5363)*
Hanlon Industries Inc...............................F 216 261-7056
Cleveland *(G-5371)*
Harrison Mch & Plastic Corp....................E 330 527-5641
Garrettsville *(G-10191)*
Hartville Plastics Inc................................G....... 330 877-9090
Hartville *(G-10694)*
HP Manufacturing Company Inc..............D....... 216 361-6500
Cleveland *(G-5421)*
Inhance Technologies LLC......................F 614 846-6400
Columbus *(G-7026)*
JPS Technologies Inc..............................F 513 984-6400
Blue Ash *(G-1797)*
JPS Technologies Inc..............................F 513 984-6400
Blue Ash *(G-1798)*
Liqui-Box Corporation.............................C....... 419 289-9696
Ashland *(G-721)*
Mega Plastics Co.....................................E 330 527-2211
Garrettsville *(G-10198)*
Milacron LLC...E 513 536-2000
Batavia *(G-1166)*
P & S Welding Co....................................G....... 330 274-2850
Mantua *(G-12557)*
P T I Inc...E 419 445-2800
Archbold *(G-663)*
Plastic Products and Supply....................G....... 330 744-5076
Youngstown *(G-21000)*
Plastic Works Inc.....................................F 419 433-6576
Huron *(G-11108)*

PRODUCT SECTION

PLASTICS: Finished Injection Molded

Preferred Solutions Inc .... F 216 642-1200
  Seven Hills *(G-16904)*
Professional Plastics Corp .... G 614 336-2498
  Dublin *(G-8968)*
Queen City Polymers Inc .... G 937 236-2710
  Dayton *(G-8456)*
Radici Plastics Usa Inc .... D 330 336-7611
  Wadsworth *(G-19271)*
Rutland Plastic Tech Inc .... G 614 846-3055
  Columbus *(G-7407)*
Samuel Strapping Systems Inc .... D 740 522-2500
  Heath *(G-10731)*
Starks Plastics LLC .... G 513 541-4591
  Cincinnati *(G-4374)*
Tahoma Enterprises Inc .... D 330 745-9016
  Barberton *(G-1108)*
Tahoma Rubber & Plastics Inc .... D 330 745-9016
  Barberton *(G-1109)*
Total Plastics Resources LLC .... G 440 891-1140
  Cleveland *(G-6192)*
United Security Seals Inc .... E 614 443-7633
  Columbus *(G-7558)*
Upl International Inc .... E 330 433-2860
  North Canton *(G-15134)*
Valley Plastics Company Inc .... E 419 666-2349
  Toledo *(G-18588)*
Wyatt Industries LLC .... G 330 954-1790
  Streetsboro *(G-17704)*
Y City Recycling LLC .... D 740 452-2500
  Zanesville *(G-21190)*

PLASTICS SHEET: Packing Materials

Automated Packg Systems Inc .... C 330 626-2313
  Streetsboro *(G-17663)*
Automated Packg Systems Inc .... C 216 663-2000
  Cleveland *(G-4770)*
Buckeye Diamond Logistics Inc .... G 937 644-2194
  Marysville *(G-12772)*
Cool Seal Usa LLC .... F 419 666-1111
  Perrysburg *(G-15935)*
Kapstone Container Corporation ...... C 330 562-6111
  Aurora *(G-886)*
Plastic Works Inc .... F 419 433-6576
  Huron *(G-11108)*
Professional Packaging Company ..... E 440 238-8850
  Strongsville *(G-17779)*
Raven Industries Inc .... G 937 323-4625
  Springfield *(G-17480)*
Western Reserve Sleeve Inc .... E 440 238-8850
  Strongsville *(G-17807)*

PLASTICS: Blow Molded

Diamond Plastics Inc .... D 419 759-3838
  Dunkirk *(G-9034)*
Klw Plastics Inc .... G 513 539-2673
  Monroe *(G-14272)*
Marshall Plastics Inc .... G 937 653-4740
  Urbana *(G-19004)*
Pinnacle Industrial Entps Inc .... C 419 352-8688
  Bowling Green *(G-1991)*
Plastic Forming Company Inc .... E 330 830-5167
  Massillon *(G-13039)*
Quality Blow Molding Inc .... D 440 458-6550
  Elyria *(G-9315)*
Roto Solutions Inc .... D 330 279-2424
  Holmesville *(G-10984)*
Steere Enterprises Inc .... E 330 633-4926
  Tallmadge *(G-18005)*
Thermoplastic Accessories Corp ...... E 614 771-4777
  Hilliard *(G-10870)*
Tigerpoly Manufacturing Inc .... B 614 871-0045
  Grove City *(G-10473)*
Tmd Wek North LLC .... C 440 576-6940
  Jefferson *(G-11241)*

PLASTICS: Cast

Polymer Tech & Svcs Inc .... E 740 929-5500
  Heath *(G-10727)*
S&V Industries Inc .... E 330 666-1986
  Medina *(G-13333)*

PLASTICS: Extruded

Akron Polymer Products Inc .... D 330 628-5551
  Akron *(G-48)*
Axion Strl Innovations LLC .... F 740 452-2500
  Zanesville *(G-21100)*
Bu E Comp Inc .... G 419 284-3381
  Bloomville *(G-1712)*
Buecomp Inc .... E 419 284-3840
  Bloomville *(G-1713)*
Cell-O-Core Co .... E 330 239-4370
  Sharon Center *(G-16948)*
Cep Holdings LLC .... G 330 665-2900
  Fairlawn *(G-9600)*
Clark Rbr Plastic Intl Sls Inc .... D 440 255-9793
  Mentor *(G-13413)*
Cleveland Specialty Pdts Inc .... E 216 281-8300
  Cleveland *(G-4977)*
D & D Plastics Inc .... F 330 376-0668
  Akron *(G-131)*
Dimex LLC .... E 740 374-3100
  Marietta *(G-12619)*
Eclipse Blind Systems Inc .... C 330 296-0112
  Ravenna *(G-16378)*
Engineered Profiles LLC .... C 614 754-3700
  Columbus *(G-6896)*
Erie Lake Plastic Inc .... F 440 333-4880
  Cleveland *(G-5189)*
Extrudex Limited Partnership .... E 440 352-7101
  Painesville *(G-15737)*
Formtech Enterprises Inc .... E 330 688-2171
  Stow *(G-17589)*
Fowler Products Inc .... F 419 683-4057
  Crestline *(G-7794)*
G & J Extrusions Inc .... G 330 753-0162
  New Franklin *(G-14690)*
Hi-Tech Extrusions Ltd .... E 440 286-4000
  Chardon *(G-3116)*
Horsemens Pride Inc .... E 800 232-7950
  Streetsboro *(G-17677)*
Hrh Door Corp .... D 440 593-5226
  Conneaut *(G-7649)*
Hudson Extrusions Inc .... E 330 653-6015
  Hudson *(G-11053)*
ICO Technology Inc .... C 330 666-3751
  Fairlawn *(G-9610)*
Imperial Plastics Inc .... D 330 927-5065
  Rittman *(G-16521)*
Inventive Extrusions Corp .... E 330 874-3000
  Bolivar *(G-1917)*
Malish Corporation .... C 440 951-5356
  Mentor *(G-13509)*
Mercury Plastics LLC .... C 440 632-5281
  Middlefield *(G-13820)*
Middlefield Plastics Inc .... C 440 834-4638
  Middlefield *(G-13826)*
Pahuja Inc .... D 614 864-3989
  Gahanna *(G-10097)*
Plastic Extrusion Tech Ltd .... E 440 632-5611
  Middlefield *(G-13846)*
Profile Plastics Inc .... E 330 452-7000
  Canton *(G-2794)*
Profusion Industries LLC .... G 800 938-2858
  Fairlawn *(G-9615)*
Roppe Holding Company .... G 419 435-6601
  Fostoria *(G-9856)*
Rowmark LLC .... D 419 425-8974
  Findlay *(G-9748)*
Rowmark LLC .... D 419 429-0042
  Findlay *(G-9749)*
Ryan Development Corp .... E 937 587-2266
  Peebles *(G-15881)*
Seagate Plastics Company .... E 419 878-5010
  Waterville *(G-19505)*
Spartech LLC .... G 419 399-4050
  Paulding *(G-15871)*
Three AS Inc .... G 419 227-4240
  Lima *(G-11951)*
Trellborg Sling Prfiles US Inc .... E 330 995-9725
  Aurora *(G-911)*
Universal Polymer & Rubber Ltd .... C 440 632-1691
  Middlefield *(G-13864)*
Vts Co Ltd .... G 419 273-4010
  Forest *(G-9790)*
West Extrusion LLC .... G 330 744-0625
  Campbell *(G-2472)*
Win Cd Inc .... F 330 929-1999
  Cuyahoga Falls *(G-7934)*
XYZ Plastics Inc .... C 440 632-5281
  Middlefield *(G-13870)*

PLASTICS: Finished Injection Molded

ABC Plastics Inc .... E 330 948-3322
  Lodi *(G-12002)*
Advanced Plastics Inc .... G 330 336-6681
  Wadsworth *(G-19222)*
Akron Porcelain & Plastics Co .... C 330 745-2159
  Akron *(G-49)*
Allied Moulded Products Inc .... C 419 636-4217
  Bryan *(G-2259)*
Allied Moulded Products Inc .... C 419 636-4217
  Bryan *(G-2260)*
Allied Moulded Products Inc .... C 419 636-4217
  Bryan *(G-2261)*
Associated Plastics Corp .... D 419 634-3910
  Ada *(G-5)*
Atc Group Inc .... D 440 293-4064
  Andover *(G-579)*
Atc Nymold Corporation .... G 440 293-4064
  Andover *(G-581)*
Atc Nymold Corporation .... G 440 293-4064
  Andover *(G-582)*
B & B Molded Products Inc .... E 419 592-8700
  Defiance *(G-8614)*
Caraustar Industries Inc .... C 330 665-7700
  Copley *(G-7679)*
Centrex Plastics LLC .... C 419 423-1213
  Findlay *(G-9666)*
CP Technologies Company .... E 614 866-9200
  Blacklick *(G-1682)*
D K Manufacturing .... D 740 654-5566
  Lancaster *(G-11562)*
D Martone Industries Inc .... E 440 632-5800
  Middlefield *(G-13790)*
Dak Enterprises Inc .... C 740 828-3291
  Marysville *(G-12780)*
Design Molded Plastics Inc .... C 330 963-4400
  Macedonia *(G-12288)*
DJM Plastics Ltd .... F 419 424-5250
  Findlay *(G-9679)*
DK Manfcturing Frazeysburg Inc ...... C 740 828-3291
  Frazeysburg *(G-9938)*
DK Manufacturing Lancaster Inc ...... D 740 654-5566
  Lancaster *(G-11568)*
Edge Plastics Inc .... C 419 522-6696
  Mansfield *(G-12435)*
Encore Plastics Corporation .... C 419 626-8000
  Sandusky *(G-16808)*
Endura Plastics Inc .... D 440 951-4466
  Kirtland *(G-11467)*
Ernie Green Industries Inc .... G 614 219-1423
  Columbus *(G-6903)*
Great Lakes McHy & Automtn LLC ... E 419 208-2004
  Fremont *(G-10026)*
Greenville Technology Inc .... A 937 548-3217
  Greenville *(G-10374)*
Hadlock Plastics LLC .... C 440 466-4876
  Geneva *(G-10221)*
Illinois Tool Works Inc .... D 937 332-2839
  Troy *(G-18674)*
Illinois Tool Works Inc .... D 519 376-8886
  Troy *(G-18675)*
International Automotive Compo .... A 419 433-5653
  Huron *(G-11099)*
Jack Gruber .... G 740 408-2718
  Cardington *(G-2874)*
Jaco Manufacturing Company .... F 440 234-4000
  Berea *(G-1613)*
Just Plastics Inc .... E 419 468-5506
  Galion *(G-10146)*
Kamco Industries Inc .... B 419 924-5511
  West Unity *(G-19971)*
Kasai North America Inc .... F 614 356-1494
  Dublin *(G-8936)*
Kennick Mold & Die Inc .... G 216 631-3535
  Cleveland *(G-5529)*
Marne Plastics LLC .... G 614 732-4666
  Columbus *(G-7152)*
Mdi of Ohio Inc .... E 937 866-2345
  Miamisburg *(G-13688)*
Meese Inc .... D 440 998-1202
  Ashtabula *(G-785)*
Myers Industries Inc .... E 440 632-1006
  Middlefield *(G-13836)*
National Molded Products Inc .... E 440 365-3400
  Elyria *(G-9299)*
Novatex North America Inc .... D 419 282-4264
  Ashland *(G-728)*
Ohio Plastics Company .... G 740 828-3291
  Newark *(G-14905)*
P P E Inc .... D 440 322-8577
  Elyria *(G-9306)*
Plas-TEC Corp .... E 419 272-2731
  Edon *(G-9187)*
Precision Custom Products Inc .... E 937 585-4011
  De Graff *(G-8605)*
Pyramid Plastics Inc .... E 216 641-5904
  Cleveland *(G-5936)*

Employee Codes: A=Over 500 employees, B=251-500
C=101-250, D=51-100, E=20-50, F=10-19, G=3-9

2019 Harris Ohio Industrial Directory

R A M Plastics Co Inc ....E.... 330 549-3107
North Lima (G-15177)
Reebar Die Casting Inc ....F.... 419 878-7591
Waterville (G-19503)
Revere Plas Systems Group LLC ....B.... 419 547-6918
Clyde (G-6393)
Sonoco Products Company ....E.... 614 759-8470
Columbus (G-7462)
Springfield Plastics Inc ....F.... 937 322-6071
Springfield (G-17496)
Stuchell Products LLC ....E.... 330 821-4299
Alliance (G-503)
T&M Plastics Co Inc ....G.... 216 651-7700
Cleveland (G-6146)
Tez Tool & Fabrication Inc ....G.... 440 323-2300
Elyria (G-9337)
Toledo Molding & Die Inc ....C.... 419 476-0581
Toledo (G-18563)
Toledo Molding & Die Inc ....D.... 419 470-3950
Toledo (G-18564)
Tom Smith Industries Inc ....C.... 937 832-1555
Englewood (G-9378)
Toth Mold & Die Inc ....F.... 440 232-8530
Cleveland (G-6193)
Tri-Craft Inc ....E.... 440 826-1050
Cleveland (G-6206)
Unique-Chardan Inc ....E.... 419 636-6900
Bryan (G-2311)
Venture Packaging Inc ....B.... 419 465-2534
Monroeville (G-14292)
Wayne Frame Products Inc ....G.... 419 726-7715
Toledo (G-18595)

PLASTICS: Injection Molded

20/20 Custom Molded Plast ....D.... 419 485-2020
Montpelier (G-14300)
Acco Brands USA LLC ....A.... 937 495-6323
Kettering (G-11426)
Accurate Plastics LLC ....F.... 330 346-0048
Kent (G-11288)
Accutech Plastic Molding Inc ....G.... 937 233-0017
Dayton (G-8004)
Advanced Plastic Systems Inc ....F.... 614 759-6550
Gahanna (G-10073)
Advantage Mold Inc ....G.... 419 691-5676
Toledo (G-18158)
All Srvice Plastic Molding Inc ....E.... 937 415-3674
Fairborn (G-9451)
All Srvice Plastic Molding Inc ....G.... 937 890-0322
Vandalia (G-19114)
All Srvice Plastic Molding Inc ....C.... 937 890-0322
Vandalia (G-19115)
Allied Custom Molded Products ....G.... 614 291-0629
Columbus (G-6571)
Allied Plastic Co Inc ....G.... 419 389-1688
Toledo (G-18165)
Amclo Group Inc ....C.... 216 791-8400
North Royalton (G-15259)
Amelia Plastics ....G.... 513 386-4926
Amelia (G-530)
American Molded Plastics Inc ....F.... 330 872-3838
Newton Falls (G-14984)
American Plastic Tech Inc ....C.... 440 632-5203
Middlefield (G-13777)
Artisan Mold Co Inc ....G.... 440 926-4511
Grafton (G-10292)
Aspec Inc ....G.... 513 561-9922
Cincinnati (G-3363)
Auld Company ....E.... 614 454-1010
Columbus (G-6629)
Automation Plastics Corp ....D.... 330 562-5148
Aurora (G-871)
Bena Inc ....G.... 419 299-3313
Van Buren (G-19071)
Bennett Plastics Inc ....E.... 740 432-2209
Cambridge (G-2427)
Berlekamp Plastics Inc ....F.... 419 334-4481
Fremont (G-9998)
Bisson Custom Plastic ....G.... 937 653-4966
Urbana (G-18979)
Bloom Industries Inc ....D.... 330 898-3878
Warren (G-19377)
Boardman Molded Intl LLC ....C.... 330 788-2400
Youngstown (G-20853)
Boardman Molded Products Inc ....D.... 330 788-2400
Youngstown (G-20854)
Brown Company of Findlay Ltd ....E.... 419 425-3002
Findlay (G-9663)
Buckeye Design & Engr Svc LLC ....G.... 419 375-4241
Fort Recovery (G-9812)

Carlisle Plastics Company Inc ....G.... 937 845-9411
New Carlisle (G-14664)
Carney Plastics Inc ....G.... 330 746-8273
Youngstown (G-20866)
Carson Industries LLC ....G.... 419 592-2309
Napoleon (G-14535)
Century Mold Company Inc ....D.... 513 539-9283
Middletown (G-13891)
Claflin Company Inc ....G.... 330 650-0582
Hudson (G-11036)
Continental Strl Plas Inc ....C.... 440 945-4800
Conneaut (G-7644)
Continental Strl Plas Inc ....B.... 419 396-1980
Carey (G-2880)
Continental Strl Plas Inc ....C.... 419 257-2231
North Baltimore (G-15043)
Continental Strl Plas Inc ....B.... 419 238-4628
Van Wert (G-19082)
Converge Group Inc ....F.... 419 281-0000
Ashland (G-698)
Cosmo Corporation ....D.... 330 359-5429
Wilmot (G-20514)
Ctc Plastics ....B.... 937 228-9184
Dayton (G-8116)
Custom Molded Products LLC ....D.... 937 382-1070
Wilmington (G-20493)
Custom Pultrusions Inc ....E.... 330 562-5201
Aurora (G-876)
D J Metro Mold & Die Inc ....G.... 440 237-1130
North Royalton (G-15268)
D M Tool & Plastics Inc ....F.... 937 962-4140
Brookville (G-2166)
D M Tool & Plastics Inc ....F.... 937 962-4140
Lewisburg (G-11790)
Deimling/Jeliho Plastics Inc ....D.... 513 752-6653
Amelia (G-536)
Dimcogray Corporation ....D.... 937 433-7600
Centerville (G-3001)
Dinesol Plastics Inc ....C.... 330 544-7171
Niles (G-15005)
Diskin Enterprises LLC ....E.... 330 527-4308
Garrettsville (G-10187)
Dlhbowles Inc ....E.... 330 479-7595
Canton (G-2663)
Dlhbowles Inc ....D.... 330 488-0716
East Canton (G-9039)
Dlhbowles Inc ....B.... 330 478-2503
Canton (G-2661)
Don-Ell Corporation ....G.... 419 841-7114
Sylvania (G-17937)
Dover High Prfmce Plas Inc ....E.... 330 343-3477
Dover (G-8821)
Doyle Manufacturing Inc ....D.... 419 865-2548
Holland (G-10926)
Dreco Inc ....C.... 440 327-6021
North Ridgeville (G-15221)
Drs Industries Inc ....D.... 419 861-0334
Holland (G-10928)
Drummond Corp ....F.... 440 834-9660
Middlefield (G-13794)
Dublin Plastics Inc ....G.... 216 641-5904
Cleveland (G-5115)
Dynamic Plastics Inc ....G.... 937 437-7261
New Paris (G-14753)
Electr-Gnral Plas Corp Clumbus ....G.... 614 871-2915
Grove City (G-10429)
Elra Industries Inc ....G.... 513 868-6228
Hamilton (G-10554)
Enginred Plstic Components Inc ....C.... 513 228-0298
Lebanon (G-11650)
Enpress LLC ....E.... 440 510-0108
Eastlake (G-9109)
Enterprise Plastics Inc ....E.... 330 346-0496
Kent (G-11320)
Evans Industries Inc ....F.... 330 453-1122
Canton (G-2669)
Fci Inc ....D.... 216 251-5200
Cleveland (G-5224)
Felicity Plastics Machinery ....E.... 513 876-7003
Felicity (G-9643)
Ferriot Inc ....C.... 330 786-3000
Akron (G-169)
Flex Technologies Inc ....D.... 330 359-5415
Mount Eaton (G-14420)
Florida Production Engrg Inc ....C.... 740 420-5252
Circleville (G-4545)
Frantz Medical Development Ltd ....C.... 440 255-1155
Mentor (G-13447)
G M R Technology Inc ....E.... 440 992-6003
Ashtabula (G-777)

Garner Industries Inc ....G.... 740 349-0238
Newark (G-14878)
Genesis Plastic Tech LLC ....D.... 440 542-0722
Solon (G-17148)
Granger Plastic Company ....E.... 513 424-1955
Middletown (G-13910)
H & H Engineered Molded Pdts ....D.... 440 415-1814
Geneva (G-10220)
Harmony Systems and Svc Inc ....D.... 937 778-1082
Piqua (G-16121)
HI Tek Mold ....G.... 440 942-4090
Mentor (G-13465)
High Tech Molding & Design Inc ....G.... 330 726-1676
Youngstown (G-20930)
Hkb Enterprises Inc ....G.... 330 733-3200
Akron (G-208)
ICO Mold LLC ....G.... 419 867-3900
Holland (G-10934)
Ieg Plastics LLC ....F.... 937 565-4211
Bellefontaine (G-1519)
Illinois Tool Works Inc ....D.... 419 633-3236
Bryan (G-2287)
Illinois Tool Works Inc ....B.... 419 636-3161
Bryan (G-2288)
Injection Molding Specialist ....G.... 440 639-7896
Painesville (G-15748)
Innovations In Plastic Inc ....G.... 216 541-6060
Cleveland (G-5460)
Innovative Plastic Molders LLC ....E.... 937 898-3775
Dayton (G-8265)
Integra Enclosures Inc ....G.... 440 269-4966
Willoughby (G-20343)
International Supply Corp ....G.... 513 793-0393
Cincinnati (G-3858)
Interpak Inc ....E.... 440 974-8999
Mentor (G-13475)
J & O Plastics Inc ....E.... 330 927-3169
Rittman (G-16522)
Jaco Manufacturing Company ....D.... 440 234-4000
Berea (G-1612)
Jay Industries Inc ....A.... 419 747-4161
Mansfield (G-12461)
Jensar Manufacturing LLC ....G.... 419 727-8320
Toledo (G-18357)
Jos-Tech Inc ....E.... 330 678-3260
Kent (G-11337)
Joslyn Manufacturing Company ....E.... 330 467-8111
Macedonia (G-12309)
Kasai North America Inc ....E.... 419 209-0470
Upper Sandusky (G-18958)
Kathom Manufacturing Co Inc ....E.... 513 868-8890
Hamilton (G-10579)
Kittyhawk Molding Company Inc ....E.... 937 746-3663
Carlisle (G-2894)
L C Liming & Sons Inc ....G.... 513 876-2555
Felicity (G-9644)
Lancaster Commercial Pdts LLC ....E.... 740 286-5081
Columbus (G-7112)
Laszeray Technology LLC ....D.... 440 582-8430
North Royalton (G-15283)
Lee Plastic Company LLC ....G.... 937 456-5720
Eaton (G-9160)
Lion Mold & Machine Inc ....G.... 330 688-4248
Stow (G-17603)
M L C Technologies Inc ....G.... 513 874-7792
Hamilton (G-10583)
Mag-Nif Inc ....D.... 440 255-9366
Mentor (G-13508)
Magnum Molding Inc ....G.... 937 368-3040
Conover (G-7665)
Mahar Spar Industries Inc ....G.... 216 249-7143
Cleveland (G-5606)
Majestic Plastics Inc ....G.... 937 593-9500
Bellefontaine (G-1522)
Matrix Cable and Mould ....G.... 513 832-2577
Cincinnati (G-3987)
Matrix Plastics Co Inc ....G.... 330 666-7730
Medina (G-13290)
Matrix Plastics Co Inc ....G.... 330 666-2395
Medina (G-13291)
McCann Tool & Die Inc ....F.... 330 264-8820
Wooster (G-20620)
Miami Valley Plastics Inc ....E.... 937 273-3200
Eldorado (G-9189)
Miniature Plastic Molding Ltd ....G.... 440 564-7210
Solon (G-17196)
Modern Mold Corporation ....G.... 440 236-9600
Columbia Station (G-6440)
Molders Choice Inc ....G.... 440 248-8500
Solon (G-17197)

PLASTICS: Molded

Company	Code	Phone
Molding Dynamics Inc Bedford (G-1427)	F	440 786-8100
Moldmakers Inc Kenton (G-11414)	F	419 673-0902
Montville Plastics & Rbr LLC Parkman (G-15812)	D	440 548-3211
Mvp Plastics Inc Middlefield (G-13835)	F	440 834-1790
NBC Industries Inc Cleveland (G-5731)	F	216 651-9800
Nebraska Industries Corp Wauseon (G-19529)	E	419 335-6010
Nissen Chemitec America Inc London (G-12065)	C	740 852-3200
Nitrojection Chesterland (G-3166)	G	440 834-8790
North Canton Plastics Inc Canton (G-2765)	E	330 497-0071
Northshore Mold Inc Cleveland (G-5786)	G	440 838-8212
Ohio Precision Molding Inc Barberton (G-1091)	E	330 745-9393
Omega Polymer Technologies Inc Aurora (G-897)	G	330 562-5201
Omega Pultrusions Incorporated Aurora (G-898)	C	330 562-5201
Orbit Manufacturing Inc Batavia (G-1175)	E	513 732-6097
P M Machine Inc Willoughby (G-20395)	F	440 942-6537
P S Plastics Inc Columbus (G-7282)	F	614 262-7070
Pace Mold & Machine LLC Massillon (G-13037)	G	330 879-1777
Paragon Plastics New Middletown (G-14751)	F	330 542-9825
Pave Technology Co Dayton (G-8417)	E	937 890-1100
Performance Plastics Ltd Cincinnati (G-4150)	E	513 321-8404
Pilot Plastics Inc Peninsula (G-15897)	E	330 920-1718
Pioneer Custom Molding Inc Pioneer (G-16088)	E	419 737-3252
Pioneer Plastics Corporation Akron (G-321)	C	330 896-2356
Plastex Industries Inc Maumee (G-13138)	E	419 531-0189
Plastic Enterprises Inc Elyria (G-9312)	E	440 324-3240
Plastic Enterprises Inc Elyria (G-9313)	G	440 366-0220
Plastic Moldings Company Llc Blue Ash (G-1830)	D	513 921-5040
Plastics Converting Solutions Medina (G-13319)	G	330 722-2537
Podnar Plastics Inc Kent (G-11363)	E	330 673-2255
Polyquest Inc Sagamore Hills (G-16619)	E	330 888-9448
Positool Technologies Inc Brunswick (G-2227)	E	330 220-4002
Possible Plastics Inc Grove City (G-10457)	G	614 277-2100
Precision Polymers Inc Reynoldsburg (G-16448)	G	614 322-9951
Precision Thrmplstc Compontts Lima (G-11962)	D	419 227-4500
Preform Technologies LLC Swanton (G-17919)	G	419 720-0355
Prime Engineered Plastics Corp Canton (G-2791)	F	330 452-5110
Proficient Plastics Inc Mentor (G-13557)	F	440 205-9700
Progressive Molding Tech Medina (G-13323)	G	330 220-7030
Proto Plastics Inc Tipp City (G-18129)	E	937 667-8416
Proto-Mold Products Co Inc Piqua (G-16157)	E	937 778-1959
Ptc Enterprises Inc Edon (G-9188)	E	419 272-2524
PVS Plastics Technology Corp Huber Heights (G-11023)	E	937 233-4376
Queen City Polymers Inc West Chester (G-19776)	E	513 779-0990
R Dunn Mold Inc Piqua (G-16158)	G	937 773-3388
Radar Love Co Findlay (G-9744)	F	419 951-4750
Rage Corporation Hilliard (G-10857)	D	614 771-4771
Raven Concealment Systems LLC North Ridgeville (G-15249)	F	440 508-9000
Recto Molded Products Inc Cincinnati (G-4256)	D	513 871-5544
Reserve Industries Inc Bay Village (G-1208)	E	440 871-2796
Resinoid Engineering Corp Hebron (G-10759)	D	740 928-6115
Retterbush Fiberglass Corp Piqua (G-16159)	E	937 778-1936
Revere Plastics Systems LLC Clyde (G-6394)	B	419 547-6918
Rez-Tech Corporation Kent (G-11374)	E	330 673-4009
Ro-MAI Industries Inc Twinsburg (G-18847)	E	330 425-9090
Ross Special Products Inc Troy (G-18700)	F	937 335-8406
Rotosolutions Inc Ashland (G-745)	F	419 903-0800
Royal Plastics Inc Mentor (G-13575)	C	440 352-1357
Saint-Gobain Hycomp LLC Cleveland (G-6027)	C	440 234-2002
Shelly Fisher Mansfield (G-12512)	D	419 522-6696
Shiloh Industries Inc Dayton (G-8504)	F	937 236-5100
Skribs Tool and Die Inc Mentor (G-13583)	F	440 951-7774
Spectrum Plastics Corporation Cuyahoga Falls (G-7921)	G	330 926-9766
Stanley Electric US Co Inc London (G-12069)	B	740 852-5200
State Tool and Die Inc Cleveland (G-6099)	G	216 267-6030
Stewart Acquisition LLC Kirtland (G-11471)	E	800 376-4466
Stewart Acquisition LLC Twinsburg (G-18860)	E	330 963-0322
Stopol Equipment Sales LLC Brunswick (G-2240)	F	440 499-0030
Sun State Plastics Inc Canton (G-2829)	E	330 494-5220
Tech II Inc Urbana (G-19014)	C	937 969-7000
Tech-Way Industries Inc Franklin (G-9925)	D	937 746-1004
Technimold Plus Inc Port Jefferson (G-16266)	F	937 492-4077
Tetra Mold & Tool Inc New Carlisle (G-14679)	F	937 845-1651
Th Plastics Inc Bowling Green (G-2001)	C	419 352-2770
Thogus Products Company Avon Lake (G-1011)	D	440 933-8850
Thomas Tool & Mold Company Westerville (G-20078)	F	614 890-4978
Tjar Innovations LLC Xenia (G-20797)	F	937 347-1999
Toledo Molding & Die Inc Bowling Green (G-2002)	F	419 354-6050
Toledo Molding & Die Inc Delphos (G-8756)	F	419 692-6022
Torsion Plastics Kent (G-11395)	F	812 453-9645
Treemen Industries Inc Boardman (G-1904)	E	330 965-3777
Triaxis Machine & Tool LLC North Royalton (G-15308)	F	440 230-0303
Trimold LLC Circleville (G-4563)	B	740 474-7591
Turbo Machine & Tool Inc Cleveland (G-6223)	F	216 651-1940
U S Development Corp Dunkirk (G-9035)	E	570 966-5990
Universal Plastics - Sajar Middlefield (G-13863)	G	440 632-5203
US Molding Machinery Co Inc Willoughby (G-20456)	E	440 918-1701
V & R Molded Products Inc Willard (G-20247)	F	419 752-4171
Venture Plastics Inc Newton Falls (G-14995)	E	330 872-5774
Venture Plastics Inc Newton Falls (G-14996)	E	330 872-6262
Vicas Manufacturing Co Inc Cincinnati (G-4480)	E	513 791-7741
Vision Color LLC West Unity (G-19975)	G	419 924-9450
Vichek Plastics Middlefield (G-13866)	G	440 632-1631
W T Inc Lima (G-11957)	F	419 224-6942
Waugs Inc Ashland (G-754)	G	440 315-4851
Weldon Plastics Corporation Twinsburg (G-18874)	G	330 425-9660
Westar Plastics Llc Bryan (G-2313)	G	419 636-1333
Wilbert Inc Bellevue (G-1551)	E	419 483-2300
Windsor Mold Inc Bellevue (G-1552)	E	419 484-2400
Windsor Mold USA Inc Bellevue (G-1553)	E	419 483-0653
World Class Plastics Inc Russells Point (G-16603)	D	937 843-3003
World Resource Solutons Corp Plain City (G-16219)	G	614 733-3737
Zehrco-Giancola Composites Inc Jefferson (G-11244)	G	440 576-9941

PLASTICS: Molded

Company	Code	Phone
Alpha Packaging Holdings Inc Cleveland (G-4675)	B	216 252-5595
American Molding Company Inc Barberton (G-1051)	G	330 620-6799
Beach Mfg Plastic Molding Div New Carlisle (G-14663)	D	937 882-6400
Cardinal Products Inc North Royalton (G-15265)	G	440 237-8280
Cobra Plastics Inc Macedonia (G-12284)	D	330 425-3669
Core Composites Cincinnati LLC Batavia (G-1133)	E	513 724-6111
Core Molding Technologies Inc Columbus (G-6820)	B	614 870-5000
Country Molding Newbury (G-14948)	G	440 564-5235
Crg Plastics Inc Dayton (G-8113)	F	937 298-2025
Don-Ell Corporation Sylvania (G-17936)	E	419 841-7114
G S K Inc Greenville (G-10371)	G	937 547-1611
Kurz-Kasch Inc Newcomerstown (G-14976)	C	740 498-8343
Kurzkasch Inc Wilm Div Newcomerstown (G-14978)	F	740 498-8345
Liqui-Box Corporation Upper Sandusky (G-18960)	E	419 209-9085
Mar-Bal Inc Chagrin Falls (G-3057)	D	440 543-7526
Mar-Bal Inc Chagrin Falls (G-3058)	E	440 543-7526
Meggitt (erlanger) LLC Cincinnati (G-4000)	D	513 851-5550
Mibtach Enterprises Inc Cincinnati (G-4021)	G	513 941-0387
Midwest Molding Inc Plain City (G-16202)	E	614 873-1572
Molded Extruded Bedford Heights (G-1475)	G	216 475-5491
Molded Fiber Glass Companies Ashtabula (G-1475)	A	440 997-5851
Molded Fiber Glass Companies Ashtabula (G-790)		440 997-5851
Molders World Inc Blue Ash (G-1823)	G	513 469-6653
Moore Industries Inc Montpelier (G-14313)	D	419 485-5572
Myers Industries Inc Akron (G-293)	E	330 253-5592
North Coast Custom Molding Inc Dunkirk (G-9035)	F	419 905-6447
Northwest Molded Plastics Edon (G-9186)	G	419 459-4414
Palpac Industries Inc Ottawa (G-15661)	F	419 523-3230
Podnar Plastics Inc Kent (G-11362)	G	330 673-2255
Priority Custom Molding Inc Beavercreek Township (G-1373)	F	937 431-8770
R and S Technologies Inc Bellevue (G-1542)	F	419 483-3691
Sentry Protection LLC Lakewood (G-11535)	G	216 228-3200

Employee Codes: A=Over 500 employees, B=251-500
C=101-250, D=51-100, E=20-50, F=10-19, G=3-9

PLASTICS: Molded

Step2 Company LLC................................B........ 866 429-5200
  Streetsboro (G-17700)
Step2 Company LLC................................B........ 419 938-6343
  Perrysville (G-16032)
Sugar Showcase ....G........ 330 792-9154
  Youngstown (G-21040)
Team Amity Molds & Plastic ....D........ 937 667-7856
  Tipp City (G-18136)
Trilogy Plastics Inc ....D........ 330 821-4700
  Alliance (G-511)
Trilogy Plastics Inc ....D........ 440 893-5522
  Chagrin Falls (G-3085)
U S Development Corp ....E........ 330 673-6900
  Kent (G-11398)
Vast Mold & Tool Co Inc ....G........ 440 942-7585
  Mentor (G-13622)
Wch Molding LLC ....E........ 740 335-6320
  Wshngtn CT Hs (G-20748)
Yanfeng US Automotive ....B........ 419 636-4211
  Bryan (G-2314)

PLASTICS: Polystyrene Foam

A K Athletic Equipment Inc ....E........ 614 920-3069
  Canal Winchester (G-2497)
ADS Ventures Inc ....G........ 614 658-0050
  Hilliard (G-10801)
Advanced Drainage Systems Inc ....D........ 614 658-0050
  Hilliard (G-10803)
All Foam Products Co ....G........ 330 849-3636
  Middlefield (G-13775)
All Foam Products Co ....G........ 330 849-3636
  Middlefield (G-13776)
Amatech Inc ....E........ 614 252-2506
  Columbus (G-6579)
Armaly LLC ....E........ 740 852-3621
  London (G-12049)
Creative Foam Dayton Mold ....G........ 937 279-9987
  Dayton (G-8111)
Dayton Molded Urethanes LLC..............D........ 937 279-9987
  Dayton (G-8139)
Deufol Worldwide Packaging LLC..........E........ 440 232-1100
  Bedford (G-1400)
Dow Chemical Company ....F........ 937 254-1550
  Dayton (G-8166)
Extol of Ohio Inc ....E........ 419 668-2072
  Norwalk (G-15392)
Gdc Inc ....F........ 574 533-3128
  Wooster (G-20596)
Hfi LLC ....B........ 614 491-0700
  Columbus (G-6995)
ICP Adhesives and Sealants Inc............F........ 330 753-4585
  Norton (G-15369)
Interior Dnnage Spcialites Inc................F........ 614 291-0900
  Columbus (G-7042)
ISO Technologies Inc ....G........ 740 928-0084
  Heath (G-10722)
IVEX Protective Packaging Inc ....E........ 937 498-9298
  Sidney (G-17046)
Jain America Foods Inc ....G........ 614 850-9400
  Columbus (G-7058)
Jain America Holdings Inc ....D........ 614 850-9400
  Columbus (G-7059)
M L B Molded Urethane Pdts LLC..........G........ 419 825-9140
  Swanton (G-17916)
Myers Industries Inc ....E........ 330 253-5592
  Akron (G-292)
Ohio Decorative Products LLC...............C........ 419 647-9033
  Spencerville (G-17311)
Ohio Foam Corporation ....G........ 419 563-0399
  Bucyrus (G-2341)
Ohio Foam Corporation ....G........ 614 252-4877
  Columbus (G-7248)
Owens Corning Sales LLC......................C........ 330 634-0460
  Tallmadge (G-17998)
Palpac Industries Inc ....F........ 419 523-3230
  Ottawa (G-15661)
Paragon Custom Plastics Inc ....E........ 419 636-6060
  Bryan (G-2304)
Plastic Forming Company Inc ....E........ 330 830-5167
  Massillon (G-13039)
Prime Industries Inc ....E........ 440 288-3626
  Lorain (G-12113)
S & A Industries Corporation ....D........ 330 733-7040
  Akron (G-364)
Scott Port-A-Fold Inc ....E........ 419 748-8880
  Napoleon (G-14561)
Smithers-Oasis Company ....F........ 330 673-5831
  Kent (G-11387)
Sonoco Prtective Solutions Inc..............D........ 419 420-0029
  Findlay (G-9759)

Toy & Sport Trends Inc ....E........ 419 748-8880
  Napoleon (G-14562)
Unique-Chardan Inc ....E........ 419 636-6900
  Bryan (G-2311)

PLASTICS: Protein

Hexa Americas Inc ....E........ 937 497-7900
  Sidney (G-17043)

PLASTICS: Thermoformed

AMD Plastics LLC ....F........ 216 289-4862
  Euclid (G-9401)
Arthur Corporation ....D........ 419 433-7202
  Huron (G-11089)
Beast Carbon Corporation ....G........ 800 909-9051
  Cincinnati (G-3384)
Comdess Company Inc ....F........ 330 769-2094
  Seville (G-16914)
Corvac Composites LLC ....E........ 248 807-0969
  Greenfield (G-10347)
Creative Plastics Intl................................F........ 937 596-6769
  Jackson Center (G-11206)
Encore Industries Inc ....C........ 419 626-8000
  Sandusky (G-16807)
First Choice Packaging Inc ....C........ 419 333-4100
  Fremont (G-10014)
Integral Design Inc ....F........ 216 524-0555
  Cleveland (G-5462)
Kurz-Kasch Inc ....D........ 740 498-8343
  Newcomerstown (G-14977)
Maverick Corporation ....F........ 513 469-9919
  Blue Ash (G-1816)
Pendaform Company ....C........ 740 826-5000
  New Concord (G-14685)
Plastikos Corporation ....E........ 513 732-0961
  Batavia (G-1176)
Premix Inc ....C........ 440 224-2181
  North Kingsville (G-15160)
Progrssive Molding Bolivar Inc ....C........ 330 874-3000
  Bolivar (G-1925)
Replex Mirror Company ....E........ 740 397-5535
  Mount Vernon (G-14504)
Rlr Industries Inc ....E........ 440 951-9501
  Mentor (G-13574)
Rochling Glastic Composites LP ....C........ 216 486-0100
  Cleveland (G-5996)
Saint-Gobain Prfmce Plas Corp..............C........ 330 296-9948
  Ravenna (G-16400)
Saint-Gobain Prfmce Plas Corp..............C........ 440 836-9000
  Solon (G-17227)
Scott Molders Incorporated ....D........ 330 673-5777
  Kent (G-11382)
Springseal Inc ....F........ 330 626-0673
  Ravenna (G-16407)
Tooling Tech Holdings LLC ....G........ 937 295-3672
  Fort Loramie (G-9809)

PLATE WORK: For Nuclear Industry

Curtiss-Wright Flow Control ....D........ 513 735-2538
  Batavia (G-1134)

PLATE WORK: Metalworking Trade

Alloy Engineering Company ....D........ 440 243-6800
  Berea (G-1589)
Hard Chrome Plating Consultant ....G........ 216 631-9090
  Cleveland (G-5374)
Mark One Manufacturing Ltd ....G........ 419 628-4405
  Minster (G-14220)
Mercury Iron and Steel Co ....F........ 440 349-1500
  Solon (G-17190)
Rezmann Karoly ....G........ 216 441-4357
  Cleveland (G-5982)

PLATEMAKING SVC: Color Separations, For The Printing Trade

Lazer Systems Inc.....................................F........ 513 641-4002
  Cincinnati (G-3935)
Pinnacle Graphics & Imaging ....F........ 216 781-1800
  Cleveland (G-5878)
Registered Images Inc ....G........ 859 781-9200
  Cincinnati (G-4257)
Stevenson Color Inc ....C........ 513 321-7500
  Cincinnati (G-4381)

PLATEMAKING SVC: Embossing, For The Printing Trade

Acme Printing Co Inc ....G........ 419 626-4426
  Sandusky (G-16792)

PLATENS, EXC PRINTERS': Rubber, Solid Or Covered

Tmac Machine Inc ....G........ 330 673-0621
  Kent (G-11394)

PLATES

Amos Media Company ....C........ 937 498-2111
  Sidney (G-17015)
Anderson & Vreeland Inc ....D........ 419 636-5002
  Bryan (G-2264)
Art-American Printing Plates ....E........ 216 241-4420
  Cleveland (G-4738)
Bock & Pierce Enterprises ....G........ 513 474-9500
  Cincinnati (G-3398)
Carey Color Inc ....D........ 330 239-1835
  Sharon Center (G-16947)
Century Graphics Inc ....E........ 614 895-7698
  Westerville (G-19983)
Csw of Ny Inc ....F........ 413 589-1311
  Sylvania (G-17935)
Custom Cntrwght Plate Proc Inc ....G........ 330 448-2347
  Masury (G-13060)
Customer Service Systems Inc ....G........ 330 677-2877
  Kent (G-11308)
Dorothy Crooker ....G........ 513 385-0888
  Cincinnati (G-3602)
E C Shaw Co ....E........ 513 721-6334
  Cincinnati (G-3616)
Earl D Arnold Printing Company ....E........ 513 533-6900
  Cincinnati (G-3624)
Econo Products Inc ....F........ 330 923-4101
  Cuyahoga Falls (G-7862)
Fine Lines Laser Engraving ....G........ 419 337-6313
  Wauseon (G-19515)
Flexoplate Inc ....E........ 513 489-0433
  Blue Ash (G-1776)
Grant John ....E........ 937 298-0633
  Dayton (G-8234)
Hadronics Inc ....D........ 513 321-9350
  Cincinnati (G-3792)
Harris Paper Crafts Inc ....F........ 614 299-2141
  Columbus (G-6983)
Jerry Pulfer ....G........ 937 778-1861
  Piqua (G-16134)
Keystone Press Inc ....E........ 419 243-7326
  Toledo (G-18367)
Mark-All Enterprises LLC ....E........ 800 433-3615
  Akron (G-268)
Master Marking Company Inc ....F........ 330 688-6797
  Stow (G-17604)
Penguin Enterprises Inc ....E........ 440 899-5112
  Westlake (G-20140)
Prime Printing Inc ....E........ 937 438-3707
  Dayton (G-8442)
Quality Rubber Stamp Inc ....G........ 614 235-2700
  Columbus (G-7365)
R W Michael Printing Co ....G........ 330 923-9277
  Akron (G-340)
Robert H Shackelford ....G........ 330 364-2221
  New Philadelphia (G-14799)
Shamrock Plastics Inc ....F........ 740 392-5555
  Mount Vernon (G-14508)
Universal Urethane Pdts Inc ....D........ 419 693-7400
  Toledo (G-18585)
West-Camp Press Inc ....D........ 614 882-2378
  Westerville (G-20082)
Westrock Cp LLC ....C........ 937 898-2115
  Dayton (G-8589)
Williams Steel Rule Die Co ....F........ 216 431-3232
  Cleveland (G-6311)
Wood Graphics Inc ....E........ 513 771-6300
  Cincinnati (G-4516)

PLATES: Paper, Made From Purchased Materials

Premier Industries Inc ....E........ 513 271-2550
  Cincinnati (G-4187)
Taylor Company ....G........ 513 271-2550
  Cincinnati (G-4408)

PLATES: Plastic Exc Polystyrene Foam

Zehrco-Giancola Composites Inc ....C........ 440 994-6317
  Ashtabula *(G-813)*

PLATES: Sheet & Strip, Exc Coated Prdts

Major Metals Company ....E........ 419 886-4600
  Mansfield *(G-12472)*
The Florand Company ....E........ 330 747-8986
  Youngstown *(G-21044)*

PLATES: Steel

Adams Fabricating Inc ....G........ 330 866-2986
  East Sparta *(G-9093)*
Charles C Lewis Company ....F........ 440 439-3150
  Cleveland *(G-4910)*
Churchill Steel Plate Ltd ....E........ 330 425-9000
  Twinsburg *(G-18753)*

PLATING & FINISHING SVC: Decorative, Formed Prdts

Mechanical Finishers Inc LLC ....E........ 513 641-5419
  Cincinnati *(G-3993)*

PLATING & POLISHING SVC

A J Oster Foils LLC ....D........ 330 823-1700
  Alliance *(G-447)*
A-Brite LP ....D........ 216 252-2995
  Cleveland *(G-4594)*
ADS Mto ....G........ 419 424-5231
  Findlay *(G-9646)*
Ak-Isg Steel Coating Company ....D........ 216 429-6901
  Cleveland *(G-4647)*
Allegheny Ludlum LLC ....E........ 330 875-2244
  Louisville *(G-12151)*
Allen Aircraft Products Inc ....E........ 330 296-9621
  Ravenna *(G-16365)*
Aluminum Extruded Shapes Inc ....C........ 513 563-2205
  Cincinnati *(G-3328)*
Arcelormittal Columbus LLC ....C........ 614 492-6800
  Columbus *(G-6613)*
Arem Co ....F........ 440 974-6740
  Mentor *(G-13393)*
Bmd Blasting ....G........ 614 580-9468
  Columbus *(G-6681)*
Carlisle and Finch Company ....E........ 513 681-6080
  Cincinnati *(G-3445)*
Carter Machine Company Inc ....G........ 419 468-3530
  Galion *(G-10125)*
Chemical Methods Inc ....E........ 216 476-8400
  Strongsville *(G-17725)*
Chrome Deposit Corporatio ....G........ 330 773-7800
  Akron *(G-116)*
Cincinnati Gearing Systems Inc ....D........ 513 527-8600
  Cincinnati *(G-3493)*
Columbus Coatings Company ....D........ 614 492-6800
  Columbus *(G-6786)*
Commercial Honing LLC ....D........ 330 343-8896
  Dover *(G-8811)*
Commercial Steel Treating Co ....F........ 216 431-8204
  Cleveland *(G-5004)*
Conley Group Inc ....G........ 330 372-2030
  Warren *(G-19388)*
Crystal Koch Finishing Inc ....G........ 440 366-7526
  Elyria *(G-9240)*
D-G Custom Chrome LLC ....D........ 513 531-1881
  Cincinnati *(G-3571)*
Die Co Inc ....E........ 440 942-8856
  Eastlake *(G-9104)*
E L Stone Company ....E........ 330 825-4565
  Norton *(G-15365)*
Electro Prime Assembly Inc ....F........ 419 476-0100
  Rossford *(G-16583)*
Electro Prime Group LLC ....D........ 419 476-0100
  Toledo *(G-18278)*
Electro Prime Group LLC ....D........ 419 666-5000
  Rossford *(G-16584)*
Etched Metal Company ....E........ 440 248-0240
  Solon *(G-17142)*
GRB Holdings Inc ....D........ 937 236-3250
  Dayton *(G-8235)*
Hall Company ....E........ 937 652-1376
  Urbana *(G-18992)*
Hartzell Mfg Co ....E........ 937 859-5955
  Miamisburg *(G-13674)*
Industrial Paint & Strip Inc ....E........ 419 568-2222
  Waynesfield *(G-19567)*

International Finishing LLC ....G........ 937 293-3340
  Dayton *(G-8273)*
J Horst Manufacturing Co ....D........ 330 828-2216
  Dalton *(G-7945)*
J M Hamilton Group Inc ....F........ 419 229-4010
  Lima *(G-11881)*
J M S Custom Finishing ....G........ 614 264-9916
  Hilliard *(G-10832)*
Jason Incorporated ....F........ 513 860-3400
  Hamilton *(G-10576)*
McGean-Rohco Inc ....D........ 216 441-4900
  Newburgh Heights *(G-14941)*
Merk Blasting ....G........ 513 813-6375
  Cincinnati *(G-4008)*
Metaltek Industries Inc ....F........ 937 323-4933
  Springfield *(G-17447)*
Metokote Corporation ....D........ 440 934-4686
  Sheffield Village *(G-16971)*
Metokote Corporation ....C........ 419 221-2754
  Lima *(G-11905)*
Micro Lapping & Grinding Co ....E........ 216 267-6500
  Cleveland *(G-5667)*
Micro Products Co Inc ....D........ 440 943-0258
  Willoughby Hills *(G-20471)*
Milestone Services Corp ....G........ 330 374-9988
  Akron *(G-282)*
Niles Manufacturing & Finshg ....C........ 330 544-0402
  Niles *(G-15024)*
Ohio Decorative Products LLC ....C........ 419 647-9033
  Spencerville *(G-17311)*
Ohio Metal Products Company ....G........ 937 228-6101
  Dayton *(G-8399)*
Ohio Metalizing LLC ....G........ 330 830-1092
  Massillon *(G-13030)*
Ohio Roll Grinding Inc ....E........ 330 453-1884
  Louisville *(G-12162)*
Oliver Chemical Co Inc ....E........ 513 541-4540
  Cincinnati *(G-4110)*
P & L Heat Trting Grinding Inc ....E........ 330 746-1339
  Youngstown *(G-20986)*
Parker Rst-Proof Cleveland Inc ....E........ 216 481-6680
  Cleveland *(G-5847)*
Parker Trutec Incorporated ....D........ 937 653-8500
  Urbana *(G-19007)*
Rack Processing Company Inc ....E........ 937 294-1911
  Moraine *(G-14388)*
Rack Processing Company Inc ....E........ 937 294-1911
  Moraine *(G-14387)*
Reifel Industries Inc ....D........ 419 737-2138
  Pioneer *(G-16095)*
Samuel Steel Pickling Company ....D........ 330 963-3777
  Twinsburg *(G-18853)*
Sawyer Technical Materials LLC ....E........ 440 951-8770
  Willoughby *(G-20424)*
Scot Industries Inc ....E........ 330 262-7585
  Wooster *(G-20651)*
Springco Metal Coatings Inc ....C........ 216 941-0020
  Cleveland *(G-6087)*
Tri-State Fabricators Inc ....E........ 513 752-5005
  Amelia *(G-550)*
Vacuum Finishing Company ....F........ 440 286-4386
  Chardon *(G-3140)*
Vectron Inc ....D........ 440 323-3369
  Elyria *(G-9343)*
Worthington Industries Inc ....C........ 513 539-9291
  Monroe *(G-14282)*
Worthington Steel Company ....C........ 614 438-3210
  Worthington *(G-20715)*
Yoder Industries Inc ....C........ 937 278-5769
  Dayton *(G-8602)*

PLATING COMPOUNDS

Plating Process Systems Inc ....G........ 440 951-9667
  Mentor *(G-13548)*
Rotech Products Incorporated ....G........ 216 476-3722
  Cleveland *(G-6006)*
Surtec Inc ....G........ 440 239-9710
  Brunswick *(G-2242)*

PLATING SVC: Chromium, Metals Or Formed Prdts

Archer Custom Chrome LLC ....G........ 216 441-2795
  Westlake *(G-20099)*
B & R Custom Chrome ....G........ 419 536-7215
  Toledo *(G-18197)*
Chromatic Inc ....F........ 216 881-2228
  Cleveland *(G-4926)*
Chrome Deposit Corporation ....E........ 513 539-8486
  Monroe *(G-14257)*

Chrome Deposit Corporation ....E........ 513 539-8486
  Monroe *(G-14258)*
Chrome Industries Inc ....G........ 216 771-2266
  Cleveland *(G-4927)*
Customchrome Plating Inc ....F........ 440 926-3116
  Grafton *(G-10296)*
Diamond Hard Chrome Co Inc ....F........ 216 391-3618
  Cleveland *(G-5089)*
Ernie Green Industries Inc ....G........ 614 219-1423
  Columbus *(G-6903)*
Hale Performance Coatings Inc ....E........ 419 244-6451
  Toledo *(G-18319)*
Master Chrome Service Inc ....E........ 216 961-2012
  Cleveland *(G-5630)*
MPC Plating LLC ....E........ 216 881-7220
  Cleveland *(G-5710)*
New Castle Industries Inc ....C........ 724 654-2603
  Youngstown *(G-20975)*
Plate-All Metal Company Inc ....G........ 330 633-6166
  Akron *(G-322)*
Quality Plating Co ....E........ 216 361-0151
  Cleveland *(G-5942)*
R A Heller Company ....F........ 513 771-6100
  Cincinnati *(G-4242)*
Raf Acquisition Co ....F........ 440 572-5999
  Valley City *(G-19058)*
United Surface Finishing Inc ....G........ 330 453-2786
  Canton *(G-2851)*
Youngstown Hard Chrome Plating ....E........ 330 758-9721
  Youngstown *(G-21077)*

PLATING SVC: Electro

Abel Metal Processing Inc ....F........ 216 881-4156
  Cleveland *(G-4597)*
Acme Industrial Group Inc ....F........ 330 821-3900
  Alliance *(G-449)*
Aetna Plating Co ....F........ 216 341-9111
  Cleveland *(G-4637)*
Akron Plating Co Inc ....F........ 330 773-6878
  Akron *(G-47)*
American Metal Coatings Inc ....E........ 216 451-3131
  Mentor *(G-13385)*
Barker Products Company ....E........ 216 249-0900
  Cleveland *(G-4792)*
Beringer Plating Inc ....G........ 330 633-8409
  Akron *(G-84)*
Bricker Plating Inc ....E........ 419 636-1990
  Bryan *(G-2271)*
Canton Plating Co Inc ....G........ 330 452-7808
  Canton *(G-2616)*
City Plating and Polishing LLC ....G........ 216 267-8158
  Cleveland *(G-4933)*
Delta Plating Inc ....E........ 330 452-2300
  Canton *(G-2655)*
Duray Plating Company Inc ....E........ 216 941-5540
  Cleveland *(G-5122)*
Electro-Metallics Co ....E........ 513 423-8091
  Middletown *(G-13904)*
Elyria Plating Corporation ....E........ 440 365-8300
  Elyria *(G-9255)*
Epd Enterprises Inc ....D........ 216 961-1200
  Cleveland *(G-5184)*
Erieview Metal Treating Co ....D........ 216 663-1780
  Cleveland *(G-5191)*
Guaranteed Fnshg Unlimited Inc ....E........ 216 252-8200
  Cleveland *(G-5358)*
Hadronics Inc ....D........ 513 321-9350
  Cincinnati *(G-3792)*
Hearn Plating Co Ltd ....F........ 419 473-9773
  Toledo *(G-18325)*
Highland Precision Plating ....G........ 937 393-9501
  Hillsboro *(G-10880)*
Kelly Plating Co ....E........ 216 961-1080
  Cleveland *(G-5526)*
Leonhardt Plating Company ....E........ 513 242-1410
  Cincinnati *(G-3938)*
Medina Plating Corp ....E........ 330 725-4155
  Medina *(G-13294)*
MPC Plastics Inc ....D........ 216 881-7220
  Cleveland *(G-5708)*
MPC Plating LLC ....E........ 216 881-7220
  Cleveland *(G-5709)*
National Plating Corporation ....E........ 216 341-6707
  Cleveland *(G-5727)*
Novavision Inc ....D........ 419 354-1427
  Bowling Green *(G-1986)*
Ohio Electro-Polishing Co Inc ....G........ 419 667-2281
  Venedocia *(G-19155)*
P & J Industries Inc ....C........ 419 726-2675
  Toledo *(G-18452)*

PLATING SVC: Electro

Plastic Platers LLC .... C 216 961-1200
  Cleveland *(G-5886)*
Plating Technology Inc .... D 937 268-6882
  Dayton *(G-8428)*
Precious Metal Plating Co .... E 440 585-7117
  Wickliffe *(G-20228)*
Roberts-Demand Corp .... G 216 581-1300
  Cleveland *(G-5993)*
Rykon Plating Inc .... G 440 933-3273
  Avon Lake *(G-1006)*
Smith Electro Chemical Co .... E 513 351-7227
  Cincinnati *(G-4346)*
Springfield Metal Finishing .... G 937 324-2353
  Springfield *(G-17494)*
Super Fine Shine Inc .... G 740 774-1700
  Chillicothe *(G-3226)*
Techniplate Inc .... F 216 486-8825
  Cleveland *(G-6155)*
Tri-State Plating & Polishing .... G 304 529-2579
  Proctorville *(G-16348)*
U S Chrome Corporation Ohio .... F 877 872-7716
  Dayton *(G-8575)*
United Hard Chrome Corporation .... F 330 453-2786
  Canton *(G-2849)*
Whitaker Finishing LLC .... E 419 666-7746
  Northwood *(G-15352)*

PLATING SVC: NEC

Automated Wheel LLC .... D 216 651-9022
  Cleveland *(G-4771)*
Best Plating Rack Corp .... F 440 944-3270
  Wickliffe *(G-20203)*
Cascade Plating Inc .... G 440 366-4931
  Elyria *(G-9232)*
Case Plating Inc .... G 440 288-8304
  Lorain *(G-12083)*
Cleveland Plating .... G 216 249-0300
  Cleveland *(G-4969)*
Custom Brass Finishing Inc .... G 330 453-0888
  Canton *(G-2641)*
Custom Nickel LLC .... G 937 222-1995
  Dayton *(G-8121)*
Durable Plating Co .... G 216 391-2132
  Cleveland *(G-5121)*
Engineering Coatings LLC .... G 419 485-0077
  Montpelier *(G-14309)*
Future Finishes Inc .... E 513 860-0020
  Hamilton *(G-10559)*
Hercules Polishing & Plating .... F 330 455-8871
  Canton *(G-2697)*
Kyron Plating Corp .... G 216 221-7275
  Cleveland *(G-5548)*
Lake City Plating LLC .... F 440 964-3555
  Ashtabula *(G-784)*
Lake County Plating Corp .... F 440 255-8835
  Mentor *(G-13494)*
Lakeside Custom Plating Inc .... G 440 599-2035
  Conneaut *(G-7652)*
Lustrous Metal Coatings Inc .... E 330 478-4653
  Canton *(G-2735)*
M&L Plating Works LLC .... G 419 255-7701
  Toledo *(G-18393)*
Mechanical Galv-Plating Corp .... E 937 492-3143
  Sidney *(G-17051)*
Metal Brite Polishing .... G 937 278-9739
  Dayton *(G-8342)*
Mmf Incorporated .... F 614 252-2522
  Columbus *(G-7187)*
Moore Chrome Products Co .... E 419 843-3510
  Sylvania *(G-17952)*
Nicks Plating Co Inc .... F 937 773-3175
  Piqua *(G-16145)*
Paxos Plating Inc .... E 330 479-0022
  Canton *(G-2782)*
Plating Perceptions Inc .... G 330 425-4180
  Twinsburg *(G-18837)*
Plating Solutions .... G 513 771-1941
  Cincinnati *(G-4167)*
Plating Technology Inc .... G 937 268-6788
  Dayton *(G-8429)*
Porter-Guertin Co Inc .... F 513 241-7663
  Cincinnati *(G-4174)*
Rawac Plating Company .... G 937 322-7491
  Springfield *(G-17481)*
Sebring Industrial Plating .... G 330 938-6666
  Sebring *(G-16895)*
Tubetech Inc .... E 330 426-9476
  East Palestine *(G-9087)*
United State Pltg Bumper Svc .... G 614 403-4666
  Worthington *(G-20706)*

Woodhill Plating Works Company .... E 216 883-1344
  Cleveland *(G-6322)*

PLAYGROUND EQPT

Adventurous Child Inc .... G 513 531-7700
  Cincinnati *(G-3303)*
Charles V Snider & Assoc Inc .... F 440 877-9151
  North Royalton *(G-15266)*
Funtown Playgrounds Inc .... G 513 871-8585
  Cincinnati *(G-3250)*
Meyer Design Inc .... E 330 434-9176
  Akron *(G-280)*
Playground Equipment Service .... G 513 481-3776
  Cincinnati *(G-4168)*
Ultrabuilt Play Systems Inc .... F 419 652-2294
  Nova *(G-15436)*

PLEATING & STITCHING FOR THE TRADE: Decorative & Novelty

Initially Yours .... G 216 228-4478
  Lakewood *(G-11521)*

PLEATING & STITCHING SVC

A Graphic Solution .... F 216 228-7223
  Cleveland *(G-4587)*
Action Sports Apparel Inc .... G 330 848-9300
  Norton *(G-15358)*
Barbs Graffiti Inc .... E 216 881-5550
  Cleveland *(G-4790)*
Big Kahuna Graphics LLC .... G 330 455-2625
  Canton *(G-2591)*
Catania Medallic Specialty .... E 440 933-9595
  Avon Lake *(G-981)*
David Brandeberry .... G 937 653-4680
  Urbana *(G-18988)*
Design Original Inc .... F 937 596-5121
  Jackson Center *(G-11207)*
Dimensions Three Inc .... G 614 539-5180
  Grove City *(G-10426)*
Fineline Imprints Inc .... E 740 453-1083
  Zanesville *(G-21135)*
Finn Graphics Inc .... E 513 941-6161
  Cincinnati *(G-3690)*
Logan Screen Printing .... G 740 385-3303
  Logan *(G-12033)*
Robs Creative Screen Printing .... G 740 264-6383
  Wintersville *(G-20541)*
Shamrock Companies Inc .... D 440 899-9510
  Westlake *(G-20158)*
Wizard Graphics Inc .... G 419 354-3098
  Bowling Green *(G-2006)*

PLUMBERS' GOODS: Rubber

Deruijter Intl USA Inc .... F 419 678-3909
  Coldwater *(G-6405)*

PLUMBING & HEATING EQPT & SPLY, WHOL: Htg Eqpt/Panels, Solar

Hess Advanced Solutions Llc .... G 937 829-4794
  Dayton *(G-8249)*
Hunters Hightech Energy Systm .... G 614 275-4777
  Columbus *(G-7012)*

PLUMBING & HEATING EQPT & SPLY, WHOLESALE: Hydronic Htg Eqpt

Accurate Mechanical Inc .... E 740 681-1332
  Lancaster *(G-11538)*

PLUMBING & HEATING EQPT & SPLYS WHOLESALERS

Carr Supply Co .... G 937 276-2555
  Dayton *(G-8076)*
Carter-Jones Lumber Company .... F 440 834-8164
  Middlefield *(G-13782)*
Clean Water Conditioning .... G 614 475-4532
  Columbus *(G-4771)*
Oatey Supply Chain Svcs Inc .... C 216 267-7100
  Cleveland *(G-5795)*
Savko Plastic Pipe & Fittings .... F 614 885-8420
  Columbus *(G-7422)*
Trumbull Manufacturing Inc .... D 330 393-6624
  Warren *(G-19452)*
US Water Company LLC .... G 740 453-0604
  Zanesville *(G-21186)*

W A S P Inc .... G 740 439-2398
  Cambridge *(G-2462)*
Waxman Industries Inc .... C 440 439-1830
  Cleveland *(G-6295)*
Wc Sales Inc .... G 419 836-2300
  Northwood *(G-15350)*
Zurn Industries LLC .... F 814 455-0921
  Hilliard *(G-10875)*

PLUMBING & HEATING EQPT & SPLYS, WHOL: Fireplaces, Prefab

Mason Structural Steel Inc .... D 440 439-1040
  Walton Hills *(G-19312)*

PLUMBING & HEATING EQPT & SPLYS, WHOL: Pipe/Fitting, Plastic

Cleveland Plastic Fabricat .... F 216 797-7300
  Euclid *(G-9409)*
Ppafco Inc .... F 614 488-7259
  Columbus *(G-7335)*

PLUMBING & HEATING EQPT & SPLYS, WHOL: Plumbing Fitting/Sply

Carr Supply Co .... G 937 316-6300
  Greenville *(G-10363)*
Columbus Pipe and Equipment Co .... F 614 444-7871
  Columbus *(G-6798)*
Empire Brass Co .... E 216 431-6565
  Cleveland *(G-5173)*
Famous Realty Cleveland Inc .... F 740 685-2533
  Byesville *(G-2385)*
Ferguson Fire Fabrication Inc .... F 614 299-2070
  Columbus *(G-6918)*
Mansfield Plumbing Pdts LLC .... A 419 938-5211
  Perrysville *(G-16030)*
Parker-Hannifin Corporation .... B 937 456-5571
  Eaton *(G-9163)*
Parker-Hannifin Corporation .... C 614 279-7070
  Columbus *(G-7294)*
Trumbull Industries Inc .... E 330 434-6174
  Akron *(G-413)*
Winsupply Inc .... F 937 346-0600
  Springfield *(G-17518)*
Zekelman Industries Inc .... C 740 432-2146
  Cambridge *(G-2463)*

PLUMBING & HEATING EQPT & SPLYS, WHOL: Plumbng/Heatng Valves

Famous Industries Inc .... E 330 535-1811
  Akron *(G-166)*
Maverick Industries Inc .... F 440 838-5335
  Brecksville *(G-2049)*
Northcoast Process Controls .... G 440 498-0542
  Cleveland *(G-5771)*

PLUMBING & HEATING EQPT & SPLYS, WHOL: Water Purif Eqpt

Chandler Systems Incorporated .... D 888 363-9434
  Ashland *(G-693)*
Enting Water Conditioning Inc .... E 937 294-5100
  Moraine *(G-14350)*
Pelton Environmental Products .... G 440 838-1221
  Lewis Center *(G-11770)*
Wayne/Scott Fetzer Company .... C 800 237-0987
  Harrison *(G-10679)*

PLUMBING & HEATING EQPT, WHOLESALE: Water Heaters/Purif

Mountain Filtration Systems .... G 419 395-2526
  Defiance *(G-8640)*

PLUMBING & HEATING EQPT/SPLYS, WHOL: Boilers, Hot Water Htg

Abbott Mechanical Services LLC .... G 419 460-4315
  Maumee *(G-13065)*

PLUMBING FIXTURES

As America Inc .... C 614 497-9384
  Groveport *(G-10483)*
As America Inc .... G 330 337-2219
  Salem *(G-16718)*
Atlantic Co .... E 440 944-8988
  Willoughby Hills *(G-20466)*

Carr Supply Co ....G....... 937 316-6300
  Greenville (G-10363)
Carr Supply Co ....G....... 937 276-2555
  Dayton (G-8076)
Cfrc Wtr & Enrgy Solutions Inc ....G....... 216 479-0290
  Cleveland (G-4906)
Dittmar Sales and Service ....G....... 740 653-7933
  Lancaster (G-11567)
Empire Brass Co ....E....... 216 431-6565
  Cleveland (G-5173)
Field Stone Inc ....D....... 937 898-3236
  Tipp City (G-18112)
Fort Recovery Industries Inc ....B....... 419 375-4121
  Fort Recovery (G-9818)
Fort Recovery Industries Inc ....E....... 419 375-3005
  Fort Recovery (G-9819)
Krendl Machine Company ....D....... 419 692-3060
  Delphos (G-8747)
Lsq Manufacturing Inc ....F....... 330 725-4905
  Medina (G-13287)
Maass Midwest Mfg Inc ....G....... 419 894-6424
  Arcadia (G-625)
Mansfield Plumbing Pdts LLC ....A....... 419 938-5211
  Perrysville (G-16030)
Next Gerenation Crimping ....G....... 440 237-6300
  North Royalton (G-15288)
Scotts Miracle-Gro Products ....E....... 937 644-0011
  Marysville (G-12812)
Trumbull Manufacturing Inc ....D....... 330 393-6624
  Warren (G-19452)
W A S P Inc ....G....... 740 439-2398
  Cambridge (G-2462)
Waxman Industries Inc ....C....... 440 439-1830
  Cleveland (G-6295)
Winsupply Inc ....F....... 937 346-0600
  Springfield (G-17518)
Zekelman Industries Inc ....C....... 740 432-2146
  Cambridge (G-2463)

PLUMBING FIXTURES: Brass, Incl Drain Cocks, Faucets/Spigots

American Brass Manufacturing ....E....... 216 431-6565
  Cleveland (G-4683)
CMI Holding Company Crawford ....D....... 419 468-9122
  Galion (G-10128)
National Brass Company Inc ....G....... 216 651-8530
  Cleveland (G-5723)

PLUMBING FIXTURES: Plastic

Add-A-Trap LLC ....G....... 330 750-0417
  Struthers (G-17812)
Bobbart Industries Inc ....E....... 419 350-5477
  Sylvania (G-17934)
Certified Walk In Tubs ....F....... 614 436-4848
  Columbus (G-6756)
Cincinnati Machines Inc ....A....... 513 536-2432
  Batavia (G-1130)
Cultured Marble Inc ....G....... 330 549-2282
  North Lima (G-15169)
Dbhl Inc ....F....... 216 267-7100
  Cleveland (G-5076)
Hancor Inc ....B....... 614 658-0050
  Hilliard (G-10827)
Lubrizol Global Management ....F....... 216 447-5000
  Brecksville (G-2048)
Mansfield Plumbing Pdts LLC ....E....... 330 496-2301
  Big Prairie (G-1675)
Mansfield Plumbing Pdts LLC ....A....... 419 938-5211
  Perrysville (G-16030)
Meese Inc ....D....... 440 998-1202
  Ashtabula (G-785)
Nibco Inc ....E....... 513 228-1426
  Lebanon (G-11676)
Righter Plumbing ....G....... 614 604-7197
  Pataskala (G-15840)
Tower Industries Ltd ....E....... 330 837-2216
  Massillon (G-13054)

PLUMBING FIXTURES: Vitreous

Aabel Plumbing Inc ....E....... 937 434-4343
  Dayton (G-7999)
Accent Manufacturing Inc ....F....... 330 724-7704
  Norton (G-15355)
As America Inc ....G....... 330 337-2219
  Salem (G-16718)
East Woodworking Company ....G....... 216 791-5950
  Cleveland (G-5140)
Mansfield Plumbing Pdts LLC ....A....... 419 938-5211
  Perrysville (G-16030)

PLUMBING FIXTURES: Vitreous China

As America Inc ....E....... 419 522-4211
  Mansfield (G-12408)
Watersource LLC ....G....... 419 747-9552
  Mansfield (G-12538)

POINT OF SALE DEVICES

A & M Creative Group Inc ....E....... 330 452-8940
  Canton (G-2555)
Outta Box Dispensers LLC ....G....... 937 221-7106
  Dayton (G-8412)

POLE LINE HARDWARE

Helical Line Products Co ....E....... 440 933-9263
  Avon Lake (G-989)
Preformed Line Products Co ....B....... 440 461-5200
  Mayfield Village (G-13174)

POLICE PROTECTION

Public Safety Ohio Department ....G....... 440 943-5545
  Willowick (G-20481)

POLISHING SVC: Metals Or Formed Prdts

A & B Deburring Company ....F....... 513 723-0444
  Cincinnati (G-3274)
Als Polishing Shop Inc ....G....... 419 476-8857
  Toledo (G-18167)
Areway Acquisition Inc ....D....... 216 651-9022
  Brooklyn (G-2111)
Century Plating Inc ....G....... 216 531-4131
  Cleveland (G-4902)
Charles J Meyers ....E....... 513 922-2866
  Cincinnati (G-3465)
Custom Polishing ....G....... 937 596-0430
  Sidney (G-17024)
Euclid Refinishing Compnay Inc ....F....... 440 275-3356
  Austinburg (G-920)
Faithful Mold Polishing Ex ....G....... 330 678-8006
  Kent (G-11321)
Finishers Inc ....G....... 937 773-3177
  Piqua (G-16115)
Gei of Columbiana Inc ....D....... 330 783-0270
  Youngstown (G-20915)
General Extrusions Inc ....D....... 330 783-0270
  Youngstown (G-20917)
Hy-Blast Inc ....F....... 513 424-0704
  Middletown (G-13912)
Indigo 48 LLC ....G....... 419 551-6931
  Montpelier (G-14310)
J J Polishing Inc ....G....... 614 214-7637
  Plain City (G-16197)
McCrary Metal Polishing Inc ....F....... 937 492-1979
  Port Jefferson (G-16265)
Miami Valley Polishing LL ....G....... 937 498-1634
  Sidney (G-17053)
Miami Valley Polishing LLC ....F....... 937 615-9353
  Piqua (G-16143)
Microsheen Corporation ....F....... 216 481-5610
  Cleveland (G-5670)
Microtek Finishing LLC ....E....... 513 766-5600
  West Chester (G-19879)
P & C Metal Polishing Inc ....E....... 513 771-9143
  Cincinnati (G-4128)
Shalmet Corporation ....G....... 440 236-8840
  Elyria (G-9326)
Sun Polishing Corp ....G....... 440 237-5525
  Cleveland (G-6118)
Tuckers Mold Polishing ....G....... 937 339-3063
  Troy (G-18716)
Wall Polishing LLC ....G....... 937 698-1330
  Ludlow Falls (G-12270)

POLYESTERS

Dupont Specialty Pdts USA LLC ....E....... 740 474-0220
  Circleville (G-4543)
Illinois Tool Works Inc ....C....... 513 489-7600
  Blue Ash (G-1791)
Maintenance Repair Supply Inc ....E....... 740 922-3006
  Midvale (G-13980)
Mar-Bal Inc ....D....... 440 543-7526
  Chagrin Falls (G-3057)
Mar-Bal Inc ....D....... 440 543-7526
  Chagrin Falls (G-3058)
Pet Processors LLc ....D....... 440 354-4321
  Painesville (G-15775)

POLYETHYLENE CHLOROSULFONATED RUBBER

Lyondell Chemical Company ....D....... 513 530-4000
  Cincinnati (G-3960)

POLYETHYLENE RESINS

Composite Technical Svcs LLC ....G....... 937 660-3783
  Kettering (G-11430)
Etna Products Incorporated ....E....... 440 543-9845
  Chagrin Falls (G-3046)
Pitt Plastics Inc ....D....... 614 868-8660
  Columbus (G-7317)

POLYMETHYL METHACRYLATE RESINS: Plexiglas

Mexichem Specialty Resins Inc ....E....... 440 930-1435
  Avon Lake (G-996)

POLYPROPYLENE RESINS

Pahuja Inc ....D....... 614 864-3989
  Gahanna (G-10097)
San Pallet LLC ....G....... 937 271-5308
  Troy (G-18702)

POLYSTYRENE RESINS

Deltech Polymers Corporation ....G....... 937 339-3150
  Troy (G-18648)
Nova Chemicals Inc ....D....... 440 352-3381
  Painesville (G-15766)
Progressive Foam Tech Inc ....C....... 330 756-3200
  Beach City (G-1214)
Queen City Foam Inc ....G....... 513 741-7722
  Cincinnati (G-4236)

POLYTETRAFLUOROETHYLENE RESINS

Crg Plastics Inc ....F....... 937 298-2025
  Dayton (G-8113)

POLYURETHANE RESINS

Hfi LLC ....B....... 614 491-0700
  Columbus (G-6995)
Louisville Molded Products ....G....... 330 877-9740
  Hartville (G-10701)
Polymer Concepts Inc ....G....... 440 953-9605
  Mentor (G-13551)

POLYVINYL CHLORIDE RESINS

Aurora Plastics LLC ....D....... 330 422-0700
  Streetsboro (G-17662)
Crane Blending Center ....E....... 614 542-1199
  Columbus (G-6835)
Kirtland Cpitl Partners III LP ....G....... 440 585-9010
  Willoughby Hills (G-20470)
Prime Conduit Inc ....F....... 216 464-3400
  Beachwood (G-1269)

POLYVINYLIDENE CHLORIDE RESINS

Great Lakes Textiles Inc ....E....... 440 914-1122
  Solon (G-17156)

PONTOONS: Rubber

Survitec Group (usa) Inc ....E....... 330 239-4331
  Sharon Center (G-16954)

POPCORN & SUPPLIES WHOLESALERS

Humphrey Popcorn Company ....F....... 216 662-6629
  Strongsville (G-17752)

PORCELAIN ENAMELED PRDTS & UTENSILS

American Trim LLC ....G....... 419 996-4703
  Lima (G-11837)
American Trim LLC ....D....... 419 738-9664
  Wapakoneta (G-19319)
American Trim LLC ....D....... 419 996-4729
  Lima (G-11838)
American Trim LLC ....D....... 419 996-4703
  Lima (G-11839)
American Trim LLC ....E....... 419 228-1145
  Lima (G-11840)
Superior Metal Products Inc ....E....... 419 228-1145
  Lima (G-11947)

POSTERS, WHOLESALE

Posterservice Incorporated .... E 513 577-7100
  Cincinnati (G-4176)

POSTS: Floor, Adjustable, Metal

Gwp Holdings Inc .... D 513 860-4050
  Fairfield (G-9501)

POTPOURRI

Rose of Sharon Enterprises .... G 937 862-4543
  Waynesville (G-19572)

POTTERY

Bosco Pup Co LLC .... G 614 833-0349
  Pickerington (G-16042)
Javanation .... F 419 584-1705
  Celina (G-2970)
Yellow Springs Pottery .... F 937 767-1666
  Yellow Springs (G-20822)

POTTING SOILS

Garick LLC .... E 216 581-0100
  Cleveland (G-5293)
Roe Transportation Entps Inc .... G 937 497-7161
  Sidney (G-17068)

POULTRY & POULTRY PRDTS WHOLESALERS

Borden Dairy Co Cincinnati LLC .... C 513 948-8811
  Cincinnati (G-3404)
Just Natural Provision Company .... G 216 431-7922
  Cleveland (G-5510)
Koch Meat Co Inc .... B 513 874-3500
  Fairfield (G-9519)
Roots Poultry Inc .... F 419 332-0041
  Fremont (G-10048)

POULTRY & SMALL GAME SLAUGHTERING & PROCESSING

Cal-Maine Foods Inc .... E 937 337-9576
  Rossburg (G-16581)
Cooper Foods .... E 419 232-2440
  Van Wert (G-19084)
Cooper Hatchery Inc .... C 419 238-4869
  Van Wert (G-19085)
Kings Command Foods LLC .... D 937 526-3553
  Versailles (G-19184)
Koch Meat Co Inc .... B 513 874-3500
  Fairfield (G-9519)
Ohio Fresh Eggs LLC .... E 937 354-2233
  Mount Victory (G-14520)
Weaver Bros Inc .... D 937 526-3907
  Versailles (G-19193)

POULTRY SLAUGHTERING & PROCESSING

Case Farms of Ohio Inc .... C 330 359-7141
  Winesburg (G-20530)
Case Farms of Ohio Inc .... F 330 878-7118
  Strasburg (G-17647)
Just Natural Provision Company .... G 216 431-7922
  Cleveland (G-5510)

POWDER: Iron

Truck Fax Inc .... G 216 921-8866
  Cleveland (G-6218)

POWDER: Metal

Additive Metal Alloys Ltd .... G 800 687-6110
  Holland (G-10914)
Bogie Industries Inc Ltd .... E 330 745-3105
  Akron (G-92)
Duffee Finishing Inc .... G 740 965-4848
  Sunbury (G-17885)
Eckart America Corporation .... D 440 954-7600
  Painesville (G-15734)
GKN Sinter Metals LLC .... F 419 238-8200
  Van Wert (G-19092)
J & K Powder Coating .... G 330 540-6145
  Mineral Ridge (G-14166)
Key Finishes LLC .... G 614 351-8393
  Columbus (G-7093)
Legacy Finishing Inc .... G 937 743-7278
  Franklin (G-9895)
Obron Atlantic Corporation .... D 440 954-7600
  Painesville (G-15767)
Powder Alloy Corporation .... E 513 984-4016
  Loveland (G-12223)
Powdermet Inc .... E 216 404-0053
  Euclid (G-9434)
Rmi Titanium Company LLC .... E 330 652-9952
  Niles (G-15028)

POWDER: Silver

Topkote Inc .... G 440 428-0525
  Madison (G-12357)

POWER GENERATORS

AEP Resources Inc .... F 614 716-1000
  Columbus (G-6548)
Babcock & Wilcox Entps Inc .... A 330 753-4511
  Barberton (G-1061)
Bwx Technologies Inc .... G 740 687-4180
  Lancaster (G-11550)
Micropower LLC .... F 513 382-0100
  Cincinnati (G-4023)

POWER SPLY CONVERTERS: Static, Electronic Applications

Bennett & Bennett Inc .... F 937 324-1100
  Dayton (G-8055)

POWER SUPPLIES: All Types, Static

Dare Electronics Inc .... E 937 335-0031
  Troy (G-18645)
Power Metrics Inc .... G 440 461-9352
  Cleveland (G-5899)
Siglent Technologies Amer Inc .... G 440 398-5800
  Solon (G-17231)
Tracewell Power Inc .... E 614 846-6175
  Westerville (G-20080)
Vertiv Group Corporation .... A 614 888-0246
  Columbus (G-7576)
Vertiv Holdings LLC .... G 614 888-0246
  Columbus (G-7577)

POWER SUPPLIES: Transformer, Electronic Type

Cletronics Inc .... F 330 239-2002
  Medina (G-13237)
Electric Service Co Inc .... E 513 271-6387
  Cincinnati (G-3632)
Norlake Manufacturing Company ..... D 440 353-3200
  North Ridgeville (G-15241)

POWER SWITCHING EQPT

Layerzero Power Systems Inc .... E 440 399-9000
  Aurora (G-890)
Te Connectivity Corporation .... C 419 521-9500
  Mansfield (G-12527)

POWER TOOLS, HAND: Drills, Port, Elec/Pneumatic, Exc Rock

Airmachinescom Inc .... G 330 759-1620
  Youngstown (G-20840)

POWER TOOLS, HAND: Hammers, Portable, Elec/Pneumatic, Chip

Corbett R Caudill Chipping Inc .... F 740 596-5984
  Hamden (G-10522)

POWER TRANSMISSION EQPT WHOLESALERS

Riverside Drives Inc .... E 216 362-1211
  Cleveland (G-5988)
Stock Fairfield Corporation .... C 440 543-6000
  Chagrin Falls (G-3078)

POWER TRANSMISSION EQPT: Mechanical

Advance Bronze Inc .... D 330 948-1231
  Lodi (G-12003)
Advanced Pneumatics Inc .... G 440 953-0700
  Mentor (G-13375)
Ban-Fam Industries Inc .... G 216 265-9588
  Cleveland (G-4788)
Bdi Inc .... F 330 498-4980
  Canton (G-2586)
Bucyrus Precision Tech Inc .... C 419 563-9950
  Bucyrus (G-2320)
Bunting Bearings LLC .... E 419 522-3323
  Mansfield (G-12417)
City Machine Technologies Inc .... E 330 740-8186
  Youngstown (G-20871)
Columbus McKinnon Corporation .... D 330 424-7248
  Lisbon (G-11965)
Custom Cltch Jint Hydrlics Inc .... F 330 431-1630
  Cleveland (G-5046)
Drive Components .... G 440 234-6200
  Brookpark (G-2144)
Dupont Specialty Pdts USA LLC ...... C 216 901-3600
  Cleveland (G-5120)
Eaton Corporation .... C 440 826-1115
  Berea (G-1604)
Eaton Hydraulics LLC .... E 419 232-7777
  Van Wert (G-19088)
Euclid Universal Corporation .... E 440 542-0960
  Akron (G-160)
General Electric Company .... D 216 883-1000
  Cleveland (G-5306)
General Metals Powder Co .... D 330 633-1226
  Akron (G-186)
Geneva Gear & Machine Inc .... F 937 866-0318
  Dayton (G-8221)
GKN Sinter Metals LLC .... C 740 441-3203
  Gallipolis (G-10166)
Hite Parts Exchange Inc .... E 614 272-5115
  Columbus (G-7003)
Lextech Industries Ltd .... G 216 883-7900
  Cleveland (G-5574)
Luk Clutch Systems LLC .... C 330 264-4383
  Wooster (G-20617)
Master Products Company .... D 216 341-1740
  Cleveland (G-5634)
Mechanical Dynamics Analis Ltd ..... E 440 946-0082
  Euclid (G-9426)
Metro Mech Inc .... G 216 641-6262
  Cleveland (G-5662)
Mfh Partners Inc .... F 440 461-4100
  Cleveland (G-5664)
Morgal Machine Tool Co .... D 937 325-5561
  Springfield (G-17451)
Nidec Minster Corporation .... G 419 628-1652
  Minster (G-14221)
Nook Industries Inc .... C 216 271-7900
  Cleveland (G-5756)
Opw Engineered Systems Inc .... G 888 771-9438
  Lebanon (G-11680)
Penn Machine Company .... E 814 288-1547
  Twinsburg (G-18829)
Poklar Power and Motion Inc .... G 513 791-5009
  Blue Ash (G-1832)
Rampe Manufacturing Company ...... F 440 352-8995
  Fairport Harbor (G-9629)
Regal Industries Inc .... G 440 352-9600
  Painesville (G-15780)
Saf-Holland Inc .... G 513 874-7888
  West Chester (G-19896)
Stevenson Machine Inc .... F 513 761-4121
  Cincinnati (G-4382)
Stripmatic Products Inc .... E 216 241-7143
  Cleveland (G-6111)
Taiho Corporation of America .... C 419 443-1645
  Tiffin (G-18086)
Webb-Stiles Company .... D 330 225-7761
  Valley City (G-19069)
Western Branch Diesel Inc .... E 330 454-8800
  Canton (G-2864)
Xtek Inc .... B 513 733-7800
  Cincinnati (G-4530)

POWER TRANSMISSION EQPT: Vehicle

Adelmans Truck Parts Corp .... E 330 456-0206
  Canton (G-2558)

POWERED GOLF CART DEALERS

Golf Car Company Inc .... F 614 873-1055
  Plain City (G-16196)

PRECAST TERRAZZO OR CONCRETE PRDTS

Lindsay Package Systems Inc .... G 330 854-4511
  Canal Fulton (G-2482)
Premere Precast Products .... F 740 533-3333
  Ironton (G-11170)

PRODUCT SECTION

PRINTING & ENGRAVING: Financial Notes & Certificates

Stress Con Industries Inc .... G 586 731-1628
  Brunswick *(G-2241)*

PRECIOUS STONES & METALS, WHOLESALE

AR Jester Co .... G 513 241-1465
  Cincinnati *(G-3353)*

PRECIPITATORS: Electrostatic

McGill Airclean LLC .... D 614 829-1200
  Columbus *(G-7163)*
McGill Corporation .... F 614 829-1200
  Groveport *(G-10504)*
Neundorfer Inc .... E 440 942-8990
  Willoughby *(G-20387)*
United McGill Corporation .... E 614 829-1200
  Groveport *(G-10516)*

PRECISION INSTRUMENT REPAIR SVCS

Beaumont Machine LLC .... F 513 701-0421
  Mason *(G-12833)*

PRERECORDED TAPE, COMPACT DISC & RECORD STORES: Records

True Dinero Records & Tech LLC ... G 513 428-4610
  Cincinnati *(G-4443)*

PRESSED FIBER & MOLDED PULP PRDTS, EXC FOOD PRDTS

Multicorr Corp .... G 502 935-1000
  Delaware *(G-8707)*
Vista Industrial Packaging LLC .... D 800 454-6117
  Columbus *(G-7586)*

PRESSES

Eae Logistics Company LLC .... G 440 417-4788
  Madison *(G-12348)*

PRESSURIZERS OR AUXILIARY EQPT: Nuclear, Metal Plate

AMF Bruns America Lp .... G 877 506-3770
  Hudson *(G-11031)*

PRESTRESSED CONCRETE PRDTS

Fabcon Companies LLC .... D 614 875-8601
  Grove City *(G-10430)*
Prestress Services Inds LLC .... E 614 871-2900
  Grove City *(G-10459)*

PRIMARY FINISHED OR SEMIFINISHED SHAPES

Dietrich Industries Inc .... C 330 372-2868
  Warren *(G-19396)*
Northeast Tubular Service Inc .... G 330 262-1881
  Wooster *(G-20634)*

PRIMARY METAL PRODUCTS

Altana .... G 440 954-7600
  Painesville *(G-15709)*
Liberty Steel Pressed Pdts LLC ...... G 330 538-2236
  North Jackson *(G-15149)*
Materion Technical Mtls Inc .... D 216 486-4200
  Cleveland *(G-5635)*
Payne Family LLC II .... G 513 861-7600
  Blue Ash *(G-1829)*

PRIMARY ROLLING MILL EQPT

Rki Inc .... C 888 953-9400
  Mentor *(G-13573)*

PRINT CARTRIDGES: Laser & Other Computer Printers

All Write Ribbon Inc .... E 513 753-8300
  Amelia *(G-529)*
Eco-Print Solutions LLC .... G 513 731-3106
  Cincinnati *(G-3629)*
Jay Tackett .... G 740 779-1715
  Frankfort *(G-9862)*
Kehler Enterprises Inc .... G 614 889-8488
  Dublin *(G-8937)*

Newwave Technologies Inc .... G 513 683-1211
  Loveland *(G-12218)*
Wood County Ohio .... G 419 353-1227
  Bowling Green *(G-2007)*

PRINTED CIRCUIT BOARDS

Accurate Electronics Inc .... C 330 682-7015
  Orrville *(G-15581)*
Adonai Technologies LLC .... G 513 560-9020
  Middletown *(G-13875)*
Alektronics Inc .... F 937 429-2118
  Beavercreek *(G-1349)*
Avcom Smt Inc .... F 614 882-8176
  Westerville *(G-20035)*
Bud Industries Inc .... G 440 946-3200
  Willoughby *(G-20289)*
C E Electronics Inc .... D 419 636-6705
  Bryan *(G-2275)*
Cartessa Corporation .... F 513 738-4477
  Shandon *(G-16940)*
Central Systems & Control .... G 440 835-0015
  Cleveland *(G-4901)*
Circle Prime Manufacturing .... E 330 923-0019
  Cuyahoga Falls *(G-7850)*
Circuit Center .... G 513 435-2131
  Dayton *(G-8091)*
Circuit Services LLC .... G 513 604-7405
  Harrison *(G-10636)*
Cleveland Coretec Inc .... G 314 727-2087
  North Jackson *(G-15144)*
Co- Ax Technology Inc .... G 440 914-9200
  Solon *(G-17128)*
Commercial Mfg Svcs Inc .... G 440 953-2701
  Mentor *(G-13420)*
Community RE Group-Comvet ...... G 440 319-6714
  Ashtabula *(G-767)*
Ddi North Jackson Corp .... G 330 538-3900
  North Jackson *(G-15145)*
Debra Harbour .... G 937 440-9618
  Troy *(G-18647)*
Flextronics International Usa .... A 513 755-2500
  Liberty Township *(G-11814)*
Interactive Engineering Corp .... E 330 239-6888
  Medina *(G-13280)*
International Trade Group Inc ...... G 614 486-4634
  Columbus *(G-7045)*
Journey Electronics Corp .... G 513 539-9836
  Monroe *(G-14269)*
L3 Technologies Inc .... E 513 943-2000
  Cincinnati *(G-3258)*
Lad Technology Inc .... E 440 461-8002
  Painesville *(G-15756)*
Levison Enterprises LLC .... E 419 838-7365
  Millbury *(G-14051)*
Libra Industries Inc .... E 440 974-7770
  Mentor *(G-13499)*
Malabar Properties LLC .... F 419 884-0071
  Mansfield *(G-12473)*
Metzenbaum Sheltered Inds Inc ... C 440 729-1919
  Chesterland *(G-3164)*
Precision Switching Inc .... G 800 800-8143
  Mansfield *(G-12502)*
Qualtech Technologies Inc .... E 440 946-8081
  Willoughby *(G-20416)*
S Wj Llcred .... G 330 938-6173
  Sebring *(G-16892)*
Tabtronics Inc .... F 937 222-9969
  Dayton *(G-8537)*
Techtron Systems Inc .... E 440 505-2990
  Solon *(G-17249)*
Tetrad Electronics Inc .... D 440 946-6443
  Willoughby *(G-20446)*
Ttm Technologies Inc .... G 330 538-3900
  North Jackson *(G-15156)*
United Circuits Inc .... F 440 926-1000
  Grafton *(G-10312)*
Versitec Manufacturing Inc .... F 440 354-4283
  Painesville *(G-15795)*
Vexos Electronic Mfg Svcs .... G 855 711-3227
  Lagrange *(G-11496)*
Visual Information Institute .... F 937 376-4361
  Xenia *(G-20801)*
Vmetro Inc .... G 281 584-0728
  Fairborn *(G-9473)*
Wurth Electronics Ics Inc .... E 937 415-7700
  Dayton *(G-8601)*

PRINTERS & PLOTTERS

Eprintworksplus .... G 513 731-3797
  Cincinnati *(G-3648)*

Gameday Vision .... F 330 830-4550
  Massillon *(G-12985)*
Intec LLC .... G 614 633-7430
  Heath *(G-10721)*
Royal Specialty Products Inc .... G 513 841-1267
  Cincinnati *(G-4284)*
Small Business Products .... G 800 553-6485
  Cincinnati *(G-4344)*

PRINTERS' SVCS: Folding, Collating, Etc

Bookmasters Inc .... C 419 281-1802
  Ashland *(G-686)*
Capitol Citicom Inc .... E 614 472-2679
  Columbus *(G-6735)*
Erd Specialty Graphics Inc .... G 419 242-9545
  Toledo *(G-18283)*
Erie Laser Ink LLC .... G 419 346-0600
  Toledo *(G-18284)*
Printing Services .... E 440 708-1999
  Chagrin Falls *(G-3070)*
Richland Blue Printcom Inc .... E 419 524-2781
  Mansfield *(G-12505)*

PRINTERS: Computer

Microcom Corporation .... E 740 548-6262
  Lewis Center *(G-11767)*

PRINTERS: Magnetic Ink, Bar Code

Hunkar Technologies Inc .... E 513 272-1010
  Cincinnati *(G-3829)*
ID Images Inc .... G 330 220-7300
  Brunswick *(G-2214)*
M C Systems Inc .... G 513 336-6007
  Mason *(G-12904)*
Paxar Corporation .... E 845 398-3229
  Mentor *(G-13544)*
Perfection Packaging Inc .... G 614 866-8558
  Gahanna *(G-10098)*

PRINTING & BINDING: Books

All Systems Colour Inc .... G 937 859-9701
  Dayton *(G-8016)*
Bip Printing Solutions LLC .... F 216 832-5673
  Beachwood *(G-1225)*
C J Krehbiel Company .... D 513 271-6035
  Cincinnati *(G-3436)*
Hf Group LLC .... A 440 729-9411
  Chesterland *(G-3160)*
Hf Group LLC .... D 440 729-9411
  Chesterland *(G-3161)*

PRINTING & BINDING: Pamphlets

Morse Enterprises Inc .... G 513 229-3600
  Mason *(G-12912)*

PRINTING & BINDING: Textbooks

Amerilam Laminating .... G 440 235-4687
  Cleveland *(G-4700)*

PRINTING & EMBOSSING: Plastic Fabric Articles

Akron Felt & Chenille Mfg Co .... F 330 733-7778
  Akron *(G-39)*
Plastic Card Inc .... D 330 896-5555
  Uniontown *(G-18929)*
Solar Arts Graphic Designs .... G 330 744-0535
  Youngstown *(G-21033)*

PRINTING & ENGRAVING: Financial Notes & Certificates

Basinger Inc .... G 614 771-8300
  Columbus *(G-6654)*
Cap City Direct LLC .... F 614 252-6245
  Columbus *(G-6729)*
Fedex Office & Print Svcs Inc .... F 937 335-3816
  Troy *(G-18657)*
Quick Tech Business Forms Inc .... E 937 743-5952
  Springboro *(G-17347)*
Watson Haran & Company Inc ..... G 937 436-1414
  Dayton *(G-8585)*

PRINTING & ENGRAVING: Invitation & Stationery

PRINTING & ENGRAVING: Invitation & Stationery

Adyl Inc	G	330 797-8700
Austintown *(G-928)*		
Papel Couture	G	614 848-5700
Columbus *(G-7290)*		
Shops By Todd Inc	G	937 458-3192
Beavercreek *(G-1340)*		

PRINTING & STAMPING: Fabric Articles

Erd Specialty Graphics Inc	G	419 242-9545
Toledo *(G-18283)*		
Hollywood Imprints LLC	F	614 501-6040
Gahanna *(G-10083)*		
Johnson Brothers Holdings LLC	G	614 868-5273
Columbus *(G-7073)*		
Pro Companies Inc	G	614 738-1222
Pickerington *(G-16057)*		
Wholesale Imprints Inc	E	440 224-3527
North Kingsville *(G-15161)*		

PRINTING & WRITING PAPER WHOLESALERS

Gvs Industries Inc	G	513 851-3606
Hamilton *(G-10565)*		
Microcom Corporation	E	740 548-6262
Lewis Center *(G-11767)*		

PRINTING INKS WHOLESALERS

Eco-Print Solutions LLC	G	513 731-3106
Cincinnati *(G-3629)*		
Kennedy Ink Company Inc	G	937 461-5600
Dayton *(G-8293)*		
Red Tie Group Inc	G	614 443-9100
Columbus *(G-7381)*		

PRINTING MACHINERY

A/C Laser Technologies Inc	F	330 784-3355
Akron *(G-24)*		
Aleris Ohio Management Inc	F	216 910-3400
Cleveland *(G-4655)*		
Anderson & Vreeland Inc	D	419 636-5002
Bryan *(G-2264)*		
Beehex Inc	G	512 633-5304
Columbus *(G-6660)*		
Capital Track Company Inc	G	614 595-5088
Columbus *(G-6734)*		
Commonwealth Aluminum Mtls LLC	G	216 910-3400
Beachwood *(G-1229)*		
FT Group Inc	E	937 746-6439
Cincinnati *(G-3716)*		
Gedico International Inc	G	937 274-2167
Dayton *(G-8218)*		
Gew Inc	G	440 237-4439
Cleveland *(G-5320)*		
Hadronics Inc	D	513 321-9350
Cincinnati *(G-3792)*		
Hotend Works Inc	G	440 787-3181
Columbia Station *(G-6438)*		
Kase Equipment	D	216 642-9040
Cleveland *(G-5517)*		
Nilpeter Usa Inc	C	513 489-4400
Cincinnati *(G-4080)*		
Ohio Graphic Supply Inc	G	937 433-7537
Dayton *(G-8397)*		
Paxar Corporation	E	845 398-3229
Mentor *(G-13544)*		
R & D Equipment Inc	F	419 668-8439
Norwalk *(G-15413)*		
Resource Graphics	G	513 205-2686
Cincinnati *(G-4261)*		
Roconex Corporation	F	937 339-2616
Troy *(G-18699)*		
Roessner Holdings Inc	G	419 356-2123
Fort Recovery *(G-9826)*		
Rotation Dynamics Corporation	F	937 746-4069
Franklin *(G-9917)*		
Schilling Graphics Inc	G	419 468-1037
Galion *(G-10154)*		
Suspension Feeder Corporation	F	419 763-1477
Fort Recovery *(G-9828)*		
Wood Graphics Inc	E	513 771-6300
Cincinnati *(G-4516)*		

PRINTING MACHINERY, EQPT & SPLYS: Wholesalers

Anderson & Vreeland Inc	D	419 636-5002
Bryan *(G-2264)*		
Boggs Graphic Equipment LLC	G	888 837-8101
Maple Heights *(G-12566)*		
Esko-Graphics Inc	D	937 454-1721
Miamisburg *(G-13665)*		
General Data Company Inc	C	513 752-7978
Cincinnati *(G-3252)*		
Monode Marking Products Inc	D	440 975-8802
Mentor *(G-13522)*		
Newfax Corporation	F	419 893-4557
Toledo *(G-18424)*		
Newfax Corporation	F	419 241-5157
Toledo *(G-18423)*		

PRINTING TRADES MACHINERY & EQPT REPAIR SVCS

A/C Laser Technologies Inc	F	330 784-3355
Akron *(G-24)*		
Glen D Lala	G	937 274-7770
Dayton *(G-8224)*		
Lazer Action Inc	G	330 630-9200
Akron *(G-249)*		

PRINTING, COMMERCIAL Newspapers, NEC

Ckm Ventures LLC	G	216 623-0370
Cleveland *(G-4935)*		
Wolfe Associates Inc	G	614 461-5000
Columbus *(G-7610)*		

PRINTING, COMMERCIAL: Bags, Plastic, NEC

Trebnick Systems Inc	E	937 743-1550
Springboro *(G-17358)*		

PRINTING, COMMERCIAL: Business Forms, NEC

Alpha Bus Forms & Prtg LLC	G	419 999-5138
Lima *(G-11835)*		
Carbonless & Cut Sheet Forms	F	740 826-1700
New Concord *(G-14683)*		
Cns Inc	G	513 631-7073
Cincinnati *(G-3533)*		
Crabar/Gbf Inc	F	419 943-2141
Leipsic *(G-11724)*		
Echographics Inc	G	440 846-2330
North Ridgeville *(G-15222)*		
PJ Bush Associates Inc	E	216 362-6700
Cleveland *(G-5881)*		
Reynolds and Reynolds Company	G	937 485-4771
Dayton *(G-8475)*		
RR Donnelley & Sons Company	B	740 928-6110
Hebron *(G-10760)*		
S F Mock & Associates LLC	F	937 438-0196
Dayton *(G-8491)*		
Smartbill Ltd	F	740 928-6909
Hebron *(G-10763)*		

PRINTING, COMMERCIAL: Calendars, NEC

Haman Enterprises Inc	F	614 888-7574
Worthington *(G-20689)*		
Proforma Systems Advantage	G	419 224-8747
Lima *(G-11922)*		

PRINTING, COMMERCIAL: Cards, Visiting, Incl Business, NEC

Bookmyer LLP	G	419 447-3883
Tiffin *(G-18051)*		

PRINTING, COMMERCIAL: Circulars, NEC

Melnor Graphics LLC	F	419 476-8808
Toledo *(G-18408)*		

PRINTING, COMMERCIAL: Decals, NEC

Boehm Inc	E	614 875-9010
Grove City *(G-10417)*		
Commercial Decal of Ohio Inc	E	330 385-7178
East Liverpool *(G-9053)*		

PRINTING, COMMERCIAL: Envelopes, NEC

Anthony Business Forms Inc	F	937 253-0072
Dayton *(G-7971)*		
McDaniel Envelope Co Inc	F	330 868-5929
Minerva *(G-14191)*		
Miami Valley Press Inc	G	937 547-0771
Greenville *(G-10381)*		
Ohio Envelope Manufacturing Co	E	216 267-2920
Cleveland *(G-5805)*		

PRINTING, COMMERCIAL: Imprinting

Better Living Concepts Inc	F	330 494-2213
Canton *(G-2590)*		
Cotton Pickin Tees & Caps	G	419 636-3595
Bryan *(G-2277)*		
Fair Publishing House Inc	F	419 668-3746
Norwalk *(G-15394)*		
Holmes Prcut/Troyer Imprinting	G	330 359-0000
Dundee *(G-9019)*		
John C Starr	G	740 852-5592
London *(G-12063)*		
Middaugh Enterprises Inc	F	330 852-2471
Sugarcreek *(G-17852)*		

PRINTING, COMMERCIAL: Invitations, NEC

Domicone Printing Inc	G	937 878-3080
Fairborn *(G-9457)*		
Doug Smith	G	740 345-1398
Newark *(G-14868)*		

PRINTING, COMMERCIAL: Labels & Seals, NEC

Bar Codes Unlimited Inc	G	937 434-2633
Dayton *(G-8051)*		
Century Marketing Corporation	F	419 354-2591
Bowling Green *(G-1960)*		
Century Marketing Corporation	C	419 354-2591
Bowling Green *(G-1961)*		
CMC Group Inc	C	419 354-2591
Bowling Green *(G-1964)*		
Collotype Labels Usa Inc	D	513 381-1480
Batavia *(G-1132)*		
Contemprary Image Labeling Inc	G	513 583-5699
Lebanon *(G-11644)*		
D&D Design Concepts Inc	F	513 752-2191
Batavia *(G-1135)*		
Federal Barcode Label Systems	G	440 748-8060
North Ridgeville *(G-15224)*		
Flex Pro Label Inc	G	513 489-4417
Blue Ash *(G-1775)*		
Geygan Enterprises Inc	F	513 932-4222
Lebanon *(G-11656)*		
Hooven - Dayton Corp	D	937 233-4473
Miamisburg *(G-13677)*		
Label Technique Southeast LLC	E	440 951-7660
Willoughby *(G-20356)*		
M PI Label Systems	G	330 938-2134
Sebring *(G-16888)*		
Miller Products Inc	G	330 335-3110
Wadsworth *(G-19254)*		
Mpi Labels of Baltimore Inc	F	330 938-2134
Sebring *(G-16890)*		
Multi-Color Corporation	G	513 459-3283
Mason *(G-12913)*		
Multi-Color Corporation	F	513 381-1480
Batavia *(G-1171)*		
Multi-Color Corporation	D	513 943-0080
Batavia *(G-1172)*		
Performance Packaging Inc	F	419 478-8805
Toledo *(G-18465)*		
Scratch-Off Systems Inc	E	216 649-7800
Brecksville *(G-2056)*		
Tech/III Inc	E	513 482-7500
Cincinnati *(G-4409)*		
The Label Team Inc	F	330 332-1067
Salem *(G-16776)*		
Triangle Label Inc	G	513 242-2822
West Chester *(G-19812)*		
Verstraete In Mold Lab	F	513 943-0080
Batavia *(G-1195)*		

PRINTING, COMMERCIAL: Letterpress & Screen

Club 513 LLC	G	800 530-2574
Cincinnati *(G-3531)*		
New Dawn Designs	G	330 759-3500
Girard *(G-10263)*		

PRODUCT SECTION

PRINTING, COMMERCIAL: Screen

PRINTING, COMMERCIAL: Literature, Advertising, NEC

Company	Code	Phone
Bottomline Ink Corporation Perrysburg (G-15923)	E	419 897-8000
Multi-Color Australia LLC Batavia (G-1170)	B	513 381-1480
Penca Design Group Ltd Painesville (G-15774)	G	440 210-4422

PRINTING, COMMERCIAL: Magazines, NEC

Company	Code	Phone
Quebecor World Johnson Hardin Cincinnati (G-4233)	A	614 326-0299

PRINTING, COMMERCIAL: Menus, NEC

Company	Code	Phone
Cleveland Menu Printing Inc Cleveland (G-4967)	E	216 241-5256

PRINTING, COMMERCIAL: Music, Sheet, NEC

Company	Code	Phone
Lorenz Corporation Dayton (G-8316)	D	937 228-6118

PRINTING, COMMERCIAL: Post Cards, Picture, NEC

Company	Code	Phone
Victory Postcards Inc Columbus (G-7583)	G	614 764-8975

PRINTING, COMMERCIAL: Promotional

Company	Code	Phone
American Imprssions Sportswear Worthington (G-20677)	G	614 848-6677
Axent Graphics LLC Brookpark (G-2137)	G	216 362-7560
Bradleys Beacons Ltd Tiffin (G-18052)	G	419 447-7560
Clear Images LLC Toledo (G-18233)	F	419 241-9347
Corporate Supply LLC Columbus (G-6824)	G	614 876-8400
Dyenamo Distributing Galion (G-10133)	F	419 462-9474
Everythings Image Inc Blue Ash (G-1768)	F	513 469-6727
Exxcite Marketing Inc Cincinnati (G-3667)	G	513 271-4550
Green Willow Inc Dayton (G-8238)	G	937 436-5290
Hyde Brothers Prtg & Mktg LLC Marietta (G-12634)	G	740 373-2054
Sensical Inc Solon (G-17229)	D	216 641-1141
Solution Ventures Inc Avon Lake (G-1008)	G	440 242-1658
Spectrum Embroidery Inc Dayton (G-8518)	G	937 847-9905
SRC Liquidation LLC Dayton (G-8521)	A	937 221-1000
Sro Prints LLC Cincinnati (G-4366)	G	865 604-0420

PRINTING, COMMERCIAL: Publications

Company	Code	Phone
Bayard Inc Moraine (G-14332)	F	937 293-1415
Brahler Inc Canton (G-2597)	G	330 966-7730
Forward Movement Publications Cincinnati (G-3707)	F	513 721-6659
Heartland Publications LLC Miamisburg (G-13675)	F	860 664-1075
Heartland Publications LLC Gallipolis (G-10167)	F	740 446-2342
Informa Media Inc Cleveland (G-5457)	A	216 696-7000
Jjkb Enterprises LLC Cincinnati (G-3873)	G	513 731-4332
ML Erectors LLC Elyria (G-9297)	G	440 328-3227
Schaffner Publication Inc Port Clinton (G-16258)	E	419 732-2154
Scriptype Publishing Inc Richfield (G-16485)	E	330 659-0303

PRINTING, COMMERCIAL: Screen

Company	Code	Phone
4d Screenprinting Ltd Cleves (G-6353)	G	513 353-1070
A Screen Printed Products Bowling Green (G-1943)	G	419 352-1535
A Special Touch Embroidery LLC Portsmouth (G-16276)	G	740 858-2241
Aardvark Screen Prtg & EMB LLC Bowling Green (G-1948)	F	419 354-6686
Aardvark Sportswear Inc Youngstown (G-20832)	G	330 793-9428
Abl Screen Printing Solon (G-17097)	G	440 914-0093
Absolute Impressions Inc Lewis Center (G-11742)	F	614 840-0599
Ace Transfer Company Springfield (G-17360)	G	937 398-1103
Adcraft Decals Inc Cleveland (G-4615)	E	216 524-2934
Advanced Incentives Inc Toledo (G-18157)	G	419 471-9088
Alberts Screen Print Inc Norton (G-15360)	C	330 753-7559
Allied Silk Screen Inc Dayton (G-8020)	G	937 223-4921
Alvin L Roepke Elmore (G-9203)	F	419 862-3891
Am Graphics Youngstown (G-20842)	G	330 799-7319
Anthony-Lee Screen Prtg Inc Crestline (G-7793)	F	419 683-1861
Ares Sportswear Ltd Hilliard (G-10805)	D	614 767-1950
Art Brands LLC Blacklick (G-1677)	E	614 755-4278
Art Tees Inc Columbus (G-6617)	G	614 338-8337
Associated Graphics Inc Plain City (G-16172)	G	614 873-1273
Benchmark Prints Fremont (G-9997)	F	419 332-7640
Big Kahuna Graphics LLC Canton (G-2591)	G	330 455-2625
Blue Ribbon Screen Graphics Avon (G-942)	G	216 226-6200
Bluelogos Inc Westerville (G-20038)	F	614 898-9971
Bob King Sign Company Inc Akron (G-90)	G	330 753-2679
Buckeye Cstm Screen Print EMB Columbus (G-6709)	F	614 237-0196
Bullseye Activewear Inc Brunswick (G-2193)	G	330 220-1720
C A I R Ohio Blue Ash (G-1743)	G	513 281-8200
Campbell Signs & Apparel LLC East Liverpool (G-9052)	F	330 386-4768
Carnegie Promotions Inc Cleveland (G-4881)	G	440 442-2099
Carroll Exhibit and Print Svcs Cleveland (G-4884)	G	216 361-2325
Casad Company Inc Coldwater (G-6404)	F	419 586-9457
Centennial Screen Printing Findlay (G-9665)	G	419 422-5548
Cleveland Printwear Inc Cleveland (G-4970)	G	216 521-5500
Cold Duck Screen Prtg & EMB Co East Palestine (G-9071)	G	330 426-1900
Columbus Humungous Apparel LLC Columbus (G-6791)	G	614 824-2657
Crabro Printing Inc Ironton (G-11163)	G	740 533-3404
Custom Apparel LLC Akron (G-127)	G	330 633-2626
Custom Deco South Inc Toledo (G-18246)	E	419 698-2900
Custom Screen Printing Twinsburg (G-18759)	G	330 963-3131
Custom Sportswear Imprints LLC Wadsworth (G-19231)	G	330 335-8326
Debandale Printing Inc Medina (G-13251)	G	330 725-5122
Digital Shorts Inc Dayton (G-8161)	G	937 228-1700
Drycal Inc Mentor (G-13433)	G	440 974-1999
Dynamic Design & Systems Inc Chagrin Falls (G-3044)	G	440 708-1010
E & E Nameplates Inc Galion (G-10134)	F	419 468-3617
Erd Specialty Graphics Inc Toledo (G-18283)	G	419 242-9545
Expert TS Wooster (G-20589)	G	330 263-4588
First Impression Wear Eaton (G-9149)	G	937 456-3900
First Stop Signs and Decals New Philadelphia (G-14769)	G	330 343-1859
Five Star Graphics Inc Girard (G-10259)	G	330 545-5077
Future Screen Inc Cleveland (G-5281)	G	440 838-5055
Gail Berner Springfield (G-17406)	G	937 322-0314
Gail Zeilmann Cleveland (G-5286)	G	440 888-4858
GCI Digital Imaging Inc Cincinnati (G-3730)	F	513 521-7446
Glauners Wholesale Inc Cleveland (G-5323)	G	216 398-7088
Glavin Industries Inc Solon (G-17149)	E	440 349-0049
Glen D Lala Dayton (G-8224)	G	937 274-7770
Good JP Ashland (G-706)	G	419 207-8484
Got Graphix Llc Fairlawn (G-9606)	F	330 703-9047
Grady McCauley Inc North Canton (G-15089)	D	330 494-9444
Graphic Plus Chillicothe (G-3190)	G	740 701-1860
Graphics To Go LLC Wilmington (G-20496)	G	937 382-4100
Graphix Junction Hudson (G-11049)	G	234 284-8392
Gym Pro LLC Waterford (G-19485)	G	740 984-4143
H & H Screen Process Inc Dayton (G-8240)	G	937 253-7520
Hartman Distributing LLC Heath (G-10719)	D	740 616-7764
Hoffee John Minerva (G-14183)	G	330 868-3553
Homestretch Inc Wapakoneta (G-19331)	G	419 738-6604
Homestretch Sportswear Inc Saint Henry (G-16663)	F	419 678-4282
Illusions Screenprinting Wooster (G-20605)	G	330 263-7770
Imagemart Inc Cleveland (G-5439)	G	216 486-4767
Industrial Screen Process Toledo (G-18346)	F	419 255-4900
Innovtive Crtive Solutions LLC Groveport (G-10494)	G	614 491-9638
J-M Designs LLC Maumee (G-13120)	G	419 794-2114
Jazz Textile Impressions Maumee (G-13121)	G	419 242-5940
Joe Paxton Columbus (G-7071)	G	614 424-9000
Jones & Assoc Advg & Design Youngstown (G-20949)	G	330 799-6876
K & J Holdings Inc Youngstown (G-20951)	G	330 726-0828
Kaufman Container Company Cleveland (G-5519)	C	216 898-2000
Kdm Signs Inc Cincinnati (G-3900)	C	513 769-1932
Kendra Screen Print Vermilion (G-19164)	G	440 967-8820
Kens His & Hers Shop Inc Newton Falls (G-14988)	G	330 872-3190
Keteli Teamwear LLC Marietta (G-12637)	G	740 373-7969
KS Designs Inc Cincinnati (G-3925)	G	513 241-5953
Lake Screen Printing Inc Lorain (G-12099)	G	440 244-5707
Lamar D Steiner Millersburg (G-14105)	G	330 466-1479
Legendary Ink Inc Columbus (G-7120)	G	614 766-5101
Lima Sporting Goods Inc Lima (G-11894)	E	419 222-1036
Locker Room Lettering Ltd Castalia (G-2940)	G	419 359-1761
Logan Screen Printing Logan (G-12033)	G	740 385-3303
Logos On Lee Cleveland (G-5583)	G	216 862-5226

Employee Codes: A=Over 500 employees, B=251-500 C=101-250, D=51-100, E=20-50, F=10-19, G=3-9

PRINTING, COMMERCIAL: Screen

Loris Printing Inc .... G 419 626-6448
  Sandusky *(G-16823)*
LSI Industries Inc .... E 513 793-3200
  Blue Ash *(G-1808)*
Magnetic Mktg Solutions LLC .... G 513 721-3801
  Cincinnati *(G-3973)*
Marazita Graphics Inc .... G 330 773-6462
  Akron *(G-267)*
Markt 740 397-5900
  Mount Vernon *(G-14490)*
Meders Special Tees .... G 513 921-3800
  Cincinnati *(G-3995)*
Metro Flex Inc .... G 937 299-5360
  Moraine *(G-14369)*
Mid Ohio Screen Print Inc .... G 614 875-1774
  Grove City *(G-10446)*
Mike B Crawford .... G 330 673-7944
  Kent *(G-11355)*
Modern Displays Inc .... G 513 471-1639
  Cincinnati *(G-4037)*
Moonshine Screen Printing Inc .... F 513 523-7775
  Oxford *(G-15697)*
Morrison Sign Company Inc .... E 614 276-1181
  Columbus *(G-7198)*
Mound Printing Company Inc .... E 937 866-2872
  Miamisburg *(G-13696)*
Niklee Co .... G 440 944-0082
  Willoughby Hills *(G-20473)*
Nordec Inc .... D 330 940-3700
  Stow *(G-17615)*
Northeastern Plastics Inc .... G 330 453-5925
  Canton *(G-2768)*
Odyssey Spirits Inc .... F 330 562-1523
  Aurora *(G-896)*
Off Contact Inc .... E 419 255-5546
  Toledo *(G-18434)*
Old Salt Tees .... G 440 463-0628
  Mentor *(G-13533)*
Painted Hill Inv Group Inc .... F 937 339-1756
  Troy *(G-18691)*
Patio Printing Inc .... G 614 785-9553
  Columbus *(G-7295)*
Perfection Printing .... F 513 874-2173
  Fairfield *(G-9547)*
Pops Printed Apparel LLC .... G 614 372-5651
  Columbus *(G-7332)*
Powell Prints LLC .... G 614 771-4830
  Hilliard *(G-10853)*
Precision Imprint .... G 740 592-5916
  Athens *(G-846)*
Premiere Printing & Signs Inc .... G 330 688-6244
  Stow *(G-17620)*
Primal Screen Inc .... E 330 677-1766
  Kent *(G-11368)*
Proline Screenwear .... G 440 205-3700
  Mentor *(G-13560)*
Promo Sparks .... G 513 844-2211
  Fairfield *(G-9552)*
Promospark Inc .... G 513 844-2211
  Fairfield *(G-9553)*
Quali Tee Design .... G 740 335-8497
  Wshngtn CT Hs *(G-20738)*
Quali-Tee Design Sports .... F 937 382-7997
  Wilmington *(G-20505)*
Qualitee Design Sportswear Co .... E 740 333-8337
  Wshngtn CT Hs *(G-20739)*
Richardson Supply Ltd .... G 614 539-3033
  Grove City *(G-10462)*
Rising Moon Custom Apparel .... G 614 882-1336
  Westerville *(G-20072)*
Rush Graphix Ltd .... G 419 448-7874
  Tiffin *(G-18079)*
Ruthie Ann Inc .... F 800 231-3567
  New Paris *(G-14755)*
Rutland Plastic Tech Inc .... G 614 846-3055
  Columbus *(G-7407)*
Schlabach Printing Ltd .... E 330 852-4687
  Sugarcreek *(G-17863)*
Screen Craft Plastics .... G 440 286-4060
  Chardon *(G-3135)*
Screen Printing Show House .... G 614 252-2202
  Columbus *(G-7433)*
Screen Printing Unlimited .... G 419 621-2335
  Sandusky *(G-16848)*
Screen Tech Graphics .... G 740 695-7950
  Saint Clairsville *(G-16650)*
Shirt Family .... G 740 706-1284
  Marietta *(G-12668)*
Sign Lady Inc .... G 419 476-9191
  Toledo *(G-18522)*

Signs By George .... G 216 394-2095
  Brookfield *(G-2109)*
Silk Screen Special TS Inc .... G 740 246-4843
  Thornville *(G-18036)*
Slater Silk Screen 419 755-8337
  Mansfield *(G-12516)*
Snyder Printing LLC .... G 740 353-3947
  Portsmouth *(G-16301)*
Spear USA Inc .... C 513 459-1100
  Mason *(G-12941)*
Specialtee Sportswear & Design .... G 614 877-0976
  Orient *(G-15578)*
Specialty Printing and Proc .... F 614 322-9035
  Columbus *(G-7468)*
Sports Express .... G 330 297-1112
  Ravenna *(G-16406)*
SRI Ohio Inc .... D 740 653-5800
  Lancaster *(G-11611)*
Srm Graphics Inc .... G 614 263-4433
  Columbus *(G-7482)*
Standout Stickers Inc 877 449-7703
  Medina *(G-13347)*
Steves Sports Inc .... G 440 735-0044
  Northfield *(G-15326)*
Studio Eleven Inc .... E 937 295-2225
  Fort Loramie *(G-9808)*
Studs N Hip Hop .... G 614 477-0786
  Columbus *(G-7496)*
T & L Custom Screening Inc .... G 937 237-3121
  Dayton *(G-8534)*
T K L Lettering .... G 937 832-2091
  Englewood *(G-9376)*
Tag .... G 614 921-1732
  Columbus *(G-7508)*
Tewell & Associates .... G 440 543-5190
  Chagrin Falls *(G-3081)*
Toledo Signs & Designs Ltd .... G 419 843-1073
  Toledo *(G-18569)*
Transfer Express Inc .... D 440 918-1900
  Mentor *(G-13613)*
Underground Sport Shop Inc .... F 513 751-1662
  Cincinnati *(G-4446)*
Unisport Inc .... F 419 529-4727
  Ontario *(G-15549)*
United Sport Apparel .... F 330 722-0818
  Medina *(G-13357)*
Uptown Dog The Inc .... G 740 592-4600
  Athens *(G-853)*
Vgu Industries Inc .... E 216 676-9093
  Cleveland *(G-6257)*
Viewpoint Graphic Design .... G 419 447-6073
  Tiffin *(G-18091)*
Vision Press Inc .... G 440 357-6362
  Painesville *(G-15796)*
Water Drop Media Inc .... G 234 600-5817
  Vienna *(G-19211)*
Youngs Screenprinting & Embro .... G 330 922-5777
  Cuyahoga Falls *(G-7935)*
Zenos Activewear Inc .... G 614 443-0070
  Columbus *(G-7626)*

PRINTING, COMMERCIAL: Tickets, NEC

Premier Southern Ticket Co Inc .... E 513 489-6700
  Cincinnati *(G-4188)*

PRINTING, LITHOGRAPHIC: Calendars

Beach Company .... F 740 622-0905
  Coshocton *(G-7722)*
Novelty Advertising Co Inc .... E 740 622-3113
  Coshocton *(G-7745)*

PRINTING, LITHOGRAPHIC: Calendars & Cards

Gb Liquidating Company Inc .... E 513 248-7600
  Milford *(G-14010)*

PRINTING, LITHOGRAPHIC: Catalogs

S F C Ltd LLC .... G 419 255-1283
  Toledo *(G-18509)*

PRINTING, LITHOGRAPHIC: Color

Evolution Crtive Solutions Inc .... E 513 681-4450
  Cincinnati *(G-3659)*
Lindsey Graphics Inc .... G 330 995-9241
  Aurora *(G-891)*
SP Mount Printing Company .... E 216 881-3316
  Cleveland *(G-6082)*

Valley Graphics .... G 330 652-0484
  Niles *(G-15038)*
West-Camp Press Inc .... E 614 895-0233
  Columbus *(G-7600)*

PRINTING, LITHOGRAPHIC: Decals

Dynamic Design & Systems Inc .... G 440 708-1010
  Chagrin Falls *(G-3044)*
Pro-Decal Inc .... G 330 484-0089
  Canton *(G-2793)*
Schilling Graphics Inc .... E 419 468-1037
  Galion *(G-10154)*
Sun Art Decals Inc .... G 440 234-9045
  Berea *(G-1626)*

PRINTING, LITHOGRAPHIC: Forms & Cards, Business

Carbonless On Demandcom .... F 330 837-8611
  Massillon *(G-12967)*
Crabar/Gbf Inc .... D 419 943-2141
  Leipsic *(G-11723)*
Crabar/Gbf Inc .... E 740 622-0222
  Coshocton *(G-7730)*
G A Spring Advertising .... G 330 343-9030
  Dover *(G-8827)*
Miami Valley Press Inc .... G 937 547-0771
  Greenville *(G-10381)*
Optimum System Products Inc .... E 614 885-4464
  Westerville *(G-20069)*
Pro Companies Inc .... G 614 738-1222
  Pickerington *(G-16057)*
Sandy Smittcamp .... G 937 372-1687
  Xenia *(G-20788)*
Victory Direct LLC .... G 614 626-0000
  Gahanna *(G-10110)*

PRINTING, LITHOGRAPHIC: Forms, Business

Betley Printing Co .... G 216 206-5600
  Cleveland *(G-4810)*
GBS Corp .... C 330 863-1828
  Malvern *(G-12391)*
Jaymac Systems Inc .... G 440 498-0810
  Solon *(G-17174)*
Print Management Partners Inc .... E 330 650-5300
  Twinsburg *(G-18839)*
Quick Tab II Inc .... D 419 448-6622
  Tiffin *(G-18076)*

PRINTING, LITHOGRAPHIC: Letters, Circular Or Form

Printers Emergency Service LLC .... G 513 421-7799
  Cincinnati *(G-4193)*

PRINTING, LITHOGRAPHIC: Offset & photolithographic printing

Corporate Dcment Solutions Inc .... F 513 595-8200
  Cincinnati *(G-3552)*
Eagle Advertising .... G 216 881-0800
  Cleveland *(G-5134)*
Graphic Solutions Company .... F 513 484-3067
  Cincinnati *(G-3778)*
Hecks Direct Mail & Prtg Svc .... E 419 661-6028
  Toledo *(G-18328)*
Kennedy Mint Inc .... D 440 572-3222
  Cleveland *(G-5528)*
Nova Creative Group Inc .... F 937 291-8653
  Dayton *(G-8388)*
Power Management Inc .... E 937 222-2909
  Dayton *(G-8430)*
Printzone .... G 513 733-0067
  Cincinnati *(G-4194)*

PRINTING, LITHOGRAPHIC: On Metal

Akron Litho-Print Company Inc .... F 330 434-3145
  Akron *(G-43)*
Concept Printing of Wauseon .... G 419 335-6627
  Wauseon *(G-19512)*
Crest Craft Company .... F 513 271-4858
  Blue Ash *(G-1754)*
Delores E OBeirn .... G 440 582-3610
  Cleveland *(G-5082)*
Genie Repros Inc .... E 216 965-0213
  Cleveland *(G-5315)*

PRODUCT SECTION   PRINTING: Commercial, NEC

Jarman Printing Company LLC	G	330 823-8585
Alliance (G-479)		
Key Press Inc	G	513 721-1203
Cincinnati (G-3907)		
Knowles Press Inc	G	330 877-9345
Hartville (G-10699)		
Meridian Arts and Graphics	F	330 759-9099
Youngstown (G-20969)		
Michael R Kelly	G	614 491-1745
Obetz (G-15511)		
Mizer Printing & Graphics	G	740 942-3343
Cadiz (G-2400)		
Queen City Reprographics	C	513 326-2300
Cincinnati (G-4240)		
Sportsartcom	G	330 903-0895
Copley (G-7697)		
Tecnocap LLC	D	330 392-7222
Warren (G-19446)		
Youngstown Pre-Press Inc	F	330 793-3690
Youngstown (G-21081)		

PRINTING, LITHOGRAPHIC: Posters

| Frame Warehouse | G | 614 861-4582 |
| Reynoldsburg (G-16440) | | |

PRINTING, LITHOGRAPHIC: Publications

| International Cntr Artfcial or | G | 440 358-1102 |
| Painesville (G-15749) | | |

PRINTING, LITHOGRAPHIC: Tags

Paxar Corporation	E	845 398-3229
Mentor (G-13544)		
Printprod Inc	F	937 228-2181
Toledo (G-18485)		
Trebnick Systems Inc	E	937 743-1550
Springboro (G-17358)		

PRINTING, LITHOGRAPHIC: Tickets

| Toledo Ticket Company | E | 419 476-5424 |
| Toledo (G-18573) | | |

PRINTING, LITHOGRAPHIC: Transfers, Decalcomania Or Dry

Mark-N-Mend Inc	G	440 951-2003
Willoughby (G-20370)		
Transfer Express Inc	D	440 918-1900
Mentor (G-13613)		

PRINTING: Book Music

| Indian River Industries | G | 740 965-4377 |
| Sunbury (G-17890) | | |

PRINTING: Books

Lsc Communications Inc	A	419 935-0111
Willard (G-20241)		
Printex Incorporated	F	740 773-0088
Chillicothe (G-3217)		
Quebecor World Johnson Hardin	A	614 326-0299
Cincinnati (G-4233)		

PRINTING: Books

Golf Marketing Group Inc	G	330 963-5155
Twinsburg (G-18788)		
Hubbard Company	E	419 784-4455
Defiance (G-8627)		
J & L Management Corporation	G	440 205-1199
Mentor (G-13479)		
Multi-Craft Litho Inc	E	859 581-2754
Blue Ash (G-1824)		
Naomi Kight	G	937 278-0040
Dayton (G-8375)		

PRINTING: Broadwoven Fabrics. Cotton

| Rapid Signs & More Inc | G | 513 553-4040 |
| New Richmond (G-14814) | | |

PRINTING: Commercial, NEC

3dlt LLC	F	513 452-3358
Cincinnati (G-3271)		
4 Over LLC	F	937 610-0629
Dayton (G-7995)		
A E Wilson Holdings Inc	G	330 405-0316
Twinsburg (G-18722)		

A Sign For The Times Inc	G	216 297-2977
Cleveland (G-4593)		
A To Z Paper Box Co	G	330 325-8722
Rootstown (G-16565)		
A Z Printing Inc	G	513 745-0700
Cincinnati (G-3283)		
Advanced Specialty Products	D	419 882-6528
Bowling Green (G-1950)		
Aero Fulfillment Services Corp	D	800 225-7145
Mason (G-12820)		
Agnone-Kelly Enterprises Inc	G	800 634-6503
Cincinnati (G-3310)		
AGS Custom Graphics Inc	G	330 963-7770
Macedonia (G-12275)		
Akos Promotions Inc	G	513 398-6324
Mason (G-12822)		
Alfacomp Inc	G	216 459-1790
Cleveland (G-4659)		
Amerigraph Llc	G	614 278-8000
Columbus (G-6589)		
Ameriprint	G	440 235-6094
Olmsted Falls (G-15528)		
Amtech Inc	G	440 238-2141
Strongsville (G-17711)		
Anderson Graphics Inc	E	330 745-2165
Barberton (G-1052)		
Appleheart	G	937 384-0430
Miamisburg (G-13641)		
Ashton LLC	F	614 833-4165
Pickerington (G-16039)		
Associated Vsual Cmmncations Inc	E	330 452-4449
Canton (G-2577)		
Atlas Printing and Embroidery	G	440 882-3537
Cleveland (G-4761)		
Austin Tape and Label Inc	D	330 928-7999
Stow (G-17570)		
Baise Enterprises Inc	G	614 443-3171
Columbus (G-6642)		
Bates Printing Inc	F	330 833-5830
Massillon (G-12962)		
Bemis Company Inc	E	330 923-5281
Akron (G-83)		
Bindery & Spc Pressworks Inc	D	614 873-4623
Plain City (G-16178)		
Bob Smith	G	513 242-7700
Blue Ash (G-1738)		
Bock & Pierce Enterprises	G	513 474-9500
Cincinnati (G-3398)		
Bohlender Engraving Company	F	513 621-4095
Cincinnati (G-3400)		
Bollin & Sons Inc	E	419 693-6573
Toledo (G-18210)		
Brakers Publishing & Prtg Svc	G	440 576-0136
Jefferson (G-11225)		
Brass Bull 1 LLC	G	740 335-8030
Wshngtn CT Hs (G-20720)		
Broadway Printing LLC	G	513 621-3429
Cincinnati (G-3419)		
Burns & Rink Enterprises LLC	G	513 421-7799
Cincinnati (G-3431)		
Bush Inc	G	216 362-6700
Cleveland (G-4854)		
C P S Enterprises Inc	F	216 441-7969
Cleveland (G-4858)		
Canvas 123 Inc	G	312 805-0563
Coventry Township (G-7766)		
Carey Color Llc/Cincinnati	G	513 241-5210
Cincinnati (G-3442)		
Century Graphics Inc	E	614 895-7698
Westerville (G-19983)		
Charles Huffman & Associates	G	216 295-0850
Warrensville Heights (G-19465)		
Cincinnati Print Solutions LLC	G	513 943-9500
Amelia (G-534)		
Cleveland Copy & Prtg Svc LLC	G	216 861-0324
Cleveland (G-4953)		
Cloverleaf Office Slutions LLC	G	614 219-9050
Hilliard (G-10817)		
Cnr Marketing Ltd	G	937 293-1030
Dayton (G-8094)		
Coloring Book Solutions LLC	F	419 281-9641
Ashland (G-695)		
Comdoc Inc	G	330 899-8000
Columbus (G-6805)		
Consolidated Graphics Group Inc	C	216 881-9191
Cleveland (G-5015)		
Consolidated Graphics Inc	C	740 654-2112
Lancaster (G-11556)		
Consolidated Web	G	216 881-7816
Cleveland (G-5018)		

Copy Source Inc	G	937 642-7140
Marysville (G-12778)		
Corporate Dcment Solutions Inc	F	513 595-8200
Cincinnati (G-3552)		
Coso Media LLC	G	330 904-5889
Hudson (G-11039)		
Creative Documents Solutions	G	740 389-4252
Marion (G-12701)		
Creative Print Solutions LLC	G	614 989-1747
Westerville (G-20042)		
Culaine Inc	G	419 345-4984
Toledo (G-18244)		
Custom Products Corporation	D	440 528-7100
Solon (G-17129)		
Customer Service Systems Inc	G	330 677-2877
Kent (G-11308)		
D & J Printing Inc	G	330 678-5868
Kent (G-11309)		
Danner Press Corp	G	330 454-5692
Canton (G-2647)		
Dayton Mailing Services Inc	E	937 222-5056
Dayton (G-8138)		
Ddg Incorporated	G	440 343-5060
Medina (G-13250)		
Dietrich Von Hildebrand Legacy	G	703 496-7821
Steubenville (G-17530)		
Digital Graphics	G	330 707-1720
Youngstown (G-20891)		
Digital Visuals Inc	G	513 420-9466
Middletown (G-13900)		
Direct Digital Graphics Inc	G	330 405-3770
Twinsburg (G-18764)		
Divine Prtg T-Shirts & More	G	419 241-8208
Toledo (G-18266)		
Dominion Labels & Forms	G	419 784-1041
Defiance (G-8622)		
DSC Supply Company LLC	G	614 891-1100
Westerville (G-20049)		
Dupli-Systems Inc	C	440 234-9415
Strongsville (G-17738)		
Durbin Minuteman Press	G	513 791-9171
Blue Ash (G-1760)		
Eagle Image Inc	F	513 662-3000
Cincinnati (G-3621)		
Eastern Graphic Arts	G	419 994-5815
Loudonville (G-12141)		
Electronic Imaging Svcs Inc	G	740 549-2487
Lewis Center (G-11759)		
Emta Inc	G	440 734-6464
North Olmsted (G-15187)		
Evolution Crtive Solutions LLC	E	513 681-4450
Cincinnati (G-3660)		
F J Designs Inc	E	330 264-1377
Wooster (G-20590)		
Fedex Office & Print Svcs Inc	E	614 898-0000
Westerville (G-20054)		
Fine Line Embroidery Company	G	440 331-7030
Rocky River (G-16547)		
Folks Creative Printers Inc	G	740 383-6326
Marion (G-12702)		
Four Ambition	G	937 239-4479
Dayton (G-8205)		
Freeport Press Inc	F	740 658-4000
New Philadelphia (G-14771)		
G Q Business Products	G	513 792-4750
Blue Ash (G-1780)		
G2 Print Plus	F	614 276-0500
Columbus (G-6943)		
Gb Liquidating Company Inc	E	513 248-7600
Milford (G-14010)		
GBS Corp	G	330 929-8050
Stow (G-17591)		
GBS Corp	C	330 494-5330
North Canton (G-15085)		
General Data Company Inc	C	513 752-7978
Cincinnati (G-3252)		
General Theming Contrs LLC	C	614 252-6342
Columbus (G-6945)		
Genesis Graphics	G	937 335-5332
Troy (G-18661)		
Genesis Quality Printing Inc	G	440 975-5700
Mentor (G-13457)		
Golden Graphics Ltd	F	419 673-6260
Kenton (G-11406)		
Grace Imaging LLC	G	419 874-2127
Perrysburg (G-15960)		
Grafisk Msknfabrik-America LLC	G	630 432-4370
Lebanon (G-11659)		
Grant John	G	937 298-0633
Dayton (G-8234)		

Employee Codes: A=Over 500 employees, B=251-500
C=101-250, D=51-100, E=20-50, F=10-19, G=3-9

2019 Harris Ohio
Industrial Directory

Graphic Info Systems Inc.......F....... 513 948-1300
Cincinnati *(G-3776)*
Graphic Paper Products Corp.......G....... 937 325-3912
Springfield *(G-17408)*
Graphic Stitch Inc.......G....... 937 642-6707
Marysville *(G-12784)*
Haines & Company Inc.......C....... 330 494-9111
North Canton *(G-15090)*
Harper Engraving & Printing Co.......D....... 614 276-0700
Columbus *(G-6982)*
Hecks Direct Mail & Prtg Svc.......E....... 419 697-3505
Toledo *(G-18327)*
Hilltop Printing.......G....... 419 782-9898
Defiance *(G-8626)*
Hkm Drect Mkt Cmmnications Inc.......E....... 440 934-3060
Sheffield Village *(G-16967)*
Hkm Drect Mkt Cmmnications Inc.......C....... 216 651-9500
Cleveland *(G-5412)*
Hollys Custom Print Inc.......E....... 740 928-2697
Hebron *(G-10748)*
Homewood Press Inc.......E....... 419 478-0695
Toledo *(G-18334)*
Horizon Ohio Publications Inc.......E....... 419 738-2128
Wapakoneta *(G-19332)*
Humtown Pattern Company.......D....... 330 482-5555
Columbiana *(G-6470)*
ID Images LLC.......F....... 513 874-5325
Fairfield *(G-9509)*
Imagine This Renovations.......G....... 330 833-6739
Navarre *(G-14577)*
Impressions - A Print Shop.......G....... 440 449-6966
Cleveland *(G-5446)*
Innomark Communications LLC.......C....... 513 285-1040
Fairfield *(G-9510)*
Instant Impressions Inc.......G....... 614 538-9844
Columbus *(G-7030)*
Intermec Technologies Corp.......F....... 513 874-5882
West Chester *(G-19726)*
International Advg Concepts.......G....... 440 331-4733
Cleveland *(G-5467)*
J & K Printing.......G....... 330 456-5306
Canton *(G-2713)*
J D B Partners Inc.......G....... 513 874-3056
Fairfield *(G-9513)*
Jack Walker Printing Co.......F....... 440 352-4222
Mentor *(G-13483)*
Jeffrey Reedy.......G....... 614 794-9292
Westerville *(G-20060)*
Joe Sestito.......G....... 614 871-7778
Grove City *(G-10437)*
Jscs Group Inc.......G....... 513 563-4900
Cincinnati *(G-3886)*
Kay Toledo Tag Inc.......D....... 419 729-5479
Toledo *(G-18363)*
Kenwel Printers Inc.......E....... 614 261-1011
Columbus *(G-7088)*
Key Marketing Group.......G....... 440 748-3479
Grafton *(G-10306)*
Keystone Printing & Copy Cat.......G....... 740 354-6542
Portsmouth *(G-16286)*
Kramer Graphics Inc.......E....... 937 296-9600
Moraine *(G-14363)*
Landen Desktop Pubg Ctr Inc.......G....... 513 683-5181
Loveland *(G-12209)*
Laughing Star Montessory.......G....... 513 683-5682
Maineville *(G-12373)*
Leeper Printing Co Inc.......G....... 419 243-2604
Toledo *(G-18380)*
Letterman Printing Inc.......G....... 513 523-1111
Oxford *(G-15696)*
Liming Printing Inc.......F....... 937 374-2646
Xenia *(G-20782)*
Locker Room Inc.......G....... 419 445-9600
Archbold *(G-656)*
Ls2 Printing.......G....... 937 544-1000
West Union *(G-19965)*
Lsc Communications Inc.......A....... 419 935-0111
Willard *(G-20241)*
Mac Printing Company.......G....... 937 393-1101
Hillsboro *(G-10884)*
Madison Graphics.......G....... 216 226-5770
Cleveland *(G-5601)*
Marbee Inc.......G....... 419 422-9441
Findlay *(G-9722)*
Marcus Uppe Inc.......D....... 216 263-4000
Cleveland *(G-5616)*
Margaret Trentman.......G....... 513 948-1700
Cincinnati *(G-3980)*
Marysville Printing Company.......G....... 937 644-4959
Marysville *(G-12800)*

Matthew Koster.......G....... 440 887-9000
Valley City *(G-19048)*
Meyers Printing & Design Inc.......G....... 937 461-6000
Dayton *(G-8344)*
Miami Graphics Services Inc.......F....... 937 698-4013
West Milton *(G-19950)*
Middleton Printing Co Inc.......G....... 614 294-7277
Gahanna *(G-10090)*
Mlp Interent Enterprises LLC.......E....... 614 917-8705
Mansfield *(G-12483)*
Miracle Custom Awards & Gifts.......G....... 330 376-8335
Akron *(G-283)*
Miracle Documents.......G....... 513 651-2222
Cincinnati *(G-4034)*
ML Advertising & Design LLC.......G....... 419 447-6523
Tiffin *(G-18069)*
Mmp Printing Inc.......E....... 513 381-0990
Cincinnati *(G-4035)*
Morse Enterprises Inc.......G....... 513 229-3600
Mason *(G-12912)*
Multi-Color Corporation.......C....... 513 396-5600
Cincinnati *(G-4054)*
Multi-Craft Litho Inc.......E....... 859 581-2754
Blue Ash *(G-1824)*
Network Printing & Graphics.......F....... 614 230-2084
Columbus *(G-7214)*
Newton Falls Printing.......G....... 330 872-3532
Newton Falls *(G-14990)*
Nilpeter Usa Inc.......C....... 513 489-4400
Cincinnati *(G-4080)*
Nomis Publications Inc.......F....... 330 965-2380
Youngstown *(G-20976)*
Ohio Legal Blank Co.......G....... 216 281-7792
Cleveland *(G-5806)*
Old Trail Printing Company.......C....... 614 443-4852
Columbus *(G-7269)*
Onetouchpoint East Corp.......D....... 513 421-1600
Cincinnati *(G-4113)*
Onnyx.......G....... 419 627-9872
Sandusky *(G-16833)*
Packaging Materials Inc.......E....... 740 432-6337
Cambridge *(G-2452)*
Park PLC Prntg Cpyg & Dgtl IMG.......G....... 330 799-1739
Youngstown *(G-20993)*
Park Press Direct.......G....... 419 626-4426
Sandusky *(G-16835)*
Peebles Creative Group Inc.......G....... 614 487-2011
Dublin *(G-8961)*
Penguin Enterprises Inc.......E....... 440 899-5112
Westlake *(G-20140)*
Pexco Packaging Corp.......E....... 419 470-5935
Toledo *(G-18468)*
Precision Business Solutions.......G....... 419 661-8700
Perrysburg *(G-16001)*
Press of Ohio Inc.......E....... 330 678-5868
Kent *(G-11367)*
Prestige Printing.......G....... 937 236-8468
Dayton *(G-8438)*
Printing Depot Inc.......G....... 330 783-5341
Youngstown *(G-21007)*
Profile Digital Printing LLC.......E....... 937 866-4241
Dayton *(G-8448)*
Proforma Advantage.......G....... 440 781-5255
Mayfield Village *(G-13175)*
Proforma Steinbacher & Assoc.......G....... 330 241-5370
Medina *(G-13322)*
Progressive Printers Inc.......D....... 937 222-1267
Dayton *(G-8450)*
PS Graphics Inc.......G....... 440 356-9656
Rocky River *(G-16553)*
Quality Print Shop Inc.......G....... 740 992-3345
Middleport *(G-13873)*
Quest Service Labs Inc.......F....... 330 405-0316
Twinsburg *(G-18843)*
Quick As A Wink Printing Co.......F....... 419 224-9786
Lima *(G-11926)*
R R Donnelley & Sons Company.......G....... 513 552-1512
West Chester *(G-19778)*
R W Michael Printing Co.......G....... 330 923-9277
Akron *(G-340)*
R&D Marketing Group Inc.......G....... 216 398-9100
Brooklyn Heights *(G-2130)*
Research and Development Group.......G....... 614 261-0454
Columbus *(G-7386)*
Reynolds and Reynolds Company.......F....... 419 584-7000
Celina *(G-2983)*
Richland Blue Printcom Inc.......G....... 419 524-2781
Mansfield *(G-12505)*
Rl Smith Printing Co.......F....... 330 747-9590
Youngstown *(G-21017)*

Robert Esterman.......G....... 513 541-3311
Cincinnati *(G-4277)*
Robert H Shackelford.......G....... 330 364-2221
New Philadelphia *(G-14799)*
Robloc Inc.......G....... 330 723-5853
Medina *(G-13329)*
Ryans Newark Leader Ex Prtg.......F....... 740 522-2149
Newark *(G-14916)*
Sandy Smittcamp.......G....... 937 372-1687
Xenia *(G-20788)*
Schilling Graphics Inc.......E....... 419 468-1037
Galion *(G-10154)*
Sevell + Sevell Inc.......G....... 614 341-9700
Columbus *(G-7441)*
Slutzkers Quickprint Center.......G....... 440 244-0330
Lorain *(G-12123)*
Small Dog Printing.......G....... 614 777-7620
Hilliard *(G-10862)*
SMS Communications Inc.......E....... 216 374-6686
Shaker Heights *(G-16937)*
Somerset Commercial Prtg Co.......G....... 740 536-7187
Rushville *(G-16597)*
Spencer-Walker Press Inc.......G....... 740 345-4494
Newark *(G-14921)*
Spencer-Walker Press Inc.......F....... 740 344-6110
Newark *(G-14920)*
Springdot Inc.......D....... 513 542-4000
Cincinnati *(G-4365)*
Stadvec Inc.......G....... 330 644-7724
Barberton *(G-1107)*
Stephen Andrews Inc.......G....... 330 725-2672
Lodi *(G-12020)*
Stolle Machinery Company LLC.......C....... 937 497-5400
Sidney *(G-17082)*
Suburban Press Inc.......E....... 216 961-0766
Cleveland *(G-6114)*
Suntwist Corp.......E....... 800 935-3534
Maple Heights *(G-12581)*
Taylor Communications Inc.......C....... 419 678-6000
Coldwater *(G-6422)*
Taylor Communications Inc.......C....... 614 277-7500
Grove City *(G-10471)*
Taylor Communications Inc.......E....... 937 221-1000
Dayton *(G-8543)*
Thomas Allen Co.......G....... 330 823-8487
Alliance *(G-506)*
Tj Metzgers Inc.......D....... 419 861-8611
Toledo *(G-18553)*
Toledo Ticket Company.......E....... 419 476-5424
Toledo *(G-18573)*
Tree Free Resources LLC.......F....... 740 751-4844
Marion *(G-12744)*
Trinity Printing Co.......F....... 513 469-1000
Cincinnati *(G-4439)*
US Government Publishing Off.......G....... 614 469-5657
Columbus *(G-7566)*
Value Added Business Svcs Co.......G....... 614 854-9755
Jackson *(G-11200)*
Visual Information Institute.......F....... 937 376-4361
Xenia *(G-20801)*
Vya Inc.......E....... 513 772-5400
Cincinnati *(G-4485)*
Ward/Kraft Forms of Ohio Inc.......D....... 740 694-0015
Fredericktown *(G-9983)*
West-Camp Press Inc.......D....... 614 882-2378
Westerville *(G-20082)*
Western Ohio Graphics.......F....... 937 335-8769
Troy *(G-18719)*
Western Roto Engravers Inc.......E....... 330 336-7636
Wadsworth *(G-19281)*
Wfsr Holdings LLC.......A....... 877 735-4966
Dayton *(G-8592)*
William J Dupps.......G....... 419 734-2126
Port Clinton *(G-16264)*
Williams Steel Rule Die Co.......F....... 216 431-3232
Cleveland *(G-6311)*
Woodrow Corp.......G....... 937 322-7696
Springfield *(G-17520)*
Yi Xing Inc.......G....... 614 785-9631
Columbus *(G-7623)*
Yockey Group Inc.......E....... 513 860-9053
West Chester *(G-19824)*
Youngstown ARC Engraving Co.......E....... 330 793-2471
Youngstown *(G-21070)*

PRINTING: Engraving & Plate

Converters/Prepress Inc.......F....... 937 743-0935
Carlisle *(G-2891)*
Northmont Sign Co Inc.......G....... 937 890-0372
Dayton *(G-8384)*

PRINTING: Letterpress

Roban Inc ....G....... 330 794-1059
  Lakemore *(G-11500)*
Sams Graphic Industries..................F....... 330 821-4710
  Alliance *(G-498)*

PRINTING: Flexographic

Admiral Products Company Inc ....E 216 671-0600
  Cleveland *(G-4619)*
Cincinnati Convertors Inc ....F 513 731-6600
  Cincinnati *(G-3487)*
Ebel-Binder Printing Co ....G....... 513 471-1067
  Cincinnati *(G-3628)*
Hawks & Associates Inc ....E 513 752-4311
  Cincinnati *(G-3254)*
Intermec Ultra Print Inc ....E 513 874-5882
  West Chester *(G-19727)*
Lazer Systems Inc..............................F 513 641-4002
  Cincinnati *(G-3935)*
Mr Label Inc ....E 513 681-2088
  Cincinnati *(G-4051)*
Novavision Inc ....D 419 354-1427
  Bowling Green *(G-1986)*
Ohio Flexible Packaging Co................F 513 494-1800
  South Lebanon *(G-17277)*
Riverside Mfg LLC..............................F 937 492-3100
  Sidney *(G-17067)*
Samuels Products Inc ....E 513 891-4456
  Blue Ash *(G-1842)*
Seneca Label Inc ....E 440 237-1600
  Cleveland *(G-6044)*
Superior Label Systems Inc................B 513 336-0825
  Mason *(G-12944)*
Thomas Products Co Inc....................E 513 756-9009
  Cincinnati *(G-4420)*
Warren Printing & Off Pdts Inc............F 419 523-3635
  Ottawa *(G-15671)*
West Carrollton Parchment.................E 513 594-3341
  West Carrollton *(G-19634)*
Wingate Packaging Inc ....E 513 745-8600
  Blue Ash *(G-1871)*

PRINTING: Gravure, Business Form & Card

Business Fnctnality Forms Svcs.........G....... 614 557-9420
  Gahanna *(G-10077)*
Wilmer ....G....... 419 678-6000
  Coldwater *(G-6424)*

PRINTING: Gravure, Color

Fx Digital Media Inc ....E 216 241-4040
  Cleveland *(G-5282)*

PRINTING: Gravure, Coupons

Clipper Magazine LLC ....G....... 937 534-0470
  Moraine *(G-14338)*

PRINTING: Gravure, Envelopes

Ohio Envelope Manufacturing Co ....E 216 267-2920
  Cleveland *(G-5805)*

PRINTING: Gravure, Forms, Business

Dupli-Systems Inc..............................C 440 234-9415
  Strongsville *(G-17738)*
Veritrack Inc.......................................F 513 202-0790
  Harrison *(G-10678)*

PRINTING: Gravure, Invitations

Miami Valley Press Inc.......................G....... 937 547-0771
  Greenville *(G-10381)*
Revenue Management Group LLC .....F 419 993-2200
  Lima *(G-11930)*

PRINTING: Gravure, Job

Cham Cor Industries Inc ....G....... 740 967-9015
  Johnstown *(G-11262)*
Graphic Paper Products Corp ....D 937 325-5503
  Springfield *(G-17407)*

PRINTING: Gravure, Labels

Admiral Products Company Inc ....E 216 671-0600
  Cleveland *(G-4619)*
Anthony Business Forms Inc ....F 937 253-0072
  Dayton *(G-7971)*
E-Z Stop Service Center ....D 330 448-2236
  Brookfield *(G-2105)*

Label Print Technologies LLC ....F 800 475-4030
  Mogadore *(G-14243)*
M PI Label Systems ....G....... 330 938-2134
  Sebring *(G-16888)*
Mpi Labels of Baltimore Inc ....F 330 938-2134
  Sebring *(G-16890)*
Retterbush Graphic and Packg ....E 513 779-4466
  West Chester *(G-19780)*
Scratch-Off Systems Inc ....E 216 649-7800
  Brecksville *(G-2056)*

PRINTING: Gravure, Rotogravure

Angstrom Graphics Inc ....C 216 271-5300
  Cleveland *(G-4716)*
Dulle Associates ....G....... 513 723-9600
  Cincinnati *(G-3612)*
Lloyd F Helber....................................E 740 756-9607
  Carroll *(G-2906)*
Multi-Color Australia LLC...................B 513 381-1480
  Batavia *(G-1170)*
Multi-Color Corporation ....D 513 943-0080
  Batavia *(G-1172)*
Ohio Gravure Technologies Inc ....E 937 439-1582
  Miamisburg *(G-13703)*
Quad/Graphics Inc ....A 513 932-1064
  Lebanon *(G-11687)*
R R Donnelley & Sons Company ....G....... 740 376-9276
  Marietta *(G-12661)*
Shamrock Companies Inc ....D 440 899-9510
  Westlake *(G-20158)*
Taylor Communications Inc ....G....... 866 541-0937
  Dayton *(G-8546)*
Taylor Communications Inc ....G....... 937 228-5800
  Dayton *(G-8545)*
W L Beck Printing & Design ....G....... 330 762-3020
  Akron *(G-430)*
Wfsr Holdings LLC............................A 877 735-4966
  Dayton *(G-8592)*

PRINTING: Laser

DCS Technologies Corporation..........E 937 743-4060
  Franklin *(G-9879)*
Laser Printing Solutions Inc ....F 216 351-4444
  Cleveland *(G-5563)*
Marketing Comm Resource Inc ....D 440 484-3010
  Willoughby *(G-20371)*
Microplex Printware Corp ....F 440 374-2424
  Bedford *(G-1426)*
Queen City Office Machine ....F 513 251-7200
  Cincinnati *(G-4238)*
True Dinero Records & Tech LLC ......G....... 513 428-4610
  Cincinnati *(G-4443)*
V I P Printing & Design......................G....... 513 777-7468
  West Chester *(G-19913)*

PRINTING: Letterpress

A-A Blueprint Co Inc..........................E 330 794-8803
  Akron *(G-23)*
Acme Printing Co Inc.........................G....... 419 626-4426
  Sandusky *(G-16792)*
Akron Litho-Print Company Inc..........F 330 434-3145
  Akron *(G-43)*
Art Printing Co Inc ....G....... 419 281-4371
  Ashland *(G-677)*
Barnhart Printing Corp ....F 330 456-2279
  Canton *(G-2585)*
Berea Printing Company ....G....... 440 243-1080
  Berea *(G-1594)*
Betley Printing Co..............................G....... 216 206-5600
  Cleveland *(G-4810)*
Boldman Printing LLC ....G....... 937 653-3431
  Urbana *(G-18980)*
Bramkamp Printing Company Inc .....E 513 241-1865
  Blue Ash *(G-1740)*
Brothers Printing Co Inc ....F 216 621-6050
  Cleveland *(G-4844)*
Cornerstone Industries Lcc ....G....... 513 871-4546
  West Chester *(G-19685)*
Cox Printing Co..................................G....... 937 382-2312
  Wilmington *(G-20491)*
Dana Graphics Inc ....G....... 513 351-4400
  Cincinnati *(G-3575)*
Dee Printing Inc.................................F 614 777-8700
  Columbus *(G-6856)*
Diocesan Publications Inc Ohio ....E 614 718-9500
  Dublin *(G-8907)*
DOV Graphics Inc..............................E 513 241-5150
  Cincinnati *(G-3605)*

Dresden Specialties Inc.....................G....... 740 452-7100
  Zanesville *(G-21131)*
Dresden Specialties Inc.....................G....... 740 754-2451
  Dresden *(G-8868)*
Earl D Arnold Printing Company ....E 513 533-6900
  Cincinnati *(G-3624)*
Eci Macola/Max LLC ....C 978 539-6186
  Dublin *(G-8911)*
Exchange Printing Company ....G....... 330 773-7842
  Akron *(G-161)*
Firelands Fas-Print LLC ....G....... 419 668-3045
  Norwalk *(G-15395)*
Foote Printing Company Inc ....F 216 431-1757
  Cleveland *(G-5260)*
Graphic Touch Inc..............................G....... 330 337-3341
  Salem *(G-16744)*
Great Lakes Printing Inc....................D 440 993-8781
  Ashtabula *(G-779)*
Heskamp Printing Co Inc ....G....... 513 871-6770
  Cincinnati *(G-3811)*
J P Quality Printing Inc ....G....... 216 791-6303
  Cleveland *(G-5485)*
Jarman Printing Company LLC ....G....... 330 823-8585
  Alliance *(G-479)*
Johnson Printing ....G....... 740 922-4821
  Uhrichsville *(G-18889)*
Kee Printing Inc..................................G....... 937 456-6851
  Eaton *(G-9156)*
Kehoe Brothers Printing Inc ....G....... 216 351-4100
  Cleveland *(G-5524)*
Keithley Enterprises Inc ....G....... 937 890-1878
  Dayton *(G-8290)*
Key Press Inc ....G....... 513 721-1203
  Cincinnati *(G-3907)*
Keystone Press Inc............................G....... 419 243-7326
  Toledo *(G-18367)*
KMS 2000 Inc ....F 330 454-9444
  Canton *(G-2727)*
Lee Corporation ....G....... 513 771-3602
  Cincinnati *(G-3937)*
Lesher Printers Inc ....E 419 332-8253
  Fremont *(G-10033)*
Lilienthal Southeastern Inc.................F 740 439-1640
  Cambridge *(G-2446)*
Lund Printing Co ....G....... 330 628-4047
  Akron *(G-262)*
Lyle Printing & Publishing Co ....E 330 337-3419
  Salem *(G-16756)*
Madison Press Inc ....G....... 216 521-3789
  Lakewood *(G-11527)*
Mariotti Printing Co LLC....................G....... 440 245-4120
  Lorain *(G-12104)*
Martin Printing Co..............................G....... 419 224-9176
  Lima *(G-11897)*
Minuteman Press of Athens LLC........G....... 740 593-7393
  Athens *(G-841)*
Nelis Printing Co................................G....... 330 757-4114
  Youngstown *(G-20974)*
Odyssey Press Inc ....F 614 410-0356
  Huron *(G-11107)*
Paragon Press ....G....... 513 281-9911
  Cincinnati *(G-4133)*
Post Printing Co.................................D 859 254-7714
  Minster *(G-14222)*
Printex Incorporated ....F 740 773-0088
  Chillicothe *(G-3217)*
R R Donnelley & Sons Company ....E 440 774-2101
  Oberlin *(G-15504)*
Rotary Printing Company ....G....... 419 668-4821
  Norwalk *(G-15414)*
Selby Service/Roxy Press Inc............G....... 513 241-3445
  Cincinnati *(G-4318)*
Shreve Printing LLC ....F 330 567-2341
  Shreve *(G-17010)*
Silica Press Inc..................................G....... 419 843-8500
  Sylvania *(G-17961)*
Sitler Printer Inc ....G....... 330 482-4463
  Columbiana *(G-6480)*
Slimans Printery Inc...........................F 330 454-9141
  Canton *(G-2818)*
Snow Printing Co Inc.........................F 419 229-7669
  Lima *(G-11941)*
South End Printing Co ....G....... 216 341-0669
  Cleveland *(G-6081)*
Star Calendar & Printing Co...............G....... 216 741-3223
  Cleveland *(G-6095)*
Star Printing Company Inc.................E 330 376-0514
  Akron *(G-386)*
Starr Printing Services Inc ....G....... 513 241-7708
  Cincinnati *(G-4375)*

Stationery Shop Inc .... G 330 376-2033
Akron *(G-387)*
Tope Printing Inc .... G 330 674-4993
Millersburg *(G-14137)*
Traxium LLC .... E 330 572-8200
Stow *(G-17637)*
William J Bergen & Co .... G 440 248-6132
Solon *(G-17261)*
Wirick Press Inc .... G 330 273-3488
Brunswick *(G-2252)*
Zech Printing Industries Inc .... E 937 748-2776
Cincinnati *(G-4532)*

PRINTING: Lithographic

1455 Group LLC .... G 330 494-9074
Canton *(G-2554)*
A Grade Notes Inc .... G 614 766-9999
Dublin *(G-8871)*
Ace Printing LLC .... G 614 855-7227
New Albany *(G-14603)*
Adcraft Decals Inc .... E 216 524-2934
Cleveland *(G-4615)*
Admark Printing Inc .... G 937 833-5111
Brookville *(G-2160)*
Affordable Bus Support LLC .... G 440 543-5547
Chagrin Falls *(G-3036)*
Albert Bramkamp Printing Co .... G 513 641-1069
Cincinnati *(G-3318)*
Alberts Screen Print Inc .... C 330 753-7559
Norton *(G-15360)*
All American Screen Printing .... G 419 475-0696
Toledo *(G-18162)*
All Print Ltd .... F 440 349-6868
Solon *(G-17101)*
All Systems Colour Inc .... G 937 859-9701
Dayton *(G-8016)*
Alliance Publishing Co Inc .... C 330 453-1304
Alliance *(G-454)*
Alt Control Print .... G 419 841-2467
Toledo *(G-18168)*
Alvito Custom Imprints .... G 614 846-8986
Worthington *(G-20676)*
Anderson Printing & Supply LLC .... G 614 891-1100
Westerville *(G-20034)*
Angstrom Graphics Inc .... C 216 271-5300
Cleveland *(G-4716)*
Anthony Business Forms Inc .... F 937 253-0072
Dayton *(G-7971)*
Arch Parent Inc .... A 440 701-7420
Mentor *(G-13392)*
Armstrong S Printing Ex LLC .... G 937 276-7794
Dayton *(G-8037)*
Art Pro Graphics .... G 216 236-6465
Seven Hills *(G-16901)*
B2 Incorporated .... G 330 244-9510
North Canton *(G-15071)*
Baise Enterprises Inc .... G 614 444-3171
Columbus *(G-6642)*
Bang Printing of Ohio Inc .... F 800 678-1222
Kent *(G-11298)*
BCT Alarm Services Inc .... G 440 669-8153
Amherst *(G-554)*
Bemis Company Inc .... E 330 923-5281
Akron *(G-83)*
Bethart Enterprises Inc .... G 513 777-8707
West Chester *(G-19660)*
Bizzy Bee Printing Inc .... G 614 771-1222
Columbus *(G-6672)*
Black River Group Inc .... D 419 524-6699
Mansfield *(G-12411)*
Bloch Printing Company .... G 330 576-6760
Copley *(G-7678)*
Blooms Printing Inc .... F 740 922-1765
Dennison *(G-8782)*
Blue Crescent Enterprises Inc .... G 440 878-9700
Strongsville *(G-17720)*
Blue Streak Services Inc .... G 216 223-3282
Cleveland *(G-4825)*
Blueserv Reprograhics LLC .... G 937 426-6410
Beavercreek *(G-1351)*
Boehr Print .... G 419 358-1350
Findlay *(G-9659)*
Bohlender Engraving Company .... F 513 621-4095
Cincinnati *(G-3400)*
Bookmasters Inc .... C 419 281-1802
Ashland *(G-686)*
Brandon Screen Printing .... F 419 229-9837
Lima *(G-11845)*
Bricolage Inc .... F 614 853-6789
Grove City *(G-10418)*
Brookville Star .... G 937 833-2545
Brookville *(G-2163)*
Buckeye Cstm Screen Print EMB .... F 614 237-0196
Columbus *(G-6709)*
Busson Digital Printing Inc .... E 330 753-8373
Wadsworth *(G-19228)*
C Massouh Printing Co Inc .... G 330 832-6334
Massillon *(G-12964)*
Canton Graphic Arts Service .... G 330 456-9868
Canton *(G-2611)*
Carriage House Printery LLC .... G 740 243-7493
Carroll *(G-2900)*
Central Ohio Printing Corp .... D 740 852-1616
London *(G-12052)*
Century Marketing Corporation .... C 419 354-2591
Bowling Green *(G-1961)*
Characters Inc .... G 937 335-1976
Troy *(G-18640)*
Child Evngelism Fellowship Inc .... E 440 218-4982
Cuyahoga Falls *(G-7849)*
Child Evngelism Fellowship Inc .... E 419 756-7799
Ontario *(G-15538)*
City of Cleveland .... F 216 664-3013
Cleveland *(G-4930)*
Cns Inc .... G 513 631-7073
Cincinnati *(G-3533)*
Commercial Prtg of Greenvill .... G 937 548-3835
Greenville *(G-10365)*
Copley Ohio Newspapers Inc .... D 330 833-2631
Massillon *(G-12969)*
Copy Cats Printing LLC .... G 440 345-5966
Cleveland *(G-5030)*
County Classifieds .... G 937 592-8847
Bellefontaine *(G-1510)*
Covap Inc .... F 513 793-1855
Blue Ash *(G-1753)*
Crabar/Gbf Inc .... F 419 943-2141
Leipsic *(G-11724)*
Culaine Inc .... G 419 345-4984
Toledo *(G-18244)*
Custom Graphics Inc .... C 330 963-7770
Macedonia *(G-12287)*
Custom Imprint .... F 440 238-4488
Strongsville *(G-17734)*
Customer Printing Inc .... F 330 629-8676
Youngstown *(G-20884)*
Customer Service Systems Inc .... G 330 677-2877
Kent *(G-11308)*
Daily Gazette .... E 937 372-4444
Xenia *(G-20764)*
Danner Press Corp .... G 330 454-5692
Canton *(G-2647)*
David A and Mary A Mathis .... G 330 837-8611
Massillon *(G-12973)*
Digital Color Intl LLC .... E 330 762-6959
Akron *(G-143)*
Directconnectgroup Ltd .... A 216 281-2866
Cleveland *(G-5097)*
Dispatch Printing Company .... E 614 885-6020
Columbus *(G-6868)*
Dixie Flyer & Printing Co .... G 937 687-0088
New Lebanon *(G-14709)*
Dla Document Services .... G 216 522-3535
Cleveland *(G-5101)*
Dla Document Services .... E 937 257-6014
Dayton *(G-7978)*
Docmann Printing & Assoc Inc .... G 440 975-1775
Solon *(G-17133)*
Dsk Imaging LLC .... F 513 554-1797
Blue Ash *(G-1759)*
Dupli-Systems Inc .... C 440 234-9415
Strongsville *(G-17738)*
Edwards Electrical & Mech .... E 614 485-2003
Columbus *(G-6885)*
Emta Inc .... G 440 734-6464
North Olmsted *(G-15187)*
Enlarging Arts Inc .... G 330 434-3433
Akron *(G-156)*
Ennis Inc .... E 800 537-8648
Toledo *(G-18282)*
Enquirer Printing Company .... G 513 241-1956
Cincinnati *(G-3643)*
Envoi Design Inc .... G 513 651-4229
Cincinnati *(G-3645)*
Etched Metal Company .... E 440 248-0240
Solon *(G-17142)*
Eugene Stewart .... G 937 898-1117
Dayton *(G-8189)*
Express Graphic Prtg & Design .... G 513 728-3344
Cincinnati *(G-3666)*
F P C Printing Inc .... G 937 743-8136
Franklin *(G-9881)*
Fair Publishing House Inc .... E 419 668-3746
Norwalk *(G-15394)*
Fedex Corporation .... G 740 687-0334
Lancaster *(G-11572)*
Fedex Office & Print Svcs Inc .... F 330 376-6002
Akron *(G-167)*
Fedex Office & Print Svcs Inc .... E 419 866-5464
Toledo *(G-18290)*
Fine Print LLC .... G 419 702-7087
Lakeside Marblehead *(G-11502)*
Fleet Graphics Inc .... G 937 252-2552
Dayton *(G-8198)*
Flowers Print Inc .... G 937 429-3823
Beavercreek *(G-1315)*
Follow Print Club On Facebook .... G 216 707-2579
Cleveland *(G-5258)*
Fortec Litho Central LLC .... G 330 463-1265
Hudson *(G-11044)*
Fourjays Inc .... G 216 741-8258
Parma *(G-15819)*
Frank J Prucha & Associates .... G 216 642-3838
Cleveland *(G-5272)*
Frankies Graphics Inc .... G 440 979-0824
Westlake *(G-20114)*
Friends Service Co Inc .... F 800 427-1704
Dayton *(G-8208)*
Friends Service Co Inc .... G 800 427-1704
Kent *(G-11322)*
Frisby Printing Company .... G 330 665-4565
Fairlawn *(G-9605)*
G S Link & Associates .... G 513 722-2457
Goshen *(G-10287)*
Gannett Co Inc .... C 740 773-2111
Chillicothe *(G-3188)*
Gannett Stllite Info Ntwrk LLC .... D 419 334-1012
Fremont *(G-10021)*
Gazette Publishing Company .... C 419 483-4190
Oberlin *(G-15495)*
Genesis Quality Printing Inc .... G 440 975-5700
Mentor *(G-13457)*
Geygan Enterprises Inc .... F 513 932-4222
Lebanon *(G-11656)*
Gordon Bernard Company LLC .... E 513 248-7600
Milford *(G-14013)*
Graphic Expressions Signs .... G 330 422-7446
Streetsboro *(G-17676)*
Graphic Paper Products Corp .... D 937 325-5503
Springfield *(G-17407)*
Graphic Print Solutions Inc .... G 513 948-3344
Cincinnati *(G-3777)*
Graphix Network .... G 740 941-3771
Waverly *(G-19547)*
Great Lakes Engraving Corp .... G 419 867-1607
Maumee *(G-13113)*
Green Leaf Printing and Design .... G 937 222-3634
Dayton *(G-8236)*
Haines & Company Inc .... C 330 494-9111
North Canton *(G-15090)*
Hawks & Associates Inc .... E 513 752-4311
Cincinnati *(G-3254)*
Herff Jones LLC .... G 740 357-2160
Lucasville *(G-12264)*
Hkm Drect Mkt Cmmnications Inc .... C 216 651-9500
Cleveland *(G-5412)*
Hollys Custom Print Inc .... E 740 928-2697
Hebron *(G-10748)*
Holmes Printing Solutions LLC .... G 330 234-9699
Fredericksburg *(G-9952)*
Horizon Ohio Publications Inc .... E 419 738-2128
Wapakoneta *(G-19332)*
Hudson Printing of Medina LLC .... G 330 591-4800
Medina *(G-13276)*
Icandi Graphics LLC .... G 330 723-8337
Medina *(G-13277)*
Info-Graphics Inc .... G 440 498-1640
Solon *(G-17169)*
Ink Well .... G 614 861-7113
Gahanna *(G-10084)*
Instant Replay .... G 937 592-0534
Bellefontaine *(G-1520)*
It XCEL Consulting LLC .... F 513 847-8261
West Chester *(G-19728)*
J&B Postal and Print Svcs LLC .... G 740 363-7653
Delaware *(G-8698)*
Jeffrey Reedy .... G 614 794-9292
Westerville *(G-20060)*
Jk Digital Publishing LLC .... E 937 299-0185
Springboro *(G-17331)*

PRODUCT SECTION

PRINTING: Offset

JM Printing G 740 412-8666
Circleville *(G-4547)*

Joe The Printer Guy LLC G 216 651-3880
Lakewood *(G-11523)*

JPS Print G 614 235-8947
Columbus *(G-7078)*

K B Printing G 614 771-1222
Columbus *(G-7081)*

Kelly Prints LLC G 440 356-6361
North Olmsted *(G-15194)*

Kem Advertising and Prtg LLC G 330 818-5061
Barberton *(G-1080)*

Kendall & Sons Company G 937 222-6996
Dayton *(G-8292)*

Keystone Printing & Copy Cat G 740 354-6542
Portsmouth *(G-16286)*

Knox County Printing Co G 740 848-4032
Galion *(G-10147)*

Kovacevic Printing Inc G 440 887-1000
Cleveland *(G-5542)*

Kuwatch Printing LLC G 513 759-5850
Liberty Twp *(G-11827)*

L & H Printing G 937 855-4512
Germantown *(G-10243)*

Lamar Proforma G 440 285-2277
Chardon *(G-3122)*

Landen Desktop Pubg Ctr Inc G 513 683-5181
Loveland *(G-12209)*

Legalcraft Inc F 330 494-1261
Canton *(G-2732)*

Lobo Awrds Screen Prtg Graphix G 740 972-9087
Marion *(G-12716)*

Loris Printing Inc G 419 626-6648
Sandusky *(G-16823)*

Lsc Communications Inc A 419 935-0111
Willard *(G-20241)*

M D M Graphics Inc G 859 816-7375
Cincinnati *(G-3962)*

M-Fischer Enterprises LLC G 419 782-5309
Defiance *(G-8634)*

Mac Printing Company G 937 393-1101
Hillsboro *(G-10884)*

McNerney & Associates LLC E 513 241-9951
Cincinnati *(G-3989)*

Mike B Crawford G 330 673-7944
Kent *(G-11355)*

Minuteman Press G 440 946-3311
Mentor *(G-13521)*

Minuteman Press G 513 772-0500
Cincinnati *(G-4031)*

Minuteman Press G 937 429-8610
Beavercreek *(G-1332)*

Minuteman Press Inc G 513 741-9056
Cincinnati *(G-4032)*

Minutman Press Frfeld Cnty LLC G 740 689-1992
Lancaster *(G-11589)*

Mp Printing & Design Inc G 740 456-2045
Portsmouth *(G-16292)*

Mullin Print Solutions G 216 383-2901
Euclid *(G-9428)*

Multi-Color Australia LLC B 513 381-1480
Batavia *(G-1170)*

Network Printing & Graphics F 614 230-2084
Columbus *(G-7214)*

Newspaper Holding Inc D 440 998-2323
Ashtabula *(G-792)*

Newton Falls Printing G 330 872-3532
Newton Falls *(G-14990)*

Nickum Enterprises Inc G 513 561-2292
Cincinnati *(G-4077)*

North Coast Litho Inc E 216 881-1952
Cleveland *(G-5767)*

Northcoast Pmm LLC F 419 540-8667
Toledo *(G-18428)*

Northeast Blueprint & Sup Co G 216 261-7500
Cleveland *(G-5773)*

Ogden Newspapers Inc C 330 841-1600
Warren *(G-19426)*

Ohio Art Company D 419 636-3141
Bryan *(G-2301)*

Omni Business Forms Inc G 513 860-0111
West Chester *(G-19883)*

Onetouchpoint East Corp D 513 421-1600
Cincinnati *(G-4113)*

Oscar Hicks G 937 435-4350
Dayton *(G-8409)*

Our Nine LLC G 614 844-6655
Columbus *(G-7280)*

Papworth Prints G 614 428-6137
Columbus *(G-7292)*

Paxar Corporation F 937 681-4541
Dayton *(G-8418)*

Peck Engraving Co E 216 221-1556
Cleveland *(G-5860)*

PIP Enterprises LLC G 740 373-5276
Marietta *(G-12654)*

Plain Dealer Publishing Co A 216 999-5000
Cleveland *(G-5883)*

Premier Printing and Packg Inc G 937 436-5290
Dayton *(G-8436)*

Premier Printing Solutions G 740 374-2836
Marietta *(G-12658)*

Press For Less Printing Firm I G 931 912-4606
Lebanon *(G-11686)*

Print Solutions Today LLC G 614 848-4500
Westerville *(G-20071)*

Print Syndicate Inc G 614 657-8318
Columbus *(G-7348)*

Print Syndicate LLC F 614 519-0341
Columbus *(G-7349)*

Print Zone G 513 733-0067
West Chester *(G-19889)*

Printers Edge Inc F 330 372-2232
Warren *(G-19434)*

Printing Express G 937 276-7794
Moraine *(G-14383)*

Printing For Less G 937 743-8268
Springboro *(G-17345)*

Printing Services E 440 708-1999
Chagrin Falls *(G-3070)*

Professional Screen Printing G 740 687-0760
Lancaster *(G-11600)*

Profile Digital Printing LLC E 937 866-4241
Dayton *(G-8448)*

Proimage Printing & Design LLC G 937 312-9544
Xenia *(G-20787)*

Promatch Solutions LLC F 937 299-0185
Springboro *(G-17346)*

Province of St John The Baptis D 513 241-5615
Cincinnati *(G-4219)*

Quick Tech Graphics Inc E 937 743-5952
Springboro *(G-17348)*

R R Donnelley & Sons Company D 330 562-5250
Streetsboro *(G-17690)*

R R Donnelley & Sons Company E 440 774-2101
Oberlin *(G-15504)*

R S Imprints F 330 872-5905
Newton Falls *(G-14992)*

R W Michael Printing Co G 330 923-9277
Akron *(G-340)*

R&D Marketing Group Inc G 216 398-9100
Brooklyn Heights *(G-2130)*

Red Vette Printing Company G 740 364-1766
Granville *(G-10337)*

Resilient Holdings Inc F 614 847-5600
Columbus *(G-7387)*

Reynolds and Reynolds Company F 419 584-7000
Celina *(G-2983)*

Ricci Anthony G 330 758-5761
Youngstown *(G-21015)*

Rl Smith Graphics LLC G 330 629-8616
Youngstown *(G-21016)*

Robs Creative Screen Printing G 740 264-6383
Wintersville *(G-20541)*

Rohrer Corporation C 440 542-3100
Solon *(G-17225)*

Rotary Forms Press Inc E 937 393-3426
Hillsboro *(G-10890)*

RPI Color Service Inc D 513 471-4040
Cincinnati *(G-4285)*

Ruda Print & Graphics G 419 331-7832
Lima *(G-11934)*

S and K Painting G 330 505-1910
Niles *(G-15036)*

Sandusky Newspapers Inc C 419 625-5500
Sandusky *(G-16845)*

Saturn Press Inc G 440 232-3344
Bedford *(G-1444)*

Schlabach Printing Ltd E 330 852-4687
Sugarcreek *(G-17863)*

Sdg News Group Inc F 419 929-3411
New London *(G-14737)*

Seifert Printing Company G 330 759-7414
Youngstown *(G-21027)*

Sensical Inc D 216 641-1141
Solon *(G-17229)*

Sfc Graphics Cleveland Ltd E 419 255-1283
Toledo *(G-18520)*

Shallow Lake Corp G 614 883-6350
Lewis Center *(G-11779)*

Shawnee Systems Inc D 513 561-9932
Cincinnati *(G-4330)*

Ship Print E Sell G 614 459-1205
Columbus *(G-7446)*

Six-3 G 614 260-5610
Columbus *(G-7456)*

Soondook LLC E 614 389-5757
Columbus *(G-7463)*

Sourcelink Ohio LLC C 937 885-8000
Miamisburg *(G-13718)*

Southeast Publications Inc F 740 732-2341
Caldwell *(G-2412)*

Spectrum Image LLC G 614 954-0102
Columbus *(G-7473)*

Sro Prints LLC G 865 604-0420
Cincinnati *(G-4366)*

Start Printing G 513 424-2121
Middletown *(G-13954)*

Stephen Andrews Inc G 330 725-2672
Lodi *(G-12020)*

Stepping Stone Enterprises Inc F 419 472-0505
Toledo *(G-18529)*

Stevenson Color Inc C 513 321-7500
Cincinnati *(G-4381)*

Stick-It Graphics LLC G 330 407-0142
New Philadelphia *(G-14801)*

Swimmer Printing Inc G 216 623-1005
Cleveland *(G-6138)*

Syndicate Printers Inc G 513 779-3625
West Chester *(G-19804)*

Taylor Communications Inc G 614 351-6868
Columbus *(G-7515)*

Taylor Communications Inc E 937 221-1000
Dayton *(G-8543)*

Taylor Communications Inc G 937 228-5800
Dayton *(G-8545)*

Tce International Ltd F 800 962-2376
Perry *(G-15914)*

Technoprint Inc F 614 899-1403
Westerville *(G-20077)*

Traxler Printing G 614 593-1270
Columbus *(G-7541)*

Tribune Printing Inc G 419 542-7764
Hicksville *(G-10785)*

Ultimate Printing Co Inc G 330 847-2941
Warren *(G-19454)*

University of Cincinnati G 513 556-5042
Cincinnati *(G-4454)*

V & C Enterprises Co G 614 221-1412
Columbus *(G-7568)*

Visual Art Graphic Services E 330 274-2775
Mantua *(G-12562)*

Vya Inc E 513 772-5400
Cincinnati *(G-4485)*

W B Mason Co Inc E 888 926-2766
Cleveland *(G-6277)*

W C Sims Co Inc G 937 325-7035
Springfield *(G-17514)*

W/S Packaging Group Inc F 740 929-2210
Heath *(G-10734)*

Weekly Villager Inc G 330 527-5761
Garrettsville *(G-10204)*

Welch Publishing Co E 419 874-2528
Perrysburg *(G-16025)*

Western Reserve Graphics G 440 729-9527
Chesterland *(G-3172)*

Westrock Commercial LLC F 419 476-9101
Toledo *(G-18598)*

Wfsr Holdings LLC A 877 735-4966
Dayton *(G-8592)*

Wholesale Printers Ltd G 440 354-5788
Painesville *(G-15799)*

Williams Executive Entps Inc G 440 887-1000
Cleveland *(G-6310)*

Woodrow Manufacturing Co E 937 399-9333
Springfield *(G-17521)*

PRINTING: Offset

1984 Printing G 510 435-8338
Westerville *(G-19976)*

21st Century Printers Inc G 513 771-4150
Cincinnati *(G-3268)*

A & D Printing Co G 440 975-8001
Willoughby *(G-20263)*

A F Krainz Co G 216 431-4341
Cleveland *(G-4586)*

A Z Printing Inc G 513 733-3900
Cincinnati *(G-3282)*

A-1 Printing Inc G 419 294-5247
Upper Sandusky *(G-18945)*

PRODUCT

Employee Codes: A=Over 500 employees, B=251-500
C=101-250, D=51-100, E=20-50, F=10-19, G=3-9

2019 Harris Ohio
Industrial Directory

1555

PRINTING: Offset

Company	Code	Phone
A-1 Printing Inc	G	419 562-3111
Bucyrus (G-2316)		
A-1 Printing Inc	G	419 468-5422
Galion (G-10121)		
A-A Blueprint Co Inc	E	330 794-8803
Akron (G-23)		
Able Printing Company	G	614 294-4547
Columbus (G-6530)		
Academy Graphic Comm Inc	E	216 661-2550
Cleveland (G-4603)		
Acme Printing Co Inc	G	419 626-4426
Sandusky (G-16792)		
Action Printing & Photography	G	419 332-9615
Fremont (G-9989)		
Action Printing Inc	G	330 963-7772
Twinsburg (G-18726)		
Activities Press Inc	E	440 953-1200
Mentor (G-13374)		
Adkins & Co Inc	G	216 521-6323
Cleveland (G-4618)		
Admiral Products Company Inc	E	216 671-0600
Cleveland (G-4619)		
Advanatage Print Solut	G	614 519-2392
Columbus (G-6543)		
Advanced Marking Systems Inc	G	330 792-8239
Youngstown (G-20837)		
Advantage Printing Inc	G	614 272-8259
Columbus (G-6546)		
Aero Printing Inc	G	419 695-2931
Delphos (G-8735)		
AGS Custom Graphics Inc	D	330 963-7770
Macedonia (G-12275)		
Akron Thermography Inc	E	330 896-9712
Akron (G-54)		
Allegra Print & Imaging	G	419 427-8095
Findlay (G-9649)		
Allegra Printing & Imaging LLC	G	440 449-6989
Westlake (G-20090)		
Allen Graphics Inc	G	440 349-4100
Solon (G-17102)		
Allen Kenard Printing Inc	F	440 323-7405
Elyria (G-9213)		
Allen Press	G	614 891-4413
Westerville (G-20033)		
Alliance Printing & Publishing	F	513 422-7611
Middletown (G-13883)		
AlphaGraphics 507 Inc	G	440 878-9700
Strongsville (G-17708)		
American Printing Inc	F	330 630-1121
Akron (G-64)		
Anderson Graphics Inc	E	330 745-2165
Barberton (G-1052)		
Angel Prtg & Reproduction Co	F	216 631-5225
Cleveland (G-4714)		
Angstrom Graphics Inc Midwest	B	216 271-5300
Cleveland (G-4717)		
Angstrom Graphics Southeast	G	216 271-5300
Cleveland (G-4718)		
Ann Printing & Promotions	G	330 399-6564
Warren (G-19371)		
Arens Corporation	E	937 473-2028
Covington (G-7781)		
Arens Corporation	G	937 473-2028
Covington (G-7782)		
Arnold Printing Inc	G	330 494-1191
Canton (G-2576)		
Art Printing Co Inc	G	419 281-4371
Ashland (G-677)		
Atkinson Printing Inc	G	330 669-3515
Wooster (G-20566)		
Avon Lake Printing	G	440 933-2078
Avon Lake (G-979)		
Avondale Printing Inc	G	330 477-1180
Canton (G-2579)		
B & B Printing Graphics Inc	F	419 893-7068
Maumee (G-13076)		
Bansal Enterprises Inc	F	330 633-9355
Akron (G-79)		
Barberton Magic Press Printing	G	330 753-9578
Barberton (G-1062)		
Barberton Printcraft	G	330 848-3000
Barberton (G-1064)		
Barnhart Printing Corp	G	330 456-2279
Canton (G-2585)		
Baseline Printing Inc	G	330 369-3204
Warren (G-19374)		
Bates Printing Inc	F	330 833-5830
Massillon (G-12962)		
Bay Business Forms Inc	F	937 322-3000
Springfield (G-17367)		
Beckman Xmo	F	614 864-2232
Columbus (G-6658)		
Belle Printing	G	937 592-5161
Bellefontaine (G-1506)		
Berea Printing Company	G	440 243-1080
Berea (G-1594)		
Bethart Enterprises Inc	F	513 863-6161
Hamilton (G-10540)		
Bill Wyatt Inc	G	330 535-1113
Mentor (G-13403)		
Bindery & Spc Pressworks Inc	D	614 873-4623
Plain City (G-16178)		
Blt Inc	F	513 631-5050
Norwood (G-15424)		
Bock & Pierce Enterprises	G	513 474-9500
Cincinnati (G-3398)		
Bodnar Printing Co Inc	G	440 277-8295
Lorain (G-12080)		
Boldman Printing LLC	G	937 653-3431
Urbana (G-18980)		
Bornhorst Printing Company Inc	G	419 738-5901
Wapakoneta (G-19325)		
Bpm Realty Inc	E	614 221-6811
Columbus (G-6692)		
Bramkamp Printing Company Inc	G	513 241-1865
Blue Ash (G-1740)		
Brass Bull 1 LLC	G	740 335-8030
Wshngtn CT Hs (G-20720)		
Brent Carter Enterprises Inc	G	513 731-1440
Cincinnati (G-3411)		
Brentwood Printing & Sty	G	513 522-2679
Cincinnati (G-3412)		
Brooke Printers Inc	G	614 235-6800
Lancaster (G-11548)		
Brothers Printing Co Inc	F	216 621-6050
Cleveland (G-4844)		
Brune Printing Co	G	419 399-2756
Paulding (G-15858)		
Buckeye Business Forms Inc	G	614 882-1890
Westerville (G-19982)		
Bucyrus Graphics Inc	F	419 562-2906
Bucyrus (G-2319)		
C Massouh Printing Co Inc	G	330 408-7330
Canal Fulton (G-2478)		
Capehart Enterprises LLC	F	614 769-7746
Columbus (G-6730)		
Capitol Square Printing Inc	G	614 221-2850
Columbus (G-6736)		
Capozzolo Printers Inc	G	513 542-7874
Cincinnati (G-3440)		
Cardinal Printing Inc	G	330 773-7300
Akron (G-103)		
Cats Printing Inc	G	216 381-8181
Cleveland (G-4892)		
Century Graphics Inc	E	614 895-7698
Westerville (G-19983)		
Charger Press Inc	F	513 542-3113
Miamitown (G-13745)		
Cincinnati Print Solutions LLC	G	513 943-9500
Amelia (G-534)		
Cincinnati Printers Co Inc	F	513 860-9053
West Chester (G-19674)		
City Printing Co Inc	E	330 747-5691
Youngstown (G-20874)		
Clark Associates Inc	G	419 334-3838
Fremont (G-10008)		
Cleveland Letter Service Inc	E	216 781-8300
Chagrin Falls (G-3013)		
Clints Printing Inc	G	937 426-2771
Beavercreek (G-1354)		
Cnb LLC	G	419 528-3109
Ontario (G-15539)		
Cold Duck Screen Prtg & EMB Co	G	330 426-1900
East Palestine (G-9071)		
Color Bar Printing Centers Inc	E	216 595-3939
Cleveland (G-4997)		
Color Process Inc	E	440 268-7100
Strongsville (G-17730)		
Consoldated Graphics Group Inc	C	216 881-9191
Cleveland (G-5015)		
Copley Ohio Newspapers Inc	C	330 364-5577
New Philadelphia (G-14765)		
Copy Right of Ohio LLC	G	614 431-1303
Plain City (G-16182)		
Cornerstone Industries Lcc	G	513 871-4546
West Chester (G-19685)		
Cornerstone Printing Inc	G	614 861-2138
Reynoldsburg (G-16433)		
COS Blueprint Inc	F	330 376-0022
Akron (G-122)		
Cowgill Printing Co	G	216 741-2076
Parma (G-15815)		
Cox Printing Co	G	937 382-2312
Wilmington (G-20491)		
Cpmm Services Group Inc	F	614 447-0165
Columbus (G-6834)		
Crabar/Gbf Inc	G	419 269-1720
Toledo (G-18242)		
Crain-Tharp Printing Inc	G	740 345-9823
Newark (G-14866)		
Creative Impressions Inc	F	937 435-5296
Dayton (G-8112)		
Crest Graphics Inc	G	513 271-2200
Blue Ash (G-1755)		
Crown Printing Inc	G	740 477-2511
Circleville (G-4541)		
Curless Printing Company	E	937 783-2403
Blanchester (G-1702)		
Curv Imaging LLC	G	614 890-2878
Westerville (G-20044)		
Cwh Graphics LLC	G	866 241-8515
Bedford Heights (G-1468)		
D M J F Inc	G	440 845-1155
Cleveland (G-5057)		
Dana Graphics Inc	G	513 351-4400
Cincinnati (G-3575)		
Dansizen Printing Co Inc	G	330 966-4962
North Canton (G-15077)		
Daubenmires Printing	G	513 425-7223
Middletown (G-13899)		
David Butler Tax Service	G	419 626-8086
Sandusky (G-16803)		
DC Reprographics Co	G	614 297-1200
Columbus (G-6854)		
Debandale Printing Inc	G	330 725-5122
Medina (G-13251)		
Deerfield Ventures Inc	G	614 875-0688
Grove City (G-10425)		
Delphos Herald Inc	D	419 695-0015
Delphos (G-8738)		
Delphos Herald Inc	D	419 695-0015
Delphos (G-8739)		
Dewitt Group Inc	F	614 847-5919
Columbus (G-6862)		
Distributor Graphics Inc	G	440 260-0024
Cleveland (G-5099)		
Doll Inc	G	419 586-7880
Celina (G-2957)		
Domicone Printing Inc	G	937 878-3080
Fairborn (G-9457)		
Donnelley Financial LLC	F	216 621-8384
Cleveland (G-5108)		
Dorothy Crooker	G	513 385-0888
Cincinnati (G-3602)		
Double b Printing LLC	G	740 593-7393
Athens (G-829)		
Doug Smith	G	740 345-1398
Newark (G-14868)		
DOV Graphics Inc	E	513 241-5150
Cincinnati (G-3605)		
Dove Graphics Inc	G	440 238-1800
Cleveland (G-5110)		
Downtown Print Shop	G	419 242-9164
Toledo (G-18268)		
Dresden Specialties Inc	G	740 452-7100
Zanesville (G-21131)		
Dresden Specialties Inc	G	740 754-2451
Dresden (G-8868)		
Duke Graphics Inc	E	440 946-0606
Willoughby (G-20310)		
Duncan Press Corporation	E	330 477-4529
Canton (G-2664)		
Durbin Minuteman Press	G	513 791-9171
Blue Ash (G-1760)		
E Bee Printing Inc	G	614 224-0416
Columbus (G-6879)		
E T & K Inc	G	440 777-7375
North Olmsted (G-15186)		
E T & K Inc	G	440 888-4780
Cleveland (G-5131)		
Eagle Printing & Graphics LLC	G	937 773-7900
Piqua (G-16113)		
Earl D Arnold Printing Company	E	513 533-6900
Cincinnati (G-3624)		
Easterdays Printing Center	G	330 726-1182
Youngstown (G-20895)		
Echographics Inc	G	440 846-2330
North Ridgeville (G-15222)		
Eg Enterprise Services Inc	F	216 431-3300
Cleveland (G-5158)		

PRINTING: Offset

Company	Code	Phone
Elyria Copy Center Inc, Elyria (G-9251)	G	440 323-4145
Engler Printing Co, Fremont (G-10013)	G	419 332-2181
Enquirer Printing Co Inc, Cincinnati (G-3642)	F	513 241-1956
Eurostampa North America Inc, Cincinnati (G-3656)	D	513 821-2275
Eveready Printing Inc, Cleveland (G-5200)	E	216 587-2389
Excelsior Printing Co, Pataskala (G-15831)	G	740 927-2934
Exchange Printing Company, Akron (G-161)	G	330 773-7842
Fairchild Printing Co, Cleveland (G-5214)	G	216 641-4192
Feld Printing Co, Cincinnati (G-3682)	G	513 271-6806
Fine Line Graphics Inc, Akron (G-170)	G	330 920-6096
Fine Line Graphics Corp, Columbus (G-6923)	G	614 486-0276
Finn Graphics Inc, Cincinnati (G-3690)	E	513 941-6161
Folks Creative Printers Inc, Marion (G-12702)	G	740 383-6326
Foote Printing Company Inc, Cleveland (G-5260)	F	216 431-1757
Franklins Printing Company, Zanesville (G-21138)	F	740 452-6375
Freeport Press Inc, New Philadelphia (G-14770)	C	330 308-3300
Fremont Quick Print, Helena (G-10771)	G	419 334-8808
Fx Digital Media Inc, Cleveland (G-5283)	G	216 241-4040
Galaxy Balloons Incorporated, Cleveland (G-5287)	C	216 476-3360
Galley Printing Inc, Brunswick (G-2208)	E	330 220-5477
Ganger Enterprises Inc, Westerville (G-19993)	G	614 776-3985
Gaspar Services LLC, Macedonia (G-12299)	G	330 467-8292
Gergel-Kellem Company Inc, Cleveland (G-5318)	D	216 398-2000
Globus Printing & Packg Co Inc, Minster (G-14216)	D	419 628-2381
Golden Graphics Ltd, Kenton (G-11406)	F	419 673-6260
Good Impressions LLC, Mount Vernon (G-14482)	G	740 392-4327
Gordons Graphics Inc, Malvern (G-12392)	G	330 863-2322
Grant John, Dayton (G-8234)	G	937 298-0633
Graphic Touch Inc, Salem (G-16744)	G	330 337-3341
Graphicsource Inc, Solon (G-17154)	G	440 248-9200
Graphtech Communications Inc, Cleveland (G-5342)	F	216 676-1020
Great Lakes Integrated Inc, Cleveland (G-5347)	D	216 651-1500
Great Lakes Lithograph, Cleveland (G-5348)	F	216 651-1500
Great Lakes Printing Inc, Ashtabula (G-779)	D	440 993-8781
Greenwood Printing & Graphics, Toledo (G-18312)	F	419 727-3275
Greg Blume, Wheelersburg (G-20182)	G	740 574-2308
Gregg Macmillan, Milford (G-14014)	G	513 248-2121
H & An LLC, Cambridge (G-2442)	G	740 435-0200
Haman Enterprises Inc, Worthington (G-20689)	F	614 888-7574
Harper Engraving & Printing Co, Columbus (G-6982)	G	614 276-0700
Harris Hawk, Mason (G-12885)	G	800 459-4295
Hartco Printing Company, Dublin (G-8921)	G	614 761-1292
Hartman Printing Co, Mount Gilead (G-14425)	G	419 946-2854
Hartmann Incorporated, Blue Ash (G-1785)	F	513 276-7318
Headlee Enterprises Ltd, Columbus (G-6496)	G	614 785-0011
Hecks Direct Mail & Prtg Svc, Toledo (G-18327)	E	419 697-3505
Hedges Printing Co, Lancaster (G-11579)	G	740 422-8500
Heitkamp & Kremer Printing, Celina (G-2967)	G	419 925-4121
Herald Inc, New Washington (G-14829)	E	419 492-2133
Heritage Press Inc, Ashland (G-709)	E	419 289-9209
Heskamp Printing Co Inc, Cincinnati (G-3811)	G	513 871-6770
Hilleary-Whitaker Inc, Columbus (G-7001)	G	614 766-4694
Holmes W & Sons Printing, Springfield (G-17419)	F	937 325-1509
Homewood Press Inc, Toledo (G-18334)	G	419 478-0695
Hoster Graphics Company Inc, Columbus (G-7009)	F	614 299-9770
HOT Graphic Services Inc, Northwood (G-15339)	E	419 242-7000
Howland Printing Inc, Cortland (G-7710)	G	330 637-8255
Hubbard Company, Defiance (G-8627)	F	419 784-4455
Hubbard Publishing Co, Bellefontaine (G-1518)	E	937 592-3060
Hummingbird Graphics LLC, Warrensville Heights (G-19470)	G	216 595-8835
Ideas & Ad Ventures Inc, Cincinnati (G-3835)	G	513 542-7154
Image Concepts Inc, Cleveland (G-5437)	F	216 524-9000
Image Print Inc, Westerville (G-19997)	G	614 776-3985
Image Print Inc, Columbus (G-7021)	G	614 430-8470
In-Touch Corp, Cleveland (G-5447)	G	440 268-0881
Ink Inc, Louisville (G-12157)	G	330 875-4789
Ink It Press, Vermilion (G-19162)	G	440 967-9062
Innomark Communications LLC, Miamisburg (G-13679)	E	937 454-5555
Inskeep Brothers Inc, Columbus (G-7028)	F	614 898-6620
Insley Printing Inc, Worthington (G-20692)	G	614 885-5973
Insta-Print Inc, Cleveland (G-5461)	G	216 741-6500
Integrity Print Solutions Inc, Akron (G-216)	G	330 818-0161
Irwin Engraving & Printing Co, Cleveland (G-5477)	G	216 391-7300
J & J Bechke Inc, Strongsville (G-17756)	G	440 238-1441
J & K Printing, Canton (G-2713)	G	330 456-5306
J & L Management Corporation, Mentor (G-13479)	G	440 205-1199
J & P Investments Inc, Cincinnati (G-3861)	F	513 821-2299
J D B Partners Inc, Fairfield (G-9513)	G	513 874-3056
J P Quality Printing Inc, Cleveland (G-5485)	G	216 791-6303
Jack Walker Printing Co, Mentor (G-13483)	F	440 352-4222
Jakprints Inc, Willowick (G-20479)	C	877 246-3132
John Kolesar and Sons Inc, Cleveland (G-5501)	G	216 221-7117
John S Swift Company Inc, Cincinnati (G-3880)	F	513 721-4147
Johnson Printing, Uhrichsville (G-18889)	G	740 922-4821
Jones Printing Services Inc, Eastlake (G-9116)	G	440 946-7300
Joseph Berning Printing Co, Cincinnati (G-3883)	F	513 721-0781
Jt Premier Printing Corp, Cleveland (G-5509)	G	216 831-8785
Kad Holdings Inc, Dublin (G-8935)	G	614 792-3399
Kahny Printing Inc, Cincinnati (G-3893)	E	513 251-2911
Kay Toledo Tag Inc, Toledo (G-18363)	D	419 729-5479
Kee Printing Inc, Eaton (G-9156)	G	937 456-6851
Keener Printing Inc, Cleveland (G-5523)	F	216 531-7595
Kehl-Kolor Inc, Ashland (G-717)	E	419 281-3107
Kehoe Brothers Printing Inc, Cleveland (G-5524)	G	216 351-4100
Keithley Enterprises Inc, Dayton (G-8290)	G	937 890-1878
Kennedy Graphics Inc, Lima (G-11883)	G	419 223-9825
Kenwel Printers Inc, Columbus (G-7088)	E	614 261-1011
Kever Incorporated, Columbus (G-7091)	G	614 552-9000
Kevin K Tidd, Sylvania (G-17948)	G	419 885-5603
Key Maneuvers Inc, Chardon (G-3119)	F	440 285-0774
Keystone Press Inc, Toledo (G-18367)	G	419 243-7326
Keystone Printing Co, East Liverpool (G-9065)	G	330 385-9519
Kimpton Printing & Spc Co, Macedonia (G-12310)	F	330 467-1640
Klingstedt Brothers Company, Canton (G-2726)	F	330 456-8319
KMS 2000 Inc, Canton (G-2727)	F	330 454-9444
L & T Collins Inc, Newark (G-14892)	G	740 345-4494
L B L Lithographers Inc, Painesville (G-15755)	F	440 350-0106
Lake Erie Graphics Inc, Brookpark (G-2151)	E	216 575-1333
Lakota Printing Inc, West Chester (G-19734)	G	513 755-3666
Lanz Printing Co Inc, Columbus (G-7115)	G	614 221-1724
Laser Images Inc, Norwalk (G-15403)	G	419 668-8348
Lasting First Impressions Inc, West Chester (G-19872)	F	513 870-6900
Lasting Impression Direct, Beachwood (G-1245)	G	216 464-1960
Laurenee Ltd LLC, Cincinnati (G-3934)	G	513 662-2225
Lee Corporation, Cincinnati (G-3937)	G	513 771-3602
Legal News Publishing Co, Cleveland (G-5572)	E	216 696-3322
Letter Shop, Greenfield (G-10354)	G	937 981-3117
Letterman Printing Inc, Oxford (G-15696)	G	513 523-1111
Lilienthal Southeastern Inc, Cambridge (G-2446)	F	740 439-1640
Liming Printing Inc, Xenia (G-20782)	F	937 374-2646
Lorain Printing Company, Lorain (G-12103)	E	440 288-6000
Lund Printing Co, Akron (G-262)	G	330 628-4047
Lyle Printing & Publishing Co, Salem (G-16756)	E	330 337-3419
Mabar Printing Service, North Baltimore (G-15045)	G	419 257-3659
Mackland Co Inc, Warren (G-19419)	G	330 399-5034
Mansfield Journal Co, New Philadelphia (G-14782)	G	330 364-8641
Marbee Inc, Findlay (G-9722)	G	419 422-9441
Marco Printed Products Co, Dayton (G-8332)	F	937 433-7030
Marco Printed Products Co Inc, Dayton (G-8333)	G	937 433-5680
Margaret Trentman, Cincinnati (G-3980)	G	513 948-1700
Mariotti Printing Co LLC, Lorain (G-12104)	G	440 245-4120
Mark Advertising Agency Inc, Sandusky (G-16827)	F	419 626-9000
Martin Printing Co, Lima (G-11897)	G	419 224-9176
Martys Print Shop, Marietta (G-12644)	G	740 373-3454
Marysville Printing Company, Marysville (G-12800)	G	937 644-4959

Employee Codes: A=Over 500 employees, B=251-500, C=101-250, D=51-100, E=20-50, F=10-19, G=3-9

2019 Harris Ohio Industrial Directory

1557

Mass-Marketing Inc .... C .... 513 860-6200 Fairfield *(G-9523)*
Master Printing Company .... E .... 216 351-2246 Cleveland *(G-5633)*
Mathews Printing Company .... F .... 614 444-1010 Columbus *(G-7158)*
Maumee Quick Print Inc .... G .... 419 893-4321 Maumee *(G-13131)*
Maximum Graphix Inc .... G .... 440 353-3301 North Ridgeville *(G-15240)*
Mc Vay Ventures Inc .... G .... 614 890-1516 Westerville *(G-20064)*
McMath & Sheets Unlimited Inc .... G .... 216 381-0010 Cleveland *(G-5646)*
Mercer Color Corporation .... G .... 419 678-8273 Coldwater *(G-6417)*
Messenger Publishing Company .... C .... 740 592-6612 Athens *(G-839)*
Metzgers .... E .... 419 861-8611 Toledo *(G-18409)*
Middaugh Enterprises Inc .... F .... 330 852-2471 Sugarcreek *(G-17852)*
Middaugh Printers .... G .... 330 852-2471 Dover *(G-8841)*
Middleton Printing Co Inc .... G .... 614 294-7277 Gahanna *(G-10090)*
Milford Printers .... E .... 513 831-6630 Milford *(G-14027)*
Milford Printers .... G .... 513 831-6630 Milford *(G-14028)*
Milo Bennett Corp .... G .... 419 874-1492 Perrysburg *(G-15977)*
Minuteman Press .... G .... 419 782-8002 Defiance *(G-8639)*
Minuteman Press .... G .... 614 337-2334 Columbus *(G-7185)*
Minuteman Press .... G .... 330 725-4121 Medina *(G-13302)*
Minuteman Press of Athens LLC .... G .... 740 593-7393 Athens *(G-841)*
Minuteman Press of Elyria .... G .... 440 365-9377 Elyria *(G-9296)*
Mmp Printing Inc .... E .... 513 381-0990 Cincinnati *(G-4035)*
Mmp Toledo .... F .... 419 472-0505 Toledo *(G-18412)*
Montview Corporation .... G .... 330 723-3409 Medina *(G-13304)*
Morse Enterprises Inc .... G .... 513 229-3600 Mason *(G-12912)*
Muir Graphics Inc .... F .... 419 882-7993 Sylvania *(G-17953)*
Multi-Craft Litho Inc .... E .... 859 581-2754 Blue Ash *(G-1824)*
Murr Corporation .... F .... 330 264-2223 Wooster *(G-20630)*
Mustang Printing .... F .... 419 592-2746 Napoleon *(G-14551)*
Nari Inc .... G .... 440 960-2280 Monroeville *(G-14289)*
National Bank Note Company .... G .... 216 281-7792 Cleveland *(G-5721)*
Nelis Printing Co .... G .... 330 757-4114 Youngstown *(G-20974)*
Newhouse & Faulkner Inc .... G .... 513 721-1660 Cincinnati *(G-4073)*
Newmast Mktg & Communications .... E .... 614 837-1200 Columbus *(G-7217)*
News Gazette Printing Company .... F .... 419 227-2527 Lima *(G-11911)*
Nomis Publications Inc .... F .... 330 965-2380 Youngstown *(G-20976)*
North Toledo Graphics LLC .... D .... 419 476-8808 Toledo *(G-18427)*
Northern Ohio Printing Inc .... E .... 216 398-0000 Cleveland *(G-5781)*
Northwest Print Inc .... G .... 419 385-3375 Perrysburg *(G-15982)*
Nta Graphics Inc .... C .... 419 476-8808 Toledo *(G-18431)*
O Connor Office Pdts & Prtg .... G .... 740 852-2209 London *(G-12066)*
Oak Printing Company .... E .... 440 238-3316 Strongsville *(G-17774)*
Odyssey Press Inc .... F .... 614 410-0356 Huron *(G-11107)*
Office Print N Copy .... G .... 740 695-3616 Saint Clairsville *(G-16642)*
Old Trail Printing Company .... C .... 614 443-4852 Columbus *(G-7269)*
Oliver Printing & Packg Co LLC .... D .... 330 425-7890 Twinsburg *(G-18823)*
Olmsted Printing Inc .... G .... 440 234-2600 Berea *(G-1621)*
One-Write Company .... E .... 740 654-2128 Lancaster *(G-11594)*
Oregon Village Print Shoppe .... F .... 937 222-9418 Dayton *(G-8407)*
Orrville Printing Co Inc .... G .... 330 682-5066 Orrville *(G-15608)*
Orwell Printing .... G .... 440 285-2233 Chardon *(G-3131)*
Page One Group .... G .... 740 397-4240 Mount Vernon *(G-14499)*
Painesville Publishing Co .... G .... 440 354-4142 Austinburg *(G-924)*
Painted Hill Inv Group Inc .... F .... 937 339-1756 Troy *(G-18691)*
Paragon Press .... G .... 513 281-9911 Cincinnati *(G-4133)*
Paragraphics Inc .... E .... 330 493-1074 Canton *(G-2778)*
Patio Printing Inc .... G .... 614 785-9553 Columbus *(G-7295)*
Patterson-Britton Printing .... G .... 216 781-7997 Cleveland *(G-5855)*
Paul Stipkovich .... G .... 330 499-7391 North Canton *(G-15110)*
Paul/Jay Associates .... G .... 740 676-8776 Bellaire *(G-1488)*
PDQ Printing Service .... F .... 216 241-5443 Cleveland *(G-5858)*
Peerless Printing Company .... F .... 513 721-4657 Cincinnati *(G-4145)*
Penguin Enterprises Inc .... E .... 440 899-5112 Westlake *(G-20140)*
Penny Printing Inc .... G .... 330 645-2955 Coventry Township *(G-7778)*
Performa La Mar Printing Inc .... G .... 440 632-9800 Middlefield *(G-13845)*
Perrons Printing Company .... E .... 440 236-8870 Columbia Station *(G-6442)*
Phil Vedda & Sons Inc .... G .... 216 671-2222 Cleveland *(G-5870)*
Pinnacle Press Inc .... F .... 330 453-7060 Canton *(G-2785)*
PIP and Huds LLC .... G .... 740 208-5519 Gallipolis *(G-10173)*
PIP Printing .... G .... 440 951-2606 Willoughby *(G-20401)*
PM Graphics Inc .... E .... 330 650-0861 Streetsboro *(G-17689)*
Pooles Printing & Office Svcs .... G .... 419 475-9000 Toledo *(G-18474)*
Porath Business Services Inc .... F .... 216 626-0060 Cleveland *(G-5896)*
Post Printing Co .... D .... 859 254-7714 Minster *(G-14222)*
POv Print Communication Inc .... G .... 440 591-5443 Chagrin Falls *(G-3068)*
Preferred Printing .... G .... 937 492-6961 Sidney *(G-17062)*
Preisser Inc .... E .... 614 345-0199 Columbus *(G-7344)*
Premier Printing Corporation .... F .... 216 478-9720 Cleveland *(G-5917)*
Pressmark Inc .... G .... 740 373-6005 Marietta *(G-12659)*
Priesman Printery .... G .... 419 898-2526 Oak Harbor *(G-15447)*
Prime Printing Inc .... E .... 937 438-3707 Dayton *(G-8442)*
Print All Inc .... G .... 419 534-2880 Toledo *(G-18484)*
Print Craft Inc .... G .... 513 931-6828 Cincinnati *(G-4191)*
Print Direct For Less 2 Inc .... E .... 440 236-8870 Columbia Station *(G-6444)*
Print Factory Pll .... G .... 330 549-9640 North Lima *(G-15176)*
Print Marketing Inc .... E .... 330 625-1500 Homerville *(G-10986)*
Print Masters Ltd .... G .... 740 450-2885 Zanesville *(G-21173)*
Print Shop Design and Print .... G .... 440 232-2391 Bedford *(G-1438)*
Print Shop of Canton Inc .... G .... 330 497-3212 Canton *(G-2792)*
Print-Digital Incorporated .... G .... 330 686-5945 Stow *(G-17621)*
Printcraft Inc .... G .... 440 599-8903 Conneaut *(G-7657)*
Printed Image .... F .... 614 221-1412 Columbus *(G-7350)*
Printers Devil Inc .... F .... 330 650-1218 Hudson *(G-11068)*
Printex Incorporated .... G .... 740 947-8800 Waverly *(G-19559)*
Printex Incorporated .... F .... 740 773-0088 Chillicothe *(G-3217)*
Printing Arts Press .... F .... 740 397-6106 Mount Vernon *(G-14502)*
Printing Center of Xenia .... G .... 937 372-1687 Xenia *(G-20786)*
Printing Connection Inc .... G .... 216 898-4878 Brookpark *(G-2154)*
Printing Express Inc .... G .... 740 532-7003 Ironton *(G-11171)*
Printing Service Company .... D .... 937 425-6100 Miamisburg *(G-13705)*
Printing System Inc .... F .... 330 375-9128 Akron *(G-331)*
Printpoint Printing Inc .... G .... 937 223-9041 Dayton *(G-8443)*
Pro Printing Inc .... G .... 614 276-8366 Columbus *(G-7351)*
Proforma Print & Imaging .... G .... 216 520-8400 Dublin *(G-8969)*
Progressive Communications .... D .... 740 397-5333 Mount Vernon *(G-14503)*
Progressive Printers Inc .... D .... 937 222-1267 Dayton *(G-8450)*
Q C Printing .... G .... 419 475-4266 Toledo *(G-18489)*
Quad/Graphics Inc .... A .... 513 932-1064 Lebanon *(G-11687)*
Quality Publishing Co .... F .... 513 863-8210 Hamilton *(G-10600)*
Quebecor World Johnson Hardin .... A .... 614 326-0299 Cincinnati *(G-4233)*
Quez Media Marketing Inc .... F .... 216 910-0202 Independence *(G-11149)*
Quick As A Wink Printing Co .... F .... 419 224-9786 Lima *(G-11926)*
R & J Bardon Inc .... G .... 614 457-5500 Columbus *(G-7370)*
R & J Printing Enterprises Inc .... F .... 330 343-1242 Dover *(G-8847)*
R & W Printing Company .... G .... 513 575-0131 Loveland *(G-12224)*
R Design & Printing Co .... G .... 614 299-1420 Columbus *(G-7374)*
R S C Sales Company .... E .... 423 581-4916 Dayton *(G-8460)*
Randd Assoc Prtg & Promotions .... G .... 937 294-1874 Dayton *(G-8464)*
Rba Inc .... G .... 330 336-6700 Wadsworth *(G-19273)*
Renco Printing Inc .... G .... 216 267-5585 Cleveland *(G-5973)*
Repro Acquisition Company LLC .... E .... 216 738-3800 Cleveland *(G-5977)*
Rhoads Printing Center Inc .... G .... 330 678-2042 Kent *(G-11375)*
Richardson Printing Corp .... D .... 740 373-5362 Marietta *(G-12663)*
Robert Becker Impressions Inc .... F .... 419 385-5303 Toledo *(G-18504)*
Robert H Shackelford .... G .... 330 364-2221 New Philadelphia *(G-14799)*
Roberts Graphic Center .... G .... 330 788-4642 Youngstown *(G-21019)*
Robin Enterprises Company .... C .... 614 891-0250 Westerville *(G-20073)*
Rutobo Inc .... G .... 614 236-2948 Columbus *(G-7408)*
Ryans Newark Leader Ex Prtg .... F .... 740 522-2149 Newark *(G-14916)*
S & S Printing Service Inc .... G .... 937 228-9411 Dayton *(G-8490)*
S Beckman Print & G .... E .... 614 864-2232 Columbus *(G-7410)*
S O S Graphics & Printing Inc .... G .... 614 846-8229 Worthington *(G-20702)*
Sanscan Inc .... G .... 330 332-9365 Salem *(G-16773)*
Schiffer Group Inc .... G .... 937 694-8185 Troy *(G-18703)*
Schuerholz Printing Inc .... G .... 937 294-5218 Dayton *(G-8496)*

PRODUCT SECTION

PRINTING: Screen, Fabric

Scorecards Unlimited LLC .... G 614 885-0796
  Columbus (G-7432)
Scratch Off Works .... G 440 333-4302
  Rocky River (G-16556)
Scrip-Safe Security Products .... E 513 697-7789
  Loveland (G-12230)
Seemless Design & Printing LLC ...... G 513 871-2366
  Cincinnati (G-4315)
Selby Service/Roxy Press Inc .... G 513 241-3445
  Cincinnati (G-4318)
Sentry Graphics Inc .... G 440 735-0850
  Northfield (G-15324)
Serv All Graphics LLC .... G 513 681-8883
  Blue Ash (G-1846)
Sharon Printing Co Inc .... G 330 239-1684
  Sharon Center (G-16953)
Sharp Enterprises Inc .... F 937 295-2965
  Fort Loramie (G-9806)
Shelby Printing Partners LLC .... E 419 342-3171
  Shelby (G-16989)
Shreve Printing LLC .... F 330 567-2341
  Shreve (G-17010)
Sidney Printing Works Inc .... G 513 542-4000
  Cincinnati (G-4333)
Sitler Printer Inc .... G 330 482-4463
  Columbiana (G-6480)
Sjpm Inc .... G 614 475-4571
  Gahanna (G-10104)
Skladany Enterprises Inc .... G 614 823-6883
  Westerville (G-20023)
Slimans Printery Inc .... F 330 454-9141
  Canton (G-2818)
Slutzkers Quickprint Center .... G 440 244-0330
  Lorain (G-12123)
Snow Printing Co Inc .... G 419 229-7669
  Lima (G-11941)
Source3media Inc .... G 330 467-9003
  Macedonia (G-12326)
South End Printing Co .... G 216 341-0669
  Cleveland (G-6081)
SPAOS Inc .... F 937 890-0783
  Dayton (G-8515)
Specialty Lithographing Co .... G 513 621-0222
  Cincinnati (G-4357)
Specialty Printing LLC .... G 937 335-4046
  Troy (G-18709)
Spencer-Walker Press Inc .... F 740 344-6110
  Newark (G-14920)
Springdot Inc .... D 513 542-4000
  Cincinnati (G-4365)
Sprint Print Inc .... G 740 622-4429
  Coshocton (G-7752)
Stapins Qick Cpy/Print Ctr LLC .... G 330 296-0123
  Ravenna (G-16410)
Star Calendar & Printing Co .... G 216 741-3223
  Cleveland (G-6095)
Star Printing Company Inc .... E 330 376-0514
  Akron (G-386)
Starr Printing Services Inc .... G 513 241-7708
  Cincinnati (G-4375)
Stationery Shop Inc .... G 330 376-2033
  Akron (G-387)
Stein-Palmer Printing Co .... G 740 633-3894
  Saint Clairsville (G-16653)
Streichers Enterprises Inc .... G 419 423-8606
  Findlay (G-9764)
Suburban Press Inc .... E 216 961-0766
  Cleveland (G-6114)
Summit Printing & Graphics .... G 330 645-7644
  Akron (G-391)
Superior Impressions Inc .... G 419 244-8676
  Toledo (G-18535)
Superprinter Inc .... G 440 277-0787
  Lorain (G-12125)
Superprinter Ltd .... G 440 277-0787
  Lorain (G-12126)
T & K Heins Corporation .... G 740 452-6006
  Zanesville (G-21184)
T D Dynamics Inc .... F 216 881-0800
  Cleveland (G-6143)
T H E B Inc .... G 216 391-4800
  Cleveland (G-6145)
Target Printing & Graphics .... G 937 228-0170
  Dayton (G-8539)
Taylor Quick Print .... G 740 439-2208
  Cambridge (G-2458)
Tcp Inc .... G 330 836-4239
  Fairlawn (G-9622)
The Gazette Printing Co Inc .... G 440 593-6030
  Conneaut (G-7660)

Timely Tours Inc .... G 419 734-3751
  Port Clinton (G-16263)
Tj Metzgers Inc .... D 419 861-8611
  Toledo (G-18553)
TL Krieg Offset Inc .... E 513 542-1522
  Cincinnati (G-4424)
Tomahawk Printing Inc .... F 419 335-3161
  Wauseon (G-19533)
Tomahawk Printing LLC .... F 419 335-3161
  Wauseon (G-19534)
Tope Printing Inc .... G 330 674-4993
  Millersburg (G-14137)
Tradewinds Prin Twear .... G 740 214-5005
  Roseville (G-16580)
Traxium LLC .... E 330 572-8200
  Stow (G-17637)
Tri-State Publishing Company .... E 740 283-3686
  Steubenville (G-17556)
True Dinero Records & Tech LLC ..... G 513 428-4610
  Cincinnati (G-4443)
Ultra Impressions Inc .... G 440 951-4777
  Mentor (G-13617)
Ultra Printing & Design Inc .... G 440 887-0393
  Cleveland (G-6228)
United Prtrs & Lithographers .... G 216 771-2759
  Cleveland (G-6235)
USA Quickprint Inc .... E 330 455-5119
  Canton (G-2854)
V I P Printing & Design .... G 513 777-7468
  West Chester (G-19913)
Variety Printing .... G 216 676-9815
  Brookpark (G-2157)
Vision Graphics .... G 330 665-4451
  Copley (G-7698)
Vision Graphix Inc .... G 440 835-6540
  Westlake (G-20169)
Vpp Industries Inc .... F 937 526-3775
  Versailles (G-19192)
Walter Graphics Inc .... G 419 522-5261
  Mansfield (G-12536)
Warren Printing & Off Pdts Inc .... F 419 523-3635
  Ottawa (G-15671)
Wasserstrom Company .... F 614 228-2233
  Columbus (G-7592)
Watkins Printing Company .... G 614 297-8270
  Columbus (G-7593)
West Bend Printing & Pubg Inc .... G 419 258-2000
  Antwerp (G-600)
West-Camp Press Inc .... D 614 882-2378
  Westerville (G-20082)
Western Ohio Graphics .... F 937 335-8769
  Troy (G-18719)
Whiskey Fox Corporation .... F 440 779-6767
  Berea (G-1632)
William J Bergen & Co .... G 440 248-6132
  Solon (G-17261)
William J Dupps .... G 419 734-2126
  Port Clinton (G-16264)
Wilson Prtg Graphics of London .... G 740 852-5934
  London (G-12072)
Wirick Press Inc .... G 330 273-3488
  Brunswick (G-2252)
X Press Printing Services Inc .... F 440 951-8848
  Willoughby (G-20461)
Xpress Print Inc .... F 330 494-7246
  Louisville (G-12172)
Yes Press Printing Co .... G 330 535-8398
  Akron (G-440)
Yespress Graphics LLC .... G 614 899-1403
  Westerville (G-20084)
Youngstown ARC Engraving Co .... E 330 793-2471
  Youngstown (G-21070)
Youngstown Letter Shop Inc .... G 330 793-4935
  Youngstown (G-21079)
Yuckon International Corp .... G 216 361-2103
  Cleveland (G-6334)
Zip Laser Systems Inc .... G 740 286-6613
  Jackson (G-11203)
Zippitycom Print LLC .... F 216 438-0001
  Cleveland (G-6344)

PRINTING: Pamphlets

Digicom Inc .... G 216 642-3838
  Brooklyn Heights (G-2120)
Society of The Precious Blood .... E 419 925-4516
  Celina (G-2984)

PRINTING: Photo-Offset

Deshea Printing Company .... G 330 336-7601
  Wadsworth (G-19234)

Gerald L Hermann Co Inc .... F 513 661-1818
  Cincinnati (G-3750)
Henry Bussman .... G 614 224-0417
  Columbus (G-6988)
Newfax Corporation .... F 419 241-5157
  Toledo (G-18423)
Newfax Corporation .... F 419 893-4557
  Toledo (G-18424)

PRINTING: Photolithographic

Acme Duplicating Co .... G 216 241-1241
  Westlake (G-20086)
Friends Service Co Inc .... D 419 427-1704
  Findlay (G-9690)

PRINTING: Rotary Photogravure

Klingstedt Brothers Company .... F 330 456-8319
  Canton (G-2726)
Toledo Tape and Label Company ..... G 419 536-8316
  Toledo (G-18572)

PRINTING: Rotogravure

Western Roto Engravers Inc .... E 330 336-7636
  Wadsworth (G-19281)

PRINTING: Screen, Broadwoven Fabrics, Cotton

Air Waves LLC .... C 740 548-1200
  Lewis Center (G-11743)
Apparel Screen Printing Inc .... G 513 733-9495
  Cincinnati (G-3352)
Atlantis Sportswear Inc .... E 937 773-0680
  Piqua (G-16101)
Designer Awards Inc .... G 937 339-4444
  Troy (G-18650)
Fryes Soccer Shoppe .... G 937 832-2230
  Englewood (G-9359)
Image Group of Toledo Inc .... E 419 866-3300
  Holland (G-10935)
Phantasm Designs .... G 419 538-6737
  Ottawa (G-15662)
Precision Imprint .... G 740 592-5916
  Athens (G-846)
Shirt Stop LLC .... G 740 574-4774
  Wheelersburg (G-20185)
Three Cord LLC .... G 419 445-2673
  Archbold (G-671)
Uptown Dog The Inc .... G 740 592-4600
  Athens (G-853)
West-Camp Press Inc .... D 216 426-2660
  Cleveland (G-6301)
Zenos Activewear Inc .... G 614 443-0070
  Columbus (G-7626)

PRINTING: Screen, Fabric

Aardvark Graphic Enterprises L .... F 419 352-3197
  Bowling Green (G-1947)
ABC Lettering & Embroidery .... G 216 321-8338
  Lakewood (G-11508)
Action Sports Apparel Inc .... G 330 848-9300
  Norton (G-15358)
American Imprssions Sportswear .... G 614 848-6677
  Worthington (G-20677)
Art Works .... G 740 425-5765
  Barnesville (G-1115)
B D P Services Inc .... D 740 828-9685
  Nashport (G-14564)
Brandon Screen Printing .... F 419 229-9837
  Lima (G-11845)
Cal Sales Embroidery .... G 440 236-3820
  Columbia Station (G-6431)
Charisma Products Inc .... G 614 846-8888
  Westerville (G-19984)
Charizma Corp .... G 216 621-2220
  Cleveland (G-4909)
Charles Wisvari .... F 740 671-9960
  Bellaire (G-1484)
David Brandeberry .... G 937 653-4680
  Urbana (G-18988)
Fineline Imprints Inc .... E 740 453-1083
  Zanesville (G-21135)
Gotcha Covered .... G 513 829-7555
  Fairfield (G-9500)
Greenfield Research Inc .... C 937 981-7763
  Greenfield (G-10350)
H & H Screen Process Inc .... G 937 253-7520
  Dayton (G-8240)

Employee Codes: A=Over 500 employees, B=251-500
C=101-250, D=51-100, E=20-50, F=10-19, G=3-9

PRINTING: Screen, Fabric

Jakes Sportswear Ltd .... G 740 746-8356
 Sugar Grove *(G-17839)*
Jetts Embroideries .... G 937 981-3716
 Greenfield *(G-10353)*
Kiwi Promotional AP & Prtg Co .... E 330 487-5115
 Twinsburg *(G-18801)*
M & H Screen Printing .... G 740 522-1957
 Newark *(G-14894)*
Madison Group Inc .... G 216 362-9000
 Cleveland *(G-5602)*
Mr Emblem Inc .... G 419 697-1888
 Oregon *(G-15561)*
Ohio State Institute of Fin .... G 614 861-8811
 Reynoldsburg *(G-16445)*
Painted Hill Inv Group Inc .... F 937 339-1756
 Troy *(G-18691)*
Peska Inc .... F 440 998-4664
 Ashtabula *(G-797)*
Pinky & Thumb LLC .... G 614 939-5216
 New Albany *(G-14634)*
Puttco Inc .... G 937 299-1527
 Dayton *(G-8453)*
Quality Rubber Stamp Inc .... G 614 235-2700
 Columbus *(G-7365)*
Quality Spt & Silk Screen Sp .... G 513 769-8300
 Cincinnati *(G-4229)*
R & A Sports Inc .... E 216 289-2254
 Euclid *(G-9438)*
Simply Canvas Inc .... E 330 436-6500
 Akron *(G-376)*
Sroufe Healthcare Products LLC .... E 260 894-4171
 Wadsworth *(G-19278)*
Swocat Design Inc .... G 440 282-4700
 Lorain *(G-12127)*
Tee Creations .... G 937 878-2822
 Fairborn *(G-9472)*
Tim L Humbert .... F 330 497-4944
 Canton *(G-2836)*
Triage Ortho Group .... G 937 653-6431
 Urbana *(G-19016)*
Vasil Co Inc .... G 419 562-2901
 Bucyrus *(G-2347)*
Vector International Corp .... G 440 942-2002
 Mentor *(G-13623)*
Wizard Graphics Inc .... G 419 354-3098
 Bowling Green *(G-2006)*
Zide Sport Shop of Ohio Inc .... F 740 373-8199
 Marietta *(G-12690)*

PRINTING: Screen, Manmade Fiber & Silk, Broadwoven Fabric

717 Inc .... G 440 925-0402
 Lakewood *(G-11507)*
B Richardson Inc .... F 330 724-2122
 Akron *(G-76)*
Cincinnati Advg Pdts LLC .... E 513 346-7310
 Cincinnati *(G-3479)*
Creatia Inc .... G 937 368-3100
 Fletcher *(G-9782)*
E & E Screen Prtg & Cstm EMB .... G 614 235-2177
 Columbus *(G-6878)*
Evolution Crtive Solutions LLC .... E 513 681-4450
 Cincinnati *(G-3660)*
Fcs Graphics Inc .... G 216 771-5177
 Cleveland *(G-5225)*
Flashions Sportswear Ltd .... G 937 323-5885
 Springfield *(G-17403)*
Great Oppurtunities Inc .... G 614 868-1899
 Columbus *(G-6969)*
Phantasm Designs .... G 419 538-6737
 Ottawa *(G-15662)*
Scenic Screen .... G 419 468-3110
 Galion *(G-10153)*
Sportsco Imprinting .... G 513 641-5111
 Cincinnati *(G-4360)*
Wayne Sporting Goods .... G 937 236-6665
 Dayton *(G-8586)*

PRINTING: Thermography

A C Hadley - Printing Inc .... G 937 426-0952
 Beavercreek *(G-1296)*
Austintown Printing Inc .... G 330 797-0099
 Youngstown *(G-20849)*
Functional Imaging Ltd .... G 740 689-2466
 Lancaster *(G-11573)*
Larmax Inc .... G 513 984-0783
 Blue Ash *(G-1803)*
Sharon Printing Co Inc .... G 330 239-1684
 Sharon Center *(G-16953)*

PRODUCTS: Petroleum & coal, NEC

Citi 2 Citi Logistics .... E 614 306-4109
 Columbus *(G-6766)*

PROFESSIONAL EQPT & SPLYS, WHOLESALE: Analytical Instruments

Consolidatd Analytical Sys Inc .... F 513 542-1200
 Cleves *(G-6359)*
Mettler-Toledo Intl Fin Inc .... G 614 438-4511
 Columbus *(G-6500)*

PROFESSIONAL EQPT & SPLYS, WHOLESALE: Bank

General Pump & Eqp Compnay .... G 330 455-2100
 Canton *(G-2682)*

PROFESSIONAL EQPT & SPLYS, WHOLESALE: Engineers', NEC

Richland Blue Printcom Inc .... G 419 524-2781
 Mansfield *(G-12505)*
S&V Industries Inc .... E 330 666-1986
 Medina *(G-13333)*
US Tsubaki Power Transm LLC .... C 419 626-4560
 Sandusky *(G-16860)*

PROFESSIONAL EQPT & SPLYS, WHOLESALE: Optical Goods

Diversified Ophthalmics Inc .... F 509 324-6364
 Cincinnati *(G-3595)*
Diversified Ophthalmics Inc .... F 803 783-3454
 Cincinnati *(G-3594)*
Essilor Laboratories Amer Inc .... E 614 274-0840
 Columbus *(G-6906)*
Hoya Optical Labs .... G 440 239-1924
 Berea *(G-1610)*

PROFESSIONAL EQPT & SPLYS, WHOLESALE: Precision Tools

Ahner Fabricating & Shtmtl Inc .... E 419 626-6641
 Sandusky *(G-16793)*
Hapco Inc .... F 330 678-9353
 Kent *(G-11331)*
Monarch Steel Company Inc .... E 216 587-8000
 Cleveland *(G-5703)*

PROFESSIONAL EQPT & SPLYS, WHOLESALE: Scientific & Engineerg

Laser Automation Inc .... F 440 543-9291
 Chagrin Falls *(G-3055)*

PROFESSIONAL INSTRUMENT REPAIR SVCS

Certon Technologies Inc .... F 440 786-7185
 Bedford *(G-1395)*
Cleveland Electric Labs Co .... E 800 447-2207
 Twinsburg *(G-18754)*
Edmonds Elevator Company .... F 216 781-9135
 Thompson *(G-18025)*
Form-A-Chip Inc .... G 937 223-4135
 Dayton *(G-8201)*
Mettler-Toledo Intl Fin Inc .... G 614 438-4511
 Columbus *(G-6500)*
UPA Technology Inc .... F 513 755-1380
 West Chester *(G-19816)*

PROFILE SHAPES: Unsupported Plastics

Advanced Composites Inc .... G 937 575-9814
 Sidney *(G-17012)*
Advanced Composites Inc .... C 937 575-9800
 Sidney *(G-17013)*
Alkon Corporation .... E 614 799-6650
 Dublin *(G-8876)*
Bobbart Industries Inc .... E 419 350-5477
 Sylvania *(G-17934)*
Dayton Technologies .... F 513 539-5474
 Monroe *(G-14259)*
Deceuninck North America LLC .... B 513 539-4444
 Monroe *(G-14260)*
Duracote Corporation .... E 330 296-9600
 Ravenna *(G-16376)*
Global Manufacturing Solutions .... F 937 236-8315
 Dayton *(G-8225)*
HP Manufacturing Company Inc .... D 216 361-6500
 Cleveland *(G-5421)*
Inventive Extrusions Corp .... E 330 874-3000
 Bolivar *(G-1917)*
Machining Technologies Inc .... E 419 862-3110
 Elmore *(G-9206)*
Meridian Industries Inc .... D 330 673-1011
 Kent *(G-11351)*
Pexco Packaging Corp .... E 419 470-5935
 Toledo *(G-18468)*
Plasto-Tech Corporation .... F 440 323-6300
 Elyria *(G-9314)*
Roach Wood Products & Plas Inc .... G 740 532-4855
 Ironton *(G-11172)*
Wurms Woodworking Company .... E 419 492-2184
 New Washington *(G-14834)*

PROGRAM ADMINISTRATION, GOVT: Workers' Compensation Office

Proficient Information Tech .... G 937 470-1300
 Dayton *(G-8447)*

PROPELLERS: Boat & Ship, Cast

Advanced Propeller Systems .... G 937 409-1038
 Dayton *(G-7968)*

PROPERTY & CASUALTY INSURANCE AGENTS

Stancorp Inc .... G 330 545-6615
 Girard *(G-10267)*

PROPRIETARY STORES, NON-PRESCRIPTION MEDICINE

Kroger Co .... D 419 423-2065
 Findlay *(G-9711)*

PROTECTION EQPT: Lightning

Amidac Wind Corporation .... G 213 973-4000
 Elyria *(G-9216)*
Burkett Industries Inc .... G 419 332-4391
 Fremont *(G-10002)*
Ohio Vly Lightning Protection .... G 937 987-0245
 New Vienna *(G-14825)*

PROTECTIVE FOOTWEAR: Rubber Or Plastic

Advantage Products Corporation .... F 513 489-2283
 Blue Ash *(G-1722)*
Calzurocom .... G 800 257-9472
 Plain City *(G-16180)*

PUBLIC RELATIONS & PUBLICITY SVCS

Dayton Weekly News .... G 937 223-8060
 Dayton *(G-8147)*
Jjkb Enterprises LLC .... G 513 731-4332
 Cincinnati *(G-3873)*
Marketing Essentials LLC .... F 419 629-0080
 New Bremen *(G-14656)*

PUBLISHERS: Atlases

Scott Fetzer Company .... F 440 892-3000
 Westlake *(G-20156)*

PUBLISHERS: Book

American Academic Press .... G 216 906-2518
 Bedford *(G-1382)*
B & S Transport Inc .... F 330 767-4319
 Navarre *(G-14572)*
Bookfactory LLC .... E 937 226-7100
 Dayton *(G-8059)*
Bookmasters Inc .... C 419 281-1802
 Ashland *(G-686)*
Carmel Trader Publishing Inc .... E 330 478-9200
 Canton *(G-2620)*
Cengage Learning Inc .... C 513 234-5967
 Mason *(G-12840)*
Conway Greene Co Inc .... G 216 619-8091
 Cleveland *(G-5026)*
Dalmatian Press LLC .... E 419 207-3600
 Ashland *(G-700)*
Eastword Publications Dev .... G 216 781-9594
 Cleveland *(G-5141)*

PRODUCT SECTION

PUBLISHERS: Miscellaneous

Elloras Cave Publishing Inc .... E 330 253-3521
  Akron *(G-151)*
Frasernet Inc .... G 216 691-6686
  Cleveland *(G-5273)*
Hubbard Company .... E 419 784-4455
  Defiance *(G-8627)*
Instruction & Design Concepts .... G 937 439-2698
  Dayton *(G-8271)*
Just Business Inc .... F 866 577-3303
  Dayton *(G-8287)*
Katherine A Stull Inc .... G 440 349-3977
  Solon *(G-17181)*
Kent State University .... F 330 672-7913
  Kent *(G-11344)*
Lachina Creative Inc .... D 216 292-7959
  Cleveland *(G-5552)*
Lloyd Library & Museum .... G 513 721-3707
  Cincinnati *(G-3949)*
Master Communications Inc .... G 208 821-3473
  Blue Ash *(G-1813)*
Matthew Bender & Company Inc ...... C 518 487-3000
  Miamisburg *(G-13686)*
McGraw-Hill Global Educatn LLC ...... B 614 755-4151
  Blacklick *(G-1690)*
McGraw-Hill School Education H ...... B 614 430-4000
  Columbus *(G-6499)*
McNamaras Pub Inc .... G 216 671-8820
  Cleveland *(G-5647)*
North Coast Media LLC .... E 216 706-3700
  Cleveland *(G-5768)*
Nurdcon LLC .... G 614 208-5898
  Canal Winchester *(G-2509)*
Ohio Psychology Pblications Inc ...... G 614 861-1999
  Columbus *(G-7256)*
One Liberty Street .... G 419 352-6298
  Bowling Green *(G-1987)*
Pardson Inc .... F 740 373-5285
  Marietta *(G-12651)*
Precision Metalforming Assn .... G 216 241-1482
  Independence *(G-11148)*
Province of St John The Baptis .... D 513 241-5615
  Cincinnati *(G-4219)*
Reynolds Industries Group LLC .... G 614 864-6199
  Blacklick *(G-1692)*
SC Solutions Inc .... G 614 317-7119
  Grove City *(G-10465)*
St Media Group Intl Inc .... D 513 421-2050
  Blue Ash *(G-1849)*
Talbot Drake Incorporated .... G 216 441-5600
  Cleveland *(G-6148)*
Tgs International Inc .... E 330 893-4828
  Millersburg *(G-14134)*
Tomahawk Entertainment Group .... G 216 505-0548
  Cleveland *(G-6180)*
Vista Research Group LLC .... G 419 281-3927
  Ashland *(G-753)*
Weaver Boos Consultants Inc .... F 419 933-5216
  Willard *(G-20248)*
Woodburn Press LLC .... G 937 293-9245
  Dayton *(G-8599)*
Zaner-Bloser Inc .... D 614 486-0221
  Columbus *(G-7624)*
Zaner-Bloser Inc .... G 608 441-5555
  Columbus *(G-7625)*

PUBLISHERS: Books, No Printing

American Legal Publishing Corp ...... E 513 421-4248
  Cincinnati *(G-3335)*
Americanhort Services Inc .... F 614 884-1203
  Columbus *(G-6588)*
Anderson Publishing Co .... D 513 474-9305
  Miamisburg *(G-13640)*
Asm International .... D 440 338-5151
  Novelty *(G-15438)*
Beevinwood Inc .... G 937 678-9910
  West Manchester *(G-19940)*
Bendon Inc .... D 419 207-3600
  Ashland *(G-685)*
CSS Publishing Co Inc .... E 419 227-1818
  Lima *(G-11850)*
Dialogue House Associates Inc .... G 216 342-5170
  Beachwood *(G-1232)*
Dreamscape Media LLC .... G 877 983-7326
  Holland *(G-10927)*
F+w Media Inc .... G 603 253-8148
  Blue Ash *(G-1771)*
F+w Media Inc .... B 513 531-2690
  Blue Ash *(G-1770)*
Gareth Stevens Publishing LP .... C 800 542-2595
  Strongsville *(G-17746)*

Gie Media Inc .... E 800 456-0707
  Cleveland *(G-5322)*
Golf Galaxy Golfworks Inc .... C 740 328-4193
  Newark *(G-14880)*
Grand Unification Press Inc .... G 330 683-1187
  Orrville *(G-15592)*
Harvey Whitney Books Company ..... G 513 793-3555
  Cincinnati *(G-3801)*
Highlights Press Inc .... G 614 487-2767
  Columbus *(G-6998)*
Indicator Advisory Corporation .... G 419 726-9000
  Toledo *(G-18345)*
Kaeden Corporation .... G 440 617-1400
  Westlake *(G-20127)*
Kelley Communication Dev .... G 937 298-6132
  Dayton *(G-8291)*
Ketman Corporation .... G 330 262-1688
  Wooster *(G-20613)*
McDonald & Woodward Pubg Co ..... G 740 321-1140
  Granville *(G-10332)*
Micropress America LLC .... G 513 746-0689
  Cincinnati *(G-4024)*
National Dirctry of Morts Inc .... G 440 247-3561
  Chagrin Falls *(G-3025)*
Neola Inc .... F 740 622-5341
  Coshocton *(G-7742)*
Northstar Publishing .... G 330 721-9126
  Medina *(G-13307)*
Orange Frazer Press Inc .... G 937 382-3196
  Wilmington *(G-20501)*
Relx Inc .... G 937 865-6800
  Miamisburg *(G-13710)*
Relx Inc .... E 937 865-6800
  Miamisburg *(G-13708)*
River Corp .... G 513 641-3355
  Cincinnati *(G-4272)*
Teachers Publishing Group .... F 614 486-0631
  Hilliard *(G-10868)*
Wolters Kluwer Clinical Drug .... D 330 650-6506
  Hudson *(G-11083)*

PUBLISHERS: Catalogs

Kennedy Catalogs LLC .... G 513 753-1518
  Batavia *(G-1157)*

PUBLISHERS: Directories, NEC

Consumer Source Inc .... G 513 621-7300
  Cincinnati *(G-3543)*
General Bar Inc .... F 440 835-2000
  Westlake *(G-20117)*
Nomis Publications Inc .... F 330 965-2380
  Youngstown *(G-20976)*
Snook Advertising Al Publisher .... F 614 866-3333
  Reynoldsburg *(G-16453)*

PUBLISHERS: Directories, Telephone

All County Phone Directories .... G 419 865-2464
  Holland *(G-10915)*
Ameritech Publishing Inc .... D 614 895-6123
  Columbus *(G-6591)*
Cbd Media Holdings LLC .... G 513 217-9483
  Cincinnati *(G-3449)*
Christian Blue Pages .... F 937 847-2583
  Miamisburg *(G-13650)*
Lanier & Associates Inc .... G 216 391-7735
  Cleveland *(G-5559)*
Local Insight Yellow Pages Inc .... C 330 650-7100
  Hudson *(G-11061)*
Supermedia LLC .... G 614 216-6566
  Westerville *(G-20027)*

PUBLISHERS: Guides

Senior Impact Publication .... F 513 791-8800
  Cincinnati *(G-4321)*
Shoppers Compass .... G 419 947-9234
  Mount Gilead *(G-14432)*

PUBLISHERS: Magazines, No Printing

Acoustical Publications Inc .... G 440 835-0101
  Bay Village *(G-1204)*
Adams Street Publishing Co .... E 419 244-9859
  Toledo *(G-18156)*
Alternative Press Magazine Inc .... E 216 631-1510
  Cleveland *(G-4678)*
Amos Media Company .... C 937 498-2111
  Sidney *(G-17015)*
Arens Corporation .... E 937 473-2028
  Covington *(G-7781)*

Arens Corporation .... G 937 473-2028
  Covington *(G-7782)*
At The Ready Publications LLC .... F 762 822-8549
  Van Wert *(G-19077)*
Baker Media Group LLC .... F 330 253-0056
  Akron *(G-78)*
Bobit Business Media Inc .... G 330 899-2200
  Uniontown *(G-18912)*
Camargo Publications Inc .... G 513 779-7177
  Cincinnati *(G-3438)*
CFM Religion Pubg Group LLC .... E 513 931-4050
  Cincinnati *(G-3461)*
Cincinnati Magazine .... G 513 421-4300
  Cincinnati *(G-3499)*
City Visitor Inc .... G 216 661-6666
  Cleveland *(G-4934)*
Columbus Bride .... D 614 888-4567
  Columbus *(G-6784)*
Crain Communications Inc .... E 216 522-1383
  Cleveland *(G-5037)*
F+w Media Inc .... B 513 531-2690
  Blue Ash *(G-1770)*
Family Motor Coaching Inc .... D 513 474-3622
  Cincinnati *(G-3672)*
Fontanelle Group Inc .... G 440 834-8900
  Burton *(G-2358)*
Generals Books .... G 614 870-1861
  Columbus *(G-6946)*
Gie Media Inc .... E 800 456-0707
  Cleveland *(G-5322)*
Great Lakes Publishing Company ..... D 216 771-2833
  Cleveland *(G-5350)*
Guitar Digest Inc .... F 740 592-4614
  Athens *(G-834)*
Harvey Whitney Books Company ..... G 513 793-3555
  Cincinnati *(G-3801)*
Jadlyn Inc .... G 330 670-9545
  Akron *(G-221)*
Kyle Publications Inc .... G 419 754-4234
  Toledo *(G-18373)*
Marketing Essentials LLC .... F 419 629-0080
  New Bremen *(G-14656)*
Meister Media Worldwide Inc .... D 440 942-2000
  Willoughby *(G-20377)*
Miller Publishing Company .... G 937 866-3331
  Miamisburg *(G-13695)*
Organic Spa Magazine Ltd .... G 440 331-5750
  Rocky River *(G-16551)*
Pardson Inc .... F 740 373-5285
  Marietta *(G-12651)*
Pink Corner Office Inc .... G 614 547-9350
  Lewis Center *(G-11772)*
Pjl Enterprise Inc .... D 937 293-1415
  Moraine *(G-14377)*
Pjl Enterprise Inc .... E 937 293-1415
  Moraine *(G-14378)*
Plus Publications Inc .... G 740 345-5542
  Newark *(G-14911)*
Province of St John The Baptis .... D 513 241-5615
  Cincinnati *(G-4219)*
Rector Inc .... G 440 892-0444
  Westlake *(G-20149)*
Sheep & Farm Life Inc .... G 419 492-2364
  New Washington *(G-14832)*
St Media Group Intl Inc .... D 513 421-2050
  Blue Ash *(G-1849)*
Standard Publishing LLC .... C 513 931-4050
  Cincinnati *(G-4371)*
Suburban Communications Inc .... E 440 632-0130
  Middlefield *(G-13855)*
Toastmasters International .... F 937 429-2680
  Dayton *(G-7991)*
Upcreek Productions Inc .... G 740 208-8124
  Bidwell *(G-1672)*
Wordcross Enterprises Inc .... F 614 410-4140
  Columbus *(G-7612)*
Xray Media Ltd .... G 513 751-9641
  Cincinnati *(G-4528)*
Z Track Magazine .... G 614 764-1703
  Dublin *(G-9013)*

PUBLISHERS: Maps

Permaguide .... E 330 456-8519
  Canton *(G-2783)*

PUBLISHERS: Miscellaneous

360 Communications LLC .... G 330 329-2013
  Akron *(G-14)*
48 Hr Books Inc .... E 330 374-6917
  Akron *(G-15)*

Employee Codes: A=Over 500 employees, B=251-500
C=101-250, D=51-100, E=20-50, F=10-19, G=3-9

Aaronyx Publishing ... G ... 419 747-2400
Mansfield *(G-12400)*
Adelphi Enterprises ... G ... 937 372-3791
Xenia *(G-20754)*
Albert Bickel ... G ... 513 530-5700
Cincinnati *(G-3317)*
Align Assess Achieve LLC ... G ... 614 505-6820
Columbus *(G-6563)*
Alonovus Corp ... D ... 330 674-2300
Millersburg *(G-14057)*
American City Bus Journals Inc ... E ... 513 337-9450
Cincinnati *(G-3331)*
American Legal Publishing Corp ... E ... 513 421-4248
Cincinnati *(G-3335)*
Ameritech Publishing Inc ... E ... 330 896-6037
Uniontown *(G-18909)*
Amos Media Company ... C ... 937 498-2111
Sidney *(G-17015)*
Anadem Inc ... G ... 614 262-2539
Columbus *(G-6598)*
Anderson Publishing Co ... D ... 513 474-9305
Miamisburg *(G-13640)*
Aquent Studios ... G ... 216 266-7551
Willoughby *(G-20280)*
At The Ready Publications LLC ... G ... 762 822-8549
Van Wert *(G-19077)*
AT&T Corp ... A ... 614 223-8236
Columbus *(G-6623)*
Bcmr Publications LLC ... G ... 740 441-7778
Gallipolis *(G-10160)*
Becker Gallagher Legal Pubg ... F ... 513 677-5044
Cincinnati *(G-3385)*
Blue Line Painting LLC ... G ... 440 951-2583
Cleveland *(G-4823)*
Ceja Publishing ... G ... 216 319-0268
Cleveland *(G-4896)*
Checkered Express Inc ... F ... 330 530-8169
Girard *(G-10255)*
Competitive Press Inc ... G ... 330 289-1968
Copley *(G-7680)*
Computer Workshop Inc ... E ... 614 798-9505
Dublin *(G-8902)*
Computercrafts ... G ... 614 231-7559
Columbus *(G-6809)*
Conquest Maps ... G ... 614 654-1627
Columbus *(G-6810)*
Copy Source Inc ... G ... 937 642-7140
Marysville *(G-12778)*
County Classifieds ... G ... 937 592-8847
Bellefontaine *(G-1510)*
Cox Publishing Hq ... G ... 937 225-2000
Dayton *(G-8108)*
Deward Publishing Co Ltd ... G ... 800 300-9778
Chillicothe *(G-3184)*
Diocesan Publications Inc Ohio ... E ... 614 718-9500
Dublin *(G-8907)*
Discover Publications ... G ... 614 785-1111
Columbus *(G-6867)*
Dodge Data & Analytics LLC ... E ... 513 763-3660
Cincinnati *(G-3598)*
Douthit Communications Inc ... D ... 419 625-5825
Sandusky *(G-16805)*
Ebsco Industries Inc ... F ... 513 398-3695
Mason *(G-12860)*
Educational Publisher Inc ... G ... 614 485-0721
Columbus *(G-6884)*
Elbern Publications ... G ... 614 235-2643
Columbus *(G-6889)*
Elloras Cave Publishing Inc ... E ... 330 253-3521
Akron *(G-151)*
Express Care ... F ... 740 266-2501
Steubenville *(G-17533)*
F and W Publications Inc ... G ... 513 531-2690
Cincinnati *(G-3668)*
Fax Medley Group Inc ... G ... 513 272-1932
Cincinnati *(G-3676)*
Fire Ball Press ... G ... 614 280-0100
Columbus *(G-6925)*
Fish Express ... G ... 513 661-3000
Cincinnati *(G-3692)*
Fleetmaster Express Inc ... C ... 419 425-0666
Findlay *(G-9688)*
Franklin Covey Co ... G ... 513 792-0099
Cincinnati *(G-3710)*
Free Bird Publications Ltd ... G ... 216 673-0229
Brunswick *(G-2206)*
Fullgospel Publishing ... F ... 216 339-1973
Shaker Heights *(G-16931)*
Gb Liquidating Company Inc ... E ... 513 248-7600
Milford *(G-14010)*
Gordon Bernard Company LLC ... E ... 513 248-7600
Milford *(G-14013)*
Gospel Trumpet Publishing ... G ... 937 548-9876
Greenville *(G-10373)*
Graphic Paper Products Corp ... D ... 937 325-5503
Springfield *(G-17407)*
Gray & Company Publishers ... G ... 216 431-2665
Cleveland *(G-5343)*
Guadalupe Publishing Inc ... G ... 614 450-2474
Etna *(G-9393)*
Haines Criss Cross ... G ... 330 494-9111
North Canton *(G-15091)*
Hanover Publishing Co ... G ... 440 838-0911
Brecksville *(G-2040)*
Hebraic Way Press Company ... G ... 330 614-4872
Alliance *(G-472)*
Herff Jones LLC ... E ... 330 678-8138
Stow *(G-17594)*
Holistic Measures ... G ... 216 261-0329
Euclid *(G-9420)*
Immigration Law Systems Inc ... G ... 614 252-3078
Columbus *(G-7023)*
Incorporated Trustees Gospel W ... D ... 216 749-1428
Cleveland *(G-5449)*
Interweave Press LLC ... G ... 513 531-2690
Blue Ash *(G-1794)*
Johnny Chin Insurance Agency ... G ... 513 777-8695
West Chester *(G-19871)*
L & S Liette Express ... G ... 419 394-7077
Saint Marys *(G-16689)*
L M Berry and Company ... A ... 937 296-2121
Moraine *(G-14364)*
Lake Publishing Inc ... G ... 440 299-8500
Mentor *(G-13495)*
Lexisnexis Group ... C ... 937 865-6800
Miamisburg *(G-13684)*
Lily Tiger Press ... E ... 513 591-0817
Cincinnati *(G-3944)*
LPC Publishing Co ... G ... 216 721-1800
Cleveland *(G-5586)*
M R I Education Foundation ... C ... 513 281-3400
Cincinnati *(G-3964)*
Masterpiece Publisher L P ... G ... 513 948-1000
Cincinnati *(G-3985)*
Matthew R Copp ... G ... 614 276-8959
Columbus *(G-7159)*
McDonald & Woodward Publishing ... G ... 740 641-2691
Newark *(G-14896)*
Mia Express Inc ... G ... 330 896-8180
Akron *(G-281)*
Nature Trek ... G ... 513 314-3916
Cincinnati *(G-4063)*
Network Communications Inc ... C ... 614 934-1919
Gahanna *(G-10095)*
New Century Sales LLC ... G ... 513 422-3631
Middletown *(G-13937)*
North Bend Express ... G ... 513 481-4623
Cincinnati *(G-4086)*
Ogr Publishing Inc ... G ... 330 757-3020
Hilliard *(G-10845)*
Ohlinger Publishing Svcs Inc ... F ... 614 261-5360
Columbus *(G-7267)*
P&M Publishing ... G ... 740 353-3300
Portsmouth *(G-16294)*
Paula and Julies Cookbooks LLC ... G ... 614 863-1193
Columbus *(G-7301)*
Pauler Communications Inc ... G ... 440 243-1229
Richfield *(G-16480)*
Pedestrian Press ... G ... 419 244-6488
Toledo *(G-18461)*
Peebles Creative Group Inc ... G ... 614 487-2011
Dublin *(G-8961)*
Pflaum Publishing Group ... G ... 937 293-1415
Moraine *(G-14376)*
Pressed Coffee Bar & Eatery ... G ... 330 746-8030
Youngstown *(G-21005)*
Province of St John The Baptis ... D ... 513 241-5615
Cincinnati *(G-4219)*
Psa Consulting Inc ... G ... 513 382-4315
Cincinnati *(G-4220)*
Puhd ... G ... 216 244-3336
Bedford *(G-1439)*
Purebred Publishing Inc ... G ... 614 339-5393
Columbus *(G-7357)*
Quaker Express Stamping Inc ... F ... 330 332-9266
Salem *(G-16768)*
Rawhide Software Inc ... G ... 419 878-0857
Bowling Green *(G-1993)*
Rcl Publishing Group LLC ... G ... 972 390-6400
Cincinnati *(G-4252)*
Recob Great Lakes Express Inc ... G ... 216 265-7940
Cleveland *(G-5966)*
Research and Development Group ... G ... 614 261-0454
Columbus *(G-7386)*
Robs Creative Screen Printing ... G ... 740 264-6383
Wintersville *(G-20541)*
S J T Enterprises Inc ... E ... 440 617-1100
Westlake *(G-20153)*
Scheel Publishing LLC ... G ... 216 731-8616
Willoughby *(G-20425)*
Scrambl-Gram Inc ... F ... 419 635-2321
Port Clinton *(G-16259)*
Sea Bird Publications Inc ... G ... 513 869-2200
Fairfield *(G-9562)*
Sei Inc ... F ... 513 942-6170
West Chester *(G-19897)*
Sevell + Sevell Inc ... G ... 614 341-9700
Columbus *(G-7441)*
Silver Maple Publications ... G ... 937 767-1259
Yellow Springs *(G-20816)*
Simon & Schuster Inc ... C ... 614 876-0371
Columbus *(G-7453)*
Singer Press ... G ... 216 595-9400
Beachwood *(G-1279)*
Snap-On Business Solutions ... B ... 330 659-1600
Richfield *(G-16489)*
Specialty Gas Publishing Inc ... G ... 216 226-3796
Cleveland *(G-6084)*
Star Brite Express Car WA ... G ... 330 674-0062
Millersburg *(G-14130)*
Starbringer Media Group Ltd ... G ... 440 871-5448
Westlake *(G-20162)*
Suburban Communications Inc ... E ... 440 632-0130
Middlefield *(G-13855)*
Success Pro Publications ... G ... 614 886-9922
Columbus *(G-7499)*
Tiny Lion Music Groups ... G ... 419 874-7353
Perrysburg *(G-16017)*
Universal Drect Flfllment Corp ... C ... 330 650-5000
Hudson *(G-11081)*
Van-Griner LLC ... G ... 419 733-7951
Cincinnati *(G-4465)*
Wizard Publications Inc ... F ... 808 821-1214
Lancaster *(G-11619)*
Zoo Publishing Inc ... E ... 513 824-8297
Blue Ash *(G-1882)*

PUBLISHERS: Music Book

Decent Hill Publishers LLC ... G ... 216 548-1255
Hilliard *(G-10824)*

PUBLISHERS: Music Book & Sheet Music

Terewell Inc ... G ... 216 334-6897
Cleveland *(G-6160)*

PUBLISHERS: Music, Sheet

American Guild of English Hand ... G ... 937 438-0085
Cincinnati *(G-3333)*
Beckenhorst Press Inc ... G ... 614 451-6461
Columbus *(G-6657)*
Lorenz Corporation ... D ... 937 228-6118
Dayton *(G-8316)*
Ludwig Music Publishing Co ... F ... 440 926-1100
Grafton *(G-10307)*

PUBLISHERS: Newsletter

Greenworld Enterprises Inc ... G ... 800 525-6999
West Chester *(G-19862)*
Pike County Paper Inc ... F ... 740 947-5522
Waverly *(G-19557)*
See Ya There Inc ... G ... 614 856-9037
Millersport *(G-14161)*

PUBLISHERS: Newspaper

Aim Media Midwest Oper LLC ... F ... 937 335-5634
Troy *(G-18633)*
American Community Newspapers ... G ... 614 888-4567
Columbus *(G-6582)*
B G News ... E ... 419 372-2601
Bowling Green *(G-1952)*
Box Seat Publishing LLC ... G ... 513 519-2812
Cincinnati *(G-3406)*
Brown Publishing Inc LLC ... G ... 513 794-5040
Blue Ash *(G-1742)*
Brv Inc ... F ... 513 977-3000
Cincinnati *(G-3427)*
Buckeye Post ... G ... 330 724-2800
Akron *(G-97)*

Catholic Diocese of Columbus..............G....... 614 224-5195
Columbus *(G-6750)*
Chronicle Telegram..............G....... 330 725-4166
Medina *(G-13236)*
Chronicle Your Life Story..............G....... 614 456-7576
Columbus *(G-6765)*
Cleveland East Ed Wns Jurnl..............G....... 216 228-1379
Cleveland *(G-4958)*
Clevelandcom..............G....... 216 862-7159
Cleveland *(G-4987)*
Crain Communications Inc..............E....... 216 522-1383
Cleveland *(G-5037)*
Dragonflies and Angels Press..............G....... 740 964-9149
Pataskala *(G-15830)*
EW Scripps Company..............E....... 513 977-3000
Cincinnati *(G-3663)*
Fire Tetrahedron Journal..............G....... 567 220-6477
Tiffin *(G-18060)*
Franklin Communications Inc..............D....... 614 459-9769
Columbus *(G-6936)*
Fresh Press LLC..............G....... 513 378-1402
Loveland *(G-12189)*
Full Gospel Baptist Times..............G....... 614 279-3307
Columbus *(G-6941)*
Gannett Stllite Info Ntwrk Inc..............D....... 513 721-2700
Cincinnati *(G-3724)*
Gannett Stllite Info Ntwrk LLC..............D....... 419 334-1012
Fremont *(G-10021)*
Gazette Publishing Company..............F....... 419 335-2010
Wauseon *(G-19517)*
Iheartcommunications Inc..............G....... 740 335-0941
Wshngtn CT Hs *(G-20728)*
Iheartcommunications Inc..............D....... 419 223-2060
Lima *(G-11876)*
James Oshea..............G....... 614 262-3188
Columbus *(G-7062)*
Journal News..............G....... 513 829-7900
Fairfield *(G-9515)*
Leaf & Thorn Press..............G....... 614 396-6055
Columbus *(G-6498)*
Lisa Arters..............G....... 330 435-1804
Creston *(G-7806)*
Lore Inc..............G....... 513 969-8481
Milford *(G-14024)*
Ls2 Printing..............G....... 937 544-1000
West Union *(G-19965)*
Marrow County Sentinel..............G....... 419 946-3010
Mount Gilead *(G-14428)*
Mature Living News Magazine..............G....... 419 241-8880
Toledo *(G-18401)*
My Way Home Finder Magazine..............G....... 419 841-6201
Toledo *(G-18420)*
Newspaper Solutions LLC..............G....... 937 694-9370
Englewood *(G-9371)*
North Coast Voice Mag..............G....... 440 415-0999
Geneva *(G-10226)*
Northeast Scene Inc..............E....... 216 241-7550
Cleveland *(G-5776)*
Ogden Newspapers of Ohio Inc..............D....... 419 448-3200
Tiffin *(G-18074)*
Ohio City Power..............G....... 216 651-6250
Cleveland *(G-5804)*
Ohio News Network..............D....... 614 460-3700
Columbus *(G-7251)*
Plain Dealer Publishing Co..............A....... 216 999-5000
Cleveland *(G-5883)*
Post..............G....... 513 768-8000
Lockland *(G-12001)*
Progressor Times..............G....... 419 396-7567
Carey *(G-2887)*
Ptr Daily LLC..............G....... 330 673-1990
Stow *(G-17622)*
Royalton Recorder..............G....... 440 237-2235
North Royalton *(G-15300)*
Sandusky Newspapers Inc..............C....... 419 625-5500
Sandusky *(G-16845)*
Scenic Valley Surplus LLC..............G....... 330 359-0555
Fredericksburg *(G-9960)*
Scioto Voice..............G....... 740 574-5400
Wheelersburg *(G-20184)*
Stumbo Publishing Co..............G....... 419 529-2847
Ontario *(G-15548)*
The Cleveland Jewish Publ Co..............F....... 216 454-8300
Beachwood *(G-1280)*
The Gazette Printing Co Inc..............G....... 440 593-6030
Conneaut *(G-7660)*
Toledo Streets Newspaper..............G....... 419 214-3460
Toledo *(G-18570)*
Toledo Sword Newspaper..............G....... 419 932-0767
Toledo *(G-18571)*
Trogdon Publishing Inc..............E....... 330 721-7678
Medina *(G-13355)*
Trumbull County Legal News..............G....... 330 392-7112
Warren *(G-19451)*
University Sports Publications..............E....... 614 291-6416
Columbus *(G-7564)*
Vindicator..............G....... 330 755-0135
Campbell *(G-2471)*
Vindicator Boardman Office..............G....... 330 259-1732
Youngstown *(G-21064)*
Weekly Brothers Cnty Line Far..............G....... 330 674-4195
Millersburg *(G-14149)*
Weekly Chatter..............G....... 740 336-4704
Belpre *(G-1587)*
Weekly Juicery..............G....... 513 321-0680
Cincinnati *(G-4494)*
Whitney House..............G....... 614 396-7846
Worthington *(G-20708)*

PUBLISHERS: Newspapers, No Printing

Act For Sneca Cnty Oprtnty Ctr..............G....... 419 447-4362
Tiffin *(G-18040)*
Akron Legal News Inc..............F....... 330 296-7578
Akron *(G-42)*
American City Bus Journals Inc..............E....... 513 337-9450
Cincinnati *(G-3331)*
American City Bus Journals Inc..............E....... 937 528-4400
Dayton *(G-8024)*
American Israelite Co..............G....... 513 621-3145
Cincinnati *(G-3334)*
American Lithuanian Press..............G....... 216 531-8150
Cleveland *(G-4691)*
Antwerp Bee-Argus..............G....... 419 258-8161
Antwerp *(G-595)*
Archbold Buckeye Inc..............F....... 419 445-4466
Archbold *(G-636)*
Arens Corporation..............E....... 937 473-2028
Covington *(G-7781)*
Arens Corporation..............G....... 937 473-2028
Covington *(G-7782)*
Boardman News..............G....... 330 758-6397
Boardman *(G-1898)*
Brookville Star..............G....... 937 833-2545
Brookville *(G-2163)*
Brothers Publishing Co LLC..............E....... 937 548-3330
Greenville *(G-10361)*
Brown Publishing Co Inc..............G....... 740 286-2187
Jackson *(G-11184)*
Chagrin Valley Publishing Co..............C....... 440 247-5335
Chagrin Falls *(G-3012)*
Chesterland News Inc..............F....... 440 729-7667
Chesterland *(G-3154)*
Cleveland Citizen Pubg Co..............G....... 216 861-4283
Cleveland *(G-4951)*
Cleveland Jewish Publ Co..............E....... 216 454-8300
Cleveland *(G-4966)*
Cleveland Jewish Publ Co Fdn..............G....... 216 454-8300
Beachwood *(G-1227)*
Columbus Messenger Company..............E....... 614 272-5422
Columbus *(G-6797)*
Columbus-Sports Publications..............F....... 614 486-2202
Columbus *(G-6804)*
Comcorp Inc..............B....... 718 981-1234
Cleveland *(G-5000)*
Coshocton Community Choir..............G....... 740 623-0554
Coshocton *(G-7725)*
Cox Newspapers LLC..............G....... 513 523-4139
Oxford *(G-15692)*
Crain Communications Inc..............D....... 330 836-9180
Akron *(G-125)*
Daily Fostoria Review Co..............C....... 419 435-6641
Fostoria *(G-9836)*
Easy Side Publishing Co Inc..............G....... 216 721-1674
Cleveland *(G-5142)*
Farmland News LLC..............F....... 419 445-9456
Archbold *(G-645)*
Fostoria Focus Inc..............F....... 419 435-6397
Fostoria *(G-9842)*
Funny Times Inc..............G....... 216 371-8600
Cleveland *(G-5277)*
Gannett Co Inc..............E....... 740 654-1321
Lancaster *(G-11574)*
Gannett Co Inc..............C....... 740 773-2111
Chillicothe *(G-3188)*
Gannett Co Inc..............E....... 419 521-7341
Marion *(G-12703)*
Gannett Co Inc..............F....... 419 332-5511
Fremont *(G-10020)*
Gannett Co Inc..............F....... 740 349-1100
Newark *(G-14877)*
Harrison News Herald Inc..............F....... 740 942-2118
Cadiz *(G-2398)*
Impact Publications..............G....... 740 928-5541
Buckeye Lake *(G-2315)*
Indian Lake Shoppers Edge..............G....... 937 843-6600
Russells Point *(G-16600)*
Leader Publications Inc..............E....... 330 665-9595
Fairlawn *(G-9612)*
Louisville Herald Inc..............G....... 330 875-5610
Louisville *(G-12160)*
Marketing Essentials LLC..............F....... 419 629-0080
New Bremen *(G-14656)*
Mickens Inc..............G....... 419 533-2401
Liberty Center *(G-11809)*
Morgan County Publishing Co..............G....... 740 962-3377
McConnelsville *(G-13209)*
Napoleon Inc..............E....... 419 592-5055
Napoleon *(G-14552)*
Nomis Publications Inc..............F....... 330 965-2380
Youngstown *(G-20976)*
North Coast Business Journal..............G....... 419 734-4838
Port Clinton *(G-16254)*
Ocm LLC..............E....... 937 247-2700
Miamisburg *(G-13701)*
Ogden Newspapers Inc..............D....... 304 748-0606
Steubenville *(G-17546)*
Ogden Newspapers Inc..............G....... 330 629-6200
Warren *(G-19425)*
Ogden Newspapers Inc..............E....... 330 332-4601
Salem *(G-16764)*
Ogden Newspapers Inc..............D....... 740 283-4711
Steubenville *(G-17547)*
Ogden Newspapers Inc..............C....... 330 841-1600
Warren *(G-19426)*
Peebles Messenger Newspaper..............G....... 937 587-1451
Peebles *(G-15880)*
Reporter Newspaper Inc..............F....... 330 535-7061
Akron *(G-346)*
Rural Urban Record Inc..............G....... 440 236-8982
Columbia Station *(G-6447)*
Sdg News Group Inc..............F....... 419 929-3411
New London *(G-14737)*
Shelby Daily Globe Inc..............E....... 419 342-4276
Shelby *(G-16988)*
Sidney Alive..............G....... 937 210-2539
Sidney *(G-17077)*
Smart Business Network Inc..............E....... 440 250-7000
Cleveland *(G-6071)*
Sugarcreek Budget Publishers..............F....... 330 852-4634
Sugarcreek *(G-17867)*
Telegram..............F....... 740 286-3604
Jackson *(G-11197)*
Toledo Journal..............G....... 419 472-4521
Toledo *(G-18560)*
Travelers Vacation Guide..............G....... 440 582-4949
North Royalton *(G-15306)*
Tribune Printing Inc..............G....... 419 542-7764
Hicksville *(G-10785)*
Voice Media Group Inc..............D....... 216 241-7550
Cleveland *(G-6268)*
Weekly Villager Inc..............G....... 330 527-5761
Garrettsville *(G-10204)*
Welch Publishing Co..............G....... 419 666-5344
Rossford *(G-16594)*
Willard Times Junction..............F....... 419 935-0184
Willard *(G-20249)*
Winkler Co Inc..............G....... 937 294-2662
Dayton *(G-8596)*

PUBLISHERS: Pamphlets, No Printing

Neola Inc..............G....... 330 926-0514
Stow *(G-17614)*

PUBLISHERS: Periodical, With Printing

American Ceramic Society..............E....... 614 890-4700
Westerville *(G-19977)*
Hacienda Publications LLC..............G....... 216 202-5440
Euclid *(G-9419)*
Incorporated Trst Gspl Wk Scty..............D....... 216 749-2100
Cleveland *(G-5448)*
SC Solutions Inc..............G....... 614 317-7119
Grove City *(G-10465)*

PUBLISHERS: Periodicals, Magazines

AGS Custom Graphics Inc..............D....... 330 963-7770
Macedonia *(G-12275)*
Alcohol & Drug Addiction Svcs..............E....... 216 348-4830
Cleveland *(G-4652)*

Employee Codes: A=Over 500 employees, B=251-500
C=101-250, D=51-100, E=20-50, F=10-19, G=3-9
2019 Harris Ohio
Industrial Directory
1563

PUBLISHERS: Periodicals, Magazines

American Heart Association Inc ....F 419 740-6180
  Maumee *(G-13070)*
Buckeye Prep Report Magazine ....G 614 855-6977
  New Albany *(G-14612)*
Center For Inquiry Inc ....G 330 671-7192
  Peninsula *(G-15890)*
Charlotte M Peters 216 798-8997
  Cleveland *(G-4912)*
City Girl Magazine LLC ....G 216 481-4110
  Cleveland *(G-4929)*
Clipper Magazine LLC 937 534-0470
  Moraine *(G-14338)*
Communication Resources Inc ....E 800 992-2144
  Canton *(G-2633)*
Crain Communications Inc ....D 330 836-9180
  Akron *(G-125)*
Dispatch Printing Company ....E 614 885-6020
  Columbus *(G-6868)*
Dominion Enterprises ....E 216 472-1870
  Cleveland *(G-5105)*
Family Values Magazine ....G 419 566-1102
  Mansfield *(G-12438)*
Graphicom Press Inc ....G 937 767-1916
  Yellow Springs *(G-20806)*
Greater Cincinnati Bowl Assn ....E 513 761-7387
  Cincinnati *(G-3780)*
In Box Publications LLC ....G 330 592-4288
  Akron *(G-215)*
Institute Mthmtical Statistics ....G 216 295-2340
  Shaker Heights *(G-16932)*
Kaleidoscope Magazine LLC ....E 216 566-5500
  Cleveland *(G-5515)*
Kent Information Services Inc ....G 330 672-2110
  Kent *(G-11342)*
Lavish Lyfe Magazine ....G 937 938-5816
  Dayton *(G-8307)*
Legal News Publishing Co ....E 216 696-3322
  Cleveland *(G-5572)*
Marketing Directions Inc ....G 440 835-5550
  Cleveland *(G-5621)*
Matthew Bender & Company Inc ....C 518 487-3000
  Miamisburg *(G-13686)*
Ohio State University ....F 614 292-1462
  Columbus *(G-7262)*
Pearson Education Inc 614 876-0371
  Columbus *(G-7303)*
Pearson Education Inc ....F 614 841-3700
  Columbus *(G-7304)*
Reel Image ....G 937 296-9036
  Dayton *(G-8468)*
Relx Inc ....F 937 865-6800
  Miamisburg *(G-13709)*
Rubber World Magazine Inc ....F 330 864-2122
  Akron *(G-357)*
Sesh Communications ....F 513 851-1693
  Cincinnati *(G-4326)*
Sterling Associates Inc ....G 330 630-3500
  Akron *(G-389)*
Target Printing & Graphics ....G 937 228-0170
  Dayton *(G-8539)*
Telex Communications Inc ....F 419 865-0972
  Toledo *(G-18546)*
University Sports Publications ....E 614 291-6416
  Columbus *(G-7564)*
Vela ....G 614 500-0150
  Salesville *(G-16784)*
Welch Publishing Co 419 874-2528
  Perrysburg *(G-16025)*

PUBLISHERS: Periodicals, No Printing

Agri Communicators Inc ....E 614 273-0465
  Columbus *(G-6551)*
American Lawyers Co Inc ....F 440 333-5190
  Westlake *(G-20092)*
Asm International ....D 440 338-5151
  Novelty *(G-15438)*
C & S Associates Inc ....E 440 461-9661
  Highland Heights *(G-10786)*
Gongwer News Service Inc ....G 614 221-1992
  Columbus *(G-6960)*
Gongwer News Service Inc ....G 614 221-1992
  Columbus *(G-6961)*
Graphic Publications Inc ....G 330 674-2300
  Millersburg *(G-14085)*
Indicator Advisory Corporation ....G 419 726-9000
  Toledo *(G-18345)*
Lorenz Corporation ....D 937 228-6118
  Dayton *(G-8316)*
Northeast Scene Inc ....E 216 241-7550
  Cleveland *(G-5776)*

Ohio Designer Craftsmen Entps ....F 614 486-7119
  Columbus *(G-7245)*

PUBLISHERS: Sheet Music

Great Works Publishing Inc ....F 440 926-1100
  Grafton *(G-10303)*
Thunder Dreamer Publishing ....G 419 424-2004
  Findlay *(G-9770)*
Willis Music Company ....F 513 671-3288
  Cincinnati *(G-4511)*

PUBLISHERS: Technical Manuals

ONeil & Associates Inc ....B 937 865-0800
  Miamisburg *(G-13704)*

PUBLISHERS: Technical Manuals & Papers

Fgm Media Inc ....G 440 376-0487
  North Royalton *(G-15272)*
Prowrite Inc 614 864-2004
  Reynoldsburg *(G-16450)*
Walter H Drane Co Inc ....G 216 514-1022
  Beachwood *(G-1285)*

PUBLISHERS: Telephone & Other Directory

B G News ....E 419 372-2601
  Bowling Green *(G-1952)*
Propress Inc ....F 216 631-8200
  Cleveland *(G-5929)*

PUBLISHERS: Television Schedules, No Printing

Virtus Stunts LLC ....G 440 543-0472
  Chagrin Falls *(G-3089)*

PUBLISHERS: Textbooks, No Printing

Leap Publishing Services Inc ....F 234 738-0082
  Stow *(G-17600)*
Neal Publications Inc ....G 419 874-4787
  Perrysburg *(G-15980)*
Scott Fetzer Company ....F 440 892-3000
  Westlake *(G-20156)*

PUBLISHERS: Trade journals, No Printing

Gardner Business Media Inc ....E 513 527-8800
  Cincinnati *(G-3727)*
Lippincott & Peto Inc ....F 330 864-2122
  Akron *(G-254)*
Lyle Printing & Publishing Co ....G 330 337-3419
  Salem *(G-16756)*
Lyle Printing & Publishing Co ....F 330 337-7172
  Salem *(G-16757)*
Relx Inc ....E 937 865-6800
  Miamisburg *(G-13708)*

PUBLISHING & BROADCASTING: Internet Only

3dnsew LLC ....G 740 618-8005
  Newark *(G-14846)*
Ahalogy ....E 314 974-5599
  Cincinnati *(G-3311)*
Clark Optimization LLC ....E 330 417-2164
  Canton *(G-2627)*
Deemsys Inc ....D 614 322-9928
  Gahanna *(G-10079)*
Dotcentral LLC ....F 330 809-0112
  Massillon *(G-12974)*
Evans Creative Group LLC ....G 614 657-9439
  Columbus *(G-6909)*
IPA Ltd ....F 614 523-3974
  Columbus *(G-7048)*
Latte Living ....G 440 364-2201
  Cleveland *(G-5564)*
Marketing Essentials LLC ....F 419 629-0080
  New Bremen *(G-14656)*
Pixslap Inc ....G 937 559-2671
  Middletown *(G-13942)*
Quadriga Americas LLC ....G 614 890-6090
  Westerville *(G-20018)*
Thickemz Entertainment LLC ....F 404 399-4255
  Cuyahoga Falls *(G-7928)*

PUBLISHING & PRINTING: Art Copy

Powerhouse Factories Inc ....F 513 719-6417
  Cincinnati *(G-4178)*

Publishing Group Ltd ....F 614 572-1240
  Columbus *(G-7356)*

PUBLISHING & PRINTING: Book Music

Swagg Productions2015llc ....F 614 815-1173
  Reynoldsburg *(G-16455)*

PUBLISHING & PRINTING: Books

Bearing Precious Seed ....G 513 575-1706
  Milford *(G-13996)*
Gardner Business Media Inc ....E 513 527-8800
  Cincinnati *(G-3727)*
Hamilton Arts Inc ....G 937 767-1834
  Yellow Springs *(G-20807)*
Kendall/Hunt Publishing Co ....D 877 275-4725
  Cincinnati *(G-3904)*
Kid Concoctions Company ....G 440 572-1800
  Strongsville *(G-17760)*
Manifest Productions LLC ....G 614 806-3054
  Columbus *(G-7147)*
Marysville Newspaper Inc ....E 937 644-9111
  Marysville *(G-12799)*
McGraw-Hill School Education H ....B 419 207-7400
  Ashland *(G-724)*
Simon & Schuster Inc ....C 614 876-0371
  Columbus *(G-7453)*
World Harvest Church Inc ....B 614 837-1990
  Canal Winchester *(G-2516)*

PUBLISHING & PRINTING: Directories, NEC

Dickman Directories Inc ....G 740 548-6130
  Lewis Center *(G-11755)*
Haines & Company Inc ....C 330 494-9111
  North Canton *(G-15090)*
Haines Publishing Inc ....D 330 494-9111
  Canton *(G-2691)*
Lsc Communications Inc ....A 419 935-0111
  Willard *(G-20241)*

PUBLISHING & PRINTING: Directories, Telephone

Berry Company ....G 513 768-7800
  Cincinnati *(G-3392)*
User Friendly Phone Book LLC ....E 216 674-6500
  Independence *(G-11154)*

PUBLISHING & PRINTING: Guides

Beaver Productions ....G 330 352-4603
  Akron *(G-82)*
Trogdon Publishing Inc ....E 330 721-7678
  Medina *(G-13355)*

PUBLISHING & PRINTING: Magazines: publishing & printing

614 Media Group LLC ....D 614 488-4400
  Columbus *(G-6513)*
A R Harding Publishing Co ....F 614 231-5735
  Columbus *(G-6516)*
Advanced Media Corporation ....F 440 260-9910
  Cleveland *(G-4629)*
Angstrom Graphics Inc ....G 216 271-5300
  Cleveland *(G-4716)*
Bluffton News Pubg & Prtg Co ....E 419 358-8010
  Bluffton *(G-1884)*
Carmel Trader Publishing Inc ....E 330 478-9200
  Canton *(G-2620)*
Cars and Parts Magazine ....C 937 498-0803
  Sidney *(G-17021)*
Cruisin Times Magazine ....G 440 331-4615
  Rocky River *(G-16544)*
Curt Harler Inc ....G 440 238-4556
  Cleveland *(G-5044)*
Downey Enterprises Inc ....G 740 587-4258
  Granville *(G-10329)*
Family Motor Coach Assn Inc ....C 513 474-3622
  Cincinnati *(G-3671)*
Highlights For Children Inc ....C 614 486-0631
  Hilliard *(G-10828)*
Horizon Communications Inc ....G 330 968-6959
  Twinsburg *(G-18792)*
Housetrends ....G 513 794-4103
  Blue Ash *(G-1789)*
Kenyon Review ....G 740 427-5208
  Gambier *(G-10182)*
Marula Publishing LLC ....G 513 549-5218
  Cincinnati *(G-3984)*

PRODUCT SECTION

PUBLISHING & PRINTING: Newspapers

Company	Code	Phone
Midwest Exposure Magazine	G	937 626-6738
Dayton (G-8352)		
Morrison Media Group-Cmj LLP	G	216 973-4005
Cleveland (G-5706)		
New Track Media LLC	F	513 421-6500
Blue Ash (G-1825)		
North Coast Minority Media LLC	E	216 407-4327
Cleveland (G-5769)		
Open House Magazine Inc	G	614 523-7775
Columbus (G-7272)		
Peninsula Publishing LLC	G	330 524-3359
Akron (G-316)		
Prehistoric Antiquities	G	937 747-2225
North Lewisburg (G-15164)		
Publishing Group Ltd	F	614 572-1240
Columbus (G-7356)		
Quad/Graphics Inc	A	513 932-1064
Lebanon (G-11687)		
Sabre Publishing	G	440 243-4300
Berea (G-1624)		
Venue Lifestyle & Event Guide	F	513 405-6822
Cincinnati (G-4475)		
Youngs Publishing Inc	F	937 259-6575
Beavercreek (G-1347)		

PUBLISHING & PRINTING: Newsletters, Business Svc

Company	Code	Phone
Matly Digital Solutions LLC	G	513 860-3435
Fairfield (G-9526)		
Questline Inc	E	614 255-3166
Dublin (G-8971)		

PUBLISHING & PRINTING: Newspapers

Company	Code	Phone
Abecs Community News	G	419 330-9658
Swanton (G-17903)		
Active Daily Living LLC	G	513 607-6769
Cincinnati (G-3295)		
Ada Herald	G	419 634-6055
Ada (G-2)		
Adams Publishing Group LLC	F	740 592-6612
Athens (G-821)		
Adult Daily Living LLC	G	330 612-7941
Coventry Township (G-7761)		
Alliance Publishing Co Inc	G	330 453-1304
Alliance (G-454)		
American Jrnl of Drmtpathology	G	440 542-0041
Solon (G-17106)		
Amos Media Company	C	937 498-2111
Sidney (G-17015)		
Ashland Publishing Co	A	419 281-0581
Ashland (G-680)		
Atrium At Anna Maria Inc	G	330 562-7777
Aurora (G-870)		
Augdon Newspapers of Ohio Inc	F	419 448-3200
Tiffin (G-18048)		
Barbara A Eisenhardt	G	614 436-9690
Columbus (G-6647)		
Becky Brisker	G	614 266-6575
Columbus (G-6659)		
Block Communications Inc	F	419 724-6212
Toledo (G-18206)		
Bloomville Gazette Inc	G	419 426-3491
Attica (G-855)		
Brecksville Broadview Gazette	E	440 526-7977
Brecksville (G-2024)		
Bryan Publishing Company	D	419 636-1111
Bryan (G-2274)		
Bryan Publishing Company	G	419 485-3113
Montpelier (G-14302)		
Buckeye Lake Shopper Reporter	G	740 246-4741
Thornville (G-18030)		
Business First Columbus Inc	E	614 461-4040
Columbus (G-6715)		
Business Journal	F	330 744-5023
Youngstown (G-20862)		
Cathie D Hubbard	E	937 593-0316
Bellefontaine (G-1509)		
Central Ohio Printing Corp	D	740 852-1616
London (G-12052)		
Cincinnati Enquirer	E	513 721-2700
Cincinnati (G-3491)		
Cincinnati Ftn Sq News Inc	F	513 421-4049
Mason (G-12841)		
Citizens USA	G	937 280-2001
Dayton (G-8092)		
Clair Zeits	G	419 643-8980
Columbus Grove (G-7633)		
Columbus Alive Inc	F	614 221-2449
Columbus (G-6783)		
Columbus Messenger Company	G	740 852-0809
London (G-12055)		
Construction Bulletin Inc	G	330 782-3733
Youngstown (G-20879)		
Consumers News Services Inc	C	740 888-6000
Columbus (G-6811)		
Consumers News Services Inc	G	614 875-2307
Grove City (G-10422)		
Coshocton Community Choir Inc	G	740 622-8571
Coshocton (G-7726)		
Cox Media Group Ohio Inc	G	937 743-6700
Dayton (G-8106)		
Cox Newspapers LLC	E	513 696-4500
Liberty Township (G-11812)		
Cox Newspapers LLC	F	937 866-3331
Miamisburg (G-13652)		
Cox Newspapers LLC	D	937 225-2000
Dayton (G-8107)		
Cox Newspapers LLC	D	513 863-8200
Liberty Township (G-11813)		
Cross Communications Inc	G	937 304-0010
Vandalia (G-19120)		
Cuyahoga Co Med Examiner S Off	G	216 721-5610
Cleveland (G-5053)		
Daily Agency Inc	F	937 456-9808
Eaton (G-9147)		
Daily Dog	G	419 708-4923
Holland (G-10924)		
Daily Gazette	E	937 372-4444
Xenia (G-20764)		
Daily Growler Inc	G	614 656-2337
Upper Arlington (G-18944)		
Daily Legal News Inc	G	330 747-7777
Youngstown (G-20885)		
Daily Needs Assistance	F	614 824-8340
Plain City (G-16184)		
Daily Needs Personal Care LLC	G	614 598-8383
Ashville (G-817)		
Daily Reporter	E	614 224-4835
Columbus (G-6846)		
Daily Squawk LLC	G	937 426-6247
Dayton (G-7976)		
Dayton City Paper New LLC	F	937 222-8855
Dayton (G-8129)		
Dayton Weekly News	G	937 223-8060
Dayton (G-8147)		
Delphos Herald Inc	D	419 695-0015
Delphos (G-8738)		
Delphos Herald Inc	G	419 399-4015
Paulding (G-15859)		
Delphos Herald Inc	G	419 695-0015
Delphos (G-8739)		
Dog Daily	G	216 624-0735
Cleveland (G-5103)		
Dow Jones & Company Inc	E	419 352-4696
Bowling Green (G-1970)		
Eastern Ohio Newspapers Inc	G	740 633-1131
Martins Ferry (G-12760)		
Erie Chinese Journal	G	216 324-2959
Twinsburg (G-18770)		
Euclid Media Group LLC	G	216 241-7550
Cleveland (G-5197)		
Fremont Discover Ltd	G	419 332-8696
Fremont (G-10018)		
Gannett Co Inc	G	740 345-4053
Newark (G-14876)		
Gannett Co Inc	D	513 721-2700
Cincinnati (G-3723)		
Gannett Co Inc	D	740 452-4561
Zanesville (G-21141)		
Gannett Co Inc	C	419 522-3311
Mansfield (G-12443)		
Gate West Coast Ventures LLC	F	513 891-1000
Blue Ash (G-1781)		
Gazette Publishing Company	G	419 483-4190
Oberlin (G-15495)		
Graphic Publications Inc	D	330 343-4377
Dover (G-8828)		
Heartland Education Community	F	330 684-3034
Orrville (G-15593)		
Heartland Publications LLC	F	740 446-2342
Gallipolis (G-10167)		
Herald Looms	G	330 948-1080
Lodi (G-12012)		
Highschoolball Inc	G	330 321-8536
Hinckley (G-10901)		
Hirt Publishing Co Inc	E	419 946-3010
Mount Gilead (G-14426)		
Hirt Publishing Co Inc	F	419 523-5709
Ottawa (G-15653)		
Holmes County Hub Inc	G	330 674-1811
Millersburg (G-14097)		
Horizon Publications Inc	G	419 628-2369
Minster (G-14217)		
Horizon Publications Inc	E	419 738-2128
Wapakoneta (G-19333)		
Huron Hometown News	G	419 433-1401
Huron (G-11097)		
Ironton Publications Inc	A	740 532-1441
Ironton (G-11166)		
Jewish Journal Monthly Mag	G	330 746-3251
Youngstown (G-20948)		
Job News USA	F	614 310-1700
Columbus (G-7070)		
Journal Register Company	C	440 951-0000
Willoughby (G-20349)		
Journal Register Company	C	440 245-6901
Lorain (G-12096)		
Kent State University	G	330 672-2586
Kent (G-11345)		
La Voz Hispania Newspaper	G	614 274-5505
Columbus (G-7109)		
Lake Community News	G	440 946-2577
Willoughby (G-20357)		
Lakewood Observer Inc	G	216 712-7070
Lakewood (G-11526)		
Legal News Publishing Co	E	216 696-3322
Cleveland (G-5572)		
Lets Golf Daily Inc	G	330 966-3373
North Canton (G-15097)		
Mansfield Journal Co	G	330 364-8641
New Philadelphia (G-14782)		
Mark Daily	G	937 369-5358
Eaton (G-9161)		
Marysville Monument Company	G	937 642-7039
Marysville (G-12798)		
Marysville Newspaper Inc	E	937 644-9111
Marysville (G-12799)		
Medina County Publications Inc	G	330 721-4040
Medina (G-13293)		
Messenger Publishing Company	C	740 592-6612
Athens (G-839)		
Mickens Inc	G	419 943-2590
Leipsic (G-11729)		
Middletownusacom	G	513 594-2831
Middletown (G-13971)		
Mirror Publishing Co Inc	E	419 893-8135
Maumee (G-13135)		
Monroe County Beacon Inc	F	740 472-0734
Woodsfield (G-20547)		
Neighborhood News Pubg Co	G	216 441-2141
Cleveland (G-5734)		
Newark Downtown Center Inc	G	740 403-5454
Newark (G-14902)		
News Watchman & Paper	F	740 947-2149
Waverly (G-19553)		
Newspaper Holding Inc	G	440 998-2323
Ashtabula (G-792)		
Newspaper Network Central OH	G	419 524-3545
Mansfield (G-12491)		
Northeast Suburban Life	E	513 248-8600
Cincinnati (G-4087)		
Ohio Community Media	G	740 848-4064
Fredericktown (G-9974)		
Ohio Newspaper Services Inc	G	614 486-6677
Columbus (G-7252)		
Ohio Newspapers Foundation	G	614 486-6677
Columbus (G-7253)		
Ohio Rights Group	G	614 300-0529
Columbus (G-7257)		
Ohio University	C	740 593-4010
Athens (G-843)		
Pataskala Post	F	740 964-6226
Pataskala (G-15837)		
Patriot	G	419 864-8411
Cardington (G-2875)		
Perry County Tribune	F	740 342-4121
New Lexington (G-14720)		
Photo Star	G	419 495-2696
Willshire (G-20482)		
Pickaway News Journal	G	740 851-3072
Circleville (G-4552)		
Plain Dealer Publishing Co	F	216 999-5000
Cleveland (G-5882)		
Plain Dealer Publishing Co	G	614 228-8200
Columbus (G-7319)		
Post Newspapers	G	330 721-7678
Medina (G-13321)		
Pride of Geneva	G	440 466-5695
Chagrin Falls (G-3069)		

Employee Codes: A=Over 500 employees, B=251-500
C=101-250, D=51-100, E=20-50, F=10-19, G=3-9

PUBLISHING & PRINTING: Newspapers

Pulse Journal .... E 513 829-7900
  Liberty Township (G-11817)
Richardson Publishing Company ...... F 330 753-1068
  Barberton (G-1102)
Robert Tuneberg .... G 440 899-9277
  Bay Village (G-1209)
Roman Cthlic Docese Youngstown .... G 330 744-8451
  Youngstown (G-21021)
Scripps Media Inc .... D 513 977-3000
  Cincinnati (G-4310)
Sesh Communications .... E 513 851-1693
  Cincinnati (G-4326)
Seven Hills Reporter .... G 216 524-9515
  Seven Hills (G-16906)
Sojourners Truth .... F 419 243-0007
  Toledo (G-18525)
Star Newspaper .... E 614 622-5930
  Columbus (G-7486)
Summit Street News Inc .... G 330 609-5600
  Warren (G-19444)
Syracuse China Company .... C 419 727-2100
  Toledo (G-18539)
The Beacon Journal Pubg Co .... C 330 996-3000
  Akron (G-400)
The Gazette Printing Co Inc .... D 440 576-9125
  Jefferson (G-11240)
Time 4 You .... G 614 593-2695
  Columbus (G-7530)
Times Bulletin Media .... F 419 238-2285
  Van Wert (G-19107)
Timothy C Georges .... G 330 933-9114
  North Canton (G-15129)
Trading Post .... G 740 922-1199
  Uhrichsville (G-18898)
Venice Cornerstone Newspaper .... G 513 738-7151
  Hamilton (G-10617)
Village Reporter .... G 419 485-4851
  Montpelier (G-14320)
Village Voice Publishing Ltd .... G 419 537-0286
  Toledo (G-18593)
Vindicator Printing Company .... D 330 744-8611
  Youngstown (G-21065)
Vindicator Printing Company .... G 330 392-0176
  Warren (G-19456)
Weirton Daily Times .... F 740 283-4711
  Steubenville (G-17557)
World Journal .... G 216 458-0988
  Cleveland (G-6325)
Your Daily Motivation Ydm Fitn ..... G 440 954-1038
  Painesville (G-15804)
Zanesville Newspaper .... G 740 452-4561
  Zanesville (G-21192)

PUBLISHING & PRINTING: Pamphlets

Communication Resources Inc .... E 800 992-2144
  Canton (G-2633)
Design Avenue Inc .... G 330 487-5280
  Twinsburg (G-18763)
J S C Publishing .... G 614 424-6911
  Columbus (G-7056)

PUBLISHING & PRINTING: Periodical Statistical Reports

City of Parma .... G 440 885-8816
  Cleveland (G-4932)

PUBLISHING & PRINTING: Posters

Posterservice Incorporated .... E 513 577-7100
  Cincinnati (G-4176)
Woodburn Press LLC .... G 937 293-9245
  Dayton (G-8599)

PUBLISHING & PRINTING: Shopping News

M Grafix LLC .... F 419 528-8665
  Mansfield (G-12471)

PUBLISHING & PRINTING: Technical Papers

Ohio Printed Products Inc .... F 330 659-0909
  Richfield (G-16478)
SC Solutions Inc .... G 614 317-7119
  Grove City (G-10465)

PUBLISHING & PRINTING: Textbooks

Spanish Lngage Productions Inc ...... G 614 737-3424
  Alexandria (G-443)

PUBLISHING & PRINTING: Trade Journals

Benjamin Media Inc .... E 330 467-7588
  Brecksville (G-2022)
Ohio Association Realtors Inc .... E 614 228-6675
  Columbus (G-7241)

PULLEYS: Metal

Industrial Pulley & Machine Co .... G 937 355-4910
  West Mansfield (G-19942)
J L R Products Inc .... F 330 832-9557
  Massillon (G-13004)

PULLEYS: Power Transmission

A J Rose Mfg Co .... C 216 631-4645
  Avon (G-936)
A J Rose Mfgco .... C 216 631-4645
  Cleveland (G-4590)
Dependable Gear Corp .... G 440 942-4969
  Eastlake (G-9103)
J L R Products Inc .... F 330 832-9557
  Massillon (G-13004)

PULP MILLS

Caraustar Industries Inc .... E 216 961-5060
  Cleveland (G-4873)
Caraustar Industries Inc .... D 740 862-4167
  Baltimore (G-1037)
Newpage Holding Corporation .... G 877 855-7243
  Miamisburg (G-13699)
Polymer Tech & Svcs Inc .... E 740 929-5500
  Heath (G-10727)
Rumpke Transportation Co LLC ...... C 513 242-4600
  Cincinnati (G-4289)
Verso Corporation .... D 901 369-4105
  Miamisburg (G-13733)
Waste Parchment Inc .... E 330 674-6868
  Millersburg (G-14147)

PULP MILLS: Mechanical & Recycling Processing

Flegal Brothers Inc .... F 419 298-3539
  Edgerton (G-9175)
Green Recycling Works LLC .... G 513 278-7111
  Cincinnati (G-3781)
Riverview Productions Inc .... G 740 441-1150
  Gallipolis (G-10174)
World Wide Recyclers Inc .... F 614 554-3296
  Columbus (G-7613)

PUMP SLEEVES: Rubber

Precision Component & Mch Inc ..... C 740 867-6366
  Chesapeake (G-3147)

PUMPS

A P O Holdings Inc .... E 330 455-8925
  Canton (G-2556)
Advanced Fuel Systems Inc .... G 614 252-8422
  Columbus (G-6545)
All - Flo Pump Company .... E 440 354-1700
  Mentor (G-13382)
Belden Brick Company .... E 330 852-2411
  Sugarcreek (G-17842)
Bergstrom Company Ltd Partnr .... E 440 232-2282
  Cleveland (G-4805)
Blue Chip Pump Inc .... G 513 871-7867
  Cincinnati (G-3396)
Chaos Entertainment .... G 937 520-5260
  Dayton (G-8086)
Cleveland Plastic Fabricat .... F 216 797-7300
  Euclid (G-9409)
Dreison International Inc .... C 216 362-0755
  Cleveland (G-5113)
Eaton-Aeroquip Llc .... D 419 891-7775
  Maumee (G-13109)
Eco-Flo Products Inc .... F 877 326-3561
  Ashland (G-703)
Electro-Mechanical Mfg Co Inc .... G 330 864-0717
  Akron (G-149)
Excel Fluid Group LLC .... F 800 892-2009
  Cleveland (G-5205)
Flow Control US Holding Corp .... G 800 843-5628
  Cincinnati (G-3698)
Flow Control US Holding Corp .... G 419 289-1144
  Ashland (G-704)
Frantz Medical Development Ltd .... D 440 205-9026
  Mentor (G-13448)
General Electric Company .... D 216 883-1000
  Cleveland (G-5306)
Giant Industries Inc .... E 419 531-4600
  Toledo (G-18305)
Gorman-Rupp Company .... G 419 755-1245
  Mansfield (G-12449)
Hugo Vglsang Maschinenbau GMBH .. E 330 296-3820
  Ravenna (G-16382)
Hurst Auto-Truck Electric .... C 216 961-1800
  Cleveland (G-5426)
Ingersoll-Rand Company .... E 419 633-6800
  Bryan (G-2291)
Keen Pump Company Inc .... E 419 207-9400
  Ashland (G-716)
M T Systems Inc .... G 330 453-4646
  Canton (G-2738)
Magnum Piering Inc .... E 513 759-3348
  West Chester (G-19874)
Neptune Chemical Pump Company .. G 513 870-3239
  West Chester (G-19748)
Pentair .... F 440 248-0100
  Solon (G-17215)
Pentair Flow Technologies LLC ...... C 419 289-1144
  Ashland (G-734)
Preferred Global Equipment LLC .... D 513 530-5800
  Cincinnati (G-4186)
Pyrotek Incorporated .... C 440 349-8800
  Aurora (G-901)
Quikstir Inc .... F 419 732-2601
  Port Clinton (G-16256)
Rumpke Transportation Co LLC ...... F 513 851-0122
  Cincinnati (G-4288)
Seepex Inc .... C 937 864-7150
  Enon (G-9386)
Stahl Gear & Machine Co .... E 216 431-2820
  Cleveland (G-6089)
Suburban Manufacturing Co .... G 440 953-2024
  Eastlake (G-9133)
Systecon LLC .... D 513 777-7722
  West Chester (G-19805)
T D Group Holdings LLC .... G 216 706-2939
  Cleveland (G-6144)
Tark Inc .... E 937 434-6766
  Dayton (G-8540)
Tolco Corporation .... D 419 241-1113
  Toledo (G-18555)
Tramec Sloan LLC .... F 419 468-9122
  Galion (G-10158)
Transdigm Inc .... F 216 291-6025
  Cleveland (G-6195)
Transdigm Inc .... E 440 352-6182
  Painesville (G-15791)
Vertiflo Pump Company .... F 513 530-0888
  Cincinnati (G-4478)
Vickers International Inc .... F 419 867-2200
  Maumee (G-13159)
Warren Rupp Inc .... C 419 524-8388
  Mansfield (G-12537)
Waterpro .... F 330 372-3565
  Warren (G-19462)

PUMPS & PARTS: Indl

A & F Machine Products Co .... E 440 826-0959
  Berea (G-1588)
Ayling and Reichert Co Consent ..... E 419 898-2471
  Oak Harbor (G-15441)
Cima Inc .... E 513 382-8976
  Hamilton (G-10546)
Crane Co .... C 330 337-7861
  Salem (G-16731)
Crane Pumps & Systems Inc .... B 937 773-2442
  Piqua (G-16108)
E R Advanced Ceramics Inc .... E 330 426-9433
  East Palestine (G-9077)
Fischer Global Enterprises LLC ...... E 513 583-4900
  Loveland (G-12187)
Flowserve Corporation .... G 513 874-6990
  Loveland (G-12188)
Flowserve Corporation .... D 937 226-4000
  Dayton (G-8200)
Fluid Automation Inc .... E 248 912-1970
  North Canton (G-15084)
Gerow Equipment Company Inc ...... E 216 383-8800
  Cleveland (G-5319)
Gorman-Rupp Company .... E 419 886-3001
  Bellville (G-12449)
Gorman-Rupp Company .... B 419 755-1011
  Mansfield (G-12448)
Gorman-Rupp Company .... B 419 755-1011
  Mansfield (G-12447)

PRODUCT SECTION — RADAR SYSTEMS & EQPT

Graphite Equipment Mfg Co ....G..... 216 271-9500
Solon *(G-17155)*
Hpc Manufacturing Inc ....G..... 440 322-8334
Lorain *(G-12095)*
Molten Mtal Eqp Innvations LLC ....E..... 440 632-9119
Middlefield *(G-13833)*
Pckd Enterprises Inc ....E..... 440 632-9119
Middlefield *(G-13844)*
Replica Engineering Inc ....F..... 216 252-2204
Cleveland *(G-5976)*
Ruthman Pump and Engineering ....G..... 513 559-1901
Cincinnati *(G-4291)*
Thieman Tailgates Inc............................D..... 419 586-7727
Celina *(G-2988)*
Valco Cincinnati Inc ....C..... 513 874-6550
West Chester *(G-19914)*

PUMPS & PUMPING EQPT REPAIR SVCS

Blue Chip Pump Inc ....G..... 513 871-7867
Cincinnati *(G-3396)*
Certified Labs & Service Inc ....G..... 419 289-7462
Ashland *(G-691)*
Ohio Electric Motor Svc LLC ....G..... 419 525-2225
Mansfield *(G-12496)*
Thirion Brothers Eqp Co LLC ....G..... 440 357-8004
Painesville *(G-15790)*
Tyler Electric Motor Repair ....G..... 330 836-5537
Akron *(G-417)*
Wm Plotz Machine and Forge Co ....F..... 216 861-0441
Cleveland *(G-6319)*

PUMPS & PUMPING EQPT WHOLESALERS

Armour Spray Systems Inc ....F..... 216 398-3838
Cleveland *(G-4735)*
Giant Industries Inc ....E..... 419 531-4600
Toledo *(G-18305)*
Gorman-Rupp Company ....G..... 419 755-1245
Mansfield *(G-12449)*
Hammelmann Corporation ....F..... 937 859-8777
Miamisburg *(G-13673)*
Motionsource International LLC............F..... 440 287-7037
Solon *(G-17198)*
Tyler Electric Motor Repair ....G..... 330 836-5537
Akron *(G-417)*

PUMPS: Domestic, Water Or Sump

Certified Labs & Service Inc ....G..... 419 289-7462
Ashland *(G-691)*
City of Newark ....F..... 740 349-6765
Newark *(G-14861)*
Hydromatic Pumps Inc............................A..... 419 289-1144
Ashland *(G-712)*
Lakecraft Inc..G..... 419 734-2828
Port Clinton *(G-16249)*
Wayne/Scott Fetzer Company ....C..... 800 237-0987
Harrison *(G-10679)*

PUMPS: Fluid Power

Alkid Corporation....................................G..... 216 896-3000
Cleveland *(G-4662)*
All - Flo Pump Company ....E..... 440 354-1700
Mentor *(G-13382)*
Custom Cltch Jint Hydrlics Inc ....F..... 216 431-1630
Cleveland *(G-5046)*
Eaton Hydraulics LLC...............................E..... 419 232-7777
Van Wert *(G-19088)*
Opw Inc ....A..... 800 422-2525
West Chester *(G-19755)*
Parker-Hannifin Corporation ....C..... 330 740-8366
Youngstown *(G-20994)*
Parker-Hannifin Corporation ....F..... 216 896-3000
Macedonia *(G-12314)*
Parker-Hannifin Corporation ....E..... 440 266-2300
Mentor *(G-13542)*
Parker-Hannifin Corporation ....F..... 216 896-3000
Cleveland *(G-5850)*
Parker-Hannifin Corporation ....B..... 216 896-3000
Cleveland *(G-5848)*
Suburban Manufacturing Co..................D..... 440 953-2024
Eastlake *(G-9133)*
Vertiflo Pump Company ....F..... 513 530-0888
Cincinnati *(G-4478)*

PUMPS: Gasoline, Measuring Or Dispensing

Field Stone Inc ....D..... 937 898-3236
Tipp City *(G-18112)*

PUMPS: Hydraulic Power Transfer

Bosch Rexroth Corporation ....B..... 330 263-3300
Wooster *(G-20573)*
Eaton Corporation ....B..... 440 523-5000
Cleveland *(G-5146)*
Linde Hydraulics Corporation ....E..... 330 533-6801
Canfield *(G-2532)*
Parker-Hannifin Corporation ....C..... 937 644-3915
Marysville *(G-12805)*
R & L Hydraulics Inc ....G..... 937 399-3407
Springfield *(G-17478)*

PUMPS: Measuring & Dispensing

Bandit Machine Inc ....G..... 419 281-6595
Ashland *(G-683)*
Bergstrom Company Ltd Partnr ....E..... 440 232-2282
Cleveland *(G-4805)*
Cohesant Inc..E..... 216 910-1700
Beachwood *(G-1228)*
Gojo Industries Inc ....C..... 330 255-6000
Akron *(G-189)*
Gojo Industries Inc ....C..... 330 255-6525
Stow *(G-17593)*
Gojo Industries Inc ....C..... 330 922-4522
Cuyahoga Falls *(G-7874)*
Graco Ohio Inc ....D..... 330 494-1313
North Canton *(G-15088)*
Hydro Systems Company ....E..... 513 271-8800
Milford *(G-14017)*
Hydro Systems Company ....E..... 513 271-8800
Cincinnati *(G-3832)*
Neptune Chemical Pump Company ....E..... 513 870-3239
West Chester *(G-19748)*
Porto Pump Inc ....G..... 740 454-2576
Zanesville *(G-21170)*
Precision Conveyor Technology ....F..... 440 352-3601
Perry *(G-15911)*
Seepex Inc ....C..... 937 864-7150
Enon *(G-9386)*
Tolco Corporation ....D..... 419 241-1113
Toledo *(G-18555)*
Tranzonic Companies ....B..... 216 535-4300
Richmond Heights *(G-16507)*
Valco Cincinnati Inc ....C..... 513 874-6550
West Chester *(G-19914)*
Valco Cincinnati Inc ....G..... 513 874-6550
West Chester *(G-19915)*

PUMPS: Oil Well & Field

General Electric Intl Inc ....E..... 330 963-2066
Twinsburg *(G-18783)*
Tat Pumps Inc..G..... 740 385-0008
Nelsonville *(G-14600)*
Westerman Inc ....D..... 330 262-6946
Wooster *(G-20665)*

PUMPS: Oil, Measuring Or Dispensing

Energy Manufacturing Ltd ....E..... 419 355-9304
Fremont *(G-10012)*

PUNCHES: Forming & Stamping

Cleveland Steel Tool Company..............E..... 216 681-7400
Cleveland *(G-4978)*
Dayton Progress Corporation................A..... 937 859-5111
Dayton *(G-8143)*
Miami Valley Punch & Mfg......................E..... 937 237-0533
Dayton *(G-8347)*
Porter Precision Products Co................D..... 513 385-1569
Cincinnati *(G-4173)*
Tipco Punch Inc ....E..... 513 874-9140
Hamilton *(G-10611)*
V I P Printing & Design ....G..... 513 777-7468
West Chester *(G-19913)*

PURCHASING SVCS

Canfield Industries Inc ....G..... 800 554-5071
Youngstown *(G-20864)*

PURIFICATION & DUST COLLECTION EQPT

Ceco Environmental Corp ....G..... 513 458-2606
Blue Ash *(G-1748)*
Ceco Group Global Holdings LLC..........G..... 513 458-2600
Cincinnati *(G-3453)*
Dreison International Inc......................C..... 216 362-0755
Cleveland *(G-5113)*

PURLINS: Steel, Light Gauge

Worthington Cnstr Group Inc ....G..... 216 472-1511
Cleveland *(G-6326)*
Worthington Mid-Rise Cnstr Inc ....E..... 216 472-1511
Cleveland *(G-6327)*

QUARTZ CRYSTAL MINING SVCS

Covia Holdings Corporation ....D..... 440 214-3284
Independence *(G-11123)*

QUARTZ CRYSTALS: Electronic

Quality Quartz Engineering Inc ....D..... 937 236-3250
Dayton *(G-8455)*
Quality Quartz of America Inc..............G..... 440 352-2851
Mentor *(G-13566)*
Quartz Scientific Inc ....E..... 360 574-6254
Fairport Harbor *(G-9628)*
Sawyer Technical Materials LLC ....E..... 440 951-8770
Willoughby *(G-20424)*
Schupp Advanced Materials LLC ....G..... 440 488-6416
Willoughby *(G-20426)*

QUILTING SVC & SPLYS, FOR THE TRADE

Angelics A Quilters Haven ....G..... 330 484-5480
Canton *(G-2573)*

RABBIT SLAUGHTERING & PROCESSING

Briarwood Valley Farms ....G..... 419 736-2298
Sullivan *(G-17880)*

RACEWAYS

Buckeye Raceway LLC...........................G..... 614 272-7888
Columbus *(G-6711)*
Highline Raceway LLC............................G..... 419 883-2042
Butler *(G-2375)*
Raceway Beverage LLC ....G..... 513 932-2214
Lebanon *(G-11688)*
Raceway Petroleum Inc ....G..... 440 989-2660
Lorain *(G-12115)*
State of Ohio Dayton Raceway ....G..... 937 237-7802
Dayton *(G-8526)*

RACKS & SHELVING: Household, Wood

Installed Building Pdts LLC ....E..... 614 308-9900
Columbus *(G-7029)*

RACKS: Display

Bates Metal Products Inc ....D..... 740 498-8371
Port Washington *(G-16267)*
Busch & Thiem Inc..................................E..... 419 625-7515
Sandusky *(G-16800)*
Dwayne Bennett Industries..................G..... 440 466-5724
Geneva *(G-10217)*
E2 Merchandising Inc ....E..... 513 860-5444
West Chester *(G-19849)*
Jhg Retail Services LLC ....F..... 216 447-0831
Cincinnati *(G-3872)*
Rack Processing Company Inc ....E..... 937 294-1911
Moraine *(G-14388)*
Unarco Material Handling Inc ....G..... 419 384-3211
Pandora *(G-15807)*
Zak Box Co Inc ....E..... 216 961-5636
Cleveland *(G-6337)*
Zukowski Rack Co ....G..... 440 942-5889
Willoughby *(G-20465)*

RACKS: Railroad Car, Vehicle Transportation, Steel

Smith Truck Cranes & Eqp Co ....F..... 330 929-3303
Cuyahoga Falls *(G-7919)*

RADAR SYSTEMS & EQPT

Decibel Research Inc.............................E..... 256 705-3341
Beavercreek *(G-1310)*
Dragoon Technologies Inc ....G..... 937 439-9223
Dayton *(G-8167)*
Escort Inc ....D..... 513 870-8500
West Chester *(G-19699)*
Valentine Research Inc ....E..... 513 984-8900
Blue Ash *(G-1864)*

Employee Codes: A=Over 500 employees, B=251-500
C=101-250, D=51-100, E=20-50, F=10-19, G=3-9

RADIO & TELEVISION COMMUNICATIONS EQUIPMENT

RADIO & TELEVISION COMMUNICATIONS EQUIPMENT

Accurate Electronics Inc .... C 330 682-7015
  Orrville *(G-15581)*
Commscope Technologies LLC .... C 216 272-0055
  Cleveland *(G-5006)*
Comrod Inc .... G 440 455-9186
  Westlake *(G-20107)*
Essential Pathways Ohio LLC .... G 330 518-3091
  Youngstown *(G-20900)*
Gatesair Inc .... G 513 459-3400
  Mason *(G-12875)*
Greyfield Industries Inc .... F 513 860-1785
  Trenton *(G-18620)*
Jason Wilson .... E 937 604-8209
  Tipp City *(G-18120)*
McClaflin Mobile Media LLC .... G 419 575-9367
  Bradner *(G-2014)*
Mentor Radio LLC .... G 216 265-2315
  Elyria *(G-9293)*
Ohio Semitronics Inc .... D 614 777-1005
  Hilliard *(G-10847)*
Prentke Romich Company .... C 330 262-1984
  Wooster *(G-20641)*
Rev38 LLC .... G 937 572-4000
  West Chester *(G-19781)*
Shenet LLC .... E 614 563-9600
  Columbus *(G-7445)*
Solar Con Inc .... G 419 865-5877
  Holland *(G-10958)*
T V Specialties Inc .... F 330 364-6678
  Dover *(G-8859)*
Tls Corp .... E 216 574-4759
  Cleveland *(G-6177)*
Track-It Systems .... G 513 522-0083
  Cincinnati *(G-4428)*
Transel Corporation .... G 513 897-3442
  Harveysburg *(G-10706)*
Valco Melton Inc .... E 513 874-6550
  West Chester *(G-19916)*

RADIO BROADCASTING & COMMUNICATIONS EQPT

Circle Prime Manufacturing .... E 330 923-0019
  Cuyahoga Falls *(G-7850)*
Imagine Communications Corp .... D 513 459-3400
  Mason *(G-12890)*
Manchik Engineering & Co .... G 740 927-4454
  Dublin *(G-8945)*
Maranatha Industries Inc .... G 419 263-2013
  Payne *(G-15873)*
Peterson Radio Inc .... G 937 549-3731
  Manchester *(G-12396)*
R L Drake Company .... D 937 746-4556
  Franklin *(G-9914)*

RADIO BROADCASTING STATIONS

Franklin Communications Inc .... D 614 459-9769
  Columbus *(G-6936)*
Iheartcommunications Inc .... G 740 335-0941
  Wshngtn CT Hs *(G-20728)*
Iheartcommunications Inc .... D 419 223-2060
  Lima *(G-11876)*
Sandusky Newspapers Inc .... C 419 625-5500
  Sandusky *(G-16845)*

RADIO COMMUNICATIONS: Airborne Eqpt

Quasonix Inc .... E 513 942-1287
  West Chester *(G-19775)*

RADIO COMMUNICATIONS: Carrier Eqpt

J Com Data Inc .... G 614 304-1455
  Pataskala *(G-15833)*
L-3 Cmmncations Nova Engrg Inc .... C 877 282-1168
  Mason *(G-12901)*

RADIO RECEIVER NETWORKS

Analynk Wireless LLC .... G 614 755-5091
  Columbus *(G-6599)*
Envision Radio MII .... F 216 831-3761
  Beachwood *(G-1236)*
Globecom Technologies Inc .... G 330 408-7008
  Canal Fulton *(G-2480)*

RADIO REPAIR & INSTALLATION SVCS

Peterson Radio Inc .... G 937 549-3731
  Manchester *(G-12396)*

RADIO, TELEVISION & CONSUMER ELECTRONICS STORES: Eqpt, NEC

House of Hindenach .... G 419 422-0392
  Findlay *(G-9707)*
Phantasm Vapors LLC .... G 513 248-2431
  Milford *(G-14032)*

RADIO, TV & CONSUMER ELEC STORES: Automotive Sound Eqpt

Electra Sound Inc .... D 216 433-9600
  Parma *(G-15817)*

RADIO, TV & CONSUMER ELEC STORES: High Fidelity Stereo Eqpt

ABC Appliance Inc .... E 419 693-4414
  Oregon *(G-15552)*
Bose Corporation .... G 614 475-8565
  Columbus *(G-6688)*
Tune Town Car Audio .... G 419 627-1100
  Sandusky *(G-16857)*

RADIO, TV/CONSUMER ELEC STORES: Antennas, Satellite Dish

Gadgets Manufacturing Co .... G 937 686-5371
  Huntsville *(G-11087)*

RADIOS WHOLESALERS

Peterson Radio Inc .... G 937 549-3731
  Manchester *(G-12396)*
T V Specialties Inc .... F 330 364-6678
  Dover *(G-8859)*

RAILINGS: Prefabricated, Metal

A & T Ornamental Iron Company .... G 937 859-6006
  Miamisburg *(G-13635)*
AT&f Advanced Metals LLC .... E 330 684-1122
  Cleveland *(G-4756)*
Beacon Metal Fabricators Inc .... F 216 391-7444
  Cleveland *(G-4798)*
Glas Ornamental Metals Inc .... G 330 753-0215
  Barberton *(G-1074)*
Hayes Bros Ornamental Ir Works .... F 419 531-1491
  Toledo *(G-18324)*

RAILINGS: Wood

L & L Ornamental Iron Co .... F 513 353-1930
  Cleves *(G-6369)*
LAtelier Custom Woodworking .... G 234 759-3359
  North Lima *(G-15175)*
Premium Panel & Tread .... G 330 695-9979
  Fredericksburg *(G-9955)*
Ufp Hamilton LLC .... F 513 285-7190
  Hamilton *(G-10616)*

RAILROAD CAR CUSTOMIZING SVCS

Transco Railway Products Inc .... E 419 726-3383
  Toledo *(G-18582)*

RAILROAD CAR RENTING & LEASING SVCS

Andersons Inc .... C 419 893-5050
  Maumee *(G-13072)*
Andersons Inc .... G 419 536-0460
  Toledo *(G-18184)*

RAILROAD CAR REPAIR SVCS

Andersons Inc .... C 419 893-5050
  Maumee *(G-13072)*
Andersons Inc .... G 419 536-0460
  Toledo *(G-18184)*
Jk-Co LLC .... E 419 422-5240
  Findlay *(G-9710)*
Norfolk Southern Corporation .... E 419 697-5070
  Oregon *(G-15563)*

RAILROAD CARGO LOADING & UNLOADING SVCS

Dale Lute Logging .... G 740 352-1779
  Mc Dermott *(G-13192)*
Fairway Carts Parts & More LLC .... G 234 209-9008
  North Canton *(G-15081)*

RAILROAD CROSSINGS: Steel Or Iron

Bridge Components Inds Inc .... G 614 873-0777
  Columbus *(G-6698)*

RAILROAD EQPT

A Stucki Company 412 424-0560
  North Canton *(G-15067)*
Amsted Industries Incorporated .... C 614 836-2323
  Groveport *(G-10481)*
Amsted Rail Company Inc .... F 614 836-2323
  Groveport *(G-10482)*
Buck Equipment Inc .... E 614 539-3039
  Grove City *(G-10419)*
Dayton-Phoenix Group Inc .... C 937 496-3900
  Dayton *(G-8151)*
Dennis Lavender .... G 740 344-3336
  Newark *(G-14867)*
George R Silcott Railway Equip .... G 614 885-7224
  Worthington *(G-20687)*
Gunderson Rail Services LLC .... E 330 792-6521
  Youngstown *(G-20927)*
Johnson Bros Rubber Co Inc .... E 419 752-4814
  Greenwich *(G-10404)*
K & G Machine Co .... E 216 732-7115
  Cleveland *(G-5512)*
L B Foster Company .... G 330 652-1461
  Mineral Ridge *(G-14168)*
Nolan Company .... G 330 453-7922
  Canton *(G-2762)*
Nolan Company .... G 740 269-1512
  Bowerston *(G-1942)*
Prime Manufacturing Corp .... G 937 496-3900
  Dayton *(G-8441)*
R H Little Co .... G 330 477-3455
  Canton *(G-2800)*
Sperling Railway Services Inc .... F 330 479-2004
  Canton *(G-2821)*
Transco Railway Products Inc .... D 330 872-0934
  Newton Falls *(G-14994)*
Trinity Highway Products Llc .... F 419 227-1296
  Lima *(G-11953)*
Wabtec Corporation .... G 440 238-5350
  Strongsville *(G-17803)*

RAILROAD EQPT & SPLYS WHOLESALERS

Amsted Industries Incorporated .... C 614 836-2323
  Groveport *(G-10481)*
Buck Equipment Inc .... E 614 539-3039
  Grove City *(G-10419)*
Ysd Industries Inc .... D 330 792-6521
  Youngstown *(G-21086)*

RAILROAD EQPT: Brakes, Air & Vacuum

Westinghouse A Brake Tech Corp .... D 419 526-5323
  Mansfield *(G-12540)*

RAILROAD EQPT: Cars & Eqpt, Dining

Standard Car Truck Company .... D 740 775-6450
  Chillicothe *(G-3223)*

RAILROAD EQPT: Cars & Eqpt, Interurban

Engines Inc of Ohio .... D 740 377-9874
  South Point *(G-17283)*

RAILROAD EQPT: Cars & Eqpt, Train, Freight Or Passenger

Rail Road Corporation .... G 614 771-2102
  Columbus *(G-7376)*

RAILROAD EQPT: Cars, Rebuilt

Jk-Co LLC .... E 419 422-5240
  Findlay *(G-9710)*
Norfolk Southern Corporation .... E 419 697-5070
  Oregon *(G-15563)*
Rescar Companies Inc .... F 630 963-1114
  Minerva *(G-14200)*

PRODUCT SECTION

RECREATIONAL & SPORTING CAMPS

RAILROAD EQPT: Locomotives & Parts, Indl
Good Day Tools LLC .... G 513 578-2050
Cincinnati *(G-3770)*

RAILROAD MAINTENANCE & REPAIR SVCS
Simpson & Sons Inc .... F 513 367-0152
Harrison *(G-10670)*
Tmt Inc .... C 419 592-1041
Perrysburg *(G-16018)*

RAILROAD RELATED EQPT
Youngstown Bending Rolling .... F 330 799-2227
Youngstown *(G-21071)*

RAILROAD RELATED EQPT: Railway Track
Ohio Valley Trackwork Inc .... F 740 446-0181
Bidwell *(G-1667)*

RAILROAD TIES: Concrete
KSA Limited Partnership .... E 740 776-3238
Portsmouth *(G-16289)*

RAILROAD TIES: Wood
Koppers Ind Inc .... G 740 776-2149
Portsmouth *(G-16287)*

RAILS: Rails, Rerolled Or Renewed
Cincinnati Barge Rail Trml LLC .... G 513 227-3611
Cincinnati *(G-3482)*

RAILS: Rails, rolled & drawn, aluminum
Pandrol Inc .... E 419 592-5050
Napoleon *(G-14555)*

RAMPS: Prefabricated Metal
Homecare Mattress Inc .... F 937 746-2556
Franklin *(G-9889)*
Jh Industries Inc .... E 330 963-4105
Twinsburg *(G-18797)*
Overhead Door Corporation .... F 419 294-3874
Upper Sandusky *(G-18970)*
Upside Innovations LLC .... G 513 889-2492
West Chester *(G-19912)*
Wyse Industrial Carts Inc .... F 419 923-7353
Wauseon *(G-19539)*

RAZORS, RAZOR BLADES
Edgewell Per Care Brands LLC .... D 440 835-7500
Westlake *(G-20111)*
Procter & Gamble Company .... B 513 983-1100
Cincinnati *(G-4198)*
Procter & Gamble Company .... C 513 983-1100
Cincinnati *(G-4199)*
Procter & Gamble Company .... E 513 266-4375
Cincinnati *(G-4200)*
Procter & Gamble Company .... F 513 871-7557
Cincinnati *(G-4201)*
Procter & Gamble Company .... B 419 998-5891
Lima *(G-11920)*
Procter & Gamble Company .... F 513 482-6789
Cincinnati *(G-4203)*
Procter & Gamble Company .... B 513 672-4044
West Chester *(G-19767)*
Procter & Gamble Company .... B 513 627-7115
Cincinnati *(G-4205)*
Procter & Gamble Company .... C 513 634-9600
West Chester *(G-19768)*
Procter & Gamble Company .... C 513 634-9110
West Chester *(G-19769)*
Procter & Gamble Company .... C 513 934-3406
Oregonia *(G-15573)*
Procter & Gamble Company .... C 513 627-7779
Cincinnati *(G-4207)*
Procter & Gamble Company .... B 513 945-0340
Cincinnati *(G-4208)*
Procter & Gamble Company .... C 513 622-1000
Mason *(G-12926)*

REACTORS: Current Limiting
Unity Cable Technologies Inc .... G 419 322-4118
Toledo *(G-18584)*

REACTORS: Saturable
Arisdyne Systems Inc .... F 216 458-1991
Cleveland *(G-4732)*

REAL ESTATE AGENCIES & BROKERS
Brent Bleh Company .... G 513 721-1100
Cincinnati *(G-3410)*
Coldwell Family Tree Farm .... G 330 506-9012
Salineville *(G-16786)*
Lenz Inc .... E 937 277-9364
Dayton *(G-8311)*
Wedco LLC .... G 513 309-0781
Mount Orab *(G-14452)*

REAL ESTATE AGENCIES: Buying
Sawmill Road Management Co LLC ... E 937 342-9071
Springfield *(G-17490)*

REAL ESTATE AGENCIES: Commercial
E L Ostendorf Inc .... G 440 247-7631
Chagrin Falls *(G-3016)*

REAL ESTATE AGENCIES: Leasing & Rentals
Lloyd F Helber .... E 740 756-9607
Carroll *(G-2906)*

REAL ESTATE AGENCIES: Residential
Ruscilli Real Estate Services .... F 614 923-6400
Dublin *(G-8976)*

REAL ESTATE AGENTS & MANAGERS
American Dreams Inc .... G 740 385-4444
Thornville *(G-18029)*
Daily Agency Inc .... F 937 456-9808
Eaton *(G-9147)*
Hitti Enterprises Inc .... F 440 243-4100
Cleveland *(G-5410)*
Holiday Homes Inc .... F 513 353-9777
Harrison *(G-10646)*
Muehlenkamp Properties Inc .... E 513 745-0874
Cincinnati *(G-4053)*
Open House Magazine Inc .... G 614 523-7775
Columbus *(G-7272)*
Rona Enterprises Inc .... G 740 927-9971
Pataskala *(G-15841)*
V&P Group International LLC .... F 703 349-6432
Cincinnati *(G-4461)*
Wellington Wllams Wrldwide LLC .... G 423 805-6198
Troy *(G-18718)*

REAL ESTATE INVESTMENT TRUSTS
Sun Communities Inc .... G 740 548-1942
Lewis Center *(G-11782)*

REAL ESTATE OPERATORS, EXC DEVELOPERS: Commercial/Indl Bldg
Afc Company .... F 330 533-5581
Canfield *(G-2519)*
At Holdings Corporation .... A 216 692-6000
Cleveland *(G-4755)*
Caravan Packaging Inc .... F 440 243-4100
Cleveland *(G-4875)*
David A Waldron & Associates .... G 330 264-7275
Wooster *(G-20583)*
DRDC Realty Inc .... G 419 478-7091
Toledo *(G-18269)*
Garland Industries Inc .... G 216 641-7500
Cleveland *(G-5294)*
Garland/Dbs Inc .... C 216 641-7500
Cleveland *(G-5295)*
Judy Mills Company Inc .... E 513 271-4241
Cincinnati *(G-3887)*
North Coast Holdings Inc .... G 330 535-7177
Akron *(G-299)*
Park Corporation .... B 216 267-4870
Cleveland *(G-5841)*
S-P Company Inc .... F 330 482-0200
Columbiana *(G-6479)*
Snyder Manufacturing Co Ltd .... G 330 343-4456
Dover *(G-8856)*
Three AS Inc .... G 419 227-4240
Lima *(G-11951)*
U S Development Corp .... E 330 673-6900
Kent *(G-11398)*

REAL ESTATE OPERATORS, EXC DEVELOPERS: Property, Retail
Perry County Tribune .... F 740 342-4121
New Lexington *(G-14720)*

REALTY INVESTMENT TRUSTS
Standard Energy Company .... G 614 885-1901
Columbus *(G-7484)*

RECEIVERS: Radio Communications
CDI Industries Inc .... E 440 243-1100
Cleveland *(G-4895)*

RECHROMING SVC: Automobile Bumpers
Prince Plating Inc .... D 216 881-7523
Cleveland *(G-5922)*

RECLAIMED RUBBER: Reworked By Manufacturing Process
Goldsmith & Eggleton LLC .... F 203 855-6000
Wadsworth *(G-19243)*
Lake Erie Rubber Recycling LLC .... G 440 570-6027
Strongsville *(G-17761)*
Midwest Elastomers Inc .... D 419 738-8844
Wapakoneta *(G-19343)*
Sparton Enterprises Inc .... E 330 745-6088
Norton *(G-15375)*
Tahoma Enterprises Inc .... D 330 745-9016
Barberton *(G-1108)*
Tahoma Rubber & Plastics Inc .... D 330 745-9016
Barberton *(G-1109)*

RECORD BLANKS: Phonographic
Musicol Inc .... G 614 267-3133
Columbus *(G-7203)*

RECORDING TAPE: Video, Blank
US Video .... G 440 734-6463
North Olmsted *(G-15202)*

RECORDS & TAPES: Prerecorded
Belkin Production .... E 440 247-2722
Chagrin Falls *(G-3009)*
Beverly Snider .... G 614 837-5817
Columbus *(G-6665)*
Magstor Inc .... G 614 433-0011
Columbus *(G-7146)*

RECORDS OR TAPES: Masters
Q C A Inc .... F 513 681-8400
Cincinnati *(G-4223)*

RECOVERY SVC: Iron Ore, From Open Hearth Slag
Masters Group Inc .... G 440 893-1900
Chagrin Falls *(G-3059)*
Stein Inc .... F 440 526-9301
Cleveland *(G-6104)*
Stein Inc .... D 216 883-7444
Cleveland *(G-6105)*
Waterford Tank Fabrication Ltd .... D 740 984-4100
Beverly *(G-1663)*

RECOVERY SVC: Silver, From Used Photographic Film
Metals Recovery Services LLC .... G 614 870-0364
Columbus *(G-7173)*

RECOVERY SVCS: Metal
Able Alloy Inc .... F 216 251-6110
Cleveland *(G-4599)*
Shaneway Inc .... G 330 868-2220
Minerva *(G-14201)*
Umicore Spclty Mtls Recycl LLC .... D 440 833-3000
Wickliffe *(G-20233)*

RECREATIONAL & SPORTING CAMPS
Prairie Lane Corporation .... G 330 262-3322
Wooster *(G-20639)*

RECREATIONAL DEALERS: Camper & Travel Trailers

RECREATIONAL DEALERS: Camper & Travel Trailers
All Power Equipment LLC ....F 740 593-3279
   Athens *(G-822)*
Cecil Caudill Trailer Sls Inc ....F 740 574-0704
   Franklin Furnace *(G-9933)*
Isaacs Jr Floyd Thomas ....G 513 899-2342
   Morrow *(G-14412)*

RECREATIONAL SPORTING EQPT REPAIR SVCS
Balbo Industries Inc ....G 440 333-0630
   Rocky River *(G-16543)*

RECREATIONAL VEHICLE PARTS & ACCESS STORES
Mitchs Welding & Hitches ....G 419 893-3117
   Maumee *(G-13136)*
Steves Vans & Accessories LLC ....G 740 374-3154
   Marietta *(G-12676)*

RECREATIONAL VEHICLE REPAIR SVCS
L A Productions Co LLC ....G 330 666-4230
   Akron *(G-243)*

RECTIFIERS: Electronic, Exc Semiconductor
Darrah Electric Company ....E 216 631-0912
   Cleveland *(G-5067)*

RECYCLABLE SCRAP & WASTE MATERIALS WHOLESALERS
Aci Industries Ltd ....E 740 368-4160
   Delaware *(G-8648)*
Ascendtech Inc ....E 216 458-1101
   Willoughby *(G-20282)*
Edw C Levy Co ....E 330 484-6328
   Canton *(G-2665)*
Imperial Alum - Minerva LLC ....D 330 868-7765
   Minerva *(G-14184)*
Midwest Iron and Metal Co ....D 937 222-5992
   Dayton *(G-8353)*
Rnw Holdings Inc ....E 330 792-0600
   Youngstown *(G-21018)*

RECYCLING: Paper
Greif Packaging LLC ....C 330 879-2101
   Massillon *(G-12992)*
Itran Electronics Recycling ....G 330 659-0801
   Richfield *(G-16474)*
SMA Plastics LLC ....G 330 627-1377
   Carrollton *(G-2929)*
Verso Paper Holding LLC ....B 877 855-7243
   Miamisburg *(G-13735)*

REELS: Cable, Metal
Alert Stamping & Mfg Co Inc ....E 440 232-5020
   Bedford Heights *(G-1458)*
Hykon Manufacturing Company ....G 330 821-8889
   Alliance *(G-477)*
New American Reel Company LLC ....G 419 258-2900
   Antwerp *(G-599)*

REELS: Fiber, Textile, Made From Purchased Materials
Howard B Claflin Co ....G 330 928-1704
   Cuyahoga Falls *(G-7880)*

REELS: Wood
Singleton Reels Inc ....E 330 274-2961
   Mantua *(G-12559)*
Sonoco Products Company ....E 614 759-8470
   Columbus *(G-7462)*

REFINERS & SMELTERS: Aluminum
Continental Metal Proc Co ....F 216 268-0000
   Cleveland *(G-5021)*
Continental Metal Proc Co ....E 216 268-0000
   Cleveland *(G-5022)*
Imco Recycling of Ohio LLC ....C 740 922-2373
   Uhrichsville *(G-18888)*
Real Alloy Specialty Products ....F 440 563-3487
   Rock Creek *(G-16533)*
Real Alloy Specialty Products ....E 440 322-0072
   Elyria *(G-9318)*

REFINERS & SMELTERS: Brass, Secondary
G A Avril Company ....F 513 641-0566
   Cincinnati *(G-3719)*
I Schumann & Co LLC ....C 440 439-2300
   Bedford *(G-1414)*
Oakwood Industries Inc ....D 440 232-8700
   Bedford *(G-1433)*

REFINERS & SMELTERS: Copper
Sam Dong Ohio Inc ....D 740 363-1985
   Delaware *(G-8721)*

REFINERS & SMELTERS: Copper, Secondary
Echo Environmental Waverly LLC ....F 740 286-2810
   Waverly *(G-19545)*
River Smelting & Ref Mfg Co ....E 216 459-2100
   Cleveland *(G-5987)*

REFINERS & SMELTERS: Gold
Quality Gold Inc ....B 513 942-7659
   Fairfield *(G-9554)*

REFINERS & SMELTERS: Gold, Secondary
Panama Jewelers LLC ....G 440 376-6987
   Painesville *(G-15771)*

REFINERS & SMELTERS: Lead, Secondary
Victory White Metal Company ....E 216 271-1400
   Cleveland *(G-6261)*

REFINERS & SMELTERS: Nonferrous Metal
A & B Iron & Metal Company ....F 937 228-1561
   Dayton *(G-7997)*
A J Oster Foils LLC ....D 330 823-1700
   Alliance *(G-447)*
Aci Industries Ltd ....E 740 368-4160
   Delaware *(G-8648)*
Agmet LLC ....F 216 663-8200
   Cleveland *(G-4641)*
Aleris Rolled Pdts Sls Corp ....G 216 910-3400
   Cleveland *(G-4656)*
Aleris Rolled Products Inc ....E 216 910-3400
   Beachwood *(G-1221)*
Aleris Rolled Products Inc ....D 740 983-2571
   Ashville *(G-814)*
Aleris Rolled Products Inc ....G 740 922-2540
   Uhrichsville *(G-18879)*
Applied Materials Finishing ....E 330 336-5645
   Wadsworth *(G-19227)*
City Scrap & Salvage Co ....E 330 753-5051
   Akron *(G-118)*
Cohen Brothers Inc ....E 513 422-3696
   Middletown *(G-13895)*
Emerald Transformer Ppm LLC ....F 800 908-8800
   Twinsburg *(G-18768)*
Fpt Cleveland LLC ....C 216 441-3800
   Cleveland *(G-5270)*
Franklin Iron & Metal Corp ....C 937 253-8184
   Dayton *(G-8206)*
Fusion Automation Inc ....G 440 602-5595
   Willoughby *(G-20326)*
Garden Street Iron & Metal ....E 513 853-3700
   Cincinnati *(G-3726)*
Gold 2 Green Ltd ....G 304 551-1172
   Bridgeport *(G-2075)*
Grandview Materials Inc ....G 614 488-6998
   Lewis Center *(G-11761)*
HC Starck Inc ....B 216 692-3990
   Cleveland *(G-5382)*
I H Schlezinger Inc ....E 614 252-1188
   Columbus *(G-7016)*
Lake County Auto Recyclers ....G 440 428-2886
   Painesville *(G-15757)*
Masters Group Inc ....G 440 893-1900
   Chagrin Falls *(G-3059)*
Materion Brush Inc ....A 419 862-2745
   Elmore *(G-9208)*
Metal Shredders Inc ....F 937 866-0777
   Miamisburg *(G-13689)*
Metalico Akron Inc ....E 330 376-1400
   Akron *(G-279)*
Midwest Iron and Metal Co ....D 937 222-5992
   Dayton *(G-8353)*
National Bronze Mtls Ohio Inc ....E 440 277-1226
   Lorain *(G-12106)*
Ohio Valley Alloy Services Inc ....E 740 373-1900
   Marietta *(G-12649)*
Old Rar Inc ....E 216 910-3400
   Beachwood *(G-1256)*
Polymet Corporation ....E 513 874-3586
   West Chester *(G-19763)*
Precision Strip Inc ....C 419 674-4186
   Kenton *(G-11418)*
R L S Corporation ....E 740 773-1440
   Chillicothe *(G-3219)*
Real Alloy Holding LLC ....G 216 755-8900
   Beachwood *(G-1270)*
Real Alloy Recycling LLC ....E 346 444-8540
   Beachwood *(G-1271)*
Real Alloy Recycling LLC ....D 216 755-8900
   Beachwood *(G-1272)*
Real Alloy Specialty Pdts LLC ....A 216 755-8836
   Beachwood *(G-1273)*
Real Alloy Specification LLC ....G 216 755-8900
   Beachwood *(G-1275)*
Rm Advisory Group Inc ....E 513 242-2100
   Cincinnati *(G-4274)*
Rmi Titanium Company LLC ....G 330 471-1844
   Canton *(G-2807)*
Rnw Holdings Inc ....E 330 792-0600
   Youngstown *(G-21018)*
Rumpke Transportation Co LLC ....C 513 242-4600
   Cincinnati *(G-4289)*
Sawbrook Steel Castings Co ....D 513 554-1700
   Cincinnati *(G-4302)*
Thyssenkrupp Materials NA Inc ....E 216 883-8100
   Independence *(G-11152)*
W R G Inc ....E 216 351-8494
   Cleveland *(G-6279)*
Wall Colmonoy Corporation ....F 937 278-9111
   Cincinnati *(G-4487)*

REFINERS & SMELTERS: Rhenium, Primary
H C Starck Inc ....B 216 692-3990
   Euclid *(G-9418)*

REFINERS & SMELTERS: Silicon, Primary, Over 99% Pure
Globe Metallurgical Inc ....C 740 984-2361
   Waterford *(G-19484)*

REFINERS & SMELTERS: Zirconium
Zircoa Inc ....C 440 248-0500
   Cleveland *(G-6345)*

REFINING LUBRICATING OILS & GREASES, NEC
American Ultra Specialties Inc ....F 330 656-5000
   Hudson *(G-11030)*
Fiske Brothers Refining Co ....D 419 691-2491
   Toledo *(G-18295)*
Wallover Oil Hamilton Inc ....F 513 896-6692
   Hamilton *(G-10620)*

REFINING: Petroleum
Aecom Energy & Cnstr Inc ....C 419 698-6277
   Oregon *(G-15553)*
Blanchard Refining Company LLC ....G 419 422-2121
   Findlay *(G-9657)*
Blanchard Terminal Company LLC ....G 419 422-2121
   Findlay *(G-9658)*
Blaster Chemical Co Inc ....G 216 901-5800
   Cleveland *(G-4818)*
BP Products North America Inc ....G 937 461-3621
   Dayton *(G-8060)*
BP Products North America Inc ....F 419 537-9540
   Toledo *(G-18212)*
BP Products North America Inc ....G 419 636-2249
   Bryan *(G-2270)*
Citgo Petroleum Corporation ....G 419 698-8055
   Oregon *(G-15558)*
Cyberutility LLC ....G 216 291-8723
   Cleveland *(G-5055)*
Husky Energy ....F 614 766-5633
   Dublin *(G-8926)*
Isp Lima LLC ....E 419 998-8700
   Lima *(G-11880)*

PRODUCT SECTION

K2 Petroleum & Supply LLC ....G....... 937 503-2614
  Cincinnati *(G-3891)*
Koch Knight LLC ....D....... 330 488-1651
  East Canton *(G-9041)*
Lima Refining Company ....B....... 419 226-2300
  Lima *(G-11890)*
Lima Refining Company ....D....... 419 226-2300
  Lima *(G-11891)*
Marathon Oil Company ....E....... 419 422-2121
  Findlay *(G-9718)*
Marathon Petroleum Coporation ....D....... 419 422-2121
  Findlay *(G-9720)*
Marathon Petroleum Corporation ....B....... 419 422-2121
  Findlay *(G-9721)*
Ohio Biofuels ....G....... 614 886-6518
  Cincinnati *(G-4099)*
Pbf Energy Partners LP ....E....... 419 698-6724
  Toledo *(G-18459)*
Seneca Petroleum Co Inc ....F....... 419 691-3581
  Toledo *(G-18518)*
Standard Oil Company ....E....... 419 698-6200
  Oregon *(G-15568)*
Sunoco Inc ....E....... 216 912-2579
  Akron *(G-393)*
Troy Valley Petroleum ....G....... 937 604-0012
  Dayton *(G-8570)*
Vertex Refining OH LLC ....E....... 281 486-4182
  Norwalk *(G-15416)*

REFLECTIVE ROAD MARKERS, WHOLESALE

Lightle Enterprises Ohio LLC ....G....... 740 998-5363
  Frankfort *(G-9863)*

REFRACTORIES: Brick

Minteq International Inc ....E....... 330 343-8821
  Dover *(G-8843)*
Plibrico Company LLC ....E....... 740 682-7755
  Oak Hill *(G-15458)*

REFRACTORIES: Cement

Castruction Company Inc ....F....... 330 332-9622
  Salem *(G-16724)*

REFRACTORIES: Clay

A N H ....G....... 513 576-6240
  Batavia *(G-1121)*
Afc Company ....F....... 330 533-5581
  Canfield *(G-2519)*
Bowerston Shale Company ....E....... 740 269-2921
  Bowerston *(G-1939)*
Glen-Gery Corporation ....E....... 419 468-5002
  Iberia *(G-11113)*
Glen-Gery Corporation ....D....... 419 845-3321
  Caledonia *(G-2416)*
Harbisonwalker Intl Inc ....E....... 330 326-2010
  Windham *(G-20524)*
Harbisonwalker Intl Inc ....D....... 440 234-8002
  Cleveland *(G-5373)*
Harbisonwalker Intl Inc ....E....... 513 576-6240
  Batavia *(G-1152)*
Harbisonwalker Intl Inc ....D....... 330 868-4141
  Minerva *(G-14181)*
I Cerco Inc ....D....... 740 982-2050
  Crooksville *(G-7816)*
Lakeway Mfg Inc ....E....... 419 433-3030
  Huron *(G-11103)*
Magneco/Metrel Inc ....E....... 330 426-9468
  Negley *(G-14590)*
Minteq International Inc ....E....... 330 343-8821
  Dover *(G-8843)*
Nock and Son Company ....F....... 440 871-5525
  Cleveland *(G-5754)*
Nock and Son Company ....F....... 740 682-7741
  Oak Hill *(G-15457)*
Resco Products Inc ....E....... 330 372-3716
  Warren *(G-19438)*
Resco Products Inc ....D....... 330 488-1226
  East Canton *(G-9044)*
Selas Heat Technology Co LLC ....E....... 800 523-6500
  Streetsboro *(G-17697)*
Specialty Ceramics Inc ....D....... 330 482-0800
  Columbiana *(G-6481)*
Stebbins Engineering & Mfg Co ....E....... 740 922-3012
  Uhrichsville *(G-18895)*
Summitville Tiles Inc ....E....... 330 868-6463
  Minerva *(G-14203)*

Whitacre Greer Company ....E....... 330 823-1610
  Alliance *(G-515)*

REFRACTORIES: Graphite, Carbon Or Ceramic Bond

E I Ceramics LLC ....D....... 513 772-7001
  Cincinnati *(G-3617)*
Global Graphite Group LLC ....G....... 216 538-0362
  Independence *(G-11132)*
Refractory Specialties Inc ....E....... 330 938-2101
  Sebring *(G-16891)*
Veitsch-Radex America LLC ....D....... 440 969-2300
  Ashtabula *(G-811)*

REFRACTORIES: Nonclay

A & M Refractories Inc ....E....... 740 456-8020
  New Boston *(G-14645)*
Allied Mineral Products Inc ....B....... 614 876-0244
  Columbus *(G-6573)*
Allstates Refr Contrs LLC ....F....... 419 878-4691
  Waterville *(G-19489)*
Ets Schaefer LLC ....E....... 330 468-6600
  Macedonia *(G-12292)*
Ets Schaefer LLC ....E....... 330 468-6600
  Beachwood *(G-1237)*
I Cerco Inc ....D....... 740 982-2050
  Crooksville *(G-7816)*
Impact Armor Technologies LLC ....F....... 216 706-2024
  Cleveland *(G-5442)*
Johns Manville Corporation ....B....... 419 878-8111
  Waterville *(G-19498)*
Magneco/Metrel Inc ....E....... 330 426-9468
  Negley *(G-14590)*
Martin Marietta Materials Inc ....E....... 513 701-1140
  West Chester *(G-19740)*
Momentive Prfmce Mtls Qrtz Inc ....C....... 440 878-5700
  Strongsville *(G-17765)*
Nock and Son Company ....F....... 440 871-5525
  Cleveland *(G-5754)*
Ohio Vly Stmpng-Assemblies Inc ....E....... 419 522-0983
  Mansfield *(G-12498)*
Old Es LLC ....E....... 330 468-6600
  Macedonia *(G-12312)*
Pyromatics Corp ....F....... 440 352-3500
  Mentor *(G-13561)*
Resco Products Inc ....E....... 740 682-7794
  Oak Hill *(G-15459)*
Ruscoe Company ....E....... 330 253-8148
  Akron *(G-358)*
Saint-Gobain Ceramics Plas Inc ....A....... 330 673-5860
  Stow *(G-17624)*
US Refractory Products LLC ....E....... 440 386-4580
  North Ridgeville *(G-15258)*
Vacuform Inc ....E....... 330 938-9674
  Sebring *(G-16898)*
Wahl Refractory Solutions LLC ....D....... 419 334-2658
  Fremont *(G-10063)*
Zircoa Inc ....C....... 440 248-0500
  Cleveland *(G-6345)*

REFRIGERATION & HEATING EQUIPMENT

A A S Amels Sheet Meta L Inc ....E....... 330 793-9326
  Youngstown *(G-20830)*
Anatrace Products LLC ....E....... 419 740-6600
  Maumee *(G-13071)*
Arthurs Refrigeration ....G....... 740 532-0206
  Ironton *(G-11161)*
Bard Manufacturing Company Inc ....D....... 419 636-1194
  Bryan *(G-2267)*
Beckett Air Incorporated ....D....... 440 327-9999
  North Ridgeville *(G-15209)*
Bennett Mechanical Systems LLC ....E....... 513 292-3506
  Franklin *(G-9871)*
Bessamaire Sales Inc ....E....... 440 439-1200
  Twinsburg *(G-18740)*
Bodor Vents LLC ....E....... 513 348-3853
  Blue Ash *(G-1739)*
C Nelson Manufacturing Co ....E....... 419 898-3305
  Oak Harbor *(G-15442)*
Carrier Corporation ....E....... 937 275-0645
  Dayton *(G-8077)*
Central Heating & Cooling Inc ....E....... 330 782-7100
  Youngstown *(G-20868)*
Cold Control LLC ....G....... 614 564-7011
  Westerville *(G-19986)*
Cryogenic Equipment & Svcs Inc ....F....... 513 761-4200
  Cincinnati *(G-3561)*
Csafe LLC ....G....... 937 312-0114
  Moraine *(G-14340)*

REFRIGERATION EQPT: Complete

Daikin Applied Americas Inc ....G....... 614 351-9862
  Westerville *(G-20045)*
Dmtco LLC ....G....... 937 324-0061
  Springfield *(G-17389)*
Dyoung Enterprise Inc ....D....... 440 918-0505
  Willoughby *(G-20312)*
Ellis & Watts Global Inds Inc ....E....... 513 752-9000
  Batavia *(G-1142)*
Emerson Network Power ....G....... 614 841-8054
  Ironton *(G-11164)*
Famous Industries Inc ....D....... 740 685-2592
  Byesville *(G-2384)*
Famous Industries Inc ....C....... 740 397-8842
  Mount Vernon *(G-14481)*
Fire From Ice Ventures LLC ....F....... 419 944-6705
  Solon *(G-17144)*
Gould Group LLC ....G....... 740 807-4294
  Hilliard *(G-10825)*
Liebert North America Inc ....E....... 614 888-0246
  Columbus *(G-7125)*
Mahle Behr USA Inc ....A....... 937 369-2000
  Dayton *(G-8327)*
Maverick Innvtive Slutions LLC ....E....... 419 281-7944
  Ashland *(G-722)*
Molecular Dimensions Inc ....G....... 419 740-6600
  Maumee *(G-13137)*
Mv Group Inc ....G....... 419 776-1133
  Toledo *(G-18419)*
Prime Manufacturing Corp ....G....... 937 496-3900
  Dayton *(G-8441)*
Professional Supply Inc ....F....... 419 332-7373
  Fremont *(G-10046)*
RSI Company ....F....... 216 360-9800
  Beachwood *(G-1277)*
Space Dynamics Corp ....E....... 513 792-9800
  Blue Ash *(G-1847)*
T J F Inc ....F....... 419 878-4400
  Waterville *(G-19506)*
Taiho Corporation of America ....C....... 419 443-1645
  Tiffin *(G-18086)*
Tempest Inc ....E....... 216 883-6500
  Cleveland *(G-6158)*
Ten Dogs Global Industries LLC ....D....... 513 752-9000
  Batavia *(G-1189)*
Thermo King Corporation ....F....... 478 625-7241
  Chagrin Falls *(G-3031)*
Trane US Inc ....E....... 513 771-8884
  Cincinnati *(G-4429)*
Trane US Inc ....C....... 614 473-3131
  Columbus *(G-7536)*
Trane US Inc ....C....... 614 497-6300
  Groveport *(G-10515)*
Trane US Inc ....D....... 614 473-8701
  Columbus *(G-7537)*
Variflow Equipment Inc ....G....... 513 245-0420
  Cincinnati *(G-4467)*
Vortec Corporation ....E....... 513 891-7485
  Blue Ash *(G-1866)*

REFRIGERATION EQPT & SPLYS WHOLESALERS

Modern Ice Equipment & Sup Co ....E....... 513 367-2101
  Cincinnati *(G-4038)*

REFRIGERATION EQPT & SPLYS, WHOLESALE: Beverage Dispensers

Dj Beverage Innovations Inc ....G....... 614 769-1569
  Plain City *(G-16188)*
International Beverage Works ....G....... 614 798-5398
  Columbus *(G-7043)*

REFRIGERATION EQPT & SPLYS, WHOLESALE: Commercial Eqpt

Hattenbach Company ....E....... 330 744-2732
  Youngstown *(G-20929)*
Hattenbach Company ....D....... 216 881-5200
  Cleveland *(G-5380)*

REFRIGERATION EQPT: Complete

CFC Startec LLC ....G....... 330 688-8316
  Stow *(G-17575)*
Hobart Corporation ....E....... 937 332-3000
  Troy *(G-18671)*
Hobart Corporation ....C....... 937 332-2797
  Piqua *(G-16128)*
Northeastern Rfrgn Corp ....E....... 440 942-7676
  Willoughby *(G-20390)*

Employee Codes: A=Over 500 employees, B=251-500
C=101-250, D=51-100, E=20-50, F=10-19, G=3-9

REFRIGERATION EQPT: Complete

NRC Inc ....E 440 975-9449
  Willoughby *(G-20391)*
Refrigeration Industries Corp ....F 740 377-9166
  South Point *(G-17293)*
So-Low Environmental Eqp Co ....E 513 772-9410
  Cincinnati *(G-4350)*

REFRIGERATION REPAIR SVCS

Northeastern Rfrgn Corp ....E 440 942-7676
  Willoughby *(G-20390)*

REFRIGERATORS & FREEZERS WHOLESALERS

Arthurs Refrigeration ....G 740 532-0206
  Ironton *(G-11161)*

REFUGEE SVCS

Jeffco Sheltered Workshop ....E 740 264-4608
  Steubenville *(G-17539)*

REFUSE SYSTEMS

A & B Iron & Metal Company ....F 937 228-1561
  Dayton *(G-7997)*
Capital City Oil Inc ....G 740 397-4483
  Mount Vernon *(G-14473)*
Metalico Akron Inc ....E 330 376-1400
  Akron *(G-279)*
Rumpke Transportation Co LLC ....F 513 851-0122
  Cincinnati *(G-4288)*
Troo Clean Enviromental LLC ....G 304 215-4501
  Saint Clairsville *(G-16656)*
Waste Water Pollution Control ....F 330 263-5290
  Wooster *(G-20663)*

REGISTERS: Air, Metal

Hart & Cooley Inc ....C 937 832-7800
  Englewood *(G-9361)*

REGULATION & ADMIN, GOVT: Facility Licensing & Inspection

National Welding & Tanker Repr ....G 614 875-3399
  Grove City *(G-10449)*

REGULATORS: Generator Voltage

Staco Energy Products Co ....G 937 253-1191
  Miamisburg *(G-13719)*

REGULATORS: Power

Vertiv Corporation ....A 614 888-0246
  Columbus *(G-7575)*

REHABILITATION SVCS

Clovernook Center For The Bli ....C 513 522-3860
  Cincinnati *(G-3530)*

RELAYS & SWITCHES: Indl, Electric

Control Electric Co ....E 216 671-8010
  Columbia Station *(G-6434)*
Controllix Corporation ....F 440 232-8757
  Walton Hills *(G-19309)*
Rogers Industrial Products Inc ....E 330 535-3331
  Akron *(G-353)*
Utility Relay Co Ltd ....E 440 708-1000
  Chagrin Falls *(G-3087)*

RELAYS: Control Circuit, Ind

Industrial and Mar Eng Svc Co ....F 740 694-0791
  Fredericktown *(G-9971)*
Omega Tek Inc ....G 419 756-9580
  Mansfield *(G-12499)*

RELAYS: Electronic Usage

Innovative Integrations Inc ....G 216 533-5353
  Mesopotamia *(G-13633)*
Te Connectivity Corporation ....C 419 521-9500
  Mansfield *(G-12527)*

RELIGIOUS SPLYS WHOLESALERS

Novak J F Manufacturing Co LLC ....G 216 741-5112
  Cleveland *(G-5790)*

REMOVERS & CLEANERS

Cahill Services Inc ....G 216 410-5595
  Lakewood *(G-11514)*
Dolgencorp LLC ....G 740 289-4790
  Piketon *(G-16069)*
Hytek Coatings Inc ....G 513 424-0131
  Middletown *(G-13913)*
Janet Sullivan ....G 419 658-2333
  Ney *(G-14997)*
Roger Hoover ....G 330 857-1815
  Orrville *(G-15616)*

REMOVERS: Paint

ABRA Auto Body & Glass LP ....G 513 367-9200
  Harrison *(G-10627)*
ABRA Auto Body & Glass LP ....G 513 247-3400
  Cincinnati *(G-3289)*
ABRA Auto Body & Glass LP ....G 513 755-7709
  West Chester *(G-19635)*
Treved Exteriors ....G 513 771-3888
  Cincinnati *(G-4432)*

RENT-A-CAR SVCS

Precision Coatings Systems ....E 937 642-4727
  Marysville *(G-12806)*

RENTAL SVCS: Business Machine & Electronic Eqpt

Pitney Bowes Inc ....D 203 426-7025
  Brecksville *(G-2054)*
Pitney Bowes Inc ....G 216 351-2598
  Cleveland *(G-5880)*
Pitney Bowes Inc ....D 740 374-5535
  Marietta *(G-12655)*

RENTAL SVCS: Costume

Akron Design & Costume Co ....G 330 644-4849
  Coventry Township *(G-7762)*
Costume Specialists Inc ....E 614 464-2115
  Columbus *(G-6825)*
Costume Specialists Inc ....G 614 464-2115
  Columbus *(G-6826)*
Promo Costumes Inc ....F 740 383-5176
  Marion *(G-12728)*
Stagecraft Costuming Inc ....F 513 541-7150
  Cincinnati *(G-4369)*

RENTAL SVCS: Eqpt, Theatrical

Schenz Theatrical Supply Inc ....F 513 542-6100
  Cincinnati *(G-4306)*

RENTAL SVCS: Home Cleaning & Maintenance Eqpt

Certon Technologies Inc ....F 440 786-7185
  Bedford *(G-1395)*

RENTAL SVCS: Motor Home

Advanced Rv LLC ....G 440 283-0405
  Willoughby *(G-20267)*

RENTAL SVCS: Musical Instrument

Loft Violin Shop ....F 614 267-7221
  Columbus *(G-7135)*
Paul Bartel ....G 513 541-2000
  Cincinnati *(G-4139)*

RENTAL SVCS: Office Facilities & Secretarial Svcs

APS Accurate Products & Svcs ....G 440 353-9353
  North Ridgeville *(G-15208)*

RENTAL SVCS: Pallet

Forklifts of Americas LLC ....G 440 821-5143
  Highland Heights *(G-10790)*

RENTAL SVCS: Saddle Horse

Victorian Farms ....G 330 628-9188
  Atwater *(G-864)*

RENTAL SVCS: Sign

A B C Sign Inc ....F 513 241-8884
  Cincinnati *(G-3278)*

RENTAL SVCS: Sound & Lighting Eqpt

Iacono Production Services Inc ....F 513 469-5095
  Blue Ash *(G-1790)*
Importers Direct LLC ....G 330 436-3260
  Akron *(G-214)*
Technical Artistry Inc ....G 614 299-7777
  Columbus *(G-7520)*

RENTAL SVCS: Sporting Goods, NEC

McSports ....G 419 586-5555
  Celina *(G-2974)*

RENTAL SVCS: Stores & Yards Eqpt

Golf Car Company Inc ....F 614 873-1055
  Plain City *(G-16196)*
Showplace Inc ....G 419 468-7368
  Galion *(G-10155)*

RENTAL SVCS: Tent & Tarpaulin

Galion Canvas Products ....F 419 468-5333
  Galion *(G-10139)*
Rainbow Industries Inc ....G 937 323-6493
  Springfield *(G-17479)*
South Akron Awning Co ....G 330 848-7611
  Akron *(G-382)*
Tarpco Inc ....F 330 677-8277
  Kent *(G-11392)*
Wolf G T Awning & Tent Co ....F 937 548-4161
  Greenville *(G-10402)*

RENTAL SVCS: Trailer

Eleet Cryogenics Inc ....E 330 874-4009
  Bolivar *(G-1913)*
Lloyd F Helber ....E 740 756-9607
  Carroll *(G-2906)*

RENTAL SVCS: Tuxedo

American Commodore Tuxedos ....G 440 324-2889
  Elyria *(G-9214)*

RENTAL SVCS: Vending Machine

Cuyahoga Vending Co Inc ....F 440 353-9595
  North Ridgeville *(G-15219)*

RENTAL SVCS: Work Zone Traffic Eqpt, Flags, Cones, Etc

A & A Safety Inc ....F 937 567-9781
  Beavercreek *(G-1348)*
A & A Safety Inc ....E 513 943-6100
  Amelia *(G-527)*
Lightle Enterprises Ohio LLC ....G 740 998-5363
  Frankfort *(G-9863)*
Paul Peterson Company ....E 614 486-4375
  Columbus *(G-7299)*
Paul Peterson Safety Div Inc ....E 614 486-4375
  Columbus *(G-7300)*

RENTAL: Portable Toilet

BJ Equipment Ltd ....F 614 497-1776
  Columbus *(G-6673)*
Pro-Kleen Industrial Svcs Inc ....E 740 689-1886
  Lancaster *(G-11599)*

RENTAL: Trucks, With Drivers

Hull Ready Mix Concrete Inc ....F 419 625-8070
  Sandusky *(G-16815)*
Mulch Madness LLC ....F 330 920-9900
  Aurora *(G-893)*

RENTAL: Video Tape & Disc

US Video ....G 440 734-6463
  North Olmsted *(G-15202)*

REPAIR SERVICES, NEC

M C Systems Inc ....G 513 336-6007
  Mason *(G-12904)*

PRODUCT SECTION

REPAIR TRAINING, COMPUTER
Corporate Elevator LLC .... F 614 288-1847
  Columbus *(G-6822)*

REPOSSESSION SVCS
Interscope Manufacturing Inc .... E 513 423-8866
  Middletown *(G-13917)*

REPRODUCTION SVCS: Video Tape Or Disk
Markeys Audio/Visual Inc .... G 419 244-8844
  Toledo *(G-18399)*

RESEARCH & DEVELOPMENT SVCS, COMMERCIAL: Engineering Lab
Morris Technologies Inc .... C 513 733-1611
  Cincinnati *(G-4047)*

RESEARCH, DEV & TESTING SVCS, COMM: Chem Lab, Exc Testing
Guild Associates Inc .... G 843 573-0095
  Dublin *(G-8920)*
Guild Associates Inc .... D 614 798-8215
  Dublin *(G-8919)*
Heraeus Precious Metals North .... E 937 264-1000
  Vandalia *(G-19127)*

RESEARCH, DEVEL & TEST SVCS, COMM: Sociological & Education
Community RE Group-Comvet .... G 440 319-6714
  Ashtabula *(G-767)*

RESEARCH, DEVELOPMENT & TEST SVCS, COMM: Cmptr Hardware Dev
Ic3d Inc .... G 614 344-0414
  Columbus *(G-7019)*
Noggin LLC .... G 440 305-6188
  Cleveland *(G-5755)*

RESEARCH, DEVELOPMENT & TEST SVCS, COMM: Research, Exc Lab
Special Mtls RES & Tech Inc .... G 440 777-4024
  North Olmsted *(G-15200)*

RESEARCH, DEVELOPMENT & TESTING SVCS, COMM: Agricultural
Lifestyle Nutraceuticals Ltd .... F 513 376-7218
  Cincinnati *(G-3941)*

RESEARCH, DEVELOPMENT & TESTING SVCS, COMM: Research Lab
Applied Sciences Inc .... E 937 766-2020
  Cedarville *(G-2943)*
Microbiological Labs Inc .... G 330 626-2264
  Streetsboro *(G-17682)*
Performnce Plymr Solutions Inc .... F 937 298-3713
  Moraine *(G-14375)*
Ronald T Dodge Co .... F 937 439-4497
  Dayton *(G-8484)*

RESEARCH, DEVELOPMENT & TESTING SVCS, COMMERCIAL: Business
Smokeheal Inc .... G 216 255-5119
  Cleveland *(G-6074)*

RESEARCH, DEVELOPMENT & TESTING SVCS, COMMERCIAL: Education
Instruction & Design Concepts .... G 937 439-2698
  Dayton *(G-8271)*

RESEARCH, DEVELOPMENT & TESTING SVCS, COMMERCIAL: Energy
Fripro Energy LLC .... G 419 865-0002
  Maumee *(G-13111)*

RESEARCH, DEVELOPMENT & TESTING SVCS, COMMERCIAL: Medical
Applied Medical Technology Inc .... E 440 717-4000
  Brecksville *(G-2020)*

RESEARCH, DEVELOPMENT & TESTING SVCS, COMMERCIAL: Physical
Fenix Magnetics Inc .... G 440 455-1142
  Westlake *(G-20113)*
Ftech R&D North America Inc .... D 937 339-2777
  Troy *(G-18659)*
H & N Instruments Inc .... G 740 344-4351
  Newark *(G-14882)*
Ivac Technologies Corp .... F 216 662-4987
  Cleveland *(G-5479)*
Leidos Inc .... D 937 431-2270
  Beavercreek *(G-1326)*
Lubrizol Advanced Mtls Inc .... E 440 933-0400
  Avon Lake *(G-993)*
Velocys Inc .... D 614 733-3300
  Plain City *(G-16215)*

RESEARCH, DVLPT & TEST SVCS, COMM: Mkt Analysis or Research
Jscs Group Inc .... G 513 563-4900
  Cincinnati *(G-3886)*

RESEARCH, DVLPT & TESTING SVCS, COMM: Mkt, Bus & Economic
Enerchem Incorporated .... G 513 745-0580
  Cincinnati *(G-3639)*
Lyondellbasell .... G 513 530-4000
  Cincinnati *(G-3961)*

RESIDENTIAL MENTAL HEALTH & SUBSTANCE ABUSE FACILITIES
Style Crest Inc .... B 419 332-7369
  Fremont *(G-10052)*

RESIDENTIAL REMODELERS
Boyce Ltd .... G 614 236-8901
  Columbus *(G-6690)*
Carr Supply Co .... G 937 316-6300
  Greenville *(G-10363)*
JC Electric .... E 330 760-2915
  Garrettsville *(G-10193)*
Winsupply Inc .... F 937 346-0600
  Springfield *(G-17518)*

RESINS: Custom Compound Purchased
Accel Corporation .... D 440 934-7711
  Avon *(G-938)*
Advanced Composites Inc .... G 937 575-9814
  Sidney *(G-17012)*
Advanced Composites Inc .... C 937 575-9800
  Sidney *(G-17013)*
Aurora Plastics LLC .... D 330 422-0700
  Streetsboro *(G-17662)*
Chemionics Corporation .... E 330 733-8834
  Tallmadge *(G-17975)*
Chromaflo Technologies Corp .... C 440 997-0081
  Ashtabula *(G-764)*
Chromaflo Technologies Corp .... C 513 733-5111
  Cincinnati *(G-3474)*
Deltech Polymers Corporation .... G 937 339-3150
  Troy *(G-18648)*
Dyneon LLC .... E 859 334-4500
  Cincinnati *(G-3614)*
Flex Technologies Inc .... E 330 897-6311
  Baltic *(G-1029)*
Freeman Manufacturing & Sup Co .... E 440 934-1902
  Avon *(G-950)*
General Color Investments Inc .... D 330 868-4161
  Minerva *(G-14180)*
Hexpol Compounding LLC .... C 440 834-4644
  Burton *(G-2360)*
Hexpol Compounding LLC .... E 440 834-4644
  Burton *(G-2361)*
Hexpol Holding Inc .... F 440 834-4644
  Burton *(G-2362)*
Killian Latex Inc .... F 330 644-6746
  Akron *(G-236)*
McCann Plastics Inc .... D 330 499-1515
  Canton *(G-2750)*
Nanosperse LLC .... G 937 296-5030
  Kettering *(G-11435)*
Omnova Solutions Inc .... C 330 628-6550
  Mogadore *(G-14246)*
Polymera Inc .... G 740 527-2069
  Hebron *(G-10758)*
Polymers By Design LLC .... G 937 361-7398
  Troy *(G-18693)*
Polyone Corporation .... C 419 668-4844
  Norwalk *(G-15412)*
Polyone Corporation .... D 440 930-1000
  Avon Lake *(G-1001)*
Polyone Corporation .... D 440 930-1000
  North Baltimore *(G-15047)*
Radici Plastics Usa Inc .... C 330 336-7611
  Wadsworth *(G-19271)*
Rutland Plastic Tech Inc .... G 614 846-3055
  Columbus *(G-7407)*
Sherwin-Williams Company .... C 330 830-6000
  Massillon *(G-13048)*
Thermafab Alloy Inc .... E 216 861-0540
  Olmsted Falls *(G-15531)*
Tymex Plastics Inc .... E 216 429-8950
  Cleveland *(G-6226)*

RESISTORS
Filnor Inc .... F 330 821-7667
  Alliance *(G-467)*

RESISTORS & RESISTOR UNITS
Asco Power Technologies LP .... C 216 573-7600
  Cleveland *(G-4744)*
Asco Power Technologies LP .... E 216 573-7600
  Cleveland *(G-4745)*

RESOLVERS
Home Resolver .... G 440 886-6758
  Cleveland *(G-5413)*

RESPIRATORS
Morning Pride Mfg LLC .... A 937 264-2662
  Dayton *(G-8367)*
Morning Pride Mfg LLC .... G 937 264-1726
  Dayton *(G-8368)*

RESTAURANT EQPT REPAIR SVCS
Harry C Lobalzo & Sons Inc .... E 330 666-6758
  Akron *(G-199)*

RESTAURANT EQPT: Carts
Cateringstone .... G 513 410-1064
  Cincinnati *(G-3448)*
Modroto .... G 800 772-7659
  Ashtabula *(G-787)*
Quadra - Tech Inc .... D 614 445-0690
  Columbus *(G-7362)*
Sotto .... G 513 977-6886
  Cincinnati *(G-4354)*

RESTAURANT EQPT: Sheet Metal
American Craft Hardware LLC .... G 440 746-0098
  Cleveland *(G-4686)*
Architectural Sheet Metals LLC .... G 216 361-9952
  Cleveland *(G-4729)*
D B S Stinless Stl Fabricators .... G 513 856-9600
  Hamilton *(G-10550)*

RESTAURANTS:Full Svc, American
Elizabeths Closet .... G 513 646-5025
  Maineville *(G-12367)*
Little Ghost Roasters .... G 614 325-2065
  Columbus *(G-7132)*
The Great Lakes Brewing Co .... D 216 771-4404
  Cleveland *(G-6164)*

RESTAURANTS:Full Svc, Barbecue
New Riegel Cafe Inc .... E 419 595-2255
  New Riegel *(G-14816)*

RESTAURANTS:Full Svc, Chinese
Magic Wok Inc .... G 419 531-1818
  Toledo *(G-18394)*

Employee Codes: A=Over 500 employees, B=251-500
C=101-250, D=51-100, E=20-50, F=10-19, G=3-9

RESTAURANTS:Full Svc, Family, Chain

Bob Evans Farms Inc .... B 614 491-2225
 New Albany *(G-14609)*
Skyline Chili Inc .... C 513 874-1188
 Fairfield *(G-9565)*

RESTAURANTS:Full Svc, Family, Independent

Amish Door Inc .... B 330 359-5464
 Wilmot *(G-20513)*
Moyer Vineyards Inc .... E 937 549-2957
 Manchester *(G-12395)*
Robert Barr .... F 740 826-7325
 New Concord *(G-14686)*

RESTAURANTS:Full Svc, Italian

Glenn Ravens Winery .... E 740 545-1000
 West Lafayette *(G-19930)*
Lloyd F Helber .... E 740 756-9607
 Carroll *(G-2906)*

RESTAURANTS:Limited Svc, Chili Stand

Gold Star Chili Inc .... E 513 631-1990
 Cincinnati *(G-3768)*

RESTAURANTS:Limited Svc, Coffee Shop

Iron Bean Inc .... F 518 641-9917
 Toledo *(G-18353)*

RESTAURANTS:Limited Svc, Fast-Food, Chain

White Castle System Inc .... B 614 228-5781
 Columbus *(G-7603)*
White Castle System Inc .... E 513 563-2290
 Cincinnati *(G-4506)*

RESTAURANTS:Limited Svc, Grill

Best Bite Grill LLC .... F 419 344-7462
 Versailles *(G-19174)*
Rivals Sports Grille LLC .... E 216 267-0005
 Middleburg Heights *(G-13769)*

RESTAURANTS:Limited Svc, Ice Cream Stands Or Dairy Bars

Country Maid Ice Cream Inc .... G 330 659-6830
 Richfield *(G-16466)*
International Brand Services ...... F 513 376-8209
 Cincinnati *(G-3856)*
Johnsons Real Ice Cream Co ...... E 614 231-0014
 Columbus *(G-7074)*
Stella Lou LLC .... F 937 935-9536
 Powell *(G-16336)*
Youngs Jersey Dairy Inc .... G 937 325-0629
 Yellow Springs *(G-20823)*

RESTAURANTS:Limited Svc, Lunch Counter

Milk & Honey .... F 330 492-5884
 Canton *(G-2755)*

RESTAURANTS:Limited Svc, Pizza

Georgetown Vineyards Inc .... E 740 435-3222
 Cambridge *(G-2440)*

RESTAURANTS:Limited Svc, Pizzeria, Chain

Miami Valley Pizza Hut Inc .... E 419 586-5900
 Celina *(G-2976)*

RESTAURANTS:Limited Svc, Pizzeria, Independent

Brinkman LLC .... F 419 204-5934
 Lima *(G-11846)*
Wal-Bon of Ohio Inc .... F 740 423-6351
 Belpre *(G-1585)*

RESTAURANTS:Limited Svc, Sandwiches & Submarines Shop

Circleville Oil Co .... G 740 477-3341
 Circleville *(G-4539)*
Perfettes Sausage LLC .... G 330 792-0775
 Youngstown *(G-20998)*

RESTAURANTS:Limited Svc, Snack Shop

Bunker Hill Cheese Co Inc .... D 330 893-2131
 Millersburg *(G-14073)*

RESTROOM CLEANING SVCS

Image By J & K LLC .... B 888 667-6929
 Maumee *(G-13118)*

RETAIL BAKERY: Bread

B L F Enterprises Inc .... F 937 642-6425
 Westerville *(G-20036)*
Norcia Bakery .... E 330 454-1077
 Canton *(G-2763)*
Schwebel Baking Company .... C 440 248-1500
 Solon *(G-17228)*
Schwebel Baking Company .... D 330 783-2860
 Hebron *(G-10762)*
Unger Kosher Bakery Inc .... E 216 321-7176
 Cleveland Heights *(G-6352)*

RETAIL BAKERY: Cakes

I Dream of Cakes .... G 937 533-6024
 Eaton *(G-9153)*
Sugar Showcase .... G 330 792-9154
 Youngstown *(G-21040)*

RETAIL BAKERY: Cookies

Cookie Bouquets Inc .... G 614 888-2171
 Columbus *(G-6817)*
Great American Cookie Company . F 419 474-9417
 Toledo *(G-18311)*

RETAIL BAKERY: Doughnuts

Crispie Creme of Chillicothe ...... E 740 774-3770
 Chillicothe *(G-3183)*
Dandi Enterprises Inc .... F 419 516-9070
 Solon *(G-17131)*
Dunkin Donuts .... G 330 336-2500
 Wadsworth *(G-19236)*
Evans Bakery Inc .... F 937 228-4151
 Dayton *(G-8190)*
Georges Donuts Inc .... G 330 963-9902
 Twinsburg *(G-18784)*
Jims Donut Shop .... G 937 898-4222
 Vandalia *(G-19131)*
Kennedys Bakery Inc .... E 740 432-2301
 Cambridge *(G-2444)*
Krispy Kreme Doughnut Corp ..... F 614 798-0812
 Columbus *(G-7101)*
Mary Ann Donut Shoppe Inc ...... E 330 478-1655
 Canton *(G-2745)*
McHappys Donuts of Parkersburg . G 740 593-8744
 Athens *(G-838)*
Schulers Bakery Inc .... E 937 323-4154
 Springfield *(G-17491)*

RETAIL BAKERY: Pastries

Meeks Pastry Shop .... G 419 782-4871
 Defiance *(G-8637)*

RETAIL BAKERY: Pies

K & B Acquisitions Inc .... F 937 253-1163
 Dayton *(G-8288)*

RETAIL BAKERY: Pretzels

Annes Auntie Pretzels .... E 614 418-7021
 Columbus *(G-6605)*
Auntie Annes .... G 330 652-1939
 Niles *(G-15000)*

RETAIL FIREPLACE STORES

Overhead Inc .... G 419 476-0300
 Toledo *(G-18443)*
Whempys Corp .... G 614 888-6670
 Worthington *(G-20707)*

RETAIL LUMBER YARDS

A & B Wood Design Assoc Inc .... G 330 721-2789
 Wadsworth *(G-19218)*
Ace Lumber Company .... F 330 744-3167
 Youngstown *(G-20835)*
Carter-Jones Lumber Company ... F 440 834-8164
 Middlefield *(G-13782)*

Clarksville Stave & Lumber Co ... G 937 376-4618
 Xenia *(G-20763)*
Conover Lumber Company Inc .... F 937 368-3010
 Conover *(G-7663)*
Crosco Wood Products .... G 937 857-0228
 Dalton *(G-7938)*
Hardwood Store Inc .... G 937 864-2899
 Enon *(G-9384)*
Hyde Park Lumber Company ...... E 513 271-1500
 Cincinnati *(G-3830)*
J D L Hardwoods .... G 440 272-5630
 Middlefield *(G-13807)*
K D Hardwoods Inc .... G 440 834-1772
 Burton *(G-2364)*
Marsh Valley Forest Pdts Ltd ..... G 440 632-1889
 Middlefield *(G-13816)*
R C Moore Lumber Co .... F 740 732-4950
 Caldwell *(G-2410)*
Regal Cabinet Inc .... E 419 865-3932
 Toledo *(G-18500)*
Salem Mill & Cabinet Co .... G 330 337-9568
 Salem *(G-16771)*
Thomas Do-It Center Inc .... D 740 446-2002
 Gallipolis *(G-10176)*

RETAIL STORES, NEC

Auntie Annes .... G 330 652-1939
 Niles *(G-15000)*
Gannons Discount Blinds .... G 216 398-2761
 Cleveland *(G-5289)*

RETAIL STORES: Air Purification Eqpt

Indoor Envmtl Specialists Inc .... F 937 433-5202
 Dayton *(G-8262)*

RETAIL STORES: Alcoholic Beverage Making Eqpt & Splys

Chappell-Zimmerman Inc .... F 330 337-8711
 Salem *(G-16725)*
General Pump & Eqp Compnay ... G 330 455-2100
 Canton *(G-2682)*
Pomacon Inc .... F 330 273-1576
 Brunswick *(G-2226)*

RETAIL STORES: Aquarium Splys

Aquatic Technology .... F 440 236-8330
 Columbia Station *(G-6428)*

RETAIL STORES: Architectural Splys

Richland Blue Printcom Inc .... G 419 524-2781
 Mansfield *(G-12505)*

RETAIL STORES: Art & Architectural Splys

GBS Corp .... E 330 929-8050
 Stow *(G-17591)*

RETAIL STORES: Artificial Limbs

Hanger Prsthetcs & Ortho Inc .... G 740 454-6215
 Zanesville *(G-21145)*
Novacare Inc .... G 216 704-4817
 Beachwood *(G-1254)*

RETAIL STORES: Audio-Visual Eqpt & Splys

Custom Automation Technologies . G 614 939-4228
 New Albany *(G-14618)*
Findaway World LLC .... D 440 893-0808
 Solon *(G-17143)*
Sound Concepts LLC .... G 513 703-0147
 Mason *(G-12940)*

RETAIL STORES: Awnings

Jacqueline L Vandyke .... G 740 593-6779
 Athens *(G-837)*
P C R Restorations Inc .... F 419 747-7957
 Mansfield *(G-12501)*

RETAIL STORES: Banners

Blang Acquisition LLC .... F 937 223-2155
 Dayton *(G-8058)*
Eastgate Custom Graphics Ltd ... G 513 528-7922
 Cincinnati *(G-3625)*

RETAIL STORES: Batteries, Non-Automotive

Battery Unlimited ....G....... 740 452-5030
  Zanesville (G-21104)
One Wish LLC ....F....... 800 505-6883
  Beachwood (G-1259)

RETAIL STORES: Business Machines & Eqpt

A/C Laser Technologies Inc ....F....... 330 784-3355
  Akron (G-24)

RETAIL STORES: Cake Decorating Splys

Cake Arts Supplies ....G....... 419 472-4959
  Toledo (G-18221)
Cake Decor ....G....... 614 836-5533
  Groveport (G-10487)
Hartville Chocolates Inc ....F....... 330 877-1999
  Hartville (G-10692)

RETAIL STORES: Children's Furniture, NEC

Foundations Worldwide Inc ....E....... 330 722-5033
  Medina (G-13264)

RETAIL STORES: Christmas Lights & Decorations

Christmas Ranch LLC ....E....... 513 505-3865
  Morrow (G-14409)
Rhc Inc ....G....... 330 874-3750
  Bolivar (G-1927)

RETAIL STORES: Cleaning Eqpt & Splys

Akron Cotton Products Inc ....G....... 330 434-7171
  Akron (G-36)
Chempure Products Corporation ....G....... 330 874-4300
  Bolivar (G-1909)
Fox Supply LLC ....G....... 419 628-3051
  Minster (G-14214)
Jeff Pendergrass ....G....... 513 575-1226
  Milford (G-14021)
Scott Fetzer Company ....E....... 216 228-2400
  Chagrin Falls (G-3075)

RETAIL STORES: Communication Eqpt

Communications Aid Inc ....F....... 513 475-8453
  Cincinnati (G-3537)
Transel Corporation ....G....... 513 897-3442
  Harveysburg (G-10706)

RETAIL STORES: Concrete Prdts, Precast

Artistic Rock LLC ....G....... 216 291-8856
  Cleveland (G-4742)
Michaels Pre-Cast Con Pdts ....F....... 513 683-1292
  Loveland (G-12215)
Snyder Concrete Products Inc ....F....... 513 539-7686
  Monroe (G-14276)

RETAIL STORES: Cosmetics

Safe 4 People Inc ....G....... 419 797-4087
  Port Clinton (G-16257)

RETAIL STORES: Decals

First Stop Signs and Decals ....G....... 330 343-1859
  New Philadelphia (G-14769)
Mike B Crawford ....G....... 330 673-7944
  Kent (G-11355)

RETAIL STORES: Drafting Eqpt & Splys

J C Equipment Sales & Leasing ....G....... 513 772-7612
  Cincinnati (G-3862)

RETAIL STORES: Educational Aids & Electronic Training Mat

Bendon Inc ....D....... 419 207-3600
  Ashland (G-685)
Health Nuts Media LLC ....G....... 818 802-5222
  Cleveland (G-5384)

RETAIL STORES: Electronic Parts & Eqpt

Mixed Logic LLC ....G....... 440 826-1676
  Valley City (G-19050)
Precision Replacement LLC ....G....... 330 908-0410
  Macedonia (G-12319)

RETAIL STORES: Engine & Motor Eqpt & Splys

Country Sales & Service LLC ....F....... 330 683-2500
  Orrville (G-15588)
DW Hercules LLC ....E....... 330 830-2498
  Massillon (G-12977)

RETAIL STORES: Farm Eqpt & Splys

Coleman Machine Inc ....G....... 740 695-3006
  Saint Clairsville (G-16628)
Gerber & Sons Inc ....E....... 330 897-6201
  Baltic (G-1030)
Jani Auto Parts Inc ....G....... 330 494-2975
  North Canton (G-15095)
R & J AG Manufacturing Inc ....F....... 419 962-4707
  Ashland (G-741)

RETAIL STORES: Farm Tractors

Miners Tractor Sales Inc ....F....... 330 325-9914
  Rootstown (G-16571)

RETAIL STORES: Fiberglass Materials, Exc Insulation

Schmelzer Industries Inc ....E....... 740 743-2866
  Somerset (G-17267)
Toledo Pro Fiberglass Inc ....G....... 419 241-9390
  Toledo (G-18567)

RETAIL STORES: Fire Extinguishers

Warren Fire Equipment Inc ....E....... 330 824-3523
  Warren (G-19459)

RETAIL STORES: Flags

Flag Lady Inc ....G....... 614 263-1776
  Columbus (G-6927)
Mel Wacker Sign Inc ....G....... 330 832-1726
  Massillon (G-13024)

RETAIL STORES: Gravestones, Finished

Ashland Monument Company Inc ....G....... 419 281-2688
  Ashland (G-678)

RETAIL STORES: Hair Care Prdts

Natural Beauty Products Inc ....F....... 513 420-9400
  Middletown (G-13935)

RETAIL STORES: Hearing Aids

Morris Maico Hearing Aid Svc ....G....... 419 232-6200
  Van Wert (G-19103)

RETAIL STORES: Hospital Eqpt & Splys

Kempf Surgical Appliances Inc ....E....... 513 984-5758
  Montgomery (G-14295)

RETAIL STORES: Ice

Haller Enterprises Inc ....F....... 330 733-9693
  Akron (G-195)
Home City Ice Company ....F....... 440 439-5001
  Bedford (G-1413)
Home City Ice Company ....E....... 614 836-2877
  Groveport (G-10493)
Home City Ice Company ....E....... 937 461-6028
  Dayton (G-8252)

RETAIL STORES: Medical Apparatus & Splys

Access To Independence Inc ....G....... 330 296-8111
  Ravenna (G-16363)
Relevium Labs Inc ....G....... 614 568-7000
  Oxford (G-15699)
Schaerer Medical Usa Inc ....F....... 513 561-2241
  Cincinnati (G-4305)

RETAIL STORES: Monuments, Finished To Custom Order

Bell Vault & Monument Works ....E....... 937 866-2444
  Miamisburg (G-13643)
Dodds Monument Inc ....F....... 937 372-2736
  Xenia (G-20767)
Drake Monument Company ....G....... 937 399-7941
  Springfield (G-17391)
Ellinger Monument Inc ....G....... 740 385-3687
  Rockbridge (G-16536)
Hirons Memorial Works Inc ....G....... 937 444-2917
  Mount Orab (G-14444)
Jackson Monument Inc ....G....... 740 286-1590
  Jackson (G-11187)
Maumee Valley Memorials Inc ....F....... 419 878-9030
  Waterville (G-19501)
Mayfair Granite Co Inc ....G....... 216 382-8150
  Cleveland (G-5636)
North Hill Marble & Granite Co ....G....... 330 253-2179
  Akron (G-301)
Piqua Granite & Marble Co Inc ....G....... 937 773-2000
  Piqua (G-16153)

RETAIL STORES: Motors, Electric

Allan A Irish ....G....... 419 394-3284
  Saint Marys (G-16675)
Big River Electric Inc ....G....... 740 446-4360
  Gallipolis (G-10161)
C and O Electric Motor Service ....G....... 614 491-6387
  Columbus (G-6718)
Carnation Elc Mtr Repr Sls Inc ....G....... 330 823-7116
  Alliance (G-460)
Franks Electric Inc ....G....... 513 313-5883
  Cincinnati (G-3711)
Lebanon Electric Motor Svc LLC ....G....... 513 932-2889
  Lebanon (G-11670)
Lemsco Inc ....G....... 419 242-4005
  Toledo (G-18381)
Wheatley Electric Service Co ....G....... 513 531-4951
  Cincinnati (G-4505)

RETAIL STORES: Orthopedic & Prosthesis Applications

Akron Orthotic Solutions Inc ....G....... 330 253-3002
  Akron (G-45)
Biocare Orthopedic Prosthetics ....G....... 614 754-7514
  Columbus (G-6671)
Capital Prosthetic Inc ....G....... 740 522-3331
  Newark (G-14859)
Hanger Prsthetcs & Ortho Inc ....G....... 740 654-1884
  Lancaster (G-11578)
Hanger Prsthetcs & Ortho Inc ....F....... 419 841-9852
  Toledo (G-18321)
Hanger Prsthetcs & Ortho Inc ....G....... 937 773-2441
  Piqua (G-16120)
Hanger Prsthetcs & Ortho Inc ....F....... 937 228-5462
  Dayton (G-8243)
Hanger Prsthetcs & Ortho Inc ....G....... 740 383-2163
  Marion (G-12709)
Hanger Prsthetcs & Ortho Inc ....G....... 740 266-6400
  Steubenville (G-17536)
Hanger Prsthetcs & Ortho Inc ....G....... 419 522-0055
  Marion (G-12708)
Leimkuehler Inc ....E....... 440 899-7842
  Cleveland (G-5573)
Presque Isle Orthotics ....G....... 216 371-0660
  Beachwood (G-1268)
Prosthetic Design Inc ....G....... 937 836-1464
  Englewood (G-9373)
Stable Step LLC ....E....... 513 825-1888
  West Chester (G-19798)

RETAIL STORES: Pet Splys

Miraclecorp Products ....D....... 937 293-9994
  Moraine (G-14372)

RETAIL STORES: Photocopy Machines

ABC Appliance Inc ....E....... 419 693-4414
  Oregon (G-15552)
Copier Resources Inc ....G....... 614 268-1100
  Columbus (G-6818)

RETAIL STORES: Picture Frames, Ready Made

Frame USA ....E....... 513 577-7107
  Cincinnati (G-3708)
House of 10000 Picture Frames ....G....... 937 254-5541
  Dayton (G-8253)

RETAIL STORES: Plumbing & Heating Splys

Carr Supply Co ....G....... 937 276-2555
  Dayton (G-8076)
Certified Walk In Tubs ....F....... 614 436-4848
  Columbus (G-6756)

RETAIL STORES: Plumbing & Heating Splys

Dbhl Inc .... F 216 267-7100
  Cleveland (G-5076)
Stevens Auto Parts & Towng .... G 740 988-2260
  Jackson (G-11195)

RETAIL STORES: Police Splys

Walter F Stephens Jr Inc .... E 937 746-0521
  Franklin (G-9930)

RETAIL STORES: Religious Goods

Incorporated Trst Gspl Wk Scty .... D 216 749-2100
  Cleveland (G-5448)
Strictly Stitchery Inc .... F 440 543-7128
  Cleveland (G-6110)

RETAIL STORES: Rock & Stone Specimens

National Lime and Stone Co .... E 740 387-3485
  Marion (G-12724)

RETAIL STORES: Rubber Stamps

Geygan Enterprises Inc .... F 513 932-4222
  Lebanon (G-11656)
Hathaway Stamp Co .... F 513 621-1052
  Cincinnati (G-3803)
Hirt Publishing Co Inc .... E 419 946-3010
  Mount Gilead (G-14426)
Kee Printing Inc .... G 937 456-6851
  Eaton (G-9156)
The Rubber Stamp Shop .... G 419 478-4444
  Toledo (G-18549)

RETAIL STORES: Safety Splys & Eqpt

Paul Peterson Safety Div Inc .... E 614 486-4375
  Columbus (G-7300)

RETAIL STORES: Sunglasses

Holte Eyeware .... G 513 321-4000
  Cincinnati (G-3820)

RETAIL STORES: Swimming Pools, Above Ground

Oliver Pool and Spa Inc .... G 740 264-5368
  Steubenville (G-17548)

RETAIL STORES: Technical Aids For The Handicapped

Steves Vans & Accessories LLC .... G 740 374-3154
  Marietta (G-12676)

RETAIL STORES: Telephone & Communication Eqpt

Securcom Inc .... E 419 628-1049
  Minster (G-14224)

RETAIL STORES: Telephone Eqpt & Systems

Ray Communications Inc .... G 330 686-0226
  Stow (G-17623)
Town Cntry Technical Svcs Inc .... F 614 866-7700
  Reynoldsburg (G-16457)

RETAIL STORES: Tents

Rainbow Industries Inc .... G 937 323-6493
  Springfield (G-17479)

RETAIL STORES: Theatrical Eqpt & Splys

Schenz Theatrical Supply Inc .... F 513 542-6100
  Cincinnati (G-4306)

RETAIL STORES: Typewriters & Business Machines

COS Blueprint Inc .... F 330 376-0022
  Akron (G-122)
Golubitsky Corporation .... G 800 552-4204
  Cleveland (G-5329)

RETAIL STORES: Vaults & Safes

National Security Products .... G 216 566-9962
  Cleveland (G-5729)

RETAIL STORES: Water Purification Eqpt

Enting Water Conditioning Inc .... E 937 294-5100
  Moraine (G-14350)
K S W C Inc .... G 440 577-1114
  Pierpont (G-16065)
Link-O-Matic Company Inc .... F 765 962-1538
  Brookville (G-2173)
US Water Company LLC .... G 740 453-0604
  Zanesville (G-21186)

RETAIL STORES: Welding Splys

AT&f Nuclear Inc .... G 216 252-1500
  Cleveland (G-4757)
C & M Welding Services LLC .... G 419 584-0008
  Celina (G-2951)
Nyeco Gas Inc .... G 419 447-2712
  Sandusky (G-16831)
Praxair Distribution Inc .... G 419 422-1353
  Lima (G-11918)
Praxair Distribution Inc .... G 513 821-2192
  Cincinnati (G-4184)
Welders Supply Inc .... F 216 241-1696
  Cleveland (G-6299)

RETREADING MATERIALS: Tire

H & H Industries Inc .... G 740 682-7721
  Oak Hill (G-15451)

REUPHOLSTERY & FURNITURE REPAIR

Fortner Upholstering Inc .... F 614 475-8282
  Columbus (G-6933)
Robert Mayo Industries .... G 330 426-2587
  East Palestine (G-9083)

REUPHOLSTERY SVCS

Central Design Services .... G 513 829-7027
  Fairfield (G-9489)
Office Magic Inc .... F 510 782-6100
  Medina (G-13310)
Wahlies Cstm Cft Drapery Uphl .... G 419 229-1731
  Lima (G-11958)

RIBBONS & BOWS

Camela Nitschke Ribbonry .... G 419 872-0073
  Perrysburg (G-15929)
Nicholas Ray Enterprises LLC .... G 330 454-4811
  Canton (G-2761)
Sylvan Studio Inc .... G 419 882-3423
  Sylvania (G-17963)

RIBBONS: Machine, Inked Or Carbon

Progressive Ribbon Inc .... E 513 705-9319
  Middletown (G-13944)

RIVETS: Metal

Jenco Manufacturing Inc .... E 216 898-9682
  Independence (G-11137)
Kre Inc .... F 216 883-1600
  Twinsburg (G-18802)
North Coast Rivet Inc .... F 440 366-6829
  Elyria (G-9301)

ROAD CONSTRUCTION EQUIPMENT WHOLESALERS

Brewpro Inc .... G 513 577-7200
  Cincinnati (G-3415)

ROAD MATERIALS: Bituminous, Not From Refineries

Road Maintenance Products .... G 740 465-7181
  Morral (G-14405)
Roof To Road LLC .... G 740 986-6923
  Williamsport (G-20261)

ROBOTS: Assembly Line

Advanced Design Industries Inc .... E 440 277-4141
  Sheffield Village (G-16965)
Air Technical Industries Inc .... E 440 951-5191
  Mentor (G-13378)
Ats Systems Oregon Inc .... B 541 738-0932
  Lewis Center (G-11747)
Computer Allied Technology Co .... G 614 457-2292
  Columbus (G-6808)
Fanuc America Corporation .... E 513 754-2400
  Mason (G-12870)
Motor Systems Incorporated .... E 513 576-1725
  Milford (G-14029)
Omega Automation Inc .... D 937 890-2350
  Dayton (G-8402)
Omega International Inc .... G 937 890-2350
  Dayton (G-8403)
Process Innovations Inc .... G 330 856-5192
  Vienna (G-19207)
Production Design Services Inc .... D 937 866-3377
  Dayton (G-8446)
Programmable Control Service .... F 740 927-0744
  Pataskala (G-15838)
Recognition Robotics Inc .... F 440 590-0499
  Elyria (G-9319)
Rennco Automation Systems Inc .... E 419 861-2340
  Holland (G-10953)
Rimrock Holdings Corporation .... E 614 471-5926
  Columbus (G-7395)
Rixan Associates Inc .... E 937 438-3005
  Dayton (G-8479)
Sas Automation LLC .... F 937 372-5255
  Xenia (G-20789)
Versatile Automation Tech Ltd .... G 330 220-2600
  Brunswick (G-2248)
Yaskawa America Inc .... C 937 847-6200
  Miamisburg (G-13742)

ROBOTS: Indl Spraying, Painting, Etc

Ats Ohio Inc .... C 614 888-2344
  Lewis Center (G-11746)
Rubberset Company .... G 800 345-4939
  Cleveland (G-6015)
Wiwa LP .... F 419 757-0141
  Alger (G-445)

ROD & BAR Aluminum

Allen Morgan Trucking & Repair .... G 330 336-5192
  Norton (G-15361)

RODS: Extruded, Aluminum

Mag Acquisitions LLC .... C 513 988-6351
  Trenton (G-18622)

RODS: Plastic

New Image Plastics Mfg Co .... G 330 854-3010
  Canal Fulton (G-2487)
Precision Fabrications Inc .... G 937 297-8606
  Sunbury (G-17897)

RODS: Rolled, Aluminum

Kaiser Aluminum Fab Pdts LLC .... C 740 522-1151
  Heath (G-10723)

RODS: Steel & Iron, Made In Steel Mills

American Posts LLC .... E 419 720-0652
  Toledo (G-18179)
Buschman Corporation .... F 216 431-6633
  Cleveland (G-4853)
Charter Manufacturing Co Inc .... A 216 883-3800
  Cleveland (G-4916)
L&H Threaded Rods Corp .... C 937 294-6666
  Moraine (G-14365)

RODS: Welding

Artistic Composite & Mold Co .... G 330 352-6632
  Litchfield (G-11984)

ROLL COVERINGS: Rubber

Niles Roll Service Inc .... F 330 544-0026
  Niles (G-15025)

ROLL FORMED SHAPES: Custom

American Roll Formed Pdts Corp .... C 440 352-0753
  Youngstown (G-20843)
Ej Usa Inc .... F 330 782-3900
  Youngstown (G-20898)
Formasters Corporation .... F 440 639-9206
  Mentor (G-13445)
Hynes Industries Inc .... C 330 799-3221
  Youngstown (G-20934)
Lion Industries LLC .... E 740 699-0369
  Saint Clairsville (G-16636)

PRODUCT SECTION

RUBBER PRDTS: Mechanical

Ontario Mechnical LLC ....E 419 529-2578
  Ontario *(G-15544)*

ROLLING MILL EQPT: Finishing

Bardons & Oliver Inc ....C 440 498-5800
  Solon *(G-17112)*
Fives Bronx Inc ....D 330 244-1960
  North Canton *(G-15083)*

ROLLING MILL EQPT: Galvanizing Lines

Multi Galvanizing LLC ....G 330 453-1441
  Canton *(G-2758)*

ROLLING MILL MACHINERY

Addisonmckee Inc ....C 513 228-7000
  Lebanon *(G-11629)*
ADS Machinery Corp ....D 330 399-3601
  Warren *(G-19362)*
Bendco Machine & Tool Inc ....F 419 628-3802
  Minster *(G-14210)*
Circle Machine Rolls Inc ....E 330 938-9010
  Sebring *(G-16885)*
E R Advanced Ceramics Inc ....E 330 426-9433
  East Palestine *(G-9077)*
Element Machinery LLC ....G 855 447-7648
  Toledo *(G-18279)*
Enprotech Industrial Tech LLC ....E 216 883-3220
  Cleveland *(G-5179)*
Formtek Inc ....D 216 292-6300
  Cleveland *(G-5263)*
Foseco Inc 440 826-4548
  Cleveland *(G-5267)*
George A Mitchell Company ....E 330 758-5777
  Youngstown *(G-20920)*
H P E Inc ....F 330 833-3161
  Massillon *(G-12993)*
Hydranamics Inc ....D 419 468-3530
  Galion *(G-10144)*
J Horst Manufacturing Co ....D 330 828-2216
  Dalton *(G-7945)*
Kottler Metal Products Co Inc ....E 440 946-7473
  Willoughby *(G-20355)*
Park Corporation ....B 216 267-4870
  Cleveland *(G-5841)*
Perfecto Industries Inc ....E 937 778-1900
  Piqua *(G-16149)*
Pines Manufacturing Inc ....E 440 835-5553
  Westlake *(G-20142)*
Pines Manufacturing Inc ....E 440 835-5553
  Westlake *(G-20141)*
Rafter Equipment Corporation ....E 440 572-3700
  Strongsville *(G-17781)*
Ridge Tool Company ....A 440 323-5581
  Elyria *(G-9320)*
Ridge Tool Manufacturing Co ....A 440 323-5581
  Elyria *(G-9322)*
Steel Eqp Specialists Inc ....E 330 829-2626
  Alliance *(G-501)*
Steel Eqp Specialists Inc ....E 330 823-8260
  Alliance *(G-502)*
Sticker Corporation ....F 440 946-2100
  Willoughby *(G-20438)*
Turner Machine Co 330 332-5821
  Salem *(G-16778)*
United Rolls Inc ....D 330 456-2761
  Canton *(G-2850)*
Warren Fabricating Corporation 330 534-5017
  Hubbard *(G-11011)*
Wauseon Machine & Mfg Inc ....D 419 337-0940
  Wauseon *(G-19537)*
Xtek Inc ....B 513 733-7800
  Cincinnati *(G-4530)*

ROLLING MILL ROLLS: Cast Steel

United Engineering & Fndry Co ....F 330 456-2761
  Canton *(G-2847)*

ROLLS & ROLL COVERINGS: Rubber

Pinnacle Roller Co ....F 513 369-4830
  Cincinnati *(G-4162)*

ROOFING MATERIALS: Asphalt

Certainteed Corporation ....C 419 499-2581
  Milan *(G-13981)*
Classic Metals Ltd ....G 330 763-1162
  Holmesville *(G-10974)*

Commercial Innovations Inc ....G 216 641-7500
  Cleveland *(G-5003)*
Garland Industries Inc ....G 216 641-7500
  Cleveland *(G-5294)*
Garland/Dbs Inc ....C 216 641-7500
  Cleveland *(G-5295)*
Johns Manville Corporation ....D 419 499-1400
  Milan *(G-13986)*
P C R Inc ....F 330 945-7721
  Akron *(G-313)*
Topps Products Inc 216 271-2550
  Cleveland *(G-6188)*
Treadstone Company ....G 216 410-3435
  Twinsburg *(G-18865)*
Tremco Incorporated ....B 216 292-5000
  Beachwood *(G-1283)*

ROOFING MATERIALS: Sheet Metal

Cincinnati Gutter Supply Inc ....G 513 825-0500
  West Chester *(G-19672)*
HCC Holdings Inc ....G 800 203-1155
  Cleveland *(G-5383)*
Interstate Contractors LLC ....E 513 372-5393
  Mason *(G-12897)*
John Baird ....G 216 440-3595
  Spencer *(G-17305)*
Oatey Supply Chain Svcs Inc ....C 216 267-7100
  Cleveland *(G-5795)*
Transtar Holding Company 800 359-3339
  Walton Hills *(G-19315)*

ROOFING MEMBRANE: Rubber

Hyload Inc ....F 330 336-6604
  Seville *(G-16916)*
Omnova Solutions Inc ....C 216 682-7000
  Beachwood *(G-1257)*
Republic Powdered Metals Inc ....D 330 225-3192
  Medina *(G-13327)*
RPM International Inc 330 273-5090
  Medina *(G-13331)*
Soprema USA Inc ....E 330 334-0066
  Wadsworth *(G-19277)*

ROOM COOLERS: Portable

All About House ....G 614 725-3595
  Columbus *(G-6564)*
Climateright LLC ....G 800 725-4628
  Columbus *(G-6775)*

ROTORS: Motor

Yamada North America Inc ....B 937 462-7111
  South Charleston *(G-17275)*

RUBBER

Advanced Elastomer Systems LP ....D 330 336-7641
  Wadsworth *(G-19221)*
All-Tra Rubber Processing ....G 330 630-1945
  Tallmadge *(G-17972)*
Bridgestone Americas Center Fo ....G 330 379-7575
  Akron *(G-94)*
Bridgestone Procurement Holdin ....A 337 882-1200
  Akron *(G-95)*
Brp Manufacturing Company ....E 800 858-0482
  Lima *(G-11847)*
Cardinal Rubber Company Inc ....E 330 745-2191
  Barberton *(G-1069)*
Concrete Sealants Inc ....E 937 845-8776
  Tipp City *(G-18109)*
Covestro LLC ....C 740 929-2015
  Hebron *(G-10740)*
East West Copolymer LLC ....C 225 267-3400
  Cleveland *(G-5139)*
Eliokem Inc ....E 330 734-1100
  Fairlawn *(G-9604)*
Flexsys America LP ....D 330 666-4111
  Akron *(G-173)*
Gdc Inc 574 533-3128
  Wooster *(G-20596)*
High Tech Elastomers Inc ....E 937 236-6575
  Vandalia *(G-19128)*
Kraton Emplyees Recreation CLB ....G 740 423-7571
  Belpre *(G-1577)*
Kraton Polymers US LLC ....B 740 423-7571
  Belpre *(G-1578)*
Meggitt (erlanger) LLC 513 851-5550
  Cincinnati *(G-4000)*
Midwest Elastomers Inc ....D 419 738-8844
  Wapakoneta *(G-19343)*

Mohican Industries Inc ....F 330 869-0500
  Akron *(G-284)*
Mondo Polymer Technologies Inc ....E 740 376-9396
  Reno *(G-16425)*
Universal Urethane Pdts Inc ....D 419 693-7400
  Toledo *(G-18585)*
Vibronic .... F 937 274-1114
  Dayton *(G-8579)*
Wayne County Rubber Inc ....E 330 264-5553
  Wooster *(G-20664)*

RUBBER BANDS

Keener Rubber Company ....E 330 821-1880
  Alliance *(G-481)*

RUBBER PRDTS

International Sources Inc ....G 440 735-9890
  Bedford *(G-1417)*

RUBBER PRDTS REPAIR SVCS

Conviber Inc ....F 330 723-6006
  Medina *(G-13241)*
Heintz Manufacturers Inc ....G 724 274-6300
  Medina *(G-13271)*

RUBBER PRDTS: Appliance, Mechanical

Canton OH Rubber Speclty Prods ....G 330 454-3847
  Canton *(G-2612)*

RUBBER PRDTS: Automotive, Mechanical

Bridgestone APM Company ....D 419 294-6989
  Upper Sandusky *(G-18946)*
Bridgestone APM Company ....F 419 294-6304
  Upper Sandusky *(G-18947)*
Cardinal Rubber Company Inc ....E 330 745-2191
  Barberton *(G-1069)*
Koneta Inc 419 739-4200
  Wapakoneta *(G-19339)*
Miller Enterprises Ohio LLC ....G 330 852-4009
  Sugarcreek *(G-17853)*
Mm Outsourcing LLC ....F 937 661-4300
  Leesburg *(G-11714)*

RUBBER PRDTS: Mechanical

Alternative Flash Inc ....E 330 334-6111
  Wadsworth *(G-19225)*
American Pro-Mold Inc ....E 330 336-4111
  Wadsworth *(G-19226)*
ARC Rubber Inc ....F 440 466-4555
  Geneva *(G-10214)*
Ashtabula Rubber Co ....C 440 992-2195
  Ashtabula *(G-763)*
Brp Manufacturing Company ....E 800 858-0482
  Lima *(G-11847)*
C & M Rubber Co Inc ....F 937 299-2782
  Dayton *(G-8069)*
Chardon Custom Polymers LLC ....F 440 285-2161
  Chardon *(G-3101)*
Clark Rbr Plastic Intl Sls Inc ....D 440 255-9793
  Mentor *(G-13413)*
Colonial Rubber Company 330 296-2831
  Ravenna *(G-16373)*
Contitech North America Inc ....F 330 664-7180
  Fairlawn *(G-9602)*
Datwyler Sling Sltions USA Inc ....D 937 387-2800
  Vandalia *(G-19122)*
Duramax Global Corp ....D 440 834-5400
  Hiram *(G-10909)*
Elbex Corporation ....D 330 673-3233
  Kent *(G-11318)*
Epg Inc 330 995-5125
  Aurora *(G-879)*
Epg Inc ....F 330 995-9725
  Streetsboro *(G-17673)*
Extruded Silicon Products Inc ....E 330 733-0101
  Mogadore *(G-14237)*
Frankes Wood Products LLC ....E 937 642-0706
  Marysville *(G-12783)*
Goodyear International Corp ....D 330 796-2121
  Akron *(G-190)*
Harwood Rubber Products Inc ....E 330 923-3256
  Cuyahoga Falls *(G-7878)*
Hygenic Acquisition Co ....C 330 633-8460
  Akron *(G-212)*
Hygenic Corporation ....C 330 633-8460
  Akron *(G-213)*

Employee Codes: A=Over 500 employees, B=251-500
C=101-250, D=51-100, E=20-50, F=10-19, G=3-9

2019 Harris Ohio
Industrial Directory

RUBBER PRDTS: Mechanical

Ier Fujikura Inc .... C 330 425-7121
  Macedonia *(G-12302)*
Jakmar Incorporated .... F 513 631-4303
  Cincinnati *(G-3867)*
Johnson Bros Rubber Co Inc .... D 419 853-4122
  West Salem *(G-19955)*
Karman Rubber Company .... E 330 864-2161
  Akron *(G-232)*
Kleen Polymers Inc .... F 330 336-4212
  Wadsworth *(G-19250)*
Lauren Manufacturing LLC .... B 330 339-3373
  New Philadelphia *(G-14781)*
Lexington Rubber Group Inc .... E 330 425-8352
  Canton *(G-2733)*
Macdivitt Rubber Company LLC .... C 440 259-5937
  Perry *(G-15909)*
Mantaline Corporation .... D 330 274-2264
  Mantua *(G-12551)*
Martin Industries Inc .... E 419 862-2694
  Elmore *(G-9207)*
Meridian Industries Inc .... D 330 673-1011
  Kent *(G-11351)*
Midlands Millroom Supply Inc .... E 330 453-9100
  Canton *(G-2753)*
Midwest Industrial Rubber Inc .... F 614 876-3110
  Hilliard *(G-10841)*
Neff-Perkins Company .... C 440 632-1658
  Middlefield *(G-13839)*
Ohio Elastomers .... G 440 354-9750
  Perry *(G-15910)*
Ottawa Rubber Company .... F 419 865-1378
  Holland *(G-10947)*
Plabell Rubber Products Corp .... F 419 691-5878
  Toledo *(G-18472)*
Polycraft Products Inc .... C 513 353-3334
  Cleves *(G-6373)*
Q Holding Company .... B 330 425-8472
  Twinsburg *(G-18842)*
Qualiform Inc .... E 330 336-6777
  Wadsworth *(G-19268)*
Quanex Ig Systems Inc .... C 740 439-2338
  Cambridge *(G-2454)*
Quanex Ig Systems Inc .... C 216 910-1519
  Akron *(G-336)*
Robin Industries Inc .... E 330 893-3501
  Berlin *(G-1644)*
Robin Industries Inc .... C 330 359-5418
  Winesburg *(G-20534)*
Robin Industries Inc .... C 330 695-9300
  Fredericksburg *(G-9958)*
Roboworld Molded Products LLC ..... G 513 720-6900
  West Chester *(G-19784)*
Rubber-Tech Inc .... F 937 274-1114
  Dayton *(G-8487)*
Saint-Gobain Prfmce Plas Corp .... B 614 889-2220
  Dublin *(G-8978)*
Shreiner Sole Co Inc .... F 330 276-6135
  Killbuck *(G-11454)*
Soffseal Inc .... E 513 934-0815
  Lebanon *(G-11697)*
Tigerpoly Manufacturing Inc .... B 614 871-0045
  Grove City *(G-10473)*
Trelleborg Wheel Systems Ameri ...... E 866 633-8473
  Akron *(G-409)*
Universal Polymer & Rubber Ltd .... E 330 633-1666
  Tallmadge *(G-18011)*
Universal Urethane Pdts Inc .... D 419 693-7400
  Toledo *(G-18585)*
Vertex Inc .... E 330 628-6230
  Mogadore *(G-14252)*
Woodlawn Rubber Co .... F 513 489-1718
  Blue Ash *(G-1875)*
Yokohama Tire Corporation .... C 440 352-3321
  Painesville *(G-15803)*

RUBBER PRDTS: Medical & Surgical Tubing, Extrudd & Lathe-Cut

Saint-Gobain Prfmce Plas Corp .... C 330 798-6981
  Akron *(G-372)*

RUBBER PRDTS: Oil & Gas Field Machinery, Mechanical

United Feed Screws Ltd .... F 330 798-5532
  Akron *(G-420)*
V & M Star LP .... E 330 742-6300
  Youngstown *(G-21057)*

RUBBER PRDTS: Reclaimed

Boomerang Rubber Inc .... E 937 693-4611
  Botkins *(G-1933)*
Chemionics Corporation .... E 330 733-8834
  Tallmadge *(G-17975)*
Econo Products Inc .... F 330 923-4101
  Cuyahoga Falls *(G-7862)*
Flexsys America LP .... D 330 666-4111
  Akron *(G-173)*
Gold Key Processing Inc .... C 440 632-0901
  Middlefield *(G-13800)*
Lanxess Corporation .... C 440 279-2367
  Chardon *(G-3123)*
Murrubber Technologies Inc .... C 330 688-4881
  Stow *(G-17609)*
Valley Rubber Mixing Inc .... F 330 434-4442
  Akron *(G-424)*

RUBBER PRDTS: Sheeting

Brp Manufacturing Company .... E 800 858-0482
  Lima *(G-11847)*
Censtar Coatings Inc .... G 330 723-8000
  West Salem *(G-19953)*

RUBBER PRDTS: Silicone

Brain Child Products LLC .... F 419 698-4020
  Toledo *(G-18215)*
Medical Elastomer Dev Inc .... E 330 425-8352
  Twinsburg *(G-18815)*

RUBBER PRDTS: Sponge

Chalfant Sew Fabricators Inc .... E 216 521-7922
  Cleveland *(G-4907)*
Miles Rubber & Packing Company ..... E 330 425-3888
  Twinsburg *(G-18820)*

RUBBER STAMP, WHOLESALE

Northmont Sign Co Inc .... G 937 890-0372
  Dayton *(G-8384)*
Quick As A Wink Printing Co .... F 419 224-9786
  Lima *(G-11926)*

RUBBER STRUCTURES: Air-Supported

Truflex Rubber Products Co .... C 740 967-9015
  Johnstown *(G-11273)*

RUST ARRESTING COMPOUNDS: Animal Or Vegetable Oil Based

Lubrizol Corporation .... E 440 357-7064
  Painesville *(G-15758)*
Magnus International Group Inc .... G 216 592-8355
  Chagrin Falls *(G-3056)*

RUST PROOFING SVC: Hot Dipping, Metals & Formed Prdts

Parker Rst-Proof Cleveland Inc .... E 216 481-6680
  Cleveland *(G-5847)*

RUST REMOVERS

Metaltek Industries Inc .... F 937 323-4933
  Springfield *(G-17447)*
Skybryte Company Inc .... G 216 771-1590
  Cleveland *(G-6070)*

RUST RESISTING

Zerust Consumer Products LLC .... G 330 405-1965
  Twinsburg *(G-18877)*

SADDLERY STORES

Old West Industries Inc .... G 513 889-0500
  Hamilton *(G-10592)*

SAFE DEPOSIT BOXES

Hamilton Safe Co .... F 513 874-3733
  Cincinnati *(G-3794)*
Hamilton Security Products Co .... C 513 874-3733
  Cincinnati *(G-3795)*
Williamson Safe Inc .... E 937 393-9919
  Hillsboro *(G-10895)*

SAFES & VAULTS: Metal

Cincy Safe Company .... E 513 900-9152
  Milford *(G-14003)*
Diebold Nixdorf Incorporated .... A 330 490-4000
  North Canton *(G-15078)*
Hamilton Fabricators Inc .... E 513 735-7773
  Batavia *(G-1151)*
Hamilton Safe Amelia .... F 513 753-5694
  Amelia *(G-540)*
Linsalata Capital Partners Fun .... G 440 684-1400
  Cleveland *(G-5579)*

SAFETY EQPT & SPLYS WHOLESALERS

All-American Fire Eqp Inc .... F 800 972-6035
  Wshngtn CT Hs *(G-20718)*
L-Mor Inc .... F 216 541-2224
  Cleveland *(G-5551)*
Municipal Signs and Sales Inc .... G 330 457-2421
  Columbiana *(G-6474)*
National Hwy Maint Systems LLC ..... G 330 922-3649
  Peninsula *(G-15896)*
Netherland Rubber Company .... F 513 733-0883
  Cincinnati *(G-4068)*
Wcm Holdings Inc .... G 513 705-2100
  Cincinnati *(G-4493)*
West Chester Holdings LLC .... C 800 647-1900
  Cincinnati *(G-4499)*

SAILBOAT BUILDING & REPAIR

Doyle Sailmaker .... G 216 486-5732
  Cleveland *(G-5111)*
Dynamic Plastics Inc .... G 937 437-7261
  New Paris *(G-14753)*
Great Midwest Yacht Co .... G 740 965-4511
  Sunbury *(G-17887)*

SAILS

R F W Holdings Inc .... G 440 331-8300
  Cleveland *(G-5951)*
Ragman Inc .... G 419 255-8068
  Toledo *(G-18497)*

SALES PROMOTION SVCS

S E Anning Company .... G 513 702-4417
  Cincinnati *(G-4295)*

SALT

Abraxus Salt Inc .... G 440 743-7669
  Cleveland *(G-4601)*
Obersons Nurs & Landscapes Inc .... F 513 894-0669
  Fairfield *(G-9538)*

SALT & SULFUR MINING

Morton International LLC .... G 513 941-1578
  Cincinnati *(G-4049)*

SALT MINING: Common

Cargill Incorporated .... C 216 651-7200
  Cleveland *(G-4877)*

SALT: Packers'

Morton Salt Inc .... F 440 354-9901
  Painesville *(G-15764)*

SAND & GRAVEL

Allen Harper .... G 740 543-3919
  Amsterdam *(G-576)*
Barrett Paving Materials Inc .... C 513 271-6200
  Middletown *(G-13970)*
Beldex Land Company LLC .... G 740 783-3575
  Dexter City *(G-8793)*
Big Bills Trucking LLC .... G 614 850-0626
  Hilliard *(G-10813)*
Bonsal American Inc .... E 513 398-7300
  Cincinnati *(G-3403)*
C F Poeppelman Inc .... E 937 448-2191
  Bradford *(G-2010)*
Clay LBC Co .... G 740 492-5055
  Newcomerstown *(G-14972)*
Covia Holdings Corporation .... D 440 214-3284
  Independence *(G-11123)*
Fisher Sand & Gravel Inc .... G 330 745-9239
  Norton *(G-15368)*

FML Resin LLC .... E 440 214-3200
Independence *(G-11129)*
FML Terminal Logistics LLC .... G 440 214-3200
Independence *(G-11131)*
Foundry Sand Service LLC .... G 330 823-6152
Sebring *(G-16886)*
Gravel Doctor of Ohio LLC .... G 844 472-8353
Millersport *(G-14159)*
Gravel-Tech .... G 513 703-3672
Morrow *(G-14410)*
Grimes Sand & Gravel .... G 740 865-3990
New Matamoras *(G-14746)*
Hanson Aggregates East .... G 513 353-1100
Cleves *(G-6363)*
Hanson Aggregates East LLC .... E 740 773-2172
Chillicothe *(G-3191)*
Hilltop Basic Resources Inc .... F 937 882-6357
Springfield *(G-17418)*
Hilltop Basic Resources Inc .... F 937 859-3616
Miamisburg *(G-13676)*
Hilltop Basic Resources Inc .... E 513 621-1500
Cincinnati *(G-3814)*
Holmes Redimix Inc .... F 330 674-0865
Millersburg *(G-14099)*
Holmes Supply Corp .... G 330 279-2634
Holmesville *(G-10980)*
James Bunnell Inc .... F 513 353-1100
Cleves *(G-6365)*
James Ryan Soloman .... G 740 659-2304
Glenford *(G-10270)*
Joe McClelland Inc .... E 740 452-3036
Zanesville *(G-21151)*
Kenmore Construction Co Inc .... E 330 832-8888
Massillon *(G-13009)*
Martin Marietta Materials Inc .... E 513 701-1140
West Chester *(G-19740)*
Medina Supply Company .... G 330 723-3681
Medina *(G-13298)*
National Lime and Stone Co .... C 419 396-7671
Carey *(G-2884)*
Oeder Carl E Sons Sand & Grav .... E 513 494-1238
Lebanon *(G-11677)*
Olen Corporation .... G 330 262-6821
Wooster *(G-20635)*
Oster Sand and Gravel Inc .... G 330 874-3322
Bolivar *(G-1920)*
Oster Sand and Gravel Inc .... G 330 833-2649
Massillon *(G-13035)*
Phillips Ready Mix Co .... D 937 426-5151
Beavercreek Township *(G-1372)*
Phoenix Asphalt Company Inc .... G 330 339-4935
Magnolia *(G-12362)*
Pioneer Sands LLC .... E 740 599-7773
Howard *(G-10997)*
Prairie Lane Corporation .... G 330 262-3322
Wooster *(G-20639)*
R W Sidley Incorporated .... E 440 564-2221
Newbury *(G-14962)*
Rjw Trucking Company Ltd .... E 740 363-5343
Delaware *(G-8720)*
Robert Perez Carpentry .... G 330 497-0043
Canton *(G-2808)*
Roger Hall .... G 740 778-2861
South Webster *(G-17299)*
Rupp Construction Inc .... F 330 855-2781
Marshallville *(G-12755)*
Shelly and Sands Inc .... E 740 453-0721
Zanesville *(G-21177)*
Shelly Company .... G 740 246-6315
Thornville *(G-18033)*
Shelly Materials Inc .... G 330 673-3646
Kent *(G-11385)*
Shelly Materials Inc .... D 740 246-6315
Thornville *(G-18035)*
Smith Concrete Co .... G 740 373-7441
Dover *(G-8854)*
Solomons Mines Inc .... G 330 337-0123
Salem *(G-16775)*
Stafford Gravel Inc .... G 419 298-2440
Edgerton *(G-9180)*
Stocker Concrete Company .... F 740 254-4626
Gnadenhutten *(G-10283)*
Streamside Materials Llc .... G 419 423-1290
Findlay *(G-9763)*
Tiger Sand & Gravel LLC .... F 330 833-6325
Massillon *(G-13052)*
Tri County Concrete Inc .... G 330 425-4464
Twinsburg *(G-18866)*
Turkeyfoot Hill Sand & Gravel .... G 330 899-1997
Akron *(G-415)*

W&W Rock Sand and Gravel .... G 513 266-3708
Williamsburg *(G-20256)*
Wayne Concrete Company .... F 937 545-9919
Medway *(G-13367)*
World Development & Conslt LLC .... G 614 805-4450
Westerville *(G-20083)*
Young Sand & Gravel Co Inc .... F 419 994-3040
Loudonville *(G-12150)*

SAND LIME PRDTS

Holmes Supply Corp .... G 330 279-2634
Holmesville *(G-10980)*

SAND MINING

Alden Sand & Gravel Co Inc .... F 330 928-3249
Cuyahoga Falls *(G-7832)*
Carl E Oeder Sons Sand & Grav .... E 513 494-1555
Lebanon *(G-11640)*
Central Ready Mix LLC .... E 513 402-5001
Cincinnati *(G-3457)*
Keeney Sand & Stone Inc .... G 440 254-4582
Painesville *(G-15752)*
L & I Natural Resources Inc .... G 513 683-2045
Loveland *(G-12208)*
Marietta Martin Materials Inc .... E 937 335-8313
Troy *(G-18686)*
Massillon Materials Inc .... E 330 837-4767
Dalton *(G-7947)*
National Lime and Stone Co .... G 330 339-2144
New Philadelphia *(G-14790)*
National Lime and Stone Co .... G 216 883-9840
Cleveland *(G-5726)*
Osborne Materials Company .... E 440 357-7026
Grand River *(G-10325)*
Phillips Companies .... F 937 426-5461
Beavercreek Township *(G-1370)*
Phillips Companies .... E 937 431-7987
Vandalia *(G-19143)*
S & S Aggregates Inc .... G 740 453-0721
Zanesville *(G-21175)*
Sant Sand & Gravel Co .... G 740 397-0000
Mount Vernon *(G-14506)*
Small Sand & Gravel Inc .... E 740 427-3130
Gambier *(G-10183)*
Technisand Inc .... G 440 285-3132
Chardon *(G-3138)*
Tipp Stone Inc .... G 937 890-4051
Dayton *(G-8559)*
Twinsburg Development Corp .... G 440 357-5562
Cleveland *(G-6224)*
Ward Construction Co .... F 419 943-2450
Leipsic *(G-11739)*

SAND: Hygrade

Fairmount Minerals LLC .... C 269 926-9450
Independence *(G-11126)*
Jim Nier Construction Inc .... F 740 289-2629
Piketon *(G-16071)*
Parry Co .... G 740 884-4893
Chillicothe *(G-3206)*
Pioneer Sands LLC .... E 740 659-2241
Glenford *(G-10271)*
Pioneer Sands LLC .... E 740 599-7773
Howard *(G-10997)*

SAND: Silica

Patriarch Trucking LLC .... G 877 875-5402
Flushing *(G-9784)*

SANDBLASTING EQPT

Hirons Memorial Works Inc .... G 937 444-2917
Mount Orab *(G-14444)*
L N Brut Manufacturing Co .... G 330 833-9045
Navarre *(G-14578)*

SANDBLASTING SVC: Building Exterior

All Ohio Companies Inc .... F 216 420-9274
Cleveland *(G-4664)*
Shur Clean Usa LLC .... G 513 341-5486
Liberty Township *(G-11820)*
X-Treme Finishes Inc .... F 330 474-0614
Medina *(G-13364)*

SANDSTONE: Dimension

Irg Operating LLC .... E 440 963-4008
Vermilion *(G-19163)*

SANITARY SVC, NEC

Ash Sewer & Drain Service .... G 330 376-9714
Akron *(G-71)*
Gerald H Smith .... G 740 446-3455
Bidwell *(G-1666)*
N-Viro International Corp .... F 419 535-6374
Toledo *(G-18421)*

SANITARY SVCS: Chemical Detoxification

A-Gas US Holdings Inc .... F 419 867-8990
Bowling Green *(G-1945)*

SANITARY SVCS: Environmental Cleanup

Alpha Omega Bioremediation LLC .... F 614 287-2600
Columbus *(G-6577)*
Envirnmntal Cmpliance Tech LLC .... G 216 634-0400
North Royalton *(G-15271)*
Samsel Rope & Marine Supply Co .... E 216 241-0333
Cleveland *(G-6029)*

SANITARY SVCS: Hazardous Waste, Collection & Disposal

Emerald Transformer Ppm LLC .... F 800 908-8800
Twinsburg *(G-18768)*
Sara Hudson .... G 850 890-1455
Dayton *(G-8493)*

SANITARY SVCS: Liquid Waste Collection & Disposal

Koski Construction Co .... G 440 997-5337
Ashtabula *(G-782)*
Stellar Industrial Tech Co .... G 740 654-7052
Lancaster *(G-11612)*

SANITARY SVCS: Refuse Collection & Disposal Svcs

Montgomerys Pallet Service .... G 330 297-6677
Ravenna *(G-16390)*

SANITARY SVCS: Rubbish Collection & Disposal

Sidwell Materials Inc .... C 740 849-2394
Zanesville *(G-21180)*

SANITARY SVCS: Waste Materials, Recycling

Fpt Cleveland LLC .... C 216 441-3800
Cleveland *(G-5270)*
Garden Street Iron & Metal .... E 513 853-3700
Cincinnati *(G-3726)*
Grasan Equipment Company Inc .... D 419 526-4440
Mansfield *(G-12452)*
Green Vision Materials Inc .... F 440 564-5500
Newbury *(G-14954)*
Homan Metals LLC .... G 513 721-5010
Cincinnati *(G-3821)*
Hope Timber Pallet Recycl Inc .... E 740 344-1788
Newark *(G-14886)*
Imco Recycling of Ohio LLC .... C 740 922-2373
Uhrichsville *(G-18888)*
Lumberjack Pallet Recycl LLC .... G 513 821-7543
Cincinnati *(G-3956)*
Magnus International Group Inc .... G 216 592-8355
Chagrin Falls *(G-3056)*
Metro Recycling Company .... G 513 251-1800
Cincinnati *(G-4017)*
Mondo Polymer Technologies Inc .... E 740 376-9396
Reno *(G-16425)*
Perma-Fix of Dayton Inc .... F 937 268-6501
Dayton *(G-8422)*
Polychem Corporation .... D 419 547-1400
Clyde *(G-6392)*
Resource Recycling Inc .... F 419 222-2702
Lima *(G-11929)*
Roe Transportation Entps Inc .... G 937 497-7161
Sidney *(G-17068)*
Rumpke Transportation Co LLC .... C 513 242-4600
Cincinnati *(G-4289)*
Shaneway Inc .... G 330 868-2220
Minerva *(G-14201)*
Synagro Midwest Inc .... F 937 384-0669
Miamisburg *(G-13722)*
Waste Parchment Inc .... E 330 674-6868
Millersburg *(G-14147)*

SANITARY WARE: Metal

Accent Manufacturing Inc ....F 330 724-7704
Norton *(G-15355)*
Agean Marble Manufacturing ....F 513 874-1475
West Chester *(G-19829)*
As America Inc ....E 419 522-4211
Mansfield *(G-12408)*
BJ Equipment Ltd ....F 614 497-1776
Columbus *(G-6673)*
Extrudex Limited Partnership ....E 440 352-7101
Painesville *(G-15737)*

SANITATION CHEMICALS & CLEANING AGENTS

Alco-Chem Inc ....E 330 253-3535
Akron *(G-56)*
Betco Corporation Ltd ....C 419 241-2156
Bowling Green *(G-1955)*
Boyd Sanitation ....G 740 697-7940
Roseville *(G-16575)*
Capital Chemical Co ....E 330 494-9535
Canton *(G-2619)*
Chester Packaging LLC ....C 513 458-3840
Cincinnati *(G-3469)*
Cincinnati - Vulcan Company ....D 513 242-5300
Cincinnati *(G-3477)*
Consolidated Coatings Corp ....E 216 514-7596
Cleveland *(G-5017)*
D C Filter & Chemical Inc ....G 419 626-3967
Sandusky *(G-16802)*
Durr Megtec LLC ....C 614 258-9501
Columbus *(G-6876)*
EMD Millipore Corporation ....C 513 631-0445
Norwood *(G-15426)*
Ferro Corporation ....D 216 577-7144
Bedford *(G-1405)*
Fuchs Lubricants Co ....E 330 963-0400
Twinsburg *(G-18777)*
Glister Inc ....G 614 252-6400
Columbus *(G-6955)*
Gojo Industries Inc ....C 330 255-6000
Akron *(G-189)*
Gojo Industries Inc ....E 330 255-6000
Cuyahoga Falls *(G-7873)*
Gojo Industries Inc ....C 330 255-6525
Stow *(G-17593)*
Gojo Industries Inc ....C 330 922-4522
Cuyahoga Falls *(G-7874)*
Henkel Corporation ....E 740 363-1351
Delaware *(G-8693)*
Henkel Corporation ....C 216 475-3600
Cleveland *(G-5392)*
Intercontinental Chemical Corp ....E 513 541-7100
Cincinnati *(G-3854)*
Jason Incorporated ....F 513 860-3400
Hamilton *(G-10576)*
Kardol Quality Products LLC ....E 513 933-8206
Blue Ash *(G-1800)*
Kcs Cleaning Service ....F 740 418-5479
Oak Hill *(G-15453)*
Klc Brands Inc ....G 201 456-4115
Cincinnati *(G-3915)*
Leonhardt Plating Company ....E 513 242-1410
Cincinnati *(G-3938)*
Malco Products Inc ....E 330 753-0361
Akron *(G-266)*
McGean-Rohco Inc ....D 216 441-4900
Newburgh Heights *(G-14941)*
Milsek Furniture Polish Inc ....G 330 542-2700
Salem *(G-16762)*
Mold Masters Intl Inc ....C 440 953-0220
Eastlake *(G-9123)*
National Colloid Company ....E 740 282-1171
Steubenville *(G-17545)*
New Vulco Mfg & Sales Co LLC ....D 513 242-2672
Cincinnati *(G-4072)*
Odortech Distributing LLC ....G 216 339-0773
Westlake *(G-20136)*
Pen Brands LLC ....E 216 674-1430
Brooklyn Heights *(G-2129)*
Pilot Chemical Company Ohio ....E 513 733-4880
Cincinnati *(G-4160)*
Pilot Chemical Corp ....E 513 424-9700
Middletown *(G-13941)*
Polynt Composites USA Inc ....E 816 391-6000
Sandusky *(G-16839)*
Reid Asset Management Company ....E 440 942-8488
Willoughby *(G-20419)*
Smart Sonic Corporation ....G 818 610-7900
Cleveland *(G-6072)*
Spc Specialty Products LLC ....G 844 475-5414
Toledo *(G-18527)*
State Industrial Products Corp ....B 877 747-6986
Cleveland *(G-6097)*
Sun Cleaners & Laundry Inc ....G 740 756-4749
Carroll *(G-2912)*
Tolco Corporation ....D 419 241-1113
Toledo *(G-18555)*
Tremco Incorporated ....B 216 292-5000
Beachwood *(G-1283)*
Univar USA Inc ....C 513 714-5264
West Chester *(G-19911)*

SASHES: Door Or Window, Metal

YKK AP America Inc ....F 513 942-7200
West Chester *(G-19823)*

SATELLITES: Communications

Great Lakes Telcom Ltd ....E 330 629-8848
Youngstown *(G-20924)*
R L Drake Holdings LLC ....F 937 746-4556
Springboro *(G-17349)*

SAW BLADES

Callahan Cutting Tools Inc ....G 614 294-1649
Columbus *(G-6724)*
Dynatech Systems Inc ....E 440 365-1774
Elyria *(G-9246)*
Form-A-Chip Inc ....G 937 223-4135
Dayton *(G-8201)*
J and S Tool Incorporated ....E 216 676-8330
Cleveland *(G-5482)*
Joes Saw Shop ....G 440 834-1196
Burton *(G-2363)*
Martindale Electric Company ....E 216 521-8567
Cleveland *(G-5628)*
Regal Diamond Products Corp ....E 440 944-7700
Wickliffe *(G-20229)*
Superion Inc ....E 937 374-0033
Xenia *(G-20793)*
Uhrichsville Carbide Inc ....F 740 922-9197
Uhrichsville *(G-18899)*

SAWDUST & SHAVINGS

McMillion Lock & Key ....G 937 473-5342
Covington *(G-7790)*
R J Dobay Enterprises Inc ....G 440 227-1005
Burton *(G-2367)*
Sugarcreek Shavings LLC ....G 330 763-4239
Sugarcreek *(G-17869)*

SAWING & PLANING MILLS

5874 Sawmill LLC ....G 614 795-1818
Dublin *(G-8870)*
Appalachia Wood Inc ....E 740 596-2551
Mc Arthur *(G-13178)*
Baillie Lumber Co LP ....E 419 462-2000
Galion *(G-10123)*
Beaver Wood Products ....E 740 226-6211
Beaver *(G-1292)*
Blankenship Lumber Inc ....G 740 372-0191
Otway *(G-15685)*
Bruewer Woodwork Mfg Co ....D 513 353-3505
Cleves *(G-6355)*
Cherokee Hardwoods Inc ....F 440 632-0322
Middlefield *(G-13784)*
Clear Run Lumber Co ....G 740 747-2665
Marengo *(G-12589)*
Coblentz Brothers Inc ....E 330 857-7211
Apple Creek *(G-602)*
Del Holdash ....G 440 427-0611
North Olmsted *(G-15185)*
DIA Enterprises Inc ....G 740 802-7075
New Bloomington *(G-14644)*
Don Puckett Lumber Inc ....F 740 887-4191
Londonderry *(G-12075)*
Dues Jersey Farm ....G 419 678-2102
Coldwater *(G-6406)*
Frickco Inc ....G 740 887-2017
South Bloomingville *(G-17270)*
Gardner Lumber Co Inc ....F 740 254-4664
Tippecanoe *(G-18148)*
Gary Brown Farm & Sawmill ....G 740 372-5022
Otway *(G-15688)*
Gross Lumber Inc ....E 330 683-2055
Apple Creek *(G-606)*
Hartzell Hardwoods Inc ....D 937 773-7054
Piqua *(G-16123)*
Hess & Gault Lumber Co ....G 419 281-3105
Ashland *(G-710)*
Hillcrest Lumber Ltd ....G 330 359-5721
Apple Creek *(G-607)*
Industrial Timber & Land Co ....G 740 596-5294
Hamden *(G-10523)*
Industrial Timber & Lumber Co ....G 800 829-9663
Beachwood *(G-1241)*
J K Logging & Chipwood Company ....G 330 738-3571
Salineville *(G-16788)*
Kaufman Mulch Inc ....G 330 893-3676
Millersburg *(G-14103)*
Knisley Lumber ....F 740 634-2935
Bainbridge *(G-1019)*
Koppers Industries Inc ....E 740 776-3238
Portsmouth *(G-16288)*
L Garbers Sons Sawmilling LLC ....G 419 335-6362
Wauseon *(G-19524)*
Lansing Bros Sawmill ....G 937 588-4291
Piketon *(G-16073)*
Lantz Lumber & Saw Shop ....G 740 286-5658
Jackson *(G-11189)*
Marathon At Sawmill ....F 614 734-0836
Columbus *(G-7149)*
Mbm Lumber ....G 937 459-7448
Union City *(G-18905)*
Millwood Lumber Inc ....E 740 254-4681
Gnadenhutten *(G-10280)*
Mohler Lumber Company ....E 330 499-5461
North Canton *(G-15102)*
Mowhawk Lumber Ltd ....E 330 698-5333
Apple Creek *(G-615)*
No Name Lumber LLC ....G 740 289-3722
Piketon *(G-16075)*
Ohio Valley Veneer Inc ....E 740 493-2901
Piketon *(G-16076)*
Omega Logging Inc ....F 330 534-0378
Hubbard *(G-11008)*
Plaza At Sawmill Pl ....G 614 889-6121
Columbus *(G-7326)*
R M Wood Co ....G 419 845-2661
Mount Gilead *(G-14431)*
Raber Lumber Co ....G 330 893-2797
Charm *(G-3142)*
Ramona Southworth ....G 740 226-8202
Beaver *(G-1293)*
Residents of Sawmill Park ....G 614 659-6678
Dublin *(G-8973)*
Roseville Hardwood ....G 740 221-8712
Roseville *(G-16579)*
Runkles Sawmill LLC ....G 937 663-0115
Saint Paris *(G-16711)*
Salt Creek Lumber Company Inc ....G 330 695-3500
Fredericksburg *(G-9959)*
Sawmill Crossing ....G 614 766-1685
Columbus *(G-7423)*
Sawmill Eye Associates Inc ....G 440 724-0396
Broadview Heights *(G-2100)*
Sawmill Eye Associates Inc ....G 614 734-2685
Columbus *(G-7424)*
Sawmill Road Management Co LLC ....E 937 342-9071
Springfield *(G-17490)*
Sawmill Station ....G 614 434-6147
Dublin *(G-8980)*
Siefker Sawmill ....G 419 339-1956
Elida *(G-9201)*
Southern Ohio Wood ....G 740 288-1825
Wellston *(G-19607)*
Stark Truss Company Inc ....E 330 756-3050
Beach City *(G-1215)*
Stephen M Trudick ....E 440 834-1891
Burton *(G-2371)*
Stony Point Hardwoods ....F 330 852-4512
Sugarcreek *(G-17865)*
Stutzman Brothers Sawmill ....G 440 272-5179
Middlefield *(G-13854)*
Summit Valley Lumber ....G 330 698-7781
Apple Creek *(G-620)*
Superior Hardwoods of Ohio ....E 740 596-2561
Mc Arthur *(G-13184)*
Superior Hardwoods of Ohio ....D 740 384-6862
Jackson *(G-11196)*
Superior Hardwoods Ohio Inc ....D 740 384-5677
Wellston *(G-19608)*
Superior Hardwoods Ohio Inc ....E 740 439-2727
Cambridge *(G-2457)*
Supply Dynamics Inc ....E 513 965-2000
Loveland *(G-12238)*

T & D Thompson Inc .... E 740 332-8515
  Laurelville (G-11627)
Taylor Lumber Worldwide Inc .... C 740 259-6222
  Mc Dermott (G-13194)
Timbermill Ltd .... G 740 862-3426
  Baltimore (G-1044)
Tusco Hardwoods LLC .... F 330 852-4281
  Sugarcreek (G-17873)
W O Hardwoods Inc .... G 740 425-1588
  Barnesville (G-1120)
Wagner Farms & Sawmill LLC .... F 419 653-4126
  Leipsic (G-11738)
Wappoo Wood Products Inc .... E 937 492-1166
  Sidney (G-17084)
Whitewater Forest Products LLC .... G 513 673-7596
  Batavia (G-1196)
Wilmington Forest Products .... G 937 382-5013
  Wilmington (G-20512)
Wooldridge Lumber Co .... D 740 289-4912
  Piketon (G-16082)
Wrights Saw Mill .... G 937 773-2546
  Piqua (G-16167)
Yoder Lumber Co Inc .... D 330 893-3131
  Sugarcreek (G-17878)

SAWING & PLANING MILLS: Custom

Facemyer Lumber Co Inc .... D 740 992-5965
  Pomeroy (G-16240)
Newberry Wood Enterprises Inc .... F 440 238-6127
  Strongsville (G-17769)
United Hardwoods Ltd .... G 330 878-9510
  Strasburg (G-17655)
Walnut Creek Lumber Co Ltd .... E 330 852-4559
  Dundee (G-9031)
Weaver Lumber Co .... G 330 359-5091
  Wilmot (G-20517)

SAWMILL MACHINES

Midwest Timber & Land Co Inc .... E 740 493-2400
  Piketon (G-16074)
Trico Enterprises LLC .... E 330 674-1157
  Millersburg (G-14138)

SAWS & SAWING EQPT

Alvords Yard & Garden Eqp .... G 440 286-2315
  Chardon (G-3098)
Rboog Industries LLC .... G 330 350-0396
  Brunswick (G-2233)
Stevens Auto Parts & Towng .... G 740 988-2260
  Jackson (G-11195)

SAWS: Hand, Metalworking Or Woodworking

Cammel Saw Company Inc .... F 330 477-3764
  Canton (G-2605)

SCAFFOLDS: Mobile Or Stationary, Metal

Hansen Scaffolding LLC .... F 513 574-9000
  West Chester (G-19863)
Sky Climber LLC .... E 740 203-3900
  Delaware (G-8725)

SCALE REPAIR SVCS

Kanawha Scales & Systems Inc .... F 513 576-0700
  Milford (G-14023)

SCALES & BALANCES, EXC LABORATORY

Etched Metal Company .... E 440 248-0240
  Solon (G-17142)
Interface Logic Systems Inc .... G 614 236-8388
  Columbus (G-7041)
K Davis Inc .... G 419 637-2859
  Gibsonburg (G-10249)
Kanawha Scales & Systems Inc .... F 513 576-0700
  Milford (G-14023)
T & S Enterprises .... E 419 424-1122
  Findlay (G-9766)

SCALES: Indl

Exact Equipment Corporation .... F 215 295-2000
  Columbus (G-6491)
Holtgrven Scale Elctronic Corp .... F 419 422-4779
  Findlay (G-9704)
Mettler-Toledo LLC .... D 614 438-4511
  Worthington (G-20695)
Mettler-Toledo LLC .... C 614 438-4390
  Worthington (G-20696)

Mettler-Toledo LLC .... C 614 841-7300
  Columbus (G-7174)
Mettler-Toledo Intl Fin Inc .... G 614 438-4511
  Columbus (G-6500)
Mettler-Toledo Intl Inc .... B 614 438-4511
  Columbus (G-6501)

SCALES: Truck

Roth Transit Inc .... G 937 773-5051
  Piqua (G-16160)

SCHOOL SPLYS, EXC BOOKS: Wholesalers

Lorenz Corporation .... D 937 228-6118
  Dayton (G-8316)
Zaner-Bloser Inc .... D 614 486-0221
  Columbus (G-7624)
Zaner-Bloser Inc .... G 608 441-5555
  Columbus (G-7625)

SCHOOLS & EDUCATIONAL SVCS, NEC

School House Winery LLC .... G 330 602-9463
  Dover (G-8851)

SCHOOLS: Vocational, NEC

Revonoc Inc .... G 440 548-3491
  Parkman (G-15813)

SCIENTIFIC EQPT REPAIR SVCS

Crystal Koch Finishing Inc .... G 440 366-7526
  Elyria (G-9240)
Instrumentors Inc .... G 440 238-3430
  Strongsville (G-17755)

SCIENTIFIC INSTRUMENTS WHOLESALERS

Science/Electronics Inc .... F 937 224-4444
  Dayton (G-8497)

SCRAP & WASTE MATERIALS, WHOLESALE: Ferrous Metal

Agmet LLC .... F 216 663-8200
  Cleveland (G-4641)
City Scrap & Salvage Co .... E 330 753-5051
  Akron (G-118)
Cohen Brothers Inc .... G 513 422-3696
  Middletown (G-13895)
Fpt Cleveland LLC .... E 216 441-3800
  Cleveland (G-5270)
Franklin Iron & Metal Corp .... C 937 253-8184
  Dayton (G-8206)
I H Schlezinger Inc .... E 614 252-1188
  Columbus (G-7016)
Induction Iron Incorporated .... G 330 501-8852
  Youngstown (G-20938)
Lake County Auto Recyclers .... G 440 428-2886
  Painesville (G-15757)
Metalico Akron Inc .... E 330 376-1400
  Akron (G-279)
Rm Advisory Group Inc .... E 513 242-2100
  Cincinnati (G-4274)

SCRAP & WASTE MATERIALS, WHOLESALE: Junk & Scrap

Lawsons Towing & Auto Wrckg .... F 216 883-9050
  Cleveland (G-5568)

SCRAP & WASTE MATERIALS, WHOLESALE: Lumber Scrap

Garick LLC .... E 216 581-0100
  Cleveland (G-5293)

SCRAP & WASTE MATERIALS, WHOLESALE: Metal

A & B Iron & Metal Company .... F 937 228-1561
  Dayton (G-7997)
Homan Metals LLC .... G 513 721-5010
  Cincinnati (G-3821)
R L S Corporation .... E 740 773-1440
  Chillicothe (G-3219)
Triple Arrow Industries Inc .... G 614 437-5588
  Marysville (G-12818)
Tungsten Sltons Group Intl Inc .... G 440 708-3096
  Chagrin Falls (G-3086)

SCRAP & WASTE MATERIALS, WHOLESALE: Nonferrous Metals Scrap

W R G Inc .... E 216 351-8494
  Cleveland (G-6279)

SCRAP & WASTE MATERIALS, WHOLESALE: Rubber Scrap

Frankes Wood Products LLC .... E 937 642-0706
  Marysville (G-12783)

SCRAP STEEL CUTTING

Geneva Liberty Steel Ltd .... E 330 740-0103
  Youngstown (G-20918)

SCREENS: Door, Metal Covered Wood

Screenmobile Inc .... G 614 868-8663
  Radnor (G-16358)

SCREENS: Door, Wood Frame

Touchstone Woodworks .... G 330 297-1313
  Ravenna (G-16413)

SCREENS: Projection

Stewart Filmscreen Corp .... E 513 753-0800
  Amelia (G-548)

SCREENS: Window, Metal

Breezeway Screens Inc .... G 740 599-5222
  Danville (G-7958)
Dale Kestler .... G 513 871-9000
  Cincinnati (G-3574)
Loxcreen Company Inc .... F 513 539-2255
  Middletown (G-13921)
Renewal By Andersen LLC .... G 614 781-9600
  Columbus (G-6506)
Thermal Industries Inc .... G 216 464-0674
  Cleveland (G-6166)

SCREENS: Window, Wood Framed

Pickens Window Service Inc .... F 513 931-4432
  Cincinnati (G-4157)

SCREENS: Woven Wire

Kimmatt Corp .... G 937 228-3811
  Dayton (G-8297)
US Screen Co .... G 419 736-2400
  Sullivan (G-17882)
Yankee Wire Cloth Products Inc .... E 740 545-9129
  West Lafayette (G-19934)

SCREW MACHINE PRDTS

Abco Bar & Tube Cutting Svc .... E 513 697-9487
  Maineville (G-12364)
Abel Manufacturing Company .... F 513 681-5000
  Cincinnati (G-3287)
Acme Machine Automatics Inc .... D 419 453-0010
  Ottoville (G-15679)
Adams Automatic Inc .... E 440 235-4416
  Olmsted Falls (G-15527)
Alco Manufacturing .... G 440 322-9166
  Amherst (G-553)
Alco Manufacturing Corp LLC .... D 440 458-5165
  Elyria (G-9210)
Amco Products Inc .... F 937 433-7982
  Dayton (G-7970)
Amerascrew Inc .... E 419 522-2232
  Mansfield (G-12404)
American Aero Components LLC .... G 937 367-5068
  Dayton (G-8022)
Amt Machine Systems Limited .... F 740 965-2693
  Columbus (G-6594)
Ashley F Ward Inc .... C 513 398-1414
  Mason (G-12829)
Atlas Machine Products Co .... G 216 228-3688
  Cleveland (G-4760)
Automatic Screw Products Co .... G 216 241-7896
  Cleveland (G-4772)
Bronco Machine Inc .... F 440 951-5015
  Willoughby (G-20288)
Bront Machining Inc .... G 937 228-4551
  Moraine (G-14336)
Chardon Metal Products Co .... E 440 285-2147
  Chardon (G-3102)

Clear Creek Screw Machine Corp..........G....... 740 969-2113
Amanda *(G-525)*

Condo Inc..........G....... 330 505-0485
Niles *(G-15004)*

Condo Incorporated..........D....... 330 609-6021
Warren *(G-19387)*

CT Ferry Screw Products I..........G....... 440 871-1617
Cleveland *(G-5041)*

D L Salkil LLC..........G....... 419 841-3341
Toledo *(G-18251)*

Day-Hio Products Inc..........E....... 937 445-0782
Dayton *(G-8127)*

Dove Machine Inc..........F....... 440 864-2645
Columbia Station *(G-6437)*

Dunham Products Inc..........F....... 440 232-0885
Walton Hills *(G-19310)*

Eastlake Machine Products Inc..........E....... 440 953-1014
Willoughby *(G-20314)*

Efficient Machine Pdts Corp..........E....... 440 268-0205
Strongsville *(G-17740)*

Elgin Fastener Group LLC..........E....... 216 481-4400
Cleveland *(G-5168)*

Elliott Oren Products Inc..........F....... 419 298-0015
Edgerton *(G-9172)*

Elliott Oren Products Inc..........E....... 419 298-2306
Edgerton *(G-9173)*

Elyria Manufacturing Corp..........D....... 440 365-4171
Elyria *(G-9252)*

Engels Machining LLC..........G....... 419 485-1500
Montpelier *(G-14308)*

Engstrom Manufacturing Inc..........F....... 513 573-0010
Mason *(G-12866)*

Eureka Screw Machine Pdts Co..........G....... 216 883-1715
Cleveland *(G-5198)*

Fairfield Machined Products..........F....... 740 756-4409
Carroll *(G-2905)*

Falmer Screw Pdts & Mfg Inc..........F....... 330 758-0593
Youngstown *(G-20903)*

Flash Industrial Tech Ltd..........G....... 440 786-8979
Cleveland *(G-5247)*

Forrest Machine Pdts Co Ltd..........E....... 419 589-3774
Mansfield *(G-12441)*

Fostoria Machine Products..........G....... 419 435-4262
Fostoria *(G-9843)*

Gent Machine Company..........E....... 216 481-2334
Cleveland *(G-5316)*

Gisco Inc..........G....... 937 773-7601
Piqua *(G-16118)*

Global Precision Parts Inc..........G....... 260 563-9030
Van Wert *(G-19093)*

Great Lakes Defense Svcs LLC..........G....... 216 272-3450
University Heights *(G-18942)*

H & E Machine Company..........F....... 614 443-7635
Columbus *(G-6972)*

H & S Precision Screw Pdts Inc..........E....... 937 437-0316
New Paris *(G-14754)*

H & W Screw Products Inc..........F....... 937 866-2577
Franklin *(G-9888)*

Hamco Manufacturing Inc..........G....... 440 774-1637
Oberlin *(G-15498)*

Harding Machine Acquisition Co..........D....... 937 666-3031
East Liberty *(G-9048)*

Hebco Products Inc..........A....... 419 562-7987
Bucyrus *(G-2333)*

Helix Linear Technologies Inc..........E....... 216 485-2263
Beachwood *(G-1240)*

Heller Machine Products Inc..........G....... 216 281-2951
Cleveland *(G-5390)*

Hept Machine Inc..........G....... 937 890-5633
Vandalia *(G-19126)*

Hi-Tech Solutions LLC..........G....... 216 331-3050
Cleveland *(G-5405)*

Houston Machine Products Inc..........E....... 937 322-8022
Springfield *(G-17422)*

Hy-Production Inc..........C....... 330 273-2400
Valley City *(G-19040)*

Hyland Machine Company..........E....... 937 233-8600
Dayton *(G-8258)*

Ilsco Corporation..........E....... 513 367-9100
Harrison *(G-10651)*

Integrity Manufacturing Corp..........E....... 937 233-6792
Dayton *(G-8272)*

J & M Cutting Tools Inc..........G....... 440 622-3900
Mentor *(G-13480)*

JAD Machine Company Inc..........F....... 419 256-6332
Malinta *(G-12380)*

Karma Metal Products Inc..........F....... 419 524-4371
Mansfield *(G-12466)*

Kernells Autmtc Machining Inc..........E....... 419 588-2164
Berlin Heights *(G-1654)*

Kohut Enterprises Inc..........G....... 440 366-6666
Independence *(G-11138)*

Krausher Machining Inc..........G....... 440 839-2828
Wakeman *(G-19285)*

Krist Krenz Machine Inc..........D....... 440 237-1800
North Royalton *(G-15281)*

Kts-Met Bar Products Inc..........G....... 440 288-9308
Lorain *(G-12097)*

Lake Erie Industries LLC..........G....... 216 255-1867
Lakewood *(G-11525)*

Lear Manufacturing Inc..........G....... 440 327-4545
North Ridgeville *(G-15238)*

Lehner Screw Machine LLC..........E....... 330 688-6616
Akron *(G-250)*

Lenco Industries Inc..........E....... 937 277-9364
Dayton *(G-8310)*

Machine Tek Systems Inc..........E....... 330 527-4450
Garrettsville *(G-10197)*

Magnetic Screw Machine Pdts..........G....... 937 348-2807
Marysville *(G-12797)*

Maumee Machine & Tool Corp..........E....... 419 385-2501
Toledo *(G-18402)*

McDaniel Products Inc..........F....... 440 967-5630
Vermilion *(G-19167)*

McDaniel Products Inc..........E....... 419 524-5841
Mansfield *(G-12478)*

Meistermatic Inc..........D....... 216 481-7773
Chesterland *(G-3163)*

Mettlr-Tledo Globl Hldings LLC..........F....... 614 438-4511
Columbus *(G-6502)*

Midwest Precision LLC..........D....... 440 951-2333
Eastlake *(G-9122)*

Morgal Machine Tool Co..........D....... 937 325-5561
Springfield *(G-17451)*

Mosher Machine & Tool Co Inc..........E....... 937 258-8070
Dayton *(G-8369)*

Murray Machine & Tool Inc..........G....... 216 267-1126
Cleveland *(G-5714)*

New Castle Industries Inc..........C....... 724 654-2603
Youngstown *(G-20975)*

Nook Industries Inc..........C....... 216 271-7900
Cleveland *(G-5756)*

Obars Machine and Tool Company..........E....... 419 535-6307
Toledo *(G-18433)*

Ohio Metal Products Company..........E....... 937 228-6101
Dayton *(G-8399)*

Ohio Screw Products Inc..........D....... 440 322-6341
Elyria *(G-9305)*

Paramont Machine Company LLC..........E....... 330 339-3489
New Philadelphia *(G-14792)*

Pfi Precision Inc..........E....... 937 845-3563
New Carlisle *(G-14677)*

Pike Machine Products Co..........E....... 216 731-1880
Euclid *(G-9433)*

Port Clinton Manufacturing LLC..........E....... 419 734-2141
Port Clinton *(G-16255)*

Precision Fittings LLC..........E....... 440 647-4143
Wellington *(G-19589)*

Profile Grinding Inc..........E....... 216 351-0600
Cleveland *(G-5928)*

Qcsm LLC..........G....... 216 531-5960
Cleveland *(G-5937)*

R T & T Machining Co Inc..........F....... 440 974-8479
Mentor *(G-13571)*

R W Screw Products Inc..........C....... 330 837-9211
Massillon *(G-13044)*

Raka Corporation..........D....... 419 476-6572
Toledo *(G-18498)*

Richland Screw Machine Pdts..........E....... 419 524-1272
Mansfield *(G-12507)*

Roehlers Machine Products..........G....... 937 354-4401
Mount Victory *(G-14522)*

Rtsi LLC..........G....... 440 542-3066
Solon *(G-17226)*

Rural Products Inc..........G....... 419 298-2677
Edgerton *(G-9179)*

S & S Machining Ltd..........F....... 419 524-9525
Mansfield *(G-12510)*

Semtorq Inc..........F....... 330 487-0600
Twinsburg *(G-18856)*

Shanafelt Manufacturing Co..........E....... 330 455-0315
Canton *(G-2814)*

Stadco Inc..........E....... 937 878-0911
Fairborn *(G-9468)*

Standby Screw Machine Pdts Co..........B....... 440 243-8200
Berea *(G-1625)*

Star Screw Machine Products..........G....... 216 361-0307
Cleveland *(G-6096)*

State Machine Co Inc..........G....... 440 248-1050
Cleveland *(G-6098)*

Superior Bar Products Inc..........G....... 419 784-2590
Defiance *(G-8644)*

Superior Products Llc..........D....... 216 651-9400
Cleveland *(G-6125)*

Supply Technologies LLC..........D....... 740 363-1971
Delaware *(G-8727)*

Swagelok Hy-Level Company..........C....... 440 238-1260
Strongsville *(G-17798)*

The Delo Screw Products Co..........F....... 740 363-1971
Delaware *(G-8728)*

Toledo Automatic Screw Co..........G....... 419 726-3441
Toledo *(G-18556)*

Toledo Screw Products Inc..........G....... 419 841-3341
Toledo *(G-18568)*

Tri-K Enterprises Inc..........G....... 330 832-7380
Canton *(G-2845)*

Triangle Machine Products Co..........E....... 216 524-5872
Cleveland *(G-6208)*

Trojon Gear Inc..........F....... 937 254-1737
Dayton *(G-8568)*

Troy Manufacturing Co..........E....... 440 834-8262
Burton *(G-2373)*

Twin Valley Metalcraft Asm LLC..........G....... 937 787-4634
West Alexandria *(G-19622)*

United Auto Worker AFL CIO..........F....... 419 592-0434
Napoleon *(G-14563)*

Usm Precision Products Inc..........D....... 440 975-8600
Wickliffe *(G-20236)*

Valley Tool & Die Inc..........D....... 440 237-0160
North Royalton *(G-15309)*

Vanamatic Company..........D....... 419 692-6085
Delphos *(G-8764)*

Vinco Machine Products Inc..........G....... 216 475-6708
Cleveland *(G-6263)*

Vulcan Products Co Inc..........F....... 419 468-1039
Galion *(G-10159)*

Warren Screw Machine Inc..........E....... 330 609-6020
Warren *(G-19460)*

Watters Manufacturing Co Inc..........G....... 216 281-8600
Cleveland *(G-6294)*

Whirlaway Corporation..........C....... 440 647-4711
Wellington *(G-19595)*

Whirlaway Corporation..........C....... 440 647-4711
Wellington *(G-19596)*

Whirlaway Corporation..........E....... 440 647-4711
Wellington *(G-19597)*

Whiteford Industries Inc..........F....... 419 381-1155
Toledo *(G-18599)*

Wood-Sebring Corporation..........G....... 216 267-3191
Cleveland *(G-6321)*

Z and M Screw Machine Products..........G....... 330 467-5822
Garrettsville *(G-10206)*

SCREW MACHINES

Ken Emerick Machine Products..........G....... 440 834-4501
Burton *(G-2365)*

Ohio CAM & Tool Co..........G....... 216 531-7900
Cleveland *(G-5803)*

Ohio Screw Products Inc..........D....... 440 322-6341
Elyria *(G-9305)*

SCREWS: Metal

Agrati - Medina LLC..........C....... 330 725-8853
Medina *(G-13218)*

Agrati - Tiffin LLC..........D....... 419 447-2221
Tiffin *(G-18041)*

Akko Fastener Inc..........F....... 513 489-8300
Blue Ash *(G-1724)*

Altenloh Brinck & Co US Inc..........D....... 419 636-6715
Bryan *(G-2263)*

Engstrom Manufacturing Inc..........F....... 513 573-0010
Mason *(G-12866)*

General Plastex Inc..........E....... 330 745-7775
Barberton *(G-1073)*

Hexagon Industries Inc..........E....... 216 249-0200
Cleveland *(G-5400)*

Ivan Extruders Co Inc..........G....... 330 644-7400
Akron *(G-220)*

Kyocera Senco Indus Tls Inc..........F....... 800 543-4596
Cincinnati *(G-3256)*

Tinnerman Palnut Engineered PR..........E....... 330 220-5100
Brunswick *(G-2246)*

W-J Inc..........G....... 440 248-8282
Solon *(G-17259)*

SCREWS: Wood

Hudson Fasteners Inc..........G....... 330 270-9500
Youngstown *(G-20933)*

PRODUCT SECTION

SECURITY EQPT STORES

SEALANTS

Company	Code	Phone
A & M Products	G	419 595-2092
Tiffin (G-18039)		
Aluminum Coating Manufacturers	E	216 341-2000
Cleveland (G-4680)		
Besten Equipment Inc	E	216 581-1166
Akron (G-87)		
Century Industries Corporation	E	330 457-2367
New Waterford (G-14838)		
Chemmasters Inc	E	440 428-2105
Madison (G-12344)		
Concrete Sealants Inc	E	937 845-8776
Tipp City (G-18109)		
Davis Caulking & Sealant LLC	G	740 286-3825
Wellston (G-19599)		
Dental Sealants	G	440 582-3466
North Royalton (G-15269)		
Egc Enterprises Inc	E	440 285-5835
Chardon (G-3110)		
Extendit Company	G	330 743-4343
Youngstown (G-20902)		
Freedom Asphalt Sealant & Line	E	937 416-1053
Miamisburg (G-13671)		
ICP Adhesives and Sealants Inc	F	330 753-4585
Norton (G-15369)		
Jetcoat LLC	E	800 394-0047
Columbus (G-7067)		
P & T Products Inc	E	419 621-1966
Sandusky (G-16834)		
Royal Adhesives & Sealants LLC	F	440 708-1212
Chagrin Falls (G-3073)		
Sealant Solutions	G	614 599-8000
Columbus (G-7435)		
Teknol Inc	D	937 264-0190
Dayton (G-8550)		
Tremco Incorporated	C	216 752-4401
Cleveland (G-6202)		
Tremco Incorporated	B	216 292-5000
Beachwood (G-1283)		
Truseal Technologies Inc	E	216 910-1500
Akron (G-414)		

SEALING COMPOUNDS: Sealing, synthetic rubber or plastic

Company	Code	Phone
Federal Process Corporation	E	216 464-6440
Cleveland (G-5227)		
Foam Seal Inc	D	216 881-8111
Cleveland (G-5256)		
Leesburg Modern Sales Inc	G	937 780-2613
Leesburg (G-11712)		
Novagard Solutions Inc	F	216 881-3890
Cleveland (G-5789)		
Premier Seals Mfg LLC	G	330 861-1060
Akron (G-328)		
Technical Rubber Company Inc	B	740 967-9015
Johnstown (G-11272)		

SEALS: Hermetic

Company	Code	Phone
Aeroseal LLC	E	937 428-9300
Centerville (G-2996)		

SEARCH & DETECTION SYSTEMS, EXC RADAR

Company	Code	Phone
Rae Systems Inc	G	440 232-0555
Walton Hills (G-19314)		

SEARCH & NAVIGATION SYSTEMS

Company	Code	Phone
Accurate Electronics Inc	C	330 682-7015
Orrville (G-15581)		
ADB Safegate Americas LLC	B	614 861-1304
Columbus (G-6542)		
Aviation Technologies Inc	G	216 706-2960
Cleveland (G-4776)		
Boeing Company	E	740 788-4000
Newark (G-14854)		
Brookpark Laboratories Inc	G	216 267-7140
Cleveland (G-4841)		
Btc Inc	E	740 549-2722
Lewis Center (G-11753)		
Btc Technology Services Inc	G	740 549-2722
Lewis Center (G-11754)		
David Boswell	E	614 441-2497
Columbus (G-6852)		
Drs Mobile Environmntl Svc	G	513 943-1111
Cincinnati (G-3246)		
Enginetics Corporation	C	937 878-3800
Huber Heights (G-11017)		
Eti Tech LLC	F	937 832-4200
Englewood (G-9358)		
Fame Tool & Mfg Co Inc	E	513 271-6387
Cincinnati (G-3670)		
Ferrotherm Corporation	C	216 883-9350
Cleveland (G-5233)		
Fluid Conservation Systems	E	513 831-9335
Milford (G-14008)		
General Dynmics Mssion Systems	E	513 253-4770
Beavercreek (G-1317)		
Grimes Aerospace Company	B	937 484-2001
Urbana (G-18990)		
Harris Corporation	C	973 284-2866
Beavercreek (G-1322)		
Heller Machine Products Inc	G	216 281-2951
Cleveland (G-5390)		
Hept Machine Inc	G	937 890-5633
Vandalia (G-19126)		
Hunter Defense Tech Inc	C	513 943-7880
Cincinnati (G-3255)		
Lake Shore Cryotronics Inc	C	614 891-2243
Westerville (G-20003)		
Lockheed Martin Corporation	G	937 429-0100
Beavercreek (G-1327)		
Lockheed Martin Corporation	B	330 796-7000
Akron (G-255)		
Lockheed Martin Corporation	G	866 562-2363
Columbus (G-7134)		
Lockheed Martin Corporation	G	937 429-0100
Beavercreek (G-1328)		
Lockheed Martin Integ	D	330 796-2800
Akron (G-257)		
Lockheed Martin Integrtd Systm	A	330 796-2800
Akron (G-258)		
Lunken Charts LLC	E	513 253-7615
Cincinnati (G-3957)		
Northrop Grumman Innovation	C	937 429-9261
Beavercreek (G-1360)		
Northrop Grumman Systems Corp	B	513 881-3296
West Chester (G-19881)		
PCC Airfoils LLC	C	216 692-7900
Cleveland (G-5857)		
Redco Instrument	G	440 232-2132
Cleveland (G-5969)		
Reuter-Stokes LLC	B	330 425-3755
Twinsburg (G-18845)		
Star Dynamics Corporation	D	614 334-4510
Hilliard (G-10864)		
Sunset Industries Inc	E	216 731-8131
Euclid (G-9444)		
Te Connectivity Corporation	C	419 521-9500
Mansfield (G-12527)		
UTC Aerospace Systems	G	330 374-3040
Uniontown (G-18937)		
Wall Colmonoy Corporation	D	513 842-4200
Cincinnati (G-4488)		
Watts Antenna Company	G	740 797-9380
The Plains (G-18024)		
Yost Labs Inc	F	740 876-4936
Portsmouth (G-16305)		

SEAT BELTS: Automobile & Aircraft

Company	Code	Phone
Tk Holdings Inc	E	937 778-9713
Piqua (G-16166)		

SEATING: Chairs, Table & Arm

Company	Code	Phone
Brocar Products Inc	E	513 922-2888
Cincinnati (G-3421)		
Gasser Chair Co Inc	E	330 534-2234
Youngstown (G-20912)		
Gasser Chair Co Inc	D	330 759-2234
Youngstown (G-20914)		

SEATING: Stadium

Company	Code	Phone
American Office Services Inc	G	440 899-6888
Westlake (G-20095)		
Ap-Alternatives LLC	F	419 267-5280
Ridgeville Corners (G-16511)		

SEATING: Transportation

Company	Code	Phone
C E White Co	E	419 492-2157
New Washington (G-14827)		

SECRETARIAL & COURT REPORTING

Company	Code	Phone
Fax Medley Group Inc	G	513 272-1932
Cincinnati (G-3676)		
Landen Desktop Pubg Ctr Inc	G	513 683-5181
Loveland (G-12209)		
Sound Communications Inc	F	614 875-8500
Grove City (G-10470)		

SECRETARIAL SVCS

Company	Code	Phone
APS Accurate Products & Svcs	G	440 353-9353
North Ridgeville (G-15208)		
Ohio Shelterall Inc	F	614 882-1110
Westerville (G-20068)		

SECURITY CONTROL EQPT & SYSTEMS

Company	Code	Phone
Aaron Smith	G	330 285-1360
Akron (G-25)		
Checkpoint Systems Inc	C	937 281-1304
Dayton (G-8087)		
Diebold Nixdorf Incorporated	A	330 490-4000
North Canton (G-15078)		
Emx Industries Inc	E	216 518-9888
Cleveland (G-5176)		
Habitec SEC Diversfd Alarm	G	419 636-1155
Bryan (G-2284)		
Henderson Partners LLC	G	614 883-1310
Columbus (G-6987)		
Honeywell International Inc	A	937 484-2000
Urbana (G-18995)		
MAI Media Group Llc	E	513 779-0604
West Chester (G-19875)		
Midwest Security Services	G	937 853-9000
Dayton (G-8354)		
Modular Security Systems Inc	E	740 532-7822
Ironton (G-11169)		
Pentagon Protection Usa LLC	F	614 734-7240
Dublin (G-8964)		
Rae Systems Inc	G	440 232-0555
Walton Hills (G-19314)		
Securcom Inc	E	419 628-1049
Minster (G-14224)		
Securtex International Inc	E	937 312-1414
Dayton (G-8500)		
Technlgy Install Partners LLC	E	888 586-7040
Cleveland (G-6156)		
Vero Security Group Ltd	G	513 731-8376
Cincinnati (G-4476)		

SECURITY DEVICES

Company	Code	Phone
Access 2 Communications Inc	G	800 561-1110
Steubenville (G-17525)		
Aysco Security Consultants Inc	E	330 733-8183
Kent (G-11297)		
Everykey Inc	G	855 666-5006
Cleveland (G-5202)		
Executive Security Systems Inc	G	513 895-2783
Cincinnati (G-3665)		
Invue Security Products Inc	C	330 456-7776
Canton (G-2711)		
J II Fire Systems Inc	G	513 574-0609
Cincinnati (G-3864)		
Lindsay Precast Inc	G	800 837-7788
Canal Fulton (G-2483)		
Mace Security Intl Inc	D	440 424-5321
Cleveland (G-5598)		
P3labs LLC	G	800 259-8059
North Canton (G-15108)		
Residential Electronic Svcs	G	740 681-9150
Lancaster (G-11601)		
Say Security Group USA LLC	F	419 634-0004
Ada (G-8)		
Stuntronics LLC	G	216 780-1413
Bedford Heights (G-1480)		
The W L Jenkins Company	F	330 477-3407
Canton (G-2835)		
Viotec LLC	G	614 596-2054
Dublin (G-9009)		

SECURITY EQPT STORES

Company	Code	Phone
American Scaffolding Inc	G	216 524-7733
Cleveland (G-4697)		
Becker Signs Inc	G	330 659-4504
Hudson (G-11033)		
Beeline Purchasing LLC	G	513 703-3733
Mason (G-12834)		
Buckeye Dimensions LLC	G	330 857-0223
Dalton (G-7936)		
Kriss Kreations	G	330 405-6102
Twinsburg (G-18803)		
Trico Enterprises LLC	E	330 674-1157
Millersburg (G-14138)		

Employee Codes: A=Over 500 employees, B=251-500
C=101-250, D=51-100, E=20-50, F=10-19, G=3-9

SECURITY PROTECTIVE DEVICES MAINTENANCE & MONITORING SVCS

Contingncy Prcrement Group LLC........G....... 513 204-9590
  Maineville *(G-12366)*
Taupe Holdings Co ....G....... 614 330-4600
  Dublin *(G-9002)*

SECURITY SYSTEMS SERVICES

Johnson Controls Inc..............................F....... 513 671-6338
  Cincinnati *(G-3882)*
Say Security Group USA LLC ....F....... 419 634-0004
  Ada *(G-8)*
Securcom Inc ....E....... 419 628-1049
  Minster *(G-14224)*
Sound Communications Inc ....F....... 614 875-8500
  Grove City *(G-10470)*

SEMICONDUCTOR CIRCUIT NETWORKS

Micro Industries Corporation..................D....... 740 548-7878
  Westerville *(G-20065)*

SEMICONDUCTORS & RELATED DEVICES

Advanced Dstrbted Gnration LLC............G....... 419 530-3792
  Maumee *(G-13066)*
Advanced Technology Products ....G....... 937 349-5221
  Mechanicsburg *(G-13210)*
Altera Corporation ....G....... 513 444-2021
  Cincinnati *(G-3326)*
Altera Corporation ....G....... 330 650-5200
  Hudson *(G-11029)*
Biometric Information MGT LLC..............G....... 614 456-1296
  Dublin *(G-8888)*
Cirrus LLC ....G....... 740 272-2012
  Delaware *(G-8667)*
Communication Concepts Inc ....G....... 937 426-8600
  Beavercreek *(G-1307)*
CPC Logistics Inc ....D....... 513 874-5787
  Fairfield *(G-9492)*
Darrah Electric Company ....E....... 216 631-0912
  Cleveland *(G-5067)*
Durr Megtec LLC ....C....... 614 258-9501
  Columbus *(G-6876)*
Em4 Inc ....G....... 216 486-6100
  Highland Heights *(G-10788)*
Gopowerx Inc ....E....... 440 707-6029
  Oberlin *(G-15497)*
Heraeus Electro-Nite Co LLC ....G....... 330 725-1419
  Medina *(G-13272)*
Hyper Tech Research Inc ....F....... 614 481-8050
  Columbus *(G-7013)*
Intel Corporation ....G....... 513 860-9686
  West Chester *(G-19723)*
Linear Asics Inc ....G....... 330 474-3920
  Twinsburg *(G-18809)*
Lucintech Inc...G....... 419 265-2641
  Toledo *(G-18390)*
Materion Brush Inc ....D....... 216 486-4200
  Mayfield Heights *(G-13167)*
Materion Corporation ....C....... 216 486-4200
  Mayfield Heights *(G-13168)*
Ohio Semitronics Inc ....D....... 614 777-1005
  Hilliard *(G-10847)*
Pepperl + Fuchs Inc...............................G....... 330 425-3555
  Twinsburg *(G-18830)*
Pepperl + Fuchs Entps Inc ....G....... 330 425-3555
  Twinsburg *(G-18831)*
SCI Engineered Materials Inc ....E....... 614 486-0261
  Columbus *(G-7429)*
Selectronics Incorporated.......................G....... 440 546-5595
  Brecksville *(G-2057)*
Signature Technologies Inc ....E....... 937 859-6323
  Miamisburg *(G-13716)*
Silfex Inc ....C....... 937 472-3311
  Eaton *(G-9166)*
Smart Commercialization Center ....G....... 440 366-4048
  Elyria *(G-9327)*
Spang & Company ....G....... 440 350-6108
  Mentor *(G-13585)*
Spb Global LLC ....G....... 419 931-6559
  Perrysburg *(G-16007)*
Special Mtls RES & Tech Inc..................G....... 440 777-4024
  North Olmsted *(G-15200)*
Tosoh SMD Inc ....C....... 614 875-7912
  Grove City *(G-10478)*
Ustek Incorporated ....F....... 614 538-8000
  Columbus *(G-7567)*
Vega Technology Group LLC ....G....... 216 772-1434
  North Canton *(G-15135)*

SENSORS: Infrared, Solid State

Madison Electric (mepco) Inc ....G....... 440 279-0521
  Chardon *(G-3124)*

SENSORS: Radiation

Integrated Sensors LLC ....G....... 419 536-3212
  Ottawa Hills *(G-15673)*

SENSORS: Temperature, Exc Indl Process

Krumor Inc...F....... 216 328-9802
  Cleveland *(G-5545)*
Lake Shore Cryotronics Inc ....C....... 614 891-2243
  Westerville *(G-20003)*
Safe-Grain Inc.......................................G....... 513 398-2500
  Loveland *(G-12229)*

SENSORS: Ultraviolet, Solid State

Transducers Direct Llc ....G....... 513 583-7597
  Loveland *(G-12240)*

SEPARATORS: Metal Plate

Almo Process Technology Inc ....G....... 513 402-2566
  West Chester *(G-19642)*

SEPTIC TANK CLEANING SVCS

Pro-Kleen Industrial Svcs Inc ....E....... 740 689-1886
  Lancaster *(G-11599)*
Reed Elvin Burl II ....G....... 937 399-3242
  Springfield *(G-17482)*

SEPTIC TANKS: Concrete

Allen Enterprises Inc ....E....... 740 532-5913
  Ironton *(G-11159)*
Bluffton Precast Concrete Co.................F....... 419 358-6946
  Bluffton *(G-1885)*
E A Cox Inc ....G....... 740 858-4400
  Lucasville *(G-12262)*
Encore Precast LLC..............................F....... 513 726-5678
  Seven Mile *(G-16907)*
J K Precast LLC ....G....... 740 335-2188
  Wshngtn CT Hs *(G-20729)*
James Kimmey......................................F....... 740 335-5746
  Wshngtn CT Hs *(G-20730)*
Lindsay Precast Inc ....G....... 800 837-7788
  Canal Fulton *(G-2483)*
Quaker City Septic Tanks LLC ....G....... 330 427-2239
  Leetonia *(G-11720)*
Reed Elvin Burl II ....G....... 937 399-3242
  Springfield *(G-17482)*
Richmond Concrete Products ....G....... 330 673-7892
  Warren *(G-19439)*
Septic Products Inc ....G....... 419 282-5933
  Ashland *(G-748)*
Stiger Pre Cast Inc.................................G....... 740 482-2313
  Nevada *(G-14601)*
Uniontown Septic Tanks Inc ....F....... 330 699-3386
  Uniontown *(G-18936)*

SEPTIC TANKS: Plastic

Hancor Inc...D....... 419 424-8225
  Findlay *(G-9701)*
Hancor Inc...B....... 614 658-0050
  Hilliard *(G-10827)*
J K Precast LLC ....G....... 740 335-2188
  Wshngtn CT Hs *(G-20729)*

SEWAGE & WATER TREATMENT EQPT

B L Anderson Co Inc..............................G....... 765 463-1518
  West Chester *(G-19654)*
City of Chardon ....F....... 440 286-2657
  Chardon *(G-3105)*
City of Troy ....F....... 937 339-4826
  Troy *(G-18641)*
Comp-U-Chem Inc.................................G....... 740 345-3332
  Newark *(G-14863)*
County of Lawrence...............................F....... 740 867-8700
  Chesapeake *(G-3144)*
De Nora Tech LLC ....D....... 440 710-5300
  Painesville *(G-15731)*
Eagle Crusher Co Inc.............................C....... 419 468-2288
  Galion *(G-10135)*
Flow-Liner Systems Ltd ....E....... 800 348-0020
  Zanesville *(G-21136)*
Greene County ....G....... 937 429-0127
  Dayton *(G-7981)*

Komar Industries Inc.............................E....... 614 836-2366
  Groveport *(G-10497)*
Pelton Environmental Products ....G....... 440 838-1221
  Lewis Center *(G-11770)*
Smart Sonic Corporation........................G....... 818 610-7900
  Cleveland *(G-6072)*
Tangent Company LLC ....G....... 440 543-2775
  Chagrin Falls *(G-3079)*
Village of Somerset................................G....... 740 743-1986
  Somerset *(G-17268)*
Village of West Alexandria ....G....... 937 839-4168
  West Alexandria *(G-19623)*
X-3-5 LLC ....G....... 513 489-5477
  Cincinnati *(G-4526)*

SEWAGE FACILITIES

City of Ravenna.....................................G....... 330 296-5214
  Ravenna *(G-16372)*

SEWAGE TREATMENT SYSTEMS & EQPT

Beckman Environmental Svcs Inc ....F....... 513 752-3570
  Batavia *(G-1127)*
City of Ravenna.....................................G....... 330 296-5214
  Ravenna *(G-16372)*
E - I Corp ....F....... 614 899-2282
  Westerville *(G-19988)*
Mack Industries PA Inc..........................F....... 330 638-7680
  Vienna *(G-19202)*
McNish Corporation ....G....... 614 899-2282
  Westerville *(G-20010)*
Oceco Inc..F....... 419 447-0916
  Tiffin *(G-18073)*

SEWER CLEANING & RODDING SVC

Beckman Environmental Svcs Inc ....F....... 513 752-3570
  Batavia *(G-1127)*
Stevens Auto Parts & Towng ....G....... 740 988-2260
  Jackson *(G-11195)*

SEWER CLEANING EQPT: Power

Best Equipment Co Inc..........................G....... 440 237-3515
  North Royalton *(G-15263)*
Electric Eel Mfg Co Inc ....E....... 937 323-4644
  Springfield *(G-17395)*

SEWING CONTRACTORS

Cold Duck Screen Prtg & EMB Co.........G....... 330 426-1900
  East Palestine *(G-9071)*
Db Rediheat Inc.....................................E....... 216 361-0530
  Cleveland *(G-5075)*
DCW Acquisition Inc..............................F....... 216 451-0666
  Cleveland *(G-5079)*

SEWING MACHINES & PARTS: Indl

Acb Three Inc..G....... 614 873-4680
  Plain City *(G-16168)*
Intelliworks Ht ....G....... 419 660-9050
  Norwalk *(G-15401)*
Omar McDowell Co ....G....... 440 808-2280
  Westlake *(G-20137)*
Rda Group LLC ....G....... 440 724-4347
  Avon *(G-962)*

SEWING, NEEDLEWORK & PIECE GOODS STORE: Quilting Matls/Splys

Quilting Creations Intl ....E....... 330 874-4741
  Bolivar *(G-1926)*

SEWING, NEEDLEWORK & PIECE GOODS STORES: Knitting Splys

Yarn Shop Inc..G....... 614 457-7836
  Columbus *(G-7621)*

SEWING, NEEDLEWORK & PIECE GOODS STORES: Notions, Incl Trim

Camela Nitschke Ribbonry ....G....... 419 872-0073
  Perrysburg *(G-15929)*

SEWING, NEEDLEWORK & PIECE GOODS STORES: Sewing & Needlework

J-M Designs LLC..................................G....... 419 794-2114
  Maumee *(G-13120)*

SHADES: Window

Cincinnati Window Shade Inc .... G 513 398-8510
Mason (G-12844)
Cincinnati Window Shade Inc .... F 513 631-7200
Cincinnati (G-3510)
Simex Inc .... G 304 665-1104
Columbus (G-7452)

SHAFTS: Shaft Collars

Southeastern Shafting Mfg .... F 740 342-4629
New Lexington (G-14723)

SHALE MINING, COMMON

Blue Jay Entps of Tscrwas Cnty .... G 330 874-2048
Bolivar (G-1907)

SHAPES & PILINGS, STRUCTURAL: Steel

A-1 Welding & Fabrication .... F 440 233-8474
Lorain (G-12077)
Brenmar Construction Inc .... D 740 286-2151
Jackson (G-11183)
Nova Structural Steel Inc .... F 216 938-7476
Cleveland (G-5788)
Steve Vore Welding and Steel .... F 419 375-4087
Fort Recovery (G-9827)

SHAPES: Extruded, Aluminum, NEC

Aerolite Extrusion Company .... D 330 782-1127
Youngstown (G-20838)
Gei of Columbiana Inc .... D 330 783-0270
Youngstown (G-20915)
General Extrusions Inc .... D 330 783-0270
Youngstown (G-20917)
I R B F Company .... G 330 633-5100
Tallmadge (G-17986)
Kit MB Systems Inc .... E 330 945-4500
Akron (G-239)
Patton Aluminum Products Inc .... F 937 845-9404
New Carlisle (G-14676)
Vari-Wall Tube Specialists Inc .... D 330 482-0000
Columbiana (G-6485)

SHAVING PREPARATIONS

Edgewell Personal Care LLC .... C 937 492-1057
Sidney (G-17034)

SHEARS

Klenk Industries Inc .... D 330 453-7857
Canton (G-2725)

SHEET METAL SPECIALTIES, EXC STAMPED

A & E Butscha Co .... G 513 761-1919
Cincinnati (G-3275)
Ahner Fabricating & Shtmtl Inc .... E 419 626-6641
Sandusky (G-16793)
All Metal Fabricators Inc .... F 216 267-0033
Cleveland (G-4663)
Allen County Fabrication Inc .... E 419 227-7447
Lima (G-11834)
Allied Fabricating & Wldg Co .... E 614 751-6664
Columbus (G-6572)
Buckeye Metal Works Inc .... F 614 239-8000
Columbus (G-6710)
C & R Inc .... E 614 497-1130
Groveport (G-10486)
Chagrin Metal Fabricating Inc .... G 440 946-6342
Eastlake (G-9101)
Columbus Steelmasters Inc .... F 614 231-2141
Columbus (G-6803)
Cramers Inc .... E 330 477-4571
Canton (G-2638)
CRC Metal Products .... G 740 966-0475
Johnstown (G-11264)
Crown Electric Engrg & Mfg LLC .... E 513 539-7394
Middletown (G-13898)
Flood Heliarc Inc .... F 614 835-3929
Groveport (G-10489)
G T Metal Fabricators Inc .... F 440 237-8745
Cleveland (G-5284)
Halls Sheet Metal Fabrication .... G 740 965-9264
Galena (G-10113)
Hartzell Mfg Co .... E 937 859-5955
Miamisburg (G-13674)
Izit Cain Sheet Metal Corp .... G 937 667-6521
Tipp City (G-18117)
J B Kepple Sheet Metal .... G 740 393-2971
Mount Vernon (G-14484)
Kirk & Blum Manufacturing Co .... C 513 458-2600
Cincinnati (G-3912)
Kuhlman Engineering Co .... F 419 243-2196
Toledo (G-18371)
Kuhn Fabricating Inc .... G 440 277-4182
Lorain (G-12098)
Lambert Sheet Metal Inc .... F 614 237-0384
Columbus (G-7111)
M3 Technologies Inc .... F 216 898-9936
Cleveland (G-5596)
Metal Technology Systems Inc .... G 513 563-1882
Cincinnati (G-4012)
Metal-Max Inc .... G 330 673-9926
Kent (G-11352)
Metlweb .... E 513 563-8822
Cincinnati (G-4016)
Midwest Fabrications Inc .... E 330 633-0191
Tallmadge (G-17993)
Midwest Metal Fabricators .... F 419 739-7077
Wapakoneta (G-19344)
Mika Metal Fabricating Co .... F 440 951-5500
Willoughby (G-20382)
Modern Manufacturing Inc .... F 513 251-3600
Cincinnati (G-4039)
Muehlenkamp Properties Inc .... E 513 745-0874
Cincinnati (G-4053)
Nufab Sheet Metal .... G 937 235-2030
Dayton (G-8391)
Paul Wilke & Son Inc .... F 513 921-3163
Cincinnati (G-4141)
S & B Metal Products Inc .... E 330 487-5790
Twinsburg (G-18852)
S & R Sheet Metal .... G 937 865-9236
Dayton (G-8489)
S L M Inc .... G 216 651-0666
Cleveland (G-6022)
Selmco Metal Fabricators Inc .... F 937 498-1331
Sidney (G-17075)
Seneca Sheet Metal Company .... F 419 447-8434
Tiffin (G-18083)
Sheet Metal Products Co Inc .... E 440 392-9000
Mentor (G-13581)
Valley Metal Works Inc .... G 513 554-1022
Cincinnati (G-4464)
Varmland Inc .... F 216 741-1510
Cleveland (G-6251)
Vicart Prcsion Fabricators Inc .... F 614 771-0080
Hilliard (G-10874)
Visual Information Institute .... F 937 376-4361
Xenia (G-20801)
Wolf Metals Inc .... G 614 461-6361
Columbus (G-7608)

SHEETING: Laminated Plastic

Great Lakes Textiles Inc .... E 440 201-1300
Bedford (G-1406)
Plaskolite LLC .... D 740 450-1109
Zanesville (G-21168)
Rochling Glastic Composites LP .... C 216 486-0100
Cleveland (G-5996)
Schneller LLC .... D 330 673-1299
Kent (G-11381)
Shamrock Plastics Inc .... F 740 392-5555
Mount Vernon (G-14508)
United Converting Inc .... G 614 863-9972
Columbus (G-7556)

SHEETS & STRIPS: Aluminum

Arconic Inc .... C 330 835-6000
Mogadore (G-14230)
Arconic Inc .... C 330 848-4000
Barberton (G-1053)
Arconic Inc .... G 330 544-7633
Niles (G-14998)

SHEETS: Hard Rubber

Novex Inc .... F 330 335-2371
Wadsworth (G-19257)

SHELLAC

Hess Advanced Technology Inc .... G 937 268-4377
Huber Heights (G-11020)
PPG Industries Inc .... E 513 576-0360
Milford (G-14033)

SHELTERED WORKSHOPS

Belco Works Inc .... B 740 695-0500
Saint Clairsville (G-16624)
Brookhill Center Industries .... C 419 876-3932
Ottawa (G-15648)
Brown Cnty Bd Mntal Rtardation .... E 937 378-4891
Georgetown (G-10237)
Carroll Hills Industries Inc .... D 330 627-5524
Carrollton (G-2917)
Cincinnati Assn For The Blind .... C 513 221-8558
Cincinnati (G-3481)
Hopewell Industries Inc .... D 740 622-3563
Coshocton (G-7737)
Hunter Defense Tech Inc .... E 216 438-6111
Solon (G-17164)
J-Vac Industries Inc .... D 740 384-2155
Wellston (G-19603)
Ken Harper .... C 740 439-4452
Byesville (G-2388)
Metzenbaum Sheltered Inds Inc .... C 440 729-1919
Chesterland (G-3164)
Monco Enterprises Inc .... A 937 461-0034
Dayton (G-8366)
R T Industries Inc .... C 937 335-5784
Troy (G-18695)

SHELVES & SHELVING: Wood

Darko Inc .... E 330 425-9805
Bedford (G-1398)

SHELVING ANGLES OR SLOTTED BARS, EXC WOOD

American Truck Equipment Inc .... G 216 362-0400
Cleveland (G-4699)

SHELVING, MADE FROM PURCHASED WIRE

Interntnal Tchncal Catings Inc .... D 614 449-6669
Columbus (G-7046)
K Effs Inc .... F 614 443-0586
Columbus (G-7082)

SHELVING: Office & Store, Exc Wood

Metrodeck Inc .... F 513 541-4370
Cincinnati (G-4018)

SHIMS: Metal

Die-Cut Products Co .... E 216 771-6994
Cleveland (G-5094)
Ohio Gasket and Shim Co Inc .... E 330 630-0626
Akron (G-307)
Spirol International Corp .... D 330 920-3655
Stow (G-17630)

SHIP BUILDING & REPAIRING: Cargo Vessels

Manitowoc Company Inc .... G 920 746-3332
Cleveland (G-5612)

SHIP BUILDING & REPAIRING: Lighthouse Tenders

Lighthouse Youth Services Inc .... F 513 961-4080
Cincinnati (G-3943)

SHIP BUILDING & REPAIRING: Tankers

Services Acquisition Co LLC .... G 330 479-9267
Dennison (G-8786)

SHIP BUILDING & REPAIRING: Tugboats

Superior Marine Ways Inc .... G 740 894-6224
South Point (G-17295)

SHIP COMPONENTS: Metal, Prefabricated

Accurate Fab LLC .... G 330 562-0065
Streetsboro (G-17656)
Navpar Inc .... G 513 738-2230
Harrison (G-10660)

SHIPBUILDING & REPAIR

Great Lakes Group .... C 216 621-4854
Cleveland (G-5346)
Oneseal Inc .... G 973 599-1155
Perrysburg (G-15989)

SHIPBUILDING & REPAIR / PRODUCT SECTION

Tack-Anew Inc ....E 419 734-4212
  Port Clinton (G-16262)
V&P Group International LLC ....F 703 349-6432
  Cincinnati (G-4461)
WH Fetzer & Sons Mfg Inc ....E 419 687-8237
  Plymouth (G-16235)

SHOE MATERIALS: Counters

Bean Counter LLC ....G 419 636-0705
  Bryan (G-2268)
Buckeye Counters ....G 330 682-0902
  Orrville (G-15585)
Classic Countertops LLC ....G 330 882-4220
  Akron (G-119)
Counter Creation Plus L L C ....G 419 826-7449
  Swanton (G-17910)
Counter Method Inc ....G 614 206-3192
  Sunbury (G-17884)
Counter Rhythm Group ....G 513 379-6587
  Columbus (G-6829)
Dicks Counter D M ....G 440 322-3312
  Elyria (G-9243)
Perfume Counter ....G 513 885-5989
  Cincinnati (G-4151)

SHOE MATERIALS: Inner Soles

Sentinel Consumer Products Inc ....D 801 825-5671
  Mentor (G-13579)

SHOE MATERIALS: Quarters

Bond Quarters Horses ....G 614 354-4028
  Freeport (G-9984)
Colonels Quarters ....G 740 385-3374
  Circleville (G-4540)
Cruise Quarters ....G 614 777-6022
  Hilliard (G-10821)
Cruise Quarters and Tours ....G 614 891-6089
  Westerville (G-20043)
Custom Floaters LLC ....G 216 536-8979
  Brookpark (G-2141)
Dewey Smith Quarter Horses ....G 682 597-2424
  Bellefontaine (G-1513)
Halvey Quarter Horses ....G 614 648-0483
  Blacklick (G-1685)
Home Quarters North Canto ....G 330 806-5336
  Hartville (G-10696)
Latin Quarter ....G 513 271-5400
  Cincinnati (G-3933)
Quarter Bistro ....G 513 271-5400
  Cincinnati (G-4232)
Quarter Mile Fabrication LLC ....G 440 298-1272
  Thompson (G-18027)
Randy R Wilson ....G 740 454-4440
  Findlay (G-9745)
Scioto Darby Quarter Horses ....G 614 464-7290
  Orient (G-15577)

SHOE MATERIALS: Rands

Ingersoll-Rand Co ....G 704 655-4000
  Hillsboro (G-10881)
McClellan Rand L ....G 614 462-4782
  Columbus (G-7162)

SHOE MATERIALS: Rubber

Remington Products Co ....C 330 335-1571
  Wadsworth (G-19274)

SHOE MATERIALS: Uppers

Upper Echelon Bar LLC ....G 513 531-2814
  Cincinnati (G-4455)
Upper Sarahsville LLC ....G 740 732-2071
  Caldwell (G-2413)

SHOE REPAIR SHOP

Charm Harness and Boot Ltd ....F 330 893-0402
  Charm (G-3141)
Maysville Harness Shop Ltd ....G 330 695-9977
  Apple Creek (G-612)

SHOE STORES

Charm Harness and Boot Ltd ....F 330 893-0402
  Charm (G-3141)
Ervin Yoder ....G 330 359-5862
  Mount Hope (G-14436)
Outdoor Army Store of Ashtabula ....F 440 992-8791
  Ashtabula (G-794)

Vances Department Store ....G 937 549-2188
  Manchester (G-12397)
Vances Department Store ....F 937 549-3033
  Manchester (G-12398)

SHOE STORES: Boots, Men's

Cobblers Corner LLC ....F 330 482-4005
  Columbiana (G-6458)
Hudson Leather Ltd ....G 419 485-8531
  Pioneer (G-16085)

SHOE STORES: Men's

Essential Pathways Ohio LLC ....G 330 518-3091
  Youngstown (G-20900)
Wagoner Stores Inc ....G 937 836-3636
  Englewood (G-9383)

SHOE STORES: Women's

Robs Creative Screen Printing ....G 740 264-6383
  Wintersville (G-20541)

SHOES & BOOTS WHOLESALERS

Sysco Guest Supply LLC ....F 440 960-2515
  Lorain (G-12128)

SHOES: Athletic, Exc Rubber Or Plastic

NTS Enterprises Ltd ....G 513 531-1166
  Cincinnati (G-4092)

SHOES: Canvas, Rubber Soled

Vans Inc ....F 419 471-1541
  Toledo (G-18589)

SHOES: Men's

Acor Orthopaedic Inc ....D 216 662-4500
  Cleveland (G-4608)
Georgia-Boot Inc ....D 740 753-1951
  Nelsonville (G-14593)
Rocky Brands Inc ....B 740 753-1951
  Nelsonville (G-14595)
Rocky Brands Inc ....D 740 753-1951
  Nelsonville (G-14596)

SHOES: Plastic Or Rubber

American Doll Accessories ....G 740 590-8458
  Coolville (G-7672)
Cobblers Corner LLC ....F 330 482-4005
  Columbiana (G-6458)
Georgia-Boot Inc ....D 740 753-1951
  Nelsonville (G-14593)
Mulhern Belting Inc ....E 201 337-5700
  Fairfield (G-9533)
Nwc HUD Corp II ....G 419 228-8400
  Lima (G-11912)
Totes Isotoner Corporation ....F 513 682-8200
  West Chester (G-19907)
Totes Isotoner Holdings Corp ....C 513 682-8200
  West Chester (G-19908)

SHOES: Women's

Acor Orthopaedic Inc ....D 216 662-4500
  Cleveland (G-4608)
Georgia-Boot Inc ....D 740 753-1951
  Nelsonville (G-14593)
Rocky Brands Inc ....B 740 753-1951
  Nelsonville (G-14595)

SHOES: Women's, Dress

Foot Petals Inc ....G 614 729-7205
  Pickerington (G-16048)

SHOT PEENING SVC

Metal Improvement Company LLC ....E 513 489-6884
  Blue Ash (G-1819)
Metal Improvement Company LLC ....E 330 425-1490
  Twinsburg (G-18817)
National Peening ....G 216 342-9155
  Bedford Heights (G-1476)

SHOWCASES & DISPLAY FIXTURES: Office & Store

Darko Inc ....E 330 425-9805
  Bedford (G-1398)

Easy Board Inc ....G 440 205-8836
  Mentor (G-13437)
Pete Gaietto & Associates Inc ....D 513 771-0903
  Cincinnati (G-4152)

SHOWER STALLS: Plastic & Fiberglass

Cfrc Wtr & Enrgy Solutions Inc ....G 216 479-0290
  Cleveland (G-4906)
Closets By Mike ....G 740 607-2212
  Zanesville (G-21120)

SHREDDERS: Indl & Commercial

Accushred LLC ....F 419 244-7473
  Toledo (G-18154)
Cintas Corporation No 2 ....G 937 236-1506
  Dayton (G-8090)

SHUTTERS, DOOR & WINDOW: Metal

A C Shutters Inc ....G 216 429-2424
  Cleveland (G-4584)
Bearded Shutter ....G 440 567-8568
  Mantua (G-12543)
Cleveland Shutters ....G 440 234-7600
  Berea (G-1597)
Installed Building Pdts LLC ....E 614 308-9900
  Columbus (G-7029)
Shutter Expressions ....G 937 626-0462
  Franklin (G-9920)
Shutterbus Ohio LLC ....G 937 726-9634
  Hilliard (G-10861)

SHUTTERS, DOOR & WINDOW: Plastic

A C Shutters Inc ....G 216 429-2424
  Cleveland (G-4584)
Tapco Holdings Inc ....F 800 771-4486
  Franklin (G-9924)

SIDING & STRUCTURAL MATERIALS: Wood

Automated Bldg Components Inc ....E 419 257-2152
  North Baltimore (G-15042)
S & J Lumber Co ....E 740 245-5804
  Thurman (G-18038)
Sphon Associates Inc ....G 614 741-4002
  Gahanna (G-10107)

SIDING MATERIALS

American Orginal Bldg Pdts LLC ....F 330 786-3000
  Akron (G-63)

SIDING: Plastic

Alsco Metals Corporation ....E 740 983-2571
  Dennison (G-8781)
Fibreboard Corporation ....C 419 248-8000
  Toledo (G-18294)
Gentek Building Products Inc ....F 800 548-4542
  Cuyahoga Falls (G-7872)
Style Crest Inc ....B 419 332-7369
  Fremont (G-10052)

SIDING: Precast Stone

Headwaters Incorporated ....F 989 671-1500
  Manchester (G-12394)

SIDING: Sheet Metal

Alsco Metals Corporation ....G 740 983-2571
  Ashville (G-815)
Alsco Metals Corporation ....E 740 983-2571
  Dennison (G-8781)
Amh Holdings LLC ....A 330 929-1811
  Cuyahoga Falls (G-7836)
Gentek Building Products Inc ....F 800 548-4542
  Cuyahoga Falls (G-7872)
Higgins Building Mtls No 2 LLC ....G 740 395-5410
  Jackson (G-11186)
Metal Sales Manufacturing Corp ....E 440 319-3779
  Jefferson (G-11234)
North Star Metals Mfg Co ....E 740 254-4567
  Uhrichsville (G-18891)
Owens Corning Sales LLC ....G 740 983-1300
  Ashville (G-819)

SIGN LETTERING & PAINTING SVCS

Akers Identity LLC ....G 330 493-0055
  Canton (G-2566)

Sign A Rama Inc....G....614 932-7005
Powell (G-16335)

SIGN PAINTING & LETTERING SHOP

All Signs and Designs LLC....G....216 267-8588
Cleveland (G-4666)
Art & Sign Corporation....G....419 865-3336
Toledo (G-18192)
Bernard R Doyles Inc....G....216 523-2288
Cleveland (G-4806)
Brent Bleh Company....G....513 721-1100
Cincinnati (G-3410)
Carroll Exhibit and Print Svcs....G....216 361-2325
Cleveland (G-4884)
Digimatics Inc....G....419 478-0804
Toledo (G-18263)
General Theming Contrs LLC....C....614 252-6342
Columbus (G-6945)
KS Designs Inc....G....513 241-5953
Cincinnati (G-3925)
Medina Signs Post Inc....G....330 723-2484
Medina (G-13297)
Ohio Shelterall Inc....F....614 882-1110
Westerville (G-20068)
Premiere Printing & Signs Inc....G....330 688-6244
Stow (G-17620)
Quick As A Wink Printing Co....F....419 224-9786
Lima (G-11926)
Signery....G....513 932-1938
Lebanon (G-11696)
Steven Mercer Inc....G....740 623-0033
Coshocton (G-7753)
Triangle Sign Co....G....513 863-2578
Hamilton (G-10615)

SIGNALS: Traffic Control, Electric

Area Wide Protective Inc....E....513 321-9889
Fairfield (G-9483)
Athens Technical Specialists....F....740 592-2874
Athens (G-824)
City Elyria Communication....G....440 322-3329
Elyria (G-9237)
City of Canton....E....330 489-3370
Canton (G-2625)
Intelligent Signal Tech....G....614 530-4784
Loveland (G-12200)
K-Hill Signal Co Inc....G....740 922-0421
Uhrichsville (G-18890)
MD Solutions Inc....G....866 637-6588
Plain City (G-16201)
Paul Peterson Company....E....614 486-4375
Columbus (G-7299)
Security Fence Group Inc....E....513 681-3700
Cincinnati (G-4314)
Union Metal Industries Corp....G....330 456-7653
Canton (G-2846)

SIGNALS: Transportation

A & A Safety Inc....F....937 567-9781
Beavercreek (G-1348)
Ds Express Carriers Inc....G....419 433-6200
Norwalk (G-15388)
Faircosa LLC....G....216 577-9909
Cleveland (G-5215)
General Dynmics Mssion Systems....E....513 253-4770
Beavercreek (G-1317)
Ohio Department Transportation....E....614 351-2898
Columbus (G-7244)
Signature Technologies Inc....E....937 859-6323
Miamisburg (G-13716)

SIGNS & ADVERTISING SPECIALTIES

1 Day Sign....G....419 475-6060
Toledo (G-18150)
A & A Safety Inc....E....513 943-6100
Amelia (G-527)
A & A Safety Inc....F....937 567-9781
Beavercreek (G-1348)
A Plus Signs & Graphix....G....330 848-4800
Akron (G-19)
Abbot Image Solutions LLC....G....937 382-6677
Wilmington (G-20483)
Accu-Sign....G....216 544-2059
Broadview Heights (G-2086)
Action Enterprise....G....740 522-1678
Newark (G-14847)
Adcraft Decals Inc....E....216 524-2934
Cleveland (G-4615)
Advertising Ideas of Ohio Inc....G....330 745-6555
Barberton (G-1049)
Affinity Disp Expositions Inc....D....513 771-2339
Cincinnati (G-3307)
Agile Sign & Ltg Maint Inc....E....440 918-1311
Eastlake (G-9098)
Akers Identity LLC....G....330 493-0055
Canton (G-2566)
Alberts Screen Print Inc....C....330 753-7559
Norton (G-15360)
All Signs and Designs LLC....G....216 267-8588
Cleveland (G-4666)
Allied Sign Company Inc....F....614 443-9656
Columbus (G-6574)
Alvin L Roepke....F....419 862-3891
Elmore (G-9203)
Am Graphics....G....330 799-7319
Youngstown (G-20842)
American Awards Inc....F....614 875-1850
Grove City (G-10414)
Applied Graphics Ltd....G....419 756-6882
Mansfield (G-12407)
Aq Productions Inc....G....614 486-7700
Dublin (G-8882)
Archer Corporation....E....330 455-9995
Canton (G-2574)
Art Tees Inc....G....614 338-8337
Columbus (G-6617)
Atlantic Sign Company Inc....E....513 383-1504
Cincinnati (G-3367)
Auld Technologies LLC....F....614 755-2853
Columbus (G-6631)
Auto Dealer Designs Inc....E....330 374-7666
Akron (G-74)
Auto Pro & Design....G....330 833-9237
Massillon (G-12961)
B & D Graphics Inc....G....513 641-0855
Cincinnati (G-3373)
Baker Plastics Inc....G....330 743-3142
Youngstown (G-20851)
Bambeck Inc....G....614 766-1000
Dublin (G-8887)
Barnes Advertising Corp....F....740 453-6836
Zanesville (G-21103)
Bates Metal Products Inc....D....740 498-8371
Port Washington (G-16267)
Becker Signs Inc....G....330 659-4504
Hudson (G-11033)
Belco Works Inc....B....740 695-0500
Saint Clairsville (G-16624)
Bench Billboard Company Inc....G....513 271-2222
Cincinnati (G-3388)
Benchmark Signs and Gifts....G....216 973-3718
Northfield (G-15313)
Bernard R Doyles Inc....G....216 523-2288
Cleveland (G-4806)
Bird Corporation....G....419 424-3095
Findlay (G-9656)
Blang Acquisition LLC....F....937 223-2155
Dayton (G-8058)
Blink Marketing Inc....G....216 503-2568
Cleveland (G-4820)
Bob King Sign Company Inc....G....330 753-2679
Akron (G-90)
Brandon Screen Printing....F....419 229-9837
Lima (G-11845)
Brent Bleh Company....G....513 721-1100
Cincinnati (G-3410)
Brown Cnty Bd Mntal Rtardation....E....937 378-4891
Georgetown (G-10237)
Buckeye Boxes Inc....C....614 274-8484
Columbus (G-6707)
Busch & Thiem Inc....E....419 625-7515
Sandusky (G-16800)
Business Idntification Systems....G....614 841-1255
Columbus (G-6716)
C A Kustoms....G....419 332-4395
Fremont (G-10003)
C JS Signs....G....330 821-7446
Alliance (G-459)
Casad Company Inc....F....419 586-9457
Coldwater (G-6404)
Cds Signs....G....513 563-7446
Cincinnati (G-3450)
Century Signs....G....419 352-2666
Bowling Green (G-1962)
Cgs Signs LLC....F....419 897-3000
Holland (G-10919)
Cline Signs LLC....G....513 396-7446
Cincinnati (G-3527)
Columbus Graphics Inc....F....614 577-9360
Reynoldsburg (G-16432)
Corporate ID Inc....G....614 841-1255
Columbus (G-6823)
Creative Blast Co....G....513 251-4177
Cincinnati (G-3558)
CTS Signs & Sales....G....419 407-5534
Oregon (G-15559)
Custom Engraving & Screen Prtg....G....440 933-2902
Avon Lake (G-983)
D & D Next Day Signs Inc....G....419 537-9595
Toledo (G-18249)
Dana Signs LLC....G....937 653-3917
Urbana (G-18987)
David Esrati....G....937 228-4433
Dayton (G-8126)
Dayton Wire Products Inc....E....937 236-8000
Dayton (G-8149)
Dee Sign Usa LLC....G....513 779-3333
West Chester (G-19692)
Dern Trophies Corp....F....614 895-3260
Westerville (G-19987)
Design Sign Inc....G....216 398-9900
Cleveland (G-5085)
Devries & Associates Inc....F....614 890-3821
Westerville (G-20047)
Devries & Associates Inc....G....614 860-0103
Westerville (G-20048)
Digimax Signs....G....513 576-0747
Milford (G-14007)
DJ Signs MD LLC....G....330 344-6643
Akron (G-144)
Dyverse Entertainment LLC....G....513 225-3301
Blue Ash (G-1761)
Eighth Floor Promotions LLC....C....419 586-6433
Celina (G-2959)
Enlarging Arts Inc....G....330 434-3433
Akron (G-156)
Etched Metal Company....E....440 248-0240
Solon (G-17142)
Ew Publishing Company....G....440 979-0025
North Olmsted (G-15188)
F J Designs Inc....E....330 264-1377
Wooster (G-20590)
Fair Publishing House Inc....E....419 668-3746
Norwalk (G-15394)
Fastsigns....G....513 489-8989
Cincinnati (G-3674)
Fastsigns....G....330 952-2626
Medina (G-13261)
Fastsigns Westerville....E....614 890-3821
Westerville (G-20053)
Fdi Cabinetry LLC....G....513 353-4500
Cleves (G-6362)
Fineline Imprints Inc....E....740 453-1083
Zanesville (G-21135)
First Stop Signs and Decals....G....330 343-1859
New Philadelphia (G-14769)
Folks Creative Printers Inc....E....740 383-6326
Marion (G-12702)
Forsvara Engineering LLC....G....937 254-9711
Dayton (G-8202)
Forty Nine Degrees LLC....F....419 678-0100
Coldwater (G-6409)
Fought Signs....G....330 262-5901
Wooster (G-20592)
Fourteen Ventures Group LLC....G....937 866-2341
West Carrollton (G-19631)
Fried Daddy....G....937 854-4542
Dayton (G-8207)
Frontier Signs & Displays Inc....G....513 367-0813
Harrison (G-10642)
Fulton Sign & Decal Inc....G....440 951-1515
Mentor (G-13452)
Gail Berner....G....937 322-0314
Springfield (G-17406)
Galaxy Balloons Incorporated....C....216 476-3360
Cleveland (G-5287)
Gallo Displays Inc....E....216 431-9500
Cleveland (G-5288)
Gary Lawrence Enterprises Inc....G....330 833-7181
Massillon (G-12986)
Gauntlet Awards & Engraving....G....937 890-5811
Dayton (G-8214)
Gedco Inc....G....330 828-2044
Dalton (G-7942)
Geograph Industries Inc....E....513 202-9200
Harrison (G-10643)
Ginos Awards Inc....E....216 831-6565
Warrensville Heights (G-19469)

PRODUCT

Employee Codes: A=Over 500 employees, B=251-500
C=101-250, D=51-100, E=20-50, F=10-19, G=3-9
2019 Harris Ohio
Industrial Directory
1587

Glavin Industries Inc...E...440 349-0049
Solon *(G-17149)*
Global Lighting Tech Inc...E...440 922-4584
Brecksville *(G-2039)*
Golden Signs and Lighting LLC...G...513 248-0895
Milford *(G-14011)*
Golf Marketing Group Inc...G...330 963-5155
Twinsburg *(G-18788)*
Grady McCauley Inc...D...330 494-9444
North Canton *(G-15089)*
Granite Industries Inc...D...419 445-4733
Archbold *(G-651)*
Graphic Detail Inc...G...330 678-1724
Kent *(G-11326)*
Great Impressions Signs Design...G...614 428-8250
Columbus *(G-6968)*
Hall Company...E...937 652-1376
Urbana *(G-18992)*
Ham Signs LLC...G...937 454-9111
Dayton *(G-8242)*
Hart Advertising Inc...F...419 668-1194
Norwalk *(G-15397)*
HP Manufacturing Company Inc...D...216 361-6500
Cleveland *(G-5421)*
HPM Business Systems Inc...G...216 520-1330
Cleveland *(G-5422)*
Identitek Systems Inc...D...330 832-9844
Massillon *(G-13002)*
Impressions To Go LLC...G...614 760-0600
Dublin *(G-8928)*
Industrial and Mar Eng Svc Co...F...740 694-0791
Fredericktown *(G-9971)*
Industrial Image...G...419 547-1417
Bellevue *(G-1537)*
Inner Products Sales Inc...G...216 581-4141
Bedford *(G-1416)*
Innovation Exhibits Inc...G...330 726-1324
Youngstown *(G-20941)*
Integral Design Inc...F...216 524-0555
Cleveland *(G-5462)*
International Installations...G...330 848-4800
Barberton *(G-1077)*
Itecgraphix Inc...G...440 951-5020
Mentor *(G-13477)*
J & D Berdine Signs Inc...G...330 468-0556
Macedonia *(G-12305)*
Jalo Inc...G...216 661-2222
Cleveland *(G-5492)*
Janeway Signs Inc...G...937 237-8433
Dayton *(G-8279)*
JCP Signs & Graphix Inc...G...740 965-3058
Galena *(G-10114)*
Jeffrey A Clark...G...419 866-8775
Holland *(G-10936)*
Joe Paxton...G...614 424-9000
Columbus *(G-7071)*
Jones & Assoc Advg & Design...G...330 799-6876
Youngstown *(G-20949)*
Judith C Zell...G...740 385-0386
Logan *(G-12029)*
Kdm Signs Inc...C...513 769-1932
Cincinnati *(G-3900)*
Kenneth J Moore...G...330 923-8313
Cuyahoga Falls *(G-7887)*
Kim Phillips Sign Co LLC...G...330 364-4280
Dover *(G-8834)*
King Retail Solutions Inc...F...513 729-5858
Hamilton *(G-10580)*
Kingsway Art & Sign...G...330 877-6241
Hartville *(G-10698)*
Kmgrafx Inc...G...513 248-4100
Loveland *(G-12206)*
Koebbeco Signs LLC...G...513 923-2974
Cincinnati *(G-3921)*
Laad Sign & Lighting Inc...F...330 379-2297
Akron *(G-244)*
Lapat Signs...G...440 277-6291
Sheffield Village *(G-16969)*
Ledge Hill Signs Limited...G...440 461-4445
Cleveland *(G-5570)*
Limelght Graphic Solutions Inc...G...614 793-1996
Dublin *(G-8942)*
Long Sign Co...G...614 294-1057
Columbus *(G-7136)*
LSI Retail Graphics LLC...D...401 766-7446
North Canton *(G-15098)*
Macray Co LLC...G...937 325-1726
Springfield *(G-17440)*
Magnetic Mktg Solutions LLC...G...513 721-3801
Cincinnati *(G-3973)*
Maines Inc...G...937 322-2084
Springfield *(G-17443)*
Marion Signs & Lighting LLC...G...352 236-0936
Columbus *(G-7151)*
Masterpiece Signs & Graphics...G...419 358-0077
Bluffton *(G-1891)*
Mayfair Granite Co Inc...G...216 382-8150
Cleveland *(G-5636)*
McQueen Advertising Inc...G...440 967-1137
Vermilion *(G-19168)*
ME Signs Inc...G...419 222-7446
Lima *(G-11898)*
Meka Signs Enterprises Inc...G...513 942-5494
West Chester *(G-19878)*
Mitchell Plastics Inc...E...330 825-2461
Barberton *(G-1086)*
Moments To Remember USA LLC...G...330 830-0839
Massillon *(G-13027)*
Moonlight Specialties...G...216 464-6444
Cleveland *(G-5705)*
Names Unlimited Corp...G...419 845-2005
Caledonia *(G-2419)*
Neon Light Manufacturing Co...G...216 851-1000
Cleveland *(G-5739)*
Next Day Signs LLC...G...614 764-7446
Columbus *(G-7219)*
Norcal Signs Inc...G...513 779-6982
West Chester *(G-19749)*
North Coast Theatrical Inc...G...330 762-1768
Akron *(G-300)*
Northmont Sign Co Inc...G...937 890-0372
Dayton *(G-8384)*
Norton Outdoor Advertising...E...513 631-4864
Cincinnati *(G-4089)*
Ohio Plastics & Safety Pdts...G...330 882-6764
New Franklin *(G-14694)*
Ohio Shelterall Inc...F...614 882-1110
Westerville *(G-20068)*
Oliver Signs & Graphics...G...330 460-2996
Valley City *(G-19057)*
Omni Media...G...216 687-0077
Cleveland *(G-5813)*
Orange Barrel Media LLC...E...614 294-4898
Columbus *(G-7275)*
Painted Hill Inv Group Inc...F...937 339-1756
Troy *(G-18691)*
Plastigraphics Inc...F...513 771-8848
Cincinnati *(G-4166)*
Pro-Decal Inc...G...330 484-0089
Canton *(G-2793)*
R & H Signs Unlimited Inc...G...937 293-3834
Dayton *(G-8457)*
R Weir Inc...G...937 438-5730
Dayton *(G-8461)*
Rapid Signs & More Inc...G...513 553-4040
New Richmond *(G-14814)*
Ray Meyer Sign Company Inc...E...513 984-5446
Loveland *(G-12226)*
Renoir Visions LLC...F...419 586-5679
Celina *(G-2982)*
Ricks Graphic Accents Inc...G...330 644-4455
Akron *(G-349)*
Rise N Shine Yard Signs...G...330 745-5868
Barberton *(G-1103)*
Roderer Enterprises Inc...G...513 942-3000
Fairfield *(G-9559)*
Roemer Industries Inc...D...330 448-2000
Masury *(G-13062)*
Rossi Concept Arts...G...330 453-6366
Canton *(G-2811)*
Royal Acme Corporation...E...216 241-1477
Cleveland *(G-6009)*
S & S Sign Co...G...614 837-1511
Canal Winchester *(G-2511)*
S T Custom Signs...G...513 733-4227
Cincinnati *(G-4298)*
S&S Sign Service...G...614 279-9722
Columbus *(G-7411)*
Sa-Mor Signs...G...937 441-4950
Wapakoneta *(G-19351)*
Sabco Industries Inc...E...419 531-5347
Toledo *(G-18510)*
Screen Images Inc...G...440 779-7356
North Olmsted *(G-15197)*
Screen Works Inc...E...937 264-9111
Dayton *(G-8499)*
Sensical Inc...D...216 641-1141
Solon *(G-17229)*
Sign A Rama...G...330 499-4653
North Canton *(G-15118)*
Sign A Rama...G...614 337-6000
Gahanna *(G-10103)*
Sign A Rama Inc...G...614 932-7005
Powell *(G-16335)*
Sign A Rama Inc...G...440 442-5002
Cleveland *(G-6064)*
Sign A Rama Inc...G...513 671-2213
Cincinnati *(G-4336)*
Sign America Incorporated...E...740 765-5555
Richmond *(G-16498)*
Sign Makers LLC...G...330 455-0909
Canton *(G-2816)*
Sign Shop...G...740 474-1499
Circleville *(G-4558)*
Sign Smith LLC...G...614 519-9144
Marengo *(G-12595)*
Sign Source USA Inc...D...419 224-1130
Lima *(G-11940)*
Sign Technologies LLC...G...937 439-3970
Dayton *(G-8507)*
Sign Write...G...937 559-4388
Beavercreek *(G-1341)*
Signed By Josette LLC...G...419 796-9632
Findlay *(G-9754)*
Signery...G...513 932-1938
Lebanon *(G-11696)*
Signery2 LLC...G...513 738-3048
Hamilton *(G-10605)*
Signline Graphics & Lettering...G...740 397-5806
Mount Vernon *(G-14513)*
Signmaster Inc...G...614 777-0670
Lewis Center *(G-11780)*
Signpost Games LLC...G...614 467-9025
Dublin *(G-8985)*
Signs N Stuff Inc...G...440 974-3151
Mentor *(G-13582)*
Signs Unlimited The Graphic...G...614 836-7446
Logan *(G-12043)*
Spotted Horse Studio Inc...G...330 533-2391
Greenford *(G-10355)*
Steel Valley Sign...G...330 755-7446
Struthers *(G-17825)*
Steven Mercer Inc...G...740 623-0033
Coshocton *(G-7753)*
Stine Consulting Inc...G...513 723-4800
Cincinnati *(G-4383)*
Summco Inc...G...330 965-7446
Youngstown *(G-21041)*
Super Sign Guys LLC...G...330 477-3887
Canton *(G-2830)*
Super Signs Inc...E...480 968-2200
North Bend *(G-15056)*
Superior Label Systems Inc...B...513 336-0825
Mason *(G-12944)*
T-Top Shoppe...G...330 343-3481
New Philadelphia *(G-14803)*
Tce International Ltd...F...800 962-2376
Perry *(G-15914)*
Ternion Inc...E...216 642-6180
Cleveland *(G-6161)*
Thatcher Enterprises Co Ltd...G...614 228-2013
Columbus *(G-7523)*
The Hartman Corp...G...614 475-5035
Columbus *(G-7525)*
Think Signs LLC...G...614 384-0333
Lewis Center *(G-11785)*
Tim Boutwell...G...419 358-4653
Bluffton *(G-1894)*
Toledo Mobile Media LLC...G...419 389-0687
Toledo *(G-18562)*
Tract Inc...G...937 427-3431
Dayton *(G-7993)*
Traffic Cntrl Sgnls Signs & MA...G...740 670-7763
Newark *(G-14930)*
Traffic Detectors & Signs Inc...G...330 707-9060
Youngstown *(G-21048)*
Tridico Silk Screen & Sign Co...G...419 526-1695
Mansfield *(G-12534)*
Triumph Signs & Consulting Inc...E...513 576-8090
Milford *(G-14046)*
Ultimate Signs and Graphics...G...740 633-8928
Martins Ferry *(G-12762)*
Unique Led Products LLC...G...440 520-4959
Northfield *(G-15329)*
Unique Straight Line & Sfety S...G...740 452-2724
Zanesville *(G-21185)*
Visionary Signs LLC...G...614 504-5899
Columbus *(G-7585)*
Visual Advantage LLC...G...714 671-0988
Perrysburg *(G-16022)*

Visual Expressions Sign Co ....G....... 440 245-6660
Lorain *(G-12136)*
Vital Signs & Advertising LLC ....G....... 937 292-7967
Bellefontaine *(G-1526)*
Westrock Cp LLC ....B....... 513 745-2400
Blue Ash *(G-1868)*
Wettle Corporation ....G....... 419 865-6923
Holland *(G-10966)*
WH Fetzer & Sons Mfg Inc ....E....... 419 687-8237
Plymouth *(G-16235)*
Williams Steel Rule Die Co......................F....... 216 431-3232
Cleveland *(G-6311)*
Wright John ....G....... 937 653-4570
Urbana *(G-19020)*
Yes Management Inc...............................G....... 330 747-8593
Columbiana *(G-6486)*

SIGNS & ADVERTISING SPECIALTIES: Artwork, Advertising

Penca Design Group Ltd ....G....... 440 210-4422
Painesville *(G-15774)*
Vision Graphix Inc ....G....... 440 835-6540
Westlake *(G-20169)*

SIGNS & ADVERTISING SPECIALTIES: Displays, Paint Process

Custom Retail Group LLC ....G....... 614 409-9720
Columbus *(G-6843)*
Ohio Displays Inc.....................................F....... 216 961-5600
Elyria *(G-9303)*

SIGNS & ADVERTISING SPECIALTIES: Letters For Signs, Metal

AG Designs LLC.......................................G....... 614 506-2849
Delaware *(G-8652)*
Engravers Gallery & Sign Co ....G....... 330 830-1271
Massillon *(G-12980)*
Hillman Group Inc ....G....... 440 248-7000
Cleveland *(G-5409)*
Interstate Sign Products Inc ....G....... 419 683-1962
Crestline *(G-7795)*
Pro Companies Inc ....G....... 614 738-1222
Pickerington *(G-16057)*
Sign City Inc ....G....... 614 486-6700
Mount Gilead *(G-14433)*
TE Signs and Ship LLC ....G....... 440 281-9340
Elyria *(G-9336)*

SIGNS & ADVERTISING SPECIALTIES: Novelties

American Executive Gifts Inc ....F....... 330 645-4396
Akron *(G-61)*
Breibach Association ....G....... 614 876-6480
Hilliard *(G-10815)*
Cdds Inc ....G....... 614 626-8747
Gahanna *(G-10078)*
Finn Graphics Inc.....................................E....... 513 941-6161
Cincinnati *(G-3690)*
Gerber Wood Products Inc ....G....... 330 857-3901
Kidron *(G-11447)*
Joseph A Panico & Sons Inc....................G....... 614 235-3188
Columbus *(G-7077)*
Power Media Inc......................................G....... 330 475-0500
Akron *(G-325)*
Quikey Manufacturing Co Inc ....C....... 330 633-8106
Akron *(G-337)*
Ruthie Ann Inc..F....... 800 231-3567
New Paris *(G-14755)*

SIGNS & ADVERTISING SPECIALTIES: Scoreboards, Electric

Industrial Electronic Service....................F....... 937 746-9750
Carlisle *(G-2893)*

SIGNS & ADVERTISING SPECIALTIES: Signs

A Sign For The Times Inc ....G....... 216 297-2977
Cleveland *(G-4593)*
Abbott Signs...G....... 937 393-6600
Hillsboro *(G-10876)*
Accutech Sign Shop ....G....... 513 385-3595
Cincinnati *(G-3291)*
Action Sign Inc..G....... 330 966-0390
Greentown *(G-10356)*
All Star Group Inc ....G....... 440 323-6060
Elyria *(G-9212)*
Atchley Signs & Graphics ....G....... 614 421-7446
Columbus *(G-6624)*
Becker Signs Inc.......................................G....... 330 659-4504
Richfield *(G-16462)*
Beebe Worldwide Graphics Sign.............G....... 513 241-2726
Blue Ash *(G-1733)*
Brockmans Signs Inc ....G....... 513 574-6163
Cincinnati *(G-3422)*
Buds Sign Shop Inc..................................F....... 330 744-5555
Youngstown *(G-20861)*
Campbell Signs & Apparel LLC ....F....... 330 386-4768
East Liverpool *(G-9052)*
Chatelain Plastics Inc...............................G....... 419 422-4323
Findlay *(G-9667)*
Classic Sign Company Inc........................G....... 419 420-0058
Findlay *(G-9670)*
Dee Sign Co..E....... 513 779-3333
West Chester *(G-19691)*
Design Masters Inc ....G....... 513 772-7175
Cincinnati *(G-3584)*
Donald Marlo ....G....... 937 836-4880
Dayton *(G-8165)*
Exchange Signs ....G....... 330 644-4552
Coventry Township *(G-7769)*
Firehouse Sign Co Inc...............................G....... 216 267-5300
Brookpark *(G-2146)*
Heres Your Sign ....G....... 740 574-1248
Franklin Furnace *(G-9935)*
Hulsman Signs..G....... 513 738-3389
Harrison *(G-10649)*
Insta Plak Inc ....F....... 419 537-1555
Toledo *(G-18349)*
Interior Graphic Systems LLC ....G....... 330 244-0100
Canton *(G-2709)*
Jerry Pulfer...G....... 937 778-1861
Piqua *(G-16134)*
Jones Old Rustic Sign...............................E....... 937 643-1695
Moraine *(G-14362)*
Kane Sign Co...G....... 330 253-5263
Akron *(G-231)*
Kessler Sign Company..............................E....... 740 453-0668
Zanesville *(G-21153)*
Kessler Sign Company..............................G....... 937 898-0633
Dayton *(G-8295)*
Kief Signs ....G....... 513 941-8800
Addyston *(G-12)*
Mel Wacker Sign Inc ....G....... 330 832-1726
Massillon *(G-13024)*
Mentor Signs & Graphics Inc....................G....... 440 951-7446
Mentor *(G-13516)*
Metromedia Technologies Inc..................D....... 330 264-2501
Wooster *(G-20624)*
Middlefield Sign Co...................................G....... 440 632-0708
Middlefield *(G-13827)*
Midwest Sign Ctr ....F....... 330 493-7330
Canton *(G-2754)*
Mike B Crawford..G....... 330 673-7944
Kent *(G-11355)*
Morrison Sign Company Inc ....E....... 614 276-1181
Columbus *(G-7198)*
Municipal Signs and Sales Inc..................G....... 330 457-2421
Columbiana *(G-6474)*
Next Day Sign..G....... 419 537-9595
Toledo *(G-18425)*
North Hill Marble & Granite Co ....F....... 330 253-2179
Akron *(G-301)*
Patriot Signage Inc ....G....... 859 655-9009
Cincinnati *(G-4138)*
Paul Peterson Safety Div Inc ....E....... 614 486-4375
Columbus *(G-7300)*
Pure Sports Design....................................G....... 937 935-5595
Middletown *(G-13946)*
Red Hot Studios ....G....... 330 609-7446
Warren *(G-19437)*
Redi-Quik Signs Inc ....G....... 614 228-6641
Columbus *(G-7382)*
Rocal Inc..D....... 740 998-2122
Frankfort *(G-9864)*
Safety Sign Company.................................E....... 440 238-7722
Strongsville *(G-17784)*
Scioto Sign Co Inc ....E....... 419 673-1261
Kenton *(G-11422)*
Sign Connection Inc ....G....... 937 435-4070
Dayton *(G-8506)*
Sign Design Wooster Inc............................G....... 330 262-8838
Wooster *(G-20654)*
Sign Graphics & Design ....G....... 513 576-1639
Milford *(G-14040)*
Sign Pro of Lima ....G....... 419 222-7767
Lima *(G-11939)*
Signage Consultants Inc ....G....... 614 297-7446
Columbus *(G-7449)*
Significant Impressions Inc ....G....... 513 874-5223
Fairfield *(G-9564)*
Signs 2 Graphics...G....... 740 493-2049
Piketon *(G-16080)*
Signs PDQ Inc ....G....... 440 951-6651
Willoughby *(G-20430)*
Standard Signs Incorporated......................F....... 330 467-2030
Macedonia *(G-12332)*
Sterling Associates Inc ....G....... 330 630-3500
Akron *(G-389)*
Unionville Center Sign Co..........................G....... 614 873-5834
Unionville Center *(G-18938)*
Vgu Industries Inc.......................................E....... 216 676-9093
Cleveland *(G-6257)*
Waterford Signs Inc.....................................G....... 740 362-7446
Delaware *(G-8731)*
Wilson Seat Company Inc ....E....... 513 732-2460
Batavia *(G-1197)*
Wurtec Manufacturing Service ....E....... 419 726-1066
Toledo *(G-18602)*

SIGNS & ADVERTSG SPECIALTIES: Displays/Cutouts Window/Lobby

Affinity Disp Expositions Inc ....C....... 513 771-2339
Cincinnati *(G-3306)*
Art & Sign Corporation...............................G....... 419 865-3336
Toledo *(G-18192)*
BDS Packaging Inc ....D....... 937 643-0530
Moraine *(G-14333)*
Benchmark Craftsman Inc ....E....... 330 975-4214
Seville *(G-16911)*
Co Pac Services Inc......................................F....... 216 688-1780
Cleveland *(G-4994)*
Downing Enterprises Inc..............................D....... 330 666-3888
Copley *(G-7683)*
Genesis Display Systems Inc ....G....... 513 561-1440
Cincinnati *(G-3748)*
Myers and Lasch Inc.....................................G....... 440 235-2050
Cleveland *(G-5716)*
Pfi Displays Inc ....E....... 330 925-9015
Rittman *(G-16527)*
Skyline Exhibits Grtr Cncnt ....G....... 513 671-4460
Cincinnati *(G-4343)*

SIGNS, ELECTRICAL: Wholesalers

Sign America Incorporated ....E....... 740 765-5555
Richmond *(G-16498)*

SIGNS, EXC ELECTRIC, WHOLESALE

Breibach Association ....G....... 614 876-6480
Hilliard *(G-10815)*
Fostoria Monument Co..................................G....... 419 435-0373
Fostoria *(G-9844)*
J-M Designs LLC..G....... 419 794-2114
Maumee *(G-13120)*
Jones & Assoc Advg & Design.......................G....... 330 799-6876
Youngstown *(G-20949)*
K Ventures Inc..F....... 419 678-2308
Coldwater *(G-6415)*
Macray Co LLC...G....... 937 325-1726
Springfield *(G-17440)*
Sign Lady Inc..G....... 419 476-9191
Toledo *(G-18522)*
Snyder Printing LLC ....G....... 740 353-3947
Portsmouth *(G-16301)*
Toledo Signs & Designs Ltd ....G....... 419 843-1073
Toledo *(G-18569)*
Water Drop Media Inc ....G....... 234 600-5817
Vienna *(G-19211)*

SIGNS: Electrical

A B C Sign Inc ....F....... 513 241-8884
Cincinnati *(G-3278)*
Ad-Pro Signs I LLC ....G....... 513 922-5046
Cincinnati *(G-3296)*
Advance Sign Group LLC ....E....... 614 429-2111
Columbus *(G-6544)*
All Signs Express Inc ....F....... 513 489-7744
Blue Ash *(G-1727)*
All Signs of Chillicothe Inc.............................G....... 740 773-5016
Chillicothe *(G-3174)*
All Star Sign Company ....E....... 614 461-9052
Columbus *(G-6568)*
American Led-Gible Inc..................................F....... 614 851-1100
Columbus *(G-6584)*

PRODUCT

Employee Codes: A=Over 500 employees, B=251-500
C=101-250, D=51-100, E=20-50, F=10-19, G=3-9

2019 Harris Ohio
Industrial Directory

1589

SIGNS: Electrical

American Metal Sign...............................G...... 267 521-2670
  Ada *(G-4)*
Architctral Identification Inc ....E...... 614 868-8400
  Gahanna *(G-10076)*
Auld Lang Signs Inc ....G...... 513 792-5555
  Blue Ash *(G-1731)*
Behrco Inc ....G...... 419 394-1612
  Saint Marys *(G-16676)*
Boyer Signs & Graphics Inc ....E...... 216 383-7242
  Columbus *(G-6691)*
Brilliant Electric Sign Co Ltd ....D...... 216 741-3800
  Brooklyn Heights *(G-2116)*
Byers Sign Co ....G...... 614 561-1224
  Columbus *(G-6717)*
Central Graphics Inc ....G...... 330 928-7080
  Cuyahoga Falls *(G-7847)*
Custom Sign Center Inc ....E...... 614 279-6700
  Columbus *(G-6844)*
Danite Holdings Ltd ....E...... 614 444-3333
  Columbus *(G-6849)*
Digimatics Inc ....G...... 419 478-0804
  Toledo *(G-18263)*
Direct Image Signs Inc ....G...... 440 327-5575
  North Ridgeville *(G-15220)*
E S Sign & Design LLC ....G...... 330 405-4799
  Twinsburg *(G-18766)*
Ellet Neon Sales & Service Inc ....G...... 330 628-9907
  Akron *(G-150)*
Federal Heath Sign Company LLC ....D...... 740 369-0999
  Delaware *(G-8678)*
Fultz Sign Co Inc ....G...... 419 225-6000
  Lima *(G-11866)*
Gardner Signs Inc ....E...... 419 385-6669
  Toledo *(G-18301)*
Gus Holthaus Signs Inc ....E...... 513 861-0060
  Cincinnati *(G-3790)*
Hendricks Vacuum Forming Inc ....E...... 330 837-2040
  Massillon *(G-12995)*
Insignia Signs Inc ....G...... 937 866-2341
  Dayton *(G-8268)*
Jacqueline L Vandyke ....G...... 740 593-6779
  Athens *(G-837)*
Jeffrey L Becht Inc ....G...... 937 264-2070
  Dayton *(G-8283)*
Letter Graphics Sign Co Inc ....G...... 330 683-3903
  Orrville *(G-15602)*
LSI Industries Inc ....E...... 513 793-3200
  Blue Ash *(G-1808)*
LSI Industries Inc ....B...... 513 793-3200
  Blue Ash *(G-1811)*
Media Sign Company ....G...... 513 564-9500
  Cincinnati *(G-3997)*
National Illmination Sign Corp ....G...... 419 866-1666
  Holland *(G-10945)*
Ohio Awning & Manufacturing Co ....E...... 216 861-2400
  Cleveland *(G-5799)*
Power Corp Sign Products Inc ....G...... 740 344-0468
  Newark *(G-14912)*
PR Signs & Service ....G...... 614 252-7090
  Columbus *(G-7340)*
Quality Channel Letters ....G...... 859 866-6500
  Miamisburg *(G-13707)*
R M Davis Inc ....G...... 419 756-6719
  Mansfield *(G-12503)*
Signs By George ....G...... 216 394-2095
  Brookfield *(G-2109)*
Signs Limited LLC ....G...... 740 282-7715
  Steubenville *(G-17551)*
Terry & Jack Neon Sign Co ....E...... 419 229-0674
  Lima *(G-11950)*
United-Maier Signs Inc ....G...... 513 681-6600
  Cincinnati *(G-4451)*
Wide Area Media LLC ....G...... 440 356-3133
  Westlake *(G-20172)*
Wilson Sign Co Inc ....F...... 937 253-2246
  Dayton *(G-8595)*

SIGNS: Neon

Canton Sign Co ....G...... 330 456-7151
  Canton *(G-2617)*
Cicogna Electric and Sign Co ....D...... 440 998-2637
  Ashtabula *(G-766)*
Columbus Sign Company ....E...... 614 252-3133
  Columbus *(G-6802)*
Kasper Enterprises Inc ....G...... 419 841-6656
  Toledo *(G-18362)*
Medina Signs Post Inc ....G...... 330 723-2484
  Medina *(G-13297)*
Moonshine Screen Printing Inc ....F...... 513 523-7775
  Oxford *(G-15697)*
Ram Z Neon ....G...... 330 788-5121
  Youngstown *(G-21013)*
Ruff Neon & Lighting Maint Inc ....F...... 440 350-6267
  Painesville *(G-15782)*
Signcom Incorporated ....E...... 614 228-9999
  Columbus *(G-7451)*
Triangle Sign Co ....G...... 513 863-2578
  Hamilton *(G-10615)*
Warren Enterprises ....G...... 330 836-6119
  Akron *(G-431)*
Wholesale Channel Letters ....G...... 440 256-3200
  Kirtland *(G-11473)*

SILICA MINING

Covia Holdings Corporation ....D...... 440 214-3284
  Independence *(G-11123)*

SILICON WAFERS: Chemically Doped

Techneglas Inc ....G...... 419 873-2000
  Perrysburg *(G-16011)*

SILICON: Pure

Ohio Valley Specialty Company ....F...... 740 373-2276
  Marietta *(G-12650)*

SILICONE RESINS

Poly-Carb Inc ....E...... 440 248-1223
  Macedonia *(G-12318)*

SILICONES

Canton OH Rubber Speclty Prods ....G...... 330 454-3847
  Canton *(G-2612)*
Chemspec ....F...... 330 896-0355
  Uniontown *(G-18914)*
Dow Silicones Corporation ....C...... 330 319-1127
  Copley *(G-7682)*
Momentive Performance Mtls Inc ....C...... 740 928-7010
  Hebron *(G-10753)*
Momentive Performance Mtls Inc ....A...... 440 878-5705
  Richmond Heights *(G-16503)*
Momentive Performance Mtls Inc ....G...... 614 986-2495
  Columbus *(G-7193)*
Momentive Prfmce Mtls Qrtz Inc ....C...... 440 878-5700
  Strongsville *(G-17765)*
Silicone Solutions Inc ....F...... 330 920-3125
  Cuyahoga Falls *(G-7917)*
Silicone Solutions Intl LLC ....G...... 419 720-8709
  Toledo *(G-18523)*
Wacker Chemical Corporation ....E...... 330 899-0847
  Canton *(G-2862)*

SILK SCREEN DESIGN SVCS

Alvin L Roepke ....F...... 419 862-3891
  Elmore *(G-9203)*
Art & Sign Corporation ....G...... 419 865-3336
  Toledo *(G-18192)*
Eastgate Custom Graphics Ltd ....G...... 513 528-7922
  Cincinnati *(G-3625)*
Galaxy Balloons Incorporated ....C...... 216 476-3360
  Cleveland *(G-5287)*
Good JP ....G...... 419 207-8484
  Ashland *(G-706)*
Heller Acquisitions Inc ....G...... 937 833-2676
  Brookville *(G-2171)*
Hollywood Imprints LLC ....F...... 614 501-6040
  Gahanna *(G-10083)*
Image Industries Inc ....G...... 937 832-7969
  Clayton *(G-4575)*
Kent Stow Screen Printing Inc ....F...... 330 923-5118
  Akron *(G-235)*
Kimpton Printing & Spc Co ....F...... 330 467-1640
  Macedonia *(G-12310)*
Liming Printing Inc ....F...... 937 374-2646
  Xenia *(G-20782)*
Lion Clothing Inc ....G...... 419 692-9981
  Delphos *(G-8751)*
Madison Graphics ....G...... 216 226-5770
  Cleveland *(G-5601)*
Marazita Graphics Inc ....G...... 330 773-6462
  Akron *(G-267)*
Newmast Mktg & Communications .....E...... 614 837-1200
  Columbus *(G-7217)*
Pelz Lettering Inc ....G...... 419 625-3567
  Sandusky *(G-16838)*
Professional Screen Printing ....G...... 740 687-0760
  Lancaster *(G-11600)*

SIGNS: Electrical (cont.)

Quali-Tee Design Sports ....F...... 937 382-7997
  Wilmington *(G-20505)*
Qualitee Design Sportswear Co ....E...... 740 333-8337
  Wshngtn CT Hs *(G-20739)*
R S C Sales Company ....E...... 423 581-4916
  Dayton *(G-8460)*
Red Barn Screen Printing & EMB ....F...... 740 474-6657
  Circleville *(G-4556)*
Roban Inc ....G...... 330 794-1059
  Lakemore *(G-11500)*
Screen Works Inc ....E...... 937 264-9111
  Dayton *(G-8499)*
Tridico Silk Screen & Sign Co ....G...... 419 526-1695
  Mansfield *(G-12534)*
Woodrow Manufacturing Co ....G...... 937 399-9333
  Springfield *(G-17521)*

SILVERWARE & PLATED WARE

Professional Award Service ....G...... 513 389-3600
  Cincinnati *(G-4216)*

SIMULATORS: Flight

Stephen Radecky ....G...... 440 232-2132
  Bedford *(G-1447)*
Technology Products Inc ....G...... 937 652-3412
  Urbana *(G-19015)*

SINK TOPS, PLASTIC LAMINATED

Malco Laminated Inc ....G...... 513 541-8300
  Cincinnati *(G-3975)*

SINTER: Iron

GKN Sinter Metals LLC ....C...... 740 441-3203
  Gallipolis *(G-10166)*
Miba Sinter USA LLC ....F...... 740 962-4242
  McConnelsville *(G-13208)*

SIZES: Indl

Ace Gasket Manufacturing Co ....G...... 513 271-6321
  Cincinnati *(G-3292)*

SKIDS

J Smokin ....G...... 330 466-7087
  Rittman *(G-16523)*
Ohio Box & Crate Inc ....F...... 440 526-3133
  Burton *(G-2366)*

SKIDS: Wood

Built-Rite Box & Crate Inc ....E...... 330 263-0936
  Wooster *(G-20577)*
Global Packaging & Exports Inc ....G...... 513 454-2020
  West Chester *(G-19716)*

SKYLIGHTS

Architectural Daylighting LLC ....G...... 330 460-5000
  Medina *(G-13225)*

SLAB & TILE: Precast Concrete, Floor

Redi Rock Structures Oki LLC ....G...... 513 965-9221
  Milford *(G-14036)*

SLAG PRDTS

Ironics Inc ....G...... 330 652-0583
  Niles *(G-15016)*
Stein Steel Mill Services Inc ....F...... 440 526-9301
  Broadview Heights *(G-2102)*

SLAG: Crushed Or Ground

Brier Hill Slag Company ....F...... 330 743-8170
  Youngstown *(G-20857)*
Harsco Corporation ....G...... 740 367-7322
  Cheshire *(G-3148)*
R W Sidley Incorporated ....G...... 330 750-1661
  Struthers *(G-17823)*
Sharon Stone Co ....G...... 740 374-3236
  Dexter City *(G-8795)*
Tms International LLC ....E...... 330 847-0844
  Warren *(G-19449)*
Trans Ash Inc ....F...... 859 341-1528
  Cincinnati *(G-4430)*

SLAUGHTERING & MEAT PACKING

American Foods Group LLC .... E 513 733-8898
  Cincinnati *(G-3332)*
Carl Rittberger Sr Inc .... E 740 452-2767
  Zanesville *(G-21116)*
Heffelfingers Meats Inc .... E 419 368-7131
  Jeromesville *(G-11250)*
John Stehlin & Sons Co Inc .... F 513 385-6164
  Cincinnati *(G-3881)*
Pine Ridge Processing .... G 740 749-3166
  Fleming *(G-9780)*
Shirer Brothers Meats .... G 740 796-3214
  Adamsville *(G-10)*
Strasburg Provision Inc .... E 330 878-1059
  Strasburg *(G-17653)*

SLINGS: Lifting, Made From Purchased Wire

Blacco Splcing Rgging Loft Inc .... G 614 444-2888
  Columbus *(G-6675)*
Tri-State Wire Rope Supply Inc .... F 513 871-8623
  Cincinnati *(G-4437)*
West Equipment Company Inc .... F 419 698-1601
  Toledo *(G-18597)*

SLIPPERS: House

Principle Business Entps Inc .... C 419 352-1551
  Bowling Green *(G-1992)*

SLOT MACHINES

Daca Vending Wholesale LLC .... G 513 753-1600
  Amelia *(G-535)*

SMOKE DETECTORS

Slap N Tickle LLC .... G 419 349-3226
  Toledo *(G-18524)*
Voice Products Inc .... F 216 360-0433
  Cleveland *(G-6269)*

SNOW PLOWING SVCS

Ioppolo Concrete Corporation .... E 440 439-6606
  Bedford *(G-1418)*
Mapledale Farm Inc .... F 440 286-3389
  Chardon *(G-3125)*

SNOW REMOVAL EQPT: Residential

R J Engineering Company Inc .... G 419 843-8651
  Toledo *(G-18494)*
Russell Hunt .... F 740 264-1196
  Steubenville *(G-17550)*

SOAP DISHES: Vitreous China

Bridgits Bath LLC .... G 937 259-1960
  Dayton *(G-8061)*

SOAPS & DETERGENTS

AIN Industries Inc .... G 440 781-0950
  Cleveland *(G-4643)*
Chester Packaging LLC .... C 513 458-3840
  Cincinnati *(G-3469)*
Cincinnati - Vulcan Company .... D 513 242-5300
  Cincinnati *(G-3477)*
Cr Brands Inc .... D 513 860-5039
  West Chester *(G-19686)*
Cresset Chemical Co Inc .... F 419 669-2041
  Weston *(G-20175)*
Emco Electric International .... G 440 878-1199
  Strongsville *(G-17742)*
Equipment Spcalists Dayton LLC .... G 937 415-2151
  Dayton *(G-8185)*
Fairy Dust Ltd Inc .... F 513 251-0065
  Cincinnati *(G-3669)*
Foam-Tex Solutions Corp .... G 216 889-2702
  Cleveland *(G-5257)*
Kardol Quality Products LLC .... E 513 933-8206
  Blue Ash *(G-1800)*
Mix-Masters Inc .... F 513 228-2800
  Lebanon *(G-11673)*
New Vulco Mfg & Sales Co LLC .... D 513 242-2672
  Cincinnati *(G-4072)*
Noveon Incorporated .... G 216 447-5000
  Brecksville *(G-2052)*
Oliver Chemical Co Inc .... G 513 541-4540
  Cincinnati *(G-4110)*
Polar Inc .... F 937 297-0911
  Moraine *(G-14380)*

Porter Hybrids Inc .... G 937 382-2324
  Wilmington *(G-20503)*
Procter & Gamble .... G 513 207-8931
  Cincinnati *(G-4197)*
St Bernard Soap Company .... B 513 242-2227
  Cincinnati *(G-4368)*
US Industrial Lubricants Inc .... G 513 541-2225
  Cincinnati *(G-4458)*
Wallover Oil Company Inc .... E 440 238-9250
  Strongsville *(G-17806)*
Washing Systems LLC .... C 800 272-1974
  Loveland *(G-12244)*

SOCIAL SERVICES, NEC

Our Voice Initiative Inc .... F 740 974-4303
  Springboro *(G-17340)*

SOCIAL SVCS: Individual & Family

County of Lake .... D 440 269-2193
  Willoughby *(G-20302)*
Ohio State University 614 293-3600
  Columbus *(G-7261)*

SOCKETS: Electric

Brooks Utility Products Group .... F 330 455-0301
  Canton *(G-2599)*

SOFT DRINKS WHOLESALERS

Central Coca-Cola Btlg Co Inc .... G 740 474-2180
  Circleville *(G-4538)*
Central Coca-Cola Btlg Co Inc .... G 330 875-1487
  Akron *(G-110)*
Central Coca-Cola Btlg Co Inc .... G 330 487-0212
  Macedonia *(G-12282)*
Coca-Cola Bottling Co Cnsld .... D 937 878-5000
  Dayton *(G-8096)*
P-Americas LLC .... E 419 227-3541
  Lima *(G-11913)*
Star Beverage Corporation Ohio .... G 216 991-4799
  Shaker Heights *(G-16938)*

SOFTWARE PUBLISHERS: Application

Acclaimd Inc .... G 614 219-9519
  Columbus *(G-6532)*
Advanced Prgrm Resources Inc .... E 614 761-9994
  Dublin *(G-8874)*
Advant-E Corporation .... F 937 429-4288
  Beavercreek *(G-1298)*
Ames Development Group Ltd .... G 419 704-7812
  Toledo *(G-18182)*
Apostrophe Apps LLC .... G 513 608-4399
  Liberty Twp *(G-11821)*
Avasax Ltd .... G 937 694-0807
  Beavercreek *(G-1350)*
Aver Inc .... G 877 841-2775
  Columbus *(G-6635)*
Baptist Heritage Revival Soc .... G 915 526-2832
  Goshen *(G-10285)*
Building Block Performance LLC .... G 614 918-7476
  Plain City *(G-16179)*
Check Yourself LLC .... G 513 685-0868
  Blue Ash *(G-1749)*
Corporate Elevator LLC .... G 614 288-1847
  Columbus *(G-6822)*
Crabware Ltd .... G 330 699-2305
  Uniontown *(G-18917)*
Dante Solutions Inc .... G 440 234-8477
  Cleveland *(G-5064)*
Delta Media Group Inc .... E 330 493-0350
  Canton *(G-2654)*
Eadhere Solutions LLC .... G 216 372-6009
  Cleveland *(G-5133)*
Eighty Six Inc .... G 800 760-0722
  Huber Heights *(G-11016)*
Equipsync LLC .... G 216 367-6640
  Cleveland *(G-5187)*
Facilities Management Ex LLC .... G 844 664-4400
  Columbus *(G-6913)*
Forcam Inc .... F 513 878-2780
  Cincinnati *(G-3702)*
Gain LLC .... G 440 396-6613
  Westerville *(G-19992)*
Gis Dynamics LLC .... G 513 847-4931
  Blue Ash *(G-1782)*
Gracie Plum Investments Inc .... E 740 355-9029
  Portsmouth *(G-16284)*
Hero Pay LLC .... G 419 771-0515
  Columbus *(G-6991)*

Hommati Franchise Network Inc .... G 833 466-6284
  Westerville *(G-20058)*
Hyland Software Inc .... A 440 788-5000
  Westlake *(G-20125)*
Idialogs LLC .... G 937 372-2890
  Xenia *(G-20777)*
Instaride Cle LLC .... G 216 801-4542
  Lakewood *(G-11522)*
Janova LLC .... F 614 638-6785
  New Albany *(G-14628)*
Kick Salsa LLC .... G 614 330-2499
  Columbus *(G-7094)*
Lift Ai LLC .... G 419 345-7831
  Ottawa Hills *(G-15674)*
List Media Inc .... G 330 995-0864
  Chagrin Falls *(G-3023)*
Lockheed Martin Corporation .... G 614 418-1930
  Columbus *(G-7133)*
Lync Corp .... E 513 655-7286
  Cincinnati *(G-3959)*
Mamsys Consulting Services .... G 440 287-6824
  Solon *(G-17187)*
Microsoft Corporation .... E 614 719-5900
  Columbus *(G-6503)*
Microsoft Corporation .... E 216 986-1440
  Cleveland *(G-5671)*
Microsoft Corporation .... D 513 339-2800
  Mason *(G-12909)*
Microstrategy Incorporated .... G 513 792-2253
  Cincinnati *(G-4027)*
Mim Software Inc .... E 216 896-9798
  Beachwood *(G-1250)*
Navistone Inc .... G 844 677-3667
  Cincinnati *(G-4065)*
New Life Chapel .... F 513 298-2980
  Cincinnati *(G-4070)*
Osisoft LLC .... G 440 442-2000
  Cleveland *(G-5823)*
Osu Labanlens .... G 614 688-2356
  Columbus *(G-7278)*
Our Voice Initiative Inc .... F 740 974-4303
  Springboro *(G-17340)*
Parthenon Global LLC .... G 888 332-5303
  Cleveland *(G-5853)*
PCC Airfolils LLC .... G 330 868-7376
  Minerva *(G-14197)*
Pmj Partners LLC .... G 201 360-1914
  Columbus *(G-7330)*
Preemptive Solutions LLC .... E 440 443-7200
  Cleveland *(G-5915)*
Proficient Information Tech .... G 937 470-1300
  Dayton *(G-8447)*
Ptc Inc .... F 513 791-0330
  Cincinnati *(G-4221)*
R & H Enterprises Llc .... G 216 702-4449
  Richmond Heights *(G-16504)*
Racedirector LLC .... G 440 940-6675
  Willoughby *(G-20417)*
Rascal House Inc .... G 216 781-0904
  Cleveland *(G-5961)*
Receet Inc .... G 513 769-1900
  Cincinnati *(G-4254)*
Rivals Sports Grille LLC .... E 216 267-0005
  Middleburg Heights *(G-13769)*
Sanctuary Software Studio Inc .... E 330 666-9690
  Fairlawn *(G-9616)*
Satelytics Inc .... G 419 419-5380
  Toledo *(G-18512)*
Secure Medical Mail LLC .... G 216 269-1971
  Cleveland *(G-6043)*
Sest Inc .... F 440 777-9777
  Westlake *(G-20157)*
Soda Pig LLC .... G 646 241-7126
  Columbus *(G-7458)*
Software Authority Inc .... G 216 236-0200
  Cleveland *(G-6077)*
Software Solutions Inc .... E 513 932-6667
  Lebanon *(G-11698)*
Spitfire Technologies LLC .... G 937 463-7729
  Dayton *(G-8520)*
Step It Up LLC .... G 720 289-1520
  Columbus *(G-7490)*
Stewardship Technology Inc .... G 866 604-8880
  Mount Vernon *(G-14515)*
Streamsavvy LLC .... G 614 256-7955
  Columbus *(G-7493)*
Strongbasics LLC .... G 716 903-6151
  Columbus *(G-7495)*
Sylvania Moose Lodge No .... F 419 885-4953
  Sylvania *(G-17964)*

Employee Codes: A=Over 500 employees, B=251-500
C=101-250, D=51-100, E=20-50, F=10-19, G=3-9

SOFTWARE PUBLISHERS: Application

Tech Solutions LLC ....G...... 419 852-7190
  Celina (G-2986)
Toccata Technologies Inc ....G...... 614 430-9888
  Powell (G-16339)
True Dinero Records & Tech LLC ....G...... 513 428-4610
  Cincinnati (G-4443)
Uninterrupted LLC ....F...... 216 771-2323
  Akron (G-418)
Vertical Data LLC ....F...... 330 289-0313
  Akron (G-425)
Wififace LLC ....G...... 419 754-4816
  Toledo (G-18600)
Wild Oak LLC ....G...... 513 769-0526
  Cincinnati (G-4509)
Willow Frog LLC ....G...... 513 861-4834
  Cincinnati (G-4512)

SOFTWARE PUBLISHERS: Business & Professional

4me Group LLC ....G...... 513 898-1083
  Terrace Park (G-18017)
Actipro Software LLC ....G...... 888 922-8477
  Broadview Heights (G-2087)
Agile Global Solutions Inc ....E...... 916 655-7745
  Independence (G-11118)
Air Force US Dept of ....B...... 937 656-2354
  Dayton (G-7969)
Alanax Technologies Inc ....G...... 216 469-1545
  Belmont (G-1564)
Application Link Inc ....F...... 614 934-1735
  Columbus (G-6609)
Apportis LLC ....G...... 614 832-8362
  Dublin (G-8881)
Assisted Patrol LLC ....G...... 937 369-0080
  Beavercreek (G-1300)
Autorentalsystemscom LLC ....G...... 513 334-1040
  Norwood (G-15423)
Avesta Systems Inc ....G...... 330 650-1800
  Hudson (G-11032)
Bass International Sftwr LLC ....G...... 877 227-0155
  Westerville (G-19980)
Bjond Inc ....G...... 614 537-7246
  Columbus (G-6674)
Casentric LLC ....G...... 216 233-6300
  Shaker Heights (G-16928)
Cincom Systems Inc ....C...... 513 459-1470
  Mason (G-12845)
Cleveland Business Supply LLC ....G...... 888 831-0088
  Broadview Heights (G-2091)
Clientrax Technology Solutions ....F...... 614 875-2245
  Grove City (G-10420)
Clinicl Otcms Mngmnt Syst LLC ....D...... 330 650-9900
  Broadview Heights (G-2092)
Cluster Software Inc ....F...... 614 760-9380
  Columbus (G-6776)
Columbus International Corp ....F...... 614 323-1086
  Columbus (G-6794)
Computer Enterprise Inc ....F...... 216 228-7156
  Lakewood (G-11515)
Contractor Tools Online LLC ....G...... 614 264-9392
  New Albany (G-14617)
Crimson Gate Consulting Co ....G...... 614 805-0897
  Dublin (G-8904)
Data Genomix Inc ....G...... 216 860-4770
  Cleveland (G-5069)
Delphia Consulting LLC ....G...... 614 421-2000
  Columbus (G-6860)
Digisoft Systems Corporation ....G...... 937 833-5016
  Brookville (G-2167)
Echo Mobile Solutions LLC ....G...... 614 282-3756
  Pickerington (G-16046)
Ela Holding Corporation ....G...... 513 200-1374
  Cincinnati (G-3631)
Field Dailies LLC ....G...... 859 379-2120
  Cincinnati (G-3687)
Healthedge Software Inc ....G...... 614 431-3711
  Powell (G-16323)
Infoaccessnet LLC ....E...... 216 328-0100
  Cleveland (G-5456)
Innerapps LLC ....G...... 419 467-3110
  Perrysburg (G-15967)
Integrity Group Consulting Inc ....G...... 614 759-9148
  Reynoldsburg (G-16444)
Jasstek Inc ....F...... 614 808-3600
  Dublin (G-8932)
Kapios LLC ....G...... 567 661-0772
  Toledo (G-18361)
King Software Systems ....G...... 330 562-1135
  Aurora (G-889)

Kronos Incorporated ....G...... 216 867-5609
  Independence (G-11140)
Lantek Systems Inc ....G...... 513 988-8708
  Mason (G-12903)
Linestream Technologies ....G...... 216 862-7874
  Cleveland (G-5578)
Mapsys Inc ....E...... 614 255-7258
  Columbus (G-7148)
Massmatrix Inc ....G...... 614 321-9730
  Yellow Springs (G-20810)
Monitored Therapeutics Inc ....G...... 614 761-3555
  Dublin (G-8948)
Netpark LLC ....F...... 614 866-2495
  Gahanna (G-10094)
Netsmart Technologies Inc ....E...... 440 942-4040
  Solon (G-17207)
Neural Holdings LLC ....G...... 734 512-8865
  Cincinnati (G-4069)
Nextmed Systems Inc ....E...... 216 674-0511
  Cincinnati (G-4076)
Ohio Cllbrtive Lrng Sltons Inc ....G...... 216 595-5289
  Beachwood (G-1255)
One Cloud Services LLC ....G...... 513 231-9500
  Cincinnati (G-4112)
Onx Holdings LLC ....F...... 866 587-2287
  Cincinnati (G-4114)
Onx USA LLC ....D...... 440 569-2300
  Cleveland (G-5815)
Oracle Corporation ....G...... 513 826-5632
  Beavercreek (G-1335)
Pakra LLC ....F...... 614 477-6965
  Columbus (G-7286)
Parallel Technologies Inc ....G...... 614 798-9700
  Dublin (G-8958)
Patriot Software LLC ....D...... 877 968-7147
  Canton (G-2780)
Pearl Tech Corporation ....G...... 614 284-8357
  Dublin (G-8960)
Perennial Software Inc ....F...... 440 247-5602
  Chagrin Falls (G-3027)
Phantom Technology LLC ....G...... 614 710-0074
  Hilliard (G-10851)
Profound Logic Software Inc ....G...... 937 439-7925
  Dayton (G-8449)
Protel Systems and Svcs LLC ....G...... 419 913-0825
  Maumee (G-13140)
Queen City Technologies ....F...... 513 253-1312
  West Chester (G-19892)
Rebiz LLC ....E...... 844 467-3249
  Cleveland (G-5965)
Research Metrics LLC ....G...... 419 464-3333
  Sylvania (G-17959)
Retail Management Products ....F...... 740 548-1725
  Lewis Center (G-11776)
Rhombus Technologies Ltd ....G...... 937 335-1840
  Troy (G-18698)
Showroom Tracker LLC ....G...... 888 407-0094
  Canton (G-2815)
Simple Vms LLC ....G...... 888 255-8918
  Cincinnati (G-4338)
Simplex-It LLC ....G...... 234 380-1277
  Stow (G-17628)
Softura Legal Solutions LLC ....G...... 614 220-5611
  Columbus (G-7460)
Spearfysh Inc ....F...... 330 487-0300
  Hudson (G-11075)
Specialized Business Sftwr Inc ....E...... 440 542-9145
  Solon (G-17235)
Symantec Corporation ....G...... 614 793-3060
  Dublin (G-9000)
Syntec LLC ....G...... 440 229-6262
  Rocky River (G-16558)
Tmw Systems Inc ....C...... 216 831-6606
  Mayfield Heights (G-13171)
Turning Technologies LLC ....G...... 330 746-3015
  Youngstown (G-21055)
Value Stream Systems Inc ....G...... 330 907-0064
  Medina (G-13359)
Veeam Software Corporation ....G...... 614 339-8200
  Columbus (G-6508)
Vertex Computer Systems Inc ....F...... 513 662-6888
  Cincinnati (G-4477)
Westmount Technology Inc ....G...... 216 328-2011
  Independence (G-11157)
Workflex Solutions LLC ....G...... 513 257-0215
  Cincinnati (G-4517)
Works International Inc ....G...... 513 631-6111
  Cincinnati (G-4518)
Workspeed Management LLC ....E...... 917 369-9025
  Solon (G-17262)

Zipscene LLC ....D...... 513 201-5174
  Cincinnati (G-4533)
Znode Inc ....F...... 888 755-5541
  Columbus (G-6509)

SOFTWARE PUBLISHERS: Computer Utilities

Asterena Corporation ....G...... 937 605-6470
  Dayton (G-8041)
Elytus Ltd ....F...... 614 824-4985
  Columbus (G-6893)
Sark Technologies LLC ....G...... 216 932-3171
  Cleveland (G-6032)

SOFTWARE PUBLISHERS: Education

360water Inc ....G...... 614 294-3600
  Columbus (G-6511)
American Grphcal Sftwr Systems ....G...... 440 729-0018
  Chesterland (G-3153)
Bullseye LLC ....G...... 216 272-7050
  Shaker Heights (G-16926)
Butler Tech Career Dev Schools ....F...... 513 867-1028
  Fairfield Township (G-9580)
Flypaper Studio Inc ....E...... 602 801-2208
  Cincinnati (G-3700)
Health Nuts Media LLC ....G...... 818 802-5222
  Cleveland (G-5384)
Jst LLC ....G...... 614 423-7815
  Westerville (G-20002)
Learning Egg LLC ....G...... 330 207-8663
  North Jackson (G-15148)
Lost Technology LLP ....G...... 513 685-0054
  West Chester (G-19739)
Noggin LLC ....G...... 440 305-6188
  Cleveland (G-5755)
Skillsoft Corporation ....D...... 216 524-5200
  Independence (G-11150)
Southwestern Ohio Instruction ....F...... 937 746-6333
  Dayton (G-8513)
Studium LLC ....G...... 614 402-0359
  Dublin (G-8997)
Vitalrock LLC ....G...... 888 596-8892
  Rocky River (G-16559)
Wellington Wllams Wrldwide LLC ....G...... 423 805-6198
  Troy (G-18718)

SOFTWARE PUBLISHERS: Home Entertainment

Cake LLC ....G...... 614 592-7681
  Dublin (G-8892)
Estreamz Inc ....E...... 513 278-7836
  Cincinnati (G-3654)
Jack A Byte Mltmdia Gaming LLC ....G...... 937 321-1716
  Englewood (G-9364)
Mirus Adapted Tech LLC ....E...... 614 402-4585
  Dublin (G-8946)
Polygon Spaceship ....G...... 440 506-0403
  Amherst (G-571)
Whatifsportscom Inc ....F...... 513 333-0313
  Blue Ash (G-1869)

SOFTWARE PUBLISHERS: NEC

252 Tattoo ....G...... 440 235-6699
  Columbia Station (G-6426)
About Time Software Inc ....F...... 614 759-6295
  Pickerington (G-16038)
Accumulus Software ....G...... 937 435-0861
  Dayton (G-8003)
Acu-Serve Corp ....G...... 330 923-5258
  Cuyahoga Falls (G-7830)
Allmax Software Inc ....G...... 419 673-8863
  Kenton (G-11401)
American Dreams Inc ....G...... 740 385-4444
  Thornville (G-18029)
Ampersand International Inc ....G...... 216 831-3500
  Beachwood (G-1223)
Apex Solutions Inc ....G...... 419 843-3434
  Toledo (G-18187)
Applied Systems Inc ....E...... 513 943-0000
  Milford (G-13994)
Arges ....G...... 440 574-1305
  Oberlin (G-15490)
Associated Software Cons Inc ....F...... 440 826-1010
  Middleburg Heights (G-13761)
Atr Distributing Company ....F...... 513 353-1800
  Cincinnati (G-3369)

Auto Des Sys Inc....E.... 614 488-7984
Upper Arlington *(G-18943)*
Automation Software & Engrg....F.... 330 405-2990
Twinsburg *(G-18737)*
Besttransportcom Inc....E.... 614 888-2378
Columbus *(G-6663)*
Callcopy Inc....G.... 614 340-3346
Columbus *(G-6725)*
Carenection LLC....G.... 614 468-6045
Columbus *(G-6743)*
Caring Things Inc....G.... 614 749-9084
Columbus *(G-6744)*
Cimx LLC....E.... 513 248-7700
Cincinnati *(G-3476)*
Citynet Ohio LLC....E.... 614 364-7881
Columbus *(G-6768)*
Coffing Corporation....F.... 513 919-2813
Liberty Twp *(G-11822)*
Columbus Incontact....G.... 801 245-8369
Columbus *(G-6792)*
Commercial Transportation Svcs....G.... 216 267-2000
Cleveland *(G-5005)*
Computer System Enhancement....G.... 513 251-6791
Cincinnati *(G-3541)*
Concept Xxi Inc....F.... 216 831-2121
Beachwood *(G-1230)*
Creative Microsystems Inc....D.... 937 836-4499
Englewood *(G-9353)*
Dakota Software Corporation....D.... 216 765-7100
Cleveland *(G-5058)*
Datatrak International Inc....E.... 440 443-0082
Mayfield Heights *(G-13162)*
Deadbolt Software....G.... 614 679-2093
Columbus *(G-6855)*
Deneb....G.... 937 223-4849
Dayton *(G-8156)*
Design & Software Intl....F.... 513 939-1800
Fairfield *(G-9493)*
Digionyx LLC....G.... 614 594-9897
London *(G-12058)*
Digital Controls Corporation....D.... 513 746-8118
Miamisburg *(G-13659)*
Drb Systems LLC....C.... 330 645-3299
Akron *(G-147)*
Eci Macola/Max LLC....C.... 978 539-6186
Dublin *(G-8911)*
Eclipse....G.... 419 564-7482
Galion *(G-10136)*
Edict Systems Inc....E.... 937 429-4288
Beavercreek *(G-1313)*
Einstruction Corp....F.... 940 565-0004
Youngstown *(G-20896)*
Einstruction Corporation....D.... 330 746-3015
Youngstown *(G-20897)*
Elynx Holdings LLC....G.... 513 612-5969
Cincinnati *(G-3633)*
EMC Corporation....E.... 216 606-2000
Independence *(G-11125)*
Empyracom Inc....E.... 330 744-5570
Canfield *(G-2526)*
Esko-Graphics Inc....D.... 937 454-1721
Miamisburg *(G-13665)*
Explorys Inc....D.... 216 767-4700
Cleveland *(G-5210)*
Finastra USA Corporation....E.... 937 435-2335
Miamisburg *(G-13668)*
Flexnova Inc....E.... 216 288-6961
Cleveland *(G-5250)*
Foundation Software Inc....D.... 330 220-8383
Strongsville *(G-17744)*
Fusionstorm....G.... 614 431-8000
Columbus *(G-6494)*
Great Migrations LLC....G.... 614 638-4632
Dublin *(G-8918)*
Guide Technologies LLC....G.... 513 631-8800
Cincinnati *(G-3789)*
Hab Inc....E.... 608 785-7650
Solon *(G-17158)*
Honeywell International Inc....D.... 513 745-7200
Cincinnati *(G-3826)*
ICC Systems Inc....G.... 614 524-0299
Sunbury *(G-17889)*
Igel Technology America LLC....F.... 954 739-9990
Cincinnati *(G-3837)*
Image Integrations Systems....F.... 419 872-0003
Perrysburg *(G-15964)*
Incessant Software Inc....G.... 614 206-2211
Lancaster *(G-11580)*
Innago LLC....G.... 330 554-3101
Hudson *(G-11055)*
Innovative Apps Ltd....G.... 330 687-2888
New Albany *(G-14626)*
Innovative Bus Cmpt Solutions....G.... 937 832-3969
Englewood *(G-9363)*
Intelligent Mobile Support Inc....F.... 440 600-7343
Solon *(G-17172)*
Intellinetics Inc....F.... 614 388-8909
Columbus *(G-7040)*
Interactive Fincl Solutions....F.... 419 335-1280
Wauseon *(G-19521)*
Intermec Technologies Corp....F.... 513 874-5882
West Chester *(G-19726)*
Intersoft Group Inc....F.... 216 765-7351
Cleveland *(G-5469)*
Investment Systems Company....G.... 440 247-2865
Chagrin Falls *(G-3022)*
Jda Software Group Inc....G.... 480 308-3000
Akron *(G-222)*
Jehm Technologies Inc....G.... 440 355-5558
Lagrange *(G-11484)*
Juniper Networks Inc....D.... 614 932-1432
Dublin *(G-8934)*
Launchvector Identity LLC....F.... 216 333-1815
Cleveland *(G-5565)*
Mae Consulting....G.... 513 531-8100
Cincinnati *(G-3970)*
Marxware Computing Services....F.... 216 661-5263
Cleveland *(G-5629)*
Mathematical Business Systems....G.... 440 237-2345
Broadview Heights *(G-2097)*
Matrix Management Solutions....C.... 330 470-3700
Canton *(G-2747)*
McGaw Technology Inc....G.... 216 521-3490
Lakewood *(G-11529)*
Merkur Group Inc....G.... 937 429-4288
Beavercreek *(G-1331)*
Miami Valley Eductl Cmpt Assn....F.... 937 767-1468
Yellow Springs *(G-20811)*
Microsoft Corporation....G.... 513 826-9630
Cincinnati *(G-4026)*
Mindcrafted Systems Inc....G.... 440 821-2245
Cleveland *(G-5692)*
Now Software Inc....G.... 614 783-4517
New Albany *(G-14632)*
Ohio Distinctive Enterprises....E.... 614 459-0453
Columbus *(G-7246)*
Omniboom LLC....G.... 833 675-3987
Hamilton *(G-10594)*
Open Text Inc....E.... 614 658-3588
Hilliard *(G-10849)*
Optimal Office Solutions LLC....G.... 201 257-8516
Cincinnati *(G-4115)*
Optimzed Prdctvity Sltions LLC....G.... 513 444-2156
Cincinnati *(G-4117)*
Oracle America Inc....G.... 650 506-7000
Dublin *(G-8957)*
Oracle America Inc....F.... 513 381-0125
Beachwood *(G-1260)*
Oracle Corporation....G.... 513 826-6000
Beachwood *(G-1261)*
Oracle Corporation....G.... 440 264-1620
Cleveland *(G-5817)*
Oracle Systems Corporation....E.... 513 826-6000
Beachwood *(G-1262)*
Oracle Systems Corporation....G.... 937 427-5495
Beavercreek *(G-1336)*
Pathfinder Computer Systems....G.... 330 928-1961
Barberton *(G-1094)*
Pathos LLC....G.... 440 497-7278
Chesterland *(G-3168)*
Patrick J Burke & Co....E.... 513 455-8200
Cincinnati *(G-4137)*
Patterson Colburne....G.... 419 866-5544
Holland *(G-10949)*
Paul/Jay Associates....G.... 740 676-8776
Bellaire *(G-1488)*
Pdmb Inc....G.... 513 522-7362
Cincinnati *(G-4144)*
Peco II Inc....D.... 614 431-0694
Columbus *(G-7305)*
Perdatum Inc....G.... 614 761-1578
Hilliard *(G-10850)*
Perfect Probate....G.... 513 791-4100
Cincinnati *(G-4146)*
Pkg Technologies Inc....G.... 513 967-2783
Lebanon *(G-11685)*
Posm Software LLC....G.... 859 274-0041
Columbus *(G-7333)*
Preferred Soft Solutions LLC....G.... 614 975-2750
Columbus *(G-7343)*
Proepo Software Ltd....G.... 937 243-3825
Wshngtn CT Hs *(G-20736)*
Profile Imaging Columbus LLC....G.... 614 222-2888
Columbus *(G-7353)*
Pwi Inc....F.... 732 212-8110
New Albany *(G-14635)*
Qc Software LLC....G.... 513 469-1424
Cincinnati *(G-4224)*
Quayle Consulting Inc....G.... 614 868-1363
Pickerington *(G-16058)*
Quest Software Inc....D.... 614 336-9223
Dublin *(G-8970)*
Reichard Software Corp....G.... 614 537-8598
Dublin *(G-8972)*
Retalix Inc....C.... 937 384-2277
Miamisburg *(G-13712)*
Revolution Group Inc....D.... 614 212-1111
Westerville *(G-20020)*
Reynolds and Reynolds Company....F.... 937 485-2805
Beavercreek *(G-1362)*
Rhino Tech Software LLC....G.... 614 456-9321
Pickerington *(G-16059)*
Rina Systems LLC....G.... 513 469-7462
Cincinnati *(G-4270)*
S L C Software Services....G.... 513 922-4303
Cincinnati *(G-4297)*
Sherwin Software Solutions....G.... 440 498-8010
Solon *(G-17230)*
Sigmatek Systems LLC....D.... 513 674-0005
Cincinnati *(G-4335)*
Softchoice Corporation....G.... 614 224-4123
Columbus *(G-7459)*
Software Management Group....E.... 513 618-2165
Cincinnati *(G-4351)*
Software To Systems Inc....G.... 513 893-4367
Fairfield *(G-9566)*
Splicenet Inc....G.... 513 563-3533
West Chester *(G-19901)*
Starwin Industries LLC....E.... 937 293-8568
Dayton *(G-8525)*
Steve Schaefer....G.... 513 792-9911
Cincinnati *(G-4380)*
Sunday School Software....G.... 614 527-8776
Hilliard *(G-10867)*
Symantec Corporation....D.... 216 643-6700
Independence *(G-11151)*
Tahoe Interactive Systems Inc....F.... 614 891-2323
Westerville *(G-20076)*
Tarigma Corporation....F.... 614 436-3734
Columbus *(G-7512)*
Tata America Intl Corp....B.... 513 677-6500
Milford *(G-14043)*
Technosoft Inc....F.... 513 985-9877
Blue Ash *(G-1857)*
Tekdog Inc....G.... 614 737-3743
Granville *(G-10338)*
Terrene Labs LLC....G.... 513 445-3539
Mason *(G-12950)*
Thinkware Incorporated....E.... 513 598-3300
Cincinnati *(G-4419)*
Timekeeping Systems Inc....F.... 216 595-0890
Solon *(G-17253)*
Trapeze Software Group Inc....G.... 905 629-8727
Beachwood *(G-1281)*
Triad Governmental Systems....E.... 937 376-5446
Xenia *(G-20799)*
United Computer Group Inc....G.... 216 520-1333
Independence *(G-11153)*
Virtual Boss Inc....G.... 419 872-7686
Perrysburg *(G-16021)*
Virtual Hold Technology LLC....D.... 330 670-2200
Akron *(G-427)*
W L Arehart Computing Systems....G.... 937 383-4710
Wilmington *(G-20510)*
Web3box Software LLC....G.... 330 794-7397
Tallmadge *(G-18014)*
Wentworth Solutions....F.... 440 212-7696
Brunswick *(G-2249)*
Wentworth Technologies LLC....F.... 440 212-7696
Brunswick *(G-2250)*

SOFTWARE PUBLISHERS: Operating Systems

Computer Zoo Inc....G.... 937 310-1474
Bellbrook *(G-1490)*
Magic Interface Ltd....G.... 440 498-3700
Solon *(G-17185)*
North Coast Security Group LLC....G.... 614 887-7255
Columbus *(G-7226)*

PRODUCT

Employee Codes: A=Over 500 employees, B=251-500
C=101-250, D=51-100, E=20-50, F=10-19, G=3-9
2019 Harris Ohio
Industrial Directory
1593

SOFTWARE PUBLISHERS: Operating Systems

Seapine Software Inc .... E 513 754-1655
  Mason (G-12938)
Tech-E-Z LLC .... G 419 692-1700
  Delphos (G-8755)

SOFTWARE PUBLISHERS: Publisher's

Capitol Citicom Inc .... E 614 472-2679
  Columbus (G-6735)
Exponentia US Inc .... E 614 944-5103
  Columbus (G-6911)
Ezshred LLC .... G 440 256-7640
  Kirtland (G-11468)
Hardmagic .... F 415 390-6232
  Marietta (G-12631)
Nsa Technologies LLC .... C 330 576-4600
  Akron (G-304)
Rawhide Software Inc .... G 419 878-0857
  Bowling Green (G-1993)

SOFTWARE TRAINING, COMPUTER

A Graphic Solution .... F 216 228-7223
  Cleveland (G-4587)
Cleveland Business Supply LLC .... G 888 831-0088
  Broadview Heights (G-2091)
Tekdog Inc .... G 614 737-3743
  Granville (G-10338)

SOLAR CELLS

Fidelux Lighting LLC .... G 404 941-4182
  Columbus (G-6493)
Fidelux Lighting LLC .... G 614 839-0250
  Columbus (G-6919)
First Solar Inc .... B 419 661-1478
  Perrysburg (G-15952)
Isofoton North America Inc .... F 419 591-4330
  Napoleon (G-14546)
Mok Industries LLC .... G 614 934-1734
  Columbus (G-7191)
Redhawk Energy Systems LLC .... G 740 927-8244
  Pataskala (G-15839)

SOLAR HEATING EQPT

Iosil Energy Corporation .... F 614 295-8680
  Groveport (G-10495)
Rbi Solar Inc .... G 513 242-2051
  Cincinnati (G-4250)
Shark Solar LLC .... G 216 630-7395
  Medina (G-13340)
Willard Kelsey Solar Group LLC .... G 419 931-2001
  Perrysburg (G-16028)

SOLDERING EQPT: Electrical, Exc Handheld

Fusion Automation Inc .... G 440 602-5595
  Willoughby (G-20326)

SOLDERING EQPT: Electrical, Handheld

Hutchinson-Stevens Inc .... G 216 281-8585
  Cleveland (G-5428)

SOLDERS

Fusion Automation Inc .... G 440 602-5595
  Willoughby (G-20326)
Metallic Resources Inc .... E 330 425-3155
  Twinsburg (G-18819)
Victory White Metal Company .... D 216 271-1400
  Cleveland (G-6260)

SOLENOIDS

Electromotive Inc .... F 330 688-6494
  Stow (G-17581)

SOLES, BOOT OR SHOE: Rubber, Composition Or Fiber

Shreiner Sole Co Inc .... F 330 276-6135
  Killbuck (G-11454)

SOLVENTS

Appalachian Solvents LLC .... G 740 680-3649
  Cambridge (G-2424)
Durr Megtec LLC .... G 614 340-4154
  Columbus (G-6877)

SOLVENTS: Organic

Mid America Chemical Corp .... G 216 749-0100
  Cleveland (G-5672)
Tedia Company Inc .... D 513 874-5340
  Fairfield (G-9567)

SONAR SYSTEMS & EQPT

Raytheon Company .... F 937 429-5429
  Beavercreek (G-1339)

SOUND EFFECTS & MUSIC PRODUCTION: Motion Picture

Swagg Productions2015llc .... F 614 815-1173
  Reynoldsburg (G-16455)

SOUND EQPT: Electric

Fernandes Enterprises LLC .... E 937 890-6444
  Dayton (G-8193)
Holland Assocts LLC DBA Archou .... F 513 891-0006
  Cincinnati (G-3818)
Mixed Logic LLC .... G 440 826-1676
  Valley City (G-19050)

SOUND RECORDING STUDIOS

Musicol Inc .... G 614 267-3133
  Columbus (G-7203)

SOUVENIR SHOPS

Modern China Inc .... E 330 938-6104
  Sebring (G-16889)

SOUVENIRS, WHOLESALE

Victory Postcards Inc .... G 614 764-8975
  Columbus (G-7583)

SOYBEAN PRDTS

Archer-Daniels-Midland Company .... E 419 435-6633
  Fostoria (G-9833)
Bunge North America Foundation .... D 740 383-1181
  Marion (G-12697)
Cargill Incorporated .... D 937 498-4555
  Sidney (G-17020)
Pioneer Hi-Bred Intl Inc .... E 419 748-8051
  Grand Rapids (G-10318)
Schlessman Seed Co .... E 419 499-2572
  Milan (G-13988)

SPACE RESEARCH & TECHNOLOGY PROGRAMS ADMINISTRATION

Weldon Pump Acquition LLC .... E 440 232-2282
  Oakwood Village (G-15489)

SPACE VEHICLE EQPT

Curtiss-Wright Controls .... E 937 252-5601
  Fairborn (G-9456)
General Electric Company .... B 513 977-1500
  Cincinnati (G-3741)
Gleason Metrology Systems Corp .... E 937 384-8901
  Dayton (G-8223)
Grimes Aerospace Company .... B 937 484-2001
  Urbana (G-18990)
Industrial Quartz Corp .... F 440 942-0909
  Mentor (G-13469)
L3 Cincinnati Electronics Corp .... A 513 573-6100
  Mason (G-12902)
Lockheed Martin Integ .... D 330 796-2800
  Akron (G-257)
Lord Corporation .... C 937 278-9431
  Dayton (G-8315)
Metalex Manufacturing Inc .... C 513 489-0507
  Blue Ash (G-1820)
Millat Industries Corp .... D 937 434-6666
  Dayton (G-8360)
Morris Bean & Company .... C 937 767-7301
  Yellow Springs (G-20812)
Sunpower Inc .... D 740 594-2221
  Athens (G-851)
Te Connectivity Corporation .... C 419 521-9500
  Mansfield (G-12527)
US Aeroteam Inc .... E 937 458-0344
  Dayton (G-8577)

SPARK PLUGS: Internal Combustion Engines

Fram Group Operations LLC .... D 419 661-6700
  Perrysburg (G-15953)

SPARK PLUGS: Porcelain

Fram Group Operations LLC .... G 937 316-3000
  Greenville (G-10369)

SPEAKER SYSTEMS

Janszen Loudspeaker Ltd .... G 614 448-1811
  Columbus (G-7063)
Phantom Sound .... F 513 759-4477
  Mason (G-12920)
Technical Artistry Inc .... G 614 299-7777
  Columbus (G-7520)

SPECIALIZED LIBRARIES

Lloyd Library & Museum .... G 513 721-3707
  Cincinnati (G-3949)

SPECIALTY FOOD STORES: Coffee

Boston Stoker Inc .... G 937 890-6401
  Vandalia (G-19118)
Generations Coffee Company LLC .... G 440 546-0901
  Brecksville (G-2038)
Iron Bean Inc .... G 518 641-9917
  Toledo (G-18353)

SPECIALTY FOOD STORES: Dried Fruit

CWC Partners LLC .... G 567 208-1573
  Findlay (G-9676)
Hershbergers Dutch Market LLP .... E 740 489-5322
  Old Washington (G-15526)

SPECIALTY FOOD STORES: Eggs & Poultry

Roots Poultry Inc .... F 419 332-0041
  Fremont (G-10048)

SPECIALTY FOOD STORES: Health & Dietetic Food

Aggregate Tersornance LLC .... G 330 418-4751
  Canton (G-2560)
Manco Inc .... G 937 962-2661
  Lewisburg (G-11795)
Premier Tanning & Nutrition .... G 419 342-6259
  Shelby (G-16986)

SPECIALTY FOOD STORES: Soft Drinks

Sunny Delight Beverage Co .... D 513 483-3300
  Blue Ash (G-1853)

SPEED CHANGERS

Great Lakes Power Products Inc .... D 440 951-5111
  Mentor (G-13462)
Peerless-Winsmith Inc .... G 614 526-7000
  Dublin (G-8963)

SPICE & HERB STORES

Gold Star Chili Inc .... E 513 231-4541
  Cincinnati (G-3767)

SPINDLES: Textile

American Precision Spindles .... G 267 436-6000
  Cleveland (G-4694)

SPONGES, ANIMAL, WHOLESALE

Armaly LLC .... E 740 852-3621
  London (G-12049)

SPONGES: Bleached & Dyed

AK Mansfield .... B 419 755-3011
  Mansfield (G-12401)

SPOOLS: Indl

P & R Specialty Inc .... E 937 773-0263
  Piqua (G-16147)

SPORTING & ATHLETIC GOODS: Bases, Baseball

Black Wing Shooting Center LLC..........G....... 740 363-7555
 Delaware *(G-8658)*

SPORTING & ATHLETIC GOODS: Basketball Eqpt & Splys, NEC

American Sports Design Company.......D....... 937 865-5431
 Centerville *(G-2997)*
Boatfun Sports Inc..............................G....... 513 379-0506
 Liberty Township *(G-11811)*
Shoot-A-Way Inc..................................F....... 419 294-4654
 Upper Sandusky *(G-18974)*

SPORTING & ATHLETIC GOODS: Bows, Archery

Lakota Industries Inc..........................G....... 937 532-6394
 Xenia *(G-20781)*

SPORTING & ATHLETIC GOODS: Camping Eqpt & Splys

M&M Great Adventures LLC ....G....... 937 344-1415
 Westerville *(G-20008)*
Rockbridge Outfitters ....G....... 740 654-1956
 Lancaster *(G-11604)*

SPORTING & ATHLETIC GOODS: Cases, Gun & Rod

Raven Concealment Systems LLC........F....... 440 508-9000
 North Ridgeville *(G-15249)*

SPORTING & ATHLETIC GOODS: Crossbows

Hunters Manufacturing Co Inc..............E....... 330 628-9245
 Mogadore *(G-14240)*

SPORTING & ATHLETIC GOODS: Darts & Table Sports Eqpt & Splys

Darting Around LLC............................G....... 330 639-3990
 Canton *(G-2649)*

SPORTING & ATHLETIC GOODS: Driving Ranges, Golf, Electronic

Mudbrook Golf Center ....G....... 419 433-2945
 Huron *(G-11105)*
Practice Center Inc ....G....... 513 489-5229
 Cincinnati *(G-4183)*

SPORTING & ATHLETIC GOODS: Dumbbells & Other Weight Eqpt

Equipment Guys Inc ....F....... 614 871-9220
 Newark *(G-14872)*

SPORTING & ATHLETIC GOODS: Fishing Bait, Artificial

Fishermans Central LLC ....G....... 330 644-5346
 New Franklin *(G-14689)*

SPORTING & ATHLETIC GOODS: Fishing Eqpt

Bay Area Products Inc..........................G....... 419 732-2147
 Port Clinton *(G-16243)*
Snakebite Snaps ....G....... 520 227-5442
 Cuyahoga Falls *(G-7920)*

SPORTING & ATHLETIC GOODS: Fishing Tackle, General

Barnett Spouting Inc............................G....... 330 644-0853
 Akron *(G-80)*
Ebsco Industries Inc ....F....... 513 398-2149
 Mason *(G-12859)*

SPORTING & ATHLETIC GOODS: Flies, Fishing, Artificial

Red Barakuda LLC...............................G....... 614 596-5432
 Columbus *(G-7380)*

SPORTING & ATHLETIC GOODS: Hooks, Fishing

Duff Farm ....G....... 740 742-2182
 Langsville *(G-11621)*

SPORTING & ATHLETIC GOODS: Hunting Eqpt

Ghostblind Industries Inc.....................G....... 740 374-6766
 Marietta *(G-12626)*
Kabler Farms ....G....... 513 732-0501
 Batavia *(G-1156)*
Lem Products Holding LLC..................E....... 513 202-1188
 West Chester *(G-19736)*

SPORTING & ATHLETIC GOODS: Indian Clubs

Country CLB Rtrment Ctr IV LLC ....G....... 740 676-2300
 Bellaire *(G-1485)*

SPORTING & ATHLETIC GOODS: Masks, Hockey, Baseball, Etc

Hofmanns Lures Inc ....G....... 937 684-0338
 Ansonia *(G-593)*

SPORTING & ATHLETIC GOODS: Pigeons, Clay Targets

Lasermark LLC....................................G....... 513 312-9889
 Dayton *(G-8306)*

SPORTING & ATHLETIC GOODS: Pools, Swimming, Exc Plastic

Bradley Enterprises Inc.......................G....... 330 875-1444
 Louisville *(G-12153)*
Imperial On-Pece Fibrgls Pools............F....... 740 747-2971
 Ashley *(G-757)*
Imperial Pools Inc ....D....... 513 771-1506
 Cincinnati *(G-3842)*
Uniwall Manufacturing Co ....F....... 330 875-1444
 Louisville *(G-12169)*

SPORTING & ATHLETIC GOODS: Pools, Swimming, Plastic

Aquapro Systems LLC ....E....... 513 315-3647
 West Chester *(G-19649)*
GL International LLC ....C....... 330 744-8812
 Youngstown *(G-20922)*

SPORTING & ATHLETIC GOODS: Reels, Fishing

Reelflyrodcom......................................G....... 937 434-8472
 Dayton *(G-8469)*

SPORTING & ATHLETIC GOODS: Shafts, Golf Club

1 Iron Golf Inc......................................G....... 419 662-9336
 Celina *(G-2948)*
Board of Park Commissioners ....G....... 216 635-3200
 Cleveland *(G-4826)*
Grey Hawk Golf Club ....E....... 440 355-4844
 Lagrange *(G-11482)*
Zwf Golf LLC.......................................E....... 937 767-5621
 Fairborn *(G-9476)*

SPORTING & ATHLETIC GOODS: Shooting Eqpt & Splys, General

Brass Tacks Corporation Ltd................G....... 614 599-7954
 Dublin *(G-8891)*
Drop Zone Ltd ....G....... 234 806-4604
 Warren *(G-19398)*
Peregrine Outdoor Products LLC.........G....... 800 595-3850
 Lebanon *(G-11683)*

SPORTING & ATHLETIC GOODS: Skateboards

Careless Heart Enterprises ....G....... 740 654-9999
 Lancaster *(G-11553)*
Konkrete City Skateboards ....G....... 513 231-0399
 Cincinnati *(G-3922)*

SPORTING & ATHLETIC GOODS: Soccer Eqpt & Splys

Soccer First Inc...................................G....... 614 889-1115
 Dublin *(G-8992)*

SPORTING & ATHLETIC GOODS: Target Shooting Eqpt

Apex Target Systems LLC...................G....... 877 224-6692
 Tiffin *(G-18044)*
Target Thompson Technology ....G....... 330 699-8000
 Uniontown *(G-18934)*

SPORTING & ATHLETIC GOODS: Targets, Archery & Rifle Shooting

Challenge Targets................................G....... 859 462-5851
 Cincinnati *(G-3462)*

SPORTING & ATHLETIC GOODS: Team Sports Eqpt

Backyard Scoreboards LLC.................G....... 513 702-6561
 Middletown *(G-13886)*
Shoot A Way Inc ....F....... 419 294-4654
 Upper Sandusky *(G-18973)*

SPORTING & ATHLETIC GOODS: Tennis Eqpt & Splys

Total Tennis Inc ....G....... 614 488-5004
 Columbus *(G-7535)*

SPORTING & ATHLETIC GOODS: Water Sports Eqpt

Kent Sporting Goods Co Inc.................D....... 419 929-7021
 New London *(G-14730)*
Rain Drop Products Llc ....E....... 419 207-1229
 Ashland *(G-742)*
Royal Spa Columbus ....G....... 614 529-8569
 Lewis Center *(G-11777)*
Wake Nation ....F....... 513 887-9253
 Fairfield *(G-9574)*

SPORTING & RECREATIONAL GOODS & SPLYS WHOLESALERS

Advantage Tent Fittings Inc ....F....... 740 773-3015
 Chillicothe *(G-3173)*
Akron Felt & Chenille Mfg Co ....F....... 330 733-7778
 Akron *(G-39)*
Balbo Industries Inc.............................G....... 440 333-0630
 Rocky River *(G-16543)*
Berry Investments Inc ....G....... 937 293-0398
 Moraine *(G-14334)*
Great Oppurtunities Inc ....G....... 614 868-1899
 Columbus *(G-6969)*
Hershberger Lawn Structures ....F....... 330 674-3900
 Millersburg *(G-14088)*
House of Awards and Sports ....G....... 419 422-7877
 Findlay *(G-9706)*
Just Basic Sports Inc ....G....... 330 264-7771
 Wooster *(G-20611)*
McSports ....G....... 419 586-5555
 Celina *(G-2974)*
Phoenix Bat Company ....G....... 614 873-7776
 Plain City *(G-16206)*
R & A Sports Inc.................................E....... 216 289-2254
 Euclid *(G-9438)*
Roy L Bayes ....G....... 614 274-6729
 Columbus *(G-7404)*
T J Target ....G....... 330 658-3057
 Doylestown *(G-8867)*
Total Tennis Inc ....G....... 614 488-5004
 Columbus *(G-7535)*
Toy & Sport Trends Inc ....E....... 419 748-8880
 Napoleon *(G-14562)*
Zebec of North America Inc ....E....... 513 829-5533
 Fairfield *(G-9579)*

SPORTING & RECREATIONAL GOODS, WHOL: Sharpeners, Sporting

Peregrine Outdoor Products LLC.........G....... 800 595-3850
 Lebanon *(G-11683)*

SPORTING & RECREATIONAL GOODS, WHOLESALE: Athletic Goods

SPORTING & RECREATIONAL GOODS, WHOLESALE: Athletic Goods

Garick LLC .... E 216 581-0100
  Cleveland *(G-5293)*

SPORTING & RECREATIONAL GOODS, WHOLESALE: Bowling

Action Sports Apparel Inc .... G 330 848-9300
  Norton *(G-15358)*
Done-Rite Bowling Service Co .... E 440 232-3280
  Bedford *(G-1402)*

SPORTING & RECREATIONAL GOODS, WHOLESALE: Fitness

Ball Bounce and Sport Inc .... B 419 289-9310
  Ashland *(G-682)*
Suarez Corporation Industries .... D 330 494-4282
  Canton *(G-2827)*

SPORTING & RECREATIONAL GOODS, WHOLESALE: Golf

Golf Galaxy Golfworks Inc .... C 740 328-4193
  Newark *(G-14880)*
Tim Boutwell .... G 419 358-4653
  Bluffton *(G-1894)*

SPORTING & RECREATIONAL GOODS, WHOLESALE: Gymnasium

A K Athletic Equipment Inc .... E 614 920-3069
  Canal Winchester *(G-2497)*

SPORTING & RECREATIONAL GOODS, WHOLESALE: Hot Tubs

Royal Spa Columbus 614 529-8569
  Lewis Center *(G-11777)*

SPORTING & RECREATIONAL GOODS, WHOLESALE: Hunting

Ghostblind Industries Inc .... G 740 374-6766
  Marietta *(G-12626)*

SPORTING & RECREATIONAL GOODS, WHOLESALE: Spa

Agean Marble Manufacturing .... F 513 874-1475
  West Chester *(G-19829)*

SPORTING GOODS

Advanced Fitness Inc .... G 513 563-1000
  Cincinnati *(G-3299)*
Al-Co Products Inc .... F 419 399-3867
  Latty *(G-11624)*
All Sport Services Corporation .... G 216 361-1965
  Cleveland *(G-4667)*
American Whistle Corporation .... F 614 846-2918
  Columbus *(G-6587)*
Americas Best Bowstrings LLC .... G 330 893-7155
  Millersburg *(G-14058)*
Arem Co .... F 440 974-6740
  Mentor *(G-13393)*
Baseball Card Corner .... G 513 677-0464
  Loveland *(G-12179)*
Battle Horse Knives LLC .... G 740 995-9009
  Cambridge *(G-2426)*
Bracemart LLC .... G 440 353-2830
  North Ridgeville *(G-15213)*
Brg Sports Inc 217 891-1429
  North Ridgeville *(G-15214)*
Camx Outdoors Inc .... G 330 474-3969
  Kent *(G-11303)*
Columbus Canvas Products Inc .... F 614 375-1397
  Columbus *(G-6785)*
Coulter Ventures Llc .... E 614 358-6190
  Columbus *(G-6828)*
Creighton Sports Center Inc .... G 740 865-2521
  New Matamoras *(G-14745)*
Daisys Pillows LLC .... G 937 776-6968
  Dayton *(G-8125)*
Galaxy Balloons Incorporated .... C 216 476-3360
  Cleveland *(G-5287)*
Golf Car Company Inc .... F 614 873-1055
  Plain City *(G-16196)*

Grey Hawk Golf LLC .... G 440 355-4844
  Lagrange *(G-11481)*
Gym Pro LLC .... G 740 984-4143
  Waterford *(G-19485)*
H & H of Milford Ohio LLC .... G 513 576-9004
  Milford *(G-14015)*
Hoistech LLC .... G 440 327-5379
  North Ridgeville *(G-15229)*
House of Awards and Sports .... G 419 422-7877
  Findlay *(G-9706)*
Just Basic Sports Inc .... G 330 264-7771
  Wooster *(G-20611)*
L A Productions Co LLC .... G 330 666-4230
  Akron *(G-243)*
Licensed Spcialty Pdts of Ohio .... G 419 800-8104
  Bradner *(G-2012)*
Line Drive Sportz-Lcrc LLC .... G 419 794-7150
  Maumee *(G-13127)*
Mc Alarney Pool Spas and Blld .... E 740 373-6698
  Marietta *(G-12646)*
McSports .... G 419 586-5555
  Celina *(G-2974)*
Meridian Industries Inc .... D 330 359-5447
  Winesburg *(G-20533)*
Neo Tactical Gear .... G 216 235-2625
  Chardon *(G-3127)*
Ohio Table Pad Company .... D 419 872-6400
  Perrysburg *(G-15986)*
R L Y Inc .... G 513 385-1950
  Cincinnati *(G-4244)*
Shooting Range Supply LLC .... G 440 576-7711
  Jefferson *(G-11237)*
Smart 3d Solutions LLC .... G 330 972-7840
  Akron *(G-379)*
Sports Monster Corp .... F 614 443-0190
  Columbus *(G-7479)*
Toy & Sport Trends Inc .... E 419 748-8880
  Napoleon *(G-14562)*
Trendco Inc .... G 216 661-6903
  North Royalton *(G-15307)*
U S Development Corp .... E 570 966-5990
  Kent *(G-11397)*
Unique-Chardan Inc .... E 419 636-6900
  Bryan *(G-2311)*
Vantage Athletic .... G 419 680-5274
  Fremont *(G-10062)*
Vf Outdoor LLC .... G 614 337-1147
  Columbus *(G-7582)*
Victory Athletics Inc .... G 330 274-2854
  Mantua *(G-12561)*
Voll Hockey Inc .... G 216 521-4625
  Lakewood *(G-11536)*
Wholesale Bait Co Inc .... F 513 863-2380
  Fairfield *(G-9576)*
Zebec of North America Inc .... E 513 829-5533
  Fairfield *(G-9579)*

SPORTING GOODS STORES, NEC

Art Tees Inc .... G 614 338-8337
  Columbus *(G-6617)*
Balbo Industries Inc .... G 440 333-0630
  Rocky River *(G-16543)*
Ernst Sporting Gds Minster LLC .... G 937 526-9822
  Versailles *(G-19179)*
Fried Daddy .... G 937 854-4542
  Dayton *(G-8207)*
Highpoint Firearms .... E 419 747-9444
  Mansfield *(G-12459)*
Hoffee John .... G 330 868-3553
  Minerva *(G-14183)*
Joe Sestito .... G 614 871-7778
  Grove City *(G-10437)*
Johndavid D Jones .... G 740 264-0176
  Wintersville *(G-20539)*
Lakeside Sport Shop Inc .... G 330 637-2862
  Cortland *(G-7711)*
Lion Clothing Co .... G 419 692-9981
  Delphos *(G-8751)*
McSports .... G 419 586-5555
  Celina *(G-2974)*
National Bullet Co .... G 800 317-9506
  Eastlake *(G-9125)*
Peska Inc .... F 440 998-4664
  Ashtabula *(G-797)*
Quality Spt & Silk Screen Sp .... G 513 769-8300
  Cincinnati *(G-4229)*
Sports Express .... G 330 297-1112
  Ravenna *(G-16406)*
Sunset Golf LLC .... E 419 994-5563
  Tallmadge *(G-18007)*

T J Target .... G 330 658-3057
  Doylestown *(G-8867)*
T K L Lettering 937 832-2091
  Englewood *(G-9376)*

SPORTING GOODS STORES: Ammunition

Reloading Supplies Corp .... G 440 228-0367
  Ashtabula *(G-802)*

SPORTING GOODS STORES: Baseball Eqpt

Phoenix Bat Company 614 873-7776
  Plain City *(G-16206)*

SPORTING GOODS STORES: Camping Eqpt

Outdoor Army Store of Ashtbula .... F 440 992-8791
  Ashtabula *(G-794)*
Vance Adams .... G 330 424-9670
  Lisbon *(G-11981)*

SPORTING GOODS STORES: Firearms

762mm Firearms LLC 440 655-8572
  Wadsworth *(G-19217)*
Apex Alliance LLC .... G 234 200-5930
  Stow *(G-17569)*
R & S Monitions Inc .... G 614 846-0597
  Columbus *(G-7371)*
Smokin Guns LLC 440 324-4003
  Elyria *(G-9329)*
TS Sales LLC .... F 727 804-8060
  Mount Gilead *(G-14435)*

SPORTING GOODS STORES: Hockey Eqpt, Exc Skates

Puck Hogs Pro Shop Inc .... G 419 540-1388
  Toledo *(G-18488)*

SPORTING GOODS STORES: Hunting Eqpt

Butera Manufacturing Inc .... F 440 516-3698
  Willoughby Hills *(G-20467)*

SPORTING GOODS STORES: Playground Eqpt

Hershberger Lawn Structures .... F 330 674-3900
  Millersburg *(G-14088)*

SPORTING GOODS STORES: Soccer Splys

Fryes Soccer Shoppe .... G 937 832-2230
  Englewood *(G-9359)*

SPORTING GOODS STORES: Team sports Eqpt

Lima Sporting Goods Inc .... E 419 222-1036
  Lima *(G-11894)*
Locker Room Inc 419 445-9600
  Archbold *(G-656)*
Wayne Sporting Goods .... G 937 236-6665
  Dayton *(G-8586)*

SPORTING GOODS: Archery

Foster Manufacturing .... G 513 735-9770
  Batavia *(G-1145)*

SPORTING GOODS: Fishing Nets

Drifter Marine Inc .... G 419 666-8144
  Perrysburg *(G-15941)*

SPORTING/ATHLETIC GOODS: Gloves, Boxing, Handball, Etc

Hillman Group Inc .... G 440 248-7000
  Cleveland *(G-5409)*

SPORTS APPAREL STORES

Aardvark Sportswear Inc .... G 330 793-9428
  Youngstown *(G-20832)*
Essential Pathways Ohio LLC .... G 330 518-3091
  Youngstown *(G-20900)*
Peregrine Outdoor Products LLC .... G 800 595-3850
  Lebanon *(G-11683)*
Quali-Tee Design Sports .... F 937 382-7997
  Wilmington *(G-20505)*

Quality Spt & Silk Screen Sp ....G........ 513 769-8300
  Cincinnati *(G-4229)*
Shoot A Way Inc ....F........ 419 294-4654
  Upper Sandusky *(G-18973)*
Silk Screen Special TS Inc ....G........ 740 246-4843
  Thornville *(G-18036)*
Sports Express ....G........ 330 297-1112
  Ravenna *(G-16406)*
Swocat Design Inc ....G........ 440 282-4700
  Lorain *(G-12127)*
T K L Lettering ....G........ 937 832-2091
  Englewood *(G-9376)*
T-Top Shoppe ....G........ 330 343-3481
  New Philadelphia *(G-14803)*
Tee Creations ....G........ 937 878-2822
  Fairborn *(G-9472)*
Trd Leathers ....G........ 216 631-6233
  Cleveland *(G-6200)*
Unisport Inc ....F........ 419 529-4727
  Ontario *(G-15549)*
Uptown Dog The Inc ....G........ 740 592-4600
  Athens *(G-853)*

SPOUTING: Plastic & Fiberglass Reinforced

C B & S Spouting Inc ....G........ 937 866-1600
  Miamisburg *(G-13646)*

SPRAYING & DUSTING EQPT

Anest Iwata Air Engrg Inc ....F........ 513 755-3100
  West Chester *(G-19644)*
Cipar Inc ....G........ 216 910-1700
  Beachwood *(G-1226)*
Paratus Supply Inc ....F........ 330 745-3600
  Barberton *(G-1093)*
Wiwa LLC ....F........ 419 757-0141
  Alger *(G-444)*

SPRAYS: Self-Defense

Mace Personal Def & SEC Inc ....E........ 440 424-5321
  Cleveland *(G-5597)*
Mace Security Intl Inc ....D........ 440 424-5321
  Cleveland *(G-5598)*

SPRINGS: Coiled Flat

Golden Spring Co Inc ....F........ 937 848-2513
  Bellbrook *(G-1495)*
Rassini Chassis Systems LLC ....D........ 419 485-1524
  Montpelier *(G-14316)*
Timac Manufacturing Company ....F........ 937 372-3305
  Xenia *(G-20796)*

SPRINGS: Cold Formed

Solon Manufacturing Company ....E........ 440 286-7149
  Chardon *(G-3137)*

SPRINGS: Leaf, Automobile, Locomotive, Etc

E & L Spring Shop ....G........ 440 632-1439
  Middlefield *(G-13796)*
Liteflex LLC ....E........ 937 836-7025
  Englewood *(G-9367)*
Liteflex LLC ....F........ 937 836-7025
  Dayton *(G-8314)*

SPRINGS: Mechanical, Precision

Kern-Liebers Usa Inc ....D........ 419 865-2437
  Holland *(G-10941)*
Spring Works Inc ....E........ 614 351-9345
  Columbus *(G-7480)*
Stalder Spring Works Inc ....F........ 937 322-6120
  Springfield *(G-17498)*
The Reliable Spring Wire Frms ....E........ 440 365-7400
  Elyria *(G-9338)*
Twist Inc ....C........ 937 675-9581
  Jamestown *(G-11221)*
Twist Inc ....E........ 937 675-9581
  Jamestown *(G-11222)*
Wire Products Company Inc ....C........ 216 267-0777
  Cleveland *(G-6316)*
Yost Superior Co ....E........ 937 323-7591
  Springfield *(G-17522)*

SPRINGS: Precision

B & P Spring Production Co ....F........ 216 486-4260
  Cleveland *(G-4783)*
Tadd Spring Co Inc ....E........ 440 572-1313
  Strongsville *(G-17799)*

SPRINGS: Steel

Accurate Tool Co Inc ....G........ 330 332-9448
  Salem *(G-16714)*
Crawford Manufacturing Company ..F........ 330 897-1060
  Baltic *(G-1026)*
Dayton Progress Corporation ....A........ 937 859-5111
  Dayton *(G-8143)*
Elyria Spring & Specialty Inc ....E........ 440 323-5502
  Elyria *(G-9256)*
Euclid Spring Company Inc ....E........ 440 943-3213
  Wickliffe *(G-20210)*
Hendrickson International Corp ....D........ 740 929-5600
  Hebron *(G-10747)*
Jamestown Industries Inc ....D........ 330 779-0670
  Youngstown *(G-20947)*
Kern-Liebers Usa Inc ....E........ 419 865-2437
  Holland *(G-10941)*
Matthew Warren Inc ....E........ 614 418-0250
  Columbus *(G-7160)*
Precision Products Group Inc ....D........ 330 698-4711
  Apple Creek *(G-617)*
Service Spring Corp ....D........ 419 838-6081
  Maumee *(G-13144)*
Tadd Spring Co Inc ....E........ 440 572-1313
  Strongsville *(G-17799)*
Torsion Control Product 248 597-9997
  Dayton *(G-8563)*
Tremac Corporation ....E........ 937 372-8662
  Xenia *(G-20798)*
Zsi Manufacturing Inc ....G........ 440 266-0701
  Painesville *(G-15805)*

SPRINGS: Torsion Bar

Napoleon Spring Works Inc ....C........ 419 445-1010
  Archbold *(G-660)*

SPRINGS: Wire

A & W Spring Co Inc ....G........ 937 222-7284
  Dayton *(G-7998)*
Aswpengg LLC ....G........ 216 292-4620
  Bedford Heights *(G-1461)*
Barnes Group Inc ....G........ 440 526-5900
  Brecksville *(G-2021)*
Barnes Group Inc ....E........ 419 891-9292
  Maumee *(G-13077)*
Bloomingburg Spring & Wire For .....E........ 740 437-7614
  Bloomingburg *(G-1709)*
Dayton Progress Corporation ....A........ 937 859-5111
  Dayton *(G-8143)*
Elyria Spring & Specialty Inc ....E........ 440 323-5502
  Elyria *(G-9256)*
Kern-Liebers Texas Inc ....E........ 419 865-2437
  Holland *(G-10940)*
Matthew Warren Inc ....E........ 614 418-0250
  Columbus *(G-7160)*
Ohio Wire Form & Spring Co ....F........ 614 444-3676
  Columbus *(G-7264)*
Precision Products Group Inc ....D........ 330 698-4711
  Apple Creek *(G-617)*
Protech Electric LLC ....F........ 937 427-0813
  Beavercreek *(G-1337)*
Regal Spring Co ....G........ 614 278-7761
  Columbus *(G-7383)*
Six C Fabrication Inc ....C........ 330 296-5594
  Ravenna *(G-16403)*
Solon Manufacturing Company ....E........ 440 286-7149
  Chardon *(G-3137)*
Spring Team Inc ....D........ 440 275-5981
  Austinburg *(G-926)*
Springtime Manufacturing ....G........ 419 697-3720
  Toledo *(G-18528)*
Supro Spring & Wire Forms Inc ....E........ 330 722-5628
  Medina *(G-13349)*
Trupoint Products ....F........ 330 204-3302
  Sugarcreek *(G-17872)*

SPRINKLER SYSTEMS: Field

Siteone Landscape Supply LLC ....G........ 330 220-8691
  Brunswick *(G-2239)*

SPRINKLING SYSTEMS: Fire Control

Cae Ransohoff Inc ....G........ 513 870-0100
  West Chester *(G-19837)*
Fire Fab Corporation ....G........ 330 759-9834
  Girard *(G-10257)*
Fire Foe Corp ....E........ 330 759-9834
  Girard *(G-10258)*
Gould Fire Protection Inc ....G........ 419 957-2416
  Findlay *(G-9694)*
Radco Fire Protection Inc ....G........ 419 476-0102
  Toledo *(G-18495)*
Viking Group Inc ....G........ 937 443-0433
  Dayton *(G-8580)*

SPROCKETS: Power Transmission

Abl Products Inc ....F........ 216 281-2400
  Cleveland *(G-4598)*
Akron Gear & Engineering Inc ....E........ 330 773-6608
  Akron *(G-41)*
Martin Sprocket & Gear Inc ....D........ 419 485-5515
  Montpelier *(G-14312)*
Robertson Manufacturing Co ....F........ 216 531-8222
  Cleveland *(G-5994)*

STACKING MACHINES: Automatic

Air Technical Industries Inc ....E........ 440 951-5191
  Mentor *(G-13378)*

STAGE LIGHTING SYSTEMS

Iacono Production Services Inc ....F........ 513 469-5095
  Blue Ash *(G-1790)*
Importers Direct LLC ....E........ 330 436-3260
  Akron *(G-214)*

STAINED GLASS ART SVCS

Whitney Stained Glass Studio ....G........ 216 348-1616
  Cleveland *(G-6306)*

STAINLESS STEEL

Acme Surface Dynamics Inc ....G........ 330 821-3900
  Alliance *(G-450)*
Aco Polymer Products Inc ....E........ 440 285-7000
  Mentor *(G-13373)*
AK Steel Corporation ....B........ 419 755-3011
  Mansfield *(G-12402)*
AK Steel Corporation ....A........ 740 829-2206
  Coshocton *(G-7717)*
AK Steel Corporation ....B........ 513 425-3694
  Middletown *(G-13877)*
Allegheny Ludlum LLC ....E........ 330 875-2244
  Louisville *(G-12151)*
Bcast Stainless Products LLC ....F........ 614 873-3945
  Plain City *(G-16176)*
Challenger Hardware Company ....F........ 216 591-1141
  Independence *(G-11122)*
Emt Trading Company LLC ....G........ 888 352-8000
  Chagrin Falls *(G-3019)*
Fulton County Processing Ltd ....D........ 419 822-9266
  Delta *(G-8771)*
Grace Metals Ltd ....G........ 234 380-1433
  Hudson *(G-11048)*
Great Lakes Mfg Group Ltd ....G........ 440 391-8266
  Rocky River *(G-16548)*
Latrobe Spcialty Mtls Dist Inc ....D........ 330 609-5137
  Vienna *(G-19199)*
Mtr Martco LLC ....D........ 513 424-5307
  Middletown *(G-13932)*
North American Steel Company ......E........ 216 475-7300
  Cleveland *(G-5759)*
North Jckson Specialty Stl LLC ....F........ 330 538-9621
  North Jackson *(G-15150)*
Premier Metal Trading LLC ....G........ 440 247-9494
  Beachwood *(G-1267)*
Qual-Fab Inc ....E........ 440 327-5000
  Avon *(G-960)*
Quality Bar Inc ....F........ 330 755-0000
  Struthers *(G-17822)*

STAINLESS STEEL WARE

Online Engineering Corporation ....G........ 513 561-8878
  Amelia *(G-545)*

STAIR TREADS: Rubber

Safeguard Technology Inc ....E........ 330 995-5200
  Streetsboro *(G-17694)*

STAIRCASES & STAIRS, WOOD

Berry Woodworking ....F........ 513 734-6133
  Amelia *(G-533)*
Carolina Stair Supply Inc ....E........ 740 922-3333
  Uhrichsville *(G-18881)*
Great Lakes Stair & Mllwk Co ....G........ 330 225-2005
  Hinckley *(G-10900)*

STAIRCASES & STAIRS, WOOD

Heartland Stairway Ltd .... G 330 279-2554
  Millersburg *(G-14087)*
Hinckley Wood Products .... F 330 220-9999
  Hinckley *(G-10902)*
Jaco Inc .... G 513 722-3947
  Loveland *(G-12202)*
Kacy Stairs .... F 740 599-5201
  Howard *(G-10996)*
L J Smith Inc .... C 740 269-2221
  Bowerston *(G-1940)*
Schreiner Cstm Stairs & Mllwk .... F 419 435-8935
  Fostoria *(G-9858)*
Shawnee Wood Products Inc .... G 440 632-1771
  Middlefield *(G-13852)*

STAMPED ART GOODS FOR EMBROIDERING

Anything Personalized .... G 330 655-0723
  Twinsburg *(G-18734)*
Graphix Junction .... G 234 284-8392
  Hudson *(G-11049)*
Vasil Co Inc .... G 419 562-2901
  Bucyrus *(G-2347)*

STAMPING: Fabric Articles

Big Kahuna Graphics LLC .... G 330 455-2625
  Canton *(G-2591)*

STAMPINGS: Automotive

A J Rose Mfg Co .... C 216 631-4645
  Avon *(G-936)*
A J Rose Mfgco .... C 216 631-4645
  Cleveland *(G-4590)*
Adval Tech US Inc .... G 216 362-1850
  Cleveland *(G-4620)*
Anchor Tool & Die Co .... B 216 362-1850
  Cleveland *(G-4709)*
Arcelormittal Tailored Blanks .... D 419 737-3180
  Pioneer *(G-16084)*
Bear Diversified Inc .... G 216 883-5494
  Cleveland *(G-4799)*
Cleveland Metal Processing Inc .... C 440 243-3404
  Cleveland *(G-4968)*
Cole Tool & Die Company .... E 419 522-1272
  Ontario *(G-15540)*
Defiance Metal Products Co .... B 419 784-5332
  Defiance *(G-8619)*
E & W Enterprises Powell Inc .... D 937 346-0800
  Springfield *(G-17393)*
Elyria Spring & Specialty Inc .... E 440 323-5502
  Elyria *(G-9256)*
Exact-Tool & Die Inc .... E 216 676-9140
  Cleveland *(G-5204)*
Falls Stamping & Welding Co .... C 330 928-1191
  Cuyahoga Falls *(G-7867)*
Falls Stamping & Welding Co .... F 216 771-9635
  Cleveland *(G-5218)*
Feintool Cincinnati Inc .... C 513 247-0110
  Blue Ash *(G-1773)*
Feintool US Operations Inc .... C 513 247-4061
  Blue Ash *(G-1774)*
Findlay Products Corporation .... C 419 423-3324
  Findlay *(G-9687)*
FMI Products LLC .... G 440 476-8262
  Valley City *(G-19037)*
Gamco Componets Group LLC .... G 440 593-1500
  Conneaut *(G-7645)*
General Motors LLC .... B 330 824-5840
  Warren *(G-19406)*
Gt Technologies Inc .... D 419 324-7300
  Toledo *(G-18314)*
Guarantee Specialties Inc .... D 216 451-9744
  Strongsville *(G-17747)*
Hayford Technologies .... D 419 524-7627
  Mansfield *(G-12455)*
Hercules Acquisition Corp .... E 419 287-3223
  Pemberville *(G-15884)*
Honda of America Mfg Inc .... F 937 644-0724
  Marysville *(G-12792)*
Hydro Extrusion North Amer LLC .... C 888 935-5759
  Sidney *(G-17045)*
Jatdco LLC .... G 440 238-6570
  Strongsville *(G-17757)*
Kirchhoff Auto Waverly Inc .... D 740 947-7763
  Waverly *(G-19550)*
L & W Inc .... D 734 397-6300
  Avon *(G-953)*
Lakepark Industries Inc .... C 419 752-4471
  Greenwich *(G-10406)*
Langenau Manufacturing Company .... F 216 651-3400
  Cleveland *(G-5558)*
Merrick Manufacturing II LLC .... G 937 222-7164
  Dayton *(G-8341)*
N N Metal Stampings Inc .... E 419 737-2311
  Pioneer *(G-16086)*
Nasg Ohio LLC .... F 419 634-3125
  Ada *(G-7)*
Nebraska Industries Corp .... E 419 335-6010
  Wauseon *(G-19529)*
Northern Stamping Co .... F 216 883-8888
  Cleveland *(G-5782)*
Northern Stamping Co .... C 216 883-8888
  Cleveland *(G-5783)*
Northern Stamping Co .... C 216 642-8081
  Cleveland *(G-5784)*
Oerlikon Friction Systems .... E 937 233-9191
  Dayton *(G-8395)*
P & A Industries Inc .... C 419 422-7070
  Findlay *(G-9738)*
Progressive Stamping Inc .... C 419 453-1111
  Ottoville *(G-15683)*
R K Industries Inc .... D 419 523-5001
  Ottawa *(G-15663)*
Select International Corp .... G 937 233-9191
  Dayton *(G-8503)*
Shiloh Industries Inc .... E 330 558-2300
  Valley City *(G-19063)*
Shiloh Industries Inc .... A 330 558-2000
  Valley City *(G-19064)*
Shiloh Industries Inc .... A 330 558-2600
  Valley City *(G-19065)*
Shiloh Industries Inc .... G 330 558-2600
  Valley City *(G-19066)*
SSP Industrial Group Inc .... G 330 665-2900
  Fairlawn *(G-9619)*
Stamco Industries Inc .... E 216 731-9333
  Cleveland *(G-6091)*
Stripmatic Products Inc .... E 216 241-7143
  Cleveland *(G-6111)*
Sunrise Cooperative Inc .... E 419 683-4600
  Crestline *(G-7801)*
T A Bacon Co .... F 216 851-1404
  Chesterland *(G-3169)*
Taylor Metal Products Co .... C 419 522-3471
  Mansfield *(G-12526)*
Tfo Tech Co Ltd .... C 740 426-6381
  Jeffersonville *(G-11248)*
Tower Automotive Operations I .... B 419 358-8966
  Bluffton *(G-1895)*
Tower Automotive Operations I .... C 419 483-1500
  Bellevue *(G-1550)*
Trucut Incorporated .... D 330 938-9806
  Sebring *(G-16896)*
TS Trim Industries Inc .... F 614 837-4114
  Canal Winchester *(G-2514)*
Valley Tool & Die Inc .... D 440 237-0160
  North Royalton *(G-15309)*
Yachiyo of America Inc .... C 614 876-3220
  Columbus *(G-7620)*
Zip Tool & Die Inc .... F 216 267-1117
  Cleveland *(G-6343)*

STAMPINGS: Metal

A J Rose Mfg Co .... C 216 631-4645
  Avon *(G-936)*
A J Rose Mfgco .... C 216 631-4645
  Cleveland *(G-4590)*
Advanced Technology Corp .... C 440 293-4064
  Andover *(G-577)*
Amcraft Inc .... G 419 729-7900
  Toledo *(G-18170)*
American Trim LLC .... A 419 228-1145
  Sidney *(G-17014)*
American Trim LLC .... D 419 739-4349
  Wapakoneta *(G-19318)*
American Truck Equipment Inc .... G 216 362-0400
  Cleveland *(G-4699)*
AMG Industries LLC .... D 740 397-4044
  Mount Vernon *(G-14467)*
Amtekco Industries Inc .... G 614 228-6525
  Columbus *(G-6597)*
Anchor Fabricators Inc .... E 937 836-5117
  Clayton *(G-4571)*
Anchor Tool & Die Co .... D 216 362-1850
  Cleveland *(G-4710)*
Anchor Tool & Die Co .... B 216 362-1850
  Cleveland *(G-4709)*
Anomatic Corporation .... B 740 522-2203
  Johnstown *(G-11255)*
Arrow Tru-Line Inc .... C 419 446-2785
  Archbold *(G-639)*
Arrow Tru-Line Inc .... D 419 636-7013
  Bryan *(G-2265)*
Art Metals Group Inc .... D 513 942-8800
  Hamilton *(G-10536)*
Artiflex Manufacturing LLC .... B 330 262-2015
  Wooster *(G-20564)*
Artisan Tool & Die Corp .... E 216 883-2769
  Cleveland *(G-4740)*
Atlantic Durant Technology Inc .... C 440 238-6931
  Strongsville *(G-17713)*
Ayling and Reichert Co Consent .... E 419 898-2471
  Oak Harbor *(G-15441)*
Barnes Group Inc .... G 440 526-5900
  Brecksville *(G-2021)*
Bates Metal Products Inc .... D 740 498-8371
  Port Washington *(G-16267)*
Bellevue Manufacturing Company .... G 419 483-3190
  Bellevue *(G-1532)*
Breitinger Company .... C 419 526-4255
  Mansfield *(G-12414)*
Brw Tool Inc .... F 419 394-3371
  Saint Marys *(G-16679)*
Buckeye Metals Industries Inc .... F 216 663-4300
  Cleveland *(G-4849)*
C & C Fabrication Inc .... G 419 354-3535
  Bowling Green *(G-1958)*
Calphalon Corporation .... D 770 418-7100
  Perrysburg *(G-15927)*
Camelot Manufacturing Inc .... F 419 678-2603
  Coldwater *(G-6403)*
Cole Tool & Die Company .... E 419 522-1272
  Ontario *(G-15540)*
Compco Industries Inc .... D 330 482-6488
  Columbiana *(G-6463)*
Contour Forming Inc .... E 740 345-9777
  Newark *(G-14864)*
Cubbison Company .... D 330 793-2481
  Youngstown *(G-20882)*
Customformed Products Inc .... F 937 388-0480
  Miamisburg *(G-13653)*
Dayton Tool Co Inc .... E 937 222-5501
  Dayton *(G-8146)*
Dayton Tractor & Crane .... G 937 317-5014
  Xenia *(G-20765)*
Defiance Stamping Co .... D 419 782-5781
  Napoleon *(G-14537)*
Delafoil Pennsylvania Inc .... D 610 327-9565
  Perrysburg *(G-15939)*
Delta Tool & Die Stl Block Inc .... F 419 822-5939
  Delta *(G-8767)*
Die-Mension Corporation .... F 330 273-5872
  Brunswick *(G-2200)*
Duro Dyne Midwest Corp .... B 513 870-6000
  Hamilton *(G-10551)*
E C Shaw Co .... E 513 721-6334
  Cincinnati *(G-3616)*
Elliott Oren Products Inc .... E 419 298-2306
  Edgerton *(G-9173)*
Elyria Spring & Specialty Inc .... E 440 323-5502
  Elyria *(G-9256)*
Ernie Green Industries Inc .... G 614 219-1423
  Columbus *(G-6903)*
Even Heat Mfg Ltd .... F 330 695-9351
  Fredericksburg *(G-9950)*
Exact-Tool & Die Inc .... E 216 676-9140
  Cleveland *(G-5204)*
F & G Tool and Die Co .... E 937 746-3658
  Franklin *(G-9880)*
Feinblanking Limited Inc .... G 513 860-2100
  West Chester *(G-19702)*
Feintool US Operations Inc .... C 513 247-4061
  Blue Ash *(G-1774)*
Findlay Products Corporation .... C 419 423-3324
  Findlay *(G-9687)*
Five Handicap Inc .... F 419 525-2511
  Mansfield *(G-12439)*
Flood Heliarc Inc .... F 614 835-3929
  Groveport *(G-10489)*
Formasters Corporation .... F 440 639-9206
  Mentor *(G-13445)*
Formetal Inc .... E 419 898-2211
  Oak Harbor *(G-15445)*
Frepeg Industries Inc .... F 440 255-8595
  Mentor *(G-13451)*
Fulton Manufacturing Inds LLC .... E 440 546-1435
  Brecksville *(G-2037)*
G & W Products LLC .... C 513 860-4050
  Fairfield *(G-9499)*

Gb Fabrication Company ....E 419 347-1835
Shelby *(G-16982)*
Gb Fabrication Company ....E 419 896-3191
Shiloh *(G-16993)*
General Technologies Inc ....E 419 747-1800
Mansfield *(G-12445)*
Gottschall Tool & Die Inc....................E 330 332-1544
Salem *(G-16743)*
Gt Technologies Inc....................D 419 324-7300
Toledo *(G-18314)*
Guardian Engineering & Mfg Co....................G 419 335-1784
Wauseon *(G-19518)*
Gwp Holdings Inc....................D 513 860-4050
Fairfield *(G-9501)*
Hayford Technologies ....D 419 524-7627
Mansfield *(G-12455)*
Hercules Acquisition Corp....................E 419 287-3223
Pemberville *(G-15884)*
Ice Industries Inc....................G 513 398-2010
Mason *(G-12889)*
International Trade Group Inc....................G 614 486-4634
Columbus *(G-7045)*
J Williams & Associates Inc....................G 330 887-1392
Westfield Center *(G-20085)*
Jet Stream International Inc....................E 330 505-9988
Niles *(G-15018)*
Jones Metal Products Company ....C 740 545-6381
West Lafayette *(G-19931)*
Kelch Manufacturing Corp....................G 440 366-5060
Elyria *(G-9282)*
Knight Manufacturing Co Inc....................G 740 676-5516
Shadyside *(G-16923)*
Langenau Manufacturing Company......F 216 651-3400
Cleveland *(G-5558)*
Larosa Die Engineering Inc....................G 513 284-9195
Cincinnati *(G-3931)*
Logan Machine Company ....D 330 633-6163
Akron *(G-259)*
Long-Stanton Mfg Company....................E 513 874-8020
West Chester *(G-19738)*
Malin Wire Co ....E 216 267-9080
Cleveland *(G-5608)*
Malin Wire Co ....G 216 267-9080
Cleveland *(G-5607)*
Matco Tools Corporation....................B 330 929-4949
Stow *(G-17605)*
McAfee Tool & Die Inc ....E 330 896-9555
Uniontown *(G-18927)*
Medina Blanking Inc....................C 330 558-2300
Valley City *(G-19049)*
Merrick Manufacturing II LLC ....G 937 222-7164
Dayton *(G-8341)*
Metal Products Company....................E 330 652-2558
Niles *(G-15021)*
Mic-Ray Metal Products Inc....................F 216 791-2206
Cleveland *(G-5665)*
Mid-America Steel Corp ....E 800 282-3466
Cleveland *(G-5674)*
Midway Products Group Inc ....G 419 422-7070
Findlay *(G-9725)*
Modern Pipe Supports Corp ....E 216 361-1666
Cleveland *(G-5700)*
Monode Steel Stamp Inc ....E 419 929-3501
New London *(G-14732)*
Monode Steel Stamp Inc ....F 440 975-8802
Mentor *(G-13523)*
Mtd Holdings Inc....................B 330 225-2600
Valley City *(G-19052)*
New Bremen Machine & Tool Co ....E 419 629-3295
New Bremen *(G-14657)*
New Can Company Inc ....G 937 547-9050
Greenville *(G-10385)*
New Holland Engineering Inc ....G 740 495-5200
New Holland *(G-14702)*
Nicholas Press Sales LLC....................G 440 652-6604
Brunswick *(G-2222)*
Niles Manufacturing & Finshg ....C 330 544-0402
Niles *(G-15024)*
Northern Stamping Co....................F 216 883-8888
Cleveland *(G-5782)*
Northern Stamping Co....................C 216 883-8888
Cleveland *(G-5783)*
Northwind Industries Inc....................E 216 433-0666
Cleveland *(G-5787)*
Norwood Medical ....G 937 228-4101
Dayton *(G-8385)*
Norwood Medical ....C 937 228-4101
Dayton *(G-8386)*
Norwood Tool Company....................C 937 228-4101
Dayton *(G-8387)*
Ohio Associated Entps LLC....................E 440 354-3148
Painesville *(G-15770)*
Ohio Stamping & Machine LLC ....C 937 322-3880
Springfield *(G-17464)*
P & A Industries Inc ....C 419 422-7070
Findlay *(G-9738)*
Pacific Manufacturing Ohio Inc ....B 513 860-3900
Fairfield *(G-9542)*
Parker-Hannifin Corporation....................F 330 336-3511
Wadsworth *(G-19262)*
Pax Machine Works Inc....................C 419 586-2337
Celina *(G-2978)*
Pettit W T & Sons Co Inc....................G 330 539-6100
Girard *(G-10264)*
Precision Die & Stamping Inc....................G 513 942-8220
West Chester *(G-19764)*
Production Products Inc ....D 734 241-7242
Columbus Grove *(G-7637)*
Progress Tool & Stamping Inc....................E 419 628-2384
Minster *(G-14223)*
Progressive Machine Die Inc ....E 330 405-6600
Macedonia *(G-12321)*
Quality Fabricated Metals Inc ....E 330 332-7008
Salem *(G-16769)*
Quality Metal Products Inc....................G 440 355-6165
Lagrange *(G-11492)*
Racelite South Coast Inc....................F 216 581-4600
Maple Heights *(G-12578)*
Range Kleen Mfg Inc....................B 419 331-8000
Elida *(G-9199)*
Rapid Machine Inc ....F 419 737-2377
Pioneer *(G-16094)*
Ratliff Metal Spinning Co Inc ....E 937 836-3900
Englewood *(G-9374)*
Rezmann Karoly....................G 216 441-4357
Cleveland *(G-5982)*
Ridge Tool Manufacturing Co ....A 440 323-5581
Elyria *(G-9322)*
Rittal Corp....................F 937 399-0500
Springfield *(G-17484)*
Rittal North America LLC ....C 937 399-0500
Urbana *(G-19010)*
Robin Industries Inc ....G 216 267-3554
Cleveland *(G-5995)*
Roemer Industries Inc ....D 330 448-2000
Masury *(G-13062)*
S-P Company Inc ....F 330 482-0200
Columbiana *(G-6479)*
Scott Fetzer Company....................C 216 267-9000
Cleveland *(G-6035)*
Shiloh Automotive Inc ....E 330 558-2600
Valley City *(G-19061)*
Shiloh Corporation....................B 330 558-2600
Valley City *(G-19062)*
Shiloh Industries Inc....................A 440 647-2100
Wellington *(G-19592)*
Shiloh Industries Inc....................A 330 558-2600
Valley City *(G-19065)*
Shiloh Industries Inc....................G 330 558-2600
Valley City *(G-19066)*
Smithville Mfg Co....................E 330 345-5818
Wooster *(G-20655)*
Stolle Properties Inc ....A 513 932-8664
Blue Ash *(G-1852)*
Stripmatic Products Inc....................E 216 241-7143
Cleveland *(G-6111)*
Suburban Manufacturing Co....................D 440 953-2024
Eastlake *(G-9133)*
Superfine Manufacturing Inc ....F 330 897-9024
Fresno *(G-10071)*
T & D Fabricating Inc ....E 440 951-5646
Eastlake *(G-9135)*
Takk Industries Inc....................F 513 353-4306
Cleves *(G-6378)*
Talent Tool & Die Inc ....E 440 239-8777
Berea *(G-1627)*
The Reliable Spring Wire Frms....................E 440 365-7400
Elyria *(G-9338)*
The W L Jenkins Company ....F 330 477-3407
Canton *(G-2835)*
Tool & Die Systems Inc ....E 440 327-5800
North Ridgeville *(G-15256)*
Treaty City Industries Inc ....F 937 548-9000
Greenville *(G-10398)*
Trucut Incorporated....................D 330 938-9806
Sebring *(G-16896)*
Twist Inc....................C 937 675-9581
Jamestown *(G-11221)*
Twist Inc....................E 937 675-9581
Jamestown *(G-11222)*
Valley Tool & Die Inc....................D 440 237-0160
North Royalton *(G-15309)*
Verhoff Machine & Welding Inc ....C 419 596-3202
Continental *(G-7669)*
W M Inc ....E 330 427-6115
Washingtonville *(G-19482)*
Weiss Industries Inc ....E 419 526-2480
Mansfield *(G-12539)*
Welage Corporation....................F 513 681-2300
Cincinnati *(G-4495)*
Willow Hill Industries LLC....................D 440 942-3003
Willoughby *(G-20459)*
Winzeler Stamping Co....................D 419 485-3147
Montpelier *(G-14322)*
Wire Products Company Inc....................C 216 267-0777
Cleveland *(G-6316)*
Wisco Products Incorporated....................E 937 228-2101
Dayton *(G-8598)*
ZF North America Inc....................D 419 726-5599
Toledo *(G-18605)*
ZF North America Inc....................E 216 750-2400
Cleveland *(G-6340)*
ZF North America Inc....................B 216 332-7100
Cleveland *(G-6341)*
Zip Tool & Die Inc....................F 216 267-1117
Cleveland *(G-6343)*

STANDS & RACKS: Engine, Metal

St Marys Iron Works Inc ....F 419 300-6300
Saint Marys *(G-16702)*

STARTERS & CONTROLLERS: Motor, Electric

MA Flynn Associates LLC ....G 513 893-7873
Hamilton *(G-10584)*

STARTERS: Electric Motor

M Technologies Inc....................F 330 477-9009
Canton *(G-2739)*

STARTERS: Motor

Charles Auto Electric Co Inc....................G 330 535-6269
Akron *(G-111)*
H W Fairway International Inc....................E 330 678-2540
Kent *(G-11330)*

STATIC ELIMINATORS: Ind

Takk Industries Inc....................F 513 353-4306
Cleves *(G-6378)*

STATIONARY & OFFICE SPLYS, WHOL: Albums, Scrapbooks/Binders

S O S Graphics & Printing Inc ....G 614 846-8229
Worthington *(G-20702)*

STATIONARY & OFFICE SPLYS, WHOLESALE: Inked Ribbons

Jay Tackett....................G 740 779-1715
Frankfort *(G-9862)*
Microcom Corporation ....E 740 548-6262
Lewis Center *(G-11767)*

STATIONARY & OFFICE SPLYS, WHOLESALE: Marking Devices

Advanced Marking Systems Inc....................G 330 792-8239
Youngstown *(G-20837)*
Dischem International Inc ....G 330 494-5210
Canton *(G-2660)*
REA Elektronik Inc....................F 440 232-0555
Bedford *(G-1440)*
The Rubber Stamp Shop ....G 419 478-4444
Toledo *(G-18549)*

STATIONARY & OFFICE SPLYS, WHOLESALE: Office Filing Splys

Corporate Supply LLC....................G 614 876-8400
Columbus *(G-6824)*

STATIONER'S SUNDRIES: Rubber

Custom Stamp Makers Inc....................G 216 351-1470
Cleveland *(G-5049)*

PRODUCT

STATIONERY & OFFICE SPLYS WHOLESALERS PRODUCT SECTION

STATIONERY & OFFICE SPLYS WHOLESALERS

AW Faber-Castell Usa Inc................D....... 216 643-4660
  Cleveland *(G-4780)*
Covap Inc..F....... 513 793-1855
  Blue Ash *(G-1753)*
Easterdays Printing Center ....G....... 330 726-1182
  Youngstown *(G-20895)*
Friends Service Co Inc....................F....... 800 427-1704
  Dayton *(G-8208)*
Friends Service Co Inc....................G....... 800 427-1704
  Kent *(G-11322)*
Friends Service Co Inc....................D....... 419 427-1704
  Findlay *(G-9690)*
Gvs Industries Inc............................G....... 513 851-3606
  Hamilton *(G-10565)*
Quick Tab II Inc................................D....... 419 448-6622
  Tiffin *(G-18076)*
Scratch-Off Systems Inc..................E....... 216 649-7800
  Brecksville *(G-2056)*
Value Added Business Svcs Co ......G....... 614 854-9755
  Jackson *(G-11200)*
Westrock Commercial LLC..............F....... 419 476-9101
  Toledo *(G-18598)*

STATIONERY ARTICLES: Pottery

Larose Industries LLC......................E....... 419 237-1600
  Fayette *(G-9634)*

STATIONERY PRDTS

CCL Label Inc..................................C....... 216 676-2703
  Cleveland *(G-4894)*
Keeler Enterprises Inc......................G....... 330 336-7601
  Wadsworth *(G-19247)*
Nature Friendly Products LLC..........E....... 216 464-5490
  Cleveland *(G-5730)*
Primary Colors Design Corp ....G....... 419 903-0403
  Ashland *(G-738)*
Westrock Mwv LLC..........................A....... 937 495-6323
  Dayton *(G-8590)*

STATIONERY: Made From Purchased Materials

American Greetings Corporation ....A....... 216 252-7300
  Cleveland *(G-4688)*
CM Paula Company..........................E....... 513 759-7473
  Mason *(G-12849)*

STATUARY & OTHER DECORATIVE PRDTS: Nonmetallic

Aquablok Ltd....................................F....... 419 402-4170
  Swanton *(G-17905)*
Aquablok Ltd....................................F....... 419 825-1325
  Swanton *(G-17906)*
Fireline Inc.......................................E....... 330 259-0647
  Youngstown *(G-20905)*
Fireline Inc.......................................C....... 330 743-1164
  Youngstown *(G-20906)*

STATUARY GOODS, EXC RELIGIOUS: Wholesalers

Mazzolini Artcraft Co Inc..................F....... 216 431-7529
  Cleveland *(G-5640)*
Wilsons Country Creations...............F....... 330 377-4190
  Killbuck *(G-11456)*

STATUES: Nonmetal

B & B Cast Stone Co Inc..................G....... 740 697-0008
  Roseville *(G-16574)*
Mazzolini Artcraft Co Inc..................F....... 216 431-7529
  Cleveland *(G-5640)*

STEAM SPLY SYSTEMS SVCS INCLUDING GEOTHERMAL

BT Investments II Inc.......................G....... 937 434-4321
  Dayton *(G-8066)*

STEEL & ALLOYS: Tool & Die

American Steel & Alloys LLC............E....... 330 847-0487
  Warren *(G-19368)*
Ernst Metal Technologies LLC..........E....... 937 434-3133
  Moraine *(G-14351)*

Esm Products Inc.............................G....... 937 492-4644
  Celina *(G-2961)*
Kind Special Alloys Us LLC..............G....... 330 788-2437
  Youngstown *(G-20953)*
L-K Industry Inc...............................E....... 937 526-3000
  Versailles *(G-19186)*
Thrift Tool Inc...................................G....... 937 275-3600
  Dayton *(G-8557)*
Unlimited Machine and Tool LLC .....F....... 419 269-1730
  Toledo *(G-18586)*
WH Fetzer & Sons Mfg Inc...............E....... 419 687-8237
  Plymouth *(G-16235)*

STEEL Electrometallurgical

Nuflux LLC.......................................G....... 330 399-1122
  Cortland *(G-7713)*

STEEL FABRICATORS

A & E Butscha Co............................G....... 513 761-1919
  Cincinnati *(G-3275)*
A & G Manufacturing Co Inc.............E....... 419 468-7433
  Galion *(G-10119)*
A+ Engineering Fabrication Inc.........F....... 419 832-0748
  Grand Rapids *(G-10314)*
A-1 Fabricators Finishers LLC..........D....... 513 724-0383
  Batavia *(G-1122)*
Accu-Tech Manufacturing Co...........F....... 330 848-8100
  Coventry Township *(G-7760)*
Ace Boiler & Welding Co Inc............G....... 330 745-4443
  Barberton *(G-1048)*
Advance Industrial Mfg Inc...............E....... 614 871-3333
  Grove City *(G-10411)*
Advance Industries Group LLC ....E....... 216 741-1800
  Cleveland *(G-4621)*
Advanced Onsight Welding Svcs......G....... 513 924-1400
  Cincinnati *(G-3302)*
Air Heater Seal Company Inc...........E....... 740 984-2146
  Waterford *(G-19483)*
Akron Rebar Co................................G....... 330 745-7100
  Akron *(G-50)*
Akron Rebar Co................................F....... 216 433-0000
  Cleveland *(G-4648)*
Albert Freytag Inc............................E....... 419 628-2018
  Minster *(G-14209)*
Alcon Industries Inc.........................D....... 216 961-1100
  Cleveland *(G-4653)*
Allied Fabricating & Wldg Co............E....... 614 751-6664
  Columbus *(G-6572)*
Alloy Fabricators Inc........................E....... 330 948-3535
  Lodi *(G-12005)*
Alloy Welding & Fabricating..............F....... 440 914-0650
  Solon *(G-17103)*
Alro Steel Corporation......................E....... 937 253-6121
  Dayton *(G-8021)*
Alron Inc..G....... 330 477-3405
  Canton *(G-2570)*
Alufab Inc..G....... 513 528-7281
  Cincinnati *(G-3240)*
Ambassador Steel Corporation.........F....... 740 382-9969
  Marion *(G-12692)*
Ameco USA Metal Fabrication..........G....... 440 899-9400
  Cleveland *(G-4682)*
American Ir Met Cleveland LLC........E....... 216 266-0509
  Cleveland *(G-4690)*
American Manufacturing Inc.............D....... 419 531-9471
  Toledo *(G-18174)*
American Metal Stamping Co LLC ...F....... 216 531-3100
  Euclid *(G-9402)*
American Mfg & Engrg Co................G....... 440 899-9400
  Westlake *(G-20094)*
American Mfg & Engrg Co................G....... 440 899-9400
  Cleveland *(G-4693)*
American Steel Assod Pdts Inc.........D....... 419 531-9471
  Toledo *(G-18180)*
Ameridian Specialty Services...........E....... 513 769-0150
  Cincinnati *(G-3339)*
Ametco Manufacturing Corp.............E....... 440 951-4300
  Willoughby *(G-20271)*
Amrod Bridge & Iron LLC................E....... 330 530-8230
  Mc Donald *(G-13196)*
Amtank Armor LLC..........................G....... 216 252-1500
  Cleveland *(G-4703)*
Amtech Tool and Machine Inc..........F....... 330 758-8215
  Youngstown *(G-20844)*
Anstine Machining Corp...................F....... 330 821-4365
  Alliance *(G-455)*
Ap-Alternatives LLC........................F....... 419 267-5280
  Ridgeville Corners *(G-16511)*
Appian Manufacturing Corp..............E....... 614 445-2230
  Columbus *(G-6608)*

Applied Energy Tech Inc..................E....... 419 537-9052
  Maumee *(G-13075)*
Arctech Fabricating Inc....................E....... 937 525-9353
  Springfield *(G-17364)*
Armor Consolidated Inc...................G....... 513 923-5260
  Mason *(G-12826)*
Armor Group Inc..............................C....... 513 923-5260
  Mason *(G-12827)*
Armor Metal Group Mason Inc..........C....... 513 769-0700
  Mason *(G-12828)*
Arrow Fabricating Co.......................E....... 216 641-0490
  Novelty *(G-15437)*
Ashco Manufacturing Inc..................G....... 419 838-7157
  Toledo *(G-18193)*
Aster Elements Inc..........................E....... 440 942-2799
  Cleveland *(G-4754)*
Astro-TEC Mfg Inc............................E....... 330 854-2209
  Canal Fulton *(G-2475)*
Avenue Fabricating Inc....................E....... 513 752-1911
  Batavia *(G-1124)*
Banks Manufacturing Company ....E....... 440 458-8661
  Grafton *(G-10293)*
Bauer Corporation............................E....... 800 321-4760
  Wooster *(G-20569)*
Bcfab Inc...E....... 419 532-2899
  Fort Jennings *(G-9791)*
Beauty Cft Met Fabricators Inc.........F....... 440 439-0710
  Bedford *(G-1389)*
Berran Industrial Group Inc..............E....... 330 253-5800
  Akron *(G-85)*
Best Process Solutions Inc..............E....... 330 220-1440
  Brunswick *(G-2192)*
Bethel Engineering and Eqp Inc.......E....... 419 568-1100
  New Hampshire *(G-14699)*
Bickers Metal Products Inc..............E....... 513 353-4000
  Miamitown *(G-13743)*
Bird Equipment LLC.........................E....... 330 549-1004
  North Lima *(G-15166)*
Bison Wldg & Fabrication Inc...........G....... 440 944-4770
  Wickliffe *(G-20205)*
Black McCuskey Souers ....G....... 330 456-8341
  Canton *(G-2593)*
Blackburns Fabrication Inc...............E....... 614 875-0784
  Columbus *(G-6677)*
Blevins Metal Fabrication Inc...........E....... 419 522-6082
  Mansfield *(G-12412)*
Breitinger Company..........................C....... 419 526-4255
  Mansfield *(G-12414)*
Brilex Industries Inc.........................C....... 330 744-1114
  Youngstown *(G-20859)*
Brilex Industries Inc.........................D....... 330 744-1114
  Youngstown *(G-20858)*
Buck Equipment Inc.........................E....... 614 539-3039
  Grove City *(G-10419)*
Buckeye Fbricators of Leetonia ....G....... 330 427-0330
  Leetonia *(G-11716)*
Buckeye Steel Inc............................F....... 740 425-2306
  Barnesville *(G-1116)*
Burghardt Metal Fabg Inc.................F....... 330 794-1830
  Akron *(G-99)*
Byer Steel Rebar Inc.......................E....... 513 821-6400
  Cincinnati *(G-3434)*
C A Joseph Co.................................F....... 330 532-4646
  Irondale *(G-11158)*
C-N-D Industries Inc........................E....... 330 478-8811
  Massillon *(G-12965)*
Camelot Manufacturing Inc..............F....... 419 678-2603
  Coldwater *(G-6403)*
CC Ironworks LLC...........................G....... 330 542-0500
  New Middletown *(G-14747)*
CCM Welding Inc.............................G....... 330 630-2521
  Akron *(G-105)*
Ceco Environmental Corp.................E....... 513 874-8915
  West Chester *(G-19838)*
Central Ohio Fabricators LLC..........E....... 740 393-3892
  Mount Vernon *(G-14474)*
Chagrin Vly Stl Erectors Inc.............F....... 440 975-1556
  Willoughby Hills *(G-20468)*
Champion Bridge Company..............E....... 937 382-2521
  Wilmington *(G-20488)*
Charles Mfg Co................................F....... 330 395-3490
  Warren *(G-19383)*
Charles Ray Evans...........................F....... 740 967-3669
  Columbus *(G-6758)*
Chattanooga Laser Cutting LLC.......E....... 513 779-7200
  Cincinnati *(G-3466)*
Chc Manufacturing Inc.....................E....... 513 821-7757
  Cincinnati *(G-3467)*
Chc Manufacturing Inc.....................G....... 614 527-1606
  Columbus *(G-6759)*

Christman Fabricators Inc ....G 330 477-8077
Canton *(G-2623)*
Cincinnati Industrial McHy Inc ....C 513 923-5600
Mason *(G-12843)*
Cincinnati Laser Cutting LLC ....E 513 779-7200
Cincinnati *(G-3498)*
Cincy Glass Inc ....G 513 241-0455
Cincinnati *(G-3514)*
Clermont Steel Fabricators LLC ....D 513 732-6033
Batavia *(G-1131)*
Cleveland City Forge Inc ....E 440 647-5400
Wellington *(G-19574)*
Clifton Steel Company ....D 216 662-6111
Maple Heights *(G-12569)*
Clipsons Metal Working Inc ....G 513 772-6393
Cincinnati *(G-3528)*
Cohen Brothers Inc ....G 513 422-3696
Middletown *(G-13895)*
Com-Fab Inc ....E 740 857-1107
Plain City *(G-16181)*
Commercial Mtal Fbricators Inc ....E 937 233-4911
Dayton *(G-8100)*
Concord Fabricators Inc ....E 614 875-2500
Grove City *(G-10421)*
Contech Engnered Solutions Inc ....F 513 645-7000
West Chester *(G-19680)*
Contech Engnered Solutions LLC ....D 513 645-7000
Middletown *(G-13896)*
Contech Engnered Solutions LLC ....C 513 645-7000
West Chester *(G-19681)*
Continental GL Sls & Inv Group ....B 614 679-1201
Powell *(G-16318)*
County of Lake ....D 440 269-2193
Willoughby *(G-20302)*
Coventry Steel Services Inc ....F 216 883-4477
Cleveland *(G-5033)*
Cramers Inc ....E 330 477-4571
Canton *(G-2638)*
Creative Fab & Welding LLC ....E 937 780-5000
Leesburg *(G-11709)*
Curtiss-Wright Flow Control ....D 513 528-7900
Cincinnati *(G-3244)*
D T Kothera Inc ....G 440 632-1651
Middlefield *(G-13792)*
Dal-Little Fabricating Inc ....G 216 883-3323
Cleveland *(G-5059)*
Davis Fabricators Inc ....E 419 898-5297
Oak Harbor *(G-15443)*
De-Ko Inc ....G 440 951-2585
Willoughby *(G-20308)*
Debra-Kuempel Inc ....D 513 271-6500
Cincinnati *(G-3579)*
Debs Welding & Fabrication ....G 330 376-2242
Akron *(G-135)*
Defiance Metal Products Wl Inc ....C 920 426-9207
Defiance *(G-8621)*
Deltec Incorporated ....E 513 732-0800
Batavia *(G-1136)*
Diamond Mfg Bluffton Ltd ....D 419 358-0129
Bluffton *(G-1888)*
Diamond Wipes Intl Inc ....G 419 562-3575
Bucyrus *(G-2325)*
Diversifd OH Vlly Eqpt & Srvcs ....F 740 458-9881
Clarington *(G-4567)*
DMC Welding Incorporated ....G 330 877-1935
Hartville *(G-10689)*
Dover Conveyor Inc ....E 740 922-9390
Midvale *(G-13976)*
Dover Tank and Plate Company ....E 330 343-4443
Dover *(G-8823)*
Dracool-Usa Inc ....E 937 743-5899
Carlisle *(G-2892)*
Dwayne Bennett Industries ....G 440 466-5724
Geneva *(G-10217)*
E B P Inc ....E 216 241-2550
Cleveland *(G-5128)*
E W Welding & Fabricating ....G 440 826-9038
Berea *(G-1603)*
E-Pak Manufacturing LLC ....D 800 235-1632
Wooster *(G-20588)*
Ebner Furnaces Inc ....D 330 335-2311
Wadsworth *(G-19237)*
Egypt Structural Steel Proc ....E 419 628-2375
Minster *(G-14213)*
Elcoma Metal Fabricating & Sls ....G 330 588-3075
Canton *(G-2666)*
Emh Inc ....E 330 220-8600
Valley City *(G-19036)*
EPI of Cleveland Inc ....G 330 468-2872
Twinsburg *(G-18769)*
Erico International Corp ....B 440 248-0100
Solon *(G-17140)*
Evers Welding Co Inc ....E 513 385-7352
Cincinnati *(G-3658)*
F M Machine Co ....E 330 773-8237
Akron *(G-163)*
Fab Shop Inc ....G 513 860-1332
Hamilton *(G-10556)*
Fabco Inc ....E 419 421-4740
Findlay *(G-9682)*
Falls Welding & Fabg Inc ....G 330 253-3437
Akron *(G-165)*
Farasey Steel Fabricators Inc ....F 216 641-1853
Cleveland *(G-5219)*
Fastfeed Corp ....G 330 948-7333
Lodi *(G-12010)*
Fenix Fabrication Inc ....E 330 745-8731
Akron *(G-168)*
Fiedeldey Stl Fabricators Inc ....E 513 353-3300
Cincinnati *(G-3684)*
Flex-Strut Inc ....D 330 372-9999
Warren *(G-19403)*
Foster Products Inc ....G 513 735-9770
Batavia *(G-1146)*
Franck and Fric Incorporated ....D 216 524-4451
Cleveland *(G-5271)*
Fulton Equipment Co ....E 419 290-5393
Toledo *(G-18299)*
G & R Welding & Machining ....G 937 323-9353
Springfield *(G-17405)*
G & W Products LLC ....C 513 860-4050
Fairfield *(G-9499)*
Galion-Godwin Truck Bdy Co LLC ....D 330 359-5495
Millersburg *(G-14084)*
Gardner Metal Craft Inc ....G 513 539-4538
Monroe *(G-14263)*
Garland Welding Co Inc ....F 330 536-6506
Lowellville *(G-12251)*
Gb Fabrication Company ....E 419 347-1835
Shelby *(G-16982)*
Gen III ....G 614 737-8744
Columbus *(G-6944)*
General Steel Corporation ....F 216 883-4200
Cleveland *(G-5314)*
George Steel Fabricating Inc ....E 513 932-2887
Lebanon *(G-11655)*
Gilson Machine & Tool Co Inc ....E 419 592-2911
Napoleon *(G-14539)*
Glenwood Erectors Inc ....G 330 652-9616
Niles *(G-15010)*
Gokoh Corporation ....F 937 339-4977
Troy *(G-18662)*
Goyal Industries Inc ....E 419 522-7099
Mansfield *(G-12451)*
Graber Metal Works Inc ....E 440 237-8422
North Royalton *(G-15274)*
Green Point Metals Inc ....E 937 743-4075
Franklin *(G-9887)*
Gregory Industries Inc ....D 330 477-4800
Canton *(G-2688)*
Grenga Machine & Welding ....F 330 743-1113
Youngstown *(G-20925)*
Gunderson Rail Services LLC ....E 330 792-6521
Youngstown *(G-20927)*
H B Products Inc ....E 937 492-7031
Sidney *(G-17042)*
Halvorsen Company ....E 216 341-7500
Cleveland *(G-5367)*
Hancock Structural Steel LLC ....F 419 424-1217
Findlay *(G-9699)*
Hanson Concrete Products Ohio ....E 614 443-4846
Columbus *(G-6980)*
Hays Fabricating & Welding ....E 937 325-0031
Springfield *(G-17412)*
Herman Manufacturing LLC ....F 216 251-6400
Cleveland *(G-5398)*
High Production Technology LLC ....F 419 591-7000
Napoleon *(G-14541)*
Holgate Metal Fab Inc ....F 419 599-2000
Napoleon *(G-14543)*
Hoppel Fabrication Specialties ....F 330 823-5700
Louisville *(G-12156)*
Horizon Metals Inc ....E 440 235-3338
Berea *(G-1609)*
Horning Steel Co ....G 330 633-0028
Tallmadge *(G-17985)*
Hr Machine LLC ....G 937 222-7644
Beavercreek *(G-1323)*
Hunkar Technologies Inc ....C 513 272-1010
Cincinnati *(G-3829)*
Hynes Industries Inc ....C 330 799-3221
Youngstown *(G-20934)*
Hyq Technologies LLC ....G 513 225-6911
Oxford *(G-15694)*
Indian Creek Fabricators Inc ....E 937 667-7214
Tipp City *(G-18116)*
Industrial Hanger Conveyor Co ....G 419 332-2661
Fremont *(G-10028)*
Industrial Mill Maintenance ....E 330 746-1155
Youngstown *(G-20939)*
Ironfab LLC ....F 614 443-3900
Columbus *(G-7049)*
Ironhead Fabg & Contg Inc ....D 419 690-0000
Toledo *(G-18354)*
J & L Specialty Steel Inc ....G 330 875-6200
Louisville *(G-12158)*
J & L Welding Fabricating Inc ....F 330 393-9353
Warren *(G-19412)*
J Horst Manufacturing Co ....D 330 828-2216
Dalton *(G-7945)*
J P Suggins Mobile Welding ....E 216 566-7131
Cleveland *(G-5486)*
J&J Precision Fabricators ....F 330 482-4964
Columbiana *(G-6472)*
Jab Sales Inc ....G 440 446-0606
Cleveland *(G-5490)*
Jayron Fabrication LLC ....G 740 335-3184
Leesburg *(G-11710)*
Jh Industries Inc ....E 330 963-4105
Twinsburg *(G-18797)*
Joe Rees Welding ....G 937 652-4067
Urbana *(G-19000)*
Johnson-Nash Metal Pdts Inc ....F 513 874-7022
Fairfield *(G-9514)*
Jomac Ltd ....G 330 627-7727
Carrollton *(G-2922)*
JR Manufacturing Inc ....C 419 375-8021
Fort Recovery *(G-9823)*
Js Fabrications Inc ....G 419 333-0323
Fremont *(G-10031)*
Kebco Precision Fabricators ....E 330 456-0808
Canton *(G-2722)*
Kecoat LLC ....F 330 527-0215
Garrettsville *(G-10195)*
Kedar D Army ....G 419 238-6929
Van Wert *(G-19097)*
Kellys Welding & Fabricating ....G 440 593-6040
Conneaut *(G-7651)*
King Wolf Enterprises LLC ....G 330 853-0450
East Liverpool *(G-9066)*
Kings Welding and Fabg Inc ....E 330 738-3592
Mechanicstown *(G-13212)*
Kirk Welding & Fabricating ....G 216 961-6403
Cleveland *(G-5538)*
Kottler Metal Products Co Inc ....E 440 946-7473
Willoughby *(G-20355)*
Kramer Power Equipment Co ....F 937 456-2232
Eaton *(G-9157)*
L & W Inc ....D 734 397-6300
Avon *(G-953)*
Langdon Inc ....E 513 733-5955
Cincinnati *(G-3930)*
Lapham-Hickey Steel Corp ....E 614 443-4881
Columbus *(G-7116)*
Laserflex Corporation ....D 614 850-9600
Hilliard *(G-10837)*
Lauren Yoakam ....G 440 365-3952
Elyria *(G-9285)*
Lazarus Steel LLC ....G 216 391-3245
Cleveland *(G-5569)*
Lefeld Welding & Stl Sups Inc ....E 419 678-2397
Coldwater *(G-6416)*
Lideco LLC ....G 330 539-9333
Vienna *(G-19200)*
Lilly Industries Inc ....E 419 946-7908
Mount Gilead *(G-14427)*
Lion Black Products LLC ....F 412 400-6980
Youngstown *(G-20960)*
Livingston & Company Ltd ....G 513 553-6430
New Richmond *(G-14811)*
Louis Arthur Steel Company ....E 440 997-5545
Geneva *(G-10225)*
Louis Arthur Steel Company ....G 440 997-5545
Uniontown *(G-18926)*
Lyco Corporation ....E 412 973-9176
Lowellville *(G-12253)*
M & H Fabricating Co Inc ....F 937 325-8708
Springfield *(G-17437)*
M & W Welding Inc ....G 614 224-0501
Columbus *(G-7139)*

Employee Codes: A=Over 500 employees, B=251-500
C=101-250, D=51-100, E=20-50, F=10-19, G=3-9

2019 Harris Ohio
Industrial Directory

1601

Machine Tool & Fab Corp ... F ... 419 435-7676
Fostoria *(G-9846)*
Magnesium Products Group Inc ... G ... 310 971-5799
Maumee *(G-13128)*
Magnum Piering Inc ... E ... 513 759-3348
West Chester *(G-19874)*
Mahoning Valley Fabricators ... F ... 330 793-8995
Austintown *(G-934)*
Manco Manufacturing Co ... G ... 419 925-4152
Maria Stein *(G-12599)*
Manifold & Phalor Inc ... E ... 614 920-1200
Canal Winchester *(G-2506)*
Manitowoc Company Inc ... G ... 920 746-3332
Cleveland *(G-5612)*
Marc Industries Inc ... G ... 440 944-9305
Willoughby *(G-20369)*
Marsam Metalfab Inc ... E ... 330 405-1520
Twinsburg *(G-18811)*
Martina Metal LLC ... E ... 614 291-9700
Columbus *(G-7155)*
Martins Steel Fabrication ... E ... 330 882-4311
New Franklin *(G-14693)*
Marysville Steel Inc ... E ... 937 642-5971
Marysville *(G-12801)*
Mason Structural Steel Inc ... D ... 440 439-1040
Walton Hills *(G-19312)*
Masonite International Corp ... G ... 937 454-9308
Vandalia *(G-19137)*
Maumee Valley Fabricators Inc ... E ... 419 476-1411
Toledo *(G-18404)*
Maverick Innvtive Slutions LLC ... E ... 419 281-7944
Ashland *(G-723)*
Mc Brown Industries Inc ... F ... 419 963-2800
Findlay *(G-9723)*
McMillen Steel LLC ... G ... 330 253-9147
Akron *(G-274)*
McNeil Group Inc ... E ... 614 298-0300
Columbus *(G-7169)*
McNeil Holdings LLC ... G ... 614 298-0300
Columbus *(G-7170)*
McWane Inc ... B ... 740 622-6651
Coshocton *(G-7739)*
Mercury Iron and Steel Co ... F ... 440 349-1500
Solon *(G-17190)*
Metal Dynamics Co ... G ... 330 601-0748
Wooster *(G-20622)*
Metal Man Inc ... G ... 614 830-0968
Groveport *(G-10506)*
Metal Sales Manufacturing Corp ... E ... 440 319-3779
Jefferson *(G-11234)*
Metlweb ... E ... 513 563-8822
Cincinnati *(G-4016)*
Miami Steel Fabricators Inc ... G ... 937 299-5550
Dayton *(G-8345)*
Mikes Welding ... G ... 937 675-6587
Jamestown *(G-11220)*
Miracle Welding Inc ... G ... 513 746-9977
Franklin *(G-9901)*
Mk Metal Products Inc ... E ... 419 756-3644
Mansfield *(G-12484)*
Mk Trempe Corporation ... E ... 937 492-3548
Sidney *(G-17055)*
Mobile Mini Inc ... F ... 614 449-8655
Columbus *(G-7188)*
Monnig Welding Co ... G ... 513 241-5156
Cincinnati *(G-4042)*
Mr Trailer Sales Inc ... G ... 330 339-7701
New Philadelphia *(G-14789)*
Nct Technologies Group Inc ... E ... 937 882-6800
New Carlisle *(G-14673)*
Neidert Fabricating Inc ... G ... 330 753-3331
Barberton *(G-1088)*
New Wayne Inc ... G ... 740 453-3454
Zanesville *(G-21162)*
Northern Boiler Company ... F ... 216 961-3033
Cleveland *(G-5777)*
Northern Manufacturing Co Inc ... C ... 419 898-2821
Oak Harbor *(G-15446)*
Northwest Installations Inc ... E ... 419 423-5738
Findlay *(G-9732)*
Northwind Industries Inc ... E ... 216 433-0666
Cleveland *(G-5787)*
Ohio Gratings Inc ... B ... 330 477-6707
Canton *(G-2772)*
Ohio Steel Industries Inc ... E ... 740 927-9500
Pataskala *(G-15836)*
Ohio Structures Inc ... E ... 330 547-7705
Berlin Center *(G-1648)*
Ohio Structures Inc ... E ... 330 533-0084
Canfield *(G-2539)*

Olson Sheet Metal Cnstr Co ... G ... 330 745-8225
Barberton *(G-1092)*
Olwin Metal Fabrication LLC ... G ... 937 277-4501
Dayton *(G-8401)*
Outotec Oyj ... E ... 440 783-3336
Strongsville *(G-17775)*
Overhead Door Corporation ... D ... 740 383-6376
Marion *(G-12727)*
Ozone Systems Svcs Group Inc ... G ... 513 899-4131
Morrow *(G-14414)*
P & L Metalcrafts LLC ... F ... 330 793-2178
Youngstown *(G-20987)*
P B Fabrication Mech Contr ... F ... 419 478-4869
Toledo *(G-18454)*
PC Campana Inc ... C ... 440 246-6500
Lorain *(G-12111)*
Pcy Enterprises Inc ... E ... 513 241-5566
Cincinnati *(G-4143)*
Pemjay Inc ... E ... 740 254-4591
Gnadenhutten *(G-10281)*
Perfections Fabricators Inc ... F ... 440 365-5850
Elyria *(G-9310)*
Perry Welding Service Inc ... F ... 330 425-2211
Twinsburg *(G-18836)*
Phillips & Sons Welding & Fabg ... G ... 440 428-1625
Geneva *(G-10228)*
Phoenix Metal Works Inc ... G ... 937 274-5555
Dayton *(G-8424)*
Pioneer Machine Inc ... G ... 330 948-6500
Lodi *(G-12018)*
Pioneer Pipe Inc ... A ... 740 376-2400
Marietta *(G-12653)*
PJs Fabricating Inc ... E ... 330 478-1120
Canton *(G-2786)*
Porters Welding Inc ... F ... 740 452-4181
Zanesville *(G-21169)*
Precision Fabg & Stamping ... G ... 740 453-7310
Zanesville *(G-21172)*
Precision International LLC ... E ... 330 793-0900
Akron *(G-327)*
Precision Steel Services Inc ... D ... 419 476-5702
Toledo *(G-18479)*
Precision Welding & Mfg ... F ... 937 444-6925
Mount Orab *(G-14449)*
Precision Welding Corporation ... E ... 216 524-6110
Cleveland *(G-5912)*
Pro Fab Industries Inc ... G ... 317 297-0461
Dundee *(G-9025)*
Pro-Fab Inc ... E ... 330 644-0044
Akron *(G-332)*
Production Support Inc ... F ... 937 526-3897
Russia *(G-16611)*
Professional Fabricators Inc ... G ... 216 362-1208
Cleveland *(G-5927)*
Pucel Enterprises Inc ... D ... 216 881-4604
Cleveland *(G-5933)*
Q S I Fabrication ... G ... 419 832-1680
Grand Rapids *(G-10319)*
Qc Industrial Inc ... G ... 740 642-5004
Chillicothe *(G-3218)*
Quality Steel Fabrication ... F ... 937 492-9503
Sidney *(G-17063)*
R L Torbeck Industries Inc ... D ... 513 367-0080
Harrison *(G-10667)*
R S V Wldg Fbrcation Machining ... F ... 419 592-0993
Napoleon *(G-14557)*
Rads LLC ... F ... 330 671-0464
Berea *(G-1623)*
Railing Crafters Ltd ... G ... 440 506-9336
Painesville *(G-15779)*
Rance Industries Inc ... F ... 330 482-1745
Columbiana *(G-6477)*
Rankin Mfg Inc ... E ... 419 929-8338
New London *(G-14735)*
RB Fabricators Inc ... F ... 330 779-0263
Youngstown *(G-21014)*
Rbm Environmental and Cnstr ... E ... 419 693-5840
Oregon *(G-15566)*
Redbuilt LLC ... E ... 740 363-0870
Delaware *(G-8719)*
Retays Welding Company ... E ... 440 327-4100
North Ridgeville *(G-15250)*
Rezmann Karoly ... G ... 216 441-4357
Cleveland *(G-5982)*
Richard Steel Company Inc ... G ... 216 520-6390
Cleveland *(G-5983)*
Ripley Metalworks Ltd ... E ... 937 392-4992
Ripley *(G-16517)*
Rittman Inc ... D ... 330 927-6855
Rittman *(G-16528)*

Riverside Steel Inc ... F ... 330 856-5299
Vienna *(G-19209)*
Riwco Corp ... F ... 937 322-6521
Springfield *(G-17486)*
RLM Fabricating Inc ... E ... 419 729-6130
Toledo *(G-18503)*
Rmi Titanium Company LLC ... G ... 330 544-9470
Niles *(G-15029)*
Robs Welding Technologies Ltd ... G ... 937 890-4963
Dayton *(G-8483)*
Romar Metal Fabricating Inc ... G ... 740 682-7731
Oak Hill *(G-15460)*
Rose Metal Industries LLC ... F ... 216 881-3355
Cleveland *(G-6002)*
Rose Metal Industries LLC ... E ... 216 426-8615
Cleveland *(G-6003)*
Royal Welding Inc ... G ... 513 829-9353
Fairfield *(G-9560)*
S & G Manufacturing Group LLC ... C ... 614 529-0100
Hilliard *(G-10859)*
Sausser Steel Company Inc ... F ... 419 422-9632
Findlay *(G-9752)*
Sautter Brothers ... G ... 419 468-7443
Galion *(G-10152)*
Schoonover Industries Inc ... E ... 419 289-8332
Ashland *(G-747)*
Seeburger Greenhouse ... G ... 419 832-1834
Grand Rapids *(G-10321)*
Shaffer Metal Fab Inc ... E ... 937 492-1384
Sidney *(G-17076)*
Sintered Metal Industries Inc ... F ... 330 650-4000
Hudson *(G-11073)*
Skinner Sales Group Inc ... E ... 440 572-8455
Medina *(G-13344)*
Snair Co ... F ... 614 873-7020
Plain City *(G-16212)*
Somerville Manufacturing Inc ... E ... 740 336-7847
Marietta *(G-12674)*
South Central Industrial LLC ... F ... 740 333-5401
Washington Court Hou *(G-19477)*
Specialty Steel Solutions ... G ... 567 674-0011
Kenton *(G-11424)*
Spradlin Bros Welding Co ... F ... 800 219-2182
Springfield *(G-17493)*
St Lawrence Holdings LLC ... E ... 330 562-9000
Maple Heights *(G-12580)*
Stainless Specialties Inc ... E ... 440 942-4242
Eastlake *(G-9130)*
Standard Welding & Steel Pdts ... F ... 330 273-2777
Medina *(G-13346)*
Starr Fabricating Inc ... D ... 330 394-9891
Vienna *(G-19210)*
Stays Lighting Inc ... G ... 440 328-3254
Elyria *(G-9331)*
Steel & Alloy Utility Pdts Inc ... E ... 330 530-2220
Mc Donald *(G-13202)*
Steel Eqp Specialists Inc ... D ... 330 823-8260
Alliance *(G-502)*
Steel It LLC ... F ... 513 253-3111
Loveland *(G-12236)*
Steel Quest Inc ... G ... 513 772-5030
Cincinnati *(G-4377)*
Steelial Wldg Met Fbrction Inc ... E ... 740 669-5300
Vinton *(G-19216)*
Steve Vore Welding and Steel ... F ... 419 375-4087
Fort Recovery *(G-9827)*
Stock Mfg & Design Co Inc ... D ... 513 353-3600
Cleves *(G-6377)*
Straightaway Fabrications Ltd ... E ... 419 281-9440
Ashland *(G-750)*
Suburban Metal Products Inc ... F ... 740 474-4237
Circleville *(G-4559)*
Suburban Stl Sup Co Ltd Partnr ... G ... 317 783-6555
Columbus *(G-7498)*
Sulecki Precision Products ... F ... 440 255-5454
Mentor *(G-13596)*
Summers Acquisition Corp ... G ... 419 423-5800
Findlay *(G-9765)*
Superior Soda Service LLC ... G ... 937 657-9700
Beavercreek *(G-1364)*
Superior Welding Co ... F ... 614 252-8539
Columbus *(G-7503)*
Surface Recovery Tech LLC ... F ... 937 879-5864
Fairborn *(G-9470)*
T & K Welding Co Inc ... G ... 216 432-0221
Cleveland *(G-6142)*
Tarrier Steel Company Inc ... E ... 614 444-4000
Columbus *(G-7514)*
Tech Dynamics Inc ... F ... 419 666-1666
Perrysburg *(G-16010)*

Tech Systems Inc....E....419 878-2100
Waterville *(G-19507)*
The Mansfield Strl & Erct Co....E....419 522-5911
Mansfield *(G-12528)*
The Mansfield Strl & Erct Co....G....419 747-6571
Mansfield *(G-12529)*
Thieman Quality Metal Fab Inc....D....419 629-2612
New Bremen *(G-14661)*
Tilton Corporation....C....419 227-6421
Lima *(G-11952)*
Transco Railway Products Inc....D....330 872-0934
Newton Falls *(G-14994)*
Tri-America Contractors Inc....E....740 574-0148
Wheelersburg *(G-20186)*
Tri-Fab Inc....E....330 337-3425
Salem *(G-16777)*
Tri-State Fabricators Inc....E....513 752-5005
Amelia *(G-550)*
Triangle Precision Industries....D....937 299-6776
Dayton *(G-8564)*
Tru-Fab Inc....F....937 435-1733
Dayton *(G-8571)*
Tru-Form Steel & Wire Inc....E....765 348-5001
Toledo *(G-18583)*
U M D Automated Systems Inc....D....740 694-8614
Fredericktown *(G-9981)*
Union Fabricating & Machine Co....G....419 626-5963
Sandusky *(G-16858)*
United Metal Fabricators Inc....E....216 662-2000
Maple Heights *(G-12582)*
Updegraff Inc....G....216 621-7600
Cleveland *(G-6241)*
Upright Steel LLC....E....216 923-0852
Cleveland *(G-6242)*
V & S Schuler Engineering Inc....D....330 452-5200
Canton *(G-2855)*
Valco Industries Inc....E....937 399-7400
Springfield *(G-17513)*
Vanscoyk Sheet Metal Corp....G....937 845-0581
New Carlisle *(G-14681)*
Verhoff Machine & Welding Inc....C....419 596-3202
Continental *(G-7669)*
Vicon Fabricating Company Ltd....E....440 205-6700
Mentor *(G-13624)*
Viking Fabricators Inc....E....740 374-5246
Marietta *(G-12687)*
Vscorp LLC....F....937 305-3562
Tipp City *(G-18144)*
W & W Custom Fabrication Inc....G....513 353-4617
Cleves *(G-6382)*
Warren Fabricating Corporation....D....330 534-5017
Hubbard *(G-11011)*
Warren Fabricating Corporation....E....330 544-4101
Niles *(G-15039)*
Wauseon Machine & Mfg Inc....D....419 337-0940
Wauseon *(G-19537)*
Wecan Fabricators LLC....G....740 667-0731
Tuppers Plains *(G-18721)*
Welage Corporation....F....513 681-2300
Cincinnati *(G-4495)*
Weldfab Inc....G....440 563-3310
Rock Creek *(G-16535)*
Welding Improvement Company....G....330 424-9666
Lisbon *(G-11982)*
Weldtec Inc....F....419 586-1200
Celina *(G-2992)*
Wernke Wldg & Stl Erection Co....F....513 353-4173
North Bend *(G-15058)*
Westerhaus Metals LLC....G....513 240-9441
Cincinnati *(G-4502)*
White Machine & Mfg Co....F....740 453-3444
Zanesville *(G-21188)*
Whole Shop Inc....F....330 630-5305
Tallmadge *(G-18015)*
Winston Campbell LLC....G....614 274-7015
Columbus *(G-7606)*
Wiseman Bros Fabg & Stl Ltd....F....740 988-5121
Beaver *(G-1295)*
Witt Industries Inc....D....513 871-5700
Mason *(G-12955)*
Woodbury Welding Inc....G....937 968-3573
Union City *(G-18906)*
Worthington Industries Inc....C....513 539-9291
Monroe *(G-14282)*
Worthngton Stelpac Systems LLC....G....937 747-2370
North Lewisburg *(G-15165)*
Ysd Industries Inc....D....330 792-6521
Youngstown *(G-21086)*
Ziegler Engineering Inc....G....440 582-8515
North Royalton *(G-15312)*
Zimmerman Shmtl Stl & Wldg....G....419 335-3806
Wauseon *(G-19540)*
Zimmerman Steel & Sup Co LLC....F....330 828-1010
Dalton *(G-7955)*

STEEL MILLS

AK Steel Corporation....B....740 450-5600
Zanesville *(G-21095)*
AK Steel Corporation....F....513 425-3593
Middletown *(G-13878)*
AK Steel Corporation....G....513 231-2552
Cincinnati *(G-3315)*
Akers America Inc....G....330 757-4100
Poland *(G-16237)*
Alba Manufacturing Inc....D....513 874-0551
Fairfield *(G-9480)*
Alro Steel Corporation....E....937 253-6121
Dayton *(G-8021)*
AM Warren LLC....G....330 841-2800
Warren *(G-19367)*
American Culvert & Fabg Co....F....740 432-6334
Cambridge *(G-2422)*
Amthor Steel Inc....G....330 759-0200
Youngstown *(G-20845)*
Arcelormittal Cleveland LLC....C....216 429-6000
Cleveland *(G-4725)*
Arcelormittal Cleveland LLC....E....216 429-6000
Cleveland *(G-4726)*
Arcelormittal USA LLC....F....740 375-2299
Marion *(G-12694)*
Arcelormittal USA LLC....D....419 347-2424
Shelby *(G-16979)*
Benjamin Steel Company Inc....E....937 233-1212
Springfield *(G-17368)*
C & R Inc....E....614 497-1130
Groveport *(G-10486)*
Canton Drop Forge Inc....B....330 477-4511
Canton *(G-2608)*
Cohen Brothers Inc....G....513 422-3696
Middletown *(G-13895)*
Community Care On Wheels....F....330 882-5506
Clinton *(G-6385)*
Contractors Steel Company....E....330 425-3050
Twinsburg *(G-18757)*
Csc Ltd....G....330 841-6011
Warren *(G-19391)*
Diversifd OH Vlly Eqpt & Srvcs....F....740 458-9881
Clarington *(G-4567)*
Eastern Automated Piping....G....740 535-8184
Mingo Junction *(G-14208)*
Egypt Structural Steel Proc....E....419 628-2375
Minster *(G-14213)*
Elster Perfection Corporation....D....440 428-1171
Geneva *(G-10218)*
Famous Industries Inc....C....740 397-8842
Mount Vernon *(G-14481)*
Franklin Iron & Metal Corp....C....937 253-8184
Dayton *(G-8206)*
Garden Street Iron & Metal....E....513 853-3700
Cincinnati *(G-3726)*
General Machine & Saw Company....D....740 382-1104
Marion *(G-12704)*
Grenga Machine & Welding....F....330 743-1113
Youngstown *(G-20925)*
Hadronics Inc....D....513 321-9350
Cincinnati *(G-3792)*
Harvard Coil Processing Inc....E....216 883-6366
Cleveland *(G-5379)*
Holgate Metal Fab Inc....F....419 599-2000
Napoleon *(G-14543)*
Humble Construction Co....E....614 888-8960
Columbus *(G-7010)*
International Steel Group....C....330 841-2800
Warren *(G-19411)*
Jck Industries....E....419 433-6277
Huron *(G-11100)*
John Maneely Company....E....724 342-6851
Niles *(G-15019)*
Lapham-Hickey Steel Corp....E....614 443-4881
Columbus *(G-7116)*
Long View Steel Corp....F....419 747-1108
Mansfield *(G-12470)*
Lukjan Metal Products Inc....C....440 599-8127
Conneaut *(G-7654)*
McWane Inc....B....740 622-6651
Coshocton *(G-7739)*
Metals USA Crbn Flat Rlled Inc....D....330 264-8416
Wooster *(G-20623)*
Metals USA Crbn Flat Rlled Inc....D....937 882-6354
Springfield *(G-17446)*
Mid-America Steel Corp....E....800 282-3466
Cleveland *(G-5674)*
Mid-Continent Coal and Coke Co....G....216 283-5700
Cleveland *(G-5675)*
Middletown Tube Works Inc....D....513 727-0080
Middletown *(G-13930)*
Ohio Gratings Inc....B....330 477-6707
Canton *(G-2772)*
Ohio Pickling & Processing LLC....D....419 241-9601
Toledo *(G-18436)*
Ohio Valley Alloy Services Inc....E....740 373-1900
Marietta *(G-12649)*
Pendleton Mold & Machine LLC....G....440 998-0041
Ashtabula *(G-796)*
Pioneer Equipment Company....F....330 857-6340
Dalton *(G-7951)*
Pioneer Pipe Inc....A....740 376-2400
Marietta *(G-12653)*
Precision Laser & Forming....F....419 943-4350
Leipsic *(G-11731)*
Precision Specialty Metals Inc....D....800 944-2255
Worthington *(G-20700)*
Precision Strip Inc....D....937 667-6255
Tipp City *(G-18127)*
Racelite South Coast Inc....F....216 581-4600
Maple Heights *(G-12578)*
Republic Steel....F....330 837-7024
Massillon *(G-13045)*
Republic Steel Inc....E....440 277-2000
Lorain *(G-12117)*
Rti Alloys....G....330 652-9952
Niles *(G-15032)*
Samuel Steel Pickling Company....D....330 963-3777
Twinsburg *(G-18853)*
Schaefer Group Inc....G....419 897-2883
Perrysburg *(G-16004)*
Sedlak....G....330 908-2200
Richfield *(G-16486)*
Sertek LLC....D....614 504-5828
Dublin *(G-8984)*
Shear Service Inc....G....216 341-2700
Cleveland *(G-6049)*
Stainless Specialties Inc....E....440 942-4242
Eastlake *(G-9130)*
Timken Receivables Corporation....G....234 262-3000
North Canton *(G-15128)*
Timkensteel Corporation....B....330 471-7000
Canton *(G-2841)*
Tms International LLC....G....513 425-6462
Middletown *(G-13958)*
Tms International LLC....G....419 747-5500
Mansfield *(G-12532)*
Tms International LLC....G....513 422-4572
Middletown *(G-13959)*
Tms International LLC....F....216 441-9702
Cleveland *(G-6178)*
Tms International Corporation....F....740 223-0091
Marion *(G-12741)*
United States Steel Corp....A....440 240-2500
Lorain *(G-12131)*
Universal Urethane Pdts Inc....D....419 693-7400
Toledo *(G-18585)*
Western Reserve Metals Inc....E....330 448-4092
Masury *(G-13064)*
Witt Industries Inc....D....513 871-5700
Mason *(G-12955)*
Wodin Inc....E....440 439-4222
Cleveland *(G-6320)*
Worthington Industries Inc....C....513 539-9291
Monroe *(G-14282)*
Worthington Industries Inc....A....614 438-3077
Worthington *(G-20712)*
Worthington Steel Company....C....614 438-3210
Worthington *(G-20715)*
Zekelman Industries Inc....C....740 432-2146
Cambridge *(G-2463)*

STEEL, COLD-ROLLED: Flat Bright, From Purchased Hot-Rolled

Clark Grave Vault Company....C....614 294-3761
Columbus *(G-6769)*
Geneva Liberty Steel Ltd....E....330 740-0103
Youngstown *(G-20918)*

STEEL, COLD-ROLLED: Sheet Or Strip, From Own Hot-Rolled

American Processing LLC....E....216 486-4600
Cleveland *(G-4695)*

STEEL, COLD-ROLLED: Sheet Or Strip, From Own Hot-Rolled

Matandy Steel & Metal Pdts LLC .... D 513 844-2277
   Hamilton *(G-10585)*
Steel Technologies LLC .... E 419 523-5199
   Ottawa *(G-15665)*
Superior Forge & Steel Corp .... D 419 222-4412
   Lima *(G-11946)*

STEEL, COLD-ROLLED: Strip NEC, From Purchased Hot-Rolled

Centaur Inc .... G 419 469-8000
   Toledo *(G-18225)*
H S Processing LP .... G 216 641-6995
   Cleveland *(G-5364)*
Heidtman Steel Products Inc .... E 419 691-4646
   Toledo *(G-18330)*
Sandvik Inc .... F 614 438-6579
   Columbus *(G-7420)*
Worthington Industries Inc .... C 614 438-3210
   Worthington *(G-20710)*
Worthington Industries Inc .... C 614 438-3113
   Columbus *(G-7615)*
Worthington Steel Company .... C 216 441-8300
   Cleveland *(G-6328)*

STEEL, COLD-ROLLED: Strip Or Wire

Bekaert Corporation .... C 330 683-5060
   Orrville *(G-15583)*
Worthington Steel Company .... C 614 438-3210
   Worthington *(G-20715)*

STEEL, COLD-ROLLED: Strip, Razor Blade, Purchd Hot-Rld Steel

Clouth Sprenger LLC .... G 937 642-8390
   Marysville *(G-12774)*

STEEL, HOT-ROLLED: Sheet Or Strip

AK Steel Corporation .... B 513 425-4200
   West Chester *(G-19640)*
AK Steel Holding Corporation .... B 513 425-5000
   West Chester *(G-19641)*
Centaur Inc .... G 419 469-8000
   Toledo *(G-18225)*
Heidtman Steel Products Inc .... E 419 691-4646
   Toledo *(G-18330)*
Ohio Steel Sheet & Plate Inc .... E 800 827-2401
   Hubbard *(G-11007)*

STEEL: Cold-Rolled

AK Steel Corporation .... B 740 450-5600
   Zanesville *(G-21095)*
AK Steel Corporation .... A 740 829-2206
   Coshocton *(G-7717)*
Akers America Inc .... G 330 757-4100
   Poland *(G-16237)*
All Ohio Threaded Rod Co Inc .... E 216 426-1800
   Cleveland *(G-4665)*
Allegheny Ludlum LLC .... E 330 875-2244
   Louisville *(G-12151)*
Alro Steel Corporation .... E 937 253-6121
   Dayton *(G-8021)*
Bar Processing Corporation .... D 330 872-0914
   Newton Falls *(G-14985)*
Bcs Metal Prep LLC .... E 440 663-1100
   Solon *(G-17114)*
Benjamin Steel Company Inc .... E 937 233-1212
   Springfield *(G-17368)*
Cincinnati Cold Drawn Inc .... G 513 874-3296
   West Chester *(G-19671)*
Consolidated Metal Pdts Inc .... E 513 251-2624
   Cincinnati *(G-3542)*
Dietrich Industries Inc .... E 614 438-3210
   Worthington *(G-20684)*
Elgin Fastener Group LLC .... E 216 481-4400
   Cleveland *(G-5168)*
Formetal Inc .... F 419 898-2211
   Oak Harbor *(G-15445)*
Independent Steel Company LLC .... E 330 225-7741
   Valley City *(G-19041)*
Lakeway Mfg Inc .... E 419 433-3030
   Huron *(G-11103)*
Lapham-Hickey Steel Corp .... D 419 399-4803
   Paulding *(G-15865)*
LLC Ring Masters .... E 330 832-1511
   Massillon *(G-13014)*
Mid-America Steel Corp .... E 800 282-3466
   Cleveland *(G-5674)*

MSC Walbridge Coatings Inc .... C 419 666-6130
   Walbridge *(G-19297)*
Raco Cutting Inc .... G 937 293-1228
   Moraine *(G-14389)*
Steel Technologies LLC .... D 440 946-8666
   Willoughby *(G-20437)*
Superior Forge & Steel Corp .... D 419 222-4412
   Lima *(G-11946)*
Tecumseh Redevelopment Inc .... G 330 659-9100
   Richfield *(G-16492)*
Western Reserve Metals Inc .... E 330 448-4092
   Masury *(G-13064)*
Worthington Industries Inc .... F 614 438-3190
   Columbus *(G-7616)*
Worthington Industries Lsg LLC .... G 614 438-3210
   Worthington *(G-20713)*

STEEL: Galvanized

Arcelormittal Obetz LLC .... E 614 492-8287
   Columbus *(G-6614)*
Arrowstrip Inc .... E 740 633-2609
   Martins Ferry *(G-12756)*
Columbus Processing Co LLC .... G 614 492-8287
   Columbus *(G-6799)*
Gregory Roll Form Inc .... D 330 477-4800
   Canton *(G-2689)*
Worthington Industries Inc .... D 419 822-2500
   Delta *(G-8780)*

STEERING SYSTEMS & COMPONENTS

American Showa Inc .... A 937 783-4961
   Blanchester *(G-1698)*
Dale Adams Enterprises Inc .... G 330 524-2800
   Twinsburg *(G-18760)*
F&P America Mfg Inc .... B 937 339-0212
   Troy *(G-18655)*
Industrial Steering Pdts Inc .... G 419 636-3300
   Bryan *(G-2290)*
Yamada North America Inc .... B 937 462-7111
   South Charleston *(G-17275)*

STENCILS

Stencilsmith LLC .... G 614 876-4350
   Hilliard *(G-10866)*

STEREOGRAPHS: Photographic Message Svcs

Octsys Security Corp .... G 614 470-4510
   Columbus *(G-7239)*

STITCHING SVCS

Wizard Graphics Inc .... G 419 354-3098
   Bowling Green *(G-2006)*

STITCHING SVCS: Custom

B Richardson Inc .... F 330 724-2122
   Akron *(G-76)*
Pelz Lettering Inc .... G 419 625-3567
   Sandusky *(G-16838)*

STONE: Cast Concrete

Rock Decor Company .... G 330 857-7625
   Orrville *(G-15615)*

STONE: Dimension, NEC

Connolly Construction Co Inc .... G 937 644-8831
   Marysville *(G-12775)*
Glens Bedford Garden Center .... G 330 305-1971
   North Canton *(G-15087)*
Heritage Marble of Ohio Inc .... E 614 436-1464
   Columbus *(G-6990)*
Jim Nier Construction Inc .... F 740 289-2629
   Piketon *(G-16071)*
North Hill Marble & Granite Co .... F 330 253-2179
   Akron *(G-301)*
Ohio Beauty Inc .... G 330 644-2241
   Akron *(G-305)*

STONE: Quarrying & Processing, Own Stone Prdts

Briar Hill Stone Company .... E 330 377-5100
   Glenmont *(G-10274)*
Cardinal Aggregate .... F 419 872-4380
   Perrysburg *(G-15931)*

Custar Stone Co .... F 419 669-4327
   Napoleon *(G-14536)*
D J Decorative Stone Inc .... G 937 848-6462
   Bellbrook *(G-1491)*
Earth Anatomy Fabrication LLC .... G 740 244-5316
   Norton *(G-15366)*
Sims-Lohman Inc .... G 330 456-8408
   North Canton *(G-15119)*
Waller Brothers Stone Company .... E 740 858-1948
   Mc Dermott *(G-13195)*

STONES, SYNTHETIC: Gem Stone & Indl Use

Cultured Marble Inc .... G 330 549-2282
   North Lima *(G-15169)*
Southwest Greens Ohio LLC .... F 614 389-6042
   Columbus *(G-7465)*

STONEWARE PRDTS: Pottery

Beaumont Brothers Stoneware .... G 740 982-0055
   Crooksville *(G-7815)*
Clay Burley Products Co .... E 740 452-3633
   Roseville *(G-16576)*
Clay Burley Products Co .... E 740 697-0221
   Roseville *(G-16577)*
Stoneware Palace Ltd .... G 614 529-6974
   Columbus *(G-7492)*

STORE FIXTURES, EXC REFRIGERATED: Wholesalers

Bobs Custom Str Interiors LLC .... G 567 316-7490
   Toledo *(G-18209)*
Starks Plastics LLC .... E 513 541-4591
   Cincinnati *(G-4374)*

STORE FIXTURES: Exc Wood

Bobs Custom Str Interiors LLC .... G 567 316-7490
   Toledo *(G-18209)*
Cap & Associates Incorporated .... C 614 863-3363
   Columbus *(G-6728)*
Dell Fixtures Inc .... E 614 449-1750
   Columbus *(G-6859)*
Heat Seal LLC .... C 216 341-2022
   Cleveland *(G-5386)*
Richard B Linneman .... E 513 922-5537
   Cincinnati *(G-4266)*

STORE FIXTURES: Wood

Allied Plastic Co Inc .... G 419 389-1688
   Toledo *(G-18165)*
Artistic Finishes Inc .... F 440 951-7850
   Willoughby *(G-20281)*
Cap & Associates Incorporated .... C 614 863-3363
   Columbus *(G-6728)*
CIP International Inc .... D 513 874-9925
   West Chester *(G-19675)*
Custom Surroundings Inc .... F 330 483-9020
   Valley City *(G-19035)*
Display Dynamics Inc .... F 937 832-2830
   Englewood *(G-9355)*
Leiden Cabinet Company LLC .... C 330 425-8555
   Twinsburg *(G-18806)*
Modern Designs Inc .... G 330 644-1771
   Coventry Township *(G-7773)*
Norton Industries Inc .... E 888 357-2345
   Lakewood *(G-11532)*
Prestige Store Interiors Inc .... D 419 476-2106
   Toledo *(G-18480)*
Richard B Linneman .... E 513 922-5537
   Cincinnati *(G-4266)*
Rivercity Woodworking Inc .... G 513 860-1900
   West Chester *(G-19783)*

STORE FRONTS: Prefabricated, Metal

Fab Tech Inc .... G 330 926-9556
   Brecksville *(G-2036)*

STORES: Auto & Home Supply

Brp Inc .... G 440 988-4398
   Amherst *(G-556)*
Doug Marine Motors Inc .... E 740 335-3700
   Wshngtn CT Hs *(G-20724)*
Knippen Chrysler Dodge Jeep .... E 419 695-4976
   Delphos *(G-8746)*
Pattons Truck & Heavy Eqp Svc .... F 740 385-4067
   Logan *(G-12039)*

PRODUCT SECTION

SURGICAL APPLIANCES & SPLYS

Public Safety Concepts LLC .... G 614 733-0200
  Plain City *(G-16208)*
Support Svc LLC .... G 419 617-0660
  Lexington *(G-11808)*
York Fabrication & Machine .... G 419 483-6275
  Bellevue *(G-1554)*

STORES: Drapery & Upholstery

M C L Window Coverings Inc .... G 513 868-6000
  Fairfield Township *(G-9584)*

STRAINERS: Line, Piping Systems

Insulpro Inc .... F 614 262-3768
  Columbus *(G-7039)*
Pipelines Inc .... G 330 448-0000
  Masury *(G-13061)*

STRAPPING

Alacriant Inc .... D 330 562-7191
  Streetsboro *(G-17658)*
Alacriant Inc .... E 330 562-7191
  Streetsboro *(G-17659)*
Drawn Metals Corp .... F 937 433-6151
  Dayton *(G-8168)*
North Shore Strapping Inc .... D 216 661-5200
  Brooklyn Heights *(G-2128)*
Shipping Room Products Inc .... G 216 531-4422
  Cleveland *(G-6059)*
Voss Industries LLC .... C 216 771-7655
  Cleveland *(G-6273)*
Warren Steel Specialties Corp .... G 330 399-8360
  Warren *(G-19461)*
Youngstown Specialty Mtls Inc .... G 330 259-1110
  Youngstown *(G-21082)*

STRAPS: Bindings, Textile

Db Rediheat Inc .... E 216 361-0530
  Cleveland *(G-5075)*
Ransom & Randolph .... G 419 794-1210
  Maumee *(G-13141)*

STRAPS: Braids, Textile

Amfm Inc .... E 440 953-4545
  Willoughby *(G-20272)*
Vacuflo Factory .... G 330 875-2450
  Louisville *(G-12170)*

STRAPS: Spindle Banding

Grove Engineered Products Inc .... G 419 659-5939
  Columbus Grove *(G-7635)*

STRAPS: Webbing, Woven

Champion Webbing Company Inc .... G 330 920-1007
  Cuyahoga Falls *(G-7848)*

STRUCTURAL SUPPORT & BUILDING MATERIAL: Concrete

Advantic LLC .... G 937 490-4712
  Dayton *(G-8010)*
High Concrete Group LLC .... C 937 748-2412
  Springboro *(G-17330)*
Jet Stream International Inc .... E 330 505-9988
  Niles *(G-15018)*

STUDIOS: Artist

Dimensional Works of Art .... G 330 657-2681
  Peninsula *(G-15891)*

STUDIOS: Artists & Artists' Studios

4w Services .... F 614 554-5427
  Hebron *(G-10736)*
B&D Truck Parts Sls & Svcs LLC .... G 419 701-7041
  Fostoria *(G-9835)*
Terewell Inc .... G 216 334-6897
  Cleveland *(G-6160)*

STUDS & JOISTS: Sheet Metal

Clarkwestern Dietrich Building .... F 330 372-5564
  Warren *(G-19384)*
Clarkwestern Dietrich Building .... C 513 870-1100
  West Chester *(G-19676)*
Clarkwestern Dietrich Building .... F 513 870-1100
  West Chester *(G-19677)*

J N Linrose Mfg LLC .... G 513 867-5500
  Hamilton *(G-10574)*
Matandy Steel & Metal Pdts LLC .... D 513 844-2277
  Hamilton *(G-10585)*

SUBDIVIDERS & DEVELOPERS: Real Property, Cemetery Lots Only

Patriot Holdings Unlimited LLC .... G 740 574-2112
  Wheelersburg *(G-20183)*

SUBMARINE BUILDING & REPAIR

Wadsworth Excavating Inc .... G 419 898-0771
  Oak Harbor *(G-15448)*

SUBPRESSES, METALWORKING

Central Machinery Company LLC .... F 740 387-1289
  Marion *(G-12699)*

SUGAR SUBSTITUTES: Organic

Sugar Foods Corporation .... G 513 336-9748
  Mason *(G-12943)*

SUNDRIES & RELATED PRDTS: Medical & Laboratory, Rubber

Abeon Medical Corporation .... G 440 262-6000
  Brecksville *(G-2018)*
Elastostar Rubber Corp .... E 614 841-4400
  Columbus *(G-6888)*
Fenner Dunlop Port Clinton Inc .... C 419 635-2191
  Port Clinton *(G-16247)*
Gdc Inc .... F 574 533-3128
  Wooster *(G-20596)*
Guardian Manufacturing Co LLC .... E 419 933-2711
  Willard *(G-20240)*
Hygenic Acquisition Co .... G 330 633-8460
  Akron *(G-212)*
Hygenic Corporation .... C 330 633-8460
  Akron *(G-213)*
Newell Brands Inc .... F 330 733-1184
  Kent *(G-11358)*
Sunsong North America Inc .... G 919 365-3825
  Moraine *(G-14397)*
Vulcan International Corp .... G 513 621-2850
  Cincinnati *(G-4484)*

SUNROOFS: Motor Vehicle

CR Laurence Co Inc .... G 440 248-0003
  Cleveland *(G-5036)*

SUNROOMS: Prefabricated Metal

Better Living Sunrooms NW Ohio .... G 419 692-4526
  Delphos *(G-8737)*

SUPERMARKETS & OTHER GROCERY STORES

Hershbergers Dutch Market LLP .... E 740 489-5322
  Old Washington *(G-15526)*
Ingles Logging .... G 740 379-2909
  Patriot *(G-15851)*
Nestle Prepared Foods Company .... A 440 248-3600
  Solon *(G-17203)*
Nestle Prepared Foods Company .... D 440 349-5757
  Solon *(G-17204)*

SURFACE ACTIVE AGENTS

Pilot Chemical Corp .... F 513 326-0600
  Cincinnati *(G-4161)*

SURFACE ACTIVE AGENTS: Emulsifiers, Exc Food & Pharmaceuticl

Berghausen Corporation .... E 513 541-5631
  Cincinnati *(G-3389)*

SURGICAL & MEDICAL INSTRUMENTS WHOLESALERS

Ashton Pumpmatic Inc .... G 937 424-1380
  Dayton *(G-8039)*
Axon Medical LLC .... E 216 276-0262
  Medina *(G-13226)*
Rultract Inc .... G 216 524-2990
  Cleveland *(G-6017)*

Ultra-Met Company .... G 937 653-7133
  Urbana *(G-19018)*

SURGICAL APPLIANCES & SPLYS

Isomedix Inc .... G 440 354-2600
  Mentor *(G-13476)*
Marlen Manufacturing & Dev Co .... G 216 292-7060
  Bedford *(G-1424)*
Steris Corporation .... G 440 354-2600
  Mentor *(G-13589)*
Steris Corporation .... C 440 354-2600
  Mentor *(G-13591)*
Steris Corporation .... F 440 354-2600
  Mentor *(G-13593)*
Surgical Appliance Inds Inc .... C 513 271-4594
  Cincinnati *(G-4401)*

SURGICAL APPLIANCES & SPLYS

Axon Medical LLC .... E 216 276-0262
  Medina *(G-13226)*
Bulk Molding Compounds Inc .... D 419 874-7941
  Perrysburg *(G-15926)*
Cardinal Health Inc .... G 614 553-3830
  Dublin *(G-8893)*
Cardinal Health Inc .... A 614 757-5000
  Dublin *(G-8894)*
Cordis Corporation .... A 614 757-5000
  Dublin *(G-8903)*
Dayton Artificial Limb Clinic .... G 937 836-1464
  Englewood *(G-9354)*
Deco Tools Inc .... E 419 476-9321
  Toledo *(G-18256)*
Dentronix Inc .... E 330 916-7300
  Cuyahoga Falls *(G-7860)*
Dj International Inc .... G 440 260-7593
  Berea *(G-1602)*
Doling & Associates Dental Lab .... E 937 254-0075
  Dayton *(G-8164)*
Ethicon Inc .... C 513 786-7000
  Blue Ash *(G-1766)*
Florida Invacare Holdings LLC .... G 800 333-6900
  Elyria *(G-9261)*
Foot Logic Inc .... G 330 699-0123
  Uniontown *(G-18919)*
Francisco Jaume .... G 740 622-1200
  Coshocton *(G-7734)*
Frohock-Stewart Inc .... E 440 329-6000
  North Ridgeville *(G-15226)*
Geauga Rhabilitation Engrg Inc .... F 216 536-0826
  Chardon *(G-3114)*
Gelok International Corp .... F 419 352-1482
  Dunbridge *(G-9015)*
Gendron Wheel LLC .... G 419 445-6060
  Archbold *(G-649)*
Guardian Manufacturing Co LLC .... E 419 933-2711
  Willard *(G-20240)*
Hanger Prsthetcs & Ortho Inc .... G 440 605-0232
  Mayfield Heights *(G-13165)*
Hanger Prsthetcs & Ortho Inc .... G 513 421-5653
  Cincinnati *(G-3797)*
Hanger Prsthetcs & Ortho Inc .... G 440 892-6665
  Westlake *(G-20121)*
Hanger Prsthetcs & Ortho Inc .... G 937 325-5404
  Springfield *(G-17411)*
Hanger Prsthetcs & Ortho Inc .... F 937 643-1557
  Moraine *(G-14358)*
Hanger Prsthetcs & Ortho Inc .... G 330 821-4918
  Canton *(G-2692)*
Hanger Prsthetcs & Ortho Inc .... F 614 481-8338
  Columbus *(G-6979)*
Hanger Prsthetcs & Ortho Inc .... G 740 354-4775
  Portsmouth *(G-16285)*
Healthtech Products .... G 419 271-1761
  Elyria *(G-9265)*
Integrated Med Solutions Inc .... D 440 269-6984
  Mentor *(G-13473)*
Invacare Canadian Holdings Inc .... G 440 329-6000
  Elyria *(G-9270)*
Invacare Canadian Holdings LLC .... G 440 329-6000
  Elyria *(G-9271)*
Invacare Corporation .... F 440 329-6000
  North Ridgeville *(G-15231)*
Invacare Corporation (tw) .... E 440 329-6000
  North Ridgeville *(G-15232)*
Invacare Holdings LLC .... G 440 329-6000
  Elyria *(G-9275)*
Invacare Respiratory Corp .... E 440 329-6000
  Elyria *(G-9278)*
Jones Metal Products Company .... C 740 545-6381
  West Lafayette *(G-19931)*

Employee Codes: A=Over 500 employees, B=251-500
C=101-250, D=51-100, E=20-50, F=10-19, G=3-9

2019 Harris Ohio Industrial Directory

SURGICAL APPLIANCES & SPLYS

Jones Metal Products Company .... E 740 545-6341
  West Lafayette *(G-19932)*
Kempf Surgical Appliances Inc .... E 513 984-5758
  Montgomery *(G-14295)*
Leimkuehler Inc .... E 440 899-7842
  Cleveland *(G-5573)*
Marlen Manufacturing & Dev Co .... E 216 292-7546
  Bedford *(G-1425)*
Meridian Industries Inc .... D 330 673-1011
  Kent *(G-11351)*
New Wave Prosthetics Inc .... G 614 782-2361
  Grove City *(G-10451)*
Optimus LLC .... E 513 918-2320
  Cincinnati *(G-4116)*
Orthohlix Surgical Designs Inc .... G 330 869-9562
  Akron *(G-312)*
Pcp Champion .... G 937 392-4301
  Ripley *(G-16516)*
Philips Medical Systems Clevel .... B 440 247-2652
  Cleveland *(G-5871)*
S K M L Inc .... G 330 220-7565
  Valley City *(G-19059)*
Schaerer Medical Usa Inc .... F 513 561-2241
  Cincinnati *(G-4305)*
Smith & Nephew Inc .... E 513 821-5888
  Cincinnati *(G-4345)*
Smith & Nephew Inc .... G 614 793-0581
  Dublin *(G-8986)*
Surgical Appliance Inds Inc .... E 937 392-4301
  Ripley *(G-16518)*
Thomas Products Co Inc .... E 513 756-9009
  Cincinnati *(G-4420)*
Tilt 15 Inc .... D 330 239-4192
  Sharon Center *(G-16955)*
Tranzonic Companies .... B 216 535-4300
  Richmond Heights *(G-16507)*
Wright Solutions LLC .... G 937 938-8745
  Dayton *(G-8600)*

SURGICAL EQPT: See Also Instruments

3M Company .... B 513 248-1749
  Milford *(G-13991)*
Atricure Inc .... C 513 755-4100
  Mason *(G-12830)*
Ethicon Endo-Surgery Inc .... A 513 337-7000
  Blue Ash *(G-1765)*
Ethicon US LLC .... E 513 337-7000
  Blue Ash *(G-1767)*
Gqi Inc .... G 330 830-9805
  Massillon *(G-12989)*
Heartbeat Company LLC .... G 614 423-5646
  Westerville *(G-20057)*
Mill-Rose Company .... C 440 255-9171
  Mentor *(G-13520)*
Rsb Spine LLC .... F 216 241-2804
  Cleveland *(G-6014)*
Rultract Inc .... G 216 524-2990
  Cleveland *(G-6017)*
Scottcare Corporation .... E 216 362-0550
  Cleveland *(G-6041)*
United States Endoscopy .... G 440 639-4494
  Mentor *(G-13619)*

SURGICAL IMPLANTS

Bahler Medical Inc .... E 614 873-7600
  Plain City *(G-16174)*
Caro Medical LLC .... G 937 604-8600
  Springboro *(G-17324)*
Hammill Manufacturing Co .... D 419 476-0789
  Maumee *(G-13115)*
Mosher Medical Inc .... G 330 668-2252
  Akron *(G-289)*
Osteosymbionics LLC .... F 216 881-8500
  Cleveland *(G-5824)*
Spinal Balance Inc .... G 419 530-5935
  Swanton *(G-17922)*

SURVEYING & MAPPING: Land Parcels

Barr Engineering Incorporated .... E 614 714-0299
  Columbus *(G-6650)*
Dlz Ohio Inc .... C 614 888-0040
  Columbus *(G-6871)*

SURVEYING INSTRUMENTS WHOLESALERS

Zaenkert Surveying Essentials .... G 513 738-2917
  Okeana *(G-15522)*

SUSPENSION SYSTEMS: Acoustical, Metal

One Wish LLC .... F 800 505-6883
  Beachwood *(G-1259)*
Wall Technology Inc .... E 715 532-5548
  Toledo *(G-18594)*

SVC ESTABLISH EQPT, WHOLESALE: Carpet/Rug Clean Eqpt & Sply

Jeff Pendergrass .... G 513 575-1226
  Milford *(G-14021)*

SVC ESTABLISHMENT EQPT & SPLYS WHOLESALERS

AIN Industries Inc .... G 440 781-0950
  Cleveland *(G-4643)*
Friends Service Co Inc .... F 800 427-1704
  Dayton *(G-8208)*
Friends Service Co Inc .... G 800 427-1704
  Kent *(G-11322)*
Vandalia Massage Therapy .... G 937 890-8660
  Vandalia *(G-19149)*

SVC ESTABLISHMENT EQPT, WHOL: Cleaning & Maint Eqpt & Splys

Tranzonic Companies .... C 216 535-4300
  Richmond Heights *(G-16506)*

SVC ESTABLISHMENT EQPT, WHOL: Concrete Burial Vaults & Boxes

Baxter Burial Vault Service .... E 513 641-1010
  Cincinnati *(G-3382)*
Bell Burial Vault Co .... G 513 896-9044
  Hamilton *(G-10539)*
Shaw Wilbert Vaults LLC .... G 740 498-7438
  Newcomerstown *(G-14982)*

SVC ESTABLISHMENT EQPT, WHOLESALE: Beauty Parlor Eqpt & Sply

Beauty Systems Group LLC .... G 740 456-5434
  New Boston *(G-14646)*
Sally Beauty Supply LLC .... G 330 823-7476
  Alliance *(G-497)*

SVC ESTABLISHMENT EQPT, WHOLESALE: Firefighting Eqpt

A-1 Sprinkler Company Inc .... D 937 859-6198
  Miamisburg *(G-13636)*
Action Coupling & Eqp Inc .... D 330 279-4242
  Holmesville *(G-10972)*
Antram Fire Equipment .... G 330 525-7171
  North Georgetown *(G-15139)*
Fire Safety Services Inc .... F 937 686-2000
  Huntsville *(G-11086)*
Merrick Manufacturing II LLC .... G 937 222-7164
  Dayton *(G-8341)*
Sutphen Corporation .... C 800 726-7030
  Dublin *(G-8999)*
United Fire Apparatus Corp .... G 419 645-4083
  Cridersville *(G-7813)*
Warren Fire Equipment Inc .... G 937 866-8918
  Miamisburg *(G-13738)*

SVC ESTABLISHMENT EQPT, WHOLESALE: Restaurant Splys

Martin-Brower Company LLC .... B 513 773-2301
  West Chester *(G-19741)*
Wasserstrom Company .... B 614 228-6525
  Columbus *(G-7591)*

SVC ESTABLISHMENT EQPT, WHOLESALE: Shredders, Indl & Comm

Cummins - Allison Corp .... G 440 824-5050
  Cleveland *(G-5042)*

SWEEPING COMPOUNDS

Nwp Manufacturing Inc .... F 419 894-6871
  Waldo *(G-19303)*

SWIMMING POOL ACCESS: Leaf Skimmers Or Pool Rakes

Spa Pool Covers Inc .... G 440 235-9981
  North Royalton *(G-15302)*

SWIMMING POOL EQPT: Filters & Water Conditioning Systems

Baleco International Inc .... E 513 353-3000
  North Bend *(G-15050)*
Clean Water Conditioning .... G 614 475-4532
  Columbus *(G-6771)*

SWIMMING POOLS, EQPT & SPLYS: Wholesalers

Baleco International Inc .... E 513 353-3000
  North Bend *(G-15050)*
Bradley Enterprises Inc .... G 330 875-1444
  Louisville *(G-12153)*
Mc Alarney Pool Spas and BiIld .... E 740 373-6698
  Marietta *(G-12646)*

SWITCHBOARDS & PARTS: Power

Vacuum Electric Switch Co Inc .... G 330 374-5156
  Akron *(G-423)*

SWITCHES

Saia-Burgess Lcc .... D 937 898-3621
  Vandalia *(G-19144)*

SWITCHES: Electric Power

Temple Israel .... G 330 762-8617
  Akron *(G-399)*
Wes-Garde Components Group Inc .... G 614 885-0319
  Westerville *(G-20081)*

SWITCHES: Electric Power, Exc Snap, Push Button, Etc

Lake Shore Electric Corp .... E 440 232-0200
  Bedford *(G-1422)*

SWITCHES: Electronic

Black Box Corporation .... F 614 825-7400
  Lewis Center *(G-11751)*
Don-Ell Corporation .... E 419 841-7114
  Sylvania *(G-17936)*
Hall Company .... E 937 652-1376
  Urbana *(G-18992)*
Quality Switch Inc .... E 330 872-5707
  Newton Falls *(G-14991)*
Specialty Switch Co .... F 330 427-3000
  Youngstown *(G-21037)*

SWITCHES: Electronic Applications

Contact Industries Inc .... E 419 884-9788
  Lexington *(G-11804)*
Twinsource LLC .... F 440 248-6800
  Solon *(G-17256)*

SWITCHES: Flow Actuated, Electrical

SCC Instruments .... G 513 856-8444
  Hamilton *(G-10602)*

SWITCHES: Knife, Electric

Filnor Inc .... F 330 821-7667
  Alliance *(G-467)*

SWITCHES: Thermostatic

Great Lakes Management Inc .... E 216 883-6500
  Cleveland *(G-5349)*

SWITCHES: Time, Electrical Switchgear Apparatus

All Pack Services LLC .... F 614 935-0964
  Grove City *(G-10413)*

SWITCHGEAR & SWITCHBOARD APPARATUS

Asco Power Technologies LP .... C 216 573-7600
  Cleveland *(G-4744)*

Asco Power Technologies LP .... E 216 573-7600
Cleveland *(G-4745)*
Bud Industries Inc .... G 440 946-3200
Willoughby *(G-20289)*
CDI Industries Inc .... E 440 243-1100
Cleveland *(G-4895)*
Delta Systems Inc .... C 330 626-2811
Streetsboro *(G-17671)*
Emerson Network Power .... G 614 841-8054
Ironton *(G-11164)*
Empire Power Systems Co .... G 440 796-4401
Madison *(G-12349)*
Fabriweld Corporation .... G 419 668-3358
Norwalk *(G-15393)*
Flood Heliarc Inc .... F 614 835-3929
Groveport *(G-10489)*
General Electric Company .... D 216 883-1000
Cleveland *(G-5306)*
Ida Controls .... G 440 785-8457
Willoughby *(G-20341)*
Mercury Iron and Steel Co .... F 440 349-1500
Solon *(G-17190)*
Pacs Switchgear LLC .... E 740 397-5021
Mount Vernon *(G-14498)*
Precision Switching Inc .... G 800 800-8143
Mansfield *(G-12502)*
Roemer Industries Inc .... D 330 448-2000
Masury *(G-13062)*
Schneider Electric Usa Inc .... C 513 755-5503
Liberty Township *(G-11819)*
Schneider Electric Usa Inc .... D 513 755-5000
West Chester *(G-19792)*
Schneider Electric Usa Inc .... C 513 755-5501
Sharonville *(G-16959)*
Siemens Industry Inc .... E 419 499-4616
Milan *(G-13989)*
Siemens Industry Inc .... D 937 593-6010
Bellefontaine *(G-1525)*
Spb Global LLC .... G 419 931-6559
Perrysburg *(G-16007)*
Technology Products Inc .... G 937 652-3412
Urbana *(G-19015)*
Toledo Transducers Inc .... E 419 724-4170
Holland *(G-10962)*

SWITCHGEAR & SWITCHGEAR ACCESS, NEC

Ideal Electric Power Co .... F 419 522-3611
Mansfield *(G-12460)*

SWITCHING EQPT: Radio & Television Communications

Pole/Zero Acquisition Inc .... C 513 870-9060
West Chester *(G-19762)*

SYNAGOGUES

Temple Israel .... G 330 762-8617
Akron *(G-399)*

SYNCHROS

Ohio Synchro Swim Club .... G 614 319-4667
Hilliard *(G-10848)*

SYNTHETIC RESIN FINISHED PRDTS, NEC

Amrex Inc .... G 330 678-7050
Kent *(G-11295)*
Orbis Corporation .... B 937 652-1361
Urbana *(G-19006)*
Orbis Corporation .... C 440 974-3857
Mentor *(G-13535)*
Printing 3d Parts Inc .... G 330 759-9099
Youngstown *(G-21006)*
Reactive Resin Products Co .... E 419 666-6119
Perrysburg *(G-16003)*

SYRUPS, DRINK

Central Coca-Cola Btlg Co Inc .... C 419 476-6622
Toledo *(G-18226)*
Dominion Liquid Tech LLC .... E 513 272-2824
Cincinnati *(G-3600)*
Innovtive Cnfction Sltions LLC .... G 440 835-8001
Westlake *(G-20126)*
Slush Puppie .... D 513 771-0940
West Chester *(G-19899)*

SYRUPS, FLAVORING, EXC DRINK

Cleveland Syrup Corp .... G 330 963-1900
Twinsburg *(G-18755)*

SYRUPS: Pharmaceutical

Nostrum Laboratories Inc .... E 419 636-1168
Bryan *(G-2299)*

SYSTEMS ENGINEERING: Computer Related

Leidos Inc .... D 937 431-2270
Beavercreek *(G-1326)*
North Coast Security Group LLC .... G 614 887-7255
Columbus *(G-7226)*

SYSTEMS INTEGRATION SVCS

Advanced Prgrm Resources Inc .... E 614 761-9994
Dublin *(G-8874)*
Creative Microsystems Inc .... D 937 836-4499
Englewood *(G-9353)*
Elynx Holdings LLC .... G 513 612-5969
Cincinnati *(G-3633)*
Generic Systems Inc .... F 419 841-8460
Holland *(G-10932)*
Kc Robotics Inc .... F 513 860-4442
West Chester *(G-19729)*
Smartronix Inc .... F 216 378-3300
Northfield *(G-15325)*
Splicenet Inc .... G 513 563-3533
West Chester *(G-19901)*
Systemax Manufacturing Inc .... C 937 368-2300
Dayton *(G-8533)*

SYSTEMS INTEGRATION SVCS: Local Area Network

Juniper Networks Inc .... D 614 932-1432
Dublin *(G-8934)*
Town Cntry Technical Svcs Inc .... F 614 866-7700
Reynoldsburg *(G-16457)*

SYSTEMS INTEGRATION SVCS: Office Computer Automation

Innovative Integrations Inc .... G 216 533-5353
Mesopotamia *(G-13633)*
Westmount Technology Inc .... G 216 328-2011
Independence *(G-11157)*

SYSTEMS SOFTWARE DEVELOPMENT SVCS

CHI Corporation .... F 440 498-2300
Cleveland *(G-4920)*
Cincinnati Ctrl Dynamics Inc .... G 513 242-7300
Cincinnati *(G-3489)*
Deemsys Inc .... D 614 322-9928
Gahanna *(G-10079)*
Drb Systems LLC .... C 330 645-3299
Akron *(G-147)*
Image Integrations Systems .... F 419 872-0003
Perrysburg *(G-15964)*
List Media Inc .... G 330 995-0864
Chagrin Falls *(G-3023)*
Medforall LLC .... G 614 947-0791
Columbus *(G-7171)*
Online Mega Sellers Corp .... D 888 384-6468
Toledo *(G-18439)*
Satelytics Inc .... G 419 419-5380
Toledo *(G-18512)*

TABLE OR COUNTERTOPS, PLASTIC LAMINATED

Archer Counter Design Inc .... G 513 396-7526
Cincinnati *(G-3354)*
E J Skok Industries .... E 216 292-7533
Bedford *(G-1403)*
Form-A-Top Products Inc .... G 440 779-9452
North Olmsted *(G-15189)*
Formware Inc .... G 614 231-9387
Columbus *(G-6930)*
Helmart Company Inc .... G 513 941-3095
Cincinnati *(G-3806)*
Scio Laminated Products Inc .... E 740 945-1321
Scio *(G-16879)*
Shur Fit Distributors Inc .... E 937 746-0567
Franklin *(G-9919)*

Summit Custom Cabinets .... G 740 345-1734
Newark *(G-14927)*
Tenkotte Tops Inc .... G 513 738-7300
Harrison *(G-10677)*
Tri-Co Industries .... G 740 927-1928
Pataskala *(G-15847)*
Wilsonart LLC .... E 614 876-1515
Columbus *(G-7605)*
Youngstown Curve Form Inc .... F 330 744-3028
Youngstown *(G-21075)*

TABLETS & PADS: Newsprint, Made From Purchased Materials

Steel City Corporation .... E 330 792-7663
Ashland *(G-749)*

TABLETS: Bronze Or Other Metal

Rise Holdings LLC .... F 440 946-9646
Willoughby *(G-20422)*

TABLEWARE OR KITCHEN ARTICLES: Commercial, Fine Earthenware

Anchor Hocking Glass Company .... G 740 681-6025
Lancaster *(G-11544)*
Us Inc .... G 513 791-1162
Blue Ash *(G-1863)*
West Ohio Tool & Mfg LLC .... G 419 678-4745
Saint Henry *(G-16671)*

TABLEWARE: Vitreous China

Libbey Inc .... C 419 325-2100
Toledo *(G-18385)*

TACKS: Steel, Wire Or Cut

Robertson Incorporated .... G 937 323-3747
Springfield *(G-17488)*

TAGS & LABELS: Paper

Century Marketing Corporation .... C 419 354-2591
Bowling Green *(G-1961)*
Federal Barcode Label Systems .... G 440 748-8060
North Ridgeville *(G-15224)*
Hooven - Dayton Corp .... D 937 233-4473
Miamisburg *(G-13677)*
Kay Toledo Tag Inc .... D 419 729-5479
Toledo *(G-18363)*
Kennedy Group Incorporated .... D 440 951-7660
Willoughby *(G-20352)*
Orbytel Print and Packg Inc .... G 216 267-8734
Cleveland *(G-5818)*
Warren Printing & Off Pdts Inc .... F 419 523-3635
Ottawa *(G-15671)*

TAGS: Paper, Blank, Made From Purchased Paper

Paxar Corporation .... F 937 681-4541
Dayton *(G-8418)*

TANK & BOILER CLEANING SVCS

Rbm Environmental and Cnstr .... E 419 693-5840
Oregon *(G-15566)*

TANK REPAIR & CLEANING SVCS

Amko Service Company .... E 330 364-8857
Midvale *(G-13975)*
Kars Ohio LLC .... G 614 655-1099
Pataskala *(G-15834)*
National Welding & Tanker Repr .... G 614 875-3399
Grove City *(G-10449)*
Ohio Hydraulics Inc .... E 513 771-2590
Cincinnati *(G-4103)*
Sabco Industries Inc .... E 419 531-5347
Toledo *(G-18510)*

TANK REPAIR SVCS

Corrotec Inc .... E 937 325-3585
Springfield *(G-17379)*
Frontier Tank Center Inc .... E 330 659-3888
Richfield *(G-16471)*

TANKS & OTHER TRACKED VEHICLE CMPNTS

American Apex Corporation ....F 614 652-2000
  Plain City *(G-16171)*
Joint Systems Mfg Ctr ....G 419 221-9580
  Lima *(G-11882)*
Sugartree Square Mercantile ....G 740 345-3882
  Newark *(G-14926)*
Tencate Advanced Armor USA Inc ....D 740 928-0326
  Hebron *(G-10765)*
Tessec Manufacturing Svcs LLC ......E 937 985-3552
  Dayton *(G-8553)*
US Yachiyo Inc ....C 740 375-4687
  Marion *(G-12746)*
Weldon Pump Acquition LLC ....E 440 232-2282
  Oakwood Village *(G-15489)*

TANKS: Concrete

Star Forming Manufacturing LL ......C 330 740-8300
  Youngstown *(G-21039)*

TANKS: Cryogenic, Metal

Amko Service Company ....E 330 364-8857
  Midvale *(G-13975)*
Eleet Cryogenics Inc ....E 330 874-4009
  Bolivar *(G-1913)*
Fiba Technologies Inc ....D 330 602-7300
  Midvale *(G-13977)*

TANKS: For Tank Trucks, Metal Plate

Elliott Machine Works Inc ....E 419 468-4709
  Galion *(G-10137)*
Ironman Metalworks LLC ....G 614 907-6629
  Groveport *(G-10496)*
Jacp Inc ....G 513 353-3660
  Miamitown *(G-13747)*
Liquid Luggers LLC ....E 330 426-2538
  East Palestine *(G-9080)*
Macleod Inc ....G 513 771-9560
  Miamitown *(G-13748)*

TANKS: Fuel, Including Oil & Gas, Metal Plate

Convault of Ohio Inc ....G 614 252-8422
  Columbus *(G-6816)*
Fabstar Tanks Inc ....F 419 587-3639
  Grover Hill *(G-10518)*
North High Marathon ....G 937 444-1894
  Mount Orab *(G-14448)*

TANKS: Lined, Metal

Hamilton Tanks LLC ....F 614 445-8446
  Columbus *(G-6977)*
Modern Welding Co Ohio Inc ....E 740 344-9425
  Newark *(G-14898)*

TANKS: Military, Including Factory Rebuilding

General Dynamics Land ....B 419 221-7000
  Lima *(G-11869)*
United States Dept of Army ....D 419 221-9500
  Lima *(G-11955)*

TANKS: Plastic & Fiberglass

AB Plastics Inc ....G 513 576-6333
  Milford *(G-13992)*
Aco Polymer Products Inc ....E 440 285-7000
  Mentor *(G-13373)*
Alliance Equipment Company Inc ....F 330 821-2291
  Alliance *(G-453)*
Cpca Manufacturing LLC ....D 937 723-9031
  Dayton *(G-8109)*
Industrial Container Svcs LLC ....E 513 921-2056
  Cincinnati *(G-3843)*
Kar-Del Plastics Inc ....G 419 289-9739
  Ashland *(G-715)*
Norwesco Inc ....F 740 335-6236
  Wshngtn CT Hs *(G-20734)*
Norwesco Inc ....E 740 654-6402
  Lancaster *(G-11592)*
R L Industries Inc ....D 513 874-2800
  West Chester *(G-19777)*
RTS Companies (us) Inc ....E 440 275-3077
  Austinburg *(G-925)*

TANKS: Standard Or Custom Fabricated, Metal Plate

Aetna Plastics Corp ....G 330 274-2855
  Mantua *(G-12541)*
Buckeye Fabricating Co ....E 937 746-9822
  Springboro *(G-17323)*
Central Fabricators Inc ....E 513 621-1240
  Cincinnati *(G-3456)*
Compco Industries Inc ....D 330 482-6488
  Columbiana *(G-6463)*
Dabar Industries LLC ....F 614 873-3949
  Plain City *(G-16183)*
Enerfab Inc ....B 513 641-0500
  Cincinnati *(G-3640)*
Gaspar Inc ....D 330 477-2222
  Canton *(G-2679)*
Hason USA Corp ....E 513 248-0287
  Milford *(G-14016)*
Hershey Machine ....G 330 674-2718
  Millersburg *(G-14089)*
M & H Fabricating Co Inc ....G 937 325-8708
  Springfield *(G-17438)*
R4 Holdings LLC ....G 614 873-6499
  Plain City *(G-16210)*
Rebsco Inc ....F 937 548-2246
  Greenville *(G-10390)*
S-P Company Inc ....F 330 482-0200
  Columbiana *(G-6479)*

TANKS: Storage, Farm, Metal Plate

Rcr Partnership ....G 419 340-1202
  Genoa *(G-10235)*

TANNING SALON EQPT & SPLYS, WHOLESALE

Success Technologies Inc ....G 614 761-0008
  Powell *(G-16337)*

TANNING SALONS

Kahuna Bay Spray Tan LLC ....G 419 386-2387
  Toledo *(G-18360)*
Premier Tanning & Nutrition ....G 419 342-6259
  Shelby *(G-16986)*

TAPE DRIVES

CHI Corporation ....F 440 498-2300
  Cleveland *(G-4920)*

TAPES, ADHESIVE: Medical

Medco Labs Inc ....F 216 292-7546
  Cleveland *(G-5651)*
Mt Pleasant Pharmacy LLC ....G 216 672-4377
  Bedford *(G-1429)*

TAPES: Fabric

Piland Parts ....G 330 686-3083
  Stow *(G-17617)*

TAPES: Insulating

Denizen Inc ....F 937 615-9561
  Piqua *(G-16111)*

TAPES: Magnetic

Magnetnotes Ltd ....G 419 593-0060
  Toledo *(G-18397)*

TAPES: Plastic Coated

Buschman Corporation ....F 216 431-6633
  Cleveland *(G-4853)*
Shaheen Oriental Rug Co Inc ....F 330 493-9000
  Canton *(G-2813)*

TAPES: Pressure Sensitive

3M Company ....D 330 725-1444
  Medina *(G-13214)*
Austin Tape and Label Inc ....D 330 928-7999
  Stow *(G-17570)*
Beiersdorf Inc ....C 513 682-7300
  West Chester *(G-19835)*
Cortape Inc ....F 330 929-6700
  Cuyahoga Falls *(G-7853)*
D M V Supply Corporation ....G 330 847-0450
  Warren *(G-19393)*
Hooven - Dayton Corp ....D 937 233-4473
  Miamisburg *(G-13677)*
Progressive Labels LLC ....F 570 688-9636
  Willoughby *(G-20412)*
Shurtape Technologies LLC ....B 440 937-7000
  Avon *(G-966)*

TARPAULINS

Custom Tarpaulin Products Inc ....F 330 758-1801
  Youngstown *(G-20883)*
Electra Tarp Inc ....F 330 477-7168
  Canton *(G-2667)*
Lesch Boat Cover Canvas Co LLC ....G 419 668-6374
  Norwalk *(G-15404)*
Rainbow Industries Inc ....G 937 323-6493
  Springfield *(G-17479)*
Tarpco Inc ....F 330 677-8277
  Kent *(G-11392)*
Tri County Tarp LLC ....E 419 288-3350
  Bradner *(G-2016)*

TARPAULINS, WHOLESALE

Berlin Truck Caps Ltd ....F 330 893-2811
  Millersburg *(G-14067)*
Shur-Co LLC ....G 330 297-0888
  Ravenna *(G-16402)*

TATTOO PARLORS

252 Tattoo ....G 440 235-6699
  Columbia Station *(G-6426)*

TAX RETURN PREPARATION SVCS

David Butler Tax Service ....G 419 626-8086
  Sandusky *(G-16803)*

TECHNICAL INSTITUTE

Borman Enterprises Inc ....F 216 459-9292
  Cleveland *(G-4833)*

TECHNICAL MANUAL PREPARATION SVCS

ONeil & Associates Inc ....B 937 865-0800
  Miamisburg *(G-13704)*
Prowrite Inc ....G 614 864-2004
  Reynoldsburg *(G-16450)*
Revonoc Inc ....G 440 548-3491
  Parkman *(G-15813)*

TELECOMMUNICATION EQPT REPAIR SVCS, EXC TELEPHONES

AT&T Corp ....A 614 223-8236
  Columbus *(G-6623)*
Town Cntry Technical Svcs Inc ....F 614 866-7700
  Reynoldsburg *(G-16457)*
Vertiv Energy Systems Inc ....A 440 288-1122
  Lorain *(G-12134)*
Vertiv Group Corporation ....G 440 288-1122
  Lorain *(G-12135)*

TELECOMMUNICATION SYSTEMS & EQPT

7signal Solutions Inc ....E 216 777-2900
  Independence *(G-11116)*
AT&T Corp ....G 513 792-9300
  Cincinnati *(G-3365)*
Cutting Edge Technologies Inc ....E 216 574-4759
  Cleveland *(G-5051)*
DTE Inc ....E 419 522-3428
  Mansfield *(G-12434)*
Electrodata Inc ....F 216 663-3333
  Bedford Heights *(G-1469)*
Greyfield Industries Inc ....F 513 860-1785
  Trenton *(G-18620)*
Mitel (delaware) Inc ....E 513 733-8000
  West Chester *(G-19745)*
Peco II Inc ....D 614 431-0694
  Columbus *(G-7305)*
Pharmazell Inc ....G 440 526-6417
  Brecksville *(G-2053)*
Prentke Romich Company ....C 330 262-1984
  Wooster *(G-20641)*
Pro Oncall Technologies LLC ....F 614 761-1400
  Dublin *(G-8967)*
Tls Corp ....E 216 574-4759
  Cleveland *(G-6177)*
Vertiv Energy Systems Inc ....A 440 288-1122
  Lorain *(G-12134)*

PRODUCT SECTION

TEXTILES: Flock

Vertiv Group Corporation..................G....... 440 288-1122
  Lorain *(G-12135)*
Vertiv Group Corporation..................F....... 440 460-3600
  Cleveland *(G-6253)*
Viasat Inc.....................................D....... 216 706-7800
  Independence *(G-11155)*

TELECOMMUNICATIONS CARRIERS & SVCS: Wired

AT&T Corp.....................................A....... 614 223-8236
  Columbus *(G-6623)*
Byrd Prcurement Specialist Inc.........G....... 419 936-0019
  Swanton *(G-17908)*
Kraft Electrical Contg Inc..................E....... 614 836-9300
  Groveport *(G-10498)*
Kraftmaid Trucking Inc....................G....... 440 632-2531
  Middlefield *(G-13812)*

TELEMETERING EQPT

Advanced Telemetrics Intl................F....... 937 862-6948
  Spring Valley *(G-17315)*
Grace Automation Services Inc.........G....... 330 567-3108
  Big Prairie *(G-1674)*

TELEPHONE BOOTHS, EXC WOOD

Ray Communications Inc.................G....... 330 686-0226
  Stow *(G-17623)*

TELEPHONE CENTRAL OFFICE EQPT: Dial Or Manual

Kentrox Inc....................................D....... 614 798-2000
  Dublin *(G-8938)*

TELEPHONE EQPT INSTALLATION

Crase Communications Inc..............F....... 419 468-1173
  Galion *(G-10131)*
Johnson Brothers Holdings LLC........G....... 614 868-5273
  Columbus *(G-7073)*
Mitel (delaware) Inc.........................E....... 513 733-8000
  West Chester *(G-19745)*

TELEPHONE EQPT: Modems

Black Box Corporation.....................F....... 614 825-7400
  Lewis Center *(G-11751)*
C Dcap Modem Line........................G....... 419 748-7409
  Mc Clure *(G-13185)*
C Dcap Modem Line........................G....... 440 685-4302
  North Bloomfield *(G-15063)*
Lisa Modem..................................G....... 216 551-3365
  Cleveland *(G-5581)*
Procomsol Ltd................................G....... 216 221-1550
  Lakewood *(G-11533)*

TELEPHONE EQPT: NEC

Arnco Corporation..........................C....... 800 847-7661
  Elyria *(G-9219)*
Commercial Electric Pdts Corp.........E....... 216 241-2886
  Cleveland *(G-5002)*
Siemens Energy Inc.......................G....... 740 393-8464
  Mount Vernon *(G-14511)*

TELEPHONE SET REPAIR SVCS

DTE Inc..E....... 419 522-3428
  Mansfield *(G-12434)*

TELEPHONE STATION EQPT & PARTS: Wire

Ocs Telecom LLC...........................F....... 740 503-5939
  Hilliard *(G-10844)*

TELEPHONE SWITCHING EQPT: Toll Switching

Crase Communications Inc..............F....... 419 468-1173
  Galion *(G-10131)*

TELEPHONE: Fiber Optic Systems

Cotsworks LLC...............................E....... 440 446-8800
  Highland Heights *(G-10787)*
Preformed Line Products Co............B....... 440 461-5200
  Mayfield Village *(G-13174)*

TELEPHONE: Headsets

Headset Wholesalers Ltd................G....... 419 798-5200
  Lakeside Marblehead *(G-11503)*

TELEPHONE: Sets, Exc Cellular Radio

Minor Corporation...........................G....... 216 291-8723
  Cleveland *(G-5695)*

TELEVISION BROADCASTING & COMMUNICATIONS EQPT

Nissin Precision N Amer Inc............D....... 937 836-1910
  Englewood *(G-9372)*

TELEVISION BROADCASTING STATIONS

Block Communications Inc..............F....... 419 724-6212
  Toledo *(G-18206)*
Dispatch Printing Company..............C....... 740 548-5331
  Lewis Center *(G-11757)*
EW Scripps Company.....................E....... 513 977-3000
  Cincinnati *(G-3663)*

TELEVISION REPAIR SHOP

Electra Sound Inc...........................D....... 216 433-9600
  Parma *(G-15817)*

TELEVISION: Closed Circuit Eqpt

Diamond Electronics Inc..................C....... 740 652-9222
  Lancaster *(G-11564)*

TEMPORARY HELP SVCS

Cima Inc.......................................E....... 513 382-8976
  Hamilton *(G-10546)*
Production Design Services Inc........D....... 937 866-3377
  Dayton *(G-8446)*

TENT REPAIR SHOP

J & W Canvas Company..................G....... 330 652-7678
  Mineral Ridge *(G-14167)*

TENTS: All Materials

Celina Tent Inc..............................E....... 419 586-3610
  Celina *(G-2954)*
Embedee LLC................................G....... 419 678-7007
  Coldwater *(G-6407)*

TERMINAL BOARDS

Osborne Coinage Company.............D....... 513 681-5424
  Cincinnati *(G-4120)*

TEST BORING SVCS: Nonmetallic Minerals

Longyear Company........................E....... 740 373-2190
  Marietta *(G-12640)*

TEST BORING, METAL MINING

Hahs Factory Outlet........................E....... 330 405-4227
  Twinsburg *(G-18790)*

TESTERS: Battery

Battery Unlimited...........................G....... 740 452-5030
  Zanesville *(G-21104)*
Zts Inc..F....... 513 271-2557
  Cincinnati *(G-4534)*

TESTERS: Environmental

Auto Technology Company..............F....... 440 572-7800
  Strongsville *(G-17715)*
Blue Water Satellite Inc...................G....... 419 372-0160
  Toledo *(G-18207)*
Bry-Air Inc....................................E....... 740 965-2974
  Sunbury *(G-17883)*
Envirnmntl Cmpliance Tech LLC......G....... 216 634-0400
  North Royalton *(G-15271)*
Northcoast Environmental Labs........G....... 330 342-3377
  Streetsboro *(G-17685)*
Reuter-Stokes LLC.........................B....... 330 425-3755
  Twinsburg *(G-18845)*

TESTERS: Gas, Exc Indl Process

Compliant Healthcare Tech LLC.......F....... 216 255-9607
  Cleveland *(G-5010)*

Compliant Healthcare Tech LLC.......E....... 216 255-9607
  Cleveland *(G-5011)*

TESTERS: Liquid, Exc Indl Process

Acense LLC..................................G....... 330 242-0046
  Twinsburg *(G-18724)*

TESTERS: Physical Property

Omega Automation Inc...................D....... 937 890-2350
  Dayton *(G-8402)*
Omega International Inc..................E....... 937 890-2350
  Dayton *(G-8403)*
Plating Test Cell Supply Co..............G....... 216 486-8400
  Cleveland *(G-5890)*
Pressco Technology Inc..................D....... 440 498-2600
  Cleveland *(G-5919)*
Test Mark Industries Inc..................F....... 330 426-2200
  East Palestine *(G-9086)*

TESTERS: Water, Exc Indl Process

CST Zero Discharged Car Wash S....G....... 740 947-5480
  Waverly *(G-19543)*
Ysi Incorporated............................D....... 937 767-7241
  Yellow Springs *(G-20825)*

TESTING SVCS

Alpha Technologies Svcs LLC..........D....... 330 745-1641
  Hudson *(G-11027)*
Data Analysis Technologies.............G....... 614 873-0710
  Plain City *(G-16186)*
Orton Edward Jr Crmic Fndation.......E....... 614 895-2663
  Westerville *(G-20014)*

TEXTILE BAGS WHOLESALERS

Baggallini Inc.................................G....... 800 628-0321
  Pickerington *(G-16040)*

TEXTILE FABRICATORS

Ver Mich Ltd..................................G....... 330 493-7330
  Canton *(G-2858)*

TEXTILE FINISHING: Chem Coat/Treat, Man, Broadwoven, Cotton

Mmi Textiles Inc.............................F....... 440 899-8050
  Westlake *(G-20131)*

TEXTILE FINISHING: Chemical Coating Or Treating, Narrow

Creative Commercial Finishing.........G....... 513 722-9393
  Loveland *(G-12184)*
Southern Adhesive Coatings...........G....... 513 561-8440
  Cincinnati *(G-4355)*

TEXTILE FINISHING: Decorative, Man Fiber & Silk, Broadwoven

Wizard Graphics Inc.......................G....... 419 354-3098
  Bowling Green *(G-2006)*

TEXTILE FINISHING: Napping, Manmade Fiber & Silk, Broadwoven

Tranzonic Acquisition Corp..............A....... 216 535-4300
  Richmond Heights *(G-16505)*
Tranzonic Companies.....................C....... 440 446-0643
  Cleveland *(G-6198)*

TEXTILE: Finishing, Cotton Broadwoven

Duracote Corporation.....................E....... 330 296-9600
  Ravenna *(G-16376)*

TEXTILE: Finishing, Raw Stock NEC

Pelz Lettering Inc...........................G....... 419 625-3567
  Sandusky *(G-16838)*

TEXTILES

Mmi Textiles Inc.............................F....... 440 899-8050
  Westlake *(G-20131)*

TEXTILES: Flock

J Rettenmaier USA LP....................G....... 440 385-6701
  Oberlin *(G-15500)*

Employee Codes: A=Over 500 employees, B=251-500
C=101-250, D=51-100, E=20-50, F=10-19, G=3-9

TEXTILES: Flock

J Rettenmaier USA LP .... D 937 652-2101
Urbana *(G-18997)*

TEXTILES: Jute & Flax Prdts

Big Productions Inc .... G 440 775-0015
Oberlin *(G-15491)*
Construction Techniques Inc .... F 216 267-7310
Cleveland *(G-5019)*

TEXTILES: Tops & Top Processing, Manmade Or Other Fiber

Cusc International Ltd .... G 513 881-2000
Hamilton *(G-10549)*

TEXTILES: Tops, Combing & Converting

Tops Inc .... G 440 954-9451
Mentor *(G-13609)*

THEATRICAL LIGHTING SVCS

Iacono Production Services Inc .... F 513 469-5095
Blue Ash *(G-1790)*

THEATRICAL PRODUCTION SVCS

North Coast Theatrical Inc .... G 330 762-1768
Akron *(G-300)*

THEATRICAL SCENERY

Schell Scenic Studio Inc .... G 614 444-9550
Columbus *(G-7425)*

THEATRICAL TALENT & BOOKING AGENCIES

Thickemz Entertainment LLC .... G 404 399-4255
Cuyahoga Falls *(G-7928)*

THERMISTORS, EXC TEMPERATURE SENSORS

Measurement Specialties Inc .... F 937 427-1231
Beavercreek *(G-1358)*

THERMOCOUPLES

Blaze Technical Services Inc .... E 330 923-0409
Stow *(G-17574)*
Heraeus Electro-Nite Co LLC .... G 330 725-1419
Medina *(G-13272)*

THERMOCOUPLES: Indl Process

Cleveland Electric Labs Co .... E 800 447-2207
Twinsburg *(G-18754)*
Geocorp Inc .... E 419 433-1101
Huron *(G-11094)*
MR&e Ltd .... G 419 872-8180
Toledo *(G-18418)*

THERMOMETERS: Indl

T P F Inc .... G 513 761-9968
Cincinnati *(G-4403)*

THERMOMETERS: Medical, Digital

ARC Drilling Inc .... F 216 525-0920
Cleveland *(G-4723)*
Corcadence Inc .... G 216 702-6371
Beachwood *(G-1231)*

THERMOPLASTIC MATERIALS

Amros Industries Inc .... E 216 433-0010
Cleveland *(G-4702)*
Denney Plastics Machining LLC .... F 330 308-5300
New Philadelphia *(G-14766)*
Dow Chemical Company .... G 740 929-5100
Hebron *(G-10742)*
Dow Chemical Company .... F 937 254-1550
Dayton *(G-8166)*
Hexpol Compounding LLC .... G 440 682-4038
Mogadore *(G-14239)*
Hexpol Compounding LLC .... G 440 834-4644
Burton *(G-2361)*
Integra Enclosures Limited .... D 440 269-4966
Mentor *(G-13472)*
Polyone Corporation .... F 740 423-7571
Belpre *(G-1583)*
Polyone Corporation .... D 440 930-1000
Avon Lake *(G-1001)*
Polyone Funding Corporation .... G 440 930-1000
Avon Lake *(G-1003)*
Polyone LLC .... G 440 930-1000
Avon Lake *(G-1004)*
Ppl Holding Company .... E 216 514-1840
Cleveland *(G-5902)*

THERMOPLASTICS

Bulk Molding Compounds Inc .... D 419 874-7941
Perrysburg *(G-15926)*
McHenry Industries Inc .... E 330 799-8930
Youngstown *(G-20968)*
Plextrusions Inc .... G 330 668-2587
North Ridgeville *(G-15244)*
Techniform Industries Inc .... E 419 332-8484
Fremont *(G-10054)*

THERMOSETTING MATERIALS

Current Inc .... G 330 392-5151
Warren *(G-19392)*
Hexion Inc .... B 614 225-4000
Columbus *(G-6992)*
Hexion LLC .... D 614 225-4000
Columbus *(G-6993)*
Momentive Performance Mtls Inc ...... G 614 986-2495
Columbus *(G-7193)*

THREAD: Embroidery

Alvin L Roepke .... F 419 862-3891
Elmore *(G-9203)*

THREAD: Rubber

West & Barker Inc .... E 330 652-9923
Niles *(G-15040)*

TIES, FORM: Metal

Puritas Metal Products Inc .... F 440 353-1917
North Ridgeville *(G-15247)*
Tig Welding Specialties Inc .... G 216 621-1763
Cleveland *(G-6174)*

TILE: Brick & Structural, Clay

Armstrong World Industries Inc .... D 614 771-9307
Hilliard *(G-10806)*
Kepcor Inc .... F 330 868-6434
Minerva *(G-14186)*
LBC Clay Co LLC .... G 330 674-0674
Millersburg *(G-14106)*
Minteq International Inc .... E 330 343-8821
Dover *(G-8843)*
Morgan Advanced Ceramics Inc .... C 440 232-8604
Bedford *(G-1428)*
Resco Products Inc .... G 740 682-7794
Oak Hill *(G-15459)*
Stebbins Engineering & Mfg Co .... E 740 922-3012
Uhrichsville *(G-18895)*

TILE: Clay, Drain & Structural

Baughman Tile Company .... D 800 837-3160
Paulding *(G-15856)*
Clay Logan Products Company .... D 740 385-2184
Logan *(G-12022)*

TILE: Clay, Roof

Ludowici Roof Tile Inc .... D 740 342-1995
New Lexington *(G-14718)*
Nr Lee Restoration Ltd .... F 419 692-2233
Delphos *(G-8752)*
Terreal North America LLC .... C 888 582-9052
New Lexington *(G-14727)*

TILE: Drain, Clay

Haviland Drainage Products Co .... F 419 622-4611
Haviland *(G-10711)*

TILE: Vinyl, Asbestos

Texas Tile Manufacturing LLC .... E 713 869-5811
Solon *(G-17251)*

TILE: Wall & Floor, Ceramic

Artfinders .... G 330 264-7706
Wooster *(G-20563)*
Ironrock Capital Incorporated .... D 330 484-4887
Canton *(G-2712)*
Wccv Floor Coverings LLC .... E 330 688-0114
Peninsula *(G-15901)*

TILE: Wall, Ceramic

Florida Tile Inc .... G 513 891-1122
Blue Ash *(G-1777)*
Florida Tile Inc .... G 614 436-2511
Columbus *(G-6928)*
Florida Tile Inc .... G 937 293-5151
Miamisburg *(G-13669)*

TIMING DEVICES: Electronic

Automatic Timing & Controls .... G 614 888-8855
New Albany *(G-14606)*

TIN

Tin Indian Performance .... G 216 214-5485
Uniontown *(G-18935)*
Tin Shed LLC .... G 330 636-2524
Willard *(G-20246)*
Tin Wizard Heating and Cooling .... G 330 468-7884
Macedonia *(G-12337)*
Tin-Sau LLC .... G 419 586-8886
Celina *(G-2989)*

TIN-BASE ALLOYS, PRIMARY

Gdc Industries LLC .... G 937 367-7229
Beavercreek *(G-1316)*

TIRE & INNER TUBE MATERIALS & RELATED PRDTS

American Airless Inc .... E 614 552-0146
Reynoldsburg *(G-16428)*
Grove Engineered Products Inc .... G 419 659-5939
Columbus Grove *(G-7635)*
Troy Engineered Components and .... G 937 335-8070
Dayton *(G-8569)*
Truflex Rubber Products Co .... C 740 967-9015
Johnstown *(G-11273)*
Yrp Industries Inc .... G 330 533-2524
Youngstown *(G-21085)*

TIRE & TUBE REPAIR MATERIALS, WHOLESALE

Myers Industries Inc .... E 330 253-5592
Akron *(G-292)*
Technical Rubber Company Inc .... B 740 967-9015
Johnstown *(G-11272)*

TIRE CORD & FABRIC

Akro Polychem Inc .... G 330 864-0360
Fairlawn *(G-9592)*
ARC Abrasives Inc .... D 800 888-4885
Troy *(G-18638)*
Cleveland Canvas Goods Mfg Co ...... D 216 361-4567
Cleveland *(G-4948)*
Mfh Partners Inc .... F 440 461-4100
Cleveland *(G-5664)*

TIRE CORD & FABRIC: Indl, Reinforcing

Midwest Precision Products .... F 440 237-9500
Cleveland *(G-5683)*

TIRE DEALERS

A & A Discount Tire .... G 330 863-1936
Carrollton *(G-2914)*
Bkt USA Inc .... F 330 836-1090
Fairlawn *(G-9598)*
Garro Tread Corporation .... G 330 376-3125
Akron *(G-181)*
Goodyear Tire & Rubber Company ... C 216 265-1800
Cleveland *(G-5332)*
Gregs Eagle Tire Co Inc .... G 330 837-1983
Massillon *(G-12990)*
Mid-Wood Inc .... F 419 257-3331
North Baltimore *(G-15046)*
Q T Columbus LLC .... G 800 758-2410
Columbus *(G-7359)*
QT Equipment Company .... E 330 724-3055
Akron *(G-334)*

PRODUCT SECTION

TIRE INNER-TUBES

Goodyear Tire & Rubber Company .... A 330 796-2121
  Akron *(G-191)*

TIRE RECAPPING & RETREADING

Goodyear Tire & Rubber Company .... A 330 796-2121
  Akron *(G-191)*

TIRE SUNDRIES OR REPAIR MATERIALS: Rubber

31 Inc .... D 740 498-8324
  Newcomerstown *(G-14968)*
PPG Industries Inc .... G 614 921-9228
  Hilliard *(G-10854)*
Technical Rubber Company Inc .... B 740 967-9015
  Johnstown *(G-11272)*

TIRES & INNER TUBES

B & S Transport Inc .... F 330 767-4319
  Navarre *(G-14572)*
Bkt USA Inc .... F 330 836-1090
  Fairlawn *(G-9598)*
Buckman Machine Works Inc .... G 330 525-7665
  Homeworth *(G-10987)*
Continental Tire Americas LLC .... G 419 633-4221
  Bryan *(G-2276)*
Cooper Tire & Rubber Company .... D 419 424-4384
  Findlay *(G-9674)*
Goodrich Corporation .... G 216 429-4655
  Brooklyn Heights *(G-2122)*
Goodyear Tire & Rubber Company .... C 216 265-1800
  Cleveland *(G-5332)*
Gregs Eagle Tire Co Inc .... G 330 837-1983
  Massillon *(G-12990)*
Intertex World Resources Inc .... G 770 214-5551
  Canton *(G-2710)*
Titan Tire Corporation .... B 419 633-4221
  Bryan *(G-2309)*
Umd Contractors Inc .... F 740 694-8614
  Fredericktown *(G-9982)*
Ws Trading LLC .... G 800 830-4547
  Galena *(G-10118)*

TIRES & TUBES WHOLESALERS

B & S Transport Inc .... F 330 767-4319
  Navarre *(G-14572)*
Chestnut Holdings Inc .... G 330 849-6503
  Akron *(G-114)*
Goodyear International Corp .... E 330 796-2121
  Akron *(G-190)*
Rhino Rubber LLC .... F 877 744-6603
  North Canton *(G-15115)*

TIRES: Auto

Chemspec Ltd .... F 330 896-0355
  Uniontown *(G-18915)*
Cooper Tire & Rubber Company .... A 419 423-1321
  Findlay *(G-9672)*
Cooper Tire & Rubber Company .... E 419 424-4202
  Findlay *(G-9673)*
Cooper Tire Vhcl Test Ctr Inc .... E 419 423-1321
  Findlay *(G-9675)*

TIRES: Indl Vehicles

Trelleborg Wheel Systems Ameri .... E 866 633-8473
  Akron *(G-409)*

TIRES: Plastic

Rhino Rubber LLC .... F 877 744-6603
  North Canton *(G-15115)*

TITANIUM MILL PRDTS

Rmi Titanium Company LLC .... G 330 652-9955
  Niles *(G-15031)*
Rmi Titanium Company LLC .... E 330 652-9952
  Niles *(G-15028)*
Tailwind Technologies Inc .... E 937 778-4200
  Piqua *(G-16164)*
Titanium Contractors Ltd .... G 513 256-2152
  Cincinnati *(G-4422)*
Titanium Lacrosse LLC .... F 614 562-8082
  Lewis Center *(G-11786)*
Titanium Metals Corporation .... E 610 968-1300
  Warrensville Heights *(G-19473)*

Titanium Sales Group LLC .... G 614 204-6098
  Dublin *(G-9004)*
Titanium Trout LLC .... G 440 543-3187
  Chagrin Falls *(G-3083)*
Water Star Inc .... F 440 996-0800
  Painesville *(G-15797)*

TOBACCO & PRDTS, WHOLESALE: Cigars

Moosehead Cigar Company Llc .... G 513 266-7207
  Fairfield *(G-9530)*

TOBACCO & TOBACCO PRDTS WHOLESALERS

Butt Hut of America Inc .... G 419 443-1997
  Tiffin *(G-18053)*

TOBACCO STORES & STANDS

Boston Stoker Inc .... G 937 890-6401
  Vandalia *(G-19118)*
Smoke Rings Inc .... G 419 420-9966
  Findlay *(G-9757)*

TOBACCO: Chewing & Snuff

Great Midwest Tobacco Inc .... G 513 745-0450
  Cincinnati *(G-3779)*
Smoke Rings Inc .... G 419 420-9966
  Findlay *(G-9757)*

TOBACCO: Cigarettes

Butt Hut of America Inc .... G 419 443-1997
  Tiffin *(G-18053)*
Itg Brands LLC .... G 614 431-0044
  Columbus *(G-7053)*

TOBACCO: Cigars

Cigars of Cincy .... G 513 931-5926
  Cincinnati *(G-3475)*
Guari Inc .... G 330 733-4005
  Akron *(G-192)*
Moosehead Cigar Company Llc .... G 513 266-7207
  Fairfield *(G-9530)*

TOBACCO: Smoking

Hookah Rush .... G 614 267-6463
  Columbus *(G-7007)*

TOILET PREPARATIONS

Barbasol LLC .... E 419 903-0738
  Ashland *(G-684)*
Bocchi Laboratories Ohio LLC .... B 614 741-7458
  New Albany *(G-14610)*
Procter & Gamble Far East Inc .... C 513 983-1100
  Cincinnati *(G-4210)*
Procter & Gamble Mfg Co .... F 513 983-1100
  Cincinnati *(G-4212)*

TOILETRIES, COSMETICS & PERFUME STORES

Bath & Body Works LLC .... B 614 856-6000
  Reynoldsburg *(G-16430)*
Olfactorium Corp Inc .... G 216 663-8831
  Cleveland *(G-5811)*

TOILETRIES, WHOLESALE: Toiletries

Nehemiah Manufacturing Co LLC .... E 513 351-5700
  Cincinnati *(G-4066)*
Walter F Stephens Jr Inc .... E 937 746-0521
  Franklin *(G-9930)*

TOMBSTONES: Cut Stone, Exc Finishing Or Lettering Only

Van Wert Memorials LLC .... G 419 238-9067
  Van Wert *(G-19110)*

TOMBSTONES: Terrazzo Or Concrete, Precast

Ellinger Monument Inc .... G 740 385-3687
  Rockbridge *(G-16536)*

TOOL & DIE STEEL

Applied Innovations .... G 330 837-5694
  Massillon *(G-12960)*
B & G Tool Company .... G 614 451-2538
  Columbus *(G-6640)*
Burn-Rite Mold & Machine Inc .... G 330 956-4143
  Canton *(G-2602)*
Carter Scott-Browne .... E 513 398-3970
  Mason *(G-12839)*
Deaks Form Tools Inc .... G 440 286-2353
  Chardon *(G-3108)*
Die Services Ltd .... G 216 883-5800
  Cleveland *(G-5093)*
Latrobe Specialty Mtls Co LLC .... D 419 335-8010
  Wauseon *(G-19525)*
Louis G Freeman Co .... E 419 334-9709
  Fremont *(G-10037)*
Maull Tool & Die Supply Llc .... G 513 646-4229
  Loveland *(G-12213)*
Metaldyne Pwrtrain Cmpnnts Inc .... C 330 486-3200
  Twinsburg *(G-18818)*
New Age Design & Tool Inc .... F 440 355-5400
  Lagrange *(G-11490)*
Nichidai America Corporation .... E 419 423-7511
  Findlay *(G-9730)*
OReilly Precision Products .... E 937 526-4677
  Russia *(G-16610)*
Precision Wood & Metal Co .... G 419 221-1512
  Lima *(G-11919)*
Quality Tool Company .... E 419 476-8228
  Toledo *(G-18490)*
R&D Machine Inc .... F 937 339-2545
  Troy *(G-18696)*
Robs Welding Technologies Ltd .... G 937 890-4963
  Dayton *(G-8483)*
S & J Precision Inc .... G 937 296-0068
  Moraine *(G-14391)*
Seilkop Industries Inc .... E 513 353-3090
  Miamitown *(G-13751)*
West Motorsports Inc .... G 330 350-0375
  Akron *(G-434)*

TOOL REPAIR SVCS

Harbor Freight Tools Usa Inc .... E 937 415-0770
  Dayton *(G-8244)*
Lawrence Industries Inc .... C 216 518-7000
  Cleveland *(G-5566)*
T M Industries Inc .... G 330 627-4410
  Carrollton *(G-2930)*

TOOLS & EQPT: Used With Sporting Arms

C-H Tool & Die .... G 740 397-7214
  Mount Vernon *(G-14471)*

TOOLS: Carpenters', Including Levels & Chisels, Exc Saws

Eric Mondene .... G 740 965-2842
  Galena *(G-10111)*
Your Carpenter Inc .... G 216 241-6434
  Cleveland *(G-6333)*

TOOLS: Hand

Acme Company .... D 330 758-2313
  Poland *(G-16236)*
Amcraft Inc .... G 419 729-7900
  Toledo *(G-18170)*
ASG .... F 216 486-6163
  Cleveland *(G-4748)*
CB Manufacturing & Sls Co Inc .... D 937 866-5986
  Dayton *(G-8079)*
Cleveland Iron Workers Members .... G 216 687-2290
  Cleveland *(G-4965)*
Cornwell Quality Tools Company .... D 330 628-2627
  Mogadore *(G-14232)*
Desmond-Stephan Mfgcompany .... G 937 653-7181
  Urbana *(G-18989)*
Eaton Electric Holdings LLC .... B 440 523-5000
  Cleveland *(G-5151)*
Edgerton Forge Inc .... E 419 298-2333
  Edgerton *(G-9171)*
Electric Eel Mfg Co Inc .... E 937 323-4644
  Springfield *(G-17395)*
Empire Plow Company Inc .... E 216 641-2290
  Cleveland *(G-5175)*
Everhard Products Inc .... C 330 453-7786
  Canton *(G-2670)*

Employee Codes: A=Over 500 employees, B=251-500
C=101-250, D=51-100, E=20-50, F=10-19, G=3-9

TOOLS: Hand

Falcon Industries Inc ....E 330 723-0099
  Medina *(G-13260)*
File Sharpening Company Inc ....E 937 376-8268
  Xenia *(G-20772)*
Furukawa Rock Drill USA Co Ltd ....E 330 673-5826
  Kent *(G-11325)*
Fusion Automation Inc ....G 440 602-5595
  Willoughby *(G-20326)*
Harbor Freight Tools Usa Inc ....E 937 415-0770
  Dayton *(G-8244)*
J and S Tool Incorporated ....E 216 676-8330
  Cleveland *(G-5482)*
Klawhorn Industries Inc ....G 330 335-8191
  Wadsworth *(G-19249)*
Knight Ergonomics Inc ....F 440 746-0044
  Brecksville *(G-2045)*
Komar Industries Inc ....E 614 836-2366
  Groveport *(G-10497)*
Martin Sprocket & Gear Inc ....D 419 485-5515
  Montpelier *(G-14312)*
Matco Tools Corporation ....B 330 929-4949
  Stow *(G-17605)*
Midwest Knife Grinding Inc ....F 330 854-1030
  Canal Fulton *(G-2486)*
Myers Industries Inc ....E 440 632-1006
  Middlefield *(G-13836)*
North Coast Holdings Inc ....G 330 535-7177
  Akron *(G-299)*
Panacea Products Corporation ....D 614 429-6320
  Columbus *(G-7288)*
Rex International USA Inc ....E 800 321-7950
  Ashtabula *(G-803)*
Ridge Tool Company ....A 440 323-5581
  Elyria *(G-9320)*
Ridge Tool Manufacturing Co ....A 440 323-5581
  Elyria *(G-9322)*
Sewer Rodding Equipment Co ....E 419 991-2065
  Lima *(G-11937)*
Simon Ellis Superabrasives ....G 937 226-0683
  Dayton *(G-8508)*
Simonds International LLC ....E 978 424-0100
  Kimbolton *(G-11457)*
Stanley Access Tech LLC ....C 440 461-5500
  Cleveland *(G-6093)*
Stanley Industrial & Auto LLC ....C 614 755-7089
  Westerville *(G-20024)*
Stanley Industrial & Auto LLC ....D 614 755-7000
  Westerville *(G-20025)*
Step2 Company LLC ....B 866 429-5200
  Streetsboro *(G-17700)*
Step2 Company LLC ....B 419 938-6343
  Perrysville *(G-16032)*
Stride Tool LLC ....C 440 247-4600
  Solon *(G-17238)*
Sumitomo Elc Carbide Mfg Inc ....F 440 354-0600
  Grand River *(G-10326)*
Summit Tool Company ....D 330 535-7177
  Akron *(G-392)*
Toolovation LLC ....G 216 514-3022
  Cleveland *(G-6185)*

TOOLS: Hand, Engravers'

F & B Engraving Tls & Sup LLC ....G 937 332-7994
  Piqua *(G-16114)*

TOOLS: Hand, Jewelers'

Abhushan LLC ....G 614 789-0632
  Dublin *(G-8872)*
Silver Expressions ....G 740 687-0144
  Lancaster *(G-11608)*
Sterling Jewelers Inc ....G 614 799-8000
  Dublin *(G-8995)*

TOOLS: Hand, Masons'

Chrisnik Inc ....G 513 738-2920
  Okeana *(G-15516)*
E Z Grout Corporation ....E 740 749-3512
  Malta *(G-12381)*

TOOLS: Hand, Mechanics

Oldforge Tools Inc ....E 330 535-7177
  Akron *(G-310)*
S & H Industries Inc ....E 216 831-0550
  Cleveland *(G-6018)*
S & H Industries Inc ....E 216 831-0550
  Bedford *(G-1442)*
Tribus Innovations LLC ....G 509 992-4743
  Englewood *(G-9379)*

TOOLS: Hand, Plumbers'

Bartter & Sons ....G 419 651-0374
  Jeromesville *(G-11249)*
Calvin Lanier ....E 937 952-4221
  Dayton *(G-8074)*

TOOLS: Hand, Power

Air Tool Service Company ....F 440 701-1021
  Mentor *(G-13379)*
Aircraft Dynamics Corporation ....F 419 331-0371
  Elida *(G-9193)*
Apex Tool Group LLC ....C 937 222-7871
  Dayton *(G-8033)*
Black & Decker (us) Inc ....G 614 895-3112
  Columbus *(G-6676)*
Black & Decker Corporation ....E 440 842-9100
  Cleveland *(G-4816)*
Campbell Hausfeld LLC ....C 513 367-4811
  Cincinnati *(G-3439)*
Chicago Pneumatic Tool Co LLC ....G 704 883-3500
  Broadview Heights *(G-2090)*
ET&f Fastening Systems Inc ....F 800 248-2376
  Solon *(G-17141)*
Furukawa Rock Drill Usa Inc ....F 330 673-5826
  Kent *(G-11324)*
Furukawa Rock Drill USA Co Ltd ....E 330 673-5826
  Kent *(G-11325)*
Galaxy Products Inc ....G 419 843-7337
  Sylvania *(G-17940)*
Hall-Toledo Inc ....F 419 893-4334
  Maumee *(G-13114)*
Huron Cement Products Company ....E 419 433-4161
  Huron *(G-11096)*
Ingersoll-Rand Company ....E 419 633-6800
  Bryan *(G-2291)*
Michabo Inc ....G 419 893-4334
  Maumee *(G-13133)*
Npk Construction Equipment Inc ....D 440 232-7900
  Bedford *(G-1432)*
Ohio Drill & Tool Co ....E 330 525-7717
  Homeworth *(G-10989)*
Rex International USA Inc ....E 800 321-7950
  Ashtabula *(G-803)*
Ridge Tool Company ....A 440 323-5581
  Elyria *(G-9320)*
Ridge Tool Manufacturing Co ....A 440 323-5581
  Elyria *(G-9322)*
Selbro Inc ....F 419 483-9918
  Bellevue *(G-1544)*
Senco Brands Inc ....E 513 388-2833
  Cincinnati *(G-4320)*
Senco Brands Inc ....D 513 388-2000
  Cincinnati *(G-3262)*
Sensource Global Sourcing LLC ....G 513 659-8283
  Cincinnati *(G-3263)*
Sewer Rodding Equipment Co ....E 419 991-2065
  Lima *(G-11937)*
Stanley Access Tech LLC ....C 440 461-5500
  Cleveland *(G-6093)*
Stanley Bittinger ....G 740 942-4302
  Cadiz *(G-2401)*
Stanley Industrial & Auto LLC ....D 614 755-7000
  Westerville *(G-20025)*
Suburban Manufacturing Co ....D 440 953-2024
  Eastlake *(G-9133)*
Sumitomo Elc Carbide Mfg Inc ....F 440 354-0600
  Grand River *(G-10326)*
Superior Pneumatic & Mfg Inc ....F 440 871-8780
  Cleveland *(G-6122)*
TC Service Co ....E 440 954-7500
  Willoughby *(G-20441)*
Technidrill Systems Inc ....F 330 678-9980
  Kent *(G-11393)*
Triad Capital Aat LLC ....G 440 236-4163
  Columbia Station *(G-6451)*
Uhrichsville Carbide Inc ....F 740 922-9197
  Uhrichsville *(G-18899)*
White Industrial Tool Inc ....F 330 773-6889
  Akron *(G-435)*
Wolf Machine Company ....C 513 791-5194
  Blue Ash *(G-1874)*
Wyeth-Scott Company ....G 740 345-4528
  Newark *(G-14933)*
X-Press Tool Inc ....E 330 225-8748
  Brunswick *(G-2254)*
Zagar Inc ....E 216 731-0500
  Cleveland *(G-6336)*

TOOLS: Soldering

Luma Electric Company ....G 419 843-7842
  Sylvania *(G-17949)*

TOOTHPASTES, GELS & TOOTHPOWDERS

Good Earth Good Eating LLC ....G 513 256-5935
  Cincinnati *(G-3771)*

TOWELS: Fabric & Nonwoven, Made From Purchased Materials

Lawnview Industries Inc ....C 937 653-5217
  Urbana *(G-19003)*
Saturday Knight Ltd ....D 513 641-1400
  Cincinnati *(G-4300)*

TOWELS: Paper

Procter & Gamble Paper Pdts Co ....E 513 983-2222
  Cincinnati *(G-4214)*

TOWERS, SECTIONS: Transmission, Radio & Television

American Tower Acquisition ....F 419 347-1185
  Shelby *(G-16977)*
K & L Die & Manufacturing ....G 419 895-1301
  Greenwich *(G-10405)*
Warmus and Associates Inc ....F 330 659-4440
  Bath *(G-1203)*

TOWERS: Cooling, Sheet Metal

Obr Cooling Towers Inc ....E 419 243-3443
  Rossford *(G-16588)*

TOWING & TUGBOAT SVC

Superior Marine Ways Inc ....G 740 894-6224
  South Point *(G-17295)*

TOWING SVCS: Marine

Great Lakes Group ....C 216 621-4854
  Cleveland *(G-5346)*

TOYS

Advance Novelty Incorporated ....G 419 424-0363
  Findlay *(G-9647)*
Ajj Enterprises LLC ....F 513 755-9562
  West Chester *(G-19830)*
AW Faber-Castell Usa Inc ....D 216 643-4660
  Cleveland *(G-4780)*
Cornpentry ....G 513 741-0594
  Cincinnati *(G-3551)*
Ink Factory Inc ....G 330 799-0888
  Youngstown *(G-20940)*
Iron Wind Metals Co LLC ....G 513 870-0606
  Cincinnati *(G-3859)*
Jackpot Festival & Gaming ....E 216 531-3500
  Cleveland *(G-5491)*
Little Cottage Company ....G 330 893-4212
  Dundee *(G-9021)*
Pioneer National Latex Inc ....D 419 289-3300
  Ashland *(G-736)*
RPM Consumer Holding Company ....G 330 273-5090
  Medina *(G-13330)*
S Toys Holdings LLC ....A 330 656-0440
  Streetsboro *(G-17693)*
Step2 Company LLC ....B 866 429-5200
  Streetsboro *(G-17700)*
Step2 Company LLC ....B 419 938-6343
  Perrysville *(G-16032)*
The Guardtower Inc ....F 614 488-4311
  Columbus *(G-7524)*
Unique-Chardan Inc ....E 419 636-6900
  Bryan *(G-2311)*
Vacuum Finishing Company ....F 440 286-4386
  Chardon *(G-3140)*
Wells Manufacturing Co Llc ....F 937 987-2481
  New Vienna *(G-14826)*

TOYS & HOBBY GOODS & SPLYS, WHOLESALE: Arts/Crafts Eqpt/Sply

AW Faber-Castell Usa Inc ....D 216 643-4660
  Cleveland *(G-4780)*
Larose Industries LLC ....E 419 237-1600
  Fayette *(G-9634)*

PRODUCT SECTION — TRANSFORMERS: Electric

Ramon Robinson .... G 330 883-3244
  Vienna (G-19208)

TOYS & HOBBY GOODS & SPLYS, WHOLESALE: Balloons, Novelty

Galaxy Balloons Incorporated .... C 216 476-3360
  Cleveland (G-5287)

TOYS & HOBBY GOODS & SPLYS, WHOLESALE: Dolls

Huston Gifts Dolls and Flowers .... G 740 775-9141
  Chillicothe (G-3193)
Middleton Llyd Dolls Inc .... G 740 989-2082
  Coolville (G-7674)

TOYS & HOBBY GOODS & SPLYS, WHOLESALE: Educational Toys

Bendon Inc .... D 419 207-3600
  Ashland (G-685)

TOYS & HOBBY GOODS & SPLYS, WHOLESALE: Playing Cards

H & H of Milford Ohio LLC .... G 513 576-9004
  Milford (G-14015)

TOYS & HOBBY GOODS & SPLYS, WHOLESALE: Toys & Games

Advance Novelty Incorporated .... G 419 424-0363
  Findlay (G-9647)

TOYS & HOBBY GOODS & SPLYS, WHOLESALE: Toys, NEC

Ball Bounce and Sport Inc .... B 419 289-9310
  Ashland (G-682)

TOYS & HOBBY GOODS & SPLYS, WHOLESALE: Video Games

Lasermark LLC .... G 513 312-9889
  Dayton (G-8306)

TOYS, HOBBY GOODS & SPLYS WHOLESALERS

Mini Graphics Inc .... G 513 563-8600
  Cincinnati (G-4030)
Toy & Sport Trends Inc .... E 419 748-8880
  Napoleon (G-14562)
Wooden Horse .... G 740 503-5243
  Baltimore (G-1046)

TOYS: Dolls, Stuffed Animals & Parts

Datatex Media Dolls .... G 216 598-1000
  Cleveland (G-5070)

TOYS: Kites

Premier Kites & Designs Inc .... G 888 416-0174
  Portsmouth (G-16296)

TOYS: Rubber

Pioneer National Latex Inc .... D 419 289-3300
  Ashland (G-736)
Plan B Toys Ltd .... G 614 751-6605
  Groveport (G-10510)

TRADE SHOW ARRANGEMENT SVCS

Publishing Group Ltd .... F 614 572-1240
  Columbus (G-7356)
Relx Inc .... E 937 865-6800
  Miamisburg (G-13708)

TRAILERS & PARTS: Boat

Hitch-Hiker Mfg Inc .... F 330 542-3052
  New Middletown (G-14750)
Loadmaster Trailer Company .... F 419 732-3434
  Port Clinton (G-16250)
Lux Corporation .... G 419 562-7978
  Bucyrus (G-2338)

TRAILERS & PARTS: Truck & Semi's

All A Cart Manufacturing Inc .... F 614 443-5544
  Worthington (G-20675)
American Mnfcturing Operations .... G 419 269-1560
  Toledo (G-18176)
Bair Bodies & Trailers Inc .... G 330 343-4853
  Dover (G-8806)
Bell Logistics Co .... E 740 702-9830
  Chillicothe (G-3177)
Brothers Equipment Inc .... G 216 458-0180
  Cleveland (G-4843)
Bruce High Performance Tran .... E 440 357-8964
  Painesville (G-15720)
David Ogilbee .... G 740 929-2638
  Hebron (G-10741)
Diamond Trailers Inc .... E 513 738-4500
  Shandon (G-16941)
Engineered MBL Solutions Inc .... F 513 724-0247
  Batavia (G-1144)
Extreme Trailers LLC .... G 330 440-0026
  Dover (G-8825)
Great Dane LLC .... E 614 876-0666
  Hilliard (G-10826)
H & H Equipment Inc .... G 330 264-5400
  Wooster (G-20601)
High Tech Prfmce Trlrs Inc .... D 440 357-8964
  Painesville (G-15746)
J & L Body Inc .... F 216 661-2323
  Brooklyn Heights (G-2126)
Jerry Tadlock .... G 937 544-2851
  West Union (G-19963)
Jsm Express Inc .... G 216 331-2008
  Euclid (G-9423)
Kenan Advantage Group Inc .... E 614 878-4050
  Columbus (G-7085)
Larry Moore .... G 740 697-7085
  Roseville (G-16578)
Longriders Trucking Company .... G 740 975-7863
  Mount Vernon (G-14489)
Lyons .... G 440 224-0676
  Kingsville (G-11460)
M & W Trailers Inc .... F 419 453-3331
  Ottoville (G-15682)
Mac Manufacturing Inc .... A 330 823-9900
  Alliance (G-483)
Mac Manufacturing Inc .... C 330 829-1680
  Salem (G-16759)
Mac Steel Trailer Ltd .... E 330 823-9900
  Alliance (G-484)
Mac Trailer Manufacturing Inc .... C 330 823-9900
  Alliance (G-485)
Mac Trailer Service Inc .... E 330 823-9190
  Alliance (G-486)
Majestic Trailers Inc .... F 330 798-1698
  Akron (G-265)
Martin Allen Trailer LLC .... G 330 942-0217
  Brunswick (G-2220)
Moritz International Inc .... E 419 526-5222
  Mansfield (G-12487)
Navarre Trailer Sales Inc .... G 330 879-2406
  Navarre (G-14583)
Paccar Inc .... A 740 774-5111
  Chillicothe (G-3205)
Rock Line Products Inc .... G 419 738-4400
  Wapakoneta (G-19349)
Saf-Holland Inc .... E 513 874-7888
  West Chester (G-19896)
Shilling Transport .... G 330 948-1105
  Lodi (G-12019)
Trailer One Inc .... F 330 723-7474
  Medina (G-13354)
Trailex Inc .... F 330 533-6814
  Canfield (G-2551)
Tri County Wheel and Rim Ltd .... G 419 666-1760
  Northwood (G-15348)
Wabash National Corporation .... D 419 434-9409
  Findlay (G-9774)

TRAILERS & TRAILER EQPT

Blue Ribbon Trailers Ltd .... F 330 538-4114
  North Jackson (G-15142)
Cleveland Hdwr & Forging Co .... E 216 641-5200
  Cleveland (G-4962)
D & A Custom Trailer Inc .... G 740 922-2205
  Uhrichsville (G-18883)
Fitchville East Corp .... E 419 929-1510
  New London (G-14729)
Hawkline Nevada LLC .... E 937 444-4295
  Mount Orab (G-14442)
Interstate Truckway Inc .... E 614 771-1220
  Columbus (G-7047)
Rankin Mfg Inc .... E 419 929-8338
  New London (G-14735)
Transglobal Inc .... G 419 396-9079
  Carey (G-2890)

TRAILERS OR VANS: Horse Transportation, Fifth-Wheel Type

Mr Trailer Sales Inc .... G 330 339-7701
  New Philadelphia (G-14789)
Pegasus Vans & Trailers Inc .... E 419 625-8953
  Sandusky (G-16837)

TRAILERS: Bodies

East Manufacturing Corporation .... B 330 325-9921
  Randolph (G-16360)
East Manufacturing Corporation .... B 330 325-9921
  Randolph (G-16361)
Gerich Fiberglass Inc .... E 419 362-4591
  Mount Gilead (G-14424)
Haulette Manufacturing Inc .... D 419 586-1717
  Celina (G-2966)
Heritage Manufacturing Inc .... G 217 854-2513
  Akron (G-206)
J W Devers & Son Inc .... F 937 854-3040
  Trotwood (G-18628)
L C Smith Co .... G 440 327-1251
  Elyria (G-9283)
Quick Loadz Delivery Sys LLC .... E 888 304-3946
  Nelsonville (G-14594)
R J Cox Co .... G 937 548-4699
  Arcanum (G-631)
Stahl/Scott Fetzer Company .... C 419 864-8045
  Cardington (G-2876)
Stahl/Scott Fetzer Company .... C 800 277-8245
  Wooster (G-20658)

TRAILERS: Camping, Tent-Type

Isaacs Jr Floyd Thomas .... G 513 899-2342
  Morrow (G-14412)

TRAILERS: Semitrailers, Missile Transportation

Ds Express Carriers Inc .... G 419 433-6200
  Norwalk (G-15388)
Pdi Ground Support Systems Inc .... D 216 271-7344
  Solon (G-17214)

TRAILERS: Semitrailers, Truck Tractors

4w Services .... F 614 554-5427
  Hebron (G-10736)
Nelson Manufacturing Company .... D 419 523-5321
  Ottawa (G-15660)

TRANSDUCERS: Electrical Properties

D C M Industries Inc .... F 937 254-8500
  Dayton (G-8124)
Guitammer Company .... G 614 898-9370
  Westerville (G-19995)
Ohio Semitronics Inc .... D 614 777-1005
  Hilliard (G-10847)

TRANSDUCERS: Pressure

Omega Engineering Inc .... E 740 965-9340
  Sunbury (G-17896)
Sensotec LLC .... G 614 481-8616
  Hilliard (G-10860)

TRANSFORMERS: Distribution

Darrah Electric Company .... E 216 631-0912
  Cleveland (G-5067)

TRANSFORMERS: Distribution, Electric

Clark Substations LLC .... E 330 452-5200
  Canton (G-2628)
Tesa Inc .... G 614 847-8200
  Lewis Center (G-11784)

TRANSFORMERS: Electric

Control Transformer Inc .... E 330 637-6015
  Cortland (G-7706)
Delta Transformer Inc .... G 513 242-9400
  Cincinnati (G-3581)

Employee Codes: A=Over 500 employees, B=251-500
C=101-250, D=51-100, E=20-50, F=10-19, G=3-9

TRANSFORMERS: Electric

Nautilus Hyosung America Inc .... G 937 203-4900
  Miamisburg *(G-13697)*
Schneider Electric Usa Inc .... D 513 755-5000
  West Chester *(G-19792)*
Transcontinental Electric LLC .... G 614 496-4379
  Columbus *(G-7538)*
Vida Ve Corp .... G 614 203-2607
  Dublin *(G-9008)*

TRANSFORMERS: Furnace, Electric

Ajax Tocco Magnethermic Corp .... C 330 372-8511
  Warren *(G-19364)*

TRANSFORMERS: Ignition, Domestic Fuel Burners

Alfred J Buescher Jr .... G 216 752-3676
  Cleveland *(G-4660)*

TRANSFORMERS: Machine Tool

Pioneer Transformer Company .... G 419 737-2304
  Pioneer *(G-16090)*

TRANSFORMERS: Meters, Electronic

Spectre Sensors Inc .... G 440 250-0372
  Westlake *(G-20160)*

TRANSFORMERS: Power Related

Acuity Brands Lighting Inc .... B 740 349-4343
  Newark *(G-14848)*
Contact Industries Inc .... E 419 884-9788
  Lexington *(G-11804)*
Custom Coil & Transformer Co .... E 740 452-5211
  Zanesville *(G-21126)*
Eaton Electric Holdings LLC .... G 440 523-5000
  Cleveland *(G-5151)*
Eaton Leasing Corporation .... G 216 382-2292
  Beachwood *(G-1235)*
Energy Developments Inc .... G 440 774-6816
  Oberlin *(G-15494)*
Fishel Company .... D 614 850-4400
  Columbus *(G-6926)*
Fostoria Bshngs Inslators Corp .... G 419 435-7514
  Fostoria *(G-9839)*
Fostoria Bushings Inc .... G 419 435-7514
  Fostoria *(G-9840)*
General Electric Company .... D 216 883-1000
  Cleveland *(G-5306)*
Hannon Company .... D 330 456-4728
  Canton *(G-2693)*
Japlar Group Inc .... F 513 791-7192
  Cincinnati *(G-3870)*
Lake Shore Electric Corp .... E 440 232-0200
  Bedford *(G-1422)*
Matlock Electric Co Inc .... E 513 731-9600
  Cincinnati *(G-3986)*
Morlan & Associates Inc .... E 614 889-6152
  Hilliard *(G-10842)*
Norlake Manufacturing Company .... D 440 353-3200
  North Ridgeville *(G-15241)*
Ohio Semitronics Inc .... D 614 777-1005
  Hilliard *(G-10847)*
Otc Services Inc .... D 330 871-2444
  Louisville *(G-12163)*
Peak Electric Inc .... G 419 726-4848
  Toledo *(G-18460)*
Precision Switching Inc .... G 800 800-8143
  Mansfield *(G-12502)*
Qualtek Electronics Corp .... C 440 951-3300
  Mentor *(G-13567)*
Schneider Electric Usa Inc .... B 513 523-4171
  Oxford *(G-15700)*
Siemens Industry Inc .... G 937 593-6010
  Bellefontaine *(G-1525)*
Specialty Magnetics LLC .... G 330 468-8434
  Macedonia *(G-12327)*

TRANSFORMERS: Specialty

LTI Power Systems .... E 440 327-5050
  Elyria *(G-9290)*

TRANSFORMERS: Voltage Regulating

Transformer Associates Limited .... G 330 430-0750
  Canton *(G-2844)*
Voltage Regulator Sales & Svcs .... G 937 878-0673
  Fairborn *(G-9474)*

TRANSLATION & INTERPRETATION SVCS

Advanced Translation/Cnsltng .... E 440 716-0820
  Westlake *(G-20087)*
Asist Translation Services .... F 614 451-6744
  Columbus *(G-6620)*
Technical Translation Services .... F 440 942-3130
  Willoughby *(G-20443)*

TRANSMISSION FLUID, MADE FROM PURCHASED MATERIALS

Koki Laboratories Inc .... E 330 773-7669
  Akron *(G-241)*

TRANSMISSIONS: Motor Vehicle

A & H Automotive Industries .... G 614 235-1759
  Columbus *(G-6514)*
Ada Technologies Inc .... B 419 634-7000
  Ada *(G-3)*
Comprehensive Logistics Co Inc .... E 440 934-3517
  Avon *(G-945)*
Custom Cltch Jint Hydrlics Inc .... F 216 431-1630
  Cleveland *(G-5046)*
Dayton Superior Pdts Co Inc .... G 937 332-1930
  Troy *(G-18646)*
FCA US LLC .... A 419 661-3500
  Perrysburg *(G-15949)*
Gear Star American Performance .... G 330 434-5216
  Akron *(G-183)*
Metro Mech Inc .... G 216 641-6262
  Cleveland *(G-5662)*

TRANSPORTATION EQPT & SPLYS, WHOLESALE: Boats, Non-Rec

Duck Water Boats Inc .... G 330 602-9008
  Dover *(G-8824)*

TRANSPORTATION EQPT & SPLYS, WHOLESALE: Combat Vehicles

Unity Cable Technologies Inc .... G 419 322-4118
  Toledo *(G-18584)*

TRANSPORTATION EQPT & SPLYS, WHOLESALE: Tanks & Tank Compnts

Eleet Cryogenics Inc .... E 330 874-4009
  Bolivar *(G-1913)*

TRANSPORTATION EQPT & SPLYS WHOLESALERS, NEC

Dircksen and Associates Inc .... G 614 238-0413
  Columbus *(G-6865)*
Omsi Transmissions Inc .... G 330 405-7350
  Twinsburg *(G-18826)*

TRANSPORTATION EQUIPMENT, NEC

Besl Specialized Carrier .... G 740 599-6305
  Danville *(G-7957)*
Cleveland Wheels .... D 440 937-6211
  Avon *(G-944)*

TRANSPORTATION PROGRAM REGULATION & ADMIN, GOVT: State

Ohio Department Transportation .... E 614 351-2898
  Columbus *(G-7244)*
Transportation Ohio Department .... G 740 927-2285
  Pataskala *(G-15846)*

TRANSPORTATION SVCS, AIR, NONSCHEDULED: Air Cargo Carriers

Grand Aire Inc .... E 419 861-6700
  Swanton *(G-17913)*

TRANSPORTATION SVCS, NEC

Anro Logistics Inc .... G 614 428-7490
  Westerville *(G-19978)*

TRANSPORTATION SVCS: Railroads, Steam

Covia Holdings Corporation .... D 440 214-3284
  Independence *(G-11123)*

TRANSPORTATION: Air, Scheduled Passenger

Grand Aire Inc .... E 419 861-6700
  Swanton *(G-17913)*
Ruhe Sales Inc .... F 419 943-3357
  Leipsic *(G-11736)*

TRANSPORTATION: Deep Sea Foreign Freight

Faircosa LLC .... G 216 577-9909
  Cleveland *(G-5215)*

TRANSPORTATION: Horse-Drawn

Victorian Farms .... G 330 628-9188
  Atwater *(G-864)*

TRAPS: Animal, Iron Or Steel

Butera Manufacturing Inc .... F 440 516-3698
  Willoughby Hills *(G-20467)*
Butera Manufacturing Inds .... G 216 761-8800
  Cleveland *(G-4855)*

TRAVEL TRAILERS & CAMPERS

Airstream Inc .... B 937 596-6111
  Jackson Center *(G-11205)*
Capitol City Trailers Inc .... D 614 491-2616
  Obetz *(G-15507)*
Cecil Caudill Trailer Sls Inc .... F 740 574-0704
  Franklin Furnace *(G-9933)*
D W Truax Enterprise Inc .... G 740 695-2596
  Saint Clairsville *(G-16631)*
Gerich Fiberglass Inc .... E 419 362-4591
  Mount Gilead *(G-14424)*
Hybrid Trailer Co LLC .... G 419 433-3022
  Huron *(G-11098)*

TRAVELER ACCOMMODATIONS, NEC

Amish Door Inc .... B 330 359-5464
  Wilmot *(G-20513)*
John Purdum .... G 513 897-9686
  Waynesville *(G-19569)*
Norstar Aluminum Molds Inc .... D 440 632-0853
  Middlefield *(G-13841)*

TRAYS: Plastic

Fastformingcom LLC .... F 330 927-3277
  Rittman *(G-16520)*

TRAYS: Rubber

Grypmat Inc .... G 419 953-7607
  Celina *(G-2964)*

TROPHIES, NEC

All American Trophy .... G 614 231-8824
  Columbus *(G-6565)*
B & B Trophies & Awards .... G 330 225-6193
  Brunswick *(G-2190)*
Ginos Awards Inc .... E 216 831-6565
  Warrensville Heights *(G-19469)*
Lawnview Industries Inc .... C 937 653-5217
  Urbana *(G-19003)*
Regal Trophy & Awards Company .... G 877 492-7531
  Sidney *(G-17064)*
Tempo Manufacturing Company .... G 937 773-6613
  Piqua *(G-16165)*

TROPHIES, PLATED, ALL METALS

Behrco Inc .... G 419 394-1612
  Saint Marys *(G-16676)*

TROPHIES, STAINLESS STEEL

Hr Machine LLC .... G 937 222-7644
  Beavercreek *(G-1323)*

TROPHIES, WHOLESALE

Behrco Inc .... G 419 394-1612
  Saint Marys *(G-16676)*
Dern Trophies Corp .... F 614 895-3260
  Westerville *(G-19987)*
Sharonco Inc .... G 419 882-3443
  Sylvania *(G-17960)*

PRODUCT SECTION

TRUCK PARTS & ACCESSORIES: Wholesalers

TROPHIES: Metal, Exc Silver

Company Front Awards .... G ...... 440 636-5493 Middlefield (G-13786)	
Dern Trophies Corp .... F ...... 614 895-3260 Westerville (G-19987)	
Hit Trophy Inc .... G ...... 419 445-5356 Archbold (G-653)	
Mid Ohio Trophy & Awards .... G ...... 419 756-2266 Mansfield (G-12480)	
P S Superior Inc .... F ...... 216 587-1000 Cleveland (G-5833)	
Ray Rieser Trophy Co .... G ...... 614 279-1128 Columbus (G-7379)	

TROPHY & PLAQUE STORES

American Awards Inc .... F 614 875-1850
   Grove City (G-10414)
Auld Crafters Inc .... G 614 221-6825
   Columbus (G-6630)
B & B Trophies & Awards .... G 330 225-6193
   Brunswick (G-2190)
Behrco Inc .... G 419 394-1612
   Saint Marys (G-16676)
Designer Awards Inc .... G 937 339-4444
   Troy (G-18650)
Fineline Imprints Inc .... E 740 453-1083
   Zanesville (G-21135)
Fried Daddy .... G 937 854-4542
   Dayton (G-8207)
Gauntlet Awards & Engraving ...... G 937 890-5811
   Dayton (G-8214)
Greg Blume .... G 740 574-2308
   Wheelersburg (G-20182)
Gym Pro LLC .... G 740 984-4143
   Waterford (G-19485)
Hit Trophy Inc .... G 419 445-5356
   Archbold (G-653)
Initially Yours .... G 216 228-4478
   Lakewood (G-11521)
Jakes Sportswear Ltd .... F 740 746-8356
   Sugar Grove (G-17839)
Joe Paxton .... G 614 424-9000
   Columbus (G-7071)
John C Starr .... G 740 852-5592
   London (G-12063)
L S Manufacturing Inc .... G 614 885-7988
   Worthington (G-20694)
M & M Engraving .... G 216 749-7166
   Cleveland (G-5591)
Mid Ohio Trophy & Awards .... G 419 756-2266
   Mansfield (G-12480)
Minotas Trophies & Awards .... G 440 720-1288
   Cleveland (G-5696)
Miracle Custom Awards & Gifts ... G 330 376-8335
   Akron (G-283)
Play All LLC .... G 440 992-7529
   Ashtabula (G-799)
Quali-Tee Design Sports .... F 937 382-7997
   Wilmington (G-20505)
Qualitee Design Sportswear Co ... E 740 333-8337
   Wshngtn CT Hs (G-20739)
Ray Rieser Trophy Co .... G 614 279-1128
   Columbus (G-7379)
Sun Shine Awards .... F 740 425-2504
   Barnesville (G-1119)
The Hartman Corp .... G 614 475-5035
   Columbus (G-7525)

TRUCK & BUS BODIES: Ambulance

Alterntive Spport Appratus LLC ... G 740 922-2727
   Midvale (G-13973)
La Boit Specialty Vehicles .... E 614 231-7640
   Gahanna (G-10088)
Life Star Rescue Inc .... E 419 238-2507
   Van Wert (G-19101)

TRUCK & BUS BODIES: Automobile Wrecker Truck

Miller Industries Inc .... G 937 293-2223
   Dayton (G-8362)
Rke Trucking Co .... F 614 891-1786
   Westerville (G-20021)

TRUCK & BUS BODIES: Bus Bodies

Gerich Fiberglass Inc .... E 419 362-4591
   Mount Gilead (G-14424)

TRUCK & BUS BODIES: Car Carrier

Kilar Manufacturing Inc .... E 330 534-8961
   Hubbard (G-11004)

TRUCK & BUS BODIES: Cement Mixer

Kimble Mixer Company .... D 330 308-6700
   New Philadelphia (G-14779)
McNeilus Truck and Mfg Inc .... G 614 868-0760
   Gahanna (G-10089)
McNeilus Truck and Mfg Inc .... E 513 874-2022
   Fairfield (G-9528)

TRUCK & BUS BODIES: Dump Truck

Daniel Wagner .... G 740 942-2928
   Cadiz (G-2397)
Friesen Transfer Ltd .... G 614 873-5672
   Plain City (G-16193)
Kruz Inc .... E 330 878-5595
   Dover (G-8835)

TRUCK & BUS BODIES: Garbage Or Refuse Truck

Arts Rolloffs & Refuse Inc .... G 419 991-3730
   Lima (G-11843)

TRUCK & BUS BODIES: Motor Vehicle, Specialty

Bush Specialty Vehicles Inc .... F 937 382-5502
   Wilmington (G-20487)
Columbus Mobility Specialist .... G 614 825-8996
   Worthington (G-20681)
Willard Machine & Welding Inc .... F 330 467-0642
   Macedonia (G-12338)

TRUCK & BUS BODIES: Tank Truck

Bosserman Automotive Engrg LLC ... G 419 722-2879
   Findlay (G-9660)
Marengo Fabricated Steel Ltd ...... F 800 919-2652
   Marengo (G-12593)
Reberland Equipment Inc .... G 330 698-5883
   Apple Creek (G-618)
Tremcar USA Inc .... D 330 878-7708
   Strasburg (G-17654)

TRUCK & BUS BODIES: Truck Beds

Able Industries Inc .... G 614 252-1050
   Columbus (G-6528)
Crosco .... G 330 477-1999
   Canton (G-2639)
Zie Bart Rhino Linings Toledo ...... G 419 841-2886
   Toledo (G-18606)

TRUCK & BUS BODIES: Truck Cabs, Motor Vehicles

Valco Industries Inc .... E 937 399-7400
   Springfield (G-17513)

TRUCK & BUS BODIES: Truck, Motor Vehicle

Altec Industries Inc .... F 205 408-2341
   Cuyahoga Falls (G-7833)
Brown Industrial Inc .... E 937 693-3838
   Botkins (G-1934)
Elliott Machine Works Inc .... E 419 468-4709
   Galion (G-10137)
Kaffenbarger Truck Eqp Co .... C 937 845-3804
   New Carlisle (G-14669)
Neiss Body & Equipment Corp .... G 330 828-2409
   Dalton (G-7948)
Proform Group Inc .... E 614 332-9654
   Columbus (G-7354)
Schodorf Truck Body & Eqp Co ... E 614 228-6793
   Columbus (G-7426)
Venco Venturo Industries LLC ..... E 513 772-8448
   Cincinnati (G-4473)

TRUCK & BUS BODIES: Utility Truck

Q T Columbus LLC .... G 800 758-2410
   Columbus (G-7359)
QT Equipment Company .... E 330 724-3055
   Akron (G-334)

TRUCK & BUS BODIES: Van Bodies

Ellis & Watts Intl LLC .... G 513 752-9000
   Batavia (G-1143)
Ford Motor Company .... A 440 933-1215
   Avon Lake (G-986)

TRUCK BODIES: Body Parts

Brothers Body and Eqp LLC .... F 419 462-1975
   Galion (G-10124)
Cota International Inc .... F 937 526-5520
   Versailles (G-19177)
Dan Patrick Enterprises Inc .... G 740 477-1006
   Circleville (G-4542)
H & H Truck Parts LLC .... G 216 642-4540
   Cleveland (G-5362)
Kaffenbarger Truck Eqp Co .... E 513 772-6800
   Cincinnati (G-3892)
Kimble Custom Chassis Company ... D 877 546-2537
   New Philadelphia (G-14778)
Mancor Ohio Inc .... E 937 228-6141
   Dayton (G-8329)
Mancor Ohio Inc .... D 937 228-6141
   Dayton (G-8330)
Silverado Trucks & Accessories ... G 937 492-8862
   Sidney (G-17080)
Wilson Seat Company Inc .... E 513 732-2460
   Batavia (G-1197)

TRUCK BODY SHOP

Q T Columbus LLC .... G 800 758-2410
   Columbus (G-7359)
QT Equipment Company .... E 330 724-3055
   Akron (G-334)

TRUCK DRIVER SVCS

Industrial Repair & Mfg Inc .... D 419 822-4232
   Delta (G-8774)

TRUCK GENERAL REPAIR SVC

Dalin Auto Service .... G 440 997-3301
   Ashtabula (G-770)
Dan Patrick Enterprises Inc .... G 740 477-1006
   Circleville (G-4542)
Knippen Chrysler Dodge Jeep .... E 419 695-4976
   Delphos (G-8746)
M & W Trailers Inc .... F 419 453-3331
   Ottoville (G-15682)
Top Notch Fleet Services LLC ..... G 419 260-4057
   Maumee (G-13155)

TRUCK PAINTING & LETTERING SVCS

Design Masters Inc .... G 513 772-7175
   Cincinnati (G-3584)
Ham Signs LLC .... G 937 454-9111
   Dayton (G-8242)
Mike B Crawford .... G 330 673-7944
   Kent (G-11355)
Sign Lady Inc .... G 419 476-9191
   Toledo (G-18522)

TRUCK PARTS & ACCESSORIES: Wholesalers

Adelmans Truck Parts Corp .... E 330 456-0206
   Canton (G-2558)
Adelmans Truck Parts Corp .... F 216 362-0500
   Canton (G-2559)
Buyers Products Company .... C 440 974-8888
   Mentor (G-13408)
Buyers Products Company .... G 440 974-8888
   Mentor (G-13410)
Dan Patrick Enterprises Inc .... G 740 477-1006
   Circleville (G-4542)
East Manufacturing Corporation ... B 330 325-9921
   Randolph (G-16360)
Kaffenbarger Truck Eqp Co .... C 937 845-3804
   New Carlisle (G-14669)
Malone Specialty Inc .... F 440 255-4200
   Mentor (G-13510)
Mytee Products Inc .... F 440 591-4301
   Aurora (G-894)
Perkins Motor Service Ltd .... E 440 277-1256
   Lorain (G-12112)
Silverado Trucks & Accessories ... G 937 492-8862
   Sidney (G-17080)
Youngstown-Kenworth Inc .... E 330 534-9761
   Hubbard (G-11014)

Employee Codes: A=Over 500 employees, B=251-500
C=101-250, D=51-100, E=20-50, F=10-19, G=3-9

TRUCKING & HAULING SVCS: Animal & Farm Prdt

Pro-Pet LLC .... G 419 394-3374
  Saint Marys *(G-16695)*

TRUCKING & HAULING SVCS: Contract Basis

Kmj Leasing Ltd .... E 614 871-3883
  Orient *(G-15575)*

TRUCKING & HAULING SVCS: Garbage, Collect/Transport Only

Werlor Inc .... E 419 784-4285
  Defiance *(G-8647)*

TRUCKING & HAULING SVCS: Hazardous Waste

Sara Hudson .... G 850 890-1455
  Dayton *(G-8493)*

TRUCKING & HAULING SVCS: Heavy Machinery, Local

J & A Machine .... G 330 424-5235
  Lisbon *(G-11970)*

TRUCKING & HAULING SVCS: Liquid, Local

Mac Oil Field Service Inc .... F 330 674-7371
  Millersburg *(G-14109)*

TRUCKING & HAULING SVCS: Machinery, Heavy

L A Productions Co LLC .... G 330 666-4230
  Akron *(G-243)*

TRUCKING & HAULING SVCS: Mail Carriers, Contract

Glenn Michael Brick .... F 740 391-5735
  Flushing *(G-9783)*

TRUCKING, ANIMAL

Yemaneh Musie .... G 614 506-3687
  Columbus *(G-7622)*

TRUCKING, AUTOMOBILE CARRIER

Akron Centl Engrv Mold Mch Inc .... E 330 794-8704
  Akron *(G-34)*
Jatdco LLC .... G 440 238-6570
  Strongsville *(G-17757)*

TRUCKING, DUMP

Carl E Oeder Sons Sand & Grav .... E 513 494-1555
  Lebanon *(G-11640)*
Edw C Levy Co .... E 419 822-8286
  Delta *(G-8769)*
Kirby and Sons Inc .... F 419 927-2260
  Upper Sandusky *(G-18959)*
Roe Transportation Entps Inc .... G 937 497-7161
  Sidney *(G-17068)*
Silverado Trucks & Accessories .... G 937 492-8862
  Sidney *(G-17080)*

TRUCKING: Except Local

Bc Investment Corporation .... G 330 262-3070
  Wooster *(G-20570)*
Buckeye Energy Resources Inc .... G 740 452-9506
  Zanesville *(G-21113)*
Chagrin Vly Stl Erectors Inc .... F 440 975-1556
  Willoughby Hills *(G-20468)*
Custom Built Crates Inc .... E 513 248-4422
  Milford *(G-14006)*
Ds Express Carriers Inc .... G 419 433-6200
  Norwalk *(G-15388)*
Euclid Chemical Company .... E 800 321-7628
  Cleveland *(G-5193)*
Faircosa LLC .... G 216 577-9909
  Cleveland *(G-5215)*
Flegal Brothers Inc .... F 419 298-3539
  Edgerton *(G-9175)*
Oeder Carl E Sons Sand & Grav .... E 513 494-1238
  Lebanon *(G-11677)*

Parobek Trucking Co .... G 419 869-7500
  West Salem *(G-19957)*

TRUCKING: Local, With Storage

M G Q Inc .... E 419 992-4236
  Tiffin *(G-18067)*
Resource Recycling Inc .... F 419 222-2702
  Lima *(G-11929)*

TRUCKING: Local, Without Storage

Collier Well Eqp & Sup Inc .... F 330 345-3968
  Wooster *(G-20580)*
Corbett R Caudill Chipping Inc .... F 740 596-5984
  Hamden *(G-10522)*
De Milta Sand and Gravel Inc .... F 440 942-2015
  Willoughby *(G-20307)*
Erichar Inc .... G 216 402-2628
  Cleveland *(G-5188)*
Fairway Carts Parts & More LLC .... E 234 209-9008
  North Canton *(G-15081)*
Haul-Away Containers Inc .... G 440 546-1879
  Richfield *(G-16473)*
Hershberger Manufacturing .... E 440 272-5555
  Windsor *(G-20526)*
M & R Redi Mix Inc .... G 419 445-7771
  Pettisville *(G-16034)*
Mm Outsourcing LLC .... F 937 661-4300
  Leesburg *(G-11714)*
Olen Corporation .... G 740 745-5865
  Saint Louisville *(G-16674)*
Parobek Trucking Co .... G 419 869-7500
  West Salem *(G-19957)*
R J Dobay Enterprises Inc .... G 440 227-1005
  Burton *(G-2367)*
Rjw Trucking Company Ltd .... E 740 363-5343
  Delaware *(G-8720)*
Roth Transit Inc .... G 937 773-5051
  Piqua *(G-16160)*
Third Party Service Ltd .... F 419 872-2312
  Perrysburg *(G-16015)*
Ward Construction Co .... F 419 943-2450
  Leipsic *(G-11739)*

TRUCKS & TRACTORS: Industrial

Belden Brick Company .... E 330 852-2411
  Sugarcreek *(G-17842)*
Canton Elevator Inc .... D 330 833-3600
  North Canton *(G-15076)*
Cincinnati Barge Rail Trml LLC .... G 513 227-3611
  Cincinnati *(G-3482)*
City Machine Technologies Inc .... F 330 747-2639
  Youngstown *(G-20870)*
Crescent Metal Products Inc .... C 440 350-1100
  Mentor *(G-13426)*
Dragon Products LLC .... E 330 345-3968
  Wooster *(G-20586)*
Eagle Industrial Truck Mfg LLC .... E 734 442-1000
  Swanton *(G-17912)*
Falls Welding & Fabg Inc .... G 330 253-3437
  Akron *(G-165)*
Fame Tool & Mfg Co Inc .... E 513 271-6387
  Cincinnati *(G-3670)*
Foerster Instruments Inc .... F 330 332-9100
  Salem *(G-16739)*
Forte Indus Eqp Systems Inc .... E 513 398-2800
  Mason *(G-12871)*
G & T Manufacturing Co .... F 440 639-7777
  Mentor *(G-13453)*
General Electric Company .... B 513 977-1500
  Cincinnati *(G-3741)*
Gradall Industries Inc .... C 330 339-2211
  New Philadelphia *(G-14773)*
Grand Harbor Yacht Sales & Svc .... G 440 442-2919
  Cleveland *(G-5339)*
Harsco Corporation .... E 740 387-1150
  Marion *(G-12710)*
Hobart Brothers LLC .... A 937 332-5439
  Troy *(G-18669)*
Jh Industries Inc .... E 330 963-4105
  Twinsburg *(G-18797)*
Kinetic Technologies Inc .... F 440 943-4111
  Wickliffe *(G-20214)*
Lange Precision Inc .... F 513 530-9500
  Blue Ash *(G-1802)*
Martin Sprocket & Gear Inc .... D 419 485-5515
  Montpelier *(G-14312)*
Miller Products Inc .... E 330 308-5934
  New Philadelphia *(G-14786)*

Miners Tractor Sales Inc .... F 330 325-9914
  Rootstown *(G-16571)*
Mitchs Welding & Hitches .... G 419 893-3117
  Maumee *(G-13136)*
Parobek Trucking Co .... G 419 869-7500
  West Salem *(G-19957)*
Perfecto Industries Inc .... E 937 778-1900
  Piqua *(G-16149)*
Pollock Research & Design Inc .... E 330 332-3300
  Salem *(G-16767)*
Pucel Enterprises Inc .... D 216 881-4604
  Cleveland *(G-5933)*
Saf-Holland Inc .... G 513 874-7888
  West Chester *(G-19896)*
Scott-Randall Systems Inc .... F 937 446-2293
  Sardinia *(G-16873)*
Snair Co .... F 614 873-7020
  Plain City *(G-16212)*
Sroka Inc .... E 440 572-2811
  Strongsville *(G-17794)*
Stock Fairfield Corporation .... C 440 543-6000
  Chagrin Falls *(G-3078)*
Sweet Manufacturing Company .... E 937 325-1511
  Springfield *(G-17501)*
Tarpco Inc .... E 330 677-8277
  Kent *(G-11392)*
Trailer Component Mfg Inc .... E 440 255-2888
  Mentor *(G-13612)*
Transco Railway Products Inc .... E 419 726-3383
  Toledo *(G-18582)*
Waltco Lift Corp .... C 330 633-9191
  Tallmadge *(G-18013)*
Webb-Stiles Company .... D 330 225-7761
  Valley City *(G-19069)*
Youngstown-Kenworth Inc .... E 330 534-9761
  Hubbard *(G-11014)*

TRUCKS, INDL: Wholesalers

Tri-Mac Mfg & Svcs Co .... F 513 896-4445
  Hamilton *(G-10613)*

TRUCKS: Forklift

Foerster Systems Inc .... F 330 332-9100
  Salem *(G-16740)*
Forklifts of Americas LLC .... G 440 821-5143
  Highland Heights *(G-10790)*
Freedom Forklift Sales LLC .... G 330 289-0879
  Akron *(G-177)*
Integrity Industrial Eqp Inc .... G 937 238-9275
  Huber Heights *(G-11021)*
Marlow-2000 Inc .... F 216 362-8500
  Cleveland *(G-5625)*
Precision Equipment Llc .... G 330 220-7600
  Brunswick *(G-2228)*

TRUCKS: Indl

Chemtrans Logistics Inc .... G 419 447-8041
  Tiffin *(G-18056)*
Elliott Machine Works Inc .... E 419 468-4709
  Galion *(G-10137)*
Grand Aire Inc .... E 419 861-6700
  Swanton *(G-17913)*
Newsafe Transport Service Inc .... F 740 387-1679
  Marion *(G-12725)*
Surplus Freight Inc .... F 614 235-7660
  Gahanna *(G-10108)*
Triumphant Enterprises Inc .... E 513 617-1668
  Goshen *(G-10290)*
Yemaneh Musie .... G 614 506-3687
  Columbus *(G-7622)*

TRUNKS

Trunk Show .... G 330 565-5326
  Youngstown *(G-21054)*

TRUSSES & FRAMING: Prefabricated Metal

Shrock Prefab LLC .... F 740 599-9401
  Danville *(G-7965)*

TRUSSES: Wood, Floor

Khempco Bldg Sup Co Ltd Partnr .... D 740 549-0465
  Delaware *(G-8700)*

TRUSSES: Wood, Roof

Automated Bldg Components Inc .... E 419 257-2152
  North Baltimore *(G-15042)*

PRODUCT SECTION

TUNGSTEN CARBIDE POWDER

Buckeye Components LLC .... E 330 482-5163
  Columbiana *(G-6456)*
Building Concepts Inc .... F 419 298-2371
  Edgerton *(G-9169)*
Columbus Roof Trusses Inc .... E 614 272-6464
  Columbus *(G-6800)*
Columbus Roof Trusses Inc .... F 740 763-3000
  Newark *(G-14862)*
Contract Building Components .... E 937 644-0739
  Marysville *(G-12777)*
Dutchcraft Truss Component Inc .... F 330 862-2220
  Minerva *(G-14178)*
Fifth Avenue Lumber Co .... D 614 833-6655
  Canal Winchester *(G-2503)*
Four Js Bldg Components LLC .... F 740 886-6112
  Scottown *(G-16881)*
M & G Truss Rafters .... G 740 667-3166
  Coolville *(G-7673)*
Miller Truss LLC .... G 440 321-0126
  Middlefield *(G-13830)*
Ohio Valley Truss Co .... E 937 393-3995
  Hillsboro *(G-10887)*
Ohio Valley Truss Co .... E 937 393-3995
  Hillsboro *(G-10888)*
Pioneer Homes Inc .... G 419 737-2371
  Pioneer *(G-16089)*
Proline Truss .... F 419 895-9980
  Shiloh *(G-16999)*
R & L Truss Inc .... F 419 587-3440
  Grover Hill *(G-10519)*
Redbuilt LLC .... E 740 363-0870
  Delaware *(G-8719)*
Schilling Truss Inc .... F 740 984-2396
  Beverly *(G-1662)*
Stark Truss Company Inc .... D 330 478-2100
  Canton *(G-2825)*
Stark Truss Company Inc .... E 740 335-4156
  Washington Court Hou *(G-19478)*
Stark Truss Company Inc .... D 419 298-3777
  Edgerton *(G-9181)*
Stark Truss Company Inc .... E 330 756-3050
  Beach City *(G-1215)*
Stark Truss Company Inc .... F 330 478-2100
  Canton *(G-2824)*
Thomas Do-It Center Inc .... D 740 446-2002
  Gallipolis *(G-10176)*
Truss Worx LLC .... G 419 363-2100
  Rockford *(G-16541)*
Waynedale Truss & Panel Co .... G 330 683-4471
  Dalton *(G-7953)*
Waynedale Truss and Panel Co .... E 330 698-7373
  Apple Creek *(G-622)*

TRUST MANAGEMENT SVC, EXC EDUCATIONAL, RELIGIOUS & CHARITY

Americanhort Services Inc .... F 614 884-1203
  Columbus *(G-6588)*

TUB CONTAINERS: Plastic

Plas-Tanks Industries Inc .... E 513 942-3800
  Hamilton *(G-10596)*

TUBE & PIPE MILL EQPT

Atkore Plastic Pipe Corp .... D 330 627-8002
  Carrollton *(G-2916)*
Formtek Inc .... D 216 292-4460
  Cleveland *(G-5264)*
Graebener Group Tech Ltd .... G 419 591-7033
  Napoleon *(G-14540)*
Kusakabe America Corporation .... G 216 524-2485
  Cleveland *(G-5547)*
Pipeline Automation Syste Inc .... G 419 462-8833
  Galion *(G-10150)*

TUBE & TUBING FABRICATORS

Addition Mfg Tech LLC .... G 513 228-7000
  Lebanon *(G-11630)*
Beaverson Machine Inc .... G 419 923-8064
  Delta *(G-8766)*
Benjamin Steel Company Inc .... E 937 233-1212
  Springfield *(G-17368)*
Chardon Metal Products Co .... E 440 285-2147
  Chardon *(G-3102)*
Cleveland Plastic Fabricat .... F 216 797-7300
  Euclid *(G-9409)*
Dekay Fabricators Inc .... G 330 793-0826
  Youngstown *(G-20888)*

Ever Roll Specialties Co .... E 937 964-1302
  Springfield *(G-17399)*
Fabcraft Inc .... G 440 286-6700
  Chardon *(G-3111)*
H-P Products Inc .... E 330 875-7193
  Louisville *(G-12155)*
Hycom Inc .... E 330 753-2330
  Barberton *(G-1076)*
Hydra-TEC Inc .... G 330 225-8797
  Brunswick *(G-2213)*
Hydro Tube Enterprises Inc .... D 440 774-1022
  Oberlin *(G-15499)*
Kenley Enterprises LLC .... E 419 630-0921
  Bryan *(G-2293)*
Machine Dynamics & Engrg Inc .... D 330 868-5603
  Minerva *(G-14190)*
Moss Vale Inc .... F 513 939-1970
  Fairfield *(G-9531)*
Parker-Hannifin Corporation .... B 937 456-5571
  Eaton *(G-9163)*
S E Anning Company .... G 513 702-4417
  Cincinnati *(G-4295)*
S-P Company Inc .... F 330 482-0200
  Columbiana *(G-6479)*
Sanoh America Inc .... E 419 425-2600
  Findlay *(G-9751)*
Stam Inc .... E 440 974-2500
  Mentor *(G-13587)*
Tomco Machining Inc .... F 937 264-1943
  Dayton *(G-8560)*
Unison Industries LLC .... D 937 426-4676
  Alpha *(G-518)*
Unity Tube Inc .... F 330 426-4282
  East Palestine *(G-9088)*
US Tubular Products Inc .... D 330 832-1734
  North Lawrence *(G-15163)*
Woodsage Corporation .... D 419 476-3553
  Holland *(G-10967)*

TUBES: Finned, For Heat Transfer

Fin Tube Products Inc .... F 330 334-3736
  Wadsworth *(G-19240)*

TUBES: Generator, Electron Beam, Beta Ray

Fripro Energy LLC .... G 419 865-0002
  Maumee *(G-13111)*

TUBES: Hard Rubber

Usui International Corporation .... E 513 448-0410
  Cincinnati *(G-4459)*

TUBES: Paper

A T Tube Company Inc .... G 330 336-8706
  Wadsworth *(G-19219)*
Acme Spirally Wound Paper Pdts .... F 216 267-2950
  Cleveland *(G-4607)*
Advanced Paper Tube Inc .... F 216 281-5691
  Cleveland *(G-4630)*
Caraustar Industrial and Con .... E 330 868-4111
  Minerva *(G-14177)*
Caraustar Industries Inc .... E 330 665-7700
  Copley *(G-7679)*
Erdie Industries Inc .... D 440 288-0166
  Lorain *(G-12090)*
Ohio Paper Tube Co .... F 330 478-5171
  Canton *(G-2774)*

TUBES: Paper Or Fiber, Chemical Or Electrical Uses

Newkor Inc .... E 216 631-7800
  Cleveland *(G-5750)*

TUBES: Steel & Iron

Crest Bending Inc .... E 419 492-2108
  New Washington *(G-14828)*
Kirtland Capital Partners LP .... E 216 593-0100
  Beachwood *(G-1244)*
Phillips Mfg and Tower Co .... D 419 347-1720
  Shelby *(G-16985)*
Systems Jay LLC Nanogate .... F 419 747-1096
  Mansfield *(G-12524)*
Universal Metals Cutting Inc .... G 330 580-5192
  Canton *(G-2852)*

TUBES: Wrought, Welded Or Lock Joint

Tubetech Inc .... E 330 426-9476
  East Palestine *(G-9087)*
United Tube Corporation .... D 330 725-4196
  Medina *(G-13358)*
Welded Tubes Inc .... G 216 378-2092
  Orwell *(G-15637)*

TUBING: Copper

Arem Co .... F 440 974-6740
  Mentor *(G-13393)*

TUBING: Electrical Use, Quartz

Unity Cable Technologies Inc .... G 419 322-4118
  Toledo *(G-18584)*

TUBING: Flexible, Metallic

Tubular Techniques Inc .... G 614 529-4130
  Hilliard *(G-10872)*
Wayne Trail Technologies Inc .... D 937 295-2120
  Fort Loramie *(G-9811)*

TUBING: Glass

Glasstech Inc .... C 419 661-9500
  Perrysburg *(G-15959)*
Techneglas Inc .... G 419 873-2000
  Perrysburg *(G-16012)*

TUBING: Plastic

Akron Polymer Products Inc .... D 330 628-5551
  Akron *(G-48)*
Alkon Corporation .... D 419 355-9111
  Fremont *(G-9990)*
Dlhbowles Inc .... D 330 488-0716
  East Canton *(G-9039)*
Dlhbowles Inc .... B 330 478-2503
  Canton *(G-2661)*
Kentak Products Company .... G 330 386-3700
  East Liverpool *(G-9062)*
Kentak Products Company .... E 330 382-2000
  East Liverpool *(G-9063)*
Kentak Products Company .... G 330 532-6211
  East Liverpool *(G-9064)*
Normandy Products Company .... D 440 632-5050
  Middlefield *(G-13840)*
Quality Poly Corp .... F 330 453-9559
  Canton *(G-2796)*

TUBING: Rubber

Eagle Elastomer Inc .... E 330 923-7070
  Peninsula *(G-15893)*
Meridian Industries Inc .... D 330 359-5447
  Winesburg *(G-20533)*
Meridian Industries Inc .... D 330 673-1011
  Kent *(G-11351)*
Meteor Sealing Systems LLC .... G 330 343-9595
  Dover *(G-8840)*
Sml Inc .... G 330 668-6555
  Akron *(G-380)*
Trico Group LLC .... G 216 589-0198
  Cleveland *(G-6212)*
Trico Group Holdings LLC .... G 216 274-9027
  Cleveland *(G-6213)*

TUBING: Seamless

Mid-Ohio Tubing LLC .... G 419 883-2066
  Butler *(G-2376)*
Mid-Ohio Tubing LLC .... G 419 886-0220
  Bellville *(G-1559)*

TUGBOAT SVCS

Shelly Materials Inc .... G 330 673-3646
  Kent *(G-11385)*
Shelly Materials Inc .... D 740 246-6315
  Thornville *(G-18035)*

TUNGSTEN CARBIDE POWDER

Castlebar Corporation .... G 330 451-6511
  Canton *(G-2621)*
Tungsten Sltons Group Intl Inc .... G 440 708-3096
  Chagrin Falls *(G-3086)*

TUNGSTEN MILL PRDTS

Castlebar Corporation..........G....... 330 451-6511
Canton *(G-2621)*
H C Starck Inc..........B....... 216 692-3990
Euclid *(G-9418)*
Rhenium Alloys Inc..........D....... 440 365-7388
North Ridgeville *(G-15251)*

TURBINE GENERATOR SET UNITS: Hydraulic, Complete

Kw River Hydroelectric I LLC..........G....... 513 673-2251
Cincinnati *(G-3927)*

TURBINES & TURBINE GENERATOR SET UNITS, COMPLETE

Northel Usa LLC..........G....... 740 973-0309
Newark *(G-14904)*

TURBINES & TURBINE GENERATOR SETS

Alin Machining Company Inc..........D....... 740 223-0200
Marion *(G-12691)*
Arete Innovative Solutions LLC..........G....... 513 503-2712
Morrow *(G-14408)*
Argosy Wind Power Ltd..........G....... 440 539-1345
Aurora *(G-869)*
Babcock & Wilcox Company..........E....... 330 753-4511
Barberton *(G-1060)*
Babcock & Wilcox Company..........E....... 740 687-6500
Lancaster *(G-11546)*
Camfil USA Inc..........G....... 937 773-0866
Piqua *(G-16106)*
Eaton Leasing Corporation..........G....... 216 382-2292
Beachwood *(G-1235)*
Fluidpower Assembly Inc..........G....... 419 394-7486
Saint Marys *(G-16685)*
GE Aircraft Engines..........G....... 513 868-9906
Fairfield Township *(G-9581)*
General Electric Company..........F....... 513 243-9317
West Chester *(G-19712)*
Metalex Manufacturing Inc..........C....... 513 489-0507
Blue Ash *(G-1820)*
Pfpc Enterprises Inc..........B....... 513 941-6200
Cincinnati *(G-4155)*
R H Industries Inc..........E....... 216 281-5210
Cleveland *(G-5952)*
Siemens Energy Inc..........B....... 740 393-8897
Mount Vernon *(G-14510)*

TURBINES & TURBINE GENERATOR SETS & PARTS

Aero Propulsion Support Inc..........E....... 513 367-9452
Harrison *(G-10628)*

TURBINES: Gas, Mechanical Drive

On-Power Inc..........E....... 513 228-2100
Lebanon *(G-11679)*

TURBINES: Hydraulic, Complete

Fluid System Service Inc..........G....... 216 651-2450
Cleveland *(G-5254)*
Fusion Incorporated..........E....... 440 946-3300
Willoughby *(G-20327)*
Parker Triad Store..........D....... 937 293-4080
Moraine *(G-14374)*

TURBINES: Steam

Siemens Energy Inc..........E....... 740 504-1947
Mount Vernon *(G-14512)*
Steam Turb Alte Reso..........E....... 740 387-5535
Marion *(G-12737)*

TURBO-SUPERCHARGERS: Aircraft

Meak Solutions Llc..........G....... 440 796-8209
Mentor *(G-13513)*

TURNSTILES

Controlled Access Inc..........F....... 330 273-6185
Hinckley *(G-10899)*

TWINE PRDTS

R C Packaging Systems..........F....... 248 684-6363
Mentor *(G-13568)*

TYPE: Rubber

Farmed Materials Inc..........G....... 513 680-4046
Cincinnati *(G-3673)*

TYPESETTING SVC

21st Century Printers Inc..........G....... 513 771-4150
Cincinnati *(G-3268)*
A-A Blueprint Co Inc..........E....... 330 794-8803
Akron *(G-23)*
Activities Press Inc..........E....... 440 953-1200
Mentor *(G-13374)*
Advanced Translation/Cnsltng..........E....... 440 716-0820
Westlake *(G-20087)*
AGS Custom Graphics Inc..........D....... 330 963-7770
Macedonia *(G-12275)*
Alfacomp Inc..........G....... 216 459-1790
Cleveland *(G-4659)*
Anderson Graphics Inc..........E....... 330 745-2165
Barberton *(G-1052)*
Anthony Business Forms Inc..........F....... 937 253-0072
Dayton *(G-7971)*
Applied Graphics Ltd..........G....... 419 756-6882
Mansfield *(G-12407)*
Art Printing Co Inc..........G....... 419 281-4371
Ashland *(G-677)*
Art Tees Inc..........G....... 614 338-8337
Columbus *(G-6617)*
Asist Translation Services..........F....... 614 451-6744
Columbus *(G-6620)*
Baise Enterprises Inc..........G....... 614 444-3171
Columbus *(G-6642)*
Bill Wyatt Inc..........G....... 330 535-1113
Mentor *(G-13403)*
Bindery & Spc Pressworks Inc..........D....... 614 873-4623
Plain City *(G-16178)*
Black River Group Inc..........D....... 419 524-6699
Mansfield *(G-12411)*
Blt Inc..........F....... 513 631-5050
Norwood *(G-15424)*
Bock & Pierce Enterprises..........G....... 513 474-9500
Cincinnati *(G-3398)*
Boldman Printing LLC..........G....... 937 653-3431
Urbana *(G-18980)*
Bookmasters Inc..........C....... 419 281-1802
Ashland *(G-686)*
Brass Bull 1 LLC..........G....... 740 335-8030
Wshngtn CT Hs *(G-20720)*
Brothers Publishing Co LLC..........E....... 937 548-3330
Greenville *(G-10361)*
Camelot Typesetting Company..........G....... 216 574-8973
Cleveland *(G-4864)*
Canton Graphic Arts Service..........G....... 330 456-9868
Canton *(G-2611)*
Capozzolo Printers Inc..........G....... 513 542-7874
Cincinnati *(G-3440)*
Carlisle Prtg Walnut Creek Ltd..........E....... 330 852-9922
Sugarcreek *(G-17846)*
Clints Printing Inc..........G....... 937 426-2771
Beavercreek *(G-1354)*
Cold Duck Screen Prtg & EMB Co..........G....... 330 426-1900
East Palestine *(G-9071)*
Colortech Graphics & Printing..........F....... 614 766-2400
Columbus *(G-6780)*
Consoldated Graphics Group Inc..........C....... 216 881-9191
Cleveland *(G-5015)*
Copley Ohio Newspapers Inc..........C....... 330 364-5577
New Philadelphia *(G-14765)*
Cornerstone Industries Lcc..........G....... 513 871-4546
West Chester *(G-19685)*
COS Blueprint Inc..........F....... 330 376-0022
Akron *(G-122)*
Crabar/Gbf Inc..........F....... 419 943-2141
Leipsic *(G-11724)*
Customer Service Systems Inc..........G....... 330 677-2877
Kent *(G-11308)*
Daily Gazette..........E....... 937 372-4444
Xenia *(G-20764)*
Daubenmires Printing..........G....... 513 425-7223
Middletown *(G-13899)*
Debandale Printing Inc..........G....... 330 725-5122
Medina *(G-13251)*
Dorothy Crooker..........G....... 513 385-0888
Cincinnati *(G-3602)*
Dove Cds Inc..........G....... 330 928-9160
Tallmadge *(G-17981)*
Earl D Arnold Printing Company..........E....... 513 533-6900
Cincinnati *(G-3624)*
Easterdays Printing Center..........G....... 330 726-1182
Youngstown *(G-20895)*
Emta Inc..........G....... 440 734-6464
North Olmsted *(G-15187)*
Eugene Stewart..........G....... 937 898-1117
Dayton *(G-8189)*
Fedex Office & Print Svcs Inc..........E....... 937 436-0677
Dayton *(G-8192)*
Fedex Office & Print Svcs Inc..........E....... 614 621-1100
Columbus *(G-6917)*
Fedex Office & Print Svcs Inc..........F....... 614 575-0800
Reynoldsburg *(G-16439)*
Fedex Office & Print Svcs Inc..........E....... 216 573-1511
Cleveland *(G-5228)*
Fedex Office & Print Svcs Inc..........E....... 419 866-5464
Toledo *(G-18290)*
Flexoplate Inc..........E....... 513 489-0433
Blue Ash *(G-1776)*
Frank J Prucha & Associates..........G....... 216 642-3838
Cleveland *(G-5272)*
Franklins Printing Company..........F....... 740 452-6375
Zanesville *(G-21138)*
Gazette Publishing Company..........C....... 419 483-4190
Oberlin *(G-15495)*
Genesis Quality Printing Inc..........G....... 440 975-5700
Mentor *(G-13457)*
Geygan Enterprises Inc..........F....... 513 932-4222
Lebanon *(G-11656)*
Graphic Image..........G....... 937 320-0302
Beavercreek *(G-1318)*
Graphic Touch Inc..........G....... 330 337-3341
Salem *(G-16744)*
Greg Blume..........G....... 740 574-2308
Wheelersburg *(G-20182)*
Harlan Graphic Arts Svcs Inc..........E....... 513 251-5700
Cincinnati *(G-3798)*
Hecks Direct Mail & Prtg Svc..........E....... 419 697-3505
Toledo *(G-18327)*
Hilleary-Whitaker Inc..........G....... 614 766-4694
Columbus *(G-7001)*
Hkm Drect Mkt Cmmnications Inc..........C....... 216 651-9500
Cleveland *(G-5412)*
Homewood Press Inc..........E....... 419 478-0695
Toledo *(G-18334)*
Hubbard Publishing Co..........E....... 937 592-3060
Bellefontaine *(G-1518)*
Image Industries Inc..........G....... 937 832-7969
Clayton *(G-4575)*
Imprints..........F....... 330 650-0467
Hudson *(G-11054)*
Jack Walker Printing Co..........F....... 440 352-4222
Mentor *(G-13483)*
Kad Holdings Inc..........G....... 614 792-3399
Dublin *(G-8935)*
Keener Printing Inc..........F....... 216 531-7595
Cleveland *(G-5523)*
Kehl-Kolor Inc..........E....... 419 281-3107
Ashland *(G-717)*
Kevin K Tidd..........G....... 419 885-5603
Sylvania *(G-17948)*
Keystone Press Inc..........G....... 419 243-7326
Toledo *(G-18367)*
Keystone Printing & Copy Cat..........G....... 740 354-6542
Portsmouth *(G-16286)*
La Dua Inc..........G....... 440 243-9600
Lakewood *(G-11524)*
Landen Desktop Pubg Ctr Inc..........G....... 513 683-5181
Loveland *(G-12209)*
Laurenee Ltd LLC..........G....... 513 662-2225
Cincinnati *(G-3934)*
Lee Corporation..........G....... 513 771-3602
Cincinnati *(G-3937)*
Legal News Publishing Co..........E....... 216 696-3322
Cleveland *(G-5572)*
Liming Printing Inc..........F....... 937 374-2646
Xenia *(G-20782)*
Lund Printing Co..........G....... 330 628-4047
Akron *(G-262)*
M Web Type Inc..........G....... 614 272-8973
Columbus *(G-7141)*
Margaret Trentman..........G....... 513 948-1700
Cincinnati *(G-3980)*
Middleton Printing Co Inc..........G....... 614 294-7277
Gahanna *(G-10090)*
Mmp Printing Inc..........E....... 513 381-0990
Cincinnati *(G-4035)*
Montview Corporation..........G....... 330 723-3409
Medina *(G-13304)*
Multi-Craft Litho Inc..........E....... 859 581-2754
Blue Ash *(G-1824)*
Nari Inc..........G....... 440 960-2280
Monroeville *(G-14289)*

PRODUCT SECTION

VACUUM CLEANERS: Household

Network Printing & Graphics ....F 614 230-2084
 Columbus *(G-7214)*
Newfax Corporation ....F 419 241-5157
 Toledo *(G-18423)*
Newspaper Holding Inc ....D 440 998-2323
 Ashtabula *(G-792)*
Old Trail Printing Company ....C 614 443-4852
 Columbus *(G-7269)*
Onetouchpoint East Corp ....D 513 421-1600
 Cincinnati *(G-4113)*
Orrville Printing Co Inc ....G 330 682-5066
 Orrville *(G-15608)*
Our Fifth Street LLC ....G 614 866-4065
 Pickerington *(G-16055)*
Painesville Publishing Co ....G 440 354-4142
 Austinburg *(G-924)*
Paul/Jay Associates ....G 740 676-8776
 Bellaire *(G-1488)*
Penguin Enterprises Inc ....E 440 899-5112
 Westlake *(G-20140)*
Performa La Mar Printing Inc ....G 440 632-9800
 Middlefield *(G-13845)*
Pooles Printing & Office Svcs ....G 419 475-9000
 Toledo *(G-18474)*
Preisser Inc ....E 614 345-0199
 Columbus *(G-7344)*
Prime Printing Inc ....E 937 438-3707
 Dayton *(G-8442)*
Printed Image ....F 614 221-1412
 Columbus *(G-7350)*
Printing Arts Press ....F 740 397-6106
 Mount Vernon *(G-14502)*
Progressive Communications ....D 740 397-5333
 Mount Vernon *(G-14503)*
Quick As A Wink Printing Co ....F 419 224-9786
 Lima *(G-11926)*
Quick Tab II Inc ....D 419 448-6622
 Tiffin *(G-18076)*
Quick Tech Graphics Inc ....E 937 743-5952
 Springboro *(G-17348)*
R & W Printing Company ....G 513 575-0131
 Loveland *(G-12224)*
R W Michael Printing Co ....G 330 923-9277
 Akron *(G-340)*
Registered Images Inc ....G 859 781-9200
 Cincinnati *(G-4257)*
Ricci Anthony ....G 330 758-5761
 Youngstown *(G-21015)*
River Corp ....G 513 641-3355
 Cincinnati *(G-4272)*
Robert Esterman ....G 513 541-3311
 Cincinnati *(G-4277)*
Robin Enterprises Company ....C 614 891-0250
 Westerville *(G-20073)*
Robs Creative Screen Printing ....G 740 264-6383
 Wintersville *(G-20541)*
Royal Acme Corporation ....E 216 241-1477
 Cleveland *(G-6009)*
Ryans Newark Leader Ex Prtg ....F 740 522-2149
 Newark *(G-14916)*
S O S Graphics & Printing Inc ....G 614 846-8229
 Worthington *(G-20702)*
Sandy Smittcamp ....G 937 372-1687
 Xenia *(G-20788)*
Sharon Printing Co Inc ....G 330 239-1684
 Sharon Center *(G-16953)*
Sjpm Inc ....G 614 475-4571
 Gahanna *(G-10104)*
South End Printing Co ....G 216 341-0669
 Cleveland *(G-6081)*
Spencer-Walker Press Inc ....F 740 344-6110
 Newark *(G-14920)*
St Media Group Intl Inc ....D 513 421-2050
 Blue Ash *(G-1849)*
Stationery Shop Inc ....G 330 376-2033
 Akron *(G-387)*
Stumbo Publishing Co ....G 419 529-2847
 Ontario *(G-15548)*
Suburban Press Inc ....E 216 961-0766
 Cleveland *(G-6114)*
Target Printing & Graphics ....G 937 228-0170
 Dayton *(G-8539)*
Technical Translation Services ....F 440 942-3130
 Willoughby *(G-20443)*
Tim L Humbert ....F 330 497-4944
 Canton *(G-2836)*
Ulrich Rubber Stamp Company ....G 419 339-9939
 Elida *(G-9202)*
W L Beck Printing & Design ....G 330 762-3020
 Akron *(G-430)*

Watkins Printing Company ....E 614 297-8270
 Columbus *(G-7593)*
West-Camp Press Inc ....D 614 882-2378
 Westerville *(G-20082)*
Western Roto Engravers Inc ....E 330 336-7636
 Wadsworth *(G-19281)*
Wfsr Holdings LLC ....A 877 735-4966
 Dayton *(G-8592)*
Winkler Co Inc ....G 937 294-2662
 Dayton *(G-8596)*
Youngstown ARC Engraving Co ....E 330 793-2471
 Youngstown *(G-21070)*

TYPESETTING SVC: Computer

Henderson Builders Inc ....G 419 665-2684
 Gibsonburg *(G-10248)*
Heritage Press Inc ....E 419 289-9209
 Ashland *(G-709)*
Plott Graphic Directions Inc ....G 614 475-0217
 Columbus *(G-7329)*
Wolters Kluwer Clinical Drug ....D 330 650-6506
 Hudson *(G-11083)*

ULTRASONIC EQPT: Cleaning, Exc Med & Dental

Cleaning Tech Group LLC ....C 877 933-8278
 West Chester *(G-19842)*
Magnus Engineered Eqp LLC ....E 440 942-8488
 Willoughby *(G-20366)*
Smart Sonic Corporation ....G 818 610-7900
 Cleveland *(G-6072)*

UMBRELLAS & CANES

Tmb Enterprises LLC ....F 419 243-2189
 Holland *(G-10961)*

UNDERCOATINGS: Paint

Custom Powdercoating LLC ....G 937 972-3516
 Dayton *(G-8122)*
Kars Ohio LLC ....G 614 655-1099
 Pataskala *(G-15834)*

UNIFORM SPLY SVCS: Indl

Cintas Corporation ....A 513 459-1200
 Cincinnati *(G-3518)*
Cintas Corporation ....D 513 631-5750
 Cincinnati *(G-3519)*
Cintas Corporation No 2 ....D 330 966-7800
 Canton *(G-2624)*
Cintas Sales Corporation ....B 513 459-1200
 Cincinnati *(G-3520)*

UNIFORM STORES

Fechheimer Brothers Company ....C 513 793-5400
 Blue Ash *(G-1772)*
K Ventures Inc ....F 419 678-2308
 Coldwater *(G-6415)*
Kip-Craft Incorporated ....D 216 898-5500
 Cleveland *(G-5537)*

UNISEX HAIR SALONS

Fantastic Sams Hair Care Salon ....G 740 456-4296
 Portsmouth *(G-16282)*
Hair & Nail Impressions ....G 937 399-0221
 Springfield *(G-17409)*

UNIVERSITY

Kent State University ....F 330 672-7913
 Kent *(G-11344)*
Kent State University ....G 330 672-2586
 Kent *(G-11345)*
Ohio State University ....F 614 292-1462
 Columbus *(G-7262)*
Ohio State University ....E 614 292-7656
 Columbus *(G-7259)*
Ohio State University ....E 614 292-4139
 Columbus *(G-7260)*
Ohio University ....C 740 593-4010
 Athens *(G-843)*
University of Cincinnati ....G 513 556-5042
 Cincinnati *(G-4454)*

UNSUPPORTED PLASTICS: Floor Or Wall Covering

Koroseal Interior Products LLC ....C 330 668-7600
 Fairlawn *(G-9611)*

UPHOLSTERY WORK SVCS

Berlin Boat Covers ....G 330 547-7600
 Berlin Center *(G-1645)*
Casco Mfg Solutions Inc ....D 513 681-0003
 Cincinnati *(G-3447)*
Tops Inc ....G 440 954-9451
 Mentor *(G-13609)*

USED CAR DEALERS

Cars and Parts Magazine ....C 937 498-0803
 Sidney *(G-17021)*
Core Automotive Tech LLC ....G 614 870-5000
 Columbus *(G-6819)*
Dawn Enterprises Inc ....E 216 642-5506
 Cleveland *(G-5072)*
Knippen Chrysler Dodge Jeep ....E 419 695-4976
 Delphos *(G-8746)*
United Ignition Wire Corp ....G 216 898-1112
 Cleveland *(G-6234)*

USED MERCHANDISE STORES: Musical Instruments

Fifth Avenue Fret Shop LLC ....G 614 481-8300
 Columbus *(G-6920)*

USED MERCHANDISE STORES: Rare Books

The Bookseller Inc ....G 330 865-5831
 Akron *(G-401)*

UTENSILS: Cast Aluminum

Quality Match Plate Co ....F 330 889-2462
 Southington *(G-17302)*

UTENSILS: Cast Aluminum, Cooking Or Kitchen

Calphalon Corporation ....D 770 418-7100
 Perrysburg *(G-15927)*
Calphalon Corporation ....E 419 666-8700
 Perrysburg *(G-15928)*
Range Kleen Mfg Inc ....B 419 331-8000
 Elida *(G-9199)*

UTENSILS: Household, Cooking & Kitchen, Metal

American Craft Hardware LLC ....G 440 746-0098
 Cleveland *(G-4686)*
Compco Columbiana Company ....G 330 482-0200
 Columbiana *(G-6462)*

UTILITY TRAILER DEALERS

Custom Way Welding Inc ....F 937 845-9469
 New Carlisle *(G-14665)*
Jerry Tadlock ....G 937 544-2851
 West Union *(G-19963)*
Lux Corporation ....G 419 562-7978
 Bucyrus *(G-2338)*
Mr Trailer Sales Inc ....G 330 339-7701
 New Philadelphia *(G-14789)*
Navarre Trailer Sales Inc ....G 330 879-2406
 Navarre *(G-14583)*
OReilly Equipment LLC ....G 440 564-1234
 Newbury *(G-14961)*

VACUUM CLEANER STORES

ABC Appliance Inc ....E 419 693-4414
 Oregon *(G-15552)*
Carbonless & Cut Sheet Forms ....F 740 826-1700
 New Concord *(G-14683)*

VACUUM CLEANERS: Household

GMI Holdings Inc ....B 330 821-5360
 Mount Hope *(G-14437)*
H-P Products Inc ....E 330 875-7193
 Louisville *(G-12155)*
Powerclean Equipment Company ......F 513 202-0001
 Cleves *(G-6374)*

Employee Codes: A=Over 500 employees, B=251-500
C=101-250, D=51-100, E=20-50, F=10-19, G=3-9

Rent A Mom Inc....F.... 216 901-9599
Seven Hills *(G-16905)*
Scott Fetzer Company....B.... 216 228-2403
Cleveland *(G-6036)*
Scott Fetzer Company....E.... 216 252-1190
Cleveland *(G-6037)*
Scott Fetzer Company....B.... 440 871-2160
Cleveland *(G-6038)*
Scott Fetzer Company....C.... 440 439-1616
Harrison *(G-10669)*
Scott Fetzer Company....D.... 216 281-1100
Cleveland *(G-6039)*
Scott Fetzer Company....D.... 216 433-7797
Cleveland *(G-6040)*
Scott Fetzer Company....C.... 440 871-2160
Avon Lake *(G-1007)*
Scott Fetzer Company....E.... 216 228-2400
Chagrin Falls *(G-3075)*
Stanley Steemer Intl Inc....C.... 614 764-2007
Dublin *(G-8994)*
Western/Scott Fetzer Company....C.... 440 871-2160
Westlake *(G-20170)*
Western/Scott Fetzer Company....E.... 440 892-3000
Westlake *(G-20171)*

VACUUM CLEANERS: Indl Type

Dinkmar Inc....G.... 419 468-8516
Galion *(G-10132)*
Hi-Vac Corporation....G.... 740 374-2306
Marietta *(G-12632)*

VALUE-ADDED RESELLERS: Computer Systems

Quayle Consulting Inc....G.... 614 868-1363
Pickerington *(G-16058)*

VALVE REPAIR SVCS, INDL

Aj Fluid Power Sales & Sup Inc....G.... 440 255-7960
Mentor *(G-13380)*

VALVES

Aswpengg LLC....G.... 216 292-4620
Bedford Heights *(G-1461)*
Brooks Manufacturing....G.... 419 244-1777
Toledo *(G-18216)*
Buckeye BOP LLC....G.... 740 498-9898
Newcomerstown *(G-14971)*
Michael N Wheeler....F.... 740 377-9777
South Point *(G-17288)*
Northcoast Process Controls....G.... 440 498-0542
Cleveland *(G-5771)*
Oylair Specialty....G.... 614 873-3968
Plain City *(G-16205)*

VALVES & PARTS: Gas, Indl

Honeywell International Inc....A.... 937 484-2000
Urbana *(G-18995)*

VALVES & PIPE FITTINGS

Air Tool Service Company....F.... 440 701-1021
Mentor *(G-13379)*
Alloy Bllows Prcision Wldg Inc....D.... 440 684-3000
Cleveland *(G-4674)*
Bowes Manufacturing Inc....F.... 216 378-2110
Solon *(G-17117)*
Calvin J Magsig....G.... 419 862-3311
Elmore *(G-9204)*
Crane Pumps & Systems Inc....B.... 937 773-2442
Piqua *(G-16107)*
Cylinders & Valves Inc....G.... 440 238-7343
Strongsville *(G-17736)*
Eaton Corporation....C.... 330 274-0743
Aurora *(G-877)*
Edward W Daniel LLC....E.... 440 647-1960
Wellington *(G-19577)*
Fcx Performance Inc....E.... 614 324-6050
Columbus *(G-6916)*
General Aluminum Mfg Company....C.... 419 739-9300
Wapakoneta *(G-19330)*
H P E Inc....F.... 330 833-3161
Massillon *(G-12993)*
Ill Williams LLC....G.... 440 721-8191
Chardon *(G-3118)*
Impaction Co....G.... 440 349-5652
Solon *(G-17167)*
Kirtland Capital Partners LP....E.... 216 593-0100
Beachwood *(G-1244)*
Knappco Corporation....C.... 816 741-0786
West Chester *(G-19731)*
Lsq Manufacturing Inc....F.... 330 725-4905
Medina *(G-13287)*
Machine Component Mfg....F.... 330 454-4566
Canton *(G-2740)*
Mack Iron Works Company....E.... 419 626-3712
Sandusky *(G-16826)*
Northcoast Valve and Gate Inc....G.... 440 392-9910
Mentor *(G-13530)*
Nupro Company....C.... 440 951-9729
Willoughby *(G-20392)*
O E M Hydraulics Inc....G.... 740 454-1201
Zanesville *(G-21164)*
Oceco Inc....F.... 419 447-0916
Tiffin *(G-18073)*
Opw Engineered Systems Inc....G.... 888 771-9438
Lebanon *(G-11680)*
Piersante and Associates....G.... 330 533-9904
Canfield *(G-2540)*
Precision Fittings LLC....E.... 440 647-4143
Wellington *(G-19589)*
Robbins & Myers Inc....B.... 937 327-3111
Springfield *(G-17487)*
Robeck Fluid Power Co....D.... 330 562-1140
Aurora *(G-903)*
Ruthman Pump and Engineering....E.... 937 783-2411
Blanchester *(G-1706)*
Stelter and Brinck Inc....E.... 513 367-9300
Harrison *(G-10672)*
Stephens Pipe & Steel LLC....C.... 740 869-2257
Mount Sterling *(G-14465)*
Superior Holding LLC....G.... 216 651-9400
Cleveland *(G-6121)*
Superior Products LLC....D.... 216 651-9400
Cleveland *(G-6126)*
Superior Products Llc....D.... 216 651-9400
Cleveland *(G-6125)*
Swagelok....G.... 440 349-5657
Solon *(G-17239)*
Swagelok Company....E.... 440 944-8988
Willoughby Hills *(G-20476)*
Swagelok Company....F.... 440 442-6611
Cleveland *(G-6133)*
Swagelok Company....D.... 440 349-5934
Solon *(G-17242)*
Tech Tool Inc....F.... 330 674-1176
Millersburg *(G-14133)*
Thogus Products Company....D.... 440 933-8850
Avon Lake *(G-1011)*
Tylok International Inc....D.... 216 261-7310
Cleveland *(G-6225)*
Waxman Industries Inc....C.... 440 439-1830
Cleveland *(G-6295)*
William Powell Company....D.... 513 852-2000
Cincinnati *(G-4510)*
Zeiger Industries....E.... 330 484-4413
Canton *(G-2868)*

VALVES & REGULATORS: Pressure, Indl

Manico Inc....G.... 440 946-5333
Willoughby *(G-20367)*
Rogers Industrial Products Inc....E.... 330 535-3331
Akron *(G-353)*
Swagelok Company....D.... 440 248-4600
Willoughby Hills *(G-20475)*
Swagelok Company....A.... 440 248-4600
Solon *(G-17240)*
Swagelok Company....D.... 440 349-5652
Solon *(G-17241)*
Swagelok Company....E.... 440 349-5836
Solon *(G-17243)*
Tylok International Inc....D.... 216 261-7310
Cleveland *(G-6225)*
William Powell Company....D.... 513 852-2000
Cincinnati *(G-4510)*

VALVES: Aerosol, Metal

Accurate Mechanical Inc....E.... 740 681-1332
Lancaster *(G-11538)*
Humble Construction Co....E.... 614 888-8960
Columbus *(G-7010)*
J Feldkamp Design Build Ltd....E.... 513 870-0601
Cincinnati *(G-3863)*
Mab Fabrication Inc....G.... 855 622-3221
Harrison *(G-10656)*
North American Steel Company....E.... 216 475-7300
Cleveland *(G-5759)*
Tosoh SMD Inc....G.... 614 875-7912
Grove City *(G-10477)*

VALVES: Aircraft

Auto-Valve Inc....E.... 937 854-3037
Dayton *(G-8043)*
Manufacturing Division Inc....G.... 330 533-6835
Canfield *(G-2534)*

VALVES: Aircraft, Fluid Power

Taiyo America Inc....F.... 419 300-8811
Saint Marys *(G-16703)*

VALVES: Aircraft, Hydraulic

Aerocontrolex Group Inc....D.... 440 352-6182
Painesville *(G-15706)*
Parker-Hannifin Corporation....C.... 419 542-6611
Hicksville *(G-10781)*
Valvole America LLC....G.... 330 464-8872
Medina *(G-13360)*

VALVES: Control, Automatic

Fisher Controls Intl LLC....G.... 513 285-6000
West Chester *(G-19703)*
Flow Technology Inc....C.... 513 745-6000
Cincinnati *(G-3699)*
Precision Q Systems LLC....G.... 614 286-5142
Westerville *(G-20070)*
Superb Industries Inc....D.... 330 852-0500
Sugarcreek *(G-17870)*
Valvole America LLC....G.... 330 464-8872
Medina *(G-13360)*

VALVES: Engine

Eaton Usev Holding Company....G.... 216 523-5000
Cleveland *(G-5153)*
Federal-Mogul Valve Train Inte....F.... 330 460-5828
Brunswick *(G-2203)*

VALVES: Fluid Power, Control, Hydraulic & pneumatic

Aj Fluid Power Sales & Sup Inc....G.... 440 255-7960
Mentor *(G-13380)*
Cfrc Wtr & Enrgy Solutions Inc....G.... 216 479-0290
Cleveland *(G-4906)*
Dana Limited....B.... 419 887-3000
Maumee *(G-13099)*
DNC Hydraulics LLC....F.... 419 963-2800
Rawson *(G-16421)*
Hy-Production Inc....C.... 330 273-2400
Valley City *(G-19040)*
National Aviation Products Inc....F.... 330 688-6494
Stow *(G-17610)*
National Machine Company....C.... 330 688-6494
Stow *(G-17611)*
Parker-Hannifin Corporation....B.... 216 896-3000
Cleveland *(G-5848)*
Parker-Hannifin Corporation....F.... 216 896-3000
Cleveland *(G-5850)*
Ruthman Pump and Engineering....G.... 513 559-1901
Cincinnati *(G-4291)*
SMC Corporation of America....E.... 330 659-2006
Richfield *(G-16488)*
Valv-Trol Company....F.... 330 686-2800
Stow *(G-17640)*
Valveco Inc....D.... 330 337-9535
Salem *(G-16779)*

VALVES: Gas Cylinder, Compressed

Kaplan Industries Inc....F.... 513 386-7762
Harrison *(G-10654)*
Kaplan Industries Inc....E.... 856 779-8181
Harrison *(G-10655)*

VALVES: Hard Rubber

Vertex Inc....E.... 330 628-6230
Mogadore *(G-14252)*

VALVES: Indl

Alkon Corporation....E.... 614 799-6650
Dublin *(G-8876)*
Bosch Rexroth Corporation....B.... 330 263-3300
Wooster *(G-20573)*
Canfield Industries Inc....G.... 800 554-5071
Youngstown *(G-20864)*
Cincinnati Valve Company....F.... 513 471-8258
Cincinnati *(G-3508)*

Cincinnati Valve Company ....F 513 471-8258
  Cincinnati *(G-3509)*
Clark-Reliance Corporation ....G 440 572-7408
  Strongsville *(G-17727)*
Cleveland Valve & Gauge Co LLC ....G 216 362-1702
  Cleveland *(G-4982)*
Curtiss-Wright Flow Control ....D 513 735-2538
  Batavia *(G-1134)*
Curtiss-Wright Flow Control ....D 513 528-7900
  Cincinnati *(G-3244)*
Curtiss-Wright Flow Ctrl Corp ....E 440 838-7690
  Brecksville *(G-2028)*
Dayton Air Control Pdts LLC ....G 937 254-4441
  Moraine *(G-14343)*
Keen Manufacturing Inc ....G 330 427-0045
  Washingtonville *(G-19480)*
Maass Midwest Mfg Inc ....G 419 894-6424
  Arcadia *(G-625)*
Machine Component Mfg ....F 330 454-4566
  Canton *(G-2740)*
Nupro Company ....C 440 951-9729
  Willoughby *(G-20392)*
Parker-Hannifin Corporation ....C 419 542-6611
  Hicksville *(G-10781)*
Parker-Hannifin Corporation ....C 937 644-3915
  Marysville *(G-12805)*
Phoenix Partners LLC ....E 734 654-2201
  Ottawa Hills *(G-15675)*
Richards Industries Inc ....C 513 533-5600
  Cincinnati *(G-4268)*
Russments Inc ....G 513 602-5035
  Cincinnati *(G-4290)*
Ruthman Pump and Engineering ....E 937 783-2411
  Blanchester *(G-1706)*
Sdh Flow Controls LLC ....G 513 624-7001
  Cincinnati *(G-4312)*
Seawin Inc ....D 419 355-9111
  Fremont *(G-10050)*
Sherwood Valve LLC ....E 216 264-5023
  Cleveland *(G-6057)*
Transdigm Inc ....G 216 706-2939
  Cleveland *(G-6196)*
Vickers International Inc ....F 419 867-2200
  Maumee *(G-13159)*
Waxman Industries Inc ....C 440 439-1830
  Cleveland *(G-6295)*
Xomox Corporation ....E 513 947-1200
  Batavia *(G-1199)*

VALVES: Nuclear Power Plant, Ferrous

Alkon Corporation ....D 419 355-9111
  Fremont *(G-9990)*

VALVES: Plumbing & Heating

Xomox Corporation ....E 936 271-6500
  Cincinnati *(G-4527)*

VALVES: Regulating & Control, Automatic

Hunt Valve Company Inc ....E 330 337-9535
  Salem *(G-16748)*
Hunt Valve Company Inc ....E 330 337-9535
  Salem *(G-16749)*
Sherwood Valve LLC ....D 216 264-5028
  Cleveland *(G-6058)*
Viking Group Inc ....G 937 443-0433
  Dayton *(G-8580)*

VALVES: Regulating, Process Control

Akron Steel Fabricators Co ....E 330 644-0616
  Coventry Township *(G-7764)*
Clark-Reliance Corporation ....C 440 572-1500
  Strongsville *(G-17726)*
Digital Automation Associates ....G 419 352-6977
  Bowling Green *(G-1969)*
Hearth Products Controls Co ....F 937 436-9800
  Dayton *(G-7982)*
Xomox Corporation ....G 513 745-6000
  Blue Ash *(G-1880)*

VALVES: Water Works

Zal Air Products Inc ....G 440 237-7155
  Cleveland *(G-6338)*

VAN CONVERSIONS

Key Mobility Services Ltd ....G 937 374-3226
  Xenia *(G-20780)*

Mobile Conversions Inc ....F 513 797-1991
  Amelia *(G-544)*
National Fleet Svcs Ohio LLC ....F 440 930-5177
  Avon Lake *(G-997)*
Steves Vans & Accessories LLC ....G 740 374-3154
  Marietta *(G-12676)*

VANADIUM ORE MINING, NEC

AMG Vanadium LLC ....G 740 435-4600
  Cambridge *(G-2423)*

VARIETY STORES

Dolgencorp LLC ....G 740 289-4790
  Piketon *(G-16069)*
Wagoner Stores Inc ....G 937 836-3636
  Englewood *(G-9383)*

VARNISHES, NEC

David E Easterday and Co Inc ....F 330 359-0700
  Wilmot *(G-20515)*
Superior Printing Ink Co Inc ....G 216 328-1720
  Cleveland *(G-6124)*

VASES: Pottery

Annies Mud Pie Shop LLC ....G 513 871-2529
  Cincinnati *(G-3348)*

VAULTS & SAFES WHOLESALERS

National Security Products ....G 216 566-9962
  Cleveland *(G-5729)*

VEHICLES: All Terrain

All Power Equipment LLC ....F 740 593-3279
  Athens *(G-822)*
GSE Production and Support LLC ....G 972 329-2646
  Swanton *(G-17914)*
Kolpin Outdoors Corporation ....G 330 328-0772
  Cuyahoga Falls *(G-7889)*
Polaris Industries Inc ....E 937 283-1200
  Wilmington *(G-20502)*
Premier Uv Products LLC ....G 330 715-2452
  Cuyahoga Falls *(G-7907)*
Wholecycle Inc ....E 330 929-8123
  Peninsula *(G-15902)*

VEHICLES: Recreational

Aerodynamic Systems ....G 440 463-8820
  Chagrin Falls *(G-3035)*
Kedar D Army ....G 419 238-6929
  Van Wert *(G-19097)*
L & R Racing Inc ....E 330 220-3102
  Brunswick *(G-2218)*
R V Spa LLC ....G 440 284-4800
  Elyria *(G-9316)*
Rv Xpress Inc ....G 937 418-0127
  Piqua *(G-16161)*
Thor Industries Inc ....E 937 596-6111
  Jackson Center *(G-11217)*

VENDING MACHINE OPERATORS: Cigarette

Priority Vending Inc ....G 216 361-4100
  Cleveland *(G-5923)*

VENDING MACHINE OPERATORS: Sandwich & Hot Food

Sanese Services Inc ....E 330 494-5900
  Warren *(G-19441)*

VENDING MACHINES & PARTS

Giant Industries Inc ....E 419 531-4600
  Toledo *(G-18305)*
Innovative Vend Solutions LLC ....E 866 931-9413
  Dayton *(G-8267)*
Michele Mellen ....G 740 369-1422
  Powell *(G-16328)*
Reeces Las Vegas Supplies ....G 937 274-5000
  Dayton *(G-8467)*
Tranzonic Companies ....B 216 535-4300
  Richmond Heights *(G-16507)*
Ve Global Vending Inc ....F 216 785-2611
  Cleveland *(G-6252)*

VENETIAN BLIND REPAIR SHOP

Miles Pk Vntian Blind Shds Mfg ....G 216 239-0850
  Beachwood *(G-1248)*

VENETIAN BLINDS & SHADES

Miles Pk Vntian Blind Shds Mfg ....G 216 239-0850
  Beachwood *(G-1248)*
Shade Youngstown & Aluminum Co .....G 330 782-2373
  Youngstown *(G-21028)*

VENTILATING EQPT: Metal

Famous Industries Inc ....E 330 535-1811
  Akron *(G-166)*

VENTILATING EQPT: Sheet Metal

Burt Manufacturing Company Inc ....C 330 762-0061
  Akron *(G-100)*
L C Systems Inc ....G 614 235-9430
  Dublin *(G-8940)*
R & S Sheet Metal LLC ....G 330 857-0225
  Dalton *(G-7952)*
Thermo Vent Manufacturing Inc ....F 330 239-0239
  Medina *(G-13351)*

VENTURE CAPITAL COMPANIES

Linsalata Capital Partners Fun ....G 440 684-1400
  Cleveland *(G-5579)*
Victoria Ventures Inc ....E 330 793-9321
  Youngstown *(G-21063)*

VESSELS: Process, Indl, Metal Plate

AT&f Advanced Metals LLC ....E 330 684-1122
  Cleveland *(G-4756)*
Columbiana Boiler Company LLC ....E 330 482-3373
  Columbiana *(G-6460)*
Columbiana Holding Co Inc ....D 330 482-3373
  Columbiana *(G-6461)*

VETERINARY PHARMACEUTICAL PREPARATIONS

Berlin Industries Inc ....F 330 549-2100
  Youngstown *(G-20852)*
Scicompro - LLC ....G 513 680-8686
  Mason *(G-12937)*

VETERINARY PRDTS: Instruments & Apparatus

Rockdale Systems LLC ....G 513 379-3577
  Cincinnati *(G-4280)*
Suarez Corporation Industries ....D 330 494-4282
  Canton *(G-2827)*

VIBRATORS, ELECTRIC: Beauty & Barber Shop

HK Technologies ....G 330 337-9710
  Cleveland *(G-5411)*

VIBRATORS: Concrete Construction

Minnich Manufacturing Co Inc ....E 419 903-0010
  Mansfield *(G-12482)*

VIBRATORS: Interrupter

Karrier Company Inc ....G 330 823-9597
  Alliance *(G-480)*

VIDEO & AUDIO EQPT, WHOLESALE

Sound Concepts LLC ....G 513 703-0147
  Mason *(G-12940)*
Technical Artistry Inc ....G 614 299-7777
  Columbus *(G-7520)*

VIDEO TAPE PRODUCTION SVCS

Master Communications Inc ....G 208 821-3473
  Blue Ash *(G-1813)*
World Harvest Church Inc ....B 614 837-1990
  Canal Winchester *(G-2516)*

VIDEO TRIGGERS EXC REMOTE CONTROL TV DEVICES
Ops Wireless ....G....... 419 396-4041
  Carey *(G-2886)*

VIDEO TRIGGERS: Remote Control TV Devices
Universal Electronics Inc ....D....... 330 487-1110
  Twinsburg *(G-18869)*

VINYL RESINS, NEC
BCi and V Investments Inc ....D....... 330 538-0660
  North Jackson *(G-15141)*
Polyone Corporation ....D....... 440 930-1000
  North Baltimore *(G-15047)*

VISES: Machine
Bee Jax Inc ....G....... 330 373-0500
  Warren *(G-19375)*

VISUAL COMMUNICATIONS SYSTEMS
Findaway World LLC ....D....... 440 893-0808
  Solon *(G-17143)*

VITAMINS: Pharmaceutical Preparations
Eyescience Labs LLC ....G....... 614 885-7100
  Powell *(G-16321)*
Libido Edge Labs LLC ....G....... 740 344-1401
  Newark *(G-14893)*

VOCATIONAL REHABILITATION AGENCY
Quadco Rehabilitation Center ....D....... 419 445-1950
  Archbold *(G-665)*
Quadco Rehabilitation Ctr Inc ....B....... 419 682-1011
  Stryker *(G-17832)*

VOCATIONAL TRAINING AGENCY
Hard Chrome Plating Consultant ....G....... 216 631-9090
  Cleveland *(G-5374)*
Jeffco Sheltered Workshop ....E....... 740 264-4608
  Steubenville *(G-17539)*

WALL & CEILING SQUARES: Concrete
Armstrong World Industries Inc ....E....... 740 967-1063
  Johnstown *(G-11257)*

WALL COVERINGS: Rubber
Koroseal Interior Products LLC ....C....... 330 668-7600
  Fairlawn *(G-9611)*

WALLPAPER & WALL COVERINGS
4 Walls Com LLC ....F....... 216 432-1400
  Cleveland *(G-4581)*
Wolff House Art Papers Inc ....G....... 740 501-3766
  Mount Vernon *(G-14519)*

WALLS: Curtain, Metal
Midwest Curtainwalls Inc ....D....... 216 641-7900
  Cleveland *(G-5680)*
YKK AP America Inc ....F....... 513 942-7200
  West Chester *(G-19823)*

WAREHOUSING & STORAGE FACILITIES, NEC
Ballreich Bros Inc ....C....... 419 447-1814
  Tiffin *(G-18050)*
Comprehensive Logistics Co Inc ....E....... 330 793-0504
  Youngstown *(G-20877)*
Kuhlman Corporation ....C....... 419 897-6000
  Maumee *(G-13124)*
Lefco Worthington LLC ....E....... 216 432-4422
  Cleveland *(G-5571)*
Littler Corporation ....G....... 330 848-8847
  Barberton *(G-1081)*
SH Bell Company ....E....... 412 963-9910
  East Liverpool *(G-9068)*
Vista Industrial Packaging LLC ....D....... 800 454-6117
  Columbus *(G-7586)*

WAREHOUSING & STORAGE, REFRIGERATED: Cold Storage Or Refrig
Youngs Locker Service Inc ....F....... 740 599-6833
  Danville *(G-7967)*

WAREHOUSING & STORAGE, REFRIGERATED: Frozen Or Refrig Goods
Oiler Processing ....G....... 740 892-2640
  Utica *(G-19026)*
Pettisville Meats Inc ....F....... 419 445-0921
  Pettisville *(G-16036)*

WAREHOUSING & STORAGE: Farm Prdts
Growmark Fs LLC ....F....... 330 386-7626
  East Liverpool *(G-9057)*

WAREHOUSING & STORAGE: General
Aero Fulfillment Services Corp ....D....... 800 225-7145
  Mason *(G-12820)*
Alegre Inc ....F....... 937 885-6786
  Miamisburg *(G-13639)*
Efco Corp ....E....... 614 876-1226
  Columbus *(G-6886)*
G & J Pepsi-Cola Bottlers Inc ....D....... 740 593-3366
  Athens *(G-831)*
Klosterman Baking Co ....F....... 513 398-2707
  Mason *(G-12899)*
Ohio Valley Alloy Services Inc ....E....... 740 373-1900
  Marietta *(G-12649)*

WAREHOUSING & STORAGE: General
Atotech USA Inc ....D....... 216 398-0550
  Cleveland *(G-4762)*
Cincinnati Barge Rail Trml LLC ....G....... 513 227-3611
  Cincinnati *(G-3482)*
Cooper Tire Vhcl Test Ctr Inc ....F....... 419 423-1321
  Findlay *(G-9675)*
Dayton Bag & Burlap Co ....F....... 937 253-1722
  Dayton *(G-8128)*
Fuchs Lubricants Co ....G....... 330 963-0400
  Twinsburg *(G-18777)*
Growmark Fs LLC ....F....... 330 386-7626
  East Liverpool *(G-9057)*
Ingersoll-Rand Company ....G....... 419 633-6800
  Bryan *(G-2291)*
Malleys Candies Inc ....E....... 216 529-6262
  Cleveland *(G-5609)*
Matandy Steel & Metal Pdts LLC ....D....... 513 844-2277
  Hamilton *(G-10585)*
Michigan Sugar Company ....G....... 419 423-1666
  Findlay *(G-9724)*
P-Americas LLC ....C....... 330 746-7652
  Youngstown *(G-20990)*
Parker-Hannifin Corporation ....A....... 216 531-3000
  Cleveland *(G-5849)*
Performance Packaging Inc ....F....... 419 478-8805
  Toledo *(G-18465)*
Precision Strip Inc ....D....... 937 667-6255
  Tipp City *(G-18127)*
Precision Strip Inc ....C....... 419 674-4186
  Kenton *(G-11418)*
SH Bell Company ....E....... 412 963-9910
  East Liverpool *(G-9068)*
Taylor Communications Inc ....G....... 614 351-6868
  Columbus *(G-7515)*
Tmarzetti Company ....C....... 614 277-3577
  Grove City *(G-10474)*
Victory White Metal Company ....E....... 216 271-1400
  Cleveland *(G-6261)*

WAREHOUSING & STORAGE: Self Storage
Cusc International Ltd ....G....... 513 881-2000
  Hamilton *(G-10549)*
John D Oil and Gas Company ....G....... 440 255-6325
  Mentor *(G-13486)*
McMillion Lock & Key ....G....... 937 473-5342
  Covington *(G-7790)*
Route 14 Storage Inc ....G....... 330 296-0084
  Ravenna *(G-16399)*

WARM AIR HEATING & AC EQPT & SPLYS, WHOL: Dust Collecting
R & S Sheet Metal LLC ....G....... 330 857-0225
  Dalton *(G-7952)*

WARM AIR HEATING & AC EQPT & SPLYS, WHOL: Elec Heating Eqpt
Torok Supply Company ....G....... 330 799-6677
  Youngstown *(G-21047)*

WARM AIR HEATING & AC EQPT & SPLYS, WHOLESALE Air Filters
Cincinnati A Flter Sls Svc Inc ....E....... 513 242-3400
  Cincinnati *(G-3478)*
Swift Filters Inc ....E....... 440 735-0995
  Oakwood Village *(G-15484)*

WARM AIR HEATING & AC EQPT & SPLYS, WHOLESALE Furnaces, Elec
Bcast Stainless Products LLC ....F....... 614 873-3945
  Plain City *(G-16176)*

WARM AIR HEATING/AC EQPT/SPLYS, WHOL Warm Air Htg Eqpt/Splys
Air-Rite Inc ....E....... 216 228-8200
  Cleveland *(G-4645)*
Anson Co ....G....... 216 524-8838
  Bedford *(G-1383)*
Shape Supply Inc ....G....... 513 863-6695
  Hamilton *(G-10604)*
Wood Stove Shed ....G....... 419 562-1545
  Bucyrus *(G-2351)*

WASHCLOTHS & BATH MITTS, FROM PURCHASED MATERIALS
Vss Store Operations LLC ....G....... 800 411-5116
  Reynoldsburg *(G-16460)*

WASHERS
Buck Eye Pressure Wash ....G....... 419 385-9274
  Toledo *(G-18218)*
Die-Cut Products Co ....E....... 216 771-6994
  Cleveland *(G-5094)*
Pressure Washer Mfrs Assn ....G....... 216 241-7333
  Cleveland *(G-5920)*
Pro Roof Washers ....G....... 440 521-2622
  Cleveland *(G-5924)*
T and D Washers LLC ....G....... 419 562-5500
  Bucyrus *(G-2344)*

WASHERS: Metal
Andre Corporation ....E....... 574 293-0207
  Mason *(G-12824)*
Atlas Bolt & Screw Company LLC ....C....... 419 289-6171
  Ashland *(G-681)*
Master Products Company ....D....... 216 341-1740
  Cleveland *(G-5634)*

WASHERS: Rubber
Clearly Visible Mobile Wash ....G....... 440 543-9299
  Chagrin Falls *(G-3040)*
Die-Cut Products Co ....E....... 216 771-6994
  Cleveland *(G-5094)*

WASHERS: Spring, Metal
Connell Limited Partnership ....D....... 877 534-8986
  Northfield *(G-15316)*
Solon Manufacturing Company ....E....... 440 286-7149
  Chardon *(G-3137)*

WASHING MACHINES: Household
Whirlpool Corporation ....B....... 419 547-7711
  Clyde *(G-6397)*

WATCH & CLOCK STORES
Quality Gold Inc ....B....... 513 942-7659
  Fairfield *(G-9554)*

WATCH REPAIR SVCS
White Jewelers ....G....... 330 264-3324
  Wooster *(G-20667)*

WATER HEATERS
RAD Technologies Incorporated ....F....... 513 641-0523
  Cincinnati *(G-4246)*

PRODUCT SECTION

U S Thermal Inc .... G 513 777-7763
  West Chester (G-19814)

WATER PURIFICATION EQPT: Household

CST Zero Discharged Car Wash S .... G 740 947-5480
  Waverly (G-19543)
De Nora Holdings Us Inc .... B 440 710-5300
  Painesville (G-15729)
K2 Pure Solutions LP .... G 925 526-8112
  Uniontown (G-18922)
Pentair Flow Technologies LLC .... C 419 289-1144
  Ashland (G-734)
Pentair Flow Technologies LLC .... G 419 281-9918
  Ashland (G-735)
R D Baker Enterprises Inc .... G 937 461-5225
  Dayton (G-8458)

WATER PURIFICATION PRDTS: Chlorination Tablets & Kits

Clearwater One LLC .... F 216 554-4747
  Cleveland (G-4943)
Hikma Pharmaceuticals USA Inc .... E 614 276-4000
  Columbus (G-7000)

WATER SOFTENER SVCS

Delta Control Inc .... G 937 277-3444
  Dayton (G-8154)
US Water Company LLC .... G 740 453-0604
  Zanesville (G-21186)

WATER SOFTENING WHOLESALERS

R D Baker Enterprises Inc .... G 937 461-5225
  Dayton (G-8458)

WATER SPLY: Irrigation

ATI Irrigation LLC .... G 937 750-2976
  Troy (G-18639)

WATER SUPPLY

American Water Services Inc .... G 440 243-9840
  Strongsville (G-17709)
Aqua Pennsylvania Inc .... G 440 257-6190
  Mentor On The Lake (G-13631)
City of Athens .... E 740 592-3344
  Athens (G-825)
City of Middletown .... F 513 425-7781
  Middletown (G-13894)
City of Troy .... F 937 339-4826
  Troy (G-18641)
Greene County .... G 937 429-0127
  Dayton (G-7981)
Samco Technologies Inc .... G 216 641-5288
  Newburgh Heights (G-14944)
Victory White Metal Company .... E 216 271-1400
  Cleveland (G-6261)

WATER TREATMENT EQPT: Indl

Ameriwater LLC .... E 937 461-8833
  Dayton (G-8030)
Aqua Pennsylvania Inc .... G 440 257-6190
  Mentor On The Lake (G-13631)
Buckeye Field Supply Ltd .... G 513 312-2343
  Cincinnati (G-3428)
City of Athens .... E 740 592-3344
  Athens (G-825)
City of Marietta .... E 740 374-6864
  Marietta (G-12615)
City of Middletown .... F 513 425-7781
  Middletown (G-13894)
City of Xenia .... F 937 376-7269
  Xenia (G-20762)
County of Lake .... F 440 428-1794
  Madison (G-12345)
Imet Corporation .... G 440 799-3135
  Cleveland (G-5441)
J & K Wade Ltd .... G 419 352-6163
  Bowling Green (G-1977)
K S W C Inc .... G 440 577-1114
  Pierpont (G-16065)
Larrys Water Conditioning .... G 419 887-0290
  Maumee (G-13126)
Layne Heavy Civil Inc .... E 513 424-7287
  Middletown (G-13919)
Link-O-Matic Company Inc .... F 765 962-1538
  Brookville (G-2173)

Mt Vernon Cy Wastewater Trtmnt .... F 740 393-9502
  Mount Vernon (G-14495)
N-Viro International Corp .... F 419 535-6374
  Toledo (G-18421)
Neil Barton .... G 614 889-9933
  Dublin (G-8953)
Norwalk Wastewater Eqp Co .... E 419 668-4471
  Norwalk (G-15411)
Or-Tec Inc .... G 216 475-5225
  Maple Heights (G-12576)
Reynolds & Co Inc .... G 937 592-8300
  Bellefontaine (G-1524)
Samco Technologies Inc .... G 216 641-5288
  Newburgh Heights (G-14944)
Samsco Corp .... F 216 400-8207
  Cleveland (G-6028)
St John Ltd Inc .... G 614 851-8153
  Galloway (G-10181)
Tipton Environmental Intl Inc .... F 513 735-2777
  Batavia (G-1190)
Trionetics Inc .... F 216 812-3570
  Brooklyn Heights (G-2133)
Under Pressure Systems Inc .... G 330 602-4466
  New Philadelphia (G-14807)
Veolia Water Technologies Inc .... D 937 890-4075
  Vandalia (G-19150)
Waste Water Pollution Control .... F 330 263-5290
  Wooster (G-20663)
Water & Waste Water Eqp Co .... G 440 542-0972
  Solon (G-17260)
Willow Water Treatment Inc .... G 440 254-6313
  Painesville (G-15800)

WATER: Distilled

Distillata Company .... D 216 771-2900
  Cleveland (G-5098)

WATER: Pasteurized & Mineral, Bottled & Canned

Natural Country Farms Inc .... G 330 753-2293
  Akron (G-294)

WATER: Pasteurized, Canned & Bottled, Etc

Creekside Springs LLC .... E 330 679-1010
  Salineville (G-16787)

WATERPROOFING COMPOUNDS

Republic Powdered Metals Inc .... D 330 225-3192
  Medina (G-13327)
RPM International Inc .... D 330 273-5090
  Medina (G-13331)
Truco Inc .... B 216 631-1000
  Cleveland (G-6219)
Water Warriors Inc .... G 513 288-5669
  Cincinnati (G-4491)

WEATHER STRIP: Sponge Rubber

Canton OH Rubber Speclty Prods .... G 330 454-3847
  Canton (G-2612)

WEATHER STRIPS: Metal

M-D Building Products Inc .... B 513 539-2255
  Middletown (G-13922)

WEIGHING MACHINERY & APPARATUS

Advance Weight System Inc .... F 440 926-3691
  Grafton (G-10291)
Hobart Corporation .... E 937 332-3000
  Troy (G-18671)
Hobart Corporation .... C 937 332-2797
  Piqua (G-16128)

WELDING & CUTTING APPARATUS & ACCESS, NEC

Accurate Machining & Welding .... G 937 584-4518
  Sabina (G-16615)
Airgas .... G 330 345-1257
  Wooster (G-20555)
Firelands Manufacturing LLC .... F 419 687-8237
  Plymouth (G-16231)
J T E Corp .... G 937 454-1112
  Dayton (G-8275)
Lima Equipment Co .... G 419 222-4181
  Lima (G-11888)

WELDING EQPT & SPLYS WHOLESALERS

Lincoln Electric Holdings Inc .... C 216 481-8100
  Cleveland (G-5577)
Luvata Ohio Inc .... D 740 363-1981
  Delaware (G-8704)
M B Industries Inc .... G 419 738-4769
  Wapakoneta (G-19341)
Miller Weldmaster Corporation .... C 330 833-6739
  Navarre (G-14580)
O E Meyer Co .... G 419 332-6931
  Fremont (G-10041)
Otto Konigslow Mfg Co .... C 216 851-7900
  Cleveland (G-5826)
Postle Industries Inc .... E 216 265-9000
  Cleveland (G-5897)
Quality Components Inc .... F 440 255-0606
  Mentor (G-13563)
Weld-Action Company Inc .... G 330 372-1063
  Warren (G-19463)

WELDING EQPT

Accurate Manufacturing Company .... E 614 878-6510
  Columbus (G-6534)
Aerowave Inc .... G 440 731-8464
  Elyria (G-9209)
AK Fabrication Inc .... F 330 458-1037
  Canton (G-2565)
American Weldquip Inc .... F 330 239-0317
  Sharon Center (G-16943)
Campbell Hausfeld LLC .... C 513 367-4811
  Cincinnati (G-3439)
Dennis Corso Co Inc .... G 330 673-2411
  Kent (G-11312)
Fusion Incorporated .... E 440 946-3300
  Willoughby (G-20328)
Halls Welding & Supplies Inc .... G 330 385-9353
  East Liverpool (G-9058)
Harris Calorific Inc .... G 216 383-4107
  Cleveland (G-5375)
Hobart Brothers Company .... E 937 773-5869
  Piqua (G-16127)
Hobart Brothers Company .... G 937 332-5338
  Troy (G-18667)
Hobart Brothers Company .... G 937 332-5023
  Troy (G-18668)
Hobart Brothers LLC .... A 937 332-5439
  Troy (G-18669)
Imax Industries Inc .... F 440 639-0242
  Painesville (G-15747)
Lincoln Electric Intl Holdg Co .... E 216 481-8100
  Euclid (G-9424)
Mansfield Welding Services LLC .... G 419 594-2738
  Oakwood (G-15471)
Nelson Stud Welding Inc .... B 440 329-0400
  Elyria (G-9300)
Owen & Sons .... G 513 726-5406
  Seven Mile (G-16908)
Peco Holdings Corp .... F 937 667-4451
  Tipp City (G-18126)
Polymet Corporation .... E 513 874-3586
  West Chester (G-19763)
Process Development Corp .... E 937 890-3388
  Dayton (G-8445)
Process Equipment Co Tipp City .... D 937 667-4451
  Tipp City (G-18128)
Select-Arc Inc .... C 937 295-5215
  Fort Loramie (G-9805)
Semtorq Inc .... G 330 487-0600
  Twinsburg (G-18856)
Sherbrooke Metals .... E 440 942-3520
  Willoughby (G-20429)
Spiegelberg Manufacturing Inc .... E 440 324-3042
  Strongsville (G-17792)
Stryver Mfg Inc .... E 937 854-3048
  Trotwood (G-18630)
Taylor - Winfield Corporation .... D 330 259-8500
  Hubbard (G-11010)
Taylor-Winfield Tech Inc .... E 330 259-8500
  Youngstown (G-21043)
Tokin America Corporation .... G 513 644-9743
  West Chester (G-19810)
Westside Supply Co Inc .... G 216 267-9353
  Brookpark (G-2159)
Wonder Weld Inc .... G 614 875-1447
  Orient (G-15579)

WELDING EQPT & SPLYS WHOLESALERS

Airgas Usa LLC .... E 937 228-8594
  Dayton (G-8013)
Airgas Usa LLC .... F 419 228-2828
  Lima (G-11831)

WELDING EQPT & SPLYS WHOLESALERS

Airgas Usa LLC .... G 440 232-6397
  Oakwood Village *(G-15477)*
Bickett Machine and Supply Inc .... G 740 353-5710
  Portsmouth *(G-16278)*
Delille Oxygen Company .... G 937 325-9595
  Springfield *(G-17386)*
Halls Welding & Supplies Inc .... G 330 385-9353
  East Liverpool *(G-9058)*
Jerrys Welding Supply Inc .... G 937 364-1500
  Hillsboro *(G-10883)*
Lefeld Welding & Stl Sups Inc .... E 419 678-2397
  Coldwater *(G-6416)*
Matheson Tri-Gas Inc .... F 513 727-9638
  Middletown *(G-13925)*
Matheson Tri-Gas Inc .... F 419 865-8881
  Holland *(G-10943)*
Matheson Tri-Gas Inc .... G 330 425-4407
  Twinsburg *(G-18812)*
Praxair Distribution Inc .... F 937 283-3400
  Wilmington *(G-20504)*
Praxair Distribution Inc .... G 419 422-1353
  Lima *(G-11918)*
Praxair Distribution Inc .... G 513 821-2192
  Cincinnati *(G-4184)*
Salem Welding & Supply Company ..... G 330 332-4517
  Salem *(G-16772)*
Sausser Steel Company Inc .... F 419 422-9632
  Findlay *(G-9752)*
T & D Fabricating Inc .... G 440 951-5646
  Eastlake *(G-9135)*
Weld-Action Company Inc .... G 330 372-1063
  Warren *(G-19463)*
Welders Supply Inc .... G 216 241-1696
  Cleveland *(G-6299)*
Weldparts Inc .... G 513 530-0064
  Blue Ash *(G-1867)*
Wright Brothers Inc .... E 513 731-2222
  Cincinnati *(G-4520)*

WELDING EQPT & SPLYS: Gas

Rexarc International Inc .... E 937 839-4604
  West Alexandria *(G-19620)*

WELDING EQPT & SPLYS: Generators, Arc Welding, AC & DC

Lincoln Electric Company .... A 216 481-8100
  Cleveland *(G-5575)*

WELDING EQPT & SPLYS: Resistance, Electric

Weldparts Inc .... G 513 530-0064
  Blue Ash *(G-1867)*

WELDING EQPT & SPLYS: Spot, Electric

Retek Inc .... G 440 937-6282
  Avon *(G-963)*

WELDING EQPT & SPLYS: Wire, Bare & Coated

Lincoln Electric Holdings Inc .... A 440 255-7696
  Mentor *(G-13500)*
Techalloy Inc .... E 216 481-8100
  Euclid *(G-9446)*

WELDING EQPT REPAIR SVCS

ARS Recycling Systems LLC .... F 330 536-8210
  Lowellville *(G-12249)*
Hannon Company .... E 740 453-0527
  Zanesville *(G-21146)*
Hannon Company .... F 330 343-7758
  Dover *(G-8829)*
Lyco Corporation .... E 412 973-9176
  Lowellville *(G-12253)*
Quality Components Inc .... F 440 255-0606
  Mentor *(G-13563)*
Unified Screening & Crushing .... G 937 836-3201
  Englewood *(G-9380)*

WELDING EQPT: Electric

Fanuc America Corporation .... E 513 754-2400
  Mason *(G-12870)*
Production Products Inc .... D 734 241-7242
  Columbus Grove *(G-7637)*
Tech-Sonic Inc .... F 614 792-3117
  Columbus *(G-7519)*

WELDING EQPT: Electrical

Izit Cain Sheet Metal Corp .... G 937 667-6521
  Tipp City *(G-18117)*
Technical Sales & Solution .... G 614 793-9612
  Dublin *(G-9003)*

WELDING MACHINES & EQPT: Ultrasonic

Cecil C Peck Co .... F 330 785-0781
  Akron *(G-108)*

WELDING REPAIR SVC

A & C Welding Inc .... E 330 762-4777
  Peninsula *(G-15888)*
A & G Manufacturing Co Inc .... E 419 468-7433
  Galion *(G-10119)*
A Metalcraft Associates Inc .... G 937 693-4008
  Botkins *(G-1931)*
Abbott Tool Inc .... E 419 476-6742
  Toledo *(G-18153)*
Advanced Onsight Welding Svcs .... G 513 924-1400
  Cincinnati *(G-3302)*
Advanced Welding Co .... E 937 746-6800
  Franklin *(G-9867)*
Advanced Wldg Fabrication Inc .... G 440 724-9165
  Avon Lake *(G-978)*
Aetna Welding Co Inc .... G 216 883-1801
  Cleveland *(G-4638)*
Aircraft Welding Inc .... G 440 951-3863
  Willoughby *(G-20268)*
Airgas Usa LLC .... G 614 308-3730
  Columbus *(G-6554)*
Albright Radiator Inc .... G 330 264-8886
  Wooster *(G-20561)*
All American Indus Svcs LLC .... G 440 255-7525
  Mentor *(G-13383)*
All American Welding Co .... G 614 224-7752
  Columbus *(G-6566)*
All Do Weld & Fab LLC .... G 740 477-2133
  Circleville *(G-4536)*
All-Type Welding & Fabrication .... E 440 439-3990
  Cleveland *(G-4669)*
Allied Fabricating & Wldg Co .... E 614 751-6664
  Columbus *(G-6572)*
Alloy Unlimited Weld .... G 330 506-8375
  Canfield *(G-2520)*
AMP-Tech Inc .... G 419 652-3444
  Nova *(G-15430)*
Amptech Machining & Welding .... G 419 652-3444
  Nova *(G-15431)*
Apollo Welding & Fabg Inc .... E 440 942-0227
  Willoughby *(G-20276)*
ARC Gas & Supply LLC .... E 216 341-5882
  Cleveland *(G-4724)*
ARC Solutions Inc .... F 419 542-9272
  Hicksville *(G-10775)*
Arctech Fabricating Inc .... E 937 525-9353
  Springfield *(G-17364)*
Arnolds Repair Shop .... G 740 373-5313
  Marietta *(G-12604)*
Athens Mold and Machine Inc .... D 740 593-6613
  Athens *(G-823)*
Auglaize Welding Company Inc .... E 419 738-4422
  Wapakoneta *(G-19323)*
Automation Welding System .... G 330 263-1176
  Wooster *(G-20567)*
B & B Welding .... G 419 968-2743
  Middle Point *(G-13756)*
B & R Fabricators & Maint Inc .... F 513 641-2222
  Cincinnati *(G-3375)*
Baker Built Products Inc .... G 419 965-2646
  Ohio City *(G-15514)*
Baker Crane Service Ltd .... G 740 453-5868
  Zanesville *(G-21101)*
Baker Welding Llc .... G 614 252-6100
  Columbus *(G-6644)*
Baughmans Machine & Weld Shop ..... G 330 866-9243
  Waynesburg *(G-19562)*
Bayloff Stmped Pdts Knsman Inc .... D 330 876-4511
  Kinsman *(G-11463)*
Bear Welding Services LLC .... F 740 630-7538
  Caldwell *(G-2403)*
Bens Welding Service Inc .... G 937 878-4052
  Fairborn *(G-9452)*
Blackwood Sheet Metal Inc .... G 614 291-3115
  Columbus *(G-6678)*
Blevins Metal Fabrication Inc .... E 419 522-6082
  Mansfield *(G-12412)*
Bob Lanes Welding Inc .... F 740 373-3567
  Marietta *(G-12609)*

PRODUCT SECTION

Breitinger Company .... C 419 526-4255
  Mansfield *(G-12414)*
Broadway Welding & Fabrication .... G 513 821-0004
  Cincinnati *(G-3420)*
Brocks Welding & Repair Svc .... G 740 453-3943
  Zanesville *(G-21111)*
Bse Welding & Fabricating LLC .... F 419 547-1043
  Vickery *(G-19194)*
Buckeye State Welding & Fabg .... E 440 322-0344
  Elyria *(G-9227)*
Buckeye Welding .... G 330 674-0944
  Millersburg *(G-14072)*
Byron Products Inc .... D 513 870-9111
  Fairfield *(G-9486)*
C & M Welding Services LLC .... G 419 584-0008
  Celina *(G-2951)*
C & R Inc .... E 614 497-1130
  Groveport *(G-10486)*
C O Welding & Fabrication Inc .... G 419 394-3293
  Saint Marys *(G-16680)*
C Stoneman Corporation .... G 440 942-3325
  Eastlake *(G-9100)*
C-N-D Industries Inc .... E 330 478-8811
  Massillon *(G-12965)*
Camelot Manufacturing Inc .... F 419 678-2603
  Coldwater *(G-6403)*
Cardinal Welding Inc .... G 330 426-2404
  East Palestine *(G-9069)*
Carol J Guiler .... G 614 252-6920
  Columbus *(G-6745)*
Carter Manufacturing Co Inc .... E 513 398-7303
  Mason *(G-12838)*
Case-Maul Manufacturing Co .... F 419 524-1061
  Mansfield *(G-12422)*
Certified Welding Co .... F 216 961-5410
  Cleveland *(G-4904)*
Chipmatic Tool & Machine Inc .... F 419 862-2737
  Elmore *(G-9205)*
Chore Anden .... G 330 695-2300
  Fredericksburg *(G-9945)*
City Machine Technologies Inc .... E 330 747-2639
  Youngstown *(G-20870)*
Cleveland Jsm Inc .... D 440 876-3050
  Strongsville *(G-17729)*
Cleveland Welding & Fabg LLC .... G 440 364-5137
  Cleveland *(G-4983)*
Clipsons Metal Working Inc .... G 513 772-6393
  Cincinnati *(G-3528)*
Cmt Machining & Fabg LLC .... F 937 652-3740
  Urbana *(G-18983)*
Columbus Pipe and Equipment Co ..... F 614 444-7871
  Columbus *(G-6798)*
Compton Metal Products Inc .... D 937 382-2403
  Wilmington *(G-20490)*
Comptons Precision Machine .... F 937 325-9139
  Springfield *(G-17378)*
Connaughton Wldg & Fence LLC .... G 513 867-0230
  Hamilton *(G-10547)*
County Wide Welding LLC .... G 440 564-1333
  Newbury *(G-14949)*
Creative Fab & Welding LLC .... E 937 780-5000
  Leesburg *(G-11709)*
Creative Fabrication Ltd .... G 740 262-5789
  Richwood *(G-16508)*
Creative Mold and Machine Inc .... E 440 338-5146
  Newbury *(G-14950)*
Crest Bending Inc .... E 419 492-2108
  New Washington *(G-14828)*
Custom Machine Inc .... E 419 986-5122
  Tiffin *(G-18057)*
Custom Way Welding Inc .... F 937 845-9469
  New Carlisle *(G-14665)*
Custom Weld & Machine Corp .... G 330 452-3935
  Canton *(G-2643)*
D & G Welding Inc .... G 419 445-5751
  Archbold *(G-643)*
D & M Welding & Radiator .... G 740 947-9032
  Waverly *(G-19544)*
Dalin Auto Service .... G 440 997-3301
  Ashtabula *(G-770)*
Davenport Service Group Inc .... G 440 487-9353
  Mentor *(G-13429)*
David Cox .... G 740 254-4858
  Gnadenhutten *(G-10277)*
Dayton Brick Company Inc .... F 937 293-4189
  Moraine *(G-14344)*
Dbcr Inc .... E 330 920-1900
  Cuyahoga Falls *(G-7859)*
Delta Machine & Tool Co .... F 216 524-2477
  Cleveland *(G-5083)*

Des Eck Welding G 330 698-7271
Apple Creek (G-603)
Diamond Welding Co Inc G 216 251-1679
Cleveland (G-5090)
Diversified Welding Services G 419 382-1433
Toledo (G-18265)
Dover Fabrication and Burn Inc G 330 339-1057
Dover (G-8820)
Dover Machine Co F 330 343-4123
Dover (G-8822)
Drabik Manufacturing Inc F 216 267-1616
Cleveland (G-5112)
Ds Welding LLC G 330 893-4049
Millersburg (G-14079)
Duco Tool & Die Inc F 419 628-2031
Minster (G-14212)
Duray Machine Co Inc F 440 277-4119
Amherst (G-561)
Durisek Enterprises Inc G 216 281-3898
Cleveland (G-5123)
Dynamic Specialties Inc G 440 946-2838
Mentor (G-13435)
Dynamic Weld Corporation E 419 582-2900
Osgood (G-15642)
E & M Liberty Welding Inc G 330 866-2338
Waynesburg (G-19563)
E & R Welding Inc F 440 329-9387
Berlin Heights (G-1653)
E L Davis Inc G 419 268-2004
Celina (G-2958)
E W Welding & Fabricating G 440 826-9038
Berea (G-1603)
Eagle Machine and Welding Inc G 740 345-5210
Newark (G-14869)
Eagle Wldg & Fabrication Inc E 440 946-0692
Willoughby (G-20313)
East End Welding Company C 330 677-6000
Kent (G-11317)
Euclid Welding Co Inc G 216 289-0714
Maple Heights (G-12572)
Fab-Tech Machine Inc G 937 473-5572
Covington (G-7785)
Fabrication Shop Inc F 419 435-7934
Fostoria (G-9837)
Fabrication Unlimited LLC G 937 492-3166
Sidney (G-17039)
Falls Stamping & Welding Co C 330 928-1191
Cuyahoga Falls (G-7867)
Fosbel Inc C 216 362-3900
Cleveland (G-5265)
Fosbel Holding Inc E 216 362-3900
Cleveland (G-5266)
Fred Winner G 419 582-2421
New Weston (G-14845)
Fredrick Welding & Machining F 614 866-9650
Reynoldsburg (G-16441)
Friess Welding Inc F 330 644-8160
Coventry Township (G-7770)
G B Welding & Metal Fabg Co G 937 444-2091
Fayetteville (G-9639)
Garland Welding Co Inc F 330 536-6506
Lowellville (G-12251)
Gaspar Inc D 330 477-2222
Canton (G-2679)
General Technologies Inc E 419 747-1800
Mansfield (G-12445)
General Tool Company C 513 733-5500
Cincinnati (G-3747)
George Steel Fabricating Inc E 513 932-2887
Lebanon (G-11655)
Gilson Machine & Tool Co Inc E 419 592-2911
Napoleon (G-14539)
Glenridge Machine Co E 440 975-1055
Willoughby (G-20332)
Gmp Welding & Fabrication Inc F 513 825-7861
Cincinnati (G-3766)
Greber Machine Tool Inc G 440 322-3685
Elyria (G-9264)
Greggs Specialty Services F 419 478-0803
Toledo (G-18313)
Gurina Company G 614 279-3891
Columbus (G-6971)
H & H Machine Shop Akron Inc E 330 773-3327
Akron (G-193)
Habco Tool and Dev Co Inc E 440 946-5546
Mentor (G-13463)
Hardline Welding LLC G 330 858-6289
Kent (G-11332)
Harris Welding and Machine Co F 419 281-8351
Ashland (G-707)
Harris Welding and Machine Co G 419 281-9623
Ashland (G-708)
Hartley Machine Inc G 330 821-0343
Alliance (G-471)
HI Tecmetal Group Inc E 216 881-8100
Cleveland (G-5402)
HI Tecmetal Group Inc E 440 946-2280
Willoughby (G-20337)
HI Tecmetal Group Inc E 440 373-5101
Wickliffe (G-20213)
Hi-Tek Manufacturing Inc C 513 459-1094
Mason (G-12886)
Highs Welding Inc G 937 464-3029
Belle Center (G-1499)
Hobart Bros Stick Electrode C 937 332-5375
Troy (G-18666)
Hoffman Machining & Repair LLC G 419 547-9204
Clyde (G-6389)
Holdren Brothers Inc F 937 465-7050
West Liberty (G-19936)
Holdsworth Industrial Fabg G 330 874-3945
Bolivar (G-1916)
Hyneks Machine and Welding G 419 281-7966
Ashland (G-713)
Independent Machine & Wldg Inc G 937 339-7330
Troy (G-18676)
Innovative Wldg & Design LLC G 330 581-1316
Alliance (G-478)
J & A Machine G 330 424-5235
Lisbon (G-11970)
J & L Welding Fabricating Inc F 330 393-9353
Warren (G-19412)
J & S Industrial Mch Pdts Inc D 419 691-1380
Toledo (G-18356)
J A B Welding Service Inc F 740 453-5868
Zanesville (G-21150)
J P Suggins Mobile Welding E 216 566-7131
Cleveland (G-5486)
James G Morehouse G 513 752-2236
Milford (G-14020)
Jerl Machine Inc D 419 873-0270
Perrysburg (G-15969)
Jerrys Welding Supply Inc G 937 364-1500
Hillsboro (G-10883)
JMw Welding and Mfg E 330 484-2428
Canton (G-2719)
Johns Welding & Towing Inc F 419 447-8937
Tiffin (G-18063)
Jrs Hydraulic & Welding G 614 497-1100
Columbus (G-7079)
K & J Machine Inc F 740 425-3282
Barnesville (G-1117)
K-M-S Industries Inc E 440 243-6680
Brookpark (G-2150)
Kedar D Army G 419 238-6929
Van Wert (G-19097)
Kellys Welding & Fabricating G 440 593-6040
Conneaut (G-7651)
Kendel Welding & Fabrication G 330 834-2429
Massillon (G-13008)
Kings Welding and Fabg Inc E 330 738-3592
Mechanicstown (G-13212)
Kirbys Auto & Truck Repair G 513 934-3999
Lebanon (G-11669)
Kirk Welding & Fabricating G 216 961-6403
Cleveland (G-5538)
Kottler Metal Products Co Inc E 440 946-7473
Willoughby (G-20355)
Kramer Power Equipment Co F 937 456-2232
Eaton (G-9157)
Kys Welding & Fabrication G 513 702-9081
Loveland (G-12207)
L B Industries Inc E 330 750-1002
Struthers (G-17820)
Lakecraft Inc G 419 734-2828
Port Clinton (G-16249)
Lanes Welding & Repair G 740 397-2525
Mount Vernon (G-14488)
Laserflex Corporation D 614 850-9600
Hilliard (G-10837)
Liberty Casting Company LLC E 740 363-1941
Delaware (G-8703)
Lima Sheet Metal Machine & Mfg E 419 229-1161
Lima (G-11893)
Logan Welding Inc G 740 385-9651
Logan (G-12034)
Long-Stanton Mfg Company E 513 874-8020
West Chester (G-19738)
Lostcreek Tool & Machine Inc F 937 773-6022
Piqua (G-16138)
Lukens Blacksmith Shop G 513 821-2308
Cincinnati (G-3955)
Lunar Tool & Mold Inc F 440 237-2141
North Royalton (G-15285)
M & M Concepts Inc G 937 355-1115
West Mansfield (G-19943)
M & W Welding Inc G 614 224-0501
Columbus (G-7139)
Mad Metal Wldg Fabrication LLC G 614 256-4163
Columbus (G-7144)
Maintenance and Repair Fabg Co G 330 478-1149
Massillon (G-13017)
Majestic Tool and Machine Inc E 440 248-5058
Solon (G-17186)
Manufacturing Concepts F 330 784-9054
Tallmadge (G-17990)
Marsam Metalfab Inc E 330 405-1520
Twinsburg (G-18811)
Martin Welding LLC F 937 687-3602
New Lebanon (G-14711)
Mc Elwain Industries Inc F 419 532-3126
Ottawa (G-15658)
McDannald Welding & Machining G 937 644-0300
Marysville (G-12802)
McIntosh Machine G 937 687-3936
New Lebanon (G-14712)
MCO Welding G 330 401-6130
Stone Creek (G-17562)
Mecca Rebuilding & Welding Co G 419 476-8133
Toledo (G-18405)
Mercers Welding Inc G 330 533-3373
Canfield (G-2536)
Meta Manufacturing Corporation E 513 793-6382
Blue Ash (G-1818)
Microweld Engineering Inc F 614 847-9410
Worthington (G-20697)
Mike Loppe F 937 969-8102
Tremont City (G-18616)
Mikes Automotive LLC G 937 233-1433
Dayton (G-8358)
Mikes Welding G 937 675-6587
Jamestown (G-11220)
Miller Welding Inc G 330 364-6173
Dover (G-8842)
Millwrght Wldg Fbrication Svcs F 740 533-1510
Kitts Hill (G-11475)
Mitchell Welding LLC G 740 259-2211
Lucasville (G-12266)
Monnig Welding Co G 513 241-5156
Cincinnati (G-4042)
Montgomery & Montgomery LLC G 330 858-9533
Akron (G-285)
National Welding & Tanker Repr G 614 875-3399
Grove City (G-10449)
National Welding & Tanker Repr G 614 875-3399
Grove City (G-10450)
New Tech Welding Inc G 937 426-4801
Beavercreek (G-1334)
Norman Noble Inc C 216 761-2133
Cleveland (G-5758)
Northwind Industries Inc E 216 433-0666
Cleveland (G-5787)
Oaks Welding Inc G 330 482-4216
Columbiana (G-6475)
Oceco Inc F 419 447-0916
Tiffin (G-18073)
Ohio Hydraulics Inc E 513 771-2590
Cincinnati (G-4103)
Ohio State University E 614 292-4139
Columbus (G-7260)
Ohio Trailer Inc F 330 392-4444
Warren (G-19428)
Ohio Trailer Supply Inc G 614 471-9121
Columbus (G-7263)
Paul Wilke & Son Inc F 513 921-3163
Cincinnati (G-4141)
Penco Tool LLC E 440 998-1116
Ashtabula (G-795)
Pentaflex Inc C 937 325-5551
Springfield (G-17470)
Perry Welding Service Inc F 330 425-2211
Twinsburg (G-18836)
Phillips & Sons Welding & Fabg G 440 428-1625
Geneva (G-10228)
Phillips Mfg and Tower Co D 419 347-1720
Shelby (G-16985)
Phoenix Industries & Apparatus F 513 722-1085
Loveland (G-12221)
Phoenix Welding Solutions LLC G 330 569-7223
Garrettsville (G-10200)

Employee Codes: A=Over 500 employees, B=251-500
C=101-250, D=51-100, E=20-50, F=10-19, G=3-9
2019 Harris Ohio
Industrial Directory
1625

WELDING REPAIR SVC

Precision Mtal Fabrication Inc...............D...... 937 235-9261
  Dayton *(G-8434)*
Precision Reflex Inc..................................F...... 419 629-2603
  New Bremen *(G-14659)*
Precision Welding Corporation............E...... 216 524-6110
  Cleveland *(G-5912)*
Pro Fab Welding Service LLC...............G...... 937 272-2142
  Moraine *(G-14384)*
Product Tooling Inc.................................G...... 740 524-2061
  Sunbury *(G-17898)*
Prout Boiler Htg & Wldg Inc...................E...... 330 744-0293
  Youngstown *(G-21008)*
Quality Welding Inc................................E...... 419 483-6067
  Bellevue *(G-1541)*
Quality Wldg & Fabrication LLC...........D...... 419 225-6208
  Lima *(G-11925)*
Quick Service Welding & Mch Co.........F...... 330 673-3818
  Kent *(G-11372)*
R S V Wldg Fbrcation Machining...........F...... 419 592-0993
  Napoleon *(G-14557)*
Ray Townsend..G...... 440 968-3617
  Montville *(G-14325)*
Rbm Environmental and Cnstr..............E...... 419 693-5840
  Oregon *(G-15566)*
RI Alto Mfg Inc..F...... 740 914-4230
  Marion *(G-12730)*
Ridge Machine & Welding Co...............G...... 740 537-2821
  Toronto *(G-18611)*
RJR & Associates Inc............................G...... 419 237-2220
  Fayette *(G-9636)*
Robert Alten Inc.....................................G...... 740 653-2640
  Lancaster *(G-11603)*
Robert E Moore......................................G...... 513 367-0006
  Harrison *(G-10668)*
Rodney Wells...G...... 740 425-2266
  Barnesville *(G-1118)*
Romar Metal Fabricating Inc.................G...... 740 682-7731
  Oak Hill *(G-15460)*
Rose Metal Industries LLC...................F...... 216 881-3355
  Cleveland *(G-6002)*
Rush Welding & Machine Inc................G...... 740 354-7874
  Portsmouth *(G-16297)*
S & S Spring Shop................................G...... 800 619-4652
  Mount Perry *(G-14458)*
Salem Welding & Supply Company......G...... 330 332-4517
  Salem *(G-16772)*
Sat Welding LLC....................................G...... 614 747-2641
  Columbus *(G-7421)*
Sauerwein Welding................................G...... 513 563-2979
  Cincinnati *(G-4301)*
Schmidt Machine Company..................E...... 419 294-3814
  Upper Sandusky *(G-18972)*
Schwab Welding Inc..............................G...... 513 353-4262
  Cincinnati *(G-4308)*
Selinick Co..G...... 440 632-1788
  Middlefield *(G-13851)*
Selzer Tool & Die Inc............................G...... 440 365-4124
  Elyria *(G-9325)*
Semtorq Inc..F...... 330 487-0600
  Twinsburg *(G-18856)*
Simpson & Sons Inc..............................F...... 513 367-0152
  Harrison *(G-10670)*
Slabe Tool Company.............................G...... 740 439-1647
  Cambridge *(G-2456)*
Slade Gardner.......................................G...... 440 355-8015
  Lagrange *(G-11493)*
Smith Springs Inc..................................G...... 800 619-4652
  Mount Perry *(G-14459)*
Smp Welding LLC..................................F...... 440 205-9353
  Mentor *(G-13584)*
Somerville Manufacturing Inc...............E...... 740 336-7847
  Marietta *(G-12674)*
Spradlin Bros Welding Co.....................G...... 800 219-2182
  Springfield *(G-17493)*
Steubenville Truck Center Inc..............E...... 740 282-2711
  Steubenville *(G-17554)*
Steve Vore Welding and Steel.............F...... 419 375-4087
  Fort Recovery *(G-9827)*
Stryker Welding.....................................G...... 419 682-2301
  Stryker *(G-17835)*
Suburban Metal Products Inc...............F...... 740 474-4237
  Circleville *(G-4559)*
Superior Weld and Fabg Co Inc..........G...... 216 249-5122
  Cleveland *(G-6128)*
Systech Handling Inc............................F...... 419 445-8226
  Archbold *(G-670)*
T & L Welding LLC.................................G...... 937 498-9170
  Sidney *(G-17083)*
T & R Welding Systems Inc..................F...... 937 228-7517
  Dayton *(G-8535)*

T&T Welding...G...... 513 615-1156
  Loveland *(G-12239)*
Tbone Sales LLC...................................E...... 330 897-6131
  Baltic *(G-1033)*
Temperature Controls Company..........F...... 330 773-6633
  Akron *(G-398)*
Tendon Manufacturing Inc....................E...... 216 663-3200
  Cleveland *(G-6159)*
Thomas Entps of Georgetown..............G...... 937 378-6300
  Georgetown *(G-10238)*
Tig Welding Specialties Inc..................G...... 216 621-1763
  Cleveland *(G-6174)*
Timothy Sasser......................................G...... 740 260-9499
  Byesville *(G-2394)*
Tonys Wldg & Fabrication LLC............E...... 740 333-4000
  Wshngtn CT Hs *(G-20746)*
Tri-State Plating & Polishing................G...... 304 529-2579
  Proctorville *(G-16348)*
Triangle Precision Industries...............D...... 937 299-6776
  Dayton *(G-8564)*
Tru-Fab Technology Inc........................F...... 440 954-9760
  Willoughby *(G-20451)*
TW Tank LLC..G...... 419 334-2664
  Fremont *(G-10058)*
Two M Precision Co Inc........................E...... 440 946-2120
  Willoughby *(G-20454)*
Valley Machine Tool Co Inc..................E...... 513 899-2737
  Morrow *(G-14417)*
Van Burens Welding & Machine...........G...... 740 787-2636
  Glenford *(G-10273)*
Viking Fabricators Inc..........................E...... 740 374-5246
  Marietta *(G-12687)*
Waldock Eqp Sls & Svc Inc..................G...... 419 426-7771
  Attica *(G-860)*
Warlock Inc..G...... 614 471-4055
  Columbus *(G-7590)*
Wayne Trail Technologies Inc..............D...... 937 295-2120
  Fort Loramie *(G-9811)*
Webers Body & Frame..........................G...... 937 839-5946
  West Alexandria *(G-19624)*
Weldfab Inc..G...... 440 563-3310
  Rock Creek *(G-16535)*
Welding Consultants Inc......................G...... 614 258-7018
  Columbus *(G-7598)*
Welding Equipment Repair Co............G...... 330 536-2125
  Lowellville *(G-12257)*
Weldments Inc.......................................F...... 937 235-9261
  Dayton *(G-8588)*
Wenrick Machine and Tool Corp.........F...... 937 667-7307
  Tipp City *(G-18145)*
Westerman Acquisition Co LLC..........E...... 330 264-2447
  Wooster *(G-20666)*
Wg Mobile Welding LLC........................G...... 440 720-1940
  Highland Heights *(G-10800)*
Whitt Machine Inc.................................F...... 513 423-7624
  Middletown *(G-13967)*
Wiederhold Wldg & Fabrication...........G...... 513 875-3755
  Fayetteville *(G-9642)*
Wonder Weld Inc...................................G...... 614 875-1447
  Orient *(G-15579)*
Worleys Machine & Fab Inc.................G...... 740 532-3337
  Hanging Rock *(G-10624)*

WELDING SPLYS, EXC GASES: Wholesalers

Airgas Usa LLC.....................................G...... 440 232-6397
  Oakwood Village *(G-15477)*
Delille Oxygen Company.......................E...... 614 444-1177
  Columbus *(G-6857)*
Retek Inc..G...... 440 937-6282
  Avon *(G-963)*

WELDING TIPS: Heat Resistant, Metal

Arete Innovative Solutions LLC...........G...... 513 503-2712
  Morrow *(G-14408)*
Ben James Enterprises Inc..................G...... 330 477-9353
  Canton *(G-2589)*
Ohio Laser LLC.....................................E...... 614 873-7030
  Plain City *(G-16204)*

WELDMENTS

A H Marty Co Ltd..................................F...... 216 641-8950
  Cleveland *(G-4588)*
A-1 Welding & Fabrication....................F...... 440 233-8474
  Lorain *(G-12077)*
All American Welding Co......................G...... 614 224-7752
  Columbus *(G-6566)*
American Tank & Fabricating Co.........C...... 216 252-1500
  Cleveland *(G-4698)*

Dj S Weld..G...... 330 432-2206
  Uhrichsville *(G-18885)*
Fred Winner...G...... 419 582-2421
  New Weston *(G-14845)*
Loveman Steel Corporation..................D...... 440 232-6200
  Bedford *(G-1423)*
M & M Certified Welding Inc................F...... 330 467-1729
  Macedonia *(G-12311)*

WELL CURBING: Concrete

Creative Curbing America LLC...........G...... 419 738-7668
  Wapakoneta *(G-19327)*

WET CORN MILLING

Tate Lyle Ingrdnts Amricas LLC.........D...... 937 235-4074
  Dayton *(G-8542)*

WHEELCHAIR LIFTS

Access To Independence Inc..............G...... 330 296-8111
  Ravenna *(G-16363)*
Key Mobility Services Ltd..................G...... 937 374-3226
  Xenia *(G-20780)*
Serving Veterans Mobility Inc.............G...... 937 746-4788
  Franklin *(G-9918)*
Steves Vans & Accessories LLC........G...... 740 374-3154
  Marietta *(G-12676)*

WHEELCHAIRS

American Ride Wheelchair Coach.......G...... 216 276-1700
  Cleveland *(G-4696)*
Columbus Prescr Rehabilitation..........G...... 614 294-1600
  Westerville *(G-20040)*
Healthwares Manufacturing.................F...... 513 353-3691
  Cleves *(G-6364)*
Invacare Corporation.............................F...... 440 329-6000
  Elyria *(G-9274)*
Invacare Corporation.............................A...... 440 329-6000
  Elyria *(G-9272)*
Invacare Corporation.............................D...... 800 333-6900
  Elyria *(G-9273)*
Invacare Holdings Corporation............G...... 440 329-6000
  Elyria *(G-9276)*
Invacare International Corp..................G...... 440 329-6000
  Elyria *(G-9277)*
Reliable Wheelchair Trans...................G...... 216 390-3999
  Beachwood *(G-1276)*
Wilson Mobility LLC...............................G...... 216 921-9457
  Cleveland *(G-6312)*

WHEELS

Ferguson Fire Fabrication Inc.............F...... 614 299-2070
  Columbus *(G-6918)*
Rocknstarr Holdings LLC....................E...... 330 509-9086
  Youngstown *(G-21020)*

WHEELS & BRAKE SHOES: Railroad, Cast Iron

Amsted Industries Incorporated..........C...... 614 836-2323
  Groveport *(G-10481)*
Engines Inc of Ohio...............................D...... 740 377-9874
  South Point *(G-17283)*

WHEELS & GRINDSTONES, EXC ARTIFICIAL: Abrasive

Everett Industries LLC.........................E...... 330 372-3700
  Warren *(G-19401)*
Regal Diamond Products Corp............E...... 440 944-7700
  Wickliffe *(G-20229)*
Schumann Enterprises Inc...................E...... 216 267-6850
  Cleveland *(G-6033)*
Unisand Incorporated............................E...... 330 722-0222
  Medina *(G-13356)*

WHEELS & PARTS

Ernie Green Industries Inc..................G...... 614 219-1423
  Columbus *(G-6903)*
Marion Industries Inc............................A...... 740 223-0075
  Marion *(G-12718)*
Martin Wheel Co Inc.............................D...... 330 633-3278
  Tallmadge *(G-17992)*
Pacific Industries USA Inc...................E...... 513 860-3900
  Fairfield *(G-9541)*

PRODUCT SECTION — WIRE & WIRE PRDTS

WHEELS, GRINDING: Artificial
Action Super Abrasive Pdts Inc ....E....... 330 673-7333
  Kent (G-11289)
Performance Superabrasives LLC ....G....... 440 946-7171
  Mentor (G-13547)

WHEELS: Abrasive
Buckeye Abrasive Inc ....F....... 330 753-1041
  Barberton (G-1067)
Research Abrasive Products Inc ....E....... 440 944-3200
  Wickliffe (G-20230)

WHEELS: Buffing & Polishing
B & P Polishing Inc ....F....... 330 753-4202
  Barberton (G-1057)
United Buff & Supply Co Inc ....G....... 419 738-2417
  Wapakoneta (G-19357)
Wright Buffing Wheel Company ....G....... 330 424-7887
  Lisbon (G-11983)

WHEELS: Disc, Wheelbarrow, Stroller, Etc, Stamped Metal
Axis Corporation ....F....... 937 592-1958
  Bellefontaine (G-1505)
Ibi Brake Products Inc ....G....... 440 543-7962
  Chagrin Falls (G-3052)

WHEELS: Iron & Steel, Locomotive & Car
Plymouth Locomotive Svc LLC ....G....... 419 896-2854
  Shiloh (G-16997)
Xtek Inc ....B....... 513 733-7800
  Cincinnati (G-4530)

WHEELS: Railroad Car, Cast Steel
Engines Inc of Ohio ....D....... 740 377-9874
  South Point (G-17283)

WHEELS: Water
Muller Engine & Machine Co ....G....... 937 322-1861
  Springfield (G-17454)

WHITING MINING: Crushed & Broken
Ayers Limestone Quarry Inc ....F....... 740 633-2958
  Martins Ferry (G-12757)

WICKING
Community Action Program Corp ....F....... 740 374-8501
  Marietta (G-12617)

WINCHES
American Power Pull Corp ....G....... 419 335-7050
  Wauseon (G-19509)
David Round Company Inc ....E....... 330 656-1600
  Streetsboro (G-17668)
Malta Dynamics LLC ....F....... 740 749-3512
  Waterford (G-19488)
Wyeth-Scott Company ....G....... 740 345-4528
  Newark (G-14933)

WINDINGS: Coil, Electronic
Adkel Corp ....G....... 740 452-6973
  Zanesville (G-21094)
M2m Imaging Corporation ....F....... 440 684-9690
  Cleveland (G-5595)

WINDMILLS: Electric Power Generation
Surenergy LLC ....F....... 419 626-8000
  Sandusky (G-16851)

WINDMILLS: Farm Type
Ohio Windmill & Pump Co Inc ....G....... 330 547-6300
  Berlin Center (G-1649)

WINDOW & DOOR FRAMES
A B Siemer Inc ....B....... 614 888-8855
  Columbus (G-6515)
Desco Corporation ....G....... 614 888-8855
  New Albany (G-14622)
Dj & Woodies Vinyl Frontier ....G....... 740 623-2818
  Coshocton (G-7731)

Midwest Curtainwalls Inc ....D....... 216 641-7900
  Cleveland (G-5680)

WINDOW FRAMES & SASHES: Plastic
Champion Opco LLC ....B....... 513 327-7338
  Cincinnati (G-3463)
Therma-Tru Corp ....D....... 419 740-5193
  Maumee (G-13152)
Vinylmax Corporation ....D....... 800 847-3736
  Hamilton (G-10618)
Vinylume Products Inc ....D....... 330 799-2000
  Youngstown (G-21067)

WINDOW FRAMES, MOLDING & TRIM: Vinyl
Builder Tech Wholesale LLC ....G....... 419 535-7606
  Toledo (G-18219)
Comfort Line Ltd ....D....... 419 729-8520
  Toledo (G-18236)
Duo-Corp ....E....... 330 549-2149
  North Lima (G-15170)
Great Lakes Window Inc ....A....... 419 666-5555
  Walbridge (G-19294)
Ipm Inc ....G....... 419 248-8000
  Toledo (G-18351)
Laird Plastics Inc ....F....... 614 272-0777
  Columbus (G-7110)
Larmco Windows Inc ....E....... 216 502-2832
  Cleveland (G-5562)
Modern Builders Supply Inc ....C....... 419 241-3961
  Toledo (G-18414)
O A R Vinyl Windows & Siding ....G....... 440 636-5573
  Middlefield (G-13842)
Owens Corning ....A....... 419 248-8000
  Toledo (G-18446)
Owens Corning Sales LLC ....A....... 419 248-8000
  Toledo (G-18448)
Soft-Lite LLC ....C....... 330 528-3400
  Streetsboro (G-17698)
Solutions In Polycarbonate LLC ....G....... 330 572-2860
  Medina (G-13345)
Stanek E F and Assoc Inc ....C....... 216 341-7700
  Macedonia (G-12333)
Tsp Inc ....E....... 513 732-8900
  Batavia (G-1191)
Vinyl Design Corporation ....E....... 419 283-4009
  Holland (G-10965)

WINDOW FURNISHINGS WHOLESALERS
Cincinnati Window Shade Inc ....F....... 513 631-7200
  Cincinnati (G-3510)

WINDOW SCREENING: Plastic
Gateway Industrial Pdts Inc ....F....... 440 324-4112
  Elyria (G-9263)

WINDOWS: Frames, Wood
American Woodwork Specialty Co ....E....... 937 263-1053
  Dayton (G-8029)
Bay World International Inc ....E....... 419 525-2222
  Mansfield (G-12410)

WINDOWS: Wood
M21 Industries LLC ....D....... 937 781-1377
  Dayton (G-8319)
Ply Gem Industries Inc ....C....... 937 492-1111
  Sidney (G-17060)
Yoder Window & Siding Ltd ....F....... 330 695-6960
  Fredericksburg (G-9962)

WINDSHIELD WIPER SYSTEMS
Commercial Vehicle Group Inc ....A....... 614 289-5360
  New Albany (G-14615)
Visible Solutions Inc ....G....... 440 925-2810
  Westlake (G-20168)

WINDSHIELDS: Plastic
Few Atmtive GL Applcations Inc ....G....... 234 249-1880
  Wooster (G-20591)

WINE & DISTILLED ALCOHOLIC BEVERAGES WHOLESALERS
Victoria Ventures Inc ....E....... 330 793-9321
  Youngstown (G-21063)

WINE CELLARS, BONDED: Wine, Blended
Georgetown Vineyards Inc ....E....... 740 435-3222
  Cambridge (G-2440)
Muirfield Wine Company LLC ....G....... 614 799-9222
  Dublin (G-8949)

WIRE
Advance Industries Group LLC ....E....... 216 741-1800
  Cleveland (G-4621)
AJD Holding Co ....D....... 330 405-4477
  Twinsburg (G-18728)
Bekaert Corporation ....C....... 330 683-5060
  Orrville (G-15583)
Bekaert Corporation ....E....... 330 683-5060
  Orrville (G-15584)
Bekaert Corporation ....E....... 330 835-5124
  Fairlawn (G-9595)
Bekaert Corporation ....G....... 330 867-3325
  Fairlawn (G-9596)
Bekaert North America MGT Corp ....E....... 330 867-3325
  Fairlawn (G-9597)
Brushes Inc ....E....... 216 267-8084
  Cleveland (G-4848)
Cambridge Cable Service Co ....G....... 740 685-5775
  Byesville (G-2380)
D C Controls LLC ....G....... 513 225-0813
  West Chester (G-19848)
Falcon Fab and Finishes LLC ....G....... 740 820-4458
  Lucasville (G-12263)
Hawthorne Wire Ltd ....F....... 216 712-4747
  Lakewood (G-11519)
Injection Alloys Incorporated ....E....... 513 422-8819
  Middletown (G-13914)
Madsen Wire Products Inc ....E....... 937 829-6561
  Dayton (G-8322)
Merchants Metals LLC ....G....... 513 942-0268
  West Chester (G-19743)
Radix Wire & Cable LLC ....G....... 216 731-9191
  Cleveland (G-5955)

WIRE & CABLE: Aluminum
Mac Its LLC ....F....... 937 454-0722
  Vandalia (G-19133)
Max Mighty Inc ....F....... 937 862-9530
  Spring Valley (G-17317)

WIRE & CABLE: Nonferrous, Aircraft
Cory Electronics ....G....... 440 951-9424
  Mentor (G-13424)

WIRE & CABLE: Nonferrous, Building
Ribbon Technology Corporation ....F....... 614 864-5444
  Gahanna (G-10100)

WIRE & WIRE PRDTS
4-Sure Wire Products Inc ....G....... 440 563-9263
  Rock Creek (G-16531)
Alabama Sling Center Inc ....F....... 440 239-7000
  Cleveland (G-4649)
Alcan Corporation ....G....... 440 460-3307
  Cleveland (G-4650)
Amanda Bent Bolt Company ....C....... 740 385-6893
  Logan (G-12021)
Bloomingburg Spring & Wire For ....E....... 740 437-7614
  Bloomingburg (G-1709)
Busch & Thiem Inc ....E....... 419 625-7515
  Sandusky (G-16800)
C & F Fabrications Inc ....E....... 937 666-3234
  East Liberty (G-9046)
Canron Manufacturing Inc ....F....... 330 497-1131
  Greentown (G-10357)
Clamps Inc ....E....... 419 729-2141
  Toledo (G-18232)
Columbus McKinnon Corporation ....D....... 330 424-7248
  Lisbon (G-11965)
Dayton Superior Corporation ....E....... 815 732-3136
  Miamisburg (G-13656)
Dayton Wire Products Inc ....E....... 937 236-8000
  Dayton (G-8149)
Die Co Inc ....E....... 440 942-8856
  Eastlake (G-9104)
Dolin Supply Co ....E....... 304 529-4171
  South Point (G-17282)
Eagle Wire Works Inc ....F....... 216 341-8550
  Cleveland (G-5136)
Efco Corp ....E....... 614 876-1226
  Columbus (G-6886)

Employee Codes: A=Over 500 employees, B=251-500
C=101-250, D=51-100, E=20-50, F=10-19, G=3-9

WIRE & WIRE PRDTS

PRODUCT SECTION

Elyria Spring & Specialty Inc .... E .... 440 323-5502 Elyria (G-9256)	
Engineered Wire Products Inc .... E .... 330 469-6958 Warren (G-19400)	
Engineered Wire Products Inc .... C .... 419 294-3817 Upper Sandusky (G-18953)	
Ever Roll Specialties Co .... E .... 937 964-1302 Springfield (G-17399)	
Falcon Fab and Finishes LLC .... G .... 740 820-4458 Lucasville (G-12263)	
Fence One Inc .... F .... 216 441-2600 Cleveland (G-5229)	
Friends Ornamental Iron Co .... G .... 216 431-6710 Cleveland (G-5275)	
Gateway Concrete Forming Svcs .... 513 353-2000 Miamitown (G-13746)	
General Chain & Mfg Corp .... E .... 513 541-6005 Cincinnati (G-3740)	
Illinois Tool Works Inc .... 216 292-7161 Bedford (G-1415)	
Industrial Wire Co Inc .... G .... 216 781-2230 Cleveland (G-5455)	
Industrial Wire Co Inc .... E .... 330 723-7471 Medina (G-13278)	
Industrial Wire Rope Sup Inc .... E .... 513 941-2443 Cincinnati (G-3846)	
J B Kepple Sheet Metal .... G .... 740 393-2971 Mount Vernon (G-14484)	
Malin Wire Co .... E .... 216 267-9080 Cleveland (G-5607)	
Marik Spring Inc .... F .... 330 564-0617 Tallmadge (G-17991)	
Mazzella Lifting Tech Inc .... D .... 440 239-7000 Cleveland (G-5638)	
McM Ind Co Inc .... F .... 216 292-4506 Cleveland (G-5644)	
McM Ind Co Inc .... E .... 216 641-6300 Cleveland (G-5645)	
Meese Inc .... D .... 440 998-1202 Ashtabula (G-785)	
Mueller Electric Company Inc .... E .... 216 771-5225 Akron (G-290)	
Ohio Wire Form & Spring Co .... F .... 614 444-3676 Columbus (G-7264)	
Options Plus Incorporated .... F .... 740 694-9811 Fredericktown (G-9975)	
Organized Living Inc .... E .... 513 489-9300 Cincinnati (G-4118)	
Panacea Products Corporation .... D .... 614 429-6320 Columbus (G-7288)	
Panacea Products Corporation .... E .... 614 850-7000 Columbus (G-7287)	
Parker-Hannifin Corporation .... F .... 330 336-3511 Wadsworth (G-19262)	
Pittsburgh Wire & Cable .... G .... 740 886-0202 Proctorville (G-16344)	
Polymet Corporation .... E .... 513 874-3586 West Chester (G-19763)	
Premier Manufacturing Corp .... D .... 216 941-9700 Cleveland (G-5916)	
Production Plus Corp .... F .... 740 983-5178 Ashville (G-820)	
Pwp Inc .... E .... 216 251-2181 Ashland (G-740)	
Qualtek Electronics Corp .... E .... 440 951-3300 Mentor (G-13567)	
Range One Products & Fabg .... F .... 330 533-1151 Canfield (G-2542)	
RFS Fabrication .... 419 547-0650 Clyde (G-6395)	
Rural Iron Works LLC .... G .... 419 647-4617 Spencerville (G-17313)	
Saxon Products Inc .... 419 241-6771 Toledo (G-18513)	
Schweizer Dipple Inc .... D .... 440 786-8090 Cleveland (G-6034)	
Spring Team Inc .... D .... 440 275-5981 Austinburg (G-926)	
Starr Fabricating Inc .... D .... 330 394-9891 Vienna (G-19210)	
Stephens Pipe & Steel LLC .... C .... 740 869-2257 Mount Sterling (G-14465)	
T & R Welding Systems Inc .... F .... 937 228-7517 Dayton (G-8535)	
Therm-O-Link Inc .... D .... 330 527-2124 Garrettsville (G-10203)	
Top Knotch Products Inc .... 419 543-2266 Cleveland (G-6186)	
Tyler Haver Inc .... E .... 440 974-1047 Mentor (G-13615)	
Ver-Mac Industries Inc .... E .... 740 397-6511 Mount Vernon (G-14517)	
W J Egli Company Inc .... F .... 330 823-3666 Alliance (G-512)	
Wire Products Company Inc .... D .... 216 267-0777 Cleveland (G-6315)	
Wrwp LLC .... 330 425-3421 Twinsburg (G-18875)	
WS Tyler Screening Inc .... E .... 440 974-1047 Mentor (G-13630)	
Yost Superior Co .... E .... 937 323-7591 Springfield (G-17522)	

WIRE CLOTH & WOVEN WIRE PRDTS, MADE FROM PURCHASED WIRE

Ofco Inc .... D 740 622-5922
Coshocton (G-7746)
Unified Screening & Crushing .... G 937 836-3201
Englewood (G-9380)

WIRE FABRIC: Welded Steel

S & S Wldg Fabg Machining Inc .... E 330 392-7878
Newton Falls (G-14993)

WIRE FENCING & ACCESS WHOLESALERS

Agratronix LLC .... E 330 562-2222
Streetsboro (G-17657)
D&M Fencing LLC .... G 419 604-0698
Spencerville (G-17308)
Richards Whl Fence Co Inc .... E 330 773-0423
Akron (G-348)
Security Fence Group Inc .... E 513 681-3700
Cincinnati (G-4314)

WIRE MATERIALS: Aluminum

Alcan Corporation .... E 440 460-3307
Cleveland (G-4650)

WIRE MATERIALS: Copper

Alcan Corporation .... E 440 460-3307
Cleveland (G-4650)
American Wire & Cable Company .... E 440 235-1140
Olmsted Twp (G-15532)
Commconnect .... G 937 414-0505
Dayton (G-8099)
Republic Wire Inc .... D 513 860-1800
West Chester (G-19779)

WIRE MATERIALS: Steel

Advance Wire Forming Inc .... F 216 432-3250
Cleveland (G-4624)
American Wire & Cable Company .... E 440 235-1140
Olmsted Twp (G-15532)
Bayloff Stmped Pdts Knsman Inc .... D 330 876-4511
Kinsman (G-11463)
Contour Forming Inc .... E 740 345-9777
Newark (G-14864)
Custom Cltch Jint Hydrlics Inc .... F 216 431-1630
Cleveland (G-5046)
D M L Steel Tech .... F 513 737-9911
Liberty Twp (G-11823)
Dayton Superior Corporation .... C 937 866-0711
Miamisburg (G-13655)
Engineered Wire Products Inc .... C 419 294-3817
Upper Sandusky (G-18953)
File Sharpening Company Inc .... E 937 376-8268
Xenia (G-20772)
Freudenberg-Nok Sealing Tech .... F 877 331-8427
Milan (G-13983)
G & S Bar and Wire LLC .... E 260 747-4154
Wooster (G-20595)
Genesis Steel Corp .... G 740 282-2300
Steubenville (G-17535)
Glebus Alloys LLC .... F 330 867-9999
Stow (G-17592)
Hawthorne Wire Services Ltd .... G 216 712-4747
Lakewood (G-11520)
JR Manufacturing Inc .... C 419 375-8021
Fort Recovery (G-9823)
McHenry Industries Inc .... E 330 799-8930
Youngstown (G-20968)
Midwestern Industries Inc .... C 330 837-4203
Massillon (G-13026)
Noco Company .... B 216 464-8131
Solon (G-17208)
Partners Manufacturing Group .... G 419 468-8516
Galion (G-10149)
Polymet Corporation .... E 513 874-3586
West Chester (G-19763)
Republic Steel Wire Proc LLC .... E 440 996-0740
Solon (G-17222)
Republic Wire Inc .... D 513 860-1800
West Chester (G-19779)
Summit Engineered Products .... F 330 854-5388
Canal Fulton (G-2493)
Tru-Form Steel & Wire Inc .... E 765 348-5001
Toledo (G-18583)
Unison Industries LLC .... F 937 426-0621
Alpha (G-517)

WIRE PRDTS: Ferrous Or Iron, Made In Wiredrawing Plants

American Spring Wire Corp .... C 216 292-4620
Bedford Heights (G-1460)
Fenix LLC .... F 419 739-3400
Wapakoneta (G-19328)
Seneca Wire Group Inc .... G 419 435-9261
Wapakoneta (G-19353)

WIRE PRDTS: Steel & Iron

Falcon Fab and Finishes LLC .... G 740 820-4458
Lucasville (G-12263)
North Shore Strapping Inc .... E 216 661-5200
Brooklyn Heights (G-2128)
Radix Wire & Cable LLC .... G 216 731-9191
Cleveland (G-5955)
Trupoint Products .... F 330 204-3302
Sugarcreek (G-17872)

WIRE WINDING OF PURCHASED WIRE

Providence Rees Inc .... E 614 833-6231
Columbus (G-7355)

WIRE, FLAT: Strip, Cold-Rolled, Exc From Hot-Rolled Mills

American Spring Wire Corp .... C 216 292-4620
Bedford Heights (G-1460)
Hynes Industries Inc .... C 330 799-3221
Youngstown (G-20934)

WIRE: Barbed

All-State Belting LLC .... G 614 497-4281
Columbus (G-6569)

WIRE: Communication

Astro Industries Inc .... E 937 429-5900
Beavercreek (G-1301)
AT&T Corp .... G 513 792-9300
Cincinnati (G-3365)
Ohio Associated Entps LLC .... E 440 354-3148
Painesville (G-15770)
Xponet Inc .... E 440 354-6617
Painesville (G-15801)

WIRE: Magnet

HM Wire International Inc .... G 330 244-8501
Canton (G-2700)
Master Magnetics Inc .... F 740 373-0909
Marietta (G-12645)

WIRE: Mesh

Midwestern Industries Inc .... C 330 837-4203
Massillon (G-13026)

WIRE: Nonferrous

Alcan Corporation .... E 440 460-3307
Cleveland (G-4650)
American Wire & Cable Company .... E 440 235-1140
Olmsted Twp (G-15532)
Arnco Corporation .... C 800 847-7661
Elyria (G-9219)
Calvert Wire & Cable Corp .... G 330 494-3248
North Canton (G-15075)
Composite Concepts Inc .... G 440 247-3844
Mason (G-12852)
Connectors Unlimited Inc .... E 440 357-1161
Painesville (G-15724)
Electra - Cord Inc .... D 330 832-8124
Massillon (G-12979)
Electrovations Inc .... E 330 274-3558
Aurora (G-878)

PRODUCT SECTION

Legrand North America LLC ....B....... 937 224-0639
  Dayton *(G-8309)*
Mueller Electric Company Inc ....E....... 216 771-5225
  Akron *(G-290)*
Murphy Industries Inc ....E....... 740 387-7890
  Marion *(G-12722)*
Radix Wire Co ....D....... 216 731-9191
  Cleveland *(G-5956)*
Radix Wire Co ....D....... 216 731-9191
  Cleveland *(G-5957)*
Radix Wire Company ....E....... 330 995-3677
  Aurora *(G-902)*
Schneider Electric Usa Inc ....B....... 513 523-4171
  Oxford *(G-15700)*
Scott Fetzer Company ....C....... 216 267-9000
  Cleveland *(G-6035)*
Therm-O-Link Inc ....D....... 330 527-2124
  Garrettsville *(G-10203)*
Therm-O-Link Inc ....G....... 330 393-7600
  Warren *(G-19447)*
Therm-O-Link of Texas Inc ....G....... 330 393-4300
  Warren *(G-19448)*
Veteran Industries LLC ....G....... 937 751-2133
  Columbus *(G-7581)*
Vulkor Incorporated ....E....... 330 393-7600
  Warren *(G-19457)*

WIRE: Steel, Insulated Or Armored

Euclid Steel & Wire Inc ....F....... 216 731-6744
  Lakewood *(G-11516)*
Marlin Thermocouple Wire Inc ....E....... 440 835-1950
  Cleveland *(G-5624)*
Ram Sensors Inc ....G....... 440 835-3540
  Westlake *(G-20148)*
Ram Sensors Inc ....F....... 440 835-3540
  Cleveland *(G-5959)*

WIRE: Wire, Ferrous Or Iron

Solon Specialty Wire Co ....E....... 440 248-7600
  Solon *(G-17234)*

WIRING DEVICES WHOLESALERS

Astro Industries Inc ....E....... 937 429-5900
  Beavercreek *(G-1301)*

WOMEN'S & CHILDREN'S CLOTHING WHOLESALERS, NEC

Fine Line Embroidery Company ....G....... 440 331-7030
  Rocky River *(G-16547)*
McCc Sportswear Inc ....E....... 513 583-9210
  West Chester *(G-19876)*
West Chester Holdings LLC ....C....... 800 647-1900
  Cincinnati *(G-4499)*
Zimmer Enterprises Inc ....E....... 937 428-1057
  Dayton *(G-8604)*

WOMEN'S & GIRLS' SPORTSWEAR WHOLESALERS

Barbs Graffiti Inc ....E....... 216 881-5550
  Cleveland *(G-4790)*
Design Original Inc ....F....... 937 596-5121
  Jackson Center *(G-11207)*
Precision Imprint ....G....... 740 592-5916
  Athens *(G-846)*
R & A Sports Inc ....E....... 216 289-2254
  Euclid *(G-9438)*
Unisport Inc ....F....... 419 529-4727
  Ontario *(G-15549)*

WOMEN'S SPORTSWEAR STORES

Locker Room Lettering Ltd ....G....... 419 359-1761
  Castalia *(G-2940)*
Sports Express Inc ....G....... 330 297-1112
  Ravenna *(G-16406)*

WOOD & WOOD BY-PRDTS, WHOLESALE

77 Coach Supply Ltd ....E....... 330 674-1454
  Millersburg *(G-14053)*
Cindoco Wood Products Co ....G....... 937 444-2504
  Mount Orab *(G-14440)*
Gross Lumber Inc ....E....... 330 683-2055
  Apple Creek *(G-606)*

WOOD CHIPS, PRODUCED AT THE MILL

Miller Logging Inc ....E....... 330 279-4721
  Holmesville *(G-10983)*

WOOD EXTRACT PRDTS

Oak Chips Inc ....E....... 740 947-4159
  Waverly *(G-19554)*

WOOD PRDTS

County Line Wood Working LLC ....G....... 330 316-3057
  Baltic *(G-1025)*
George & Underwood LLP ....G....... 513 409-5631
  Lebanon *(G-11653)*
Global Wood Products LLC ....G....... 440 442-5859
  Highland Heights *(G-10791)*
Gregoire Moulin ....G....... 614 861-4582
  Reynoldsburg *(G-16442)*
Growers Choice Ltd ....G....... 330 262-8754
  Shreve *(G-17001)*
Kennewegs Wood Products ....G....... 330 832-1540
  Massillon *(G-13010)*
R M Wood Co ....G....... 419 845-2661
  Mount Gilead *(G-14431)*
Rework Furnishings LLC ....F....... 614 300-5021
  Columbus *(G-7390)*

WOOD PRDTS: Applicators

Woodcor America Inc ....G....... 614 277-2930
  Columbus *(G-7611)*

WOOD PRDTS: Door Trim

Mohican Wood Products ....G....... 740 599-5655
  Butler *(G-2377)*

WOOD PRDTS: Engraved

Minotas Trophies & Awards ....G....... 440 720-1288
  Cleveland *(G-5696)*
Solid Dimensions Inc ....G....... 419 663-1134
  Norwalk *(G-15415)*

WOOD PRDTS: Furniture Inlays, Veneers

Wurms Woodworking Company ....E....... 419 492-2184
  New Washington *(G-14834)*

WOOD PRDTS: Ladders & Stepladders

Bc Investment Corporation ....G....... 330 262-3070
  Wooster *(G-20570)*

WOOD PRDTS: Laundry

Dalton Wood Products Inc ....G....... 330 682-0727
  Orrville *(G-15589)*

WOOD PRDTS: Moldings, Unfinished & Prefinished

Clark Wood Specialties Inc ....G....... 330 499-8711
  Clinton *(G-6384)*
Cox Interior Inc ....F....... 270 789-3129
  Norwood *(G-15425)*
Custom Carving Source LLC ....G....... 513 407-1008
  Cincinnati *(G-3563)*
J McCoy Lumber Co Ltd ....E....... 937 587-3423
  Peebles *(G-15879)*
J McCoy Lumber Co Ltd ....G....... 937 544-2968
  West Union *(G-19962)*
K D Hardwoods Inc ....G....... 440 834-1772
  Burton *(G-2364)*
Laborie Enterprises LLC ....G....... 419 686-6245
  Portage *(G-16270)*
Seneca Millwork Inc ....E....... 419 435-6671
  Fostoria *(G-9859)*

WOOD PRDTS: Mulch Or Sawdust

American Wood Fibers Inc ....E....... 740 420-3233
  Circleville *(G-4537)*
BR Mulch Inc ....G....... 937 667-8288
  Tipp City *(G-18102)*
Chromascape Inc ....G....... 330 998-7574
  Twinsburg *(G-18752)*
Garick LLC ....E....... 216 581-0100
  Cleveland *(G-5293)*
Hope Timber & Marketing Group ....F....... 740 344-1788
  Newark *(G-14884)*
Hope Timber Mulch Inc ....G....... 740 344-1788
  Newark *(G-14885)*
Mulch Madness LLC ....F....... 330 920-9900
  Aurora *(G-893)*
National Pallet & Mulch LLC ....F....... 937 237-1643
  Dayton *(G-8378)*
Roe Transportation Entps Inc ....G....... 937 497-7161
  Sidney *(G-17068)*

WOOD PRDTS: Mulch, Wood & Bark

Cedar Products LLC ....G....... 937 892-0070
  Peebles *(G-15877)*
Gayston Corporation ....C....... 937 743-6050
  Miamisburg *(G-13672)*
Hauser Services Llc ....E....... 440 632-5126
  Middlefield *(G-13804)*
Irvine Wood Recovery Inc ....E....... 513 831-0060
  Miamiville *(G-13752)*
Kaufman Mulch Inc ....G....... 330 893-3676
  Millersburg *(G-14103)*
Latham Lumber & Pallet Co Inc ....F....... 740 493-2707
  Latham *(G-11623)*
Mad River Topsoil Inc ....G....... 937 882-6115
  Springfield *(G-17441)*
Mulch Man ....E....... 937 866-5370
  Dayton *(G-7987)*
Scotts Company LLC ....B....... 937 644-0011
  Marysville *(G-12809)*
Yoder Lumber Co Inc ....D....... 330 893-3121
  Millersburg *(G-14153)*

WOOD PRDTS: Novelties, Fiber

F J Designs Inc ....E....... 330 264-1377
  Wooster *(G-20590)*
Good Wood Inc ....G....... 740 484-1500
  Belmont *(G-1566)*

WOOD PRDTS: Panel Work

S & S Panel ....G....... 330 412-6735
  Orrville *(G-15617)*

WOOD PRDTS: Plugs

Sealco Inc ....G....... 740 922-4122
  Uhrichsville *(G-18893)*

WOOD PRDTS: Reed, Rattan, Wicker & Willow ware, Exc Furnitr

Buhi Imports ....G....... 440 224-0013
  North Kingsville *(G-15159)*

WOOD PRDTS: Saddle Trees

Red Lion Nursery Inc ....G....... 937 704-9840
  Lebanon *(G-11689)*

WOOD PRDTS: Signboards

Blang Acquisition LLC ....F....... 937 223-2155
  Dayton *(G-8058)*
Heartland Design Concepts ....G....... 419 774-0199
  Mansfield *(G-12456)*
Lehner Signs Inc ....G....... 614 258-0500
  Columbus *(G-7122)*
R T Communications Inc ....G....... 330 726-7892
  Youngstown *(G-21011)*
Signature Sign Co ....F....... 216 426-1234
  Cleveland *(G-6065)*

WOOD PRDTS: Survey Stakes

Lawnview Industries Inc ....C....... 937 653-5217
  Urbana *(G-19003)*
Zaenkert Surveying Essentials ....G....... 513 738-2917
  Okeana *(G-15522)*

WOOD PRDTS: Trophy Bases

Company Front Awards ....G....... 440 636-5493
  Middlefield *(G-13786)*
Hit Trophy Inc ....G....... 419 445-5356
  Archbold *(G-653)*
L S Manufacturing Inc ....G....... 614 885-7988
  Worthington *(G-20694)*

WOOD PRDTS: Veneer Work, Inlaid

Decorative Veneer Inc ....G....... 216 741-5511
  Cleveland *(G-5080)*

Employee Codes: A=Over 500 employees, B=251-500
C=101-250, D=51-100, E=20-50, F=10-19, G=3-9

WOOD PRDTS: Washboards, Wood & Part Wood

Columbus Washboard Company Ltd....G....... 740 380-3828
 Logan *(G-12023)*

WOOD PRDTS: Weather Strip, Wood

Action Industries Ltd..........................F....... 216 252-7800
 Strongsville *(G-17705)*

WOOD PRDTS: Wrappers, Excelsior

IVEX Protective Packaging Inc..............E....... 937 498-9298
 Sidney *(G-17046)*

WOOD PRODUCTS: Reconstituted

Profile Products LLC...........................F....... 330 452-2630
 Canton *(G-2795)*

WOOD TREATING: Millwork

Couch Business Development Inc........F....... 937 253-1099
 Dayton *(G-8104)*
Joseph Sabatino.................................G....... 330 332-5879
 Salem *(G-16751)*

WOOD TREATING: Structural Lumber & Timber

Clark Rm Inc......................................E....... 419 425-9889
 Findlay *(G-9669)*
Luxus Products LLC...........................G....... 937 444-6500
 Mount Orab *(G-14446)*
Ufp Hamilton LLC..............................F....... 513 285-7190
 Hamilton *(G-10616)*
Urbn Timber LLC................................G....... 614 981-3043
 Columbus *(G-7565)*

WOODWORK & TRIM: Exterior & Ornamental

Lehman & Sons..................................G....... 330 857-7404
 Orrville *(G-15601)*

WOODWORK & TRIM: Interior & Ornamental

Hoover Group.....................................G....... 419 525-3159
 Shiloh *(G-16994)*
LE Smith Company.............................D....... 419 636-4555
 Bryan *(G-2295)*
Pete Emmert Co.................................G....... 740 455-3924
 Nashport *(G-14569)*
Pleasant Valley Wdwkg LLC................G....... 440 636-5860
 Middlefield *(G-13847)*
Richardson Woodworking....................G....... 614 893-8450
 Blacklick *(G-1693)*
Turnwood Industries Inc.....................E....... 330 278-2421
 Hinckley *(G-10907)*

WOODWORK: Carved & Turned

Baker McMillen Co.............................D....... 330 923-8300
 Stow *(G-17572)*
Crosco Wood Products.......................G....... 330 857-0228
 Dalton *(G-7938)*
Mark Nelson......................................F....... 740 282-5334
 Steubenville *(G-17542)*
Mollard Conducting Batons Inc...........F....... 330 659-7081
 Bath *(G-1202)*
Smith P K Woodcarving LLC................G....... 513 271-7077
 Louisville *(G-12167)*
Todd W Goings..................................G....... 740 389-5842
 Marion *(G-12743)*

WOODWORK: Interior & Ornamental, NEC

Cincinnati Wood Products Co.............G....... 513 542-0569
 Cincinnati *(G-3511)*
Joe P Fischer Woodcraft.....................G....... 513 530-9600
 Blue Ash *(G-1796)*
Mandi A Tripp....................................G....... 740 380-1216
 Rockbridge *(G-16537)*
Sawdust...G....... 740 862-0612
 Baltimore *(G-1043)*
Sylvan Forge Inc................................G....... 440 237-3626
 North Royalton *(G-15303)*
V & W Woodcraft................................G....... 330 674-0073
 Millersburg *(G-14141)*

WOODWORK: Ornamental, Cornices, Mantels, Etc.

Reserve Millwork Inc..........................E....... 216 531-6982
 Bedford *(G-1441)*

WOOL: Felted

Ohio Table Pad of Indiana...................E....... 419 872-6400
 Perrysburg *(G-15987)*

WORD PROCESSING EQPT

Cap Data Supply Inc...........................G....... 216 252-2280
 Cleveland *(G-4869)*

WORK EXPERIENCE CENTER

TAC Industries Inc.............................B....... 937 328-5200
 Springfield *(G-17502)*

WOVEN WIRE PRDTS, NEC

Mazzella Lifting Tech Inc....................F....... 513 772-4466
 Cincinnati *(G-3988)*
Roy I Kaufman Inc..............................G....... 740 382-0643
 Marion *(G-12731)*
Utility Wire Products Inc....................F....... 216 441-2180
 Cleveland *(G-6247)*

WREATHS: Artificial

Horse Hill Wreath Company................G....... 937 272-0701
 Sugarcrk Twp *(G-17879)*
Season of Wreath...............................G....... 330 936-7498
 Canton *(G-2812)*
Wreaths & Masn Jars By Krissi...........G....... 419 250-6606
 Holland *(G-10970)*

WRENCHES

Bergman Safety Spanner Co Inc..........G....... 419 691-1462
 Northwood *(G-15334)*
Buckeye Gear Co................................F....... 216 292-7998
 Chagrin Falls *(G-3038)*
Norbar Torque Tools Inc....................F....... 440 953-1175
 Willoughby *(G-20389)*
Wright Tool Company.........................C....... 330 848-0600
 Barberton *(G-1114)*

X-RAY EQPT & TUBES

Comet Technologies USA Inc..............F....... 234 284-7849
 Hudson *(G-11038)*
Control-X Inc.....................................G....... 614 777-9729
 Columbus *(G-6815)*
Dentsply Sirona Inc............................D....... 419 865-9497
 Maumee *(G-13108)*
Metro Design Inc...............................F....... 440 458-4200
 Elyria *(G-9295)*
North Coast Medical Eqp Inc..............G....... 440 243-2722
 Berea *(G-1619)*
Philips Medical Systems Clevel...........B....... 440 247-2652
 Cleveland *(G-5871)*
Yxlon...G....... 234 284-7862
 Hudson *(G-11084)*

X-RAY EQPT REPAIR SVCS

Metro Design Inc...............................F....... 440 458-4200
 Elyria *(G-9295)*

YARN & YARN SPINNING

Specilty Fbrics Converting Inc............E....... 706 637-3000
 Fairlawn *(G-9618)*
Yarn Shop Inc....................................G....... 614 457-7836
 Columbus *(G-7621)*

YARN: Manmade & Synthetic Fiber, Twisting Or Winding

US Greentech....................................G....... 513 371-5520
 Cincinnati *(G-4457)*